THE SERIALS DIRECTORY

AN INTERNATIONAL REFERENCE BOOK

Editorial Advisory Board

Susan A. Cady
Associate Director
of Technical Services
Linderman Library
Lehigh University Libraries

Mary Elizabeth Clack
Serial Records Librarian
Harvard College Library

Genevieve Clay
Head, Central Serials
Eastern Kentucky University
Crabbe Library

Claude Daris
Head of Serials Department
Universite Libre de Bruxelles
Belgium

Kenneth E. Dowlin
Director, San Francisco Public Library
City Librarian
Main Library Civic Center

Ludo Holans
Librarian
Campus Bibliotheekdienst
Katholieke Universiteit Leuven
Belgium

Sul H. Lee
Dean, University Libraries
University of Oklahoma

Lois N. Upham
Uncle Remus Regional Library
Madison, Georgia

The 9th Edition of *The Serials Directory: An International Reference Book* was compiled and published by EBSCO Publishing, division of EBSCO Industries, Inc.

J.T. Stephens, President-EBSCO Industries, Inc.
Tim Collins, Vice President, Division General Manager-EBSCO Publishing
Mary Beth Vanderpoorten, M.S.L.S., Vice President-EBSCO Subscription Services, General Manager-Title Information

EDITORIAL / PRODUCTION

Leanne Wofford, Editorial Manager
Jill Hinds, Special Projects Editor
Stefanie Letanosky, Titles Editor

Jean Bowick, Editorial Assistant
Joe B. Crowe, Editorial Assistant
Kathy Entrekin, Editorial Assistant

Loyd McIntosh, Editorial Assistant
Mona Powell, Editorial Assistant
Kelly Rogers, Editorial Assistant

Database and publishing software
provided by Syscomp, Inc., Atlanta, Georgia, using Advanced Revelation®

Typesetting software provided by
Laser Solutions, Inc., Atlanta, Georgia using FrameMaker®

THE SERIALS DIRECTORY

AN INTERNATIONAL REFERENCE BOOK

NINTH EDITION 1995

VOLUME IV

Newspapers
Indexes

Division of EBSCO Industries Inc., Birmingham, Alabama

Published by EBSCO Publishing
division of EBSCO Industries, Inc.
P.O. Box 1943, Birmingham, AL 35201-1943   USA

Copyright © 1995 by EBSCO Industries, Inc.
Printed and bound in the United States of America.

All rights reserved. Reproduction of this Directory, in whole or in part, by any method, without prior written permission of the publisher is prohibited.

Direct all editorial inquiries to EBSCO Publishing, P.O. Box 1943, Birmingham, AL 35201-1943.

Direct all other inquiries to EBSCO Publishing, 83 Pine Street, PO Box 2250, Peabody, MA 01960-7250

International Standard Book Number (5-Volume Set) 0-913956-86-4
International Standard Book Number (Volume-1) 0-913956-81-3
International Standard Book Number (Volume-2) 0-913956-82-1
International Standard Book Number (Volume-3) 0-913956-83-X
International Standard Book Number (Volume-4) 0-913956-84-8
International Standard Book Number (Volume-5) 0-913956-85-6

International Standard Serial Number 0886-4179

Every effort has been made to ensure the accuracy of information in *The Serials Directory* and since no payment has been made for the inclusion of any entries, the publisher cannot accept liability for errors or omissions, regardless of the cause.

CONTENTS

Preface vii
User's Guide ix
Filing Rules.. xvi
Subject Headings... xvii
Subject Cross References xxi
Tables xxxvii
    Frequency... xxxviii
    Document Delivery xxxviii
    Wire Services... xxxix
    Country of Publication by Code............................ xl
    Country of Publication by Country xli
    Unit of Currency xlii
    Indexes/Abstracts...................................... xliii

Volume 1
    Serial Listings (A–Em) 3
Volume 2
    Serial Listings (En-L)................................... 1923
Volume 3
    Serial Listings (M-Z) 3475
Volume 4
    Newspapers
        US Newspapers..................................... 5625
        International Newspapers 5777
    Alphabetical Title Index................................ 5815
Volume 5
    ISSN Index.. 7607
    Peer Reviewed Index 7987
    Serials on CD-ROM Index.............................. 8051
    Serials Online Index................................... 8075
    Book Review Index 8113
    Advertising Accepted Index............................. 8275
    Controlled Circulation Index 8465
    Copyright Clearance Center Index...................... 8601
    New Title Index 8675

PREFACE

At EBSCO Publishing it is our goal to produce the primary serial reference source available. We have directed our energies toward obtaining the most up-to-date and accurate information on every title -- from the most familiar to the most obscure. In working toward this goal, several additions and changes have been made to the newest edition of *The Serials Directory: An International Reference Book*.

Eight new bibliographic elements are included in this edition to provide information professionals with a means for quick and easy serial research. In the newspaper section, Full and Half-page ad rates are now listed along with Publication Size, Wire Service Affiliations, and a notation for the inclusion of Photographs. Also included is data on document delivery availability/vendors, "Acid Free" notations and both Internet and E-mail addresses when provided by the publisher.

This edition of *The Serials Directory* contains approximately 151,000 serial titles with up to 60 bibliographic elements available for each one. Included in Volumes I, II and III are over 6,500 new titles, 2,800 titles available on CD-ROM or an online database, 10,600 titles registered with the Copyright Clearance Center, 24,000 serials publishing book reviews, and over 27,000 serials accepting advertising. This Edition contains verified information for over 100,000 serial titles representing approximately 65,000 publishers worldwide.

EBSCO Publishing is a sister division to EBSCO Subscription Services; therefore, gaining access to serial information on an ongoing basis is more simplified. EBSCO remains in constant contact with publishers throughout the world ensuring the accuracy of title and publisher information as well as providing the latest pricing and subscription data.

Information found in *The Serials Directory* is maintained through four sources. First, through the internal EBSCO Subscription Services database, updated daily as a result of continuous contact with publishers worldwide. The second source is The Library of Congress' CONSER file of which EBSCO is an affiliate member. The CONSER file is maintained by the National Serials Data Program, National Library of Canada, National Library of Medicine, Chemical Abstracts Service, and the National Agricultural Library. The third source is The ISSN Register (formerly ISDS) which provides extensive coverage of international serials. The fourth source for data is direct correspondence with thousands of publishers throughout the world.

With this edition, you will receive two cumulative Updates throughout 1995 to keep you abreast of changes in title status, publisher and subscription addresses, format changes or additions, price and frequency changes, as well as information on new titles. With a subscription to *The Serials Directory: EBSCO CD-ROM*, you will receive four quarterly updated discs containing all historical serial data that may not be included in the print version.

Our other international offering is *The Index and Abstract Directory: An International Guide to Services and Serials Coverage*. This valuable reference tool, which is now contained in two volumes, consists of information on over 950 "active" Indexing/Abstracting services and includes bibliographic information on the more than 56,000 serials that are monitored by each.

You will also find that we go beyond just providing reference products alone. As always, we will continue to offer free serials research to any of our customers needing assistance in locating the more ambiguous serial publications. We receive thousands of calls each year and have proven very successful in pinpointing the answers to a variety of serials questions.

At EBSCO Publishing, we continue to grow -- to change -- to improve. *The Serials Directory* and the *Index and Abstract Directory* reflect this growth and, combined with EBSCO's valued reputation within the library community, provide the highest standard of quality available in serials reference.

Leanne Wofford
Editorial Manager

EBSCO Publishing, PO Box 1943, Birmingham, AL 35201-1943 USA
(800)826-3024 / (205)980-2773 / FAX (205)995-1582

USER'S GUIDE

USER'S GUIDE

How to Use The Serials Directory.
Twelve sections comprise The Serials Directory. Each of these sections allows the user to access information easily. The following is a brief explanation of each section.

- **Serial Listings (Subjects A-Z)** (Volumes I, II and III)
- **Newspaper Listings** (Volume IV)
- **Alphabetical Title Index** (Volume IV)
- **ISSN Index** (Volume V)
- **Peer Reviewed Index** (Volume V)
- **Serials Available on CD-ROM Index** (Volume V)
- **Serials Available Online Index** (Volume V)
- **Book Review Index** (Volume V)
- **Advertising Accepted Index** (Volume V)
- **Controlled Circulation Index** (Volume V)
- **Copyright Clearance Center Index** (Volume V)
- **New Title Index** (Volume V)

● Serial Listings—
The Serial Listings are arranged alphabetically by subject category. Titles given under each subject heading are in alphabetical order (See Filing Rules—page xvi). The Serial Listing arrangement enables the user to quickly locate the relevant subject area and to review all serial titles relating to that subject. There are over 18,000 "see notes" throughout the 146 major subject headings and 330 subheadings in the Serial Listings. These notes refer the user from related subject areas to the primary subject heading under which the full title listing appears. See pages xvii-xxxvi for a list of subject headings and subject cross references.

● Newspaper Listings—
This section lists all US and international newspapers included in our database. US newspapers will be listed alphabetically by state. International titles will follow and are arranged alphabetically, by country. Newspaper listings can be found in the Alphabetical Title Index as well as the ISSN Index along with the regular listings in Volume IV.

● Alphabetical Title Index—
Arranged alphabetically by title, this index lists the primary title, along with Country of Publication/ISSN, and MARC control number, when available.

The following notations are made in the Alphabetical Title Index:

1. New Titles— Titles are denoted with a bullet "●". Bullets will appear in both the Serial Listing, as well as the Alphabetical Title Index. This edition includes over 6,500 new titles which began publication after 1992 and were active at the time data was secured for publication.

2. Ceased Titles— Titles that have ceased publication and do not have a "succeeding entry." Ceased titles are denoted with "*CEASED*" in bold italics, following the primary title in the Serial Listing, as well as the Alphabetical Title Index. Ceased titles are included in the Directory for two consecutive editions after EBSCO is notified of the status change. This edition contains over 4,700 cessations.

3. Title Changes— Titles which have a succeeding entry, MARC field 785. These entries are included in the Alphabetical Title Index with a reference to the current title(s). Title changes are included in the Directory for two consecutive editions based on the "ending date of publication," MARC field 008/11-14. This edition contains over 4,840 title changes. See the User's Guide/Sample Listing for more information.

4. Suspended Titles— Titles for which EBSCO has received notification of suspension. Suspended titles are denoted in both the Serial Listing and the index with "*SUSPENDED*" in bold italics, following the primary title. These titles will remain suspended until EBSCO is notified otherwise.

5. Preceding Entries— Preceding entries print with a "see" note to the primary title provided the primary title has a MARC publication start date (008/7-10) later than 1992. Preceding entries will remain in the Directory for two consecutive editions with a reference to the newer title(s).

6. Main Entry - Corporate Name— A corporate name used as a main entry, this element prints in the Alphabetical Title Index as another access point to the publication in question. To further aid the user, the Main Entry-Corporate Name is listed with a "see" note to the primary title in the Serial Listings. Over 24,000 Main Entry-Corporate Names are included in the Directory.

USER'S GUIDE

- **ISSN Index—**

The ISSN Index contains current as well as preceding ISSN's, arranged in numerical order. The ISSN will be followed by a "see" note giving the title under which the ISSN will appear. The preceding ISSN is included with a "see" note to the primary title provided the MARC publication start date (field 008/7-10) is later than 1992. Preceding ISSN will appear in italicized typeface in order to distinguish it from the current ISSN. The page number for which the Serial Listing appears prints in boldface. There are over 100,400 titles included in the ISSN Index.

- **Peer Reviewed Index—**

Arranged alphabetically by title, the Peer Reviewed Index lists all active serials found in Volumes I, II and III which contain peer reviewed articles. Country of Publication/ISSN and MARC control number are provided, when available. The page number for which the Serial Listing appears prints in boldface. There are over 8,800 titles included in the Peer Reviewed Index.

- **Serials Available on CD-ROM Index—**

Arranged alphabetically by title, this index lists all active serial titles in Volumes I, II and III that are available on CD-ROM, either as the primary format, or as an "additional" available format. Included in this index are the Country of Publication/ISSN and publisher address/telephone number(s) when available. The page number for which the Serial Listing appears prints in boldface. There are over 1,300 titles included in the Serials Available on CD-ROM Index.

- **Serials Available Online Index—**

Arranged alphabetically by title, this index lists all active serials found in Volumes I, II and III that are available online, either as the primary format, or as an "additional" available format. Included in this index are the Country of Publication/ISSN and publisher address/telephone number(s) when available. The page number for which the Serial Listing appears prints in boldface. There are over 2,500 titles included in the Serials Available Online Index.

- **Book Review Index—**

Arranged alphabetically by title, this index lists all active serials found in Volumes I, II and III that contain book reviews. Included in this index are Country of Publication/ISSN and the quantity of book reviews published "per year" (unless otherwise specified). The page number for which the Serial Listing appears prints in boldface. There are over 24,000 titles included in the Book Review Index.

- **Advertising Accepted Index—**

Arranged alphabetically by title, this index contains all active serials found in Volumes I, II and III that accept advertising. The Country of Publication/ISSN and advertising manager/telephone number(s) are also provided, when supplied by the publisher. The page number for which the Serial Listing appears prints in boldface. There are over 27,000 titles included in the Advertising Accepted Index.

- **Controlled Circulation Index—**

Arranged alphabetically by title, this index lists all active titles in the Directory that have a controlled circulation. The Country of Publication/ISSN and circulation figures [printing in brackets] are provided when available. The page number for which the Serial Listing appears prints in boldface. There are over 19,000 titles included in the Controlled Circulation Index.

- **Copyright Clearance Center Index—**

Arranged alphabetically by title, this index lists all active serials found in Volumes I, II and III that are registered with the Copyright Clearance Center (CCC). The Country of Publication/ISSN are provided when available. The page number for which the Serial Listing appears prints in boldface. There are over 10,600 titles included in the Copyright Clearance Center Index.

- **New Title Index—**

Arranged by subject, then alphabetically by title, this index consists of all active titles that have a MARC "beginning date" of "1992" or greater, as well as, "non-MARC" titles where the start date has been verified by the publisher. Country of Publication/ISSN follow the title, with the page number on which the Serial Listing appears. There are over 6,500 titles included in the New Title Index.

USER'S GUIDE/SAMPLE LISTING

SAMPLE LISTING

Country of Publication/ISSN
● **KEY TITLE.** *CEASED/SUSPENDED.* (TITLE STATEMENT). [Abbreviated Title]. **Main/Conf** Main Entry—Meeting. **Main/Corp** Main Entry—Corporate Name. **Added/Corp** Added Entry—Corporate Name. **Series/Conf** Series Statement—Meeting Name. **VFOAT** Varying Form of a Title. **VAT** Variant Access Title. Date of Publication. Type of Serial. Language(s). Frequency. Price. Publisher Name & Address. **Tel** Telephone/Telex Number/Fax/Internet Address/Email Address. (subscription address:) **ED** Editor. **LC** Library of Congress Classification. **DD** Dewey Decimal Classification. **UDC** Universal Decimal Classification. **NLM** National Library of Medicine Classification. **CODEN** CODEN Designation. **[CCC]** Copyright Clearance Center. Index Availability. cum. index (Cumulative Index Availability). **Bk Rev** (Book reviews published), (Qty: Quantity Published). **Photos** [Photographs published]. **Ad Acc** (Advertising accepted), **Adv. Mgr**: Advertising Manager. **Tel** Telephone. Full Page (B&W) - Full page black and white ad rates. Half Page (B&W) - Half page black and white ad rates. Full Page (Color) - Full page color ad rates. Half Page (Color) - Half page color ad rates. **Pub. Size** [Publication trim size]. **Wire Svcs** [Newspaper wire services]. **Pr Rev.** (Peer Reviewed or Refereed). **Acid Free** [Acid free paper]. Circulation. (ctrl) - Controlled circulation. Document Delivery Available. Additional Physical Forms Available. *Preceding Entry-Title, Preceding Entry-ISSN. Succeeding Entry-Title, Succeeding Entry-ISSN.*
   Desc: Descriptive listing.
      Ind/Abst Indexes/Abstracts. Dates of Coverage. Full Text. Full/Selective Coverage

SERIAL LISTING CONTENTS

For the purpose of defining a serial, the definition as given in the USMARC Bibliographic Format is used: a bibliographic item issued in successive parts bearing numerical or chronological designations and intended to be continued indefinitely. Serials include periodicals; newspapers; annuals (reports, yearbooks, etc.); the journals, memoirs, proceedings, transactions, etc., of societies; and numbered monographic series, etc.

The following data elements (when available) are shown in order of appearance within a listing. Some definitions are taken in part from USMARC Formats Bibliographic Data.

Country of Publication. A two letter code indicating the place of publication, production, or execution. See Country of Publication Table, Page xxxvi for additions/changes.

ISSN. International Standard Serial Number, a unique identification number assigned to a serial title by national centers under the auspices of the ISSN Register (formerly ISDS).

●Denotes new titles beginning after 1992, that were active at the time data was secured for publication.

Key Title. Key Title is assigned by various national centers under the auspices of the ISSN Register (formerly International Serials Data System /ISDS). It is formed from title information transcribed from a piece of the serial and is constructed with qualifiers to make it unique when necessary. Since serial titles are taken from both the CONSER and ISSN Register databases, the primary title has not been altered to differentiate the alternative format from the original. In cases where CONSER or the ISSN Register has included a notation for the alternative format within the primary title, the primary title will reflect that notation. Serials in an alternative format (microfiche, microfilm, CD-ROM, etc.) are included in the Directory. Also in cases where multiple language entries appear, the user must refer to the primary language of the publication to ensure that the correct title is located. These titles may appear to be identical with the primary language being the only unique qualifier.

Ceased. This element is present only when a title has ceased publication. This does not include titles that have a succeeding entry or have had a title change. The word "*CEASED*" in bold italics, follows the primary title in the Serial Listing. Ceased titles are included in the Directory for two consecutive editions after the actual date of cessation. This edition contains over 4,700 cessations.

Suspended. Denotes temporary suspension of a title. The word "*SUSPENDED*" in bold italics, follows the primary title in the Serial Listing to denote suspended titles. These titles remain suspended in the database until the publisher notifies EBSCO otherwise.

Title Statement. Title Statement is present only when it differs from Key Title in any way, other than initial articles and prepositions. It consists of the title proper (including short title and alternative title, the numerical designation of a part/section and the name of a part/section) and may also contain the medium, remainder of title, other title information, and the statement of responsibility/remainder of title page transcription. Title Statement will follow Key Title in uppercase and will be enclosed in parentheses.

Abbreviated Title. Assigned by the ISSN Register (formerly ISDS), in accordance with ISO 4-1984, Documentation - Rules for the Abbreviation of Title Words and Titles of Publications and List of Serial Title Word Abbreviations. The Abbreviated Title is based on the Key Title and files in [brackets].

USER'S GUIDE/SAMPLE LISTING

Main Entry-Meeting. A meeting or conference name used as a main entry. Main entry under a meeting name is assigned to works that contain proceedings, reports, etc. Main Entry-Meeting will be preceded by the prefix "**Main/Conf**" in boldface.

Main Entry-Corporate Name. A corporate name used as a main entry. Main entry under corporate name is assigned to works that represent the collective thought of a body, including conference and meeting names that are entered subordinately to a corporate body. Main Entry-Corporate Name is preceded by the prefix "**Main/Corp**" in boldface.

Added Entry-Corporate Name. Contains a corporate heading used as main entry. A corporate body is identified by a name that acts or may act as an entity. Included in this definition are: associations, institutions, business firms, governments and their agencies, ships, churches and programs. The Added Entry-Corporate Name will be preceded by a prefix of "**Added/Corp**" in boldface.

Series Statement-Meeting Name. Series statement entered under a named conference or meeting. Series Statement-Meeting is preceded by "**Series/Conf**" in boldface.

Varying Form of a Title. Titles which may appear on different parts of a serial, or consisting of portions of the title proper or alternative forms of titles. Varying Form of a Title differs substantially from Key Title/Title Statement and contributes to the further identification of the serial. It is preceded by the prefix "**VFOAT**" in boldface. Additional titles are separated by commas.

Variant Access Title. A variant form of the title that does not appear on the serial. It is used when the title contains an initialism, non-roman alphabet character, etc. It provides additional access for searching purposes when access is not provided by any other title. Variant Access Title is preceded by the prefix of "**VAT**" in boldface. Additional titles are separated by commas.

Dates of Publication and Volume Information. Beginning (and ending) dates of publication and volume designation. The date may consist of the year, month, or day; month or season and year; or year alone, depending upon the frequency of publication and the usage of the publisher. Dates may appear in the vernacular and/or may be abbreviated.

Type of Serial. Indicates if the serial is a periodical, monographic series, or newspaper. When available, more specific types will be used such as bibliography, catalog, bulletin, directory, government publication, newsletter, proceedings, trade publication, consumer publication, corporate report, academic scholarly publication and abstracting/indexing publication.

Language(s). If the serial is published in more than one language, the predominant language will appear first and any additional languages will follow in parentheses (including languages for translations, summaries, tables of contents, etc.) with appropriate explanation if necessary.

Frequency. Indicated by a two letter code - see Frequency Table, page xxxviii. Exceptions to frequency are noted and in parentheses following code.

Price. The current annual subscription price at the time information was secured for publication. Prices are usually given in US dollars and currency of Country of Publication, if other than US. Exceptions are noted and explained.

Publisher Name and Address/Telecommunications Numbers. The complete name and address of the publisher when available. Telephone, telex and/or facsimile number as well as Internet and E-mail addresses are given for serials. Preceded by a prefix of "**Tel**" in boldface.

Subscription Address. The complete name and subscription/fulfillment address. Telecommunication numbers are listed when available.

Editor(s). Name, address and telephone number(s), when available. Preceded by a prefix of "**ED**" in boldface.

Library of Congress Classification. Contains an LC class/call number, shelf number, or pseudo-call-number assigned by The Library of Congress or one of its authorized agencies. Preceded by a prefix of "**LC**" in boldface.

Dewey Decimal Classification. Assigned according to the Dewey Decimal schedules maintained by The Library of Congress. Preceded by a prefix of "**DD**" in boldface.

Universal Decimal Classification. Derived from the Dewey Decimal Classification, the UDC differs in arrangement and philosophy. The UDC is distinguished from the DDC by its extensive expansions. Preceded by a prefix of "**UDC**" in boldface.

National Library of Medicine Classification. Contains either a complete NLM call number or an NLM classification number. Preceded by a prefix of "**NLM**" in boldface.

CODEN Designation. Abbreviation for periodical titles, which is assigned by the CODEN section of Chemical Abstracts Service. It is a unique identifier for scientific and technical publications. Preceded by a prefix of "**CODEN**" in boldface.

Copyright Clearance Center. [**CCC**] indicates titles registered with the Copyright Clearance Center. The Copyright Clearance Center has been authorized to give photocopy permission and to collect any pre-set royalty fees set by the publisher.

Index Availability. Shows the existence of an index, or a table of contents issued as an index, and the method of acquisition.

Cumulative Index Availability. Specifies if a cumulative index, or a table of contents issued as a cumulative index, is published.

USER'S GUIDE/SAMPLE LISTING

Appears in abbreviated form as "cum. index."

Book Reviews. If book reviews are published, "**Bk Rev**" will appear in the Serial Listing.

Book Review Quantity. Quantity of book reviews published "per year," unless otherwise specified. Quantity is preceded by "Qty:" and prints in parentheses.

Photos. If photographs are included within the serial, "**Photos**" will appear in the listing.

Advertising. If advertising is accepted in a serial, the abbreviation "**Ad Acc**" will appear in boldface.

Advertising Manager/Telephone. Lists the name and telephone number of the Advertising Manager, when available. Advertising Manager name is preceded by "**Adv Mgr**:" in boldface. Telephone is preceded by the prefix "**Tel**" in boldface.

Advertising Rates. Advertising rates for full and half-page ads. (B&W) designates rates for ads in black and white. (Color) designates ads printed in color.

Publication Size. The trim size of the serial or newspaper. Preceded by the abbreviation **Pub. Size**. Common publication sizes include Tabloid, Standard and Broadsheet.

Wire Services. Lists the news and photograph wire services affiliated with any given newspaper. These are preceded by a prefix of "**Wire Svcs**" in boldface. A chart of abbreviations used can be found on page xxxix.

Peer Reviewed. If a journal is peer reviewed or refereed, the abbreviation "**Pr Rev**" will appear.

Acid Free. If a publication is available on acid free paper, "**Acid Free**" will be seen in boldface.

Circulation. Annual circulation of publication, unless noted otherwise. Multiple circulation figures are separated by a comma.

Controlled Circulation. If circulation of a serial is controlled by the publisher, the abbreviation "ctrl" in parentheses follows the circulation figures. If no circulation figures are given, but the publisher has notified us that circulation is controlled, "ctrl circ" will appear.

Document Delivery. Indicates the availability of that serial for document delivery through the specified service(s). Refer to the chart on page xxxviii.

Additional Physical Forms Available. Additional media in which a serial is published, other than its original or conventional form.

Preceding Entry - Title/Preceding Entry - ISSN. The immediate predecessor(s) for the title, along with ISSN, appears in italics. Depending on indicators taken from the CONSER 780 field, a title's preceding entry will be preceded by one of the following: Continues, Continues in part, Supersedes, Supersedes in part, Formed by the union of... and..., Absorbed, Absorbed in part, or Separated from. If the title Continues in part, another title which is current, both titles will then be listed. Additional titles and ISSN are separated by semicolons and are preceded by one of the above, in boldface.

Succeeding Entry Title/Succeeding Entry - ISSN. The immediate successor(s) for the serial title (along with corresponding ISSN) will be listed. Multiple titles and ISSN are separated by semicolons, and preceded by a prefix of one of the following: Continued by, Continued in part by, Superseded by, Superseded in part by, Absorbed by, Absorbed in part by, Split into... and..., Merged with... to form..., Merged into, or Changed back to. In cases where CONSER did not give an ending date or a title was only continued "in part" both titles will be listed.

Descriptive Listing. Description of content submitted by publisher or by CONSER. Descriptions may have been edited for clarity. Description is preceded by "**Desc:**" in boldface.

Indexes/Abstracts. Specifies the publication(s) in which a serial has been indexed and/or abstracted. These are preceded by a prefix of "**Ind/Abst**" in boldface. Over 920 "active" Indexing/Abstracting services are used for the purposes of this Directory and can be found within the Serial Listings. See Indexes/Abstracts Abbreviations Table on page xliii.

Dates of Coverage. Dates of coverage are included for each index or abstract, when available. Dates are enclosed in parentheses and follow the abbreviation as used in the Serial Listing for each Indexing/Abstracting service. If no dates are provided by the Indexing/Abstracting service publisher, and we have been notified that a serial is no longer covered by a particular service, question marks will be used to notify the user that coverage of the particular serial by the service has been discontinued.

Full Text. Specifies if a journal is covered by an Indexing/Abstracting service in "Full Text." Full Text coverage indicates that all articles in the journal are indexed/abstracted completely, with any pertinent graphics, charts etc. For the purposes of this Directory, "Full Text" and "Full Image" are treated as if they were the same. These will be coded in the Serial Listing as [Full Txt.]. This notation will follow the dates of coverage in the Serial Listing.

Full/Selective Coverage — Full coverage indicates that journals are indexed/abstracted cover to cover. Selective coverage specifies serials in which the Indexing / Abstracting service selects only articles relevant to their publication. These will be coded in the Serial Listing as [Full Cov.] or [Select. Cov.]. This notation will follow the dates of coverage, when available, or will precede the Index or Abstract abbreviation when no dates of coverage are noted in the Serial Listing.

FILING RULES

A. General Rules— Filing is word for word with exceptions noted below. The order of characters applies the principle "nothing files before something," with numerals before letters, file A to Z.

1. Spaces, hyphens, diagonal slashes, and periods are filed as blanks:

AAG-AAG
AAG Directory / Association of American Geographers
AAG Newsletter
AAHA Directory of Membership

2. Variant spellings are filed as written:

Ageing and Society
Aging and Aging Disorders

B. Special Rules and Exceptions.

1. Modified letters and diacritics— Modified letters are written as their plain English alphabet equivalents.

2. Punctuation— Punctuation and non-alphabetic symbols (except those noted in A above) are ignored for filing purposes:

"A" Magazine
A Magyar Talalkozo Kronikaja
A.N.A. Audiologia Protesica

3. Abbreviations— Filed exactly as written.

Dr. McBirnie's Newsletter
St. Louis Review
U.N. Observer & International Report
U.S. Census Report

4. Numerals— Filed character by character according to the numeric value of each string of characters.
Numerals precede letters:

33 Metal Producing
35/70; Journal of the Feature Film Industry
35MM Photography London England : 1983)
36 Cities : Real Estate Forecast and Review

5. Initials, initialisms, acronyms— Those in which each letter is separated by a space, dash, hyphen, period, or diagonal slash are regarded as a series of separate words. Those in which characters are separated by other marks or symbols, or which are not separated in any way, are regarded as single words:

A. C. C. L. Union List of Serials
A C E Q-A C G R Information
A/C Flyer, The
A.C.G.C.-Information : Bulletin d'Information de l'Association des Cadres et Gerants des Colleges du Quebec
A C I S
A. C. L. : Agence Cambodge Laos

6. Initial Articles— The following words are ignored when they appear at the beginning of an entry.

A	Eine	Hio	'n
al	Eit	Hin	Na
An	el-	Hinar	Nje
As	El	Hinir	Nji
Az	Els	Hinn	O
Bir	En	Ho	Os
Das	Et	Hoi	't
De	Ett	I	Ta
Dei	Gl'	Il	The
Den	Gli	Ka	To
Der	ha-	Ke	Um
Di	Hai	L'	Uma
Die	He	La	Un
Dos	he-	Las	Un'
Een	Heis	Le	Una
Eene	Hen	Les	Une
Egy	Hena	Lo	Uno
Ei	Henas	Los	Y
Ein	Het	Mia	Yr

Exceptions— Titles composed entirely of words on the list above are filed as written, as well as place names.
Hence:

A Tavola
A to Z of Who is Who in Australia's History, The
A Traverso

7. Names and prefixes— A prefix that is part of the name of a person or place is treated as a separate word unless it is joined to the rest of the name:

De Paul Law Review
McCall's Book for Brides
Van Buren Register

SUBJECT HEADINGS

The following section lists the subject headings used throughout the Directory. The list is arranged alphabetically, by subject, with the major subject (printing in boldface) followed by specific subheadings within the same category.

CROSS REFERENCES

This section combines all subject headings into one alphabetical list, regardless of whether it is a general, main subject or specific, subordinate subject. Cross references from a subject or topic not used in the Directory are made to that which is used. "See also" notes from one subject to a similar subject are included as well.

SUBJECT HEADINGS

Aeronautics, Astronautics 3
Agriculture 42
   Agricultural Equipment 158
   Crop Production and Soil 161
   Dairy Industry 191
   Feed Grain and Milling 199
   Livestock and Poultry 204
Animal Welfare 225
Anthropology 227
Antiques 248
Archaeology 253
Architecture 286
Arts, The 311
   Art 335
   Crafts and Decorative Arts 369
   Graphic Arts 376
   Performing Arts 383
Astrology 389
Astronomy 391
Beauty and Cosmetics 402
Bibliographies 406
Bicycles and Bicycling 427
Biographies 429
Biology 439
   Biochemistry 479
   Biophysics 494
   Botany 496
   Cytology and Histology 531
   Embryology 541
   Genetics 541
   Marine Biology 552
   Microbiology 558
   Microscopy 572
   Mycology 574
   Physiology 577
Birth Control 587
Boats and Boating 591
Building and Construction 597
   Carpentry and Woodwork 633
Business 636
   Accounting 735
   Advertising and Public Relations .. 753
   Banking and Finance 768
   Chamber of Commerce 817
   Commerce 821
   General Management 858
   Investments 890
   Marketing 920
   Personnel Management 938
   Purchasing 948
   Retail 952
Chemistry 958
   Analytical Chemistry 1012
   Chemical Technology 1020
   Crystallography 1031
   Electrochemistry 1033
   Inorganic Chemistry 1035
   Organic Chemistry 1038
   Physical and Theoretical Chemistry . 1049
Children and Youth Interests 1059
Civil Defense 1072
Classical Studies 1073
Clothing Industry and Fashion 1081
College and School Publications ... 1088
   Alumni 1096

Communication 1103
   Broadcasting 1125
   Postal Communications 1144
   Telecommunications 1148
Computers 1169
   Artificial Intelligence 1210
   Automation 1217
   Computer Assisted Instruction ... 1222
   Computer Crimes and Security ... 1225
   Computer Engineering 1227
   Computer Games 1230
   Computer Graphics and Design .. 1231
   Computer Industry and Industry
     Directories 1235
   Computer Music 1240
   Computer Networks 1240
   Computer Sales, Service
     and Supply 1244
   Computer Systems 1246
   Cybernetics 1250
   Data Base Management 1252
   Data Processing 1255
   Desktop Publishing 1263
   Hardware 1264
   Microcomputers, Personal
     Computers 1265
   Minicomputers 1273
   Online Computing and
     Information 1274
   Optical Storage, CD-ROM
     Applications 1276
   Programs and Programming 1277
   Simulation 1282
   Software 1283
   Word Processing 1292
Consumer Interests 1293
Copyright, Intellectual Property ... 1300
Dance 1310
Dentistry 1314
Drug Abuse and Alcoholism 1338
Earth Sciences 1351
   Geology 1364
   Geophysics 1402
   Hydrology 1412
   Meteorology 1419
   Mineralogy 1437
   Oceanography 1445
   Petrology 1458
Economics 1459
   Cooperatives 1541
   Economic History, Conditions ... 1544
   Economic Theory 1589
   Industry and Production 1596
   International Economics 1632
   Labor 1642
Education 1720
   Adult and Continuing Education .. 1799
   Early Childhood and
     Primary Education 1802
   Higher Education 1806
   Physical Education and
     Training 1854
   School Organization and
     Administration 1859
   Special Education and
     Rehabilitation 1874
   Teaching and Curriculum 1887
   Vocational Education 1909

Emigration and Immigration 1918
Encyclopedias and General
   Reference Books 1923
Energy 1930
Engineering 1963
   Chemical Engineering 2007
   Civil Engineering 2018
   Electricity, Electrical
     Engineering, Electronics 2034
   Hydraulic Engineering 2087
   Industrial Engineering
     and Design 2096
   Materials Engineering and
     Mechanics 2100
   Mechanical Engineering and
     Machinery 2108
   Mines and Mining Engineering ... 2132
   Nuclear Engineering 2153
Environmental Issues 2159
   Conservation and Natural
     Resources 2185
   Ecology 2210
   Pollution and Waste
     Management 2222
Ethics 2248
Ethnic Interests 2253
Family and Marriage 2276
Fire Prevention 2287
Fish and Fisheries 2293
Folklore 2318
Food and Food Industry 2325
   Beverage Industry 2363
Forestry 2373
   Lumber and Wood 2399
Funeral Service 2406
Gardening and Horticulture 2407
   Florist Trade 2434
Genealogy and Heraldry 2436
   Archives 2478
General Interest 2484
   General Interest-Africa 2497
   General Interest-Asia 2501
   General Interest-Australia
     and Oceania 2510
   General Interest-Central
     America 2511
   General Interest-Europe 2513
   General Interest-Middle East ....
   General Interest-North America ... 2526
   General Interest-South America ... 2551
Geography 2553
   Cartography 2580
Gifts, Toys 2583
Glass and Ceramics 2585
Health and Personal Fitness 2595
Heating, Plumbing, and
   Refrigeration 2602
History(General) 2609
   History of Africa 2636
   History of Asia 2644
   History of Australia and
     Oceania 2668
   History of Europe 2671
   History of North, South, and
     Central America 2717
   History of the Middle East 2767

SUBJECT HEADINGS

Hobbies	2770
Numismatics	2779
Philately	2784
Home Economics	2788
Homosexuality	2793
Horses and Horsemanship	2796
Hotels/Motels	2803
Household Hardware and Appliances	2810
Housing and Urban Development	2812
Humanities	2841
Hypnosis	2857
Industrial Health and Safety	2858
Insurance	2872
Interior Design	2898
Home Furnishings	2904
International Assistance and Development	2907
Jewelry	2913
Clocks and Watches	2916
Journalism	2917
Law	2926
Banking Law	3084
Civil Law	3088
Constitutional Law	3091
Corporate Law	3094
Criminal Law	3104
Environmental Law	3109
Estate Planning	3117
Family Law	3119
International Law	3122
Judicial Systems	3138
Labor Law	3143
Law Enforcement and Criminology	3156
Legal Aid	3179
Maritime Law	3180
Military Law	3182
Leather and Fur Industry	3183
Library and Information Sciences	3186
Linguistics	3260
Literary and Political Reviews	3337
Literature	3357
Poetry	3459
Manufacturing	3475
Mathematics	3490
Medical Science and Technology	3543
Allergy and Immunology	3662
Anatomy	3678
Anesthesiology	3680
Biotechnology	3685
Cardiology	3697
Communicable Diseases	3711
Dermatology	3717
Emergency Medicine	3723
Endocrinology	3726
Epidemiology	3733
Family Practice	3736
Forensic Medicine, Medical Jurisprudence	3739
Gastroenterology	3743
Geriatrics	3748
Gynecology and Obstetrics	3755
Hematology	3769
Homeopathy	3774
Hospital Administration and Medical Centers	3775
Internal Medicine	3794
Musculoskeletal System	3802
Neoplasma, Neoplastic	3808
Neurology	3825
Nuclear Medicine	3847
Nursing	3849
Ophthalmology	3871
Orthopedics	3880
Otorhinolaryngology	3885
Pathology	3891
Pediatrics	3899
Physicians and Medical Personnel	3912
Podiatry	3917
Psychiatry	3918
Radiology	3938
Respiratory System	3947
Sports Medicine	3953
Surgery	3957
Toxicology	3978
Tropical Medicine	3985
Urology and Nephrology	3987
Men's Interests	3994
Metals and Metallurgy	3996
Welding	4026
Metrology and Standardization	4029
Military and Defense	4033
Motion Picture	4062
Motorcycles	4080
Museums and Galleries	4083
Music	4098
Natural History	4161
Naval Science, Navigation	4174
New Age Publications	4185
Newspapers	5625
Nutrition and Dietetics	4186
Occupations and Careers	4201
Office Equipment and Services	4210
Optometry	4214
Packaging	4217
Paints and Painting	4222
Paleontology	4226
Paper and Pulp Industry	4232
Parapsychology and Occultism	4240
Pest Control	4243
Petroleum and Natural Gas	4248
Pets	4285
Pharmacy and Pharmacology	4288
Philanthropy	4334
Philosophy	4339
Photography and Video	4366
Physical Therapy	4378
Physically Impaired	4382
Physics	4395
Analytic and Experimental Mechanics	4427
Heat	4430
Light, Optics, Radiation	4432
Magnetism	4443
Nuclear Physics	4445
Sound	4451
Plastics	4453
Political Science	4461
Civil Rights	4503
International Relations	4514
Socialism, Communism, Anarchism, Utopianism	4539
Population Studies	4549
Printing Industry	4563
Psychology	4570
Public Administration	4623
Civil Service	4701
Parks and Recreation	4705
Public Finance and Taxation	4708
Public Utilities	4759
Public Health and Safety	4763
Publishing	4811
Books and Bookmaking	4822
Real Estate	4833
Recreation, Leisure	4848
Games and Amusements	4856
Outdoor Life	4868
Sports	4881
Religion and Theology	4931
Bible	5013
Buddhism	5020
Catholicism	5022
Eastern Christian Churches	5039
Hinduism	5040
Islam, Bahaism, Theosophy	5041
Judaism	5045
Protestantism	5054
Restaurants	5070
Romance and Adventure	5073
Rubber	5075
Science and Technology	5078
Security Systems and Alarms	5176
Senior Citizens	5177
Sewing and Needlework	5182
Sexual Life	5186
Social Sciences	5189
Societies and Clubs	5228
Sociology	5237
Manners and Customs	5267
Social Services and Welfare	5269
Sound Recordings and Systems	5315
Statistics	5320
Textiles	5347
Theater	5361
Tobacco	5372
Transportation	5375
Automobiles	5403
Railroads	5429
Roads and Traffic	5438
Ships and Shipping	5447
Travel and Tourism	5458
Veterinary Sciences	5501
Water Resources	5528
Women's Interests	5550
Zoology	5572
Entomology	5604
Ornithology	5614

SUBJECT HEADINGS

The 117 subject headings listed below all contain a sub-heading for "Abstracting, Bibliographies, and Statistics." This sub-heading, which follows the major heading in the Serial Listing, contains serials which abstract and/or index publications in the applicable subject area. Bibliographies and statistical publications pertaining to each subject are also included.

Subject	Page
Aeronautics, Astronautics	3
Agriculture	42
Anthropology	227
Antiques	248
Archaeology	253
Architecture	286
Arts, The	311
Astronomy	391
Bicycles and Bicycling	427
Biographies	429
Biology	439
Birth Control	587
Boats and Boating	591
Building and Construction	597
Business	636
Chemistry	958
Children and Youth Interests	1059
Classical Studies	1073
Clothing Industry and Fashion	1081
Communication	1103
Computers	1169
Consumer Interests	1293
Copyright, Intellectual Property	1300
Dance	1310
Dentistry	1314
Drug Abuse and Alcoholism	1338
Earth Sciences	1351
Economics	1459
Education	1720
Encyclopedias and General Reference Books	1923
Energy	1930
Engineering	1963
Environmental Issues	2159
Ethnic Interests	2253
Family and Marriage	2276
Fire Prevention	2287
Fish and Fisheries	2293
Folklore	2318
Food and Food Industry	2325
Forestry	2373
Gardening and Horticulture	2407
Genealogy and Heraldry	2436
General Interest	2484
Geography	2553
Glass and Ceramics	2585
Health and Personal Fitness	2595
History (General)	2609
Hobbies	2770
Homosexuality	2793
Horses and Horsemanship	2796
Hotels/Motels	2803
Household Hardware and Appliances	2810
Housing and Urban Development	2812
Humanities	2841
Industrial Health and Safety	2858
Insurance	2872
International Assistance and Development	2907
Journalism	2917
Law	2926
Library and Information Sciences	3186
Linguistics	3260
Literary and Political Reviews	3337
Literature	3357
Manufacturing	3475
Mathematics	3490
Medical Science and Technology	3543
Metals and Metallurgy	3996
Metrology and Standardization	4029
Military and Defense	4033
Motion Picture	4062
Motorcycles	4080
Museums and Galleries	4083
Music	4098
Natural History	4161
Naval Science, Navigation	4174
New Age Publications	4185
Newspapers	5625
Nutrition and Dietetics	4186
Occupations and Careers	4201
Packaging	4217
Paints and Painting	4222
Paleontology	4226
Paper and Pulp Industry	4232
Parapsychology and Occultism	4240
Pest Control	4243
Petroleum and Natural Gas	4248
Pharmacy and Pharmacology	4288
Philosophy	4339
Photography and Video	4366
Physically Impaired	4382
Physics	4395
Plastics	4453
Political Science	4461
Population Studies	4549
Printing Industry	4563
Psychology	4570
Public Administration	4623
Public Health and Safety	4763
Publishing	4811
Real Estate	4833
Recreation, Leisure	4848
Religion and Theology	4931
Restaurants	5070
Rubber	5075
Science and Technology	5078
Social Sciences	5189
Sociology	5237
Sound Recordings and Systems	5315
Textiles	5347
Theater	5361
Tobacco	5372
Transportation	5375
Travel and Tourism	5458
Veterinary Sciences	5501
Water Resources	5528
Women's Interests	5550
Zoology	5572

SUBJECT CROSS REFERENCES

Abortion –See **Medical Science and Technology -- Gynecology and Obstetrics** pg 3755

Abrasives –See **Metals and Metallurgy** pg 3996

Accessories –See **Clothing Industry and Fashion** pg 1081

Accident Prevention –See **Industrial Health and Safety** pg 2858; **Public Health and Safety** pg 4763; **Transportation -- Roads and Traffic** pg 5438

Accounting –pg 735; see also Law pg 2926; Public Administration -- Public Finance and Taxation pg 4708

Acoustics –See **Physics -- Sound** pg 4451

Acquired Immune Deficiency Syndrome (AIDS) –See **Medical Science and Technology -- Allergy and Immunology** pg 3662; see also Medical Science and Technology -- Communicable Diseases pg 3711; Public Health and Safety pg 4763

Acting –See **Motion Picture** pg 4062; **The Arts -- Performing Arts** pg 383; **Theater** pg 5361

Actuarial Science –See **Insurance** pg 2872

Acupuncture –See **Medical Science and Technology** pg 3543

Addictions –See **Drug Abuse and Alcoholism** pg 1338; see also Psychology pg 4570

Adhesives –See **Chemistry -- Physical and Theoretical Chemistry** pg 1049; see also Chemistry -- Chemical Technology pg 1020; Engineering -- Chemical Engineering pg 2007; Engineering -- Materials Engineering and Mechanics pg 2100; Metals and Metallurgy -- Welding pg 4026; Paints and Painting pg 4222; Plastics pg 4453

Administrative Law –See **Law -- Constitutional Law** pg 3091

Adoption –See **Sociology -- Social Services and Welfare** pg 5269

Adult and Continuing Education –pg 1799

Adventure –See **Romance and Adventure** pg 5073

Advertising –See **Business -- Advertising and Public Relations** pg 753

Advertising and Public Relations –pg 753

Aerobics –See **Health and Personal Fitness** pg 2595

Aerodynamics –See **Aeronautics, Astronautics** pg 3

Aeronautics, Astronautics –pg 3; see also Military and Defense pg 4033; Transportation pg 5375

Aerospace Medicine –See **Aeronautics, Astronautics** pg 3; **Medical Science and Technology** pg 3543

Aesthetics –See **The Arts -- Art** pg 335; see also Philosophy pg 4339

Africa –See **General Interest -- General Interest-Africa** pg 2497; **History(General) -- History of Africa** pg 2636

African Studies –See **History(General) -- History of Africa** pg 2636; **Literature** pg 3357

Aging –See **Medical Science and Technology -- Geriatrics** pg 3748; **Sociology -- Social Services and Welfare** pg 5269; see also Senior Citizens pg 5177

Agricultural Aviation –See **Aeronautics, Astronautics** pg 3; see also Agriculture pg 42

Agricultural Chemistry –See **Agriculture** pg 42; see also Chemistry pg 958

Agricultural Economics –See **Agriculture** pg 42; see also Economics pg 1459

Agricultural Engineering –See **Agriculture** pg 42; see also Engineering pg 1963

Agricultural Equipment –pg 157

Agricultural Marketing –See **Agriculture** pg 42; see also Business -- Marketing pg 920

Agricultural Meteorology –See **Earth Sciences -- Meteorology** pg 1419; see also Agriculture pg 42

Agriculture –pg 42; see also Food and Food Industry pg 2325; Gardening and Horticulture pg 2407

Agronomy –See **Agriculture** pg 42; see also Agriculture -- Crop Production and Soil pg 161

AIDS –See **Medical Science and Technology -- Allergy and Immunology** pg 3662; see also Medical Science and Technology -- Communicable Diseases pg 3711; Public Health and Safety pg 4763

Air Cargo –See **Transportation** pg 5375; see also Aeronautics, Astronautics pg 3

Air Conditioning –See **Heating, Plumbing, and Refrigeration** pg 2810

Air Force –See **Aeronautics, Astronautics** pg 3; **Military and Defense** pg 4033

Air Pollution –See **Environmental Issues -- Pollution and Waste Management** pg 2222

Air Travel –See **Aeronautics, Astronautics** pg 3; **Travel and Tourism** pg 5458

Airplanes –See **Aeronautics, Astronautics** pg 3

Airports –See **Aeronautics, Astronautics** pg 3

Alarm/Security Systems –See **Engineering -- Electricity, Electrical Engineering, Electronics** pg 2034

Alcoholic Beverages –See **Food and Food Industry -- Beverage Industry** pg 2363

Alcoholism –See **Drug Abuse and Alcoholism** pg 1338

Alimony –See **Law -- Family Law** pg 3119

Allergy and Immunology –pg 3662

Almanacs –See **Encyclopedias and General Reference Books** pg 1923

Alumni –pg 1096

Amateur Radio –See **Communication -- Broadcasting** pg 1125; see also Communication pg 1103

American Studies –See **History(General) -- History of North, South, and Central America** pg 2717

Amusements –See **Recreation, Leisure -- Games and Amusements** pg 4856

Analytic and Experimental Mechanics –pg 4427

Analytical Chemistry –pg 1012

Anarchism –See **Political Science -- Socialism, Communism, Anarchism, Utopianism** pg 4539

Anatomy –See **Medical Science and Technology -- Anatomy** pg 3543; see also Biology -- Embryology pg 541; Medical Science and Technology -- Pathology pg 3891

Anesthesia –See **Medical Science and Technology -- Anesthesiology** pg 3680; see also Medical Science and Technology -- Surgery pg 3957; Pharmacy and Pharmacology pg 4288

Anesthesiology –pg 3680; see also Medical Science and Technology -- Surgery pg 3957

Angiology –See **Medical Science and Technology -- Cardiology** pg 3697

Anglo-Saxon Studies –See **History(General) -- History of Europe** pg 2671; **Literature** pg 3357

Animal Husbandry –See **Agriculture** pg 42; **Veterinary Sciences** pg 5501

Animal Science –See **Veterinary Sciences** pg 5501; see also Zoology pg 5572

SUBJECT CROSS REFERENCES

Animal Welfare –pg 225; see also Ethics pg 2248

Animals –See **Horses and Horsemanship** pg 2796; **Pets** pg 4285; see also Veterinary Sciences pg 5501; Zoology pg 5572

Anthropology –pg 227; see also Archaeology pg 253; Paleontology pg 4226; Sociology pg 5237

Antibiotics –See **Medical Science and Technology** pg 3543; **Pharmacy and Pharmacology** pg 4288; see also Chemistry pg 958

Antiques –pg 248; see also Hobbies pg 2770; Museums and Galleries pg 4083

Antitrust Law –See **Law -- Corporate Law** pg 3094

Anxiety –See **Medical Science and Technology -- Psychiatry** pg 3918; see also Psychology pg 4570

Apartments –See **Housing and Urban Development** pg 2812

Apparel –See **Clothing Industry and Fashion** pg 1081; see also Business -- Retail pg 952; Textiles pg 5347

Appliances –See **Household Hardware and Appliances** pg 2810

Applied Mechanics –See **Engineering -- Materials Engineering and Mechanics** pg 2100; **Physics -- Analytic and Experimental Mechanics** pg 4427; see also Engineering -- Mechanical Engineering and Machinery pg 2108

Apprenticeship –See **Economics -- Labor** pg 1642

Aquaculture –See **Fish and Fisheries** pg 2293; see also Biology pg 439; Biology -- Marine Biology pg 552

Archaeology –pg 253; see also Anthropology pg 227; History(General) pg 2609; Paleontology pg 4226

Archery –See **Recreation, Leisure -- Sports** pg 4881

Architecture –pg 286; see also Building and Construction pg 597; Engineering pg 1963; Interior Design pg 2898

Archives –pg 2478; see also History(General) pg 2609; Library and Information Sciences pg 3186

Army –See **Military and Defense** pg 4033

Aromatherapy –See **Beauty and Cosmetics** pg 402

Art –pg 335; see also Humanities pg 2841

Art Galleries –See **Museums and Galleries** pg 4083; see also The Arts -- Art pg 335

Art History –See **The Arts -- Art** pg 335; see also Humanities pg 2841; Museums and Galleries pg 4083; The Arts pg 311

Arthritis –See **Medical Science and Technology -- Musculoskeletal System** pg 3802

Artificial Intelligence –pg 1210; see also Computers -- Automation pg 1217; Science and Technology pg 5078

Arts and Sciences –See **The Arts** pg 311; see also Humanities pg 2841; Social Sciences pg

Asbestos –See **Building and Construction** pg 597; **Engineering -- Mines and Mining Engineering** pg 2132; see also Public Health and Safety pg 4763

Asia –See **General Interest -- General Interest-Asia** pg 2501; **History(General) -- History of Asia** pg 2644

Asian Studies –See **History(General) -- History of Asia** pg 2644; **Literature** pg 3357

Associations –See **Societies and Clubs** pg 5228

Asthma –See **Medical Science and Technology -- Respiratory System** pg 3947

Astrology –pg 389

Astronautics –See **Aeronautics, Astronautics** pg 3

Astronomy –pg 391

Atheism –See **Philosophy** pg 4339

Athletic Clubs –See **Health and Personal Fitness** pg 2595; see also Recreation, Leisure -- Sports pg 4881

Athletics –See **Recreation, Leisure -- Sports** pg 4881; see also Health and Personal Fitness pg 2595

Atlas –See **Geography** pg 2553

Atmospheric Science –See **Earth Sciences -- Meteorology** pg 1419; see also Science and Technology pg 5078

Atomic Energy –See **Energy** pg 1930; **Engineering -- Nuclear Engineering** pg 2153

Attorney General –See **Law -- Judicial Systems** pg 3138

Audio-Visual Education –See **Education -- Teaching and Curriculum** pg 1887

Audiology –See **Medical Science and Technology -- Otorhinolaryngology** pg 3885

Auditing –See **Business -- Accounting** pg 735; see also Public Administration -- Public Finance and Taxation pg 4708

Audubon Society –See **Environmental Issues -- Conservation and Natural Resources** pg 2185; see also Natural History pg 4161

Australia –See **General Interest -- General Interest-Australia and Oceania** pg 2510; **History(General) -- History of Australia and Oceania** pg 2668

Authors –See **Biographies** pg 429; **Literature** pg 3357; see also Literature -- Poetry pg 3459; Publishing pg 4811

Automation –pg 1217

Automobile Racing –See **Recreation, Leisure -- Sports** pg 4881

Automobiles –pg 5403

Aviation –See **Aeronautics, Astronautics** pg 3

Bacteriology –See **Biology** pg 439; **Biology -- Microbiology** pg 558

Badminton –See **Recreation, Leisure -- Sports** pg 4881

Bahaism –See **Religion and Theology -- Islam, Bahaism, Theosophy** pg 5041

Bakers and Bakeries –See **Food and Food Industry** pg 2325

Balkan Studies –See **History(General) -- History of Europe** pg 2671

Banking –See **Business -- Banking and Finance** pg 768

Banking and Finance –pg 768; see also Business -- Cooperatives pg 1541; Business -- Investments pg 890; Economics pg 1459; Public Administration -- Public Finance pg 4708

Banking Law –pg 3084; see also Business -- Banking and Finance pg 768; Law -- Corporate Law pg 3094

Bankruptcy –See **Law -- Banking Law** pg 3084; see also Business -- Banking and Finance pg 768

Baptist –See **Religion and Theology -- Protestantism** pg 5054

Baseball –See **Recreation, Leisure -- Sports** pg 4881

Baseball Cards –See **Hobbies** pg 2770; **Recreation, Leisure -- Sports** pg 4881

Beauty and Cosmetics –pg 402

Beekeeping –See **Agriculture** pg 42

Behavior Therapy –See **Psychology** pg 4570

Behavioral Science –See **Medical Science and Technology -- Psychiatry** pg 3918; **Psychology** pg 4570; see also Sociology pg 5237

SUBJECT CROSS REFERENCES

Belizean Studies –See **History(General) -- History of North, South, and Central America** pg 2717

Beverage Industry –pg 2363

Bible –pg 5013

Bibliographies –pg 406; see also Library and Information Sciences pg 3186

Bicycles and Bicycling –pg 427

Bilingual –See **Education -- Special Education and Rehabilitation** pg 1874; **Linguistics** pg 3260; see also Education pg 1720

Biochemistry –pg 479

Bioengineering –See **Medical Science and Technology -- Biotechnology** pg 3685

Biofeedback –See **Psychology** pg 4570; see also Biology -- Physiology pg 577; Medical Science and Technology pg 3543

Biographies –pg 429

Biology –pg 439; see also Medical Science and Technology pg 3543; Zoology pg 5572

Biomechanics –See **Medical Science and Technology -- Biotechnology** pg 3685

Biomedical Engineering –See **Medical Science and Technology -- Biotechnology** pg 3685

Biomedicine –See **Medical Science and Technology -- Biotechnology** pg 3685

Biophysics –pg 494

Biotechnology –pg 3685

Birds –See **Zoology -- Ornithology** pg 5614; see also Environmental Issues -- Conservation and Natural Resources pg 2185; Natural History pg 4161

Birth Control –pg 587; see also Population Studies pg 4549

Blind –See **Physically Impaired** pg 4382; see also Education -- Special Education and Rehabilitation pg 1874; Medical Science and Technology -- Ophthalmology pg 3871; Sociology -- Social Services and Welfare pg 5269

Blood –See **Medical Science and Technology -- Hematology** pg 3769

Blood Groups –See **Medical Science and Technology -- Hematology** pg 3769

Blood Preservation –See **Medical Science and Technology -- Hematology** pg 3769

Blood Transfusions –See **Medical Science and Technology -- Hematology** pg 3769; see also Medical Science and Technology pg 3543; Medical Science and Technology -- Internal Medicine pg 3794; Medical Science and Technology -- Surgery pg 3957

Boats and Boating –pg 591

Bodybuilding –See **Health and Personal Fitness** pg 2595; see also Recreation, Leisure -- Sports pg 4881

Books and Bookmaking –pg 4822

Booksellers –See **Publishing -- Books and Bookmaking** pg 4822; see also Publishing pg 4811

Botany –pg 496; see also Agriculture -- Crop Production and Soil pg 161; Gardening and Horticulture pg 2407

Bowling –See **Recreation, Leisure -- Sports** pg 4881

Boxing –See **Recreation, Leisure -- Sports** pg 4881

Brahmanism –See **Hinduism** pg 5040

Braille –See **Physically Impaired** pg 4382; see also Education -- Special Education and Rehabilitation pg 1874

Breast-feeding –See **Medical Science and Technology -- Gynecology and Obstetrics** pg 3755; see also Medical Science and Technology -- Pediatrics pg 3899

Breweries –See **Food and Food Industry -- Beverage Industry** pg 2363

Bricks –See **Building and Construction** pg 597

Bride –See **Family and Marriage** pg 2276

Bridges –See **Transportation** pg 5375; see also Engineering -- Civil Engineering pg 2018; Transportation -- Roads and Traffic pg 5438

British Studies –See **History(General) -- History of Europe** pg 2671; **Literature** pg 3357

Broadcasting –pg 1125

Buddhism –pg 5020

Budget –See **Public Administration -- Public Finance and Taxation** pg 4708; see also Business -- Banking and Finance pg 768

Building and Construction –pg 597; see also Engineering -- Civil Engineering pg 2018; Housing and Urban Development pg 2812

Burns –See **Medical Science and Technology** pg 3543

Buses –See **Transportation** pg 5375

Business –pg 636

Business Education –See **Business** pg 636; see also Education pg 1720

Business Law –See **Business** pg 636; **Law -- Corporate Law** pg 3094; see also Law -- International Law pg 3122

Buying –See **Business -- Purchasing** pg 948

Cable Television –See **Communication -- Broadcasting** pg 1125

CAD/CAM –See **Computers -- Computer Graphics and Design** pg 1231; see also Computers -- Computer Engineering pg 1227

Calligraphy –See **The Arts -- Graphic Arts** pg 376

Cameras –See **Photography and Video** pg 4366; see also Hobbies pg 2770; Motion Picture pg 4062

Camping –See **Recreation, Leisure -- Outdoor Life** pg 4868

Canadian Studies –See **History(General) -- History of North, South, and Central America** pg 2717

Cancer –See **Medical Science and Technology -- Neoplasma, Neoplastic** pg 3808

Candy –See **Food and Food Industry** pg 2325

Canning and Preserving –See **Food and Food Industry** pg 2325; see also Gardening and Horticulture pg 2407

Canoeing –See **Boats and Boating** pg 591

Canon Law –See **Religion and Theology** pg 4931

Cardiology –pg 3697; see also Medical Science and Technology -- Hematology pg 3769

Careers –See **Occupations and Careers** pg 4201

Cargo –See **Transportation** pg 5375

Caribbean Studies –See **History(General) -- History of North, South, and Central America** pg 2717

Carpentry and Woodwork –pg 633; see also Hobbies pg 2770; Interior Design -- Home Furnishings pg 2904

Carpet, Rugs –See **Interior Design -- Home Furnishings** pg 2904

Cartography –pg 2580

Cartoons –See **The Arts -- Graphic Arts** pg 376; see also Recreation, Leisure -- Games and Amusements pg 4856

Catalogues –See **Bibliographies** pg 406

Catalysis –See **Chemistry -- Physical and Theoretical Chemistry** pg 1049

SUBJECT CROSS REFERENCES

Catalysts —See **Chemistry -- Physical and Theoretical Chemistry** pg 1049

Catering —See **Food and Food Industry** pg 2325; **Hotels/Motels** pg 2803; **Restaurants** pg 5070

Catholicism —pg 5022

Cattle —See **Agriculture -- Livestock and Poultry** pg 204; see also Agriculture pg 42; Agriculture -- Dairy Industry pg 191; Veterinary Sciences pg 5501

Caves —See **Earth Sciences -- Geophysics** pg 1402; see also Earth Sciences -- Geology pg 1364

CD-ROM —See **Computers -- Optical Storage, CD-ROM Applications** pg 1276

Celebrity Interests —See **General Interest** pg 2484; see also Motion Picture pg 4062

Celtic Studies —See **History(General) -- History of Europe** pg 2671; **Literature** pg 3357

Cement —See **Building and Construction** pg 597; **Chemistry -- Chemical Technology** pg 1020; see also Engineering -- Civil Engineering pg 2018; Industry and Production pg 1596

Cemeteries —See **Funeral Service** pg 2406

Central America —See **General Interest -- General Interest-Central America** pg 2511; **History(General) -- History of North, South, and Central America** pg 2717

Ceramics —See **Glass and Ceramics** pg 2585

Cereals —See **Agriculture -- Feed Grain and Milling** pg 199; see also Food and Food Industry pg 2325

Cerebral Palsy —See **Medical Science and Technology -- Neurology** pg 3825

Chamber of Commerce —pg 817

Charities —See **Philanthropy** pg 4334; see also Sociology -- Social Services and Welfare pg 5269

Chemical Engineering —pg 2007; see also Chemistry pg 958; Chemistry -- Chemical Technology pg 1020

Chemical Technology —pg 1020; see also Chemistry pg 958; Engineering -- Chemical Engineering pg 2007; Medical Science and Technology -- Biotechnology pg 3685

Chemistry —pg 958; see also Engineering -- Chemical Engineering pg 2007

Chemotherapy —See **Medical Science and Technology -- Neoplasma, Neoplastic** pg 3808; see also Pharmacy and Pharmacology pg 4288

Chess —See **Recreation, Leisure -- Games and Amusements** pg 4856

Child Development —See **Education -- Early Childhood and Primary Education** pg 1802

Child Psychology —See **Psychology** pg 4570

Child Welfare —See **Sociology -- Social Services and Welfare** pg 5269

Children and Youth Interests —pg 1059

China, Tableware —See **Glass and Ceramics** pg 2585; see also Gifts, Toys pg 2583

Chinese Studies —See **History(General) -- History of Asia** pg 2644; **Literature** pg 3357

Chiropractor —See **Medical Science and Technology -- Musculoskeletal System** pg 3802; **Physical Therapy** pg 4378

Christianity —See **Religion and Theology** pg 4931

Chromatography —See **Chemistry -- Analytical Chemistry** pg 1012; see also Chemistry pg 958

Churches —See **Religion and Theology** pg 4931; see also Religion and Theology -- Eastern Christian Churches pg 5039; Religion and Theology -- Protestantism pg 5054

Cinema —See **Motion Picture** pg 4062

Cinematography —See **Photography and Video** pg 4366; see also Motion Picture pg 4062

Citrus Industry —See **Agriculture -- Crop Production and Soil** pg 161; **Food and Food Industry** pg 2325; **Gardening and Horticulture** pg 2407

City Directory —See **Geography** pg 2553

City Planning —See **Housing and Urban Development** pg 2812

Civil Defense —pg 1072

Civil Engineering —pg 2018

Civil Law —pg 3088

Civil Rights —pg 4503

Civil Service —pg 4701; see also Public Administration pg 4623

Classical Studies —pg 1073; see also Archaeology pg 253; History(General) pg 2609; Linguistics pg 3260; Literature pg 3357

Climatology —See **Earth Sciences -- Meteorology** pg 1419

Clinical Medicine —See **Medical Science and Technology** pg 3543; **Medical Science and Technology** pg 3543

Clocks —See **Jewelry -- Clocks and Watches** pg 2916

Clocks and Watches —pg 2916

Clothing Industry and Fashion —pg 1081; see also Leather and Fur Industry pg 3183; Textiles pg 5347

Clubs —See **Societies and Clubs** pg 5228

Coaching —See **Recreation, Leisure -- Sports** pg 4881

Coal —See **Earth Science -- Mineralogy** pg 1437; see also Energy pg 1930; Engineering -- Mines and Mining Engineering pg 2132

Coast Guard —See **Naval Science, Navigation** pg 4174

Coins —See **Hobbies -- Numismatics** pg 2779

Collectors and Collecting —See **Antiques** pg 248; see also Hobbies pg 2770

College and School Publications —pg 1088; see also Education -- Higher Education pg 1806

Colleges and Universities —See **Education -- Higher Education** pg 1806; see also College and School Publications pg 1088

Combustion —See **Chemistry -- Physical and Theoretical Chemistry** pg 1049; **Energy** pg 1930; **Engineering** pg 1963

Comics —See **Recreation, Leisure -- Games and Amusements** pg 4856

Commerce —pg 821

Commercial Art —See **The Arts -- Graphic Arts** pg 376

Commercial Law —See **Law -- Corporate Law** pg 3094

Commodities —See **Business -- Commerce** pg 821

Common Law —See **Law -- Civil Law** pg 3088

Communicable Diseases —pg 3711; See also **Medical Science and Technology -- Epidemiology** pg 3733; Public Health and Safety pg 248

Communication —pg 1103

Communism —See **Political Science -- Socialism, Communism, Anarchism, Utopianism** pg 4539

Community Affairs —See **Public Administration** pg 4623

SUBJECT CROSS REFERENCES

Community Development –See **Housing and Urban Development** pg 2812

Compact Disc –See **Computers -- Optical Storage, CD-ROM Applications** pg 1276

Company Law –See **Law -- Corporate Law** pg 3094

Comparative Law –See **Law -- International Law** pg 3122

Composite Materials –See **Engineering -- Materials Engineering and Mechanics** pg 2100

Computer Architecture –See **Computers -- Computer Graphics and Design** pg 1231

Computer Assisted Instruction –pg 1222; see also Education -- Teaching and Curriculum pg 1887

Computer Crimes –See **Computers -- Computer Crimes and Security** pg 1225

Computer Crimes and Security –pg 1225

Computer Directories –See **Computers -- Computer Industry and Industry Directories** pg 1235

Computer Engineering –pg 1227

Computer Games – pg 1230; see also Recreation, Leisure -- Games and Amusements pg 4856

Computer Graphics and Design –pg 1231

Computer Industry –See **Computers -- Computer Industry and Industry Directories** pg 1235

Computer Industry and Industry Directories –pg 1235; see also Computers -- Computer Sales, Service and Supply pg 1244

Computer Music –pg 1240; see also Music pg 4098

Computer Networks –pg 1240

Computer Products –See **Computers -- Computer Sales, Service and Supply** pg 1244

Computer Sales, Service and Supply –pg 1244

Computer Science –See **Computers** pg 1169

Computer Simulation –See **Computers -- Simulation** pg 1282

Computer Systems –pg 1246

Computers –pg 1169

Confectioners –See **Food and Food Industry** pg 2325

Congress –See **Public Administration** pg 4623

Conservation and Natural Resources –pg 2185; see also Environmental Issues -- Ecology pg 2210; Natural History pg 4161; Public Administration -- Parks and Recreation pg 4705; Water Resources pg 5528

Constitutional Law –pg 3091

Construction –See **Building and Construction** pg 597; see also Engineering -- Civil Engineering pg 2018

Consumer Interests –pg 1293; see also Economics pg 1459

Consumer Protection –See **Consumer Interests** pg 1293; see also Law -- Corporate Law pg 3094

Contact Lenses –See **Medical Science and Technology -- Ophthalmology** pg 3871; **Optometry** pg 4214

Continuing Education –See **Education -- Adult and Continuing Education** pg 1799

Contraception –See **Birth Control** pg 587

Contractors –See **Building and Construction** pg 597; **Engineering -- Civil Engineering** pg 2018; see also Architecture pg 286

Conventions –See **Business -- Advertising and Public Relations** pg 753; **Science and Technology** pg 5078

Cookbooks, Cooking –See **Home Economics** pg 2788

Cooperatives –pg 1541; see also Agriculture pg 42; Business -- Banking and Finance pg 768

Copyright, Intellectual Property –pg 1300

Corporate Law –pg 3094

Corporation Law –See **Law -- Corporate Law** pg 3094

Corrosion –See **Engineering -- Chemical Engineering** pg 2007; see also Metals and Metallurgy pg 3996

Cosmetic Surgery –See **Medical Science and Technology -- Surgery** pg 3957

Cosmetics –See **Beauty and Cosmetics** pg 402

Cotton –See **Agriculture -- Crop Production and Soil** pg 161; see also Textiles pg 5347

Counseling –See **Psychology** pg 4570; see also Family and Marriage pg 2276; Religion and Theology pg 4931; Sociology -- Social Services and Welfare pg 5269

Court Rules –See **Law -- Judicial Systems** pg 3138

Courts –See **Law -- Judicial Systems** pg 3138

Crafts and Decorative Arts –pg 369; see also Gifts, Toys pg 2583; Glass and Ceramics pg 2585; Hobbies pg 2770; Sewing and Needlework pg 5182

Credit Unions –See **Business -- Banking and Finance** pg 768

Crime Prevention –See **Law -- Law Enforcement and Criminology** pg 3156

Crime Statistics –See **Law -- Law Enforcement and Criminology** pg 3156; see also Statistics pg 5320

Criminal Justice –See **Law -- Law Enforcement and Criminology** pg 3156; see also Law -- Criminal Law pg 3104

Criminal Law –pg 3104; see also Law -- Law Enforcement and Criminology pg 3156

Criminal Procedure –See **Law -- Judicial Systems** pg 3138; **Law -- Law Enforcement and Criminology** pg 3156; see also Law -- Criminal Law pg 3104

Criminology –See **Law -- Law Enforcement and Criminology** pg 3156

Croatian Studies –See **History(General) -- History of Europe** pg 2671

Crop Production and Soil –pg 161

Crystallography –pg 1031

Currency –See **Business -- Banking and Finance** pg 768; **Business -- Investments** pg 890; see also Economics -- International Economics pg 1632

Curriculum –See **Education -- Teaching and Curriculum** pg 1887

Customs –See **Sociology -- Manners and Customs** pg 5267

Customs and Excise –See **Public Administration -- Public Finance and Taxation** pg 4708; see also Law pg 2926

Cybernetics –pg 1250

Cystic Fibrosis –See **Medical Science and Technology -- Musculoskeletal System** pg 3802

Cytology –See **Biology -- Cytology and Histology** pg 531

Cytology and Histology –pg 531

Dairy Industry –pg 191

Dance –pg 1310; see also The Arts -- Performing Arts pg 383

Data Base Management –pg 1252

Data Processing –pg 1255

Data Protection –See **Computers -- Computer Crimes and Security** pg 1225

Daycare –See **Sociology -- Social Services and Welfare** pg 5269

SUBJECT CROSS REFERENCES

Deaf –See **Physically Impaired** pg 4382; see also Medical Science and Technology -- Otorhinolaryngology pg 3885

Decorative Arts –See **The Arts -- Crafts and Decorative Arts** pg 369

Defense –See **Military and Defense** pg 4033; see also Civil Defense pg 1072

Demography –See **Population Studies** pg 4549; see also Statistics pg 5320

Dentistry –pg 1314

Department Stores –See **Business -- Retail** pg 952; see also Business -- Marketing pg 920

Dermatology –pg 3717

Desktop Publishing –pg 1263; see also Publishing pg 4811

Diabetes –See **Endocrinology** pg 3726

Diagnostic Imaging –See **Medical Science and Technology -- Radiology** pg 3938

Dialysis –See **Medical Science and Technology -- Urology and Nephrology** pg 3987; see also Medical Science and Technology pg 3543; Medical Science and Technology -- Internal Medicine pg 3794

Dictionaries –See **Encyclopedias and General Reference Books** pg 1923

Dietetics –See **Nutrition and Dietetics** pg 4186

Directories –See **Encyclopedias and General Reference Books** pg 1923

Disarmament –See **Military and Defense** pg 4033; see also Law -- International Law pg 3122

Divorce –See **Family and Marriage** pg 2276; **Law -- Family Law** pg 3119

Doctrinal Theology –See **Religion and Theology** pg 4931

Dog Racing –See **Recreation, Leisure -- Sports** pg 4881

Domestic Relations –See **Law -- Family Law** pg 3119

Drama –See **Theater** pg 5361; see also The Arts -- Performing Arts pg 383

Drink –See **Food and Food Industry -- Beverage Industry** pg 2363

Drug Abuse and Alcoholism –pg 1338

Dyes and Dyeing –See **Chemistry -- Chemical Technology** pg 1020; **Textiles** pg 5347; see also The Arts -- Crafts and Decorative Arts pg 369

Early Childhood and Primary Education –pg 1802

Early Childhood Education –See **Education -- Early Childhood and Primary Education** pg 1802

Earth Sciences –pg 1351

Eastern Christian Churches –pg 5039

Ecology –pg 2210; see also Natural History pg 4161

Economic Conditions –See **Economics -- Economic History, Conditions** pg 1544

Economic History –See **Economics -- Economic History, Conditions** pg 1544

Economic History, Conditions –pg 1544

Economic Theory –pg 1589

Economics –pg 1459

Editing –See **Publishing** pg 4811; see also Journalism pg 2917; Literature pg 3357

Education –pg 1720

Educational Psychology –See **Education -- Teaching and Curriculum** pg 1887; **Psychology** pg 4570; see also Education pg 1720; Education -- Special Education and Rehabilitation pg 1874

Elections –See **Political Science** pg 4461; see also Public Administration pg 4623

Electric Power –See **Engineering -- Electricity, Electrical Engineering and Electronic** pg 2034

Electricity, Electrical Engineering, Electronics –pg 2034; see also Energy pg 1930; Heating, Plumbing and Refrigeration pg 2602; Public Administration -- Public Utilities pg 4759; Sound Recordings and Systems pg 5315

Electrochemistry –pg 1033; see also Chemistry -- Analytical Chemistry pg 1012; Chemistry -- Physical and Theoretical Chemistry pg 1049

Electronic Publishing –See **Desktop Publishing** pg 1263

Electronics –See **Engineering -- Electricity, Electrical Engineering, Electronics** pg 2034

Embroidery –See **Sewing and Needlework** pg 5182

Embryology –pg 541; see also Medical Science and Technology -- Anatomy pg 3678

Emergencies –See **Medical Science and Technology -- Emergency Medicine** pg 3723

Emergency Health Services –See **Medical Science and Technology -- Emergency Medicine** pg 3723

Emergency Medicine –pg 3723

Emigration and Immigration –pg 1918

Employment Law –See **Law -- Labor Law** pg 3143

Encyclopedias and General Reference Books –pg 1923

Endocrinology –pg 3726

Energy –pg 1930; see also Engineering -- Electricity, Electrical Engineering, Electronics pg 2034; Engineering -- Nuclear Engineering pg 2153; Petroleum and Natural Gas pg 4248; Physics -- Nuclear Physics pg 4445; Public Administration -- Public Utilities pg 4759

Engineering –pg 1963; see also Computers -- Artificial Intelligence pg 1210

Entomology –pg 5604

Environmental Health –See **Environmental Issues** pg 2159; see also Public Health and Safety pg 4763

Environmental Issues –pg 2159

Environmental Law –pg 3109; see also Environmental Issues pg 2159

Environmental Protection –See **Environmental Issues** pg 2159; see also Environmental Issues -- Pollution and Waste Management pg 2222

Environmental Studies –See **Environmental Issues** pg 2159; see also Environmental Issues -- Conservation and Natural Resources pg 2185; Environmental Issues -- Ecology pg 2210; Environmental Issues -- Pollution and Waste Management pg 2222

Environmental Technology –See **Environmental Issues** pg 2159; see also Science and Technology pg 5078

Environmental Waste Management –See **Environmental Issues** pg 2159

Enzymes –See **Biology -- Biochemistry** pg 479

Epidemiology –pg 3733; see also Medical Science and Technology -- Epidemiology pg 3711; Public Health and Safety pg 4763

Epilepsy –See **Medical Science and Technology -- Neurology** pg 3825

Episcopal –See **Religion and Theology -- Protestantism** pg 5054

Ergonomics –See **Engineering -- Mechanical Engineering and Machinery** pg 2108; see also Computers -- Cybernetics pg 1250

Esperanto –See **Linguistics** pg 3260; see also Education -- Teaching and Curriculum pg 1887

SUBJECT CROSS REFERENCES

Estate Planning –pg 3117; see also Business -- Banking and Finance pg 768; Business -- Investments pg 890

Ethics –pg 2248

Ethnic Interests –pg 2253

Ethnology –See **Anthropology** pg 227

Europe –See **General Interest-Europe** pg 2513; **History(General) -- History of Europe** pg 2671

European Studies –See **History(General) -- History of Europe** pg 2671; **Literature** pg 3357

Evangelism –See **Religion and Theology** pg 4931

Exceptional Children –See **Education -- Special Education and Rehabilitation** pg 1874

Exercise –See **Health and Personal Fitness** pg 2595

Exhibits/Exhibitions –See **Business -- Advertising and Public Relations** pg 753; **Science and Technology** pg 5078

Experimental Mechanics –See **Physics -- Analytic and Experimental Mechanics** pg 4427

Expert Systems –See **Computers -- Artificial Intelligence** pg 1210

Expositions –See **Business -- Advertising and Public Relations** pg 753; **Recreation, Leisure -- Games and Amusements** pg 4856; **Science and Technology** pg 5078

Fabric –See **Textiles** pg 5347; see also Clothing Industry and Fashion pg 1081; Sewing and Needlework pg 5182

Fairs –See **Recreation, Leisure -- Games and Amusements** pg 4856

Family and Marriage –pg 2276; see also Home Economics pg 2788

Family Law –pg 3119

Family Medicine –See **Medical Science and Technology -- Family Practice** pg 3736

Family Physicians –See **Medical Science and Technology -- Family Practice** pg 3736; see also Medical Science and Technology -- Physicians and Medical Personnel pg 3912

Family Planning –See **Birth Control** pg 587; **Family and Marriage** pg 2276

Family Practice –pg 3736

Fashion –See **Clothing Industry and Fashion** pg 1081

Federal Aid to Education –See **Education -- Higher Education** pg 1806; see also Education -- School Organization and Administration pg 1859

Federal Employees –See **Public Administration -- Civil Service** pg 4701

Federal Government –See **Public Administration** pg 4623; see also Political Science pg 4461

Feed Grain and Milling –pg 199

Feminism –See **Women's Interests** pg 5550

Fencing –See **Recreation, Leisure -- Sports** pg 4881

Fertility –See **Birth Control** pg 587; **Population Studies** pg 4549; see also Biology -- Physiology pg 577; Medical Science and Technology -- Gynecology and Obstetrics pg 3755

Fertilizers –See **Agriculture -- Crop Production and Soil** pg 161; **Chemistry -- Chemical Technology** pg 1020

Fiber Optics –See **Communication -- Telecommunications** pg 1148; **Physics -- Light, Optics, Radiation** pg 4432

Fiction –See **Literature** pg 3357; see also Literary and Political Reviews pg 3337

Films and Filmmaking –See **Motion Picture** pg 4062; see also Photography and Video pg 4366

Finance –See **Business -- Banking and Finance** pg 768; **Public Administration -- Public Finance and Taxation** pg 4708

Fire Prevention –pg 2287

Fish and Fisheries –pg 2293

Fishing –See **Fish and Fisheries** pg 2293

Floor Coverings –See **Building and Construction** pg 597; **Interior Design -- Home Furnishings** pg 2904

Florist Trade –pg 2434

Flowers –See **Gardening and Horticulture -- Florist Trade** pg 2434

Fluid Mechanics –See **Engineering -- Hydraulic Engineering** pg 2087; **Physics -- Analytic and Experimental Mechanics** pg 4427

Folk Music –See **Folklore** pg 2318; **Music** pg 4098

Folklore –pg 2318; see also History(General) pg 2609; Literature pg 3357; Sociology -- Manners and Customs pg 5267

Food and Food Industry –pg 2325; see also Agriculture pg 42; Home Economics pg 2788; Restaurants pg 5070

Food Production –See **Agriculture -- Crop Production and Soil** pg 3475; see also Food and Food Industry pg 2325

Football –See **Recreation, Leisure -- Sports** pg 4881

Footwear –See **Clothing Industry and Fashion** pg 1081; see also Leather and Fur Industry pg 3183

Foreign Affairs –See **International Relations** pg 4514; see also Law -- International Law pg 3122

Foreign Trade –See **Business -- Commerce** pg 821; see also Economics -- International Economics pg 1632

Forensic Medicine –See **Medical Science and Technology -- Forensic Medicine, Medical Jurisprudence** pg 3739

Forensic Medicine, Medical Jurisprudence –pg 3739

Forestry –pg 2373; see also Environmental Issues -- Conservation and Natural Resources pg 2185; Gardening and Horticulture pg 2407; Paper and Pulp Industry pg 4232

Franchises –See **Business** pg 636

Fraternities –See **Societies and Clubs** pg 5228

Freight –See **Transportation** pg 5375; see also Aeronautics, Astronautics pg 3; Business -- Commerce pg 821; Transportation - Ships and Shipping pg 5447; Transportation -- Railroads pg 5429

French Studies –See **History(General) History of Europe** pg 2671; **Literature** pg 3357

Frozen Foods –See **Food and Food Industry** pg 2325

Fruit –See **Agriculture -- Crop Production and Soil** pg 161; **Food and Food Industry** pg 2325; **Gardening and Horticulture** pg 2407

Fuel –See **Petroleum and Natural Gas** pg 4248; see also Energy pg 1930; Engineering -- Electricity, Electrical Engineering, Electronics pg 2034

Fund Raising –See **Philanthropy** pg 4334; see also Sociology -- Social Services and Welfare pg 5269

Funeral Service –pg 2406

Fungi –See **Biology -- Mycology** pg 574

Fur –See **Leather and Fur Industry** pg 3183

Furniture –See **Interior Design -- Home Furnishings** pg 2904; see also Antiques pg 248; Building and Construction -- Carpentry and Woodwork pg 633; Interior Design pg 2898

Galleries –See **Museums and Galleries** pg 4083

SUBJECT CROSS REFERENCES

Gambling –See **Recreation, Leisure -- Games and Amusements** pg 4856; see also Psychology pg 4570; Public Administration pg 4623

Games and Amusements –pg 4856; see also Children and Youth Interests pg 1059

Gardening and Horticulture –pg 2407

Gastroenterology –pg 3743

Gay/Lesbian –See **Homosexuality** pg 2793

Genealogy and Heraldry –pg 2436; see also History(General) pg 2609

General Interest –pg 2484

General Interest-Africa –pg 2497

General Interest-Asia –pg 2501

General Interest-Australia and Oceania –pg 2510

General Interest-Central America –pg 2511

General Interest-Europe –pg 2513

General Interest-Middle East –pg 2525

General Interest-North America –pg 2526

General Interest-South America –pg 2551

General Management –pg 858

General Management and Administration –See **Business -- General Management** pg 858

General Practice –See **Medical Science and Technology -- Family Practice** pg 3736

General Reference Books –See **Encyclopedias and General Reference Books** pg 1923

Genetic Engineering –See **Medical Science and Technology -- Biotechnology** pg 3685; see also Biology -- Genetics pg 541

Genetics –pg 541

Geochemistry –See **Chemistry** pg 958

Geodesy –See **Earth Sciences -- Geophysics** pg 1402; **Geography** pg 2553

Geography –pg 2553; see also Travel and Tourism pg 5458

Geology –pg 1364

Geophysics –pg 1402

Geriatrics –pg 3748; see also Senior Citizens pg 5177

Germanic Studies –See **History(General) -- History of Europe** pg 2671; **Literature** pg 3357

Gifted Children –See **Education -- Special Education and Rehabilitation** pg 1874

Gifts, Toys –pg 2583; see also Glass and Ceramics pg 2585; Recreation, Leisure -- Games and Amusements pg 4856; The Arts -- Crafts and Decorative Arts pg 369

Glass and Ceramics –pg 2585; see also The Arts -- Crafts and Decorative Arts pg 369

Golf –See **Recreation, Leisure -- Sports** pg 4881

Government –See **Public Administration** pg 4623; see also Political Science pg 4461

Government Employees –See **Public Administration -- Civil Service** pg 4701

Graphic Arts –pg 376; see also Printing Industry pg 4563

Grocery Trade –See **Food and Food Industry** pg 2325

Guns –See **Recreation, Leisure -- Sports** pg 4881; see also Military and Defense pg 4033

Gymnastics –See **Recreation, Leisure -- Sports** pg 4881

Gynecology and Obstetrics –pg 3755

Handicrafts –See **The Arts -- Crafts and Decorative Arts** pg 369

Hardware –pg 1264; **Household Hardware and Appliances** pg 2810; see also Building and Construction pg 597

Hazardous Waste –See **Environmental Issues -- Pollution and Waste Management** pg 2222; see also Environmental Issues pg 2159

Health and Personal Fitness –pg 2595; see also Physical Education and Training pg 1854; Recreation, Leisure -- Sports pg 4881

Hearing Disorders –See **Medical Science and Technology -- Otorhinolaryngology** pg 3885; **Physically Impaired** pg 4382

Heat –pg 4430

Heating, Plumbing, and Refrigeration –pg 2602; see also Electricity, Electrical Engineering, Electronics pg 2034; Household Hardware and Appliances pg 2810

Helicopters –See **Aeronautics, Astronautics** pg 3

Helminthology –See **Zoology** pg 5572

Hematologic Diseases –See **Medical Science and Technology -- Hematology** pg 3769

Hematology –pg 3769; see also Biology -- Physiology pg 577; Medical Science and Technology -- Cardiology pg 3697; Medical Science and Technology -- Internal Medicine pg 3794

Hemodialysis –See **Medical Science and Technology -- Hematology** pg 3769

Heraldry –See **Genealogy and Heraldry** pg 2436

Herbs and Spices –See **Food and Food Industry** pg 2325; see also Gardening and Horticulture pg 2407

Heredity –See **Biology -- Genetics** pg 541

Higher Education –pg 1806

Hinduism –pg 5040

Histology –See **Biology -- Cytology and Histology** pg 531

History of Africa –pg 2636

History of Asia –pg 2644

History of Australia and Oceania –pg 2668

History of Europe –pg 2671

History of North, South, and Central America –pg 2717

History of the Middle East –pg 2767

History(General) –pg 2609

Hobbies –pg 2770; see also Recreation, Leisure -- Sports pg 4881; Sewing and Needlework pg 5182; The Arts -- Crafts and Decorative Arts pg 369

Hockey –See **Recreation, Leisure -- Sports** pg 4881

Home and Gardening Publications –See **Gardening and Horticulture** pg 2407

Home Computing –See **Computers -- Microcomputers, Personal Computers** pg 1265

Home Economics –pg 2788; see also Family and Marriage pg 2276

Home Furnishings –pg 2904; see also Building and Construction -- Carpentry and Woodwork pg 633; Interior Design pg 2898

Homeopathy –pg 3774

Homosexuality –pg 2793

Hormones –See **Endocrinology** pg 3726; see also Biology -- Biochemistry pg 479; Biology -- Physiology pg 577

Horse Racing –See **Horses and Horsemanship** pg 2796; see also Recreation, Leisure -- Sports pg 4881

Horses and Horsemanship –pg 2796; see also Recreation, Leisure -- Sports pg 4881

Horticulture –See **Gardening and Horticulture** pg 2407; see also Agriculture -- Crop Production and Soil pg 161; Biology -- Botany pg 496; Forestry pg 2373

SUBJECT CROSS REFERENCES

Hospital Administration –See **Medical Science and Technology -- Hospital Administration and Medical Centers** pg 3775

Hospital Administration and Medical Centers –pg 3775

Hospitals –See **Medical Science and Technology -- Hospital Administration and Medical Centers** pg 3775

Hotels/Motels –pg 2803; see also Travel and Tourism pg 5458; see also Restaurants pg 5070

Household Hardware and Appliances –pg 2810; see also Electricity, Electrical Engineering, Electronics pg 2034; Heating, Plumbing, and Refrigeration pg 2602

Housing and Urban Development –pg 2812; see also Building and Construction pg 597; Real Estate pg 4833

Human Sexuality –See **Sexual Life** pg 5186

Humane Society –See **Animal Welfare** pg 225

Humanities –pg 2841; see also Social Sciences pg 5189; The Arts pg 311

Hunting –See **Recreation, Leisure -- Outdoor Life** pg 4868

Hydraulic Engineering –pg 2087; see also Earth Sciences -- Hydrology pg 1412; Energy pg 1930; Water Resources pg 5528

Hydrobiology –See **Biology -- Marine Biology** pg 552; see also Earth Sciences -- Oceanography pg 1445

Hydrology –pg 1412; see also Engineering -- Hydraulic Engineering pg 2087; Water Resources pg 5528

Hygiene –See **Industrial Health and Safety** pg 2858; **Public Health and Safety** pg 4763

Hypertension –See **Medical Science and Technology -- Cardiology** pg 3697; see also Medical Science and Technology -- Internal Medicine pg 3794

Hypnosis –pg 2857

Immigration –See **Emigration and Immigration** pg 1918

Immunology –See **Medical Science and Technology -- Allergy and Immunology** pg 3662

Imports/Exports –See **Business -- Commerce** pg 821

Income Tax –See **Public Administration -- Public Finance and Taxation** pg 4708; see also Business -- Accounting pg 735

Industrial Arts –See **Education -- Vocational Education** pg 1909; see also Science and Technology pg 5078

Industrial Design –See **Engineering -- Industrial Engineering and Design** pg 2096; see also Manufacturing pg 3475

Industrial Engineering and Design –pg 2096

Industrial Health and Safety –pg 2858

Industrial Medicine –See **Industrial Health and Safety** pg 2858

Industry –See **Economics -- Industry and Production** pg 1596

Industry and Production –pg 1596

Infectious Diseases –See **Medical Science and Technology -- Communicable Diseases** pg 3711; see also Medical Science and Technology -- Epidemiology pg 3733; Public Health and Safety pg 4763

Information Retrieval –See **Library and Information Sciences** pg 3186

Information Science –See **Library and Information Sciences** pg 3186

Inheritance –See **Law -- Estate Planning** pg 3117

Inorganic Chemistry –pg 1035

Insecticide –See **Pest Control** pg 4243

Insects –See **Zoology -- Entomology** pg 5604; see also Pest Control pg 4243

Insulation –See **Building and Construction** pg 597; see also Engineering -- Electricity, Electrical Engineering, Electronics pg 2034

Insurance –pg 2872

Insurance Law –See **Insurance** pg 2872; **Law -- Corporate Law** pg 3094

Integrated Circuits –See **Engineering -- Electricity, Electrical Engineering, Electronics** pg 2034

Intellectual Property –See **Copyright, Intellectual Property** pg 1300

Intensive Care –See **Medical Science and Technology** pg 3543; see also Medical Science and Technology -- Nursing pg 3849

Interior Design –pg 2898; see also Architecture pg 286

Internal Medicine –pg 3794

International Assistance and Development –pg 2907; see also Economics -- International Economics pg 1632; Sociology -- Social Services and Welfare pg 5269

International Economics –pg 1632

International Law –pg 3122; see also Political Science -- International Relations pg 4514

International Relations –pg 4514; see also History(General) pg 2609; Law -- International Law pg 3122; Military and Defense pg 4033

Invertebrates/Vertebrates –See **Zoology** pg 5572

Investing –See **Business -- Investments** pg 890

Investments –pg 890; see also Business -- Banking and Finance pg 768

Irish Slavonic Studies –See **History(General) -- History of Europe** pg 2671; **Literature** pg 3357

Irish Studies –See **History(General) -- History of Europe** pg 2671; **Literature** pg 3357

Irrigation –See **Engineering -- Hydraulic Engineering** pg 2087; see also Agriculture -- Crop Production and Soil pg 161

Islam –See **Religion and Theology -- Islam, Bahaism, Theosophy** pg 5041

Islam, Bahaism, Theosophy –pg 5041

Jails –See **Law -- Law Enforcement and Criminology** pg 3156

Jewelry –pg 2913

Journalism –pg 2917; see also Communication -- Broadcasting pg 1125; Publishing pg 4811

Judaism –pg 5045; see also Ethnic Interests pg 2253

Judges –See **Law -- Judicial Systems** pg 3138

Judicial Ethics –See **Law -- Judicial Systems** pg 3138

Judicial Statistics –See **Law -- Judicial Systems** pg 3138

Judicial Systems –pg 3138

Judo/Karate –See **Recreation, Leisure -- Sports** pg 4881; see also Health and Personal Fitness pg 2595

Juvenile Delinquency –See **Law -- Law Enforcement and Criminology** pg 3156; see also Sociology -- Social Services and Welfare pg 5269

Kidneys –See **Medical Science and Technology -- Urology and Nephrology** pg 3987

Kindergarten –See **Education -- Early Childhood and Primary Education** pg 1802

Knitting –See **Sewing and Needlework** pg 5182; see also Textiles pg 5347

SUBJECT CROSS REFERENCES

Korean Studies —See **History(General) -- History of Asia** pg 2644; see also Literature pg 3357

Labels/Labelling —See **Packaging** pg 4217

Labor —pg 1642; see also Business -- Personnel Management pg 938; Industrial Health and Safety pg 2858

Labor Law —pg 3143; see also Law pg 2926; see also Economics -- Labor pg 1642

Labor Unions —See **Economics -- Labor** pg 1642

LAN (Local Area Networks) —See **Computers -- Computer Networks** pg 1240

Land —See **Economics** pg 1459; **Environmental Issues -- Conservation and Natural Resources** pg 2185; **Public Administration** pg 4623; **Real Estate** pg 4833; see also Geography pg 2553

Landscape Architecture —See **Gardening and Horticulture** pg 2407

Language —See **Linguistics** pg 3260

Lasers —See **Physics -- Light, Optics, Radiation** pg 4432; see also Chemistry pg 958; Engineering pg 1963; Medical Science and Technology -- Surgery pg 3957; Physics pg 4395

Latin American Studies —See **History(General) -- History of North, South, and Central America** pg 2717; see also Literature pg 3357

Laundry —See **Chemistry -- Chemical Technology** pg 1020; see also Textiles pg 5347

Law —pg 2926; see also Public Administration pg 4623

Law Enforcement —See **Law -- Law Enforcement and Criminology** pg 2926

Law Enforcement and Criminology —pg 3156

Law Offices —See **Law** pg 2926; see also Business -- General Management pg 858

Learning Disabilities —See **Education -- Special Education and Rehabilitation** pg 1874

Leather and Fur Industry —pg 3183; see also Clothing Industry and Fashion pg 1081

Legal Aid —pg 3179

Legislation —See **Law** pg 2926; see also Public Administration pg 4623

Leisure —See **Recreation, Leisure** pg 4848

Leukemia —See **Medical Science and Technology -- Neoplasma, Neoplastic** pg 3808; see also Medical Science and Technology -- Internal Medicine pg 3794

Library and Information Sciences —pg 3186; see also Archives pg 2478; Bibliographies pg 406

Life/Death —See **Philosophy** pg 4339

Light, Optics, Radiation —pg 4432

Linguistics —pg 3260; see also Literature pg 3357

Liquor —See **Food and Food Industry -- Beverage Industry** pg 2363

Literacy —See **Education -- Special Education and Rehabilitation** pg 1874

Literary and Political Reviews —pg 3337; see also Literature pg 3357

Literary Criticism —See **Literary and Political Reviews** pg 3337

Literary Theory —See **Literary and Political Reviews** pg 3337

Literature —pg 3357; see also Linguistics pg 3260; Literary and Political Reviews pg 3337; Romance and Adventure pg 5073

Livestock and Poultry —pg 204

Local Area Networks —See **Computers -- Computer Networks** pg 1240

Local Government —See **Political Science** pg 4461; **Public Administration** pg 4623; **Public Administration** pg 4708

Lotteries —See **Public Administration** pg 4623

Lumber and Wood —pg 2399; see also Paper and Pulp Industry pg 4232

Lutheran —See **Religion and Theology -- Protestantism** pg 5054

Machinery —See **Engineering -- Mechanical Engineering and Machinery** pg 2108

Macroeconomics —See **Economics -- Economic Theory** pg 1589; see also Economics pg 1459; Economics -- International Economics pg 1632

Magic —See **Recreation, Leisure -- Games and Amusements** pg 4856; see also Parapsychology and Occultism pg 4240

Magnetic Resonance Imaging —See **Medical Science and Technology -- Radiology** pg 3938

Magnetism —pg 4443

Mainframe Computing —See **Computers -- Data Processing** pg 1255

Manners and Customs —pg 5267

Manufacturing —pg 3475; see also Industry and Production pg 1596

Maps and Mapmaking —See **Geography -- Cartography** pg 2580

Marine Biology —pg 552; see also Earth Sciences -- Oceanography pg 1445; Zoology pg 5572

Marine Engineering —See **Engineering** pg 1963

Marine Pollution —See **Environmental Issues -- Pollution and Waste Management** pg 2222

Marine Toxins —See **Biology -- Marine Biology** pg 552

Marines —See **Naval Science, Navigation** pg 4174

Maritime Law —pg 3180

Marketing —pg 920

Marriage —See **Family and Marriage** pg 2276

Marriage Law —See **Law -- Family Law** pg 3119

Martial Arts —See **Health and Personal Fitness** pg 2595

Marxism —See **Political Science -- Socialism, Communism, Anarchism, Utopianism** pg 4539; see also Sociology pg 5237

Masonry —See **Building and Construction** pg 597

Materials Engineering and Mechanics —pg 2100

Mathematical Geography —See **Geography** pg 2553

Mathematics —pg 3490

Matrimonial Actions —See **Law -- Family Law** pg 3119

Meat —See **Food and Food Industry** pg 2325; see also Agriculture -- Livestock and Poultry pg 204

Mechanical Engineering and Machinery —pg 2108

Media —See **Communication** pg 1103; see also Journalism pg 2917

Medical Centers —See **Medical Science and Technology -- Hospital Administration and Medical Centers** pg 3775

Medical Jurisprudence —See **Medical Science and Technology -- Forensic Medicine, Medical Jurisprudence** pg 3739

Medical Malpractice —See **Law** pg 2926; see also Medical Science and Technology pg 3543

Medical Personnel —See **Medical Science and Technology -- Physicians and Medical Personnel** pg 3912

Medical Science and Technology —pg 3543; see also Public Health and Safety pg 4763

xxx

SUBJECT CROSS REFERENCES

Medieval Studies –See **History(General) -- History of Europe** pg 2671; see also Classical Studies pg 1073

Meetings –See **Business** pg 636

Memory –See **Psychology** pg 4570

Men's Interests –pg 3994

Mental Health –See **Medical Science and Technology -- Psychiatry** pg 3918; **Psychology** pg 4570; **Public Health and Safety** pg 4763; **Sociology -- Social Services and Welfare** pg 5269

Mentally Disabled –See **Education -- Special Education and Rehabilitation** pg 1874; see also Medical Science and Technology -- Psychiatry pg 3918; Psychology pg 4570

Mergers/Acquisitions –See **Business** pg 636

Metabolic Diseases –See **Medical Science and Technology -- Allergy and Immunology** pg 3662

Metallurgy –See **Metals and Metallurgy** pg 3996

Metals and Metallurgy –pg 3996; see also Mines and Mining Engineering pg 2132

Meteorology –pg 1419

Methodist –See **Religion and Theology -- Protestantism** pg 5054

Metrology and Standardization –pg 4029

Microbiology –pg 558

Microcomputers –See **Computers -- Microcomputers, Personal Computers** pg 1265

Microcomputers, Personal Computers –pg 1265

Microscopy –pg 572

Midwifery –See **Medical Science and Technology -- Gynecology and Obstetrics** pg 3755

Migration –See **Emigration and Immigration** pg 1918; **Population Studies** pg 4549; see also Economics -- Labor pg 1642; Zoology pg 5572

Military Administration –See **Military and Defense** pg 4033

Military and Defense –pg 4033; see also Political Science -- International Relations pg 4514

Military History –See **Military and Defense** pg 4033

Military Law –pg 3182

Military Medicine –See **Medical Science and Technology** pg 3543; see also Military and Defense pg 4033

Milling –See **Agriculture -- Feed Grain and Milling** pg 199

Mineralogy –pg 1437

Mines and Mining Engineering –pg 2132; see also Earth Sciences -- Mineralogy pg 1437; Metals and Metallurgy pg 4026; Petroleum and Natural Gas pg 4248

Minicomputers –pg 1273; see also Computers -- Microcomputers, Personal Computers pg 1265

Mobile Homes –See **Building and Construction** pg 597; **Housing and Urban Development** pg 2812; **Transportation** pg 5375

Money –See **Business -- Banking and Finance** pg 768; **Economics** pg 1459

Monuments –See **History(General)** pg 2609; see also Architecture pg 286; The Arts -- Art pg 335

Mormons –See **Religion and Theology** pg 4931

Morphology –See **Biology -- Botany** pg 496

Motels –See **Hotels/Motels** pg 2803

Motion Picture –pg 4062

Motorcycles –pg 4080

Mountain Climbing –See **Recreation, Leisure -- Outdoor Life** pg 4868; see also Recreation, Leisure -- Sports pg 4881

Movies –See **Motion Picture** pg 4062

Multiple Sclerosis –See **Medical Science and Technology -- Neurology** pg 3825

Muscular Dystrophy –See **Medical Science and Technology -- Musculoskeletal System** pg 3802; see also Medical Science and Technology -- Neurology pg 3825

Musculoskeletal System –pg 3802

Museums and Galleries –pg 4083; see also Natural History pg 4161; The Arts -- Art pg 335

Music –pg 4098; see also Computers -- Computer Music pg 1240; Sound Recordings and Systems pg 5315; The Arts -- Performing Arts pg 383

Music Therapy –See **Medical Science and Technology** pg 3543; **Music** pg 4098; see also Psychology pg 4570

Mutual Funds –See **Business -- Investments** pg 890; see also Business -- Banking and Finance pg 768

Mycology –pg 574; see also Biology -- Botany pg 496

Mysticism –See **Parapsychology and Occultism** pg 4240; see also Literature pg 3357; Religion and Theology pg 4931

Mythology –See **Folklore** pg 2318

Narcotics –See **Drug Abuse and Alcoholism** pg 1338; see also Law -- Law Enforcement and Criminology pg 3156; Pharmacy and Pharmacology pg 4288

Natural Gas –See **Petroleum and Natural Gas** pg 4248

Natural History –pg 4161; see also Biology pg 4570; Environmental Issues -- Conservation and Natural Resources pg 2185; Environmental Issues -- Ecology pg 2185

Natural Resources –See **Environmental Issues -- Conservation and Natural Resources** pg 2185

Naturalist –See **Natural History** pg 4161; see also Environmental Issues -- Ecology pg 2210

Naval Architecture –See **Architecture** pg 286; **Naval Science and Navigation** pg 4174

Naval Science, Navigation –pg 4174; see also Transportation -- Ships and Shipping pg 5447

Navigation –See **Naval Science, Navigation** pg 4174

Navy –See **Naval Science, Navigation** pg 4174

Needlework –See **Sewing and Needlework** pg 5182

Neoplasma –See **Medical Science and Technology -- Neoplasma, Neoplastic** pg 3808

Neoplasma, Neoplastic –pg 3808; see also Medical Science and Technology -- Radiology pg 3938

Neoplastic –See **Medical Science and Technology -- Neoplasma, Neoplastic** pg 3808

Nephrology –See **Medical Science and Technology -- Urology and Nephrology** pg 3987

Neural Networks –See **Computers -- Artificial Intelligence** pg 1210

Neurology –pg 3825; see also Medical Science and Technology -- Psychiatry pg 3918; Psychology pg 4570

New Age Publications –pg 4185

Newspapers –pg 5625

Noise Control –See **Environmental Issues** pg 2159

North America –See **General Interest -- General Interest-North America** pg 2526; **History(General) -- History of North, South, and Central America** pg 2717

Nuclear Engineering –pg 2153

Nuclear Medicine –See **Medical Science and Technology -- Internal Medicine** pg 3794; Medical Science and Technology -- Radiology pg 3938

SUBJECT CROSS REFERENCES

Nuclear Physics –pg 4445

Nuclear Waste –See **Environmental Issues -- Pollution and Waste Management** pg 2222

Numismatics –pg 2779

Nursing –pg 3849; see also Medical Science and Technology -- Surgery pg 3849

Nursing Homes –See **Medical Science and Technology -- Hospital Administration and Medical Centers** pg 3775; see also Sociology -- Social Services and Welfare pg 5269

Nutrition and Dietetics –pg 4186; see also Food and Food Industry pg 2325

Nutritional Disorders –See **Nutrition and Dietetics** pg 4186

Obstetrics –See **Medical Science and Technology -- Gynecology and Obstetrics** pg 3755

Occultism –See **Parapsychology and Occultism** pg 4240

Occupational Health –See **Industrial Health and Safety** pg 2858

Occupational Therapy –See **Industrial Health and Safety** pg 2858; see also Education -- Special Education and Rehabilitation pg 1874; Medical Science and Technology -- Psychiatry pg 3918

Occupations and Careers –pg 4201; see also Economics -- Labor pg 1642; Education -- Special Aspects of Education pg 1874

Ocean Engineering –See **Engineering -- Hydraulic Engineering** pg 2087; see also Earth Sciences -- Oceanography pg 1445

Oceania –See **General Interest -- General Interest-Australia and Oceania** pg 2510; see also History(General) -- History of Australia and Oceania pg 2668

Oceanography –pg 1445

Office Equipment and Services –pg 4210; see also Computers pg 1169

Oil –See **Petroleum and Natural Gas** pg 4248

Oncology –See **Medical Science and Technology -- Neoplasma, Neoplastic** pg 3808

Online Computing and Information –pg 1274

Opera –See **The Arts -- Performing Arts** pg 383; see also Music pg 4098

Ophthalmology –pg 3871

Optical Storage, CD-ROM Applications –pg 1276

Optics –See **Physics -- Light, Optics, Radiation** pg 4432

Optometry –pg 4214

Oral Surgery –See **Medical Science and Technology -- Surgery** pg 3957; see also Dentistry pg 1314

Organic Chemistry –pg 1038

Oriental Studies –See **History(General) -- History of Asia** pg 2644; see also Literature pg 3357

Ornithology –pg 5614; see also Natural History pg 4161

Orthodontics –See **Dentistry** pg 1314

Orthopedics –pg 3880

Otorhinolaryngology –pg 3885

Outdoor Life –pg 4868; see also Environmental Issues -- Conservation and Natural Resources pg 2185; Fish and Fisheries pg 2293; Recreation, Leisure -- Sports pg 4881

Pacific Studies –See **History(General) -- History of Australia and Oceania** pg 2671; see also Literature pg 3357

Packaging –pg 4217

Pain –See **Medical Science and Technology -- Neurology** pg 3825

Paints and Painting –pg 4222

Paleontology –pg 4226

Paper and Pulp Industry –pg 4232

Parachuting –See **Recreation, Leisure -- Sports** pg 4881

Paramedics –See **Medical Science and Technology -- Emergency Medicine** pg 3723

Parapsychology and Occultism –pg 4240

Parenting –See **Family and Marriage** pg 2276

Parks –See **Environmental Issues -- Conservation and Natural Resources** pg 2185; Recreation, Leisure pg 4848

Parks and Recreation –pg 4705; see also Environmental Issues -- Conservation and Natural Resources pg 2185

Parliament/House of Commons –See **Public Administration** pg 4623; see also Political Science pg 4461

Patents –See **Copyright, Intellectual Property** pg 1300

Pathology –pg 3891; see also Medical Science and Technology -- Anatomy pg 3678

Pediatric Surgery –See **Medical Science and Technology -- Pediatrics** pg 3899; see also Medical Science and Technology -- Surgery pg 3957

Pediatrics –pg 3899

Penology –See **Law -- Law Enforcement and Criminology** pg 3156

Pensions –See **Business -- Investments** pg 890; see also Economics -- Labor pg 1642; Insurance pg 2872

Performing Arts –pg 383; see also Motion Picture pg 4062; Music pg 4098; The Arts -- Dance pg 1310; Theater pg 5361

Perfumes –See **Beauty and Cosmetics** pg 402; see also Chemistry -- Chemical Technology pg 1020

Perinatology –See **Medical Science and Technology -- Gynecology and Obstetrics** pg 3755; see also Medical Science and Technology -- Pediatrics pg 3899

Personal Computers –See **Computers -- Microcomputers, Personal Computers** pg 1265

Personal Hygiene –See **Health and Personal Fitness** pg 2595

Personnel Management –pg 938; see also Economics -- Labor pg 1642

Pest Control –pg 4243

Petroleum and Natural Gas –pg 4248; see also Energy pg 1930; Engineering -- Mines and Mining Engineering pg 2132

Petrology –pg 1458

Pets –pg 4285

Pharmaceutical Industry –See **Pharmacy and Pharmacology** pg 4288

Pharmacy and Pharmacology –pg 4288; see also Medical Science and Technology -- Toxicology pg 3978

Philanthropy –pg 4334; see also Sociology -- Social Services and Welfare pg 5269

Philately –pg 2784

Philology –See **Linguistics** pg 3260; see also Classical Studies pg 1073

Philosophy –pg 4339

Phonetics –See **Linguistics** pg 3260

Photography and Video –pg 4366

Physical and Theoretical Chemistry –pg 1049

Physical Education –See **Education -- Physical Education and Training** pg 2595; **Education -- Physical Education and Training** pg 1854; see also Health and Personal Fitness pg 2595

Physical Education and Training –pg 1854

Physical Fitness –See **Health and Personal Fitness** pg 2595

Physical Therapy –pg 4378

Physical Training –See **Education -- Physical Education and Training** pg 1854

SUBJECT CROSS REFERENCES

Physically Impaired –pg 4382; see also Education -- Special Education and Rehabilitation pg 1874; Sociology -- Social Services and Welfare pg 5269

Physician's Assistants –See **Medical Science and Technology -- Physicians and Medical Personnel** pg 3912

Physicians –See **Medical Science and Technology -- Physicians and Medical Personnel** pg 3912; see also Medical Science and Technology -- Family Practice pg 3736

Physicians and Medical Personnel –pg 3912

Physics –pg 4395

Physiology –pg 577

Phytopathology –See **Biology -- Botany** pg 496; **Gardening and Horticulture** pg 2407

Planned Parenthood –See **Birth Control** pg 587; see also Family and Marriage pg 2276

Plant Breeding –See **Biology -- Botany** pg 496; see also Agriculture -- Crop Production and Soil pg 161; Gardening and Horticulture pg 2407

Plant Culture –See **Gardening and Horticulture** pg 2407

Plastic Surgery –See **Medical Science and Technology -- Surgery** pg 3957

Plastics –pg 4453; see also Engineering -- Materials Engineering and Mechanics pg 2100

Plays –See **Literature** pg 3357; **The Arts -- Performing Arts** pg 383; **Theater** pg 5361

Plumbing –See **Heating, Plumbing, and Refrigeration** pg 2602

Podiatry –pg 3917

Poetry –pg 3459; see also Literary and Political Reviews pg 3337

Political Reviews –See **Literary and Political Reviews** pg 3337

Political Science –pg 4461; see also Military and Defense pg 4033; Public Administration pg 4623

Polling –See **Public Administration** pg 4623; see also Sociology pg 5237; Statistics pg 5320

Pollution and Waste Management –pg 2222; see also Earth Sciences -- Ecology pg 2210; Environmental Issues -- Ecology pg 2210

Polymers –See **Chemistry -- Organic Chemistry** pg 1038; see also Paints and Painting pg 4222; Plastics pg 4453

Population Studies –pg 4549; see also Birth Control pg 587; Statistics pg 5320

Portable Computers –See **Computers -- Microcomputers, Personal Computers** pg 1265

Postage Stamps –See **Hobbies -- Philately** pg 2784

Postal Communications –pg 1144; see also Public Administration -- Civil Service pg 4701

Pottery –See **Glass and Ceramics** pg 2585

Poultry –See **Agriculture -- Livestock and Poultry** pg 204

Poverty –See **Sociology -- Social Services and Welfare** pg 5269; see also International Assistance and Development pg 2907

Power –See **Engineering -- Electricity, Electrical Engineering, Electronics** pg 2034

Powerlifting –See **Health and Personal Fitness** pg 2595; see also Recreation, Leisure -- Sports pg 4881

Practical Theology –See **Religion and Theology** pg 4931

Presbyterian –See **Religion and Theology -- Protestantism** pg 5054

Preschool Education –See **Education -- Early Childhood and Primary Education** pg 1802

Preventive Medicine –See **Medical Science and Technology** pg 3543; see also Public Health and Safety pg 4763

Primary Care –See **Medical Science and Technology -- Family Practice** pg 3736

Primary Education –See **Education -- Early Childhood and Primary Education** pg 1802

Printing Industry –pg 4563; see also The Arts -- Graphic Arts pg 376

Prisons –See **Law -- Law Enforcement and Criminology** pg 3156

Private Schools –See **Education** pg 1720

Probation –See **Law -- Law Enforcement and Criminology** pg 3156

Production –See **Economics -- Industry and Production** pg 1596

Programs and Programming –pg 1277; see also Computers -- Software pg 1283

Protestantism –pg 5054

Psychiatry –pg 3918; see also Medical Science and Technology -- Neurology pg 3825; Psychology pg 4570

Psychoanalysis –See **Medical Science and Technology -- Psychiatry** pg 3918; **Psychology** pg 4570

Psychology –pg 4570; see also Medical Science and Technology -- Psychiatry pg 3918; Sociology pg 5237

Psychopathology –See **Medical Science and Technology -- Psychiatry** pg 3918

Psychosomatic Medicine –See **Medical Science and Technology** pg 3543; **Psychology** pg 4570

Psychotherapy –See **Medical Science and Technology -- Psychiatry** pg 3918; see also Family and Marriage pg 2276; Psychology pg 4570

PTA –See **Education -- School Organization and Administration** pg 1859

Public Administration –pg 4623; see also Political Science pg 4461

Public Affairs –See **Public Administration** pg 4623

Public Finance and Taxation –pg 4708; see also Law pg 2926

Public Health and Safety –pg 4763; see also Environmental Issues -- Pollution and Waste Management pg 2222; Medical Science and Technology -- Communicable Diseases pg 3711; Medical Science and Technology -- Epidemiology pg 3733

Public Opinion –See **Sociology** pg 5237

Public Relations –See **Business -- Advertising and Public Relations** pg 753

Public Transportation –See **Transportation** pg 5375; see also Public Administration pg 4623

Public Utilities –pg 4759

Publishing –See **Computers -- Desktop Publishing** pg 1263; Journalism pg 2917

Pulp Industry –See **Paper and Pulp Industry** pg 4232

Puppetry –See **The Arts -- Performing Arts** pg 383

Purchasing –pg 948

Puzzles –See **Recreation, Leisure -- Games and Amusements** pg 4856

Quarries –See **Engineering -- Mines and Mining Engineering** pg 2132; see also Industrial Health and Safety pg 2858

Race Relations –See **Sociology** pg 5237; see also Ethnic Interests pg 2253

Radiation –See **Physics -- Light, Optics, Radiation** pg 4432

Radio –See **Communication -- Broadcasting** pg 1125

SUBJECT CROSS REFERENCES

Radiology –pg 3938; see also Medical Science and Technology -- Neoplasma, Neoplastic pg 3808; Medical Science and Technology -- Nuclear Medicine pg 3847

Railroads –pg 5429

Rationalism –See **Philosophy** pg 4339

Real Estate –pg 4833; see also Housing and Urban Development pg 2812

Record Industry –See **Music** pg 4098; see also Communication -- Broadcasting pg 1125; Sound Recordings and Systems pg 5315

Recreation, Leisure –pg 4848; see also Hobbies pg 2770; Travel and Tourism pg 5458

Recreational Vehicles –See **Transportation** pg 5375; see also Recreation, Leisure pg 4848

Recycling –See **Environmental Issues -- Pollution and Waste Management** pg 2222

Red Cross –See **Sociology -- Social Services and Welfare** pg 5269; see also Medical Science and Technology pg 3543

Reformed Church –See **Religion and Theology -- Protestantism** pg 5054

Refrigeration –See **Heating, Plumbing, and Refrigeration** pg 2602

Regional Planning –See **Housing and Urban Development** pg 2812

Rehabilitation –See **Education -- Special Education and Rehabilitation** pg 1874; **Physically Impaired** pg 4382; see also Drug Abuse and Alcoholism pg 1338; Physical Therapy pg 4378; Sociology -- Social Services and Welfare pg 5269

Religion and Theology –pg 4931

Religious Education –See **Religion and Theology** pg 4931

Religious Music –See **Music** pg 4098

Research –See **Science and Technology** pg 5078; see also Education -- Higher Education pg 1806

Residential Homes –See **Housing and Urban Development** pg 2812

Resorts –See **Hotels/Motels** pg 2803; **Travel and Tourism** pg 5458

Respiratory System –pg 3947

Restaurants –pg 5070; see also Food and Food Industry pg 2325; Hotels/Motels pg 2803

Retail –pg 952

Rheumatology –See **Medical Science and Technology -- Musculoskeletal System** pg 3802; see also Pharmacy and Pharmacology pg 4288

Roads and Traffic –pg 5438

Robotics –See **Computers -- Artificial Intelligence** pg 1210; see also Computers -- Automation pg 1217

Roman Catholic Church –See **Religion and Theology -- Catholicism** pg 5022

Romance and Adventure –pg 5073; see also Literature pg 3357

Rubber –pg 5075

Rugby –See **Recreation, Leisure -- Sports** pg 4881

Running –See **Health and Personal Fitness** pg 2595

Safety –See **Industrial Health and Safety** pg 2858; see also Public Health and Safety pg 4763

Safety Engineering –See **Engineering -- Industrial Engineering and Design** pg 2096

Sailing –See **Boats and Boating** pg 591

Salary/Wages –See **Economics** pg 1459; **Economics -- Labor** pg 1642

Sanitation/Municipal Engineering –See **Environmental Issues -- Pollution and Waste Management** pg 2222; **Public Health and Safety** pg 4763; see also Environmental Issues -- Conservation and Natural Resources pg 2185; Environmental Issues -- Ecology pg 2210

Scholarships –See **Education -- Higher Education** pg 1806

School Counseling –See **Education -- Special Education and Rehabilitation** pg 1874

School Law/Legislation –See **Education -- School Organization and Administration** pg 1859

School Organization and Administration –pg 1859

Science –See **Science and Technology** pg 5078

Science and Technology –pg 5078; see also Chemistry -- Chemical Technology pg 1020; Engineering pg 1963

Science Fiction –See **Literature** pg 3357; see also Literary and Political Reviews pg 3337

Scuba Diving –See **Recreation, Leisure -- Sports** pg 4881

Sculpture –See **The Arts -- Art** pg 335; see also Architecture pg 286

Secondary Education –See **Education** pg 1720

Securities Law –See **Law -- Corporate Law** pg 3094

Security –See **Computers -- Computer Crimes and Security** pg 1225

Security Systems and Alarms –pg 5176; see also Engineering -- Electricity, Electrical Engineering, Electronics pg 2034

Sedimentology –See **Earth Sciences -- Geology** pg 1364; see also Earth Sciences -- Geophysics pg 1402

Seismology –See **Earth Sciences -- Geophysics** pg 1402

Semantics –See **Linguistics** pg 3260

Senior Citizens –pg 5177; see also Medical Science and Technology -- Geriatrics pg 3748; Sociology -- Social Services and Welfare pg 5269

Sewage –See **Environmental Issues -- Pollution and Waste Management** pg 2222; see also Water Resources pg 5528

Sewing and Needlework –pg 5182; see also Hobbies pg 2770; The Arts -- Crafts and Decorative Arts pg 369

Sexual Life –pg 5186

Sexually Transmitted Diseases –See **Medical Science and Technology -- Communicable Diseases** pg 3711; **Public Health and Safety** pg 4763

Ship Design –See **Engineering** pg 1459; **Naval Science, Navigation** pg 4174; see also Transportation -- Ships and Shipping pg 5447

Shipbuilding –See **Naval Science, Navigation** pg 4174; **Transportation -- Ships and Shipping** pg 5447

Ships and Shipping –pg 5447; see also Business -- Commerce pg 821; Naval Science, Navigation pg 4174

Shoes –See **Clothing Industry and Fashion** pg 1081

Simulation –pg 1282

Skiing –See **Recreation, Leisure -- Sports** pg 4881

Slavery –See **Civil Rights** pg 4503

Slavic Studies –See **History(General) -- History of Europe** pg 2671; **Literature** pg 3357

Small Business –See **Business** pg 636; see also Economics pg 1459

Smoking –See **Public Health and Safety** pg 4763; **Tobacco** pg 5372

Soap Operas –See **General Interest** pg 2484

Soccer –See **Recreation, Leisure -- Sports** pg 4881

Social Sciences –pg 5189; see also Humanities pg 2841

SUBJECT CROSS REFERENCES

Social Security –See **Sociology -- Social Services and Welfare** pg 5269; see also Economics -- Labor pg 1642; Insurance pg 2872

Social Services –See **Sociology -- Social Services and Welfare** pg 5269

Social Services and Welfare –pg 5269

Socialism –See **Political Science -- Socialism, Communism, Anarchism, Utopianism** pg 1589

Socialism, Communism, Anarchism, Utopianism –pg 4539

Societies and Clubs –pg 5228

Sociology –pg 5237

Software –pg 1283; see also Computer Industry and Industry Directories pg 1235; Programs and Programming pg 1277

Soil –See **Agriculture -- Crop Production and Soil** pg 161

Solar Energy –See **Energy** pg 1930; see also Engineering -- Mechanical Engineering and Machinery pg 2108

Sound –pg 4451

Sound Recordings and Systems –pg 5315; see also Engineering -- Electricity, Electrical Engineering, Electronics pg 2034; Music pg 4098

South America –See **General Interest -- General Interest-South America** pg 2551; **History(General) -- History of North, South, and Central America** pg 2717

Special Education –See **Education -- Special Education and Rehabilitation** pg 1874

Special Education and Rehabilitation –pg 1874

Spectroscopy –See **Physics -- Light, Optics, Radiation** pg 4432

Speech Disorders –See **Medical Science and Technology – Otorhinolaryngology** pg 3885; see also Education -- Special Education and Rehabilitation pg 1874; Physically Impaired pg 4382

Speech Pathology –See **Physically Impaired** pg 4382; see also Education -- Special Education and Rehabilitation pg 1874

Speleology –See **Earth Sciences -- Geophysics** pg 1402

Sports –pg 4881; see also Recreation, Leisure -- Games and Amusements pg 4856; Recreation, Leisure -- Health and Personal Fitness pg 2595; Recreation, Leisure -- Outdoor Life pg 4868

Sports Medicine –pg 3953

Stained Glass –See **Glass and Ceramics** pg 2585

Standardization –See **Metrology and Standardization** pg 4029

State Government –See **Public Administration** pg 4623; see also Public Administration -- Public Finance and Taxation pg 4708

Statistics –pg 5320

Stomatology –See **Dentistry** pg 1314

Stress –See **Medical Science and Technology** pg 3543; **Psychology** pg 4570

Sugar –See **Agriculture -- Crop Production and Soil** pg 161; see also Food and Food Industry pg 2325

Surface Chemistry –See **Chemistry -- Physical and Theoretical Chemistry** pg 1049

Surgeons –See **Medical Science and Technology -- Physicians and Medical Personnel** pg 3912

Surgery –pg 3957

Surveying –See **Engineering -- Civil Engineering** pg 2018; **Geography** pg 2553

Swimming –See **Recreation, Leisure -- Sports** pg 4881

Tax Planning –See **Law -- Estate Planning** pg 3117

Taxation –See **Public Administration -- Public Finance and Taxation** pg 4708; see also Business -- Accounting pg 735; Law -- Estate Planning pg 3117

Taxidermy –See **Hobbies** pg 2770

Tea –See **Food and Food Industry -- Beverage Industry** pg 2363; see also Agriculture pg 42

Teaching and Curriculum –pg 1887

Teaching Materials –See **Education -- Teaching and Curriculum** pg 1887

Technical Education –See **Education -- Vocational Education** pg 1909

Technology –See **Science and Technology** pg 5078

Telecommunications –pg 1148

Telegraph –See **Communication -- Telecommunications** pg 1148

Telephone –See **Communication -- Telecommunications** pg 1148

Telephone Directories –See **Communication -- Telecommunications** pg 1148

Television –See **Communication -- Broadcasting** pg 1125

Tennis –See **Recreation, Leisure -- Sports** pg 4881

Textbooks –See **Education** pg 1720

Textiles –pg 5347; see also Clothing Industry and Fashion pg 1081

The Arts –pg 311

Theater –pg 5361; see also The Arts -- Performing Arts pg 383

Theology –See **Religion and Theology** pg 4931

Theoretical Chemistry –See **Chemistry -- Physical and Theoretical Chemistry** pg 1049

Theosophy –See **Religion and Theology -- Islam, Bahaism, Theosophy** pg 5041

Thrombosis –See **Medical Science and Technology -- Internal Medicine** pg 3794; see also Medical Science and Technology -- Cardiology pg 3697; Medical Science and Technology -- Hematology pg 3769; Medical Science and Technology -- Pathology pg 3891

Tobacco –pg 5372

Total Quality Management –See **Business -- General Management** pg 858; **Business -- Personnel Management** pg 938

Tourism –See **Travel and Tourism** pg 5458

Toxicology –pg 3978; see also Pharmacy and Pharmacology pg 4288

Toys –See **Gifts, Toys** pg 2583

Track and Field –See **Recreation, Leisure -- Sports** pg 4881

Trade –See **Business -- Commerce** pg 821

Trade Regulation –See **Business -- Commerce** pg 821; see also Law -- Corporate Law pg 3094

Trade Schools –See **Education -- Vocational Education** pg 1909

Trade Shows –See **Business -- Advertising and Public Relations** pg 753

Trade Unions –See **Economics -- Labor** pg 1642

Trademarks –See **Copyright, Intellectual Property** pg 1300

Traffic –See **Transportation -- Roads and Traffic** pg 5438

Transportation –pg 5375; see also Business -- Commerce pg 821

Travel and Tourism –pg 5458; see also Geography pg 2553; Recreation, Leisure pg 4848

Trees –See **Gardening and Horticulture** pg 2407; see also Forestry pg 2373

Tropical Diseases –See **Medical Science and Technology -- Tropical Medicine** pg 3985

Tropical Medicine –pg 3985

Trucks and Trucking –See **Transportation** pg 5375

Trustees –See **Law -- Estate Planning** pg 3117

SUBJECT CROSS REFERENCES

Trusts –See **Law -- Estate Planning** pg 3117

Ukrainian Studies –See **History(General) -- History of Europe** pg 2671; see also Literature pg 3357

Ultrafication –See **Medical Science and Technology -- Hematology** pg 3769

Ultrasonic Therapy –See **Medical Science and Technology -- Radiology** pg 3938

Ultrasound –See **Medical Science and Technology -- Radiology** pg 3938

Unemployment –See **Economics -- Labor** pg 1642; see also Law pg 2926

Unions –See **Economics -- Labor** pg 1642

Universities and Colleges –See **Education -- Higher Education** pg 1806; see also College and School Publications pg 1088

Urban Development –See **Housing and Urban Development** pg 2812

Urinary Tract –See **Medical Science and Technology -- Urology and Nephrology** pg 3987

Urology –See **Medical Science and Technology -- Urology and Nephrology** pg 3987

Urology and Nephrology –pg 3987

Utopianism –See **Political Science -- Socialism, Communism, Anarchism, Utopianism** pg 4539

Vacations –See **Travel and Tourism** pg 5458; see also Recreation,Leisure pg 4848

Veterans –See **Military and Defense** pg 4033; see also Naval Science, Navigation pg 4174

Veterinary Sciences –pg 5501; see also Zoology pg 5572

Video –See **Communication -- Broadcasting** pg 1125; **Photography and Video** pg 4366; see also Motion Picture pg 4062

Video Games/Arcades –See **Recreation, Leisure -- Games and Amusements** pg 4856

Virology –See **Biology -- Microbiology** pg 558

Virtual Reality –See **Computers -- Artificial Intelligence** pg 1210; see also Computers -- Automation pg 1217

Visual Arts –See **The Arts -- Art** pg 335

Vitamins –See **Nutrition and Dietetics** pg 4186

Vocational Education –pg 1909

Vocational Guidance –See **Education -- Vocational Education** pg 1909; see also Occupations and Careers pg 4201

Volcanoes –See **Earth Sciences -- Geophysics** pg 1402

Volunteer Work –See **Philanthropy** pg 4334

Voting –See **Political Science** pg 4461; see also Public Administration pg 4623

WAN (Wide Area Networks) –See **Computer** pg 1240

War –See **History(General)** pg 2609; see also Political Science pg 4461

Waste Management –See **Environmental Issues -- Pollution and Waste Management** pg 2222

Watches –See **Jewelry -- Clocks and Watches** pg 2916

Water Pollution –See **Environmental Issues -- Pollution and Waste Management** pg 2222; see also Water Resources pg 5528

Water Resources –pg 5528; see also Earth Sciences -- Hydrology pg 1412; Engineering -- Hydraulic Engineering pg 2087; Environmental Issues -- Conservation and Natural Resources pg 2185

Water Utilities –See **Public Administration -- Public Utilities** pg 4759; see also Water Resources pg 5528

Weaponry –See **Military and Defense** pg 4033

Weather –See **Earth Sciences -- Meteorology** pg 1419

Weightlifting –See **Health and Personal Fitness** pg 2595; see also Recreation, Leisure -- Sports pg 4881

Weights and Measures –See **Metrology and Standardization** pg 4029

Welding –pg 4026

Welfare –See **Sociology -- Social Services and Welfare** pg 5269

Western Australian Studies –See **History(General) -- History of Australia and Oceania** pg 2668

Who's Who –See **Biographies** pg 429

Wide Area Networks –See **Computers -- Computer Networks** pg 1240

Wildlife –See **Environmental Issues -- Conservation and Natural Resources** pg 2185; see also Environmental Issues -- Ecology pg 2210; Recreation, Leisure -- Outdoor Life pg 4868

Wills –See **Law -- Estate Planning** pg 3117

Wine –See **Food and Food Industry -- Beverage Industry** pg 2363

Women's Interests –pg 5550

Wood –See **Forestry -- Lumber and Wood** pg 2399

Woodwork –See **Building and Construction -- Carpentry and Woodwork** pg 633

Word Processing –pg 1292

Workmen's Compensation –See **Economics -- Labor** pg 1642; see also Insurance pg 2872

World Politics –See **Political Science** pg 4461

Wrestling –See **Recreation, Leisure -- Sports** pg 4881

Writing –See **Journalism** pg 2917; see also Literature pg 3357

Yachts and Yachting –See **Boats and Boating** pg 591; see also Travel and Tourism pg 5458

Yearbooks –See **Encyclopedias and General Reference Books** pg 1923

Youth –See **Children and Youth Interests** pg 1059

Zoning –See **Housing and Urban Development** pg 2812; **Law** pg 2926; see also Real Estate pg 4833

Zoology –pg 5572; see also Veterinary Sciences pg 5501

TABLES

Frequency
Document Delivery
Wire Services
Country of Publication
Unit of Currency
Indexes/Abstracts

FREQUENCY TABLE

an	Annual		sa	Semiannual
be	Biennial		sm	Semimonthly
bm	Bimonthly		sw	Semiweekly
bw	Biweekly		te	Triennial
da	Daily		tm	Three times a month
ir	Irregular		tq	Tri-quarterly
mo	Monthly		tw	Three times a week
qt	Quarterly		wk	Weekly

Additional frequencies may appear in the Serial Listing when provided by the publisher.

DOCUMENT DELIVERY

The following document supplier notations, when noted in a Serial Listing, indicate the availability of that serial for document delivery through the specified service. Permission has been granted by the copyright owner and is subject to change without notice. Only the portion in boldface will appear in the listing.

ADONIS™
ADONIS B.V.
Spuistraat 112D
1012VA Amsterdam, The Netherlands

Article Express International
Engineering Information Inc.
469 Union Avenue
Westbury, New York 11590

Ask*IEEE
(in cooperation with EBSCOdoc™)
1722 Gilbreth Road
Burlingame, CA 94010

BIOSIS Document Express™
(in cooperation with EBSCOdoc™)
1722 Gilbreth Road
Burlingame, CA 94010

BLDSC
British Library Document Supply Centre - Customer Services
Boston Spa, Wetherby
LS23 7BQ, United Kingdom

CASDDS ®
Chemical Abstracts Service Document Delivery Service
PO Box 3012
Columbus, Ohio 43210-0012

Documents on Demand
Congressional Information Service
4520 East-West Highway
Bethesda, MD 20814-3389

FAXON Xpress
FAXON Research Services, Inc.
15 Southwest Park
Westwood, MA 02090

Haworth Document Delivery Service
The Haworth Press, Inc.
10 Alice Street
Binghamton, New York 13904-1580

Magazine Collection™
Information Access Company
362 Lakeside Drive
Foster City, CA 94404

Petroleum Abstracts Document Delivery Service
University of Tulsa
600 South College
Tulsa, OK 74104-3189

Quick Copies
Williams and Wilkins Company
428 East Preston Street
Baltimore, MD 21202-3993

SWETSCAN-SWETDOC
Swets & Zeitlinger bv
Hereweg 347, PO Box 830
2160 SZ Lisse, The Netherlands

The Genuine Article®
Institute for Scientific Information
3501 Market Street
Philadelphia, PA 19104

The Uncover Company
3801 East Florida Avenue
Suite 200
Denver, CO 80210

UMI Article Clearinghouse
300 North Zeeb Road
PO Box 1346
Ann Arbor, MI 48106-1346

WIRE SERVICES

The following abbreviations represent the news and photograph wire services found in the Directory. Each code is followed by the complete name of the service.

CODE:	SERVICE:
AF	Agence France Presse
AN	Alternet
AP	Associated Press
API	Associated Press International
BU	British United Press
CA	Canadian Press
CH	Chicago Tribune - New York
CN	Capital News
CM	Christian Science Monitor
CO	Copley News Service
CP	Colorado Press
CQ	Congressional Quarterly
CS	Catholic News Service
CT	Chicago Sun Times
CP	China and Taiwan News Age
CU	Canadian United Press
DJ	Dow Jones
EI	Empire Information Service
ER	Editorial Research Service
FN	Federation News Service
GN	Gannett News Service
GP	Georgia Press Association
HH	Hearst Headline Service
HN	Harris News Service
IT	Independent Television Network
IM	Iowa Medialink
JT	Jewish Telegraphic Agency
KF	King Features
KN	Knight News Service
KR	Knight-Ridder
LA	Los Angeles Times
LO	London Daily News
LT	Times of London
MG	Manchester Guardian
ML	MediaLink
MN	Morris News Service
MP	Montana Press Association
NC	NEWSCOM
NE	Newspaper Enterprises Association
NF	Newsfinder
NM	Notimex
NN	Newhouse News Service
NP	NNAP
NU	News USA
NW	National Weather Service
NY	New York Times
ON	Ottawa News Service
PN	Pacific News Service
RN	Reuters News Service
SH	Scripps-Howard Newspaper Alliance-Scripps Howard News Service
SS	SportsStats
WN	World News
WP	Washington Post Writer's Guild
WS	Women's News Service
WW	Women's Wear Daily

COUNTRY OF PUBLICATION TABLE

The following lists of country codes have been taken directly from the USMARC Bibliographic Format, with the exception being that the United States and Canada state and province codes have been grouped under their respective countries, rather than being listed individually.

COUNTRY OF PUBLICATION BY CODE

Code	Country
AA	Albania
AE	Algeria
AF	Afghanistan
AG	Argentina
AI	Armenia
AJ	Azerbaijan
AM	Anguilla
AN	Andorra
AO	Angola
AQ	Antigua and Barbuda
AS	American Samoa
AT	Australia
AU	Austria
AW	Aruba
AY	Antarctica
BA	Bahrain
BB	Barbados
BD	Burundi
BE	Belgium
BF	Bahamas
BG	Bangladesh
BH	Belize
BI	British Indian Ocean Territory
BL	Brazil
BM	Bermuda Islands
BN	Bosnia Hercegovina
BO	Bolivia
BP	Solomon Islands
BR	Burma
BS	Botswana
BT	Bhutan
BU	Bulgaria
BV	Bouvet Island
BW	Byelarus
BX	Brunei
CB	Cambodia
CC	China
CD	Chad
CE	Sri Lanka
CF	Congo (Brazzaville)
CG	Zaire
CH	China (Republic: 1949)
CI	Croatia
CJ	Cayman Islands
CK	Colombia
CL	Chile
CM	Cameroon
CN	Canada
CP	Canton and Enderbury Islands
CQ	Comoros
CR	Costa Rica
CS	Czechoslovakia
CU	Cuba
CV	Cape Verde
CW	Cook Islands
CX	Central African Republic
CY	Cyprus
DK	Denmark
DM	Benin
DQ	Dominica
DR	Dominican Republic
EC	Ecuador
EG	Equatorial Guinea
ER	Estonia
ES	El Salvador
ET	Ethiopia
FA	Faroe Islands
FG	French Guiana
FI	Finland
FJ	Fiji
FM	Micronesia (Federated States)
FP	French Polynesia
FR	France
FS	Terres Australes et Antarctiques Francaises
FT	Djibouti
GB	Kiribati
GD	Grenada
GH	Ghana
GI	Gibralter
GL	Greenland
GM	Gambia
GO	Gabon
GP	Guadeloupe
GR	Greece

Code	Country
GS	Georgia (Republic)
GT	Guatemala
GU	Guam
GV	Guinea
GW	Germany
GY	Guyana
GZ	Gaza Strip
HK	Hong Kong
HM	Heard and McDonald Islands
HO	Honduras
HT	Haiti
HU	Hungary
IC	Iceland
IE	Ireland
II	India
IO	Indonesia
IQ	Iraq
IR	Iran
IS	Israel
IT	Italy
IV	Ivory Coast
IY	Iraq-Saudi Arabia Neutral Zone
JA	Japan
JI	Johnson Atoll
JM	Jamaica
JO	Jordan
KE	Kenya
KG	Kyrgyzstan
KN	Korea (North)
KO	Korea (South)
KU	Kuwait
KZ	Kazakhstan
LB	Liberia
LE	Lebanon
LH	Liechtenstein
LI	Lithuania
LO	Lesotho
LS	Laos
LU	Luxembourg
LV	Latvia
LY	Libya
MC	Monaco
MF	Mauritius
MG	Madagascar
MH	Macao
MJ	Montserrat
MK	Oman
ML	Mali
MM	Malta
MP	Mongolia
MQ	Martinique
MR	Morocco
MU	Mauritania
MV	Moldova
MW	Malawi
MX	Mexico
MY	Malaysia
MZ	Mozambique
NA	Netherlands Antilles
NE	Netherlands
NG	Niger
NL	New Caledonia
NN	Vanuatu
NO	Norway
NP	Nepal
NQ	Nicaragua
NR	Nigeria
NU	Nauru
NW	Northern Mariana Islands
NX	Norfolk Island
NZ	New Zealand
OT	Mayotte
PC	Pitcairn Island
PE	Peru
PF	Paracel Islands
PG	Guinea-Bissau
PH	Philippines
PK	Pakistan
PL	Poland
PN	Panama
PO	Portugal
PP	Papua New Guinea
PR	Puerto Rico
PW	Palau

Code	Country
PY	Paraguay
QA	Qatar
RE	Reunion
RH	Zimbabwe
RM	Romania
RW	Rwanda
RU	Russia (Republic)
SA	South Africa
SE	Seychelles
SF	Sao Tome and Principe
SG	Senegal
SH	Spanish North Africa
SI	Singapore
SJ	Sudan
SL	Sierra Leone
SM	San Marino
SO	Somalia
SP	Spain
SQ	Swaziland
SR	Surinam
SS	Western Sahara
SU	Saudi Arabia
SW	Sweden
SX	Namibia
SY	Syria
SZ	Switzerland
TA	Tajikstan
TC	Turks and Caicos Islands
TG	Togo
TH	Thailand
TI	Tunisia
TK	Turkmenistan
TL	Tokelau Islands
TO	Tonga
TR	Trinidad and Tobago
TS	Trucial States (United Arab Emirates)
TU	Turkey
TZ	Tanzania
UA	Egypt
UC	United States Misc. Caribbean Islands
UG	Uganda
UK	United Kingdom (Including Scotland)
UN	Ukraine
UP	United States Misc. Pacific Islands
UR	USSR
US	United States
UV	Burkina Faso
UY	Uruguay
UZ	Uzbekistan
VB	Virgin Islands (British V.I.)
VC	Vatican City
VE	Venezuela
VI	Virgin Islands (U.S.)
VM	Vietnam
WF	Wallis and Futuna
WJ	West Bank of the Jordan River
WK	Wake Island
WS	Western Samoa
XA	Christmas Island (Indian Ocean)
XB	Cocos (Keeling) Islands
XC	Maldives
XD	Saint Kitts-Nevis
XE	Marshall Islands
XF	Midway Island
XH	Niue
XJ	Saint Helena
XK	Saint Lucia
XL	Saint Pierre and Miquelon
XM	Saint Vincent and the Grenadines
XN	Macedonia
XO	Slovakia
XP	Spratly Islands
XR	Czech Republic
XS	Falkland Islands
XV	Slovenia
YE	Yemen
YU	Yugoslavia
ZA	Zambia

COUNTRY OF PUBLICATION TABLE

COUNTRY OF PUBLICATION BY COUNTRY

Country	Code	Country	Code	Country	Code
Afghanistan	AF	Greenland	GL	Paracel Islands	PF
Albania	AA	Grenada	GD	Paraguay	PY
Algeria	AE	Guadeloupe	GP	Peru	PE
American Samoa	AS	Guam	GU	Philippines	PH
Andorra	AN	Guatemala	GT	Pitcairn Island	PC
Angola	AO	Guinea	GV	Poland	PL
Anguilla	AM	Guinea-Bissau	PG	Portugal	PO
Antarctica	AY	Guyana	GY	Puerto Rico	PR
Antigua and Barbuda	AQ	Haiti	HT	Qatar	QA
Argentina	AG	Heard and McDonald Islands	HM	Reunion	RE
Armenia	AI	Honduras	HO	Romania	RM
Aruba	AW	Hong Kong	HK	Russia (Republic)	RU
Australia	AT	Hungary	HU	Rwanda	RW
Austria	AU	Iceland	IC	Saint Helena	XJ
Azerbaijan	AJ	India	II	Saint Kitts-Nevis	XD
Bahamas	BF	Indonesia	IO	Saint Lucia	XK
Bahrain	BA	Iran	IR	Saint Pierre and Miquelon	XL
Bangladesh	BG	Iraq	IQ	Saint Vincent and the Grenadines	XM
Barbados	BB	Iraq-Saudi Arabia Neutral Zone	IY	San Marino	SM
Belgium	BE	Ireland	IE	Sao Tome and Principe	SF
Belize	BH	Israel	IS	Saudi Arabia	SU
Benin	DM	Italy	IT	Senegal	SG
Bermuda Islands	BM	Ivory Coast	IV	Seychelles	SE
Bhutan	BT	Jamaica	JM	Sierra Leone	SL
Bolivia	BO	Japan	JA	Singapore	SI
Bosnia Hercegovina	BN	Johnson Atoll	JI	Slovakia	XO
Botswana	BS	Jordan	JO	Slovenia	XV
Bouvet Island	BV	Kazakhstan	KZ	Solomon Islands	BP
Brazil	BL	Kenya	KE	Somalia	SO
British Indian Ocean Territory	BI	Kiribati	GB	South Africa	SA
Brunei	BX	Korea (North)	KN	Spain	SP
Bulgaria	BU	Korea (South)	KO	Spanish North Africa	SH
Burkina Faso	UV	Kuwait	KU	Spratly Island	XP
Burma	BR	Kyrgyzstan	KG	Sri Lanka	CE
Burundi	BD	Laos	LS	Sudan	SJ
Byelarus	BW	Latvia	LV	Surinam	SR
Cambodia	CB	Lebanon	LE	Swaziland	SQ
Cameroon	CM	Lesotho	LO	Sweden	SW
Canada	CN	Liberia	LB	Switzerland	SZ
Canton and Enderbury Islands	CP	Libya	LY	Syria	SY
Cape Verde	CV	Liechtenstein	LH	Tajikistan	TA
Cayman Islands	CJ	Lithuania	LI	Tanzania	TZ
Central African Republic	CX	Luxembourg	LU	Terres Australes et Antarctiques Francaises	FS
Chad	CD	Macao	MH		
Chile	CL	Macedonia	XN	Thailand	TH
China	CC	Madagascar	MG	Togo	TG
China (Republic: 1949)	CH	Malawi	MW	Tokelau Islands	TL
Christmas Island (Indian Ocean)	XA	Malaysia	MY	Tonga	TO
Cocos (Keeling) Islands	XB	Maldives	XC	Trinidad and Tobago	TR
Colombia	CK	Mali	ML	Trucial States (United Arab Emirates)	TS
Comoros	CQ	Malta	MM		
Congo (Brazzaville)	CF	Marshall Islands	XE	Tunisia	TI
Cook Islands	CW	Martinique	MQ	Turkey	TU
Costa Rica	CR	Mauritania	MU	Turkmenistan	TK
Croatia	CI	Mauritius	MF	Turks and Caicos Islands	TC
Cuba	CU	Mayotte	OT	Uganda	UG
Cyprus	CY	Mexico	MX	Ukraine	UN
Czech Republic	XR	Micronesia (Federated States)	FM	United Kingdom (Including Scotland)	UK
Czechoslovakia	CS	Midway Island	XF		
Denmark	DK	Moldova	MV	United States	US
Djibouti	FT	Monaco	MC	United States (Misc. Caribbean Islands)	UC
Dominica	DQ	Mongolia	MP		
Dominican Republic	DR	Montserrat	MJ	United States (Misc. Pacific Islands)	UP
Ecuador	EC	Morocco	MR	Uruguay	UY
Egypt	UA	Mozambique	MZ	USSR	UR
El Salvador	ES	Namibia	SX	Uzbekistan	UZ
Equatorial Guinea	EG	Nauru	NU	Vanuatu	NN
Estonia	ER	Nepal	NP	Vatican City	VC
Ethiopia	ET	Netherlands	NE	Venezuela	VE
Falkland Islands	XS	Netherlands Antilles	NA	Vietnam	VM
Faroe Islands	FA	New Caledonia	NL	Virgin Islands (British V.I.)	VB
Fiji	FJ	New Zealand	NZ	Virgin Islands (U.S.)	VI
Finland	FI	Nicaragua	NQ	Wake Island	WK
France	FR	Niger	NG	Wallis and Futuna	WF
French Guiana	FG	Nigeria	NR	West Bank of the Jordan River	WJ
French Polynesia	FP	Niue	XH	Western Sahara	SS
Gabon	GO	Norfolk Island	NX	Western Samoa	WS
Gambia	GM	Northern Mariana Islands	NW	Yemen	YE
Gaza Strip	GZ	Norway	NO	Yugoslavia	YU
Georgia (Republic)	GS	Oman	MK	Zaire	CG
Germany	GW	Pakistan	PK	Zambia	ZA
Ghana	GH	Palau	PW	Zimbabwe	RH
Gibralter	GI	Panama	PN		
Greece	GR	Papua New Guinea	PP		

UNIT OF CURRENCY TABLE

In the Serial Listing, prices are given in country of publication currency and are one-year library subscription rates, unless designated otherwise.

Country	Currency	Country	Currency	Country	Currency
Afghanistan	afghanin	Greece	Greek drachma	Papua New Guinea	kina
Albania	lek	Guadeloupe	French franc	Paraguay	guarani
Algeria	Algerian dinar	Guatemala	quetzal	Peru	sole
Angola	kwanza	Guyana	Guyana dollar	Philippines	peso
Antigua and Barbuda	East Caribbean dollar	Haiti	gourde	Papua New Guinea	kina
Argentina	peso argentino	Honduras	lempira	Paraguay	guarani
Australia	Australian dollar	Hong Kong	Hong Kong dollar	Peru	sole
Austria	schilling	Hungary	forint	Philippines	peso
Bahamas	Bahamian dollar	Iceland	krona	Poland	zloty
Bangladesh	taka	India	rupee	Portugal	escudo
Barbados	Barbados dollar	Indonesia	rupiah	Qatar	Qatar riyal
Belgium	Belgian franc	Iran	rial	Reunion	French franc
Bermuda Islands	Bermuda dollar	Iraq	Iraqi dinar	Romania	lei
Bolivia	peso	Ireland	Irish pound	Rwanda	Rwanda franc
Botswana	pula	Israel	shekel	San Marino	Italian lira
Brazil	cruzeiro	Italy	lira	Saudi Arabia	Saudi riyal
Belize	Belize dollar	Ivory Coast	CFA franc	Senegal	CFA franc
Benin	CFA franc	Jamaica	Jamaican dollar	Sierra Leone	leone
Bulgaria	lev	Japan	yen	Singapore	Singapore dollar
Burkina Faso	CFA franc	Jordan	Jordanian dinar	Somalia	Somali shilling
Burma	kyat	Kenya	Kenya shilling	South Africa	South African rand
Cameroon	CFA franc	Korea (North)	won	Southern Yemen	dinar
Canada	Canadian dollar	Korea (South)	won	Spain	pesata
Cayman Islands	cordoba/dollar	Kuwait	Kuwaiti dinar	Sri Lanka	rupee
Central African Republic	CFA franc	Lebanon	Lebanese pound	Sudan	Sudanese pound
		Liberia	U.S. dollar	Surinam	Surinam guilder
		Libya	Libyan dinar	Swaziland	emalangeni
Chad	CFA franc	Liechtenstein	Swiss franc	Sweden	krona
Chile	peso	Luxembourg	Luxembourg franc	Switzerland	franc
China	renminbi yuan	Madagascar	Malagasy franc	Syria	Syrian pound
China (Republic: 1949)	New Taiwan dollar	Malawi	Malawi kwacha	Tanzania	Tanzanian shilling
		Malaysia	ringgit	Thailand	baht
Colombia	peso	Mali	CFA franc	Togo	CFA franc
Cook Islands	New Zealand dollar	Malta	Maltese pound	Trinidad and Tobago	Trinidad and Tobago dollar
Costa Rica	colon	Martinique	French franc		
Cuba	peso	Mauritius	Mauritian rupee	Tunisia	Tunisian dinar
Cyprus	Cyprus pound	Mexico	peso	Turkey	Turkish lira
Czechoslovakia	korona	Monaco	French franc	Uganda	Uganda shilling
Benin	CFA franc	Morocco	dirham	United Kingdom	pound sterling
Denmark	krone	Mozambique	meticais	United States	U.S. dollar
Djibouti	Djibouti franc	Nauru	Australian dollar	Uruguay	new peso
Dominican Republic	peso	Nepal	Nepalese rupee	USSR	ruble
Ecuador	sucre	Netherlands	guilder	Vatican City	lira
Egypt	Egyptian pound	New Caledonia	CFP franc	Venezuela	bolivare
El Salvador	colon	New Zealand	New Zealand dollar	Vietnam	dong
Ethiopia	Ethiopian birr	Nicaragua	cordoba	Yemen (Yemen (Sana))	riyal
Fiji	Fiji dollar	Niger	CFA franc		
Finland	fim (finnmark)	Nigeria	naira	Yugoslavia	dinar
France	French franc	Norway	krone	Zaire	CFA franc
Gambia	dalasi	Oman	rial	Zambia	Zambian kwacha
Germany	mark	Pakistan	rupee	Zimbabwe	Zimbabwean dollar
Ghana	cedi	Panama	balboa		

INDEXES/ABSTRACTS TABLE

The following is a list of all publications which may index, or contain an abstract of, titles in the Directory. The Abbreviated Title in boldface is the abbreviation of the index or abstract as used in the Serial Listing. The complete title of the index or abstract follows. Succeeding information or a Ceased/Suspended indicator will follow the complete title for those serials where it applies. For services that share the same journal source list, a reference will be made to that service which will appear in the Serial Listing. This table includes over 1,300 Indexing/Abstracting services, 921 of which are active.

A.I.D. RES. DEV. ABSTR.
[US/0096-1507]
A.I.D. RESEARCH AND DEVELOPMENT ABSTRACTS.
(*Continues* A.I.D. Reference Center. A.I.D. Research Abstracts.)

ABC POL SCI
[US/0001-0456]
ABC POL SCI. ADVANCE BIBLIOGRAPHY OF CONTENTS: POLITICAL SCIENCE & GOVERNMENT.

ABI/INFORM ONDISC
[US/1062-5127]
ABI/INFORM ONDISC.

ABI/INFORM ONDISC: EXPR. ED.
[US]
ABI/INFORM ONDISC: EXPRESS EDITION [COMPUTER FILE].

ABI/INFORM GLOB. ED.
[US]
ABI/INFORM GLOBAL EDITION [COMPUTER FILE].

ABR. CATHOL. PERIOD. LIT. INDEX
[US/0737-3457]
ABRIDGED CATHOLIC PERIODICAL AND LITERATURE INDEX, THE.

ABR. INDEX MED.
[US/0001-3331]
ABRIDGED INDEX MEDICUS.
(*Continues* American Medical Association. Abridged Index Medicus.)

ABR. READ. GUIDE PERIOD. LIT.
[US/0001-334X]
ABRIDGED READERS' GUIDE TO PER ODICAL LITERATURE.

ABS INT. GUIDE CLASSICAL STUD.
[US]
ABS INTERNATIONAL GUIDE TO CLASSICAL STUDIES.
(*Continued by* International Guide to Classical Studies (1966).)

ABSTR. ABSTR. BOOK REV. CUR. LEG. PERIOD.
[US]
ABSTRACTS : ABSTRACTS OF BOOK REVIEWS IN CURRENT LEGAL PERIODICALS.
(*Continues* Abstracts of Book Reviews in Current Legal Periodicals.)

ABSTR. AIT REP. PUBL. ENERGY
[TH/0857-6181]
ABSTRACTS OF AIT REPORTS AND PUBLICATIONS ON ENERGY.
(*Continues* Abstracts of AIT Reports and Publications on Renewable Energy Resources.)

ABSTR. ANTHROPOL.
[US/0001-3455]
ABSTRACTS IN ANTHROPOLOGY.

ABSTR. BIOCOMMER.
[UK/0263-6778]
ABSTRACTS IN BIOCOMMERCE.

ABSTR. BOOK REV. CURR. LEG. PERIOD.
[US/0362-1065]
ABSTRACTS OF BOOK REVIEWS IN CURRENT LEGAL PERIODICALS.
(*Continued by* Abstracts : Abstracts of Book Reviews in Current Legal Periodicals.)

ABSTR. BULL. INST. PAP. SCI. TECH.
[US/1047-2088]
ABSTRACT BULLETIN OF THE INSTITUTE OF PAPER SCIENCE AND TECHNOLOGY.
(*Continues* Institute of Paper Chemistry (Appleton, Wis.) Abstract Bulletin of the Institute of Paper Chemistry.)

ABSTR. BULL. INST. PAPER CHEM.
[US]
ABSTRACT BULLETIN OF THE INSTITUTE OF PAPER CHEMISTRY.
(*Continued by* Abstract Bulletin of the Institute of Paper Science and Technology.)

ABSTR. CLIN. CARE GUIDEL.
[US/1042-4423]
ABSTRACTS OF CLINICAL CARE GUIDELINES.

ABSTR. CRIMINOL. PENOL.
[NE/0001-3684]
ABSTRACTS ON CRIMINOLOGY AND PENOLOGY.
(*Continued by* Criminology & Penology Abstracts.)

ABSTR. ENGL. STUD.
[US/0001-3560]
ABSTRACTS OF ENGLISH STUDIES.
(Suspended)

ABSTR. ENTOMOL.
[US/0001-3579]
ABSTRACTS OF ENTOMOLOGY.
***Refer to Biological Abstracts for complete source list.

ABSTR. FOLK. STUD.
[US/0001-3587]
ABSTRACTS OF FOLKLORE STUDIES.
(Ceased)

ABSTR. GRAPHIC ARTS TECH. FOUND.
[US]
ABSTRACTS (GRAPHIC ARTS TECHNICAL FOUNDATION).
(*Continues* Graphic Arts Abstracts (Pittsburgh, PA. : 1968).)

ABSTR. HEALTH CARE MANAGE. STUD.
[US/0194-4908]
ABSTRACTS OF HEALTH CARE MANAGEMENT STUDIES.
(*Continues* Abstracts of Hospital Management Studies.)

ABSTR. HEALTH ENVIRON. POLLUTANTS
[US/0044-5819]
ABSTRACTS ON HEALTH EFFECTS OF ENVIRONMENTAL POLLUTANTS.
(Ceased)

ABSTR. HOSPIT. MANAGE. STUD.
[US/0001-3595]
ABSTRACTS OF HOSPITAL MANAGEMENT STUDIES.
(*Continued by* Abstracts of Health Care Management Studies.)

ABSTR. HUM. COMPUT. INTERACT.
[US/1042-0193]
ABSTRACTS IN HUMAN-COMPUTER INTERACTION.
(Suspended)

ABSTR. HYG.
[UK/0001-3692]
ABSTRACTS ON HYGIENE.
(*Continued by* Abstracts on Hygiene and Communicable Diseases.)

ABSTR. HYG. COMMUN. DIS.
[UK/0260-5511]
ABSTRACTS ON HYGIENE AND COMMUNICABLE DISEASES.
(*Continues* Abstracts on Hygiene.)
***Refer to Tropical Diseases Bulletin for complete source list.

ABSTR. J. EARTHQ. ENG.
[US/0363-5732]
ABSTRACT JOURNAL IN EARTHQUAKE ENGINEERING.

ABSTR. MIL. BIBLIOGR.
[AG]
ABSTRACTS OF MILITARY BIBLIOGRAPHY.
(*Continues* Resumenes Analiticos Sobre Defensa y Seguridad Nacional.)

ABSTR. NEW WORLD ARCHAEOL.
[US]
ABSTRACTS OF NEW WORLD ARCHAEOLOGY.
(Ceased)

ABSTR. NORTH AM. GEOL.
[US/0001-3625]
ABSTRACTS OF NORTH AMERICAN GEOLOGY.
(Ceased)

ABSTR. OF MYCOL.
[US/0001-3617]
ABSTRACTS OF MYCOLOGY.
***Refer to Biological Abstracts for complete source list.

ABSTR. PHOTOGR. SCI. ENG. LIT.
[US/0001-3633]
ABSTRACTS OF PHOTOGRAPHIC SCIENCE & ENGINEERING LITERATURE.
(*Continues* Monthly Abstract Bulletin from the Kodak Research Laboratories; ANSCO Abstracts.)

ABSTR. POP. CULT.
[US/0147-2615]
ABSTRACTS OF POPULAR CULTURE.
(Ceased)

ABSTR. RES. PASTOR. CARE COUNS.
[US/0733-2599]
ABSTRACTS OF RESEARCH IN PASTORAL CARE AND COUNSELING.
(*Continues* Pastoral Care and Counseling Abstracts.)

INDEXES/ABSTRACTS TABLE

ABSTR. SOC. GERONTOL.
[US/1047-4862]
ABSTRACTS IN SOCIAL GERONTOLOGY.
(*Continues* Current Literature on Aging.)

ABSTR. SOC. WORK.
[US/0001-3412]
ABSTRACTS FOR SOCIAL WORKERS.
(*Continued by* Social Work Research & Abstracts.)

ABSTR. TROP. AGRIC.
[NE/0304-5951]
ABSTRACTS ON TROPICAL AGRICULTURE.
(*Supersedes* Tropical Abstracts.)

ABSTR. WORLD MED.
[UK]
ABSTRACTS OF WORLD MEDICINE.
(*Absorbed* Abstracts of World Surgery, Obstetrics and Gynaecology.)

ACAD. ABSTR.
[US/1056-7496]
ACADEMIC ABSTRACTS.

ACAD. ABSTR. FULL TEXT ELITE
[US/1060-6750]
ACADEMIC ABSTRACTS FULL TEXT ELITE.

ACAD. IND. [COMPUTER FILE]
[US]
ACADEMIC INDEX. [COMPUTER FILE].

ACAD. SEARCH
[US/1071-2720]
ACADEMIC SEARCH.

ACCESS
[US/0095-5698]
ACCESS (SYRACUSE).
(*Absorbed* Monthly Periodical Index.)

ACCESS INDEX LITTLE MAG.
[US/0363-065X]
ACCESS INDEX TO LITTLE MAGAZINES.
(Ceased)

ACCOUNT. ART.
[US]
ACCOUNTING ARTICLES.

ACCOUNT. DATA PROCESS. ABSTR.
[UK/0001-4796]
ACCOUNTING + DATA PROCESSING ABSTRACTS.
(*Continued by* Accounting + Finance Abstracts.)

ACCOUNT. INDEX
[US]
ACCOUNTANTS INDEX.
(*Continued by* Accounting & Tax Index.)

ACCOUNT. INDEX SUPPL.
[US/0748-7975]
ACCOUNTANTS' INDEX. SUPPLEMENT.
(*Continued by* Accounting & Tax Index.)

ACCOUNT. TAX DATAB.
[US]
ACCOUNTING AND TAX DATABASE [ONLINE DATABASE].

ACCOUNT. TAX INDEX
[US/1063-0287]
ACCOUNTING AND TAX INDEX.
(*Continues* Accountants' Index. Supplement.)
***Refer to Accounting and Tax Database for complete source list.

ACCUMU. VET. INDEX
[US/0567-7033]
ACCUMULATIVE VETERINARY INDEX.
(Ceased)

ACID RAIN ABSTR.
[US/0882-1402]
ACID RAIN ABSTRACTS.
(*Absorbed by* Environment Abstracts.)

ACM GUIDE COMPUT. LIT.
[US/0149-1199]
ACM GUIDE TO COMPUTING LITERATURE.
(*Continues* Computing Reviews. Bibliography and Subject Index of Current Computing Literature.)

ACOUST. ABSTR.
[UK/0001-4974]
ACOUSTICS ABSTRACTS.

ADOLESC. MENT. HEALTH ABSTR.
[US]
ADOLESCENT MENTAL HEALTH ABSTRACTS.
(Ceased)

ADONIS
[NE]
ADONIS CD-ROM.

AERO. DEF. MARK. TECHNOL.
[US/0885-2286]
AEROSPACE/DEFENSE MARKETS & TECHNOLOGY.
(*Continues* Defense Markets & Technology.)

AESIS Q.
[AT/0313-704x]
AESIS QUARTERLY.

AFR. ABSTR.
[UK/0568-1200]
AFRICAN ABSTRACTS.
(Ceased)

AGBIOTECH NEWS INF.
[UK/0954-9897]
AGBIOTECH NEWS AND INFORMATION.

AGRIC. ENG. ABSTR.
[UK/0308-8863]
AGRICULTURAL ENGINEERING ABSTRACTS.

AGRIC. ENVIRON. BIOTECHNOL. ABSTR.
[US/1063-1151]
AGRICULTURAL & ENVIRONMENTAL BIOTECHNOLOGY ABSTRACTS.
(*Continues in part* Biotechnology Research Abstracts.)
***Refer to Biotechnology Research Abstracts for complete source list.

AGRIC. INDEX
[US/0196-5883]
AGRICULTURAL INDEX.
(*Continued by* Biological & Agricultural Index.)

AGRICOLA
[US/1050-6810]
AGRICOLA.

AGRINDEX
[IT/0254-8801]
AGRINDEX.

AGROFOR. ABSTR.
[UK/0952-1453]
AGROFORESTRY ABSTRACTS.

AIDS ABSTR.
[US/1066-1107]
AIDS ABSTRACTS (ATLANTA, GA.).

AIR POLLUT. TITLES
[US/0002-2497]
AIR POLLUTION TITLES.
(Ceased)

AIR UNIV. LIBR. INDEX MIL. PERIOD.
[US/0002-2586]
AIR UNIVERSITY LIBRARY INDEX TO MILITARY PERIODICALS.
(*Continues* Air University Periodical Index.)

AIR UNIV. PERIOD. INDEX
[US]
AIR UNIVERSITY PERIODICAL INDEX.
(*Continued by* Air University Library Index to Military Periodicals.)

ALCOHOL CLIN. UPDATE
[US/0740-1035]
ALCOHOL CLINICAL UPDATE.
(Ceased)

ALCOHOL. DIG.
[US/0093-7010]
ALCOHOLISM DIGEST.
(Ceased)

ALTERN. PRESS INDEX
[US/0002-662X]
ALTERNATIVE PRESS INDEX.

ALUM. IND. ABSTR.
[US/1066-0623]
ALUMINIUM INDUSTRY ABSTRACTS.
(*Continues* World Aluminum Abstracts.)

AM. BIBLIOGR. SLAVIC EAST EUROP. STUD.
[US/0094-3770]
AMERICAN BIBLIOGRAPHY OF SLAVIC AND EAST EUROPEAN STUDIES.
(*Continues* American Bibliography of Russian and East European Studies.)

AM. HIST. LIFE
[US/0002-7065]
AMERICA, HISTORY AND LIFE (SANTA BARBARA, CALIF. : 1989).
(*Formed by the union of* America, History and Life. Part A, Article Abstracts and Citations *and* America, History and Life. Part B, Index to Book Reviews America, History and Life. Part C, American History Bibliography, Books, Articles and Dissertations America, History and Life. Part D, Annual Index.)

AM. HIST. LIFE PART B
[US/0002-7065]
AMERICA: HISTORY AND LIFE. PART B: INDEX TO BOOK REVIEWS.
(*Merged with* America, History and Life. Part A, Article Abstracts and Citations; America, History and Life. Part C, American History Bibliography, Books, Articles and Dissertations *and* America, History and Life. Part D, Annual Index *to form* America, History and Life.)

AM. HUMANIT. INDEX
[US/0361-0144]
AMERICAN HUMANITIES INDEX, THE.

AM. INDIAN INDEX
[US/0569-5244]
AMERICAN INDIAN INDEX.
(Ceased)

AM. STAT. INDEX
[US/0091-1658]
AMERICAN STATISTICS INDEX.

ANAL. ABSTR.
[UK/0003-2689]
ANALYTICAL ABSTRACTS.
(*Continues* British Abstracts. Section C, Analysis and Apparatus.)

INDEXES/ABSTRACTS TABLE

ANBAR ACCOUNT. FINAN. ABSTR.
[UK/0961-2742]
ANBAR ACCOUNTING & FINANCE ABSTRACTS.
(*Continues* Accounting + Data Processing Abstracts.)

ANBAR MANAG. SERV. ABSTR.
[UK]
ANBAR MANAGEMENT SERVICES ABSTRACTS.
(***Superseded in part by*** Accounting + Data Processing Abstracts; Marketing + Distribution Abstracts; Personnel + Training Abstracts **and** Top Management Abstracts.)

ANBAR MARK. DISTR. ABSTR.
[UK/0305-0661]
ANBAR MARKETING & DISTRIBUTION ABSTRACTS.
(*Continues* Marketing + Distribution Abstracts.)

ANBAR TOP MANAG. ABSTR.
[UK]
ANBAR TOP MANAGEMENT ABSTRACTS.
(*Continues* Top Management Abstracts.)

ANIM. BEHAV. ABSTR.
[US/0301-8695]
ANIMAL BEHAVIOR ABSTRACTS.
(*Continues* Animal Behaviour Abstracts.)

ANIM. BREED. ABSTR.
[UK/0003-3499]
ANIMAL BREEDING ABSTRACTS.
(***Formed by the union of*** Imperial Bureau of Animal Breeding and Genetics. Quarterly Bulletin **and** Imperial Bureau of Animal References to Literature Contained in Periodicals Received.)

ANIM. DISEASE OCCURR.
[UK/0144-3879]
ANIMAL DISEASE OCCURRENCE.
(Ceased)

ANNALS BEHAV. MED.
[US/0883-6612]
ANNALS OF BEHAVIORAL MEDICINE.
(*Continues* Behavioral Medicine Update; **Absorbed** Behavioral Medicine Abstracts.)

ANNOT. BIBLIOGR. ECON. GEOL.
[US/0003-5076]
ANNOTATED BIBLIOGRAPHY OF ECONOMIC GEOLOGY.
(Ceased)

ANNU. BIBLIOGR. ENGL. LANG. LIT.
[UK/0066-3786]
ANNUAL BIBLIOGRAPHY OF ENGLISH LANGUAGE AND LITERATURE.
(*Continues* Bibliography of English Language and Literature.)

ANNU. INDEX POP. MUSIC REC. REV.
[US/0092-3486]
ANNUAL INDEX TO POPULAR MUSIC RECORD REVIEWS.
(*Continues* Annual Index to Popular Music Record Reviews.)

ANNU. LEG. BIBLIOGR.
[US/0073-0793]
ANNUAL LEGAL BIBLIOGRAPHY.
(Ceased)

ANTHROPOL. INDEX
[UK/0003-5467]
ANTHROPOLOGICAL INDEX TO CURRENT PERIODICALS IN THE LIBRARY OF THE ROYAL ANTHROPOLOGICAL INSTITUTE.
(*Continues* Anthropological Index to Current Periodicals in the Museum of Mankind (Library Incorporating the Royal Anthropological Institute Library).)

ANTHROPOL. LIT.
[US/0190-3373]
ANTHROPOLOGICAL LITERATURE.
(*Continues* Anthropological Literature (Cambridge, Mass. : 1984).)

ANTHROPOL. LIT. MICRO.
[US/0190-3373]
ANTHROPOLOGICAL LITERATURE.
(*Continued by* Anthropological Literature (Cambridge, Mass. : 1989).)

APAIS, AUST. PUBLIC AFF. INF. SER.
[AT/0727-8926]
APAIS. AUSTRALIAN PUBLIC AFFAIRS INFORMATION SERVICE.

API ABSTR. HEALTH ENVIRON.
[US]
API ABSTRACTS. HEALTH & ENVIRONMENT.
(*Continued by* Literature Abstracts. Health & Environment.)

API ABSTR. OIL. CHEM.
[US]
API ABSTRACTS : OILFIELD CHEMICALS.
(*Continued by* Literature & Patent Abstracts. Oilfield Chemicals.)

APIBIZ
[US]
APIBIZ [ONLINE DATABASE].
***Refer to Petroleum/Energy Business News Index for complete source list.

APIC. ABSTR.
[UK/0003-648X]
APICULTURAL ABSTRACTS.

APILIT
[US]
APILIT [ONLINE DATABASE].
***Refer to Literature & Patent Abstracts Oilfield Chemicals for a complete source list.

APPL. ECOL. ABSTR.
[UK/0305-3040]
APPLIED ECOLOGY ABSTRACTS.
(*Continued by* Ecology Abstracts.)

APPL. MECH. REV.
[US/0003-6900]
APPLIED MECHANICS REVIEWS.

APPL. SCI. TECHNOL. INDEX
[US/0003-6986]
APPLIED SCIENCE & TECHNOLOGY INDEX.
(*Continues in part* Industrial Arts Index.)

APPL. SOC. SCI. INDEX ABSTR.
[UK/0950-2238]
ASSIA. APPLIED SOCIAL SCIENCES INDEX & ABSTRACTS.

AQUALINE ABSTR.
[UK/0263-5534]
AQUALINE ABSTRACTS.
(*Continues* Water Research Centre (Great Britain). WRC Information.)

AQUAREF
[CN]
AQUAREF.
(*Continues* Canadian Environment; Environnement.)

AQUAT. SCI. FISH. ABSTR.
[UK/0044-8516]
AQUATIC SCIENCES & FISHERIES ABSTRACTS.
(**Split into** Aquatic Sciences and Fisheries Abstracts. Part 1, Biological Sciences and Living Resources **and** Aquatic Sciences and Fisheries Abstracts. Part 2, Ocean Technology, Policy and Non-Living Resources.)

AQUAT. SCI. FISH. ABSTR. (COMPUTER FILE)
[US/1064-0460]
AQUATIC SCIENCES & FISHERIES ABSTRACTS (CD-ROM ED.).

AQUAT. SCI. FISH. ABSTR. PART 1
[US/0140-5373]
AQUATIC SCIENCES AND FISHERIES ABSTRACTS. PART 1 : BIOLOGICAL SCIENCES AND LIVING RESOURCES.
(*Continued in part by* Aquatic Sciences and Fisheries Abstracts. Part 3, Aquatic Pollution and Environmental Quality.)
***Refer to Aquatic Science & Fisheries Abstracts [Computer File]: ASFA / Cambridge Scientific Abstracts for complete source list.

AQUAT. SCI. FISH. ABSTR. 2, OCEAN TECHNOL. POLICY NON-LIVING RESOUR.
[US/0140-5381]
AQUATIC SCIENCES AND FISHERIES ABSTRACTS. PART 2 : OCEAN TECHNOLOGY, POLICY AND NON-LIVING RESOURCES.
(*Continued in part by* Aquatic Sciences and Fisheries Abstracts. Part 3, Aquatic Pollution and Environmental Quality.)
***Refer to Aquatic Sciences & Fisheries Abstracts [Computer File] : ASFA / Cambridge Scientific Abstracts for complete source list.

AQUAT. SCI. FISHER. ABSTR. 3, AQUAT. POLLUT. ENVIRO. QUAL.
[US/1045-6031]
AQUATIC SCIENCES AND FISHERIES ABSTRACTS. PART 3 : AQUATIC POLLUTION AND ENVIRONMENTAL QUALITY.
(*Continues in part* Aquatic Sciences and Fisheries Abstracts. Part 1, Biological Sciences & Living Resources **and** Aquatic Sciences and Fisheries Abstracts. Part 2, Ocean Technology, Policy and Non-Living Resources.)
***Refer to Aquatic Sciences & Fisheries Abstracts [Computer File] : ASFA / Cambridge Scientific Abstracts for complete source list.

ARCHIT. PERIOD. INDEX
[UK/0266-4380]
API. ARCHITECTURAL PERIODICALS INDEX.
(***Supersedes*** Royal Institute of British Architects. RIBA Library Bulletin; Royal Institute of British Architects. RIBA Annual Review of Periodical Articles.)

ARCT. BIBLIOGR.
[CN/0066-6947]
ARCTIC BIBLIOGRAPHY.
(Ceased)

ARECO Q. INDEX PERIOD. LIT. AGING
[US/0734-5569]
ARECO'S QUARTERLY INDEX TO PERIODICAL LITERATURE ON AGING.
(*Continued by* Index to Periodical Literature on Aging.)

ART ARCHAEOL. TECH. ABSTR.
[US/0004-2994]
ART AND ARCHAEOLOGY TECHNICAL ABSTRACTS.
(*Continues* I.I.C. Abstracts.)

ART DES. PHOTO
[UK/0306-817X]
ART, DESIGN, PHOTO.
(Ceased)

ART INDEX
[US/0004-3222]
ART INDEX.

INDEXES/ABSTRACTS TABLE

ART INTELL. ABSTR.
[US/0882-1410]
ARTIFICIAL INTELLIGENCE ABSTRACTS.
(**Ceased**)

ARTBIBLIOGR. CURR. TITLES
[UK/0307-9961]
ARTBIBLIOGRAPHIES. CURRENT TITLES.

ARTBIBLIOGR. MOD.
[UK/0300-466X]
ARTBIBLIOGRAPHIES MODERN.
(**Continues** LOMA; Literature on Modern Art.)

ARTS HUMANIT. CITATION INDEX
[US/0162-8445]
ARTS & HUMANITIES CITATION INDEX (PRINT ED.).

ASCATOPICS
[US/0730-8574]
ASCATOPICS.
(**Continued by** Research Alert.)

ASCE
[US/0730-3149]
ASCE.
(**Continued by** ASCE Annual Combined Index.)

ASCE ANNU. COMB. INDEX
[US/0742-1753]
ASCE ANNUAL COMBINED INDEX.
(**Continues** American Society of Civil Engineers. ASCE.)

ASCE PUBL. INF.
[US/0734-1962]
ASCE PUBLICATIONS INFORMATION.
(**Continues** ASCE Publications Abstracts.)

ASIA.-PAC. ECON. LIT.
[UK/0818-9935]
ASIAN-PACIFIC ECONOMIC LITERATURE.

ASSIA PLUS
[UK]
ASSIA PLUS [COMPUTER FILE].
***Refer to Applied Social Sciences Index & Abstracts for complete source list.

ASTIS BIBLIOGR.
[CN/0226-1685]
ASTIS BIBLIOGRAPHY.

ASTIS CURR. AWARE. BULL.
[CN/0705-8454]
A S T I S CURRENT AWARENESS BULLETIN.
(**Continues** Arctic Institute of North America. Library Accessions.)

ASTRON. ASTROPHYS. ABSTR.
[GW/0067-0022]
ASTRONOMY AND ASTROPHYSICS ABSTRACTS.
(**Continues** Astronomischer Jahresbericht.)

AUST. EDUC. INDEX
[AT/0004-9026]
AUSTRALIAN EDUCATION INDEX.

AUST. LEG. MON. DIG.
[AT/0004-9646]
AUSTRALIAN LEGAL MONTHLY DIGEST.

AUST. LIBR. INF. SCI. ABSTR.
[AT/0810-9265]
ALISA. AUSTRALIAN LIBRARY AND INFORMATION SCIENCE ABSTRACTS.

AUST. SCI. INDEX
[AT/0005-0229]
AUSTRALIAN SCIENCE INDEX.
(**Continues** C.S.I.R.O. Science Abstracts.)

AUTOM. SUBJ. CITATION ALERT
[US]
AUTOMATIC SUBJECT CITATION ALERT.
(**Continued by** Research Alert.)

AVERY INDEX ARCHIT. PERIOD. SUPPL.
[US/0588-540X]
AVERY INDEX TO ARCHITECTURAL PERIODICALS. SUPPLEMENT.
(**Continued by** Avery Index to Architectural Periodicals. Supplement / Columbia University.)

AVERY INDEX ARCHIT. PERIOD. SUPPL. COLUM. UNIV.
[US/0196-0008]
AVERY INDEX TO ARCHITECTURAL PERIODICALS. SECOND EDITION. REVISED AND ENLARGED. SUPPLEMENT.
(**Continues** Avery Library. Avery Index to Architectural Periodicals. Supplement.)

AVIAT. TRADESCAN
[US/0899-1928]
AVIATION TRADESCAN.

BEHAV. ABSTR.
[UK/0262-236X]
BEHAVIOURAL ABSTRACTS.
(**Ceased**)

BEHAV. MED. ABSTR.
[US/0197-7717]
BEHAVIORAL MEDICINE ABSTRACTS.
(**Absorbed by** Annals of Behavioral Medicine.)

BER. BIOCHEM. BIOL.
[GW/0005-9013]
BERICHTE BIOCHEMIE UND BIOLOGIE.
(**Continues** Berichte uber die Wissenschaftliche Biologie.)

BHA : BIBLIO. HIST. ART
[FR/1150-1588]
BIBLIOGRAPHY OF THE HISTORY OF ART : BHA.
(**Formed by the union of** Repertoire International de la Litterature de l'Art **and** Repertoire d'Art et d'Archeologie.)

BHI PLUS
[UK/0966-8772]
BHI PLUS [COMPUTER FILE].
***Refer to British Humanities Index for complete source list.

BIBLIOGR. AGRIC.
[US/0006-1530]
BIBLIOGRAPHY OF AGRICULTURE.
(**Continues** Bibliography of Agriculture with Subject Index.)
***Refer to AGRICOLA for complete source list.

BIBLIOGR. BRAS. CIEN. INF.
[BL/0102-2865]
BIBLIOGRAFIA BRASILEIRA DE CIENCIA DA INFORMACAO.
(**Ceased**)

BIBLIOGR. BRAS. MED.
[BL/0067-6675]
BIBLIOGRAFIA BRASILEIRA DE MEDICINA.
(**Continues** Indice-Catalogo Medico Brasileiro.)

BIBLIOGR. CARTO.
[GW/0340-0409]
BIBLIOGRAPHIA CARTOGRAPHICA.
(**Supersedes** Bibliotheca Cartographica.)

BIBLIOGR. ENGL. LIT.
[UK]
BIBLIOGRAPHY OF ENGLISH LANGUAGE AND LITERATURE.
(**Continued by** Annual Bibliography of English Language and Literature.)

BIBLIOGR. HIST. MED.
[US/0067-7280]
BIBLIOGRAPHY OF THE HISTORY OF MEDICINE.
***Refer to Index Medicus for complete source list.

BIBLIOGR. INDEX GEOL.
[US/0098-2784]
BIBLIOGRAPHY AND INDEX OF GEOLOGY.
(**Continues** Bibliography and Index of Geology Exclusive of North America; **Absorbed** Bibliography of North American Geology.)
***Refer to GeoRef [Computer File] for complete source list.

BIBLIOGR. INDEX GEOL. EXCLUS. NORTH AM.
[US/0376-1673]
BIBLIOGRAPHY AND INDEX OF GEOLOGY EXCLUSIVE OF NORTH AMERICA.
(**Continued by** Bibliography and Index of Geology.)

BIBLIOGR. INDEX HEALTH EDUC. PERIOD.
[US/0278-2340]
BIBLIOGRAPHIC INDEX OF HEALTH EDUCATION PERIODICALS : BIHEP.
(**Ceased**)

BIBLIOGR. INDEX MICROPALEONTOLOGY
[US/0300-7227]
BIBLIOGRAPHY AND INDEX OF MICROPALEONTOLOGY.
***Refer to GeoRef [Computer File] for complete source list.

BIBLIOGR. MISSION.
[IT]
BIBLIOGRAFIA MISSIONARIA.
(**Continued by** Bibliographia Missionaria.)

BIBLIOGR. MISSION.
[VC/0394-9869]
BIBLIOGRAPHIA MISSIONARIA / PONTIFICAL MISSIONARY LIBRARY OF THE CONGREGATION FOR THE EVANGELIZATION OF PEOPLES.
(**Continues** Bibliografia Missionaria.)

BIBLIOGR. NORTH AM. GEOL.
[US/0740-6347]
BIBLIOGRAPHY OF NORTH AMERICAN GEOLOGY.
(**Absorbed by** Bibliography and Index of Geology.)

BIOBUSINESS
[US]
BIOBUSINESS.

BIOCONT. NEWS INF.
[UK/0143-1404]
BIOCONTROL NEWS AND INFORMATION.

BIODETER. ABSTR.
[UK/0951-0621]
BIODETERIORATION ABSTRACTS.
(**Separated from** International Biodeterioration.)

BIOENG. ABSTR.
[US/0093-8378]
BIOENGINEERING ABSTRACTS.
(**Continued by** Engineering Index Bioengineering Abstracts.)

INDEXES/ABSTRACTS TABLE

BIOENG. ABSTR.
[US/1068-5693]
BIOENGINEERING ABSTRACTS (1993).
(*Continues* Engineering Index Bioengineering and Biotechnology Abstracts.)

BIOGR. INDEX
[US/0006-3053]
BIOGRAPHY INDEX.

BIOL. ABSTR. RRM
[US/0192-6985]
BIOLOGICAL ABSTRACTS / RRM.
(*Continues* Bioresearch Index.)
***Refer to Biological Abstracts for complete source list.

BIOL. ABSTR.
[US/0006-3169]
BIOLOGICAL ABSTRACTS.
(*Formed by the union of* Abstracts of Bacteriology *and* Botanical Abstracts.)

BIOL. ABSTR. ON COMPACT DISC
[US/1058-4129]
BIOLOGICAL ABSTRACTS ON COMPACT DISC.
***Refer to Biological Abstracts for complete source list.

BIOL. AGRIC. INDEX
[US/0006-3177]
BIOLOGICAL & AGRICULTURAL INDEX.
(*Continues* Agricultural Index.)

BIOL. DIG.
[US/0095-2958]
BIOLOGY DIGEST.

BIOSTATISTICA
[US/1041-7648]
BIOSTATISTICA (DAVENPORT, IOWA).

BIOTECHNOL. ABSTR.
[UK/0262-5318]
DERWENT BIOTECHNOLOGY ABSTRACTS.
(*Continued by* Biotechnology Abstracts.)

BIOTECHNOL. ABSTR.
[UK]
BIOTECHNOLOGY ABSTRACTS.
(*Continues* Derwent Biotechnology Abstracts.)
***Refer to PESTDOC for complete source list.

BIOTECHNOL. RES. ABSTR.
[US/0733-5709]
BIOTECHNOLOGY RESEARCH ABSTRACTS.
(*Continued in part by* Medical & Pharmaceutical Biotechnology Abstracts *and* Agricultural & Environmental Biotechnology Abstracts.)

BLACK INF. INDEX
[US/0045-2173]
BLACK INFORMATION INDEX.
(Ceased)

BMT ABSTR.
[UK/0268-9650]
BMT ABSTRACTS : BRITISH MARITIME TECHNOLOGY ABSTRACTS.
(*Continues* Journal of Abstracts of the British Ship Research Association.)

BOOK REV. DIGEST
[US/0006-7326]
BOOK REVIEW DIGEST.
(*Continues* Cumulative Book Review Digest.)

BOOK REV. INDEX
[US/0524-0581]
BOOK REVIEW INDEX.

BOOK REV. MON.
[US/0006-7342]
BOOK REVIEWS OF THE MONTH.
(Ceased)

BOSTON GLOBE INDEX
[US/0893-2727]
BOSTON GLOBE INDEX (1987), THE.
(*Continues* Bell & Howell Newspaper Index to the Boston Globe.)

BOWNE DIG. CORP. SEC. LAWYERS
[US/0896-906X]
BOWNE DIGEST FOR CORPORATE & SECURITIES LAWYERS.
(*Continues* Abstracts of Legal Periodicals (Corporate & Securities Ed.).)

BR. ARCHAEOL. ABSTR.
[UK/0007-0270]
BRITISH ARCHAEOLOGICAL ABSTRACTS.
(*Continued by* British Archaeological Bibliography.)

BR. ARCHAEOL. BIBLIOGR.
[UK/0964-7104]
BRITISH ARCHAEOLOGICAL BIBLIOGRAPHY.
(*Continues* British Archaeological Abstracts.)

BR. CERAM. ABSTR.
[UK/0300-4570]
BRITISH CERAMIC ABSTRACTS.
(*Continued by* World Ceramics Abstracts.)

BR. EDUC. INDEX
[UK/0007-0637]
BRITISH EDUCATION INDEX.

BR. HUMANIT. INDEX
[UK/0007-0815]
BRITISH HUMANITIES INDEX.
(*Supersedes in part* Subject Index to Periodicals.)

BR. TECHNOL. INDEX
[UK/0007-1889]
BRITISH TECHNOLOGY INDEX.
(*Continued by* Current Technology Index.)

BULL. ANAL. ENTOMOL. MED. VET.
[FR/0007-4098]
BULLETIN ANALYTIQUE D'ENTOMOLOGIE MEDICALE ET VETERINAIRE.
(Ceased)

BULL. SIGNAL.
[FR]
BULLETIN SIGNALETIQUE.
(Ceased)

BUS. ASAP
[US]
BUSINESS ASAP [COMPUTER FILE].

BUS. DATELINE
[US]
BUSINESS DATELINE.

BUS. EDUC. INDEX
[US/0068-4414]
BUSINESS EDUCATION INDEX.

BUS. INDEX
[US/0273-3684]
BUSINESS INDEX.

BUS. PERIOD. INDEX
[US/0007-6961]
BUSINESS PERIODICALS INDEX.
(*Continues in part* Industrial Arts Index.)

BUS. SOURCE
[US]
BUSINESS SOURCE. [COMPUTER FILE].

CA QUICK SEARCH
[US]
CA QUICK SEARCH [COMPUTER FILE].
***Refer to Concrete Abstracts for complete source list.

CA SEL., ACID RAIN ACID AIR
[US/0885-0097]
CA SELECTS: ACID RAIN & ACID AIR.
***Refer to Chemical Abstracts for complete source list.

CA SEL., ADHESIVES
[US/0162-7686]
CA SELECTS: ADHESIVES.
***Refer to Chemical Abstracts for complete source list.

CA SEL., AIDS RELAT. IMMUNODEFIC.
[US/1040-7111]
CA SELECTS: AIDS & RELATED IMMUNODEFICIENCIES.
***Refer to Chemical Abstracts for complete source list.

CA SEL., AIR POLLUT. BOOKS REV.
[US/0895-5980]
CA SELECTS: AIR POLLUTION (BOOKS & REVIEWS).
***Refer to Chemical Abstracts for complete source list.

CA SEL., ALKYL. CATAL.
[US/0895-5964]
CA SELECTS: ALKYLATION & CATALYSTS.
***Refer to Chemical Abstracts for complete source list.

CA SEL., ALUMIN. LITH. ALUMIN. CER. ALLOYS
[US/1066-1166]
CA SELECTS: ALUMINUM-LITHIUM & ALUMINUM-CERIUM ALLOYS.
***Refer to Chemical Abstracts for complete source list.

CA SEL., ALZHEIMER'S DIS. RELAT. MEM. DYSFUNC.
[US/1047-8183]
CA SELECTS: ALZHEIMER'S DISEASE & RELATED MEMORY DYSFUNCTIONS.
***Refer to Chemical Abstracts for complete source list.

CA SEL., AMINO ACIDS PEP. PROT.
[US/0275-701X]
CA SELECTS: AMINO ACIDS, PEPTIDES & PROTEINS.
***Refer to Chemical Abstracts for complete source list.

CA SEL., ANALYT. ELECTROCHEM.
[US/0160-8959]
CA SELECTS: ANALYTICAL ELECTROCHEMISTRY.
***Refer to Chemical Abstracts for complete source list.

CA SEL., ANIMAL LONG. AGING
[US/0162-7694]
CA SELECTS: ANIMAL LONGEVITY & AGING.
***Refer to Chemical Abstracts for complete source list.

CA SEL., ANTI INFLAM. AGENTS ARTHRIT.
[US/0148-2394]
CA SELECTS: ANTI-INFLAMMATORY AGENTS & ARTHRITIS.
***Refer to Chemical Abstracts for complete source list.

CA SEL., ANTIBAC. AGENTS
[US/1045-8522]
CA SELECTS: ANTIBACTERIAL AGENTS.
(*Continues* CA Selects. Bactericides, Disinfectants & Antiseptics.)
***Refer to Chemical Abstracts for complete source list.

CA SEL., ANTIOXID.
[US/0275-7028]
CA SELECTS: ANTIOXIDANTS.
***Refer to Chemical Abstracts for complete source list.

INDEXES/ABSTRACTS TABLE

CA SEL., ANTITUMOR AGENTS
[US/0148-2386]
CA SELECTS: ANTITUMOR AGENTS.
***Refer to Chemical Abstracts for complete source list.

CA SEL., ARTIF. SWEETEN.
[US/0890-1813]
CA SELECTS: ARTIFICIAL SWEETENERS.
***Refer to Chemical Abstracts for complete source list.

CA SEL., ASYMMET. SYNTH. INDUC.
[US/0890-183X]
CA SELECTS: ASYMMETRIC SYNTHESIS & INDUCTION.
***Refer to Chemical Abstracts for complete source list.

CA SEL., AT. SPECTROSC.
[US/0195-4911]
CA SELECTS: ATOMIC SPECTROSCOPY.
***Refer to Chemical Abstracts for complete source list.

CA SEL., ATHEROSCL. HEART DIS.
[US/0148-2378]
CA SELECTS: ATHEROSCLEROSIS & HEART DISEASE.
***Refer to Chemical Abstracts for complete source list.

CA SEL., AUTOM. CHEM. ANAL.
[US/0740-0683]
CA SELECTS: AUTOMATED CHEMICAL ANALYSIS.
***Refer to Chemical Abstracts for complete source list.

CA SEL., B-LACTAM ANTIB.
[US/0148-2459]
CA SELECTS: B-LACTAM ANTIBIOTICS.
***Refer to Chemical Abstracts for complete source list.

CA SEL., BACTER. DISINFECT. ANTISEP.
[US/0890-1848]
CA SELECTS: BACTERICIDES, DISINFECTANTS & ANTISEPTICS.
(*Continued by* CA Selects: Antibacterial Agents.)

CA SEL., BATTER. FUEL CELLS
[US/0162-7708]
CA SELECTS: BATTERIES & FUEL CELLS.
***Refer to Chemical Abstracts for complete source list.

CA SEL., BIOGEN. AMINES NERV. SYST.
[US/0162-7716]
CA SELECTS: BIOGENIC AMINES & THE NERVOUS SYSTEM.
***Refer to Chemical Abstracts for complete source list.

CA SEL., BIOL. INFO. TRANSF.
[US/0162-7724]
CA SELECTS: BIOLOGICAL INFORMATION TRANSFER.
(Ceased)

CA SEL., BISMUTH CHEM.
[US/1061-5342]
CA SELECTS: BISMUTH CHEMISTRY.
***Refer to Chemical Abstracts for complete source list.

CA SEL., BLOCK GRAFT POLYM.
[US/0734-8851]
CA SELECTS: BLOCK & GRAFT POLYMERS.
***Refer to Chemical Abstracts for complete source list.

CA SEL., BLOOD COAG.
[US/0162-7732]
CA SELECTS: BLOOD COAGULATION.
***Refer to Chemical Abstracts for complete source list.

CA SEL., CARBOHYDR. (CHEM. ASP.)
[US/0740-0756]
CA SELECTS: CARBOHYDRATES (CHEMICAL ASPECTS).
***Refer to Chemical Abstracts for complete source list.

CA SEL., CARBON FIBER COMPOS.
[US/0895-5956]
CA SELECTS: CARBON FIBER COMPOSITES.
***Refer to Chemical Abstracts for complete source list.

CA SEL., CARBON GRAPH. FIB.
[US/0890-1856]
CA SELECTS: CARBON & GRAPHITE FIBERS.
***Refer to Chemical Abstracts for complete source list.

CA SEL., CARBON HETERO. NMR
[US/0190-9401]
CA SELECTS: CARBON & HETEROATOM NMR.
(*Continues in part* CA Selects. Nuclear Magnetic Resonance, Chemical Aspects.)
***Refer to Chemical Abstracts for complete source list.

CA SEL., CARCIN. MUT. TERATO.
[US/0148-2408]
CA SELECTS: CARCINOGENS, MUTAGENS & TERATOGENS.
***Refer to Chemical Abstracts for complete source list.

CA SEL., CATAL. (APPL. PHYS. ASP.)
[US/0146-440X]
CA SELECTS: CATALYSIS (APPLIED AND PHYSICAL ASPECTS).
***Refer to Chemical Abstracts for complete source list.

CA SEL., CATAL. (ORG. REACT.)
[US/0146-4396]
CA SELECTS: CATALYSIS (ORGANIC REACTIONS).
***Refer to Chemical Abstracts for complete source list.

CA SEL., CATAL. KINET. ANAL.
[US/0890-1864]
CA SELECTS: CATALYTIC & KINETIC ANALYSIS.
***Refer to Chemical Abstracts for complete source list.

CA SEL., CATAL. REGEN.
[US/0734-8800]
CA SELECTS: CATALYST REGENERATION.
***Refer to Chemical Abstracts for complete source list.

CA SEL., CERAM. MATER. J.
[US/0895-5948]
CA SELECTS: CERAMIC MATERIALS (JOURNALS).
***Refer to Chemical Abstracts for complete source list.

CA SEL., CERAM. METER. PAT.
[US/0885-0100]
CA SELECTS: CERAMIC MATERIALS (PATENTS).
***Refer to Chemical Abstracts for complete source list.

CA SEL., CHELATING AGENTS
[US/0734-8797]
CA SELECTS: CHELATING AGENTS.
***Refer to Chemical Abstracts for complete source list.

CA SEL., CHEM. ENG. OPER.
[US/1040-712X]
CA SELECTS: CHEMICAL ENGINEERING OPERATIONS.
***Refer to Chemical Abstracts for complete source list.

CA SEL., CHEM. HAZ. HEALTH SAFETY
[US/0190-9398]
CA SELECTS: CHEMICAL HAZARDS, HEALTH, & SAFETY.
(*Continues* CA Selects. Chemical Hazards.)
***Refer to Chemical Abstracts for complete source list.

CA SEL., CHEM. INSTRUM.
[US/0195-4938]
CA SELECTS: CHEMICAL INSTRUMENTATION.
***Refer to Chemical Abstracts for complete source list.

CA SEL., CHEM. IR OS RH RU
[US/1040-7146]
CA SELECTS: CHEMISTRY OF IR, OS, RH, & RU.
***Refer to Chemical Abstracts for complete source list.

CA SEL., CHEM. PROCESS. APPAR.
[US/0195-4946]
CA SELECTS: CHEMICAL PROCESSING APPARATUS.
***Refer to Chemical Abstracts for complete source list.

CA SEL., CHEM. VAPOR DEPOS.
[US/0885-0119]
CA SELECTS. CHEMICAL VAPOR DEPOSITION.
***Refer to Chemical Abstracts for complete source list.

CA SEL., CHEMILUMIN.
[US/1040-7138]
CA SELECTS: CHEMILUMINESCENCE.
***Refer to Chemical Abstracts for complete source list.

CA SEL., COAL SCI. PROC. CHEM.
[US/0146-4426]
CA SELECTS: COAL SCIENCE & PROCESS CHEMISTRY.
***Refer to Chemical Abstracts for complete source list.

CA SEL., COAT. INKS REALT. PROD.
[US/0275-7036]
CA SELECTS: COATINGS, INKS, & RELATED PRODUCTS.
***Refer to Chemical Abstracts for complete source list.

CA SEL., COLLOIDS (APPL. ASP.)
[US/0160-8967]
CA SELECTS: COLLOIDS (APPLIED ASPECTS).
(*Continued by* CA Selects. Colloids (Macromolecular Aspects).)

CA SEL., COLLOIDS (MACROMOL. ASP.)
[US/0190-9444]
CA SELECTS: COLLOIDS (MACROMOLECULAR ASPECTS).
(*Supersedes in part* CA Selects. Colloids (Applied Aspects).)
***Refer to Chemical Abstracts for complete source list.

CA SEL., COLLOIDS (PHYSICO. ASP.)
[US/0160-8975]
CA SELECTS: COLLOIDS (PHYSICOCHEMICAL ASPECTS).
***Refer to Chemical Abstracts for complete source list.

CA SEL., COLOR SCI.
[US/0885-0127]
CA SELECTS: COLOR SCIENCE.
***Refer to Chemical Abstracts for complete source list.

CA SEL., COLOR. DYES
[US/0734-8789]
CA SELECTS: COLORANTS & DYES.
***Refer to Chemical Abstracts for complete source list.

CA SEL., COMPOS. MATER. (CERAM.)
[US/1066-1158]
CA SELECTS: COMPOSITE MATERIALS (CERAMIC).
***Refer to Chemical Abstracts for complete source list.

CA SEL., COMPOS. MATER. (MET.)
[US/1066-114X]
CA SELECTS: COMPOSITE MATERIALS (METALLIC).
***Refer to Chemical Abstracts for complete source list.

CA SEL., COMPOS. MATER. (POLYM.)
[US/1040-7154]
CA SELECTS: COMPOSITE MATERIALS (POLYMERIC).
***Refer to Chemical Abstracts for complete source list.

CA SEL., COMPUT. CHEM.
[US/0160-9025]
CA SELECTS: COMPUTERS IN CHEMISTRY.
***Refer to Chemical Abstracts for complete source list.

INDEXES/ABSTRACTS TABLE

CA SEL., CONDUCT. POLYM.
[US/0885-0135]
CA SELECTS: CONDUCTIVE POLYMERS.
***Refer to Chemical Abstracts for complete source list.

CA SEL., CONTROL. RELEASE TECHNOL.
[US/0740-0748]
CA SELECTS: CONTROLLED RELEASE TECHNOLOGY.
***Refer to Chemical Abstracts for complete source list.

CA SEL., CORROS.
[US/0146-4434]
CA SELECTS: CORROSION.
***Refer to Chemical Abstracts for complete source list.

CA SEL., CORROS.-INHIB. COAT.
[US/0749-7296]
CA SELECTS: CORROSION-INHIBITING COATINGS.
***Refer to Chemical Abstracts for complete source list.

CA SEL., COSMET. CHEM.
[US/0275-7044]
CA SELECTS: COSMETIC CHEMICALS.
***Refer to Chemical Abstracts for complete source list.

CA SEL., COSMOCHEM.
[US/0195-4954]
CA SELECTS: COSMOCHEMISTRY.
(Ceased)

CA SEL., CROSSLINK. REACT.
[US/0740-0721]
CA SELECTS: CROSSLINKING REACTIONS.
***Refer to Chemical Abstracts for complete source list.

CA SEL., CRYS. GROWTH
[US/0162-7740]
CA SELECTS: CRYSTAL GROWTH.
***Refer to Chemical Abstracts for complete source list.

CA SEL., DETER. SOAPS, SURFAC.
[US/0162-7767]
CA SELECTS: DETERGENTS, SOAPS, & SURFACTANTS.
***Refer to Chemical Abstracts for complete source list.

CA SEL., DISTILL. TECHNOL.
[US/0275-7052]
CA SELECTS: DISTILLATION TECHNOLOGY.
***Refer to Chemical Abstracts for complete source list.

CA SEL., DRILL. MUDS
[US/0749-730X]
CA SELECTS: DRILLING MUDS.
***Refer to Chemical Abstracts for complete source list.

CA SEL., DRUG COSMET. TOXIC.
[US/0162-7775]
CA SELECTS: DRUG & COSMETIC TOXICITY.
***Refer to Chemical Abstracts for complete source list.

CA SEL., DRUG DELIV. SYST. DOS. FORMS
[US/1040-7162]
CA SELECTS: DRUG DELIVERY SYSTEMS & DOSAGE FORMS.
***Refer to Chemical Abstracts for complete source list.

CA SEL., ELECT. AUG. SPECTRO.
[US/0146-4450]
CA SELECTS: ELECTRON & AUGER SPECTROSCOPY.
***Refer to Chemical Abstracts for complete source list.

CA SEL., ELECT. SPIN RESON. (CHEM. ASP.)
[US/0146-4469]
CA SELECTS: ELECTRON SPIN RESONANCE (CHEMICAL ASPECTS).
***Refer to Chemical Abstracts for complete source list.

CA SEL., ELECTR. CONDUCT. ORG.
[US/0885-0143]
CA SELECTS: ELECTRICALLY CONDUCTIVE ORGANICS.
***Refer to Chemical Abstracts for complete source list.

CA SEL., ELECTROCHEM. ORG. SYNTH.
[US/0734-8770]
CA SELECTS: ELECTROCHEMICAL ORGANIC SYNTHESIS.
***Refer to Chemical Abstracts for complete source list.

CA SEL., ELECTROCHEM. REAC.
[US/0146-4442]
CA SELECTS: ELECTROCHEMICAL REACTIONS.
***Refer to Chemical Abstracts for complete source list.

CA SEL., ELECTRODEPOSIT.
[US/0162-7783]
CA SELECTS: ELECTRODEPOSITION.
***Refer to Chemical Abstracts for complete source list.

CA SEL., ELECTRON. CHEM. MATER.
[US/0885-0151]
CA SELECTS: ELECTRONIC CHEMICALS & MATERIALS.
***Refer to Chemical Abstracts for complete source list.

CA SEL., ELECTROPHOR.
[US/0195-4962]
CA SELECTS: ELECTROPHORESIS.
***Refer to Chemical Abstracts for complete source list.

CA SEL., EMULS. POLYM.
[US/0195-4970]
CA SELECTS: EMULSION POLYMERIZATION.
***Refer to Chemical Abstracts for complete source list.

CA SEL., EMULSIF. & DEMULSIF.
[US/0734-8754]
CA SELECTS: EMULSIFIERS & DEMULSIFIERS.
***Refer to Chemical Abstracts for complete source list.

CA SEL., ENERGY REV. BOOKS
[US/0162-7791]
CA SELECTS: ENERGY REVIEWS & BOOKS.
***Refer to Chemical Abstracts for complete source list.

CA SEL., ENGINE EXH.
[US/0160-9033]
CA SELECTS: ENGINE EXHAUST.
(Ceased)

CA SEL., ENHANC. PETRO. RECOV.
[US/0734-8746]
CA SELECTS: ENHANCED PETROLEUM RECOVERY.
***Refer to Chemical Abstracts for complete source list.

CA SEL., ENVIRON. POLLUT.
[US/0160-9041]
CA SELECTS: ENVIRONMENTAL POLLUTION.
***Refer to Chemical Abstracts for complete source list.

CA SEL., ENZYM. APPL.
[US/0895-593X]
CA SELECTS: ENZYME APPLICATIONS.
***Refer to Chemical Abstracts for complete source list.

CA SEL., ENZYM. ASSAYS
[US/0895-5808]
CA SELECTS: ENZYME ASSAYS.
***Refer to Chemical Abstracts for complete source list.

CA SEL., EPOXY RESINS
[US/0275-7060]
CA SELECTS: EPOXY RESINS.
***Refer to Chemical Abstracts for complete source list.

CA SEL., FATS OILS
[US/0275-7079]
CA SELECTS: FATS & OILS.
***Refer to Chemical Abstracts for complete source list.

CA SEL., FERMENT. CHEM.
[US/0740-0713]
CA SELECTS: FERMENTATION CHEMICALS.
***Refer to Chemical Abstracts for complete source list.

CA SEL., FIBER OPT. OPT. COMMUN.
[US/0890-1872]
CA SELECTS: FIBER OPTICS & OPTICAL COMMUNICATION.
***Refer to Chemical Abstracts for complete source list.

CA SEL., FIBER-REINFOR. PLAST.
[US/0734-869X]
CA SELECTS: FIBER-REINFORCED PLASTICS.
***Refer to Chemical Abstracts for complete source list.

CA SEL., FLAMMABIL.
[US/0162-7805]
CA SELECTS: FLAMMABILITY.
***Refer to Chemical Abstracts for complete source list.

CA SEL., FLAV. FRAGR.
[US/0148-2327]
CA SELECTS: FLAVORS & FRAGRANCES.
***Refer to Chemical Abstracts for complete source list.

CA SEL., FLUID. SOLIDS TECHNOL.
[US/0195-4989]
CA SELECTS: FLUIDIZED SOLIDS TECHNOLOGY.
***Refer to Chemical Abstracts for complete source list.

CA SEL., FLUOROPOLY.
[US/0895-5921]
CA SELECTS: FLUOROPOLYMERS.
***Refer to Chemical Abstracts for complete source list.

CA SEL., FOOD DRUGS COSMET.
[US/1051-3914]
CA SELECTS: FOOD, DRUGS, & COSMETICS.
***Refer to Chemical Abstracts for complete source list.

CA SEL., FOOD FEED ANAL.
[US/0895-5913]
CA SELECTS: FOOD & FEED ANALYSIS.
***Refer to Chemical Abstracts for complete source list.

CA SEL., FOOD TOXIC.
[US/0162-7813]
CA SELECTS: FOOD TOXICITY.
***Refer to Chemical Abstracts for complete source list.

CA SEL., FORENS. CHEM.
[US/0362-9880]
CA SELECTS: FORENSIC CHEMISTRY.
***Refer to Chemical Abstracts for complete source list.

CA SEL., FORMUL. CHEM.
[US/0890-1880]
CA SELECTS: FORMULATION CHEMISTRY.
***Refer to Chemical Abstracts for complete source list.

CA SEL., FREE RADIC.
[US/0885-016X]
CA SELECTS: FREE RADICALS.
(**Continued by** CA Selects: Free Radicals (Organic Aspects).)

CA SEL., FREE RADIC. (BIOCHEM. ASP.)
[US/0895-5905]
CA SELECTS: FREE RADICALS (BIOCHEMICAL ASPECTS).
***Refer to Chemical Abstracts for complete source list.

INDEXES/ABSTRACTS TABLE

CA SEL., FREE RADIC. (ORG. ASP.)
[US/0895-5972]
CA SELECTS: FREE RADICALS (ORGANIC ASPECTS).
(*Continues* CA Selects. Free Radicals.)
***Refer to Chemical Abstracts for complete source list.

CA SEL., FUEL LUBR. ADDIT.
[US/0195-4997]
CA SELECTS: FUEL & LUBRICANT ADDITIVES.
***Refer to Chemical Abstracts for complete source list.

CA SEL., FUNGICID.
[US/0160-9068]
CA SELECTS: FUNGICIDES.
***Refer to Chemical Abstracts for complete source list.

CA SEL., GAS CHROMAT.
[US/0146-4477]
CA SELECTS: GAS CHROMATOGRAPHY.
***Refer to Chemical Abstracts for complete source list.

CA SEL., GAS. WASTE TREAT.
[US/0160-9076]
CA SELECTS: GASEOUS WASTE TREATMENT.
***Refer to Chemical Abstracts for complete source list.

CA SEL., GEL PERM. CHROMAT.
[US/0146-4485]
CA SELECTS: GEL PERMEATION CHROMATOGRAPHY.
***Refer to Chemical Abstracts for complete source list.

CA SEL., GEOCHEM.
[US/1066-5730]
CA SELECTS: GEOCHEMISTRY.
***Refer to Chemical Abstracts for complete source list.

CA SEL., HEAT-RESIST. ABLAT. POLYM.
[US/0162-7821]
CA SELECTS: HEAT-RESISTANT & ABLATIVE POLYMERS.
***Refer to Chemical Abstracts for complete source list.

CA SEL., HERBIC.
[US/0160-9084]
CA SELECTS: HERBICIDES.
***Refer to Chemical Abstracts for complete source list.

CA SEL., HIGH PERFORM. LIQ. CHROMATOGR.
[US/0195-5217]
CA SELECTS: HIGH PERFORMANCE LIQUID CHROMATOGRAPHY.
(*Continues* CA Selects. High Speed Liquid Chromatography.)
***Refer to Chemical Abstracts for complete source list.

CA SEL., HOT-MELT ADHES.
[US/0895-5891]
CA SELECTS: HOT-MELT ADHESIVES.
***Refer to Chemical Abstracts for complete source list.

CA SEL., HYPERTENS. ANTIHYPERTENS.
[US/1051-3922]
CA SELECTS: HYPERTENSION & ANTIHYPERTENSIVES.
***Refer to Chemical Abstracts for complete source list.

CA SEL., INFR. SPECTRO. (ORG. ASP.)
[US/0190-9428]
CA SELECTS: INFRARED SPECTROSCOPY (ORGANIC ASPECTS).
(*Continues in part* CA Selects. Infrared Spectroscopy.)
***Refer to Chemical Abstracts for complete source list.

CA SEL., INFR. SPECTRO. (PHYSICOCHEM. ASP.)
[US/0190-9436]
CA SELECTS: INFRARED SPECTROSCOPY (PHYSICOCHEMICAL ASPECTS).
(*Continues in part* CA Selects. Infrared Spectroscopy.)
***Refer to Chemical Abstracts for complete source list.

CA SEL., INIT. POLYMER.
[US/0734-8843]
CA SELECTS: INITIATION OF POLYMERIZATION.
***Refer to Chemical Abstracts for complete source list.

CA SEL., INORG. ANAL. CHEM.
[US/0275-7087]
CA SELECTS: INORGANIC ANALYTICAL CHEMISTRY.
***Refer to Chemical Abstracts for complete source list.

CA SEL., INORG. CHEM. REACT.
[US/0275-7095]
CA SELECTS: INORGANIC CHEMICALS & REACTIONS.
***Refer to Chemical Abstracts for complete source list.

CA SEL., INORG. FLOUR. CHEM.
[US/0195-5004]
CA SELECTS: INORGANIC FLOURINE CHEMISTRY.
(Ceased)

CA SEL., INORG. ORGANOMET. REACT. MECHAN.
[US/0195-5012]
CA SELECTS: INORGANIC & ORGANOMETALLIC REACTION MECHANISMS.
***Refer to Chemical Abstracts for complete source list.

CA SEL., INSECTIC.
[US/0160-9092]
CA SELECTS: INSECTICIDES.
***Refer to Chemical Abstracts for complete source list.

CA SEL., ION CHROMATOGR.
[US/0890-1899]
CA SELECTS: ION CHROMATOGRAPHY.
***Refer to Chemical Abstracts for complete source list.

CA SEL., ION EXCHANGE
[US/0146-4493]
CA SELECTS: ION EXCHANGE.
***Refer to Chemical Abstracts for complete source list.

CA SEL., ION-CONTAIN. POLYM.
[US/0195-5020]
CA SELECTS: ION-CONTAINING POLYMERS.
***Refer to Chemical Abstracts for complete source list.

CA SEL., ISOMERI. CATAL.
[US/0895-5883]
CA SELECTS: ISOMERIZATION & CATALYSTS.
***Refer to Chemical Abstracts for complete source list.

CA SEL., LASER APPL.
[US/0195-5039]
CA SELECTS: LASER APPLICATIONS.
***Refer to Chemical Abstracts for complete source list.

CA SEL., LASER-INDUC. CHEM REACT.
[US/0885-0178]
CA SELECTS: LASER-INDUCED CHEMICAL REACTIONS.
***Refer to Chemical Abstracts for complete source list.

CA SEL., LASERS MASERS
[US/0195-5047]
CA SELECTS: LASERS & MASERS.
(Ceased)

CA SEL., LIQ. CRYST.
[US/0148-2351]
CA SELECTS: LIQUID CRYSTALS.
***Refer to Chemical Abstracts for complete source list.

CA SEL., LIQ. WASTE TREAT.
[US/0160-9106]
CA SELECTS: LIQUID WASTE TREATMENT.
***Refer to Chemical Abstracts for complete source list.

CA SEL., LUBR. GREAS. LUBRICAT.
[US/0734-8738]
CA SELECTS: LUBRICANTS, GREASES & LUBRICATION.
***Refer to Chemical Abstracts for complete source list.

CA SEL., MACROCYCL. ANTIBIOT.
[US/0195-5055]
CA SELECTS: MACROCYCLIC ANTIBIOTICS.
(Ceased)

CA SEL., MASS SPECTRO.
[US/0362-9872]
CA SELECTS: MASS SPECTROMETRY.
***Refer to Chemical Abstracts for complete source list.

CA SEL., MEM. REC. DEVICES MATER.
[US/0890-1821]
CA SELECTS: MEMORY & RECORDING DEVICES & MATERIALS.
***Refer to Chemical Abstracts for complete source list.

CA SEL., MEMBR. SEP.
[US/1040-7197]
CA SELECTS: MEMBRANE SEPARATION.
***Refer to Chemical Abstracts for complete source list.

CA SEL., METAL. GLASS.
[US/1062-8681]
CA SELECTS: METALLIC GLASSES.
***Refer to Chemical Abstracts for complete source list.

CA SEL., METALLO ENZ. METALLO COENZ.
[US/0160-9114]
CA SELECTS: METALLO ENZYMES & METALLO COENZYMES.
***Refer to Chemical Abstracts for complete source list.

CA SEL., MOLEC. MODEL. (BIOCHEM. ASP.)
[US/1059-2784]
CA SELECTS: MOLECULAR MODELING (BIOCHEMICAL ASPECTS).
***Refer to Chemical Abstracts for complete source list.

CA SEL., NAT. PROD. SYNTH.
[US/0740-0691]
CA SELECTS: NATURAL PRODUCT SYNTHESIS.
***Refer to Chemical Abstracts for complete source list.

CA SEL., NEW ANTIBIOT.
[US/0895-5875]
CA SELECTS: NEW ANTIBIOTICS.
***Refer to Chemical Abstracts for complete source list.

CA SEL., NEW BOOKS CHEM.
[US/0148-2416]
CA SELECTS: NEW BOOKS IN CHEMISTRY.
***Refer to Chemical Abstracts for complete source list.

CA SEL., NEW PLAST.
[US/0734-8673]
CA SELECTS: NEW PLASTICS.
***Refer to Chemical Abstracts for complete source list.

CA SEL., NITROGEN FIXAT.
[US/1047-8108]
CA SELECTS: NITROGEN FIXATION.
***Refer to Chemical Abstracts for complete source list.

CA SEL., NONLINEAR OPT. MATER.
[US/0895-5867]
CA SELECTS: NONLINEAR OPTICAL MATERIALS.
***Refer to Chemical Abstracts for complete source list.

INDEXES/ABSTRACTS TABLE

CA SEL., NOV. PESTIC. HERBIC.
[US/0749-7318]
CA SELECTS: NOVEL PESTICIDES & HERBICIDES.
***Refer to Chemical Abstracts for complete source list.

CA SEL., NOVEL NAT. PROD.
[US/0734-872X]
CA SELECTS: NOVEL NATURAL PRODUCTS.
***Refer to Chemical Abstracts for complete source list.

CA SEL., NOVEL POLYM. PAT.
[US/0734-8819]
CA SELECTS: NOVEL POLYMERS FROM PATENTS.
***Refer to Chemical Abstracts for complete source list.

CA SEL., NOVEL SULFUR HETEROCYCL.
[US/0275-7109]
CA SELECTS: NOVEL SULFUR HETEROCYCLES.
***Refer to Chemical Abstracts for complete source list.

CA SEL., OMEGA THREE FAT. ACID. FISH OIL
[US/1052-1984]
CA SELECTS: OMEGA THREE FATTY ACIDS & FISH OIL.
***Refer to Chemical Abstracts for complete source list.

CA SEL., OPT. PHOTOSENSIT. MATER.
[US/0195-5063]
CA SELECTS: OPTICAL & PHOTOSENSITIVE MATERIALS.
***Refer to Chemical Abstracts for complete source list.

CA SEL., OPTIMIZ. ORG. REACT.
[US/0195-5071]
CA SELECTS: OPTIMIZATION OF ORGANIC REACTIONS.
***Refer to Chemical Abstracts for complete source list.

CA SEL., ORAGNOPHOS. CHEM.
[US/0162-783X]
CA SELECTS: ORGANOPHOSPHORUS CHEMISTRY.
***Refer to Chemical Abstracts for complete source list.

CA SEL., ORG. ANAL. CHEM.
[US/0275-7117]
CA SELECTS: ORGANIC ANALYTICAL CHEMISTRY.
***Refer to Chemical Abstracts for complete source list.

CA SEL., ORG. OPT. MATER.
[US/0885-0186]
CA SELECTS: ORGANIC OPTICAL MATERIALS.
***Refer to Chemical Abstracts for complete source list.

CA SEL., ORG. REACT. MECHAN.
[US/0162-7848]
CA SELECTS: ORGANIC REACTION MECHANISMS.
***Refer to Chemical Abstracts for complete source list.

CA SEL., ORG. STEREOCHEM.
[US/0195-508X]
CA SELECTS: ORGANIC STEREOCHEMISTRY.
***Refer to Chemical Abstracts for complete source list.

CA SEL., ORG.-TRANS. MET. COMPL.
[US/0160-9130]
CA SELECTS: ORGANO-TRANSITION METAL COMPLEXES.
***Refer to Chemical Abstracts for complete source list.

CA SEL., ORGANOBOR. CHEM. BORAN.
[US/0195-5098]
CA SELECTS: ORGANOBORON CHEMISTRY & BORANES.
(Ceased)

CA SEL., ORGANOFLOUR. CHEM.
[US/0160-905X]
CA SELECTS: ORGANOFLUORINE CHEMISTRY.
***Refer to Chemical Abstracts for complete source list.

CA SEL., ORGANOMET. ORG. SYNTH.
[US/0895-5859]
CA SELECTS: ORGANOMETALLICS IN ORGANIC SYNTHESIS.
***Refer to Chemical Abstracts for complete source list.

CA SEL., ORGANOSIL. CHEM.
[US/0362-9899]
CA SELECTS: ORGANOSILICON CHEMISTRY.
***Refer to Chemical Abstracts for complete source list.

CA SEL., ORGANOSUL. CHEM. J.
[US/1040-7189]
CA SELECTS: ORGANOSULFUR CHEMISTRY (JOURNALS).
***Refer to Chemical Abstracts for complete source list.

CA SEL., ORGANOTIN CHEM.
[US/0195-5101]
CA SELECTS: ORGANOTIN CHEMISTRY.
***Refer to Chemical Abstracts for complete source list.

CA SEL., OXID. CATAL.
[US/1040-7170]
CA SELECTS: OXIDATION CATALYSTS.
***Refer to Chemical Abstracts for complete source list.

CA SEL., OXIDE SUPERCOND.
[US/1040-7219]
CA SELECTS: OXIDE SUPERCONDUCTORS.
***Refer to Chemical Abstracts for complete source list.

CA SEL., PAINT ADDIT.
[US/0734-8762]
CA SELECTS: PAINT ADDITIVES.
***Refer to Chemical Abstracts for complete source list.

CA SEL., PAP. CHEM.
[US/1040-7200]
CA SELECTS: PAPER CHEMISTRY.
***Refer to Chemical Abstracts for complete source list.

CA SEL., PAP. THIN-LAY. CHROMATOGR.
[US/0146-4515]
CA SELECTS: PAPER & THIN-LAYER CHROMATOGRAPHY.
***Refer to Chemical Abstracts for complete source list.

CA SEL., PAPER ADDIT.
[US/0734-8711]
CA SELECTS: PAPER ADDITIVES.
***Refer to Chemical Abstracts for complete source list.

CA SEL., PHARM. ANAL.
[US/0890-1902]
CA SELECTS: PHARMACEUTICAL ANALYSIS.
***Refer to Chemical Abstracts for complete source list.

CA SEL., PHARM. CHEM. (PAT.)
[US/0890-1929]
CA SELECTS: PHARMACEUTICAL CHEMISTRY (PATENTS).
***Refer to Chemical Abstracts for complete source list.

CA SEL., PHARM. CHEM. J.
[US/0890-1910]
CA SELECTS: PHARMACEUTICAL CHEMISTRY (JOURNALS).
***Refer to Chemical Abstracts for complete source list.

CA SEL., PHASE TRANSF. CATAL.
[US/0885-0194]
CA SELECTS: PHASE TRANSFER CATALYSIS.
***Refer to Chemical Abstracts for complete source list.

CA SEL., PHOTOBIOCHEM.
[US/0148-2335]
CA SELECTS: PHOTOBIOCHEMISTRY.
***Refer to Chemical Abstracts for complete source list.

CA SEL., PHOTOCHEM.
[US/0362-9856]
CA SELECTS: PHOTOCHEMISTRY.
***Refer to Chemical Abstracts for complete source list.

CA SEL., PHOTOCHEM. ORG. SYNTH.
[US/0885-0208]
CA SELECTS: PHOTOCHEMICAL ORGANIC SYNTHESIS.
***Refer to Chemical Abstracts for complete source list.

CA SEL., PHOTORESIS.
[US/0885-0216]
CA SELECTS: PHOTORESISTS.
***Refer to Chemical Abstracts for complete source list.

CA SEL., PHOTOSENSIT. POLYM.
[US/0749-7326]
CA SELECTS: PHOTOSENSITIVE POLYMERS.
***Refer to Chemical Abstracts for complete source list.

CA SEL., PLAS. REACT. ION ETCHING
[US/0749-7334]
CA SELECTS: PLASMA & REACTIVE ION ETCHING.
***Refer to Chemical Abstracts for complete source list.

CA SEL., PLAST. ADDIT.
[US/0734-8681]
CA SELECTS: PLASTICS ADDITIVES.
***Refer to Chemical Abstracts for complete source list.

CA SEL., PLAST. FABR. USES
[US/0275-7125]
CA SELECTS: PLASTICS FABRICATION & USES.
***Refer to Chemical Abstracts for complete source list.

CA SEL., PLAST. FILMS
[US/0195-511X]
CA SELECTS: PLASTIC FILMS.
***Refer to Chemical Abstracts for complete source list.

CA SEL., PLAST. MANUF. PROCESS.
[US/0275-7133]
CA SELECTS: PLASTICS MANUFACTURING & PROCESSING.
***Refer to Chemical Abstracts for complete source list.

CA SEL., PLAT. PALLAD. CHEM.
[US/0890-1937]
CA SELECTS: PLATINUM & PALLADIUM CHEMISTRY.
***Refer to Chemical Abstracts for complete source list.

CA SEL., POLLUT. MONIT.
[US/0160-9149]
CA SELECTS: POLLUTION MONITORING.
***Refer to Chemical Abstracts for complete source list.

CA SEL., POLYACRYL. J.
[US/0890-1945]
CA SELECTS: POLYACRYLATES (JOURNALS).
***Refer to Chemical Abstracts for complete source list.

CA SEL., POLYEST.
[US/0734-8703]
CA SELECTS: POLYESTERS.
***Refer to Chemical Abstracts for complete source list.

CA SEL., POLYIMIDES
[US/0895-5840]
CA SELECTS: POLYIMIDES.
***Refer to Chemical Abstracts for complete source list.

CA SEL., POLYM. BLENDS
[US/0734-8827]
CA SELECTS: POLYMER BLENDS.
***Refer to Chemical Abstracts for complete source list.

CA SEL., POLYM. DEGRAD.
[US/0734-8835]
CA SELECTS: POLYMER DEGRADATION.
***Refer to Chemical Abstracts for complete source list.

INDEXES/ABSTRACTS TABLE

CA SEL., POLYM. KINET. PROCESS CONTROL
[US/0885-0224]
CA SELECTS: POLYMERIZATION KINETICS & PROCESS CONTROL.
***Refer to Chemical Abstracts for complete source list.

CA SEL., POLYM. MORPHOL.
[US/0195-5128]
CA SELECTS: POLYMER MORPHOLOGY.
***Refer to Chemical Abstracts for complete source list.

CA SEL., POLYURETH.
[US/0740-0705]
CA SELECTS: POLYURETHANES.
***Refer to Chemical Abstracts for complete source list.

CA SEL., PORPHYR.
[US/0195-5136]
CA SELECTS: PORPHYRINS.
***Refer to Chemical Abstracts for complete source list.

CA SEL., PROSTAGLAND.
[US/0148-2343]
CA SELECTS: PROSTAGLANDINS.
***Refer to Chemical Abstracts for complete source list.

CA SEL., PROT. MAG. RESON.
[US/0190-941X]
CA SELECTS: PROTON MAGNETIC RESONANCE.
(*Continues in part* CA Selects. Nuclear Magnetic Resonance, Chemical Aspects.)
***Refer to Chemical Abstracts for complete source list.

CA SEL., PSYCHOBIOCHEM.
[US/0362-9848]
CA SELECTS: PSYCHOBIOCHEMISTRY.
***Refer to Chemical Abstracts for complete source list.

CA SEL., QUAT. AMMON. COMP.
[US/0890-1953]
CA SELECTS: QUATERNARY AMMONIUM COMPOUNDS.
***Refer to Chemical Abstracts for complete source list.

CA SEL., RADIAT. CHEM.
[US/0146-4523]
CA SELECTS: RADIATION CHEMISTRY.
***Refer to Chemical Abstracts for complete source list.

CA SEL., RADIAT. CURING
[US/0749-7342]
CA SELECTS: RADIATION CURING.
***Refer to Chemical Abstracts for complete source list.

CA SEL., RAMAN SPECTROS.
[US/0148-2432]
CA SELECTS: RAMAN SPECTROSCOPY.
***Refer to Chemical Abstracts for complete source list.

CA SEL., RECOV. RECYCL. WASTES
[US/0160-9157]
CA SELECTS: RECOVERY & RECYCLING OF WASTES.
***Refer to Chemical Abstracts for complete source list.

CA SEL., SELEN. TELLUR. CHEM.
[US/0749-7350]
CA SELECTS: SELENIUM & TELLURIUM CHEMISTRY.
***Refer to Chemical Abstracts for complete source list.

CA SEL., SHAPE MEM. ALLOYS
[US/1062-869X]
CA SELECTS: SHAPE MEMORY ALLOYS.
***Refer to Chemical Abstracts for complete source list.

CA SEL., SILICAS SILICAT.
[US/0890-1961]
CA SELECTS: SILICAS & SILICATES.
***Refer to Chemical Abstracts for complete source list.

CA SEL., SILOX. SILIC.
[US/0895-5832]
CA SELECTS: SILOXANES & SILICONES.
***Refer to Chemical Abstracts for complete source list.

CA SEL., SILVER CHEM.
[US/0148-2440]
CA SELECTS: SILVER CHEMISTRY.
***Refer to Chemical Abstracts for complete source list.

CA SEL., SOL. ENERGY
[US/0148-236X]
CA SELECTS: SOLAR ENERGY.
***Refer to Chemical Abstracts for complete source list.

CA SEL., SOLID RADIOACT. WASTE TREAT.
[US/0160-9165]
CA SELECTS: SOLID & RADIOACTIVE WASTE TREATMENT.
***Refer to Chemical Abstracts for complete source list.

CA SEL., SOLID STATE NMR
[US/0895-5824]
CA SELECTS: SOLID STATE NMR.
***Refer to Chemical Abstracts for complete source list.

CA SEL., SOLV. EXTRACT.
[US/0146-4531]
CA SELECTS: SOLVENT EXTRACTION.
***Refer to Chemical Abstracts for complete source list.

CA SEL., SPECTROCHEM. ANAL.
[US/0885-0232]
CA SELECTS: SPECTROCHEMICAL ANALYSIS.
***Refer to Chemical Abstracts for complete source list.

CA SEL., STEROIDS (BIOCHEM. ASP.)
[US/0160-9173]
CA SELECTS: STEROIDS (BIOCHEMICAL ASPECTS).
***Refer to Chemical Abstracts for complete source list.

CA SEL., STEROIDS (CHEM. ASP.)
[US/0160-9181]
CA SELECTS: STEROIDS (CHEMICAL ASPECTS).
***Refer to Chemical Abstracts for complete source list.

CA SEL., STRESS CORROS.-MET.
[US/1066-1174]
CA SELECTS: STRESS CORROSION - METALS.
***Refer to Chemical Abstracts for complete source list.

CA SEL., STRUCT.-ACT. RELAT.
[US/0895-5816]
CA SELECTS: STRUCTURE-ACTIVITY RELATIONSHIPS.
***Refer to Chemical Abstracts for complete source list.

CA SEL., SUBSTIT. EFFECTS LIN. FREE ENERGY RELAT.
[US/0162-7856]
CA SELECTS: SUBSTITUENT EFFECTS & LINEAR FREE ENERGY RELATIONSHIPS.
(Ceased)

CA SEL., SURF. ANAL.
[US/0195-5152]
CA SELECTS: SURFACE ANALYSIS.
***Refer to Chemical Abstracts for complete source list.

CA SEL., SURF. CHEM. (PHYSICOCHEM. ASP.)
[US/0146-454X]
CA SELECTS: SURFACE CHEMISTRY (PHYSICOCHEMICAL ASPECTS).
***Refer to Chemical Abstracts for complete source list.

CA SEL., SYNFUELS
[US/0195-5160]
CA SELECTS: SYNFUELS.
***Refer to Chemical Abstracts for complete source list.

CA SEL., SYNTH. HIGH POLYM.
[US/0275-7168]
CA SELECTS: SYNTHETIC HIGH POLYMERS.
***Refer to Chemical Abstracts for complete source list.

CA SEL., SYNTH. MACROCY. COMP.
[US/0195-5179]
CA SELECTS: SYNTHETIC MACROCYCLIC COMPOUNDS.
***Refer to Chemical Abstracts for complete source list.

CA SEL., TECH. CERAM.
[US/1062-8703]
CA SELECTS: TECHNICAL CERAMICS.
***Refer to Chemical Abstracts for complete source list.

CA SEL., THERM. ANAL.
[US/0195-5187]
CA SELECTS: THERMAL ANALYSIS.
***Refer to Chemical Abstracts for complete source list.

CA SEL., THERMOCHEM.
[US/0162-7864]
CA SELECTS: THERMOCHEMISTRY.
***Refer to Chemical Abstracts for complete source list.

CA SEL., TRACE ELEM. ANAL.
[US/0160-919X]
CA SELECTS: TRACE ELEMENT ANALYSIS.
***Refer to Chemical Abstracts for complete source list.

CA SEL., ULTRAFILTR.
[US/0195-5195]
CA SELECTS: ULTRAFILTRATION.
***Refer to Chemical Abstracts for complete source list.

CA SEL., ULTRAVIOL. VISI. SPECTRO.
[US/0195-5209]
CA SELECTS: ULTRAVIOLET & VISIBLE SPECTROSCOPY.
***Refer to Chemical Abstracts for complete source list.

CA SEL., WATER TREAT.
[US/0740-073X]
CA SELECTS: WATER TREATMENT.
***Refer to Chemical Abstracts for complete source list.

CA SEL., WATER-BASED COAT.
[US/0749-7369]
CA SELECTS: WATER-BASED COATINGS.
***Refer to Chemical Abstracts for complete source list.

CA SEL., X-RAY ANAL. SPECTRO.
[US/0162-7872]
CA SELECTS: X-RAY ANALYSIS & SPECTROSCOPY.
***Refer to Chemical Abstracts for complete source list.

CA SEL., ZEOLITES
[US/0190-4949]
CA SELECTS: ZEOLITES.
***Refer to Chemical Abstracts for complete source list.

CALCIUM CALCIF. TISSUE ABSTR.
[US/1069-5540]
CALCIUM AND CALCIFIED TISSUE ABSTRACTS.
(*Continues* Calcified Tissue Abstracts.)

CALIF. PERIOD. INDEX
[US/0730-1367]
CALIFORNIA PERIODICALS INDEX.
(Ceased)

CALIF. PERIOD. MICROFI.
[US]
CALIFORNIA PERIODICALS ON MICROFILM.
(Ceased)

INDEXES/ABSTRACTS TABLE

CAN. BUS. INDEX
[CN/0227-8669]
CANADIAN BUSINESS INDEX.
(*Merged with* Canadian News Index *and* Canadian Magazine Index (Toronto, Ont.) *to form* Canadian Index (Toronto, Ont.).)

CAN. BUS. PERIOD. INDEX
[CN/0318-6717]
CANADIAN BUSINESS PERIODICALS INDEX.
(*Continued by* Canadian Business Index.)

CAN. CURR. LAW
[CN/0835-9768]
CANADIAN CURRENT LAW.
(*Split into* Jurisprudence (Scarborough, Ont.); Legislation (Scarborough, Ont.) *and* Canadian Legal Literature.)

CAN. EDUC. INDEX
[CN/0008-3453]
CANADIAN EDUCATION INDEX.
(*Absorbed* Directory of Education Studies in Canada.)

CAN. ENVIRON.
[CN]
CANADIAN ENVIRONMENT.
(*Continued by* AQUAREF.)

CAN. ESSAY LIT. INDEX
[CN/0316-0696]
CANADIAN ESSAY AND LITERATURE INDEX.
(**Ceased**)

CAN. INDEX
[CN/1192-4160]
CANADIAN INDEX (TORONTO).
(*Formed by the union of* Canadian Business Index *and* Canadian News Index Canadian Magazine Index (Toronto, Ont.).)

CAN. LEGAL LIT.
[CN/0832-9257]
CANADIAN LEGAL LITERATURE.
(*Continues in part* Canadian Current Law (1988).)

CAN. LIT. INDEX
[CN/0838-6021]
CANADIAN LITERATURE INDEX.
(**Ceased**)

CAN. MAG. INDEX
[CN/0829-8777]
CANADIAN MAGAZINE INDEX.
(*Merged with* Canadian Business Index *and* Canadian News Index *to form* Canadian Index (Toronto, Ont.).)

CAN. NEWS INDEX
[CN/0225-7459]
CANADIAN NEWS INDEX TORONTO.
(*Merged with* Canadian Business Index *and* Canadian Magazine Index (Toronto, Ont.) *to form* Canadian Index (Toronto, Ont.).)

CAN. PERIOD. INDEX
[CN/0008-4719]
CANADIAN PERIODICAL INDEX (1964).
(*Continues* Canadian Index to Periodicals and Documentary Films.)

CAN., MICROFICHE
[CN/0225-3216]
CANADIANA. MICROFICHE.
(**Ceased**)

CANON LAW ABSTR.
[UK/0008-5650]
CANON LAW ABSTRACTS.

CATCH. TRADE NAME INDEX : CATNI
[UK]
CATCHWORD AND TRADE NAME INDEX : CATNI.
***Refer to Current Technology Index for complete source list.

CATHOL. PERIOD. INDEX
[US/0363-6895]
CATHOLIC PERIODICAL INDEX.
(*Continued by* Catholic Periodical and Literature Index.)

CATHOL. PERIOD. LIT. INDEX
[US/0008-8285]
CATHOLIC PERIODICAL AND LITERATURE INDEX, THE.
(*Continues* Catholic Periodical Index; *Absorbed* Guide to Catholic Literature.)

CCLP CONTENTS CURR. LEG. PERIOD.
[US/0300-7391]
CCLP. CONTENTS OF CURRENT LEGAL PERIODICALS.
(*Continued by* Legal Contents.)

CERAM. ABSTR.
[US/0095-9960]
CERAMIC ABSTRACTS.
(*Continues in part* American Ceramic Society. Journal of the American Ceramic Society.)

CHEM INFORM
[GW/0931-7597]
CHEM INFORM.
(*Continues* Chemischer Informationsdienst.)

CHEM. ABSTR.
[US/0009-2258]
CHEMICAL ABSTRACTS.
(*Supersedes* Review of American Chemical Research.)

CHEM. BUS. BULL.
[UK]
CHEMICAL BUSINESS BULLETINS.

CHEM. BUS. NEWSBASE
[UK]
CHEMICAL BUSINESS NEWSBASE [ONLINE DATABASE].

CHEM. BUS. UPDATE
[UK/0950-6144]
CHEMICAL BUSINESS UPDATE.

CHEM. ENG. ABSTR.
[UK/0262-6438]
CHEMICAL ENGINEERING ABSTRACTS.
(*Continued by* Process & Chemical Engineering.)

CHEM. HAZARDS IND.
[UK/0265-5721]
CHEMICAL HAZARDS IN INDUSTRY.

CHEM. IND. NOTES
[US/0045-639X]
CHEMICAL INDUSTRY NOTES.
(*Supersedes* Plastics Industry Notes.)

CHEM. INF. DIENST.
[GW/0009-2975]
CHEMISCHER INFORMATIONSDIENST.
(*Continued by* Chem Inform.)

CHEM. TITLES
[US/0009-2711]
CHEMICAL TITLES.

CHEMORECEPT. ABSTR.
[US/0300-1261]
CHEMORECEPTION ABSTRACTS.

CHICAGO PSYCHOANAL. LIT. INDEX.
[US/0009-3661]
CHICAGO PSYCHOANALYTIC LITERATURE INDEX.
(**Ceased**)

CHICANO INDEX
[US/1044-3487]
CHICANO INDEX, THE.
(*Continues* Chicano Periodical Index.)

CHICOREL INDEX MENT. HEALTH BOOK REV.
[US/0149-4090]
CHICOREL INDEX TO MENTAL HEALTH BOOK REVIEWS.
(*Continues* Mental Health Book Review Index.)

CHILD DEV. ABSTR. BIBLIOGR.
[US/0009-3939]
CHILD DEVELOPMENT ABSTRACTS AND BIBLIOGRAPHY.
(*Continues* Selected Child Development Abstracts Currently Published in the Journal of Nervous and Mental Disease, the Wistar Institute Bibliographic Service, American Journal of Diseases of Children, Archives of Neurology and Psychiatry, Psychological Abstracts, Physiological Abstracts, Biological Abstracts, Chemical Abstracts, Endocrinology.)

CHILD. LIT. ABSTR.
[UK/0306-2015]
CHILDREN'S LITERATURE ABSTRACTS.

CHILD. MAG. GUIDE
[US/0743-9873]
CHILDREN'S MAGAZINE GUIDE.
(*Continues* Subject Index to Children's Magazines.)

CHRIST. PERIOD. INDEX
[US/0069-3871]
CHRISTIAN PERIODICAL INDEX.

CIS ABSTR.
[US/0302-7651]
CIS ABSTRACTS.
(*Continued by* Safety and Health at Work.)

CIS INDEX PUBL. U.S. CONGR.
[US/0007-8514]
CIS INDEX TO PUBLICATIONS OF THE UNITED STATES CONGRESS.

CIV. STRUCT. ENG. ABSTR.
[US/1063-7338]
CIVIL AND STRUCTURAL ENGINEERING ABSTRACTS.
(**Ceased**)

CLARK'S DIG.-ANNOT.
[US]
CLARK'S DIGEST-ANNOTATOR.
(*Continued by* New York Law Journal Digest-Annotator.)

CLASSIFIED ABSTR. ARCH. ALCOHOL LIT.
[US]
CLASSIFIED ABSTRACT ARCHIVE OF THE ALCOHOL LITERATURE.
(**Ceased**)

CLIN. BEHAV. THERAPY REV.
[US/0162-2269]
CLINICAL BEHAVIOR THERAPY REVIEW.
(**Ceased**)

COAL ABSTR.
[UK/0309-4979]
COAL ABSTRACTS.
(**Ceased**)

INDEXES/ABSTRACTS TABLE

COLL. STUD. PERS. ABSTR.
[US/0010-1168]
COLLEGE STUDENT PERSONNEL ABSTRACTS.
(*Continued by* Higher Education Abstracts.)

COMB. CUMUL. INDEX CARDIOL.
[US/0747-5330]
COMBINED CUMULATIVE INDEX TO CARDIOLOGY.
(Ceased)

COMB. CUMUL. INDEX OB. GYN.
[US/0884-8092]
COMBINED CUMULATIVE INDEX TO OBSTETRICS AND GYNECOLOGY.

COMB. CUMUL. INDEX PEDIATR.
[US/0190-4981]
COMBINED CUMULATIVE INDEX TO PEDIATRICS.

COMM. FISH. ABSTR.
[US/0010-2970]
COMMERCIAL FISHERIES ABSTRACTS.
(*Continued by* Marine Fisheries Abstracts.)

COMMUN. ABSTR.
[US/0162-2811]
COMMUNICATION ABSTRACTS.

COMMUNITY DEV. ABSTR.
[US]
COMMUNITY DEVELOPMENT ABSTRACTS.
(Ceased)

COMMUNITY MENT. HEALTH REV.
[US/0363-1605]
COMMUNITY MENTAL HEALTH REVIEW.
(*Continued by* Prevention in Human Services.)

COMPEND. PLUS
[US/1063-8709]
COMPENDEX PLUS.
***Refer to Engineering Index for complete source list.

COMPUMATH CIT. INDEX
[US/0730-6199]
COMPUMATH CITATION INDEX : CMCI.

COMPUT-A-CAL
[US/0742-5686]
COMPUT-A-CAL.
(Ceased)

COMPUT. ABSTR.
[UK/0010-4469]
COMPUTER ABSTRACTS.
(*Continues* Computer Bibliography.)

COMPUT. ASAP
[US]
COMPUTER ASAP [ONLINE DATABASE].

COMPUT. BUS.
[US/0732-8346]
COMPUTER BUSINESS (LOS ANGELES, CALIF.).

COMPUT. CONTENTS
[US/0747-0193]
COMPUTER CONTENTS.
(Ceased)

COMPUT. CONTROL ABSTR.
[UK/0036-8113]
COMPUTER & CONTROL ABSTRACTS.
(*Continues* Control Abstracts.)
***Refer to INSPEC [Online Database] for a complete source list.

COMPUT. DATABASE
[US]
COMPUTER DATABASE [ONLINE DATABASE].

COMPUT. IND. UPDATE
[US/0744-0081]
COMPUTER INDUSTRY UPDATE.

COMPUT. INF. SYST.
[US/0010-4507]
COMPUTER & INFORMATION SYSTEMS.
(*Continued by* Computer and Information Systems Abstracts Journal.)

COMPUT. INF. SYST. ABSTR. J.
[US/0191-9776]
COMPUTER AND INFORMATION SYSTEMS ABSTRACTS JOURNAL.
(*Continued by* Computer and Information Systems Abstracts.)

COMPUT. LIT. INDEX
[US/0270-4846]
COMPUTER LITERATURE INDEX.
(*Continues* Quarterly Bibliography of Computers and Data Processing.)

COMPUT. REV.
[US/0010-4884]
COMPUTING REVIEWS.

COMPUT. REV. INDEX
[US/1040-5003]
COMPUTER REVIEW INDEX.

COMPUT. REV., BIBLIOGR. SUBJ. INDEX CURR. COMPUT. LIT.
[US/0149-1202]
COMPUTING REVIEWS. BIBLIOGRAPHY AND SUBJECT INDEX OF CURRENT COMPUTING LITERATURE.
(*Continued by* ACM Guide to Computing Literature.)

CONCR. ABSTR.
[US/0045-8007]
CONCRETE ABSTRACTS.

CONSTR. INDEX
[US/0892-2047]
CONSTRUCTION INDEX.

CONSUM. HEALTH NUTR. INDEX
[US/0883-1963]
CONSUMER HEALTH & NUTRITION INDEX.

CONSUM. INDEX PROD. EVAL. INF. SOURCE
[US/0094-0534]
CONSUMERS INDEX TO PRODUCT EVALUATIONS AND INFORMATION SOURCES.

CONTENTS CONTEMP. MATH. J.
[US/0010-759X]
CONTENTS OF CONTEMPORARY MATHEMATICAL JOURNALS.
(*Merged with* New Publications - American Mathematical Society *to form* Contents of Contemporary Mathematical Journals and New Publications.)

CONTENTS CONTEMP. MATH. J. NEW PUBL.
[US]
CONTENTS OF CONTEMPORARY MATHEMATICAL JOURNALS AND NEW PUBLICATIONS.
(*Continued by* Current Mathematical Publications.)

CONTENTS CURR. LEG. PERIOD.
[US/0300-7391]
CONTENTS OF CURRENT LEGAL PERIODICALS.
(*Continued by* CCLP. Contents of Current Legal Periodicals.)

CONTENTS PAGES EDUC.
[UK/0265-9220]
CONTENTS PAGES IN EDUCATION.

CONTENTS RECENT ECON. J.
[UK]
CONTENTS OF RECENT ECONOMICS JOURNALS.
(Ceased)

CORROS. ABSTR.
[US/0010-9339]
CORROSION ABSTRACTS.
(*Supersedes in part* Corrosion.)

COT. TROP. FIBR. ABSTR. BIBLIOGR.
[UK]
COTTON AND TROPICAL FIBRES ABSTRACTS BIBLIOGRAPHY.
(*Continues* Cotton and Tropical Fibres Abstracts.)

CRIM. JUSTICE ABSTR.
[US/0146-9177]
CRIMINAL JUSTICE ABSTRACTS.
(*Continues* Crime and Delinquency Literature.)

CRIM. JUSTICE PERIOD. INDEX
[US/0145-5818]
CRIMINAL JUSTICE PERIODICAL INDEX.

CRIM. PENOL. POLICE SCI. ABSTR.
[NE/0928-8759]
CRIMINOLOGY, PENOLOGY AND POLICE SCIENCE ABSTRACTS.
(*Formed by the union of* Criminology & Penology Abstracts *and* Police Science Abstracts.)

CRIME DELINQ. ABSTR.
[US/0045-902X]
CRIME AND DELINQUENCY ABSTRACTS.
(*Continues* International Bibliography on Crime and Delinquency.)

CRIME DELINQ. LIT.
[US/0037-1327]
CRIME AND DELINQUENCY LITERATURE.
(*Continued by* Criminal Justice Abstracts.)

CRIMINOL. PENOL. ABSTR.
[NE/0166-6231]
CRIMINOLOGY & PENOLOGY ABSTRACTS.
(*Merged with* Police Science Abstracts *to form* Criminology, Penology, and Police Science Abstracts.)

CROP PHYSIOL. ABSTR.
[UK/0306-7556]
CROP PHYSIOLOGY ABSTRACTS.

CSA NEURO. ABSTR.
[US/0141-7711]
CSA NEUROSCIENCES ABSTRACTS.

CTI PLUS
[UK]
CTI PLUS [COMPUTER FILE].
***Refer to Current Technology Index for complete source list.

CUMUL. INDEX MED.
[US/0090-1423]
CUMULATED INDEX MEDICUS.
(*Continues* Quarterly Cumulative Index Medicus.)
***Refer to Index Medicus for complete source list.

CUMUL. INDEX NURS. ALLIED HEALTH LIT.
[US/0146-5554]
CUMULATIVE INDEX TO NURSING & ALLIED HEALTH LITERATURE.
(*Continued in part by* Nursing and Allied Health Index.)

CUMUL. INDEX NURS. LIT.
[US/0011-3018]
CUMULATIVE INDEX TO NURSING LITERATURE.
(*Continued by* Cumulative Index to Nursing & Allied Health Literature.)

INDEXES/ABSTRACTS TABLE

CURR. ABSTR. CHEM. INDEX CHEM.
[US/0161-455X]
CURRENT ABSTRACTS OF CHEMISTRY AND INDEX CHEMICUS.
(*Continued by* Index Chemicus : IC.)

CURR. ADV. APPL. MICROBIOL. BIOTECHNOL.
[UK/0964-8712]
CURRENT ADVANCES IN APPLIED MICROBIOLOGY & BIOTECHNOLOGY.
(*Continues* Current Advances in Microbiology.)
***Refer to Current Awareness in Biological Sciences : CABS for complete source list.

CURR. ADV. BIOCHEM.
[UK/0741-1618]
CURRENT ADVANCES IN BIOCHEMISTRY.
(*Continued by* Current Advances in Protein Biochemistry.)

CURR. ADV. CANCER RES.
[UK/0895-9803]
CURRENT ADVANCES IN CANCER RESEARCH.
***Refer to Current Awareness in Biological Sciences : CABS for complete source list.

CURR. ADV. CELL DEV. BIOL.
[UK/0741-1626]
CURRENT ADVANCES IN CELL AND DEVELOPMENTAL BIOLOGY.
(*Continues in part* Current Awareness in Biological Sciences.)
***Refer to Current Awareness in Biological Sciences : CABS for complete source list.

CURR. ADV. CLIN. CHEM.
[UK/0885-1980]
CURRENT ADVANCES IN CLINICAL CHEMISTRY.
(*Continues* Current Clinical Chemistry.)
***Refer to Current Awareness in Biological Sciences : CABS for complete source list.

CURR. ADV. ECOL. ENVIRON. SCI.
[UK/0955-6648]
CURRENT ADVANCES IN ECOLOGICAL & ENVIRONMENTAL SCIENCES.
(*Continues* Current Advances in Ecological Sciences.)
***Refer to Current Awareness in Biological Sciences : CABS for complete source list.

CURR. ADV. ECOL. SCI.
[UK/0306-3291]
CURRENT ADVANCES IN ECOLOGICAL SCIENCES.
(*Continued by* Current Advances in Ecological & Environmental Sciences.)

CURR. ADV. ENDOCRIN.
[UK/0741-1634]
CURRENT ADVANCES IN ENDOCRINOLOGY.
(*Continues in part* Current Awareness in Biological Sciences.)

CURR. ADV. ENDOCRIN. METAB.
[UK/0964-8720]
CURRENT ADVANCES IN ENDOCRINOLOGY AND METABOLISM.
(*Continues* Current Advances in Physiology.)
***Refer to Current Awareness in Biological Sciences : CABS for complete source list.

CURR. ADV. GENET. MOL. BIOL.
[UK/0741-1642]
CURRENT ADVANCES IN GENETICS & MOLECULAR BIOLOGY.
(*Continues* Current Advances in Genetics.)
***Refer to Current Awareness in Biological Sciences : CABS for complete source list.

CURR. ADV. IMMUNOL.
[UK/0741-1650]
CURRENT ADVANCES IN IMMUNOLOGY.
(*Continued by* Current Advances in Immunology & Infectious Diseases.)

CURR. ADV. IMMUNOL. INFECT. DISEAS.
[UK/0964-8747]
CURRENT ADVANCES IN IMMUNOLOGY & INFECTIOUS DISEASES.
(*Continues* Current Advances in Immunology.)
***Refer to Current Awareness in Biological Sciences : CABS for complete source list.

CURR. ADV. MICROBIOL.
[UK/0741-1669]
CURRENT ADVANCES IN MICROBIOLOGY.
(*Continued by* Current Advances in Applied Microbiology & Biotechnology.)

CURR. ADV. NEUROSCI.
[UK/0741-1677]
CURRENT ADVANCES IN NEUROSCIENCE.
(*Continues in part* Current Awareness in Biological Sciences.)
***Refer to Current Awareness in Biological Sciences : CABS for complete source list.

CURR. ADV. PHARMACOL. TOXICOL.
[UK/0741-1685]
CURRENT ADVANCES IN PHARMACOLOGY & TOXICOLOGY.
(*Continued by* Current Advances in Toxicology.)

CURR. ADV. PHYSIOL.
[UK/0741-1693]
CURRENT ADVANCES IN PHYSIOLOGY.
(*Continued by* Current Advances in Endocrinology & Metabolism.)

CURR. ADV. PLANT SCI.
[UK/0306-4484]
CURRENT ADVANCES IN PLANT SCIENCE.
***Refer to Current Awareness in Biological Sciences : CABS for complete source list.

CURR. ADV. PROT. BIOCHEM.
[UK/0965-0504]
CURRENT ADVANCES IN PROTEIN BIOCHEMISTRY.
(*Continues* Current Advances in Biochemistry.)
***Refer to Current Awareness in Biological Sciences : CABS for complete source list.

CURR. ADV. PROT. CHEM.
[UK/0965-0504]
CURRENT ADVANCES IN PROTEIN CHEMISTRY.
(*Continues* Current Advances in Biochemistry.)
***Refer to Current Awareness in Biological Sciences : CABS for complete source list.

CURR. ADV. TOXICOL.
[UK/0965-0512]
CURRENT ADVANCES IN TOXICOLOGY.
(*Continues* Current Advances in Pharmacology & Toxicology.)
***Refer to Current Awareness in Biological Sciences : CABS for complete source list.

CURR. AUST. NEW Z. LEG. LIT. INDEX
[AT]
CURRENT AUSTRALIAN AND NEW ZEALAND LEGAL LITERATURE INDEX.
(Ceased)

CURR. AWARE. BIOL. SCI., CABS
[UK/0733-4443]
CURRENT AWARENESS IN BIOLOGICAL SCIENCES.
(*Continued in part by* Current Advances in Neuroscience; Current Advances in Cell & Developmental Biology.)

CURR. AWARENESS LIBR. LIT., CALL
[US/0091-5270]
CURRENT AWARENESS-LIBRARY LITERATURE : CALL.
(Ceased)

CURR. BIOTECHNOL.
[UK/0960-5037]
CURRENT BIOTECHNOLOGY.
(*Continues* Current Biotechnology Abstracts.)

CURR. BIOTECHNOL. ABSTR.
[UK/0264-3391]
CURRENT BIOTECHNOLOGY ABSTRACTS.
(*Continued by* Current Biotechnology.)

CURR. BOOK REV. CITATIONS
[US/0360-1250]
CURRENT BOOK REVIEW CITATIONS.
(Ceased)

CURR. CHEM. REACT.
[US/0163-6278]
CURRENT CHEMICAL REACTIONS.

CURR. CONTENTS
[US/0272-1430]
CURRENT CONTENTS.
(*Continued by* Current Contents of Pharmaceutical Publications.)

CURR. CONTENTS AFR.
[UK/0721-5207]
CURRENT CONTENTS AFRICA.
(*Continues* CCA, Current Contents Afrika.)

CURR. CONTENTS AGRIC. BIOL. ENVIRON. SCI.
[US/0090-0508]
CURRENT CONTENTS. AGRICULTURE, BIOLOGY, & ENVIRONMENTAL SCIENCES.
(*Continues* Current Contents. Agricultural, Food & Veterinary Sciences.)

CURR. CONTENTS AGRIC. FOOD VET. SCI.
[US/0011-3379]
CURRENT CONTENTS : AGRICULTURAL, FOOD AND VETERINARY SCIENCES.
(*Continued by* Current Contents. Agriculture, Biology & Environmental Sciences.)

CURR. CONTENTS ARTS HUMANIT.
[US/0163-3155]
CURRENT CONTENTS. ARTS & HUMANITIES.

CURR. CONTENTS BEHAV. SOC. EDUC. SCI.
[US/0011-3387]
CURRENT CONTENTS: BEHAVIORAL, SOCIAL & EDUCATIONAL SCIENCES.
(*Continued by* Current Contents. Social & Behavioral Sciences.)

CURR. CONTENTS BEHAV. SOC. MANAGE. SCI.
[US/0590-384X]
CURRENT CONTENTS: BEHAVIORAL, SOCIAL & MANAGEMENT SCIENCES.
(*Continued by* Current Contents. Behavioral, Social & Educational Sciences.)

CURR. CONTENTS CLIN. MED.
[US/0891-3358]
CURRENT CONTENTS. CLINICAL MEDICINE.
(*Continues* Current Contents. Clinical Practice.)

CURR. CONTENTS CLIN. PRACT.
[US/0091-1704]
CURRENT CONTENTS. CLINICAL PRACTICE.
(*Continued by* Current Contents. Clinical Medicine.)

INDEXES/ABSTRACTS TABLE

CURR. CONTENTS EDUC.
[US/0590-3866]
CURRENT CONTENTS. EDUCATION.
(*Absorbed by* Current Contents: Behavioral, Social & Management Sciences.)

CURR. CONTENTS ENG. TECH. APPL. SCI.
[US/0095-7917]
CURRENT CONTENTS. ENGINEERING, TECHNOLOGY & APPLIED SCIENCES.
(*Continues* Current Contents: Engineering & Technology.)

CURR. CONTENTS ENG. TECH.
[US/0011-3395]
CURRENT CONTENTS: ENGINEERING & TECHNOLOGY.
(*Continued by* Current Contents. Engineering, Technology & Applied Sciences.)

CURR. CONTENTS LIFE SCI.
[US/0011-3409]
CURRENT CONTENTS. LIFE SCIENCES.
(*Continues* Current Contents. Your Weekly Guide to the Chemical, Pharmaco-Medical & Life Sciences.)

CURR. CONTENTS PHARM. PUBL.
[US/0272-1422]
CURRENT CONTENTS OF PHARMACEUTICAL PUBLICATIONS.
(*Superseded by* Current Contents of Pharmaco-Medical Publications.)

CURR. CONTENTS PHARM.-MED. PUBL.
[US/0272-1414]
CURRENT CONTENTS OF PHARMACO-MEDICAL PUBLICATIONS.
(*Continued by* Current Contents: Your Weekly Survey of Chemical, Pharmacological & Clinical Publications.)

CURR. CONTENTS PHYS. CHEM. EARTH SCI.
[US/0163-2574]
CURRENT CONTENTS. PHYSICAL, CHEMICAL & EARTH SCIENCES.
(*Continues* Current Contents. Physical and Chemical Sciences.)

CURR. CONTENTS PHYS. CHEM. SCI.
[US/0011-3417]
CURRENT CONTENTS. PHYSICAL & CHEMICAL SCIENCES.
(*Continued by* Current Contents. Physical, Chemical & Earth Sciences.)

CURR. CONTENTS SOC. BEHAV. SCI.
[US/0092-6361]
CURRENT CONTENTS. SOCIAL & BEHAVIORAL SCIENCES.
(*Continues* Current Contents. Behavioral, Social & Educational Sciences.)

CURR. CONTENTS YOUR WKLY. GUIDE CHEM. PHARM.-MED. LIFE SCI.
[US/0272-1503]
CURRENT CONTENTS: YOUR WEEKLY GUIDE OF THE CHEMICAL, PHARMACO-MEDICAL & LIFE SCIENCES.
(*Continued by* Current Contents. Life Sciences.)

CURR. CONTENTS YOUR WKLY. SURV. CHEM. PHARMACOL. CLIN. PUBL.
[US/0272-1449]
CURRENT CONTENTS: YOUR WEEKLY SURVEY OF CHEMICAL, PHARMACOLOGICAL & CLINICAL PUBLICATIONS.
(*Continued by* Current Contents. Your Weekly Guide to the Chemical, Pharmaco-Medical & Life Sciences.)

CURR. DIG. POST SOV. PRESS
[US/1067-7542]
CURRENT DIGEST OF THE POST-SOVIET PRESS, THE.
(*Continues* Current Digest of the Soviet Press.)

CURR. GEOGR. PUBL.
[US/0011-3514]
CURRENT GEOGRAPHICAL PUBLICATIONS.

CURR. INDEX J. EDUC.
[US/0011-3565]
CURRENT INDEX TO JOURNALS IN EDUCATION.

CURR. INDEX STAT.
[US/0364-1228]
CURRENT INDEX TO STATISTICS.

CURR. LAW INDEX
[US/0196-1780]
CURRENT LAW INDEX.

CURR. LIT. AGING
[US/0011-3662]
CURRENT LITERATURE ON AGING.
(*Continued by* Abstracts in Social Gerontology.)

CURR. LIT. BLOOD
[US/0001-7108]
CURRENT LITERATURE OF BLOOD.
(Ceased)

CURR. LIT. FAM. PLAN.
[US/0092-6000]
CURRENT LITERATURE IN FAMILY PLANNING.
(*Continues* Acquisitions List - Katharine Dexter McCormick Library.)

CURR. LIT. SCI. SCI.
[II]
CURRENT LITERATURE ON SCIENCE OF SCIENCE.
(*Supersedes* Index to Literature on Science of Science.)

CURR. MATH. PUBL.
[US/0361-4794]
CURRENT MATHEMATICAL PUBLICATIONS.
(*Continues* Contents of Contemporary Mathematical Journals and New Publications.)
***Refer to Mathematical Reviews for complete source list.

CURR. MIL. POL. LIT.
[UK/0954-3589]
CURRENT MILITARY & POLITICAL LITERATURE.
(*Continues* Current Military Literature.)

CURR. PAP. COMPUT. CONTROL
[UK/0011-3794]
CURRENT PAPERS ON COMPUTERS & CONTROL.
(*Continues* Current Papers on Control.)
***Refer to INSPEC [Online Database] for complete source list.

CURR. PAP. ELECTR. ELECTRON. ENG.
[UK/0011-3778]
CURRENT PAPERS IN ELECTRICAL & ELECTRONICS ENGINEERING.
(*Continues* Current Papers in Eletrotechnology.)
***Refer to INSPEC [Online Database] for complete source list.

CURR. PAP. PHYS.
[UK/0011-3786]
CURRENT PAPERS IN PHYSICS.
***Refer to INSPEC [Online Database] for complete source list.

CURR. PHYS. INDEX
[US/0098-9819]
CURRENT PHYSICS INDEX.

CURR. PRIMATE REF.
[US/0590-4102]
CURRENT PRIMATE REFERENCES.
(*Supersedes* Unverified Primate References.)

CURR. REF. FISH RES.
[US/0739-540X]
CURRENT REFERENCES IN FISH RESEARCH.

CURR. TECHNOL. INDEX
[UK/0260-6593]
CURRENT TECHNOLOGY INDEX : CTI.
(*Continues* British Technology Index.)

CURR. THOUGHTS TRENDS
[US/1054-8688]
CURRENT THOUGHTS AND TRENDS.
(*Continues* Current Christian Abstracts.)

CURR. TITL. DENT.
[DK/0903-3483]
CURRENT TITLES IN DENTISTRY.

CURR. TITLES ELECTROCHEM.
[II/0300-4376]
CURRENT TITLES IN ELECTROCHEMISTRY.
(*Absorbed* Electrochemical News.)

DAIRY SCI. ABSTR.
[UK/0011-5681]
DAIRY SCIENCE ABSTRACTS.

DATA PROCESS. DIG.
[US/0011-6858]
DATA PROCESSING DIGEST.

DEEP-SEA OCEANOGR. ABSTR.
[UK/0011-7471]
DEEP-SEA RESEARCH AND OCEANOGRAPHIC ABSTRACTS.
(*Continued by* Deep-Sea Research.)

DEEP-SEA RES.
[UK/0146-6291]
DEEP-SEA RESEARCH.
(*Continued by* Deep-Sea Research. Part A. Oceanographic Research Papers.)

DEEP-SEA RES., B, OCEANOGR. LIT. REV.
[UK/0198-0254]
DEEP-SEA RESEARCH. PART B. OCEANOGRAPHIC LITERATURE REVIEW.
(*Continued by* Oceanographic Literature Review.)

DENT. ABSTR.
[US/0011-8486]
DENTAL ABSTRACTS (CHICAGO).

DESALIN. ABSTR.
[IS/0011-9202]
DESALINATION ABSTRACTS.
(*Continued by* Desalination and Recycling Abstracts.)

DESALIN. RECYC. ABSTR.
[IS/0011-9172]
DESALINATION AND RECYCLING ABSTRACTS.
(*Continues* Desalination Abstracts.)

DEV. DISABIL. ABSTR.
[US/0191-1600]
DEVELOPMENTAL DISABILITIES ABSTRACTS.
(*Continues* Mental Retardation & Developmental Disabilities Abstracts.)

DEV. MED. CHILD NEUROL.
[UK/0012-1622]
DEVELOPMENTAL MEDICINE & CHILD NEUROLOGY.
(*Continued in part by* American Academy For Cerebral Palsy & Developmental Medicine. Meeting. Abstracts.)

INDEXES/ABSTRACTS TABLE

DIABETES LIT. INDEX
[US/0012-1819]
DIABETES LITERATURE INDEX.
(*Supersedes* Diabetes-Related Literature Index.)

DOANE INF. CENT. INDEX. SYST. SUBJ. INDEX
[US]
DICIS, DOANE INFORMATION CENTER INDEXING SYSTEM : SUBJECT INDEX.
(Ceased)

DOK. GEFAHRDUNG ALKOHOL, RAUCH., DROGEN, ARZNEIMITTEL
[GW/0341-8022]
DOKUMENTATION GEFAHRDUNG DURCH ALKOHOL, RAUCHEN, DROGEN, ARZNEIMITTEL.
(*Continues* Dokumentation Drogengefahrdung und Alkoholmissbrauch.)

DOK. RAUMENTWICKL.
[GW]
DOKUMENTATION ZUR RAUMENTWICKLUNG.
(*Continues* Documentatio Geographica.)

DSH ABSTR.
[US/0011-5150]
DSH ABSTRACTS.
(Ceased)

ECOL. ABSTR.
[UK/0305-196X]
ECOLOGICAL ABSTRACTS.

ECOLOGY ABSTR.
[US/0143-3296]
ECOLOGY ABSTRACTS.
(*Continues* Applied Ecology Abstracts.)

ECON. LIT. INDEX
[US]
ECONOMIC LITERATURE INDEX.

ECONLIT
[US]
ECONLIT [COMPUTER FILE].
***Refer to Economic Literature Index for a complete source list.

EDUC. ADM. ABSTR.
[US/0013-1601]
EDUCATIONAL ADMINISTRATION ABSTRACTS.

EDUC. INDEX
[US/0013-1385]
EDUCATION INDEX.

EDUC. TECHNOL. ABSTR.
[UK/0266-3368]
EDUCATIONAL TECHNOLOGY ABSTRACTS.

EI PAGE ONE
[US]
EI PAGE ONE [COMPUTER FILE].

ELECT. COMM. ABSTR.
[US/1069-5303]
ELECTRONICS AND COMMUNICATIONS ABSTRACTS.
(*Continues* Electronics & Communications Abstracts Journal.)

ELECTR. ELECTRON. ABSTR.
[UK/0036-8105]
ELECTRICAL & ELECTRONICS ABSTRACTS.
(*Continues* Science Abstracts. Electrical & Electronics Abstracts.)
***Refer to INSPEC [Online Database] for a complete source list.

ELECTROANAL. ABSTR.
[SZ/0013-4775]
ELECTROANALYTICAL ABSTRACTS.
(*Continues* Journal of Electroanalytical Chemistry. Abstracts Section.)

ELECTRON. COMMUN. ABSTR. J.
[US/0361-3313]
ELECTRONICS AND COMMUNICATIONS ABSTRACTS JOURNAL (RIVERDALE, MD.).
(*Continued by* Electronics and Communications Abstracts.)

ELECTRON. PUB. ABSTR.
[UK/0739-2907]
ELECTRONIC PUBLISHING ABSTRACTS.
(*Continued by* World Publishing Monitor.)

EMBASE LIST J. INDEXED
[NE]
EMBASE LIST OF JOURNALS INDEXED.
(*Continues* List of Journals Abstracted (1983).)
***Refer to EMBASE [Online Database] for complete source list.

EMBASE
[NE]
EMBASE [ONLINE DATABASE].

EMPLOY. RELAT. ABSTR.
[US]
EMPLOYMENT RELATIONS ABSTRACTS.
(*Continued by* Work Related Abstracts.)

ENERGY INDEX
[US/0094-6281]
ENERGY INDEX.
(*Absorbed by* Energy Information Abstracts Annual.)

ENERGY INF. ABSTR.
[US/0147-6521]
ENERGY INFORMATION ABSTRACTS.
(Ceased)

ENERGY INF. ABSTR. ANNU.
[US/0739-3679]
ENERGY INFORMATION ABSTRACTS ANNUAL.
(*Absorbed* Energy Index.)
***Refer to Energy Information Abstracts for complete source list.

ENERGY RES. ABSTR.
[US/0160-3604]
ENERGY RESEARCH ABSTRACTS.
(*Continues* ERDA Energy Research Abstracts.)

ENG. INDEX
[US/0739-4624]
ENGINEERING INDEX (1919), THE.
(*Continued by* Engineering Index Annual.)

ENG. INDEX ANNU.
[US/0360-8557]
ENGINEERING INDEX ANNUAL.
(*Continues* Engineering Index (New York, N.Y. : 1919).)

ENG. INDEX BIOENG. ABSTR.
[US/0736-6213]
ENGINEERING INDEX BIOENGINEERING ABSTRACTS.
(*Continued by* Engineering Index Bioengineering and Biotechnology Abstracts.)

ENG. INDEX ENERGY ABSTR.
[US/0093-8408]
ENGINEERING INDEX ENERGY ABSTRACTS.
. ***Refer to Engineering Index Annual for a complete source list.

ENG. INDEX MON.
[US/0742-1974]
ENGINEERING INDEX MONTHLY.
(*Continues* Engineering Index Monthly and Author Index.)
***Refer to Engineering Index Annual for a complete source list.

ENG. INDEX MON. AUTHOR INDEX
[US/0162-3036]
ENGINEERING INDEX MONTHLY AND AUTHOR INDEX.
(*Continued by* Engineering Index Monthly (1984).)

ENG. MATER. ABSTR.
[US/0951-9998]
ENGINEERED MATERIALS ABSTRACTS.

ENTOMOL. ABSTR.
[US/0013-8924]
ENTOMOLOGY ABSTRACTS.

ENVIRO ENERGYLINE PLUS
[US/1076-6464]
ENVIRO/ENERGYLINE ABSTRACTS PLUS.
(*Continued by* Environment Abstracts.)
***Refer to Environment Abstracts and Energy Information Abstracts for complete source list.

ENVIRON.
[CN/0709-8847]
ENVIRONNEMENT (MONTREAL).
(*Continues* Journal l'Environnement.)

ENVIRON. ABSTR.
[US/0093-3287]
ENVIRONMENT ABSTRACTS.
(*Continues* Environment Information Access; *Absorbed* Acid Rain Abstracts.)

ENVIRON. ABSTR.
[US]
ENVIRONMENT ABSTRACTS [COMPUTER FILE].
(*Continues* Enviro/Energyline Abstracts Plus.)
***Refer to Environment Abstracts and Energy Information Abstracts for complete source list.

ENVIRON. ABSTR. ANNU.
[US/0000-1198]
ENVIRONMENT ABSTRACTS ANNUAL.
(*Absorbed* Environment Index and Acid Raid Abstracts Annual.)
***Refer to Environment Abstracts for complete source list.

ENVIRON. ENG. ABSTR.
[US/1063-7346]
ENVIRONMENTAL ENGINEERING ABSTRACTS.
(Ceased)

ENVIRON. INDEX
[US/0090-791X]
ENVIRONMENT INDEX.
(*Absorbed by* Environment Abstracts Annual.)

ENVIRON. PERIOD. BIBLIOGR.
[US/0145-3815]
ENVIRONMENTAL PERIODICALS BIBLIOGRAPHY.
(*Continues* Environmental Periodicals.)

ERGON. ABSTR.
[UK/0046-2446]
ERGONOMICS ABSTRACTS.
(*Continues* Ergonomics Abstracts (1959).)

ETHNIC STUD. BIBLIOGR.
[US/0149-1555]
ETHNIC STUDIES BIBLIOGRAPHY.
(Ceased)

INDEXES/ABSTRACTS TABLE

ETHNOARTS INDEX
[US/0893-0120]
ETHNOARTS INDEX.
(*Continues* Tribal Arts Review.)

EUR. RES.
[NE/0304-4297]
EUROPEAN RESEARCH.
(*Continued by* Marketing and Research Today.)

EXCEPT. CHILD EDUC. RESOUR.
[US/0160-4309]
EXCEPTIONAL CHILD EDUCATION RESOURCES.
(*Continues* Exceptional Child Education Abstracts.)

EXCEPT. CHILD EDUC. ABSTR.
[US/0014-4010]
EXCEPTIONAL CHILD EDUCATION ABSTRACTS.
(*Continued by* Exceptional Child Education Resources.)

EXCEPT. HUM. EXP.
[US/1053-4768]
EXCEPTIONAL HUMAN EXPERIENCE.
(*Continues* Parapsychology Abstracts International.)

EXCERPTA MED. LIST J. ABSTR.
[US]
EXCERPTA MEDICA : LIST OF JOURNALS ABSTRACTED.
(*Continued by* List of Journals Abstracted.)

EXCERPTA MED., SECT. 06B, ARTHR. RHEUM.
[NE]
EXCERPTA MEDICA. SECTION 06B. ARTHRITIS AND RHEUMATISM.
(Ceased)

EXCERPTA MEDICA., SECT. 1, ANATOM. ANTHROPOL. EMBRYOL. HISTOL.
[NE/0014-4053]
EXCERPTA MEDICA. SECTION 1. ANATOMY, ANTHROPOLOGY, EMBRYOLOGY AND HISTOLOGY.
***Refer to EMBASE [Online Database] for complete source list.

EXCERPTA MED., SECT. 2, PHYSIOL.
[NE/0367-1089]
EXCERPTA MEDICA. SECTION 2A. PHYSIOLOGY.
(*Continues* Excerpta Medica. Section 2A. Physiology.)
***Refer to EMBASE [Online Database] for complete source list.

EXCERPTA MED., SECT. 2A, PHYSIOL.
[NE/0367-1089]
EXCERPTA MEDICA. SECTION 2A. PHYSIOLOGY.
(*Continued by* Excerpta Medica. Section 2. Physiology.)

EXCERPTA MED., SECT. 3, ENDOCRINOL.
[NE/0014-407X]
EXCERPTA MEDICA. SECTION 3. ENDOCRINOLOGY.
(*Continues* Excerpta Medica. Section 3. Endocrinology, Experimental and Clinical.)
***Refer to EMBASE [Online Database] for complete source list.

EXCERPTA MED., SECT. 4, MICROBIOL.
[NE/0167-4285]
EXCERPTA MEDICA. SECTION 4. MICROBIOLOGY.
(*Continued by* Excerpta Medica. Section 4, Microbiology, Bacteriology, Mycology, Parasitology, and Virology.)

EXCERPTA MED., SECT. 4, MICROBIOL. BACTERIOL. MYCOL. PARASITOL. VIROL.
[NE]
EXCERPTA MEDICA. SECTION 4. MICROBIOLOGY, BACTERIOLOGY, MYCOLOGY, PARASITOLOGY, AND VIROLOGY.
(*Continues* Excerpta Medica. Section 4, Microbiology; *Absorbed* Virology.)
***Refer to EMBASE [Online Database] for complete source list.

EXCERPTA MED., SECT. 5, GEN. PATHOL. PATHOLOGIC. ANAT.
[NE/0014-4096]
EXCERPTA MEDICA. SECTION 5. GENERAL PATHOLOGY AND PATHOLOGICAL ANATOMY.
***Refer to EMBASE [Online Database] for complete source list.

EXCERPTA MED., SECT. 6, INTERN. MED.
[NE/0014-410X]
EXCERPTA MEDICA. SECTION 6. INTERNAL MEDICINE.
***Refer to EMBASE [Online Database] for complete source list.

EXCERPTA MED., SECT. 7, PEDIATR. PEDIATR. SUR.
[NE/0373-6512]
EXCERPTA MEDICA. SECTION 7. PEDIATRICS AND PEDIATRIC SURGERY.
(*Continues* Excerpta Medica. Section 7. Pediatrics.)
***Refer to EMBASE [Online Database] for complete source list.

EXCERPTA MED., SECT. 8, NEUROL. NEUROSURG.
[NE/0014-4126]
EXCERPTA MEDICA. SECTION 8. NEUROLOGY AND NEUROSURGERY.
(*Continues* Excerpta Medica. Section 8A. Neurology and Neurosurgery.)
***Refer to EMBASE [Online Database] for complete source list.

EXCERPTA MED., SECT. 8A, NEUROL. NEUROSURG.
[NE/0014-4126]
EXCERPTA MEDICA. SECTION 8A. NEUROLOGY AND NEUROSURGERY.
(*Continued by* Excerpta Medica. Section 8. Neurology and Neurosurgery.)

EXCERPTA MED., SECT. 9, SURG.
[NE/0014-4134]
EXCERPTA MEDICA. SECTION 9. SURGERY.
(*Continued by* Excerpta Medica. Section 28, Urology.)

EXCERPTA MED., SECT. 9B, ORTHO. TRAUMATOL.
[NE]
EXCERPTA MEDICA. SECTION 9B. ORTHOPAEDICS AND TRAUMATOLOGY.
(*Continued by* Orthopedic Surgery.)

EXCERPTA MED., SECT. 10, OBSTETR. GYNECOL.
[NE/0014-4142]
EXCERPTA MEDICA. SECTION 10. OBSTETRICS AND GYNECOLOGY.
***Refer to EMBASE [Online Database] for complete source list.

EXCERPTA MED., SECT. 12, OPHTHALMOL.
[NE/0014-4169]
EXCERPTA MEDICA. SECTION 12. OPHTHALMOLOGY.
***Refer to EMBASE [Online Database] for complete source list.

EXCERPTA MED., SECT. 13, DERMATOL.
[NE/0014-4177]
EXCERPTA MEDICA. SECTION 13. DERMATOLOGY AND VENEREOLOGY.
***Refer to EMBASE [Online Database] for complete source list.

EXCERPTA MED., SECT. 14, RADIOL.
[NE/0014-4185]
EXCERPTA MEDICA. SECTION 14. RADIOLOGY.
***Refer to EMBASE [Online Database] for complete source list.

EXCERPTA MED., SECT. 16, CANCER
[NE/0014-4207]
EXCERPTA MEDICA. SECTION 16. CANCER.
(*Continues* Cancer, Experimental and Clinical.)
***Refer to EMBASE [Online Database] for complete source list.

EXCERPTA MED., SECT. 17, PUBL. HEALTH SOC. MED EPIDEM.
[NE]
EXCERPTA MEDICA. SECTION 17. PUBLIC HEALTH, SOCIAL MEDICINE AND EPIDEMIOLOGY.
(*Continues* Excerpta Medica. Section 17, Public Health, Social Medicine and Hygiene.)
***Refer to EMBASE [Online Database] for complete source list.

EXCERPTA MED., SECT. 17, PUBL. HEALTH SOC. MED. HYG.
[NE/0014-4215]
EXCERPTA MEDICA. SECTION 17. PUBLIC HEALTH, SOCIAL MEDICINE AND HYGIENE.
(*Continued by* Excerpta Medica. Section 17, Public Health, Social Medicine and Epidemiology.)

EXCERPTA MED., SECT. 18, CARDIOVASC. DISEAS. CARDIOVASC. SURG.
[NE/0014-4223]
EXCERPTA MEDICA. SECTION 18. CARDIOVASCULAR DISEASES AND CARDIOVASCULAR SURGERY.
(*Continues* Excerpta Medica. Section 18. Cardiovascular Diseases.)
***Refer to EMBASE [Online Database] for complete source list.

EXCERPTA MED., SECT. 19, REHABIL. PHYS. MED.
[NE/0014-4231]
EXCERPTA MEDICA. SECTION 19. REHABILITATION AND PHYSICAL MEDICINE.
(*Continues* Excerpta Medica. Section 19. Rehabilitation.)
***Refer to EMBASE [Online Database] for complete source list.

EXCERPTA MED., SECT. 20, GERONTOL. GERIATR.
[NE/0014-424X]
EXCERPTA MEDICA. SECTION 20. GERONTOLOGY AND GERIATRICS.
***Refer to EMBASE [Online Database] for complete source list.

INDEXES/ABSTRACTS TABLE

EXCERPTA MED., SECT. 21, DEVELOP. BIOL. TERATOL.
[NE/0014-4258]
EXCERPTA MEDICA. SECTION 21. DEVELOPMENTAL BIOLOGY AND TERATOLOGY.
(*Continues* Excerpta Medica. Section 21. Human Developmental Biology.)
***Refer to EMBASE [Online Database] for complete source list.

EXCERPTA MED., SECT. 22, HUMAN GENET.
[NE/0014-4266]
EXCERPTA MEDICA. SECTION 22. HUMAN GENETICS.
(*Continues* Human Genetics Abstracts.)
***Refer to EMBASE [Online Database] for complete source list.

EXCERPTA MED., SECT. 23, NUCL. MED.
[NE/0014-4274]
EXCERPTA MEDICA. SECTION 23. NUCLEAR MEDICINE.
***Refer to EMBASE [Online Database] for complete source list.

EXCERPTA MED., SECT. 24, ANESTHESIOL.
[NE/0014-4282]
EXCERPTA MEDICA. SECTION 24. ANESTHESIOLOGY.
***Refer to EMBASE [Online Database] for complete source list.

EXCERPTA MED., SECT. 25, HEMATOL.
[NE/0014-4290]
EXCERPTA MEDICA. SECTION 25. HEMATOLOGY.
***Refer to EMBASE [Online Database] for complete source list.

EXCERPTA MED., SECT. 26, IMMUNOL. SEROL. TRANSPLANT.
[NE/0014-4304]
EXCERPTA MEDICA. SECTION 26. IMMUNOLOGY, SEROLOGY AND TRANSPLANTATION.
(*Supersedes in part* Excerpta Medica. Section 4, Medical Microbiology, Immunology and Serology.)
***Refer to EMBASE [Online Database] for complete source list.

EXCERPTA MED., SECT. 27, BIOPHYS. BIOENG. MED. INSTRUMEN.
[NE/0014-4312]
EXCERPTA MEDICA. SECTION 27. BIOPHYSICS, BIOENGINEERING AND MEDICAL INSTRUMENTATION.
(*Continues* Excerpta Medica. Section 27. Medical Instrumentation.)
***Refer to EMBASE [Online Database] for complete source list.

EXCERPTA MED., SECT. 28, UROL.
[NE]
EXCERPTA MEDICA. SECTION 28. UROLOGY.
(*Continued by* Excerpta Medica. Section 28, Urology and Nephrology.)

EXCERPTA MED., SECT. 28, UROL. NEPHROL.
[NE/0014-4320]
EXCERPTA MEDICA. SECTION 28. UROLOGY AND NEPHROLOGY.
(*Continues* Excerpta Medica. Section 28, Urology.)
***Refer to EMBASE [Online Database] for complete source list.

EXCERPTA MED., SECT. 29, CLIN. BIOCHEM.
[NE/0300-5372]
EXCERPTA MEDICA. SECTION 29. CLINICAL BIOCHEMISTRY.
(*Continues* Excerpta Medica. Section 29. Biochemistry.)
***Refer to EMBASE [Online Database] for complete source list.

EXCERPTA MED., SECT. 30, CLIN. EXPER. PHARMACOL.
[NE]
EXCERPTA MEDICA. SECTION 30. CLINICAL AND EXPERIMENTAL PHARMACOLOGY.
(*Formed by the union of* Excerpta Medica. Section 30, Pharmacology *and* Excerpta Medica. Section 130, Clinical Pharmacology.)
***Refer to EMBASE [Online Database] for complete source list.

EXCERPTA MED., SECT. 30, PHARMACOL.
[IE/0167-9643]
EXCERPTA MEDICA. SECTION 30. PHARMACOLOGY.
(*Continued in part by* Excerpta Medica. Section 130, Clinical Pharmacology; *Merged into* Excerpta Medica. Section 30. Clinical and Experimental Pharmacology.)
***Refer to EMBASE [Online Database] for complete source list.

EXCERPTA MED., SECT. 32, PSYCH.
[NE/0014-4363]
EXCERPTA MEDICA. SECTION 32. PSYCHIATRY.
(*Continues* Excerpta Medica. Section 8B, Psychiatry.)
***Refer to EMBASE [Online Database] for complete source list.

EXCERPTA MED., SECT. 35, OCCUPAT. HEALTH INDUSTR. MED.
[NE/0014-4398]
EXCERPTA MEDICA. SECTION 35. OCCUPATIONAL HEALTH AND INDUSTRIAL MEDICINE.
***Refer to EMBASE [Online Database] for complete source list.

EXCERPTA MED., SECT. 36, HEALTH POLICY ECON. MANAG.
[NE]
EXCERPTA MEDICA. SECTION 36. HEALTH POLICY, ECONOMICS, AND MANAGEMENT.
(*Continues* Health Economics and Hospital Management.)
***Refer to EMBASE [Online Database] for complete source list.

EXCERPTA MED., SECT. 37, DRUG LIT. INDEX
[NE/0167-9171]
EXCERPTA MEDICA. SECTION 37. DRUG LITERATURE INDEX.
(*Continues* Drug Literature Index.)

EXCERPTA MED., SECT. 38, ADVERSE REACT. TITLES
[NE/0167-9090]
EXCERPTA MEDICA. SECTION 38. ADVERSE REACTIONS TITLES.
(*Continues* Adverse Reactions Titles.)
***Refer to EMBASE [Online Database] for complete source list.

EXCERPTA MED., SECT. 40, DRUG DEPEND. ALCOHOL ABUSE ALCOHOL.
[NE/0304-4041]
EXCERPTA MEDICA. SECTION 40. DRUG DEPENDENCE, ALCOHOL ABUSE, AND ALCOHOLISM.
(*Continues* Excerpta Medica. Section 40, Drug Dependence.)
***Refer to EMBASE [Online Database] for complete source list.

EXCERPTA MED., SECT. 46, ENVIRON. HEALTH POLLUT. CONT.
[NE/0300-5194]
EXCERPTA MEDICA. SECTION 46. ENVIRONMENTAL HEALTH AND POLLUTION CONTROL.
(*Continues* Environmental Health and Pollution Control.)
***Refer to EMBASE [Online Database] for complete source list.

EXCERPTA MED., SECT. 50, EPILEP. ABSTR.
[NE/0303-8459]
EXCERPTA MEDICA. SECTION 50. EPILEPSY ABSTRACTS.
(*Continues* Epilepsy Abstracts.)
***Refer to EMBASE [Online Database] for complete source list.

EXCERPTA MED., SECT. 52, TOXICOL.
[NE/0167-8353]
EXCERPTA MEDICA. SECTION 52. TOXICOLOGY.
(*Continues in part* Excerpta Medica. Section 30, Pharmacology and Toxicology.)
***Refer to EMBASE [Online Database] for complete source list.

EXCERPTA MED., SECT. 54, AIDS
[NE/0922-6532]
EXCERPTA MEDICA. SECTION 54. AIDS (ACQUIRED IMMUNE DEFICIENCY SYNDROME).
(Ceased)

EXCERPTA MED., SECT. 65, CANCER IMMUNOL. LIT. INDEX
[NE/0304-3789]
EXCERPTA MEDICA. SECTION 65. CANCER IMMUNOLOGY. LITERATURE INDEX.
***Refer to EMBASE [Online Database] for complete source list.

EXCERPTA MED., SECT. 130, CLINIC. PHARMACOL.
[NE/0921-4496]
EXCERPTA MEDICA. SECTION 130. CLINICAL PHARMACOLOGY.
(*Separated from* Excerpta Medica. Section 30, Pharmacology.)

EXCERPTA MED., SECT. 151, MYCOBACTER. DISEAS. LEPROSY TUBERCUL. RELATED SUBJ.
[NE/0168-8944]
EXCERPTA MEDICA. SECTION 151. MYCOBACTERIAL DISEASES--LEPROSY, TUBERCULOSIS, AND RELATED SUBJECTS.
(*Continues* Excerpta Medica. Section 51, Mycobacterial Diseases--Leprosy, Tuberculosis, and Related Subjects.)

EXPAND. ACAD. INDEX
[US]
EXPANDED ACADEMIC INDEX [COMPUTER FILE].

INDEXES/ABSTRACTS TABLE

F & S INDEX CORP. IND.
[US/0014-567X]
F & S INDEX OF CORPORATIONS AND INDUSTRIES.
(*Continued by* Predicasts F & S Index United States (Annual Edition).)

F & S INDEX PLUS TEXT, INT.
[US/1065-5956]
F & S INDEX PLUS TEXT. INTERNATIONAL.

F & S INDEX PLUS TEXT, U.S.
[US/1065-5964]
F & S INDEX PLUS TEXT. UNITED STATES.
***Refer to F&S Index Plus Text International for complete source list.

FABA BEAN ABSTR.
[UK/0260-8456]
FABA BEAN ABSTRACTS.
(Ceased)

FAMLI, FAM. MED. LIT. INDEX
[CN/0227-2393]
FAMLI : FAMILY MEDICINE LITERATURE INDEX.
(Ceased)

FARM GARD. INDEX
[US/0736-9980]
FARM & GARDEN INDEX.
(Ceased)

FDA CLIN. EXP. ABSTR.
[US/0429-9442]
FDA CLINICAL EXPERIENCE ABSTRACTS.
(Ceased)

FED. PRINT
[US/0891-2769]
FED IN PRINT.
(*Continued by* Fed in Print: Economics and Banking Topics.)

FED. PRINT ECON. BANK. TOP.
[US]
FED IN PRINT: ECONOMICS AND BANKING TOPICS.
(*Continues* Fed in Print: Business and Banking Topics.)

FED. TAX ARTIC.
[US]
FEDERAL TAX ARTICLES: INCOME, ESTATE, GIFT, EXCISE, EMPLOYMENT TAXES.

FERT. ABSTR.
[US/0015-0290]
FERTILIZER ABSTRACTS.
(Ceased)

FIELD CROP ABSTR.
[UK/0015-069X]
FIELD CROP ABSTRACTS.

FILM LIT. INDEX
[US/0093-6758]
FILM LITERATURE INDEX.

FISH REV.
[US/1042-6299]
FISHERIES REVIEW (FORT COLLINS, COLO.).
(*Continues* Sport Fishery Abstracts; **Absorbed** Fish Health News.)

FLUID ABSTR. CIVIL ENG.
[UK/0962-7170]
FLUID ABSTRACTS. CIVIL ENGINEERING.
(*Formed by the union of* Civil Engineering Hydraulics Abstracts; Industrial Aerodynamics Abstracts; Offshore Engineering Abstracts **and** World Ports & Harbours Abstracts (Incorporating International Dredging Abstracts).)

FLUID ABSTR. PROC. ENG.
[UK/0962-7162]
FLUID ABSTRACTS. PROCESS ENGINEERING.
(*Formed by the union of* Fluid Flow Measurements Abstracts; Fluid Power Abstracts; Fluid Sealing Abstracts; Pipelines Abstracts; Pumps and Other Fluids Machinery Abstracts; Solid-Liquid Flow Abstracts; Computer-Aided Process Control Abstracts **and** Mixing and Separation Technology Abstracts.)

FLUIDEX
[UK]
FLUIDEX [ONLINE DATABASE].

FOOD SCI. TECHNOL. ABSTR.
[UK/0015-6574]
FOOD SCIENCE AND TECHNOLOGY ABSTRACTS.

FOODS ADLIBRA
[US/0146-9304]
FOODS ADLIBRA (1975).

FOR. ABSTR.
[UK/0015-7538]
FORESTRY ABSTRACTS.

FOR. PROD. ABSTR.
[UK/0140-4784]
FOREST PRODUCTS ABSTRACTS.

FOREIGN LANG. INDEX
[US/0048-5810]
FOREIGN LANGUAGE INDEX.
(*Continued by* PAIS Foreign Language Index.)

FRESH. AQUA. CONTENTS TABLES
[IT]
FRESHWATER AND AQUACULTURE CONTENTS TABLES. ACTUALITES DES EAUX DOUCES ET DE L'AQUACULTURE.

FUNK & SCOTT ANNU. INDEX CORP. LIB.
[US]
FUNK & SCOTT ANNUAL INDEX OF CORPORATIONS & INDUSTRIES, THE.
(*Continued by* F & S Index of Corporations and Industries.)

FUNK & SCOTT INDEX CORP. IND.
[US/0532-8705]
FUNK & SCOTT INDEX OF CORPORATIONS AND INDUSTRIES.
(*Continued by* Funk & Scott Annual Index of Corporations & Industries.)

FUT. SURV.
[US/0190-3241]
FUTURE SURVEY.
(*Continues* Public Policy Book Forecast.)

GARDEN LIT.
[US/1061-3722]
GARDEN LITERATURE.

GAS ABSTR.
[US/0016-4844]
GAS ABSTRACTS.

GASTROENTEROL. ABSTR. CITATIONS
[US/0016-5093]
GASTROENTEROLOGY: ABSTRACTS & CITATIONS.
(Ceased)

GEN. BUSINESSFILE
[US]
GENERAL BUSINESSFILE [COMPUTER FILE].

GEN. PERIOD. INDEX
[US]
GENERAL PERIODICALS INDEX [COMPUTER FILE].

GEN. PERIOD. ONDISC
[US/1064-8380]
GENERAL PERIODICALS ONDISC (RESEARCH 1 ED.).
***Refer to Newspaper and Periodical Abstracts for complete source list.

GEN. SCI. INDEX
[US/0162-1963]
GENERAL SCIENCE INDEX.

GEN. SCI. SOURCE
[US/1073-1954]
GENERAL SCIENCE SOURCE.

GENEALOGICAL PERIOD. ANNU. INDEX
[US/0072-0593]
GENEALOGICAL PERIODICAL ANNUAL INDEX.

GENET. ABSTR.
[US/0016-674X]
GENETICS ABSTRACTS.

GEO ABSTR.
[UK]
GEO ABSTRACTS.
(*Continued by* Geographical Abstracts : Physical Geography; Geographical Abstracts. Human Geography.)

GEOGR. ABSTR.
[UK]
GEOGRAPHICAL ABSTRACTS.
(*Continued by* Geo Abstracts.)

GEOGR. ABSTR. HUMAN GEOGR.
[UK/0953-9611]
GEOGRAPHICAL ABSTRACTS. HUMAN GEOGRAPHY.
(*Formed by the union of* Geographical Abstracts. C, Economic Geography (1986); Geographical Abstracts. D, Social and Historical Geography **and** Geographical Abstracts. F, Regional and Community Planning.)

GEOGR. ABSTR. PHYS. GEOGR.
[UK/0954-0504]
GEOGRAPHICAL ABSTRACTS : PHYSICAL GEOGRAPHY.
(*Formed by the union of* Geographical Abstracts. A, Landforms and the Quaternary; Geographical Abstracts. B, Climatology and Hydrology; Geographical Abstracts. E, Sedimentology **and** Geographical Abstracts. G, Remote Sensing, Photogrammetry, and Cartography.)

GEOL. ABSTR.
[UK/0954-0512]
GEOLOGICAL ABSTRACTS.
(*Formed by the union of* Geological Abstracts. Economic Geology; Geological Abstracts. Geophysics & Tectonics Abstracts; Geological Abstracts. Palaeontology & Stratigraphy **and** Geological Abstracts. Sedimentary Geology.)

GEOL. ABSTR. ECON. GEOL.
[UK]
GEOLOGICAL ABSTRACTS. ECONOMIC GEOLOGY.
(**Merged with** Geological Abstracts. Geophysics & Tectonics Abstracts; Geological Abstracts. Palaeontology & Stratigraphy **and** Geological Abstracts. Sedimentary Abstracts **to form** Geological Abstracts.)

GEOL. ABSTR. GEOPHYS. TECTON.
[UK/0262-0847]
GEOLOGICAL ABSTRACTS. GEOPHYSICS & TECTONICS.
(**Merged with** Geological Abstracts. Economic Geology; Geological Abstracts. Palaeontology & Stratigraphy **and** Geological Abstracts. Sedimentary Geology **to form** Geological Abstracts.)

INDEXES/ABSTRACTS TABLE

GEOL. ABSTR. PALAEON. STRAT.
[UK/0268-8018]
GEOLOGICAL ABSTRACTS. PALAEONTOLOGY & STRATIGRAPHY.
(*Merged with* Geological Abstracts. Economic Geology; Geological Abstracts. Geophysics & Tectonics Abstracts and Geological Abstracts. Sedimentary Geology *to form* Geological Abstracts.)

GEOL. ABSTR. SEDIMEN. GEOL.
[UK/0268-8026]
GEOLOGICAL ABSTRACTS. SEDIMENTARY GEOLOGY.
(*Merged with* Geological Abstracts. Economic Geology; Geological Abstracts. Geophysics & Tectonics Abstracts and Geological Abstracts. Palaeontology & Stratigraphy *to form* Geological Abstracts.)

GEOPHYS. ABSTR.
[UK/0309-4332]
GEOPHYSICAL ABSTRACTS.
(*Continued by* Geological Abstracts. Geophysics & Tectonics Abstracts.)

GEOREF
[US/0197-7482]
GEOREF (CD-ROM).

GEOSCI. ABSTR.
[US/0435-5628]
GEOSCIENCE ABSTRACTS.
(*Supersedes* Geological Abstracts.)

GEOSCI. DOC.
[UK/0016-8483]
GEOSCIENCE DOCUMENTATION.

GEOTECH. ABSTR.
[US/0016-8491]
GEOTECHNICAL ABSTRACTS.
(Ceased)

GERONTOL. ABSTR.
[US/0736-4342]
GERONTOLOGICAL ABSTRACTS.
(Ceased)

GRAPH. ARTS ABSTR.
[US/0017-3282]
GRAPHIC ARTS ABSTRACTS.
(*Continued by* Abstracts (Graphic Arts Technical Foundation).)

GRAPH. ARTS BULL. INST. PAP. SCI. TECHNOL.
[US/1064-9638]
GRAPHIC ARTS BULLETIN OF THE INSTITUTE OF PAPER SCIENCE AND TECHNOLOGY.
(*Continues* Graphic Arts Literature Abstracts.)

GRAPH. ARTS LIT. ABSTR.
[US/0090-8207]
GRAPHIC ARTS LITERATURE ABSTRACTS.
(*Continued by* Graphic Arts Bulletin of the Institute of Paper Science and Technology.)

GUIDE PERFORM. ARTS
[US/0072-873X]
GUIDE TO THE PERFORMING ARTS.
(*Absorbed* Guide to Dance Periodicals.)

GUIDE REV. BOOKS HISP. AM.
[US/0716-0348]
GUIDE TO REVIEWS OF BOOKS FROM AND ABOUT HISPANIC AMERICA.
(Ceased)

GUIDE SOC. SCI. RELIG.
[US/1054-0946]
GUIDE TO SOCIAL SCIENCE AND RELIGION.
(*Continues* Guide to Social Science and Religion in Periodical Literature.)

GUIDE SOC. SCI. RELIG. PERIOD. LIT.
[US/0017-5307]
GUIDE TO SOCIAL SCIENCE AND RELIGION IN PERIODICAL LITERATURE.
(*Continued by* Guide to Social Science and Religion.)

HEALTH DEVICES ALERTS
[US/0163-0458]
HEALTH DEVICES ALERTS.

HEALTH INDEX
[US]
HEALTH INDEX [COMPUTER FILE].

HEALTH PERIOD. DATABASE
[US]
HEALTH PERIODICALS DATABASE [ONLINE DATABASE].

HEALTH PLAN. ADMINIS.
[US/1065-0679]
HEALTH PLANNING AND ADMINISTRATION.

HEALTH SAF. SCI. ABSTR.
[US/0892-9351]
HEALTH AND SAFETY SCIENCE ABSTRACTS.
(*Continues* Safety Science Abstracts Journal.)

HEALTH SERV. ABSTR.
[UK/0268-0459]
HEALTH SERVICE ABSTRACTS.
(*Formed by the union of* Current Literature on Health Services; Current Literature on General Medical Practice and Hospital Abstracts.)

HEALTH SOURCE
[US/1063-9810]
HEALTH SOURCE (PEABODY, MASS.).

HELMINTHOL. ABSTR.
[UK/0957-6789]
HELMINTHOLOGICAL ABSTRACTS.
(*Continues* Helminthological Abstracts. Series A, Animal and Human Helminthology.)

HELMINTHOL. ABSTR. SER. A, ANIM. HUM. HELMINTHOL.
[UK/0300-8339]
HELMINTHOLOGICAL ABSTRACTS. SERIES A, ANIMAL AND HUMAN HELMINTHOLOGY.
(*Continued by* Helminthological Abstracts.)

HELMINTHOL. ABSTR. SER. B, PLANT NEMATOLOGY
[UK/0300-8320]
HELMINTHOLOGICAL ABSTRACTS. SERIES B, PLANT NEMATOLOGY.
(*Continued by* Nematological Abstracts.)

HERB. ABSTR.
[UK/0018-0602]
HERBAGE ABSTRACTS.
(*Continued by* Grasslands and Forage Abstracts.)

HIGH. EDUC. ABSTR.
[US/0748-4364]
HIGHER EDUCATION ABSTRACTS.
(*Continues* College Student Personnel Abstracts.)

HIGHW. RES. ABSTR.
[US/0018-1730]
HIGHWAY RESEARCH ABSTRACTS.
(*Continued by* Transportation Research Abstracts.)

HIGHW. RES. ABSTR.
[US/1050-0804]
HIGHWAY RESEARCH ABSTRACTS (1990).
(*Continues* HRIS Abstracts.)

HILITES
[US]
HILITES DATABASE [ONLINE DATABASE].

HISP. AM. PERIOD. INDEX
[US/0270-8558]
HISPANIC AMERICAN PERIODICALS INDEX (LOS ANGELES, CALIF.).

HIST. ABSTR.
[US/0018-2435]
HISTORICAL ABSTRACTS.
(*Split into* Historical Abstracts. Part A, Modern History Abstracts *and* Historical Abstracts. Part B, Twentieth Century Abstracts.)

HIST. ABSTR., PART A, MOD. HIST. ABSTR.
[US/0363-2717]
HISTORICAL ABSTRACTS. PART A, MODERN HISTORY ABSTRACTS.
(*Continues in part* Historical Abstracts.)
***Refer to America: History and Life for complete source list.

HIST. ABSTR., PART B, TWENT. CENTURY ABSTR.
[US/0363-2725]
HISTORICAL ABSTRACTS. PART B, TWENTIETH CENTURY ABSTRACTS.
(*Continues in part* Historical Abstracts.)
***Refer to America: History and Life for complete source list.

HIST. SOURCE
[US/1063-9799]
HISTORY SOURCE.
(*Merged into* Humanities Source CD-ROM.)

HORTIC. ABSTR.
[UK/0018-5280]
HORTICULTURAL ABSTRACTS.

HOSPIT. ABSTR.
[UK/0018-5507]
HOSPITAL ABSTRACTS.
(*Merged with* Current Literature on Health Services and Current Literature on General Medical Practice *to form* Health Service Abstracts.)

HOSPIT. HEALTH ADMIN. INDEX
[US/1077-1719]
HOSPITAL AND HEALTH ADMINISTRATION INDEX.
(*Continues* Hospital Literature Index.)

HOSPIT. LIT. INDEX
[US/0018-5736]
HOSPITAL LITERATURE INDEX.
(*Continued by* Hospital and Health Administration Index.)

HOSPIT. MANAGE. REV.
[US/0737-903X]
HOSPITAL MANAGEMENT REVIEW.

HRIS ABSTR.
[US/0017-6222]
HRIS ABSTRACTS.
(*Continued by* Highway Research Abstracts (Washington, D.C. : 1990).)

HTFS DIG.
[UK/0952-2654]
HTFS DIGEST (1987).
(*Continues* Heat Transfer & Fluid Flow Digest; *Absorbed* Fouling Prevention Research Digest.)

INDEXES/ABSTRACTS TABLE

HUM. GENOME ABSTR.
[US/1045-4470]
HUMAN GENOME ABSTRACTS.

HUM. RESOUR. ABSTR.
[US/0099-2453]
HUMAN RESOURCES ABSTRACTS.
(*Continues* Poverty and Human Resources Abstracts.)

HUM. RIGHTS INTERN. REP.
[US/0275-049X]
HUMAN RIGHTS INTERNET REPORTER.
(*Continues* Human Rights Internet Newsletter.)

HUMANIT. INDEX
[US/0095-5981]
HUMANITIES INDEX.
(*Supersedes in part* Social Sciences & Humanities Index.)

HUMANIT. SOURCE
[US/1073-1962]
HUMANITIES SOURCE.
(*Absorbed* History Source CD-ROM.)

HUNGAR. LIBR. INFO. SCI. ABSTR.
[HU/0046-8304]
HUNGARIAN LIBRARY AND INFORMATION SCIENCE ABSTRACTS.

IAG, LIT. AUTO.
[NE/0376-9666]
IAG - LITERATURE ON AUTOMATION.
(*Continued by* New Literature on Automation.)

IMAGING ABSTR.
[US/0896-100X]
IMAGING ABSTRACTS.
(*Continues* Photographic Abstracts.)

IMMUNOL. ABSTR.
[US/0307-112X]
IMMUNOLOGY ABSTRACTS.

IND. ARTS INDEX
[US/0275-1682]
INDUSTRIAL ARTS INDEX.
(*Split into* Business Periodicals Index *and* Applied Science & Technology Index.)

IND. HYG. DIG.
[US/0019-8382]
INDUSTRIAL HYGIENE DIGEST.

INDEX AM. PERIOD. VERSE
[US/0090-9130]
INDEX OF AMERICAN PERIODICAL VERSE.

INDEX BLACK PERIOD.
[US/0899-6253]
INDEX TO BLACK PERIODICALS.
(*Continues* Index to Periodical Articles by and About Blacks.)

INDEX BOOK REV. HUMANIT.
[US/0073-5892]
INDEX TO BOOK REVIEWS IN THE HUMANITIES.
(**Ceased**)

INDEX BOOK REV. RELIG.
[US/0887-1574]
INDEX TO BOOK REVIEWS IN RELIGION.
(*Continues in part* Religion Index One. Periodicals.)

INDEX BUS. REPORTS
[UK]
INDEX TO BUSINESS REPORTS.
(*Continues* Index to Special Reports in UK Newspapers and Selected Periodicals.)

INDEX CAN. LEG. PERIOD. LIT.
[CN/0316-8891]
INDEX TO CANADIAN LEGAL PERIODICAL LITERATURE.

INDEX CHEM.
[US/0891-6055]
INDEX CHEMICUS (1987).
(*Continues* Current Abstracts of Chemistry and Index Chemicus (Philadelphia, Pa. : 1978).)

INDEX DENT. LIT.
[US/0019-3992]
INDEX TO DENTAL LITERATURE.
(*Continues* Index to Dental Literature in the English Language.)

INDEX ECON. ARTIC. J. COLLECT. VOL.
[US/0536-647X]
INDEX OF ECONOMIC ARTICLES IN JOURNALS AND COLLECTIVE VOLUMES.
(*Formed by the union of* Index of Economic Journals *and* Index of Economic Articles in Collective Volumes.)
***Refer to Journal of Economic Literature for complete source list.

INDEX ECON. J.
[US/0893-9527]
INDEX OF ECONOMIC JOURNALS.
(*Merged with* Index of Economic Articles in Collective Volumes *to form* Index of Economic Articles in Journals and Collective Volumes.)

INDEX FOREIGN LEG. PER.
[UK/0019-400X]
INDEX TO FOREIGN LEGAL PERIODICALS.

INDEX FREE PERIOD.
[US/0147-5630]
INDEX TO FREE PERIODICALS.
(*Merged into* Matter of Fact.)

INDEX IEEE PUBL.
[US/0099-1368]
INDEX TO IEEE PUBLICATIONS.
(*Supersedes* Institute of Electrical and Electronics Engineers. Index to IEEE Periodicals.)

INDEX INF.
[US/0073-5930]
INDEX TO HOW TO DO IT INFORMATION.

INDEX ISLAM.
[UK]
INDEX ISLAMICUS.
(*Continues* Index Islamicus. Supplement.)

INDEX ISLAM. LIT.
[UK]
INDEX OF ISLAMIC LITERATURE.

INDEX JEW. PERIOD.
[US/0019-4050]
INDEX TO JEWISH PERIODICALS.

INDEX LEG. PERIOD.
[US/0019-4077]
INDEX TO LEGAL PERIODICALS.

INDEX LIT. AM. INDIAN
[US/0091-7346]
INDEX TO LITERATURE ON THE AMERICAN INDIAN.
(**Ceased**)

INDEX MATH. PAP.
[US/0019-3917]
INDEX OF MATHEMATICAL PAPERS.
(**Ceased**)

INDEX MED.
[US/0019-3879]
INDEX MEDICUS (1960).
(*Continues* Current List of Medical Literature; *Absorbed* Monthly Bibliography of Medical Reviews.)

INDEX NEW Z. PERIOD.
[NZ]
INDEX TO NEW ZEALAND PERIODICALS.
(**Ceased**)

INDEX PERIOD. ARTIC. BLACKS
[US/0161-8245]
INDEX TO PERIODICAL ARTICLES BY AND ABOUT BLACKS.
(*Continued by* Index to Black Periodicals.)

INDEX PERIOD. ARTIC. NEGROES
[US/0073-5973]
INDEX TO PERIODICAL ARTICLES BY AND ABOUT NEGROES.
(*Continued by* Index to Periodical Articles by and About Blacks.)

INDEX PERIOD. ARTIC. RELAT. LAW
[US/0019-4093]
INDEX TO PERIODICAL ARTICLES RELATED TO LAW.

INDEX PERIOD. LIT. AGING
[US/0882-3405]
INDEX TO PERIODICAL LITERATURE ON AGING.
(*Continues* ARECO's Quarterly Index to Periodical Literature on Aging.)

INDEX PHILIP. PERIOD.
[PH/0073-599X]
INDEX TO PHILIPPINE PERIODICALS.

INDEX RELIG. PERIOD. LIT.
[US/0019-4107]
INDEX TO RELIGIOUS PERIODICAL LITERATURE.
(*Continued by* Religion Index One. Periodicals.)

INDEX SCI. REV.
[US/0360-0661]
INDEX TO SCIENTIFIC REVIEWS.

INDEX U.S. GOV. PERIOD.
[US/0098-4604]
INDEX TO U.S. GOVERNMENT PERIODICALS.
(**Ceased**)

INDEX VET.
[UK/0019-4123]
INDEX VETERINARIUS.

INDIAN GEOSCI. ABSTR.
[II]
INDIAN GEOSCIENCE ABSTRACTS.

INDIAN LIBR. SCI. ABSTR.
[II/0019-5790]
INDIAN LIBRARY SCIENCE ABSTRACTS.

INDIAN SCI. ABSTR.
[II/0019-6339]
INDIAN SCIENCE ABSTRACTS.
(*Continues* Bibliography of Scientific Publications of South and South East Asia.)

INDICE AGRICOLA AM. LAT. CARIBE
[CR/0304-0119]
INDICE AGRICOLA DE AMERICA LATINA Y EL CARIBE.
(*Continues* Bibliografia Agricola Latinoamericana y del Caribe.)

INDICE HIST. ESP.
[SP/0537-3522]
INDICE HISTORICO ESPANOL.

INDEXES/ABSTRACTS TABLE

INDICE MED. ESP.
[SP]
INDICE MEDICO ESPANOL.

INF. INSTRUC. TECHNOL.
[US]
INFORMATION & INSTRUCTION TECHNOLOGIES.

INF. MANAGE. TECHNOL.
[UK]
INFORMATION MANAGEMENT & TECHNOLOGY.
(*Continues* Information Media & Technology.)

INF. SCI. ABSTR.
[US/0020-0239]
INFORMATION SCIENCE ABSTRACTS.
(*Continues* Documentation Abstracts and Information Science Abstracts.)

INFO-SOUTH ABSTR.
[US/1059-5910]
INFO-SOUTH ABSTRACTS.

INFOBANK
[IO]
INFOBANK.

INFOMAT INT. BUS.
[US]
INFOMAT INTERNATIONAL BUSINESS [ONLINE DATABASE].

INIS ATOMINDEX
[AU/0004-7139]
INIS ATOMINDEX.
(*Continued by* INIS Atomindex.)

INIS ATOMINDEX [MICRO.]
[AU]
INIS ATOMINDEX [MICROFORM].
(*Continues* INIS Atomindex.)

INS. PERIOD. INDEX
[US/0074-073X]
INSURANCE PERIODICALS INDEX.

INSPEC
[UK]
INSPEC [ONLINE DATABASE].

INT. ABSTR. BIOL. SCI.
[UK/0020-5818]
INTERNATIONAL ABSTRACTS OF BIOLOGICAL SCIENCES.
(*Continued by* Current Awareness in Biological Sciences : CABS.)

INT. ABSTR. OPER. RES.
[UK/0020-580X]
INTERNATIONAL ABSTRACTS IN OPERATIONS RESEARCH.

INT. AEROSP. ABSTR.
[US/0020-5842]
INTERNATIONAL AEROSPACE ABSTRACTS.
(*Supersedes in part* Aerospace Engineering.)

INT. BIBLIOGR. BOOK REV.
[GW]
INTERNATIONAL BIBLIOGRAPHY OF BOOK REVIEWS.
(*Continued by* Internationale Bibliographie der Rezensionen Wissenschaftlicher Literatur (Osnabruck, Germany : 1984).)

INT. BIBLIOGR. HIST. RELIG.
[NE/0538-5105]
INTERNATIONAL BIBLIOGRAPHY OF THE HISTORY OF RELIGIONS.
(Ceased)

INT. BIBLIOGR. PERIOD. LIT.
[GW]
INTERNATIONAL BIBLIOGRAPHY OF PERIODICAL LITERATURE.
(*Continued by* Internationale Bibliographie der Zeitschriftenliteratur aus Allen Gebieten des Wissens (Osnabruck, Germany : 1984).)

INT. BIBLIOGR. REZEN. WISSEN. LIT.
[GW/0020-918X]
INTERNATIONALE BIBLIOGRAPHIE DER REZENSIONEN WISSENSCHAFTLICHER LITERATUR.
(*Continues* Internationale Bibliographie der Rezensionen.)

INT. BIBLIOGR. SOCIOL.
[UK/0085-2066]
INTERNATIONAL BIBLIOGRAPHY OF SOCIOLOGY.
(*Continues in part* Current Sociology (Paris, France).)

INT. BIBLIOGR. ZEITSCHRIFTENLITERATUR ALLEN GEBIETEN WISSENS
[GW]
INTERNATIONALE BIBLIOGRAPHIE DER ZEITSCHRIFTENLITERATUR AUS ALLEN GEBIETEN DES WISSENS.
(*Continues* Internationale Bibliographie der Zeitschriftenliteratur.)

INT. BUILD. SERV. ABSTR.
[UK/0140-4237]
INTERNATIONAL BUILDING SERVICES ABSTRACTS.
(*Continues* Thermal Abstracts.)

INT. CIVIL ENG. ABSTR.
[IE/0332-4095]
INTERNATIONAL CIVIL ENGINEERING ABSTRACTS.
(*Continues* Institution of Civil Engineers (Great Britain). I.C.E. Abstracts.)

INT. COPPER INF. BULL.
[UK/0309-2216]
INTERNATIONAL COPPER INFORMATION BULLETIN.
(*Formed by the union of* Selected Abstracts of Recent Literature on Copper and Copper Alloys **and** Kupfer-Mitteilungen.)

INT. DEV. ABSTR.
[UK/0262-0855]
INTERNATIONAL DEVELOPMENT ABSTRACTS.
(*Absorbed* International Development Index.)

INT. EXEC.
[US/0020-6652]
INTERNATIONAL EXECUTIVE.

INT. GUIDE CLASSICAL STUD.
[US/0020-6849]
INTERNATIONAL GUIDE TO CLASSICAL STUDIES.
(*Continues* ABS International Guide to Classical Studies.)

INT. INDEX
[US/0363-0382]
INTERNATIONAL INDEX.
(*Continued by* Social Sciences & Humanities Index.)

INT. INDEX FILM PERIOD.
[US/0000-0388]
INTERNATIONAL INDEX TO FILM PERIODICALS.

INT. INDEX MULTI MEDIA INF.
[US/0094-6818]
INTERNATIONAL INDEX TO MULTI-MEDIA INFORMATION.
(*Continues* Film Review Index.)

INT. INDEX PERIOD.
[US]
INTERNATIONAL INDEX TO PERIODICALS.
(*Continued by* International Index.)

INT. LABOUR DOC.
[SZ/0020-7756]
INTERNATIONAL LABOUR DOCUMENTATION.
(*Continues* International Labour Office. Library. International Labour Documentation.)

INT. NURS. INDEX
[US/0020-8124]
INTERNATIONAL NURSING INDEX.

INT. PACKAG. ABSTR.
[UK/0260-7409]
INTERNATIONAL PACKAGING ABSTRACTS.
(*Continues* PIRA Packaging Abstract.)

INT. PET. ABSTR.
[UK/0309-4944]
INTERNATIONAL PETROLEUM ABSTRACTS.
(*Continued by* International Petroleum Abstracts Incorporating Offshore Abstracts.)

INT. PHARM. ABSTR.
[US/0020-8264]
INTERNATIONAL PHARMACEUTICAL ABSTRACTS.

INT. POLIT. SCI. ABSTR.
[FR/0020-8345]
INTERNATIONAL POLITICAL SCIENCE ABSTRACTS.

INT. POLYM. SCI. TECH.
[UK/0307-174X]
INTERNATIONAL POLYMER SCIENCE AND TECHNOLOGY.
(*Formed by the union of* Soviet Plastics **and** Soviet Rubber Technology.)

INT. RISK CONTROL REV.
[US/0739-389X]
INTERNATIONAL RISK CONTROL REVIEW.
(*Continued by* International Loss Control Review.)

INT. ZEITSCHRIFTENSCHAU BIBELWISS. GRENZGEB.
[GW/0074-9745]
INTERNATIONALE ZEITSCHRIFTENSCHAU FUER BIBELWISSENSCHAFT UND GRENZGEBIETE.

IOWA DRUG INF. SERV.
[US]
IOWA DRUG INFORMATION SERVICE.

IRR. DRAIN. ABSTR.
[UK/0306-7327]
IRRIGATION AND DRAINAGE ABSTRACTS / COMMONWEALTH AGRICULTURAL BUREAUS.

ISMEC BULL.
[US/0306-0039]
ISMEC BULLETIN.
(*Continued by* ISMEC, Mechanical Engineering Abstracts.)

ISMEC MECH. ENG. ABSTR.
[US/0896-7113]
ISMEC, MECHANICAL ENGINEERING ABSTRACTS.
(*Continued by* Mechanical Engineering Abstracts.)

J. ABSTR. ARTIC. INT. EDUC.
[US/1064-0746]
JOURNAL OF ABSTRACTS (AND ARTICLES) IN INTERNATIONAL EDUCATION.
(*Continues* Journal of Abstracts in International Education.)

INDEXES/ABSTRACTS TABLE

J. ABSTR. BR. SHIP RES. ASSOC.
[UK/0141-903X]
JOURNAL OF ABSTRACTS OF THE BRITISH SHIP RESEARCH ASSOCIATION.
(*Continued by* BMT Abstracts.)

J. ABSTR. INT. EDUC.
[US/0094-2383]
JOURNAL OF ABSTRACTS IN INTERNATIONAL EDUCATION.
(*Continued by* Journal of Abstract (and Articles) in International Education.)

J. CONTENTS QUAN. METHODS
[UK/0142-5951]
JOURNAL CONTENTS IN QUANTITATIVE METHODS.

J. ECON. ABSTR.
[US/0364-281X]
JOURNAL OF ECONOMIC ABSTRACTS.
(*Continued by* Journal of Economic Literature.)

J. ECON. LIT.
[US/0022-0515]
JOURNAL OF ECONOMIC LITERATURE.
(*Continues* Journal of Economic Abstracts.)

J. FERROCEMENT
[TH/0125-1759]
JOURNAL OF FERROCEMENT.

J. PLAN. LIT.
[US/0885-4122]
JOURNAL OF PLANNING LITERATURE.

J. WATCH
[US/0896-7210]
JOURNAL WATCH.

JAZZ INDEX
[GW/0344-5399]
JAZZ INDEX.
(Ceased)

JMR ABSTR.
[US/1066-2375]
JMR ABSTRACTS.
(*Absorbed by* MRS Bulletin.)

JR. HIGH MAG. ABSTR.
[US/1045-5493]
JUNIOR HIGH MAGAZINE ABSTRACTS.
(Ceased)

KEY ABSTR., ADV. MATER.
[UK/0950-4753]
KEY ABSTRACTS. ADVANCED MATERIALS.
***Refer to INSPEC [Online Database] for complete source list.

KEY ABSTR., ANTENNAS PROPAG.
[UK/0950-4761]
KEY ABSTRACTS. ANTENNAS & PROPAGATION.
(*Continues in part* Key Abstracts. Communication Technology.)
***Refer to INSPEC [Online Database] for complete source list.

KEY ABSTR., ARTIF. INTELL.
[UK/0950-477X]
KEY ABSTRACTS. ARTIFICIAL INTELLIGENCE.
(*Continues* Key Abstracts. Systems Theory.)
***Refer to INSPEC [Online Database] for complete source list.

KEY ABSTR., BUS. AUTOMAT.
[UK/0954-9153]
KEY ABSTRACTS. BUSINESS AUTOMATION.
(*Continues* IT Focus.)
***Refer to INSPEC [Online Database] for complete source list.

KEY ABSTR., COMPUT. COMMUN. STOR.
[UK/0950-4788]
KEY ABSTRACTS. COMPUTER COMMUNICATIONS & STORAGE.
***Refer to INSPEC [Online Database] for complete source list.

KEY ABSTR., COMPUT. ELECTRON. POWER
[UK/0950-4796]
KEY ABSTRACTS. COMPUTING IN ELECTRONICS AND POWER.
***Refer to INSPEC [Online Database] for complete source list.

KEY ABSTR., ELECTR. MEAS. INSTRUM.
[UK/0307-7977]
KEY ABSTRACTS : ELECTRICAL MEASUREMENTS AND INSTRUMENTATION.
(*Continued by* Key Abstracts. Electronic Instrumentation.)

KEY ABSTR., ELECTRON. CIRC.
[UK/0306-557X]
KEY ABSTRACTS. ELECTRONIC CIRCUITS.
***Refer to INSPEC [Online Database] for complete source list.

KEY ABSTR., ELECTRON. INSTRUM.
[UK/0950-480X]
KEY ABSTRACTS. ELECTRONIC INSTRUMENTATION.
(*Continues* Key Abstracts. Electrical Measurements and Instrumentation.)
***Refer to INSPEC [Online Database] for complete source list.

KEY ABSTR., FACTORY AUTOMAT.
[UK]
KEY ABSTRACTS. FACTORY AUTOMATION.
***Refer to INSPEC [Online Database] for complete source list.

KEY ABSTR., HIGH-TEMP. SUPERCONDUC.
[UK/0953-1262]
KEY ABSTRACTS. HIGH-TEMPERATURE SUPERCONDUCTORS.
***Refer to INSPEC [Online Database] for complete source list.

KEY ABSTR., HUMAN-COMPUT. INTERACT.
[UK]
KEY ABSTRACTS. HUMAN-COMPUTER INTERACTION.
***Refer to INSPEC [Online Database] for complete source list.

KEY ABSTR., MACH. VISION
[UK/0952-7052]
KEY ABSTRACTS. MACHINE VISION.
***Refer to INSPEC [Online Database] for complete source list.

KEY ABSTR., MEAS. PHYS.
[UK/0950-4818]
KEY ABSTRACTS. MEASUREMENTS IN PHYSICS.
(*Continues* Key Abstracts. Physical Measurements and Instrumentation.)
***Refer to INSPEC [Online Database] for complete source list.

KEY ABSTR., MICROELECTRON. PRINT. CIRC.
[UK/0952-7060]
KEY ABSTRACTS. MICROELECTRONICS AND PRINTED CIRCUITS.
***Refer to INSPEC [Online Database] for complete source list.

KEY ABSTR., MICROWAVE TECHNOL.
[UK/0952-7079]
KEY ABSTRACTS. MICROWAVE TECHNOLOGY.
***Refer to INSPEC [Online Database] for complete source list.

KEY ABSTR., NEUR. NETWORKS
[UK]
KEY ABSTRACTS. NEURAL NETWORKS.
***Refer to INSPEC [Online Database] for complete source list.

KEY ABSTR., OPTOELECTRON.
[UK/0950-4826]
KEY ABSTRACTS. OPTOELECTRONICS.
(*Continues in part* Key Abstracts. Solid State Devices.)
***Refer to INSPEC [Online Database] for complete source list.

KEY ABSTR., PHYS. MEAS. INSTRUM.
[UK/0307-7969]
KEY ABSTRACTS : PHYSICAL MEASUREMENTS AND INSTRUMENTATION.
(*Continued by* Key Abstracts. Measurements in Physics.)

KEY ABSTR., POWER SYST. APPL.
[UK/0950-4834]
KEY ABSTRACTS. POWER SYSTEMS AND APPLICATIONS.
(*Continues* Key Abstracts. Power Transmission and Distribution.)
***Refer to INSPEC [Online Database] for complete source list.

KEY ABSTR., ROBOT. CONTROL
[UK/0950-4842]
KEY ABSTRACTS. ROBOTICS & CONTROL.
(*Continues* Key Abstracts. Industrial Power and Control Systems.)
***Refer to INSPEC [Online Database] for complete source list.

KEY ABSTR., SEMICOND. DEVICES
[UK/0950-4850]
KEY ABSTRACTS. SEMICONDUCTOR DEVICES.
(*Continues in part* Key Abstracts. Solid State Devices.)
***Refer to INSPEC [Online Database] for complete source list.

KEY ABSTR., SOFTW. ENG.
[UK/0950-4869]
KEY ABSTRACTS. SOFTWARE ENGINEERING.
***Refer to INSPEC [Online Database] for complete source list.

KEY ABSTR., TELECOM.
[UK/0950-4877]
KEY ABSTRACTS. TELECOMMUNICATIONS.
(*Continues* Key Abstracts. Communication Technology.)
***Refer to INSPEC [Online Database] for complete source list.

KEY ECON. SCI.
[NE]
KEY TO ECONOMIC SCIENCE.
(*Continued by* Key to Economic Science and Managerial Sciences.)

KEY ECON. SCI. MANAGE. SCI.
[NE/0165-4748]
KEY TO ECONOMIC SCIENCE AND MANAGERIAL SCIENCES.
(*Continues* Key to Economic Science.)

KEY WORD INDEX WILDL. RES.
[SZ]
KEY-WORD-INDEX OF WILDLIFE RESEARCH.

INDEXES/ABSTRACTS TABLE

KEY WORD INDEX MED. LIT.
[US/0145-9716]
KEY-WORD INDEX FOR THE MEDICAL LITERATURE.
(*Continues* Keyword Index in Internal Medicine.)

KEYWORD INDEX INTERN. MED.
[US/0097-0220]
KEYWORD INDEX IN INTERNAL MEDICINE.
(*Continued by* Key-Word Index for the Medical Literature.)

LAB. HAZARDS BULL.
[UK/0261-2917]
LABORATORY HAZARDS BULLETIN.

LABORDOC
[SZ]
LABORDOC [ONLINE DATABASE].

LANG. LANG. BEHAV. ABSTR.
[US/0023-8295]
LANGUAGE AND LANGUAGE BEHAVIOR ABSTRACTS : LLBA.
(*Continued by* Linguistics and Language Behavior Abstracts.)

LANG. TEACH.
[UK/0261-4448]
LANGUAGE TEACHING.
(*Continues* Language Teaching & Linguistics. Abstracts.)

LANG. TEACH. LINGUIST. ABSTR.
[UK/0306-6304]
LANGUAGE TEACHING & LINGUISTICS ABSTRACTS.
(*Continued by* Language Teaching.)

LAW OFFICE INF. SERV.
[US/0164-5390]
LAW OFFICE INFORMATION SERVICE.
(Ceased)

LEAD ABSTR.
[US/0023-9569]
LEAD ABSTRACTS.
(*Continued by* Leadscan.)

LEADSCAN
[UK/0950-1584]
LEADSCAN.
(*Continues* Lead Abstracts (London, England : 1962).)

LEFT INDEX
[US/0733-2998]
LEFT INDEX.

LEG. CONTENTS, LC
[US/0279-5787]
LEGAL CONTENTS : LC.
(*Continues* CCLP, Contents of Current Legal Periodicals.)

LEG. INF. MANAGE. INDEX
[US/0747-9298]
LEGAL INFORMATION MANAGEMENT INDEX.

LEG. RESOUR. INDEX
[US/0272-9296]
LEGAL RESOURCE INDEX.

LEGALTRAC
[US]
LEGALTRAC [COMPUTER FILE].

LEIS. RECREAT. TOUR. ABSTR.
[UK/0261-1392]
LEISURE, RECREATION, AND TOURISM ABSTRACTS.
(*Continues* Rural Recreation and Tourism Abstracts.)

LEUKEMIA ABSTR.
[US/0024-1466]
LEUKEMIA ABSTRACTS.
(Ceased)

LIBR. INF. SCI. ABSTR.
[UK/0024-2179]
LIBRARY & INFORMATION SCIENCE ABSTRACTS.
(*Supersedes* Library Science Abstracts.)

LIBR. LIT.
[US/0024-2373]
LIBRARY LITERATURE.

LIBR. SCI. ABSTR.
[UK/0459-262X]
LIBRARY SCIENCE ABSTRACTS.
(*Continued by* Library & Information Science Abstracts.)

LIFE SCI. COLLECT.
[US/0891-3889]
PERIODICALS SCANNED AND ABSTRACTED. LIFE SCIENCES COLLECTION.

LINGUIST. LANG. BEHAV. ABSTR.
[US/0888-8027]
LINGUISTICS AND LANGUAGE BEHAVIOR ABSTRACTS.
(*Continues* Language and Language Behavior Abstracts; **Absorbed** Reading Abstracts.)

LISA PLUS
[UK/0966-8799]
LISA PLUS [COMPUTER FILE].
***Refer to Library and Information Science Abstracts for complete source list.

LIST J. ABSTR.
[NE/0923-5582]
LIST OF JOURNALS ABSTRACTED.
(*Continued by* EMBASE List of Journals Indexed.)

LIT. ABSTR., CATAL. CATAL.
[US/1065-0539]
LITERATURE ABSTRACTS. CATALYSTS & CATALYSIS.
(*Continued by* Literature Abstracts. Catalysts/Zeolites.)

LIT. ABSTR., HEALTH ENVIRON.
[US/1065-0490]
LITERATURE ABSTRACTS. HEALTH & ENVIRONMENT.
(*Continues* API Abstracts. Health & Environment.)

LIT. ABSTR., PET. REFIN. PETROCHEM.
[US/1065-0512]
LITERATURE ABSTRACTS. PETROLEUM REFINING & PETROCHEMICALS.
(*Continues* Petroleum Refining and Petrochemicals.)

LIT. ABSTR., PET. SUBSTIT.
[US/1065-0504]
LITERATURE ABSTRACTS. PETROLEUM SUBSTITUTES.
(*Continues* Petroleum Substitutes.)

LIT. ABSTR., TRANSP. STORAGE
[US/1065-0520]
LITERATURE ABSTRACTS. TRANSPORTATION & STORAGE.
(*Continues* Transportation and Storage.)

LIT. ANALY. MICROCOMPUT. PUBL.
[US/0735-9721]
LITERATURE ANALYSIS OF MICROCOMPUTER PUBLICATIONS : LAMP.
(Ceased)

LIT. CRIT. REGIST.
[US/0733-2165]
LITERARY CRITICISM REGISTER.

LIT. PAT. ABSTR., OILFIELD CHEM.
[US/1065-0547]
LITERATURE & PATENT ABSTRACTS. OILFIELD CHEMICALS.
(*Continued in part by* Literature Abstracts. Oilfield Chemicals **and** Patent Abstracts. Oilfield Chemicals.)

LOMA LIT. MOD. ART
[US/0090-7235]
LOMA; LITERATURE ON MODERN ART.
(*Continued by* ARTbibliographies Modern.)

MAG. ARTIC. SUMMAR.
[US/0895-3376]
MAGAZINE ARTICLE SUMMARIES (PRINT ED.).
(*Continues* Popular Magazine Review.)

MAG. ARTIC. SUMMAR. CD-ROM
[US/1041-1151]
MAGAZINE ARTICLE SUMMARIES (CD-ROM ED.).

MAG. ARTIC. SUMMAR. ELITE
[US/1060-6769]
MAGAZINE ARTICLE SUMMARIES FULL TEXT ELITE.

MAG. ARTIC. SUMMAR. SELECT
[US/1058-0255]
MAGAZINE ARTICLE SUMMARIES FULL TEXT SELECT.

MAG. ASAP PLUS
[US]
MAGAZINE ASAP PLUS [COMPUTER FILE].

MAG. ASAP SEL.
[US]
MAGAZINE ASAP SELECT [COMPUTER FILE].

MAG. EXPRESS
[US]
MAGAZINE EXPRESS [COMPUTER FILE].

MAG. INDEX
[US]
MAGAZINE INDEX, THE.

MAG. INDEX PLUS
[US]
MAGAZINE INDEX PLUS [COMPUTER FILE].

MAG. INDEX SEL. MICROFICHE
[US]
MAGAZINE INDEX SELECT MICROFICHE.

MAG. INDEX. SEL.
[US]
MAGAZINE INDEX SELECT [COMPUTER FILE].

MAG. SEARCH
[US/1071-2739]
MAGAZINE SEARCH.

MAGYAR KONYV. SZAK. BIBLIO.
[HU/0133-736X]
MAGYAR KONYVTARI SZAKIRODALOM BIBLIOGRAFIAJA, A.

MAIZE ABSTR.
[UK/0267-2987]
MAIZE ABSTRACTS.
(*Continues* Maize Quality Protein Abstracts.)

MANAGE. BIBLIOGR. REV.
[UK/0309-0582]
MANAGEMENT BIBLIOGRAPHIES & REVIEWS.
(*Continues* Business Education.)

MANAGE. CONTENTS
[US/0360-2400]
MANAGEMENT CONTENTS.
(Ceased)

INDEXES/ABSTRACTS TABLE

MANAGE. CONTENTS
[US]
MANAGEMENT CONTENTS [ONLINE DATABASE].

MANAGE. INDEX
[US]
MANAGEMENT INDEX.
(Ceased)

MANAGE. MARKET. ABSTR.
[UK/0308-2172]
MANAGEMENT AND MARKETING ABSTRACTS.

MANAGE. RES.
[US/0099-2224]
MANAGEMENT RESEARCH.
(*Continues* Bi-Monthly Review of Management Research.)

MANUF. PROCESS ENG. ABSTR.
[US/1063-7354]
MANUFACTURING AND PROCESS ENGINEERING ABSTRACTS.
(Ceased)

MAR. FISH. ABSTR.
[US/0735-3782]
MARINE FISHERIES ABSTRACTS.
(*Continues* Commercial Fisheries Abstracts.)

MAR. SCI. CONTENTS TABLES
[IT/0025-3308]
MARINE SCIENCE CONTENTS TABLES. ACTUALITES DES SCIENCES DE LA MER. INDICES DE REVISTAS SOBRE CIENCIAS MARINAS.
(*Continues* Current Contents in Marine Sciences; *Continues in part* International Marine Science.)

MARK. ADVERT. REF. SERV.
[US]
MARKETING AND ADVERTISING REFERENCE SERVICE [ONLINE DATABASE].

MARK. DISTR. ABSTR.
[UK]
MARKETING + DISTRIBUTION ABSTRACTS.
(*Continued by* Anbar Marketing & Distribution Abstracts.)

MARK. INF. GUIDE
[US/0025-374X]
MARKETING INFORMATION GUIDE.
(*Continues* Marketing Information Guide (Washington : 1961).)

MARK. RES. ABSTR.
[UK/0025-3596]
MARKET RESEARCH ABSTRACTS.

MARK. RES. TODAY
[NE/0923-5957]
MARKETING AND RESEARCH TODAY : THE JOURNAL OF THE EUROPEAN SOCIETY FOR OPINION AND MARKETING RESEARCH.
(*Continues* European Research.)

MASS SPECT. BULL.
[UK/0025-4738]
MASS SPECTROMETRY BULLETIN.

MATER. SCI. ENG. ABSTR.
[US/1063-732X]
MATERIALS SCIENCE AND ENGINEERING ABSTRACTS.
(Ceased)

MATH. REV.
[US/0025-5629]
MATHEMATICAL REVIEWS.

MECH. ENG. ABSTR.
[US/1063-7311]
MECHANICAL ENGINEERING ABSTRACTS.
(*Continues* ISMEC, Mechanical Engineering Abstracts.)

MED. ABSTR. NEWSL.
[US/0730-7810]
MEDICAL ABSTRACTS NEWSLETTER.

MED. ELECTRON. COMMUN. ABSTR.
[UK/0025-7222]
MEDICAL ELECTRONICS AND COMMUNICATIONS ABSTRACTS.
(Ceased)

MED. PHARM. BIOTECHNOL. ABSTR.
[US/1063-1178]
MEDICAL & PHARMACEUTICAL BIOTECHNOLOGY ABSTRACTS.
(*Continues in part* Biotechnology Research Abstracts.)
***Refer to Biotechnology Research Abstracts for complete source list.

MED. REV. DIG.
[US/0363-7778]
MEDIA REVIEW DIGEST.
(*Continues* Multi Media Reviews Index.)

MED. SOCIOECON. RES. SOURCE.
[US/0025-7540]
MEDICAL SOCIOECONOMIC RESEARCH SOURCES.
(*Supersedes* Weekly Bulletin *and* Index to Medical Socioeconomic Literature.)

MEDOC
[US/0097-9732]
MEDOC.
(Ceased)

MENT. HEALTH BOOK REV. INDEX
[US/0076-6445]
MENTAL HEALTH BOOK REVIEW INDEX.
(*Continued by* Chicorel Index to Mental Health Book Reviews.)

MENT. RETARD. ABSTR.
[US/0025-9691]
MENTAL RETARDATION ABSTRACTS.
(*Continued by* Mental Retardation & Developmental Disabilities Abstracts.)

MENT. RETARD. DEV. DISABIL. ABSTR.
[US/0361-3798]
MENTAL RETARDATION & DEVELOPMENTAL DISABILITIES ABSTRACTS.
(*Continued by* Developmental Disabilities Abstracts.)

MET. ABSTR.
[UK/0026-0924]
METALS ABSTRACTS.
(*Formed by the union of* Metallurgical Abstracts *and* Review of Metal Literature.)

MET. ABSTR. INDEX
[UK/0026-0932]
METALS ABSTRACTS INDEX.
(*Formed by the union of* Metallurgical Abstracts *and* Review of Metal Literature.)
***Refer to Metals Abstracts for complete source list.

MET. FINISHING ABSTR.
[UK/0026-0584]
METAL FINISHING ABSTRACTS.
(*Continued by* Surface Treatment Technology Abstracts.)

METEOROL. GEOASTROPHYS. ABSTR.
[US/0026-1130]
METEOROLOGICAL AND GEOASTROPHYSICAL ABSTRACTS.
(*Continues* Meteorological Abstracts and Bibliography.)

METEOROL. GEOASTROPHYS. ABSTR. [CD-ROM]
[US/1066-2707]
METEOROLOGICAL & GEOASTROPHYSICAL ABSTRACTS.
***Refer to Meteorological and Geoastrophysical Abstracts for a complete source list.

METHODIST PERIOD. INDEX
[US]
METHODIST PERIODICAL INDEX.
(*Continued by* United Methodist Periodical Index.)

METHODS ORGAN. SYNTH.
[UK/0265-4245]
METHODS IN ORGANIC SYNTHESIS.

MICROBIOL. ABSTR. SECT. A
[US/0300-838X]
MICROBIOLOGY ABSTRACTS. SECTION A : INDUSTRIAL & APPLIED MICROBIOLOGY.
(*Continues* Microbiology Abstracts. Section A. Industrial Microbiology.)

MICROBIOL. ABSTR. SECT. B
[US/0300-8398]
MICROBIOLOGY ABSTRACTS. SECTION B, BACTERIOLOGY.
(*Continues* Microbiology Abstracts. Section B: General Microbiology and Bacteriology.)

MICROBIOL. ABSTR. SECT. C
[US/0301-2328]
MICROBIOLOGY ABSTRACTS. SECTION C, ALGOLOGY, MYCOLOGY & PROTOZOOLOGY.

MICROCOMPUT. IND. UPDATE
[US/0741-6016]
MICROCOMPUTER INDUSTRY UPDATE.

MICROCOMPUT. INDEX
[US/8756-7040]
MICROCOMPUTER INDEX.
(*Continued by* Microcomputer Abstracts.)

MID. SEARCH
[US/1071-2755]
MIDDLE SEARCH.
(*Continues* Junior Search.)

MIDDLE EAST ABSTR. INDEX
[US/0162-766X]
MIDDLE EAST, ABSTRACTS AND INDEX.

MIDDLE EAST J.
[US/0026-3141]
MIDDLE EAST JOURNAL, THE.

MINERAL. ABSTR.
[UK/0026-4601]
MINERALOGICAL ABSTRACTS.

MINPROC
[CN/0828-8461]
MINPROC : MINERAL PROCESSING ABSTRACTS.
(Ceased)

MINTEC, MIN. TECHNOL. ABSTR.
[CN/0823-0773]
MINTEC : MINING TECHNOLOGY ABSTRACTS.
(Ceased)

INDEXES/ABSTRACTS TABLE

MISSIONALIA
[SA/0256-9507]
MISSIONALIA.
(*Formed by the union of* Lux Mundi (Pretoria, South Africa) *and* Missionaria.)

MLA INT. BIBL. BOOKS ARTIC. MOD. LANG. LIT.
[US/0024-8215]
MLA INTERNATIONAL BIBLIOGRAPHY OF BOOKS AND ARTICLES ON THE MODERN LANGUAGES AND LITERATURES (COMPLETE ED.).
(*Continues* MLA International Bibliography of Books and Articles on the Modern Languages and Literatures.)

MOD. MED.
[US/0026-8070]
MODERN MEDICINE (MINNEAPOLIS).

MON. PERIOD. INDEX
[US/0197-6567]
MONTHLY PERIODICAL INDEX.
(*Absorbed by* Access.)

MOSHER PERIOD. INDEX
[US/0194-0716]
MOSHER PERIODICAL INDEX.
(*Continues* Subject Index to Select Periodical Literature.)

MRS BULL.
[US/0883-7694]
MRS BULLETIN.
(*Absorbed* JMR Abstracts.)

MULTI MEDIA REV. INDEX
[US/0091-5858]
MULTI MEDIA REVIEWS INDEX.
(*Continued by* Media Review Digest.)

MULTICULT. EDUC. ABSTR.
[UK/0260-9770]
MULTICULTURAL EDUCATION ABSTRACTS.

MUSCULAR DYSTROPHY ABSTR.
[US/0027-3732]
MUSCULAR DYSTROPHY ABSTRACTS.
(**Ceased**)

MUSEUM ABSTR.
[UK/0267-8594]
MUSEUM ABSTRACTS.

MUSIC ARTIC. GUIDE
[US/0027-4240]
MUSIC ARTICLE GUIDE.

MUSIC INDEX
[US/0027-4348]
MUSIC INDEX, THE.

N. Y. LAW J. DIG.-ANNOT.
[US/0745-4406]
NEW YORK LAW JOURNAL DIGEST-ANNOTATOR.
(*Continues* Clark's Digest-Annotator.)

NAPRALERT
[US]
NAPRALERT [ONLINE DATABASE].

NAT. PROD. UPDATES
[UK/0950-1711]
NATURAL PRODUCT UPDATES.

NATL. NEWSP. INDEX
[US/0273-3676]
NATIONAL NEWSPAPER INDEX.

NEMATOL. ABSTR.
[UK/0957-6797]
NEMATOLOGICAL ABSTRACTS.
(*Continues* Helminthological Abstracts. Series B, Plant Nematology.)

NEW LIT. AUTOMAT.
[NE]
NEW LITERATURE ON AUTOMATION.
(*Continues* IAG-Literature on Automation.)

NEW PERIOD. INDEX
[US/0146-5716]
NEW PERIODICALS INDEX.
(**Ceased**)

NEW TESTAM. ABSTR.
[US/0028-6877]
NEW TESTAMENT ABSTRACTS.

NEWSP. ABSTR.
[US/1064-993X]
NEWSPAPER ABSTRACTS ONDISC.

NEWSP. ABSTR.
[US]
NEWSPAPER ABSTRACTS.

NEWSP. PERIOD. ABSTR.
[US]
NEWSPAPER & PERIODICAL ABSTRACTS [ONLINE DATABASE].

NEXIS
[US]
NEXIS.

NONWOVENS ABSTR.
[UK/9036-1234]
NONWOVENS ABSTRACTS.

NUCL. ACIDS ABSTR.
[US/1070-2466]
NUCLEIC ACIDS ABSTRACTS (1994).
(*Continues* Cambridge Scientific Biochemistry Abstracts, Part 2: Nucleic Acids.)

NUCL. SCI. ABSTR.
[US/0029-5612]
NUCLEAR SCIENCE ABSTRACTS.
(*Continues* Abstracts of Declassified Documents; Guide to Published Research on Atomic Energy.)

NUMIS. LIT.
[US/0029-6031]
NUMISMATIC LITERATURE.

NURS. ABSTR.
[US/0195-3354]
NURSING ABSTRACTS.

NURS. ALLIED HEALTH INDEX
[US/0744-8732]
NURSING AND ALLIED HEALTH INDEX.
(*Absorbed by* Cumulative Index to Nursing & Allied Health Literature.)

NURS. DIG.
[US/0091-4215]
NURSING DIGEST.
(*Continued by* Nursing Dimensions.)

NURS. DIMEN.
[US/0164-0232]
NURSING DIMENSIONS.
(*Continues* Nursing Digest.)

NUTR. ABSTR. REV.
[UK/0029-6619]
NUTRITION ABSTRACTS AND REVIEWS.
(*Split into* Nutrition Abstracts and Reviews. Series A. Human and Experimental *and* Nutrition Abstracts and Reviews. Series B, Livestock Feeds and Feeding.)

NUTR. ABSTR. REV., SER. A, HUM. EXP.
[UK/0309-1295]
NUTRITION ABSTRACTS AND REVIEWS. SERIES A: HUMAN & EXPERIMENTAL.
(*Continues in part* Nutrition Abstracts and Reviews.)

NUTR. ABSTR. REV., SER. B, LIVE FEEDS AND FEED.
[UK/0309-135X]
NUTRITION ABSTRACTS AND REVIEWS. SERIES B. LIVESTOCK FEEDS AND FEEDING.
(*Continues in part* Nutrition Abstracts and Reviews.)

NUTR. RES. NEWSL.
[US/0736-0037]
NUTRITION RESEARCH NEWSLETTER.

OCCUP. MENT. HEALTH
[US/0090-1679]
OCCUPATIONAL MENTAL HEALTH.
(*Supersedes* Occupational Mental Health News.)

OCCUP. MENT. HEALTH NOTES
[US/0029-795X]
OCCUPATIONAL MENTAL HEALTH NOTES.
(*Superseded by* Occupational Mental Health.)

OCEAN. ABSTR.
[US/0748-1489]
OCEANIC ABSTRACTS (BETHESDA, MD.).
(*Continues* Oceanic Abstracts with Indexes.)

OCEAN. ABSTR. INDEXES
[US/0093-6901]
OCEANIC ABSTRACTS WITH INDEXES.
(*Continued by* Oceanic Abstracts (Bethesda, Md.).)

OCEANIC CIT. J. ABSTR.
[US]
OCEANIC CITATION JOURNAL WITH ABSTRACTS / OCEANIC RESEARCH INSTITUTE.
(*Merged with* Oceanic Index *to form* Oceanic Abstracts with Indexes.)

OCEANIC INDEX CIT. J. ABSTR.
[US]
OCEANIC INDEX CITATION JOURNAL WITH ABSTRACTS.
(*Continued by* Oceanic Citation Journal with Abstracts.)

OCEANOGR. LIT. REV.
[UK/0967-0653]
OCEANOGRAPHIC LITERATURE REVIEW.
(*Continues* Deep-Sea Research. Part B, Oceanographic Literature Review.)

OLD TESTAM. ABSTR.
[US/0364-8591]
OLD TESTAMENT ABSTRACTS.

ONCOG. GROWTH FACTORS ABSTR.
[US/1043-8963]
ONCOGENES AND GROWTH FACTORS ABSTRACTS.

OPER. PROD. MANAGE. ABSTR.
[UK]
OPERATIONS & PRODUCTION MANAGEMENT ABSTRACTS.
(*Continues* Management Services and Production Abstracts.)

OPER. RES. MANAG. SCI.
[US/0030-3658]
OPERATIONS RESEARCH/MANAGEMENT SCIENCE.

ORAL RES. ABSTR.
[US/0030-4212]
ORAL RESEARCH ABSTRACTS.
(**Ceased**)

ORNAMENTAL HORT.
[UK/0305-4934]
ORNAMENTAL HORTICULTURE.

INDEXES/ABSTRACTS TABLE

ORTHO. SUR.
[NE/0014-4371]
ORTHOPEDIC SURGERY.
(*Continues* Orthopedics and Traumatology.)
***Refer to EMBASE [Online Database] for complete source list.

OZARK PERIOD. INDEX
[US/0275-9713]
OZARK PERIODICAL INDEX.

PAIS BULL.
[US/0898-2201]
PAIS BULLETIN.
(*Merged with* PAIS Foreign Language Index *to form* PAIS International in Print.)

PAIS FOREIGN LANG. INDEX
[US/0896-792X]
PAIS FOREIGN LANGUAGE INDEX.
(*Merged with* PAIS Bulletin *to form* PAIS International in Print.)

PAIS INT. PRINT
[US/1051-4015]
PAIS INTERNATIONAL IN PRINT.
(*Formed by the union of* PAIS Bulletin *and* PAIS Foreign Language Index.)

PAP. BOARD ABSTR.
[UK/0307-0778]
PAPER & BOARD ABSTRACTS.
(*Continues in part* Kenley Abstracts.)

PARAPSYCHOL. ABSTR. INT.
[US/0740-7629]
PARAPSYCHOLOGY ABSTRACTS INTERNATIONAL.
(*Continued by* Exceptional Human Experience.)

PASTOR. CARE COUNS. ABSTR.
[US]
PASTORAL CARE AND COUNSELING ABSTRACTS.
(*Continued by* Abstracts of Research in Pastoral Care and Counseling.)

PEACE RES. ABSTR. J.
[US/0031-3599]
PEACE RESEARCH ABSTRACTS JOURNAL.

PERIODEX
[CN]
PERIODEX: INDEX ANALYTIQUE DE PERIODIQUES DE LANGUE FRANCAISE.
(*Merged with* Radar *to form* Point de Repere.)

PERSON. MANAGE. ABSTR.
[US/0031-577X]
PERSONNEL MANAGEMENT ABSTRACTS.

PERSON. TRAIN. ABSTR.
[UK/0305-067X]
PERSONNEL + TRAINING ABSTRACTS.
(*Continues in part* Anbar Management Services Abstracts.)

PESTDOC
[UK]
PESTDOC.

PET. ABSTR.
[US/0031-6423]
PETROLEUM ABSTRACTS (TULSA, OKLA.).

PET. ENERGY BUS. NEWS INDEX
[US/0098-7743]
PETROLEUM/ENERGY BUSINESS NEWS INDEX.

PET. REFIN. PETROCHEM.
[US]
PETROLEUM REFINING AND PETROCHEMICALS.
(*Continued by* Literature Abstracts. Petroleum Refining & Petrochemicals.)

PET. SUBS.
[US]
PETROLEUM SUBSTITUTES.
(*Continued by* Literature Abstracts. Petroleum Substitutes.)

PHARM. NEWS INDEX
[US/0362-4439]
PHARMACEUTICAL NEWS INDEX.

PHILIP. ABSTR.
[PH/0031-7438]
PHILIPPINE ABSTRACTS.
(*Continued by* Philippine Science & Technology Abstracts.)

PHILIP. SCI. TECHNOL. ABSTR.
[PH/0115-8724]
PHILIPPINE SCIENCE & TECHNOLOGY ABSTRACTS.
(*Continues* Philippine Science and Technology Abstract Bibliography.)

PHILOS. INDEX
[US/0031-7993]
PHILOSOPHER'S INDEX.

PHOTOGR. ABSTR.
[UK/0031-8701]
PHOTOGRAPHIC ABSTRACTS.
(*Continued by* Imaging Abstracts.)

PHYS. ABSTR.
[UK/0036-8091]
PHYSICS ABSTRACTS.
(*Continues* Science Abstracts. Physics Abstracts.)
***Refer to INSPEC [Online Database] for a complete source list.

PHYS. BRIEFS
[UK/0170-7434]
PHYSICS BRIEFS.
(*Supersedes* Physikalische Berichte.)

PHYS. EDUC. INDEX
[US/0191-9202]
PHYSICAL EDUCATION INDEX (CAPE GIRARDEAU).

PHYS. MED. BIOL.
[UK/0031-9155]
PHYSICS IN MEDICINE & BIOLOGY.

PHYSIC. MEDLINE PLUS
[US/1065-6545]
PHYSICIAN'S MEDLINE PLUS.

PIG NEWS INF.
[UK/0143-9014]
PIG NEWS AND INFORMATION.

PINPOINTER
[AT/0031-9910]
PINPOINTER.
(Ceased)

PLANT BREED. ABSTR.
[UK/0032-0803]
PLANT BREEDING ABSTRACTS.

PLANT GROW. REG. ABSTR.
[UK/0305-9154]
PLANT GROWTH REGULATOR ABSTRACTS.

POINT REPERE
[CN/0822-8833]
POINT DE REPERE (MONTREAL).
(*Continued by* Repere.)

POLICE SCI. ABSTR.
[NE/0166-6282]
POLICE SCIENCE ABSTRACTS.
(*Merged with* Criminology & Penology Abstracts *to form* Criminology, Penology, and Police Science Abstracts.)

POLLUT. ABSTR. INDEXES
[US/0032-3624]
POLLUTION ABSTRACTS WITH INDEXES.

POLYMER CONTENTS
[UK/0883-153X]
POLYMER CONTENTS.
(*Continues* PRA Report: Polymer Contents.)

POP. MAG. REV.
[US/0740-3763]
POPULAR MAGAZINE REVIEW : PMR.
(*Continued by* Magazine Article Summaries.)

POP. PERIOD. INDEX
[US/0092-9727]
POPULAR PERIODICAL INDEX.
(Ceased)

POPUL. INDEX
[US/0032-4701]
POPULATION INDEX.
(*Continues* Population Literature.)

POTATO ABSTR.
[UK/0308-7344]
POTATO ABSTRACTS.

POULT. ABSTR.
[UK/0306-1582]
POULTRY ABSTRACTS.

POVER. HUM. RESOUR.
[US/0032-5864]
POVERTY & HUMAN RESOURCES.
(*Continued by* Poverty and Human Resources Abstracts.)

POVER. HUM. RESOUR. ABSTR.
[US/0094-4394]
POVERTY & HUMAN RESOURCES ABSTRACTS.
(*Continued by* Human Resources Abstracts.)

PREDICASTS
[US/0032-7166]
PREDICASTS.
(*Continued by* Predicasts Forecasts.)

PREDICASTS F & S INDEX INT.
[US/0270-4528]
PREDICASTS F & S INDEX INTERNATIONAL.
(*Continued by* F&S Index International (Foster City, Calif.).)
***Refer to Predicasts Forecasts for a complete source list.

PREDICASTS F&S INDEX, U. S. ANNU. ED.
[US/0277-9676]
PREDICASTS F&S INDEX. UNITED STATES ANNUAL EDITION.
(*Continued by* F&S Index United States Annual.)

PREDICASTS FORECASTS
[US/0278-0135]
PREDICASTS FORECASTS.
(*Continues* Predicasts.)

PREV. HUM. SERV.
[US/0270-3114]
PREVENTION IN HUMAN SERVICES.
(*Continues* Community Mental Health Review.)

PRIM. SEARCH
[US/1065-2485]
PRIMARY SEARCH.

PRINT. ABSTR.
[UK/0031-109X]
PRINTING ABSTRACTS.

INDEXES/ABSTRACTS TABLE

PROC. CHEM. ENG.
[UK/0960-5045]
PROCESS AND CHEMICAL ENGINEERING.
(*Continues* Chemical Engineering Abstracts.)

PROMT
[US/0161-8032]
PROMT / PREDICASTS OVERVIEW OF MARKETS AND TECHNOLOGY.
(*Formed by the union of* Chemical Market Abstracts *and* EMA, Equipment Market Abstracts.)

PROTOZOOLOG. ABSTR.
[UK/0309-1287]
PROTOZOOLOGICAL ABSTRACTS.

PSYCHEDELIC REV.
[US/0033-2631]
PSYCHEDELIC REVIEW.
(Ceased)

PSYCHOANAL. ABSTR.
[US/1066-9884]
PSYCHOANALYTIC ABSTRACTS.
(*Continues* Psycscan. Psychoanalysis.)

PSYCHOL. ABSTR.
[US/0033-2887]
PSYCHOLOGICAL ABSTRACTS.

PSYCHOL. READ. GUIDE
[SZ/0300-0443]
PSYCHOLOGICAL READER'S GUIDE.
(Ceased)

PSYCHOPHARMACOLOGY ABSTR.
[US/0033-3166]
PSYCHOPHARMACOLOGY ABSTRACTS.
(Ceased)

PSYCINFO
[US]
PSYCINFO.

PSYCLIT
[US]
PSYCLIT DATABASE.

PSYCSCAN PSYCHOANAL.
[US/0889-5236]
PSYCSCAN: PSYCHOANALYSIS.
(*Continued by* Psychoanalytic Abstracts.)

PSYCSCAN: APPL. EXP. ENG. PSYCH.
[US/0891-0685]
PSYCSCAN: APPLIED EXPERIMENTAL AND ENGINEERING PSYCHOLOGY.

PSYCSCAN: APPL. PSYCH.
[US/0271-7506]
PSYCSCAN. APPLIED PSYCHOLOGY.

PSYCSCAN: CLIN. PSYCH.
[US/0197-1484]
PSYCSCAN. CLINICAL PSYCHOLOGY.

PSYCSCAN: DEVELOP. PSYCH.
[US/0197-1492]
PSYCSCAN. DEVELOPMENTAL PSYCHOLOGY.

PSYCSCAN: LD/MR
[US/0730-1928]
PSYCSCAN. LD/MR.

PSYCSCAN: NEUROPSYCH.
[US/1058-6660]
PSYCSCAN. NEUROPSYCHOLOGY.

PTS NEWSL. DATABASE
[US]
PTS NEWSLETTER DATABASE [ONLINE DATABASE].

PUBLIC ADM. ABSTR. INDEX ARTIC. INDIA
[II/0033-331X]
PUBLIC ADMINISTRATION ABSTRACTS AND INDEX OF ARTICLES (INDIA).
(Ceased)

PUBLIC AFF. INF. SERV. BULL.
[US/0033-3409]
PUBLIC AFFAIRS INFORMATION SERVICE BULLETIN.
(*Continued by* PAIS Bulletin (Annual).)

Q. BIBLIOGR. COMPUT. DATA PROCESS.
[US/0048-6132]
QUARTERLY BIBLIOGRAPHY OF COMPUTERS AND DATA PROCESSING.
(*Continued by* Computer Literature Index.)

Q. INDEX ISLAM.
[UK/0308-7395]
QUARTERLY INDEX ISLAMICUS.
***Refer to Index Islamicus for complete source list.

QUAL. CONTROL APPL. STAT.
[US/0033-5207]
QUALITY CONTROL AND APPLIED STATISTICS.

RAPRA ABSTR.
[UK/0033-6750]
RAPRA ABSTRACTS.
(*Formed by the union of* Plastics. RAPRA Abstracts *and* Rubbers. RAPRA Abstracts.)

READ. ABSTR.
[US/0361-6118]
READING ABSTRACTS.
(*Continued by* Linguistics and Language Behavior Abstracts.)

READ. GUIDE ABSTR.
[US/0899-1553]
READERS' GUIDE ABSTRACTS (PRINT EDITION).
(*Continued by* Readers' Guide Abstracts (School and Public Library Ed. : Monthly).)

READ. GUIDE ABSTR.
[US/1058-1219]
READERS' GUIDE ABSTRACTS (SCHOOL AND PUBLIC LIBRARY ED.).
(*Continued by* Readers' Guide Abstracts Select Edition.)

READ. GUIDE ABSTR. SELECT ED.
[US]
READERS' GUIDE ABSTRACTS SELECT EDITION.
(*Continues* Readers' Guide Abstracts School and Public Library Edition.)

READ. GUIDE PERIOD. LIT.
[US/0034-0464]
READERS' GUIDE TO PERIODICAL LITERATURE.
(*Continues* Monthly Cumulative Index to ... Important Periodicals; *Absorbed* Cumulative Index to a Selected List of Periodicals (Annual).)

RECENT. PUBL. ARTIC.
[US/0145-5311]
RECENTLY PUBLISHED ARTICLES - AMERICAN HISTORICAL ASSOCIATION.
(Ceased)

RECIPE PERIOD. INDEX
[US/0743-3484]
RECIPE PERIODICAL INDEX.
(Ceased)

REF. BOOK REV. INDEX
[US]
REFERENCE BOOK REVIEW INDEX.
(Ceased)

REF. SOURCES
[US/0163-3546]
REFERENCE SOURCES.
(Ceased)

REF. UPD. BASIC ED.
[US]
REFERENCE UPDATE BASIC EDITION [COMPUTER FILE].

REF. UPD. CLINICAL ED.
[US]
REFERENCE UPDATE CLINICAL EDITION [COMPUTER FILE].

REF. UPD. DELUXE ED.
[US]
REFERENCE UPDATE DELUXE EDITION [COMPUTER FILE].

REFER. Z.
[RU]
REFERATIVNYI ZHURNAL: ORGANIZATSIIA I BEZOPASNOST DOROZHNOGO DVIZHENIIA.

REHABIL. LIT.
[US/0034-3579]
REHABILITATION LITERATURE.
(Ceased)

RELIG. INDEX ONE PERIOD.
[US/0149-8428]
RELIGION INDEX ONE. PERIODICALS.
(*Continued in part by* Index to Book Reviews in Religion.)

RELIG. PERIOD. INDEX
[US/0034-4117]
RELIGIOUS PERIODICALS INDEX.
(Ceased)

RELIG. THEOL. ABSTR.
[US/0034-4044]
RELIGIOUS AND THEOLOGICAL ABSTRACTS.

REPERT. ANAL. ARTIC. REV. QUE.
[CN/0315-2316]
RADAR: REPERTOIRE ANALYTIQUE D'ARTICLES DE REVUES DU QUEBEC.
(*Merged with* Periodex *to form* Point de Repere.)

RES. ALERT
[US]
RESEARCH ALERT.
(*Continues* Ascatopics.)

RES. HIGH. EDUC. ABSTR.
[UK/0034-5326]
RESEARCH INTO HIGHER EDUCATION ABSTRACTS.

RESOURCE/ONE ONDISC
[US]
RESOURCE/ONE ONDISC [COMPUTER FILE].

REV. AGRIC. ENTOMOL.
[UK/0957-6762]
REVIEW OF AGRICULTURAL ENTOMOLOGY.
(*Continues* Review of Applied Entomology. Series A, Agricultural.)

REV. APPL. ENTOMOL. SER. A, AGRIC.
[UK/0305-0076]
REVIEW OF APPLIED ENTOMOLOGY. SERIES A: AGRICULTURAL.
(*Continued by* Review of Agricultural Entomology.)

INDEXES/ABSTRACTS TABLE

REV. APPL. ENTOMOL. SER. B, MED. VET.
[UK/0305-0084]
REVIEW OF APPLIED ENTOMOLOGY. SERIES B, MEDICAL AND VETERINARY.
(*Continued by* Review of Medical and Veterinary Entomology.)

REV. MED. VET. ENTOMOL.
[UK/0957-6770]
REVIEW OF MEDICAL AND VETERINARY ENTOMOLOGY.
(*Continues* Review of Applied Entomology. Series B, Medical and Veterinary.)

REV. MED. VET. MYCOLOGY
[UK/0034-6624]
REVIEW OF MEDICAL AND VETERINARY MYCOLOGY.
(*Continues* Annotated Bibliography of Medical Mycology.)

REV. PLANT PATHOL.
[UK/0034-6438]
REVIEW OF PLANT PATHOLOGY.
(*Continues* Review of Applied Mycology.)

RIBA LIB. BULL.
[UK]
RIBA LIBRARY BULLETIN.
(*Superseded by* Architectural Periodicals Index.)

RILA, INT. REP. LIT. ART
[US/0145-5982]
RILA : INTERNATIONAL REPERTORY OF THE LITERATURE OF ART.
(*Merged with* Repertoire d'Art et d'Archeologie **to form** Bibliography of the History of Art.)

RILM ABSTR.
[US/0033-6955]
RILM ABSTRACTS.

RINGDOC
[UK]
RINGDOC.
***Refer to PESTDOC for complete source list.

RISK ABSTR.
[CN/0824-3336]
RISK ABSTRACTS.

ROBOMATIX REPORT.
[US/0748-1624]
ROBOMATIX REPORTER.
(*Continued by* Robotics Abstracts.)

ROBOTICS ABSTR.
[US/0000-1139]
ROBOTICS ABSTRACTS.
(*Continues* Robomatix Reporter.)

ROMANT. MOVE.
[US/0557-2738]
ROMANTIC MOVEMENT.

ROTHS AM. POETRY ANNUAL
[US/1040-5461]
ROTH'S AMERICAN POETRY ANNUAL.
(*Formed by the union of* Annual Survey of American Poetry; Annual Index to Poetry in Periodicals **and** American Poetry Index.)

RURAL EXT. EDUC. TRAIN. ABSTR.
[UK/0140-4776]
RURAL EXTENSION, EDUCATION AND TRAINING ABSTRACTS.
(Ceased)

RURAL RECREAT. TOUR. ABSTR.
[UK/0308-0137]
RURAL RECREATION AND TOURISM ABSTRACTS.
(*Continued by* Leisure, Recreation and Tourism Abstracts.)

SAF. HEALTH WORK
[SZ/1010-7053]
SAFETY AND HEALTH AT WORK : ILO-CIS BULLETIN.
(*Continues* International Occupational Safety and Health Information Centre. CIS Abstracts.)

SAF. SCI. ABSTR.
[US/0092-542X]
SAFETY SCIENCE ABSTRACTS.
(*Continued by* Safety Science Abstracts Journal.)

SAF. SCI. ABSTR. J.
[US/0160-1342]
SAFETY SCIENCE ABSTRACTS JOURNAL.
(*Continued by* Health and Safety Science Abstracts.)

SAGE FAM. STUD. ABSTR.
[US/0164-0283]
SAGE FAMILY STUDIES ABSTRACTS.

SAGE PUBLIC ADM. ABSTR.
[US/0094-6958]
SAGE PUBLIC ADMINISTRATION ABSTRACTS.

SAGE RACE RELAT. ABSTR.
[UK/0307-9201]
SAGE RACE RELATIONS ABSTRACTS.
(*Continues* Race Relations Abstracts.)

SAGE URBAN STUD. ABSTR
[US/0090-5747]
SAGE URBAN STUDIES ABSTRACTS.

SCHOOL ORGAN. MANAGE. ABSTR.
[UK/0261-2755]
SCHOOL ORGANISATION & MANAGEMENT ABSTRACTS.

SCI. ABSTR. PHYS. ABSTR.
[UK]
SCIENCE ABSTRACTS. PHYSICS ABSTRACTS.
(*Continued by* Science Abstracts. Series A, Physics Abstracts.)

SCI. ABSTR. SECT. A. PHYS. ABSTR.
[UK]
SCIENCE ABSTRACTS. SECTION A, PHYSICS ABSTRACTS / EDITED AND ISSUED MONTHLY BY THE INSTITUTION OF ELECTRICAL ENGINEERS, IN ASSOCIATION WITH THE PHYSICAL SOCIETY, THE AMERICAN PHYSICAL SOCIETY, THE AMERICAN INSTITUTE OF ELECTRICAL ENGINEERS.
(*Continued by* Science Abstracts. Physics Abstracts.)

SCI. ABSTR. SER. A, PHYS. ABSTR.
[UK]
SCIENCE ABSTRACTS. SERIES A, PHYSICS ABSTRACTS.
(*Continued by* Physics Abstracts.)

SCI. CIT. INDEX
[US/0036-827X]
SCIENCE CITATION INDEX (PRINT ED.).

SCI. CIT. INDEX ABSTR.
[US/1061-1290]
SCIENCE CITATION INDEX WITH ABSTRACTS.
***Refer to Science Citation Index (US/0036-827X) for a complete source list.

SCI. CIT. INDEX [CD-ROM]
[US/1044-6052]
SCIENCE CITATION INDEX (COMPACT DISC ED.).
***Refer to Science Citation Index (US/0036-827X) for a complete source list.

SCI. CIT. INDEX, ABR. ED.
[US/0737-2108]
SCIENCE CITATION INDEX. ABRIDGED EDITION.
(Ceased)

SCI. FICT. FANTASY BOOK REV. INDEX
[US/1046-1922]
SCIENCE FICTION AND FANTASY BOOK REVIEW INDEX.
(*Continues* Science Fiction Book Review Index.)

SCI. RES. ABSTR. J.
[US/0731-0943]
SCIENCE RESEARCH ABSTRACTS JOURNAL.
(*Absorbed by* Solid State Abstracts Journal.)

SCI. RES. ABSTR. J. PART A.
[US/0194-7486]
SCIENCE RESEARCH ABSTRACTS JOURNAL. PART A: SUPERCONDUCTIVITY, MAGNETOHYDRODYNAMICS AND PLASMAS, THEORETICAL PHYSICS.
(*Merged with* Science Research Abstracts Journal. Part B: Laser and Electro-Opticreviews, Quantum Electronics and Unconventional Energy Sources **to form** Science Research Abstracts Journal.)

SCISEARCH
[US]
SCISEARCH [ONLINE DATABASE].

SEA ABSTR.
[PH]
SEA ABSTRACTS.

SEED ABSTR.
[UK/0141-0180]
SEED ABSTRACTS.

SEL. PHILIP. PERIOD. INDEX
[PH/0037-1335]
SELECTED PHILIPPINE PERIODICAL INDEX.
(Ceased)

SEL. WATER RESOUR. ABSTR.
[US/0037-136X]
SELECTED WATER RESOURCES ABSTRACTS (WASHINGTON, D.C.).
(Ceased)

SELEC. COOP. INDEX MANAGE. PERIOD.
[FI/0782-2979]
SCIMP SELECTIVE CO-OPERATIVE INDEX OF MANAGEMENT PERIODICALS.
(Ceased)

SEVENTH-DAY ADVENTIST PERIOD. INDEX
[US/0270-3599]
SEVENTH-DAY ADVENTIST PERIODICAL INDEX.

SHIP ABSTR.
[NO/0346-1025]
SHIP ABSTRACTS.
(*Absorbed by* Journal of Abstracts of the British Ship Research Association.)

SHOCK VIBR. DIG.
[US/0583-1024]
SHOCK AND VIBRATION DIGEST, THE.

SMALL ANIM. ABSTR. BIBLIOGR.
[UK]
SMALL ANIMAL ABSTRACTS BIBLIOGRAPHY.
(*Continues* Small Animal Abstracts.)

SOC. PLANN. POLICY DEV. ABSTR.
[US/1042-8380]
SOCIAL PLANNING, POLICY & DEVELOPMENT ABSTRACTS.
(*Continues* Social Welfare, Social Planning/Policy & Social Development.)

INDEXES/ABSTRACTS TABLE

SOC. RES. METHODOL. ABSTR.
[NE/0167-8477]
SOCIAL RESEARCH METHODOLOGY ABSTRACTS.
(*Continues in part* SRM Abstract Bulletin.)

SOC. SCI. CIT. INDEX
[US/0091-3707]
SOCIAL SCIENCES CITATION INDEX (PRINT ED.).

SOC. SCI. HUMANIT. INDEX
[US/0037-7899]
SOCIAL SCIENCES & HUMANITIES INDEX.
(*Split into* Social Sciences Index *and* Humanities Index.)

SOC. SCI. INDEX
[US/0094-4920]
SOCIAL SCIENCES INDEX.
(*Supersedes in part* Social Sciences & Humanities Index.)

SOC. SCI. INDEX FULLTEXT
[US]
SOCIAL SCIENCES INDEX / FULLTEXT.

SOC. SCI. SOURCE
[US/1063-9802]
SOCIAL SCIENCE SOURCE.

SOC. WELF. SOC. PLAN./POLICY SOC. DEV.
[US/0195-7988]
SOCIAL WELFARE, SOCIAL PLANNING/POLICY & SOCIAL DEVELOPMENT.
(*Continued by* Social Planning, Policy & Development Abstracts.)

SOC. WORK ABSTR.
[US/1070-5317]
SOCIAL WORK ABSTRACTS.
(*Continues in part* Social Work Research and Abstracts.)

SOC. WORK RES.
[US/1070-5309]
SOCIAL WORK RESEARCH.
(*Continues in part* Social Work Research and Abstracts.)
***Refer to Social Work Abstracts for a complete source list.

SOC. WORK RES. ABSTR.
[US/0148-0847]
SOCIAL WORK RESEARCH & ABSTRACTS.
(*Split into* Social Work Abstracts *and* Social Work Research.)

SOCIOL. ABSTR.
[US/0038-0202]
SOCIOLOGICAL ABSTRACTS.

SOCIOL. EDUC. ABSTR.
[UK/0038-0415]
SOCIOLOGY OF EDUCATION ABSTRACTS.

SOFT. ABSTR. ENG.
[IE/0790-150X]
SOFTWARE ABSTRACTS FOR ENGINEERS : SAFE.

SOILS FERT.
[UK/0038-0792]
SOILS AND FERTILIZERS.
(*Supersedes* Imperial Bureau of Soil Science. Monthly Letter.)

SOLID STATE ABSTR. J.
[US/0038-108X]
SOLID STATE ABSTRACTS JOURNAL.
(*Continued by* Solid State and Superconductivity Abstracts.)

SOLID STATE SUPERCOND. ABSTR.
[US/0896-5900]
SOLID STATE AND SUPERCONDUCTIVITY ABSTRACTS.
(*Continues* Solid State Abstracts Journal.)

SORGHUM MILL. ABSTR.
[UK/03082970]
SORGHUM AND MILLETS ABSTRACTS.
(Ceased)

SOUTH. BAPTIST PERIOD. INDEX
[US/0081-3028]
SOUTHERN BAPTIST PERIODICAL INDEX.

SOYABEAN ABSTR.
[UK/0141-0172]
SOYABEAN ABSTRACTS.

SPEC. EDUC. NEEDS ABSTR.
[UK/0954-0822]
SPECIAL EDUCATIONAL NEEDS ABSTRACTS.

SPIN
[US]
SPIN.

SPORT DISCUS
[US]
SPORT DISCUS [COMPUTER FILE].

SPORT FISH. ABSTR.
[US/0038-786X]
SPORT FISHERY ABSTRACTS.
(*Continued by* Fisheries Review.)

SPORTSEARCH
[US/0882-553X]
SPORTSEARCH.

STAT. REF. INDEX
[US/0885-6834]
STATISTICAL REFERENCE INDEX.

STAT. THEORY METHOD ABSTR.
[UK/0039-0518]
STATISTICAL THEORY AND METHOD ABSTRACTS.
(*Continues* International Journal of Abstracts: Statistical Theory and Method.)

STUD. WOMEN ABSTR.
[UK/0262-5644]
STUDIES ON WOMEN ABSTRACTS.

SUBJ. INDEX CHILD. MAG.
[US/0039-4351]
SUBJECT INDEX TO CHILDREN'S MAGAZINES.
(*Continued by* Children's Magazine Guide.)

SUBJ. INDEX PERIOD.
[UK]
SUBJECT INDEX TO PERIODICALS.
(*Split into* British Humanities Index *and* British Technology Index.)

SUBJ. INDEX SEL. PERIOD. LIT.
[US/0194-0708]
SUBJECT INDEX TO SELECT PERIODICAL LITERATURE.
(*Continued by* Mosher Periodical Index.)

SUG. INDUS. ABSTR.
[UK/0957-5022]
SUGAR INDUSTRY ABSTRACTS / [CAB INTERNATIONAL, BUREAU OF HORTICULTURE AND PLANTATION CROPS IN ASSOCIATION WITH TATE & LYLE PLC].
(*Continues* Tate & Lyle's Sugar Industry Abstracts.)

SURF. TREAT. TECHNOL. ABSTR.
[UK]
SURFACE TREATMENT TECHNOLOGY ABSTRACTS.
(*Continues* Metal Finishing Abstracts.)

TECH. DATA DIG.
[US]
TECHNICAL DATA DIGEST.
(Ceased)

TECH. EDUC. ABSTR.
[UK/0040-0920]
TECHNICAL EDUCATION ABSTRACTS.
(*Continued by* Technical Education & Training Abstracts.)

TECH. EDUC. TRAIN. ABSTR.
[UK]
TECHNICAL EDUCATION & TRAINING ABSTRACTS.
(*Continues* Technical Education Abstracts.)

TELEGEN ABSTR.
[US/0000-118X]
TELEGEN ABSTRACTS.
(*Continues* Telegen Reporter.)

TELEGEN REPORT.
[US/0743-8443]
TELEGEN REPORTER.
(*Continued by* Telegen Abstracts.)

TERMITE ABSTR.
[UK/0144-5995]
TERMITE ABSTRACTS.
(Ceased)

TEXT. TECHNOL. DIG.
[US/0040-5191]
TEXTILE TECHNOLOGY DIGEST.

THEOL. RELIG. INDEX
[UK]
THEOLOGICAL AND RELIGIOUS INDEX.
(Ceased)

THEOR. CHEM. ENG.
[UK/0960-5053]
THEORETICAL CHEMICAL ENGINEERING.
(*Continues* Theoretical Chemical Engineering Abstracts.)

THEOR. CHEM. ENG. ABSTR.
[UK/0040-5787]
THEORETICAL CHEMICAL ENGINEERING ABSTRACTS.
(*Continued by* Theoretical Chemical Engineering.)

TOM GEN. INDEX
[US]
TOM GENERAL INDEX.

TOP MANAGE. ABSTR.
[UK/0049-4100]
TOP MANAGEMENT ABSTRACTS.
(*Continued by* Anbar Top Management Abstracts.)

TOPICATOR
[US/0040-9340]
TOPICATOR.

TOXICOL. ABSTR.
[US/0140-5365]
TOXICOLOGY ABSTRACTS.

TRADE IND. ASAP
[US]
TRADE & INDUSTRY ASAP [ONLINE DATABASE].

TRADE IND. INDEX
[US]
TRADE & INDUSTRY INDEX [ONLINE DATABASE].

INDEXES/ABSTRACTS TABLE

TRANS. AM. SOC. CIV. ENG.
[US/0066-0604]
TRANSACTIONS OF THE AMERICAN SOCIETY OF CIVIL ENGINEERS.

TRANSP. RES. ABSTR.
[US/0095-2648]
TRANSPORTATION RESEARCH ABSTRACTS.
(*Absorbed in part by* HRIS Abstracts.)

TRANSP. STORAGE
[US]
TRANSPORTATION AND STORAGE.
(*Continued by* Literature Abstracts. Transportation & Storage.)

TROP. ABSTR.
[NE/0041-3208]
TROPICAL ABSTRACTS.
(*Superseded by* Abstracts on Tropical Agriculture.)

TROP. DIS. BULL.
[UK/0041-3240]
TROPICAL DISEASES BULLETIN.
(*Supersedes* Bulletin of the Sleeping Sickness Bureau and the Kala Azar Bulletin.)

U.S. POLIT. SCI. DOC.
[US/0148-6063]
UNITED STATES POLITICAL SCIENCE DOCUMENTS.
(*Absorbed* Asian Studies Indexed Journal Reference Guide.)

UMI ABI/INFORM--BUS. PERIOD. ONDISC
[US/1064-5381]
UMI ABI/INFORM--BUSINESS PERIODICALS ONDISC.

UNITED METHODIST PERIOD. INDEX
[US/0041-7319]
UNITED METHODIST PERIODICAL INDEX.
(*Continues* Methodist Periodical Index.)

URBAN AFF. ABSTR.
[US/0300-6859]
URBAN AFFAIRS ABSTRACTS.

VET. BULL.
[UK/0042-4854]
VETERINARY BULLETIN (LONDON).
(*Supersedes* Tropical Veterinary Bulletin; *Absorbed* Veterinary Reviews.)

VETDOC
[UK]
VETDOC.
***Refer to PESTDOC for complete source list.

VIROL. ABSTR.
[US/0042-6830]
VIROLOGY ABSTRACTS.
(*Continued by* Virology and AIDS Abstracts.)

VIROL. AIDS ABSTR.
[US/0896-5919]
VIROLOGY & AIDS ABSTRACTS.
(*Continues* Virology Abstracts.)

VIS. INDEX
[US/0049-6510]
VISION INDEX.
(Ceased)

VITIS VITIC. ENOL. ABSTR.
[GW/0175-8292]
VITIS, VITICULTURE AND ENOLOGY ABSTRACTS.
(*Separated from* Vitis.)

VOCAT. SEARCH
[US/1071-2747]
VOCATIONAL SEARCH.

WALL STREET J. INDEX
[US/0083-7075]
WALL STREET JOURNAL INDEX.
(Ceased)

WATER POLLUT. ABSTR.
[UK/0043-1281]
WATER POLLUTION ABSTRACTS.
(*Merged with* Water Research Association Library List *to form* WRC Information.)

WEED ABSTR.
[UK/0043-1729]
WEED ABSTRACTS.

WEST. HIST. Q.
[US/0043-3810]
WESTERN HISTORICAL QUARTERLY.

WHEAT BARLEY TRIT. ABSTR.
[UK/0265-7880]
WHEAT, BARLEY AND TRITICALE ABSTRACTS.
(*Continues* Triticale Abstracts.)

WILDL. REV.
[US/0043-5511]
WILDLIFE REVIEW (FORT COLLINS).

WILSON BUS. ABSTR.
[US/1057-6533]
WILSON BUSINESS ABSTRACTS.

WOMEN MANAG. REV. ABSTR.
[UK/0955-8357]
WOMEN IN MANAGEMENT REVIEW & ABSTRACTS.
(*Continued by* Women in Management Review.)

WOMEN MANAGE. REV.
[UK/0964-9425]
WOMEN IN MANAGEMENT REVIEW.
(*Continues* Women in Management Review & Abstracts.)

WOMEN STUD. ABSTR.
[US/0049-7835]
WOMEN STUDIES ABSTRACTS.

WORK RELAT. ABSTR.
[US/0273-3234]
WORK RELATED ABSTRACTS.
(*Continues* Employment Relations Abstracts.)

WORLD AGRIC. ECON. RURAL SOCIOL. ABSTR.
[UK/0043-8219]
WORLD AGRICULTURAL ECONOMICS AND RURAL SOCIOLOGY ABSTRACTS.

WORLD ALUM. ABSTR.
[US/0002-6697]
WORLD ALUMINUM ABSTRACTS.
(*Continued by* Aluminium Industry Abstracts.)

WORLD CERAM. ABSTR.
[UK/0957-8897]
WORLD CERAMICS ABSTRACTS.
(*Continues* British Ceramic Abstracts.)

WORLD FISH. ABSTR.
[IT/0043-8472]
WORLD FISHERIES ABSTRACTS.
(Ceased)

WORLD PUBL. MONIT.
[UK/0960-653X]
WORLD PUBLISHING MONITOR.
(*Continues* Electronic Publishing Abstracts.)

WORLD SURF. COAT. ABSTR.
[UK/0043-9088]
WORLD SURFACE COATINGS ABSTRACTS.
(*Continues* Review of Current Literature Relating to the Paint, Colour, Varnish and Allied Industries.)

WORLD TEXT. ABSTR.
[UK/0043-9118]
WORLD TEXTILE ABSTRACTS.
(*Supersedes* Textile Abstracts.)

WRC INF.
[UK/0306-6649]
WRC INFORMATION.
(*Continued by* Aqualine Abstracts.)

WRIT. AM. HIST.
[US/0364-2887]
WRITINGS ON AMERICAN HISTORY.
(Ceased)

ZENTRALBL. MATH. IHRE GRENZGEB.
[GW/0044-4235]
ZENTRALBLATT FUER MATHEMATIK UND IHRE GRENZGEBIETE.
(*Superseded in part by* Zentralblatt fuer Mechanik.)

ZOOL. REC.
[UK/0144-3607]
ZOOLOGICAL RECORD (LONDON).
(*Continues* Record of Zoological Literature.)

US Newspapers

The following section lists all newspapers in the directory that originated in the United States. These are arranged by state then alphabetically by title within each state. Full and half-page ad rates will be given for color and/or black and white ads depending on what is accepted by the publisher. Publication size, affiliate wire services, and a notation for photographs will also be listed when provided.

ALABAMA

US
ABBEVILLE HERALD. (1918)-. Newspaper. English. wk. Abbevile Herald, PO Box 609, Abbeville AL 36310-0609. **Tel** (205)585-2331. **ED** J. Edward Dodd III. **Ad Acc. Circ:** 2,100. ***Continues*** *Southeast Alabamian.*

US
ADVERTISER-GLEAM, THE. VFOAT Advertiser Gleam. Vol. 70, No. 19 (Oct. 1948)-. Newspaper. English. sw (Wed. & Sat.). $17.00 Marshall County; $32.00 others. Advertiser-Gleam, 2218 Taylor Street, PO Box 190, Guntersville AL 35976. **Tel** (205)582-3232. **ED** Sam Harvey (editor's address: PO Box 190, Guntersville, AL 35976). **Ad Acc, Adv Mgr:** Don Woodward. **Circ:** 12,249. available on microfilm. ***Formed by the union of*** *Guntersville Advertiser and Democrat* ***and*** *Guntersville Gleam.*

US/0738-7741
ALABAMA BAPTIST, THE. Added/Corp Alabama Baptist State Convention. (1874)-. Newspaper. English. wk (No publication on July 4 and Christmas). $9.45 (Jefferson County, Alabama); $9.36 (other counties in Alabama); $9.00 other. The Alabama Baptist, 3310 Independence Drive, Birmingham AL 35209. **Tel** (205)870-4720. **ED** Hudson Baggett. **Bk Rev. Photos. Ad Acc, Adv Mgr:** Bobbie Maxwell, **Tel** (205)870-4720. Full Page (B&W) $1,320.00. Half Page (B&W) $660.00. **Pub. Size:** Tabloid. **Circ:** 123,000. ***Continues*** *Southern and Alabama Baptist.*
Desc: Publishes Baptist news for churches 2nd individuals.

US/0745-323X
ALABAMA JOURNAL, THE. ***Ceased.*** (ALABAMA JOURNAL.). **VFOAT** Montgomery Alabama Journal; Montgomery Alabama Journal and the Times. Vol. 52, No. 344 (Sept. 9, 1940)-V. 57, No. 313 (Aug. 14, 1945)-(Apr. 1993). Newspaper. English. da. Alabama Journal, PO Box 1000, Montgomery AL 36192. **Tel** (205)262-1611. **ED** Bill Brown. **Bk Rev. Ad Acc. Circ:** 20,686 (ctrl). available on microfilm from University Microfilms International (UMI). ***Continues*** *Alabama Journal and the Times.*

US/0273-9593
ALABAMA MESSENGER, THE. Added/Corp Assemblies of God. Alabama District Council. (19??)-. Periodical. English. wk. $10.00. Alabama Messenger, 706 Frank Nelson Building, Birmingham AL 35203. **Tel** (205)252-3672. **ED** Karen W. Abercrombie. **Ad Acc. Circ:** 1,500.
Desc: Contains general news.

US/0738-5110
ALEXANDER CITY OUTLOOK, THE. VFOAT Alexander City Outlook and the Goodwater Enterprise Chronicle; Alexander City Outlook and the Alexander City Chronicle; Alexander City Outlook (Semi-weekly). Jan. (1892)-. Newspaper. English. da (Published Tue. - Fri. & Sun.). $72.00 Alexander City, Tallapoosa & Coosa counties; $86.00 others. Tallapoosa Publishers Inc., PO Box 999, Alexander City AL 35010-0999. **Tel** (205)234-4281. **ED** K. A. Turner. **Photos. Ad Acc, Adv Mgr:** Billy McGhee. **Pub. Size:** Broadsheet. **Wire Svcs.:** AP. **Circ:** 6,200 (morning), 6,200 (Sunday). ***Absorbed*** *Enterprise-Chronicle (Goodwater, Ala.)* ***and*** *Alexander City Chronicle and the Alexander City Outlook.*

US/0746-2115
ANDALUSIA STAR-NEWS, THE. VFOAT Andalusia Star News. Vol. 37, No. 1 (Nov. 1948)-. Newspaper. English. da. Andalusia Star-News, 209 Dunson Street, Andalusia AL 36420-3705. **Tel** (205)222-2402, FAX (205)222-6597. **ED** Stephen Weeks. **Ad Acc. Pub. Size:** Standard. **Circ:** 6,500 (morning). ***Formed by the union of*** *Andalusia Star (Andalusia, Ala. : 1926)* ***and*** *Covington News (Andalusia, Ala. : 1924).*

US
ANNISTON STAR, THE. Vol. 37, No. 189 (Mar. 15, 1919)-. Newspaper. English. da. $8.00 (per month). Anniston Star, PO Box 189, Anniston AL 36202-0189. **Tel** (205)236-1551, FAX (205)231-0027. **ED** H. Brandt Ayers, Joe Distelheim (Executive Editor). **Bk Rev. Photos. Ad Acc, Adv Mgr:** Hershel Victory. Full Page (B&W) $2382.63. Half Page (B&W) $1191.32. Full Page (Color) $2630.43. Half Page (Color) $1439.12. **Wire Svcs.:** AP, NY. **Circ:** 32,000. available on microfilm from University Microfilms International (UMI); available on an online database (file 635/Full-Text) from DIALOG. Documents available from UMI Article Clearinghouse. ***Continues*** *Anniston Star and the Daily Hot Blast.*
Ind/Abst Bus. Dateline (Dec. 15, 1991-) [Full Txt.].

US
ARAB TRIBUNE, THE. (1958)-. Newspaper. English. Fifty-two times a year (Wed.). $13.00 Arab and Marshall County; $17.00 others in Alabama; $21.00 other. Arab Tribune, South Brindlee Mountain Parkway, PO Box 605, Arab AL 35016. **Tel** (205)586-3188, FAX (205)586-3190. **ED** David Moore. **Ad Acc. Circ:** 6,800.

US/0739-1307
ATHENS LC NEWS COURIER. VFOAT Athens L.C. News Courier; Athens News Courier. Vol. 86, No. 1 (Oct. 7, 1968)-. Newspaper. English. da (except Sat. and Mon.). $48.40 Limestone County; $74.37 other. Athens News Courier, 410 West Green Street, Athens AL 35611. **Tel** (205)232-2720. **ED** Robert C Bryan. **Circ:** 7,915. ***Formed by the union of*** *Alabama Courier (Athens, Ala.)* ***and*** *Athens LC News Leader.*
Desc: Limestone County's only daily newspaper. Published 5 days each week, Tuesday through Friday and Sunday, it brings the most indepth coverage of local news, sports and more as well as money saving advertisements from local merchants.

US/0746-1968
ATMORE ADVANCE, THE. Vol. 1, No. 1, (Oct. 6, 1927)-. Newspaper. English. wk (Sun. and Wed.). Atmore Advance, PO Drawer 28, Atmore AL 36504-0028. **Tel** (205)368-2123, FAX (205)368-2124. **ED** Michelle Gerlach. **Circ:** 3,900.

US/1071-1279
AUBURN PLAINSMAN, THE. (19??)-. Newspaper. English. Thirty-five times a year (Not published between quarters or on holidays of the university). $20.00. Auburn Plainsman, Attn: Circulation Joy Bufford, Basement Union Building, Auburn AL 36849. **Tel** (205)844-4130, FAX (205)844-9114. **ED** Jan Clifford, (editor's address: B-100 Union Building, Auburn University, AL 36849-5343 phone: (205)844-9021). **Ad Acc. Circ:** 19.500 (ctrl). available on microfiche from Ralph Draughon Library. ***Continues*** *Plainsman (Auburn, Ala.).*

US/0744-5318
AZALEA CITY NEWS & REVIEW. VFOAT Azalea City News and Review. Vol. 6, No. 15 (April 27, 1979)-. Newspaper. English. wk. $14.00. TJP Publishing Company, PO Box 1467, Mobile AL 36633-1467. **ED** Pat McArthur. **Bk Rev. Ad Acc. Circ:** 7,500.
Desc: An alternative to the local daily paper; provides in-depth news coverage, with features, sports, a food page, extensive arts coverage and comics.

US
BALDWIN TIMES, THE. (April 1895)-. Newspaper. English. sw. Baldwin Times, PO Box 519, Bay Minette AL 36507. **Tel** (205)937-2511. **ED** Steve Mitchell. **Circ:** 4,800. ***Continues*** *Daphne Times.*

US/0899-0050
BIRMINGHAM NEWS, THE. VFOAT Birmingham News. Birmingham Age-Herald. Vol. 7, No. 144 (Sept. 2, 1894)-. Newspaper. English. da. $59.98 (Mon.-Fri.), $123.60 (evening & Sun.), $123.60 (morning, evening, & Sun.), $63.62 (Sat. & Sun.) (carrier), $156.00 (evening, Mon-Fri.), $248.40 (evening & Sun.), $386.00 (morning, evening & Sun.), $83.20 (Sun.) (mail); $120.00 (combined with Birmingham Post-Herald, Sunday edition) (carrier) Montgomery. The Birmingham News / Post Herald, City Prepaid Department, 2200 4th Avenue North, Birmingham AL 35202. **Tel** (205)325-2299. **ED** Jim Jacobson. **Pub. Size:** Broadsheet. **Wire Svcs.:** AP. **Circ:** 168,398 daily, 213,630 Sunday. available on microfilm from University Microfilms International (UMI). ***Continues*** *Daily News (Birmingham, Ala.);* ***Absorbed*** *Birmingham Ledger.*
Ind/Abst PROMT.

US/1040-1571
BIRMINGHAM POST-HERALD. VFOAT Birmingham Post Herald; Saturday. (May 13, 1950)-. Newspaper. English. da. $165.20 (morning, Mon.-Fri.), $248.40 (combined with Sunday edition) mail; $59.98 (morning, Mon.-Fri.), $123.60 (combined with Sunday edition) carrier; $120.00 (combined with Birmingham News Sunday edition) (carrier), Montgomery. The Birmingham News / Post Herald, City Prepaid Department, 2200 4th Avenue North, Birmingham AL 35202. **Tel** (205)325-2299. **ED** James Denley. **Bk Rev. Ad Acc. Circ:** 61,418. available on microfilm. ***Formed by the union of*** *Birmingham Post* ***and*** *Birmingham Age-Herald.*

US/0006-3754
BIRMINGHAM WORLD; A STANDARD RACE JOURNAL. (1928)-. Newspaper. English. Fifty-two times a year. $26.00. Birmingham World, 407 15th Street North, Birmingham AL 35203. **Tel** (205)251-6523. **ED** Marcel Hopson Sr. **Bk Rev. Ad Acc. Circ:** 37,000 (ctrl).
Desc: Non partisan independent philosophy, non-sectarian general news reporting features, and independent political persuasion.

US/1056-3288
BLOUNT COUNTIAN, THE. (BLOUNT COUNTIAN.). Vol. 1, No. 1 (Jan. 3, 1990)-. Newspaper. English. wk. $12.00 (in county), $20.00 (out of county). Southern Democrat, 3rd Stree Washington Avenue, Oneonta AL 35121. **Tel** (205)625-3231. **ED** Molly Howard Ryan. **Photos. Ad Acc, Adv Mgr:** Ricky Hicks. Full Page (B&W) $677.25. Half Page (B&W) $330.75. Full Page (Color) $777.25. Half Page (Color) $430.75. **Pub. Size:** Broadsheet. **Circ:** 7,000 paid, 13,000 total. ***Continues*** *Southern Democrat.*

US
BREWTON STANDARD, THE. Vol. 19, No. 30 (Jan. 1906)-. Newspaper. English. sw. $30.00 (residents) within 35 miles radius of Brewton; $34.00 others in Alabama; $34.00 others states. Brewton Standard, PO Box 887, Brewton AL 36427-0887. **Tel** (205)867-4876, FAX (205)867-4877. **ED** Harris A. Pippen III. **Ad Acc. Circ:** 5,000. ***Continues*** *Standard Gauge.* ***Absorbed in part by*** *Pine Belt News.*

US/0741-3319
BUTLER COUNTY NEWS (GEORGIANA, ALA.). (THE BUTLER COUNTY NEWS.). (1911)-. Newspaper. English. wk. $9.50. Butler County News, PO Box 488, Georgianna AL 36033. **Tel** (205)376-2325. **ED** R. Pride Jr. **Circ:** 2,200.

US
CALL-NEWS DISPATCH, THE. ***Title Change.*** **VFOAT** Call News Dispatch. Vol. 1, No. 1 (Jan. 10, 1963)-(19??). Newspaper. English. wk. Washington County News / Alabama, 305 Jordan Street, PO Box 510, Chatom AL 36518. **Tel** (205)847-2599. **ED** Frank Harwell. **Ad Acc. Circ:** 3,300 (ctrl). ***Formed by the union of*** *Washington County News (St. Stephens, Ala.)* ***and*** *Citronelle Call.* ***Continued by*** *Washington County News.*

US/1045-7496
CATHOLIC WEEK, THE. ***Title Change.*** **Added/Corp** Catholic Church. Diocese of Mobile-Birmingham (Ala.). Catholic Church. Diocese of Mobile (Ala.). Vol. 1, No. 1 (Dec. 16, 1934)-. Newspaper. English. wk. PO Box 349, 400 Government Street, Mobile AL 36601. **Tel** (205)432-3529. **ED** Anna B Crow. ***Continued by*** *One Voice.*

US
CENTRAL ALABAMA INDEPENDENT ADVERTISER AND THE UNION-BANNER, THE. Vol. 5, No. 35 (Aug. 1975)-. Newspaper. English. sw. $18.00. PO Box 1379, Clanton AL 35045. **Tel** (205)755-5747, FAX (205)755-5857. **ED** Michael R Kelley. **Ad Acc. Circ:** 13,000. ***Formed by the union of*** *Central Alabama Independent Advertiser* ***and*** *Union-Banner.*

US
CENTREVILLE PRESS, THE. (189?)-. Newspaper. English. wk. $26.05 Centreville, Alabama; $36.00 other. Bibb Publications, PO Box 127, Centerville AL 35042. **Tel** (205)926-9769. **ED** Bob Tribble (Publisher). **Ad Acc. Circ:** 4,395. ***Continues*** *County Press.*
Desc: Covers news concerning Bibb County, it's municipalities and the southern-metro region of Birmingham.

US
CHEROKEE COUNTY HERALD, THE. Vol. 1, No. 1 (Mar. 23, 1938)-. Newspaper. English. wk. $12.00, $10.00 (local). Cherokee County Herald, 107 West 1st Avenue, Centre AL 35960-1998. **Tel** (205)927-5037. **ED** Paul W. Dale. **Bk Rev. Ad Acc. Circ:** 4,500.

US/0888-451X
CHILTON COUNTY NEWS (CLANTON, ALA. : 1986). (CHILTON COUNTY NEWS.). (1986)-. Newspaper. English. wk. $25.00 Chilton County; $32.50 other. Chilton County News, Box 189, Clanton AL 35045-0189. **Tel** (205)755-0110. **ED** Bob Tucker. **Ad Acc. Circ:** 2,000 (ctrl). ***Continues*** *Chilton County News and Peacheroo, 0884-5476.*

US
CHOCTAW ADVOCATE, THE. VFOAT Choctaw Alliance. Vol. 9, No. 35 (Aug. 1901)-. Newspaper. English. wk. $25.00. Choctaw Advocate, 210 North Mulberry Street, PO Box 475, Butler AL 36904. **Tel** (205)459-2858, (205)459-2836, FAX (205)459-3000. **ED** Tommy J. Campbell. **Bk Rev. Photos. Ad Acc, Adv Mgr:** Lee Mosley. Full Page (B&W) $429.00. Half Page (B&W) $215.00. Full Page (Color) $489.00. Half Page (Color) $275.00. **Pub. Size:** Standard. **Wire Svcs.:** AP. **Circ:** 4,400. available in microform. ***Continues*** *Choctaw Alliance.*

US/1050-2084
CLANTON ADVERTISER, THE. VFOAT Advertiser. (Jan. 1990)-. Newspaper. English. tw. Clanton Newspapers, 1109 Seventh Street North, PO Box 1379, Clanton AL 35045. ***Continues*** *Independent Advertiser (Clanton, Ala.).*

US
CLARKE COUNTY DEMOCRAT, THE. VFOAT Democrat. Vol. 11, No. 31 (Nov. 22, 1866)-. Newspaper. English. wk. $13.91 County; $16.05 out of County; $18.00 out of state. Clarke County Democrat, James A. Cox, 261 North Jackson, Grove Hill AL 36451. **Tel** (205)275-3375, FAX (205)275-3060. **ED** James A. Cox. **Circ:** 4,800 (paid). ***Continues*** *Clarke County Journal.*

US/1053-9123
CLAY TIMES-JOURNAL, THE. (CLAY TIMES-JOURNAL.). **VFOAT** Clay Times Journal. Vol. 1, No. 1 (Sept. 6, 1990)-. Newspaper. English. wk (published on Thursdays). $20.00. Clay Times-Journal, PO Box 97, Lineville AL 36266. **Tel** (205)396-5760. **ED** David Proctor and Linda McDonald (Managing Editor). Index available. cum. index. **Bk Rev**. **Photos**. **Ad Acc**, **Adv Mgr:** David Proctor & Linda McDonald. Full Page (B&W) $400.00. Half Page (B&W) $200.00. Full Page (Color) $485.00. Half Page (Color) $250.00. **Pub. Size:** Standard. **Circ:** 3,400. ***Formed by the union of*** *Ashland Progress* ***and*** *Lineville Tribune.*
Desc: Newspaper on local events, sports, and features.

US
CLAYTON RECORD, THE. (1897)-. Newspaper. English. wk. $12.00 (Alabama residents); $15.00 (other). Clayton Record, PO Box 69, Clayton AL 36016. **Tel** (205)775-3254. **ED** Bertie G. Parish. **Circ:** 2,500. ***Continues*** *Clayton Courier.*

US
CLEBURNE NEWS (HEFLIN, ALA.). (THE CLEBURNE NEWS.). (1911)-. Newspaper. English. wk. $15.00 Cleburn County; $18.00 other. Cleburne News, 515 Ross Street, PO Box 6, Heflin AL 36264. **Tel** (205)463-2872. **ED** Henry A. Jackson. **Bk Rev**. **Ad Acc**. ***Continues*** *Cleburne County News.*

US/0739-9219
COMMUNITY PRESS (MILLBROOK, ALA.). (THE COMMUNITY PRESS.). Vol. 1, No. 1 (Oct. 13, 1977)-. Newspaper. English. Fifty-two times a year (Thurs.). $12.00. Community Press, PO Box 568, Millbrook AL 36054. **Tel** (205)285-6000. **ED** Mary S. Goodwyn. **Ad Acc**. **Circ:** 1,850 (ctrl).

US
CULLMAN TIMES, THE. 60th Year, No. 430 (Jan. 1963)-. Newspaper. English. da (except Sat. and Mon.). $58.40 Cullman county; 84.37 other. Cullman Times, 400 4th Avenue SE, Cullman AL 35055. **Tel** (205)734-2131. **ED** Dale Greer. **Circ:** 9,639 daily, 11,727 Sunday. ***Continues*** *Daily Times Democrat.*

US/0739-523X
CULLMAN TRIBUNE, THE. Vol. 20, No. 38 (Dec. 1895)-. Newspaper. English. wk. $15.00 Cullman & surrounding counties, $25.00 other. Cullman Tribune, 219 Second Avenue Southeast, Cullman AL 35055. **Tel** (205)739-1351. **ED** Delton Blalock. Index available. **Photos**. **Ad Acc**, **Adv Mgr:** Barbara Blalock. Full Page (B&W) $645.00. Half Page (B&W) $325.00. Full Page (Color) $725.00. Half Page (Color) $405.00. **Pub. Size:** Broadsheet. **Circ:** 13,400 (ctrl). ***Continues*** *Alabama Tribune (Cullman, Ala.).*

US/0739-9677
DADEVILLE RECORD, THE. .51st year, No. 31 (Sept. 8, 1949)-. Newspaper. English. wk. $10.00 Tallapoosa County; $13.00 other. Dadeville Record, PO Box 999, Dadeville AL 36853. **Tel** (205)234-4281. **ED** Michael Anderson. **Circ:** 1,988. ***Separated from*** *Tallapoosa Record;* ***Absorbed*** *Camp Hill News (Camp Hill, Ala.); Lake Martin News.*

US/1059-6461
DAILY HOME. **VFOAT** Daily Home Sylacauga News. Jan. 24 (1966)-. Newspaper. English. da. $90.00. Daily Home, PO Box 977, Talladega AL 35160. **Tel** (205)362-1000. **ED** Edgar L. Fowler, Carol Pappas (Managing Editor). **Bk Rev**. **Photos**. **Ad Acc**, **Adv Mgr:** Sandy Carden. Full Page (B&W) $1151.97. Half Page (B&W) $589.38. Full Page (Color) $1251.72. Half Page (Color) $689.13. **Pub. Size:** Broadsheet. **Wire Svcs.:** AP. **Circ:** 10,000 paid daily, 41,000 Wednesday TMC. ***Continues*** *Talladega Daily Home and Our Mountain Home;* ***Absorbed*** *Sylacauga News; Sylacauga daily advance.*

US/0893-0759
DAILY MOUNTAIN EAGLE. Vol. 1, No. 1 (May 2, 1960)-. Newspaper. English. ir (Sunday through Friday). $71.10 all except state of Alabama; $45.90 Walker County, Alabama; $66.60 all except Walker County in state of Alabama. Daily Mountain Eagle, 1301 East 19th Street, PO Box 1469, Jasper AL 35501. **Tel** (205)221-2840, FAX (205)221-2421. **ED** Douglas Pearson. **Bk Rev**. **Ad Acc**. **Circ:** 12,553 (ctrl). ***Continues*** *Mountain Eagle (Jasper, Ala.);* ***Absorbed*** *Walker County Times (Jasper, Ala.).*

US
DAILY SENTINEL (SCOTTSBORO, ALA.). (THE DAILY SENTINEL.). Vol. 1, No. 1 (July 1970)-. Newspaper. English. da (except Mon. and Sat.). Scottsboro Daily Sentinel, PO Box 220, Scottsboro AL 35768. **Tel** (205)259-1020. **ED** James K Harkness. ***Continues*** *Sentinel-Age.*

US
DECATUR DAILY (1927). (THE DECATUR DAILY.). **VFOAT** Decatur (Ala.) Daily. Vol. 14, No. 284 (Feb. 1927)-. Newspaper. English. da. $108.00 (carrier), $132.00 (mail) Alabama; $143.00 other. Decatur Daily, PO Box 2213, Decatur AL 35609-2213. **Tel** (205)353-4612. **ED** Barrett C. Shelton Jr. **Circ:** 26,100. ***Continues*** *Albany-Decatur Daily.*

US
DEMOCRAT-REPORTER, THE. **VFOAT** Democrat Reporter. Vol. 1, No. 1 (Feb. 1911)-. Newspaper. English. wk. $17.50. Democrat-Reporter, PO Box G, Linden AL 36748. **Tel** (205)295-5224. **ED** Goodloe Sutton, Jean Sutton (Managing Editor). **Bk Rev**. **Photos**. **Ad Acc**, **Adv Mgr:** Linda Williams. Full Page (B&W) $516.00. Half Page (B&W) $258.00. Full Page (Color) $616.00. Half Page (Color) $358.00. **Pub. Size:** Standard. **Circ:** 4,125. ***Formed by the union of*** *Linden Reporter (Linden, Ala.)* ***and*** *Marengo Democrat (Linden, Ala.).*
Desc: Covers general news.

US
DEMOPOLIS TIMES, THE. (1904)-. Newspaper. English. wk. $40.00 Alabama; $48.00 other. Boone Newspapers, PO Box 860, Demopolis AL 36732. **Tel** (205)289-4017. **ED** Danny Smith. **Ad Acc**. **Circ:** 2,800.

US/0745-855X
DOTHAN EAGLE, THE. (190?)-. Newspaper. English. da (published Sunday through Saturday). $123.60 by mail; $117.60 by carrier for Fort Rucker, AL. Dothan Eagle, PO Box 1968, Dothan AL 36301. **Tel** (205)792-3141. **ED** Doug Bradford. **Circ:** 22,624 daily, 26,221 Sunday.

US
EAGLE. ***Title Change.*** **VFOAT** Sunday Eagle; Wednesday Eagle; Lee County Eagle. Newspaper. English. sw. Auburn Bulletin Inc., 122 Tichenor Ave., Auburn AL 36830. **Tel** (205)821-7150. ***Continues*** *Auburn Bulletin & the Lee County Eagle, 0746-5521.* ***Continued by*** *Lee County Eagle, 1050-3846.*

US
EAST LAUDERDALE NEWS. (197?)-. Newspaper. English. wk. East Lauderdale News, PO Box 179, Rogersville AL 35652-0179. **Tel** (205)247-5565, FAX (205)247-1902. **ED** James Cox. **Ad Acc**. **Circ:** 4,500.

US
EASTERN SHORE COURIER. Vol. 79, No. 50 (May 1974)-. Newspaper. English. sw. Eastern Shore Courier, PO Box 549, Fairhope AL 36533. **Tel** (205)928-2321. **ED** Vickie Fildes Plunkett. **Circ:** 4,100. ***Continues*** *Fairhope Courier.*

US
ELBA CLIPPER, THE. (June 1897)-. Newspaper. English. wk. $14.50. Elba Clipper, PO Drawer A, Elba AL 36323. **Tel** (205)897-2823. **ED** Marvin McIlwain. **Photos**. **Ad Acc**, **Adv Mgr:** Ferrin Cox, **Tel** (205)897-2823. Full Page (B&W) $416.67. Half Page (B&W) $208.34. Full Page (Color) $496.67. Half Page (Color) $288.34. **Pub. Size:** Standard. **Circ:** 3,200. available in microform.

US
ENTERPRISE LEDGER (ENTERPRISE, ALA. : 1977). (THE ENTERPRISE LEDGER.). Vol. 78, No. 147 (June 22, 1977)-. Newspaper. English. da. $9.80 per month. Enterprise Ledger, PO Box 1140, 106 North Edwards Street, Enterprise AL 36331. **Tel** (205)347-9533. **ED** Sarah Stephens. **Bk Rev**, (Qty: 1-5). **Photos**. **Ad Acc**, **Adv Mgr:** Kelly Speigner. Full Page (B&W) $869.46. Half Page (B&W) $434.73. Full Page (Color) $996.46. Half Page (Color) $561.73. **Pub. Size:** Standard. **Circ:** 9,500 daily, 10,300 Wednesday, 10,800 Sunday. ***Continues*** *Daily Ledger (Enterprise, Ala.).*

US
EUFAULA TRIBUNE, THE. (1929)-. Newspaper. English. sw (published Wednesday and Sunday). $24.95 Barbour county; $27.95 other. Eufaula Tribune, 514 East Barbour Street, Eufaula AL 36072. **Tel** (205)687-3506. **ED** Joel P. Smith. **Ad Acc**, **Adv Mgr:** Jack Jackson. **Circ:** 6,200 (ctrl).

US
EVERGREEN COURANT, THE. Vol. 1, No. 41 (July 1896)-. Newspaper. English. wk. $20.00. Evergreen Courant, PO Box 440, Evergreen AL 36401. **Tel** (205)578-1492, FAX (205)578-1496. **ED** Robert Bozeman. **Photos**. **Ad Acc**. Full Page (B&W) $2.50 per column inch. Half Page (B&W) $2.50 per column inch. **Circ:** 3,800. ***Continues*** *Courant (Evergreen, Ala.);* ***Absorbed*** *Conecuh Record.*

US
FLORALA NEWS, THE. (1919)-. Newspaper. English. wk. $16.05. Florala News, 421 South Fifth Street, Florala AL 36442. **Tel** (205)858-3342. **ED** Larry Woodham. **Ad Acc**. **Circ:** 3,000. ***Continues*** *Florala News-Democrat.*

US
FRANKLIN COUNTY TIMES. Vol. 77, No. 42 (Oct. 18, 1956)-. Newspaper. English. sw (104/year). $30.00 local counties; $39.00 other. Franklin County Newspapers Inc., PO Box 1088, Russellville AL 35653. **Tel** (205)332-1881. **ED** Ken Lightsey. **Circ:** 5,400. ***Continues*** *Franklin Citizen-Times.*

US
GADSDEN TIMES (GADSDEN, ALA. : 1925). (THE GADSDEN TIMES.). **VFOAT** Gadsden Times and News Journal. Vol. 58, No. 231 (Jan. 1, 1925)-. Newspaper. English. ds. $24.00 (3 months), $48.00 (6 months), $96.00 (one year) daily only; $27.00 (3 months), $54.00 (6 months), $108.00 (one year) daily and Sunday; $18.00 (3 months), $36.00 (6 months), $72.00 (one year) Sunday only. Gadsden Times, PO Box 188, Gadsden AL 35999. **Tel** (205)547-7521. **ED** A. Shaw. **Ad Acc**. **Circ:** 30,341. ***Continues*** *Gadsden Daily Times-News;* ***Absorbed*** *Gadsden Evening Star.*
Desc: General interest newspaper for the city of Gadsden and surrounding areas. Contains current events, local news, sports, lifestyle section, editorials, etc.

US
GENEVA COUNTY REAPER. (191?)-. Newspaper. English. wk. $16.00. Geneva Publications Inc., PO Box 160, Geneva AL 36340. **Tel** (205)684-2280, FAX (205)684-3099. **ED** James Specht, Sherrie Farabee (Managing Editor). **Photos**. **Ad Acc**, **Adv Mgr:** Mable Ruttlen. Full Page (B&W) $838.50. Half Page (B&W) $419.25. Full Page (Color) $913.50. Half Page (Color) $494.25. **Pub. Size:** Broadsheet. **Circ:** 3,300 (ctrl). ***Continues*** *Geneva Reaper.*

US/0889-518X
GREENE COUNTY DEMOCRAT (EUTAW, ALA.), THE. (GREENE COUNTY DEMOCRAT.). (1???)-. Newspaper. English. wk. $15.00 Greene County; $18.00 other in Alabama; $20.00 other. Greene County Democrat, Box 598, Eutaw AL 35462. **Tel** (205)372-3373, FAX (205)372-2243. **ED** Carol Zippert. **Bk Rev**, (Qty: 12). **Photos**. **Ad Acc**, **Adv Mgr:** Laddi Jones & Ed Jordan. Full Page (B&W) $877.50. Half Page (B&W) $438.75. Full Page (Color) $917.50. Half Page (Color) $478.75. **Pub. Size:** Broadsheet. **Circ:** 3,500 (ctrl). available in microform. ***Continues*** *Eutaw Mirror.*
Desc: Records information in Greene County, Alabama. It emphasis on the African american news.

US
GREENE COUNTY INDEPENDENT. (198?)-. Newspaper. English. wk. $16.00 Greene County; $18.00 other. Greene County Independent, 106 Main Street, Eutaw AL 35462. **Tel** (205)372-2232. **ED** Leewanna Parker. **Bk Rev**. **Photos**. **Ad Acc**, **Adv Mgr:** Betty Banks. Full Page (B&W) $387.00. Half Page (B&W) $241.75. **Pub. Size:** Standard. **Circ:** 1,200.

US
GREENSBORO WATCHMAN. (Sept. 1886)-. Newspaper. English. wk. $16.50 Hale County; $18.50 others in Alabama; $20.50 others. Greensboro Watchman, PO Drawer 550, Greensboro AL 36744. **Tel** (205)624-8323. **ED** Edward E. Lowry Jr (Editor-in-Chief) and Wille L. Arrington (Managing Editor). **Bk Rev**. **Photos**. **Ad Acc**, **Adv Mgr:** Ed Lowry. Full Page (B&W) $623.70. Half Page (B&W) $311.85. Full Page (Color) $$788.70. **Pub. Size:** Standard. **Circ:** 3,000. ***Continues*** *Southern Watchman (Greensboro, Ala.).*
Desc: Covers general local news interests for Greensboro, Alabama and Hale County..

US
GREENVILLE ADVOCATE. **VFOAT** Weekly Advocate. Vol. 9, No. 5 (Dec. 1873)-. Newspaper. English. wk. $15.00 (local), $20.00 other. Greenville Advocate - Alabama, PO Box 507, 103 Hickory Street, Greenville AL 36037. **Tel** (205)382-3111. **ED** Bill Hardin. **Photos**. **Ad Acc**. Full Page (B&W) $451.50. Half Page (B&W) $231.00. **Pub. Size:** Broadsheet. **Circ:** 4,850. available on microfilm and microfiche. ***Continues*** *Greenville Weekly Advocate.*

US
HAMILTON PROGRESS, THE. Began in 1893?. Newspaper. English. wk. Hamilton Progress, PO Box 950, Hamilton AL 35570. **Tel** (205)921-7898. **ED** Les Walters. **Circ:** 5,000.

US
HANCEVILLE HERALD, THE. (197?)-. Newspaper. English. wk. $19.63 (one year), $31.40 (two year). Hanceville Herald, PO Box 880, Hanceville AL 35077. **Tel** (205)352-4775. **ED** Ginger Grantham. **Ad Acc**. **Circ:** 4,000.

US
HARTFORD NEWS-HERALD, THE. **VFOAT** Hartford News Herald. Vol. 80, No. 20 (Feb. 14, 1980)-. Newspaper. English. wk. $18.19 Alabama; $36.04 other. Hartford News Herald, Box 69, Hartford AL 36344. **Tel** (205)588-2996. ***Continues*** *News-Herald (Hartford, Ala.).*

US
HARTSELLE ENQUIRER, THE. **VFOAT** Enquirer. Vol. 1, No. 1 (May 25, 1933)-. Newspaper. English. wk. $26.00 Morgan County & all within 20 miles of Hartselle; $32.00 Alabama; $34.00 US. Hartselle Enquirer, PO Box 929, Hartselle AL 35640. **Tel** (205)773-6566.

US
HEADLAND OBSERVER, THE. (196?)-. Newspaper. English. wk. $16.00. Headland Observer, Highway 431 North, Rout 2 Box 707, Headland AL 36345. **Tel** (205)693-3326, FAX (205)693-5224. **ED** Terry Grimes, Rick Thomason (Managing Editor). **Photos**. **Ad Acc**, **Adv Mgr:** Betty Rowland. Full Page (B&W) $464.00.

Half Page (B&W) $226.80. Full Page (Color) $524.00. Half Page (Color) $286.80. **Pub. Size:** Broadsheet. **Circ:** 1,926 (ctrl).

US
HUNTSVILLE NEWS. (196?)-. Newspaper. English. da (Mon.-Sat.). $90.00 Alabama; $111.00 other. Huntsville Times, PO Box 1487, West Station, Huntsville AL 35807. **Tel** (205)532-4000. **ED** Lee Woodward. **Circ:** 13,034. available on microfilm from University Microfilms International (UMI).

US
HUNTSVILLE TIMES, THE. Vol. 21, No. 220 (Dec. 5, 1931)-. Newspaper. English. da. $144.00 per year (mail); $9.85 per month (carrier). Huntsville Times, PO Box 1487, West Station, Huntsville AL 35807. **Tel** (205)532-4000. **ED** Patrick McCauley. **Bk Rev. Photos. Ad Acc, Adv Mgr:** J. Michael Venable, **Tel** (205)532-4450. Full Page (B&W) $4,541.04; $4,726.26 (Sunday). Half Page (B&W) $2,270.52; $2,363.13 (Sunday). Full Page (Color) $5,016.04; $5,201.26 (Sunday). Half Page (Color) $2,745.52; $2,838.13 (Sunday). **Pub. Size:** Broadsheet. **Wire Svcs.:** AP. **Circ:** 58,919 daily, 84,910 Sunday, 16,778 Morning, 75,698 Combination Daily (ctrl). available on microfilm from University Microfilms International (UMI). ***Continues*** *Huntsville Daily Times.*

US
INDEPENDENT (ROBERTSDALE, ALA.). (THE INDEPENDENT.). (197?)-. Newspaper. English. wk. $21.95 Alabama; $23.95 US. The Independent / Roberstdale, PO Box 509, Robertsdale AL 36567. **Tel** (205)947-7318. **ED** Jeffrey R. Dute, John Underwood (Associate Editor). **Photos. Ad Acc, Adv Mgr:** Jeniece Hooper, **Tel** (205)947-7712. **Pub. Size:** Broadsheet. **Circ:** 6,100 (ctrl).

US/1041-2662
ISLANDER (GULF SHORES, ALA.), THE. (THE ISLANDER.). (197?)-. Newspaper. English. wk. Islander, PO Box 1128, Canal Vielage Road, Gulf Shores AL 36542. **Tel** (205)968-6414. **ED** Francis Coleman.

US
JACKSONVILLE NEWS (JACKSONVILLE, ALA.). (THE JACKSONVILLE NEWS.). (Nov. 1936)-. Newspaper. English. wk. $14.00 Calhoun County; $20.00 US. Jacksonville News / Alabama, 203 Pelham Road South, Jacksonville AL 36265. **Tel** (205)435-5021. **ED** Phillip A. Sanguinetti and Julia Brock (Managing Editor). **Bk Rev,** (Qty: 12). **Photos. Ad Acc, Adv Mgr:** Roy Roberts. Full Page (B&W) $662.29. Half Page (B&W) $331.14. Full Page (Color) $757.29. Half Page (Color) $426.14. **Pub. Size:** Broadsheet. **Circ:** 3,000. available in microform.

US
JOURNAL RECORD (HAMILTON, AL.). (THE JOURNAL-RECORD.). **VFOAT** Journal Record. Vol. 6, No. 14 (June 5, 1975)-. Newspaper. English. wk. Moore Publishing, PO Box 430, Haleyville AL 35565. **Tel** (205)486-9461, FAX (205)486-4849. **Ad Acc. Circ:** 8,500. ***Formed by the union of*** *Marion County Journal* ***and*** *Winfield Record.*

US
LAMAR DEMOCRAT AND THE SULLIGENT NEWS. (VERNON, AL.), THE. (THE LAMAR DEMOCRAT AND THE SULLIGENT NEWS.). Vol. 56, No. 23 (Apr. 3, 1952)-. Newspaper. English. wk. $12.00 in county; $15.00 other in Alabama; $20.00 others. Vernon Lamar Democrat, PO Box 587, Vernon AL 35592. **Tel** (205)695-7029, FAX (205)699-9501. **ED** Howard L. Reeves. **Ad Acc, Adv Mgr:** Tammy Bardon. Full Page (B&W) $300.00. Half Page (B&W) $150.00. Full Page (Color) $375.00. Half Page (Color) $225.00. **Pub. Size:** Standard. **Circ:** 3,300. ***Formed by the union of*** *Lamar Democrat (Vernon, Ala.)* ***and*** *Sulligent News.*

US/1050-3846
LEE COUNTY EAGLE, THE. VFOAT Lee County/Eagle; Eagle. (19??)-. Newspaper. English. wk. $25.00 Lee county, 27.50 other. Auburn Bulletin Inc., 122 Tichenor Ave., Auburn AL 36830. **Tel** (205)821-7150. ***Continues*** *Eagle (Auburn, Ala.).*

US
LEEDS NEWS, THE. Vol. 1, No. 1 (May 25, 1939)-. Newspaper. English. wk (Thursdays). $16.00 (local), $21.00 (other). Leeds News, 720 Parkway Drive Southeast, Leeds AL 35094. **Tel** (205)699-2214, FAX (205)699-3157. **ED** Rebecca Gunter (Editor-in-Chief) and David Poynor (Managing Editor). **Photos. Ad Acc, Adv Mgr:** Stephen A. Adams. Full Page (B&W) $586.95. Half Page (B&W) $300.30. Full Page (Color) $651.95. Half Page (Color) $365.30. **Pub. Size:** Broadsheet. **Circ:** 3,398. available in microform from Leeds Public Library.

US
LOWNDES SIGNAL, THE. Vol. 1, No. 1 (April 16, 1925)-. Newspaper. English. wk (52 issues - published on Thursdays). $12.96 Lowndes County; $16.20 Alabama; $18.36 US. Lowndes Signal, PO Drawer 384, Fort Deposit AL 36032. **Tel** (205)227-4411, FAX (205)227-3441. **ED** Frieda B. Cross. **Photos. Ad Acc, Adv Mgr:** Trey Cross. Full Page (B&W) $296.10. Half Page (B&W) $148.05. Full Page (Color) $381.10. Half Page (Color) $233.05. **Pub. Size:** Standard. **Circ:** 1,800 paid.

US
LUVERNE JOURNAL (AND NEWS), THE. (1954)-. Newspaper. English. wk. $17.00. Luverne Journal, 406 Forest Avenue, Luverne AL 36049. **Tel** (205)335-3541. **ED** Alvin Bland. **Photos. Ad Acc, Adv Mgr:** James Morgan. **Pub. Size:** Standard. **Circ:** 3,400. ***Continues*** *Luverne Journal (Luverne, Ala. : 1949).*

US/0889-4205
MADISON COUNTY RECORD. (196?)-. Newspaper. English. Fifty-two times a year (Thurs.). $25.00 Madison County; $31.50 others. Madison County Record, PO Box 175, Madison AL 35758. **Tel** (205)772-8666. **ED** Richard A. Haston. **Bk Rev. Ad Acc. Circ:** 11,000.

US
MARION TIMES-STANDARD, THE. VFOAT Marion Times Standard; Times Standard; Times-Standard. Vol. 1, No. 1 (Feb. 8, 1917)-. Newspaper. English. wk. $34.30 Alabama; $40.00 other. Marion Times Standard, 220 Jackson Street, Marion AL 36756. **Tel** (205)683-6318. ***Formed by the union of*** *Marion Standard* ***and*** *Marion Times (Marion, Ala.);* ***Absorbed*** *Messenger (Marion, Ala.).*

US/1044-0070
MESSENGER (TROY, ALA.), THE. (THE MESSENGER.). Vol. 121, No. 166 (July 1, 1987)-. Newspaper. English. da. $96.00. The Troy Messenger, PO Box 727, Troy AL 36081. **Tel** (205)566-4270. ***Continues*** *Troy Messenger, 0746-3278.*

US
MOBILE BEACON & ALABAMA CITIZEN, THE. VFOAT Mobile Beacon and Alabama Citizen. (1966)-. Newspaper. English. wk. $20.00. Beacon & Alabama Citizen, PO Box 1407, Mobile AL 36633. **Tel** (205)479-0629. **ED** Cleretta Blackmon. **Bk Rev. Photos. Ad Acc, Adv Mgr:** Cleretta Blackmon. Full Page (B&W) $1,064.70. Half Page (B&W) $532.50. Full Page (Color) $1,189.70. Half Page (Color) $594.85. **Pub. Size:** Broadsheet. **Circ:** 5,048. available on microfiche from The State Historical Society of Wisconsin. ***Formed by the union of*** *Alabama Citizen (Tuscaloosa, Ala.)* ***and*** *Mobile Beacon (Mobile, Ala.).*

US
MOBILE REGISTER, THE. VFOAT Mobile Sunday Register; Mobile Press Register; Mobile Daily Register; Mobile County Register. Vol. 83, No. 100 (May 26, 1903)-. Newspaper. English. da. The Mobile Press Register, PO Box 2488, Mobile AL 36630. available on microfilm from University Microfilms International (UMI); and University Microfilms International (UMI). ***Continues*** *Daily Register (Mobile AL).*

US/0884-8750
MONROE JOURNAL, THE. (19??)-. Newspaper. English. wk. $20.00 residents of Monroe and adjacent counties in Alabama; $23.50 Alabama; $26.00 US. Monroe Journal, PO Box 826, Monroeville AL 36460. **Tel** (205)575-3282, FAX (205)575-3284. **ED** Steve Stewart. **Ad Acc. Circ:** 6,500. available on microfilm.
Desc: Covers general interest news of the local community.

US/0892-4457
MONTGOMERY ADVERTISER (1987), THE. (THE MONTGOMERY ADVERTISER.). **VFOAT** Montgomery Advertiser & the Alabama Journal; Sunday Montgomery Advertiser. 160th Year, No. 1 (Jan. 2, 1987)-. Newspaper. English. da. $144.56 (daily and Sunday) 52 weeks. Montgomery Advertiser, 200 Washington Avenue, PO Box 1000, Montgomery AL 36101-1000. **Tel** (205)262-1611, FAX (205)261-1584. **ED** Bill Brown. **Bk Rev. Ad Acc.** ctrl circ. available on microfilm from University Microfilms International (UMI). Documents available from UMI Article Clearinghouse. ***Continues*** *Advertiser (Montgomery, Ala.), 0745-3221.* **Ind/Abst** Bus. Dateline [Full Txt.].

US
MONTGOMERY INDEPENDENT, THE. Vol. 1, No. 1 (Feb. 1964)-. Newspaper. English. wk. $19.90. Montgomery Independent, 6005C Monticello Drive, Montgomery AL 36117. **Tel** (205)213-7323. **ED** Tom Johnson (Editor-in-Chief) and Wendy Lewis (Managing Editor). **Photos. Ad Acc, Adv Mgr:** Alan Cutler. Full Page (B&W) $500.00. Half Page (B&W) $255.00. Full Page (Color) $575.00. Half Page (Color) $330.00. **Pub. Size:** Standard. **Circ:** 8,500 (ctrl).

US
MOULTON ADVERTISER, THE. Vol. 105, No. 1 (Jan. 1933)-. Newspaper. English. wk. Moulton Advertiser, PO Box 517, Moulton AL 35650. **Tel** (205)974-1114. **ED** Luke Slaton. **Circ:** 4,684. ***Continues*** *Advertiser (Moulton, Ala.).*

US/0885-1662
NEW TIMES (MOBILE, ALA.), THE. (THE NEW TIMES.). (1981)-. Newspaper. English. wk. $11.00, $9.00 (senior citizens and students). Mobile New Times, 156 South Broad Street, Mobile AL 36602-0356. **Tel** (205)432-0356, FAX (205)456-9928. **ED** Vivian D. Figures. **Ad Acc. Circ:** 21,500 (ctrl).

US
NEWS, THE. (1865)-. Newspaper. English. wk. $19.00 Macon County, AL; $24.00 Alabama; $26.00 other. Tuskegee News, PO Box 60, Tuskegee AL 36083. **Tel** (205)727-3020, FAX (205)727-3036. **ED** Jennifer Suppa. **Ad Acc. Pr Rev. Circ:** 5000. available on microfilm.
Desc: Community newspaper featuring mostly local news with some state and national views.

US/0747-4512
NEWS HERALD (SARALAND, ALA.), THE. ***Ceased.*** (THE NEWS HERALD.). (1958)-(1985). Newspaper. English. wk. Mobile County Publications, PO Box 5809, Saraland AL 56571.

US/0164-9108
NORTH JACKSON PROGRESS. (1977)-. Newspaper. English. sw. North Jackson Progress, PO Drawer 625, Stevenson AL 35772-9988. **Tel** (205)437-2395, FAX (205)437-0253. **ED** Larry O. Glass. **Ad Acc. Circ:** 4,000.

US
NORTH JEFFERSON NEWS, THE. (1970)-. Newspaper. English. wk. $16.00 Jefferson County; $21.00 other. North Jefferson News, PO Box 849, 125 Bell Street, Gardendale AL 35071. **Tel** (205)631-8716, FAX (205)631-9902. **ED** Tim Lasseter. **Photos. Ad Acc, Adv Mgr:** Mona Richards. Full Page (B&W) $677.25. Half Page (B&W) $346.50. Full Page (Color) $742.25. Half Page (Color) $441.50. **Pub. Size:** Standard. **Circ:** 3,176.
Desc: Provides news and general interest articles concerning the northern section of Jefferson County, Alabama. Special interest is given to local school, church, and community activities.

US
NORTHWEST ALABAMIAN (HALEYVILLE, ALA.). (THE NORTHWEST ALABAMIAN.). 7th Year, No. 238 (Jan. 1969)-. Newspaper. English. sw. Northwest Alabamian, PO Box 430, Haleyville AL 35565. **Tel** (205)486-9461. **ED** Les Walters. **Circ:** 8,896. ***Continues*** *Daily Northwest Alabamian.*

US
ONE VOICE. Vol. 1, No. 1 (Jan. 1, 1971)-. Newspaper. English. wk. $12.00. Birmingham Catholic Press Inc, 5333 1st Avenue North, PO Box 10822, Birmingham AL 35202. **Tel** (205)838-8305. **ED** Rev. John T. Iboe. ***Separated from*** *Catholic Week, 1045-7496.*
Desc: For circulation of the Diocese of Birmingham.

US/1044-7539
OPELIKA AUBURN NEWS. (THE OPELIKA-AUBURN NEWS.). (August 1969)-. Newspaper. English. da (Sun.-Fri.). $82.00 (one year), $63.85 (nine months). Opelika-Auburn News, PO Drawer 2208, Opelika AL 36801-2208. **Tel** (205)749-6271, FAX (205)749-1228. **ED** Steve F. McPhaul and Richard Walker (Managing Editor). **Bk Rev. Photos. Ad Acc, Adv Mgr:** Jack Nolan. Full Page (B&W) $1,226.79. Half Page (B&W) $627.66. Full Page (Color) $1,376.79. Half Page (Color) $777.66. **Pub. Size:** Broadsheet. **Wire Svcs.:** AP. **Circ:** 14,000. available in microform. ***Continues*** *Opelika Daily News.*

US
OPP NEWS, THE. Vol. 22, No. 31 (March 1943)-. Newspaper. English. wk. $21.00. Opp News, PO Box 409, Opp AL 36467. **Tel** (205)493-3595, FAX (205)493-4901. **ED** Tracey D. Nelson. **Photos. Ad Acc, Adv Mgr:** Jennifer Cosby. Full Page (B&W) $693.00. Half Page (B&W) $363.00. Full Page (Color) $768.00. Half Page (Color) $438.00. **Pub. Size:** Standard. **Circ:** 5,300. ***Continues*** *Opp Weekly News.*

US
PHENIX CITIZEN (1973). (THE PHENIX CITIZEN.). **VFOAT** Phenix Citizen Herald. Vol. 21, No. 35 (Jan. 22, 1976)-. Newspaper. English. wk. $31.40. Phenix Citizen, PO Box 1267, Phenix City AL 36868. **Tel** (205)298-0679. **ED** John C. Kuykendall. **Ad Acc. Circ:** 1,600. ***Continues*** *Phenix-Citizen Herald.*

US/0893-0767
PICKENS COUNTY HERALD. VFOAT Pickens County Herald and West Alabamian. Vol. 138, No. 40 (Oct. 2, 1986)-. Newspaper. English. wk. $16.00 Pickens County; $24.00 other. Pickens County Herald, Highway 17, Junkin Building, Carrollton AL 35447. **Tel** (205)367-2217, FAX (205)367-2217. **ED** Doug Sanders Jr. **Photos. Ad Acc, Adv Mgr:** Brian Hood. Full Page (B&W) $496.65. Half Page (B&W) $248.32. Full Page (Color) $586.65. Half Page (Color) $338.32. **Circ:** 4,500. ***Continues*** *Pickens County Herald and West Alabamian, 0746-0473.*

US/0890-6017
PIEDMONT JOURNAL-INDEPENDENT, THE. VFOAT Journal Independent. Vol. 4, No. 52 (Dec. 24, 1985)-. Newspaper. English. wk (Published on Wednesdays). $13.91 (one year), $26.43 (two year).

Piedmont Journal Independent, 115 North Center Avenue, Piedmont AL 36272-2013. **Tel** (205)447-2837, FAX (205)447-2837. **ED** Lane Weatherbee. **Photos**. **Ad Acc, Adv Mgr:** Carol Weatherbee. Full Page (B&W) $508.52. Half Page (B&W) $274.63. Full Page (Color) $608.27. Half Page (Color) $369.63. **Circ:** 3,450 paid. ***Continues*** *Journal-Independent.*
Desc: Provides coverage of local news, weather, sports and entertainment for Piedmont, Alabama.

●US/1061-1908
PRATT CITY COMMUNITY NEWSPAPER. (1992)-. English. qt. $6.00. Pratt City Community Newspaper, PO Box 370171, Birmingham AL 35237. ***Continues*** *Pratt City Community Newsletter, 1055-0321.*

US/1044-0380
PRATTVILLE PROGRESS (PRATTVILLE, ALA.), THE. (THE PRATTVILLE PROGRESS.). Vol. 102, No. 8 (Jan. 20, 1987)-. Newspaper. English. ir (published Tues., Thurs. and Fri.). $24.00. Progress / Prattville, PO Drawer C, Prattville AL 36067. **Tel** (205)365-6739. ***Continues*** *Progress (Prattville, Ala.), 0745-7596.*

US
RANDOLPH LEADER, THE. Vol. 91, No. 1 (Oct. 6, 1982)-. Newspaper. English. wk. Randolph Leader, 321 East Main Street, Roanoke AL 36274. **Tel** (205)863-2819. **ED** John W Stevenson. **Circ:** 6,200. ***Formed by the union of*** *Roanoke Leader* ***and*** *Randolph Press.*

US
RED BAY NEWS (RED BAY, ALA. : 1963). (THE RED BAY NEWS.). (1963)-. Newspaper. English. wk. $16.00 selected counties, Alabama; $22.00 other. Red Bay News, PO Box 1339, Red Bay AL 35582. **Tel** (205)356-2148. **ED** Fred Childers. **Photos**. **Ad Acc, Adv Mgr:** LaVale Mills. Full Page (B&W) $525.00. Half Page (B&W) $261.22. Full Page (Color) $625.00. Half Page (Color) $361.22. **Circ:** 2,954. ***Continues*** *Franklin Citizen (Russellville, Ala. : 1956).*

US/0890-1724
SAND MOUNTAIN REPORTER. **VFOAT** Reporter; Sand Mountain Reporter Combined with the Albertville Herald; Reporter. Vol. 1, No. 1 (Aug. 5, 1955)-. Newspaper. English. ir (154 issues per year). $22.50. Sand Mountain Reporter, PO Box 190, Albertville AL 35950. **Tel** (205)878-1311, FAX (205)878-2104. **ED** Avis Holderfield. **Bk Rev**. **Photos**. **Ad Acc, Adv Mgr:** Debra Hedgepath. Full Page (B&W) $845.00. Half Page (B&W) $432.30. Full Page (Color) $1,070.00. Half Page (Color) $657.30. **Pub. Size:** Broadsheet. **Circ:** 13,500. ***Absorbed*** *Albertville Herald.*

US/1043-9129
SELMA TIMES-JOURNAL, THE. **VFOAT** Selma Times Journal. Vol. 1, No. 1 (March 1920)-. Newspaper. English. da (Sun.-Fri.). Selma Times-Journal, PO Box 611, 1018 Water Street, Selma AL 36702-0611. **Tel** (205)875-2110. **ED** David Roundtree. **Circ:** 10,663. ***Formed by the union of*** *Selma Times* ***and*** *Selma Journal.*

US/0896-615X
SHADES VALLEY SUN, THE. ***Ceased.*** **VFOAT** Sun. (1945)-?. Newspaper. English. wk. Cook Publications Inc, PO Box 10567, Birmingham AL 35202. **Tel** (205)991-8700. **ED** Pat Bray. **Circ:** 9,900.

US/1063-9489
SHELBY COUNTY REPORTER (1955). (SHELBY COUNTY REPORTER.). Vol. 113, No. 8 (Nov. 1955)-. Newspaper. English. wk. $26.95. Shelby County Newspapers, Inc., PO Box 947, Columbiana AL 35051. **Tel** (205)669-3131, FAX (205)669-4217. **ED** Kim N. Price. **Bk Rev**. **Photos**. **Ad Acc, Adv Mgr:** Terri Quarles. Full Page (B&W) $1612.50. Half Page (B&W) $806.25. Full Page (Color) additional $90.00 per color. Half Page (Color) additional $90.00 per color. **Pub. Size:** Broadsheet. **Pr Rev**. **Circ:** 10,258. available on microfilm (library). ***Continues*** *Shelby County Reporter-Democrat;* ***Absorbed*** *Shelby County Times-Herald.*
Desc: General interest articles limited to Shelby County and surrounding areas.

US/0890-8168
SOUTH ALABAMIAN (JACKSON, ALA.), THE. (THE SOUTH ALABAMIAN.). Vol. 1, No. 1 (Sept. 3, 1887)-. Newspaper. English. wk. $13.91 (one year), $25.68 (two year) Clark and Washington Counties; $22.00 (one year), $40.00 (two year) other. The South Alabamian, PO Box 68, 1064 Coffeeville Road, Jackson AL 36545. **Tel** (205)246-4494, FAX (205)246-7486. **ED** Mike Breedlove, Scott Morris (Managing Editor). **Photos**. **Ad Acc, Adv Mgr:** Cammie Breedlove. Full Page (B&W) $409.00. Half Page (B&W) $240.00. Full Page (Color) $519.00. Half Page (Color) $350.00. **Pub. Size:** Standard. **Circ:** 4,678.

US
SOUTHERN STAR. (1867)-. Newspaper. English. wk. $21.00. Southern Star Inc, PO Box 1729, Ozark AL 36361. **Tel** (205)774-2715, FAX (205)774-9619. **ED** Joe Adams. **Bk Rev**. **Photos**. **Ad Acc, Adv Mgr:** Charlie Dawkins. Full Page (B&W) $548.25. Half Page (B&W) $274.13. Full Page (Color) $648.25. Half Page (Color) $374.13. **Pub. Size:** Standard. **Circ:** 4,800.

US/1044-1964
ST. CLAIR NEWS-AEGIS. **VFOAT** St. Clair News Aegis; Saint Clair News-Aegis; Saint Clair News Aegis; Pell City News the Southern Aegis. Vol. 43, No. 46 (Jan. 3, 1952); 79th Year, No. 2 (Jan. 10, 1952)-. Newspaper. English. wk. $16.00 (St. Clair County); $21.00 other. St. Clair News-Aegis, PO Box 748, Pell City AL 35125. **Tel** (205)884-2310, FAX (205)884-2312. **ED** Randy Grider. **Ad Acc**. **Circ:** 3,549 (ctrl). ***Formed by the union of*** *Pell City News* ***and*** *Southern Aegis (Ashville, Ala.);* ***Absorbed*** *St. Clair Observer.*

US
STANDARD AND TIMES LAUDERDALE COUNTY NEWS, THE. **VFOAT** Standard and Times and Lauderdale County News. (19??)-. Newspaper. English. wk. $12.00 Colbert county; $14.00 others counties in Alabama; $16.00 others. Standard and Times, PO Box 470, Tuscumbia AL 35674. **Tel** (205)383-8471, FAX (205)383-8476. **ED** Jan Crawford Jr. (editor's address: PO Box 1419, Tuscumbia, AL 25674). **Ad Acc, Adv Mgr:** Estelle W., **Tel** (250)383-8471. **Circ:** 5,500. ***Continues in part*** *Standard & Times.*

US
SUMTER COUNTY JOURNAL. (19??)-. Newspaper. English. wk. Sumter County Journal, 2 Main Street, York AL 36925. **Tel** (205)392-5251, FAX (205)392-7006. **ED** Tommy McGrau. **Bk Rev**. **Ad Acc, Adv Mgr:** Judi Johnston. **Circ:** 2,700. ***Absorbed*** *Our Southern Home.*

US
TALLASSEE TRIBUNE, THE. (1919)-. Newspaper. English. wk. Tallassee Tribune, 301 Gilmer Avenue, Tallassee AL 36078. **Tel** (205)283-6568, FAX (205)283-6569. **ED** Jack Venable. **Ad Acc**. **Circ:** 4,000.

US
THOMASVILLE TIMES (THOMASVILLE, ALA.). (THE THOMASVILLE TIMES.). Began in 1921. Newspaper. English. wk. Thomasville Times, Box 367, Thomasville AL 36784. **Tel** (205)636-2214. **ED** Jackie H Bozeman. **Circ:** 3,600.

US
THRIFTY NICKEL WEEKLY NEWSPAPER. BIRMINGHAM. (1982)-. Newspaper. English. Fifty-two times a year (Thursdays). Free. Thrifty Nickel, 619 Robert Jemison Road Suite 200, Birmingham AL 35209. **Tel** (205)942-2555, FAX (205)942-5770. **ED** Rob Puckett, Abraham Manear (Managing Editor). **Photos**. **Ad Acc, Adv Mgr:** Elizabeth Laird. Full Page (B&W) $1519.00. Half Page (B&W) $787.00. Full Page (Color) $1969.00. Half Page (Color) $1237.00. **Pub. Size:** Tabloid. **Circ:** 70,000 (unpaid, weekly).
Desc: An advertising newspaper serving Birmingham and the 10-county surrounding area.

US
TIMES-JOURNAL (FORT PAYNE, ALA.). (THE TIMES-JOURNAL.). **VFOAT** Times Journal. Vol. 80, No. 42 (Sept. 4, 1958)-. Newspaper. English. da. $70.00. Times-Journal, Box 349, Fort Payne AL 35967. **Tel** (205)845-2550. **ED** Gary Gengozian. **Circ:** 6,571. ***Formed by the union of*** *Fort Payne Journal* ***and*** *Times-New Era.*

US
TIMES-RECORD, THE. **VFOAT** Times Record. Vol. 1, No. 1 (Aug. 24, 1977)-. Newspaper. English. wk. Moore Publishing, PO Box 430, Haleyville AL 35565. **Tel** (205)486-9461, FAX (205)486-4849. **Ad Acc**. **Circ:** 4,700.

US/0743-152X
TIMESDAILY (REGIONAL ED.). (TIMESDAILY.). **VFOAT** Times Daily. Vol. 114, No. 226 (Aug. 14, 1983)-. Newspaper. English. da (365 issues per year). $156.00 (mail), $123.00 (carrier). Times Daily, 219 West Tennessee Street, Florence AL 35630. **Tel** (205)766-3444. ***Continues*** *Times Tri-Cities Daily.*

US/0743-1511
TIMESDAILY (SHOALS EDITION). (TIMESDAILY.). **VFOAT** Times Daily. Began with: Vol. 114, No. 226 (Aug. 14, 1983). Newspaper. English. da. $78.00. Times Daily, 219 West Tennessee Street, Florence AL 35630. **Tel** (205)766-3444. ***Continues*** *Times Tri-Cities Daily.*

US/0889-0676
TRI-CITY LEDGER (FLOMATON), THE. (THE TRI-CITY LEDGER.). **VFOAT** Tri City Ledger; Ledger. Began with Nov. 10 (1971)-. Newspaper. English. wk. Tri-City Ledger, PO Drawer F, Flomaton AL 36441. **Tel** (205)296-3491. **ED** James G. Thornton Jr. **Circ:** 3,000.

US
TUSCALOOSA NEWS, THE. Vol. 96, No. 350 (July 7, 1929)-. Newspaper. English. da. $208.00. Tuscaloosa News, PO Drawer 1, Tuscaloosa AL 35402. **Tel** (205)340-0505. **ED** Charles Land. **Ad Acc**. **Circ:** 39,900. ***Continues*** *Tuscaloosa News and Times-Gazette.*

US
UNION SPRINGS HERALD. Herald Vol. 3, No. 40 (July 30, 1873)-. Newspaper. English. wk. Union Springs Herald, PO Box 600, Union Springs AL 36089. **Tel** (205)738-2360, FAX (205)738-2342. **ED** Thomas May. **Ad Acc**. **Circ:** 3,900. ***Continues*** *Union Springs Herald and Times.*

US
VALLEY TIMES-NEWS, THE. **VFOAT** Valley Times News. Vol. 1, No. 1 (June 1956)-. Newspaper. English. da (Mon.-Fri.). Valley Times-News, 220 North 12th Street, Lanett AL 36863. **Tel** (205)644-1101. **ED** Mark T Walls. ***Continues*** *Valley Daily Times-News.*

US
WASHINGTON COUNTY NEWS. (19??)-. Newspaper. English. Fifty-two times a year. $15.00 Alabama; $22.00 other. Washington County News / Alabama, 305 Jordan Street, PO Box 510, Chatom AL 36518. **Tel** (205)847-2599. **ED** Frank Harwell. **Photos**. **Ad Acc, Adv Mgr:** Pauline Jackson. **Pub. Size:** Standard. **Circ:** 3,600 (ctrl). ***Continues*** *Call-News Dispatch.*

US/0889-0080
WESTERN STAR (BESSEMER, ALA.), THE. (THE WESTERN STAR.). (198?)-. Newspaper. English. wk. $21.00 Alabama; $29.00 other. Western Star, PO Box 1900, Bessemer AL 35021. **Tel** (205)424-7827. **ED** John Calure. **Bk Rev**, (Qty: 12). **Photos**. **Ad Acc, Adv Mgr:** Cathy Calure. Full Page (B&W) $838.50. Half Page (B&W) $419.25. Full Page (Color) $913.50. Half Page (Color) $544.25. **Pub. Size:** Broadsheet. **Circ:** 11,500. ***Absorbed*** *Bessemer Advertiser.*

US
WETUMPKA HERALD, THE. Vol. 30, No. 10 (Aug. 1927)-. Newspaper. English. wk. $16.00 Elmore County; $20.00 Alabama; $24.00 US. Wetumpka Herald, 300 Green Street, PO Box 29, Wetumpka AL 36092-0029. **Tel** (205)567-7811, FAX (205)567-3284. **ED** Gerald M. Williams, Ellen T. Williams (Managing Editor). **Bk Rev**, (Qty: 42). **Photos**. **Ad Acc, Adv Mgr:** JoAnn Lambert, **Tel** (205)567-2266. Full Page (B&W) $657.90. Half Page (B&W) $336.60. Full Page (Color) $907.90. Half Page (Color) $586.60. **Pub. Size:** Standard. **Circ:** 4,100 (ctrl). ***Continues*** *Weekly Herald (Wetumpka, Ala.).*

US
WILCOX PROGRESSIVE ERA. **VFOAT** Progressive Era. Vol. 11, No. 48 (Aug. 29, 1900); Vol. 1, no. 2 (Sept. 5, 1900)-. Newspaper. English. wk. $20.00. Wilcox Progressive Era, PO Box 100, Camden AL 36726-0100. **Tel** (205)682-4422, FAX (205)682-5163. **ED** M. Hollis Curl. **Bk Rev**, (Qty: 6). **Photos**. **Ad Acc, Adv Mgr:** Melissa Dove. **Pub. Size:** Standard. **Wire Svcs.:** AP. **Circ:** 2,300. ***Formed by the union of*** *Wilcox New Era* ***and*** *Wilcox Progress.*

ALASKA

US/0194-6870
ANCHORAGE DAILY NEWS. (1946)-. Newspaper. English. da. $300.00 (daily and Sun.), $120.00 (Sun.) mail; $18.00 (Sun.) carrier. Anchorage Daily News, PO Box 14, 9001 Mail Subs, Anchorage AK 99514. **Tel** (907)257-4400, FAX (907)279-8170. **ED** Howard Weaver. **Ad Acc**. **Circ:** 60,000 Daily, 78,000 Sunday (ctrl). available on an online database (file 737/Full-Text) from DIALOG.
Desc: National and international news; covers Alaska and the Anchorage area.
Ind/Abst PROMT.

US
ANCHORAGE TIMES. ***Ceased.*** Vol. 62, No. 1 (Jan. 2, 1976)-(June 1992). Newspaper. English. da. Anchorage Times Publishing Company, PO Box 40, Anchorage AK 99510. **Tel** (907)263-9000. **ED** William J Tobin. **Bk Rev**. **Ad Acc**. **Circ:** 35,524 daily, 45,267 Sunday (ctrl). available on microfilm from University Microfilms International (UMI). ***Continues*** *Anchorage Daily Times.*

US/0897-9502
ARCTIC SOUNDER, THE. **VFOAT** Sounder. (1986)-. Newspaper. English. Fifty-two times a year (Thursdays). $45.00 (one year); $90.00 (two years). Alaska Newspapers Inc., 503 East 6th Avenue, Anchorage AK 99501. **Tel** (907)272-9830, FAX (907)272-9512. **ED** John Woodbury, Jim Paulin (Managing Editor). **Bk Rev**. **Photos**. **Ad Acc, Adv Mgr:** Doris Anderson, **Tel** (907)442-2716. Full Page (B&W) $862.50. Half Page (B&W) $431.25. Full Page (Color) $1012.50. Half Page (Color) $506.25. **Pub. Size:** Tabloid. **Wire Svcs.:** AP. **Circ:** 2,120. available on microfilm.

US
BRISTOL BAYTIMES. (19??)-. Newspaper. English. wk. $45.00. Alaska Newspapers Inc., 503 East 6th Avenue, Anchorage AK 99501. **Tel** (907)272-9830, FAX (907)272-9512. **ED** John Woodbury, Michael Berger (Managing Editor). **Bk Rev**. **Photos**. **Ad Acc**, **Adv Mgr:** Tanya Holman, **Tel** (907)842-5572. Full Page (B&W) $862.50. Half Page (B&W) $431.25. Full Page (Color) $1012.50. Half Page (Color) $506.25. **Pub. Size:** Tabloid. **Wire Svcs.:** AP. **Circ:** 1,720.

US/8750-3336
CHILKAT VALLEY NEWS. Newspaper. English. wk. Chilkat Valley News, Main Street, Box 630, Haines AK 99827. **Tel** (907)766-2688. **ED** Janis Marston. **Circ:** 1,300. ***Continues*** *Lynn Canal News.*

US/0740-963X
COPPER VALLEY VIEWS. (19??)-. Newspaper. English. Fifty-two times a year (Wed.). Sun Forest Productions, Box 229, HC 60, Copper Center AK 99573. **Tel** (907)822-3742. **ED** Lily Gallatin.

US/1048-8766
CORDOVA TIMES, THE. Vol. 33 No. 17 (Jan. 20, 1947)-. Newspaper. English. wk. $45.00. Alaska Newspapers Inc., 503 East 6th Avenue, Anchorage AK 99501. **Tel** (907)272-9830, FAX (907)272-9512. **ED** John Woodbury, Sandra Medearis (Managing Editor). **Bk Rev**. **Photos**. **Ad Acc**, **Adv Mgr:** Joy Landaluce, **Tel** (907)424-7181. Full Page (B&W) $862.50. Half Page (B&W) $431.25. Full Page (Color) $1012.50. Half Page (Color) $506.25. **Pub. Size:** Tabloid. **Wire Svcs.:** AP. **Circ:** 1,294. available in microform from The Library of Congress Photoduplication Service. ***Continues*** *Cordova Daily Times.*

US
DAILY SENTINEL (SITKA, ALASKA). (THE DAILY SENTINEL.). (Sept. 11, 1939)-. Newspaper. English. da (Mon.-Fri.). $99.00 Alaska; $111.00 other. Daily Sitka Sentinel, Box 799, Sitka AK 99835. **Tel** (907)747-3219, FAX (907)747-8898. **ED** Thad Poulson. **Circ:** 2,765.

US
DUTCH HARBOR FISHERMAN. (19??)-. Newspaper. English. wk. $45.00. Alaska Newspapers Inc., 503 East 6th Avenue, Anchorage AK 99501. **Tel** (907)272-9830, FAX (907)272-9512. **ED** John Woodbury, Soren Wuerth (Managing Editor). **Bk Rev**. **Photos**. **Ad Acc**, **Adv Mgr:** Deidre Fellner, **Tel** (907)581-2092. Full Page (B&W) $862.50. Half Page (B&W) $431.25. Full Page (Color) $1012.50. Half Page (Color) $506.25. **Pub. Size:** Tabloid. **Wire Svcs.:** AP. **Circ:** 1,132. available in microform.

US/8750-5495
FAIRBANKS DAILY NEWS-MINER. **VFOAT** Fairbanks Daily News Miner. (Aug. 1909)-. Newspaper. English. da. $298.00. Fairbanks Publishing Company, PO Box 70710, Fairbanks AK 99707. **Tel** (907)456-6666, FAX (907)452-5054. **LC** 7044. **DD** 183900. **Bk Rev**, (Qty: 52). **Photos**. **Ad Acc**, **Adv Mgr:** Marilyn Romano, **Tel** (907)456-6661 ext. 257. Full Page (B&W) $1733.76. Half Page (B&W) $866.88. Full Page (Color) $2145.76. Half Page (Color) $1278.88. **Pub. Size:** Standard. **Wire Svcs.:** AP, NY. **Circ:** 17,037 evening, 21,367 Sunday (ctrl). available on microfilm from University Microfilms International (UMI). ***Formed by the union of*** *Fairbanks Daily News;* *Tanana Miner* ***and*** *Tanana Tribune.*

US
HOMER NEWS. (19??)-. Newspaper. English. Fifty-two times a year (Thurs.). $38.00 Alaska; $30.00 Kenai, Peninsula & Burrough; $48.00 others. Homer News, 3482 Landings Street, Homer AK 99603. **Tel** (907)235-7767. **ED** Mark Turner. **Photos**. **Ad Acc**, **Adv Mgr:** Jane Alberts. Full Page (B&W) $600.00. Half Page (B&W) $300.00. Full Page (Color) $900.00. Half Page (Color) $600.00. **Pub. Size:** Tabloid. **Circ:** 4,000 (ctrl).
Desc: General news and information in Homer, Alaska.

US
JUNEAU EMPIRE. Vol. 74, No. 29 (Feb. 11, 1980)-. Newspaper. English. da. $198.00. Juneau Empire, 3100 Channel Drive, Juneau AK 99801-7814. **Tel** (907)586-3746. **ED** Larry Persily (editor's phone: (907)586-3740). **Bk Rev**. **Ad Acc**, **Adv Mgr:** Robin Paul, **Tel** (907)586-3740. **Circ:** 8,000. available on microfilm from University Microfilms International (UMI). ***Continues*** *Southeast Alaska Empire.*

US/0274-581X
KETCHIKAN DAILY NEWS. (THE KETCHIKAN DAILY NEWS.). Vol. 19, No. 222 (Aug. 1, 1947)-. Newspaper. English. da (Sun.-Fri.). $140.00. Ketchikan Daily News, Box 7900, Ketchikan AK 99901. **Tel** (907)225-3157. **ED** Brooks Dareff (Managing Editor). **Bk Rev**. **Ad Acc**. **Circ:** 4,600 (morning), 5,080 (Sunday). ***Continues*** *Ketchikan Daily Alaska Fishing News.*
Desc: Local, national and international news.

US/0740-2112
KODIAK DAILY MIRROR, THE. (19??)-. Newspaper. English. da (Monday-Friday). $96.00. Kodiak Daily Mirror, 1419 Selig, Kodiak AK 99615. **Tel** (907)486-3227, FAX (907)486-3088. **ED** Andy Hall, Nancy Freeman (Managing Editor). **Photos**. **Ad Acc**, **Adv Mgr:** Amy Willis. Full Page (B&W) $537.85. **Wire Svcs.:** AP. **Circ:** 3,500 (ctrl). available in microform.

US/0745-9106
NOME NUGGET (NOME, ALASKA : 1938). (THE NOME NUGGET.). Vol. 39, No. 2 (Jan. 5, 1938)-. Newspaper. English. Fifty-one times per year (Thurs.). Nome Nugget, PO Box 610, Nome AK 99672. **Tel** (907)443-5235. **ED** Nancy L. McGuire. Index available. **Ad Acc**. **Circ:** 3,000 (ctrl). available on microfilm from The State Historical Society of Wisconsin. ***Continues*** *Nome News.*
Desc: Alaska news, local and statewide. Concentrates on Nome/northwest Alaska area news.

US/0747-3729
PIONEER, ALL-ALASKA WEEKLY, THE. ***Ceased.*** **VFOAT** All-Alaska Weekly; Pioneer; All Alaska Weekly. (19??)-(19??). Newspaper. English. wk. All Alaska Weekly, PO Box 970, Fairbanks AK 99701.

US/0743-8303
PRUDHOE BAY JOURNAL. (198?)-. Newspaper. English. bw. $17.50. Prudhoe Bay Publishing, PO Box 80969, Fairbanks AK 99708.

US
SEWARD PHOENIX LOG. (19??)-. Newspaper. English. wk. $45.00. Alaska Newspapers Inc., 503 East 6th Avenue, Anchorage AK 99501. **Tel** (907)272-9830, FAX (907)272-9512. **ED** John Woodbury, Eric Fry (Managing Editor). **Bk Rev**. **Photos**. **Ad Acc**, **Adv Mgr:** Claire Rodgers, **Tel** (907)224-8070. Full Page (B&W) $862.50. Half Page (B&W) $431.25. Full Page (Color) $1012.50. Half Page (Color) $506.25. **Pub. Size:** Tabloid. **Wire Svcs.:** AP. **Circ:** 2,183. available in microform.

US/0745-872X
SKAGWAY NEWS, THE. (198?)-. Newspaper. English. sm (24 issues). $30.00. Skagway News, PO Box 1898, Skagway AK 99840-0498. **Tel** (907)983-2354. **ED** William J. Brady. **Circ:** 414.

US
TUNDRA DRUMS, THE. Vol. 12, No. 25 (Sept. 20, 1984)-. Newspaper. English. Fifty-two times a year (Published on Thusdays). $45.00. Alaska Newspapers Inc., 503 East 6th Avenue, Anchorage AK 99501. **Tel** (907)272-9830, FAX (907)272-9512. **ED** John Woodbury, Jay Barrett (Managing Editor). **Bk Rev**. **Photos**. **Ad Acc**, **Adv Mgr:** Natalia Akerlund, **Tel** (907)543-3500. Full Page (B&W) $862.50. Half Page (B&W) $431.25. Full Page (Color) $1012.50. Half Page (Color) $506.25. **Pub. Size:** Tabloid. **Wire Svcs.:** AP. **Circ:** 4,437. available on microfilm. ***Continues*** *Drums (Bethel, Alaska).*

US/0049-4801
TUNDRA TIMES. Vol. 1, No. 1 (Oct. 1, 1962)-. Newspaper. English. wk. $30.00 US; $55.00 others. Eskimo Indian Aleut Publishing Company, PO Box 92247, Anchorage AK 99509-2247. **Tel** (907)274-2512, FAX (907)277-7217. **ED** Anna M. Pickett. **Bk Rev**, (Qty: 5-10). **Photos**. **Ad Acc**, **Adv Mgr:** Debi Smith. **Pub. Size:** Tabloid. **Circ:** 4,000. available on microfilm (from The Library of Congress Photoduplication Service).
Desc: News and opinions on issues of concern to Alaska Natives.

US
VALDEZ VANGUARD. Vol. 1, No. 1 (Dec. 1, 1975)-. Newspaper. English. wk. $45.00. Alaska Newspapers Inc., 503 East 6th Avenue, Anchorage AK 99501. **Tel** (907)272-9830, FAX (907)272-9512. **ED** John Woodbury, Tony Bickert (Managing Editor). **Bk Rev**. **Photos**. **Ad Acc**, **Adv Mgr:** Linda Wakefield, **Tel** (907)835-2211. Full Page (B&W) $862.50. Half Page (B&W) $431.25. Full Page (Color) $1012.50. Half Page (Color) $506.25. **Pub. Size:** Tabloid. **Wire Svcs.:** AP. **Circ:** 1,581. available in microform.

US/0192-8589
VALLEY SUN (WASILLA), THE. (THE VALLEY SUN.). Newspaper. English. wk. Valley Publications Inc, PO Box 1780, Wasilla AK 99687. **Tel** (907)376-5225. **ED** Jim Springer.

US
WRANGELL SENTINEL. (1909)-. Newspaper. English. wk (Thurs.). $27.50 Wrangell; $31.00 others. Wrangell Sentinel, PO Box 798, Wrangell AK 99929. **Tel** (907)874-2301. **ED** Allen L. Bird. **Bk Rev**, (Qty: 3-4). **Photos**. **Ad Acc**, **Adv Mgr:** Sara Bird. Full Page (B&W) $504.24. Half Page (B&W) $252.12. Full Page (Color) $611.24. Half Page (Color) $359.12. **Pub. Size:** Tabloid. available in microform from the publisher.

ARIZONA

US/0888-546X
ARIZONA DAILY STAR. Vol. 1, No. 1 (June 25 [i.e. 26], 1879)-. Newspaper. English. da. Tucson Citizen, 4850 South Park Avenue, PO Box 26887, Tucson AZ 85726. **Tel** (602)573-4511, (800)695-4492. **ED** Michael E. Pulitzer. **LC** 7069-X. available on microfilm from University Microfilms International (UMI); available on an online database (file 635/Full-Text) from DIALOG. Documents available from UMI Article Clearinghouse.
Ind/Abst Bus. Dateline (Dec. 20, 1991-) [Full Txt.].

US/1054-9536
ARIZONA DAILY SUN (FLAGSTAFF, ARIZ.). (ARIZONA DAILY SUN.). [Ariz. dly. sun]. **VFOAT** Arizona Sun; Daily Sun. Vol. 1 (1946)-. Newspaper. English. da (Sunday-Friday 312 issues per year). $215.00. Arizona Daily Sun, PO Box 1849, 417 West Santa Fe Avenue, Flagstaff AZ 86002. **Tel** (602)774-4545. **ED** Burt L Lyons. **Circ:** 11,162.

US/1053-5616
ARIZONA JEWISH POST. **Added/Corp** Jewish Federation of Southern Arizona. Newspaper. English. bw. The Arizona-Post, 635 North Craycroft Road/#202, Tucson AZ 85711-1451. **Tel** (602)791-9962. ***Continues*** *Arizona post, 0744-1509.*

US/0892-8711
ARIZONA REPUBLIC. **VFOAT** Republic. No. 177 (Nov. 11, 1930)-. Newspaper. English. ds. $254.40 Arizona; $367.00 California, Colorado, Nevada, New Mexico & Utah; $426.40 US; $803.20 other. Phoenix Newspapers Inc., 120 East Van Buren Street, Phoenix AZ 85001. **Tel** (602)271-8503, (602)271-8000. **DD** 071. **Bk Rev**. **Ad Acc**. **Circ:** 315,000 Daily, 507,000 Sunday. available on microfilm from Southwest Micropublishing International; available on an online database (files 493,635/Full-Text) from DIALOG. Documents available from UMI Article Clearinghouse. ***Continues*** *Arizona Republican.*
Ind/Abst Bus. Dateline (Jan. 1 1990-) [Full Txt.]; PROMT.

US/0270-0425
ARIZONA SENIOR WORLD, THE. **VFOAT** Senior World of Arizona; Senior World/Arizona. Vol. 1, (Mar. 1979)-. Periodical. English. Twelve times a year. $14.95. Arizona Senior World, 2207 South 48th Street, Suite A, Tempe AZ 85282. **Tel** (602)438-1566, FAX (602)438-0369. **ED** Gilbert Moore. **Bk Rev**, (Qty: 24). **Photos**. **Ad Acc**, **Adv Mgr:** Jamie Hastings. Full Page (B&W) $5760.00. Half Page (B&W) $3280.00. Full Page (Color) $7110.00. Half Page (Color) $4630.00. **Pub. Size:** Tabloid. **Circ:** 200,000 (ctrl).
Desc: Newspaper targeted to the 50 year and over market.

US
ARIZONA SILVER BELT. (May 2, 1878)-. Newspaper. English. Fifty-two times a year. Copper Belt Printing & Publishing Company, PO Box 31, Globe AZ 85501. **Tel** (602)425-7121. **ED** Tom E. Anderson. **Bk Rev**. **Ad Acc**. **Circ:** 7,262.

US
BISBEE DAILY REVIEW. Began in Jan. 1901?. Newspaper. English. da (Sun.-Fri.). Bisbee Daily Review, 12 Main Street, Bisbee AZ 85603. **Tel** (602)432-2231. **ED** Lee James. **Circ:** 2,514.

US/0895-2450
BISBEE OBSERVER, THE. Vol. 1, No. 1 (April 25, 1985)-. Newspaper. English. wk. $22.00. The Bisbee Observer, 7 Bisbee Road, Suite L, Bisbee AZ 85603. **Tel** (602)432-7254. **ED** Larry Ketchum. **Photos**. **Ad Acc**, **Adv Mgr:** Laura Swan. Full Page (B&W) $341.25. Half Page (B&W) $170.63. Full Page (Color) $441.25. Half Page (Color) $270.63. **Pub. Size:** Tabloid. **Wire Svcs.:** AP. **Circ:** 2,300.

●US/1065-3880
BUCKEYE INDEPENDENT, THE. Vol. 1, No. 1 (Mar. 31, 1992)-. Newspaper. English. Fifty-two times a year. Buckeye Independent Printing and Publishing, 626 East Monroe Avenue, Buckeye AZ 85326-0230. **Tel** (602)386-4346.

US
BUCKEYE VALLEY NEWS. (19??)-. Newspaper. English. wk. $13.95 (in county), $15.95 (other). Buckeye Valley News, PO Box 217, Buckeye AZ 85326. **Tel** (602)386-4426. **ED** Sharon Butler. **Bk Rev**. **Photos**. **Ad Acc**, **Adv Mgr:** Rhoda Sylvester. **Pub. Size:** Standard. **Circ:** 2,600.

US/1054-2876
BUGLE (COTTONWOOD, ARIZ.), THE. (THE BUGLE.). (19??)-. Newspaper. English. sw. $35.00 Arizona; $42.00 other. The Independent/Bugle Call, PO Box 1979, Camp Verde AZ 86322. **Tel** (602)567-4101. ***Continues*** *Bugle Call (Cottonwood, Ariz.), 0894-301X.*

US
CASA GRANDE DISPATCH. (19??)-. Newspaper. English. da (Published Monday thru Saturday). $130.00 Pinal County; $140.00 others in Arizona; $150.00 others. Casa Grande Dispatch, 200 West 2nd Avenue, PO Box 639, Casa Grande AZ 85222. **Tel** (602)836-7461. **ED** Jim Fickess. **Circ:** 7,484.

US
COURIER, THE. **VFOAT** Prescott Courier. (19??)-. Newspaper. English. da. $112.00 Yavapai County; $142.00 US; $310.00 other. Western Newspapers, PO Box 429, Cottonwood AZ 86326. **Tel** (602)634-2241. **(Subscription address:** Western Newspapers, PO Box 312, Prescott, AZ 86302) **ED** Jim Garner. **Ad Acc, Adv Mgr:** Pam Carpenter. **Circ:** 14,031 daily, 15,430 Sunday.

US/0743-8397
DAILY TERRITORIAL, THE. (19??)-. Newspaper. English. da (Mon.-Fri.). $90.00 in-county, $100.00 other. The Daily Territorial, PO Box 35250, 1 West Orange Grove, Tucson AZ 85740. **Tel** (602)297-1107, FAX (602)297-6253. **ED** Cheri Cross. **Ad Acc, Adv Mgr:** David Stoler. **Circ:** 1,492 (ctrl). ***Continues*** *Daily Reporter (Tucson, Ariz.).*
Desc: Political, business and economic issues covered. Court, legals, special lists published on a daily basis.

US
DOUGLAS DAILY DISPATCH. **VFOAT** Doutlas Dispatch. (April 1903)-. Newspaper. English. da (Mon. - Fri.). Douglas Daily Dispatch, PO Drawer H, Douglas AZ 85607. **Tel** (602)364-3424. **ED** Gary Dillard. **LC** 7071. **Bk Rev**. **Ad Acc**. **Circ:** 3,500. ***Continues*** *Douglas Dispatch.*

US
EATERN AIZONA COURIER. Newspaper. English. wk (published Wednesday). $22.00 Graham, Greenlee, North Cochise coutnies, $28.00 other Arizona and New Mexico, $35.00 other. Eastern Arizona Courier, 203 East Main Street, PO Box N, Safford AZ 85548. **Tel** (602)428-2560, FAX (602)428-5396. **ED** Lawrence Blaskey. **Bk Rev**. **Ad Acc**. ctrl circ.

US/1059-0633
ESSENTIAL NEWS. [Essent. news]. Vol. 8, No. 1 (Sept. 1991)-. Newspaper. English. Twelve times a year. Essential News Inc. / Bear Essential News for Kids, 209 East Baseline Road, Suite E 203, PO Box 26908, Tempe AZ 85285. **Tel** (602)345-7323. **DD** 070. ***Continues*** *Bear Essential News for Kids.*

US/8750-3026
FOOTHILLS SENTINEL. (1984)-. Periodical. English. Fifty-two times a year (Wed.). Foothills Sentinel, PO Box 1569, Cave Creek AZ 85331. **Tel** (602)488-3624. **ED** Linda Ritchie and Marianne Lasby. Index available. **Bk Rev**. **Ad Acc**. **Circ:** 3,500 (ctrl). ***Formed by the union of*** *Black Mountain News; Black Canyon Express, 0745-6670* ***and*** *Pinnacle Peak/Rio Verde View.*

US
GILA BEND SUN NEWSPAPER. English. wk. $16.00 (Maricopa Co residents); $19.00 (other). Gila Bend Sun, PO Box Z, Gila Bend AZ 85337. **Tel** (602) 683-2393.

US/8750-5363
HOLBROOK TRIBUNE-NEWS AND SNOWFLAKE HERALD. **VFOAT** Holbrook Tribune News and Snowflake Herald; Snowflake Herald; Holbrook Tribune-News. (19??)-. Newspaper. English. sw (Wed. & Fri.). $20.00 Holbrook County; $26.00 Arizona; $34.00 others. Holbrook Tribune News, PO Box L, Holbrook AZ 86025. **Tel** (602)524-6203. **ED** Paul Barger (Editor in Chief), F. Payne (Managing Editor). **Photos**. **Ad Acc, Adv Mgr:** Matthew Barger. Full Page (B&W) $466.20. Half Page (B&W) $245.70. Full Page (Color) $551.20. Half Page (Color) $330.70. **Pub. Size:** Standard. **Circ:** 5,002.

US/1070-5848
JEWISH NEWS OF GREATER PHOENIX. Vol. 45, No. 33 (May 7, 1993)-. Newspaper. English. wk. $39.00. Phoenix Jewish News, Inc., PO Box 26590, Phoenix AZ 85068. **Tel** (602)870-9470, FAX (602)870-9470. **ED** Florence Eckstein. **Bk Rev**. **Ad Acc**. **Pub. Size:** Tabloid. **Circ:** 6,500. available in microform. ***Continues*** *Greater Phoenix Jewish News, 0747-444X.*
Desc: Articles of interest to the Jewish community.

US/0744-3285
JOURNAL (CAMP VERDE, ARIZ.), THE. (THE JOURNAL.). (198?)-. Newspaper. English. Fifty-two times a year. $14.00 Yavapai County; $19.00 other. The Journal / Camp Verde, PO Box 2048, Camp Verde AZ 86322. **Tel** (602)567-3341. **ED** Tony Brossart; Telephone: (602)282-7795. **Bk Rev**. **Ad Acc**. **Circ:** 3,100 (ctrl).

US/1068-1884
LAKE HAVASU CITY HERALD. (19??)-. Newspaper. English. sw. $26.00 Lake Havasu City; $34.00 US; $55.00 Canada. Lake Havasu City Herald, 2225 West Acoma Boulevard, Lake Havasu City AZ 86403. **Tel** (602)855-2197.

US
LAKE POWELL CHRONICLE. Vol. 1, No. 1 (Aug. 1965)-. Newspaper. English. wk. Lake Powell Chronicle, PO Box 1716, 3 Elm Street Mall, Page AZ 86040-1716. **Tel** (602)645-8888. **ED** Julia P. Betz. **Circ:** 3,400.

US
MESA TRIBUNE. Newspaper. English. da. $161.00 Arizona; $185.00 other. Cox Arizona Publications, PO Box 1547, Mesa AZ 85211. **Tel** (602)898-6500. available on an online database (file 635/Full-Text) from DIALOG. Documents available from UMI Article Clearinghouse.
Ind/Abst Bus. Dateline (Dec. 22, 1991-) [Full Txt.].

US
MOHAVE COUNTY MINER (KINGMAN, ARIZ. : 1931). (MOHAVE COUNTY MINER.). **VFOAT** Mohave County Miner and our Mineral Wealth. (1931)-. Newspaper. English. da (Sun.-Fri.). Mohave County Miner, PO Box 3909, Kingman AZ 86402-3909. **Tel** (602)753-6397, FAX (602)753-5661. **ED** Tim Weideraenders, Wayne Russel (News Manager). **LC** 7072. **Bk Rev**, (Qty: 6-8). **Photos**. **Ad Acc, Adv Mgr:** Kathi Wright. Full Page (B&W) $993.30. Half Page (B&W) $485.10. Full Page (Color) $1,116.02. Half Page (Color) $562.94. **Pub. Size:** Standard. **Wire Svcs.:** AP. **Circ:** 6,350. available on microfilm and microfiche. ***Continues*** *Mohave County Miner and our Mineral Wealth.*

US/0746-9764
MOHAVE DAILY MINER AND KINGMAN DAILY MINER, THE. **VFOAT** Mohave Daily Miner. (Jan. 1, 1984)-. Newspaper. English. da. Mohave Daily Miner and Kingman Daily Miner, PO Box 3909, Kingman AZ 86401. **Tel** (602)753-6397. ***Continues*** *Kingman Daily Miner, 0742-485X.*

US/0164-9078
MOHAVE VALLEY NEWS. ***Title Change.*** (1978)-(19??). Newspaper. English. sw. Mohave Valley News, PO Box 567, Bullhead City AZ 86430. ***Continued by*** *Mohave Valley Daily News, 1061-8589.*

US
NAVAJO TIMES (WINDOW ROCK, ARIZ. : 1987). (NAVAJO TIMES.). **Added/Corp** Navajo Tribe. Vol. 15, No. 1 (May 22, 1987)-. Newspaper. English. Fifty-two times a year. $35.00. Navajo Times, PO Box 310, Window Rock AZ 86515. **Tel** (602)871-6641, (602)870-6642, FAX (602)871-7359. **ED** Tommy Arviso Jr. **Photos**. **Ad Acc, Adv Mgr:** Gene Tapahe, **Tel** (602)871-7358. Full Page (B&W) $882.00. Half Page (B&W) $441.00. Full Page (Color) $952.00. Half Page (Color) $511.00. **Pub. Size:** Standard. available in microform. ***Continues*** *Navajo Times Today, 8750-3468.*

US/0279-3962
NEW TIMES (PHOENIX, ARIZ.). (NEW TIMES.). Vol. 12, No. 33 (Apr. 8-14, 1981)-. Newspaper. English. Fifty-two times a year (Wed.). New Times / The Valley News, PO Box 2510, Phoenix AZ 85002. **Tel** (602)271-0040, FAX (602)495-9954. **ED** Jana Bommersbach. **Bk Rev**. **Ad Acc**. **Circ:** 135,000 (ctrl). available on microfilm and microfiche from University Microfilms International (UMI). ***Continues*** *N.T. (Tempe, Ariz. : 1976), 0273-9836.*
Desc: Local news and arts.

US/0888-3963
ORO VALLEY TERRITORIAL. ***Ceased.*** **VFOAT** Territorial. Vol. 1, No. 1 (Dec. 1985)-(19??). Newspaper. English. wk. The Daily Territorial, PO Box 35250, 1 West Orange Grove, Tucson AZ 85740. **Tel** (602)297-1107, FAX (602)297-6253.

US/8750-1260
ORO VALLEY VOICE. Vol. 11, No. 26 (July 1984)-. Newspaper. English. wk. $7.50. Oro Valley Voice, PO Box 3003, Tucson AZ 85702. **Tel** (602)884-9880. **ED** Theodore C Turpin. ***Continues*** *Oro Valley Voice/Call, 0746-9144.*

US
PHOENIX GAZETTE. (Nov. 14, 1946)-. Newspaper. English. da (Mon. - Sat.). $150.40 Arizona; $224.20 California, Colorado, Nevada, New Mexico and Utah; $263.80 US; $561.20 other. Phoenix Newspapers Inc., 120 East Van Buren Street, Phoenix AZ 85001. **Tel** (602)271-8503, (602)271-8000. **ED** Lynne Holt. **Circ:** 99,532. available on an online database (files 492,635/Full-Text) from DIALOG. Documents available from UMI Article Clearinghouse. ***Continues*** *Phoenix Evening Gazette.*
Ind/Abst Bus. Dateline (Jan. 1, 1990-) [Full Txt.].

US
PRESCOTT EVENING COURIER. Began in Aug. 1920. Newspaper. English. da. Prescott Evening Courier, 147 North Cortez, PO Box 312, Prescott AZ 86301. **ED** Susan Coffroth. **Circ:** 13,074. ***Continues*** *Prescott Morning Courier.*

US/0194-9748
PRESCOTT'S WEEKLY. (19??)-. Newspaper. English. wk. Prescotts Weekly, 129 North Cortez, Prescott AZ 86301. **Tel** (602)778-3100. **Ad Acc**.

US/0739-0122
QUA'TOQTI. [Qua' toqti]. **VFOAT** Eagle's Cry. **VAT** Qua' Toqti. Began with July 19, 1973 issue. Newspaper. English. wk. $17.00 US; $25.00 other. Qua'Toqti, PO Box 266, Kykotsmovi AZ 86039. **Tel** (602)734-2425. **ED** Abbot Sekaquaptewa.

US/0888-0271
SCOTTSDALE PROGRESS. **VFOAT** Scottsdale (Ariz.) Progress. (198?)-. Newspaper. English. da (Mon.-Sat.). $109.20 Arizona; $124.80 other. Scottsdale Publishing Inc, PO Box 1150, Scottsdale AZ 85252. **Tel** (602)941-2300. **ED** Jonathon Marshall. **Circ:** 18,981. ***Continues*** *Scottsdale Daily Progress.*

US/1044-7555
SEDONA RED ROCK NEWS. **VFOAT** Red Rock News. (19??)-. Newspaper. English. wk. $26.00 Sedona; $37.00 other. Sedona Red Rock News, PO Box 619, Sedona AZ 86336. **Tel** (602)282-7795, FAX (602)282-6011. **ED** Tom Brossart. **Bk Rev**. **Ad Acc**. **Circ:** 7,200 (ctrl). ***Continues*** *Red Rock News.*

US/8750-3891
SIERRA VISTA HERALD. **VFOAT** Sierra Vista Herald and Bisbee Review. (1984)-. Newspaper. English. da (Sun.-Fri.). $93.60 Cochise county, Arizona; $95.00 other Arizona; $100.00 other. Sierra Vista Herald, 102 Fab Avenue, Sierra Vista AZ 85635. **Tel** (602)458-9440. **ED** H. Lee James. **Circ:** 5,531. ***Continues*** *Sierra Vista Herald-Dispatch, 0746-0422.*

US
SOL (PHOENIX, ARIZ. : 1939). (EL SOL.). Began in (1939)-. Newspaper. Spanish. wk. $18.00. El Sol, 4001 North 3rd Street, Suite 465, Phoenix AZ 85012. **Tel** (602)234-3464. **ED** Orona Marcos. **Bk Rev**. **Ad Acc**. **Circ:** 15,000 (ctrl).
Desc: Articles and information of national interest, for the Hispanic public as well as local, from medical, editorial and sports, through horoscope and spectacles.

US
TEMPE DAILY NEWS. Sept. 17, 1887-. Newspaper. English. da. Tempe Daily News, Box 3099, Tempe AZ 85281. **Tel** (602)829-4700. **ED** Hal DeKeyser. **Circ:** 10,534. ***Continues*** *Salt River Valley News.*

US
TIMES OF FOUNTAIN HILLS, THE. English. wk (Published Thursday). $19.00 Maricopa county, $26.50 US, $55.00 other. The Times of Fountain Hills, PO Box 17869, Fountain Hills AZ 85269. **Tel** (602)837-1925.

US/0899-6687
TODAY NEWS. ***Title Change.*** (19??)-(19??). Newspaper. English. tw. Today News, 1890 W Acoma Blvrd, Lake Havasu City AZ 86403. **Tel** (602)855-6397. ***Continues*** *Today on the Colorado River, 0745-8657.* ***Continued by*** *Today's Daily News, 1068-1876.*

US/1068-1876
TODAY'S DAILY NEWS. (LAKE HAVASU CITY). (TODAY'S DAILY NEWS.). (19??)-. Newspaper. English. da (Tues.- Fri. and Sun.). $52.00 local, $95.00 other. Today's Daily News, 1890 West Acoma Boulevard, Lake Havasu City AZ 86403-2959. **Tel** (602)855-6397. **ED** Stan Usinowicz. **Ad Acc, Adv Mgr:** John Schneider. Full Page (B&W) $6.95 per cubic inch. Half Page (B&W) $6.95 per cubic inch. Full Page (Color) Add $80.00. Half Page (Color) $6.95 per cubic inch. **Pub. Size:** Standard. **Wire Svcs.:** AP. **Circ:** 8,250. ***Continues*** *Today News, 0899-6687.*

US/0888-5478
TUCSON CITIZEN (1977). (TUCSON CITIZEN.). Vol. 107, No. 130 (June 1, 1977)-. Newspaper. English. da. $78.00. Tucson Citizen, 4850 South Park Avenue, PO Box 26887, Tucson AZ 85726. **Tel** (602)573-4511, (800)695-4492. **ED** C. Donald Hatfield, Ricardo Pimental (Managing Editor). **Bk Rev**. **Photos**. **Ad Acc, Adv Mgr:** Sam Adkins, **Tel** (602)573-4398. Full Page (B&W) $5910.78. Half Page (B&W) $2955.39. Full Page (Color) $7044.78. Half Page (Color) $4089.39. **Pub. Size:** Standard. **Wire Svcs.:** GN, AP, UPI. **Circ:** 55,796. available on an online database (file 635/Full-Text) from DIALOG. Documents available from UMI Article Clearinghouse. ***Continues*** *Tucson Daily Citizen.*
Ind/Abst Bus. Dateline (Dec. 10, 1991-) [Full Txt.].

US/0745-5321
VALLEY-FOOTHILLS NEWS, THE. **VFOAT** Valley & Foothills News. Newspaper. English. wk. Valley-Foothills News, 11351 Foothills Boulevard, Yuma AZ 85365. **Tel** (602)342-1332. **ED** Michael R Bush. **Ad Acc**. **Circ:** 10,000. ***Continues*** *Valley and Foothills News.*
Desc: Free-distribution newspaper covering east Yuma, Mesa and Arizona counties.

US
VERDE INDEPENDENT, THE. (1948)-. Newspaper. English. sw (104 per year). $35.00 Arizona; $42.00 other. Western Newspapers, PO Box 429, Cottonwood AZ 86326. **Tel** (602)634-2241. **ED** Dan Engler. **LC** 7070. **Ad Acc, Adv Mgr:** Kathy Bartlett. **Circ:** 4,900 (ctrl).

US
WILLIAMS NEWS. (1891)-. Newspaper. English. wk. $18.50 Arizona; $24.50 other. Williams News, 118 South 3rd Street, PO Box 667, Williams AZ 86046. **Tel** (602)635-4426, FAX (602)635-4785. **ED** Jerry Herrmann. **LC** 7086. **Bk Rev**, (Qty: 10). **Photos**. **Ad Acc, Adv Mgr:** Joyce McNelly. Full Page (B&W) $882.00. Half Page (B&W) $441.00. Full Page (Color) $1,062.00. Half Page (Color) $1,062. **Pub. Size:** Standard. **Circ:** 5,020 (ctrl).

US/8750-5711
WINSLOW MAIL, THE. (1932)-. Newspaper. English. sw. $30.00 Winslow; $36.00 Arizona; $44.00 other. Navajo County Publishers Inc., PO Box AW, Winslow AZ 86047. **Tel** (602)289-2467. **Circ:** 6,400. ***Continues*** *Winslow Daily Mail.*

ARKANSAS

US
ADVANCE-MONTICELLONIAN. VFOAT Advance Monticellonian. (1920)-. Newspaper. English. wk. Advance Monticellonian, 314 North Main, PO Box 486, Monticello AR 71655-0486. **Tel** (501)367-5325. ***Formed by the union of*** *Advance (Monticello, Ark.)* ***and*** *Monticellonian.*

US/0882-2522
AMERICAN NATIVE PRESS. Added/Corp American Native Press Archives. American Indian and Alaska Native Periodicals Research Clearinghouse. American Indian and Alaska Native Newspapers and Periodicals Research Project. University of Arkansas at Little Rock. No. 1 (Fall 1983)-. Periodical. English. Three times a year. Free. American Native Press, 2801 South University Avenue, Little Rock AR 72204. **Tel** (501)569-3610. **LC** PN4883; .A44. **DD** 071.

US/1060-4332
ARKANSAS DEMOCRAT GAZETTE. VFOAT Arkansas Democrat-Gazette. (Oct. 19, 1991)-. Newspaper. English. da. Arkansas Democrat Gazette, PO Box 8008, Little Rock AR 72203. **Tel** (501)378-3456, (800)846-1121. available on microfilm from University Microfilms International (UMI). ***Formed by the union of*** *Arkansas Democrat (Little Rock, Ark. : Daily)* ***and*** *Arkansas Gazette (Little Rock, Ark. : 1889).* **Ind/Abst** PROMT.

US
ASHLEY NEWS OBSERVER, THE. Vol. 40, No. 24 (June 11, 1980)-. Newspaper. English. wk. $18.00 Ashley County; $30.00 other. Ashley News Observer, 102 Pine, PO Box 798, Crossett AR 71635. **Tel** (501)364-5186. **ED** Larry Johnson, Larry Wittnebert. **Photos. Ad Acc, Adv Mgr:** Charlotte Johnson. Full Page (B&W) $784.32. Half Page (B&W) $392.16. Full Page (Color) $884.32. Half Page (Color) $492.16. **Pub. Size:** Broadsheet. ***Continues*** *News Observer (Crossett, Ark.).*

US
AUGUSTA ADVOCATE, THE. Vol. 97, No. 25 (Aug. 2, 1956)-. Newspaper. English. wk. Augusta Advocate, 116 Main, PO Box 494, Augusta AR 72006-0494. **Tel** (501)731-2561. ***Continues*** *Advocate (Augusta, Ark.).*

US
BANNER-NEWS, THE. VFOAT Banner News; Daily Banner-News. 99th Year, No. 47 (Jan 5, 1977)-. Newspaper. English. da. Magnolia Banner News, 134 South Washington, Magnolia AR 71753-3523. **Tel** (501)234-5130, FAX (501)234-2551. **ED** Chris Gilliam. **Ad Acc, Adv Mgr:** Susan Carmichael. **Circ:** 5,000. ***Continues*** *Daily Banner-News.*

US
BATESVILLE GUARD. VFOAT Batesville Daily Guard. (1924)-. Newspaper. English. da. Batesville Guard, 258 West Main Street, Batesville AR 72501-6730. **Tel** (501)793-2383, FAX (501)793-9268. **ED** Jeff Porter. **Ad Acc. Circ:** 9,703. ***Continues*** *Batesville Daily Guard.*

US/0745-7707
BAXTER BULLETIN. Vol. 1, No. 1 (Dec. 20, 1901)-. Newspaper. English. da (Mon.-Sat.). $65.00. Baxter County Newspapers Inc, 16 West 6th Steet, Mountain Home AR 72653. **Tel** (501)425-3133, FAX (501)425-5091. **ED** Bob Quarles, Linda Leicht (Managing Editor). **Bk Rev. Photos. Ad Acc, Adv Mgr:** Eddie Majeste. Full Page (B&W) $835.38. Half Page (B&W) $417.69. Full Page (Color) $925.38. Half Page (Color) $507.69. **Pub. Size:** Broadsheet. **Wire Svcs.:** AP. **Circ:** 10,500 daily.

US
BEEBE NEWS, THE. (1948)-. Newspaper. English. wk. Beebe News, PO Box O, Beebe AR 72012. **Tel** (501)882-5414.

US
BENTON COUNTY DAILY RECORD. Vol. 103, No. 195 (Aug. 28, 1988)-. Newspaper. English. da. Benton County Daily Record, 209 NW A Street, Bentonville AR 72712-5291. **Tel** (501)271-3713, FAX (501)273-7777. **ED** Susan Scantlin. **Ad Acc. Circ:** 8,100. ***Continues*** *Benton County Daily Democrat.*

US
BENTON COURIER, THE. Vol. 95, No. 164 (Aug. 19, 1971)-. Newspaper. English. da. Benton Courier, 1 Courier Place, Benton AR 72015. **Tel** (501)778-8228, FAX (501)776-1230. **ED** Judy Smith. **Ad Acc, Adv Mgr:** Rebecca Windburn. **Circ:** 9,600. ***Continues*** *Benton Daily Courier.*

US
BRINKLEY ARGUS, THE. VFOAT Brinkley Sunday Argus. (1883)-. Newspaper. English. sw. Brinkley Newspapers, 308 West Cedar, Brinkley AR 72021-2710. **Tel** (501)734-1056, FAX (501)734-2302. **Circ:** 3,400. ***Absorbed*** *Citizen (Brinkley, Ark.).*

US
CAMDEN NEWS, THE. Vol. 10, No. 125 (Sept. 22, 1929)-. Newspaper. English. da. $65.00 Ouschita County; $68.00 other. Camden News, PO Box 798, Camden AR 71701. **Tel** (501)836-8192, FAX (501)837-1414. **ED** James Waller. **Photos. Ad Acc, Adv Mgr:** Sue Parnell. Full Page (B&W) $850.11. Half Page (B&W) $425.06. Full Page (Color) $940.11. Half Page (Color) $515.06. **Circ:** 5,520. ***Continues*** *Camden Evening News.*

US
CONWAY COUNTY PETIT JEAN COUNTRY HEADLIGHT. VFOAT Petit Jean Country Headlight. Vol. 103, No. 11 (July 28, 1982)-. Newspaper. English. wk. Conway Petit Jean Country Headlight, PO Box 540, Morrilton AR 72110-0540. **Tel** (501)354-2451. ***Continues*** *Petit Jean Country Headlight (Morrilton, Ark. : 1973).*

US/0745-6956
COURIER DEMOCRAT. ***Title Change.*** (1983)-(1994). Newspaper. English. da (Sun.-Fri.). Courier Democrat, 201 East 2nd Street, Russellville AR 72801. **Tel** (501)968-5252. **ED** Bill Newsom. ***Continues*** *Daily Courier-Democrat.* ***Continued by*** *Courier (Russellville, Ark.), 1075-1866.*

US/0746-9527
COURIER NEWS. (THE COURIER NEWS.). **VFOAT** Sunday's Courier News. Vol. 63, No. 85 (June 20, 1968)-. Newspaper. English. ds. $90.60. Blytheville Courier News, Box 1108, Blytheville AR 72316-1108. **Tel** (501)763-4461, FAX (501)763-6874. **ED** Cynthia Jardon (editor-in-chief) and Sheila McCall (managing editor). **Photos. Ad Acc, Adv Mgr:** Christine Moore. Full Page (B&W) $677.25. Half Page (B&W) $330.75. Full Page (Color) $787.25. Half Page (Color) $440.75. **Pub. Size:** Broadsheet. **Wire Svcs.:** AP. **Circ:** 5,600. available on an online database (file 635/Full-Text) from DIALOG; available in microform from Southwest Micropublishing International. ***Continues*** *Blytheville Courier News.*

US
DAILY CITIZEN, THE. 128th Year, No. 5 (Sept. 6, 1981)-. Newspaper. English. da. $81.00. Daily Citizen / Searcy, PO Box 1379, 3000 East Race Street, Searcy AR 72143. **Tel** (501)268-8621. **ED** Tommy Jackson. **Bk Rev,** (Qty: 52). **Photos. Ad Acc, Adv Mgr:** Phil Weaver. Full Page (B&W) $1,228.08. Half Page (B&W) $614.04. Full Page (Color) $1,353.08. Half Page (Color) $739.04. **Pub. Size:** Standard. **Wire Svcs.:** AP. **Circ:** 7,300 (evening), 7,600 (Sunday). available in microform. ***Continues*** *Searcy Daily Citizen.*

US
DAILY SIFTINGS HERALD, THE. VFOAT Siftings Herald. Vol. 8, No. 184 (June 25, 1929)-. Newspaper. English. da. Southern Standard, 205 South 26th Street, Arkadelphia AR 71923. **Tel** (501)246-5525. **ED** Lewis Delavan. **Ad Acc, Adv Mgr:** Tim Hart. **Circ:** 3,514. ***Continues*** *Siftings Herald (Arkadelphia, Ark. : Daily);* ***Absorbed*** *Southern Standard (Arkadelphia, Ark.).*

US/8750-5274
DAILY WORLD (HELENA, ARK.), THE. (THE DAILY WORLD.). (19??)-. Newspaper. English. da (except Saturday). $60.00 per year. Daily World / Helena, AR, PO Box 340, Helena AR 72342. **Tel** (501)338-9181, FAX (501)338-9184. **ED** Bill Glenn. **Bk Rev,** (Qty: 20). **Photos. Ad Acc, Adv Mgr:** Ann Puckett. Full Page (B&W) $548.10. Half Page (B&W) $302.40. Full Page (Color) $633.10. Half Page (Color) $387.40. **Pub. Size:** Broadsheet. **Wire Svcs.:** AP. **Circ:** 5,500 (paid). available on microfilm and microfiche. ***Continues*** *Helena-West Helena World.*

US
DE QUEEN BEE. VFOAT Daily Citizen; De Queen Advertiser. (1897)-. Newspaper. English (Choctaw). wk. De Queen Bee, PO Box 1000, De Queen AR 71832-1000. **Tel** (501)642-2111, FAX (501)642-3138. **ED** Billy Ray McKelvy. **Ad Acc. Circ:** 2,100. ***Absorbed*** *Times-Record (Horatio, Ark.)* ***and*** *Horatio Times.*

US
DUMAS CLARION, THE. (1929)-. Newspaper. English. wk. $15.00. Dumas Clarion, PO Box C, Dumas AR 71639-0220. **Tel** (501)382-4925, FAX (501)382-6461. **ED** Charlotte Schexwayder (Editor-in-Chief) and Terry Hawkins (Managing Editor). **Photos. Ad Acc, Adv Mgr:** Glenda Ward. Full Page (B&W) $580.50. Half Page (B&W) $290.25. Full Page (Color) $680.50. Half Page (Color) $390.25. **Pub. Size:** Standard. **Circ:** 4,000.

US
EL DORADO NEWS-TIMES. VFOAT El Dorado News Times. (May 1, 1974)-. Newspaper. English. da. El Dorado News Times, 111 North Madison Avenue, El Dorado AR 71730-6124. **Tel** (501)862-6611, FAX (501)862-5226. **ED** George Arnold. **Ad Acc, Adv Mgr:** Betty Pattings. **Circ:** 11,238. ***Formed by the union of*** *El Dorado Daily News* ***and*** *El Dorado Times (El Dorado, Ark. : Daily).*

US
ENGLAND DEMOCRAT, THE. (1934)-. Newspaper. English. wk. England Democrat, PO Drawer 250, England AR 72046-0250. **Tel** (501)842-3111.

US
EVENING TIMES. Vol. 1, No. 1 (June 17, 1957)-. Newspaper. English. da. $76.00. Crittenden Publishing Company, PO Box 459, West Memphis AR 72303. **Tel** (501)735-1010, FAX (501)735-1020. **ED** Kay Brockwell. **Bk Rev,** (Qty: 5/year). **Photos. Ad Acc, Adv Mgr:** Bob Bruce. **Wire Svcs.:** AP. available in microform from Bell & Howell.

US/8750-4995
FORDYCE NEWS-ADVOCATE. VFOAT Fordyce News Advocate; News Advocate; News-Advocate. Vol. 40, No. 32 (Feb. 1, 1945)-. Newspaper. English. wk. $14.00. Fordyce News-Advocate, 304 Spring Street, PO Box 559, Fordyce AR 71742. **Tel** (501)352-3144. **ED** William R. Whitehead Jr. **Photos. Ad Acc, Adv Mgr:** Ann Mathews. Full Page (B&W) $630.00. Half Page (B&W) $315.00. **Pub. Size:** Standard. **Circ:** 3,186 paid. available on microfilm. ***Formed by the union of*** *Advocate (Fordyce, Ark.)* ***and*** *Fordyce Weekly News (Fordyce, Ark. : 1942).*

US
GLENWOOD HERALD, THE. (1925)-. Newspaper. English. wk. Glenwood Herald, 204 Broadway, PO Box L, Glenwood AR 71943. **Tel** (501)356-2111.

US
GRAVETTE NEWS-HERALD, THE. VFOAT Gravette News Herald. Vol. 15, No. 15 (Dec. 18, 1908)-Vol. 20, no. 17 (Dec. 26, 1913); 20th Year, No. 18 (Jan 2, 1914)-. Newspaper. English. wk. $21.00 Benton County Arkansas, MacDonald County Missouri, Delaware County Oklahoma; $26.00 other. Gravette News Herald, Box 640, Gravette AR 72736. **Tel** (501)787-5300. ***Continues*** *Gravett News.*

US
GREEN FOREST TRIBUNE, THE. Vol. 98, No. 76 (Aug. 24, 1988)-. Newspaper. English. wk. Carroll County Newspapers, PO Box 232, Berryville AR 72616. **Tel** (501)423-6636, FAX (501)423-6640. **ED** Ken O'Toole. **Circ:** 1,825. ***Continues*** *Tribune (Green Forest, Ark. : 1987).*

US
HARRISON DAILY TIMES. 11th Year, No. 11 (October 12, 1929)-. Newspaper. English. da. Daily Times / Harrison, PO Box 40, Harrison AR 72601. **Tel** (501)741-2325. ***Continues*** *Daily Times (Harrison, Ark.).*

US/1061-9542
HERALD-LEADER (SILOAM SPRINGS, ARK.). (THE HERALD-LEADER.). **VFOAT** Herald Leader. Vol. 100, No. 45 (Sept. 4, 1991)-. Newspaper. English. sw. The Herald-Leader, 101 Mt. Olive, Siloam Springs AR 72761. ***Formed by the union of*** *Herald and Democrat (Siloam Springs, Ark. : 1916)* ***and*** *News Leader (Siloam Springs, Ark.).*

US/0891-5601
JACKSONVILLE NEWS. ***Title Change.*** **VFOAT** News. Vol. 29 No. 35 (Oct. 8, 1986)-(19??). Newspaper. English. da. Jacksonville Patriot, PO Box 5329, Jacksonville AR 72078. **Tel** (501)982-6506. **ED** Bryce Marshall. **Circ:** 17,536. ***Continues*** *Jacksonville Daily News (Jacksonville, Ark. : 1982).* ***Continued by*** *Jacksonville Patriot, 1064-7260.*

US/1064-7260
JACKSONVILLE PATRIOT. (19??)-. Newspaper. English. da. $36.00. Jacksonville Patriot, PO Box 5329, Jacksonville AR 72078. **Tel** (501)982-6506. **ED** Mark Magie, Bill Rutherford (Managing Editor). **Bk Rev,** (Qty: 12). **Photos. Ad Acc, Adv Mgr:** Susie Magie. **Pub. Size:** Broadsheet. ***Continues*** *Jacksonville News, 0891-5601.*

US
JONESBORO SUN, THE. 66th Year, No. 105 (Apr. 7, 1968)-. Newspaper. English. da. Jonesboro Sun Newspaper, PO Box 1249, Jonesboro AR 72403. **Tel** (501)935-5525. Documents available from UMI Article Clearinghouse. ***Continues*** *Jonesboro Evening Sun.* **Ind/Abst** Bus. Dateline (April 2, 1992-) [Full Txt.].

US
MALVERN DAILY RECORD. Vol. 1 No. 1 (Oct. 7, 1916)-. Newspaper. English. da (Mon.-Fri.). $69.00. Malvern Daily Record, 219 Locust Street, PO Box 70, Malvern AR 72104. **Tel** (501)337-7523, FAX (501)337-1226. **ED** Stephanie Brawner. **LC** 7087-X. **Bk Rev,** (Qty: 4). **Photos. Ad Acc, Adv Mgr:** Richard Folds. Full Page (B&W) $806.25. Half Page (B&W) $428.40. Full Page (Color) $886.25. Half Page (Color)

$508.40. **Pub. Size:** Broadsheet. **Wire Svcs.:** AP. **Circ:** 6,000. available on microfilm from Arkansas History Commission.

US/0747-1513
MENA STAR, THE. **VFOAT** Mena Star. Weekend Edition. Vol. 88, No. 1 (Jan. 5, 1986)-. Newspaper. English. da (Tues.-Fri.). Mena Star, Box 1307, 501 Mena Street, Mena AR 71953. **Tel** (501)394-1900. **ED** Derwood Brett. **Circ:** 4,550. ***Continues*** *Mena Evening Star.*

US/1053-9689
MORNING NEWS (SPRINGDALE, ARK.), THE. (MORNING NEWS.). Vol. 104, No. 5 (May 1, 1990)-. Newspaper. English. da. Springdale News, 514 East Emma Avenue, Springdale AR 72764. **Tel** (501)751-6200. ***Continues*** *Springdale News, 0745-7715.*

US
MOUNTAIN ECHO, THE. **VFOAT** Mountain Echo and the Arkansas Miner. Vol. 1, No. 1 (Mar. 5, 1886)-. Newspaper. English. wk. Mountain Echo, PO Box 528, Yellville AR 72687-0528. **Tel** (501)449-4257, FAX (501)449-6605. **ED** Ray Davis. **Ad Acc, Adv Mgr:** Tony Mack. **Circ:** 2,500. ***Absorbed*** *Arkansas Miner.*

US
NEVADA COUNTY PICAYUNE. ***Title Change.*** (Oct. 1885)-?. Newspaper. English. wk. Nevada County Picayune, 125 West Main Street, Prescott AR 71857. **Tel** (501)887-2002. **ED** John Ragsdale. **Circ:** 2,800. ***Continues*** *Nevada Picayune.* ***Merged with*** *Weekly Times (Prescott, Ark.)* ***to form*** *Times-Picayune (Prescott, Ark.).*

US/1066-3355
NORTHWEST ARKANSAS TIMES (FAYETTEVILLE, AR.). (NORTHWEST ARKANSAS TIMES.). Vol. 77, No. 195 (July 8, 1937)-. Newspaper. English. da. $78.00. Northwest Arkansas Times, Drawer D, Fayetteville AR 72701. **Tel** (501)442-6242, FAX (501)442-5477. **ED** John H. Walker. **Bk Rev. Photos. Ad Acc, Adv Mgr:** Carmen Collen, **Tel** (501)447-1735. Full Page (B&W) $1,207.44. Half Page (B&W) $710.15. Full Page (Color) $1,345.44. Half Page (Color) $848.15. **Pub. Size:** Standard. **Wire Svcs.:** AP. **Circ:** 13,960. available in microform from Crest Information Technologies. ***Continues*** *Fayetteville Daily Democrat;* ***Absorbed*** *Progressive Star; Lincoln Sun.*

US
PINE BLUFF COMMERCIAL. Began with Aug. 1, 1887 issue. Newspaper. English. da. Pine Bluff Commercial, 421 West Barraque, PO Box 7806, Pine Bluff AR 71611. **Tel** (501)534-8803. **ED** E Freeman III. **Circ:** 21,085. available on microfilm. ***Continues*** *Pine Bluff Weekly Commercial.*

US
POCAHONTAS STAR HERALD. (1907)-. Newspaper. English. wk. $11.00 local; $22.00 other. Pocahontas Star Herald, 109 North Van Bibber, Pocahontas AR 72455. **Tel** (501)892-4451, FAX (501)892-4453. **ED** Kathy Cheyne. **Photos. Ad Acc, Adv Mgr:** Becky Blisener, **Tel** (501)892-4451. Full Page (B&W) $403.77. Half Page (B&W) $216.72. Full Page (Color) $503.77. Half Page (Color) $316.72. **Circ:** 5,780 (paid). ***Formed by the union of*** *Pocahontas Star* ***and*** *News-Herald (Pocahontas, Ark.);* ***Absorbed*** *Randolph County Clipper.*

US/0885-9086
PRESS ARGUS-COURIER. **VFOAT** Press Argus Courier. Newspaper. English. sw. $24.00. Press Argus-Courier, 100 North 11th Street, PO Box 369, Van Buren AR 72956. **Tel** (501)474-5215. **ED** Glen A Phillips Jr. **Ad Acc. Circ:** 8,000. ***Continues*** *Press Argus, 0746-3219.*
Desc: Primary focus on Crawford County's communities and residents.

US
SENTINEL-RECORD, THE. **VFOAT** Sentinel Record. (1900)-. Newspaper. English. da. $8.50 (per month). Sentinel-Record Incorporated, PO Box 580, Hot Springs National Park AR 71902. **Tel** (501)623-7711, FAX (501)623-2984. **ED** Melinda Gassaway (Editor-in-Chief) and Isabelle Peregrin (Managing Editor). **Bk Rev. Photos. Ad Acc, Adv Mgr:** Floyd Emerson. Full Page (B&W) $1,388.04. Half Page (B&W) $694.02. Full Page (Color) $1,613.04. Half Page (Color) $919.02. **Pub. Size:** Standard. **Wire Svcs.:** AP. available in microform. ***Formed by the union of*** *Morning Sentinel (Hot Springs, Ark.)* ***and*** *Hot Springs Record.*

US
SHERIDAN HEADLIGHT, THE. **VFOAT** Sheridan Weekly Headlight. (1927)-. Newspaper. English. wk. Sheridan Headlight, 101 East Center Street, Sheridan AR 72150. **Tel** (501)942-2142, FAX (942)2143. **ED** Melody Smith. **Ad Acc. Circ:** 3,475. ***Continues*** *Sheridan Weekly Headlight.*

US
SOUTHWEST TIMES RECORD. Vol. 87, No. 208 (May 18, 1969)-. Newspaper. English. da. $103.80 (daily edition only) Arkansas and Oklahoma; $132.60 (daily edition only) other; $133.20 (daily and Sunday editions) Oklahoma and Arkansas; $163.20 (daily and Sunday editions) other. Southwest Times Record, 920 Rogers Avenue, PO Box 1359, Fort Smith AR 72902. **Tel** (501)785-7767. **ED** Jack Moseley (phone: (501)785-7742). **Ad Acc, Adv Mgr:** Mr. Beasley, **Tel** (501)785-7726. **Circ:** 42,541. ***Formed by the union of*** *Southwest American* ***and*** *Fort Smith Times-Record.*

US
STAR PROGRESS, THE. **VFOAT** Star-Progress. Vol. 57, No. 5 (Oct. 9, 1930)-. Newspaper. English. wk. Berryville Star Progress, Oakview Drive, Berryville AR 72616. **Tel** (501)423-6636, FAX (501)423-6640. **ED** Ken O'Toole. **Bk Rev. Ad Acc, Adv Mgr:** Judith Hurler. **Circ:** 3,900. ***Continues*** *North Arkansas Star (Berryville, Ark. : 1921).*

US
STONE COUNTY CITIZEN. Vol. 1, No. 1 (Mar. 12, 1986)-. Newspaper. English. wk. Stone County Citizen, PO Box 6, Mountain View AR 72560. **Tel** (501)269-8626.

US/1066-3983
STONE COUNTY LEADER (1956). (STONE COUNTY LEADER.). **VFOAT** Stone County Leader and the Mountain View Herald. Vol. 5, No. 28 (Oct. 18, 1956)-. Newspaper. English. wk. Stone County Leader, 103 West Main Street, Mountain View AR 72560. **Tel** (501)269-3841, FAX (501)269-2171. **ED** James R. Fraser. **Ad Acc. Circ:** 2,700. ***Continues*** *Stone County Leader-and the Mountain View Herald.*

US
STUTTGART DAILY LEADER, THE. Vol. 105-60 (Nov. 6, 1989)-. Newspaper. English. da. Stuttgart Daily Leader, 111 West Sixth Street, Stuttgart AR 72160-4243. **Tel** (501)673-8533, FAX (501)673-3671. **ED** Stephen Bell. **Ad Acc, Adv Mgr:** Gene Austin. **Circ:** 4,188. ***Continues*** *Daily Leader (Stuttgart, Ark. : 1982).*

US/1050-5105
SUN-TIMES (HEBER SPRINGS, ARK.). (SUN-TIMES.). **VFOAT** Sun Times; Cleburne County Sun-Times. 102nd Year, No. 7 (Apr. 4, 1990)-. Newspaper. English. Twice a week. $24.00 (in county), $34.00 (out of county). Sun Times / Heber Springs, PO Box 669, Heber Springs AR 72543-0190. **Tel** (501)362-2425, FAX (501)362-5877. **ED** Randy Kemp. **Bk Rev. Photos. Ad Acc, Adv Mgr:** John Jennings. Full Page (B&W) $693.00. Half Page (B&W) $347.00. Full Page (Color) $738.00. Half Page (Color) $392.00. **Pub. Size:** Broadsheet. **Wire Svcs.:** AP. **Circ:** 5,100 paid. ***Formed by the union of*** *Arkansas Sun* ***and*** *Cleburne County Times (Heber Springs, Ark. : 1940).*

US
TEXARKANA GAZETTE. (1926)-. Newspaper. English. ds. $114.00. Texarkana Gazette, PO Box 621, Texarkana AR 75501. **Tel** (903)794-3311, FAX (903)792-7183. **ED** Les Minor. **Photos. Ad Acc, Adv Mgr:** Rick Meredith. Full Page (B&W) $1896.30. Half Page (B&W) $955.50. Full Page (Color) $2061.30. Half Page (Color) $1120.50. **Wire Svcs.:** SH, AP. **Circ:** 33,203 (ctrl). available on microfilm from Microfilm Center, Inc. ***Absorbed*** *Four States Press;* ***Absorbed in part*** *Texarkana Press.*

US
TIMES DISPATCH, THE. **VFOAT** Times Dispatch and the Walnut Ridge Blade. (1910)-. Newspaper. English. wk. Times Dispatch, 225 West Main Street, Walnut Ridge AR 72476. **Tel** (501)886-2464. **ED** John Bland. **LC** 7087-X. **Circ:** 6,810. ***Absorbed*** *Blade (Walnut Ridge, Ark.); Lawrence County News.*

US
TIMES-HERALD (FORREST CITY, ARK.). (TIMES-HERALD.). **VFOAT** Times Herald. 113-84 (Mar. 1, 1984)-. Newspaper. English. da. $48.00 Forrest City & surrounding areas; $69.50 other. Forrest City Times Herald, PO Box 1699, Forrest City AR 72335. **Tel** (501)633-3130, FAX (501)633-0599. **ED** Weston Lewey. **Ad Acc, Adv Mgr:** Truman Beasley. **Circ:** 41,667. ***Continues*** *Forrest City Times-Herald (Forrest City, Ark. : 1980).*

US/8750-3921
TIMES OF NORTHEAST BENTON COUNTY, THE. **VFOAT** Times. 19th Year, No. 39 (Sept. 26, 1984)-. Newspaper. English. wk. Times of Northeast Benton County, PO Box 25, Pea Ridge AR 72751. **Tel** (501)451-1196. **ED** E. Calvin Beisner. ***Continues*** *Times of Pea Ridge Country.*

US
TIMES-PICAYUNE, THE. ***Title Change.*** **VFOAT** Times Picayune. Newspaper. English. wk. Nevada County Picayune, 125 West Main Street, Prescott AR 71857. **Tel** (501)887-2002. Documents available from UMI Article Clearinghouse. ***Formed by the union of*** *Weekly Times (Prescott, Ark.)* ***and*** *Nevada County Picayune (Prescott, Ark. : 1885).* ***Continued by*** *Nevada County Picayune (Prescott, Ark. : 1906).*
Ind/Abst Newsp. Abstr.

US
TRI-CITY TRIBUNE. **VFOAT** Tri City Tribune. Vol. 1, No. 1 (Nov. 10, 1988)-. Newspaper. English. wk. $18.00. Tri City Tribune, PO Box 490, Marked Tree AR 72365-0490. **Tel** (501)358-2993. **ED** John Boxley. **Bk Rev,** (Qty: 12). **Photos. Ad Acc, Adv Mgr:** Judy Chase. Full Page (B&W) $415.80. Half Page (B&W) $207.90. **Pub. Size:** Standard. **Circ:** 2,000. ***Continues*** *Marked Tree Tribune.*

US
TRUMANN DEMOCRAT, THE. (1931)-. Newspaper. English. wk. Trumann Democrat, 217 Highway 63 South, Trumann AR 72472-3503. **Tel** (501)483-6317, FAX (501)483-6031. **ED** Charles Nix. **Bk Rev,** (Qty: 20). **Photos. Ad Acc, Adv Mgr:** John Hampton. Full Page (B&W) $383.00. Half Page (B&W) $215.00. Full Page (Color) $483.00. Half Page (Color) $315.00.

US
VAN BUREN COUNTY DEMOCRAT. **VFOAT** Van Buren Co. Democrat. (1909)-. Newspaper. English. wk. $12.00 Van Buren County; $15.00 others in Arkansas; $20.00 others. Van Buren County Democrat, 114 South Court, PO Box 119, Clinton AR 72031. **Tel** (501)745-5175, FAX (501)745-8865. **ED** Jay Jackson. **Photos. Ad Acc.** Full Page (B&W) $580.50. Half Page (B&W) $292.50. Full Page (Color) $680.50. Half Page (Color) $392.50. **Pub. Size:** Standard. **Circ:** 4,800. ***Absorbed*** *Van Buren County News.*

US/8750-5177
WHITE COUNTY RECORD (JUDSONIA, ARK.). (THE WHITE COUNTY RECORD.). Began in 1878. Newspaper. English. wk. $10.00. White County Record, PO Box 578, Judsonia AR 72081. **Tel** (501)724-3863. **ED** Gregg Cornett. **Ad Acc. Circ:** 1,850 (ctrl). available on microfilm. ***Formed by the union of*** *Judsonia Weekly Advance* ***and*** *Bald Knob Eagle.*

US
WHITE RIVER JOURNAL. Vol. 1, No. 1 (Aug. 15, 1907)-. Newspaper. English. wk. $15.00. White River Journal, PO Box 1051, Des Arc AR 72040-1051. **Tel** (501)256-4254. **ED** Dean L. Walls. **Photos. Ad Acc, Adv Mgr:** Dean Walls. Full Page (B&W) $588.00. Half Page (B&W) $294.00. Full Page (Color) $688.00. Half Page (Color) $394.00. **Pub. Size:** Broadsheet. **Circ:** 2,700. available in microform from Arkansas History Commission.

US
WYNNE PROGRESS, THE. **VFOAT** Weekly Progress; Weekly Star-Progress. (1904)-. Newspaper. English. wk. $21.50. Wynne Progress, 702 North Falls Boulevard, PO Box 308, Wynne AR 72396-2209. **Tel** (501)238-2375. **ED** David Nichol. **Photos. Ad Acc, Adv Mgr:** Brandon Boger. Full Page (B&W) $756.00. Half Page (B&W) $378.00. Full Page (Color) $876.00. Half Page (Color) $498.00. **Pub. Size:** Broadsheet. **Circ:** 4,300. available in microform.

CALIFORNIA

US/0164-5234
20 DE MAYO. **VAT** Veinte de Mayo. (1969)-. Newspaper. Spanish. wk. $30.00. 20 de Mayo Spanish Newspaper, 1824 Sunset Boulevard, Suite 202, Los Angeles CA 90026. **Tel** (213)483-8511, FAX (213)483-6474. **ED** Abel Perez (Editor-in-Chief) and Orlando Atienza (Managing Editor). **Bk Rev,** (Qty: 10). **Photos. Ad Acc, Adv Mgr:** P. Cacheiro. Full Page (B&W) $800.00. Half Page (B&W) $400.00. **Pub. Size:** Tabloid. **Circ:** 25,000 weekly.
Desc: A Spanish newspaper with a variety of subjects including politics, sports and social events, and others. Oriented to the Hispanic community of Southern California.

US/0494-3384
29ER, THE. **Added/Corp** Office and Professional Employees Union. Local no. 29. **VAT** Twenty-Niner. (19??)-. Periodical. English. mo. The Twenty-Niner, 1475 Powell Street, PO Box 8466, Emeryville CA 94662.

US
ALAMEDA TIMES STAR. **VFOAT** Times Alameda Star; Alameda Times-Star; Sunday Review and Sunday Alameda Times-Star; Sunday Review Alameda Times-Star Edition; Alameda Times-Star Edition of the Sunday Review. Vol. 94, No. 154 (June 30, 1958)-. Newspaper. English. da. $94.00 Alameda; $190.00 other. Alameda Times Star, PO Box 2 447, Alameda CA 94501. **Tel** (415)523-1200. **ED** Thomas Tuttle. **Ad Acc, Adv Mgr:** Sharon Kinkade. **Circ:** 9,500. ***Continues*** *Times-Star (Alameda, Calif.).*

US/0889-0730
ALMANAKH PANORAMA. [Almanakh panorama]. **VFOAT** Almanac Panorama; Panorama. (1980)-. Newspaper. Russian. wk. $58.00 US; $65.00 Canada; $110.00 Commonwealth of Independent States; $96.00 other. Almanac Press Inc., 501 South Fairfax Avenue, Suite 206, Los Angeles CA 90036. **Tel** (818)981-7194. **(Subscription address:** Almanac Panorama, PO Box 480264, Los Angeles CA 90048.**)** **ED**

Alexander Polovets, Lilia Sokolov (Managing Editor). Index available. **Bk Rev**, (Qty: 5-6). **Photos. Ad Acc, Adv Mgr:** Angela Nersesian. Full Page (B&W) $1350.00. Half Page (B&W) $720.00. available on microfilm from The Library of Congress Photoduplication Service.

US/8750-8257
ALPINE SUN. (19??)-. Newspaper English. wk. $15.00. Alpine Sun, PO Box 1089, Alpine CA 92001. **Tel** (619)445-3288. **ED** Jay Harn. **Photos. Ad Acc, Adv Mgr:** Teresa Harn. Full Page (B&W) $375.00. Half Page (B&W) $250.00. **Pub. Size:** Tabloid. **Circ:** 2,200 paid weekly.

US/1045-8336
AMADOR LEDGER DISPATCH. VFOAT Amador Ledger Dispatch. Vol. 134, No. 11 (June 7, 1989)-. Newspaper. English. tw. $40.00. Amador Ledger Dispatch, 10776 Argonaut Lane, Jackson CA 95642. **Tel** (209)223-1767, FAX (209)223-1264. **ED** Kathleen Newton (Editor-in-Chief) and Joe Evans (Managing Editor). **Photos. Ad Acc, Adv Mgr:** Jerry Behrens. Full Page (B&W) $1,375.92. Half Page (B&W) $687.96. Full Page (Color) $1,435.92. Half Page (Color) $747.96. **Pub. Size:** Broadsheet. **Wire Svcs.:** CO. **Circ:** 8,979. ***Formed by the union of*** *Amador Ledger and the Amador Record, 1042-7619; Amador Dispatch, 8750-5010* ***and*** *Amador Progress News and the Ione Valley Echo, 8750-5002.*

US
ANGELES MESA WAVE. Vol. 54, No. 46 (Jan 1978)-. Newspaper. English. wk. Angeles Mesa Wave, 2621 West 54th Street, Los Angeles CA 90043. **Tel** (310)290-3000. **ED** Alice Marshall. **Circ:** 14,100. ***Continues*** *Angeles Mesa News Advertiser-Press.*

US/0744-5830
ANTELOPE VALLEY PRESS. VFOAT Valley Press. (19??)-. Newspaper. English. ir (Published Sun., Tues., Thurs., and Fri.). Antelope Valley Newspapers, PO Box 880, Palmdale CA 93550. **Tel** (805)273-2700 ext. 113. **ED** Lamont Odett. **Ad Acc. Circ:** 58 150 (ctrl). available on microfilm. Documents available from UMI Article Clearinghouse.
Desc: General news and features at local, state and national levels with emphasis on local and sports features.
Ind/Abst Bus. Dateline (Dec. 22, 1991-) [Full Txt.].

US/0883-6124
ANZA VALLEY OUTLOOK. Newspaper. English. wk. Anza Valley Outlook, PO Box 1050, Anza CA 92306.

US
APPEAL DEMOCRAT, THE. Vol. 124, No. 146 (July 12, 1990)-. Newspaper. English. da. $88.75. Marysville Appeal-Democrat, 1530 Ellis Lake Drive, Marysville CA 95901. **Tel** (916)741-1123. ***Continues*** *Yuba-Sutter Appeal-Democrat.*

US
ARCATA UNION, THE. Vol. 1, No. 1 (July 31, 1886)-. Newspaper. English. da. $24.00. Hadley Newspapers Inc, PO Drawer X, Arcata CA 95521. **Tel** (707)822-3661.

US/0044-894X
ARMENIAN OBSERVER, THE. (Dec. 1970)-. Newspaper. English. Fifty-two times a year. Armenian Observer, 6646 Hollywood Boulevard, Suite 207, Los Angeles CA 90028. **Tel** (310)467-6767. available on microfilm from The Library of Congress Photoduplication Service.

US/0195-2056
ASIANWEEK. VFOAT Asian Week. Vol. 1, No. 1 (Aug. 18, 1979)-. Newspaper. English. Fifty-one times per year (Friday). $28.00. Asian Week, 811 Sacramento Street, San Francisco CA 94108. **Tel** (415)397-0220, FAX (415)397-7258. **ED** Linda Sherry (editor's address: 809 Sacramento Street, San Francisco, CA 94108) and Gerard Lim (Managing Editor). Index available. **Bk Rev**, (Qty: 51). **Photos. Ad Acc, Adv Mgr:** Jaccueline Rodina. Full Page (B&W) $1,455.30. Half Page (B&W) $750.75. **Pub. Size:** Tabloid. **Circ:** 30,000. available on microfilm from Bay Microfilm, Inc; available on CD-ROM from Ethnic News Watch; available on an online database from Mead News Service.
Desc: Covers a wide variety of news, analysis and commentary of special interest to Asian Americans. Subjects include people, news, arts, books, sports, politics and many more.

US/0004-4229
ASPAREZ. (ASBAREZ.). **Added/Corp** Armenian Revolutionary Federation Central Committee of Western U.S. **VFOAT** Asbarez Daily Newspaper; Asbarez. (Aug. 14, 1908)-. Newspaper. Armenian (English). da (250 issues per year). $84.00 US; $250.00 Canada; $1500.00 other. Asbarez, 419 West Colorado Street, Glendale CA 91204. **Tel** (818)500-9363, FAX (818)956-1106. **ED** John Kossakian. **Bk Rev. Photos. Ad Acc, Adv Mgr:** Salpi Khouri, **Tel** (818)500-9555. Full Page (B&W) $400.00. Half Page (B&W) $240.00. Full Page (Color) $1,250.00. Half Page (Color) $750.00. **Wire Svcs.:** RN. **Circ:** 10,000 (ctrl). available on microfilm and microfiche.
Desc: News about the US Armenia Communities, Armenian Republic and Armenian communities worldwide.

US
ATASCADERO NEWS. Began in 1921. Newspaper. English. sw. Atascadero News, PO Box 6068, Atascadero CA 93423. **Tel** (805)466-2585. **ED** Lon Allan. **Circ:** 6,125.

US
ATWATER SIGNAL. (19??)-. Newspaper. English. wk. Atwater Signal, 927 Atwater Boulevard, Atwater CA 95301-4398. **Tel** (209)358-6431, FAX (209)357-2968. **ED** David J. Wickenhauser. **Ad Acc. Circ:** 12,150.

US
AUBURN JOURNAL. VFOAT Sunday Journal. Vol. 87, No. 26 (Oct. 29, 1959)-. Newspaper. English. da. $125.00. Auburn Journal, PO Box 5957, Auburn CA 95603. **Tel** (916)885-2471. **ED** Mark Craddock. **Bk Rev**, (Qty: 52). **Photos. Ad Acc, Adv Mgr:** Debbie Dragon. Full Page (B&W) $1625.00. Half Page (B&W) $812.00. Full Page (Color) $1725.00. Half Page (Color) $912.00. **Pub. Size:** Standard. **Wire Svcs.:** AP. **Circ:** 13,650 daily & Sunday. ***Continues*** *Auburn Journal and Placer County Republican.*

US/0746-9888
BAKER VALLEY NEWS. (19??)-. Newspaper. English. Twenty-four times a year. $25.00. Baker Valley News, PO Box 84, Baker CA 92309. **Tel** (619)733-4349.

US/0276-5837
BAKERSFIELD CALIFORNIAN, THE. Vol. 19, No. 131 (Jan. 3, 1908)-. Newspaper. English. da (and Sunday). $122.28 (daily and Sunday); $120.00 (weekend only). Bakersfield Californian, PO Bin 440, Bakersfield CA 93302. **Tel** (805)395-7330, FAX (805)395-7499. **ED** Donald Fritts and Virginia F. Cowenhove. **Circ:** 83,818 daily, 93,319 Sunday. ***Continues*** *Bakersfield Californian and the Daily Californian.*
Ind/Abst PROMT.

US
BAY AREA REPORTER : B.A.A. VFOAT BAA. Vol. 1, No. 1 (Apr. 1, 1971)-. Periodical. English. wk. $125.00 (for postage). Bay Area Reporter, 395 9th Street, San Francisco CA 94103. **Tel** (415)861-5019.

US/0888-6016
BAYRUT TAYMZ. VFOAT Beirut Times. (198?)-. Periodical. Arabic (English). wk. $38.00 (one year); $76.00 (first class). Beirut Times, PO Box 93475, Los Angeles CA 90093. **Tel** (213)469-4354, FAX (213)469-4988. **ED** Michel Bou Abssi. Index available. cum. index. **Bk Rev. Photos. Ad Acc, Adv Mgr:** Amale Paige, **Tel** (213)469-4354. Full Page (B&W) $1,100.00. Half Page (B&W) $550.00. **Pub. Size:** Standard. **Circ:** 15,000 (ctrl). available in microform from Data Microfilming Corporation.
Desc: Independent, informative, social, political newspapers published in English and Arabic to serve the Arab American Community in the USA and Canada and abroad.

US/0892-645X
BEVERLY HILLS COURIER, THE. (1965)-. Newspaper. English. Fifty-two times a year. $75.00. Beverly Hills Courier, 8840 West Olympia Boulevard, Beverly Hills CA 90211. **Tel** (310)278-1322, FAX (310)271-5118. **ED** March Schwartz, Simon-Jacques Ifergan (Managing Editor). **Bk Rev**, (Qty: 10-12). **Photos. Ad Acc, Adv Mgr:** Sande Schwartz. Full Page (B&W) $1960.00. Half Page (B&W) $980.00. Full Page (Color) $3920.00. Half Page (Color) $1960.00. **Pub. Size:** Tabloid. **Circ:** 48,000 (ctrl).
Desc: Community newspaper covering all the news and entertainment and social events in Beverly Hills and neighboring areas.

●US/1073-6867
BIG BEAR GRIZZLY. (1993)-. Newspaper. English. Big Bear Grizzly, PO Box 1789, Big Bear Lake CA 92315. **Tel** (714)866-3456. ***Continues*** *Big Bear Life & the Grizzly.*

US
BIOWORLD TODAY. (BIOWORLD TODAY DAILY BIOTECHNOLOGY NEWSPAPER FAX SERVICE.). Newspaper. English. $734.00 US; $784.00 Canada; $1234.00 Western Europe; $1434.00 Eastern Europe; $1734.00 other. BioWorld, 217 South B Street, San Mateo CA 94401. **Tel** (415)696-6555.
Ind/Abst Abstr. BioCommer.

US
CALIFORNIA ADVOCATE, THE. VFOAT Central California Advocate. (1967)-. Newspaper. English. Twenty-four times a year. $20.00. California Advocate, PO Box 11826, Fresno CA 93775. **Tel** (209)268-0941. **ED** Pauline Kimber.

US/0008-0950
CALIFORNIA COURIER, THE. (19??)-. Periodical. English. Fifty-two times a year. $39.00. California Courier, PO Box 5390, Glendale CA 91201. **Tel** (818)409-0949, FAX (818)500-7372. **ED** Harut Sassounian (Editor-in-Chief) and Serge Samoniantz (Managing Editor). **NLM** W1 CA346. **Bk Rev**, (Qty: 10-15). **Photos. Ad Acc, Adv Mgr:** S. Samoniantz. Full Page (B&W) $435.00. Half Page (B&W) $240.00. **Pub. Size:** Tabloid. **Circ:** 3,000.
Desc: News, views, and interviews with particular focus on the Armenian-American community.

US/0008-1124
CALIFORNIA GRANGE NEWS. Added/Corp California State Grange. (19??)-. Periodical. English. mo. California Grange News, 2101 Stockton Boulevard, Sacramento CA 95817. **Tel** (916)454-5805. **ED** J D Hartz. **Circ:** 30,000.

US/0739-4438
CALIFORNIA INTERMOUNTAIN NEWS. (1935)-. Newspaper. English. wk. $4.95. California Intermountain News, 6708 Melrose Avenue, Los Angeles CA 90038. **Tel** (213)937-3386. **ED** Rebecca Ozrelic.

US/0748-5727
CALIFORNIA SENIOR CITIZEN. (197?)-. Periodical. English. mo. $5.00. California Senior Citizen, 4805 Alta Canyada Road, Lacanada CA 91011. **Tel** (818)790-0651, FAX (818)687-4001. **ED** Carol Osmon. **Bk Rev**, (Qty: 4). **Photos. Ad Acc, Adv Mgr:** Carol Osmon. Full Page (B&W) $1,300.00. Half Page (B&W) $744.00. Full Page (Color) $1,500.00. Half Page (Color) $944.00. **Pub. Size:** Tabloid. **Circ:** 69,000 (ctrl). ***Continues*** *California Senior Citizen News, 0008-1531.*
Desc: Opportunities and services available for senior citizens. Legislative news, investment columns and travel.
Ind/Abst Calif. Period. Index (19??-); Calif. Period. Microfi. (19??-).

US/0890-1473
CALIFORNIA STAATS-ZEITUNG. [Calif. Staats-Ztg.]. (18??)-. Newspaper. German. Fifty-two times a year. $22.00 California; $35.00 other. California Staats-Zeitung, 1201 North Alvarado, PO Box 26308, Los Angeles CA 90026. **Tel** (213)413-5500, FAX (213)413-5469. **ED** Stephanie Teichmann. **DD** 053. **Bk Rev. Photos. Ad Acc.** Full Page (B&W) $2,200.00. Half Page (B&W) $1,100.00. Full Page (Color) $2,350.00. Half Page (Color) $1,250.00. ctrl circ.

US
CALIFORNIAN, THE. No. 81 (Apr. 4, 1990)-. Newspaper. English. da. $142.00 Monterey County; $154.00 other. Salinas Californian, PO Box 1091, Salinas CA 93901. **Tel** (408)424-2221, (408)649-6626, FAX (408)424-0117. **ED** Michael Chihak. **Ad Acc. *Continues*** *Salinas Californian.*

US/0898-1817
CALIFORNIAN (EL CAJON, CALIF.), THE. (THE CALIFORNIAN.). **VFOAT** Californian of East County. Vol. 96, No. 9 (Jan. 12, 1988)-. Newspaper. English. da. Californian Publishers, PO Box 1565, El Cajon CA 92022. **Tel** (619)442-4404. ***Continues*** *Daily Californian.*

US/1045-5868
CALIFORNIAN (TEMECULA, CALIF.), THE. (THE CALIFORNIAN.). Vol. 29, No. 26 (July 30, 1987)-. Newspaper. English. da. $52.00. The Californian, PO Box 970, Temecula CA 92390. **Tel** (714)676-5771. **Photos. Ad Acc, Adv Mgr:** Paula Patton, **Tel** (909)676-4315. Full Page (Color) $290.00. **Pub. Size:** Standard. **Wire Svcs.:** NY, AP. available in microform. ***Continues*** *Californian and the Valley Press.*

US/0746-9926
CANYON CRIER NEWS. VFOAT Canyon Crier; Los Angeles Canyon Crier News. Newspaper. English. wk. Canyon Crier News, 10215 Riverside Drive, Toluca Lake CA 91602. **Tel** (310)762-2171. **ED** Colleen Dunn.

US
CARMEL PINE CONE AND CARMEL VALLEY OUTLOOK, THE. 67th Year, No. 14 (Apr. 2, 1981)-. Newspaper. English. wk. $60.00. Carmel Pine Cone, Box G-1, Carmel CA 93921. **Tel** (408)624-0162. **ED** Doug Thompson. **Bk Rev**, (Qty: 25). **Ad Acc, Adv Mgr:** Karen Carlson. ctrl circ. ***Formed by the union of*** *Carmel Pine Cone (Carmel, Calif. : 1962)* ***and*** *Carmel Valley Outlook.*

US/0884-6189
CATHEDRAL CITY POST. VFOAT Post. Vol. 6, No. 18 (July 31, 1985)-. Newspaper. English. sw (Wed. & Fri.). Cathedral City Post, PO Box 459, Palm Desert CA 92261. **Tel** (619)346-1181, FAX (619)773-5400. **ED** Jamie Pricer. **Ad Acc. Circ:** 5,125. ***Continues*** *Cathedral Citizen, 0745-5496.*
Desc: Articles cover local news, sports, government, lifestyles, and entertainment.

US
CERES COURIER. (19??)-. Newspaper. English. Twice a week. $30.00. Ceres Courier, 2940 4th Street, Ceres CA 95307-3223. **Tel** (209)537-5032, FAX (209)537-0543. **ED** Jeff Benziger. **Bk Rev**, (Qty: 12). **Photos. Ad Acc, Adv Mgr:** Douglas Cox. Full Page (B&W) $1094.94. Half Page (B&W) $547.47. **Pub. Size:** Standard. **Circ:** 13,000.

US/0746-5548
CHICO ENTERPRISE-RECORD. (THE CHICO ENTERPRISE-RECORD.). **VFOAT** Chico Enterprise Record. (Dec. 6, 1948)-. Newspaper. English.

ds. $100.00. Enterprise Publishing Company / California, Box 9, Chico CA 95927-0009. **Tel** (916)891-1234. **ED** Jack Winning. **Bk Rev**. **Ad Acc**. **Circ:** 27,208 (ctrl). ***Formed by the union of*** *Chico Enterprise (Chico, Calif. : 1911)* ***and*** *Chico Record.*

US/0279-9758
CHUGAN KWANGGO. **VFOAT** Korean Street Journal. Newspaper. Korean. wk. Jugan-Kwangki Company, 2836 West 8th Street, Los Angeles CA 90005.

US/1067-4357
CIVIC CENTER NEWSOURCE. **VFOAT** Civic Center News Source. (1991)-. Newspaper. English. wk. $32.48. Metropolitan News-Enterprise, PO Box 60859, Los Angeles CA 90060. **Tel** (213)628-4384, FAX (213)687-3886. **Ad Acc**.

US
CLOVERDALE WEEKLY REVEILLE. (1879)-. Newspaper. English. wk (Published Wednesdays). $27.70 Sonoma California; 33.50 other. Cloverdale Weekly Reveille, PO Box 157, Cloverdale CA 95425. **Tel** (707)894-3339. **ED** Bonny J. Hanchett, Robert Lyons (Managing Editor). **Photos**. **Ad Acc**. **Pub. Size:** Broadsheet. **Circ:** 8,600. available in microform.

US/1068-5944
CLOVIS INDEPENDENT (CLOVIS, CALIF. 1946), THE. (THE CLOVIS INDEPENDENT.). Vol. 29, No. 17 (July 25, 1946)-. Newspaper. English. wk. $21.00. Clovis Independent, PO Box 189, Clovis CA 93613. **Tel** (209)298-8081, FAX (209)298-0459. **ED** Earl Wright Jr. (Editor-in-Chief) and Paula Lloyd (Managing Editor). **Photos**. **Ad Acc**, **Adv Mgr:** Deborah Brown. Full Page (B&W) $1,408.68. Half Page (B&W) $704.34. **Pub. Size:** Standard. **Circ:** 3,500. available in microform. ***Continues*** *Clovis Independent and Tribune.*

US
COALINGA RECORD. Vol. 30, No. 10 (Mar. 15, 1945)-. Newspaper. English. sw. Central California Publishing, 339 D Street, Lemoore CA 93245. **Tel** (209)924-5361, FAX (209)924-6220. **ED** Sam Ezell. **Ad Acc**, **Adv Mgr:** Jeff Rice. **Circ:** 26,680. ***Continues*** *Coalinga Daily Record.*

US/0746-3871
COLUSA COUNTY FARMER, THE. Newspaper. English. wk. $7.50. Colusa County Farmer, 555 7th Street, Williams CA 95987. **Tel** (916)473-5384. **ED** Donna A Curt.

US/0897-8743
COLUSA COUNTY SUN HERALD. **VFOAT** Colusa County Sun-Herald. No. 57 (Mar. 23, 1987)-. Newspaper. English. ir (Published only on Monday, Wednesday, and Friday). $60.00 Colusa County; $63.00 other. Colusa Sun Herald, PO Box 89, Colusa CA 95932. **Tel** (916)458-2123. **Bk Rev**, (Qty: 156). **Ad Acc**. ctrl circ. ***Continues*** *Coulsa Sun Herald, 0889-5163.*

US/0885-7989
COMMERCIAL NEWS INTERNATIONAL. [Commer. news int.]. Vol. 204, No. 81 (July 1985)-. Newspaper. English. bw. Commercial News / San Francisco, 99 South Van Ness Avenue, San Francisco CA 94103. **Tel** (415)621-7012. **ED** Roger Lindahl. **DD** 380. available on microfilm from Bay Microfilm, Inc. ***Continues*** *Commercial News (San Francisco, Calif.), 0884-0148.*

US/0192-0235
CONTRA COSTA TIMES. (19??)-. Newspaper. English. ds. $190.00 California; $214.00 other. Contra Costa Times, 2640 Shadelands Drive, Walnut Creek CA 94598. **Tel** (510)935-2525. **(Subscription address:** Circulation Department, PO Box 5501, Walnut Creek, CA 94596 USA**)** **ED** Ernest Hines. **Circ:** 88,255 daily, 93,918 Sunday.

US
CORNING OBSERVER, THE. **VFOAT** Corning (California) Daily Observer; Corning (California) Observer; Corning Daily Observer. Vol. 29, No. 16 (Dec. 14, 1916)-. Newspaper. English. da. Tri-County Newspapers, PO Box 731, Willows CA 95988-0731. **Tel** (916)934-6800, FAX (916)934-6815. **ED** Martha Coe. **Circ:** 8,500. ***Continues*** *Observer;* ***Absorbed*** *Corning Advance.*

US/0745-3930
CORONA-NORCO INDEPENDENT. **VFOAT** Corona Norco Independent; Independent; Daily Independent. (19??)-. Newspaper. English. da (Mon.-Fri.). Corona-Norco Independent, 823 South Main Street, PO Box 1029, Corona CA 91270. **ED** Sherry Skufca. **Circ:** 7,000. ***Continues*** *Daily Independent (Corona, Calif.).*

US/0195-0126
COSTA MESA NEWS. (197?)-. Newspaper. English. wk. $42.35. Costa Mesa News, 1609 Babcock Ave, Newport Beach CA 92663. **Tel** (714)631-8120. **ED** John Trausch. **Circ:** 2,000.

US/0192-0111
COUNTRY ALMANAC, THE. (1966)-. Newspaper. English. wk (52 issues). $20.00 Menlo Park; $30.00 others. Country Almanac / Menlo Park's Alamanac, 855 Oak Grove Avenue, PO Box 98, Menlo Park CA 94025. **Tel** (415)328-1600. **ED** Tom Gibboney, and Richard Hine (Managing Editor). **Photos**. **Ad Acc**, **Adv Mgr:** Jennifer Brown. Full Page (B&W) $1,46.00. Half Page (B&W) $590.00. **Pub. Size:** Tabloid. **Circ:** 21,000 (ctrl).
Desc: Community interest is the theme for this weekly newspaper.

US/1058-5737
CRESTLINE COURIER-NEWS. **VFOAT** Crestline Courier News. (19??)-. Newspaper. English. wk. Crestline Courier News, 607 Forest Shade, PO Drawer 3307, Crestline CA 92325. **Tel** (714)338-1893. ***Formed by the union of*** *Mountain Courier-News, 0745-6220* ***and*** *Rim of the World News.*

US/1050-2300
DAILY CALIFORNIAN. Newspaper. English. da (Mon.-Fri.). $50.00. Daily Californian, 2150 Dwight Way, Berkeley CA 94704. **Tel** (510)849-2482. **ED** James Herron. **Bk Rev**. **Ad Acc**. **Circ:** 25,000 (ctrl).
Desc: City of Berkeley and University of California at Berkeley news and information.

US
DAILY DEMOCRAT. DAVIS EDITION. Began publication in 1966?. English. da. $57.00 (in town), $66.00 (mailed). Daily Democrat, PO Box 730, Woodland CA 95776. **Tel** (916)662-5421. **ED** Dave Liebber. Index available. **Bk Rev**. **Ad Acc**. **Circ:** 12,500.
Desc: Covers community news, AP and is non-partisan.

US/0747-1890
DAILY DEMOCRAT (WOODLAND, CALIF.). (THE DAILY DEMOCRAT.). (19??)-. Newspaper. English. da. Daily Democrat, PO Box 730, Woodland CA 95776. **Tel** (916)662-5421. **ED** Dave Liebber. Index available. **Bk Rev**. **Ad Acc**. **Circ:** 12,500.

US
DAILY FACTS, THE. (1890)-. Newspaper. English. da. Daily Facts, 700 Brookside Avenue, Redlands CA 92373. **Tel** (909)793-3221. **ED** Jim Mattson. **Ad Acc**, **Adv Mgr:** David Berkowitz. **Circ:** 9,500.

US/0746-7370
DAILY LEDGER (ANTIOCH, CALIF.). ***Title Change.*** (DAILY LEDGER.). **VFOAT** Sunday Daily Ledger, Post Dispatch; Daily Ledger, Post Dispatch; Sunday Daily Ledger-Post Dispatch; Daily Ledger-Post Dispatch. Newspaper. English. da. California Delta Newspapers, PO Box 2299, Antioch CA 94531-2299. **Tel** (415)757-2525. ***Continues*** *Antioch Daily Ledger.* ***Merged with*** *Pittsburg Postdispatch, 0746-7389* ***to form*** *Daily Ledger, Post Dispatch, 1054-8459.*

US/1054-8459
DAILY LEDGER, POST DISPATCH. ***Title Change.*** Vol. 120, No. 196 (Oct. 1, 1990)-(199?). Newspaper. English. da. California Delta Newspapers, PO Box 2299, Antioch CA 94531-2299. **Tel** (415)757-2525. ***Formed by the union of*** *Daily Ledger (Antioch, Calif.), 0746-7370* ***and*** *Pittsburg PostDispatch, 0746-7389.* ***Continued by*** *Ledger Dispatch, 1078-5620.*

US/0745-5364
DAILY MIDWAY DRILLER. Newspaper. English. da (Mon.-Fri.). $45.00. Daily Midway Driller, 800 Center Street, Taft CA 92806. **Tel** (805)763-3171. **ED** Doug Keeler. **Circ:** 4,342. ***Continues*** *Taft Daily Midway Driller.*

US
DAILY NEWS (RED BLUFF, CALIF.). (THE DAILY NEWS.). Began in 1885. Newspaper. English. da (Mon.-Sat.). Red Bluff Daily News, PO Box 220, Red Bluff CA 96080. **Tel** (916)527-2151. **ED** Donald Reynolds. **Circ:** 8,697.

US/0746-6188
DAILY NEWS (WHITTIER, CALIF.), THE. ***Title Change.*** (THE DAILY NEWS.). (19??)-(19??). Newspaper. English. da. San Gabriel Valley Tribune, 1210 Azusa Canyon Road, West Covina CA 91790. **Tel** (818)962-8811. **ED** Bill Bell. **Circ:** 18,127. ***Continued by*** *Whittier Daily News, 1069-2819.*

US/1042-8496
DAILY PRESS (1988). (DAILY PRESS.). (198?)-. Newspaper. English. da. $93.60. Victor Valley Publishing Company, PO Box 1389, Victorville CA 92393-0964. **Tel** (619)241-7744, FAX (619)241-7145. **ED** Steve Williams (Editor-in-Chief) and John Iddings (Managing Editor). **Bk Rev**, (Qty: varies). **Photos**. **Ad Acc**, **Adv Mgr:** Dean Strella, **Tel** (619)951-6260. Full Page (B&W) $2,969.58. Half Page (B&W) $1,484.79. Full Page (Color) $3,344.58. Half Page (Color) $1,859.79. **Pub. Size:** Broadsheet. **Wire Svcs.:** AP, KR. **Circ:** 27,625. available on microfilm. ***Continues*** *Victor Valley Daily Press, 0739-0173.*
Desc: Local daily newspaper covering California's Victor Valley.

US/0746-5858
DAILY REPUBLIC (FAIRFIELD, CALIF.). (THE DAILY REPUBLIC.). 106th Year, No. 56 (Oct. 2, 1961)-. Newspaper. English. da. $125.00. Daily Republic, 1250 Texas Street, PO Box 47, Fairfield CA 94533. **Tel** (707)425-4646. **ED** Bill Buchannen. **Circ:** 15,398. ***Continues*** *Solano Republican and Solano County Courier.*

US
DAILY REVIEW, THE. **VFOAT** Sunday Review. Vol. 57, No. 270 (July 12, 1949)-. Newspaper. English. da. $180.00. Daily Review / Hayward, Box 5050, Hayward CA 94540. **Tel** (415)783-6111. **Bk Rev**. **Ad Acc**, **Adv Mgr:** H.R. Autz, **Tel** (510)293-2302. **Circ:** 41,782 (ctrl). available on microfiche. ***Continues*** *Daily Hayward Review;* ***Absorbed*** *Morning News.*

US
DAVIS ENTERPRISE. (Jan. 1, 1898)-. Newspaper. English. da. $79.79. The Davis Enterprise, PO Box 1470, 325 G Street, Davis CA 95617. **Tel** (916)756-0800, FAX (916)756-6707. **ED** Debbie Davis. **Ad Acc**, **Adv Mgr:** Allison Perkes Felch. Full Page (B&W) $1,373.40. Half Page (B&W) $686.70. Full Page (Color) $1,502.40. Half Page (Color) $815.70. **Pub. Size:** Standard. **Wire Svcs.:** AP. **Circ:** 11,000. available in microform from Bay Microfilm, Inc.

US/1074-410X
DELANO RECORD. (1908)-. Newspaper. English. wk (Thurs.). $17.00, Kern & Tulare counties, California; $19.00 other California); $22.00 other US. Delano Record, PO Box 938, Delano CA 93216. **Tel** (805)725-0600, FAX (805)725-4373. **ED** Bob Schettler. **Ad Acc**, **Adv Mgr:** L. Lemons. **Circ:** 4,650 (ctrl).

US/0745-5585
DESERT POST. Vol. 18, No. 7 (Nov. 6-12, 1980)-. Newspaper. English. sw. Palm Desert Post, 74-405 Highway 111, Palm Desert CA 92260. **Tel** (619)346-1181. ***Continues*** *Palm Desert Post.*

US/0746-5599
DESERT TRAIL, THE. Newspaper. English. wk. $12.00 in San Bernardino County; $17.00 in California; $22.00 other. Desert Trail, PO Box 159, Twentynine Palms CA 92277. **Tel** (619)367-3577. **ED** Kathy Dutro. **Circ:** 4,400.

US/0745-6654
DINUBA SENTINEL. (19??)-. Newspaper. English. wk (published Thursday). $20.00. Dinuba Sentinel, PO Box 247, Dinuba CA 93618. **Tel** (209)591-4632. **ED** Bob Raison. **Photos**. **Ad Acc**, **Adv Mgr:** Bob Raison. Full Page (B&W) $1,132.74. Half Page (B&W) $566.37. Full Page (Color) $1,267.74. Half Page (Color) $701.37. **Pub. Size:** Standard.

US/0739-0181
DIXON TRIBUNE, THE. **VFOAT** Dixon California Tribune. (Nov. 14, 1874)-. Newspaper. English. Fifty-two times a year (Thurs.). Dixon Tribune, 145 East A Street, Dixon CA 95620. **Tel** (916)678-5594, (707)447-1686, FAX (707)448-6528. **ED** Dennis Hall. **Circ:** 5,000.

US
DOWNTOWN NEWS. (19??)-. Newspaper. English. wk. $75.00. Downtown News, 1264 West 1st Street, Los Angeles CA 90026. **Tel** (213)481-1448. **ED** Sue Laris Eastin (Editor-in-Chief) and Jack Skelley (Managing Editor). **Bk Rev**. **Photos**. **Ad Acc**, **Adv Mgr:** Maria Flannigan. Full Page (B&W) $2,418.00. Half Page (B&W) $1,344.00. Full Page (Color) $2,668.00. Half Page (Color) $1,594.00. **Pub. Size:** Broadsheet. available in microform. Documents available from UMI Article Clearinghouse.
Ind/Abst Bus. Dateline (Jan. 20, 1992-) [Full Txt.].

US
EASTSIDE SUN. (19??)-. English (Spanish). wk. $70.00. Eastern Group Publications, PO Box 33803, Los Angeles CA 90033. **Tel** (213)263-5743, FAX (213)263-9169. **ED** Dolores Sanchez (Editor-in-Chief) and Tony Castro (Managing Editor). **Bk Rev**. **Photos**. **Ad Acc**, **Adv Mgr:** Jonathan Sanchez. Full Page (B&W) $2,772.00. Half Page (B&W) $1,386.00. Full Page (Color) $3,172.00. Half Page (Color) $1,586.00. **Pub. Size:** Broadsheet. **Wire Svcs.:** CU. **Circ:** 63,000 (ctrl).

US/0194-6412
EASY READER. (19??)-. Periodical. English. wk. $12.00 US; $15.00 other. Easy Reader, 1233 Hermosa Avenue, Hermosa Beach CA 90254. **Tel** (310)372-4611. **ED** Kevin Cody. **Bk Rev**. **Ad Acc**. **Circ:** 60,000 (ctrl).
Desc: Community paper for South Bay cities.

US/0893-3502
EL CHICANO (COLTON, CALIF.). (EL CHICANO.). **VFOAT** Chicano de San Bernardino. Vol. 1, No. 1 (Apr. 1968)-. Newspaper. English (Spanish). wk. $25.00 San Bernadino Counties; $40.00 other. El Chicano, PO Box 6247, San Bernadino CA 92412. **Tel** (909)381-3898, FAX (909)384-0406. **ED** Lynette Juneman. **Ad Acc**, **Adv Mgr:** Christine Donelan. **Circ:** 10,000. available on microfilm from University Microfilms International (UMI).
Desc: Covers Mexican-Americans, local community news.

US/8750-6289
EL DORADO GAZETTE, GEORGETOWN GAZETTE & TOWN CRIER. **VFOAT** El Dorado Gazette; El Dorado Gazette and Georgetown Gazette and Town Crier; El Dorado Gazette & Georgetown Gazette & Town Crier. **VAT** El Dorado Gazette, Georgetown Gazette and Town Crier. (19??)-. Newspaper. English. wk. $15.00 (in county), $20.00 (out of county). El Dorado Gazette, Gazette Building, PO Box 49, Georgetown CA 95634. **Tel** (916)333-4481, FAX (916)333-0152. **ED** Thomas Daly. **Bk Rev**, (Qty: 12). **Photos**. **Ad Acc**, **Adv Mgr:** Megan Costa. Full Page (B&W) $420.00. Half Page (B&W) $214.00. Full Page (Color) $570.00. Half Page (Color) $364.00. **Pub. Size:** Standard. **Circ:** 1,500. ***Continues*** *Georgetown Gazette & Town Crier.*

US/1064-1998
EL SOL (SALINAS, CALIF.). (EL SOL.). (November 13, 1968)-. Newspaper. Spanish (English). wk. $50.00. El Sol / California, PO Box 1610, Salinas CA 93902. **Tel** (408)757-8118, FAX (408)757-1006. **ED** Oscar Panodi. Index available (bound in 52nd issue). **Bk Rev**, (Qty: 10). **Photos**. **Ad Acc**. Full Page (B&W) $1638.00. Half Page (B&W) $819.00. Full Page (Color) $1788.00. Half Page (Color) $969.00. **Pub. Size:** Standard. **Circ:** 13,000.
Desc: Local, national and international news, sports page, entertainment page, religious page, classified adds, and social page.

US/0888-0212
ENTERPRISE NEWS (PIXLEY, CALIF.). ***Ceased.*** (ENTERPRISE NEWS.). Vol. 76, No. 41 (March 1986)-(19??). Newspaper. English. Fifty-two times a year (Thurs.). Enterprise News, 1303 Glenwood, Delano CA 93215. **Tel** (209)757-3124 (Mon., Wed., & Fri.), . **ED** Dick Palmquist. **Circ:** 900. ***Formed by the union of*** *Terra Bella News, 0740-2066* ***and*** *Pixley Enterprise, 0739-8980.*

US/1067-4365
ESCONDIDO NEWS-REPORTER. **VFOAT** Escondido News Reporter. (198?)-. Newspaper. English. sw. $40.00. Metropolitan News Co., 210 South Juniper Street, Suite 205, Escondido CA 92025.

US/1072-1827
FARMERSVILLE HERALD (FARMERSVILLE, CALIF.). (FARMERSVILLE HERALD.). (19??)-. Newspaper. English. Fifty-two times a year (Published on Wed.). $20.00 (one year); $33.00 (two years); $46.00 (three years). Mineral King Publishing Inc., PO Box 7, Exeter CA 93221. **Tel** (209)592-3171, FAX (209)592-3171. **ED** Jerry Newton. **Ad Acc**, **Adv Mgr:** V. Spencer, **Tel** (209)592-3171.
Desc: Community news, sports, and agriculture information.

US/0747-3397
FISH SNIFFER (NORTHERN CALIFORNIA-NEVADA ED.), THE. (THE FISH SNIFFER.). [Fish sniff.]. (19??)-. Periodical. English. bw. $27.50. The Fish Sniffer, PO Box 994, Elk Grove CA 95624. **Tel** (916)685-2245. **ED** Hal Bonslett. **DD** 799. **Bk Rev**. **Ad Acc**. **Circ:** 20,000.

US/0886-8840
FORT BRAGG ADVOCATE-NEWS. **VFOAT** Fort Bragg Advocate News; Advocate News; Advocate-News. No. 39 (Sept. 26, 1985)-. Newspaper. English. wk. $17.00 in county; $26.00 others. Fort Bragg Advocate-News, PO Box 1188, 450 North Franklin Street, Fort Bragg CA 95437. **Tel** (707)964-5642. **ED** Karel Reynolds. **Photos**. **Ad Acc**, **Adv Mgr:** Bill Bodany, **Tel** (707)964-5642. Full Page (B&W) $750.78. Half Page (B&W) $366.66. Full Page (Color) $860.78. Half Page (Color) $476.66. **Pub. Size:** Standard. **Circ:** 15,400 (ctrl). ***Continues*** *Advocate-News (Fort Bragg, Calif. : 1982), 0746-0236.*

US
FREE LANCE. (May 5, 1986)-. Newspaper. English. da. $139.00 San Benito County; $154.00 other. Gavilan Newspapers, PO Box 22365, Gilroy CA 95021. **Tel** (408)842-6411. ***Continues*** *Evening Free Lance.*

US/0884-9641
FREE VENICE BEACHHEAD. **Added/Corp** Beachhead Collective. **VFOAT** Beachhead. (19??)-. Periodical. English. Twelve times a year. Free Venice Beachhead, PO Box 504, Venice CA 90294. **Tel** (310)396-0811. **Bk Rev**. **Ad Acc**. **Circ:** 10,000.
Desc: Alternative community newspaper; primarily political articles, poems and items of local interest. Priorities are articles about Venice and articles by Venetian authors.

US/1057-3682
FREEDOM SPEECH. (FREEDOM [OF] SPEECH.). [Freedom speech]. **VFOAT** Freedom of Speech; Freedom Speech. (1991)-. Newspaper. English. mo. $30.00. Freedom of Speech, PO Box 134, Carmel CA 93921. **ED** Pual Laub. **DD** 071. **Photos**. **Ad Acc**, **Adv Mgr:** Jean Bolrmon, **Tel** (408)626-6600. Full Page (B&W) $550.00. Half Page (B&W) $325.00. Full Page (Color) $750.00. Half Page (Color) $459.00. **Pub. Size:** Tabloid. **Wire Svcs.:** KF.

US/0889-6070
FRESNO BEE, THE. **VFOAT** Sunday Morning Fresno Bee. Vol. 106, No. 19113 (Sept. 10, 1975)-. Newspaper. English. da. $292.70 Fresno & Madera counties, $292.83 residents of Fresno City, $292.01 others counties in California, $282.00 others by mail, $135.12 by carrier (daily & Sunday); $117.12 residents of Fresno City, $117.05 Fresno & Madera counties, $116.66 other counties in California, $111.00 others by mail (Sunday). McClatchy Newspapers, PO Box 11016, Fresno CA 93786. **Tel** (209)441-6396. **ED** Beverly Kees. Index available. **Bk Rev**. **Ad Acc**. **Circ:** 140,402 daily, 164,403 Sunday. available on microfilm from Bay Microfilm, Inc; available on an online database (file 739/Full-Text) from DIALOG. ***Continues*** *Fresno Bee and the Fresno Republican.*
Desc: News coverage of Central California.

US
GALT HERALD, THE. (191?)-. Newspaper. English. sw. $19.00. Galt Herald, PO Box 307, Galt CA 95632. **Tel** (209)745-1551. ***Continues*** *Weekly Witness (Galt, Calif.).*

US/8750-4766
GATOS TIMES-OBSERVER (GENERAL NEWS ED.), LOS. (LOS GATOS TIMES-OBSERVER.). **VFOAT** Los Gatos Times Observer; Times Observer; Times-Observer. (19??)-. Newspaper. English. ir (Tues., Thurs. & Sat.). Pennisula Community Newspapers, PO Box 1685, Cupertino CA 95015. **Tel** (408)255-7500. **ED** Michael Bailey. **Circ:** 13,784.

US/1071-3476
GLENDALE NEWS-PRESS (1993). (GLENDALE NEWS-PRESS.). **VFOAT** Glendale News Press. (19??)-. Newspaper. English. da. $111.00. Leader Newspapers, 111 North Isabel Street, PO Box 911, Glendale CA 91209. **Tel** (818)241-4141. ***Continues*** *News-Press (Glendale, Calif.), 0746-3340.*

US
GRIDLEY HERALD, THE. Vol. 1, No. 1 (Oct. 29, 1880)-. Newspaper. English. sw (Wed. and Fri.). $24.00 (in county), $28.00 (out of county). Gridley Herald, PO Box 68, Gridley CA 95948. **Tel** (916)846-3661, FAX (916)846-4519. **Photos**. **Ad Acc**, **Adv Mgr:** John Skaggs. Full Page (B&W) $574.05. Half Page (B&W) $310.40. Full Page (Color) $649.05. Half Page (Color) $385.40. **Pub. Size:** Standard. **Circ:** 3,300 paid.

US/0741-126X
GUOJI RIBAO. (KUO CHI JIH PAO - INTERNATIONAL DAILY NEWS.). **VFOAT** International Daily News. (19??)-. Newspaper. Chinese. da (except holidays and Chinese New Year). $129.90 California, $140.00 other. International Daily News, 870 Monterey Pass Road, Monterey Park CA 91754. **Tel** (213)265-1317 ext. 240. **ED** Pyng-Yee Sheu (Editor in Chief) and Simon Chen (Managing Editor). **Bk Rev**, (Qty: 12). **Photos**. **Ad Acc**, **Adv Mgr:** Fred King. Full Page (B&W) $844.00. Half Page (B&W) $424.00. Full Page (Color) $1443.00. Half Page (Color) $721.00. **Wire Svcs.:** AP. **Circ:** 100,000 (ctrl). available in microform from Data Microfilming Corporation.
Desc: Articles on: sports, local news, community services, international news and entertainment section.

US
HALF MOON BAY REVIEW AND PESCADERO PEBBLE. (1???)-. Newspaper. English. wk. $30.00. Half Moon Bay Review, 714 Kelly Avenue, Box 68, Half Moon Bay CA 94019. **Tel** (415)726-4424, FAX (415)726-7054. **ED** John Toth, Marc DesJardins (Managing Editor). **Bk Rev**. **Photos**. **Ad Acc**. Full Page (B&W) $1074.00. Half Page (B&W) $537.00. **Pub. Size:** Broadsheet.

US
HANFORD SENTINEL, THE. Vol. 193, No. 54 (Sept. 2, 1960)-. Newspaper. English. da. $181.00 Kings County; $205.00 other. Hanford Sentinel, PO Box 9, 418 West 8th Street, Hanford CA 93232. **Tel** (209)582-0471, FAX (209)582-8631. **ED** Leah Leach. **Ad Acc**, **Adv Mgr:** Bob Randall. **Circ:** 13,743. ***Continues*** *Hanford Sentinel the Journal.*

US/0746-4312
HANGUK ILBO, ROSUENJELSU. **VFOAT** Korea Times Los Angeles Edition; Hanguk Ilbo; Korea Times. (19??)-. Newspaper. Korean. da. $135.00 California; $180.00 other. Korea Times / Los Angeles, CA, 141 North Vermont Avenue, Los Angeles CA 90004. **Tel** (213)487-8907.

US/0747-8356
HANGUK ILBO, SAEN PURANSISUKO. **VFOAT** Korea Times San Francisco Edition; Hanguk Ilbo; Korea Times. (19??)-. Newspaper. Korean. da (Except Mon.). $14.50. The Korea Times San Francisco, 679 Bryant Street, PO Box 77250, San Francisco CA 94107-7250. **Tel** (415)777-1133, FAX (415)777-1336. **ED** Uoo Kang. **Photos**. **Ad Acc**, **Adv Mgr:** Michael Kang. Full Page (B&W) $700.00. Half Page (B&W) $400.00. **Pub. Size:** Standard. **Wire Svcs.:** AP.

US
HAWTHORNE WAVE. Vol. 63, No. 36 (Aug. 1981)-. Newspaper. English. wk. Hawthorne Wave, 2621 West 54th Street, Los Angeles CA 90043. **Tel** (310)290-3000. **ED** Russ Hudson. **Circ:** 20,050. ***Continues in part*** *Inglewood Hawthorne Wave.*

US/0017-8810
HEALDSBURG TRIBUNE-ENTERPRISE AND SCIMITAR. Periodical. English. sw. $17.75. Healdsburg Tribune, PO Box 518, Healdsburg CA 95448. **Tel** (707)433-4451. **ED** Guion Kovner. **Bk Rev**. **Ad Acc**. **Circ:** 7,377 (ctrl). available on microfilm.
Desc: Community newspaper serving Healdsburg, Windsor and Geyserville, California.

US
HEMET NEWS, THE. (1893)-. Newspaper. English. da. $56.03 (by carrier), $104.00 (by mail). Hemet News, 474 West Esplanade Avenue, San Jacinto CA 92583. **Tel** (714)487-2231, FAX (714)487-2250. **ED** Scott Moore. **Bk Rev**. **Ad Acc**, **Adv Mgr Tel** (909)487-2211. **Pr Rev**. **Circ:** 17,500 (ctrl). available on microfiche.

US/8750-2038
HERALD-DISPATCH (LOS ANGELES, CALIF. : 1981). (HERALD-DISPATCH.). **VFOAT** Herald Dispatch. Vol. 28, No. 62 (June 1981)-. Newspaper. English. wk (published Thursdays). $40.00. Herald-Dispatch, PO Box 19027A, Los Angeles CA 90019. **Tel** (310)291-9486, FAX (213)291-2123. **ED** Lela A. Ward-Oliver. **DD** 071. **Bk Rev**. **Ad Acc**, **Adv Mgr:** L. Holoman. **Circ:** 35,000 (ctrl). ***Continues*** *Weekend Herald-Dispatch.*

US/1046-865X
HERALD (HAYWARD, CALIF.), THE. ***Title Change.*** (HERALD.). [Herald]. (198?)-(19??). Newspaper. English. da. Alameda Newspaper, Inc, 116 West Winton Avenue, Haywood CA 94544-1211. **DD** 071. ***Continues*** *Tri-Valley Herald, 8750-9946.* ***Continued by*** *Valley Herald (Hayward, Calif.), 1049-2518.*

US/0889-3101
HERALD (MONTEREY, CALIF.), THE. (THE HERALD.). **VFOAT** Sunday Herald. 64th year, No. 290 (Mar. 31, 1986)-. Newspaper. English. da. $102.96 (Sunday only), $231.72 (daily & Sunday) by mail; $128.76 (daily & Sunday) carrier. Monterey Peninsula Herald Company, 8 Upper Ragsdale Road, PO Box 271, Monterey CA 93940. **Tel** (408)372-8401. **ED** Reginald Henry. **Circ:** 33,167. ***Continues*** *Monterey Peninsula Herald.*
Desc: Daily newspaper.

US/0746-2301
HI-DESERT STAR. **VFOAT** Hi Desert Star. Newspaper. English. tw. $12.00 in county; $17.00 in California; $22.00 other. H Paradis, 7333 Apache Tr., Yucca Valley CA 92284. **ED** Art Mitz. **Circ:** 10,100.

US
HISPANO (SACRAMENTO, CALIF.). (EL HISPANO.). (1969)-. Newspaper. Spanish (English). Fifty-two times a year (Wednesdays). $28.00. El Hispano, PO Box 2856, Sacramento CA 95812. **Tel** (916)442-0267, FAX (916)446-9221. **ED** Bel Larenas (editor's address: 928 Second Street, Suite 300, Sacramento, CA 95814). **Photos**. **Ad Acc**. Full Page (B&W) $1234.80. Half Page (B&W) $617.40. Full Page (Color) $1384.80. Half Page (Color) $767.40. **Pub. Size:** Standard. **Wire Svcs.:** AP, NM. **Circ:** 35,000. ***Continues*** *Hispanoamericano.*

US/0300-8800
HOLLAND REPORTER, THE. (1961)-. Newspaper. Dutch (English). wk. Holland Reporter, 3680 Division Street, Los Angeles CA 90065.

US/0746-777X
HUMBOLDT BEACON AND FORTUNA ADVANCE, THE. **VFOAT** Humboldt Beacon. Newspaper. English. sw. $16.50 Humboldt County; $21.00 other. The Humboldt Beacon Inc, 928 Main Street, Fortuna CA 95540. **Tel** (707)725-6166. **Ad Acc**. **Circ:** 15,500. ***Formed by the union of*** *Humboldt Beacon* ***and*** *Fortuna Advance.*

US/0194-6021
HUNTINGTON BEACH INDEPENDENT. (19??)-. Newspaper. English. da. $84.00. Huntington Beach Independent, PO Box 1560, Costa Mesa CA 92626. **Tel** (714)842-1444.

US
IDYLLWILD TOWN CRIER. Vol. 25, No. 40 (Sept. 3, 1971)-. Newspaper. English. wk. $24.00 (in county), $28.00 (out of county). Idyllwild Town Crier, PO Box 157, Idyllwild CA 92349. **Tel** (909)659-2145, FAX (909)659-2071. **ED** Gary Hutner. **Photos**. **Ad Acc**, **Adv Mgr:** Lisa Swett. Full Page (B&W) $362.70. Half Page (B&W) $185.25. Full Page (Color) $437.70. Half Page (Color) $260.25. **Pub. Size:** Tabloid. **Circ:** 4,000 (ctrl). ***Continues*** *Town Crier (Idyllwild, Calif. : 1969).*

US
IMPERIAL VALLEY PRESS. **VFOAT** Imperial Valley Press and El Centro Progress; Post-Press; Imperial Valley News-Press; Imperial Valley Press/The

Brawley News. Vol. 7, No. 14 (July 17, 1907)-. Newspaper. English. da. $79.60 Imperial County; $92.80 US. Imperial Valley Press, PO Box 2770, El Centro CA 92244. **Tel** (619)352-2211, (619)337-3400, FAX (619)353-3003. **ED** J. R. "Dick" Fitch, and Susan Giller (Managing Editor). **Bk Rev**. **Photos**. **Ad Acc, Adv Mgr:** John Yanni. Full Page (B&W) $1,869.00. Half Page (B&W) $935.00. Full Page (Color) $2,164.00. Half Page (Color) $1,230.00. **Pub. Size:** Broadsheet. **Wire Svcs.:** AP. **Circ:** 17,181 (Mon. & Fri.), 18,311 (Sun.). available in microform. ***Continues*** *Imperial Valley Press and the Imperial Press;* ***Absorbed*** *El Centro Daily Standard* ***and*** *Morning Daily El Centro Progress.*

US/0883-721X
INDIA-WEST. [India west]. **VFOAT** India West. Vol. 1 (Nov. 1975)-. Newspaper. English. wk. $30.00 (one year); $56.00 (two years). India West Publications, 5901 Christie Avenue, Suite 301, Emeryville CA 94608-1934. **Tel** (415)652-3552, FAX (415)652-0265. **ED** Bina Murarka (Editor-in-Chief) and Atul Vaidya (Managing Editor). **DD** 071. **Bk Rev**. **Photos**. **Ad Acc, Adv Mgr:** Prem Dutt, **Tel** (510)652-9064. Full Page (B&W) $600.00. Half Page (B&W) $300.00. Full Page (Color) $1,000.00. Half Page (Color) $500.00. **Pub. Size:** Tabloid. **Wire Svcs.:** RN. **Circ:** 10,000 (ctrl). available in microform.
Desc: Contains news from India, and news and features covering the Indian community settled in the U.S. Includes India politics, Indo-US relations, features on Indians successful in business, science and academia in the U.S., book and film reviews, sports, and trades.

US
INGLEWOOD WAVE. Vol. 63, No. 36 (Aug. 1981)-. Newspaper. Caucasian. wk. Inglewood Wave, 2621 West 54th Street, Los Angeles CA 90043. **Tel** (310)290-3000. **ED** Alice Marshall. **Circ:** 27,060. ***Continues in part*** *Inglewood Hawthorne Wave.*

US/0274-7464
INTER-CITY EXPRESS (OAKLAND, CALIF.). (INTER-CITY EXPRESS.). (19??)-. Periodical. English. da (260 issues). $130.00. Daily Journal Corporation, 915 East First Street, Los Angeles CA 90012. **Tel** (213)229-5300, FAX (213)680-3682. **ED** Gerald L. Salzman. Index available. **Bk Rev**. **Ad Acc**. **Circ:** 126,659 (ctrl). available on microfilm.

US
INYO REGISTER. No. 168 (Mar. 1, 1985)-. Newspaper. English. tw. Chalfant Press, 450 East Line Street, PO Box 787, Bishop CA 93514. **Tel** (717)873-3535. ***Continues*** *Inyo Register & Independent and Owens Valley Progress-Citizen.*

US/0195-4822
IRVINE WORLD NEWS, THE. (Jan. 1970)-. Newspaper. English. wk. Free to Irvine California; $60.00 other. Irvine World News, PO Box C 19512, Irvine CA 92713. **Tel** (714)261-2435. **ED** Jean Keevil.

US/0746-5432
JINSHAN SHIBAO. (CHIN-SHAN SHIH PAO = CHINESE TIMES.). [Jinshan shibao]. **VFOAT** Chinese Times; Chin Shan Shih Pao. (1924)-. Newspaper. Chinese. da (Mon.-Sat.). $108.50 (1 year), $206.15 (2 year). Chinese Times, 686 Sacramento Street, San Francisco CA 94111. **Tel** (415)982-0136, FAX (415)982-3387. **ED** Man-Kai Lee. **LC** 7002. **DD** 071. **Bk Rev**, (Qty: 2). **Ad Acc**. **Circ:** 15,000 (ctrl). available on microfilm from University Microfilms International (UMI).

US/8756-2200
JORNAL PORTUGUES (SAN PABLO, CALIF.). (JORNAL PORTUGUES.). [J. port.]. **VFOAT** Portuguese Journal. Vol. 1, No. 1 (July 1, 1932)-. Newspaper. Portuguese (English). wk (Published on Thursdays). $25.00 residents of California; $30.00 elsewhere US; $50.00 other. Portuguese Journal, 1912 Church Lane, San Pablo CA 94806. **Tel** (415)237-0888. **ED** Albert S. Lemos, Maria C. Leal (Managing Editor). **DD** 071. **Bk Rev**, (Qty: 20 per year). **Photos**. **Ad Acc, Adv Mgr:** Magda Bettencourt. Full Page (B&W) $400.00. Half Page (B&W) $200.00. **Pub. Size:** Tabloid. **Circ:** 2,500 paid. available in microform from University of California at Berkeley. ***Formed by the union of*** *Jornal de Noticias (San Francisco, Calif.); Colonia Portuguesa* ***and*** *Imparcial (Sacamento, Calif.).*
Desc: Emphasis on Portuguese Americans.

US/0195-2889
JOURNAL FRANCAIS D'AMERIQUE. [J. fr. Am.]. Vol. 1 (Sept./Oct. 1979)-. Periodical. French. bw. $37.00. Francepress Inc., 1051 Divisadero Street, San Francisco CA 94115. **Tel** (415)921-5100, 800 851-7785, FAX (415)921-0213. **ED** Anne Prah-Perochon. **DD** 944. **Bk Rev**, (Qty: 20). **Ad Acc, Adv Mgr:** A. Kautmann. **Circ:** 25,000 (ctrl). ***Continues*** *Californien.*
Desc: Covers all the news from France including politics, business, culture, cinema, literature, travel and more.

US/1056-4616
JUNTA TRIBUNE-DEMOCRAT, LA. **VFOAT** La Junta Tribune Democrat; La Junta (Colorado) Tribune-Democrat. 48th Year, No. 104 (June 1, 1944)-. Newspaper. English. da. $62.00. La Junta Democrat Publishing Co., 422 Colorado Avenue, La Junta CA 81050. **Tel** (303)384-4475. ***Formed by the union of*** *La Junta Daily Democrat* ***and*** *La Junta Daily Tribune.*

US
JURUPA THIS WEEK. (19??)-. Newspaper. English. wk. $13.00 Riverside County; $15.00 other. Jurupa This Week, PO Box 720, Mira Loma CA 91752. **Tel** (909)681-0586, FAX (909)360-9180. **ED** Bob Umphress. **Photos**. **Ad Acc, Adv Mgr:** Bob Umphress. Full Page (B&W) $180.00. Half Page (B&W) $100.00. **Pub. Size:** Tabloid. **Circ:** 400.

US/1066-9353
KAMAI FORUM. (199?)-. Newspaper. English. Thirty times a year. $30.00. Kamai Forum, 1916 East 1st Street, Los Angeles CA 90033. **Tel** (213)264-5767. ***Continues*** *Kashu Mainichi, 0893-8962.*

US/0893-8962
KASHU MAINICHI. ***Title Change.*** **VFOAT** California Daily News. (1931)-(19??). Newspaper. Japanese (English). da (Monday-Friday). Kashi Mainichi, 915 East 1st Street, Los Angeles CA 90012-4083. **Tel** (310)636-1168, FAX (310)626-0131. **ED** Jitsuo Kikunaga and Hiro E. Hishiki. **Ad Acc**. **Circ:** 7,000 (ctrl). ***Continued by*** *Kamai Forum.*
Desc: General information newspaper.

US
KERMAN NEWS, THE. (19??)-. Newspaper. English. wk. Kerman News, PO Box 336, Kerman CA 93630-0336. **Tel** (209)846-6689.

US
KOREA CENTRAL DAILY (U.S. EDITION). (THE KOREA CENTRAL DAILY.). (19??)-. Newspaper. Korean (English). da. The Korea Central Daily, 690 Wilshire Place, Los Angeles CA 90005. **Tel** (213)389-2500.

US/0749-0143
KURISUCHYON HEROLDU. **VFOAT** Christian Herald. Began in 1977. Newspaper. Korean. wk. $40.00. Christian Herald, 801 South Wilton Place, Los Angeles CA 90005. **DD** 071.

US/0192-1940
L.A. WEEKLY. **VFOAT** LA Weekly. **VAT** Los Angeles Weekly. (1978)-. Periodical. English. wk (Thursdays). $30.00 (six months); $52.00 (one year). Los Angeles Weekly / Department of Circulation, PO Box 5720, 6657 San Fernando Road, Glendale CA 91221-5720. **Tel** (818)545-0396, FAX (818)545-0641. **ED** Sue Horton (Editor-in-Chief) and Mary Melton (Managing Editor). **Bk Rev**. **Photos**. **Ad Acc**, **Adv Mgr Tel** (213)465-9909. **Pub. Size:** Tabloid. **Circ:** 170,000.
Desc: Brings LA's active young population the information they need about news, entertainment, culture, and lifestyle. Coverage includes every area from politics to health.

US/0744-8759
LA MESA COURIER. (19??)-. Newspaper. English. Fifty-two times a year (Thurs.). La Mesa Courier, PO Box 216, La Mes CA 92041. **Tel** (909)461-1021. **ED** Debra Buehn. **Circ:** 2,000.

US/0192-0324
LA MIRADA LAMPLIGHTER. Newspaper. English. sw. 8800 National Avenue, South Gate CA 90280. **Tel** (714)537-7510.

US/0746-4304
LAKE COUNTY RECORD-BEE. **VFOAT** Lake County Record Bee; Lake County Record-Bee Weekender; Lake County Record Bee Weekender. 91st Year, No. 51 (May 4, 1961)-. Newspaper. English. da (Except Sun. & Mon.). $52.55 (carrier); $62.21 (mail). Lake County Publishing Company, PO Box 849, Lakeport CA 95453. **Tel** (707)263-5636, FAX (707)263-0600. **ED** John Lawman, and Cliff Larimer (Managing Editor). **Photos**. **Ad Acc, Adv Mgr:** Roy Dufrain and Ursula Gallas. Full Page (B&W) $824.04. Half Page (B&W) $418.32. Full Page (Color) $924.04. Half Page (Color) $518.32. **Pub. Size:** Standard. **Wire Svcs.:** AP. **Circ:** 8,200. ***Formed by the union of*** *Lakeport Press & Record* ***and*** *Lake County Bee (Lakeport, Calif. : 1895).*

US/0745-1350
LAKE ELSINORE VALLEY SUN-TRIBUNE. **VAT** Lake Elsinore Valley Sun Tribune. (19??)-. Newspaper. English. Fifty-two times a year. Lake Elsinore Valley Sun, PO Box B, Lake Elsinore CA 92330-3038. **Tel** (909)674-1535. **ED** Tom McCann. **Ad Acc**. **Circ:** 15,000 (ctrl).

US/0193-9904
LAS VIRGENES ENTERPRISE. (19??)-. Newspaper. English. Fifty-two times a year. Las Virgenes Enterprise, Box 27, Calabasas CA 91302. **ED** Rodger Sterling.

US
LASSEN COUNTY TIMES. English. wk. $18.00 Lassen County, $25.00 California, $28.00 other. Lassen County Times, 800 Main Street, Susanville CA 96130. **Tel** (916) 257-5321.

US/1072-1800
LINDSAY GAZETTE. (190?)-. Newspaper. English. wk. $15.00 Tulare County; $17.00 other. Lindsay Gazette, PO Box 308, Lindsay CA 93247. **Tel** (209)562-2585.

US
LODI NEWS-SENTINEL. **VFOAT** Lodi News Sentinel. 55th Year, No. 5 (June 24, 1935)-. Newspaper. English. da. $74.00 San Jocquin & Sacramento counties; $80.00 California; $92.00 other. Lodi News Sentinel, PO Box 1360, Lodi CA 95241. **Tel** (209)369-2761. ***Formed by the union of*** *Lodi News* ***and*** *Lodi Sentinel.*

US
LOMPOC RECORD, THE. Vol. 1, No. 1 (Apr. 10, 1875)-. Newspaper. English. wk (Sun.-Fri.). Lompoc Record, 115 North H Street, Lompoc CA 93436. **Tel** (805)736-2313. **ED** Don Han. **Circ:** 9,995.

US
LONG BEACH COMMUNITY NEWS. Vol. 1, No. 1 (June 6, 1891)-. wk. $23.00. Long Beach Community News, PO Box 92825, Long Beach CA 90809-2825. **Tel** (310)597-5185. **ED** Terry L McAlpine. **Ad Acc**. **Circ:** 12,000.
Desc: Reports community news.

US
LONG BEACH PRESS-TELEGRAM. (Sept. 1, 1924)-. Newspaper. English. ds. $114.00. Long Beach Press-Telegram, 604 Pine Avenue, Long Beach CA 90844. **Tel** (310)436-3676. ***Formed by the union of*** *Long Beach Telegram* ***and*** *Long Beach Press.*

US/8750-4588
LOS ALTOS TOWN CRIER. **VFOAT** Town Crier. (19??)-. Newspaper. English. wk. $20.00. Los Altos Town Crier, 138 Main Street, Los Altos CA 94022. **ED** Paul Nuberg, Bruce Barton (Managing Editor). **Bk Rev**, (Qty: 50). **Photos**. **Ad Acc, Adv Mgr:** Susan Glaze. Full Page (B&W) $877.00. Half Page (B&W) $495.00. **Pub. Size:** Tabloid. **Circ:** 16,500.

US/0890-4340
LOS ANGELES SENTINEL. (Aug. 27, 1933)-. Newspaper. English. Fifty-two times a year (Thurs.). Los Angeles Sentinel, 1112 East 43rd Street, Los Angeles CA 90011. **Tel** (213)299-3800. **ED** Kenneth Thomas. **Circ:** 27,856. available on microfilm from University Microfilms International (UMI). Documents available from UMI Article Clearinghouse. ***Continues*** *Eastside News.*
Ind/Abst Newsp. Abstr.

US/0458-3035
LOS ANGELES TIMES, THE. [Los Angeles times]. **VFOAT** Los Angeles Daily Times. Vol. 10, No. 119 (Oct. 23, 1886)-. Newspaper. English (Spanish). ds. $546.00 US; $832.00 other. Los Angeles Times, Times Mirror Square, Los Angeles CA 90053. **Tel** (714)237-5000, (800)528-4637. **(Subscription address:** Los Angeles Times, Box 60186, Mail Subscriptions, Los Angeles CA 90053.**) LC** 7114-X. Index available. cum. index. **Bk Rev**. **Ad Acc**. **Circ:** 1,200,000. available on microfilm and CD-ROM from VU-TEXT; NEXIS; DIALOG; and University Microfilms International (UMI); available on an online database (files 630,635/Full-Text) from DIALOG. Documents available from UMI Article Clearinghouse. ***Continues*** *Los Angeles Daily Times.*
Ind/Abst Art Archaeol. Tech. Abstr.; Bus. Dateline; Health Ref. Cent. (1987-) [Select. Cov.]; Infobank (Jan. 1969-); Mark. Advert. Ref. Serv.; Natl. Newsp. Index (Oct. 1982-); Newsp. Abstr.; Newsp. Abstr.; NEXIS (1985-); PROMT.

US
LOS BANOS ENTERPRISE, THE. (18??)-. Newspaper. English. wk. Los Banos Enterprise, 1253 West I Street, Los Banos CA 93635-3999. **Tel** (209)826-3831, FAX (209)826-2005. **ED** Kae Reed. **Ad Acc**. **Circ:** 5,532.

US/0748-4704
LOS GATOS WEEKLY. (19??)-. Newspaper. English. wk. $28.00. Los Gatos Weekly, PO Box 65, Los Gatos CA 95031. **Tel** (408)354-3666.

●US/1065-8262
LUSOAMERICANO CALIFORNIA. [LusoAmericano Calif.]. No. 1 (Sept. 9, 1992)-. Newspaper. English. wk. $25.00. Luso Americano Co., 21378 Mission Boulevard, Hayward CA 94541. **DD** 071.

US/8750-9571
MADERA TRIBUNE. **VFOAT** Madera Tribune Weekender. Vol. 88, No. 145 (Dec. 15, 1978)-. Newspaper. English. da (Except Sun. & holidays). Madera Tribune, PO Box 269, Madera CA 93637. **Tel** (209)674-2424. **ED** Jerry J. Herrmann. **Circ:** 8,600. ***Continues*** *Madera Daily Tribune (Madera, Calif. : 1960).*

US/0191-7307
MALIBU SURFSIDE NEWS, THE. (19??)-. Newspaper. English. Fifty-two times a year. $15.00 California; $30.00 others. Malibu Surfside News, PO Box 903, Malibu CA 90265-0903. **Tel** (310)457-2112, FAX (310)457-9908. **ED** Anne Soble. Index available. **Bk Rev**. **Photos**. **Ad Acc, Adv Mgr:** C. Stoddard. Full Page (B&W) $790.00. Half Page (B&W) $490.00. **Pub. Size:**

Tabloid. **Circ:** 12,600 (ctrl).
Desc: Community news featuring interests in environmental and political issues.

US/1050-4931
MALIBU TIMES. (May 1946)-. Newspaper. English. wk. $35.00. Malibu Times, PO Box 1127, Malibu CA 90265. **Tel** (213)456-5507. **ED** Arnold G. York. **Photos**. **Ad Acc**, **Adv Mgr:** Gloria Neiman and Mary Abbott. Full Page (B&W) $1,071.00. Half Page (B&W) $781.00. **Pub. Size:** Broadsheet. **Circ:** 13,200 (ctrl).

US/1044-4416
MANILA TIMES INTERNATIONAL. [Manila times int.]. (199?)-. Newspaper. English. wk. $25.00. Manila Times International, 2323 Beverly Boulevard/Suite 205, Los Angeles CA 90057. **DD** 909. ***Continues*** *Manila Times Weekly, 1040-5593.*

US/0745-2748
MANTECA BULLETIN. (19??)-. Bulletin. English. ds. $90.00. Manteca Bulletin, PO Box 912, Manteca CA 95336. **Tel** (209)239-3531. **ED** Earl Wright Jr. **Circ:** 5,671.

US/0891-5164
MARIN INDEPENDENT JOURNAL. VFOAT Sunday Marin Independent Journal. Vol. 124, No. 26 (Apr. 22, 1985)-. Newspaper. English. da. $105.41. Marin Independent Journal, PO Box 151790, San Rafael CA 94915. **Tel** (415)883-8600 ext. 400 or ext.402. **ED** Mike Townsend (phone: (415)382-7203). **Bk Rev**. **Ad Acc**. **Circ:** 40,214 daily, 43,083 Sunday (ctrl). available on microfilm. ***Continues*** *Independent Journal (San Rafael, Calif.).*

US/0746-4320
MARINA NEWS (LONG BEACH, CALIF.). (THE MARINA NEWS.). **VFOAT** Marina/Seal Beach News; Marina, Seal Beach News; Marina/Seal Beach News-Huntington Beach News. Newspaper. English. wk. $10.00. Long Beach Marina News, PO Box 92825, Long Beach CA 90809-2825. **Tel** (310)438-9941. **ED** William H Quinn. **Circ:** 24,000.

US
MARIPOSA WEEKLY GAZETTE AND MINER. VFOAT Mariposa Weekly Gazette. Vol. 122, No. 46 (Feb. 3, 1977)-. Newspaper. English. wk. $16.50. DJ Campbell, PO Box 38, Mariposa CA 95338. **Tel** (209)966-2500, (209)966-2509, FAX (209)966-3384. **ED** C. Ruth Campbell. **Ad Acc. Circ:** 5,000 (ctrl). ***Continues*** *Mariposa Weekly Gazette (Mariposa, Calif. : 1977).*

US
MARTINEZ NEW GAZETTE. English. da (Tues. thru Sat.). $68.00 residents of Martinez, $80.00 others (mail); $44.00 (carrier). Martinez New Gazette, PO Box 151, Martinez CA 94553. **Tel** (415)228-6400.

US
MENDOCINO BEACON, THE. VFOAT Mendocino Coast Beacon. Vol. 1, No. 1 (Oct. 6, 1877)-. Newspaper. English. wk. $17.00 Mendocino County; $26.00 other. Mendocino Beacon, PO Box 225, Mendocino CA 95460. **Tel** (707)937-5874. **ED** Kate Lee. **Bk Rev**. **Ad Acc. Circ:** 2,400 (ctrl).

●US/1065-8416
MENDOCINO COUNTY OUTLOOK. VFOAT Outlook. Issue 1 (Aug. 7, 1992)-. Newspaper. English. bw. Free. Mendocino County Outlook, 660 Harrison Street, Fort Bragg CA 95437.

US
MERCED SUN-STAR. (1925)-. Newspaper. English. da. $92.03 Merced County; $141.60 California; $156.00 other. Lesher Newspapers Inc, PO Box 739, Merced CA 95341. **Tel** (209) 722-1511. **ED** Norman Martin II. **Bk Rev**. **Ad Acc. Circ:** 21,000 (ctrl). ***Formed by the union of*** *Merced Evening Sun* ***and*** *Merced Morning Star.*

US
MERCURY-REGISTER. VFOAT Mercury Register. Vol. 114, No. 231 (Oct. 1, 1987)-. Newspaper. English. da. $106.53 Butte County; $138.00 other. Oroville Mercury Register, PO Box 651, Oroville CA 95965. **Tel** (916)533-3131. **ED** Roger Aylworth. **Ad Acc**, **Adv Mgr:** Lonnie Steedman. **Circ:** 8,663. ***Continues*** *Oroville Mercury-Register (Oroville, Calif. : 1961).*

US/0897-2281
METROPOLITAN NEWS-ENTERPRISE. VFOAT Metropolitan News Enterprise. Vol. 87, No. 88 (Thursday, Sept. 10, 1987)-. Newspaper. English. ir (252 issues per year). $172.12. Metropolitan News-Enterprise, PO Box 60859, Los Angeles CA 90060. **Tel** (213)628-4384, FAX (213)687-3886. **Ad Acc. *Formed by the union of*** *Metropolitan News, 0893-9071* ***and*** *Enterprise.*
Desc: Provides intensive coverage of law and the courts.

US/0888-7764
MEXICAN AMERICAN SUN. (1945)-. Newspaper. English (Spanish). wk. $72.00. Eastern Group Publications, PO Box 33803, Los Angeles CA 90033. **Tel** (213)263-5743, FAX (213)263-9169. **ED** Dolores Sanchez (editor's address: 3643 East 1st Street, Los Angeles CA 90063) and Tony Castro (Managing Editor). **Bk Rev**. **Photos**. **Ad Acc**, **Adv Mgr:** Jonathan Sanchez. Full Page (B&W) $22.00. Half Page (B&W) $22.00. Full Page (Color) $25.97. Half Page (Color) $25.97. **Pub. Size:** Broadsheet. **Wire Svcs.:** CN. **Circ:** 68,000 (ctrl).
Desc: Covers hispanic and community news.

US/0745-6212
MILPITAS POST. (19??)-. Newspaper. English. wk. $17.00. Milpitas Post, 1615 A South Mail Street, Milpitas CA 95035. **Tel** (408)262-2454. **ED** Rod Vincenzi. **Ad Acc**, **Adv Mgr:** Linda Schmitz. **Pub. Size:** Tabloid. **Circ:** 17,352.

US
MODESTO BEE, THE. Vol. 98, No. 250 (Oct. 19, 1975)-. Newspaper. English. da. $10.50 per month. Modesto Bee, 14th & H Streets, PO Box 3928, Modesto CA 95352. **Tel** (209)578-2000. **ED** Sanders Lamont, Mark Vasche (Managing Editor). **Bk Rev**. **Photos**. **Ad Acc**, **Adv Mgr:** Gary Moore, **Tel** (209)578-2080. **Pub. Size:** Standard. **Wire Svcs.:** AP, RN, MNS. **Circ:** 83,680 daily, 92,310 Sunday. available in microform from VU-TEXT. ***Continues*** *Modesto Bee and News-Herald.*

US
MODOC COUNTY RECORD, THE. Vol. 60, No. 41 (Mar. 10, 1960)-. Newspaper. English. wk. $22.00. Modoc County Record, PO Box 531, Alturas CA 96101. **Tel** (916)233-2632, FAX (916)233-5113. **ED** Rick Holloway. **Photos**. **Ad Acc**, **Adv Mgr:** Karen Badmark. Full Page (B&W) $504.00. Half Page (B&W) $252.00. Full Page (Color) $504.00 plus $100.00 per color. Half Page (Color) $252.00 plus $100.00 per color. **Pub. Size:** Standard. **Circ:** 4,500. available in microform. ***Continues*** *Modoc County Record and Alturas Plaindealer.*

US/1065-1152
MOJAVE DESERT NEWS, THE. (19??)-. Newspaper. English. wk. $20.00 Kern county, other California, $35.00 US, $85.00 other. Mojave Desert News, PO Box 937, Mojave CA 93501. **Tel** (619)373-4812.

US/8750-4863
MONTECITO LIFE. (198?)-. Newspaper. English. wk (Published on Thursdays). South Coast Community Newspapers, PO Box 1670, Goleta CA 93116-1670. **Tel** (805)683-1955, FAX (805)964-8371. **ED** Jeffrey Veen. **Circ:** 2,850.

US
MORGAN HILL TIMES, SAN MARTIN NEWS. VFOAT Morgan Hill Times and San Martin News. Vol. 48, No. 56 (May 9, 1947)-. Newspaper. English. wk. $30.25 California; $70.25 other. Morgan Hill Times, 30 East Third Street, Morgan Hill CA 95037. **Tel** (408)683-4551. ***Continues*** *Times (Morgan Hill, Calif.).*

US/1064-6477
MOUNT SHASTA HERALD. VFOAT Mount Shasta, Calif. Herald. Vol. 1, No. 1 (Sept. 13, 1887)-. Newspaper. English. wk. $25.50. Southern Siskiyou Newspapers, PO Box 127, 316 Chestnut Street, Mount Shasta CA 96067. **Tel** (916)926-5214, FAX (916)926-4166. **ED** Darlene Moss. **Photos**. **Ad Acc**, **Adv Mgr:** Genny Axtman. Full Page (B&W) $883.65. Half Page (B&W) $445.25. Full Page (Color) $948.65. Half Page (Color) $505.25. **Pub. Size:** Standard. available in microform.

US/0745-6220
MOUNTAIN COURIER-NEWS. VFOAT Mountain Courier News. Newspaper. English. wk. Allen P McCombs, PO Drawer 1670-A, Crestline CA 92325.

US
MOUNTAIN DEMOCRAT AND PLACERVILLE TIMES. Vol. 134, No. 94 (Aug. 4, 1989)-. Newspaper. English. tw. Mother Lode Printing and Publishing Company, 447 Main Street, Placerville CA 95667. ***Continues*** *Mountain Democrat (Placerville, Calif. : 1987).*

US/0278-4394
MOUNTAIN MESSENGER, THE. VFOAT Mountain Messenger and the Independent Messenger. (1855)-. Newspaper. English. Fifty-two times a year. The Mountain Messenger, PO Drawer A, Downieville CA 95936-0395. **Tel** (916)289-3262. **ED** Liz Fisher and Fred Cochran. ***Continues*** *Gibonsville Trumpet.*

US
MOUNTAIN NEWS AND MOUNTAINEER. English. Fifty-two times a year (Thurs.). $21.55 San Bernadino County; $28.00 others in California; $43.10 others in US. Mountain News California, PO Box 2609, Blue Jay CA 92317. **Tel** (714)336-3555. **Circ:** 7,500.

US/0745-8584
MYRTLE BEACH JOURNAL, THE. *Ceased.* (1982)-(1992). Newspaper. English. wk. Myrtle Beach Journal, PO Box 2443, Myrtle Beach CA 29577. **Tel** (803)448-9715. **ED** Chad Buffkin. **Bk Rev**. **Ad Acc**.

US/0744-6942
NAPA COUNTY RECORD AND NAPA VALLEY NEWS. VFOAT Napa County Record; Napa Valley News. (19??)-. Newspaper. English. wk. $18.00. Napa County Record, 520 3rd Street, PO Box 88, Napa CA 94558. **Tel** (707)252-8877, FAX (707)226-3707. **ED** Melodie Antiy. **Bk Rev**, (Qty: 13). **Photos**. **Ad Acc**, **Adv Mgr:** David Barker. Full Page (B&W) $595.00. Half Page (B&W) $300.00. **Pub. Size:** Broadsheet. **Circ:** 9,800.
Desc: Local interest publication concerning the Napa Valley area.

US
NAPA VALLEY REGISTER, THE. No. 244 (Apr. 15, 1991)-. Newspaper. English. da. $120.00 in county (by mail); $144.00 other (by mail). Napa Register, PO Box 150, Napa CA 94558. **Tel** (707)226-3711. **ED** Doug Ernst. **Ad Acc**, **Adv Mgr:** Micheal Stansfield. **Circ:** 21,123. ***Continues*** *Napa Register (Napa, Calif. : 1984).*

US/0739-1617
NATIONAL EDUCATOR, THE. [Nat. educ.]. (19??)-. Periodical. English. mo. $20.00. National Educator, PO Box 333, 1051 South Lemon Street #E, Fullerton CA 92632. **Tel** (714)871-2950, FAX (714)871-5353. **ED** James Townsend. **Bk Rev**, (Qty: 12). **Photos**. **Ad Acc**, **Adv Mgr:** Max Goldberg. Full Page (B&W) $400.00. Half Page (B&W) $250.00. **Pub. Size:** Tabloid. **Circ:** 65,000.
Desc: Non-affiliated conservative newspaper.

US/8750-8729
NEVADA COUNTY INDEPENDENT MESSENGER, THE. VFOAT Independent Messenger. Newspaper. English. wk. The Independent Messenger, Drawer A, Downieville CA 95936-0395. **Tel** (916)289-3262. **ED** F Cochran. **Circ:** 3,600.

US/1054-5891
NEW KOREA (LOS ANGELES, CALIF.). ***Ceased.*** (THE NEW KOREA.). (19??)-(19??). Newspaper. Korean (English). wk. New Korea, 2936 West 8th Street, Los Angeles CA 90005. **Tel** (213)382-9345, FAX (213)382-1678. **ED** Woon-Ha Kim. cum. index. **Ad Acc. Circ:** 3,000 (ctrl).

US/0747-4180
NEWS-PILOT. VFOAT News Pilot. Newspaper. English. da. News-Pilot, 5215 Torrance Boulevard, Torrance CA 90509.

US/0893-9004
NEWS-REVIEW (INYOKERN, CALIF.), THE. (THE NEWS-REVIEW.). **VFOAT** News Review. (19??)-. Newspaper. English. wk. $24.00. Inyokern News Review, 109 North Sanders, Ridgecrest CA 93555. **Tel** (619)371-4301, FAX (619)371-4304. **ED** Patti Cosner. **Bk Rev**. **Photos**. **Ad Acc**, **Adv Mgr:** Pat Farris. Full Page (B&W) $432.00. Half Page (B&W) $216.00. Full Page (Color) $497.00. Half Page (Color) $281.00. **Pub. Size:** Tabloid. available in microform.

US/1056-5124
NGOUI VIET DAILY NEWS. ENGLISH SECTION. (19??)-. Newspaper. Vietnamese (English). wk (Thurs.). $120.00. Nguoi Viet Daily News, 14891 Moran Street, Westminster CA 92683. **Tel** (714)892-9414, FAX (714)894-1381. **Ad Acc**. ctrl circ.

US/0739-2443
NICHI BEI TIMES. (NICHI BEI TIMES. JAPANESE AMERICAN DAILY. NICHI BEI JIJI.). **VFOAT** Japanese American Daily; Nichi Bei Jiji. (May 23, 1946)-. Periodical. Japanese (English). da. $107.40. Nichi Bei Times Co, PO Box 3098, San Francisco CA 91319. **Tel** (415)921-6920, FAX (415)921-0770. **ED** Iwao Nanekawa. **Photos**. **Ad Acc**, **Adv Mgr:** Mr. Tsutomu Umezu, **Tel** (415)921-6820. Full Page (B&W) $2000.00. Half Page (B&W) $1100.00. **Pub. Size:** Standard. **Circ:** 8,000.

US/0194-0074
NOR KIANK. VFOAT Nor Gyank Armenian Weekly; Nor Gyank; New Life; Nor Gyank, New Life. (197?)-. Periodical. Armenian (English and French). wk (52 issues). $50.00 US; $55.00 Canada; $300.00 other. Nor Gyank, PO Box 1694, Glendale CA 91209. **Tel** (818)240-9996, (818)240-9997, FAX (818)240-1917. **ED** Krikor Smenian. **Bk Rev**. **Ad Acc. Circ:** 10,000 (ctrl).
Desc: Published news about the Armenian community and of general interest to Armenians in addition to literary work, book reviews, and editorials.

US
NOR OR. VFOAT New Day. (1923)-. Newspaper. Armenian. sw. $50.00. Nor Or Publishing Company, 1901 North Allen Avenue, Altadena CA 91001-3421. **Tel** (818)797-6320, FAX (818)469-8198. **ED** Hagop Boghossian. **LC** 7002. **Photos**. **Ad Acc**. Full Page (B&W) $250.00. Half Page (B&W) $120.00. **Pub. Size:** Standard. **Circ:** 2,000. available on microfilm from University of California at Berkeley. ***Continues*** *Nor Giank-Siswan.*

US/1059-5694
NORTH COUNTY BLADE-CITIZEN, THE. VFOAT Blade Citizen; North County Blade Citizen; Blade-Citizen. (1989)-. Newspaper. English. da. North

County Blade Citizen, PO Box 7006, Solana Beach CA 92075-0988. **Tel** (619)755-1127. ***Formed by the union of*** *Citizen (Solana Beach, Calif.), 0746-0058; Costan, 0744-7825* ***and*** *Del Mar Citizen, 8750-8796.*

US
NOVATO ADVANCE. (1922)-. Newspaper. English. wk. $45.60 Marin County; $48.60 other. Marin Publishing Co., PO Box 8, Novato CA 94947. **Tel** (415)892-1516.

US
OAKDALE LEADER. (188?)-. Newspaper. English. wk. Live Oak Publishing, 122 South Third, Oakdale CA 95361. **Tel** (209)847-3021, FAX (209)847-9750. **ED** Steve Breen. **Ad Acc, Adv Mgr:** John Burden. **Circ:** 9,059.

US
OAKLAND POST. **VFOAT** Oakland Sunday Post. (June 8, 1963)-. Newspaper. English (Spanish). sw (104 issues). $80.00 US; $83.50 other (includes postage). Post Newspaper Group, 630 20th Street, Oakland CA 94612. **Tel** (510)763-1120, (510)287-8200, FAX (510)763-9670. **ED** Gail Berkley. **Bk Rev. Ad Acc. Circ:** 49,500 (ctrl). available on microfilm.

US/1068-5936
OAKLAND TRIBUNE (OAKLAND, CALIF. 1991). (OAKLAND TRIBUNE.). (Feb. 27, 1991)-. Newspaper. English. da. $260.00 (daily & Sunday),$165.88 (Sunday only) + sales tax, $169.00 (daily & Sunday for Santa Mateo & Santa Clara counties) by mail; $126.65 (daily & Sunday) by carrier. Alameda Newspaper Group, PO Box 5050, Circulation Department, Hayward CA 94544. **Tel** (510) 208-6300, FAX (510) 293-2319. ***Continues*** *Tribune (Oakland, Calif.), 0745-3841.*

US
OJAI AND VALLEY NEWS, THE. **VFOAT** Ojai and the Ojai Valley News; Ojai Valley News; Ojai Valley News and Oaks Gazette. (1958)-. Newspaper. English. $60.00 in county; $70.00 other. Ojai Valley News, PO Box 277, Ojai CA 93023. **Tel** (805)646-1476. ***Formed by the union of*** *Ojai; Ojai Valley News* ***and*** *Oaks Gazette.*

US/0276-590X
OPINION (LOS ANGELES, CALIF.), LA. (LA OPINION.). Vol. 1, No. 1 (Sept. 16, 1926)-. Newspaper. Spanish. ds. $160.00 (daily and Sunday), $88.00 (Sunday only). La Opinion, PO Box 15268, Los Angeles CA 90015. **Tel** (213)896-2222, telex 910 3213516. **ED** Sergio Munoz. Index available. **Bk Rev. Ad Acc. Circ:** 72,442. available on microfilm from Bay Microfilm, Inc.
Desc: An independent newspaper on general interests.

US/0030-4298
ORANGE COUNTY JEWISH HERITAGE. (19??)-. Newspaper. English. wk. $25.00 US; $49.00 others. Heritage Publishing Company, 2130 South Vermont Avenue, Los Angeles CA 90007. **Tel** (213)737-2122. **ED** Dan Brin.

US/0192-0421
ORANGE COUNTY NEWS. Newspaper. English. wk. $85.00. Orange County News, 9872 Chapman/Suite 8, Garden Grove CA 92640. **Tel** (714)530-7622. **ED** Dave Royue. **Circ:** 52,000.

US/0886-4934
ORANGE COUNTY REGISTER, THE. Vol. 80, No. 215 (May 19, 1985)-. Newspaper. English. ds. $658.00 US; $1570.00 other. Orange County Register, 625 North Grand Avenue, Santa Ana CA 92701. **Tel** (714)835-1234, (714)972-9800. **ED** N. Christian Anderson. **Circ:** 317,331. available on microfilm from University Microfilms International (UMI). ***Continues*** *Register (Santa Ana, Calif.), 0746-8628.*
Ind/Abst PROMT.

US
ORANGE COVE NEWS. (19??)-. Newspaper. English. wk. Reedley Exponent News, 1130 G Street, Reedley CA 93654-3004. **Tel** (209)638-2244, FAX (209)638-5021.

US/1059-2369
ORGANIZER (SAN FRANCISCO, CALIF.), THE. (THE ORGANIZER.). [Organizer]. **Added/Corp** Socialist Organizer (San Francisco, Calif.). Vol. 1, No. 1 (May 1991)-. Newspaper. English. mo. $12.00. The Organizer, 4017 24th Street, #19, San Francisco CA 94114. **LC** HD4802; .O74. **DD** 071.

US/0898-5375
OUTLOOK (SANTA MONICA, CALIF.), THE. (THE OUTLOOK.). 112th Year, No. 1 (Jan. 1, 1987)-. Newspaper. English. da. $88.00 (carrier). Santa Monica Outlook, 5215 Torrance Boulevard, Torrance CA 90509. **Tel** (213)540-5511. **ED** Jim Box, Skip Rimer (Managing Editor). **Photos. Ad Acc, Adv Mgr:** Paul Wrosch. Full Page (B&W) $2315.55. Half Page (B&W) $1177.00. **Pub. Size:** Broadsheet. **Wire Svcs.:** AP, HH, SH, NY. **Circ:** 26,000. ***Continues*** *Evening Outlook, 0889-826X.*

US/0895-3457
PACIFIC BEACH LIGHT. ***Ceased.*** **VFOAT** Light. Vol. 1, No. 1 (Jan. 1987)-?. Newspaper. English. wk. Pacific Beach Light, 450 Pearl Street, PO Box 1927, La Jolla CA 92038.

US/0030-8579
PACIFIC CITIZEN, THE. **Added/Corp** Japanese American Citizen's League. New American Citizen's League of San Francisco. National Japanese American Citizens League. (Nov. 1931)-. Newspaper. English. Forty-Five times a year. Pacific Citizen, 2 Coral Circle, Suite 204, Monterey Park CA 91755. **Tel** (213)725-0083. **ED** Harry K. Honda. **Bk Rev. Ad Acc. Circ:** 21,918. available on microfilm from Bay Microfilm, Inc. ***Continues*** *Nikkei Shimin.*
Desc: Emphasizes issues affecting Japanese-Americans and their activities, contributions and personal achievements.

US/0746-8423
PACIFIC GROVE, PEBBLE BEACH TRIBUNE. **VFOAT** Pacific Grove-Pebble Beach Tribune. (19??)-. Newspaper. English. wk. $12.00. Monterey County Media, 305 Forest Avenue, Pacific Grove CA 93950. **Tel** (408)649-1311.

US/0048-2641
PACIFIC SUN. Year 5, No. 1 (Jan. 4, 1967)-. Newspaper. English. wk. $15.00 (6 months), $25.00 (1 year). Pacific Sun, 2 Corte Madera, Mill Valley CA 94941. **Tel** (415)383-4500. **ED** Stephen McNamara. **Bk Rev. Ad Acc. Circ:** 35,700 (ctrl). ***Continues*** *Pacific Sun and Tamalpais Times.*
Desc: A newsmagazine focusing on local events and issues.

US
PALM SPRINGS DESERT SUN. (1927)-. Newspaper. English. da (Mon.-Sat.). The Desert Sun / Palm Springs Desert Sun, PO Box 2735, Palm Springs CA 92263. **ED** James Lycett. **Circ:** 25,478. ***Continues*** *Coachella Valley Sun; Indio Daily News.*

US/0199-1159
PALO ALTO WEEKLY. Vol. 1 (Oct. 1979)-. Newspaper. English. tw. $40.00 (one year), $70.00 (two years). Palo Alto Weekly, 703 High Street, Palo Alto CA 94302. **Tel** (415)326-8210. **ED** Paul Gullixson. **Bk Rev**, (Qty: 12). **Ad Acc. Circ:** 45,000 (ctrl). available on microfilm from Bay Microfilm, Inc; available via Internet.
Desc: General interest news magazine.

US/1069-2827
PASADENA STAR-NEWS. **VFOAT** Pasadena Star News; Star News; Star-News. (Mar. 1, 1916)-. Newspaper. English. da. $127.00 (daily and Sunday). Star News, 525 East Colorado Boulevard, Pasadena CA 91109. **Tel** (818)962-8811. **ED** Patty Burnett. **Bk Rev. Ad Acc. Circ:** 39,510.
Desc: Daily newspaper for Pasadena, California.

US/0195-0134
PASO ROBLES COUNTRY NEWS, THE. (19??)-. Newspaper. English. wk. $15.00. Paso Robles Country News, 945 Spring Street, Paso Robles CA 93446. **Tel** (805)238-6937. **ED** Sheena Berwick, Scott Steepleton (Managing Editor). **Photos. Ad Acc, Adv Mgr:** Mary Baldwin, **Tel** (805)237-6060. Full Page (B&W) $748.00. Half Page (B&W) $399.20. Full Page (Color) $748.00 plus $126.00 per color. Half Page (Color) $399.20 plus $126.00 per color. **Pub. Size:** Tabloid.

US/0031-5044
PEOPLE'S WORLD (BERKELEY). (PEOPLE'S WORLD.). (19??)-. Newspaper. English. wk. Pacific Publication Foundation, 620 York Street, San Francisco CA 94110. **Tel** (415)848-1373. **ED** Carl Bloice. **Bk Rev. Ad Acc. Circ:** 8,000.
Desc: General left political newspaper.

US
PERRIS PROGRESS, THE. Vol. 82, No. 48 (Dec. 1, 1982)-. Newspaper. English. wk (published on Wed.). $17.54. Perris Progress, PO Box 128, Perris CA 92572. **Tel** (714)657-2181. **Photos. Ad Acc. Pub. Size:** Standard. ***Continues*** *Perris Progress Sun City Sun.*

US
PHILIPPINE NEWS. 6th Year, No. 33 (May 2, 1967)-. Newspaper. English. Fifty-two times a year (Wed.). Philippine News, 148 South Spruce Avenue, South San Francisco CA 94080. **Tel** (415)872-3000, FAX (415)872-0217. available on microfilm. ***Continues*** *Manila Chronicle.*

US
PIONEER, THE. **VFOAT** Shelley Pioneer. (Aug. 29, 1974)-. Newspaper. English. wk (Published on Thursdays). The Filipino American, 2741 Fruitridge Road, Sacramento CA 95820. **Ad Acc, Adv Mgr:** Irv Smith. **Circ:** 1,525. ***Continues*** *Shelley Pioneer.*

US/0746-7389
PITTSBURG POSTDISPATCH, THE. ***Title Change.*** (PITTSBURG POSTDISPATCH.). **VFOAT** Pittsburg Post Dispatch; Sunday Daily Ledger, Post Dispatch; Daily Ledger, Post Dispatch; Sunday Daily Ledger-Post Dispatch; Daily Ledger-Post Dispatch; Post Dispatch. Newspaper. English. da. California Delta Newspapers, PO Box 2299, Antioch CA 94531-2299. **Tel** (415)757-2525. ***Merged with*** *Daily Ledger (Antioch, Calif), 0746-7370* ***to form*** *Daily Ledger, Post Dispatch, 1054-8459.*

●US
PLACER HERALD, THE. (1992)-. Newspaper. English. wk. $12.87 Placer County; $21.45 other. Placer Herald, Auburn Journal, PO Box 1488, Auburn CA 95603. **Tel** (916)885-2471. ***Continues*** *Placer Rocklin Herald.*

US/0747-220X
PRESS DEMOCRAT (SANTA ROSA, CALIF.). (THE PRESS DEMOCRAT.). **VFOAT** Democrat-Republican. No. 242 (Oct. 9, 1928)-. Newspaper. English. da (Sun.-Fri.). $128.70 by carrier, $216.32 by mail (daily & Sun.). Santa Rosa Press Democrat, PO Box 569, Santa Rosa CA 95402. **Tel** (707)546-2020. **ED** Bruce Kyse (Editor in Chief), Bob Swofford (Managing Editor). **Bk Rev. Photos. Ad Acc, Adv Mgr:** Ken Svanum, **Tel** (707)526-8577. Full Page (B&W) $5166.00. Half Page (B&W) $2583.00. **Pub. Size:** Standard. **Wire Svcs.:** AP, NY, LA, WP. **Circ:** 77,707 daily, 85,640 Sunday. available in microform from Bay Microfilm, Inc. ***Absorbed*** *Santa Rosa Republican (Santa Rosa, Calif. : Daily).*

US/0746-4258
PRESS-ENTERPRISE (RIVERSIDE, CALIF.). (THE PRESS-ENTERPRISE.). **VFOAT** Press Enterprise; Saturday Press-Enterprise; Sunday Press-Enterprise. (Oct. 1, 1983)-. Newspaper. English. da. $95.68. Press-Enterprise / California, PO Box 792, 3512 14th Street, Riverside CA 92502. **Tel** (909)684-1200, FAX (909)782-6034. **ED** Marcia McQuern, Mel Opotowsky (Managing Editor). **Ad Acc, Adv Mgr:** David Cornwall, **Tel** (909)782-7670. Full Page (B&W) $44.80 (per inch). Half Page (B&W) $45.30 (per inch). Full Page (Color) $564.00. Half Page (Color) $564.00. **Pub. Size:** Standard. **Wire Svcs.:** SH, KR, AP, NY. **Circ:** 163,004 (morning, paid). ***Formed by the union of*** *Morning Press-Enterprise* ***and*** *Evening Press-Enterprise.*

US
PRESS-TELEGRAM. **VFOAT** Press Telegram. Newspaper. English. da. Press-Telegram, 604 Pine Avenue, Long Beach CA 90844. **Tel** (310)435-1161. **ED** Larry Allison. **Circ:** 130,999. ***Continues*** *Independent Press-Telegraph.*

US
RAFU SHIMPO. **VFOAT** L.A. Japanese Daily; L.A. Japanese Daily News; Los Angeles Japanese Daily News. (1903)-. Newspaper. Japanese (English). da. $60.00. La Japanese Daily News, 259 So Los Angeles Street, Los Angeles CA 90012. **Tel** (213)629-2231, FAX (213)687-0737. **ED** Naomi Hirahara (English) and Yukikazu Nagashimo (Japanese) Editor-in-Chief's. **Bk Rev. Photos. Ad Acc, Adv Mgr:** Mr. Ubukata. Full Page (B&W) $1,680.00 (English) & $2,080.00 (Japanese). Half Page (B&W) $840.00 (English) & $960.00 (Japanese). **Pub. Size:** Standard. **Circ:** 22,000.

US/0884-6170
RANCHO MIRAGE POST. **VFOAT** Post. Vol. 9, No. 18 (Wednesday, July 31, 1985)-. Newspaper. English. sw (Wed. & Fri.). $22.00 Riverside County, California; $45.00 other. Rancho Mirage Post, PO Box 459, Palm Desert CA 92261. **Tel** (619)346-1181. **ED** Dave Stephens. **Circ:** 4,125. ***Continues*** *Rancho Mirage Chronicle, 0745-5577.*

US/0891-8627
RANDOM LENGTHS (SAN PEDRO, CALIF.). (RANDOM LENGTHS.). (Winter 1979)-. Newspaper. English. sm. $19.95. Random Lengths, 1117 South Pacific Avenue, PO Box 731, San Pedro CA 90733. **Tel** (310)519-1442, FAX (310)832-9490. **ED** James Allen (Editor-in-Chief) and M. Easterbrooke (Managing Editor). **Bk Rev**, (Qty: varies). **Photos. Ad Acc, Adv Mgr:** Tom Davidson. Full Page (B&W) $900.00. Half Page (B&W) $575.00. Full Page (Color) $1,300.00. Half Page (Color) $850.00. **Pub. Size:** Tabloid. **Wire Svcs.:** PN, AN. **Circ:** 30,000 (ctrl). available on videocassette.
Desc: Newspaper of general circulation for the LA Harbor area. Includes news, fine dining, health and fitness, business news and real estate information.

US
READER (SAN DIEGO, CALIF.). (READER.). Vol. 1, No. 1 (Oct. 5, 1972)-. Newspaper. English. wk. $135.00 domestic only. San Diego Reader, PO Box 80803, San Diego CA 92138. **Tel** (619)231-7821, FAX (619)231-0489. **ED** Jim Holman. Index available. cum. index. **Ad Acc. Circ:** 130,000 (ctrl).
Desc: Features stories on theater, movie, film, restaurant, reviews, and entertainment listings.

US/0747-1521
RECORD-GAZETTE. **VFOAT** Record Gazette. 61st Year, No. 93 (May 9, 1968)-. Newspaper. English. da (Monday - Friday). $85.00. Record-Gazette, 218 North Murray Street, Banning CA 92220. **Tel** (714)849-4586. **ED** Henry Aceuedo. **Circ:** 3,518. ***Continues*** *Daily Record-Gazette.*

US
RECORD SEARCHLIGHT. Vol. 124, No. 52 (May 12, 1975)-. Newspaper. English. da. $156.00 (daily and Sunday). Record Searchlight, PO Box 492397, Redding CA 96049. **Tel** (916)243-2424 ext.306. **ED** Robert Edkin. **Ad Acc**, **Adv Mgr:** Bill Dawson. **Circ:** 39,379. ***Continues*** *Redding Record-Searchlight and the Courier Free Press.*

US
RECORDER (SAN FRANCISCO, CALIF.). (THE RECORDER.). **VFOAT** San Francisco Legal Newspaper. (19??)-. Newspaper. English. ir. $325.00. American Lawyer Media LP / California, PO Box 421378, San Francisco CA 94142. **Tel** (415)749-5400. **Desc:** Legal newspaper for San Francisco, California area.

US
RED BLUFF TEHAMA COUNTY DAILY NEWS. Vol. 86, No. 98 (Feb. 26, 1969)-. Newspaper. English. da. Daily News / Red Bluff, 545 Diamond Avenue, Red Bluff CA 96080-4302. **Tel** (916)527-2151, FAX (916)527-3719. **ED** Bill Goodyear. **Ad Acc**. **Circ:** 39,379. ***Continues*** *Red Bluff Daily News (Red Bluff, Calif. : 1935).*

US/0195-0533
REDWOOD CITY ALMANAC. Vol. 1 (July 3, 1979)-. Newspaper. English. wk. $12.00 San Mateo County; $48.00 other. Redwood City Almanac, PO Box 5347, Redwood City CA 94063. **Tel** (415)364-9500. **ED** Bob Distefano. **Bk Rev**. **Ad Acc**. **Circ:** 4,000. **Desc:** Coverage of Redwood City, San Carlos, and Belmont areas including information on the city council, planning commission, Port of Redwood City, San Mateo County government.

US
REEDLEY EXPONENT, THE. (18??)-. Newspaper. English. wk. Reedley Exponent News, 1130 G Street, Reedley CA 93654-3004. **Tel** (209)638-2244, FAX (209)638-5021.

US/0746-5688
REPORTER (LONG BEACH, CALIF.), THE. (THE REPORTER.). (198?)-. Newspaper. English. sw (104 per year). $25.00. The Reporter / Long Beach, CA, PO Box 4278, Long Beach CA 90804. **Tel** (213)438-5641. **ED** Craig Pfanstiel. **Circ:** 700. ***Continues*** *Long Beach Reporter.*

US/0746-4193
REPORTER (VACAVILLE, CALIF.). (REPORTER.). (19??)-. Newspaper. English. da. Vacaville Reporter, PO Box 1509, Vacaville CA 95688. **Tel** (707)448-8566. ***Continues*** *Vacaville Reporter.*

US/1052-5300
REVIEW-HERALD, THE. **VFOAT** Review Herald. Vol. 15, No. 8 (Feb. 19, 1987)-. Newspaper. English. sw. $43.00. Chalfant Press, 450 East Line Street, PO Box 787, Bishop CA 93514. **Tel** (717)873-3535. ***Formed by the union of*** *Review (Bishop, Calif.), 0746-780X* ***and*** *Mono Herald & Bridgeport Chronicle-Union.*

US
RICHMOND POST. (1963)-. Newspaper. English. wk. $75.00 US; $100.00 other. Richmond Post, 630 20th Street, Oakland CA 94612. **Tel** (510)673-1120. **ED** Gail Berkley. **Bk Rev**. **Ad Acc**. **Circ:** 13,661 (ctrl). available on microfilm.

US
RIVER NEWS HERALD & ISLETON JOURNAL, THE. **VFOAT** River News Herald & Isleton Journal; River News-Herald and Isleton Journal. (19??)-. Newspaper. English. wk. $21.00 Solano County; $28.00 other. River News Herald, PO Box 786, Rio Vista CA 94571. **Tel** (707)374-6431. ***Formed by the union of*** *River News-Herald* ***and*** *Isleton Journal.*

US/8750-7986
RIVERSIDE COUNTY RECORD-NEWS. **VFOAT** Riverside County Record News; Record News. Newspaper. English. wk. $12.00 Riverside County; $14.00 Southern California; $18.00 other. Riverside County Record-News, PO Box 3187, Riverside CA 92519-3187. **Tel** (909)685-6191. **ED** Allen P McCombs. **Circ:** 750. ***Continues*** *Riverside County Record.*

US/8750-3417
ROPERS SPORTS NEWS. (19??)-. Periodical. English. Twelve times a year. $20.00. Ropers Sports News, 24060 North Ray Road, Lodi CA 95242. **Tel** (209)333-2924, FAX (209)368-9512.

US
ROSEVILLE PRESS-TRIBUNE. **VFOAT** Roseville Press Tribune; Roseville, California Press-Tribune. (19??)-. Newspaper. English. sw. $84.00 Placer County; $104.00 other. Roseville Press Tribune, 188 Cirby Way, Roseville CA 95678. **Tel** (916)786-6500, FAX (916)783-1183. **ED** Nick Baptista. **Ad Acc**. **Circ:** 12,000.

US
RUSSKAIA ZHIZN. **Added/Corp** Russian American Anticommunist Organization. **VFOAT** Russian Life; Russian Life Daily. Vol. 22, No. 1 (Jan. 1, 1942)-. Newspaper. Russian. da (161 issues per year). $90.00. Russian Life / California, 2458 Sutter Street, San Francisco CA 94115. **Tel** (415)921-5380, FAX (415)921-8726. **Photos**. **Ad Acc**, **Adv Mgr:** Anna Zeltzer. Full Page (B&W) $864.00. Half Page (B&W) $432.00. **Circ:** 1,200 (ctrl). ***Continues*** *Russkie Novosti (San Francisco, Calif. : 1940).*

US/0890-5738
SACRAMENTO BEE, THE. Vol. 103, No. 16,950 (Mar. 6, 1908)-. Newspaper. English. ds. $11.58 per month. Sacramento Bee, 2100 Q Street, PO Box 15779, Sacramento CA 95852. **Tel** (916)321-1111, (800)284-3233. **ED** Gregory Favre and Rick Rodriguez (Mananging Editor). **LC** 7135. **Bk Rev**. **Photos**. **Ad Acc**, **Adv Mgr:** Lisa Leonard, **Tel** (916)321-1476. Full Page (B&W) $13,815.00. Half Page (B&W) $6,908.00. Full Page (Color) $15,672.00. Half Page (Color) $8,765.00. **Pub. Size:** Broadsheet. **Wire Svcs.:** RN, LA, AP, SH. **Circ:** 260,952 daily, 314,762 Sunday. available on microfilm from Bay Microfilm, Inc; available on an online database (files 496,635/Full-Text) from DIALOG. Documents available from UMI Article Clearinghouse. ***Continues*** *Evening Bee;* ***Absorbed*** *Sacramento Star.* **Ind/Abst** Bus. Dateline; PROMT.

US/0036-2212
SACRAMENTO OBSERVER, THE. (1962)-. Newspaper. English. wk. $35.00. Observer Publishing Company / Sacramento, PO Box 209, Sacramento CA 95801. **Tel** (916)452-4781, FAX (916)452-7744. **ED** William H. Lee, Kathryn C. Lee (Managing Editor). **Bk Rev**, (Qty: 52). **Photos**. **Ad Acc**, **Adv Mgr:** Joe Stinson. **Circ:** 49,600 (ctrl). available in microform from Bay Microfilm, Inc.

US
SAN BERNARDINO COUNTY SUN, THE. Vol. 113, No. 112 (Apr. 22, 1986)-. Newspaper. English. da. $218.52 San Bernardino County; $247.00 other. San Bernardino Sun, 399 North D Street, San Bernardino CA 92401. **Tel** (909)889-9666, (800)922-0922, FAX (909)885-8741. **ED** Arnold Garson. **Ad Acc**, **Adv Mgr:** John Bennett. **Circ:** 87,993. ***Continues*** *Sun (San Bernardino, Calif. : 1978).*

US
SAN DIEGO DAILY TRANSCRIPT. (19??)-. Newspaper. English. da. $130.68. San Diego Daily Transcript, 2131 3rd Avenue, PO Box 85469, San Diego CA 92138. **Tel** (619)232-4381 Ext. 207.

US
SAN DIEGO DAILY TRANSCRIPT. Newspaper. English. da. $126.24. San Diego Daily Transcript, 2131 3rd Avenue, PO Box 85469, San Diego CA 92138. **Tel** (619)232-4381 Ext. 207. available on an online database (file 635/Full-Text) from DIALOG. Documents available from UMI Article Clearinghouse. **Ind/Abst** Bus. Dateline (Jan. 28, 1991-) [Full Txt.].

US
SAN DIEGO TRIBUNE. ***Title Change.*** (Nov. 6, 1989)-(199?). Periodical. English. da. Union-Tribune Publishing Company, PO Box 191, San Diego CA 92112. **Tel** (619)299-3131, (800)244-6397. ***Continues*** *Tribune (San Diego, Calif.).* ***Merged with*** *San Diego Union (San Diego, Calif. : 1918)* ***to form*** *San Diego Union-Tribune (San Diego, Calif. : 1992), 1063-102X.*

US
SAN DIEGO UNION (SAN DIEGO, CALIF. : 1930). ***Title Change.*** (THE SAN DIEGO UNION.). (19??)-(19??). Newspaper. English. da. Union-Tribune Publishing Company, PO Box 191, San Diego CA 92112. **Tel** (619)299-3131, (800)244-6397. **ED** Gerald L Warren. **Bk Rev**. **Ad Acc**. **Circ:** 271,270 daily, 439,860 Sunday (ctrl). available on microfilm from University Microfilms International (UMI); and University Microfilms International (UMI). ***Continues*** *San Diego Union and Daily Bee.* ***Merged with*** *San Diego Tribune* ***to form*** *San Diego Union-Tribune (San Diego, Calif. : 1992), 1063-102X.*

●US/1063-102X
SAN DIEGO UNION-TRIBUNE (1992). (THE SAN DIEGO UNION-TRIBUNE.). [S. Diego union-trib.]. **VFOAT** San Diego Union Tribune; Union-Tribune. No. 1 (Feb. 2, 1992)-. Newspaper. English. ds. $202.00. Union-Tribune Publishing Company, PO Box 191, San Diego CA 92112. **Tel** (619)299-3131, (800)244-6397. ***Formed by the union of*** *San Diego Union (San Diego, Calif.: 1930)* ***and*** *San Diego Tribune.* **Ind/Abst** PROMT.

US
SAN DIMAS PRESS, THE. Oct. (1911)-. Newspaper. English. wk. San Dimas Press, PO Box 2708, Pomona CA 91769. **Tel** (909)622-5005. **ED** Jim Fulton. **LC** 7114-X. **Circ:** 9,111. available on microfilm. ***Continues*** *San Dimas Eagle.*

US
SAN FERNANDO VALLEY SUN. (19??)-. Newspaper. English. sw. $45.00. San Fernando Valley Sun, 314 Chatsworth Drive, San Fernando CA 91340. **Tel** (213)365-3111.

US
SAN FRANCISCO BAY TIMES. (19??)-. English. ir (every other Thursday). $36.00 (18 issues), $54.00 (26 issues). San Francisco Bay Times, 288 7th Street, San Francisco CA 94103. **Tel** (415)626-8121. **ED** Kim Corsaro. **Bk Rev**. **Photos**. **Ad Acc**, **Adv Mgr:** Bob Gordon.

US
SAN FRANCISCO CHRONICLE. **VFOAT** Sunday Chronicle; San Francisco Sunday Chronicle; San Francisco Sunday Examiner & Chronicle; San Francisco Sunday Examiner and Chronicle. Vol. 10, No. 27 (Aug. 15, 1869)-. Newspaper. English. ds. $306.00 California, Nevada, Oregon; $318.00 Arizona, Colorado, Idaho, Montana, New Mexico, Utah, Washington State; $336.00 US; $744.00 other. San Francisco Newspaper Agency, 925 Mission Street, San Francisco CA 94103. **Tel** (415)777-5700, (800)227-4423. **ED** Richard Thieriot. Index available. **Bk Rev**. **Ad Acc**. **Circ:** 569,185. available on microfilm from MCI; available in microform from University Microfilms International (UMI); available on an online database (file 640/Full-Text) from DIALOG. Documents available from UMI Article Clearinghouse. ***Continues*** *Daily Morning Chronicle (San Francisco, Calif.).* **Ind/Abst** Infobank (Jan. 1969-); Newsp. Abstr.; PROMT.

US
SAN FRANCISCO EXAMINER, THE. **VFOAT** San Francisco Examiner and News Call Bulletin; San Francisco Sunday Examiner & Chronicle. Vol. 76, No. 87 (March 28, 1902)-. Newspaper. English. ds. $306.00 California, Nevada, Oregon; $318.00 Arizona, Colorado, Idaho, Montana, New Mexico, Utah, Washington State; $336.00 US; $744.00 other. San Francisco Newspaper Agency, 925 Mission Street, San Francisco CA 94103. **Tel** (415)777-5700, (800)227-4423. **ED** Will Hearst. **Circ:** 145,014. available on microfilm from University Microfilms International (UMI); available on an online database (file 732/Full-Text) from DIALOG. ***Continues*** *Examiner (San Francisco, Calif. : 1889).* **Ind/Abst** Abstr. Res. Pastor. Care Couns.; PROMT.

US
SAN FRANCISCO JOURNAL, THE. Vol.1 (1976)-. Newspaper. English. wk. $10.00. San Francisco Journal, 1600 Armstrong Avenue, San Francisco CA 94124. **Tel** (415)822-1155. **LC** x.

US/0199-462X
SAN FRANCISCO JOURNAL. CHINESE EDITION, THE. ***Ceased.*** (SHIH TAI PAO.). **VFOAT** The San Francisco Journal. (1972)-Vol. 15 (1986). Newspaper. Chinese. da. San Francisco Journal, 1600 Armstrong Avenue, San Francisco CA 94124. **Tel** (415)822-1155. **Ad Acc**. **Circ:** 6,000. **Desc:** Newspaper representing the Chinese-American community. News coverage includes national and international news, sports, and entertainment.

US
SAN FRANCISCO POST. **VFOAT** San Francisco Sunday Post. Began in 1963. Newspaper. English. sw. $75.00 US; $100.00 other. San Francisco Post, 630 20th Street, Oakland CA 94612. **Tel** (510)763-1120, FAX (510)763-9670. **ED** Gail Berkley. **Bk Rev**. **Ad Acc**. **Circ:** 18,289 (ctrl). available on microfilm.

US/0191-8192
SAN FRANCISCO PROGRESS, THE. ***Ceased.*** Newspaper. English. tw. San Francisco Progress, 909 Montgomery Street/#200, San Francisco CA 94133. **Tel** (415)982-8022. **ED** Marvin Johnson. **Ad Acc**. **Circ:** 626,828 (ctrl). **Desc:** General interest newspaper concentrating on Bay area and San Francisco news, sports and entertainment. Legal advertising vehicle for city and county of San Francisco.

US
SAN FRANCISCO SENTINEL. (198?)-. Periodical. English. wk. $65.00. San Francisco Sentinel, 500 Hayes Street, San Francisco CA 94102. **Tel** (415)861-8100. ***Continues*** *Sentinel U.S.A.*

US/8755-9595
SAN GABRIEL VALLEY DAILY TRIBUNE. **VFOAT** San Gabriel Valley Tribune. (19??)-. Newspaper. English. da. $208.00 California; $286.00 US; $486.20 other. San Gabriel Valley Tribune, 1210 Azusa Canyon Road, West Covina CA 91790. **Tel** (818)962-8811. **ED** Joe Blackstock. **Circ:** 59,769.

US
SAN JACINTO VALLEY REGISTER. ***Ceased.*** (19??)-(19??). Newspaper. English. wk. San Jacinto Valley Register, PO Box 427, San Jacinto CA 92383. **Tel** (714)654-7327.

US/0747-2099
SAN JOSE MERCURY NEWS. (Aug. 29, 1983)-. Newspaper. English. ds. $360.00 California;

$450.00 other US; $975.00 other. San Jose Mercury News, 750 Ridder Park Drive, San Jose CA 95190. **Tel** (408)920-5000, (408)920-5609. **ED** Robert Ingle. **Circ:** 268,967 daily, 314,033 Sunday. available on microfilm from University Microfilms International (UMI); available on an online database (file 634/Full-Text) from DIALOG. ***Formed by the union of*** *San Jose Mercury (San Jose, Calif. : 1950)* ***and*** *San Jose News.*
Ind/Abst Comput. Database; PROMT.

US/0036-4185
SAN JOSE POST-RECORD, THE. VFOAT San Jose Post Record. (199?)-. Newspaper. English. ir (250 issues). $105.00. Daily Journal Corporation, 915 East First Street, Los Angeles CA 90012. **Tel** (213)229-5300, FAX (213)680-3682. **ED** Gerald L. Salzman. Index available. **Bk Rev**. **Ad Acc**.
Desc: Legal and real estate news for San Jose, California.

US
SAN LUIS OBISPO COUNTY TELEGRAM-TRIBUNE. (19??)-. Newspaper. English. da. $85.00 San Luis Obispo County; $105.00 outside county. County Telegram-Tribune, PO Box 112, San Luis Obispo CA 93401. **Tel** (805)781-7800, FAX (805)781-7870. **ED** Jeff Fairbanks. **Bk Rev**, (Qty: 12). **Photos**. **Ad Acc, Adv Mgr:** Devon Goetz, **Tel** (805)781-7849. Full Page (B&W) $16.24. Half Page (B&W) $16.24. Full Page (Color) $22.35. Half Page (Color) $22.35. **Pub. Size:** Broadsheet. **Wire Svcs.:** AP, SH. **Circ:** 32,500. available in microform.

US/0273-9259
SAN MARCOS COURIER. (19??)-. Newspaper. English. wk. $25.00 (by carrier). Press Courier, PO Box 2168, Vista CA 92083. **Tel** (619)724-7161. **ED** Nancy Richards. **Ad Acc**. **Circ:** 11,100 (ctrl).
Desc: News and information on people and happenings in San Marcos, California.

US
SAN MARCOS NEWS REPORTER. (19??)-. Newspaper. English. wk. $36.00. San Marcos News Reporter, 815 West San Marcos Boulevard, San Marcos CA 92069. **Tel** (619)471-8701. **ED** William Willoughby. **Ad Acc, Adv Mgr:** M. Ferdo. **Circ:** 10,000. ***Continues*** *San Marcos Outlook.*

US
SANGER HERALD. Newspaper. English. wk. Reedley Exponent News, 1130 G Street, Reedley CA 93654-3004. **Tel** (209)638-2244, FAX (209)638-5021. **ED** Bud Brockett. **Ad Acc, Adv Mgr:** Cheri Chastain. **Circ:** 3,000.

US
SANTA BARBARA NEWS & REVIEW (MICROFICHE). (SANTA BARBARA NEWS & REVIEW.). V.1- Feb. 11, 1972-. Newspaper. English. wk. $9.75. Santa Barbara News & Review, 607 State Street, Santa Barbara CA 93101. **Tel** (805)963-9411. **ED** Marianne Partridge. **Circ:** 34,837.

US
SANTA BARBARA NEWS-PRESS (1932). (SANTA BARBARA NEWS-PRESS.). **VFOAT** Santa Barbara News Press. (1932)-. Newspaper. English. da. $179.00 Santa Barbara county; $244.00 other US, Canada, and Mexico; $530.00 other. Santa Barbara News Press, PO Box 1359, Santa Barbara CA 93102. **Tel** (805)564-5200, FAX (805)966-6258. **ED** Allen Parsons and Tom Bolton (Managing Editor). **LC** 7205. **Bk Rev**. **Photos**. **Ad Acc, Adv Mgr:** John Leonard, **Tel** (805)564-5248. Full Page (B&W) $3528.00. Half Page (B&W) $1764.00. Full Page (Color) $4092.00 (full color). Half Page (Color) $2328.00 (full color). **Pub. Size:** Broadsheet. **Wire Svcs.:** AP, NY. **Circ:** 49,537 daily, 57,030 Sunday. available on microfilm from University Microfilms International (UMI). ***Formed by the union of*** *Morning Press* ***and*** *Santa Barbara Daily News.*

US
SANTA CRUZ SENTINEL (SANTA CRUZ, CALIF. : DAILY). (SANTA CRUZ SENTINEL.). 100th Year, No. 143 (June 17, 1956)-. Newspaper. English. da. Santa Cruz Sentinel Publishers Company / Department of Circulation, PO Box 638, Santa Cruz CA 95061. **Tel** (408)423-4242, (408)458-0111. **ED** Bruce McPherson. **Circ:** 27,882 (daily), 31,025 (Sunday). Documents available from UMI Article Clearinghouse. ***Continues*** *Santa Cruz Sentinel-News.*
Ind/Abst Bus. Dateline (Jan. 4, 1992-) [Full Txt.].

US/0745-6166
SANTA MARIA TIMES. VFOAT Times. Newspaper. English. da. $71.50. Santa Maria Times, PO Box 400, Santa Maria CA 93456. **Tel** (805)925-2691, FAX (805)928-5657. **ED** Don Brown. **Ad Acc**. **Circ:** 21,066. available on microfilm.

US
SANTA PAULA CHRONICLE. *Ceased.* (1887)-(19??). Newspaper. English. da (Mon.-Fri). Santa Paula Chronicle, 116 North 10th Street, Santa Paula CA 93060. **Tel** (805)525-5555. **ED** Robert Vincent.

US/0745-6255
SARATOGA NEWS. (19??)-. Newspaper. English. wk. $17.00 Santa Clara County; $30.00 other. Saratoga News, 14375 Saratoga Avenue, Suite E2, Saratoga CA 95070. **Tel** (408)867-6397. **ED** Mary Barnett. **Ad Acc**. **Circ:** 8,405 (ctrl).
Desc: Newspaper for the San Jose area.

US
SELMA ENTERPRISE, THE. 62nd Year, No. 12 (June 19, 1947)-. Newspaper. English. wk. $18.00. Selma Enterprise, 2045 Grant Street, Selma CA 93662-3593. **Tel** (209)896-1976, FAX (209)896-9160. **ED** Timothy Sheehan. **Photos**. **Ad Acc, Adv Mgr:** Gerald Latham. Full Page (B&W) $1424.00. Half Page (B&W) $693.00. Full Page (Color) $1514.00. Half Page (Color) $783.00. **Pub. Size:** Standard. **Circ:** 4,150. ***Continues*** *Selma Enterprise and the Selma Irrigator.*

US/0888-238X
SERICHAI. [Serichai]. **VFOAT** Sereechai Newspaper. (198?)-. Newspaper. Thai (English). Fifty-two times a year. $52.00. Sereechai Newspaper, 1241 North Vineth Street, Suite 20, Los Angeles CA 90038. **ED** Khanitha Angkabsee (Editor-in-Chief) and Siriwan Plsuttipong (Managing Editor). **DD** 071. **Photos**. **Ad Acc, Adv Mgr:** Siriwan Plsuttipong. Full Page (B&W) $400.00. Half Page (B&W) $200.00. Full Page (Color) $1,000.00. Half Page (Color) $500.00. **Pub. Size:** Standard. ***Continues*** *Serichon, 0747-3990.*

US/1060-2526
SF WEEKLY (SAN FRANCISCO, CALIF.). (SF WEEKLY.). [SF wkly.]. **VFOAT** San Francisco Weekly. (198?)-. Newspaper. English. wk. $80.00. SF Weekly, 425 Brannan Street, San Francisco CA 94107. **Tel** (415)541-0700, FAX (415)777-1839. **ED** Andrew O'Hehir. **DD** 051. **Ad Acc**. **Circ:** 80,000.

US/0749-7679
SHAONIEN ZHONGGUO (SAN FRANCISCO, CALIF.). (SHAO NIEN CHUNG-KUO.). [Shaonien Zhongguo]. **VFOAT** Young China; Young China Daily; Shao Nien Chung Kuo; Shao Nien Chung-kuo Cheng pao. (August 19, 1910)-. Newspaper. Chinese (English). da. Young China Publishing Company, 49-51 Hangah Street, San Francisco CA 94108. **Tel** (415)982-6161, FAX (415)982-1979. **ED** Peter S. Hsu. **DD** 071. **Bk Rev**. **Ad Acc**. **Circ:** 43,000 (ctrl).

US/0747-5071
SHIJIE RIBAO (SAN FRANCISCO, CALIF.). (SHIH CHEIH JIH PAO.). **VFOAT** Chinese World; World Journal. (1891)-. Newspaper. Chinese. da (except holidays). $133.00. World Journal Bookstore, 231 Adrian Road, Millbrae CA 94030. **Tel** (415)692-9936. **ED** Min-Sheing Su, Chia-Cheng Wang (Managing Editor). **Photos**. **Ad Acc, Adv Mgr:** Shirley Chan. Full Page (B&W) $1020.00. Half Page (B&W) $510.00. Full Page (Color) $1824.00. Half Page (Color) $912.00. **Pub. Size:** Standard. **Circ:** 40,000 daily. ***Continues*** *Hsien Cheng Pao;* ***Formed by the union of*** *Wen Hsing Jih Pao.*

US
SIERRA SUN. Vol. 1, Nov. (1978)-. Newspaper. English. wk (52 issues). $42.17. Sierra Sun Newspaper, PO Box 2973, Truckee CA 95734. **Tel** (916)587-6061. **ED** Herb Swett. **Circ:** 4,038. ***Continues*** *Sierra Sun-Bonanza.*

US
SISKIYOU DAILY NEWS. VFOAT Daily Siskiyou News. Vol. 65, No. 1 (Oct. 6, 1941)-. Newspaper. English. da. $7.50 (per month). Yreka Siskiyou News, Box 129, Yreka CA 96097. **Tel** (916)842-5777, FAX (916)842-6787. **ED** Dale D. Andreasen (Editor-in-Chief) and Rebecca Weathers (Managing Editor). **Photos**. **Ad Acc, Adv Mgr:** Eric Grooters. Full Page (B&W) $890.10. Half Page (B&W) $445.05. Full Page (Color) $990.10. Half Page (Color) $545.05. **Pub. Size:** Standard. **Wire Svcs.:** AP. **Circ:** 6,140. available in microform from Bay Microfilm, Inc. ***Formed by the union of*** *Siskiyou News* ***and*** *Yreka Journal (Yreka, Calif. : 1941 : Semiweekly).*

US/8755-9498
SONOMA INDEX-TRIBUNE, THE. VFOAT Sonoma Index Tribune. Newspaper. English. sw. Sonoma Index-Tribune, PO Box C, Sonoma CA 95476. **Tel** (707)938-2111. **ED** Robert M Lynch.

US
SOUTHEAST WAVE STAR. Began in 1938?. Newspaper. English. wk. Southeast Wave Star, 2621 West 54th Street, Los Angeles CA 90043. **Tel** (310)290-3000. **ED** Alice Marshall. **Circ:** 16,075.

US
SOUTHSIDE JOURNAL WAVE. Began in 1937?. Newspaper. English. wk. Southside Journal Wave, 2621 West 54th Street, Los Angeles CA 90043. **Tel** (310)290-3000. **ED** Alice Marshall. **Circ:** 19,950.

US
SOUTHWEST NEWS WAVE. Began in 1953?. Newspaper. English. wk. Southwest News Wave, 2621 West 54th Street, Los Angeles CA 90043. **Tel** (310)290-3000. **ED** Alice Marshall. **Circ:** 9,600.

US
SOUTHWEST TOPICS WAVE. Began in 1942?. Newspaper. English. wk. Southwest Topics Wave, 2621 West 54th Street, Los Angeles CA 90043. **Tel** (310)290-3000. **ED** Alice Marshall. **Circ:** 30,865.

US
SOUTHWEST WAVE. (April 1920)-. Newspaper. English. wk. $55.00 (six months), $78.00 (one year). Central News Wave Publications, 2621 West 54th Street, Los Angeles CA 90043. **Tel** (213)290-3000. **ED** Alice Marshall. **Ad Acc**. **Circ:** 277,000 (ctrl).

US
SOUTHWESTERN SUN WAVE. (1947)-. Newspaper. English. wk. Southwestern Sun Wave, 2621 West 54th Street, Los Angeles CA 90043. **Tel** (310)290-3000. **ED** Alice Marshall. **Circ:** 22,875.

US
STOCKTON DAILY EVENING RECORD. ***Title Change.*** **VFOAT** Stockton Daily Record; Stockton Evening Record; Stockton Record. (March 2, 1904)-(19??). Newspaper. English. da. The Stockton Record, 530 East Market, Stockton CA 95202. **Tel** (209)948-1702 ext 322. **ED** Phillip Bookman. **Circ:** 52,728. available on microfilm from University Microfilms International (UMI). ***Continues*** *Daily Record;* ***Absorbed*** *Evening Mail.* ***Continued by*** *Stockton Record (Stockton, Calif.).*

US
STOCKTON RECORD (STOCKTON, CALIF.). (THE STOCKTON RECORD.). **VFOAT** Saturday Stockton Record; Sunday Stockton Record; Sunday Record. Vol. 81, No. 77 (June 23, 1975)-. Newspaper. English. da. $10.50. The Stockton Record, 530 East Market, Stockton CA 95202. **Tel** (209)948-1702 ext 322. **ED** Betty Liddick and Jim Gold. **Bk Rev**. **Photos**. **Ad Acc, Adv Mgr:** Dave Winegarden, **Tel** (209)546-8238. **Pub. Size:** Broadsheet. **Wire Svcs.:** GN, AP. **Circ:** 53,764 (daily), 59,631 (Sunday). ***Continues*** *Stockton Evening and Sunday Record.*

US/0890-0930
SUN-REPORTER, THE. VFOAT Sun Reporter. (1943)-. Newspaper. English. Fifty-two times a year. San Francisco Sun-Reporter, 1366 Turk Street, San Francisco CA 94115. **Tel** (415)931-5778, FAX (415)931-0214. **ED** Amelia Ashley-Ward. **LC** 7114-X. **Bk Rev**. **Ad Acc, Adv Mgr:** J Castle. **Circ:** 11,187 (ctrl). available on microfilm.
Desc: News, stories, feature articles, and editorials dedicated to the interests and concerns of the Bay Area Black communities.

US/0192-0278
SUNNYVALE VALLEY JOURNAL. Newspaper. English. wk. Peninsula Newspapers Inc, 355 West Olive Avenue No. 204, Sunnyvale CA 94086. **Tel** (408)739-3093. **ED** Michael Kidder. **Circ:** 30,624.

US/8750-3948
TAHOE DAILY TRIBUNE AND THE LAKE TAHOE NEWS. VFOAT Tahoe Daily Tribune; Lake Tahoe News. Vol. 26, No. 125 (June 22, 1984)-. Newspaper. English. da. $163.00. Tahoe Daily Tribune, PO Box 1358, South Lake Tahoe CA 95705. **Tel** (916)541-3880, FAX (916)541-0373. **ED** John Stearns. **Ad Acc, Adv Mgr:** Marianne Archibald. **Circ:** 9,051. ***Formed by the union of*** *Tahoe Daily Tribune* ***and*** *Lake Tahoe News.*

US
TAHOE WORLD. Vol. 8, No. 348 (April 1970)-. Newspaper. English. wk. Tahoe World Publishing Company, PO Box 138, Tahoe City CA 95730. **Tel** (916)583-3488. **ED** Christine Dufour. **Circ:** 5,507. ***Continues*** *Tahoe City World.*

US/0743-5355
TAIWAN GONGLUNBAO. (TAI-WAN KUNG LUN PAO.). [Taiwan gonglunbao]. **VFOAT** Tai Wan Kung Lun Pao; Taiwan Tribune. (July 24, 1981)-. Newspaper. Chinese. sw. Taiwan Tribune Publishing Corporation, PO Box 297, Temple City CA 91780-0297. **Tel** (818)443-5673. **Ad Acc**.
Ind/Abst Hum. Rights Intern. Rep.

US
TEHACHAPI NEWS, THE. Vol. 46, No. 1 (Oct. 11, 1935)-. Newspaper. English. wk. Tehachapi News Inc, PO Box 230, Tehachapi CA 93581-0230. **Tel** (805)822-6828, FAX (805)822-4053. **ED** Fred Covzens. **Ad Acc, Adv Mgr:** Al Crisaui. **Circ:** 9,500. ***Continues*** *Tehachapi News and the Mojave-Randsburg Record-Times.*

US/0191-7145
TEMPLE CITY TIMES. (19??)-. Newspaper. English. sw. Temple City Times, 10 North 1st Avenue, Arcadia CA 91006. **Tel** (818)287-0419. **ED** Richard Singer. **Circ:** 7,663.

US
TIMES STANDARD, THE. VFOAT Times-Standard. Vol. 111, No. 130 (June 1, 1967)-. Newspaper. English. da. $129.00 (one year). Humboldt Newspapers Inc, PO Box 3580, Eureka CA 95501. **Tel** (707)442-1711, FAX (707)445-3117. **ED** Rex Wilson. **Bk**

Rev, (Qty: 50). **Photos**. **Ad Acc, Adv Mgr:** Gary Siegal. Full Page (B&W) E2328.77. Half Page (B&W) $1178.45. Full Page (Color) $2908.77. Half Page (Color) $1748.45. **Pub. Size:** Broadsheet. **Wire Svcs.:** AP. **Circ:** 22,248. available on microfilm from Crest Information Technologies. ***Formed by the union of*** *Humboldt Times (Eureka, Calif. : 1892)* ***and*** *Humboldt Standard (Eureka, Calif. : 1913).*

US/1051-5739
TRI-VALLEY HERALD (1990). (TRI-VALLEY HERALD.). **VFOAT** Tri Valley Herald. (1990)-. Newspaper. English. da. $73.84 (by carrier), $180.00 (by mail). Herald / California, 4770 Willow Road, Pleasanton CA 94588. **Tel** (415)734-8522. ***Continues*** *Valley Herald (Hayward, Calif.), 1049-2518.*

US
TRIBUNE NEWS WAVE. Vol. 52, No. 38 (Jan 1978)-. Newspaper. English. wk. Tribune News Wave, 2621 West 54th Street, Los Angeles CA 90043. **Tel** (310)290-3000. **ED** Alice Marshall. **Circ:** 20,725. ***Continues*** *Tribune News Advertiser-Press.*

US
TRINITY WEEKLY JOURNAL. **VFOAT** Trinity Journal; Weekly Trinity Journal. (Jan. 1856)-. English. wk. $22.00. Trinity Weekly Journal, PO Box 340, Weaverville CA 96093. **Tel** (916)623-2055. **ED** Mike Wenninger. **Photos**. **Ad Acc, Adv Mgr:** Fran Wittmann. Full Page (B&W) $504.00. Half Page (B&W) $252.00 Full Page (Color) $594.00. Half Page (Color) $342.00. **Pub. Size:** Standard. **Circ:** 8,250.

US/8750-2542
TRIUMPH (LOS ANGELES, CALIF.). (THE TRIUMPH.). V. 1, No. 1 (Sept. 1984)-. Periodical. English. bm. The Triumph, 741 Gayley Avenue, Los Angeles CA 90024.

US
TURLOCK JOURNAL. Vol. 75, No. 166 (May 23, 1979)-. Newspaper. English. da. Turlock Journal, PO Box 800, Turlock CA 95381. **Tel** (209)634-9141, FAX (209)632-8813. **ED** Bob Crawford. **Ad Acc**. **Adv Mgr:** Ted Emory. **Circ:** 9,241. ***Continues*** *Turlock Daily Journal (Turlock, Calif. : 1923).*

US/0892-6441
TUSTIN NEWS, THE. (19??)-. Newspaper. English. Fifty-two times a year. $17.24 Oryco County; $20.47 other. The Tustin News, PO Box 486, Tustin CA 92681. **Tel** (714)544-4110. **ED** William A. Moses II.

US
U : THE NATIONAL COLLEGE NEWSPAPER. Periodical. English. Eight times a year (publ Sep. through Jun.). $18.00. American Collegiate Network, 1800 Century Park East, Los Angeles CA 90067. **Tel** (310)551-1381, FAX (310)551-1659. **ED** Ari Cheren and Kelley Tuthill. **Ad Acc, Adv Mgr:** Greg Dickson. **Circ:** 1.5 million (ctrl).

US
UKIAH DAILY JOURNAL. Vol. 1, No. 1 (Apr. 19, 1954)-. Newspaper. English. da. $145.00. Ukiah Daily Journal, PO Box 749, Ukiah CA 95482. **Tel** (707)468-0123, FAX (707)468-5780. **ED** Jim Smith. **Ad Acc. Circ:** 8,561. ***Continues*** *Redwood Journal Press-Dispatch.*

US
UNION, THE. **VFOAT** Sacramento Sunday Union. 141st Year, Vol. 281 (July 3, 1991)-. Newspaper. English. da. Sacramento Union, 301 Capitol Mall, Sacramento CA 95814. **Tel** (916)440-0501, FAX (916)440-0524. **ED** Kenneth Harvey. **Ad Acc, Adv Mgr:** Richard Larimer. **Circ:** 83,300 (daily). ***Continues*** *Sacramento Union (Sacramento, Calif. : 1903).*

US/1050-7906
UNION (1987), THE. (THE UNION.). Vol. 123, No. 20 (Nov. 19, 1987)-. Newspaper. English. da. $108.00. Union / Grass Valley, PO Box 1025, Grass Valley CA 95945. **Tel** (916)273-9561, FAX (916)273-9566. **ED** Jack Moorhead. **Ad Acc. Circ:** 16,800. ***Continues*** *Union and the Nevada County Nugget, 0747-1211.*

US
UNION DEMOCRAT, THE. 127th Year, No. 165 (Feb. 24, 1981)-. Newspaper. English. da. $58.00. Union Democrat, 84 South Washington Street, Sonora CA 95370. **Tel** (209)532-7151, FAX (209)532-5139. **ED** Harvey C. McGee. **Ad Acc, Adv Mgr:** Bud Vogel. **Circ:** 12,784. ***Continues*** *Daily Union Democrat (Sonora, Calif. : 1963).*

US
UNION (GRASS VALLEY-NEVADA CITY, CALIF.). ***Title Change.*** (THE UNION.). Newspaper. English. da (Mon.-Sat.). The Union, 11464 Sutton Way, PO Box 1025, Grass Valley CA 95945. **Tel** (916)273-9561. **ED** Jack Moorhead. **Circ:** 13,664. ***Continued by*** *Union and the Nevada County Nugget, 0747-1211.*

US/0889-8154
UNIVERSITY CITY LIGHT. (198?)-. Newspaper. English. wk. $16.00 San Diego County, $24.50 other. University City Light, 450 Pearl Street, PO Box 1927, La Jolla CA 92038. **Tel** (619)459-4201, FAX (619)459-0977. **ED** Cynthia Queen (Editor-in-Chief) and Brad Graves (Managing Editor). **Bk Rev**, (Qty: 12). **Photos**. **Ad Acc, Adv Mgr:** Leah Hansen. **Pub. Size:** Standard. **Circ:** 5,417. ***Continues*** *Light II, 8750-2755.*

US/0898-4581
UPTOWN SAN DIEGO EXAMINER. (19??)-. Newspaper. English. tw. $25.00. Uptown San Diego Examiner, PO Box 4368, San Diego CA 92164-4368. **Tel** (619)295-5432. **ED** J. Specht. **Photos**. **Ad Acc. Circ:** 2,000.

US
VACAVILLE REPORTER. ***Title Change.*** Vol. 1, No. 1 (March 10, 1883)-(19??). Newspaper. English. wk. Vacaville Reporter, PO Box 1509, Vacaville CA 95688. **Tel** (707)448-8566. **LC** 7114-X. available on microfilm from Bay Microfilm, Inc. ***Continued by*** *Reporter (Vacaville, Calif.), 0746-4193.*

US
VALLEJO TIMES-HERALD. **VFOAT** Vallejo Times Herald. 109th Year, No. 1 (Jan. 1, 1985)-. Newspaper. English. da. $203.08. Vallejo Times Herald, 440 Curtola Parkway, Vallejo CA 94590. **Tel** (707)644-1141, FAX (707)643-5217. **ED** Colleen Truelsen. **Ad Acc. Circ:** 23,445. ***Continues*** *Times-Herald (Vallejo, Calif.).*

US/0745-6336
VALLEY NEWS (APPLE VALLEY, CALIF.). (THE VALLEY NEWS.). **VFOAT** News. Newspaper. English. wk. $10.50. Valley News, PO Box 1147, Apple Valley CA 92307. **Tel** (909)247-6700. **ED** Jenny Jones. **Circ:** 3,000.

US
VENTURA COUNTY STAR-FREE PRESS. **VFOAT** Ventura County Star Free Press. (19??)-. Newspaper. English. da. $190.80 Ventura County; $226.80 other. Ventura County Newspapers, PO Box 6711, Ventura CA 93003. **Tel** (805)650-2900, FAX (805)650-2944. **ED** John R. Irby and Joe Howry (Managing Editor). **Bk Rev**. **Photos**. **Ad Acc, Adv Mgr:** Harvey Hopkins, **Tel** (805)655-1780. Full Page (B&W) $37.39 (per inch). Half Page (B&W) $18.70 (per inch). Full Page (Color) $3.50 (1 extra color). **Pub. Size:** Standard. **Wire Svcs.:** AP, NY, LA, DJ, SH. **Circ:** 53,325. ***Formed by the union of*** *Ventura County Star* ***and*** *Ventura Free Press.*

US
VISALIA TIMES-DELTA. **VFOAT** Visalia Times Delta. Vol. 1, No. 1 (Mar. 1, 1928)-. Newspaper. English. da (except Sunday). $149.28 California; $141.00 other. Visalia Times-Delta, PO Box 31, Visalia CA 93279. **Tel** (209)734-5821. **ED** Burton Swope (editor's address: 330 North West Street, Visalia, CA 93279). **LC** 7210. **Bk Rev**, (Qty: 20/year). **Ad Acc. Circ:** 21,019 (ctrl). available on microfilm from University Microfilms International (UMI). ***Formed by the union of*** *Visalia Daily Times* ***and*** *Visalia Morning Delta.*

US/0893-3464
VISTA PRESS, THE. (19??)-. Newspaper. English. ir (twice weekly Wed. & Sat.). $45.00. Press Courier, PO Box 2168, Vista CA 92083. **Tel** (619)724-7161. **ED** Nancy Richards. **Ad Acc, Adv Mgr:** Helen Woods. **Circ:** Wed.-8,500, Sat.-13,100 (ctrl).
Desc: News and information on people and happenings in Vista, California.

US
VOZ LIBRE, LA. Vol. 1 No. 1 (Oct. 1981)-. Newspaper. Spanish. wk. La Voz Libre, 3107 West Beverly Boulevard/Suite 1, Los Angeles CA 90057. **Tel** (213)388-2903. **ED** Angel M. Prada. **Circ:** 37,000.

US
WATSONVILLE REGISTER-PAJARONIAN. **VFOAT** Watsonville Register Pajaronian; Register-Pajaronian; Register Pajaronian. (19??)-. Newspaper. English. da. Watsonville Register Pajaronian, 1000 Main Street, Watsonville CA 95076-3732. **Tel** (408)761-7300, FAX (408)722-8386. **ED** Bud O'Brien. **Ad Acc. Circ:** 12,000.

US/1064-6469
WEED PRESS. **VFOAT** Weed, Calif. Press. (19??)-. Newspaper. English. wk. $19.50 Siskiyou County; $25.50 US. Southern Siskiyou Newspapers, PO Box 127, 316 Chestnut Street, Mount Shasta CA 96067. **Tel** (916)926-5214, FAX (916)926-4166. **ED** Darlene Moss. **Photos**. **Ad Acc, Adv Mgr:** Genny Axtman. Full Page (B&W) $6.50 per column inch. Half Page (B&W) $6.70 per column inch. Full Page (Color) $6.50 per column inch plus $60.00. Half Page (Color) $6.70 per column inch plus $60.00. **Pub. Size:** Standard. **Circ:** 13,250. available in microform.

US/8750-4316
WEEKEND DESERT POST. **VFOAT** Desert Post. Newspaper. English. wk. Desert Post, PO Box 459, Palm Desert CA 92261.

US/0746-6323
WEST COUNTY TIMES. Newspaper. English. da. $42.00. Lesher Communications Inc, 2640 Shadelands Drive, Walnut Creek CA 94598.

US/1069-2819
WHITTIER DAILY NEWS. **VFOAT** Daily News. (19??)-. Newspaper. English. da. $208.00 California; $286.00 US; $486.20 other. San Gabriel Valley Tribune, 1210 Azusa Canyon Road, West Covina CA 91790. **Tel** (818)962-8811. ***Continues*** *Daily News (Whittier, Calif.), 0746-6188.*

US
WILLOWS JOURNAL. Vol. 1, No. 1 (Oct. 1, 1982)-. Newspaper. English. tw. $30.00. Tri-County Newspapers, PO Box 731, Willows CA 95988-0731. **Tel** (916)934-6800, FAX (916)934-6815. **ED** Martha Coe, Brooks Mencher (Managing Editor). **Bk Rev**. **Photos**. **Ad Acc, Adv Mgr:** Patricia Begrin, **Tel** (916)934-6804. Full Page (B&W) $774.00. Half Page (B&W) $387.00. Full Page (Color) $864.00. Half Page (Color) $477.00. **Pub. Size:** Standard. **Circ:** 8,000. ***Continues*** *Willows Daily Journal (Willows, Calif. : 1972).*

US/0192-1932
WILSHIRE CENTER'S LARCHMONT CHRONICLE. **VFOAT** Larchmont Chronicle. (1964)-. Newspaper. English. mo. $19.50. Larchmont Chronicle, 542 1/2 North Larchmont Boulevard, Los Angeles CA 90004. **Tel** (213)462-2241. **ED** Jane Gilman. **Bk Rev**. **Photos**. **Ad Acc, Adv Mgr:** Dawne P. Goodwin. Full Page (B&W) $1128.00. Half Page (B&W) $652.00. Full Page (Color) $1370.00. Half Page (Color) $902.00. **Circ:** 20,000 (ctrl).
Desc: Local newspaper covering residents and issues relevant to Hancock Park area of Los Angeles and immediate surroundings.

US
WINTERS EXPRESS. Began in 1883. Newspaper. English. wk. $6.50. Winters Express, 312 Railroad Avenue, Winters CA 95694. **Tel** (916)795-4551. **ED** Charles Wallace. **Circ:** 1,757. available on microfilm from Bay Microfilm, Inc.

US/1072-1819
WOODLAKE ECHO AND THE THREE RIVERS CURRENT. (WOODLAKE ECHO). **VFOAT** Woodlake Echo; Three Rivers Current. (19??)-. Newspaper. English. Fifty-two times a year (Published on Wed.). $15.00 (one year); $28.00 (two years); $41.00 (three years). Mineral King Publishing Inc., PO Box 7, Exeter CA 93221. **Tel** (209)592-3171, FAX (209)592-3171. **ED** Jerry Newton. **Ad Acc, Adv Mgr:** V. Spencer, **Tel** (209)592-3171.
Desc: Community news, sports, and agriculture information.

US/0890-8710
YOMIURI SHIMBUN (NEW YORK, N.Y.). (THE YOMIURI SHIMBUN = THE YOMIURI SHIMBUN.). **VFOAT** Yomiuri Shimbun. (19??)-. Newspaper. Japanese. da. $670.00. Yomuiri America, 19600 Magellin Drive, Torrance CA 90502. **Tel** (213)352-3900. **DD** 952. available on an online database (file 772,799/Full-Text) from DIALOG.

COLORADO

US
APPLEWOOD TRANSCRIPT. Newspaper. English. wk (published Wednesdays). $26.00 Golden, Colorado area; $36.00 other. Transcript Newspapers / Colorado, 1000 10th Street, PO Box 987, Golden CO 80402. **Tel** (303)279-5541, FAX (303)279-7157. **ED** Jacque Scott. **Ad Acc, Adv Mgr:** John Tracy. **Circ:** 8,000 (ctrl).

US/1060-5207
ARVADA JEFFERSON SENTINEL, THE. (19??)-. Newspaper. English. wk. $26.00. Jefferson Sentinels, 1224 Wadsworth Boulevard, Lakewood CO 80215. **Tel** (303)239-9890. **ED** Ben Miller. **Ad Acc. Circ:** 19,000 (ctrl). available on microfilm. ***Continues*** *Arvada Sentinel, 0899-2452.*

US
ASPEN DAILY NEWS. (19??)-. Newspaper. English. da. Free. Ute City Tea Party Ltd, PO Box DD, Aspen CO 81612. **Tel** (303)925-2220, FAX (303)449-9358. **ED** Curtis Robinson. **Bk Rev**, (Qty: 1-2). **Photos**. **Ad Acc, Adv Mgr:** Cassandra Davenport. Full Page (B&W) $399.00. Half Page (B&W) $216.13. Full Page (Color) $599.00. Half Page (Color) $416.30. **Pub. Size:** Tabloid. **Wire Svcs.:** AP. **Circ:** 12,000.

US
ASPEN TIMES, THE. **VFOAT** Aspen Times Incorporating the Snowmass Villager. (Jan. 14, 1927)-. Newspaper. English. wk. $28.00 Roaring Fork Valley; $42.00 other US; $88.00 other. Aspen Times, PO Box E,

Aspen CO 81612. **Tel** (303)925-3414. available on microfilm. ***Continues*** *Aspen Daily Times (Aspen, Colo. : 1926);* ***Absorbed*** *Snowmass Villager.*

US
AURORA SENTINEL. **VFOAT** Aurora Sentinel Weekender. Vol. 70, No. 7 (Feb. 28, 1979)-. Newspaper. English. wk. Sentinel Publishing, 1730 South Abilene, Aurora CO 80012. **Tel** (303)750-7555, FAX (303)750-7699. **ED** Jack Bacon. **Ad Acc, Adv Mgr:** Jim Gourley. **Circ:** 8,000. available on microfilm. ***Continues*** *Aurora Advocate Sentinel.*

US
BENT COUNTY DEMOCRAT. (1886)-. Newspaper. English. Fifty-two times a year. $16.00 Bent County Colorado; $19.00 others in Colorado; $22.00 others. Bent County Democrat, PO Box 467, Las Animas CO 81054. **Tel** (719)456-1333. **ED** Jack Lowes. **Ad Acc.** ctrl circ.

US
BROOMFIELD ENTERPRISE. Vol. 12, No. 3 (Nov. 13, 1986)-Vol. 13, No. 1 (Oct. 29, 1987); 13th Year, 2nd Issue (Nov. 5, 1987)-. Newspaper. English. Fifty-two times a year (Thursday). $52.00. Boulder Publishing Company, Inc., 28 Garden Center 4A, Broomfield CO 80020. **ED** Noralee Taylor, (editor's address: 26 Garden Center, 4A, Broomfield, CO 80020, phone: (303)466-3636). **Photos. Ad Acc, Adv Mgr Tel** 466-3636. Full Page (B&W) $784.55. Half Page (B&W) $392.28. Full Page (Color) $819.55. Half Page (Color) $427.28. **Pub. Size:** Tabloid. available on microfilm. ***Continues*** *Broomfield Enterprise Sentinel.*
Desc: News coverage of Broomfield, Boulder, Adams, Jefferson and Weld counties.

US
BRUSH-MORGAN COUNTY NEWS-TRIBUNE. **VFOAT** Brush Morgan County News Tribune. Vol. 88, No. 9 (Mar. 3, 1982)-. Newspaper. English. wk. Brush News Tribune, 109 Clayotn, Brush CO 80723-2101. **Tel** (303)842-5516, FAX (303)842-5519. **ED** Paula Stonebraker. **Ad Acc. Circ:** 2,300. available on microfilm. ***Continues*** *Brush News-Tribune.*

US/0192-0197
CANYON COURIER WEEKENDER, THE. **VFOAT** Weekender. (197?)-. Newspaper. English. wk. $18.00 in county; $21.00 others. Canyon Courier, PO Box 430, Evergreen CO 80439. **Tel** (303)674-5534, FAX (303)674-4104. **ED** Tony Messenger. **Bk Rev. Photos. Ad Acc.** Full Page (B&W) $560.00. Half Page (B&W) $307.00. Full Page (Color) $660.00. Half Page (Color) $407.00. **Pub. Size:** Tabloid. **Wire Svcs.:** AP. **Circ:** 8,600 (ctrl).
Desc: News of Evergreen.

US
CHRONICLE-NEWS, THE. **VFOAT** Evening Chronicle-News; Daily Chronicle-News; Sunday Chronicle-News; Chronicle-News and Evening Picketwire; Chronicle News and Evening Picketwire; Chronicle News; Evening Chronicle News; Daily Chronicle News. Vol. 11, No. 204 (Aug. 1, 1898)-Vol. 59, No. 153-. Newspaper. English. da. $36.00 Colorado; $37.00 other. The Chronicle News, PO Box 763, Trinidad CO 81082. **Tel** (303)846-3311. **ED** Cosette Henritze. **Ad Acc, Adv Mgr:** Annette Girom. **Circ:** 3,203. available on microfilm. ***Formed by the union of*** *Daily News (Trinidad, Colo.)* ***and*** *Morning Chronicle (Trinidad, Colo.);* ***Absorbed*** *Evening Picketwire.*

US
CLEAR CREEK COURANT, THE. Vol. 11, No. 24 (Jan. 18, 1984)-. Newspaper. English. wk. $22.00 Clear Creek County; $27.00 other US. Clear Creek Courant, 1634 Miner Street, PO Box 2020, Idaho Springs CO 80452-2020. **Tel** (303)567-4491, (800)310-4491, FAX (303)567-4492. **ED** Cary Stiff and Carol Wilcox. **Ad Acc, Adv Mgr:** J. Reichwein. **Circ:** 2,100 (ctrl). available on microfilm. ***Continues*** *Clear Creek Courant & Evergreen Today.*

US/0190-8235
COLORADO LABOR ADVOCATE. **Added/Corp** Colorado AFL-CIO. (192?)-. Newspaper. English (Spanish). Twenty-three times a year. $12.00 Colorado; $15.00 other. Denver Labor Center Annex, 35 West 4th Avenue, Denver CO 80223. **Tel** (303)744-1731, FAX (303)238-1904. **ED** Michael K. Osborn. **Bk Rev. Ad Acc. Circ:** 22,000.
Desc: Labor and nation news in Colorado.

US
COLORADO SPRINGS GAZETTE-TELEGRAPH. **VFOAT** Colorado Springs Gazette Telegraph; Colorado Springs Morning Gazette Telegraph; Gazette Telegraph; Morning Issue of the Colorado Springs Gazette-Telegraph; Evening Issue of the Colorado Springs Gazette-Telegraph. 74th Year, No. 25040 (Feb. 5, 1946)-. Newspaper. English. da. $144.00 El Paso, Teller Park, Fremont, Pueblo, Elbert and Lincoln counties in Colorado; $216.00 other. Colorado Springs Gazette, 30 South Prospect Street, Colorado Springs CO 80901. **Tel** (719)632-5511, FAX (719)636-0224, (719)636-0202. **ED** Jon Stepleton, Wayne Stewart (Managing Editor). **Photos. Ad Acc, Adv Mgr:** Doug Barnett, **Tel** (719)636-0113. Full Page (B&W) $7821.27 (daily), $8942.28 (Sunday). Half Page (B&W) $3819.69 (daily), $4367.16 (Sunday). Full Page (Color) $8190.27 (daily), $9359.28 (Sunday). Half Page (Color) $4188.69 (daily), $4784.16 (Sunday). **Pub. Size:** Standard. **Wire Svcs.:** SH, AP, KR. available on microfilm. ***Formed by the union of*** *Colorado Springs Gazette* ***and*** *Colorado Springs Evening Telegraph.*

US
COLORADO STATESMAN, THE. (197?)-. Newspaper. English. wk. $39.00. Colorado Statesman, Drawer 18129, Capitol Hill, Denver CO 80218. **Tel** (303)837-8600. ***Continues*** *Colorado Democrat.*

US
CORTEZ SENTINEL, THE. Vol. 57, No. 3 (Mar. 11, 1985)-. Newspaper. English. wk. Cortez Newspapers, PO Drawer O, Cortez CO 81321. **Tel** (303)565-8527. **ED** Byron McKelvie. **Ad Acc, Adv Mgr:** Jeanne Scrivner. available on microfilm. ***Continues*** *Monday Cortez Sentinel.*

US/0745-9920
COUNTRY PRESS. (19??)-. Newspaper. English. wk. The Country Press, PO Box 5024, Durango CO 81301.

US
DAILY CAMERA (BOULDER, COLO.: 1973). (THE DAILY CAMERA.). **VFOAT** Sunday Camera. 83rd Year, No. 203 (Oct. 7, 1973)-. Newspaper. English. da. Boulder Daily Camera, PO Box 898, Boulder CO 80306. **Tel** (303)442-1202 ext.262. available on microfilm from Colorado Historical Society. ***Continues*** *Boulder Daily Camera.*

US/1067-4241
DAILY NEWS-PRESS. (CASTLE ROCK, COLO. : 1987). ***Title Change.*** **VFOAT** Daily News Press; Douglas County Daily News-Press; News-Press. 95th Year, No. 196 (May 18, 1987)-(Oct. 3, 1992). Newspaper. English. da. Douglas County Publishing Company, 319 Perry Street, Castle Rock CO 80104. **Tel** (303)688-3128. available on microfilm. ***Continues*** *Douglas County Daily News-Press, 0746-5602.* ***Continued by*** *Douglas County News-Press (Castle Rock, Colo. : 1992), 1067-425X.*

US/1054-3457
DAILY RECORD (1989). (DAILY RECORD.). **VFOAT** Canon City, Colorado, Daily Record. 115th year, No. 160 (July 6, 1989)-. Newspaper. English. da. Canon City Daily Record, 523 Main Street, Canon City CO 81212. **Tel** (303)275-7565. available on microfilm. ***Continues*** *Canon City Daily Record.*

US
DAILY SENTINEL (GRAND JUNCTION, COLO.). (THE DAILY SENTINEL.). (Nov. 20, 1893)-. Newspaper. English. da. The Daily Sentinel, 734 South Seventh Street, Box 668, Grand Junction CO 81502. **Tel** (303)242-5050. **ED** David L. McLean. **Circ:** 28,876 daily, 32,877 Sunday. ***Absorbed*** *Grand Junction Morning News.*

US
DAILY TIMES-CALL. **VFOAT** Daily Times Call; Longmont Daily Times-Call. 111th Year, No. 85 (Apr. 9, 1981)-. Newspaper. English. da. $118.00. Longmont Daily Times Call, 350 Terry Street, Longmont CO 80501. **Tel** (303)776-2244, FAX (303)678-8615. **ED** Keith Briscoe. **Ad Acc, Adv Mgr:** Mike Gugliotto. **Circ:** 19,409. ***Continues*** *Longmont Daily Times-Call (Longmont, Colo. : 1964).*

US/0891-9704
DELTA COUNTY INDEPENDENT. **VFOAT** Delta Sunday Independent. Vol. 49, No. 6 (Feb. 8, 1940)-Vol. 55, No. 46 (Nov. 14, 1946)- 65th year, No. 41 (Nov. 21, 1946)- 86th year, No. 86 (Dec. 15, 1969)- Vol. 86, No. 87 (Dec. 18, 1969)-. Newspaper. English. wk. $20.00. Delta County Independent, PO Box 809, Delta CO 81416. **Tel** (303)874-4421. **ED** Randy Sunderland (editor), Pat Sunderland (managing editor). **Photos. Ad Acc, Adv Mgr:** Linda Storm. Full Page (B&W) $819.00. Half Page (B&W) $409.50. Full Page (Color) $919.00. Half Page (Color) $509.00. **Pub. Size:** Broadsheet. **Circ:** 5,600. available on microfilm. ***Continues*** *Delta County Daily Independent;* ***Absorbed*** *Paonian-Herald; North Fork Times (Paonia, Colo. : 1974).*

US/0898-1701
DENVER HERALD DISPATCH. **VFOAT** Herald Dispatch. Vol. 62, No. 23 (June 4, 1987)-. Newspaper. English. wk. Denver Herald Dispatch, 47 South Federal Boulevard, Denver CO 80219-2000. **Tel** (303)936-7778, FAX (303)839-5891. **ED** J. Ivanhoe Rosenberg. **Ad Acc. Circ:** 17,500. ***Continues*** *Herald Disparch (Denver, Colo.).*

US
DENVER POST (1901). (THE DENVER POST.). **VFOAT** Sunday Denver Post. 9th year (Jan. 1, 1901)-(June 14, 1929); Vol. 37, No. 317 (June 15, 1929)-. Newspaper. English. ds. $181.44 Kansas, Nebraska, New Mexico and Wyoming; $175.15 Colorado; $286.00 other US. Denver Post, 1560 Broadway, Denver CO 80202. **Tel** (303)832-3232, (800)543-5543. **ED** Chuck Green. **LC** 7217. **Circ:** 227,105 daily, 425,454 Sunday. available on microfilm from University Microfilms International (UMI); available on an online database (file 635/Full-Text) from DIALOG. Documents available from UMI Article Clearinghouse. ***Continues*** *Denver Evening Post;* ***Absorbed*** *Denver Evening News.*
Ind/Abst Bus. Dateline; Newsp. Abstr.; PROMT.

US/0889-5155
DOLORES STAR. (THE DOLORES STAR.). **VFOAT** Dolores Star Diamond Jubilee. (1901)-. Newspaper. English. wk. $17.00. Dolores Star, PO Box 660, Dolores CO 81323. **Tel** (303)882-4486. **ED** Melinda H. Green. **Photos. Ad Acc, Adv Mgr:** Sam Green. Full Page (B&W) $160.00. Half Page (B&W) $90.00. **Pub. Size:** Tabloid. **Circ:** 1,050. available on microfilm. ***Continues*** *Silver Star.*

US
DURANGO HERALD, THE. **VFOAT** Durango-Cortez Herald; Durango Cortez Herald. Vol. 9, No. 144 (July 25, 1960)-. Newspaper. English. ds. $56.00. Durango Herald, PO Drawer A, Durango CO 81301. **Tel** (303)247-3504. **ED** Morley Ballantine, Dan Partridge (Managing Editor). **Bk Rev. Photos. Ad Acc, Adv Mgr:** Sharon Hermes. Full Page (B&W) $819.00. Half Page (B&W) $409.50. Full Page (Color) $819.00 plus $95.00 per color. Half Page (Color) $409.50 plus $95.00 per color. **Pub. Size:** Broadsheet. **Wire Svcs.:** AP. available on microfilm. ***Continues*** *Durango Herald-News.*

US
EAGLE VALLEY ENTERPRISE. Vol. 22, No. 32 (May 23, 1919)-. Newspaper. English. Twice a week. $14.00 in County; $20.00 Colorado; $24.00 other. Eagle Valley Enterprise, 11 Eagle Park East Drive, Eagle CO 81631. **Tel** (303)328-6656, FAX (303)328-6393. **ED** G. Nikoloch, Scott Miller (Managing Editor). **Bk Rev,** (Qty: 6). **Photos. Ad Acc, Adv Mgr:** Kimberly Reed. Full Page (B&W) $400.00. Half Page (B&W) $200.00. Full Page (Color) $750.00. Half Page (Color) $350.00. **Pub. Size:** Tabloid. **Circ:** 2,500. available on microfilm. ***Continues*** *Eagle Valley Enterprise and Western Slope Enterprise.*

US/0745-774X
EDGEWATER TRIBUNE. (1983)-. Newspaper. English. sm (2nd and 4th Thursday of each month). $12.00. Edgewater Tribune, 2252 Lamar Street, Edgewater CO 80214-1157. **Tel** (303)232-7083, FAX (303)234-9345. **ED** Doni Brune, Mark Brune (Managing Editor). **Bk Rev. Photos. Ad Acc.** Full Page (B&W) $195.00. Half Page (B&W) $100.00. **Circ:** 150.

US/1058-9899
ENGLEWOOD HERALD, THE. Issue 48 (Aug. 8, 1991)-. Newspaper. English. wk. The Englewood Herald, 2329 West Main Street, PO Box 649, Littleton CO 80160. available on microfilm. ***Continues*** *Englewood Sentinel, 0745-9610.*

US
ESTES PARK TRAIL-GAZETTE, THE. **VFOAT** Estes Park Trail Gazette; Estes Park Trail Gazette Succeeding the Estes Park Trail and the Mountain Gazette. Vol. 1, No. 19 (June 2, 1971)-. Newspaper. English. sw. $24.00 Larimer, Weld & Boulder Counties; $32.00 Colorado; $38.00 other. Estes Park Trail Gazette, PO Box 1707, Estes Park CO 80517. **Tel** (303)586-3356, FAX (303)586-9532. **ED** Tim Asbury. **Ad Acc. Circ:** 5,500. available on microfilm. ***Continues*** *Trail-Gazette.*

US/0274-7308
FENCE POST, THE. Vol. 1, No. 1 (June 2, 1980)-. Newspaper. English. wk (Published on Mondays). $14.00. McMillen Publishing Company, PO Box 369, 421 Main Street, Windsor CO 80550. **Tel** (303)224-5405. **ED** Andrea Koutonen. **Circ:** 9,100.

US
FLAGLER NEWS, THE. Newspaper. English. wk. Flagler News, 317 Main Avenue, Flagler CO 80815. **Tel** (303)765-4466. **ED** Clyde B Coulter. **Circ:** 1,350.

US
FLORENCE CITIZEN, THE. Vol. 93, No. 1 (Apr. 26, 1990)-. Newspaper. English. wk. Florence Citizen, 200 South Pikes Peak, Florence CO 81226. **Tel** (719)784-6383. **ED** Bob Wood. **Ad Acc. Circ:** 1,500. ***Continues*** *Citizen (Florence, Colo. : 1988).*

US
FORT COLLINS COLORADOAN. (Mar. 11, 1984)-. Newspaper. English. da. $166.00 Colorado; $205.00 others. Fort Collins Newspapers, PO Box 1577, Fort Collins CO 80522. **Tel** (303)224-7778. **ED** Dave Greiling. **Photos. Ad Acc, Adv Mgr:** Bob Williams, **Tel** (303)224-7702. **Pub. Size:** Standard. **Wire Svcs.:** AP, GN. **Circ:** 27,055 (daily), 33,318 (Sunday). available on microfilm. ***Continues*** *Coloradoan (Fort Collins, Colo.).*

US/0744-3870
FORT COLLINS REVIEW. ***Title Change.*** **VFOAT** Fort Collins Triangle Review; Triangle Review. Vol. 8, No. 46 (Nov. 18, 1981)-(199?). Newspaper. English. wk. Fort Collins Review, PO Box 2063, Fort Collins CO 80522. **Tel** (303)221-2000. ***Continues*** *Review (Fort Collins, Colo.), 0164-419X.* ***Continued by*** *Fort Collins Triangle Review, 1076-4631.*

US/1076-4631
FORT COLLI RIANGLE REVIEW. (199?)-. Newspape glish. wk. Fort Collins Review, PO Box 2063, Fort Collins CO 80522. **Tel** (303)221-2000. ***Continues*** *Fort Collins Review (Fort Collins, Colo. : 1981), 0744-3870.*

US/1056-2419
FORT LUPTON PRESS (1981). (FORT LUPTON PRESS.). Vol. 83, No. 52 (Sept. 24, 1981)-. Newspaper. English. sw. Metro West Publishing, PO Box 646, Brighton CO 80601. **Tel** (303)659-1141. **ED** Chuck Ballou. **Circ:** 5,300. available on microfilm. ***Continues*** *New Fort Lupton Press.*

US
FORT MORGAN TIMES, THE. Vol. 47, No. 210 (May 1, 1931)-. Newspaper. English. da. $70.00 Colorado; $74.00 other. Fort Morgan Times, PO Box 4000, Fort Morgan CO 80701. **Tel** (303)867-5651, FAX (303)867-7448. **ED** Robert W. Spencer Jr. **Ad Acc, Adv Mgr:** Harold Bohm. **Circ:** 5,249. available on microfilm. ***Continues*** *Fort Morgan Times and the Evening Times.*

US
FREE WEEKLY, THE. ***Ceased.*** Vo . 51, No. 17 (Nov. 11, 1987)- (199?). Newspaper. English. wk. Free Weekly Newspaper, PO Box 339, Glenwood Springs CO 81602. **Tel** (303)945-7493. ***Continues*** *Free Weekly Newspaper.*

US
GLENWOOD POST. Vol. 81, No. 31 (Aug. 4, 1971)-. Newspaper. English. Six issues per week (pulbished Mon.-Sat.). $96.00 (zone 1 & 2), $99.00 (zone 3), $102.00 (zone 4), $105.00 (zone 5), $108.00 (zone 6), $110.00 (zone 7), $114.00 (zone 8). Glenwood Post, PO Box 550, Glenwood Springs CO 81602. **Tel** (303)945-8515, FAX (303)945-4487. **ED** Gary Dickson, Dennis Webb (Managing Editor). **Bk Rev**, (Qty: 6-12). **Photos**. **Ad Acc, Adv Mgr:** Bob Zanella. Full Page (B&W) $935.25. Half Page (B&W) $467.63. Full Page (Color) 1,010.25. Half Page (Color) $542.00. **Pub. Size:** Broadsheet. **Wire Svcs.:** AP. **Circ:** 5,200 (ctrl). ***Continues*** *Glenwood Post with Which is Merged the Glenwood Avalnche-Echo and Glenwood Daily Post.*

US/0746-6382
GOLDEN TRANSCRIPT, THE. Vol. 117, No. 82 (Nov. 1, 1983)-. Newspaper. English. sw (published Tuesdays and Thursdays). $26.00 Jefferson County, Colorado; $36.00 other. Transcript Newspapers / Colorado, 1000 10th Street, PO Box 987, Golden CO 80402. **Tel** (303)279-5541, FAX (303)279-7157. **ED** Jacque Scott. **Ad Acc, Adv Mgr:** John Tracy. **Circ:** 4,400 (ctrl). available on microfilm. ***Continues*** *Colorado Transcript (Golden, Colo : 1979).*

US
GREELEY TRIBUNE. **VFOAT** Greeley Daily Tribune; Greeley Daily Tribune and the Greeley Republican. Vol. 70, No. 93 (Feb. 9, 1978)-. Newspaper. English. da. $112.00 Weld County; $124.00 other. Greeley Daily Tribune, PO Box 1138, Greeley CO 80631. **Tel** (303)352-0211 ext 277. ***Continues*** *Greeley Tribune and the Greeley Republican.*

US/0892-1113
GUNNISON COUNTRY TIMES, THE. V. 42, No. 33 (Aug. 1975)-V. 42, No. 45 (Nov. 1975)-. Newspaper. English. wk. Gunnison Country Times, 218 North Wisconsin, Gunnison CO 81230. **Tel** (303)641-1414. **ED** Tom Reed. **Circ:** 4,600. ***Formed by the union of*** *Gunnison Courier (Gunnison, Colo. : 1965); Gunnison County Globe* ***and*** *Gunnison News Champion (Gunnison, Colo. : 1947).*

US/0884-3120
HANGUK ILBO, TENBO. **VFOAT** Korea Times, Denver Edition. Newspaper. Korean. wk. Korea Times / Aurora, Colorado, 1454 South Vaughn Circle, Aurora CO 80012.

US
HAXTUN HERALD, THE. Vol. 1, No. 1 (Nov. 13, 1975)-. Newspaper. English. wk. $18.00. Haxtun Herald, PO Box 128, Haxtun CO 80731. **Tel** (303)774-6118, FAX (303)774-6437. **ED** Jean Gray. **Photos**. **Ad Acc, Adv Mgr:** Holly Barnett. Full Page (B&W) $623.70. Half Page (B&W) $311.85. Full Page (Color) $693.70. Half Page (Color) $381.85. **Circ:** 1,500. available on microfilm.

US
HAYDEN VALLEY PRESS, THE. (1965)-. Newspaper. English. wk. Hayden Valley Press, 126 Walnut Street, Hayden CO 81639. **Tel** (303)824-7031, FAX (303)824-6810. **ED** Stefka White. **Ad Acc. Circ:** 770. available on microfilm.

US
HIGH TIMBER TIMES. (1977)-. Newspaper. English. wk. $17.00 Jefferson & Park Counties in Colorado; $21.00 other. High Timber Times, 43 Mt. Evans Boulevard, Pine CO 80470. **Tel** (303)838-4884, (303)674-5534, FAX (303)838-6007. **ED** Tony Messenger. **Bk Rev**. **Photos**. **Ad Acc, Adv Mgr:** John Ellis. Full Page (B&W) $329.00. Half Page (B&W) $171.00. Full Page (Color) $429.00. Half Page (Color) $271.00. **Pub. Size:** Tabloid. **Wire Svcs.:** AP. **Circ:** 2,500. available on microfilm.

US
HOLYOKE ENTERPRISE (HOLYOKE, COLO.). ***Title Change.*** (THE HOLYOKE ENTERPRISE.). (1913)-?. Newspaper. English. wk. The Holyoke Enterprise, PO Box 297, Holyoke CO 80734. ***Continues*** *Holyoke Enterprise Formerly Phillips County Herald.* ***Continued by*** *Phillips County Herald.*

US/0278-7202
INDIAN TIMES. **Added/Corp** White Buffalo Council of American Indians. (1???)-. Periodical. English. Twelve times a year. White Buffalo Coun Amer Indian, PO Box 4131, Santa Fe Stn., Denver CO 80204. **LC** Discard.

US/0047-0511
INTERMOUNTAIN JEWISH NEWS. Vol. 11, No. 42 (Oct. 1925)-. Newspaper. English. wk. $42.50 one year; $80.00 two years. Intermountain Jewish News, 1275 Sherman Street, Suite 214, Denver CO 80203. **Tel** (303)861-2234, FAX (303)832-6942. **ED** Miriam Goldberg. **Bk Rev**. **Ad Acc. Circ:** 9,773. available on microfilm. ***Continues*** *Denver Jewish News.*

US
JOURNAL-ADVOCATE. **VFOAT** Journal Advocate. (Sept. 12, 1984)-. Newspaper. English. da. $71.00. Journal Advocate / Sterling, 504 North Third Street, Sterling CO 80751-3203. **Tel** (303)522-1990, FAX (303)522-2320. **ED** Jeff Rice. **Bk Rev**. **Photos**. **Ad Acc, Adv Mgr:** Myron House. Full Page (B&W) $953.31. Half Page (B&W) $480.35. Full Page (Color) $95.00 (each color). Half Page (Color) $95.00 (each color). **Pub. Size:** Standard. **Wire Svcs.:** AP. **Circ:** 5,700. available in microform from Colorado Historical Society. ***Continues*** *Sterling Journal-Advocate.*

US
JULESBURG ADVOCATE. Vol. 14, No. 9 (Mar. 1, 1972)-. Newspaper. English. wk. $20.00. Julesburg Advocate, PO Box 46, Julesburg CO 80737. **Tel** (303)474-3388, FAX (303)474-3389. **ED** Sandi Austin. **Photos**. **Ad Acc.** Full Page (B&W) $464.40. Half Page (B&W) $232.20. **Circ:** 1,870 paid. ***Continues*** *Julesburg Grit-Advocate.*

●US/1071-0620
KIDS CUE. [kids cue]. (Apr. 1992)-. Periodical. English. Eleven times a year (Except July). $5.00 library; $5.50 others. Kids Cue, 10120 West Fair Avenue, Littleton CO 80127. **Tel** (303)972-1930. **ED** Shelley Poland. **DD** 363. **Circ:** 160.
Desc: Environmental newspaper written and illustrated by kids.

US
LAKE CITY SILVER WORLD. Vol. 11, No. 1 (May 20, 1988)-. Newspaper. English. Fifty-two times a year. $15.00 Hinsdale & Gunnison counties; $23.00 others. Silver World, PO Box 100, Lake City CO 81235. **Tel** (303)944-2515. **ED** Grant E. Houston. **Ad Acc. Circ:** 1,200 (ctrl). ***Continues*** *Silver World (Lake City, Colo. : 1978).*

US/1060-5215
LAKEWOOD JEFFERSON SENTINEL (1991), THE. (THE LAKEWOOD JEFFERSON SENTINEL.). (199?)-. Newspaper. English. wk. $26.00. Jefferson Sentinels, 1224 Wadsworth Boulevard, Lakewood CO 80215. **Tel** (303)239-9890. **ED** Ben Miller. **Ad Acc. Circ:** 19,000 (ctrl). ***Continues*** *Lakewood Sentinel (Denver, Colo. : 1990), 1053-6337.*

US/1053-6337
LAKEWOOD SENTIN 90). ***Title Change.*** (LAKEWOOD SENTIN...). Vol. 67, Issue 7 (Sept. 20, 1990)-(199?). Newspaper. English. wk. Jefferson Sentinels, 1224 Wadsworth Boulevard, Lakewood CO 80215. **Tel** (303)239-9890. available on microfilm. ***Continues*** *Lakewood Jefferson Sentinel, 0892-2535.* ***Continued by*** *Lakewood Jefferson Sentinel (Lakewood, Colo. : 1991), 1060-5215.*

US
LAMAR DAILY NEWS AND HOLLY CHIEFTAIN, THE. **VFOAT** Lamar Daily News; Lamar (Co.) Daily News. Vol. 80, No. 255 (Aug. 6, 1987)-. Newspaper. English. da. $84.00. Lamar Daily News, 310 South Fifth Street, Box 1217, Lamar CO 81052-1217. **Tel** (719)336-2266, FAX (719)336-2526. **ED** Tom Betz, Ava Betz (Managing Editor). **Bk Rev**. **Photos**. **Ad Acc, Adv Mgr:** Sandee Leighty. Full Page (B&W) $662.76. Half Page (B&W) $389.34. **Pub. Size:** Broadsheet. **Wire Svcs.:** AP. **Circ:** 3,800. available in microform. ***Formed by the union of*** *Holly Chieftain* ***and*** *Lamar Daily News (Lamar, Colo. : 1982).*

US
LEADVILLE HERALD DEMOCRAT. 112th Year, No. 2 (Jan. 11, 1990)-. Newspaper. English. wk. Leadville Herald Democrat, 717 Harrison Avenue, Leadville CO 80461. **Tel** (719)486-0641. **ED** Christine Barnett. **Ad Acc.** available on microfilm. ***Continues*** *Herald Democrat (Leadville, Colo.).*

US/0899-6318
LIFE AT KEN-CARYL. (19??)-. Newspaper. English. bw. Ken-Caryl Ranch Master Association, The Ranch House, 7676 South Continental Divide Road, Littleton CO 80127. **Tel** (303)979-1876.

US/0897-8395
LITTLETON TIMES. (198?)-. Newspaper. English. wk. Littleton Times, 5870 South Curtice, c/o G. Peacock, Middleton CO 80120. **Tel** (303)797-3841.

US
LOUISVILLE TIMES. **VFOAT** Lafayette News; Louisville Times / Lafayette News. (19??)-. Newspaper. English. sw. $22.00. Louisville Times, 916 Main Street, Louisville CO 80027. **Tel** (303)666-6576. **ED** Cynthia Campbell. **Photos**. **Ad Acc, Adv Mgr:** Doug Conarroe. Full Page (B&W) $430.00. Half Page (B&W) $250.00. Full Page (Color) $750.00. Half Page (Color) $450.00. **Pub. Size:** Tabloid. **Circ:** 3,400 paid. available on microfilm.

US
LOVELAND DAILY REPORTER-HERALD. **VFOAT** Loveland Daily Reporter Herald; Loveland Reporter-Herald; Loveland Reporter Herald. 82nd Year, No. 233 (Oct. 3, 1962)-. Newspaper. English. da (Except Sunday). $90.00. Loveland Reporter Herald, 201 East 5th Street, PO Box 59, Loveland CO 80537. **Tel** (303)669-5050. **ED** Robert Rummel and Ken Amundson (Managing Editor). **Bk Rev**. **Photos**. **Ad Acc, Adv Mgr:** Sally Lee. **Pub. Size:** Broadsheet. **Wire Svcs.:** AP, LA. **Circ:** 17,500. ***Continues*** *Loveland Reporter Herald;* ***Absorbed*** *Berthoud Bulletin.*

US
LOWRY AIRMAN. (1957)-. Newspaper. English. wk. Sentinel Publishing, 1730 South Abilene, Aurora CO 80012. **Tel** (303)750-7555, FAX (303)750-7699. **ED** Jack Bacon. **Ad Acc, Adv Mgr:** Jim Gourley. **Circ:** 14,500. available on microfilm.

US
MEEKER HERALD, THE. Vol. 1, No. 2 (Aug. 1885)-. Newspaper. English. wk. $25.00. Meeker Herald, PO Box 720, Meeker CO 81641-0720. **Tel** (303)878-4017, FAX (303)878-4016. **ED** Mike Cook (Editor in Chief), Steve Anderson (Managing Editor). **Bk Rev**, (Qty: varies). **Photos**. **Ad Acc, Adv Mgr:** Lisa Cook. Full Page (B&W) $400.00. Half Page (B&W) $227.00. Full Page (Color) $450.00. Half Page (Color) $277.00. **Pub. Size:** Broadsheet. **Wire Svcs.:** AP. **Circ:** 2,325. available on microfilm.

US/0745-791X
MINERAL COUNTY MINER, THE. Newspaper. English. wk. Mineral County Miner, Box 219, Creede CO 81130. **Tel** (303)658-2603. **ED** Steve Haynes. **Circ:** 1,850.

US
MONTE VISTA JOURNAL, THE. **VFOAT** Monte Vista Tribune; San Luis Valley Graphic. Vol. 47, No. 48 (Nov. 30, 1945)-. Newspaper. English. wk. Valley Publishing, 229 Adams Street, Monte Vista CO 81144. **Tel** (719)852-3531, FAX (719)852-3387. **ED** Ray James. **Circ:** 2,078. available on microfilm. ***Continues*** *Monte Vista Journal with Which is Consolidated the Monte Vista Tribune.*

US
MONTEZUMA VALLEY JOURNAL. **VFOAT** Cortez Montezuma Valley Journal. (1964)-. Newspaper. English. wk. $28.00. Montezuma Valley Journal, 37 East Main Street, Drawer O, Cortez CO 81321. **Tel** (303)565-8527. **ED** Byron McKelvie. **Ad Acc, Adv Mgr:** Jeanne Scrivner. available on microfilm. ***Continues*** *Cortez Montezuma Valley Journal.*

US
MONTROSE DAILY PRESS. Vol. 6, No. 293 (June 19, 1914)-. Newspaper. English. da. $36.00. Montrose Daily Press, 535 South First Street, Montrose CO 81401. **Tel** (303)249-3444, FAX (303)249-3331. **ED** Richard E. Day. **Ad Acc. Circ:** 6,800. available on microfilm. ***Continues*** *Montrose Daily Press and Daily Western Empire.*

US
MOUNTAIN MAIL. Vol. 76, No. 148 (Jan. 2, 1956)-. Newspaper. English. da. $42.00. Mountain Mail, 125 East Second Street, Salida CO 81201-2114. **Tel** (719)539-6691, FAX (719)539-6630. **ED** Merle I. Baranczyk (Editor in Chief), Cheryl Hoeppner (Managing Editor). **Photos. Ad Acc, Adv Mgr:** Vicki Sue Vigil. Full Page (B&W) $416.00. Half Page (B&W) $208.00. Full Page (Color) $473.00. Half Page (Color) $265.00. **Pub. Size:** Standard. **Circ:** 2,943. available on microfilm. ***Continues*** *Salida Daily Mail-Record.*

US
NEWS-REPORTER. VFOAT News Reporter. 79th Year, No. 7 (Apr. 13, 1989)-. Newspaper. English. wk (Thurs.). $19.00 (in state), $22.00 (other). Akron News Reporter, 69 Main Street, Akron CO 80720-1439. **Tel** (303)345-2296, FAX (303)345-6638. **ED** Karen Ashley. **Photos. Ad Acc, Adv Mgr:** Bonnie Miller. Full Page (B&W) $437.50. Half Page (B&W) $225.75. Full Page (Color) $487.50. Half Page (Color) $275.75. **Pub. Size:** Broadsheet. **Circ:** 2,378 (paid, weekly). ***Continues*** *Akron News-Reporter.*

US/1052-5572
NEWSPAPERS & TECHNOLOGY. [Newsp. technol.]. **VFOAT** Newspapers and Technology. Vol. 1, No. 1 (Feb. 1989)-. Periodical. English. mo. Free on request. Citizen Publishing Inc., 4800 Wadsworth Boulevard Suite 309, Wheat Ridge CO 80003. **Tel** (303)456-4880, FAX (303)456-4870. **ED** Brad Moritz, Jeff Konrade-Helm (Managing Editor). **DD** 070. **Photos. Ad Acc, Adv Mgr:** Mary Van Meter. **Pub. Size:** Tabloid. **Wire Svcs.:** AP. ctrl circ.
Ind/Abst Abstr. Bull. Inst. Pap. Sci. Tech.

US
NORTHGLENN-THORNTON SENTINEL. (19??)-. English. Fifty-two times a year (Thurs.). $24.00. Metro North Newspapers, PO Box 215, c/o Bruce G. Harper, Westminister CO 80030-0215. **Tel** (303)426-6000, FAX (303)430-1676. **ED** Bruce G. Harper (General Manager), Marilyn Petterson (Managing Editor). **Bk Rev**, (Qty: 25). **Photos. Ad Acc, Adv Mgr:** Scott Bumgardner. Full Page (B&W) $675.75. Half Page (B&W) $339.20. Full Page (Color) $825.75 (spot color). Half Page (Color) $489.20 (spot color). **Pub. Size:** Tabloid. **Circ:** 5,500 (ctrl).

US
OLD LYONS RECORDER, THE. Vol. 19, No. 41 (July 16, 1987)-. Newspaper. English. Fifty-two times a year. $16.00 Boulder County; $28.00 others in Colorado; $40.00 others. Old Lyons Recorder, PO Box 1729, Lyons CO 80540. **Tel** (303)823-6625, FAX (303)823-6633. **ED** Walt Kinnerman. **Bk Rev**, (Qty: varies). **Ad Acc. Pr Rev. Circ:** 2,500. ***Continues*** *Lyons Recorder (Lyons, Colo. : 1981).*
Desc: Community interest.

US
OURAY COUNTY PLAINDEALER. Vol. 102, No. 46 (Apr. 24, 1980)-. Newspaper. English. wk. $33.00 (one year), $49.00 (two year). Ouray Newspapers, 333 6th Avenue, Ouray CO 81427. **Tel** (303)325-4412. **ED** Marcia Wood. **Ad Acc. Circ:** 2,000. ***Continues*** *Ouray County Plaindealer and Ouray Herald.*

US
PALISADE TRIBUNE & VALLEY REPORT, THE. VFOAT Palisade Tribune and Valley Report. Vol. 85, No. 42 (Oct. 15, 1987)-. Newspaper. English. wk. $28.00. Palisade Tribune, PO Box 8, Palisade CO 81526. **Tel** (303)464-5614. **ED** D. Coba. **Photos. Ad Acc, Adv Mgr:** Cindy O'Keeffe. Full Page (B&W) $480.00. Half Page (B&W) $240.00. **Pub. Size:** Tabloid. **Wire Svcs.:** CP. **Circ:** 4,000. available on microfilm. ***Continues*** *Palisade Tribune.*

US
PIKES PEAK JOURNAL, THE. (19??)-. Newspaper. English. wk. $12.00 Colorado; $30.00 other. Pikes Peak Journal, 22 Ruston Avenue, Manitou Springs CO 80829. **Tel** (719)685-9201. **ED** John G. Graham. **Ad Acc. Circ:** 2,500. ***Continues*** *Manitou Springs Journal.*

US
PUEBLO CHIEFTAIN. VFOAT Pueblo Daily Chieftain; Pueblo Chieftain and Sunday Star-Journal; Pueblo Chieftain and Sunday Star Journal; Pueblo Star-Journal and the Sunday Chieftain; Pueblo Star Journal and the Sunday Chieftain. (Sept. 8, 1889)-. Newspaper. English. da. $144.00 Colorado; $168.00 other. Star Journal Publishing Company / Colorado, PO Box 4040, Pueblo CO 81003. **Tel** (719)544-3520. **ED** Robert Rawlings. **Ad Acc, Adv Mgr:** Jack Wyss. **Circ:** 51,500. available on microfilm. ***Continues*** *Pueblo Daily Chieftain (Pueblo, Colo. : 1887);* ***Absorbed*** *Pueblo Star-Journal.*

US
ROCKY FORD DAILY GAZETTE, THE. (April 19, 1954)-. Newspaper. English. da. $20.00 Otero & Crowley Counties; $40.00 other. Rocky Ford Daily Gazette, PO Box 430, Rocky Ford CO 81067. **Tel** (719)254-3351, FAX (719)254-3354. **ED** J.R. Thompson (Managing Editor). **Ad Acc. Circ:** 3,400. available on microfilm.

US
ROCKY MOUNTAIN NEWS (DENVER, COLO. : 1937). (ROCKY MOUNTAIN NEWS.). Vol. 78, No. 213 (Aug. 1, 1937)-Vol. 80, No. 130 (May 10, 1939); 80th Year, No. 131 (May 11, 1939)-. Newspaper. English. da. $190.00 New Mexico, Kansas, Utah, Nebraska, Wyoming, Colorado; $286.00 US. Rocky Mountain News, PO Box 719, Circulation Department, Denver CO 80201. **Tel** (303)892-5310, (303)892-6397. **ED** Ralph Looney. **Circ:** 332,114 daily, 373,206 Sunday. available on microfilm from University Microfilms International (UMI); available on an online database (file 641/Full-Text) from DIALOG. ***Continues*** *Denver Rocky Mountain News.*

US
SILVERTON STANDARD AND THE MINER, THE. VFOAT Silverton Standard. (Nov. 1889)-. Newspaper. English. wk. $26.00. Silverton Standard and Miner, PO Box 8, Silverton CO 81433-0187. **Tel** (303)387-5477. **ED** Jon Denious. **Photos. Ad Acc, Adv Mgr:** Sharon Denious. Full Page (B&W) $325.00. Half Page (B&W) $162.50. **Circ:** 1,413. ***Continues*** *Silverton Standard.*

US
SKY-HI NEWS. VFOAT Sky Hi News. Vol. 46, No. 45 (Sept. 7, 1989)-. Newspaper. English. wk. $14.00 Grand City; $19.50 other. Johnson Media, PO Box 409, Granby CO 80446. **Tel** (303)887-3334, FAX (303)887-3204. **ED** Patrick Brower. **Ad Acc. Circ:** 3,601. available on microfilm. ***Continues*** *Granby Sky-Hi News.*

US
STEAMBOAT PILOT, THE. Vol. 64, No. 42 (May 16, 1946)-. Newspaper. English. wk. $42.00 Routt County; $56.00 other. Steamboat Pilot, Box 4488, Steamboat Springs CO 80477. **Tel** (303)879-1502, FAX (303)879-2888. **ED** Deb Ward. **Ad Acc. Circ:** 7,000. available on microfilm. ***Continues*** *Steamboat Pilot with Which is Combined the Routt County Sentinel and Oak Creek Times-Leader.*

US
TELLURIDE TIMES-JOURNAL, THE. VFOAT Telluride Times Journal. Vol. 26, No. 25 (June 2, 1988)-. Newspaper. English. Fifty-two times a year (Thurs.). $24.00. Telluride Times-Journal, PO Box 1765, Telluride CO 81435. **Tel** (303)728-4301, (303)728-4488, FAX (303)728-6090. **ED** James Davidson. **Bk Rev. Photos. Ad Acc, Adv Mgr:** Bruce Kinsey. Full Page (B&W) $500.00. Half Page (B&W) $270.00. **Pub. Size:** Tabloid. **Circ:** 3,703 (paid), 645 (free). ***Formed by the union of*** *Telluride Times* ***and*** *Telluride Mountain Journal.*

US
TRIBUNE, THE. (1977)-. Newspaper. English. wk. $15.00 Colorado; $22.00 US. Tribune / Monument, PO Box 488, Monument CO 80132. **Tel** (719)481-3423. **ED** William Kezziah. **Ad Acc. Circ:** 3,500.

US
VAIL TRAIL, THE. Vol. 1, No. 1 (Oct. 1965)-. Newspaper. English. wk. Vail Trail, PO Drawer 6200, Vail CO 81658-6200. **Tel** (303)827-4004, FAX (303)827-5374. **ED** Allen Best (Managing Editor). **Ad Acc. Circ:** 14,000. available on microfilm.

US/1047-1170
VALLEY COURIER (ALAMOSA, COLO.). (THE VALLEY COURIER.). Vol. 27, No. 231 (Oct. 3, 1955)-. Newspaper. English. da. $105.00. Alamosa Valley Courier, PO Box 1099, Alamosa CO 81101. **Tel** (719)589-2553, FAX (719)589-6573. **ED** Catherine Gray Beuten. **Photos. Ad Acc, Adv Mgr:** Keith Cerny. Full Page (B&W) $967.50. Half Page (B&W) $483.75. Full Page (Color) $1,317.50. Half Page (Color) $833.75. **Pub. Size:** Standard. **Wire Svcs.:** AP. **Circ:** 4,895. available on microfilm. ***Continues*** *San Luis Valley Courier (Alamosa, Colo. : 1955).*

US
VALLEY JOURNAL, THE. Vol. 14, No. 49 (Dec. 10, 1987)-. Newspaper. English. wk. Valley Journal / Carbondale, 36 North 4th Street, Carbondale CO 81623-2031. **Tel** (303)963-3211, FAX (303)963-3259. **ED** Lynn Burton (Managing Editor). **Ad Acc. Circ:** 5,000. available on microfilm. ***Continues*** *Roaring Fork Valley Journal (Carbondale, Colo. : 1977).*

US
VILLAGER, THE. (1982)-. Newspaper. English. Fifty-two times a year (Thurs.). $26.00. The Villager Newspaper Group, 8933 East Union #230, Greenwood Village CO 80111. **Tel** (303)773-8313. **ED** Robert Sweeney (Editor in Chief), Cheryl Ghrist (Managing Editor). **Photos. Ad Acc, Adv Mgr:** Gerri Sweeney. Full Page (B&W) $2112.00. Half Page (B&W) $1056.00. Full Page (Color) $2237.00. Half Page (Color) $1181.00. **Pub. Size:** Tabloid. **Circ:** 8,000.
Desc: An locally-owned, legal, community newspaper for Arapahoe County.

US/0746-0988
VOZ (DENVER, COLO.). (LA VOZ.). Vol. 14, No. (1988)-. Newspaper. English (Spanish). wk. $24.00 (one year), $45.00 other. Santa Fe Publishing, PO Box 12068, Denver CO 80212. **Tel** (303)936-8556, FAX (303)922-9632. ***Continues*** *Voz Hispana de Colorado.*

US
WEEKLY REGISTER-CALL (CENTRAL CITY, COLO. : 1861). (WEEKLY REGISTER-CALL.). **VFOAT** Weekly Register Call. Vol. 16, No. 47 (June 23, 1878)-. Newspaper. English. Fifty-two times a year. $15.00 Gilpin County; $18.00 other. Weekly Register-Call, PO Box 609, Central City CO 80427. **Tel** (303)582-5333. **ED** Charlotte Taylor. **Bk Rev. Ad Acc, Adv Mgr:** Debra Soucy. **Tel** (303)582-5395. **Circ:** 1,100 (ctrl). available on microfilm. ***Continues*** *Weekly Central City Register (Central City, Colo. : 1878).*
Desc: Local news and legal publication for the Gilpin County, Colorado, area.

US
WESTMINISTER WINDOW. (19??)-. Newspaper. English. Fifty-two times a year (Thurs.). $24.00. Metro North Newspapers, PO Box 215, c/o Bruce G. Harper, Westminister CO 80030-0215. **Tel** (303)426-6000, FAX (303)430-1676. **ED** Marilyn Petterson. **Bk Rev**, (Qty: 25). **Photos. Ad Acc, Adv Mgr:** Scott Bumgardner. Full Page (B&W) $675.75. Half Page (B&W) $339.20. Full Page (Color) $1,075.75. Half Page (Color) $739.20. **Pub. Size:** Tabloid. **Circ:** 12,000 (ctrl).
Desc: A community interest newspaper with community, school, and local news.

US/0194-7710
WESTWORD. (1977)-. Periodical. English. wk (Wed.). $50.00 (by mail). Westword Corporation, PO Box 5790, Denver CO 80217. **Tel** (303)296-7744, FAX (303)296-5416. **ED** Patricia Calhoun, Andy Van de Voorde (Managing Editor). **Photos. Ad Acc, Adv Mgr:** Amy Cobb. Full Page (B&W) $2627.00. Half Page (B&W) $1313.00. Full Page (Color) $2852.00. Half Page (Color) $1538.00. **Pub. Size:** Standard. **Circ:** 110,000 (ctrl).

US/1060-5223
WHEAT RIDGE JEFFERSON SENTINEL, THE. Vol. 22, No. 7 (Sept. 19 1991)-. Newspaper. English. wk. $26.00. Jefferson Sentinels, 1224 Wadsworth Boulevard, Lakewood CO 80215. **Tel** (303)239-9890. **ED** Ben Miller. **Ad Acc. Circ:** 19,000 (ctrl). available on microfilm. ***Continues*** *Wheat Ridge sentinel, 0747-2021.*

US
WINTER PARK MANIFEST. Vol. 7, No. 50 (Mar. 1, 1984)-. Newspaper. English. wk. Winter Park Manifest, PO Box 409, Winter Park CO 80482-0409. **Tel** (303)726-5721, FAX (303)726-8789. **ED** Bruce Rubin. **Circ:** 4,000. ***Continues*** *Manifest (Winter Park, Colo.).*

US
WRAY GAZETTE, THE. (Mar. 6, 1903)-. Newspaper. English. wk. $18.00 Yuma County; $21.00 other. Wray Gazette Inc., PO Box 7, Wray CO 80758. **Tel** (303)332-4846, FAX (303)332-4065. **ED** Ronald C. Rieb. **Photos. Ad Acc, Adv Mgr:** Jeanette B. Rieb. **Pub. Size:** Standard. **Circ:** 3,084. ***Absorbed*** *Wray Rattler* ***and*** *Colorado Patriot.*

US
YUMA PIONEER, THE. (1886)-. Newspaper. English. wk. $16.00. Yuma Pioneer, PO Box 326, Yuma CO 80759. **Tel** (303)848-2174, FAX (303)848-2895. **ED** Anthony Rayl (Editor in Chief), Roger Chance (Managing Editor). **Photos. Ad Acc, Adv Mgr:** Mary Lynne Groshans. Full Page (B&W) $390.60. Half Page (B&W) $195.30. **Pub. Size:** Broadsheet. **Circ:** 2,800. available in microform.

CONNECTICUT

US/0746-7605
ADVERTISER (NEW MILFORD, CONN.). (ADVERTISER.). (19??)-. Newspaper. English. wk. New Milford Advertiser, 132 Danbury Road, New Milford CT 06776. **Tel** (203)354-2261, FAX (203)354-2645. **ED** Art Cummings. **Bk Rev. Ad Acc. Circ:** 26,000 (free).

US/0279-5167
ADVOCATE (STAMFORD, CONN.), THE. (THE ADVOCATE.). **VFOAT** Sunday Advocate. No. 279 (Mar. 7, 1974)-(Apr. 10, 1982); Vol. 154, No. 132 (Apr. 11, 1982)-. Newspaper. English. da. $171.60 (Fairfield County), $174.20 (rest of Connecticut), $187.20 (other) daily and Sunday (mail); $132.60 daily and Sunday (carrier). Stamford Advocate, 75 Tressor Boulevard, PO Box 9307, Stamford CT 06904. **Tel** (203)324-9799, FAX (203)964-2345. **ED** Kenneth Brief. **Bk Rev. Ad Acc. Circ:** 31,000 Daily, 44,000 Sunday. ***Continues*** *Stamford Advocate (Stamford, Conn. : 1922).*
Desc: General interest community newspaper.

US
AVON NEWS. (1981)-. Newspaper. English. wk. $25.00 Connecticut; $45.00 other. Imprint Publications /

Connecticut, PO Box 2, 20 Isham Road, West Hartford CT 06107. **Tel** (203)236-3571, FAX (203)236-0490. **ED** Laura Manente. **Ad Acc, Adv Mgr:** Frank Chilinski. **Circ:** 1,800.

US
BETHEL HOME NEWS, THE. (1965)-. Newspaper. English. wk. $30.00. Acorn Press Inc., PO Box 1019, Ridgefield CT 06877. **Tel** (203)438-6544, FAX (203)438-3395. **ED** Sue Wolf and Jack Sanders (Managing Editor). **Photos. Ad Acc, Adv Mgr:** Jim DeFillipo. Full Page (B&W) $882.00. Half Page (B&W) $441.00. Full Page (Color) $982.00. Half Page (Color) $541.00. **Pub. Size:** Broadsheet.

US/0746-9632
BLOOMFIELD JOURNAL, THE. (197?)-. Newspaper. English. wk. $23.00 Connecticut; $43.00 other. Imprint Publications / Connecticut, PO Box 2, 20 Isham Road, West Hartford CT 06107. **Tel** (203)236-3571, FAX (203)236-0490. **ED** Laura Manente. **Ad Acc, Adv Mgr:** Frank Chilinski. **Circ:** 2,400 (ctrl).
Desc: Content is comprised of local news.

US/0888-1901
BRANFORD REVIEW, THE. VFOAT Sunday Branford Review Shoreliner; Weekend Branford Review Shoreliner; Branford Review North Branford Review; Branford (Conn.) Review. Vol. 35, No. 1 (Jan. 16, 1958)-Vol. 48, No. 22 (May 29, 1975) ; 47th Year, No. 23 (June 5, 1975)-. Newspaper. English. sw. $40.00 New Haven County; $60.00 US; $110.00 other. Shore Line Newspapers, 120 North Fair Street, Guildford CT 06437. **Tel** (203)453-2711. **ED** Marianne Cipriano. **Circ:** 4,455. ***Continues in part*** *Suburban Spokesman.*

US/1049-9164
BRIDGEPORT POST, THE. ***Title Change.*** **VFOAT** Bridgeport Sunday Post. Vol. 47, No. 106 (May 4, 1906)-Vol. 109, No. 153 (June 1, 1992). Newspaper. English. da. Post Publishing Company, 410 State Street, Bridgeport CT 06602. **Tel** (203)333-0161, FAX (203)367-8158. **ED** Charles Betts. **Circ:** 61,890 daily, 91,642 Sunday. ***Continues*** *Bridgeport Standard American;* ***Absorbed*** *Bridgeport Telegram.* ***Continued by*** *Connecticut Post (Bridgeport, Conn.).*

US
BRISTOL PRESS, THE. Began with March 1871 issue. Newspaper. English. da. Bristol Press, 99 Main Street, Bristol CT 06010-1903. **Tel** (203)584-0501. **ED** Donald Goranson Jr. **Circ:** 20,105.

US
BROOKFIELD JOURNAL, THE. Vol. 1, No. 1 (Mar. 7, 1957)-. Newspaper. English. wk. $19.95 Fairfield County; $29.95 Connecticut; $31.95 US; $47.95 other. Houstonic Valley Publishing Co, PO Box 1139, New Milford CT 06776. **Tel** (203)354-2261, FAX (914)225-1914, (203)354-2645.

US
CATHOLIC TRANSCRIPT, THE. **Added/Corp** Catholic Church. Diocese of Hartford (Conn.) Catholic Church. Archdiocese of Hartford (Conn.) Catholic Church. Diocese of Norwich (Conn.) Catholic Church. Diocese of Bridgeport (Conn.). Vol. 1, No. 1 (June 17, 1898)-. Newspaper. English. wk. $25.00. The Catholic Transcript, 785 Asylum Avenue, Hartford CT 06105-2886. **Tel** (203) 527-1175, FAX (203)547-NEWS. **ED** Janet Alampi (Managing Editor). **Bk Rev** (Qty: 12). **Photos. Ad Acc, Adv Mgr:** Roy J. Rowland. Full Page (B&W) $867.20. Half Page (B&W) $433.60. Full Page (Color) $1,462.20. Half Page (Color) $1,028.60. **Pub. Size:** Tabloid. **Wire Svcs.:** CS. **Circ:** 15,204. ***Continues*** *Connecticut Catholic.*

US
CHESHIRE HERALD. Vol. 1, No. 1 (Feb. 4, 1953)-. Newspaper. English. wk. $15.00 New Haven County; $19.00 US. True Publishing Inc, PO Box 247, Cheshire CT 06410. **Tel** (203)272-5316, FAX (203)250-7145. **ED** Clarke Hammersly. **Photos. Ad Acc, Adv Mgr:** Joseph Jakubisyn. Full Page (B&W) $382.08. Half Page (B&W) $197.16. Full Page (Color) $432.08. Half Page (Color) $247.16. **Circ:** 6,800 paid.

US
CHRONICLE, THE. Vol. 89, No. 19 (Jan. 23, 1971)-. Newspaper. English. da. $125.50 Local. The Chronicle / Willimantic, PO Box 148, Willimantic CT 06226. **Tel** (203)423-8466. available on microfilm. ***Continues*** *Willimantic Daily Chronicle.*

US/0191-5134
CITIZEN NEWS. (19??)-. Newspaper. English. sw (Wednesday & Friday). $30.00 Connecticut; $45.00 other. Brooks Community News, 136 Main Street, Westport CT 06880-3304. **Tel** (203)226-6311, FAX (203)227-6864. **Circ:** 11,402.

US
CLINTON RECORDER. VFOAT Saturday Clinton Recorder; Weekend East; Recorder. Vol. 93, No. 9 (Feb. 28, 1974)-Vol. 94, No. 22 (May 29, 1975) ; 94th Year, No. 23 (June 5, 1975)-. Newspaper. English. sw. $22.00 New Haven County; $50.00 US; $100.00 other. Shore Line Newspapers, 120 North Fair Street, Guildford CT 06437. **Tel** (203)453-2711. **ED** Don Merrill. **Ad Acc. Circ:** 6,000. ***Continues*** *Recorder (Clinton, Conn.).*

●US/1070-874X
CONNECTICUT POST (BRIDGEPORT, CONN.). (CONNECTICUT POST.). Vol. 1, No. 1 (June 2, 1992)-. Newspaper. English. da. $291.20 within 150 miles of Bridgeport; $319.80 other. Post Publishing Company, 410 State Street, Bridgeport CT 06602. **Tel** (203)333-0161, FAX (203)367-8158. **ED** Robert H. Laska. **Ad Acc, Adv Mgr:** Paul Ward. **Circ:** 70,690. ***Continues*** *Bridgeport Post.*

US/0744-3862
DARIEN NEWS-REVIEW. VFOAT Darien News Review. **VAT** Darien News Review. Vol. 10, No. 9 (March 4, 1982)-. Newspaper. English. wk. $12.00. Darien News Corporation, 6 Squab Lane, Darien CT 06820. **Tel** (203)226-6311. **ED** Janet H. Cummings and Diana Barnard. **Ad Acc. Circ:** 8,800. ***Formed by the union of*** *Darien News (Darien, Conn.), 0192-0154* ***and*** *Darien Review (Darien, Conn. : 1915).*
Desc: Hometown newspaper covering the cultural, political and athletic news of Darien. Includes a classified section, weekly features.

US/0744-0499
DAY (NEW LONDON, CONN.), THE. (THE LONDON DAY.). (1963)-. Newspaper. English. da (Except six holidays per year). $155.00 (weekdays & Sun.), $125.00 (weekdays) Connecticut; $158.00 (weekdays & Sun.), $127.00 (weekdays) New England states; $175.00 (weekdays & Sun.), $140.00 (weekdays) other US. Day Publishing Company, 47-53 Main Street, New London CT 06320. **Tel** (203)442-2200. **ED** Reid McCluggage. **Ad Acc. Circ:** 38,500 daily, 42,500 Sunday. available on microfilm. ***Continues*** *New London Evening Day.*

US/8750-9156
EAST HARTFORD GAZETTE, THE. VFOAT Gazette. (1???)-. Newspaper. English. Fifty-two times a year (Fri.). $20.00 inside East Hartford; $30.00 outside East Hartford. East Hartford Gazette, 7 Franklin Square, New Britten CT 06051. **Tel** (203)225-4608 ext. 333. **ED** Andrew Nelson. **Circ:** 21,000.

US/8750-3123
ENFIELD PRESS (1984), THE. (THE ENFIELD PRESS.). **VFOAT** Press. (1984)-. Newspaper. English. wk (Publish on Thursday). $13.60 Connecticut; $21.60 other. Enfield Press, PO Box 1141, Enfield CT 06083. **Tel** (203)745-3348. **ED** Frank Poirot. **Ad Acc, Adv Mgr Tel** (413)562-4181. **Circ:** 3,400 (ctrl). ***Continues*** *Press (Enfield, Conn. 1984), 0746-9780.*
Desc: Content is comprised of local news.

US/0192-3110
FAIRPRESS. ***Ceased.*** **VAT** Fair Press. Vol. 2, No. 23 (Jan. 10, 1973)-Vol. 22, No. 21 (Feb. 4, 1993). Newspaper. English. wk. Fairpress Inc, PO Box 5700, 200 Westport Avenue, Norwalk CT 06856. **Tel** (203)846-3451. **ED** John Schwing. **Bk Rev. Ad Acc. Circ:** 62,072 (ctrl). ***Continues*** *Westport-Weston Fairpress.*
Desc: Section one covers politics, environment and business. Section two covers fashion, the home, food and cars. Includes classifieds and a tab on theater, dance, film and books.

US
FARMINGTON NEWS, THE. (198?)-. Newspaper. English. wk. $25.00 Connecticut; $45.00 other. Imprint Publications / Connecticut, PO Box 2, 20 Isham Road, West Hartford CT 06107. **Tel** (203)236-3571, FAX (203)236-0490. **ED** Laura Manente. **Ad Acc, Adv Mgr:** Frank Chilinski. **Circ:** 1,800 (ctrl).

US/0191-7463
FOOTHILLS TRADER. (19??)-. Newspaper. English. wk. $25.00. Foothills Trader, Central Avenue, New Hartford CT 06057. **Tel** (203)379-7517. **ED** Lillian J. Ludlam. **Bk Rev. Ad Acc. Circ:** 35,000.

US
GLASTONBURY CITIZEN, THE. Vol. 1, No. 1 (Nov. 2, 1950)-. Newspaper. English. wk. $18.00 Connecticut; $20.00 US. Glastonbury Citizen, PO Box 373, Glastonbury CT 06033. **Tel** (203)633-4691, FAX (203)657-3258. **ED** Cathleen Stack. **Ad Acc, Adv Mgr:** Carol Saucier. **Circ:** 8,111.

US/0746-8539
GREENWICH NEWS. (1983)-. Newspaper. English. wk. Free to Greenwich, Connecticut residents; $12.00 other states in the US; $15.00 other. Greenwich News Inc, PO Box 7879, Greenwich CT 06836-7979. **ED** Larry Fellows. **Circ:** 20,519.

US/0192-8503
HARTFORD ADVOCATE. Vol. 2, No. 1 (Sept. 3, 1975)-. Newspaper. English. wk. $70.00. Advocate Publishing, 30 Arbor Street, Hartford CT 06106-1209. **Tel** (203)232-4501, FAX (203)232-6132. **ED** Janet Reynolds. **Circ:** 58,810. ***Continues*** *Valley Advocate (Hartford, Conn.).*

US/1047-4153
HARTFORD COURANT, THE. Vol. 50, No. 161, July 9 (1887)-. Newspaper. English. da. $187.20 (daily), $98.80 (Sunday), $286.00 (daily and Sunday) by mail US; $405.60 (daily), $176.80 (Sunday), $582.40 (daily and Sunday) by mail other; $93.60 daily by carrier; $166.40 daily and Sunday by carrier. Hartford Courant, 285 Broad Street, Hartford CT 06115. **Tel** (203)241-6574, (203)525-5555. **[CCC]. Circ:** 226,319 daily, 308,111 Sunday. available on microfilm from University Microfilms International (UMI). ***Continues*** *Hartford Daily Courant;* ***Absorbed*** *Globe (Hartford, Conn.).*
Ind/Abst PROMT.

US
HERALD, THE. VFOAT Herald Extra; New Britain Herald. (1976)-. Newspaper. English. da (except Sunday). $154.00. Herald Publishing Company / New Britain, 1 Herald Square, PO Box 2050, New Britain CT 06050. **Tel** (203)225-4601 ext. 238, AFTER HOURS (203)225-4603, FAX (203)225-4601 ext. 238. **ED** Judith W. Brown, William Millerick (Managing Editor). **Bk Rev. Photos. Ad Acc.** Full Page (B&W) $2,534.85. Half Page (B&W) $1,267.43. Full Page (Color) $2890.50. Half Page (Color) $1,445.00. **Pub. Size:** Broadsheet. **Wire Svcs.:** AP, SH. **Circ:** 41,000. available on microfilm. ***Continues*** *New Britain Herald.*
Desc: Central Connecticut and greater Hartford's largest afternoon newspaper for local, national and worldwide news.

US
HOUR, THE. Vol. 100, No. 179 (Aug. 2, 1971)-. Newspaper. English. da. $110.00 Fairfield Co., CT; $134.00 other. Hour Publishing Company, PO Box 790, Norwalk CT 06852. **Tel** (203)846-3281, FAX (203)846-9897. ***Continues*** *Norwalk Hour (Norwalk, Conn. : 1901).*

US
LAKEVILLE JOURNAL, THE. VFOAT Canaan Journal. (1897)-. Newspaper. English. wk. $26.50. Lakeville Journal, Bissell Street, Lakeville CT 06039-0353. **Tel** (203)435-9873. **ED** Robert Hatch, Kathryn Boughton (Managing Editor). **Bk Rev. Photos. Ad Acc, Adv Mgr:** Anna Mae Kupferer. Full Page (B&W) $1462.65. Half Page (B&W) $781.33. Full Page (Color) $1612.65. Half Page (Color) $881.33. **Pub. Size:** Broadsheet. **Circ:** 6,588 paid. available in microform from New England Micrographics, Inc.

US/0888-3017
LEDGER (RIDGEFIELD, CONN.), THE. (THE LEDGER.). **Added/Corp** Schult, Eric. **VFOAT** NY Ledger; N.Y. Ledger. (19??)-. Newspaper. English. wk (52 issues per year). $30.00. Acorn Press Inc., PO Box 1019, Ridgefield CT 06877. **Tel** (203)438-6544, FAX (203)438-3395. **ED** Rose Fisk and Jack Sanders (Managing Editor). **Photos. Ad Acc, Adv Mgr:** Jim DeFillipo. Full Page (B&W) $630.00. Half Page (B&W) $315.00. Full Page (Color) $730.00. Half Page (Color) $415.00. **Pub. Size:** Broadsheet. **Circ:** 1,700. ***Continues*** *Lewisboro Ledger.*

US/0744-6705
LITCHFIELD COUNTY TIMES, THE. Vol. 1, No. 1 (Nov. 13, 1981)-. Newspaper. English. wk. $30.00. Litchfield County Times, 32 Main Street, New Milford CT 06776. **Tel** (203)355-8706. **ED** Ken Paul and Douglas Clement. **Bk Rev. Photos. Ad Acc, Adv Mgr:** Marty Sweeney, **Tel** (203)355-4141. Full Page (B&W) $1,499.40. Half Page (B&W) $850.50. **Pub. Size:** Broadsheet. **Circ:** 16,000. available in microform.
Desc: A weekly newspaper covering major news stories in Litchfield County. Includes a feature/life section and a business/real estate/classified section.

US
LITCHFIELD ENQUIRER. Vol. 3, No. 33 (Jan. 1829)-. Newspaper. English. wk. Litchfield Enquirer, 132 Danbury Road, New Milford CT 06776. **Tel** (203)354-2261. **ED** Robert S Mellis. **Circ:** 2,458. ***Continues*** *Litchfield County Post.*

US/0746-3693
LONGMEADOW NEWS. Newspaper. English. wk. Longmeadow News, PO Box 941, Enfield CT 08062. **Tel** (203)745-3348. **ED** Bette Quatrale. **Circ:** 1,768.

US
MIDDLETOWN PRESS, THE. (June 2, 1919)-. Newspaper. English. da. $120.00. Middletown Press, PO Box 471, Middletown CT 06457. **Tel** (203)347-3331, FAX (203)347-3380. **ED** David Scribner. **LC** 7002. **Ad Acc, Adv Mgr:** Tom Howard. **Circ:** 18,526. ***Continues*** *Evening Press (Middletown, Conn.).*

US
MILFORD CITIZEN, THE. VFOAT Sunday Milford Citizen; Sunday Citizen. Vol. 1, No. 1 (May 25, 1894)-. Newspaper. English. da. $125.00. Citizen Publications, PO Box 589, 349 New Haven Avenue, Milford CT 06460. **Tel** (203)876-6800. ***Absorbed*** *Milford News (Milford, Conn.)* ***and*** *Chronicle (Devon, Conn.).*

US
MONROE COURIER. (19??)-. Newspaper. English. wk. $20.00 Fairfield County; $30.00 other. Monroe Courier, PO Box 216, Monroe CT 06468. **Tel** (203)268-6234, FAX (202)452-1068. **ED** Lorraine Bukowski. **Ad Acc**, **Adv Mgr:** Robin Glowa.

US
NAUGATUCK DAILY NEWS. Vol. 1, No. 42 (Aug. 12, 1895)-Vol. 67, No. 265 (Nov. 10, 1952) ; 67th Year, No. 266 (Nov. 11, 1952)-. Newspaper. English. da. $96.00. Naugatuck Daily News, 195 Water Street, Naugatuck CT 06770. **Tel** (203)729-2228, FAX (203)729-9099. **ED** Jean Wertz (Managing Editor). **Ad Acc**. **Circ:** 4,788. ***Continues*** *Naugatuck News.*

US
NEW CANAAN ADVERTISER. (190?)-Vol. 53, No. 31 (Mar. 2, 1961) ; 53rd Year, No. 32 (Mar. 9, 1961)-. Newspaper. English. wk. $20.00 Connecticut; $25.00 other. Hersam Publishing Company, PO Box 605, New Canaan CT 06840. **Tel** (203)966-9541, FAX (203)966-8006. **ED** Edmund J. Chrowtowski. **Ad Acc**. **Circ:** 6,535.

US/0192-8511
NEW HAVEN ADVOCATE. (Sept. 3, 1975)-. Newspaper. English. Fifty-two times a year (Thursdays). $40.00. New Haven Advocate, One Long Worth Drive, New Haven CT 06511. **Tel** (203)789-0010. **ED** Bob LaRussa. **Circ:** 50,000.

US
NEW HAVEN REGISTER, THE. **VFOAT** New Haven Register, New Haven Journal-Courier. (1961)-. Newspaper. English. da. $127.40. New Haven Register Inc, 40 Sargent Drive, New Haven CT 06511. **Tel** (203)789-5200. **(Subscription address:** New Haven Register, PO Box 9702, New Haven CT 06536.**)** **ED** Thomas P. Geyer and David Butler. **Bk Rev**. **Ad Acc**. **Circ:** 103,400 daily, 138,856 Sunday. available on microfilm from New England Micrographics, Inc.; available on an online database (file 635/Full-Text) from DIALOG. Documents available from UMI Article Clearinghouse. ***Continues*** *New Haven Evening Register (New Haven, Conn. : 1874);* ***Absorbed*** *Journal-Courier (New Haven, Conn.).*
Ind/Abst Bus. Dateline (Dec. 19, 1991-) [Full Txt.].

US
NEW MILFORD TIMES, THE. **VFOAT** Washington, New Preston News. (191?)-. Newspaper. English. wk. $24.95 Litchfield County; $34.95 Connecticut; $36.95 US; $52.95 other. Houstonic Valley Publishing Co, PO Box 1139, New Milford CT 06776. **Tel** (203)354-2261, FAX (914)225-1914, (203)354-2645. **ED** Arthur Cummings. **Ad Acc**, **Adv Mgr:** Bernie Schraer. ***Absorbed*** *New Milford Gazette.*

US/0745-0796
NEWINGTON TOWN CRIER. Vol. 12, No. 7 (Feb. 18, 1971)-. Newspaper. English. Fifty-two times a year. $33.00 Connecticut; $53.00 other. Imprint Publications / Connecticut, PO Box 2, 20 Isham Road, West Hartford CT 06107. **Tel** (203)236-3571, FAX (203)236-0490. **ED** Joyce Rossignol. **Bk Rev**. **Ad Acc**. **Circ:** 4,700 (ctrl). ***Continues*** *Town Crier (Newington, Conn.).*

US/1044-4106
NEWS-TIMES (DANBURY, CONN.), THE. (THE NEWS-TIMES.). **VFOAT** News Times; Sunday, News-Times. Vol. 80, No. 236 (Oct. 7, 1963)-. Newspaper. English. da. $135.00 Connecticut; $150.00 other (daily and Sunday by mail). The News-Times, Circulation Department, 333 Main Street, Danbury CT 06810. **Tel** (203)744-5100, FAX (203)792-4211. ***Continues*** *Danbury News-Times (Danbury, Conn. : Daily).*

US
NORWICH BULLETIN. **VFOAT** Norwich Sunday Record; Norwich Bulletin-Record; Norwich Bulletin Record; Sunday Bulletin; Morning Bulletin, Weekly Courier; Morning Bulletin; Norwich Bulletin and Courier; Norwich Bulletin, Norwich Courier. (1895)-. Newspaper. English. da (except Sunday). $138.00. Norwich Bulletin, 66 Franklin Street, Norwich CT 06360. **Tel** (203)887-9211. **ED** William F. Mungo. **LC** 7002. **Circ:** 34,638 daily, 38,286 Sunday. available on an online database (file 635/Full-Text) from DIALOG. Documents available from UMI Article Clearinghouse. ***Continues*** *Norwich Morning Bulletin;* ***Absorbed*** *Norwich Courier-Cooley's Weekly; Norwich Evening Record; News (Groton, Conn.).*
Ind/Abst Bus. Dateline (Dec. 30, 1991-) [Full Txt.].

US
OBSERVER, THE. Vol. 1, No. 1 (Dec. 3, 1975)-. Newspaper. English. wk. $15.00. Southington Observer, PO Box 648, Southington CT 06489. **Tel** (203)621-6751, FAX (203)621-1841. **ED** Robert Zarnetsky. **Photos**. **Ad Acc**, **Adv Mgr:** Anthony J. Urillo, **Tel** (203)628-9645. Full Page (B&W) $882.00. Half Page (B&W) $441.00. Full Page (Color) $982.00. **Pub. Size:** Broadsheet. **Circ:** 5,205.

US
OBSERVER-PATRIOT, THE. ***Ceased.*** **VFOAT** Observer Patriot; Times/Observer. Vol. 94, No. 37 (Sept. 19, 1979)-(Sept. 1994). Newspaper. English. wk. Observer Patriot, PO Box 249, Putnam CT 06260. **Tel** (203)928-7943, FAX (203)928-1768. **ED** Christine Bates. **Ad Acc**. **Circ:** 4,224. ***Continues*** *Windham County Observer, Putnam Patriot.*

US
PICTORIAL GAZETTE, THE. **VFOAT** Weekend East. (199?)-. Newspaper. English. sw. Pictorial Gazette, PO Box O, Old Saybrook CT 06475. **Tel** (203)388-3441, FAX (203)388-5613. ***Continues*** *Pictorial Gazette West.*

US
PISCATAQUIS OBSERVER, THE. Began with Nov. 26, 1847 issue. Newspaper. English. wk. Northeast Publishing Company, PO Box 362, 26 Long Hill Road, Guilford CT 06437. **Tel** (800)972-2001, (203)453-3717. **LC** 8007-X. available on microfilm from University Microfilms International (UMI). ***Continues*** *Piscataquis Farmer.*

US
POST, THE. Vol. 46, No. 36 (Jan. 3, 1991)-. Newspaper. English. wk. $21.00 New Haven County; $55.00 other. Shore Line Newspapers, 120 North Fair Street, Guilford CT 06437. **Tel** (203)453-2711. ***Formed by the union of*** *Wallingford Post.*

US/0890-1147
PUTNAM COUNTY COURIER (CARMEL, N.Y. : 1852). ***Title Change.*** (PUTNAM COUNTY COURIER.). **VFOAT** Putnam Courier. Vol. 11, No. 1 (Jan. 10, 1852)-Vol. 152, No. 22 (June 2, 1993). Newspaper. English. wk. Houstonic Valley Publishing Co, PO Box 1139, New Milford CT 06776. **Tel** (203)354-2261, FAX (914)225-1914, (203)354-2645. **ED** Howard O Burr. **Ad Acc**. **Circ:** 9,000 (ctrl). ***Continues*** *Democratic Courier (Carmel, N.Y.).* ***Merged with*** *Putnam Trader (Carmel, N.Y.)* ***to form*** *Putnam Courier-Trader.*
Desc: News of local government, recreational and cultural activities. Official newspaper for Putnam County, all legal notices.

●US
PUTNAM COURIER-TRADER, THE. **VFOAT** Putnam Courier Trader; Courier-Trader; Courier Trader. (June 10, 1993)-. Newspaper. English. wk. $18.00 (1 year), $31.00 (2 year), $44.00 (3 year) in-county; $28.00 (1 year), $51.00 (2 year), $74.00 (3 year) other Connecticut; $30.00 (1 year), $55.00 (2 year), $80.00 (3 year) other. Houstonic Valley Publishing Co, PO Box 1139, New Milford CT 06776. **Tel** (203)354-2261, FAX (914)225-1914, (203)354-2645. **ED** Barbara Gallo-Farrel. **Ad Acc**. **Circ:** 7,500 (ctrl). ***Formed by the union of*** *Putnam County Courier* ***and*** *Putnam Trader (Carmel, N.Y.).*

US
RECORD-JOURNAL. **VFOAT** Record Journal. 113th Year, No. 207 (Sept. 2, 1980)-. Newspaper. English. da. $169.00 New Haven County; $221.00 other. Meriden Record Journal, Crown Street Square, PO Box 915, Meriden CT 06450. **Tel** (203)235-1661, (203)634-3933, FAX (203)639-0210. **ED** Eliot White. **Ad Acc**. **Circ:** 30,958. ***Continues*** *Morning Record and Journal.*

US
REDDING PILOT, THE. Vol. 1, No. 1 (Oct. 12, 1966)-. Newspaper. English. wk (Wednesdays). $30.00. Acorn Press Inc., PO Box 1019, Ridgefield CT 06877. **Tel** (203)438-6544, FAX (203)438-3395. **ED** Claire Bronson and Jack Sanders (Managing Editor). **Photos**. **Ad Acc**, **Adv Mgr:** J. DeFillipo. Full Page (B&W) $882.00. Half Page (B&W) $641.00. Full Page (Color) $982.00. **Pub. Size:** Broadsheet.

US/0746-8180
REGISTER CITIZEN. **VFOAT** Citizen. Vol. 111, No. 1 (Jan. 3, 1984)-. Newspaper. English. da. $107.00 Torrington, Connecticut; $118.00 other. Register Citizen, 190 Water Street, Torrington CT 06790. **Tel** (203)489-3121. **Circ:** 16,421. ***Absorbed*** *Winsted Citizen; Register (Torrington, Conn.).*

US
REMINDER. (19??)-. Newspaper. English. wk. Reminder, 130 Old Town Road, Vernon CT 06066. **Tel** (203)875-3366, FAX (203)875-2089. **ED** Kenneth Hovland Jr. **Circ:** 116,646. ***Continues*** *Rockville Reminder.*

US
RIDGEFIELD PRESS. (19??)-. Newspaper. English. wk. $30.00. Acorn Press Inc., PO Box 1019, Ridgefield CT 06877. **Tel** (203)438-6544, FAX (203)438-3395. **ED** Mark Reid and Jack Sanders (Managing Editor). **Photos**. **Ad Acc**, **Adv Mgr:** Jim DeFillipo. Full Page (B&W) $882.00. Half Page (B&W) $441.00. Full Page (Color) $982.00. Half Page (Color) $541.00. **Pub. Size:** Broadsheet. **Circ:** 6,500. ***Continues*** *Press (Ridgefield, Conn.).*

US
ROCKY HILL POST, THE. Vol. 12, No. 45 (Nov. 9, 1972)-. Newspaper. English. wk. $23.00 Connecticut; $43.00 other. Imprint Publications / Connecticut, PO Box 2, 20 Isham Road, West Hartford CT 06107. **Tel** (203)236-3571, FAX (203)236-0490. **ED** Laura Manente. **Ad Acc**. **Circ:** 1,500.

US/0887-7912
SHORE LINE TIMES. **VFOAT** Sunday Shore Line Times Shoreliner; Weekend Shore Line Times Shoreliner. (1877)-. Newspaper. English. sw. $30.00 New Haven County; $50.00 others US; $100.00 other. Shore Line Newspapers, 120 North Fair Street, Guildford CT 06437. **Tel** (203)453-2711. **ED** John Peterson. **Circ:** 27,345. ***Continues*** *Shore Line Times and County Chronicle.*

US/0891-9542
SIMSBURY NEWS, THE. (1986)-. Newspaper. English. wk. $25.00 Connecticut; $35.00 other. Imprint Publications / Connecticut, PO Box 2, 20 Isham Road, West Hartford CT 06107. **Tel** (203)236-3571, FAX (203)236-0490. **ED** Laura Manente. **Bk Rev**. **Ad Acc**, **Adv Mgr:** Frank Chilinski. **Circ:** 2,300 (ctrl).
Desc: Content is comprised of local news.

US
STRATFORD BARD, THE. (197?)-. Newspaper. English. wk. $28.00 Fairfield; $60.00 other. Elm City Citizens Newspapers, 349 New Haven Avenue, Milford CT 06460. **Tel** (203)876-6800. ***Absorbed*** *Stratford Town News.*

US
TRUMBULL TIMES, THE. Vol. 1, No. 1 (June 18, 1959)-. Newspaper. English. wk. $34.50 Fairfield County; $40.00 other. Hometown Publications, PO Box 298, Trumbull CT 06611. **Tel** (203)268-6234, FAX (203)452-1068.

US/0193-1474
VOICES (SOUTHBURY). (VOICES.). (19??)-. Newspaper. English. wk. $36.00. Voices, PO Box 383, Southbury CT 06488. **Tel** (203)263-2116. **ED** Mary Jane Musgat. **Ad Acc**. **Circ:** 22,510 (ctrl).
Desc: Specializes in total local news for a market of 57,000.

US/1057-1272
WEST HARTFORD NEWS. Vol. 15, No. 41 (July 2, 1947)-. Newspaper. English. wk. $32.00 Connecticut; $52.00 other. Imprint Publications / Connecticut, PO Box 2, 20 Isham Road, West Hartford CT 06107. **Tel** (203)236-3571, FAX (203)236-0490. **ED** Keith Griffin. **Ad Acc**, **Adv Mgr:** Frank Chilinski. **Circ:** 10,000 (ctrl). ***Continues*** *West Hartford Metropolitan News.*

US
WEST HAVEN NEWS. Vol. 7, No. 11 (Mar. 31, 1977)-. Newspaper. English. wk. $28.20. Elm City Citizens Newspapers, 349 New Haven Avenue, Milford CT 06460. **Tel** (203)876-6800. **ED** Linda Bouvier. **Ad Acc**, **Adv Mgr:** Bill Flaucher. **Circ:** 15,000. ***Continues*** *West Haven City News.*

US
WESTON FORUM, THE. Vol. 1, No. 1 (Aug. 5, 1970)-. Newspaper. English. wk. Free (Weston, CT). Acorn Press Inc., PO Box 1019, Ridgefield CT 06877. **Tel** (203)438-6544, FAX (203)438-3395. **ED** Sybil Blau and Jack Sanders (Managing Editor). **Photos**. **Ad Acc**, **Adv Mgr:** Jim DeFillipo. Full Page (B&W) $882.00. Half Page (B&W) $441.00. Full Page (Color) $982.00. Half Page (Color) $541.00. **Pub. Size:** Broadsheet. ***Continues*** *Weston Voice.*

US
WETHERSFIELD POST. **VFOAT** Wethersfield-Rocky Hill Post; Wethersfield Rocky Hill Post. Vol. 1, No. 1 (Sept. 10, 1959)-. Newspaper. English. wk. $25.00 Connecticut; $45.00 other. Imprint Publications / Connecticut, PO Box 2, 20 Isham Road, West Hartford CT 06107. **Tel** (203)236-3571, FAX (203)236-0490. **ED** Kim Sirois. **Ad Acc**, **Adv Mgr:** Frank Chilinski. **Circ:** 3,625 (ctrl).

US
WILTON BULLETIN. (193?)-. Newspaper. English. wk. $30.00 Fairfield County; $35.00 other US; $90.00 other. Acorn Press Inc., PO Box 1019, Ridgefield CT 06877. **Tel** (203)438-6544, FAX (203)438-3395. **ED** Greg Bartlett. **Ad Acc**, **Adv Mgr:** Jim DeFillipo. **Circ:** 4,600.

US
WINDSOR JOURNAL, THE. **VFOAT** Windsor Edition of the Journals. Vol. 1, No. 1 (Sept. 13, 1973)-. Newspaper. English. wk. $25.00 Connecticut; $45.00 other. Imprint Publications / Connecticut, PO Box 2, 20 Isham Road, West Hartford CT 06107. **Tel** (203)236-3571, FAX (203)236-0490. **ED** Melanie Winters.

Ad Acc, **Adv Mgr**: Frank Chilinski. **Circ**: 2,400 (ctrl). **Continues** Windsor Locks Journal (Windsor Locks, Conn. : Windsor Ed.).

US
WINDSOR LOCKS JOURNAL, THE. Vol. 105, No. 3 (Jan. 20, 1984)-. Newspaper. English. wk. $25.00 Connecticut; $45.00 other. Imprint Publications / Connecticut, PO Box 2, 20 Isham Road, West Hartford CT 06107. **Tel** (203)236-3571, FAX (203)236-0490. **ED** Laura Manente. **Ad Acc, Adv Mgr**: Frank Chilinski. **Circ**: 1,400 (ctrl). **Continues** Windsor Locks Journal Observer.

US/0890-2240
YALE DAILY NEWS. (1???)-. Newspaper. English. da (Mon.-Fri.). $45.00 (students); $55 00 (local); $65.00 (others). Yale Daily News Publishing Co., Inc., 202 York Street, PO Box 209007, New Haven CT 06520. **Tel** (203)432-2424, FAX (203)432-1323. **ED** Jeffery Glasser (Editor-in-Chief), A. LaCroix and S. Sagan (Managing Editor). **Bk Rev**. **Photos**. **Ad Acc, Adv Mgr**: Anastasia Katsetos, **Tel** (203)432-2401. Full Page (B&W) $1,764.00. Half Page (B&W) $882.00. Full Page (Color) $2,564.00. Half Page (Color) $1,682.00. **Pub. Size**: Broadsheet. **Wire Svcs.**: AP. **Circ**: 3,500. available on microfilm from Yale University Photographic Services. **Desc**: College newspaper run by undergraduates at Yale. Covers all the news at Yale: art, sports, with a listing of events and speakers. The oldest collegiate daily newspaper.

DELAWARE

US
CHRONICLE (MILFORD, DEL.). (THE CHRONICLE.). Vol. 96 No. 1 (Oct. 3, 1974)-. Newspaper. English. wk. $21.00. Chronicle / Milford, PO Box 297, Milford DE 19963. **Tel** (302)422-1200, FAX (302)422-1211. **ED** Ronald MacArthur. **Photos**. **Ad Acc, Adv Mgr**: Jerry Miller. **Pub. Size**: Broadsheet. **Circ**: 8,000. **Continues** Milford Chronicle.

US/0740-2023
DELAWARE COAST PRESS. VFOAT Coast Press. (1949)-. Newspaper. English. wk. $32.00. Delaware Coast Press, PO Box 309, Rehoboth Beach DE 19971. **Tel** (302)227-9466, FAX (302)227-9469. **ED** Terry Plowman. **Photos**. **Ad Acc, Adv Mgr**: Jane Meleady. Full Page (B&W) $562.25. Full Page (Color) $28.13. Full Page (Color) $697.25. Half Page (Color) $416.13. **Pub. Size**: Tabloid. available in microform. **Continues** Public Press and the Delaware Coast News.

US/0745-8096
DELAWARE STATE NEWS AND MARYLAND STATE NEWS. VFOAT Delaware State News, Maryland State News and Daily Eagle; Delaware State News, Maryland State News; Delaware State News; Maryland State News; State News & Daily Eagle. Vol. 77, No. 246 (Oct. 20, 1972)-. Newspaper. English. da. $78.00 one year (Sunday by mail), $208.00 one year (daily & Sunday by mail) $100.00 one year (daily & Sunday by carrier), $130.00 one year (daily by mail). Delaware State News, PO Box 737, Dover DE 19903. **Tel** (302)674-3600. **ED** Frank Fantini. **Circ**: 24,078 daily, 31,247 Sunday. available on microfilm from University Microfilms International (UMI). **Continues** Delaware State News; **Absorbed** Daily Eagle.

US/0191-5037
DOVER POST. (1???)-. Newspaper. English. Fifty-two times a year (Wed.). $43.80. Dover Post Company, 609 East Division Street, PO Box 664, Dover DE 19901. **Tel** (302)678-3616.

US/0747-0975
HARRINGTON JOURNAL, THE. (191?)-. Newspaper. English. wk. $23.50 Delaware; $22.00 other. Harrington Journal, 15 Commerce Street, PO Box 239, Harrington DE 19952. **Tel** (302)398-3206.

US/1072-1568
LEADER (1993), THE. (THE LEADER.). (19??)-. Newspaper. English. sw. $35.00 (East Coast). Seaford Leader, 616 Water Street, Seaford DE 19973. **Tel** (302)629-5505. **Continues** Leader and State Register.

US
NEWARK POST, THE. (June 5, 1985)-. Newspaper. English. wk. $14.95. Chesapeake Publishing Corporation / Delaware, Robscott Building, 153 East Chestnut Hill Road, Newark DE 19713. **Tel** (302)737-9724, FAX (302)737-9019. **ED** Marty Valania. **Photos**. **Ad Acc, Adv Mgr**: Tina Winibell. Full Page (B&W) $926.10. Half Page (B&W) $485.10. Full Page (Color) $1176.10. Half Page (Color) $735.40. **Pub. Size**: Broadsheet. **Wire Svcs.**: AP. **Circ**: 12,000. **Continues** Newark Weekly Post.

US/1042-4121
NEWS JOURNAL (WILMINGTON, DEL.), THE. (THE NEWS JOURNAL.). VFOAT Sunday News Journal. (Jan. 3, 1989)-. Newspaper. English. wk (published Monday through Saturday). $171.60 US and Canada; $359.75 other. News-Journal Company, 950 West Basin Road, New Castle DE 19720. **Tel** (800)235-9100, (302)324-2500, FAX (302)324-2945. **ED** John Walson and Valerie Bender (Managing Editor). **Bk Rev**. **Photos**. **Ad Acc, Adv Mgr**: Kitty Burns Esenberg, **Tel** (302)324-2617. Full Page (B&W) $12,337.00 (daily) & $13.984.00 (Sunday). Half Page (B&W) $6,169.00 (daily) & $6,992.00 (Sunday). Full Page (Color) $12,883.00 (daily) & $14,584.00 (Sunday). Half Page (Color) $6,715.00 (daily) & $7,592.00 (Sunday). **Pub. Size**: Broadsheet. **Wire Svcs.**: AP. available on microfilm from University Microfilms International (UMI). **Formed by the union of** Morning News (Wilmington, Del. : 1966) **and** Evening Journal (Wilmington, Del. : 1960).

US/0891-8716
REVIEW, THE. (THE REVIEW / UNIVERSITY OF DELAWARE, STUDENT CENTER.). Added/Corp University of Delaware. Vol. 42, No. 23 (May 7, 1926)-. Newspaper. English. sm. The Review / University of Delaware, B1 Student Center, Newark DE 19716. **Tel** (302)451-2771. **ED** Tobias Naegele. available on microfilm. **Continues** University of Delaware Review.

US
WAVE. (19??)-. English. wk (Wed.). $35.00. Wave, PO Box 1467, Bethany Beach DE 19930. **Tel** (302)537-1881. **ED** James Cresson. **Photos**. **Ad Acc, Adv Mgr**: Susan Lyons. Full Page (B&W) $568.75. Half Page (B&W) $284.38. Full Page (Color) $568.75 plus $135.00 per color. Half Page (Color) $284.38 plus $135.00 per color. **Pub. Size**: Tabloid. **Circ**: 11,500 (ctrl). **Continues** Delmarva News, 0740-2031.

DISTRICT OF COLUMBIA

US/1062-2985
ANACOSTIA GRAPE VINE, THE. (THE ANACOSTIA GRAPE VINE : SERVING THE ANACOSTIA RIVER COMMUNITIES.). [Anacostia grape vine]. (1991)-. Newspaper. English. mo. Free. The Anacostia Grape Vine, 3510 Brothers Place Southeast, Suite 4, Washington DC 20032. **Tel** (202)889-8463. **DD** 071.

US/0147-2828
BLACK PRESS INFORMATION HANDBOOK. 1974/75-. English. $5.00 per issue. National Newspapers Publishers Association, 770 National Press Building, Washington DC 20004. **LC** PN4882.5; .B56. **DD** 071/.3.

US/0746-3812
C-SPAN UPDATE. **Title Change**. **Added/Corp** C-SPAN. VFOAT C SPAN Update. (19??)-(199?). Newspaper. English. wk. C-SPAN, PO Box 75298, Washington DC 20013. **Tel** (202)737-3220. **ED** Kate Howpford and Mark West. **Circ**: 20,000. **Continued by** American Caucus, 1061-8570. **Desc**: An "insider's" newspaper for viewers of C-SPAN, the cable satellite public affairs network. the newspaper offers C-SPAN's TV schedule and background stories on the public affairs process.

US/0411-0137
CAPITAL SPOTLIGHT, THE. (THE CAPITAL SPOTLIGHT : WASHINGTON'S AWARD WINNING NEWSPAPER.). [Cap. spotlight]. (195?)-. Newspaper. English. wk. $25.00. Capitol Spotlight, 2112 New Hampton Avenue NW, Suite 515, Washington DC 20009. **Tel** (202)628-0700, FAX (202)745-7860. **ED** Barry A. Murray. **DD** 071. **Ad Acc**. **Circ**: 50,000.

US
GEORGETOWN CURRENT. (19??)-. English. bw. $42.00. Current Newspapers, 5125 MacArthur Boulevard, Suite 10, Washington DC 20016. **Tel** (202)244-7223. **ED** Geoffrey Edwards. **Bk Rev**. **Photos**. **Ad Acc, Adv Mgr**: Simone Diggs. Full Page (B&W) $2,170.00. Half Page (B&W) $1,120.00. **Circ**: 65,000.

US/0887-9400
INTOWNER, THE. VFOAT In Towner. (19??)-. Newspaper. English. Twelve times a year. $25.00 US; $35.00 other. Intowner Publishing Corporation, 1627 17th Street Northwest, 2nd Floor, Washington DC 20009. **Tel** (202)234-1717. **ED** P. L. Wolfe. **Ad Acc, Adv Mgr**: Mr. Wolfe. **Circ**: 30,000 (ctrl). **Desc**: Community newspaper serving downtown residential neighborhoods in Washington DC.

US
IRAN TIMES, THE. VFOAT International Iran Times. (1970)-. Newspaper. Persian (English). wk. $95.00 (institutions), $75.00 (individuals) US; $95.00 (institutions), $80.00 (individuals) Canada; $155.00 (individuals) Europe; $165.00 other. The Iran Times, 2727 Wisconsin Avenue NW, Washington DC 20007. **Tel** (202)659-9868, (202)659-2118, FAX (202)337-7449, telex 440434. **ED** Javad Khakbaz. **Bk Rev**, (Qty: 45050). **Ad Acc**.

US/1041-7281
MIJU HAN'GUK ILBO. VFOAT Korea Times; Han'Guk Ilbo. (198?)-. Newspaper. Korean. da. $12.00 per month. Korea Times / Washington, DC, 6120 Kansas Avenue Northwest, Washington DC 20011. **Tel** (202)722-5400, FAX (202)723-3718. **ED** Tae Hee Yoo, Suk Hee Yoo (Managing Editor). **Bk Rev**. **Photos**. **Ad Acc, Adv Mgr**: Yang Ho Lee, **Tel** (202)723-3060. Full Page (B&W) $600.00. Half Page (B&W) $300.00. **Pub. Size**: Standard. **Circ**: 15,000. **Continues** Han'Guk Ilbo, Wosington, 0883-6647.

US/1061-5881
NATIONAL CHRONICLE (WASHINGTON, D.C.), THE. (THE NATIONAL CHRONICLE.). [Natl. chron.]. Vol. 1, No. 1 (July 6, 1990)-. Newspaper. English. wk. $30.00. McCain Media, 1134 11th Street NW, Washington DC 20001. **DD** 071. **Continues** Metro Chronicle.

●US/1064-3699
NEWS DIMENSIONS. [News dimens.]. (1992)-. Newspaper. English. wk. $29.00. News Dimensions, 1221 Mass. Avenue NW, Suite 522, Washington DC 20005. **DD** 071.

US/0192-1231
NEWSPAPERS IN MICROFORM: FOREIGN COUNTRIES. Ceased. (NEWSPAPERS IN MICROFORM. FOREIGN COUNTRIES / [COMPILED AND EDITED BY THE CATALOG MANAGEMENT AND PUBLICATION DIVISION, LIBRARY OF CONGRESS].). [Newsp. microform foreign ctries.]. **Added/Corp** Library of Congress. Catalog Management and Publication Division. Library of Congress. Catalog Publication Division. VFOAT Foreign Countries. Issue 1 (1948/72)-(199?). Catalog. English. ir. Library of Congress / Cataloging Distribution Service, Washington DC 20541-5017. **Tel** (800)255-3666, (202)707-6100, FAX (202)707-1334. **LC** Z6945; .U515a; PN4731. **DD** 011/.35; 016.070/9. **Continues in part** Library of Congress. Newspapers on Microfilm. **Desc**: Brings under bibliographic control master and service copies of foreign newspapers that have been microformed.

US/0093-6464
NEWSPAPERS RECEIVED CURRENTLY IN THE LIBRARY OF CONGRESS. [Newsp. received curr. Libr. Congr.]. **Main/Corp** Library of Congress. Serial & Government Publications Division. 7th Ed.-. English. be. Library of Congress, 101 Independence Avenue SE, Washington DC 20540. **Tel** (202)287-5000. **LC** Z6945.U5; N42; PN4731. **DD** 016.07. **Continues** Newspapers Received Currently in the Library of Congress, 0093-6464.

●US
OUTLOOK FOR FARM COMMODITY PROGRAM SPENDING, THE. **Added/Corp** United States. Congressional Budget Office. Began with fiscal years (1988-1993)-. Newspaper. English. Congressional Budget Office, 2nd and D Streets SW, Washington DC 20515. **Tel** (202)226-2115.

US
PHILIPPINES TODAY (WASHINGTON, D.C. : 1983). (PHILIPPINES TODAY). Vol. 1, No. 1 (Aug. 23, 1983)-. Newspaper. English. bw. Philippines Today, Editorial Offices, 1617 Massachusetts Avenue NW, Washington DC 20036.

US/8750-9326
PREGONERO (WASHINGTON, D.C.), EL. (EL PREGONERO.). **Added/Corp** Centro Catolico Hispano (Washington, D.C.). (1977)-. Newspaper. English (Spanish). wk. $4.50 US; $6.00 other. El Pregonero, 5001 Eastern Avenue, PO Box 4464, Washington DC 20017. **Tel** (301)853-4504. **ED** Oscar Reyes. **Bk Rev**. **Ad Acc**. **Circ**: 6,000. **Desc**: An official publication of the Catholic Archdiocese of Washington D.C. for the general hispanic reader.

US/1045-7585
PROUT PRESS (WASHINGTON, D.C.). (THE PROUT PRESS.). [Prout press]. Newspaper. English. sw. $25.00 (membership) US; $52.50 other. Proutist Universal Inc, 1354 Montague Street NW, Box 56466, Washington DC 20011. **Tel** (202)829-2278, FAX (202)829-0462. **ED** D Dhruva and A Brahmananda. **DD** 071. **Bk Rev**. **Circ**: 2,500. **Desc**: News and views from the Prout perspective.

●US/1062-2721
ROCK CREEK CURRENT, THE. (THE ROCK CREEK CURRENT: SERVING THE COMMUNITIES OF MOUNT PLEASANT, ADAMS MORGAN, DUPONT CIRCLE, LOGAN CIRCLE & FOGGY BOTTOM.). [Rock Creek curr.]. (1992)-. Newspaper. English. bw. $42.00. Current Newspapers, 5125 MacArthur Boulevard, Suite 10, Washington DC 20016. **Tel** (202)244-7223. **ED** Geoffrey Edwards. **DD** 071. **Bk Rev. Photos. Ad Acc, Adv Mgr:** Simone Diggs. Full Page (B&W) $2,170.00. Half Page (B&W) $1,120.00. **Circ:** 65,000.

US/0191-6270
SPOTLIGHT (WASHINGTON), THE. (THE SPOTLIGHT.). Vol. 2, No. 16 (April 19, 1976)-. Newspaper. English. wk. $36.00 (1 year), $66.00 (2 year) US; $27.00 (1 year), $50.00 (2 year) senior citizens US; $64.00 (1 year), $122.00 (2 year) other. Liberty Lobby, 300 Independence Avenue SE, Washington DC 20003. **Tel** (202)546-5611. **ED** Vincent Ryan. **Bk Rev. Ad Acc. Circ:** 150,000 (ctrl). available on microfilm and microfiche from University Microfilms International (UMI). ***Continues*** *National Spotlight (Washington, D.C.).*
Desc: Exclusive news for consumers, taxpayers and voters, covering populist politics, defense, security, fiscal responsibility and many other areas.

US/1046-5693
TRILOGY. [Trilogy]. Newspaper. English. Free to students. University of the District of Columbia, 4200 Connecticut Avenue NW, Building 38 Room 301, Washington DC 20008. **DD** 071.

US/0278-9892
WASHINGTON BLADE, THE. (198?)-. Periodical. English. wk. $30.00 one year. Washington Blade, 1408 U Street Northwest, 2nd Floor, Washington DC 20009-3916. **Tel** (202)234-5400 (advertising), (202) 797-7000, FAX (202)797-7104. **ED** Lisa M. Keen. **Bk Rev. Ad Acc. *Continues*** *Blade 0192-0383.*

US/0741-9414
WASHINGTON INFORMER, THE. VFOAT Informer. (19??)-. Newspaper. English. wk. $15.00 (1 year), $25.00 (2 year). Washington Informer Newspaper Company Limited, 3117 Martin Luther King Southeast, Washington DC 20032. **Tel** (202)561-4100, FAX (202)574-3785. **ED** Dr. Calvin Rolark and Denise Rolark Barnes. **Bk Rev**, (Qty: 10). **Ad Acc. Circ:** 17,000 (ctrl).
Desc: Newspaper focusing on the African-American in the Washington metropolitan area.

US/0740-5421
WASHINGTON POST (NATIONAL WEEKLY ED.), THE. (THE WASHINGTON POST.). [Wash. post]. **VFOAT** Washington Post National Weekly Edition. Vol. 1, No. 1 (Nov. 7, 1983)-. Newspaper. English. wk. $39.00. Washington Post, 1150 15th Street NW, Washington DC 20071. **Tel** (202)334-6000. **(Subscription address:** CDS / SIFD Agency Control, 1901 Bell Avenue, Des Moines A 50315.**)**
Ind/Abst Curr. Thoughts Trends.

US/0190-8286
WASHINGTON POST (WASHINGTON, D.C. : 1974). (THE WASHINGTON POST.). [Washington post]. 97th year, No. 27 (Jan. 1, 1974)-. Newspaper. English. ds. $658.10 (includes sales tax) Maryland; $627.24 US; $1043.24 other. The Washington Post Company, 1150 15th Street Northwest, Washington DC 20071. **Tel** (202)334-5950. **ED** Ben Bradlee. **DD** 071. **Bk Rev. Ad Acc. Circ:** 761,142 daily, 1,096,725 Sun. available on microfilm from University Microfilms International (UMI). Documents available from UMI Article Clearinghouse. ***Continues*** *Washington Post, Times Herald.*
Ind/Abst Account. Tax Datab. (Feb. 1988-) [Full Txt.]; AGRICOLA [Select. Cov.]; Art Archaeol. Tech. Abstr.; Bus. Dateline; F&S Index Plus Text, Int. [Select. Cov.]; Health Ref. Cent. (1987-) [Select. Cov.]; Index Period. Artic. Relat. Law; Infobank (Jan. 1974-); Natl. Newsp. Index (Oct. 1982-); Newsp. Abstr.; Newsp. Abstr.; NEXIS (Jan. 1977-); PROMT; Sage Race Relat. Abstr.

US/1052-696X
WASHINGTON REPORTER (WASHINGTON, D.C.), THE. (THE WASHINGTON REPORTER.). (1991)-. Newspaper. English. da. Selectively distributed. Our Newspaper Company, 918-16th Street NW, Washington DC 20006.

US/0732-8494
WASHINGTON TIMES (WASHINGTON, D.C. : 1982), THE. (THE WASHINGTON TIMES.). [Wash. times]. Vol. 1, No. 1 (May 17, 1982)-. Newspaper. English. da (Mon.-Fri.). $59.95. The Washington Times Corporation, 3400 New York Avenue Northeast, Washington DC 20002. **Tel** (202)635-4000, (800)822-2822. available on an online database (files 635,717/Full-Text) from DIALOG. Documents available from UMI Article Clearinghouse.
Ind/Abst Bus. Dateline; Newsp. Abstr.; PROMT.

FLORIDA

US/0745-9971
AMERIKAN UUTISET. [Am. uut.]. Vol. 29, No. 96 (Aug. 16, 1960)-. Newspaper. Finnish (English). Fifty-two times a year. $32.00 US. Amerikan Uutiset Inc., PO Box 8147, Lantana FL 33465. **Tel** (407)588-9770, FAX (407)588-3229. **ED** Sakri Viklund. **DD** 058. **Bk Rev**, (Qty: 10). **Photos. Ad Acc.** Full Page (B&W) $820.00. Half Page (B&W) $360.00. Full Page (Color) $1,200.00. Half Page (Color) $700.00. **Pub. Size:** Broadsheet. **Circ:** 2,400. ***Continues*** *Minnesota Uutiset.*

US/0163-027X
AVON PARK SUN. (19??)-. Newspaper. English. wk. Avon Park Sun, PO Box 1117, Avon Park FL 33825.

US/1059-647X
BEACHES LEADER, THE. (19??)-. Newspaper. English. sw. $19.17. Leader Group, 1114 Beaches Boulevard, PO Box 50129, Jacksonville FL 32240. **Tel** (904)249-9033. **ED** Kathleen Feindt Bailey. **Bk Rev**, (Qty: 6). **Photos. Ad Acc, Adv Mgr:** Linda Borgstede. Full Page (B&W) $1,061.67. Half Page (B&W) $530.83. Full Page (Color) $1,101.67. Half Page (Color) $570.83. **Pub. Size:** Broadsheet. **Circ:** 11,500. available in microform.

US/0191-5479
BONITA BANNER. (19??)-. Newspaper. English. Twice a week. $41.60. Bonita Banner, PO Box 40, Bonita Springs FL 33959. **Tel** (813)992-2110, FAX (813)992-7819. **ED** Don Goodwin. **Photos. Ad Acc, Adv Mgr:** Steve Akers. Full Page (B&W) $1121.40. Half Page (B&W) $560.70. Full Page (Color) Full Color $200.00. Half Page (Color) Full Color $200.00. **Pub. Size:** Broadsheet. **Circ:** 33,000.

US
BRADENTON HERALD, THE. (1926)-. Newspaper. English. da. $244.00. Bradenton Herald, 102 Manatee Avenue West, Bradenton FL 34205. **Tel** (813)748-0411, FAX (813)745-7097. **ED** Wayne Poston. **Ad Acc, Adv Mgr:** Ed Gruwell. **Circ:** 48,894. ***Continues*** *Evening Herald (Bradenton, Florida).*

US
BRANDON NEWS. (19??)-. Newspaper. English. wk. Free. Sunbelt Newspapers Inc., 3901 Coconut Palm Drive, Suite 111, Tampa FL 33619. **Tel** (813)664-0264, FAX (813)626-1503. **ED** Lee Lamemberger. **Photos. Ad Acc, Adv Mgr:** Susie Howell. Full Page (B&W) $908.65. Half Page (B&W) $454.33. Full Page (Color) $1,133.65. Half Page (Color) $679.33. **Pub. Size:** Tabloid. **Circ:** 37,350 (ctrl).

US/1053-4504
BREEZE (CAPE CORAL, FLA.), THE. (THE BREEZE.). (1990)-. Newspaper. English. wk. The Breeze Corporation, 2510 Del Prado Boulevard, Cape Coral FL 33904. Documents available from UMI Article Clearinghouse. ***Continues*** *Cape Coral Daily Breeze, 1046-8609.*
Ind/Abst Bus. Dateline (Dec. 20, 1991-) [Full Txt.].

US/0889-0412
CANADA NEWS (AUBURNDALE, FLA.). (CANADA NEWS.). (198?)-. Newspaper. English. wk (from Nov. to April, 26 issues). $23.40. Canada News, 2725 Thornhill Road, PO Box 1729, Auburndale FL 33823. **Tel** (813)967-6450, (800)535-6788, FAX (813)967-1954. **ED** Joe Braddy. **DD** 072. **Photos. Ad Acc, Adv Mgr:** Andy Steinbergs. Full Page (B&W) $880.75. Half Page (B&W) $440.38. Full Page (Color) $1380.00. Half Page (Color) $690.00. **Pub. Size:** Standard. **Wire Svcs.:** CA. ***Continues*** *Canada News Inc., 0745-8363.*
Desc: Canadian news, business, and sports.

US/1044-0399
CHARLOTTE SUN HERALD. ***Title Change.*** Newspaper. English. da. Sun Coast Media Group Inc, 23170 Harborview Road, Charlotte Harbor FL 33980-2198. ***Continues*** *Charlotte Sun and Herald-News, 1042-8984.* ***Continued by*** *Sun Herald (Charlotte Ed), 1055-7806.*

US
CITRUS COUNTY CHRONICLE. ***Ceased.*** (1???)-(19??). Newspaper. English. da. Citrus County Chronicle, PO Box 1899, Inverness FL 32651-1899.

US/0191-7323
COLLIER COUNTY STAR NEWS, THE. Newspaper. English. da. $109.00. Naples Daily News, 1075 Central Avenue, Naples FL 33941. **Tel** (813)262 3161.

US/0896-0283
COURIER JOURNAL (JUPITER, FLA.), THE. (THE COURIER JOURNAL.). **VFOAT** Courier-Journal. (19??)-. Newspaper. English. sw. Jupiter Courier Journal, PO Box 1486, Jupiter FL 33458-1486.

US
COURIER (PLANT CITY, FL). (COURIER.). (19??)-. Newspaper. English. wk. Free. Sunbelt Newspapers Inc., 3901 Coconut Palm Drive, Suite 111, Tampa FL 33619. **Tel** (813)664-0264, FAX (813)626-1503. **ED** Lee Lamemberger. **Photos. Ad Acc, Adv Mgr:** Sherry Wheeler. Full Page (B&W) $698.70. Half Page (B&W) $349.35. Full Page (Color) $923.70. Half Page (Color) $574.35. **Pub. Size:** Tabloid. **Circ:** 4,486.

US/0896-1042
DAILY COMMERCIAL (LEESBURG LAKE/SUMTER EDITION). (DAILY COMMERCIAL.). Newspaper. English. da. Daily Commercial, 212 East Main, Leesburg FL 32748. ***Continues*** *Leesburg/Commercial, 0163-0296.*

US
DAILY PALM BEACH NEWS, THE. VFOAT Palm Beach Daily News. (1894)-. Newspaper. English. da (276 issues, daily Sept.-May, twice weekly in summer). $64.50 (home delivery), $133.35 (by mail). Palm Beach News, 265 Royal Poinciana Way, Palm Beach FL 33480-4063. **Tel** (407)820-3800, FAX (407)655-4594. **ED** Linda Rawls (Editor in Chief), Elizabeth Wells (Managing Editor). **Photos. Ad Acc, Adv Mgr:** Donna Moore, **Tel** (407)820-3820. Full Page (B&W) $4186.35. Half Page (B&W) $2093.18. Full Page (Color) $5253.70. Half Page (Color) $3160.53. **Pub. Size:** Standard. **Circ:** 9,500 (daily), 11,500 (morning, paid).

US
DELAND SUN NEWS. (19??)-. Newspaper. English. $72.00. DeLand Sun News, PO Box 1119, DeLand FL 32720. **Tel** (904)734-3661.

US/0744-3234
DIARIO LAS AMERICAS. (July 4, 1953)-. Newspaper. Spanish. da (except Monday). $73.14 Miami, Florida; $111.00 other. Diario Los Americas, 2900 Northwest 39th Street, Miami FL 33142-5193. **Tel** (305)633-3341, FAX (305)635-7668. **ED** Horacio Aguirre. **Bk Rev. Ad Acc. Circ:** 64,093 (ctrl). available on microfilm.
Desc: Newspaper with complete news coverage and features such as food section, travel, business, sports, lifestyle, social real estate, editorials, movie reviews, etc.

US/0744-3226
DOLPHIN DIGEST. (19??)-. Periodical. English. Twenty-eight times a year (Published weekly (during football season), Monthly Feb.- July). $84.95 one year; $58.95 two year; $82.95 three year; $130.00 Subscription per year. Curtis Publishing Company, PO Box 526600, Miami FL 33252. **Tel** (305)662-6646, (800)334-4005. **ED** Andy Cohen, (phone: (305)594-0508). **Ad Acc, Adv Mgr:** K. Keidel, **Tel** (305)594-0508. **Circ:** 25,000.
Desc: Information on the Miami Dolphins.

US/8750-5339
EVENING TIMES (WEST PALM BEACH, FLA.), THE. (THE EVENING TIMES.). (19??)-. Newspaper. English. da. $49.40. Palm Beach Post, 2751 South Dixie Highway, West Palm Beach FL 33416. **Tel** (407)820-4231.

US/1063-9942
FAMUAN (TALLAHASSEE, FLA.), THE. (THE FAMUAN : THE VOICE OF THE STUDENTS OF FLORIDA A & M UNIVERSITY.). **Added/Corp** Florida Agricultural and Mechanical University. (19??)-. Periodical. English. Twenty-four times a year (Thursday). $20.00. Florida A & M University, Tucker Hall 309, C/O Dr. G. Workman, Tallahassee FL 32307. **Tel** (904)599-3159, FAX (904)561-2570. **ED** Gale A. Workman, (phone: (904)599-3840). **Bk Rev**, (Qty: varies). **Ad Acc. Circ:** 5,000.

US
FERNANDINA BEACH NEWS-LEADER. (19??)-. English. Fifty-two times a year. $15.00 Naussau County; $30.00 other. Fernandina Beach News-Leader, 511 Ask Street, PO Box 766, Fernandina Beach FL 32034. **Tel** (904)261-3696. **ED** Steve Nichols. **Ad Acc, Adv Mgr:** Mike H., **Tel** (904)261-3696. **Pr Rev. Circ:** 11,000 (ctrl).

US
FLORIDA FLAMBEAU, THE. Added/Corp Florida. State University. (1914)-. English. da (Mon.-Fri.). $100.00. The Florida Flambeau Foundation, PO Box U 7001, Tallahassee FL 32306. **Tel** (904)681-6692. **ED** Glen Torbert (Editor-in-Chief) and Che Odom (Managing Editor). **Bk Rev. Photos. Ad Acc, Adv Mgr:** Rose Rodriguez, **Tel** (904)681-6692 ext. 29. **Pub. Size:** Tabloid. **Wire Svcs.:** NY.

US/8756-6427
FLORIDA KEYS KEYNOTER. (19??)-. Newspaper. English. sw. Florida Keys Keynoter, 3015 Overseas Highway, Marathon FL 33050.

US/0745-9971
AMERIKAN UUTISET. [Am. uut.]. Vol. 29, No. 96 (Aug. 16, 1960)-. Newspaper. Finnish (English). Fifty-two times a year. $32.00 US. Amerikan Uutiset Inc., PO Box 8147, Lantana FL 33465. **Tel** (407)588-9770, FAX (407)588-3229. **ED** Sakri Viklund. **DD** 058. **Bk Rev**, (Qty: 10). **Photos**. **Ad Acc**. Full Page (B&W) $820.00. Half Page (B&W) $360.00. Full Page (Color) $1,200.00. Half Page (Color) $700.00. **Pub. Size:** Broadsheet. **Circ:** 2,400. ***Continues*** *Minnesota Uutiset.*

US/0163-027X
AVON PARK SUN. (19??)-. Newspaper. English. wk. Avon Park Sun, PO Box 1117, Avon Park FL 33825.

US/1059-647X
BEACHES LEADER, THE. (19??)-. Newspaper. English. sw. $19.17. Leader Group, 1114 Beaches Boulevard, PO Box 50129, Jacksonville FL 32240. **Tel** (904)249-9033. **ED** Kathleen Feindt Bailey. **Bk Rev**, (Qty: 6). **Photos**. **Ad Acc, Adv Mgr:** Linda Borgstede. Full Page (B&W) $1,061.67. Half Page (B&W) $530.83. Full Page (Color) $1,101.67. Half Page (Color) $570.83. **Pub. Size:** Broadsheet. **Circ:** 11,500. available in microform.

US/0191-5479
BONITA BANNER. (19??)-. Newspaper English. Twice a week. $41.60. Bonita Banner, PO Box 40, Bonita Springs FL 33959. **Tel** (813)992-2110, FAX (813)992-7819. **ED** Don Goodwin. **Photos**. **Ad Acc, Adv Mgr:** Steve Akers. Full Page (B&W) $1121.40. Half Page (B&W) $560.70. Full Page (Color) Full Color $200.00. Half Page (Color) Full Color $200.00. **Pub. Size:** Broadsheet. **Circ:** 33,000.

US
BRADENTON HERALD, THE. (1926)-. Newspaper. English. da. $244.00. Bradenton Herald, 102 Manatee Avenue West, Bradenton FL 34205. **Tel** (813)748-0411, FAX (813)745-7097. **ED** Wayne Poston. **Ad Acc, Adv Mgr:** Ed Gruwell. **Circ:** 48,894. ***Continues*** *Evening Herald (Bradenton, Florida).*

US
BRANDON NEWS. (19??)-. Newspaper. English. wk. Free. Sunbelt Newspapers Inc., 3901 Coconut Palm Drive, Suite 111, Tampa FL 33619. **Tel** (813)664-0264, FAX (813)626-1503. **ED** Lee Lamemberger. **Photos**. **Ad Acc, Adv Mgr:** Susie Howell. Full Page (B&W) $908.65. Half Page (B&W) $454.33. Full Page (Color) $1,133.65. Half Page (Color) $679.33. **Pub. Size:** Tabloid. **Circ:** 37,350 (ctrl).

US/1053-4504
BREEZE (CAPE CORAL, FLA.), THE. (THE BREEZE.). (1990)-. Newspaper. English. wk. The Breeze Corporation, 2510 Del Prado Boulevard, Cape Coral FL 33904. Documents available from UMI Article Clearinghouse. ***Continues*** *Cape Coral Daily Breeze, 1046-8609.*
Ind/Abst Bus. Dateline (Dec. 20, 1991-) [Full Txt.].

US/0889-0412
CANADA NEWS (AUBURNDALE, FLA.). (CANADA NEWS.). (198?)-. Newspaper. English. wk (from Nov. to April, 26 issues). $23.40. Canada News, 2725 Thornhill Road, PO Box 1729, Auburndale FL 33823. **Tel** (813)967-6450, (800)535-6788, FAX (813)967-1954. **ED** Joe Braddy. **DD** 072. **Photos**. **Ad Acc, Adv Mgr:** Andy Steinbergs. Full Page (B&W) $880.75. Half Page (B&W) $440.38. Full Page (Color) $1380.00. Half Page (Color) $690.00. **Pub. Size:** Standard. **Wire Svcs.:** CA. ***Continues*** *Canada News Inc., 0745-8363.*
Desc: Canadian news, business, and sports.

US/1044-0399
CHARLOTTE SUN HERALD. ***Title Change.*** Newspaper. English. da. Sun Coast Media Group Inc, 23170 Harborview Road, Charlotte Harbor FL 33980-2198. ***Continues*** *Charlotte Sun and Herald-News, 1042-8984.* ***Continued by*** *Sun Herald (Charlotte Ed), 1055-7806.*

US
CITRUS COUNTY CHRONICLE. ***Ceased.*** (1???)-(19??). Newspaper. English. da. Citrus County Chronicle, PO Box 1899, Inverness FL 32651-1899.

US/0191-7323
COLLIER COUNTY STAR NEWS, THE. Newspaper. English. da. $109.00. Naples Daily News, 1075 Central Avenue, Naples FL 33941. **Tel** (813)262 3161.

US/0896-0283
COURIER JOURNAL (JUPITER, FLA.), THE. (THE COURIER JOURNAL.). **VFOAT** Courier-Journal. (19??)-. Newspaper. English. sw. Jupiter Courier Journal, PO Box 1486, Jupiter FL 33458-1486.

US
COURIER (PLANT CITY, FL). (COURIER.). (19??)-. Newspaper. English. wk. Free. Sunbelt Newspapers Inc., 3901 Coconut Palm Drive, Suite 111, Tampa FL 33619. **Tel** (813)664-0264, FAX (813)626-1503. **ED** Lee Lamemberger. **Photos**. **Ad Acc, Adv Mgr:** Sherry Wheeler. Full Page (B&W) $698.70. Half Page (B&W) $349.35. Full Page (Color) $923.70. Half Page (Color) $574.35. **Pub. Size:** Tabloid. **Circ:** 4,486.

US/0896-1042
DAILY COMMERCIAL (LEESBURG LAKE/SUMTER EDITION). (DAILY COMMERCIAL.). Newspaper. English. da. Daily Commercial, 212 East Main, Leesburg FL 32748. ***Continues*** *Leesburg/Commercial, 0163-0296.*

US
DAILY PALM BEACH NEWS, THE. VFOAT Palm Beach Daily News. (1894)-. Newspaper. English. da (276 issues, daily Sept.-May, twice weekly in summer). $64.50 (home delivery), $133.35 (by mail). Palm Beach News, 265 Royal Poinciana Way, Palm Beach FL 33480-4063. **Tel** (407)820-3800, FAX (407)655-4594. **ED** Linda Rawls (Editor in Chief), Elizabeth Wells (Managing Editor). **Photos**. **Ad Acc, Adv Mgr:** Donna Moore, **Tel** (407)820-3820. Full Page (B&W) $4186.35. Half Page (B&W) $2093.18. Full Page (Color) $5253.70. Half Page (Color) $3160.53. **Pub. Size:** Standard. **Circ:** 9,500 (daily), 11,500 (morning, paid).

US
DELAND SUN NEWS. (19??)-. Newspaper. English. $72.00. DeLand Sun News, PO Box 1119, DeLand FL 32720. **Tel** (904)734-3661.

US/0744-3234
DIARIO LAS AMERICAS. (July 4, 1953)-. Newspaper. Spanish. da (except Monday). $73.14 Miami, Florida; $111.00 other. Diario Los Americas, 2900 Northwest 39th Street, Miami FL 33142-5193. **Tel** (305)633-3341, FAX (305)635-7668. **ED** Horacio Aguirre. **Bk Rev**. **Ad Acc**. **Circ:** 64,093 (ctrl). available on microfilm.
Desc: Newspaper with complete news coverage and features such as food section, travel, business, sports, lifestyle, social real estate, editorials, movie reviews, etc.

US/0744-3226
DOLPHIN DIGEST. (19??)-. Periodical. English. Twenty-eight times a year (Published weekly (during football season), Monthly Feb.- July). $84.95 one year; $58.95 two year; $82.95 three year; $130.00 Subscription per year. Curtis Publishing Company, PO Box 526600, Miami FL 33252. **Tel** (305)662-6646, (800)334-4005. **ED** Andy Cohen, (phone: (305)594-0508). **Ad Acc, Adv Mgr:** K. Keidel, **Tel** (305)594-0508. **Circ:** 25,000.
Desc: Information on the Miami Dolphins.

US/8750-5339
EVENING TIMES (WEST PALM BEACH, FLA.), THE. (THE EVENING TIMES.). (19??)-. Newspaper. English. da. $49.40. Palm Beach Post, 2751 South Dixie Highway, West Palm Beach FL 33416. **Tel** (407)820-4231.

US/1063-9942
FAMUAN (TALLAHASSEE, FLA.), THE. (THE FAMUAN : THE VOICE OF THE STUDENTS OF FLORIDA A & M UNIVERSITY.). **Added/Corp** Florida Agricultural and Mechanical University. (19??)-. Periodical. English. Twenty-four times a year (Thursday). $20.00. Florida A & M University, Tucker Hall 309, C/O Dr. G. Workman, Tallahassee FL 32307. **Tel** (904)599-3159, FAX (904)561-2570. **ED** Gale A. Workman, (phone: (904)599-3840). **Bk Rev**, (Qty: varies). **Ad Acc**. **Circ:** 5,000.

US
FERNANDINA BEACH NEWS-LEADER. (19??)-. English. Fifty-two times a year. $15.00 Naussau County; $30.00 other. Fernandina Beach News-Leader, 511 Ask Street, PO Box 766, Fernandina Beach FL 32034. **Tel** (904)261-3696. **ED** Steve Nichols. **Ad Acc, Adv Mgr:** Mike H., **Tel** (904)261-3696. **Pr Rev.** **Circ:** 11,000 (ctrl).

US
FLORIDA FLAMBEAU, THE. Added/Corp Florida. State University. (1914)-. English. da (Mon.-Fri.). $100.00. The Florida Flambeau Foundation, PO Box U 7001, Tallahassee FL 32306. **Tel** (904)681-6692. **ED** Glen Torbert (Editor-in-Chief) and Che Odom (Managing Editor). **Bk Rev**. **Photos**. **Ad Acc, Adv Mgr:** Rose Rodriguez, **Tel** (904)681-6692 ext. 29. **Pub. Size:** Tabloid. **Wire Svcs.:** NY.

US/8756-6427
FLORIDA KEYS KEYNOTER. (19??)-. Newspaper. English. sw. Florida Keys Keynoter, 3015 Overseas Highway, Marathon FL 33050.

US
FLORIDA SENTINEL BULLETIN. Bulletin. English. wk. $44.00. Florida Sentinel Bulletin, 2207 21st Ave., Tampa FL 36605. **Tel** (813)248-1921.

US/0740-2325
FLORIDA TIMES-UNION (JACKSONVILLE, FLA. : 1910). (THE FLORIDA TIMES-UNION.). [Fla. times-union]. **VFOAT** Sunday Times Union; Florida Times Union. Vol. 45 (April 5, 1910)-. Newspaper. English. da (including Sat., Sun. and holidays). $65.00 (Mon.-Fri.), $52.00 (Sun.), $117.00 (daily & Sun.), $83.20 (daily), carrier. Florida Publishing Company, 1 Riverside Avenue, PO Box 1949F, Jacksonville FL 32231. **Tel** (904)359-4111, (800)553-0541. **ED** Fred Hartmann. **DD** 071. **Bk Rev**. **Ad Acc**. **Circ:** 156,967 daily, 224,291 Sunday. available on microfilm from Recordak Corp. ***Continues*** *Semi-Weekly Times-Union.*
Ind/Abst PROMT.

US/1051-8304
FLORIDA TODAY. Vol. 20, No. 157 (Aug. 26, 1985)-. Newspaper. English. da. $2.50 per week (Daily/Sunday). Cape Publications Inc., PO Box 419000, Melbourne FL 32941. **Tel** (407)242-3500, FAX (800)633-8449. ***Continues*** *Today.*

US/0744-8147
FORT LAUDERDALE NEWS. VFOAT News, Sun-Sentinel; News/Sun-Sentinel; Fort Lauderdale News and Sun-Sentinel. (19??)-. Newspaper. English. da. $426.00. News and Sun Sentinel Company, PO Box 14488, Fort Lauderdale FL 33302. **Tel** (305)356-4000, (305)761-4000, FAX (305)356-4559. **ED** Gene Cryer. **Circ:** 57,000.

US/0199-2945
FORT MYERS BEACH OBSERVER. VFOAT Observer. (19??)-. Newspaper. English. wk. Ogden Newspapers / Florida, 15501 McGregor Boulevard, Fort Myers FL 33908. **Tel** (813)482-7111, FAX (813)482-6365. **ED** Prudy Board. **Ad Acc**. **Circ:** 10,000.

US
FORT MYERS NEWS-PRESS. VFOAT Fort Myers News Press. (1931)-. Newspaper. English. da. $195.00. Fort Myers News Press, PO Box 10, Ft Myers FL 33902. **Tel** (813)334-2351. **ED** Ron Thornburg. **Circ:** 63,597 daily, 80,788 Sunday. ***Continues*** *Fort Myers Tropical News.*

US
FROSTPROOF NEWS, THE. (1915)-. Periodical. English. wk. $15.70. Frostproof News, Box 67, Frostproof FL 33843. **Tel** (813)635-2171. **ED** Sonny Stalbs (Editor-in-Chief) and Amy Stealy (Managing Editor). **Photos**. **Ad Acc, Adv Mgr:** Amy Stealy. Full Page (B&W) $275.00. Half Page (B&W) $327.60. Full Page (Color) $340.00. Half Page (Color) $92.60. **Pub. Size:** Standard. **Circ:** 2,000 (ctrl).
Desc: Community newspaper serving Frostproof, Florida.

US/0016-3724
GACETA (TAMPA, FLA.), LA. (LA GACETA.). (1922)-. Newspaper. English (Italian and Spanish). Fifty-two times a year (Published on Fri.). $15.00 Tampa & Hillsborough County; $20.00 others in Florida; $25.00 others. Gaceta Publishing Company, PO Box 5536, Tampa FL 33675. **Tel** (813)247-2962, (813)248-3921.

US
GADSDEN COUNTY TIMES. (1955)-. English. wk. $21.40 Gadsden County, Fla.; $32.10 other Fla.; $30.00 other. Gadsden County Times, PO Box 790, Quincy FL 32351. **Tel** (904)627-7649. **ED** Alice D. Smith. **Ad Acc, Adv Mgr:** Bev Kirk.

US/0163-4925
GAINESVILLE SUN. (June 24, 1963)-. Newspaper. English. da. $137.00. Gainesville Sun, PO Box 147147, Gainesville FL 32614. **Tel** (904)378-1416. **ED** Ed Johnson. **Circ:** 51,917. available on microfilm from University Microfilms International (UMI). ***Continues*** *Gainesville Daily Sun.*

US/0745-4120
GLADES COUNTY DEMOCRAT. Newspaper. English. wk. Glades County Democrat, PO Box 70, Moore Haven FL 33471.

US
GULF COUNTY BREEZE. (19??)-. Newspaper. English. wk. $9.00 Gulf County, Florida; $12.00 other Florida; $17.00 other. Gulf County Breeze, PO Box 218, 2nd Street and Osceola, Wewachitchka FL 32465. **Tel** (904)639-2706. **ED** Edward A. Bandjough. **Bk Rev**. **Ad Acc**. **Circ:** 1,450.

US
HAVANA HERALD. (19??)-. Newspaper. English. Fifty-two times a year. $16.48. Havana Herald, 103 West 7th Avenue, Havana FL 32333. **Tel** (904)539-6586. **ED** Nick Bert, Billy Blackman (Managing Editor). **Bk Rev**, (Qty: 10). **Photos**. **Ad Acc**. Full Page (B&W) $496.65. Half Page (B&W) $248.33. Full Page (Color) $596.65. Half Page (Color) $348.33. **Pub. Size:** Broadsheet. **Circ:** 2,800.

US/0746-1046
HIGH SPRINGS HERALD. VFOAT Herald. (19??)-. Newspaper. English. wk. $12.72. High Springs Herald, PO Box 745, High Springs FL 32643. **Tel** (904)454-1297, FAX (904)454-4559. **ED** Ronald DuPont Jr. **Photos**. **Ad Acc, Adv Mgr:** Carol Chidlow. Full Page (B&W) $579.60. Half Page (B&W) $289.80. Full Page (Color) $619.60. Half Page (Color) $329.80. **Pub. Size:** Broadsheet. **Circ:** 3,400. ***Continues*** *Herald (High Springs, Fla.).*
Desc: General news, information and advertising of interest to readers of the area.

US
HIGHLANDER, THE. VFOAT Semi-Weekly Highlander. (19??)-. Newspaper. English. sw. Lake Wales Daily, 33 West Orange Avenue, Lake Wales FL 33853-4176. **ED** Max Robinson. **Ad Acc. Circ:** 5,100.

US
HIGHLANDS PRESS. (19??)-. Newspaper. English. wk. $24.00. Highlands Press, PO Box 956, Highland City FL 33846. **Tel** (813)425-3411. **ED** William M. Histed (Editor-in-Chief) and Bill Histed Jr. (Managing Editor). **Bk Rev**. **Photos**. **Ad Acc, Adv Mgr:** Barbara Wagoner. Full Page (B&W) $300.00. Half Page (B&W) $200.00. Full Page (Color) $350.00. Half Page (Color) $250.00. **Pub. Size:** Standard. available in microform.

US
HOLMES COUNTY ADVERTISER. Newspaper. English. wk (Published Wednesdays). $19.08 Florida residents; $18.00 other. Holmes County Advertiser, 112 East Virginia Advertiser, Bonifay FL 32425. **Tel** (904)547-2270, FAX (904)547-9200. **ED** Kathy Foster.

US
JACKSON COUNTY FLORIDAN. VFOAT Floridan. (Sept. 1934)-. Newspaper. English. da. $80.00. Jackson County Floridan, PO Box 520, 104 Lafayette, Marianna FL 32446. **Tel** (904)526-3614, FAX (904)482-4478. **ED** Chris Day. **Ad Acc. Circ:** 5,600 daily, 6,300 Sunday. ***Continues*** *Marianna Floridan* ***and*** *Times-Courier,.*

US/0743-0914
JACKSONVILLE JOURNAL. ***Ceased.*** Vol. 35, No. 290 (June 6, 1922 1922)-Ceased Nov. 1988. Newspaper. English. da (Mon.-Fri.). Florida Publishing Company, 1 Riverside Avenue, PO Box 1949F, Jacksonville FL 32231. **Tel** (904)359-4111, (800)553-0541. **ED** Fred Hartmann. **Circ:** 41,935. ***Continues*** *Florida Metropolis.*

US
KEY WEST CITIZEN, THE. (1879)-. Newspaper. English. da (Sun.-Fri.). $115.70. Key West Citizen, PO Box 1800, Key West FL 33041. **Tel** (305)294-6641. **ED** Winston Burrell (Editor in Chief). **LC** 7448-X. **Bk Rev**, (Qty: 12-14). **Photos**. **Ad Acc, Adv Mgr:** Randy Erikson. Full Page (B&W) $1328.70. Half Page (B&W) $679.80. **Pub. Size:** Standard. **Wire Svcs.:** AP. **Circ:** 6,818 daily, 8,520 Sunday. available in microform.

US
LAKE ALFRED PRESS. (19??)-. Newspaper. English. wk. $24.00. Lake Alfred Press, PO Box 756, 815 South Lake Shore Way, Lake Alfred FL 33850. **Tel** (813)425-3411. **ED** William M. Histed (Editor-in-Chief) and Bill Histed Jr. (Managing Editor). **Bk Rev**, (Qty: 25). **Photos**. **Ad Acc, Adv Mgr:** Barbara Wagoner. Full Page (B&W) $350.00. Half Page (B&W) $225.00. Full Page (Color) $400.00. Half Page (Color) $300.00. **Pub. Size:** Standard. available in microform.

US
LAKE WALES DAILY, THE. (19??)-. Newspaper. English. da. Lake Wales Daily, 33 West Orange Avenue, Lake Wales FL 33853-4176.

US
LAKE WORTH HERALD, THE. (1912)-. Newspaper. English. wk. $16.00. Lake Worth Herald, 130 South H Street, Lake Worth FL 33460. **Tel** (407)585-9387. **LC** 7002.

US/0163-0288
LEDGER (LAKELAND), THE. (THE LEDGER.). (19??)-. Periodical. English. da. $140.40. Lakeland Ledger Publishing Company, West Lime and Missouri Avenue, Lakeland FL 33802. **Tel** (813)687-7000 or, 800 282-3200. **ED** Louis Michael Perez. **Circ:** 62,333 daily, 77,958 Sunday. available on microfilm from University Microfilms International (UMI).

US/0892-2969
LOG (DESTIN, FLA.). (THE LOG.). Newspaper. English. sw. $15.00 Okaloosa and Walton counties, $20.00 others in Florida and out of state. The Log, PO Box 957, Destin FL 32541.

US
MADISON COUNTY CARRIER. Newspaper. English. Twice a week (52 weekly publications, Carrier on Weds., Enterprise Recorder on Fri.). $32.10 Madison County, $35.31 other Florida, $33.00 other. Madison County Carrier, PO Drawer 772, Madison FL 32340. **Tel** (904)973-4141. **ED** Harvey Greene. **Ad Acc. Circ:** 3,500.

US/0898-865X
MIAMI HERALD (MIAMI, FLA.). (THE MIAMI HERALD.). [Miami her.]. (1910)-. Newspaper. English. ds. $358.40. Miami Herald Publishing Company, 1 Herald Plaza, Miami FL 33132. **Tel** (305)350-2111, (800)825-6245. **ED** Heath Meriwether. **DD** 071. **Circ:** 458,759 daily, 559,758 Sunday. available on microfilm from University Microfilms International (UMI); available on an online database (file 702/Full-Text) from DIALOG. ***Continues*** *Morning News-Record.*
Ind/Abst Infobank (Jan. 1969-); PROMT.

US/1064-6442
MIAMI HURRICANE, THE. (THE MIAMI HURRICANE / UNIVERSITY OF MIAMI.). **Added/Corp** University of Miami. (19??)-. Newspaper. English. sw (Tues. & Fri.). $30.00. Miami Hurricane, PO Box 248132, Attn: Subs Dept., Coral Gables FL 33124. **Tel** (305) 284-4401, FAX (305) 284-4404.

US
MIAMI NEWS, THE. ***Ceased.*** 62nd Year, No. 175 (Nov. 4, 1957)-Ceased (Dec. 1988). Newspaper. English. da. Miami Herald, PO Box 522190, Miami FL 33152. available on microfilm from University Microfilms International (UMI); and Dakota Microfilm Service. ***Continues*** *Miami Daily News (1930).*

US/0735-6064
MIAMI NEWSPAPERS INDEX. ***Ceased.*** (Jan. 1982)-Ceased (Dec. 1991). English. mo. Miami Dade Public Library, 101 Flagler Street, Miami FL 33130. **Tel** (305)375-2665. available on microfilm.

US/0739-0319
MIAMI TIMES, THE. (1923)-. Newspaper. English. Fifty-two times a year. $45.00. Miami Times, 900 NW 54th Street, Miami FL 33147. **Tel** (305)757-1147. **ED** H.F.S. Reeves.

US/0889-2296
MIAMI TODAY. (1983)-. Newspaper. English. wk. $54.00. Miami Today, PO Box 1368, Miami FL 33101. **Tel** (305)358-2663. **ED** Michael Lewis. **Bk Rev**, (Qty: 50). **Photos**. **Ad Acc, Adv Mgr:** Alicia Coya. Full Page (B&W) $4300.00. Half Page (B&W) $2550.00. Full Page (Color) $5300.00. Half Page (Color) $3550.00. **Pub. Size:** Tabloid. **Wire Svcs.:** AP. **Circ:** 35,000 (ctrl). available on microfilm from University Microfilms International (UMI).

US/0746-5297
MONTICELLO NEWS (MONTICELLO, FLA.). (MONTICELLO NEWS.). Newspaper. English. sw. Monticello News, 100 North Jefferson Street, Monticello FL 32344.

US
MULBERRY PRESS. (1909)-. Newspaper. English. wk (Thurs.). $24.00 (one year). Mulberry Press, 1020 North Church Avenue, Highway 37 North, Mulberry FL 33860-2040. **Tel** (813) 425-3411. **ED** William M. Histed (Editor-in-Chief) and Bill Histed Jr. (Managing Editor). **Bk Rev**, (Qty: 20). **Photos**. **Ad Acc, Adv Mgr:** Barbara Wagoner. Full Page (B&W) $350.00. Half Page (B&W) $225.00. Full Page (Color) $400.00. Half Page (Color) $295.00. **Pub. Size:** Standard. available in microform.

US/1045-8093
NEW AMERICAN PRESS, THE. Vol. 8, No. 11 (Mar. 3-6, 1988)-. Newspaper. English. wk. $20.80. New American Publishing, PO Box 13626, Pensacola FL 32591. **Tel** (904)432-8410. **ED** A. LeRoy-Herbert and Walter LeRoy. **Bk Rev**, (Qty: 10). **Ad Acc, Adv Mgr:** Al LeRoy, **Tel** (904)434-3973. **Circ:** 34,000. ***Continues*** *Pensacola New American.*

US/8750-5029
NEWS-GAZETTE (SAINT CLOUD, FLA.). (NEWS-GAZETTE.). **VFOAT** News Gazette. 92nd Year, 33rd Ed. (Oct. 18, 1984)-. Newspaper. English. wk. $30.00. News-Gazette / Florida, PO Drawer 422068, Kissimmee FL 32742-2068. **Tel** (407)846-7600, FAX (407)846-8516. **ED** William Orben (Editor-in-Chief) and Tom Germond (Managing Editor). **Photos**. **Ad Acc, Adv Mgr:** Paula Stark. Full Page (B&W) $1,067.00. Half Page (B&W) $550.00. Full Page (Color) $1,142.00. Half Page (Color) $625.00. **Pub. Size:** Broadsheet. **Wire Svcs.:** CO, UPI. **Circ:** 29,000. ***Formed by the union of*** *St. Cloud News (Saint Cloud, Fla.)* ***and*** *Kissimmee Gazette.*

US/0163-4011
NEWS-LEADER. ***Title Change.*** (19??)-. Newspaper. English. da. South Dade News Leader, PO Box 900340, Homestead FL 33090. **Tel** (305)245-2311, FAX (305)248-0596. ***Continued by*** *South Dade News Leader, 1048-5406.*

US/1074-8342
NEWS-SUN (SEBRING, FLA.), THE. (THE NEWS-SUN.). (19??)-. Newspaper. English. sw (104 per year). $34.00. Sebring News-Sun, 2227 US 27 South, Sebring FL 33870. **Tel** (813)385-6155. ***Continues*** *Sebring News, 0163-3988.*

US/0898-168X
NORTHWEST FLORIDA DAILY NEWS. **VFOAT** Daily News. (198?)-. Newspaper. English. da. $130.00. Northwest Florida News, PO Box 2949, Fort Walton Beach FL 32549. **Tel** (904)863-1212. ***Continues*** *Playground Daily News.*

US/0163-3201
OCALA STAR-BANNER. (1???)-. Newspaper. English. da. $127.20 (including tax) Florida, $120.00 other (Sat. and Sun. by mail); $190.80 (including tax) Florida, $180.00 other (daily and Sun. by mail). Ocala Star Banner, PO Box 490, Ocala FL 32678. **Tel** (800)541-2171, (904)867-4010. **ED** Bernard Watts. **Circ:** 37,788 daily, 43,333 Sunday. available on microfilm from University Microfilms International (UMI).

US/0744-6055
ORLANDO SENTINEL, THE. 106th Year, No. 116 (April 26, 1982)-. Newspaper. English. da. Orlando Sentinel, PO Box 2833, Orlando FL 32802. **Tel** (407)420-5000, FAX (407)420-5765. **ED** L. John Haile Jr. **Circ:** 242,755 daily, 314,195 Sunday. available on microfilm from University Microfilms International (UMI); available on an online database (file 705/Full-Text) from DIALOG. ***Continues*** *Sentinel Star.*
Ind/Abst PROMT.

US/1070-860X
ORLANDO SPECTATOR, THE. VFOAT Spectator. (19??)-. Newspaper. English. bm (6 issues). $12.00. The Orlando Spectator, PO Box 540957, Orlando FL 32854-0957. **Tel** (407)263-7768. **ED** Benjamin Bruckner-Markeson, Michael Camarata, Suzannah Luna, John Perez. **Bk Rev**, (Qty: 3-4). **Photos**. **Ad Acc.** Full Page (B&W) $195.00. Half Page (B&W) $110.00. Full Page (Color) $245.00 (spot color), $392.00 (full color). Half Page (Color) $160.00 (spot color), $310.00 (full color). **Pub. Size:** Tabloid. **Wire Svcs.:** PN. **Circ:** 5,000.
Desc: Alternative, left-wing community newspaper offering news and views on local, national and international issues.

US/0163-5050
PALATKA DAILY NEWS. (19??)-. Newspaper. English. da. $3.25 (per month). Palatka Daily News, PO Box 777, Palatka FL 32077. **Tel** (904)328-2721. available on microfilm from University Microfilms International (UMI).

US
PALM BEACH POST, THE. (1908)-. Newspaper. English. da. 303.78 Florida; 287.16 others. Palm Beach Post, 2751 South Dixie Highway, West Palm Beach FL 33416. **Tel** (407)820-4231. **(Subscription address:** Palm Beach Post, PO Box 24700, Palm Beach FL 33416.**) ED** Thomas A. Kelly. **Circ:** 102,247 daily, 164,717 Sunday. available on an online database (file 712/Full-Text) from DIALOG.

US
PENSACOLA NEWS JOURNAL. Vol. 1 (June 1985)-. Newspaper. English. da. $3.00 (per week). Pensacola News Journals Inc, One News Journal Plaza, Pensacola FL 32501. **Tel** (904)435-8500, (904)435-8526. **ED** Curtis Coghlan (Editor-in-Chief) and Mike Ryan (Managing Editor). **Bk Rev**. **Photos**. **Ad Acc, Adv Mgr:** Kit Carson, **Tel** (904)435-8667. **Pub. Size:** Broadsheet. **Wire Svcs.:** AP, KR, GN. **Circ:** 61,725 (Mon.-Fri.), 71,630 (Sat.), 84,345 (Sun.) (ctrl). available on microfilm from University Microfilms International (UMI). ***Formed by the union of*** *Pensacola News* ***and*** *Pensacola Journal.*
Desc: News, features and editorial opinion.

US/0747-0967
PERRY NEWS-HERALD. VFOAT Perry News Herald. Newspaper. English. sw. $8.00 Taylor County; $15.00 other. Perry News-Herald, PO Box 888, 123 South Jefferson Street, Perry FL 32347. **Tel** (904)584-7819. **ED** Sharon Carrol. **Circ:** 9,000.

US/0745-5631
PINELLAS PARK NEWS. Vol. 1 No. 1 (Feb. 3, 1983)-. Newspaper. English. wk. $5.00 in county, $6.50 others in Florida, $9.00 others. Pinellas Park News, PO Box 1700, Pinellas Park FL 33564. **Tel** (813)541-6485.

US
PLAYGROUND DAILY NEWS (MICROFICHE). ***Title Change.*** (PLAYGROUND DAILY NEWS.). **VFOAT** Fort Walton Beach Playground News. (Sept. 3, 1962)-(19??). Newspaper. English. da. Playground News, PO Box 2949, Fort Walton Beach FL 32549. ***Continues*** *Playground News.* ***Continued by*** *Northwest Florida Daily News.*

US
POMPANO LEDGER. (19??)-. English. wk. $13.78 in the county ; $26.50 others outside the county. Pompano Ledger, 660 South Federal Highway, Suite 100, Pompano Beach FL 33062. **Tel** (305)946-7277. **ED** Edward Foley (Editor-in-Chief) and Ralph Rieht (Managing Editor). **Bk Rev**. **Photos**. **Ad Acc, Adv Mgr:** Karen Foley. Full Page (B&W) $1,670.55. Half Page (B&W) $835.28. Full Page (Color) $2,070.55. Half Page (Color) $1,035.28. **Pub. Size:** Standard. **Wire Svcs.:** AP.

US
PORK CITY PRESS. (19??)-. Newspaper. English. wk. $24.00. Pork City Press, PO Box 444, Pork City FL 33868. **Tel** (813)956-4033. **ED** William M. Histed (Editor-in-Chief) and Bill Histed Jr. (Managing Editor). **Bk Rev**. **Photos**. **Ad Acc, Adv Mgr:** Barbara Wagoner. Full Page (B&W) $350.00. Half Page (B&W) $225.00. Full Page (Color) $400.00. Half Page (Color) $300.00. **Pub. Size:** Standard. available in microform.

US/0888-756X
PRENSA (ORLANDO, FLA.), LA. (LA PRENSA.). (198?)-. Newspaper. Spanish. wk. $20.00. La Prensa Newspaper / Longwood, FL, 685 South County Road 427, Longwood FL 32750. **Tel** (407)767-0070. **ED** Dora Casanova de Toro. **Bk Rev**. **Ad Acc, Adv Mgr:** Sandra Gonzalez. **Pr Rev. Circ:** 40,000 (ctrl).

Desc: International, national, state and local news. General information of interest for the Spanish community.

US/0740-4166
REPORTER. ROCKLEDGE EDITION, THE. (THE REPORTER.). Vol. 3, No. 1 (Apr. 7, 1983)-. Newspaper. English. wk (Published on Thursdays). $15.00. Rockledge Reporter, 550-8 Gus Hipp Boulevard, Rockledge FL 32315-3137. **Tel** (407)636-5332, FAX (407)636-5675. **ED** Chris Beytes. **Ad Acc. Circ:** 4,900. ***Continues*** *Rockledge Reporter.*

US/0893-3642
SANFORD HERALD (SANFORD, FLA.). (19??)-. Newspaper. English. da (Sun.-Fri.). $69.00. Sanford Herald, 300 North French Avenue, Sanford FL 32771. **Tel** (305)322-2611. **ED** Thomas Giordano. ***Continues*** *Evening Herald (Sanford, Fla.).*

US/0273-5857
SANTA ROSA FREE PRESS. VFOAT Free Press. Newspaper. English. wk. Santa Rosa Free Press, 531 West Elva, Milton FL 32344.

US/8750-2070
SEMINOLE OUTLOOK. Newspaper. English. wk. $18.00. Outlook Newspapers, PO Box 1149, Oviedo FL 32765. **ED** Frank Garner. **Ad Acc. Circ:** 5,000 (ctrl). ***Continues*** *Outlook (Oviedo, Fla.).*

US/0891-8252
SEMINOLE TRIBUNE, THE. Added/Corp Seminole Tribe of Florida. (198u)-. Newspaper. English. bw. $15.00. Seminole Tribune, 6333 Northwest 30th Street, Hollywood FL 33024. **Tel** (305)964-1875. **ED** Betty Mae Jumper, Twila Perkins, and Barbara Billie. Index available. **Bk Rev. Ad Acc. Circ:** 5,000. ***Continues*** *Alligator Times.*

US/1048-5406
SOUTH DADE NEWS LEADER. (19??)-. Newspaper. English. sw (104 issues). $52.00. South Dade News Leader, PO Box 900340, Homestead FL 33090. **Tel** (305)245-2311, FAX (305)248-0596. **ED** Yoland Ulrich. **Ad Acc, Adv Mgr:** M. Davis. **Circ:** 12,000 (ctrl). available on microfilm.
Desc: General interest newspaper.

US/1041-1577
ST. AUGUSTINE RECORD, THE. VFOAT Saint Augustine Record. (Nov. 24, 1935)-. Newspaper. English. ir. $89.04 (home delivery), $120.00 (mail). St Augustine Record, PO Drawer 1630, St Augustine FL 32084. **Tel** (904)829-6562, FAX 904-829-6664. **ED** Adrian Pratt. **LC** 7488-X. **Photos. Ad Acc, Adv Mgr:** Jason Borcharot. Full Page (B&W) $1657.65. Half Page (B&W) $828.23. Full Page (Color) $1897.65 Half Page (Color) $1068.83. **Pub. Size:** Broadsheet. **Wire Svcs.:** KR, AP, MNS. **Circ:** 14,000 (ctrl). available on microfilm from University Microfilms International (UMI). ***Continues*** *Evening Record (Saint Augustine, Fla.).*

US
ST. PETERSBURG TIMES. VFOAT Saint Petersburg Times; St. Petersburg Daily Times. (Oct. 1892)-. Newspaper. English. ds. $234.00. St. Petersburg Times, PO Box 1121, St Petersburg FL 33731. **Tel** (813)895-1181, (800)333-7505. **ED** Andrew Barnes. **Ad Acc. Circ:** 226,706 daily, 350,400 Sunday. available on microfilm from University Microfilms International (UMI); available on an online database (file 735/Full-Text) from DIALOG. ***Continues*** *West Hillsborough Times;* ***Absorbed*** *Evening Independent (Saint Petersburg, Fla.).*
Ind/Abst PROMT.

US
STUART NEWS, THE. (1913)-. Newspaper. English. da. $190.00. Stuart News, PO Box 9009, Stuart FL 33495-9009. **Tel** (407)287-1550, FAX (407)221-4250. **ED** Thomas E. Weber Jr., Nancy Smith (Managing Editor). **Bk Rev**, (Qty: 40). **Photos. Ad Acc.** Full Page (B&W) $2710.29. Half Page (B&W) $1260.60. Full Page (Color) $3160.29. Half Page (Color) $1710.60 **Pub. Size:** Broadsheet. **Wire Svcs.:** AP. available on an online database (file 635/Full-Text) from DIALOG. Documents available from UMI Article Clearinghouse.
Ind/Abst Bus. Dateline (Jan. 19, 1992-) [Full Txt.].

US/0747-0304
SUMTER JOURNAL, THE. (198?)-. Newspaper. English. wk. $10.00 in Florida, $15.00 other states. The Sumter Journal, PO Box 90, Lake Panaskoffkee FL 33538. **Tel** (904)793-6222. **ED** Ed Lasky and Jim Burris. **Ad Acc. Circ:** 8,000 (ctrl).

US/1055-7806
SUN HERALD (CHARLOTTE ED.). (199?)-. Newspaper. English. da. Sun Coast Media Group Inc, 23170 Harborview Road, Charlotte Harbor FL 33980-2198. ***Continues*** *Charlotte Sun Herald. 1044-0399.*

●US/1068-7939
SUN HERALD (ENGLEWOOD ED.). (SUN HERALD.). (1993)-. Newspaper. English. da. $84.00. Englewood Sun Times, 167 West Dearborn, Englewood FL 34223-3237. **Tel** (813)474-5521. ***Continues*** *Englewood Sun Times, 1051-9351.*

US/0744-8139
SUN-SENTINEL (FORT LAUDERDALE, FLA.). (SUN-SENTINEL.). **VFOAT** Sun Sentinel. (19??)-. Newspaper. English. da. $426.00. News and Sun Sentinel Company, PO Box 14488, Fort Lauderdale FL 33302. **Tel** (305)356-4000, (305)761-4000, FAX (305)356-4559. **ED** Earl Maucker, Ellen Soeteber (Managing Editor). **Photos.** Full Page (B&W) $28072.00. Half Page (B&W) $14036.00. Full Page (Color) $31592.00. Half Page (Color) $15796.00. **Pub. Size:** Broadsheet. **Wire Svcs.:** AP, KR, UPI. **Circ:** 157,195. available on an online database (file 497,635/Full-Text) from DIALOG.
Ind/Abst PROMT.

US/0746-2182
SUNDAY NEWS SUN. Vol. 1, No. 1 (June 12, 1983)-. Newspaper. English. wk. $29.26 Sebriing Florida, $46.30 Florida, $44.00 other. Sebring News-Sun, 2227 US 27 South, Sebring FL 33870. **Tel** (813)385-6155.

US/0747-2358
TACO TIMES. (19??)-. Newspaper. English. sm (24 issues per year). $10.00. Taco Times, PO Box 25, Perry FL 32347.

US/0744-4400
TALLAHASSEE ADVERTISER, THE. Periodical. English. wk. Tallahassee Advertiser, PO Box 3696, Tallahassee FL 32315-3696.

US/0738-5153
TALLAHASSEE DEMOCRAT. (1914)-. Newspaper. English. da. $218.40 (by mail), $127.92 (by carrier) daily and Sunday; $159.12 (by mail), $127.92 (by carrier) daily; $91.00, Sunday only; $180.96, Monday-Saturday; $258.44, daily and Sunday; (Florida subscribers add sales tax or provide tax exempt number). Tallahassee Democrat, North Magnolia Drive, Box 990, Tallahassee FL 32302. **Tel** (904)599-2100, (800)999-2271, FAX (904)599-2347. **ED** Bob Stiff. **Ad Acc. Circ:** 54,556 daily, 67,394 Sunday. available on microfilm from University Microfilms International (UMI).

US
TAMPA DAILY TIMES, THE. 1893-. Newspaper. English. da. Tampa Daily Times, 202 South Parker Street, Tampa FL 33602. **Tel** (813)272-7711. available on microfilm from University of Florida.

US/1042-3761
TAMPA TRIBUNE, THE. VFOAT Tampa Tribune and the Tampa Times; Tampa Tribune-Times; Tampa Tribune Times. 64th Year, No. 152 (June 1, 1958)-. Newspaper. English. ds. $314.59 Florida; $296.00 US. Tampa Tribune, PO Box 191, Tampa FL 33601. **Tel** (813)272-7405, (813)272-7765. **ED** A. Paul Hogan. **Circ:** 207,671 daily, 283,991 Sunday. available on microfilm from University Microfilms International (UMI); and University Microfilms International (UMI). ***Continues*** *Tampa Morning Tribune.*
Ind/Abst PROMT.

US/0889-2245
TWIN CITY NEWS (CHATTAHOOCHEE, FLA.). (THE TWIN CITY NEWS.). **VFOAT** News. (19??)-. Newspaper. English. Fifty-two times a year (Thurs.). $13.50 Gadsen & Jackson counties; $16.85 others. Twin City News, PO Box 505, Chattahoochee FL 32324. **Tel** (904)663-2255, FAX (904)663-8102. **ED** Stanley J. Ramsey. Index available. cum. index. **Bk Rev**, (Qty: 10). **Photos. Ad Acc.** Full Page (B&W) $441.00. Half Page (B&W) $220.50. Full Page (Color) $531.00. Half Page (Color) $310.50. **Pub. Size:** Broadsheet. **Circ:** 2,000. ***Continues*** *Chattahochee News.*

US/0745-6263
VENICE GONDOLIER, THE. (19??)-. Periodical. English. sw. Sun Coast Media Group, 200 East Venice Avenue, Venice FL 33595.

US
VERO BEACH PRESS JOURNAL. (1919)-. English. da. $95.00. Vero Beach Press Journal, PO Box 1268, Vero Beach FL 32960. **Tel** (407)562-2315. **ED** J. J. Schumann Jr. **Circ:** 20,925 daily, 22,244 Sunday.

US
VOYAGER. Vol. 1, No. 1- (May 1968)-. Newspaper. English. wk. $15.00. Voyager, University of West Florida/Building 22, Pensacola FL 32514. **Bk Rev. Ad Acc. Circ:** 4,000.

US
WAKULLA COUNTY NEWS. (1898)-. Periodical. English. wk. News Publishing, PO Box 307, Crawfordville FL 32327-0307. **Tel** (904)926-7102. **ED** Stacie Phillips.

US/0279-795X
WASHINGTON COUNTY NEWS (CHIPLEY, FLA.). (WASHINGTON COUNTY NEWS.). (19??)-. Newspaper. English. sw (Each Mon. and Thurs.). $26.50, Washington, Holmes, and Jackson Counties; $31.80 other. Washington County News / Florida, PO Box 627, Chipley FL 32428. **Tel** (904)638-0212, (904)638-4242. **ED** M. Pujol.

US
WEEKLY CHALLENGER. (1966)-. Newspaper. English. wk. $40.00. Weekly Challenger, 2500 9th Street South, St Petersburg FL 33705. **Tel** (813)896-2922.

US
WEEKLY FLORIDA TIMES UNION, THE. (1865)-. Newspaper. English. wk. Florida Publishing Company, 1 Riverside Avenue, PO Box 1949F, Jacksonville FL 32231. **Tel** (904)359-4111, (800)553-0541.

US/0199-574X
WEEKLY WORLD NEWS. Vol. 1 (Oct. 16, 1979)-. Newspaper. English. wk. $24.95. Weekly World News, 600 South East Coast Avenue, Lantana FL 33642. **Tel** (305)586-0201. **(Subscription address:** CDS / SIFD Agency Control, 1901 Bell Avenue, Des Moines IA 50315.**) ED** Joe West. **Ad Acc. Circ:** 1,000,000.

US
WEST ORANGE TIMES. (19??)-. Newspaper. English. Fifty-two times a year. $17.50 Orange County; $27.50 other. West Orange Times, PO Box 309, Winter Garden FL 32787. **Tel** (305)656-2121. **Bk Rev**, (Qty: 200/year). **Ad Acc, Adv Mgr:** Andrew Bailey. **Circ:** 8,000.

●US
WESTSIDE GAZETTE. THURSDAY. (1993)-. English. Fifty-two times a year. $22.50. Westside Gazette, PO Box 5304, Ft. Lauderdale FL 33310. **Tel** (305)523-5115. **ED** Yvonne Henry. **Ad Acc, Adv Mgr:** Sonia Henry, **Tel** (305)523-5115. **Circ:** 35,000 (ctrl).

US
WINTER HAVEN DAILY CHIEF. (1911)-. Newspaper. English. ds. $142.08 (includes 6% sales tax) Florida; $150.00 other. Winter Haven News Chief, PO Box 1440, 650 Sixth Street SW, Winter Haven FL 33881. **Tel** (813)294-7731, FAX (813)294-2008.

US
WINTER HAVEN DAILY NEWS-CHIEF. (19??)-. Periodical. English. da. $150.00 Florida (includes sales tax); $142.08 other. Winter Haven News Chief, PO Box 1440, 650 Sixth Street SW, Winter Haven FL 33881. **Tel** (813)294-7731, FAX (813)294-2008. **ED** Gary Maitland. **Ad Acc, Adv Mgr:** Rick Etzkorn. **Circ:** 11,113.

US/1064-3613
WINTER PARK-MAITLAND OBSERVER. Vol. 1, No. 1, Jan. 26, (1989)-. Newspaper. English. wk. $24.00. Winter Park-Maitland Observer, PO Box 2426, Winter Park FL 32790. **Tel** (407)628-8500. **ED** Gerhard J.W. Munster (Editor-in-Chief) and Carole Arthurs (Managing Editor). Index available. cum. index. **Bk Rev**, (Qty: 12). **Photos. Ad Acc, Adv Mgr:** G. Munster. Full Page (B&W) $800.00. Half Page (B&W) $400.00. Full Page (Color) $915.00. Half Page (Color) $515.00. **Pub. Size:** Tabloid. **Circ:** 3,000 (ctrl).

US/0745-9203
WINTER PARK OUTLOOK. ***Title Change.*** **VFOAT** Outlook. Newspaper. English. wk. Outlook Newspapers, PO Box 1149, Oviedo FL 32765. **(Subscription address:** PO Box 1269, Winter Park, FL 32790**) ED** Frank Garner. **Ad Acc. Circ:** 5,000 (ctrl). ***Continued by*** *Winter Park Sun Outlook, 1051-967X.*

US
WINTER PARK SUN HERALD. (19??)-. English. wk (52 issues - published on Thursdays). $8.00 Florida; $9.00 other. Winter Park Sun Herald, PO Box 416, Winter Park FL 32790. **Tel** (407)647-1217.

US/1051-967X
WINTER PARK SUN OUTLOOK. Newspaper. English. wk. $26.00 (home delivery), $52.00 (mail). Outlook Newspapers, PO Box 1149, Oviedo FL 32765. ***Continues*** *Winter Park Outlook, 0745-9203.*

US
ZEPHYRHILLS NEWS. (1911)-. Newspaper. English. wk. Zephyrhills News, 611 5th Avenue, Zephyrhills FL 34283.

GEORGIA

US/0191-7269
ACWORTH NEIGHBOR, THE. Vol. 1, No. 49 (Dec. 12, 1968)-. Newspaper. English. wk. Neighbor Newspapers Inc., PO Box 449, 580 Fairground Street, Marietta GA 30061. **Tel** (404)428-9411, FAX (404)422-9533. ***Continues*** *Acworth Post.*

US/0746-0716
ADEL NEWS TRIBUNE. (ADEL NEWS-TRIBUNE.). Vol. 95, No. 1, (July 6, 1983)-. Newspaper. English. wk. $19.08 in county, $26.50 Georgia; $30.00 other. Adel News Tribune, PO Box 312, Adel GA 31620. **Tel** (912)896-2233. **ED** Ann G. Knight (editor), Charles Shiver (managing editor). **Photos. Ad Acc, Adv Mgr:** Grace Day. Full Page (B&W) $483.75.

Half Page (B&W) $254.77. Full Page (Color) $558.75. Half Page (Color) $329.77. **Pub. Size:** Standard. **Wire Svcs.:** GP. available on microfiche from University Library. ***Formed by the union of*** *Adel News* ***and*** *Cook County Tribune.*

US
ALBANY DAILY HERALD (ALBANY, GA.). ***Title Change.*** (THE ALBANY DAILY HERALD.). **VFOAT** Albany Herald. (1891)-?. Newspaper. English. da. The Albany Daily Herald, PO Box 48, Albany GA 31702. **Tel** (912)888-9322. **ED** James H Gray. **Bk Rev. Ad Acc. Circ:** 37,937 daily, 44,421 Sunday. ***Continued by*** *Albany Herald (Albany, GA.).*

US
ALBANY HERALD. VFOAT Albany Sunday Herald. (190?)-. Newspaper. English. da. The Albany Daily Herald, PO Box 48, Albany GA 31702. **Tel** (912)888-9322. ***Continues*** *Albany Daily Herald (Albany, Ga.).*

US/0745-7898
ALMA TIMES-STATESMAN. (1983)-. Newspaper. English. wk. Alma Newspapers Inc, PO Box 428, Alma GA 31510-0428. **Tel** (912)632-7201. ***Formed by the union of*** *Alma Times* ***and*** *Statesman.*

US/0191-8494
ALPHARETTA NEIGHBOR, THE. Vol. 6, No. 51 (Dec. 19, 1968)-. Newspaper. English. wk (52 per year). $55.00. Alpharetta Neighbor, 580 Fairground Street, Marietta GA 30060. **Tel** (404)428-9411. ***Continues*** *Alpharetta Sun.*

US
AMERICUS TIMES-RECORDER. VFOAT Americus Times Recorder; Americus Daily Times-Recorder. Vol. 1, No. 13 (Apr. 19, 1891)-. Newspaper. English. da. $62.00. Americus Times Recorder, PO Box 1247, Americus GA 31709. **ED** Beth Alston. **Ad Acc, Adv Mgr:** Jeff Masters. **Circ:** 7,584. ***Continues*** *Times-Recorder (Americus, Ga. : Daily).*

US/0898-3712
ATHENS DAILY NEWS, ATHENS BANNER-HERALD. VFOAT Athens Daily News/Athens Banner Herald; Athens Daily News and Athens Banner-Herald; Athens Banner-Herald and Athens Daily News; Athens Daily News/Athens Banner-Herald. (198?)-. Newspaper. English. ds. $104.00. Athens Newspapers, PO Box 912, Athens GA 30613. **Tel** (706)549-0123, FAX (706)543-5234. **ED** Rick Parham. **Bk Rev**, (Qty: 15). **Ad Acc, Adv Mgr:** Frank Moss, **Tel** (706)208-2308. Full Page (B&W) $2113.32. Half Page (B&W) $1056.66. Full Page (Color) $2304.57. Half Page (Color) $1247.91. **Pub. Size:** Broadsheet. **Wire Svcs.:** KR, AP. available in microform. ***Continues*** *Banner-Herald/The Daily News, 0745-9904.*

US/0744-4001
ATHENS OBSERVER, THE. VFOAT Observer. Vol. 1, No. 1 (Jan. 3, 1974)-. Newspaper. English. wk. The Athens Observer, PO Box 112, 228 North Lumpkin, Athens GA 30613. **Tel** (404)548-6346. **ED** Merrill Morris and Phil Sanderlin. **Bk Rev. Ad Acc. Circ:** 6,000 (ctrl).
Desc: Contents include: local news, sports, features, opinion, entertainment, TV, calendar events, and classifieds.

US
ATLANTA CONSTITUTION (ATLANTA, GA. : 1897). (THE ATLANTA CONSTITUTION.). **VFOAT** Atlanta Journal and the Atlanta Constitution; Atlanta Journal the Atlanta Constitution. Vol. 14 (Sept. 15, 1881)-. Newspaper. English. ds. $264.84 (tax exempt schools, universities & libraries in Canada). Atlanta Journal Constitution, PO Box 4689, Atlanta GA 30302. **Tel** (404)526-5151, (800)944-7363. **ED** Jim Minter. **Circ:** 255,636. available in microform from University Microfilms International (UMI); available on an online database (files 635,713) from DIALOG. Documents available from UMI Article Clearinghouse. ***Continues*** *Daily Constitution (Atlanta, Ga.).*
Ind/Abst Bus. Dateline (June 1, 1990-) [Full Txt.]; PROMT.

US
ATLANTA DAILY WORLD. Vol. 5, No. 36 (March 18, 1932)-. Newspaper. English. da. $65.00. Atlanta Daily World, 145 Auburn Avenue, Atlanta GA 30335-1201. **Tel** (404)659-1110. **ED** C.A. Scott and Portia Scott (Managing Editor). **Bk Rev. Photos. Ad Acc, Adv Mgr:** J.R. Simmons. Full Page (B&W) $1,499.40. Half Page (B&W) $749.70. **Pub. Size:** Standard. **Wire Svcs.:** API, UPI, NP. **Circ:** 18,000 (Sun.), 16,000 (weekdays). available on microfilm. ***Continues*** *Atlanta World.*

US
ATLANTA INQUIRER, THE. Vol. 1, No. 1 (July 31, 1960)-. Newspaper. English. wk. $28.20. Atlanta Inquirer, PO Box 92367, Atlanta GA 30314. **Tel** (404)523-6086.

US/0892-3345
ATLANTA JEWISH TIMES, THE. VFOAT Jewish Times. Vol. 63, No. 1 (Jan. 2, 1987)-. Newspaper. English. Fifty-two times a year (Friday). $31.50 Georgia; $39.50 other states; $95.00 others. Atlanta Jewish Times, 1575 Northside Drive Northwest, Suite 470, Atlanta GA 30318. **Tel** (800)875-6621, (404)352-2400, FAX (404)355-9388. **ED** Neil Rubin (Managing Editor). Index available. cum. index (1929-1987). **Bk Rev**, (Qty: 12). **Photos. Ad Acc, Adv Mgr:** Dan Chorgnec, **Tel** (404)352-2400. Full Page (B&W) $1,045.00. Half Page (B&W) $570.00. Full Page (Color) $1,526.00. Half Page (Color) $1,020.00. **Pub. Size:** Tabloid. **Wire Svcs.:** AP, JT. **Circ:** 10,000 (ctrl). ***Continues*** *Southern Israelite, 0038-4224.*
Desc: Features local, national and international news. Includes opinion and comment of the Jewish interest and import.

US
ATLANTA JOURNAL (ATLANTA, GA. : 1889). (THE ATLANTA JOURNAL.). **VFOAT** Atlanta Journal and the Atlanta Constitution; Atlanta Journal the Atlanta Constitution; Juvenile Journal. Vol. 6, No. 33 (April 8, 1889)-. Newspaper. English. ds. $529.68 postal zones 1 & 2; $618.24 postal zone 3; $710.40 postal zones 4 & 5; $863.52 postal zones 6, 7, & 8. Atlanta Journal Constitution, PO Box 4689, Atlanta GA 30302. **Tel** (404)526-5151, (800)944-7363. **ED** Jim Minter. **Circ:** 185,375. available on microfilm from University Microfilms International (UMI). Documents available from UMI Article Clearinghouse. ***Continues*** *Evening Journal (Atlanta, Ga.);* ***Absorbed*** *Atlanta Georgian (Atlanta, Ga. : 1912).*
Ind/Abst Newsp. Abstr.

US
ATLANTA VOICE, THE. (1966)-. Newspaper. English. Fifty-two times a year. $39.00. Atlanta Voice, 633 Pryer Street Southwest, Atlanta GA 30312. **Tel** (404)524-6426, FAX (404)523-7853. **ED** Stan Washington. Index available. cum. index. **Bk Rev**, (Qty: 10). **Photos. Ad Acc, Adv Mgr:** Malcolm Caldwell, **Tel** (404)524-6426 Ext. 29. Full Page (B&W) $3,780.00. Half Page (B&W) $1,890.00. Full Page (Color) $4,620.00. Half Page (Color) $2,310.00. **Pub. Size:** Tabloid. **Wire Svcs.:** API. **Circ:** 103,000 (ctrl). available on microfilm from University Microfilms International (UMI).

US/0747-1343
AUGUSTA CHRONICLE (1885), THE. (THE AUGUSTA CHRONICLE.). **VFOAT** Augusta Chronicle Augusta Herald. (May 7, 1885)-. Newspaper. English. da. $114.00 Georgia & South Carolina; $180.00 other. Augusta Chronicle Herald, PO Box 1928, Augusta GA 30913. **Tel** (706)722-5620. **ED** W. S. Morris III. **LC** 7501. **Circ:** 62,630. available on microfilm. ***Continues*** *Chronicle & Constitutionalist (Augusta, Ga. : 1882).*

US/0746-4657
AUGUSTA FOCUS. Newspaper. English. wk. Augusta Focus, PO Box 10112, Augusta GA 30903. ***Continues*** *Black Focus, 0746-1496.*

US/0191-7382
AUSTELL NEIGHBOR, THE. (19??)-. Newspaper. English. wk. Neighbor Newspapers Inc., PO Box 449, 580 Fairground Street, Marietta GA 30061. **Tel** (404)428-9411, FAX (404)422-9533. **ED** Rodney Shumake. **Circ:** 7,025.

US
BAXLEY NEWS-BANNER, THE. VFOAT Baxley News Banner. Vol. 59, No. 44 (Nov. 12, 1942)-. Newspaper. English. wk. $17.00 Appling county, $24.00 other Georgia, $26.00 other. Baxley News Banner, PO Box 409, Baxley GA 31513. **Tel** (912)367-2468. ***Continues*** *Baxley News-Banner (Baxley Herald).*

US
BERRIEN PRESS, THE. (1958)-. Newspaper. English. wk. $18.40 Berrien County; $20.50 Georgia; $22.60 other. Berrien Press, PO Box 666, Nashville GA 31639. **Tel** (912)686-3523.

US/0746-9330
BLACKSHEAR TIMES, THE. (1876)-. Newspaper. English. wk (Tuesday). $22.00. Blackshear Times, PO Box 410, Blackshear GA 31516. **Tel** (912)449-6693. **ED** Robert M. Williams Jr. **Bk Rev. Photos. Ad Acc, Adv Mgr:** Cheryl Williams. Full Page (B&W) $451.50. Half Page (B&W) $225.75. Full Page (Color) $501.50. Half Page (Color) $275.75. **Pub. Size:** Broadsheet.

US
BLADE, THE. Vol. 121, No. 5 (Jan. 31, 1979)-. Newspaper. English. wk. Blade / Swainsboro, PO Box 938, Swainsboro GA 30401-0938. **Tel** (912)237-9971, FAX (912)237-9451. **ED** William Rogers. **Ad Acc. Circ:** 6,000. ***Continues*** *Swainsboro Forest-Blade.*

US
BRUNSWICK NEWS, THE. VFOAT Brunswick Daily News. (Sept. 30, 1906)-. Newspaper. English. da. $76.00. Brunswick News, PO Box 1557, Brunswick GA 31521. **Tel** (912)265-1104, FAX (912)264-4973. **ED** C. H. Leavy III (Editor-in- Chief) and H. Rowland (Managing Editor). **Bk Rev. Photos. Ad Acc, Adv Mgr:** Ron Walden, **Tel** (912)265-8320. Full Page (B&W) $903.42. Half Page (B&W) $451.71. Full Page (Color) $993.42. Half Page (Color) $541.71. **Pub. Size:** Broadsheet. **Wire Svcs.:** AP. **Circ:** 16,874. available on microfilm. ***Continues*** *Brunswick Daily News;* ***Absorbed*** *Brunswick Banner.*

US
CAIRO MESSENGER, THE. Vol. 1, No. 1 (Jan. 15, 1904)-. Newspaper. English. wk. $11.55. Messenger Publication Co., PO Box 30, Cairo GA 31728. **Tel** (912)377-2032.

US
CALHOUN TIMES AND GORDON COUNTY NEWS. Vol. 107, No. 12 (Oct. 31, 1976)-. Newspaper. English. sw. Rome News-Tribune, 305 East 6th Avenue, Rome GA 30161. **Tel** (706)291-6397, FAX (706)234-6478. ***Formed by the union of*** *Calhoun Times (Calhoun, Ga. : 1894)* ***and*** *Gordon County News.*

US/1055-6559
CAMDEN COUNTY TRIBUNE. Vol. 1, No. 1 (Apr. 14, 1950)-. Newspaper. English. wk. $15.00. Camden County Tribune, PO Box 470, St Marys GA 31558. **Tel** (912)882-4927, (912)882-4926. **ED** Linn Hudson. **Photos. Ad Acc, Adv Mgr:** Tina Thompson. Full Page (B&W) $580.50. Half Page (B&W) $283.50. **Pub. Size:** Standard.

US
CAMILLA ENTERPRISE, THE. (1902)-. Newspaper. English. wk. $24.38. Camilla Enterprise, 13 South Scott Street, PO Box 365, Camilla GA 31730-1705. **Tel** (912)336-5265, FAX (912)336-8476. **ED** Roger Ann Jones. **Photos. Ad Acc, Adv Mgr:** Sherie Kegrns. Full Page (B&W) $509.55. Half Page (B&W) $254.78. Full Page (Color) $609.55. Half Page (Color) $354.78. **Pub. Size:** Standard. **Circ:** 3,600.

US/1056-8271
CEDARTOWN STANDARD (1950). (THE CEDARTOWN STANDARD.). **VFOAT** Daily Standard; Cedartown Daily Standard. Vol. 5, No. 51 (July 10, 1950)-. Newspaper. English. sw. Rome News-Tribune, 305 East 6th Avenue, Rome GA 30161. **Tel** (706)291-6397, FAX (706)234-6478. **ED** Mike Colombo. **Ad Acc, Adv Mgr:** Wilson Adam. **Circ:** 3,400. ***Continues*** *Daily Standard (Cedartown, Ga. : 1946).*

US/0199-7416
CHAMBLEE DEKALB NEIGHBOR, THE. Vol. 11, No. 8 (Feb. 20, 1980)-. Newspaper. English. wk. Neighbor Newspapers Inc., PO Box 449, 580 Fairground Street, Marietta GA 30061. **Tel** (404)428-9411, FAX (404)422-9533. ***Continues*** *Chamblee Neighbor, 0192-0723.*

US
CHARLTON COUNTY HERALD. (1898)-. Newspaper. English. wk. Charlton County Herald, POBox 398, Folkston GA 31537-0398. **Tel** (912)496-3585, FAX (912)496-4585. **ED** David Thompson. **Ad Acc. Circ:** 2,495.

US
CHATSWORTH TIMES. (1913)-. Newspaper. English. wk. Chatsworth Times, PO Box 130, Chatsworth GA 30705-0130. **Tel** (706)695-4646, FAX (706)695-7181. **ED** Albert Edwards. **Ad Acc. Circ:** 4,704.

US
CHATTOOGA PRESS, THE. (198?)-. Newspaper. English. wk. Chattooga Press, PO Box 485, Summerville GA 30747. **Tel** (706)857-5433. **Ad Acc.**

US
CHEROKEE TRIBUNE, THE. Vol. 60, No. 36 (Sept. 13, 1973)-. Newspaper. English. sw. $36.00 Canton County; $39.00 other. Cherokee Tribune, 64 Academy Street, Canton GA 30114. **Tel** (404)479-1441, FAX (404)479-3505. **ED** Rebecca Johnston. ***Continues*** *North Georgia Tribune.*

US
CHIEFTAIN, THE. (1983)-. Newspaper. English. wk. Community Newspapers / Georgia, PO Box 1555, Cornelia GA 30531-6555. **Tel** (706)778-4215, FAX (706)778-4114. **Circ:** 11,100.

US/0883-7007
CITIZEN GEORGIAN, THE. VFOAT Citizen and Georgian; Citizen & Georgian. Newspaper. English. wk. The Citizen & Georgian, PO Box 387, Montezuma GA 31063. ***Continues*** *Macon County Citizen.*

US/0192-074X
CLAYTON NEIGHBOR, THE. Newspaper. English. wk. $50.00. Neighbor Newspapers Inc., PO Box 449, 580 Fairground Street, Marietta GA 30061. **Tel** (404)428-9411, FAX (404)422-9533.

US/0199-7270
CLAYTON SUN. (19??)-. Newspaper. English. wk. $15.00. Clayton Sun, 5477 Riverdale Road, College Park GA 30349. **Tel** (404)996-6400. **ED** Phil Herman. **Ad Acc, Adv Mgr:** J. Hewitt. ***Continues*** *Henry and Clayton Sun, 0192-0782.*

US
CLAYTON TRIBUNE, THE. (18??)-. Newspaper. English. wk. $20.50 Rabun County; $23.50 other. Clayton Tribune, PO Box 425, Clayton GA 30525. **Tel** (404)782-3312.

US/1047-6636
COASTAL COURIER (HINESVILLE, GA.), THE. (THE COASTAL COURIER.). Vol. 112, No. 1 (Oct. 2, 1980)-. Newspaper. English. sw (Weds. and Fri.). $39.00 Liberty County, Georgia; $41.00 other US; $46.00 other. Coastal Courier, PO Box 498, Hinesville GA 31313. **Tel** (912)876-0156, FAX (912)368-6329. **ED** Pat Watkins. **Ad Acc, Adv Mgr:** Matt Newton. **Circ:** 5,500. ***Formed by the union of*** *Byron County News* ***and*** *Liberty County Herald;* ***Absorbed*** *Hinesville Star.*

US/1053-7511
COLUMBIA NEWS-TIMES, THE. VFOAT Columbia News Times. Vol. 68, No. 29 (Feb. 15, 1989)-. Newspaper. English. wk. $15.90. Columbia Publishing Company / Georgia, PO Box 4178, Martinez GA 30907. **Tel** (706)863-6165, FAX (706)863-9080. **ED** Karl N. Haywood (Editor-in-Chief) and Paul Floeckher (Managing Editor). **Bk Rev**, (Qty: 10). **Photos. Ad Acc, Adv Mgr:** Gainette Haywood. Full Page (B&W) $693.00. Half Page (B&W) $346.50. Full Page (Color) $753.00. Half Page (Color) $406.50. **Pub. Size:** Broadsheet. **Circ:** 15,500. available in microform. ***Continues*** *News-Times (Martinez, Ga.), 0747-0665.*

US/0898-3860
COLUMBUS LEDGER-ENQUIRER. VFOAT Columbus Ledger Enquirer. (1988). Newspaper. English. da. $237.00 (daily and Sunday by mail); $151.32 (daily and Sunday by carrier) $134.16 (daily by mail); 102.96 (Sunday by mail); $70.20 (daily by carrier). Columbus Enquirer, 17 West 12th Street, Columbus GA 31902. ***Formed by the union of*** *Columbus Ledger* ***and*** *Columbus Enquirer (Metro Edition), 8750-8389.*

US
COLUMBUS TIMES, THE. (1970)-. Newspaper. English. wk. $19.10. Columbus Times, PO Box 2845, Columbus GA 31902. **Tel** (706)324-2404, FAX (706)596-0657. **ED** Helmut Gertjegerdes. **Bk Rev**, (Qty: 30 per year). **Photos. Ad Acc.** Full Page (B&W) $1836.96. Half Page (B&W) $939.84. **Pub. Size:** Standard. **Circ:** 20,056 paid.

US
COMMERCE NEWS, THE. (1???)-. Newspaper. English. wk. Jackson Herald Inc, PO Box 908, Jefferson GA 30549-0908. **Tel** (706)367-5233, FAX (706)367-8056. **ED** Helen Buffington. **Ad Acc, Adv Mgr:** Scott Buffington. **Circ:** 4,300.

US
CORDELE DISPATCH AND THE WILCOX COUNTY CHRONICLE, THE. Vol. 54, No. 59 (Jan. 11, 1971)-. Newspaper. English. da. Cordele Dispatch, 306 13th Avenue West, Cordele GA 31015-2348. **Tel** (912)273-2277, FAX (912)273-7239. **ED** Terri Blackwell. **Ad Acc. Circ:** 5,827. ***Formed by the union of*** *Cordele Dispatch* ***and*** *Wilcox County Chronicle.*

US
COURIER HERALD, THE. VFOAT Dublin Courier Herald. Vol. 67, No. 178 (June 1, 1981)-. Newspaper. English. da. $85.00. Dublin Courier Herald, Drawer B, Court Square Station, Dublin GA 31040. **Tel** (912)272-5522, FAX (912)272-2189. **ED** Dubose Porter. **Ad Acc. Circ:** 12,200. ***Continues*** *Dublin Courier Herald (Dublin, Ga. : 1942).*

US/1049-4936
COVINGTON NEWS (COVINGTON, GA.), THE. (THE COVINGTON NEWS.). (Dec. 2, 1908)-. Newspaper. English. sw. $20.00. Covington News, PO Box 1249, Covington GA 30209-1249. **Tel** (404)787-6397, FAX (404)786-6451. **ED** Ron Stokes. **Ad Acc. Circ:** 8,100. ***Absorbed*** *Citizen-Observer (Rockdale, Ga.).*

US/0889-8685
CREATIVE LOAFING (1978). (CREATIVE LOAFING.). **VFOAT** Atlantan/Creative Loafing. Vol. 6, Issue 47 (April 29, 197?)-. Newspaper. English. Fifty-two times a year (Published on Wed.). $48.00. Creative Loafing News Atlanta, 750 Willoughby Way, Atlanta GA 30312. **Tel** (404)688-5623, FAX (404)522-1532. **ED** Deborah Eason, and Tony Paris (Managing Editor). **Bk Rev. Photos. Ad Acc, Adv Mgr:** Howard Landsman. Full Page (B&W) $3,028.00. Half Page (B&W) $1,636.00. Full Page (Color) $3,253.00. Half Page (Color) $1,861.00. **Pub. Size:** Tabloid. **Circ:** 120,000 (ctrl). ***Absorbed*** *Atlantan/Creative Loafing.*
Desc: Carries news, features, entertainment listings, calendar of events, coverage of arts, movies, sports, advertising and classifieds.

US
DAILY NEWS. VFOAT Sunday Daily News. (July 15, 1991)-. Newspaper. English. da. Gwinnett Daily News, 3414 Peachtree Road Northeast, Suite 1100, Atlanta GA 30326-1167. ***Continues*** *Gwinnett Daily News.*

US
DAILY SUN (WARNER ROBINS, GA.). (THE DAILY SUN.). **VFOAT** Sunday Sun. Vol. 1, No. 1 (Nov. 3, 1969)-. Newspaper. English. da. Warner Robins Daily Sun, PO Box 6129, Warner Robins GA 31095-6129. **Tel** (912)923-6432, FAX (912)328-7682. **ED** H.A. Johnson. **Ad Acc, Adv Mgr:** Gary McDuffy. **Circ:** 10,075.

US/1049-6750
DAILY TRIBUNE NEWS (CARTERSVILLE, GA.), THE. (THE DAILY TRIBUNE NEWS.). Vol. 1, No. 1 (May 6, 1946)-. Newspaper. English. da. $71.00. Daily Tribune News, PO Box 70, Cartersville GA 30120. **Tel** (404)382-4545. **Bk Rev. Photos. Ad Acc, Adv Mgr:** Barbara Dolken. Full Page (B&W) $848.82. Half Page (B&W) $424.41. Full Page (Color) $1029.42. Half Page (Color) $514.71. **Pub. Size:** Broadsheet. **Wire Svcs.:** AP. **Circ:** 10,200 evening paid.

US/8750-1376
DALLAS NEW ERA, THE. Vol. 16, No. 18 (Mar. 25, 1898)-. Newspaper. English. wk (Thurs.). $8.00. Dallas New Era, PO Box 530, Dallas GA 30132-0530. **Tel** (404)445-3379. **ED** T. E. Parker. **Photos. Ad Acc, Adv Mgr:** Annette Manning. **Circ:** 6,700. ***Continues*** *New Era (Dallas, Ga.).*

US
DARIEN NEWS, THE. Vol. 1, No. 1 (June 8, 1951)-. Newspaper. English. wk. $15.00 (local), $20.00 (in state), $25.00 (out of state). Darien News, PO Box 496, Darien GA 31305. **Tel** (912)437-4251, FAX (912)437-2299. **ED** Kathleen Russell. **Bk Rev**, (Qty: 3-4). **Photos. Ad Acc.** Full Page (B&W) $451.50. Half Page (B&W) $225.75. Full Page (Color) $571.50. Half Page (Color) $345.75. **Pub. Size:** Standard. **Circ:** 3,000.

US/0199-6010
DECATUR DEKALB NEIGHBOR, THE. Vol. 1, No. 1 (Feb. 20, 1980)-. Newspaper. English. wk. $50.00. Neighbor Newspapers Inc., PO Box 449, 580 Fairground Street, Marietta GA 30061. **Tel** (404)428-9411, FAX (404)422-9533.

US
DECATUR-DEKALB NEWS/ERA. 31st year, No. 1 (Jan. 4, 1979)-. Newspaper. English. wk. $15.75. Decatur Dekalb News/Era, 150 East Ponce de Leon Avenue, Suite 100, Decatur GA 30030. **Tel** (404)373-4488. **ED** John Sell (phone: (404)292-3536). **Ad Acc, Adv Mgr:** J. Crane. **Circ:** 10,600. available on microfilm from University Library. ***Absorbed*** *Lithonia Observer;* ***Formed by the union of*** *DeKalb New Era (Decatur, Ga. : 1967)* ***and*** *Decatur-Dekalb News.*
Desc: Community newspaper and business news.

US/0199-7289
DORAVILLE DEKALB NEIGHBOR, THE. (19??)-. Newspaper. English. wk. Neighbor Newspapers Inc., PO Box 449, 580 Fairground Street, Marietta GA 30061. **Tel** (404)428-9411, FAX (404)422-9533. ***Continues*** *Doraville Neighbor, 0192-0707.*

US
DOUGLAS COUNTY SENTINEL. VFOAT West Georgia Sentinel. (190?)-. Newspaper. English. sw. $45.00 Douglas County; $50.00 other. Douglas County Sentinel, PO Box 1586, Douglasville GA 30133. **Tel** (404)942-6571.

US
DOUGLAS ENTERPRISE, THE. Vol. 16, No. 23 (Oct. 7, 1905)-. Newspaper. English. wk (Sunday and Wednesday). $24.50 local; $55.00 other. Douglas Enterprise, 1823 South Peterson Avenue, PO Box 551, Douglas GA 31533. **Tel** (912)384-2323, FAX (912)383-0218. **ED** Thomas Frier Jr. and Jim Merrit (Managing Editor). **Bk Rev. Photos. Ad Acc, Adv Mgr:** Jim Merritt. Full Page (B&W) $472.50. Half Page (B&W) $252.00. Full Page (Color) $532.50. Half Page (Color) $312.00. **Pub. Size:** Standard. **Circ:** 8,100. available on microfilm (from GSU). ***Formed by the union of*** *Douglas Weekly Breeze* ***and*** *Coffee County Gazette.*

US/0192-0758
DOUGLAS NEIGHBOR, THE. Newspaper. English. wk. Neighbor Newspapers Inc., PO Box 449, 580 Fairground Street, Marietta GA 30061. **Tel** (404)428-9411, FAX (404)422-9533.

US/0199-7408
DUNWOODY DEKALB NEIGHBOR, THE. Vol. 11, No. 7 (Feb. 20, 1980)-. Newspaper. English. wk. $50.00. Neighbor Newspapers Inc., PO Box 449, 580 Fairground Street, Marietta GA 30061. **Tel** (404)428-9411, FAX (404)422-9533. ***Continues*** *Dunwoody Neighbor, 0192-0650.*

US
EARLY COUNTY NEWS (BLAKELY, GA. : 1859). (EARLY COUNTY NEWS.). Began in 1859. Newspaper. English. wk. Early County News, PO Box 748, Blakely GA 31723.

US/0191-5029
EAST COBB NEIGHBOR, THE. (1977)-. Newspaper. English. wk. $60.00. Neighbor Newspapers Inc., PO Box 449, 580 Fairground Street, Marietta GA 30061. **Tel** (404)428-9411, FAX (404)422-9533.

US
ELBERTON STAR, THE. Vol. 100, No. 67 (Sept. 1, 1987)-. Newspaper. English. wk. $16.00. The Elberton Star - The Elberton Beacon Inc, 10 Oliver Street, Elberton GA 30635. **Tel** (404)283-3100, FAX (404)283-7841. **ED** Jim Rainey. **Bk Rev**, (Qty: 50). **Photos. Ad Acc, Adv Mgr:** Amanda Slaughterback. Full Page (B&W) $642.60. Half Page (B&W) $321.30. Full Page (Color) $717.00. Half Page (Color) $396.00. **Pub. Size:** Broadsheet. **Circ:** 5,500. ***Continues*** *Elberton Star, The Elberton Beacon.*

US
FAYETTE COUNTY NEWS, THE. (19??)-. Newspaper. English. wk. Fayette County News, PO Box 96, Fayetteville GA 30214. **Tel** (404)461-6317.

US/0192-0669
FAYETTE NEIGHBOR, THE. (1978)-. Newspaper. English. wk. $50.00. Neighbor Newspapers Inc., PO Box 449, 580 Fairground Street, Marietta GA 30061. **Tel** (404)428-9411, FAX (404)422-9533. **ED** Bobby Nesbitt. **Circ:** 14,054.

US/0747-2242
FORSYTH COUNTY NEWS, THE. (19??)-. Newspaper. English. sw. Forsyth County News, 107 Dahlonega Street, Cumming GA 30130.

US
FRANKLIN COUNTY CITIZEN. Vol. 1, No. 1 (Aug. 5, 1971)-. Newspaper. English. wk. Community Newspapers / Georgia, PO Box 1555, Cornelia GA 30531-6555. **Tel** (706)778-4215, FAX (706)778-4114. **Circ:** 5,300. ***Formed by the union of*** *Carnesville Herald and Advance; Royston Record* ***and*** *Lavonia Times and Gauge (Lavonia, Ga. : 1941).*

US/0730-1138
GEORGIA GAZETTE (SAVANNAH, GA.: 1978), THE. (THE GEORGIA GAZETTE.). (1978)-. Newspaper. English. wk. $15.00. Georgia Gazette & Journal, PO Box 9925, 21 West York Street, Savannah GA 31412. **Tel** (912)236-7757.

US/0746-3324
GRIFFIN DAILY NEWS. VFOAT Daily News. Vol. 53, No. 51 (Sept. 24, 1924)-. Newspaper. English. da. Griffin Daily News, 323 East Solomon Street, Griffin GA 30223. **Tel** (404)227-3276. ***Continues*** *Griffin Daily News and Sun.*

●US/1076-4852
GWINNETT POST-TRIBUNE. VFOAT Gwinnett Post Tribune. (Oct. 18, 1992)-. Newspaper. English. wk. $17.50 Gwinnett County; $22.50 other. Gwinnett Post Tribune, PO Box 1286, Lawrenceville GA 30246. **Tel** (404)339-5848. ***Continues*** *Gwinnett Home Weekly.*

US/0746-4169
HARALSON GATEWAY-BEACON, THE. VFOAT Haralson Gateway Beacon. Vol. 1, No. 1 (Sept. 1, 1983)-. Newspaper. English. wk (Published on Thursdays). Worrell Enterprises, PO Box 757, Villa Rica GA 30180. **Tel** (404)459-5166. **ED** Julianne Foster. **Ad Acc, Adv Mgr:** Glenn Smith. **Circ:** 5,600. ***Formed by the union of*** *Bremen Gateway; Haralson County Tribune* ***and*** *Tallapoosa Journal-Beacon.*

US
HARBOR SOUND, THE. Vol. 2, No. 29 (Oct. 12, 1983)-. Newspaper. English. wk. $30.00. Harbor Sound, 1326 Newcastle Street, Brunswick GA 31520. **Tel** (912)264-4521, FAX (912)264-4531. **ED** James Dryden. **Photos. Ad Acc, Adv Mgr:** Jim Dryden. Full Page (B&W) $459.00. Half Page (B&W) $238.50. Full Page (Color) $519.00. Half Page (Color) $278.50. **Pub. Size:** Tabloid. **Circ:** 27,000.

US
HAWKINSVILLE DISPATCH AND NEWS, THE. Began Jan. 2, 1890. Newspaper. English. wk. Hawkinsville Dispatch and News, Hawkinsville GA 31036. ***Formed by the union of*** *Hawkinsville Dispatch (Hawkinsville, GA.)* ***and*** *Hawkinsville News.*

US/1045-6678
HENRY HERALD, THE. (198?)-. Newspaper. English. sw. $18.00 (in-county), $26.00 (out-of-county). Henry Herald, PO Box 233, McDonough GA 30253. **Tel** (404)957-9161, FAX (404)954-0282. **ED** Larry Stanford. **Ad Acc. Circ:** 10,500. ***Continues*** *Henry County Herald, 8750-9962.*

US/0192-0677
HENRY NEIGHBOR, THE. (1978)-. Newspaper. English. wk. Neighbor Newspapers Inc., PO Box 449, 580 Fairground Street, Marietta GA 30061. **Tel** (404)428-9411, FAX (404)422-9533.

US
HERALD-LEADER, THE. **VFOAT** Herald Leader. Vol. 63, No. 52 (Nov. 27, 1980)-. Newspaper. English. wk. $30.00. Herald Leader / Fitzgerald, 202-204 East Central Avenue, Fitzgerald GA 31750-2502. **Tel** (912)423-9331, FAX (912)423-6533. **ED** Gerald W. Pryor and Barbara Ashe (Managing Editor). **Photos**. **Ad Acc, Adv Mgr:** Becky Anderson. Full Page (B&W) $441.00. Half Page (B&W) $252.00. Full Page (Color) $491.00. Half Page (Color) $302.00. **Pub. Size:** Standard. **Circ:** 5,915. ***Continues*** *Fitzgerald Herald and Leader.*

US/0899-627X
HERALD (RINCON, GA.), THE. (THE HERALD.). (19??)-. Newspaper. English. wk. $18.00 Effingham County, GA; $21.00 other Georgia; $25.00 other. Springfield Herald, PO Drawer 799, Rincon GA 31326. **Tel** (912)826-5012. **ED** Charles Cockran and Ginny Anderson. **Bk Rev**, (Qty: 5). **Photos**. **Ad Acc**. Full Page (B&W) $677.25. Half Page (B&W) $338.63. Full Page (Color) $742.25. Half Page (Color) $403.63. **Pub. Size:** Broadsheet.

US
HERALD-TRIBUNE, THE. Vol. 52, No. 31 (June 5, 1969)-. Newspaper. English. wk. Cartersville Newspapers, PO Box 70, Cartersville GA 30120-4545. **Tel** (404)382-2211, FAX (404)382-2711. **ED** Lewis Justus. **Circ:** 7,621. ***Formed by the union of*** *Bartow Herald* ***and*** *Weekly Tribune News.*

US
HOUSTON HOME JOURNAL. ***Title Change.*** Vol. 54, No. 33 (Aug. 14, 1924)-(1994). Newspaper. English. wk. Houston Home Journal, PO Box Drawer M, Perry GA 31069. ***Continues*** *Home Journal (Perry, Ga. : 1901).* ***Merged with*** *Perry Times (Perry, Ga.), 1050-7132* ***to form*** *Houston Times-Journal, 1075-1874.*

●US/1075-1874
HOUSTON TIMES-JOURNAL. **VFOAT** Houston Times Journal. Vol. 124, No. 16 (Feb. 23, 1994)-. Newspaper. English. sw. Evans Newspapers Inc., 535 General Courtney Hodges Boulevard, Perry GA 31069. **Ad Acc**. ***Formed by the union of*** *Houston Home Journal (Perry, Ga. : 1924)* ***and*** *Perry Times (Perry, Ga.), 1050-7132.*

US
ISLANDER, THE. (19??)-. Newspaper. English. wk. $12.50. Islander / St. Simons, PO Box 20539, St. Simons GA 31522-0139. **Tel** (912)638-2765, FAX (912)638-2764. **ED** E.J. Permar, M.J. Perman (Managing Editor). **Bk Rev**, (Qty: 52). **Photos**. **Ad Acc**. Full Page (B&W) $270.00. Half Page (B&W) $140.00. Full Page (Color) $320.00. Half Page (Color) $190.00. **Pub. Size:** Tabloid. **Circ:** 2,500 paid.

US
JACKSON HERALD. Vol. 1, No. 1 (Feb. 25, 1881)-. Newspaper. English. wk. Jackson Herald Inc, PO Box 908, Jefferson GA 30549-0908. **Tel** (706)367-5233, FAX (706)367-8056. **ED** Mrs. Herman Buffington. **Bk Rev**. **Ad Acc, Adv Mgr:** Scott Buffington. **Circ:** 8,500. ***Continues*** *Forest News (Jefferson, Ga.).*

US
JEFF DAVIS LEDGER. Vol 31, No. 3 (Jan. 19, 1983)-. Newspaper. English. wk. $21.00. Hazlehurst Jeff Davis Ledger, 104 Latimer Street, Hazlehurst GA 31539. **Tel** (912)375-4225, FAX (912)375-3704. **ED** Thomas H. Purser. **Photos**. **Ad Acc, Adv Mgr:** Kay Purser. Full Page (B&W) $504.00. Half Page (B&W) $252.00. Full Page (Color) $544.00. Half Page (Color) $292.00. **Circ:** 3,800. ***Continues*** *Jeff Davis County Ledger.*

US/8755-9501
JEFFERSON REPORTER, THE. (19??)-. Newspaper. English. sw. $13.00 in county; $15.00 others in Georgia; $18.00 others. Jefferson Reporter, 202 Estelle Street, PO Box 277, Wrens GA 30833. **Tel** (706)547-6629, FAX $706)547-2259. **ED** Joyce Drinkwater. **Photos**. **Ad Acc, Adv Mgr:** Joyce Drinkwater. Full Page (B&W) $327.60. Half Page (B&W) $163.80. Full Page (Color) $367.60. Half Page (Color) $203.80. **Pub. Size:** Standard. **Circ:** 2,200.

US
JEKYLL'S GOLDEN ISLANDER. Vol. 1, No. 1 (Nov. 2, 1972)-. Newspaper. English. sm. Jekyll's Golden Islander, 5000 D Altama Avenue, Brunswick GA 31525. **Tel** (912)267-7878.

US
JOURNAL, THE. (19??)-. Newspaper. English. wk. Journal / Albany, 118 Roosevelt, PO Box 1628, Albany GA 31703. **Tel** (912)436-6134. ***Continues*** *Albany Journal (Albany, Ga.).*

US/0191-7072
KENNESAW NEIGHBOR, THE. (19??)-. Newspaper. English. wk (Published on Thursdays). Neighbor Newspapers Inc., PO Box 449, 580 Fairground Street, Marietta GA 30061. **Tel** (404)428-9411, FAX (404)422-9533. **ED** Rodney Shumake. **Circ:** 11,625.

US/1064-6876
LAKE OCONEE FREE PRESS, THE. Vol. 1, No. 1 (May 15, 1989)-. Newspaper. English. wk. $10.60. Lake Oconee Free Press, PO Drawer 191, Madison GA 30650.

US/8750-250X
LEADER-TRIBUNE (FORT VALLEY, GA.), THE. (THE LEADER-TRIBUNE.). **VFOAT** Leader Tribune. (192?)-. Newspaper. English. wk (Wed.). $18.00. Peach Publications Company Inc., PO Box 1060, Fort Valley GA 31030. **Tel** (706)846-3188. **ED** Chuck and Cindy Morley. **Photos**. **Ad Acc, Adv Mgr:** Maria Kitchens. **Pub. Size:** Broadsheet. **Circ:** 3,456. ***Continues*** *Leader-Tribune and Peachland Journal.*

US
LUDOWICI NEWS, THE. (1922)-. Newspaper. English. wk. Ludowici News, 252 West Walnut Street, Ludowici GA 31316. **Tel** (912)545-2103, FAX (912)545-2521. **ED** Ronnie Robins. **Bk Rev**. **Ad Acc**. **Circ:** 1,156.

US/0192-2483
MABLETON NEIGHBOR, THE. Newspaper. English. wk. Neighbor Newspapers Inc., PO Box 449, 580 Fairground Street, Marietta GA 30061. **Tel** (404)428-9411, FAX (404)422-9533.

US/1054-2485
MACON TELEGRAPH. 164th Year, No. 316 (Nov. 12, 1990)-. Newspaper. English. da. $142.00 per year (Mon.-Sun.); $84.00 per year (Mon.-Sat.); $70.00 per year (Mon.-Fri.); $75.96 per year (Sat.-Sun.); $62.40 per year (Sunday only). Macon Telegraph Publishing Company, 120 Broadway, Macon GA 31213. **Tel** (912)744-4200. **ED** Richard D. Thomas. **Bk Rev**, (Qty: 6-12). **Ad Acc, Adv Mgr:** Alton Brown, **Tel** (912)-477-8434. **Circ:** 75,000 daily, 104 Sunday'. available on an online database (file 635/Full-text) from DIALOG. Documents available from UMI Article Clearinghouse. ***Continues*** *Macon Telegraph and News (Macon, Ga. : 1983), 0746-3782.*
Desc: Local, state, national, international news, features, sports and advertising.
Ind/Abst Bus. Dateline (Dec. 16, 1991-) [Full Txt.].

US
MADISONIAN, THE. Vol. 89, No. 52 (Dec. 26, 1957)-. Newspaper. English. wk. Madison Newspapers, PO Box 191, Madison GA 30650-0191. **Tel** (706)342-2424, FAX (706)342-1300. **ED** Adelaide Ponder. **Ad Acc, Adv Mgr:** Sara Speer. **Circ:** 4,564. ***Continues*** *Madisonian Combined with the Morgan County News.*

US
MANCHESTER STAR-MERCURY. **VFOAT** Manchester Star Mercury. Vol. 17, No. 3 (Jan. 19, 1983)-. Newspaper. English. wk. $18.00. Peach Publications Company Inc., PO Box 1060, Fort Valley GA 31030. **Tel** (706)846-3188. **ED** Mike Hale. **Photos**. **Ad Acc, Adv Mgr:** Mike Hale, **Tel** (706)846-3188. **Pub. Size:** Broadsheet. **Circ:** 3,826. available in microform. ***Continues*** *Star Mercury.*

US/8750-4618
MARIETTA DAILY JOURNAL (MARIETTA, GA.), THE. (THE MARIETTA DAILY JOURNAL.). Vol. 78, No. 185 (Sept.18, 1944)-. Newspaper. English. da (Sun.-Fri.). $88.30 carrier, $120.00 mail. Marietta Daily Journal, 580 Fairground Street, Box 449, Marietta GA 30060. **Tel** (404)428-9411. **ED** Bobby Nesbit. **Circ:** 27,201. available on an online database (file 635/Full-Text) from DIALOG. Documents available from UMI Article Clearinghouse. ***Continues*** *Marietta Journal (Marietta, Ga. : 1918).*
Ind/Abst Bus. Dateline (Dec. 23, 1991-) [Full Txt.].

US
MCDUFFIE PROGRESS, THE. (1901)-. Newspaper. English. sw. McDuffie Progress, 101 Church Street, Thomson GA 30824. **Tel** (404)595-1601. **ED** Tray Hutchinson. **Ad Acc**. **Circ:** 4,300.

US
MERIWETHER VINDICATOR, THE. Vol. 14, No. 2 (Dec. 25, 1885)-. Newspaper. English. wk. PO Box A, Greenville GA 31827. ***Continues*** *Meriwether County Vindicator (Greenville, Ga. : 1872).*

US
MOULTRIE OBSERVER, THE. Vol. 14, No. 248 (Feb. 15, 1919)-. Newspaper. English. da. $88.00. Observer Publishing Co. / Moultrie, Moultrie Observer, 25 North Main Street, Moultrie GA 31768. **Tel** (912)985-4545, FAX (912)985-3569. **ED** Dwain Walden. **Ad Acc, Adv Mgr:** Velda Duke. **Circ:** 7,750. ***Continues*** *Daily Observer (Moultrie, Ga.).*

US/0194-2050
MULTI-COUNTY STAR. Newspaper. English. wk. Multi-County Star, PO Box 1278, Covington GA 30209.

US/1051-4147
MUNDO HISPANICO (ATLANTA, GA.). (MUNDO HISPANICO.). [Mundo hisp.]. (1979)-. Newspaper. Spanish (English). bm. $50.00. Mundo Hispanico, PO Box 13808, Station K, Atlanta GA 30324. **Tel** (404)881-0441, FAX (404)881-6085. **ED** Lino Dominguez. **DD** 975. **Bk Rev**. **Photos**. **Ad Acc, Adv Mgr:** Tabiola Dorrh. Full Page (B&W) $962.50. Half Page (B&W) $490.00. **Pub. Size:** Tabloid. **Wire Svcs.:** AP. **Circ:** 21,000 unpaid (ctrl). available on CD-ROM.
Desc: Bilingual Hispanic community newspaper for the state of Georgia.

US/0883-2536
NEWNAN TIMES-HERALD, THE. **VFOAT** Newnan Times Herald. Vol. 1, No. 1 (Dec. 24, 1947)-. Newspaper. English. wk. $26.50. Newnan Times-Herald, 16 Jefferson Street, PO Box 1052, Newnan GA 30264. **Tel** (404)253-1576, FAX (404)253-2538. **ED** Ellen Corker and Marianne Thomasson (Managing Editor). **Bk Rev**, (Qty: 52). **Photos**. **Ad Acc, Adv Mgr:** Lamar Truitt. Full Page (B&W) $709.50. Half Page (B&W) $354.75. Full Page (Color) $799.50. Half Page (Color) $444.75. **Pub. Size:** Standard. **Wire Svcs.:** AP. available in microform. ***Formed by the union of*** *Newnan Times* ***and*** *Newnan Herald (Newnan, Ga. : 1915).*

US
NEWS LEADER, THE. (1978)-. Newspaper. English. wk. Morris Communications Corporation, PO Box 936, Augusta GA 30903-0936. **Tel** (706)724-0851, FAX (706)722-7403. **ED** Dennis Sodomka. **Ad Acc, Adv Mgr:** Don Bailey. **Circ:** 2,800.

US
NEWS-REPORTER (WASHINGTON, GA.). (THE NEWS-REPORTER.). **VFOAT** News Reporter; Washington News-Reporter; Wilkes County News. Vol. 3, No. 17 (June 6, 1919)-. Newspaper. English. wk. News-Reporter, 116 West Robert Toombs Avenue, Washington GA 30673. ***Formed by the union of*** *Washington Reporter (Washington, Ga.)* ***and*** *Wilkes County News.*

US
NORTH GEORGIA NEWS, THE. (1922)-. Newspaper. English. wk. Free to zip code 35012; $18.00 other. North Georgia News, PO Box 2029, Blairsville GA 30512. **Tel** (404)745-6343.

US
NORTHEAST GEORGIAN. (19??)-. Newspaper. English. wk. $13.50 Habersham, White and Banks couties, $20.00 other. Northeast Georgian, PO Box 1555, Cornelia GA 30531. **Tel** (404)778-4215.

US/0192-0731
NORTHSIDE NEIGHBOR, THE. (Mar. 1968)-. Newspaper. English. wk. $50.00. Neighbor Newspapers Inc., PO Box 449, 580 Fairground Street, Marietta GA 30061. **Tel** (404)428-9411, FAX (404)422-9533. **ED** Bobby Nesbitt. **Circ:** 24,228.

US/0192-0685
PAULDING NEIGHBOR, THE. Newspaper. English. wk. Neighbor Newspapers Inc., PO Box 449, 580 Fairground Street, Marietta GA 30061. **Tel** (404)428-9411, FAX (404)422-9533.

US/1060-3646
PELHAM JOURNAL, THE. **VFOAT** Pelham Semi-Weekly Journal; Home Lance. Vol. 1, No. 1 (Oct. 10, 1902)-. Newspaper. English. wk. $10.60 Georgia; $15.90 US. Pelham Journal, PO Box 472, Pelham GA 31779. **Tel** (912)294-3661. ***Formed by the union of*** *South Georgia Home* ***and*** *Free Lance.*

US
POST-SEARCH LIGHT, THE. **VFOAT** Post Search Light; Post Searchlight. (1915)-. Newspaper. English. sw. Post-Search Light, 301 North Crawford Street, Bainbridge GA 31717-3612. **Tel** (912)246-2827, FAX (912)246-7665. **ED** James E. Smith. **Ad Acc**. **Circ:** 6,250. ***Formed by the union of*** *Bainbridge Post* ***and*** *Bainbridge Searchlight.*

US/0191-5525
POWDER SPRINGS NEIGHBOR. (1969)-. Newspaper. English. wk. Neighbor Newspapers Inc., PO Box 449, 580 Fairground Street, Marietta GA 30061. **Tel** (404)428-9411, FAX (404)422-9533.

US
PRESS-SENTINEL, THE. **VFOAT** Press Sentinel. Vol. 114, No. 1 (Feb. 3, 1977)-. Newspaper. English. sw. $14.95 Wayne County; $24.95 other. Press Sentinel / Jesup, PO Box 607, Jesup GA 31545. **Tel** (912)427-3757. **ED** Joan Matthews. **Ad Acc**. **Circ:** 7,200. ***Formed by the union of*** *Wayne County Press (Jesup, Ga.)* ***and*** *Jesup Sentinel (Jesup, Ga. : 1913).*

US/1050-1401
ROCKDALE CITIZEN, THE. Vol. 1, No. 1 (July 30, 1953)-. Newspaper. English. da. $60.00. Rockdale Citizen, 969 South Main Street, PO Box 136, Conyers GA 30207. **Tel** (404)483-7108. **ED** Fred Turner. **Bk Rev**, (Qty: 10). **Photos**. **Ad Acc, Adv Mgr:** Jane Patterson. Full Page (B&W) $739.35. Half Page (B&W) $396.68. Full Page (Color) $888.35. Half Page (Color) $491.68. **Pub. Size:** Broadsheet. **Wire Svcs.:** AP. ***Absorbed*** *Conyers News.*

US/0199-6282
ROCKDALE NEIGHBOR, THE. Vol. 1- (Feb. 1980)-. Newspaper. English. wk. Neighbor Newspapers Inc., PO Box 449, 580 Fairground Street, Marietta GA 30061. **Tel** (404)428-9411, FAX (404)422-9533.

US/0192-2637
ROSWELL NEIGHBOR, THE. Vol. 6, No. 51 (Dec. 19, 1968)-. Newspaper. English. wk. $50.00. Neighbor Newspapers Inc., PO Box 449, 580 Fairground Street, Marietta GA 30061. **Tel** (404)428-9411, FAX (404)422-9533. **Continues** Roswell Herald.

US/0747-3710
SANDERSVILLE PROGRESS, THE. Vol. 8, No. 41 (Mar. 2, 1917)-. Newspaper. English. wk (Published on Thursdays). Sandersville Georgian Inc, PO Box 431, Sandersville GA 31082-0431. **Tel** (912)552-3161, FAX (912)552-5177. **ED** Robert Garrett. **Ad Acc, Adv Mgr:** Melissa Brown. **Circ:** 5,100. **Continues** Sandersville Georgian (Sandersville, Ga. : 1909); **Absorbed** Sandersville Georgian (Sandersville, Ga. : 1971).

US/0192-0715
SANDY SPRINGS NEIGHBOR, THE. (1968)-. Newspaper. English. wk. $50.00. Neighbor Newspapers Inc., PO Box 449, 580 Fairground Street, Marietta GA 30061. **Tel** (404)428-9411, FAX (404)422-9533.

US/8750-4685
SAVANNAH EVENING PRESS. VFOAT Savannah Morning News and Savannah Evening Press. (1931)-. Newspaper. English. da (except New Years Day, Memorial Day, July 4th, Labor Day, Thanksgiving, and Christmas). $60.00 Georgia and South Carolina; $74.00 other. Savannah Evening Press, PO Box 1088 Savannah GA 31402. **Tel** (912)236-9511. **ED** Wallace M. Davis Jr. **LC** 7002. **Bk Rev. Ad Acc. Circ:** 22,000. **Continues** Savannah Press.

US/8750-8273
SAVANNAH MORNING NEWS, SAVANNAH EVENING PRESS (COASTAL EMPIRE ED.). (SAVANNAH MORNING NEWS, SAVANNAH EVENING PRESS.). VFOAT Savannah Evening Press; Savannah Morning News; Savannah News Press; Savannah News-Press. (19??)-. Newspaper. English. da. $66.00 Georgia and South Carolina; $90.00 Others. Savannah Evening Press, PO Box 1088, Savannah GA 31402. **Tel** (912)236-9511. **ED** W. M. Davis Jr. **Circ:** 74,283.

US/0191-5487
SMYRNA NEIGHBOR, THE. Newspaper. English. wk. Neighbor Newspapers Inc., PO Box 449, 580 Fairground Street, Marietta GA 30061. **Tel** (404)428-9411, FAX (404)422-9533. **ED** Bobby Nesbitt. **Circ:** 10,599.

US
SOPERTON NEWS, THE. (1914)-. Newspaper. English. wk. $20.50 (one year), $31.00 (two year). Soperton News, PO Box 537, Main and Second Streets, Soperton GA 30457. **Tel** (912)529-6624. **ED** James T. Windsor. **LC** 7488-X. **Ad Acc. Circ:** 3,950.

US/0199-6029
SOUTH DEKALB NEIGHBOR, THE. Vol. 1 (Feb. 1980)-. Newspaper. English. wk. $50.00. Neighbor Newspapers Inc., PO Box 449, 580 Fairground Street, Marietta GA 30061. **Tel** (404)428-9411, FAX (404)422-9533. **Circ:** 28,340.

US/0192-0693
SOUTH FULTON NEIGHBOR, THE. (19??)-. Newspaper. English. wk. $50.00. Neighbor Newspapers Inc., PO Box 449, 580 Fairground Street, Marietta GA 30061. **Tel** (404)428-9411, FAX (404)422-9533.

US/0192-0774
SOUTHSIDE AND FAYETTE SUN. (19??)-. Newspaper. English. wk. Southside and Fayette Sun, 1614 Thompson Avenue, East Point GA 30344.

US/0746-4665
STATESBORO HERALD. Vol. 1, no. 1 (Dec. 21, 1970)-. Newspaper. English. da. $102.00. Statesboro Herald, Box 888, 1 Herald Square, Statesboro GA 30458. **Tel** (912)764-9031. **Continues** Bulloch Herald and the Bulloch Times.

US
STONE MOUNTAIN DEKALB NEIGHBOR. Newspaper. English. wk. Neighbor Newspapers Inc., PO Box 449, 580 Fairground Street, Marietta GA 30061. **Tel** (404)428-9411, FAX (404)422-9533. **Continues** Stone Mountain Neighbor.

US
SUMMERVILLE NEWS, THE. Vol. 9, No. 32 (Oct. 14, 1896)-. Newspaper. English. wk. Summerville News, PO Box 310, Summerville GA 30747-0310. **Tel** (706)857-2494, FAX (706)857-2393. **ED** Tommy Toles. **Ad Acc. Circ:** 7,800. **Continues** Chattooga News.

US/8750-5312
SYLVESTER LOCAL NEWS, THE. VFOAT Sylvester, Ga. Local News. Newspaper. English. wk. Sylvester Local News, PO Box 387, Sylvester GA 31791. **Continues** Sylvester Local.

US/0885-6567
TALBOTTON NEW ERA. Newspaper. English. wk. Talbotton New Era, PO Box 248, Talbotton GA 31827.

US
TELFAIR TIMES, THE. Vol. 32, No. 7 (Feb. 6, 1985)-. Newspaper. English. wk $10.00 Telfair County; $15.00 other. Telfair Times, PO Box 459, Helena GA 31037. **Tel** (912)868-5776. **Continues** Telfair Times Combined with the Lumber City Log.

US/1050-6012
THIS WEEK IN PEACHTREE CITY. VFOAT This Week. (1974)-. Newspaper. English. tw. This Week in Peachtree City, 111 Petrol Point, PO Box 2468, Peachtree City GA 30269. **Tel** (404)487-7729. available on microfilm.

US
THOMASTON TIMES AND THE FREE PRESS, THE. Vol. 108, No. 12 (Mar. 31, 1977)-. Newspaper. English. sw. Thomaston Times, PO Box 430, Thomaston GA 30286-2755. **Tel** (706)647-5414, FAX (706)647-2833. **ED** Cy Woods. **Ad Acc. Circ:** 6,000. Formed by the union of Thomaston Times and Free Press (Thomaston, Ga.).

US/0746-4894
THOMASVILLE TIMES-ENTERPRISE. VFOAT Thomasville Times Enterprise; Times Enterprise; Times-Enterprise. Vol. 35, No. 275 (Jan. 2, 1925)-. Newspaper. English. da (Mon.-Sat.). $83.40. Thomasville Times Enterprise, PO Box 650, Thomasville GA 31792. **Tel** (912)226-2400. **ED** Charles Blanton III. **Circ:** 11,358. **Continues** Daily Times-Enterprise.

US/1065-2884
TIFTON GAZETTE (DAILY), THE. (THE TIFTON GAZETTE.). Vol. 65, No. 1 (Sept. 14, 1979)-. Newspaper. English. da. $7.50 per month. Tifton Gazette, PO Box 708, Tifton GA 31793. **Tel** (912)382-4321, FAX (912)387-7322. **ED** James McKee, Mike Jones (Managing Editor). **Photos. Ad Acc, Adv Mgr:** Randy Blalock. Full Page (B&W) $1052.64. Half Page (B&W) $565.02. Full Page (Color) $1183.64. Half Page (Color) $629.52. **Pub. Size:** Broadsheet. **Wire Svcs.:** AP. **Circ:** 9,431 paid. available in microform. **Continues** Daily Tifton Gazette.

US
TIMES, THE. Vol. 26, No. 208 (Sept. 1, 1972)-. Newspaper. English. ds $135.72. Gainesville Times, PO Box 838, Gainesville GA 30503. **Tel** (404)532-1234, FAX (404)532-0457. **ED** Johnny Vardeman (editor-in-chief) and John Druckenmiller (managing editor). **Bk Rev** (Qty: 12/year). **Photos. Ad Acc, Adv Mgr:** Rebecca Ladewig. Full Page (B&W) $2486.00. Half Page (B&W) $1243.00. Full Page (Color) $2724.00. Half Page (Color) $1470.00. **Pub. Size:** Broadsheet. **Wire Svcs.:** AP, GN. **Circ:** 22,500. **Continues** Daily Times (Gainesville, Ga.).

US/1049-9458
TIMES-GEORGIAN (CARROLLTON, GA.). (TIMES-GEORGIAN.). VFOAT Times Georgian. Vol. 113, No. 109 (May 7, 1985)-. Newspaper. English. da. $55.00 Carroll County; $61.00 adjoining counties; $67.00 other. Carroll Publishing Co, PO Box 460, Carrollton GA 30117. **Tel** (404)834-6631, FAX (404)834-9991. **ED** Julianne Foster. **Ad Acc, Adv Mgr:** Bill Chaple. **Circ:** 10,172. **Continues** Daily Times-Georgian, 8750-5193.

US
TIMES JOURNAL SPOTLIGHT. VFOAT Times-Journal Spotlight. Vol. 103, No. 24 (June 12, 1975)-. Newspaper. English. wk. $10.92 Dodge County; $14.56 Georgia; $18.72 other. Times Journal Spotlight, PO Drawer 707, 227 College Street, Eastman GA 31023. **Tel** (912)374-5562. **Continues** New Times Journal Spotlight.

US
TOCCOA RECORD, THE. (1901)-. Newspaper. English. wk. $8.32 Toccoa; $12.48 Georgia; $15.60 other. Toccoa Record, PO Drawer 1069, 151 West Doyle Street, Toccoa GA 30577. **Tel** (404)886-9476. **Continues** Southern Record (Toccoa, Ga.).

US
TRUE CITIZEN, THE. Vol. 1, No. 1 (Apr. 28, 1882)-. Newspaper. English. wk. $16.00 Burk County, Georgia; $21.00 other Georgia; $27.00 other US; $37.80 other. The True Citizen, PO Box 948, Waynesboro GA 30830. **Tel** (404)554-2111. **Continues** Burke News.

US
UNION RECORDER. VFOAT Union-Recorder; Union Recorder the Baldwin News. Vol. 56, No. 39 (Apr. 6, 1886)-. Newspaper. English. da. $72.80. Milledgeville Union Recorder, PO Box 1010, Milledgeville GA 31061-1010. **Tel** (912)452-0567, FAX (912)452-9033. **ED** Susan Patterson (Editor-in-Chief) and Dan Baker (Managing Editor). **Photos. Ad Acc, Adv Mgr:** Percy Canon. Full Page (B&W) $1,070.00. Half Page (B&W) $522.90. Full Page (Color) $1,169.70. Half Page (Color) $621.90. **Pub. Size:** Standard. **Wire Svcs.:** AP, KR. **Circ:** 8,500. **Continues** Union and Recorder (Milledgeville, Ga. : 1872).

US
VALDOSTA DAILY TIMES, THE. (Oct. 16, 1905)-. Newspaper. English. da. $120.00. Valdosta Daily Times, PO Box 968, Valdosta GA 31601. **Tel** (912)244-1880, FAX (912)244-2560. **ED** Jerry Cruy. **Bk Rev. Photos. Ad Acc, Adv Mgr:** Bill Wallace. Full Page (B&W) $1168.74. Half Page (B&W) $610.82. Full Page (Color) $1329.74. Half Page (Color) $771.82. **Pub. Size:** Standard. **Wire Svcs.:** AP. **Circ:** 19,280. available in microform from University Microfilms International (UMI). **Continues** Valdosta Times.

US/0895-7312
VILLA RICAN, THE. (19??)-. Newspaper. English. wk. Worrell Enterprises, PO Box 757, Villa Rica GA 30180. **Tel** (404)459-5166. **Absorbed** Villa Rica Breeze.

US
WALKER COUNTY MESSENGER. (187?)-. Newspaper. English. sw. Walker County Messenger, 120 East Patton Street, La Fayette GA 30728. **Tel** (404)638-1859.

US/0893-410X
WALTON TRIBUNE, THE. (1900)-. Newspaper. English. sw. $25.00 Walton County, GA; $30.00 US; $37.00 other. Monroe Newspapers Inc., PO Box 808, Monroe GA 30655. **Tel** (404)267-8371. **ED** Audrey A. Barrow. **Ad Acc. Circ:** 5,800 (ctrl). **Desc:** Covers local and county news.

US
WARRENTON CLIPPER (WARRENTON, GA. : 1876). (THE WARRENTON CLIPPER.). (187?)-. Newspaper. English. wk. $22.60 Georgia; $24.70 other. Warrenton Clipper, PO Box 306, Warrenton GA 30828. **Continues** Georgia Clipper (Warrenton, Ga.).

US
WAYCROSS JOURNAL-HERALD. VFOAT Waycross Journal Herald. Began with Oct. 1, (1914)-. Newspaper. English. da. $114.00 (mail). Waycross Journal Herald, PO Box 219, Waycross GA 31501. **Tel** (912)283-2244, FAX (912)283-0740. **ED** Jack Williams. **Ad Acc, Adv Mgr:** David Tanner. **Circ:** 13,435. **Continues** Waycross Daily Journal and Evening Herald.

US
WINDER NEWS, THE. Vol. 32, No. 23 (Oct. 8, 1925)-. Newspaper. English. wk. $24.00. Winder News, PO Drawer C, Winder GA 30680. **Tel** (404)867-7557, FAX (404)867-1034. **ED** LeAnne Bell. **Bk Rev,** (Qty: 4). **Photos. Ad Acc, Adv Mgr:** Debbie Burgamy. Full Page (B&W) $995.40. Half Page (B&W) $497.70. Full Page (Color) $1085.40. Half Page (Color) $587.70. **Pub. Size:** Broadsheet. **Circ:** 6,700. **Continues** Winder News and the Barrow Times; **Absorbed** Winder Leader.

US/0747-3737
WRIGHTSVILLE HEADLIGHT, THE. VFOAT Wrightsville Headlight and the Johnson County News. (19??)-. Newspaper. English. wk. $15.90 Johnson County; $23.85 others in Georgia; $30.00 others. Wrightsville Headlight, PO Box 290, Wrightsville GA 31096. **Tel** (912)864-3528, FAX (912)864-2166. **ED** Brenda Hollingsworth. **Bk Rev,** (Qty: 2-4). **Photos. Ad Acc, Adv Mgr:** Sherry Lanier. Full Page (B&W) $387.00. Half Page (B&W) $189.00. Full Page (Color) $462.80. Half Page (Color) $264.00. **Pub. Size:** Standard. **Circ:** 2,150. available in microform. **Absorbed** Johnson County News (Wrightsville, Ga.).

HAWAII

US/0744-4028
GARDEN ISLAND, THE. Newspaper. English. da (except Thurs.). Kaua'i Publishing Company, 3137 Kuhio Hwy, Lihue HI 96766. **Tel** (808)245-3681. **ED** John M Uyeno. **Circ:** 9,407.

US
HA UY DI THI BAO. VFOAT Hawaii News. (Mar. 15, 1990)-. Newspaper. Vietnamese. mo. Ha Uy Di Thi Bao, PO Box 8404, Honolulu HI 96830.

US/0884-3139
HANGUK ILBO, HAWAI. VFOAT Korea Times, Hawaii. Newspaper. Korean. da. Korea Times / Honolulu, 1839 South King Street, Honolulu HI 96826.

US
HAWAII FILIPINO NEWS HONOLULU, HAWAII : 1985). Ceased. (HAWAII FILIPINO NEWS.). VFOAT Filipino News. Vol. 9, No. 11 (Oct. 1-15, 1985)-Ceased ?. Newspaper. English (English). sm.

Hawaii Filipino News, 275 Puuhale Road, Honolulu HI 96819. **Tel** (808)841-1886. ***Continues*** *Hawaii News (Honolulu, Hawaii).*

US/8750-913X
HAWAII HERALD (1969). (THE HAWAII HERALD.). Vol. 1, No. 1 (May 16, 1980)-. Newspaper. English. sm. $20.00. The Hawaii Herald, PO Box 17429, Honolulu HI 96817. **Tel** (808)845-2255, FAX (808)847-7215. **ED** Arnold T Hiura. Index available. cum. index. **Bk Rev. Ad Acc. Circ:** 7,500 (ctrl). available on microfiche. ***Continues*** *Hawaii Herald (Honolulu, Hawaii : 1969), 8750-913X.*
Desc: Covers cultural, historical and contemporary issues affecting Japanese Americans in Hawaii.

US
HAWAII HOCHI, THE. VFOAT Hawai Hochi. Vol. 27, No. 10 (Jan. 11, 1952)-. Newspaper. English (Japanese). da. Hawaii Hochi, 917 Kokea Street, Honolulu HI 96817. **Tel** (808)845-2255. ***Continues*** *Hawaii Herald (Honolulu, Hawaii : 1942).*

US
HAWAII MARINE. Added/Corp Kaneohe Marine Corps Air Station (Hawaii). Joint Public Affairs Office. (1973)-. Newspaper. English. wk. Free to residents of government housing at air station. RFD Publications Inc, 46-016 Alaloa Street, Kaneohe HI 96744. **Tel** (808)235-5881. ***Continues*** *Windward Marine.*

US
HAWAII NAVY NEWS. Newspaper. English. wk. RFD Publications Inc, 46-016 Alaloa Street, Kaneohe HI 96744. **Tel** (808)235-5881.

US
HAWAII NEWS. Vol. 8, No. 18 (Feb. 1-16, 1985)-. Newspaper. English (English). sm. $10.00 (24 issues), $20.00 (48 issues) add $15.00 postage and handling other. Creative Publishing Pacific Inc, 275 Puuhale Road, Honolulu HI 96818. ***Continues*** *Hawaii Filipino News (Honolulu, Hawaii : 1977), 0732-9970.*

US
HAWAIIAN FALCON. Newspaper. English. wk. Laissez Faire Group Inc, 1290 Maunakea Street/Suite 309, Honolulu HI 96817.

US/1053-0045
HILO TIMES, THE. VFOAT Hiro Taimusu. Began in 1955?. Newspaper. Japanese (Japanese). sm. Hilo Times, 639 Kilauea Avenue, Hilo HI 96720.

US
HILO TRIBUNE HERALD. (1895)-. Newspaper. English. da. Hilo Tribune Herald, PO Box 767, Hilo HI 96720.

US/1072-7191
HONOLULU ADVERTISER, THE. VFOAT Sunday Advertiser; Sunday Star-Bulletin & Advertiser; Sunday Star Bulletin and Advertiser. 64th Year, No. 12,249 (March 31, 1921)-. Newspaper. English. da. Hawaii Newspaper Agency Inc. / Department of Circulation, PO Box 3350, Honolulu HI 96801. **Tel** (808)525-8000, (808)525-7657, FAX (808)525-7423. cum. index. **Circ:** 85,186. available on microfilm from University Microfilms International (UMI); available on an online database (file 635/Full-Text) from DIALOG. Documents available from UMI Article Clearinghouse. ***Continues*** *Pacific Commercial Advertiser (Honolulu, Hawaii : 1885).*
Ind/Abst Bus. Dateline (Dec. 11, 1991-) [Full Txt.].

US
HONOLULU STAR-BULLETIN. VFOAT Honolulu Star Bulletin; Saturday Star Bulletin; Sunday Star Bulletin; Sunday Star-Bulletin & Advertiser; Sunday Star Bulletin and Advertiser. Vol. 20, No. 6318 (July 1, 1912)-. Newspaper. English. ds. $338.00 US and Pacific Islands; $1,220.00 US and Canada (air mail); $626.60 (ship mail), $2,948.00 (air mail) other. Hawaii Newspaper Agency Inc. / Department of Circulation, PO Box 3350, Honolulu HI 96801. **Tel** (808)525-8000, (808)525-7657, FAX (808)525-7423. **ED** John Flanagan (Editor in Chief) and David Shapiro (Managing Editor). **Bk Rev**, (Qty: 50-75). **Photos. Ad Acc, Adv Mgr:** Howard Mullenary, **Tel** (808)525-7658. Full Page (B&W) $7742.28. Half Page (B&W) $4221.53. Full Page (Color) $8634.28. Half Page (Color) $5113.53. **Pub. Size:** Standard. **Circ:** 96,000. available on microfilm from University of Hawaii Microfilm; and University Microfilms International (UMI); available on an online database (file 635/Full-Text) from DIALOG. Documents available from UMI Article Clearinghouse. ***Formed by the union of*** *Hawaiian Star* ***and*** *Evening Bulletin (Honolulu, Hawaii).*
Ind/Abst Bus. Dateline (Nov. 26, 1991-) [Full Txt.].

US/1057-414X
HONOLULU WEEKLY. Vol. 1, Issue 1 (July 17, 1991)-. Newspaper. English. wk. $50.00. Honolulu Weekly, 1200 College Walk, Suite 212, Honolulu HI 96817. **Tel** (808)528-1475, FAX (808)528-3144. **ED** Christine Whalen. **Bk Rev**, (Qty: 10). **Photos. Ad Acc, Adv Mgr:** Laurie Carlson. Full Page (B&W) $1,760.00. Half Page (B&W) $950.00. Full Page (Color) $2,000.00. Half Page (Color) $1,260.00. **Pub. Size:** Broadsheet. **Wire Svcs.:** AN.

US
LAHAINA NEWS, THE. Summer 1979. Newspaper. English. wk. $10.00 Hawaii, $12.00 US and Canada. Lahaina News, PO Box 221, Lahaina HI 96761.

US
LANAIAN (LANAI CITY, HAWAII : 1978). (THE LANAIAN.). Began with Nov. 1978 issue. Newspaper. English. mo. Lanai Community Services Council, PO Box 327, Lanai City HI 96763.

US/8750-457X
MAUI NEWS, THE. VFOAT Semi-Weekly Maui News; Daily Maui News. Vol. 1, No. 1 (Feb. 17, 1900)-. Newspaper. English. da (except Sat., Christmas Day, and New Years' Day). Maui Publishing Company, PO Box 550, Wailuku Maui HI 96793-0550. **Tel** (808)244-3981. **ED** Nora I Cooper. **Circ:** 18,000.

US
NORTH OAHU PLANET. Vol. 1, No. 18 (Oct. 10/23 1990)-. Newspaper. English. bw. North Oahu Planet, 66-250 Kam Highway, Suite 214, Haleiwa HI 96712. ***Continues*** *North Oahu Press.*

US/0030-8552
PACIFIC BUSINESS NEWS. [Pac. bus. news]. Vol. 1, No. 1 (March 18, 1963)-. Newspaper. English. Fifty-two times a year (Mon.). Crossroads Press Inc., PO Box 833, Honolulu HI 96808. **Tel** (808)521-0021. available on microfilm from University Microfilms International (UMI); available on an online database (files 635,648/Full-Text) from DIALOG. Documents available from UMI Article Clearinghouse.
Ind/Abst Acad. Search (July 1993-); Bus. Dateline; Bus. Index (Jan. 1985-Dec. 1985); Bus. Source (Jul. 1993-); Gen. BusinessFile (Jan. 1985-Dec. 1985); Gen. Period. Index (Jan. 1985-Dec. 1985); INFO-SOUTH Abstr.; Mag. Search; PROMT; Trade Ind. ASAP [Full Txt.]; Trade Ind. Index [Full Txt.].

US
SUN-FLYER. VAT Sun Flyer. (1984)-. Newspaper. English. wk. Free. RFD Publications Inc, 46-016 Alaloa Street, Kaneohe HI 96744. **Tel** (808)235-5881. **ED** Theodore Kurrus. **Circ:** 4,708.

US/0744-4591
WEST HAWAII TODAY. Vol. 1, No. 1 (July 31, 1968)-. Newspaper. English. da. West Hawaii Today, PO Box 789, Kailua Kona HI 96745. **Tel** (808)329-9311, FAX (808)329-4860. **ED** Reed Flickinger. **Bk Rev. Ad Acc. Circ:** 15,500. ***Continues*** *Kona Weekly Tribune-Herald.*

IDAHO

US
ABERDEEN TIMES, THE. (1911)-. Newspaper. English. wk (Published on Wednesdays). $20.00 Idaho; $24.00 other. Aberdeen Times, PO Box X, Aberdeen ID 83210. **Tel** (208)397-4440, FAX (208)226-5295. **ED** Farhana Hibbert. **Bk Rev. Photos. Ad Acc.** Full Page (B&W) $602.00. Half Page (B&W) $308.00. Full Page (Color) $702.00. Half Page (Color) $408.00.

US
ADVOCATE, THE. (Nov. 1986)-. Newspaper. English. wk (Published on Wednesdays). The Advocate / Idaho, 112 Main, Cascade ID 83611. **Tel** (208)382-3233, FAX (208)382-6728. **ED** Michael Stewart. **Bk Rev. Ad Acc. Circ:** 2,400.

US/0890-1511
ARCO ADVERTISER, THE. Vol. 1, No. 1 (March 12, 1909)-. Newspaper. English. Fifty-two times a year (Thurs.). $14.50 Local; $17.00 others. Arco Advertiser, PO Box 803, Arco ID 83213-0803. **Tel** (208)527-3038, FAX (208)527-8210. **ED** Donald L. Cammack, and C. L. Cammack (Managing Editor). **Bk Rev. Photos. Ad Acc, Adv Mgr:** Tom Cammack. Full Page (B&W) $472.50. Half Page (B&W) $236.25. **Pub. Size:** Standard. **Circ:** 1,844.
Desc: A traditional community newspaper which reaches the adult population in our trade area.

US/0896-1409
ARGONAUT (MOSCOW, IDAHO). (THE ARGONAUT.). Periodical. English. sw. University of Idaho Student Union Building, Moscow ID 83843. ***Continues*** *Idaho Argonaut.*

US/1047-6822
BONNER COUNTY DAILY BEE. Vol. 23, No. 87 (Oct. 3, 1988)-. Newspaper. English. da. Bonner County Daily Bee, 310 Church, Sandpoint ID 83864. **Tel** (208)263-9534, FAX (208)263-9091. **ED** David Keys. **Bk Rev. Ad Acc, Adv Mgr:** James Thompson. **Circ:** 32,000. ***Continues*** *Sandpoint Daily Bee.*

US/1064-9298
BONNERS FERRY HERALD. Vol. 14, No. 27 (Dec. 31, 1904)-. Newspaper. English. sw (Published on Wednesdays & Fridays). $25.50 Boundary County; $27.50 other Idaho; $29.50 other. Bonners Ferry Herald, PO Box 539, Bonners Ferry ID 83805. **Tel** (208)267-5521, FAX (208)267-5523. **ED** David Keys. **Bk Rev. Ad Acc. Circ:** 2,200. ***Continues*** *Kootenai Herald;* ***Absorbed*** *Kootenai Valley Sentinel and the Bonners Ferry Times (Bonners Ferry, Idaho : 1935).*

US
BUHL HERALD, THE. (June 25, 1909)-. Newspaper. English. wk (Published on Wednesdays). Buhl Herald Inc, 124 South Broadway, PO Box 312, Buhl ID 83316. **Tel** (208)543-4335, FAX (208)543-6834. **ED** Sandra Wisecaver. **Bk Rev. Ad Acc. Circ:** 3,200. ***Continues*** *Filer Films.*

US
CARIBOU COUNTY SUN. VFOAT Caribou County Sun and Soda Springs Sun. Vol. 24, No. 20 (Mar. 31, 1955)-. Newspaper. English. wk. $16.00 (in county), $20.00 (out of county). Caribou County Sun, PO Box 815, Soda Springs ID 83276. **ED** Mark Steele. **Photos. Ad Acc.** Full Page (B&W) $554.70. Half Page (B&W) $277.35. Full Page (Color) $554.70 plus $150.00. Half Page (Color) $277.35 plus $150.00. **Pub. Size:** Standard. **Circ:** 2,900. ***Continues*** *Caribou County Sun and the Soda Springs Sun.*

US/0747-248X
CENTRAL IDAHO STAR-NEWS, THE. VFOAT Central Idaho Star News; Star-News. (19??)-. Newspaper. English. wk. $19.80 Adams & Valley counties, Idaho; $23.50 other Idaho; $28.50 other. Star-News / Idaho, PO Box 985, 1000 First Street, McCall ID 83638. **Tel** (208)634-2123. **ED** Tom Grote. **Bk Rev. Photos. Ad Acc, Adv Mgr:** Tom Grote. **Pub. Size:** Broadsheet. **Circ:** 4,000. available in microform.

US
CENTRAL IDAHO STAR-NEWS, THE. VFOAT Central Idaho Star News. Vol. 9, No. 38 (July 7, 1977)-. Newspaper. English. wk (Published on Thursdays). Central Idaho Publishing, 1000 First Street, McCall ID 83638. **Tel** (208)634-2123, FAX (208)634-4950. **ED** Tom Grote. **Bk Rev. Ad Acc. Circ:** 4,000. ***Continues*** *Star-News (Cascade, Idaho).*

US
CLEARWATER TRIBUNE. Vol. 11, No. 6 (May 5, 1922)-. Newspaper. English. wk. $23.50. Clearwater Tribune, PO Box 71, Orofino ID 83544. **ED** Cloann McNall and Marcie Stanton (Managing Editor). **Photos. Ad Acc, Adv Mgr:** Marty Donner, **Tel** (208)476-4571. Full Page (B&W) $459.90. Half Page (B&W) $229.95. Full Page (Color) $509.90. Half Page (Color) $254.95. **Pub. Size:** Standard. ***Formed by the union of*** *Clearwater Republican* ***and*** *Orofino Tribune.*

US
COTTONWOOD CHRONICLE. Vol. 25, No. 38 (Sept. 21, 1917)-. Newspaper. English. wk (Published on Thursdays). $18.00. Cottonwood Chronicle, 503 King Street, Box 157, Cottonwood ID 83522. **Tel** (208)962-3851, FAX (208)962-7131. **ED** Greg Wherry. **Bk Rev. Photos. Ad Acc, Adv Mgr:** Pat Wherry. Full Page (B&W) $211.25. Half Page (B&W) $105.63. **Pub. Size:** Tabloid. **Circ:** 1,000. ***Continues*** *Camas Prairie Chronicle.*

US
EAST COUNTY CHRONICLE. Vol. 1, No. 1 (July 30, 1982)-. Newspaper. English. wk (Published on Fridays). East County Chronicle, 113 North Main, Kimberly ID 83341. **Tel** (208)423-6401. **ED** Dwaine R. Anderson. **Bk Rev. Ad Acc. Circ:** 5,000 (ctrl).

US
FREMONT COUNTY HERALD-CHRONICLE. VFOAT Fremont County Herald Chronicle. Vol. 87, No. 34 (June 5, 1986)-. Newspaper. English. sw (Published on Tuesdays & Thursdays). $15.75 Fremont County; $18.90 other. Herald Chronicle / Idaho, PO Box Z, Ashton ID 83420. **Tel** (208)652-3261. ***Formed by the union of*** *Fremont County Chronicle-News;* ***Absorbed*** *Ashton Herald.*

US
GOODING COUNTY LEADER. VFOAT Gooding County Leader and Gooding Independent. Vol. 57, No. 38 (July 15, 1965)-. Newspaper. English. wk (Published on Wednesdays). Gooding County Leader, 200 Main Street, Gooding ID 83330. **Tel** (208)934-4449. **ED** Mary Ann Hagen. **Bk Rev. Ad Acc. Circ:** 1,200. ***Continues*** *Gooding Leader.*

US
IDAHO COUNTY FREE PRESS. VFOAT Free Press. Vol. 1, No. 1 (June 18, 1886)-. Newspaper. English. wk. Idaho County Free Press, 318 East Main Street, Grangeville ID 83530. ***Absorbed*** *Grangeville Globe.*

US
IDAHO ENTERPRISE, THE. Vol. 56, No. 17 (May 6, 1930)-. Newspaper. English. wk (Published on Thursdays). Idaho Enterprise, PO Box 205, Malad City ID 83252. **Tel** (208)766-4773, FAX (208)766-4774. **ED** Kris Jones. **Bk Rev. Ad Acc. Circ:** 1,250. ***Continues*** *Oneida County Enterprise.*

US/0279-8964
IDAHO MOUNTAIN EXPRESS. (THE IDAHO MOUNTAIN EXPRESS.). **VFOAT** Mountair Express; Express. (Nov. 27, 1974)-. Newspaper. English. wk. $29.00. Idaho Mountain Express, PO Box 1013, Ketchum ID 83340. **Tel** (208)726-8060, FAX (208)726-2329. **ED** Pam Morris. **Bk Rev. Photos. Ad Acc.** Full Page (B&W) $660.00. Half Page (B&W) $330.00. Full Page (Color) $735.00 (one color). Half Page (Color) $405.00 (one color). **Pub. Size:** Tabloid. **Wire Svcs.:** NF. **Desc:** Local news and features for the Sun Valley and Wood River Valley areas of Idaho.

US
IDAHO PRESS-TRIBUNE. VFOAT Idaho Press Tribune. Vol. 1, No. 1 (July 1, 1980)-. Newspaper. English. da. Idaho Press-Tribune, 1618 North Midland, Nampa ID 83651. **Tel** (208)467-9251. **ED** Jack D. Pearson. **Bk Rev. Ad Acc, Adv Mgr:** John Rybarczyk. **Circ:** 18,500. ***Formed by the union of*** *Idaho Free Press;* ***Absorbed*** *News-Tribune (Caldwell, Idaho).*

US
IDAHO STATE JOURNAL. Began in 1922. Newspaper. English. da (Sun.-Fri.). $90.00. Tribune Journal Publishing Company, Box 431, Pocatello ID 83204. **Tel** (208)232-4161. **ED** Lyle Olson. **Bk Rev. Ad Acc. Circ:** 20,200.

US
IDAHO STATESMAN, THE. (June 1, 1969)-. Newspaper. English. ds. $156.00. Idaho Statesman, PO Box 40, 1200 North Curtis Road, Boise ID 83707. **Tel** (800)635-8934, FAX (208)377-6449 (News), (208)377-6309 (Advertising). **ED** John A. Costa, Carolyn Washburn (Managing Editor). **Photos. Ad Acc, Adv Mgr:** Debbie Pantenburg, **Tel** (208)377-6358. Full Page (B&W) $$3802.00. Half Page (B&W) $1910.00. Full Page (Color) $4405.00. Half Page (Color) $2495.00. **Wire Svcs.:** AP, GN. **Circ:** 54,744 daily, 71,007 Sunday. available in microform from University Microfilms International (UMI). ***Continues*** *Idaho Daily Statesman.* **Ind/Abst** PROMT.

US/8755-9080
IDAHONIAN. ***Title Change.*** Vol. 81, No. 157 (May 28, 1974)-(19??). Newspaper. English. da. Idahonian, 409 South Jackson Street, Moscow ID 83843. ***Continues*** *Daily Idahonian.* ***Continued by*** *Moscow Pullman Daily News, 1061-8597.*

US
KELLOGG EVENING NEWS, THE. 37th Year, No. 1 (Mar. 12, 1924)-. Newspaper. English. da. $40.00. Kellogg Evening News, PO Box 149, Kellogg ID 83837. **Tel** (208)784-0201.

US
KENDRICK GAZETTE, THE. (1987)-. Newspaper. English. wk (Published on Thursdays). Kendrick Gazette, PO Box 177, Kendrick ID 83537. **Tel** (208)289-5731. **ED** William A. Roth. **Bk Rev. Ad Acc. Circ:** 900.

US
KUNA-MELBA NEWS. VFOAT Kuna Melba News. (1982)-. Newspaper. English. wk (Published on Wednesdays). $14.00. Kuna-Melba News, Box 373, Kuna ID 83634. **Tel** (208)466-3557. **ED** Earl Maggard. **Bk Rev. Photos. Ad Acc.** Full Page (B&W) $412.50. Half Page (B&W) $206.25. **Pub. Size:** Tabloid.

US/0892-2586
LEWISTON MORNING TRIBUNE. VFOAT Sunday Tribune; Lewiston Tribune. (1899)-. Newspaper. English. da. $144.00 (daily & Sunday by mail). Tribune Publishing Company / Lewiston, PO Box 1387, Lewiston ID 83501. **Tel** (208)743-9411. **ED** A. L. Alford Jr (Editor in Chief), Wayne Hollingshead (Managing Editor). **Bk Rev. Photos. Ad Acc, Adv Mgr:** Rob Minervini. Full Page (B&W) $1515.75. Half Page (B&W) $740.25. **Pub. Size:** Standard. **Wire Svcs.:** AP, NY. **Circ:** 23,778 daily, 24,768 Sunday.

US
LINCOLN COUNTY JOURNAL. Vol. 49, No. 32 (Aug. 14, 1931)-. Newspaper. English. wk (Published on Wednesdays). Lincoln County Journal, PO Box 704, Shosone ID 83352. **Tel** (208)886-2740. **ED** P. Nance. **Bk Rev. Ad Acc. Circ:** 1,000. ***Continues*** *Shoshone Journal.*

US/0893-3812
MORNING NEWS (BLACKFOOT, IDAHO), THE. (THE MORNING NEWS.). Vol. 82, No. 155 (Apr. 1, 1983)-. Newspaper. English. da (312 issues per year). $86.00. Blackfoot News, PO Box 70, Blackfoot ID 83221. **Tel** (208)785-1100. **ED** Michael O'Donnell. **Bk Rev**, (Qty: 1 per month). **Photos. Ad Acc, Adv Mgr:** Leslie Bare. Full Page (B&W) $6.85 (per inch). Half Page (B&W) $6.85 (per inch). Full Page (Color) $80.00 (per color). Half Page (Color) $80.00 (per color). **Pub. Size:** Broadsheet. **Wire Svcs.:** AP. available in microform. ***Continues*** *Morning News of Southeastern Idaho, 0745-712X.*

US/1061-8597
MOSCOW PULLMAN DAILY NEWS. VFOAT Moscow-Pullman Daily News. (19??)-. Newspaper. English. da (312 issues per year - not published on Sundays). $147.00. News Review Publishing Compnay, PO Box 8187, Moscow ID 83843. **Tel** (208)882-5561. ***Continues*** *Idahonian, 8755-9080.*

US
MOUNTAIN HOME NEWS. VFOAT News; Mtn. Home News. Vol. 56, No. 31 (Aug. 8, 1946)-. Newspaper. English. Fifty-two times a year (Wed.). $25.00 Idaho; $35.00 others. Mountain Home News, PO Box O, Mountain Home ID 83647. **Tel** (208)587-3331, FAX (208)587-9205. **ED** Kelly Everitt. **Ad Acc. Pr Rev. Circ:** 4,200 (ctrl). ***Continues*** *Mountain Home Republican.*

US
NEWS-EXAMINER, THE. VFOAT News Examiner. Vol. 18, No. 35 (Sept. 16, 1937)-. Newspaper. English. wk (Published on Thursdays). News-Examiner / Montpelier, 847 Washington, Montpelier ID 83254. **Tel** (208)847-0552. **ED** Rosa Moosman. **Bk Rev. Ad Acc. Circ:** 2,500. ***Formed by the union of*** *Montpelier Examiner* ***and*** *Bear Lake County News;* ***Absorbed*** *Paris Post, (Paris, Idaho : 1941).*

US
NORTH SIDE NEWS. Vol. 1, No. 1 (Nov. 12, 1908)-. Newspaper. English. wk. North Side News, PO Box 468, Jerome ID 83338. **LC** 7568. ***Absorbed*** *Jerome County Journal.*

US/8750-6823
OWYHEE AVALANCHE (HOMEDALE, IDAHO : 1985). (THE OWYHEE AVALANCHE.). Vol. 1, No. 1 (Jan. 2, 1985)-. Newspaper. English. wk. Owyhee Avalanche, PO Box 97, Homedale ID 83628. ***Formed by the union of*** *Owyhee Chronicle* ***and*** *Owyhee Nugget.*

US
PARMA REVIEW, THE. Vol. 1, No. 1 (Dec. 3, 1909)-. Newspaper. English. wk (Published on Wednesdays). Parma Review, PO Box 540, Parma ID 83660-0540. **Tel** (208)722-6737. **ED** Greg Szymanski. **Circ:** 1,500.

US
POST FALLS TRIBUNE. Vol. 69, No. 22 (Oct. 28, 1963)-. Newspaper. English. wk. Post Falls Tribune, 318 Spokane Street, Post Falls ID 83661-0520. **Tel** (208)773-7502, FAX (208)773-7002. **ED** Kerri Thoreson. ***Continues*** *Tribune (Rathdrum, Idaho);* ***Absorbed*** *Lake Valley times.*

US
POST-REGISTER, THE. VFOAT Post Register. Vol. 1, No. 1 (Nov. 1, 1931)-Vol. 20, No. 18 (Nov. 21, 1950): Vol. 20, No. 19 (Nov. 22, 1950)-. Newspaper. English. da (Sun.-Fri.). The Post Register, PO Box 1800, Idaho Falls ID 83401. **Tel** (208)522-1800. **ED** J. Robb Brady. **Circ:** 24,662 daily, 25,406 Sunday. ***Formed by the union of*** *Idaho Falls Post* ***and*** *Times-Register (Idaho Falls, Idaho).*

US
POWER COUNTY PRESS, THE. (1937)-. Newspaper. English. wk. $20.00. Power County Press, PO Box 547, American Falls ID 83211. **Tel** (208)226-5294. **ED** Brett Crumpton. **LC** 7560. **Photos. Ad Acc, Adv Mgr:** Leslie Lusk. Full Page (B&W) $632.10. Half Page (B&W) $316.05. Full Page (Color) $732.10. Half Page (Color) $416.00. **Pub. Size:** Broadsheet. ***Formed by the union of*** *American Falls Press* ***and*** *Power County Booster.*

US/0740-3348
PRIEST RIVER TIMES. Vol. 1, No. 1 (Apr. 16, 1914)-Vol. 31, No. 35 (Aug. 31, 1944); 31st Year, No. 36 (Sept. 7, 1944)-. Newspaper. English. wk (Published on Wed.). $25.00. Priest River Times, PO Box 10, Priest River ID 83856. **Tel** (208)448-2431. **ED** Marylyn Cork (News Editor), Linda Ramsey (Managing Editor). **Photos. Ad Acc, Adv Mgr:** Jeanine Hinchleff. Full Page (B&W) $793.55. Half Page (B&W) $396.68. Full Page (Color) $968.55. Half Page (Color) $571.68. **Pub. Size:** Standard.

US
RECORDER HERALD. No. 21 (Sept. 4, 1929)-. Newspaper. English. wk. $22.00. Recorder Herald, PO Box 310, Salmon ID 83467. **Tel** (208)756-2221, FAX (208)756-2222. **ED** Rachel Snook (Editor-in-Chief) and Rick Hodges (Managing Editor). **Photos. Ad Acc, Adv Mgr:** Sheila Hodges. Full Page (B&W) $674.10. Half Page (B&W) $337.05. Full Page (Color) $809.10. Half Page (Color) $472.05. **Pub. Size:** Broadsheet. available in microform. ***Continues*** *Lemhi County Recorder Herald.*

US
RED APPLE BULLETIN. (1969)-. Bulletin. English. wk (Published on Thursdays). Red Apple Bulletin, PO Box 48, New Plymouth ID 83655. **Tel** (208)278-3735. **ED** Hazel Brown. **Bk Rev. Ad Acc. Circ:** 1,100.

US
REXBURG STANDARD/JOURNAL, THE. VFOAT Rexburg Standard Journal. Vol. 97, No. 36 (Aug. 28, 1984)-. English. sw (Published on Tuesdays & Thursdays). Standard-Journal Inc, PO Box 10, Rexburg ID 83440-0010. **Tel** (208)356-5441, FAX (208)356-8312. **ED** Cathy Coon. **Ad Acc, Adv Mgr:** Garph Lords. **Circ:** 5,674. ***Formed by the union of*** *Rexburg Standard* ***and*** *Rexburg Journal.*

US
SANDPOINT DAILY BEE. Newspaper. English. da. $96.00. Sandpoint Daily Bee, PO Box 159, Sandpoint ID 83864. **Tel** (208)263-9534, FAX (208)263-9091. **ED** Bill Buley. **Ad Acc, Adv Mgr:** Herb, **Tel** 263-9534. **Circ:** 6,000 (ctrl).

US/0197-7954
SHO-BAN NEWS, THE. Added/Corp Shoshone-Bannock Tribes. **VFOAT** Sho Ban News. Vol. 1 No. 1 (Dec. 11, 1976)-. Newspaper. English. Fifty-two times a year (Thurs.). Fort Hall Business Council, PO Box 900, Fort Hall ID 83203. **Tel** (208)238-3888. **ED** Laverne Sheppard. Index available. **Ad Acc. Circ:** 2,400 (ctrl). ***Continues*** *Sho-Ban News (Fort Hall, Idaho : 1970).* **Desc:** Local, national and Indian news.

US/1044-9353
SHOSHONE NEWS-PRESS. VFOAT Shoshone County News-Press; Shoshone News Press. Vol 4, No. 104 (Oct. 2, 1988)-. Newspaper. English. da. $8.00 (per month) carrier; $8.50 (per month) motor route. Shoshone News-Press / Wallace Miner, 401 Main Street, Kellogg ID 83837-2630. **Tel** (208)783-1107. **ED** Daniel Drewry (Editor-in-Chief) and Darrel Beehner (Managing Editor). **Photos. Ad Acc, Adv Mgr:** Judy Binkley, **Tel** (208)783-1107. Full Page (B&W) $709.50. Half Page (B&W) $346.80. Full Page (Color) $829.50. Half Page (Color) $466.50. **Pub. Size:** Broadsheet. available in microform. ***Continues*** *Shoshone County News-Press.*

US/0744-866X
SILHOUETTE (IDAHO FALLS, IDAHO), THE. (THE SILHOUETTE.). **Added/Corp** International Handgun Metallic Silhouette Association. (19??)-. Periodical. English. mo (with Jan./Feb. and Nov./Dec. issues combined). $20.00. International Handgun Metallic Silhouette, Box 1609, Idaho Falls ID 83403. **Tel** (208)524-0880.

US
SOUTH IDAHO PRESS. VFOAT SIP. Vol. 64, no. 1 (Apr. 1, 1968)-. Newspaper. English. da. South Idaho Press, 230 East Main Street, Burley ID 83318. ***Formed by the union of*** *Reminder Morning News* ***and*** *World (Burley, Idaho).*

US
ST. MARIES GAZETTE-RECORD. VFOAT A.St. Maries gazette record; A.Saint Maries gazette-record; A.Saint Maries gazette record. **VAT** Saint Maries Gazette-Record. Vol. 13, No. 18 (June 4, 1918)-Vol. 64, No. 28 (July 10, 1969) ; 64th year, No. 28 (July 17, 1969)-. Newspaper. English. wk. Gazette-Record, 127 South 7th Street, Saint Maries ID 83861. ***Formed by the union of*** *St. Maries Gazette* ***and*** *Record (Saint Maries, Idaho).*

US/0889-9851
TETON VALLEY NEWS. Vol. 1, No. 1 (Apr. 15, 1909)-. Newspaper. English. wk. $15.00 Teton County; $20.00 others. Teton Valley News, PO Box 49, Driggs ID 83422. **Tel** (208)354-8101. **ED** Debbi Barracato. **Bk Rev**, (Qty: 10). **Photos. Ad Acc, Adv Mgr:** Eileen Foster. Full Page (B&W) $384.00. Half Page (B&W) $192.00. Full Page (Color) $518.40. Half Page (Color) $259.20. **Pub. Size:** Tabloid. **Circ:** 2,600.

US
TIMES-NEWS (TWIN FALLS, IDAHO). (THE TIMES-NEWS.). **VFOAT** Times News. Vol. 24, No. 262 (Feb. 16, 1942)-. Newspaper. English. da. Twin Falls Times News, PO Box 548, 132 3rd Street West, Twin Falls ID 83301. **Tel** (208)733-0931. ***Formed by the union of*** *Twin Falls News (Twin Falls, Idaho)* ***and*** *Idaho Evening Times.*

US
TWIN FALLS TIMES-NEWS. VFOAT Twin Falls Times News. (Feb. 6, 1942)-. Newspaper. English. da. $182.00. Twin Falls Times News, PO Box 548, 132 3rd Street West, Twin Falls ID 83301. **Tel** (208)733-0931. **ED** Clark Walworth. **Ad Acc. Circ:** 22,000 (ctrl). ***Formed by the union of*** *Idaho Evening Times; Twin Falls News.*

US
UPPER COUNTY NEWS-REPORTER, THE. VFOAT Upper County News Reporter. Vol. 35, No. 18 (Dec. 7, 1923)-. Newspaper. English. wk (Published on Wednesdays). Upper County News-Reporter, PO Box 9, Cambridge ID 83610. **Tel** (208)257-3515. **ED** R. Stuart Dopf. **Bk Rev. Ad Acc. Circ:** 1,100. ***Formed by the union of*** *Midvale Reporter;* ***Absorbed*** *Cambridge News (Cambridge, Idaho : 1922).*

US
VALLEY NEWS. Vol. 74, issue 28 (Oct. 21, 1976)-. Newspaper. English. wk (Published on Thursdays). Valley

News / Meridian, 815 East First Street, Meridian ID 83642. **Tel** (208)888-5130. **ED** Helen Alidjani. **Bk Rev. Ad Acc. Circ:** 2,000. ***Continues*** *Valley News-Times.*

US/0883-671X
WALLACE MINER, THE. Vol. 1, No. 1 (Feb. 21, 1907)-. Newspaper. English. wk. $40.00 (one year); $72.00 (first class). Shoshone News-Press / Wallace Miner, 401 Main Street, Kellogg ID 83837-2630. **Tel** (208)783-1107. **ED** Daniel Drewry (Editor-in-Chief) and Darrel Bechner (Managing Editor). **Photos. Ad Acc, Adv Mgr:** Judi Binkley, **Tel** (208)783-1107. Full Page (B&W) $541.80. Half Page (B&W) $270.90. Full Page (Color) $661.80. Half Page (Color) $390.90. **Pub. Size:** Broadsheet. **Wire Svcs.:** AP. ***Absorbed*** *Kellogg Wardner News (Kellogg, Idaho : 1924).*

US
WEISER SIGNAL-AMERICAN, THE. **VFOAT** Signal American; Weiser Signal American. No. 34 (Sept. 30, 1985)-. Newspaper. English. sw (Published on Mondays & Wednesdays). $30.00 local; $45.00 other. Weiser Signal American, PO Box 709, Weiser ID 83672. **Tel** (208)549-1717, FAX (208)549-1718. **ED** Steve Wherry. **Photos. Ad Acc, Adv Mgr:** James R. Simpson. Full Page (B&W) $837.90. Half Page (B&W) $418.95. Full Page (Color) $125.00. **Pub. Size:** Broadsheet. **Circ:** 3,000 (evening, paid). ***Formed by the union of*** *Weiser Signal (Weiser, Idaho : 1925).*

US
WOOD RIVER JOURNAL. Vol. 87, No. 1 (Jan. 2, 1969)-. Newspaper. English. wk. Wood River Journal, 112 South Main, Hailey ID 83333. **Tel** (208)788-3444. **Bk Rev. Ad Acc. Circ:** 11,000. ***Continues*** *Hailey Times.*

ILLINOIS

US
ADVOCATE, THE. Vol. 87, No. 51 (Jan. 18, 1979)-. Newspaper. English. wk (Published on Thursdays). Clifton Advocate, 330 North Fourth, Box 548, Clifton IL 60927. **Tel** (815)694-2122, FAX (815)694-3770. **ED** Therese Simoneau. **Circ:** 2,207. ***Continues*** *Clifton Chebanse Ashkum Advocate.*

US/0744-527X
ALGONQUIN COUNTRYSIDE. **VFOAT** Countryside. (198?)-. Newspaper. English. wk. Barrington Press Inc, 200 James Street, Barrington IL 60010. ***Continues*** *Fox Valley Countryside, 0194-1224.*

US/1047-9317
ALTAMONT NEWS, THE. Began in 1881. Newspaper. English. sw. Altamont News, 111 North Main Street, Altamont IL 62411. available on microfilm. ***Absorbed*** *Altamont Herald.*

US
AMBOY NEWS, THE. (18??)-. Newspaper. English. wk. $14.00. Amboy News, PO Box 162, Amboy IL 61310. **Tel** (815)857-2311. **ED** David L. Volz. **Photos. Ad Acc.** Full Page (B&W) $2.14 per column inch. Half Page (B&W) $2.14 per column inch. **Pub. Size:** Broadsheet. **Circ:** 2,250. ***Absorbed*** *Amboy Journal.*

US/0745-6557
AMERIKA WOCHE. **VFOAT** America Week. Vol. 10, No. 22 (June 3, 1982)-. Newspaper. German. Fifty-two times a year. $39.50. Amerika Woche, 4732 North Lincoln, Chicago IL 60625. **Tel** (312)275-5054, FAX (312)275-0596. **ED** Mario Schiefelbein. **Bk Rev. Photos. Ad Acc, Adv Mgr:** Rita Hetz. Full Page (B&W) $1250.00. Half Page (B&W) $650.00. Full Page (Color) $1750.00. Half Page (Color) $1150.00. **Pub. Size:** Tabloid. **Circ:** 25,000 (ctrl). ***Absorbed*** *America Herold und Sonntagspost; Buffalo Voklsfreund; California Freie Presse; Cincinnati Kurier; Deutsche Wochen Schrift; Milwaukee-Herold; Volkszeitung-Tribune; Welt-Post.*

US/0745-5453
AMERIKANSKI SLOVENEC (CHICAGO, ILL.). (AMERIKANSKI SLOVENEC.). **VFOAT** Amerikanski Slovenec Glasilo K.S.J. Jednote. Vol. 34., No. 121 (Aug. 4, 1925)-. Newspaper. English (Slovenian). bw. $10.00 US; $14.00 other. American Slovenian Catholic Union, 2439 Glenwood Avenue, Joliet IL 60435. **Tel** 741-2001. **Circ:** 12,000 (ctrl). available on microfilm from The Library of Congress Photoduplication Service. ***Continues*** *Amerikanski Slovenec Edinost.*
Desc: Official organ of the American Slovenian Catholic Union, a fraternal insurance society.

US
AREA NEWS, THE. Vol. 58, No. 27 (May 1, 1963)-. Newspaper. English. wk (Published on Wednesdays). Area News / Chicago, 112-116 West Chestnut Street, Gillespie IL 62033. **Tel** (217)839-2130, FAX (217)839-2139. **ED** G.L. Dufnor. **Bk Rev. Ad Acc. Circ:** 3,175. ***Continues*** *Gillespie News.*

US
ARLINGTON HEIGHTS HERALD. (19??)-. Newspaper. English. wk. Arlington Heights Herald, 217 West Campbell, Arlington Heights IL 60006.

US
ARTHUR GRAPHIC-CLARION, THE. **VFOAT** Arthur Graphic Clarion. Vol. 19, No. 25 (Nov. 3, 1905)-. Newspaper. English. wk (Published on Thursdays). Arthur Graphic Clarion, 113 East Illinois Street, Arthur IL 61911. **Tel** (217)543-2151, FAX (217)543-2152. **ED** Allen Mann & Lowell Cutsinger. **Bk Rev. Ad Acc, Adv Mgr:** Phylis Burkfield. **Circ:** 3,000. ***Formed by the union of*** *Arthur Graphic* ***and*** *Arthur Clarion.*

US
ASHTON GAZETTE, THE. (1???)-. Newspaper. English. wk. Ashton Gazette, 813 Main Stret, Ashton IL 61006. **Tel** (815)453-2551. **ED** David W. Townsend. **Bk Rev. Ad Acc. Circ:** 1,000.

US
ASTORIA SOUTH FULTON ARGUS, THE. **VFOAT** Astoria Argus. (197?)-. Newspaper. English. wk (Published on Wednesdays). Astoria South Fulton Argus, 100 North Pearl, Astoria IL 61501. **Tel** (309)329-2151, FAX (309)329-2344. **ED** Thomas B. Stevens. **Bk Rev. Ad Acc, Adv Mgr:** Erma Geiman. **Circ:** 2,500. ***Formed by the union of*** *Astoria Argus-Searchlight* ***and*** *Table Grove Herald.*

US
ATWOOD HERALD, THE. (1???)-. Newspaper. English. wk (Published on Thursdays). Atwood Herald, 107 North Main, Atwood IL 61913. **Tel** (217)578-3213. **ED** Doris Elmore. **Bk Rev. Ad Acc. Circ:** 1,000.

US
AUBURN CITIZEN. Vol. 2, No. 1(Apr. 29, 1875)-. Newspaper. English. wk (Published on Thursdays). Auburn Citizen, 110 North Fifth Street, Auburn IL 62615. **Tel** (217)438-6155, FAX (217)438-6156. **ED** Joe Michelich. **Bk Rev. Ad Acc. Circ:** 1,600. ***Continues*** *Auburn Herald (Auburn, Ill.).*

US
AUGUSTA EAGLE, THE. (Oct. 30, 1884)-. Newspaper. English. wk. $13.00 (Illinois), $16.00 (out of state). Augusta Eagle, PO Box 257, Augusta IL 62311. **Tel** (217)392-2715. **ED** John T. Flack and Lea A. Flack. **Photos. Ad Acc.** Full Page (B&W) $218.40. Half Page (B&W) $109.20. **Pub. Size:** Standard. **Circ:** 1,600 (ctrl). available in microform.

US
BACK OF THE YARDS JOURNAL. (19??)-. Newspaper. English. wk (Published on Wednesdays). Back of the Yards Journal, 4625 South Ashland Avenue, Chicago IL 60609. **Tel** (312)927-7203. **ED** Susan Strohacker. **Bk Rev. Ad Acc. Circ:** 48,000.

US/1066-7970
BEECHER CITY JOURNAL. (THE BEECHER CITY JOURNAL.). (19??)-. Newspaper. English. wk. Beecher City Journal, 219 North Illinois, Belleville IL 62220. **Tel** (618)277-7000. **ED** P. J. Ryan. **Bk Rev. Ad Acc. Circ:** 1,700. ***Absorbed*** *Stewardson Clipper* ***and*** *Cowden Reflector.*

US
BELLEVILLE DAILY NEWS-DEMOCRAT. ***Ceased.*** (18??)-(19??). Newspaper. English. da (except Sunday). Belleville News Democrat, 120 South Illinois Street, Belleville IL 62220. **Tel** (618)234-1000, FAX (618)234-9597. **ED** Greg Edwards. **Circ:** 42,927 daily, 52,043 Sunday.

US/8750-1058
BELLEVILLE NEWS-DEMOCRAT. (THE BELLEVILLE NEWS-DEMOCRAT.). **VFOAT** Belleville News Democrat. Vol. 128, No. 173 (July 24, 1983)-. Newspaper. English. da. $3.25 per week. Belleville News Democrat, 120 South Illinois Street, Belleville IL 62220. **Tel** (618)234-1000, FAX (618)234-9597. **ED** Greg Edwards. **Photos. Ad Acc, Adv Mgr:** Dave Baur. Full Page (B&W) $3597.00. Half Page (B&W) $1798.00. Full Page (Color) $3807.00. Half Page (Color) $2008.00. **Pub. Size:** Broadsheet. **Wire Svcs.:** CO, AP. **Circ:** 51,232 paid daily, 62,617 paid Sunday. ***Continues*** *News-Democrat (Belleville, Ill.).*

US
BENTON NEWS, THE. (19??)-. Newspaper. English. da. Benton News / Illinois, 11-115 East Church, Benton IL 62812. **Tel** (618)438-5611, FAX (618)435-2413. **ED** Danny Malkovich. **Bk Rev. Ad Acc, Adv Mgr:** Paula Kerkemeyer. **Circ:** 4,800.

US/0006-0410
BEVERLY REVIEW, THE. (19??)-. Newspaper. English. wk. $16.00. Beverly Review, 1739 W 99th Street, Chicago IL 60643. **Tel** (312)238-3366. **ED** Robert Olszewski and Jerry Moore (Managing Editor). **Photos. Ad Acc.** Full Page (B&W) $532.00. Half Page (B&W) $266.00. Full Page (Color) $612.00 (1 color). Half Page (Color) $346.00. **Pub. Size:** Tabloid. **Circ:** 6,100. ***Continues*** *Weekly Review (Blue Island, Ill.).*

US/0745-4813
BI-STATE REPORTER. **VFOAT** Lakeland Newspapers. Newspaper. English. wk. $49.00. Antioch News Reporter, PO Box 819, Antioch IL 60002-0819. **Tel** (312)226-8161. **ED** William H Schroeder, Charles Johnston and Gloria Davis. **Bk Rev. Ad Acc. Circ:** 8,521 (ctrl).
Desc: Serves west Kenosha County Wisconsin, part of Lakeland newspaper group.

US
BLUE MOUND LEADER. (18??)-. Newspaper. English. wk. $13.50. Blue Mound Leader, PO Box 318, Blue Mound IL 62513. **Tel** (217)692-2323. **ED** Cindy Stuart. **Photos. Ad Acc, Adv Mgr:** Cindy Stuart. **Pub. Size:** Tabloid. **Circ:** 800.

US
BRAIDWOOD INDEX, THE. (19??)-. Newspaper. English. wk. Braidwood Index, 111 South Water Street, Wilmington IL 60481. **Tel** (815)476-7966, FAX (815)476-7002. **ED** George Fisher. **Bk Rev. Ad Acc, Adv Mgr:** Pam Divine. **Circ:** 13,300.

US
BREESE JOURNAL, THE. (1921)-. Newspaper. English. Fifty-two times a year. $18.50 US; $15.00 Clinton County Illinois; $42.50 others. Breese Journal, PO Box 405, Breese IL 62230. **Tel** (618)526-7211. **ED** Dave Mahlandt, (editor's address: 625 North 2nd Street, Breese, IL 62230). **LC** 7580. **Ad Acc. Circ:** 5,600 (ctrl). available on microfilm.

US
BRIDGEPORT LEADER. Vol. 81, No. 1 (Jan. 5, 1978)-. Newspaper. English. wk. Bridgeport Leader, PO Box 317, Bridgeport IL 62417. **Tel** (618)945-2111. **ED** Louis Valbert. **Bk Rev. Ad Acc. Circ:** 3,200. ***Continues*** *Leader Times (Bridgeport, Ill.).*

US
BRIDGEPORT NEWS. **VFOAT** Bridgeport and McKinley Park News. Vol. 1, No. 1 (Aug. 31, 1939)-. Newspaper. English. wk. Bridgeport News, 3252 South Halsted Street, Chicago IL 60608. **Tel** (312)842-5883.

US
BRIGHTON PARK AND MCKINLEY PARK LIFE. **VFOAT** Brighton Park & McKinley Park Life; Brighton Park Life; McKinley Park Life; Brighton Park McKinley Park Life. (19??)-. Newspaper. English. wk. Brighton Park Life, 2949 West 43rd Street, Chicago IL 60632-2554. **Tel** (312)523-3663.

US
BUNKER HILL GAZETTE-NEWS, THE. **VFOAT** Bunker Hill Gazette News. Vol. 40, No. 6 (Feb. 10, 1905)-. Newspaper. English. wk. Bunker Hill Gazette News, 150 North Washington, Bunker Hill IL 62014-9501. **Tel** (618)585-4411. ***Formed by the union of*** *Bunker Hill News (Bunker Hill, Ill.)* ***and*** *Bunker Hill Gazette (Bunker Hill, Ill.).*

US/0894-1181
BUREAU COUNTY REPUBLICAN, THE. **VFOAT** Bureau County Record; Bureau County's Republican. Vol. 1, No. 1 (Jan. 14, 1858)-. Newspaper. English. bw. Bureau County Republican, 316 South Main Street, Princeton IL 61356. ***Continues*** *Princetonian.*

US
CALHOUN NEWS, THE. Vol. 1, No. 1 (Apr. 1, 1915)-. Newspaper. English. wk. $13.00 Illinois, $18.00 other. The Calhoun News, 310 South County Road, Hardin IL 62047. **Tel** (618)576-2321. **Ad Acc, Adv Mgr:** Mary Buchanan, **Tel** (618)576-2244. **Pub. Size:** Broadsheet. **Circ:** 2,700. available in microform. ***Continues*** *Calhoun County Republican (Hardin, Ill.).*

US
CAMBRIDGE CHRONICLE, THE. **VFOAT** Chronicle; Henry County Chronicle. Vol. 31, No. 10 (Jan. 3, 1889)-. Newspaper. English. wk. Cambridge Chronicle, 119 West Exchange, Cambridge IL 61238. **Tel** (309)937-3303. ***Continues*** *Chronicle (Cambridge, Ill.).*

US
CARLINVILLE DEMOCRAT, THE. **VFOAT** Carlinville Weekly Democrat; Weekly Carlinville Democrat. Vol. 11, No. 30 (Mar. 28, 1867)-. Newspaper. English. wk. $17.00 Macoupin County; $19.00 other. ALA Enterprises Inc., 118 North West Street, PO Box 490, Carlinville IL 62626. **Tel** (217)854-2561, FAX (217)854-3366. **ED** Edward J. Albracht (Editor-in-Chief) and Thomas Hatalla (Managing Editor). **Photos. Ad Acc, Adv Mgr:** Laurie Flori. Full Page (B&W) $412.80. Half Page (B&W) $206.40. Full Page (Color) $462.80. Half Page (Color) $231.40. **Pub. Size:** Standard. **Circ:** 2,500. available in microform. ***Continues*** *Carlinville Free Democrat.*

US
CARROLL COUNTY REVIEW. Vol. 1, No. 1 (May 7, 1970)-. Newspaper. English. wk. Carroll County Review, 809 Main Street, PO Box 369, Thomson IL 61285-0369. **Tel** (815)259-2131. ***Formed by the union of*** *Lanark Gazette* ***and*** *Chadwick Review Shannon Reporter Thomson Review.*

US/1059-8162
CENTRALIA SENTINEL. 126th Year, Vol. 106, No. 21 (Apr. 4, 1989)-. Newspaper. English. da. Centralia Sentinel, PO Box 627, 232 East Broadway, Centralia IL 62801. **Tel** (618)532-5604. ***Continues*** *Centralia Evening Sentinel.*

US
CHICAGO CRUSADER, THE. **VFOAT** New Crusader. Vol. 41, No. 32 (Jan. 2, 1982)-. Newspaper. English. Fifty-two times a year (Thurs.). Jefferson Leavell Publishing Company Inc., 6429 South Martin Luther King Drive, Chicago IL 60637. **Tel** (312)752-2500. **ED** Dorothy Leavell. **Bk Rev**. **Ad Acc. Circ:** 50,000 (ctrl). available on microfilm from Bell & Howell. ***Continues*** *New Crusader (Chicago, Ill.).*

US/0745-7014
CHICAGO DEFENDER (1973). (CHICAGO DEFENDER.). Vol. 18, No. 8 (Feb. 19, 1973)-. Newspaper. English. da. $55.47 (six months). Chicago Daily Defender, 2400 Michigan Avenue, Chicago IL 60616. **Tel** (312)225-2400. **ED** John H Sengstacke. **Bk Rev**, (Qty: 12 per year). **Photos**. **Ad Acc, Adv Mgr:** Joseph Gilmore. Full Page (B&W) $1561.70. Half Page (B&W) $780.85. Full Page (Color) $1864.20. Half Page (Color) $1083.35. **Pub. Size:** Standard. **Wire Svcs.:** UPI. available in microform. Documents available from UMI Article Clearinghouse. ***Continues*** *Chicago Daily Defender (Chicago, Ill. : Daily).*
Ind/Abst Newsp. Abstr.

US
CHICAGO INDEPENDENT BULLETIN. Vol. 2, No. 18 (Nov. 15, 1973)-. Bulletin. English. wk. $20.00. Chicago Independent Bulletin, 2042 West 95th Street, Chicago IL 60643. **Tel** (312)783-1040. ***Continues*** *Southeast Independent Bulletin.*

US/1054-1365
CHICAGO JEWISH STAR. Vol. 1, No. 1 (Feb. 22/Mar. 7, 1991)-. Newspaper. English. sw. $25.00. Star Media Group, Inc., PO Box 268, Skokie IL 60076-0268. **Tel** (708)674-7827, FAX (708)674-0014. **ED** D. Wertheimer. **Photos**. **Ad Acc.** Full Page (B&W) $1,488.00. Half Page (B&W) $744.00. **Pub. Size:** Tabloid. **Wire Svcs.:** JT. **Circ:** 25,000.

US
CHICAGO POST, THE. (19??)-. Newspaper. English. bw. $20.00. Chicago Post, PO Box 478369, Chicago IL 60647. **Tel** (312)772-3300. **ED** James Boratyn. **Photos**. **Ad Acc, Adv Mgr:** James Boratyn. Full Page (B&W) $1,400.00. Half Page (B&W) $700.00. **Pub. Size:** Tabloid. **Circ:** 45,000.

US
CHICAGO SHORELAND NEWS, THE. (198?)-. Newspaper. English. wk. Chicago Shoreland News, 11740 South Elizabeth, Chicago IL 60643-5120. **Tel** (312)568-7091, FAX (312)928-6056. **ED** Al Johnson, Terry Johnson (Managing Editor). **Bk Rev**. **Photos**. **Ad Acc.** Full Page (B&W) $905.00. Half Page (B&W) $452.90. Full Page (Color) $1115.00. Half Page (Color) $652.00. **Pub. Size:** Tabloid. **Wire Svcs.:** NP. ***Continues*** *Chicago Shoreland.*

US
CHICAGO SUN-TIMES. **VFOAT** Chicago Sun Times; Chicago Sunday Sun Times. Vol. 12, No. 78 (May 4, 1959)-. Newspaper. English. da. Chicago Sun-Times, 401 North Wabash Avenue, Chicago IL 60611 **Tel** (312)321-4924, FAX (312)321-4924. **ED** Frank Devine. **Ad Acc. Circ:** 612,686 daily, 625,935 Sunday. ***Continues*** *Chicago Daily Sun Times.*
Desc: Daily newspaper for the Chicago area.
Ind/Abst Mark. Advert. Ref. Serv.; PROMT.

US
CHICAGO TRIBUNE (CHICAGO, ILL. : 1963). (CHICAGO TRIBUNE.). 116th Year, No. 48 (Feb. 17, 1963)-. Newspaper. English. da. Price varies. Chicago Tribune, 777 West Chicago Avenue, Department 300, Chicago IL 60610. **Tel** (312)222-5350. **ED** Jack Fuller. Index available. **Bk Rev**. **Ad Acc. Circ:** 744,969 daily, 1,112,200 Sun. (ctrl). available in microform from University Microfilms International (UMI); available on an online database (file 632/Full-Text) from DIALOG. Documents available from UMI Article Clearinghouse. ***Continues*** *Chicago Daily Tribune (Chicago, Ill. : 1872).*
Desc: This newspaper, published continuously since June 10, 1847, features investigative reporting.
Ind/Abst Infobank (Jan. 1969-); Mark. Advert. Ref. Serv.; Newsp. Abstr.; Newsp. Abstr.; PROMT.

US
CHICAGO WEEKEND. (1974)-. Newspaper. English. wk. Chicago Citizen, 412 East 87th Street, Chicago IL 60619-6004. **Tel** (312)487-7700.

US
CHICAGOLAND JOB SOURCE. English. wk. $29.95. PO Box 7125, North Suburban IL 61099-7125.
Desc: A quality employment newspaper, with a large variety of career news and helpwanted advertisements from across the country. A great source for patrons.

US
CHILLICOTHE BULLETIN, THE. (1???)-. Bulletin. English. wk. Tazewell Publishing Company, 100 Detroit Avenue, PO Box 250, Morton IL 61550-1532. **Tel** (309)263-2211.

US
CHRISMAN LEADER. Vol. 1, No. 1 (Mar. 26, 1970)-. Newspaper. English. wk. Chrisman Leader, 148 West Madison, Chrisman IL 61924-1118. **Tel** (217)269-2811.

US
CICERO LIFE. (19??)-. Newspaper. English. tw. Life Printing & Publishing Co., PO Box 100, La Grange Park IL 60525-0100. **Tel** (708)579-4242, FAX (708)579-4226. **ED** William Conkis. **Ad Acc, Adv Mgr:** Pete Manning. **Circ:** 61,000.

US
CISSNA PARK NEWS, THE. (1906)-. Newspaper. English. wk. $20.00. Baier Publishing Company, PO Box 8, Cissna Park IL 60924-0008. **Tel** (815)457-2245. **ED** Rick A. Baier. **Bk Rev**, (Qty: 15). **Photos**. **Ad Acc.** Full Page (B&W) $200.00. Half Page (B&W) $100.00. **Pub. Size:** Tabloid. **Circ:** 2,072. ***Continues*** *Cissna Park Express.*

US
CLINTON COUNTY NEWS. (19??)-. Newspaper. English. wk. $17.50. Rube Yelvington Enterprises Inc., PO Box C, Mascoutah IL 62258-0189. **Tel** (618)566-8282. **ED** Pamela Rensing. **Bk Rev**, (Qty: 15). **Photos**. **Ad Acc, Adv Mgr:** Jeff Forsythe. Full Page (B&W) $500.00. Half Page (B&W) $250.00. Full Page (Color) $550.00. Half Page (Color) $275.00. **Pub. Size:** Broadsheet. **Wire Svcs.:** SS. available in microform.

US
CLINTON DAILY JOURNAL. No. 195 (Jan. 2, 1980)-. Newspaper. English. da. Clinton Daily Journal, PO Box 615, Clinton IL 61727-0615. **Tel** (217)935-3171, FAX (217)935-6086. **ED** Kevin Barlow. **Ad Acc, Adv Mgr:** Terrie Baker. **Circ:** 3,783. ***Continues*** *Clinton Daily Journal and Public.*

US
COAL CITY COURANT, THE. (19??)-. Newspaper. English. wk. Bailey Printing & Publishing, PO Box 99, Coal City IL 60416-0099. **Tel** (815)634-2102.

US/0010-1125
COLLEGE PRESS SERVICE. (19??)-. Periodical. English. ir (published mid-August to mid-May). $120.00 (subscribers who receive CPS weekly service); $180.00 (subscribers who receive CPS 2 or more weekly service). Tribune Media Services, 435 North Michigan Avenue, Chicago IL 60611. **Tel** (800)637-4082, FAX (312)222-2581. **ED** Diana Smith. **Circ:** 600. available on microfilm and microfiche from University Microfilms International (UMI).
Desc: Provides in-depth news and feature stories, editorial cartoons, photos, movie reviews and crossword puzzles all year long. Available once or twice a week, by mail and electronically.

US/0883-6574
COLLINSVILLE HERALD (COLLINSVILLE, ILL.), THE. (THE COLLINSVILLE HERALD.). (Sept. 15, 1879)-. Newspaper. English. wk. $14.50 in county; $28.00 others. Madison County Publications Inc., 113 East Clay Street, PO Box 389, Collinsville IL 62234. **Tel** (618)344-0264. **ED** Martin Richter (Editor-in-Chief) and Scott Queen (Managing Editor). **LC** 7639. **Photos**. **Ad Acc, Adv Mgr:** Doug Cooper. Full Page (B&W) $1,023.00. Half Page (B&W) $511.50. Full Page (Color) $1,108.00. Half Page (Color) $596.50. **Pub. Size:** Broadsheet. **Circ:** 9,347. ***Continues*** *Weekly Herald (Collinsville, Ill.).*

US/0191-7439
COMMAND POST. Vol. 1, No. 1 (Mar. 29, 1968)-. Newspaper. English. wk. Command Post, 612 East State Street, O'Fallon IL 62269. ***Continues*** *Broadcaster (Scott Air Force Base, Ill.).*

US/0742-8286
COMMERCIAL-NEWS (DANVILLE, ILL.), THE. (THE COMMERCIAL-NEWS.). **VFOAT** Commercial news; Sunday commercial-news. **VAT** Commercial News. (19??)-. Newspaper. English. da (except Sunday). $148.00. Commercial-News, 17 West North Street, Danville IL 61832. ***Continues*** *Danville Commercial-News.*

US/1061-3218
COUNTRY COURIER (HINCKLEY, ILL.). (COUNTRY COURIER.). (1991)-. Newspaper. English. wk. $20.00. Country Courier, 180 North May, PO Box 1241, Hinckley IL 60520. **Tel** (815)286-7761. **ED** Richard Manser. **Photos**. **Ad Acc, Adv Mgr:** Dolores Bastian. Full Page (B&W) $400.00. Half Page (B&W) $220.00. **Pub. Size:** Tabloid. **Circ:** 1,260 (USPS), 960 (paid), 150 (dealer sales), 160 (schools). available on microfilm from University Microfilms International (UMI).

US/1054-7940
COUNTRYSIDE (BARRINGTON, ILL.). (COUNTRYSIDE.). (19??)-. Newspaper. English. wk. $17.95. Pioneer Press, 1232 Central, Wilmette IL 60091. **Tel** (708)251-4300. ***Continues*** *Buffalo Grove Countryside, 0888-0204.*

●US
COURIER, THE. (Feb. 3, 1992)-. Newspaper. English. da. $96.52 Logan and adjoining counties in Illinois; $104.84 Illinois; $122.52 US; $187.00 other. Lincoln Courier, 601 Pulaski Street, PO Box 40, Lincoln IL 62656. **Tel** (217)732-2101. ***Continues*** *Lincoln Courier (Lincoln, Ill. : 1968).*

US
DAILY CLAY COUNTY ADVOCATE-PRESS, THE. Vol. 1, No. 1 (Aug. 6, 1979)-. Newspaper. English. da. Daily Clay County Advocate Press, 105 West North Avenue, Flora IL 62839-1613. **Tel** (618)662-2108. **ED** Jack Thatcher. **Ad Acc. Circ:** 4,100. ***Formed by the union of*** *Flora Daily News-Record* ***and*** *Clay County Advocate-Press.*

US/8750-7552
DAILY DISPATCH (MOLINE, ILL.). ***Title Change.*** (THE DAILY DISPATCH.). **VFOAT** Dispatch; Sunday Dispatch. (19??-19??). Newspaper. English. da. Moline Dispatch Publishing Company, 1720 5th Avenue, Moline IL 61265. **Tel** (309)764-4344. ***Continued by*** *Dispatch (Moline, Ill.), 1064-9220.*

US
DAILY GAZETTE NEWSPAPER. English. da. $98.80 (one year). Daily Gazette, 312 Second Avenue, Sterling IL 61701. **Tel** (815) 625-3600.

US/8750-6769
DAILY ILLINI (CHAMPAIGN-URBANA, ILL.), THE. (THE DAILY ILLINI.). (19??)-. Newspaper. English. da. Daily Illini, University of Illinois, 620 East John Street, Champaign IL 61820.

US
DAILY TIMES, THE. 123rd Year, 50th Day (Mar. 1, 1967)-. Newspaper. English. da (Published Mon.-Sat.). $78.00. Ottawa Daily Times, 110 West Jefferson, Ottawa IL 61350. **Tel** (815)433-2003, FAX (815)433-1626. **ED** James E. Malley Jr. (Editor-in-Chief) and Lonny Cain (Managing Editor). **Photos**. **Ad Acc, Adv Mgr:** Joan Heyers, **Tel** (815)433-2000. Full Page (B&W) $1,302.90. Half Page (B&W) $651.45. Full Page (Color) $1,427.90. Half Page (Color) $776.45. **Pub. Size:** Broadsheet. **Wire Svcs.:** AP. **Circ:** 13,600. available in microform from University Microfilms International (UMI). ***Continues*** *Daily Republican-Times.*

US/0747-3869
DANSKE PIONEER, DEN. **VFOAT** Dansk Pioneer. (Aug. 1, 1872)-. Newspaper. Danish (English). bw. $20.00. Bertelsen Publishing Company, 36 Elmwood Parkway, Elmwood Park IL 60635. **ED** H Miller. ***Absorbed*** *Dansk Tidende.*

US/0192-0073
DEERFIELD LIFE. **VFOAT** Deerfield Life and the Deerfield Star; Deerfield Lake County Life. (196?)-. Newspaper. English. wk. Lerner-Life Newspapers, 5158 Main Street, Skokie IL 60077. ***Absorbed*** *Lincolnshire Lake County Life.*

US
DELAVAN TIMES, THE. 63rd Year, No. 30 (July 25, 1929)-. Newspaper. English. wk. $16.00. Delavan Times, 314 Locust Street, Delavan IL 61734. **Tel** (309)244-7111. **ED** Ruth Larimore. **Photos**. **Ad Acc. Pub. Size:** Tabloid. **Circ:** 1,475 paid. available in microform. ***Continues*** *Delavan Times the Delavan Advertiser-Times;* ***Absorbed*** *Tribune (Delavan, Ill.).*

US/0744-6586
DENNI HLASATEL. **VFOAT** Nedelni Hlasatel; Czechoslovak Daily Herald. Vol. 1, No. 1 (April 4, 1891)-. Newspaper. Czech (Slovak). da (Tues. thru Thurs., except holidays). Denni Hlastel Print & Publishing Company, 1545 West 18th Street, Chicago IL 60608. **Tel** (312)863-5315. **ED** Josef Kucera. **Ad Acc. Circ:** 9,000. available on microfiche; available on microfilm.
Desc: Preserves Czechoslovak heritage, calling attention to the situation in Czechoslovakia.

US/0895-0148
DES PLAINES EDITION OF THE TIMES. **VFOAT** Des Plaines Times; Chicago Suburban Times. (Aug. 1985)-. Newspaper. English. wk. $33.15 Cook County; $66.30 other. Des Plaines Publishing Company, 1000 Executive Way, Des Plaines IL 60018. **Tel** (708)824-1111. **ED** John Meyer (Editor-in-Chief) and Joyce Diebel (Managing Editor). **Photos**. **Ad Acc, Adv Mgr:** Bill Tapper. Full Page (B&W) $2,576.00. Half Page (B&W) $1,480.50. Full Page (Color) $2,781.00. Half Page (Color) $1,685.00. **Pub. Size:** Broadsheet. **Circ:** 10,473. ***Continues*** *Des Plaines Times, 0745-8681.*
Desc: Community news, features, photos and advertising.

US/0889-4612
DIXON TELEGRAPH (DIXON, ILL. : 1985). (THE DIXON TELEGRAPH.). **VFOAT** Dixon (Ill.) Telegraph. (1985)-. Newspaper. English. da. $70.00 Leg, Ogle, Bureau and Whitside counties; $80.00 other. Dixon Telegraph, Dixon IL 61021. **Tel** (815)284-2222. ***Continues*** *Dixon Evening Telegraph.*

US
DRAUGAS. **VFOAT** Lithuanian Daily Friend; Lithuanian World-Wide Daily. (1917)-. Newspaper. Lithuanian (Lithuanian). da. $65.00 (Saturday); $100.00 (daily). Lithuanian Catholic Press, 4545 West 63rd Street, Chicago IL 60629. **Tel** (312)585-8284, FAX (312)585-8284. **ED** D. Bindokas (phone: (312)585-9500). **Bk Rev. Ad Acc, Adv Mgr:** Nijole. **Circ:** 6,200. available on microfilm from The Library of Congress Photoduplication Service. ***Continues*** *Savaitinis Draugas.*

US/0742-6615
DZIENNIK ZWIAZKOWY. **VFOAT** Zgoda; Polish Daily Zgoda. (Jan. 9, 1908)-. Newspaper. Polish (English). da. $80.00 US & Canada; $135.00 others. Alliance Printers and Publishers Inc., 5711 North Milwaukee Avenue, Chicago IL 60646. **Tel** (312)763-3343, FAX (312)763-3825. **ED** Wojciech Bialasiewicz, Elizabeth Glinka (Managing Editor). **Bk Rev**, (Qty: 10-20). **Photos. Ad Acc, Adv Mgr:** Wanda Such. Full Page (B&W) $700.00. Half Page (B&W) $420.00. **Pub. Size:** Broadsheet. **Wire Svcs.:** RN, AP. **Circ:** 22,000 (ctrl). available on microfilm from The Library of Congress Photoduplication Service. ***Absorbed*** *Dziennik Narodowy.*

US
EAST DUBUQUE REGISTER. Vol. 1, No. 1 (Feb. 2, 1894)-. Newspaper. English. wk. East Dubuque Register, 141 Saninawa Avenue, East Dubuque IL 61025.

US/0046-0966
EAST ST. LOUIS MONITOR. **VFOAT** East Saint Louis Monitor. (196?)-. Newspaper. English. wk. $40.00. East St. Louis Monitor, 1501 State Street, East St. Louis IL 62205. **Tel** (618)271-0468. **ED** Ernest Mercer. Full Page (B&W) $1,883.40. Half Page (B&W) $941.70. available on microfilm.

US/0895-0105
EDGEBROOK EDITION OF THE TIMES REVIEW. **VFOAT** Edgebrook Times Review; Times Review. (Dec. 1985)-. Newspaper. English. wk. $33.15. Des Plaines Publishing Company, 1000 Executive Way, Des Plaines IL 60018. **Tel** (708)824-1111. **ED** John Meyer (Editor-in-Chief) and Joyce Diebel (Managing Editor). **Photos. Ad Acc, Adv Mgr:** Bill Tapper. Full Page (B&W) $2,576.00. Half Page (B&W) $1,480.50. Full Page (Color) $2,781.00. Half Page (Color) $1,685.00. **Pub. Size:** Broadsheet. **Circ:** 3,454.

US/0895-0091
EDISON-NORWOOD EDITION OF THE TIMES REVIEW. **VFOAT** Edison Norwood Edition of The Times Review. (1986)-. Newspaper. English. wk. $33.15. Des Plaines Publishing Company, 1000 Executive Way, Des Plaines IL 60018. **Tel** (708)824-1111. **ED** John Meyer (Editor-in-Chief) and Joyce Diebel (Managing Editor). **Photos. Ad Acc, Adv Mgr:** Bill Tapper. Full Page (B&W) $2,576.00. Half Page (B&W) $1,480.50. Full Page (Color) $2,781.00. Half Page (Color) $1,685.00. **Pub. Size:** Broadsheet. **Circ:** 9,223. ***Continues*** *Edison Norwood Review.*

US
ELGIN COURIER-NEWS, THE. **VFOAT** Elgin Courier News. Began in (1925)-. Newspaper. English. da. $109.20. Elgin Daily Courier News, PO Box 531, 300 Lake Street, Elgin IL 60120. **Tel** (800)445-3538, (312)888-7721. ***Formed by the union of*** *Elgin Daily News* ***and*** *Elgin Daily Courier.*

US/1044-7733
EVANSTON REVIEW, THE. Vol. 1, No. 1 (June 4, 1925)-. Newspaper. English. wk (52 issues). $34.95 (Cooke County), $36.75 other. Pioneer Press, 1232 Central, Wilmette IL 60091. **Tel** (708)251-4300. **LC** 7645.

•US/1063-0570
EXPRESS (CHICAGO, ILL.). (EXPRESS : CHICAGO POLISH DAILY NEWS.). [Express]. (1992)-. Newspaper. Polish. da. $75.00. Alfa Publishing Company, 4854 West Addison Avenue, Chicago IL. **DD** 051.

US/0890-2682
FOCUS ON THE NEWS. [Focus news]. (19??). Periodical. English. Thirty-five times a year (Sept.- May, excluding 2 weeks in Dec.,& 1 week in Mar.). $85.00. Key Publications / Northbrook, PO Box 313, Northbrook IL 60065. **Tel** (312)272-8898. **DD** 051.

US/8750-7455
FOREST PARK NEWS. Newspaper. English. wk. $6.25. Pioneer Press, 1232 Central, Wilmette IL 60091. **Tel** (708)251-4300.

US
FREEPORT JOURNAL-STANDARD. ***Title Change.*** **VFOAT** Freeport Journal Standard. Began with Oct. 19, 1913 issue. Newspaper. English. da. Journal-Standard, 27 South State Street, Freeport IL 61032. ***Merged with*** *Freeport Daily Journal* ***to form*** *Freeport Evening Standard.*

US/0747-282X
GALVA NEWS, THE. Vol. 39, No. 1 (Jan. 5, 1915)-. Newspaper. English. wk. $15.00 in Illinois; $17.00 other. Galesburg Printing and Publishing Company, Box GG, Galva IL 61434. **Tel** (309)932-2103. **ED** Randy Rodgers. **LC** 7651. **Ad Acc. Circ:** 2,687. available on microfilm. ***Continues*** *Galva Standard;* ***Absorbed*** *Altona Record-News.*
Desc: Local government, schools, and feature news material. Local sports and commentary section.

US
GAZETTE-DEMOCRAT, THE TALK AND COBDEN REVIEW, THE. **VFOAT** Gazette Democrat, The Talk and Cobden Review; Talk; Cobden Review. Vol. 119, No. 11 (Apr. 11, 1968)-. Newspaper. English. wk (Published on Thursdays). Anna Gazette Democrat, 112 Lafayette Street, Anna IL 62906-1544. **Tel** (618)833-2158, FAX (618)833-5813. **ED** Geof Skinner. **Circ:** 5,800. ***Continues*** *Gazette-Democrat and The Anna Talk.*

US
GIRARD GAZETTE, THE. Vol. 1, No. 1 (Jan. 18, 1879)-. Newspaper. English. wk. $21.00. Girard Gazette, 174 West Center Street, Girard IL 62640. **Tel** (217)965-3355, FAX (217)965-4512. **ED** Norris Jones. **LC** 7652. **Photos. Ad Acc, Adv Mgr:** Nathan Jones. Full Page (B&W) $750.00. Half Page (B&W) $400.00. **Pub. Size:** Broadsheet. available on microfilm.

US
GLASFORD GAZETTE. Began with Jan. 1899 issue. Newspaper. English. wk. Glasford Gazette, 401 Main Street, Glasford IL 61533.

US/0747-3311
GLENCOE NEWS/VOICE. **VFOAT** Glencoe News Voice. (198?)-. Newspaper. English. wk. Pioneers Press, 1232 Centrl, Wilmette IL 60091. **Tel** (708)251-4300. ***Continues*** *Glencoe Mail Advertiser.*

US/0745-9815
GLENVIEW NEWS/VOICE. **VFOAT** Glenview News Voice. Vol. 1, No. 1 (June 8, 1983)-. Newspaper. English. wk. Pioneers Press, 1232 Centrl, Wilmette IL 60091. **Tel** (708)251-4300.

US
GOLDEN PRAIRIE NEWS. Vol. 1, No. 11 (Mar. 17, 1977)-. Newspaper. English. wk (Published on Thursdays). $15.00. Golden Prairie News, 301 South Chestnut, Assumption IL 62510. **Tel** (217)226-3721, FAX (217)226-3579. **ED** Willard Raymond. **Photos. Ad Acc, Adv Mgr:** Angela Pamery. Full Page (B&W) $336.00. Half Page (B&W) $175.00. Full Page (Color) $400.00. Half Page (Color) $235.00. **Pub. Size:** Standard. **Circ:** 2,200 weekly paid. ***Continues*** *Moweaqua News.*

US
GREENVILLE ADVOCATE (GREENVILLE, ILL.). ***Title Change.*** (THE GREENVILLE ADVOCATE.). Vol. 1, No. 1 (Feb. 11, 1858)-?. Newspaper. English. sw. Greenville Advocate - Illinois, 305 South 2nd Street, Greenville IL 62246. **ED** Duane L Reeves. **Ad Acc. Circ:** 5,050 (ctrl). ***Absorbed*** *Greenville Item.* ***Continued by*** *American Courier (Greenville, Ill.).*

US/0745-810X
GURNEE PRESS. (GURNEE PRESS : A LAKELAND NEWSPAPER.). **VFOAT** Lakeland Newspapers. (19??)-. Newspaper. English. wk. $20.00. Lakeland Newspapers, 30 South Whitney Street, Grayslake IL 60030. **Tel** (708)223-8161, FAX (708)223-8810. **ED** Rhonda Burke. **Bk Rev. Photos. Ad Acc, Adv Mgr:** Jill DePasquale. Full Page (B&W) $600.00. Half Page (B&W) $300.00. Full Page (Color) $655.00. Half Page (Color) $355.00. **Pub. Size:** Standard. **Circ:** 4,714.

US/0274-5801
HANGUK ILBO (CHICAGO, ILL.). (HANGUK ILBO.). **VFOAT** Hanguk Ilbo; Korea Times; Korea Times Chicago. (1965)-. Newspaper. Korean. da. Korea Times Inc., 4447 North Kedzie Avenue, Chicago IL 60625. **Tel** (312)463-1050.

US
HARVARD HERALD, THE. 53rd Year, No. 13 (Jan. 25, 1940)-. Newspaper. English. wk. Harvard Herald, 201 South Ayer Street, Harvard IL 60033. **LC** 7655. available on microfilm from University Microfilms International (UMI). ***Continues*** *Harvard Herald Independent.*

US
HERALD, THE. Vol. 96, No. 45 (Nov. 11, 1981)-. Newspaper. English. wk. $17.50. Herald Publications, 314 East Church, Mascoutah IL 62258. **Tel** (618)566-8282. **ED** Pamela Rensing. **Bk Rev**, (Qty: 15). **Photos. Ad Acc, Adv Mgr:** Jeff Forsythe. Full Page (B&W) $500.00. Half Page (B&W) $250.00. Full Page (Color) $550.00. Half Page (Color) $275.00. **Pub. Size:** Broadsheet. **Wire Svcs.:** SS. available in microform. ***Continues*** *Mascoutah Herald.*

US
HERALD, THE. (19??)-. Newspaper. English. wk (Published on Tuesdays). Bourbonnais Herald, 390 North Convent Avenue, Bourbonnais IL 60914-2016. **Tel** (815)933-1131, FAX (815)933-3785. **ED** Toby Olszewski. **Circ:** 32,200.

US/8750-0957
HIGHLAND NEWS LEADER. **VFOAT** News Leader. Vol. 21, No. 50 (Aug. 16, 1921)-. Newspaper. English. sw. $26.00. Highland News Leader, 822 Broadway, PO Box 250, Highland IL 62249. **Tel** (618)654-2366. **ED** Adam Koishor. **Photos. Ad Acc, Adv Mgr:** Gay Bentlage. Full Page (B&W) $871.72. Half Page (B&W) $512.78. Full Page (Color) $961.72. Half Page (Color) $602.78. **Pub. Size:** Broadsheet. available on microfilm. ***Absorbed*** *Highland News (Highland, Ill.); Highland Leader.*

US/0191-5460
HIGHLAND PARK LIFE. Newspaper. English. wk. Learner Newspaper, 7519 North Ashland, Chicago IL 60625. **Tel** (312)761-7200.

US/1053-2846
HIGHLAND PARK NEWS (HIGHLAND PARK, ILL.). (HIGHLAND PARK NEWS.). (19??)-. Newspaper. English. wk. Pioneers Press, 1232 Centrl, Wilmette IL 60091. **Tel** (708)251-4300. ***Continues*** *Highland Park News/Voice, 0746-0813.*

US
HLASATEL. **VFOAT** Bohemian Herald. (June 1, 1892)-. Newspaper. Czech (Slovak). wk. $60.00. Denni-Hlastel Print and Publishing Company, 6426 West Cermak Road, Berwyn IL 60402. **Tel** (708)749-1891, FAX (708)749-1935. **ED** Josef Kucera Sr. (Editor-in-Chief) and Josef Kucera Jr. (Managing Editor). **LC** 7602-A. **Photos. Ad Acc, Adv Mgr:** Josef Kucera and Martha Jerabek. Full Page (B&W) $400.00. Half Page (B&W) $200.00. **Pub. Size:** Tabloid. **Circ:** 5,000. available on microfiche; available on microfilm.
Desc: Preserve history of Czechoslovakia and calls attention to current situations there.

US
ILLINOIAN-STAR DAILY. **VFOAT** Illinoian Star Daily. No. 29 (May 11, 1982)-. Newspaper. English. $23.40. Beardstown Illinoian Star, 1210 Wall Street, Beardstown IL 62618-2399. **Tel** (217)323-1010, FAX (217)323-5402. **ED** Sally Lael. **Bk Rev. Photos. Ad Acc, Adv Mgr:** Lillian Mitchell. Full Page (B&W) $618.24. Half Page (B&W) $388.08. Full Page (Color) $683.24. Half Page (Color) $453.08. **Pub. Size:** Broadsheet. **Circ:** 2,200. ***Continues*** *Illinoian-Star (Beardstown, Ill. : Daily).*

US/0199-7823
ILLINOIS TIMES. (Sept. 18, 1975)-. Newspaper. English. Fifty-two times a year. $30.00. Illinois Times, PO Box 3524, Springfield IL 62708. **Tel** (217)753-2226, FAX (217)753-2281. **ED** Fletcher F. Farrar, William Furry (Managing Editor). **Bk Rev**, (Qty: 12). **Photos. Ad Acc, Adv Mgr:** Simon Mulverhill. Full Page (B&W) $1050.00. Half Page (B&W) $694.00. Full Page (Color) $1050.00 plus $125.00 per color. Half Page (Color) $694.00 plus $125.00 per color. **Pub. Size:** Tabloid. **Wire Svcs.:** AN. **Circ:** 33,000 weekly unpaid. available in microform.
Desc: Ideas in the area of downstate Illinois.

•US
JOURNAL, THE. (June 10, 1992)-. Newspaper. English. sw. $23.40. Sun Publications / IL, 9 West Jackson Avenue, PO Box 269, Naperville IL 60566. **Tel** (312)355-0063. ***Continues*** *Daily Journal (Wheaton, Ill.).*

US
JOURNAL STAR, THE. Vol. 117, No. 94 (Oct. 2, 1971)-. Newspaper. English. da. Peoria Journal Star, 1 News Plaza, Peoria IL 61643. **Tel** (309)686-3000. **ED** Marge Fanning. **Bk Rev. Ad Acc. Circ:** 99,197 daily, 114,536 Sunday (ctrl). available on microfilm. Documents available from UMI Article Clearinghouse. ***Continues*** *Peoria Journal Star.*
Ind/Abst Bus. Dateline (Dec. 17, 1991-) [Full Txt.].

US
KANKAKEE DAILY JOURNAL. Newspaper. English. $75.00 Illinois and Indiana; $100.00 other. Kankakee Daily Journal, 8 Dearborn Square, Kankakee IL 60901. **Tel** (815)937-3322. available on an online database (file 635/Full-Text) from DIALOG. Documents available from UMI Article Clearinghouse.
Ind/Abst Bus. Dateline (Dec. 12, 1991-) [Full Txt.].

US
KENDALL COUNTY RECORD (YORKVILLE, ILL. : 1864 : WEEKLY). (KENDALL COUNTY RECORD.). (May 1864)-. Newspaper. English. wk. Kendall County Record, 222 Bridge Street, Yorkville IL 60506.

US
LACON HOME JOURNAL (LACON, ILL. : 1866 : WEEKLY). (THE LACON HOME JOURNAL.). **VFOAT** Lacon Semi-Weekly Home Journal. New Series, Vol. 27, No. 1 (June 27, 1866)-. Newspaper. English. Fifty-two times a year (Thurs.). $23.00. Home Journal, 204 South Washington Street, Lacon IL 61540. **Tel** (309)246-2865. **ED** William H. Sondag. **LC** 7663. **Photos. Ad Acc.** Full Page (B&W) $280.00. Half Page (B&W) $140.00. Full Page (Color) $380.00. Half Page

(Color) $240.00. **Pub. Size:** Tabloid. **Circ:** 1,650 (ctrl). ***Continues*** *Illinois Gazette (Lacon, Ill.);* ***Absorbed*** *Marshall County Record (Lacon, Ill.).*

US/0744-7973
LAKE FORESTER. **VFOAT** Lake Forester, with News of Lake Bluff. (19??)-. Newspaper. English. Fifty-two times a year. $39.95 Lake County Illinois; $41.50 other. Pioneer Press, 1232 Central, Wilmette IL 60091. **Tel** (708)251-4300. **ED** Cathy Backer. **Circ:** 5,655.

US/8750-6998
LEMONT METROPOLITAN. **VFOAT** MET. Newspaper. English. wk. $15.00, $8.00 (Belngbrook). Lemont Metropolitan, 223 Main Street, Lemont IL 60439. **Tel** (312)257-5300. **ED** Jan Protko. **Ad Acc. Circ:** 3,800. available on microfilm.

US/0195-2528
LEYDEN STAR-SENTINEL. (19??)-. Newspaper. English. wk. West Suburban Press Inc., 130-D Broadway, Melrose Park IL 60160.

US/0744-852X
LIBERTYVILLE REVIEW. (19??)-. Newspaper. English. Fifty times a year. $24.95 Lake County Illinois; $26.50 other. Pioneer Press, 1232 Central, Wilmette IL 60091. **Tel** (708)251-4300. **ED** Robert Miodonski. **Circ:** 2,580.

US
MACOUPIN COUNTY ENQUIRER. Vol. 28, No. 52 (Dec. 27, 1899); Vol. 39, No. 1 (Jan. 3, 1900)-Vol. 77, No. 25 (June 24, 1937); Vol. 66, No. 26 (July 1, 1937); Vol. 80, No. 8 (Feb. 22, 1951); Vol. 100, No. 1 (Mar. 1, 1951)-. Newspaper. English. Fifty-two times a year (Thurs.). $17.00 (in county), $19.00 (out of county). MaCoupin County Enquirer, 125 East Main Street, Carlinville IL 62626. **Tel** (217)854-2534, FAX (217)854-2535. **ED** Chris Schmitt. **Photos. Ad Acc, Adv Mgr:** Mary Schmitt. Full Page (B&W) $415.00. Half Page (B&W) $215.00. Full Page (Color) $465.00. Half Page (Color) $265.00. **Pub. Size:** Broadsheet. **Circ:** 4,400 paid, 600 unpaid. ***Formed by the union of*** *Macoupin Enquirer* ***and*** *Macoupin County Herald.*

US
MATTOON JOURNAL GAZETTE. (Oct. 13, 1986)-. Newspaper. English. da. $52.00. Mattoon Journal Gazette, 100 Broadway, Mattoon IL 61938. **Tel** (217)235-5656. ***Continues*** *Journal Gazette (Mattoon, Ill.).*

US/0745-3744
MELROSE PARK HERALD WITH NEWS OF STONE PARK. **VFOAT** Melrose Park Herald. Newspaper. English. wk. Pioneer Press, 1232 Central, Wilmette IL 60091. **Tel** (708)251-4300. **ED** Tom Ganz. **Circ:** 2,797. ***Continues*** *Herald.*

US/0270-4641
MEMBERSHIP DIRECTORY - SUBURBAN NEWSPAPERS OF AMERICA. **Main/Corp** Suburban Newspapers of America, Chicago, Ill. Directory. English. Suburban Newspapers of America, Chicago IL 60610. **Tel** FAX (312)565-4658. **LC** Z6944.C64; S9A; PN4888.C594. **DD** 071/.3. **Ad Acc.** ctrl circ.

US/0193-7251
MORTON GROVE CHAMPION. (1???)-. Periodical. English. Fifty-two times a year. $22.95 Cook County, Illinois; $23.95 other. Pioneer Press, 1232 Central, Wilmette IL 60091. **Tel** (708)251-4300. **ED** Geoff Pounds. **Circ:** 4,085.

US/0194-9381
MORTON GROVE LIFE. Vol. 20, No. 33 (Apr. 6, 1967)-. Newspaper. English. wk. Lerner-Life Newspapers, 5158 Main Street, Skokie IL 60077. ***Continues*** *Life (Skokie, Ill. : Morton Grove Ed.).*

US/0747-458X
MOUNT OLIVE HERALD, THE. Newspaper. English. wk. Mt Olive Herald, 305 East Maine Street, Mt Olive IL 62069.

US/0747-2595
MOUNT PROSPECT TIMES. **VFOAT** Mt. Prospect Times. (1948)-. Newspaper. English. wk. $33.15. Des Plaines Publishing Company, 1000 Executive Way, Des Plaines IL 60018. **Tel** (708)824-1111. **ED** John Meyer (Editor-in-Chief) and Joyce Diebel (Managing Editor). **Photos. Ad Acc, Adv Mgr:** Bill Tapper. Full Page (B&W) $2,576.00. Half Page (B&W) $1,480.50. Full Page (Color) $2,781.00. Half Page (Color) $1,685.00. **Pub. Size:** Broadsheet. **Circ:** 5,981 (ctrl). ***Continues*** *Suburban (Mt. Prospect, Ill.), 0279-7887.*
Desc: Community newspaper.

US/0746-8938
MUNDELEIN NEWS. (198?)-. Newspaper. English. wk. Lakeland Newspapers, 30 South Whitney Street, Grayslake IL 60030. **Tel** (708)223-8161, FAX (708)223-8810. **Ad Acc, Adv Mgr:** Jill DePasquale. **Circ:** 3,162. ***Continues*** *Fremont Patriot.*

US/0744-8538
MUNDELEIN REVIEW. (19??)-. Newspaper. English. Fifty-two times a year. $24.95 Lake County Illinois; $26.50 other. Pioneer Press, 1232 Central, Wilmette IL 60091. **Tel** (708)251-4300. **ED** Robert Miodonski. **Circ:** 1,511.

US/0745-5445
NAUJIENOS. **VFOAT** Lithuanian Daily News. Began Feb. 9, 1914. Newspaper. Lithuanian (Lithuanian). da (Mon.-Sat.). Lithuanian News Publishing Company, 1739 South Halsted Street, Chicago IL 60608. **Tel** (312)421-6100. **Circ:** 18,500.

US/0028-1778
NEAR NORTH NEWS. (195?)-. Newspaper. English. wk. $25.00. Near North News Inc., 222 West Ontario Street, Suite 502, Chicago IL 60610-3095. **Tel** (312)787-2677, FAX (312)787-2680. **ED** Arnie Matanky. **Bk Rev**, (Qty: 15). **Photos. Ad Acc.** Full Page (B&W) $806.40. Half Page (B&W) $504.00. Full Page (Color) $956.40. Half Page (Color) $654.00. **Pub. Size:** Tabloid. **Circ:** 7,500.
Desc: Community newspaper of Chicago's neighborhoods, with emphasis on arts, politics, entertainment and business.

US
NEW METRO NEWS. (199?)-. English. wk. $32.00. New Metro News, 501 East 32nd Street, Apartment 501, Chicago IL 60616. **Tel** (312)791-0880. Index available (free). ***Continues*** *Chicago Metro News.*

US
NEWS, THE. (1925)-. Newspaper. English. wk. Skokie News, 7870 Lincoln Avenue, Skokie IL 60077. **LC** 7689.

US/1042-3354
NEWS-GAZETTE (CHAMPAIGN, ILL.). (THE NEWS-GAZETTE.). **VFOAT** News Gazette. 134th Year, No. 155 (Jan. 1, 1986)-. Newspaper. English. da (Except Christmas). $116.50 (daily & Sun.), selected counties in Illinois; $177.35 (daily & Sun.), other. Champaign News-Gazette, PO Box 677, 15 Main Street, Champaign IL 61820. **Tel** (217)351-5266, (217)351-5252, FAX (217)351-5291. **ED** John R. Foreman (Editor-in-Chief) and John Beck (Managing Editor). **Bk Rev. Photos. Ad Acc, Adv Mgr:** Sue Trippiedi, **Tel** (217)351-5282. **Pub. Size:** Broadsheet. **Wire Svcs.:** AP. **Circ:** 45,000 (Mon.-Sat.), 52,300 (Sunday). available on microfilm. ***Continues*** *Champaign-Urbana News-Gazette (Champaign, Ill. : 1965).*

US/0744-141X
NEWS PROGRESS (SULLIVAN, ILL.). (NEWS PROGRESS.). (19??)-. Newspaper. English. sw (103 per year). $17.50 Moultrie County; $22.50 other. Sullivan News Progress, PO Box A, Sullivan IL 61951. **Tel** (217)728-7381.

US/0194-8628
NILES LIFE, THE. (19??)-. Newspaper. English. wk. Lerner-Life Newspapers, 5158 Main Street, Skokie IL 60077.

US/0744-5393
NILES SPECTATOR. (19??)-. Newspaper. English. wk. Pioneer Press, 1232 Central, Wilmette IL 60091. **Tel** (708)251-4300.

US/1054-7932
NORRIDGE HARWOOD HEIGHTS NEWS. (19??)-. Newspaper. English. wk. $11.95. Pioneer Press, 1232 Central, Wilmette IL 60091. **Tel** (708)251-4300. **ED** Carroll M. Salman. **Ad Acc, Adv Mgr:** Julie Ross. **Circ:** 3400. ***Continues*** *Norridge News, 0885-7814.*
Desc: We cover news of Norridge and Harwood Heights, IL such as: Village Government, schools, park district, township and politics, as well as people.

US/0885-7814
NORRIDGE NEWS. ***Title Change.*** (1985)-?. Newspaper. English. wk. Pioneer Press, 1232 Central, Wilmette IL 60091. **Tel** (708)251-4300. ***Continues*** *Citizen.* ***Continued by*** *Norridge Harwood Heights News, 1054-7932.*

US/0191-6300
NORTHBROOK LIFE. (1968)-. Newspaper. English. wk. Lerner-Life Newspapers, 5158 Main Street, Skokie IL 60077. **ED** Gary Roberts. **Circ:** 5,792.

US/0745-9777
NORTHBROOK NEWS/VOICE. **VFOAT** Northbrook News Voice. Vol. 1, No. 1 (June 9, 1983)-. Newspaper. English. wk. Pioneers Press, 1232 Centrl, Wilmette IL 60091. **Tel** (708)251-4300. ***Continues*** *Northbrook News-Advertiser, 0191-6432.*

US/0744-9550
NORTHBROOK STAR. (19??)-. Newspaper. English. Fifty-two times a year. $39.95 Cook County Illinois; $41.50 other. Pioneer Press, 1232 Central, Wilmette IL 60091. **Tel** (708)251-4300. **ED** Ellen Shubart. **Circ:** 7,495.

US
OAK LEAVES. **VFOAT** Mid-Week Oak Leaves; Mid Week Oak Leaves; Sunday Oak Leaves; Oak Leaves-Forest Leaves; Oak Leaves Forest Leaves; Oak-Forest Leaves; Oak Forest Leaves. Vol. 21, No. 4 (Jan. 24, 1902)-. Newspaper. English. Three times a year. $29.95. Pioneer Press, 1232 Central, Wilmette IL 60091. **Tel** (708)251-4300. **ED** Peter Neill. **LC** 7672. **Ad Acc. Circ:** 13,314. available on microfilm. ***Formed by the union of*** *Oak Park Times; Oak Park Vindicator;* ***Continues in part*** *Proviso Vindicator.*

US/1045-3059
OGLE COUNTY LIFE, ROCK VALLEY SHOPPER, THE. (OGLE COUNTY LIFE, ROCK VALLEY SHOPPER.). **VFOAT** Ogle County Life/Rock Valley Shopper; Rock Valley Shopper. Newspaper. English. wk. Ogle County Life, PO Box 378, Oregon IL 61061-0378. ***Continues*** *Ogle County Life, 8750-2496.*

US
OLNEY DAILY MAIL. Began with April 15, 1898 issue. Newspaper. English. da. Olney Daily Mail, PO Box 340, Olney IL 62450. ***Continues*** *Daily Mail (Olney, Ill.);* ***Absorbed*** *Olney Advocate; Olney Times (Olney, Ill. : 1883); Noble News (Noble, Ill.).*

US
PANTAGRAPH (BLOOMINGTON, ILL.). (THE PANTAGRAPH.). Newspaper. English. da. Pantagraph, 301 West Washington Street, Bloomington IL 61701. available on microfilm from University Microfilms International (UMI). ***Continues*** *Daily Pantagraph (Bloomington, Ill. : 1945).*

US/0744-5385
PARK RIDGE ADVOCATE. Newspaper. English. wk. Pioneer Press, 1232 Central, Wilmette IL 60091. **Tel** (708)251-4300. **ED** Chuck Hutchcraft. **Circ:** 7,694.

US/0895-013X
PARK RIDGE EDITION OF THE TIMES HERALD. **VFOAT** Park Ridge Times Herald; Times Herald. (August 1985)-. Newspaper. English. wk. $33.15. Des Plaines Publishing Company, 1000 Executive Way, Des Plaines IL 60018. **Tel** (708)824-1111. **ED** John Meyer (Editor-in-Chief) and Joyce Diebel (Managing Editor). **Photos. Ad Acc, Adv Mgr:** Bill Tapper. Full Page (B&W) $2,576.00. Half Page (B&W) $1,480.50. Full Page (Color) $2,781.00. Half Page (Color) $1,685.00. **Pub. Size:** Broadsheet. **Circ:** 9,307. ***Continues*** *Park Ridge Herald.*

US/0745-7863
PEKIN DAILY TIMES. Vol. 1, No. 1 (Jan. 3, 1881)-. Newspaper. English. da (except Sun. and holidays). $77.00 (one year). The Pekin Daily Times, PO Box 430, Pekin IL 61555. **Tel** (309)346-1111. **ED** Robert W. Marshall. **Circ:** 16,477.

US/0162-8976
PRAIRIE SUN. (1977)-. Periodical. English. Forty-Four times a year. Prairie Sun, 1109 West Main Street, Peoria IL 61606. available on microfilm from Bell & Howell.

US/1043-3236
PRESS (ELMHURST, ILL. : OAK BROOK ED.). (THE PRESS.). 1989-. Newspaper. English. sw. $21.00 (Oak Brook or Oakbrook Terrace), $35.00 other. Press Publications, 122 South York Street, Elmhurst IL 60126. ***Continues*** *Oak Brook Press, 8750-9296.*

US/0195-251X
PROVISO STAR-SENTINEL. (19??)-. Newspaper. English. wk. West Suburban Press Inc., 130-D Broadway, Melrose Park IL 60160.

US/0746-6358
QUINCY HERALD-WHIG, THE. **VFOAT** Herald-Whig. (June 1, 1926)-. Newspaper. English. da. Quincy Herald-Whig, 130 South 5th Street, Quincy IL 62301. **Tel** (217)223-5100. **ED** Joe Conover. **Circ:** 27,900 daily, 31,746 Sunday. available on an online database (file 635/Full-Text) from DIALOG. Documents available from UMI Article Clearinghouse. ***Formed by the union of*** *Quincy Herald* ***and*** *Whig Journal.*
Ind/Abst Bus. Dateline (Dec. 29, 1991-) [Full Txt.].

US
READER. **VFOAT** Chicago Reader. Vol. 1, No. 1 (Oct. 1, 1971)-. Newspaper. English. wk. $50.00. Chicago Reader Inc, 11 East Illinois, Chicago IL 60611. **Tel** (312)828-0350.

US/8750-2380
REPORTER (CASEY, ILL.). (THE REPORTER.). Newspaper. English. sw. Clark County Publishing Company, 216 South Central Avenue, Casey IL 62420.

US/0193-3485
REVOLUTIONARY WORKER. **Added/Corp** Revolutionary Communist Party, USA. (19??)-. Newspaper. English (Spanish). wk. $52.00 (institutions), $31.20 (individuals). RCP Publications, PO Box 3486, Merchandise Mart, Chicago IL 60654. **Tel** (312)327-1689.
Desc: The newspaper of the Revolutionary Communist

Illinois

Party, U.S.A. In-depth, serious, yet often irreverently humorous analysis of current events. Follows and reports on revolutionary movements and popular upsurges worldwide.

US/0744-5369
RIVER GROVE MESSENGER. *Ceased.*
Ceased (Dec. 1990). Newspaper. English. wk. Pioneer Press, 1232 Central, Wilmette IL 60091. **Tel** (708)251-4300. **ED** Andy Blaser. **Circ:** 1,666.

US
ROCKFORD REGISTER STAR. **VFOAT**
Sunday Register Star. (Jan. 2, 1979)-. Newspaper. English. da. Rockford Newspapers Inc., 99 East State Street, Rockford IL 61104. **Tel** (815)987-1200. **ED** Charles Morris. **Circ:** 70,192 daily, 86,485 Sunday. *Formed by the union of Morning Star (Rockford, Ill.) and Rockford Register-Republic.*

US/0894-7465
ROCKTON-ROSCOE HERALD. *Title Change.* **VFOAT** Rockton Roscoe Herald. Newspaper. English. wk. North Central Associated Publishers Inc, 416 Center Street, Durand IL 61024. *Continued by Rockton Herald.*

US/0895-0113
ROSEMONT EDITION OF THE TIMES.
VFOAT Rosemont Times; Times. (Aug. 1985)-. Newspaper. English. Fifty-two times a year (Wed.). $43.00 Illinois; $80.00 others. Des Plaines Publishing Company, 1000 Executive Way, Des Plaines IL 60018. **Tel** (708)824-1111. *Continues Rosemont Times.*

US/0744-5407
ROSEMONT PROGRESS. *Ceased.*
Newspaper. English. wk. Pioneer Press, 1232 Central, Wilmette IL 60091. **Tel** (708)251-4300. **ED** Deborah Roberts. **Circ:** 252.

US/8750-2348
SANDARA. (SANDARA : AMERIKOS LIETUVIU TAUTINES SANDAROS ORGANAS.). [Sandara]. **VFOAT** League. Began publication in 1913. Newspaper. Lithuanian. mo. $10.00. Sandara, 840 West 33rd Street, Chicago IL 60608. **DD** 071.

US/0744-5377
SCHILLER PARK INDEPENDENT. *Ceased.*
(19??)-?. Newspaper. English. wk. Pioneer Press, 1232 Central, Wilmette IL 60091. **Tel** (708)251-4300. **ED** Deborah Roberts. **Circ:** 1,232.

US/0037-2331
SENTINEL (CHICAGO, ILL.). (SENTINEL.). (19??)-. Periodical. English. Fifty-two times a year. $48.95. The Sentinel / Chicago, Illinois, 150 North Michigan Avenue, Suite 3130, Chicago IL 60601. **Tel** (312)407-0060. **ED** Jack I. Fishbein. **Bk Rev. Ad Acc. Circ:** 50,000 (ctrl).

US/1061-320X
SESSER-VALIER TIMES. **VFOAT** Sesser Valier Times. (1991)-. Newspaper. English. bw. Sesser-Valier Times, 113 East Franklin, Sesser IL 62884-0658.

US/0192-2742
SMOKIE REVIEW. Newspaper. English. wk. Pioneer Press, 1232 Central, Wilmette IL 60091. **Tel** (708)251-4300.

US
SOUTH SHORE SCENE. (Sept. 1961)-. Newspaper. English. wk. South Shore Scene, PO Box 49007, Chicago IL 60649-3610. **Tel** (312)363-0441.

US/0038-4704
SOUTHWEST NEWS-HERALD. **VAT** Southwest News-Herald. Newspaper. English. wk. $15.00. Southwest News-Herald, 6225 South Kedzie Avenue, Chicago IL 60629.

US/0746-5181
STAR (CHICAGO HEIGHTS AREA [ED.]), THE. (THE STAR.). (19??)-. Newspaper. English. sw. $53.20. Star Publications, 1526 Otto Boulevard, Chicago Heights IL 60411. **Tel** (708)755-6161, **FAX** (708)755-0095. **ED** Lester Sons. **Ad Acc, Adv Mgr:** Jay Frederickson. **Circ:** 14,640. *Continues Chicago Heights Star.*

US/8750-5932
STAR (CHICAGO HEIGHTS, ILL.), THE. (THE STAR.). (19??)-. Newspaper. English. sw. Chicago Heights Star, 1526 Otto Boulevard, Chicago Heights IL 60411. **Tel** (312)755-6161.

US
STAR-COURIER, THE. **VFOAT** Star Courier. Vol. 42, No. 218 (Sept. 17, 1948)-. Newspaper. English. da. Kewanee Star Courier, 105 East Central Boulevard, Kewanee IL 61443. **Tel** (309)852-2181. *Continues Kewanee Star-Courier.*

US/0746-5742
STAR (FRANKFORT, ILL.), THE. (THE STAR.). (19??)-. Newspaper. English. sw. varies ($25.20 to #37.20). Frankfort-Mokena Star, 1526 Otto Boulevard, Chicago Heights IL 60411. **Tel** (708)755-6161. **ED** Lester Sons. **Bk Rev. Ad Acc. Circ:** 70,000 (ctrl). available on microfilm. *Continues Frankfort-Mokena Star.*
Desc: Nineteen separate community newspapers.

US/0746-5173
STAR (HARVEY-MARKHAM AREA ED.), THE. (THE STAR.). (19??)-. Newspaper. English. sw. The Star Williams Press Inc, 154th and Broadway/Suite 201, Harvey IL 60426. *Formed by the union of Harvey Star-Tribune and Markham Star-Tribune.*

US/0746-5157
STAR (TINLEY PARK ED.), THE. (THE STAR.). (19??)-. Newspaper. English. sw. Tinley Park Star, 1526 Otto Boulevard, Chicago Heights IL 64117. *Continues Star Herald.*

US
STATE JOURNAL-REGISTER, THE.
VFOAT State Journal Register. Vol. 143, No. 234 (July 1, 1974)-. Newspaper. English. da. State Journal Register, PO Box 19486, Springfield IL 62794. **Tel** (217)788-1450, (800)397-2472. **ED** Edward H. Armstrong. **Circ:** 69,349 daily; 71,834 Sunday. *Formed by the union of Illinois State Journal (Springfield, Ill. : 1889) and Illinois State Register (Springfield, Ill. : 1889).*

US/0885-6389
SUN (BOLINBROOK EDITION). (THE SUN.). Newspaper. English. wk. The Sun / Illinois, 349 North Schmidt Road, Bolingbrook IL 60439. *Continues Beacon Sun.*

US/8750-2003
SUN (LAGRANGE, ILL.), THE. (THE SUN.). Newspaper. English. wk. $13.50. Sun Newspapers Inc, 500 East Avenue, Lagrange IL 60525. **DD** 071.

US/0897-456X
TELEGRAPH (ALTON, ILL.), THE.
(TELEGRAPH.). **VFOAT** Alton Evening Telegraph; Alton Telegraph. (1986)-. Newspaper. English. da. Alton Telegraph, 111 East Broadway, Alton IL 62002. **Tel** (618)463-2500, **FAX** (618)463-9829. *Continues Alton Telegraph (Alton, Ill. : 1852 : Daily).*

US
TIMES-COURIER. **VFOAT** Times Courier. No. 285 (May 5, 1977)-. Newspaper. English. da. Charleston Times Courier, 307 Sixth Street, Charleston IL 61920-1558. **Tel** (217)345-7085, **FAX** (217)345-7090. **ED** Betty Boyer. **Ad Acc, Adv Mgr:** Bob Yamamoto. **Circ:** 7,432. *Continues Coles County Daily Times-Courier.*

US
TIMES-LEADER, THE. **VFOAT** Times Leader. (July 1, 1933)-. Newspaper. English. wk. $22.00 (in county), $26.00 (out of county). Times-Leader / Illinois, PO Box 479, McCleansboro IL 62859. **LC** 7666. **Photos. Ad Acc, Adv Mgr:** Kathy Metcalf. Full Page (B&W) $679.40. Half Page (B&W) $339.70. Full Page (Color) $779.40. Half Page (Color) $449.70. available on microfilm from University Microfilms International (UMI). *Formed by the union of McLeansboro Leader and McLeansboro Times.*

US/0745-5542
TIMES-PRESS (STREATOR, ILL.).
(TIMES-PRESS.). **VAT** Times Press. Newspaper. English. da. $37.00 in Illinois, $43.00 other. Times-Press, 115 Oak Street, Streator IL 61364. *Continues Streator Daily Times Press.*

US
TIMES-RECORD, THE. **VFOAT** Times Record. Newspaper. English. wk. Times-Record, 113-115 South College Avenue, Aledo IL 61231. available on microfilm. *Formed by the union of Aledo Times and Aledo Weekly Record.*

US
TRIBUNE (SCRANTON, PA.). (THE TRIBUNE.). (June 30, 1977)-. Newspaper. English. da. Scranton Gillette Communications Inc., 380 East Northwest Highway, Des Plaines IL 60016-2282. **Tel** (708)298-6622, **FAX** (708)390-0408. *Continues Scranton Tribune (Scranton, Pa. : 1936).*

US
UNION BANNER. Vol. 107, No. 33 (Jan. 14, 1970)-. Newspaper. English. wk. $15.00 (in county), $25.00 (other). Union Banner, 105 East Main Street, Carlyle IL 62231. **Tel** (618)594-3131. **ED** Warren Dempsey. **Photos. Ad Acc, Adv Mgr:** Mike Langham. Full Page (B&W) $451.50. Half Page (B&W) $225.75. Full Page (Color) $526.50. Half Page (Color) $300.75. **Pub. Size:** Broadsheet. **Circ:** 6,700 (paid). available in microform. *Continues Carlyle Union Banner.*

US/0746-8768
VERNON NEWS/VOICE. **VFOAT** Vernon News Voice. (198?)-. Newspaper. English. wk. $11.50. Pioneers Press, 1232 Centrl, Wilmette IL 60091. **Tel** (708)251-4300.

US/0745-8118
WARREN-NEWPORT PRESS.
(WARREN-NEWPORT PRESS : A LAKELAND NEWSPAPER.). **VFOAT** Lakeland Newspapers. (19??)-. Newspaper. English. wk. Lakeland Newspapers, 30 South Whitney Street, Grayslake IL 60030. **Tel** (708)223-8161, **FAX** (708)223-8810. **Photos. Ad Acc, Adv Mgr:** Jill DePasquale. **Circ:** 2,791.

US/0744-4524
WEEKLY INDIA TRIBUNE. **VFOAT** India Tribune. (19??)-. Newspaper. English. sm. $20.00. India Tribune Publishers Inc, 2702 West Peterson Avenue, Chicago IL 60659. **Tel** 583-6150. **ED** Prashant Shah. **Bk Rev. Ad Acc. Circ:** 15,000 (ctrl).

US/0192-0286
WHEELING LIFE. Vol. 5, No. 27 (June 22, 1978)-. Newspaper. English. wk. Lerner-Life Newspapers, 5158 Main Street, Skokie IL 60077. *Continues in part Wheeling Buffalo Grove Life.*

US/0745-0044
WILMETTE LIFE. (19??)-. Newspaper. English. Fifty-two times a year. $39.95 Cook County Illinois; $41.50 other. Pioneer Press, 1232 Central, Wilmette IL 60091. **Tel** (708)251-4300. **ED** Pat Schneider. **Circ:** 7,708.

US/0745-9750
WILMETTE NEWS/VOICE. **VFOAT** Wilmette News Voice. Vol. 1, No. 1 (June 9, 1983)-. Newspaper. English. wk. Pioneers Press, 1232 Centrl, Wilmette IL 60091. **Tel** (708)251-4300. *Continues Wilmette News-Advertiser, 0191-5878.*

US
WINCHESTER TIMES (WINCHESTER, ILL. : 1865 : WEEKLY). (THE WINCHESTER TIMES.). Began Sept. 14, 1865. Newspaper. English. wk. Winchester Times, 4 South Hill Street, Winchester IL 62694.

US/0273-6993
WINFIELD PRESS, THE. Newspaper. English. wk. Winfield Press, Box P, West Chicago IL 60185.

US/0745-9742
WINNETKA NEWS/VOICE. **VFOAT** Winnetka News Voice. Vol. 1, No. 1 (June 9, 1983)-. Newspaper. English. wk. Pioneers Press, 1232 Centrl, Wilmette IL 60091. **Tel** (708)251-4300. *Continues Winnetka News-Advertiser, 0191-6440.*

US/0747-2838
WROVA REPORTER, THE. **VFOAT** W.R.O.V.A. Reporter. Newspaper. English. wk. WROVA Reporter, 210 South Exchange Street, Galva IL 61434.

INDIANA

US
ADVANCE-LEADER (LIGONIER, IND.).
(ADVANCE-LEADER.). Vol. 97, No. 46 (May 14, 1975)-. Newspaper. English. wk. $25.00. Advance-Leader, PO Box 30, Ligonier IN 46767-0030. **ED** Gary Kauffman. **Circ:** 1,080. *Formed by the union of Cromwell Advance and Ligonier Leader.*

US
AKRON MENTONE NEWS, THE. Vol. 78, No. 37 (Sept. 12, 1968)-. Newspaper. English. wk. Akron Mentone News, PO Box 229, Rochester IN 46975. *Formed by the union of Akron News and Mentone News (Mentone, Ind. : 1964).*

US/8750-6513
ALBION NEW ERA, THE. Vol. 4, No. 11 (Jan. 6, 1876)-. Newspaper. English. wk. $25.00. Albion New Era, PO Box 25, Albion IN 46701. **Tel** (219)636-2727. *Continues New Era (Albion, Ind.).*

●US/1063-553X
ALEXANDRIA TIMES-TRIBUNE (1992), THE. (THE ALEXANDRIA TIMES-TRIBUNE.). **VFOAT** Alexandria times tribune; Times tribune. Vol. 106, No. 19 (May 13, 1992)-. Newspaper. English. wk. Alexandria Times Tribune, 116 East Church Street, PO Box 330, Alexandria IN 46001-2006. **Tel** (317)724-4469. *Continues Alexandria, In. Times-Tribune.*

US/0893-908X
ANDERSON HERALD-BULLETIN. **VFOAT** Anderson Herald Bulletin. Vol. 118, No. 1 (Apr. 5, 1987)-. Bulletin. English. da. Anderson Herald Bulletin, 1133 Jackson Street, Anderson IN 46016-1433. **Tel** (317)643-5371, **FAX** (317)649-3271. **ED** Elliot Tompkin. **Ad Acc, Adv Mgr:** Linda Millisor. **Circ:** 34,700 (morning), 35,200 (Sun.). *Formed by the union of Anderson Herald (Anderson, Ind. : Daily) and Anderson Daily Bulletin (Anderson, Ind. : 1918).*

US/0194-3545
BANNER-GAZETTE, THE. **VFOAT** Banner Gazette. Vol. 29, No. 54 (June 3, 1954)-. Newspaper. English. wk (Wed.). $15.00. Banner-Gazette, PO Box 38, Pekin IN 47165. **ED** Mark Grigsby. **Photos. Ad Acc, Adv Mgr:** John C. Roberts, **Tel** (812)967-3176. Full Page (B&W) $476.80. Half Page (B&W) $238.40. Full

Indiana

Page (Color) $556.80. Half Page (Color) $278.40. **Pub. Size:** Tabloid. *Formed by the union of Palmyra Gazette and Pekin Banner.*

US
BENTON REVIEW, THE. (1879)-. Newspaper. English. wk. Benton Review, Box 668, Fowler IN 47944. *Continues Benton Democrat (Fowler, Ind.); Absorbed Republican-Leader (Fowler, Ind.).*

US
BERNE TRI-WEKLY NEWS. VFOAT Berne Tri Weekly News. Vol. 80, No. 193 (Aug. 16, 1976)-. Newspaper. English. tw. Berne Tri-Weekly News, 153 South Jefferson Street, Berne IN 46711. *Continues Adams County Sun & Berne Daily Witness.*

US
BLOOMFIELD NEWS, THE. (1875)-. Newspaper. English. Fifty-two times a year. $41.00. Bloomfield News, 29 West Main Street, PO Box 311, Bloomfield IN 47424. **Tel** (812)384-4684.

US
BLUFFTON NEWS-BANNER. Vol. 13, No. 58 (Jan. 10, 1942)-. Newspaper. English. da. Bluffton News-Banner, 125 North Johnson Street, Bluffton IN 46714. *Continues Evening News-Banner.*

US
BOONVILLE STANDARD (BOONVILLE, IND. : 1906). (THE BOONVILLE STANDARD.). No. 41 (April 6, 1906)-. Newspaper. English. wk. Boonville Standard, 204 West Locust Street, Boonville IN 47601. *Continues Republican Standard (Boonville, Ind.).*

US
BOSWELL ENTERPRISE, THE. Began with Jan. 27, 1921 issue. Newspaper. English. wk. Boswell Enterprise, Box N, Boswell IN 47921. *Continues Boswell Argus; Absorbed Benton County Tribune (Fowler, Ind.).*

US/1042-5225
BOURBON NEWS-MIRROR (1971). (BOURBON NEWS-MIRROR.). VFOAT Bourbon News Mirror. Vol. 101, No. 29 (July 22, 1971)-. Newspaper. English. wk. $12.00. Bourbon News-Mirror, Box 47, Bourbon IN 46504. **ED** S. Krepp. **Photos. Ad Acc, Adv Mgr:** Full Page (B&W) $286.38. Half Page (B&W) $146.52. Full Page (Color) $361.38. Half Page (Color) $221.52. **Pub. Size:** Standard. **Circ:** 1,400. *Continues News-Mirror (Bourbon, Ind. : 1947).*

US
BRAZIL TIMES, THE. Vol. 87, No. 284 (Sept. 15, 1975)-. Newspaper. English. da. $78.00. Brazil Times, 100 Times Square, Brazil IN 47834. **Tel** (814)446-2216, FAX (814)446-0938. **ED** James Dressler. **Bk Rev**, (Qty: 50). **Photos. Ad Acc, Adv Mgr:** Larry Knight. Full Page (B&W) $703.05. Half Page (B&W) $351.53. Full Page (Color) $768.05. Half Page (Color) $416.53. **Pub. Size:** Broadsheet. **Wire Svcs.:** AP. **Circ:** 5,400. *Continues Brazil Daily Times.*

US
BROOKVILLE AMERICAN (BROOKVILLE, IND. : 1873). (THE BROOKVILLE AMERICAN.). Vol. 22, No. 44 (Oct. 1873)-. Newspaper. English. wk. $13.00 Indiana; $16.00 US. Whitewater Publications Inc., PO Box 38, Brookville IN 47012. **ED** John L. Estredge, Gary L. Wolf (Managing Editor). **Photos. Ad Acc, Adv Mgr:** Donald G. Siuty. Full Page (B&W) $441.00. Half Page (B&W) $220.50. Full Page (Color) $506.00. Half Page (Color) $285.50. **Circ:** 1,050. *Continues Brookville Weekly American*

US
BROOKVILLE DEMOCRAT, THE. 57th Year, No. 3 (Jan. 17, 1895)-. Newspaper. English. wk. $13.00 (one year); $24.00 (two years). Whitewater Publications Inc., PO Box 38, Brookville IN 47012. **ED** Gary L. Wolf (Editor-in-Chief) and John L. Estridge (Managing Editor). **Photos. Ad Acc, Adv Mgr:** Donald Goutz, **Tel** (317)647-4221. **Pub. Size:** Broadsheet. **Circ:** 5,650. *Continues Franklin Democrat (Brookville, Ind. : 1859).*

US
BROWN COUNTY DEMOCRAT (NASHVILLE, IND.). (BROWN COUNTY DEMOCRAT.). Began in 1883. Newspaper. English. wk. Brown County Democrat, 136 North Van Buren Street, Nashville IN 47448. *Continues Jacksonian Democrat.*

US
BUTLER BULLETIN, THE. 1st Year, No. 1 (March 31, 1976)-1st Year, No. 51 (March 23, 1977). Bulletin. English. wk. Butler Bulletin, 108 East Main Street, Butler IN 46721. *Absorbed Record-Herald (Butler, Ind. : 1976).*

US
CALUMET PRESS, THE. (1959)-. Newspaper. English. wk. Calumet Press, 8411 Kennedy Avenue, Highland IN 46322. **ED** Jeanne Larson. **Photos. Ad Acc, Adv Mgr:** Bill Palmateer, **Tel** (219)838-0717. Full Page (B&W) $846.72. Half Page (B&W) $483.84. Full Page (Color) $914.76. Half Page (Color) $551.44. **Pub. Size:** Tabloid.

US
CARMEL DAILY LEDGER, THE. No. 166 (July 2, 1990)-. Newspaper. English. da. Noblesville Daily Ledger, 957 East Logan Street, Noblesville IN 46060. **Tel** (317)773-1210. *Continues Daily Ledger (Noblesville, Ind. : 1989).*

US
CARROLL COUNTY COMET. Vol. 1, No. 1 (Feb. 6, 1974)-. Newspaper. English. wk. Carroll Papers Inc, PO Box 26, Flora IN 46929-0026. *Formed by the union of Journal-Citizen and Hoosier Democrat.*

US
CASTLETON BANNER, THE. Vol. 16, No. 4 (Nov. 4, 1981)-. Newspaper. English. wk. Topic Newspapers, 9615 College Avenue, Indianapolis IN 46280-1627. **Tel** (317)844-3311, FAX (317)575-8651. *Continues North East Topics.*

US
CEDAR LAKE JOURNAL. (19??)-. Newspaper. English. wk. $9.00 Lake County, Indiana; $10.00 other. Pilcher Publishing, PO Box 248, Lowell IN 46356. **Tel** (219)696-7711.

US
CHESTERTON TRIBUNE, THE. Vol. 14, No. 33 (Nov. 27, 1897)-. Newspaper. English. da. Chesterton Tribune, PO Box 558, Chesterton IN 46304. **Tel** (219)926-1131, FAX (219)926-6389. **ED** Warren Canright. **Ad Acc, Adv Mgr:** Bill Mathe. **Circ:** 4,900. *Continues Westchester Tribune.*

US
CHRONICLE TRIBUNE (MARION, IND.). (CHRONICLE TRIBUNE.). Vol. 38, No. 203 (Mar. 30, 1968)-. Newspaper. English. da. Marion Chronicle Tribune, 610 South Adams Street, Marion IN 46952. **Tel** (317)664-5111. **ED** Terry Eberle. **Circ:** 20,790 daily, 24,700 Sunday. *Formed by the union of Leader-Tribune (Marion, Ind.) and Marion Chronicle (Marion, Inc. : Daily).*

US
CLARION (MILLTOWN, IND.). (THE CLARION.). Began in 1940. Newspaper. English. wk. The Clarion, 301 North Capitol Avenue, Corydon IN 47112.

US
CLARION NEWS. Periodical. English. wk. O'Bannon Publishing Company, Corydon IN.

US
CLARK COUNTY JOURNAL. Vol. 64, No. 44 (Nov. 4, 1920)-. Newspaper. English. wk. News & Journal Inc, PO Box 867, Jeffersonville IN 47130. **Tel** (812)283-6636. *Continues National Democrat and The Citizen-Record.*

US
COLLEGE CORNER NEWS. Began in 1901. Newspaper. English. wk. Oxford Press Inc, 11 East Union Street, Liberty IN 47353.

US
COLUMBUS HERALD (COLUMBUS, IND. : WEEKLY). (THE COLUMBUS HERALD.). Began in 1881. Newspaper. English. wk. Columbus Herald, 333 2nd Street, Columbus IN 47201. *Absorbed Columbus Daily Herald; Columbus Weekly Star.*

US
COMMERCIAL-REVIEW (PORTLAND, IND. : DAILY : 1922). (THE COMMERCIAL-REVIEW.). VFOAT Commercial Review. Vol. 29, No. 159 (May 26, 1922)-. Newspaper. English. da. $75.00. Commercial-Review, 309 West Main Street, Portland IN 47371. **ED** Jack Ronald, Tom Casey (Managing Editor). **Photos. Ad Acc, Adv Mgr:** Don Gillespie, **Tel** (219)726-8141. Full Page (B&W) $598.50. Half Page (B&W) $289.25. Full Page (Color) $678.50. Half Page (Color) $369.25. **Pub. Size:** Broadsheet. **Wire Svcs.:** AP. **Circ:** 6,000. *Continues Portland Commercial-Review; Absorbed Republican (Portland, Ind.) and Graphic (Portland, Ind. : 1956).*

US
CONNERSVILLE NEWS-EXAMINER. VFOAT Connersville News and Examiner; Connersville News Examiner. Vol. 32, No. 177 (Jan. 2, 1920)-. Newspaper. English. da. Connersville Publishing Co., Inc., 406 Central Avenue, Connersville IN 47331. **Tel** (317)825-0585, FAX (317)825-4599. **ED** Robert L. Powers, Gary Hufferd (Managing Editor). **Bk Rev. Photos. Ad Acc, Adv Mgr:** Diane Howell, **Tel** (317)825-0581. **Circ:** 9,152. *Formed by the union of Evening News (Connersville, Ind.) and Connersville Daily Examiner.*

US
CORYDON DEMOCRAT (CORYDON, IND. : 1880). (THE CORYDON DEMOCRAT.). Vol. 23, No. 2 (March 25, 1879)-. Newspaper. English. wk. $21.50 Crawford, Floyd, Washington, & Harrison counties; $25.00 Indiana; $36.00 other. Obannon Publishing Co. Inc., 301 North Capitol Avenue, PO Box 220, Corydon IN 47112. **Tel** (812)738-2211. *Continues Democrat (Corydon, Ind.).*

US
COURIER-TIMES, THE. VFOAT Courier Times. 111th Year, Issue No. 217 (Sept. 10, 1951)-. Newspaper. English. da. Courier-Times Inc, PO Box 369, New Castle IN 47362. *Continues New Castle Courier-Times.*

US
CROWN POINT REGISTER, THE. VFOAT Register. (Aug. 1857)-. Newspaper. English. wk. Crown Point Register, 15 North Court, Crown Point IN 46307. *Continues Lake County Herald (Crown Point, Ind. : 1856); Absorbed Crown Point Herald (Crown Point, Ind. : 1872).*

US
CRUSADER (CENTERVILLE, IND.). (THE CRUSADER.). VFOAT Centerville Crusader. Vol. 13, No. 20 (July 18, 1979)-. Newspaper. English. wk. $14.00. Crusader, PO Box 26, Centerville IN 47330. **Tel** (317)855-5262. **Photos. Ad Acc, Adv Mgr:** Peggy Patterson. Full Page (B&W) $280.00. Half Page (B&W) $150.00. **Pub. Size:** Standard. available in microform. *Continues New Crusader (Centerville, Ind.).*

US
CYNTHIANA ARGUS, THE. Began in 1890. Newspaper. English. wk. Cynthiana Argus, PO Box 128, Cynthiana IN 47612. *Absorbed Mt. Vernon Republican (Mount Vernon, Ind. : 1938).*

US
DAILY CLINTONIAN, THE. (1912)-. Newspaper. English. da. $68.00. Daily Clintonian, 422 South Main Street, Clinton IN 47842. **ED** J. Carey and G. Carey (Managing Editor). **Photos. Ad Acc, Adv Mgr:** B. Bartlett, **Tel** (317)832-2443. Full Page (B&W) $529.20. Half Page (B&W) $264.60. **Pub. Size:** Broadsheet. **Wire Svcs.:** AP. **Circ:** 5,560. available in microform. *Continues Clintonian (Clinton, Ind.).*

US
DAILY JOURNAL (FRANKLIN, IND.). (THE DAILY JOURNAL.). Vol. 1, No. 1 (July 22, 1963)-. Newspaper. English. da. $93.00 (one year by mail). Daily Journal / Franklin, Box 699, Franklin IN 46131. **Tel** (317)736-7101. *Absorbed Franklin Evening Star.*

US
DALE NEWS, THE. (May 26, 1960)-. Newspaper. English. wk. $13.00. Dubois-Spencer Counties Publishing Company, 113 West 6th Street, PO Box 38, Ferdinand IN 47532. **ED** Richard P. Treffer. **Bk Rev**, (Qty: 10/year). **Photos. Ad Acc, Adv Mgr:** Kathy Treffer, **Tel** (812)367-2041. Full Page (B&W) $345.75. Half Page (B&W) $173.25. **Pub. Size:** Standard. **Circ:** 1,700 paid.

US
DEARBORN COUNTY REGISTER (LAWRENCEBURG, INC. : 1954). (THE DEARBORN COUNTY REGISTER.). VFOAT Register. Vol. 118, No. 40 (Sept. 30, 1954)-. Newspaper. English. wk. Dearborn County Register, 126 West High Street, Lawrenceburg IN 47025. *Continues Lawrenceburgh Register.*

US/0894-2307
DECATUR DAILY DEMOCRAT. Vol. 5, No. 60 (March 11, 1907)-. Newspaper. English. da. Decatur Daily Democrat, 131 2nd Street, Decatur IN 46733. *Continues Daily Democrat (Decatur, Ind.).*

US
EAST ALLEN COURIER. Vol. 24, No. 1 (Jan. 7, 1982)-Vol. 24, No. 6 (Feb. 11, 1982)-. Newspaper. English. wk. East Allen Courier, Box 77, Grabill IN 46741-0077. *Formed by the union of Woodburn Booster and Cedar Creek Courier.*

US
EAST CHICAGO GLOBE. Began in 1891. Newspaper. English. wk. East Chicago Globe, 2005 Broadway, East Chicago IN 46312.

US
EAST SIDE HERALD INDIANAPOLIS, IND.). (THE EAST SIDE HERALD.). Began in (1953?)-. Newspaper. English. wk. East Side Herald, 4309 East Michigan Street, Indianapolis IN 46201. *Continues Indianapolis Herald (Indianapolis, Ind. : 1938).*

US/0746-7516
ELKHART TRUTH, THE. VFOAT Truth. Vol. 15, No. 178 (Mar. 13, 1906)-. Newspaper. English. da. Truth Publishing Company Inc., 421 South Second Street, Elkhart IN 46516. **Tel** (219)294-1661. **ED** John F. Dillie. **LC** 7002. **Bk Rev. Photos. Ad Acc, Adv Mgr. Circ:** 30,000. available on an online database (file 635/Full-Text) from DIALOG. Documents available from UMI Article Clearinghouse. *Continues Elkart Daily Truth; Absorbed Elkhart Review (Elkhart, Ind. : Daily : 1918).*
Ind/Abst Bus. Dateline (Dec. 17, 1991-) [Full Txt.].

US
EVANSVILLE COURIER, THE. VFOAT Sunday Courier and Journal; Sunday Courier and Press; Sunday Courier & Press; Sunday Courier. Vol. 25, No. 233 (Apr. 2, 1888)-. Newspaper. English. da. $106.80 (one year) daily; $76.20 (one year) Sunday only; $183.00 (one year) daily & Sunday;. Evansville Courier Company,

PO Box 268, Evansville IN 47702. **Tel** (812)464-7500, (800)288-3100. **ED** Bill D. Jackson. **LC** 7002. **Circ:** 63,026. ***Continues*** *Evansville Daily Courier.*

US/0896-6249
EVANSVILLE PRESS. **VFOAT** Sunday Courier and Press. (July 22, 1906)-. Newspaper. English. da (Except Sunday). $106.80. Evansville Courier Company, PO Box 268, Evansville IN 47702. **Tel** (812)464-7500, (800)288-3100. **ED** Tom Tuley. **LC** 7002. **Bk Rev. Ad Acc. Circ:** 42,000 (ctrl).
Desc: General-circulation evening and Sunday newspapers.

US
EVENING NEWS (JEFFERSONVILLE, IND. : 1924). (THE EVENING NEWS.). Vol. 52, No. 172 (June 7, 1924)-. Newspaper. English. da. $78.00. Park Newspapers / Indiana, PO Box 867, Jeffersonville IN 47130-0867. **Tel** (812)283-6636, FAX (812)284-7080. **ED** Don Newton, John Gilkey (Managing Editor). **Bk Rev**, (Qty: 52). **Photos. Ad Acc, Adv Mgr:** Donna Barrett. Full Page (B&W) $1322.00. Half Page (B&W) $662.00. Full Page (Color) $1422.00. Half Page (Color) $762.00. **Pub. Size:** Broadsheet. **Wire Svcs.:** AP. **Circ:** 12,800 evening paid. ***Continues*** *The Evening News and the Jeffersonville Star.*

US
EVENING STAR (AUBURN, IND.). (THE EVENING STAR.). Began in Feb. 1913. Newspaper. English. da. Evening Star, PO Box 431, Auburn IN 46706. ***Formed by the union of*** *Auburn Daily Courier* ***and*** *Evening Dispatch (Auburn, Ind.);* ***Absorbed*** *Auburn Courier (Auburn, Ind. : 1909); Auburn Dispatch.*

US
EVENING WORLD (BLOOMFIELD, IND.). (THE EVENING WORLD.). Began in 1942?. Newspaper. English. da. Bloomfield News, 29 West Main Street, PO Box 311, Bloomfield IN 47424. **Tel** (812)384-4684. ***Continues*** *Greene County World.*

US/0745-7227
EVENING WORLD (SPENCER, IND.). (EVENING WORLD.). **VFOAT** Spencer Evening World. Began with June 29, 1927 issue. Newspaper. English. da. Evening World - IN, PO Box 226, Spencer IN 47460.

US
FERDINAND NEWS, THE. Vol. 1, No. 1 (May 25, 1906)-. Newspaper. English. wk. $16.00. Ferdinand News, 113 West 6th Street, PO Box 38, Ferdinand IN 47532. **Tel** (812)367-2041. **ED** Richard P. Tretter. **Bk Rev**, (Qty: 10). **Photos. Ad Acc, Adv Mgr:** Kathy Tretter. Full Page (B&W) $387.00. Half Page (B&W) $189.00. **Pub. Size:** Standard. **Circ:** 3,100. available in microform.

US
FISHERS SUN-HERALD. **VFOAT** Fishers Sun Herald. Vol. 1 No. 1 (Nov. 12 1980)-. Newspaper. English. wk. Topic Newspapers, 9615 College Avenue, Indianapolis IN 46280-1627. **Tel** (317)844-3311, FAX (317)575-8651. ***Continues*** *Sheridan Topics.*

US/1060-5495
FOUNTAIN COUNTY NEIGHBOR. (19??)-. Newspaper. English. bw. $39.00 local; $50.00 Indiana. Fountain County Neighbor, PO Box 30, Attica IN 47918. **ED** Kirk Johannesen. **Photos. Ad Acc, Adv Mgr:** Judy Buchley, **Tel** (317)762-2411. Full Page (B&W) $588.00. Half Page (B&W) $294.00. **Pub. Size:** Broadsheet. available in microform. ***Continues*** *Star Tribune (Attica, Ind.), 8750-6548.*

US/0747-1793
FRANCESVILLE TRIBUNE. Began in 1897. Newspaper. English. wk (51 issues a year). Francesville Tribune, PO Box 458, Francesville IN 47946. **Tel** (219)567-2221. **ED** Darlene J Ames. **Circ:** 1,004.

US/8750-7390
FRANKLIN CHALLENGER. (198?)-. Newspaper. English. wk. $12.00. Challenger Newspapers, PO Box 708, Greenwood IN 46142-3573. **Tel** (317)888-3376, FAX (317)888-3377. **ED** Don Guerrettiz. **Bk Rev**, (Qty: 2). **Photos. Ad Acc.** Full Page (B&W) $160.00. Half Page (B&W) $80.00. Full Page (Color) $235.00. Half Page (Color) $155.00. **Pub. Size:** Tabloid.

US
GARRETT CLIPPER (GARRETT, IND. : 1919). (GARRETT CLIPPER.). Vol. 36, No. 8 (Dec. 18, 1919)-. Newspaper. English. sw. Garrett Clipper, Box 59, Garrett IN 46738. ***Continues*** *Garrett Weekly Clipper.*

US
GARY AMERICAN, THE. 1st Year, No. 1 (March 22, 1928)-. Newspaper. English. Twenty-four times a year. Gary American / Fred Harris Editor, 2268 Broadway, Gary IN 46407. **Tel** (219-883-4903. ***Continues*** *Gary Colored American;* ***Absorbed*** *Gary Sun (Gary, Ind. : 1929).*

US
GARY CRUSADER. (1960)-. Newspaper. English. wk (Published on Thursdays). Gary Crusader, 1549 Broadway, Gary IN 46407-3106. **Tel** (219)885-4357, FAX (219)883-3317. **ED** David Denson. **Ad Acc. Circ:** 26,000. available on microfilm from University Microfilms International (UMI).

US
GEIST GAZETTE. Vol. 1, No. 1 (May 18, 1988)-. Newspaper. English. wk. Topic Newspapers, 9615 College Avenue, Indianapolis IN 46280-1627. **Tel** (317)844-3311, FAX (317)575-8651. **ED** Pat White. **Ad Acc, Adv Mgr:** John McNatt.

US
GIVEAWAY, THE. (1937)-. Newspaper. English. wk (Wed.). $15.00. The Giveaway, PO Box 38, Pekin IN 47165. **ED** Mark Grigsby. **Photos. Ad Acc, Adv Mgr:** John C. Roberts, **Tel** (812)967-3176. Full Page (B&W) $528.80. Half Page (B&W) $264.40. Full Page (Color) $608.80. Half Page (Color) $304.40. **Pub. Size:** Tabloid.

US/8750-3867
GOSHEN NEWS, THE. Vol. 117, No. 218 (Sept. 16, 1954)-. Newspaper. English. da (except Sunday and holidays). News Printing Company Inc. / Goshen News, Goshen IN 46526-0569. **Tel** (219)533-2151. **ED** Robert Conrad. **Circ:** 14,216. ***Continues*** *News-Democrat (Goshen, Ind.).*

US
GRAPHIC (RICHMOND, IND.). (THE GRAPHIC.). Began in 1961. Newspaper. English. wk. The Graphic, 621 West 1st Street, Richmond IN 47374. ***Continues*** *West Side Enterprise.*

US
GREENSBURG DAILY NEWS. (Jan. 1, 1894)-. Newspaper. English. da. $104.00. Greensburg Daily News, 135 South Franklin, Greensburg IN 47240. **Tel** (812)663-3111, FAX (812)663-2985. **ED** Jeff Emsweller. **Bk Rev. Photos. Ad Acc, Adv Mgr:** Pamela Jackson Abel. Full Page (B&W) $923.64. Half Page (B&W) $478.59. Full Page (Color) $1018.64. Half Page (Color) $573.59. **Pub. Size:** Broadsheet. **Wire Svcs.:** AP. **Circ:** 6,700. available on microfilm. ***Formed by the union of*** *Greensburg Daily Review.*

US
GREENSBURG TIMES, THE. (1928)-. Newspaper. English. wk. $39.00. Greensburg Daily News, 135 South Franklin, Greensburg IN 47240. **Tel** (812)663-3111, FAX (812)663-2985. **ED** Jeff Emsweller. **Photos. Pub. Size:** Broadsheet. ***Absorbed*** *St. Paul Record;* ***Continues*** *Greensburg Evening Times.*

US/1068-6673
GREENWOOD AND SOUTHSIDE CHALLENGER, THE. **VFOAT** Challenger. (1972)-. Newspaper. English. wk. $15.00. Challenger Newspapers, PO Box 708, Greenwood IN 46142-3573. **Tel** (317)888-3376, FAX (317)888-3377. **ED** Don Guerrettaz. **Bk Rev**, (Qty: 2). **Photos. Ad Acc.** Full Page (B&W) $320.00. Half Page (B&W) $176.00. Full Page (Color) $400.00. Half Page (Color) $250.00. **Pub. Size:** Tabloid. **Circ:** 1,100.

US
GREENWOOD GAZETTE, THE. (Oct. 28, 1986)-. Newspaper. English. wk. $78.00. The Greater Greenwood Business Journal, 128 South Park Boulevard, Greenwood IN 46143. **Tel** (317)882-8796, FAX (317)882-8830. **ED** Brian Kelly (Editor-in-Chief) and Jane Palmer & Johannah Pollert (Managing Editor). **Bk Rev**, (Qty: 12). **Photos. Ad Acc, Adv Mgr:** Brian Kelly. Full Page (B&W) $1,095.00. Half Page (B&W) $550.00. Full Page (Color) $1,170.00. Half Page (Color) $625.00. **Pub. Size:** Broadsheet. **Circ:** 14,000.

US
HAMILTON NEWS (HAMILTON, IND.). (THE HAMILTON NEWS.). Vol. 1, No. 1 (July 12, 1901)-. Newspaper. English. wk. Hamilton News Inc, PO Box 205, Hamilton IN 46742.

US
HARRISON POST, THE. Newspaper. English. wk. Harrison Post, 7962 Pendleton Pike, Lawrence IN 46226. ***Continues*** *Harrisonian (Indianapolis, Ind.).*

US
HARTFORD CITY NEWS-TIMES. **VFOAT** Hartford City News Times. Vol. 44, No. 6 (Feb. 15, 1937)-. Newspaper. English. da. $125.00. Hartford City News-Times, 123 South Jefferson Street, Hartford City IN 47348. **Tel** (317)248-0110, FAX (317)348-0112. **ED** Chris Landis. **Photos. Ad Acc, Adv Mgr:** Connie Murray. Full Page (B&W) $684.99. Half Page (B&W) $342.50. Full Page (Color) $734.99. Half Page (Color) $392.50. **Pub. Size:** Broadsheet. **Wire Svcs.:** AP. available in microform. ***Formed by the union of*** *Hartford City News (Hartford City, Ind. : 1917)* ***and*** *Hartford City Times Gazette.*

US/0887-476X
HEIGHTS HERALD. **VFOAT** Cicero Heights Herald. Vol. 5, No. 8 (Dec. 18, 1985)-. Newspaper. English. wk. $7.50. Topic Newspapers, 9615 College Avenue, Indianapolis IN 46280-1627. **Tel** (317)844-3311, FAX (317)575-8651. ***Continues*** *Northern Heights Herald.*

US/0193-4910
HENDRICKS COUNTY FLYER. (March 1965)-. Newspaper. English. wk. Hendricks County Flyer, PO Box 6, Plainfield IN 46168. **Tel** (317)839-5129. **ED** Tim Evans. **Photos. Ad Acc, Adv Mgr:** Mike Schaefer. Full Page (B&W) $9.75 per inch. Half Page (Color) $9.75 per inch. **Pub. Size:** Standard.

US
HENRY COUNTY NEWS REPUBLICAN, THE. Vol. 47, No. 51 (Oct. 5, 1978)-. Newspaper. English. wk. Henry County News Republican, 206 South 14th Street, New Castle IN 47362. ***Continues*** *News-Republican (New Castle, Ind.).*

US
HERALD (JASPER, IND.). (THE HERALD.). (Feb 1, 1977)-. Newspaper. English. da. $38.00. Jasper Dubois County Daily, PO Box 31, Jasper IN 47546. **Tel** (812)482-2424. ***Continues*** *Dubois County Daily Herald.*

US
HERALD-PRESS (HUNTINGTON, IND.). (THE HERALD-PRESS.). **VFOAT** Huntington Herald-Press. (1929)-. Newspaper. English. da. $20.80 Huntington; $22.75 (route); $31.98 (mail). Herald-Press, 7 North Jefferson Street, PO Box 860, Huntington IN 46750. **Tel** (219)356-6700, FAX (219)356-9026. **ED** Mike Perkins. **Photos. Ad Acc, Adv Mgr:** Claude Good. Full Page (B&W) $882.00. Half Page (B&W) $502.74. Full Page (Color) $977.00. Half Page (Color) $597.74. **Pub. Size:** Broadsheet. **Wire Svcs.:** AP. **Circ:** 7,091. ***Continues*** *Huntington Herald-Press.*

US
HERALD-REPUBLICAN (ANGOLA, IND.). (HERALD-REPUBLICAN.). **VFOAT** Herald Republican. No. 22 (June 1, 1983)-. Newspaper. English. wk. Herald-Republican, 12 Monument Place, Angola IN 46703. ***Continues*** *Steuben County Herald-Republican.*

US/1044-4246
HERALD-TIMES (BLOOMINGTON, IND.), THE. (THE HERALD-TIMES.). **VFOAT** Herald Times; Sunday Herald-Times; Sunday Herald Times. Vol. 112, No. 305 (May 8, 1989)-. Newspaper. English. da. $146.40 Brown, Greene, Jackson, Lawrence, Monroe, Morgan and Owen counties; $195.00 other. Herald-Times Inc, 1900 South Walnut, Bloomington IN 47401. **Tel** (812)336-4200, (800)422-0070. **ED** Robert Zaltsberg. **Circ:** 42,403. ***Continues*** *Herald-Telephone, 0745-7936.*

US/0746-2042
HERALD-TRIBUNE, THE. (THE HERALD-TRIBUNE.). **VAT** Herald Tribune. Vol. 1, No. 1 (Feb. 20, 1930)-. Newspaper. English. wk. Herald-Tribune, PO Box 89, Batesville IN 47006. ***Formed by the union of*** *Batesville Herald* ***and*** *Batesville Tribune.*

US
HOBART GAZETTE (HOBART, IND. : 1939). (THE HOBART GAZETTE.). Vol. 50, No. 29 (Jan. 19, 1939)-. Newspaper. English. wk. Hobart Gazette, 413 Main Street, Hobart IN 46342. ***Formed by the union of*** *Hobart Index Combined with The Commonwealth* ***and*** *Hobart News-Gazette (Hobart, Ind.).*

US
INDIANA HERALD (INDIANAPOLIS, IND.). (INDIANA HERALD.). (1960)-. Newspaper. English. wk. $9.50. OL Tandy, 723 North West Street, Indianapolis IN 46202. **Tel** (317)634-8117. ***Continues*** *Indiana Herald-Times.*

US
INDIANA NEWSPAPER DIRECTORY AND RATE BOOK. **Added/Corp** Hoosier State Press Association. (19??)-. Periodical. English. an. $22.50 Indiana; $21.50 other. Hoosier State Press Association Inc, 1542 Consolidate Building, 115 North Penn, Indianapolis IN 46204. **Tel** (317)637-3966. **ED** Grace A. Falvey. Index available (bound in issue). **Ad Acc.**

US
INDIANAPOLIS NEWS (INDIANAPOLIS, IND. : 1876). (THE INDIANAPOLIS NEWS.). **VFOAT** Indianapolis Daily News. Whole No. 2001 (May 9, 1876)-. Newspaper. English. da (except Sunday). $95.00. Indianapolis Newspapers Inc, PO Box 145, Indianapolis IN 46206. **Tel** (317)633-9142 or (800)669-7827. **ED** Harvey Jacobs. **LC** 7701-X. **Circ:** 124,292. available on microfilm from University Microfilms International (UMI). ***Continues*** *Evening News (Indianapolis, Ind.);* ***Absorbed*** *Indianapolis (Indianapolis, Ind. : 1899);* ***Absorbed in part*** *Indianapolis Sentinel (Indianapolis, Ind. : 1905).*

US
INDIANAPOLIS RECORDER, THE. Vol. 13, No. 28 (Jan. 15, 1910)-. Newspaper. English. Fifty-two times a year. $26.00 Indiana; $31.00 other. Indianapolis Recorder, 2901 North Tacoma Avenue, Indianapolis IN

46218. **Tel** (317)924-5143. **ED** Eunice Trotter. **LC** 7002. **Ad Acc. Circ:** 11,212. available on microfilm. ***Continues*** *Recorder (Indianapolis, Ind.).*

US
INDIANAPOLIS STAR, THE. **VFOAT** Indianapolis Sunday Star. Vol. 4, No. 364 (June 4, 1907)-. Newspaper. English. da. $200.00 Indiana, $244.00 others (daily & Sunday by mail); $166.00 (daily & Sunday by carrier); $91.00 Indiana, $101.00 others (Sunday & by mail); $62.00 (Sunday & by carrier); $119.00 Indiana, $153.00 others (daily by mail); $88.00 (daily by carrier. Indianapolis Newspapers Inc, PO Box 145, Indianapolis IN 46206. **Tel** (317)633-9142 or (800)669-7827. **ED** John H. Lyst. **Circ:** 229,595 daily, 400,150 Sunday. available on microfilm from University Microfilms International (UMI). ***Continues*** *Indianapolis Morning Star.*
Ind/Abst PROMT.

US
INFO (GARY, IND.). (INFO.). Began in (1963)-. Newspaper. English. wk. Info Printing Inc / New Jersey, PO Box M-587, Gary IN 46401-0587. **Tel** (219)882-6711. available on microfilm.

US/1055-775X
JACKSON COUNTY BANNER (BROWNSTOWN, IND.). (THE JACKSON COUNTY BANNER.). **VFOAT** Banner. Vol. 121, No. 79 (Jan. 2, 1990)-. Newspaper. English. sw. Jackson County Banner, 116 East Cross Street, PO Box G, Brownstown IN 47220-2011. **Tel** (812)358-2111. ***Continues*** *Banner (Brownstown, Ind.).*

US/0896-2790
JASONVILLE LEADER, THE. **VFOAT** Jasonville Leader-Worthington Times. Began in 1902. Newspaper. English. wk. Jasonville Leader, 241 West Main, Jasonville IN 47438.

US
JOURNAL AND COURIER (LAFAYETTE, IND.). (JOURNAL AND COURIER.). Vol. 53, No. 44 (Feb. 21, 1972)-. Newspaper. English. da. $117.00 (daily), $156.00 (daily & Sun.), Lafayette residents; $208.00 (daily & Sun.) other Indiana; $234.00 (daily & Sun.) other;. Journal and Courier, 217 North Sixth Street, Lafayette IN 47901. **Tel** (317)423-5512. **ED** Judi Austin. **LC** 7002. **Circ:** 35,620 daily, 37,062 Sunday. ***Continues*** *Lafayette Journal and Courier.*

US
JOURNAL (ELLETTSVILLE, IND.). (THE JOURNAL.). Vol. 18, No. 35 (Feb. 14, 1957)-. Newspaper. English. wk. $16.00 in county; $22.00 other. The Journal Publishing Company, Inc., PO Box 98, Ellettsville IN 47429. **Tel** (812)876-2254, FAX (812)876-2853. **ED** Gina M. Hawkins. **Photos. Ad Acc, Adv Mgr:** Jane Fiscus. Full Page (B&W) $404.25. Half Page (B&W) $202.13. Full Page (Color) $479.25. Half Page (Color) $277.13. **Pub. Size:** Standard. ***Continues*** *Ellettsville Journal.*

US/0734-3701
JOURNAL-GAZETTE (FORT WAYNE, IND.), THE. (THE JOURNAL-GAZETTE.). **VFOAT** Journal Gazette; Fort Wayne Journal-Gazette. Nov. 10, (1944)-. Newspaper. English. wk. $78.00 (1 year); $83.20 (2 year); $88.40 (3 year). Fort Wayne Newspapers Inc., PO Box 100, Fort Wayne IN 46801. **Tel** (219)461-8394 or (219)461-8464, FAX (219)461-8749. **ED** Craig Klugman. **LC** 7002. **Ad Acc. Circ:** 63,000 daily, 135,000 Sunday. Documents available from UMI Article Clearinghouse. ***Continues*** *Ft. Wayne Journal-Gazette.*
Desc: Newspaper based in Fort Wayne, Indiana.
Ind/Abst Bus. Dateline (Dec. 24, 1991-) [Full Txt.].

US
JOURNAL (ODON, IND.). (THE JOURNAL.). Vol. 109, No. 7 (March 1981)-. Newspaper. English. wk. $15.00 (in county), $18.00 (out of county). Journal / Odon, 102 West Main Street, Odon IN 47562. **Tel** (812)636-7350. **ED** John L. Myers. **Photos. Ad Acc.** Full Page (B&W) $359.00. Half Page (B&W) $189.00. Full Page (Color) $409.00. Half Page (Color) $239.00. **Pub. Size:** Broadsheet. **Circ:** 2,600. available in microform. ***Continues*** *Odon Journal.*

US
JOURNAL-REVIEW. **VFOAT** Journal Review. Vol. 45 No. 158 (Apr 18, 1974)-. Newspaper. English. da. Journal-Review, 119 North Green Street, Crawfordsville IN 47933. ***Continues*** *Crawfordsville Journal and Review.*

US
KANKAKEE VALLEY NEWS-POST, THE. **VFOAT** Kankakee Valley Post News. Vol. 41, No. 30 (July 29, 1971)-. Newspaper. English. wk. Kankakee Valley News-Post, 827 South Halleck Street, De Motte IN 46310. ***Formed by the union of*** *Kankakee Valley Post* ***and*** *Jasper County News (Rensselaer, Ind.).*

US/1060-6173
KNOX COUNTY DAILY NEWS (BICKNELL, IND. : 1991). (THE KNOX COUNTY DAILY NEWS.). Vol. 73, No. 1, Jan. 11 (1991)-. Newspaper. English. da. $49.50. Knox County Daily News, 310 North Main, Bicknell IN 47512. **ED** William Menke. **Bk Rev. Ad Acc. Circ:** 21,800. ***Absorbed in part by*** *Morning News-Report.*
Desc: Local, state and national news.

US/0746-2034
KOKOMO TRIBUNE (KOKOMO, IND. : 1966). (THE KOKOMO TRIBUNE.). Vol. 117, No. 62 (Nov. 3, 1966)-. Newspaper. English. da (except Memorial Day, Labor Day, Christmas and New Year's). $104.00 (mail); $114.00 Kokomo; $127.00 suburban area of Kokomo (carrier). Kokomo Tribune, 300 North Union Street, PO Box 9014, Kokomo IN 46904. **Tel** (317)459-3121. **ED** John C. Wiles. **LC** 7701-X. **Circ:** 27,346 daily, 28,339 Sunday. ***Continues*** *Kokomo Tribune, The Kokomo Dispatch.*

US
LA PORTE HERALD-ARGUS, THE. **VFOAT** La Porte Herald Argus. Vol. 38, No. 41 (Oct. 20, 1924)-. Newspaper. English. da (except Sunday and holidays). $108.00. La Porte PUblishing Company, 701 State Street, La Porte IN 46350. **Tel** (219)362-2161. **ED** Mark Johnson. **LC** 7002. **Bk Rev. Photos. Ad Acc, Adv Mgr:** Thomas Avery. Full Page (B&W) $1038.45. Half Page (B&W) $519.23. Full Page (Color) $1238.45. Half Page (Color) $719.23. **Pub. Size:** Broadsheet. **Wire Svcs.:** SH, AP. **Circ:** 13,500 paid. ***Formed by the union of*** *Daily Herald (La Porte, Ind.)* ***and*** *Laporte Daily Argus;* ***Absorbed*** *La Porte Times (La Porte, Ind. : 1925).*

US
LAFAYETTE LEADER (LAFAYETTE, IND. : 1952). (THE LAFAYETTE LEADER.). **VFOAT** New Lafayette Leader. Vol. 80, No. 17 (April 25, 1952)-. Newspaper. English. wk. $48.00. Lafayette Leader, 22 North Second Street, PO Box 710, Lafayette IN 47902. **Tel** (317)423-2624, FAX (317)423-4495. **ED** Lynn Holland. **Photos. Ad Acc, Adv Mgr:** Kim Critchlow. **Pub. Size:** Tabloid. **Circ:** 5,000. ***Continues*** *Friday Lafayette Leader.*
Desc: Community newspaper.

US
LAGRANGE STANDARD. **VFOAT** La Grange Standard. (1857)-. Newspaper. English. wk. $33.00. Lagrange Publishing Company, PO Box 148, Lagrange IN 46761-0148. **Tel** (219)463-2167. **Ad Acc. Circ:** 6,000.

US
LAKE COUNTY STAR (CROWN POINT, IND.). (THE LAKE COUNTY STAR.). Began in Oct. 1880. Newspaper. English. wk. Lake County Star / Indiana, 15 North Court, Crown Point IN 46307. ***Continues*** *Crown Point Herald (Crown Point, Ind. : 1878).*

US/1044-2839
LAKE STATION HERALD. Newspaper. English. wk. Lake Station Herald, 3161 East 84th Place, Merrillville IN 46410. ***Continues*** *Herald (Gary, Ind. : East Gary Ed.).*

US
LAWRENCE TIMES, THE. Vol. 11, No. 47 (Nov. 4, 1981)-. Newspaper. English. wk. Topic Newspapers, 9615 College Avenue, Indianapolis IN 46280-1627. **Tel** (317)844-3311, FAX (317)575-8651. ***Continues*** *Lawrence Topics.*

US
LAWRENCE TOWNSHIP JOURNAL, THE. Vol. 29, No. 31 (Dec. 6, 1973)-. Newspaper. English. wk. Lawrence Township Journal, 7962 Pendleton Pike, Lawrence IN 46226. ***Continues*** *Lawrence Journal (Indianapolis, Ind.).*

US
LOWELL TRIBUNE, THE. (Dec. 1885)-. Newspaper. English. Fifty-two times a year (Wed.). Pilcher Publishing, PO Box 248, Lowell IN 46356. **Tel** (219)696-7711.

US
MADISON COURIER (MADISON, IND : 1892 : DAILY). (THE MADISON COURIER.). Vol. 45, No. 273 (March 12, 1892)-. Newspaper. English. da. $70.00. Madison Courier, 310 Courier Square, Madison IN 47250. **ED** Jane Jacobs, Graham Taylor (Managing Editor). **Photos. Ad Acc, Adv Mgr:** Edward Eggers, **Tel** (812)265-3641. Full Page (B&W) $1119.72. Half Page (B&W) $572.88. Full Page (Color) $1213.84. Half Page (Color) $667.00. **Wire Svcs.:** AP. available on microfilm from Crest Information Technologies. ***Continues*** *Madison Daily Courier (Madison, Ind. : 1869).*

US
MAIL-JOURNAL, THE. **VFOAT** Mail Journal. Vol. 1, No. 1 (Feb. 15, 1962)-. Newspaper. English. wk. Mail-Journal, 206 South Main Street, Milford IN 46542. ***Formed by the union of*** *Milford Mail* ***and*** *Syracuse-Wawase Journal;* ***Absorbed*** *Pierceton Press.*

US/0024-9009
MAKEDONSKA TRIBUNA. **Added/Corp** Macedonian Patriotic Organization. Central Committee. Macedono-Bulgarian Orthodox Churches of the U.S.A. and Canada. **VFOAT** Macedonian Tribune. Vol. 1, No. 1 (Feb. 10, 1927)-. Newspaper. Macedonian (English). bw. $15.00 US; $20.00 others; $75.00 (airmail). Macedonian Patriotic Organization, 124 West Wayne, Fort Wayne IN 46802-2504. **Tel** (219)422-5900, FAX (219)422-1349. **Bk Rev. Photos. Ad Acc.** Full Page (B&W) $500.00. Half Page (B&W) $250.00. **Pub. Size:** Tabloid. **Circ:** 1,500 (ctrl). available on microfilm from The Library of Congress Photoduplication Service.

US/1043-9587
MERRILLVILLE HERALD, THE. (Jan. 12, 1983)-. Newspaper. English. wk. Merrillville Herald, 3161 East 84th Place, Merrillville IN 46410. ***Continues*** *Herald (Gary, Ind. : Glen Park Ed.).*

US
MIDDLEBURY INDEPENDENT (MIDDLEBURY, IND. : 1974). (MIDDLEBURY INDEPENDENT.). 86th Year, No. 2 (March 15, 1974)-. Newspaper. English. wk. $8.50. Middlebury Independent, 103 North Main, Middlebury IN 46540. **ED** Michael Sullivan. **Ad Acc. Circ:** 1,200. ***Continues*** *Independent (Middlebury, Ind.).*

US
MIDDLETOWN NEWS (MIDDLETOWN, IND. : 1913). (THE MIDDLETOWN NEWS.). Vol. 29, No. 50 (Dec. 12, 1913)-. Newspaper. English. wk. $15.75. Middletown News, 469 Locust Street, Middletown IN 47356. **Tel** (317)354-2221, FAX (317)354-2221. **ED** Jack N. White (Editor-in-Chief) and Cheryl Hines (Managing Editor). **Bk Rev**, (Qty: 2). **Photos. Ad Acc, Adv Mgr:** Jack White. Full Page (B&W) $251.30. Half Page (B&W) $125.65. Full Page (Color) $311.30. Half Page (Color) $185.65. **Pub. Size:** Tabloid. **Circ:** 1,757. available in microform. ***Continues*** *Tri-County News (Middletown, Ind.).*

US/8750-829X
MISHAWAKA ENTERPRISE (MISHAWAKA, IND. : 1985). (THE MISHAWAKA ENTERPRISE.). Vol. 130, No. 7 (Feb. 14, 1985)-. Newspaper. English. wk. $7.50 St. Joseph county, $10.50 other. Mishawaka Enterprise, PO Box 584, Mishawaka IN 46544. ***Continues*** *Mishawaka Enterprise Record.*

US
MITCHELL TRIBUNE, THE. Began on July 27, 1889. Newspaper. English. wk. Mitchell Tribune, Box 248, Mitchell IN 47446.

US/1060-5231
MOROCCO COURIER, THE. (1876)-. Newspaper. English. wk. $23.50. Courier / Morocco Indiana, PO Box 138, Morocco IN 47963. **ED** William Kaye. **Bk Rev. Photos. Ad Acc, Adv Mgr:** Sally Snow. **Pub. Size:** Broadsheet. ***Absorbed*** *Kentland Democrat.*

US
MUNCIE EVENING PRESS. Vol. 1, No. 1 (March 27, 1905)-. Newspaper. English. da. Muncie Evening Press, High and Jackson Streets, Muncie IN 47302. ***Formed by the union of*** *Evening Times (Muncie, Ind.)* ***and*** *Muncie Daily Herald.*

US
MUNCIE STAR, THE. Vol. 68, No. 245 (Dec. 29, 1944)-. Newspaper. English. da. The Muncie Star, PO Box 2408, Muncie IN 47307. **Tel** (317)747-5700. **ED** W. W. Spurgeon Jr. **LC** 7745. **Circ:** 29,089 daily, 34,178 Sunday. ***Continues*** *Muncie Morning Star (Muncie, Ind. : 1904).*

US
NAPPANEE ADVANCE-NEWS. **VFOAT** Nappanee Advance News. Vol. 28, No. 40 (June 2, 1920)-. Newspaper. English. wk. Nappanee Advance-News, 158 Market Street, Nappanee IN 46550. ***Formed by the union of*** *Nappanee Advance* ***and*** *Nappanee News.*

US/0164-470X
NASA NADA. [Nasa nada]. **VFOAT** Our Hope. Periodical. Serbo-Croatian (Roman) (English). wk. Nasa Nada-Our Hope, 1414 West 119th Place, Crown Point IN 46307.

US/0888-0379
NATIONAL JEWISH POST & OPINION (INDIANAPOLIS, INC. : 1984). (THE NATIONAL JEWISH POST & OPINION.). [Natl. Jew. post. opin.]. **VFOAT** National Jewish Post and Opinion; Jewish Post and Opinion. (March 21, 1984)-. Newspaper. English. wk. $36.00 (one year); $64.00 (two years); $91.00 (three years). Jewish Post and Opinion, 2120 North Meridian Street, Indianapolis IN 46202. **Tel** (317)927-7800, FAX (317)927-7807. **ED** Gabriel Cohen (Editor-in-Chief) and Ed Stattmann (Managing Editor). **DD** 071. **Bk Rev**, (Qty: 10). **Photos. Ad Acc, Adv Mgr:** Sam Schulman, **Tel** (317)927-7800. Full Page (B&W) $1,176.00. Half Page (B&W) $588.00. **Pub. Size:** Tabloid. ***Continues*** *Jewish Post and Opinion, 0021-6658.*

US/0896-3150
NEW HEAVEN, NEW EARTH. ***Ceased.*** [New heaven new earth]. **VFOAT** New Heaven/New Earth. Vol. 1, No. 1 (Jan. 1983)-(1992). Newspaper. English. mo

Indiana

(except for August). New Heaven/New Earth, 107 South Greenlawn, South Bend IN 46617. **ED** Jeanne DeCeller. **DD** 205. **Bk Rev. Ad Acc. Circ:** 3,000 (ctrl).
Desc: A magazine for christians who want to live out their lives as christians in the world but not of the world.

US
NEW WOLCOTT ENTERPRISE, THE. Vol. 1, No. 1 (July 27, 1967)-. Newspaper. English. wk. $14.00 Indiana; $16.00 other. New Wolcott Enterprise, PO Box 78, Wolcott IN 47995. **Tel** (219)279-2167. **ED** Richard M. Wheeler, Barb Lawson (Managing Editor). **Photos. Ad Acc.** Full Page (B&W) $160.00. Half Page (B&W) $90.00. **Circ:** 900 paid.

US
NEWBURGH REGISTER (NEWBURGH, IND.). (THE NEWBURGH REGISTER.). VFOAT Chandler News. (1916)-. Newspaper. English. wk. Newburgh Register, PO Box 535, Newburgh IN 47630-0535.

US
NEWS (CLAY CITY, IND.). (THE NEWS.). Vol. 65, No. 48 (Dec. 1, 1976)-. Newspaper. English. wk. $16.00 in county; $23.00 others. Clay City News, 717 Main Street, PO Box 38, Clay City IN 47841. **ED** Rhonda Riggle. **Photos. Ad Acc, Adv Mgr:** Rhonda Riggle. **Tel** (812)939-2163. Full Page (B&W) $477.75. Half Page (B&W) $238.88. **Continues** Clay County Today.

US/1047-6016
NEWS-DISPATCH (MICHIGAN CITY, IND.). (NEWS-DISPATCH.). VFOAT News Dispatch. Vol. 1, No. 1 (June 6, 1938)-. Newspaper. English. da. News-Dispatch, 121 West Michigan Boulevard, Michigan City IN 46360. **Formed by the union of** Michigan City News (Michigan City, Ind. : 1922) **and** Evening Dispatch (Michigan City, Ind.).

US
NEWS (FARMERSBURG, IND.). (THE NEWS.). Vol. 46, No. 20 (March 25, 1948)-. Newspaper. English. wk. The News / Farmersburg, PO Box 371, Farmersburg IN 47850. **Formed by the union of** Farmersburg News; Hymera News **and** Shelburn News.

US/1060-6165
NEWS-REPORT (BICKNELL, IND.). (NEWS-REPORT.). VFOAT News Report. (Sept. 28, 1991)-. Newspaper. English. wk. News-Report, 310 North Main, Bicknell IN 47512. **Continues** Morning News-Report, 1054-707X.

US
NEWS-SENTINEL (FORT WAYNE, IND.). (THE NEWS-SENTINEL.). VFOAT News-Sentinel; News Sentinel; A.Sunday news and sentinel; A.Sunday news sentinel. (Dec. 11, 1925)-. Newspaper. English. da (Mon.-Sat.). $78.00 (1 year); $104.00 (2 year): $109.20 (3 year). Fort Wayne Newspapers Inc, PO Box 100, Fort Wayne IN 46801. **Tel** (219)461-8222. **ED** Stewart Spencer. **LC** 7002. **Circ:** 57,603. **Continues** Fort Wayne News-Sentinel.

US
NEWS-SUN (FAIRMOUNT, IND.). (THE NEWS-SUN.). VFOAT News Sun. Newspaper. English. wk. News Sun / Indiana, 122 South Main Street, Fairmount IN 46928. **Formed by the union of** Fairmount News (Fairmount, Ind.) **and** Summitville Sun.

US/8750-0876
NEWS-SUN (KENDALLVILLE, IND.). (THE NEWS-SUN.). VFOAT News Sun. (July 2, 1984)-. Newspaper. English. da. Kendallville Publishing Company, 112 North Main Street, Kendallville IN 46755. **Tel** (219)347-0400. **Continues** Kendallville News-Sun.

US/0887-0837
NEWS (TELL CITY, IND.). (THE NEWS.). Vol. 1, No. 1 (April 5, 1977)-. Newspaper. English. sw. The News / Indiana, 537 Main Street, Tell City IN 47586. **Formed by the union of** Cannelton News (Cannelton, Ind. : 1972) **and** Tell City News (Tell City, Ind. 1967).

US
NEWTON COUNTY ENTERPRISE. Vol. 1, No. 1 (April 30, 1891)-. Newspaper. English. wk. $20.00 (in county), $65.00 (out of state). Newton County Enterprise, 305 East Graham Street, Kentland IN 47951. **Tel** (219)474-5532, **FAX** (219)474-5354. **ED** Carla Waters. **Photos. Ad Acc, Adv Mgr:** Eric Drain. Full Page (B&W) $231.00. Half Page (B&W) $115.50. **Pub. Size:** Tabloid. **Continues** Kentland Gazette; **Absorbed** Newton Gazette (Kentland, Ind.).

US
NOBLESVILLE DAILY LEDGER. (1888)-. Newspaper. English. da. Noblesville Daily Ledger, 957 East Logan Street, Noblesville IN 46060. **Tel** (317)773-1210. **Continues** Ledger (Noblesville, Ind.); **Absorbed** Noblesville Telegraph.

US
NORTH MERIDIAN OBSERVER. Vol. 27, No. 33 (June 15, 1988)-. Newspaper. English. wk. Topic Newspapers, 9615 College Avenue, Indianapolis IN 46280-1627. **Tel** (317)844-3311, **FAX** (317)575-8651. **Continues** Washington Patriot (Indianapolis, Ind.).

US
NORTH SIDE TOPICS, BROAD RIPPLE-GLENDALE, THE. Vol. 70, No. 4 (Feb. 27, 1991)-. Newspaper. English. wk. The North Side Topics, 9615 North College Avenue, Indianapolis IN 46280. **Continues** Broad Ripple-Glendale North Side Topics.

US
NORTH VERNON PLAIN DEALER, THE. VFOAT North Vernon (Indiana) Plain Dealer. Vol. 92, No. 25 (Sept. 9, 1954)-. Newspaper. English. wk. $21.00. North Vernon Plain Dealer & Sun, 528 East O & M Avenue, PO Box 410, North Vernon IN 47265. **Tel** (812)346-3973. **ED** Barbara King. **Photos. Ad Acc, Adv Mgr:** Paula Lamb. Full Page (B&W) $516.60. Half Page (B&W) $258.30. Full Page (Color) $586.60. Half Page (Color) $328.30. **Pub. Size:** Standard. **Circ:** 6,880 (ctrl). **Continues** Plain Dealer, Republican, News.

US
NORTH VERNON SUN. (1873)-. Newspaper. English. wk. $21.00. North Vernon Plain Dealer & Sun, 528 East O & M Avenue, PO Box 410, North Vernon IN 47265. **Tel** (812)346-3973. **ED** Barbara King. **Photos. Ad Acc, Adv Mgr:** Paula Lamb. Full Page (B&W) $516.60. Half Page (B&W) $258.30. Full Page (Color) $586.60. Half Page (Color) $328.30. **Pub. Size:** Standard. **Circ:** 5,806 (ctrl). **Continues** North Vernon Weekly Sun.

US
NORTHEAST REPORTER. (19??)-. Newspaper. English. wk. Northeast Reporter, 4309 East Michigan Street, Indianapolis IN 46201.

US
NORTHERN STAR (LAKE VILLAGE, IND.). (THE NORTHERN STAR.). Vol. 1, No. 1 (Feb. 4, 1976)-. Newspaper. English. wk. Northern Star, Lake Village IN 46349. **Continues** Villager (Lake Village, Ind.).

US
OAKLAND CITY JOURNAL. Newspaper. English. wk. Oakland City Journal, PO Box 187, Oakland City IN 47660.

US
OBSERVER, THE. Vol. 2, No. 15 (Feb. 5, 1948)-. Newspaper. English. wk. The Observer / Indiana, Box 307, Kewanna IN 46939. **Continues** Kewanna Observer.

US
OHIO COUNTY NEWS (RISING SUN, IND.). (THE OHIO COUNTY NEWS.). 34th year, No. 23 (Dec. 5, 1912)-. Newspaper. English. wk. Ohio County News, 235 Main Street, Rising Sun IN 47040. **Continues** Rising Sun Local.

US
OSGOOD JOURNAL, THE. Vol. 43, No. 13 (March 17, 1909)-. Newspaper. English. wk. $29.00. Osgood Journal, 115 Washington Street, Versailles IN 47042. **ED** Laura Creech (Editor-in-Chief) and Linda Chandler (Managing Editor). **Bk Rev. Photos. Ad Acc, Adv Mgr:** Linda Chandler. **Tel** (812)689-6364. Full Page (B&W) $535.50. Half Page (B&W) $267.75. Full Page (Color) $610.50. Half Page (Color) $342.75. **Pub. Size:** Broadsheet. **Circ:** 5,150. **Continues** Ripley Journal (Osgood, Ind. : 1901).

US
OSSIAN JOURNAL, THE. (1914)-. Newspaper. English. wk. $3.50. Ossian Journal, 105 North Jefferson, Ossian IN 46777. **ED** James Barbieri. **Photos. Ad Acc, Adv Mgr:** Nila Dafform. Full Page (B&W) $441.00. Half Page (B&W) $220.50. Full Page (Color) $511.00. Half Page (Color) $290.50. **Pub. Size:** Broadsheet. **Wire Svcs.:** AP. **Continues** Ossian News.

US
PALLADIUM-ITEM. 1972-. Newspaper. English. da. Palladium-Item, 1175 North A Street, Richmond IN 47374. **Continues** Palladium-Item and Sun-Telegram.

US
PAOLI NEWS, THE. Began in 1893. Newspaper. English. wk. Paoli News, PO Box 190, Paoli IN 47454. **Continues** Paoli Weekly News.

US
PAOLI REPUBLICAN, THE. Began in 1878?. Newspaper. English. wk. Paoli Republican, PO Box 190, Paoli IN 47454. **Continues** Republican (Paoli, Ind.).

US/1044-7822
PARKE COUNTY SENTINEL. (1977)-. Newspaper. English. wk. $20.00 (in-state), $22.00 (out-of-state). Parke County Sentinel, 125 West High Street, Rockville IN 47872. **Tel** (317)569-2018. **ED** Larry Bemis. **Photos. Ad Acc, Adv Mgr:** Jane Moss. Full Page (B&W) $2.70 per column inch. Half Page (B&W) $2.80 per column inch. **Pub. Size:** Broadsheet. **Formed by the union of** Rockville Tribune **and** Rockville Republican (Rockville, Ind.).

US
PERU DAILY TRIBUNE (PERU, IND. : 1980). (PERU DAILY TRIBUNE.). Vol. 60, No. 75 (July 14, 1980)-. Newspaper. English. da. Peru Daily Tribune, 26 West 3rd Street, Peru IN 46970. **Continues** Peru Tribune.

US
PHAROS-TRIBUNE, THE. VFOAT Pharos Tribune. May 9, 1976-. Newspaper. English. da. Pharos-Tribune, 517 East Broadway, Logansport IN 46947. **Continues** Pharos-Tribune & Press.

US
PIKE REGISTER. Vol. 10, No. 5 (June 24, 1981)-. Newspaper. English. wk. Topic Newspapers, 9615 College Avenue, Indianapolis IN 46280-1627. **Tel** (317)844-3311, **FAX** (317)575-8651. **Continues** North West Topics.

US
PLAINFIELD MESSENGER (PLAINFIELD, IND. : 1984). (THE PLAINFIELD MESSENGER.). Vol. 117, No. 76 (Sept. 20, 1984)-. Newspaper. English. wk. Plainfield Messenger, 202 North Mill Street, Plainfield IN 46168. **Continues** Messenger (Plainfield, Ind.).

US
POSEY COUNTY NEWS & THE TIMES. VFOAT Posey County News. Vol. 108, No. 48 (Nov. 14, 1990)-. Newspaper. English. $18.00. Posey County News, Box 250, Poseyville IN 47633-0250. **Tel** (812)874-2813, **FAX** (812)985-7989. **ED** Jim Kohlmeyer. **Bk Rev. Photos. Ad Acc, Adv Mgr:** Jim Kohlmeyer. Full Page (B&W) $726.00. Half Page (B&W) $363.00. Full Page (Color) $776.00. Half Page (Color) $413.00. **Pub. Size:** Standard. **Circ:** 4,800. **Formed by the union of** Posey County News **and** Times (New Harmony, Ind.).

US/8750-3492
POST-TRIBUNE (GARY, IND.). (THE POST-TRIBUNE.). VFOAT Post Tribune; Sunday Post-Tribune; Sunday Post Tribune. Vol. 55, No. 151 (March 2, 1964)-. Newspaper. English. da. Post Tribune, 1065 Broadway, Gary IN 46402. **Tel** (219)881-3015, **FAX** (219)881-3005. **ED** Bety Cox, (phone: (219)881-3150). **LC** 7002. **Ad Acc, Adv Mgr:** Todd Brownrout, **Tel** (219)881-3166. **Circ:** 75,000 daily, 88,000 Sunday (ctrl). **Continues** Gary Post-Tribune.

US
PRESS-DISPATCH, THE. VFOAT Press Dispatch. Vol. 81, No. 21 (April 6, 1967)-. Newspaper. English. wk. $14.00 Indiana, $31.00 other. Press-Dispatch, PO Box 68, Petersburg IN 47567. **ED** Frank Heuring (Editor in Chief), Andy Heuring (Managing Editor). **Photos. Ad Acc, Adv Mgr:** John Heuring. Full Page (B&W) $453.60. Half Page (B&W) $226.80. Full Page (Color) $533.00. Half Page (Color) $306.80. **Pub. Size:** Tabloid. **Formed by the union of** Pike County Dispatch **and** Petersburg Press (Petersburg, Ind.).

US
PRINCETON DAILY CLARION (PRINCETON, IND. : 1960). (PRINCETON DAILY CLARION.). July 5, 1960-. Newspaper. English. da. Princeton Daily Clarion, PO Box 321, Princeton IN 47670. **Continues** Princeton Clarion-Democrat.

US
PROGRESS-EXAMINER, THE. VFOAT Progress Examiner. Vol. 21, No. 16 (Nov. 22, 1900)-. Newspaper. English. wk. Progress-Examiner, PO Box 225, Orleans IN 47452. **Formed by the union of** Orleans Progress **and** Examiner (Orleans, Ind.).

US
PULASKI COUNTY JOURNAL. Vol. 80, No. 1 (Jan. 3, 1957)-. Newspaper. English. wk. $17.00 US; $37.00 North America; $47.00 other. Pulaski County Journal, PO Box 19, Winamac IN 46996. **Tel** (219)946-6628. **ED** Douglas F Haley. **Bk Rev. Ad Acc. Circ:** 3,400 (ctrl). **Formed by the union of** Pulaski County Democrat **and** Winamac Republican (Winamac, Ind. : 1867); **Absorbed** Pulaski County Press.

US
PURDUE EXPONENT, THE. Added/Corp Purdue Student Publishing Foundation. Purdue University. VFOAT Exponent. (1???)-. Newspaper. English. ir. Purdue Exponent, PO Box 2506, West Lafayette IN 47906. **Tel** (317)743-1111. **ED** Tim Mathew. **LC** LH1.P9; E7. **Ad Acc. Circ:** 20,000 (ctrl).
Desc: The largest college newspaper in Indiana, 10th in size in the nation. It has received awards for the classified section, art, copy and layout.

US
REGIONAL NEWS (LA CROSSE, IND.). (THE REGIONAL NEWS.). Began in 1955. Newspaper. English. wk. Regional News, PO Box 358, La Crosse IN 46348. **Continues** La Crosse Sentinel; **Absorbed** Wanatah Mirror.

US
REMINGTON PRESS (REMINGTON, IND.). (THE REMINGTON PRESS.). Began in 1888. Newspaper. English. wk. Remington Press, Box 129, Remington IN 47977. ***Continues*** *Remington News (Remington, Ind.).*

US
REPORTER (MARTINSVILLE, IND.). (REPORTER.). 85th Year, No. 16 (Jan. 18, 1974)-. Newspaper. English. da. Reporter / Martinsville, 60 South Jefferson Street, Martinsville IN 46151. ***Continues*** *Martinsville Daily Reporter;* ***Absorbed*** *Morgan County Gazette (Martinsville, Ind. : 1970).*

US
REPUBLIC (COLUMBUS, IND.). (THE REPUBLIC.). (Jan. 3, 1967)-. Newspaper. English. da. Columbus Republic, 333 2nd Street, Columbus IN 47201. **Tel** (800)876-7811. ***Continues*** *Evening Republican (Columbus, Ind.).*

US
REPUBLICAN (DANVILLE, IND.). (THE REPUBLICAN.). Vol. 12, No. 27 (April 6, 1893)-. Newspaper. English. wk. $12.00 per year. Hendricks County Republican Inc, PO Box 149, Danville IN 46122. **Tel** (317)745-2777. **ED** Betty Jean Weesner. **Photos**. **Ad Acc.** Full Page (B&W) $462.00. Half Page (B&W) $231.00. **Pub. Size:** Standard. **Circ:** 1,700 (paid). available on microfilm and microfiche from Danville Public Library. ***Continues*** *Hendricks County Republican.*

US
REVIEW-REPUBLICAN, THE. **VFOAT** Review Republican. New Ser., V. 1, No. 1 (Oct. 22, 1914)-. Newspaper. English. wk. Review-Republican, 26 North Monroe, Williamsport IN 47993. ***Formed by the union of*** *Warren Review* ***and*** *Warren Republican (williamsport, Ind. : 1854).*

US
RISING SUN RECORDER, THE. **VFOAT** Centennial Daily Recorder. Began with Vol. 41, No. 2051 (Jan. 9, 1874). Newspaper. English. wk. Rising Sun Recorder, 235 Main Street, Rising Sun IN 47040. ***Continues*** *Ohio County Recorder.*

US
ROCHESTER SENTINEL (ROCHESTER, IND. : DAILY : 1961). (THE ROCHESTER SENTINEL.). Vol. 103, No. 1 (Jan. 3, 1961)-. Newspaper. English. da. $84.00. Rochester Sentinel, 118 East 8th Street, Rochester IN 46975. **ED** W.S. Wilson. **Photos**. **Ad Acc**, **Adv Mgr:** Arthur Hoffman. Full Page (B&W) $619.20. Half Page (B&W) $302.40. **Pub. Size:** Broadsheet. **Wire Svcs.:** AP. **Circ:** 4,900. available in microform from University Microfilms International (UMI). ***Continues*** *News-Sentinel (Rochester, Ind.).*

US
ROYAL CENTER RECORD. **VFOAT** Royal Center Record. (1890)-. Newspaper. English. wk. Royal Centre Record, PO Box 156, Royal Center IN 46978.

US/8756-6443
RUSHVILLE REPUBLICAN (RUSHVILLE, IND. : 1930 : DAILY). (RUSHVILLE REPUBLICAN.). **VFOAT** Rushville Evening Daily Republican. Vol. 26, No. 282 (Feb. 10, 1930)-. Newspaper. English. da. Rushville Republican, 219 North Perkins Street, Rushville IN 46173. ***Absorbed*** *Carthage Citizen;* ***Continues*** *Daily Republican (Rushville, Ind.).*

US
SALEM DEMOCRAT (SALEM, IND. : 1874). (THE SALEM DEMOCRAT.). Vol. 26, No. 26 (July 1, 1874)-. Newspaper. English. Fifty-two times a year (Thurs.). Leader Publication Company, PO Box 509, Salem IN 47167. **Tel** (812)883-3281. ***Continues*** *Washington Democrat (Salem, Ind. : 1873).*

US
SALEM LEADER (SALEM, INC. : 1959). (THE SALEM LEADER.). 80th year, No. 26 (June 25, 1959)-. Newspaper. English. wk. $19.50 Salem County, Indiana; $28.50 other Indiana; $34.50 other US. Leader Publication Company, PO Box 509, Salem IN 47167. **Tel** (812)883-3281. ***Continues*** *Salem Republican-Leader.*

US/0740-4573
SCOTT COUNTY JOURNAL (SCOTTSBURG, IND.), THE. (THE SCOTT COUNTY JOURNAL.). Vol. 31, No. 13 (March 4, 1914)-. Newspaper. English. wk. Scott County Journal, 39 East Wardell, Scottsburg IN 47170. **Tel** (812)752-2611. ***Continues*** *Scott County Journal and Scott County Democrat.*

US
SEYMOUR DAILY TRIBUNE. Vol. 39, No. 189 (Aug. 9, 1920)-. Newspaper. English. da. Seymour Daily Tribune, 1215 East Tipton Street, Seymour IN 47274. ***Formed by the union of*** *Seymour Daily Democrat (Seymour, Ind. : 1912)* ***and*** *Seymour Daily Republican.*

US/8750-0213
SHERIDAN NEWS, THE. Began in 1896?. Newspaper. English. wk. Topic Newspapers, 9615 College Avenue, Indianapolis IN 46280-1627. **Tel** (317)844-3311, FAX (317)575-8651. ***Absorbed*** *Weekly Sun (Sheridan, Ind.);* ***Continues*** *Sheridan Enterprise.*

US
SHOALS NEWS, THE. Vol. 27, No. 20 (May 14, 1915)-. Newspaper. English. wk. Shoals News, PO Box 218, Shoals IN 47581. ***Continues*** *News (Shoals, Ind.).*

US
SOUTH BEND TRIBUNE, THE. **VFOAT** South Bend Saturday Tribune. 29th Year (May 26, 1902)-. Newspaper. English. da. South Bend Tribune Corporation, 225 West Colfax Avenue, South Bend IN 46626. **Tel** (219)233-6161, FAX (219)239-2642. **ED** Jack McGann. **Bk Rev**. **Ad Acc**. **Circ:** 106,000 daily, 125,000 Sunday (ctrl). available on microfilm from University Microfilms International (UMI); available on an online database (file 635/Full-Text) from DIALOG. Documents available from UMI Article Clearinghouse. ***Continues*** *South-Bend Daily Tribune.*
Ind/Abst Bus. Dateline (Dec. 26, 1991-) [Full Txt.].

US
SOUTH BEND TRIBUNE IRISH SPORTS REPORTS. English. Twenty-two times a year (During the football season). $28.00 (one year); $50.00 (two years); $72.00 (three years). South Bend Tribune Corporation, 225 West Colfax Avenue, South Bend IN 46626. **Tel** (219)233-6161, FAX (219)239-2642. **ED** Bill Bilinski. **Ad Acc**, **Adv Mgr:** Smith, **Tel** (219)235-6161. **Circ:** 20,000.
Desc: News about the Notre Dame sports mainly football.

US
SOUTH GIBSON STAR-TIMES. **VFOAT** South Gibson Star Times. (1991)-. Newspaper. English. wk. $12.00 Gibson County; $16.00 others. South Gibson Star-Times, PO Box 70, Fort Branch IN 47648-0070. **Tel** (812)753-3553, FAX (812)753-4251. **ED** Mike Rasche. **Photos**. **Ad Acc**, **Adv Mgr:** John Heuring. Full Page (B&W) $216.00. Half Page (B&W) $115.20. Full Page (Color) $281.00. Half Page (Color) $180.20. **Pub. Size:** Broadsheet. **Circ:** 2,578. ***Formed by the union of*** *Fort Branch Times, 8605-8819* ***and*** *Owensville Star-Echo (Owensville Ind. : 1991), 0934-9019.*

US
SOUTHSIDE CHALLENGER, THE. (1973)-. Newspaper. English. wk. Challenger Newspapers, PO Box 708, Greenwood IN 46142-3573. **Tel** (317)888-3376, FAX (317)888-3377. **ED** Don Guerretaz (Editor-in-Chief) and Jeff Narmore (Managing Editor). **Bk Rev**, (Qty: 2). **Photos**. **Ad Acc**, **Adv Mgr:** Don Guerreta. Full Page (B&W) $400.00. Half Page (B&W) $225.00. Full Page (Color) $475.00. Half Page (Color) $300.00. **Pub. Size:** Tabloid.

US
SPENCER COUNTY JOURNAL-DEMOCRAT, THE. **VFOAT** Journal-Democrat. Vol. 132, No. 3 (March 5, 1987)-. Newspaper. English. wk. Spencer County Journal-Democrat, 541 Main Street, Rockport IN 47635. ***Continues*** *Journal & Democrat.*

US
SPOTLIGHT (INDIANAPOLIS, IND.). (THE SPOTLIGHT.). Vol. 1, No. 1 (Feb. 16, 1939)-. Newspaper. English. wk. $45.00. The Spotlight / Indiana, 4217 South Meridian, Indianapolis IN 46217. **Tel** (317)788-4554. **ED** Jerry L. Cosby, B. Scott Mohr (Managing Editor). **Bk Rev**. **Photos**. **Ad Acc**, **Adv Mgr:** Ron Douglas. Full Page (B&W) $795.00. Half Page (B&W) $440.00. **Pub. Size:** Broadsheet.

US
SPRINGS VALLEY HERALD. (Oct. 7 1903)-. Newspaper. English. Fifty-two times a year. $15.95. Springs Valley Herald, PO Box 311, 211 College Street, French Lick IN 47432. **Tel** (812)936-9630. **ED** Ruth Marshall. **Bk Rev**, (Qty: 1). **Photos**. **Ad Acc**. **Circ:** 3,000 (ctrl).

US
STAR-ECHO, THE. **VFOAT** Owensville Star-Echo. Newspaper. English. wk. Star-Echo, Box 248, Owensville IN 47665-0248. ***Continues*** *Owensville Star-Echo.*

US
STAR-JOURNAL (HOPE, IND.). (THE STAR-JOURNAL.). **VFOAT** Star Journal. 1943-. Newspaper. English. wk. Star-Journal, PO Box 65, Hope IN 47246. ***Continues*** *Hope Star-Journal (Hope, Ind.).*

US/8750-6548
STAR TRIBUNE (ATTICA, IND.). ***Title Change.*** (STAR TRIBUNE.). Vol. 134, No. 1 (Jan. 2, 1985)-(19??). Newspaper. English. sw. Tribune Star Publishing Co Inc / Indiana, PO Box 149, Terre Haute IN 47808. **Tel** (812)231-4288. ***Formed by the union of*** *Fountain County Star* ***and*** *Ledger Tribune.* ***Continued by*** *Fountain County Neighbor, 1060-5495.*

US
SULLIVAN DAILY TIMES, THE. **VFOAT** Sullivan Times-Democrat. Vol. 3, No. 234 (March 24, 1906)-. Newspaper. English. da. Sullivan Daily Times, 115 West Jackson Street, Sullivan IN 47882. ***Continues*** *Sullivan Evening Times;* ***Absorbed*** *Sullivan Democrat (Sullivan, Ind. : 1854).*

US
SWITZERLAND DEMOCRAT. Began in 1904. Newspaper. English. wk. Switzerland Democrat, 111 West Market Street, Vevay IN 47043. **ED** Craig McCall. **Circ:** 1,500. ***Formed by the union of*** *Vevay Democrat* ***and*** *Vevay Times.*

US/8755-934X
TERRE HAUTE GAZETTE (TERRE HAUTE, IND. : WEEKLY). (THE TERRE HAUTE GAZETTE.). Vol. 1, No. 1 (Oct. 31, 1984)-. Newspaper. English. wk. LA Beckley, 1313 Wabash Avenue, Terre Haute IN 47807. ***Continues*** *Macksville Gazette, 0747-0584.*

US
TIMES (FRANKFORT, IND.). (THE TIMES.). (June 16, 1975)-. Newspaper. English. da. $100.00 by carrier; $115.00 by mail. Frankfort Times Inc, 251 East Clinton Street, Frankfort IN 46041. **Tel** (317)659-4622. ***Continues*** *Frankfort Times (Frankfort, Ind. : Daily).*

US
TIMES-MAIL, THE. **VFOAT** Times Mail; Sunday Herald-Times; Sunday Herald Times. Vol. 92, No. 239 (May 16, 1977)-. Newspaper. English. da (daily & Sundays). Times-Mail, 813 16th Street, PO Box 849, Bedford IN 47421. **Tel** (812)275-3355. ***Continues*** *Daily Times-Mail.*

US
TIMES (MOORESVILLE, IND.). (THE TIMES.). Vol. 62, No. 17 (Dec. 7, 1950)-. Newspaper. English. wk. $16.00. The Times / Mooresville, Indiana, 23 East Main Street, Mooresville IN 46158. **ED** Steve Heath. **Photos**. **Ad Acc**, **Adv Mgr:** Sharon Clipp, **Tel** (317)831-0280. Full Page (B&W) $806.25. Half Page (B&W) $403.13. Full Page (Color) $876.25. Half Page (Color) $473.13. **Pub. Size:** Broadsheet. **Circ:** 6,800 weekly paid. ***Continues*** *Mooresville Times.*

US
TIMES-UNION (WARSAW, IND.). (TIMES-UNION.). **VFOAT** Times Union. 118th Year, No. 18 (Jan. 22, 1972)-. Newspaper. English. da (Mon.-Sat.). Reub Williams & Sons Inc., PO Box 1448, Warsaw IN 46580. **Tel** (219)267-3111. ***Continues*** *Warsaw Times-Union.*

US/0746-0619
TIPTON COUNTY TRIBUNE. **VFOAT** Tipton Tribune. Vol. 84, No. 3 (Jan. 4, 1980)-. Newspaper. English. da (except Sun. and holidays). Tipton County Tribune, 317 South Anderson Street, Elwood IN 46036. **Tel** (317)675-2115. **ED** Tom Carey. **Circ:** 3,400. ***Continues*** *Tribune (Tipton, Ind.).*

US
TRI-COUNTY BANNER. **VFOAT** Tri County Banner. Vol. 114, No. 39 (Sept. 27, 1978)-. Newspaper. English. wk. Tri-County Banner, 103 East Main Street, Knightstown IN 46148. ***Continues*** *Banner (Knightstown, Ind.).*

US
TRI-COUNTY NEWS (SOUTH BEND, IND.). (TRI-COUNTY NEWS.). (1941)-. Newspaper. English. wk. Tri-County News / South Bend, Indiana, 1410 South Michigan Street, South Bend IN 46613. ***Continues*** *South Side Free Press.*

US
TRI-COUNTY NEWS (WASHINGTON, IND.). (TRI-COUNTY NEWS.). **VFOAT** Tri County News. Vol. 1, No. 1 (Nov. 10, 1981)-. Newspaper. English. wk. Tri-County News / Indiana, PO Box 9, Washington IN 47501.

US
TRIBUNE (NEW ALBANY, IND.). (THE TRIBUNE.). **VFOAT** Sunday Ledger-Tribune. 79th Year, No. 33 (Feb. 15, 1967)-. Newspaper. English. da. New Albany Tribune, West 2nd Street and Market, New Albany IN 47150. **Tel** (812)944-6481. ***Continues*** *New Albany Tribune.*

US
TRIBUNE-NEWS (SOUTH WHITLEY, IND.). (TRIBUNE-NEWS.). **VFOAT** Tribune News. Vol. 90, No. 35 (Feb. 5, 1976)-. Newspaper. English. wk. Tribune-News, 113 South State Street, South Whitley IN 46787. ***Continues*** *South Whitley Tribune.*

US/0745-9599
TRIBUNE-STAR, THE. **VFOAT** Tribune Star. **VAT** Tribune Star. Vol. 1, No. 1 (May 16, 1983)-. Newspaper. English. da. The Tribune-Star, 721 Wabash Avenue, PO Box 149, Terre Haute IN 47808-0149. **Tel** (812)231-4288, FAX (812)231-4234. **ED** Robert Schumaker. **Bk Rev**. **Ad Acc**. **Circ:** 37,000 (ctrl). available on microfilm. ***Formed by the union of*** *Terre Haute Tribune* ***and*** *Star (Terre Haute, Ind.).*
Desc: Newspaper of record in eight-county area that comprises the Wabash Valley between Indiana and Illinois.

Indiana

TWIN CITY JOURNAL-REPORTER.
VFOAT Twin City Journal Reporter. Vol. 87, No. 21 (May 22, 1975)-. Newspaper. English. wk. $15.00. Community Newspapers Inc., 239 East Main Street, Gas City IN 46933. **Tel** (317)674-0070. **ED** Cynthia E. Payne. **Photos**. **Ad Acc**, **Adv Mgr**: Marvin Stang. Full Page (B&W) $419.25. Half Page (B&W) $208.00. Full Page (Color) $469.00. Half Page (Color) $258.00. **Pub. Size**: Broadsheet. **Circ**: 1,750 (ctrl). available in microform. *Formed by the union of* Reporter (Gas City, Ind.); Gas City Journal *and* Jonesboro Journal (Jonesboro, Ind.). **Desc**: Covers community news.

VERSAILLES REPUBLICAN (VERSAILLES, IND. : 1893). (THE VERSAILLES REPUBLICAN.). Vol. 37, No. 42 (May 18, 1893)-. Newspaper. English. wk. $29.00. Versailles Republican, 115 South Washington Street, Versailles IN 47042. **ED** Laura Creech (Editor-in-Chief) and Linda Chandler (Managing Editor). **Bk Rev**. **Photos**. **Ad Acc**, **Adv Mgr**: Linda Chandler. Full Page (B&W) $535.50. Half Page (B&W) $267.75. Full Page (Color) $610.50. Half Page (Color) $342.75. **Pub. Size**: Broadsheet. **Circ**: 5,200. *Continues* Republican (Versailles, Ind.); *Absorbed* Milan Commercial.

VEVAY REVEILLE-ENTERPRISE, THE.
VAT Vevay Reveille Enterprise. Vol. 106 No. 10 (Mar 9 1922)-. Newspaper. English. wk. Vevay Reveille-Enterprise, PO Box 157, Vevay IN 47043. **ED** Craig McCall. **Circ**: 3,500. *Formed by the union of* Vevay Reveille *and* Vevay Enterprise.

VINCENNES SUN-COMMERCIAL, THE.
VFOAT Vincennes Sun Commercial. Vol. 1, No. 19 (Feb. 1, 1931)-. Newspaper. English. da. $144.00. Vincennes Sun-Commercial, 702 Main Street, Vincennes IN 47591. **Tel** (812)886-9955, FAX (812)885-2235. **ED** Mikael N. Wright. **Ad Acc**, **Adv Mgr**: V. Kopp. **Circ**: 16,000 Sunday, 14,000 daily (ctrl). *Formed by the union of* Vincennes Sun *and* Vincennes Commercial (Vincennes, Ind. : Daily).

WABASH PLAIN DEALER (WABASH, IND. : DAILY : 1937). **VFOAT** Wabash Times Star. Vol. 74, No. 297 (Jan. 16, 1937)-. Newspaper. English. da. Wabash Plain Dealer, 123 West Canal Street, Wabash IN 46992. *Continues* Wabash Plain Dealer, and Times-Star.

WAKARUSA TRIBUNE, THE. (Sept. 1893)-. Newspaper. English. wk. $18.20. Wakarusa Tribune, PO Box 507, Wakarusa IN 46573. **Tel** (219)862-2179, FAX (219)293-3705. **ED** Bill L. Nich (Editor-in-Chief) and Molly McGarrett (Managing Editor). **Bk Rev**, (Qty: 15). **Photos**. **Ad Acc**, **Adv Mgr**: Ginger Rodgers. Full Page (B&W) $294.40. Half Page (B&W) $147.20. Full Page (Color) $369.40. Half Page (Color) $222.20. **Pub. Size**: Tabloid. **Circ**: 1,390.

WASHINGTON TIMES-HERALD (WASHINGTON, IND.). (THE WASHINGTON TIMES-HERALD.). **VFOAT** Washington Times Herald. Vol. 1, No. 1 (June 1, 1964)-. Newspaper. English. da. $6.00 (per month). Washington Times-Herald, 102 East Vantrees Street, Washington IN 47501. **Tel** (812)254-0480, FAX (812)254-7517. **ED** Melody Maust. **Bk Rev**. **Photos**. **Ad Acc**, **Adv Mgr**: Don Brown. Full Page (B&W) $617.91. Half Page (B&W) $321.93. **Pub. Size**: Standard. **Wire Svcs.**: AP. *Formed by the union of* Washington Daily Times (Washington, Ind.) *and* Washington Herald (Washington, Ind. : 1905).

WAYNEDALE NEWS. (1967)-. Newspaper. English. bw. Waynedale News, 2700 L Huntington Road, Fort Wayne IN 46809.

WEEKLY HERALD (MADISON, IND. : 1974). (THE WEEKLY HERALD.). (19??)-. Newspaper. English. wk. $19.00. Madison Courier, 310 Courier Square, Madison IN 47250. **ED** Jane Jacobs. **Photos**. *Continues* Madison Weekly Herald (Madison, Ind. : 1940).

WEST SIDE MESSENGER (BROWNSBURG, IND.). (THE WEST SIDE MESSENGER.). Newspaper. English. wk. Mid-State Newspapers Inc, 516 East Main Street, Brownsburg IN 46112. *Continues* West Side Messenger-Indianapolis Courier.

WESTFIELD ENTERPRISE. Vol. 4, No 15 (June 24, 1981)-. Newspaper. English. wk. Topic Newspapers, 9615 College Avenue, Indianapolis IN 46280-1627. **Tel** (317)844-3311, FAX (317)575-8651. *Continues* Westfield Topics.

WESTSIDE ENTERPRISE, THE. (1968)-. Periodical. English. wk. Indy Suburban Newspapers, PO Box 602, Greenfield IN 46140-0602. **Tel** (317)462-7368, FAX (317)462-7779. **ED** Jim Thomas. **Circ**: 12,000.

WESTVILLE INDICATOR. Vol. 1, No. 1 (May 6, 1882)-. Newspaper. English. wk. $17.00 (in county), $20.00 (out of county). Westville Indicator, 9852 West Street Road 2, Westville IN 46391. **Tel** FAX (219)785-2442. **Photos**. **Ad Acc**. Full Page (B&W) $627.00. Half Page (B&W) $316.00. **Circ**: 5,200. available in microform.

US/0886-4330
ZIONSVILLE TIMES SENTINEL. Vol. 124 No. 28 (Sept. 4, 1985)-. Newspaper. English. wk. Zionsville Times Sentinel, 58 North Main Street, Zionsville IN 46077. *Formed by the union of* Zionsville Main Street; Zionsville Times *and* Zionsville Sentinel Dispatch.

IOWA

US/0746-1119
AD-EXPRESS AND DAILY IOWEGIAN AND CITIZEN. **VFOAT** Daily Iowegian and Citizen; Ad-Express and Iowegian and Citizen; Centerville Iowegian. **VAT** Ad Express and Daily Iowegian and Citizen. Vol. 100, No. 66 (July 11, 1983)-. Newspaper. English. da. Centerville Daily Iowegian, 105 North Main Street, Centerville IA 52544-1732. **Tel** (515)856-6336, FAX (515)856-8118. **ED** Steve Dunn. **Ad Acc**. **Circ**: 4,000. available on microfilm from University Microfilms International (UMI). *Continues* Daily Iowegian and Citizen.

ADAIR COUNTY FREE PRESS (GREENFIELD, IOWA : 1984). (ADAIR COUNTY FREE PRESS.). Vol. 94, No. 39 (Feb. 22, 1984)-. Newspaper. English. wk. $27.00. Adair County Free Press, 108 East Iowa Street, Greenfield IA 50849. **ED** Ken Sidey. **Photos**. **Ad Acc**, **Adv Mgr**: Kristine Morken-Houl. **Tel** (515)743-6121. Full Page (B&W) $486.00. Half Page (B&W) $292.00. **Pub. Size**: Standard. **Circ**: 3,000 (weekly). *Continues* Adair County Free Press and The Greenfield Transcript.

ADAIR NEWS (WITH THE CASEY VINDICATOR), THE. Vol. 90, No. 39 (Dec. 2, 1971)-. Newspaper. English. wk. Adair News, 403 Audubon Street, Adair IA 50002. **ED** W E Littler Jr. *Formed by the union of* Adair News *and* Casey Vindicator.

AFTON STAR-ENTERPRISE, THE. **VFOAT** Afton Star Enterprise; Star-Enterprise. (1897)-. Newspaper. English. wk. $17.50 Iowa; $22.50 others. Afton Star-Enterprise Publishing Company, 274 North Douglas, PO Box 128, Afton IA 50830. **Tel** (515)347-8721. **ED** Donna G. Haight. **Photos**. **Ad Acc**, **Adv Mgr**: Mary Lou Cheers. Full Page (B&W) $178.75. Half Page (B&W) $89.38. **Pub. Size**: Tabloid. **Circ**: 1,158. *Formed by the union of* Afton Enterprise *and* Afton Star.

ALBIA UNION-REPUBLICAN, THE. **VFOAT** Albia Union Republican; Albia Union and Republican. Vol. 62, No. 2 (Jan. 4, 1923)-. Newspaper. English. wk. Albia Newspapers, 109-111 Benton Avenue East, Albia IA 52531-2034. **Tel** (515)932-7121, FAX (515)932-2822. **ED** Carol Beronich-Jones. **Ad Acc**, **Adv Mgr**: Mary Ann Crall. **Circ**: 3,600. *Continues* Albia Union and Republican.

ALGONA UPPER DES MOINES, THE.
VFOAT Algona (IA.) Upper Des Moines. Vol. 31, No. 1 (Jan. 4, 1933)-. Newspaper. English. wk. Algona Upper Des Moines, PO Box 400, Algona IA 50511. *Continues* Upper Des Moines Republican; *Absorbed* Fenton Reporter.

ALLAMAKEE JOURNAL AND LANSING MIRROR. **VFOAT** Allamakee Journal. (Nov. 30, 1922)-. Newspaper. English. wk. Allamakee Journal and Lansing Mirror, Lansing IA 52151. *Formed by the union of* Allamakee Journal *and* Lansing Mirror (Lansing, Iowa : 1874).

ALTOONA HERALD-MITCHELLVILLE INDEX, THE. **VFOAT** Altoona Herald Mitchellville Index. Vol. 86, No. 27 (Jan. 9, 1975)-. Newspaper. English. wk. Altoona Herald-Mitchellville Index, 116 2nd Street Southeast, Altoona IA 50009. *Formed by the union of* Altoona Herald *and* Mitchellville Index.

ANAMOSA JOURNAL-EUREKA, THE.
VFOAT Anamosa Journal Eureka. Vol. 111, No. 48 (Dec. 5 1979)-. Newspaper. English. wk. Anamosa Journal-Eureka, 113 North Ford Street, Anamosa IA 52205. *Formed by the union of* Anamosa Eureka *and* Anamosa Journal.

ANKENY PRESS CITIZEN. **VFOAT** Ankeny Press Citizen/Crier. Mar. 25, (1986)-. Newspaper. English. wk. $11.00 Polk County, IA; $17.00 other Iowa; $25.00 other. Ankeny Press Citizen, 602 Southwest Third Street, Ankeny IA 50021. **Tel** (515)964-0639. *Continues* Ankeny Press Citizen/Crier.

US/8756-6400
ATLANTIC NEWS-TELEGRAPH. **VFOAT** Atlantic News Telegraph. Vol. 33, No. 223 (Jan. 2, 1912)-. Newspaper. English. da. $70.50. Atlantic News-Telegraph, PO Box 230, Atlantic IA 50022. **Tel** (712)243-2624. **ED** M.D. Griggs, Christy Stinger (Managing Editor). **Photos**. **Ad Acc**, **Adv Mgr**: Kim Johnson. Full Page (B&W) $838.50. Half Page (B&W) $419.25. Full Page (Color) $943.50. Half Page (Color) $471.75. **Pub. Size**: Broadsheet. **Wire Svcs.**: AP. **Circ**: 5,500. *Formed by the union of* Atlantic Evening News *and* Atlantic Daily Telegraph (Atlantic, Iowa : 1911).

AURELIA SENTINEL. Began in March 1881. Newspaper. English. wk. Aurelia Sentinel, Aurelia IA 51005. *Continues* Aurelia Independent.

BANCROFT REGISTER. Began in 1882. Newspaper. English (German). wk. Bancroft Register, PO Box 38, Bancroft IA 50517-0038.

BEACON-FORUM. **VFOAT** Beacon Forum. Vol. 97, No. 42 (Oct. 14, 1981)-. Newspaper. English. wk. Beacon Forum, 500 Church Street, Eldon IA 52554. **Tel** (515)652-7612. **ED** Donna Garber. **Bk Rev**. **Ad Acc**. **Circ**: 1,000. *Formed by the union of* Eldon Forum (Eldon, Iowa : 1921) *and* Batavia Beacon.

US/1061-4516
BEACON (SPIRIT LAKE, IOWA). (THE BEACON.). Vol. 113, No. 44, Nov. 3 (1983)-. Newspaper. English. wk. The Beacon / Iowa, PO Box A, Spirit Lake IA 51360. *Continues* Spirit Lake Beacon.

BEDFORD TIMES-PRESS, THE. **VFOAT** Bedford Times Press. Vol. 60 No. 1 (Jan. 7, 1932)-. Newspaper. English. wk. Bedford Times-Press, 313 Main Street, Bedford IA 50833. **ED** Originally edited by: J.W. Brown, Jr. (managing editor). *Absorbed* Taylor County Herald (Bedford, Iowa); *Formed by the union of* Bedford Free Press *and* Times-Republican (Bedford, Iowa : 1925).

BELLE PLAINE UNION (BELLE PLAINE, IOWA : 1922). (THE BELLE PLAINE UNION.). **VFOAT** Union. No. 3882 (Jan. 5, 1922)-. Newspaper. English. wk. Belle Plaine Union, 832 12th Street, Belle Plaine IA 52208. *Continues* Belle Plaine Union and Herald; *Absorbed* Keystone Bulletin; Belle Plaine Gazette.

BETTENDORF NEWS. **VFOAT** Bettendorf News and Bettendorf Press. Vol. 33, No. 48 (Mar. 16, 1961)-. Newspaper. English. wk. $20.00. Bettendorf News, PO Box L, Bettendorf IA 52722-1512. **Tel** (319)355-2644, FAX (319)355-0956. **ED** Deirdre Cox Baker. **Photos**. **Ad Acc**. Full Page (B&W) $487.50. Half Page (B&W) $243.75. Full Page (Color) $537.50. Half Page (Color) $293.75. **Pub. Size**: Tabloid. **Circ**: 2,500. available in microform. *Continues* Bettendorf Press.

BLOOMFIELD DEMOCRAT (BLOOMFIELD, IOWA : 1922). (BLOOMFIELD DEMOCRAT.). 53rd Year, No. 37 (Sept. 21, 1922)-. Newspaper. English. wk. Bloomfield Democrat, 207-209 South Madison, Bloomfield IA 52537. *Continues in part* Combined Issue of the Davis County Republican and Bloomfield Democrat; *Continues* Davis County Republican (Bloomfield, Iowa : 1922).

US/0899-8698
BREMER COUNTY INDEPENDENT (1959). (BREMER COUNTY INDEPENDENT.). **VFOAT** Independent. Vol. 103, No 6 (Feb. 25, 1959)-. Newspaper. English. wk. Waverly Newspapers, 311 West Bremer, Waverly IA 50677. **Tel** (319)352-3334, FAX (319)352-5135. **ED** Ray Locke. **Photos**. **Ad Acc**, **Adv Mgr**: Jayne Thomas Hall. **Pub. Size**: Broadsheet. **Circ**: 6,400. *Formed by the union of* Waverly Journal (Waverly, Iowa) *and* Bremer County Independent and Waverly Republican.

BRITT NEWS-TRIBUNE, THE. **VFOAT** Britt News Tribune. Vol. 25, No. 14 (Oct. 17, 1918)-.

Newspaper. English. wk. Britt News-Tribune, Box 128, Britt IA 50423. ***Formed by the union of*** *Britt News* ***and*** *Britt Tribune (Britt, Iowa : 1885).*

US
BUFFALO CENTER TRIBUNE. Began in May 1892. Newspaper. English. wk. Buffalo Center Tribune, 124 North Main Street, Buffalo Center IA 50424. ***Absorbed*** *Buffalo Center Globe.*

US/0746-8512
CALHOUN COUNTY ADVOCATE. VFOAT Rockwell City Advocate. 106th year, No. 20 (Jan. 4, 1984)-. Newspaper. English. wk. $13.50 Calhoun and surrounding counties. Calhoun County Advocate, 430 Main Street, Rockwell City IA 50579. ***Continues*** *Advocate (Rockwell City, Iowa).*

US
CARLISLE CITIZEN, THE. VFOAT Carlisle Citizen Newspapers, Inc. Began in 1925. Newspaper. English. wk. Carlisle Citizen, PO Box 370, Carlisle IA 50047.

US
CARROLL TODAY NEWS. VFOAT Carroll Today; Today News Extra; Carroll Today News Extra; Carroll Today Weekender News. Vol. 8, No. 12 (Feb. 11, 1989)-. Newspaper. English. bw. $22.50. Carroll Communications, 526 North Carroll, Carroll IA 51401. **ED** Mary Russelmain, Duanne Winn. **Bk Rev. Photos. Ad Acc.** Full Page (B&W) $425.00. Half Page (B&W) $220.00. **Pub. Size:** Broadsheet. ***Continues*** *Carroll Today.*

US/8750-5665
CEDAR FALLS CITIZEN, THE. Dec. 8, 1984-. Newspaper. English. wk. Cedar Falls Citizen, PO Box 726, 222 Main Street, Cedar Falls IA 50613. ***Continues*** *Cedar Falls Sun, 0747-2323.*

US/0746-5645
CEDAR VALLEY TIMES (VINTON, IOWA : 1971). (THE CEDAR VALLEY TIMES.). **VFOAT** Times. Vol. 85, No. 89 (Jan. 4, 1972)-Vol. 87, No. 259 (Sept. 1, 1972). Newspaper. English. da. Cedar Valley Times, 108-110 East 5th Street, Vinton IA 52349. ***Continues*** *Cedar Valley Daily Times.*

US
CHALLIS MESSENGER, THE. Vol. 31, No. 37 (Mar. 19, 1912)-. Newspaper. English. wk. $21.00. Challis Messenger, PO Box 405, Challis IA 83226. **Tel** (208)879-4445. **ED** Peggy Parks. **Photos. Ad Acc, Adv Mgr:** Peggy Parks. Full Page (B&W) $316.00. Half Page (B&W) $158.00. Full Page (Color) $416.00. Half Page (Color) $258.00. **Pub. Size:** Tabloid. **Circ:** 1,900. available in microform. ***Continues*** *Silver Messenger.*

US
CHARITON HERALD-PATRIOT, THE. VFOAT Chariton Herald Patriot; Herald-Patriot. Vol. 1, No. 1 (Oct. 7, 1909)-. Newspaper. English. $34.00. Chariton Newspapers, Box 651, Chariton IA 50049. **ED** Keith Isley. **Photos. Ad Acc, Adv Mgr:** Norral Lowe, **Tel** (515)774-2137. Full Page (B&W) $580.50. Half Page (B&W) $290.25. **Circ:** 3,650. ***Formed by the union of*** *Chariton Herald* ***and*** *Chariton Patriot (Chariton, Iowa : 1870).*

US
CHARITON LEADER (CHARITON, IOWA : 1904). (THE CHARITON LEADER.). **VFOAT** Leader. Vol. 33 No. 14 (Apr 7, 1904)-. Newspaper. English. wk. $34.00. Chariton Newspapers, Box 651, Chariton IA 50049. **ED** Keith Isley. **Photos. Ad Acc, Adv Mgr:** Norral Lowe, **Tel** (515)774-2137. Full Page (B&W) $580.50. Half Page (B&W) $290.25. **Circ:** 3,650. available in microform. ***Continues*** *Chariton Democrat (Chariton, Iowa : 1885).*

US/1049-7242
CHARLES CITY PRESS (1951). (CHARLES CITY PRESS.). Vol. 55, No. 128 (Aug. 6, 1951)-. Newspaper. English. da. $61.00. Charles City Press, 801 Riverside, Charles City IA 50616-2015. **Tel** (515)228-3211, FAX (515)228-2641. **ED** Dave Ruble. **Ad Acc. Circ:** 3,321 (evening). ***Continues*** *Charles City Press and Evening Intelligencer (Charles City, Iowa : 1949).*

US/0747-4776
CHEROKEE DAILY TIMES. VFOAT Daily Times. Vol. 24, No. 66 (Nov. 16, 1951)-. Newspaper. English. da (except Sundays and holidays). $56.50 local, $66.50 others. Cherokee Daily Times, PO Box 281, Cherokee IA 51012. **Tel** (712)225-5111. **ED** David Yoder. **Circ:** 3,400. ***Continues*** *Cherokee Times (Cherokee, Iowa : 1870).*

US
CLARINDA, IOWA HERALD-JOURNAL, THE. VFOAT Clarinda, Iowa Herald Journal. Vol. 114, No. 65 (Aug. 14, 1972)-. Newspaper. English. sw. Clarinda Herald-Journal, 215 East Washington Street, Clarinda IA 51632. ***Continues*** *Clarinda Herald-Journal.*

US
CLARKSVILLE STAR, THE. Began in 1870?. Newspaper. English. wk. Clarksville Star, Box 788, Clarksville IA 50619. ***Continues*** *Star of the West (Clarksville, Iowa).*

US
CLAYTON COUNTY REGISTER, THE. VFOAT Register. Vol. 49, No. 38 (Sept. 23, 1926)-. Newspaper. English. wk. Clayton County Register, 106 Cedar Street, Elkader IA 52043. **Tel** (319)245-1311. **ED** Robert Andersen. **Ad Acc. Circ:** 2,900. ***Formed by the union of*** *Clayton County Messenger* ***and*** *Elkader Register (Elkader, Iowa : 1918);* ***Absorbed*** *Volga City News; Monona Leader.*

US
CLEARFIELD CHRONICLE, THE. Began in 1959. Newspaper. English. wk. Clearfield Chronicle, PO Box 155, Clearfield IA 50840.

US
CLINTON HERALD, THE. VFOAT Daily Herald; Clinton Daily Herald. (1???)-. Newspaper. English. da. $114.00. Clinton Herald, 221 6th Ave. South, Clinton IA 52732. **Tel** (319)242-7101. **LC** 7002. ***Continues*** *Clinton Daily Herald;* ***Absorbed*** *Clinton Advertiser (Clinton, Iowa).*

US/0164-6915
COLLECTORS JOURNAL (VINTON). (COLLECTORS JOURNAL.). (197?)-. Periodical. English. wk. $28.00. Collectors Journal, 421 First Avenue, Box 601, Vinton IA 52349-0601. **Tel** (319)472-4613. **ED** Cristina McCormick. **Bk Rev. Photos. Ad Acc, Adv Mgr:** Leann Jones, **Tel** (319)472-4763. Full Page (B&W) $578.88. Half Page (B&W) $313.92. **Pub. Size:** Standard. **Circ:** 8,000.

US/0747-2889
COLUMBUS GAZETTE (COLUMBUS JUNCTION, IOWA), THE. (THE COLUMBUS GAZETTE.). **VFOAT** Columbus Gazette and Columbus Safeguard. Vol. 75, No. 20 (Sept. 13, 1962)-. Newspaper. English. wk. $21.00. Columbus Gazette, 209 Main Street, Columbus Junction IA 52738. **Tel** (319)728-2413. **ED** Mark Sheafer. **Photos. Ad Acc, Adv Mgr:** Tammy Virzi. Full Page (B&W) $483.75. Half Page (B&W) $247.50. Full Page (Color) $513.75. Half Page (Color) $277.50. **Pub. Size:** Broadsheet. available in microform. ***Continues*** *Columbus Gazette and Columbus Safeguard.*

US
CRESTON NEWS ADVERTISER (CRESTON, IOWA : 1928 : DAILY). (CRESTON NEWS ADVERTISER.). **VFOAT** News Advertiser. 49th Year, No. 142 (Sept. 6, 1928)-. Newspaper. English. da. $105.00. Creston News Advertiser, 503 West Adams Street, Creston IA 50801. **Tel** (515)782-2141, FAX (515)782-6628. **ED** Jeff Young (Managing Editor). **Photos. Ad Acc, Adv Mgr:** Roger Lanning. Full Page (B&W) $824.31. Half Page (B&W) $412.16. Full Page (Color) $1019.31. Half Page (Color) $607.16. **Pub. Size:** Broadsheet. **Wire Svcs.:** AP. available in microform from Bell & Howell. ***Formed by the union of*** *Creston Evening News* ***and*** *Creston Daily Advertiser (Creston, Iowa : 1923);* ***Absorbed*** *Creston Weekly Times.*

US
DAILY FREEMAN-JOURNAL, THE. VFOAT Daily Freeman Journal. (Oct. 15, 1917)-. Newspaper. English. da. Freeman-Journal Publishing Company, 720 2nd Street, Webster City IA 50595. **ED** Originally edited by: W.F. Hunter. Documents available from UMI Article Clearinghouse. ***Formed by the union of*** *Daily Freeman-Tribune* ***and*** *Evening Journal (Webster City, Iowa);* ***Absorbed*** *Webster City Tribune; Webster City Graphic (Webster City, Iowa : 1951); Public Press (Webster City, Iowa).*
Ind/Abst Bus. Dateline (April 22, 1992-) [Full Txt.].

US
DAILY GATE CITY (KEOKUK, IOWA : 1957). (THE DAILY GATE CITY.). 111th Year, No. 250 (Oct. 22, 1957)-. Newspaper. English. da. Daily Gate City, 1016 Main Street, Keokuk IA 52632. ***Continues*** *Daily Gate City and Constitution-Democrat (Keokuk, Iowa : 1940).*

US
DAILY IOWAN, THE. (1901)-. Newspaper. English. da. The Daily Iowan, 111 Communications Center, Iowa City IA 52240. **Tel** (319)335-5786. ***Formed by the union of*** *S.U.I. Quill* ***and*** *Vidette-Reporter (Iowa City, Iowa : 1881).*

US/1046-1833
DAILY NONPAREIL (1976), THE. (THE DAILY NONPAREIL.). **VFOAT** Nonpareil. 119th Year, No. 330 (Nov. 25, 1976)-. Newspaper. English. da. Daily Nonpareil, 117 Pearl Street, Council Bluffs IA 51501. **ED** Frank Lane. ***Continues*** *Council Bluffs Nonpareil (Council Bluffs, Iowa : 1920).*

US/1074-4487
DAILY REGISTER (OELWEIN, IOWA). (DAILY REGISTER.). (19??)-. Newspaper. English. da. $83.00 (mail); $109.20 (carrier). Oelwein Publishing Company, 16-20 East Charles Street, Oelwein IA 50662. **Tel** (319)283-2144. **ED** Dick Palmer. **Photos. Ad Acc, Adv Mgr:** Jeff Swor, **Tel** (218)624-3665. Full Page (B&W) $1,270.65. Half Page (B&W) $835.28. Full Page (Color) $1,386.15. Half Page (Color) $950.78. **Circ:** 48,800 (unpaid), 2,650 (paid). ***Continues*** *Register (Oelwein, Iowa).*

US/0746-0872
DAILY REPORTER (SPENCER, IOWA), THE. (THE DAILY REPORTER.). (19??)-. Newspaper. English. da. Spencer Daily Reporter, 416 1st Avenue West, Spencer IA 51301.

US/0893-7915
DAILY TRIBUNE (AMES, IOWA), THE. (THE DAILY TRIBUNE.). **VFOAT** Ames Daily Tribune Weekender Edition. Vol. 119, No. 232 (April 2, 1987)-. Newspaper. English. da. Daily Tribune / Ames, Box 380, Ames IA 50010. ***Continues*** *Ames Daily Tribune (Ames, Iowa : 1986).*

US
DALLAS COUNTY NEWS (ADEL, IOWA). ***Title Change.*** (DALLAS COUNTY NEWS.). **VFOAT** Adel News. (1872)-. Newspaper. English. wk. Dallas County News, Box 156, Adel IA 50003. ***Absorbed*** *Dallas County Republican; Dallas County Record; Dexfield Review-Sentinel.* ***Continued by*** *Dexfield Review-Sentinel.*

US
DAYTON REVIEW (DAYTON, IOWA). (THE DAYTON REVIEW.). Vol. 7, No. 1 (Jan. 9, 1885)-. Newspaper. English. wk. $16.00 Iowa; $17.00 others. Dayton Review, Main and Skillet Streets, Box 6, Dayton IA 50530-0006. **Tel** (515)547-2811, FAX (515)547-2337. **ED** James A. Diehl. Index available. cum. index. **Bk Rev**, (Qty: 12). **Photos. Ad Acc, Adv Mgr:** James A. Diehl. Full Page (B&W) $192.00. Half Page (B&W) $108.00. Full Page (Color) $247.00. Half Page (Color) $163.00. **Pub. Size:** Tabloid. **Circ:** 1,079. ***Continues*** *Dayton Weekly Review.*

US
DECORAH JOURNAL. VFOAT Decorah Journal and Press. (187?)-. Newspaper. English. wk. $30.00. Decorah Newspapers, 107 East Water Street, PO Box 350, Decorah IA 52101. **Tel** (319)382-4221, FAX (319)382-5949. **ED** Richard Fromm. **Photos. Ad Acc, Adv Mgr:** Ken Eicle. Full Page (B&W) $710.00. Half Page (B&W) $355.00. **Pub. Size:** Broadsheet. **Circ:** 6,500. available in microform. ***Continues*** *Decorah Bee & Journal;* ***Absorbed*** *Decorah Bee.*

US
DECORAH PUBLIC OPINION (DECORAH, IOWA : 1954). (DECORAH PUBLIC OPINION.). **VFOAT** Decorah Public Opinion, Decorah Republican and Calmar Courier. Vol. 59, No. 7 (Feb. 15, 1954)-. Newspaper. English. wk. $30.00. Decorah Newspapers, 107 East Water Street, PO Box 350, Decorah IA 52101. **Tel** (319)382-4221, FAX (319)382-5949. **ED** Richard Fromm. **Photos. Ad Acc, Adv Mgr:** Ken Eicle. Full Page (B&W) $710.00. Half Page (B&W) $355.00. **Pub. Size:** Broadsheet. **Circ:** 6,500. available in microform. ***Continues*** *Decorah Public Opinion, Decorah Republican and Calmar Courier.*

US/1042-119X
DEMOCRAT (EMMETSBURG, IOWA). (THE DEMOCRAT.). 94th year, No. 2 (Jan. 12, 1978)-. Newspaper. English. wk. The Democrat, Box 73, Emmetsburg IA 50536. ***Continues*** *Emmetsburg Democrat.*

US
DENISON REVIEW, THE. VFOAT Denison, Ia., Review. Began with May 3, 1867 issue. Newspaper. English. wk. $50.00. Denison Review, 1410 Broadway, Denison IA 51442. **Tel** (712)263-2121, FAX (712)263-2125. **ED** Charles Signs. **Bk Rev. Ad Acc. Circ:** 5,800 (ctrl). ***Absorbed*** *Journal (Denison, Iowa).*

US
DES MOINES COUNTY NEWS. (198?)-. Newspaper. English. wk. Louisa Publishing Company / West Burlington, PO Box 177, West Burlington IA 52655. ***Continues*** *Des Moines County DMC News.*

US
DES MOINES REGISTER, THE. VFOAT Des Moines Sunday Register. Vol. 68, No. 93 (Oct. 1, 1916)-. Newspaper. English. da. Des Moines Register, PO Box 957, Des Moines IA 50304. **Tel** (515)284-8000. **ED** James P. Gannon. **DD** 071/.7758. **Circ:** 221,869 daily, 364,727 Sunday. available on microfilm from University Microfilms International (UMI). ***Continues*** *Des Moines Register and Leader;* ***Absorbed*** *Des Moines Tribune.*
Ind/Abst PROMT.

US
DIAGONAL PROGRESS (DIAGONAL, IOWA : 1979). (THE DIAGONAL PROGRESS.). Vol. 1, No. 1 (July 26, 1979)-. Newspaper. English. wk. Diagonal Progress, PO Box 1, Diagonal IA 50845.

Iowa

US
DIAMOND TRAIL NEWS. Vol. 1, No. 1 (Aug. 6, 1975)-. Newspaper. English. wk. $16.00 Iowa. Diamond Trail News, 303 7th Avenue, Sully IA 50251. **Tel** (515)594-4488, FAX (515)594-4498. **ED** Margaret F Vanderweedt. **Bk Rev. Photos. Ad Acc.** Full Page (B&W) $229.20. Half Page (B&W) $113.60. **Pub. Size:** Tabloid. **Circ:** 1,800 (ctrl).

US
DONNELLSON STAR, THE. Began Sept. 24, 1970. Newspaper. English. wk. Donnellson Star, PO Box 340, Donnellson IA 52625. *Continues Donnellson Review.*

US
DOON PRESS. Vol. 1, No. 1 (June 18, 1964)-. Newspaper. English. wk. Doon Press, Doon IA 51235. **Ad Acc. Circ:** 3,800. available on microfilm.

US/0012-6918
DUBUQUE LEADER, THE. Added/Corp Dubuque Federation of Labor. Vol. 13, No. 8 (Jan. 3, 1919)-. Newspaper. English. wk. $12.00 per year. Dubuque Leader, 1527 Central, Dubuque IA 52001. **Tel** (319)556-6625. **ED** William R. Winders. **Photos. Ad Acc.** Full Page (B&W) $445.50. Half Page (B&W) $222.75. **Pub. Size:** Tabloid. **Circ:** 5,000 (paid). available on microfilm and microfiche. *Continues Labor Leader (Dubuque, Iowa).*

US
DUNLAP REPORTER (DUNLAP, IOWA : 1913). (THE DUNLAP REPORTER.). **VFOAT** Weekly Dunlap Reporter. Vol. 44, No. 13 (July 11, 1913)-. Newspaper. English. wk. $17.00. Dunlap Reporter, 114 Iowa Avenue, Dunlap IA 51529. **Tel** (712)643-5380. **ED** Doris Bingham. **Photos. Ad Acc, Adv Mgr:** Agnes Morris. Full Page (B&W) $410.00. Half Page (B&W) $205.00. Full Page (Color) $480.00. Half Page (Color) $275.00. **Pub. Size:** Broadsheet. **Circ:** 1,400. *Continues Dunlap Reporter and Herald.*

US
DYERSVILLE COMMERCIAL. VFOAT Commercial. Began in March 1873. Newspaper. English. wk. Dyersville Commercial, PO Box 128, Dyersville IA 52040-0128.

US
DYSART REPORTER, THE. Vol. 1, No. 1 (March 22, 1878). Newspaper. English. wk. Dysart Reporter, 317 Main Street, Dysart IA 52224.

US
EAGLE GROVE EAGLE AND GOLDFIELD CHRONICLE. VFOAT Eagle Grove Eagle Consolidated with the Eagle Grove Times and Goldfield Chronicle; Eagle Grove Eagle. Vol. 38, No. 4 (Jan. 27, 1927)-. Newspaper. English. wk. Eagle Grove Eagle, 314 West Broadway, Eagle Grove IA 50533. *Formed by the union of Eagle Grove Eagle and Goldfield Chronicle and Eagle Grove Times (Eagle Grove, Iowa : 1923).*

US
ECLIPSE-NEWS-REVIEW, THE. VFOAT Eclipse News-Review; Eclipse News Review. Vol. 96, No. 26 (Feb. 26, 1969)-. Newspaper. English. wk (Wednesday). $20.00. Eclipse-News-Review, 503 Coates Street, Parkersburg IA 50665. **Tel** (319)346-1461. **ED** Leon Thorne. **Bk Rev. Photos. Ad Acc.** Full Page (B&W) $748.00. Half Page (B&W) $374.00. Full Page (Color) $783.00. Half Page (Color) $409.00. **Pub. Size:** Broadsheet. **Circ:** 2,436. *Continues Parkersburg Eclipse and the New Hartford Review, Consolidated (Parkersburg, Iowa : 1964).*

US
EDDYVILLE TRIBUNE, THE. (1886)-. Newspaper. English. wk. Big Grove Publications, PO Box 9, Fremont IA 52561-0009. **Tel** (515)933-4241. **ED** Nancy Annis. **Circ:** 700.

US
ELDORA HERALD-LEDGER, THE. VFOAT Eldora Herald Ledger. Vol. 66, No. 14 (April 2, 1931)-. Newspaper. English. wk. Eldora Herald-Ledger, Eldora IA 50627. *Formed by the union of Eldora Herald (Eldora, Iowa : 1910) and Hardin County Ledger; Absorbed Union Star (Union, Iowa).*

US
ELK HORN-KIMBALLTON REVIEW. VFOAT Elk Horn Kimballton Review. Began in 1924. Newspaper. English. wk. Elk Horn-Kimballton Review, Elk Horn IA 51531.

US
ESSEX INDEPENDENT, THE. (1894)-. Newspaper. English. wk. $18.00. Essex Independent, Box 59, Essex IA 51638-0059. **ED** Gregg K. Knowles (Editor-in-Chief) and Bob Jackson (Managing Editor). **Photos. Ad Acc, Adv Mgr:** Bob Jackson, **Tel** (712)379-3313. Full Page (B&W) $455.11. Half Page (B&W) $227.56. Full Page (Color) $515.11. Half Page (Color) $287.56. **Pub. Size:** Broadsheet. **Circ:** 508.

US/0747-0754
ESTHERVILLE DAILY NEWS. VFOAT Daily News. 59th Year, No. 232 (July 10, 1947)-. Newspaper. English. da. $52.00. Estherville Daily News, 10 North 7th Street, Estherville IA 51334. Documents available from UMI Article Clearinghouse. *Continues Estherville Daily News Combining the Vindicator & Republican.* **Ind/Abst** Bus. Dateline (Jan. 6, 1992-) [Full Txt.].

US
EVENING SENTINEL (SHENANDOAH, IOWA). (THE EVENING SENTINEL.). **VFOAT** Shenandoah Evening Sentinel. Vol. 45, No. 30 (May 5, 1926)-. Newspaper. English. da. Evening Sentinel, 118 South Elm Street, Shenandoah IA 51601. *Continues Evening Sentinel-World.*

US/1061-4508
FAIRFIELD LEDGER (1966). (FAIRFIELD LEDGER.). **VFOAT** Fairfield Daily Ledger. Vol. 117, No. 193, Aug. 17 (1966)-. Newspaper. English. da. Fairfield Ledger, 112 East Broadway, Fairfield IA 52556. *Continues Fairfield Daily Ledger (Fairfield, Iowa : 1923).*

US
FONTANELLE OBSERVER (FONTANELLE, IOWA : 1904). (THE FONTANELLE OBSERVER.). **VFOAT** Observer. Vol. 41, No. 14 (April 14, 1904)-. Newspaper. English. wk. Fontanelle Observer, PO Box 248, Fontanelle IA 50846-0248. *Continues Observer (Fontanelle, Iowa).*

US
FOREST CITY SUMMIT (FOREST CITY, IOWA : 1947). (FOREST CITY SUMMIT.). **VFOAT** Summit. Vol. 80, No. 41 (Oct. 9, 1947)-. Newspaper. English. wk (published on Tuesdays). $22.00 Forest City; $25.00 Iowa and Minnesota; $27.00 other. Forest City Summit, PO Box 350, Forest City IA 50436. **Tel** (515)582-2112, FAX (515)582-4442, . **ED** Cynthia Carter. **Ad Acc. Circ:** 3,600. *Continues Summit (Forest City, Iowa).*

US/0746-4266
FORT MADISON DAILY DEMOCRAT. VFOAT Democrat; Daily Democrat. (1???)-. Newspaper. English. da. Fort Madison Daily Democrat, 1226 Avenue H, Fort Madison IA 52627.

US
FREMONT GAZETTE. (1890)-. Newspaper. English. Fifty-two times a year. $31.00 Wapello County; $34.00 others in Iowa; $40.00 others. Mother Wit Publications Inc., PO Box 697, Ottumwa IA 52501. **Tel** (515)682-3745. *Absorbed Fremont Record; Oskaloosa Tribune-Press (Oskaloosa, Iowa : 1960).*

US
FREMONT-MILLS BEACON-ENTERPRISE (TABOR, IOWA : 1981). (THE FREMONT-MILLS BEACON-ENTERPRISE.). **VFOAT** Fremont Mills Beacon Enterprise. Vol. 99, No. 28 (June 4, 1981)-. Newspaper. English. wk. Beacon-Enterprise, PO Box 299, Tabor IA 51653. *Continues Beacon-Enterprise.*

US
GARNER LEADER AND SIGNAL AND GARNER HERALD, THE. VFOAT Leader and Signal. Vol. 72, No. 8 (April 19, 1944)-. Newspaper. English. wk. 365 State Street, Garner IA 50438. *Continues Garner Leader and Garner Signal and Garner Herald; Absorbed Klemme Times.*

US/1066-0291
GAZETTE (CEDAR RAPIDS, IOWA), THE. (THE GAZETTE.). **VFOAT** Cedar Rapids Gazette. Vol. 97, No. 201 (July 29, 1979)-. Newspaper. English. da. $86.00 Iowa; $147.16 other US. Cedar Rapids Gazette, PO Box 511, Cedar Rapids IA 52406. **Tel** (319)398-8333, FAX (319)398-8395. **ED** Joe Hladky. **Bk Rev. Ad Acc, Adv Mgr:** David Storey, **Tel** (319)398-8208. available on microfilm from University Microfilms International (UMI). *Continues Cedar Rapids Gazette.*

US
GAZETTE (NEOLA, IOWA). (GAZETTE.). Vol. 8, No. 42 (April 15, 1982)-. Newspaper. English. wk. $16.00. Gazette, Box 7, Neola IA 51559. **Tel** (712)485-2276. **ED** Maureen R. Olsen. **Photos. Ad Acc.** Full Page (B&W) $364.76. Half Page (B&W) $203.18. **Pub. Size:** Standard. **Circ:** 1,863. *Continues Neola Gazette-Reporter, Minden-Shelby News.*

US/0746-6196
GLIDDEN GRAPHIC, THE. (March 14, 1890)-. Newspaper. English. wk. Glidden Graphic, PO Box 607, Glidden IA 51443.

US
GOWRIE NEWS, THE. Vol. 1, No. 1 (March 28, 1889)-. Newspaper. English. wk. Gowrie News, Box C, Gowrie IA 50543.

US
GREENE RECORDER, THE. Vol. 73, No. 1 (Aug. 8, 1956)-. Newspaper. English. wk. Greene Recorder, 219 North 2nd Street, Greene IA 50636. *Continues Iowa Recorder.*

US
GUTHRIE CENTER TIMES (GUTHRIE CENTER, IOWA : 1952). (GUTHRIE CENTER TIMES.). Vol. 71 No. 22 (Sept. 11, 1952)-. Newspaper. English. wk. $24.00. Guthrie Center Times, Box 217, Guthrie Center IA 50115. **Tel** (515)747-3511, FAX (515)747-2208. **ED** Scott Gonzales and Daryl Ames (Managing Editor). **Photos. Ad Acc.** Full Page (B&W) $509.12. Half Page (B&W) $260.48. Full Page (Color) $549.12. Half Page (Color) $300.48. **Pub. Size:** Standard. **Wire Svcs.:** IM. **Circ:** 2,201 (ctrl). available on microfiche; available on diskette; available on videocassette. *Continues Guthrie County Times (Guthrie Center, Iowa : 1950); Absorbed Guthrian.*

US
HARDIN COUNTY TIMES, THE. Vol. 71, No. 23 (June 1, 1948)-. Newspaper. English. wk. Hardin County Times, 406 Stevens Street, Iowa Falls IA 50126. **ED** Carl Hamilton. *Continues New Times (Alden, Iowa).*

US
HARLAN NEWS-ADVERTISER. VFOAT Harlan News Advertiser. Vol. 66, No. 27 (July 4, 1935)-. Newspaper. English. wk. Harlan News-Advertiser, 1114 7th Street, Harlan IA 51537. *Continues Harlan Republican.*

US
HARLAN TRIBUNE, THE. VFOAT Harlan (Iowa) Tribune. Vol. 1, No. 1 (June 11, 1879)-. Newspaper. English. wk. Harlan Tribune, 1114 7th Street, Harlan IA 51537.

US
HARTLEY SENTINEL, THE. Vol. 1, No. 1 (June 13, 1912)-. Newspaper. English. wk. Hartley Sentinel, 71 1st Street Southeast, Hartley IA 51346.

US
HAWK EYE, THE. 136th Year, No. 19 (July 31, 1972)-. Newspaper. English. da. $144.00. Hawk Eye, 800 South Main Street, Burlington IA 52601. **Tel** (319)759-8461, 800 397-1708. **ED** Bill Mertens (editor), Dale Alison (managing editor). **Bk Rev. Photos. Ad Acc, Adv Mgr:** Nelson H. Showalter. Full Page (B&W) $1,328.70. Half Page (B&W) $664.35. **Pub. Size:** Broadsheet. **Wire Svcs.:** AP. available on microfiche. *Continues Burlington Hawk-Eye (Burlington, Iowa : 1960).*

US
IDA COUNTY COURIER, THE. Vol. 1, No. 1 (Nov. 11, 1975)-. Newspaper. English. wk. Ida County Courier, 210 2nd Street, Ida Grove IA 51445.

US
IDA COUNTY PIONEER RECORD. VFOAT Pioneer Record. Vol. 56, No. 1 (May 19, 1927)-. Newspaper. English. Fifty-two times a year (Thrus.). $14.95. Ida County Pioneer Record, PO Box 31, Ida Grove IA 51445. **Tel** (712)364-2022. **ED** Steve Merrill (Editor-in-Chief) and Judy Bowman (Managing Editor). **Photos. Ad Acc.** Full Page (B&W) $412.00. Half Page (B&W) $206.00. Full Page (Color) $482.00. Half Page (Color) $276.00. **Pub. Size:** Broadsheet. *Formed by the union of Ida County Pioneer and Ida Grove Record.*

US
INDEPENDENT DEMOCRAT (WAVERLY). (INDEPENDENT DEMOCRAT.). (19??)-. Newspaper. English. bw. $40.00 Bremer & Butler counties; $56.00 other. Waverly Newspapers, 311 West Bremer, Waverly IA 50677. **Tel** (319)352-3334, FAX (319)352-5135. **ED** Ray Locke. **Photos. Ad Acc, Adv Mgr:** Jayne Thomas Hall. **Pub. Size:** Broadsheet. **Circ:** 6,400.

US
IOWA CITY PRESS-CITIZEN. VFOAT Iowa City Press Citizen. (Nov. 1 1920)-. Newspaper. English. da. Iowa City Press-Citizen, 319 East Washington Street, Iowa City IA 52240. *Formed by the union of Iowa City Daily Press and Iowa City Daily Citizen.*

US
IOWA FALLS CITIZEN. VFOAT Citizen, Iowa Falls, Iowa. Vol. 45, No. 43 (Oct. 26, 1933)-. Newspaper. English. wk. Iowa Falls Citizen, 406 Stevens Street, Iowa Falls IA 50126. **ED** T B Purcell. *Continues Hardin County Citizen.*

US
IOWA STATE DAILY. Added/Corp Iowa State College. Iowa State University. **VFOAT** Daily. Vol. 77, No. 1 (Sept. 20, 1947)-. Newspaper. English. da. $58.00. Iowa State Daily Publications, Iowa State University, 108 Hamilton Hall, Ames IA 50011. **Tel** (515)294-4120. **ED** Colleen Bradford (Editor-in-Chief) and Jason Howland (Managing Editor). **Photos. Ad Acc, Adv Mgr:** Kathy Davis, **Tel** (515)294-4121. Full Page (B&W) $1,008.00. Half Page (B&W) $504.00. Full Page (Color) $1,088.00.

Half Page (Color) $584.00. **Pub. Size:** Standard. **Wire Svcs.:** AP. available in microform. ***Continues*** *Iowa State Daily Student.*

US
JEFFERSON BEE, THE. Vol. 6, No. 20 (June 7, 1872)-. Newspaper. English. wk. Jefferson Bee, 214 North Wilson Avenue, Jefferson IA 50129. ***Continues*** *Bee (Jefferson, Iowa);* ***Absorbed*** *Souvenir (Jefferson, Iowa).*

US
JEFFERSON HERALD (JEFFERSON, IOWA). (THE JEFFERSON HERALD.). Vol. 21, No. 45 (Nov. 7, 1917)-. Newspaper. English. wk. Jefferson Herald, 214 North Wilson Avenue, Jefferson IA 50129. ***Continues*** *Free Lance (Jefferson, Iowa).*

US
JESUP CITIZEN HERALD. VFOAT Citizen Herald. Vol. 78, No. 50 (Dec. 13, 1978)-. Newspaper. English. wk. $19.50. Jesup Citizen Herald, 930 6th Street, Jesup IA 50648. **Tel** (319)827-1128, FAX (319)827-1125. **ED** Kim Edward-Adams. **Photos. Ad Acc.** Full Page (B&W) $625.65. Half Page (B&W) $312.83. **Pub. Size:** Broadsheet. **Circ:** 1,320. available on microfilm. ***Continues*** *Citizen Herald.*

US
JOURNAL-EXPRESS. VFOAT Saturday Journal-Express; Journal Express; Knoxville Journal-Express. Vol. 131, No. 39 (Sept. 22, 1986)-. Newspaper. English. sw. $25.00. Edwards Publishing Company, PO Box 458, Knoxville IA 50138. **ED** Darcy Maile. **Photos. Ad Acc, Adv Mgr:** Don Abens, **Tel** (515)842-2155. Full Page (B&W) $903.00. Half Page (B&W) $448.00. Full Page (Color) $988.00. Half Page (Color) $533.00. **Pub. Size:** Broadsheet. ***Formed by the union of*** *Knoxville Journal (Knoxville, Iowa : 1874)* ***and*** *Knoxville Express.*

US
KALONA NEWS, THE. Vol. 1, No. 1 (Nov. 19, 1891)-. Newspaper. English. wk. $22.00 Iowa $30.00 US. Kalona News, Box 329, Kalona IA 52247. **Tel** (319)656-2273, FAX (319)656-2299. **ED** Ronald Slechta. **Bk Rev**, (Qty: 2). **Photos. Ad Acc.** Full Page (B&W) $4.00 per column inch. Half Page (B&W) $4.00 per column inch. Full Page (Color) $4.00 per column inch plus $100.00 per color. Half Page (Color) $4.00 per column inch plus $100.00 per color. **Pub. Size:** Broadsheet. **Circ:** 3,250.

US
KEOSAUQUA EAGLE. Began with Dec. 4, 1875 issue. Newspaper. English. wk. Keosauqua Eagle, Box 18, Keota IA 52248.

US
LAKE MILLS GRAPHIC, THE. Vol. 18, No. 1 (Sept. 1, 1892)-. Newspaper. English. wk. Lake Mills Graphic, 204 North Mill Street, Lake Mills IA 50450. ***Continues*** *Star (Lake Mills, Iowa).*

US
LAKE PARK NEWS (LAKE PARK, IOWA : 1976). (THE LAKE PARK NEWS.). Vol. 84, No. 34 (April 8, 1976)-. Newspaper. English. wk. Lake Park News, PO Box 157, Lake Park IA 51347. ***Separated from*** *Dickinson County Mail News.*

US
LAKE VIEW RESORT (LAKE VIEW, IOWA : 1910). (LAKE VIEW RESORT.). Vol. 21, No. 41 (Feb. 3, 1910)-. Newspaper. English. wk. $15.00. Lake View Resort, Box 798, Lake View IA 51450. **ED** Tessie McKinney (Editor-in-Chief) and Marcia Haakenson (Managing Editor). **Photos. Ad Acc, Adv Mgr:** Deb Druivenga, **Tel** (712)657-8588 or (712)664-2830. Full Page (B&W) $231.00. Half Page (B&W) $115.50. **Pub. Size:** Tabloid. ***Continues*** *Lake View Argus.*

US
LAMONI CHRONICLE, THE. Vol. 7, No. 42 (April 4, 1901). Newspaper. English. wk. Lamoni Chronicle, PO Box 40, Lamoni IA 50140. ***Continues*** *College City Chronicle.*

US
LEETOWN NEWS. VFOAT Lee Town News. Vol. 1, No. 1 (Dec. 14, 1961)-. Newspaper. English. wk. Des Moines Lee Town News, PO Box 4826, Des Moines IA 50306. **Tel** (515)262-1724, FAX (515)262-1825. **ED** Rick Hawbaker. **Bk Rev. Ad Acc, Adv Mgr:** Dennis Cook. **Circ:** 10,100. ***Absorbed*** *Highland Park News (Des Moines, Iowa).*

US
LENOX TIME TABLE. VFOAT Lenox Time-Table. Began with Oct. 2, 1874 issue. Newspaper. English. wk. Lenox Time Table, Box 145, Lenox IA 50851. ***Absorbed*** *New Times (Lenox, Iowa).*

US
LEON JOURNAL-REPORTER, THE. VFOAT Leon Journal Reporter. Vol. 1, No. 1 (March 13, 1930)-. Newspaper. English. wk. Leon Journal-Reporter, 114 North Main Street, Leon IA 50144. ***Formed by the union of*** *Decatur County Journal* ***and*** *Leon Reporter (Leon, Iowa : 1887).*

US/1051-6433
LIBERAL OPINION WEEK. [Liberal opin. week]. **VFOAT** Liberal Opinion. (1990)-. Periodical. English. wk. $42.00 (one year), $21.00 (6 months). Liberal Opinion Week, PO Box 468, Vinton IA 52349-0468. **ED** Regina Huelman. **LC** E840; .L44. **DD** 320.973. **Photos. Ad Acc, Adv Mgr:** Tim Stephany, **Tel** (515)282-8220. **Pub. Size:** Standard. **Wire Svcs.:** NC. ***Continues*** *Opinion Week, 1050-1002.*

US
LIME SPRINGS HERALD (LIME SPRINGS, IOWA : 1932). (LIME SPRINGS HERALD.). Vol. 51, No. 5 (Feb. 4, 1932)-. Newspaper. English. wk. Lime Springs Herald, Main Street, Lime Springs IA 52155. ***Continues*** *Sun-Herald (Chester, Iowa : 1906).*

US
LINN NEWS-LETTER. VFOAT Linn News Letter; Linn Weekly News-Letter; Linn Weekly News Letter. Vol. 89, No. 48 (Oct. 5, 1972)-. Newspaper. English. wk. Linn News-Letter, Box A, Central City IA 52214. **ED** R. C. Sutton. ***Formed by the union of*** *Central City News-Letter and the Springville New Era* ***and*** *Coggon Monitor.*

US
LOGAN HERALD-OBSERVER. VFOAT Logan Herald Observer. Vol. 59, No. 35 (Sept. 2, 1943)-. Newspaper. English. wk. $20.00. Logan Herald-Observer, PO Box 148, Logan IA 51546. **Tel** (712)644-2705. **ED** Gerald D Bloom. **Circ:** 2,275. available on microfilm. ***Formed by the union of*** *Logan Observer* ***and*** *Harrison County Herald (Logan, Iowa).*

US
LONE TREE REPORTER (LONE TREE, IOWA : 1981). (LONE TREE REPORTER.). Vol. 89, No. 10 (Feb. 5, 1981)-. Newspaper. English. wk. Lone Tree Reporter, Box 235, Lone Tree IA 52755. **ED** Bill Crawford. ***Continues*** *Reporter (Lone Tree, Iowa).*

US
LYON COUNTY NEWS (GEORGE, IOWA). (THE LYON COUNTY NEWS.). **VFOAT** George News. (July 1915)-. Newspaper. English. wk. $15.50 (in county), $17.50 (out of county). Lyon County News, Box 68, George IA 51237. **Tel** (712)475-3351. **ED** Faye Trei. **Photos. Ad Acc.** Full Page (B&W) $406.35. Half Page (B&W) $203.18. Full Page (Color) $456.35. Half Page (Color) $253.18. **Pub. Size:** Standard. **Circ:** 1,450 (ctrl). ***Continues*** *George News.*

US
LYON COUNTY REPORTER (ROCK RAPIDS, IOWA : 1956). (THE LYON COUNTY REPORTER.). Vol. 72 No. 10 (Jan. 2, 1956)-. Newspaper. English. wk. Lyon County Reporter Inc, 310 1st Avenue, Rock Rapids IA 51246. ***Continues*** *Lyon County Reporter and The Lyon County Leader.*

US
MALVERN LEADER (MALVERN, IOWA : 1883). (THE MALVERN LEADER.). **VFOAT** Leader. Vol. 9, No. 10 (Nov. 15, 1883)-. Newspaper. English. wk. Malvern Leader, Box 129, Malvern IA 51551. **Bk Rev. Ad Acc. Circ:** 1,200 (ctrl). ***Continues*** *Malvern Republican Leader.*

US
MANCHESTER PRESS, THE. Vol. 1, No. 1 (June 16, 1871)-. Newspaper. English. wk. Manchester Press, 109 East Delaware Street, Manchester IA 52057. ***Absorbed*** *Manchester Democrat-Radio.*

US
MANLY SIGNAL (MANLY, IOWA : 1921). (MANLY SIGNAL.). Vol. 6, No. 17 (Nov. 24, 1921)-. Newspaper. English. wk. Manly Signal, Manly IA 50456. ***Continues*** *Manly Signal and The Kensett News.*

US
MANNING MONITOR. VFOAT Carroll County Monitor. Began Nov. 17, 1881. Newspaper. English (German). wk. L&V Publishing Company Inc, 411 Main Street, Manning IA 51455. ***Absorbed*** *Free Press (Manning, Iowa); Manning Herald.*

US
MARS DAILY SENTINEL, LE. VFOAT Lemars Daily Sentinel; Le Mars, Iowa, Daily Sentinel. Vol. 87, No. 34 (Aug. 18, 1958)-. Newspaper. English. da (Mon.-Fri.). Le Mars Sentinel / Iowa, 41 First Avenue Northeast, Le Mars IA 51031. **Tel** (712)546-7031. **ED** Wayne Dominowski. **Bk Rev. Ad Acc. Circ:** 4,300. ***Absorbed*** *LeMars Globe-Post and the Floyd Valley News;* ***Continues*** *Le Mars Sentinel (Le Mars, Iowa : 1957).* **Desc:** General local news.

US/0747-3591
MEDIAPOLIS NEWS (MEDIAPOLIS, IOWA : 1984). (MEDIAPOLIS NEWS.). Vol. 110, No. 20 (May, 17, 1984)-. Newspaper. English. wk. Mediapolis News, 635 Main Street, Mediapolis IA 52637. **ED** Fran Brolley. ***Continues*** *Mediapolis New Era, 0747-2897.*

US/0740-6991
MESSENGER (FORT DODGE, IOWA), THE. (THE MESSENGER.). **VFOAT** Messenger Weekender. 124th Year, No. 78 (April 2, 1979)-. Newspaper. English. da. $126.46. Ogden Newspapers Inc., PO Box 659, Fort Dodge IA 50501. **Tel** (515)573-2141. **ED** Larry W Johnson. **Bk Rev. Ad Acc. Circ:** 20,301 (ctrl). ***Continues*** *Fort Dodge Messenger (Fort Dodge, Iowa : 1974).*

US
MIDLAND TIMES (WYOMING, IOWA : 1973). (MIDLAND TIMES.). Feb. 23, 1973-. Newspaper. English. wk. Midland Times, Box 87, Wyoming IA 52362.

US
MILFORD MAIL, THE TERRIL RECORD, THE. VFOAT Terril Record. Vol. 92, No. 15 (April 8, 1976)-. Newspaper. English. wk. Mid-American Publishing Company, 108 3rd Street, #350, Des Moines IA 50309. **Tel** FAX (515)282-0125. ***Separated from*** *Dickinson County Mail News.*

US
MISSOURI VALLEY TIMES-NEWS. VFOAT Missouri Valley Times News; Missouri Valley Times-News Mid-Week Issue; Missouri Valley Times News Mid-Week Issue; Missouri Valley Times-News Weekender Edition; Missouri Valley Times News Weekender Edition; Valley Times News; Valley Times-News. Vol. 2, No. 1 (Jan. 2, 1980)-. Newspaper. English. sw. $31.50. Missouri Valley Times-News, 501 East Erie Street, PO Box 159, Missouri Valley IA 51555. **ED** Peter H. Graham. **Photos. Ad Acc, Adv Mgr:** Charles Hickman, **Tel** (712)642-2791. Full Page (B&W) $785.40. Half Page (B&W) $392.70. Full Page (Color) $860.40. Half Page (Color) $467.00. **Pub. Size:** Broadsheet. ***Continues*** *Valley Times-News (Missouri Valley, Iowa).*

US/0746-7540
MITCHELL COUNTY PRESS-NEWS, THE. VFOAT Press-News. Vol. 91, No. 29 (July 19, 1956)-. Newspaper. English. wk. Mitchell County Press-News, PO Box 60, Osage IA 50461. ***Continues*** *Mitchell County Press and The Osage News Consolidated.*

US
MONROE COUNTY NEWS (ALBIA, IOWA : 1902). (MONROE COUNTY NEWS.). Vol. 23, No. 17 (April 24, 1902)-. Newspaper. English. wk. Monroe County News, 111 Benton Avenue East, Albia IA 52531. ***Continues*** *Monroe County News and Albia Democrat.*

US
MONROE LEGACY, THE. (19??)-. Newspaper. English. wk. $13.50 Jasper & Marion Counties; $14.50 Iowa; $15.50 US. Monroe Legacy, 209 North Commerce, Monroe IA 50170. **Tel** (515)259-2708. **Photos. Ad Acc, Adv Mgr:** Kathleen Burman. **Pub. Size:** Tabloid. ***Continues*** *The Monroe Mirror.*

US
MONTICELLO EXPRESS. Vol. 1, No. 1 (July 10, 1865)-. Newspaper. English. wk. Monticello Express, PO Box 191, Monticello IA 52310. ***Absorbed*** *Monticello Times (Monticello, Iowa).*

US
MOULTON TRIBUNE (MOULTON, IOWA : 1981). (MOULTON TRIBUNE.). Vol. 98, No. 33 (Aug. 19, 1981)-. Newspaper. English. wk. Moulton Tribune, PO Box 468, Moravia IA 52571. ***Continues*** *Moulton Weekly Tribune.*

US
MOUNT AYR RECORD-NEWS. VFOAT Record-News; Mount Ayr Record News; Record News. Vol. 42, No. 1 (March 5, 1907)-. Newspaper. English. wk. $17.50 (in county), $24.00 (Iowa and Missouri), $27.00 (other). Mount Ayr Record-News, PO Box 346, Mount Ayr IA 50854. **ED** H. Alan Smith. **Photos. Ad Acc, Adv Mgr:** Helen Terry, **Tel** (515)464-2440. Full Page (B&W) $315.00. Half Page (B&W) $157.50. **Pub. Size:** Broadsheet. **Wire Svcs.:** IM. **Circ:** 2,800 (paid, weekly) (ctrl). available on microfilm. ***Formed by the union of*** *Ringgold Record (Mount Ayr, Iowa)* ***and*** *Twice-A-Week News.*

US
MOUNT PLEASANT NEWS, THE. (1875)-. Newspaper. English. da. $70.00 Iowa; $84.00 others. Mount Pleasant News, 215 West Monroe Street, Mount Pleasant IA 52641. **Tel** (319)385-3131. **ED** Larry K. Marlow (Editor-in-Chief) and John Sloca (Managing Editor). **Photos. Ad Acc, Adv Mgr:** Doug Kofoed. Full Page (B&W) $526.32. Half Page (B&W) $272.19. Full Page (Color) $597.32. Half Page (Color) 342.19. **Pub. Size:** Standard. **Wire Svcs.:** AP. ***Continues*** *Mt. Pleasant Daily News;* ***Absorbed*** *Mt. Pleasant Republican (Mount Pleasant, Iowa : 1899); Mt. Pleasant Free Press.*

US
MUSCATINE JOURNAL (MUSCATINE, IOWA: 1960). (THE MUSCATINE JOURNAL.). Sept. 29, 1960-. Newspaper. English. da (260 issues per year).

Iowa

$111.55. Muscatine Journal, 301 East 3rd Street, PO Box 809, Muscatine IA 52761. **Tel** 800-383-3189. *Continues Muscatine Journal and News-Tribune.*

US
NASHUA REPORTER AND WEEKLY NASHUA POST, THE. **VFOAT** Nashua Reporter. Vol. 26, No. 15 (Dec. 5, 1918)-. Newspaper. English. wk. $19.00 local area; $21.00 others. Reporter and Weekly Post, 216 Main Street, Nashua IA 50658. **ED** Carmen Conklin (Editor-in-Chief) and Wanda Orric (Managing Editor). **Bk Rev. Photos. Ad Acc, Adv Mgr:** Wanda Orric, **Tel** (515)435-4151. Full Page (B&W) $312.00. Half Page (B&W) $156.00. **Pub. Size:** Broadsheet. **Circ:** 1,300. available in microform. *Formed by the union of Weekly Nashua Post and Nashua Reporter (Nashua, Iowa : 1894).*

US/0747-430X
NEVADA JOURNAL (NEVADA, IOWA). (NEVADA JOURNAL.). **VFOAT** Nevada (Iowa) Journal. 90th Year, No. 60 (June 5, 1984)-. Newspaper. English. wk. $28.00. Nevada Newspapers Inc, PO Box 89, Nevada IA 50201. **Tel** (515)382-2161, FAX (515)382-4299. **ED** Annette Forbes (Editor-in-Chief) and Craig Ducker (Managing Editor). **Photos. Ad Acc, Adv Mgr:** Annette Forbes. Full Page (B&W) $741.75. Half Page (B&W) $370.88. Full Page (Color) $853.75. Half Page (Color) $482.88. **Pub. Size:** Standard. **Circ:** 2,927. available in microform. *Continues Nevada Evening Journal (Nevada, Iowa : 1928).*

US
NEW HAMPTON TRIBUNE (NEW HAMPTON, IOWA : 1937). (THE NEW HAMPTON TRIBUNE.). Vol. 61, No. 1 (Jan. 7, 1937)-. Newspaper. English. wk. New Hampton Tribune, 10 North Chestnut Avenue, New Hampton IA 50659. *Continues New Hampton Tribune-Gazette; Absorbed Lawler Dispatch.*

US
NEW LONDON JOURNAL, THE. Vol. 1, No. 1 (July 8, 1915)-. Newspaper. English. wk. New London Journal, 102 Main Street, New London IA 52645. *Formed by the union of Henry County Times (New London, Iowa : 1912) and New London Advertiser; Absorbed Danville Enterprise.*

US
NEW SHARON STAR, THE. Vol. 1, No. 1 (Jan. 22, 1873)-. Newspaper. English. wk. New Sharon Star, Box 90, New Sharon IA 50207.

US
NORTH IOWA TIMES (1867). (NORTH IOWA TIMES.). Vol. 11, No. 24 (Feb. 27, 1867)-. Newspaper. English. wk. North Iowa Times, PO Box M, McGregor IA 52157. *Continues Weekly North Iowa Times; Absorbed McGregor News (McGregor, Iowa : 1871).*

US
NORTH SCOTT PRESS, THE. (Jan. 31, 1968)-. Newspaper. English. wk. $22.00. Eldridge North Scott Press, 214 North Second Street, Eldridge IA 52748-1208. **Tel** (319)285-8111, FAX (319)285-8114. **ED** William Tubbs, Scott Campbell (Managing Editor). **Photos. Ad Acc, Adv Mgr:** Jayne Carstersen. **Pub. Size:** Tabloid. **Circ:** 5,500. available in microform.

US/0886-8808
OBSERVER (DE WITT, IOWA. NATIONAL ED.). (OBSERVER.). **VFOAT** Wednesday Observer; Saturday Observer; DeWitt Observer; A.Press-gazette. Vol. 118, No. 49 (Jan. 5, 1983)-. Newspaper. English. sw (Wed. & Sat.). $30.00. De Witt Observer, 512 7th Street, De Witt IA 52742-1610. **Tel** (319)659-3121, FAX (319)659-3778. **ED** Mary Rueter. **Photos. Ad Acc, Adv Mgr:** Jean Bormann. Full Page (B&W) $271.00. Half Page (B&W) $174.00. Full Page (Color) $331.00. Half Page (Color) $234.00. **Pub. Size:** Tabloid. **Wire Svcs.:** IM. **Circ:** 4,700. available in microform. *Continues Dewitt Observer.*

US
OCHEYEDAN PRESS-THE MELVIN NEWS, THE. **VFOAT** Ocheyedan Press, The Melvin News. Vol. 84, No. 20 (April 13, 1978)-. Newspaper. English. wk. Ocheyedan Press-Melvin News, Box 456, Ocheyedan IA 51354. *Formed by the union of Ocheyedan Press (Ocheyedan, Iowa : 1947) and Melvin News.*

US/0899-6520
ONAWA DEMOCRAT (ONAWA, IOWA : 1967). (THE ONAWA DEMOCRAT.). **VFOAT** Onawa, Iowa Weekly Democrat. March 2, 1967-. Newspaper. English. wk. Onawa Democrat, 720 Iowa Avenue, Onawa IA 51040. *Continues Onawa Weekly Democrat (Onawa, Iowa : 1937).*

US
ONAWA SENTINEL. **VFOAT** Onawa, Monona County, Sentinel. (March 1885)-. Newspaper. English. wk. Onawa Sentinel, Box 180, Onawa IA 51040. *Absorbed Onawa Gazette; Blencoe Herald; Whiting Argus; Soldier Sentinel.*

US
OPINION-TRIBUNE, THE. (1???)-. Newspaper. English. wk (Published on Wednesdays). Glenwood Opinion Tribune, PO Box 191, Glenwood IA 51534-1741. **Tel** (712)527-3191, FAX (712)527-3193. **ED** Joe Foreman. **Circ:** 3,750.

US
OSCEOLA COUNTY GAZETTE-TRIBUNE, THE. **VFOAT** Osceola County Gazette Tribune. Vol. 111, No. 25 (Sept. 21, 1982)-. Newspaper. English. sw. Sibley Publishing Company, 201 9th Street, Sibley IA 51249. **ED** Rosalie Peters. *Formed by the union of Osceola County Tribune (Sibley, Iowa : 1974) and Sibley Gazette (Sibley, Iowa : 1966).*

US/0745-6247
OSCEOLA SENTINEL-TRIBUNE. **VFOAT** Osceola Sentinel Tribune. 124th year, No. 4 (Jan. 27, 1983)-. Newspaper. English. wk. Clarke County Publishing, 115 East Washington Street, Osceola IA 50213. *Formed by the union of Osceola Sentinel (Osceola, Iowa : 1890) and Osceola Tribune.*

US/0898-2066
OSKALOOSA HERALD (OSKALOOSA, IOWA : 1977). (OSKALOOSA HERALD.). 127th Year, No. 157 (March 5, 1977)-. Newspaper. English. da. Oskaloosa Herald, Box 530, Oskaloosa IA 52577. *Continues Oskaloosa Daily Herald (Oskaloosa, Iowa : 1972).*

US
OSSIAN BEE, THE. **VFOAT** Bee. (1885)-. Newspaper. English. wk. $10.00 Iowa; $15.00 others. Ossian Bee, Box 96, Ossian IA 52161. **ED** Dirk Amundsen. **Photos. Ad Acc, Adv Mgr:** Dirk Amundsen, **Tel** (319)532-9113. Full Page (B&W) $308.70. Half Page (B&W) $154.35. Full Page (Color) $368.70. Half Page (Color) $214.35. **Pub. Size:** Standard. available in microform from Iowa Historical Society.

US/0886-4209
OTTUMWA COURIER. Vol. 99, No. 154 (Sept. 30, 1960)-. Newspaper. English. da. Ottumwa Courier, 213 East 2nd Street, Ottumwa IA 52501. *Continues Ottumwa Daily Courier.*

US
PAULLINA TIMES-SUTHERLAND COURIER (PAULLINA ED.). (PAULLINA TIMES-SUTHERLAND COURIER.). **VFOAT** Paullina Times Sutherland Courier. Vol. 101, No. 34 (June 14, 1984)-. Newspaper. English. wk. $14.00 (tri-county area); $16.00 other Iowa; $20.00 other. Paullina Times - Sutherland Courier, 144 East Broadway, Paullina IA 51046. **Tel** (712)448-3622. **ED** Mike Otto. **Photos. Ad Acc.** Full Page (B&W) $325.00. Half Page (B&W) $175.00. **Pub. Size:** Broadsheet. **Circ:** 1,600. *Formed by the union of Paullina Times and Sutherland Courier.*

US/0746-7222
PERRY CHIEF (PERRY, IOWA : 1983). Title Change. (THE PERRY CHIEF.). Vol. 1, No. 1 (Dec. 1, 1983)-. Newspaper. English. wk. Chief Printing Company, 1323 2nd Street, Perry IA 50220. *Continued by Perry Daily Chief (Perry, Iowa : 1919).*

US/0892-1261
PIONEER HERALD, THE. Vol. 1, No. 1 (Sept. 7, 1977)-. Newspaper. English. wk. Pioneer Herald, Box 280, Mechanicville IA 52306.

US
PIONEER-REPUBLICAN OF IOWA COUNTY, THE. **VFOAT** Pioneer-Republican; Pioneer Republican. Vol. 70, No. 32 (Sept. 22, 1927)-. Newspaper. English. wk. Pioneer-Republican, 100 West Main Street, Marengo IA 52301. **ED** Originally edited by: Mortimer Goodwin. *Formed by the union of Marengo Republican and Marengo Pioneer and The Marengo Democrat.*

US
PLAINSMAN-CLARION, THE. **VFOAT** Clarion-Plainsman. Vol. 5, No. 27 (July 5, 1979)-. Newspaper. English. wk. Louisa Publishing Company / Richland, PO Box 188, Richland IA 52585. **ED** Sallie Hinshaw. *Formed by the union of Calrion (Packwood, Iowa) and Richland Plainsman.*

US
POCAHONTAS RECORD-DEMOCRAT. **VFOAT** Pocahontas Record Democrat. Vol. 48, No. 23 (Sept. 3, 1931)-. Newspaper. English. wk. Wagner Publishing Company, 218 North Main Street, Pocahontas IA 50574. *Formed by the union of Pocahontas Record and Pocahontas Democrat; Absorbed Arrow (Rolfe, Iowa : 1986) and Fonda Times (Fonda, Iowa : 1917).*

US
POSTVILLE HERALD. 26th year, No. 32 (June 7, 1918)-. Newspaper. English. wk. Postville Herald, PO Box 580, Postville IA 52162-0580. *Continues Iowa Volks-Blatt.*

US
QUAD-CITY TIMES. (1974)-. Newspaper. English. da. $132.60 Sunday only; $166.40 Daily but not Sunday; $244.40 Daily & Sunday. Quad City Times, PO Box 3828, Davenport IA 52808. **Tel** (319)383-2200, FAX (319)383-2433. **ED** Forrest Kilmer. **Circ:** 58,427 daily, 82,271 Sunday. available on microfilm. Documents available from UMI Article Clearinghouse. *Continues Times-Democrat.*
Ind/Abst Bus. Dateline [Full Txt.].

US
RAKE REGISTER, THE. Began Aug. 3, 1900. Newspaper. English. wk. Rake Register, Box 83, Rake IA 50465.

US/0895-3287
RECORD-HERALD AND INDIANOLA TRIBUNE, THE. **VFOAT** Record Herald and Indianola Tribune. Vol. 54, No. 35-B (March 2, 1945)-. Newspaper. English. wk. $26.00. Record-Herald and Indianola Tribune, PO Box 259, Indianola IA 50125. **ED** Tom Hawley, Deb Belt (Managing Editor). **Photos. Ad Acc, Adv Mgr:** Brian Weber, **Tel** (515)961-2511. Full Page (B&W) $674.10. Half Page (B&W) $337.05. Full Page (Color) $734.10. Half Page (Color) $397.05. **Pub. Size:** Broadsheet. **Wire Svcs.:** AP. available in microform. *Formed by the union of Record-Herald (Indianola, Iowa) and Indianola Tribune (Indianola, Iowa : 1923).*

US
REINBECK COURIER. Vol. 22, No. 19 (April 25, 1902)-. Newspaper. English. wk. $20.00 Iowa; $23.00 others. Reinbeck Courier, 406 Grundy Avenue, Reinbeck IA 50669. **Tel** FAX (319)345-6767. **ED** Leroy A. Moser (Editor-in-Chief) and Gregg A. Moser (Managing Editor). **Photos. Ad Acc, Adv Mgr:** Gregg Moser, **Tel** (319)345-2031. Full Page (B&W) $505.68. Half Page (B&W) $252.84. Full Page (Color) $555.68. Half Page (Color) $302.84. **Pub. Size:** Broadsheet. **Circ:** 1,680. *Continues Grundy Courier (Reinbeck, Iowa); Absorbed Farm Bureau Courier.*

US
REMSEN BELL-ENTERPRISE. **VFOAT** Remsen Bell Enterprise; Bell-Enterprise. (1901)-. Newspaper. English. wk. $16.00. Remsen Bell-Enterprise, 257 Washington Street, Remsen IA 51050. **Tel** (712)786-1196. **ED** Noel Ahmann. **Photos. Ad Acc.** Full Page (B&W) $302.40. Half Page (B&W) $151.20. Full Page (Color) $379.40. Half Page (Color) $228.20. **Pub. Size:** Standard. *Formed by the union of Remsen Bell and Enterprise (Remsen, Iowa).*

US/1042-1203
REPORTER (EMMETSBURG, IOWA). (THE REPORTER.). 101st Year, No. 2 (Jan. 10, 1978)-. Newspaper. English. wk. The Reporter / Iowa, Box 73, Emmetsburg IA 50536. *Continues Emmetsburg Reporter.*

US
RINGSTED DISPATCH. Began in March 1901. Newspaper. English. wk. Ringsted Dispatch, Ringsted IA 50578.

US
SANBORN PIONEER, THE. Vol. 11, No. 10 (Feb. 17, 1882)-. Newspaper. English. wk. Sanborn Pioneer, Box 280, Sanborn IA 51248. *Formed by the union of Sanborn Cycle and O'Brien Pioneer.*

US
SCHLESWIG LEADER, THE. Began in Oct. 1903. Newspaper. English (German). wk. Schleswig Leader, Schleswig IA 51461. *Continues Schleswig Herold; Absorbed Kiron Weekly News.*

US
SEYMOUR HERALD, THE. Vol. 1, No. 1 (Sept. 19, 1918)-. Newspaper. English. wk. $16.00 in county; $19.00 out of county. Seymour Herald, 116 North 4th Street, Seymour IA 52590. **Tel** (515)898-7554. **ED** Karen S. Young, Ken Bank (Managing Editor). **Photos. Ad Acc.** Full Page (B&W) $320.00. Half Page (B&W) $160.00. **Circ:** 1,600. available in microform. *Formed by the union of Seymour Leader and Seymour Democrat (Seymour, Iowa).*

US
SIDNEY ARGUS-HERALD, THE. **VFOAT** Sidney Argus Herald; Argus Herald, Sidney, Iowa; Sidney Argus; Argus-Herald, Sidney, Iowa. Vol. 12, No. 1 (Sept. 22, 1927)-. Newspaper. English. wk. $25.00. Sidney Argus-Herald, Box 190, Sidney IA 51652. **ED** Dennis Bateman (Editor-in-Chief) and Ellen West Longman (Managing Editor). **Bk Rev. Photos. Ad Acc, Adv Mgr:** Ellen Longman, **Tel** (712)374-2251. Full Page (B&W) $446.04. Half Page (B&W) $223.02. Full Page (Color) $491.04. Half Page (Color) $268.02. **Pub. Size:** Broadsheet. available in microform from Iowa Historical Society. *Formed by the union of Sidney Argus and Fremont County Herald (Sidney, Iowa : 1885).*

US
SIOUX CENTER NEWS. Vol. 39, No. 24 (Aug. 20, 1930)-. Newspaper. English. wk. Sioux Center News, 32 3rd Street Northwest, Sioux Center IA 51250. ***Continues*** *Sioux Center Nieuwsblad.*

US
SIOUX CITY JOURNAL (SIOUX CITY, IOWA : 1887). ***Title Change.*** (SIOUX CITY JOURNAL.). **VFOAT** Sioux City Sunday Journal. (Sept. 1887)-. Newspaper. English. da. Sioux City Newspapers Inc, PO Box 118, 6th and Pavonia Streets, Sioux City IA 51105. **Tel** (712)279-5068. **ED** Cal Olson. **Circ:** 51,845. ***Continues*** *Sioux City Daily Journal;* ***Absorbed*** *Sioux City Tribune (Sioux City, Iowa : 1884).* ***Merged with*** *Sioux City Tribune (Sioux City, Iowa : 1929)* ***to form*** *Sioux City Tribune and the Sioux City Journal.*

US
SIOUX COUNTY CAPITAL-DEMOCRAT, THE. **VFOAT** Sioux County Capital Democrat; Capital-Democrat. Vol. 100, No. 45 (Jan. 6, 1983)-. Newspaper. English. wk. $19.00 in county, $25.00 out of county. Sioux County Capital-Democrat, 113 Central Avenue, Orange City IA 51041. **Tel** (712)737-4266. **ED** Doug Marks. **Photos. Ad Acc, Adv Mgr:** Dennis Hartog. Full Page (B&W) $688.00. Half Page (B&W) $344.00. Full Page (Color) $773.00. Half Page (Color) $429.00. **Pub. Size:** Broadsheet. **Circ:** 2,300. ***Formed by the union of*** *Democrat (Alton, Iowa)* ***and*** *Sioux County Capital (Orange City, Iowa : 1959).*

US
SIOUX COUNTY INDEX-REPORTER, THE. **VFOAT** Sioux County Index Reporter. Vol. 87, No. 1 (Nov. 9, 1967)-. Newspaper. English. wk. Sioux County Index-Reporter, 1217 Main Street, Hull IA 51239. ***Formed by the union of*** *Boyden Reporter* ***and*** *Sioux County Index.*

US
SIOUX RAPIDS BULLETIN-PRESS. **VFOAT** Sioux Rapids Bulletin Press. Began in Sept. 1943?. Bulletin. English. wk. Sioux Rapids Bulletin-Press, PO Box T, Sioux Rapids IA 50585. ***Formed by the union of*** *Sioux Rapids Press* ***and*** *Bulletin Board (Sioux Rapids, Iowa);* ***Absorbed*** *Rembrandt Booster.*

US
SOLON ECONOMIST (SOLON, IOWA : 1981). (THE SOLON ECONOMIST.). Vol. 61, No. 10 (March 12, 1981)-. Newspaper. English. wk. Solon Newspapers Inc, Box 249, Solon IA 52333. **ED** Marietta Beuter. ***Continues*** *Economist (Solon, Iowa).*

US
SOUTH HAMILTON RECORD/NEWS (JEWELL, IOWA : 1978). (SOUTH HAMILTON RECORD/NEWS.). **VFOAT** Record-News. Vol. 2, No. 48 (Oct. 5, 1978)-. Newspaper. English. wk. $16.00 Hamilton & adjoining counties; $20.00 other. South Hamilton Record/News, PO Box 130, Jewell IA 50130. **Tel** (515)827-5931, FAX (515)827-5760. **ED** Scott Ervin. **Photos. Ad Acc. Pub. Size:** Standard. **Circ:** 1,000. ***Continues*** *Record/News (Jewell, Iowa).*

US
SOUTHERN COUNTY NEWS, THE. (1966)-. Newspaper. English. wk. $20.00 Iowa; $25.00 others. Southern County News, PO Box 96, Thornton IA 50479-0096. **Tel** (515)998-2712. **ED** Wm. F. Scharader. **Photos. Ad Acc, Adv Mgr:** Wm. F. Scharader. Full Page (B&W) $250.00. Half Page (B&W) $150.00. Full Page (Color) $295.00. Half Page (Color) $195.00. **Pub. Size:** Broadsheet. **Circ:** 864. ***Continues*** *Thornton Enterprise.*

US
STORY CITY HERALD (STORY CITY, IOWA : 1892). (THE STORY CITY HERALD.). (1892)-. Newspaper. English. wk. $20.00 Iowa; $22.00 US. Story City Herald, 423 Broad Street, Story City IA 50248. **Tel** (515)733-4318, FAX (515)733-4319. **ED** Eloise Thorson. **Photos. Ad Acc, Adv Mgr:** Tricia Sawyer. **Pub. Size:** Standard. **Circ:** 2,300 paid. available on microfilm. ***Continues*** *Story City News;* ***Absorbed*** *Roland Record (Roland, Iowa : 1898).*

US
STRAWBERRY POINT PRESS-JOURNAL. **VFOAT** Strawberry Point Press Journal. Began in 1964?. Newspaper. English. wk. Press-Journal, 107 West Mission Street, Strawberry Point IA 52076. ***Continues*** *Clayton County Press-Journal.*

US
STUART HERALD, THE. Vol. 30, No. 1 (Dec. 7, 1900)-. Newspaper. English. wk. $18.00. Stuart Herald, Box D, Stuart IA 50250. **Tel** (515)523-1010, FAX (515)523-2825. **ED** Vicki Taylor. **Photos. Ad Acc, Adv Mgr:** Norma Thurman. Full Page (B&W) $441.00. Half Page (B&W) $245.00. **Pub. Size:** Broadsheet. available in microform from Iowa Historical Society. ***Continues*** *Stuart Locomotive;* ***Absorbed*** *Earlham Echo.*

US
SUMNER GAZETTE (SUMNER, IOWA). (THE SUMNER GAZETTE.). Vol. 1, No. 1 (Jan. 5, 1881)-. Newspaper. English. wk. Sumner Gazette, 106 East 1st Street, Sumner IA 50674. ***Absorbed*** *Sumner Herald; Westgate Herald.*

US
SUN (MOUNT VERNON, IOWA : 1979). (THE SUN.). Vol. 3, No. 9 (Feb. 1, 1979)-. Newspaper. English. wk. The Sun / Iowa, 104 2nd Avenue North, Mount Vernon IA 52314. **ED** Sara K Gaarde. ***Continues*** *Sun Hawkeye-Record-Herald.*

US
SUN-NEWS (LOWDEN, IOWA). (SUN-NEWS.). **VFOAT** Sun News. Vol. 1, No. 1 (Jan. 1, 1976)-. Newspaper. English. wk. $15.00. Sun-News, 518 Main Street, Lowden IA 52255. **Tel** (319)944-5387, FAX (319)886-6466. **ED** Pat Kroemer (Editor-in-Chief) and Sally Taylor (Managing Editor). **Photos. Ad Acc, Adv Mgr:** Pat Kroemer. Full Page (B&W) $255.36. Half Page (B&W) $127.68. **Pub. Size:** Tabloid. **Circ:** 1,150. ***Formed by the union of*** *Lowden News (Lowden, Iowa : 1935)* ***and*** *North Cedar Press.*

US
SWEA CITY HERALD-PRESS, THE. **VFOAT** Swea City Herald Press. Began in April 1986. Newspaper. English. wk. Community Publications, PO Box 428, Swea City IA 50590. ***Formed by the union of*** *Swea City Herald* ***and*** *Swea City Press.*

US
TAMA NEWS-HERALD, THE. **VFOAT** Tama News Herald. Vol. 1, No. 1 (Jan. 8, 1925)-. Newspaper. English. wk. $24.00 Tama County; $27.00 Iowa; $33.00 others. Tama News-Herald, 220-224 West 3rd Street, Tama IA 52339. **Tel** (515)484-2841. **ED** Nancy Dostal. **Photos. Ad Acc, Adv Mgr:** Maraly Hotchkiss. Full Page (B&W) $440.00. Half Page (B&W) $285.60. Full Page (Color) $480.00. Half Page (Color) $325.60. **Pub. Size:** Broadsheet. **Circ:** 3,600. ***Formed by the union of*** *Tama Herald* ***and*** *Tama News.*

US/1041-293X
TELEGRAPH HERALD (1935). (THE TELEGRAPH-HERALD.). **VFOAT** Telegraph Herald; Telegraph. Vol. 95 No. 89 (May 7, 1935)-. Newspaper. English. da (Sun.-Fri.). $156.00. Dubuque Telegraph-Herald, PO Box 688, Dubuque IA 52004-0688. **Tel** (319)588-5620, (800)553-4801. **ED** Brian Cooper (Editor-in-Chief) and Soren Nielsen (Managing Editor). **Bk Rev**, (Qty: 2). **Photos. Ad Acc, Adv Mgr:** Jim Hart. Full Page (B&W) $2,910.15. Half Page (B&W) $1,449.50. Full Page (Color) $3,135.15. Half Page (Color) $1,674.50. **Pub. Size:** Broadsheet. **Wire Svcs.:** AP. **Circ:** 33,899 daily, 38,870 Sunday. available on microfiche from Crest Information Technologies. ***Continues*** *Telegraph-Herald and Times-Journal.*

US
THOMPSON COURIER (THOMPSON, IOWA : 1926). (THE THOMPSON COURIER.). (1926)-. Newspaper. English. wk. Thompson Courier, Box 318, Thompson IA 50478. ***Continues*** *Thompson Journal.*

US
TIMES HERALD (CARROLL, IOWA). (THE TIMES HERALD.). **VFOAT** Daily Times Herald. (Aug. 3, 1987)-. Newspaper. English. da. Times Herald / Iowa, PO Box 546, Carroll IA 51401. ***Continues*** *Carroll Daily Times Herald.*

US
TIMES-PLAIN DEALER, THE. **VFOAT** Times Plain Dealer; Times-Plain Dealer (The Howard County Times and Cresco Plain Dealer Consolidated); Howard County Times and Cresco Plain Dealer. Vol. 85, No. 32 (Aug. 8, 1951)-. Newspaper. English. wk. $32.00. Times-Plain Dealer, Box 350, Cresco IA 52136. **Tel** (319)547-3601, FAX (319)547-4602. **ED** Kenneth Becker (Editor in Chief) and H. Denis Moore (Managing Editor). **Bk Rev**, (Qty: 2-3). **Photos. Ad Acc, Adv Mgr:** H.D. Moore. Full Page (B&W) $437.31. Half Page (B&W) $246.00. Full Page (Color) $492.31. Half Page (Color) $301.00. **Pub. Size:** Broadsheet. **Circ:** 3,662 (weekly, Wed. morning). ***Continues*** *Times-Plain Dealer and The Howard County Times and Cresco Plain Dealer Consolidated.*
Desc: General news and advertising for the community.

US
TIMES-REPUBLICAN (CORYDON, IOWA : 1973). (THE TIMES-REPUBLICAN.). **VFOAT** Times Republican. Vol. 101, No. 10 (April 5, 1973)-. Newspaper. English. wk. Times-Republican / Iowa, PO Box 258, Corydon IA 50060. ***Continues*** *Times-Republican, Wayne County Democrat.*

US
TIMES-REPUBLICAN (MARSHALLTOWN, IOWA : 1974). (TIMES-REPUBLICAN.). **VFOAT** Times Republican; Times-Republican Morning Star; Times Republican Morning Star; Marshalltown Times Republican; Marshalltown Times-Republican. Vol. 100, No. 30 (Feb. 4, 1974)-. Newspaper. English. da. Marshalltown Times Republican, 135 West Main Street, Marshalltown IA 50158. **Tel** (515)753-6611. **ED** Paul G. Norris Jr. ***Continues*** *Marshalltown Times-Republican.*

US
TIPTON CONSERVATIVE AND ADVERTISER, THE. **VFOAT** Conservative Advertiser. Vol. 95, No. 3 (Jan. 15, 1970)-. Newspaper. English. wk. $21.00. Conservative Publishing Company, Box 271, Tipton IA 52772. **Tel** (319)886-2131. **ED** Stuart Clark (Editor-in-Chief) and Sally Taylor (Managing Editor). **Photos. Ad Acc, Adv Mgr:** Sally Taylor. Full Page (B&W) $610.00. Half Page (B&W) $243.00. Full Page (Color) $660.00. Half Page (Color) $393.00. **Pub. Size:** Broadsheet. **Circ:** 4,800 (ctrl). ***Formed by the union of*** *Tipton Conservative* ***and*** *Tipton Advertiser & The Bennett Gazette.*

US/0745-7405
TITONKA TOPIC. ***Title Change.*** Vol. 1, No. 1 (Jan. 26, 1899)-?. Newspaper. English. wk. Titonka Topic, Box 329, Titonka IA 50480. ***Continued by*** *Woden Watchman.*

US
TRAER STAR-CLIPPER, THE. ***Title Change.*** **VFOAT** Traer Star Clipper. 36th Year, No. 19 (May 7, 1909)-. Newspaper. English. wk. Traer Star-Clipper, 625 2nd Street, Traer IA 50675. ***Continued by*** *Star Clipper.*

US
TREYNOR RECORD, THE. (19??)-. Newspaper. English. wk. Treynor Record, Box 517, Treynor IA 51575.

US/0890-4626
TRI-COUNTY NEWS (ZEARING, IOWA. 1986), THE. (THE TRI-COUNTY NEWS.). (Nov. 1968)-. Newspaper. English. Fifty-two times a year (Thurs.). Tri-County News / Iowa, 111 West Main Street, PO Box 156, Zearing IA 50278. **Tel** (515)487-7661. ***Continues*** *New Tri-County News.*

US
TRI-COUNTY TIMES, THE. **VFOAT** Times. (Nov. 9, 1972)-. Newspaper. English. wk. $15.00. Tri County Times, PO Box 237, 312 Main Street, Slater IA 50244. **ED** E. W. Rood. **Photos. Ad Acc, Adv Mgr:** Sharon Rood, **Tel** (515)685-3416. Full Page (B&W) $602.70. **Pub. Size:** Broadsheet. **Circ:** 4,700. ***Continues*** *Slater News.*

US
VAN BUREN REGISTER (KEOSAUGUA, IOWA : 1982). (THE VAN BUREN REGISTER.). Aug. 19, 1982-. Newspaper. English. wk. Van Buren Register, PO Box 477, Keosaugua IA 52565. ***Continues*** *Van Buren County Register (Keosaugua, Iowa : 1975).*

US/0894-2552
WASHINGTON EVENING JOURNAL, THE. Vol. 55, No. 97 (June 7, 1948)-. Newspaper. English. da. Washington Evening Journal, PO Box 471, Washington IA 52353. ***Continues*** *Evening Journal (Washington, Iowa).*

US/8750-0868
WATERLOO COURIER CEDAR FALLS. **VFOAT** Courier. Vol. 126, No. 158 (July 1, 1984)-. Newspaper. English. da (except Sat.). $166.00 Iowa; $192.00 other. WH Hartman Company, PO Box 540, Waterloo IA 50704. **Tel** (319)291-1400. ***Continues*** *Waterloo Courier, The Cedar Falls Record, 0746-181X.*

US
WAUKON DEMOCRAT (WAUKON, IOWA : 1945). (THE WAUKON DEMOCRAT.). Vol. 67, No. 23 (June 7, 1945)-. Newspaper. English. wk. Waukon Democrat, 15 1st Street Northwest, Waukon IA 52172. ***Continues*** *Democrat (Waukon, Iowa : 1899).*

US
WAUKON REPUBLICAN-STANDARD. **VFOAT** Waukon Republican Standard. Vol. 78, No. 23 (June 5, 1945)-. Newspaper. English. wk. Waukon Republican-Standard, 15 1st Street Northwest, Waukon IA 52172. ***Continues*** *Waukon Republican and Standard.*

US
WAVERLY DEMOCRAT, THE. Vol. 1, No. 1 (Feb. 27, 1880)-. Newspaper. English. wk. Waverly Democrat, 309 West Bremer, Waverly IA 50677. ***Absorbed*** *Waverly Phoenix.*

US
WEST BRANCH TIMES (WEST BRANCH, IOWA : 1889). (WEST BRANCH TIMES.). Vol. 11, No. 27 (April 11, 1889)-. Newspaper. English. wk. $22.00 Iowa; $27.00 other. West Branch Times Inc., PO Box 368, West Branch IA 52358. **Tel** (319)643-2131. **ED** Mike Owen. **Ad Acc. Pub. Size:** Full Page (B&W) $272.00. Half Page (B&W) $147.20. Full Page (Color) $332.00. Half Page (Color) $197.20. **Pub. Size:** Tabloid. ***Continues*** *Local Record (West Branch, Iowa).*

US
WEST LYON HERALD, THE. Newspaper. English. wk. West Lyon Herald, Main Street, Inwood IA 51240. ***Continues*** *Inwood Herald.*

US
WILLIAMSBURG JOURNAL TRIBUNE WILLIAMSBURG, IOWA 1972. (WILLIAMSBURG JOURNAL TRIBUNE.). **VFOAT** Journal Tribune; Journal-Tribune and Williamsburg Shopper Consolidated. Vol. 76, No. 43 (Oct. 26, 1972)-. Newspaper. English. wk. Williamsburg Journal Tribune, PO Box 690, Williamsburg IA 52361. **ED** Reid K. Beveridge. ***Continues*** *Williamsburg Journal Tribune and Williamsburg Shopper, Consolidated.*

US/0746-6315
WILTON-DURANT ADVOCATE NEWS. **VFOAT** Wilton Durant Advocate News. Vol. 88, No. 42 (Oct. 14, 1982)-. Newspaper. English. wk. Advocate News, 101 West 4th Street, Wilton IA 52778. ***Continues*** *Advocate News (Wilton, Iowa).*

US
WRIGHT COUNTY MONITOR. Began with March 31, 1869 issue. Newspaper. English. wk. Wright County Monitor, 107 2nd Avenue Northeast, Clarion IA 50525. ***Absorbed*** *Goldfield Gazette.*

KANSAS

US/0890-345X
ABILENE REFLECTOR-CHRONICLE. **VFOAT** Abilene Reflector Chronicle; Abilene Daily Reflector-Chronicle. Vol. 73, No. 54 (May 1, 1942)-Vol. 100, No. 268 (Jan. 13, 1973)- Vol. 55, No. 1 (May 1, 1942)-Vol. 85, No. 216 (Jan. 13, 1973); (Jan. 15, 1973)-. Newspaper. English. da. Abilene Reflector-Chronicle, PO Box 8, Abilene KS 67410. **Tel** (913)263-1000, FAX (913)263-7645. **Bk Rev. Ad Acc. Circ:** 4,823 (ctrl). ***Formed by the union of*** *Abilene Daily Chronicle (Abilene, Kan. : 1933)* ***and*** *Abilene Daily Reflector.*

US
ALMENA PLAINDEALER (ALMENA, KAN. : 1905). (ALMENA PLAINDEALER.). Vol. 18, No. 35 (Nov. 9, 1905)-. Newspaper. English. wk. Almena Plaindealer, PO Box 278, Almena KS 67622-0278. ***Continues*** *Norton County Plaindealer.*

US
ANDERSON COUNTIAN, THE. Vol. 32, No. 4 (Nov. 15, 1923)-. Newspaper. English. wk. Garnett Publishing Company, PO Box 409, Garnett KS 66032. ***Continues*** *Greeley Graphic.*

US/0746-6447
ANDOVER ADVOCATE, THE. Vol. 1, No. 1 (July 16, 1975)-. Newspaper. English. wk. $15.00 Kansas; $18.00 other elsewhere. Jackalope Publishing Company, Box 443, Andover KS 67002. **ED** Dave Kratzer. **Ad Acc. Circ:** 1,000. available on microfilm.
Desc: Lively coverage of all facets of small town Kansas.

US
ANDOVER JOURNAL, THE. Vol. 1, No. 1 (March 17, 1971)-. Newspaper. English. wk. Andover Journal, Box 271, Andover KS 67002-0271. **ED** David E Dullea. available on microfilm from University Microfilms International (UMI).

US
ANTHONY REPUBLICAN AND THE ANTHONY BULLETIN (ANTHONY, KAN. : 1973). (THE ANTHONY REPUBLICAN AND THE ANTHONY BULLETIN.). Anthony Republican, Vol. 96, No. 13 (Mar. 21, 1973)-. Newspaper. English. wk. $18.00 Kansas; $22.00 others. Anthony Republican and Bulletin, 121 East Main Street, Anthony KS 67003. **Tel** (316)842-5129, FAX (316)842-5120. **ED** Jim Dunn (Editor-in-Chief) and Vera L. Dunn (Managing Editor). **Photos. Ad Acc, Adv Mgr:** Jim Dunn. Full Page (B&W) $352.50. Half Page (B&W) $202.50. **Pub. Size:** Standard. **Circ:** 3,090. ***Continues*** *Anthony Republican (Anthony, Kan. : 1967).*

US
ARK VALLEY NEWS, THE. Began in 1975?. Newspaper. English. wk. Ark Valley News, 206 West Main Street, Valley Center KS 67147. ***Absorbed*** *Valley Center Index.*

US/0888-8485
ARKANSAS CITY TRAVELER (ARKANSAS CITY, KAN. : 1970). (ARKANSAS CITY TRAVELER.). 99th Year, No. 183 (March 23, 1970)-. Newspaper. English. da (except Sunday). Arkansas City Traveler, PO Box 741, Arkansas City KS 67005. **Tel** (316)442-4200. **ED** Kim Benedict. Index available. cum. index. **Bk Rev. Ad Acc. Circ:** 7,000 (ctrl). available in microform. ***Continues*** *Arkansas City Daily Traveler.*

US
ATCHISON DAILY GLOBE (ATCHISON, KAN. : 1884). (THE ATCHISON DAILY GLOBE.). **VFOAT** Atchison Sunday Globe. Sept. 1, 1884-. Newspaper. English. da. Atchison Daily Globe, 1015-25 Main Street, Atchison KS 66002. available on microfilm from University Microfilms International (UMI). ***Continues*** *Atchison Globe.*

US
AUGUSTA DAILY GAZETTE, THE. Vol. 4, No. 129 (Nov. 13, 1905)-. Newspaper. English. da. $64.34. Augusta Daily Gazette, PO Box 9, Augusta KS 67010. **Tel** (316)775-2218, FAX (316)775-3220. **ED** Carter Zerbe, Michael McDermott (Managing Editor). **Photos. Ad Acc, Adv Mgr:** Len Hudson. **Pub. Size:** Broadsheet. **Wire Svcs.:** AP. **Circ:** 3,250. ***Continues*** *Daily Gazette (Augusta, Kan.);* ***Absorbed*** *Augusta Weekly Gazette; Augusta Bugle.*
Desc: News and information for a general readership.

US/0745-9335
BALDWIN LEDGER, THE. Vol. 98, Issue 34 (June 2, 1983)-. Newspaper. English. wk. $22.50 (local). Baldwin Ledger, Box 66, Baldwin City KS 66006. **ED** Doris Miller. **Bk Rev**, (Qty: 40-50). **Photos. Ad Acc, Adv Mgr:** Christopher Miller, **Tel** (913)594-6424. Full Page (B&W) $567.00. Half Page (B&W) $283.50. Full Page (Color) add $100.00. Half Page (Color) add $100.00. **Pub. Size:** Broadsheet. ***Continues*** *Tele-News;* ***Continues in part*** *Telegraphics.*

US
BASEHOR SENTINEL. **VFOAT** Basehor News. Vol. 1, No. 1 (Nov. 19, 1970)-. Newspaper. English. wk. $12.75. Basehor Sentinel, PO Box 247, Basehor KS 66007. **ED** Clausie W. Smith. **Bk Rev. Photos. Ad Acc, Adv Mgr:** Angela Skwark. Full Page (B&W) $645.00. Half Page (B&W) $330.00. Full Page (Color) $705.00. Half Page (Color) $390.00. **Pub. Size:** Standard.

US/0455-6000
BAXTER SPRINGS CITIZEN. Vol. 77, No. 1 (May 27, 1948)-. Newspaper. English. sw (104 issues per year). $32.00. Baxter Springs Citizen, PO Box 657, Baxter Springs KS 66713. **Tel** (316)856-2115, FAX (316)856-3162. **ED** Jeff Nichols (Editor-in-Chief) and Brent Fisher (Managing Editor). **Bk Rev**, (Qty: 15-20). **Photos. Ad Acc, Adv Mgr:** Jeff Nichols. **Pub. Size:** Standard. available on microfilm. ***Continues*** *Baxter Springs Citizen and Herald.*

US
BELLE PLAINE NEWS. Vol. 1, No. 15 (March 13, 1880)-. Newspaper. English. wk. $20.00 Kansas; $32.00 other. Belle Plaine News, 431 West Merchant, Belle Plaine KS 67013. **Tel** (316)488-2234, telex (316)488-3241. **ED** Marian Phipps and Carol Cole (Managing Editor). **Bk Rev. Photos. Ad Acc, Adv Mgr:** Carol Cole. Full Page (B&W) $245.00. Half Page (B&W) $122.50. Full Page (Color) $320.00. Half Page (Color) $197.50. **Pub. Size:** Tabloid. **Circ:** 1,000 (paid). ***Continues*** *Belle Plaine Home News;* ***Absorbed*** *Belle Plaine Defender.*

US/0740-0985
BELLEVILLE TELESCOPE (BELLEVILLE, KAN. : 1923). (THE BELLEVILLE TELESCOPE.). Vol. 53, No. 23 (Feb. 8, 1923)-. Newspaper. English. wk. $28.59. Belleville Telescope, 1817 East US 81 Frontage Road, Belleville KS 66935. **Tel** (913)527-2244, FAX (913)527-2225. **ED** Mark L. Miller, Deb Madachek (Managing Editor). **Photos. Ad Acc.** Full Page (B&W) $504.00. Half Page (B&W) $252.00. Full Page (Color) $654.00. Half Page (Color) $402.00. **Pub. Size:** Standard. **Circ:** 5,600 paid. ***Continues*** *Belleville Telescope and the Belleville Freeman;* ***Absorbed*** *Republic County Democrat* ***and*** *Republic County News and the Republic City News.*

US/8750-1791
BELOIT DAILY CALL, THE. (THE BELOIT DAILY NEWS.). Vol. 4, No. 230 (June 30, 1905)-. Newspaper. English. da. $115.00 (by mail); $78.00 (by carrier). Beloit Daily News, 149 State Street, Beloit KS 67420-0309. **Tel** (608)362-6962. **ED** Gary W. Hilt. **Ad Acc. Circ:** 3,000 (ctrl). ***Continues*** *Daily Call (Beloit, Kan.).*

US
BLADE-EMPIRE. **VFOAT** Blade Empire. Vol. 79, No. 3 (May 31, 1979)-. Newspaper. English. da. $51.98. Blade-Empire Publishing Company, Box 309, Concordia KS 66901-0309. **ED** Brad Lowell, Jim Lowell (Managing Editor). **Photos. Ad Acc, Adv Mgr:** Joni Regnier, **Tel** (913)243-2424. Full Page (B&W) $612.36. Half Page (B&W) $306.18. Full Page (Color) $672.23. Half Page (Color) $376.18. **Pub. Size:** Broadsheet. **Wire Svcs.:** AP. available on microfilm from University Microfilms International (UMI). ***Continues*** *Concordia Blade-Empire.*

US
BLUE VALLEY GAZETTE (STANLEY, KAN.). (THE BLUE VALLEY GAZETTE.). Vol. 4, No. 52 (Jan. 26, 1984)-. Newspaper. English. wk. Blue Valley Gazette, 7713 West 151st Street, Stanley KS 66223. ***Continues*** *Blue Valley Gazette and Country Life Weekly.*

US
BONNER SPRINGS-EDWARDSVILLE CHIEFTAIN. **VFOAT** Bonner Springs Edwardsville Chieftain. Vol. 79, No. 40 (Jan. 23, 1975)-. Newspaper. English. wk. Chieftain, 128 Oak Street, Bonner Springs KS 66012. ***Continues*** *Bonner Springs Chieftain (Bonner Springs, Kan. : 1965).*

US/0897-4551
CALDWELL MESSENGER (CALDWELL, KAN. 1942), THE. (THE CALDWELL MESSENGER.). **VFOAT** Caldwell Messenger Border Queen; Border Queen the Caldwell Messenger. Vol. 56, No. 1 (Sept. 1942)-. Newspaper. English. da. $16.50 local; $19.00 out of state. Caldwell Messenger, PO Box 313, Caldwell KS 67022. **Tel** (316)845-2320, FAX (316)845-6461. **ED** Damon Weber. **Bk Rev**, (Qty: 3-4). **Photos. Ad Acc.** Full Page (B&W) $380.55. Half Page (B&W) $190.30. **Pub. Size:** Standard. available on microfilm and microfiche (from the Kansas Historical Society and the Kansas Press Association). ***Continues in part*** *Caldwell Daily Messenger and The Caldwell News.*

US
CANEY CHRONICLE (CANEY, KAN. : 1958). (CANEY CHRONICLE.). Vol. 36, No. 170 (June 2, 1958)-. Newspaper. English. sw. Caney Chronicle, 202 West 4th Street, Caney KS 67333. ***Continues*** *Caney Daily Chronicle (Caney, Kan. : 1931).*

US
CANTON PILOT, THE. Vol. 1, No. 1 (March 2, 1899)-. Newspaper. English. wk. Canton Pilot, 112 North Main Street, Canton KS 67428. ***Formed by the union of*** *Canton Argus* ***and*** *Canton Leader.*

US/0892-1148
CAPPER'S. ***Title Change.*** Vol. 109, No. 1 (Jan. 1987)-. Newspaper. English. bw. Capper Publications, 616 Jefferson, Topeka KS 66607. **Tel** (913)295-1111. **ED** Nancy Peavler. **Ad Acc. Circ:** 399,000. ***Continued by*** *Capper's Weekly, 0008-5936.*
Desc: A news and human interest magazine for families of prospering towns, ranches, and farms in America's heartland.

US
CEDAR VALE MESSENGER, THE. Began in 1921. Newspaper. English. wk. Cedar Vale Messenger, PO Box F, Sedan KS 67361. available on microfilm from University Microfilms International (UMI). ***Absorbed*** *County Liner and Cedar Vale Commercial.*

US
CHANUTE TRIBUNE (CHANUTE, KAN. : 1946). (THE CHANUTE TRIBUNE.). Vol. 54 No. 241 (Jan. 24, 1946)-. Newspaper. English. da. $5.25 per month. Chanute Publishing Company, 15 North Evergreen Street, Chanute KS 66720. **Tel** (316)431-4100, FAX (316)431-2635. **ED** Tom Bell, Stu Butchen (Managing Editor). **Photos. Ad Acc, Adv Mgr:** Jo Anne Johnson. Full Page (B&W) $664.35. Half Page (B&W) $332.18. **Pub. Size:** Broadsheet. **Wire Svcs.:** AP, HN. **Circ:** 5,100. available in microform. ***Continues*** *Chanute Tribune and The Daily Timesett.*

US
CHAPMAN ADVERTISER AND THE ENTERPRISE JOURNAL, THE. Sept. 1, 1977-. Newspaper. English. wk. Chapman Advertiser and Enterprise Journal, 436 North Marshall, Chapman KS 67431. ***Formed by the union of*** *Chapman Advertiser* ***and*** *Enterprise Journal (Enterprise, Kan. : 1922).*

US
CHASE COUNTY LEADER-NEWS. **VFOAT** Chase County Leader News. Vol. 81, No. 44 (Jan. 2, 1952)-. Newspaper. English. wk. Chase County Leader-News, Box 340, Cottonwood Falls KS 66845. available on microfilm from University Microfilms International (UMI). ***Formed by the union of*** *Chase County Leader (1871)* ***and*** *Chase County News.*

US
CHENEY SENTINEL, THE. Vol. 1 No. 1 (Mar. 1 1894)-. Newspaper. English. wk. $22.00 Kansas; $30.00 others in Kansas; $34.00 others. Cheney Sentinel, Box 507, Cheney KS 67025. **Tel** (316)542-3111, FAX (316)542-3283. **ED** Paul Rhodes (Editor-in-Chief) and Gail Haverkamp (Managing Editor). **Bk Rev. Photos. Ad Acc, Adv Mgr:** Arla Tanner. Full Page (B&W) $395.00. Half Page (B&W) $220.00. Full Page (Color) $470.00. Half Page (Color) $295.00. **Pub. Size:** Standard. ***Absorbed*** *Garden Plain Tribune; Viola Sentinel.*

US
CITIZEN-PATRIOT, THE. **VFOAT** Citizen Patriot. Vol. 32, No. 28 (Jan. 1911/1912)-. Newspaper. English. wk. Rawlins County Publishing Company, Box 26, Atwood KS 67730. ***Continues*** *Republican Citizen and the Atwood Patriot;* ***Absorbed*** *Square Deal (Atwood, Kan.); Herndon Nonpareil (Herndon, Kan. : 1908); McDonald Standard.*

US
CLARK COUNTY CLIPPER (ASHLAND, KAN. : 1976). (THE CLARK COUNTY CLIPPER.). Vol. 93, No. 25 (Nov. 11, 1976)-. Newspaper. English. wk. Clark County Clipper, Box 457, Ashland KS 67831. available on microfilm from University Microfilms International (UMI). ***Continues in part*** *Clark County Clipper combined with The Minneola Record.*

US
CLAY CENTER DISPATCH (1930). (THE CLAY CENTER DISPATCH.). Vol. 37, No. 139 (May 24, 1930)-. Newspaper. English. da. Clay Center Publishing Company, PO Box 519, Clay Center KS 67432. available on microfilm from University Microfilms International (UMI). ***Continues*** *Dispatch-Republican.*

US
CLEARWATER TIMES (CLEARWATER, KAN. : 1963). (THE CLEARWATER TIMES.). Vol. 1, No. 1 (Nov. 7, 1963)-. Newspaper. English. wk. Clearwater Times, Box 549, Clearwater KS 67026.

US
CLYDE REPUBLICAN (CLYDE, KAN. : 1986). (CLYDE REPUBLICAN.). Vol. 107, No. 46 (May 8, 1986)-. Newspaper. English. wk. $13.00. Clyde Republican, PO Box 397, Clyde KS 66938-0397. **Tel** (913)446-2201. **ED** Margene Cash. **Photos**. **Ad Acc**, **Adv Mgr:** Ann Carlson. Full Page (B&W) $315.00. Half Page (B&W) $157.50. **Pub. Size:** Standard. ***Continues*** *Republican (Clyde, Kan.).*

US
COFFEY COUNTY REPORTER, THE. Vol. 96, No. 52 (Oct. 17, 1975)-. Newspaper. English. wk. Coffey County Reporter, PO Drawer A, Burlington KS 66839. ***Continues*** *Leroy Reporter.*

US/0745-838X
COFFEY COUNTY TODAY. **VFOAT** Today. Vol. 1, No. 1 (May 2, 1983)-. Newspaper. English. tw. $42.00. Coffey County Today, 324 Hudson Street, Burlington KS 66839. **Tel** (316)364-5325. **ED** Marie Petterson. **Bk Rev**, (Qty: 10). **Photos**. **Ad Acc**, **Adv Mgr:** B. J. Peterson. Full Page (B&W) $546.84. Full Page (Color) $621.84. **Pub. Size:** Standard. **Circ:** 2,400. available in microform. ***Continues*** *Daily Republican (Burlington, Kan.).*
Desc: Concentrates on Coffey County news.

US/0746-8202
COFFEYVILLE JOURNAL (COFFEYVILLE, KAN. : 1964). (THE COFFEYVILLE JOURNAL.). Vol. 72, No. 32 (July 7, 1964)-. Newspaper. English. da. Coffeyville Journal, PO Box 849, Coffeyville KS 67337-0849. ***Continues*** *Coffeyville Daily Journal (Coffeyville, Kan. : 1895).*

US
COLBY FREE PRESS AND THE PRAIRIE DRUMMER, THE. Vol. 93, No. 20 (Oct. 6, 1981)-. Newspaper. English. da. Free Press and Prairie Drummer KS 67701. ***Continues*** *Colby Free Press (Colby, Kan. : 1980).*

US/8756-6044
COLUMBUS DAILY ADVOCATE. **VFOAT** Daily Advocate. Newspaper. English. da. $24.00, $19.50 trade territory outside Columbus by mail in advance, $33.50 outside Cherokee county. Columbus Daily Advocate, 215 South Kansas Street, Columbus KS 66725.

US
COUNCIL GROVE REPUBLICAN (COUNCIL GROVE, KAN. : DAILY). (COUNCIL GROVE REPUBLICAN.). 52nd year, No. 2 (Sept. 1, 1924)-. Newspaper. English. da. Council Grove Republican, 208 West Main Street, Council Grove KS 66846. ***Formed by the union of*** *Daily Guard (Council Grove, Kan.)* ***and*** *Council Grove Republican (Council Grove, Kan. : Weekly).*

US
COURIER-TRIBUNE (SENECA, KAN.). (THE COURIER-TRIBUNE.). **VFOAT** Courier Tribune; Semiweekly Courier-Tribune; Semiweekly Courier Tribune. Vol. 56, No. 44 (August 7, 1919)-. Newspaper. English. wk. $15.00. Courier-Tribune, 512 Main Street, Seneca KS 66538. **ED** Dan Diehl. **Photos**. **Ad Acc**, **Adv Mgr:** Janet Diehl, **Tel** (913)336-2175. Full Page (B&W) $504.00. Half Page (B&W) $252.00. Full Page (Color) $604.00. Half Page (Color) $352.00. **Pub. Size:** Standard. **Circ:** 3,250 (weekly). ***Formed by the union of*** *Seneca Tribune* ***and*** *Courier-Democrat (Seneca, Kan.);* ***Absorbed*** *Seneca Times.*

US
COWLEY COUNTY REPORTER, THE. Vol. 89, No. 46 (Nov. 16, 1967)-. Newspaper. English. Fifty times a year (Thurs.). $14.65 in county; $19.00 other. Cowley County Reporter, PO Box 97, Burden KS 67019. **Tel** (316)438-2370. **ED** Ann Alexander. **Photos**. **Ad Acc**, **Adv Mgr:** Ann Alexander. Full Page (B&W) $220.50. Half Page (B&W) $110.25. **Pub. Size:** Standard. **Circ:** 650. available on microfilm from University Microfilms International (UMI). ***Continues*** *Burden Times.*

US
DAILY REPORTER, THE. Vol. 3, No. 29 (June 5, 1963)-. Newspaper. English. da. $72.00. Derby Daily Reporter, 201 South Baltimore, Derby KS 67037-1405. **Tel** (316)788-2835, FAX (316)788-0854. **ED** Jim Stephenson, Sam Foster (Managing Editor). **Bk Rev**. **Photos**. **Ad Acc**, **Adv Mgr:** Faye Osenbaugh. Full Page (B&W) $847.98. Half Page (B&W) $423.99. Full Page (Color) $922.98. Half Page (Color) $498.99. **Pub. Size:** Broadsheet. **Wire Svcs.:** AP. **Circ:** 2,000 evening paid. ***Continues*** *Derby Reporter;* ***Absorbed*** *Daily Reporter (Derby, Kan. : 1979).*

US/0745-743X
DAILY UNION (JUNCTION CITY, KAN.). (DAILY UNION.). No. 12 (July 15, 1974)-. Newspaper. English. da. Junction City Union / Kansas, 814 North Washington Street, Junction City KS 66441. **Tel** (913)762-5000. ***Continues*** *Junction City Union.*

US
DELPHOS REPUBLICAN, THE. Vol. 1, No. 1 (Dec. 3, 1888)-. Newspaper. English. wk. Delphos Republican, Box 457, Glasco KS 67445.

US
DIGHTON HERALD (DIGHTON, KAN. : 1916). (THE DIGHTON HERALD.). Vol. 31, No. 37 (Dec. 1, 1916)-. Newspaper. English. wk. $15.89 Lane County; $16.94 other Kansas; $19.00 other. Dighton Herald, PO Box 637, Dighton KS 67839. **Tel** (316)397-5347. **ED** Jim W. Gardner. **Photos**. **Ad Acc**. Full Page (B&W) $346.50. Half Page (B&W) $165.00. Full Page (Color) $396.50. Half Page (Color) $215.50. **Pub. Size:** Standard. ctrl circ. ***Formed by the union of*** *Dighton News* ***and*** *Journal-Herald (Dighton, Kan.);* ***Absorbed*** *Healy Homestead.*

US/1057-0578
DIRECTORY OF POLITICAL PERIODICALS. ***Title Change.*** [Dir. polit. period.]. **Added/Corp** Government Research Service. (1991)-(199?). Directory. English. an (Feb.). Government Research Service, 701 Jackson, Suite 304B, Topeka KS 66603. **Tel** (913)232-7720, (800)346-6898, FAX (913)232-1615. **LC** Z7165.U5; D597; JK1. **DD** 016.324/0973. ***Continues*** *Directory of Political Newsletters, 1052-9896.* ***Continued by*** *Directory of Political Newsletters, 1071-796X.*
Desc: These are newsletters, journals, and newspapers that focus on the people, politics and government of Washington D. C. and the states.

US/0889-3489
DODGE CITY DAILY GLOBE, THE. **VFOAT** Daily Globe. (1911)-. Newspaper. English. da. Dodge City Globe, 705 2nd Avenue, Dodge City KS 67801. **Tel** (316)225-4151.

US
DOWNS NEWS AND TIMES, THE. **VFOAT** Downs News & Times. Vol. 90, No. 44 (Oct. 29, 1970)-. Newspaper. English. wk. Downs News and Times, Downs KS 67437. ***Continues*** *News and Times.*

US
EDNA SUN, THE. Vol 1, No. 1 (Nov. 24, 1894)-. Newspaper. English. wk. Edna Sun, Box 225, Edna KS 67342.

US/1053-9999
EL DORADO TIMES, THE. Vol. 1, No. 1 (Dec. 1, 1919)-. Newspaper. English. da. Times Publishing Company / El Dorado Times, PO Box 694, 114 North Vine Street, El Dorado KS 67042. **Tel** (814)870-1808. ***Formed by the union of*** *Walnut Valley Times (El Dorado, Kan. 1902)* ***and*** *El Dorado Republican (El Dorado, Kan. : 1885);* ***Absorbed*** *El Dorado Republican (El Dorado, Kan. : 1883); Butler County News and Butler Free-Lance; Douglass Tribune.*

US
ELLINWOOD LEADER. Vol. 3, No. 27 (Sept. 17, 1896)-. Newspaper. English (German). wk. Ellinwood Publishing Inc, Box 487, Ellinwood KS 67526. ***Continues*** *Claflin Leader;* ***Absorbed*** *Ellinwood Advocate.*

US
ELLIS COUNTY STAR, THE. Vol. 15, No. 34 (April 2, 1964)-. Newspaper. English. wk. $20.00. Ellis County Star, 708 Main Street, Hays KS 67601. **Tel** (913)625-7358. **ED** Pat Taylor. **Bk Rev**. **Photos**. **Ad Acc**, **Adv Mgr:** Pat Taylor. Full Page (B&W) $189.00. **Pub. Size:** Standard. ***Continues*** *Ellis County Farmer.*

US
ELLIS REVIEW (ELLIS, KAN. : 1930). (THE ELLIS REVIEW.). Vol. 46, No. 24 (March 6, 1930)-. Newspaper. English. wk. Ellis Review, 1018 Washington Street, Ellis KS 67637. **ED** Joleen Fisher. **Photos**. **Ad Acc**. Full Page (B&W) $226.80. Half Page (B&W) $131.79. **Pub. Size:** Standard. **Circ:** 1,400. ***Continues*** *Ellis Review-Headlight (Ellis, Kan. : 1906).*

US
ELLSWORTH REPORTER. **VFOAT** Ellsworth Daily Reporter. (Dec. 7, 1871)-. Newspaper. English. wk. $24.00. Ellsworth Reporter, PO Box 7, Ellsworth KS 67439. **Tel** (913)472-3103, FAX (913)472-3268. **ED** Kent Gaston (Editor-in-Chief) Joel Smits (Managing Editor). **Photos**. **Ad Acc**, **Adv Mgr:** Karl Gaston. Full Page (B&W) $350.00. Half Page (B&W) $200.00. Full Page (Color) $425.00. Half Page (Color) $260.00. **Pub. Size:** Broadsheet. **Circ:** 2,900 (ctrl). available on microfilm. ***Absorbed*** *Ellsworth Messenger; Holyrood Buston News/Gazette.*
Desc: General news and sports.

US
EMPORIA GAZETTE (EMPORIA, KAN. : 1899). (THE EMPORIA GAZETTE.). Vol. 8, No. 4099 (April 20, 1899)-. Newspaper. English. da (Except Sundays & holidays). $63.25 Emporia KS; $71.50 Within 45 miles of Emporia KS; $112.80 others. Emporia Gazette, Emporia KS 66801. **Tel** (316)342-4800, FAX (316)342-8108. available on microfilm from University Microfilms International (UMI). ***Continues*** *Emporia Daily Gazette;* ***Absorbed*** *Northern Star (Admire, Kan.).*

US
ERIE RECORD (ERIE, KAN. : 1904). (THE ERIE RECORD.). **VFOAT** Erie Record and Walnut Eagle. Vol. 29 No. 12 (Dec. 16, 1904)-. Newspaper. English. wk. $12.00 local; $16.00 other. Erie Record, PO Box 156, Erie KS 66733. **ED** Leah Kensinger. **Photos**. **Ad Acc**. Full Page (B&W) $352.17. Half Page (B&W) $176.09. Full Page (Color) $392.17. Half Page (Color) $216.09. **Pub. Size:** Broadsheet. available in microform. ***Continues*** *Erie Republican Record;* ***Absorbed*** *Erie Sentinel (Erie, Kan. : 1917); Walnut Eagle.*

US
EUREKA HERALD, THE. Vol. 86, No. 2 (July 2, 1953)-. Newspaper. English. wk (Published on Fridays). Eureka Herald, PO Box 590, Eureka KS 67045-1512. **Tel** (316)583-5721. **ED** Richard W. Clasen. **Ad Acc**. **Circ:** 3,600. ***Continues*** *Eureka Herald and the Eureka Messenger;* ***Absorbed*** *Greenwood Pioneer-Post.*

US
EVEREST WORLD, THE. Vol. 1, No. 1 (Jan. 24, 1963)-. Newspaper. English. wk. $14.00 (carrier), $18.00 (airmail. Everest World, 607 Utah Street, Everest KS 66434. **Tel** (913)742--3237. **ED** Virginia Regier. **Photos**. **Ad Acc**, **Adv Mgr:** Becky Williams. Full Page (B&W) $123.50. Half Page (B&W) $61.75. Full Page (Color) $198.50. Half Page (Color) $136.75. **Pub. Size:** Tabloid. **Circ:** 500.

US
FORT RILEY POST, THE. **VFOAT** Post. Vol. 1, No. 1 (Nov. 6, 1959)-. Newspaper. English. wk. $15.00. Fort Riley Post, 814 North Washington Street, Junction City KS 66441. **Tel** (913)762-5000, FAX (913)762-4584. **ED** John D. Montgomery. **Bk Rev**, (Qty: 1-2). **Photos**. **Ad Acc**, **Adv Mgr:** Doris Peterson, **Tel** (913)762-5000. Full Page (B&W) $1,548. Half Page (B&W) $792.00. Full Page (Color) $1,718. Half Page (Color) $962.00. **Pub. Size:** Broadsheet. **Circ:** 10,935. available on microfilm and microfiche. ***Continues*** *Fort Riley Traveler.*

US/8755-3171
FORT SCOTT TRIBUNE, THE. **VFOAT** Tribune. 97th Year, No. 127 (May 3, 1982)-. Newspaper. English. da (except Sundays and holidays). $40.06 Kansas; $42.56 other. The Fort Scott Tribune, PO Box 150, Fort Scott KS 66701. **Tel** (316)223-1460. **ED** Tom Eblen. ***Continues*** *Fort Scott Daily Tribune and Fort Scott Daily Monitor.*

US
GARDEN CITY TELEGRAM (GARDEN CITY, KAN. : 1953). (GARDEN CITY TELEGRAM.). Vol. 24, No. 95 (March 3, 1953)-. Newspaper. English. da. $98.00. Telegram Publishing Company, PO Box 958, Garden City KS 67846. **Tel** (316)275-0106. **ED** Jim Bloom, Carol Crupper (Managing Editor). **Bk Rev**. **Photos**. **Ad Acc**, **Adv Mgr:** Kent O'Toole. Full Page (B&W) $825.60. Half Page (B&W) $412.80. Full Page (Color) $905.60. Half Page (Color) $492.80. **Pub. Size:** Broadsheet. **Wire Svcs.:** HN. ***Continues*** *Garden City Daily Telegram.*

US
GARNETT REVIEW, THE. Vol. 51, No. 88 (Sept. 16, 1915)-. Newspaper. English. wk. Garnett Publishing Company, PO Box 409, Garnett KS 66032. **ED** W O Champe. ***Continues*** *Garnett Evening Review and Journal-Plaindealer;* ***Absorbed*** *Colony Free Press (Colony Kan. : 1925).*

US
GIRARD PRESS, THE. (July 15, 1871)-. Newspaper. English. wk (Published on Wednesdays). $13.72 Kansas; $18.99 others. Girard Press, PO Box 126, Girard KS 66743-0126. **Tel** (316)724-4426, FAX (316)724-4493. **ED** Ed McKechnie and Andra Bryan (Managing Editor). **Bk Rev**. **Photos**. **Ad Acc**, **Adv Mgr:** Tammy Merrett. Full Page (B&W) $374.00. Half Page (B&W) $191.00. **Pub. Size:** Broadsheet. **Circ:** 2,600. ***Continues*** *Girard Weekly Press;* ***Absorbed*** *Independent News (Girard, Kan.)* ***and*** *McCune Herald.*

US
GLASCO SUN (GLASCO, KAN. : 1937). (THE GLASCO SUN.). Vol. 54, No. 31 (Aug. 19, 1937)-. Newspaper. English. wk. $16.94. Glasco Sun, Box 457, Glasco KS 67445. **Tel** (913)568-2565. **ED** Royanne Tatro. **Photos**. **Ad Acc**. Full Page (B&W) $294.00. Half Page (B&W) $147.00. ***Continues*** *Sun (Glasco, Kan. : 1919).*

US/0893-0562
GOODLAND DAILY NEWS, THE. Vol. 1, No. 1 (Oct. 3, 1932)-. Newspaper. English. da. Goodland Daily News, 1205 Main Street, Goodland KS 67735. ***Absorbed*** *Goodland News-Republic.*

US/0891-7078
GREAT BEND TRIBUNE (1972). (GREAT BEND TRIBUNE.). Vol. 97, No. 11 (Aug. 24, 1972)-. Newspaper. English. da. $91.80. Great Bend Tribune, PO Box 228, Great Bend KS 67530. **Tel** (316)792-1211. **ED** Cleon Rickel. **Bk Rev**, (Qty: 5). **Photos**. **Ad Acc, Adv Mgr:** Debbie Piland. **Pub. Size:** Standard. **Wire Svcs.:** AP. **Circ:** 11,862 daily, 12,099 Sunday. ***Continues*** *Great Bend Daily Tribune (Great Bend, Kan. : 1950).*

US
GREELEY COUNTY REPUBLICAN AND THE GREELEY COUNTY NEWS. Vol. 48, No. 18 (May 4, 1933)-. Newspaper. English. wk. PO Box 610, Tribune KS 67879. ***Continues*** *Greeley County Republican.*

US/0017-4289
GRIT (NATIONAL ED.). (GRIT.). Vol. 25, No. 52 (Nov. 24, 1907)-. Newspaper. English. bm. $26.00 US; $32.00 (includes postage) other. Capper's, 1503 Southwest 42nd Street, Topeka KS 66609. **Tel** (913)274-4366. **ED** Al Elmer. **Ad Acc. Circ:** 380,945. ***Continues in part*** *Pennsylvania Grit.*
Desc: Focuses on family issues.

●US/1065-3740
HARVEY COUNTY INDEPENDENT, THE. Vol. 114, No. 8 (Aug. 20, 1992)-. Newspaper. English. wk. The Harvey County Independent, PO Box 71, Halstead KS 67056. ***Formed by the union of*** *Halstead Independent (Halstead, Kan. : 1892)* ***and*** *Burrton Graphic (Burrton, Kan. : 1893);* ***Continues*** *Sedgewick Pantagraph (Sedgewick, Kan. : 1947).*

US
HASKELL COUNTY MONITOR-CHIEF, THE. **VFOAT** Haskell County Monitor Chief. Vol. 70, No. 40 (Jan. 3, 1957)-. Newspaper. English. wk. $16.94 (Haskell County, Kansas), $19.06 (other). Haskell County Monitor-Chief, PO Box 700, Sublette KS 67877. **Tel** (316)675-2204, FAX (316)675-8717. **ED** Charity Horinek (Managing Editor). **Bk Rev**, (Qty: 5-10). **Photos**. **Ad Acc, Adv Mgr:** Doris Birney. Full Page (B&W) $598.50. Half Page (B&W) $299.25. **Pub. Size:** Broadsheet. ***Formed by the union of*** *Sublette Monitor* ***and*** *Satanta Chief.*

US
HAYS DAILY NEWS, THE. Vol. 1, No. 1 (Nov. 11, 1929)-. Newspaper. English. da (Except Sat.). $80.36 Kansas, $78.17 others (mail); $75.54 Hays Kansas, $93.90 others (carrier). Hays Daily News, PO Box 857, Hays KS 67601. **Tel** (913)628-1081. **ED** Kay Berenson. **LC** 7803-X. **Ad Acc, Adv Mgr:** Mike Haas, **Tel** (913)628-1081. **Circ:** 14,000 (ctrl).

US
HERINGTON TIMES (HERINGTON, KAN. : 1973). (THE HERINGTON TIMES.). Vol. 84, No. 15 (Sept. 6, 1973)-. Newspaper. English. Fifty-two times a year (Wed.). Herington Times, PO Box 310, Herington KS 67449. **Tel** (913)258-2211. **ED** Larry L. Byers. **Ad Acc.** ***Continues*** *Herington Advertiser-Times;* ***Absorbed*** *Hope Diapatch (Hope, Kan. : 1904); White City Register.*

US
HESSTON RECORD, THE. Vol. 1, No. 1 (Dec. 8, 1932)-. Newspaper. English. Fifty-two times a year. $30.50 Harvey County; $35.00 US; $33.00 other. The Hesston Record, 109 N Main Street, PO Box 340, Hesston KS 67062. **Tel** (316)327-4831. **ED** Robert L. Latta. **Ad Acc. Circ:** 1,250.

US
HIAWATHA DAILY WORLD HIAWATHA, KAN. : 1908). (THE HIAWATHA DAILY NEWS.). No. 259 (Nov. 4, 1910). Newspaper. English. da. Hiawatha Daily News, 607 Utah Street, Hiawatha KS 66434. ***Absorbed*** *Brown County World (Hiawatha, Kan. : 1884).*

US/0018-1471
HIGH PLAINS JOURNAL, THE. Vol. 69, No. 1 (Jan. 6, 1949)-. Newspaper. English. Fifty-two times a year. $56.00. High Plains Journal, Box 760, Dodge City KS 67801. **Tel** (316)227-7171, FAX (316)227-7173. **ED** Galen Hubbs (Editor-in-Chief) and Doug Rich (Managing Editor). **Photos**. **Ad Acc, Adv Mgr:** Tom Taylor. Full Page (B&W) $7,358.00. Half Page (B&W) $3,679.00. Full Page (Color) $8,978.00. Half Page (Color) $5,299.00. **Pub. Size:** Tabloid. **Wire Svcs.:** AP, KR, NF. **Circ:** 57,314. available in microform. ***Continues*** *Dodge City Journal.*

US
HIGHLAND VIDETTE (HIGHLAND, KAN.). (HIGHLAND VIDETTE.). Vol. 3, No. 38 (Nov. 29, 1894)-. Newspaper. English. wk. Highland Vidette, PO Box 98, Highland KS 66035-0098. ***Continues*** *Vidette (Highland, Kan.).*

US
HILL CITY TIMES, THE. Vol. 49, No. 39 (March 27, 1930)-. Newspaper. English. wk. Hill City Publishing Company, PO Box 308, Hill City KS 67642. ***Formed by the union of*** *Reveille-New Era* ***and*** *Hill City Republican;* ***Absorbed*** *Bogue Messenger; Mortland Monitor.*

US
HOISINGTON DISPATCH, THE. Vol. 1, No. 1 (Mar. 7, 1889)-. Newspaper. English. wk (Published on Thursdays). Hoisington Dispatch, 104 North Main, Hoisington KS 67544-2502. **Tel** (316)653-4154. **ED** Luke Brown. **Ad Acc. Circ:** 2,200.

US
HOLTON RECORDER (HOLTON, KAN. : 1908). (THE HOLTON RECORDER.). Vol. 40, No. 45 (Jan. 2, 1908)-. Newspaper. English. sw. Holton Recorder, 109 West 4th Street, Holton KS 66436. ***Continues*** *Recorder-Tribune;* ***Absorbed*** *Jackson County Signal; Jackson County Clipper.*

US
HORTON HEADLIGHT (HORTON, KAN. : 1933). (THE HORTON HEADLIGHT.). Vol. 47, No. 97 (August 24, 1933)-. Newspaper. English. wk. $12.00 Atchison and Brown counties; $14.00 other. Headlight Publishing Company, 133 West 8th Street, Horton KS 66439. **ED** Susan Hegley. **Photos**. **Ad Acc, Adv Mgr:** Renee Wilburn, **Tel** 486-2512. Full Page (B&W) $378.00. Half Page (B&W) $189.00. available on microfilm from University Microfilms International (UMI). ***Continues*** *The Horton Headlight-Commercial.*

US
HOWARD COURANT-CITIZEN, THE. **VFOAT** Howard Courant Citizen. Vol. 72, No. 5 (Jan. 29, 1942)-. Newspaper. English. wk. Howard Courant-Citizen, 125 South Wabash Street, Howard KS 67349. ***Formed by the union of*** *Courant (Howard, Kan.)* ***and*** *Citizen (Howard, Kan.).*

US/1041-2921
HOXIE SENTINEL (HOXIE, KAN. : 1931). (THE HOXIE SENTINEL.). Vol. 49, No. 29 (Nov. 19, 1931)-. Newspaper. English. wk. Hoxie Sentinel, Box 78, Hoxie KS 67740. ***Continues*** *Hoxie Sentinel and The Sheridan County News.*

US
HUTCHINSON NEWS (HUTCHINSON, KAN. : 1957). (THE HUTCHINSON NEWS.). Vol. 85, No. 289 (April 1957)-. Newspaper. English. da. $120.96. The Hutchinson News, PO Box 190, Hutchinson KS 67504. **Tel** (316)662-3311, FAX (316)662-4186 (ads), (316)694-5767 (news). **ED** Wayne Lee, Roger Verdon (Managing Editor). **LC** 7818. Index available. **Photos**. **Ad Acc, Adv Mgr:** Debbie Lemen. Full Page (B&W) $2741.25. Half Page (B&W) $1402.50. **Wire Svcs.:** AP, SH, LA, NY. **Circ:** 45,000 (ctrl). available in microform. Documents available from UMI Article Clearinghouse. ***Continues*** *Hutchinson News-Herald (Hutchinson, Kan. : 1943).*
Ind/Abst Bus. Dateline (Feb. 9, 1992-) [Full Txt.].

US
HUTCHINSON RECORD, THE. Vol. 9, No. 10 (Oct. 17, 1930)-. Newspaper. English. wk. The Hutchinson Record, PO Box 38, Turon KS 67583-0038. ***Formed by the union of*** *South Hutchinson Record* ***and*** *Langdon Leader and The Penalosa Times.*

US
INDEPENDENCE DAILY REPORTER (INDEPENDENCE, KAN. : 1927). (INDEPENDENCE DAILY REPORTER.). 46th year, No. 171 (March 30, 1927)-. Newspaper. English. da. Independence Publishing Company, PO Box 869, Independence KS 67301. ***Continues*** *Independence Daily Reporter and the Independence Daily Free Press.*

US
INDEPENDENCE NEWS (INDEPENDENCE, KAN.). (THE INDEPENDENCE NEWS.). Began Dec. 4, 1948. Newspaper. English. wk. Independence News, 210 West Main Street, Independence KS 67301.

US/0889-308X
INFORM LETTER (WICHITA, KAN.), THE. (THE INFORM LETTER / THE INTERNATIONAL REFERENCE ORGANIZATION IN FORENSIC MEDICINE.). **Added/Corp** International Reference Organization in Forensic Medicine. **VAT** International Reference Organization in Forensic Medicine Letter. (19??)-. Periodical. English. Four times a year (Jan., Apr., July, Oct.). $30.00 one year; $50.00 two years; $75.00 three years. International Reference Org Forensic Medical & Society, PO Box 8282, Wichita KS 67208. **Tel** (316)685-7612, FAX (316)685-8625. **DD** 614. ***Continues*** *Inform.*

US
INMAN REVIEW AND BUHLER NEWS, THE. Vol. 86 No. 27 (July 5, 1973)-. Newspaper. English. wk. Inman Review and Buhler News, PO Box 720, Moundridge KS 67107. ***Continues*** *Inman Review.*

US
IOLA REGISTER (IOLA, KAN. : 1939). (THE IOLA REGISTER.). Vol. 42, No. 161 (May 2, 1939)-. Newspaper. English. da (except Sun.). $55.65 Allen County, Kansas; $78.50 other Kansas; $74.76 other. Iola Register, 302 South Washington Street, Iola KS 66749. **Tel** (316)365-2111, FAX (316)365-6289. **ED** Emerson Lynn. **Photos**. **Ad Acc, Adv Mgr:** Jack Hastings. Full Page (B&W) $593.40. Half Page (B&W) $303.15. Full Page (Color) $653.40. Half Page (Color) $333.15. **Pub. Size:** Broadsheet. **Wire Svcs.:** AP. ***Continues*** *Iola Daily Register (Iola, Kan. : 1899).*

US
JACKSONIAN (CIMARRON, KAN. : 1937). (THE JACKSONIAN.). Vol. 50, No. 18 (May 6, 1937)-. Newspaper. English. wk. The Jacksonian, Box 528, Cimarron KS 67835. ***Formed by the union of*** *Copeland Chronicle* ***and*** *Jacksonian and The Gray County Record.*

US
JEWELL COUNTY RECORD (MANKATO, KAN.). (JEWELL COUNTY RECORD.). Vol. 50, No. 23 (Dec. 26, 1940)-. Newspaper. English. wk. Jewell County Record, PO Box 305, Mankato KS 66956. ***Continues*** *Western Advocate (Mankato, Kan.);* ***Absorbed*** *Burr Oak Herald.*

US
JEWELL COUNTY REPUBLICAN. Began in 1879. Newspaper. English. wk. Jewell County Republican, PO Box 98, Jewell KS 66949.

US
JOHNSON COUNTY SUN. Vol. 24, No. 43 (June 6, 1973)-. Newspaper. English. sw (104 issues per year - published on Wednesdays & Fridays). $63.51 Johnson County, Kansas; $68.80 other. Johnson County Sun, I-435 and Metcalf Overland Park, Shawnee Mission KS 66212. **Tel** (913)381-1010. ***Continues*** *Johnson County Scout.*

US
JOURNAL-FREE PRESS, THE. **VFOAT** Journal Free Press. Vol. 63, No. 44 (March 1, 1933)-. Newspaper. English. wk. Journal-Free Press, 403 Market Street, Osage City KS 66523. ***Formed by the union of*** *Osage City Free Press (Osage City, Kan. : 1913)* ***and*** *Osage County Journal;* ***Absorbed*** *Reading Herald.*

US
KANSAS CHIEF, THE. 62nd year, No. 27 (Nov. 21, 1918)-. Newspaper. English. wk. Kansas Chief, 113 South Main Street, Troy KS 66087. ***Continues*** *Weekly Kansas Chief;* ***Absorbed*** *White Cloud Press.*

US/0022-8524
KANSAS CITY JEWISH CHRONICLE. Vol. 1, No. 1 (Jan. 2, 1920)-. Newspaper. English. wk. Sun Publications / Kansas City Jewish Chronicle, 7373 West 107th Street, Overland Park KS 66212-2500. **Tel** (913)381-1010, FAX (913)382-9889.

US
KANSAS CITY KANSAN, THE. Vol. 1, No. 1 (Apr. 3, 1916)-. Newspaper. English. da (Sun.-Fri.). $62.35. The Kansas City Kansan, 901 North 8th Street, Kansas City KS 66101. **Tel** (913)371-4300 ext. 60. **ED** Patrick Lowry. **LC** 7002. **Photos**. **Ad Acc, Adv Mgr:** Joie Millenbruch. Full Page (B&W) $1,309.90. Half Page (B&W) $651.45. Full Page (Color) $1,384.90. Half Page (Color) $726.45. **Pub. Size:** Standard. **Wire Svcs.:** AP. **Circ:** 12,888 (evening, Tuesday thru Friday and Sunday morning). available in microform from Bell & Howell's Underground Newspaper Collection. ***Absorbed*** *Kansas City Globe (Kansas City, Kan. : 1917).*

US
KANSAS WORKS. (1989)-. Newspaper. English. mo. $15.00. Kanhistique, Box 7, Ellsworth KS 67439. **Tel** (913)472-3103, FAX (913)472-3268. **ED** Edna Lee. **Bk Rev**, (Qty: 12). **Photos**. **Ad Acc, Adv Mgr:** Karl Gaston. Full Page (B&W) $190.50. Half Page (B&W) $110.00. Full Page (Color) $250.00. Half Page (Color) $170.00. **Pub. Size:** Tabloid. **Circ:** 1,400 (ctrl). available in microform.

US
KIOWA COUNTY SIGNAL (GREENSBURG, KAN. : 1936). (THE KIOWA COUNTY SIGNAL.). **VFOAT** Kiowa County Signal and The Greensburg News. Vol. 50, No. 9 (Nov. 12, 1936)-. Newspaper. English. wk. Kiowa County Signal, Box 368, Greensburg KS 67054. ***Continues*** *Progressive-Signal Magazine;* ***Absorbed*** *Greensburg News (Greensburg, Kan.); Haviland Journal.*

US
KIOWA NEWS (KIOWA, KAN. : 1983).
(THE KIOWA NEWS.). Vol. 90, No. 4 (Jan. 27, 1983)-. Newspaper. English. wk. Kiowa News, 614 Main Street, Kiowa KS 67070. **ED** Rex Zimmerman. ***Continues*** *Kiowa News Review and Record.*

US
LAWRENCE DAILY JOURNAL-WORLD.
VFOAT Lawrence Daily Journal World; Journal World; Daily Journal World. Journal Vol. 55, No. 43 (Feb. 20, 1911)-V. 55, No. 65 (Mar. 16, 1911)-. Newspaper. English. da. $103.95 Lawrence, Kansas; $127.75 adjoining counties; $147.00 all others in Kansas; $157.00 other. Lawrence Daily Journal World, Box 888, 609 New Hampshire, Lawrence KS 66044. **Tel** (913)843-1000. **ED** Dolph C Simons Jr. **LC** 7002. **Ad Acc. Circ:** 18,746 daily, 19,145 Sunday (ctrl). ***Formed by the union of*** *Lawrence Daily World* ***and*** *Lawrence Daily Journal.*
Desc: General circulation newspaper with news emphasis on Lawrence and area communities, including the University of Kansas.

US
LEADER COURIER, THE. VFOAT
Leader-Courier. Vol. 5, No. 52 (Nov. 28, 1889)-. Newspaper. English. wk (Published on Fridays). Leader Courier / Kansas, 140 North Main, Kingman KS 67068-1301. **Tel** (316)532-3151, FAX (316)532-3152. **ED** Robert McQuin. **Ad Acc, Adv Mgr:** Sarah Solomon. **Circ:** 3,450. ***Formed by the union of*** *Kingman Leader* ***and*** *Kingman Weekly Courier.*

US/1050-5806
LEADER (LANSING, KAN.), THE. (THE LEADER.). Vol. 3, No. 18 (Mar. 29, 1973)-. Newspaper. English. wk (Published on Thursdays). Lansing Leader, 102 East Olive, Lansing KS 66043-1222. **Tel** (913)727-1291, FAX (913)727-2320. **ED** Cathy Gripka. **Ad Acc. Circ:** 1,100. ***Continues*** *Lansing Leader.*

US/0194-9799
LEAVEN (KANSAS CITY), THE. (THE LEAVEN.). **Added/Corp** Catholic Church. Archdiocese of Kansas City in Kansas. Vol. 1, No. 1 (July 6, 1979)-. Newspaper. English. wk (Sept.-May, except last week in Dec.). $8.00. The Leaven / Kansas, 2220 Central, Box 2329, Kansas City KS 66110. ***Continues*** *Eastern Kansas Register, 0012-883X.*

US
LEAVENWORTH TIMES LEAVENWORTH, KAN. : 1878). (THE LEAVENWORTH TIMES.). Vol. 37, No. 4 (Nov. 28, 1878)-. Newspaper. English. da (6 days a week). $111.96. Leavenworth Times, PO Box 144, Leavenworth KS 66048. **Tel** (913)682-0305. **ED** Tom Johanning Meier. ***Continues*** *Daily Leavenworth Times (Leavenworth, Kan. : 1877);* ***Absorbed*** *Evening Standard (Leavenworth, Kan. : 1897); Leavenworth Post (Leavenworth, Kan : 1906); Leavenworth Times (Leavenworth, Kan. : 1880).*

US
LEAWOOD SUN, THE. (June 27, 1966)-. Newspaper. English. sw (Published on Wednesdays & Fridays). Sun Publications / Kansas City Jewish Chronicle, 7373 West 107th Street, Overland Park KS 66212-2500. **Tel** (913)381-1010, FAX (913)382-9889. **ED** Mark Reddig & Jack Lovelace. **Circ:** 6,950.

US
LEBANON TIMES, THE. Vol. 16, No. 1 (May 7, 1903)-. Newspaper. English. wk. $9.97 local; $11.01 elsewhere Kansas; $11.50 other. Lebanon Times, PO Box 158, Lebanon KS 66952. **Tel** (913)389-6631. **ED** Phyllis Bell (editor's phone: (913)454-3514). **Photos. Ad Acc.** Full Page (B&W) $252.00. Half Page (B&W) $126.00. **Pub. Size:** Standard. **Circ:** 600. available in microform from Kansas State Historical Society. ***Formed by the union of*** *Lebanon Criterion* ***and*** *Lebanon Journal (Lebanon, Kan.).*

US
LEBO ENTERPRISE, THE. Vol. 1, No. 1 (May 28, 1891)-. Newspaper. English. wk. Lebo Enterprise, PO Drawer A, Burlington KS 66839.

US
LEDGER, THE. English. wk. $17.45. Moundridge Journal, PO Box 720, Moundridge KS 67107. **Tel** (316)345-6353. **Ad Acc. Pr Rev.** ctrl circ. ***Continues*** *Moundridge Journal.*

US
LEOTI STANDARD. Vol. 5, No. 1 (Nov. 7, 1889)-. Newspaper. English. wk. Leoti Standard, PO Box N, Leoti KS 67861. ***Continues*** *Wichita Standard;* ***Absorbed*** *Western Kansan (Leoti, Kan.).*

US
LINCOLN SENTINEL-REPUBLICAN, THE. VFOAT Lincoln Sentinel Republican. Vol. 38, No. 46 (Nov. 26, 1925)-. Newspaper. English. wk. Lincoln Sentinel-Republican, PO Box 67, Lincoln KS 67455. ***Formed by the union of*** *Lincoln Sentinel* ***and*** *Lincoln Republican (Lincoln, Kan.);* ***Absorbed*** *Lincoln County News (Lincoln, Kan. : 1932).*

US
LINDSBORG NEWS-RECORD, THE.
VFOAT Lindsborg News Record. Vol. 42, No. 29 (May 7, 1920)-. Newspaper. English. wk. Bethany Printing Company, 114 South Main Street, Lindsborg KS 67456. ***Continues*** *Lindsborg News and The Lindsborg Record;* ***Absorbed*** *Gypsum Advocate.*

US
LOGAN REPUBLICAN (LOGAN, KAN. : 1911). (THE LOGAN REPUBLICAN.). **VFOAT** Prairie View News. Vol. 5, No. 49 (Feb. 2, 1911)-. Newspaper. English. wk. Logan Republican, PO Box 97, Logan KS 67646-0097. ***Continues*** *Logan Republican and The Prairie View News.*

US
LONGTON ELK CITY NEWS-SUN, THE.
VFOAT News-Sun. Vol. 75, No. 1 (Jan. 4, 1974)-. Newspaper. English. wk. Star Publishing Company / Kansas, PO Box F, Sedan KS 67361. ***Formed by the union of*** *Longton News and Elk Falls Reflector* ***and*** *Elk City Sun (Elk City, Kan. : 1907).*

US/8750-6378
LOUISBURG HERALD, THE. VFOAT Herald. (July 4, 1876)-. Newspaper. English. wk. $19.15. The Louisburg Herald, Box 99, Louisburg KS 66053. **Tel** (913)837-4321, FAX (913)837-4322. **ED** Donna Doyle. **LC** 7845. **Bk Rev**, (Qty: 52). **Photos. Ad Acc, Adv Mgr:** Larry Roth. Full Page (B&W) $346.50. Half Page (B&W) $173.25. Full Page (Color) $376.50. Half Page (Color) $203.25. **Pub. Size:** Broadsheet. **Circ:** 2,000.

US
LUCAS-SYLVAN NEWS. VFOAT Lucas Sylvan News. Vol. 68, No. 68 (Jan. 6, 1966)-. Newspaper. English. wk. $15.89 Kansas; $17.25 US. Lucas-Sylvan News, PO Box 337, Lucas KS 67648. **Photos. Ad Acc, Adv Mgr:** Carolyn Schultz, **Tel** (913)525-6355. Full Page (B&W) $150.40. Half Page (B&W) $75.20. **Pub. Size:** Tabloid. available in microform. ***Formed by the union of*** *Lucas Independent* ***and*** *Sylvan Grove News.*

US/1040-1504
LYONS DAILY NEWS (1929). (LYONS DAILY NEWS.). Vol. 24, No. 68 (May 13, 1929)-. Newspaper. English. da. $36.00 Kansas; $58.00 others. Lyons Publishing Company / Lyons, KS, 210 West Commercial Street, Lyons KS 67554. **ED** John Sauler. **Photos. Ad Acc, Adv Mgr:** Paul Jonet, **Tel** (316)257-2368. Full Page (B&W) $554.00. Half Page (B&W) $277.00. Full Page (Color) $654.00. Half Page (Color) $377.00. **Pub. Size:** Standard. **Wire Svcs.:** AP. **Circ:** 2,564. ***Continues*** *Lyons Daily News and the Lyons Republican;* ***Absorbed*** *Chase Index.*

US
MACKSVILLE ENTERPRISE. (1904)-. Newspaper. English. wk. Enterprise Publishing Company / Kansas, PO Box 187, Macksville KS 67557. ***Formed by the union of*** *Macksville Argus* ***and*** *Macksville Index.*

US
MADISON NEWS (MADISON, KAN. : 1915). (THE MADISON NEWS.). Began in 1911. Newspaper. English. wk. Madison News, PO Box 248, Madison KS 66860. **Tel** (316)437-2433. **Ad Acc. Circ:** 927 (ctrl). ***Continues*** *Live Stock Belt.*

US
MANHATTAN MERCURY (MANHATTAN, KAN. : 1954). (THE MANHATTAN MERCURY.). 46th year, No. 203 (Oct. 3, 1954)-. Newspaper. English. da. Seaton Publishing Company, 318 North 5th Street, Manhattan KS 66502. ***Continues*** *Manhattan Mercury-Chronicle.*

US
MARION COUNTY RECORD (MARION, KAN. : 1957). (MARION COUNTY RECORD.). Vol. 88, No. 1 (Sept. 12, 1957)-. Newspaper. English. wk. Hoch Publishing Company Inc, 117 South 3rd Street, Marion KS 66861. ***Continues*** *Marion Record-Review.*

US
MARYSVILLE ADVOCATE, THE. Vol. 61, No. 1 (April 1946)-. Newspaper. English. wk. $22.00 local; $33.00 other. Advocate Publishing Company Inc, PO Box 271, Marysville KS 66508. **Tel** (913)562-2317, FAX (913)562-5589. **ED** Howard Kessirger. **LC** 7851. **Photos. Ad Acc, Adv Mgr:** Randy Meerian. Full Page (B&W) $567.00. Half Page (B&W) $283.50. Full Page (Color) $637.00. Half Page (Color) $353.50. **Pub. Size:** Standard. **Circ:** 5,600. available on microfilm from Marysville Public Library. ***Continues*** *Advocate and Democrat;* ***Absorbed*** *Marshall County News.*

US/0889-2156
MENNONITE WEEKLY REVIEW. Vol. 1, No. 1 (Sept. 18, 1923)-. Newspaper. English. wk. Herald Publishing Company / Kansas, Box 568, 129 West Sixth, Newton KS 67114. **Tel** (316)283-3670. **ED** Robert M. Schrag. **Bk Rev**, (Qty: 50). **Ad Acc. Circ:** 11,000.

US
MERRIAM SUN, THE. (19??)-. Newspaper. English. sw (Published on Wednesdays & Fridays). Sun Publications / Kansas City Jewish Chronicle, 7373 West 107th Street, Overland Park KS 66212-2500. **Tel** (913)381-1010, FAX (913)382-9889. **ED** Mark Reddig & Jack Lovelace. **Circ:** 16,126.

US
MIAMI REPUBLICAN, THE. (1871)-. Newspaper. English. wk. $29.00. Miami Republican, 121 South Pearl Street, Paola KS 66071. **ED** Phil McLaughlin. **Photos. Ad Acc, Adv Mgr:** Lori, **Tel** (913)294-2311. Full Page (B&W) $554.40. Half Page (B&W) $277.20. Full Page (Color) $624.40. Half Page (Color) $347.20. **Pub. Size:** Broadsheet. **Wire Svcs.:** AP. **Circ:** 6,000. available in microform. ***Continues*** *Miami County Republican;* ***Absorbed*** *Republican Citizen (Paola, Kan.).*

US
MILTONVALE RECORD, THE. Vol. 1, No. 1 (Feb. 1, 1901)-. Newspaper. English. wk. $14.00. Miltonvale Record, 12 Spruce Street, Miltonvale KS 67466. **Tel** (913)427-2680. **ED** Richard Phelps. **Photos. Ad Acc, Adv Mgr:** Richard Phelps. Full Page (B&W) $252.00. Half Page (B&W) $126.00. **Pub. Size:** Broadsheet. **Circ:** 850 (ctrl). available on microfilm.

US
MINNEAPOLIS MESSENGER. VFOAT Messenger. Vol. 9, No. 8 (Sept. 1883)-. Newspaper. English. wk. Minneapolis Messenger, 108 North Concord Street, Minneapolis KS 67467. ***Formed by the union of*** *Sentinel (Minneapolis, Kan.)* ***and*** *Ottawa County Index (Minneapolis, Kan. : 1880).*

US
MINNEOLA RECORD (MINNEOLA, KAN. : 1976). (THE MINNEOLA RECORD.). Vol. 65, No. 1 (Nov. 11, 1976)-. Newspaper. English. wk. $14.69 local; $15.50 other. Minneola Record, PO Box 456, Minneola KS 67865. **Tel** (316)885-4710, FAX (316)635-2643. **ED** Amber Woodruff. **Photos. Ad Acc, Adv Mgr:** Jane Unruh. Full Page (B&W) $130.00. Half Page (B&W) $65.00. **Pub. Size:** Tabloid. available in microform. ***Continues in part*** *Clark County Clipper combined with The Minneola Record.*

US
MOLINE ADVANCE (MOLINE, KAN. : 1978). (THE MOLINE ADVANCE.). Vol. 67, No. 22 (June 1, 1978)-. Newspaper. English. wk. Moline Advance, 125 South Wabash Street, Howard KS 67349. ***Continues*** *Elk County Reporter.*

US
MORNING SUN, THE. Vol. 88, No. 68 (Oct. 1, 1973)-. Newspaper. English. da (313 issues). $81.00 (Pittsburgh, Kansas), $99.00 (Bourbon, Crawford, Cherokee, Barton, and Jasper counties) US; $116.00 other. Morning Sun, PO Drawer H, Pittsburg KS 66762. **Tel** (316)231-2600, FAX (316)231-0645. **ED** Kurt Johnson. **Ad Acc. Circ:** 12,000 (ctrl). ***Continues*** *Pittsburg Headlight-Sun.*

US
MOUNDRIDGE JOURNAL. ***Title Change.*** Vol. 16, No. 8 (Apr. 25, 1902)-. Newspaper. English. wk. Moundridge Journal, PO Box 720, Moundridge KS 67107. **Tel** (316)345-6353. **ED** Jean Herr. **Circ:** 1,275. ***Continues*** *Journal (Moundridge, Kan.).* ***Continued by*** *The Ledger.*

US
MULVANE NEWS, THE. Vol. 1, No. 1 (July 30, 1903)-. Newspaper. English. wk. Mulvane News, 204 West Main Street, Mulvane KS 67110. ***Absorbed*** *Mulvane Record.*

US
NEODESHA SUN-REGISTER, THE. VFOAT Neodesha Sun Register. Vol. 103, No. 69 (Sept. 4, 1986)-. Newspaper. English. wk. $20.85 Kansas; $23.00 others. The Neodesha Derrick, 509 Main Street, Neodesha KS 66757. **Tel** (316)325-3000, FAX (316)325-2636. **ED** JoAnne Harper. **Photos. Ad Acc, Adv Mgr:** Dorothy Campbell. Full Page (B&W) $441.00. Half Page (B&W) $220.50. Full Page (Color) $471.00. Half Page (Color) $250.50. **Pub. Size:** Standard. **Circ:** 1,800. available in microform. ***Formed by the union of*** *Neodesha Register* ***and*** *Neodesha Sun (Neodesha, Kan. : 1979).*

US
NESS COUNTY NEWS. VFOAT Ness County News and Ness City Times. Vol. 1, No. 1 (Nov. 22, 1884)-Vol. 1, No. 52 (Nov. 14, 1885)-. Newspaper. English. wk. $19.00. Ness County News, PO Box C, Ness City KS 67560. **ED** John Clarke. **Photos. Ad Acc.** Full Page (B&W) $239.40. Half Page (B&W) $119.70. Full Page (Color) $299.40. Half Page (Color) $179.70. **Circ:** 2,700. available in microform. ***Absorbed*** *Ness City Times* ***and*** *Ransom Record.*

US
NEWTON KANSAN (NEWTON, KAN. : 1952). (THE NEWTON KANSAN.). Vol. 68, No. 19 (March 1, 1952)-. Newspaper. English. da (except Sundays). $72.71 local Kansas; $94.43 other Kansas; $120.00 other. Newton Kansan, 121 West 6th Street, PO Box 268, Newton KS 67114. **Tel** (316)283-1500, FAX (316)283-2471. **ED** Robert Anderson. Index available. **Bk Rev. Ad Acc. Circ:** 7,800 (ctrl). ***Continues*** *Evening*

Kansan-Republican; ***Absorbed*** *Newton Journal (Newton, Kan. : 1904); Harvey County News Newton, Kan. : 1932.* **Desc:** Local and national news coverage.

US
NORTON DAILY TELEGRAM (NORTON, KAN. : 1928). (THE NORTON DAILY TELEGRAM.). Vol. 21 No. 179 (Sept. 22, 1928)-. Newspaper. English. da. Norton Daily Telegram, 215 South Kansas Street, Norton KS 67654. ***Continues*** *Norton Telegram (Norton, Kan. : 1923);* ***Absorbed*** *Norton Courier.*

US
OAKLEY GRAPHIC, THE. Vol. 1 No. 1 (Nov. 22, 1889)-. Newspaper. English. wk. Graphic Publishing Company, 118 Center Street, Oakley KS 67748. ***Absorbed*** *Logan County Clipper; Winona Press.*

US
OBERLIN HERALD (OBERLIN, KAN. : 1951). (THE OBERLIN HERALD.). Vol. 72, No. 29 (Jan. 4, 1951)-. Newspaper. English. wk. $25.00. Oberlin Herald, 170 South Penn Avenue, Oberlin KS 67749. **Tel** (913)475-2206, FAX (913)475-2800. **ED** Steve Haynes, Connie Gratel (Managing Editor). **Photos. Ad Acc, Adv Mgr:** Stan Chupin. Full Page (B&W) $504.00. Half Page (B&W) $252.00. Full Page (Color) $574.00. Half Page (Color) $322.00. **Pub. Size:** Standard. **Circ:** 2,857. available in microform. ***Continues*** *Oberlin Herald and The Oberlin Times.*

US/0886-9871
OLATHE DAILY NEWS, THE. Vol. 26, No. 236 (Jan. 1, 1986)-. Newspaper. English. da (Tuesday-Sunday). $79.86 trade territory; $124.71 elsewhere Kansas; $138.70 elsewhere US. Olathe Daily News, PO Box 130, Olathe KS 66061. **Tel** (913)764-2211. ***Continues*** *Daily News of Johnson County.*

US/1040-6077
OSAGE COUNTY CHRONICLE (BURLINGAME, KAN. : 1983). (THE OSAGE COUNTY CHRONICLE.). Vol. 120, No. 29 (April 7, 1983)-. Newspaper. English. Fifty-two times a year. $18.50. Incunabula Inc. / Osage County Chronicle, 107 East Santa Fe, PO Box 65, Burlingame KS 66413. **ED** K. Kurt Kessinger. **Bk Rev. Photos. Ad Acc, Adv Mgr:** Kurt Kessinger, **Tel** (913)654-3621. Full Page (B&W) $535.35. Half Page (B&W) $267.75. Full Page (Color) $610.35. Half Page (Color) $342.75. **Pub. Size:** Broadsheet. **Circ:** 5,100. available in microform from Kansas State Historical Society. ***Formed by the union of*** *Enterprise-Chronicle* ***and*** *Citizen-Times (Overbrook, Kan.).*

US
OSAWATOMIE GRAPHIC-NEWS, THE. **VFOAT** Osawatomie Graphic News. Vol. 44, No. 26 (July 23, 1931)-. Newspaper. English. wk (Published on Thursdays). Osawatomie Graphic News, 635 Main Street, Osawatomie KS 66064-1420. **Tel** (913)755-4151, FAX (913)755-6544. **ED** Carol Chitwood. **LC** 7853. **Ad Acc. Circ:** 5,200. ***Continues*** *Osawatomie Graphic and the Osawatomie News.*

US/1040-9033
OSBORNE COUNTY FARMER (OSBORNE, KAN. : 1958). (OSBORNE COUNTY FARMER.). [Osborne Cty. farmer]. Vol. 84, No. 19 (March 5, 1958)-. Newspaper. English. wk. Osborne County Farmer, 210 West Main Street, Osborne KS 67473. ***Continues*** *Osborne Farmer-Journal.*

US
OSKALOOSA INDEPENDENT, THE. **VFOAT** Winchester Press. Vol. 14, No. 38 (May 9, 1874)-. Newspaper. English. wk. Oskaloosa Independent, PO Box 278, Oskaloosa KS 66066. ***Continues*** *Independent (Oskaloosa, Kan.);* ***Absorbed*** *Jefferson County Tribune; Winchester Star.*

US
OTTAWA HERALD, THE. Vol. 20, No. 50 (Jan. 17, 1916)-. Newspaper. English. da. Ottawa Herald, 104 South Cedar Street, Ottawa KS 66067. ***Continues*** *Evening Herald and the Ottawa Daily Republic.*

US
OVERLAND PARK SUN, THE. Vol. 1, No. 1 (May 13, 1965)-. Newspaper. English. sw (Published on Wednesdays & Fridays). Sun Publications / Kansas City Jewish Chronicle, 7373 West 107th Street, Overland Park KS 66212-2500. **Tel** (913)381-1010, FAX (913)382-9889. **ED** Mark Reddig & Jack Lovelace. **Circ:** 23,021.

US
PARSONS NEWS, THE. **VFOAT** Parsons and Labette County News. Vol. 7, No. 40 (March 4, 1948)-. Newspaper. English. wk. $16.95. Parsons News, 1930 Clark Street, Parsons KS 67357. **Tel** (316)421-2990. **ED** Toni Tippet, Ron Riley (Managing Editor). **Bk Rev**, (Qty: 10y). **Photos. Ad Acc, Adv Mgr:** Silva Staten. Full Page (B&W) $312.00. Half Page (B&W) $192.00. Full Page (Color) $450.00. Half Page (Color) $292.00. **Pub. Size:** Tabloid. ***Continues*** *Parsons Visitor;* ***Absorbed*** *St. Paul Journal (St. Paul, Kan.).*

US
PARSONS SUN (PARSONS, KAN. : 1929). (THE PARSONS SUN.). Vol. 56, No. 204 (Jan. 16, 1929)-. Newspaper. English. da. $74.52. Parsons Sun Publishing Company, PO Box 836, 220 South 18th Street, Parsons KS 67357. **Tel** (316)421-2000, FAX (316)421-9214. **ED** Bruce Buchanan. **Ad Acc. Circ:** 7,700 (ctrl). ***Continues*** *Parsons Daily Sun (Parsons, Kan. : 1906).*

US
PHILLIPS COUNTY REVIEW (PHILLIPSBURG, KAN. : 1945). (THE PHILLIPS COUNTY REVIEW.). **VFOAT** Review. Vol. 24, No. 32 (May 17, 1945)-. Newspaper. English. wk. Boyd Printing Company Inc, PO Box 446, Phillipsburg KS 67661. ***Continues*** *Phillips County Review and The Phillips County Leader.*

US/0898-4360
PLAINDEALER (WICHITA, KAN. 1919), THE. (THE PLAINDEALER.). (1919)-. Newspaper. English. Twelve times a year. $12.00. Plaindealer Publishing Inc, 3830 South Meridian, Wichita KS 67217. **Tel** (316)522-8228, FAX (316)522-7989. **ED** Lynne Baker. **Bk Rev. Ad Acc, Adv Mgr:** Linda Powell. **Circ:** 15,300.
Desc: Covers local, national and international events within the labor movement for its readers in South-Central Kansas. It features articles on legislation, the workplace, labor history, labor and the arts, health and issues of concern to retired workers. Deadline for news/advertising, 20th of each month except September issue (August 10th) and December issue (November 10th).

US
PLAINVILLE TIMES (PLAINVILLE, KAN. : 1904). (PLAINVILLE TIMES.). Vol. 1, No. 1 (Dec. 1, 1904)-. Newspaper. English. wk. Plainville Times, 400 West Mill Street, Plainville KS 67663. ***Absorbed*** *Plainville Gazette; Palco News.*

US/1048-3675
PRATT TRIBUNE (PRATT, KAN. : 1964). (THE PRATT TRIBUNE.). Vol. 46, No. 290 (Jan. 27, 1964)-. Newspaper. English. da (Mon.-Fri. and Sat. morning). $91.00. Pratt Tribune, PO Box 909, Pratt KS 67124. **Tel** (316)672-5511. **ED** Charles G Barnes and Donald W Ball. **Ad Acc. Circ:** 3,436. available on microfilm. ***Continues*** *Pratt Daily Tribune;* ***Absorbed*** *Sawyer News (Sawyer, Kan. : 1925).*
Desc: Contains local and wire service news.

US
ROELAND PARK SUN, THE. (Mar. 27, 1969)-. Newspaper. English. sw (Published on Wednesdays & Fridays). Free. Sun Publications / Kansas City Jewish Chronicle, 7373 West 107th Street, Overland Park KS 66212-2500. **Tel** (913)381-1010, FAX (913)382-9889. **ED** Jack Lovelace. **Bk Rev. Ad Acc, Adv Mgr:** Peggy Flora. **Circ:** 102,106.

US
ROOKS COUNTY RECORD (STOCKTON, KAN. : 1931). (ROOKS COUNTY JOURNAL.). 52nd year, No. 15 (April 9, 1931)-. Newspaper. English. wk. Rooks County Journal, PO Box 506, Stockton KS 67669. ***Continues*** *Stockton Review and Rooks County Record;* ***Absorbed*** *Woodston Argus.*

US
RUSH COUNTY NEWS (LA CROSSE, KAN.). (THE RUSH COUNTY NEWS.). Vol. 45, No. 9 (June 5, 1941)-. Newspaper. English. wk. $19.50. Rush County News, PO Box 60, La Crosse KS 67548. **Tel** (913)222-2555, FAX (913)222-2557. **ED** Duane Engel (Editor-in-Chief) and Mary Engel (Managing Editor). **LC** 7824. **Photos. Ad Acc, Adv Mgr:** Duane Engel, **Tel** (913)222-2555. Full Page (B&W) $509.55. Half Page (B&W) $254.00. Full Page (Color) $569.55. Half Page (Color) $314.00. **Pub. Size:** Standard. **Circ:** 2,300 (ctrl). available on microfilm. ***Formed by the union of*** *La Crosse Chieftain* ***and*** *La Crosse Republican (La Crosse, Kan.);* ***Absorbed*** *McCracken Enterprise (McCracken, Kan. : 1904).*

US
RUSSELL DAILY NEWS. Began with May 1948 issue?. Newspaper. English. da. Russell Daily News, 802 North Maple Street, Russell KS 67665. ***Continues*** *Russell County News (Russell, Kan.).*

US
RUSSELL RECORD (RUSSELL, KAN. : 1905). (THE RUSSELL RECORD.). Vol. 33, No. 14 (April 8, 1905)-. Newspaper. English. wk. Russell Record, 802 North Maple Street, Russell KS 67665. ***Continues*** *Record (Russell, Kan.);* ***Absorbed*** *Russell Informer.*

US
SABETHA HERALD (SABETHA, KAN. : 1905). (THE SABETHA HERALD.). Vol. 29, No. 2 (Nov. 30, 1905)-. Newspaper. English. sw. Sabetha Herald, 1024 Main Street, Sabetha KS 66534. ***Continues*** *Sabetha Republican-Herald;* ***Absorbed*** *Sabetha Republican; Sabetha Star.*

US/0745-127X
SALINA JOURNAL, THE. Vol. 40 No. 245 (Oct. 13, 1925)-. Newspaper. English. da. Salina Journal Inc. / Kansas, 333 South 4th Street, PO Box 740, Salina KS 67402. **Tel** (913)823-6363, (800)827-6363. **ED** Harris Rayl. **LC** 7857. **Circ:** 29,244 daily, 32,606 Sunday. ***Formed by the union of*** *Salina Evening Journal* ***and*** *Salina Daily Union.*

US
SCANDIA JOURNAL. Vol. 5, No. 1 (Jan. 7, 1882)-. Newspaper. English. wk. Scandia Journal, PO Box 98, Scandia KS 66966. ***Continues*** *Republic County Journal;* ***Absorbed*** *Scandia Independent.*

US
SEDAN TIMES-STAR, THE. **VFOAT** Sedan Times Star. Vol. 37, No. 48 (Nov. 25, 1909)-. Newspaper. English. wk. Sedan Times-Star, PO Box F, Sedan KS 67361. available on microfilm from University Microfilms International (UMI). ***Continues*** *Weekly Times-Star and Sedan Lance;* ***Absorbed*** *Advertiser-Journal (Sedan, Kan.).*

US
SHERMAN COUNTY HERALD. Vol. 18, No. 34 (Nov. 29, 1933)-. Newspaper. English. wk. Sherman County Herald, 1205 Main Street, Goodland KS 67735. ***Continues*** *Brewster Herald.*

US
SIGNAL-ENTERPRISE, THE. **VFOAT** Signal Enterprise. Vol. 59, No. 46 (Aug. 19, 1943)-. Newspaper. English. wk. Signal-Enterprise, 323 Missouri Street, Alma KS 66401. ***Formed by the union of*** *Alma Signal* ***and*** *Alma Enterprise.*

US
SOLOMON VALLEY POST. Vol. 1, No. 1 (Oct. 30, 1973)-. Newspaper. English. wk. Solomon Valley Post, 114 North Hersey Street, Beloit KS 67420.

US
SOUTH HAVEN NEW ERA (SOUTH HAVEN, KAN. : 1941). (SOUTH HAVEN NEW ERA.). Vol. 56, No. 34 (Oct. 2, 1941)-. Newspaper. English. wk. South Haven New Era, South Haven KS 67140. ***Continues*** *New Era (South Haven, Kan.).*

US/0745-8916
SOUTHWEST DAILY TIMES, THE. Vol. 50, No. 165 (Oct. 30, 1935)-. Newspaper. English. da (Except Saturday). $84.00. Southwest Daily Times, PO Box 889, Liberal KS 67905. **Tel** (316)624-2541. **ED** Jim Elsberry (Editor-in-Chief) and Jeff Burkhead (Managing Editor). **LC** 7844. **Photos. Ad Acc, Adv Mgr:** Jodie Harless. Full Page (B&W) $1,033.20. Half Page (B&W) $516.60. **Pub. Size:** Standard. **Wire Svcs.:** AP. **Circ:** 7,913. ***Continues*** *Liberal News (Liberal, Kan.).*

US
SPEARVILLE NEWS (SPEARVILLE, KAN. : 1899). (THE SPEARVILLE NEWS.). **VFOAT** News. Vol. 1, No. 1 (April 7, 1899)-. Newspaper. English. wk. Spearville News, PO Box 127, Spearville KS 67876.

US
ST. MARYS STAR (ST. MARYS, KAN. : 1978). (THE ST. MARYS STAR.). **VFOAT** Saint Marys Star. 95th Year, No. 23-A (June 6, 1978)-. Newspaper. English. wk. $21.95 St. Marys County; $22.87 Kansas; $25.65 others. St. Marys Star, PO Box 190, Saint Marys KS 66536-0190. **Tel** (913)437-2935, FAX (913)437-2095. **ED** Anita H. Janssen. **Photos. Ad Acc, Adv Mgr:** Carla Opliger. Full Page (B&W) $180.00. Half Page (B&W) $94.00. Full Page (Color) $65.00. Half Page (Color) $65.00. **Pub. Size:** Tabloid. available in microform. ***Continues*** *St. Marys Star and Valley Ho!.*

US
STAFFORD COURIER. Vol. 1, No. 1 (Dec. 18, 1902)-. Newspaper. English. wk. Stafford Courier, PO Box 276, Stafford KS 67578. ***Absorbed*** *Stafford County Republican (Stafford, Kan. : 1896); Hudson Herald; Turon Bulletin.*

US/0888-1189
TILLER AND TOILER (1986), THE. (THE TILLER AND TOILER.). (198?)-. Periodical. English. da. $39.00 (Pawnee and adjoining counties), $41.25 (others). Larned Tiller and Toiler, 115 West Fifth Street, Larned KS 67550-3084. **Tel** (913)285-3111. **ED** John M. Settle. **Ad Acc, Adv Mgr:** Dennis Martin. **Circ:** 3,000 (evening). ***Continues*** *Larned Tiller and Toiler, 0745-4872.*

US/1067-1994
TOPEKA CAPITAL-JOURNAL (TOPEKA, KAN. : MORNING ED.). (THE TOPEKA CAPITAL-JOURNAL.). **VFOAT** Topeka Capital Journal; Topeka Sunday Capital-Journal. Vol. 106, No. 307 (Sept. 2, 1980)-. Newspaper. English. da. Topeka Capital Journal, 616 Jefferson, Topeka KS 66607. **Tel** (913)295-1111, FAX (913)295-1198. **ED** Lee Porter. **Circ:** 67,500. available on microfilm. Documents available from UMI Article Clearinghouse. ***Formed by the union of*** *Topeka Daily Capital* ***and*** *Topeka State Journal (Topeka, Kan. : Daily).*
Ind/Abst Bus. Dateline (Jan. 1, 1992-) [Full Txt.].

US
ULYSSES NEWS, THE. Vol. 46 No. 27 (Oct. 7, 1937)-. Newspaper. English. wk. Ulysses News, PO Box 706, Ulysses KS 67880. **Tel** (316)356-1201. **ED** Keith Stephens. **LC** 7803-X. **Bk Rev**. **Ad Acc**. **Circ:** 3,350 (ctrl). ***Continues*** *Grant County Republican.*
Desc: A community newspaper.

US/0746-4967
UNIVERSITY DAILY KANSAN. Vol. 9, No. 1 (Jan. 16, 1912)-. Newspaper. English. da (published 5 days a week except summer & school breaks). $90.00. University Daily Kansan, 119 Flint Hall, Lawrence KS 66045. **Tel** (913)864-4358, FAX (913)864-5261. **Photos**. **Ad Acc**, **Adv Mgr:** (913)864-7661. Full Page (B&W) $842.55. Half Page (B&W) $383.60. Full Page (Color) $1,037.55. Half Page (Color) $578.60. **Pub. Size:** Broadsheet. **Wire Svcs.:** AP. **Circ:** 15,300. ***Continues*** *Kansas.*

US
VALLEY FALLS VINDICATOR, THE. No. 1 (Dec. 12, 1924)-. Newspaper. English. wk. Valley Falls Vindicator, PO Box 187, Valley Falls KS 66088. ***Continues*** *Farmers' Vindicator.*

US
WAMEGO TIMES (WAMEGO, KAN. : 1917). (THE WAMEGO TIMES.). Vol. 30, No. 28 (Feb. 9, 1917)-. Newspaper. English. wk. $22.60 Kansas; $25.00 other. Wamego Times, PO Box 247, Wamego KS 66547. **Tel** (913)456-7838. ***Continues*** *Wamego Weekly Times.*

US
WASHINGTON COUNTY NEWS (WASHINGTON, KAN.). (WASHINGTON COUNTY NEWS.). Vol. 1, No. 1 (May 21, 1936)-. Newspaper. English. wk. Washington County News / Kansas, PO Box 316, Washington KS 66968.

US
WATERVILLE TELEGRAPH (WATERVILLE, KAN. : 1880). (WATERVILLE TELEGRAPH.). Vol. 11, No. 27 (Jan. 16, 1880)-. Newspaper. English. wk. Waterville Telegraph, PO Box 39, Waterville KS 66548. ***Continues*** *Blue Valley Telegraph.*

US
WATHENA TIMES, THE FRIDAY TROY REPUBLICAN, THE. **VFOAT** Friday Troy Republican. Vol. 40, No. 27 (Nov. 16, 1923)-. Newspaper. English. wk. $13.50. Wathena Times, PO Box 368, Wathena KS 66090. **ED** Dana Foley. **Photos**. **Ad Acc**. Full Page (B&W) $440.00. Half Page (B&W) $200.00. Full Page (Color) $490.00 spot color. Half Page (Color) $250.00 spot color. **Pub. Size:** Standard. **Circ:** 1,850. available on microfilm from University Microfilms International (UMI). ***Continues in part*** *Wathena Times.*

US
WAVERLY GAZETTE (WAVERLY, KAN. : 1898). (THE WAVERLY GAZETTE.). Vol. 2, No. 41 (Jan. 7, 1898)-. Newspaper. English. wk. $28.00. Waverly Gazette, 324 Hudson Street, Burlington KS 66839. **ED** Marle Petterson. **Bk Rev**, (Qty: 10). **Photos**. **Ad Acc**, **Adv Mgr:** B. J. Peterson, **Tel** (316-264-5325. Full Page (B&W) $432.18. Full Page (Color) $507.18. **Pub. Size:** Standard. **Circ:** 1,500. available on microfilm from University Microfilms International (UMI). ***Continues*** *Post-Gazette (Waverly, Kan.).*

US
WELLINGTON DAILY NEWS, THE. **VFOAT** Daily News. Vol. 1, No. 1 (Sept. 2, 1901)-. Newspaper. English. da. Wellington Daily News, PO Box 368, Wellington KS 67152. ***Absorbed*** *Wellington Journal (Wellington, Kan.); Sumner County News.*

US
WEST SEDGWICK COUNTY NEWS-SENTINEL, THE. Vol. 8, No. 33 (March 3, 1977)-. Newspaper. English. wk. West Sedgwick County News-Sentinel, 431 Merchants Street, Belle Plaine KS 67013. ***Formed by the union of*** *West Sedgwick County News* ***and*** *Goddard Sentinel.*

US
WESTERN KANSAS WORLD. 7th Year, No. 4 (March 21, 1985)-. Newspaper. English. wk. $15.00 Kansas; $21.00 others. Western Kansas World, PO Box 218, Wa Keeney KS 67672. **Tel** (913)743-2155. **ED** Jerry Millard. **LC** 7881. **Bk Rev**, (Qty: 6). **Photos**. **Ad Acc**, **Adv Mgr:** Jerry Millard. Full Page (B&W) $283.50. Half Page (B&W) $141.75. Full Page (Color) $348.50. Half Page (Color) $206.75. **Pub. Size:** Standard. **Circ:** 2,375. ***Continues*** *Wa-Keeney Weekly World;* ***Absorbed*** *Trego County Republican; Collyer Advance.*

US
WESTERN STAR (COLDWATER, KAN.). (THE WESTERN STAR.). Began in 1884. Newspaper. English. wk. The Western Star Inc, PO Box 518, Coldwater KS 67029-0518. ***Absorbed*** *Echo-Advocate; Coldwater Enterprise; Stock Journal.*

US
WESTERN TIMES (SHARON SPRINGS, KAN. : 1934). (THE WESTERN TIMES.). Vol. 48, No. 50 (Aug. 30, 1934)-. Newspaper. English. wk. $18.88 Wallace & Bordering counties; $20.98 others in Kansas; $23.00 others. Western Times, 209 North Main Street, Po Box 279, Sharon Springs KS 67758. **Tel** (913)852-4900, FAX (913)852-4804. **ED** Barry Walker (Editor-in-Chief) and Jackie Walker (Managing Editor). **Photos**. **Ad Acc**, **Adv Mgr:** Jackie Walker or Julie Samuelson. **Pub. Size:** Standard. **Circ:** 1,265. ***Continues*** *Western Times and The Wallace County News.*

US
WESTMORELAND RECORDER (WESTMORELAND, KAN. : 1919). (WESTMORELAND RECORDER.). Vol. 35, No. 7 (May 8, 1919)-. Newspaper. English. wk. Westmoreland Recorder, PO Box 128, Westmoreland KS 66549-0128. ***Continues*** *Westmoreland Recorder and The Westmoreland Signal.*

US/1046-3127
WICHITA EAGLE (1989), THE. (WICHITA EAGLE.). (Sept. 3, 1989)-. Newspaper. English. da. $107.64 (US), $79.04 (Kansas & Oklahoma & Missouri), Sunday only; $193.44 (US), $162.24 (Kansas & Oklahoma & Missouri), Daily; $179.40 Morning & Sunday Carrier; $301.08 (US); $250.64 (Kansas & Oklahoma & Missouri), Daily & Sunday Mail subscription. The Wichita Eagle-Beacon, Box 820, Attention: Mail Desk, Wichita KS 67201. **Tel** (800)825-6397. available on an online database (file 723/Full-Text) from DIALOG. ***Continues*** *Wichita Eagle-Beacon, 0892-872X.*
Ind/Abst PROMT.

US/1048-3365
WICHITA JOURNAL. Vol. 91, No. 40 (Oct. 5, 1974)-. Newspaper. English. wk (published on Thursdays). $31.71. American Publishing Co. of Kansas Inc., PO Box 190, Derby KS 67037. **Tel** (316)788-2835, FAX (316)788-0854. **ED** Jimmie R. Stephenson, Mary Gardner (Managing Editor). **Photos**. **Ad Acc**, **Adv Mgr:** Faye Osenbaugh. Full Page (B&W) $364.00. Half Page (B&W) $182.00. Full Page (Color) $439.00. Half Page (Color) $257.00. **Pub. Size:** Tabloid. **Wire Svcs.:** AP. ctrl circ. ***Continues*** *Harper's Wichita Journal.*

US
WILSON COUNTY CITIZEN. Vol. 3, No. 27 (June 6, 1873)-. Newspaper. English. sw. Wilson County Citizen, 706 Madison Street, Fredonia KS 66736. **ED** J S Gilmore. ***Continues*** *Neodesha Citizen;* ***Absorbed*** *Fredonia Chronicle; Fredonia Daily Citizen.*

US
WILSON WORLD, THE. Vol. 36, No. 18 (March 6, 1913)-. Newspaper. English. wk. Wilson World, PO Box 526, Wilson KS 67490. ***Continues*** *Wilson Echo.*

US/0889-6747
WINFIELD DAILY COURIER (1931), THE. (THE WINFIELD DAILY COURIER.). Vol. 91, No. 10 (Apr. 0, 1931)-. Newspaper. English. ir (312 issues). $60.95 Kansas residents, $84.95 other. Winfield Daily Courier, PO Box 543, Winfield KS 67156. **Tel** (316-221-1050. available on microfilm from University Microfilms International (UMI). ***Continues*** *Winfield Daily Courier and The Winfield Daily Free Press.*

US
WYANDOTTE WEST. (1968)-. Newspaper. English. wk. $17.49. Wyandotte West, PO Box 12003, Kansas City KS 66102. **ED** Murrel W. Bland and Jack Root (News Editor). **Photos**. **Ad Acc**, **Adv Mgr:** Carol A. Bland, **Tel** (915)788-5565. Full Page (B&W) $627.20. Half Page (B&W) $313.60. Full Page (Color) $1,027.20. Half Page (Color) $713.60. **Pub. Size:** Tabloid. **Circ:** 3,000. available in microform from Kansas State Historical Society.

US
YATES CENTER NEWS (YATES CENTER, KAN. : 1948). (THE YATES CENTER NEWS.). Vol. 70, No. 38 (Jan. 1, 1948)-. Newspaper. English. wk. $20.00 US; $30.00 North America; $25.00 other. Yates Center News, PO Box 285, Yates Center KS 66783. **Ad Acc**. **Circ:** 2,100 (ctrl). available on microfilm. ***Continues*** *Yates Center News and the Woodson County Post;* ***Absorbed*** *Toronto Republican.*

KENTUCKY

US
ADVANCE-YEOMAN. **VFOAT** Advance Yeoman; Weekly Advance Combined with the Ballard Yeoman; Weekly Advance-the Ballard Yeoman. Vol. 1, No. 1 (Sept. 5, 1947)-. Newspaper. English. wk. $20.00 in county; $25.00 others. Advance-Yeoman, PO Box 8, Wickliffe KY 42087. **Tel** (502)335-3193, FAX (502)335-3560. **ED** Teresa Sullivan. **Photos**. **Ad Acc**, **Adv Mgr:** Brian Wyatt, **Tel** (502)442-7389. **Pub. Size:** Standard. available in microform. ***Formed by the union of*** *Ballard Yeoman* ***and*** *Weekly Advance (La Center, KY.).*

US/0889-0056
ADVOCATE-MESSENGER, THE. [Advocate-messenger]. **VFOAT** Advocate Messenger; Kentucky Advocate. Vol. 112, No. 162 (Jan. 3, 1978)-. Newspaper. English. da. $127.60. The Advocate Messenger, Box 149, Danville KY 40422. **Tel** (606)236-2551. **DD** 071. ***Continues*** *Danville Advocate-Messenger.*

US
BATH COUNTY NEWS-OUTLOOK. **VFOAT** Bath County News Outlook; News Bath County Outlook. (192?)-. Newspaper. English. wk. $12.00 Bath County; $16.00 others in Kentucky; $18.00 others. Bath County News-Outlook, PO Box 577, Owingsville KY 40360. **Tel** (606)674-2181. **ED** Ken Metz. **Photos**. **Ad Acc**, **Adv Mgr:** Margaret Metz. Full Page (B&W) $535.50. Half Page (B&W) $267.75. Full Page (Color) $625.50. Half Page (Color) $357.75. **Pub. Size:** Broadsheet. ***Continues*** *Owingsville Outlook.*

US
BEREA CITIZEN, THE. 60th year, No. 1 (July 3, 1958)-. Newspaper. English. wk. Berea Citizen, PO Box 207, Berea KY 40403. ***Continues*** *Citizen (Berea, Ky.).*

US/0891-2327
BIG SANDY NEWS (LOUISA, KY. : 1974). (THE BIG SANDY NEWS.). Vol. 88, No. 51 (May 2, 1974)-. Newspaper. English. wk (Wed.). $15.50 Kentuky; $18.00 other. Big Sandy Publishing Company, PO Box 766, Ricky Skaggs Boulevard, Louisa KY 41230-0766. **Tel** (606)638-4581, FAX (606)638-9949. **ED** Marjorie P. Hale, Jerry Pennington (Managing Editor). **Photos**. **Ad Acc**. Full Page (B&W) $283.50. Half Page (B&W) $144.90. Full Page (Color) $358.50. Half Page (Color) $219.90. **Pub. Size:** Standard. **Circ:** 4,300. available in microform. ***Continues*** *Big Sandy News and the Lawrence County Recorder.*

US
BOONE COUNTY RECORDER, THE. Vol. 1, No. 1, (Sept. 23, 1875)-. Newspaper. English. Fifty-two times a year. $18.02 Boone County; $20.14 surrounding counties in Kentucky; $23.32 others in Kentucky; $27.56 others in US; $34.98 others. Boone County Recorder, 7736 US 42, Suite D4, Florence KY 41042. **Tel** (606)283-0404, FAX (606)283-2536. **ED** Amy Charley. **Ad Acc**, **Adv Mgr:** Sandra Cupps. **Circ:** 7,000 (ctrl).

US
BOONEVILLE SENTINEL. **VFOAT** Sentinel. Vol. 1, No. 1 (Dec. 9, 1976)-. Newspaper. English. wk. $12.00. Booneville Sentinel, PO Box 43, Booneville KY 41314. **Tel** (606)593-6627.

US/0747-0282
BOURBON COUNTY CITIZEN, THE. Vol. 1, No. 1 (Jan. 21, 1984)-. Newspaper. English. wk. Bourbon County Citizen, 123 West 8th Street, PO Box 158, Paris KY 40361. **Tel** (606)987-1870.

US/1040-9017
BOURBON TIMES (PARIS, KY.). (THE BOURBON TIMES.). Vol. 1, No. 1 (July 6, 1988)-. Newspaper. English. wk. Bourbon Times Inc., 1306 Main Street, PO Box 777, Paris KY 40361. **Tel** (606)987-6397.

US
BRACKEN COUNTY NEWS, THE. (1927)-. Newspaper. English. wk. $12.00 Bracken County; $15.00 elsewhere Kentucky; $18.00 other. Bracken County News, PO Box 68, Brooksville KY 41004. **ED** Libby Estill. **Photos**. **Ad Acc**, **Adv Mgr:** Kathy Bay, **Tel** (606)735-2198. Full Page (B&W) $315.00. Half Page (B&W) $157.50. Full Page (Color) $315.00 plus $75.00 per color. Half Page (Color) $157.50 plus $75.00 per color. **Pub. Size:** Standard. **Circ:** 2,750.

US/0745-7006
BUTLER COUNTY BANNER. ***Title Change.*** **VFOAT** Banner. Vol. 1, No. 1 (Nov. 30, 1982)-Vol.10, No. 30 (June 24, 1992). Newspaper. English. wk. Butler County Banner, PO Box 219, Morgantown KY 42261. **Tel** (502)526-4151. ***Merged with*** *Green River Republican* ***to form*** *Butler County Banner and the Green River Republican, 1064-895X.*

●US/1064-895X
BUTLER COUNTY BANNER AND THE GREEN RIVER REPUBLICAN, THE. **VFOAT** Green River Republican and the Butler County Banner; Butler County Banner. Vol. 10, No. 3 (July 1, 1992)-. Newspaper. English. wk. $8.00 (Butler & surrounding counties), $10.00 (KY), $12.00 (elsewhere). Butler County Banner, PO Box 219, Morgantown KY 42261. **Tel** (502)526-4151. ***Formed by the union of*** *Butler County Banner, 0745-7006* ***and*** *Green River Republican.*

US
CADIZ RECORD, THE. (18??)-. Newspaper. English. wk. $18.00 in county; $20.00 Kentucky; $28.00 US. Cadiz Record, PO Box 311, Nunn Blvd., Cadiz KY 42211. **Tel** (502)522-6605, FAX (502)522-3001. **ED** Matt

Kentucky

Sanders. **Photos. Ad Acc, Adv Mgr:** Jan Witty. Full Page (B&W) $470.85. Half Page (B&W) $240.90. Full Page (Color) $475.00 plus color charge. Half Page (Color) $240.90 plus color charge. **Pub. Size:** Broadsheet. available in microform. **Continues** Kentucky Telephone.

US
CALDWELL COUNTY TIMES. Title Change. (19??-1992). Newspaper. English. wk. Caldwell County Times, 607 West Washington Street, Princeton KY 42445. **Merged with** Princeton Leader **to form** Times-Leader (Princeton, Ky.).

US
CAMPBELL COUNTY RECORDER, THE. Vol. 4, No. 23 (Jan. 21, 1982)-. Newspaper. English. wk. Campbell County Recorder, 654 Highland Avenue/Suite 27, Fort Thomas KY 41075. **Continues** Campbell County News.

US
CARLISLE COUNTY NEWS, THE. Began in 1894. Newspaper. English. wk. Carlisle County News, PO Box 309, Bardwell KY 42023-0309.

US
CARLISLE MERCURY, THE. Began in Jan. 1867. Newspaper. English. wk. Carlisle Mercury, 234 North Locust Street, Carlisle KY 40311.

US
CASEY COUNTY NEWS, THE. (Mar. 17, 1904)-. Newspaper. English. wk. Casey County News, PO Box 40, Liberty KY 42539. **Tel** (606)787-7171.

US
CENTRAL KENTUCKY NEWS-JOURNAL. VFOAT Central Kentucky News Journal. Vol. 1, No. 1 (Sept. 6, 1974)-. Newspaper. English. sw. $29.95 Taylor, Green, and Adair counties, Kentucky; $40.25 other Kentucky; $47.00 other. Central Kentucky News Journal, PO Box 1138, Campbellsville KY 42718. **Tel** (502)465-8111, FAX (502)465-2500. **ED** Stan McKinney. **Bk Rev. Ad Acc, Adv Mgr:** Cheryl Caulk. ctrl circ. available on microfilm. **Formed by the union of** News-Journal (Campbellsville, KY.) **and** Central Kentucky News.

US
CENTRAL RECORD (LANCASTER, KY.). (THE CENTRAL RECORD.). Newspaper. English. wk. Central Record, 106 Richmond Street, Lancaster KY 40444.

US
CITIZEN-ADVERTISER, THE. VFOAT Citizen Advertiser. Vol. 3, No. 21 (Sept. 22, 1966)-. Newspaper. English. wk. Citizen-Advertiser, 123 West 8th Street, Paris KY 40361. **Continues** Paris Advertiser and Kentuckian-Citizen.

US
CITIZEN-TIMES, THE. VFOAT Citizen Times. (Oct. 10, 1918)-. Newspaper. English. wk. $12.00 (counties); $15.00 others. Citizen Times, PO Box 308, Scottsville KY 42164. **Tel** (502)237-3441, FAX (502)237-4840. **ED** Robert B. Pitchford. **Ad Acc, Adv Mgr:** Quinn Wood. **Pub. Size:** Standard. **Circ:** 5,400. **Formed by the union of** Citizen (Scottsville, Ky.) **and** Allen County Times (Scottsville, Ky.).

US
CITIZEN VOICE & TIMES. VFOAT Citizen Voice and Times. Vol. 66, No. 1 (Jan. 3, 1985)-. Newspaper. English. wk. Citizen Voice & Times, 108 Court Street, Irvine KY 40336. **Continues** Estill County Citizen Voice & Times.

US
CLAY CITY TIMES, THE. Vol. 6, No. 36 (Nov. 28, 1901)-. Newspaper. English. wk. $11.08 Powell County; $14.31 Kentucky; $18.50 other. Jerlene Rose, PO Box 606, Clay Rose KY 40312. **Absorbed** Menifee County Journal.

US/0899-1839
COMMONWEALTH-JOURNAL (SOMERSET, KY.), THE. (THE COMMONWEALTH-JOURNAL.). VFOAT Commonwealth-Journal. Vol. 1, No. 1 (Jan. 3, 1966)-. Newspaper. English. da. $76.96. Commonwealth-Journal, 110-112 East Mount Vernon Street, Somerset KY 42501. **Bk Rev. Photos. Ad Acc, Adv Mgr:** David Trimble, **Tel** (606)678-8191. Full Page (B&W) $7.50 per inch. Half Page (B&W) $7.50 per inch. Full Page (Color) $85.00 one color. Half Page (Color) $85.00 one color. **Pub. Size:** Standard. **Wire Svcs.:** AP. **Formed by the union of** Somerset Journal (Somerset, Ky.) Commonwealth (Somerset, Ky.) **and** Commonwealth (Somerset, Ky.).

US
COURIER-JOURNAL (LOUISVILLE, KY. : KENTUCKY ED.). (THE COURIER-JOURNAL.). VFOAT Courier Journal. Vol. 248, No. 133 (May 13, 1979)-. Newspaper. English. da. Price varies. Louisville Courier Journal, 525 West Broadway, Louisville KY 40202. **Tel** (800)765-4011. available on microfilm from University Microfilms International (UMI); and University Microfilms International (UMI) from UMI Article Clearinghouse. **Continues** Courier-Journal (Louisville, KY. : 1869 : Daily).
Ind/Abst Bus. Dateline; PROMT.

US
CRITTENDEN PRESS, THE. (1919)-. Newspaper. English. wk. Crittenden Press, PO Box 191, Marion KY 42064-0191. **Tel** (502)965-3191. **Ad Acc. Circ:** 4,500. **Continues** Crittenden Record-Press (Marion, Ky. : 1909); **Absorbed** Marion Reporter (Marion, Ky. : 1954).

US
CUMBERLAND COUNTY NEWS, THE. (19??)-. Newspaper. English. wk. $12.98. Cumberland County News, PO Box 307, Burkesville KY 42717-0307. **ED** Joe Trotter. **Photos. Ad Acc, Adv Mgr:** Bruce Henson, **Tel** (502)864-3891. Full Page (B&W) $327.60. Half Page (B&W) $182.70. Full Page (Color) $412.60. Half Page (Color) $267.70. **Pub. Size:** Broadsheet. **Continues** Cumberland News (Burkesville, KY.).

US
CYNTHIANA DEMOCRAT, THE. Began in 1868. Newspaper. English. wk. Cynthiana Democrat, PO Box 160, Cynthiana KY 41031. **Absorbed** Log Cabin (Cynthiana, Ky.); Robertson County News.

US/0744-6837
DAILY INDEPENDENT (ASHLAND, KY), THE. (THE DAILY INDEPENDENT.). VFOAT Sunday Independent. Vol. 86, No. 74 (March 1, 1982)-. Newspaper. English. da. (except Christmas). $72.45. Ashland Publishing Indpendent, PO Box 311, Ashland KY 41101. **Tel** (606)329-1717. **ED** Paul Sierer. **Circ:** 23,446. **Continues** Ashland Daily Independent; **Absorbed** Ashland Daily Commercial.

US/1041-7095
DAILY NEWS (MIDDLESBORO, KY. 1981). (DAILY NEWS.). Vol. 69, No. 69 (June 17, 1981)-. Newspaper. English. da. Middlesboro Daily News, PO Box 579, Middlesboro KY 40965. **Tel** (606)248-1010. **Continues** Middlesboro Daily News.

US
DAWSON SPRINGS PROGRESS, THE. (19??)-. Newspaper. English. wk. Dawson Springs Progress, PO Box 404, Dawson Springs KY 42408. **Tel** (502)797-3271. **ED** Jed Dillingham and Scott Dillingham (Managing Editor). **Photos. Ad Acc, Adv Mgr:** Faye Winfrey. Full Page (B&W) $302.40. Half Page (B&W) $158.40. Full Page (Color) $392.40 (one color). Half Page (Color) $248.40 (one color). **Pub. Size:** Broadsheet. **Circ:** 3,000. available in microform.

US
DIXIE NEWS. Began in 1962. Newspaper. English. wk. Dixie News, 6603 Dixie Highway, Florence KY 41042.

US
EDMONSON NEWS. Vol. 6, No. 1 (Sept. 22, 1932)-. Newspaper. English. wk. Edmonson News, PO Box 69, Brownsville KY 42210. **Continues** Edmonson County News.

US/0891-8694
FALMOUTH OUTLOOK, THE. VFOAT Outlook. Vol. 1, No. 1 (June 21, 1907)-. Newspaper. English. Fifty-two times a year. $19.50 in county; $26.50 Kentucky; $33.00 US. Outlook Publications, 210 Main Street, Falmouth KY 41040. **Tel** (606)654-3333, FAX (606)654-4365. **ED** Deborrah Dennie. **Photos. Ad Acc.** Full Page (B&W) $548.25. Half Page (B&W) $274.13. **Pub. Size:** Standard. **Pr Rev. Circ:** 4,650 (ctrl). available on microfilm.
Desc: News stories, club meetings, pictures, and general information covering Pendleton County and the surrounding area.

US
FLEMINGSBURG GAZETTE (FLEMINGSBURG, KY. : 1978). (FLEMINGSBURG GAZETTE.). April 12, 1978-. Newspaper. English. wk. $17.00 Fleming County, Kentucky; $25.00 other Kentucky; $30.00 other. Flemingsburg Gazette, PO Box 32, Flemingsburg KY 41041. **Tel** (606)845-9211. **Continues** Fleming Gazette.

US
FLOYD COUNTY TIMES. Newspaper. English. wk. Prestonburg Publishing Company, PO Box 391, Prestonburg KY 41653.

US
FRANKLIN FAVORITE, THE. Newspaper. English. wk. Franklin Favorite, 103 North High Street, Franklin KY 42134.

US
FULTON LEADER. (Oct. 12, 1989)-. Newspaper. English. sw. Fulton Publishing Company, PO Box 327, Fulton KY 42041. **Continues** Fulton Daily Leader.

US
GALLATIN COUNTY NEWS, THE. (1926)-. Newspaper. English. wk. Gallatin County News, 211 3rd Street, Warsaw KY 41095.

US/0886-5965
GEORGETOWN GRAPHIC. Title Change. Vol. 35, No. 50 (Nov. 7, 1985)-Vol. 43, No. 27 (July 3, 1993). Newspaper. English. wk. Georgetown Graphic, PO Box 808, Georgetown KY 40324. **Continues** Graphic (Georgetown, KY.). **Merged with** Georgetown News (Georgetown, Ky. : 1993) **to form** Georgetown News-Graphic.

US
GEORGETOWN NEWS & TIMES, THE. Title Change. VFOAT Georgetown News and Times. (Jan. 18, 1978)-Vol. 125, No. 52 (Dec. 30, 1992). Newspaper. English. wk. Georgetown News and Times, 218 East Main Street, Georgetown KY 40324. **Formed by the union of** Georgetown News (Georgetown, Ky.) **and** Georgetown Times (Georgetown, Ky. : 1884). **Continued by** Georgetown News (Georgetown, Ky. : 1993).

US
GLASGOW DAILY TIMES, THE. Vol. 92, No. 106 (April 2, 1957)-. Newspaper. English. da. Glasgow Publishing Corporation, PO Box 179, Glasgow KY 42141. **Tel** (502)678-5171. **Continues** Glasgow Times and the Evening Journal.

US
GLASGOW REPUBLICAN, THE. Vol. 4, No. 40 (June 5, 1896)-. Newspaper. English. wk. Glasgow Republican, PO Box 399, Glasgow KY 42142-0179. **Tel** (502)678-5171, FAX (502)678-5052. **ED** Frances Bastien. **Ad Acc. Circ:** 949. **Continues** Glasgow Weekly Republican.

US
GLEANER (HENDERSON, KY.). (THE GLEANER.). 88th Yr., No. 203 (April 28, 1973)-. Newspaper. English. da. The Gleaner, 455 Klutey Park Plaza, Henderson KY 42420. **Continues** Gleaner-Journal.
Ind/Abst Seventh-Day Adventist Period. Index (1971-).

US
GRANT COUNTY NEWS (WILLIAMSTOWN, KY.). (THE GRANT COUNTY NEWS.). Began in 1906. Newspaper. English. wk. Grant County News, PO Box 247, Williamstown KY 41097. **Tel** (606)824-3344.

US
GRAYSON COUNTY NEWS-GAZETTE. VFOAT Grayson County News Gazette. Vol. 1, No. 1 (July 21, 1977)-. Newspaper. English. wk. Grayson County News-Gazette, 208 South Main Street, Leitchfield KY 42754. **Formed by the union of** Grayson County News (Leitchfield, KY.) **and** Leitchfield Gazette.

US
GRAYSON JOURNAL-ENQUIRER. VFOAT Grayson Journal Enquirer. Vol. 51, No. 36 (Sept. 6, 1973)-. Newspaper. English. wk. $15.00 (Carter County), $28.00 (Kentucky), $30.00 (others). Grayson Journal-Enquirer, Box 578, Grayson KY 41143. **Tel** (606)474-5101. **Continues** Journal-Enquirer.

US
GREEN RIVER REPUBLICAN. Title Change. Vol.111, No. 23 (1889)-(June 24, 1992). Newspaper. English. wk. Green River Republican, PO Box 369, Morgantown KY 42261. **Merged with** Butler County Banner, 0745-7006 **to form** Butler County Banner and the Green River Republican, 1064-895X.

US
GREENSBURG RECORD-HERALD (1941). (GREENSBURG RECORD-HERALD.). 46th Year, No. 16 (April 18, 1941)-. Newspaper. English. wk. Greensburg Record-Herald, PO Box 130, Greensburg KY 42743. **Continues** Record-Herald (Greensburg, Ky.).

US
HANCOCK CLARION, THE. Vol. 1, No. 1 (Mar. 4, 1893)-. Newspaper. English. wk. $15.00 Hancock County; $19.00 others. Hancock Clarion, Main Street, PO Box 39, Hawesville KY 42348. **Tel** (502)927-6945, FAX (502)927-6947. **ED** Donn K. Wimmer. **Photos. Ad Acc, Adv Mgr:** Kathy Sabelhaus. **Pub. Size:** Broadsheet. **Circ:** 4,000.

US/1041-7109
HARLAN DAILY ENTERPRISE, THE. (Aug. 3, 1928)-. Newspaper. English. da. $105.00. Harlan Daily Enterprise, PO Box E, Harlan KY 40831. **Tel** (606)573-4510. **Continues** Harlan Enterprise (Harlan, KY.).

US
HARRODSBURG HERALD, THE. Newspaper. English. wk. Harrodsburg Herald, PO Box 68, Harrodsburg KY 40330.

Kentucky

US/1075-4628
HART COUNTY NEWS-HERALD. Vol. 1, No. 1 (Sept. 5, 1989)-. Newspaper. English. wk. Hart County Herald, PO Box 340, Horse Cave KY 42749-0340. **Tel** (502)786-1929, FAX (502)786-4470. **ED** A.C. Wilson Jr., Daniel Martin (Managing Editor). **Photos. Ad Acc.** Full Page (B&W) $3.45 per column inch. Half Page (B&W) $3.45 per column inch. Full Page (Color) $3.45 per colum inch plus $100.00. Half Page (Color) $3.45 per column inch plus $100.00. **Pub. Size:** Standard. *Formed by the union of Hart County News and Hart County Herald.*

US
HAZARD HERALD-VOICE. VFOAT Hazard Herald Voice; Herald-Voice; Herald Voice; Hazard Herald. Vol. 73, No. 51 (March 1, 1984)-. Newspaper. English. Fifty-two times a year. $15.00. Hazard Herald-Voice, PO Box 869, Hazard KY 41702. **Tel** (606)436-5771, FAX (606)436-3140. **ED** Jack Thomas. **Bk Rev. Photos. Ad Acc, Adv Mgr:** Wilma Thomas. Full Page (B&W) $712.00. Half Page (B&W) $375.00. Full Page (Color) $805.00. Half Page (Color) $470.00. **Pub. Size:** Standard. **Circ:** 4,985. *Continues Herald-Voice (Hazard, Ky.).*

US/0883-752X
HAZARD TIMES, THE. Began in 1985. Newspaper. English. wk. $10.50. The Hazard Times, PO Box 1239, Hazard KY 41701. **Tel** (606)439-5189. **ED** Billy Kilburn. **Bk Rev. Ad Acc. Circ:** 9,763.
Desc: A publication enhancing the life in Appalachian while keeping the residents up on current events.

US
HERALD LEDGER. Vol. 61, No. 1 (Aug. 4, 1966)-. Newspaper. English. wk. $12.72 Eddyville KY; $14.31 other Kentucky; $15.12 other. Herald Ledger, 116 Commerce Street, Eddyville KY 42038. **Tel** (502)388-2269. *Formed by the union of Lyon County Herald and Lakeside Ledger.*

US/0889-9711
HERALD-NEWS (EDMONTON, KY.), THE. (THE HERALD-NEWS.) VFOAT Herald News. 88th Year, No. 52 (July 15, 1986)-. Newspaper. English. sw. $14.98. Herald-News / Edmonton, PO Box 87, Edmonton KY 42129. **Tel** (502)432-3291, FAX (502)432-4414. **ED** Clay Scott. **Photos. Ad Acc, Adv Mgr:** Kandis Shive. Full Page (B&W) $308.70. Half Page (B&W) $173.25. **Pub. Size:** Broadsheet. **Circ:** 2,447. *Continues Edmonton Herald-News.*

US
HICKMAN COUNTY GAZETTE, THE. 1904-. Newspaper. English. wk. Hickman County Gazette, PO Box 100, Clinton KY 42031. *Continues Twice a Week Gazette.*

US
HICKMAN COURIER, THE. (1859)-. Newspaper. English. wk. Hickman Courier, PO Box 70, Hickman KY 42050-0070.

US/8750-7609
INTERIOR JOURNAL (1984). (THE INTERIOR JOURNAL.) Vol. 125, No. 40 (Nov. 1, 1984)-. Newspaper. English. wk. $12.75 Kentucky; $24.75 other. The Interior Journal, PO Box 196, Stanford KY 40484. **Tel** (606)365-2104. **ED** Thomas J. Moore. **Photos. Ad Acc, Adv Mgr:** Sharmon P. Moore. Full Page (B&W) $396.90. Half Page (B&W) $198.45. Full Page (Color) $446.90. Half Page (Color) $248.45. **Pub. Size:** Broadsheet. **Circ:** 4,314 (ctrl). available in microform. *Continues Interior Journal & Lincoln County Post, 8750-1554.*
Desc: General interest newspaper.

US
JESSAMINE JOURNAL (NICHOLASVILLE, KY.). (THE JESSAMINE JOURNAL.) (188?)-. Newspaper. English. wk. Jessamine Journal, 131 East Brown Street, Nicholasville KY 40356. *Continues Journal-Courier (Nicholasvilke, KY.); Absorbed Jessamine News-Week; Jessamine County Star.*

US
JOURNAL-ENTERPRISE, THE. VFOAT Journal Enterprise. Vol. 41, No. 37 (July 1, 1943)-. Newspaper. English. wk. $12.00 Webster & surrounding counties; $15.00 Kentucky; $18.00 other. Journal-Enterprise, PO Box 190, Providence KY 42450. **Tel** (502)667-2068, FAX (502)667-9160. **ED** Charles Hust. **Photos. Ad Acc.** Full Page (B&W) $451.50. Half Page (B&W) $220.50. Full Page (Color) $511.50. Half Page (Color) $280.50. **Pub. Size:** Standard. **Circ:** 4,660. *Formed by the union of Dixon Journal and Providence Enterprise; Absorbed Clay Tribune.*

US
KENTON COUNTY RECORDER, THE. VFOAT The Recorder Newspapers and the News Enterprise; The Recorder Newspapers. Vol. 12 No. 5 (Aug. 1, 1991)-. Newspaper. English. wk. Recorder Newspapers, 7736 US 42, Suite D4, Florence KY 41042. *Continues Kenton County Recorder and News Enterprise.*

US
KENTUCKY NEW ERA (HOPKINSVILLE, KY. : DAILY). (KENTUCKY NEW ERA.) Vol. 57, No. 98 (March 12, 1945)-. Newspaper. English. da. $108.00. Kentucky New Era, PO Box 729, 1618 East 9th Street, Hopkinsville KY 42240. **Tel** (502)886-4444. **Ad Acc.** *Continues Daily Kentucky New Era.*

US/8750-0760
KENTUCKY STANDARD, THE. Vol. 1, No. 1 (Dec. 15, 1900)-. Newspaper. English. sw. $30.00 Nelson County; $37.00 Kentucky; $50.00 other. Standard Publishing Company Inc. / Kentucky, 110 West Stephen Foster Avenue, Bardstown KY 40004. **Tel** (502)348-9003. **ED** Teresa Englert and David Greer. **Circ:** 8,200.

US/8750-3689
LAKE NEWS, THE. Newspaper. English. wk. $9.50. Lake News, PO Box 498, Calvert City KY 42029. **Tel** (502)395-5858. **ED** Loyd W Ford. **Bk Rev. Ad Acc. Circ:** 4,500.
Desc: General interest newspaper located in a top tourist and resort area adjacent to the largest developed man-made lake in the world.

US
LARUE COUNTY HERALD NEWS, THE. VFOAT Herald News. Vol. 82, No. 41 (March 23, 1967)-. Newspaper. English. wk. $15.00, $13.95 (Kentucky), $11.55 (local). LaRue County Herald News, PO Box 239, Hodgenville KY 42748. **Tel** (502)358-3118. **ED** Celin C McDonald. **Bk Rev. Ad Acc. Circ:** 4,000 (ctrl). *Continues Herald-News (Hodgenville, KY.).*

US
LEBANON ENTERPRISE, THE. (18??)-. Newspaper. English. wk. Lebanon Enterprise, PO Box 679, Lebanon KY 40033. **Tel** (502)692-2118. *Absorbed Marion Falcon.*

US
LEDGER-INDEPENDENT, THE. VFOAT Ledger Independent. (April 1, 1969)-. Newspaper. English. wk. $79.00 Mason, Fleming, Bracken, Robertson, Lewis, Adams, & Brown; $99.00 others. Maysville Publishing Corporation, PO Box 518, Maysville KY 41056. **Tel** (606)564-9091. *Continues Public Ledger The Daily Independent.*

US
LESLIE COUNTY NEWS (HYDEN, KY.). (THE LESLIE COUNTY NEWS.) Vol. 1 (Dec. 1963)-. Newspaper. English. wk. $15.75 Leslie County; $21.00 other. Leslie County News, PO Box 967, Hyden KY 41749. **Tel** (606)672-2841.

US/0899-1820
LETCHER COUNTY COMMUNITY NEWS-PRESS. VFOAT Letcher County Community News Press. Vol. 29, No. 18 (May 3, 1988)-. Newspaper. English. wk. $26.00. Superior Printing & Publishing Company, PO Box 156, Cromona KY 41810. *Continues Letcher County Community Press.*

US
LEWIS COUNTY HERALD. Vol. 61, No. 1 (Apr. 18, 1957)-. Newspaper. English. wk. Free, Kentucky and Ohio; $8.00 other. Lewis County Herald, 206 Main Street, Vanceburg KY 41179. *Formed by the union of Nezperce Herald; Absorbed Lewis County Register.*

US
LEWIS COUNTY HERALD. Began in 1924. Newspaper. English. wk. Lewis County Herald, 206 Main Street, Vanceburg KY 41179. *Continues Sun (Vanceburg, KY. : 1917).*

US/0745-4260
LEXINGTON HERALD-LEADER. VFOAT Lexington Herald Leader. VAT Lexington Herald Leader. Vol. 1, No. 1 (Jan. 3, 1983)-. Newspaper. English. da. $236.20 Kentucky; $257.00 others (daily & Sunday by mail); $101.00 Kentucky, $112.00 others (Sunday only by mail); $$181.60 (daily & Sunday by mail). Lexington Herald-Leader Company, 100 Midland Avenue, Lexington KY 40508. **Tel** (606)231-3100. **ED** John Carroll. **Circ:** 111,162 daily, 136,969 Sunday. available on microfilm; available on an online database (file 721/Full-Text) from DIALOG. *Formed by the union of Lexington Herald (Lexington, Ky. : 1904) and Lexington Leader (Lexington, Ky. : Daily).*

US
LICKING VALLEY COURIER. (19??)-. Newspaper. English. wk. Morgan County Publishing Company, PO Box 187, West Liberty KY 41472.

US
LIVINGSTON LEDGER. (196?)-. Newspaper. English. wk. Livingston Ledger, PO Box 127, Smithland KY 42081.

US
LOGAN LEADER (RUSSELLVILLE, KY.). Title Change. (THE LOGAN LEADER.) Vol. 1, No. 1 (May 1, 1968)-(1992). Newspaper. English. wk. Park Newspapers / Kentucky, 120 Public Square, Russellville KY 42276. *Merged with News-Democrat (Russellville, Ky.) to form News-Democrat & Leader, 1066-8071.*

US
LOUISVILLE DEFENDER, THE. (1933)-. Newspaper. English. wk. $16.96 Kentucky; $18.20 other. Louisville Defender, PO Box 1558, Louisville KY 40201. **Tel** (502)772-2591. **ED** Yvonne Coleman. **Ad Acc, Adv Mgr:** V. Woodson. ctrl circ. available in microform from University of Florida.
Desc: Weekly publication covering events and subjects that affect the African American Community. Content is strong in an unbiased manner, showing the positive side and role models.

US
MANCHESTER ENTERPRISE, THE. (193?)-. Newspaper. English. wk. $23.00 Clay County, Kentucky; $28.00 other. Manchester Enterprise / Kentucky, PO Box 217, Manchester KY 40962. **Tel** (606)598-6174.

US
MAYFIELD MESSENGER (MAYFIELD, KY. : 1923). (THE MAYFIELD MESSENGER.) Vol. 23, No. 134 (Sept. 7, 1923)-. Newspaper. English. da. Mayfield Messenger, PO Box 709, Mayfield KY 42066. **Tel** (502)247-5223. *Continues Daily Messenger (Mayfield, KY.).*

US
MCCREARY COUNTY RECORD. Newspaper. English. wk. McCreary County Record, PO Box 9, Whitley City KY 42653.

US
MCLEAN COUNTY NEWS. (18??)-. Newspaper. English. wk. McLean County News, PO Box 266, Calhoun KY 42327.

US
MEADE COUNTY MESSENGER (BRANDENBURG, KY. : 1987). (THE MEADE COUNTY MESSENGER.) Vol. 95, No. 28 (July 15, 1987)-. Newspaper. English. wk. Meade County Messenger, PO Box 612, Brandenburg KY 40108-0612. *Continues Messenger (Brandenburg, KY.).*

US
MESSENGER INQUIRER. VFOAT Messenger-Inquirer; Messenger and Inquirer. No. 285 (Dec. 5, 1954)-. Newspaper. English. da. $135.20 (daily and Sunday) Kentucky and Southern Indiana; $140.40 (daily and Sunday) other; $65.00 (Sunday) Kentucky; $70.20 (Sunday) other. Owensboro Publishing Company, PO Box 1480, Owensboro KY 42302. **Tel** (502)926-0123. **ED** John S Hager. **Circ:** 32,262 daily, 33,769 Sunday. available on an online database (file 635/Full-Text) from DIALOG. *Formed by the union of Owensboro Messenger (1919) and Owensboro Inquirer.*

US
MESSENGER (MADISONVILLE, KY.). (THE MESSENGER.) Vol. 54, No. 230 (Jan. 30, 1965)-. Newspaper. English. da. Madisonville Publishing Company, 221 South Main Street, Madisonville KY 42431. *Continues Madisonville Messenger.*

US
MOUNTAIN ADVOCATE (BARBOURVILLE, KY.). (THE MOUNTAIN ADVOCATE.) VFOAT Barbourville (KY.) Advocate. Vol. 83, No. 31 (April 23, 1987)-. Newspaper. English. wk. $12.00. Mountain Advocate, PO Box 190, Barbourville KY 40906. **Tel** (606)546-9225, FAX (606)546-3175. **ED** David Cole. **Bk Rev,** (Qty: 5). **Photos. Ad Acc, Adv Mgr:** Carolyn Kennedy. Full Page (B&W) $419.25. Half Page (B&W) $235.43. Full Page (Color) $469.25. Half Page (Color) $285.43. **Pub. Size:** Standard. **Circ:** 7,200. available in microform. *Continues Barbourville Mountain Advocate.*

US
MOUNTAIN EAGLE, THE. Began in 1907. Newspaper. English. wk. $11.00. T E Gish, Tunnel Hill, Whitesburg Letcher County KY 41858. **Tel** (606)633-2252.

US
MT. STERLING ADVOCATE, THE. VFOAT Mount Sterling Advocate; Advocate; Mt. Sterling Advocate the Sentinel Democrat; Mount Sterling Advocate the Sentinel Democrat. (1890)-. Newspaper. English. wk. $27.00. Mt Sterling Advocate, 40 South Bank Street, Mount Sterling KY 40353. **Tel** (606)498-2222, FAX (606)498-2228. **ED** Doug Taylor. **Bk Rev. Photos. Ad Acc, Adv Mgr:** Doug Taylor. Full Page (B&W) $988.14. Half Page (B&W) $494.07. **Pub. Size:** Broadsheet. **Circ:** 5,950. available in microform. *Absorbed Sentinel Democrat; Daily News (Mount Sterling, KY.).*

US
MURRAY LEDGER & TIMES, THE. VFOAT Murray Ledger and Times. Vol. 94, No. 295 (Dec. 14, 1973)-. Newspaper. English. da. $59.50. Murray Ledger & Times, 1001 Whitnell Avenue, Box 1040, Murray KY 42071. **Tel** (502)759-1916. **ED** Greg Travis. Index available. cum. index. **Bk Rev. Ad Acc. Circ:** 7,800 (ctrl). *Continues Ledger & Times.*

US/0894-8100
NEW VOICE (LOUISVILLE, KY.). ***Title Change.*** (THE NEW VOICE.). Vol. 37, No. 7 (April 1, 1987)-(1994). Newspaper. English. wk. New Voice, 3818 Shelbyville Road, Louisville KY 40207. ***Continues*** *East End Voice.* ***Continued by*** *Voice-Tribune, 1076-7398.*

●US/1066-8071
NEWS-DEMOCRAT & LEADER. VFOAT News Democrat and Leader; News Democrat & Leader. Vol. 195, No. 44 (Nov. 2, 1992)-. Newspaper. English. sw. Park Communications of Kentucky, 120 Public Square, PO Box 270, Russellville KY 42276. **Tel** (502)726-8394. ***Formed by the union of*** *Logan Leader (Russellville, Ky.)* ***and*** *News-Democrat (Russellville, Ky.).*

US
NEWS-DEMOCRAT (CARROLLTON, KY.). (THE NEWS-DEMOCRAT.). **VFOAT** News Democrat. Began in April 1930?. Newspaper. English. wk. News-Democrat, PO Box 60, Carrollton KY 41008. ***Formed by the union of*** *Carrollton Democrat* ***and*** *Carrollton News.*

US
NEWS-DEMOCRAT (RUSSELLVILLE, KY.). ***Title Change.*** (THE NEWS-DEMOCRAT.). **VFOAT** News Democrat. Began with June 14, 1912 issue?. Newspaper. English. wk. Park Newspapers / Kentucky, 120 Public Square, Russellville KY 42276. ***Formed by the union of*** *Logan County News (Russellville, KY.)* ***and*** *Democrat (Russellville, KY.).* ***Merged with*** *Logan Leader (Russellville,Ky.); News-Democrat & Leader.*

US
NEWS-ENTERPRISE ELIZABETHTOWN, KY.). (THE NEWS-ENTERPRISE.). **VFOAT** News Enterprise. Vol. 1, No. 1 (July 2, 1974)-. Newspaper. English. da. $125.00. News-Enterprise, 408 West Dixie Street, Elizabethtown KY 42701. **Tel** (508)769-2312. ***Formed by the union of*** *Elizabethtown News* ***and*** *Hardin County Enterprise.*

US
NEWS JOURNAL. ***Title Change.*** **VFOAT** Corbin/Whitley News-Journal; Corbin! This Week News Journal; Whitley Republican/Corbin! This Week News Journal. Vol. 84, No. 9 (Feb. 27, 1991)-Vol. 87, No. 18 (May 4, 1994). Newspaper. English. wk. Whitley Republican News Journal, PO Box 418, Williamsburg KY 40769. **Tel** (606)528-9767, FAX (606)528-9779. ***Continues*** *Corbin! This Week.* ***Merged with*** *News Journal (Williamsburg, Ky. : Whitley Republican Ed.); News Journal (Williamsburg, Ky. : 1994).*

US
NEWS JOURNAL. (19??)-. Newspaper. English. wk. $19.10. Whitley Republican News Journal, PO Box 418, Williamsburg KY 40769. **Tel** (606)528-9767, FAX (606)528-9779. **ED** Susie Hart, and Linda Carpenter (Managing Editor). **Photos. Ad Acc, Adv Mgr:** Don Estep. Full Page (B&W) $771.42. Half Page (B&W) $376.74. Full Page (Color) $836.42. Half Page (Color) $441.74. **Pub. Size:** Broadsheet. **Circ:** 6,306. ***Continues*** *News Journal (Williamsburg KY : Corbin! This Week Ed.); News Journal (Williamsburg KY : Whitley Republican Ed.).*

US
NEWS JOURNAL. ***Title Change.*** **VFOAT** Corbin/Whitley News-Journal; Whitley Republican News Journal; Whitley Republican, Corbin! This Week News Journal. Vol. 84, No. 9 (Feb. 27, 1991)-Vol. 87, No. 18 (May 4, 1994). Newspaper. English. wk. Whitley Republican News Journal, PO Box 418, Williamsburg KY 40769. **Tel** (606)528-9767, FAX (606)528-9779. ***Continues*** *Whitley Republican.* ***Merged with*** *News Journal (Williamsburg, Ky. : Corbin! This Week Ed.); News Journal (Williamsburg, Ky. : 1994).*

US
NEWSWEEK (SHIVELY, KY.). ***Title Change.*** (THE NEWSWEEK.). Vol. 20, No. 29 (July 19, 1973)-Vol. 36, No. 20 (May 21, 1992). Newspaper. English. wk. The Newsweek, 4639 Dixie Highway, Shively KY 40216. ***Continues*** *Shively Newsweek.* ***Continued by*** *Southwest Newsweek, 1064-1645.*

US
OLDHAM ERA (LAGRANGE, KY.). (THE OLDHAM ERA.). Vol. 36, No. 43 (June 23, 1910)-. Newspaper. English. wk. $30.50 Oldham County; $37.50 other Kentucky; $46.00 other. Oldham Era, PO Box 5, La Grange KY 40031. **Tel** (502)222-7183. ***Continues*** *Oldham County Era.*

US
OLIVE HILL TIMES (OLIVE HILL, KY.). (THE OLIVE HILL TIMES.). Newspaper. English. wk. Olive Hill Times, PO Box 484, Olive Hill KY 41164.

US/1050-0030
PADUCAH SUN (1978), THE. (THE PADUCAH SUN.). (June 26, 1978)-. Newspaper. English. ds. $11.40 per month. The Paducah Sun, PO Box 2300, Paducah KY 42002. **Tel** (502)443-1771. **ED** James Paxton, Karl Harrison (Managing Editor). **Photos. Ad Acc, Adv Mgr:** Jana Thomasson. Full Page (B&W) $1778.63. Half Page (B&W) $957.60. Full Page (Color) $1963.63. Half Page (Color) $1142.60. **Wire Svcs.:** AP. **Circ:** 29,922 daily, 33,771 Sunday. ***Continues*** *Sun-Democrat (Paducah, Ky. : 1962).*

US
PAINTSVILLE HERALD, THE. (1902)-. Newspaper. English. wk. $28.50 Kentucky; $32.00 other. Paintsville Herald, PO Box 1547, Paintsville KY 41240. **Tel** (606)789-5315.

US
PARK CITY DAILY NEWS. VFOAT Daily News. (1920)-. Newspaper. English. da. $118.72 Allen, Warren, Barren, Todd, Ohio, Muhlenberg, Hart, Edmondson, Simpson, Logan, Butler, Grayson, Metcalfe, Monroe Counties in Kentucky; $125.08 others in Kentucky; $130.00 others. Park City Daily News, PO Box 929, Bowling Green KY 42101. **Tel** (502)781-1700. **ED** J Ray Gaines (502)781-1700. **Circ:** 24,519. ***Continues*** *News-Democrat-Messenger.*

US
PINEVILLE SUN. VFOAT Pineville Sun and the Cumberland Courier. Vol. 83, No. 52 (May 23, 1991)-. Newspaper. English. wk. Associated Publications Inc. / Kentucky, PO Box 250, Pineville KY 40977. ***Continues*** *Pineville Sun-Cumberland Courier.*

US/0746-8806
PIONEER NEWS (SHEPHERDSVILLE, KY.), THE. (THE PIONEER-NEWS.). **VFOAT** Pioneer News. Began 1882-. Newspaper. English. sw. $7.50 Bullitt, Jefferson, Spencer & Nelson counties, $10.50 other. Pioneer-News, 1105 Beech Street, Shepherdsville KY 40165. ***Absorbed*** *Salt River Valley News; North Bullitt Postboy; Mt. Washington Star.*

US
PRINCETON LEADER, THE. ***Title Change.*** Vol. 69, No. 1 (July 4, 1940)-Vol. 120, No. 52 (Apr. 29, 1992). Newspaper. English. wk. Princeton Leader, PO Box 529, Princeton KY 42445. **ED** Chip Hutcheson. **Ad Acc. Circ:** 3,500 (ctrl). ***Continues*** *Twice-A-Week Leader.* ***Merged with*** *Caldwell County Times* ***to form*** *Times-Leader (Princeton, Ky.).*

US/1055-9531
PROGRESS (CAVE CITY, KY. 1988), THE. (THE PROGRESS.). **VFOAT** Barren County Progress. Vol. 10. No. 9 (Mar. 3, 1988)-. Newspaper. English. wk. $6.95 in county; $16.00 others in Kentucky; $20.00 others. Barren County Progress, 609 East Broadway, Cave City KY 42127. **ED** A. C. Wilson Jr. **Photos. Ad Acc, Adv Mgr:** A. C. Wilson Jr., **Tel** $502)773-3401. Full Page (B&W) $593.40. Half Page (B&W) $303.60. Full Page (Color) $693.40. Half Page (Color) $403.60. **Circ:** 4,706 (paid), $3,700 (free). ***Formed by the union of*** *Barren County Progress (Cave City, Ky. : 1987).*

US/0746-8474
RECORD (LOUISVILLE, KY.), THE. (THE RECORD : LOUISVILLE ARCHDIOCESAN NEWSPAPER.). Began publication in Feb. 1879. Periodical. English. wk. $12.00 US; $15.00 other. The Daily Record Inc., PO Box 1062, Louisville KY 40201. **Tel** (502)583-4771, (800)666-6966. **ED** J E Deurr. **Ad Acc. Circ:** 61,000.

US
RICHMOND REGISTER (RICHMOND, KY.). (THE RICHMOND REGISTER.). **VFOAT** Richmond Daily Register. Vol. 62 (June 22, 1978)-. Newspaper. English. da. Richmond Register, PO Box 99, Richmond KY 40475. ***Continues*** *Richmond Daily Register.*

US/8750-1651
RUSSELL COUNTY NEWS (JAMESTOWN, KY.), THE. (RUSSELL COUNTY NEWS.). (May 1, 1913)-. Newspaper. English. Fifty-two times a year. $22.00 area counties; $26.00 other. Russell County News / Kentucky, PO Box 27, Jamestown KY 42629. **Tel** (502)343-2565.

US
SALYERSVILLE INDEPENDENT. VFOAT Independent. Vol. 1, No. 1 (May 6, 1921)-. Newspaper. English. wk. Salyersville Independent, PO Box 29, Salyersville KY 41465. **Tel** (606)349-2915.

US
SEBREE BANNER, THE. VFOAT Banner. (19??)-. Newspaper. English. wk. $9.54. Sebree Banner, PO Box 36, Sebree KY 42455. **Tel** (502)835-9521. **ED** Tony Catlett. Index available. **Photos. Ad Acc, Adv Mgr:** Betty P. Catlett, **Tel** (502)835-7521. Full Page (B&W) $346.50. Half Page (B&W) $173.25. Full Page (Color) $396.50. Half Page (Color) $253.25. **Pub. Size:** Broadsheet. **Circ:** 3,500 (ctrl). available in microform from University of Kentucky. ***Continues*** *Green River News.*

US/0898-9311
SENTINEL-ECHO (LONDON, KY.), THE. (THE SENTINEL-ECHO.). **VFOAT** Sentinel Echo. Vol. 12, No. 38 (Feb. 6, 1919)-. Newspaper. English. sw. Sentinel-Echo, 123 West 5th Street, London KY 40741. ***Continues*** *London Sentinel and Mountain Echo.*

US
SENTINEL-NEWS, THE. VFOAT Sentinel News. Vol. 1, No. 1 (Feb. 7, 1972)-. Newspaper. English. sw. Sentinel-News, 702 Washington Street, Shelbyville KY 40065. ***Formed by the union of*** *Shelby News (Shelbyville, KY. : 1886)* ***and*** *Shelby Sentinel (Shelbyville, KY.).*

US
SENTINEL (RADCLIFF, KY.). (THE SENTINEL.). Vol. 1, No. 1 (May 11, 1961)-. Newspaper. English. wk. The Sentinel / Radcliff, Kentucky, 1558 Hill Street, Radcliff KY 40160. **Tel** (502)351-4407. **ED** O.J. Royalty. **Photos. Ad Acc, Adv Mgr:** Sandy Bowen. Full Page (B&W) $469.56. Half Page (B&W) $234.78. Full Page (Color) $554.56. Half Page (Color) $319.78. **Pub. Size:** Standard. **Circ:** 3,501. ***Continues*** *West Point New Era.*

●US/1064-1645
SOUTHWEST NEWSWEEK, THE. (1992)-. Newspaper. English. wk. $11.00. Southwest Newsweek, 4447 Dixie Highway, Shively KY 40216-2605. **Tel** (502)448-4581, FAX (502)448-4583. ***Continues*** *Newsweek (Shively, Ky.).*

US
SPRINGFIELD SUN, THE. Vol. 1, No. 1 (Nov. 30, 1904)-. Newspaper. English. wk. Springfield Sun, 117 Cross Street, Springfield KY 40069.

US
STATE JOURNAL, THE. 14th year, No. 36 (June 20, 1912)-. Newspaper. English. da. $97.15 Kentucky; $107.00 others. The State Journal / Kentucky, 321 West Main, Frankfort KY 40601. **Tel** (502)227-4556. **ED** Carl West. **Bk Rev. Ad Acc. Circ:** 11,500. ***Continues*** *Frankfort News Journal.* **Ind/Abst** Bus. Index (Jan. 1985-Dec. 1985); Gen. BusinessFile (Jan. 1985-Dec. 1985); Gen. Period. Index (Jan. 1985-Dec. 1985); Mag. Search.

US
STURGIS NEWS, THE. (1???)-. Newspaper. English. wk. Sturgis News, 615 Adams Street, Sturgis KY 42459.

US/0744-883X
SUNDAY INDEPENDENT, THE. Newspaper. English. wk. Ashland Publishing Indpendent, PO Box 311, Ashland KY 41101. **Tel** (606)329-1717. **ED** Paul Sierer. **Circ:** 25,658.

US
TIMES-ARGUS (CENTRAL CITY, KY). (THE TIMES-ARGUS.). **VFOAT** Times Argus. Began in 1906. Newspaper. English. wk (Published on Wednesdays). $9.40 local counties; $11.50 others in Kentucky; $13.00 other. Central City Publishing Corporation, PO Box 31, 202 West Broad Street, Central City KY 42330. **Tel** (502)754-2331. **ED** Mark Stone. **LC** 7885-X. **Ad Acc. Circ:** 3,000.

US
TIMES JOURNAL (RUSSELL SPRINGS, KY.). (THE TIMES JOURNAL.). 1st Year, No. 1 (Oct. 13, 1949)-. Newspaper. English. wk. $14.39 Russell Springs; $20.00 other in Kentucky; $28.00 others in US; $80.00 others. Russell County Newspapers Inc., PO Box 190, Russell Springs KY 42642. **Tel** (502)866-3191, FAX (502)866-3198. **ED** Dave Cazalet (Editor-in-Chief) and Ed Cahill (Managing Editor). **Photos. Ad Acc, Adv Mgr:** Kathy Haynes-Ellis. Full Page (B&W) $510.30. Half Page (B&W) $264.60. **Pub. Size:** Broadsheet. **Circ:** 4,133. available in microform from University of Kentucky.

●US
TIMES-LEADER, THE. VFOAT Times Leader. Vol. 1, No. 1 (May 6, 1992)-. Newspaper. English. wk. $24.00 Princeton County; $29.00 others in Kentucky; $36.00 others. Times Leader / Kentucky, PO Box 439, Princeton KY 42445. **Tel** (502)365-2141, FAX (502)365-7299. **ED** Chip Hutcheson. **Photos. Ad Acc, Adv Mgr:** Chip Hutcheson. Full Page (B&W) $372.81. Half Page (B&W) $200.64. Full Page (Color) $492.81. Half Page (Color) $320.64. **Pub. Size:** Broadsheet. **Wire Svcs.:** AP. **Circ:** 6,000. available in microform. ***Formed by the union of*** *Caldwell County Times* ***and*** *Princeton Leader.*

US
TIMES-NEWS. VFOAT Times News. Vol. 106, No. 44 (Oct. 30, 1980)-. Newspaper. English. wk. Andy Anderson Company, PO Box 226, Hartford KY 42347-0226. **Tel** (502)298-7100. **ED** Dave McBride and Carolyn Hillard. **Circ:** 7,000. ***Formed by the union of*** *Ohio County Times* ***and*** *Ohio County News (Hartford, Ky.).*

US
TIMES TRIBUNE (CORBIN, KY.). (TIMES TRIBUNE.). **VFOAT** Times-Tribune. Vol. 89, No. 27 (Feb. 2, 1981)-. Newspaper. English. da. $102.00. The Tribune Times, PO Box 516, Corbin KY 40701. **Tel** (606)528-2464. **ED** Joseph E. Harbwich, Debra Legg

(Managing Editor). **Bk Rev**. **Photos**. **Ad Acc**, **Adv Mgr:** Rochelle Stadlin. Full Page (B&W) $1,388.04. Half Page (B&W) $649.02. Full Page (Color) $1,548.04. Half Page (Color) $854.02. **Pub. Size:** Broadsheet. **Wire Svcs.:** AP. available on microfilm from University Microfilms International (UMI). ***Continues*** *Corbin Times-Tribune (Corbin, Ky.).*

US
TODD COUNTY STANDARD, THE.
Newspaper. English. wk. Todd County Standard, PO Box 308, Elkton KY 42220.

US
TOMPKINSVILLE NEWS, THE. Began in 1903. Newspaper. English. wk. Tompkinsville News, 105 Main Street, Tompkinsville KY 42167.

US
TRI-CITY NEWS, THE. **VFOAT** Tri City News. Vol. 1, No. 1 (Mar. 15, 1929)-. Newspaper. English. wk. $22.00 Kentucky, $24.50 other. Tri City News, PO Box 490, Cumberland KY 40823. **Tel** (606)589-2588.

US/1046-302X
TRIBUNE-COURIER (1989).
(TRIBUNE-COURIER.). **VFOAT** Tribune Courier. (May 1989)-. Newspaper. English. wk (Wednesdays). $20.00. Kentucky Waterland Press Inc, Tribune Courier, PO Box 410, Benton KY 42025. **Tel** (502)527-3162, FAX (502)527-4567. **ED** Greg Travis. **Photos**. **Ad Acc**, **Adv Mgr:** Terri Dunnigan, **Tel** (501)527-4565. Full Page (B&W) $541.80. Half Page (B&W) $270.90. Full Page (Color) $616.80. Half Page (Color) $345.90. **Pub. Size:** Broadsheet. **Wire Svcs.:** AP. available in microform. ***Continues*** *Marshall County's Tribune-Courier.*

US
TROUBLESOME CREEK TIMES. Vol. 1, No. 1 (June 5, 1980)-. Newspaper. English. wk. $13.00 Knott County, Kentucky; $15.00 other Kentucky; $20.00 other. Knott County Publishing Company Inc, PO Box 700, Hindman KY 41822. **Tel** (606)785-5135.

US
UNION COUNTY ADVOCATE (MORGANFIELD, KY.). (THE UNION COUNTY ADVOCATE.). Vol. 1, No. 1 (April 17, 1924)-. Newspaper. English. wk. Munford Publishing Company, PO Box 370, Morganfield KY 42437-0370. ***Continues*** *Union Local.*

US
WAYNE COUNTY OUTLOOK, THE. Vol. 1, No. 1 (May 26, 1904)-. Newspaper. English. wk. Monticello Publishing Company, PO Box 432, Monticello KY 42633. **Tel** (606)348-3338.

US
WEST KENTUCKY NEWS. Vol. 19, No. 50 (Feb. 25, 1987)-. Newspaper. English. wk. $20.00 Kentucky; $25.00 others. Kentucky Publishing Company / Paducah, Kentucky, PO Box 1135, Paducah KY 42002. **Tel** (502)442-7389, FAX (502)442-5220. **ED** Connee Lown (Editor-in-Chief) and Melissa Jones (Managing Editor). **Photos**. **Ad Acc**, **Adv Mgr:** Greg LeNeave. Full Page (B&W) $1,367.40. Half Page (B&W) $724.00. **Pub. Size:** Broadsheet. **Circ:** 21,500. available in microform from University of Kentucky. ***Continues*** *Kentucky Shopper News.*

US
WHITLEY REPUBLICAN, THE. ***Title Change.*** **VFOAT** Corbin! This Week, Whitley Republican. (19??)-(199?). Newspaper. English. wk. Whitley Republican News Journal, PO Box 418, Williamsburg KY 40769. **Tel** (606)528-9767, FAX (606)528-9779. ***Continued by*** *News Journal (Williamsburg, Ky. : Whitley Republican Ed.).*

US
WINCHESTER SUN (WINCHESTER, KY. : 1912). (THE WINCHESTER SUN.). Vol. 1, No. 1 (March 1, 1912)-. Newspaper. English. da. $127.20. Winchester Sun, 20 Wall Street, PO Box 4300, Winchester KY 40392. **Tel** (606)744-3123. **ED** William S. Blakeman. **Bk Rev**, (Qty: 10-12). **Photos**. **Ad Acc**, **Adv Mgr:** Ann Laurence. Full Page (B&W) $709.50. Half Page (B&W) $370.87. Full Page (Color) $791.50. Half Page (Color) $450.87. **Pub. Size:** Standard. **Wire Svcs.:** AP. **Circ:** 7,000. available in microform.

US
WOLFE COUNTY NEWS, THE. Newspaper. English. wk. Wolfe County News, PO Box 187, West Liberty KY 41472.

US
WOODFORD SUN. Vol. 10, No. 1 (Feb. 8, 1877)-. Newspaper. English. wk (published on Thursday). $15.00 residents of Woodford County, Kentucky; $18.00 Kentucky; $24.00 other. Woodford Sun, PO Box 29, Versailles KY 40383. **Tel** (606)873-4131, FAX (606)873-0300. **ED** H. Moss Vance. **Photos**. **Ad Acc**, **Adv Mgr:** Robert H. Atres. Full Page (B&W) $623.70. Half Page (B&W) $311.85. Full Page (Color) $693.70. Half Page (Color) $381.85. **Pub. Size:** Standard. ***Formed by the union of*** *Midway Sun* ***and*** *Woodford Weekly.*

LOUISIANA

US
ABBEVILLE MERIDIONAL. Vol. 51, No. 1 (Jan. 5, 1906 [i.e. 1907]-Vol.. 99, No. 52 (Dec. 24, 1949) ; Vol. 97, No. 1 (Dec. 31, 1949)-Vol. 118, No. 85 (Jan. 6, 1972) ; 116th year, No. 3 (Jan. 10, 1972)-. Newspaper. English. da. $49.95 Abbeville; $72.00 others. Abbeville Meridional, Abbeville LA 70510. **Tel** (318)893-4223. ***Continues*** *Meridional;* ***Absorbed*** *Kaplan Journal (Kaplan, La. : 1935); Abbeville Progress; Kaplan Times; Gueydan News; Vermilion Post.*

●US/1061-3978
ADVOCATE (BATON ROUGE, LA.), THE.
(THE ADVOCATE.). **VFOAT** Saturday; Sunday Advocate. 67th Year, No. 168 (Jan. 13, 1992)-. Newspaper. English. da. $116.48. The Advocate, PO Box 588, Baton Rouge LA 70821-0588. **Tel** (504)383-1111, FAX (504)388-0219. **ED** David C. Manship, Linda C. Lightfoot (Managing Editor). **Bk Rev**, (Qty: 1,000 per year). **Photos**. **Ad Acc**, **Adv Mgr:** Donald R. Stewart. Full Page (B&W) $4391.10. Half Page (B&W) $2195.55. Full Page (Color) $4716.10. Half Page (Color) $2520.55. **Pub. Size:** Standard. **Wire Svcs.:** AP, KR, LA, NY. available in microform from University Microfilms International (UMI). ***Continues*** *Morning Advocate (Baton Rouge, La.), 1056-2125.*

US
ALEXANDRIA DAILY TOWN TALK, THE.
VFOAT Daily Town Talk. (Mar. 17, 1883)-. Newspaper. English. da (Except Christmas). $132.00 (zip codes beginning with 713 or 714); $144.00 other. Alexandria Daily Town Talk, PO Box 7558, Alexandria LA 71306. **Tel** (318)487-6327. **ED** Jim Butler. **LC** 7949-X. **Bk Rev**. **Ad Acc**, **Adv Mgr:** Bill Heintzler, **Tel** (318)487-6391. **Circ:** 39,773 daily, 41,270 Sunday (ctrl). available on microfilm. ***Continues*** *Daily Town Talk (Alexandria, La. : 1892).*

US
ALEXANDRIA NEWS WEEKLY. (1976)-. Newspaper. English. wk. $15.00. Alexandria News Weekly, PO Box 608, Alexandria LA 71301. ***Continues*** *Alexandria Weekly News.*

US
ASSUMPTION PIONEER, THE. **VFOAT** Pionnier de l'Assomption. Vol. 37, No. 40 (March 23, 1895)-. Newspaper. English (French). wk. Assumption Pioneer, PO Drawer 428, Napoleanville LA 70390. **Tel** (504)369-7153, FAX (504)369-7153. **ED** Philip Gianelloni. **Ad Acc**. **Circ:** 2,600 (ctrl). available on microfilm. ***Continues*** *Pioneer of Assumption.*

US
BASTROP DAILY ENTERPRISE, THE.
(1952)-. Periodical. English. da. Enterprise / Bastrop, PO Box 311, Bastrop LA 71221-0311. **Tel** (318)281-4421, FAX (318)283-1699. **ED** Dan Strack. **Ad Acc**, **Adv Mgr:** Robert Godfrey. **Circ:** 6,000.

US/1044-3630
BATON ROUGE DAILY NEWS. **VFOAT** Daily News. (198?)-. Newspaper. English. da. $240.00. Newspress Inc. / Baton Rouge Daily News, 8252 West El Cajon Drive, Baton Rouge LA 70815. **ED** Mike Cannon (Editor-in-Chief) and Chris Vaughn (Managing Editor). **Photos**. **Ad Acc**, **Adv Mgr:** Bill Richard, **Tel** (504)927-6242. Full Page (B&W) $156.00. Half Page (B&W) $72.00. **Pub. Size:** Tabloid. ***Continues*** *Baton Rouge Daily Legal News.*

US
BEAUREGARD DAILY NEWS. Vol. 41, No. 1 (Mar. 1, 1987)-. Newspaper. English. da. $41.20 Beauregard, Vernon, Calcasieu, & Allen Counties (includes 1% sales tax); $51.50 Louisiana; $55.00 other. Beauregard Daily News, PO Box 698, Deridder LA 70634. **Tel** (318)462-0616. ***Continues*** *Beauregard News.*

US
BIENVILLE DEMOCRAT RINGGOLD RECORD, THE. **VFOAT** Bienville Democrat. Vol. 67, No. 29 (July 17, 1980)-. Newspaper. English. wk. $10.00. Bienville Democrat, 117 North Maple, Arcadia LA 71001. ***Formed by the union of*** *Bienville Democrat* ***and*** *Ringgold Record.*

US/0747-4733
BOSSIER PRESS-TRIBUNE. **VFOAT** Bossier Press Tribune. Began in 1984. Newspaper. English. wk. $12.00 Bossier parrish, $15.00 other. Bossier Newspaper Publishing Company, PO Box 6267, Bossier City LA 71171-6267. ***Formed by the union of*** *Bossier Press* ***and*** *Bossier Tribune.*

US
CADDO CITIZEN. No. 11 (Mar. 14, 1974) No. 10 (Mar. 6, 1985); 73rd yr., No. 11 (Mar. 13, 1985)-. Newspaper. English. wk. $8.50 Vivian area; $10.00 US; $18.00 other. Caddo Citizen, PO Box 312, Vivian LA 71082. **Tel** (318)375-3294. ***Continues*** *Vivian's Caddo Citizen.*

US
CONCORDIA SENTINEL, THE. (188?)-. Newspaper. English. sw. Hanna Publishing, PO Box 312, Ferriday LA 71334-2503. **Tel** (318)539-3646, FAX (318)539-3647. **ED** Rod Elrod. **Circ:** 4,500.

US/0888-7586
CONTRABAND. **Added/Corp** McNeese State University. McNeese State College. Vol. 1, (Sept. 1939)-. Newspaper. English. wk. $24.00. McNeese State University, Box 92940, Lake Charles LA 70609-2940. **Tel** (318)475-5593. **ED** Seth Hopkins. **Bk Rev**, (Qty: 5). **Photos**. **Ad Acc**, **Adv Mgr:** Richard Allen. Full Page (B&W) $967.50. Half Page (B&W) $472.50. **Pub. Size:** Standard. **Circ:** 4,500-5,000.

US
COUSHATTA CITIZEN, THE. Vol. 1, No. 1 (Dec. 9, 1871)-. Newspaper. English. wk. Coushatta Citizen, PO Drawer F, Tinggold Avenue, Coushatta LA 71019. **Tel** (318)932-4201.

US
CROWLEY POST-SIGNAL, THE. **VFOAT** Crowley Post Signal. Vol. 1, No. 1 (Mar. 1, 1974)-. Newspaper. English. da. $62.40. Crowley Post Signal, 602 North Parkerson Avenue, Crowley LA 70526. **ED** Milo Nickel, Harold Gonzales (Managing Editor). **Bk Rev**, (Qty: 12). **Ad Acc**, **Adv Mgr:** Glenn Boudreux. Full Page (B&W) $774.00. Half Page (B&W) $396.00. Full Page (Color) $874.00. Half Page (Color) $496.00. **Pub. Size:** Broadsheet. **Wire Svcs.:** AP. available in microform from Louisiana State University Library. ***Formed by the union of*** *Crowley Daily Signal* ***and*** *Crowley Post Herald.*

US
DAILY COMET, THE. Vol. 81, No. 11 (June 3, 1968)-. Newspaper. English. da. Daily Comet, 705 West 5th Street, Thibodaux LA 70301-3148. **Tel** (504)447-4055, FAX (504)448-7606. **ED** Colley Charpentier. **Ad Acc**, **Adv Mgr:** Alan Rini. **Circ:** 14,000. ***Formed by the union of*** *Lafourche Comet* ***and*** *Lafourche Press-News.*

US
DAILY NEWS. **VFOAT** Sunday News. Vol. 36, No. 155 (Nov. 6, 1962)-. Newspaper. English. da. Daily News / Bogalusa, 525 Avenue V, Bogalusa LA 70427-0820. **Tel** (504)732-2565, FAX (504)732-4006. **ED** Lou Major. **Ad Acc**. **Circ:** 7,600 daily, 8,500 Sunday. ***Continues*** *Bogalusa Daily News.*

US/0194-5327
DAILY RECORD (NEW ORLEANS), THE.
(THE DAILY RECORD.). (19??)-. Newspaper. English. ir (256 per year). $108.00. The Daily Record LA, 931 Canal Street/Suite 518, New Orleans LA 70112. **Tel** (504)581-5926.

US
DAILY REVIEW, THE. Vol. 96, No. 1 (Mar. 3, 1963)-. Newspaper. English. da. $36.40 local; $80.00 other. Morgan City Daily Review, 1014 Front Street, Morgan City LA 70380-3226. **Tel** (504)384-8370. **ED** Doyle E. Shirley, Steve Shirley (Managing Editor). **Photos**. **Ad Acc**, **Adv Mgr:** Andy Shirley. Full Page (B&W) $722.40. Half Page (B&W) $352.80. Full Page (Color) $822.40. Half Page (Color) $452.80. **Pub. Size:** Broadsheet. **Wire Svcs.:** AP. **Circ:** 6,345 evening paid. ***Continues*** *Morgan City Review (Morgan City, La. : 1920).*

US
DAILY WORLD. Vol. 16, No. 229 (Nov. 17, 1955)-. Newspaper. English. da. $74.00 St. Landry Parish & balance of the ABC Trading Zone; $78.00 Louisiana; $84.00 US. Daily World / Opelousas, PO Box 1179, Opelousas LA 70570. **Tel** (318)942-8852. ***Continues*** *Opelousas Daily world.*

US/0164-9027
DENHAM SPRINGS AND LIVINGSTON PARISH NEWS. **VFOAT** Denham Springs-Livingston Parish News. Vol. 79, No. 21 (Sept. 19, 1977)-. Newspaper. English. sw. Denham Springs News, PO Box 458, Denham Springs LA 70726. **Tel** (504)665-5176, FAX (5504)665-0167. ***Continues*** *Denham Springs News.*

US
DEQUINCY NEWS, THE. **VFOAT** De Quincy News. (Mar. 1923)-. Newspaper. English. wk. $14.56. De Quincy News, PO Box 995, De Quincy LA 70633. **Tel** (318)786-8004, FAX (318)786-8131. **ED** Jerry Wise. **Bk Rev**, (Qty: 20). **Photos**. **Ad Acc**, **Adv Mgr:** Jeffra DeViney. Full Page (B&W) $466.20. Half Page (B&W) $233.10. Full Page (Color) $591.20. Half Page (Color) $358.10. **Pub. Size:** Standard. **Circ:** 3,900. available in microform.

US
DONALDSONVILLE CHIEF (DONALDSONVILLE, LA. : 1871). (THE DONALDSONVILLE CHIEF.). (Sept. 16, 1871)-. Newspaper. English. wk. $22.66 LA; $24.50 other. Donaldsonville Chief, PO Box 309, Donaldsonville LA 70346. **Tel** (504)473-3101.

US/0889-0684
ENTERPRISE (PONCHATOULA, LA.). (THE ENTERPRISE.). **VFOAT** Ponchatoula Enterprise. Vol. 1, No. 1 (Mar. 11, 1921)-. Newspaper. English. wk. $8.00 (one year), $12.00 (two year) Tangiphoa Parish; $14.00 other. The Enterprise / Louisiana, PO Box 218, Ponchatoula LA 70454. **Tel** (504)386-6537. **ED** Don Ellzey. **Ad Acc**, **Adv Mgr:** Sharyn Brecheen. **Circ:** 2,000.

US/0885-8233
EUNICE NEWS, THE. **VFOAT** Eunice (LA.) News. Vol. 48, No. 8 (Nov. 29, 1951)-. Newspaper. English. da. Eunice News, Eunice LA 70535. **Tel** (318)457-3061. ***Continues*** *New Era and Clarion-News.*

US
FRANKLIN SUN (WINNSBORO, LA.). (THE FRANKLIN SUN.). Vol. 96, No. 29 (Nov. 20, 1952)-. Newspaper. English. wk. $18.00 Local; $24.00 others in Louisiana; $30.00 others. The Franklin Sun, 604 Prairie Street, PO Box 550, Winnsboro LA 71295. **Tel** (318)435-4521, FAX (318)435-9220. **ED** Rod Elrod. **LC** 8006. **Photos**. **Ad Acc**, **Adv Mgr:** Monica Huff. Full Page (B&W) $504.00. Half Page (B&W) $252.00. Full Page (Color) $554.00. Half Page (Color) $302.00. **Circ:** 6,000. ***Continues*** *Franklin Sun-Franklin Parish News.*

US/0279-6589
GAMBIT (NEW ORLEANS, LA.). (GAMBIT.). (19??)-. Periodical. English. wk. $52.00. Gambit - New Orleans Weekly, 4141 Bienville, New Orleans LA 70119. **Tel** (504)486-5900. **ED** Allen Johnson. **Ad Acc**, **Adv Mgr:** Susan Crichton. **Circ:** 37,000.

US
GREATER AVOYELLES JOURNAL, THE. **VFOAT** Avoyelles Journal. (1978)-. Newspaper. English. sw. Avoyelles Journal, 100 North Main Street, Marksville LA 71351. **Tel** (318)253-5413. **ED** Randy DeCuir. **Ad Acc**. **Circ:** 16,800.

US
HAMMOND VINDICATOR, THE. (19??)-. Newspaper. English. Fifty-two times a year (Thurs.). Hammond Vindicator, 105 South Cate Avenue, PO Box 2838, Hammond LA 70401. **Tel** (504)345-4321. **ED** Harrell L. Griffin. **LC** 7946-X. **Bk Rev**. **Ad Acc**. **Circ:** 4,500. ***Continues*** *Southern Vindicator.*

US
HOUMA DAILY COURIER. **VFOAT** Houma Daily Courier and the Terrebonne Press. Vol. 105, No. 7 (Jan. 9, 1983)-. Newspaper. English. da. Houma Courier and Terrebonne Press, PO Box 2717, Houma LA 70361. **Tel** (504)879-1557. ***Continues*** *Houma Daily Courier and the Terrebonne Press.*

US/0895-2132
JEFFERSON PARISH TIMES & DEMOCRAT / KENNER CITY NEWS. **VFOAT** Jefferson Parish Times and Democrat/Kenner City News; Kenner City News. Vol. 44, No. 46 (Nov. 13, 1986)-. Newspaper. English. wk. Jefferson Business of New Orleans, PO Box 354, Gretna LA 70054. **Tel** (504)362-4310. ***Formed by the union of*** *Jefferson Business Jefferson Parish Times the Jefferson Democrat* ***and*** *City News (Kenner, La.), 0887-4344;* ***Absorbed*** *West Bank Guide. July 6, 1989.*

US/1051-0591
KENNER/METAIRIE LIVING. **VFOAT** Kenner Metairie Living. Vol. 4, No. 1 (Feb. 1990)-. Newspaper. English. mo. $12.00. Kenner/Metairie Living, Concourse Place Building/Suite 110, 1940 I-10 Service Road, Kenner LA 70065. ***Continues*** *Kenner Living.*

US/0890-8087
KENTWOOD LEDGER, THE. Vol. 1, No. 1 (June 30, 1966)-. Newspaper. English. wk. $30.00. Kentwood Ledger, PO Box AD, Kentwood LA 70444. **Tel** (504)229-8607.

US
KENTWOOD NEWS. (19??)-. Newspaper. English. wk. $8.50 Washington Parish, LA and Pike County, MS; $9.50 (one year), $18.00 (two year), $24.00 (three year) other. Kentwood News, PO Box K, Kentwood LA 70444. **Tel** (504)229-7541.

US/0739-1196
LAKE CHARLES AMERICAN-PRESS. **VFOAT** Lake Charles American Press; Lake Charles American Press the Southwest Citizen. 18th Year, No. 5448 (July 19, 1912)-. Newspaper. English. da. Lake Charles American, 327 Broad Street, PO Box 2893, Lake Charles LA 70601. **Tel** (318)494-4040. **ED** Jim Beam. **Bk Rev**. **Ad Acc**. **Circ:** 39,582 daily, 44,397 Sunday. available on microfilm. ***Continues*** *Lake Charles Daily American Press;* ***Absorbed*** *Southwest Citizen.*

US
LEESVILLE DAILY LEADER. Vol. 87, No. 78 (June 12, 1984)-. Newspaper. English. da. The Leesville Leader, PO Box 619, Leesville LA 71446. **Tel** (318)239-3444. ***Continues*** *Leesville Leader.*

US
LEMON-AID. **Added/Corp** Consumer Protection Center, Baton Rouge, La. Vol. 1 (1973)-. Newspaper. English. ir. Consumer Protection Center, PO Box 1471, Baton Rouge LA 70821. **Tel** (504)389-3454.
Ind/Abst Can. Index (?-?).

US
LOUISIANA WEEKLY, THE. Vol. 1, No. 3 (Oct. 10, 1925)-. Newspaper. English. Fifty-two times a year. $18.00. Louisiana Publications, 1001 Howard Avenue, Suite 2600, New Orleans LA 70113. **Tel** (504)524-5563. **ED** Henry Dejoie Sr., Henry Dejoie Jr. (Managing Editor). **Bk Rev**, (Qty: 3 to 4). **Photos**. **Ad Acc**, **Adv Mgr:** Bertel Dejoie. Full Page (B&W) $1440.00. Half Page (B&W) $720.04. **Pub. Size:** Standard. available on microfilm. ***Continues*** *New Orleans Herald (New Orleans, La. : 1925).*

US/1056-2125
MORNING ADVOCATE (BATON ROUGE, LA.). ***Title Change.*** (MORNING ADVOCATE.). **VFOAT** Sunday Advocate. (July 1925)-67th Year, No. 167 (Jan. 12, 1992). Newspaper. English. da. Morning Advocate, PO Box 588, Baton Rouge LA 70821. **Tel** (504)383-1111, FAX (504)388-0371. **ED** James Hughes. **Circ:** 81,598 daily, 136,979 Sunday. available on microfilm. ***Continued by*** *Advocate (Baton Rouge, La.), 1061-3978.*

US
NAAWP NEWS : PUBLICATION OF THE NATIONAL ASSOCIATION FOR THE ADVANCEMENT OF WHITE PEOPLE. **Main/Corp** National Association for the Advancement of White People. **VFOAT** N.A.A.W.P. News. **VAT** National Association for the Advancement of White People News. No. 1 (1980)-. Periodical. English. Eight times a year. National Association for Advancement of White People / NAAWP News, Box 10625, New Orleans LA 70181. **Tel** (504)831-6986. **ED** David Duke. **Bk Rev**. **Circ:** 15,000.

US
NATCHITOCHES TIMES, THE. Vol. 1, No. 1 (Mar. 13, 1903)-. Newspaper. English. sw. $38.40. The Natchitoches Times, PO Box 448, 904 Highway 1 South, Natchitoches LA 71457. **Tel** (318)352-3618. **ED** Steve Colwell. **LC** 7962. **Circ:** 7,206.

US
NEWS-DIGEST (AMITE, LA.). (THE NEWS-DIGEST.). **VFOAT** News Digest. Began in 1935?. Newspaper. English. wk. $25.00. News-Digest, 133 East Oak Street, Amite LA 70422. **ED** Harrell L Griffin. **Ad Acc**. **Circ:** 1,500. ***Continues*** *Amite News-Digest.*

US
OBSERVER, THE. (1958)-. Newspaper. English. wk. $15.00 Louisiana & Mississippi; $16.00 other. Observer / Baker, PO Box 517, Baker LA 70714. **Tel** (504)775-2315.

US/0746-7478
OUACHITA CITIZEN, THE. Newspaper. English. sw. $15.00 Ouachita parish, $20.00 other. Ouachita Citizen, 810 Natchitoches Street, West Monroe LA 71291. ***Continues*** *Citizen.*

US
PONCHATOULA TIMES, THE. 90th Year, No. 17 (Aug. 27, 1981)-90th Year, No. 21 (Sept. 24, 1981); 1st Year, No. 1 (Oct. 1, 1981)-. Newspaper. English. Fifty-two times a year. $13.00. The Ponchatoula Times, 145 West Pine Suite A, PO Box 743, Ponchatoula LA 70454-0743. **Tel** (504)386-2877. **ED** Bryan McHahon. Index available. cum. index (In office bound copy). **Bk Rev**, (Qty: 24 per year). **Photos**. **Ad Acc**. Full Page (B&W) $509.55. Half Page (B&W) $254.78. Full Page (Color) $509.55 plus $100.00 per color. Half Page (Color) $254.78 plus $100.00 per color. **Pub. Size:** Broadsheet. **Circ:** 5,225. available in microform from Southeastern Louisiana University.

US
RAYNE ACADIAN TRIBUNE. 195?- . Newspaper. English. sw. $18.00. Acadian Tribune Inc, South Adams Street, Rayne LA 70578. **Tel** (318)334-3186. **ED** Steven Bandy. **Ad Acc**. **Circ:** 3,980 (ctrl). ***Continues*** *Rayne Tribune.*

US/0746-7567
RAYNE INDEPENDENT, THE. Newspaper. English. wk. $7.00 with Acadia parish, $9.00 outside Acadia parish. Rayne Independent, 201E South 1st Street, Rayne LA 70578.

US
REVEILLE, THE. **Added/Corp** Louisiana State University, Baton Rouge. **VFOAT** Daily Reveille; Summer Reveille. Vol. 1 (Jan. 14, 1897)-. Newspaper. English. da. $13.00. Louisiana State University / School of Journalism, Baton Rouge LA 70803.

US/0747-1955
RIVER PARISHES GUIDE. **VFOAT** River Parishes Guide West St. Charles Guide. Vol. 14, No. 44 (June 22, 1983)-. Newspaper. English. sw. Louisiana Sportsman Magazine / Louisiana, PO Box 1199, Boutte LA 70039. **Tel** (504)758-7217, FAX (504)758-7000. ***Continues*** *River Parishes Guide and West St. Charles Guide.*

US/0891-8708
RUSTON DAILY LEADER, THE. **VFOAT** Ruston-Daily Leader; Ruston (La.) Daily Leader. Vol. 28, No. 30 (May 3, 1932)-. Newspaper. English. da (Sun.-Fri.). $88.00. The Ruston Daily Leader, PO Box 520, Ruston LA 71270-0520. **Tel** (318)255-4353. **ED** Nancy Bergeron. **Circ:** 7,526. available on microfilm. ***Continues*** *Daily Leader (Ruston, La.).*

US/0739-0017
SABINE INDEX (MANY, LA. : 1879). (THE SABINE INDEX.). Vol. 1, No. 1 (Sept. 6, 1879)-. Newspaper. English. wk. $13.13 Parish; $26.26 other. Sabine Index, 850 San Antonio Avenue, PO Box 850, Many LA 71449. **Tel** (318)256-3495. **ED** Larry Morris. Index available. **Ad Acc**. **Circ:** 6,000 (ctrl).

●US
SAC NEWS MONTHLY. (199?)-. Newspaper. English. Twelve times a year. $20.00. SAC News Monthly, PO Box 159, Bogalusa LA 70429. **Tel** (800)825-3722, FAX (504)732-3744. **ED** Wayne Smith. **Bk Rev**. **Ad Acc**, **Adv Mgr Tel** (800)825-3722. **Circ:** 3,000 (ctrl). ***Absorbed*** *Art & Crafts Catalyst;* ***Continues*** *National Arts & Crafts Network.*
Desc: A newspaper that lists thousands of art and craft shows nationwide.

US
SHREVEPORT JOURNAL (SHREVEPORT, LA. : 1895). (THE SHREVEPORT JOURNAL.). Began Jan. 7, 1895. Newspaper. English. da. Shreveport Journal, 222 Lake Street, Shreveport LA 71130.

US
ST. TAMMANY FARMER. **VFOAT** Saint Tammany Farmer. (Nov. 1874)-. Newspaper. English. wk. $15.00 and $20.00. St. Tammany Farmer, PO Box 269, Covington LA 70434. **Tel** (504)892-2323, FAX (504)892-2325. **ED** Ron Barthet. **LC** 7946-X. **Photos**. **Ad Acc**, **Adv Mgr:** Vera Hardman. Half Page (B&W) $277.83. Full Page (Color) $483.30. Half Page (Color) $383.83. **Pub. Size:** Broadsheet. available in microform.

US/0745-5526
ST. TAMMANY NEWS-BANNER, THE. **VFOAT** Saint Tammany News-Banner; St. Tammany News Banner. **VAT** St. Tammany News Banner. Vol. 12, No. 40 (Jan. 28, 1976)-. Newspaper. English. sw (Sun. & Wed.). $35.00 St. Tammany Parish; $45.00 other. St. Tammany News-Banner, PO Drawer 90, Covington LA 70434. **Tel** (504)892-7980. ***Formed by the union of*** *Banner (Mandeville, La.)* ***and*** *St. Tammany News.*

US
TANGI TALK. Vol. 18, No. 50 (Mar. 25, 1948)-. Newspaper. English. wk. $11.69 local. Tangi Talk, PO Box 637, Amite LA 70422. **Tel** (504)748-6343. ***Continues*** *Tangi Talk and the Amite Progress.*

US/1055-3053
TIMES-PICAYUNE (NEW ORLEANS, LA. 1986), THE. (TIMES-PICAYUNE.). **VFOAT** Times Picayune; Times-Picayune Incorporating the States-Item. **VAT** Times Picayune. No. 250 (Oct. 1, 1986)-. Newspaper. English. da. $144.00 Louisiana and Mississippi; $180.00 US; $456.00 other (daily only). Times-Picayune Publishing Corporation, 3800 Howard Avenue, New Orleans LA 70140. **Tel** (800)925-0000, (504)822-6660. **Ad Acc**. ***Continues*** *Times-Picayune the States-Item.*
Ind/Abst PROMT.

US
TIMES (SHREVEPORT, LA.). (THE TIMES.). June 17, 1979-. Newspaper. English. da. Newspaper Production Company, 222 Lake Street, Shreveport LA 71130. **Tel** (318)459-3200. **ED** Raymond L McDaniel. **Circ:** 77,508 daily, 110,549 Sunday. ***Continues*** *Shreveport Times (Shreveport, La. : 1889 : Daily);* ***Absorbed*** *Shreveport Journal (Shreveport, La. : 1902).*

US/8750-6785
VILLE PLATTE GAZETTE, THE. Vol. 71, No. 6 (Jan. 14, 1985)-. Newspaper. English. bw. $25.00. Evangeline Publishing Company, 145 Court Street, PO Box 220, Ville Platte LA 70586. **Tel** (318)363-2103. **ED** David Ortepo, Jeff Guillard (Managing Editor). **Bk Rev**, (Qty: 12). **Photos**. **Ad Acc**, **Adv Mgr:** Jerry Matt. Full Page (B&W) $635.00. Half Page (B&W) $325.00. Full Page (Color) $725.00. Half Page (Color) $415.00. **Pub. Size:** Broadsheet. **Circ:** 4,100 paid. ***Continues*** *Gazette (Ville Platte, La).*

US
WATCHMAN, THE. **VFOAT** East Feliciana Watchman. Vol. 91, No. 16 (Apr. 2, 1970)-. Newspaper. English. wk. $24.00 Louisiana; $39.00 US. Louisiana Suburban Press Inc., 5240 Groom Road, Baker LA 70714. **Tel** (504)683-5195, (504)683-5196. ***Continues*** *East Feliciana Watchman.*

MAINE

US/0892-8738
BANGOR DAILY NEWS. (THE BANGOR DAILY NEWS.). **VFOAT** Maine Weekend. (June 18, 1889)-. Newspaper. English. da (Mon.-Sat.). $195.00. Bangor Daily News, 491 Main Street, PO Box 1329, Bangor ME 04402. **Tel** (207)990-8000, FAX (207)941-9476. **ED** Robert A. Kelleter, Nancy S. Remsen. **DD** 071. **Photos**. **Ad Acc, Adv Mgr:** Wayne A. Lawton, **Tel** (207)990-8261. Full Page (B&W) $3780.00. Half Page (B&W) $1890.00. Full Page (Color) $4360.00. Half Page (Color) $2470.00. **Pub. Size:** Broadsheet. **Circ:** 83,276 (ctrl). available on microfilm from University Microfilms International (UMI). **Absorbed** *Bangor Daily Whig & Courier.*
Desc: Sections include national, international, state and local news, sports, home improvements, editorial, financial, obituaries, TV and radio schedules, classified ads and amusements.

US
BAR HARBOR TIMES, THE. Began in 1925?. Newspaper. English. wk. $21.00 Hancock County; $27.00 Maine; $42.00 US; $70.00 other. Courier Publications / Maine, One Park Drive, Box 249, Rockland ME 04841. **Tel** (207)594-4401. **Continues** *Bar Harbor Times and Bar Harbor Record.*

US
BOOTHBAY REGISTER. Vol. 1, No. 1 (Dec. 9, 1876)-. Newspaper. English. wk. Boothbay Register, 95 Townsend Avenue, Boothbay Harbor ME 04538.

US
BRIDGTON NEWS, THE. Began in Sept. 1870. Newspaper. English. wk. Bridgton News, 42 Main Street, Bridgton ME 04009.

US
CAMDEN HERALD, THE. (1869)-. Newspaper. English. wk. Camden Herald, PO Box 248, Camden ME 04843.

US
CASTINE PATRIOT. English. wk (51 issues per year). $20.00 Maine; $25.00 other. Castine Patriot, PO Box 205, Castine ME 04421. **Tel** (207)326-4383. **ED** Nathaniel W. Barrows (Editor's telephone: 207-367-2325). **Ad Acc, Adv Mgr:** W. Sewall, **Tel** (207)367-2200. **Circ:** 1,000.

US/0192-4524
COASTAL JOURNAL. (19??)-. Newspaper. English. wk. Coastal Publishing Company, PO Box 575, Bath ME 04530. **Tel** (207)443-6241. **ED** Richard Denzer and Mary Denzer. **Circ:** 21,000.

US
COURIER-GAZETTE, THE. **VFOAT** A.Courier gazette. (1882)-. Newspaper. English. tw. Courier Publications / Maine, One Park Drive, Box 249, Rockland ME 04841. **Tel** (207)594-4401. **LC** 7002. available on microfilm from Graphic Microfilm Division. **Formed by the union of** *Rockland Courier and Rockland Gazette.*

US/8750-961X
EASTERN GAZETTE (1985), THE. (THE EASTERN GAZETTE.). (1985)-. Newspaper. English. wk. $26.00. Eastern Gazette, PO Box 306, Dexter ME 04930. **ED** Bob Shank, Michele Lancaster (Managing Editor). **Bk Rev,** (Qty: 5). **Photos**. **Ad Acc.** Full Page (B&W) $393.75. Half Page (B&W) $225.00. Full Page (Color) $423.75. Half Page (Color) $255.00. **Pub. Size:** Tabloid. **Circ:** 13,500. **Continues** *Gazette (Dexter, ME.).*

US
ELLSWORTH AMERICAN. (1854)-. Newspaper. English. wk (Thursday). $10.00. Ellsworth American, Box 509, Ellsworth ME 04605. **Tel** (207)667-2576, FAX (207)667-7656. **ED** James Russell Wiggins (Editor-in-Chief) and Katherine Heidinger (Managing Editor). **Bk Rev,** (Qty: 52). **Photos**. **Ad Acc, Adv Mgr:** Terry L. Young. Full Page (B&W) $1100.00. Half Page (B&W) $698.25. Full Page (Color) $1275.00. Half Page (Color) $873.25. **Pub. Size:** Broadsheet. **Circ:** 12,000. **Continues** *Ellsworth Herald.*

US
FRANKLIN JOURNAL AND FARMINGTON CHRONICLE, THE. (March 1919)-. Newspaper. English. sw. $25.00 Maine; $35.00 others. The Franklin Journal and Farmington Chronicle, PO Box 750, Farmington ME 04938. **ED** Janet K. Warner (Editor-in-Chief) and Dan Fellini (Managing Editor). **Photos**. **Ad Acc, Adv Mgr:** Carol A. Lanier, **Tel** (207)778-2075. Full Page (B&W) $784.35. Half Page (B&W) $392.18. Full Page (Color) $878.85. Half Page (Color) $439.43. **Pub. Size:** Broadsheet. **Circ:** 5,336. available on microfilm. **Formed by the union of** *Franklin Journal and Farmington Chronicle.*

US/1064-0657
KATAHDIN TIMES. (19??)-. Newspaper. English. wk. $34.00 Maine; $38.00 US; $44.00 other. Eastern Publ. Limited, Box 330, Millinocket ME 04462. **Tel** (207)723-8118, FAX (207)723-4434. **ED** Barbara M. Waters. **Bk Rev**. **Photos**. **Ad Acc, Adv Mgr:** Robin Stevens. Full Page (B&W) $793.35. Half Page (B&W) $396.68. Full Page (Color) $883.35. Half Page (Color) $486.68. **Pub. Size:** Broadsheet. **Circ:** 4,400.

US/0745-2039
KENNEBEC JOURNAL (AUGUSTA, ME. : 1975). (KENNEBEC JOURNAL.). Vol. 150, No. 7 (Jan. 8, 1975)-. Newspaper. English. da (Monday - Saturday). $168.00. Kennebec Journal, 274 Western Avenue, Augusta ME 04330. **Tel** (207)623-3811, FAX (207)623-3811. **ED** Alan Buncher. **Ad Acc, Adv Mgr:** Molly Evans. **Circ:** 19,134. available on microfilm from University Microfilms International (UMI). **Continues** *Daily Kennebec Journal.*

US
LEWISTON JOURNAL. **VFOAT** Sunday Sun-Journal. Oct. 15, (1979)-. Newspaper. English. Fifty-two times a year. $76.00. Lewiston Sun, PO Box 4400, Lewiston ME 04243. **Tel** (207)784-5411, (800)482-0753. **Circ:** 12,397. available on microfilm. **Continues** *Lewiston Evening Journal.*

US/0025-0783
MAINE TIMES. (Oct. 4, 1968)-. Newspaper. English. wk. $25.00 (1 year), $43.50 (2 year), $58.50 (3 year) US; $45.00 (1 year), $83.50 (2 year), $118.50 (3 year) other. Maine Times, One Main Street, Topsham ME 04086. **Tel** (207)729-0126, FAX (207)729-2699. **ED** Peter W. Cox. **Bk Rev**. **Ad Acc**. **Circ:** 20,000. available on microfilm from University Microfilms International (UMI).
Desc: Newspaper focusing on current issues and news of Maine with particular emphasis on environment, regional industries, coastal development and cultural affairs.

US
PORTLAND PRESS HERALD, THE. **VFOAT** Sunday Press Herald; Sunday Press Herald and Maine Farmer; Portland Sunday Telegram and Sunday Press Herald; Portland Sunday Telegram. (Nov. 21, 1921)-. Newspaper. English. da (Except Sunday). $120.00 Maine (morning edition by carrier); $158.00 Maine, $226.00 others (daily by mail subs.); $103.00 Maine, $111.40 other (Sunday edition by mail). Guy Gannett Publishing Company, PO Box 11350, Portland ME 04101. **Tel** (207)780-9000. **ED** John K. Murphy. Index available. cum. index. **Bk Rev**. **Ad Acc**. **Pr Rev**. **Circ:** 62,183 (ctrl). available on microfilm. **Formed by the union of** *Portland Daily Press and Portland Herald.*

US/0034-5075
REPUBLICAN JOURNAL (BELFAST, ME.). (THE REPUBLICAN JOURNAL.). (Feb. 6, 1829)-. Newspaper. English. wk. $18.00 (libraries); $39.00 US; $60.00 other. Courier Publications / Maine, One Park Drive, Box 249, Rockland ME 04841. **Tel** (207)594-4401. **ED** Polly Saltonstall. **Ad Acc**. **Circ:** 8,500 (ctrl). available on microfilm. **Continues** *Waldo Democrat.*

US/0747-1432
SUNDAY SUN-JOURNAL. **VFOAT** Sunday; Sunday Sun Journal. Vol. 1, No. 1 (Oct. 2, 1983)-. Newspaper. English. wk. Lewiston Sun, PO Box 4400, Lewiston ME 04243. **Tel** (207)784-5411, (800)482-0753. **Circ:** 41,103.

US
SUNDAY TELEGRAM, THE. (1887)-. Newspaper. English. wk. Guy Gannett Publishing Company, PO Box 11350, Portland ME 04101. **Tel** (207)780-9000. Index available. cum. index. **Bk Rev**. **Ad Acc**. ctrl circ.

US/0747-1300
TIMES RECORD (BRUNSWICK, ME), THE. (THE TIMES RECORD.). (1967)-. Newspaper. English. da (5 days a week). $105.00. Brunswick Publishing Co. / Maine, Box 10, Industry Road, Brunswick ME 04011. **Tel** (207)729-3311, FAX (207)729-5728. **ED** Campbell Niven, and Martin McKenna (Managing Editor). **Bk Rev**. **Photos**. **Ad Acc, Adv Mgr:** John Bamford. Full Page (B&W) $1,147.50. Half Page (B&W) $567.00. Full Page (Color) $1,347.50. Half Page (Color) $767.00. **Pub. Size:** Broadsheet. **Wire Svcs.:** AP. **Circ:** 14,000. **Formed by the union of** *Bath Times and Brunswick Record.*

US
YORK COUNTY COAST STAR. Newspaper. English. wk (published Wednesday). $28.00 York County, $36.00 US; $75.00 other. York County Coast Star, PO Box 979, Kennebunk ME 04043. **Tel** (207)985-2961. **ED** Ralph Hall. **Bk Rev**. **Ad Acc**. ctrl circ.

MARYLAND

US
AEGIS, THE. Vol. 113, No. 39 (Sept. 25, 1969)-. Newspaper. English. Fifty-two times a year. $26.00. Aegis Newspaper, Box 189, Belair MD 21014. **Tel** (301)879-9592. **ED** Ted Hendricks, (phone: (410)879-1710). **Photos**. **Ad Acc, Adv Mgr:** Kay Kline, **Tel** (410)838-4409. Full Page (B&W) $125.00. Full Page (Color) $325.00. **Pub. Size:** Broadsheet. **Circ:** 36,000. **Continues** *Aegis the Harford Gazette and the Democratic Ledger.*

US/0278-6605
AFRICAN NEWSPAPER INDEX, THE. [Afr. newsp. index]. Vol. 1, No. 1-. English. sa. $125.00 US; $155.00 other. Current Documents and Information, PO Box 3714, Langley Park MD 20787. **ED** Elizabeth N Yang. **LC** Z3503; .A365; DT3. **DD** 960/.05. **Circ:** 205.

US
AFRO-AMERICAN (BALTIMORE, MD. : NATIONAL ED.). (THE AFRO-AMERICAN.). **VFOAT** Afro American. 55th year, No. 33 (March 29, 1947)-. Newspaper. English. wk. Afro-American Company of Baltimore City, 628 North Eutaw Street, Baltimore MD 21201. **Tel** (410)728-8200, FAX (410)383-3213. available on microfilm. Documents available from UMI Article Clearinghouse.
Ind/Abst Newsp. Abstr.

US
BALTIMORE AFRO-AMERICAN. Newspaper. English. wk. Afro-American Company of Baltimore City, 628 North Eutaw Street, Baltimore MD 21201. **Tel** (410)728-8200, FAX (410)383-3213.

US
BALTIMORE CHRONICLE. (1977)-. Newspaper. English. mo. Baltimore Chronicle, 30 West 25th Street, Baltimore MD 21218. **Tel** (410)243-4141. **ED** Laurence Kraus. **Ad Acc**. **Circ:** 28,000. **Continues** *City Dweller (Baltimore, Md.).*

US
BALTIMORE ENTERPRISE AND INNER HARBOR NEWS, THE. (1987)-. Newspaper. English. wk. Baltimore Enterprise, 1205 South Charles Street, Baltimore MD 21230. **Tel** (301)752-0711. **Continues** *Enterprise (Baltimore, Md. : 1939).*

US/1041-0872
BALTIMORE MESSENGER (1985), THE. (THE BALTIMORE MESSENGER). Vol. 22, No. 34 (Aug. 28, 1985)-. Newspaper. English. wk. Baltimore Messenger, 409 Washington Avenue, Baltimore MD 21204. **Tel** (301)338-7632. **ED** Leu Lazaride. **Photos**. **Ad Acc, Adv Mgr:** Mark Iacurra. **Pub. Size:** Tabloid. available in microform. **Continues** *Messenger (Baltimore, Md.),* 0191-6211.

US
BANNER / CAMBRIDGE. Newspaper. English. da (Published Monday through Friday). $95.00. The Banner / Cambridge MD, PO Box 580, Cambridge MD 21613. **Tel** (301)228-3131.

US
BOWIE BLADE-NEWS, THE. **VFOAT** Bowie Blade News. Vol. 19, No. 5 (Feb. 6, 1980)-. Newspaper. English. wk. $18.20. Capital Gazette Newspapers Inc., 2000 Capital Drive, Annapolis MD 21401. **Tel** (301)268-5000. **Formed by the union of** *Bowie Blade (Bowie, Md. : 1979) and Bowie News (Bowie, Md.).*

US
CALVERT INDEPENDENT. Vol. 1, No. 1 (Oct. 24, 1940)-. Newspaper. English. wk. $15.00 Calvert County; $18.24 other. Prince Fredrick Calvert Independent, PO Box 910, Prince Fredrick MD 20678. **Tel** (301)535-1575.

US
CAPITAL, THE. **VFOAT** Sunday Capital. Vol. 97, No. 146 (June 22, 1981)-. Newspaper. English. ds. $166.00. Capital Gazette Newspapers Inc., 2000 Capital Drive, Annapolis MD 21401. **Tel** (301)268-5000. **ED** Edward Casey. **Circ:** 39,848. **Continues** *Evening Capital (Annapolis, Md. : 1922).*

US/0746-1658
CAROLINE COUNTY TIMES-RECORD, THE. **VFOAT** Times-Record. **VAT** Caroline County Times Record. Vol. 1, No. 1 (August 3, 1983)-. Newspaper. English. wk. Chesapeake Publishing Corporation / Maryland, 1 Airpark Drive, Box 600, Easton MD 21601. **Tel** (410)479-3174. **Formed by the union of** *Federalsburg Times (Federalsburg, Md. : 1964) and County Record (Denton, Md.).*

US/0746-7494
CARROLL COUNTY TIMES. **VFOAT** Neighborhoods of Carroll. Vol. 45, No. 27 (July 5, 1956)-. Newspaper. English. da (Mon.-Sat.). $60.75. Carroll

County Times, 12 Carroll Street, PO Box 346, Westminister MD 21157-0346. **Tel** (301)857-9413 or, (301)875-7494. **ED** Charles E. Bracken. **Ad Acc. Circ:** 20,000. ***Continues*** *Times (Westminster, MD.);* ***Absorbed*** *Pilot (Union Bridge, Md.); Democratic Advocate (Westminster, Md.).*

US/0748-5263
CATONSVILLE TIMES. 98th Year, No. 51 (Sept. 12, 1979)-. Newspaper. English. wk. $16.80 Baltimore county residents. Patuxent Publishing Corporation, 10750 Little Patuxent Parkway, Columbia MD 21044. **Tel** (410)730-3620, FAX (410)730-7053. **Photos. Ad Acc.** Full Page (B&W) $32.50 per column inch (Classified Ads). **Pub. Size:** Tabloid. **Circ:** 7,800. ***Continues*** *Catonsville Times and Herald Argus-Baltimore Countian.*

US/1046-2058
CECIL WHIG, THE. Began with Aug. 7, 1841 issue. Newspaper. English. wk. Cecil Whig, 601 Bridge Street, Elkton MD 21921. **Tel** (301)398-3311. **ED** Donald Herring. **Circ:** 15,130. ***Absorbed*** *Cecil Democrat (Elkton, Md. : 1850).*

US
CITIZEN RECORD. Vol. 1, No. 1 (Nov. 4, 1983)-. Newspaper. English. wk. The Citizen / Maryland, Route 2 Box 584, Frostburg MD 21532. ***Continues*** *Citizen (Frostburg, Md.), 0746-5424.*

US/0195-0843
CITY PAPER. Vol. 4, No. 3 (March 1979)-. Newspaper. English. mo. $20.00. City Paper, 800 North Charles Street/Suite 350, Baltimore MD 21201. **Tel** (301)539-5200. **ED** Russ Smith. **Bk Rev. Ad Acc. Circ:** 86,000 (ctrl).
Desc: Baltimore's largest weekly. Circulates Metro Area, targets young adult readers with an emphasis on news, art, and entertainment.

US/0740-3410
CITY PAPER (BALTIMORE, MD.). (CITY PAPER.). Vol. 2, No. 11 (Feb. 10, 1978)-. Newspaper. English. wk. $20.00. City Paper, 800 North Charles Street/Suite 350, Baltimore MD 21201. **Tel** (301)539-5200. ***Continues*** *City Squeeze.*

US/0192-7841
COLUMBIA FLIER. Vol. 1, No. 1 (June 18, 1969)-. Newspaper. English. wk. Free locally. Patuxent Publishing Corporation, 10750 Little Patuxent Parkway, Columbia MD 21044. **Tel** (410)730-3620, FAX (410)730-7053. **ED** Thomas Graham. **Bk Rev. Photos. Ad Acc.** Full Page (B&W) $29.55 per column inch (Classified Ads). **Pub. Size:** Tabloid. **Circ:** 34,000 (ctrl).
Desc: Concerns opinion, news, education, health, religion, community service, business, marketplace, villages, people, teens music; homelife, recreation, sports, theater, real estate, classifieds, art and cinema.

US
CUMBERLAND TIMES-LAW. VFOAT Cumberland Times News. Vol. 50, No. 165 (April 21, 1988)-. Newspaper. English. da. $153.60 Maryland, West Virginia, Virginia, Pennsylvania, Washington DC; $164.20 other. Cumberland Times News, PO Box 1662, Cumberland MD 21502. **Tel** (301)722-4600. ***Continues*** *Cumberland News (Cumberland, MD.).*

US
DAILY BANNER, THE. VFOAT Cambridge Daily Banner; Daily Banner and Cambridge Record. (Sept. 1897)-. Newspaper. English. da. $70.00. Daily Banner, PO Box 580, Cambridge MD 21613. ***Absorbed*** *Cambridge Chronicle (Cambridge, Md. : 1871); Cambridge Record.*

US
DAILY MAIL (HAGERSTOWN, MD.). (THE DAILY MAIL.). **VFOAT** Hagerstown Daily Mail. Began with Sept. 1, 1890 issue. Newspaper. English. da (Mon.-Fri.). Herald-Mail Company, Box 439, Hagerstown MD 21741. **Tel** (301)733-5123. **ED** James Schurz. **Circ:** 22,015.

US
DAILY RECORD, THE. Vol. 1, No. 1 (Oct. 2, 1888)-. Newspaper. English. da (303 issues per year - not published on Sundays or holidays). $139.00. Baltimore Daily Record, 11 East Saratoga Street, Baltimore MD 21202. available on microfilm.

US
DAILY TIMES (SALISBURY, MD.). (THE DAILY TIMES.). **VFOAT** Sunday Times. Vol. 42, No. 8 (Dec. 11, 1964)-. Newspaper. English. da. $169.00. Daily Times / Salisbury, PO Box 1937, Salisbury MD 21801. **Tel** (410)749-7171, FAX (410)543-8736. **ED** Mel Toadvine. **Bk Rev. Photos. Ad Acc, Adv Mgr:** Clyde Pinson. Full Page (B&W) $2457.45. Half Page (B&W) $1228.73. Full Page (Color) $27748.45 (one color). Half Page (Color) $1531.73 (one color). **Pub. Size:** Broadsheet. **Wire Svcs.:** AP. **Circ:** 28,840 morning, 32,293 Sunday. available on microfilm from Crest Information Technologies. ***Continues*** *Salisbury Times.*

US
DAMASCUS COURIER-GAZETTE, THE. VFOAT Damascus Courier Gazette. Vol. 6, No. 13 (Feb. 2, 1983)-. Newspaper. English. wk. $50.00 Montgomery County, MD; $75.00 other. The Gazette Newspapers, PO Caller 6006, Gaithersburg MD 20884. **Tel** (301)948-3120. ***Continues*** *Courier, Damascus, Mt. Airy.*

US
DIAMONDBACK, THE. Vol. 1, No. 1 (June 9, 1921)-. Newspaper. English. da. $55.00 (one year); $95.00 (two years). Diamondback, 3136 South Campus Dining Hall, College Park MD 20742. **Tel** (301)314-8000, FAX (301)314-8358. **ED** Patty Logve (Editor-in-Chief) and Akweli Parker (Managing Editor). **Bk Rev**, (Qty: 20). **Photos. Ad Acc, Adv Mgr:** Chris Stelzig. Full Page (B&W) $1,606.50. Half Page (B&W) $803.25. **Pub. Size:** Broadsheet. **Wire Svcs.:** AP. **Circ:** 20,000. ***Continues*** *University Review (College Park, Md.).*

US
DUNDALK EAGLE, THE. Vol. 1, No. 1 (May 15, 1969)-. Newspaper. English. wk. $10.50 Maryland; $20.00 others. Dundalk Eagle, 4 North Center Place, Dundalk MD 21222-4300. **Tel** (410)288-6060, FAX (410)288-2712. **ED** Kimbel Oelke (Editor-in-Chief) and Deborah Cornery (Managing Editor). **Photos. Ad Acc, Adv Mgr:** Kim Boone. Full Page (B&W) $1,260.00. Half Page (B&W) $630.00. Full Page (Color) $1,380.00. Half Page (Color) $750.00. **Pub. Size:** Tabloid. **Circ:** 26,000.

US
EAST BALTIMORE GUIDE, THE. No. 7 (Apr. 29, 1971)-. Newspaper. English. wk. $7.00. Guide Publications / Maryland, 526 Conkling Street, Baltimore MD 21224. **Tel** (301)732-6600. ***Continues*** *Baltimore Guide.*

US
ENQUIRER-GAZETTE, THE. VFOAT Enquirer Gazette. Vol. 38, No. 4 (Feb. 6, 1925)-. Newspaper. English. wk. $15.00. Enquirer Gazette, PO Box 30, Upper Marlboro MD 20870. **Tel** (301)627-2833. ***Formed by the union of*** *Marlboro' Gazette, and Prince George's Advertiser* ***and*** *Prince George's Enquirer and Southern Maryland Advertiser.*

US
ENTERPRISE, THE. Vol. 60, No. 35 (Oct. 31, 1947)-. Newspaper. English. sw (published Wednesday and Fri.). $34.00 St. Marys coutny, $44.00 other. Enterprise Newspaper, PO Box 700, Lexinton Park MD 20653. **Tel** (301)862-2111. **ED** Rick Boyd. **Ad Acc, Adv Mgr:** Dave Palmer. ***Continues*** *St. Mary's Enterprise.*

US
EVENING SUN (BALTIMORE, MD.). (THE EVENING SUN.). Vol. 1, No. 1 (April 18, 1910)-. Newspaper. English. da (Monday-Friday). $90.00. Baltimore Sun, PO Box 17111, Baltimore MD 21297. **Tel** 800 829-8000. **Circ:** 175,643. available on microfilm from University Microfilms International (UMI).

US
FREDERICK POST, THE. (1913)-. Newspaper. English. da (Mon.-Sat.). $88.85 (zip codes 200-214, 217, 220-223, 172-174, and 254); $93.30 Maryland; $106.85 other. Frederick News Post, PO Box 578, 200 East Patrick Street, Frederick MD 21701. **Tel** (301)662-1177. **ED** Tom Mills. **Circ:** 22,860. ***Continues*** *Evening Post.*

US/0195-2447
GAITHERSBURG GAZETTE, THE. ***Title Change.*** Vol. 23, No. 36 (Sept. 30, 1982)-. Newspaper. English. wk. The Gazette Newspapers, PO Caller 6006, Gaithersburg MD 20884. **Tel** (301)948-3120. **ED** Terry Holland, Pat Royce, Bill Pritchard, and Amy Fickling. **Ad Acc. Circ:** 131,000. ***Continued by*** *Gazette (Gaithersburg, MD).*
Desc: News and information pertinent to the local community, county and state. Sports, family, school, entertainment, political issues, etc.

US
GREENBELT NEWS REVIEW. Vol. 19, No. 7 (Sept. 23, 1954)-. Newspaper. English. wk. $30.00. Greenbelt News Review, PO Box 68, Greenbelt MD 20768-0068. **Tel** (301)441-2662. **ED** Mary Lou Williamson, Elaine Skolnile (Managing Editor). **Photos. Ad Acc.** Full Page (B&W) $420.00. Half Page (B&W) $210.00. **Pub. Size:** Tabloid. **Circ:** 10,400 weekly unpaid. available in microform. ***Continues*** *Greenbelt Cooperator (Greenbelt, Md.).*

US
HANCOCK NEWS, THE. (July 2, 1914)-. Newspaper. English. wk. $12.00. Hancock News, 263 Pennsylvania, Hancock MD 21750. **Tel** (301)678-6255.

US/0748-5298
HOWARD COUNTY TIMES (COLUMBIA, MD.). (HOWARD COUNTY TIMES.). **VFOAT** Ellicott City Times. Vol. 118, No. 32 (Nov. 12, 1958)-. Newspaper. English. wk (Thurs.). $16.80. Patuxent Publishing Corporation, 10750 Little Patuxent Parkway, Columbia MD 21044. **Tel** (410)730-3620, FAX (410)730-7053. **ED** Tom Graham. **Photos. Ad Acc.** Full Page (B&W) $32.50 per column inch (Classified Ads). **Pub. Size:** Tabloid. **Circ:** 20,500. ***Continues*** *Ellicott City Times.*

US/0739-831X
HUAFU YOUBAO. (HUA FU YU PAO = WASHINGTON CHINA POST.). **VFOAT** Washington China Post. No. 1 (April/May 1983)-. Periodical. Chinese. wk (Published on Friday). $30.00. Washington China Post, PO Box 2284, Kensington MD 20895. **Tel** (310)231-5258.

US
JEFFERSONIAN, THE. (1911)-. Newspaper. English. wk (Thursday). $13.65. Patuxent Publishing Corporation, 10750 Little Patuxent Parkway, Columbia MD 21044. **Tel** (410)730-3620, FAX (410)730-7053. **Photos. Ad Acc.** Full Page (B&W) $15.45 per column inch (Classified Ads). **Pub. Size:** Broadsheet. **Circ:** 6,000. ***Absorbed*** *New Era (Towson, Md.); Democrat and Journal (Towson, Md.).*

US
KENT COUNTY NEWS. Vol. 1, No. 1 (Feb. 1, 1946)-. Newspaper. English. wk. Price varies according to postal code. Kent Publishing Company, 217 High Street, Chestertown MD 21620. **Tel** (410)778-2011, FAX (410)778-6522. **ED** Trisha McGee. **Ad Acc, Adv Mgr:** Mary Burton. **Circ:** 9,200. ***Formed by the union of*** *Kent News (Chestertown, Md.)* ***and*** *Chestertown Transcript.*

US/0748-528X
LAUREL LEADER. Vol. 85, No. 43 (June 25, 1981)-. Newspaper. English. wk (Thursday). Free locally. Patuxent Publishing Corporation, 10750 Little Patuxent Parkway, Columbia MD 21044. **Tel** (410)730-3620, FAX (410)730-7053. **Photos. Ad Acc.** Full Page (B&W) $18.00 per column inch (Classified Ads). **Pub. Size:** Tabloid. **Circ:** 30,000. ***Continues*** *News Leader (Laurel, Md.).*

US
MARYLAND TIMES-PRESS. VFOAT Maryland Times Press. Vol. 65, No. 41 (Nov. 3, 1988)-. Newspaper. English. wk. $18.90 Worcester County, MD; $26.25 other. Atlantic Publications, PO Box 479, Ocean City MD 21842. **Tel** (301)289-6834, FAX (410)289-6838. **ED** Stewart Dobson. **Ad Acc, Adv Mgr:** Sue Lathbery. ctrl circ. ***Formed by the union of*** *Maryland Coast Press* ***and*** *Ocean City Times.*

US
MONTGOMERY COUNTY SENTINEL. (1985)-. Newspaper. English. wk. $12.00. Montgomery County Sentinel, PO Box 1272, Rockville MD 20850. **Tel** (301)948-4630. ***Continues*** *Sentinel Montgomery County.*

US
MORNING HERALD, THE. VFOAT Herald Mail. (Dec. 1895)-. Newspaper. English. da. $159.00. Herald-Mail Company, Box 439, Hagerstown MD 21741. **Tel** (301)733-5123. **ED** Fred Temby, John League (Managing Editor). **LC** 8145. **Ad Acc, Adv Mgr:** Terry McDaniel. Full Page (B&W) $3125.67. Half Page (B&W) $1602.85. Full Page (Color) $3325.67. Half Page (Color) $1802.85. **Pub. Size:** Standard. **Wire Svcs.:** AP. **Circ:** 23,000 morning, 17,000 evening, 41,000 weeking (ctrl). available on microfiche; available on microfilm and microfiche. ***Formed by the union of*** *Daily Herald and Torch Light* ***and*** *Morning News (Hagerstown, Md.).*

US
NEWS (FREDERICK, MD.). (THE NEWS.). **VFOAT** Daily News. (Oct. 15, 1883)-. Newspaper. English. da (Mon.-Sat.). Frederick News Post, PO Box 578, 200 East Patrick Street, Frederick MD 21701. **Tel** (301)662-1177. **ED** Tom Mills. **LC** 7002. **Circ:** 15,489. ***Continues*** *Daily News (Frederick, MD.).*

US/0739-0955
NORTHWEST STAR. (19??)-. Newspaper. English. wk. $10.00. Northwest Star, 23 Walker Avenue, Circulation Department, Baltimore MD 21208. **Tel** (301)653-3800.

US/1041-0880
OWINGS MILLS TIMES. Vol. 1, No. 1 (Apr. 3, 1986)-. Newspaper. English. wk (Thursday). Free locally. Patuxent Publishing Corporation, 10750 Little Patuxent Parkway, Columbia MD 21044. **Tel** (410)730-3620, FAX (410)730-7053. **ED** Karen Yenick (Editor's Address: 410 Washington Avenue, Towson, MD 21204). **Photos. Ad Acc, Adv Mgr:** Tim Biringer, **Tel** (410)337-2455. Full Page (B&W) $18.00 per column inch (Classified Ads). **Pub. Size:** Tabloid. **Circ:** 32,000. ***Absorbed*** *Owings Mills, Pikesville, Randallstown, Reisterstown Flier, 0898-123X.*

US
PEEKE REPORT / METRO WASHINGTON DC EDITION / (MONDAY ONLY, BY MAIL). (19??)-. Newspaper. English. ir (48 issues per volume). $350.00. Peeke Loanfax Inc., 101 Chestnut Street, Suite 200, Gaithersburg MD 20878. **Tel** (301) 840-5752, FAX (301) 670-2881. **ED** Victor Peeke and Linda Parkhill (Editor-in-Chief) and Donna Smith (Managing Editor). **Ad Acc.**

US
PHS GRANTS POLICY MEMORANDUM. **Main/Corp** United States. Public Health Service. **VFOAT**

Public Health Service Grants Policy Memorandum. No. 1- Jan. 22, 1974-. Periodical. English. U.S. Public Health Service, 5600 Fishers Lane, Rockville MD 20857.

US/0194-2182
POTOMAC ALMANAC. (1957)-. Newspaper. English. wk. $27.00. Potomic Almanac Inc, 9910 River Road, Potomac MD 20854. **Tel** (301)983-3350. **ED** Leslie Leven and Joe Klem. **Bk Rev. Ad Acc. Circ:** 33,000 (ctrl).
Desc: Community newspaper including news, education, lifestyle, business and sports.

US/0883-7104
RANDALLSTOWN NEWS. Newspaper. English. wk. $13.50. Randallstown News, PO Box 247, Reisterstown MD 21136. **Tel** (301)356-2030. **ED** Curtis Updike. **Ad Acc. Circ:** 10,119 (ctrl). available in microform.
Desc: An independent community newspaper.

US/0893-0805
RICHMOND AFRO-AMERICAN AND RICHMOND PLANET (RICHMOND, VA. : 1941). (RICHMOND AFRO-AMERICAN AND RICHMOND PLANET.). **VFOAT** Richmond Afro American and Richmond Planet. 50th year, No. 13 (Nov. 15, 1941)-. Newspaper. English. wk. Afro-American Company of Baltimore City, 628 North Eutaw Street, Baltimore MD 21201. **Tel** (410)728-8200, FAX (410)383-3213. ***Continues*** *Richmond Afro-American.*

US/8756-6397
SOMERSET HERALD (PRINCESS ANNE, MD. : 1985). (SOMERSET HERALD.). **VFOAT** Marylander & Herald. Vol. 159, No. 40 (Jan. 2, 1985)-. Newspaper. English. Fifty-two times a year (Wed.). $18.90 local, $31.50 other. Somerset Herald, PO Box 310, Princess Anne MD 21853. **Tel** (410)651-1600. **ED** Darel LaPrade, Richard Crumbacker (Managing Editor). **Bk Rev**, (Qty: 12). **Photos. Ad Acc, Adv Mgr:** Tom Sexton. Full Page (B&W) $693.00. Half Page (B&W) $385.00. Full Page (Color) $828.00. Half Page (Color) $520.00. **Pub. Size:** Broadsheet. **Circ:** 3,200. ***Continues*** *Marylander and Herald.*
Desc: Covers entire Somerset county area and community news.

US/1065-2345
STAR-DEMOCRAT (EASTON, MD.), THE. (THE STAR-DEMOCRAT.). **VFOAT** Star Democrat; Sunday Star. (June 9, 1961)-. Newspaper. English. da (Mon.-Fri.). $119.70 (Sun.-Fri.), $102.90 (Mon.-Fri.), $88.20 (Sun.) (1 year). Star Democrat, PO Box 600, 1 Airpark Drive, Easton MD 21601. **Tel** (301)822-1500, FAX (301)820-6519. **ED** Denise Riley, Barbara Sauers (Managing Editor). **Bk Rev**, (Qty: 50-75). **Photos. Ad Acc, Adv Mgr:** David Fike. Full Page (B&W) $1770.00. Half Page (B&W) $885.00. Full Page (Color) $1895.00. Half Page (Color) $1010.00. **Pub. Size:** Broadsheet. **Wire Svcs.:** AP. **Circ:** 16,500 (ctrl). available in microform from University Microfilms International (UMI). ***Continues*** *Easton Star-Democrat.*

US
STATE REGISTER AND THE LEADER. **VFOAT** Leader & State Register. (19??)-. Newspaper. English. wk. Chesapeake Publishing Corporation / Maryland, 1 Airpark Drive, Box 600, Easton MD 21601. **Tel** (410)479-3174.

US
SUN (BALTIMORE, MD. : 1837). (THE SUN.). **VFOAT** Baltimore Sun. Vol. 1, No. 1 (May 17, 1837)-. Newspaper. English. da (except Sunday). $90.00. Baltimore Sun, PO Box 17111, Baltimore MD 21297. **Tel** 800 829-8000. **Circ:** 585,651. available on microfilm from University Microfilms International (UMI).
Ind/Abst PROMT.

US/8755-2663
U.S. PRESS. [U.S. press]. **VFOAT** US Press. **VAT** United States Press. Began in 1984?. Newspaper. English. wk. $26.00. US Press, PO Box 1789, Hyattsville MD 20788-0789. **DD** 071.

US/0734-7456
USA TODAY (ARLINGTON, VA.). (USA TODAY.). [USA today]. **VFOAT** U.S.A. Today. **VAT** United States of America Today (Arlington, Va.). Vol. 1, No. 1 (Sept. 15, 1982)-. Newspaper. English. da (Mon.-Fri.). $118.00 (library and institution) US. USA Today, PO Box 4179, Silver Springs MD 20914. **Tel** (301)622-7474. **DD** 071. **Ad Acc. Circ:** 1,324,223. Documents available from UMI Article Clearinghouse.
Desc: The only national newspaper that provides comprehensive coverage of news from all 50 states. Organized in four concise and easy-to-read sections, News, Money, Sports and Life.
Ind/Abst Account. Tax Datab. (Jan. 1989-); Foods Adlibra; Gen. Period. Index (19??-); Middle East Abstr. Index; Newsp. Period. Abstr. (1989-); PROMT; Resource/One Ondisc (1991-); TOM Gen. Index.

US/0894-8194
USAE. (USAE.). [USAE]. **VAT** United States Association Executive. (198?)-. Periodical. English. wk. $95.00. United States Association Executive (USAE), 4341 Montgomery Avenue, Bethesda MD 20814. **Tel** (301)951-1881, (800)627-USAE, FAX (301)656-2845. **ED** George Coustautine. **DD** 061. **Photos. Ad Acc, Adv Mgr:** Ross Heller. Full Page (B&W) $2,350.00. Half Page (B&W) $1,485.00. **Pub. Size:** Tabloid. **Pr Rev.** ***Continues*** *U.S. Association Executive (National Edition), 0740-2678.*
Desc: National news for and about Association Executives, hotels, and convention bureaus.

US
VALLEY REGISTER, THE. (1856)-. Newspaper. English. wk. $10.00. Valley Register Inc., 121 125 West Main Street, Middletown MD 21769. **ED** John Saxon. **LC** 7002. **Circ:** 1,500. ***Continues*** *Catoctin Whig.*

US
WASHINGTON AFRO-AMERICAN AND THE WASHINGTON TRIBUNE. **VFOAT** Washington Afro American and the Washington Tribune; Washington Afro American; Afro-American; Afro American. **VAT** Washington Afro American and the Washington Tribune. (May 12, 1964)-. Newspaper. English. Fifty-two times a year. $27.82 (one year), $49.22 (two years), $62.06 (three years). Afro-American Newspapers, 2915 North Charles Street, Baltimore MD 21218. **Tel** (410)554-8200, FAX (410)554-8213. **(Subscription address:** Washington Afro-American Newspapers, 1612 14th Street Northwest, Washington, DC 20009, phone: (202)332-0080**) DD** 071. **Ad Acc.** ctrl circ. ***Continues*** *Washington Afro-American.*

US
WORCESTER COUNTY MESSENGER. Vol. 4, No. 1 (May 1, 1980)-. Newspaper. English. wk. $18.00 Worcester County, MD; $30.00 other. Worcester County Messenger, PO Box 388, Pocomoke MD 21851. **Tel** (410)957-1700. ***Formed by the union of*** *Worcester Democrat (Pocomoke City, Md. : 1953)* ***and*** *Democratic Messenger (Snow Hill, Md.).*

MASSACHUSETTS

US/0192-8910
AMESBURY NEWS. Vol. 1, No. 1 (May 24, 1962)-. Newspaper. English. wk. North Shore Weeklies, 2 Washington Street, Box 192, Ipswich MA 01938. **Tel** (508)356-5141, FAX (508)356-9188. ***Continues*** *Amesbury Daily News.*

US
ANDOVER TOWNSMAN, THE. (Oct. 14, 1887)-. Newspaper. English. wk. $30.00. Andover Townsman, 89 North Main Street, PO Box 1986, Andover MA 01810. **Tel** (508)475-1943.

US
ARLINGTON ADVOCATE. (Dec. 30, 1871)-. Newspaper. English. wk. $25.00 (in county), $42.50 (other). Harte Hanks Communications Newspapers, 580 Winter Street, Waltham MA 02154. **Tel** (617)729-8100, (617)487-7200.

US/0004-234X
ARMENIAN MIRROR-SPECTATOR, THE. **VFOAT** Armenian Mirror Spectator. Vol. 7, No. 28 (Jan. 4, 1939)-. Newspaper. English. wk (except two weeks during July). $40.00. Baikar Association Inc, 755 Mt Auburn Street, Watertown MA 02172. **Tel** (617)924-4420, FAX (617)924-3860, telex 928436. **ED** Ara Kalaydjian. **Bk Rev. Ad Acc. Circ:** 3,300 (ctrl). ***Formed by the union of*** *Armenian Mirror* ***and*** *Armenian Spectator.*
Desc: We cover the North American Armenian community news of cultural, social, political and religious activities.

US/0004-2374
ARMENIAN WEEKLY, THE. Began in 1969. Periodical. English. wk. $40.00 North America; $95.00 (airmail) other. Hairenik Association Inc, 80 Bigelow Avenue, Watertown MA 02172-2012. **Tel** (617)926-3974, FAX (617)926-1750. **ED** Muriel Parseghian. **Bk Rev. Ad Acc. Circ:** 2,500 (ctrl). available on microfilm from University Microfilms International (UMI). ***Continues*** *Hairenik.*

US
ATHOL DAILY NEWS. Vol. 1, No. 1 (Nov. 1, 1934)-. Newspaper. English. da. Athol Daily News, 225 Exchange Street, Athol MA 01331. **Tel** (508)249-3535. **ED** Barney Cummings. **Bk Rev. Ad Acc, Adv Mgr:** Bernard Cunningham. **Circ:** 6,000 (evening). ***Absorbed*** *Athol Chronicle; Athol Transcript.*

US
AUBURN NEWS, THE. (Oct. 6, 1949)-. Newspaper. English. wk. $15.00 Massachusetts; $17.50 other. Auburn News, 475 Washington Street, Auburn MA 01501. **Tel** (617)832-5876.

US/0744-7221
BARNSTABLE PATRIOT. **VFOAT** Barnstable Patriot and Commercial Advertiser. Vol. 17, No. 842 (Sept. 9, 1846)-. Newspaper. English. Fifty-two times a year. $15.75 (one year), $30.00 (two years). Barnstable Patriot, PO Box 1208, Hyannis MA 02601. **Tel** (508)771-1427, FAX (508)790-3997. **ED** David B. Shill II, (editor's address: 712 Main Street, Hyannis, MA 02601, phone: (508)771-1427). **LC** 8160-X. **Bk Rev**, (Qty: 5). **Photos. Ad Acc, Adv Mgr:** Lucinda Harrison. Full Page (B&W) $1,118.88. Half Page (B&W) $604.80. **Pub. Size:** Broadsheet. **Circ:** 2,750. available in microform. ***Continues*** *Barnstable Patriot, and Commercial Advertiser.*
Desc: Coverage of the town government, sports, people, and local county news.

US
BARRE GAZETTE (BARRE, MASS. : 1839). (BARRE GAZETTE.). (1839)-. Newspaper. English. wk (published Thursday). $18.00. Bizarre Gazette, PO Box 448, Barre MA 01005. **Tel** (617)355-4000. **ED** Clarke W Hammersley. **LC** 8160-X. **Bk Rev. Ad Acc. Circ:** 1,850 (ctrl). available on microfilm. ***Continues*** *Barre Weekly Gazette;* ***Absorbed*** *Barre Patriot.*
Desc: Covers local news; items of interest to families, young and old; welcomes editorials, news, photos and illustrations.

US
BAY STATE BANNER. **VFOAT** Banner. Began with V. 1, Sept. 25, 1965. Newspaper. English. wk. $15.00. Banner Publications Inc, 925 Washington Street, Dorchester MA 02124. **Tel** (617)288-4900. **ED** M B Miller. **Bk Rev. Ad Acc. Circ:** 11,500. available on microfilm.
Desc: Community newspaper of greater Boston's African american community.

US/0744-7930
BEACON (ACTON, MASS.), THE. (THE BEACON.). (Oct. 22, 1981)-. Newspaper. English. Fifty-two times a year. $24.00 Middlesex County; $36.00 others. Beacon Communications Corp., 20 Main Street, Acton MA 01720. **Tel** (800)842-1317, (508)264-9300. ***Continues*** *Assabet Valley Beacon.*

US
BEDFORD MINUTE-MAN. **VFOAT** Bedford Minute Man. Vol. 1, No. 1 (Oct. 31, 1957)-. Newspaper. English. Fifty-two times a year. $24.00 Middlesex County; $36.00 others. Beacon Communications Corp., 20 Main Street, Acton MA 01720. **Tel** (800)842-1317, (508)264-9300.

US
BELMONT CITIZEN HERALD. (Apr. 7, 1988)-. Newspaper. English. wk. Century Newspapers Inc., 27 Waterfield Street, Winchester MA 01890-1804. **Tel** (617)729-8100, FAX (617)729-3837. ***Formed by the union of*** *Belmont Citizen* ***and*** *Belmont Herald.*

US
BERKSHIRE COURIER (GREAT BARRINGTON, MASS. : 1848). (THE BERKSHIRE COURIER.). **VFOAT** Courier. Newspaper. English. wk. Berkshire Courier, PO Box 150, Great Barrington MA 01230. ***Continues*** *Berkshire Courier and Housatonic Mirror;* ***Absorbed*** *Berkshire News (Great Barrington, Mass.).*

US/0895-8793
BERKSHIRE EAGLE, THE. **VFOAT** Berkshire Morning Eagle. Vol. 64, No. 206 (Jan. 2, 1956)-. Newspaper. English. da. $180.00. Eagle Publishing Co. / Pittsfield, MA, PO Box 1171, Pittsfield MA 01202. **Tel** (413)447-7311. ***Continues*** *Berkshire Evening Eagle.*

US
BEVERLY TIMES, THE. **VFOAT** Beverly Peabody Times. Vol. 71, No. 173 (Apr. 29, 1964)-. Newspaper. English. da. $99.20 (by carrier), $104.40 (by motor route). Beverly Times / Department of Circulation, 32 Dunham Road, Beverly MA 01915. **Tel** (508)927-6800. **ED** Paul Briand. **Photos. Ad Acc, Adv Mgr:** David Lodge, **Tel** (508)922-1234. Full Page (B&W) $2,186.10. Half Page (B&W) $1,093.05. Full Page (Color) $2,311.10. Half Page (Color) $1,218.05. **Pub. Size:** Broadsheet. **Wire Svcs.:** AP. available in microform. ***Continues*** *Beverly Evening Times.*

US
BILLERICA MINUTE-MAN. **VFOAT** Billerica Minute Man. (1973)-. Newspaper. English. Fifty-two times a year. $20.00 Middlesex County; $30.00 others. Beacon Communications Corp., 20 Main Street, Acton MA 01720. **Tel** (800)842-1317, (508)264-9300.

US
BILLERICA NEWS, THE. Vol. 1, No. 1 (Feb. 2, 1928)-. Newspaper. English. wk. North Shore Weeklies, 2 Washington Street, Box 192, Ipswich MA 01938. **Tel** (508)356-5141, FAX (508)356-9188. **Ad Acc, Adv Mgr:** John Vistorino. **Circ:** 180,508.

US/0745-8673
BLACKSTONE VALLEY TRIBUNE. **VFOAT** Weekend Blackstone Valley Tribune. Vol. 14, No. 17 (May 4, 1983)-. Newspaper. English. sw. Blackstone Valley Tribune, 60 Church Street, Whitinsville MA 01588. ***Continues*** *Blackstone Valley Tribune/Advertiser.*

US/0743-1791
BOSTON GLOBE, THE. **VFOAT** Boston Sunday Globe. Vol. 177, No. 116 (Apr. 25, 1960)-. Newspaper. English. ds. $324.00 Massachusetts, Vermont, New Hampshire, Rhode Island, Maine and Connecticut; $426.00 other US; $915.00 other. Globe Newspaper Company, PO Box 2378, Boston MA 02107. **Tel** (617)929-2720. **ED** John S. Driscoll. **Circ:** 516,284 daily, 805,099 Sunday. available on microfilm from University Microfilms International (UMI); available on an online database (files 631,635/Full-Text) from DIALOG. Documents available from UMI Article Clearinghouse. ***Continues*** *Boston Daily Globe (Boston, Mass. : 1872).* **Ind/Abst** Bus. Dateline (June 1, 1990-) [Full Txt.]; Newsp. Abstr.; Newsp. Abstr.; PROMT; Boston Globe Index.

US/0738-5854
BOSTON HERALD (1982), THE. (THE BOSTON HERALD.). **VFOAT** Sunday Boston Herald. Vol. 12, No. 355 (Dec. 21, 1982)-Vol. 12, No. 365 (Dec. 31, 1982); Vol. 12, No. 365 (Jan. 1, 1983); Vol. 1, No. 2 (Jan. 2, 1983)-. Newspaper. English. da. $140.40 (daily) Bedford Massachusett, $124.80 (Mon-Sat), by carrier; $153.00 US, $357.00 others (daily), $86.70 US, $142.80 others (Sunday), $239.70 US, $499.80 others (daily & Sunday) by mail. Boston Herald, PO Box 2096, One Herald Square, Boston MA 02106. **Tel** (617)426-3000, FAX (617)482-3507. **ED** Joseph Robinowitz. **Circ:** 359,527. available on microfilm from University Microfilms International (UMI); available on an online database (file 635/Full-text) from DIALOG. ***Continues*** *Boston Herald American.*

US/8750-1961
BOSTON JEWISH TIMES, THE. (1983)-. Newspaper. English. bw. $12.00. Boston Jewish Times, 15 School Street, Boston MA 02108. **Tel** (617)367-9100, FAX (617)367-9310. **ED** Robert Israel (Managing Editor). **Bk Rev. Photos. Ad Acc, Adv Mgr:** Eleanor Grosser, **Tel** (617)367-9100 ext.36. Full Page (B&W) $480.00. Half Page (B&W) $240.00. Full Page (Color) $1130.00 (full color). Half Page (Color) $890.00 (full color). **Pub. Size:** Tabloid. **Circ:** 9,000. available in microform. ***Continues*** *Jewish Times, 0021-6771.*
Desc: The interpretation of international, national and local events as seen through eyes of identifying American Jews.

US/0163-3015
BOSTON PHOENIX, THE. **VFOAT** Phoenix. Vol. 2, No. 4 (Jan. 23, 1973)-. Newspaper. English. wk. $41.50 (one year), $78.00 (two year) US; $43.50 (one year), $80.00 (two year) Canada; $45.50 (one year), $82.00 (two year) other. The Boston Phoenix, c/o Stephen M Mindich, 100 Massachusetts Avenue, Boston MA 02115. **Tel** (617)536-5390. **ED** Richard M Gaines. **Bk Rev. Ad Acc. Circ:** 128,000 (ctrl). available on microfilm from University Microfilms International (UMI). ***Continues*** *Boston Phoenix After Dark.*
Desc: Newspaper covering politics, arts, lifestyle topics and special interest areas.

US/0745-2055
BOSTON TAB, THE. **VFOAT** Tab. (Sept. 1981)-. Newspaper. English. wk. $15.00. Tab Newspapers, 1254 Chestnut Street, Newton MA 02164. **Tel** (617)969-0340. **ED** David Luberoff. **Circ:** 24,482.

US/0895-2590
BOURNE COURIER. Newspaper. English. wk. $13.00 Barnstable County, $18.00 other. Bourne Courier, PO Box 157, Bourne MA 02532. **ED** Sharon Cowan.

US
BRAINTREE FORUM AND OBSERVER. Vol. 100, No. 39 (Sept. 21, 1978)-. Newspaper. English. wk. $13.00. Braintree Forum, 354 Washington Street, Braintree MA 02184. ***Continues*** *Braintree Observer and Sunday Forum.*

●US
BRIDGEWATER TOWNSMAN, THE. Vol. 9, No. 36 (Oct. 13, 1992)-. Newspaper. English. wk. Mariner Newspapers, 165 Enterprise Drive, PO Box 682, Marshfield MA 02050-0905. **Tel** (617)837-3500, FAX (617)837-9619. ***Continues*** *Townsman (Bridgewater, Mass.).*

US
BROOKLINE CITIZEN. Began (Mar. 22, 1984)-. Newspaper. English. wk. Brookline Citizen, 2 Summit Avenue, Brookline MA 02146. **Tel** (617)232-7000, FAX (617)232-4305. **ED** Dan Greenfield. **Ad Acc. Circ:** 12,000. ***Continues*** *Brookline Chronicle Citizen.*

US/0745-2071
BROOKLINE TAB, THE. **VFOAT** Tab, Brookline Edition. Vol. 1, No. 1 (Apr. 25, 1979)-. Newspaper. English. Fifty-two times a year. $10.00 Brookline; $43.00 other. Tab Newspapers, 1254 Chestnut Street, Newton MA 02164. **Tel** (617)969-0340.

US
BURLINGTON NEWS, THE. (1957)-. English. wk. $12.00 Middlesex County; $16.00 other. Burlington News, PO Box 8, 120 Cambridge Street, Burlington MA 01803. **Tel** (617)272-2369.

US
CAMBRIDGE CHRONICLE. (Dec. 10, 1970)-. Newspaper. English. wk. $21.00. Bay State Community Newspapers, 360 Summer Street, PO Box 312, Sommerville MA 02144. **Tel** (617)625-6300. **ED** John Breneman and George Donnelly (Managing Editor). **Photos. Ad Acc, Adv Mgr:** Edwin Vargas. Full Page (B&W) $2192.40. Half Page (B&W) $1096.20. Full Page (Color) $2362.40. Half Page (Color) $1266.20. **Circ:** 6,500 (paid), 6,000 (unpaid). available in microform. ***Continues*** *Cambridge Chronicle and the Cambridge Sun.*

US/0745-2063
CAMBRIDGE TAB, THE. **VFOAT** Tab. (Sept. 1981)-. Newspaper. English. Fifty-two times a year. $10.00 Cambridge; $43.00 other. Tab Newspapers, 1254 Chestnut Street, Newton MA 02164. **Tel** (617)969-0340. **ED** David Luberoff. **Circ:** 20,874.

US/0192-8465
CAPE COD NEWS (SANDWICH, MASS.). (CAPE COD NEWS.). (19??)-. Newspaper. English. wk (Published Wed.). $25.00 one year. Cape Cod Newspapers, PO Box 39, Orleans MA 02653. **Tel** (508)255-2121.

US/0747-1467
CAPE COD TIMES. **VFOAT** Sunday Cape Cod Times. (19??)-. Newspaper. English. da. $221.00. Cape Cod Times, 319 Main Street, Hyannis MA 02601. **Tel** (508)775-1200. **ED** William Breisky. **Circ:** 44,188 daily, 52,499 Sunday.

US
CAPE CODDER, THE. Vol. 1, No. 1 (Jan. 31, 1946)-. Newspaper. English. sw (Published on Tues., Wed.). $26.00 Cape Cod MA; $37.50 US; $57.00 others. Cape Cod Newspapers, PO Box 39, Orleans MA 02653. **Tel** (508)255-2121.

US
CARVER REPORTER. Vol. 1, No. 1 (Nov. 17 1988)-. Newspaper. English. wk. $27.00. MPG Newspapers, 9 Long Pond Road, Plymouth MA 02360. **Tel** (508)746-5555, FAX (508)747-2148. **ED** Mark Pothier. **Photos. Ad Acc, Adv Mgr:** Gary Higgins. Full Page (B&W) $53.20. Half Page (B&W) $262.00. Full Page (Color) $681.00. Half Page (Color) $340.60. **Pub. Size:** Tabloid. **Circ:** 4,266. available on microfilm and microfiche.

US
CHELMSFORD INDEPENDENT. (Jan. 20, 1980)-. Newspaper. English. wk. $20.00 Middlesex County; $30.00 other. Beacon Communications Corp., 20 Main Street, Acton MA 01720. **Tel** (800)842-1317, (508)264-9300.

US/1054-6529
CHELSEA RECORD (CHELSEA, MASS.), THE. (THE CHELSEA RECORD.). Vol. 57, No. 229 (Sept. 16, 1948)-. Newspaper. English. sw. $60.00. Chelsea Record, PO Box 292, Chelsea MA 02150. **Tel** (617)884-2416. ***Continues*** *Chelsea Evening Record.*

US/0882-7729
CHRISTIAN SCIENCE MONITOR (1983), THE. (THE CHRISTIAN SCIENCE MONITOR.). [Christ. Sci. monitor]. **Added/Corp** Christian Science Publishing Society. Vol. 75, No. 218 (Oct. 3, 1983)-. Newspaper. English. da (except Saturday, Sunday and holidays). $168.00. Christian Science Publishing Society, One Norway Street, Boston MA 02115. **Tel** (617)450-2678, (617)450-2504. **(Subscription address:** CDS / SIFD Agency Control, 1901 Bell Avenue, Des Moines IA 50315.**) ED** J. Anthony Periton (Editor in Chief), John Dillin (Managing Editor), David Cook (Editor). **DD** 071. **CODEN** CSMOBF. **[CCC].** Index available. cum. index. **Bk Rev. Photos. Ad Acc, Adv Mgr:** Nick Drinker, **Tel** (617)450-2652. Full Page (B&W) $4500.00. Half Page (B&W) $2700.00. Full Page (Color) $5000.00. Half Page (Color) $3000.00. **Pub. Size:** Tabloid. **Wire Svcs.:** AP, RN. **Circ:** 95,000. available on microfilm from University Microfilms International (UMI); available on CD-ROM; available on an online database (files 635,715,771,772 - Full-Text) from DIALOG. Documents available from UMI Article Clearinghouse. ***Formed by the union of*** *Christian Science Monitor (Eastern Edition); Christian Science Monitor (Central Edition); Christian Science Monitor (New England Edition)* ***and*** *Christian Science Monitor (Pacific Edition).*
Desc: Pulitzer prize-winning newspaper reporting on global issues. Correspondents worldwide write on political, cultural, social, economic, religious trends and topics.
Ind/Abst AGRICOLA [Select. Cov.]; Art Archaeol. Tech. Abstr.; BioBusiness (1987-); Book Rev. Digest; Book Rev. Index; Bus. Dateline; Fut. Surv.; Gen. Period. Index; Health Ref. Cent. (1987-) [Select. Cov.]; Index Period. Artic. Relat. Law; Infobank (1983-); Music Index (-19??); Natl. Newsp. Index (1983-); Newsp. Abstr.; Newsp. Abstr.; NEXIS (1983-); Numis. Lit.

US
CLINTON DAILY ITEM. Vol. 1, No. 1 (July 17, 1893)-. Newspaper. English. wk. $96.20. Clinton Daily Item, 156 Church Street, Clinton MA 01510-2506. **Tel** (508)368-0176, FAX (508)368-1151. **ED** Jan Gottesman. **Bk Rev. Photos. Ad Acc, Adv Mgr:** Joan Marino. Full Page (B&W) $882.00. Half Page (B&W) $441.00. Full Page (Color) $967.00. Half Page (Color) $526.00. **Pub. Size:** Broadsheet. **Wire Svcs.:** AP. **Circ:** 4,846.

US
COHASSET MARINER. (1978)-. Newspaper. English. wk. Mariner Newspapers, 165 Enterprise Drive, PO Box 682, Marshfield MA 02050-0905. **Tel** (617)837-3500, FAX (617)837-9619.

US
CONCORD JOURNAL. Vol. 34, No. 25 (June 23, 1960)-. Newspaper. English. Fifty-two times a year (Publishes on Thurs.). $24.00 Middlesex County; $36.00 others. Beacon Communications Corp., 20 Main Street, Acton MA 01720. **Tel** (800)842-1317, (508)264-9300. ***Continues*** *Concord Journal and the Colonial.*

US/8750-8249
DAILY EVENING ITEM. Began with Dec. 8, 1877 issue. Newspaper. English. da (Mon.-Sat.). $91.20. Hastings and Sons Publishing Company, 38 Exchange Street, Lynn MA 01901. **Tel** (617)593-7700. **ED** John S Morgan. **Circ:** 29,333.

US/0739-3504
DAILY HAMPSHIRE GAZETTE. (1890)-. Newspaper. English. Six issues per week (published Mon. through Sat.). $160.00. H. S. Gere & Sons Inc, 115 Conz Street, Northampton MA 01060. **Tel** (413)584-5000, FAX (413)585-5222. **ED** Jim Foudy (editor-in-chief), Lou Groccia (managing editor). **LC** 8160-X. **Bk Rev. Photos. Ad Acc, Adv Mgr:** Bill Knittle. Full Page (B&W) $1567.35. Half Page (B&W) $789.75. **Pub. Size:** Standard. **Wire Svcs.:** AP, LA. **Circ:** 22,491 (ctrl). available on an online database (file 635/Full-Text) from DIALOG.

US
DAILY NEWS-MERCURY, THE. **VFOAT** Daily news Mercury. No. 1 (Oct. 30, 1989)-. Newspaper. English. da. $120.00. Malden Publications, 277 Commercial Street, Malden MA 02148. **Tel** (617)321-8000. ***Formed by the union of*** *Malden Evening News; Malden Evening News (Everett ed.); Medford Daily Mercury* ***and*** *Melrose Evening News.*

US/0744-2114
ENTERPRISE (BROCKTON, MASS.). (THE ENTERPRISE.). Newspaper. English. da. Enterprise Publishing Company / Massachusetts, 60 Main Street, Brockton MA 02403. **Tel** (508)586-6200. ***Continues*** *Brockton Enterprise & Brockton Times, 0279-4683.*

US/0747-0142
ENTERPRISE (FALMOUTH, MASS.), THE. (THE ENTERPRISE.). (19??)-. Newspaper. English. sw. $42.00 Cape Cod; $45.00 other. Enterprise / Massachusetts, 50 Depot Avenue, Falmouth MA 02540. **Tel** (508)548-4700.

US/0740-0837
GARDNER NEWS (1983), THE. (THE GARDNER NEWS.). Vol. 4, No. 298 (Nov. 21, 1900)-. Newspaper. English. da (Except Sundays). $138.00. Gardner News, 309 Central Street, Gardner MA 01440. **Tel** (508)632-8000. ***Continues*** *Gardner Daily News.*

US/0740-2090
GAZETTE (HAVERHILL, MASS.). (GAZETTE.). **VFOAT** Haverhill, Mass., Gazette. Newspaper. English. da. $72.00. Haverhill Publishing Company, 447 West Lowell Avenue, Haverhill MA 01830.

US/8750-0485
HALIFAX REPORTER, PLYMPTON REPORTER. (HALIFAX REPORTER.). **VFOAT** Halifax Reporter. (1984)-. Newspaper. English. wk. $18.00. MPG Newspapers, 9 Long Pond Road, Plymouth MA 02360. **Tel** (508)746-5555, FAX (508)747-2148. **ED** Mark Pothier. **Photos. Ad Acc, Adv Mgr:** Gary Higgins. Full Page (B&W) $487.20. Half Page (B&W) $243.00. Full Page (Color) $637.00. Half Page (Color) $318.60. **Pub. Size:** Tabloid. **Circ:** 1,243. ***Continues in part*** *Silver Lake News, 0746-6064.*

US/0747-4040
HANSON REPORTER. ***Ceased.*** (1984)-(199?). Newspaper. English. wk. MPG Communications, PO Box 959, Plymouth MA 02360. **Tel** (617)746-5555. ***Continues in part*** *Silver Lake News, 0746-6064.*

US
HARVARD CRIMSON, THE. (Oct. 23, 1891)-. Newspaper. English. da (during the academic year, except Sunday). $35.00 (Cambridge, MA); $59.00 (others). Harvard Crimson, 14 Plympton Street, Cambridge MA 02138. **Tel** (617)495-7890. **ED** Joe Kahn. **LC** LH1.H3; C5. **DD** 378.744/4. **Bk Rev. Ad Acc. Circ:** 3,500 (ctrl). ***Continues*** *Daily Crimson.*
Desc: Harvard University and Cambridge's only daily paper. Covers university, city, national and international news.

US
HELLENIC CHRONICLE, THE. (1950)-. Newspaper. English. wk. $20.00 (1 year) $35.00 (2 year) US; $45.00 (1 year), $85.00 (2 year) Canada; $55.00 (1 year), $90.00 (2 year) other. Hellenic Publishing Corporation, 324 Newbury Street, Boston MA 02115. **Tel** (617)262-4500.

US
HOLYOKE DAILY TRANSCRIPT HOLYOKE TELEGRAM. (Jan. 1927)-. Newspaper. English. wk. $161.00. Holyoke Transcript-Telegram Publishing Company, 120 Whiting Farms Road, Holyoke MA 01040. **Tel** (413)536-2300. **ED** Tom Schumaker. **LC** 8160-X. **Circ:** 23,888.

US/0745-9262
HYDE PARK TRIBUNE, THE MATTAPAN TRIBUNE. (HYDE PARK TRIBUNE.). **VFOAT** Hyde Park Tribune/Mattapan Tribune; Mattapan Tribune. **VAT** Hyde Park Tribune, Mattapan Tribune. (Sept. 1980)-. Newspaper. English. Fifty-two times a year (Thursdays). $15.00 Hyde Park; $18.00 other. Hyde Park Tribune, PO Box 67, Hyde Park MA 02136-0067. **Tel** (617)361-6500, FAX (617)361-8909. **ED** David Johnson, (phone: (617)361-6500). **Ad Acc, Adv Mgr:** K. Willette. **Circ:** 5,869 (ctrl). ***Formed by the union of*** *Hyde Park Tribune* ***and*** *Mattapan Tribune.*
Desc: Covers the local news.

US/0891-8686
INQUIRER AND MIRROR. Began in 1865. Newspaper. English. wk. Marie Griffin, 1 Milestone, Nantucket MA 02554. **Tel** (508)228-0001. **ED** Marianne Griffin. **Circ:** 9,775. ***Formed by the union of*** *Nantucket Inquirer (Nantucket, Mass. : 1840)* ***and*** *Nantucket Weekly Mirror.*

US/0745-9254
JAMAICA PLAIN CITIZEN ROXBURY CITIZEN. **VFOAT** Jamaica Plain Citizen and Roxbury Citizen; Roxbury Citizen. (19??)-. Newspaper. English. Fifty-two times a year (Thursdays). $15.00 Suffolk County; $18.00 others. Hyde Park Tribune, PO Box 67, Hyde Park MA 02136-0067. **Tel** (617)361-6500, FAX (617)361-8909. **ED** David Johnson, (phone (617)361-6500). **Ad Acc, Adv Mgr:** K. Willette. ***Continues*** *Jamaica Plain Citizen.*
Desc: Covers the local news and current events.

US
JEWISH ADVOCATE, THE. **VFOAT** Connecticut Hebrew Record; Springfield Hebrew Record; Springfield Review. Vol. 9, No. 12 (May 28, 1909)-. Newspaper. English. wk (published on Thursday). $26.00 Massachusetts, Maine, New Hampshire, Vermont, Rhode Island, Connecticut; $30.00 US; $43.00 other. Jewish Advocate, 15 School Street, Boston MA 02108. **Tel** (617)367-9100, FAX (617)367-9310. **ED** Robert Israel. **Bk Rev**, (Qty: 12). **Photos**. **Ad Acc, Adv Mgr:** Eleanor Grosser, **Tel** (617)367-9100 ext. 36. Full Page (B&W) $3,213.00. Half Page (B&W) $1,606.50. Full Page (Color) $3,863.00. Half Page (Color) $2,256.50. **Pub. Size:** Standard. **Wire Svcs.:** AP, JT. available on microfilm from University Microfilms International (UMI). ***Continues*** *Boston Advocate (Boston, Mass. : 1905);* ***Absorbed*** *Connecticut Hebrew Record.*

US/0747-2692
KINGSTON REPORTER. Vol. 1, No 1 (Feb. 9, 1984)-. Newspaper. English. wk. $27.00. MPG Newspapers, 9 Long Pond Road, Plymouth MA 02360. **Tel** (508)746-5555, FAX (508)747-2148. **ED** Mark Pothier. **Photos**. **Ad Acc, Adv Mgr:** Gary Higgins. Full Page (B&W) $531.20. Half Page (B&W) $265.60. Full Page (Color) $681.20. Half Page (Color) $340.60. **Pub. Size:** Tabloid. **Circ:** 5,434. available on microfilm and microfiche. ***Continues in part*** *Silver Lake News, 0746-6064.*

US/0746-4479
KYRIAKATIKA NEA. **VFOAT** Greek Sunday News. Vol. 1, No. 1 (1953)-. Newspaper. English (Greek, Modern). Twelve times a year. Greek Sunday News, 231 Harrison Avenue, Boston MA 02111. **Tel** (617)426-1948. **ED** William Harris. **Bk Rev**. **Ad Acc**. **Circ:** 250,000 (ctrl).

US
LANDMARK, THE. Vol. 8, No. 37 (Oct. 6, 1983)-. Newspaper. English. Fifty times a year. $20.00. The Landmark / Holden MA, PO Box 546, Holden MA 01521. **Tel** (508)829-5981, FAX (508)829-5981. **ED** Joanne Root. **Photos**. **Ad Acc, Adv Mgr:** Kathleen Puffer. Full Page (B&W) $652.80. Half Page (B&W) $326.40. Full Page (Color) $120.00. Half Page (Color) $401.40. **Pub. Size:** Standard. **Circ:** 7,604 (ctrl). available in microform from New England Micrographics, Inc. ***Continues*** *Holden Landmark.*

US
LAWRENCE EAGLE-TRIBUNE. **VFOAT** Lawrence Eagle Tribune; Sunday Eagle-Tribune. 93rd Year (Sept. 28, 1959)-. Newspaper. English. da (except Christmas). $92.00 (Sunday only); $158.00 (daily). Eagle-Tribune Publishing Company, Box 100, Lawrence MA 01842. **Tel** (617)685-1000, FAX (617)685-1588. **ED** Daniel Warner (Editor-in-Chief) and Gerry Molina (Managing Editor). Index available. **Photos**. **Ad Acc, Adv Mgr:** Vincent Cottone. Full Page (B&W) $2,799.30. Half Page (B&W) $1,399.65. Full Page (Color) $2,989.30. Half Page (Color) $1,589.65. **Pub. Size:** Broadsheet. **Wire Svcs.:** AP, SH. **Circ:** 55,515 (daily), 60,217 (Sundays) (ctrl). available on microfilm from New England Micrographics, Inc. Documents available from UMI Article Clearinghouse. ***Formed by the union of*** *Lawrence Daily Eagle* ***and*** *Evening Tribune (Lawrence, Mass.);* ***Absorbed*** *Lawrence Sunday Sun.*
Desc: Carries news ranging from the Lawrence area to international areas.
Ind/Abst Bus. Dateline (Dec. 31, 1991-) [Full Txt.].

US
LEXINGTON MINUTE-MAN. **VFOAT** Lexington Minute Man. Vol. 62, No. 10 (Feb. 2, 1933)-. Newspaper. English. Fifty-two times a year. $24.00 Middlesex County; $36.00 others. Beacon Communications Corp., 20 Main Street, Acton MA 01720. **Tel** (800)842-1317, (508)264-9300. **LC** 7002. ***Continues*** *Lexington Townsman and Lexington Times-Minute-Man, 8906-2266.*

US
LINCOLN JOURNAL. Vol. 1, No. 1 (Sept. 5, 1985)-. Newspaper. English. Fifty-two times a year (Published on Thurs.). $24.00 Middlesex County; $36.00 others. Beacon Communications Corp., 20 Main Street, Acton MA 01720. **Tel** (800)842-1317, (508)264-9300.

US/0744-7949
LITTLETON INDEPENDENT, THE. Vol. 25, No. 37 (July 28, 1977)-. Newspaper. English. wk (Published on Thurs.). $24.00 Middlesex County; $36.00 others. Beacon Communications Corp., 20 Main Street, Acton MA 01720. **Tel** (800)842-1317, (508)264-9300. **ED** Nancy Tuttle. **Circ:** 1,624. ***Continues*** *Independent.*

US/8750-1449
MARTHA'S VINEYARD TIMES, THE. Vol. 1, Issue 1 (Thursday, May 3, 1984)-. Newspaper. English. wk. $35.00 (third class); $75.00 (first class). Martha's Vineyard Times, PO Box 518, Vineyard Haven MA 02568-0518. **Tel** (508)693-6100, FAX (508)693-6000. **ED** Doug Cabral. **Bk Rev**, (Qty: 6). **Photos**. **Ad Acc, Adv Mgr:** Don Lyons and Nelson Sigelman. Full Page (B&W) $885.00. Half Page (B&W) $443.00. **Pub. Size:** Tabloid. **Circ:** 12,000 (ctrl). available in microform from the publisher.
Desc: Dedicated to the interests and concerns of those living on Martha's Vineyard.

US/0890-0434
MASSACHUSETTS DAILY COLLEGIAN, THE. **VFOAT** Collegian. (1890)-. Newspaper. English. da (Sept.-May). $85.00 (1 year), $50.00 (1 semester) daily delivery; $30.00 (1 year), $20.00 (1 semester) weekly delivery. The Massachusetts Daily, University of Massachusetts, 113 Campus Center, Amherst MA 01003. **Tel** (413)545-3500. **ED** Michelle Bayliss. cum. index. **Bk Rev**. **Ad Acc, Adv Mgr:** Danielle Yaniro, **Tel** (413)545-3500. **Circ:** 20,000 (ctrl). available on microfilm.

US
MAYNARD BEACON, THE. Vol. 40, No. 51 (Jan. 3, 1991)-. Newspaper. English. wk. $24.00 (1 year), $42.00 (2 year) Middlesex County, Massachusetts; $36.00 (1 year), $65.00 (2 year) other. Beacon Communications Corp., 20 Main Street, Acton MA 01720. **Tel** (800)842-1317, (508)264-9300. ***Continues*** *Beacon (Acton, Mass.).*

US
MIDDLEBORO GAZETTE (MIDDLEBORO, MASS. : 1870). (THE MIDDLEBORO GAZETTE.). Began in 1870. Newspaper. English. wk. Middleboro Gazette, 6 South Main Street, Middleboro MA 02346. ***Continues*** *Middleborough Gazette, and Old Colony Advertiser.*

US/0895-7681
NATICK BULLETIN (1982). (NATICK BULLETIN.). [Natick bull.]. Began May 1982. Bulletin. English. wk. Natick Bulletin, 2 Summer Street, Natick MA 01760. ***Continues*** *Natick Bulletin and Sun.*

US
NEWSWEEKLY. **VFOAT** Chelmsford Newsweekly; Chelmsford-Westford-Tyngsboro Newsweekly; Chelmsford Westford Tyngsboro Newsweekly. Vol. 35, No. 45 (Mar. 6, 1975)-. Newspaper. English. wk. $18.00. Chelmsford Newsweekly Inc., 5 North Road, PO Box 100, Chelmsford MA 01824. **Tel** (508)256-3311. ***Continues*** *Chelmsford Newsweekly.*

US/0739-3849
NEWTON GRAPHIC, THE. Vol. 11, No. 1 (Oct. 21, 1882)-. Newspaper. English. wk. $25.00 (in county), $42.50 (out of county). Transcript Newspapers Inc, 420 Washington Street, Dedham MA 02026. **ED** Andrea Haynes, Ellen Ishkanian (Managing Editor). **Photos**. **Ad Acc, Adv Mgr:** Susan Robinson, **Tel** (617)487-7255. Full Page (B&W) $681.75. Half Page (B&W) $340.88. **Pub. Size:** Tabloid. ***Continues*** *Newton Republican (Newton, Mass.)* ***and*** *Town Crier (Newton, Mass.).*

US/0745-2047
NEWTON TAB, THE. **VFOAT** Tab, Newton Edition. Vol. 1, No. 1 (Apr. 25, 1979)-. Newspaper. English. Fifty-one times per year. $10.00 Newton Massachusetts; $43.00 other. Tab Newspapers, 1254 Chestnut Street, Newton MA 02164. **Tel** (617)969-0340.

US
NORTH SHORE : SUNDAY. (Aug. 14, 1977)-. Newspaper. English. wk. $30.00. North Shore Weeklies Inc., 2 Washington Street, PO Box 192, Ipswich MA 01938.

US
NORWOOD YOUNG AMERICA TIMES. **VFOAT** Norwood Times. Vol. 96, No. 25 (Oct. 14, 1982)-. Newspaper. English. wk. Norwood Times, 601 Washington Street, Norwood MA 02062. **Tel** 769-1725. available on microfilm. ***Continues*** *Norwood Times.*

US
OLD COLONY MEMORIAL. **VFOAT** Old Colony Memorial, Plymouth Rock, and The Old Colony Sentinel. Vol. 51, No. 18 (May 2, 1872)-. Newspaper. English. wk. $30.00. Old Colony Memorial, Long Pond Road, PO Box 959, Plymouth MA 02360. **Tel** (508)746-5555, FAX (508)747-2148. **ED** Mark Pothier. **Photos**. **Ad Acc, Adv Mgr:** Gary Higgins. Full Page (B&W) $2,124.00. Half Page (B&W) $1,071.00. Full Page (Color) $2,292.00. Half Page (Color) $1,221.00. **Pub. Size:** Broadsheet. **Pr Rev. Circ:** 12,861. available on microfilm and microfiche. ***Continues*** *Old Colony Memorial and Plymouth Rock (Plymouth, Mass. : 1872);* ***Absorbed*** *Old Colony Sentinel; Plymouth Free Press; Plymouth Observer; Marshfield News (Marshfield, Mass.); Kingston News (Kingston, Mass.)* ***and*** *Duxbury News.*

US
PATRIOT LEDGER (CITY EDITION), THE. (THE PATRIOT LEDGER.). Vol. 126, No. 206 (Sept. 10, 1962)-. Newspaper. English. ir (308 per year). $130.00 public libraries; $260.00 other. George M Prescott Publishing Company, 400 Crown Colony Drive, Quincy MA 02169. **Tel** (617)786-7200, FAX (617)786-7092. **ED** Bill Ketter (editor's phone: (617)786-7013). **Bk Rev**, (Qty: 100/year). **Ad Acc, Adv Mgr:** George White, **Tel** (617)786-7175. **Circ:** 86,000. ***Continues*** *Patriot Ledger (Quincy, Mass.).*

US
PATRIOT LEDGER (SOUTH EDITION), THE. (THE PATRIOT LEDGER.). Vol. 126, No. 206 (Sept. 10, 1962)-. Newspaper. English. ir (308 per year). $130.00 public libraries; $260.00 other. George M Prescott Publishing Company, 400 Crown Colony Drive, Quincy MA 02169. **Tel** (617)786-7200, FAX (617)786-7092. **ED** Bill Ketter (editor's phone: (617)786-7013). **Bk Rev**, (Qty: 100/year). **Ad Acc, Adv Mgr:** George White, **Tel** (617)786-7175. **Circ:** 86,000. ***Continues*** *Patriot Ledger (Quincy, Mass.).*

US
PATRIOT LEDGER (SUBURBAN EDITION), THE. (THE PATRIOT LEDGER.). Vol. 153, No. 208 (Sept. 11, 1989)-. Newspaper. English. ir (308 per year). $130.00 public libraries; $260.00 other. George M Prescott Publishing Company, 400 Crown Colony Drive, Quincy MA 02169. **Tel** (617)786-7200, FAX (617)786-7092. **ED** Bill Ketter (editor's phone: (617)786-7013). **Bk Rev**, (Qty: 100/year). **Ad Acc, Adv Mgr:** George White, **Tel** (617)786-7175. **Circ:** 86,000. ***Continues*** *Patriot Ledger (Quincy, Mass. : West Ed.).*

US/0746-6056
PEMBROKE REPORTER. (1983)-. Newspaper. English. wk. $18.00. MPG Newspapers, 9 Long Pond Road, Plymouth MA 02360. **Tel** (508)746-5555, FAX (508)747-2148. **ED** Mark Pothier. **Photos**. **Ad Acc, Adv Mgr:** Gary Higgins. Full Page (B&W) $487.20. Half Page (B&W) $243.60. Full Page (Color) $637.20. Half Page (Color) $318.60. **Pub. Size:** Tabloid. **Circ:** 1,448. ***Continues in part*** *Silver Lake News, 0746-6064.*

US/0746-3928
PORTUGUESE TIMES (NEW BEDFORD, MASS.). (PORTUGUESE TIMES.). (1971)-. Newspaper. Portuguese (Portuguese). wk. $15.00 Rhode Island, Massachusetts, Maine, New Hampshire, Vermont, Connecticut, New Jersey, Pennsylvania, and New York); $20.00 (all other US states); $55.00 (Canada); $65.00 (other). Portuguese Times, Box N-1288/1501 Acushnet Avenue, New Bedford MA 02746. **Tel** (508) 997-3118, FAX (508) 990-1231, telex 9102400449. **ED** Manuel Ferreira. **Bk Rev**. **Ad Acc**. **Circ:** 17,000 (ctrl).
Desc: Foreign language news.

US/0888-0107
POST-GAZETTE (BOSTON, MASS.). (POST-GAZETTE.). **VFOAT** Post Gazette. Vol. 66, No. 9 (1962)-. Newspaper. Italian (English). wk (publ Fri.). $20.00 US, $30.00 other. Post-Gazette, 5 Prince Street, Boston MA 02113. **Tel** (617)227-8929. **ED** Pamela Donnaruma (phone: (617)227-8929). **Bk Rev**, (Qty: 26). **Photos**. **Ad Acc**. Full Page (B&W) $1,600.00. Half Page (B&W) $800.00. **Pub. Size:** Tabloid. **Circ:** 16,900 (ctrl). available on microfilm. ***Continues*** *Gazzetta (Boston, Mass.).*

US
PROVINCETOWN ADVOCATE. VFOAT Advocate. Newspaper. English. wk. Provincetown Advocate, 100 Bradford Street, Provincetown MA 02657. **ED** J M Crocker. ***Continues*** *Provincetown Advocate, and Cape Cod Advertiser.*

US
QUINCY SUN, THE. Vol. 1, No. 1 (Sept. 26, 1968)-. Newspaper. English. wk. $12.00 Quincy; $14.00 rest of MA, $17.00 other. Quincy Sun Publ Co, 1372 Hancock St., Quincy MA 02169. **Tel** (617)471-3100.

US/1059-4779
RAIVAAJA (FITCHBURG, MASS.). (RAIVAAJA.). **VFOAT** Pioneer. Began in Jan. (1905). Newspaper. Finnish (English). wk. $20.00. Raivaaja Publishing Company, Box 600, Fitchburg MA 01420. **Tel** (508)343-3822.

US
RECORDER (GREENFIELD, MASS.). (THE RECORDER.). (1967)-. Newspaper. English. da (Mon.-Sat.). $140.00. Recorder Publishing Company Inc., 14 Hope Street, Greenfield MA 01301. **Tel** (413)772-0261, FAX (413)774-5511. **ED** Tim Blogg and George Folcier (Managing Editor). **Bk Rev**. **Photos**. **Ad Acc, Adv Mgr:** Rich Foley. Full Page (B&W) $1,037.34. Half Page (B&W) $537.60. Full Page (Color) $1,143.34. Half Page (Color) $643.60. **Pub. Size:** Standard. **Wire Svcs.:** AP, LA, CO. **Circ:** 15,200. ***Continues*** *Greenfield Recorder-Gazette.*

US/0738-9108
SOUTH END NEWS (BOSTON, MASS.). (SOUTH END NEWS.). Vol. 1, No. 1 (Feb. 15, 1980)-. Newspaper. English. wk. $20.00. South End News, 1523 Washington Street, Boston MA 02118. **Tel** (617)266-6670.

US/0192-4869
SOUTH SHORE NEWS (WEST HANOVER, MASS.). (SOUTH SHORE NEWS.). (1???)-. Newspaper. English. wk. $30.00. South Shore News, 65 Grove Street, Rockland MA 02370. **Tel** (617)878-5100, FAX (617)878-1318. **ED** Eraina Rubin. **Bk Rev**, (Qty: 6). **Photos**. **Ad Acc, Adv Mgr:** Paul A. Mark. Full Page (B&W) $1872.00. Half Page (B&W) $936.00. Full Page (Color) $2097.00. Half Page (Color) $1161.00. **Pub. Size:** Tabloid. **Circ:** 51,090.

US/0745-3574
STANDARD-TIMES (NEW BEDFORD, MASS.), THE. (THE STANDARD-TIMES.). **VFOAT** Standard Times; Sunday Standard Times. **VAT** Standard Times (New Bedford, Mass.). (1932)-. Newspaper. English. da. Standard Times Publishing Company Inc, 555 Pleasant Street, PO Box D912, New Bedford MA 02742. **Tel** (617)997-7411. **ED** James M. Ragsdale. **Circ:** 46,996. available on an online database (file 635/Full-Text) from DIALOG. ***Formed by the union of*** *Evening Standard (New Bedford, Mass.)* ***and*** *New Bedford Times (New Bedford, Mass. : 1902).*

US
STONEHAM INDEPENDENT, THE. Vol. 38, No. 29 (July 18, 1908)-. Newspaper. English. wk. $20.00 (one year), $37.00 (two years)-(Stoneham, MA); $22.00 (other in MA); $24.00 (east of Mississippi River); $25.00 (west of Mississippi River). Stoneham Independent, 377 Main St, Stoneham MA 02180. **Tel** (617)438-1660, FAX (617)438-6762. **ED** Jeffrey Gutridge. **Ad Acc, Adv Mgr:** Jon Haggesty, **Tel** (617)438-1660. **Circ:** 5,000 (ctrl). ***Continues*** *Independent (Stoneham, Mass.).*

US/0194-276X
SUBURBAN NEWS (READING), THE. (THE SUBURBAN NEWS.). (197?)-. Newspaper. English. wk. $16.95. Suburban News / Massachusetts, 100 Main St., Reading MA 01867. **Tel** (617)944-4444, FAX (617)944-4494. **ED** Rose Thompson. **Bk Rev**, (Qty: 10). **Photos**. **Ad Acc, Adv Mgr:** Paul Mack. Full Page (B&W) $1,915.20. Half Page (B&W) $957.60. Full Page (Color) $2,040.20. Half Page (Color) $1,082.60. **Pub. Size:** Standard. **Circ:** 30,950.

US/1053-7805
SUN CHRONICLE (ATTLEBORO, MASS.). (THE SUN CHRONICLE.). Vol. 1, No. 1 (March 1971)-. Newspaper. English. da. $80.00. The Sun Chronicle, PO Box 600, Attleboro MA 02703. ***Formed by the union of*** *Attleboro Sun* ***and*** *North Attleboro Evening Chronicle.*

US
SUN (LOWELL, MASS. : 1946). (THE SUN.). **VFOAT** Lowell Sun; Lowell Sunday Sun. Vol. 91, No. 45 (Feb. 24, 1969)-. Newspaper. English. ds. $275.45 US and US possessions; $471.15 other. Lowell Sun Publishing Company, PO Box 1477, Lowell MA 01853. **Tel** (508)459-1300. **ED** Clement C. Costello. **Circ:** 56,247. ***Continues*** *Lowell Sun (Lowell, Mass. : 1943).*

US/0191-281X
SUNDAY REPUBLICAN (SPRINGFIELD, MASS.). (THE SUNDAY REPUBLICAN.). Vol. 98 No. 30 (Apr 11, 1976)-. Newspaper. English. wk (Published on Sundays). $78.00. Springfield Newspapers / Massachusetts, 1860 Main Street, Springfield MA 01102. **Tel** (413)788-1000. available on microfilm from University Microfilms International (UMI); and University Microfilms International (UMI). ***Continues*** *Springfield Sunday Republican (Springfield, Mass : 1947).*

US/0893-3634
SWAMPSCOTT REPORTER, THE. Vol. 1, No. 1 (Aug. 26, 1965)-. Newspaper. English. Fifty-two times a year (Thurs.). $22.00 Massachusetts; $30.00 others. North Shore Weeklies, 2 Washington Street, Box 192, Ipswich MA 01938. **Tel** (508)356-5141, FAX (508)356-9188. **ED** Christopher Hill. **Ad Acc**. **Circ:** 4,000.
Desc: Contains local news and features.

US
TAUNTON DAILY GAZETTE. Vol. 1, No. 1 (June 10, 1848)-. Newspaper. English. da. $125.00 (by mail). Taunton Daily Gazette, PO Box 111, 5-19 Cohannet Street, Taunton MA 02780. **Tel** (508)822-7121. available in microform (from General Microfilm of New England Dec. 1848 & 1893, Feb. 1894 and Dec. 1974).

US/0148-9607
TECH, THE. (1881)-. Newspaper. English. ir (68 issues). $20.00. The Tech, PO Box 29, MIT Branch, Cambridge MA 02139. **Tel** (617)253-1541. **ED** Andrew Fish. **LC** T171; .M45. Index available. **Bk Rev**. **Ad Acc**. **Circ:** 9,000 (ctrl).
Desc: MIT's oldest and largest student newspaper. Covers campus, local and national news.

US/1050-4184
TELEGRAM & GAZETTE. VFOAT Telegram and Gazette; Sunday Telegram. Vol. 1, No. 1 (April 17, 1989)-. Newspaper. English. ds. $205.40 Worcester County; $286.00 New England; $299.00 elsewhere US. Worcester Telegram & Gazette, 20 Franklin Street, Worcester MA 01613. **Tel** (508)793-9276. **Ad Acc**. **Circ:** 112,256. ***Formed by the union of*** *Worcester Telegram* ***and*** *Evening Gazette (Worcester, Mass.).*

US/0747-2900
TIMES (WEBSTER, MASS.), THE. (THE TIMES.). Vol. 126, No. 5 (Apr. 18, 1984)-. Newspaper. English. wk. $21.50. The Times / Massachusetts, PO Box 900, Webster MA 01570. **Tel** (508)943-4800, FAX (508)987-0002. **ED** Martin Fey. **Photos**. **Ad Acc, Adv Mgr:** Ernest Mayotte. Full Page (B&W) $860.00. Half Page (B&W) $430.00. Full Page (Color) $985.00. Half Page (Color) $555.00. **Pub. Size:** Tabloid. **Circ:** 6,061. available in microform. ***Continues in part*** *Webster Times (Webster, Mass. : 1934).*

US
TRANSCRIPT. (Nov. 15, 1969)-. Newspaper. English. da. North Adams Transcript, 124 American Legion Drive, North Adams MA 01247. ***Continues*** *North Adams Transcript (North Adams, Mass. : Daily).*

US
UNION-NEWS. VFOAT Union News; Sunday Republican. (June 1, 1987)-. Newspaper. English. da. $156.00. Springfield Newspapers / Massachusetts, 1860 Main Street, Springfield MA 01102. **Tel** (413)788-1000.

US
VINEYARD GAZETTE, THE. Vol. 1, No. 1 (May 14, 1846)-. Newspaper. English. Twice a week. $33.00 (in county). Vineyard Gazette, PO Box 66, Edgartown MA 02539. **Tel** (508)627-4311, FAX (508)627-7444. **ED** Richard Reston, Nis Kildegaard (Managing Editor). **LC** 8275. **Bk Rev**, (Qty: 2-3). **Photos**. **Ad Acc, Adv Mgr:** Eileen Holley. Full Page (B&W) $1499.00. Half Page (B&W) $845.00. **Pub. Size:** Broadsheet. **Circ:** 12,626 paid (ctrl). available on microfilm.

US/0099-9660
WALL STREET JOURNAL. EASTERN EDITION, THE. (THE WALL STREET JOURNAL.). [Wall St. j., East. ed.]. Vol. 153, No. 32 (Feb. 16, 1959)-. Academic Scholarly Publication. English. da. $149.00. Dow Jones and Company Inc, 200 Burnett Road, Chicopee MA 01021. **Tel** (413)592-7761, (800)568-7625. **CODEN** WSJOAF. **[CCC].** available on microfilm from University Microfilms International (UMI). Documents available from UMI Article Clearinghouse, CASDDS, Documents on Demand. ***Continues*** *Wall Street Journal (New York, N.Y. : 1889).*
Ind/Abst Acad. Search (July 1993-); AGRICOLA [Select. Cov.]; Art Archaeol. Tech. Abstr.; Aviat. Tradescan [Select. Cov.]; BioBusiness (1987-); Book Rev. Index; Bus. Index; Chem. Abstr.; Chem. Ind. Notes; Comput. Bus. (19??-); Energy Inf. Abstr.; Environ. Abstr.; F&S Index Plus Text, Int. [Select. Cov.]; Foods Adlibra; Garden Lit. (1992-); Gen. BusinessFile; Gen. Period. Index; Health Ref. Cent. (1987-) [Select. Cov.]; INFO-SOUTH Abstr.; Infobank (Jan. 1969-); Int. Aerosp. Abstr.; Mag. Index Plus; Mark. Advert. Ref. Serv.; Natl. Newsp. Index (1979-); Newsp. Period. Abstr. (1989-); Predicasts; PROMT; Public Aff. Inf. Serv. Bull.; Text. Technol. Dig.; Trade Ind. Index.

US
WALL STREET JOURNAL. MIDWEST EDITION, THE. (THE WALL STREET JOURNAL.). [Wall St. j.]. Vol. 32, No. 292 (Oct. 1, 1951)-. Newspaper. English. da. $149.00. Dow Jones and Company Inc, 200 Burnett Road, Chicopee MA 01021. **Tel** (413)592-7761, (800)568-7625. available on microfilm from University Microfilms International (UMI). ***Continues*** *Chicago Journal of Commerce Edition of the Wall Street Journal.*
Ind/Abst Wall Street J. Index; Work Relat. Abstr.

US/0193-2241
WALL STREET JOURNAL. WESTERN EDITION, THE. (THE WALL STREET JOURNAL.). [Wall Str. j., West. ed.]. (1978)-. Newspaper. English. da. $149.00. Dow Jones and Company Inc, 200 Burnett Road, Chicopee MA 01021. **Tel** (413)592-7761, (800)568-7625. **[CCC].**
Ind/Abst Chicano Index; Consum. Health Nutr. Index; Natl. Newsp. Index (1979-); Wall Street J. Index.

US
WELLESLEY TOWNSMAN, THE. (198?)-. Newspaper. English. Fifty-two times a year. $20.00 Wellesley Mass.; $27.00 others. Townsman Publishing Company, One Crest Road, Lock Box D, Wellesley MA 02181. **Tel** (617)235-4000. ***Continues*** *Townsman (Wellesley, Mass.).*

US/0893-3782
WESTBOROUGH NEWS, THE. (19??)-. Newspaper. English. wk. $10.00. The Westborough News, PO Box 1153, 10 East Main Street, Westborough MA 01581. **Tel** (508) 366-1511, FAX (508) 366-5265. **ED** Phyllis T. Jones, Joy Nelson (Managing Editor). Index available. **Bk Rev**, (Qty: 3). **Photos**. **Ad Acc**. Full Page (B&W) $720.00. Half Page (B&W) $360.00. **Pub. Size:** Tabloid. **Circ:** 3,700.

US/0744-7957
WESTFORD EAGLE. (1981)-. Newspaper. English. Fifty-two times a year. $24.00 Middlesex County; $36.00 others. Beacon Communications Corp., 20 Main Street, Acton MA 01720. **Tel** (800)842-1317, (508)264-9300. ***Continues*** *Eagle (Acton, Mass.).*

US
WINCHENDON COURIER, THE. (Nov. 1878)-. Newspaper. English. wk. F. W. Ward, Winchendon MA.
Desc: General interest newspaper for Winchendon, MA.

MICHIGAN

US/0191-7064
ADVISOR NEWSPAPER. UTICA-SHELBY EDITION, THE. (THE ADVISOR NEWSPAPER.). Newspaper. English. wk. The Advisor, PO Box 168, Utica MI 48087. **Tel** (313)731-1000.

US/8750-9008
ALBION RECORDER, THE. Newspaper. English. da (Mon.-Fri.). The Albion Recorder, 111 West Center Street, Albion MI 49224. **Tel** (517)629-3984. **ED** Jeff Aesen. **Circ:** 15,100. ***Continues*** *Albion Evening Recorder.*

US/0746-8172
ALCONA COUNTY REVIEW. (19??)-. Newspaper. English. Fifty-two times a year. $12.00 Alcona County; $15.00 other. Alcona County Review, PO Box 548, Harrisville MI 48740. **Tel** (517)724-6384.

US
ALPENA NEWS. English. da. $98.75 Alpena, Alcona, Montmorency, Presque Isle, and Iosco Counties; $121.25 Michigan; $138.75 other. Alpena News, PO Box 367, Alpena MI 49707. **Tel** (517)354-3111. Documents available from UMI Article Clearinghouse.
Ind/Abst Bus. Dateline (Dec. 31, 1991-) [Full Txt.].

US
ANN ARBOR NEWS, THE. Newspaper. English. da. $100.00, $90.00 (within the state). Ann Arbor News, 340 East Huron Street, PO Box 1147, Ann Arbor MI 48106-1147. **Tel** (313)994-6989, FAX EDITORIAL(313)994-6879, ADVERTISING(313)994-6725. **ED** Edward PetyKiewicz. Index available. cum. index. **Bk Rev**. **Ad Acc**. **Circ:** 48,701 daily, 58,726 Sunday. available on microfilm. ***Continues*** *Ann Arbor Times News.*
Desc: Full service daily newspaper.

●US
ANTRIM COUNTY NEWS. (19??)-. English. Fifty-two times a year (published on Thurs.). $22.00

Antrim County; $25.00 others. Antrim County News, PO Box 337, Bellaire MI 49615. **Tel** (616)533-8523. **ED** Marge Fleet.

US
ARGUS (EDWARDSBURG, MICH.).
(THE ARGUS.). (Oct. 23, 1875)-. Newspaper. English. wk. $28.00. Edwardsburg Argus, PO Box 123, Cassopolis MI 49031. **Tel** (616)663-2100.

US/0890-3751
ARMADA TIMES.
(1???)-. Newspaper. English. wk. $15.00 Michigan; $35.00 others. Armada Times, PO Box 915, 23061 Main Street, Armada MI 48005. **Tel** (810)784-5551, FAX (810)784-8710. **ED** Kathleen Steffen. **Photos. Ad Acc, Adv Mgr:** Jim Misener, **Tel** (810)784-5551. **Pub. Size:** Standard. **Circ:** 2,200.

US
ATHENAI.
VFOAT Detroit Athens. Began in 1928. Newspaper. Greek, Modern. wk. 520 Morroe Avenue, Detroit MI 48226.

US/0199-0950
AUCTION EXCHANGE, THE.
(197?)-. Periodical. English. Fifty times a year (Mondays; Not on Christmas & New Years). $7.50 (one year); $14.00 (two years). The Auction Exchange, 211 East Gannister Street, Plainwell MI 49080. **Tel** (616)685-1343.

US
BAY CITY TIMES (1935).
(THE BAY CITY TIMES.). Newspaper. English. da. Booth Newspapers Inc, 311 Fifth Avenue, Bay City MI 48706. **Tel** (517)895-8551. **ED** Robert H Longstaff. **Circ:** 39,650 daily, 47,389 Sunday. available on microfilm from University Microfilms International (UMI). ***Continues*** *Bay City Times-Tribune.*

US/8750-7188
BAY VOICE, THE.
(198?)-. Newspaper. English. wk. Bay Voice, 31950 23 Mile Road, New Baltimore MI 48047. **Tel** (313)949-7900. **ED** Tom Stanton. **Bk Rev. Ad Acc. Circ:** 12,000.

US
BELL & HOWELL NEWSPAPER INDEX TO THE CHICAGO SUN-TIMES / COMPILED AND PUBLISHED BY THE INDEXING CENTER, MICRO PHOTO DIVISION, BELL & HOWELL COMPANY.
Added/Corp Bell & Howell Co. Indexing Center. **VFOAT** Bell and Howell's Newspaper Index to the Chicago Sun-Times; Index to the Chicago Sun-Times. (19??)-. English. University Microfilms International, 300 North Zeeb Road, Ann Arbor MI 48106-1346. **Tel** (313)761-4700, (800)521-0600 Exts. 2490, 2491, FAX (313)973-1540. **LC** AI21.C44; B44. **DD** 071/.73/11. ***Continues*** *Bell & Howell's Newspaper Index to the Chicago Sun-Times, 0195-6442.*

US/0195-6418
BELL & HOWELL'S NEWSPAPER INDEX TO THE LOS ANGELES TIMES.
[Bell Howell's newsp. index Los Angeles times]. **Main/Corp** Bell & Howell Co. Indexing Center. **Added/Corp** Bell & Howell Co. Indexing Center Index to the Los Angeles Times. **VAT** Bell and Howell's Newspaper Index to the Los Angeles Times. (19??)-. Newspaper. English. Thirteen times a year. $680.00. University Microfilms International, 300 North Zeeb Road, Ann Arbor MI 48106-1346. **Tel** (313)761-4700, (800)521-0600 Exts. 2490, 2491, FAX (313)973-1540. **ED** Andrew Horvay. **LC** AI21.L65; B44a. **DD** 071.94/94.

US
BIRMINGHAM ECCENTRIC, THE.
(May 1878)-. Newspaper. English. Four times a year (Mon. & Thurs.). $65.00. Observer & Eccentric Newspaper, 36251 Schoolcraft Road, Livonia MI 48150. **Tel** (313)591-2300. **LC** 8408.

US
BLISSFIELD ADVANCE.
(April 9, 1874)-. Newspaper. English. wk. $18.00 local; $28.00 other. Blissfield Advance, 121 Newspaper Street, Blissfield MI 49228. **Tel** (517)486-2400. **ED** Walt Walkowski. **Bk Rev. Photos. Ad Acc, Adv Mgr:** Paul Heidbreder, **Tel** (517)486-4290. Full Page (B&W) $504.00. Half Page (B&W) $260.00. **Pub. Size:** Broadsheet. **Circ:** 2,492 paid.

US
BRIGHTON ARGUS.
(1880)-. Newspaper. English. Fifty-two times a year. $14.00 local; $21.00 other. Sliger/Livingston Publications, PO Box 899, Brighton MI 48116. **Tel** (313)227-4442.

US
BRONSON JOURNAL.
English. wk. $15.00 Branch County, Michigan; $20.00 other. Bronson Journal, Post Office Box 38, Bronson MI 49028. **Tel** (517)369-5085.

US
BROOKLYN EXPONENT.
Began Sept. 1881. Newspaper. English. wk. Brooklyn Exponent, 160 South Main Street, Brooklyn MI 49230.

US
CADENCE.
Newspaper. English. wk (published Wed.). $25.00. Cadence, 705 Bagley Southeast, Grand Rapids MI 49341. **Tel** (616)454-9456.

US/0745-3655
CADILAC EVENING NEWS.
(19??)-. Newspaper. English. da. Cadillac Evening News, 130 North Mitchell, PO Box 640, Cadillac MI 49601. **Tel** (616)775-6565.

US/0192-6446
CANTON EAGLE, THE.
(1???)-. Newspaper. English. wk (52 issues). $26.00 US; $28.00 other. Associated Newspapers Inc, 35540 Michigan Avenue West, Wayne MI 48184. **Tel** (313)729-4000. **ED** Susan Willett and Ray Day. **Ad Acc. Circ:** 4,143 (ctrl).

US
CHARLEVOIX COURIER.
(19??)-. Newspaper. English. wk. $32.45 Charlevoix & Antrim & Emmet counties in Michigan; $43.80 others. Charlevoix Courier, PO Box 17, Charlevoix MI 49720. **Tel** (616)547-6558, FAX (616)547-4992. **ED** L. Scott Swanson.

US/0746-665X
CHEBOYGAN DAILY TRIBUNE.
(1???)-. Newspaper. English. da. $88.00 Cheboygan; $142.00 others. Cheboygan Daily Tribune, PO Box 290, 308-10 North Main Street, Cheboygan MI 49721. **Tel** (616)627-7144, FAX (616)627-5331. **ED** Jillian Bogater. **Ad Acc, Adv Mgr:** Roy Trahan.

US/1042-6906
CITIZEN (HAMTRAMCK, MICH.), THE.
(THE CITIZEN.). (19??)-. Newspaper. English. wk. $18.00 (in county), $24.00 (out of county). Hamtramck Citizen, 11901 Joseph Campau, Hamtramck MI 48212. **Tel** (313)365-9500. **ED** Karen Spang, Charles Sercombe (Managing Editor). **Photos. Ad Acc, Adv Mgr:** Chris Stamatel. Full Page (B&W) $1285.00. Half Page (B&W) $665.00. Full Page (Color) $1350.00. Half Page (Color) $720.00. **Pub. Size:** Broadsheet. **Circ:** 10,000 paid.

US
CLINTON COUNTY NEWS.
Vol. 1, No. 1 (Nov. 3, 1949)-. Newspaper. English. wk. $17.50 Michigan; $27.50 other. Clinton County News, 215 North Clinton, Saint Johns MI 48879. **Tel** (517)224-2361, FAX (517)224-4452. **ED** Al Wilson. **Photos. Ad Acc, Adv Mgr:** Preston Odette. Full Page (B&W) $400.32. Half Page (B&W) $208.80. Full Page (Color) $485.32. Half Page (Color) $293.80. **Pub. Size:** Tabloid. **Circ:** 13,604.

US/0745-6794
COLDWATER DAILY REPORTER.
(COLDWATER DAILY REPORTER.). (1???)-. Newspaper. English. da (Mon.-Sat.). Coldwater Daily Reporter, 15 West Pearl Street, Coldwater MI 49036. **Tel** (517)278-2318. **ED** Mike Morrissey. **Circ:** 7,365.

US/0193-077X
COMMUNITY CRIER, THE.
(19??)-. Newspaper. English. wk (Weds.). $30.00. Community Crier, 821 Penniman Street, Plymouth MI 48170. **Tel** (313)453-6900, FAX (313)453-6917. **ED** W. Edward Wendover, Robert Kirkbride (Managing Editor). **Photos. Ad Acc, Adv Mgr:** Jack Armstrong. Full Page (B&W) $1232.00. Half Page (B&W) $723.00. **Pub. Size:** Tabloid. **Circ:** 19,655. available in microform.
Desc: Provides community coverage in Plymouth, Canton, and Northville Michigan.

US/8750-4561
COUNTY PRESS (LAPEER, MICH.).
(THE COUNTY PRESS.). (19??)-. Newspaper. English. sw (Wed. & Sun.). The County Press, Lapeer MI 48446. **Tel** (313)664-0811. **ED** Pam Brannon. **Circ:** 19,783. ***Continues*** *Lapeer County Press.*

US
DAILY MINING GAZETTE, THE.
(Sept. 14, 1899)-. Newspaper. English. da. $135.52. Mining Gazette Company, 206 Shelden Avenue, Houghton MI 49931. **LC** 8401-X. ***Continues*** *Houghton Daily Mining Gazette.*

US/0899-6342
DAILY NEWS (GREENVILLE, MICH.), THE.
(THE DAILY NEWS.). (1923)-. Newspaper. English. da. $93.00 Iowa; $105.00 other. The Daily News / Greenville, Michigan, 109 North Lafayette Street, Greenville MI 48838. **Tel** (616)754-9301. ***Continues*** *Greenville Independent.*

US
DAILY PRESS (ESCANABA, MICH.).
(THE DAILY PRESS.). (1977)-. Newspaper. English. da (Mon.-Sat.). Daily Press / Michigan, 600 Ludington Street, Escanaba MI 49829. **Tel** (906)786-2021, (800)743-0609 ext.86. **ED** Robert B. Gregg and Peggy Bryson. **Bk Rev. Ad Acc. Circ:** 11,450, 19,950 (Tuesday). available on microfilm. ***Continues*** *Escanaba Daily Press.*

US/1041-9977
DAILY TRIBUNE (MOUNT CLEMENS, MICH.).
(DAILY TRIBUNE.). (1902)-. Newspaper. English. da. $131.00 (one year). Daily Tribune / Royal Oak, PO Box 80003, Royal Oak MI 48067. **Tel** (313)541-3000, FAX (313)541-0195.

US/0192-4516
DAVISON INDEX, THE.
(1???)-. Newspaper. English. wk. Davison Index, 220 North Main Street, Davison MI 48423.

US/0193-0230
DEARBORN TIMES-HERALD.
Newspaper. English. sw. $24.00. Dearborn Times-Herald, 13730 Michigan Avenue, Dearborn MI 48126. **Tel** (313)584-4000. **ED** Scott Bewick. Index available. **Ad Acc. Circ:** 27,000 (ctrl).

US/0893-2441
DENVER POST INDEX (1987), THE.
(THE DENVER POST INDEX.). [Denver post index]. **Added/Corp** University Microfilms International. (1987)-. Newspaper. English. an. $680.00. University Microfilms International, 300 North Zeeb Road, Ann Arbor MI 48106-1346. **Tel** (313)761-4700, (800)521-0600 Exts. 2490, 2491, FAX (313)973-1540. **ED** Andrew Horvay. **LC** AI21.D44; B44. **DD** 071/.88/83. ***Continues*** *Bell & Howell Newspaper Index to the Denver Post, 0195-6434.*

US/1055-2758
DETROIT FREE PRESS (DETROIT, MICH., 1858).
(DETROIT FREE PRESS.). **VFOAT** Detroit News and Free Press. Vol. 22, No. 60 (Aug. 18, 1858)-. Newspaper. English. da. $600.00. Detroit Newspapers, 615 West LaFayette Boulevard, Detroit MI 48226. **Tel** (313)222-6400, (313)222-2419. **ED** Heath Moriwetton, Bob McGruden (Managing Editor). **LC** 8415. Index available. **Bk Rev**, (Qty: 100). **Photos. Ad Acc, Adv Mgr:** Richard McClennen. **Pub. Size:** Standard. **Wire Svcs.:** KR, AP. **Circ:** 656,477 daily, 747,268 Sunday. available on microfilm from University Microfilms International (UMI); available on an online database (file 498/Full-Text) from DIALOG. ***Continues*** *Detroit Daily Free Press (Detroit, Mich. : 1851).*
Ind/Abst PROMT.

US/1055-2715
DETROIT NEWS (DETROIT, MICH.), THE.
(THE DETROIT NEWS.). **VFOAT** Detroit News Tribune; Detroit Tribune; Detroit Sunday News; Detroit News Detroit Free Press; Detroit News and Free Press. Vol. 33, No. 1 (Aug. 23, 1905)-. Newspaper. English. da. $494.00 (daily & Sunday), $343.20 (daily), $150.80 (Sunday) Michigan; $530.40 (daily & Sunday), $371.80 (daily), $158.60 (Sunday) US; $572.00 (daily & Sunday), $400.40 (daily), $171.60 (Sunday) Canada; $1261.00 (daily & Sunday), $876.20 (daily), $384.80 (Sunday) other. Detroit Newspapers, 615 West LaFayette Boulevard, Detroit MI 48226. **Tel** (313)222-6400, (313)222-2419. **ED** Lionel Linder. **Bk Rev. Ad Acc. Circ:** 680,800 daily, 839,841 Sunday. available on microfilm from University Microfilms International (UMI); available on an online database (file 635/Full-Text) from DIALOG. Documents available from UMI Article Clearinghouse. ***Formed by the union of*** *Evening News (Detroit, Mich. : 1873)* ***and*** *Detroit Tribune;* ***Absorbed*** *Detroit Journal (Detroit, Mich. : 1888); Detroit Times.*
Desc: International, national and local news, plus features and editorial comment.
Ind/Abst Bus. Dateline; Newsp. Abstr.; PROMT.

US/0893-2433
DETROIT NEWS INDEX, THE.
[Detroit news index]. **Added/Corp** University Microfilms International. (Jan. 1987)-. English. mo (with quarterly and annual cumulations). $680.00. University Microfilms International, 300 North Zeeb Road, Ann Arbor MI 48106-1346. **Tel** (313)761-4700, (800)521-0600 Exts. 2490, 2491, FAX (313)973-1540. **ED** Andrew Horvay. **LC** AI21.D46; B44. **DD** 071. ***Continues*** *Bell & Howell Newspaper Index to the Detroit News, 0195-637X.*
Desc: Comprehensive subject index; includes access by personal and corporate name headings; informative abstracts.

US
DEXTER LEADER, THE.
(Jan. 1, 1869)-. Newspaper. English. wk. $20.00. Dexter Leader, 300 North Main, Chelsea MI 48118-1502. **Tel** (313)475-1371. **ED** Walter P. Leonard. **Photos. Ad Acc.** Full Page (B&W) $309.60. Half Page (B&W) $184.80. Full Page (Color) $434.60. Half Page (Color) $309.80. **Pub. Size:** Standard. ***Absorbed*** *Dexter News (Dexter, Mich.).*

US
DOWAGIAC DAILY NEWS.
(Feb. 6, 1897)-. Newspaper. English. da. $88.00. Dowagiac Daily News, 205 Spaulding Street, Dowagiac MI 49047. **Tel** (616)782-2101.

US/0194-7303
DOWNRIVER NEWS-HERALD, THE.
VAT Downriver News Herald. (19??)-. Newspaper. English. Twice a week. $42.00. News-Herald Newspapers, PO Box 40, Wyandotte MI 48192. **ED** Karl Ziomek, Joe Hoshaw (Managing Editor). **Photos. Ad Acc, Adv Mgr:** Bill Dillingham. Full Page (B&W) $6411.30. Half Page

(B&W) $3205.65. Full Page (Color) $6361.30. Half Page (Color) $3655.65. **Pub. Size:** Broadsheet. **Circ:** 92,003 Wednesday controlled circulation, 58,536 paid.

US/0747-4156
EATON COUNTY NEWSCHRONICLE. **VFOAT** Eaton County News Chronicle; Newschronicle. Vol. 130, No. 20 (May 17, 1984)-. Newspaper. English. wk. Eaton County Newschronicle, 239 S Chochrane Street, Charlotte MI 48813. ***Continues*** *Charlotte Republican Tribune.*

US
EVENING NEWS (SAULT SAINTE MARIE, MICH.). (THE EVENING NEWS.). (19??)-. Newspaper. English. da (Sun. thru Fri.). The Evening News - Michigan, 109 Arlington Street, Sault Sainte Marie MI 49783. **Tel** (906)632-2235.

US/0747-4113
EXPRESS (BANGOR, MICH.), THE. (THE EXPRESS.). Vol. 1, No. 48 (March 1984)-. Newspaper. English. wk. Express Newspapers, Inc., 404 West Monroe Street, Bangor MI 49013. ***Continues*** *Bangor Trust Express, 0745-9521.*

US/0745-211X
FARMERS' ADVANCE, THE. (198?)-. Newspaper. English. wk. $28.00 Michigan, Indiana, & Ohio; $33.00 other US; $56.00 other. Farmers' Advance, 331 E. Bell, Camden MI 49232. **Tel** (517)368-0365. **ED** Kris Roelof. **Bk Rev**. **Ad Acc**. **Circ:** 20,000. ***Continues*** *Farmers' Advance News, 0273-7949.*

US/0888-6199
FARMINGTON OBSERVER. (19??)-. Newspaper. English. sw. Observer-Eccentric, PO Box 503, 805 East Maple, Birmingham MI 48009. **Tel** (313)644-1100. **Ad Acc, Adv Mgr:** Mark Lewis, **Tel** (313)591-2300. **Circ:** 18,400 (ctrl).

US
FENNVILLE HERALD. English. wk. $16.00 (MI residents); $19.00 (other). Fennville Herald, PO Box 189, Allegan MI 49010. **Tel** (616) 673-5534.

US
FLINT JOURNAL (1935). (THE FLINT JOURNAL.). **VFOAT** Saturday A.M. Flint Journal. (June 2, 1935)-. Newspaper. English. da. $136.00 Michigan; $142.00 other. Flint Journal, 200 East First Street, Flint MI 48502. **Tel** (313)766-6280, FAX (313)767-9480. **ED** Thomas L. Lindley. **LC** 7002. **Bk Rev**. **Ad Acc, Adv Mgr:** R. Samuel. **Circ:** 107,130 daily: 123,937 (Sun.). available on microfilm from University Microfilms International (UMI). Documents available from UMI Article Clearinghouse. ***Continues*** *Flint Daily Journal.*
Desc: Serves Genesee County and parts of seven other counties in Central/Eastern Michigan. Politically independent, it is the fourth largest newspaper in Michigan.
Ind/Abst Bus. Dateline (Feb. 4, 1992-) [Full Txt.].

US/0747-1718
FLUSHING OBSERVER, THE. (19??)-. Newspaper. English. sw (Thurs. & Fri.). Flint Advance Newspapers Inc., PO Box 497, Swartz Creek MI 48473. **Tel** (313)733-2239.

US/0191-6920
FOWLERVILLE REVIEW, THE. (June 19, 1874)-. Newspaper. English. wk. Sliger/Livingston Publications, PO Box 899, Brighton MI 48116. **Tel** (313)227-4442.

US
GARDEN CITY OBSERVER. English. sw. $36.40 Garden City, Michigan; $55.00 others in Michigan; $80.00 others in US. Observer-Eccentric, PO Box 503, 805 East Maple, Birmingham MI 48009. **Tel** (313)644-1100. **ED** Leonard Poger. **Ad Acc, Adv Mgr:** Mark Lewis, **Tel** (313)591-2300. **Circ:** 8,800 (ctrl).

US/1071-0019
GLADWIN COUNTY RECORD AND BEAVERTON CLARION, THE. **VFOAT** Gladwin County Record; Beaverton Clarion. (19??)-. Newspaper. English. wk (Wed.). $15.00 Gladwin County; $17.00 others in Michigan; $19.00 others. Gladwin County Record, PO Box 425, 700 East Cedar Avenue, Gladwin MI 48624. **Tel** (517)426-9411, FAX (517)426-2023. **ED** Ron Pruystas. **Photos**. **Ad Acc, Adv Mgr:** Dick Malosh. Full Page (B&W) $709.50. Half Page (B&W) $354.75. Full Page (Color) $809.50. Half Page (Color) $454.75. **Pub. Size:** Broadsheet. **Circ:** 7,500. available in microform.

US/0747-1742
GRAND BLANC NEWS, THE. (19??)-. Newspaper. English. sw (Thurs. and Sun.). $70.00. Flint Advance Newspapers, PO Box 497, Swartz Creek MI 48473. **Tel** (313)733-2239.

US/1043-593X
GRAND LEDGE INDEPENDENT. Began in 1869. Newspaper. English. wk. Peter Cantine Publications, 219 South Bridge Street, Grand Ledge MI 48837.

US/0746-617X
GRAND MARAIS PILOT & PICTURED ROCKS REVIEW, THE. **VFOAT** Grand Marais Pilot and Pictured Books Review. (19??)-. Newspaper. English. sm (24 issues per year). $16.00. Grand Marais Pilot, PO Box 336, Grand Marais MI 49839. **Tel** (906)494-2391.

US
GRAND RAPIDS PRESS, THE. Nov. 1, 1913)-. Newspaper. English. da. $172.00 (MI residents), $226.00 (other) Daily & Sunday by mail; $74.00 (MI residents), $106.00 (other) Sunday by mail; $108.00 Mon.-Fri. by carrier; $144.00 daily and Sunday by mail. Grand Rapids Press, 155 Michigan Street NW, % Mail Subscription Department, Grand Rapids MI 49503. **Tel** (616) 459-1400, (616) 459-1411. **ED** Michael Lloyd. **LC** 7002. **Circ:** 135,998 daily, 179,604 Sunday. available on microfilm from University Microfilms International (UMI). ***Continues*** *Grand Rapids Evening Press.*
Ind/Abst PROMT.

US
HOLLAND EVENING SENTINEL (HOLLAND, MICH. : 1952). ***Title Change.*** (THE HOLLAND EVENING SENTINEL.). (1952)-?. Newspaper. English. da. Holland Evening Sentinel, 54-56 West 8th Street, Holland MI 49423. **Tel** (616)392-2311, FAX (616)392-3526. ***Continues*** *Holland Daily Sentinel (Holland, Mich. : 1929).* ***Continued by*** *Holland Sentinel (Holland, Mich. : 1977), 1050-4044.*

US/1050-4044
HOLLAND SENTINEL (1977), THE. (THE HOLLAND SENTINEL.). (April 1, 1977)-. Newspaper. English. da (except on Christmas). $99.50 (Holland, MI home delivery); $156.00 (other, mail delivery). Holland Evening Sentinel, 54-56 West 8th Street, Holland MI 49423. **Tel** (616)392-2311, FAX (616)392-3526. **ED** Susan Sopel. **Bk Rev**, (Qty: varies). **Ad Acc, Adv Mgr:** Margaret Van Sant. **Circ:** 19,769 (ctrl). ***Continues*** *Holland Evening Sentinel (Holland, Mich. : 1952).*

US/0891-1398
HOMER INDEX, THE. (1871)-. Newspaper. English. wk. $25.00. Homer Index, 122 East Main Street, PO Box 236, Homer MI 49245. **Tel** (517)568-4646.

US/0893-2476
HOUSTON POST INDEX, THE. [Houst. post index]. **Added/Corp** University Microfilms International. (Jan. 1987)-. Periodical. English. mo (with quarterly and annual cumulations). $680.00. University Microfilms International, 300 North Zeeb Road, Ann Arbor MI 48106-1346. **Tel** (313)761-4700, (800)521-0600 Exts. 2490, 2491, FAX (313)973-1540. **ED** Andrew Horvay. **LC** AI21.H68; B44. **DD** 071. cum. index. ***Continues*** *Bell & Howell Newspaper Index to the Houston Post, 0195-6388.*
Desc: Comprehensive subject index; includes access by personal and corporate headings; informative abstracts.

US
ILE CAMERA. Newspaper. English. Fifty-two times a year (Fri.). $20.00. Ile Camera, PO Box 233, Grosse Ile MI 48138. **Tel** (313)676-0515, FAX (313)676-0638. **ED** Sheila Ryan McAfee. **Ad Acc, Adv Mgr:** L. Atkinson.

US/8750-8230
INDEPENDENT (FENTON, MICH.). ***Suspended.*** (THE INDEPENDENT.). (19??)-(19??). Newspaper. English. Fifty-two times a year (Wed.). Independent / Fenton Michigan, 112 East Ellen Street, Fenton MI 48430. **Tel** (313)629-2203.

US/1062-4260
INGHAM COUNTY NEWS. **VFOAT** Ingham Co. News. Vol. 1, No. 1 (June 23, 1859)-. Newspaper. English. Fifty-two times a year. Ingham County News, PO Box 160, Mason MI 48854. **Tel** (517)676-9393.

US
IRON MOUNTAIN NEWS, THE. Began in 1921. Newspaper. English. da. Iron Mountain Publishing Company, 215 East Ludington, Iron Mountain MI 49801.

US
IRONWOOD DAILY GLOBE. Began with Nov. 20, 1919 issue. Newspaper. English. da. Ironwood Daily Globe, 118 East McLeod Avenue, Ironwood MI 49938.

US
JACKSON CITIZEN PATRIOT, THE. **VFOAT** Sunday Citizen Patriot. (1917)-. Newspaper. English. da. $145.00 (MI residents); $170.00 (other). Jackson Citizen Patriot, 214 South Jackson Street, Jackson MI 49204. **Tel** (517) 787-2300. **ED** Robert D Ludwig. **LC** 8431. **Circ:** 38,187 daily, 42,330 Sunday. available on microfilm from University Microfilms International (UMI). ***Formed by the union of*** *Jackson Citizen Press* ***and*** *Jackson Daily Patriot.*

US
KALAMAZOO GAZETTE (1916). (THE KALAMAZOO GAZETTE.). (Nov. 1916)-. Newspaper. English. da. $84.00 (Sunday, by mail), $160.00 (daily, by mail), $186.00 (daily & Sunday, by mail), $112.80 (daily & Sunday, by carrier), $84.00 (Saturday & Sunday by mail). Kalamazoo Gazette, 401 South Burdick Street, Kalamazoo MI 49003. **Tel** (616)345-3511. **ED** James R. Mosby Jr. **LC** 7002. **Circ:** 63,355 daily, 75,890 Sunday. available on microfilm from University Microfilms International (UMI). ***Continues*** *Gazette-Telegraph.*

US
LAKE COUNTY STAR, THE. (May 1, 1873)-. Newspaper. English. Fifty-two times a year (Thurs.). $23.00 Lake County, Michigan; $30.00 others in Michigan; $35.00 others. Lake County Star / Michigan, PO Box 399, 821 Michigan Avenue, Baldwin MI 49304. **Tel** (616)745-4635.

US/0274-9742
LANSING STATE JOURNAL. Vol. 126, No. 120 (August 25, 1980)-. Newspaper. English. da. $169.00. Gannet Corporation, 120 East Lenawee Street, Lansing MI 48919. **Tel** (517)377-1203. **(Subscription address:** Lansing State Journal, 120 E Lenawee, Lansing MI 48919.**) ED** Zack Binkley, Roni Rucher-Waters (Managing Editor). **Bk Rev**, (Qty: 52). **Photos**. **Ad Acc, Adv Mgr:** Stan Howard. Full Page (B&W) $3300.00. Half Page (B&W) $1650.00. Full Page (Color) $3850.00. Half Page (Color) $1925.00. **Wire Svcs.:** AP. **Circ:** 72,000 daily, 93,000 Sunday (ctrl). available on microfilm from Bell & Howell. ***Continues*** *State Journal (Lansing, Mi. : 1911).*

US/0192-5768
LINCOLN PARKER, THE. Newspaper. English. wk. Mellus News Herald, 1 Heritage Place/Suite 100, Southgate MI 48195-3047.

US/8750-040X
MACKINAC ISLAND TOWN CRIER. **VFOAT** Town Crier. Newspaper. English. wk. MacKinac Island Town Crier, Box 532, MacKinac Island MI 49757. **Tel** (906)847-3788. **ED** Wesley H Maurer Jr. **UDC** 977.8. **Bk Rev**. **Ad Acc**. **Circ:** 4,500.
Desc: Covers history of the region, British-American occupation of Fort Mackinac and of Fort Michdomackinae, Mackinaw city, founding of St Ignaee by Father Marquette, and reports of the community today.

US/1071-1406
MACOMB DAILY, THE. (1964)-. Newspaper. English. da (312 per year). $128.00. The Macomb Daily, PO Box 707 / Circulation, Mt. Clemens MI 48046. **Tel** (313)469-4510. ***Continues*** *Monitor Leader.*

US
MANCHESTER ENTERPRISE. (Oct. 17, 1867)-. Newspaper. English. wk. $25.00 Washtenaw County, Michigan; $28.00 other. Manchester Enterprise, PO Box 37, Manchester MI 48158. **Tel** (313)428-8173.

US
MAYVILLE MONITOR. (19??)-. English. Fifty-two times a year. $12.00 Tuscola County, MI; $14.00 other in Michigan; $17.00 others in US. Mayville Monitor, PO Box 299, 6071 Fulton Street, Mayville MI 48744. **Tel** (517)843-6441, FAX (517)843-6441. **ED** Gale Langford (Editor-in-Chief) and Debra Langford (Managing Editor). **Bk Rev**. **Photos**. **Ad Acc**. Full Page (B&W) $262.50. Half Page (B&W) $131.25. Full Page (Color) $337.50. Half Page (Color) $206.25. **Pub. Size:** Tabloid. **Circ:** 1,400.
Desc: General community news.

US
MENOMINEE HERALD-LEADER, THE. **VFOAT** Menominee Herald Leader; Daily Herald-Leader. Vol. 11, No. 264 (April 2, 1908)-. Newspaper. English. da. $95.00 Marinette & Menominee counties in Michigan; $108.50 US. Eagle Printing Company, PO Box 10, Menominee MI 49858. **Tel** (906)863-5544. **LC** 7002. ***Continues*** *Daily Herald-Leader (Menominee, Mich. : 1904).*

US/0746-4045
METRO TIMES (DETROIT, MICH.), THE. (THE METRO TIMES.). **VFOAT** Detroit Metro Times. (19??)-. Periodical. English. wk. $40.00 (3rd class), $100.00 (1st class). Metro Times, 733 St. Antoine, Detroit MI 48226. **Tel** (313)961-4060, FAX (313)961-6598. **ED** Ron Williams, Desiree Cooper (Managing Editor). **Bk Rev**, (Qty: 25). **Photos**. **Ad Acc, Adv Mgr:** Rick Ficorelli. Full Page (B&W) $2015.00. Half Page (B&W) $1120.00. Full Page (Color) $2140.00. Half Page (Color) $1245.00. **Pub. Size:** Standard. **Wire Svcs.:** AN. **Circ:** 100,000 weekly unpaid (ctrl). ***Continues*** *Detroit Metro Times, 0279-2370.*
Desc: Serves metropolitan Detroit with local news and investigative reporting, entertainment reviews, arts commentary, and a comprehensive calendar.

US
MICHIGAN CHRONICLE, THE. (1936)-. Newspaper. English. Fifty-two times a year. $25.00 (one year); $46.00 (two year). Michigan Chronicle Publishing Company, 479 Ledyard Street, Detroit MI 48201. **Tel** (313)963-5522, FAX (313)963-8788. **ED** Robert E. McTyre, Carol Archer (Managing Editor). **Bk Rev**. **Photos**. **Ad Acc, Adv Mgr:** Sherry Hatcher, **Tel** (313)963-5522 ext. 246. Full Page (B&W) $3725.82. Half Page (B&W) $1862.91. Full Page (Color) additional $925.00 (full color). Half Page (Color) additional $925.00 (full color). **Pub. Size:** Broadsheet. **Circ:** 40,000. available on microfiche (Detroit Public Library) from the

Michigan

publisher. Documents available from UMI Article Clearinghouse.
Ind/Abst Newsp. Abstr.

US/1072-2041
MICHIGAN CITIZEN. (19??)-. Newspaper. English. wk. $21.00. Michigan Citizen, PO Box 03560, Highland Park MI 48203. **Tel** (313)869-0033, FAX (313)869-0430. **ED** Teresa M. Kelly. **Bk Rev**, (Qty: 40). **Ad Acc, Adv Mgr**: Mark Hicks. **Circ**: 45,300 (ctrl). available on CD-ROM from Ethnic News Watch; available on an online database from Mead Data Central.

US/0745-967X
MICHIGAN DAILY, THE. (19??)-. Newspaper. English. da. $160.00. Board for Student Publications, 420 Maynard Street, Ann Arbor MI 48109. **Tel** (313)764-0560. **ED** Jessie Halliday (Editor-in-Chief) and David Shepardson (Managing Editor). **Bk Rev. Photos. Ad Acc, Adv Mgr**: Harris Winters, **Tel** (313)764-0554. **Pub. Size**: Standard. **Wire Svcs.**: AP, WP, LA. **Circ**: 45,000 (readership), 16,500 (daily).

US/0147-7110
MICHIGAN FREE PRESS. (Jan. 9, 1974)-. Periodical. English. wk. $25.00 (institutions), $10.00 (individuals and sponsors). Michigan Free Press, 124 East Washington, Ann Arbor MI 48104.

US
MILFORD TIMES, THE. Began (Feb. 18, 1871)-. Newspaper. English. wk. $22.00 Oakland County. Milford Times, PO Box 339, Milford MI 48042. **Tel** (313)685-1509.

US/0898-4964
MINING JOURNAL (1954). (THE MINING JOURNAL.). (Jan. 1, 1954)-. Newspaper. English. da (Except legal holidays). $130.00 (carrier); $137.80 (motor route); $148.20 others. The Mining Journal / Department of Circulation, PO Box 430, Marquette MI 49855. **Tel** (906)228-2500 ext. 204. **ED** Dave Edwards. cum. index. **Photos. Ad Acc, Adv Mgr**: Gail England. Full Page (B&W) $1,304.19. Half Page (B&W) $660.48. Full Page (Color) $1404.19. Half Page (Color) $710.48. **Pub. Size**: Broadsheet. **Wire Svcs.**: AP. **Circ**: 18,386 (ctrl). available in microform. **Continues** Daily Mining Journal (Marquette, Mich. : 1884).

US/0746-4495
MISSOULIAN (MISSOULA, MONT. 1961). (THE MISSOULIAN.). VFOAT Missoulian-Sentinel; Sunday Missoulian. 89th Year, No. 114 (Sept. 13, 1961)-. Newspaper. English. ir. University Microfilms International, 300 North Zeeb Road, Ann Arbor MI 48106-1346. **Tel** (313)761-4700, (800)521-0600 Exts. 2490, 2491, FAX (313)973-1540. **ED** Bradley Hurd. cum. index. **Bk Rev. Ad Acc. Circ**: 29,000 (ctrl). available on microfilm from University Microfilms International (UMI). Documents available from UMI Article Clearinghouse. **Continues** Daily Missoulian (Missoula, Mont. : 1904). **Desc**: Covers World, national, state, regional and local news. Contents include: editorial and opinion pages; syndicated and local columnists; features; entertainment news; book, movie, film, video, theater, and dance reviews; comics; daily and weekly TV schedules.
Ind/Abst Bus. Dateline (Dec. 21, 1991-) [Full Txt.].

US
MORNING SUN. (19??)-. Newspaper. English. da. $117.00 carrier; $99.00 by mail Isabella, Montcalm, Mecosta, Midland & Clare counties; $114.00 other. Mount Pleasant Morning Sun, PO Box 447, Mount Pleasant MI 48858. **Tel** (517)772-2971.

US
MUNISING NEWS. (1896)-. Newspaper. English. wk. $25.00 (1 year), $50.00 (2 year). Munising Publishing Company, 113 West Superior Street, Munising MI 49862. **ED** Rob Wright.

US
MUSKEGON CHRONICLE, THE. VFOAT Muskegon Chronicle and the Muskegon Times with the Muskegon News; Sunday Chronicle. (March 1913)-. Newspaper. English. da. $11.50 Michigan. Muskegon Chronicle, 981 Third Street, PO Box 59, Muskegon MI 49443. **Tel** (616)722-0320, FAX (616)728-3330 advertising, (616)722-2552 editorial. **ED** D. Gunnar Carlson, John Stephenson (Managing Editor). **LC** 7002. **Photos. Ad Acc, Adv Mgr**: Kevin Newton. Full Page (B&W) $3187.80. Half Page (B&W) $1593.90. Full Page (Color) $3477.80. Half Page (Color) $1883.90. **Pub. Size**: Standard. **Wire Svcs.**: AP. **Circ**: 47,358 daily, 51,004 Sunday. available on microfilm from University Microfilms International (UMI). **Continues** Muskegon News Chronicle.

US/0194-3014
NORTHERN MICHIGAN NEWS. Newspaper. English. wk. Northern Michigan News, 130 North Mitchell Street, Cadillac MI 49601.

US/1050-2467
NORTHVILLE RECORD (NORTHVILLE, MICH. : 1871). (THE NORTHVILLE RECORD.). (1871)-. Newspaper. English. wk. $22.00 Wayne, Oakland, Livingston, Washtenaw & Igham counties; $27.00 Michigan; $30.00 other. Northville Record, PO Box 899, Brighton MI 48116. **Tel** (517)548-2000. **Continues** Wayne County Record (Northville, Mich.).

US/1071-2607
NORWAY CURRENT, THE. (19??)-. Newspaper. English. wk. $25.00. Norway Publications, PO Box 66, Norway MI 49870. **Tel** (906)563-5212, FAX (906)563-5904. **ED** L. A. Underhill (Editor-in-Chief) and V. L. (Managing Editor). **Bk Rev. Ad Acc, Adv Mgr**: L. A. Underhill. Full Page (B&W) $283.20. Half Page (B&W) $141.60. Full Page (Color) $358.20. Half Page (Color) $216.60. **Pub. Size**: Tabloid. **Circ**: 1,500 (ctrl). **Continues** New Norway Current.

US
OAKLAND PRESS. Newspaper. English. da. $156.00 Oakland County, $260.00 other. Oakland Press, PO Box 436009, Pontiac MI 48343. **Tel** (313)332-8181. available on an online database (file 635/Full-Text) from DIALOG. Documents available from UMI Article Clearinghouse.
Ind/Abst Bus. Dateline (Dec. 14, 1991-) [Full Txt.].

US
OBSERVER ECCENTRIC. Newspaper. English. sw. $36.40 Oakland County; $40.00 Macomb & Wayne Counties; $55.00 Michigan; $80.00 remaining US; $150.00 Canada. Observer-Eccentric, PO Box 503, 805 East Maple, Birmingham MI 48009. **Tel** (313)644-1100. **ED** Dave Varga. **Ad Acc, Adv Mgr**: Mark Lewis, **Tel** (313)591-2300. **Circ**: 16,000 (ctrl).

US/0471-1688
OFFICIAL MICHIGAN. (19??)-. Newspaper. English. Fifty-two times a year. Official Michigan, PO Box 275, 3078 Main Street, Marlette MI 48453. **Tel** (517)635-3000, FAX (517)635-3000). **ED** Emmett Robinson.

US
OGEMAW COUNTY HERALD. Newspaper. English. Fifty-two times a year (Thursdays). $18.00 West Branch; $25.00 other Michigan; $30.00 other US. Ogemaw County Herald, PO Box 247, West Branch MI 48661. **Tel** (517)345-0044. **ED** Kristine Persinger (editor's address: 215 West Noughton, West Branch, MI 48661). **Ad Acc, Adv Mgr**: R. Eaton. **Circ**: 6,750.

US
ONAWAY OUTLOOK. Newspaper. English. wk (Published on Wednesday). $19.00 Isle County, $20.00 Michigan, $21.00 other. Presque Isle County Newspaper, PO Box 50, 104 South 3rd Street, Roger City MI 49779. **Tel** (517)734-2105.

US
ONTONAGON HERALD. (19??)-. Newspaper. English. wk (Wed.). $28.00. Ontonagon Herald, 326 River Street, Ontonagon MI 49953. **Tel** (906)884-2826, FAX (906)884-2939. **ED** Maureen Kilmer. **Bk Rev**, (Qty: 26). **Photos. Ad Acc. Pub. Size**: Standard.

US
OWOSSO ARGUS-PRESS, THE. VFOAT Owosso Argus Press. (1919)-. Newspaper. English. da. $81.00. The Argus-Press, 201 East Exchange Street, Owosso MI 48867. **Tel** (517)725-5136, FAX (517)725-6376. **ED** Richard E. Campbell, Joseph R. Peacock (Managing Editor). **LC** 7002. **Bk Rev**, (Qty: 12). **Photos. Ad Acc, Adv Mgr**: Thomas E. Campbell. Full Page (B&W) $1225.50. Half Page (B&W) $612.75. Full Page (Color) $1500.50. Half Page (Color) $897.75. **Pub. Size**: Broadsheet. **Wire Svcs.**: AP. **Circ**: 12,500 evening paid. available in microform from University Microfilms International (UMI). **Formed by the union of** Owosso Evening Argus **and** Press-American.

US/0895-8580
PENASEE GLOBE. Vol. 103 No. 1 (Sept. 23 1987)-. Newspaper. English. Fifty-two times a year. Wayland Printing Company, 133 East Superior Street, PO Box 445, Wayland MI 49348. **Tel** (616)792-2271. **Formed by the union of** Wayland Globe **and** Penasee Press.

US
PETOSKEY NEWS REVIEW. (19??)-. English. da. $19.75. Petoskey News Review, 319 State Street, PO Box 528, Petoskey MI 49770. **Tel** (616)347-2544, FAX (616)347-6833. **ED** Ken Winter (Editor-in-Chief) and Kendall P. Stanley (Managing Editor). **Photos. Ad Acc, Adv Mgr**: Tari Calouette. **Pub. Size**: Broadsheet. **Wire Svcs.**: AP. **Circ**: 11,245. available on microfilm from University Microfilms International (UMI).

US/0192-7906
PINCKNEY POST AND WHITMORE LAKER, THE. (197?)-. Newspaper. English. wk. Sliger/Livingston Publications, PO Box 899, Brighton MI 48116. **Tel** (313)227-4442.

US/8750-5533
PIONEER (BIG RAPIDS, MICH.), THE. (THE PIONEER.). (19??)-. Newspaper. English. ir (309 issues per year). $78.00 Mecosta Co., MI; $96.00 other MI; $130.00 other US. The Pioneer, 502 North State Street, Big Rapids MI 49307. **ED** Judy Hale. **Ad Acc, Adv Mgr Tel** (616)796-4831. **Circ**: 5,500.

US
PORT HURON TIMES HERALD. Began with Apr. 4, 1910 issue. Newspaper. English. da. The Times Herald Company, Port Huron MI 48060. **Tel** (313)985-7171. **ED** Gordon T Weller. **LC** 8401-X. **Circ**: 27,225 daily, 32,007 Sunday. **Formed by the union of** Port Huron Daily Times **and** Port Huron Daily Herald.

US
PRESQUE ISLE COUNTY ADVANCE. Newspaper. English. wk. $21.00 Presque, Isle, Alpena Montmorency, and Cheboygan counties, $22.00 Michigan, $23.00 other. Presque Isle County Newspaper, PO Box 50, 104 South 3rd Street, Roger City MI 49779. **Tel** (517)734-2105.

US/0192-6519
PRESS ADVERTISER (PONTIAC), THE. (THE PRESS ADVERTISER.). Newspaper. English. da. $145.44. Oakland Press, PO Box 436009, Pontiac MI 48343. **Tel** (313)332-8181.

US/0194-245X
REMINDER. ZONE ONE. BRANDON, GROVELAND, ATLAS AND HADLEY TOWNSHIPS, THE. (THE REMINDER.). (19??)-. Newspaper. English. wk (Published on Mondays). Free. Reminder Newspapers, 7151 Ortonville Road, Clarkston MI 48346. **Tel** (313)625-9346, FAX (313)625-1214. **Bk Rev. Ad Acc. Circ**: 116,900.

US/0194-1917
ROCHESTER ECCENTRIC. (197?)-. Newspaper. English. sw (Mon. & Thurs). $65.00. Observer & Eccentric Newspaper, 36251 Schoolcraft Road, Livonia MI 48150. **Tel** (313)591-2300. **ED** Robert Sklar. **Circ**: 8,131.

US/0747-1815
ROCKFORD SQUIRE, THE. (1984)-. Newspaper. English. wk (Wednesday). $17.00. Cadence, 705 Bagley Southeast, Grand Rapids MI 49341. **Tel** (616)454-9456. **ED** R C Allen. **Circ**: 2,250.

US/0192-8082
ROMEO-WASHINGTON ADVISOR NEWSPAPER, THE. VFOAT Advisor Newspaper. (1???)-. Newspaper. English. Fifty-four issues per year (Monday). $36.00. The Advisor, PO Box 168, Utica MI 48087. **Tel** (313)731-1000.

US
SAGINAW NEWS (1929). (THE SAGINAW NEWS.). (Jan. 1, 1929)-. Newspaper. English. da. c/o Saginaw News, 203 South Washington Avenue, Marsha Jacobs, Saginaw MI 48605. **Tel** (517)752-7171, (517)776-9616. **ED** Paul C. Chaffee. **LC** 7002. **Photos. Ad Acc, Adv Mgr**: Charles Kretschmer. Full Page (B&W) $3696.00. Half Page (B&W) $1848.00. Full Page (Color) $4346.00. Half Page (Color) $2173.00. **Wire Svcs.**: AP. **Circ**: 56,931 daily, 62,683 Sunday. available on microfilm from University Microfilms International (UMI). **Continues** Saginaw Daily News.

US
SALINE REPORTER. (19??)-. English. Fifty-two times a year (Wed.). $14.00 Washtenaw County; $17.00 others. Saline Reporter, 106 West Michigan Avenue, Saline MI 48176. **Tel** (313)429-5572.

US/0191-6874
SANILAC COUNTY ADVISOR. (197?)-. Periodical. English. sw. Sanilac County Advisor, 432 South Sandusky Road, Sandusky MI 48471.

US/0745-2128
SENTINEL-STANDARD. VAT Sentinel Standard. (19??)-. Newspaper. English. da. $84.00. Ionia Sentinel Standard, 114 North Depot Street, Ionia MI 48846. **Tel** (616)527-2100. **Continues** Ionia Sentinel-Standard.

US/0746-9055
SHIAWASSEE COUNTY JOURNAL. (1???)-. Newspaper. English. wk (Published on Thursdays). $15.00, $10.00 (senior citizens). A O R Inc,

Michigan

219 North Saginaw Street, Durand MI 48429-0168. **Tel** (517)288-3164, FAX (517)288-4666. **ED** Keith Salisbury. **Circ:** 1,200.

US
SOUTH HAVEN DAILY TRIBUNE. (1899)-. Newspaper. English. da. $82.80. South Haven Tribune, 950 Bailey Avenue, Suite 4, South Haven MI 49090. **Tel** (616)637-1104. **ED** Jeff Hogan. **Photos**. **Ad Acc**, **Adv Mgr:** Michael Eastman. Full Page (B&W) $891.00. Half Page (B&W) $445.50. Full Page (Color) $931.00. Half Page (Color) $525.50. **Pub. Size:** Broadsheet. **Wire Svcs.:** AP. available in microform.

US
SOUTHFIELD ECCENTRIC. English. sw. $24.20 Oakland County; $40.00 Macomb & Wayne Counties; $55.00 all others in MI; $80.00 others. Observer-Eccentric, PO Box 503, 805 East Maple, Birmingham MI 48009. **Tel** (313)644-1100. **ED** Joe Bauman. **Ad Acc**, **Adv Mgr:** Mark Lewis, **Tel** (313)591-2300.

US
ST. IGNACE NEWS. (19??)-. Newspaper. English. wk. $34.00. St. Ignace News, 359 Regon Street, Saint Ignace MI 49781. **Tel** (906)643-9150, FAX (906)643-9122. **ED** Gary Heinlew. **Ad Acc**, **Adv Mgr:** Richard Hayden. **Circ:** 6,000.

US
STATE LINE OBSERVER. Began in 1875. Newspaper. English. wk. State Line Observer, 120 North Street, Morenci MI 49256.

US
STATE NEWS. English. da. $55.00. Michigan State University / 345 Student Services Building, East Lansing MI 48824-1113. **Tel** (517)355-3447. **ED** Matt Helms (517)355-8252. Index available. **Bk Rev**, (Qty: 180). **Ad Acc**, **Adv Mgr:** D. Decoste, **Tel** (517)353-6400. **Circ:** 36,000. available on microform.
 Desc: News of Michigan State University and nearby communities.

US/0747-3230
STURGIS JOURNAL (MICHIGAN EDITION). (STURGIS JOURNAL.). (19??)-. Newspaper. English. da. Sturgis Journal, 209 John Street, Sturgis MI 49091. **Tel** (616)651-5407. **Continues** Sturgis Daily Journal (Michigan Edition).

US/0194-2751
SUBURBAN NEWS (FLINT), THE. (THE SUBURBAN NEWS.). (19??)-. Newspaper. English. sw (104 per year). $70.00. Flint Advance Newspapers, PO Box 497, Swartz Creek MI 48473. **Tel** (313)733-2239.

US
TECUMSEH HERALD (TECUMSEH, MICH. : 1850). (THE TECUMSEH HERALD.). (May 25, 1850)-. Newspaper. English. wk. $27.00 Linawee county; $29.00 other. Tecumseh Herald, PO Box 213, Tecumseh MI 49286. **Tel** (517)423-2175.

US
TOWN MEETING. (19??)-. Newspaper. English. wk (Wed.). $25.00. Elk Rapids Town Meeting, PO Box 335, Elk Rapids MI 49629. **Tel** (616)264-9711. **ED** Lori Robinson. **Photos**. **Ad Acc**, **Adv Mgr:** Lynn Genow. Full Page (B&W) $240.00. Half Page (B&W) $120.00. Full Page (Color) $270.00. Half Page (Color) $150.00. **Pub. Size:** Tabloid. **Circ:** 2,050.

US/1062-4279
TOWNE COURIER. (19??)-. Newspaper. English. wk (Published on Wednesdays). $26.00 Ingham County, $30.00 others in Michigan, $40.00 other. Ingham County News, PO Box 160, Mason MI 48854. **Tel** (517)676-9393.

US
TRAVERSE CITY RECORD EAGLE. (19??)-. Newspaper. English. da. $181.05. Traverse City Record Eagle, 120 W Front Street, Traverse City MI 49684. **Tel** (616)946-2000. **ED** John True (Editor-in-Chief) and Deb Flemming (Managing Editor). **Bk Rev**. **Photos**. **Ad Acc**, **Adv Mgr:** Don Beem and Patrice Lynch. Full Page (B&W) $2,096.25. Half Page (B&W) $1,048.12. **Pub. Size:** Standard. **Wire Svcs.:** AP. **Circ:** 27,000 (daily), 40,000 (Sunday). available in microform.

US/0194-892X
TRI-COUNTY NEWS (FENTON). (TRI-COUNTY NEWS.). (19??)-. Newspaper. English. sw (Published on Wed. & Sun.). $34.00 Finton Linden Holly & Davidburg counties; $49.00 others. Tri-County News / Michigan, PO Box F, Fenton MI 48430. **Tel** (313)629-2069.

US/0193-0249
VASSAR PIONEER TIMES, THE. VFOAT Pioneer Times. (1???)-. Newspaper. English. wk. $19.00 in Tusola County, $21.00 in Michigan, $23.00 other. Huron Daily Tribune, 211 North Heisterman, Bad Axe MI 48413. **Tel** (517)296-6461.

US/1041-1534
WASHINGTON POST INDEX (ANN ARBOR, MICH.). (THE WASHINGTON POST INDEX.). [Wash. post index]. **Added/Corp** University Microfilms International. (Jan. 1989)-. Newspaper. English. mo. $895.00. University Microfilms International, 300 North Zeeb Road, Ann Arbor MI 48106-1346. **Tel** (313)761-4700, (800)521-0600 Exts. 2490, 2491, FAX (313)973-1540. **ED** Andrew Horvay. LC Al21.W33; W372. DD 071/.53. **Formed by the union of** Official Washington Post Index, 0193-9580 **and** Official Washington Post Index (Annual), 0193-9580.

US/0747-1726
WEST VALLEY NEWS, THE. (19??)-. Newspaper. English. sw. $55.00 Genesse County, $60.00 other Michigan, $65.00, other. Flint Advance Newspapers, PO Box 497, Swartz Creek MI 48473. **Tel** (313)733-2239.

US/0192-6497
WESTLAND EAGLE, THE. Newspaper. English. wk. Associated Newspapers Inc, 35540 Michigan Avenue West, Wayne MI 48184. **Tel** (313)729-4000.

US
YPSILANTI PRESS. English. ds. $109.45 US; $133.20 other. Ypsilanti Press, 20 East Michigan Avenue, Ypsilanti MI 48197.

MINNESOTA

US/0745-3450
AGRI NEWS. [Agri news]. (19??)-. Newspaper. English. Fifty-two times a year (Tues.). Post Bulletin Company, PO Box 6118, 18 First Avenue Southwest, Rochester MN 55903. **Tel** (507)285-7600. **ED** Kelly J. Boldan. **Ad Acc**. **Circ:** 21,800 (ctrl). available on microfilm.
 Desc: An agricultural newspaper for southern Minnesota and northern Iowa. Features the news of importance to farm households and agribusinesses in the 38 county coverage area.

US
AITKIN INDEPENDENT AGE. Began 1883. Newspaper. English. wk. Aitkin Independent Age, PO Box 259, Aitkin MN 56431. **Formed by the union of** Aitkin Independent **and** Aitkin Age; **Absorbed** Aitkin Republican.

US/1051-7421
ALBERT LEA TRIBUNE, THE. VFOAT Daily and Sunday Albert Lea Tribune. Vol. 91, No. 192 (Aug. 15, 1988)-. Newspaper. English. da. Albert Lea Tribune, PO Box 16, Albert Lea MN 56007. **Tel** (507)373-1411. available on microfilm. **Continues** Tribune (Albert Lea, Minn. : 1988).

US/0898-526X
ALDEN ADVANCE. Newspaper. English. Alden Advance, PO Box 485, Alden MN 56009.

US
ALEXANDRIA ECHO PRESS. (199?)-. Newspaper. English. bw. $37.00. Alexandria Newspaper, PO Box 549, Alexandria MN 56308. **Tel** (612)763-3133, FAX (612)763-3258. **ED** Al Edenloff. **Bk Rev**. **Photos**. **Ad Acc**, **Adv Mgr:** Jody Hanson. **Circ:** 10,700 paid. **Continues** Alexandria Lake Region Press.

US/0747-0363
AMERICAN (BLACKDUCK, MINN.), THE. (THE AMERICAN.). Vol. 71, No. 1 (Dec. 2, 1971)-. Newspaper. English. wk. $26.00. The American, 209 Main Street, PO Box M, Blackduck MN 56630. **ED** Paula Bouman (Editor-in-Chief) and Jeanne Scham) Managing Editor). **Photos**. **Ad Acc**, **Adv Mgr:** Cindy Fisher-Preuett, **Tel** (218)835-4211. Full Page (B&W) $341.85. Half Page (B&W) $173.25. Full Page (Color) $378.85. Half Page (Color) $208.25. **Pub. Size:** Broadsheet. available in microform. **Continues** Blackduck American and Kelliher Independent.

US
ANOKA COUNTY UNION, THE. VFOAT Anoka Union. Vol. 4, No. 47 (July 22, 1869)-. Newspaper. English. wk (Published on Fridays). A B C Newspapers, PO Box 99, Anoka MN 55303-0099. **Tel** (612)421-4444, FAX (612)421-4315. **ED** Peter Bodley. LC 8447. **Ad Acc**, **Adv Mgr:** Hugh Campbell. **Circ:** 5,800. available on microfilm. **Continues** Anoka Weekly Union; **Absorbed** Fridley Free Press (Fridley, Minn. : 1950). **Continued in part by** Anoka County Suburban Life.

US
APPLETON PRESS. Newspaper. English. Appleton Press, 241 West Snelling, Appleton MN 56208.

US
ASKOV AMERICAN. Vol. 1, No. 1 (Sept. 17, 1914)-. Newspaper. English. Fifty-two times a year. $26.00 Pine County Minnesota; $30.00 other. Askov American, PO Box 275, Kontor Building, Askov MN 55704. **Tel** (612)838-3130. **ED** David Heiller. **Bk Rev**, (Qty: 5). **Photos**. **Ad Acc**, **Adv Mgr:** David Heiller. Full Page (B&W) $300.00. Half Page (B&W) $180.00. Full Page (Color) $375.00. Half Page (Color) $255.00. **Pub. Size:** Broadsheet. **Circ:** 1,800 (ctrl). **Absorbed** Pine County Farmer.

US
AUSTIN HERALD. (19??)-. Newspaper. English. da. Austin Daily Herald, 310 Northeast Second Street, Austin MN 55912. **Tel** (507)433-8851. **ED** Ed E. Smith. **Circ:** 8,762.

US
BAGLEY FARMERS INDEPENDENT. Newspaper. English. wk. Bagley Farmers Independent, Bagley MN 56621. **Tel** (218)694-6265. **ED** James E Golda. **Circ:** 2,950. **Continues** Bagley Independent; **Absorbed** Gonvick Banner; Bagley Herald.

US
BARNESVILLE RECORD-REVIEW, THE. VFOAT Barnesville Record Review. Vol. 1, No. 1 (Sept. 17, 1903)-. Newspaper. English. Fifty-two times a year (Tues.). Barnesville Record Review, PO Box 70, Barnesville MN 56514. **Tel** (218)354-2606. **ED** Eugene A. Prim. **Bk Rev**. **Ad Acc**. **Circ:** 2,000 (ctrl). **Formed by the union of** Barnesville Record and Review (Barnesville, Minn.); **Absorbed** Red River Valley News (Glyndon, Minn. : 1878).

US
BATTLE LAKE REVIEW. (May 1884)-. Newspaper. English. wk. $27.00. Review Enterprises Inc, PO Box 98, Battle Lake MN 56515. **Tel** (218)864-5952, FAX (218)864-5212. **ED** Jon A. Tamke. **Photos**. **Ad Acc**. Full Page (B&W) $453.60. Half Page (B&W) $226.80. Full Page (Color) $528.60. Half Page (Color) $301.80. **Pub. Size:** Broadsheet. available on microfilm. **Absorbed** Ashby-Dalton Post.

US
BAUDETTE REGION, THE. (1913)-. Newspaper. English. wk. $19.00 Minnesota; $25.50 others. Baudette Region, PO Drawer C, Baudette MN 56623. **Tel** (218)634-1722. **ED** John C. Oren. **Bk Rev**, (Qty: 3-10). **Photos**. **Ad Acc**, **Adv Mgr:** John Oren. Full Page (B&W) $295.00. Half Page (B&W) $175.44. Full Page (Color) $370.00. Half Page (Color) $250.00. **Pub. Size:** Broadsheet. **Circ:** 2,385 (ctrl). available in microfilm. **Continues** Rainy River Region; **Absorbed** Northern News (Spooner, Minn.).
 Desc: Covers Lake of the Woods and northwestern Koochiching counties in far Northern Minnesota.

US
BECKER COUNTY RECORD, THE. Vol. 111, No. 39 (Sept. 27, 1982)-. Newspaper. English. wk. Becker County Record, 511 Washington Avenue, Detroit Lakes MN 56501. available on microfilm. **Continues** Record (Detroit Lakes : 1977).

US
BENTON COUNTY NEWS. Newspaper. English. Benton County News, 220 Broadway, Foley MN 56329.

US
BIRD ISLAND UNION. Newspaper. English. Bird Island Union, PO Box 160, Bird Island MN 55310.

US
BIWABIK TIMES. Newspaper. English. wk. Biwabik Times, PO Box 169, Biwabik MN 55708. **Tel** (218)865-6265. **ED** Kitty Anderson. Index available. **Ad Acc**. **Circ:** 1,500.
 Desc: Newspaper and printing.

US
BRAINERD DISPATCH. (19??)-. Newspaper. English. da (daily except Sat.). Brainerd Daily Dispatch / Department of Cirulation, 215 South 6th Street, Brainerd MN 56401. **Tel** (218)829-4705, FAX (218)829-7735. **ED** Roy Miller. **Bk Rev**. **Ad Acc**. **Circ:** 14,500 (week days),. available on microfilm.
 Desc: Daily newspaper serving central Minnesota.

US
BREWSTER TRIBUNE. (19??)-. Newspaper. English. wk (Wed.). $5.00. Heron Lake News, Box 227, Heron Lake MN 56137. **Tel** (507)793-2327.

US
BROOKLYN CENTER POSTNEWS. VFOAT Brooklyn Center Post News. Vol. 33, No. 41 (Jan. 26, 1989)-. Newspaper. English. wk. $14.50 Minnesota; $15.50 other. Post Publishing Co., 4080 West Broadway Avenue #113, Minneapolis MN 55722-5605. **Tel** (612)537-8484. available on microfilm. **Continues** Brooklyn Center Post.

US/0193-3000
BURNSVILLE CURRENT, THE. (19??)-. Newspaper. English. Fifty-two times a year (Wed.). $25.00. Current Newspaper Inc, 1209 East Cliff Road, Burnsville MN 55337. **Tel** (612)890-4456. **ED** Edward Shur (Editor-in-Chief) and Yvonne Klinnett (Managing Editor). **Photos**. **Ad Acc**, **Adv Mgr:** Paul Johnson, **Tel**

(612)896-4700. Full Page (B&W) $1,480.00. Half Page (B&W) $744.00. Full Page (Color) $1,645.00. Half Page (Color) $901.00. **Pub. Size:** Tabloid. **Circ:** 19,000.

US
BYRON REVIEW. Newspaper. English. Byron Review, PO Box 39, Byron MN 55920.

US
CAMBRIDGE STAR, THE. (1952)-. Newspaper. English. wk. Cambridge Star, 741 2nd Avenue Southeast, Cambridge MN 55008. available on microfilm. ***Continues*** *North Star (Cambridge, Minn.);* ***Absorbed*** *Braham Journal.*

US/0745-7251
CANBY NEWS. Vol. 88, No. 11 (Oct. 14, 1965)-. Newspaper. English. wk (Published on Wednesdays). Canby News, 123 First Street East, Canby MN 56220-1342. **Tel** (507)223-5303, FAX (507)223-5404. **ED** Bridget M. Buesing. **Ad Acc. Circ:** 3,400 available on microfilm. ***Continues*** *Canby News and the Canby Press.*

US
CANNON FALLS BEACON. (Aug. 1876)-. Newspaper. English. wk. $18.00. Cannon Falls Beacon, 120 South 4th Street, Cannon Falls MN 55009. **Tel** (507)263-3991. **ED** Dick Dalton. **Photos. Ad Acc, Adv Mgr:** Dave Templin. Full Page (B&W) $496.65. Half Page (B&W) $270.90. **Pub. Size:** Broadsheet. **Circ:** 4,136 weekly. available on microfilm. ***Absorbed*** *Lewis' Ledger.*

US
CARVER COUNTY NEWS. Newspaper. English. Carver County News, 101 Lewis Avenue North, Watertown MN 55388.

US
CHASKA HERALD. 126th year, No. 47 (July 27, 1989)-. Newspaper. English. wk. Chaska Herald, PO Box 113, Chaska MN 55318-0113. **Tel** (612)448-2650. available on microfilm. ***Continues*** *Carver County Herald.*

US
CHISAGO COUNTY PRESS. Vol. 8, No. 28 (May 11, 1905)-. Newspaper. English. Fifty-two times a year. $29.50. Chisago County Press, PO Box 748, Lindstrom MN 55045-0748. **Tel** (612)257-5115, FAX (612)257-5500. **ED** John Silver, Denise Martin (Managing Editor). **Photos. Ad Acc, Adv Mgr:** Ellen Glemna. Full Page (B&W) $540.32. Half Page (B&W) $285.12. Full Page (Color) $630.32. Half Page (Color) $375.12. **Pub. Size:** Standard. **Circ:** 4,000 (ctrl). available on microfilm. ***Formed by the union of*** *Center City Press; Medborgaren (Lindstrom, Minn.)* ***and*** *Chisago County Courier;* ***Absorbed*** *Chisago County News (Center City, Minn.).* **Desc:** Coverage of area news and events.

US
CHRONICLE. (19??)-. Newspaper. English. Fifty-two times a year (Wed.). $25.00. Current Newspaper Inc, 1209 East Cliff Road, Burnsville MN 55337. **Tel** (612)890-4456. **ED** Edward Shur (Editor-in-Chief) and Yvonne Klinnelt (Managing Editor). **Bk Rev. Photos. Ad Acc, Adv Mgr:** Paul Johnson, **Tel** (612)896-4700. Full Page (B&W) $1,488.00. Half Page (B&W) $744.00. Full Page (Color) $1,643.00. Half Page (Color) $899.00. **Pub. Size:** Tabloid. **Circ:** 15,400. ***Continues*** *Eagan Chronicle.*

US
COOK COUNTY NEWS-HERALD, THE. **VFOAT** Cook County News Herald. (1909)-. Newspaper. English. Fifty-two times a year. $20.00. Cook County News Herald, PO Box 757, Grand Marais MN 55604. **Tel** (218)387-1025. **ED** Jack Becklund. **LC** 8468. **Photos. Ad Acc, Adv Mgr:** Hal Kettunen. Full Page (B&W) $529.00. Full Page (Color) $589.00. **Pub. Size:** Broadsheet. **Circ:** 4,983 paid. available on microfilm from The University of Minnesota Historical Society. ***Formed by the union of*** *Cook County Herald* ***and*** *Grand Marais News.*

US
COON RAPIDS HERALD. 97th year, No. 24 (May 17, 1963)-. Newspaper. English. wk. $10.00 Minnesota; $13.00 others. Anoka Union Shopper Inc, PO Box 99, Anoka MN 55303. **Tel** (612)421-4444. available on microfilm. ***Continues*** *Coon Rapids Herald-Life.*

US
COTTONWOOD COUNTY CITIZEN AND THE WINDOM REPORTER. [MICROFILM]. (19??)-. Newspaper. English. Cottonwood County Citizen / Windom Reporter, 260 10th Street, Windom MN 56101.

US/0744-8627
COUNTRY TIMES. Newspaper. English. wk. Spencer-Davis Publishing, PO Box 276, Amboy MN 56010. ***Continues*** *Herald, 0277-3910.*

US
CROOKSTON TIMES. (19??)-. Newspaper. English. da. $48.00 Polk & Red Lake Counties; $65.00 Minnesota & North Dakota; $95.00 other. Crookston Times Printing Company, 124 South Broadway, Crookston MN 56716. **Tel** (218)281-2730.

US
CRYSTAL ROBBINSDALE POSTNEWS. **VFOAT** Crystal Robbinsdale Post News. Vol. 76 No. 41 (Jan. 26, 1989)-. Newspaper. English. Fifty-two times a year (Wed.). $40.00. Post Publishing Co., 4080 West Broadway Avenue #113, Minneapolis MN 55722-5605. **Tel** (612)537-8484. available on microfilm. ***Continues*** *North Hennepin Post.*

US/1045-487X
DAILY GLOBE (WORTHINGTON, MINN.). (DAILY GLOBE.). **VFOAT** Worthington Daily Globe. 112th Year, No. 248 (June 1, 1985)-. Newspaper. English. da. $112.50. Worthington Daily Globe, 300 11th Street, Worthington MN 56187. **ED** Ron Lindsay. **Ad Acc, Adv Mgr:** Denise McMillen, **Tel** (507)376-9711. **Circ:** 13,915. available on microfilm. ***Continues*** *Worthington Daily Globe, 0738-7539.*

US
DAILY JOURNAL. 99th Year, No. 67 (Mar. 20, 1972)-. Newspaper. English. da. Fergus Falls Journal, 914 East Channing Avenue, Fergus Falls MN 56537. available on microfilm. ***Continues*** *Fergus Falls Daily Journal.*

US
DAILY JOURNAL, THE. **VFOAT** International Falls Daily Journal. Vol. 22, No. 235 (Apr. 6, 1933)-. Newspaper. English. da. $85.20. North Star Publishing Company, PO Box 951, International Falls MN 56649. **ED** Arlin Albrecht (Editor-in-Chief) and Tom Klein (Managing Editor). **Bk Rev**, (Qty: 25). **Photos. Ad Acc, Adv Mgr:** Harry Swendsen, **Tel** (218)285-7411. Full Page (B&W) $722.40. Half Page (B&W) $364.00. Full Page (Color) $797.40. Half Page (Color) $439.00. **Pub. Size:** Standard. **Wire Svcs.:** AP. **Circ:** 4,400. ***Continues*** *International Falls Daily Journal.*

US/8750-2895
DAKOTA COUNTY TRIBUNE. **VFOAT** Tribune. Vol. 28, No. 51 (Feb. 9, 1912)-. Newspaper. English. Fifty-two times a year. Dakota County Tribune, PO Box 1439, Burnsville MN 55337. **Tel** (612)894-1111, FAX (612)894-1859. **ED** Joseph Clay and Daniel Clay. **Ad Acc. Circ:** 2,000. available on microfilm from The University of Minnesota Historical Society. ***Continues*** *Dakota County Tribune and Farmington Herald;* ***Absorbed*** *Lakeville Leader.*

US
DAWSON SENTINEL. Vol. 14, No. 15 (Mar. 4, 1898)-. Newspaper. English. wk. Dawson Sentinel, PO Box P, Dawson MN 56232. available on microfilm. ***Continues*** *Sentinel (Dawson, Minn.).*

US
DETROIT LAKES TRIBUNE. Newspaper. English. Detroit Lakes Tribune, 511 Washington Avenue, Detroit Lakes MN 56501. ***Continues*** *Detroit News Tribune;* ***Absorbed*** *Frazee Press.*

US/1048-8774
DISTRIBUTOR SALES. ***Ceased.*** [Distrib. sales]. Vol. 1, No. 1 (Jan. 1990)-Ceased (Jan. 1991). Periodical. English. mo. Advanstar Communications Inc., 131 West First Street, Duluth MN 55802. **Tel** (218)723-9477, (800)346-0085. **DD** 658. ***Continues*** *Paper Sales, 0031-1170.*

US
DODGE CENTER STAR-RECORD. Newspaper. English. Dodge Center Star-Record, PO Box 279, Dodge Center MN 55927. ***Formed by the union of*** *Dodge County Star* ***and*** *Dodge Center Record with the Clarement News.*

US
DODGE COUNTY INDEPENDENT. (1949)-. Newspaper. English. Fifty-two times a year. $18.00. Kasson Dodge County, 105 First Avenue Northwest, Kasson MN 55944. **Tel** (507)634-7503. **ED** Randy Carlsen. **Photos. Ad Acc, Adv Mgr:** Marcia Seland, **Tel** (507)634-7503. Full Page (B&W) $300.00. Half Page (B&W) $175.00. Full Page (Color) $325.00. **Circ:** 2,300. ***Continues*** *Dodge County Republican and the Mantorville Express;* ***Absorbed*** *Mantorville Express (Mantorville, Minn. : 1953).*

US
DULUTH BUDGETEER, THE. (Oct. 1931)-. Newspaper. English. wk. $15.00. Duluth Budgeteer, 5807 Grand Avenue, Duluth MN 55807. **Tel** (218)624-3665, FAX (218)624-7927. **ED** Dick Palmer. **Bk Rev. Photos. Ad Acc, Adv Mgr:** Jeff Swor. Full Page (B&W) $1,270.65. Half Page (B&W) $835.28. Full Page (Color) $1,386.15. Half Page (Color) $950.78. **Pub. Size:** Broadsheet. **Circ:** 48,800 (unpaid), 2,650 (paid).

US/0896-9418
DULUTH NEWS-TRIBUNE (1987), THE. (THE DULUTH NEWS-TRIBUNE.). **VFOAT** Duluth News Tribune. Vol. 118, No. 242 (Dec. 6, 1987)-. Newspaper. English. da. $177.84. Duluth News-Tribune, PO Box 169000, Duluth MN 55816. **Tel** (218)723-5252. ***Continues*** *News-Tribune and Herald, 0889-4620.*

US
EASTERN ITASCAN, THE. (19??)-. Newspaper. English. wk. $18.00. Eastern Itascan, 310 Central Street, Nashwauk MN 55769. **ED** Bill Proznik (Editor-in-Chief) and Deborah Oftelie (Managing Editor). **Bk Rev. Photos. Ad Acc, Adv Mgr:** Leanne Stanley, **Tel** (218)885-2100. Full Page (B&W) $201.60. Half Page (B&W) $109.20. Full Page (Color) $216.60. Half Page (Color) $114.20. **Pub. Size:** Standard. available in microform. ***Continues*** *Nashwauk Herald.*

US/0891-0731
ECM POST-REVIEW, THE. **VFOAT** ECM Post Review; East Central Minnesota Post-Review. **VAT** East Central Minnesota Post-Review. Vol. 103, No. 43 (July 13, 1978)-. Newspaper. English. Fifty-two times a year (Thursday). East Central MN Post-Review, PO Box 366, 612 Main Hall, North Branch MN 55056. **Tel** (612)674-7025, FAX (612)674-7026. **ED** Twyla Ring. **Ad Acc. Circ:** 2,400. available on microfilm. ***Continues*** *Post-Review.*

US
EDGERTON ENTERPRISE. (1883)-. Newspaper. English. wk. $18.00 local; $23.00 US. Edgerton Enterprise, 831 Main Street, PO Box 397, Edgerton MN 56128. **Tel** (507)442-6161, FAX (507)442-6161. **ED** Melvin DeBoer, Liz DeBoer (Managing Editor). **LC** 8461. **Photos. Ad Acc.** Full Page (B&W) $390.00. Half Page (B&W) $208.00. **Pub. Size:** Broadsheet. **Circ:** 1,995 paid. available on microfilm.

US/0746-7087
ELY ECHO. Vol. 1, No. 1 (Oct. 25, 1972)-. Newspaper. English. wk. $18.00, St. Louis County; $26.00 other Minnesota; $35.00 other US; $50.00 other. Ely Echo, 2 East Sheridan Street, Ely MN 55731-1278. **Tel** (218)365-3141. **ED** Bob Cary. **Bk Rev. Ad Acc. Circ:** 4,000. available on microfilm.

US
ENTERPRISE AND DISPATCH. Vol. 1, No. 1 (Jan. 7, 1987)-. Newspaper. English. wk. Cardan Inc, PO Box 340, Dassel MN 55325. available on microfilm. ***Formed by the union of*** *Cokato Enterprise* ***and*** *Dassel Dispatch.*

US
ERSKINE ECHO, THE. (1899)-. Newspaper. English. wk (published Thursdays). $15.00. Erskine Echo, 309 1st Street, Erskine MN 56535. **Tel** (218)687-3775. **ED** Robert M. Hole. Index available. cum. index. **Bk Rev**, (Qty: 10). **Photos. Ad Acc, Adv Mgr:** Robert M. Hole. Full Page (B&W) $325.00. Half Page (B&W) $162.50. Full Page (Color) $405.00. Half Page (Color) $242.50. **Pub. Size:** Broadsheet. **Circ:** 1,100 (ctrl). available on microfilm; available on diskette. ***Continues*** *Erskine Enterprise;* ***Absorbed*** *Mentor Herald.*

US
FAIRFAX STANDARD. Newspaper. English. Fairfax Standard, 102 Southeast 1st Street, Fairfax MN 55332. ***Absorbed*** *Fairfax Crescent.*

US
FAIRMONT SENTINEL. (19??)-. Newspaper. English. da. Fairmont Sentinel, PO Box 681, Fairmont MN 56031. **Tel** (218)235-3303, FAX (507)235-3718. **ED** Bryan Welch (Editor-in-Chief) and Bola Steeuson (Managing Editor). **Photos. Ad Acc, Adv Mgr:** Gary Audersen, **Tel** (507)235-3303. Full Page (B&W) $1,300.32. Half Page (B&W) $650.16. Full Page (Color) $1500.32. Half Page (Color) $850.16. **Pub. Size:** Broadsheet. **Wire Svcs.:** AP. **Circ:** 10,000. available on microfilm from University Microfilms International (UMI).

US/1045-7429
FARIBAULT COUNTY REGISTER (1989). (FARIBAULT COUNTY REGISTER.). Vol. 121, No. 32 (July 24, 1989)-. Newspaper. English. wk. $24.50 (non-local). Tuff Publishing, 111 North Main Street, Blue Earth MN 56013. available on microfilm. ***Continues*** *Post Ambassador, 0747-2307.*

US/0889-8898
FARIBAULT DAILY NEWS. **VFOAT** Daily News. (Dec. 1, 1914)-. Newspaper. English. da (except Sunday and holidays). $65.95. Faribault News, 514 Central Avenue, Faribault MN 55021. **Tel** (507)334-4383. **ED** Michael Cooper. **LC** 7002. **Circ:** 8,753. available on microfilm. ***Continues*** *Faribault Daily News Republican and Pilot.*

US
FERTILE JOURNAL. Newspaper. English. wk. $13.00. Fertile Journal, Fertile MN 56540. **Tel** (218)945-6843. ***Absorbed*** *Winger Enterprise.*

US
FOCUS. **VFOAT** Fridley Focus. Vol. 4, No. 9 (Sept. 14, 1987)-. Newspaper. English. wk. $25.00. Minnesota Suburban Publications, 7831 East Bush Lake Road, Bloomington MN 55435. **Tel** (612)896-4700. available on microfilm. ***Continues in part*** *Focus (Edina, Minn. : Fridley Columbia Heights ed.).*

US
FOCUS. **VFOAT** Columbia Heights Focus. (Sept. 14, 1987)-. Newspaper. English. wk. $25.00. Minnesota

Minnesota

Suburban Publications, 7831 East Bush Lake Road, Bloomington MN 55435. **Tel** (612)896-4700. available on microfiche. *Continues* Focus (Edina, Minn. : Fridley Columbia Heights Ed.).

US
FRAZEE FORUM. (Jan. 8, 1960)-. Newspaper. English. Fifty-two times a year (Thurs.). Frazee Forum, PO Box 187, Frazee MN 56544. **Tel** (218)334-3566. **ED** Jerold J. Brenk. **Ad Acc. Circ:** 1,625. available on an online database, CD-ROM, magnetic tape, and microfilm.

US
FREE PRESS. Vol. 86, No. 289 (Feb. 21, 1973)-. Newspaper. English. da. $177.00 (one year). The Free Press, 418 South 2nd Street, Mankato MN 56001. **Tel** (507)625-4451, FAX (507)388-4355. **Ad Acc. Circ:** 26,000 (ctrl). available on microfilm. *Continues* Mankato Free Press (Mankato, Minn. : 1931).

US
FREE PRESS TRIBUNE-TRESS. VFOAT Free Press Tribune Press; Tribune Press Free Press. Vol. 26, No. 16 (Apr. 19, 1983)-. Newspaper. English. sw. Chisholm Free Press Publishers, 216 West Lake Street, Chisholm MN 55719-1716. **Tel** (218)254-4432, FAX (218)254-4902. available on microfilm. *Formed by the union of* Free Press (Chisholm, Minn.) *and* Tribune-Press (Chisholm, Minn.).

US/0892-5364
FULL-COURT PRESS, THE. Vol. 1, No. 1 (Nov. 1986)-. Periodical. English. Twelve times a year. $18.00. Full-Court Press, PO Box 605, Renville MN 56284. **Tel** (612)329-8182. **ED** Kevin Mulder. **Bk Rev**. **Ad Acc.** ctrl circ.
 Desc: Minnesota basketball news.

US/0742-1591
GAYLORD HUB, THE. VFOAT Hub. (Mar. 1886)-. Newspaper. English. Fifty-two times a year. Gaylord Hub, PO Box 208, Gaylord MN 55334. **Tel** (612)237-2476. **ED** James E. Deis. **Circ:** 2,260. available on microfilm from The University of Minnesota Historical Society.

US
GAZETTE. Vol. 92, No. 47 (July 31, 1974)-. Newspaper. English. wk. Red Lake Falls Gazette, PO Box 370, Red Lake Falls MN 56750. available on microfilm. *Continues* Red Lake Falls Gazette.

US
GLENCOE ENTERPRISE. Began in 1880. Newspaper. English. wk. $14.00 US; $18.00 other. Glencoe Enterprise, 831 11th Street, Glencoe MN 55336. **Tel** (612)864-4715. **ED** Annamarie Tudhope. **Circ:** 4,500. *Continues* McLeod County Enterprise; *Absorbed* McLeod County Republic.

US/0744-544X
GRAND RAPIDS HERALD-REVIEW. VFOAT Grand Rapids Herald Review; Grand Rapids Review; A.Grand Rapids herald. Vol. 4, No. 39 (May 23, 1896)-. Newspaper. English. sw. Grand Rapids Herald Review, 406 Pokegama Avenue North, Grand Rapids MN 55744. **Tel** (218)326-6623. available on microfilm. *Formed by the union of* Grand Rapids Herald *(Grand Rapids, Minn.) and* Iron and Lumber Review; *Absorbed* Bigfork Times; Keewatin Chronicle; Grand Rapids Magnet. *Absorbed in part by* Itasca County Independent.

US
GRYGLA EAGLE, THE. (1973)-. Newspaper. English. wk. Richards Publishing Company, PO Box 159, Gonvick MN 56644-0159. **Tel** (218)487-5225, FAX (218)487-5251. available on microfilm.

US
GUSTAVIAN WEEKLY. Newspaper. English. Gustavus Adolphus College, Saint Peter MN 56082.

US
HALSTAD VALLEY JOURNAL. Ceased. (1884)-Ceased (July 1987). Newspaper. English. wk. Valley Journal, Box 267, Halstad MN 56548. **Tel** (218)456-2133. **ED** Harold V Nelson. **Bk Rev**. **Ad Acc. Circ:** 3,517 (ctrl).
 Desc: General interest publication featuring people, organizations and things in the Red River Valley of northwest Minnesota and eastern North Dakota.

US
HANSKA HERALD, THE. (1901)-. Newspaper. English. wk. Hanska Herald, Hanska MN 56041. available on microfilm.

US
HASTINGS STAR GAZETTE. Vol. 12, No. 18 (Jan. 8, 1981)-. Newspaper. English. wk. Hastings Star Gazette, 745 Spiral Boulevard, PO Box 277, Hastings MN 55033-3651. **Tel** (612)437-6153. available on microfilm. *Formed by the union of* Hastings Gazette (Hastings, Minn. : Weekly) *and* Hastings Star.

US
HAWLEY HERALD, THE. Vol. 35, No. 41 (Feb. 17, 1927)-. Newspaper. English. wk. $17.50 Clay and Beckers counties, Minnesota; $22.50 other. Hawley Herald, Hawley MN 56549. **Tel** (218)483-3306. **ED** Robert A. Brekken. **Ad Acc. Circ:** 2,250. *Continues* Clay County Herald.

US
HENDRICKS PIONEER, THE. (1900)-. Newspaper. English. wk. Hendricks Pioneer, 108 North Main Street, Hendricks MN 56136. available on microfilm.

US
HIBBING TRIBUNE. 1901. Newspaper. English. da (Sun.-Fri.). $52.00. Hibbing Daily Tribune, 2142 1st Avenue, Hibbing MN 55746. **Tel** (218)262-1011. **ED** Alan Zoon. **Ad Acc. Circ:** 11,832 daily, 19,211 Sunday. *Continues* Hibbing Tribune; *Absorbed* Hibbing Daily News.

US
HINCKLEY NEWS. (Mar. 4, 1921)-. Newspaper. English. Fifty-two times a year. $24.00 Hinckley; $34.00 other. Hinckley News, 115 Main Street, Hinckley MN 55037. **Tel** (612)384-6188. available on microfilm. *Continues* Hinckley Enterprise.

US
HOWARD LAKE HERALD. Newspaper. English. Howard Lake Herald, PO Box 190, Howard Lake MN 55349.

US
HUTCHINSON LEADER. (July 17, 1880)-. Newspaper. English. Twenty-six times a year. The Hutchinson Leader, 36 Washington Avenue West, Hutchinson MN 55350. **Tel** (218)587-5000. **ED** Cathy Nevanen. LC 7002. **Ad Acc. Circ:** 6,000 (ctrl). available on microfilm. *Absorbed* Hutchinson Press; Hutchinson Banner.

US/8750-2267
ISANTI COUNTY NEWS. VFOAT American-News. Newspaper. English. wk. $14.00 (residents of Minnesota), $10.00 (senior citizens), $30.00 (out of state). Isanti County News, Box 352, Cambridge MN 55008. **Tel** (612)689-4862. **(Subscription address:** Box 160, Isanti, MN 55040) **Ad Acc. Circ:** 3,400. *Continues* Isanti News.

US
JACKSON COUNTY PILOT. (Sept. 1889)-. Newspaper. English. Fifty-two times a year (Thurs.). $23.00 (Jackson County, MI); $30.95 other. Jackson County Pilot, 302 Second Street, Jackson MN 56143. **Tel** (504)847-3771. **ED** Rosalie Block. **Bk Rev**. **Photos**. **Ad Acc, Adv Mgr:** Dallas Luhmann. Full Page (B&W) $427.42. Half Page (B&W) $226.51. **Pub. Size:** Broadsheet. available on microfilm. *Absorbed* Jackson Republic.

US
JANESVILLE ARGUS. (19??)-. Newspaper. English. wk. $24.00. Janesville Argus, PO Box 220, Janesville MN 56048-0220. **Tel** (507)234-6651, FAX (507)234-6390. **ED** Judy A. Winter. **Photos**. **Ad Acc**. Full Page (B&W) $412.80. Half Page (B&W) $206.40. Full Page (Color) $487.80. Half Page (Color) $281.40. **Pub. Size:** Broadsheet. **Circ:** 1,313 (paid, weekly).

US/0744-3110
JASPER JOURNAL, THE. Vol. 1, No. 1 (July 17, 1888)-. Newspaper. English. wk. Pipestone Publishing Company, 101 2nd Street Northeast, PO Box 470, Pipestone MN 56164. **Tel** (507)348-4176. **ED** Elaine Sestak. **Photos**. **Ad Acc, Adv Mgr:** Delores Quissel. Full Page (B&W) $213.75. Half Page (B&W) $106.88. Full Page (Color) $285.75. Half Page (Color) $181.88. **Pub. Size:** Tabloid. **Circ:** 1,015.
 Desc: A community newspaper.

US
JORDAN INDEPENDENT. Newspaper. English. wk. Jordan Independent, 109 Rice Street, Jordan MN 55352. *Absorbed* Peoples Weekly (Jordan, Minn.).

US/1059-1338
JOURNAL (NEW ULM, MINN.). (THE JOURNAL.). 77th year, No. 101, Dec. 2 (1974)-. Newspaper. English. da (except Mon.). $55.25. New Ulm Journal, Markstrasse North 303, New Ulm MN 56073. **Tel** (507)359-2911. **ED** Kevin Sweeney. **Ad Acc. Circ:** 11,000. available on microfilm. *Continues* New Ulm Daily Journal.

US
KANABEC COUNTY TIMES. Newspaper. English. Kanabec County Times, 36 North Union Street, Mora MN 55051.

US
KARLSTAD NORTH STAR NEWS. Newspaper. English. Karlstad North Star News, 204 South Main Street, Karlstad MN 56732. *Formed by the union of* Karlstad Advocate; Lake Bronson Budget; Lancaster Herald (Lancaster, Minn.) *and* Kennedy Star.

US
KENYON LEADER. Began in 1885. Newspaper. English. wk. Kenyon Leader, 638 2nd Street, Kenyon MN 55946.

US
KERKHOVEN BANNER, THE. (Aug. 14, 1896)-. Newspaper. English. wk. Kerkhoven Banner, PO Box 148, Kerkhoven MN 56252. available on microfilm. *Absorbed* Murdock Independent.

US
KIMBALL TRI-COUNTY NEWS. Newspaper. English. Kimball Tri-County News, PO Box 220, Kimball MN 55353.

US
KITTSON COUNTY ENTERPRISE. Vol. 1, No. 1 (Sept. 26, 1882)-. Newspaper. English. $28.00. Northern Media, 109 3rd Street South, Hallock MN 56728. **Tel** (218)843-2868, FAX (218)843-2312. **ED** Keith Axvig (Editor-in-Chief) and Gail Norland (Managing Editor). **Photos**. **Ad Acc, Adv Mgr:** Gail Norland. Full Page (B&W) $465.37. Half Page (B&W) $232.68. Full Page (Color) $555.37. Half Page (Color) $322.68. **Pub. Size:** Broadsheet. **Circ:** 2,200. available in microform. *Absorbed* People's Press (Hallock, Minn.).

US
LAKE CITY GRAPHIC. Newspaper. English. Lake City Graphic, 107 South Lakeshore Drive, Lake City MN 55041.

US
LAKE COUNTY NEWS-CHRONICLE. VFOAT Lake County News Chronicle. Vol. 1, No. 1 (Sept. 25, 1974)-. Newspaper. English. wk. $17.00 yearly residents of Lake County, $22.00 seasonal residents, $21.00 other Minnesota, $23.00 other. Lake County News Chronicle, PO Box 158, Two Harbors MN 55616. **Tel** (218)834-2141. available on microfilm. *Formed by the union of* Two Harbors Chronicle and Times *and* Silver Bay News.

US
LAKE CRYSTAL TRIBUNE. No. 15 (Dec. 1, 1921)-. Newspaper. English. wk. Lake Crystal Tribune, Lake Crystal MN 56055. *Continues* Lake Crystal Union.

US
LAKE LILLIAN CRIER. Vol. 1 No. 1 (May 6, 1949)-. Newspaper. English. wk. Lake Lillian Crier, PO Box 98, Lake Lillian MN 56253. available on an online database, CD-ROM, magnetic tape, and microfilm; available on microfilm.

US
LAKE PARK JOURNAL. Vol. 30, No. 35 (Sept. 1, 1927)-. Newspaper. English. Fifty-two times a year. Lake Park Journal, Lake Park MN 56554. **Tel** (218)238-5828. **ED** Gerald W. Schlueter. **Ad Acc. Circ:** 1,000. available on microfilm. *Continues* Becker County Journal.

US
LAKEFIELD STANDARD. Newspaper. English. Lakefield Standard, PO Box 248, Lakefield MN 56150. *Absorbed* Lakefield Herald.

US
LAKER, THE. (19??)-. Newspaper. English. Fifty-two times a year. The Laker, PO Box 82, Mound MN 55364. **Tel** (612)472-1140.

US
LAMBERTON NEWS. Vol. 10, No. 52 (Nov. 14, 1929)-. Newspaper. English. wk. $15.00 local; $20.00 outside Minnesota. Lamberton News, 218 East Main Street, Lamberton MN 56152. **ED** Joseph G. Dietl. **Photos**. **Ad Acc**. Full Page (B&W) $387.00. Half Page (B&W) $193.50. **Pub. Size:** Standard. **Circ:** 1,775. available on microfilm. *Continues* Northern Light (Lamberton, Minn.).

US
LE CENTER LEADER. Newspaper. English. Le Center Leader, 60 East Minnesota Street, Le Center MN 56057.

US
LE ROY INDEPENDENT, THE. Began in 1875. Newspaper. English. wk. Le Roy Independent, Le Roy MN 55951.

US
LE SUEUR NEWS-HERALD. VFOAT Le Sueur News Herald. 103rd Year, No. 29 (July 21, 1983)-. Newspaper. English. wk. Le Sueur News-Herald, 101 Bridge Street, Le Sueur MN 56058. available on microfilm. *Continues* News-Herald (Le Sueur, Minn.).

US
LEADER-RECORD, THE. VFOAT Leader Record. Vol. 54, No. 38 (June 20, 1956)-. Newspaper. English. wk. Richards Publishing Company, PO Box 159, Gonvick MN 56644-0159. **Tel** (218)487-5225, FAX (218)487-5251. available on microfilm. *Formed by the union of* Gonvick Record *and* Clearbrook Leader.

US
LEWISON JOURNAL. (1930)-. Newspaper. English. wk. Mack Publishing Co. / Minnesota, 409 West Broadway, Plainview MN 55964-1257. **Tel** (507)534-3121. available on microfilm.

Minnesota

US
LITTLE CANADA PRESS. (19??)-. Newspaper. English. wk. Press Publications Inc, 4779 Bloom Avenue, White Bear Lake MN 55110. **Tel** (612)429-7781, FAX (612)429-1242. **ED** Bob Snell. **Photos. Ad Acc, Adv Mgr:** Michelle Larson. Full Page (B&W) $696.60. Half Page (B&W) $361.20. Full Page (Color) $696.00 plus $130.00 per color. Half Page (Color) $361.20 plus $130.00 per color. **Pub. Size:** Broadsheet. *Separated from North Surburban Press.*

US
LITTLEFORK TIMES. Newspaper. English. Littlefork Times, 1305 Sherburne Avenue, St Paul MN 55104.

US
MADELIA TIMES-MESSENGER. VFOAT Madelia Times Messenger. (1903)-. Newspaper. English. wk. Madelia Media Inc, PO Box 159, Madelia MN 56062. **LC** 8476. available on microfilm. *Formed by the union of Madelia Times and Madelia Messenger.*

US
MADISON WESTERN GUARD. Newspaper. English. Madison Western Guard, PO Box 183, Madison MN 56256.

US
MAHNOMEN PIONEER, THE. (April 1910)-. Newspaper. English. Fifty-two times a year. Mahnomen Pioneer, PO Box 219, Mahnomen MN 56557. **Tel** (218)935-5296. **LC** 8477. *Continues Mahnomen Plaintalk; Absorbed Mahnomen Free Press; Waubun Forum.*

US
MAPLE LAKE MESSENGER. Newspaper. English. Maple Lake Messenger, PO Box J, Maple Lake MN 55358.

US
MAPLEWOOD REVIEW. Vol. 1, No. 1 (June 5, 1962)-. Newspaper. English. wk. $16.00. T R Lillie, 2515 East 7th Avenue, North St Paul MN 55109. **Tel** (612)777-8800, FAX (612)777-8288. **ED** MaryLee Haggert (Editor-in-Chief) and Holly Swanson (Managing Editor). **Photos. Ad Acc, Adv Mgr:** Paula Greene. **Pub. Size:** Broadsheet. **Circ:** 1,000 (paid), 135,000 (unpaid). available on microfilm.

US
MCINTOSH TIMES, THE. (1888)-. Newspaper. English. wk. $20.00, $15.00 (Polk County) US; $25.00 Canada. McIntosh Times, McIntosh MN 56556. **Tel** (218)563-3585. **ED** Richard Richards. **Bk Rev. Ad Acc. Circ:** 1,700 (ctrl). *Absorbed Fosston Journal.*
Desc: Small town newspaper servicing merchants and advertisers.

US
MELROSE BEACON. Newspaper. English. Melrose Beacon, PO Box 186, Melrose MN 56352.

US
MESABI DAILY NEWS. VFOAT Mesabi Sunday News; Sunday Mesabi Daily News. Vol. 53, No. 120 (July 2, 1945)-. Newspaper. English. da. Mesabi Daily News, 704 7th Avenue South, PO Box 956, Virginia MN 55792. **LC** 8515. *Continues Virginia Daily Enterprise; Absorbed Eveleth News (Eveleth, Minn. : 1961).*

US/0747-1734
MILAN STANDARD WATSON JOURNAL, THE. Newspaper. English. wk. Milan Standard Watson Journal, PO Box 190, Milan MN 56262.

US
MILLE LACS COUNTY TIMES. Newspaper. English. Mille Lacs County Times, 225 Southwest 2nd Street, Milaca MN 56353.

US
MILLE LACS MESSENGER, THE. Vol. 1, No. 1 (Oct. 25, 1928)-. Newspaper. English. Fifty-two times a year (Wed.). $20.00. Messenger Publications, PO Box 26, Isle MN 56342. **Tel** (612)676-3123. **ED** Jim Boden. **Photos. Ad Acc, Adv Mgr:** Kevin Anderson, Patrice O'Leary. Full Page (B&W) $297.00. Half Page (B&W) $151.53. **Pub. Size:** Standard. **Circ:** 6,000. *Formed by the union of Isle Advance and Onamia Herald.*

US/0738-9868
MINNEAPOLIS STAR AND TRIBUNE INDEX (MINNEAPOLIS, MINN.).
(MINNEAPOLIS STAR AND TRIBUNE INDEX.). May 1982-. Periodical. English. mo. $165.00. Minneapolis Public Library and Information Center, 300 Nicollet Mall, Minneapolis MN 55401. **LC** Al21; .M53. **DD** 071/.76/579. *Continues Minneapolis Tribune and Minneapolis Star Index.*

US
MINNESOTA DAILY, THE. Added/Corp University of Minnesota. Vol. 1, No. 1 (May 1, 1900)-. Newspaper. English. da. $80.00. University of Minnesota Daily Business Office, 2301 University Avenue Southeast, Minneapolis MN 55414-3070. **Tel** (612)627-0480, FAX (612)627-4159. **ED** Pam Louwagie (Editor-in-Chief) and Matt McKinney (Managing Editor). **Bk Rev.** (Qty: 75). **Photos. Ad Acc, Adv Mgr:** Michael Armel. Full Page (B&W) $919.60. Half Page (B&W) $458.60. Full Page (Color) $1,069.60. Half Page (Color) $608.60. **Pub. Size:** Tabloid. **Wire Svcs.:** AP. **Circ:** 60,000 (ctrl). available on microfilm. *Continues Ariel (Minneapolis, Minn.).*
Desc: General, University of Minnesota, state, national and world news, with literary content.

US
MINNESOTA LAKE TRIBUNE. Newspaper. English. Minnesota Lake Tribune, PO Box 308, Minnesota Lake MN 56068.

US
MINNESOTA UNITED METHODIST LEADER. (19??)-. Newspaper. English. bw. $10.00. Minnesota United Methodist Reporter, 122 West Franklin Avenue, Room 400, Minneapolis MN 55404. **Tel** (612)870-0058, FAX (612)870-1260. **ED** Mary Edlund. **Photos. Pub. Size:** Standard. *Continues Minnesota United Methodist Reporter, 0893-4142.*

US/0893-4142
MINNESOTA UNITED METHODIST REPORTER. *Title Change.* [Minn. United Methodist report.]. **Added/Corp** United Methodist Church (U.S.). Minnesota Conference. VFOAT United Methodist Reporter. (1??)-(19??). Periodical. English. Twenty-six times a year. Minnesota United Methodist Reporter, 122 West Franklin Avenue, Room 400, Minneapolis MN 55404. **Tel** (612)870-0058, FAX (612)870-1260. **ED** Mary Edlund. **DD** 287. **Ad Acc. Circ:** 4,500 (ctrl). *Continued by Minnesota United Methodist Leader.*

US
MONTGOMERY MESSENGER. Newspaper. English. Montgomery Messenger, 310 1st Street South, Montgomery MN 56069.

US/0746-2980
MOOSE LAKE STAR GAZETTE (1983). *Title Change.* (MOOSE LAKE STAR GAZETTE.). VFOAT Moose Lake Star-Gazette. Vol. 88, No. 62 (Aug. 22, 1983)-?. Newspaper. English. sw. Moose Lake Star Gazette, 308 Elm Street, Moose Lake MN 55767. available on microfilm. *Continues Star-Gazette (Moose Lake, Minn.), 0744-7094. Absorbed by Evergreen Shopper.*

US
MORGAN MESSENGER, THE. Vol. 2, No. 25 (Oct. 15, 1891)-. Newspaper. English. wk. $17.00. Morgan Messenger, PO Box 38, Morgan MN 56266-0038. **Tel** (507)249-3130, FAX (507)249-3130. **ED** Walter M. Olson. **Photos. Ad Acc, Adv Mgr:** Arlene Olson. Full Page (B&W) $283.50. Half Page (B&W) $141.75. Full Page (Color) $323.50 (one color). Half Page (Color) $181.75. **Pub. Size:** Broadsheet. **Circ:** 1,180 (paid). available on microfilm. *Continues Messenger (Morgan, Minn.).*

US
MORRIS SUN. Newspaper. English. Morris Sun, 108 East 6th Street, Morris MN 56267.

US
MORRIS SUN-TRIBUNE. (1???)-. Newspaper. English. bw. $24.00 local; $34.00 other. Morris Sun-Tribune, Box 470, Morris MN 56267. **Tel** (612)589-2525. **ED** James Morrison. **Photos. Ad Acc, Adv Mgr:** Anne Erichson. Full Page (B&W) $516.00. Half Page (B&W) $258.00. Full Page (Color) $596.00. Half Page (Color) $338.00. **Pub. Size:** Broadsheet. **Circ:** 3,820. *Continues Morris Tribune.*

US/1066-0887
NATIONAL DIRECTORY OF COMMUNITY NEWSPAPERS (1992). *Title Change.* (NATIONAL DIRECTORY OF COMMUNITY NEWSPAPERS.). [Natl. dir. community newsp.]. **Added/Corp** American Newspaper Representatives, Inc. 72nd Edition (1992)-(1993). Monographic series. English. an. $75.00. American Newspaper Representatives, Inc., 1000 Shelard Parkway, Suite 360, Minneapolis MN 55426. **Tel** (612)545-1116, FAX (612)545-1481. **LC** Z6951; .N27; PN4867. **DD** 071/3. **Ad Acc, Adv Mgr:** Gwen Smith. *Continues Directory of Community Newspapers, 1045-1102. Continued by Directory of Community Newspapers (Minneapolis, Minn. : 1994), 1078-4381.*

US
NEW HOPE GOLDEN VALLEY POSTNEWS. VFOAT New Hope Golden Valley Post News. Vol. 26, No. 41 (Jan. 26, 1989)-. Newspaper. English. wk. Post Publishing Co., 4080 West Broadway Avenue #113, Minneapolis MN 55722-5605. **Tel** (612)537-8484. available on microfilm. *Continues New Hope-Golden Valley Post.*

US
NEW YORK MILLS HERALD. Newspaper. English. New York Mills Herald, PO Box 158, New York Mills MN 56567.

US
NEWS, THE. Vol. 85 No. 41 (Apr. 23, 1986)-. Newspaper. English. wk. Raymond News, 204 Spicer Avenue, Raymond MN 56282. **Tel** (612)967-4244. available on microfilm. *Continues Raymond News.*

US/8750-4693
NEWS HERALD (EAGLE BEND, MINN.), THE. *Title Change.* (THE NEWS HERALD.). VFOAT Eagle Bend News, Bertha Herald; Eagle Bend Bertha News Herald. (1984-1992). Newspaper. English. wk. News Herald / Minnesota, PO Box 248, Eagle Bend MN 56446. *Formed by the union of Eagle Bend News; Bertha Herald. Merged with Clarissa Independent to form Independent News Herald, 1065-0628.*

US
NOBLES COUNTY REVIEW. VFOAT Nobles County Review and Continuing the Wilmont Tribune. (1923)-. Newspaper. English. Fifty-two times a year (Thurs.). Nobles County Review, PO Box 536, c/o Ray Bohn, Adrian MN 56110. **Tel** (507)483-2213. **ED** Merolyn Salter. **Circ:** 1,800. *Continues Nobles County Democrat; Absorbed Wilmont Tribune.*

US
NORMAN COUNTY INDEX. (Apr. 1883)-. Newspaper. English. Fifty-two times a year (Tues.). Norman County Index, 307 West Main Street, PO Box 148, Ada MN 56510. **Tel** (218)784-2541. **ED** Ross D. Pfund. available on microfilm. *Continues Ada Alert; Absorbed Norman County Herald; Norman County Banner; Puhler's Red River Valley Journal.*

US/0892-1792
NORTH SUBURBAN PRESS. *Title Change.* Vol. 6, No. 42 (June 2, 1981)-(19??). Newspaper. English. wk. Press Publications Inc, 4779 Bloom Avenue, White Bear Lake MN 55110. **Tel** (612)429-7781, FAX (612)429-1242. **ED** Sue Roethele. Index available. cum. index. **Ad Acc. Circ:** 52,000 (ctrl). available on microfilm. *Continues Vadnais Heights/Little Canada Free Press (White Bear, Minn. : 1981). Split into Little Canada Press; Shoreview Press and Vadnais Heights Press.*
Desc: Local news in Northeast suburbs of twin cities. Also classified ads, advertising and legal notices.

US
NORTHEASTER. (19??)-. Periodical. English. sm (24 issues). $8.00. Minneapolis Northeaster, 1909 Central Avenue Northeast, Minneapolis MN 55418. **Tel** (612)788-9003. **ED** Tim Fuehrer. **Ad Acc. Circ:** 30,000 (ctrl).
Desc: Community newspapers for Northeast Minneapolis, St. Anthony, and Columbia Heights-Minnesota area. Distinguished in investigative reporting and aggressive local advertising.

US/1053-542X
NORTHFIELD NEWS, THE. VFOAT News, Northfield, Minn. Vol. 4, No. 1 (Nov. 15, 1879)-. Newspaper. English. Fifty-two times a year. Northfield News, PO Box 58, Northfield MN 55057. **Tel** (507)645-5615. **LC** 7002. *Continues Dundas News; Absorbed Northfield Independent; Rice County Journal.*

US
NORTHWOODS PRESS. Vol. 28, No. 35 (Aug. 31, 1989)-. Newspaper. English. wk. Hubbard County Independent, PO Box 105, Nevis MN 56467. available on microfilm. *Continues Independent (Nevis, Minn.).*

US/0897-4977
OJIBWE TIMES, THE. VFOAT Times. (Jan. 1988)-. Newspaper. English. wk. $36.00. Native American Press / Minnesota, 1819 Bemidji Avenue, Bemidji MN 56001. **Tel** (218)751-1655. *Continues Red Lake Times.*

US
OKLEE HERALD. Newspaper. English. Oklee Herald, PO Box 8, Oklee MN 56742.

US
OLIVIA TIMES-JOURNAL. VFOAT Olivia Times Journal. Vol. 69, No. 48 (July 10, 1941)-. Newspaper. English. Fifty-two times a year. $24.00 Olivia County; $28.00 others in Minnesota; $32.00 others. Olivia Publishing Inc., 816 East Lincoln, Olivia MN 56277. **Tel** (612)523-2032, FAX (612)523-2033. **ED** Patricia Kelly. **Photos. Ad Acc, Adv Mgr:** Rose He Hig. Full Page (B&W) $389.80. Half Page (B&W) $221.99. Full Page (Color) $389.80. Half Page (Color) $296.99. **Pub. Size:** Broadsheet. **Circ:** 1,800. available in microform. *Formed by the union of Olivia Times and Renville County Journal.*
Desc: Carries news and advertising.

US
ORACLE, THE. Vol. 63, No. 23 (Apr. 28, 1950)-. Newspaper. English. wk. Hamline University, 1536 Hewitt, Saint Paul MN 55104. available on microfilm.

US
ORTONVILLE INDEPENDENT. Newspaper. English. Ortonville Independent, PO Box 336, Ortonville MN 56278. ***Absorbed*** *Ortonville Journal Star.*

US
PELICAN RAPIDS PRESS. (1897)-. Newspaper. English. wk. Pelican Rapids Press, PO Box L, Pelican Rapids MN 56572. available on microfilm.

US
PERHAM ENTERPRISE-BULLETIN. **VFOAT** Perham Enterprise Bulletin. Began June 1913. Bulletin. English. wk. Perham Enterprise-Bulletin, PO Box 288, Perham MN 56573. ***Formed by the union of*** *Perham Enterprise; Perham Bulletin;* ***Absorbed*** *Perham Graphic.*

US
PILOT INDEPENDENT. (May 20, 1976)-. Newspaper. English. wk. Walker Pilot, PO Box 190, Walker MN 56484. available on microfilm. ***Formed by the union of*** *Cass County Independent* ***and*** *Walker Pilot.*

US/0892-2012
PINE CITY PIONEER. **VFOAT** Pioneer. Vol. 83 No. 26 (May 23, 1968)-. Newspaper. English. wk. $24.00. Pine City Pioneer, 405 East 2nd Avenue, Pine City MN 55063. **Tel** (612)629-6771. **ED** Cindy Rolain. **Ad Acc. Circ:** 2,900 (ctrl). available on microfilm. ***Continues*** *Pine Poker-Pioneer.*
Desc: Hard news and human interest features pertinent to Pine City and surrounding areas. Includes sports, coming events, ect.

US
PINE COUNTY COURIER. Vol. 1, No. 1 (Dec. 27, 1894)-. Newspaper. English. wk. $15.00 Pine, Kanabec, and Aitkin counties, Minnesota; $22.00 other. Sunset Hill Publications Inc., PO Box 230, Sandstone MN 55072-0230. **Tel** (612)245-2368, FAX (612)245-2438. **ED** Donna Sostak. **Bk Rev**, (Qty: 5). **Photos. Ad Acc, Adv Mgr:** Patty McQuiston. Full Page (B&W) $176.00. Half Page (B&W) $88.00. Full Page (Color) $240.00. Half Page (Color) $168.00. **Pub. Size:** Tabloid. **Circ:** 2,000.

US
PINE RIVER JOURNAL. (Aug. 1935)-. Newspaper. English. wk. $22.00. Pine River Journal, PO Box 520, Pine River MN 56474. **ED** Louis Hoglund (Editor-in-Chief) and Jodi Wallin (Managing Editor). **Bk Rev**, (Qty: 14). **Photos. Ad Acc, Adv Mgr:** Debbie Hughes, **Tel** (218)587-2360. Full Page (B&W) $360.00. Half Page (B&W) $180.00. Full Page (Color) $450.00. Half Page (Color) $270.00. **Pub. Size:** Tabloid. **Circ:** 2,331. available in microform.

US/0899-1812
PIONEER (BEMIDJI, MINN.), THE. (THE PIONEER.). Vol. 69, No. 18 (May 11, 1971)-. Newspaper. English. da. $96.00. Nielson and Pioneer St, PO Box 455, Bemidji MN 56601-0455. **Tel** (218)751-3740. **ED** Omar Forberg (Editor-in-Chief) and Brad Swenson (Managing Editor). **Bk Rev**, (Qty: 6). **Photos. Ad Acc, Adv Mgr:** Jeff Haverson. Full Page (B&W) $1,045.80. Half Page (B&W) $522.90. Full Page (Color) $1,115.80. Half Page (Color) $592.90. **Pub. Size:** Broadsheet. **Wire Svcs.:** AP. **Circ:** 8,676 (a.m.). available on microfilm from Crest Information Technologies. ***Continues*** *Bemidji Daily Pioneer.*

US
PIPESTONE COUNTY STAR. Vol. 8, No. 25 (Feb. 18, 1887)-. Newspaper. English. wk. $32.00. Pipestone Publishing Company, 101 2nd Street Northeast, PO Box 470, Pipestone MN 56164. **Tel** (507)348-4176. **ED** Mark Fode. **Photos. Ad Acc, Adv Mgr:** Ray Fuder, **Tel** (507)825-3333. Full Page (B&W) $677.25. Half Page (B&W) $338.63. Full Page (Color) $747.25. Half Page (Color) $408.63. **Pub. Size:** Broadsheet. available on microfilm. ***Continues*** *Pipestone Semi-Weekly Star;* ***Absorbed*** *Pipestone Leader.*

US
PLYMOUTH POSTNEWS. **VFOAT** Plymouth Post News. Vol. 26, No. 41 (Jan. 26, 1989)-. Newspaper. English. wk. Post Publishing Co., 4080 West Broadway Avenue #113, Minneapolis MN 55722-5605. **Tel** (612)537-8484. available on microfilm. ***Continues*** *Plymouth Post.*

US
POPE COUNTY TRIBUNE. Newspaper. English. Pope County Tribune, 108 South Franklin, Glenwood MN 56334. ***Absorbed*** *Glenwood Herald; Villard Grit.*

US
PRESS, THE. ***Title Change.*** (ALEXANDRIA LAKE REGION PRESS). Vol. 47, No. 35 (Jan. 11, 1991)-(199?). Newspaper. English. Fifty-two times a year (Fri.). Alexandria Newspaper, PO Box 549, Alexandria MN 56308. **Tel** (612)763-3133, FAX (612)763-3258. **ED** Hollan Lommen. available on microfilm. ***Continues*** *Lake Region Press.* ***Continued by*** *Alexandria Echo Press.*

US/8750-0698
PRINSBURG NEWS. **VFOAT** Raymond-Prinsburg News. Newspaper. English. wk. $15.00. Raymond-Prinsburg News, 204 Spicer Avenue, Raymond MN 56282. **Tel** (612)967-4244. **ED** Bill Paterson. **Bk Rev. Ad Acc. Circ:** 1,100 (ctrl).
Desc: Weekly newspaper in west central Minnesota.

US
PROCTOR JOURNAL, THE. Vol. 77, No. 9 (Aug. 26, 1982)-. Newspaper. English. wk. Proctor Journal, 215 5th Street, Proctor MN 55810. **Tel** (218)624-3344. available on microfilm. ***Continues*** *Journal (Proctor, Minn.).*

US/0892-1806
QUAD COMMUNITY PRESS. Vol. 1, No. 1 (Oct. 26, 1982)-. Newspaper. English. wk. $25.00. Quad Community Press, 4779 Bloom Avenue, White Bear Lake MN 55110. **Tel** (612)429-7781, FAX (612)429-1242. **ED** Bob Snell. Index available. cum. index. **Photos. Ad Acc, Adv Mgr:** Michelle Larson. Full Page (B&W) $864.30. Half Page (B&W) $454.73. Full Page (Color) $994.30. Half Page (Color) $584.73. **Pub. Size:** Broadsheet. **Circ:** 52,000 (ctrl). available on microfilm.
Desc: Local news in Northeast suburbs of Twin Cities. Also classified ads, advertising and legal notices.

US
RAMSEY COUNTY REVIEW. Vol. 27, No. 30 (Oct. 10, 1946)-. Newspaper. English. wk. T R Lillie, 2515 East 7th Avenue, North St Paul MN 55109. **Tel** (612)777-8800, FAX (612)777-8288. **ED** Raymond Enright. **Circ:** 2,172. available on microfilm. ***Continues*** *North St. Paul Courier.*

US
RED WING REPUBLICAN EAGLE. Vol. 84, No. 37 (Nov. 24, 1969)-. Newspaper. English. da. $94.00. Red Wing Republican Eagle, PO Box 82, Red Wing MN 55066. **Tel** (612)388-8235. **ED** James Pumarlo. **Bk Rev. Photos. Ad Acc, Adv Mgr:** Mary Foley. Full Page (B&W) $1371.27. Half Page (B&W) $685.64. Full Page (Color) $1481.28. Half Page (Color) $740.64. **Pub. Size:** Standard. **Wire Svcs.:** AP. **Circ:** 8,059 (ctrl). available on microfilm. ***Continues*** *Daily Republican Eagle.*
Desc: Local, regional, state and national news; advertising suited to local needs.

US
REDWOOD FALLS REDWOOD GAZETTE. Newspaper. English. Redwood Gazette, 140 East 2nd Street, Redwood Falls MN 56283.

US
RENVILLE COUNTY STAR FARMER NEWS. **VFOAT** Star Farmer News. Vol. 101, No. 35 (Oct. 4, 1989)-. Newspaper. English. wk. $22.00. Renville Star Farmer, PO Box 468, Renville MN 56284. **Tel** (612)329-3324. **ED** Daniel A. Licklider. **Photos. Ad Acc, Adv Mgr:** Rich McCube. **Pub. Size:** Broadsheet. **Circ:** 2,199 paid. available on microfilm. ***Formed by the union of*** *Renville Star-Farmer* ***and*** *Sacred Heart News.*

US
REPORTER. **VFOAT** Mankato State Reporter; MSU Reporter. Vol. 50, No. 7 (Aug. 2, 1978)-. Newspaper. English. sw. $25.00. Mankato State University, Box 38, Mankato MN 56001. **Tel** (507)387-1776, FAX (507)389-5812. **ED** Robb Murray. **Bk Rev. Photos. Ad Acc, Adv Mgr:** Leslie Knight. Full Page (B&W) $292.50. Half Page (B&W) $146.25. Full Page (Color) $357.50. Half Page (Color) $211.25. **Pub. Size:** Tabloid. **Circ:** 7,500. available on microfilm from the publisher. ***Continues*** *Mankato State University Reporter.*

US
ROSEAU TIMES-REGION. Newspaper. English. Roseau Times-Region, 106 West Center Street, Roseau MN 56751. ***Formed by the union of*** *Roseau County Times* ***and*** *Roseau Region;* ***Absorbed*** *Roseau Forum; Herald-Rustler.*

US
SAILOR. **VFOAT** Eden Prairie Sailor. (1984)-. Newspaper. English. wk. Minnesota Suburban Publications, 7831 East Bush Lake Road, Bloomington MN 55435. **Tel** (612)896-4700. available on microfilm. ***Continues*** *Eden Prairie Sailor.*

US
SAINT PAUL LEGAL LEDGER. Vol. 1, No. 1 (May 21, 1927)-. Newspaper. English. da. $90.00. Saint Paul Legal Ledger, 46 E 4th Street, 640 Minnesota Building, St Paul MN 55101-1163. **Tel** (612)222-0059. **ED** Samuel E. Lewis Jr. **Photos. Ad Acc.** Full Page (B&W) $432.00. Half Page (B&W) $216.00. **Pub. Size:** Tabloid. **Wire Svcs.:** AP. **Circ:** 600 (mornings) (ctrl).
Desc: Business and legal newspaper.

US/1050-0405
SAINT PAUL PIONEER PRESS (SAINT PAUL, MINN. : 1990 : A.M. ED.). (SAINT PAUL PIONEER PRESS.). **VFOAT** St. Paul Pioneer Press; Pioneer Press. Vol. 141, No. 333 (March 26, 1990)-. Newspaper. English. da. St Paul Pioneer Press Dispatch, 345 Cedar Street, Saint Paul MN 55101. **Tel** (800)678-7737, (612)222-5011. available on an online database (file 701/Full-Text) from DIALOG. ***Continues*** *St. Paul Pioneer Press Dispatch (Saint Paul, Minn. : A.M. Ed.), 0892-1083.*
Ind/Abst Foods Adlibra; PROMT.

US
SAINT PETER HERALD. **VFOAT** St. Peter Herald; St. Peter Times Herald. Vol. 1, No. 1 (Oct. 17, 1884)-. Newspaper. English. Fifty-two times a year (Thurs., & except the week of Christmas). Saint Peter Herald, PO Box 520, Saint Peter MN 56082. **Tel** (507)931-4520. ***Absorbed*** *St. Peter New Times; Saint Peter Free Press (Saint Peter, Minn. : 1894);* ***Absorbed in part*** *Saint Peter Tribune.*

US
SAUK CENTRE HERALD, THE. Vol. 19, No. 48 (Apr. 29, 1886)-. Newspaper. English. wk. Sauk Centre Publishers Inc, 522 Sinclair Lewis Avenue, Sauk Centre MN 56378. available on microfilm. ***Continues*** *Sauk Centre Herald and Melrose Tribune;* ***Absorbed*** *Sauk Centre News; Sauk Centre Avalanche.*

US
SHAKOPEE VALLEY NEWS, THE. Vol. 1, No. 1 (Dec. 11, 1941)-Vol. 14, No. 50 (Aug. 11, 1960); Vol. 99, No. 47 (Aug. 18, 1960)-. Newspaper. English. Fifty-two times a year. Shakopee Valley News, PO Box 8, Shakopee MN 55379. **Tel** (612)445-3333. ***Absorbed*** *Shakopee Argus-Tribune.*

US
SHOREVIEW PRESS. (19??)-. Newspaper. English. wk. Press Publications Inc, 4779 Bloom Avenue, White Bear Lake MN 55110. **Tel** (612)429-7781, FAX (612)429-1242. **ED** Bob Snell. **Photos. Ad Acc, Adv Mgr:** Michelle Larson. Full Page (B&W) $903.00. Half Page (B&W) $467.63. Full Page (Color) $903.00 plus $130.00 per color. Half Page (Color) $467.63 plus $130.00 per color. **Pub. Size:** Broadsheet. ***Separated from*** North Surburban Press.

US
SLEEPY EYE HERALD-DISPATCH. Newspaper. English. wk. $24.00. Sleepy Eye Herald-Dispatch, 109 East Main Street, Sleepy Eye MN 56085. **Tel** (507)794-3511. **ED** Mark W Beito. **Ad Acc. Circ:** 4,000.

US
SOUTH CROW RIVER NEWS. Vol. 26, No. 36 (Jan. 30, 1989)-. Newspaper. English. wk. South Crow River News, 33 2nd Street Northeast, Osseo MN 55369. available on microfilm from The University of Minnesota Historical Society. ***Continues*** *Crow River News (Rockford, Minn. : South Ed.).*

US
SPRING GROVE HERALD. Newspaper. English. Spring Grove Herald, PO Box 68, Spring Grove MN 55974.

US
SPRINGFIELD ADVANCE-PRESS. **VFOAT** Springfield Advance Press. (1918)-. Newspaper. English. wk. $29.00. Springfield Advance-Press, 13 South Marshall Avenue, Springfield MN 56087. **ED** Dorts Weber. **Bk Rev**, (Qty: 48). **Photos. Ad Acc, Adv Mgr:** Peter Hedstrom. Full Page (B&W) $451.50. Half Page (B&W) $225.75. Full Page (Color) $491.50. Half Page (Color) $265.75. **Circ:** 2,400. ***Formed by the union of*** *Springfield Free Press* ***and*** *Springlield Advance.*

US
ST. CHARLES PRESS. **VFOAT** A.Saint Charles press. Vol. 64, No. 3 (Jan. 5, 1939)-. Newspaper. English. wk. Saint Charles Press, PO Box 617, Saint Charles MN 55972. available on microfilm. ***Continues*** *Inter-County Press.*

US/0899-5028
ST. CLOUD TIMES. **VFOAT** Saint Cloud Times; St. Cloud (Minn.) Times. 127th Year/295 (May 22, 1988)-. Newspaper. English. da. Saint Cloud Times, PO Box 768, 3000 7th Street North, Saint Cloud MN 56302. **Tel** (612)255-8700. available on microfilm. Documents available from UMI Article Clearinghouse. ***Continues*** *St. Cloud Daily Times (St. Cloud, Minn. : 1941), 0742-7913.*
Ind/Abst Bus. Dateline (Jan. 13, 1992-) [Full Txt.].

US/0892-1784
ST. CROIX VALLEY PRESS. **VFOAT** Saint Croix Valley Press. Vol. 3, No. 49 (Jan. 20, 1981)-. Newspaper. English. wk. Press Publications Inc, 4779 Bloom Avenue, White Bear Lake MN 55110. **Tel** (612)429-7781, FAX (612)429-1242. **ED** Bob Snell. Index available. cum. index. **Photos. Ad Acc, Adv Mgr:** Michelle Larson. Full Page (B&W) $494.00. Half Page (B&W) $264.00. Full Page (Color) $624.00. Half Page (Color) $394.00. **Pub. Size:** Tabloid. **Circ:** 52,000 (ctrl). ***Continues*** *St. Croix Valley Free Press.*
Desc: Local news in Northeast suburbs of the Twin Cities. Also classified ads, advertising and legal notices.

US
ST. PAUL RECORDER. **VFOAT** Saint Paul Recorder. Vol. 1, No. 1 (Aug. 10, 1934)-. Newspaper. English. Fifty-two times a year. St Paul Recorder, 3744 4th Avenue South, Minneapolis MN 55409. **Tel** (612)827-4021. **ED** Launa Q. Newman. **Ad Acc. Circ:** 10,000.

US
STAPLES WORLD. (19??)-. Newspaper. English. wk. $22.00. Staples World, 224 4th Street North, Staples MN 56479. **Tel** (218)894-1112, FAX (218)894-3570. **ED** Brenda Halvorson. **Bk Rev**, (Qty: 6). **Photos**. **Ad Acc**, **Adv Mgr:** Gary Mueller. Full Page (B&W) $528.90. Half Page (B&W) $270.60. **Pub. Size:** Broadsheet. **Circ:** 3,000.

US/0895-2825
STAR TRIBUNE (MINNEAPOLIS, MINN.). (STAR TRIBUNE.). Vol. 6, No 149 (Aug. 31, 1987)-. Newspaper. English. ds. $286.00. Star Tribune / Minnesota, 425 Portland Avenue South, Minneapolis MN 55488. **Tel** (800)775-4344, (612)673-4000. **CODEN** STMIED. available on microfilm. ***Continues in part*** *Minneapolis Star and Tribune, 0744-5458.*
Ind/Abst Foods Adlibra; PROMT.

US
STEARNS-MORRISON ENTERPRISE. Newspaper. English. Stearns-Morrison Enterprise, PO Box 310, Albany MN 56307.

US
STEWARTVILLE STAR. (May 1, 1891)-. Newspaper. English. Fifty-two times a year. $20.00. Stewartville Star / Stewartville Publishing Company, PO Box 35, Stewartville MN 55976. **Tel** (507)533-4271, (507)533-4272. **ED** Sandy Forstner. **Photos**. **Ad Acc**. Full Page (B&W) $490.00. Half Page (B&W) $260.00. Full Page (Color) $565.00. Half Page (Color) $335.00. **Pub. Size:** Standard. ***Absorbed*** *Dover Independent.*

US
STILLWATER EVENING GAZETTE. (Dec. 11, 1959)-. Newspaper. English. da. Stillwater Daily Gazette, 102 South 2nd Street, Stillwater MN 55082. available on microfilm. ***Continues*** *Stillwater Daily Gazette.*

US/0747-1653
SWIFT COUNTY MONITOR-NEWS. **VFOAT** Swift County Monitor News. Vol. 98 No. 38 (Feb. 22, 1984)-. Newspaper. English. wk (Published on Wednesdays). Swift County Monitor News, PO Box 227, 101 South 12th Street, Benson MN 56215-1844. **Tel** (612)843-4111, FAX (612)843-3246. **ED** Reed Anfinson. **Ad Acc**. **Circ:** 32,000. available on microfilm. ***Formed by the union of*** *Swift County News* ***and*** *Swift County Monitor.*

US/8750-3883
THIEF RIVER FALLS TIMES. (19??)-. Newspaper. English. sw. $22.00 Minnesota; $38.00 others. Thief River Falls Times, 324 North Main Avenue, Thief River Falls MN 56701. **Tel** (218)681-4450, FAX (218)681-4455. **ED** Marvin Lundin. **Bk Rev**. **Photos**. **Ad Acc**, **Adv Mgr:** Ken Kohler. Full Page (B&W) $516.00. Half Page (B&W) $258.00. Full Page (Color) $564.50. Half Page (Color) $282.25. **Pub. Size:** Broadsheet. **Circ:** 6,325 (ctrl). available on microfilm.
Desc: Local and regional community news of Northwest Minnesota.

US
THIRTEEN TOWNS, THE. (1884)-. Newspaper. English. Fifty-two times a year (Wed.). $16.00 local; $20.00 others. Thirteen Towns, Box 505, Fosston MN 56542. **Tel** (218)435-1313, FAX (218)435-1309. **ED** David S. Carr. **Photos**. **Ad Acc**, **Adv Mgr:** Peter Carr. **Pub. Size:** Standard. **Circ:** 3,249 (ctrl). available on microfilm.

US
TIMES, THE. Vol. 81, No. 12 (Aug. 2, 1984)-. Newspaper. English. wk. Forest Lake Times, 880 Southwest 15th Street, Forest Lake MN 55025. **Tel** (612)464-4601, FAX (612)464-4605. **ED** Cliff Buchan. **Photos**. **Ad Acc**, **Adv Mgr:** Roxanne Muehlberg. Full Page (B&W) $459.00. **Pub. Size:** Tabloid. available on microfilm. ***Continues*** *Forest Lake Times.*

US/1068-1817
TOMORROW'S NATION. ***Ceased.*** **VFOAT** Today's Perspective from Tomorrow's Nation. Vol. 1 (Sept. 1993)-(19??). Periodical. English. Nine times a year (September thru May). Writer Publications, PO Box 718, Grand Rapids MN 55744. **Tel** (218)326-8025. **ED** Roxanne Kain. **Ad Acc**. ctrl circ.
Desc: The Heart and Mind of America's Teens.

US
TRACY HEADLIGHT-HERALD. Newspaper. English. Tracy Headlight-Herald, 207 4th Street, Tracy MN 56175. ***Formed by the union of*** *Tracy Headlight* ***and*** *Tracy Weekly Herald.*

US
TRI-COUNTY RECORD. (1915)-. Newspaper. English. Tri-County Record, PO Box 429, Rushford MN 55971. ***Absorbed*** *Peterson Herald; Rushford Star-Republican.*

US
TWIN VALLEY TIMES AND GARY GRAPHIC, THE. **VFOAT** Twin Valley Times and Continuing the Gary Graphic. Vol. 94 No. 48 (Aug 1 1989)-. Newspaper. English. wk. Twin Valley Times, 101-103 West Main Street, PO Box 478, Twin Valley MN 56584-0478. available on microfilm. ***Continues*** *Twin Valley Times and Continuing the Gary Graphic.*

US
ULEN UNION, THE. (Oct. 1896)-. Newspaper. English. Fifty-two times a year (Wed.). $20.00. Ulen Union, PO Box 248, Ulen MN 56585. **Tel** (218)596-8813. **ED** David G. Evans. **Photos**. **Ad Acc**, **Adv Mgr:** David Evans. Full Page (B&W) $410.22. Half Page (B&W) $205.11. Full Page (Color) $530.22. Half Page (Color) 265.11. **Pub. Size:** Standard.

US
UMD STATESMAN. **Main/Corp** University of Minnesota, Duluth. **Added/Corp** University of Minnesota, Duluth. **VFOAT** UMD Statesman; Statesman; Duluth Statesman. Vol. 15, No. 1 (Oct. 8, 1947)-. Newspaper. English. wk. University of Minnesota at Duluth, 2400 Oakland Avenue, Duluth MN 55812. **Tel** (218)726-7112. **ED** Jerome Paul Guidinger. **Circ:** 6,000. ***Continues*** *Duluth Statesman.*

US/8750-1562
UNION ADVOCATE. **Added/Corp** St. Paul AFL-CIO Trades and Labor Assembly. Vol. 69, No. 47 (Nov. 25, 1965)-. Newspaper. English. sm. $12.50. Union Advocate, 411 Main Street, Room 416, St. Paul MN 55102. **Tel** (612)227-0106, FAX (612)293-1989. **ED** Barbara Kucera. **Photos**. **Ad Acc**. Full Page (B&W) $14.87 per column inch. Half Page (B&W) $14.87 per column inch. **Pub. Size:** Tabloid. available on microfilm. ***Continues*** *Minnesota Union Advocate.*

US
VADNAIS HEIGHTS PRESS. (19??)-. Newspaper. English. wk. Press Publications Inc, 4779 Bloom Avenue, White Bear Lake MN 55110. **Tel** (612)429-7781, FAX (612)429-1242. **ED** Bob Snell. **Photos**. **Ad Acc**, **Adv Mgr:** Michelle Larson. Full Page (B&W) $625.65. Half Page (B&W) $325.73. Full Page (Color) $625.65 plus $130.00 per color. Half Page (Color) $325.73 plus $130.00 per color. **Pub. Size:** Broadsheet. ***Separated from*** *North Surburban Press.*

US
WACONIA PATRIOT. Newspaper. English. Waconia Patriot, 124 West Main Street, Waconia MN 55387.

US
WADENA PIONEER JOURNAL. **VFOAT** Pioneer-Journal; Pioneer Journal; Wadena Pioneer Journal and the Wadena Nws. Vol. 20, No. 16 (Aug. 6, 1897); Vol. 106, No. 43 (Jan. 25, 1984). Newspaper. English. wk. $14.00 Wadena area, $19.00 others in Minnesota, $24.00 outside Minnesota. Wadena Pioneer Journal, PO Box 31, Wadena MN 56482. **LC** 8516. available on microfilm. ***Formed by the union of*** *Wadena County Pioneer* ***and*** *Wadena County Journal;* ***Absorbed*** *Wadena Tribune (Wadena, Minn. : 1885); Wadena News (Wadena, Minn. : 1910); Inter-County Tab.*

US/1068-168X
WANDERER (SAINT PAUL, MINN. : 1931). (THE WANDERER.). Vol. 1 (1931)-Vol. 37, No. 42, (Oct. 19, 1967)-. Newspaper. English. wk (Thursdays). $35.00 US; $42.00 other. The Wanderer Printing Company, 201 Ohio Street, St Paul MN 55107. **Tel** (612)224-5733. **ED** A J Matt Jr. **Bk Rev**. **Ad Acc**. **Circ:** 36,500 (ctrl). available on microfilm.
Desc: News, reviews, and commentary history, philosophy, theology, politics, religions, and other topics as they affect the Roman Catholic Church.

US
WARREN SHEAF. Vol. 1, No. 1 (Dec. 1, 1880)-. Newspaper. English. Fifty-two times a year. Warren Sheaf, Box 45, Warren MN 56762. **Tel** (218)745-5174. **ED** E. Neil Mattson. **Ad Acc**. **Circ:** 3,450. ***Absorbed*** *Warren Register; Marshall County Star.*

US
WARROAD PIONEER. (Aug. 31, 1911)-. Newspaper. English. wk. $19.00. Warroad Pioneer, PO Box E, Warroad MN 56763. **ED** Tony Rogers. **Bk Rev**, (Qty: 10-20). **Photos**. **Ad Acc**, **Adv Mgr:** Pam Pederson. Full Page (B&W) $419.25. Half Page (B&W) $204.75. **Pub. Size:** Standard. available on microfilm. ***Continues*** *Warroad Plaindealer.*

US/0745-8177
WASECA COUNTY NEWS. Vol. 1, No. 1 (July 1, 1982)-. Newspaper. English. Twice a week. $30.00 Minnesota; $40.00 other. Waseca County News, 108 2nd Avenue Northwest, Waseca MN 56093. **Tel** (507)835-3380, FAX (507)835-3435. **ED** Tom West, Lisa Meyers (Managing Editor). **Bk Rev**, (Qty: 3). **Photos**. **Ad Acc**, **Adv Mgr:** Cheryl Neid. Full Page (B&W) $563.73. Half Page (B&W) $307.40. Full Page (Color) $663.73. Half Page (Color) $407.40. **Pub. Size:** Broadsheet. **Wire Svcs.:** AP. available on microfilm.

US
WASHINGTON COUNTY BULLETIN, THE. Vol. 10, No. 1 (Aug. 1, 1968)-. Newspaper. English. wk. $32.00. Bulletin Publishing Corporation, 7163 E Pt Douglas Road, Cottage Grove MN 55016. **Tel** (612)459-3434. available on microfilm. ***Continues*** *South Washington County Bulletin.* ***Continued in part by*** *Woodbury Bulletin.*

US/1059-4744
WEEKLY REVIEW (EMMONS, MINN.), THE. ***Title Change.*** (THE WEEKLY REVIEW : VOICE OF SOUTHERN FREEBORN COUNTY.). Vol. 1, No. 1 (Thursday, Oct. 3, 1991)-(199?). Newspaper. English. wk. The Weekly Review / Minnesota, PO Box 113, Emmons MN 56029. ***Absorbed*** *Leader-Press (Glenville, Minn.).* ***Continued by*** *Freeborn County Weekly Review, 1068-1795.*

US
WELLS MIRROR. Newspaper. English. Wells Mirror, 40 West Franklin, Wells MN 56097. ***Absorbed*** *Forum-Advocate.*

US/0892-1326
WHITE BEAR PRESS, THE. Vol. 19, No. 2 (Apr. 9, 1914)-. Newspaper. English. wk (Thurs.). Press Publications Inc, 4779 Bloom Avenue, White Bear Lake MN 55110. **Tel** (612)429-7781, FAX (612)429-1242. **ED** Bob Snell. **LC** 7002. cum. index. **Photos**. **Ad Acc**, **Adv Mgr:** Michelle Larson. Full Page (B&W) $1960.80. Half Page (B&W) $1025.55. Full Page (Color) $1960.80 plus $130.00 per color. Half Page (Color) $1155.50. **Pub. Size:** Broadsheet. **Circ:** 15,000 (ctrl). available on microfilm. ***Continues*** *White Bear Life;* ***Absorbed*** *White Bear Lake Area Free Press.*
Desc: Local news in Northeast suburbs of twn cities. Also classified ads, advertising, and legal notices.

US/0744-7582
WILLIAMS NORTHERN LIGHT. ***Title Change.*** Vol. 1, No. 1 (Feb. 3, 1916)-(19??). Newspaper. English. wk. Williams Northern Light, PO Box 157, Williams MN 56686. available on microfilm. ***Continued by*** *Northern Light, 1054-1667.*

US
WINONA COURIER. **Added/Corp** Catholic Church. Diocese of Winona (Minn.). (Nov. 1910)-. Periodical. English. Twenty-six times a year. $15.00. Diocese of Winona, PO Box 53, Winona MN 55987. **Tel** (507)454-4369. **ED** Ivan Kubista. **Bk Rev**. ctrl circ. available on microfilm.

US/0273-9941
WINONA DAILY NEWS. **VFOAT** Winona Sunday News. Vol. 1, No. 1 (Sept. 14, 1916)-. Newspaper. English. da. $167.50. Winona Daily News, PO Box 147, Winona MN 55987. **Tel** (507)454-6804. **ED** Stan Schmidt. **LC** 8520. **Circ:** 14,804. ***Continues*** *Winona Republican-Herald.*

US
WINSTED JOURNAL. Newspaper. English. wk. Winsted Journal, PO Box 129, Winsted MN 55395. **Tel** (612)485-2535. **ED** Dale E Kovar. **Circ:** 1,695.

US
WOOD LAKE NEWS. Vol. 1, No. 1 (Nov. 8, 1900)-. Newspaper. English. wk. Wood Lake News, Wood Lake MN 56297. available on microfilm from The University of Minnesota Historical Society. ***Absorbed*** *Wood Lake Ledger.*

US
WRIGHT COUNTY JOURNAL-PRESS. **VFOAT** Wright County Journal Press. Vol. 44, No. 50 (Dec. 4, 1930)-. Newspaper. English. Fifty-two times a year. $20.00 (Residents of Minnesota; $23.00 other. Wright County Journal Press, 108 Central Avenue, Buffalo MN 55313. **Tel** (612)682-1221. **ED** James P. McDonnell Jr. available on microfilm. ***Formed by the union of*** *Buffalo Journal* ***and*** *Wright County Press;* ***Absorbed*** *Waverly Star and Tribune.*

MISSISSIPPI

US/1055-3061
ABERDEEN EXAMINER (ABERDEEN, MISS.: 1866). (THE ABERDEEN EXAMINER.). **VFOAT** Weekly Examiner. (April 28, 1866)-. Newspaper. English. wk. $28.00 Monroe County Mississippi; $32.00 other Mississippi; $38.00 other. Aberdeen Examiner, 209 Commerce Street, PO Box 279, Aberdeen MS 39730. **Tel** (601)369-4507. **LC** 8525. ***Absorbed*** *Aberdeen News Herald.*

US/0899-0085
AMORY ADVERTISER (1957), THE. (THE AMORY ADVERTISER.). Vol. 37, No. 40 (Jan. 24, 1957)-. Newspaper. English. Fifty-two times a year. $23.00 Monroe, Itawamba, Lee, Chickasaw, Clay, Lowndes, Counties in Mississippi & Lamar Alabama; $26.00 others in Mississippi; $29.00 other. Amory Advertiser, 113 South Main Street, PO Box 519, Amory MS 38821. **Tel** (601)256-5647. ***Continues*** *Amory News-Advertiser (Amory, Miss. : 1940).*

US
BANNER INDEPENDENT, THE. Vol. 60, No. 30 (Oct. 31, 1957)-. Newspaper. English. wk. Banner Independent, PO Box 10, Booneville MS 38829. ***Formed by the union of*** *Booneville Independent* ***and*** *Booneville Banner.*

US
BELZONI BANNER, THE. Began with Jan. 31, 1914 issue. Newspaper. English. wk. Belzoni Banner, 115 Jackson Street, Belzoni MS 39038. ***Formed by the union of*** *Belzoni Journal* ***and*** *Delta New Era.*

US
BOLIVAR COMMERCIAL, THE. Began with March 30, 1917 issue. Newspaper. English. da. $48.00 US; $60.00 North America. Bolivar Commercial, PO Box 1050, Cleveland MS 38732. **Tel** (601)843-4241. **ED** Norman C Van Liew and Wayn Nicholas. **Ad Acc. Circ:** 7,025.

US
CALHOUN COUNTY JOURNAL (BRUCE, MISS.). (THE CALHOUN COUNTY JOURNAL.). Began with Aug. 13, 1953 issue. Newspaper. English. wk. Calhoun County Journal, PO Box 278, Bruce MS 38915-0278.

US
CARTHAGINIAN (CARTHAGE, MISS. : 1872). (THE CARTHAGINIAN.). **VFOAT** Carthage-Mississippian; Carthage Mississippian. (1872)-. Newspaper. English. wk. Carthaginian, PO Box 457, Carthage MS 39051-0457. **Tel** (601)267-4501. **ED** Mildred Dearman. **Circ:** 5,700. ***Absorbed*** *Mississippian (Carthage, Miss.).*

US
CHOCTAW COMMUNITY NEWS. (1969)-. Newspaper. English (Choctaw). Twelve times a year. Free. Choctaw Community News, Route 7 Box 21, Philadelphia MS 39350. **Tel** (601)656-5251. **ED** Julie Kelsey. **Bk Rev. Circ:** 5,400 (ctrl). available on microfilm.
Desc: Tribal information and news of the Mississippi band of Choctaw Indians.

US
CHOCTAW PLAINDEALER. Vol. 1, No. 1 (Aug. 26, 1887)-. Newspaper. English. wk. Choctaw Plaindealer, PO Box 910, Ackerman MS 39735-0910. **Tel** (601)285-6248. ***Absorbed*** *Ackerman Record.*

US/0744-9526
CLARION-LEDGER, THE. (CLARION-LEDGER.). **VFOAT** Clarion Ledger. (May 8, 1941)-. Newspaper. English. da. $216.00 (Mississippi), $240.00 (other) daily and Sunday by mail; $150.00 (primary market counties - Adams, Attala, Claiborne, Copiah, Covington, Franklin, Hinds, Holmes, Humphreys, Issaquena, Jasper, Jefferson, Davis, Jones, Lauderdale, Lawrence, Leake, Leflore, Lincoln, Madison, Neshoba, Newton, Pike, Rankin, Scott, Sharkey, Simpson, Smith, Walthall, Warren, Washington, and Yazoo), $156.00 (other) daily and Sunday by carrier; $120.00 (Mississippi), $132.00 (other) weekend edition by mail; $132.00 (Mississippi), $144.00 (other) daily by mail; $96.00 (primary market counties), $99.00 (other) daily by carrier. Mississippi Publishing Company, PO Box 40, 311 East Pearl Street, Jackson MS 39225. **Tel** (601)961-7000, (800)367-3384. **ED** John Johnson and Bennie Ivory. **Bk Rev. Ad Acc. Circ:** 98,829. available on microfilm from University Microfilms International (UMI). ***Continues*** *Daily Clarion-Ledger.*
Ind/Abst PROMT.

US/0746-3421
CLARION-LEDGER, JACKSON DAILY NEWS, THE. **VFOAT** Clarion Ledger, Jackson Daily News. Oct. 3, 1954-. Newspaper. English. sw. Mississippi Publishing Company, PO Box 40, 311 East Pearl Street, Jackson MS 39225. **Tel** (601)961-7000, (800)367-3384. **ED** David Hardin. **Circ:** 114,552. available on microfilm.

US
CLARKE COUNTY TRIBUNE, THE. Began in 1910. Newspaper. English. wk. $16.00 Clark and Wayne coutnies, $18.00 other Mississippi, $20.00 other. Quitman Clark County Reporter, 101 Main Street, Quitman MS 39355. **Tel** (601)776-3726.

US
CLARKSDALE PRESS REGISTER, THE. **VFOAT** Clarksdale Register Clarksdale Daily Press. 41st Year, No. 153 (June 15, 1949)-. Newspaper. English. da. $90.00 US. Delta Press Publishing Compnay Inc, Box 1119, Clarksdale MS 38614. **Tel** (601)627-2201. ***Formed by the union of*** *Clarksdale Daily Register and Daily News* ***and*** *Clarksdale Daily Press.*

US
COFFEEVILLE COURIER, THE. Began in 1891. Newspaper. English. wk. Coffeeville Courier, 1119 Main Street, Coffeeville MS 38922. ***Continues*** *Coffeeville Times.*

US/1044-9922
COLUMBIAN-PROGRESS, THE. **VFOAT** Columbian Progress. (Sept. 26, 1935)-. Newspaper. English. wk. Columbian-Progress, PO Box 1171, Columbia MS 39429-1171. **Tel** (601)736-2611. ***Formed by the union of*** *Columbian* ***and*** *Marion County Progress.*

US/0746-7729
COMMERCIAL DISPATCH, THE. (March 12, 1922)-. Newspaper. English. da. $96.00. Commercial Dispatch Publishing Company, PO Box 511, Columbus MS 39703. **Tel** (601)328-2424, FAX (601)329-8937. **ED** Birney Imes, Jr., Joseph Ammerman (Managing Editor). **LC** 7002. **Photos. Ad Acc, Adv Mgr:** George Turner, **Tel** (601)328-2427. Full Page (B&W) $987.00. Half Page (B&W) $493.00. Full Page (Color) $1087.00. Half Page (Color) $543.00. **Pub. Size:** Broadsheet. **Wire Svcs.:** AP. **Circ:** 14,300 weekday, 16,000 Sunday. ***Formed by the union of*** *Columbus Commercial* ***and*** *Columbus Dispatch (Columbus, Miss. : 1919).*

US
CONSERVATIVE (CARROLLTON, MISS.). (THE CONSERVATIVE.). Began with Jan. 29, 1881 issue. Newspaper. English. wk. The Conservative / Carrollton, PO Box 345, Carrollton MS 38917. ***Continues*** *Mississippi Conservative.*

US
COPIAH COUNTY COURIER. Vol. 69, No. 39 (Jan. 1, 1964)-. Newspaper. English. Fifty-two times a year (Wed.). $14.00 Copiah County; $16.00 others in Mississippi; $20.00 others. Copiah County Courier, Box 351, Hazlehurst MS 39083. **Tel** (601)894-3141. **ED** Jim Lambert. **Photos. Ad Acc, Adv Mgr:** Cardyn Runnells. Full Page (B&W) $681.12. Half Page (B&W) $340.56. Full Page (Color) $891.12. Half Page (Color) $550.56. **Pub. Size:** Standard. **Circ:** 4,400. ***Formed by the union of*** *Copiah County News (Hazlehurst, Miss. : 1935)* ***and*** *Hazlehurst Courier.*

US
DAILY CORINTHIAN, THE. **VFOAT** Corinthian. (1895)-. Newspaper. English. da. Daily Corinthian, PO Box 109, Corinth MS 38834. **Tel** (601)287-6111.

US
DAILY LEADER (BROOKHAVEN, MISS.). (THE DAILY LEADER.). Vol. 86, No. 1 (Sept. 30, 1968)-. Newspaper. English. wk. Daily Leader, 123 North Railroad Avenue, Brookhaven MS 39601. ***Continues*** *Leader-Advertiser.*

US/1066-7512
DAILY SENTINEL-STAR, THE. **VFOAT** Daily Sentinel Star. 93rd yr., No. 154 (Nov. 19, 1946)-. Newspaper. English. da. $79.00. Grenada Daily Sentinel Star, 158 Green Street, Grenada MS 38901. **Tel** (601)226-4323. ***Continues*** *Grenada Daily Star;* ***Absorbed*** *Grenada Sentinel (Grenada, Miss. : 1871); Grenada County Weekly.*

US
DAILY TIMES-LEADER (WEST POINT, MISS.). (DAILY TIMES-LEADER.). **VFOAT** Daily Times Leader. (1935)-. Newspaper. English. da. Daily Times-Leader, 227 Court Street, PO Box 1176, West Point MS 39773. **Tel** (601)494-1422. ***Continues*** *West Point Times Leader;* ***Absorbed*** *Times-Herald.*

US
DEER CREEK PILOT (ROLLING FORK, MISS. : 1886). (THE DEER CREEK PILOT.). **VFOAT** Sharkey Tribune. (1886)-. Newspaper. English. wk (52 issues). $18.00. Deer Creek Pilot, PO Box 398, Rolling Fork MS 39159. **Tel** (601)873-4354. ***Continues*** *Weekly Pilot.*

US
DELTA DEMOCRAT-TIMES, THE. **VFOAT** Delta Democrat Times. (Sept. 1, 1938)-. Newspaper. English. da (Sun.-Fri.). $132.00 Mississippi; $146.40 other US. Greenville Delta Democrat, 988 North Broadway, Greenville MS 38701-2349. **Tel** (601)335-1155, FAX (601)335-2860. **ED** Ken Cazalas. **Ad Acc. Circ:** 17,000 (evening and Sun.). ***Formed by the union of*** *Daily Democrat-Times* ***and*** *Delta Star (Greenville, Miss.).*

US/0746-0538
DELTA WEEKLY. Newspaper. English. wk. Delta Democrat-Publishing Company, 988 North Broadway, Greenville MS 38702-1618.

US
DESOTO COUNTY TRIBUNE, THE. Vol. 5, No. 37 (Aug. 11, 1977)-. Newspaper. English. wk. $19.50. DeSoto County Tribune, PO Box 486, Olive Branch MS 38654. **Tel** (601)895-6220. **ED** D.W. Jones. **Bk Rev,** (Qty: 52). **Photos. Ad Acc, Adv Mgr:** Tam Ratcliff. Full Page (B&W) $1032.00. Half Page (B&W) $516.00. Full Page (Color) $1132.00. Half Page (Color) $616.00. **Pub. Size:** Broadsheet. ***Continues*** *Olive Branch Tribune.*

US/1064-4784
DESOTO TIMES (1981). (DESOTO TIMES.). Vol. 86, No. 29 (July 16, 1981)-. Newspaper. English. Fifty-two times a year. $18.50 Desoto County; $27.00 other. Desoto Times, PO Box 100, Hernando MS 38632. **Tel** (601)429-6397, FAX (601)429-5229. **ED** William Bailey. **Ad Acc, Adv Mgr:** Tawanda Tanxersley. **Circ:** 6,000 (ctrl). ***Continues*** *North Mississippi Times.*

US
ENTERPRISE-JOURNAL (MCCOMB, MISS.). (ENTERPRISE-JOURNAL.). **VFOAT** Enterprise Journal. 71st Year, No. 24 (June 29, 1959)-. Newspaper. English. da. $90.00. Enterprise-Journal, Circulation Dept., PO Box 910, McComb MS 39648. **Tel** (601)684-2713. ***Continues*** *McComb Enterprise-Journal.*

US
ENTERPRISE-TOCSIN, THE. **VFOAT** Enterprise Tocsin. (195?)-. Newspaper. English. wk. Indianola Publishing Company, Box 650, Indianola MS 38751. **Tel** (601)887-2848. ***Formed by the union of*** *Indianola Enterprise* ***and*** *Sunflower Tocsin.*

US
FRANKLIN ADVOCATE, THE. Vol. 1 No. 1 (Mar 12, 1891)-. Newspaper. English. wk. $22.50. Franklin Advocate, PO Box 576, Meadville MS 39653-0576. **Tel** (601)384-2484. **ED** David Webb, Mary Lou Webb (Managing Editor). **Bk Rev. Photos. Ad Acc.** Full Page (B&W) $752.50. Half Page (B&W) $376.75. Full Page (Color) $952.50. Half Page (Color) $576.75. **Pub. Size:** Standard. **Wire Svcs.:** UPI, AP, CA. **Circ:** 3,550. available in microform from Franklin County Library.

US
GEORGE COUNTY TIMES, THE. Began in 1910. Newspaper. English. wk. George County Times, PO Box 238, Lucedale MS 39452. ***Continues*** *Plaindealer.*

US
GREENE COUNTY HERALD. (Sept. 1, 1898)-. Newspaper. English. wk. Greene County Herald, PO Box 220, Leakesville MS 39451. **Tel** (601)394-5070.

US
GREENWOOD COMMONWEALTH (GREENWOOD, MISS. : 1976). (THE GREENWOOD COMMONWEALTH.). Vol. 80, No. 261 (Nov. 2, 1976)-. Newspaper. English. da. $96.00. Greenwood Commonwealth, PO Box 8050, Greenwood MS 38930. **Tel** (601)453-5312. **ED** John Emmerick, Steve Stewart (Managing Editor). **Photos. Ad Acc, Adv Mgr:** Larry Alderman. Full Page (B&W) $883.65. Half Page (B&W) $441.83. Full Page (Color) $1003.65. Half Page (Color) $561.83. **Wire Svcs.:** AP, NY. **Circ:** 8,797 paid (ctrl). ***Continues*** *Commonwealth (Greenwood, Miss. : 1974).*

US
HATTIESBURG AMERICAN. (Oct. 2 1917)-. Newspaper. English. da. $110.00. Hattiesburg American, 825 North Main Street, PO Box 1111, Hattiesburg MS 39401. **Tel** (601)582-4312. **ED** Edward 'Buddy' Baker. **LC** 7002. Index available. **Bk Rev. Ad Acc. Circ:** 25,000 (ctrl). ***Continues*** *Hattiesburg News.*
Desc: General interest newspaper.

US
HOLMES COUNTY HERALD. Began in 1959. Newspaper. English. wk. Holmes County Herald, 308 Court Square, Lexington MS 39095. ***Absorbed*** *Durant Plaindealer.*

US
ITAWAMBA COUNTY TIMES. Vol. 1, No. 1 (Dec. 2, 1943)-. Newspaper. English. wk. $15.00 Itawamba & adjoining counties; $20.00 other. Itawamba County Times, PO Box 1549, 106 West Main Street, Fulton MS 38843. **Tel** (601)862-3141, FAX (601)862-7804. **ED** Rubye Del Harden (Editor-in-Chief) and Don Hill (Managing Editor). **Photos. Ad Acc, Adv Mgr:** Terry Miller. Full Page (B&W) $574.05. Half Page (B&W) $287.03. Full Page (Color) $674.05. Half Page (Color) $387.03. **Pub. Size:** Standard. **Circ:** 5,500. ***Absorbed*** *Fulton News Beacon.*
Desc: Weekly newspaper published in Fulton, MS. Contains local news, features, & advertising.

US/0047-1704
JACKSON ADVOCATE. (1939)-. Newspaper. English. wk. $25.00. The Jackson Advocate, PO Box 3708, Jackson MS 39207. **Tel** (601)948-4122. **ED** Charles Tisdale, Alice Thomas (Managing Editor). **Bk Rev,** (Qty: 52). **Photos. Ad Acc, Adv Mgr:** O.J.Daniels. Full Page (B&W) $2520.00. Half Page (B&W) $1260.00. Full Page (Color) $2820.00. Half Page (Color) $1560.00. **Pub. Size:** Standard. **Wire Svcs.:** NP. **Circ:** 26,000 (ctrl).

US
JACKSON DAILY NEWS (JACKSON, MISS. : 1907). (JACKSON DAILY NEWS.). V. 15, No. 120 (May 16, 1907)-. Newspaper. English. da (Mon.-Fri.). Mississippi Publishing Company, PO Box 40, 311 East Pearl Street, Jackson MS 39225. **Tel** (601)961-7000, (800)367-3384. **ED** David Hardin. **Circ:** 33,160. available on microfilm from University Microfilms International (UMI). ***Continues*** *Jackson Evening News.*

US
JASPER COUNTY NEWS (BAY SPRINGS, MISS.), THE. (THE JASPER COUNTY NEWS.). Began in 1917. Newspaper. English.

wk. Jasper County News, PO Box 449, Bay Springs MS 39422. ***Formed by the union of*** *Bay Springs News* ***and*** *Jasper County Review.*

US/0893-3693
JEFFERSON COUNTY CHRONICLE. ***Title Change.*** Vol. 1, No. 1 (Nov. 27, 1986)-Vol. 127, No. 28 (July 15-21, 1992). Newspaper. English. wk. Jefferson County Chronicle, Box 757, Fayette MS 39069. **Tel** (601)786-6397. **ED** B N Shaw. **Circ:** 1,925. ***Absorbed by*** *Fayette Chronicle (Fayette, Miss. : 1866).*

US
KEMPER COUNTY MESSENGER. (1932)-. Newspaper. English. wk. $18.00. Kemper County Messenger, PO Box 546, DeKalb MS 39328. **ED** Jeff Jowers. **Photos. Ad Acc, Adv Mgr:** Jayne Jowers, **Tel** (601)743-5760. Full Page (B&W) $378.00. Half Page (B&W) $189.00. Full Page (Color) $438.00. Half Page (Color) $249.00. **Pub. Size:** Broadsheet. **Circ:** 2,200. ***Absorbed*** *Kemper Herald (DeKalb, Miss. : 1921); DeKalb Sentinel.*

US
LAUREL LEADER-CALL (LAUREL, MISS. : 1936). (THE LAUREL LEADER-CALL.). **VFOAT** Laurel Leader Call; Leader-Call. Vol. 36, No. 81 (Jan. 25, 1936)-. Newspaper. English. da (Mon.-Sat.). $99.00 Mississippi; $106.00 other. Laurel Leader-Call, 130 Beacon Street, Laurel MS 39440. **Tel** (601)428-0551. **ED** William E. England Jr. **LC** 7002. **Circ:** 10,031. ***Continues*** *Laurel Daily Leader; Morning Call (Laurel, Miss.).*

US
MACON BEACON (MACON, MISS. : 1860). (MACON BEACON.). Began in 1860. Newspaper. English. wk. Beacon, PO Box 32, Macon MS 39341. **Tel** (601)726-4747. **ED** Mrs J W Robbins. **Circ:** 3,520. ***Continues*** *Union Beacon.*

US
MADISON COUNTY HERALD (CANTON, MISS. : 1906). (THE MADISON COUNTY HERALD.). (1906)-. Newspaper. English. Fifty-two times a year. $22.00 Madison County; $25.00 others. Madison County Herald, PO Box 291, Canton MS 39046. **Tel** (601)859-1221. ***Continues*** *Canton Times (Canton, Miss.).*

US
MAGNOLIA GAZETTE (MAGNOLIA, MISS. : 1872). (THE MAGNOLIA GAZETTE.). (Dec. 7, 1872)-. Newspaper. English. Fifty-two times a year (Wed.). $30.00 Pike County, MS; $40.00 others. Magnolia Gazette, PO Box 152, Magnolia MS 39652. **Tel** (601)783-2441.

US/1064-9549
MERIDIAN STAR (1914), THE. (THE MERIDIAN STAR.). **VFOAT** Star. (1914)-. Newspaper. English. da. $135.00 within Laud County, MS; $156.00 other. Meridian Star, PO Box 14, Meridian MS 39301. **Tel** (601)693-1551. **ED** James B Skewes. **Circ:** 23,125 daily, 26,528 Sunday. ***Continues*** *Evening Star.*

US
METEOR (CRYSTAL SPRINGS, MISS. : 1889). (THE METEOR.). Began in 1889. Newspaper. English. wk. The Meteor, 238 East Georgetown Street, Crystal Springs MS 39059. ***Continues*** *Crystal Springs Meteor.*

US
MISSISSIPPI ENTERPRISE, THE. (1938)-. Newspaper. English. ir. Mississippi Enterprise, PO Box 3442, Jackson MS 39207. **Tel** (601) 353-8300.

US/1059-7166
MISSISSIPPI PRESS (PASCAGOULA, MISS.), THE. (THE MISSISSIPPI PRESS.). **VFOAT** Mississippi Press Register. Vol. 120, No. 242, Sept. 1 (1966)-. Newspaper. English. da. Mississippi Press, 405 Delmas Avenue, Pascagoula MS 39567. **Tel** (601)762-1111. available on microfilm from University Microfilms International (UMI). ***Continues*** *Mississippi Press and The Chronicle.*

US
MONITOR-HERALD, THE. **VFOAT** Monitor Herald. Vol. 23, No. 3 (Oct. 13, 1921)-. Newspaper. English. wk. Monitor-Herald, PO Box 69, Calhoun City MS 38916-0069. ***Formed by the union of*** *Calhoun Monitor* ***and*** *Dixie Herald.*

US/0888-8744
NATCHEZ DEMOCRAT (1916), THE. (THE NATCHEZ DEMOCRAT.). Vol. 51, New Series No. 1 (Aug. 1, 1916)-. Newspaper. English. da (except Monday). $149.00. Natchez Newspapers, PO Box 1447, Natchez MS 39121. **Tel** (601)442-9101. **ED** Dolph Tillofson. **LC** 8525-X. **Ad Acc. Circ:** 13,520. ***Continues*** *Natchez News-Democrat.*
Desc: General interest daily newspaper.

US
NESHOBA DEMOCRAT, THE. (1881)-. Newspaper. English. wk. $25.00. Philadelphia Neshoba Democrat, PO Box 30, Philadelphia MS 39350. **Tel** (601)656-4000. **ED** Stanley Dearman. **Bk Rev. Photos. Ad Acc, Adv Mgr:** Charlie Howell. Full Page (B&W) $516.00. Half Page (B&W) $258.00. Full Page (Color) $616.00. Half Page (Color) $358.00. **Pub. Size:** Broadsheet. **Circ:** 7,000 paid, 7,071 total market coverage.

US
NEW ALBANY GAZETTE (NEW ALBANY, MISS.). (THE NEW ALBANY GAZETTE.). **VFOAT** New Albany Gazette and Union County Times. (1890)-. Newspaper. English. sw (104 issues per year). Price varies within Missippi; $55.00 other US. New Albany Gazette, 713 Carter Avenue, PO Box 300, New Albany MS 38652. ***Absorbed*** *Union County Times.*

US
NEWS-COMMERCIAL, THE. **VFOAT** News Commercial. Vol. 35, No. 21 (Feb. 12, 1937)-. Newspaper. English. wk. $14.00 (Covington County), $17.00 (other Mississippi); $19.00 other. News-Commercial, PO Box 1299, Collins MS 39428. **Tel** (601)765-8275, FAX (601)765-6952. **ED** Jamie Arrington. **Bk Rev**, (Qty: 12). **Photos. Ad Acc.** Full Page (B&W) $430.00. Half Page (B&W) $215.00. **Pub. Size:** Standard. **Circ:** 3,142 paid (ctrl). ***Formed by the union of*** *Collins Commercial* ***and*** *Covington County News.*

US
NEWTON RECORD, THE. Vol. 1, No. 1 (Dec. 5, 1901)-. Newspaper. English. wk. $20.00 in county; $25.00 Mississippi; $30.00 US. Newton Record, PO Box 60, Newton MS 39345. **ED** J.E. Strange. **LC** 7002. **Photos. Ad Acc.** Full Page (B&W) $554.70. Half Page (B&W) $283.80. Full Page (Color) $637.70. Half Page (Color) $363.86. **Pub. Size:** Broadsheet. **Circ:** 2,300. available in microform.

US/0744-5431
NORTHEAST MISSISSIPPI DAILY JOURNAL. **VFOAT** Daily Northeast Mississippi Journal; Daily Journal. Vol. 100, No. 149 (Sept. 22, 1973)-. Newspaper. English. da. $117.00. Northeast Mississippi Daily, PO Box 909, Tupelo MS 38802. **Tel** (601)842-2611. **ED** Tom Pittman. **Bk Rev. Ad Acc. Circ:** 35,383 (ctrl). ***Continues*** *Tupelo Daily Journal.*
Desc: Contains local features, world briefs, and obituaries. Other articles/information concerns sports, music, movies, people, and business.

US
NORTHSIDE SUN, THE. Began in 1967. Newspaper. English. wk. Warren Publishing Company, PO Box 16708, Jackson MS 39236.

US
OCEAN SPRINGS RECORD. (August 1965)-. Newspaper. English. wk. $19.75 Jackson; $27.75 others. Ocean Springs Record, 715 Cox Avenue, Ocean Springs MS 39564. **ED** James Ricketts. **Photos. Ad Acc, Adv Mgr:** Peter Logan, **Tel** (601)875-2791. Full Page (B&W) $674.67. Half Page (B&W) $361.68. Full Page (Color) $734.67. Half Page (Color) $421.68. **Pub. Size:** Standard.

US
OKOLONA MESSENGER. Began in 1900. Newspaper. English. wk. Okolona Messenger, 249 Main Street, Okolona MS 38860. ***Continues*** *Chickasaw Messenger (Okolona, Miss. : 1880).*

US
OXFORD EAGLE. Vol. 1, No. 1 (Feb. 11, 1876)-. Newspaper. English. da (260 issues). $63.00 Lafayette County; $72.00 other. Oxford Eagle, PO Box 866, Oxford MS 38655. **Tel** (601)234-4331. ***Absorbed*** *Lafayette County Press.*

US
PANOLIAN (BATESVILLE, MISS. : 1914). (THE PANOLIAN.). Vol. 33, No. 39 (Nov. 5, 1914)-. Newspaper. English. wk. The Panolian, 218 Watt Street, Batesville MS 38606. ***Continues*** *Weekly Panolian (Batesville, Miss. : 1905).*

US/0747-1904
PEARL PRESS, THE. Began with Sept. 8, 1983 issue. Newspaper. English. wk. Pearl Press, 212 North Bierdeman Road, Pearl MS 39208.

US
PICAYUNE ITEM, THE. (1916)-. Newspaper. English. da. $45.00 Pearl River County, MS; $55.00 other. Picayune Item, PO Box 580, Picayune MS 39466. **Tel** (601)798-4766.

US
PONTOTOC PROGRESS, THE. Began in 1929?. Newspaper. English. wk. Pontotoc Progress, 12 East Jefferson Street, Pontotoc MS 38863.

US
PORT GIBSON REVEILLE (PORT GIBSON, MISS.: 1890). (THE PORT GIBSON REVEILLE.). New Series. Vol. 15, No. 10 (June 6, 1890)-. Newspaper. English. wk. $14.00 Mississippi; $19.50 others. Claiborne Publishing Company Inc., PO Box 1002, Port Gibson MS 39150. **Tel** (601)437-5103, FAX (601)437-4410. **ED** Edgar T. Crisler Jr. **Bk Rev. Photos. Ad Acc, Adv Mgr:** Janice G. Bufkin. Full Page (B&W) $475.48. Half Page (B&W) $187.74. **Pub. Size:** Standard. **Circ:** 2,450. available on microfilm. ***Continues*** *Southern Reveille (Port Gibson, Miss. : 1876).*

US/0742-8316
PRENTISS HEADLIGHT, THE. Newspaper. English. wk. Prentiss Headlight, PO Drawer 1257, Prentiss MS 39474.

US
RANKIN COUNTY NEWS. Vol. 114, No. 12 (Nov. 30, 1961)-. Newspaper. English. wk. $15.00 (in county), $20.00 (other). Rankin County News, PO Box 107, Brandon MS 39042. **Tel** (601)825-8333, FAX (601)825-8334. **ED** Marcus Bowers. **Bk Rev. Photos. Ad Acc.** Full Page (B&W) $580.50. Half Page (B&W) $283.50. **Pub. Size:** Standard. **Circ:** 6,000. available in microform. ***Continues*** *Brandon News.*

US/0893-3286
REFLECTOR (1983), THE. (THE REFLECTOR.). **Added/Corp** Mississippi State University. Student Association. Vol. 96, No. 1 (Aug. 30, 1983)-. Newspaper. English. Fifty times a year (Tues.- Fri. during school year). $10.00 (fall & spring semester) $20.00 (two years). The Reflector, PO Drawer 5407, Student Media Center, Mississippi State MS 39762. **Tel** (601)325-2374, FAX (601)325-8985. **ED** Terri Tabor (Editor-in-Chief) and Jason Cother (Managing Editor). **Bk Rev**, (Qty: 12). **Photos. Ad Acc, Adv Mgr:** Pratap Velagapudi, **Tel** (601)325-7907. Full Page (B&W) $756.00. Half Page (B&W) $396.00. Full Page (Color) $816.00. Half Page (Color) $456.00. **Pub. Size:** Broadsheet. **Wire Svcs.:** WP. **Circ:** 13,000. ***Continues*** *Mississippi State University's Reflector.*

US
RICHTON DISPATCH, THE. (1906)-. Newspaper. English. wk. $12.00 Perry County, Mississippi; $13.00 Mississippi; $12.00 other. Richton Dispatch, PO Drawer X, Richton MS 39476. **Tel** (601)788-6031, FAX (601)788-6031. **ED** Larry A. Wilson, Mrs. Dean Wilson (Managing Editor). **Photos. Ad Acc. Pub. Size:** Standard. **Circ:** 1,600 (ctrl). ***Absorbed*** *Augusta Telephone and The Perry County Review* ***and*** *Perry County News.*

US
SCOTT COUNTY TIMES (FOREST, MISS.). (SCOTT COUNTY TIMES.). Vol. 1, No. 1 (Nov. 30, 1939)-. Newspaper. English. wk. Scott County Times, PO Box 89, Forest MS 39074. ***Absorbed*** *Morton Tribune (Morton, Miss.), 0896-3339.*

US
SEA COAST ECHO, THE. Began with Jan. 9, 1892 issue. Newspaper. English. wk. Sea Coast Echo, 124 Court Street, Bay St Louis MS 39520.

US
SIMPSON COUNTY NEWS. (1902)-. Newspaper. English. wk (Thurs.). $14.00 in county; $16.00 others in Mississippi; $20.00 others. Simpson County News, PO Box 97, Mendenhall MS 39114. **Tel** (601)847-2525. **ED** Pat Brown. **Photos. Ad Acc, Adv Mgr:** Jean Butler, **Tel** (601)849-3434. Full Page (B&W) $771.42. Half Page (B&W) $394.68. Full Page (Color) $851.42. Half Page (Color) $474.68. **Pub. Size:** Standard. ***Continues*** *Westville News (Westville, Miss. : 1894).*

US
SMITH COUNTY REFORMER, THE. (1892)-. Newspaper. English. wk. $15.00. Smith County Reformer, PO Box 187, Raleigh MS 39153. **Tel** (601)782-4358, FAX (601)764-3106. **Photos. Ad Acc, Adv Mgr:** Brenda Ingram, **Tel** (601)785-6525. Full Page (B&W) $567.00. Half Page (B&W) $283.50. Full Page (Color) $657.00. Half Page (Color) $373.50. **Pub. Size:** Standard.

US
SOUTH-REPORTER. **VFOAT** South Reporter; Southern Reporter. Vol. 55, No. 1 (Jan. 2, 1920)-. Newspaper. English. wk. $20.00. Holly Springs South Reporter, PO Box 278, Holly Springs MS 38635-0278. **Tel** (601)252-4261, FAX (601)252-3388. **ED** Walter W. Webb. **Photos. Ad Acc, Adv Mgr:** Betty Webb. Full Page (B&W) $472.50. Half Page (B&W) $248.85. Full Page (Color) $572.50. Half Page (Color) $348.85. **Pub. Size:** Broadsheet. **Wire Svcs.:** AP. **Circ:** 5,200. ***Formed by the union of*** *South (Holly Springs, Miss.)* ***and*** *Holly Springs Reporter (Holly Springs, Miss. : 1893).*

US/0893-3790
SOUTHERN HERALD (LIBERTY, MISS.), THE. (THE SOUTHERN HERALD.). (1866)-. Newspaper. English. wk. $15.00 in county; $20.00 other. The Southern Herald, PO Box D, Liberty MS 39645. **Tel** (601)657-4818. **ED** Richard Stratton, Lyne Jackson (Managing Editor). **Bk Rev. Photos. Ad Acc.** Full Page (B&W) $360.00. Half Page (B&W) $180.00. Full Page (Color) $450.00. Half Page (Color) $270.00. **Pub. Size:** Broadsheet. **Circ:** 1,100. ***Continues*** *Amite Democrat.*

US
SOUTHERN REPORTER (SARDIS, MISS.). (SOUTHERN REPORTER.). (18??)-. Newspaper. English. Fifty-two times a year. $18.00 Panola County; $20.00 other. Southern Reporter, PO Box 157, Sardis MS 38666-0157. **Tel** (601)487-1551.

US
SOUTHERN SENTINEL (RIPLEY, MISS.). (SOUTHERN SENTINEL.). Began in 1879. Newspaper. English. wk. Southern Sentinel, PO Box 558, Ripley MS 38663.

US/1048-4116
STAR-HERALD (KOSCIUSKO, MISS.), THE. (THE STAR-HERALD.). **VFOAT** Star Herald. Began in 1920. Newspaper. English. wk. The Star-Herald, 319 North Madison Street, Kosciusko MS 39090. ***Formed by the union of*** *Star Ledger (Kosciusko, Miss.)* ***and*** *Kosciusko Herald.*

US
STAR JOURNAL (GULFPORT, MISS.). (THE STAR JOURNAL.). Began in 1976. Newspaper. English. wk. Gulf Coast Media Inc, PO Drawer BB, Gulfport MS 39502.

US/1044-3657
STARKVILLE DAILY NEWS. (Oct. 31, 1960)-. Newspaper. English. da. Starkville Daily News, PO Drawer 1068 C, Starkville MS 39759. **Tel** (601)323-1642. ***Continues*** *Starkville News.*

US
STONE COUNTY ENTERPRISE. (19??)-. Newspaper. English. Fifty-two times a year. $23.00 Stone County; $26.00 elsewhere Mississippi; $28.00 other. Stone County Enterprise, PO Box 157, Wiggins MS 39301. **Tel** (601)928-4802. **ED** Don Groves. **Photos**. **Ad Acc, Adv Mgr:** Christy Groves. Full Page (B&W) $516.60. Half Page (B&W) $258.30. **Pub. Size:** Standard. **Circ:** 2,950. ***Continues*** *Wiggins Enterprise.*

US
SUN HERALD (BILOXI, MISS.). (THE SUN HERALD.). Vol. 102, No. 1 (Oct. 1, 1985)-. Newspaper. English. da. $10.75 (per month). Gulf Publishing Company / Mississippi, PO Box 4567, Biloxi MS 39531. **Tel** (601)896-2498, FAX (601)896-2104. **ED** Michael Torps, Andrea Yeager (Managing Editor). **Photos**. **Ad Acc, Adv Mgr:** Stone Ellis. Full Page (B&W) $3076.00. Half Page (B&W) $1538.00. **Pub. Size:** Standard. **Wire Svcs.:** SH, WP. **Circ:** 49,022 daily, 53,389 Sunday. available in microform from University Microfilms International (UMI). ***Formed by the union of*** *Sun (Biloxi, Miss.)* ***and*** *Daily Herald.*

US
SUNFLOWER COUNTY NEWS. Vol. 1, No. 1 (Aug. 31, 1956)-. Newspaper. English. wk. Sunflower County News, PO Box 126, Drew MS 38737.

US
TATE COUNTY DEMOCRAT, THE. Vol. 36, No. 5 (Jan. 29, 1925)-. Newspaper. English. wk. Tate County Democrat, 219 East Main Street, Senatobia MS 38668. ***Continues*** *Senatobia Democrat.*

US
TAYLORSVILLE POST, THE. (Dec. 1984)-. Newspaper. English. wk. $13.00 Smith County, Mississippi; $16.00 other Mississippi; $19.00 other. Taylorsville Post, PO Box 100, Taylorsville MS 39168. **Tel** (601)785-4333.

US
TERRY HEADLIGHT, THE. Began with Sept. 8, 1923 issue. Newspaper. English. wk. Terry Headlight, PO Box 157, Terry MS 39170.

US/0746-3901
TIMES-POST. **VAT** Times Post. (Jan. 9, 1913)-. Newspaper. English. wk. $18.00 Chickasaw, MS and adjoining counties; $25.00 other. Times Post, PO Box 629, Houston MS 38851. **Tel** (601)456-3771. **ED** Kenny Hoblitzell. **Bk Rev**. **Ad Acc**. **Circ:** 4,500. ***Formed by the union of*** *Houston Post (Houston, Miss. : 1909)* ***and*** *Chickasaw County Times (Houston, Miss.).*
Desc: General interest newspaper.

US
TISHOMINGO COUNTY NEWS. THE VIDETTE AND BELMONT NEWS. No. 14 (Oct. 2, 1969)-. Newspaper. English. Fifty-two times a year. $15.00. Tishomingo County News, PO Box 70, Iuka MS 38852. **Tel** (601)423-3666. ***Formed by the union of*** *Vidette and The Belmont News* ***and*** *Tishomingo County News.*

US
TUNICA TIMES-DEMOCRAT, THE. **VFOAT** Tunica Times Democrat. Vol. 15, No. 49 (Nov. 1, 1923)-. Newspaper. English. Fifty-two times a year. $16.00 Tunica, Tate, Desoto, Panola Panola Quitman & Coahoma; $20.00 others in Mississippi; $24.00 others. Tunica Times - Democrat, PO Box 308, Tunica MS 38676. **Tel** (601)363-1511, FAX (601)363-1511. **ED** Lou Erwin. **Ad Acc, Adv Mgr:** Anita Reed, **Tel** (601)363-2503. **Circ:** 2,100. ***Continues*** *Tunica Times.*

US/0738-9930
TYLERTOWN TIMES, THE. (Oct. 25, 1907)-. Newspaper. English. wk. $10.00 in county, $14.00 elsewhere. Tylertown Times, PO Box 72, Tylertown MS 39667. **Tel** (601)876-5111.

US/0884-8912
VICKSBURG EVENING POST. **VFOAT** Vicksburg Sunday Post Herald; Vicksburg Sunday Post. Vol. 1, No. 1 (May 4, 1883)-. Newspaper. English. da. $85.00 Mississippi; $112.00 other. Vicksburg Evening Post, PO Box 951, Vicksburg MS 39180. **Tel** (601)636-4545. **ED** Louis P. Cashman III, Charles D. Mitchell (Managing Editor). **Photos**. **Ad Acc, Adv Mgr:** David Gillis. Full Page (B&W) $1190.00. Half Page (B&W) $595.35. Full Page (Color) $1300.00. Half Page (Color) $705.35. **Pub. Size:** Broadsheet. **Wire Svcs.:** AP. **Circ:** 15,553 paid.

US
WAYNE COUNTY NEWS, THE. Vol. 1, No. 1 (Nov. 28, 1918)-. Newspaper. English. wk. $12.00 Wayne County, $16.00 other. Wayne County News, PO Box 509, Waynesboro MS 39367-0509. **Tel** (601)735-4341. ***Continues*** *Waynesboro News-Beacon.*

US
WEBSTER PROGRESS-TIMES, THE. **VFOAT** Webster Progress Times; Webster Progress Times and the Maben News Press; Webster Progress-Times and the Maben News Press. Vol. 40, No. 26 (Feb. 1, 1968)-. Newspaper. English. wk. $18.00-$24.00. Webster Progress-Times, 124 Dunn Street, Eupora MS 39744. **Tel** (601)258-7532, FAX (601)258-6474. **ED** Jim Laird. **Photos**. **Ad Acc, Adv Mgr:** Tim James. Full Page (B&W) $400.00. Half Page (B&W) $245.10. Full Page (Color) $450.00. Half Page (Color) $300.00. **Pub. Size:** Broadsheet. ***Formed by the union of*** *Webster Progress; Tri-County Times (Eupora, Miss.)* ***and*** *Maben News Pres.*

US
WILKAMITE RECORD, THE. **VFOAT** Wilk Amite Record. Vol. 55, No. 36 (June 7, 1946)-. Newspaper. English. wk. $18.50. Wilkamite Record, PO Box 130, Gloster MS 39638. **ED** David Webb, Mary Lou Webb (Managing Editor). **Bk Rev**. **Photos**. **Ad Acc**. Full Page (B&W) $602.00. Half Page (B&W) $301.00. **Pub. Size:** Standard. **Circ:** 2,000 weekly paid. available in microform. ***Continues*** *Gloster Record.*

US
WINONA TIMES, THE. Began in 1884. Newspaper. English. wk. $22.00. Winona Times, PO Box 151, Winona MS 38967. **Tel** (601)283-1131.

US/8750-9385
WINSTON COUNTY JOURNAL, THE. (THE WINSTON COUNTY JOURNAL.). **VFOAT** Winston Co Journal. Vol. 1, No. 1 (Sept. 23, 1892)-. Newspaper. English. wk. $15.00 Winston and adjoining counties, $22.00 other. Winston County Journal, 199 North Carolina Avenue, Louisville MS 39339.

US
WOODVILLE REPUBLICAN (WOODVILLE, MISS. : 1861). (WOODVILLE REPUBLICAN.). (18??)-. Newspaper. English. wk. $13.00 Woodville County; $15.00 others in Mississippi; $17.00 others. Woodville Republican, PO Box 696, Woodville MS 39669. **ED** Andy Lewis. **Photos**. **Ad Acc, Adv Mgr:** Lili Lewis, **Tel** (601)888-4293. Full Page (B&W) $493.92. Half Page (B&W) $246.96. Full Page (Color) $593.92. Half Page (Color) $346.96. **Pub. Size:** Standard. available in microform.

US
YAZOO HERALD, THE. Vol. 109, No. 33 (July 2, 1980)-. Newspaper. English. sw. Yazoo Herald, PO Box 720, Yazoo City MS 39194. ***Continues*** *Yazoo Daily Herald.*

MISSOURI

US
ATCHISON COUNTY MAIL, THE. Vol. 2, No. 47 (July 15, 1880)-. Newspaper. English. wk. Atchison County Mail, 300 Main Street, Rock Port MO 64482. **Tel** (816)744-6245, FAX (816)744-2645. **ED** Bill Farmer (Editor-in-Chief) and W. C. Farmer (Managing Editor). **Bk Rev**. **Photos**. **Ad Acc, Adv Mgr:** Bill Farmer. Full Page (B&W) $387.00. Half Page (B&W) $198.00. Full Page (Color) $437.00. Half Page (Color) $248.00. **Pub. Size:** Broadsheet. available in microform. ***Continues*** *Democratic Mail;* ***Absorbed*** *Atchison County Journal; Westboro Enterprise; Atchison County Independent.*

US/1041-1275
AURORA ADVERTISER (AURORA, MO. : 1914), THE. (THE AURORA ADVERTISER.). [Aurora advert.]. 28th year, No. 29 (Mar. 27, 1914)-. Newspaper. English. tw. $26.00 Lawrence County, $29.00 other. The Aurora Advertiser, PO Box 509, Aurora MO 65605. **Tel** (417)678-2115. ***Continues*** *Aurora Advertiser and Southwest Miner;* ***Absorbed*** *Miller News-Herald; Marionville Free Press.*

US/0194-1542
BARRY COUNTY ADVERTISER. Vol. 1, No. 1 (Dec. 13, 1967)-. Newspaper. English. wk. $20.00. Barry County Advertiser, 904 West Street, Cassville MO 65625. **Tel** (417)847-3155, telex (417)847-4523. **ED** Irene Horner. **Bk Rev**. **Ad Acc**. **Circ:** 10,000.

US/0746-1569
BATES COUNTY NEWS-HEADLINER, THE. Newspaper. English. wk. Bates County News-Headliner, 611 West Ft Scott, Butler MO 64730.

US
BELLE BANNER, THE. Vol. 1, No. 1 (Nov. 30, 1923)-. Newspaper. English. wk. $17.61 Maries, Osage, Gastonode counties; $20.28 others in Missouri; $20.00 others in US; $30.00 others. Tri-County Newspapers / Missouri, 307 South Alvarado Avenue, PO Box 711, Belle MO 65013. **Tel** (314)859-3328, FAX (314)859-6274. **ED** Ron Lewis. **Photos**. **Ad Acc, Adv Mgr:** Ron Lewis. Full Page (B&W) $227.35. Half Page (B&W) $151.75. **Pub. Size:** Broadsheet. **Circ:** 2,000.

US
BETHANY REPUBLICAN-CLIPPER. **VFOAT** Bethany Republican Clipper. Vol. 56, No. 50 (Feb. 6, 1929)-. Newspaper. English. wk. $25.00. Bethany Republican Clipper, 214 16th Street, Bethany MO 64424. **Tel** (816)425-6325, FAX (816)425-3441. **ED** Phillip Conger. **Bk Rev**, (Qty: 20). **Photos**. **Ad Acc, Adv Mgr:** Kathy Conger. Full Page (B&W) $549.00. Half Page (B&W) $262.00. Full Page (Color) $613.00. Half Page (Color) $326.00. **Pub. Size:** Broadsheet. **Wire Svcs.:** ML. **Circ:** 4,000. available in microform from Missouri State Historical Society. ***Formed by the union of*** *Bethany Republican (Bethany, Mo.)* ***and*** *Bethany Clipper (Bethany, Mo. : 1905);* ***Absorbed*** *Harrison County Times; Cainsville News; Tribune (Gilman City, Mo.).*

US
BLAND COURIER, THE. Began in 1904. Newspaper. English. wk. Bland Courier, Bland MO 65014.

US
BOLIVAR HERALD-FREE PRESS. **VFOAT** Bolivar Herald Free Press. Vol. 95, No. 38 (Nov. 30, 1967)-. Newspaper. English. wk. $21.00 Polk County, Missouri; $36.00 other Missouri; $52.00 other. Bolivar Herald Free Press, PO Box 330, Bolivar MO 65613. **Tel** (417)326-7636. ***Formed by the union of*** *Bolivar Herald; Bolivar Free Press* ***and*** *Polk County Times;* ***Absorbed*** *Fair Play Advocate (Fair Play, Mo. : 1965).*

US/0162-6701
BOWLING GREEN TIMES, THE. (1876)-. Newspaper. English. wk. Bowling Green Times, 106 West Main Street, Bowling Green MO 63334. **Tel** (314)324-2222. **ED** Mike Branson. **Circ:** 3,352. ***Continues*** *Pike County Express;* ***Absorbed*** *Bowling Green Jeffersonian.*

●US/1063-6994
BRANSON TRI-LAKES DAILY NEWS. **VFOAT** Tri-Lakes Branson Daily News. Vol. 81, No. 21 (May 1, 1992)-. Newspaper. English. da. Tri Lakes Newspapers Inc., PO Box 1900, Branson MO 65616. **Tel** (417)334-3161. ***Formed by the union of*** *Branson Beacon and White River Leader; Southwest Missourian, 0193-1016* ***and*** *Taney County Republican.*

US
BRUNSWICKER (BRUNSWICK, MO. : 1916). (THE BRUNSWICKER.). Newspaper. English. wk. The Brunswicker, 118 East Broadway, Brunswick MO 65236. ***Continues*** *Weekly Brunswicker (Brunswick, MO. : 1866);* ***Absorbed*** *Brunswick Argus.*

US
CALIFORNIA DEMOCRAT. (1871)-. Newspaper. English. wk (Published on Wednesdays). California Democrat / Missouri, PO Box 126, California MO 65018-0126. **Tel** (314)796-2135, FAX (314)796-4220. **ED** Grant Chapman. **Ad Acc**. **Circ:** 4,000. ***Continues*** *Moniteau County Democrat;* ***Absorbed*** *California Dispatch* ***and*** *Moniteau County Herald.*

US
CALL (KANSAS CITY, MO. : 1933 : CITY ED.). (THE CALL.). Vol. 15, No. 26 (Oct. 20, 1933)-. Newspaper. English. Fifty-two times a year. The Call / Missouri, 1715 East 18th Street, Kansas City MO 64108. **Tel** (816)842-3804. ***Continues*** *Kansas City Call;* ***Absorbed*** *Call (Kansas City, Mo. : 1933 : Tulsa Ed.).*

US
CAMERON CITIZEN OBSERVER, THE. Vol. 68, No. 211 (Jan. 6, 1975)-. Newspaper. English. wk. Cameron Citizen Observer, PO Box 70, Cameron MO 64429-0070. **Tel** (816)632-6543, FAX (816)632-4508. ***Formed by the union of*** *Cameron News-Observer; Cameron Sun (Cameron, Mo. : 1973)* ***and*** *Cameron Citizen.*

US
CARTHAGE PRESS. Vol. 82, No. 280 (Nov. 29, 1966)-. Newspaper. English. da. Carthage Evening Press, PO Box 678, Carthage MO 64836. ***Continues*** *Carthage Evening Press.*

US
CASSVILLE DEMOCRAT (CASSVILLE, MO. : 1871). (CASSVILLE DEMOCRAT.). (1871)-. Newspaper. English. wk. $8.00 in county; $18.50 others. Cassville Democrat, 600 Main Street, PO Box 486, Cassville MO 65625. **Tel** (419)847-2610, FAX (419)847-3092. **ED** Bob Mitchell. **Photos**. **Ad Acc**, **Adv Mgr:** Darlene Wierman. Full Page (B&W) $370.44. Half Page (B&W) $185.22. Full Page (Color) $450.44. Half Page (Color) $265.22. **Pub. Size:** Standard.

US
CEDAR COUNTY REPUBLICAN AND STOCKTON JOURNAL. Vol. 56, No. 47 (Nov. 19, 1942)-. Newspaper. English. wk. Cedar County Republican & Stockton Journal, PO Box C, Stockton MO 65785-0626. **Tel** (417)276-4211. ***Continues*** *Cedar County Republican (Stockton, Mo.).*

US/0883-7112
CENTRAL MISSOURI NEWS. ***Title Change.*** Vol. 1, No. 1 (April 17, 1985)-?. Newspaper. English. wk. Central Missouri News, 901 West Main Street, Sedalia MO 65301. ***Continued by*** *Pettis County Local Times-News.*

US
CENTRAL WEST END JOURNAL. (Oct. 3, 1984)-. Newspaper. English. wk. $150.00. Suburban Newspapers / Missouri, 1714 Deer Tracks Trail, St. Louis MO 63131. **Tel** (314)821-2462.

US
CENTRALIA FIRESIDE GUARD. (1885)-. Newspaper. English. wk. Centralia Fireside Guard, 118 West Sneed Street, Centralia MO 65240. ***Continues*** *Our Fireside Guard (Centralia, Mo. : 1871);* ***Absorbed*** *Hallsville Top; Sturgeon Missouri Leader (Sturgeon, Mo. : 1935).*

US
CLARENCE COURIER (CLARENCE, MO. : 1946. (THE CLARENCE COURIER.). Vol. 66, No. 3 (Jan. 16, 1946)-. Newspaper. English. wk. $16.00 Missouri; $19.00 others. Clarence Courier, 106 East Maple Street, Clarence MO 63437. **Photos**. **Ad Acc**, **Adv Mgr:** Dennis Williams, **Tel** (816)699-2344. Full Page (B&W) $191.75. Half Page (B&W) $103.25. **Pub. Size:** Tabloid. ***Continues*** *Independant-Courier (Clarence, Mo.).*

US
CLAY DISPATCH-TRIBUNE. (1979)-. Newspaper. English. wk. Townsend Communications, 7007 Northeast Parvin Road, PO Box 12338, Kansas City MO 64117-1532. **Tel** (816)454-9660.

US
CLINTON DAILY DEMOCRAT, THE. Began in 1886. Newspaper. English. da. Clinton Daily Democrat, PO Box 586, Clinton MO 64735.

US
CLINTON EYE, THE. Began in 1885. Newspaper. English. wk. Clinton Eye, PO Box 586, Clinton MO 64735. ***Absorbed*** *Urich Herald-Montrose Tidings.*

US
COLUMBIA DAILY TRIBUNE. Vol. 3, No. 114 (Jan. 26, 1904)-. Newspaper. English. da. $94.44. Columbia Daily Tribune, PO Box 798, Columbia MO 65201. **ED** Henry J. Waters III, Jim Robertson (Managing Editor). **Photos**. **Ad Acc**. Full Page (B&W) $951.30. Half Page (B&W) $475.65. **Pub. Size:** Broadsheet. **Wire Svcs.:** AP, KR. available on microfilm. ***Continues*** *Daily Tribune (Columbia, Mo.).*

US/0747-1874
COLUMBIA MISSOURIAN. No. 236 (June 1, 1923)-. Newspaper. English. da. $84.00 Missouri; $96.00 other. Columbia Missourian Publishing, Box 917, Columbia MO 65205. **Tel** (314)442-3161. **ED** George Kennedy. Index available. cum. index. **Bk Rev**, (Qty: 312). **Ad Acc**, **Adv Mgr:** Jack Swartz. **Circ:** 5,527 (ctrl). ***Continues*** *Columbia Evening Missourian.*

US
COMMONWEALTH, THE. (188?)-. Newspaper. English. Fifty-two times a year. $13.75 Greene County; $14.75 Missouri; $20.00 others. Ash Grove Commonwealth, PO Box 277, Ash Grove MO 65604. **Tel** (471)672-2322. **ED** F. Dal Mason. **Ad Acc**. ctrl circ. ***Absorbed*** *Ash Grove Advance.*

US
CONSTITUTION-TRIBUNE (CHILLICOTHE, MO. : 1985). (CONSTITUTION-TRIBUNE.). **VFOAT** Constitution Tribune. Vol. 125, No. 250 (Dec. 19, 1985)-. Newspaper. English. da. Constitution-Tribune, 818 Washington Street, Chillicothe MO 64601. ***Continues*** *Chillicothe Constitution-Tribune (Chillicothe, MO. : Daily).*

US
COURIER JOURNAL. **VFOAT** Courier-Journal. Began in 1975?. Newspaper. English. wk. Jefferson County Publications, 998 East Gannon Drive, Festus MO 63028-4105. **Tel** (314)296-1800. **ED** Liz Irwin. **Ad Acc**, **Adv Mgr:** Mary Sue Roberts. **Circ:** 22,315.

US
CUBA FREE PRESS, THE. (July 21, 1960)-. Newspaper. English. wk. $14.00 Crawford County; $17.50 Missouri; $23.25 other. Cuba Free Press, PO Box 568, Cuba MO 65453. **Tel** (314)885-7460.

US
CURRENT LOCAL, THE. (1884)-. Newspaper. English. wk (Thurs.). $30.00. The Current Local, PO Box 100, Van Buren MO 63965. **Tel** (314)323-4515.

US/1061-7116
DAILY AMERICAN REPUBLIC. Vol. 25, No.33 (Mar. 5, 1934)-. Newspaper. English. da. $69.00 Butler County; $84.00 other Missouri and Arkansas; $144.00 other. Daily American Republic, PO Box 7C, Poplar Bluff MO 63901. **Tel** (314)785-1414. ***Continues*** *American Republic (Poplar Bluff, Mo.).*

US
DAILY CAPITAL NEWS. **VFOAT** Sunday News and Tribune. Began in 1910. Newspaper. English. da. Daily Capital News, 210 Monroe Street, Jefferson City MO 65102.

US/1047-7160
DAILY DUNKLIN DEMOCRAT, THE. Vol. 69, No. 12a (Apr. 2, 1956)-. Newspaper. English. wk. $63.00. Daily Dunklin Democrat, 203 First Street, Kennett MO 63857-2052. **Tel** (314)888-4505, FAX (314)888-5114. **ED** Buo Hunt, and Lyman Skyles (Managing Editor). **Bk Rev**, (Qty: 12). **Photos**. **Ad Acc**, **Adv Mgr:** Terri Coleman. Full Page (B&W) $1,064.75. Half Page (B&W) $532.33. Full Page (Color) $1,149.75. Half Page (Color) $617.33. **Pub. Size:** Broadsheet. **Wire Svcs.:** AP. **Circ:** 7,500. available in microform. ***Continues*** *Twice-a-Week Dunklin Democrat.*

US
DAILY RECORD & THE KANSAS CITY DAILY NEWS PRESS. (19??)-. Newspaper. English. Five issues per week (Mon. - Fri., July 1 through June 30). $67.21 Missouri; $63.00 others. Daily Record & Kansas City News Press, 3611 Troost, Kansas City MO 64109. **Tel** (816)931-2002, FAX (816)561-6675. **ED** Garrett L. Smalley Jr. (Editor-in-Chief) and Pamela Weaver (Managing Editor). **Photos**. **Ad Acc**, **Adv Mgr:** Pam Weaver. Full Page (B&W) $1,411.20. Half Page (B&W) $705.60. **Pub. Size:** Broadsheet. **Circ:** 600. available in microform.

US/0746-9934
DEMOCRAT-LEADER (FAYETTE, MO.). (THE DEMOCRAT-LEADER.). **VFOAT** Democrat Leader. (1897)-. Newspaper. English. wk. $32.00 (combined with Fayette Advertiser). The Democrat-Leader, 202 East Morrison, PO Box 32, Fayette MO 65248-0032. **Tel** (816)248-2235, FAX (816)248-1200. **ED** H. Denny Davis. **Bk Rev**. **Photos**. **Ad Acc**. Full Page (B&W) $375.48. Half Page (B&W) $185.48. Full Page (Color) $465.48. Half Page (Color) $276.48. **Pub. Size:** Standard. **Circ:** 2,400. available on microfilm from Missouri State Historical Society. ***Formed by the union of*** *Semi-Weekly Democrat-Banner* ***and*** *Howard County Leader.*
Desc: A general newspaper.

US
DEMOCRAT-NEWS (FREDERICKTOWN, MO.). (THE DEMOCRAT-NEWS.). **VFOAT** Democrat News. (1897)-. Newspaper. English. wk. $24.00. Democrat-News, 110 North Mine La Motte, Fredericktown MO 63645. **Tel** (314)783-3366, FAX (314)783-6890. **ED** Mary Cissell (Editor-in-Chief) and Alan Kopitsky (Managing Editor). **Photos**. **Ad Acc**, **Adv Mgr:** Laura Yount. Full Page (B&W) $472.50. Half Page (B&W) $236.25. **Pub. Size:** Broadsheet. available in microform. ***Formed by the union of*** *Madison County Democrat (Fredericktown, Mo.)* ***and*** *Fredericktown News.*

US
ENTERPRISE-COURIER. **VFOAT** Enterprise Courier; Enterprise Courier and Charleston Times. Vol. 14, No. 16 (Apr. 22, 1915)-. Newspaper. English. wk. Charleston Enterprise Courier, 206 South Main Street, Box 69, Charleston MO 63834-1640. **Tel** (314)683-3351, FAX (314)683-2217. **ED** Jim Anderson. **Ad Acc**. **Circ:** 3,000. ***Formed by the union of*** *Weekly Enterprise (Charleston, Mo.)* ***and*** *Charleston Courier (Charleston, Mo. : 1902);* ***Absorbed*** *Charleston Republican; Charleston Times; Charleston Democrat.*

US
EXAMINER, THE. **VFOAT** Examiner Weekend. Vol. 59, No. 46 (July 14, 1963)-. Newspaper. English. da. Independence / Missouri, 410 South Liberty Street, Independence MO 64051. **Tel** (816)254-8600. ***Continues*** *Independence Examiner.*

US/0746-9942
FAYETTE ADVERTISER, THE. (Dec. 13, 1916)-. Newspaper. English. wk. $24.00. The Democrat-Leader, 202 East Morrison, PO Box 32, Fayette MO 65248-0032. **Tel** (816)248-2235, FAX (816)248-1200. **ED** H. Denny Davis. **Bk Rev**. **Photos**. **Ad Acc**. Full Page (B&W) $375.48. Half Page (B&W) $185.48. Full Page (Color) $465.48. Half Page (Color) $276.48. **Circ:** 2,400. ***Continues*** *Howard County Advertiser (Fayette, Mo. : 1863).*

US
FLORISSANT VALLEY REPORTER, THE. Vol. 43, No. 43 (Jan. 27, 1966)-. Newspaper. English. Fifty-two times a year. $9.95 St. Louis City & in county; $14.95 others. Reynolds Publishing Co. Inc., PO Box 69, Florrissant MO 63032. **Tel** (314)839-1111. **ED** David Reynolds. **Bk Rev**. **Photos**. **Ad Acc**. Full Page (B&W) $720.00. Half Page (B&W) $360.00. Full Page (Color) $780.00. Half Page (Color) $420.00. **Pub. Size:** Tabloid. **Circ:** 5,000 (ctrl). ***Continues*** *Reporter (Florissant, Mo.).*

US
FRANKLIN COUNTY TRIBUNE. Vol. 72, No. 1 (Mar. 12, 1937)-. Newspaper. English. Fifty-two times a year. $10.00 Franklin County, $13.00 others in Missouri; $15.00 others. Franklin County Tribune, PO Box 111, Union MO 63084. **Tel** (314)583-2545. **ED** Mark Samuels. **Ad Acc**, **Adv Mgr:** Jeannie York, **Tel** (314)583-2545. **Circ:** 2,000. ***Continues*** *Republican Tribune (Union, Mo.).*

US/8750-6696
FULTON SUN, THE. Vol. 108 No. 174 (Jan. 2 1985)-. Newspaper. English. da. $50.00. Waters Publications Inc, 5th and Ravine Streets, Fulton MO 65251. **Tel** (314)642-7272. **ED** Kent Davy. **Bk Rev**. **Ad Acc**. **Circ:** 4,900. ***Continues*** *Kingdom Daily Sun-Gazette.*
Desc: An independent newspaper.

US/0746-1666
HOME PRESS, THE. Newspaper. English. wk. Home Press, PO Box 150, La Plata MO 63549. ***Continues*** *Macon County Home Press.*

US
INDEPENDENT DE SOTO PRESS. Began in 1869. Newspaper. English. Independent De Soto Press, 116 North Main Street, De Soto MO 63020.

US
JEFFERSON CITY POST-TRIBUNE. **VFOAT** Jefferson City Post Tribune. (May 5, 1927)-. Newspaper. English. da. $92.00 Missouri; $130.00 other US. News Tribune Compnay, PO Box 420, Jefferson City MO 65102. **Tel** (314)636-3131. **LC** 7002. ***Formed by the union of*** *Jefferson City Tribune (Jefferson city, Mo. : 1924)* ***and*** *Daily Post (Jefferson City Mo.).*

US
JOPLIN GLOBE. 19th Year, No. 36 (Sept. 19, 1914)-. Newspaper. English. da. Joplin Globe Publishing Company, 117 East 4th Street, PO Box 7, Joplin MO 64802. **Tel** (417)623-3480. **ED** James R. Ellis. **Bk Rev**. **Ad Acc**. **Circ:** 37,000 daily, 45,000 Sunday (ctrl). available on microfilm. Documents available from UMI Article Clearinghouse. ***Continues*** *Joplin Daily Globe;* ***Absorbed*** *Joplin News-Herald.*
Ind/Abst Bus. Dateline (Dec. 21, 1991-) [Full Txt.].

US/0745-1067
KANSAS CITY STAR, THE. (Sept. 1885)-. Newspaper. English. da (Except Saturday). $182.33 Kansas, $184.91 Missouri, $208.96 others (morning edition only); $212.21 Kansas, $215.24 Missouri, $232.52 other states including APO & FPO addresses, $507.92 other (morning & Sunday); $163.99 Kansas, $166.30 Missouri, (morning & Sunday carrier delivery); $166.59 Kansas, $168.95 Missouri, $176.56 other states including APO & FPO addresses, $288.64 other (Sunday). Kansas City Star, 1729 Grand Avenue, Kansas City MO 64108. **Tel** (816)234-4141, (800)726-2340. **ED** Joe McGaff. **LC** 7002. **Circ:** 220,758 daily, 399,157 Sunday. available on microfilm from University Microfilms International (UMI). ***Continues*** *Kansas City Evening Star (Kansas City, Mo. : 1883).*
Ind/Abst PROMT.

US
LA BELLE STAR, THE. Began in 1883. Newspaper. English. wk. La Belle Star, PO Box 66, La Belle MO 63447.

US/0745-9300
LAMAR DEMOCRAT. Vol. 78, No. 110 (July 3, 1978)-. Newspaper. English. wk. $37.50 (local); $53.75 others. Lamar Democrat, PO Box 458, Lamar MO 64759. **Tel** (417)682-5529. **ED** Douglas D. Davis (Editor-in-Chief) and Opal Sims (Managing Editor). **Bk Rev**, (Qty: 1 or 2). **Photos**. **Ad Acc**, **Adv Mgr:** Stephanie Morgan. Full Page (B&W) $580.50. Half Page (B&W) $288.00. Full Page (Color) $665.50. Half Page (Color) $373.00. **Pub. Size:** Standard. **Circ:** 3,400 (ctrl). available on microfilm. ***Continues*** *Democrat (Lamar, Mo.).*
Desc: Orientation to local news.

US
LANDMARK (PLATTE CITY, MO.). (THE LANDMARK.). (1865)-. Newspaper. English. wk (Fri.). $13.00. The Landmark, PO Box 410, Platte City MO

64079. **Tel** (816)431-2313. **ED** Ivan Foley. **Photos. Ad Acc, Adv Mgr Tel** Ivan Foley. Full Page (B&W) $275.00. Half Page (B&W) $175.00. Full Page (Color) $350.00. Half Page (Color) $250.00. **Pub. Size:** Broadsheet. **Circ:** 1,750 (weekly). ***Absorbed*** *Platte County Reveille.*

US
LIFE LINE. Newspaper. English. $15.00 US; $30.00 foreign. Patillo Enterprises, Rt. 1 Box 153, Knob Noster MO 65336. **Tel** (816)563-5804.
Desc: Newspaper containing mail order marketing.

US
LOUISIANA PRESS-JOURNAL, THE.
VFOAT Louisiana Press Journal. Vol. 91, No. 23 (Aug. 17, 1945)-. Newspaper. English. wk (Wednesday). $17.00 Pike county and adjoining counties in Missouri; $26.00 other. Louisiana Press Journal, PO Box 466, Louisiana MO 63353. **Tel** (314)754-5566. ***Continues*** *Louisiana Press-Journal and Twice-a-Week Times;* ***Absorbed*** *Clarksville Sentinel (Clarksville, Mo. : 1928).*

US
MARSHFIELD MAIL, THE. (1892)-. Newspaper. English. wk. $19.50 area counties of Missouri; $25.00 other. Marshfield Mail, Box A, Marshfield MO 65706. **Tel** (417)468-2013, FAX (417)859-7930. **ED** Gordon E. Nordquist, Deana A. Barker (Managing Editor). **Bk Rev**, (Qty: 52). **Photos. Ad Acc, Adv Mgr:** Rita Ritterhouse, **Tel** (417)859-2014. Full Page (B&W) $409.50. Half Page (B&W) $204.75. Full Page (Color) $470.50. Half Page (Color) $269.75. **Pub. Size:** Standard. **Circ:** 5,500. available on microfilm and microfiche.

US
MEXICO LEDGER. 114th Year, No. 103 (Apr. 30, 1968)-. Newspaper. English. da (except Sun.). $74.00 Mexico, MO; $83.00 other. Mexico Ledger, PO Box 8, Mexico MO 65265. **Tel** (314)581-1111. **Bk Rev**. ctrl circ. available on microfilm. ***Continues*** *Mexico Evening Ledger.*

US
NEVADA HERALD, THE. Began in 1888. Newspaper. English. wk. Southwest Mail Printing Company, 131 South Cedar, Nevada MO 64772.

US/0893-3448
NEWS-LEADER (SPRINGFIELD, MO.). (THE NEWS-LEADER.). **VFOAT** News Leader; Springfield News-Leader; Springfield News Leader. Vol. 97, No. 57, (March 23, 1987)-. Newspaper. English. da. Springfield Newspapers Inc / Missouri, MPO Box 798, 651 Boonville Avenue, Springfield MO 65801. **Tel** (417)836-1100. **ED** Bill Southerland. **Circ:** 56,069 Saturday, 92,277 Sunday. ***Continues*** *Springfield News-Leader.*

US
NORBORNE DEMOCRAT-LEADER.
VFOAT Norborne Democrat Leader. Began in 1902. Newspaper. English. wk. Norborne Democrat-Leader, 106 South Pine Street, Norborne MO 64668. ***Formed by the union of*** *Norborne Democrat* ***and*** *Norborne Leader (Norborne, Mo. : 1904).*

US
OFALLON COUNTY JOURNAL. English. ir. $225.00. Ofallon County Journal, PO Box 69, Ofallon MO 63336. **Tel** (314)272-4949.

US/0890-2690
OZARK VISITOR. (OZARK VISITOR. THE SCHOOL OF THE OZARKS.). [Ozark visit.]. **Added/Corp** School of the Ozarks. (19??)-. Periodical. English. Four times a year (Jan., Apr., July, Oct.). Free. College of the Ozarks, PO Box 17, Point Lookout MO 65726-0017. **Tel** (417)334-6411, FAX (417)335-2618. **ED** Camille F. Howell. **DD** 378. **Photos. Pub. Size:** Standard. **Circ:** 180,000 unpaid (ctrl).
Desc: A newsletter about the Ozarks in Point Lookout, MO. It features things about the schools, programs, new service, and many more things.

US/0899-5737
PLATTE COUNTY GAZETTE (1988), THE. (THE PLATTE COUNTY GAZETTE.). Vol. 104, No. 23 (June 8, 1988)-. Newspaper. English. wk. $15.00. Platte County Gazette, PO Box 12086, Parkville MO 64152. **Tel** (816)741-9530, FAX (816)741-9593. **ED** Janelle Gann Moon and Jason Offutt (Managing Editor). **Photos. Ad Acc, Adv Mgr:** Carol Allen, **Tel** (816)781-1044. **Pub. Size:** Broadsheet. ***Continues*** *Northland Gazette, 0885-6923.*

US
POST-TELEGRAPH (PRINCETON, MO.). (THE POST-TELEGRAPH.). **VFOAT** Post Telegraph. Vol. 72, No. 37 (Nov. 23, 1944)-. Newspaper. English. Fifty-one times per year (Thurs.). $20.50. Post Telegraph / Missouri, PO Box 286, 704 East Main Street, Princeton MO 64673. **Tel** (816)748-3266, FAX (816)748-3267. **ED** Preston Cole (Editor-in-Chief) and Patsy Cole (Managing Editor). **Photos. Ad Acc, Adv Mgr:** Carrie Haouck. Full Page (B&W) $468.56. Half Page (B&W) $234.28. Full Page (Color) $528.56. Half Page (Color) $264.28. **Pub. Size:** Tabloid. available in microform. ***Formed by the union of*** *Princeton Post (Princeton, Mo.)* ***and*** *Princeton Telegraph.*

US
PUXICO PRESS. Vol. 19, No. 19 (Oct. 15, 1986)-. Newspaper. English. Fifty-two times a year (Wed.). $12.50 Stoddard, Wayne, Butler & Bollinger counties; $16.50 others in Missouri; $17.50 others. Puxico Press, PO Box 277, Puxico MO 63960. **Tel** (314)222-3243. **ED** Cletis Ellinghouse. **Ad Acc.** ***Continues*** *Puxico Weekly Press.*

US/8750-7625
RALLS COUNTY HERALD-ENTERPRISE, THE. ***Title Change.*** **VFOAT** Ralls County Herald Enterprise. Newspaper. English. wk. Ralls County Herald-Enterprise, PO Box 426, New London MO 63459. **Tel** (314)985-5531. ***Merged with*** *Ralls County Herald-Record* ***to form*** *Twainland Enterprise.*

US
RAYTOWN DISPATCH. **VFOAT** Dispatch-Tribune. Vol. 55, No. 5 (Nov. 11, 1981)-. Newspaper. English. Fifty-two times a year. $30.00 (one year). Raytown Dispatch, PO Box 12338, Kansas City MO 64116. ***Continues*** *Raytown News (Raytown, Mo. : 1926).*

US
REYNOLDS COUNTY COURIER (ELLINGTON, MO.). (REYNOLDS COUNTY COURIER.). Vol. 100, No. 26 (Jan. 6, 1977)-. Newspaper. English. wk. $17.00. Reynolds County Courier, PO Box 130, Ellington MO 63638. **Tel** (314)663-2243, FAX (314)663-2763. **ED** Harold T Ellinghouse. **Ad Acc. Circ:** 2,900 (ctrl). ***Continues*** *Courier-Press (Ellington, MO.).*

US
SALISBURY PRESS-SPECTATOR.
VFOAT Salisbury Press Spectator. Began in 1871. Newspaper. English. wk. Salisbury Press Spectator, 111 South Broadway, Salisbury MO 65281. ***Formed by the union of*** *Salisbury Press (Salisbury, MO. : 1870)* ***and*** *Salisbury Spectator;* ***Absorbed*** *Salisbury Democrat.*

US
SHANNON COUNTY CURRENT WAVE.
VFOAT Current Wave. Vol. 105, No. 11 (June 8, 1978)-. Newspaper. English. wk. $16.00 Shannon County; $18.00 surrounding counties; $22.00 Missouri; $24.00 other. Current Wave, PO Box J, Eminence MO 65466. **Tel** (314)226-3335. **ED** Roger Dillon. **Photos. Ad Acc, Adv Mgr:** Rita Johnson. Full Page (B&W) $315.00. Half Page (B&W) $170.00. **Pub. Size:** Standard. **Circ:** 2,000. ***Continues*** *Current Wave (Eminence, Mo. : 1884).*

US/0746-4452
SOUTHEAST MISSOURIAN. Began with Mar. 8, 1918 issue. Newspaper. English. da (except Saturday). $102.00. Southeast Missourian, PO Box 699, Cape Girardeau MO 63701. **Tel** (314)335-6611, FAX (314)334-4454. **ED** Joni Adams and Ken Newton. **Ad Acc. Circ:** 39,000. ***Continues*** *Cape Girardeau Southeast Missourian (Cape Girardeau, MO. : Daily).*
Desc: Contains news and local features.

US
ST. CHARLES JOURNAL. **VFOAT** Saint Charles Journal. Vol. 1, No. 1 (Dec. 5, 1957)-. Newspaper. English. tw. $225.00. St. Charles Journal, PO Box 720, St. Charles MO 63302. **Tel** (314)946-6111.

●US/1063-4312
ST. JOSEPH NEWS-PRESS (1992). (ST. JOSEPH NEWS-PRESS.). **VFOAT** Saint Joseph News Press. Vol. 147, No. 365 (Apr. 5, 1992)-. Newspaper. English. da. St. Joseph News Press Gazette / Department of Circulation, PO Box 29, St. Joseph MO 64502. **Tel** (816)279-5671. ***Continues*** *St. Joseph News-Press/Gazette, 0899-711X.*

US/0899-711X
ST. JOSEPH NEWS-PRESS/GAZETTE.
Title Change. **VFOAT** Saint Joseph News Press Gazette. Vol. 144, No. 49 (July 1, 1988)-Vol. 147, No. 345 (Apr. 4, 1992). Newspaper. English. da. St Joseph Gazette, Ninth and Edmonds Streets, St Joseph MO 64502. **Tel** (816)279-5671. ***Formed by the union of*** *St. Joseph News-Press* ***and*** *St. Joseph Gazette (Saint Joseph, Mo. : 1902).* ***Continued by*** *St. Joseph News-Press (Saint Joseph, Mo. : 1992), 1063-4312.*

US
ST. LOUIS ARGUS. Began publication in 1912?. Newspaper. English. wk. $10.00. Argus, 4595 Dr Martin Luther King Drive, St Louis MO 63113.

US/0036-2948
ST. LOUIS COUNTIAN, THE. **VFOAT** Saint Louis Countian. **VAT** Saint Louis Countian. Vol. 1, No. 1 (Jan. 25, 1919)-. Newspaper. English. da. $168.00 one year;. Saint Louis Daily Record, PO Box 88910, St Louis MO 63188. **Tel** (314)421-1880. **ED** Will Connaghan. **Ad Acc. Circ:** 1,800 (ctrl). available on microfilm from University Microfilms International (UMI). ***Continues*** *Kirkwood Courier.*
Desc: A newspaper for credit information, business leads and more.

US
ST. LOUIS POST-DISPATCH. **VAT** Saint Louis Post-Dispatch. (Mar. 8, 1879)-. Newspaper. English. ds. $223.83 Missouri; $214.00 Arkansas & Illinois; $293.00 US; $694.00 other. Saint Louis Post-Dispatch, 900 North Tucker Boulevard, St Louis MO 63101. **Tel** (314)340-8808. **ED** William F. Woo (Editor-in-Chief) and Foster Davis (Managing Editor). **LC** 8638. **Bk Rev**, (Qty: 200). **Photos. Ad Acc, Adv Mgr:** Tom Rees, **Tel** (314)340-8577. **Pub. Size:** Standard. **Wire Svcs.:** AP, KR, LA, RN, SH, WP. **Circ:** 378,255 daily, 560,618 Sunday. available on microfilm; available on an online database (file 494/Full-Text) from DIALOG. Documents available from UMI Article Clearinghouse. ***Continues*** *St. Louis Post and Dispatch (Saint Louis, Mo. : 1878);* ***Absorbed*** *Banner-News (Saint Charles, Mo.).*
Ind/Abst Newsp. Abstr.; PROMT.

US
ST. LOUIS SENTINEL. (1968)-. Newspaper. English. wk. $25.00. Woods Printing Company, 2900 North Market Street, St Louis MO 63106. **Tel** (314)531-2101, FAX (314)531-4442. **ED** Michael C. Williams. **Bk Rev**, (Qty: 50). **Photos. Ad Acc, Adv Mgr:** O. Smith. Full Page (B&W) $2273.09. Half Page (B&W) $1136.52. Full Page (Color) $2523.09. Half Page (Color) $1386.52. **Pub. Size:** Broadsheet. **Wire Svcs.:** API, NP. **Circ:** 70,000 (ctrl). available in microform.

US
STEELVILLE STAR-CRAWFORD MIRROR. **VFOAT** Steelville Star Crawford Mirror. Vol. 115, No. 19 (July 2, 1986)-. Newspaper. English. wk. $10.62 local; $12.22 Missouri; $14.50 US. Crawford Mirror, PO Box 100, Steelville MO 65565. **Tel** (314)775-5454, FAX (314)885-3803. **ED** Ava Viehman, Mary Ann Baumann (Managing Editor). **Photos. Ad Acc, Adv Mgr:** Delma Pascoe. Full Page (B&W) $113.75. Half Page (B&W) $56.88. Full Page (Color) $208.75. Half Page (Color) $151.88. **Pub. Size:** Tabloid. ***Formed by the union of*** *Steelville Star* ***and*** *Crawford Mirror.*

US
TARKIO AVALANCHE, THE. (1884)-. Newspaper. English. wk. $18.00 local; $24.00 other. Tarkio Avalanche, 107 North 3rd Street, Tarkio MO 64491. **Photos. Ad Acc, Adv Mgr:** Will Johnson, **Tel** 736-4411. **Pub. Size:** Broadsheet. **Wire Svcs.:** AP. ***Absorbed*** *Independent (Tardio, Mo.).*

US/0746-1712
TRI-COUNTY JOURNAL. Newspaper. English. wk. Suburban Newspapers / Missouri, 1714 Deer Tracks Trail, St. Louis MO 63131. **Tel** (314)821-2462.

US
UNTERRIFIED DEMOCRAT. Began in 1866. Newspaper. English. wk. Unterrified Democrat, PO Box 119, Linn MO 65051-0119. ***Absorbed*** *Meta Herald.*

US/0744-2394
VALLEY HORSE NEWS, THE. Periodical. English. mo. Valley Horse News, 525 North Commercial, St Clair MO 63077.

US/0743-8052
WASHINGTON MISSOURIAN. **VFOAT** Washington Tabloid Missourian. Vol. 1, No. 1 (Aug. 6, 1926)-. Newspaper. English. sw. Missourian Publishing Company, 14 West Main Street, PO Box 336, Washington MO 63090. **Tel** (314)239-7701. ***Continues*** *Franklin County Observer (Washington, Mo. : 1861);* ***Absorbed*** *Buyer's Guide (Washington, Mo.); Washington Citizen.*

US/0893-6048
WEEKLY AMERICAN (POPLAR BLUFF, MO.). (THE WEEKLY AMERICAN.). Newspaper. English. wk. Weekly American, 208 Poplar Street, Poplar Bluff MO 63901.

US/0738-8055
WEEKLY WESTPORT REPORTER, THE. (19??)-. Newspaper. English. Fifty-two times a year. $20.00. Westport Reporter Inc., 3837 Walnut Street, Kansas City MO 64111. **Tel** (816)531-1555, FAX (816)931-2345. **ED** Sarah P. Reddoch. **Ad Acc.**
Desc: A shopper newspaper.

US
WEST PLAINS DAILY QUILL. Began in 1903. Newspaper. English. da. West Plains Daily Quill, 125 North Jefferson Street, West Plains MO 65775. ***Absorbed*** *Journal-Gazette (West Plains, Mo. : 1947).*

MONTANA

US
AGRI-NEWS (BILLINGS, MONT.). (AGRI-NEWS.). **VFOAT** Agri News. Vol. 15, No. 11 (Oct. 29, 1982)-. Newspaper. English. Fifty-two times a year. $15.00 (one year); $20.00 (two years); $25.00 (three years). Agri News, PO Box 30755, Billings MT 59107. **Tel** (406)259-5406, FAX (406)259-6888. **ED** Chuck Rightmire (editor's address: 2227 Spruce, Billings, MT 59101, phone: (406)259-4589). **Photos. Ad Acc, Adv Mgr:** Donna Owen. Full Page (B&W) $950.40. Half Page (B&W) $475.20. Full Page (Color) $1,090.40. Half Page (Color) $615.20. **Pub. Size:** Tabloid. **Wire Svcs.:** AP. **Circ:** 20,000. **Continues** Montwyo Agri-News.
Desc: This publication is devoted exclusively to agriculture and agri-business concentrated in Montana and Wyoming.

US
ANACONDA LEADER, THE. Vol 1, No. 1 (Dec. 17, 1970)-. Newspaper. English. sw. Anaconda Leader, 121 Main Street, Anaconda MT 59711. available on microfilm from University Microfilms International (UMI).

US
BEARTOOTH WEEKLY. Vol. 4, Nc. 45 (Nov. 1, 1983)-. Newspaper. English. wk. Beartooth Weekly, PO Box 2228, Red Lodge MT 59068. **Continues** Red Lodge Weekly.

US/0897-8735
BIG HORN COUNTY NEW. (19??)-. Newspaper. English. Fifty-two times a year. News Montana Inc., 204 North Center, Hardin MT 59034. **Tel** (406)655-1008, (800)767-1008. **Continues** Hardin Herald, 0740-2600.

US/0740-1981
BIG TIMBER PIONEER (1983), THE. (THE BIG TIMBER PIONEER.). **VFOAT** Pioneer. Vol. 95, No. 18 (Jan. 5, 1983)-. Newspaper. English. Fifty-two times a year. Big Timber Pioneer, PO Box 190, Big T mber MT 59011. **Tel** (406)932-5298. **Continues** Pioneer (Big Timber, Mont.).

US
BILLINGS GAZETTE (BILLINGS, MONT. : DAILY : 1914). (THE BILLINGS GAZETTE.). Vol. 13, No. 50 (Jan. 1, 1914)-. Newspaper. English. ds. $218.10 Yellowstone County, Montana; $245.60 Wyoming, North Dakota and Montana; $318.90 other. The Billings Gazette, PO Box 36300, Billings MT 59107. **Tel** (406)657-1200, (800)669-6397, FAX (406)657-1345. **ED** Richard Wesnick. **Bk Rev. Ad Acc. Circ:** 57,620 daily, 60,144 Sunday. available on microfilm from University Microfilms International (UMI); available on an online database (file 635/Full-Text) from DIALOG. Documents available from UMI Article Clearinghouse. **Continues** Billings Daily Gazette.
Desc: General interest newspaper.
Ind/Abst Bus. Dateline.

US
BOZEMAN DAILY CHRONICLE. Vol. 1, No. 1 (Dec. 4, 1911)-. Newspaper. English. da. $10.C0 per month. Bozeman Daily Chronicle, PO Box 1188, Bozeman MT 59771. **Tel** (406)587-4491. **ED** Bill Wilke. **Photos. Ad Acc, Adv Mgr:** Mike Smit. Full Page (B&W) $1200.00. Half Page (B&W) $600.00. Full Page (Color) $1200.00 plus $90.00 per color. Half Page (Color) $600.00 plus $90.00 per color. **Pub. Size:** Broadsheet. **Wire Svcs.:** AP. **Circ:** 13,100 daily, 15,200 Sunday. **Absorbed** Bozeman Courier.

US
CARBON COUNTY NEWS (RED LODGE, MONT. : 1936). (CARBON COUNTY NEWS.). Vol. 13, No. 10 (May 8, 1936)-. Newspaper. English. wk. Carbon County News, PO Box 970. Red Lodge MT 59068. **Continues** Red Lodge Daily News Combined With Carbon County News; **Absorbed** Picket-Journal; Bridger News.

US
CASCADE COURIER, THE. Vol. 1, No. 1 (Jan. 21, 1910)-. Newspaper. English. wk. $16.00 Cascade County; $18.00 others. Cascade Courier, PO Box 308, Cascade MT 59421. **Tel** (406)468-9231, FAX (406)468-9231. **ED** Pat Travis. **Bk Rev. Photos. Ad Acc, Adv Mgr:** Ellen & Pat Travis. Full Page (B&W) $200.00. Half Page (B&W) $100.00. Full Page (Color) $290.00. Half Page (Color) $190.00. **Pub. Size:** Tabloid.

US
CHOTEAU ACANTHA, THE. Vol. 10, No. 29 (March 24, 1904)-. Newspaper. English. wk. Choteau Acantha, 119 1st Avenue Northwest, Choteau MT 59422. **Continues** Dupuyer Acantha; **Absorbed** Choteau Montanan (Choteau, Mont. : 1913); Teton Citizen.

US
CUT BANK PIONEER PRESS. Vol. 1, No. 1 (July 16, 1909)-. Newspaper. English. wk. Cut Bank Pioneer Press, 217 West Main Street, Cut Bank MT 59427. **Absorbed** Cut Bank Tribune.

US
DAILY INTER LAKE, THE. VFOAT Inter Lake. Began with April 13, 1908. Newspaper. English. da. Daily Inter Lake, 727 East Idaho, Kalispell MT 59901. **Absorbed** Kalispell Journal.

US/1046-1590
DAILY NEWS (HAVRE, MONT.), THE. (THE DAILY NEWS.). (May 13, 1985)-. Newspaper. English. da (except weekends). $98.00 Hill County, Montana; $110.00 other Montana; $122.00 other. Havre Daily News, PO Box 431, Havre MT 59501. **Tel** (406)265-6795. **ED** Steve Miller. **Photos. Ad Acc, Adv Mgr:** Paula Carmean. Full Page (B&W) $4.95 per inch. Half Page (B&W) $5.04 per inch. **Wire Svcs.:** AP. available on microfilm. **Continues** Havre Daily News, 0745-7782.

US
DANIELS COUNTY LEADER. (Feb. 9, 1922)-. Newspaper. English. Fifty-two times a year (Thurs.). Daniels County Leader, PO Box 850, Scobey MT 59263. **Tel** (406)487-5303. **Continues** Whitetail Courier [non-extant]; **Absorbed** Scobey Sentinel; Daniels County Free Press.

US
EKALAKA EAGLE (EKALAKA, MONT. : 1923). (THE EKALAKA EAGLE.). Vol. 15, No. 1 (Jan. 5, 1923)-. Newspaper. English. wk. Ekalaka Eagle, PO Box 66, Ekalaka MT 59324. **Continues** Ekalaka Eagle and Beaver Valley Press.

US
FAIRFIELD TIMES, THE. Began in 1916. Newspaper. English. wk. Fairfield Times, PO Box 578, Fairfield MT 59436.

US
FLATHEAD COURIER, THE. Vol. 1, No. 1 (April 14, 1910)-. Newspaper. English. wk. Flathead Courier, PO Box 1091, Polsom MT 59860. **Absorbed** Lake Shore Sentinel (Polson, Mont.).

US
GLACIER REPORTER, THE. Vol. 23, No. 24 (August 21, 1953)-. Newspaper. English. wk. Glacier Reporter, PO Box R, Browning MT 59417. **Continues** Browning Chief.

US
GLASGOW COURIER, THE. VFOAT Glasgow Courier and Valley County Nnews; Glasgow-Fort Peck Courier; Glasgow Fort Peck Courier. Vol. 10, No. 13 (August 8, 1913)-. Newspaper. English. Fifty-two times a year. Glasgow Courier, PO Box 151, c/o R. B. Helland, Glasgow MT 59230. **Tel** (406)228-9301. **LC** 8654. **Continues** Valley County Independent; **Absorbed** Glasgow Times; Glasgow Messenger; Valley County News (Glasgow, Mont. : 1904); Opheim Observer.

US
GLENDIVE RANGER-REVIEW. VFOAT Glendive Ranger Review; Ranger-Review. Vol. 14, No. 69 (Nov. 16, 1975)-. Newspaper. English. wk. $36.00 (carrier), $45.00 (mail) Montana; $47.50 other. Glendive Ranger-Review, PO Box 61, Glendive MT 59330. **Tel** (406)365-3303. **ED** Craig Elliott. **Bk Rev. Photos. Ad Acc, Adv Mgr:** Pat Boese. Full Page (B&W) $451.50. Half Page (B&W) $232.20. Full Page (Color) $501.50. Half Page (Color) $282.20. **Continues** Ranger-Review.

US
GREAT FALLS TRIBUNE (GREAT FALLS, MONT. : 1921). (GREAT FALLS TRIBUNE.). 32nd year, (Jan. 11, 1921)-. Newspaper. English. da. $167.20 (daily & Sunday); $143.20 (daily by mail); $105.00 (Sunday by mail) Montana; $220.20 (daily & Sunday by mail), $185.20 (daily by mail), $129.00 (Sunday by mail) other. Great Falls Tribune, PO Box 5468, Great Falls MT 59403. **Tel** (406)791-1400, (800)438-6600, FAX (406)791-1431. **ED** Dennis Ryerson. **Ad Acc. Circ:** 35,000 daily, 42,000 Sunday. available on microfilm from University Microfilms International (UMI). **Continues** Great Falls Daily Tribune; **Absorbed** Great Falls Leader (Great Falls, Mont. : 1909 : Daily).

US
HARLEM NEWS (HARLEM, MONT. : 1908). (THE HARLEM NEWS.). Vol. 5, No. 14 (June 18, 1908)-. Newspaper. English. wk. Harlem News, PO Box 278, Harlem MT 59526. **Continues** Milk River Valley News.

US
HERALD-NEWS (WOLF POINT, MONT.). (THE HERALD-NEWS.). **VFOAT** Herald News. Vol. 27, No. 51 (Jan. 18, 1940)-. Newspaper. English. wk. Herald-News / Wolf Point, PO Box 639, Wolf Point MT 59201. **Tel** (406)653-2222. **Formed by the union of** Wolf Point Herald **and** Roosevelt County News.

US/0746-3359
HIGH COUNTRY INDEPENDENT PRESS. Vol. 1, No. 1 (Feb. 2, 1983)-. Newspaper. English. wk. $15.00 in county, $20.00 in-state; $25.00 out-of-state. High Country Independent Press MT 59714. **Tel** (406)388-6762. **ED** Devon Ann Sorlie and Glenn F Sorlie. **Ad Acc. Circ:** 5,300 (ctrl). **Formed by the union of** Belgrade Independent Press **and** High Country News (Bozeman, Mont.).
Desc: Local News of small towns in Western Gallatin county and rural areas.

US
HUNGRY HORSE NEWS. Vol. 2, No. 35 (April 2, 1948)-. Newspaper. English. wk. $21.00 Flathead county and Glacier Park; $25.00 Montana; $30.00 other. Hungry Horse News, PO Box 189, Columbia Falls MT 59912. **Tel** (406)892-2151. **Continues** Hungry Horse News and Columbian.

US
INDEPENDENT-OBSERVER (CONRAD, MONT.). (INDEPENDENT-OBSERVER.). **VFOAT** Independent Observer; Conrad Independent-Observer. Vol. 18, No. 35 (Dec. 21, 1922)-. Newspaper. English. wk. $19.00. Independent-Observer / Conrad, PO Box 966, Conrad MT 59425. **Tel** (406)278-5562. **ED** Jack Lee. **Photos. Ad Acc, Adv Mgr:** Pat Loran. Full Page (B&W) $553.11. Half Page (B&W) $283.14. Full Page (Color) $703.11. Half Page (Color) $433.14. **Pub. Size:** Broadsheet. **Formed by the union of** Conrad Independent **and** Conrad Observer; **Absorbed** Pondera County News; Valerian.

US
INDEPENDENT-RECORD (HELENA, MONT.). (THE INDEPENDENT-RECORD.). **VFOAT** Independent Record. Vol. 1, No. 1 (Nov. 22, 1943)-. Newspaper. English. da. Independent-Record, 317 Allen Street, Helena MT 59604. **Formed by the union of** Helena Independent (Helena, Mont. : 1875) **and** Montana Record-Herald.

US
KALISPELL'S WEEKLY NEWS. VFOAT Kalispell's News; Kalispell News. 76th Year, No. 37 (April 1, 1965)-. Newspaper. English. wk. $18.00 Flathead County; $20.00 Montana; $26.00 US; $40.00 other. Kalispell's News, PO Box 669, Kalispell MT 59901. **Tel** (406)755-6767. **Ad Acc. Continues** News (Kalispell, Mont.).

US
LAUREL OUTLOOK. Vol. 1, No. 1 (July 14, 1909)-. Newspaper. English. Fifty-two times a year. $19.00. Laurel Outlook, PO Box 278, Laurel MT 59044. **Tel** (406)628-4412. **ED** Steven Barlow. **Bk Rev**, (Qty: 25 per year). **Photos. Ad Acc, Adv Mgr:** Milton E. Wester. Full Page (B&W) $655.20. Half Page (B&W) $327.60. Full Page (Color) $730.20. Half Page (Color) $402.60. **Pub. Size:** Standard. **Wire Svcs.:** AP.

US
LEWISTOWN NEWS-ARGUS. VFOAT Lewistown News Argus. Vol. 92, No. 1 (Sept. 3, 1972)-. Newspaper. English. sw. $25.96 Central Montana; $35.72 Montana; $42.88 other. Lewistown News Argus, PO Box 900, Lewistown MT 59457. **Tel** (406)538-3401. **Continues** Lewistown Daily News (Lewistown, Mont. : 1947).

US
LIVINGSTON ENTERPRISE (LIVINGSTON, MONT. : DAILY). (LIVINGSTON ENTERPRISE.). **VFOAT** Sunday Enterprise. Vol. 4 No. 194 (May 4, 1914)-. Newspaper. English. da. $97.50 (Park County, MT); $112.60 (other counties, MT); $118.00 (other). Livingston Enterprise, PO Box 606, Livingston MT 59047. **Tel** (406)222-2000. **Formed by the union of** Livingston Daily Post **and** Daily Enterprise (Livingston, Mont. : 1910).

US
MEAGHER COUNTY NEWS (WHITE SULPHUR SPRINGS, MONT. : 1934). (THE MEAGHER COUNTY NEWS.). Vol. 34, No. 12 (July 4, 1934)-. Newspaper. English. wk. Meagher County News, PO Box 349, White Sulphur Springs MT 59645. **Continues** Meagher Republican.

US/0891-8988
MILES CITY STAR. Vol. 47, No. 113 (Oct. 5, 1957)-. Newspaper. English. da. $94.00 Montana; $99.75 other. Miles City Star, PO Box 1216, Miles City MT 59301. **Tel** (406)232-0450. **Continues** Miles City Daily Star.

US
MONTANA STANDARD (BUTTE, MONT. : 1967). (THE MONTANA STANDARD.). 91st Year, No. 299 (May 26, 1967)-. Newspaper. English. da. Montana Standard, PO Box 627, 25 West Granite Street, Butte MT 59701. **Tel** (406)496-5556, (800)877-1074.

available on microfilm from University Microfilms International (UMI). ***Continues*** *Montana Standard and The Butte Daily Post.*

US
PHILIPSBURG MAIL, THE. Began with Jan. 28, 1887 issue. Newspaper. English. wk. Philipsburg Mail, PO Box 160, Philipsburg MT 59858.

US
PHILLIPS COUNTY NEWS (MALTA, MONT. : 1928). (PHILLIPS COUNTY NEWS.). Vol. 5, No. 10 (July 5, 1928)-. Newspaper. English. wk. Phillips County News, PO Box 850, Malta MT 59538. ***Continues*** *Phillips County News and the Enterprise.*

US
PLENTYWOOD HERALD. (1908)-. Newspaper. English. Fifty-two times a year. $25.00 in state; $28.00 other. Plentywood Herald, Box 297, Plentywood MT 59254. **Tel** (406)765-1150. **ED** Joe Nistler. **Photos**. **Ad Acc, Adv Mgr:** Tim Polk. Full Page (B&W) $495.60. Half Page (B&W) $247.80. Full Page (Color) $535.60. Half Page (Color) $287.80. **Pub. Size:** Standard. ***Absorbed*** *Medicine Lake Wave.*

US
RAVALLI REPUBLIC. VFOAT Ravalli Republic and the Western News. Vol. 87, No. 117 (June 16, 1975)-. Newspaper. English. da (five days a week). $72.00 Ravalli; $81.00 others. Ravalli Republic, 232 Main Street, Hamilton MT 59840. **Tel** (406)363-3300. **ED** Drake Kiewit. **Ad Acc, Adv Mgr:** Cindi. **Circ:** 5,200. ***Continues*** *Ravalli Daily Republic;* ***Absorbed*** *Western News (Hamilton, Mont.).*

US
RIVER PRESS, THE. Vol. 1, No. 1 (Oct. 27, 1880)-. Newspaper. English. wk. River Press, PO Box 69, Fort Benton MT 59442.

US/8750-2097
ROSEBUD COUNTY PRESS. Vol. 2, No. 8 (Apr. 6, 1979)-. Newspaper. English. wk. $20.00 (in county), $22.00 (out of county, in state), $24.00 (out of state). Rosebud County Press, PO Box 734, Colstrip MT 59323-0734. **ED** Patricia Corley. **Bk Rev. Photos. Ad Acc, Adv Mgr:** Pearl Ryckman, **Tel** (406)356-2149. Full Page (B&W) $2.40 per column inch. Half Page (B&W) $2.75 per column inch. Full Page (Color) add $60.00 per color. Half Page (Color) add $60.00 per color. **Pub. Size:** Standard. ***Continues*** *Colstrip Comments.*

US/0890-9660
ROUNDUP RECORD-TRIBUNE & WINNETT TIMES. VFOAT Roundup Record Tribune and Winnett Times. 73th Year, No. 41 (Jan. 8, 1986)-. Newspaper. English. wk. $18.00. Roundup Record Tribune, PO Box 747, Roundup MT 59072. **ED** Eric N. Rasmussen. **Bk Rev**, (Qty: 20). **Photos**. **Ad Acc, Adv Mgr Tel** (406)323-1105. Full Page (B&W) $440.00. Half Page (B&W) $250.00. Full Page (Color) $505.00. Half Page (Color) $315.00. **Pub. Size:** Broadsheet. ***Formed by the union of*** *Roundup Record-Tribune, 0742-8294* ***and*** *Winnett Times, 0746-5610.*

US
SANDERS COUNTY LEDGER (THOMPSON FALLS, MONT. : 1959). (SANDERS COUNTY LEDGER.). Vol. 53, No. 47 (Jan. 29, 1959)-. Newspaper. English. wk. $17.00 - $24.00. Sanders County Ledger, PO Box 219, Thompson Falls MT 59873. **ED** Tom Eggensperger. **Bk Rev. Photos. Ad Acc, Adv Mgr:** Sherry Hagerman-Benton, **Tel** (406)827-4375. Full Page (B&W) $300.00. Half Page (B&W) $150.00. Full Page (Color) $400.00. Half Page (Color) $250.00. **Pub. Size:** Standard. **Circ:** 3,000. ***Continues*** *Sanders County Independent-Ledger.*

US
SEARCHLIGHT (CULBERTSON, MONT.). (THE SEARCHLIGHT.). **VFOAT** Culbertson Searchlight; Searchlight and Culbertson Republican. Vol. 1, No. 1 (April 24, 1902)-. Newspaper. English. wk. $17.00. The Searchlight / Montana, PO Box 496, Culbertson MT 59218. **Tel** (406)787-5821. **ED** Ila Mae Torbregd. **Photos**. **Ad Acc**. Full Page (B&W) $192.50. Half Page (B&W) $96.25. **Pub. Size:** Standard. **Wire Svcs.:** MP. available in microform from Montana Historical Society. ***Absorbed*** *Culbertson Republican; Valley Tribune; Froid Tribune; Big Muddy Journal.*

US
SHELBY PROMOTER, THE. VFOAT Shelby Promoter and Tribune of Shelby. (May 15, 1912)-. Newspaper. English. wk. $30.00. Shelby Promoter, 119 Maple Street, Shelby MT 59474. **ED** Sharon Dunham and John F. Kavanagh (Managing Editor). **Photos. Ad Acc, Adv Mgr:** Cindy Combs, **Tel** (406)434-5171. Full Page (B&W) $492.66. Half Page (B&W) $262.08. Full Page (Color) $567.66 (1 spot color). Half Page (Color) $337.08 (1 spot color). **Pub. Size:** Standard. ***Absorbed*** *Montana Courier; Tribune of Shelby.*

US
SIDNEY HERALD-LEADER. English. Sidney Herald, 121 North Central Avenue, Sidney MT 59270. **Tel** (406)482-2403.

US
SILVER STATE POST, THE. Vol. 36, No. 47 (March 12, 1925)-. Newspaper. English. wk. Silver State Post, 312 Missouri Avenue, Deer Lodge MT 59722. ***Formed by the union of*** *Silver State (Deer Lodge, Mont.)* ***and*** *Powell County Post;* ***Absorbed*** *Evening Bulletin.*

US
THREE FORKS HERALD AND MANHATTAN INTERMOUNTAIN PRESS. VFOAT Three Forks Herald. Vol. 61, No. 40 (July 3, 1969)-. Newspaper. English. wk. PO Box 586, Three Forks MT 59752. ***Formed by the union of*** *Three Forks Herald* ***and*** *Manhattan Inter-Mountain Press.*

US/0889-5627
TIMES CLARION (HARLOWTON, MONT.), THE. (THE TIMES CLARION.). **VFOAT** Times-Clarion. 58th Year, No. 39 (April 1, 1976)-. Newspaper. English. wk. $20.00. Times Clarion, PO Box 307, Harlowton MT 59036-0307. **Tel** (406)632-5633, FAX (406)632-5644. **ED** Gerald Miller. **Bk Rev**, (Qty: 10). **Photos**. **Ad Acc, Adv Mgr:** Julie Killorn. **Pub. Size:** Standard. **Wire Svcs.:** AP. **Circ:** 1,625 (paid). ***Formed by the union of*** *Harlowton Times* ***and*** *Eastern Montana Clarion.*

US/8750-2925
TOBACCO VALLEY NEWS. Vol. 1, No. 1 (July 14, 1960)-. Newspaper. English. wk. $10.50 in county, $11.50 in Montana, $12.50 other. Tobacco Valley News, PO Box 307, Eureka MT 59917.

US
TOWNSEND STAR. Vol. 1, No. 1 (April 24, 1897)-. Newspaper. English. wk. $22.00. Townsend Star, PO Box M, Townsend MT 59644. **Tel** (406)266-3333, FAX (406)266-5440. **ED** Jeff Stoffer. **Photos. Ad Acc.** Full Page (B&W) $443.00. Half Page (B&W) $234.00. Full Page (Color) $663.00. Half Page (Color) $454.00. **Pub. Size:** Broadsheet. **Circ:** 1,500 (paid). ***Absorbed*** *Townsend Forum and Townsend Messenger.*

US/0745-0362
WESTERN NEWS (LIBBY, MONT.), THE. (THE WESTERN NEWS.). Vol. 33, No. 2 (June 15, 1933)-. Newspaper. English. Fifty-two times a year (Wed.). Western News, PO Box 1377, Libby MT 59923. **Tel** (406)293-4124. **ED** June McMahon. **Bk Rev. Ad Acc. Circ:** 4,550 (ctrl). ***Continues*** *Western News and the Libby Times;* ***Absorbed*** *Troy Tribune; Eureka Mirror; Kootenai Valley Call.*
Desc: Surrounding news, weddings, engagements, interesting articles from surrounding areas.

US
WHITEFISH PILOT, THE. Vol. 1, No. 1 (Jan. 23, 1904)-. Newspaper. English. wk. Whitefish Pilot, PO Box 488, Whitefish MT 59937. ***Absorbed*** *Daily Reminder.*

US
WIBAUX PIONEER-GAZETTE, THE. VFOAT Wibaux Pioneer Gazette. (1919)-. Newspaper. English. wk. $19.00. Wibaux Pioneer-Gazette, 118 South Wibaux Street, Wibaux MT 59353. **ED** Frank Datta. **Photos. Ad Acc, Adv Mgr:** F. Datta, **Tel** (406)795-2218. Full Page (B&W) $178.75. Half Page (B&W) $89.40. Full Page (Color) $255.00. Half Page (Color) $165.00. **Pub. Size:** Tabloid. **Circ:** 1,000. available in microform. ***Formed by the union of*** *Wibaux Pioneer* ***and*** *Beaver Valley Gazette.*

NEBRASKA

US/0746-6439
AINSWORTH STAR-JOURNAL. VFOAT Ainsworth Star Journal. Newspaper. English. wk. $10.50. Ainsworth Star-Journal, 327 North Main Street, Ainsworth NE 69210.

US
ARTHUR ENTERPRISE, THE. Began in 1911. Newspaper. English. wk. Arthur Enterprise, PO Box 165, Arthur NE 69121.

US
BEATRICE DAILY SUN. (1902)-. Newspaper. English. da. $78.00. Beatrice Daily Sun, PO Box 847, Beatrice NE 68310. **ED** Dennis M. DeRossett (Editor-in-Chief) and Anita Meyer (Managing Editor). **Photos. Ad Acc, Adv Mgr:** Ron Sohl, **Tel** (402)223-5233. Full Page (B&W) $883.65. Half Page (B&W) $445.25. Full Page (Color) $973.65. Half Page (Color) $535.25. **Pub. Size:** Broadsheet. **Wire Svcs.:** AP. **Circ:** 9,600. available in microform from Crest Information Technologies.

US/0193-0389
BELLEVUE LEADER. (19??)-. Newspaper. English. Fifty-two times a year. $18.00. Bellevue Leader, 604 Fort Crook Road North, Bellevue NE 68005. **Tel** (402)733-7300, FAX (402)733-9116. **ED** Ron Petak. **Photos. Ad Acc, Adv Mgr:** Ron Stadie. Full Page (B&W) $1771.00. Half Page (B&W) $885.80. **Pub. Size:** Broadsheet. **Circ:** 24,000.

US/0746-1437
DOUGLAS COUNTY POST-GAZETTE. VFOAT Post-Gazette. (19??)-. Newspaper. English. wk. $18.75. Douglas County Post Gazette, 113 Hillrise, Elkhorn NE 68022-1604. **Tel** (402)289-2329, FAX (402)289-0861. **ED** Penny Overmann, Mark Thiessen (Managing Editor). **Photos. Ad Acc.** Full Page (B&W) $823.90. Half Page (B&W) $411.95. Full Page (Color) $908.90. Half Page (Color) $496.95. **Pub. Size:** Broadsheet. **Circ:** 2,400 paid, 5,400 free, 7,800 total market coverage. available in microform. ***Continues*** *Douglas County Gazette.*

US
FALLS CITY JOURNAL, THE. Began in 1881?. Newspaper. English. da. Falls City Journal, PO Box 128, Falls City NE 68355. **Tel** (402)245-2431. **ED** George W Schock. ***Continues*** *Globe-Journal.*

US/1049-8338
FREMONT TRIBUNE. (1868)-. Newspaper. English. da. $98.90 Fremont Area; $114.40 other. Fremont Tribune, Box 9, Fremont NE 68025. **Tel** (402)721-5000.

US
GORDON JOURNAL. Newspaper. English. Fifty-two times a year (Wed.). $16.00 Sheridan County & surrounding counties; $21.00 others. Gordon Journal, PO Box 270, Gordon NE 69343-0270. **Tel** (308)282-0118. **ED** Susanne Evans. **Bk Rev**, (Qty: 6). **Ad Acc, Adv Mgr:** Neal Ziller, **Tel** (308)282-0118. ctrl circ.

US/1049-3018
GRAND ISLAND INDEPENDENT. (19??)-. Periodical. English. da. $78.00 (local counties), $97.00 (elsewhere in Neb.), 109.00 (elsewhere in U.S.). Grand Island Daily Independent, Grand Island NE 68802. Documents available from UMI Article Clearinghouse. ***Formed by the union of*** *Grand Island Daily Independent (Regular ed.), 0748-5387* ***and*** *Grand Island Daily Independent (Mail ed.), 0748-5379.*
Ind/Abst Bus. Dateline (Feb. 2, 1992-) [Full Txt.].

US
HASTINGS DAILY TRIBUNE. (1???)-. Newspaper. English. da. $90.00 Nebraska; $108.00 other. Hastings Tribune, PO Box 788, Hastings NE 68901. **Tel** (402)462-2131.

US
KEARNEY DAILY HUB, THE. (1873)-. Newspaper. English. da. $86.00 Buffalo, Hall, Kearney, Dawson, Phelps and Custer counties; $95.50 other. Kearney Daily Hub, Box 1988, Kearney NE 68847. **Tel** (308)237-2152.

US
LINCOLN DAILY STAR, THE. Began with Oct. 2, 1902 issue. Newspaper. English. da (except Sun.). Journal Star Printing Company, 926 P Street, PO Box 81609, Lincoln NE 68508. **Tel** (402)475-4200. **ED** Tom White. **Circ:** 36,818.

US/1054-7983
LINCOLN JOURNAL (LINCOLN, NEB.). (LINCOLN JOURNAL.). **VFOAT** Sunday Journal and Star; Sunday Journal-Star; Lincoln Journal-Star. (Apr. 11, 1977)-. Newspaper. English. da. $142.60 (one year). Journal Star Printing Company, 926 P Street, PO Box 81609, Lincoln NE 68508. **Tel** (402)475-4200. **ED** Gary Seacrest, Bob Mayer, Dick Herman and Diane White. **Bk Rev. Ad Acc. Circ:** 43,752 (ctrl). ***Continues*** *Lincoln Evening Journal (Lincoln, Neb. : 1973).*

US/0746-0961
LOUISVILLE MESSENGER, THE. (19??)-. Newspaper. English. sw (Mon. & Thurs.). Louisville Messenger, PO Box 218, Louisville NE 68037. **Tel** (402)234-6695.

US
MCCOOK DAILY GAZETTE. (1924)-. Newspaper. English. ir (309 issues per year). $69.00 Decatur, Norton, Rawlins, and Cheyenne Cos. in KS and Dundy, Hitchcock, Furnas, Chase, Hayes, and Frontier in Nebraska; $89.00 other. McCook Daily Gazette, West 1st and E Streets, McCook NE 69001. **Tel** (308)345-4500. **ED** Jack Rogers. **Ad Acc. Circ:** 7,900 (ctrl).

US
NEBRASKA DAILY NEWS-PRESS. VFOAT Nebraska daily News Press; Nebraska City News-Press; Nebraska City News Press. (192?)-. Newspaper. English. da. $70.00. Nebraska Daily News-Press, 123 8th Street, Nebraska City NE 68410. **Tel** (402)873-3334, FAX (402)873-5436. **ED** Dan Swanson. **Photos. Ad Acc, Adv Mgr:** Greg Dillon. Full Page (B&W) $851.40. Half Page (B&W) $438.60. Full Page (Color) $901.40. Half Page (Color) $458.60. **Pub. Size:** Broadsheet. **Wire Svcs.:** AP. **Circ:** 2,850 (paid), 13,500 (free).

US/0028-1913
NEBRASKA NEWSPAPER. Added/Corp Nebraska Press Association. Nebraska. University. School of Journalism. (1948)-. Periodical. English. bm.

$10.50. Nebraska Press Association, 1120 K Street, Lincoln NE 68508-2853. **Tel** (402)476-2851, FAX (402)476-2942. **ED** Gary Seacrest. **LC** PN4700; .N39. **DD** 071/.82. **Photos. Ad Acc, Adv Mgr:** Mary Burt, **Tel** (402)476-2851. Full Page (B&W) $342.00. Half Page (B&W) $171.00. Full Page (Color) $412.00. Half Page (Color) $241.00. **Pub. Size:** Standard. **Circ:** 430.
Desc: Gives information concerning the events happening in the Nebraska newspaper industry.

US
NORFOLK DAILY NEWS. Newspaper. English. da. $75.00 Nebraska; $85.00 other. Norfolk Daily News, PO Box 977, Norfolk NE 68701. **Tel** (402)371-1020. Documents available from UMI Article Clearinghouse.
Ind/Abst Bus. Dateline (Feb. 6, 1992-) [Full Txt.].

US
OMAHA STAR, THE. (July 9, 1939)-. Periodical. English. wk. $26.00. Omaha Star, 2216 North 24th, PO Box 11128, Omaha NE 68110. **Tel** (402)346-4041. **ED** Marquerita L. Washington. **Bk Rev. Photos. Ad Acc, Adv Mgr:** Preston Love Sr. Full Page (B&W) $2,046.80. Half Page (B&W) $1,023.40. **Pub. Size:** Broadsheet.

US
OMAHA WORLD-HERALD (OMAHA, NB : 1954 : SUNRISE ED.). (OMAHA WORLD-HERALD.). **VFOAT** Omaha World Herald. Vol. 90, No. 1 (Oct. 2, 1954)-. Newspaper. English. da. $59.80. Omaha World Herald / Mail Subscription Department, World Herald World, 14th and Dodge, Omaha NE 68102. **Tel** (402)444-1000. **ED** G. Woodson Howe. **Bk Rev. Ad Acc. Circ:** 224,000 (ctrl). available on microfilm from University Microfilms International (UMI). ***Continues*** *Morning World-Herald (Omaha, Neb. : 1937).*
Ind/Abst PROMT.

US/0883-1394
PAPILLION TIMES. (1874)-. Newspaper. English. Fifty-two times a year. Papillion Times Printing Company, PO Box 145, Papillion NE 68046. **Tel** (402)339-3331.

US
PAWNEE REPUBLICAN. Began with Dec. 8, 1872 issue. Newspaper. English. wk. Pawnee Republican, PO Box 11, Pawnee NE 68420. ***Continues*** *Pawnee Tribune (Pawnee, Neb. : 1867);* ***Absorbed*** *Pawnee Tribune (Pawnee, Neb. : 1876); Pawnee Chief.*

US
PLATTSMOUTH EVENING JOURNAL. (1904)-. Newspaper. English. sw. $15.00 Cass, Otto, Douglas, Lancaster, Sarpy Counties; $20.00 US. Plattsmouth Journal, PO Box 250, 410 Main Street, Plattsmouth NE 68048. **Tel** (402)296-2141.

US
SCHUYLER SUN, THE. (1875)-. Newspaper. English. wk. Schuyler Sun, 1112 C Street, Schuyler NE 68661. ***Continues*** *Schuyler Register.*

US
SCOTTSBLUFF DAILY STAR-HERALD. VFOAT Scottsbluff Daily Star Herald. (July 1, 1924)-. Newspaper. English. da. Scottsbluff Daily Star-Herald, 1405 Broadway, Scottsbluff NE 69361. **LC** 8686. ***Continues*** *Scottsbluff Star-Herald;* ***Absorbed*** *Daily Tribune.*

US
SIDNEY TELEGRAPH (SIDNEY, NEB. : 1951). (THE SIDNEY TELEGRAPH.). (1???)-. Newspaper. English. da. $65.00. Sidney Telegraph, 809 Illinois Street, Sidney NE 69162. **ED** Don Evans (Editor-in-Chief) and Gordon Tustin (Managing Editor). **Photos. Ad Acc, Adv Mgr:** Sue Kilgore, **Tel** (308)254-5555. Full Page (B&W) $917.19. Half Page (B&W) $458.59. Full Page (Color) $1,007.19. Half Page (Color) $548.59. **Pub. Size:** Standard. **Wire Svcs.:** AP. available in microform.

US
SUNDAY JOURNAL AND STAR. Jan. 10, 1932-. Newspaper. English. wk. Journal Star Printing Company, 926 P Street, PO Box 81609, Lincoln NE 68508. **Tel** (402)475-4200. ***Continues*** *Sunday State Journal and Lincoln Sunday Star.*

US
SUNDAY WORLD-HERALD (OMAHA, NEB. : 1937). (SUNDAY WORLD-HERALD.). **VFOAT** Sunday World Herald. Vol. 52, No. 50 (Aug. 29, 1937)-. Newspaper. English. wk. World-Herald Square, Omaha NE 68102. **Tel** (402)444-1000. **ED** G Woodson Howe. **Circ:** 283,783. available on microfilm. ***Continues*** *Omaha World-Herald (Omaha, Neb. : 1928 : Sunday Ed.).*

US/0740-0969
SUPERIOR EXPRESS, THE. (19??)-. Newspaper. English. wk. $14.00 (local). Superior Express, 148 East 3rd Street, Superior NE 68978. **Tel** (402)879-3291. **ED** Bill Blauvelt. **Photos. Ad Acc, Adv Mgr:** Sherri Nun. Full Page (B&W) $378.00. Half Page (B&W) $200.00. **Pub. Size:** Broadsheet. **Circ:** 4,000.

US/0747-4008
TELEGRAPH (NORTH PLATTE, NEB.). (TELEGRAPH.). (19??)-. Newspaper. English. da. North Platte Telegraph, Box 370, 621 North Chestnut Street, North Platte NE 69101. **Tel** (800)658-4244. ***Continues*** *North Platte Telegraph.*

US/8750-3484
WALTHILL CITIZEN, THE. Newspaper. English. wk. Walthill Citizen, PO Box 7, Walthill NE 68067.

US/1060-3026
WINNEBAGO INDIAN NEWS. Added/Corp Winnebago Tribe of Nebraska. Vol. 5, No. 8 (Aug. 8, 1991)-. Newspaper. English. bw. $5.00 (in state), $10.00 (out-of-state). Winnebago Indian News, PO Box 687, Winnebago NE 68071. available on microfilm. ***Continues*** *WIN (Winnebago, Neb.), 1056-1323.*

NEVADA

US
BATTLE MOUNTAIN BUGLE. No. 1 (May 27, 1976)-. Newspaper. English. wk. $17.00. Battle Mountain Bugle, 163 Broad Street, Battle Mountain NV 89820. **Tel** (702)635-2230.

US
BOULDER CITY NEWS (1948). (BOULDER CITY NEWS.). Vol. 11, No. 22 (Feb. 4, 1948)-. Newspaper. English. wk. $35.00 west of Mississippi River; $38.00 east of Mississippi. HBC Publications, PO Box 90430, Henderson NV 89009. **Tel** (702)565-1881. ***Continues*** *Boulder City Daily News.* ***Continued in part by*** *Henderson Home News.*

US
CARSON VALLEY CHRONICLE. (19??)-. Newspaper. English. wk. Free. Carson Valley Chronicle, 200 Batch Street, PO Box 2288, Carson City NV 89701. **Tel** (702)882-2111, FAX (702)882-6664. **ED** Don Ham and Patt Quinn Davis (Managing Editor). **Bk Rev**, (Qty: 12). **Photos. Ad Acc, Adv Mgr:** Loren Abbott, **Tel** (702)882-2111 ext.269. Full Page (B&W) $1,154.55. Half Page (B&W) $419.25. Full Page (Color) $1,290.55. Half Page (Color) $555.25. **Pub. Size:** Standard. **Circ:** 19,275.

US/0896-9353
COMSTOCK CHRONICLE. (1987)-. Newspaper. English. Fifty-two times a year. $17.50. Comstock Chronicle, PO Box 530, Virginia City NV 89440. **Tel** (702)847-0765, FAX (702)847-0765. **ED** Martin Lane. **Bk Rev**, (Qty: 10). **Photos. Ad Acc, Adv Mgr:** Nick Nicosia. Full Page (B&W) $300.00. Half Page (B&W) $150.00. **Pub. Size:** Tabloid. available on microfilm.

US/0899-9538
DAILY SPARKS TRIBUNE, THE. (198?)-. Newspaper. English. da. Sparks Tribune / Nevada, 1000 C Street, PO Box 887, Sparks NV 89431. **Tel** (702)358-8061. ***Continues*** *Sparks Tribune, 0891-513X.*

US/0746-7419
DEATH VALLEY GATEWAY GAZETTE. VFOAT Gateway Gazette. Vol. 1, No. 1 (July 22, 1983)-. Newspaper. English. wk. $15.00 US; $30.00 other. Gateway Gazette, PO Box 2765, Pahrump NV 89041. **Tel** (702)553-2707. **ED** Bob and Helaine Lowe. **Bk Rev. Ad Acc. Circ:** 5,500.

US
ELKO DAILY FREE PRESS. 49th Year, No. 71 (June 15, 1931)-. Newspaper. English. da (Published 6 days a week). $84.50. Free Press Publishing Company, 3720 Idaho Street, Elko NV 89801. **Tel** (702)738-3118, FAX (702)738-2215. **ED** Rex Steninger. **Photos. Ad Acc, Adv Mgr:** Glenas Bir. Full Page (B&W) $1032.00. Full Page (Color) $1032.00 plus $150.00 per color. **Pub. Size:** Standard. **Wire Svcs.:** AP. **Circ:** 7,500 paid. available on microfiche. ***Continues*** *Elko Free Press (1919).*
Desc: Carries local and national news.

US
ELKO INDEPENDENT (1915). (ELKO INDEPENDENT.). **VFOAT** Weekly Elko Independent. Vol. 48, No. 74 (March 30, 1915)-. Newspaper. English. wk. $18.00 Nevada; $21.00 other. Elko Independent, 276 11th Street, Elko NV 89801. **Tel** (702)738-3611, FAX (702)738-1453. **ED** Kay Thompson. **Bk Rev. Photos. Ad Acc, Adv Mgr:** Sean Thompson. Full Page (B&W) $567.50. Half Page (B&W) $283.50. **Pub. Size:** Standard. ***Continues*** *Daily Independent (Elko, Nev.).*

US
ELY DAILY TIMES (1961). (ELY DAILY TIMES.). Vol. 41, No. 347 (July 17, 1961)-. Newspaper. English. da. Ely Daily Times, 655 Aultman Street, Ely NV 89301. ***Continues*** *Daily Times (Ely, Nev.).*

US
EUREKA SENTINEL (EUREKA, NEV. : 1902). (THE EUREKA SENTINEL.). (Jan. 18, 1902)-. Newspaper. English. wk. $19.00. Central Nevada Newspapers, PO Box 193, Tonopah NV 89049. **Tel** (702) 482-3365. **ED** William G Roberts. **Bk Rev. Ad Acc. Circ:** 550 (ctrl). ***Continues*** *Eureka Weekly Sentinel (Eureka, Nev. : 1887).*

US
GREEN VALLEY NEWS. English. wk. $25.00. HBC Publications, PO Box 90430, Henderson NV 89009. **Tel** (702)565-1881.

US
HENDERSON HOME NEWS. (Jan. 15, 1950)-. Newspaper. English. sw. $30.00 west of Mississippi; $35.00 east of Mississippi. HBC Publications, PO Box 90430, Henderson NV 89009. **Tel** (702)565-1881. **ED** John Dailey. **LC** 8694. **Bk Rev. Ad Acc. Circ:** 7,890 (ctrl). ***Continues in part*** *Boulder City News.*
Desc: Local news.

US
HUMBOLDT SUN. Vol. 1, No. 1 (Jan. 19, 1972)-. Newspaper. English. sw. $35.00. Humboldt Sun, PO Box 3000, Winnemucca NV 89446. **Tel** (702)623-5011, FAX (702)623-5243. **ED** Susan Brockus. **Bk Rev. Photos. Ad Acc. Pub. Size:** Broadsheet. **Circ:** 5,000 (paid, semiweekly). available on microfilm from Bay Microfilm, Inc; and University Microfilms International (UMI).

US
LAHONTAN VALLEY NEWS AND FALLON EAGLE STANDARD. Vol. 81, No. 51 (Jan. 8, 1985)-. Newspaper. English. da (Except national holidays). $89.00. Lahontan Valley Printing Inc., 60 West Center Street, PO Box 1297, Fallon NV 89406. **Tel** FAX (702)423-0474. ***Formed by the union of*** *Lahontan Valley News* ***and*** *Eagle Standard.*

•US/1071-2186
LAS VEGAS BUSINESS PRESS. VFOAT Business Press. (1993)-. Newspaper. English. wk. $48.00. Las Vegas Business Press, 5300 West Sahara, Suite 101, Las Vegas NV 89102. **Tel** (702)871-6780. available on an online database (file 635/Full Text) from DIALOG. Documents available from UMI Article Clearinghouse.
Ind/Abst Bus. Dateline (May 1986-) [Full Txt.].

US
LAS VEGAS REVIEW-JOURNAL. VFOAT Las Vegas Review Journal; Las Vegas Review-Journal and Boulder City Journal. Vol. 41, No. 73 (April 3, 1949)-. Newspaper. English. da. $30.00 (Sunday), $33.00 (daily), $36.00 (daily & Sunday). Las Vegas Review Journal, 1111 West Bonanza Road, Las Vegas NV 89125. **Tel** (702)383-0473, FAX (702)383-4699. **ED** Tom Keevil and Thomas Mitchell and Charles Zobell (Managing Editor). **Bk Rev. Photos. Ad Acc, Adv Mgr:** Jack Harpster, **Tel** (702)383-0388. Full Page (Color) $610.00. **Pub. Size:** Standard. **Wire Svcs.:** AP, KR, LA. **Circ:** 108,687 daily, 124,939 Sunday. available on microfilm. ***Continues*** *Las Vegas Evening Review-Journal and Boulder City Journal.*

US
LAS VEGAS SUN. VFOAT Sunday Las Vegas Sun. Vol. 2, No. 183 (Jan. 1, 1952)-. Newspaper. English. da. $30.00 (Sunday), $28.00 (daily), $32.40 (daily & Sunday). Las Vegas Sun, PO Box 70, 1111 West Bonanza Road, Las Vegas NV 89125. **Tel** (702)385-3111. **ED** H. M. Greenspun. **Circ:** 62,735 daily, 97,369 Sun., 38,512 daily & Sun. available on microfilm from University Microfilms International (UMI). ***Continues*** *Las Vegas Morning Sun.*

US/8755-3260
LINCOLN COUNTY RECORD (PIOCHE, NEV. : 1968). (LINCOLN COUNTY RECORD.). **VFOAT** Record. Vol. 98, No. 27 (June 6, 1968)-. Newspaper. English. wk. $10.00 Lincoln county; $15.00 other. Lincoln County Record, 1001 Ranch, Caliente NV 89008. **Tel** (702)726-3333. **ED** Connie Simkins. **Bk Rev**, (Qty: 12). **Photos. Ad Acc.** Full Page (B&W) $325.00. Half Page (B&W) $200.00. Full Page (Color) $400.00. Half Page (Color) $270.00. **Pub. Size:** Tabloid. **Circ:** 1,600 (weekly,paid) (ctrl). available in microform from Bay Microfilm, Inc.

US
LOVELOCK REVIEW-MINER. VFOAT Lovelock Review Miner. Vol. 22, No. 20 (May 24, 1929)-. Newspaper. English. wk (Published on Thursdays). $18.00 Lovelock County; $25.00 Utah; $30.00 US. Lovelock Tribune Inc, PO Box 620, Lovelock NV 89419. **Tel** (702)273-7245. **ED** Gwen Carter. **Ad Acc. Circ:** 1,500 (ctrl). ***Continues*** *Review-Miner.*
Desc: Local newspaper serving all of Pershing County, Nevada.

US
MASON VALLEY NEWS. VFOAT Mason Valley News & Yerington Times. Vol. 1, No. 1 (March 19, 1909)-.

Newspaper. English. wk. Emerson Publishing Company, PO Box DD, Yerington NV 89447. ***Absorbed*** *Tri-Town Times.*

US
MINERAL COUNTY INDEPENDENT AND HAWTHORNE NEWS. **VFOAT** Mineral County Independent-News. Vol. 3, No. 22 (July 24, 1935)-. Newspaper. English. wk. PO Box 1277, Hawthorne NV 89415. ***Formed by the union of*** *Mineral County Independent* ***and*** *Hawthorne News.*

US
NEVADA APPEAL (CARSON CITY, NEV. : 1968). (NEVADA APPEAL.). Vol. 104, No. 220 (Sept. 1, 1968)-. Newspaper. English. da (except Sat.). $234.00 (daily & Sunday by mail). Nevada Appeal, PO Box 2288, Carson City NV 89702. **Tel** (702)882-2111, FAX (702)882-6664. **ED** Don Ham and Patt Quinn-Davis (Managing Editor). **Bk Rev**, (Qty: 12). **Photos. Ad Acc, Adv Mgr:** Loren Abbott, **Tel** (702)882-2111 ext. 269. Full Page (B&W) $1,154.55. Half Page (B&W) $419.25. Full Page (Color) $1,290.55. Half Page (Color) $555.25. **Pub. Size:** Standard. **Wire Svcs.:** AP. **Circ:** 10,268. available in microform. ***Continues*** *Carson City Nevada Appeal (Carson City, Nev. : 1955).*

US
NEVADA APPEAL. CHRONICLE EDITION. Vol. 57, No. 31 (Feb. 1, 1984)-. Newspaper. English. wk. Nevada Appeal, PO Box 2288, Carson City NV 89702. **Tel** (702)882-2111, FAX (702)882-6664. ***Continues*** *Carson Chronicle (Carson City, Nev. : 1969).*

US/0192-3129
NORTH LAKE TAHOE BONANZA. (May 5, 1976)-. Newspaper. English. sw (Wed. and Fri.). $38.00. North Lake Tahoe Bonanza, PO Box 7820, Incline Village NV 89450. **Photos. Ad Acc, Adv Mgr:** Lucy Karnes, **Tel** (702)831-4666. **Pub. Size:** Standard. available in microform.

US/8755-4631
RECORD-COURIER (GARDNERVILLE, NEV.). (THE RECORD-COURIER.). **VFOAT** Record Courier. Vol. 24, No. 8 (April 8, 1904)-. Newspaper. English. sw. $39.00. Record-Courier, 1218 West Eddy Street, Gardnerville NV 89410. **Tel** (702)782-5121, (702)882-2553, FAX (702)882-2556. **ED** Sheila Gardner. **Ad Acc, Adv Mgr:** Toni. ctrl circ. ***Formed by the union of*** *Courier (Gardnerville, Nev.)* ***and*** *Record (Gardnerville, Nev.).*

US
REESE RIVER REVEILLE (AUSTIN, NEV. : 1950). ***Ceased.*** (REESE RIVER REVEILLE.). Vol. 128, No. 7 (May 13, 1950)-(19??). Newspaper. English. wk. Central Nevada Newspapers, PO Box 193, Tonopah NV 89049. **Tel** (702) 482-3365. **ED** William G Roberts. **Bk Rev. Ad Acc. Circ:** 500 (ctrl). available on microfilm from Bell & Howell. ***Continues*** *Reese River Reveille and Austin Sun.*

US/0745-1415
RENO GAZETTE-JOURNAL. **VFOAT** Reno Gazette Journal; Sunday Reno Gazette-Journal; Sunday Reno Gazette Journal. (Oct. 1, 1983)-. Newspaper. English. da. $39.00 (12 weeks). Reno Newspapers Inc., 955 Kuenzli, PO Box 22000, Reno NV 89520-2000. **Tel** (702)788-6200, (800)648-5048, FAX (702)788-6458 newsroom, (702)788-6436 advertising. **ED** Ward Bushee, Tonia Cunning (Managing Editor). **Photos. Ad Acc, Adv Mgr:** John Zidich, **Tel** (702)788-6236. Full Page (B&W) $3738.42. Half Page (B&W) $1825.74. Full Page (Color) $4343.42. Half Page (Color) $2430.74. **Pub. Size:** Standard. **Wire Svcs.:** AP, LA, WP, GN. **Circ:** 60,976 daily, 72,398 Sunday. available in microform from Nevada Historical Society. ***Formed by the union of*** *Nevada State Journal (Reno, Nev. : 1907)* ***and*** *Reno Evening Gazette, 0745-1431.*

US
TONOPAH TIMES-BONANZA AND GOLDFIELD NEWS. **VFOAT** Goldfield News and Tonopah Times Bonanza. (Jan. 4, 1957)-. Newspaper. English. wk. $19.00 Nye County residents; $20.00 other. Central Nevada Newspapers, PO Box 193, Tonopah NV 89049. **Tel** (702) 482-3365. **ED** William G. Roberts. **Bk Rev. Ad Acc. Circ:** 3,200 (ctrl). ***Formed by the union of*** *Tonopah Times-Bonanza* ***and*** *Goldfield News and Beatty Bulletin.*

NEW HAMPSHIRE

US/0192-8597
1590 BROADCASTER. **VAT** One Thousand Five Hundred and Ninety Broadcaster. (19??)-. Newspaper. English. wk (Wed.). $20.00. 1590 Broadcaster, PO Box 548, Nashua NH 03061-0548. **Tel** (603)882-1590, FAX (603)883-4344. **ED** Maurice R. Parent. **Photos. Ad Acc, Adv Mgr:** Maurice Parent. Full Page (B&W) $1,092.00. Half Page (B&W) $546.00. Full Page (Color) $1,292.00. Half Page (Color) $746.00. **Pub. Size:** Tabloid. **Circ:** 64,000.

US
ARGUS-CHAMPION, THE. **VFOAT** Argus Champion. Vol. 148, No. 49 (Dec. 8, 1971)-. Newspaper. English. wk. $25.00. Argus-Champion, PO Box 509, Newport NH 03773. **Tel** (603)863-1776, FAX (603)863-0066. **ED** Jeff Shippee. **Bk Rev**, (Qty: 10). **Photos. Ad Acc, Adv Mgr:** Robert Shemphe. Full Page (B&W) $844.95. Half Page (B&W) $451.75. Full Page (Color) $879.95. Half Page (Color) $486.75. **Pub. Size:** Standard. available in microform. ***Continues*** *Argus-Champion and Newport-Lake Sunapee Times.*

US/1074-3499
BERLIN REPORTER, THE. Vol. 1, No. 1 (Oct. 8, 1897)-. Newspaper. English. da. Berlin Reporter, 151 Main Street, Berlin NH 03570. **Tel** (603)752-1200, FAX (603)752-2339. **ED** Ben Gagnon. **Ad Acc, Adv Mgr:** Lucille Jalbert. **Circ:** 6,500.

US
CARROLL COUNTY INDEPENDENT CARROLL COUNTY PIONEER. **VFOAT** Carroll County Independent and Pioneer; Carroll County Independent and Carroll County Pioneer. Vol. 40, No. 47 (July 18, 1924)-. Newspaper. English. wk. $18.00 New Hampshire; $22.00 other. Carroll County Independent Inc, Center Ossipee NH 03814. **Tel** (603)539-4111. ***Continues*** *Carroll County Pioneer.*

US
CONCORD MONITOR (CONCORD, N.H. : 1970). (CONCORD MONITOR.). No. 192 (Aug. 18, 1970)-. Newspaper. English. da. $221.00 Merrimack County; $239.20 other. Concord Monitor, 3 North State Street, PO Box 1177, Concord NH 03301. **Tel** (603)224-5301. **ED** Michael Pride. **Ad Acc. Circ:** 21,479. ***Continues*** *Concord Daily Monitor (Concord, N.H. : 1946).*

US
COOS COUNTY DEMOCRAT, THE. Vol. 1, No. 1 (Aug. 27, 1884)-. Newspaper. English. wk. $24.00. North Country Publishing Company, 79 Main Street, PO Box 28, Lancaster NH 03584. **Tel** (603)788-4939. **ED** John D. Harrigan (Editor-in-Chief) and Gene Ehlert (Managing Editor). **Photos. Ad Acc, Adv Mgr:** Sue Hikel. Full Page (B&W) $1,008.00. Half Page (B&W) $504.00. Full Page (Color) $1,108.00. Half Page (Color) $604.00. **Pub. Size:** Broadsheet. available in microform. ***Absorbed*** *Groveton Enterprise; Whitefield Times; Jefferson Times* ***and*** *Lancaster Gazette (Lancasster, N.H.).*

US
COURIER, THE. (Oct. 11, 1984)-. Newspaper. English. wk. $25.00. White Mountain Publishing, 146 Union Street, Littleton NH 03561. **Tel** (603)444-3927, FAX (603)444-3920. **ED** Olivia Garfield. **Photos. Ad Acc, Adv Mgr:** Georgia Golden. Full Page (B&W) $535.50. Half Page (B&W) $286.65. Full Page (Color) $635.50. Half Page (Color) $386.65. **Circ:** 7,000. ***Continues*** *Littleton Courier.*

US
DERRY NEWS, THE. **VFOAT** Derry Twice Weekly News; Derry News & Salem Enterprise; Derry-Salem News Enterprise; Derry News-Salem Enterprise. Vol. 83, No. 9 (May 2, 1963)-. Newspaper. English. sw. $32.00. Derry News, 46 West Broadway, Derry NH 03038. **Tel** (603)432-3363. **ED** Robert Wallack (Editor-in-Chief) and Carol Settino (Managing Editor). **Photos. Ad Acc, Adv Mgr:** Ellen Wolslegel, **Tel** (603)437-7000. Full Page (B&W) $1,373.40. Half Page (B&W) $686.70. Full Page (Color) $1,498.40. Half Page (Color) $811.70. **Pub. Size:** Broadsheet. **Circ:** 11,000. ***Continues*** *Derry News & Salem Enterprise.*

US
EAGLE TIMES. **VFOAT** Sunday Eagle Times. Vol. 1, No. 1 (Nov. 1, 1974)-. Newspaper. English. da. $171.00. Eagle Times Claremont New Hampshire, 19 Sullivan Street, Claremont NH 03743. **Tel** (603)542-5121. ***Formed by the union of*** *Daily Eagle (Claremont, N.H.)* ***and*** *Springfield Bellows Falls Times Reporter.*

US/8750-6386
EVENING CITIZEN (LACONIA, N.H.), THE. (THE EVENING CITIZEN.). **VFOAT** Laconia, N.H., Evening. Vol. 58, No. 21 (Jan. 26, 1984)-. Newspaper. English. da. $119.20. Citizen Publishing Company, PO Box 40, Laconia NH 03246. **Tel** (603)524-3806, (800)852-0411. **ED** Larry Smith. **Circ:** 10,881. ***Continues*** *Laconia Evening Citizen.*

US/0886-3962
EXETER NEWS-LETTER (1867), THE. (THE EXETER NEWS-LETTER.). **VFOAT** Exeter News Letter; Exeter Newsletter. Vol. 36, No. 44 (Jan. 14, 1867)-. Newspaper. English. sw. $32.00. Exeter News-Letter, PO Box 250, 255 Water Street, Exeter NH 03833-0250. **Tel** (603)772-6000. **ED** Robert M Herbert. **Bk Rev. Ad Acc. Circ:** 6,630. available on microfilm. ***Continues*** *Exeter News-Letter and Rockingham Advertiser;* ***Absorbed*** *Chronicle (Seabrook, N.H.).*

US/0892-6026
FOSTER'S DAILY DEMOCRAT. (June 18, 1873)-. Newspaper. English. ir (305 issues per year). $124.00 New Hampshire and Maine; $130.00 US. Foster's Daily Democrat, 333 Central Avenue, Dover NH 03820. **Tel** (603)742-4455. **LC** 7002.

US
HAMPTON UNION, THE. Vol. 82, No. 12 (Oct. 6, 1982)-. Newspaper. English. wk. Rockingham County Newspapers, PO Box 250, Exeter NH 03833-0250. **Tel** (603)772-6000. ***Continues*** *Hampton Union and the Bordertown News.*

US/0193-0532
IRREGULAR & MOUNT WASHINGTON VALLEY NEWS, THE. ***Title Change.*** **VFOAT** Irregular. (197?)-(19??). Newspaper. English. wk. PO Box 728, North Conway NH 03860. ***Continued by*** *Irregular (North Conway, N.H.).*

US
KEENE SENTINEL, THE. No. 197 (Aug. 22, 1972)-. Newspaper. English. da. Keene Evening Sentinel, 60 West Street, Keene NH 03431. **Tel** (603)352-1234. ***Continues*** *Keene Evening Sentinel.*

US/1062-5070
MANCHESTER JOURNAL (MANCHESTER, VT.), THE. (THE MANCHESTER JOURNAL.). (May 28, 1861)-. Newspaper. English. Fifty-two times a year. Free. Southern New Hampshire Publishers, 177 East Industrial Drive, Manchester NH 03103. **Tel** (603)668-7330. available on microfilm.
Ind/Abst Acad. Search (19??-19??); Bus. Index (Jan. 1985-Dec. 1985); Gen. BusinessFile (Jan. 1985-Dec. 1985); Gen. Period. Index (Jan. 1985-Dec. 1985).

US
MEREDITH NEWS, THE. (July 1880)-. Newspaper. English. wk. $26.00. Meredith News, PO Box 729, Meredith NH 03253. **Tel** (603)279-4516, FAX (603)279-3331. **ED** Rudy VanVeghten. **LC** 8701-X. **Photos. Ad Acc, Adv Mgr:** David French. Full Page (B&W) $405.00. Half Page (B&W) $202.50. Full Page (Color) $475.00. Half Page (Color) $277.50. **Circ:** 4,500. ***Continues*** *Meredith Weekly News.*

US
MILFORD CABINET AND WILTON JOURNAL, THE. Vol. 170, No. 23 (Dec. 7, 1972)-. Newspaper. English. wk. Milford Cabinet, PO Box 180, Milford NH 03055. **Tel** (603)673-3100. ***Continues*** *Milford Cabinet.*

US
NASHUA DAILY TELEGRAPH. ***Title Change.*** **VFOAT** Daily Evening Telegraph; Daily Nashua Telegraph. Vol. 1, No. 1 (March 1, 1869)-Vol. 36, No. 299 (Feb. 19, 1904). Newspaper. English. da (and Sunday). Nashua Telegraph, PO Box 1008, Nashua NH 03061. **Tel** (603)882-2741. **(Subscription address:** PO Box 1008, Nashua, NH 03061**) ED** Ken Frizell. **LC** 8701-X. **Circ:** 32,575. ***Continued by*** *Nashua Telegraph (Nashua, N.H. : Daily).*

US
NEW HAMPSHIRE BUSINESS JOURNAL. (1985)-. Newspaper. English. mo. $9.00. New Hampshire Business Journal, PO Box 2393, Concord NH 03301. **Tel** (603)224-6566. **ED** Jane Holiday (Editor-in-Chief) and Barb Johnson (Managing Editor). Full Page (B&W) $950.00. Half Page (B&W) $425.00. Full Page (Color) $1,650.00. Half Page (Color) $950.00. **Pub. Size:** Tabloid. available in microform.
Ind/Abst Acad. Search (Jan. 1994-); Bus. Index (Jan. 1985-Dec.1985); Gen. BusinessFile (Jan. 1985-Dec. 1985); Gen. Period. Index (Jan. 1985-Dec. 1985).

US/0892-8703
NEW HAMPSHIRE SUNDAY NEWS. Vol. 1, No. 1 (Oct. 6, 1946)-. Newspaper. English. wk. $6.00 (4 weeks), $18.85 (13 weeks), $36.40 (26 weeks), $70.20 (52 weeks) by mail New Hampshire; $6.80 (4 weeks), $21.45 (13 weeks), $41.60 (26 weeks), $80.60 (52 weeks) by mail continental US; $195.00 (New Hampshire), $221.00 (US) by mail combined with Manchester Union Leader; $10.00 (8 weeks), $16.25 (13 weeks), $31.72 (26 weeks), $62.40 (52 weeks) by carrier; $26.80 (8 weeks), $43.55 (13 weeks), $83.20 (26 weeks), $162.24 (52 weeks) by carrier combined with Manchester Union Leader. The Union Leader, PO Box 9555, Manchester NH 03108. **Tel** (603)668-4321, (800)562-8218. **ED** J W McQuaid. **DD** 071. **Circ:** 85,779. available on microfilm from University Microfilms International (UMI).

US
NEWS MESSENGER. (March 22, 1989)-. Newspaper. English. wk. Hillsboro News Messenger, PO Box 917, Hillsboro NH 03244-0918. **Tel** (603)464-3388. ***Continues*** *Messenger Outlook.*

US/1049-2399
OSSIPEE VALLEY TIMES. **VFOAT** Times. (1990)-. Newspaper. English. wk. $15.00. Read Advertising, PO Box 806, Wolfeboro Falls NH 03896. ***Continues*** *Carroll County Times (Wolfeboro Falls, N.H.).*

US
PETERBOROUGH TRANSCRIPT, THE. **VFOAT** Peterboro's Transcript. Vol. 6, No 1 (May 24, 1854)-. Newspaper. English. wk. $20.00 New Hampshire; $24.00 others. The Peterborough Transcript, 43 Grove Street, Peterborough NH 03458. **ED** Marsha Morrow. **Bk Rev**, (Qty: 12). **Photos**. **Ad Acc**, **Adv Mgr:** Cher Powers, **Tel** (603)924-3333. Full Page (B&W) $623.70. Half Page (B&W) $346.50. Full Page (Color) $703.70. Half Page (Color) $426.50. **Pub. Size:** Standard. ***Continues*** *Contoocook Transcript;* ***Absorbed*** *Jaffrey Recorder-Transcript.*

US/0746-6218
PORTSMOUTH HERALD, THE. (1936)-. Newspaper. English. da. $97.00. The Portsmouth Herald, 111 Maplewood Avenue, Portsmouth NH 03801. **Tel** (603)436-1800. **ED** J. Whiteman. **LC** 7002. **Bk Rev**. **Ad Acc**. **Circ:** 13,000. ***Continues*** *Portsmouth Herald and Times;* ***Absorbed*** *New Hampshire Gazette.*
Desc: General local news, national and syndicated news and pictures.

US/1070-745X
RECORD ENTERPRISE (PLYMOUTH, N.H.), THE. (THE RECORD ENTERPRISE.). (19??)-. Newspaper. English. wk. $21.00 Merrimack, Bilknap & Grafton counties; $26.00 others. White Mountain Publishing, 146 Union Street, Littleton NH 03561. **Tel** (603)444-3927, (800)639-3061, FAX (603)444-3920. **ED** Brian McCarthy (Editor-in-Chief) and Bill York (Managing Editor). **Photos**. **Ad Acc**, **Adv Mgr:** Georgia Golden. Full Page (B&W) $326.25. Half Page (B&W) $163.13. **Pub. Size:** Tabloid. **Circ:** 6,000. ***Formed by the union of*** *Record Citizen* ***and*** *Enterprise (Bristol, N.H.).*

US
SALEM OBSERVER. Vol. 19, No. 17 (Sept. 5, 1984)-. Newspaper. English. wk. $18.00 New Hampshire; $21.00 others in New Hampshire; $24.00 others. Salem Observer, 380 Main Street, PO Box 720, Salem NH 03079. **Tel** (603)893-4356. **ED** Monique Dusamed. **Photos**. **Ad Acc**, **Adv Mgr:** Armend Beliyeau. Full Page (B&W) $1,103.76. Half Page (B&W) $551.88. Full Page (Color) $1,253.76. Half Page (Color) $626.88. ***Continues*** *Observer (Salem, N.H.).*

US
UNION LEADER (MANCHESTER, N.H. : STATE EDITION), THE. (THE UNION LEADER.). **VFOAT** Manchester (N.H.) Union Leader. 118th Year, No. 153 (Sept. 24, 1980)-. Newspaper. English. da (except Sunday). $12.00 (4 weeks), $36.66 (13 weeks), $70.20 (26 weeks), $124.80 (52 weeks) by mail New Hampshire; $13.20 (4 weeks), $40.56 (13 weeks), $78.00 (26 weeks), $140.40 (52 weeks) by mail continental US; $195.00 (New Hampshire), $221.00 (US) by mail combined with New Hampshire Sunday News; $16.80 (8 weeks), $27.30 (13 weeks), $51.48 (26 weeks), $99.84 (52 weeks) by carrier; $26.80 (8 weeks), $43.55 (13 weeks), $83.20 (26 weeks), $162.24 (52 weeks) by carrier combined with New Hampshire Sunday News. The Union Leader, PO Box 9555, Manchester NH 03108. **Tel** (603)668-4321, (800)562-8218. **ED** J W McQuaid. **Circ:** 68,838. available on microfilm from University Microfilms International (UMI). ***Continues*** *Manchester New Hampshire Union Leader (Manchester, N.H. : State Ed.).*

US
VALLEY NEWS. Vol. 1, No. 1 (June 9, 1952)-. Newspaper. English. da. Valley News / New Hampshire, 7 Interchange Drive, West Lebanon NH 03784. **Tel** (603)298-8711. **ED** Jim Fox. **Ad Acc**, **Adv Mgr:** Terri Dudley. **Circ:** 19,000.

US/1053-1572
WORLDWISE (HANOVER, N.H.). (WORLDWISE.). [WorldWise]. **VFOAT** World Wise. Vol. 1, No. 1 (Nov. 1, 1989)-. Newspaper. English. Nine times a year. $19.95 US; $23.00 Canada and Mexico; $25.00 other. South North News Service Inc., 4 West Wheelock, Department CS, Hanover NH 03755. **Tel** (603)643-5071, FAX (603)643-9599. **ED** Peter B. Martin. **DD** 990. **Photos**. **Ad Acc**, **Adv Mgr:** Grace Kelly, **Tel** same as publisher. **Circ:** 26,000.
Desc: Newspaper on the current events of the world.

NEW JERSEY

US/1042-6965
AMERICA OGGI. [Am. oggi]. **VFOAT** Oggi. Vol. 1, No. 1 (Nov. 14, 1988)-. Newspaper. Italian. da (Sat./Sun. issue combined). $200.00. America Oggi, 41 Bergenline Avenue, Westwood NJ 07675. **Tel** (201)358-6692. **ED** Andrea Mantineo. **DD** 085. **Bk Rev**, (Qty: 50). **Photos**. **Ad Acc**, **Adv Mgr:** Louis d'Alo, **Tel** (201)358-6582. **Pub. Size:** Standard. **Wire Svcs.:** AP. **Circ:** 60,000 (daily, morning) (ctrl). available in microform from New York Public Library.
Desc: Newspaper for Italian-Americans.

US
ASBURY PARK PRESS. **VFOAT** Asbury Park Sunday Press. 95th Year, No. 230 (Sept. 1974)-. Newspaper. English. da. $106.60 Sunday only; $182.00 daily; $115.20 carrier; $275.60 daily & Sunday. Asbury Park Press, 3601 Highway 66, Box 1550, Neptune NJ 07754. **Tel** (908)922-6000 ext. 2216. **ED** E. Donald Lass. cum. index. **Bk Rev**. **Ad Acc**. **Circ:** 140,000 daily, 210,000 Sunday (ctrl). available on microfilm from Norton Micro Images; and University Microfilms International (UMI). ***Continues*** *Asbury Park Evening Press.*
Desc: Newspaper serving Monmouth and Ocean counties with general news and advertising.

US/0192-5741
ATOM TABLOID. MIDDLESEX COUNTY EDITION, THE. (THE ATOM TABLOID.). Newspaper. English. wk. Atom Tabloid, 219 Central Avenue, Rahway NJ 07065.

US
BEACH HAVEN TIMES. Began in 1923. Newspaper. English. wk. Manahawkin Newspapers Inc, 345 East Bay Avenue, Manahawkin NJ 08050. available on microfilm from Micro-Graphic Corp.

US/0194-6307
BEACHCOMBER, THE. (19??)-. Periodical. English. wk. Free in Southern Ocean County, $12.00 others. Beachcomber, 21st Street and Central Avenue, Ship Bottom NJ 08008.

US/1044-4289
BEACON (1989), THE. (THE BEACON.). (May 1989)-. Newspaper. English. wk. Princeton Packet Inc, PO Box AF, Circulation Department, Princeton NJ 08542. **Tel** (609)924-3244, FAX (609)921-2714. **ED** Richard Willever. **Ad Acc**, **Adv Mgr:** Martin Hilson. **Circ:** 3,287. ***Continues*** *Beacon and Lambertville Record Combined with New Hope News, 0746-5831.*

US
BELLEVILLE POST. (1982)-. Newspaper. English. wk. Worrall Community Newspapers Inc., 266 Liberty Street, Bloomfield NJ 07003-0110. **Tel** (201)743-4040, FAX (201)680-8848. **ED** David Worrall. **Bk Rev**. **Ad Acc**. **Circ:** 12,000.

US
BELLEVILLE TIMES NEWS, THE. (1945)-. Newspaper. English. wk. Belleville Times News, 155A Washington Avenue, Belleville NJ 07109. **Tel** (201)759-3200. **ED** Anthony Buccino. **Bk Rev**. **Ad Acc**. **Circ:** 12,500. ***Continues*** *Belleville News (Belleville, N.J.).*

US/0094-7989
BERGEN COUNTY HISTORY. **Added/Corp** Bergen County Historical Society. (1970)-. English. $3.25. Bergen County Historical Society, Box 55, River Edge NJ 07661. **Tel** (201)343-9492. **LC** F142.B4; B42. **DD** 917.49/21/034.

US
BLAIRSTOWN PRESS (BLAIRSTOWN, N.J. : 1877). (THE BLAIRSTOWN PRESS.). Vol. 1, No. 1 (Feb. 7, 1877)-. Newspaper. English. wk. Blairstown Press, Route 94/Box 425, Blairstown NJ 07825.

US/1047-3351
BOUND BROOK CHRONICLE (1971). (BOUND BROOK CHRONICLE.). No. 26 (July 1, 1971)-. Newspaper. English. wk. Somerset Press Inc, 15 Maiden Lane, Bound Brook NJ 08805. available on microfilm from University Microfilms International (UMI). ***Continues*** *Bound Brook Chronicle, State Centre-Record and Somerset Advocate.*

US
BRIDGETON EVENING NEWS. Began with Feb. 1, 1879 issue. Newspaper. English. da. $98.40. Bridgeton Evening News, 100 East Commerce Street, Bridgeton NJ 08302. **Tel** (609)451-1000, FAX (609)451-7214. **ED** Dean R Schofield and Eillen Bennett. Index available. **Bk Rev**. **Ad Acc**. **Circ:** 12,240. available on microfilm from University Microfilms International (UMI).

US
BURLINGTON COUNTY TIMES (WILLINGBORO, N.J.). (BURLINGTON COUNTY TIMES.). (July 10, 1961)-. Newspaper. English. da. $140.00. Burlington County Times, Route 130, Willingboro NJ 08046. **Tel** (609)871-8001. available on microfilm from University Microfilms International (UMI); available on an online database (file 635/Full-Text) from DIALOG. Documents available from UMI Article Clearinghouse. ***Continues*** *Levittown Times.*
Ind/Abst Bus. Dateline (Nov. 22, 1991-) [Full Txt.].

US
CALDWELL PROGRESS (1942). (CALDWELL PROGRESS.). (Jan. 1942)-. Newspaper. English. wk. $16.00. Caldwell Progress, 6 Brookside Avenue, Caldwell NJ 07006. **ED** Jean E. Conlon. **Photos**. **Ad Acc**, **Adv Mgr:** Roger White. Full Page (B&W) $1,200.00. **Pub. Size:** Standard. ***Continues*** *Caldwell Progress-The Verona News.*

US
CAPE MAY COUNTY HERALD. **VFOAT** Herald-Lantern-Dispatch; Herald Lantern Dispatch. (19??)-. Newspaper. English. wk. Seawave Corporation, PO Box 430, Cape May NJ 08210.

US
CAPE MAY STAR AND WAVE. Began with May 17, 1919 issue. Newspaper. English. wk. Cape May Star and Wave, 513 Washington Mall, Cape May NJ 08204. **ED** F Mervyn Kent. ***Continues*** *Star and Wave (Cape May, N.J. : 1919).*

US
CENTRAL NEW JERSEY HOME NEWS, THE. **VFOAT** Home News. (April 1, 1985)-. Newspaper. English. da. Central New Jersey Home News, PO Box 551, New Brunswick NJ 08903. **Tel** 800 288-2472. **ED** Watson Sims. **Circ:** 58,994. available on microfilm from University Microfilms International (UMI). ***Continues*** *Home News (New Brunswick, N.J. : 1970).*

US/8750-1392
CENTRAL POST, THE. (1959)-. Newspaper. English. wk. $60.00 New Jersey; $42.00 other. Central Post / New Jersey, PO Box AF, Princeton NJ 08542. **Tel** (201)329-9214.

US/0745-7030
CENTRAL RECORD (MEDFORD, N.J.). (THE CENTRAL RECORD.). (Dec. 4, 1896)-. Newspaper. English. wk. 416.00. Central Record / New Jersey, PO Box 127, Medford NJ 08055. **Tel** (609)654-5000, FAX (609)654-8237. **ED** Patricia E. Haughey and Josephy A. Panella. **Photos**. **Ad Acc**, **Adv Mgr:** Elain Kern. Full Page (B&W) $1,050.00. Half Page (B&W) $577.00. Full Page (Color) $1,165.00. Half Page (Color) $692.00. **Pub. Size:** Broadsheet.

US
CITIZEN OF MORRIS COUNTY, THE. **VFOAT** Citizen. Vol. 16, No. 49 (Feb. 21, 1962)-. Newspaper. English. wk (Published on Wednesdays). Citizen of Morris County, PO Box 7, Denville NJ 07834-0007. **Tel** (201)627-0400, FAX (201)627-0403. **ED** Audry Davie. **Ad Acc**. **Circ:** 6,200. available on microfilm. ***Formed by the union of*** *Mountain Lakes Citizen; Montville Citizen; Parsippany-Troy Hills Citizen; Citizen of Morris County (Denville, N.J.); Boonton Ed.; Denville Citizen* ***and*** *Rockaway Citizen.*

US/0745-8150
COMMUNITY NEWS (BROWNS MILLS, N.J.), THE. (THE COMMUNITY NEWS.). (March 17, 1983)-. Newspaper. English. wk. $17.00 in county; $20.00 other. Community News / Browns Mills, PO Box 119, Browns Mills NJ 08015. **Tel** (609)893-4585, FAX (609)893-5839. **ED** Marie Reynolds. **Bk Rev**. **Ad Acc**. **Circ:** 2,500 (ctrl).
Desc: News of government and society in Pemberton Township and Pemberton Boro, New Jersey.

US/0891-7272
COURIER (MIDDLETOWN, N.J.), THE. (THE COURIER.). (19??)-. Newspaper. English. wk (except Christmas). $16.00 New Jersey; $20.00 other. John Famulary Publishing, PO Box 399, Middletown NJ 07748. **Tel** (908) 957-0070, FAX (908)671-0814. **ED** Bonnie Walling. **Bk Rev**. **Photos**. **Ad Acc**. Full Page (B&W) $720.00. Half Page (B&W) $360.00. Full Page (Color) $845.00. Half Page (Color) $485.00. **Pub. Size:** Tabloid. **Circ:** 11,500 (ctrl).

US/0895-8785
COURIER-NEWS (BRIDGEWATER, N.J.). (THE COURIER-NEWS.). **VFOAT** Courier News. Began in 1961. Newspaper. English. da. Courier-News, 1201 US Highway 22 West, Bridgewater NJ 08807. ***Continues*** *Plainfield Courier-News.*

US/1050-432X
COURIER-POST (CHERRY HILL, N.J.). (COURIER-POST.). **VFOAT** Courier Post. Vol. 74, No. 191 (Sept. 9, 1949)-. Newspaper. English. da. Camden Courier Post, PO Box 5300, Cherry Hill NJ 08034. **Tel** (609)663-6000. **ED** William Chanin. **Circ:** 104,225. available on microfilm from University Microfilms International (UMI). ***Formed by the union of*** *Morning Post (Camden, N.J.)* ***and*** *Evening Courier (Camden, N.J.).*

US/1061-5563
CRANBURY PRESS, THE. July 17 (1885)-. Newspaper. English. wk. Princeton Packet Inc, PO Box AF, Circulation Department, Princeton NJ 08542. **Tel** (609)924-3244, FAX (609)921-2714. available on microfilm from New Jersey State Library; and Rutgers University Libraries.

US
CRANFORD CHRONICLE (1979). (THE CRANFORD CHRONICLE.). Vol. 86, No. 11 (March 15, 1979)-. Newspaper. English. wk. $25.00 (in Cranford county); $28.00 (rest of New Jersey); $30.00 other. Cranford Chronicle, PO Box 757, Bedminster NJ 07921. **Tel** (908)781-6000, FAX (201)276-6220. **ED** Patricia Anderson. **Bk Rev**. **Ad Acc**. ctrl circ. available on microfilm. ***Continues*** *Cranford Citizen and Chronicle (1958).*

US
DAILY JOURNAL (ELIZABETH, N.J.). ***Ceased.*** (THE DAILY JOURNAL.). Issue No. 28,283 (June 1, 1960)-Issue No. 5,172 (Sept. 27, 1972)-(1992). Newspaper. English. da (except Sunday). Daily Journal / Elizabeth, 295 North Broad Street, Elizabeth NJ 07207. **Tel** (201)354-5000. **ED** Phil Read. **Circ:** 34,395. available on microfilm from University Microfilms International (UMI). ***Continues*** *Elizabeth Daily Journal.*

US
DAILY RECORD (PARSIPPANY, N.J.). (DAILY RECORD.). Vol. 72, No. 46 (Aug. 30, 1971)-. Newspaper. English. da. $221.00. Daily Record / Parsippany, 629 Parsippany Road, Parsippany NJ 07054. **Tel** (201)428-6200, FAX (201)428-7280. **ED** William M Donnellon, Larry Miller, Loretta Boeche, Jack Bowie. **Bk Rev. Ad Acc. Circ:** 63,000 daily, 74,000 Sunday (ctrl). available on microfilm from University Microfilms International (UMI); available on an online database (file 635/Full-Text) from DIALOG. ***Continues*** *Morris County's Daily Record.*
Desc: Emphasizes local news and covers highlights of state, national and world news. Circulates in one of the nation's fastest growing and most affluent areas - Morris County, northern Somerset County and southern Sussex County.

US
DAILY TARGUM, THE. Vol. 112, No. 1 (Sept. 2, 1980)-. Newspaper. English. da. Rutgers University / Department of Italian, 18 Seminary Place, New Brunswick NJ 08903. **Tel** (908)932-7031. ***Continues*** *Rutgers Daily Targum.*

US
DELAWARE VALLEY NEWS. Began with Oct. 27, 1933 issue. Newspaper. English. wk. Delaware Valley News, PO Box 244, Frenchtown NJ 08825. available on microfilm from Micro-Graphic Corp.; and New Jersey State Library. ***Continues*** *Delaware Valley News: The Frenchtown Star;* ***Absorbed*** *Milford Leader.*

US
EAST ORANGE RECORD. (1899)-. Newspaper. English. wk. $22.00 (one year), $39.00 (two year). Worrall Newspapers, Box 849, 170 Scotland Road, Orange NJ 07051. **Tel** (201)674-8000, FAX (201)674-2038. **ED** James C. Sheil. **LC** 8775. **Photos. Ad Acc, Adv Mgr:** Erik Kent, **Tel** (908)686-7700. **Pub. Size:** Broadsheet. available in microform.

US/0746-7036
EGG HARBOR NEWS, THE. (19??)-. Newspaper. English. wk. $21.00. Times Graphics Newspapers, PO Box 231, 69 73 E W Jersey Avenue, Pleasantville NJ 08232. **Tel** (609)641-3100.

US
GAZETTE LEADER. (April 1977)-. Newspaper. English. Fifty-two times a year (Published on Wed.). $15.00 in county; $17.50 other. Gazette Leader Publications, 1212 Atlantic Avenue, PO Box 469, Wildwood NJ 08260. **Tel** (609)522-3423, FAX (609)522-7451. **ED** Steve Erlanger and Rob Seitzinger (Managing Editor). **Bk Rev**, (Qty: 12). **Photos. Ad Acc.** Full Page (B&W) $1440.00. Half Page (B&W) $720.00. Full Page (Color) $1490.00. Half Page (Color) $770.00. **Pub. Size:** Tabloid. **Pr Rev. Circ:** 15,000 (ctrl). available on microfilm from New Jersey State Library; and Micro-Graphic Corp.; available on microfiche from Cape Cod Country Library. ***Formed by the union of*** *Wildwood Leader* ***and*** *Cape May Co. Gazette.*

US
GLEN RIDGE PAPER. Began with April 19, 1935 issue. Newspaper. English. wk. $16.50 (Essex County). Glen Ridge Paper, PO Box 147, Glen Ridge NJ 07028. **Tel** (201)674-2038. **ED** Donald Veleber. **Bk Rev. Ad Acc.** ctrl circ.

US
GLOUCESTER COUNTY TIMES. (1975)-. Newspaper. English. da. $169.00. Gloucester County Times, 309 South Broad Street, Woodbury NJ 08096. **Tel** (609)845-3300 ext. 303. **ED** William Long. **Circ:** 28,971. ***Continues*** *Woodbury Daily Times.*

US
HERALD-NEWS (PASSAIC, N.J.). (THE HERALD-NEWS.). **VFOAT** Herald News. Began with April 4, 1932 issue. Newspaper. English. da. 988 Main Avenue, Passaic NJ 07055. available on microfilm from University Microfilms International (UMI). ***Formed by the union of*** *Daily Herald (Passaic, N.J.)* ***and*** *Daily News (Passaic, N.J.).*

US
HILLSBOROUGH BEACON. Vol. 20, No. 13 (Apr. 11, 1974)-. Newspaper. English. wk. Hillsborough Beacon, PO Box 695, Belle Mead NJ 08502. ***Continues*** *South Somerset News.*

US
HILLSIDE TIMES, THE. BEgan with Nov. 1, 1924 issue. Newspaper. English. wk. Hillside Times, 1443 North Broad Street, Hillside NJ 07205.

US/0018-7844
HUNTERDON COUNTY DEMOCRAT. (1847)-. Newspaper. English. wk. $29.00 (one year), $75.00 (three year) Hunterdon County; $35.00 (one year), $85.00 (three year) N. J. & PA; $39.00 (one year) $100.00 (three year) other. Hunterdon County Democrat, PO Box 32, Flemington NJ 08822. **Tel** (908)782-4747 Ext 289, FAX (908)782-6572. **ED** Jay Langley, (phone: (908)782-4747 Ext. 640). **LC** 8768-X. **Ad Acc, Adv Mgr:** A. Angreli, **Tel** (908)782-4747 Ext 631. **Circ:** 24,362 (ctrl). ***Continues*** *Hunterdon Democrat;* ***Absorbed*** *Democrat (Flemington, N.J.); Democrat-Advertiser.*

US/0746-3863
HUNTERDON REVIEW AND THE HIGH BRIDGE GAZETTE. ***Title Change.*** **VFOAT** Hunterdon Review; High Bridge Gazette. Vol. 73, No. 20 (May 14, 1969)-(19??). Newspaper. English. wk. Recorder Publishing Company / New Jersey, 17 Morristown Road, Bernardsville NJ 07924. **Tel** (201)766-6960. ***Formed by the union of*** *Hunterdon Review* ***and*** *High Bridge Gazette.* ***Continued by*** *Hunterdon Review (Lebanon, N.J.), 1059-8715.*

US/1059-8715
HUNTERDON REVIEW (LEBANON, N.J.). (HUNTERDON REVIEW.). (19??)-. Newspaper. English. wk. $16.00 Hunterdon county, $25.00 other New Jersey, $30.00 other. Hunterdon Review, 17 19 Morristown Road, Bernardsville NJ 07924. **Tel** (201)766-3900. ***Continues*** *Hunterdon Review and the High Bridge Gazette, 0746-3863.*

US/0747-4075
INDEPENDENT PRESS (BLOOMFIELD, N.J.). (THE INDEPENDENT PRESS.). (19??)-. Newspaper. English. wk. $22.00. Worrall Community Newspapers Inc., 266 Liberty Street, Bloomfield NJ 07003-0110. **Tel** (201)743-4040, FAX (201)680-8848. **ED** Jim Sheil and Russell Roemmele (Managing Editor). **Bk Rev. Photos. Ad Acc, Adv Mgr:** Peter Worrall, **Tel** (908)686-7700. **Pub. Size:** Standard. ctrl circ. available in microform.
Desc: Local coverage of Bloomfield New Jersey.

US
IRVINGTON HERALD. Vol. 41, No. 1 (Apr. 17, 1952)-. Newspaper. English. wk. $18.00 Essex County; $22.50 New Jersey; $26.50 other. Worrall Community Newspapers, 1291 Stuyvesant Avenue, Union NJ 07083. **Tel** (908)686-7700. ***Continues*** *Irvington Herald and Irvington Times.*

US
ITALIAN TRIBUNE NEWS. Vol. 53, No. 16 (Apr. 12, 1984)-. Newspaper. English. Fifty-two times a year (Thurs.). Free to schools and libraries; $20.00 others. Ace Alagna, 427 Bloomfield Avenue, Newark NJ 07107. **Tel** (201)485-6000, FAX (201)485-8967. **ED** William Madden and Joan Alagna (Managing Editor). **Bk Rev**, (Qty: 25). **Photos. Ad Acc, Adv Mgr:** David Aaron. Full Page (B&W) $869.40. Half Page (B&W) $434.70. Full Page (Color) $1,069.40. Half Page (Color) $634.70. **Pub. Size:** Tabloid. **Circ:** 40,000 (ctrl). ***Continues*** *Italian Tribune (Newark, N.J. : 1978).*
Desc: General news geared toward Italian American community.

US
ITALIAN VOICE, THE. **VFOAT** La Voce Italiana. (June 4, 1932)-. Newspaper. English. wk. $27.00. Emile Augusto Publishing Co., PO Box 9, Totowa NJ 07512. **Tel** (201)942-5028.

US
ITEM OF MILLBURN AND SHORT HILLS, THE. Vol. 86, No. 52 (Dec. 31, 1975)-. Newspaper. English. wk. $16.50. The Item, 100 Millburn Avenue, Millburn NJ 07041. **Tel** (201)376-1200. **ED** Carter J. Bennett. **Photos. Ad Acc, Adv Mgr:** Tracy Dupuis. Full Page (B&W) $1260.00. Half Page (B&W) $630.00. Full Page (Color) $1260.00 plus an additional $200.00 per color. Half Page (Color) $630.00 plus an additional $200.00 per color. **Pub. Size:** Broadsheet. **Circ:** 5,800. available on microfilm from New Jersey State Library. ***Continues*** *Item (Millburn, N.J.).*

US
JERSEY JOURNAL AND JERSEY OBSERVER, THE. **VFOAT** Jersey Journal. 86th year, No. 78 (August 2, 1952)-. Newspaper. English. da. Jersey Journal, 30 Journal Square, Jersey City NJ 07306. ***Continues*** *Jersey Journal including all of the News Services, Features and Local News of the Jersey Observer.*

US/8750-8664
KENILWORTH LEADER. (19??)-. Newspaper. English. Fifty-two times a year. $10.00 Union County; $24.50 others. Worral Community Newspapers, 1291 Stuyvesant Avenue, Union NJ 07083. **Tel** (201)686-7700, FAX (201)686-4169.

US/0747-4377
LACEY BEACON. **VFOAT** Beacon. (1???)-. Newspaper. English. wk. Manahawkin Newspapers Inc, 345 East Bay Avenue, Manahawkin NJ 08050.

US/0746-1771
LAWRENCE LEDGER, THE. Began in 1969. Newspaper. English. sw. Princeton Packet Inc, PO Box AF, Circulation Department, Princeton NJ 08542. **Tel** (609)924-3244, FAX (609)921-2714.

US/0745-6816
LEADER (POINT PLEASANT BEACH, N.J.). (THE LEADER.). (June 23, 1955)-. Newspaper. English. wk. $17.50. The Leader / New Jersey, PO Box 1771, Point Pleasant Beach NJ 08742. **Tel** (908)899-1000, FAX (908)899-2135. **ED** Camille Thomas; Al Muzer and Jeannie Tomaselli (Managing Editors). **Bk Rev**, (Qty: 4-6 per year). **Photos. Ad Acc, Adv Mgr:** Tom Bateman. Full Page (B&W) $775.00. Half Page (B&W) $450.00. **Pub. Size:** Broadsheet. available in microform. ***Continues*** *Ocean County Leader South Monmouth News.*

US/0898-9052
LUSOAMERICANO (NEWARK, N.J.). (LUSO AMERICANO.). [LusoAmericano]. **VFOAT** LusoAmericano; Luso-Americano. (19??)-. Newspaper. Portuguese (English and Portuguese). sw. $35.00. Luso Americano, 88 Ferry Street, Newark NJ 07105. **Tel** (201)589-4600, FAX (201)589-3848, telex 139099. **ED** Antonio S. Matinho and Fernando Santos (Managing Editor). **DD** 071. **Bk Rev**, (Qty: 12). **Photos. Ad Acc, Adv Mgr:** David Matinho. Full Page (B&W) $450.00. Half Page (B&W) $240.00. Full Page (Color) $650.00. Half Page (Color) $440.00. **Pub. Size:** Tabloid. **Wire Svcs.:** RN. **Circ:** 15,000 (ctrl). available in microform. ***Continues*** *New Jersey Luso-Americano.*

US
MADISON EAGLE, THE. Began with May 1, 1891 issue. Newspaper. English. wk. Madison Eagle, PO Box 160, Madison NJ 07940. ***Continues*** *Madison Weekly Eagle.*

US/1058-6857
MANVILLE NEWS, THE. Began with Aug. 15 (1933). Newspaper. English. wk. Princeton Packet Inc, PO Box AF, Circulation Department, Princeton NJ 08542. **Tel** (609)924-3244, FAX (609)921-2714.

US
MAPLE SHADE PROGRESS. (Nov. 4, 1916)-. Newspaper. English. wk (Published on Thursdays). Progress Publications Inc, 306-08 East Main Street, Maple Shade NJ 08052-2626. **Tel** (609)779-7788. **ED** Frank Gerkens, Jr. **Ad Acc, Adv Mgr:** Barbara Bethard. **Circ:** 5,200.

US/0747-3222
MERCER MESSENGER. Newspaper. English. wk. Mercer Messenger, 2667 Nottingham Way, Hamilton NJ 08619. ***Continues*** *Mercer County Messenger and Hamilton Life.*

US
MESSENGER-PRESS. **VFOAT** Messenger Press. Vol. 70, No. 25 (July 6, 1972)-. Newspaper. English. wk. $27.00 Hunterdon, Somerset, Middlesex, Mercer & Monmouth Counties; $18.00 New Jersey; $27.00 other. Princeton Packet Inc, PO Box AF, Circulation Department, Princeton NJ 08542. **Tel** (609)924-3244, FAX (609)921-2714. **ED** Joan Walling. **Ad Acc. Circ:** 4,800 (ctrl). available on microfilm. ***Continues*** *Allentown Messenger, Millstone Press.*

US/0747-2390
METUCHEN, EDISON REVIEW. **VFOAT** Metuchen/Edison Review. Newspaper. English. wk. $15.00 (Middlesex county), $18.00 (out of county), $22.00 (out of state). The Metuchen, Edison Review, PO Box 804, Edison NJ 08818-0804. **Tel** (201)494-7727, FAX (201)968-0591. **(Subscription address:** PO Box 699, Somerville, NJ 08876) **ED** Jean Whiston. **Bk Rev. Ad Acc. Circ:** 8,000.
Desc: General weekly newspaper serving Edison Township and (borough of) Metuchen, New Jersey.

US/0746-8350
MONITOR (TRENTON, N.J.), THE. (THE MONITOR.). (19??)-. Periodical. English. wk (except week of July 4 and Christmas). $20.00. Newspaper of Diocese Trenton, PO Box 3095, 315 Lowell Avenue, Trenton NJ 08619. **Tel** (609)586-7400. **ED** Joseph M. Donadiev. **Bk Rev. Ad Acc, Adv Mgr:** James Cassidy.

US
MONTCLAIR TIMES, THE. (Feb. 17, 1877)-. Newspaper. English. wk. $17.00. Montclair Times, 114 Valley Road, Montclair NJ 07042. **ED** Cindy Smith. **Photos. Ad Acc, Adv Mgr:** Sara Singleton, **Tel** (201)746-1100. Full Page (B&W) $1638.00. Half Page (B&W) $819.00. Full Page (Color) $1638.00 plus an additional $200.00 per color. Half Page (Color) $819.00 plus an additional $200.00 per color. **Pub. Size:** Broadsheet. **Circ:** 12,300.

US/0195-2498
MT. OLIVE CHRONICLE. **VAT** Mount Olive Chronicle. Vol. 1- (Sept. 6, 1979)-. Newspaper. English. wk. Mt Olive Chronicle, PO Box 174, Budd Lake NJ 07828.

New Jersey

US
NEW EGYPT PRESS, THE. Began in 1900. Newspaper. English. wk. The New Egypt Press, PO Box 188, New Egypt NJ 08533. **Continues** Advertiser (New Egypt, N.J.).

US
NEW JERSEY 50 PLUS. (19??)-. English. Twelve times a year. $10.00. Village Crier, 1830 Highway 9, Toms River NJ 08753. **ED** Edward Jasin. **Bk Rev**, (Qty: 24). **Photos**. **Ad Acc**, **Adv Mgr**: Patricia Jasin, **Tel** (908)240-3000. Full Page (B&W) $1,200.00. Half Page (B&W) $600.00. Full Page (Color) $1,540.00. Half Page (Color) $940.00. **Pub. Size**: Tabloid. **Circ**: 75,000. **Continues** Village Crier.

US/0893-3677
NEW JERSEY HERALD (1960), THE. (THE NEW JERSEY HERALD.). **VFOAT** New Jersey Sunday Herald. 131st Year, No. 21 (Nov. 10, 1960)-. Newspaper. English. ds. $135.00 New Jersey, New York and Pennsylvania; $153.50 other. The New Jersey Herald, PO Box 10, 2 Spring Street, Newton NJ 07860. **Tel** (201)383-1500. **ED** Randy Bergmann. **Circ**: 19,217 daily, 26,522 Sunday. **Continues** New Jersey Herald and the Sussex Register-Sussex County Independent.

US/1060-0167
NEW YORK GUARDIAN, THE. **VFOAT** The NY Guardian and the LI Guardian; The N.Y. and the L.I. Guardian. Vol. 1, No. 1 (May/June 1991)-. Newspaper. English. mo. $27.00 one year; $45.00 two years. Guardian / New Jersey, PO Box 3000, Denville NJ 07834. **Tel** (718)229-8209, **FAX** (718)229-8134. **ED** Christopher Ruddy. **Bk Rev**. **Ad Acc**. **Circ**: 25,000.

US/8750-3913
NEWS BEACON (FAIR LAWN, N.J.). (THE NEWS BEACON.). (1959)-. Newspaper. English. wk. $9.00. Shopper Publications, 12-38 River Road, Fair Lawn NJ 07410. **Tel** (201)791-8400.

US
NEWS-RECORD OF MAPLEWOOD AND SOUTH ORANGE. **VFOAT** News Record of Maplewood and South Orange. Vol. 82, No. 10 (Oct. 3, 1968)-. Newspaper. English. wk. News Record of Maplewood and South Orange, 463 Valley Street, PO Box 158, Maplewood NJ 07040. **Tel** (201)763-0700. **ED** Don Veleber. **Bk Rev**. **Ad Acc**, **Adv Mgr**: Steve Ward. **Circ**: 6,745. **Continues** News-Record of Maplewood and South Orange, New Jersey.

US/0191-5908
NEWS TRANSCRIPT. (Jan. 31, 1979)-. Newspaper. English. wk. $22.00. Greater Media Inc, 25 Kilmer Drive, Suite 109, Morganville NJ 07751. **Tel** (908)972-6740. **ED** Jeanette Blair. **Circ**: 34,215. available on microfilm. **Continues** Colonial News Transcript.

US/1069-2681
NEWS TRIBUNE (WOODBRIDGE, N.J.). (THE NEWS TRIBUNE.). (19??)-. Newspaper. English. da. $230.00 daily & Sunday. News Tribune / New Jersey, 1 Hoover Way, Woodbridge NJ 07095. **Tel** (908)442-0400.

US
NEWSPAPER FUND ADVISER UPDATE. (19??)-. English. Twice a year (During school year). Free. Dow Jones Newspaper Fund Inc., PO Box 300, Princeton NJ 08543-0300. **Tel** (609)452-2820, **FAX** (609)520-5804. **ED** George Taylor and Linda Waller. **Bk Rev**, (Qty: 4y). **Photos**. **Pub. Size**: Tabloid. **Circ**: 1,500.

US/0895-8807
NORTH JERSEY HERALD & NEWS, THE. **VFOAT** North Jersey Herald and News; Herald & News; Herald and News. (Sept. 21, 1987)-. Newspaper. English. da. $156.00 (with Sunday), $130.00 (without Sunday). North Jersey Herald & News, 988 Main Avenue, Passaic NJ 07055. **Tel** (201)365-3200. **Formed by the union of** News (Paterson, N.J.) **and** North Jersey Herald-News.

US/0745-8908
NORTH JERSEY PROSPECTOR, THE. Newspaper. English. wk. $15.00. North Jersey Prospector, 85 Crooks, Clifton NJ 07011. **Tel** (201)773-8300. **Bk Rev**. **Ad Acc**. **Circ**: 59,600 (ctrl). **Continues** Independent-Prospector.

US/0191-4936
NORTH JERSEY SUBURBANITE, THE. **VFOAT** Suburbanite. Newspaper. English. wk. North Jersey Suburbanite, 50 Piermont Road, Cresskill NJ 07626.

US/0746-5416
OCEAN COUNTY OBSERVER. (1??)-. Newspaper. English. ds. $119.20 local Delaware; $127.00 other. Ocean County Observer, CN 2449 Robbins Street, Toms River NJ 08754. **Tel** (908)349-3000.

US/1053-4555
OCEAN COUNTY REVIEW. **VFOAT** Review. (1913)-. Newspaper. English. wk. $15.00. Ocean County Review, PO Box 8, Seaside Heights NJ 08751. **Tel** (201)793-0147.

US/0300-6786
POST EAGLE. (1962)-. Newspaper. English. wk. $22.00. Post Publishing Company Inc, 800 Van Hutten Avenue, Clifton NJ 07013. **Tel** (201)473-5414. **ED** Chester Grabowski, Christine Grabowski (Managing Editor). Index available. **Bk Rev**. **Photos**. **Ad Acc**. Full Page (B&W) $560.00. Half Page (B&W) $280.00. Full Page (Color) $640.00. Half Page (Color) $360.00. **Pub. Size**: Tabloid. **Circ**: 16,500 (ctrl). available in microform.

US
PRESS (ATLANTIC CITY, N.J. : 1971). (THE PRESS.). **VFOAT** Sunday Press. (Sept. 25, 1971)-. Newspaper. English. da. $239.80 (by mail), $154.96 (home delivery). South Jersey Publishing Company, 1000 West Washington Avenue, Pleasantville NJ 08232. **Tel** (609)272-1100. **ED** Charles Reynolds. **Circ**: 81,129 daily, 90,151 Sunday. available on microfilm from Bell & Howell. **Continues** Atlantic City Press.

US/0746-178X
PRINCETON PACKET, THE. No. 18 (May 3, 1956)-. Newspaper. English. sw. Princeton Packet Inc, PO Box AF, Circulation Department, Princeton NJ 08542. **Tel** (609)924-3244, **FAX** (609)921-2714. **Continues** Lawrence-Pennington Echo; **Absorbed** Princeton Packet and the Hopewell Herald.

US
RAHWAY NEWS-RECORD. **VFOAT** Rahway News Record. Vol. 124, No. 31 (Feb. 7, 1946)-. Newspaper. English. wk. Rahway News-Record, 219 Central Avenue, Rahway NJ 07065. **Formed by the union of** Rahway News **and** Rahway Record.

US/0191-703X
RANDOLPH REPORTER, THE. Newspaper. English. wk. Randolph Reporter, 1225 Sussex Turnpike, Mount Freedom NJ 07970.

US
RECORD (HACKENSACK, N.J.). (THE RECORD.). **VFOAT** Sunday Record. Vol. 66, No. 85 (Sept. 14, 1960)-. Newspaper. English. da (except Sat.). Record / Hackensack, New Jersey, 150 River Street, Hackensack NJ 07601. **Tel** (201)646-4270. **Circ**: 161,969 daily, 227,205 Sunday. available on microfilm from University Microfilms International (UMI). **Continues** Bergen Evening Record.
Ind/Abst PROMT.

US
REGISTER-NEWS (BORDENTOWN, N.J.). (REGISTER-NEWS.). **VFOAT** Register News. Began with Vol. 122, No. 9 (May 26, 1966). Newspaper. English. wk. Register-News / Bordentown, 137 Farnsworth Avenue, Bordentown NJ 08505. available on microfilm from Norton Micro Images. **Formed by the union of** Bordentown Register **and** Florence Township News.

US/0884-4704
REGISTER (SHREWSBURY, N.J.), THE. (THE REGISTER.). **VFOAT** Sunday Register. (198?)-. Newspaper. English. da. Red Bank Register, 1 Register Plaza, Shrewsbury NJ 07701. **ED** Arthur Z. Kamin. **Circ**: 21,110. **Continues** Daily Register (Shrewsbury, N.J.), 8750-6491.

US/0194-3537
SENTINEL (EAST BRUNSWICK, N.J. : 1973). (SENTINEL.). Vol. 54, No. 9 (Feb. 28, 1973)-. Newspaper. English. wk. Sentinel Publishing Company, Edgeboro Road, East Brunswick NJ 08816. available on microfilm from Norton Micro Images. **Continues** Sentinel Spokesman.

US
SHIELD FOR CIVIL SERVICE NEWS, THE. Ceased. **VFOAT** Shield. Vol. 8, No. 3 (Feb. 1942)-?. Newspaper. English. wk. The Shield, 155 Broad Avenue, Fort Lee NJ 07022. **Tel** (201)941-4400. **Continues** Shield for Civil Service News of New Jersey.

US
SOMERSET MESSENGER GAZETTE. Vol. 1, No. 1 (Jan. 6, 1931)-. Newspaper. English. wk. Somerset Messenger Gazette, East Main and Warren Streets, Somerville NJ 08876. **Formed by the union of** Somerset Messenger; Unionist-Gazette **and** Somerset Democrat (Somerville, N.J.).

US/1041-2514
SOUTH AMBOY CITIZEN (SOUTH AMBOY, N.J. 1884), THE. (THE SOUTH AMBOY CITIZEN.). (1884)-. Newspaper. English. ir (every other Thurs.). $10.00. South Amboy Citizen, PO Box 3095, South Amboy NJ 08879. **ED** Joe Sainato. **Bk Rev**, (Qty: 3). **Photos**. **Ad Acc**, **Adv Mgr**: Jim Gotti. Full Page (B&W) $816.00. Half Page (B&W) $408.00. Full Page (Color) $966.00. Half Page (Color) $558.00. **Pub. Size**: Tabloid. **Circ**: 4,014. available in microform.

US
STAR-GAZETTE (HACKETTSTOWN, N.J.). (THE STAR-GAZETTE.). **VFOAT** Star Gazette. Vol. 4, No. 38 (Sept. 12, 1974)-. Newspaper. English. wk. Star Gazette / New Jersey, PO Box 500, Hackettstown NJ 07840. **Tel** (908)852-1212. available on microfilm from New Jersey State Library. **Formed by the union of** Hackettstown Gazette (1971) **and** Star (Washington, N.J. : 1971).

US
STAR-LEDGER (NEWARK, N.J. : 1964). (STAR-LEDGER.). **VFOAT** Star Ledger; Sunday Star-Ledger; Sunday Star Ledger. Vol. 51, No. 91 (May 19, 1964)-. Newspaper. English. da. $345.00 (daily), $180.00 (Sunday), $525.00 (daily and Sunday). Star Ledger, Mail Subscription Department, Star Ledger Plaza, PO Box 148, Newark NJ 07101. **Tel** (201)877-4053, (800)242-0850. **ED** Mort Pye. **Photos**. **Ad Acc**, **Adv Mgr**: Fred Marks. Full Page (B&W) $24473.63. Half Page (B&W) $13211.73. **Pub. Size**: Standard. **Circ**: 460,330 daily, 678,743 Sunday. available on microfilm from University Microfilms International (UMI). **Continues** Newark Star-Ledger.
Ind/Abst PROMT.

US/0193-6492
SUBURBAN NEWS. Newspaper. English. wk. Suburban News / New Jersey, PO Box 2309, Westfield NJ 07091. **Tel** (908)396-4500.

US/0746-052X
SUBURBAN NEWS (FRANKLIN LAKES, N.J. : 1981). (SUBURBAN NEWS.). Began in 1981?. Newspaper. English. wk. Pennysaver Inc, 795 Susquehanna Avenue, Franklin Lakes NJ 07417. **Continues** United Suburban News, 0274-6646.

US/0274-6964
SVOBODA (JERSEY CITY). (SVOBODA : UKRAINSKYI SHCHODENNYK.). [Svoboda]. **Added/Corp** Ukrainian National Association. **VFOAT** Liberty; Liberty : Ukrainian Daily; Ukrainian Daily; Ukrainian Weekly. (1893)-. Newspaper. Ukrainian (English). da. $30.00 members; $55.00 non-members. Ukrainian National Association Inc, 30 Montgomery Street, PO Box 76, Jersey City NJ 07303. **Tel** (201)451-2200. **ED** Zenon Snylyk. **LC** 8777. **Bk Rev**. **Photos**. **Ad Acc**, **Adv Mgr**: Maria Szeparowycz, **Tel** (201)434-0237. Full Page (B&W) $1,800.00. Half Page (B&W) $900.00. **Pub. Size**: Broadsheet. **Circ**: 14,000 (ctrl). available on microfilm.
Ind/Abst MLA Int. Bibl. Books Artic. Mod. Lang. Lit.

US/8750-9083
TIMES (TRENTON, N.J. PRINCETON METRO ED.), THE. (THE TIMES.). No. 165 (Feb. 11, 1985)-. Newspaper. English. da. $28.08 (daily), $17.42 (Sunday); $45.50 (daily and Sun.) Three months; $56.16 (daily), $34.84 (Sunday), $91.00 (daily and Sun.) Six months; $112.32 (daily), $69.68 (Sunday), $182.00 (daily and Sun.) One year. Trenton Times Newspapers, 500 Perry Street, PO Box 847, Trenton NJ 08605. **Tel** (609)989-5454, (609)989-5656. **ED** Richard Bilotti and Linda Cunningham. **Bk Rev**. **Ad Acc**. **Circ**: 63,870 daily, 81,396 Sunday. available on microfilm from University Microfilms International (UMI). **Continues in part** Trenton Times (Trenton, N.J.: 1976).

US/0890-9830
TODAY'S SUNBEAM. Began in (1972)-. Newspaper. English. da. $109.00. Sunbeam Publishing Company, 93 5th Street, Salem NJ 08079. **Tel** (609)935-1500. **Formed by the union of** Monitor-Register; Penns Grove Sun; Pennsville Progress; Salem Standard and Jerseyman **and** Salem Sunbeam.

US/0191-7056
TOWN TOPICS (PRINCETON, N.J.). (TOWN TOPICS.). Vol. 1, No. 1 (March 1946)-. Newspaper. English. wk. Town Topics, PO Box 664, Princeton NJ 08542. **Tel** (609)924-2200. **ED** Donald C. Stuart and Dan D. Coyle.

US/1064-3567
TRENTONIAN (TRENTON, N.J.), THE. (THE TRENTONIAN.). (1945)-. Newspaper. English. da. $156.00 New Jersey, Delaware, and District of Columbia; $182.00 other. Trentonian, 600 Perry Street, Trenton NJ 08602. **Tel** (609)989-7800 ext. 235. **ED** Gail Baldwin. **Ad Acc**, **Adv Mgr**: M Gebhart, **Tel** (609)989-7800, ext. 218. **Circ**: 68,391 daily, 64,989 Sunday (ctrl). available on

microfilm from University Microfilms International (UMI); available on an online database (file 635/Full-Text) from DIALOG. Documents available from UMI Article Clearinghouse.
Ind/Abst Bus. Dateline (Jan. 12, 1992-) [Full Txt.].

US
TRIBUNA DE NEW YORK & NEW JERSEY, LA. **VFOAT** Tribuna de New York and New Jersey; Tribuna. (1988)-. Newspaper. Spanish. bm. $25.00. La Tribuna de New York & New Jersey, PO Box 805, Union City NJ 07087. **Tel** (201)617-1360, FAX (201)619-0042. **ED** Lionel Rodriguez. **Bk Rev.** **Photos.** **Ad Acc, Adv Mgr:** Soraya Molenaar. Full Page (B&W) $1562.40. Half Page (B&W) $781.20. Full Page (Color) $1687.40. Half Page (Color) $906.00. available in microform. ***Continues*** *Tribuna de North Jersey.*

US/0882-9616
TUCKERTON BEACON (TUCKERTON, N.J. : 1985). (TUCKERTON BEACON.). Vol. 95, No. 29 (March 21, 1985)-. Newspaper. English. wk. $20.00. Manahawkin Newspapers Inc, 345 East Bay Avenue, Manahawkin NJ 08050. **ED** Jan Zollenger. **Photos.** **Ad Acc, Adv Mgr:** Tim Wallace. **Tel** (609)597-3211. Full Page (B&W) $1082.00. Half Page (B&W) $545.00. Full Page (Color) $1325.00. Half Page (Color) $788.00. **Pub. Size:** Standard. **Circ:** 4,700 (weekly). ***Continues*** *More Tuckerton News.*

US
VALLEY STAR (ENGLEWOOD, N.J.). (THE VALLEY STAR.). Newspaper. English. wk. Valley Star, 35A West Street, Englewood NJ 07631.

US/1066-1204
VILLAGE CRIER (TOMS RIVER, N.J.), THE. ***Title Change.*** (THE VILLAGE CRIER.). (19??)-(19??). Periodical. English. mo. Village Crier, 1830 Highway 9, Toms River NJ 08753. **ED** Edward Jasin. **Bk Rev**, (Qty: 24). **Photos.** **Ad Acc, Adv Mgr:** Patricia Jasin, **Tel** (908)240-3000. **Pub. Size:** Tabloid. **Circ:** 75,000. ***Continued by*** *New Jersey 50 Plus.*

US
VINELAND TIMES JOURNAL. Began with Feb. 27, 1942 issue. Newspaper. English. da. Vineland Times Journal, 891 East Oak Street, Vineland NJ 08360. available on microfilm from University Microfilms International (UMI). ***Formed by the union of*** *Evening Journal (Vineland, N.J.)* ***and*** *Evening Times (Vineland, N.J.).*

US
WEST ESSEX TRIBUNE. Vol. 1, No. 1 (July 6, 1929)-. Newspaper. English. wk. $17.00 Essex County; $20.00 New Jersey; $23.00 other. West Essex Tribune, 495 South Livingston Avenue, PO Box 65, Livingston NJ 07039-0065. **Tel** (201)992-1771, FAX (201)992-7015. **ED** E. Christopher Cone (Editor in Chief), Nancy B. Dinar (Managing Editor). **Photos.** **Ad Acc, Adv Mgr:** Judith Dressel. Full Page (B&W) $1171.80. Half Page (B&W) $585.90. **Pub. Size:** Broadsheet. available on microfilm.
Desc: Weekly community newspaper of Livingston, New Jersey.

US
WESTFIELD LEADER, THE. (Sept. 1890)-. Newspaper. English. wk. $16.00. Westfield Leader, PO Box 250, Westfield NJ 07091. **ED** Paul Peyton, Kurt Bauer (Managing Editor). **Bk Rev.** **Photos.** **Ad Acc.** **Pub. Size:** Standard. available on microfilm from Norton Micro Images.

US
WOMAN'S NEWSPAPER. Issue No. 46 (Jan. 1986)-. Newspaper. English. mo. $10.00. The Woman's Newspaper of Princeton Inc, PO Box 1303, Princeton NJ 08542. ***Continues*** *Woman's Newspaper of Princeton.*
Desc: Covers topics of interest to women - including health, business, law, politics, and arts.

US/1048-2237
YUMA DAILY SUN, THE. (198?)-. Newspaper. English. da. Yuma Daily Sun, PO Box 271, Caldwell NJ 07006. **Tel** (602)783-3333. ***Continues*** *Yuma Daily Sun and Arizona Sentinel, 0893-343X.*

NEW MEXICO

US
ALAMOGORDO DAILY NEWS. (Dec. 5, 1954)-. Newspaper. English. da (313 issues per year). $84.00 (carrier); $114.00 (mail). Alamogordo Daily News, PO Box 870, Alamogordo NM 88310. **Tel** (505)437-7120, (505)437-2974. **ED** Don McKinney. **Photos.** **Ad Acc, Adv Mgr:** Milly House. **Pub. Size:** Standard. **Wire Svcs.:** AP. available on microfilm. ***Continues*** *Alamogordo News (1920).*

US
ALBUQUERQUE JOURNAL (ALBUQUERQUE, N.M. : 1926). (ALBUQUERQUE JOURNAL.). **VFOAT** Sunday Journal. Vol. 189, No. 81 (June 20, 1926)-. Newspaper. English. da. $214.00 New Mexico, $241.00 US, $379.00 others, by mail, $133.00 by carrier, (mornings & Sundays); $73.00 New Mexico, $88.00 US, $102.16 others (Sundays only) by mail. Albuquerque Publishing Company, 7777 Jefferson Northeast, Albuquerque NM 87103. **Tel** (800)641-3451, (505)823-7777. **(Subscription address:** PO Box J-T, Albuquerque, New Mexico 87103) **ED** Jerry Crawford. **Ad Acc.** **Circ:** 115,000. available on microfilm. ***Continues*** *Albuquerque Morning Journal (Albuquerque, N.M. : 1903).*
Ind/Abst PROMT.

US
ALBUQUERQUE TRIBUNE, THE. (Feb. 20, 1933)-. Newspaper. English. da (except Sunday). $141.00 New Mexico; $153.00 US; $259.80 other. Albuquerque Publishing Company, 7777 Jefferson Northeast, Albuquerque NM 87103. **Tel** (800)641-3451, (505)823-7777. **ED** Tim Gallagher (Editor in Chief) and Neal Pattison (Managing Editor). **Photos.** **Ad Acc, Adv Mgr:** Scott Daskins, **Tel** (505)823-3301. **Pub. Size:** Broadsheet. **Wire Svcs.:** SH, AP, WP, NY. **Circ:** 34,000. available in microform. ***Formed by the union of*** *New Mexico State Tribune* ***and*** *Albuquerque Journal (Albuquerque, N.M. : Evening Ed.).*

US
ARTESIA DAILY PRESS. Vol. 1, No. 1 (June 2, 1954)-. Newspaper. English. da. Artesia Daily Press, PO Drawer 179, Artesia NM 88210. **Tel** (505)746-3524. ***Absorbed*** *Artesia Advocate.*

US
CARLSBAD CURRENT-ARGUS. Vol. 65, No. 259 (Sept. 2, 1951)-. Newspaper. English. da. $108.00 Eddy County, New Mexico; $132.00 other. Carlsbad Current Argus, PO Drawer 1629, Carlsbad NM 88220. **Tel** (505)887-5501. available on microfilm. ***Continues*** *Daily Current-Argus.*

US/1071-3506
CIBOLA COUNTY BEACON. Vol. 51, No. 108 (June 6, 1990)-. Newspaper. English. da. $79.00. Cibola Beacon, PO Box 579, Grants NM 87020. **Tel** (505)287-4411, FAX (505)287-7822. **ED** J. D. Meisner. **Ad Acc, Adv Mgr:** Ken Wingat. **Circ:** 3,500. ***Continues*** *Grants Daily Beacon.*

US
CLOVIS NEWS-JOURNAL. **VFOAT** Clovis News Journal; Clovis New Mexico News-Journal. (April 1, 1929)-. Newspaper. English. da (except Sat.). $96.00. Clovis News-Journal, PO Box 1689, Clovis NM 88101. **Tel** (505)763-3431. **ED** Bill Salter. **LC** 7002. **Bk Rev.** **Ad Acc, Adv Mgr:** Mikie Bohannan. **Circ:** 10,000 (daily). ***Formed by the union of*** *Clovis News* ***and*** *Clovis Journal.*

US
DAILY TIMES. Vol. 99, No. 14 (Aug. 14, 1986)-. Newspaper. English. da. $7.00 per month. Farmington Daily Times, PO Box 450, Farmington NM 87401. **Tel** (505)325-4545. **ED** Jack Swickard, Ralph Damiani (Managing Editor). **Photos.** **Ad Acc, Adv Mgr:** Bill Standley. Full Page (B&W) $1251.00. Half Page (B&W) $640.00. Full Page (Color) $1491.00. Half Page (Color) $880.00. **Pub. Size:** Broadsheet. **Wire Svcs.:** AP. available on microfilm. ***Continues*** *Farmington Daily Times (Farmington, N.M. : 1978).*

US/0011-7633
DEFENSOR CHIEFTAIN. (EL DEFENSOR CHIEFTAIN.). **VFOAT** Socorro Chieftain; Defensor-Socorro Chieftain; Chieftain-El Defensor. Vol. 93, No. 161 (Nov. 3, 1959)-. Newspaper. English. sw. Tres Verdes Inc, PO Box Q, Socorro NM 87801. **Tel** (505)835-0520. **ED** Gwen Roath. **Bk Rev**, (Qty: 6 per year). **Ad Acc, Adv Mgr Tel** (505)835-0520. **Circ:** 2,850 (ctrl). available on microfilm. ***Formed by the union of*** *Socorro Chieftain (Socorro, N.M. : 1902)* ***and*** *Defensor (Socorro, N.M.).*
Desc: Newspaper serving high tech and college community; explosives, mining technology and radioastronomy.

US/0738-8349
DEMING HEADLIGHT (1956). (THE DEMING HEADLIGHT.). Vol. 74, No. 3 (Jan. 6, 1956)-. Newspaper. English. da. $54.00. Deming Newspaper Inc, 219 East Maple, Deming NM 88030. **Tel** (505)546-2611. **ED** Tom Field. **Bk Rev.** **Photos.** **Ad Acc, Adv Mgr:** Rachel Baldwin. Full Page (B&W) $614.88. Half Page (B&W) $357.84. Full Page (Color) $674.88. Half Page (Color) $417.84. **Pub. Size:** Broadsheet. **Wire Svcs.:** AP. available on microfilm from Southwest Micropublishing International. ***Continues in part*** *Deming Graphic and the Deming Headlight.*

US/0746-1399
GUADALUPE COUNTY COMMUNICATOR. **VFOAT** Communicator. (198?)-. Newspaper. English. wk (published Thursday). $12.00 in-county, $15.00 elsewhere. Guadalupe County Communicator, PO Box 403, Santa Rosa NM 88435. **Tel** (505)472-3555.

US
HEALTH CITY SUN. Vol. 53, No. 6 (Oct. 3, 1980)-. Newspaper. English. Fifty-two times a year. $10.00 (one year); $18.00 (two years); $26.00 (three years). Health City Sun, PO Box 517, Albuquerque NM 87103. **Tel** (505)242-3010, FAX (505)842-5464. **ED** Moira Martin, and Alicia Alvarez (Managing Editor). **Bk Rev**, (Qty: 20). **Photos.** **Ad Acc, Adv Mgr:** A. D. Collado. Full Page (B&W) $700.00. Half Page (B&W) $350.00. Full Page (Color) $825.00. Half Page (Color) $450.00. **Pub. Size:** Tabloid. **Circ:** 2,000 (ctrl). ***Continues*** *Health City Sun and the News Chieftain.*

US
HERALD, THE. Vol. 33, No. 21 (Jan. 29, 1965)-. Newspaper. English. Fifty-two times a year. $18.00 (residents of Sierra County New Mexico), $25.00 (others). Herald Publishing Company Inc., 1204 North Date, Truth or Consequences NM 87901. **Tel** (505)894-2143, FAX (505)894-7824. **ED** Jim Streicher. **Ad Acc.** **Circ:** 4,600. ***Continues*** *Hot Springs Herald (Hot Springs, N.M. : 1922).*

US
HOBBS DAILY NEWS-SUN. Vol. 9, No. 1 (May 3, 1937)-. Newspaper. English. da (311 issues per year). $108.00. Hobbs Daily News Sun, PO Box 860, Hobbs NM 88240. **Tel** (505)393-2123. ***Continues*** *Hobbs New Mexico Daily News and Sun.*

US
HOBBS FLARE, THE. Newspaper. English. wk. Hobbs Flare, PO Box 1095, Hobbs NM 88240.

US
INDEPENDENT. **VFOAT** Gallup Daily Independent. Vol. 75, No. 236 (Oct. 16, 1964)-. Newspaper. English. da. Gallup Independent, PO Box 1210, Gallup NM 87305. **Tel** (505)863-6811, (800)545-3817. ***Continues*** *Gallup Daily Independent.*

US/0885-8527
LAS CRUCES BULLETIN. Bulletin. English. wk. $18.00. 1210 East Madrid Avenue, PO Box 637, Las Cruces NM 88004. **Tel** (505)524-8061. **ED** Stephen C Klinger. **Bk Rev.** **Ad Acc.** **Circ:** 20,200 (ctrl).
Desc: Community weekly newspaper.

US
LAS CRUCES SUN-NEWS. **VFOAT** Las Cruces Sun News. (March 6, 1939)-. Newspaper. English. da. $83.00. Sunshine Press Inc, PO Box 1749, Las Cruces NM 88004. **Tel** (505)523-4581. ***Continues*** *Las Cruces Daily News and Rio Grande Farmer;* ***Absorbed*** *Las Cruces Citizen.*

US
LAS VEGAS OPTIC. 88th Year, No. 106 (May 2, 1967)-. Newspaper. English. da (Mon. - Fri.). $59.40. Las Vegas Optic, PO Box 2607, Las Vegas NM 87701. **Tel** (505)425-6796, FAX (505)425-1005. **ED** Sharon Vander Meer. **Bk Rev.** **Photos.** **Ad Acc, Adv Mgr:** Anna Huie. Full Page (B&W) $967.50. Half Page (B&W) $487.50. Full Page (Color) $1071.50. Half Page (Color) $591.50. **Pub. Size:** Broadsheet. **Wire Svcs.:** AP. **Circ:** 4,600 (ctrl). available in microform. ***Continues*** *Las Vegas Daily Optic (East Las Vegas, N.M. : 1921).*

US/0893-3456
LOS ALAMOS MONITOR. **VFOAT** Monitor. (March 7, 1963)-. Newspaper. English. da. Monitor / New Mexico, PO Box 1268, Los Alamos NM 87544. **Tel** (505)662-5951. **ED** Gary Jasinek.

US
NAVAJO NATION MESSENGER, THE. **VFOAT** Messenger. (19??)-. Newspaper. English. wk. Free. Gallup Independent, PO Box 1210, Gallup NM 87305. **Tel** (505)863-6811, (800)545-3817. **ED** Ted Ricshton (Editor in Chief), Vicki Raum (Managing Editor). **Bk Rev.** **Photos.** **Ad Acc, Adv Mgr:** Bob Zollinger. Full Page (B&W) $516.00. Half Page (B&W) $258.00. **Pub. Size:** Standard. **Wire Svcs.:** AP, NY. **Circ:** 12,000.

US/0193-5356
NEW MEXICO INDEPENDENT, THE. Vol. 80, No. 37 (July 2, 1976)-. Newspaper. English. wk. $50.00. Independent Publishing Company Inc, PO Box 10, Bernalillo NM 87004. **Tel** (505)843-6440. ***Continues*** *Independiente and the New Mexico Independent.*

US/1049-7374
OBSERVER (RIO RANCHO, N.M.), THE. (THE OBSERVER.). (198?)-. Periodical. English. Fifty-two times a year (Wed.). $30.00. Wick Communications Inc., PO Box 15878, Rio Rancho NM 87174. **Tel** (505)892-8080, FAX (505)892-5719. **ED** Michael J. Ryan, Cord McQueen (Managing Editor). **Bk Rev**, (Qty: 3). **Photos.** **Ad Acc, Adv Mgr:** Marlsa Gilles. Full Page (B&W) $1161.00. Half Page (B&W) $585.00. Full Page (Color) $1311.00. Half Page (Color) $735.00. **Circ:** 17,500 (ctrl). available on microfilm. ***Continues*** *Rio Rancho Observer, 0897-4799.*

US
PORTALES NEWS-TRIBUNE. **VFOAT** Portales News Tribune. Vol. 1, No. 2 (Feb. 11, 1957)-. Newspaper. English. da. Portales News-Tribune, 101 East 1st Street, PO Box 848, Portales NM 88130. **Tel** (505)356-4481. available on microfilm. ***Formed by the union of*** *Portales Daily News* ***and*** *Portales Daily Tribune.*

US
QUAY COUNTY SUN, THE. (19??)-. Newspaper. English. bw. $32.00. Quay County Sun, PO Box 1408, Tucumcari NM 88401. **Tel** (505)461-1952. **ED** Ron Wilmot, Kristie Saatmann (Managing Editor). **Photos. Ad Acc, Adv Mgr:** Linda Griggs. Full Page (B&W) $434.00. Half Page (B&W) $222.00. Full Page (Color) $534.00. Half Page (Color) $322.00. **Pub. Size:** Standard. **Circ:** 3,600. available in microform.

US/0896-1093
RATON RANGE (1985). (RATON RANGE.). **VFOAT** Range; Raton Daily Range. (1975)-. Newspaper. English. sw (Tues. & Fri.). $40.00. Raton Range, 208 South 3rd Street, Raton NM 87740. **Tel** (505)445-2721, FAX (505)445-2723. **ED** David Mullings. **Ad Acc, Adv Mgr:** Paula Pachoruk. ctrl circ. ***Continues*** *Range (Raton, N.M.).*

US
RIO GRANDE SUN. (Oct. 4, 1956)-. Newspaper. English. wk. $15.00 New Mexico; $20.00 other. Rio Grande Sun, PO Box 238, North Railroad Avenue, Espanola NM 87532. ***Absorbed*** *Espanola Valley News.*

US
ROSWELL DAILY RECORD, THE. Vol. 1, No. 143 (Sept. 1, 1903)-. Newspaper. English. da. Roswell Daily Record, PO Box 1897, Roswell NM 88201. **Tel** (505)622-7730. **ED** Jerry McCormick (phone: (505)622-7710). **Bk Rev. Ad Acc, Adv Mgr:** J Pettit, **Tel** (505)622-7710. ctrl circ. available on microfilm. ***Continues*** *Roswell Morning Record;* ***Absorbed*** *Roswell Evening News; Roswell Morning Dispatch.*
Desc: Southern New Mexico's only morning newspaper giving local reports for the town of Roswell.

US/0744-5555
ROUND UP (UNIVERSITY PARK, N.M.). (ROUND UP.). **Added/Corp** New Mexico State University. New Mexico State University of Agriculture, Engineering, and Science New Mexico. College of Agriculture and Mechanic Arts, State College. Vol. 1 (Sept. 4, 1907)-. Newspaper. English. Three times a year. Round Up / New Mexico, New Mexico State University, Box CC, University Park NM 88003. **Tel** (505)646-4501, FAX (505)646-6022. **ED** Wade Wilson. Index available. **Bk Rev. Ad Acc. Pr Rev. Circ:** 10,000 (ctrl). ***Formed by the union of*** *College Weekly* ***and*** *New Mexico Collegian.*
Desc: Primarily of interest to students or alumni of New Mexico State University. Contains local and state news and a wire service as well as university news, syndicated cartoonists/columnists, student staff and writers.

US/0745-5402
RUIDOSO NEWS. Vol. 1, No. 1 (May 17, 1946)-. Newspaper. English. sw. Ruidoso News, PO Box 128, Ruidoso NM 88345-0128. **Tel** (505)257-4001. available on microfilm.

US
SANTA FE NEW MEXICAN, THE. **VFOAT** New Mexican. (19??)-. Newspaper. English. da. $143.00. Santa Fe New Mexican, PO Box 2048, Santa Fe NM 87504. **Tel** (505)983-3309, (800)873-3372. **ED** Rob Dezn. **Bk Rev. Photos. Ad Acc, Adv Mgr:** Virginia Sohn-Shihi, **Tel** (505)986-3006. **Pub. Size:** Broadsheet. **Wire Svcs.:** AP, LA. available in microform. ***Continues*** *New Mexican (Santa Fe, N.M. : 1951).*

US/0744-477X
SANTA FE REPORTER, THE. (1974)-. Newspaper. English. Fifty-two times a year. $31.00 one year; $56.00 two years; $80.00 three years. Santa Fe Reporter, PO Box 2306, Santa Fe NM 87504. **Tel** (505)988-5541. **ED** Robert Mayer. **Photos. Ad Acc, Adv Mgr:** Andrew Strong Jordan. Full Page (B&W) $1,153.00. Half Page (B&W) $578.00. Full Page (Color) $2,001.00. Half Page (Color) $1,282.00. **Pub. Size:** Tabloid. **Circ:** 25,000 (ctrl).

US/0894-783X
SANTA ROSA NEWS (1987). (SANTA ROSA NEWS.). 63rd Year, No. 41 (Jan. 1, 1987)-. Newspaper. English (Spanish). wk. $15.00 in county; $20.00 others. Santa Rosa News, 108 Fifth Street, Santa Rosa NM 88435. **Tel** (505)472-5454. **ED** Darrel Freeman. **Photos. Ad Acc, Adv Mgr:** Virginia Freeman. Full Page (B&W) $529.20. Half Page (B&W) $264.60. Full Page (Color) $604.20. Half Page (Color) $302.10. **Pub. Size:** Broadsheet. **Circ:** 2,200. available on microfilm. ***Continues*** *News (Santa Rosa, N.M. : 1986), 0887-0810.*

US
SIERRA COUNTY SENTINEL. Vol. 1, No. 1 (Mar. 2, 1967)-. Newspaper. English. wk. $25.00. Sierra County Sentinel, PO Box 351, Truth or Consequences NM 87901-0351. **Tel** (505)894-3088. **ED** Myrna Baird. **Bk Rev. Photos. Ad Acc. Wire Svcs.:** AP. **Circ:** 4,300.

US/0891-7981
SILVER CITY DAILY PRESS (1963). (SILVER CITY DAILY PRESS.). **VFOAT** Silver City Daily Press and Independent. Vol. 68, No. 295 (June 19, 1963)-. Newspaper. English. da. Silver City Daily Press, Box 740, Silver City NM 88061. **Tel** (505)388-1576. available on microfilm. ***Continues*** *Silver City Daily Press and Independent.*

US
TAOS NEWS. (July 30, 1959)-. Newspaper. English. Fifty-two times a year (Thurs.). $32.00 Taos Valley & Moreno Valley; $40.00 others in New Mexico; $45.00 others. Taos Publishing Co., PO Box U, Taos NM 87571. **Tel** (505)758-2241. **ED** Billie Blair. **Circ:** 7,909. ***Continues*** *El Crepusculo de la Libertad.*

US
UNION COUNTY LEADER, THE. (1929)-. Newspaper. English. Fifty-two times a year (Published on Wed.). $24.00. Union County Leader, PO Box 486, Clayton NM 88415. **Tel** (505)374-2587, FAX (505)374-8117. **ED** Nick Payton. **Bk Rev**, (Qty: 6). **Photos. Ad Acc.** Full Page (B&W) $651.59. Half Page (B&W) $325.79. Full Page (Color) $970.15. Half Page (Color) $644.36. **Pub. Size:** Broadsheet. **Circ:** 2,750 (ctrl).
Desc: General local news.

US/1071-3492
VALENCIA COUNTY NEWS-BULLETIN. **VFOAT** News Bulletin; Valencia County News Bulletin. (Jan. 1977)-. Bulletin. English. sw. $18.00 Valencia County; $32.00 other. Valencia County News Bulletin, PO Box 25, Belen NM 87002. **Tel** (505)864-4472. available on microfilm. ***Formed by the union of*** *News-Bulletin (Belen, N.M.)* ***and*** *Valencia County News.*

NEW YORK

US
ADIRONDACK DAILY ENTERPRISE. (1927)-. Newspaper. English. da. $90.00. Adirondack Daily Enterprise, PO Box 318, Saranac Lake NY 12983. **Tel** (518)891-2600. **ED** John Penney. **Bk Rev. Photos. Ad Acc, Adv Mgr:** Catherine Moore. Full Page (B&W) $737.10. Half Page (B&W) $368.55. **Pub. Size:** Broadsheet. **Wire Svcs.:** AP. Documents available from UMI Article Clearinghouse. ***Continues*** *Adirondack Enterprise.*
Ind/Abst Bus. Dateline (Nov. 22, 1991-) [Full Txt.].

US/0745-7332
ADIRONDACK ECHO. Vol. 1, No. 1 (Nov. 16, 1950)-. Newspaper. English. wk. $18.50. Adirondack Echo, PO Box 188, Crosby Boulevard, Old Forge NY 13420. **Tel** (315)369-2213. ***Continues*** *Adirondack Arrow.*

US
ADVOCATE, THE. **VFOAT** Advocate, Combining Camillus Advocate, Elbridge Courier, Jordan Leader. Vol. 46, No. 20 (Aug. 1, 1972)-. Newspaper. English. wk. $21.00. Camillus Advocate, Box 7, Camillus NY 13031. **Tel** (315)637-3121. **ED** Jim Arnold (Editor-in-Chief) and Kate Loomis Smith (Managing Editor). **Bk Rev. Photos. Ad Acc, Adv Mgr:** Tania Grashof, **Tel** (315)635-3921. **Pub. Size:** Broadsheet. **Circ:** 3,400. ***Formed by the union of*** *Camillus Advocate; Elbridge Courier* ***and*** *Jordan Leader.*

US/1044-7199
AFRO TIMES (BROOKLYN, N.Y.). (AFRO TIMES.). [Afro times]. **VFOAT** Afro-American Times. Vol. 1, No. 23 (July 18, 1987)-. Newspaper. English. wk. $24.00. Challenge Group, 1360 Fulton Street, Brooklyn NY 11216. **Tel** (718)636-9500, FAX (718)857-9115. **ED** Thomas H. Watkins, Dawn Phillip (Managing Editor). **DD** 071. **Bk Rev. Photos. Ad Acc, Adv Mgr:** Jean Wells. Full Page (B&W) $3,855.60. **Pub. Size:** Standard. **Wire Svcs.:** AP, RN, UPI. **Circ:** 54,000. available on microfilm. ***Continues*** *Afro-American Times.*

US
AKRON BUGLE. Vol. 1, No. 1 (July 2, 1981)-. Newspaper. English. wk. $16.00 North America; $14.00 US; $14.00 other. Akron Bugle, 7263 Downey Road, Akron NY 14001-9714. **Tel** (716)542-9615. **ED** Marilyn J. Kasperek. **Bk Rev. Ad Acc. Circ:** 1,650 (ctrl).
Desc: Local, weekly newspaper serving the residents of Akron Central School District, town of Newstead, and adjoining towns with articles and information of local interest.

US/0300-5453
AL-HUDA AL-JADIDAH. **VFOAT** The New Al-Hoda. (19??)-. Newspaper. Arabic. bw. Stephen Fares Travel, 34 West 28th Street, New York NY 10001. **Tel** (212)686-7398. ***Continues*** *Hoda.*

US
ALBION ADVERTISER. Vol. 1, No. 1 (Nov. 8, 1929)-. Newspaper. English. wk. Albion Advertiser, 8 East Bank Street, Albion NY 14411. ***Absorbed*** *Orleans Republican American and Weekly News.*

US
ALFRED SUN, THE. **VFOAT** Daily Alfred Sun. (Dec. 6, 1883)-. Newspaper. English. wk. $20.00 Allegany County; $22.00 other. Alfred Sun, PO Box 811, Alfred NY 14802. **Tel** (607)587-8110, FAX (607)587-8110. **ED** David L. Snyder. **Bk Rev. Photos. Ad Acc.** Full Page (B&W) $175.00. Half Page (B&W) $90.00. Full Page (Color) $200.00. Half Page (Color) $105.00. **Pub. Size:** Tabloid. **Circ:** 900. available on microfilm from University Microfilms International (UMI).

US
ALGEMEINER JOURNAL, DER. (197?)-. Newspaper. Yiddish (English). wk. $45.00 (surface mail); $200.00 (airmail). Algemeiner Journal, 211 63rd Street, Brooklyn NY 11220. **Tel** (718)492-6420. **ED** Gershon Jacobson. **Bk Rev. Photos. Ad Acc.** Full Page (B&W) $5,400.00. Half Page (B&W) $2,700.00. **Pub. Size:** Broadsheet.
Desc: Covers all news, features, theatre, and books on newsstands from coast to coast.

US/0890-6025
ALTAMONT ENTERPRISE (1983), THE. (THE ALTAMONT ENTERPRISE.). **VFOAT** Altamont Enterprise and Albany County Post. (1983)-. Newspaper. English. wk. $22.50 Albany County, NY; $24.00 other. Altamont Enterprise, PO Box 654, Altamont NY 12019. **Tel** (518)861-6641, FAX (518)861-5105. **ED** Christopher Sanford. **Bk Rev. Photos. Ad Acc. Pub. Size:** Standard. **Circ:** 7,250. available in microform. ***Continues*** *Altamont Enterprise and Albany County Post.*
Desc: Coverage of local news in six towns and three school districts in Albany County, New York.

US/0276-1904
AM-POL EAGLE. (19??)-. Periodical. English. Fifty-two times a year (Thurs.). $19.50. Am-Pol Eagle, 3343 Harlan Road, Cheektowoga NY 14225. **Tel** (716)835-9454, FAX (716)835-9457. **ED** Renee Harzewski (Editor-in-Chief) and Roger Purchalski (Managing Editor). **Bk Rev. Photos. Ad Acc, Adv Mgr:** James Lasky, **Tel** (716)835-9457. Full Page (B&W) $526.40. Half Page (B&W) $263.20. **Pub. Size:** Tabloid.
Desc: Caters to Polish-American population of Western New York.

US/0194-7990
AMERIKAI MAGYAR SZO. **VFOAT** Magyar Szo. (1952)-. Newspaper. Hungarian (English). wk. $30.00. Amerikai Magyar Szo, 130 East 16th Street, New York NY 10003. **Tel** (212)254-0397, FAX (212)254-0397. **ED** Joseph Garai. **DD** 071. **Bk Rev. Ad Acc.** Full Page (B&W) $400.00. Half Page (B&W) $250.00. **Pub. Size:** Tabloid. ctrl circ.

US
AMHERST BEE, THE. (March 20, 1879)-. Newspaper. English. wk. $24.00. Bee Publications, PO Box 150, Buffalo NY 14231. **Tel** (716)632-4700.

US
AMITYVILLE RECORD, THE. (May 4, 1904)-. Newspaper. English. Fifty-two times a year. $19.00 Suffolk County; $24.00 others. Amityville Record, 85 Broadway, Amityville NY 11701. **Tel** (516)264-0077, FAX (516)798-5296. **ED** Carolyn James. **Photos. Ad Acc, Adv Mgr:** Alfred James. Full Page (B&W) $300.00. Half Page (B&W) $180.00. Full Page (Color) $325.00. Half Page (Color) $205.00. **Pub. Size:** Standard. **Circ:** 3,500. available in microform.

US/0746-102X
ARCADE HERALD. Vol. 78, No. 1 (Aug. 20, 1981)-. Newspaper. English. Fifty-one times per year. $20.00 Erie Wyoming & Cattaragus counties in New York; $22.00 others. Arcade Herald Inc, 12 Liberty Street, Arcade NY 14009. **Tel** (716)492-2525. **ED** Kathleen Mason. **Ad Acc, Adv Mgr:** Amy Gordon. Full Page (B&W) $360.00. Half Page (B&W) $205.00. **Pub. Size:** Standard. **Circ:** 4,900 (ctrl). ***Continues*** *Tri-County Times.*

US/0004-2358
ARMENIAN REPORTER, THE. [Armen. rep.]. Vol. 1, No. 1 (Nov. 2, 1967)-. Newspaper. English. Fifty times a year (Except 2 weeks in July). $60.00 surface mail; $120.00 airmail. Armenian Reporter International, PO Box 600, Fresh Meadow NY 11365. **Tel** (718)380-1200, FAX (718)380-8057. **ED** Edward K. Bogosian (Editor-in-Chief) and Aris Sevag (Managing Editor). **Bk Rev**, (Qty: 40). **Photos. Ad Acc, Adv Mgr:** Arlene Bogosian. Full Page (B&W) $500.00. Half Page (B&W) $300.00. **Pub. Size:** Standard. **Wire Svcs.:** AP, UPI. **Circ:** 5,000. available on microfilm from The Library of Congress Photoduplication Service.
Desc: Covers and reports all the news pertaining to the Armenian community and people.

US/0004-7813
AUFBAU (NEW YORK, N.Y.). (AUFBAU : NACHRICHTENBLATT DES GERMAN-JEWISH CLUB, INC., NEW YORK, N. Y.). [Aufbau]. **Added/Corp** German-Jewish Club. New World Club. **VFOAT** Reconstruction. Vol. 1, No. 1 (Dec. 1, 1934)-. Newspaper. German. Six times a year. $48.50 (one year), $84.00 (two years) US; $54.00 Canada & Mexico; $58.00 Israel; $68.00 Europe; $56.00 South America; $74.00 other. New World Club Inc, 2121 Broadway, New York NY

10023. **Tel** (212)873-7400, FAX (212)496-5736. **ED** Henry Marx. **Bk Rev. Ad Acc. Circ:** 30,000.
Desc: Emphasis on political and cultural articles.

US
BALDWINSVILLE MESSENGER. English. wk (Wed.). $32.00 (New York residents outside of 13027 zip code); $30.00 (other New York residents); $40.00 (other). Brown Newspapers, PO Box 270, 7-9-11 East Geness Street, Baldwinsville NY 13027. **Tel** (315)635-3921.

US
BALLSTON JOURNAL (BALLSTON SPA, N.Y. : 1952). (BALLSTON JOURNAL.). Vol. 14, No. 131 (April 3, 1952)-. Newspaper. English. wk. Ballston Journal, 72 West High Street, Ballston Spa NY 12020. **Tel** (518)885-4341. **ED** Charles Hogan. **Circ:** 7,591. ***Continues*** *Ballston Spa Journal.*

US
BAYSIDE TIMES. (1935)-. Newspaper. English. wk. $15.00. Queens Publishing Corporation, 214 41st Avenue, Bayside NY 11361. **Tel** (718)229-0300, FAX (718)225-7117. **ED** Steven Bleuh, Roz Liston (Managing Editor). **Photos. Ad Acc, Adv Mgr:** Howard Swengler. Full Page (B&W) $960.00. Half Page (B&W) $480.00. Full Page (Color) $1110.00. Half Page (Color) $630.00. **Pub. Size:** Standard. **Circ:** 11,900.

US
BEACON (BABYLON, N.Y.). (THE BEACON.). Vol. 6, No. 44 (Aug. 31, 1972)-. Newspaper. English. wk. The Babylon Beacon, 65 Deer Park Avenue, PO Box L, Babylon NY 11702. **Tel** (516)587-5612. available on microfilm from Berhan Industries, Ltd. ***Continues*** *Babylon Beacon.*

US
BEACON FREE PRESS. (19??)-. Newspaper. English. wk. $25.00. Southern Dutchess News, 84 East Main Street, Wappingers Falls NY 12590. **Tel** (914)297-3723, FAX (914)297-6810. **ED** Bill Parsons. **Photos. Ad Acc, Adv Mgr:** Audrey Morgenstern. Full Page (B&W) $724.50. Half Page (B&W) $362.25. Full Page (Color) $849.50. Half Page (Color) $487.25. **Pub. Size:** Broadsheet. **Circ:** 8,300 (ctrl). available in microform.
Desc: Local, community and school news. Also government, politics sports, police reports, horoscope, and comics.

US
BELLMORE LIFE. (19??)-. Newspaper. English. wk. Bellmore Life, 2717 Grand Avenue, Bellmore NY 11710. **Tel** (516)826-0333.

US
BELLMORE MERRICK OBSERVER. Newspaper. English. Fifty-two times a year. $7.00. Bellmore Merrick Observer, 2262 Centre Avenue, Bellmore NY 11710. **Tel** (516)679-9888. **ED** Jackson Pokress (editor's address: 508 Atlanta Avenue North, Messapequa, NY 11758). cum. index. **Ad Acc, Adv Mgr:** Wilma Pokress.

US/0745-936X
BIG RED NEWS. ***Title Change.*** **VFOAT** Big Red. (19??)-(19??). Periodical. English. Fifty-two times a year. Smith Haj Publishing, 15 East 40th Street, Suite 402, New York NY 10016. **Tel** (212)213-8585. ***Continues*** *Week-End Big Red.* ***Continued by*** *New York Beacon.*

US
BOONVILLE HERALD AND ADIRONDACK TOURIST. VFOAT Boonville Herald. Vol. 32, No. 10 (May 7, 1885)-. Newspaper. English. Fifty-two times a year. $16.00 Oneida, Lewis, Hamilton and Herkimer Counties; $18.00 others. Boonville Herald, PO Box 372, East Schuyler Street, Boonville NY 13309. **Tel** (315)942-4449. **ED** Irene S. Lansing, and Sandra Hrim (Managing Editor). **Photos. Ad Acc, Adv Mgr:** Teresa Freeman, **Tel** (315)942-4449. Full Page (B&W) $400.00. Half Page (B&W) $250.00. Full Page (Color) $460.00. Half Page (Color) $310.00. **Pub. Size:** Broadsheet. **Circ:** 3,400 (ctrl). available on microfiche. ***Continues*** *Boonville Herald (Boonville, N.Y.).*
Desc: Cover news in Oneida, Lewis, Herkimer and Hamilton Counties.

US
BRIGHTON PITTSFORD POST. English. wk. $25.00 (one year); $42.00 (two year); $54.00 (three year). Wolfe Publications, 666 Phillips Road, Victor NY 14564. **Tel** (716) 924-4040, FAX (716) 924-7734.

US
BROCKPORT POST, THE. Vol. 1, No. 1 (Oct. 1973)-. Newspaper. English. Fifty-two times a year. $25.00. Wolfe Publications, 666 Phillips Road, Victor NY 14564. **Tel** (716) 924-4040, FAX (716) 924-7734.

US
BRONX PRESS-REVIEW. VFOAT Bronx Press Review; Press-Review; Press Review. (1940)-. Newspaper. English. wk. $18.00 (1 year), $35.00 (2 year). Parkchester Publishing Company Inc, 1924 Cross Bronx Express Way, Bronx NY 10472. **Tel** (212)823-5200, FAX (212)823-7108. **ED** Gerald Doyle. available on microfilm from New York Public Library.

US/8750-4499
BRONX TIMES REPORTER. (1981)-. Newspaper. English. wk. $5.00 Bronx county; $25.00 other. Bronx Times Reporter, 3711 East Tremont Avenue, Bronx NY 10465. **Tel** (212)597-1116, FAX (212)518-0038. **ED** John Collazzi. **Bk Rev**, (Qty: 6). **Photos. Ad Acc, Adv Mgr:** Evelyn Perreira, **Tel** (718)597-1116. Full Page (B&W) $750.00. Half Page (B&W) $375.00. Full Page (Color) $950.00. **Pub. Size:** Standard. **Circ:** 17,000 (ctrl).
Desc: Bronx based local community newspaper.

US/0744-7728
BROOKLYN COURIER. ***Title Change.*** Newspaper. English. wk. Courier Life Inc, 1733 Sheepshead Bay Road, Brooklyn NY 11235. **Tel** (718)769-4400. ***Continued by*** *Bay Ridge Courier.*

US/0740-2260
BROOKLYN GRAPHIC, THE. VFOAT Graphic. (19??)-. Newspaper. English. Fifty-two times a year. $20.00 (one year); $30.00 (two year). Courier Life Inc., 1733 Sheepshead Bay Road, Brooklyn NY 11235. **Tel** (718)769-4400.

US/0007-2346
BROOKLYN HEIGHTS PRESS & COBBLE HILL NEWS. VFOAT Brooklyn Heights Press and Cobble Hill News. 1965-. Newspaper. English. wk. 129 Montague Street, Brooklyn NY 11201. **ED** Edmund J Pinto. ***Continues*** *Brooklyn Heights Press.*

US/0885-839X
BROOKLYN PAPER, THE. VFOAT BH-BWN. Newspaper. English. wk. Brooklyn Paper, 26 Court Street, Brooklyn NY 11242. ***Continues*** *Brooklyn Heights Paper, 8756-1832.*

US/0740-2643
BROOKLYN RECORD. ***Ceased.*** (19??)-(19??). Newspaper. English. wk. Brooklyn Record, 44 Court Street, Brooklyn NY 11201.

US
BUFFALO JEWISH REVIEW. (1912)-. Newspaper. English. wk. Buffalo Jewish Review, 15 East Mohawk Street, Buffalo NY 14203. **Tel** (716)854-2192. available on microfilm. ***Continues*** *American Jewish Review.*

US/0745-2691
BUFFALO NEWS, THE. Vol. 204, No. 182 (Oct. 9, 1982)-. Newspaper. English. da. $263.00. Buffalo Evening News, 1 News Plaza, PO Box 100, Buffalo NY 14240. **Tel** 800 777-8640 ext. 4530, FAX (716)856-5150, telex 916430. **ED** Murray B. Light, Foster L. Spencer and Leonard W. Halpert. Index available. **Bk Rev. Ad Acc. Circ:** 317,651 daily, 371,016 Sunday. available on microfilm from University Microfilms International (UMI); available on an online database (files 635,733/Full-Text) from DIALOG. Documents available from UMI Article Clearinghouse. ***Continues*** *Buffalo Evening News.*
Ind/Abst Bus. Dateline (Nov. 25, 1991-) [Full Txt.]; PROMT.

US
CALEDONIA ADVERTISER. VFOAT Caledonia Advertiser Including the Churchville Times; Scottsville News. (1878)-. Newspaper. English. wk. $17.95. The Keith Press, 3096 Main Street, Caledonia NY 14423. ***Continues*** *Tri-County Weekly (Caledonia, N.Y.).*

US
CANARSIE COURIER. Newspaper. English. wk. $11.50 New York; $17.00 other. Canarsie Courier, 1142 East 92nd Street, Brooklyn NY 11236. **Tel** (718)257-0600. **ED** Charles Rogers. **Ad Acc, Adv Mgr:** R.Sito.

US
CARROLL GARDENS COBBLE HILL NEWSPAPER, THE. VFOAT The Carroll Gardens/Cobble Hill Newspaper; Newspaper. (19??)-. Newspaper. English. qt. Brooklyn Paper Publications, 26 Court Street, Brooklyn NY 11242-0009. **Tel** (718)834-9350, FAX (718)834-9278. **ED** Paul Toomey. **Ad Acc, Adv Mgr:** Celia Weintraub. **Circ:** 8,300.

US/0889-8715
CARTHAGE REPUBLICAN TRIBUNE. (CARTHAGE REPUBLICAN-TRIBUNE.). **VFOAT** Carthage Republican Tribune. 63rd Year, No. 36 (Jan. 18, 1923)-. Newspaper. English. wk (Weds.). $20.00 (in county), $24.00 (other) US; $30.00 (other). Carthage Republican-Tribune, Box 549, Carthage NY 13619. **Tel** (315)493-1270. **ED** Ray Hansen. **Photos. Ad Acc, Adv Mgr:** Charles Howlett, **Tel** (315)788-3638. **Pub. Size:** Standard. ctrl circ. available on microfilm from Bell & Howell. ***Continues*** *Carthage Republican and the Carthage Tribune;* ***Absorbed*** *North Country Advance; Theresa Gleaner.*

US
CATO CITIZEN, THE. Vol. 47, No. 15 (Jan. 22, 1940)-. Newspaper. English. wk. $15.00. Wayuga Community Newspapers, Inc., PO Box 199, Red Creek NY 13143-0199. **Tel** (315)594-2506, FAX (315)594-6331. **ED** Charles Itzin (Editor in Chief), Chris Palermo (Managing Editor). **Photos. Ad Acc, Adv Mgr:** Charles Palermo, **Tel** (315)754-6229. Full Page (B&W) $408.00. Half Page (B&W) $204.00. Full Page (Color) $438.00. Half Page (Color) $234.00. **Pub. Size:** Tabloid. **Wire Svcs.:** El. ***Continues*** *Cato Citizen and Tri-County Leader.*

US
CATSKILL MOUNTAIN NEWS. Vol. 8, No. 41 (Sept. 1902)-. Newspaper. English. wk (Wed.). $48.50. Catskill Mountain Publishing Corporation, PO Box 290, Margeretville NY 12455. **Tel** (914)586-2601. **Ad Acc.** ***Continues*** *Catskill Mountain News and Margaretville Messenger;* ***Absorbed*** *Utilitarian.*

US
CAZENOVIA REPUBLICAN. Vol. 1, No. 1 (May 3, 1854)-. Newspaper. English. wk. $21.00. Cazenovia Republican, PO Box 301, Cazenovia NY 13035. **ED** Jim Arnold, and Robyn Larwood (Managing Editor). **Bk Rev. Photos. Ad Acc, Adv Mgr:** Barbara Dukette, **Tel** (315)655-3415. Full Page (B&W) $575.00. Half Page (B&W) $295.00. Full Page (Color) $690.00. Half Page (Color) $355.00. **Pub. Size:** Broadsheet. available in microform.

US/8750-104X
CENTRAL ISLIP NEWS (1984). (CENTRAL ISLIP NEWS.). Newspaper. English. wk. Central Islip News, PO Box 160, Central Islip NY 11722.

US/0009-1049
CHALLENGE (NEW YORK, N.Y.). (CHALLENGE / DESAFIO.). [Challenge]. **Added/Corp** Progressive Labor Party. **VFOAT** Desafio. No. 1 (June 11, 1964)-. Newspaper. English (Spanish). Forty-six times a year. $35.00 (institutions), $15.00 (individuals). Progressive Labor Party, GPO Box 808, Brooklyn NY 11202. **Tel** (212)629-0002. **ED** Louis Castro. **LC** E838; .C5. **DD** 335. **Photos. Pub. Size:** Standard. **Circ:** 10,000. available on microfilm and microfiche from University Microfilms International (UMI).
Ind/Abst Urban Aff. Abstr.

US/1040-8886
CHALLENGER (BUFFALO, N.Y.), THE. (THE CHALLENGER.). (19??)-. Newspaper. English. wk. $15.00. Challenger Publishing Company Inc, 1301 Fillmore Avenue, Buffalo NY 14211. **Tel** (716)897-0442. **ED** Al-Nisa Barbara Banks. **Bk Rev. Ad Acc.** ctrl circ. ***Continues*** *Buffalo Challenger.*
Desc: Community newspaper distributed throughout the Buffalo area with emphasis on local, national and international events as they impact African-Americans and other minorities.

US
CHATEAUGAY RECORD AND FRANKLIN COUNTY DEMOCRAT. (198?)-. Newspaper. English. wk. $16.00 Franklin City, New York; $23.00 US; $29.00 other. Chateaugay Record Printing, 10 West Main Street, Chateaugay NY 12920. **Tel** (518)497-6142. ***Continues*** *Chateaugay Record.*

US/1064-4644
CHATHAM COURIER, THE ROUGH NOTES, THE. VFOAT Chatham Courier-Rough Notes. No. 46 (Feb. 16, 1967)-. Newspaper. English. wk. $28.00. Chatham Courier Company, PO Box 355, Chatham NY 12037. **Tel** (518)392-4141. **ED** Anne M. Sheehan. **Bk Rev. Photos. Ad Acc, Adv Mgr:** James Fleming, **Tel** (518)392-5151. Full Page (B&W) $638.40. Half Page (B&W) $319.20. Full Page (Color) $713.40. Half Page (Color) $394.20. **Pub. Size:** Tabloid. **Circ:** 7,500. ***Formed by the union of*** *Chatham Courier* ***and*** *Rough Notes (Valatie, N.Y.).*

US/0746-0414
CHAUTAUQUAN DAILY, THE. (THE CHAUTAUQUAN DAILY / CHAUTAUQUA INSTITUTION.). **Added/Corp** Chautauqua Institution. Vol. 31, No. 1 (June 28, 1906)-. Periodical. English. da. $22.00 New York; $27.50 others. Chautauquan Daily, Chautauque Institution, Chautauqua NY 14722. **Tel** (909)357-6206. **(Subscription address:** Chautauguan Daily, PO Box 1065, Chautauguan NY 14722.) **ED** Joan Hutter, and B. Shilling (Managing Editor). **Photos. Ad Acc, Adv Mgr:** Barney Shilling. **Pub. Size:** Standard. **Pr Rev. Circ:** 3,000. available on microfilm from University Microfilms International (UMI). ***Continues*** *Chautauqua Assembly Herald.*
Desc: Contains coverage of the arts and subjects of the day. Includes world affairs, and articles on the family.

US
CHEEKTOWAGA TIMES. (Jan. 10, 1946)-. Newspaper. English. Fifty-one times per year (Thurs.). $25.00. Cheektowaga Times, 343 Maryvale Drive, Cheektowaga NY 14225. **Tel** (716)892-5323, FAX (716)892-4925. **ED** Eve Allis, Margaret Bourdette. **Photos. Ad Acc.** Full Page (B&W) $622.40. Half Page (B&W) $311.20. Full Page (Color) $722.40. Half Page (Color) $411.20. **Pub. Size:** Standard. **Circ:** 5,600. available in microform.

US/1064-4091
CHEMUNG VALLEY REPORTER. (Apr. 14, 1887)-. Newspaper. English. wk (Thurs.). $18.00 Chemung County, New York; $20.00 other. Chemung Valley Reporter, 205 South Main Street, PO Box 474, Horseheads NY 14845. **Tel** (607)739-3001. **ED** Martha Horton, Linda Gudas (Managing Editor). **Photos. Ad Acc, Adv Mgr:** Marian Grushetsky. **Pub. Size:** Tabloid. **Circ:** 1,500 (ctrl). ***Continues*** *Horseheads Journal (Horseheads, N.Y. : 1886).*

US/0746-7761
CHIEF CIVIL SERVICE LEADER, THE. **VFOAT** Civil Service Leader; Chief-Leader. (198?)-. Newspaper. English. wk. $20.00 US; $25.00 other. New York Civil Service Employees Publishing Company Inc, 150 Nassau Street, New York NY 10038. **Tel** (212)962-2690. ***Continues*** *Chief, 0009-3807.*

US
CHINA PRESS. (19??)-. Newspaper. English. da (312 per year). $100.00 US; $1850.00 other. China Press, 15 Mercer Street, New York NY 10013. **Tel** (212) 274-8282.

US
CHITTENANGO, BRIDGEPORT TIMES. (Apr. 2, 1975)-. Newspaper. English. wk. $21.00. Chittenango Bridgeport Times, PO Box 210, 216 Genesee Street, Chittenango NY 13037. **Tel** (315)687-3887. **ED** Jim Arnold, and Marcia Skramko (Managing Editor). **Bk Rev. Photos. Ad Acc, Adv Mgr:** Diane Connors. Full Page (B&W) $415.00. Half Page (B&W) $211.00. Full Page (Color) $497.00. Half Page (Color) $255.00. **Pub. Size:** Broadsheet. available in microform. ***Continues*** *Madison County Times.*

US/0743-7056
CHOSON ILBO (MIJU PAN). (CHOSON ILBO = CHOSUN ILBO.). **VFOAT** Chosun Ilbo; Chosun Ilbo New York. (19??)-. Newspaper. Korean. da. $165.00. Choson Ilbo, 40-22 College PT Boulevard, Room 14-B, Flushing NY 11354. **Tel** (718)463-4443, FAX (718)359-2067. **ED** Mr. Han Young Sik. cum. index. **Bk Rev**, (Qty: 306). **Ad Acc, Adv Mgr:** Elaine Kim, **Tel** (718)463-4443. **Pr Rev. Circ:** 30,000.
Desc: A Korean newspaper that list many articles such as, politics, areas affairs, art, economics, sports, education, health, religion, home and refined articles like the New York Times.

US
CHRONICLE-EXPRESS. **VFOAT** Chronicle Express. Vol. 103, No. 2 (Jan. 13, 1926)-. Newspaper. English. wk (Published on Wednesday). $24.00. Chronicle Express / New York, 138 Main Street, Penn Yan NY 14527. **Tel** (315)536-4422. **ED** Tim Jones. **Ad Acc, Adv Mgr:** Ken Miller. ctrl circ. ***Formed by the union of*** *Penn Yan Express; Yates County Chronicle* ***and*** *Rushville Chronicle and Gorham New Age.*

US/0738-7520
CITIZEN (AUBURN, N.Y.), THE. (THE CITIZEN.). Vol. 45, No. 215 (Nov. 2, 1975)-. Newspaper. English. da (daily except Saturday and holidays). $176.00 (one year). Auburn Publishers Company, 25 Dill Street, Auburn NY 13021. **Tel** (315)253-5311. **ED** Susan Gadock (phone: (315)253-5311 Ext. 230). **Ad Acc, Adv Mgr:** Charles Kolsky. **Circ:** 15,787 daily, 16,226 Sunday (ctrl). ***Continues*** *Citizen-Advertiser.*

US
CITY NEWSPAPER. Vol. 9, No. 7 (Nov. 1, 1979)-. Newspaper. English. wk. WMT Publications, 250 North Goodman Street, Rochester NY 14607. ***Formed by the union of*** *City/West* ***and*** *City/East (Rochester, N.Y.).*

US/8750-2720
CITY SUN, THE. Vol. 1, No. 1 (June 6, 1984)-. Newspaper. English. wk (except Christmas and New Year's). $40.00. The City Sun, PO Box 560, Brooklyn NY 11202. **Tel** (718)624-5959, FAX (718)596-7429. **ED** Andrew W. Cooper, and Stefani Zinerman (Managing Editor). **Bk Rev**, (Qty: 6). **Photos. Ad Acc, Adv Mgr:** Barbara Sealy Rhoden. Full Page (B&W) $3,400.00. Full Page (Color) $3,800.00. **Pub. Size:** Standard. **Circ:** 56,863 (ctrl).

US
CLINTON COURIER (CLINTON, N.Y.). ***Title Change.*** (THE CLINTON COURIER.). Vol. 3, No. 1 (Sept. 8, 1859)-(195?). Newspaper. English. wk. Clinton Courier, 32 College Street, Clinton NY 13323. ***Continues*** *Clinton Courier and Oneida Chief;* ***Absorbed*** *Clinton Advertiser (Clinton, N.Y.).* ***Continued by*** *Courier (Clinton, N.Y.).*

•US
COLUMBIA COUNTY INDEPENDENT, THE. **VFOAT** Independent. (1992)-. Newspaper. English. sw. $42.00. The Independent / New York, Box 246, Hillsdale NY 12529. **Tel** (518)325-4400, FAX (518)325-4497. **ED** Vicki Simons (Editor-in-Chief) and Ray Fashona (Managing Editor). **Photos. Ad Acc, Adv Mgr:** Charles Schram. Full Page (B&W) $812.00. Half Page (B&W) $406.00. **Pub. Size:** Tabloid. **Circ:** 9,050. ***Continues*** *Twice Weekly Independent.*

US
COLUMBIA SPECTATOR. (1877)-. Newspaper. English. da. $85.00. Columbia University Spectator Publishing Co., 1125 Amsterdam Avenue/2nd Floor, New York NY 10025. **Tel** (212)280-4771. **ED** Sara Just. **Bk Rev. Ad Acc. Circ:** 10,000 (ctrl).
Desc: College newspaper covering New York City and University affairs as well as the arts spectator.

US/0746-7508
COMMACK NEWS. (19??)-. Newspaper. English. wk. $15.00. Commack News, PO Box 277, Commack NY 11725. **Tel** (516)265-2100. **ED** David Ambro, Jennifer Paley (Managing Editor). **Photos. Ad Acc, Adv Mgr:** Jen Paley. **Pub. Size:** Standard. **Circ:** 4,125.

US/0192-5253
COMMERCIAL NEWS. Newspaper. English. wk. Commercial News / Saratoga Springs, 20 Lake Avenue, Saratoga Springs NY 12866.

US
CORNELL DAILY SUN. **VFOAT** Cornell Sun. Vol. 3, No. 2 (Sept. 25, 1882)-. Newspaper. English. da. $29.95 Ithaca; $45.00 other. Cornell Daily Sun, 119 South Cayuga Street, Ithaca NY 14850. **Tel** (607)273-3606. **ED** Marc Lacey. **Bk Rev. Ad Acc. Circ:** 5,550. ***Continues*** *Cornell Sun.*
Desc: Reports the news in Ithaca and at Cornell. A member of AP and UPI, with review and sports sections.

US
CORNWALL LOCAL (CORNWALL, N.Y. : 1923). (THE CORNWALL LOCAL.). Began with Vol. 33, No. 29 (Nov. 1, 1923). Newspaper. English. wk. News of the Highlands Inc, 35 Hasbrouck Avenue, Cornwall NY 12518. ***Continues*** *Cornwall Press.*

US/0745-9823
CORTLAND DEMOCRAT (1877), THE. (THE CORTLAND DEMOCRAT.). (July 1877)-. Newspaper. English. wk. Cortland Democrat, 12 Central Avenue, PO Box 426, Cortland NY 13045. **Tel** (607)753-00610. ***Continues*** *Cortland County Democrat;* ***Absorbed*** *Dryden Herald.*

US
CORTLAND STANDARD. No. 79 (Apr. 4, 1921)-. Newspaper. English. da. Cortland Standard, PO Box 5548, Cortland NY 13045. **Tel** (607)756-5665. ***Continues*** *Cortland Standard and Homer Republican (Cortland, N.Y. : Daily).*

US/0192-1126
COUNTRY SHOPPER, THE. (19??)-. Periodical. English. mo. Free. Country Shopper, PO Box 190, Pound Ridge NY 10576. **Tel** (914)764-4678, FAX (914)764-4662. **ED** Jan Powell. **Bk Rev. Ad Acc, Adv Mgr:** Charles Seaman. **Circ:** 8,000.

US
COURIER, THE. ***Title Change.*** (195?)-(19??). Newspaper. English. wk. Clinton Courier, 32 College Street, Clinton NY 13323. ***Continues*** *Clinton Courier (Clinton, N.Y. : 1859).* ***Continued by*** *Clinton Courier (Clinton, N.Y. : 1985).*

US
COURIER-OBSERVER. Newspaper. English. da (Tues., thru Sat.). $77.00 (five days) St. Lawrence county in New York; $86.00 (five days) others; $94.00 (six days). Courier-Observer, 71 Market Street, Postdam NY 13676. **Tel** (315)769-2451.

US/0738-7709
COURIER-STANDARD-ENTERPRISE. **VAT** Courier, Standard, Enterprise. (Oct. 18, 1977)-. Newspaper. English. wk. $14.00 county, $15.50 elsewhere in NY state, $19.00 other. Courier-Standard-Enterprise, PO Box 351, Fort Plain NY 13339. **Tel** (518)993-2321. ***Continues*** *Canajoharie Courier; Fort Plains Standard; St Johnsville Enterprise.*

US/0746-9969
CUBA PATRIOT AND FREE PRESS. (197?)-. Newspaper. English. wk. $29.00. Cuba Patriot and Free Press, 34 West Main Street, Cuba NY 14727. **Tel** (716)968-2580. ***Continues*** *Patriot and Free Press.*

US/1060-4723
DAILY ARGUS (WHITE PLAINS, N.Y.), THE. (DAILY ARGUS.). (1892)-. Newspaper. English. da. price vaies due to area. Gannett Surburban Newspaper, 1 Gannett Drive, White Plains NY 10604. **Tel** 800 942-1010.

US/0746-8865
DAILY CHALLENGE. **VFOAT** New York Daily Challenge. (1972)-. Newspaper. English. da. $48.00. New York Daily Challenge, 1360 Fulton Street, Brooklyn NY 11216. **Tel** (718)636-9500, FAX (718)857-9115. **ED** Thomas H. Watkins, Jr. and Dawad Philip (Managing Editor). **Photos. Ad Acc, Adv Mgr:** Jean Wells. Full Page (B&W) $3,855.60. Half Page (B&W) $1,927.80. Full Page (Color) $4,241.16. Half Page (Color) $2,120.58. **Pub. Size:** Tabloid. **Wire Svcs.:** UPI, RN. **Circ:** 77,776 (daily). available on microfilm from New York Public Library.

US
DAILY COURIER-OBSERVER. **VFOAT** Daily Courier Observer; Courier-Observer; Courier Observer; Journal-Courier-Observer; Journal Courier Observer. Vol. 1, No. 1 (May 2, 1989)-. Newspaper. English. da (Tues. thru Sat.). $90.00 St. Lawrence County in New York; $98.00 others. Potsdam Courier Observer, PO Box 5205, 71 Market Street, Potsdam NY 13676. **Tel** (315)265-6000. ***Formed by the union of*** *Courier and Freeman* ***and*** *Massena Observer.*

US/0746-4932
DAILY FREEMAN (KINGSTON, N.Y. 1969), THE. (THE DAILY FREEMAN.). **VFOAT** Sunday Freeman. Vo. 99, No. 50 (Dec. 15, 1969)-. Newspaper. English. da. $169.80 (daily and Sunday). Daily Freeman, 79 97 Hurley Avenue, Kingston NY 12401. **Tel** (914)331-5691, FAX (914)338-0672. **ED** Ira Fusfeld. **Circ:** 21,107 daily, 27,258 Sunday. ***Continues*** *Kingston Daily Freeman.*

US/1050-0340
DAILY GAZETTE (1990), THE. (DAILY GAZETTE.). **VFOAT** Sunday Gazette. (Jan. 1, 1990)-. Newspaper. English. da. $3.15 (1 week), $12.60 (1 month), $37.80 (3 months), $81.90 (6 months) $163.80 (1 year). Daily Gazette Company, 2345 Maxon Road, Schenectady NY 12301. **Tel** (518) 374-4141, FAX (518) 395-3089, (518) 395-3029. ***Continues*** *Schenectady Gazette (Schenectady, N.Y. : 1902).*

US/1060-4553
DAILY ITEM (WHITE PLAINS, N.Y.), THE. (THE DAILY ITEM.). Aug. 17 (1931)-. Newspaper. English. da. $288.00. Westchester Rockland Newspapers Inc, 1 Gannett Drive, White Plains NY 10604. available on microfilm. ***Continues*** *Port Chester Daily Item.*

US
DAILY MESSENGER (CANANDAIGUA, N.Y.). (THE DAILY MESSENGER.). (191?)-. Newspaper. English. da. $61.00. Canandaigua Messenger Inc, PO Box 344, Canandaigua NY 14424. **Tel** (716)394-0770. **ED** Thomas R. Miller. **Circ:** 11,750. available on microfilm from University Microfilms International (UMI). ***Continues*** *Ontario Messenger and Repository.*

US
DAILY NEWS, THE. Vol. 4, No. 974 (Aug. 17, 1881)-. Newspaper. English. da. Batavia Daily News, 2 Apollo Drive, Batavia NY 14020. **Tel** (716)343-8000. ***Continues*** *Batavia Daily News.*

US
DAILY NEWS (NEW YORK, N.Y. : 1920). (DAILY NEWS.). **VFOAT** Sunday News; Combined New York Morning Newspapers. Vol. 2, No. 87 (Oct. 5, 1920)-Vol. 61, No. 289 (May 28, 1980)-. Newspaper. English. da. $379.00 (daily and Sunday), $278.20 (daily), $100.80 (Sunday) US and possessions. Kingston Newspaper Mailing Company, CPO Box 1517, Kingston NY 12401. **Tel** (914)331-1865, (800)724-0661. available on microfilm. Documents available from UMI Article Clearinghouse. ***Continues*** *News (New York, N.Y. : 1919).*
Ind/Abst Bus. Dateline.

US
DAILY SENTINEL (ROME, N.Y.). (DAILY SENTINEL.). Vol. 95 (May 5, 1976)-. Newspaper. English. da (Mon.-Sat.). $119.60. Rome Sentinel Company, PO Box 471, Rome NY 13440. **Tel** (315)337-4000, FAX (315)337-4704. **ED** George B. Waters (Editor in Chief), Dave C. Swanson (Managing Editor). **Photos. Ad Acc, Adv Mgr:** Ronald D. O'Neil, **Tel** (315)337-1438. Full Page (B&W) $1354.50. Half Page (B&W) $677.25. **Pub. Size:** Broadsheet. **Wire Svcs.:** AP. **Circ:** 18,500 (daily) (ctrl). available on microfilm from University Microfilms International (UMI). ***Continues*** *Rome Daily Sentinel (Rome, N.Y. : 1881).*
Desc: Daily newspaper about Rome, New York.

US
DAILY STAR (ONEONTA, NEW YORK). (THE DAILY STAR.). **VFOAT** Oneonta Star. Vol. 83, No. 285 (May 28, 1974)-. Newspaper. English. ir (307 per year). $113.52. Daily Star, 102 Chestnut Street, Oneonta NY 13820. **Tel** (607)432-1000, FAX (607)432-5847. **ED** Gary Grossman. **Bk Rev. Ad Acc. Circ:** 19,101. available on microfilm from University Microfilms International (UMI). ***Continues*** *Oneonta Star (Oneonta, N.Y. : 1940).*
Desc: A newspaper focusing on local news of Otsego, Delaware, Chenango and Schoharie counties of upstate New York.

US/0745-0206
DELAWARE COUNTY TIMES. Vol. 139, No. 39 (Oct. 5, 1978)-. Newspaper. English. Fifty-two times a year. $25.00 Delaware Co. New York; $27.50 others. Delaware County Times, 56 Main Street, Delhi NY 13753. **Tel** (607)746-2176. **ED** K. O. Wilson. **Ad Acc. Circ:** 2,000. ***Continues*** *Delaware Republican-Express.*
Desc: Weekly newspaper disseminating local news.

US
DEMOCRAT AND CHRONICLE. **VFOAT** Democrat Chronicle; Rochester Democrat and Chronicle;

Rochester Democrat and Chronicle, Rochester Herald; Sunday Democrat and Chronicle. Vol. 52, No. 257 (Sept. 13, 1884)-. Newspaper. English. da. $180.00 (by mail). Rochester Democrat and Chronicle, 55 Exchange Boulevard, Rochester NY 14614. **Tel** (800)666-6686, (716)232-7100. **ED** Barbara Henry. **Ad Acc. Circ:** 128,869 daily, 256,933 Sunday. available on microfilm from University Microfilms International (UMI); and Remington Rand, Inc. ***Continues*** *Rochester Democrat and Chronicle (Rochester, N.Y. : Daily);* ***Absorbed*** *Rochester Herald (Rochester, N.Y.).*
Ind/Abst PROMT.

US/0746-4460
DEPEW BEE. 95th Year, No. 42 (Oct. 13, 1983)-. Newspaper. English. Fifty-two times a year. $31.00. Bee Publications, PO Box 150, Buffalo NY 14231. **Tel** (716)632-4700. ***Continues*** *Depew Herald.*

US/0742-9428
DIARIO, LA PRENSA, EL. VFOAT Diario la Prensa. Vol. 16, No. 4,771 (June 14, 1963)-. Newspaper. Spanish. da. $266.13 (daily and Sunday), $80.60 (Sunday), $185.53 (daily). El Diario / La Prensa, 143-155 Varick Street, New York NY 10013. **Tel** (212)807-4643. **ED** Manuel De Dois Unanue, Javier Martinez De Pizon and Rossana Rosado. **Circ:** 70,000. available on microfilm. ***Continues*** *Diario de Nueva York, La Prensa.*
Desc: Provides the Hispanic community with news and information from Latin America as well as the local New York metropolitan area.

US
DUNDEE OBSERVER (DUNDEE, N.Y. : 1971). (DUNDEE OBSERVER.). Began with Feb. 4, 1971. Newspaper. English. wk. Finger Lakes Radio Inc, Water Street, Dundee NY 14837. ***Continues*** *Viewpoint Finger Lakes.*

US
DUNKIRK EVENING OBSERVER. ***Title Change.*** Newspaper. English. da. The Evening Observer, PO Box 391, Dunkirk NY 14048. **Tel** (716)366-3000. ***Continues*** *Evening Observer (Dunkirk, N.Y. : 1904).* ***Continued by*** *Evening Observer (Dunkirk, N.Y. : 1990).*

US/0745-9831
EAGLE (CAMBRIDGE, N.Y.), THE. (THE EAGLE.). (Oct. 21, 1981)-. Newspaper. English. wk. $22.00 Washington county; $23.00 others. The Eagle, 128 West Main Street, Cambridge NY 12816. **ED** R. Franklin Farrell (Editor-in-Chief) and Richard Farrell Jr. (Managing Editor). **Bk Rev**, (Qty: 3). **Photos. Ad Acc, Adv Mgr:** Richard Farrell, **Tel** (518)677-5158. Full Page (B&W) $450.00. Half Page (B&W) $225.00. Full Page (Color) $520.00. Half Page (Color) $295.00. **Pub. Size:** Tabloid.

US/0898-2945
EAST AURORA BEE. (19??)-. Newspaper. English. wk (published on Thursday). $10.00 within zip code 14052; $20.00 other. Bee Publications, PO Box 150, Buffalo NY 14231. **Tel** (716)632-4700.

US
EAST HAMPTON STAR, THE. VFOAT East-Hampton Star; East Hampton Star; Star. Vol. 1, No. 1 (Dec. 26, 1885)-. Newspaper. English. wk. $36.00. East Hampton Star, 153 Main Street, East Hampton NY 11937. **Tel** (516)324-0002, FAX (516)324-7943. **ED** Helen Rattray and Jack Otter (Managing Editor). **Bk Rev**, (Qty: 52). **Ad Acc, Adv Mgr:** Greg Robinson. available in microform.

US/1053-7619
EAST ROCHESTER POST-HERALD. VFOAT East Rochester Post Herald. Vol. 56, No. 45 (May 6, 1971)-. Newspaper. English. wk. $18.00 (US); $30.00 (other). Wolfe Publications, 666 Phillips Road, Victor NY 14564. **Tel** (716) 924-4040, FAX (716) 924-7734. ***Continues*** *East Rochester Herald.*

US/0746-2093
EAST ROCKAWAY LYNNBROOK OBSERVER. (19??)-. Newspaper. English. wk. $11.00 (one year), $19.00 (two year), $25.00 (three year). East Rockaway Lynbrook Observer, PO Box A, East Rockaway NY 11518. **Tel** (561)887-1233. **ED** John J Hambel. **Ad Acc. Circ:** 3,600.

US/0747-170X
EDWARD WILLIAMS WEEKLY, THE. Vol. 159. No. 15 Mar. 16, 1984)- .Newspaper. English. wk. The Edward Williams Weekly, 179 Laburnum Crescent, Rochester NY 14620-1835. ***Continues*** *Vergennes Citizen, 0745-9440.*

US
ELLENVILLE JOURNAL, THE. (1849)-. Newspaper. English. wk. The Ellenville Journal, PO Box 546, Ellenville NY 12428. **Tel** (914)647-3061. **LC** 8829-X.

US
ELLENVILLE PRESS, THE. (1873)-. Newspaper. English. wk (published Wednesday). $14.50. The Ellenville Press, PO Box 31, 7 Cape Avenue, Ellenville NY 12428. **Tel** (914)647-7222. **ED** Bernard V. Wainer. **LC** 8829-X. ***Continues*** *South Ulster Press.*

US/1070-7328
ELMONT HERALD. (1978)-. Newspaper. English. Fifty-two times a year. $14.00 in county; $16.00 others. Elmont Herald, 591 Bauer Court, Elmont NY 11003. **Tel** (516)354-3379. **ED** Rita Mezzapelle (Editor-in-Chief) and Cathy Ferrigno (Managing Editor). **Bk Rev. Photos. Ad Acc, Adv Mgr:** Rita Mezzapelle. Full Page (B&W) $525.00. Half Page (B&W) $262.50. Full Page (Color) $655.00. Half Page (Color) $392.50. **Pub. Size:** Standard. **Circ:** 5,600.

US
ETHNIKOS KERUX. VFOAT National Herald. Vol. 1, (Apr. 2, 1915)-. Newspaper. Greek, Modern (English). da. $129.00. National Herald Inc., 41-17 Crescent Street, Long Island City NY 11101. **Tel** (718)784-5255. **Ad Acc, Adv Mgr:** Victoria Diamatard, **Tel** (718)784-5255.

US
EVENING OBSERVER, THE. ***Title Change.*** (1???)-(19??). Newspaper. English. da. The Evening Observer, PO Box 391, Dunkirk NY 14048. **Tel** (716)366-3000. **ED** Henry K. Williams IV, 10 East Second Street, Dunkirk, NY 14048 (phone: (716)366-3000). Index available (Bound in each issue). **Ad Acc, Adv Mgr:** Karl Davis, **Tel** (716)366-3000. **Circ:** 15,300. ***Continued by*** *Dunkirk Evening Observer.*

US/0747-0355
EVENING SUN (NORWICH, N.Y.). (THE EVENING SUN.). Vol. 76, No. 117 (Aug. 1, 1961)-. Newspaper. English. da. $88.40. Evening Sun - Norwich NY, 45-47 Hale Street, Norwich NY 13815. **Tel** (607)334-9086. **ED** Jeff Gening, Karen Bergamo (Managing Editor). **Photos. Ad Acc, Adv Mgr:** Russell Foote, **Tel** (607)334-3276. Full Page (B&W) $945.00. Half Page (B&W) $472.50. **Pub. Size:** Broadsheet. **Wire Svcs.:** AP. ***Continues*** *Norwich Sun.*

US
EVENING TELEGRAM (HERKIMER, N.Y.). (THE EVENING TELEGRAM.). **VFOAT** Telegram Weekender. (1898)-. Newspaper. English. da. $115.60 New York; $127.60 other. Herkimer Evening Telegram, 111-113 Green Street, Herkimer NY 13350. **Tel** (315)866-2222. **ED** Daniel Guzewich. **Bk Rev**, (Qty: 12). **Photos. Ad Acc, Adv Mgr:** Wesley Williams, **Tel** (315)866-2220. Full Page (B&W) $1074.57. Half Page (B&W) $537.29. **Pub. Size:** Broadsheet. **Wire Svcs.:** AP. **Circ:** 7,023. available in microform.

US
EVENING TIMES (LITTLE FALLS, N.Y.), THE. (THE EVENING TIMES.). **VFOAT** Little Falls Evening Times. Vol. 1, No. 1 (May 10, 1886)-. Newspaper. English. da (Published Mon. thru Sat.). $115.00. Little Falls Evening Times, 347 South 2nd Street, PO Box 1007, Little Falls NY 13365. **Tel** (315)823-3680. **ED** Mark Sisti. **Photos. Ad Acc, Adv Mgr:** Peggy Vespi and Elaine McEvoy. Full Page (B&W) $967.50. Half Page (B&W) $483.75. Full Page (Color) $1,057.50. Half Page (Color) $573.75. **Pub. Size:** Broadsheet. **Wire Svcs.:** AP. **Circ:** 7,168.

US
EVENING TRIBUNE (HORNELL, N.Y. : 1934). (THE EVENING TRIBUNE.). **VFOAT** Sunday Tribune; Spectator. Vol. 55 (Nov. 12, 1934)-. Newspaper. English. da. The Evening Tribune / New York, 85 Canisteo Street, Hornell NY 14843. **Tel** (607)324-1425. available on microfilm from University Microfilms International (UMI). ***Continues*** *Evening Tribune-Times.*

US/0746-6080
EXPRESS (MECHANICVILLE, N.Y.). (THE EXPRESS.). Vol. 1, No. 1 (June 29, 1983)-. Newspaper. English. Fifty-two times a year (Tues.). $11.00 New York; $13.00 others. The Express / New York, PO Box 608, Mechanicville NY 12118. **Tel** (518)664-3335.

US
FINGER LAKES TIMES. 83rd Year, No. 29 (July 1, 1977)-. Newspaper. English. da. $80.00. Finger Lakes Times Circulating, 218 Genesee Street, PO Box 393, Geneva NY 14456. **Tel** (315)789-3333. **ED** Donald C. Hadley. **Circ:** 19,663. available on microfilm from University Microfilms International (UMI). ***Continues*** *Geneva Times (Geneva, N.Y.).*

US
FIRE ISLAND NEWS. (19??)-. Newspaper. English. wk. $16.00. Fire Island News, PO Box 486, Ocean Beach NY 11770. **Tel** (201)226-5292 Winter, (201)516-5345 Summer, FAX (516)583-9740.

US
FLUSHING TIMES. (1947)-. Newspaper. English. wk (Thursdays). $15.00. Queens Publishing Corporation, 214 41st Avenue, Bayside NY 11361. **Tel** (718)229-0300, FAX (718)225-7117. **ED** Steven Bleuh, Roz Liston (Managing Editor). **Photos. Ad Acc, Adv Mgr:** Howard Swengler. Full Page (B&W) $720.00. Half Page (B&W) $360.00. Full Page (Color) $870.00. Half Page (Color) $510.00. **Pub. Size:** Standard. **Circ:** 5,205.

US/1051-340X
FORWARD (NEW YORK, N.Y.). (FORWARD.). [Forward]. (1990)-. Newspaper. English. wk. $32.84 US; $48.24 Canada; $54.24 other. Jewish Daily Forward, 45 East 33rd Street, New York NY 10016. **Tel** (212)889-8200. **(Subscription address:** Kable Publishers Aide, 308 East Hitt Street, Subscription Department, Mt. Morris IL 61054-1473.) **DD** 071.
Desc: Founded in 1897 in Yiddish, The Forward is now reaching out to the next generation in the English language. It combines news from full-time news bureaus in Washington, DC, Moscow, Jerusalem, and Tel Aviv, with arts pages rich in Jewish art, literature and culture.

US/0747-2757
FRANCE AMERIQUE (NEW YORK, N.Y.). (FRANCE-AMERIQUE.). [Fr. Am.]. **VFOAT** France Amerique. **VAT** France Amerique. (1827)-. Newspaper. French. wk. $42.00. Trocadero Publishing / France-Amerique, 1560 Broadway, Suite 511, New York NY 10036. **Tel** (212)221-6700, FAX (212)221-6997. **ED** Jean-Louis Turlin. **LC** AP21; .F7. **DD** 071. **Bk Rev**, (Qty: 12 per year). **Photos. Ad Acc.** Full Page (B&W) $2000.00. Half Page (B&W) $1000.00. **Pub. Size:** Tabloid. **Wire Svcs.:** AF. **Circ:** 20,000. available on microfilm. ***Absorbed*** *French American Student; Victoire (New York, N.Y.)* ***and*** *Amerique.*
Desc: French-American newspaper.

US
FULTON PATRIOT (FULTON, N.Y. : 1892). (THE FULTON PATRIOT.). **VFOAT** Patriot. (1892)-. Newspaper. English. wk. $7.00 Oswego County New York; $14.00 other. Fulton Patriot, 186 S First Street, Fulton NY 13069. **Tel** (315)592-2459. ***Continues*** *Fulton Patriot and Gazette.*

US
GLENDALE REGISTER. Began in 1946. Newspaper. English. wk. Glendale Register, 65-17 Grand Avenue, Maspeth NY 11378.

US/1065-1748
GOLD COAST GAZETTE (SEA CLIFF, N.Y.). (GOLD COAST GAZETTE.). Vol. 1, No. 1 (Sept. 27, 1991)-. Newspaper. English. wk. $18.00. KCH Publications, 147 Glen Street, Glen Cove NY 11542. **Tel** (516)671-2360, FAX (516)671-2361. **ED** Kevin Horton. **Bk Rev**, (Qty: 12). **Photos. Ad Acc, Adv Mgr:** Kevin Horton and John O'Connell. Full Page (B&W) $525.00. Half Page (B&W) $290.00. Full Page (Color) $675.00. Half Page (Color) $440.00. **Pub. Size:** Standard.

US
GOSHEN UNLIMITED NEWS. VFOAT Goshen News; Unlimited News. Vol. 4, No. 44 (Mar. 14, 1991)-. Newspaper. English. wk. Unlimited Pub. Co., Route 17K, Bullville NY 10915.

US
GRANVILLE SENTINEL (GRANVILLE, N.Y. : 1885). (THE GRANVILLE SENTINEL.). **VFOAT** Semi-Weekly Sentinel; Semi Weekly Sentinel. (188?)-. Newspaper. English. wk. $18.00 New York; $28.00 others. Granville Sentinel, 6 North Street, Granville NY 12832. **ED** John Manchester (Editor-in-Chief) and Stella Wood (Managing Editor). **Bk Rev**, (Qty: 6). **Photos. Ad Acc, Adv Mgr:** John Manchester, **Tel** (518)642-1234. Full Page (B&W) $915.90. Half Page (B&W) $457.95. Full Page (Color) $1,015.90. Half Page (Color) $557.95. **Wire Svcs.:** NY. available in microform. ***Continues*** *Semi-Weekly Sentinel (Granville, N.Y.).*

US
GRAPE BELT (1959). (THE GRAPE BELT.). Vol. 65, No. 30 (April 15, 1959)-. Newspaper. English. wk. Grape Belt, 8 East 2nd Street, Dunkirk NY 14048. ***Continues*** *Grape Belt and Chautauqua Farmer.*

US
GREECE POST, THE. Vol. 1, No. 1 (Apr. 27, 1967)-. Newspaper. English. wk. $18.00 (Monroe county, New York); $30.00 (other). Wolfe Publications, 666 Phillips Road, Victor NY 14564. **Tel** (716) 924-4040, FAX (716) 924-7734. **ED** Andrew D Wolfe, (716)924-4040, PO Box C, Fisher, NY 14453). **Ad Acc, Adv Mgr:** Catharene Gardner. **Circ:** 7,616.
Desc: Local hometown news.

US/0883-1637
GREENBURGH ENQUIRER, THE. Newspaper. English. wk. WHW Publications, PO Box 400, Hartsdale NY 10530.

US
GREENBUSH AREA NEWS. Vol. 1, No. 1 (March 18, 1970)-. Newspaper. English. wk. Greenbush Area News, PO Box 31, East Greenbush NY 12061.

US
GREENE COUNTY NEWS. VFOAT Examiner Recorder; Union News. No. 1 (March 1, 1962)-. Newspaper. English. wk. $25.00. Greene County News, 30 Church Street, Catskill NY 12414. **ED** Annabar Jensis. **Photos. Ad Acc, Adv Mgr:** Barb Cragie, **Tel** (518)943-2100. Full Page (B&W) $722.40. Half Page

New York

(B&W) $361.20. Full Page (Color) $847.40. Half Page (Color) $486.20. **Pub. Size:** Broadsheet. *Formed by the union of Greene County Examiner-Recorder and Coxsackie Union News.*

US
GREENPOINT GAZETTE.
Newspaper. English. wk (published Wednesdays). $20.00. Greenpoint Gazette, 597 Manhattan Avenue, Brooklyn NY 11222. **Tel** (718)389-6067. **ED** Ralph Carrano & Adelle Haines. **Bk Rev**, (Qty: 10). **Ad Acc**.

US/1065-1144
GREENWOOD LAKE AND WEST MILFORD NEWS.
Vol. 26, No. 39 (Jan. 3, 1989)-. Newspaper. English. wk (Published on Wednesdays). $21.00 (in county), $24.50 other. Greenwood Lake West Milford News, PO Box 1117, Greenwood Lake NY 10925. **Tel** (914)477-2575, FAX (914)477-2577. **ED** Ron Nowak. **Photos**. **Ad Acc, Adv Mgr:** Ann Chaimowitz. Full Page (B&W) $540.00. Half Page (B&W) $360.00. Full Page (Color) $715.00. Half Page (Color) $535.00. **Pub. Size:** Tabloid. ctrl circ. *Continues Greenwood Lake News.*
 Desc: Local bi-state weekly newspaper covering Passaic County, New Jersey & Orange County, New York. Contains sports, school and town news and social coverage.

US
HAMILTON COUNTY NEWS, THE.
VFOAT Hamilton County News Combined with Indian Lake Bulletin. Vol. 1, No. 14 (March 21, 1947)-. Newspaper. English. wk. $18.00 US; $35.00 other. Hamilton County News, PO Box 640, Circulation Department, Amsterdam NY 12010. **Tel** (518)548-6898. **ED** Cristine Knapp. **Ad Acc. Circ:** 3,800. available on microfilm. *Continues Hamilton County Republican (Inlet, N.Y.); Absorbed Indian Lake Bulletin.*

US
HANCOCK HERALD, THE.
VFOAT Herald. (May 10, 1873)-. Newspaper. English. wk. $23.00 Delaware County, New York; $28.00 other. Herald Association, PO Box 519, Hancock NY 13783. **ED** Sally W. Zegers (Managing Editor). **Photos**. **Ad Acc, Adv Mgr:** Millie Triff, **Tel** (607)637-3591. Full Page (B&W) $428.00. Half Page (B&W) $214.00. Full Page (Color) $468.00. Half Page (Color) $254.00. **Pub. Size:** Broadsheet. **Circ:** 2,300.

US/0273-8031
HAN'GUK ILBO NEW YORK PAN.
VFOAT Korea Times New York Edition. (198?)-. Newspaper. Korean (English). da. $200.00. Korean News / Long Island, NY, 42-22 27th Street, Long Island NY 11101. **Tel** (718)784-4500. *Continues Han'Guk Ilbo. Korea News of New York.*

US
HARLEM VALLEY TIMES.
VFOAT Dover Plains News; Sharon Messenger; Pawling Sentinel; Millerton Herald; Wassaic Record. (July 6, 1912)-. Newspaper. English. wk. $59.00 local $77.00 other. Taconic Newspapers Inc., PO Box 316, Millbrook NY 12545. **Tel** (914)677-8241. *Continues Amenia Times.*

US/0892-4163
HARRISON INDEPENDENT.
(1962)-. Newspaper. English. Fifty-two times a year. $25.00. Martinelli Publishing, 40 Larkin Plaza, Yonkers NY 10701. **Tel** (914)965-4000. **ED** Louise Montcharre. **Bk Rev**. **Photos**. **Ad Acc, Adv Mgr:** Ray Martin. Full Page (B&W) $1,680.00. Half Page (B&W) $840.00. **Pub. Size:** Standard. **Circ:** 4,108.

US/8750-1023
HAUPPAGE NEWS.
Newspaper. English. wk. Graphic Square Corporation, PO Box 108-P, One East Main Street, Bay Shore NY 11706.

US/1059-2121
HELLENIC TIMES.
[Hell. times]. (1973)-. Newspaper. English. bm. Hellenic Times, 229 8th Avenue, New York NY 10011. **DD** 071.

US
HENRIETTA POST, THE.
Vol. 1, No. 1 (Sept. 22, 1961)-. Newspaper. English. Fifty-two times a year. $25.00. Wolfe Publications, 666 Phillips Road, Victor NY 14564. **Tel** (716) 924-4040, FAX (716) 924-7734. **(Subscription address:** Wolfe Publications, PO Box C, Fishers, NY 14453)

US/1060-460X
HERALD STATESMAN.
(THE HERALD STATESMAN.). VFOAT Herald-Statesman. Vol. 49, No. 106, March 15 (1932)-. Newspaper. English. da. price varies due to area. Gannett Surburban Newspaper, 1 Gannett Drive, White Plains NY 10604. **Tel** 800 942-1010. available on microfilm from University Microfilms International (UMI). *Formed by the union of Yonkers Herald (Yonkers, N.Y. : 1884) and Yonkers Statesman (Yonkers, N.Y. : 1875).*

US/0895-5476
HICKSVILLE ILLUSTRATED NEWS.
(1987)-. Newspaper. English. wk. Anton Community Newspapers, 135 Liberty Avenue, Mineola NY 11501. **Tel** (516)747-8282 ext. 124. *Continues Mid-Island Herald (Hicksville Edition).*

US
HOME REPORTER.
Newspaper. English. wk. $70.00 New York City; $80.00 other. Home Reporter Inc, 8723 3rd Avenue, Brooklyn NY 11209. **Tel** (718)238-6600.

US/0891-561X
HUAYU KUAIBAO.
(HUA YU K UAI PAO / SINO EXPRESS.). [Huayu kuaibao]. No. 2175 (Sept. 20, 1986)-. Newspaper. Chinese. wk. $52.00. Greater Chinatown Publishing, 449 Broadway, New York NY 10013. *Continues Hu Ay U Kua Ibao, 0748-4038.*

US
HUDSON REGISTER STAR.
(19??)-. English. wk. $93.60. Record Printing & Publishin Co Inc., 364 Warren Street, Hudson NY 12534. **Tel** (518)828-1616, FAX (518)828-9437. **ED** Jack Kehrer. **Photos**. **Ad Acc, Adv Mgr:** Steven Mortefolio. Full Page (B&W) $1148.10. Half Page (B&W) $574.05. Full Page (Color) $1373.10. Half Page (Color) $799.05. **Pub. Size:** Broadsheet. **Wire Svcs.:** AP. **Circ:** 8,500 (ctrl). available in microform. *Continues Register Star.*

US/1057-7084
INDIA MONITOR.
[India monit.]. (1991)-. Newspaper. English. Twice a week. $29.00. India Monitor, 303 Fifth Avenue, Suite 1506, New York NY 10016. **Tel** (212)889-6878, FAX (212)889-6798. **Bk Rev**. **Photos**. **Ad Acc, Adv Mgr:** Yirishh Seth. Full Page (B&W) $3024.00. Half Page (B&W) $1512.00. Full Page (Color) $3024.00 plus $15.00 per color. Half Page (Color) $1512.00 plus $15.00 per color. **Pub. Size:** Broadsheet.

US/0893-3820
INDIAN TIME (ROOSEVELTOWN, N.Y.).
(INDIAN TIME.). VFOAT Indian Times. Vol. 1, No. 1 (July 1, 1983)-. Newspaper. English. Fifty-two times a year. $50.00 US; $55.00 others. Mohawk Nation, PO Box 196, Rooseveltown NY 13683. **Tel** (518)358-9531, (518)358-9535.

US
INTERLAKEN REVIEW, THE.
Vol. 18, No. 1 (July 1, 1904)-. Newspaper. English. wk. $17.00. Interlaken Review, PO Box 404, Interlaken NY 14847. **ED** Chris Kimball-Peterson. **Bk Rev**, (Qty: 3). **Photos**. **Ad Acc, Adv Mgr:** Del Hall, Jim Graney. Full Page (B&W) $398.40. Half Page (B&W) $210.24. Full Page (Color) $773.40. Half Page (Color) $585.24. **Pub. Size:** Standard. *Continues Farmer Review.*

US/0895-4534
IRISH VOICE (NEW YORK, N.Y.).
(IRISH VOICE.). [Ir. voice]. (1987)-. Newspaper. English. Fifty-two times a year. $25.00. Irish Voice, 432 Park Avenue South, Suite 1503, New York NY 10016. **Tel** (212)684-3366, FAX (212)779-1198. **ED** Debbie McGoldrick. **DD** 941. **Bk Rev**, (Qty: 52 per year). **Photos**. **Ad Acc, Adv Mgr:** Paddy McCarthy. **Pub. Size:** Standard. **Circ:** 86,000 paid.

US
IRONDEQUOIT PRESS.
Vol. 1, No. 1 (Feb. 19, 1932)-. Newspaper. English. wk (Tuesdays). $18.00 (Irondequoit, NY); $30.00 (other). Wolfe Publications, 666 Phillips Road, Victor NY 14564. **Tel** (716) 924-4040, FAX (716) 924-7734.

US/0892-2497
ISLAND DISPATCH.
(19??)-. Newspaper. English. wk (Fri.). $35.95. Niagra Frontier Publication, PO Box 130, Grand Island NY 14072-0130. **Tel** (716)773-7676, FAX (716)773-7190. **ED** Jerrie S. Page and Joelle Logue. **Ad Acc. Circ:** 3,500 (ctrl). available in microform.
 Desc: Town newspaper containing legals, current events and editorials referring to the town, schools and local organization organizations.

US
ITHACA JOURNAL (ITHACA, N.Y. : 1934).
(THE ITHACA JOURNAL.). Vol. 119, No. 1 (Jan. 2, 1934)-. Newspaper. English. da (except Sun.). $192.00. Ithaca Journal, 123-125 West State Street, Ithaca NY 14850. **Tel** (607)272-2321. **LC** 7002. **Ad Acc**. *Continues Ithaca Journal-News.*

US/0277-1187
ITHACA TIMES.
Vol. 1, (June 22, 1978)-. Newspaper. English. wk. $21.95. Ithaca Times, Box 27, Ithaca NY 14851. **Tel** (607)277-7000. **Photos**. **Ad Acc**. Full Page (B&W) $1680.00. Half Page (B&W) $840.00. Full Page (Color) $2080.00. Half Page (Color) $1240.00. **Pub. Size:** Standard. **Circ:** 19,100 (ctrl). *Formed by the union of Good Times Gazette and Ithaca New Times.*

US
JEFFERSON COUNTY JOURNAL.
Vol. 2, No. 28 (Oct. 20, 1870)-. Newspaper. English. wk. $18.00 Jefferson County; $22.00 New York; $24.00 other. Jefferson County Journal, PO Box 68, 7 Main Street, Adams NY 13605. **Tel** (315)232-2141, (315)232-4586. available on microfilm. *Continues Northern Temperance Journal.*

US/8750-3476
JERICHO TRIBUNE, THE.
Newspaper. English. wk. Litmore Publications, 81 East Barclay Street, Hicksville NY 11801. **Tel** (516)931-0012.

US/0745-0818
JEWISH JOURNAL (BROOKLYN, N.Y.).
(JEWISH JOURNAL.). (1971)-. Newspaper. English. wk (52 issues). $15.00. C A B Jewish Journal, 210 East Sunrise Highway, Valley Stream NY 11581. **Tel** (516)561-6900.

US/0021-6550
JEWISH LEDGER (ROCHESTER NY).
(THE JEWISH LEDGER.). Vol. 1, No. 1 (Sept. 27, 1924)-. Newspaper. English. wk (52 issues). $15.00. Jewish Ledger, 3385 Brighton Henrietta TL Road, Rochester NY 14623-2896. **Tel** (716)427-2434.

US
JOURNAL AND REPUBLICAN, THE.
VFOAT Journal Republican. Vol. 1, No. 1 (Jan. 4, 1860)-. Newspaper. English. wk. $23.00 New York state; $27.00 other. Journal and Republican, 7556 State Street, Lowville NY 13367. **Tel** (315)376-3525, FAX (315)376-4136. **ED** Gordon Allen. **LC** 8829-X. **Photos**. **Ad Acc, Adv Mgr:** Bonnie Franklin. Full Page (B&W) $670.32. Half Page (B&W) $335.16. **Pub. Size:** Standard. *Formed by the union of Northern Journal (Lowville, N.Y.) and Lewis County Republican.*

US/0893-5149
JOURNAL (OGDENSBURG, N.Y.), THE.
(THE JOURNAL.). VFOAT Journal-Courier-Observer; Journal Courier Observer. Vol. 26, No. 3370 (June 7, 1971)-. Newspaper. English. da. $66.00. Park Newspapers of St Lawrence Inc, PO Box 409, Ogdensburg NY 13669. **Tel** (315)393-1000, FAX (315)393-5108. **ED** Charles W. Kelly, James E. Reagen (Managing Editor). **Bk Rev**, (Qty: 5). **Photos**. **Ad Acc, Adv Mgr:** Mary McGreg. Full Page (B&W) $1030.00. Half Page (B&W) $527.30. **Wire Svcs.:** AP. **Circ:** 4,861 paid. available on microfilm. *Continues Ogdensburg Journal (Ogdensburg, N.Y.).*

US/0745-6875
KEN-TON BEE.
VAT Kenmore Tonawanda Bee. (198?)-. Newspaper. English. wk. $31.00 Erie County New York; $40.00 US. Bee Publications, PO Box 150, Buffalo NY 14231. **Tel** (716)632-4700.

US
LAIKS (BROOKLYN, N.Y. : 1949).
(LAIKS.). VFOAT Time. (1949)-. Newspaper. Latvian. sw. $65.00. Helmars Rudzitis, 7307 Third Avenue, Brooklyn NY 11209. **Tel** (718)836-6382. **ED** Ilavars Spilners. **Circ:** 10,500.

US
LAKE GEORGE MIRROR (LAKE GEORGE, N.Y. : 1890).
(LAKE GEORGE MIRROR.). Began in 1890. Newspaper. English. wk. Lake George Mirror, PO Box 130, Warrensburg NY 12885.

US
LAKE PLACID NEWS.
(May 1905)-. Newspaper. English. wk. $40.00 Essex County; $43.00 other. Lake Placid News, Box 111, Lake Placid NY 12946. **Tel** (518)523-4401. **Bk Rev**. **Photos**. **Ad Acc, Adv Mgr:** Sue Harrington, **Tel** (518)891-2600. Full Page (B&W) $693.00. Half Page (B&W) $346.50. Full Page (Color) $$768.00. Half Page (Color) $421.50. **Pub. Size:** Broadsheet. available in microform.

US/0746-4487
LANCASTER BEE.
VFOAT Lancaster, Depew; Lancaster/Depew. (1???)-. Newspaper. English. wk (Thurs.). $21.00. Bee Publications, PO Box 150, Buffalo NY 14231. **Tel** (716)632-4700.

US/1050-1983
LEADER (CORNING, N.Y.), THE.
(THE LEADER.). (19??)-. Periodical. English. da. $133.00 (Steuben County), $146.00 (elsewhere). Corning Publishers Inc, 34 West Pulteney Street, Corning NY 14830. *Continues Corning Leader.*

New York

US
LEADER-HERALD, THE. Vol. 1, No. 1 (Jan. 24, 1955)-. Newspaper. English. da. Leader-Herald, 8-10 Fulton Street, Gloversville NY 12078. **ED** W H Evans. *Formed by the union of Morning Herald (Gloversville, N.Y.) and Leader-Republican.*

US
LEADER-OBSERVER, THE. **VFOAT** Leader Observer. Vol. 6, No. 272 (Jan. 11, 1912)-. Newspaper. English. wk. Realty, 80-34 Jamaica Avenue, Woodhaven NY 11421. **Tel** (212)296-2233. *Formed by the union of Leader (Forest Parkway, N.Y.) and Observer.*

US
LEWISTON - PORTER SENTINEL. English. Two issues per month. Niagara Frontier Publications, POB 130, 2231 Grand Island Boulevard, Grand Island NY 14072-0130. **Tel** (716)773-7676, FAX (716)773-7190. **Ad Acc. Pr Rev. Circ:** 13,500 (ctrl).
Desc: Other than advertising this paper contains current events and editorials referring to town, schools, local organizations and public information notices.

US/0891-1436
LIAN HE RI BAO. (LIEN HO JIH.). **VFOAT** United Journal. (July 1952)-. Newspaper. Chinese. da. $96.00 (libraries); $216.00 other. United Journal Inc, 83-85 White Street, New York NY 10013. **Tel** (212)513-1440. **ED** Leo Lan, Simon Wong and David Chu. **Ad Acc.** *Absorbed Chung Mei Chou Pao.*
Desc: International, domestic and local news.

US
LITTLE NECK-GLEN OAKS LEDGER. *Title Change.* **VFOAT** Little Neck Glen Oaks Ledger. (1926)-(19??). Newspaper. English. wk. Little Neck-Glen Oaks Ledger, 214-11 41st Avenue, Bayside NY 11361. *Continued by Little Neck Ledger.*

US
LITTLE NECK LEDGER. (19??)-. English. wk. $415.00. Little Neck Ledger, 241-02 Bell Boulevard, 2nd Floor, Bayside NY 11361. **Tel** (718)229-0300, FAX (718)225-7117. **ED** Steven Blenh (Editor-in-Chief) and Roz Liston (Managing Editor). **Photos. Ad Acc, Adv Mgr:** Howard Sweugle. Full Page (B&W) $720.00. Half Page (B&W) $360.00. Full Page (Color) $870.00. Half Page (Color) $440.00. **Pub. Size:** Standard. **Circ:** 4,260. *Continues Little Neck Glen Oaks Ledger.*

US
LIVERPOOL SALINA CLAY REVIEW. Newspaper. English. wk. $16.00 Liverpool, Salina, and Clay, New York residents; $18.00 other New York residents; $25.00 other. Brown Newspapers, PO Box 270, 7-9-11 East Geness Street, Baldwinsville NY 13027. **Tel** (315)635-3921.

US/1046-8293
LIVINGSTON COUNTY NEWS (GENESEO, N.Y.). (LIVINGSTON COUNTY NEWS.). Vol. 1, No. 1 (May 4, 1989)-. Newspaper. English. wk. Livingston County News, 122 Main Street, Geneseo NY 14454-1230. **Tel** (716)243-0296, FAX (716)243-0348.

US
LONG ISLAND TRAVELER, MATTITUCK WATCHMAN, THE. **VFOAT** Long Island Traveler; Mattituck Watchman. (19??)-. Newspaper. English. Fifty-two times a year (Thurs.). $22.00 New York; $25.00 other. Traveler Watchman, Traveler Street, Southold NY 11971. **Tel** (516)765-3425. **ED** Pat Wood and T. Kelly. **Photos. Ad Acc.** Full Page (B&W) $1,000.00. Half Page (B&W) $500.00. Full Page (Color) $1,100.00. Half Page (Color) $550.00. **Pub. Size:** Broadsheet. **Circ:** 18,500. available on microfilm. *Formed by the union of Long Island Traveler and Mattituck Watchman.*

US
MALONE TELEGRAM. Vol. 85, No. 199 (July 30, 1990)-. Newspaper. English. da. Malone Newspapers Corporation, 387 East Main Street, Malone NY 12953. *Continues Malone Evening Telegram.*

US
MANHATTAN SPIRIT. **VFOAT** Spirit. (19??)-. Newspaper. English. wk (Thurs.). $75.00. News Communications Inc., 242 West 30th Street, 5th Floor, New York NY 10001. **Tel** (212)268-8600. **ED** Tom Allen. **Bk Rev,** (Qty: 52). **Ad Acc, Adv Mgr:** Debra Schrott. **Circ:** 76,000 (ctrl).
Desc: Weekly newspaper covering the communities of the West Side of Manhattan.

US
MASSAPEQUA POST. (19??)-. Newspaper. English. Fifty-two times a year (Wed.). $15.00 Nassau County; $20.00 others. ACJ Communications, 1045 B Park Boulevard, Massapequa Park NY 11762. **Tel** (516)798-5100, FAX (516)798-5296. **ED** Mary Capone.

US
MAYVILLE SENTINEL. Vol. 46 (Oct. 7, 1898)-. Newspaper. English. Fifty-two times a year. $29.00 Chautauqua County in New York State; $30.50 other. Mayville Sentinel, PO Box 38, Westfield NY 14787. **Tel** (716)326-3163. *Continues Mayville Sentinel and Chautauqua Era.*

US/1070-6437
MIAMI DAILY BUSINESS REVIEW. Vol. 67, No. 251 (June 4, 1993)-. Newspaper. English. da (5 days a week). $159.00. American Lawyer Media, L.P., 600 3rd Avenue, New York NY 10016. **Tel** (212)973-2800. (Subscription address: Miami Review Inc., PO Box 010589, Miami FL 33101.) *Continues Miami Review, 0888-0263.*

US/0888-0263
MIAMI REVIEW. *Title Change.* (198?)-(19??). Newspaper. English. da (260 issues per year). American Lawyer Media, L.P., 600 3rd Avenue, New York NY 10016. **Tel** (212)973-2800. available on microfilm from University Microfilms International (UMI); available on an online database (file 635/Full-Text) from DIALOG. Documents available from UMI Article Clearinghouse. *Continues Miami Review and Daily Record. Continued by Miami Daily Business Review, 1070-6437.*
Ind/Abst Bus. Dateline (June 10, 1991-) [Full Txt.]; Bus. Index (Jan. 1985-Dec. 1985); Gen. BusinessFile (Jan. 1985-Dec. 1985); Gen. Period. Index (Jan. 1985-Dec. 1985); INFO-SOUTH Abstr.; PROMT.

US/0894-0584
MID-ISLAND HERALD (PLAINVIEW-OLD BETHPAGE EDITION). (MID-ISLAND HERALD.). **VFOAT** Mid Island Herald; Plainview Old Bethpage Mid Island Herald; Plainview-Old Bethpage Mid-Island Herald. (19??)-. Newspaper. English. wk. Litmore Publications, 81 East Barclay Street, Hicksville NY 11801. **Tel** (516)931-0012.

US/0747-4741
MID-ISLAND TIMES & LEVITTOWN TIMES. **VFOAT** Mid-Island Times and Levittown Times; Mid Island Times. Newspaper. English. wk. $5.50. Litmore Publications, 81 East Barclay Street, Hicksville NY 11801. **Tel** (516)931-0012. **ED** Robert L Morgan. *Continues Mid-Island Times.*

US
MID-YORK WEEKLY, THE. Vol. 1 (June 5, 1947)-. Newspaper. English. wk. $16.00. Mid-York Weekly, 3 Madison Street, Hamilton NY 13346. **Tel** (315)824-2150, FAX (315)824-4220. **ED** Carolyn Godfrey. **Photos. Ad Acc, Adv Mgr:** Charles Mahaffy, **Tel** (315)853-6103. Full Page (B&W) $475.00. Half Page (B&W) $250.00. **Pub. Size:** Broadsheet. **Circ:** 9,000. *Formed by the union of Hamilton Republican; Madison County Leader and Earlville Standard.*

US/0026-3885
MILITANT (NEW YORK, N.Y. 1941), THE. (THE MILITANT.). [Militant]. **Added/Corp** Socialist Workers Party. Vol. 5, No. 5 (Feb. 1941)-. Newspaper. English. Forty-seven times a year. $80.00 (institutions), $45.00 (individuals) US & Canada & Japan & Latin America; $75.00 (one year), $140.00 (two years) Australia & Philippines & Pacific Islands. 408 Printing and Publishing Inc, 410 West Street, New York NY 10014. **Tel** (212)243-6392, FAX (212)727-0150. **ED** George Fyson. **DD** 071. Index available. **Bk Rev. Circ:** 8,000. available on microfilm from University Microfilms International (UMI). *Supersedes Socialist Appeal; Absorbed in part Intercontinental Press (New York, N.Y. : 1985).*
Desc: Socialist newspaper covering the national and international workers movement and liberation struggles.
Ind/Abst Altern. Press Index.

US
MILLERTON NEWS, THE. Vol. 45, No. 32 (Aug. 9, 1979)-. Newspaper. English. wk. Millerton News, Main Street, Millerton NY 12546. **Tel** (518)789-4401, (203)435-9873. **ED** Tony Adamis. **Circ:** 2,262. *Continues News (Millerton, N.Y. : 1960).*

US
MONTICELLO UNLIMITED NEWS. **VFOAT** Monticello News; Unlimited News. (Sept. 1990)-. Newspaper. English. wk. Unlimited Publishing Co., Route 17K, Bullville NY 10915.

US
MORAVIA REPUBLICAN REGISTER. **VFOAT** Moravia Republican-Register. (Feb. 1901)-. Newspaper. English. Fifty-two times a year. $12.00 Cayuga County, New York; $16.00 other. Moravia Republican Register, 6 Central Street, PO Box 591, Moravia NY 13118. **Tel** (315)497-1551. **ED** B. F. McGuerty III. **Bk Rev. Ad Acc.** ctrl circ. *Formed by the union of Moravia Republican and Moravia Valley Register; Absorbed Journal Courier (Groton, N.Y.).*
Desc: Includes local news and features of Moravia, New York.

US
MORICHES BAY TIDE. **VFOAT** Tide. Vol. 1, No. 1 (June 2, 1961)-. Newspaper. English. wk. $12.00, $10.00 (Suffolk County). Moriches Bay Tide, 640 Montauk Avenue, Shirley NY 11967. **Tel** (516)981-1000, FAX (516)681-6517. **ED** Camille Cardoza. **Bk Rev. Ad Acc. Circ:** 5,000. available on microfilm. *Absorbed Moriches Bay View.*

US/1052-1356
MOUNTAIN EAGLE (TANNERSVILLE, N.Y.), THE. (MOUNTAIN EAGLE.). (1982)-. Newspaper. English. wk. $24.00 New York; $28.00 other. The Mountain Eagle, PO Box 968 Railroad Avenue, Tannersville NY 12485. **Tel** (518)589-7007.

US
NATIONAL EXAMINER. (Mar. 16, 1830)-. Newspaper. English. wk. Globe International, PO Box 11, Rouse Point NY 12979. **Tel** (518)298-4010, (514)849-7733, FAX (514)849-8330.

US
NEW AMERICAN, THE. (1990)-. Periodical. English. wk (published on Thurs.). $48.00 (one year), $28.00 (6 months). Challenge Group, 1360 Fulton Street, Brooklyn NY 11216. **Tel** (718)636-9500, FAX (718)857-9115. **ED** Thomas H. Watkins, Jr. (Editor in Chief), Eleanor Branch (Managing Editor). **Photos. Ad Acc, Adv Mgr:** Jean Wells. Full Page (B&W) $3855.60. Half Page (B&W) $1927.80. Full Page (Color) $4241.16. Half Page (Color) $2120.58. **Pub. Size:** Tabloid. **Wire Svcs.:** UPI, RN. **Circ:** 54,374 (weekly). available in microform. *Continues Black American.*

US
NEW PALTZ NEWS COMBINED WITH THE WALLKILL VALLEY WORLD, THE. Vol. 93, No. 19 (May 7, 1980)-. Newspaper. English. wk. $24.00 Ulster County; $28.00 others. Hudson Valley Newspapers Inc., PO Box 458, Highland NY 12528. **Tel** (914)691-2000. **ED** Craig McKinney. **Photos. Ad Acc, Adv Mgr:** Barbara Walters. Full Page (B&W) $400.00. Half Page (B&W) $200.00. Full Page (Color) $500.00. Half Page (Color) $300.00. **Pub. Size:** Broadsheet. available in microform. *Formed by the union of New Paltz News and Wallkill Valley World (Wallkill, N.Y. : 1953).*

US
NEW RUSSIAN WORD. **VFOAT** New Russian Word. Newspaper. Russian. da. New Russian Word, 519 8th Avenue, 5th Floor, New York NY 10018.

US/1059-1818
NEW YORK AMSTERDAM NEWS (1962). (NEW YORK AMSTERDAM NEWS.). [N. Y. Amst. news (1962)]. **VFOAT** Amsterdam News. Vol. 30 (May 26, 1962)-. Newspaper. English. wk. $30.00 US; $40.00 other. Powell Savory Corporation, 2340 Frederic Douglass Boulevard, New York NY 10027. **Tel** (212)932-7400, FAX (212)222-3842. **ED** Willie Egyir. **Bk Rev. Ad Acc. Circ:** 50,000. available on microfilm. Documents available from UMI Article Clearinghouse. *Formed by the union of New York Amsterdam News (1962 : National Ed.) and New York Amsterdam News (1943 : City Ed.).*
Desc: Ideas on health and beauty, fashions, travel, art and entertainment. Coverage of sports, local, national and international news.
Ind/Abst Infobank (1969-); Newsp. Abstr.; Sage Race Relat. Abstr.

US
NEW YORK BEACON. (19??)-. Newspaper. English. Fifty-two times a year (Fri.). $32.00. Smith Haj Publishing, 15 East 40th Street, Suite 402, New York NY 10016. **Tel** (212)213-8585. **ED** Walter Smith. Index available. cum. index. **Bk Rev. Ad Acc, Adv Mgr:** Daye, **Tel** (212)213-8585. **Circ:** 50,000. *Continues Big Red News, 0745-936X.*

US/1051-4031
NEW YORK CARIB NEWS, THE. (NEW YORK CARIB NEWS.). [N. Y. Carib news]. **VFOAT** Carib News; Carib News, N.Y. (1983)-. Newspaper. English. wk. New York Carib News, 28 West 39th Street, New York NY 10018. **Tel** (212)944-1991. **DD** 071. *Continues Carib News Weekly, 0745-8428.*

US
NEW YORK POST (1949). (NEW YORK POST). Vol. 148, No. 308 (Nov. 14, 1949)-. Newspaper. English. da. $221.20. Kingston Newspaper Mailing Company, CPO Box 1517, Kingston NY 12401. **Tel** (914)331-1865, (800)724-0661. available on microfilm

from University Microfilms International (UMI); and New York Public Library. ***Continues*** *New York Post and the Home News.*

US/0362-4331
NEW YORK TIMES, THE. [N. Y. times]. **VFOAT** Combined New York Morning Newspapers; Combined New York Sunday Newspapers. Vol. 6, No. 1868 (Sept. 14, 1857)-. Academic Scholarly Publication. English. ds. $401.10 subscribers within zip codes 00001-24699; $573.00 subscribers within zip codes 24700-99999; $989.70 other. The New York Times, 229 West 43rd Street, New York NY 10036. **Tel** (800)631-2580, (212)556-1234, FAX (212)556-4603. **(Subscription address:** New York Times Subscriptions Department, PO Box 9564, Uniondale NY 11555-9564.**) ED** Joseph Lelyveld, Gene Roberts (Managing Editor). **CODEN** NYTIAO. **Bk Rev. Photos. Ad Acc, Adv Mgr:** Janet L. Robinson. **Pub. Size:** Broadsheet. **Wire Svcs.:** RN, AP. **Circ:** 1,001,694 daily, 1,584,259 Sun. available in microform from University Microfilms International (UMI). Documents available from UMI Article Clearinghouse, CASDDS, Documents on Demand. ***Continues*** *New-York Daily Times.*
Ind/Abst Abr. Read. Guide Period. Lit.; Acad. Abstr. Full Text Elite (Jan. 1989-); Acad. Abstr. (Jan. 1989-); Acad. Ind. [Computer File]; Acad. Search (Jan. 1989-); Account. Tax Datab. (Jan. 1989-); AGRICOLA [Select. Cov.]; Art Archaeol. Tech. Abstr.; BioBusiness; Book Rev. Index; Bus. Index; Chem. Abstr.; Chem. Ind. Notes; Comput. Bus. (19??-); Consum. Health Nutr. Index; Curr. Lit. Fam. Plan.; Energy Inf. Abstr.; Environ. Abstr.; Expand. Acad. Index (1984-); F&S Index Plus Text, Int. [Select. Cov.]; Film Lit. Index; Fut. Surv.; Gen. Period. Index; Health Ref. Cent. (1987-) [Select. Cov.]; INFO-SOUTH Abstr.; Infobank (Jan. 1969-); Mag. Artic. Summar. Elite (Jan. 1989-); Mag. Artic. Summar. Select (Jan. 1989-); Mag. Artic. Summar. CD-ROM (Jan. 1989-); Mag. Index Plus; Mag. Index. Sel.; Mag. Search; Mark. Advert. Ref. Serv.; Natl. Newsp. Index (1979-); Newsp. Period. Abstr. (1988-); Newsp. Abstr.; Newsp. Abstr.; NEXIS (June 1, 1980-); Numis. Lit.; PROMT; Read. Guide Period. Lit.; Sage Race Relat. Abstr.; Vocat. Search (Jan. 1989-).

US/0028-7814
NEW YORK TIMES LARGE TYPE WEEKLY, THE. (1967)-. Newspaper. English. wk. $70.20 US; $86.20 other. The New York Times, 229 West 43rd Street, New York NY 10036. **Tel** (800)631-2580, (212)556-1234, FAX (212)556-4603. **(Subscription address:** New York Times Subscriptions Department, PO Box 9564, Uniondale NY 11555-9564.**) Photos. Ad Acc. Wire Svcs.:** NY, RN, AP, FN.

US
NEW YORK VOICE (JAMAICA, N.Y.). (THE NEW YORK VOICE.). **VFOAT** Voice. Vol. 12, No. 55 (Apr. 23, 1971)-. Newspaper. English. wk. $35.00. The New York Voice, 75 43 Parsons Boulevard, Flushing NY 11366. **Tel** (718)264-1500. **ED** Jimmy Hicks. **Circ:** 90,000. available on microfilm from University Microfilms International (UMI). ***Continues*** *Voice (Jamaica, N.Y.).*

US/1061-7604
NEW YORKER STAATS-ZEITUNG (1991). (NEW YORKER STAATS-ZEITUNG.). [N.Y. Staats-Ztg.]. **VFOAT** New Yorker Staats Zeitung; Staats-Zeitung; Staats Zeitung; Gazette-Democrat. (Jan. 19, 1991)-. Newspaper. German. wk. $44.50. Staats-Herold Corporation, 36-30 37th Street, Lond Island City NY 11101. **Tel** (718)786-1110. **DD** 070. ***Continues*** *New Yorker Staats-Zeitung und Herold, 1050-4591.*

US/0895-5549
NEW YORKIN UUTISET. VFOAT Finnish New York News; New York News. (1906)-. Newspaper. Finnish (English). wk. $20.00 (six months); $30.00 (one year). Finnish Newspaper Company, 4422 8th Avenue, Brooklyn NY 11220. **ED** Leena Isbom. **LC** 7002. **Bk Rev,** (Qty: varies). **Photos. Ad Acc, Adv Mgr:** Eija Hendel, **Tel** (718)435-0800. Full Page (B&W) $600.00. Half Page (B&W) $300.00. **Pub. Size:** Tabloid.

US/0746-5289
NEWFIELD NEWS. Vol. 1, No. 1 (Feb. 5/11, 1973)-. Newspaper. English. wk (50 issues per year). $25.00 Tompkins County in New York State; $28.50 other. Oddyssey Publications, PO Box N, Trumansburg NY 14886. **Tel** (607)387-3181. ***Continues*** *Newfield Newsletter.*

US/0747-2188
NEWS CHRONICLE (PAWLING, N.Y.), THE. (THE NEWS CHRONICLE.). No. 32 (Aug. 18, 1982)-. Newspaper. English. wk. Housatonic Valley Publishing Company, 3 Memorial Avenue, Pawling NY 12564. ***Continues*** *Pawling-Patterson News-Chronicle (Pawling, N.Y. : 1942).*

US/0884-3910
NEWS FOR YOU (SYRACUSE, N.Y.). (NEWS FOR YOU.). [News you]. Vol. 33, No. 24 (June 12, 1985)-. Newspaper. English. wk (48 per year). $14.40. New Readers Press, PO Box 888, Syracuse NY 13210. **Tel** (800)448-8878, (315)422-9121. **ED** Marianne Ralbousky. **DD** 428. **Photos. Pub. Size:** Tabloid. Documents available from UMI Article Clearinghouse. ***Formed by the union of*** *News for You (Syracuse, N.Y. : Ed. A), 0162-8518* ***and*** *News for You (Syracuse, N.Y. : Ed. B), 0162-850X.*
Ind/Abst Mag. Artic. Summar. Elite (July 1989-); Mag. Artic. Summar. Select (July 1989-); Mag. Artic. Summar. CD-ROM (July 1989-); Mag. Search; Mid. Search (Jul. 1989-); Newsp. Period. Abstr. (1989-); Prim. Search (Jul. 1989-).

US
NEWS OF THE HIGHLANDS, THE. Vol. 1, No. 1 (March 5, 1891)-. Newspaper. English. wk. $31.00. News of the Highlands, 163-165 Main Street, PO Box 278, Highland Falls NY 10928. **Tel** (914)446-4519.

US
NEWS REVIEW (MATTITUCK, NEW YORK). (NEWS REVIEW.). English. wk (Thursday). $29.00 (Suffolk County, New York); $37.00 other. Times / Review Newspapers, 7785 Main Road, PO Box 1500, Mattituck NY 11952. **Tel** (516)298-3200, FAX (516)298-3287.

US
NEWS REVIEW (RIVERHEAD, N.Y.). (THE NEWS-REVIEW.). **VFOAT** News Review. (July 27, 1950)-. Newspaper. English. wk. News-Review / Riverhead, PO Box 720, Riverhead NY 11901. ***Formed by the union of*** *Riverhead News* ***and*** *County Review.*

US/0278-5587
NEWSDAY. NASSAU EDITION. (NEWSDAY.). **VFOAT** Sunday Newsday. (Sept. 3, 1940)-. Newspaper. English. da. $338.00 (daily & Sunday), $234.00 (daily only), $104.00 (Sunday only). Newsday Inc, 235 Pine Lawn Road, Mail Subscriptions, Melville NY 11747. **Tel** (516)843-2150, FAX (516)843-5401. **ED** Anthony Insolia. **Circ:** 603,172 daily, 666,951 Sunday. Documents available from UMI Article Clearinghouse.
Ind/Abst Bus. Dateline; PROMT.

US/0889-793X
NEWSDAY (NEW YORK ED.). (NEW YORK EDITION NEWSDAY.). **VFOAT** Newsday; New York Newsday. Vol. 44, No. 9 (Sept. 11, 1983)-. Newspaper. English. da. $338.00 (daily and Sunday), $234.00 (daily), $104.00 (Sunday) by mail. Newsday Inc, 235 Pine Lawn Road, Mail Subscriptions, Melville NY 11747. **Tel** (516)843-2150, FAX (516)843-5401. Documents available from UMI Article Clearinghouse. ***Continues*** *Newsday (Queens Ed.).*
Ind/Abst Bus. Dateline.

US
NIAGARA GAZETTE. Vol. 79, No. 188 (Sept. 27, 1972)-. Newspaper. English. sw. $90.76. Niagara Gazette, 310 Niagara Street, Niagara Falls NY 14303. **Tel** (716)282-2311 Ext 395. **ED** Mark Francis. **Circ:** 27,436 daily, 28,960 Sunday. available on microfilm from University Microfilms International (UMI). ***Continues*** *Niagara Falls Gazette (Niagara Falls, N.Y. : 1881).*

US
NIAGARA - WHEATFIELD TRIBUNE. English. wk. Niagara Frontier Publications, POB 130, 2231 Grand Island Boulevard, Grand Island NY 14072-0130. **Tel** (716)773-7676, FAX (716)773-7190. **Ad Acc. Pr Rev. Circ:** 16,500 (ctrl).
Desc: Other than advertising this paper contains current events and editorials referring to town, schools, local organizations and public information notices.

US/0895-2612
NORDEN (NEW YORK, N.Y.). (NORDEN : FINSKA AMERIKANAREN : FOLKTIDING FOR FINLANDSSVENSKARNA I AMERIKA.). [Norden]. Vol. 39, No. 18, (May 2, 1935)-. Newspaper. Swedish (English). wk (except 1st three weeks in July). $20.00. Norden News Inc, 123 West 44th Street, Suite 12C, New York NY 10036. **Tel** (212)944-0775. **ED** Erik R. Hermans. **DD** 305. **Bk Rev. Ad Acc. Circ:** 900 (ctrl). available on microfilm from New York Public Library. ***Continues*** *Finska Amerikanaren.*
Desc: Current news from Finland.

US/1059-7670
NORDSTJERNAN (1991). (NORDSTJERNAN.). [Nordstjernan]. Vol. 119, No. 38 (Oct. 10, 1991)-. Newspaper. Swedish (English). wk (except first three weeks of Aug.). $32.00 (1 year), $60.00 (2 year) US; $75.00 (1 year) (surface mail), $150.00 (1 year) (air mail) other. Swedish News Incorporated, PO Box 2143, New York NY 10185. **Tel** (212)944-0776, FAX (212)944-0763. **ED** Liif Marteussen. **DD** 305. **Bk Rev. Photos. Ad Acc, Adv Mgr:** Mette Barlsund. Full Page (B&W) $1,280.00. Half Page (B&W) $640.00. **Circ:** 6,500. ***Continues*** *Nordstjernan Svea, 0895-2620.*

US/8750-4537
NORTH CASTLE NEWS. (19??)-. Newspaper. English. Fifty-two times a year. $35.00 New York; $47.50 others. Martinelli Publishing, 40 Larkin Plaza, Yonkers NY 10701. **Tel** (914)965-4000.

US/0745-628X
NORTH COUNTRY GAZETTE. VFOAT Gazette. Newspaper. English. wk. $10.00. North Country Gazette, Route 9 Box 408, Chestertown NY 12817.

US
NORTH COUNTRYMAN, THE. VFOAT New North Countryman. Vol. 1, No. 1 (Mar. 1, 1928)-. Newspaper. English. wk. $28.00 (Essex County); $35.00 (other). Denton Publications, PO Box 338 High Street, Elizabethtown NY 12932. **Tel** (518)873-6368. **ED** Ron Longto. **Circ:** 5,000. available on microfilm.

US/8750-9245
NORTH CREEK NEWS ENTERPRISE, THE. VFOAT North Creek News-Enterprise. Vol. 15, No. 38 (Sept. 21, 1938)-. Newspaper. English. wk. $8.00 Warren county, $10.00 US; $12.00 other. North Creek News Enterprise, PO Box 85, North Creek NY 12853. ***Continues*** *North Creek Enterprise.*

US
NORTHPORT JOURNAL. Began with May 1885. Newspaper. English. wk. Northport Journal, 248 Main Street, Northport NY 11768. available on microfilm.

US/0891-6322
NORWAY TIMES. VFOAT Norwegian News; Norske Nyheter. Vol. 94, No. 1 (Jan. 5, 1984)-. Newspaper. English (Norwegian). Forty-six times a year. $42.00. Norse News Inc., 481-81 Street, Brooklyn NY 11209. **Tel** (718)238-1100, FAX (718)921-9648. **ED** Tom Roren. **Photos. Ad Acc, Adv Mgr:** Judith Anderson. Full Page (B&W) $1,000.00. **Pub. Size:** Broadsheet. available on microfilm. ***Continues*** *Nordisk Tidende.*
Desc: Politics, sports, current events, local, church news, editorial, etc.

US/0888-143X
NOTICIAS DEL MUNDO. (19??)-. Newspaper. Spanish. da (Except Sat/Sun., X-mas and New Year). $104.00. News World Communication, 401 5th Avenue, New York NY 10016. **Tel** (212)684-5656, FAX (212)889-0024. **ED** Jose Cardinali, (phone: (212)576-0303). **Ad Acc, Adv Mgr:** David Rosa. **Circ:** 32,000 (ctrl).
Desc: Provides the Hispanic community with coverage of local, national and international news.

US/0730-8949
NOVOE RUSSKOE SLOVO. [Novoe rus. slovo]. **VFOAT** New Russian Word. Vol. 10, No. 2764 (Aug. 20, 1920)-. Newspaper. Russian (Slovak). da (except Monday & Christmas). $130.00 US and Canada; $180.00 other. Novoye Russkoye Slovo, 111 Fifth Avenue, 5th Floor, New York NY 10003. **Tel** (212)387-0299 ext. 108, FAX (212)387-9050. **DD** 071. **Bk Rev. Ad Acc. Circ:** 47,000. available on microfilm from The Library of Congress Photoduplication Service. ***Continues*** *Russkie Slovo (New York, N.Y.).*
Desc: Covers political science, anti-communism, society, history of Russia, life in the former Soviet Union, problems of immigration, sports, entertainment, art, economics, etc.

US
OBSERVER. . Newspaper. English. mo. $31.00. Observer Press Inc., PO Box 85, Bard College, Annadaleon Hudson NY 12504. **Tel** (617)431-1993.
Ind/Abst Appl. Soc. Sci. Index Abstr.

US/0890-0329
OBSERVER-DISPATCH (UTICA ED.), THE. (THE OBSERVER-DISPATCH.). **VFOAT** Observer Dispatch. (Sept. 29, 1969)-. Newspaper. English. da (Sun.-Fri. except holidays). $180.00. Utica Observer Dispatch, 221 Oriskany Plaza, Utica NY 13503. **Tel** (315)792-5000. **ED** Jack Marsin. **Circ:** 30,969 daily, 61,354 Sunday. available on microfilm from University Microfilms International (UMI). ***Continues*** *Utica Observer-Dispatch.*

US
OBSERVER (NORTHPORT, N.Y.). (THE OBSERVER.). **VFOAT** Northport Observer. Vol. 39, No. 3 (March 22, 1962)-. Newspaper. English. wk. The Observer / NY, 160 Main Street, Northport NY 11768. ***Continues*** *Huntington Today, Northport Observer.*

US
OLD DUTCH POST STAR. Vol. 109, No. 52 (Dec. 24, 1989)-. Newspaper. English. wk. Lee Publications Inc, 45 Partition Street, PO Box 149, Saugerties NY 12477. **Tel** (914)246-4985. ***Continues*** *Saugerties Old Dutch Post Star.*

US/0745-4848
ONONDAGA VALLEY NEWS. (19??)-. Newspaper. English. Fifty-two times a year. $15.00. Onondaga Valley News, PO Box 4970, Syracuse NY 13221. **Tel** (315)472-7825. ***Continues*** *South Side News.*

US
ORANGE COUNTY POST. (1939)-. Newspaper. English. wk. $17.50. Spears Printing, PO Box 341, Washingtonville NY 10992. **Tel** (914)496-3611. **ED** John Spear. **Photos**. **Ad Acc**, **Adv Mgr:** Pam Lewis. Full Page (B&W) $300.00. Half Page (B&W) $165.00. Full Page (Color) $375.00. Half Page (Color) $240.00. **Pub. Size:** Tabloid. **Circ:** 2,800. ***Continues*** *Post (Washingtonville, N.Y.).*

US/0745-8398
OVID GAZETTE, THE. Newspaper. English. wk. Odyssey Publications, PO Box N, Trumansburg NY 14886. **Tel** (607)387-3181, FAX (607)387-9421.

US
PALLADIUM-TIMES, THE. VFOAT Palladium Times. Vol. 45, No. 138 (June 13, 1969)-. Newspaper. English. da. $106.60. Palladium-Times, 140 West 1st Street, Oswego NY 13126. **Tel** (315)343-3800. **ED** Bruce P. Frassinelli. **Photos**. **Ad Acc**, **Adv Mgr:** Craig Nessck. Full Page (B&W) $1004.91. Half Page (B&W) $502.46. Full Page (Color) $1163.91. Half Page (Color) $661.46. **Pub. Size:** Standard. **Wire Svcs.:** AP, SH. **Circ:** 11,000. available on microfilm from University Microfilms International (UMI). ***Continues*** *Oswego Palladium-Times.*

US/0746-1747
PENFIELD POST-REPUBLICAN. VAT Penfield Post Republican. Vol. 20, No. 14 (May 1971)-. Newspaper. English. wk (Wednesday). $18.00 (local zip codes); $30.00 (other). Wolfe Publications, 666 Phillips Road, Victor NY 14564. **Tel** (716) 924-4040, FAX (716) 924-7734. ***Continues*** *Penfield Republican.*

US
PEOPLE'S WEEKLY WORLD [MICROFORM]. VFOAT World; Nuestro Mundo. Vol. 5, No. 12 (Oct. 6, 1990)-. Newspaper. English. wk. $20.00. Long View Publishing Company, 239 West 23rd Street, New York NY 10011. **Tel** (212)924-2523, FAX (212)645-5436, telex 12-7819. **ED** Timothy Wheeler, Carolin Rummel (Managing Editor). **Bk Rev**, (Qty: 10). **Photos**. **Ad Acc**, **Adv Mgr:** Audrey West. Half Page (B&W) $370.00. **Pub. Size:** Tabloid. **Wire Svcs.:** AP. **Circ:** 46,000. available in microform. ***Continues*** *People's Daily World (New York, N.Y. : 1986).*

US/1065-1128
PERRY HERALD (1912). (PERRY HERALD.). Vol. 36 (Sept. 4, 1912)-. Newspaper. English. wk. $20.50 Wyoming County, New York; $23.50 other. Perry Herald, 12 Borden Avenue, PO Box 219, Perry NY 14530. **Tel** (716)237-2211. **ED** Susan Cady White. **Photos**. **Ad Acc**, **Adv Mgr:** Lois Taylor. **Pub. Size:** Broadsheet. available in microform. ***Continues*** *Perry Semi-Weeky herald;* ***Absorbed*** *Perry Record.*

US
PLAINWELL-THE UNION ENTERPRISE. English. Fifty-two times a year. $18.50 (one year); $33.00 (two years); $47.00 (three years). Union Enterprise / New York, PO Box 417, Plainwell NY 49080.

US
POLISH AMERICAN JOURNAL (1985 : NATIONAL ED.). (POLISH AMERICAN JOURNAL.). **VFOAT** Polonia's Voice; Polonia's Voice, Polish American Journal. Vol. 74, No. 1 (Jan. 16, 1985)-. Newspaper. English. mo. $15.00. Polish American Journal, 1275 Harlem Road, Buffalo NY 14206. **Tel** (716)893-5771, FAX (716)893-5783. **ED** Mark A. Kohan (Editor-in-Chief) and Paulette T. Kulbacki (Managing Editor). **Bk Rev**, (Qty: 3). **Photos**. **Ad Acc**, **Adv Mgr:** Kathy Sobocinski. Full Page (B&W) $1,000.00. Half Page (B&W) $600.00. Full Page (Color) $2,500.00. Half Page (Color) $2,000.00. **Pub. Size:** Tabloid. **Circ:** 18,300 (ctrl). available on an online database from Ethnic News Watch. ***Formed by the union of*** *Pol-Am Journal (Scranton, Pa. : National Ed.), 0749-0453* ***and*** *Polish American Voice, 0749-0178.*

US
POLISH AMERICAN WORLD. VFOAT Polish World American; Polish-American World; World. (1958)-. Newspaper. English. wk. $15.00. Polish American World, 3100 Grand Boulevard, Baldwin NY 11510. **Tel** (516)223-6514, FAX (516)223-6514. **ED** Hellen Poster, T.W. Poskropski (Managing Editor). **Bk Rev**, (Qty: 12). **Photos**. **Ad Acc**, **Adv Mgr:** Tom Poster. Full Page (B&W) $400.00. Half Page (B&W) $220.00. Full Page (Color) $500.00. Half Page (Color) $275.00. **Pub. Size:** Tabloid. **Circ:** 4,000 paid, 6,000 unpaid.

US/0893-4304
PORT JEFFERSON RECORD (1969). (PORT JEFFERSON RECORD.). No. 25 (Jan. 23, 1969)-. Newspaper. English. wk. Anton Community Newspapers, 135 Liberty Avenue, Mineola NY 11501. **Tel** (516)747-8282 ext. 124. **ED** Margie Freaney. **Circ:** 9,000. available on microfilm. ***Continues*** *Record (Port Jefferson, N.Y.).*

US
POST-JOURNAL, THE. VFOAT Post Journal. Vol. 25, No. 151 (April 2, 1966)-. Newspaper. English. da. $125.80 (one year). Post-Journal, 11 21 West Second Street, Jamestown NY 14701. **Tel** (716)487-1111 Ext. 262. ***Continues*** *Jamestown Post Journal.*

US
POST-STANDARD, THE. VFOAT Post Standard. Began with Jan. 1, 1899 issue. Newspaper. English. da. Post-Standard Company, Clinton Square, PO Box 4915, Syracuse NY 13201. available on microfilm from The Library of Congress Photoduplication Service. ***Formed by the union of*** *Syracuse Daily Standard (Syracuse, N.Y. : 1890)* ***and*** *Syracuse Post.*

US/0897-0505
POST-STAR (GLENS FALLS, N.Y. : 1974). (THE POST-STAR.). **VFOAT** Post Star. 70th year, 62nd issue (Feb. 12, 1974)-. Newspaper. English. da. $215.00. Glens Falls Newspapers Inc., Glens Falls NY 12801. **Tel** (518)792-3131. **ED** Jim Marshall. **Ad Acc**. ctrl circ. available on microfilm. ***Continues*** *Post-Star and Times.*

US
POUGHKEEPSIE JOURNAL (POUGHKEEPSIE, N.Y. : 1960). (POUGHKEEPSIE JOURNAL.). Vol. 175, No. 370 (Aug. 10, 1960)-. Newspaper. English. da (365 issues). $246.24. Poughkeepsie Newspapers Inc, PO Box 1231, Poughkeepsie NY 12602. **Tel** (914)454-2000 ext. 282. ***Continues*** *Poughkeepsie New Yorker.*

US/0886-8816
PRESS & SUN-BULLETIN. VFOAT Press & Sun bulletinB; Press and Sun-Bulletin; Press and Sun Bulletin. Vol. 1, No. 1 (Sept. 30, 1985)-. Bulletin. English. da. $241.64 (local), $265.80 (other) Daily & Sunday by mail. Binghamton Press Company, Vestal Parkway East, PO Box 1270, Binghamton NY 13902-9982. **Tel** (607)798-1234, (607)798-1188. **ED** Kevin Walter. **Bk Rev**, (Qty: 200). **Ad Acc**, **Adv Mgr:** Scott Putnicki. **Circ:** 70,000 Daily, 92,000 Sunday. ***Formed by the union of*** *Sun-Bulletin (Binghamton, N.Y.)* ***and*** *Evening Press (Binghamton, N.Y.).*

US/1041-4754
PRESS-REPUBLICAN. VFOAT Press Republican; Press-Extra; Press Extra. Vol. 73, No. 79 (Nov. 14, 1966)-. Newspaper. English. da. $51.35 (three months), $102.70 (six months), $176.00 (one year). Press-Republican, 170 Margaret Street, Plattsburgh NY 12901. **Tel** (800)288-7323, (415)561-2300. ***Continues in part*** *Plattsburgh Press-Republican.*

US/0749-3126
PROINE, HE. (PROINE.). [Proine]. **VFOAT** Proini. (1976)-. Newspaper. Greek, Modern (English). da (except Sundays and holidays). Petallides Publishing, 25-50 Crescent Street, Astoria NY 11102. **DD** 071. available on microfilm from New York Public Library.

US/0747-086X
QUEENSWEEK. VFOAT Queens Week. (198?)-. Newspaper. English. wk. $8.00. Queensweek Publishing Corporation, PO Box 29, Middle Village NY 11379.

US/8750-0930
RANDOM HARVEST WEEKLY. VFOAT Random Harvest. Newspaper. English. wk. Odyssey Publications, PO Box N, Trumansburg NY 14886. **Tel** (607)387-3181, FAX (607)387-9421.

US/0894-6140
READING RAINBOW GAZETTE. *Ceased.* [Read. rainbow gaz.]. Vol. 1, No. 1, 1983- Ceased (1987). Periodical. English. an. Reading Rainbow Gazette Inc, 648 Broadway/Suite 402, New York NY 10012. **DD** 372.

US
RECORD PILOT. VFOAT Glen Cove Record Pilot; Glen Cove Record-Pilot. (19??)-. Newspaper. English. wk. Anton Community Newspapers, 135 Liberty Avenue, Mineola NY 11501. **Tel** (516)747-8282 ext. 124. ***Formed by the union of*** *Record-Advance and Sea Cliff News* ***and*** *Enterprise-Pilot.*

US/1053-8976
RECORD (TROY, N.Y.). (THE RECORD.). **VFOAT** Sunday Record. (Jan. 11, 1988)-. Newspaper. English. da. $2.85 per week. Record, 501 Broadway, Troy NY 12181. **Tel** (518)270-1200, telex (518)270-1202. **ED** Rex Smith, Lisa Lewis (Managing Editor). **Bk Rev**. **Photos**. **Ad Acc**, **Adv Mgr:** Regina Burkhart, **Tel** (518)270-1241. Full Page (B&W) $3,433.00. Half Page (B&W) $1716.00. Full Page (Color) $3733.00. Half Page (Color) $2016.00. **Pub. Size:** Standard. **Wire Svcs.:** AP. **Circ:** 32,211 daily, 35,789 other. available on microfilm and microfiche from Crest Information Technologies. ***Continues*** *Times Record (Troy, N.Y.).*

US/0739-2540
RECORDER (AMSTERDAM, N.Y.). (THE RECORDER.). Vol. 98, No. 238 (May 28, 1977)-. Newspaper. English. da. Amsterdam Evening News, 1 Venner Road, Amsterdam NY 12010. **Tel** (518)843-1100. ***Continues*** *Amsterdam Evening Recorder.*

US
REGISTER HERALD (MILLBROOK, N.Y.). (THE REGISTER HERALD.). Vol. 117, No. 32 (August 13, 1981)-. Newspaper. English. wk. $29.00 (1 year) local, $35.00 (1 year) other, $49.00 (3 year) local, $67.00 (3 year) other. Register Herald, PO Box 316, Millbrook NY 12545. **Tel** (914)677-8241. ***Continues*** *Pine Plains Register Herald.*

US/0747-2374
REGISTER STAR. VFOAT Register-Star. (Feb. 1990)-. Newspaper. English. da (258 Issues per year). $130.00. Record Printing & Publishin Co Inc., 364 Warren Street, Hudson NY 12534. **Tel** (518)828-1616, FAX (518)828-9437. ***Continues*** *Evening Register Star.*

US
REPORTER DISPATCH, THE. (1917)-. Newspaper. English. ds. price varies. Gannett Surburban Newspaper, 1 Gannett Drive, White Plains NY 10604. **Tel** 800 942-1010.
Ind/Abst PROMT.

US
RIVER REPORTER, THE. VFOAT River Reporter Weekly. Vol. 1, No. 1 (Dec. 3, 1975)-. Newspaper. English. wk (Thursdays). $22.00. River Reporter, PO Box 150, Narrowsburg NY 12764. **Tel** (914)252-7414. **ED** Glenn Pontier. **Bk Rev**. **Photos**. **Ad Acc**, **Adv Mgr:** Laurie Stuart. Full Page (B&W) $340.20. Half Page (B&W) $170.10. Full Page (Color) $440.20. Half Page (Color) $270.10. **Pub. Size:** Standard. **Circ:** 4,000 (paid weekly).

US
RIVERDALE PRESS, THE. Vol. 1, No. 1 (April 20, 1950)-. Newspaper. English. wk. $19.00. Riverdale Press, 6155 Broadway, New York NY 10471-3153. **Tel** (718)543-6065, FAX (718)548-4038. **ED** Bernard L. Stein, Tom Watson (Managing Editor). **Bk Rev**, (Qty: 50). **Photos**. **Ad Acc**, **Adv Mgr:** Phyllis Steele. Full Page (B&W) $2431.80. Half Page (B&W) $1260.00. **Pub. Size:** Standard. **Circ:** 14,000 paid. available on microfilm from University Microfilms International (UMI).

US/0192-6535
ROCHESTER TIMES, THE. Newspaper. English. Rochester Times, 222 Sunrise Highway, Rochester NY 11570.

US
ROCKLAND COUNTY TIMES, THE. VFOAT Times. (Oct. 1889)-. Newspaper. English. wk. $27.50 (Rockland County); $32.50 (other). Rockland County Times, 11 New Main Street, Haverstraw NY 10927. **Tel** FAX (914)429-8990. **Ad Acc**. **Circ:** 6,000.

US
ROCKLAND JOURNAL-NEWS. VFOAT Rockland Journal News. Vol. 101, No. 241 (Jan. 1, 1991)-. Newspaper. English. da. price varies. Gannett Surburban Newspaper, 1 Gannett Drive, White Plains NY 10604. **Tel** 800 942-1010. **(Subscription address:** PO Box 427, Yorktown Heights NY 10598; telephone: (800)942-1010) ***Continues*** *Journal-News (Nyack, N.Y.).*

US/1076-3740
ROCKVILLE CENTRE'S LONG ISLAND NEWS AND THE OWL. VFOAT Long Island News and the Owl. Vol. 49, No. 35 (Aug. 28, 1964)-. Newspaper. English. wk. News and Owl, PO Box 360, Lynbrook NY 11563. **Tel** (516)536-4900. ***Continues*** *Long Island News and the Owl.*

US/0893-4401
RYE CHRONICLE, THE. Began in 1905. Newspaper. English. wk. Rye Chronicle, 40 Larkin Plaza, Yonkers NY 10701.

US
SAG HARBOR EXPRESS. Vol. 86, No. 28 (April 17, 1947)-. Newspaper. English. wk. $25.00. Coastal Publications Incorporated, PO Box 1620, Main Street, Sag Harbor, Long Island NY 11963. **Tel** (516)725-1700. **ED** Bryan Boyhan. **Ad Acc**. ***Continues*** *Sag Harbor Express and the News and the Corrector;* ***Absorbed*** *Shelter Islander.*

US/8755-9110
SALAMANCA PRESS. 115th Year, No. 108 (Sept. 1, 1981)-. Newspaper. English. da. Salamanca Press, 36 42 River Street, Salamanca NY 14779. **Tel** (716)945-1644. ***Continues*** *Salamanca Republican Press.*

US/0193-0311
SALMON RIVER NEWS. Newspaper. English. Oswego County Weeklies, North Jefferson Street, Box 1, Mexico NY 13114.

US/1071-4448
SARATOGIAN (SARATOGA SPRINGS, N.Y., 1910), THE. (THE SARATOGIAN.). **VFOAT** Saratogian Sunday. Vol. 41, No. 37 (Feb. 7, 1910)-. Newspaper. English. ds. $132.60 Saratoga; $232.00 other. Saratogian, 20 Lake Avenue, Saratoga Springs NY 12866. **Tel** (518)584-4242, FAX (518)587-7750. **ED** Barbara Lombardo. **LC** 9122. Index available. cum.

index. **Ad Acc. Circ:** 12,135 daily, 13,873 Sunday. available on microfilm from University Microfilms International (UMI). ***Continues*** *Daily Saratogian.*

US
SCARSDALE INQUIRER, THE. (July 1901)-. Newspaper. English. bw. $29.50 Westchester County New York; $35.50 other. Scarsdale Inquirer, PO Box 418, Scarsdale NY 10583. **Tel** (914)725-2500. **ED** Linda Leavitt. **Bk Rev**, (Qty: 6-8). **Ad Acc, Adv Mgr:** D White. **Circ:** 7,000.

US/0746-066X
SHELTER ISLAND REPORTER. VFOAT Shelter Island Reporter Combined with Bargain Hunter. Vol. 1, No. 1 (June 20, 1959)-. Newspaper. English. wk. $20.00 New York; $25.00 others. Shelter Island Reporter, PO Box 1000, Shelter Island NY 11965. **ED** Elizabeth Bonora. **Photos. Ad Acc, Adv Mgr:** Patricia Binder, **Tel** (516)749-1000. Full Page (B&W) $405.00. Half Page (B&W) $202.50. **Pub. Size:** Tabloid.

US
SHERBURNE NEWS, THE. Vol. 5, No. 1 (Apr. 16, 1868)-. Newspaper. English. wk. $13.00. Sherburne News, 17 East State Street, Sherburne NY 13460. **Tel** (607)674-6071. ***Continues*** *Sherburne Home News.*

US/0883-6655
SHIBAO ZHOU KAN (MEIZHOU-BAN). (SHIH PAO CHOU KAN.). **VFOAT** China Times Weekly. (1985)-. Newspaper. Chinese (Chinese). wk. $120.00. China Times Inc, 43-27 36th Street, 3rd Floor, Long Island NY 11101. **Tel** (718)937-6110, FAX (718)729-8685. **ED** Dong-Sing Liang. **DD** 071. **Photos. Ad Acc, Adv Mgr:** Hai-Hwa Yuan, **Tel** (718)937-6110. Full Page (Color) $600.00. Half Page (Color) $300.00. **Pub. Size:** Standard. **Circ:** 25,000. ***Continues*** *Chung-Kuo Shih Pao, 0733-2270.*

US/0049-0490
SILENT NEWS. (1969)-. Newspaper. English. mo. $20.00 US. Silent News Inc., PO Box 23330, Rochester NY 14620. **Tel** (716)334-7736, FAX (716)334-0962. **ED** Tom Willard (editor's telephone: (716)272-4900). **Bk Rev. Ad Acc, Adv Mgr Tel** (716)272-4900. **Circ:** 6,000 (ctrl).
Desc: The hearing impaired have a lively, colorful and diverse culture with traits that distinguish ethnic groups. Talented deaf writers, artists and photographers inform of current news, political and other issues, opinion, adaptive devices and lifestyles experienced by people without hearing.

US
SKAGIT ARGUS, THE. (Jan. 21, 1982)-. Newspaper. English. wk. Gannett Surburban Newspaper, 1 Gannett Drive, White Plains NY 10604. **Tel** 800 942-1010. ***Continues*** *Mount Vernon Argus.*

US/0745-6484
SOUTHAMPTON PRESS, THE. (SOUTHAMPTON PRESS.). (May 29, 1897)-. Newspaper. English. Fifty-one times per year. $26.00 Suffolk County; $32.00 other. Southampton Press & Publishing Company, PO Box 1207, Southampton NY 11968.

US/0192-9631
SOUTHERN DUTCHESS NEWS. Vol. 15, No. 10 (Mar. 9, 1967)-. Newspaper. English. wk. S25.00. Southern Dutchess News, 84 East Main Street, Wappingers Falls NY 12590. **Tel** (914)297-3723, FAX (914)297-6810. **ED** Albert M. Osten, Bill Parsons (Managing Editor). **Photos. Ad Acc, Adv Mgr:** Audrey Morgenstern. Full Page (B&W) $1228.50. Half Page (B&W) $693.00. Full Page (Color) $1353.50. Half Page (Color) $818.00. **Pub. Size:** Broadsheet. **Circ:** 27,000. available on microfilm. ***Continues*** *Wappingers and Southern Dutchess News.*
Desc: Local, community news, profiles, school news and reports.

US
STAR-GAZETTE (ELMIRA, N.Y.). (STAR-GAZETTE.). **VFOAT** Star Gazette; Sunday Telegram; Star-Gazette Sunday Telegram; Sunday Star-Gazette. Vol. 4, No. 308 (Jan. 23 1967)-. Newspaper. English. da (365 issues). $185.50 Star Gazette / New York, 201 Baldwin Street, Elmira NY 14902. **Tel** (607)734-5151. ***Continues*** *Star-Gazette and Advertiser.*

US
STATEN ISLAND ADVANCE. (1886)-. Newspaper. English. da. $104.00, $65.00 (Sunday only by mail). Staten Island Advance, 950 Fingerboard Road, Staten Island NY 10305. **Tel** (718)981-1234. **ED** Brian Laline, Editor's Phone: (718)981-1234 ext. 2200. **LC** 7002. **Circ:** 76,543. available on microfilm from University Microfilms International (UMI).

US/0890-9881
STATEN ISLAND REGISTER. (19??)-. Newspaper. English. Fifty-two times a year (Thurs.). $15.00 Staten Island residents; $25.00 other. Staten Island Register, 2100 Clove Road, Staten Island NY 10305. **Tel** (718)447-4727, FAX (718)816-7719 **ED** Diane Sclafani (editor's address: 2100 Clovero, Staten Island, New York 10305, phone: (718)447-4700). **Bk Rev. Ad Acc. Circ:** 20,000.

US
STEUBEN COURIER-ADVOCATE, THE. VFOAT Steuben Courier Advocate. Vol. 152, No. 30 (July 25, 1968)-. Newspaper. English. wk. $65.00. Steuben Courier - Advocate, 10 West Steuben Street, Bath NY 14810. **Tel** (607)776-2121, FAX (607)776-3967. available on microfilm from University Microfilms International (UMI). ***Continues*** *Steuben Courier and The Steuben Advocate.*

US/8750-7307
SUFFOLK COUNTY LIFE. VFOAT Suffolk Life. (19??)-. Newspaper. English. Fifty-two times a year. $20.00 Suffolk County; $27.00 other. Suffolk Life Newspapers, PO Box 167, Riverhead NY 11901. **Tel** (516)369-0820.

US/1065-1470
SUFFOLK COUNTY NEWS, THE. (1885)-. Newspaper. English. wk. $31.00. Suffolk County News Inc, 23 Candee, Sayville NY 11782. **Tel** (516)589-6200. available on microfilm. ***Continues*** *Sayville Weekly News.*

US/8750-0922
SUFFOLK SOURCE, THE. VFOAT Source. Newspaper. English. mo. $2.99. Suffolk Source, 136 Carman Street, Patchogue NY 11772.

US
SUFFOLK TIMES, THE. 112th Year, No. 23 (Dec. 26, 1969)-. Newspaper. English. wk (Thursday). $29.00 Suffolk county; $37.00 other. Times / Review Newspapers, 7785 Main Road, PO Box 1500, Mattituck NY 11952. **Tel** (516)298-3200, FAX (516)298-3287. **ED** Troy Gistavson (Editor-in Chief) and Jeff Miller (Managing Editor). **Photos. Ad Acc, Adv Mgr:** Janice Robinson. Full Page (B&W) $640.00. Half Page (B&W) $346.00. **Pub. Size:** Tabloid. ***Continues*** *Suffolk Weekly Times (Greenport, N.Y. : 1964).*

US/1072-8619
SUN (1993). (THE SUN.). Vol. 108, No. 11 (Mar. 16, 1993)-. Newspaper. English. wk. $24.00 St. Lawrence and Franklin counties; $26.00 other. Fort Covington Sun, Fort Covington NY 12937. **ED** Tom Grady. **Ad Acc, Adv Mgr:** Bob Alexsander. **Circ:** 2,000 (ctrl). ***Continues*** *Fort Covington Sun.*

US
SWISS AMERICAN REVIEW. VFOAT Amerikanische Schweizer Zeitung. Vol. 106, No. 14 (Dec. 5, 1973)-. Newspaper. German (English, French and Italian). Fifty-two times a year. $30.00. Swiss American Review, 608 5th Avenue, Room 609, New York NY 10020. **Tel** (212)247-0459. **ED** Karl Vonlanthen. **Bk Rev**, (Qty: 6). **Photos. Ad Acc, Adv Mgr:** Nadja C. Leonard, **Tel** (202)408-1200. Full Page (B&W) $999.00. Half Page (B&W) $550.00. Full Page (Color) $1,049.00. Half Page (Color) $600.00. **Pub. Size:** Standard. ctrl circ. available on microfilm. ***Continues*** *Amerikanische Schweizer Zeitung.*

US
SYRACUSE HERALD-JOURNAL. VFOAT Syracuse Herald Journal. Vol. 63, No. 18,393 (Sept. 27, 1939)-. Newspaper. English. da. Syracuse Newspapers, PO Box 4915, Syracuse NY 13221. **Tel** (315)470-0011. **ED** Timothy Bunn. **Circ:** 101,922. available on microfilm from University Microfilms International (UMI); and University Microfilms International (UMI). ***Continues*** *Syracuse Herald, Syracuse Journal.*
Ind/Abst PROMT.

US
THOUSAND ISLANDS SUN AND ON THE ST. LAWRENCE. VFOAT Thousand Islands Sun Combined With On the St. Lawrence. Vol. 52, No. 51 (Mar. 19, 1953)-. Newspaper. English. wk. $20.00 Jefferson and St. Lawrence counties; $24.00 other US; $30.00 other. Thousand Island Sun, 7 Market Street, Alexandria Bay NY 13607. **Tel** (315)482-2581. ***Formed by the union of*** *Thousand Island Sun* ***and*** *On the St. Lawrence.*

US/1053-2684
THREE VILLAGE HERALD. (1954)-. Newspaper. English. wk. $18.00 (in county), $24.00 (out of county). Three Village Herald, 60 Route 25A, Box 703, East Setauket NY 11733. **Tel** (516)751-1550, FAX (516)751-8592. **ED** Phil Holland. **Photos. Ad Acc, Adv Mgr:** Barbara Farley. Full Page (B&W) $759.00. Half Page (B&W) $380.00. **Pub. Size:** Standard. **Circ:** 8,600 paid weekly. available on microfilm from Berhan Industries, Ltd.
Desc: Covers news and features on this community and its people. Also focuses on how state, county, and federal events affect us.

US
TIMES HERALD (OLEAN, N.Y.). (TIMES HERALD.). Newspaper. English. da. Olean Times Herald Corporation, 639 Norton Drive, Olean NY 14760. **Tel** (716)372-3121. available on microfilm from University Microfilms International (UMI). ***Continues*** *Olean Times-Herald.*

US
TIMES HERALD RECORD, THE. VFOAT Sunday Record. Vol. 25, No. 212 (Mar. 2, 1981)-. Newspaper. English. da. $215.80 (daily and Sun.), $149.50 (daily) Orange, Ulster, Pike, Sullivan, and Dutchess counties; $234.80 (daily & Sun.), $160.00 (daily) other. Times Herald Record, 40 Mulberry Street, Middletown NY 10940. **Tel** (914)343-2181. **ED** Gary Grossman. **Ad Acc, Adv Mgr:** Dan Stewart. **Circ:** 86,000 Daily, 102,000 Sun. ***Continues in part*** *Times Herald Record (Middletown, N.Y. : Sullivan Ulster Tri-State Ed.).*

US
TIMES-JOURNAL. VFOAT Times Journal. 105th year, No. 13 (April 1981)-. Newspaper. English. wk. Ryder Newspapers Inc, 19 Division Street, Cobleskill NY 12043. ***Continues*** *Times-Journal, the Cobleskill Index.*

US/0746-0392
TIMES OF TI. Newspaper. English. wk. $3.45. Denton Publications, PO Box 338 High Street, Elizabethtown NY 12932. **Tel** (518)873-6368. **ED** Michael Connery. **Bk Rev. Ad Acc. Circ:** 8,900 (ctrl).
Desc: Community newspaper.

US
TIMES-UNION (ALBANY, N.Y.). (THE TIMES-UNION.). **VFOAT** Times Union; Sunday Times Union; Times Union, Out of Town News; Times-Union, Out of Town News. (Nov. 17, 1891)-. Newspaper. English. da. Times-Union / Albany New York, News Plaza, Box 1500, Albany NY 12212. **Tel** (518)454-5694. **ED** Harry Rosenfeld. **Circ:** 89,049 daily, 176,080 Sunday. available on microfilm. ***Formed by the union of*** *Albany Evening Times* ***and*** *Evening Union (Albany, N.Y.);* ***Absorbed*** *Knickerbocker News (Albany, N.Y. : 1975).*

US/0744-1851
TIMES-UNION (ROCHESTER, N.Y.). (THE TIMES-UNION.). **VFOAT** Times Union. Vol. 46, No. 170 (Sept. 30, 1963)-. Newspaper. English. da. $119.00. Rochester Times Union, 55 Exchange Street, Rochester NY 14614. **Tel** (716)232-7100 ext. 3650. **ED** Barbara Henry. **Circ:** 99,500. available on microfilm from University Microfilms International (UMI). ***Continues*** *Rochester Times-Union.*

US
TONAWANDA NEWS. (Nov. 1, 1954)-. Newspaper. English. da. Tonawanda News, 435 River Road, North Tonawanda NY 14120. **Tel** (716)693-1000. ***Continues*** *Evening News (North Tonawanda, N.Y.).*

US/0040-9979
TOWN & VILLAGE. VFOAT Town and Village. (19??)-. Newspaper. English. wk. $12.00. Hagedorn Communications, 1 Madison Avenue, 35th Floor, New York NY 10010. **Tel** (212)679-1234, FAX (212)689-2267. **ED** Charles G. Hagedorn. Index available. **Bk Rev. Ad Acc. Circ:** 10,800 (ctrl).
Desc: Local news.

US
TRI-STATE GAZETTE, THE. VFOAT Tri State Gazette. Vol. 132, No. 216 (Sept. 13, 1982)-. Newspaper. English. da (312 issues per year). $119.20. Tri-States Publishing Co., 86 Fowler Street, Port Jervis NY 12771. **Tel** (914)856-5383. **ED** Stan Hojnacki. ***Continues*** *Union-Gazette (Port Jervis, N.Y.).*

US
TRI-TOWN NEWS, THE. VFOAT Tri Town News. (1867)-. Newspaper. English. wk. Tri-Town News, PO Box 388, Sidney NY 13838. **Tel** (607)563-3526. ***Continues*** *Sidney Record and Bainbridge News;* ***Absorbed*** *Afton Enterprise and Harpursville Budget.*

US/1052-374X
TRIBUNE SYOSSET, JERICHO. (1990)-. Newspaper. English. wk. Anton Community Newspapers, 135 Liberty Avenue, Mineola NY 11501. **Tel** (516)747-8282 ext. 124. ***Continues*** *Syosset Tribune, 8756-2073.*

US
TRUMANSBURG FREE PRESS. No. 3 (Jan. 25, 1984)-. Newspaper. English. wk. $17.00. Odyssey Publications, PO Box N, Trumansburg NY 14886. **Tel** (607)387-3181, FAX (607)387-9421. **ED** Jim Bilinsk, Chris Kimball-Peterson (Managing Editor). **Bk Rev**, (Qty: 2-3). **Photos. Ad Acc, Adv Mgr:** Del Hall, Jim Graney. Full Page (B&W) $398.40. Half Page (B&W) $210.24. Full Page (Color) $773.40. Half Page (Color) $585.24. **Pub. Size:** Standard. available in microform. ***Continues*** *Free Press (Trumansburg, N.Y. : 1932).*

US
TUPPER LAKE FREE PRESS AND TUPPER LAKE HERALD. (1895)-. Newspaper. English. wk. $23.00 (in county), $24.00 (out of county). Tupper Lake Free Press, 136 Park Street, Tupper Lake NY 12986. **Tel** (518)359-2166. **ED** Sue Mitchell. **Photos. Ad Acc, Adv Mgr:** Betty Bell. Full Page (B&W) $558.00. Half Page (B&W) $279.00. Full Page (Color) $633.00. Half Page (Color) $354.00. **Pub. Size:** Broadsheet. **Circ:** 3,537 (ctrl). available on microfilm from Capitol Microfilm Services, Inc. ***Formed by the union of*** *Tupper Lake Free Press* ***and*** *Tupper Lake Herald.*
Desc: Weekly hometown newspaper.

US/0747-3788
UNION-SUN AND JOURNAL. **VFOAT** Union Sun and Journal; Union Sun Journal; Union-Sun and Journal. (191?)-. Newspaper. English. da. $125.00. Union Sun & Journal Inc, PO Box 503, 459 South Transit Road, Lockport NY 14094. **Tel** (716)439-9218. **ED** Dan Kane. **Circ:** 18,384. ***Formed by the union of*** *Lockport Union-Sun* ***and*** *Lockport Daily Journal (Lockport, N.Y. : 1871).*

US/0199-6886
USA POLONIA. (USA POLONIA; POLISH AMERICAN WEEKLY.). **VFOAT** Polish American Weekly. **VAT** United States of America Polonia. Newspaper. Polish (English). mo. $17.00. Tytan, 896 Manhattan Avenue, Brooklyn NY 11222. ***Continues*** *Tydzien.*

US/1051-7405
USA TODAY (INTERNATIONAL ED.). (USA TODAY.). (198?)-. Newspaper. English. da (260 per year). $404.34 Australia; $606.91 Japan; $272.69 UK; $331.63 France; $412.90 Germany; $600.00 Middle East and Africa; $471.29 Austria; $331.92 Italy; $361.12 Switzerland; 352.01 Belgium; $551.55 Denmark; $394.09 Finland. Gannett International, 535 Madison Avenue, New York NY 10022. **Tel** (212)715-5426, (800)872-0001, FAX (212)207-8982. **ED** John M. Simpson. **Bk Rev**, (Qty: 80). **Ad Acc**, **Adv Mgr:** Alex Clemente. **Circ:** 67,000. **Ind/Abst** Abstr. BioCommer.

US/8755-5808
VABA EESTI SONA. **VFOAT** Free Estonian Word. Vol. 1, No. 1 (June 11, 1949)-. Newspaper. Estonian. wk. $37.00. Nordic Press Inc, 243 East 34th Street, PO Box 123, New York NY 10016. **Tel** (212)686-3356. **ED** Harald Raudsenn. **Circ:** 3,800. available on microfilm from New York Public Library; and The Library of Congress Photoduplication Service.

US
VALLEY NEWS (ELIZABETHTOWN, N.Y.). (THE VALLEY NEWS.). **VFOAT** Elizabethtown Post; Essex County Republican; Adirondack Record-Post. (1948)-. Newspaper. English. wk. $18.00 Essex County; $25.00 other; $35.00 (outside US). Denton Publications, PO Box 338 High Street, Elizabethtown NY 12932. **Tel** (518)873-6368. **Circ:** 4,000. ***Absorbed*** *Independent (Elizabethtown, N.Y.).*

US/1067-7755
VALLEY NEWS (FULTON, N.Y.), THE. (THE VALLEY NEWS.). Vol. 34, No. 20 (Feb. 2, 1982)-. Newspaper. English. sw (Published on Monday and Thursday). $17.00 Oswego County; $24.00 New York State; $32.00 other. Valley News / New York, 117 Oneida Street, Fulton NY 13069. **Tel** (315)598-6397. **ED** Theresa Bennett. **Photos**. **Ad Acc**. Full Page (B&W) $460.00. Half Page (B&W) $230.00. Full Page (Color) $545.00. Half Page (Color) $290.00. **Pub. Size:** Tabloid. **Circ:** 9,000. ***Continues*** *Oswego Valley News.*

US/0889-8677
VILLAGE TIMES, THE. Vol. 1, No. 1 (April 8, 1976)-. Newspaper. English. wk. $22.00 (one year), $37.00 (two years), $52.00 (three years) Suffolk County, New York; $30.00 (one year), $53.00 (two years), $76.00 (three years) other. Village Times, PO Box 707, Setauket NY 11733. **Tel** (516)751-7744. **ED** Leah Dunaief, Ann Fossan (Managing Editor). **Photos**. **Ad Acc**, **Adv Mgr:** Kathryn Mandracchia. **Pub. Size:** Tabloid.

US/0746-7869
VORWARTS (NEW YORK, N.Y.). (FORVERTS.). [Vorwarts]. **VFOAT** Jewish Daily Forward; Forward; Vorwarts; Yiddish Forward. (April 22, 1897)-. Newspaper. Yiddish (English). wk. $36.00 US; $40.00 other. Jewish Forward, 45 East 33rd Street, New York NY 10016. **Tel** (212)889-8200, FAX (212)684-3949. **ED** Mordechai Strigter (Editor-in-Chief) and Joseph Moltek (Managing Editor). **Bk Rev**. **Photos**. **Ad Acc**, **Adv Mgr** **Tel** (212)889-8200 ext. 406. ***Absorbed*** *Forverts (Chicago, Ill.).*

US/0270-9910
WALL STREET FINAL, THE. [Wall Street final]. Periodical. English. da. $250.00. Wall Street Final, 66 Greene Street, New York NY 10012.

US
WARRENSBURG-LAKE GEORGE NEWS, THE. **VFOAT** Warrensburg Lake George News. Vol. 62, No. 44 (April 12, 1962)-. Newspaper. English. wk. $24.00. Warrensburg Lake George News, 159 Main Street, Warrensburg NY 12885. **ED** Tom Randall. **Photos**. **Ad Acc**, **Adv Mgr:** John McGuire, **Tel** (518)623-9786. Full Page (B&W) $640.00. Half Page (B&W) $320.00. Full Page (Color) $720.00. Half Page (Color) $380.00. **Pub. Size:** Tabloid. ***Continues*** *Warrensburgh News.*

US/0891-009X
WATERTOWN DAILY TIMES (WATERTOWN, N.Y. : 1929). (WATERTOWN DAILY TIMES.). Began Aug. 15, 1929. Newspaper. English. da. Johnson Newspaper Corporation, 260 Washington Street, Watertown NY 13601-3364. **Tel** (315)782-1000. **ED** John B Johnson Jr. **Circ:** 42,972. ***Continues*** *Watertown Standard.*

US
WATERVILLE TIMES (WATERVILLE, N.Y.). (WATERVILLE TIMES.). (195?)-. Newspaper. English. Fifty-two times a year. $24.00 Oneida County, New York; $26.00 other. Waterville Times, 124 East Main Street, PO Box C, Waterville NY 13480. **Tel** (315)841-4105. available on microfilm from Waterville Historical Society. ***Continues*** *Waterville Times and Hop Reporter (Waterville, N.Y. : 1937).*

US/1041-6250
WATKINS REVIEW & EXPRESS, THE. **VFOAT** Watkins Review and Express. Vol. 1, No. 1 (June 15, 1988)-. Newspaper. English. wk. $18.00 Schuyler County; $20.00 New York; $22.00 other. Watkins Review Inc, PO Box 112, Watkins Glen NY 14891. **Tel** (607)535-2711, FAX (607)535-2500. **ED** Colenda Gephart. **Photos**. **Ad Acc**, **Adv Mgr:** Joe Fazzary. Full Page (B&W) $205.00. Half Page (B&W) $110.00. Full Page (Color) $255.00. **Pub. Size:** Standard. **Circ:** 3,100. ***Formed by the union of*** *Watkins Review* ***and*** *Watkins Express.*

US/0882-7028
WAVE (ROCKAWAY BEACH, N.Y.), THE. (THE WAVE.). Vol. 86, No. 69 (Sept. 1, 1979)-. Newspaper. English. wk. $15.00 in county; $18.00 others. The Wave, 8808 Rockaway Beach Boulevard, Rockaway Beach NY 11693. **Tel** (718)634-4000, FAX (718)945-0913. **ED** George Andreassi. **Photos**. **Ad Acc**, **Adv Mgr:** Sanford Benstein. Full Page (B&W) $345.00. Half Page (B&W) $190.00. Full Page (Color) $470.00. Half Page (Color) $315.00. **Pub. Size:** Standard. available in microform. ***Continues*** *Wave of Long Island.*

US/0745-7685
WAYNE COUNTY MAIL. (1979)-. Newspaper. English. ir (approx. 50-52 per year on Thursdays). $11.00 Wayne County, New York; $12.50 other. Empire State Weeklies Inc., 2010 Empire Boulevard, Webster NY 14580. **Tel** (716)671-1533, FAX (716)671-7067. **ED** Jennifer Calus. **Ad Acc**, **Adv Mgr:** Donna Herzog, **Tel** (716)671-3554. ***Continues*** *Wayne County Mail and Ontario Register.*
Desc: Local newspaper covering the Ontario, Williamson and Sodus area. It is subscription only and deals mainly with local and school news.

US/0745-1377
WEBSTER HERALD, THE. (1899)-. Newspaper. English. Fifty-two times a year (Wed.). $15.00. Empire State Weeklies Inc., 2010 Empire Boulevard, Webster NY 14580. **Tel** (716)671-1533, FAX (716)671-7067. **ED** James Gertner (phone: (716)671-3554). **Photos**. **Ad Acc**, **Adv Mgr:** Greg Rickard. Full Page (B&W) $325.00. Half Page (B&W) $170.00. Full Page (Color) $405.00. Half Page (Color) $250.00. **Pub. Size:** Tabloid. available in microform.

US/0745-3663
WEBSTER POST, THE. Vol. 1, No. 1 (Mar. 31, 1982)-. Newspaper. English. wk. $18.00 (within local zip codes); $30.00 (others). Wolfe Publications, 666 Phillips Road, Victor NY 14564. **Tel** (716) 924-4040, FAX (716) 924-7734.

US/0885-9531
WEST SIDE SPIRIT (CITY EDITION). ***Title Change.*** (THE WEST SIDE SPIRIT.). (1986)-(19??). Periodical. English. wk. Manhattan Spirit, 363 7th Avenue/12th Floor, New York NY 10001. **Tel** (212)868-8800, FAX (212)594-0719. ***Continued by*** *The Manhattan Spirit.*

US
WESTERN QUEENS GAZETTE, THE. (1982)-. Newspaper. English. Fifty-two times a year. $20.00. Western Queens Gazette, 42-16 34th Avenue, Astoria NY 11101. **Tel** (718)361-6161. **ED** Tony Barsamian (Editor-in-Chief) and Brian Winzeworth (Managing Editor). **Bk Rev**, (Qty: 20). **Photos**. **Ad Acc**, **Adv Mgr:** Tony Brasamian. Full Page (B&W) $850.00. Half Page (B&W) $465.00. Full Page (Color) $960.00. **Pub. Size:** Tabloid. **Circ:** 60,000 (ctrl).

US
WESTFIELD REPUBLICAN. (April 25, 1855)-. Newspaper. English. wk. $21.50 Chautauqua County in New York State; $24.00 other. Westfield Republican, PO Box 38, Westfield NY 14787. **Tel** (716)326-3163, FAX (716)326-3165. **LC** 9134.

US
WHITEHALL TIMES (WHITEHALL, N.Y. : 1927). (THE WHITEHALL TIMES.). (1927)-. Newspaper. English. wk. $14.00 Vermont, Massechusettes, New York and Connencticut; $18.00 other. Whitehall Times, 6-8 North William Street, Whitehall NY 12887. **Tel** (518)499-1500. ***Continues*** *Whitehall Evening Times.*

US
WINDHAM JOURNAL, THE. Began with March 21, 1857 issue. Newspaper. English. wk. Windham Journal, Main Street, Windham NY 12496.

US
WOODSIDE HERALD. (1935)-. Newspaper. English. wk (Fri.). $15.00. Woodside Herald, 49-16 Skillman Avenue, Woodside NY 11377. **Tel** (718)426-1234.

US
WOODSTOCK TIMES. Vol. 1, No. 1 (Feb. 7, 1972)-. Newspaper. English. Fifty-two times a year (Thurs.). $35.00 Alster County; $40.00 others. Woodstock Times, PO Box 808, Woodstock NY 12498. **Tel** (914)679-7363, FAX (914)679-2841. **ED** Parry Teasdale and Mikhail Horowitz. cum. index. **Bk Rev**, (Qty: 4 times a year). **Ad Acc**. ctrl circ.

US
YOUTH AND NATION. ***Suspended.*** (1968)-. Newspaper. English. ir. $3.00. Youth & Nation, 150 5th Avenue, New York NY 10011.

NORTH CAROLINA

US
ALAMANCE NEWS, THE. **VFOAT** Alamance News and Burlington Journal. (19??)-. Newspaper. English. wk (Published on Thursdays). $15.75 Alamance, North Carolina; $26.25 other. Alamance News, PO Box 431, Graham NC 27253. **Tel** (919)228-7851.

US/8750-0221
ANGIER INDEPENDENT, THE. (1984)-. Newspaper. English. wk (Published on Tuesdays). Angier Independent, PO Box 878, Angier NC 27501-0878. **Tel** (910)639-4913, FAX (910)891-4444. **ED** Terri Flowers. **Ad Acc**. **Circ:** 4,000.

US
ASHEVILLE CITIZEN (ASHEVILLE, N.C. : 1885). ***Title Change.*** (THE ASHEVILLE CITIZEN.). **VFOAT** Asheville Citizen and Asheville Times; Sunday Citizen; Asheville Citizen-Times; Asheville Citizen Times. (1885)-Vol. 4, No. 251 (Jan. 30, 1889). Newspaper. English. da. 14 O Henry Avenue, Asheville NC 28802. **Tel** (704)254-7334. **ED** Larry Pope. **LC** 9137-X. **Circ:** 49,809. ***Continued by*** *Daily Citizen (Asheville, N.C.).*

●US/1060-3255
ASHEVILLE CITIZEN-TIMES. **VFOAT** Asheville Citizen Times. Vol. 122, No. 182 (July 1, 1991)-. Newspaper. English. da. $210.00. Asheville Citizen, PO Box 2090, Asheville NC 28802. **Tel** (800)800-4204, (704)252-5610. **ED** Larry Pope (phone: (704)252-5610). ***Formed by the union of*** *Asheville Citizen (Asheville, N.C. : 1900)* ***and*** *Asheville Times.*

US
BERTIE LEDGER-ADVANCE. **VFOAT** Bertie Ledger Advance. (1930)-. Newspaper. English. wk. $15.90 in county; $25.00 other. Martinsborough Publishers Inc, PO Drawer 69, 124 South King Street, Windsor NC 27983-0069. **Tel** (919)794-3195, FAX 919794-2835. **ED** Laura Harrell. **Photos**. **Ad Acc**, **Adv Mgr:** Cliff Clark, **Tel** (919)794-3185. Full Page (B&W) $432.15. Half Page (B&W) $211.05. Full Page (Color) $527.15. Half Page (Color) $306.05. **Pub. Size:** Standard. ***Formed by the union of*** *Bertie News-Leader; Windsor Ledger* ***and*** *Aulander Advance.*

US/1071-0574
BLOWING ROCKET, THE. (June 1932)-. Newspaper. English. wk (Fridays). $15.00 one year, $30.00 two years, $45.00 three years North Carolina; $17.00 one year, $34.00 two years, $51.00 three years others. Blowing Rocket, PO Box 1026, Blowing Rock NC 28605. **Tel** (704)295-7522, FAX (704)262-0282. **ED** Jerry Burns. **DD** 071. **Bk Rev**, (Qty: unlimited). **Photos**. **Ad Acc**, **Adv Mgr:** Jerry Burns. Full Page (B&W) $346.50. Half Page (B&W) $173.25. Full Page (Color) $446.50. Half Page (Color) $273.25. **Pub. Size:** Standard.

US/0883-1645
CALDWELL INFORMER. Newspaper. English. wk. Caldwell Informer, PO Box 225, Rhodhiss NC 28667-0225.

US
CAROLINA TIMES, THE. (1919)-. Newspaper. English. wk. Carolina Times, PO Box 3825, Durham NC 27702-3825. **Tel** (919)682-2913. **LC** 7002.

US/0045-5873
CAROLINIAN (RALEIGH), THE. (THE CAROLINIAN.). (Apr. 6, 1940)-. Newspaper. English. sw. $25.00. The Carolinian, PO Box 25308, Raleigh NC 27611. **Tel** (919)834-5558, FAX (919)832-3243. **ED** P.R. Jervay Sr., C. Michaels (Managing Editor). **Bk Rev**. **Photos**. **Ad Acc**, **Adv Mgr:** P.J. Monroe. Full Page (B&W) $1782.90. Half Page (B&W) $891.45. **Pub. Size:** Broadsheet. **Wire Svcs.:** AP. **Circ:** 14,000 (ctrl). ***Continues*** *Carolina Tribune.*

US/1074-5092
CASWELL MESSENGER, THE. Vol. 1, No. 1 (Feb. 25, 1926)-. Newspaper. English. wk (Published on

Wednesdays). $17.00 Caswell COunty, North Carolina; $21.00 other. Caswell Messenger, PO Box 100, Yanceyville NC 27379. **Tel** (919)694-4145.

●US/1070-2741
CHAPEL HILL NEWS (CHAPEL HILL, N.C. 1992). (THE CHAPEL HILL NEWS.). Vol. 70, No. 142 (Sept. 30, 1992)-. Newspaper. English. tw (Wed., Fri. & Sun.). Free (mailmen carriers in Chapel Hill area); $120.00 (others in Chapel Hill area). Chapel Hill Publishing Company, PO Box 870, Chapel Hill NC 27514. **Tel** (919)967-7045. ***Continues*** *Chapel Hill Newspaper.*

US
CHAPEL HILL NEWSPAPER, THE. ***Title Change.*** Vol. 50, No. 71 (Sept. 5, 1972)-Vol. 70, no. 141 (Sept. 27, 1992). Newspaper. English. da (except Saturday). Chapel Hill Publishing Company, PO Box 870, Chapel Hill NC 27514. **Tel** (919)967-7045. **ED** Bill McCulloch. **Bk Rev. Ad Acc. Circ:** 25,000 (ctrl). available on microfilm. ***Continues*** *Chapel Hill Weekly.* ***Continued by*** *Chapel Hill News (Chapel Hill, N.C. : 1992).*

US
CHARLOTTE OBSERVER, THE. (Apr. 3, 1916)-. Periodical. English. da. Price varies according to zip code within North Carolina; $396.20 other. Charlotte Observer, PO Box 32188, Charlotte NC 28234. **Tel** (800)532-5350, (704)358-6000, FAX (704)358-5975. ***Continues*** *Charlotte Daily Observer,.*

US
CHARLOTTE OBSERVER (CHARLOTTE, N.C. : 1916). (THE CHARLOTTE OBSERVER.). **VFOAT** Charlotte Sunday Observer. (April 3, 1916)-. Newspaper. English. da. $238.40. Charlotte Observer, PO Box 32188, Charlotte NC 28234. **Tel** (800)532-5350, (704)358-6000, FAX (704)358-5975. **ED** Rich Oppel. **Circ:** 214,700 daily, 269,435 Sunday. available on microfilm from University Microfilms International (UMI). ***Continues*** *Charlotte Daily Observer; Charlotte Daily Observer (Charlotte, N.C. : 1897).*
Ind/Abst PROMT.

US
CHARLOTTE POST, THE. (191?)-. Newspaper. English. wk. Charlotte Post, PO Box 30144, Charlotte NC 28230. **Tel** (704)376-0496.

US/1067-1773
CHATHAM NEWS (SILER CITY, N.C.), THE. (THE CHATHAM NEWS.). (1924)-. Newspaper. English. wk (Published on Thursdays). $12.00 Chatham, North Carolina; $14.00 other. Chatham News, PO Box 290, Siler City NC 27344. **Tel** (919)663-3232.

US/1067-1765
CHATHAM RECORD, THE. (Sept. 19, 1878)-. Newspaper. English. wk. Chatham Record, PO Box 458, Pittsboro NC 27312. **LC** 9137-X. ***Continues*** *Home (Pittsboro, N.C.).*

US/0746-3987
CHEROKEE SCOUT. ***Ceased.*** (188?)-(199?). Newspaper. English. wk. Cherokee Scout, PO Box 190, Murphy NC 28906. ***Continues*** *Murphy Advance.*

US/0739-0246
CHOWAN HERALD, THE. (193?)-. Newspaper. English. wk. $14.70 North Carolina; $19.00 other. Chowan Herald, PO Box 207, Edenton NC 27932. **Tel** (919)482-4418. **ED** J. P. Huskins. **Circ:** 3,950.

US
CITIZEN NEWS-RECORD (COUNTY ED.), THE. (THE CITIZEN NEWS-RECORD.). (1985)-. Newspaper. English. The Citizen News-Record, PO Box 336, Aberdeen NC 28315. ***Continues in part*** *Sandhill Citizen and News Outlook, 0746-6137.*

US/0886-3261
CITIZEN NEWS-RECORD (ROBBINS ED.), THE. (THE CITIZEN NEWS-RECORD.). **VFOAT** Citizen News Record. Vol. 84, No. 20 (Nov. 4, 1985)-. Newspaper. English. tw. $15.00 (Moore & adjoining counties), $17.00 (other). The Citizen News-Record, PO Box 336, Aberdeen NC 28315. ***Continues in part*** *Sandhill Citizen and News Outlook, 0746-6137;* ***Absorbed*** *Robbins Record; Moore County News;* ***Absorbed in part*** *News Outlook, 0192-8341.*

US
CLAYTON NEWS. (191?)-. Newspaper. English. wk. Clayton News, 222 West Main Street, Clayton NC 27520. **Tel** (919)553-7234, FAX (919)553-5858. **ED** Douglas Johnson. **Ad Acc. Circ:** 3,500.

US/1069-4722
COASTLAND TIMES, THE. (July 4, 1935)-. Newspaper. English. tw. Price varies according to postal code. Times Printing Company, PO Box 400, Manteo NC 27954. **Tel** (919)473-2105.

US
COURIER-TIMES, THE. VFOAT Courier Times. (1???)-. Newspaper. English. sw. $25.13 (in county), $38.22 (out of county). Courier Times / Roxboro, PO Box 311, Roxboro NC 27573. **Tel** (910)599-0162, FAX (910)597-2773. **ED** Neal F. Rattican. **Photos. Ad Acc.** Full Page (B&W) $612.75. Half Page (B&W) $322.50. Full Page (Color) $702.75. Half Page (Color) $412.50. **Pub. Size:** Standard. **Wire Svcs.:** AP. available in microform from the publisher.

US
COURIER-TRIBUNE, THE. VFOAT Courier Tribune. (May 1940)-. Newspaper. English. da (312 issues per year - not published on Saturdays). $98.00. Courier Tribune / Asheboro, PO Box 340, Asheboro NC 27204. **Tel** (919)625-2101. ***Formed by the union of*** *Courier (Asheboro, N.C. : 1939)* ***and*** *Randolph Tribune.*

US/1060-6130
DAILY REFLECTOR (GREENVILLE, N.C.). (THE DAILY REFLECTOR.). Began in 1882. Newspaper. English. da. Daily Reflector, 209 Cotanche Street, Greenville NC 27834.

US
DAILY SOUTHERNER. (18??)-. Newspaper. English. da. $70.00, $100.00 (by mail). Daily Southerner, Box 1199, Tarboro NC 27886. **Tel** (919)823-3106, FAX (919)823-4599. **ED** Robert Hughes (Managing Editor). **Bk Rev. Photos. Ad Acc, Adv Mgr:** Ellis W. Hooks. Full Page (B&W) $657.90. Half Page (B&W) $328.95. Full Page (Color) $732.90. Half Page (Color) $403.95. **Pub. Size:** Standard. **Wire Svcs.:** AP. **Circ:** 6,300. available on microfilm and microfiche from University Microfilms International (UMI).

US
DAILY TIMES-NEWS, THE. VFOAT Daily Times News; Times News. (1930)-. Newspaper. English. da. $123.50, Alamance County, North Carolina; $143.00 other. Daily Times News, PO Box 481, Burlington NC 27215. **Tel** (919)227-0131, FAX (919)229-2462. **ED** Don Bolden, Frank Isley (Managing Editor). **LC** 9145. **Bk Rev** (Qty: 60). **Photos. Ad Acc, Adv Mgr:** Trip Hatley, **Tel** (910)227-0131. Full Page (B&W) $1304.00. Half Page (B&W) $652.00. Full Page (Color) $1504.00. Half Page (Color) $852.00. **Pub. Size:** Tabloid. **Wire Svcs.:** AP, KR. **Circ:** 29,336 daily (paid), 30,369 Sunday (paid). available on microfilm and microfiche from Bell & Howell. ***Formed by the union of*** *Burlington Daily Times* ***and*** *Burlington News.*

US
DAVIE COUNTY ENTERPRISE-RECORD. (19??)-. Newspaper. English. wk. $18.00 North Carolina; $22.50 other. Enterprise-Record / NC, Box 525, c/o Gordan Tomlinson, Mocksville NC 27028. **Tel** (704)634-2129. **Ad Acc. Circ:** 8,000.

US/0163-3090
DISPATCH (LEXINGTON), THE. ***Ceased.*** (THE DISPATCH.). (1902)-(19??). Newspaper. English. da. The Dispatch Company, PO Box 908, Lexington NC 27292. **Tel** (704)249-3981. **ED** Ralph Simpson. **Circ:** 14,694. available on microfilm from University Microfilms International (UMI).
Ind/Abst Mag. Search.

US/0738-5137
EVENING TELEGRAM (ROCKY MOUNT, N.C.). (THE EVENING TELEGRAM.). **VFOAT** Rocky Mount Evening Telegram. (1911)-. Newspaper. English. da. $132.22. Rocky Mount Publishing Company, 150 152 Howard Street, Rocky Mount NC 27801. **Tel** (919)446-5161. ***Continues*** *Morning Telegram (Rocky Mount, N.C.);* ***Absorbed*** *Daily Record (Rocky Mount, N.C.).*

US/1052-9829
FAYETTEVILLE OBSERVER-TIMES, THE. (FAYETTEVILLE OBSERVER-TIMES.). [Fayettev. obs.-times]. **VFOAT** Fayetteville Observer Times. Vol. 175, No. 241 (Saturday, Sept. 1, 1990)-. Newspaper. English. ds. $226.24 North Carolina; $238.00 all states east of Mississippi River; $274.00 all states west of Mississippi River. Fayetteville Observer-Times, PO Box 849, Fayetteville NC 28302. **Tel** (919)323-4848. **DD** 071. available on an online database (file 635/Full-Text) from DIALOG. Documents available from UMI Article Clearinghouse. ***Formed by the union of*** *Fayetteville Times* ***and*** *Fayetteville Observer (Fayetteville, N.C. : 1896).*
Ind/Abst Bus. Dateline (Jan. 1, 1992-) [Full Txt.].

US
FRANKLIN TIMES, THE. VFOAT Times. (1870)-. Newspaper. English. sw (104 issues per year - published on Wednesdays & Saturdays). $21.00 Franklin County, North Carolina; $34.00 other counties in North Carolina; $46.00 others US. Franklin Times, PO Box 119, 109 South Bickett Boulevard, Louisburg NC 27549-0119. **Tel** (919)496-6503. **LC** 9137-X.

US
FREE PRESS, THE. VFOAT Kinston Daily Free Press. Vol. 108, No. 240 (Jan. 6, 1991)-. Newspaper. English. da. Kingston Free Press Co., Inc., 2103 North Queen Street, Kingston NC 28501. ***Continues*** *Kinston Daily Free Press.*

US/0747-1858
GREENSBORO NEWS & RECORD. ***Title Change.*** **VFOAT** Greensboro News and Record. Vol. 94, No. 77 (Mar. 17, 1984)-(1992). Newspaper. English. da. Greensboro News & Record Inc, PO Box 20848, Mail Subscriptions Department, Greensboro NC 27401. **Tel** (910)274-5280 or, 800 553-6880. **ED** Ben J. Bowers. **Circ:** 111,022 daily, 127,651 Sunday. available on an online database (file 635/Full-Text) from DIALOG. Documents available from UMI Article Clearinghouse. ***Formed by the union of*** *Greensboro Daily News, 0746-0740* ***and*** *Greensboro Record.* ***Continued by*** *News & Record (Greensboro, N.C.), 1072-0065.*
Ind/Abst AGRICOLA [Select. Cov.]; Bus. Dateline; PROMT.

US/8750-023X
HARNETT COUNTY NEWS. Newspaper. English. wk. Harnett County News, 307 North Main Street, Lillington NC 27546.

US/0747-1149
HAVELOCK PROGRESS, THE. Newspaper. English. wk. $7.00 Craven county, $8.00 other. Havelock Progress, Box 689, Havelock NC 28532.

US/1055-4467
HERALD-SUN (DURHAM, N.C.), THE. (THE HERALD-SUN). **VFOAT** Herald Sun. (Jan. 1, 1991)-. Newspaper. English. da. Herald Sun / North Carolina, 2828 Pickett Road, Durham NC 27702. **Tel** (919)419-6500. **(Subscription address:** Herald Sun / North Carolina, PO Box 2092, Durham NC 27702.) ***Formed by the union of*** *Durham Morning Herald* ***and*** *Durham Sun.*

US/0747-1491
HIGH POINT ENTERPRISE, THE. ***Ceased.*** (188?)-(19??). Newspaper. English. da. High Point Enterprise, 210 Church Avenue, High Point NC 27261. **Tel** (919)884-5700. **ED** Joe Brown. **Circ:** 31,343.

US
INDEPENDENT (RURAL HALL). (INDEPENDENT.). Newspaper. English. $12.00. Independent Publishing Co., PO Box 806, The Depot, Rural Hall NC 27045. **Tel** (919)969-6076, FAX (919)969-9390.

US
JOURNAL-PATRIOT, THE. VFOAT Journal Patriot. (1932)-. Newspaper. English. sw. Journal-Patriot, PO Box 70, North Wilkesboro NC 28659. **Tel** FAX (910)858-9864. **ED** Charles Williams. **LC** 7002. **Photos. Ad Acc, Adv Mgr:** Carolyn Sipes, **Tel** (910)838-4117. **Pub. Size:** Standard. **Circ:** 17,600 paid. ***Formed by the union of*** *Wilkes Journal* ***and*** *Wilkes Patriot.*

US/0195-0622
LEADER (RESEARCH TRIANGLE PARK, N.C.), THE. (THE LEADER.). [Leader]. **VFOAT** North Carolina Leader. Year 13, No. 30 (Apr. 12, 1979)-. Newspaper. English. Fifty-two times a year (Thursday). $26.00. Leader Newsmagazine, 20 Park Drive, Box 12054, Research Triangle Park NC 27709. **Tel** (919)549-8209. **ED** Steve Adams. **DD** 975. **Bk Rev. Ad Acc. Circ:** 8,500 (ctrl). ***Continues*** *North Carolina Leader.*
Desc: A newspaper focusing on the Research Triangle Park, its people, its research and what this means to the Triangle and to North Carolina.

US/0199-8137
MCDOWELL EXPRESS, THE. VFOAT Express; McDowell News. Vol. 1 (March 1980)-. Newspaper. English. da. $89.93 North Carolina; $95.44 others. Park Newspapers, PO Box 610, Marion NC 28752. **Tel** (704)652-3313.

US
MECKLENBURG GAZETTE, THE. (19??)-. Newspaper. English. wk (Published on Wednesdays). $12.00. Mecklenburg Gazette, PO Box 549, Davidson NC 28036. **Tel** (704)892-8809. **ED** Sam Knowlton. **Ad Acc, Adv Mgr:** Lou Sullivan. **Circ:** 4,800 (ctrl).

US
MECKLENBURG TIMES. (19??)-. English. sw (104 issues per year). $51.00. Mecklenburg Times, PO Box 36306, Charlotte NC 28236. **Tel** (704)377-6221, FAX (704)377-6214. **ED** Jill T. Purdy. **Photos. Ad Acc, Adv Mgr:** Norris Rumfelt. Full Page (B&W) $426.25. Half Page (B&W) $213.13. Full Page (Color) $526.25. Half Page (Color) $313.13. **Pub. Size:** Tabloid. **Wire Svcs.:** AP. **Circ:** 790 (ctrl).
Desc: Covers news in business, investments, careers, real estate, and computers. Also includes legal advertising and public notices.

US/0892-1814
MESSENGER (MADISON, N.C.). (THE MESSENGER.). (19??)-. Newspaper. English. wk. $18.00 (six months); $24.00 (one year) North Carolina Residents; $22.00 (six months); $32.00 (one year) others. Rockingham Newspapers Inc, PO Box 508, Madison NC 27025. **Tel** (919)548-6047. **ED** Randy Case. Index available. cum. index. **Bk Rev. Ad Acc. Circ:** 7,800 (ctrl). available on microfilm.

US
MORNING STAR. **VFOAT** Sunday Star-News; Sunday Star News. Vol. 106, No. 290 (Sept. 18, 1990)-. Newspaper. English. da. Star-News Newspapers Company, 1003 South 17th Street, Wilmington NC 28401. **Tel** (919)343-2000, FAX (919)343-2227. ***Continues*** *Wilmington Morning Star.*

US
NEWS & OBSERVER (RALEIGH, N.C. : 1894). (THE NEWS & OBSERVER.). **VFOAT** News and Observer. Vol. 37, No. 19 (Aug. 12, 1894)-. Newspaper. English. ds. $258.40 North Carolina; $311.00 other. Raleigh News & Observer, PO Box 191, Raleigh NC 27602. **Tel** (919)829-4700. **ED** Claude Sitton. **LC** 7002. **Bk Rev**. **Ad Acc**. **Circ:** 137,746 daily, 178,326 Sunday. available on microfilm from University Microfilms International (UMI); available on an online database (file 635/Full-Text) from DIALOG. ***Absorbed*** *Weekly News and Observer;* ***Continues*** *News-Observer-Chronicle.*
Ind/Abst PROMT.

●US/1072-0065
NEWS & RECORD (GREENSBORO, N.C.). (NEWS & RECORD.). **VFOAT** News and Record. Vol. 102, No. 62 (Mar. 2, 1992)-. Newspaper. English. da. Greensboro News & Record Inc, PO Box 20848, Mail Subscriptions Department, Greensboro NC 27401. **Tel** (910)274-5280 or, 800 553-6880. **ED** Ben J. Bowers. **Circ:** 111,022 daily, 127,651 Sunday. available on an online database. ***Continues*** *Greensboro News and Record, 0747-1858.*

US/8750-3980
NEWS-HERALD (MORGANTON, N.C.), THE. (THE NEWS-HERALD.). **VFOAT** News Herald; Sunday News-Herald. (Nov. 1901)-. Newspaper. English. da. $93.60. News Herald / North Carolina, PO Box 280, Morganton NC 28655. **Tel** (704)437-2161. **ED** Eugene Willard, Bill Poteat (Managing Editor). **Photos**. **Ad Acc, Adv Mgr:** Randy Hart. Full Page (B&W) $645.00. Half Page (B&W) $338.63. Full Page (Color) $930.00. Half Page (Color) $623.63. **Pub. Size:** Standard. **Wire Svcs.:** AP. ***Formed by the union of*** *Burke County News* ***and*** *Morganton Herald.*

US/1071-1716
NEWS OF ORANGE COUNTY, THE. **VFOAT** News. (1???)-. Newspaper. English. wk (Published on Wednesdays). $18.93 Orange County; $25.54 other. News of Orange County, PO Box 580, Hillsborough NC 27278. **Tel** (919)732-2171, FAX (919)732-4852. **ED** Johnathan Butler. **Photos**. **Ad Acc, Adv Mgr:** David Jones, **Tel** (919)732-2171. Full Page (B&W) $774.00. Half Page (B&W) $387.00. Full Page (Color) $924.00. Half Page (Color) $537.00. **Pub. Size:** Broadsheet. ctrl circ. available on microfilm and microfiche from Orange County Public Library.

US
NEWS REPORTER, THE. **VFOAT** Fair Tattler; News Reporter of Columbus County; News-Reporter of Columbus County. (1905)-. Newspaper. English. sm (Mon., & Wed.). $29.50 Columbus & Brunswick & Bladen & Robeson counties; $41.50 others in North Carolina; $45.00 others. News Reporter company, PO Box 707, Whiteville NC 28472-0707. **Tel** (919)642-4104. **ED** James C. High. **LC** 7002. **Ad Acc**. **Circ:** 10,152 (ctrl).
Desc: Local and county news.

US/1064-4830
NORTH CAROLINA BEACON. (1990)-. Newspaper. English. wk (52 issues). $25.00. Park Communications Inc., PO Box 14125, Research Triangle Park NC 27709. **Tel** (919)549-7340, FAX (919)549-8383. **ED** Alison Egger. **Bk Rev**, (Qty: 52). **Photos**. **Ad Acc, Adv Mgr:** Jim Tucker. Full Page (B&W) $593.69. Half Page (B&W) $296.85. Full Page (Color) $703.69. Half Page (Color) $406.85. **Circ:** 6,000 (ctrl).

US/0029-2435
NORTH CAROLINA CHRISTIAN ADVOCATE. **Added/Corp** United Methodist Church (U.S.). North Carolina Conference. United Methodist Church (U.S.). Western North Carolina Conference. **VFOAT** Christian Advocate; NC Christian Advocate. (1855)-. Newspaper. English. wk (except 1st week in Jan. and 2nd week in July). $10.00. North Carolina Christian, Box 508, Greensboro NC 27402. **Tel** (910)272-1196. **ED** C A Simonton Jr. Index available. cum. index. **Bk Rev**. **Ad Acc**. **Circ:** 18,000. ***Formed by the union of*** *Western North Carolina Christian Advocate* ***and*** *Raleigh Christian Advocate (Raleigh, N.C. : 1870).*
Desc: United Methodist Church publication; with particular emphasis on North Carolina; also national and worldwide religion news.

US/0737-8254
NORTH CAROLINA INDEPENDENT, THE. **VFOAT** NC Independent; N.C. Independent; Independent. (1983)-. Newspaper. English. Fifty times a year (publ weekly except Christmas). $29.00 (one year), $50.00 (two year) individuals; $35.00 (one year), $60.00 (two year) institutions. Carolina Independent, PO Box 2690, Durham NC 27715. **Tel** (919)286-1972, FAX (919)285-3489. **ED** Gillian Floren. **Bk Rev**, (Qty: 50). **Ad Acc, Adv Mgr:** B. Thorp. ctrl circ.

US/8750-0418
OUTER BANKS CURRENT. **VFOAT** Current. Newspaper. English. wk. Outer Banks Current, PO Box 2376, Kill Devil Hills NC 27948.

US/0891-7965
PARAGLIDE (FORT BRAGG, N.C.). (THE PARAGLIDE.). (19??)-. Newspaper. English. wk. Fort Bragg Paraglide, Box 5395, Fayetteville NC 28303. **Tel** (919)864-0666, FAX (919)864-8911. **ED** Louis H. Fogleman Jr. **Ad Acc**. **Circ:** 23,000 (ctrl). available on microfilm from The State Historical Society of Wisconsin.

US
PENDER POST. Vol. 1, No. 1 (Oct. 20, 1971)-. Newspaper. English. wk. $15.00 Pender County, NC; $20.00 other. Pender Post, PO Box 955, Burgaw NC 28425. **Tel** (919)259-9111. **ED** Patrick A. Thomas. **Ad Acc**. **Circ:** 5,500.
Desc: Weekly community newspaper focusing on state and local regional news.

US
REIDSVILLE REVIEW, THE. **VFOAT** Reidsville Semi-Weekly Review; Reidsville (N.C.) Review. Vol. 11, No. 28 (Sept. 19, 1899)-. Newspaper. English. ir (260 issues). $78.00. Reidsville Review, PO Box 2157, Reidsville NC 27320. **Tel** (919)349-4331, FAX (919)342-2513. **ED** Glenn Cook. **Ad Acc, Adv Mgr:** T. Talley. **Circ:** 7,200. ***Continues*** *Weekly Review (Reidsville, N.C.).*

US
ROANOKE BEACON, THE. Vol. 70, No. 33 (Aug. 13, 1959)-. Newspaper. English. wk. $19.03 Washington County, NC; $24.33 North Carolina; $27.03 other. Roanoke Beacon, 210 West Water Street, Plymouth NC 27962. **Tel** (919)793-2123, FAX (919)792-5365. **ED** D. N. Jones. **Bk Rev**, (Qty: 10). **Ad Acc, Adv Mgr:** Sherrie Phelps. Full Page (B&W) $405.06. Half Page (B&W) $202.53. Full Page (Color) $510.06. Half Page (Color) $307.53. **Pub. Size:** Standard. ***Continues*** *Roanoke Beacon and the Washington County News.*

US
ROBESONIAN, THE. **VFOAT** Semi-Weekly Robesonian. (1870)-. Newspaper. English. da. Robesonian Inc, Publication Circulation Department, PO Box 1028, Lumberton NC 28358. **Tel** (910)739-4322. **LC** 9137-X. ***Absorbed*** *Lumberton Daily News.*

US/0747-0738
SALISBURY POST, THE. (Feb. 20, 1984)-. Newspaper. English. da. $133.00 North Carolina; $145.00 others. Salisbury Post, PO Box 4639, Salisbury NC 28144. **Tel** (704)633-8950, FAX (704)633-7373. **ED** Elizabeth G. Cook (Editor-in-Chief) and Frank Deloache (Managing Editor). **Bk Rev**. **Photos**. **Ad Acc, Adv Mgr:** Steve Johnson. Full Page (B&W) $1,568.70. Half Page (B&W) $784.35. Full Page (Color) $1,698.70. Half Page (Color) $914.35. **Pub. Size:** Broadsheet. **Wire Svcs.:** AP. available in microform from University Microfilms International (UMI). ***Continues*** *Salisbury Evening Post.*

US
SAMPSON INDEPENDENT, THE. **VFOAT** Sunday Independent. (March 27, 1924)-. Newspaper. English. da. Sampson Independent, 303 Elizbeth Street, Clinton NC 28328-4426. **Tel** (910)592-8137, FAX (910)592-8756. **ED** Steve Mathis. **Ad Acc, Adv Mgr:** Gary Pate. **Circ:** 9,000 (evening & Sun.). ***Continues*** *News Dispatch, the Sampson Democrat;* ***Absorbed*** *Sampsonian.*

US/1043-1950
SHELBY STAR, THE. Vol. 90, No. 79 (April 2, 1984)-. English. da. Shelby Star, 315 East Graham Street, Shelby NC 28150. ***Continues*** *Shelby Daily Star.*
Desc: Cleveland county's home newspaper.

US/0744-1118
SOUTHERN POST, THE. Newspaper. English. wk. Peters Publishing Company / North Carolina, PO Box 85, Coinjock NC 27923-0085.

US
STATE PORT PILOT, THE. (1928)-. Newspaper. English. wk (Wednesday). $19.00. State Port Pilot, PO Box 10548, Southport NC 28461. **Tel** (919)457-4568, FAX (919)457-9427. **ED** Ed Harper. **Photos**. **Ad Acc, Adv Mgr:** Kim Adams, **Tel** (910)457-4568. Full Page (B&W) $567.00. Half Page (B&W) $283.50. Full Page (Color) $807.00. Half Page (Color) $523.50. **Pub. Size:** Broadsheet. **Circ:** 7,750. available in microform.

US/0745-7804
STATESVILLE RECORD & LANDMARK. **VFOAT** Statesville Record and Landmark. (195?)-. Newspaper. English. da. $93.60. Statesville Record & Landmark, PO Box 1071, Statesville NC 28677. **Tel** (704)873-1451. ***Formed by the union of*** *Statesville Daily Record* ***and*** *Landmark (Statesville, N.C.).*

US/0163-4038
SUNDAY STAR-NEWS, THE. Newspaper. English. wk. Star-News Newspapers Company, 1003 South 17th Street, Wilmington NC 28401. **Tel** (919)343-2000, FAX (919)343-2227.

US/0746-2654
THERMAL BELT NEWS JOURNAL. (19??)-. Newspaper. English. wk. Thermal Belt News Journal, PO Box 566, Columbus NC 28722.

US/1042-2323
TIMES-NEWS (HENDERSONVILLE, N.C.). (TIMES-NEWS.). **VFOAT** Times News. "ESTABLISHED 1927"--VOL. 110, NO. 263 (NOV. 1, 1985), P. 4. Newspaper. English. da. Times News Hendersonville NC, PO Box 490, Hendersonville NC 28739. **Tel** (704)692-5763. ***Formed by the union of*** *Hendersonville Times* ***and*** *Hendersonville News.*

US
TRANSYLVANIA TIMES, THE. (1931)-. Newspaper. English. sw. Transylvania Times, 100 North Broad Street, Brevard NC 28712-3796. **Tel** (704)883-8156, FAX (704)883-8158. **ED** Stella A. Trapp. **Ad Acc**. **Circ:** 8,200. ***Continues*** *Brevard News.*

US/0891-0022
TRIANGLE BUSINESS. ***Title Change.*** (198?)-(19??). Periodical. English. wk. Triangle Business, PO Box 91453, Raleigh NC 27625. available on microfilm from University Microfilms International (UMI); available on an online database (file 635/Full-Text) from DIALOG. Documents available from UMI Article Clearinghouse. ***Continued by*** *Triangle Business Journal, 1060-5096.*
Ind/Abst AGRICOLA [Select. Cov.]; Bus. Dateline (Nov. 19, 1990-) [Full Txt.].

US/1063-7702
TRIBUNE (TABOR CITY), THE. (THE TRIBUNE.). (19??)-. Newspaper. English. wk. $9.98 Columbus, Bladen, Brunswick, Robeson counties, North Carolina; $13.00 other US; $15.00 other. Tabor City Tribune, PO Box 67, Tabor City NC 28436. **Tel** (919)653-3153. ***Continues*** *Tabor City Tribune.*

US
TRYON DAILY BULLETIN, THE. Began with Jan. 31, 1928 issue. Bulletin. English. da. $35.00. Tryon Daily Bulletin Inc, Box 790, Tryon NC 28782. **Tel** (704)859-9151. **ED** Jeffrey Byrd. **Bk Rev**. **Ad Acc**. **Circ:** 4,000 (ctrl).
Desc: Local community news.

US
WALLACE ENTERPRISE. (19??)-. Newspaper. English. sw. $25.00 Duplin, Pender & Samson counties; $40.00 North Carolina; $50.00 other. Wallace Enterprise, PO Box 699, Wallace NC 28466. **Tel** (910)285-2178, FAX (910)285-3179. **ED** Sammie Carter. **Photos**. **Ad Acc, Adv Mgr:** Mary Oswald. Full Page (B&W) $582.00. Half Page (B&W) $306.38. Full Page (Color) $667.00. Half Page (Color) $391.38. **Pub. Size:** Standard. **Circ:** 7,600.

US/0745-1903
WATAUGA DEMOCRAT. (1888)-. Newspaper. English. Three times a year. $32.00. Watauga Democrat, POB 353, Boone NC 28607. **Tel** (404)264-3612. **ED** Sandy Shook. **Bk Rev**. **Ad Acc**. **Circ:** 13,300 (ctrl).
Desc: General news articles.

US/0049-7649
WILMINGTON JOURNAL (WILMINGTON, N.C.), THE. (WILMINGTON JOURNAL.). (19??)-. Newspaper. English. wk. $18.00 US; $20.00 other. Wilmington Journal, PO Box 1618, Wilmington NC 28402. **Tel** (919)762-5502, FAX (919)762-4406. **ED** Katherine Jervay Tate. **Bk Rev**. **Photos**. **Ad Acc, Adv Mgr:** Gwendolyn Hamilton. Full Page (B&W) $630.00. Half Page (B&W) $315.00. Full Page (Color) $730.00. Half Page (Color) $415.00. **Pub. Size:** Standard. **Pr Rev**. **Circ:** 6,000 (ctrl).
Desc: The only black newspaper in southeastern North Carolina. It contains information on retail sales, demography, and local commerce.

US
WINSTON-SALEM CHRONICLE. **VFOAT** Winston Salem Chronicle. Vol. 1, No. 1 (Sept. 5, 1974)-. Newspaper. English. wk. $30.92. Winston-Salem Chronicle, PO Box 1636, Earnest Pitt, Winston-Salem NC 27102. **Tel** (919)722-8624. **ED** Richard Williams. **Bk Rev**. **Photos**. **Ad Acc, Adv Mgr:** Mike Pitt. Half Page (B&W) $606.69. **Pub. Size:** Standard. **Wire Svcs.:** AP. **Circ:** 10,000 (ctrl).
Desc: Newspaper focusing on local and national community news directly affecting black community. Also contains monthly supplement, Black College Sports Review covering CIAA, MEAC, SIAC, and SWAC.

US
WINSTON-SALEM JOURNAL. **VFOAT** Winston Salem Journal; Morning Journal. (190?)-. Newspaper. English. da. $181.90 North Carolina; $171.60 other. Piedmont Publishing Company, PO Box 3159, Winston-Salem NC 27102-3159. **Tel** (919)727-7456. **ED** Joe Goodman. **LC** 7002. **Bk Rev**. **Ad Acc**. **Circ:** 95,213, 106,990101,176 Sunday. available on microfilm from University Microfilms International (UMI); available on an

online database (file 635/Full-Text) from DIALOG. Documents available from UMI Article Clearinghouse. **Continues** *Daily Journal (Winston-Salem, N.C.).* **Desc:** General news for the Winston-Salem area. **Ind/Abst** Bus. Dateline (Dec. 29, 1991-) [Full Txt.]

NORTH DAKOTA

US
BENSON COUNTY FARMERS PRESS, THE. Vol. 36, No. 27 (June 26, 1919)-. Newspaper. English. wk. $24.00 North Dakota; $30.00 others in US; $36.00 others. Benson County Farmers Press, 120 B Avenue North, Minnewaukan ND 58351-0098. **Tel** (701)473-5438. **ED** Richard M. Peterson. **Photos. Ad Acc, Adv Mgr:** Richard Peterson. Full Page (B&W) $491.40. Half Page (B&W) $245.70. Full Page (Color) $521.40. Half Page (Color) $305.70. **Pub. Size:** Standard. **Circ:** 3,046. **Continues** *North Dakota Siftings*; **Absorbed** *Esmond Bee (Esmond, N.D. : 1902); Benson County Courier.*

US
BISMARCK TRIBUNE, THE. VFOAT Bismarck Daily Tribune; Bismarck Evening Tribune. Vol. 36, No. 281 (Nov. 21, 1916)-. Newspaper. da. $162.00. Bismarck Tribune, PO Box 1498, Bismarck ND 58502. **Tel** (701)223-2500, FAX (701)223-4240. **ED** Kevin Giles. cum. index. **Photos. Ad Acc, Adv Mgr:** Lani Renneau. **Pub. Size:** Broadsheet. **Wire Svcs.:** AP, KR. **Circ:** 32,500 (a.m. Mon.-Sat.), 34,000 (a.m. Sunday) (ctrl). **Continues** *Bismarck Daily Tribune.*

US
BOWMAN FINDER. Newspaper. English. Bowman Finder, 212 South Main Street, Bowman ND 58623.

US
BURKE COUNTY TRIBUNE. Newspaper. English. Burke County Tribune, PO Box 40, Bowbells ND 58721.

US/0899-7624
CARSON PRESS, THE. Vol. 1, No. 1 (May 6, 1908)-Vol. 70, No. 9 (Mar. 3, 1983); (Mar. 10, 1983)-. Newspaper. English. wk. $23.00. Carson Press, PO Box 100, Carson ND 58533-0100. **Photos. Ad Acc, Adv Mgr:** Duane Schatz, **Tel** (701)584-2900. Full Page (B&W) $588.00. Half Page (B&W) $294.00. **Pub. Size:** Standard.

US
CASS COUNTY REPORTER. VFOAT Reporter Casselton Reporter-the Hunter Times-the Kindred Tribune. No. 4 (May 20, 1971)-. Newspaper. English. wk. $20.00 local; $27.50 other. Cass County Reporter, PO Box 190, Casselton ND 58012-0190. **Tel** (701)347-4493. **ED** Michael L. Utt. **Photos. Ad Acc, Adv Mgr:** Peggy Hanson. Full Page (B&W) $620.34. Half Page (B&W) $310.12. Full Page (Color) $700.34. Half Page (Color) $390.12. **Pub. Size:** Broadsheet. **Circ:** 3,325. available on microfilm. **Continues** *Reporter (Casselton, N.D.).*

US
CAVALIER CHRONICLE. Newspaper. English. Cavalier Chronicle, PO Box A, Cavalier ND 58220.

US
CAVALIER COUNTY REPUBLICAN. (August 1889)-. Newspaper. English. wk. Cavalier County Republican, PO Box 809, Langdon ND 58249. available on microfilm. **Absorbed** *Cavalier County Farmers Press; Milton Globe.*

US
COURANT. Vol. 96, No. 52 (Dec. 15, 1981)-. Newspaper. English. wk. Bottineau Courant, 419 Main Street, Bottineau ND 58318. available on microfi m. **Continues** *Bottineau Courant (Bottineau, N.D. : 1969).*

US
DAILY NEWS, THE. Vol. 91, No. 92 (Oct. 18, 1971)-. Newspaper. English. da (Published Tues. thru Sat.. except New Year, July 4th, Thanksgiving and Christmas). $75.00 (zones 1 and 2 with zip code prefixes 580-581, 562-567, 572, 574, 582-584), $90.00 others US; $180.00 others. The Daily News, PO Box 970, Wahpeton ND 58075. **Tel** (701)642-8585. **ED** David Youngquist. **Absorbed** *County Press (Wahpeton, N.D.);* **Formed by the union of** *Farmer-Globe* **and** *Valley Alert.*

US
DAKOTA SCIENTIST, THE. Newspaper. English. North Dakota State School of Science, Wahpeton ND 58075.

US
DICKEY COUNTY LEADER. VFOAT Dickey County Leader & Ellendale Commercial. Vol. 49, No. 49 (Mar. 26, 1931)-. Newspaper. English. Fifty-two times a year (Thurs.). $26.00 (in county), $29.00 (in state), $32.00 other. Dickey County Leader, 216 Main, Ellendale ND 58436. **Tel** (701)349-3222, FAX (701)349-3229. **Photos. Ad Acc, Adv Mgr:** Doug Robb. Full Page (B&W) $491.40. Half Page (B&W) $245.70. **Pub. Size:** Standard. **Circ:** 1,999. **Continues** *Dickey County Leader and Ellendale Commercial.*

US/1049-6718
DICKINSON PRESS (DICKINSON, N.D. 1942), THE. (THE DICKINSON PRESS.). Vol. 60, No. 4 (Feb. 17, 1942)-. Newspaper. English. da. $101.00 North Dakota; $111.00 Minnesota, South Dakota and Montana; $120.00 other. Dickinson Newspaper Inc., Box 1367, Dickinson ND 58602. **Tel** (701)225-8111. **ED** Larry Nossaman. **Bk Rev. Ad Acc. Circ:** 8,450 (ctrl). available on microfilm. **Continues** *Dickinson Press and Dickinson Recorder-Post, Richardton Times and Belfield Review.*

US
EDGELEY MAIL, THE. (July 1887)-. Newspaper. English. wk. $14.00 North Dakota; $17.00 others. Edgeley Mail, PO Box 278, Edgeley ND 58433. **ED** Robert L. Ketchum. **Photos. Ad Acc, Adv Mgr:** Robert L. Ketchum, **Tel** (701)493-2261. Full Page (B&W) $387.00. Half Page (B&W) $195.00. Full Page (Color) $462.00. Half Page (Color) $270.00. **Pub. Size:** Broadsheet. **Circ:** 1,146.

US/8750-5444
EDMORE HERALD. Newspaper. English. wk. $12.00. Ness Press Inc, PO Box 157, Fordville ND 58231. **Tel** (701)229-3641. **ED** Truman Ness. **Ad Acc. Circ:** 721.

US
EMMONS COUNTY RECORD. Vol. 1, No. 1 (June 10, 1884)-. Newspaper. English. wk. Emmons County Record, 201 North Broadway, Linton ND 38552. available on microfilm. **Absorbed** *Emmons County Free Press (Linton, N.D. : 1927) and Hazelton Independent.*

US/0274-0001
FLICKERTALES (ERIE, N.D.). (FLICKERTALES). **Added/Corp** North Dakota Wildlife Federation. (19??)-. Periodical. English. Six times a year. $10.00 (one year) Comes with North Dakota Wildlife Federation Membership. North Dakota Wildlife Federation, PO Box 7248, 1830 North 11st Street, Bismarck ND 58501. **Tel** (701)223-6610.

US/0895-1292
FORUM (FARGO, N.D.), THE. (THE FORUM.). **VFOAT** Sunday Forum. Vol. 88 No. 99 (Apr. 1, 1966)-. Newspaper. English. da (daily & Sunday). $182.98. The Forum Communications Company, PO Box 2020, Fargo ND 58107. **Tel** (701)235-7311, FAX (701)241-5487. **ED** Joseph Dill and John Lohman (Managing Editor). **Photos. Ad Acc, Adv Mgr:** Robert Hiemenz. **Pub. Size:** Standard. **Wire Svcs.:** AP, NY. **Circ:** 55,532 daily, 70,701 Sunday. available on microfilm from University Microfilms International (UMI). **Formed by the union of** *Fargo Forum, Daily Republican and Moorhead Daily News* **and** *Fargo Forum, Daily Tribune and Moorhead Daily News.*

US
GLEANER. Vol. 78, No. 40 (Oct. 3, 1968)-. Newspaper. English. wk. Northwood Gleaner, Northwood ND 58267. available on microfilm. **Continues** *Northwood Gleaner;* **Absorbed** *Larimore Pioneer (Larimore, N.D. : 1882); McVille journal.* **Continued in part by** *Larimore Pioneer (Larimore, N.D. : 1975).*

US
GOLDEN VALLEY NEWS. Vol. 1, No. 1 (Oct. 8, 1936)-. Newspaper. English. wk. $26.00. Golden Valley News, PO Box 156, 97 East Main, Beach ND 58621. **Tel** (701)872-3755, FAX (701)872-3756. **ED** Mary Melvin. **Photos. Ad Acc, Adv Mgr:** Sandy Culleim. Full Page (B&W) $468.00. Half Page (B&W) $234.00. Full Page (Color) $543.00. Half Page (Color) $309.00. **Pub. Size:** Broadsheet. **Circ:** 1,350. **Formed by the union of** *Beach Advance* **and** *Beach Review and the Sentinel Butte Review.*

US/0745-9661
GRAND FORKS HERALD. VFOAT Daily Herald; Grand Forks Daily Herald. Vol. 35, No. 210 (July 1, 1916)-. Newspaper. English. da. Grand Forks Herald, 120 North 4th Street, Grand Forks ND 58201. **Tel** (701)780-1200, (800)477-6572. available on microfilm. Documents available from UMI Article Clearinghouse. **Continues** *Grand Forks Daily Herald (Grand Forks, N.D. : 1891).* **Continued in part by** *Grand Forks Herald Farm and Home, 0741-1103.*
Ind/Abst Bus. Dateline (Dec. 7, 1991-) [Full Txt.]

US
GRANT COUNTY NEWS, THE. Vol. 16, No. 10 (Jan. 7, 1926)-. Newspaper. English. wk. $23.00. Grant County News - North Dakota, PO Box 100, Elgin ND 58533. **Photos. Ad Acc, Adv Mgr:** Duane Schatz, **Tel** (701)584-2900. Full Page (B&W) $588.00. Half Page (B&W) $294.00. **Pub. Size:** Standard. **Continues** *Elgin News;* **Absorbed** *New Leipzig Sentinel.*

US
HATTON FREE PRESS. *Title Change.* (Jan. 1905)-Vol. 64, No. 49 (Nov. 7, 1968)-Vol. 65, No. 10 (Feb 6, 1919)-?. Newspaper. English. wk. Hatton Free Press, PO Box 289, Hatton ND 58240-0289. LC 9209. available on microfilm from State Historical Society of North Dakota. **Absorbed by** *Traill County Tribune (Mayville, N.D. : 1968).*

US
HILLSBORO BANNER. Newspaper. English. Hillsboro Banner, PO Box 49, Hillsboro ND 58045.

US
JAMESTOWN SUN, THE. Vol. 1, No. 205 (Mar. 6, 1926)-. Newspaper. English. da. $93.50. Jamestown Sun, PO Box 1760, Jamestown ND 58402. **Tel** (701)252-3120. **ED** Wayne Nelson and Bruce Henke (Managing Editor). LC 7002. **Photos. Ad Acc, Adv Mgr:** Gene Keller. **Pub. Size:** Standard. **Wire Svcs.:** AP. available on microfilm from State Historical Society of North Dakota. **Continues** *Jamestown Sun and Jamestown Daily Alert.*

US/0886-6007
JOURNAL (CROSBY, N.D.), THE. (THE JOURNAL.). **VFOAT** Divide County Journal; Crosby Journal. Vol. 66, No. 21 (May 22, 1968)-. Newspaper. English. wk (Published on Wednesdays). Crosby Journal, 217 North Main Street, Crosby ND 58730-9608. **Tel** (701)965-6088. **ED** Steven J. Andrist. **Ad Acc. Circ:** 3,100. available on microfilm.

US
KENMARE NEWS. Newspaper. English. Kenmare News, PO Box 894, Kenmare ND 58746.

US
LAMOURE CHRONICLE. Vol. 49, No. 7 (Jan. 7, 1932)-. Newspaper. English. wk. $20.00. Lamoure Chronicle, PO Box 196, Lamoure ND 58458. **Tel** (701)883-5393. **ED** Gerald Harris. **Photos. Ad Acc.** Full Page (B&W) $403.00. Half Page (B&W) $211.20. Full Page (Color) $478.00. Half Page (Color) $286.20. **Pub. Size:** Standard. ctrl circ. **Continues** *LaMoure County Chronicle.*

US
LARIMORE PIONEER, THE. No. 1 (Jan. 2, 1975)-. Newspaper. English. wk. Community News Inc / North Dakota, PO Box C, Northwood ND 58267-0602. **Tel** (701)587-6126. **ED** David Pfeifle. **Ad Acc. Adv Mgr:** Arlo Sbedberg. **Circ:** 655. available on microfilm. **Continues in part** *Gleaner (Northwood, N.D.).*

US/0888-0220
LEADER-NEWS (WASHBURN, N.D.), THE. (THE LEADER-NEWS.). **VFOAT** Leader News. Vol. 96, No. 43 (Feb. 5, 1986)-. Periodical. English. wk. Leader News, PO Box 340, Washburn ND 58577-0340. **Tel** (701)462-8126, FAX (701)463-7487. **ED** Joe Froelich. **Ad Acc, Adv Mgr:** Kathy Ploughman. **Circ:** 2,500. available on microfilm. **Formed by the union of** *Washburn Leader, 8750-7250 and Wilton News, 0279-6538.*

US
LITCHVILLE BULLETIN. Vol. 1, No. 1 (May 10, 1901). Bulletin. English. wk. $15.00, $12.00 (North Dakota) US, (add $12.00 for postage) other. Litchville Bulletin, PO Box 46, Litchville ND 58461-0046. **ED** Norma R Miedema. **Ad Acc. Circ:** 1,575 (ctrl). available on microfilm from State Historical Society of North Dakota.

US
MANDAN NEWS. Vol. 14, No. 50 (Nov. 2, 1989)-. Newspaper. English. wk. Mandan News, 303 Northeast 1st Street, Mandan ND 58554. **Tel** (701)663-6823. available on microfilm. **Continues** *Morton County and Mandan News.*

US
MCLEAN COUNTY INDEPENDENT. Began in May, 1905. Newspaper. English. wk. BHG Inc, PO Box 309, Garrison ND 58540. available on microfilm from The State Historical Society of Wisconsin.

US/8750-5436
MCVILLE MESSENGER. Vol. 1, No. 1 (June 25, 1981)-. Newspaper. English. wk. Ness Press Inc, PO Box 157, Fordville ND 58231. **Tel** (701)229-3641. **ED** Gunnard Ness. **Ad Acc. Circ:** 450. available on diskette.

US
MIDWEEK EAGLE. VFOAT Midweek. (1971)-. Newspaper. English. wk. Midweek Eagle, 322 Sheyenne

North Dakota

Street, West Fargo ND 58078. **Tel** (701)282-2443, FAX (701)282-9248. **ED** Donovan C. Witham. **Ad Acc. Circ:** 44,306. available on microfilm.

US
MIDWEEK PLUS. Vol. 1, No. 1 (July 22, 1979)-. Newspaper. English. wk. Pioneer Enterprises, PO Box 457, West Fargo ND 58078-0457. **Tel** (701)282-2443, FAX (701)283-9248. **ED** Karen Huber.

US/0885-3053
MINOT DAILY NEWS, THE. VFOAT Daily Optic Reporter. Vol. 51, No. 8 (May 10, 1966)-. Newspaper. English. da (except Sun.). 123.00 Northwestern North Dakota; $135.00 rest of North Dakota; $199.00 all others in the US; $270.00 Canada. Minot Daily News, PO Box 1150, Minot ND 58702. **Tel** (701)857-1910. **ED** Mike Burbach. **Bk Rev**. **Ad Acc, Adv Mgr:** S. Baker, **Tel** (701)857-1927. **Circ:** 29,736 (ctrl). available on microfilm. *Formed by the union of Minot Daily News (and Daily Optic-Reporter) and Ward County Independent.* **Desc:** We serve the Northwest quadrant of North Dakota approximately 26,000 circulation.

US
MOTT PIONEER PRESS. Newspaper. English. Pioneer Press Company, PO Box 369, Mott ND 58646. *Absorbed Bentley Bulletin; Mott Spotlight.*

US
MOUNTRAIL COUNTY PROMOTER. Newspaper. English. Mountrail County Promoter, PO Box 99, Stanley ND 58784. *Continues Ross Promoter; Absorbed Stanley Sun; Powers Lake Herald.*

US
MOUNTRAIL COUNTY RECORD. Newspaper. English. Mountrail County Record, PO Box 8, Parshall ND 58770. *Formed by the union of Parshall Plainsman and Van Hook Reporter.*

US
NAPOLEON HOMESTEAD. (June 11, 1886)-. Newspaper. English. wk. $19.50 North Dakota; $25.00 others. Napoleon Homestead, PO Box 29, Napoleon ND 58561. **Tel** (701)754-2212. **ED** Terry Schwartzemberger. **Photos**. **Ad Acc, Adv Mgr:** Terry Schwartzemberger. Full Page (B&W) $451.50. Half Page (B&W) $226.00. Full Page (Color) $526.50. Half Page (Color) $301.00. **Pub. Size:** Broadsheet.

US/0895-5344
NELSON COUNTY ARENA (MICHIGAN, N.D. : 1919). (NELSON COUNTY ARENA.). Began March 1919?-. Newspaper. English. wk. $12.00. Ness Press Inc, PO Box 157, Fordville ND 58231. **Tel** (701)229-3641. **ED** Gunnard Ness. **Ad Acc. Circ:** 900. available on diskette.

US
PEMBINA NEW ERA. Newspaper. English. Pembina New Era, Pembina ND 58271.

US
PIERCE COUNTY TRIBUNE, THE. VFOAT Pierce County Tribune and Rugby Optimist. (1888)-. Newspaper. English. wk. $20.00 North Dakota; $26.00 others. Pierce County Tribune, 219 South Main Street, Rugby ND 58368. **ED** Mark Carlson. **Photos**. **Ad Acc, Adv Mgr:** Kim Brown, **Tel** (701)776-5252. Full Page (B&W) $459.00. Half Page (B&W) $250.80. Full Page (Color) $509.00. Half Page (Color) $300.80. **Pub. Size:** Broadsheet. **Wire Svcs.:** AP. **Circ:** 3,100. *Absorbed Rugby Optimist; Pierce County Globe and Pierce County Press (Rugby, N.D. : 1933).*

US
PLAINS REPORTER. (May 1982)-. Newspaper. English. wk. Williston Plains Reporter, PO Box 1447, Williston ND 58801. available on microfilm from State Historical Society of North Dakota. *Continues Williston Plains Reporter.*

US
RANSOM COUNTY GAZETTE, THE. (1991)-. Newspaper. English. wk. Ransom County Gazette, 310 Main Street, Lisbon ND 58054. *Continues Ransom County Gazette and Enterprise.*

US
RANSOM COUNTY GAZETTE AND ENTERPRISE, THE. Vol. 93, No. 46 (Feb. 12, 1976)-. Newspaper. English. wk. 310 Main Street, Lisbon ND 58054. *Continues Ransom County Gazette the Enterprise.*

US/0747-1181
RECORD (GRAFTON, N.D.). *Title Change.* (THE RECORD.). Vol. 93, No. 19 (June 5, 1982)-Vol. 102, No. 28 (Nov. 4, 1992). Newspaper. English. bw. The Record / North Dakota, PO Box 471, Grafton ND 58237. **Tel** (701)352-0640. available on microfilm. *Continues Grafton Record. Continued by Walsh County Record (Grafton, N.D. : 1992), 1067-5922.*

US
RENVILLE COUNTY FARMER. VFOAT Renville County Farmer and Glenburn Advance. Vol. 49, No. 42 (Oct. 5, 1950)-. Newspaper. English. wk. $27.00. Renville County Farmer, PO Box 98, Mohall ND 58761. **ED** Gloria Abrahamson. **Photos**. **Ad Acc, Adv Mgr:** Gloria Abrahamson, **Tel** (701)756-6363. Full Page (B&W) $500.00. Half Page (B&W) $250.00. Full Page (Color) $560.00. Half Page (Color) $310.00. **Pub. Size:** Broadsheet. **Circ:** 1,750. *Continues Renville County Farmer and Glenburn Advance.*

●US/1061-1029
RICHLAND COUNTY NEWS-MONITOR. VFOAT Richland County News Monitor. Vol. 101, No. 42 (Jan. 1, 1992)-. Newspaper. English. wk. Richland Publishing Company, 107 Main, Hankinson ND 58041. **Tel** (701)242-7696. *Formed by the union of Fairmount News (Fairmount, N.D. : 1965), 8750-4545; Hankinson News and Monitor (Lidgerwood, N.D. : 1981), 0744-1401.*

US
STEELE COUNTY PRESS. Newspaper. English. Steele County Press, PO Box 475, Fessenden ND 58230.

US
TELLER, THE. Vol. 83, No. 4 (May 24, 1972)-. Newspaper. English. wk (Wed.). $10.00 North Dakota residents; $14.00 other. The Teller, Box 308, Milnor ND 58060. **Tel** (701)427-9472. **ED** Richard Bradbury. available on microfilm. *Continues Sargent County Teller.*

US
TOWNER COUNTY RECORD HERALD. Newspaper. English. Towner County Record Herald, 405 Main Street, Cando ND 58324. *Formed by the union of Cando Record (Cando, N.D. : 1914) and Cando Herald.*

US
TRAILL COUNTY TRIBUNE. Vol. 87, No. 13 (Nov. 14, 1968)-. Newspaper. English. wk. Traill County Tribune, 19 East Main Street, Mayville ND 58257. *Continues Traill County Tribune and Portland Republican; Absorbed Hatton Free Press.*

US
TRI-COUNTY SUN (FORDVILLE, N.D.). (TRI-COUNTY SUN.). Began May 10, 1922-. Newspaper. English. wk. $12.00. Ness Press Inc, PO Box 157, Fordville ND 58231. **Tel** (701)229-3641. **ED** Gunnard Ness. **Ad Acc. Circ:** 800. available on diskette.

US
TURTLE MOUNTAIN STAR. Newspaper. English. wk. Turtle Mountain Star, PO Box 849, Rolla ND 58367. **Tel** (701)477-6495. **ED** Roger Bailey. *Continues Turtle Mountain Star and Rolette County Herald; Absorbed Dunseith Journal.*

US/8750-7285
UNDERWOOD NEWS, THE. Newspaper. English. wk. The Underwood News, Borlang Publishing Company, 216 Lincoln Avenue, Underwood ND 58576.

US
VALLEY CITY TIMES-RECORD (VALLEY CITY, N.D. : 1964). (VALLEY CITY TIMES-RECORD.). VFOAT Valley City Times Record; Valley City Times-Record and the Dakota Press; Valley City Times Record and the Dakota Press. Vol. 85, No. 222 (Sept. 1, 1964)-. Newspaper. English. da. Valley City Times-Record, 146 3rd Street Northeast, Valley City ND 58072. available on microfilm from State Historical Society of North Dakota. *Continues Valley City and Barnes County Times-Record.*

US
WALSH COUNTY FREE PRESS. Newspaper. English. Walsh County Free Press, PO Box 49, Park River ND 58270.

●US/1067-5922
WALSH COUNTY RECORD (1992), THE. (THE WALSH COUNTY RECORD.). Vol. 102, No. 29 (Nov. 10, 1992)-. Newspaper. English. wk. $24.00 in county; $28.00 others. Walsh County Record, Box 471, Grafton ND 58237. **Tel** (701)352-0640. **ED** John Strand. **Photos**. **Ad Acc, Adv Mgr:** Don Tuff. Full Page (B&W) $554.62. Half Page (B&W) $277.31. Full Page (Color) $639.62. Half Page (Color) $362.31. **Pub. Size:** Broadsheet. *Continues Record (Grafton, N.D.).*

US
WEST FARGO PIONEER. (Mar. 15, 1967)-. Newspaper. English. wk. West Fargo Pioneer, PO Box 457, West Fargo ND 58078. available on microfilm.

US
WESTERN CONCEPT, THE. Newspaper. English. Dickinson State College, PO Box 165, Dickinson ND 58601.

US
WESTHOPE STANDARD. Newspaper. English. Westhope Standard, PO Box 427, Westhope ND 58793.

US
WILLISTON DAILY HERALD. Vol. 72, No. 245 (June 11, 1971)-. Newspaper. English. da. $55.00. Williston Daily Herald, PO Box 1447, Williston ND 58801. **Tel** (701)572-2165. available on microfilm. *Continues Williston Herald (Williston, N.D. : Daily : 1964).*

US
WISHEK STAR. Newspaper. English. Wishek Star, PO Box 275, Wishek ND 58495.

OHIO

US/0747-3338
ADVANCE REPORTER, THE. (Jan. 1976)-. Newspaper. English. wk. $8.00 Williams and adjoining Ohio counties; $10.00 other. The Advance Reporter, Box 377, West Unity OH 43570. **Tel** (419)924-2382. **ED** Lee Spielvogel. *Formed by the union of West Unity Reporter and Stryker Advance.*

US
ADVERTISER-TRIBUNE, THE. VFOAT Advertiser Tribune. Vol. 1, No. 1 (Jan. 9, 1933)-. Newspaper. English. da. $137.00. Tiffin Advertiser-Tribune, PO Box 778, Tiffin OH 44883. **Tel** (419)447-4455. *Formed by the union of Tiffin Daily Tribune (Tiffin, Ohio : 1931) and Daily Advertiser (Tiffin, Ohio).*

US/0740-2120
ADVOCATE (NEWARK, OHIO), THE. (THE ADVOCATE.). (Oct. 12, 1970)-. Newspaper. English. da. $122.00 Newark area; $138.00 other. The Newark Advocate, 25 West Main Street, Newark OH 43055. **Tel** (614)345-4053. **ED** Roger Bartel. **Circ:** 21,271. *Continues Newark Advocate and American Tribune.*

US
AKRON BEACON JOURNAL, THE. 34th year, No. 288 (Nov. 6, 1903)-. Newspaper. English. da. $135.00 (daily and Sunday, carrier); $129.80 (Saturday and Sunday, regular mail); $254.60 (daily, regular mail); $358.60 (daily and Sunday, regualr mail), $109.00 (Sunday, regular mail) US; $504.20 (daily, regular mail); $712.20 (daily and Sunday, regular mail), $213.00 (Sunday, regular mail) other. Akron Beacon Journal, 44 East Exchange Street, Akron OH 44328. **Tel** (216)996-3000 or, 800 777-2442. **ED** Dale Allen. **Circ:** 155,023 daily, 225,741 Sunday. available on microfilm from University Microfilms International (UMI). *Continues Beacon Journal.* **Ind/Abst** PROMT.

US
ALLIANCE REVIEW (ALLIANCE, OHIO : 1924). (THE ALLIANCE REVIEW.). VFOAT Alliance Review and Leader. (Nov. 29, 1924)-. Newspaper. English. da (except Sun.). $98.00. Alliance Review, PO Box 2180, Alliance OH 44601. **Tel** (216)821-1200, FAX (216)821-8258. **ED** James Hastings (Editor-in-Chief) and Michael Patterson (Managing Editor). **Bk Rev**. **Photos**. **Ad Acc, Adv Mgr:** Don Watson. Full Page (B&W) $959.75. Half Page (B&W) $516.65. Full Page (Color) $1,039.75. Half Page (Color) $596.65. **Pub. Size:** Standard. **Wire Svcs.:** AP. available in microform from Bell & Howell. *Continues Alliance Daily Review and Daily Leader.*

US/0164-680X
AMERIŠKA DOMOVINA. VFOAT American Home. Vol. 22, No. 24 (Feb. 26, 1919)-. Newspaper. Slovenian (English). Forty-eight times a year. $25.00 US; $30.00 Canada; $35.00 other. American Home Publishing Company, 6117 St Clair Avenue, Cleveland OH 44103. **Tel** (216)431-0628, FAX (216)361-4088. *Continues Clevelandska Amerika.*

US
ANTWERP BEE-ARGUS, THE. VFOAT Antwerp Bee Argus. (1913)-. Newspaper. English. wk. $17.00. Antwerp Bee-Argus, PO Box 278, Antwerp OH 45813. **Tel** (419)258-8161. **ED** Sandra Temple. **Bk Rev**, (Qty: 6). **Photos**. **Ad Acc**. Full Page (B&W) $387.00. Half Page (B&W) $180.00. Full Page (Color) $462.00. Half Page (Color) $255.00. **Pub. Size:** Standard. **Circ:** 1,200. available in microform. *Formed by the union of Antwerp Bee (Antwerp, Ohio) and Antwerp Argus.*

US
ARCHBOLD BUCKEYE. (1905)-. Newspaper. English. Fifty-two times a year (Wed.). $27.00 Ohio; $33.00 other. Archbold Buckeye, 207 North Defiance Street, Archbold OH 43502. **Tel** (419)445-4466. **ED** David Pugh (News Editor); Sharon S. Taylor (Managing Editor). **Photos**. **Ad Acc, Adv Mgr:** Mary Huber. Full Page (B&W) $637.00. Half Page (B&W) $362.25. Full Page (Color) $637.00 ($100.00 extra per color). Half Page (Color) $362.25 ($100.00 extra per color). **Pub. Size:** Standard. **Circ:** 3,350.

US/0882-8695
ATHENS NEWS (ATHENS, OHIO). (THE ATHENS NEWS.). Began in 1979?-. Newspaper. English. sw. $60.00. Athens News, PO Box 543, Athens OH 45701. *Continues Athens 'A' News, An Alternative Newspaper.*

US
ATTICA HUB. Began with March 10, 1896 issue. Newspaper. English. wk. Seneca Publishing Inc, Box 516, Attica OH 44807.

US/0890-8591
BARBERTON HERALD. (THE BARBERTON HERALD.). (1923)-. Newspaper. English. wk. Barberton Herald, PO Box 831, Barberton OH 44203. **Tel** (216)753-1068. **ED** Dave Spice. **Circ:** 10,000. ***Absorbed*** *Barberton News; Barberton Leader.*

US/0746-262X
BEDFORD SUN BANNER. **VFOAT** Sun. Newspaper. English. wk. $23.40. Sun Newspapers, 5510 Cloverleaf Parkway, Cleveland OH 44125. **Tel** (216)524-0830, FAX (216)524-7792. **Ad Acc. Circ:** 5,442 (ctrl).

US
BEDFORD TIMES-REGISTER, THE. **VFOAT** Bedford Times Register. Began with June 18, 1959 issue. Newspaper. English. wk. Bedford Times-Register, 711 Broadway, Bedford OH 44146. ***Continues*** *Bedford Times-Register and Maple Heights Pioneer.*

US/0747-3273
BELLEFONTAINE EXAMINER. Vol. 58, No. 70 (Mar. 7, 1949)-. Newspaper. English. da. $78.00 Logan and surrounding counties in Ohio; $93.00 other. Bellefontaine Examiner, PO Box 40, Bellefontaine OH 43311. **Tel** (513)592-3060, FAX (513)592-4463. **ED** David Wagner. Index available. **Ad Acc, Adv Mgr:** Cindy Titus. **Circ:** 11,134 (ctrl). available on microfilm. ***Continues*** *Daily Examiner (Bellefontaine, Ohio).*

US/0746-4061
BETHEL JOURNAL, THE. ***Title Change.*** (1898)-(1992). Newspaper. English. wk. Bethel Journal, 115 South Main Street, Bethel OH 45106. ***Continued by*** *Bethel Journal-Press, 1066-7458.*

●US/1066-7458
BETHEL JOURNAL-PRESS, THE. **VFOAT** Bethel Journal Press. (1992)-. Newspaper. English. wk. Bethel Journal-Press, 115 South Main Street, Bethel OH 45106. ***Continues*** *Bethel Journal, 0746-4061.*

US
BLADE (TOLEDO, OHIO). (THE BLADE.). Vol. 110, No. 3 (Jan. 3, 1960)-. Newspaper. English. da (365 issues). $195.00 (daily and Sunday), $117.00 (daily only), $91.00 (Sunday only). The Blade, 541 Superior Street, Toledo OH 43660. **Tel** (419)245-6300, (419)245-6300, FAX (419)245-6391. **ED** Bernard Judy. **Circ:** 160,606 daily, 218,867 Sunday. available on microfilm from University Microfilms International (UMI). ***Continues*** *Toledo Blade (Toledo, Ohio : 1886).*
Ind/Abst PROMT.

US
BLUFFTON NEWS, THE. (July 28, 1875)-. Newspaper. English. wk. $30.00. Bluffton News, 103 North Main Street, Bluffton OH 45817. **Tel** (419)358-8010, FAX (419)358-5027. **ED** Fred Steiner. **Photos. Ad Acc.** Full Page (B&W) $516.60. Half Page (B&W) $258.30. **Pub. Size:** Standard. **Circ:** 3,000. available in microform.

US
BOOSTER, THE. (Feb. 16, 1933)-. Newspaper. English. wk (Wed.). $20.00 Franklin County; $25.00 other. Suburban News Publications, PO Box 29912, Columbus OH 43229. **Tel** (614)785-1212, FAX (614)785-1881. ***Absorbed*** *News Beechwold Clintonville.*

US
BUDGET (SUGARCREEK, OHIO : 1928). (THE BUDGET.). **VFOAT** Weekly Budget. Vol. 39, No. 19 (Sept. 6, 1928)-. Newspaper. English (Dutch). wk (Wednesday). 25.00Can$. The Budget / SugarCreek, PO Box 249, 134 North Factory Street, Sugarcreek OH 44681. **Tel** (216)852-4634, FAX (216)852-4421. **ED** George R. Smith (Editor-in-Chief), Jerry Dudek (Local Editor) and Fannie Erb (Managing Editor). **Bk Rev. Photos. Ad Acc, Adv Mgr:** Virginia Baab. **Pub. Size:** Broadsheet. **Circ:** 18,000. available on microfilm. ***Continues*** *Weekly Budget (Sugarcreek, Ohio : 1911).*
Desc: The daily happenings of Amish-Mennonites communities throughout the Americas.

US
CALL AND POST. Vol. 67, No. 32 (Aug. 7, 1982)-. Newspaper. English. wk. $35.00. PW Publishing Co., PO Box 6237, Cleveland OH 44101. **Tel** (216)791-7600. available on microfilm. ***Continues*** *Call and Post (Cleveland, Ohio : City Ed.).*

US
CALL AND POST (CINCINNATI ED.). (CALL AND POST.). (1967)-. Newspaper. English. wk. $35.00. PW Publishing Co., PO Box 6237, Cleveland OH 44101. **Tel** (216)791-7600.

US/0161-6900
CALVIN SYNOD HERALD. (CALVIN SYNOD HERALD. REFORMATUSOK LAPJA.). **Added/Corp** United Church of Christ. Calvin Synod. **VFOAT** Reformatusok Lapja. (1957)-. Periodical. English (Hungarian; summaries and/or abstracts in English and Hungarian). Six times a year. $4.00 (individuals); $6.00 (institutions). Calvin Synod Herald, PO Box 07812, Columbus OH 43207. **Tel** (614)444-1473. **ED** Paul Kantor.

US
CATHOLIC TELEGRAPH. (19??)-. Newspaper. English. wk. $22.00 US;. Catholic Telegraph, 100 East 8th Street, Cincinnati OH 45202. **Tel** (513)421-3131. **ED** Jim Stackpoole. **Bk Rev**, (Qty: 51 per year). **Ad Acc. Circ:** 24,000 (ctrl). available on microfilm from University Microfilms International (UMI).
Desc: Religious publication serving Catholic households.

US/0194-3685
CHAGRIN VALLEY TIMES, THE. Vol. 1, No. 1 (Sept. 23, 1971)-. Newspaper. English. wk. $22.50 Ohio; $26.50 others. Chagrin Valley Publishing Company, PO Box 150, Chagrin Falls OH 44022. **Tel** (216)247-5335, FAX (216)247-5615. **ED** David Lange. **Photos. Ad Acc, Adv Mgr:** Carole Vigliotti. Full Page (B&W) $1,272.00. Half Page (B&W) $636.00. Full Page (Color) $1,917.00. Half Page (Color) $958.50. **Pub. Size:** Tabloid. **Circ:** 14,000.

US
CHILLICOTHE GAZETTE (1940). (CHILLICOTHE GAZETTE.). **VFOAT** Sunday Gazette and News-Advertiser. Vol. 140, No. 1 (Jan. 1, 1940)-. Newspaper. English. da (daily except Sundays). $148.20 (within 50 mile radius of Chillicothe); $156.00 (Ohio); $171.60 (other). Chillicothe Gazette, 50 West Main Street, Chillicothe OH 45601. **Tel** (614)773-2111. ***Continues*** *Chillicothe Scioto Gazette;* ***Absorbed*** *Chillicothe News-Advertiser.*

US
CHRONICLE-TELEGRAM, THE. **VFOAT** Chronicle Telegram; Sunday Chronicle-Telegram; Elyria Chronicle-Telegram. Vol. 1, No. 1 (July 1, 1919)-. Newspaper. English. da (Except Sundays and Christmas). $171.60. Lorain County Printing & Publishing, 225 East Avenue, Elyria OH 44035. **Tel** (216)329-7000. **ED** Arnold Miller. Index available. cum. index. **Ad Acc.** ctrl circ. ***Formed by the union of*** *Elyria Chronicle (Elyria, Ohio : 1906)* ***and*** *Evening Telegram (Elyria, Ohio : 1915).*

US
CINCINNATI ENQUIRER (CINCINNATI, OHIO : 1872). (THE CINCINNATI ENQUIRER.). Vol. 36, No. 47 (Feb. 18, 1872)-. Newspaper. English. da. $322.40 (daily & Sun.), $218.40 (daily only), $104.00 (Sun. only). Cincinnati Enquirer, 312 Elm Street, Cincinnati OH 45202. **Tel** (513)721-2700, (800)876-4500. **ED** George R. Blake. **LC** 9240. **Bk Rev. Ad Acc. Circ:** 188,927 daily, 312,558 Sunday. available on microfilm from University Microfilms International (UMI); and University Microfilms International (UMI); available on an online database (file 635/Full-Text) from DIALOG. Documents available from UMI Article Clearinghouse. ***Continues*** *Cincinnati Daily Enquirer (Cincinnati, Ohio : 1852);* ***Absorbed*** *Commercial Tribune (Cincinnati, Ohio).*
Desc: A general circulation newspaper.
Ind/Abst Bus. Dateline (Nov. 15, 1990-) [Full Txt.]; PROMT.

US
CINCINNATI POST (CINCINNATI, OHIO : 1974). (THE CINCINNATI POST.). **VFOAT** Cincinnati Post and Times-Star. (Jan. 1, 1974)-. Newspaper. English. da. $218.40. Cincinnati Enquirer, 312 Elm Street, Cincinnati OH 45202. **Tel** (513)721-2700, (800)876-4500. available on microfilm from University Microfilms International (UMI); available on an online database (files 635,722/Full-Text) from DIALOG. Documents available from UMI Article Clearinghouse. ***Continues*** *Cincinnati Post and Times Star.*
Ind/Abst Bus. Dateline (Nov. 23, 1991-) [Full Txt.].

US
CIRCLEVILLE HERALD (1883 : DAILY). (THE CIRCLEVILLE HERALD.). (June 4, 1883)-. Newspaper. English. da. Circleville Herald, 220 North Court Street, PO Box 498, Circleville OH 43113. **Tel** (614)474-3131. **ED** Steve Jones. ***Absorbed*** *Daily Union-Herald (Circleville, Ohio : 1894).*

US
CLERMONT SUN (BATAVIA, OHIO : 1854). (THE CLERMONT SUN.). Newspaper. English. wk. $9.00. Clermont Sun, 465 E Main Street, Batavia OH 45103. **Tel** FAX (513)732-6344. **ED** Jean Kowalski. **Ad Acc. Circ:** 5,000. ***Continues*** *Ohio Sun (Batavia, Ohio : 1834).*
Desc: Local news of Clermont County Ohio.

US/0009-8825
CLEVELAND JEWISH NEWS, THE. Vol. 1, No. 1 (Oct. 30, 1964)-. Newspaper. English. wk. $24.00 Ohio; $28.00 others; $44.00 US & others. Cleveland Jewish Publishing Company, 3645 Warrensville Ctr., Road 230, Cleveland OH 44122. **Tel** (216)991-8300. **ED** Cynthia Detteibach. **Circ:** 14,300. ***Formed by the union of*** *Jewish Independent* ***and*** *Jewish Review and Observer.*

US/0745-435X
CLEVELAND LUTHERAN MESSENGER. ***Title Change.*** **Added/Corp** Lutheran Council of Greater Cleveland. Vol. 1 (1911)-(19??). Newspaper. English. mo (except combined July/Aug.). Cleveland Lutheran Messenger, 2057 West 30th Street, Cleveland OH 44113. **Tel** (216)281-8116. **ED** David Westcott. **Bk Rev. Ad Acc. Circ:** 12,000 (ctrl). ***Continued by*** *Lutheran Messenger (Cleveland, Ohio), 1060-3832.*
Desc: News of Cleveland Lutheran community.

US
CLYDE ENTERPRISE (CLYDE, OHIO : 1881). (THE CLYDE ENTERPRISE.). Vol. 4, No. 24 (Sept. 1, 1881)-. Newspaper. English. wk. Clyde Enterprise, 125 South Main Street, Clyde OH 43410. ***Continues*** *Clyde Enterprise and Sentinel.*

US
COLUMBUS DISPATCH, THE. Vol. 104, No. 267 (Mar. 24, 1975)-. Newspaper. English. da. $124.80 (Sun.), $192.40 (daily), $317.20 (daily & Sun.). Dispatch Printing Company, 34 South Third Street, Columbus OH 43215. **Tel** (614)461-5000. **Circ:** 248,121 daily, 371,489 Sunday. available on microfilm from University Microfilms International (UMI); available on an online database (files 495,635/Full-Text) from DIALOG. Documents available from UMI Article Clearinghouse. ***Continues*** *Columbus Evening Dispatch.*
Ind/Abst Bus. Dateline (Dec. 20, 1991-) [Full Txt.]; PROMT.

US
COMMUNITY JOURNAL-PRESS. **VFOAT** Community Journal Press. Vol. 165, No. 10 (Mar. 22, 1989)-. Newspaper. English. wk. $30.00. Press Community Newspaper, 4866 Cooper Road, Cincinnati OH 45242. **Tel** (513)745-0077. ***Formed by the union of*** *Clermont Courier-Press; Community Journal-Press South* ***and*** *Community Journal-Press North.*

US
COMMUNITY PRESS. (19??)-. Newspaper. English. wk. Press Community Newspapers, 4910 Para Drive, Cincinnati OH 45237. **Tel** (513)242-4300, FAX (513)242-2649.

US
CONTINENTAL NEWS-REVIEW, THE. **VFOAT** Continental News Review. (1916)-. Newspaper. English. wk. Continental News-Review, 201 North Main Street, Continental OH 45831.

US
COUNTYLINE, THE. (1967)-. Newspaper. English. wk. $6.80. Countyline, 127 South Walnut Street, PO Box 471, Bryan OH 43506. **Tel** (419)636-1111. **ED** Jack Bryce (Editor-in-Chief) and Lee Bryce (Managing Editor). **Ad Acc, Adv Mgr:** Lee Bryce.

US
COURIER, THE. Vol. 141, No. 1 (Jan. 2, 1976)-. Newspaper. English. da. $104.00. Findlay Publishing, 701 West Sandusky Street, Findlay OH 45840. **Tel** (419)422-5151, FAX (419)422-2937. **ED** Robert Hesse, Parker Sams (Managing Editor). **Photos. Ad Acc, Adv Mgr:** Eugene Weber. Full Page (B&W) $1306.80. Half Page (B&W) $653.40. Full Page (Color) $1431.80. Half Page (Color) $878.40. **Pub. Size:** Standard. **Wire Svcs.:** AP. **Circ:** 26,000. available in microform. ***Continues*** *Republican-Courier (Findlay, Ohio).*

US
CRESCENT-NEWS. **VFOAT** Crescent News. No. 270 (May 17, 1971)-. Newspaper. English. da. $96.00 Toledo; $101.00 Ohio; $106.00 other. Crescent News, PO Box 249, Defiance OH 43512. **ED** Robert M. Cummins. **Ad Acc, Adv Mgr:** Jim Eitniear. **Circ:** 18,000. ***Continues*** *Defiance Crescent-News (Defiance, Ohio : 1913).*

US
CRESTLINE ADVOCATE (CRESTLINE, OHIO : 1869). (CRESTLINE ADVOCATE.). (July 1869)-. Newspaper. English. wk. $18.00. Crestline Advocate, PO Box 226, Crestline OH 44827. **Tel** (419)683-3355. **ED** Joseph Petti. **Photos. Ad Acc.** Full Page (B&W) $559.86. Half Page (B&W) $279.93. Full Page (Color) $639.86. Half Page (Color) $319.93. **Pub. Size:** Standard. **Circ:** 2,300 (ctrl). available on microfilm.

US
DAILY ADVOCATE (GREENVILLE, OHIO : 1978). (THE DAILY ADVOCATE.). Vol. 95 No. 146 (Oct. 21, 1978)-. Newspaper. English. da. Daily Advocate, PO Box 220, Greenville OH 45331. ***Continues*** *Greenville Daily Advocate (Greenville, Ohio : 1968).*

US
DAILY CHIEF-UNION, THE. **VFOAT** Daily Chief Union; Chief-Union. 59th Year, No. 295 (Feb. 28, 1938)-. Newspaper. English. da. $84.00. Daily Chief-Union, 111 West Wyandot Avenue, Upper Sandusky OH 43351. **ED** Bette Snyder. **Bk Rev. Photos. Ad Acc, Adv Mgr:** Tom Martin, **Tel** (419)294-2332. Full Page (B&W) $528.90. Half Page (B&W) $269.61. Full Page (Color) $578.90. Half Page (Color) $319.61. **Pub. Size:** Standard. **Wire Svcs.:** AP.

available in microform. ***Formed by the union of*** *Daily Chief (Upper Sandusky, Ohio)* ***and*** *Daily Union (Upper Sandusky, Ohio : 1916).*

US
DAILY HERALD, THE. Vol. 118, No. 119 (Nov. 2, 1987)-. Newspaper. English. da. $104.00 Allen, Putnam, Van Wert; $108.00 other. Delphos Herald, 405 North Main Street, Delphos OH 45833. **Tel** (419)695-0015, FAX (419)692-7704. **ED** Esther Bielawski and Frank Noonan (Managing Editor). **Photos. Ad Acc, Adv Mgr:** Jane Ricker. Full Page (B&W) $735.30. Half Page (B&W) $367.65. Full Page (Color) $820.30. Half Page (Color) $452.65. **Pub. Size:** Standard. **Wire Svcs.:** UPI. **Circ:** 7,503. available in microform. ***Continues*** *Delphos Herald.*

US
DAILY JEFFERSONIAN (CAMBRIDGE, OHIO). (THE DAILY JEFFERSONIAN.). **VFOAT** Jeffersonial. Vol. 1, No. 1 (Sept. 19, 1892)-. Newspaper. English. da. Daily Jeffersonian, 821 Wheeling Avenue, Cambridge OH 43725.

US/0892-8215
DAILY RECORD (WOOSTER, OHIO), THE. (THE DAILY RECORD.). (19??)-. Newspaper. English. da (except Sunday and legal holidays). $90.50 Wooster; $92.50 others in Ohio; $97.50 others. The Daily Record, 212 East Liberty Street, Wooster OH 44691. **Tel** (216)264-1125, FAX (216)264-3756. **ED** Melody Snure (phone: (216)264-1125 ext.337). **Ad Acc, Adv Mgr:** Bob Anderson, **Tel** (216)264-1125 ext.327. **Circ:** 25,200. available on microfilm from University Microfilms International (UMI). Documents available from UMI Article Clearinghouse. ***Continues*** *Wooster Daily Record.*
Desc: Emphasis on coverage in Wayne and Holmes Counties of Ohio.
Ind/Abst Bus. Dateline (Dec. 23, 1991-) [Full Txt.].

US/0011-5487
DAILY REPORTER (COLUMBUS, OHIO). (DAILY REPORTER.). (19??)-. Newspaper. English. da (Mon.-Fri.). $80.00. Columbus Daily Reporter, 329 South Front Street, Columbus OH 43215-5094. **Tel** (614)224-4835, FAX (614)224-8649. **Photos. Ad Acc, Adv Mgr:** Dan Shillinburg. **Pub. Size:** Broadsheet. **Wire Svcs.:** AP.

US
DAILY SENTINEL (POMEROY, OHIO). (THE DAILY SENTINEL.). **VFOAT** Sunday Times-Sentinel. Vol. 6, No. 138 (Sept. 27, 1954)-. Newspaper. English. da. Pomeroy Daily Sentinel, 111 Court Street, Pomeroy OH 45769. ***Continues*** *Sentinel (Pomeroy, Ohio).*

US
DAILY STANDARD (CELINA, OHIO : 1905). (THE DAILY STANDARD.). (Dec. 4, 1905)-. Newspaper. English. da. Daily Standard / Celina, 123 East Market Street, Celina OH 45822.

US/0897-0920
DAYTON DAILY NEWS (DAYTON, OHIO : 1987). (DAYTON DAILY NEWS.). Vol. 111, No. 113 (Dec. 31, 1987)-. Newspaper. English. da. $187.20 US; $338.00 other. Dayton Newspapers Inc, 45 South Ludlow Street, Dayton OH 45402. **Tel** (513)225-2135. **ED** Betty Dietz Krebs. **Bk Rev. Ad Acc.** available on microfilm from University Microfilms International (UMI); available on an online database (file 734/Full-Text) from DIALOG. ***Continues*** *Dayton Daily News, The Journal Herald, 0890-8931.*

US/1064-2013
DELAWARE GAZETTE (DELAWARE, OHIO 1932), THE. (THE DELAWARE GAZETTE.). Vol. 114, No. 240 (Jan. 21, 1932)-. Newspaper. English. da. $110.00. Delaware Gazette, 18 East William, Delaware OH 43015. **Tel** (614)363-1161, FAX (614)363-6262. **ED** W. D. Thomson III (Editor-in-Chief) and Tom Williams (Managing Editor). cum. index. **Bk Rev**, (Qty: 5-6/yr). **Photos. Ad Acc, Adv Mgr:** Deirdre Warden. Full Page (B&W) $986.85. Half Page (B&W) $504.90. Full Page (Color) $1,076.85. Half Page (Color) $594.90. **Pub. Size:** Standard. **Wire Svcs.:** AP. **Circ:** 7,612 (ctrl). available in microform from University Microfilms International (UMI). ***Continues*** *Delaware Daily Gazette.*

US/1058-0298
DELHI PRESS. (1977)-. Newspaper. English. wk. Delhi Press, 5552 Cheviot Road, Cincinnati OH 45247. **Tel** (513)923-3111.

US
DELTA ATLAS. Began with June 6, 1885 issue. Newspaper. English. wk. Delta Atlas, 212 Main Street, Delta OH 43515.

US
DIRVA. VFOAT Field. Began in 1915. Newspaper. Lithuanian (Lithuanian). wk. American-Lithuanian Press and Radio Association, 6116 St Clair Avenue, Cleveland OH 44103. **ED** Vytautas Gedgaudas. available on microfilm from The Center for Research Libraries.

US
DUBLIN NEWS. Vol. 6, No. 43 (Feb. 26, 1986)-. Newspaper. English. wk (Wed.). $20.00 Franklin County; $25.00 other. Suburban News Publications, PO Box 29912, Columbus OH 43229. **Tel** (614)785-1212, FAX (614)785-1881. ***Continues*** *Dublin Suburbia News (Columbus, Ohio).*

US/0191-7927
DUBLIN VILLAGER. Vol. 1, No. 1 (Oct.25, 1978)-. Newspaper. English. wk. $15.00 Ohio; $18.00 other. Dublin Villager, PO Box 636, Dublin OH 43017. **Tel** (614)889-5733.

US
EARLY BIRD (ARCANUM, OHIO). (THE EARLY BIRD.). (1968)-. Newspaper. English. wk. Early Bird, 114 East George Street, Arcanum OH 45304.

US
EASTERN HILLS JOURNAL-PRESS. VFOAT Eastern Hills Journal Press. Vol. 52, No. 36 (Oct. 1, 1986)-. Newspaper. English. wk. $104.00. Press Community Newspaper, 4866 Cooper Road, Cincinnati OH 45242. **Tel** (513)745-0077. ***Continues*** *Eastern Hills Journal.*

US/0891-2300
EASTSIDE MESSENGER. Vol. 9, No. 19 (Sept. 16, 1982)-. Newspaper. English. wk (Monday). $52.00. Columbus Messenger Company, 3378 Sullivant Avenue, P. Daubel, Columbus OH 43204. **Tel** (614)272-5422, (614)852-0809, FAX (614)852-0814. **ED** Kenneth Drenton. **Photos. Ad Acc, Adv Mgr:** Bruce Russel. Full Page (B&W) $1715.20. Half Page (B&W) $857.60. Full Page (Color) $1790.20. Half Page (Color) $932.60. **Pub. Size:** Tabloid. **Circ:** 48,657. available on microfilm from Bell & Howell. ***Continues*** *Columbus Messenger (East Ed.).*

US
EDGERTON EARTH, THE. (1882)-. Newspaper. English. wk. $13.75 Williams, Stuben, Delkalb & Defance Counties; $17.00 other. Earth Publications Inc, PO Box 445, Edgerton OH 43517. **Tel** (419)298-2369.

US
EDON COMMERCIAL. (1906)-. Newspaper. English. wk. $15.75 in county; $19.00 others. Edon Commercial, PO Box 218, 113 North Michigan, Edon OH 43518. **Tel** (419)272-2413, FAX (419)298-2360. **ED** Dean and Mary Howard. **Photos. Ad Acc, Adv Mgr:** Mary Howard, **Tel** (419)298-2369. Full Page (B&W) $419.25. Half Page (B&W) $215.00. Full Page (Color) $519.24. Half Page (Color) $315.00. **Pub. Size:** Tabloid. **Circ:** 1,000 (ctrl). available on microfilm. ***Continues*** *Edon Independent.*

US/0740-1922
ELECTRON (WILLOUGHBY, OHIO), THE. (THE ELECTRON.). [Electron]. (19??)-. Newspaper. English. bm (Jan., Mar., May, July, Sept., Nov.). $12.00. The Electron, 4781 East 355 Street, Willoughby OH 44094. **Tel** (216)781-9400, FAX (216)781-0331. **ED** Denise M. Zakrajsek. **Bk Rev**, (Qty: 2-3). **Photos. Ad Acc, Adv Mgr:** Denise M. Zakrajsek. Full Page (B&W) $995.00. Half Page (B&W) $495.00. **Pub. Size:** Standard. **Circ:** 25,000.

US/0745-5550
EVENING LEADER (SAINT MARYS, OHIO). (THE EVENING LEADER.). Began in 1905?. Newspaper. English. da. $40.00 within county, $49.00 others Ohio, $54.00 others. Evening Leader, 102 East Spring Street, Saint Marys OH 45885. ***Continues*** *St. Marys Argus.*

US
EVENING REVIEW, THE. Vol. 91, No. 85 (Feb. 1, 1970)-. Newspaper. English. da. East Liverpool Review, 210 East 4th Street, East Liverpool OH 43920-3144. **Tel** (216)385-4545, FAX (216)385-7114. **ED** Gary Housey. **Ad Acc, Adv Mgr:** Lisa Lynn. **Circ:** 13,900. ***Continues*** *East Liverpool Review.*

US/0014-7826
FARM AND DAIRY (SALEM, OHIO : 1914). (FARM AND DAIRY.). (1914)-. Newspaper. English. wk. $17.00 (one year); $33.00 (two years). The Lyle Printing and Publishing Company, 185/189 East State Street, Box 38, Salem OH 44460. **Tel** (216)337-3419. **ED** Susan Crowell. **Photos. Ad Acc, Adv Mgr:** Scot Darling. Full Page (B&W) $500.00. Half Page (B&W) $250.00. Full Page (Color) $675.00. Half Page (Color) $337.50. **Pub. Size:** Tabloid. **Circ:** 19,000. ***Continues*** *Farm and Dairy Profit;* ***Absorbed*** *Record (Salem, Ohio).*
Desc: Brief research from experiment stations in agriculture, success stories concerning farmers of the tri-state area; sale and livestock market reports; farm sales, antique sales, etc.

US/1065-0083
FAYETTE REVIEW, THE. (1901)-. Newspaper. English. wk. $23.00 Fulton, Williams, Lenawee, & Hillsdale counties; $25.00 other. Fayette Review, PO Box 219, Fayette OH 43521. **Tel** (419)237-2591. **ED** Donald J Potter. **Ad Acc. Circ:** 1,300.

US
FREE PRESS STANDARD, THE. VFOAT Free Press Standard. Vol. 75, No. 11 (March 16, 1906)-. Newspaper. English. wk. $14.50 Harrison, Jefferson, Stark, Carol, and Columbiana, Ohio; $32.00 other Ohio; $40.00 other. Carrolton Free Press-Standard, PO Box 37, Carrollton OH 44615. **Tel** (216)627-5591, FAX (216)627-3195. **ED** Carol McIntire. **Ad Acc. Circ:** 8,500 (ctrl). ***Formed by the union of*** *Carroll Free Press* ***and*** *Republican-Standard;* ***Absorbed*** *Carroll Journal.*

US
GALLIPOLIS DAILY TRIBUNE, THE. Began in 1894. Newspaper. English. da. Ohio Valley Publishing Company, 452 West Haller Street, Lima OH 45801. ***Absorbed*** *Gallia Times.*

US/0746-2611
GARFIELD-MAPLE HEIGHTS SUN. VFOAT Sun. **VAT** Garfield, Maple Heights Sun. 11th year, No. 14 (Apr. 2, 1981)-. Newspaper. English. wk. $29.25. Sun Newspapers, 5510 Cloverleaf Parkway, Cleveland OH 44125. **Tel** (216)524-0830, FAX (216)524-7792. **ED** Carol Kovach. **Photos. Ad Acc.** Full Page (B&W) 2,263.85. Half Page (B&W) 1,132.00. **Circ:** 10,579 (ctrl). ***Continues*** *Southeast Sun (Cleveland Heights, Ohio).*

US
GAZETTE, THE. VFOAT Gazette and the Ashtabula County Sentinel. Vol. 115, No. 45 (Nov. 8, 1990)-. Newspaper. English. wk. $20.00 Ohio; $30.00 other. Jefferson Gazette, 46 West Jefferson Street, PO Box 166, Jefferson OH 44047. **Tel** (216)576-9115. **ED** Lucille Donley. **Ad Acc.** ctrl circ. ***Continues*** *Gazette, Ashtabula County Sentinel.*

US/0891-2270
GROVE CITY SOUTHWEST MESSENGER. VFOAT Southwest Messenger. Vol. 3, No. 21 (Jan. 23, 1984)-. Newspaper. English. wk. Free. Columbus Messenger Company, 3378 Sullivant Avenue, P. Daubel, Columbus OH 43204. **Tel** (614)272-5422, (614)852-0809, FAX (614)852-0814. **ED** Harold Stevens Jr. and Ken Drenten (Managing Editor). **Photos. Ad Acc, Adv Mgr:** Bruce Russel, **Tel** (614272-5422. Full Page (B&W) $896.00. Half Page (B&W) $448.00. Full Page (Color) $971.00. Half Page (Color) $523.00. **Pub. Size:** Tabloid. **Circ:** 17,978. available on microfilm from Bell & Howell. ***Continues*** *Grove City Messenger.*

US
GUARDIAN - WRIGHT STATE'S STUDENT NEWSPAPER. (19??)-. Newspaper. English. wk. Wright State University / Guardian, W016C Student Union, Dayton OH 45435. **Tel** (513)873-5537, FAX (513)873-5535. **ED** JoAnne Smith. **Bk Rev. Photos. Ad Acc, Adv Mgr:** Elizabeth Green. Full Page (B&W) $529.75. Half Page (B&W) $285.25. Full Page (Color) $614.75. Half Page (Color) $370.25. **Pub. Size:** Tabloid. available in microform.

US/1043-4992
HARRISON NEWS-HERALD. VFOAT Harrison News Herald. Vol. 1, No. 1 (April 4, 1968)-. Newspaper. English. sw. Harrison News-Herald, 136 South Main Street, Cadiz OH 43907. ***Formed by the union of*** *Freeport Press-Herald; SCIO Press-Herald* ***and*** *Cadiz Republican (1845).*

US/0746-8016
HARTVILLE NEWS, THE. Vol. 1, No. 1 (Sept. 12, 1930)-. Newspaper. English. wk. $22.00 in county; $24.00 others. Knowles Press Inc, 316 East Maple Street, Hartville OH 44632. **Tel** (216)877-9345, FAX (216)877-1364. **ED** Rosalee Haines (Editor-in-Chief) and Linda Sourini (Managing Editor). **Photos. Ad Acc, Adv Mgr:** Rosalee Haines. Full Page (B&W) $245.00. Half Page (B&W) $123.00. Full Page (Color) $320.00. Half Page (Color) $198.00. **Pub. Size:** Standard. **Circ:** 2,900. available in microform.

US/0890-8656
HERALD-STAR, THE. VFOAT Herald Star; Sunday Herald-Star. Vol. 163, No. 310 (June 3, 1974)-. Newspaper. English. da. $136.00. The Herald-Star, 401 Herald Square, Steubenville OH 43952. **Tel** (614)283-4711. **ED** James Smith. Index available. **Bk Rev. Ad Acc. Circ:** 22,000 (ctrl). available on microfilm. ***Continues*** *Steubenville Herald-Star.*
Desc: Daily newspaper.

US
HERALD-VOICE (BELLE CENTER, OHIO : 1928). (THE HERALD-VOICE.). **VFOAT** Herald Voice. Vol. 33, No. 18 (June 29, 1928)-. Newspaper. English. wk. Herald-Voice, 109 East Main Street, Belle Center OH 43310. ***Continues*** *Herald-Voice and Huntsville News.*

US
HILLIARD NORTHWEST NEWS. Vol. 18, No. 6 (Oct. 7, 1987)-. Newspaper. English. wk (Wed.). $20.00 Franklin County; $25.00 other. Suburban News Publications, PO Box 29912, Columbus OH 43229. **Tel** (614)785-1212, FAX (614)785-1881. ***Continues*** *Northwest News (Hilliard, Ohio).*

US/0279-5124
IRONTON TRIBUNE, THE. (19??)-. Newspaper. English. da (Tues.-Fri. and Sun.). $117.00. Ironton Tribune, PO Box 647, Ironton OH 45638. **Tel** (614)532-1441.

US
JOURNAL, THE. **VFOAT** Sunday Journal. Vol. 82, No. 294 (June 8, 1961)-. Newspaper. English. da. $170.14 (colleges), $212.68 (other) daily and Sunday editions; $117.31 (colleges), $146.64 (other) daily only. Lorain Journal Company, 1657 Broadway, Lorain OH 44052. **Tel** (216)245-6901, FAX (216)245-5637. ***Absorbed*** *Lorain Journal (Lorain, Ohio : 1957).*

US
JOURNAL AND THE NOBLE COUNTY LEADER, THE. **VFOAT** Journal-Leader; Journal Leader. Vol. 103, No. 9 (Aug. 24, 1961)-. Newspaper. English. wk. $24.00 (in county), $26.00 (out of county). Journal-Leader / Caldwell, Ohio, 309 Main Street, Caldwell OH 43724. **ED** Dave Evans. **Photos. Ad Acc, Adv Mgr:** Fred Powell, **Tel** (614)732-234-. Full Page (B&W) $602.70. Half Page (B&W) $303.4C. Full Page (Color) $662.70. Half Page (Color) $363.40. **Pub. Size:** Broadsheet. **Circ:** 5,010 weekly paid. available in microform. ***Formed by the union of*** *Journal (Caldwell, Ohio)* ***and*** *Noble County Leader.*

US
JOURNAL-HERALD (JACKSON, OHIO). (THE JOURNAL-HERALD.). **VFOAT** Journal Herald. Vol. 1, No. 1 (June 3, 1974)-. Newspaper. English. tw. Journal-Herald / Ohio, PO Box 270, Jackson OH 45640. ***Formed by the union of*** *Jackson Sun-Journal; Oak Hill Press* ***and*** *Jackson Herald (Jackson, Ohio : 1902).*

US
KENTON TIMES, THE. Vol. 6, No. 7 (Nov. 2, 1953)-. Newspaper. English. da. Kenton Times, 201 East Columbus Street, Kenton OH 43326. ***Formed by the union of*** *The Kenton Daily Democrat (Kenton, Ohio : 1892)* ***and*** *News and Republican.*

US
KENTUCKY POST (CONVINGTON KY. : 1974). (THE KENTUCKY POST.). **VFOAT** Kentucky Post and Times-Star. (Jan. 1, 1974)-. Newspaper. English. da (Mon.-Sat.). $95.40. Cincinnati Enquirer, 312 Elm Street, Cincinnati OH 45202. **Tel** (513)721-2700, (800)876-4500. **LC** 7002. available on an online database (file 722/Full-Text) from DIALOG. ***Continues*** *Kentucky Post and Times-Star.*

US/8750-8141
KETTERING-OAKWOOD TIMES, THE. **VFOAT** Kettering Oakwood Times. Vol. 29, No. 77 (Jan. 23, 1985)-. Newspaper. English. sw. $26.00. Times Publications / Ohio, 3484 Far Hills Avenue, Dayton OH 45429. **Tel** (513)294-7000. ***Continues*** *Times (Kettering, Ohio).*

US
KIDRON NEWS THE DALTON GAZETTE, THE. **VFOAT** Dalton Gazette & the Kidorn News; Dalton Gazette and the Kidron News. Vol. 40, No. 50 (Dec. 24, 1974)-. Newspaper. English. wk (Weds.). $12.50 Ohio; $13.50 US. Dalton Gazette Kidron News, PO Box 495, Dalton OH 44618. **Tel** (216)828-8401. **ED** Francis Woodruff. Index available. cum. index. **Photos. Ad Acc.** Full Page (B&W) $325.00. **Pub. Size:** Tabloid. **Circ:** 1,500 (ctrl). available on microfilm. ***Formed by the union of*** *Kidron News* ***and*** *Dalton Gazette.*

US/0744-8910
KURYER ZJEDNOCZENIA. (KURYER ZJEDNOCZENIA : OFFICIAL ORGAN OF THE UNION OF POLES IN AMERICA.). **VFOAT** Polish Courier. Began in 1939. Newspaper. Polish (English). mo. $4.00. Kuryer Publishers Company, 6805 Lansing Avenue, Cleveland OH 44105. **Tel** (216)641-9234. **ED** R Joblonski. **Circ:** 20,945. ***Formed by the union of*** *Kuryer* ***and*** *Zjednoczeniec.*

US
LANCASTER EAGLE-GAZETTE. **VFOAT** Lancaster Eagle Gazette. (March 11, 1936)-. Newspaper. English. da. Lancaster Eagle-Gazette, PO Box 848, Lancaster OH 43130. **Tel** (614)654-1321. **ED** Ron Johnson. **Circ:** 17,133. ***Formed by the union of*** *Lancaster Daily Eagle* ***and*** *Lancaster Daily Gazette;* ***Absorbed*** *Lexington Daily News.*

US
LEADER ENTERPRISE, THE. (1923)-. Newspaper. English. wk. Bryan Publishing, PO Box 471, Bryan OH 43506. **Tel** (419)636-1111. **(Subscription address:** Leadership Enterprise, PO Box 149, Montpelier OH 43543.**)** ***Formed by the union of*** *Montpelier Leader* ***and*** *Montpelier Enterprise;* ***Absorbed*** *Montpelier Daily Leader.*

US/8750-8095
LEADER (GARFIELD HEIGHTS, OHIO), THE. (THE LEADER.). **VFOAT** Garfield Hts. Leader. Newspaper. English. wk. The Leader / Ohio, 4818 Turney Road, Garfield Heights OH 44125. **Tel** (216)883-0300. **ED** William E Kleinschimdt. **Circ:** 6,300. ***Continues*** *Garfield Heights Leader.*

US
LIMA NEWS, THE. **VFOAT** Lima Sunday News. (1926)-. Newspaper. English. da. $144.00 (daily & Sunday), $120.00 (daily), $84.00(Sunday) Allen, Putnam, Auglaize, Van Wert & Hardin counties; $168.00 (daily & Sunday), $132.00 (daily), $108.00 (Sunday) US. Lima News, 121 East High Street, PO Box 690, Lima OH 45802. **Tel** (419)223-1010, FAX (419)229-0426. **ED** Ray Sullivan (Editor-in-Chief) and Jim Krumel (Managing Editor). **Ad Acc, Adv Mgr:** Ken Carpenter. **Pub. Size:** Broadsheet. **Wire Svcs.:** AP. **Circ:** 36,000 (weekday), 40,000 (Saturday morning), 46,000 (Sunday mornings). available in microform. ***Continues*** *Lima News and Times-Democrat.*

US/8750-2674
LYNCHBURG NEWS. Newspaper. English. wk. $7.50 Ohio, $10.00 other. Lynchburg News, 345 Jefferson, Greenfield OH 45123.

US/0891-2262
MADISON MESSENGER. (19??)-. Newspaper. English. wk. $52.00. Columbus Messenger Company, 3378 Sullivant Avenue, P. Daubel, Columbus OH 43204. **Tel** (614)272-5422, (614)852-0809, FAX (614)852-0814. **ED** Kristy Zurbrick. **Photos. Ad Acc, Adv Mgr:** Jim Durban. Full Page (B&W) $704.00. Half Page (B&W) $352.00. Full Page (Color) $779.00. Half Page (Color) $427.00. **Pub. Size:** Tabloid. available on microfilm from University Microfilms International (UMI).

US
MAGYAR HIRADO (NEW BRUNSWICK, N.J.). (MAGYAR HIRADO.). **VFOAT** Magyar Herald. Vol. 62, No. 45 (Nov. 5, 1970)-. Newspaper. Hungarian (English). wk. Liberty Publishing Company, 1736 East 22nd Street, Cleveland OH 44114. ***Formed by the union of*** *Magyar Hirnok; Hirado; Szabad Sajto; Fuggetlenseg* ***and*** *Bethlehemi Hirado.*

US
MARIETTA TIMES (1977). (THE MARIETTA TIMES.). Newspaper. English. da. Marietta Times, 700 Channel Lane, Marietta OH 45750. ***Continues*** *Marietta Daily Times.*

US/1069-2207
MARYSVILLE JOURNAL-TRIBUNE. **VFOAT** Journal Tribune; Marysville Journal Tribune; Journal-Tribune. Vol. 81, No. 47 (May 9, 1972)-. Newspaper. English. da (Monday-Saturday). $75.00 Union County; $60.00 Ohio; $80.00 other. Marysville Journal Tribune, 207 North Main Street, PO Box 226, Marysville OH 43040. **Tel** (513)644-9111. **ED** Daniel E. Behrens. **Ad Acc, Adv Mgr:** Peyton Rardin. **Circ:** 6,000 (ctrl). ***Continues*** *Journal-Tribune (Marysville, Ohio).*

US
MEDINA COUNTY GAZETTE (MEDINA, OHIO : 1982). (THE MEDINA COUNTY GAZETTE.). 150th year, No. 282 (Dec. 1, 1982)-. Newspaper. English. da. Medina County Gazette, 885 West Liberty Street, Medina OH 44256. ***Continues*** *Gazette (Medina, Ohio).*

US
MERCER COUNTY CHRONICLE (COLDWATER, OHIO : 1959). (MERCER COUNTY CHRONICLE.). Began with June 4, 1959 issue. Newspaper. English. wk. Mercer County Chronicle, 223 West Walnut and Market Station, Coldwater OH 45828. ***Separated from*** *Mercer County Chronicle-Journal.*

US
METRO PRESS. **VFOAT** Press. Vol. 1, No. 1 (Sept. 25, 1894)-. Newspaper. English. wk. $15.00. Metro Press, PO Box 169, Millbury OH 43447. **ED** Scott Carpenter. **Photos. Ad Acc, Adv Mgr:** Patty Toneff, **Tel** (418)836-2221. Full Page (B&W) $1,193.28. Half Page (B&W) $596.64. Full Page (Color) $1,553.28. Half Page (Color) $956.64. **Pub. Size:** Tabloid. ***Continues*** *Metro Update.*

US
MIDDLETOWN JOURNAL. Newspaper. English. ir. $124.80. Middletown Journal, PO Box 490, Middletown OH 45042. **Tel** (513)422-3611.

US
MONROE COUNTY BEACON, THE. Vol. 1, No. 1 (May 27, 1937)-. Newspaper. English. wk. $18.50 US; $23.00 other. Monroe County Beacon, 103 East Court Street, Woodsfield OH 43793-0070. **Tel** (614)472-0734. **ED** Pam Sloan.

US
MONROEVILLE SPECTATOR, THE. **VFOAT** Weekly Spectator. (Oct. 1870)-. Newspaper. English. wk. Monroeville Reporter, 40 South Main Street, Monroeville OH 44847.

US
MORROW COUNTY SENTINEL (MOUNT GILEAD, OHIO : 1859). (MORROW COUNTY SENTINEL.). (July 13, 1859)-. Newspaper. English. wk. Morrow County Sentinel, PO Box 149, Mount Gilead OH 43338. **Tel** (419)946-3010. ***Continues*** *Mount Gilead Sentinel.*

US
NEW WASHINGTON HERALD. Began publication in 1881. Newspaper. English. wk. $9.00. New Washington Herald, 625 South Kibler Street, New Washington OH 44854. **Tel** (419)492-2133, FAX (419)492-2128. **ED** Robert Bordner. **Ad Acc. Circ:** 1,300.

US
NEWCOMERSTOWN NEWS (1953). (NEWCOMERSTOWN NEWS.). Vol. 50, No. 25 (Mar. 4, 1948)-. Newspaper. English. wk. $14.00 Ohio; $16.00 US. The Jeffersonian Company, 140 West Main Street, Newcomerstown OH 43832. **Tel** (614)498-7117, FAX (614)498-5624. **ED** Ray Booth. **Bk Rev. Photos. Ad Acc, Adv Mgr:** Laura Bridges. Full Page (B&W) $399.90. Half Page (B&W) $204.75. Full Page (Color) $469.90. Half Page (Color) $274.75. **Pub. Size:** Standard. **Circ:** 3,400. ***Continues*** *Newcomerstown News and Index.*

US
NEWS-HERALD, THE. **VFOAT** News Herald. 64th Year, No. 74 (Mar. 29, 1955)-. Newspaper. English. da (Except Sundays & Holidays). $58.75 (nine months); $75.00 (one year). Conneaut News-Herald, 182 184 Broad Street, Conneaut OH 44030. **Tel** (216)593-1166. ***Continues*** *Conneaut News-Herald.*

US
NEWS JOURNAL (MANSFIELD, OHIO). (NEWS JOURNAL.). Vol. 80, No. 118 (July 2, 1964)-. Newspaper. English. da. $3.00 per week. Mansfield News Journal, 70 West 4th Street, Mansfield OH 44901. **Tel** (800)472-5547, (419)522-3311, FAX (419)522-2672. **ED** Bill Sedivy. Index available. **Photos. Ad Acc, Adv Mgr:** Ann Danuloff, **Tel** (419)522-3311. Full Page (B&W) $3502.80. Half Page (B&W) $1751.40. Full Page (Color) $4017.80. Half Page (Color) $2266.40. **Pub. Size:** Broadsheet. **Wire Svcs.:** KR. **Circ:** 50,000 (ctrl). available on microfilm and microfiche from University Microfilms International (UMI). ***Continues*** *Mansfield News-Journal.*

US
NEWS-MESSENGER, THE. **VFOAT** News Messenger. Vol. 117, No. 271 (Feb. 28, 1973)-. Newspaper. English. da. News-Messenger, 1700 Cedar Street, Fremont OH 43420. ***Continues*** *Fremont News-Messenger.*

US
NORTH BALTIMORE NEWS, THE. Vol. 1, No. 1 (April 13, 1933)-. Newspaper. English. wk. North Baltimore News, 114 North Main Street, North Baltimore OH 45872.

US
NORTHWEST-SIGNAL. **VFOAT** Northwest Signal; Northwest-Signal Digest. 109th Year, No. 37 (Sept. 7, 1960)-. Newspaper. English. da. $66.00 Henry County, Ohio; $72.00 Ohio; $78.00 other. Napoleon Inc., PO Box 567, 595 East Riverview, Napoleon OH 43545. **Tel** (419)592-5055. ***Formed by the union of*** *Northwest News (Napoleon, Ohio)* ***and*** *Henry County Signal (Napoleon, Ohio : 1865).*

US/0745-4023
NORWALK REFLECTOR (NORWALK, OHIO : DAILY). (NORWALK REFLECTOR.). 135th year, No. 131 (June 5, 1964)-. Newspaper. English. da. $91.00. Norwalk Reflector, 61 East Monroe, Norwalk OH 44857. **ED** Jim Brown, Jay Thwaite (Managing Editor). **Photos. Ad Acc, Adv Mgr:** John Ringenbeng. Full Page (B&W) $1221.63. Half Page (B&W) $610.82. Full Page (Color) $1471.63. Half Page (Color) $685.82. **Pub. Size:** Standard. **Wire Svcs.:** AP. **Circ:** 9,100. available in microform. ***Continues*** *Norwalk Reflector-Herald (Norwalk, Ohio : 1963).*

US
OHIO GRAPHIC. **VFOAT** Graphic Week. (1974)-. Newspaper. English. wk. Ohio Graphic, Eaton OH.

US
OJC THE OHIO JEWISH CHRONICLE, THE. **VFOAT** OJC Ohio Jewish Chronicle. Vol. 68, No. 39 (Sept. 20, 1990)-. Newspaper. English. wk (Published on Thursdays). $23.00. Ohio Jewish Chronicle, PO Box 30965, Columbus OH 43230. **Tel** (614)337-2055. **ED** Judith Franklin. **Bk Rev. Ad Acc, Adv Mgr:** Stephen Pinsky. ctrl circ. ***Continues*** *Ohio Jewish Chronicle.*

US
OTTAWA COUNTY EXPONENT, THE. (1881)-. Newspaper. English. Fifty-two times a year (Wednesdays). $22.00 Exponent County; $25.00 other. Exponent Publishing Co., 106 North Locust Street, Oak Harbor OH 43449. **Tel** (419)898-5361. ***Continues*** *Exponent (Oak Harbor, Ohio).*

US
PANDORA TIMES. **VFOAT** Times. Began in 1899. Newspaper. English. wk. Pandora Times, PO Box 167, Pandora OH 45877.

US
PAULDING COUNTY PROGRESS. **VFOAT** Paulding Progress. Vol. 112, No. 22 (Feb. 18, 1987)-. Newspaper. English. wk. $19.00. Paulding County Progress, PO Box 180, Paulding OH 45879. **Tel** (419)399-4015, FAX (419)399-4030. **ED** Anna Brewster. **Photos. Ad Acc, Adv Mgr:** Teri Daniels. Full Page (B&W) $554.70. Half Page (B&W) $277.35. Full Page (Color) $634.70. Half Page (Color) $357.35. **Pub. Size:** Standard. **Circ:** 3,742 (paid), 4,200 (2nd class). available in microform. ***Continues*** *Paulding Progress.*

US/1064-2021
PERRYSBURG MESSENGER-JOURNAL. **VFOAT** Perrysburg Messenger Journal. Vol. 112, No. 35 (Sept. 2, 1965)-. Newspaper. English. wk. $12.00 (Wood County), $17.00 (other). Perrysburg Messenger Journal, PO Box 267, Perrysburg OH 43551. **Tel** (419)874-4491. **ED** Robert C. Welch. **Ad Acc, Adv Mgr:** Matt Welch, **Tel** (419)874-4491. ***Formed by the union of*** *Perrysburg Journal (Perrysburg, Ohio : 1913)* ***and*** *Perrysburg Messenger.*

US/0191-7935
PHOTO STAR. Newspaper. English. wk. Photo Star, 307 State Street, Willshire OH 45898. ***Continues*** *Willshire Herald.*

US/0746-9101
PICKERINGTON TIMES-SUN, THE. **VFOAT** Pickerington Times Sun; Times Sun; Times-Sun. Vol. 7, No. 44 (Jan. 18, 1984)-. Newspaper. English. wk (Wed.). $20.00 Franklin County; $25.00 other. Suburban News Publications, PO Box 29912, Columbus OH 43229. **Tel** (614)785-1212, FAX (614)785-1881. **ED** Tim Krumlauf. **Circ:** 6,173. ***Continues*** *Times-Sun (Pickerington, Ohio), 0746-0481.*

US
PIQUA DAILY CALL (PIQUA, OHIO : 1927). (THE PIQUA DAILY CALL.). Vol. 44, No. 207 (June 17, 1927)-. Newspaper. English. da. Piqua Daily Call, 121 East Ash Street, Piqua OH 45356. ***Continues*** *Piqua Daily Call and Piqua Press-Dispatch.*

US
PLAIN DEALER (CLEVELAND, OHIO : 1961). (THE PLAIN DEALER.). **VFOAT** Sunday Plain Dealer. Vol. 120, No. 259 (Sept. 16, 1961)-. Newspaper. English. ds. $338.00 (daily & Sunday), $234.00 (daily), $130.00 (Sunday only) US; $676.00 (daily & Sunday), $468.00 (daily), $208.00 (Sunday only) other. Plain Dealer, PO Box 6730 T, Cleveland OH 44101. **Tel** (216)344-4600, FAX (216)694-6369. **ED** Thomas Vail. **Circ:** 452,343. available on microfilm from University Microfilms International (UMI); available on an online database (file 725/Full-Text) from DIALOG. ***Continues*** *Cleveland Plain Dealer (Cleveland, Ohio : 1885).* **Ind/Abst** PROMT.

US/0883-6523
POLAND LEADER. **VFOAT** Leader. Began in March 1985. Newspaper. English. wk. Phoenix Publications Inc. / Ohio, 35 West State Street, Niles OH 44446. **Tel** (216)652-5841. ***Continues*** *Poland Clarion.*

US/0746-6021
PORTAGE LAKES HERALD, THE. **VFOAT** Herald. Newspaper. English. wk. $10.00 (Summit County), $15.00 (outside Summit County). Barberton Herald, PO Box 831, Barberton OH 44203. **Tel** (216)753-1068. **Ad Acc. Circ:** 5,000 (ctrl).

US/8750-6963
PORTSMOUTH DAILY TIMES (1984), THE. (THE PORTSMOUTH DAILY TIMES.). **VFOAT** Daily Times. (1985)-. Newspaper. English. da. Thompson Brusmore Newspapers, PO Box 581, Portsmouth OH 45662. **Tel** (614)353-3101. ***Continues*** *Daily Times (Portsmouth, Ohio).*

US
PRESS-NEWS, THE. **VFOAT** Press News. Vol. 69, No. 8 (Oct. 12, 1967)-. Newspaper. English. wk. $16.50 Ohio; $18.50 other. Press News, PO Box 30170 121 W Nassau, East Canton OH 44740. **Tel** (216)488-0666. ***Formed by the union of*** *Sandy Valley Press; East Canton News* ***and*** *Observer (North Industry, Ohio).*

US
PROGRESSOR-TIMES. **VFOAT** Progressor Times. Vol. 4, No. 26 (June 30, 1971)-. Newspaper. English. wk. Progressor-Times, 109 West Findlay Street, Carey OH 43316. ***Formed by the union of*** *Carey Progressor* ***and*** *Carey Times.*

US
PUTNAM COUNTY SENTINEL (OTTAWA, OHIO : 1865). (PUTNAM COUNTY SENTINEL.). **VFOAT** Putnam Sentinel. Began with August 17, 1865 issue. Newspaper. English. wk. Putnam County Sentinel, PO Box 149, Ottawa OH 45875. ***Continues*** *Kalida Sentinel (Kalida, Ohio : 1855).*

US
PUTNAM COUNTY VIDETTE. Began in 1873. Newspaper. English. wk. Putnam County Vidette, 111 East Sycamore Street, Columbus Grove OH 45830.

US
RECORD-COURIER. **VFOAT** Record Courier. Vol. 131, No. 187 (Aug. 10, 1961)-. Newspaper. English. da. Ravenna Record Courier, 126 North Chestnut Street, Ravenna OH 44266. **Tel** (216)296-9657. **ED** Lucella Cordier. **Circ:** 23,740. ***Continues*** *Evening Record-Courier Tribune.*

US/0745-7545
REPOSITORY (CANTON, OHIO), THE. (THE REPOSITORY.). Vol. 163, No. 337 (Mar. 1, 1978)-. Newspaper. English. da. Price varies for Ohio; $97.45 other. Thomson Newspapers / Repository Division, 500 Market Avenue South, Canton OH 44702. **Tel** (216)454-5611 ext 365. **ED** Michael E. Hanke. **Ad Acc, Adv Mgr:** Michael Miller. **Circ:** 65,000 daily, 71,000 Sunday (ctrl). available on microfilm. ***Continues*** *Canton Repository (Canton, Ohio : 1939).* **Desc:** Daily newspaper for the Canton, Ohio area.

US
RIPLEY BEE (RIPLEY, OHIO : 1887). (THE RIPLEY BEE.). (1887)-. Newspaper. English. wk. $12.00. Ripley Bee, 110 Waterworks Road, Ripley OH 45167. **Tel** (513)392-4321, FAX (513)392-4124. **ED** Morgan Ross. **Photos. Ad Acc.** Full Page (B&W) $300.00. Half Page (B&W) $160.00. Full Page (Color) $450.00. Half Page (Color) $260.00. **Pub. Size:** Standard. **Circ:** 2,300. available in microform. ***Continues*** *Ripley Bee and Times.*

US
ROCKY FORK ENTERPRISE. Vol. 1, No. 1 (Aug. 15, 1963)-. Newspaper. English. wk. $15.00 (1 year), $27.00 (2 year), $40.00 (3 year) Ohio; $18.00 (1 year) other. Rocky Fork Enterprise, 110 North High Street, Gahanna OH 43230. **Tel** (614)471-1600, FAX (614)471-1764. ***Absorbed*** *Tri-Community News.*

US
ROSSFORD RECORD JOURNAL. Vol. 42, No. 5 (Jan 29, 1981)-. Newspaper. English. wk. $12.00 Wood county, $13.00 Ohio; $15.00 other. Rossford Record Journal, 117 East Second Street, Perysburg OH 43551. **Tel** (419)666-5344. **ED** Robert C. Welch. **Photos. Ad Acc, Adv Mgr:** Matt Welch, **Tel** (419)874-4491. Full Page (B&W) $619.20. Half Page (B&W) $309.60. Full Page (Color) $719.20. Half Page (Color) $409.60. **Pub. Size:** Broadsheet. **Circ:** 5,400. available in microform. ***Continues*** *Record (Rossford, Ohio).*

US/0192-9771
RURAL-URBAN RECORD. **VAT** Rural Urban Record. Newspaper. English. wk. Rural-Urban Record, 24487 Squire Road, Columbia Station OH 44028.

US
SALEM NEWS, THE. 17th Year, No. 211 (Sept. 8, 1905)-. Newspaper. English. da. Thomas Brush Moore Newspaper, 161 North Lincoln Street, Salem OH 44460. **Tel** (216)332-4601. ***Continues*** *Salem Daily News;* ***Absorbed*** *Salem Daily Herald.*

US
SANDUSKY REGISTER (SANDUSKY, OHIO : 1957). (SANDUSKY REGISTER.). Vol. 135, No. 41 (June 1, 1957)-. Newspaper. English. da. Sandusky Register, 314 West Market Street, Sandusky OH 44870. **Tel** (419)625-5500. ***Continues*** *Sandusky Register-Star-News.*

US
SEBRING TIMES, THE. (1907)-. Newspaper. English. wk. Sebring Times, 114 East Ohio, Sebring OH 44672.

US/0274-9408
SHAWNEE-CRIDERSVILLE PRESS. **VFOAT** Shawnee Cridersville Press. (August 1980)-. Newspaper. English. wk. $15.00. Daily News Printing Company, 8 Willipie Street, Wapakoneta OH 45895. ***Continues*** *Cridersville Press.*

US/0893-4592
SIGNAL (LISBON, OHIO). (THE SIGNAL.). (19??)-. Newspaper. English. wk. The Signal / Ohio, 117 A North Canal Street, PO Box, Canal Fulton OH 44614. **Tel** (216)854-4549, FAX (216)854-1928. **ED** Mark J. Knapik. Index available. cum. index. **Bk Rev. Photos. Ad Acc, Adv Mgr:** Tammy Thacker. **Pub. Size:** Broadsheet. **Circ:** 14,000 (morning) (ctrl).

US/0194-3677
SOLON TIMES, THE. Vol. 1, No. 1 (Aug. 3, 1978)-. Newspaper. English. wk. $22.50 Ohio; $26.50 others. Chagrin Solon Times, PO Box 150, Chagrin Falls OH 44022. **Tel** (216)247-5335, FAX (216)247-5335. **ED** David Lange. **Photos. Ad Acc, Adv Mgr:** Carole Vigliotti. Full Page (B&W) $1,272.00. Half Page (B&W) $636.00. Full Page (Color) $1,917.00. Half Page (Color) $958.50. **Pub. Size:** Tabloid. **Circ.** 4,000. **Desc:** Articles cover local news and features.

US/0891-2289
SOUTHEAST MESSENGER. Vol. 1, No. 1 (May 30, 1983)-. Newspaper. English. wk. $52.00. Columbus Messenger Company, 3378 Sullivant Avenue, P. Daubel, Columbus OH 43204. **Tel** (614)272-5422, (614)852-0809, FAX (614)852-0814. **ED** Becky Cassidy. **Photos. Ad Acc, Adv Mgr:** Bruce Russel, **Tel** (614)272-5422. Full Page (B&W) $1062.40. Half Page (B&W) $531.20. Full Page (Color) $1137.40. Half Page (Color) $606.20. **Pub. Size:** Tabloid. **Circ:** 29,852 (morning). available on microfilm from Bell & Howell.

US
SPIRIT OF DEMOCRACY (WOODSFIELD, OHIO : 1844). (THE SPIRIT OF DEMOCRACY.). Began with March 1, 1844 issue. Newspaper. English. wk. $18.20. Spirit of Democracy, 323 Eastern Avenue, Woodsfield OH 43793-0470. **ED** W E Moore. **Ad Acc. Circ:** 1,200 (ctrl). ***Absorbed*** *Monroe Gazette (Woodsfield, Ohio); Sentinel (Woodsfield, Ohio : 1906); Monroe County Democrat (Woodsfield, Ohio : 1937); Monroe County Republican (Woodsfield, Ohio).*

US/0744-6101
SPRINGFIELD NEWS-SUN. **VFOAT** Springfield News Sun. Vol. 1, No. 1 (May 3, 1982)-. Newspaper. English. da. Springfield Newspapers Inc / Ohio, 202 North Limestone Street, Springfield OH 45501. **Tel** (513)328-0277. **ED** Norman Pearson. **Ad Acc. Circ:** 38,000 daily, 44,000 Sunday. ***Formed by the union of*** *Springfield Daily News (Springfield, Ohio : 1909)* ***and*** *Sun (Springfield, Ohio).*

US/0744-771X
STEUBENVILLE REGISTER, THE. **Added/Corp** Catholic Church. Diocese of Steubenville (Ohio). (1945)-. Newspaper. English. bw. $12.00. The Steubenville Register, Box 160, 422 Washington Street, Steubenville OH 43952. **ED** James A. Boehm. **Photos. Ad Acc, Adv Mgr:** Janice Ward, **Tel** (614)282-6831. Full Page (B&W) $514.35. Half Page (B&W) $266.70. **Pub. Size:** Tabloid. **Wire Svcs.:** CS. **Circ:** 17,755. available in microform from University Microfilms International (UMI).

US/0192-9410
STOW SENTRY. **VFOAT** Sentry; Stow Sentry and Citizen. (1969)-. Newspaper. English. wk. Record Publishing Company / Ohio, 1619 Commerce Drive, Stow OH 44224. **Tel** (216)688-0088. ***Absorbed*** *Stow Citizen.*

US
SUNBURY NEWS, THE. Vol. 1, No. 1 (May 20, 1909)-. Newspaper. English. wk. $13.00 (OH residents); $15.00 (other). Sunbury News, PO Box 59, Sunbury OH 43074. **Tel** (614) 965-3891. **Photos. Ad Acc, Adv Mgr:** Mary Ann Pemberton. **Pub. Size:** Broadsheet. **Circ:** 3,250. available in microform. ***Continues*** *Delaware Co. News-Item.*

US
TALLMADGE EXPRESS. Vol. 4, No. 30 (Feb. 25, 1981)-. Newspaper. English. wk. Free to Talmadge residents; $20.00 other. Record Publishing Company / Ohio, 1619 Commerce Drive, Stow OH 44224. **Tel** (216)688-0088. ***Continues*** *Tallmadge Express & Circle News.*

US
TELEGRAM (MECHANICSBURG, OHIO). (THE TELEGRAM.). (19??)-. Newspaper. English. wk. The Telegram / London, Ohio, 30 South Oak Street, London OH 43140. ***Continues*** *Daily Telegram (Mechanicsburg, Ohio).*

US/8750-1503
TIMES-BULLETIN, THE. **VFOAT** Times Bulletin. Vol. 127, No. 266 (Apr. 2, 1973)-. Newspaper. English. da. $70.00 Van West County; $75.00 Ohio; $80.00 other. Times-Bulletin, PO Box 271, Van Wert OH 45891. **Tel** (419)238-2285. **ED** Larry Joseph. **Bk Rev. Ad Acc. Circ:** 8,300 (ctrl). available on microfilm. ***Continues*** *Van West Times Bulletin.*

US/0884-4135
TIMES (CANAL WINCHESTER, OHIO). (THE TIMES.). **VFOAT** Times-Sun. 31st year, No. 3 (Jan. 16, 1901)-. Newspaper. English. wk. $12.00 (in county); $15.00 other. Suburban News Publications, PO Box 29912, Columbus OH 43229. **Tel** (614)785-1212, FAX (614)785-1881. **ED** Martin Rozenman and Joe Meyer (Managing Editor). **Photos. Ad Acc, Adv Mgr:** Carol Zimmer. Full Page (B&W) $546.00. Half Page (B&W) $273.00. Full Page (Color) $681.00. Half Page (Color) $408.00. **Pub. Size:** Tabloid. **Circ:** 2,456. available in microform from University Microfilms International (UMI). ***Continues*** *Winchester Times (Canal Winchester, Ohio).*

US
TIMES-LEADER (MARTINS FERRY, OHIO). (THE TIMES-LEADER.). **VFOAT** Times Leader. (April 7, 1943)-. Newspaper. English. da. $133.50 Ohio and West Virginia; $163.00 other. Martins Ferry Times Leader, 200 South 4th Street, Martins Ferry OH 43935. **Tel** (614)633-1131. ***Continues*** *Daily Times and The Daily Leader;* ***Absorbed*** *St. Clairsville Gazette-Chronicle.*

US
TIMES RECORDER (ZANESVILLE, OHIO : 1965). (THE TIMES RECORDER.). **VFOAT** Sunday Times Recorder. 101st Year, No. 338 (Jan. 7, 1965)-. Newspaper. English. da (361 days of the year). $125.00 (one year) Ohio; $140.00 (one year) other. Zanesville Times Recorder, 34 South 4th Street, Zanesville OH 43701. **Tel** (614)452-4561. **ED** Nancy Keely. **Ad Acc, Adv Mgr:** Mike Kimmons, **Tel** (614)452-4561. ctrl circ. ***Continues*** *Times Recorder and Zanesville Signal.*
Desc: This publication is the local daily newspaper of the Zanesville, Ohio area.

US/0745-1989
TOLEDO UNION JOURNAL. Vol. 1 (1942)-. Newspaper. English. wk (48 issues per year). $10.00. Toledo Union Journal, 2300 Ashland Avenue, Toledo OH 43620. **Tel** (419)241-9126. **ED** Tom Whalen. **Circ:** 15,000.

US
TRIBUNE (COSHOCTON, OHIO). (THE TRIBUNE.). Vol. 76, No. 274 (April 1, 1986)-. Newspaper. English. ds. $117.00. The Tribune / Ohio, 115 North 6th Street, Coshocton OH 43812. **Tel** (614)622-1122, FAX (614)622-7341. **ED** Kenneth Smailes. **Photos. Ad Acc, Adv Mgr:** David Rich. Full Page (B&W) $1677.00. Half Page (B&W) $838.50. Full Page (Color) $1772.00. Half Page (Color) $933.50. **Pub. Size:** Broadsheet. **Wire Svcs.:** AP. available in microform from University Microfilms International (UMI). ***Continues*** *Coshocton Tribune (Coshocton, Ohio : 1929).*

US
TROY DAILY NEWS. VFOAT Miami Valley Sunday News. Began in 1909. Newspaper. English. da. Troy Daily News, 224 South Market Street, Troy OH 45373.

US/0882-7214
UNITED CHURCH NEWS (NATIONAL EDITION). (UNITED CHURCH NEWS.). [United church news]. Vol. 1, No. 1 (May 1985)-. Periodical. English. Ten times a year (Except January and July). $8.00. United Church of Christ / Ohio, 700 Prospective Avenue, Cleveland OH 44115. **Tel** (216)736-2150. **ED** W. Evan Golder. **DD** 205. **Ad Acc. Circ:** 100,000 (ctrl).
Desc: National publication for United Church of Christ clergy and laity. News and features on significant issues for church members and friends.

US/0194-2131
UPPER ARLINGTON NEWS, THE. (Aug. 31, 1954)-. Newspaper. English. wk. $20.00 Franklin County; $25.00 other. Suburban News Publications, PO Box 29912, Columbus OH 43229. **Tel** (614)785-1212, FAX (614)785-1881. **ED** Martin Rozenman and Joe Meyer (Managing Editor). **Photos. Ad Acc, Adv Mgr Tel** Carol Zimmer. Full Page (B&W) $764.40. Half Page (B&W) $382.20. Full Page (Color) $959.40 (spot color). Half Page (Color) $577.20 (spot color). **Pub. Size:** Tabloid. **Circ:** 22,547. available in microform from University Microfilms International (UMI).

US
URBANA DAILY CITIZEN (URBANA, OHIO : 1910). (THE URBANA DAILY CITIZEN.). (March 21, 1910)-. Newspaper. English. da. $163.00. Urbana Daily Citizen, 220 East Court Street, Urbana OH 43078. **Tel** (513)652-1331. ***Continues*** *Urbana Daily Times Citizen.*

US
UTICA HERALD (UTICA, OHIO : 1878). (THE UTICA HERALD.). (Feb. 14, 1878)-. Newspaper. English. wk. $20.00 Licking county, Martinburg and Bladensburg Ohio; $22.00 others in Ohio; $24.00 other. Utica Herald, PO Box 515, 120 South Main, Utica OH 43080. **Tel** (614)892-2771. **ED** Nelson A. Smith.

US
VERSAILLES POLICY, THE. (1875)-. Newspaper. English. wk. $18.00. Versailles Policy, 16 South Center Street, Versailles OH 45380. **ED** Scott Lanston. **Photos. Ad Acc, Adv Mgr:** Lynn Langston, **Tel** (513)526-9131. Full Page (B&W) $219.00. Half Page (B&W) $151.00. Full Page (Color) $294.00. Half Page (Color) $226.00.

US/0890-9857
VINDICATOR (YOUNGSTOWN, OHIO). (THE VINDICATOR.). Vol. 96, No. 1 (Sept. 1, 1984)-. Newspaper. English. da. The Vindicator / Ohio, PO Box 780, Youngstown OH 44501. **Tel** (216)746-6561. ***Continues*** *Youngstown Vindicator (Youngstown, Ohio : 1960).*

US
VINTON COUNTY COURIER, THE. Vol. 1, No. 1 (Aug. 4, 1971)-. Newspaper. English. wk. $20.00 (in county), $24.00 (out of county). Vinton County Courier, 106 North Market Street, PO Box 468, McArthur OH 45651. **Tel** (614)596-5393, FAX (614)286-5854. **ED** Dale Gardner. **Photos. Ad Acc, Adv Mgr:** Ardena Kessler. Full Page (B&W) $490.20. Half Page (B&W) $250.80. **Pub. Size:** Standard. available in microform. ***Continues*** *Democrat-Enquirer (McArthur, Ohio).*

US
WAPAKONETA DAILY NEWS, THE. Began with July 5, 1905 issue. Newspaper. English. da. Daily News Printing Company, 8 Willipie Street, Wapakoneta OH 45895.

US
WELLINGTON ENTERPRISE (WELLINGTON, OHIO : 1901). (THE WELLINGTON ENTERPRISE.). Began in April 1901. Newspaper. English. wk. Wellington Enterprise, PO Box 38, Wellington OH 44090. ***Continues*** *Wellington Enterprise and Observer.*

US
WELLSTON SENTRY, THE. Vol. 1, No. 1 (Aug. 3, 1971)-. Newspaper. English. sw. Wellston Sentry, PO Box 310, Wellston OH 45692.

US
WEST MILTON RECORD, THE. Began in 1892. Newspaper. English. wk. West Milton Record, PO Box 277, West Milton OH 45383.

US/8750-1872
WEST TOLEDOHERALD. VFOAT Herald. (19??)-. Newspaper. English. wk. $15.00. Allen C. Foster & Son Inc., 4444 West Alexis Road, Toledo OH 43623. **Tel** (419)475-6000. **ED** David Matile. **Photos. Ad Acc, Adv Mgr:** Thomas Nishwitz. Full Page (B&W) $1354.05. Half Page (B&W) $669.06. Full Page (Color) $1495.05. Half Page (Color) $735.06. **Pub. Size:** Broadsheet.

US/0746-9802
WESTLAKER TIMES, THE. VFOAT Times. (1983)-. Newspaper. English. wk. $26.00. Westlaker Times, PO Box 40216, Bay Village OH 44140. **Tel** (216)356-0920. **ED** E.J. Gottschaek, Mark Gottschaek (Managing Editor). **Bk Rev**, (Qty: 12 per year). **Photos. Ad Acc, Adv Mgr:** Eleaner J. Gottschaek. Full Page (B&W) $12.76 per inch. Half Page (B&W) $12.76 per inch. **Circ:** 3,000. available in microform.

US/0891-2297
WESTSIDE MESSENGER. Vol. 9, No. 19 (Sept. 6, 1982)-. Newspaper. English. wk. $52.00. Columbus Messenger Company, 3378 Sullivant Avenue, P. Daubel, Columbus OH 43204. **Tel** (614)272-5422, (614)852-0809, FAX (614)852-0814. **ED** Dan Tritschuh and Ken Drenten (Managing Editor). **Photos. Ad Acc, Adv Mgr:** Bruce Russel. Full Page (B&W) $1696.00. Half Page (B&W) $848.00. Full Page (Color) $1771.00. Half Page (Color) $923.00. **Pub. Size:** Tabloid. **Circ:** 46,828. available on microfilm from Bell & Howell. ***Continues*** *Columbus Messenger (West Ed.).*

US/8750-4650
XENIA DAILY GAZETTE, THE. (1984)-. Newspaper. English. da. $70.00. Chew Publishing Company, PO Box 400, Xenia OH 45385. ***Continues*** *Daily Gazette, 0747-0525.*

US
YELLOW SPRINGS NEWS. 12th Year, No. 19 (Sept. 21, 1905)-. Newspaper. English. wk. $33.00. Yellow Springs News, PO Box 187, Yellow Springs OH 45387. **ED** Amy Harper. **Photos. Ad Acc, Adv Mgr:** Karen Hernandez, **Tel** (513)767-7373. Full Page (B&W) $591.00. Half Page (B&W) $288.75. **Pub. Size:** Standard. **Circ:** 1,750. ***Continues*** *News (Yellow Springs, Ohio).*

OKLAHOMA

US
ALTUS TIMES, THE. (19??)-. Newspaper. English. da. Altus Times, 218-20 West Commerce Street, Altus OK 73521-3810. **Tel** (405)482-1221, FAX (405)482-5709. **ED** Rick Lomenick. **Ad Acc. Circ:** 6,796.

US
ALVA REVIEW-COURIER, THE. VFOAT Alva Review Courier. (19??)-. Newspaper. English. da. $59.00. Alva Review Courier, 620 Choctaw, Alva OK 73717-1600. **Tel** (405)327-2200, FAX (405)327-2454. **ED** Marione Martin. **Photos. Ad Acc, Adv Mgr:** Maggie Yates. Full Page (B&W) $280.00. Half Page (B&W) $140.00. Full Page (Color) $355.00. Half Page (Color) $215.00. **Pub. Size:** Tabloid. **Wire Svcs.:** AP. **Circ:** 1,860. ***Continues*** *Daily Alva Review-Courier.*

US/0744-1398
ANADARKO DAILY NEWS, THE. (1???)-. Newspaper. English. da. $66.00. Anadarko Daily News, PO Box 548, Anadarko OK 73005. **Tel** (405)247-3331, FAX (405)247-5571. **ED** Carolyn N. McBride (Editor-in-Chief) and Jack Stone (Managing Editor). **Bk Rev**, (Qty: 8-10). **Photos. Ad Acc, Adv Mgr:** Vic Brian. **Pub. Size:** Broadsheet. **Wire Svcs.:** AP. **Circ:** 5,976. available in microform from Oklahoma Historical Society.

US/0746-1623
ARGUS-TIMES, THE. VAT Argus Times. Vol. 80, No. 5 (Aug. 4, 1983)-. Newspaper. English. wk. Dan Connally, PO Box 1234, Guymon OK 73942-1234. ***Formed by the union of*** *Argus (Texhoma, Okla.)* ***and*** *Texhoma Times.*

US
ATOKA COUNTY TIMES, THE. VFOAT Atoka County Graphic; Atoka County Sunday Times. (1950)-. Newspaper. English. wk. $16.05 Atoka County; $21.40 Oklahoma; $25.00 other. Atoka County Times, PO Box 310, Atoka OK 74525. **Tel** (405)889-3319.

US/0883-7015
BARTLESVILLE EXAMINER-ENTERPRISE. VFOAT Bartlesville Examiner Enterprise; Examiner-Enterprise; Bartlesville, Oklahoma Examiner-Enterprise. (1???)-. Newspaper. English. da. Bartlesville Examiner, 300 East Frank Phillips Boulevard, PO Box 1278, Bartlesville OK 74005. **Tel** (918)336-1600.

US
BLACKWELL JOURNAL-TRIBUNE. VFOAT Blackwell Journal-Tribune; Blackwell Daily Journal Tribune. (1904)-. Newspaper. English. da. $66.00 Oklahoma; $90.00 others. Blackwell Journal Tribune, Box 760, Blackwell OK 74631. **Tel** (405)363-3370. **ED** Dayle E. McGaha. **Photos. Ad Acc, Adv Mgr:** Lamar Allen. Full Page (B&W) $709.50. Half Page (B&W) $354.75. Full Page (Color) $789.50. Half Page (Color) $434.75. **Pub. Size:** Broadsheet. **Wire Svcs.:** AP. **Circ:** 3,250. available on microfilm from Oklahoma Historical Society; and Microfilm Center, Inc. ***Formed by the union of*** *Blackwell Journal* ***and*** *Blackwell Morning Tribune.*

US
CHICKASHA DAILY EXPRESS, THE. (Jan. 1, 1900)-. Newspaper. English. da (Published daily except Saturday). $82.00. Chickasha Daily Express, PO Drawer E, Chickasha OK 73018. **Tel** (405)224-2600.

US
CHICKASHA STAR, THE. (19??)-. Newspaper. English. wk. Chickaska Star, PO Box 610, Chickaska OK 73018.

US/0745-7561
CITIZEN (JAY, OKLA.). (THE CITIZEN.). Began in 1983. Newspaper. English. wk. $6.18 Delaware, Mayes, Cherokee counties, $7.21 elsewhere in Oklahoma, $6.18 McDonald county, MO, $6.18 Benton county, AR, $9.00 elsewhere in US. The Citizen / Oklahoma, PO Box 660, Jay OK 74346. ***Continues*** *Jay Citizen.*

US
CLAREMORE DAILY PROGRESS. (1909)-. Newspaper. English. da (Tues., Fri., and Sun.). $66.00. Claremore Daily Progress, 315 West Will Rogers, Claremore OK 74017. **Tel** (918)341-1101. **ED** Dave Story (Editor-in-Chief) and Pat Reeder (Managing Editor). **LC** 9347-X. **Photos. Ad Acc, Adv Mgr:** Dave Kucifer, **Tel** (918)341-1195. Full Page (B&W) $741.75. Half Page (B&W) $390.00. Full Page (Color) $821.75. Half Page (Color) $470.00. **Pub. Size:** Standard. **Wire Svcs.:** AP. available on microfilm from University Microfilms International (UMI); and Oklahoma Historical Society.

US
CLINTON DAILY NEWS. (1929)-. Newspaper. English. da. $63.00 Oklahoma; $75.00 other. Clinton Daily News, 522 Avant Avenue, Clinton OK 73601. **Tel** (405)323-5151, FAX (405)323-5159. **ED** Charles Engleman. **Ad Acc, Adv Mgr:** Carla Miller. **Circ:** 5,326. ***Continues*** *Custer County Post-Dispatch;* ***Absorbed*** *Custer County Chronicle (Clinton, Okla. : 1927).*

US
COALGATE RECORD-REGISTER, THE. VFOAT Coalgate Record Register. Newspaper. English. wk. Coalgate Record-Register, 6 North Main Street, Coalgate OK 74538. ***Formed by the union of*** *Coal County Register* ***and*** *Coalgate Record.*

US/0746-4789
COUNTRY CONNECTION, THE. Newspaper. English. wk. $7.50 Oklahoma, $8.00 other. PO Box 206, Eakly OK 73033.

US
CUSHING CITIZEN, THE. (1907)-. Newspaper. English. da. $53.00. Cushing Citizen, 115 South Cleveland, Cushing OK 74023-3719. **Tel** (918)225-3333, FAX (918)225-1050. **ED** Terry Hoggatt. **Bk Rev**, (Qty: 6). **Photos. Ad Acc, Adv Mgr:** Brian Hammock. Full Page (B&W) $617.49. Half Page (B&W) $308.70. Full Page (Color) $692.40. Half Page (Color) $385.70. **Pub. Size:** Broadsheet. **Wire Svcs.:** AP. **Circ:** 3,200.

US/1065-7894
DAILY ARDMOREITE, THE. VFOAT Sunday Ardmoreite-Press; Sunday Ardmoreite Press. (Oct. 28, 1893)-. Newspaper. English. da. PO Box 1328, Ardmore OK 73401. **Tel** (405)223-2200. **ED** Bill Stauffer. **LC** 7002. **Circ:** 13,369 daily, 15,991 Sunday. available on microfilm from Microfilm Center, Inc.; and Oklahoma Historical Society.

US
EDMOND EVENING SUN, THE. VFOAT Edmond Sunday. Vol. 86, No. 37 (Dec. 12, 1976)-. Newspaper. English. da. $73.00. Edmond Sun, PO Box 2470, Edmond OK 73084. **Tel** (405)341-2121, FAX (405)340-7363. **ED** Carol Hartzog. **Bk Rev**, (Qty: 20). **Photos**. **Ad Acc**, **Adv Mgr:** Jack Hovorka, **Tel** (405)341-2121 ext. 130. Full Page (B&W) $1,161.00. Half Page (B&W) $580.50. Full Page (Color) $1,231.00. Half Page (Color) $650.00. **Pub. Size:** Standard. **Wire Svcs.:** AP. **Circ:** 10,200 (weekdays), 10,800 (Sundays). available in microform from Oklahoma Historical Society. ***Continues*** *Edmond Sun (Edmond, Okla. : 1900);* ***Absorbed*** *Edmond Booter.*

US
ELK CITY DAILY NEWS, THE. (1901)-. Newspaper. English. da. $63.00 locally and in county; $84.00 others. Elk City Daily News, 200-206 West Broadway, PO Box 1037, Elk City OK 73644. **Tel** (405)225-3000. **ED** Larry R. Wade (Editor-in-Chief) and Bob Fisher (Managing Editor). **LC** 9347-X. **Bk Rev**. **Photos**. **Ad Acc**, **Adv Mgr:** Sharon Penny. **Pub. Size:** Standard. **Wire Svcs.:** AP. **Circ:** 5,126 (Mon., Tues., Thurs., & Sun.), 10,036 (Wed. & Sat). available on microfilm from Microfilm Center, Inc. ***Continues*** *Elk City News-Democrat.*

US
ENID MORNING NEWS, THE. VFOAT News. Began with Feb. 1923 issue. Newspaper. English. da. 227 West Broadway, Enid OK 73701. **Tel** (405)233-6600. **ED** Todd Garber. **Circ:** 18,481 daily, 26,157 Sunday. available on microfilm from University Microfilms International (UMI); and Microfilm Center, Inc. ***Continues*** *Enid Daily News.*

US
FAIRVIEW REPUBLICAN. (1???)-. Newspaper. English. wk. Fairview Republican, PO Box 497, Fairview OK 73737-0497. **Tel** (405)227-4439, FAX (405)227-4430. **ED** Dave Altman. **Ad Acc**. **Circ:** 3,300.

US
FREDERICK LEADER, THE. Began in 1917. Newspaper. English. da. Frederick Leader, 304-306 West Grand, Frederick OK 73542.

US
GROVE SUN, THE. (1904)-. Newspaper. English. sw. $16.96 Delaware County; $23.32 Oklahoma; $22.00 US. Sun / Grove, PO Box 969, 14 West 3rd Street, Grove OK 74344. ***Continues*** *Grove Messenger;* ***Absorbed*** *Delaware County News* ***and*** *Jay Record.*

US
GUTHRIE DAILY LEADER, THE. Began in 1892. Newspaper. English. da. Guthrie Daily Leader, 107-109 West Harrison, Guthrie OK 73044. ***Absorbed*** *Oklahoma State Capital (Guthrie, Okla. : Daily); Weekly Oklahoma State Capital (Guthrie, Okla. : 1893).*

US
HEAVENER LEDGER. Began in 1904. Newspaper. English. wk. Heavener Ledger, 507 East 1st Street, Heavener OK 74937.

US
HENNESSEY CLIPPER. Vol. 1, No. 1 (June 13, 1890)-. Newspaper. English. wk. Hennessey Clipper, 117 South Main Street, Hennessey OK 73742.

US
HERALD-DEMOCRAT (BEAVER, OKLA.). (THE HERALD-DEMOCRAT.). VFOAT Herald Democrat. Vol. 37, No. 1 (July 17, 1924)- = v. 15, no. 6-. Newspaper. English. wk. Herald-Democrat, 108 South Douglas, Beaver OK 73932. ***Continues*** *Beaver Herald and Democrat;* ***Absorbed*** *Forgan Advocate.*

US
HOMINY NEWS-PROGRESS, THE. VFOAT Hominy News Progress. Vol. 1, No. 1 (Nov. 4, 1971)-. Newspaper. English. wk. Hominy News Progress, 115 West Main, PO Box 38, Hominy OK 74035-1031. **Tel** (918)885-2101. ***Formed by the union of*** *Hominy News* ***and*** *Hominy Progress (Hominy, Okla.).*

US
HUGO DAILY NEWS, THE. (1913)-. Newspaper. English. da. Hugo Daily News, 128 East Jackson, Hugo OK 74743-4082. **Tel** (405)326-3311, FAX (405)326-6397. **ED** Stan Stamper. **Ad Acc**, **Adv Mgr:** Linda Packard. **Circ:** 3,100.

US
KINGFISHER FREE PRESS, THE. (June 1913)-. Newspaper. English. sw. $26.00. Kingfisher Free Press, PO Box 209, Kingfisher OK 73750. **ED** Gary Reid. **LC** 9349. **Photos**. **Ad Acc**, **Adv Mgr:** Barry Reid. Full Page (B&W) $541.80. Half Page (B&W) $270.90. Full Page (Color) $606.80. Half Page (Color) $335.90. **Pub. Size:** Standard. available on microfilm from Oklahoma Historical Society. ***Continues*** *Kingfisher Weekly Star and Free Press.*

US
KIOWA INDIAN NEWS. VFOAT Kiowa News; Gkaoy Gkoot Pighgyah. Vol. 4, No. 5 (Oct. 1976)-. Newspaper. English. mo. Kiowa Indian News, PO Box 361, Carnegie OK 73015. available on microfilm. ***Continues*** *Kiowa Tribal Newsletter.*

US/0745-9017
LAKE EUFAULA WORLD. Newspaper. English. wk. Lake Eufaula World, Route 4/Box 183, Eufaula OK 74432.

US/0889-566X
LAWTON CONSTITUTION, THE. VFOAT Lawton Constitution & Morning Press. (1911)-. Newspaper. English. da. Lawton Publishing Company, PO Box 2069, Lawton OK 73502. **Tel** (405)353-0620. available on microfilm from Microfilm Center, Inc. ***Continues*** *Constitution Democrat (Lawton, Okla.).*

US/0746-3235
LAWTON MORNING PRESS. ***Ceased.*** **VFOAT** Press. (19??)-(19??). Newspaper. English. da. Lawton Publishing Company, PO Box 2069, Lawton OK 73502. **Tel** (405)353-0620.

US/0896-4661
LOGAN COUNTY NEWS (CRESCENT, OKLA.). (THE LOGAN COUNTY NEWS.). VFOAT News. Began in 1902. Newspaper. English. wk. Logan County News, 108 North Grand, Crescent OK 73028.

US
MADILL RECORD, THE. (191?)-. Newspaper. English. wk. $15.00 local; $25.00 Oklahoma & Texas; $30.00 US. Madill Record, 211 Plaza, Madill OK 73446. **ED** Wilbert Wiggs. **Bk Rev**. **Photos**. **Ad Acc**, **Adv Mgr:** Sam McKenzie. Full Page (B&W) $4.00 per inch. Half Page (B&W) $4.00 per inch. Full Page (Color) $4.00 per inch plus $80.00. Half Page (Color) $4.00 per inch plus $80.00. **Pub. Size:** Broadsheet. available in microform.

US
MCALESTER NEWS-CAPITAL, THE. **VFOAT** McAlester News Capital. (1896)-. Newspaper. English. da. McAlester News Capital, 500 South Second Street, McAlester OK 74502. **Tel** (918)423-1700, FAX (918)426-3081. **ED** Don Luke. **Ad Acc**, **Adv Mgr:** Kay Coffee. **Circ:** 12,500.

US
MCCURTAIN GAZETTE. (1905)-. Newspaper. English. ir (Published on Tuesday-Friday & Sunday). $44.00. McCurtain Daily Gazette, 107 South Central, Idabel OK 74745. **Tel** (405)286-3321, FAX (405)286-2208. **ED** Bruce Willingham. **LC** 7002. **Ad Acc**, **Adv Mgr:** Margie Jones. **Circ:** 6,200 evening, 8,600 Sunday. available on microfilm from Oklahoma Historical Society. ***Continues*** *Signal.*

US
MIAMI NEWS-RECORD. VFOAT Miami News Record. Began in 1900. Newspaper. English. da. Miami News-Record, PO Box 940, Miami OK 74354.

US/8750-5908
MIDTOWN NEWS. VFOAT Midtownnews. Newspaper. English. wk. Midtown News, PO Box 61310, Oklahoma City OK 73146-1310. ***Continues*** *Northwest Quill.*

US/0747-1947
MOORE AMERICAN, THE. (19??)-. Monographic series. English. wk. $26.50 Oklahoma, $36.00 other. Engleman Newspapers, PO Box 6739, Moore OK 73153. **Tel** (405)794-5555. ***Continues*** *Monitor.*

US
MUSKOGEE DAILY PHOENIX AND TIMES-DEMOCRAT. VFOAT Muskogee Daily Phoenix and Times Democrat. Vol. 70, No. 130 (May 31, 1971)-. Newspaper. English. Fifty-two times a year. $10.75 (per month). Oklahoma Press Publishing Co., 214 Wall Street, PO Box 1968, Muskogee OK 74401. **Tel** (918)684-2888, FAX (918)684-2878. **ED** George Beuge. **Bk Rev**. **Photos**. **Ad Acc**, **Adv Mgr:** DeAnn Anderson, **Tel** (918)684-2804. Full Page (B&W) $2,191.71. Half Page (B&W) $1,121.34. Full Page (Color) $2,451.71. Half Page (Color) $1,381.34. **Pub. Size:** Broadsheet. **Wire Svcs.:** AP, GN, NE. **Circ:** 20,000 (ctrl). available in microform from Oklahoma Historical Society. ***Formed by the union of*** *Muskogee Daily Phoenix* ***and*** *Muskogee Times-Democrat.*
Desc: General daily newspaper, oriented to local news.

US
MUSKOGEE-PHOENIX. English. Fifty-two times a year. $117.30 Oklahoma, $129.00 others daily & Sunday. Oklahoma Press Publishing Co., 214 Wall Street, PO Box 1968, Muskogee OK 74401. **Tel** (918)684-2888, FAX (918)684-2878.

US/0161-8016
NATIONAL REPORTER (BIXBY). (NATIONAL REPORTER.). Periodical. English. mo. $10.00 US; $12.00 Canada. Lost Treasure Inc, PO Box 1589, Grove OK 74344. **Tel** (918)496-8169.

US
NEW CHEROKEE ADVOCATE, THE. Vol. 1, No. 1 (May 3, 1950)-. Newspaper. English (Cherokee). mo. $12.50. Cherokee Nation of Oklahoma, PO Box 948, Tahlequah OK 74465. **Tel** (918)456-0671, FAX (918)456-6485. **ED** Lynn Howard (Editor-in-Chief) and Marsha Harlan (Managing Editor). **Photos**. **Ad Acc**. **Pub. Size:** Standard. available in microform.

US
NORMAN TRANSCRIPT (NORMAN, OKLA.). (THE NORMAN TRANSCRIPT.). (1913)-. Newspaper. English. da. Norman Transcript, PO Drawer 1058, 215 East Commanche, Norman OK 73069. **Tel** (405)321-1800.

US/8750-3719
NORTH CADDO COUNTY NEWS, THE. Newspaper. English. wk. Richard and Susan Hume, 108 East Main, Hinton OK 73047. **ED** Richard W Hume. **Circ:** 1,860.

US/8750-393X
OKARCHE CHIEFTAIN, THE. VAT Oklahoma Arapacho Cheyenne Chieftain. Newspaper. English. wk. Okarchie Chieftain, PO Box 468, Okarche OK 73762.

US/0030-171X
OKLAHOMA DAILY, THE. **Added/Corp** University of Oklahoma. (1916)-. Newspaper. English. da (Monday - Friday). $60.00 (Semester); $150.00 (1 year). University of Oklahoma / Oklahoma Daily, 860 Van Vleet Oval, Room 149A, Norman OK 73019-0270. **Tel** (405)325-2521, FAX (405)325-7517. **ED** (phone: (405)325-5190), Editor's changes each semester. **Ad Acc**, **Adv Mgr:** Susan Sasso, **Tel** (405)325-2521. **Circ:** 14,550 fall/spring (ctrl).

US/0745-385X
OKLAHOMA EAGLE, THE. (1922)-. Newspaper. English. wk. $21.00. Oklahoma Eagle Publishing Company, PO Box 3267, Tulsa OK 74101. **Tel** (918)582-7124. **ED** Mike Staniford. **Bk Rev**. **Photos**. **Ad Acc**, **Adv Mgr:** Jerry Goodwin. Full Page (B&W) $1386.00. Half Page (B&W) $693.00. Full Page (Color) add $125.00 per color. Half Page (Color) add $125.00 per color. **Pub. Size:** Broadsheet. **Circ:** 13,000 paid.

US/0746-7559
PERRY DAILY JOURNAL, THE. Began in 1914. Newspaper. English. da. Perry Daily Journal, 714 Delaware Street, Perry OK 73077.

US
PONCA CITY NEWS, THE. (1897)-. Newspaper. English. da (except Sat.). $89.00. Ponca City Publishing Co., 300 North 3rd Street, PO Box 191, Ponca City OK 74602. **Tel** (405)765-3311, FAX (405)762-6397. **ED** Allan W. Muchmore (Editor-in-Chief) and Foster Johnson (Managing Editor). **Photos**. **Ad Acc**, **Adv Mgr:** Elec Rains. Full Page (B&W) $1,032.00. Half Page (B&W) $516.00. Full Page (Color) $1,112.00. Half Page (Color) $596.00. **Pub. Size:** Broadsheet. **Wire Svcs.:** AP. **Circ:** 12,500 (paid, Sunday), 14,000 (paid) (ctrl). available in microform.

US
PURCELL REGISTER, THE. VFOAT Purcell Weekly Register. Vol. 1, No. 1 (Nov. 23, 1887)-. Newspaper. English. wk. $12.00. Purcell Register, 225 West Main Street, PO Box 191, Purcell OK 73080. **ED** John D. Montgomery (Editor-in-Chief) and Bill Moakley (Managing Editor). **Photos**. **Ad Acc**, **Adv Mgr:** Vickie Foreaker, **Tel** (405)527-2126. Full Page (B&W) $598.50. Half Page (B&W) $313.50. **Pub. Size:** Broadsheet. available in microform.

US/8750-8508
REVIEW (SHIDLER, OKLA.), THE. (THE REVIEW.). Vol. 60, No. 25 (Feb. 21, 1985)-. Newspaper. English. wk. $15.00. The Review / Oklahoma, PO Box 6, Shidler OK 74652. **ED** Brenda Lawless. **Photos**. **Ad Acc**, **Adv Mgr:** Brenda Lawless, **Tel** (918)793-3841. Full Page (B&W) $375.00. Half Page (B&W) $250.00. **Pub. Size:** Standard. ***Continues*** *Shidler Review.*

US
SAND SPRINGS LEADER. Began in 1914. Newspaper. English. wk. Sand Springs Leader, 303 North McKinley, Sand Springs OK 74063.

US
SENTINEL LEADER, THE. Began in 1904. Newspaper. English. wk. Sentinel Leader, PO Box 37, Sentinel OK 73664.

US
SHAWNEE NEWS-STAR. VFOAT Shawnee News Star. (1944)-. Newspaper. English. da. Shawnee News Company, PO Box 1688, Shawnee OK 74802. **Tel** (405)273-4200. **ED** John Tucker. **Circ:** 13,555 daily, 14,692 Sunday. available on microfilm from Oklahoma Historical Society. ***Formed by the union of*** *Shawnee Morning News* ***and*** *Shawnee Evening Star.*

US/1056-7550
SHAWNEE SUN (SHAWNEE, OKLA.), THE. (THE SHAWNEE SUN.). (1991)-. Newspaper. English. wk. The Shawnee Sun, 114 North Broadway, Shawnee OK 74801-3578.

US
TONKAWA NEWS, THE. (1898)-. Newspaper. English. wk. $16.50. Tonkawa News, 108 North 7th Street, Tonkawa OK 74653. **ED** Lyle Becker. **Bk Rev**, (Qty: 12). **Photos**. **Ad Acc**, **Adv Mgr:** Lyle Becker, **Tel** $405)628-2532. Full Page (B&W) $580.50. Half Page (B&W) $290.25. Full Page (Color) $660.50. Half Page (Color) $370.25. **Pub. Size:** Broadsheet. available in microform from Oklahoma Historical Society.

US/0745-5747
TULSA BUSINESS CHRONICLE. ***Ceased.*** Vol. 1, No. 1 (Sept. 13, 1982)-(1992). Newspaper. English. wk. Tulsa Business Chronicle, 315 South Boulder Avenue, Tulsa OK 74103. **Tel** (918)581-8560. **(Subscription address:** PO Box 1770, Tulsa OK 74102**)** **ED** Bill Sansing and John Stancavage. **Ad Acc**. **Circ:** 2,000. available on an online database (file 635/Full-Text) from DIALOG. Documents available from UMI Article Clearinghouse.
Desc: Contains local business features, new business, real estate, stock tips, local stock listing, corporate ladder, legals, and columns by editors.
Ind/Abst Bus. Dateline; Bus. Index (Jan. 1985-Dec. 1985); Gen. BusinessFile (Jan. 1985-Dec. 1985); Gen. Period. Index (Jan. 1985-Dec. 1985).

US
TULSA TRIBUNE, THE. ***Ceased.*** Vol. 16, No. 85 (Jan. 1, 1920)-(1992). Newspaper. English. da. The Tulsa Tribune, 315 South Boulder, PO Box 1770, Tulsa OK 74102. **Tel** (918)581-8400, FAX (918)583-3550. **ED** J L Jones. **LC** 7002. **Circ:** 75,405. available on microfilm from University Microfilms International (UMI). ***Continues*** *Tulsa Tribune-Democrat.*

US/8750-5959
TULSA WORLD (TULSA, OKLA.). (TULSA WORLD.). Vol. 72, No. 266 (June 9, 1977)-. Newspaper. English. da. $126.00 Oklahoma; $145.50 Kansas & Missouri; $138.00 other US; $160.00 other. World Publishing Company / Tulsa, PO Box 1770, 315 South Boulder, Tulsa OK 74102. **Tel** (918)581-8596, FAX (918)583-3550. **ED** Robert Haring. **Circ:** 131,816 daily, 231,473 Sunday. available on microfilm from University Microfilms International (UMI); available on an online database (file 635/Full-Text) from DIALOG. Documents available from UMI Article Clearinghouse. ***Continues*** *Tulsa Daily World (Tulsa, Okla. : 1927).*
Ind/Abst Bus. Dateline; PROMT.

US
VINITA DAILY JOURNAL. Began in 1918. Newspaper. English. da. Vinita Daily Journal, 138-140 South Wilson, Vinita OK 74301.

US
WAKITA HERALD, THE. Began in 1897. Newspaper. English. wk. Wakita Herald, 117 South Locust, Wakita OK 73771.

US/8750-0701
WAURIKA NEWS-DEMOCRAT. **VFOAT** Waurika News Democrat; News Democrat. (191?)-. Newspaper. English. wk. Waurika News-Democrat Publishing Company, 117 West Broadway, Waurika OK 73573. **Tel** (405)228-2316.

US/0746-4339
WELEETKAN, THE. 1st Year, No. 1 (May 9, 1975)-. Newspaper. English. wk. $13.55. Weleetkan, Box 427, 108 West 9th Street, Weleetkan OK 74880. **Tel** (405)786-2224, FAX (405)452-3329. **ED** William C. Mayer. **Photos**. **Ad Acc**, **Adv Mgr:** Polly Everett or Ronda Clinesmith. Full Page (B&W) $283.50. Half Page (B&W) $141.75. Full Page (Color) $358.50. Half Page (Color) $216.75. **Pub. Size:** Standard. available in microform.

US/0883-8755
WOODWARD NEWS. **VFOAT** News. Newspaper. English. da. $25.00. Woodward News, 1222 10th Street, Woodward OK 73802. ***Continues*** *Woodward Journal, 0746-4010.*

OREGON

US
ARGUS OBSERVER. (19??)-. Newspaper. English. da (Sunday - Friday). $108.00 Malheur, Baker, Payette & Washington counties; $145.80 other. Argus Observer / Oregon, PO Box 130, 1160 Southwest 4th Street, Ontario OR 97914. **Tel** (503)889-5387. **Ad Acc**.

US
BAKER CITY HERALD. (19??)-. Newspaper. English. da. Baker City Herald / Oregon, PO Box 807, Baker OR 97814. **Tel** (503)523-3673. ***Continues*** *Democrat Herald, 8756-6419.*

US
BEND BULLETIN, THE. **VFOAT** Bend Bulletin and Central Oregon Press. (1???)-. Bulletin. English. da. $154.00. Bend Bulletin, 1526 NW Hill Street, Bend OR 97701. **Tel** (503)385-5800. **ED** Robert Chandler. **Ad Acc**. **Circ:** 24,800.

US
CANBY HERALD. Newspaper. English. wk (Published on Wednesdays). $28.00 Clackamas & North Marion counties in Oregon; $31.00 other counties in Oregon; $35.00 others in US. Canby Herald, PO Box 250, Canby OR 97013. **Tel** (503)266-6831.

US/0740-3704
CAPITAL PRESS. (19??)-. Periodical. English. wk (Published on Friday). $30.00 (one year), $45.00 (two year). Press Publishing Company / Oregon, PO Box 2048, Salem OR 97308. **Tel** (503)364-4431. **ED** Carolyn Homen. **Ad Acc**, **Adv Mgr:** Mr. Schultz, **Tel** (503)364-4798. **Circ:** 36,000.

US/0739-9758
CHRONICLE (CRESWELL, OR.). (THE CHRONICLE.). (1???)-. Newspaper. English. wk. $15.00 in county; $18.00 others. Lane Community Newspapers, PO Box 428, Creswell OR 97426. **ED** Gerri O'Rourke. **Photos**. **Ad Acc**, **Adv Mgr:** Gerri O'Rourke, **Tel** $503)895-2197. Full Page (B&W) $388.50. Half Page (B&W) $194.25. Full Page (Color) $488.50. Half Page (Color) $294.25. **Pub. Size:** Tabloid. **Circ:** 3,400.

US/0746-0260
CLACKAMAS COUNTY REVIEW, THE. (19??)-. Newspaper. English. wk. $18.00 Clackamas County, $23.00 Oregon, $28.00 other. Clackamas County Review, PO Box 1520, Clackamas OR 97015. **Tel** (503)656-4101. ***Continues*** *New Review.*

US/0746-3995
CORVALLIS GAZETTE-TIMES. **VFOAT** Corvallis Gazette Times. (1???)-. Newspaper. English. da. $166.40 Oregon; $156.00 Benton County, Oregon; $172.90 other US; $390.00 other. Corvallis Gazette-Times, PO Box 368, Corvallis OR 97330. **Tel** (503)753-2641. **ED** Dan Shryock. **Ad Acc**. **Circ:** 14,000.

US
COTTAGE GROVE SENTINEL. Newspaper. English. Fifty-two times a year. $16.80 Lane & Douglas counties; $24.00 others. Cottage Grove Sentinel, 116 North 6th Street, Cottage Grove OR 97424. **Tel** (503)942-3325, FAX (503)942-3328. **ED** Jody Rolnick.

US/0739-5078
DAILY ASTORIAN, THE. (19??)-. Newspaper. English. da. $6.00 (per month) local; $7.00 (per month) other. Astorian Budget Publishing Company, PO Box 210, Astoria OR 97103. **Tel** (503)325-3211, FAX (503)325-6573. **ED** Stephen Forrester, Dan Carter. **Bk Rev**, (Qty: 25). **Photos**. **Ad Acc**, **Adv Mgr:** Charles Swift. Full Page (B&W) $1253.70. Half Page (B&W) $626.85. Full Page (Color) $1343.70. Half Page (Color) $716.85. **Pub. Size:** Standard. **Wire Svcs.:** AP.

US/0747-3443
DALLES CHRONICLE, THE. **VFOAT** Chronicle. (April 1948)-. Newspaper. English. da. $97.00. Dalles Chronicle, 414 Federal Street, The Dalles OR 97058. **Tel** (503)296-2141. **ED** Tom Stevenson. **LC** 9356. **Photos**. **Ad Acc**, **Adv Mgr:** Skop Tschanz. Full Page (B&W) $1,360.95. Half Page (B&W) $679.42. Full Page (Color) $1,444.95. Half Page (Color) $763.42. **Pub. Size:** Standard. **Wire Svcs.:** AP. available on microfilm from University Microfilms International (UMI). ***Continues*** *Dalles Daily Chronicle.*

US/8756-6419
DEMOCRAT HERALD (BAKER, OR.). ***Title Change.*** (DEMOCRAT HERALD.). (19??)-(19??). Newspaper. English. da. Baker City Herald / Oregon, PO Box 807, Baker OR 97814. **Tel** (503)523-3673. **ED** Gary Middleton. **Circ:** 3,067. ***Continued by*** *Baker City Herald.*

US
DRAIN ENTERPRISE. (19??)-. English. Fifty-two times a year. $10.50 Douglas County. Drain Enterprise, PO Box 26, Drain OR 97435. **Tel** (503)836-2241. **ED** Sue Anderson, Betty Anderson (Managing Editor). **Photos**. **Ad Acc**. Full Page (B&W) $184.00. Half Page (B&W) $92.00. **Pub. Size:** Tabloid. **Circ:** 1,600. available in microform.

US
EAST OREGONIAN. (19??)-. Newspaper. English. da (312 issues per year - no Sunday edition). $144.00 Oregon; $168.00 other. East Oregonian, PO Box 1089, Pendleton OR 97801. **Tel** (503)276-2211, FAX (503)278-2688, (503)276-8314. **ED** Bill Crampton. **Photos**. **Ad Acc**, **Adv Mgr:** Al Donnelly. Full Page (B&W) $1457.70. Half Page (B&W) $728.85. Full Page (Color) $1552.70. Half Page (Color) $823.85. **Pub. Size:** Standard. **Wire Svcs.:** AP, NY.

US/0747-4067
ENTERPRISE (BOARDMAN, OR.), THE. (THE ENTERPRISE.). (198?)-. Newspaper. English. wk. The Enterprise / Oregon, PO Box 21, Boardman OR 97818-0021. **Tel** (503)481-7881. **ED** Donna Schmidt. **Circ:** 310.

US/0746-6404
FOODDAY UPDATE. **VFOAT** Food Day Update. (19??)-. Newspaper. English. wk. Oregonian Publishing Company, 1320 South West Broadway, Portland OR 97201. **Tel** (503)221-8109. ***Continues*** *Fooday.*

US
GRANTS PASS DAILY COURIER. Newspaper. English. da (312 issues per year - no Sunday edition). $90.00 Josephine county; $117.00 others. Grants Pass Daily Courier, PO Box 1468, 409 7th Street Southeast, Grants Pass OR 97526. **Tel** (503)474-3702.

US
GRESHAM OUTLOOK. English. sw (Wed. & Sat.). $34.00 residents in Muttnomah County; $38.00 others. Gresham Outlook, PO Box 747, Gresham OR 97030. **Tel** (503)661-3200.

US
HEADLIGHT HERALD. Newspaper. English. wk (Published on Wednesdays). $20.00 Tillamook county; $30.00 other. Headlight Herald, PO Box 444, Tillamook OR 97141. **Tel** (503)842-7535.

US/8750-4782
HERMISTON HERALD AND BUYER'S BONUS, THE. **VFOAT** Hermiston Herald. (19??)-. Newspaper. English. wk (Published on Tuesdays). $18.50 Umatilla and Morrow Counties, $38.50 other. Hermiston Herald, PO Box 46, Hermiston OR 97838. **Tel** (503)567-6457, FAX (503)567-6479. **ED** David Kennard. **Ad Acc**, **Adv Mgr:** Dan Zimmerman. **Circ:** 4,200 (ctrl).

US/8750-5479
HILLSBORO ARGUS (HILLSBORO, OR.). (HILLSBORO ARGUS.). (1???)-. Newspaper. English. sw (Tues. & Thurs.). $28.00. Hillsboro Argus, 150 South 3rd Street, Hillsboro OR 97123. **ED** Val Hess. **Bk Rev**, (Qty: 5). **Photos**. **Ad Acc**, **Adv Mgr:** Kent Johnson, **Tel** (503)648-1131. Full Page (B&W) $1,083.60. Half Page (B&W) $541.80. Full Page (Color) $1,193.60. Half Page (Color) $596.80. **Pub. Size:** Standard. **Circ:** 14,750.

US/0746-5823
HOOD RIVER NEWS. (1???)-. Newspaper. English. sw. Hood River News, PO Box 390, Hood River OR 97031. **Tel** (503)386-1234.

US/0889-2369
LAKE OSWEGO REVIEW. (19??)-. Newspaper. English. Fifty-two times a year (Thurs.). $22.00 Lake Oswego, Portland Oregon area; $33.00 others in Oregon; $39.00 others. Lake Oswego Review, 111 A Avenue, PO Box 548, Lake Oswego OR 97034. **Tel** (503)635-8811.

US
LEBANON EXPRESS. Newspaper. English. wk (Published on Fridays). $16.50 Lebanon, Oregon; $25.00 others. Lebanon Express Inc, PO Box 459, Lebanon OR 97355. **Tel** (503)258-3151.

US/0892-3353
LINCOLN COUNTY LEADER. Began in 1893. Newspaper. English. sw. Newport News Publishing Company, PO Box 965, Newport OR 97365. **Tel** (503)265-8571, FAX (503)265-3103.

US
MADRAS PIONEER, THE. (1904)-. Newspaper. English. wk. $18.00 (in county), $24.00 (out of county). Madras Pioneer, PO Box W, Madras OR 97741. **ED** Tony Ahern, Sue Matheny (Managing Editor). **Photos**. **Ad Acc**, **Adv Mgr:** Shannon Ahern. Full Page (B&W) $504.00. Half Page (B&W) $264.60. Full Page (Color) $589.00. Half Page (Color) $349.60. **Pub. Size:** Broadsheet. **Circ:** 3,587 paid, 75 unpaid.

US
NEWS GUARD. Newspaper. English. wk (52 issues per year). $25.00. News Guard, PO Box 848, Lincoln City OR 97367. **Tel** (503)994-2178.

US
NEWS REGISTER. (19??)-. Newspaper. English. Twice a week (Wed., & Sat.). $48.00 (carrier) local; $70.00 other. News-Register Publishing Company Inc., 611 3rd Street, McMinnville OR 97128. **Tel** (503)472-5114. **ED** Jeb Baldine, (editor's address: P. O. Box 727, McMinnville, OR 97128, phone: (503)472-5114), Yvette Saarinen (Managing Editor). **Photos**. **Ad Acc**, **Adv Mgr:** Rick McDonald. Full Page (B&W) $1168.00. Half Page (B&W) $584.00. Full Page (Color) $1568.00. Half Page (Color) $984.00. **Pub. Size:** Standard. **Circ:** 10,200. available in microform.

US/0888-2010
NEWS TIMES (NEWPORT, OR.). (NEWS TIMES.). (1???)-. Newspaper. English. sw. $52.00 Lincoln County; $104.00 others. Newport News Publishing Company, PO Box 965, Newport OR 97365. **Tel** (503)265-8571, FAX (503)265-3103. **ED** Leslie O'Donnell. **Ad Acc**, **Adv Mgr:** Rhonda Persyn. **Circ:** 10,500 (ctrl).

US/0894-444X
NORTHWEST LABOR PRESS. **VFOAT** Labor Press. Vol. 88 No. 9 (May 1, 1987)-. Periodical. English.

Twenty-four times a year. $12.50 one year. Northwest Labor Press, PO Box 13150, Portland OR 97213. **Tel** (503)288-3311. **ED** Michael Gutwig, (phone: (503)288-3311). **Ad Acc. *Continues*** *Oregon/Washington Labor Press, 0889-3195.*

US/8750-1317
OREGONIAN (PORTLAND, OR. 1937), THE. (THE OREGONIAN.). **VFOAT** Sunday Oregonian. Vol. 76, No. 23,803 (Feb. 15, 1937)-. Newspaper. English. da. $293.80 (daily & Sunday) US; $699.40 (daily & Sunday) other. Oregonian Publishing Company, 1320 South West Broadway, Portland OR 97201. **Tel** (503)221-8109. **ED** Sandra Rowe. **Photos. Ad Acc, Adv Mgr:** Denny Atkin, **Tel** (503)221-8279. Full Page (B&W) $7151.76. Half Page (B&W) $1329.90. Full Page (Color) $7716.76. Half Page (Color) $1894.90. **Pub. Size:** Broadsheet. **Circ:** 335,200 daily, 408,126 Sunday. available on microfilm from University Microfilms International (UMI); available on an online database (files 635,704/Full-Text) from DIALOG. Documents available from UMI Article Clearinghouse. ***Continues*** *Morning Oregonian.*
Ind/Abst Bus. Dateline (Dec. 20, 1991-) [Full Txt.]; PROMT.

US
PORTLAND OBSERVER. (1970)-. Newspaper. English. wk (Wed.). $35.00. Portland Observer, PO Box 3137, Portland OR 97208. **Tel** (503)288-0033. **ED** Joyce Washington. **Bk Rev**, (Qty: 10). **Photos. Ad Acc, Adv Mgr:** Chuck Washington, **Tel** (503)288-1897. Full Page (B&W) $1,764.00. Half Page (B&W) $822.00. Full Page (Color) $1,914.00. Half Page (Color) $1,032.00. **Pub. Size:** Standard. ctrl circ.

US/0747-0029
PROGRESS (WELLS, NEV.). (PROGRESS.). Vol. 1, No. 1 (Sept. 15, 1983)-. Newspaper. English. Fifty-two times a year (Tues.). Steven & Janet Juenke, 1945 Northwest 13th Street, Gresham OR 97030. **Tel** (702)752-3540.

US/0739-8557
REGISTER-GUARD, THE. VFOAT Register Guard. 116th Year, No. 324 (Sept. 12, 1983)-. Newspaper. English. da. The Register-Guard, PO Box 10188, Eugene OR 97440. **Tel** (503)485-1234. **ED** A. F. Baker Jr. **Circ:** 69,551 (daily), 73,094 (Sunday). available on microfilm from University Microfilms International (UMI). Documents available from UMI Article Clearinghouse. ***Continues*** *Eugene Register-Guard.*
Ind/Abst Bus. Dateline (Dec. 20, 1991-) [Full Txt.].

US
SANDY POST. Newspaper. English. wk. $15.00 Clackamas & Sandy counties; $16.00 Multonmah county; $18.00 others in Oregon; $20.00 Washington state; $23.00 others. Outlook Publishing Company, PO Box 68, Sandy OR 97055. **Tel** (503)668-5548.

US
SKANNER, THE. (Oct. 9, 1975)-. Newspaper. English. wk. $35.00. Portland Skanner, PO Box 5455, Portland OR 97228. **Tel** (503)287-3562, FAX (503)284-5677. **ED** Bobbie D. Foster. **Bk Rev. Photos. Ad Acc, Adv Mgr:** Ted Banks, **Tel** (503)287-3562 ext. 507. Half Page (B&W) $2,950.00. Half Page (Color) $3,300.00. **Pub. Size:** Standard. **Wire Svcs.:** AP. **Circ:** 20,000. available in microform.

US/0744-785X
SOUTH COAST WEEK. (19??)-. Newspaper. English. wk. Free. Southwestern Oregon Publishing Company, PO Box 1840, Coos Bay OR 97420. **Tel** (503)269-1222, (800)437-6397. **Photos. Ad Acc, Adv Mgr:** Juan Mejia. Full Page (B&W) $1,580.25. Half Page (B&W) $819.79. Full Page (Color) $1,660.25. Half Page (Color) $909.79. **Pub. Size:** Standard. **Circ:** 12,735.

US/0739-5507
STATESMAN JOURNAL. VFOAT Statesman-Journal; Sunday Statesman Journal; Sunday Statesman-Journal. (July 1, 1980)-. Newspaper. English. da. $138.00. Statesman-Journal Newspaper, PO Box 13009, Salem OR 97309. **Tel** (503)399-6622, FAX (503)399-6808. **ED** Mike Whitehead, Kristin Gilger (Managing Editor). **Bk Rev. Photos. Ad Acc, Adv Mgr:** Lorna Danielson, **Tel** (503)399-6645. Full Page (B&W) $5289.00. Half Page (B&W) $2644.50. **Pub. Size:** Standard. **Wire Svcs.:** AP. **Circ:** 60,066 daily, 71,900 Sunday. available on microfilm from University Microfilms International (UMI). ***Formed by the union of*** *Oregon Statesman (Salem, OR. : 1916)* ***and*** *Capital Journal (Salem, Or.).*

US
SUN TRIBUNE. (19??)-. Newspaper. English. wk. $15.00 Douglas County; $20.00 other. Sun Tribune, PO Box 430, Sutherlin OR 97479-0430. **Tel** (503)459-2261, FAX (503)459-1542. **ED** Linda Schnell. **Photos. Ad Acc, Adv Mgr:** Tolley Evans. **Pub. Size:** Tabloid. **Circ:** 900.

US/0746-1100
THIS WEEK MAGAZINE (PORTLAND, ORE.). (THIS WEEK MAGAZINE.). **VFOAT** This Week. (198?)-. Periodical. English. wk (Published on Wednesdays). Free. This Week Magazine, 9600 Southwest Boeckman Road, Wilsonville OR 97070. **Tel** (503)682-1881, FAX (503)682-2133. **ED** Don Campbell. **Bk Rev. Ad Acc, Adv Mgr:** Ken Raddle. **Circ:** 508,570. ***Continues*** *This Week (Portland, Ore.).*

US/0194-9640
TIDINGS, WEST LINN. (197?)-. Newspaper. English. wk. West Linn Tidings, 111 A Avenue, Lake Oswego OR 97034. ***Continues*** *West Linn, Wilsonville Review, 0194-8601.*

US/8750-0841
TIGARD TIMES. VFOAT Times. (19??)-. Newspaper. English. wk. $32.00 Tri-County Portland area; $43.00 Oregon; $49.00 other. Times Newspaper / Oregon, PO Box 370, Beaverton OR 97075. **Tel** (503)620-9797.

US/0745-7588
UMPQUA FREE PRESS. (198?)-. Newspaper. English. Fifty-two times a year. Umpqua Free Press, 119 South Main Street, PO Box 729, Myrtle Creek OR 97457. **Tel** (503)863-5233. **ED** Robert F. Scherer. **Ad Acc. Circ:** 3,400. ***Continues*** *Mail (Myrtle Creek, OR.).*

US/8750-0795
VALLEY TIMES (TIGARD, OR.). (VALLEY TIMES.). **VFOAT** Times. (19??)-. Newspaper. English. wk. Times Newspaper / Oregon, PO Box 370, Beaverton OR 97075. **Tel** (503)620-9797.

US
WILLAMETTE WEEK. Vol. 1, No. 1 (Nov. 16, 1974)-. Newspaper. English. Fifty-two times a year. $40.00 Oregon & Washington & Idaho; $55.00 others. City of Roses Newspaper Company, 2 North West 2nd Street, Portland OR 97209. **Tel** (503)243-2122. **ED** Mark Zusman. **Ad Acc, Adv Mgr:** Meeker, **Tel** (503)243-2122. **Circ:** 65,000 (ctrl).

US/0894-7481
WOODWORKER, THE. ***Ceased.*** (THE WOODWORKER : OFFICIAL PUBLICATION OF IWA-U.S., AFL-CIO.). [Woodworker]. **Added/Corp** International Woodworkers of America-U.S. Vol. 1, No. 1 (May 29, 1987)-(19??). Newspaper. English (Spanish). mo. IWA-US, 25 Cornell Avenue, Gladstone OR 97027. **Tel** (503)656-1475, FAX (503)657-2254. **ED** Glenn Blaylock. **DD** 331. Index available. **Circ:** 25,000 (ctrl). ***Continues*** *International Woodworker, 0020-9139.*
Desc: Covers labor issues.
Ind/Abst Index Inf.

US/1062-8495
WORLD (COOS BAY, OR.), THE. (THE WORLD.). (187?)-. Newspaper. English. da. $90.00 Coos, Curry & Western Douglas Counties; $114.00 US. Southwestern Oregon Publishing Company, PO Box 1840, Coos Bay OR 97420. **Tel** (503)269-1222, (800)437-6397. **ED** Don Brown (Editor-in-Chief) and Charles Kocher (Managing Editor). **Photos. Ad Acc, Adv Mgr:** Juna Mejia, **Tel** (503)269-1222. Full Page (B&W) $1,361.00. Half Page (B&W) $712.72. Full Page (Color) $1,441.00. Half Page (Color) $802.72. **Pub. Size:** Standard. **Wire Svcs.:** AP. **Circ:** 17,600 (ctrl). available in microform.

PENNSYLVANIA

US
ABINGTON JOURNAL (CLARKS SUMMIT, PA.). (THE ABINGTON JOURNAL.). (1948)-. Newspaper. English. wk. $18.00 in county; $22.00 others. Abington Journal, 406 South State Street, Clarks Summit PA 18411. **ED** Kenneth Books. **Photos. Ad Acc, Adv Mgr:** Ron Bartizek, **Tel** (717)586-7822. Full Page (B&W) $664.35. Half Page (B&W) $324.45. Full Page (Color) $749.35. Half Page (Color) $409.45. **Pub. Size:** Broadsheet. **Circ:** 3,500. ***Continues*** *Abington Press;* ***Absorbed*** *Voice (Clarks Summit, PA.).*

US
ADVANCE LEADER, THE. Vol. 74, No. 40 (Oct. 4, 1972)-. Newspaper. English. wk. Gateway Press Inc / Pennsylvania, 610 Beatty Road, Monroeville PA 15146. **Tel** (412)856-7400. **ED** Edith Hughes. **Ad Acc, Adv Mgr:** Mark Caruso. ***Continues*** *Allegheny Valley Advance Leader.*

US
ADVANCE OF BUCKS COUNTY, THE. (Apr. 3, 1975)-. Newspaper. English. wk. $17.50. Intercounty Newspaper Group / Pennsylvania, 6220 Ridge Avenue, Philadelphia PA 19128. **Tel** (215)483-7300, FAX (215)483-2073. **ED** Art Thompson, Nancy Pickering (Managing Editor). **Photos. Ad Acc, Adv Mgr:** Jane Parr, **Tel** (215)968-2244. Full Page (B&W) $667.20. Half Page (B&W) $333.60. Full Page (Color) $1167.20. Half Page (Color) $833.60. **Pub. Size:** Tabloid. **Circ:** 6,000. ***Continues*** *Delaware Valley Advance (Langhorne, Pa.).*

US
ADVERTISER, THE. (1965)-. Newspaper. English. wk. Publix Publications, 3801 Washington Road, McMurray PA 15317-2953. **Tel** (412)941-7725, FAX (412)941-8685. **ED** Debbie Popp. **Ad Acc, Adv Mgr:** Karen Strickland. **Circ:** 34,641.

US
ADVISOR, THE. VFOAT Ad Visor. Vol. 1, No. 1 (June, 1978)-. Newspaper. English. wk. $18.60. Laurel Group Press, PO Box 222, Scottdale PA 15683. **Tel** (412)547-5722, FAX $412)887-5115. **ED** Jonna Stairs. **Photos. Ad Acc, Adv Mgr:** Charles Hixson. **Pub. Size:** Standard.

US
ALBION NEWS, THE. VFOAT Albion Semi-Weekly News; Albion Weekly News. Vol. 1, No. 1 (Dec. 31, 1901)-. Newspaper. English. wk. $16.00 local; $27.00 other. Albion News, 16 Market Street, Albion PA 16401. **ED** Vickie Canfield Peters. **Photos. Ad Acc, Adv Mgr:** Peggy Fails, **Tel** (814)756-4133. Full Page (B&W) $275.00. Half Page (B&W) $156.00. Full Page (Color) $400.00. Half Page (Color) $281.00. **Pub. Size:** Tabloid. **Circ:** 3,250. available in microform.

US
ALLEGHENY TIMES. (Aug. 18, 1986)-. Newspaper. English. da. Allegheny Times, 894 Beavergrade Road, Coraopolis PA 15108. **Tel** (412)269-1144. **ED** Dennis Dible. **Ad Acc. Circ:** 2,500.

US
ALLIED NEWS. No. 11 (Mar. 14, 1972)-. Newspaper. English. wk. Grove City Allied News, 113 North Broad Street, Grove City PA 16127-1636. **Tel** (412)458-5010. **ED** Lynda Guthrie. **Ad Acc. Circ:** 4,300. ***Formed by the union of*** *Allied News (Grove City, Pa. : Mercer Dispatch Ed.); Allied News (Grove City, Pa. : Lakeview Breeze Ed.); Allied News (Grove City, Pa. : Grove City Reporter-Herald Ed.)* ***and*** *Allied News (Grove City, Pa. : Slippery Rock Signal Ed.).*

US/0193-581X
ALMANAC (MCMURRAY), THE. (THE ALMANAC.). (1968)-. Newspaper. English. wk. McMurray Almanac, 3801 Washington Road, McMurray PA 15317.

US
ALTOONA MIRROR. VFOAT Saturday Mirror,. Vol. 4, No. 1 (June 16, 1888)-. Newspaper. English. da. Altoona Mirror Thomson Division, PO Box 2008, Altoona PA 16603. **Tel** (814)946-7411. **LC** 7002.

US
AMBLER GAZETTE, THE. (1882)-. Newspaper. English. wk (52 issues). $26.00. Montgomery Publishing Company, 290 Commerce Drive, Fort Washington PA 19034. **Tel** (215)542-0200, FAX (215)643-9475. **ED** Fred Behringer (Editor-in-Chief) and Gillian Gordon (Managing Editor). **LC** 9377. **Photos. Ad Acc, Adv Mgr:** Mike Fisher, **Tel** (215)542-0200 ext. 271. Full Page (B&W) $2,580.00. Half Page (B&W) $1,290.00. Full Page (Color) $2,665.00. Half Page (Color) $1,375.00. **Pub. Size:** Broadsheet. **Circ:** 12,056. ***Continues*** *Fort Washington Times.*

US
APOLLO NEWS-RECORD. VFOAT Apollo News Record. (19??)-. Newspaper. English. wk. Apollo News-Record, PO Box 158, Apollo PA 15613-0158.

US
BARNESBORO STAR, THE. Began July 1, 1904. Newspaper. English. wk. Barnesboro Star, 520 Philadelphia Avenue, Barnesboro PA 15714. ***Continues*** *Sentinel (Barnesboro, PA.).*

US
BEAVER COUNTY TIMES (SOUTHERN ED.). (BEAVER COUNTY TIMES.). (Sept. 20, 1982)-. Newspaper. English. da. $165.00 (one year). Beaver County Times, PO Box 400, Beaver PA 15009. **Tel** (412)775-3200. **ED** Dennis D. Dible. **Ad Acc, Adv Mgr:** Robert Woelfez, **Tel** (412)775-3200. **Circ:** 47,312 - daily, 58,866 - Sunday. ***Continues in part*** *Beaver County Times (Beaver Valley Home Ed.).*

US
BEDFORD COUNTY INQUIRER. VFOAT Bedford Inquirer; Bedford County Inquirer Combined with the Everett Republican. 162nd Year, No. 3 (July 12, 1974)-. Newspaper. English. wk. Inquirer Publishing Company, PO Box 671, Bedford PA 15522. **ED** Sarah L. Frear. **Photos. Ad Acc, Adv Mgr Tel** (814)623-1151. **Pub. Size:** Broadsheet. **Circ:** 365. available in microform. ***Continues*** *Bedford Inquirer (Bedford, PA. : 1959).*

US/0744-8457
BEDFORD GAZETTE (BEDFORD, PA.). (THE BEDFORD GAZETTE.). **VFOAT** Bedford Daily Gazette. Vol. 1, No. 1 (Sept. 1805)-. Newspaper. English. da. Inquirer Publishing Company, PO Box 671, Bedford PA 15522.

US
BENNETTS VALLEY NEWS, THE. (1953)-. Newspaper. English. wk. Bennetts Valley News, PO Box 158, Weedville PA 15868-0158. **Tel** (814)787-4454. **ED** James Leonard. **Circ:** 1,000.

US
BETHLEHEM BULLETIN. Vol. 1, No. 1 (Nov. 19, 1926)-. Bulletin. English. wk. Bethlehem Bulletin, 4th and Polk Streets, Bethlehem PA 18015. **ED** Richard Ernest Fowler. ***Absorbed*** *Hellertown Tribune; Fountain Hill News-Telegram.*

US
BOTSCHAFT, DIE. (19??)-. Newspaper. English (Germanic). Fifty-two times a year (Wed.). $24.00. Brookshire Publications, 200 Hazel Street Lancaster PA 17603. **Tel** (717)392-1321, FAX (717)392-2078. **Ad Acc, Adv Mgr:** Carla, **Tel** (717)392-1321. **Circ:** 7,000 (ctrl).

US
BOYERTOWN AREA TIMES, THE. Vol. 125, No. 17 (Sept. 24, 1981)-. Newspaper. English. wk. Berks - Mont Newspapers Inc., 124 North Chestnut Street, Boyertown PA 19512-1123. **Tel** (215)367-6041, FAX (215)369-0233. **ED** Deborah Fetterman. **Ad Acc, Adv Mgr:** Jim Davidheiser. **Circ:** 6,500. ***Continues*** *Times of the Boyertown Area.*

US
BRADFORD ERA, THE. **VFOAT** Yankee Doodler. Vol. 10, No. 264 (Oct. 10, 1887)-. Newspaper. English. da. Bradford Publishing Inc, PO Box 365, Bradford PA 16701. **Tel** (814)368-3173. ***Continues*** *Daily Era (Bradford, PA.);* ***Absorbed*** *Bradford Evening Star (Bradford, PA. : 1943).*

US
BRADFORD JOURNAL (BRADFORD, PA. : 1973). (BRADFORD JOURNAL.). **VFOAT** New Bradford Journal. Vol. 33, No. 37 (Nov. 15, 1973)-. Newspaper. English. wk. $23.00 in county; $33.00 others. Bradford Journal, PO Box 17, Bradford PA 16701. **ED** G. Nichols (Editor-in-Chief) and Deb Nichols (Managing Editor). **Bk Rev**, (Qty: 4). **Photos**. **Ad Acc, Adv Mgr:** G. Nichols. Full Page (B&W) $532.80. Half Page (B&W) $266.40. Full Page (Color) $582.80. Half Page (Color) $316.40. **Pub. Size:** Tabloid. ***Continues in part*** *Bradford Journal, McKean County Miner, Mount Jewett Echo.*

US
BREEZE (ROCKLEDGE, PA.). (THE BREEZE.). Vol. 17, No. 5 (Sept. 2, 1943)-. Newspaper. English. Intercounty Newspaper Group, 54 Park Avenue, Philadelphia PA 19111. ***Continues*** *Breeze of Lower Montgomery County.*

US/1047-0670
BRIDGEVILLE AREA NEWS. Vol. 51, No. 6131 (May 5, 1977)-. Newspaper. English. wk. $22.50 Allegheny county, $34.00 other. Gateway Publications, 705 5th Avenue, Coraopolis PA 15108. **Tel** (412)264-4140. ***Continues*** *Bridgeville News.*

US
BRISTOL PILOT. No. 1 (March 20, 1986)-. Newspaper. English. wk. Intercounty Newspaper Group / Pennsylvania, 6220 Ridge Avenue, Philadelphia PA 19128. **Tel** (215)483-7300, FAX (215)483-2073. **ED** George Beetham. **Ad Acc, Adv Mgr:** Jane Parr, **Tel** (215)968-2244. **Circ:** 5,000 weekly.

US
BROAD TOP BULLETIN. Vol. 1, No. 1 (March 13, 1947)-. Newspaper. English. wk. $12.50. Broad Top Bulletin, 900 6th Street, Saxton PA 16678. **Tel** (814)635-2851. **ED** Jon Baughman. **Photos**. **Ad Acc, Adv Mgr:** Chris Hodge. Full Page (B&W) $409.50. Half Page (B&W) $204.75. Full Page (Color) $459.50. Half Page (Color) $254.75. **Pub. Size:** Broadsheet. **Circ:** 3,150.

US/1054-755X
BROCKWAY RECORD, THE. ***Title Change.*** **VFOAT** Brockwayville Record. (1925-199?). Newspaper. English. wk. Indiana Printing and Publishing Company, 682 Main Street, Brockway PA 15824. ***Continues*** *Brockwayville Record.* ***Continued by*** *County Neighbors (Punxsutawney, Pa.), 1065-268X.*

US
BROOKVILLE AMERICAN (BROOKVILLE, PA.). (THE BROOKVILLE AMERICAN.). **VFOAT** American. Vol. 1, No. 1 (March 6, 1918)-. Newspaper. English. wk. Brookville American, 175 Main Street, Brookville PA 15825.

US
BUCKS-MONT COURIER (HARLEYSVILLE, PA. : NORTH PENN ED.). (BUCKS-MONT COURIER.). **VFOAT** Bucks Mont Courier. Vol. 35, No. 19 (June 4, 1985)-. Newspaper. English. wk. $50.00. Bucks-Mont Courier, PO Box 204, Harleysville PA 19438. **ED** Susan Lapp. **Photos**. **Ad Acc, Adv Mgr:** Susan Lapp, **Tel** 721-9100. Full Page (B&W) $1,575.36. Half Page (B&W) $787.68. Full Page (Color) $1,760.00. Half Page (Color) $862.00. **Pub. Size:** Tabloid. ***Continues in part*** *Bucks-Mont Courier (Harleysville, PA. : 1965).*

US/0744-401X
BUTLER EAGLE (BUTLER, PA. : DAILY). (BUTLER EAGLE.). **VFOAT** Butler Daily Eagle. Vol. 3, No. 25 (June 16, 1904)-. Newspaper. English. da (except Sunday and 5 holidays). $48.00. Eagle Printing Company Inc, 114 West Diamond Street, Butler PA 16001. **Tel** 800 842-8098 ext. 231. **ED** John Laing Wise Jr. **Circ:** 30,955. ***Continues*** *Butler Daily Eagle;* ***Absorbed*** *Butler Eagle (Butler, Pa. : Weekly).*

US/0744-2289
BYZANTINE CATHOLIC WORLD, THE. **Added/Corp** Catholic Church. Exarchate of Pittsburgh (Pa.) Catholic Church. Eparchy of Pittsburgh (Pa.) Catholic Church. Archeparchy of Munhall (Pa.) Catholic Church. Eparchy of Parma (Ohio). **VFOAT** World. Vol. 1, No. 1 (June 17, 1956)-. Newspaper. English (Slovak and Hungarian). bw (26 issues). $10.00. Byzantine Catholic World, PO Box 1215, Pittsburgh PA 15214. **Tel** (412)281-0380. available on microfilm from University of Chicago Library. ***Continued in part by*** *Horizons (Parma, Ohio).*

US
CALL, THE. **VFOAT** Call and Orwigsburg News. Vol. 78, No. 37 (Sept. 11, 1969)-. Newspaper. English. wk. The Call Newspapers Inc., 960 East Main Street, Schuylkill Haven PA 17972-9752. **Tel** (717)385-3120, FAX (717)385-0725. **ED** LaJeune Steidle. **Circ:** 5,000. ***Continues*** *Call and the Orwigsburg News.*

US
CAMERON COUNTY ECHO. **VFOAT** Echo. Vol. 1, No. 16 (Aug. 1, 1963)-. Newspaper. English. wk. Cameron County Echo, PO Box 308, Emporium PA 15834. ***Continues*** *Area Shoppers' News.*

US
CANTON INDEPENDENT-SENTINEL, THE. **VFOAT** Canton Independent Sentinel. Seventy First Year, No. 21 (Sept. 18, 1941)-. Newspaper. English. wk. $22.00. Independent-Sentinel, PO Box 128, Canton PA 17714. **Tel** (717)673-5151, FAX (717)4315. **ED** John Shaffer. **Photos**. **Ad Acc, Adv Mgr:** Janie Riggs. Full Page (B&W) $352.80. Half Page (B&W) $176.40. Full Page (Color) $417.80. Half Page (Color) $208.90. **Pub. Size:** Broadsheet. **Circ:** 2,000. available in microform. ***Formed by the union of*** *Canton Independent* ***and*** *Canton Sentinel (Canton, PA. : 1907).*

US/0746-3510
CARBONDALE NEWS (CARBONDALE, PA. : 1961). (CARBONDALE NEWS.). **VFOAT** Carbondale (Pa.) News. Vol. 89, No. 1 (Jan. 5, 1961)-. Newspaper. English. wk. $10.00 Carbondale area, $11.00 elsewhere in Pennsylvania, $13.00 out of state. Carbondale News, 41 North Church Street, Carbondale PA 18407. ***Continues*** *Carbondale Daily News.*

US
CATASAUQUA DISPATCH, THE. Began in 1872. Newspaper. English. wk. Dispatch Printery, 420 Howertown Road, Catasauqua PA 18032.

US/0164-9418
CATHOLIC LIGHT, THE. **Added/Corp** Catholic Church. Diocese of Scranton (Pa.). (190?)-. Newspaper. English. bw. $6.00 US; $8.00 other. Catholic Light, PO Box 708, Scranton PA 18501. **Tel** (717)346-8915. **ED** Arthur F. Perry. **Ad Acc. Circ:** 52,631. available on microfilm from University Microfilms International (UMI). ***Continues*** *Diocesan Record.*

US
CATHOLIC STANDARD AND TIMES, THE. **VFOAT** Standard and Times. Vol. 1, No. 1 (Dec. 7, 1895)-. Newspaper. English. wk. Catholic Standard & Times, 222 North Seventeenth Street, Philadelphia PA 19103. **Tel** (215)587-2469. ***Formed by the union of*** *Catholic Standard (Philadelphia, Pa.)* ***and*** *Catholic Times (Philadelphia, Pa.).*

US/0745-483X
CENTRE DAILY TIMES. Vol. 37, No. 1 (Apr. 2, 1934)-. Newspaper. English. da (except certain holidays). $34.97 (per 13 weeks). Centre Daily Times, PO Box 89, State College PA 16804. **Tel** (814)238-5000, FAX (814)237-5966. **ED** Cecil Bentley, Cindy Burton (Managing Editor). **Photos**. **Ad Acc, Adv Mgr:** Gene Kneller, **Tel** (814)231-4650. Full Page (B&W) $1644.75. Half Page (B&W) $828.75. Full Page (Color) $1844.75. Half Page (Color) $1038.75. **Pub. Size:** Broadsheet. **Wire Svcs.:** AP, KR, LA, WP. **Circ:** 23,000 daily, 29,000 Sunday. ***Continues*** *State College Times.*

US
CHESTER COUNTY PRESS. Vol. 105, No. 30 (Sept. 16, 1970)-. Newspaper. English. wk. $15.00. Ad Pro Inc., PO Box 520, Oxford PA 19363. **Tel** (610)932-2444, FAX (610)932-2246. **ED** Monika Weiss (Editor-in- Chief and Steve Ennen (Managing Editor). **Bk Rev**, (Qty: 6). **Photos**. **Ad Acc, Adv Mgr:** Alan Turns. Full Page (B&W) $1,323.00. Half Page (B&W) $661.50. Full Page (Color) $1,523.00. Half Page (Color) $861.50. **Pub. Size:** Standard. **Circ:** 15,000. available in microform. ***Formed by the union of*** *Oxford Press (Oxford, Pa.)* ***and*** *Avon Grove News.*

US/0009-3394
CHESTNUT HILL LOCAL, THE. **Added/Corp** Chestnut Hill Community Association. (1958)-. Newspaper. English. wk. $15.00. Chestnut Hill Community Association, 8434 Germantown Avenue, Philadelphia PA 19118. **Tel** FAX (215)248-8814. **ED** Marie R. Jones. **Photos**. **Ad Acc, Adv Mgr:** Frank Moeschlin, **Tel** (215)248-8815. Full Page (B&W) $978.40. Half Page (B&W) $489.70. Full Page (Color) $1028.40. Half Page (Color) $539.00. **Pub. Size:** Tabloid. available on microfilm and microfiche.

US/1053-489X
CITIZEN-STANDARD, THE. **VFOAT** Citizen Standard; Valley Citizen. Vol. 1, No. 1 (Sept. 10, 1975)-. Newspaper. English. wk. $17.00, $19.00 (out-of-area). Citizen Standard, 100 West Main Street, Valley View PA 17983. **Tel** (717)682-9081, FAX (717)682-8734. **ED** Andrew Heintzelman. **Circ:** 4,500. ***Formed by the union of*** *Valley Citizen (Valley View, Pa. : 1974)* ***and*** *Standard (Lykens, Pa.).*

US
CLARION NEWS, THE. **VFOAT** Clarion News Combined with the Republican; Clarion News Combined with the Democrat. 125th year, No. 45 (Nov. 3, 1965)-. Newspaper. English. sw. Western Pennsylvania Newspaper Company, 645 Main Street, Clarion PA 16214. ***Formed by the union of*** *Republican (Clarion, Pa.)* ***and*** *Democrat (Clarion, Pa.).*

US
COLUMBIA DAILY NEWS. ***Title Change.*** **VFOAT** Columbia Daily News and Daily Spy; Daily News. (1888)-(1923). Newspaper. English. da. Columbia Daily News, 341 Chestnut Street, Columbia PA 17512. ***Absorbed*** *Columbia Daily Spy.* ***Continued by*** *Columbia News.*

US/8750-0590
CONNEAUTVILLE COURIER (CONNEAUTVILLE, PA. : 1871). (THE CONNEAUTVILLE COURIER.). **VFOAT** Courier and Record. Began in 1871?. Newspaper. English. wk. Conneautville Courier, 1012 Main Street, Conneautville PA 16406. ***Continues*** *Record and Courier.*

US
CORRY JOURNAL. Vol. 82, No. 126 (May 28, 1983)-. Newspaper. English. da. Corry Journal, 28 West South Street, Corry PA 16407-1810. **Tel** (814)665-8291, FAX (814)664-2288. **ED** Kevin Downey. **Ad Acc. Circ:** 4,363 (evening). ***Continues*** *Corry Evening Journal.*

●US/1065-268X
COUNTY NEIGHBORS (PUNXSUTAWNEY, PA.). (COUNTY NEIGHBORS.). Vol. 1, Issue 1 (Aug. 12, 1992)-. Newspaper. English. wk. American Publishing Co., 111 North Findley Street, Punxsutawney PA 15767. ***Continues*** *Brockway Record, 1054-755X.*

US/8750-4049
COURIER-EXPRESS (DUBOIS, PA. : 1964). (THE COURIER-EXPRESS.). **VFOAT** Courier Express. Vol. 85, No. 144 (June 18, 1964)-. Newspaper. English. da. Courier-Express, 50-58 West Long Avenue, Dubois PA 15801. ***Continues*** *Dubois Courier Express.*

US/0745-7499
CRESSON & GALLITZIN MAINLINER, THE. (CRESSON GALLITZIN MAINLINER.). **VFOAT** Mainliner. (Oct. 22, 1975)-. Newspaper. English. wk. $15.95 Pennsylvania, $16.95 elsewhere. Cresson Gallitzin Mainliner, PO Box 395, Portage PA 15946-0395. ***Continues*** *Mainliner & Dispatch.*

US/8750-247X
DAILY AMERICAN (SOMERSET, PA.), THE. (THE DAILY AMERICAN.). **VFOAT** Daily American and the Berlin Record, Combined with the Somerset Bulletin, the Somerset Standard, and the Boswell News. Vol. 48, No. 3 (July 3, 1976)-. Newspaper. English. da (except Sundays and Holidays). Somerset Newspapers, 334 West Main Street, Somerset PA 15501. **Tel** (814)445-9621. **ED** Keith A Curtis. **Circ:** 11,063. ***Continues*** *Somerset Daily American.*

US
DAILY COURIER (CONNELLSVILLE, PA.). (THE DAILY COURIER.). Vol. 73, No. 59 (Jan. 21, 1974)-. Newspaper. English. da. Daily Courier, 127 North Apple Street, Connellsville PA 15425. ***Continues*** *Courier (Connellsville, PA. : Daily).*

US
DAILY ITEM (SUNBURY, PA.). (THE DAILY ITEM.). **VFOAT** Sunbury Daily Item. Vol. 30, No. 202 (Aug. 26, 1968)-. Newspaper. English. da. Daily Item, 200 Market Street, Sunbury PA 17801. ***Continues*** *Sunbury Daily Item (Sunbury, PA. : 1937).*

US/0163-3082
DAILY LOCAL NEWS (WEST CHESTER). (DAILY LOCAL NEWS.). **VFOAT** West Chester Local News. Vol. 1, No. 1 (Nov. 19, 1872)-. Newspaper. English. da (except Sundays and holidays). $40.00. Daily Local News, 250 North Bradford Avenue, Box 517, West Chester PA 19380. **Tel** (215)696-1776. **ED** William H. Dean. **LC** 9375-X. **Circ:** 38,549 daily, 39,837 Sunday.

US
DAILY NEWS (HUNTINGDON, PA.). (THE DAILY NEWS.). Vol. 1, No. 1 (Jan. 31, 1922)-. Newspaper. English. da. Huntingdon Daily News, 325 Penn Street, Huntingdon PA 16652. **ED** Joseph F Biddle.

US/0746-8563
DAILY NEWS (LEBANON, PA.), THE. (THE DAILY NEWS.). (Mar. 23, 1981)-. Newspaper. English. da. $122.20. Lebanon News Publishing Company, PO Box 600, Lebanon PA 17042. **Tel** (717)272-5611. **ED** Richard Scaife. **Circ:** 24,760. ***Continues*** *Lebanon Daily News (Lebanon, PA. : 1971).*

US
DAILY NEWS (MCKEESPORT, PA.). (THE DAILY NEWS.). (1896)-. Newspaper. English. da (except Sun.). $108.10. Daily News Publishing Company, PO Box 128, McKeesport PA 15134. **ED** Thomas D. Mansfield. **Circ:** 30,219. ***Continues*** *McKeesport Daily News.*

US
DAILY PRESS (SAINT MARYS, PA.). (THE DAILY PRESS.). Began in 1910. Newspaper. English. da. Daily Press, PO Box 353, St Marys PA 15857. **ED** James A Dippold.

US
DAILY REVIEW (TOWANDA, PA.). (THE DAILY REVIEW.). 42nd Yr., No. 11,895 (May 17, 1921)-. Newspaper. English. da. Daily Review, 116 Main Street, Towanda PA 18848. ***Continues*** *Towanda Daily Review.*

US
DAILY TIMES (PRIMOS, PA.). (THE DAILY TIMES.). **VFOAT** Sunday Times; Delaware County Daily Times; Delaware County Sunday Times. (Sept. 8, 1985)-. Newspaper. English. da. $158.60. Delaware County Daily Times, 500 Mildred Avenue, Primos PA 19018. **Tel** (215)284-7200. **ED** Andrew Reynolds, Linda DeMeggio (Managing Editor). **Bk Rev**. **Photos**. **Ad Acc, Adv Mgr:** Elaine Lyon. Full Page (B&W) $2545.05. Half Page (B&W) $1272.53. Full Page (Color) $2820.05. Half Page (Color) $1410.03. **Pub. Size:** Tabloid. **Wire Svcs.:** AP. ***Continues*** *Delaware County Daily Times.*

US
DALLAS POST, THE. **VFOAT** Post. (19??)-. Newspaper. English. wk. $18.00 in county; $22.00 others. Bartsen Media Inc., PO Box 366, Dallas PA 18612. **Tel** (717)675-5211. **ED** Ronald Bartizek. **Photos**. **Ad Acc, Adv Mgr:** Ron Bartizek. Full Page (B&W) $664.35. Half Page (B&W) $324.45. Full Page (Color) $749.35. Half Page (Color) $409.45. **Pub. Size:** Broadsheet. **Circ:** 3,000. ***Continues*** *Dallas Weekly Post.*

US
DANVILLE NEWS (DANVILLE, PA.). (THE DANVILLE NEWS.). Vol. 67, No. 105 (Jan. 4, 1965)-. Newspaper. English. da (except Sun.). $75.00. Stauffer Media Inc, PO Box 200, Danville PA 17821. **Tel** (717)275-3235, FAX (717)275-7624. **ED** Pamela Christine. **Bk Rev**. **Photos**. **Ad Acc, Adv Mgr:** Donna Keefer. Full Page (B&W) $748.20. Half Page (B&W) $374.10. Full Page (Color) $823.20. Half Page (Color) $449.10. **Pub. Size:** Broadsheet. **Wire Svcs.:** AP. **Circ:** 9,000. available on microfilm from University Microfilms International (UMI). ***Continues*** *Daily Danville News (Danville, PA.).*

US
DERRICK (OIL CITY, PA.). (THE DERRICK.). No. 28,034 (July 10, 1954)-. Newspaper. English. da. The Derrick, PO Box 928, Oil City PA 16301. ***Continues*** *Oil City Derrick (Oil City, Pa. : Daily).*

US
ECHO PILOT. **VFOAT** Echo-Pilot. (Sept. 13, 1893)-. Newspaper. English. wk. Echo Pilot, PO Box 159, Greencastle PA 17225. ***Continues*** *Pilot (Greencastle, PA. : 1892); Valley Echo (Greencastle, PA.).*

US
ELIZABETHTOWN CHRONICLE (ELIZABETHTOWN, PA. : 1989). (ELIZABETHTOWN CHRONICLE.). Vol. 120, No. 8 (Jan. 5, 1989)-. Newspaper. English. wk. $18.00. Elizabethtown Chronicle, PO Box 189, Elizabethtown PA 17022-0189. **Tel** (717)367-7152, FAX (717)367-3655. **ED** John Reid (Editor-in-Chief) and Karen Putt (Managing Editor). **Photos**. **Ad Acc, Adv Mgr:** Dave Wagner. Full Page (B&W) $625.65. Half Page (B&W) $349.80. Full Page (Color) $700.65. Half Page (Color) $424.80. **Pub. Size:** Broadsheet. **Circ:** 3,500. ***Continues*** *Chronicle (Elizabethtown, PA.).*

US
ELKLAND JOURNAL (ELKLAND, PA. : 1956). (ELKLAND JOURNAL.). 80th Yr., No. 14 (April 5, 1956)-. Newspaper. English. wk. Elkland Journal, 221 East River Street, Elkland PA 16920. ***Continues*** *Elkland Journal and Cowanesque Valley News.*

US
ELLWOOD CITY LEDGER. Began in 1919. Newspaper. English. da. Ellwood City Ledger, 835 Lawrence Avenue, Ellwood City PA 16117.

US
EPHRATA REVIEW, THE. **VFOAT** Saturday Review. (Feb. 10, 1873)-. Newspaper. English. wk. Ephrata Review, 1 East Main Street, Ephrata PA 17522. **Tel** (717)733-6397, FAX (717)733-6058. **ED** Andrew Fasnacht. **Photos**. **Ad Acc, Adv Mgr:** Doug Dussinger. **Circ:** 9,000 paid. available in microform. ***Continues*** *Saturday Review (Ephrata, Pa.);* ***Absorbed*** *Ephrata Ensign* ***and*** *Denver Press.*

US
ERIE DAILY TIMES, THE. **VFOAT** Erie Times-News; Times-News; Erie Sunday Times. (Apr. 12, 1888)-. Newspaper. English. da. Times Publishing Company / Pennsylvania, 205 West 12th Street, Erie PA 16534. **Tel** (814)870-1600. **ED** Ed Mead. **Bk Rev**. **Photos**. **Ad Acc, Adv Mgr:** Al Haskins, **Tel** (814)870-1657. **Pub. Size:** Broadsheet. **Wire Svcs.:** AP. **Circ:** 75,000 combined, 105,000 Sunday (ctrl). available in microform.
Desc: A daily newspaper of general interest.

US/1055-8403
EVENING HERALD (SHEHANDOAH, PA. : 1969). (EVENING HERALD.). 94th Year, No. 82 (April 7, 1969)-. Newspaper. English. da. Evening Herald - Shenandoah Pennsylvania, Ringtown Road, Shenandoah PA 17976. ***Formed by the union of*** *Record American (Mahoney City, Pa.)* ***and*** *Evening Herald, and Ashland Daily News.*

US/0887-7939
EVENING NEWS (HARRISBURG, PA.), THE. (THE EVENING NEWS.). **VFOAT** Sunday Patriot News; Patriot the Evening News. No. 1 (Feb. 15, 1917)-. Newspaper. English. da. Patriot News Company, PO Box 1437, Harrisburg PA 17101. **Tel** (717)255-8277. **ED** Ronald Minard. **Bk Rev**. **Ad Acc**. **Circ:** 54,180. available on microfilm from University Microfilms International (UMI). ***Continues*** *News (Harrisburg, Pa.).*

US/0746-4843
EVENING TIMES (SAYRE, PA.). (THE EVENING TIMES.). (Jan. 29, 1917)-. Newspaper. English. da (312 issues per year). $126.00. The Evening Times, 201 North Lehigh Avenue, Sayre PA 18840. **Tel** (717)888-9643. **ED** G R Sample. **Ad Acc**. **Circ:** 9,000. available in microform. ***Continues*** *Daily Times-Record;* ***Absorbed*** *Evening News (Athens, PA.)* ***and*** *Athens Gazette (Athens, PA. : 1870).*

US
EXPRESS (LOCK HAVEN, PA. : 1971). (THE EXPRESS.). Vol. 90, No. 201 (Oct. 23, 1971)-. Newspaper. English. da. The Express / Lock Haven Pennsylvania, PO Box 208, 9-11 West Main Street, Lock Haven PA 17745. **Tel** (717)748-6791. ***Continues*** *Express with the Jersey Shore Evening News.*

US/1062-3620
EXPRESS-TIMES, THE. **VFOAT** Express Times. (Nov. 5, 1991)-. Newspaper. English. wk. $244.00, $309.00 (outside PA, NJ). The Express-Times, PO Box 391, Easton PA 18044-0391. **Tel** 800 360-3602. ***Formed by the union of*** *Globe-Times (Bethlehem, Pa.)* ***and*** *Express (Easton, Pa.).*

US
FAR NORTHEAST CITIZEN-SENTINEL, THE. **VFOAT** Far Northeast Citizen Sentinel. Began in 1968. Newspaper. English. wk. 1102 Churchill Road, Philadelphia PA 19118.

US/1054-4240
FEATURE NEWS PUBLICITY OUTLETS. [Feature news public. outlets]. **VFOAT** FNPO. No. 2 (1989)-. Periodical. English. sa. $70.00. Morgan-Rand Publications Inc., 1800 Byberry Road 800, Huntingdon Valley PA 19006. **Tel** (215)938-5511, FAX (215)988-0402. **DD** 071. ***Continues*** *Family Page Directory, 0889-373X.*

US
FOREST PRESS (TIONESTA, PA. : 1953). (THE FOREST PRESS.). (1953)-. Newspaper. English. wk. $21.00. Forest Press, PO Box 366, Tionesta PA 16353. **ED** Edwin R. Patrick and Virginia Patrick (Managing Editor). **Photos**. **Ad Acc, Adv Mgr:** Leslie Holt, **Tel** 755-4900. Full Page (B&W) $243.00. Half Page (B&W) $117.00. Full Page (Color) $324.00. Half Page (Color) $207.00. **Pub. Size:** Tabloid. ***Continues*** *Forest Republican (Tionesta, PA.).*

US
FREE PRESS-COURIER (GALETON ED.). (THE FREE PRESS-COURIER.). **VFOAT** Free Press Courier. Eighty-Third Year, No. 22 (June 1, 1961)-. Newspaper. English. wk. Tioga Printing Corporation, PO Box 515, Westfield PA 16950. ***Continues in part*** *Free Press-Courier.*

US
FULTON COUNTY NEWS (MCCONNELLSBURG, PA.). (THE FULTON COUNTY NEWS.). **VFOAT** Fulton County News the Fulton County Journal. Began in 1899. Newspaper. English. wk. $17.00. Fulton County News, PO Box 635, McConnellsburg PA 17233. **Tel** (717)485-4513. **ED** Jamie S Greathend. **Bk Rev**. **Ad Acc**. **Circ:** 6,400 (ctrl). ***Absorbed*** *Fulton County Journal the Fulton Democrat.*

US
GERMANTOWN COURIER. Vol. 1, No. 1 (Dec. 4, 1936)-. Newspaper. English. wk. Philadelphia Suburban Newspapers, 311 East Lancaster Avenue, Ardmore PA 19003. **Tel** (215)848-4300. **ED** Rick Linsk. **Circ:** 26,007. ***Absorbed*** *Germantown Telegraph (Germantown, PA. : 1840).*

US
GERMANTOWN PAPER, THE. Vol. 1, No. 1 (Jan. 3, 1979)-. Newspaper. English. wk. $48.00. Intercounty Newspaper Group / Pennsylvania, 6220 Ridge Avenue, Philadelphia PA 19128. **Tel** (215)483-7300, FAX (215)483-2073. **ED** Marshall Rothman. **Photos**. **Ad Acc, Adv Mgr:** James Mitchell, **Tel** (215)885-4111. Full Page (B&W) $667.20. Half Page (B&W) $333.60. **Pub. Size:** Tabloid. **Circ:** 15,000 weekly.

US
GETTYSBURG TIMES. Began Jan. 1, 1904. Newspaper. English. da. Gettysburg Times, 18 Carlisle Street, Gettysburg PA 17325. ***Absorbed*** *New Oxford Item.*

US
GIRARD HOME NEWS. Vol. 7, No. 22 (May 27, 1943)-. Newspaper. English. wk. Girard Home News, 106 South 7th Street, Philadelphia PA 19106. ***Continues*** *Girard Avenue Home News.*

US
GREENSBURG TRIBUNE-REVIEW. (19??)-. English. da (360 per year). $213.20. Greensburg Tribune-Review, Cabin Hill Drive, Greensburg PA 15601. **Tel** (412)834-1151.

US/0744-7302
HERALD (SHARON, PA.), THE. (THE HERALD.). (1909)-. Newspaper. English. da (except Sunday, New Year's Day, Memorial Day, Independence Day, Labor Day, Thanksgiving, and Christmas). $78.00. Sharon Herald, PO Box 51, Sharon PA 16146. **Tel** (412)981-6100. **ED** J. A. Dunlap. **Circ:** 27,056. available on microfilm from Bell & Howell. ***Continues*** *Sharon Herald (Sharon, Pa. : Daily).*

US
HERALD (SHARPSBURG, PA. : 1953). (THE HERALD.). 62nd Year, No. 1 (Dec. 28, 1939)-. Newspaper. English. wk. The Herald / Pennsylvania, 1024 Main Street, Sharpsburg PA 15215. ***Continues*** *Sharpsburg and Etna Herald.*

US
HERALD-STANDARD (UNIONTOWN, PA. : 1980). (HERALD-STANDARD.). **VFOAT** Herald Standard. (Jan. 26, 1980)-. Newspaper. English. da. $2.85 (weekly) mail. Herald-Standard, 8-18 East Church Street, Uniontown PA 15401. **ED** Michael Ellis and Gloria Pasinski (Managing Editor). **Bk Rev**, (Qty: 4). **Photos**. **Ad Acc, Adv Mgr:** Maureen Lorichak, **Tel** (412)439-7582. Full Page (B&W) $2392.95 (daily). Half Page (B&W) $1205.75 (daily). Full Page (Color) $2617.95. Half Page (Color) $1430.75. **Pub. Size:** Broadsheet. **Wire Svcs.:** AP. **Circ:** 32,500 (AM). available in microform. ***Absorbed*** *Morning Herald (Uniontown, PA.).*

US
HOME NEWS (BATH, PA.). (THE HOME NEWS.). Vol. 1, No. 1 (Dec. 11, 1942)-. Newspaper. English. wk. $15.00. Home News, 120 South Walnut Street, Bath PA 18014. **Tel** (215)837-0107, FAX (215)837-0482. **ED** William Halbfoerster (Editor-in-Chief) and David Halbfoerster (Managing Editor). **Photos**. **Ad Acc, Adv Mgr:** Kevin Halbfoerster. Full Page (B&W) $245.00. Half Page (B&W) $122.50. Full Page (Color) $295.00. Half Page (Color) $172.50. **Pub. Size:** Tabloid. **Circ:** 4,200.

US
INDEPENDENT-OBSERVER (SCOTTDALE, PA.). (THE INDEPENDENT-OBSERVER.). **VFOAT** Independent Observer. Vol. 47, No. 7 (Jan. 22, 1926)-. Newspaper. English. wk. $23.60. Independent Observer, 229 Pittsburgh Street, Scottdale PA 15683. **Tel** (412)887-6101, FAX (412)887-5115. **ED** Dirk Kaufman. **Photos**. **Ad Acc, Adv Mgr:** Bob Cummingham or Peggy Milliron, **Tel** (412)887-6102. **Pub. Size:** Standard. ***Formed by the union of*** *Scottdale Independent* ***and*** *Scottdale News-Observer.*

US
INDIANA GAZETTE (INDIANA, PA.). (INDIANA GAZETTE.). Vol. 78 No. 111 (Jan. 2, 1982)-. Newspaper. English. da (Except holidays). $103.95 Indiana, Armstrong, Clearfield, Cambria, Jefferson, & Westmoreland counties; $134.95 others. Indiana Evening Gazette, PO Box 10, Indiana PA 15701. **Tel** (412)465-5555. ***Continues*** *Indiana Evening Gazette.*

US
INTELLIGENCER. (Vol. 98, No. 111 (May 10, 1988)-. Newspaper. English. da. Intelligencer, 333 North Broad Street, Box 858, Doylestown PA 18901. **Tel** (215)345-3000. Documents available from UMI Article Clearinghouse. ***Continues*** *Daily Intelligencer (Doylestown, Pa.).*
Ind/Abst Bus. Dateline (Dec. 27, 1991-) [Full Txt.].

US/0889-4140
INTELLIGENCER JOURNAL. **VFOAT** Daily Intelligencer Journal; Lancaster Daily Intelligencer Journal. Vol. 64, No. 229 (May 26, 1928)-. Newspaper. English. da. $51.00. Lancaster Newspapers Inc, 8 West King Street, PO Box 1328, Lancaster PA 17603. **Tel** (717)291-8611. **ED** William R Schultz and William H Cody. **Ad Acc. Circ:** 43,523. available on an online database (file 635/Full-Text) from DIALOG. Documents available from UMI Article Clearinghouse. ***Continues*** *Lancaster Intelligencer. News Journal.*
Desc: Local (Lancaster County) general interest daily newspaper.
Ind/Abst Bus. Dateline (Dec. 23, 1991-) [Full Txt.].

US/0746-5971
JEANNETTE SPIRIT, THE. Newspaper. English. wk. $13.00. Jeannette Spirit, 310 Clay Avenue, Jeannette PA 15644. **Tel** (412)887-7400. **ED** Gregory L Stock. **Ad Acc. Circ:** 2,500.
Desc: Articles cover local and community news.

US
JEFFERSONIAN-DEMOCRAT (BROOKVILLE, PA.). (THE JEFFERSONIAN-DEMOCRAT.). **VFOAT** Jeffersonian Democrat. Vol. 8, No. 16 (April 22, 1885)- = Whole No. 366-. Newspaper. English. wk. Jeffersonian-Democrat, 175 Main Street, Brookville PA 15825. ***Continues*** *Brookville Democrat (Brookville, PA.).*

US
JEWISH TIMES. Vol. 8, No. 32 (Oct. 27, 1983)-. Newspaper. English. wk (Thursday). $15.97. Jewish Times / Huntingdon Valley, 103A Tomlinson Road, Huntingdon Valley PA 19006. **Tel** (215)938-1177, FAX (215)677-2264. **ED** Matthew Schuman. **Bk Rev. Photos. Ad Acc, Adv Mgr:** Larry Salomon. **Wire Svcs.:** JT. **Circ:** 30,000 (ctrl). ***Continues*** *Jewish Times of the Greater Northeast.*

US
JOHNSONBURG PRESS, THE. **VFOAT** Press. Began in 1896. Newspaper. English. wk. Johnsonburg Press, 517 Market Street, Johnsonburg PA 15845.

US
JOURNAL-HERALD (WHITE HAVEN, PA.). (THE JOURNAL-HERALD.). **VFOAT** Journal Herald. Vol. 1, No. 1 (Sept. 10, 1981)-. Newspaper. English. wk. $15.00. Journal-Herald / Pennsylvania, 211 Main Street, White Haven PA 18661. **ED** Clara Holder (Editor-in-Chief) and Ruth Isenberg (Managing Editor). **Bk Rev. Photos. Ad Acc, Adv Mgr:** Seth Isenberg, **Tel** (717)443-9131. Full Page (B&W) $250.00. Half Page (B&W) $140.00. Full Page (Color) $375.00. Half Page (Color) $200.00. **Pub. Size:** Broadsheet. **Circ:** 1,800. ***Formed by the union of*** *Journal (White Haven, PA.)* ***and*** *Weatherly Herald.*

US
JUNIATA NEWS. (1934)-. Newspaper. English. wk. $47.00. Juniata News, 2241 North 5th Street, Philadelphia PA 19133. **Tel** (215)739-8197, FAX (215)739-9290. **ED** Gerard Lineman. **Photos. Ad Acc, Adv Mgr:** Thomas Lineman. Full Page (B&W) $412.50. Half Page (B&W) $206.25. **Pub. Size:** Tabloid. **Circ:** 10,000.

US
JUNIATA SENTINEL (MIFFLINTOWN, PA. : 1955). (THE JUNIATA SENTINEL.). **VFOAT** Juniata Sentinel and Republican. Began in 1955?. Newspaper. English. wk. Juniata Sentinel, PO Box 127, Mifflintown PA 17059. ***Continues*** *Juniata Sentinel and Republican.*

US
KANE REPUBLICAN (KANE, PA. : 1912). (THE KANE REPUBLICAN.). **VFOAT** Daily Republican. Vol. 18, No. 195 (Aug. 29, 1912)-. Newspaper. English. da. Kane Republican, 200 North Fraley Street, Kane PA 16735. ***Continues*** *Kane Daily Republican.*

US/1052-8547
KEYSTONE GAZETTE (BELLEFONTE, PA. : 1989). (THE KEYSTONE GAZETTE.). (Dec. 1, 1989)-. Newspaper. English. wk. Keystone Gazette, PO Box 746, Bellefonte PA 16823-0746. **ED** George Giokas. ***Continues*** *Centre Democrat (Bellefonte, PA. : 1848), 0747-0118.*

US
LANCASTER NEW ERA. **VFOAT** Lancaster New Era and Examiner; New Era. (Aug. 30, 1923)-. Newspaper. English. da. $83.50. Lancaster Newspapers Inc, 8 West King Street, PO Box 1328, Lancaster PA 17603. **Tel** (717)291-8611. **ED** Robert J. Kozak and Peter C. Mekeel. Index available. **Ad Acc. Circ:** 55,393. available on an online database (file 635/Full-Text) from DIALOG. Documents available from UMI Article Clearinghouse. ***Continues*** *Lancaster New Era and Examiner.*
Desc: Local (Lancaster County), general interest, daily newspaper.
Ind/Abst Bus. Dateline (Dec. 12, 1991-) [Full Txt.].

US
LATROBE BULLETIN. Vol. 1, No. 1 (Dec. 18, 1902)-. Bulletin. English. da. Latrobe Bulletin, 1211 Ligonier Street, Latrobe PA 15650.

US
LEADER (PHILADELPHIA, PA.). (THE LEADER.). Began in 1963. Newspaper. English. wk. Intercounty Newspaper Group / Philadelphia, 2923 Cheltenham Avenue, Philadelphia PA 19150.

US
LEADER-TIMES. **VFOAT** Leader Times. Vol. 76, No. 275 (Nov. 20, 1964)-. Newspaper. English. da (Monday - Saturday). $120.00 (one year) Armstrong County, PA, $125.00 (one year) others (by mail); $101.00 (one year) by carrier. Leader-Times, 115-121 North Grant Avenue, Kittanning PA 16201. **Tel** (412)543-1303. ***Continues*** *Daily Leader-Times.*

US
LEADER-VINDICATOR, THE. **VFOAT** Leader Vindicator; New Bethlehem Leader Vindicator; Leader-Vindicator Merged with the Record. Vol. 34, No. 18 (Jan. 3, 1929)-. Newspaper. English. wk. $20.00 Pennsylvania; $40.00 others. Leader-Vindicator, 435 Broad Street, New Bethlehem PA 16242. **ED** James R. Shaffer (Editor-in-Chief) and Jos P. Shaw (Managing Editor). **Bk Rev. Photos. Ad Acc, Adv Mgr:** Jas R. Shaffer, **Tel** (814)275-3131. Full Page (B&W) $630.00. Half Page (B&W) $315.00. **Pub. Size:** Standard. **Circ:** 5,500. available in microform. ***Formed by the union of*** *New Bethlehem Vindicator* ***and*** *New Bethlehem Leader;* ***Absorbed*** *Record (Rimersburg, Pa.).*

US
LIGONIER ECHO, THE. Vol. 1, No. 1 (Sept. 5, 1888)-. Newspaper. English. wk. Ligonier Echo, 112 West Main Street, Ligonier PA 15658. ***Absorbed*** *Ligonier American.*

US
LUMINARY (MUNCY, PA.). (THE LUMINARY.). Vol. 106, No. 1 (Sept. 26, 1946)-. Newspaper. English. wk. The Luminary, PO Box 267, Muncy PA 17756. ***Continues*** *Muncy Luminary (Muncy, PA. : 1939).*

US
MAIN LINE TIMES. Vol. 9, No. 72 (Feb. 16, 1939)-. Newspaper. English. wk (Wednesdays). $43.80 local. ACME Newspapers, 311 East Lancaster Avenue, Ardmore PA 19003. **Tel** (215)642-4300. ***Continues*** *tMain Line Daily Times.*

US
MCKEAN COUNTY MINER (SMETHPORT, PA. : 1974). (MCKEAN COUNTY MINER.). Vol. 140, No. 2 (Jan. 10, 1974)-. Newspaper. English. wk. $23.00 in county; $33.00 others. McKean County Miner, PO Box 17, Bradford PA 16701. **ED** G. Nichols (Editor-in-Chief) and Deb Nichols (Managing Editor). **Bk Rev,** (Qty: 2). **Photos. Ad Acc, Adv Mgr:** G. Nichols, **Tel** (814)362-6563. Full Page (B&W) $532.80. Half Page (B&W) $266.40. Full Page (Color) $582.80. Half Page (Color) $316.40. **Pub. Size:** Tabloid. ***Continues in part*** *McKean County Miner and The Mount Jewett Echo;* ***Continues*** *Mount Jewett Echo (Mount Jewett, PA. : 1974).*

US/0747-2412
MEADVILLE TRIBUNE (1955). (THE MEADVILLE TRIBUNE.). Vol. 71, No. 270 (July 1955)-. Newspaper. English. da. Meadville Tribune, 947 Federal Court, Meadville PA 16335. **Ad Acc. Circ:** 16,500. ***Formed by the union of*** *Evening Republican* ***and*** *Tribune-Republican.*

US/0164-5102
MERCHANT (HARRISBURG), THE. (THE MERCHANT.). Periodical. English. mo. Free to members, $9.00 nonmembers. PRA, 22 South 3rd Street, Harrisburg PA 17101.

US
MERCURY (POTTSTOWN, PA.). (THE MERCURY.). **VFOAT** Sunday Mercury. Vol. 42, No. 205 (May 29, 1973)-. Newspaper. English. da (360 issues per year). $244.00. The Mercury, Hanover and King Streets, Pottstown PA 19464. **Tel** (610)323-3000, FAX (610)970-4492. **ED** Walt Herring (Editor-in-Chief) and Jack Croft (Managing Editor). **Bk Rev. Photos. Ad Acc, Adv Mgr:** 52. Full Page (B&W) $1,901.00. Half Page (B&W) $950.00. Full Page (Color) $2,111.00. Half Page (Color) $1,160.00. **Pub. Size:** Broadsheet. **Wire Svcs.:** AP. **Circ:** 30,000. ***Continues*** *Pottstown Mercury (Pottstown, PA. : 1937).*

US
MIDWEEKER. **VFOAT** Pocono-Anthracite Midweeker. Vol. 1, No. 1 (June 15, 1983)-. Newspaper. English. wk. Pocono-Anthracite Communications, Lansford PA.

US
MIFFLINBURG TELEGRAPH. Vol. 1, No. 1 (June 10, 1862)-. Newspaper. English. wk. $8.00. Mifflinburg Telegraph, 358 Walnut Street, Mifflinburg PA 17844. **Tel** (717)966-2255, FAX (717)966-9706. **ED** Vanessa Bilger. **Photos. Ad Acc, Adv Mgr:** John Stamm. Full Page (B&W) $280.00. Half Page (B&W) $140.00. **Pub. Size:** Tabloid. **Circ:** 750. available in microform.

US/0747-2943
MILLCREEK SUN, THE. (1982)-. Newspaper. English. Fifty-two times a year (Wed.). $18.00 Millcreek County; $34.00 others. Brown Thompson Newspapers, PO Box 151, Millcreek Sun Paper, Union City PA 16438. **Tel** (814)438-7666.

US
MILTON STANDARD, THE. **VFOAT** Milton Standard Combined Temporarily with Union County Journal. 72nd Yr., No. 21,909 (May 3, 1961)-. Newspaper. English. da. Milton Standard, 19 Arch Street, Milton PA 17847. ***Continues*** *Milton Evening Standard (Milton, PA. : 1941).*

US/0884-5557
MORNING CALL (ALLENTOWN, PA.), THE. (THE MORNING CALL.). Vol. 98, No. 74 (Mar. 15, 1939)-. Newspaper. English. ds. $319.28. Morning Call, 6th and Linden Streets, Allentown PA 18105. **Tel** (215)820-6612. **ED** Lawrence Hymans. **LC** 7002. **Circ:** 132,806 daily, 174,210 Sunday. ***Continues*** *Allentown Morning Call (Allentown, Pa. : 1921).*

US
MORNING NEWS (ERIE, PA.). (MORNING NEWS.). **VFOAT** Times-News. Vol. 9, No. 153 (July 7, 1964)-. Newspaper. English. da. Times Publishing Company / Pennsylvania, 205 West 12th Street, Erie PA 16534. **Tel** (814)870-1600. **ED** Ed Mead (Editor-in-Chief) and Jeff Pinski (Managing Editor). **Bk Rev,** (Qty: 20). **Photos. Ad Acc, Adv Mgr:** John Anderson, **Tel** (814)870-1655. **Pub. Size:** Broadsheet. **Wire Svcs.:** AP. **Circ:** 28,426. available in microform. ***Continues*** *Erie Morning News.*

US
MORRISONS COVE HERALD. Vol. 46, No. 32 (March 6, 1931)-. Newspaper. English. wk. Morrisons Cove Herald, 113 North Market Street, Martinsburg PA 16662. ***Continues*** *Martinsburg Herald (Martinsburg, PA. : 1903).*

US
MOUNT PLEASANT JOURNAL (MOUNT PLEASANT, PA.). (MOUNT PLEASANT JOURNAL.). **VFOAT** Mt. Pleasant Journal; Journal. Vol. 1, No. 1 (June 5, 1873)-. Newspaper. English. wk. $16.00 West Moreland County; $26.00 Pennsylvania; $29.00 US. Mount Pleasant Journal, 23 South Church Street, Mount Pleasant PA 15666. **Tel** (412)547-5722.

US
MOUNT UNION TIMES (MOUNT UNION, PA. : 1873). (MOUNT UNION TIMES.). **VFOAT** People's Era. Began in Feb. 1873. Newspaper. English. wk. Mount Union Times, 325 Penn Street, Mount Union PA 16652.

US
MOUNTAINEER-HERALD, THE. **VFOAT** Mountaineer Herald. 99th Year, No. 14 (Sept. 11, 1952)-. Newspaper. English. wk. $20.80. Mountaineer-Herald, 113 South Center Street, Edensburg PA 15931. **Tel** (814)472-9544. **ED** Kathleen Nikolishen. **Photos. Ad Acc, Adv Mgr:** David Thompson, **Tel** (814)472-8240. **Pub. Size:** Standard. **Circ:** 3,200. ***Continues*** *Edensburg Mountaineer-Herald.*

US
MOUNTAINTOP EAGLE, THE. Vol. 1, No. 1 (Oct. 30, 1969)-. Newspaper. English. wk. Mountaintop Eagle, PO Box 10, Mountaintop PA 18707. ***Continues*** *Mountain View.*

US
MURRYSVILLE AREA STAR. Vol. 13 No. 18 (Oct. 10 1984)-. Newspaper. English. wk. Gateway Press Inc., 610 Beatty Road, Monroeville PA 15146. **Tel** (412)856-7400. ***Continues*** *Star (Monroeville, Pa.).*

US/0746-4037
NANTY-GLO JOURNAL, THE. Vol. 1, No. 1 (May 5, 1921)-. Newspaper. English. wk. $15.95 Pennsylvania residents, $16.95 other. Nanty-Glo Journal, PO Box 395, Portage PA 15946-0395.

US
NEW CASTLE NEWS. Began in 1890. Newspaper. English. da. New Castle News, 35 North Mercer Street, New Castle PA 16103. ***Continues*** *City News.*

US/1047-8051
NEW PITTSBURGH COURIER (CITY ED.). (NEW PITTSBURGH COURIER.). **VFOAT** Pittsburgh Courier; New Courier; Pittsburgh New Courier. (Oct. 15, 1966)-. Newspaper. English. sw (Wed. & Sat.). $40.00 Pennsylvania & Ohio & West Virginia; $45.00 others. New Pittsburgh Courier, PO Box 2939, Pittsburgh PA 15230-9939. **Tel** (412)481-8302. **ED** John H. Sengstacke (Editor-in-Chief) and Ed Davis (Managing Editor). **Bk Rev**, (Qty: 12). **Photos**. **Ad Acc**, **Adv Mgr:** Donna Walker, **Tel** (412)481-8302. Full Page (B&W) $5,060.16. Half Page (B&W) $2,530.08. Full Page (Color) $5,810.16. Half Page (Color) $3,280.08. **Pub. Size:** Broadsheet. **Wire Svcs.:** AP. **Circ:** 24,000. available in microform from Ethnic News Watch. ***Continues*** *Pittsburgh Courier (City Ed. : 1955).*

US/1047-806X
NEW PITTSBURGH COURIER (NATIONAL ED.). (NEW PITTSBURGH COURIER.). [New Pittsbg. cour.]. **VFOAT** Pittsburgh New Courier; Pittsburgh Courier; A.New courier; A.Courier. Vol. 58, No. 44 (Nov. 4, 1966)-. Newspaper. English. Twice a week (Wed. and Sat.). $28.00 (one year); $37.00 (two year); $48.00 (three year). New Pittsburgh Courier, PO Box 2939, Pittsburgh PA 15230-9939. **Tel** (412)481-8302. **DD** 071. **Bk Rev**. **Ad Acc**, **Adv Mgr:** D. Walker. **Circ:** 24,000. ***Continues*** *Pittsburgh Courier (Pittsburgh, Pa. : 1955 : National ed.).*
Desc: Acts as vehicle for Afro-American expression.

US
NEWS-CHRONICLE (SHIPPENSBURG, PA.). (THE NEWS-CHRONICLE.). **VFOAT** News Chronicle. Vol. 1, No. 1 (Sept. 6, 1927)-. Newspaper. English. sw. $31.20 (carrier); $41.60 (mail). The News Chronicle Company, PO Box 100, Road 1, Shippensburg PA 17257. **Tel** (717)532-4101, FAX (717)532-3020. **ED** Jim Curtis. **Bk Rev**, (Qty: 26). **Photos**. **Ad Acc**, **Adv Mgr:** Steve Helm, **Tel** (717)532-4101. Full Page (B&W) $690.15. Half Page (B&W) $345.08. Full Page (Color) $755.15. Half Page (Color) $410.08. **Pub. Size:** Broadsheet. available in microform. ***Formed by the union of*** *Shippensburg News* ***and*** *Chronicle (Shippensburg, PA.).*

US
NEWS-CITIZEN (VANDERGRIFT, PA.). (THE NEWS-CITIZEN.). **VFOAT** News Citizen. Newspaper. English. wk. $16.00. News-Citizen, 203 Walnut Street, Vandergrift PA 15690. **Tel** (412)567-5656. **Circ:** 6,000 (ctrl). available on microfilm.

US
NEWS-HERALD (FRANKLIN, PA). (THE NEWS-HERALD.). **VFOAT** News Herald. 43rd Year, No. 13196 (May 5, 1919)-. Newspaper. English. da. $82.00. Venango Newspapers, Inc., PO Box 889, Oil City PA 16301. **Tel** (814)676-7444. **LC** 7000. ***Absorbed*** *Blizzard (Oil City, Pa.);* ***Formed by the union of*** *Franklin Evening News* ***and*** *Venango Daily Herald.*

US
NEWS-ITEM (COMBINED ED.). (THE NEWS-ITEM.). **VFOAT** News Item. Vol. 1, No. 283 (Sept. 2, 1969)-. Newspaper. English. da. News-Item, 707 North Rock Street, Shamokin PA 17872. ***Formed by the union of*** *News-Item (Shamokin Area Ed.)* ***and*** *News-Item (Mount Carmel Area Ed.).*

US
NEWS OF DELAWARE COUNTY (UPPER DARBY, PA. : MARPLE-NEWTOWN--SPRINGFIELD ED.). (NEWS OF DELAWARE COUNTY.). (19??)-. Newspaper. English. Fifty-two times a year (Published on Wed.). $23.40. ACME Newspapers, 311 East Lancaster Avenue, Ardmore PA 19003. **Tel** (215)642-4300.

US/0889-3810
NEWS-SUN (NEWPORT, PA.), THE. (THE NEWS-SUN.). **VFOAT** News Sun. 80th Year, No. 9 (Feb. 26, 1948)-. Newspaper. English. wk. News Sun / Pennsylvania, 19 South 3rd Street, Newport PA 17074. ***Continues*** *Weekly News-Sun.*

US/8750-5916
NORTH HILLS NEWS RECORD. Newspaper. English. tw. North Hills News Record, 137 Commonwealth Drive, Warrendale PA 15035. **ED** Ronald Wayne. **Circ:** 15,718.

US
NORTHEAST TIMES (PHILADELPHIA, PA. : 1971). (NORTHEAST TIMES.). Vol. 5, No. 49 (April 14, 1971)-. Newspaper. English. wk. $35.00 (six months). Northeast Times, 8001 Roosevelt Boulevard, Suite 404, Philadelphia PA 19152. **Tel** (215)332-3300, FAX (215)355-4812. **ED** John Scowlon (Editor-in-Chief) and Fred Gusoff (Managing Editor). **Photos**. **Ad Acc**, **Adv Mgr:** Timothy Smylie, **Tel** (215)355-9009 ext. 121. Full Page (B&W) $1,500.00. Full Page (Color) $1,995.00. **Pub. Size:** Standard. **Circ:** 257,000. ***Continues*** *Times Northeast.*

US/0891-0693
OBSERVER-REPORTER. **VFOAT** Observer Reporter. No. 671 (May 1, 1967)-. Newspaper. English. da (except holidays). Observer Reporter / Pennsylvania, 122 South Main Street, Washington PA 15301. **Tel** (412)222-2200. **ED** John Crouse. **Circ:** 38,134. ***Formed by the union of*** *Washington Reporter (Washington, Pa. : Daily)* ***and*** *Washington Observer (Washington, Pa. : Daily);* ***Absorbed*** *Democrat-Messenger.*

US
OLNEY TIMES. (Sept. 20, 1929)-. Newspaper. English. wk. $60.00. Olney Times, 5703 North 5th Street, Philadelphia PA 19120. **Tel** (215)424-0700, FAX (215)424-4082. **ED** Thomas Reilly Jr. **Photos**. **Ad Acc**, **Adv Mgr:** Melissa Reilly. Full Page (B&W) $494.00. Half Page (B&W) $290.00. Full Page (Color) $600.00. **Pub. Size:** Standard. **Circ:** 25,000.

US/1041-4029
PATRIOT (HARRISBURG, PA. : DAILY). (THE PATRIOT). (April 1891)-. Newspaper. English. da. Patriot News Company, PO Box 1437, Harrisburg PA 17101. **Tel** (717)255-8277. **ED** Ronald Minard. **Bk Rev**. **Ad Acc**. **Circ:** 50,425 daily, 94,740 Saturday. available on microfilm from University Microfilms International (UMI). ***Continues*** *Daily Morning Patriot (Harrisburg, PA. : 1889).*

US/0745-2586
PENNSYLVANIA BEACON, THE. Vol. 1, No. 1 (August 4, 1982)-. Newspaper. English. wk. Pennsylvania Beacon, 3600 Vartan Way, Harrisburg PA 17110.

US/0192-8406
PENNY SAVER (LANCASTER), THE. (THE PENNY SAVER.). (19??)-. Newspaper. English. Fifty-two times a year. $12.00. Brookshire Publications, 200 Hazel Street, Lancaster PA 17603. **Tel** (717)392-1321, FAX (717)392-2078.

US
PERRY COUNTY TIMES, THE. **VFOAT** Times. (188?)-. Newspaper. English. wk. $17.00. Perry County Times, PO Box 128, New Bloomfield PA 17068. **ED** Wade Fowler (Editor-in-Chief) and Gary Thomas (Managing Editor). **Photos**. **Ad Acc**, **Adv Mgr:** Rick White, **Tel** (717)582-4305. Full Page (B&W) $468.27. Half Page (B&W) $234.14. Full Page (Color) $868.27. Half Page (Color) $634.14. **Circ:** 5,580. ***Continues*** *New Bloomfield, Pa. Times.*

US/0733-6349
PHILADELPHIA CITY PAPER. **VFOAT** City Paper. (19??)-. Newspaper. English. wk. $52.00. Philadelphia City Paper, 206 South 13th Street, Philadelphia PA 19107. **Tel** (215)735-8444. **ED** Chris Hill, Violette Phillips. Index available. **Bk Rev**. **Ad Acc**. **Circ:** 88,000 (ctrl).
Desc: Covers national news, local politics, music, entertainment, the arts, and reviews of records, books, and movies.

US
PHILADELPHIA DAILY NEWS (PHILADELPHIA, PA. : 1925). (PHILADELPHIA DAILY NEWS.). **VFOAT** Daily News. Vol. 1, No. 1 (March 31, 1925)-Vol. 49, No. 223 (Dec. 20, 1973)-. Newspaper. English. da. $192.00. Philadelphia Newspapers Inc., PO Box 8500 6800, Philadelphia PA 19178. **Tel** (215)854-4790. available on microfilm from University Microfilms International (UMI); available on an online database (file 731/Full-Text) from DIALOG. ***Continues*** *Daily News (Philadelphia, PA : 1884).*

US
PHILADELPHIA GAY NEWS. **VFOAT** PGN; P G N. Vol. 8, No. 49 (Oct. 18, 1984)-. Newspaper. English. wk. $115.00. Gay News, 254 South 11th Street, Philadelphia PA 19107. **Tel** (215)625-8501, FAX (215)625-8501. **ED** Al Patrick, Mark Segal (Managing Editor). **Bk Rev**, (Qty: 4). **Photos**. **Ad Acc**, **Adv Mgr:** Tony Lombardo. Full Page (B&W) $1040.00. Half Page (B&W) $520.00. Full Page (Color) $1040.00 plus $100.00 per color. Half Page (Color) $520.00 plus $100.00 per color. **Wire Svcs.:** AP. **Circ:** 15,000 (ctrl). ***Continues*** *Gay News (Philadelphia, PA.).*

US/0885-6613
PHILADELPHIA INQUIRER (1969), THE. (THE PHILADELPHIA INQUIRER.). [Phila. inq.]. Vol. 281, No. 165 (Dec. 12, 1969)-. Newspaper. English. da. $192.00 (daily by mail). Philadelphia Newspapers Inc., PO Box 8500 6800, Philadelphia PA 19178. **Tel** (215)854-4790. **ED** Eugene Roberts Jr. **DD** 071. **Circ:** 504,946 daily, 985,582 Sunday. available on microfilm from University Microfilms International (UMI); and Bell & Howell; available on an online database (file 633/Full-Text) from DIALOG. ***Continues*** *Philadelphia Inquirer Public Ledger.*
Ind/Abst Art Archaeol. Tech. Abstr.; PROMT.

US/0890-8435
PHILADELPHIA NEW OBSERVER, THE. **VFOAT** New Observer. Vol. 4, No. 50 (Dec. 8, 1979)-. Newspaper. English. wk. $30.00. The Philadelphia New Observer Inc, Box 30092, 1930 Chestnut Street/Suite 900, Philadelphia PA 19103. **Tel** (215)665-8400, FAX (215)665-8914. **ED** J. Hugo Warren III. **Bk Rev**. **Photos**. **Ad Acc**, **Adv Mgr:** Frank Green. Full Page (B&W) $2304.00. Half Page (B&W) $1152.00. Full Page (Color) $3804.00. Half Page (Color) $1902.00. **Pub. Size:** Broadsheet. **Circ:** 20,000 (ctrl). available in microform from Free Library of Philadelphia. ***Continues*** *New Observer.*
Desc: Minority-oriented newspaper, all positive news format.

US/0746-956X
PHILADELPHIA TRIBUNE (1884). (THE PHILADELPHIA TRIBUNE.). (Nov. 2, 1884)-. Newspaper. English. sw. $47.00 (1 year), $90.00 (2 year); $13.00 (6 months, once a week), $22.00 (1 year, once a week), $25.00 (6 months, twice a week), $44.00 (1 year, twice a week), $38.00 (1 year, senior citizens) libraries and schools. Philadelphia Tribune, 520026 South 16th Street, Philadelphia PA 19146. **Tel** (215)893-4050, FAX (215)735-3612. **ED** Paul Burnett. **LC** 7002. **Ad Acc**. **Circ:** 25,000 Tuesday, 18,000 Friday (ctrl). available on microfilm.

US
PIKE COUNTY DISPATCH (MILFORD, PA.). (PIKE COUNTY DISPATCH.). **VFOAT** Pike County Dispatch and Port Jervis News. 130th Yr., No. 49 (Sept. 19, 1957)-. Newspaper. English. wk. Pike County Dispatch, 105 West Catharine Street, Milford PA 18337. ***Continues*** *Milford Dispatch and Pike County Press.*

US
PITT NEWS, THE. Vol. 24, No. 5 (Oct. 1932)-. Newspaper. English. wk. University of Pittsburgh / 441 William Pitt Union, Pittsburgh PA 15260. ***Continues*** *Pitt Weekly.*

US/1068-624X
PITTSBURGH POST-GAZETTE (PITTSBURGH, PA. 1978). (PITTSBURGH POST-GAZETTE.). **VFOAT** Post-Gazette; Pittsburgh Post Gazette; A.Post gazette; A.Pittsburgh Post-gazette and the best of the Press. Vol. 51, No. 133 (Jan. 2, 1978)-. Newspaper. English. da. $240.00 US; $360.00 other. Pittsburgh Post-Gazette, PO Box 566, Pittsburgh PA 15230. **Tel** (412)263-1659. available on microfilm from University Microfilms International (UMI); available on an online database (files 635,718/Full-Text) from DIALOG. Documents available from UMI Article Clearinghouse. ***Continues*** *Pittsburgh Post-Gazette, Sun-Telegraph;* ***Absorbed*** *Pittsburgh Press.*
Ind/Abst Bus. Dateline (July 30, 1990-) [Full Txt.].

US
PITTSBURGH PRESS, THE. ***Title Change.*** **VFOAT** Pittsburgh Press; Pittsburgh Press and Daily News. Vol. 4, No. 250 (Oct. 19, 1887)-Vol. 109, No. 2 (July 28, 1992). Newspaper. English. da (except legal holidays). Pittsburgh Post-Gazette, PO Box 566, Pittsburgh PA 15230. **Tel** (412)263-1659. **LC** 7002. available on microfilm; available on an online database (file 718/Full-Text) from DIALOG. ***Continues*** *Evening Penny Press (Pittsburgh, Pa.);* ***Absorbed*** *Evening Record (Allegheny, Pa.); Pittsburg Daily News.* ***Absorbed by*** *Pittsburgh Post-Gazette (Pittsburgh, Pa. : 1978), 1068-624X.*
Ind/Abst PROMT.

US
PORTAGE DISPATCH (PORTAGE, PA. : 1948). (THE PORTAGE DISPATCH.). No. 21 (May 7, 1948)-. Newspaper. English. wk. Portage Dispatch, PO Box 395, Portage PA 15946-0395. available on microfilm. ***Continues*** *Cambria Dispatch.*

US/1043-4291
POST (MIDDLEBURG, PA. 1976), THE. (THE POST.). Vol. 113, No. 10 (March 4, 1976)-. Newspaper. English. wk. The Post / Middleburg, 29 West Market Street, Middleburg PA 17842. ***Continues*** *Middleburg Post.*

US/0895-6839
POTTER LEADER-ENTERPRISE. **VFOAT** Potter Leader Enterprise; Leader-Enterprise; Leader Enterprise. Vol. 113, No. 21 (Sept. 2, 1987)-. Newspaper. English. wk. $23.00. Leader Publishing Company, 6 West 2nd Street, PO Box 29, Coudersport PA 16915-0671. **Tel** (814)274-8044, FAX (814)274-8120. **ED** Paul Heimel. **Ad Acc**. **Circ:** 10,500 (ctrl). available in microform. ***Formed by the union of*** *Potter Enterprise (Coudersport, PA. : 1950), 0888-6253* ***and*** *Potter County Leader.*
Desc: Covers local and county news.

US
POTTSVILLE REPUBLICAN (POTTSVILLE, PA. : 1942). (POTTSVILLE REPUBLICAN.). Vol. 114, No. 114 (March 11, 1942)-. Newspaper. English. da (except Sun.). Pottsville Republican, 111 Mahantongo Street, Pottsville PA 17901.

Tel (717)622-3456. **ED** Douglas Costello. **Circ:** 28,718. available on microfilm. ***Continues*** *Pottsville Evening Republican;* ***Absorbed*** *Pottsville Journal.*

US
PRESS AND JOURNAL, THE. VFOAT Middletown Press and Journal. Nov. 3, 1944-. Newspaper. English. wk. Press and Journal, 20 South Union Street, Middletown PA 17057. ***Formed by the union of*** *Middletown Press (Middletown, PA.)* ***and*** *Middletown Journal (Middletown, PA. : 1870).*

US/0746-0724
PRESS-ENTERPRISE (BLOOMSBURG, PA.). (PRESS-ENTERPRISE.). **VFOAT** Press Enterprise. Vol. 83, No. 88 (July 1, 1983)-. Newspaper. English. da (Mon.-Sat.). $110.00. Press-Enterprise / Pennsylvania, PO Box 747, 3185 Lackawanna Avenue, Bloomsburg PA 17815. **Tel** (800)228-3483, (717)784-2121. **Photos. Ad Acc, Adv Mgr:** Sandy Bower, **Tel** (717)387-1234 ext. 1216. Full Page (B&W) $1082.31. Half Page (B&W) $566.31. Full Page (Color) $1194.31. Half Page (Color) $678.31. **Pub. Size:** Broadsheet. **Circ:** 22,000 net paid. available in microform. ***Formed by the union of*** *Berwick Enterprise (Berwick, Pa. : 1907)* ***and*** *Morning Press (Bloomsburg, Pa.).*

US
PROGRESS (CLEARFIELD, PA. : 1946). (THE PROGRESS.). Vol. 40, No. 151 (June 27, 1946)-. Newspaper. English. da (312 issues). The Clearfield Progress, PO Box 291, Clearfield PA 16830. **Tel** (814)765-5581. ***Continues*** *Clearfield Progress.*

US
PUBLIC OPINION (CHAMBERSBURG, PA. : 1974 : DAILY). (PUBLIC OPINION.). No. 217 (April 3, 1974)-. Newspaper. English. da. McClure Newspapers Inc, 77 North 3rd Street, Chambersburg PA 17201. ***Continues*** *Public Opinion, Franklin Repository.*

US
READING EAGLE. 16th Year, No. 219 (Sept. 3, 1883)-. Newspaper. English. da. The Reading Eagle, PO Box 582, Reading PA 19603. **Tel** (215)373-4221. **ED** Edward A Taggert. **Circ:** 35,188 daily, 111,638 Sunday. ***Continues*** *Reading Daily Eagle.*

US
READING TIMES (READING, PA. : 1923). (READING TIMES.). **VFOAT** Times. Vol. 65, No. 199 (March 1, 1923)-. Newspaper. English. da. Reading Eagle Company, 345 Penn Street, Reading PA 19603. **Tel** (215)373-4421. **ED** Edward A. Taggert. **Circ:** 44,950. ***Continues*** *Reading News-Times.*

US/0199-0438
RECORD ADVERTISER. Newspaper. English. wk. Record Advertiser, 549 South Main Street, Shrewsbury PA 17361.

US
RECORD-ARGUS (GREENVILLE, PA. : 1985). (THE RECORD-ARGUS.). **VFOAT** Record Argus. 136th year, No. 233 (Oct. 3, 1985)-. Newspaper. English. da. Record-Argus, 10 Penn Avenue, Greenville PA 16125. ***Continues*** *Greenville Record-Argus*

US
RECORD (COATESVILLE, PA.). (THE RECORD.). Vol. 66, No. 108 (Feb. 2, 1974)-. Newspaper. English. da. Community Service Publishing Company, 204 East Lincoln Highway, Coatesville PA 19320. ***Continues*** *Coatesville Record.*

US
RECORD HERALD. VFOAT Record Herald. Vol. 27, No. 306 (Mar. 16, 1921)-. Newspaper. English. da (Except Sundays and six holidays). $81.00. Waynesboro Record Herald, Waynesboro PA 17268. ***Continues*** *Record-Herald and Blue Ridge Zephyr.*

US/0747-2161
RECORD-OUTLOOK, THE. VFOAT Record Outlook. Vol. 1, No. 1 (July 15, 1932)-. Newspaper. English. wk. $18.00. Observer Publishing Company, 116 East Lincoln Avenue, PO Box 117, McDonald PA 15057. **Tel** (412)926-2111, FAX (412)926-2123. **ED** Eliza A. Northrop. **Photos. Ad Acc, Adv Mgr:** Carolyn Windows. Full Page (B&W) $727.02. Half Page (B&W) $363.51. Full Page (Color) $797.02. Half Page (Color) $433.51. **Pub. Size:** Broadsheet. **Circ:** 4,280. available in microform. ***Formed by the union of*** *McDonald Record* ***and*** *M'Donald Outlook (McDonald, Pa. : 1892).*

US
RECORD (RENOVO, PA.). (THE RECORD.). 1974-. Newspaper. English. wk. The Record / Pennsylvania, 129 5th Street, Renovo PA 17764. ***Continues*** *Renovo Record (Renovo, PA. : Daily).*

US
REPORTER ARGUS. VFOAT Port Allegany Reporter-Argus. Vol. 112, No. 22 (Nov. 13, 1985)-. Newspaper. English. wk. $19.50. Leader Publishing Company Inc, 6 West 2nd Street, PO Box 29, Port Allegany PA 16743-0129. **Tel** (814)642-2811, FAX (814)642-7169. **(Subscription address:** 4 North Main Street, PO Box 129, Port Allegany, PA 16743-0129) **ED** George Petrisek, Paul Heimel. **Ad Acc. Circ:** 2,800 (ctrl). ***Continues*** *Port Allegany Reporter, Port Allegany Argus (Port Allegany, PA. : 1985).*
Desc: Local and county issues.

US/0890-8443
REPORTER (LANSDALE, PA.), THE. (THE REPORTER.). 109th Yr., Issue 55 (Jan. 2, 1979)-. Newspaper. English. da. $176.00 US (by mail). Equitable Publishing Company, 307 Derstine Avenue, Lansdale PA 19446. **Tel** (215)855-8440. **ED** Eric Wolferman. **Circ:** 18,359. ***Continues*** *North Penn Reporter.*

US
REPUBLIC (MEYERSDALE, PA.). (THE REPUBLIC.). (Nov. 4, 1974)-. Newspaper. English. wk. The Republic / Pennsylvania, 301 North Street, Meyersdale PA 15552. ***Continues*** *Meyersdale Republican.*

US
REYNOLDSVILLE STAR, THE. 54th Year of publication, No. 39 (Feb. 22, 1946)-. Newspaper. English. wk. Reynoldsville Star, 511 Main Street, Reynoldsville PA 15851. ***Continues*** *Star (Reynoldsville, PA.).*

US
RIDGWAY RECORD. Vol. 15, No. 148 (May 25, 1918)-. Newspaper. English. da. Ridgway Record, PO Box T, Ridgway PA 15853. ***Continues*** *Ridgway Daily Record.*

US
ROCKET-COURIER. VFOAT Rocket Courier. No. 36 (Sept. 15, 1877)-. Newspaper. English. wk. Rocket-Courier, PO Box 187, Wyalusing PA 18853. ***Formed by the union of*** *Wyalusing Rocket* ***and*** *Wyoming County Courier.*

US
SCRANTON TIMES (SCRANTON, PA. : 1891 : DAILY). (THE SCRANTON TIMES.). Vol. 21, No. 104 (July 27, 1891)-. Newspaper. English. da. Scranton Times, Penn Avenue at Spruce Street, PO Box 3311, Scranton PA 18501. **Tel** (717)348-9190. **ED** Edwin Rogers and Robert Borke. **LC** 7002. **Ad Acc. Circ:** 85,000. available on microfilm from University Microfilms International (UMI). Documents available from UMI Article Clearinghouse. ***Continues*** *Scranton Daily Times (Scranton, Pa. : 1891).*
Ind/Abst Bus. Dateline (Jan. 9, 1992-) [Full Txt.].

US
SCRANTONIAN, THE. VFOAT Scrantonian, The Scranton Tribune. (1897)-. Newspaper. English. wk. Scrantonian, 338 North Washington Avenue, Scranton PA 18501.

US
SELINSGROVE TIMES-TRIBUNE, THE. VFOAT Selinsgrove Times Tribune. 145th Yr., No. 42 (Aug. 6, 1959)-. Newspaper. English. wk. Selinsgrove Times-Tribune, PO Box 30, Selinsgrove PA 17870. ***Continues*** *Selinsgrove Times and the Snyder County Tribune.*

US/0887-0802
SENTINEL (CARLISLE, PA.), THE. (THE SENTINEL.). (July 2, 1984)-. Newspaper. English. da. $104.00. Cumberland Publishers Inc, PO Box 130, Carlisle PA 17013. **Tel** (717)243-3121. **ED** Carol Talley (Editor-in-Chief) and Kurth Wanfried (Managing Editor). Index available. **Photos. Ad Acc, Adv Mgr:** Steve Crowley, **Tel** (717)243-2611 ext. 244. Full Page (B&W) $1,362.24. Half Page (B&W) $739.86. Full Page (Color) $1,502.24. Half Page (Color) $879.86. **Pub. Size:** Standard. **Wire Svcs.:** AP. **Circ:** 18,000. available in microform. ***Continues*** *Evening Sentinel (Carlisle, PA.).*

US
SENTINEL (LEWISTOWN, PA.). (THE SENTINEL.). Dec. 16, 1920-. Newspaper. English. da. Lewiston Sentinel, 6th & Summit Drive, Pleasant Acre, Lewistown PA 17044. **Tel** (717)248-6741. ***Continues*** *Daily Sentinel (Lewistown, PA. : 1903).*

US/0747-1610
SENTINEL (SHILLINGTON, PA.), THE. (THE SENTINEL.). Began in 1984. Newspaper. English. wk. Berks-Mont Newspapers, Inc. / Shillington, Shillington PA 19607.

US
SERIAL ARTICLES PUBLISHED IN NEWSPAPERS / STATE LIBRARY OF PENNSYLVANIA, LIBRARY SERVICES DIVISION, NEWSPAPER SECTION. **Added/Corp** State Library of Pennsylvania. Newspaper Section. (June 9, 1983)-. English. mo. State Library of Pennsylvania, PO Box 1601, Harrisburg PA 17105. **LC** AI3; .S47. **DD** 071/.48. ctrl circ. ***Continues*** *Articles Published in a Series ... .*

US/0739-6236
SERVICE DEALER'S NEWSLETTER. SDN. VFOAT SDN. Vol. 1, No. 1 (Apr. 1984)-. Newsletter. English. mo. $58.00. SDN Service Dealer, 1400 Easton Road, Roslyn PA 19001. **Tel** (800)673-7808 (215)657-3010, FAX (212)659-2199. **ED** Alvin E. Brooks. Index Bound in First Issue (Bound in January issue). cum. index. **Bk Rev.**
Desc: A newsletter for business and personal insights for service dealers & managers.

US/1047-0697
SEWICKLEY HERALD (1968), THE. (THE SEWICKLEY HERALD.). **VFOAT** Sewickley Herald, The Record. Vol. 69, No. 6 (Feb. 8, 1968)-. Newspaper. English. Fifty-two times a year. $32.50 (Allegheny County Pennsylvania); $44.00 other. Gateway Publications, 705 5th Avenue, Coraopolis PA 15108. **Tel** (412)264-4140. **ED** Mike May. **Ad Acc. Circ:** 4,000 (ctrl). available on microfilm. ***Continues*** *Herald (Sewickley, Pa. : 1955).*

US/0199-6819
SLOVAK V AMERIKE. VFOAT Daily Slovak American; Dennik Slovak v Amerike; Slovak American. Began with Dec. 21, 1889 issue. Newspaper. Slovak (English). mo. $15.00 US; $20.00 other. Michael J Krajsa, Box 350, Middletown PA 17057. **Tel** (717)944-0461, FAX 717-944-3107. **ED** Joseph C Krajsa. **Bk Rev. Ad Acc. Circ:** 1,200 (ctrl). available on microfilm from The Library of Congress Photoduplication Service.

US
SOUDERTON INDEPENDENT. (April 1881)-. Newspaper. English. wk. $17.00. Souderton Independent, 21 South Front Street, Box 459, Souderton PA 18964. **Tel** (215)723-5188, FAX (215)723-8779. **ED** Fred Behringer (Editor-in-Chief) and Barbara McClennen (Managing Editor). **Photos. Ad Acc, Adv Mgr:** John Derr, **Tel** (215)723-4801. Full Page (B&W) $928.80. Full Page (Color) $1,013.80. **Circ:** 6,900. available on microfilm.

US
SOUTH HILLS RECORD. VFOAT Record; Mt. Oliver Record. Vol. 49, No. 31 (Dec. 5, 1952)-. Newspaper. English. wk. Gateway Publications, 705 5th Avenue, Coraopolis PA 15108. **Tel** (412)264-4140. ***Continues*** *Hill Top Record and the South Hills Economist.*

US
SOUTH PITTSBURGH REPORTER. VFOAT Reporter. Vol. 31, No. 13 (Jan. 6, 1971)-. Newspaper. English. wk. $32.00. South Pittsburgh Reporter, PO Box 4285, Pittsburgh PA 15203. **ED** Roberta F Smith. **Photos. Ad Acc, Adv Mgr:** W. T. Smith, **Tel** (412)481-0266. Full Page (B&W) $379.68. Half Page (B&W) $189.84. Full Page (Color) $479.68. Half Page (Color) $289.84. **Pub. Size:** Tabloid. **Circ:** 12,000. ***Continues*** *Reporter (Pittsburgh, Pa.).*

US
SOUTHWEST GLOBE-TIMES. VFOAT Southwest Globe Times. Newspaper. English. wk. Southwest Globe-Times, 6330 Paslhall Avenue, Philadelphia PA 19142. ***Continues*** *Southwest Phila. Globe Times.*

US
SPIRIT (PUNXSUTAWNEY, PA.). (THE SPIRIT.). Vol. 94, No. 308 (Sept. 12, 1967)-. Newspaper. English. da. $102.00 local counties; $140.00 other. Spirit Publishing Company, 111 North Findley Street, Punxsutawney PA 15767. **Tel** (814)938-8740. **ED** David R. Divelbiss. ***Continues*** *Punxsutawney Spirit (Punxsutawney, PA. : Daily).*

US
STANDARD OBSERVER (IRWIN, PA. : 1979). (THE STANDARD OBSERVER.). **VFOAT** Daily Standard-Observer. Vol. 5, No. 1065 (July 18, 1979)-. Newspaper. English. da. Westmoreland Journals Inc, PO Box 280, Irwin PA 15642. ***Continues*** *Daily Standard-Observer.*

US
STANDARD-SPEAKER. VFOAT Hazleton Standard-Speaker. Vol. 114 No. 32,282 (June 20, 1980)-. Newspaper. English. da. Standard-Speaker, 21 North Wyoming Street, Hazleton PA 18201. available on microfilm from Bell & Howell. ***Continues*** *Hazleton Standard-Speaker.*

US
SUBURBAN GAZETTE. (19??)-. Newspaper. English. wk. $20.00 local; $32.00 other. Suburban Gazette, 421 Locust Street, McKees Rocks PA 15136. **Tel** (412)331-2645. **Photos. Ad Acc, Adv Mgr:** James Dinaudo. Full Page (B&W) $650.00. Half Page (B&W) $325.00. **Pub. Size:** Standard. ***Continues*** *McKees Rocks Gazette.*

US
SULLIVAN REVIEW (DUSHORE, PA. : 1958). (THE SULLIVAN REVIEW.). **VFOAT** Sully. Vol. 81, No. 43 (Oct. 24, 1958)-. Newspaper. English. wk. Towanda Printing Company, PO Box 305, Dushore PA 18614. available in microform from Bell & Howell. ***Continues*** *Sullivan Review Gazette and Herald.*

US
SUN (HUMMELSTOWN, PA.). (THE SUN.). Vol. 99, No. 4 (Aug. 5, 1970)-. Newspaper. English. wk. $14.00 Pennsylvania; $17.00 others. The Sun / Pennsylvania, 115-117 South Water Street, PO Box C,

Hummelstown PA 17036. **Tel** (717)566-3251, FAX (717)566-6196. **ED** William S. Jackson and Rosemary Jackson (Managing Editor). **Bk Rev**, (Qty: 5-10). **Photos**. **Ad Acc**, **Adv Mgr:** Rosemary Jackson. Full Page (B&W) $619.20. Half Page (B&W) $309.60. Full Page (Color) $699.20. Half Page (Color) $389.60. **Pub. Size:** Broadsheet. **Circ:** 6,564. available on microfilm. ***Continues*** *Hummelstown Sun.*
Desc: Newspaper serving Hershey, Hummelstown and lower Dauphin county.

US
SUNDAY DISPATCH (PITTSON, PA.). (SUNDAY DISPATCH.). Vol. 1 No. 1 (Feb. 9, 1947)-. Newspaper. English. wk. Sunday Dispatch, 109 New Street, Pittston PA 18640.

US
SUNDAY INDEPENDENT (WILKES-BARRE, PA.). (SUNDAY INDEPENDENT.). Began with May 1914 issue?. Newspaper. English. wk. Sunday Independent, 90 East Market Street, Wilkes-Barre PA 18701. ***Continues*** *Independent (Wilkes-Barre, PA.).*

US
SUNDAY NEWS (LANCASTER, PA.). (SUNDAY NEWS.). **VFOAT** Lancaster Sunday News. (Sept. 1923)-. Newspaper. English. wk. $51.00. Lancaster Newspapers Inc, 8 West King Street, PO Box 1328, Lancaster PA 17603. **Tel** (717)291-8611. **ED** David M Hennigan. **Ad Acc. Circ:** 100,691.
Desc: Local, general interest Sunday newspaper.

US
SUNDAY TIMES (SCRANTON, PA. : 1966). (THE SUNDAY TIMES.). **VFOAT** New Sunday Times. Vol. 1, No. 1 (Oct. 9, 1966)-. Newspaper. English. wk. Sunday Times, Pennsylvania Avenue & Spruce Street, Scranton PA 18501. **Tel** (717)342-9151. available on microfilm from University Microfilms International (UMI).

US
SUSQUEHANNA COUNTY INDEPENDENT, THE. VFOAT Independent. 169th Year, No. 45 (Nov. 6, 1985)-. Newspaper. English. wk. Susquehanna County Independent, Montrose PA 18801. ***Formed by the union of*** *Montrose Independent* ***and*** *Susquehanna County Press.*

US
TELEGRAPH (BROWNSVILLE, PA.). (THE TELEGRAPH.). Vol. 54, No. 288 (Dec. 12, 1969)-. Newspaper. English. da. $60.00. Brownsville Telegraph, 16-18 Bridge Street, Brownsville PA 15417. **Tel** (412)785-5000. ***Continues*** *Brownsville Telegraph.*

US/0746-4606
TIMES-CHRONICLE. VFOAT Times Chronicle; Times-Chronicle; Jenkintown Times Chronicle. Vol. 1, No. 39 (Dec. 29, 1894)-. Newspaper. English. wk. $26.00. Montgomery Publishing Company, 290 Commerce Drive, Fort Washington PA 19034. **Tel** (215)542-0200, FAX (215)643-9475. **ED** Fred Behringer (Editor-in-Chief) and Warren Patton (Managing Editor). **Photos**. **Ad Acc**, **Adv Mgr:** Leslie Hamada, **Tel** (215)885-1345. Full Page (B&W) $2,347.80. Half Page (B&W) $1,173.90. Full Page (Color) $2,432.80. Half Page (Color) $1,258.90. **Pub. Size:** Broadsheet. available in microform. ***Continues*** *Jenkintown Times;* ***Absorbed*** *Jenkintown Journal.*

US
TIMES HERALD (NORRISTOWN, PA.). (THE TIMES HERALD.). No. 255 (April 14, 1952)-. Newspaper. English. da (360 issues per year). $155.68. Times Herald / Pennsylvania, PO Box 591, Norristown PA 19404. **Tel** (215)272-2500. **ED** Jim Strommen. **Ad Acc. Circ:** 30,000 (ctrl). ***Continues*** *Norristown Times Herald.*

US/0896-4084
TIMES LEADER (WILKES-BARRE, PA.). (THE TIMES LEADER). **VFOAT** Sunday Times Leader. (March 29, 1982)-. Newspaper. English. da. $93.60 Pennsylvania; $132.00 others. Times Leader / Pennsylvania, 15 North Main Street, Wilkes Barre PA 18711. **Tel** (717)829-7100. **ED** Cliff Schechtmna (phone: (717)829-7252). **Bk Rev**. **Ad Acc**, **Adv Mgr:** Dennis Shealey, **Tel** (717)829-7122. **Circ:** 48,000 (Mon. - Fri.), 55,000 (Saturday), 79,000 (Sunday). available on microfilm from University Microfilms International (UMI). ***Continues*** *Wilkes-Barre Times Leader (Wilkes-Barre, PA. : 1978), 0199-0519.*

US
TIMES-NEWS (LEHIGHTON, PA.). (THE TIMES-NEWS.). **VFOAT** Times News. 89th year, No. 267 (Feb. 16, 1972)-. Newspaper. English. da. $105.00. Times News / Pennsylvania, PO Box 239, Lehighton PA 18235. **ED** Bob Perfitt and Bob Urban (Managing Editor). **Ad Acc**, **Adv Mgr:** Don Reese, **Tel** (610)377-2051. Full Page (B&W) $1291.50. Half Page (B&W) $645.75. Full Page (Color) $1391.50 (1 color). Half Page (Color) $745.75 (1 color). **Pub. Size:** Broadsheet. **Wire Svcs.:** AP. **Circ:** 16,500 (evening). ***Continues*** *Times News-Record & Courier.*

US
TIMES-SUN, THE. VFOAT Times Sun. 95th Year, No. 15 (Jan. 3, 1973)-. Newspaper. English. wk. Times-Sun, 201-208 1st Street, West Newton PA 15089. ***Continues*** *West Newton Times-Sun.*

US
TITUSVILLE HERALD, THE. Vol. 48, No. 222 (Feb. 26, 1913)-. Newspaper. English. da. $108.00. Titusville Herald, 209 West Spring Street, Titusville PA 16354. **Tel** (814)827-3634, FAX (814)827-9647. **ED** Michael Sample (Editor-in-Chief) and John Yates (Managing Editor). **LC** 9618. **Photos**. **Ad Acc**, **Adv Mgr:** Michael Sample. Full Page (B&W) $774.00. Half Page (B&W) $387.00. Full Page (Color) $854.00. Half Page (Color) $467.00. **Pub. Size:** Broadsheet. **Wire Svcs.:** AP. **Circ:** 4,753. ***Continues*** *Titusville Morning Herald.*

US/8755-9315
TODAY'S SPIRIT. Vol. 100, No. 22 (Feb. 6, 1973)-. Newspaper. English. wk. $26.00. Montgomery Publishing Company, 290 Commerce Drive, Fort Washington PA 19034. **Tel** (215)542-0200, FAX (215)643-9475. **ED** Fred Behringer (Editor-in-Chief) and Andrew Hussie (Managing Editor). **Photos**. **Ad Acc**, **Adv Mgr:** Herbert Hoover, **Tel** (215)675-3430. Full Page (B&W) $2,347.80. Half Page (B&W) $1,173.90. Full Page (Color) $2,432.80. Half Page (Color) $1,258.90. **Pub. Size:** Broadsheet. available in microform. ***Continues*** *Public Spirit (Hatboro, Pa.).*

US/0888-9996
TOWN AND COUNTRY (LANSDALE, PA.). (TOWN AND COUNTRY.). Vol. 1, No. 1 (April 1, 1899)-. Newspaper. English. wk. $36.00 Pennsylvania, $41.00 other. Town and Country, PO Box 5, Pennsburg PA 18073. **Tel** (215)679-9561.

US/1055-9590
TRIBORO BANNER. Vol. 1, No. 1 (Aug. 13, 1970)-. Newspaper. English. wk. $15.50. Triboro Banner, 105 South Main Street, Taylor PA 18517. **Tel** (717)562-3511, FAX (717)562-7785. **ED** Shirley Helbing. **Photos**. **Ad Acc**, **Adv Mgr:** Carol Carey. Full Page (B&W) $300.00. Half Page (B&W) $150.00. Full Page (Color) $325.00. Half Page (Color) $175.00. **Pub. Size:** Standard. **Circ:** 6,000 (ctrl).

US
TRIBUNE-DEMOCRAT (JOHNSTOWN, PA.). (THE TRIBUNE-DEMOCRAT). **VFOAT** Tribune Democrat. (1952)-. Newspaper. English. da. Johnstown Tribune Publishing, 425 Locust Street, Johnstown PA 15907. **Tel** (814)532-5000. available on microfilm. ***Formed by the union of*** *Johnstown Tribune (Johnstown, Pa. : 1891 : Daily)* ***and*** *Johnstown Democrat (Johnstown, Pa. : Daily).*

US
TRIBUNE-REVIEW (GREENSBURG, PA.). (TRIBUNE-REVIEW.). **VFOAT** Tribune Review; Sunday Tribune-Review. Newspaper. English. da. Tribune-Review, Cabin Hill Drive, Greensburg PA 15602.

US
TRIBUNE-REVIEW (GREENSBURG, PA. : ALLEGHENY EAST ED.). (TRIBUNE-REVIEW.). **VFOAT** Tribune Review. Vol. 98, No. 162 (Aug. 1, 1983)-. Newspaper. English. da. Tribune-Review, Cabin Hill Drive, Greensburg PA 15602. ***Continues in part*** *Tribune-Review (Greensburg, PA. : Jeannette Ed.).*

US
TRIBUNE-REVIEW (GREENSBURG, PA. : FAY-WEST ED.). (TRIBUNE-REVIEW.). **VFOAT** Tribune Review; Sunday Tribune-Review. Vol. 98, No. 162 (Aug. 1, 1983)-. Newspaper. English. da. Tribune-Review, Cabin Hill Drive, Greensburg PA 15602. ***Continues in part*** *Tribune-Review (Greensburg, PA: Jeannette Ed.).*

US
TRIBUNE-REVIEW (GREENSBURG, PA. : WESTERN ED.). (TRIBUNE-REVIEW.). Vol. 98, No. 162 (Aug. 1, 1983)-. Newspaper. English. da. Tribune-Review Building, Cabin Hill Drive, Greensburg PA 15602. ***Continues*** *Tribune-Review (Greensburg, PA. : Jeannette Ed.).*

US/1062-5844
TRIBUNE (SCRANTON, PA. 1990), THE. (THE TRIBUNE.). (May 22, 1990)-. Newspaper. English. da. $132.20 (inside PA), $148.20 (outside PA). The Tribune, Scranton Times, PO Box 3311, Scranton PA 18505. ***Formed by the union of*** *Morning Times (Scranton, Pa.), 1045-8123* ***and*** *Scrantonian Tribune.*

US
TROY GAZETTE-REGISTER. VFOAT Troy Gazette Register. Began in Jan. 1905. Newspaper. English. wk. Troy Gazette-Register, 11 Canton Street, Troy PA 16947. ***Formed by the union of*** *Troy Gazette (Troy, PA.)* ***and*** *Troy Register.*

US
TYRONE DAILY HERALD. VFOAT Tyrone Herald. Began with April 16, 1887 issue. Newspaper. English. da. Tyrone Herald Company, 1018 Penna Avenue, Turbotville PA 16686.

US
UNION PRESS-COURIER. VFOAT Union Press Courier. Vol. 2, No. 22 (Oct. 1, 1936)-. Newspaper. English. wk. Union Press-Courier, 452 Magee Avenue, Patton PA 16668. ***Formed by the union of*** *Union Press (Patton, PA.)* ***and*** *Patton Courier.*

US/1056-4853
VALLEY GAZETTE, THE. VFOAT Panther Valley Gazette. 1st Issue (July 1972)-. Newspaper. English. mo. $14.00. Gazette Publications Inc, 102 West Water Street, Lansford PA 18232. **Tel** (717)645-4692. **ED** Edward Gildea. **Bk Rev**. **Photos**. **Ad Acc**, **Adv Mgr:** Ed Gildea. Full Page (B&W) $120.00. Half Page (B&W) $60.00. **Pub. Size:** Tabloid. **Circ:** 1,800 (ctrl).
Desc: Local history of the anthracite area, nostalgia, feature articles, photos, reminiscence, columns, etc.

US
VALLEY INDEPENDENT (MONESSEN, PA. : COMBINED ED.). (THE VALLEY INDEPENDENT.). (1960)-. Newspaper. English. da. Valley Independent, Eastgate 19, Monessen PA 15062. ***Formed by the union of*** *Valley Independent (Charleroi, PA. : Westmoreland-Fayette Counties Ed.)* ***and*** *Valley Independent (Charleroi, PA. : Washington County Ed.).*

US
VALLEY NEWS DISPATCH. 80th Year, No. 290 (Nov. 1, 1971)-. Newspaper. English. da. Valley News Dispatch, 210 Fourth Avenue, Tarentum PA 15084. **Tel** (412)224-4321. ***Formed by the union of*** *Daily Dispatch, The Valley Daily News* ***and*** *Valley Daily News, Daily Dispatch.*

US
VILLAGER (MOSCOW, PA.). (THE VILLAGER.). **VFOAT** Villager, The Shopper's Guide & News. Vol. 11, No. 6 (Aug. 5, 1965)-. Newspaper. English. wk. The Villager / Pennsylvania, PO Box 362, Moscow PA 18444. ***Continues*** *Shopper's Guide and News.*

US/0899-479X
WAYNE INDEPENDENT, THE. VFOAT Wayne Semi-Weekly Independent. Vol. 1, No. 1 (Feb. 7, 1878)-. Newspaper. English. tw. Wayne Independent, 220 8th Street, Honesdale PA 18431. available on microfilm.

US
WAYNESBURG REPUBLICAN (WAYNESBURG, PA. : 1870). (THE WAYNESBURG REPUBLICAN.). Vol. 14, No. 2 (June 15, 1870)-. Newspaper. English. wk. Waynesburg Republican, 122 South Main Street, Waynesburg PA 15301. ***Continues*** *Waynesburg Repository.*

US
WEEKLY BULLETIN (DILLSBURG, PA.). (WEEKLY BULLETIN.). Vol. 53, No. 8 (Dec. 21, 1928)-. Bulletin. English. wk. Weekly Bulletin, 2-4 North Baltimore Street, Dillsburg PA 17019. ***Continues*** *Weekly Bulletin and Tri-County Farm News.*

US
WEEKLY COLLEGIAN. Vol. 1, No. 1 (Sept. 12, 1979)-. Newspaper. English. wk (33 times while classes are in session). $22.25. Collegian Inc., 123 South Burrowes Street, State College PA 16801-3882. **Tel** (814)865-2531. **Photos**. **Ad Acc.** Full Page (B&W) $470.85. Half Page (B&W) $240.90. Full Page (Color) $595.85. Half Page (Color) $365.90. **Pub. Size:** Broadsheet. **Circ:** 3,000.
Desc: News for Penn State's branch campuses and alumni.

US
WEEKLY RECORDER, THE. Vol. 89, No. 1 (Jan. 3, 1977)-. Newspaper. English. wk. $18.00 Pennsylvania; $20.00 others. Weekly Recorder, 246 Main Street, PO Box F, Claysville PA 15323. **Tel** (412)663-7742. **ED** Douglas R. Teagarden. **Photos**. **Ad Acc**, **Adv Mgr:** Susan Burd. Full Page (B&W) $208.00. Half Page (B&W) $104.00. Full Page (Color) $258.00. Half Page (Color) $154.00. **Pub. Size:** Tabloid. **Circ:** 3,500. ***Continues*** *McGuffey Recorder.*

US
WELLSBORO GAZETTE (WELLSBORO, PA. : 1984). (THE WELLSBORO GAZETTE.). **VFOAT** Gazette. 109th Yr., No. 7 (Jan. 4, 1984)-. Newspaper. English. Fifty-two times a year. $30.00 Tioga County; $34.00 other. Wellsboro Gazette, PO Box 118, Wellsboro PA 16901. **Tel** (717)724-2287. ***Continues*** *Wellsboro Gazette Combined with Mansfield Advertiser (Combined Edition).*

US/0747-4024
WEST MIFFLIN AREA RECORD. VFOAT West Mifflin Area. Began in 1984. Newspaper. English. wk. West Mifflin Area Record, 3623 Brownsville Road, Pittsburgh PA 15227.

US/1056-3083
WILLIAMSPORT SUN-GAZETTE. VFOAT Williamsport Sun Gazette. 154th Year, No. 214 (Sept. 12, 1955)-. Newspaper. English. da. $117.00. Williamsport Sun-Gazette, 252 West 4th Street, Williamsport PA 17701. **Tel** (717)326-1551, FAX (717)323-0948. **ED** David Troisi (Editor-in-Chief) and Jeff Durham (Managing Editor). **Bk Rev. Photos. Ad Acc, Adv Mgr:** John Yahner. Full Page (B&W) $3,221.93. Half Page (B&W) $1,610.96. Full Page (Color) $3,646.93. Half Page (Color) $2,035.96. **Pub. Size:** Broadsheet. **Wire Svcs.:** AP. **Circ:** 33,272 (evening), 41.968 (Sunday). available in microform from University Microfilms International (UMI). Documents available from UMI Article Clearinghouse. ***Formed by the union of*** *Gazette and Bulletin* ***and*** *Williamsport Sun.*
Ind/Abst Bus. Dateline (Dec. 29, 1991-) [Full Txt.].

US/0746-4592
WILLOW GROVE GUIDE. (1925)-. Newspaper. English. wk. Willow Grove Guide, PO Box N, Willow Grove PA 19090.

US/1043-4313
YORK DAILY RECORD (YORK, PA. : 1973). (YORK DAILY RECORD.). Mar. 13, 1973-. Newspaper. English. da. York Daily Record, 1750 Industrial Highway, York PA 17402. **Tel** (717)757-4842, FAX (717)755-4457. **ED** Sam Fosdick. **Bk Rev. Ad Acc. Circ:** 41,000 (ctrl). ***Continues*** *Daily Record (York, Pa. : 1971).*

US/1050-267X
YORK DISPATCH, THE. VFOAT York Evening Dispatch. V. 20, No. 55 (Feb. 2, 1886)-. Newspaper. English. da. $180.00. York Dispatch, 15 17 East Philadelphia Street, York PA 17401. **Tel** (717)854-1575. **ED** Nancy Conway. **Ad Acc. Circ:** 42,000 Daily. ***Continues*** *Evening Dispatch (York, Pa. : 1878).*
Desc: World, national, state and local news and feature stories. Includes editorial opinion pieces and syndicated features.

RHODE ISLAND

US
BARRINGTON TIMES. Vol. 1, No. 1 (Jan. 23, 1958)-. Newspaper. English. wk. $29.95 Barrington; $39.00 Rhode Island, Maine, New Hampshire, Vermont, Massachusetts, Connecticut; $43.00 other. Barrington Times, Box 227, Barrington RI 02806. **Tel** (401)245-6000.

●US/1073-6468
CALL (WOONSOCKET, RI), THE. (THE CALL.). (1993)-. Newspaper. English. da. $153.40. Woonsocket Call, 75 Main Street, Woonsocket RI 02895. **Tel** (401)762-3000. ***Continues*** *Woonsocket Call.*

●US/1069-9473
CHARIHO TIMES (1993), THE. (THE CHARIHO TIMES.). (1993)-. Newspaper. English. wk. $24.00. Wilson Newspapers, 187 Main Street, Wakefield RI 02879. **Tel** (401)789-9744. **Photos. Ad Acc, Adv Mgr:** Laurie Ramaker. Full Page (B&W) $504.00 -$693.00. Half Page (B&W) $252.00 - $346.50. Full Page (Color) $629.00 - $818.00. Half Page (Color) $378.00 - $471.50. **Pub. Size:** Broadsheet. **Circ:** 3,000. ***Continues in part*** *Narragansett Times (Wakefield, R.I. : 1889), 1040-1938.*

US
CRANSTON HERALD. Vol. 55, No. 14 (June 15, 1977)-. Newspaper. English. wk. $18.00. Cranston Herald, 1944 Warwick Avenue, Warwick RI 02889 **Tel** (401)732-3100, FAX (401)732-3110. **ED** Steve Lowenthal. **Bk Rev. Photos. Ad Acc, Adv Mgr:** Alice Stanelun. Full Page (B&W) $806.25. Half Page (B&W) $403.12. Full Page (Color) $931.25. Half Page (Color) $528.12. **Pub. Size:** Standard. **Circ:** 4,500. available in microform. ***Continues*** *Cranston Herald-Today.*

US
EAST GREENWICH PENDULUM, THE. Vol. 134, No. 11 (Aug. 20, 1987)-. Newspaper. English. wk. $29.00 Rhode Island; $37.00 other. Wilson Publishing Co, PO Box 350, East Greenwich RI 02818. **Tel** (401)884-4662. ***Continues*** *Rhode Island Pendulum.*

US
EAST PROVIDENCE POST. VFOAT Post. Vol. 1, No. 1 (Nov. 3, 1955)-. Newspaper. English. wk. $12.00 Rhode Island; $14.00 New England; $18.00 other. East Providence Post, 1175 Warren Avenue, East Providence RI 02914. **Tel** (401)434-7210.

US
EVENING BULLETIN (PROVIDENCE, R.I.). (THE EVENING BULLETIN.). Vol. 1, No. 1 (Jan. 26, 1863)-. Bulletin. English. da. Providence Journal Company, 75 Fountain Street, Providence RI 02903. **Tel** (401)277-7508. **Circ:** 115,127. available on microfilm from University Microfilms International (UMI).

US
EVENING TIMES (PAWTUCKET, R.I. : 1978). (THE EVENING TIMES.). **VFOAT** Pawtucket Saturday Times. Vol. 363, No. 24 (Jan. 30, 1978)-. Newspaper. English. da. Times - Rhode Island, 23 Exchange Street, Pawtucket RI 02860. **Tel** (401)722-4000. available on microfilm from Graphic Microfilm Division. ***Continues*** *Pawtucket Times (Pawtucket, R.I. : 1920).*

US
KENT COUNTY DAILY TIMES, THE. Vol. 95, No. 75 (Mar. 30, 1987)-. Newspaper. English. da. $156.00. Kent County Daily Times, 1353 Main Street, West Warnick RI 02893. **Tel** (401)821-7400. ***Continues*** *Pawtuxet Valley Daily Times.*

US/1053-2560
NEWPORT DAILY NEWS. *Ceased.* Vol. 1, No. 1 (May 4, 1846)-Ceased (June 1989). Newspaper. English. da. Newport Daily News, 101 Malbone Road, Newport RI 02840. available in microform from Bell & Howell.

US
NEWPORT MERCURY. Vol. 230, No. 1 (Jan. 2, 1987)-. Newspaper. English. wk. $35.00. Edward A. Sherman Publishing Co, 101 Malbone Road, Newport RI 02840. **Tel** (401)849-3300. ***Continues*** *Newport Mercury and Weekly News.*

US
NEWPORT NAVALOG. Added/Corp United States Naval Training Station (Newport, R.I.). **VFOAT** Navalog. (1944)-. Newspaper. English. wk. Edward A. Sherman Publishing Co, 101 Malbone Road, Newport RI 02840. **Tel** (401)849-3300. **ED** David Offer. **Ad Acc, Adv Mgr:** Mary Jane Mann. **Circ:** 7,500. ***Continues*** *Newport Recruit and Service Schools' Log.*

US
NEWPORT THIS WEEK. Vol. 1, No. 1 (June 7, 1974)-. Newspaper. English. wk. $60.00 (first class); $16.00 (third class). Newport This Week, PO Box 159, Newport RI 02840. **Tel** (401)847-7766, FAX (401)846-4974. **ED** John Pantalone. **Bk Rev. Photos. Ad Acc, Adv Mgr:** James Maraziti. Full Page (B&W) $595.00. Half Page (B&W) $375.00. **Pub. Size:** Tabloid. **Circ:** 10,000.

US
OBSERVER, THE. Vol. 1, No. 1 (Mar. 16, 1956)-. Newspaper. English. wk. $19.50 Rhode Island; $35.00 US. Observer Publications / Greenville, PO Box 950, Greenville RI 02828. **Tel** (401)949-2700. ***Absorbed*** *Lincoln-Cumberland Observer (Ashton, R.I.)* ***and*** *North Smithfield-Burrillville Observer.*

US/0887-8226
PROVIDENCE BUSINESS NEWS. [Provid. bus. news]. Vol. 1, No. 1 (May 5, 1986)-. Newspaper. English. wk. $52.00. Providence Business News, 300 Richmond Street, Providence RI 02903. **Tel** (401)273-2201, FAX (401)274-0670, (401)274-0270. **ED** Frank Prosnitz, Donald DeMaio (Managing Editor). **DD** 338. Index available. **Bk Rev**, (Qty: 12). **Photos. Ad Acc, Adv Mgr:** John Lamp. Full Page (B&W) $3086.00. Half Page (B&W) $1667.00. Full Page (Color) $3686.00. Half Page (Color) $2267.00. **Pub. Size:** Tabloid. **Wire Svcs.:** AP. **Circ:** 4,500 paid, 6,000 unpaid (ctrl). available on an online database (file 635/Full-Text) from DIALOG. Documents available from UMI Article Clearinghouse.
Ind/Abst Bus. Dateline (Sept. 16, 1991-) [Full Txt.].

US
PROVIDENCE JOURNAL, THE. VFOAT Providence Sunday Journal; Providence Journal-Bulletin; Providence Journal Bulletin. Vol. 92, No. 35 (Feb. 10, 1920); Vol. 159, No. 187 (Sept. 26, 1988); Vol. 16, No. 188 (Sept. 27, 1988)-. Newspaper. English. da (312 issues per year). $187.20 (daily only); $312.00 (daily and Sunday by mail); $31.20 (Saturday by mail). Providence Journal Company, 75 Fountain Street, Providence RI 02903. **Tel** (401)277-7508. **LC** 7002. **Circ:** 94,220 daily, 260,926 Sunday. available on microfilm from University Microfilms International (UMI). Documents available from UMI Article Clearinghouse. ***Continues*** *Providence Daily Journal.*
Ind/Abst Bus. Dateline (Feb. 1, 1988-) [Full Txt.]; PROMT.

US/8750-5452
PROVIDENCE VISITOR (1984), THE. (THE PROVIDENCE VISITOR : OFFICIAL NEWSPAPER OF THE DIOCESE OF PROVIDENCE SINCE 1875.). **Added/Corp** Catholic Church. Diocese of Providence (R.I.). Vol. 110, No. 23 (July 12, 1984)-. Newspaper. English. wk (except 1st & 3rd weeks of July and August). $15.00 US; Free to libraries; $18.00 other. Visitor Printing Company, 184 Broad Street, Providence RI 02903. **Tel** (401)272-1010, FAX (401)421-8418. **ED** Stanley T. Nakowicz, Michael Brown (Managing Editor). **Bk Rev**, (Qty: 5-6/year). **Photos. Ad Acc.** Full Page (B&W) $1008.00. Half Page (B&W) $504.00. Full Page (Color) $1058.00. Half Page (Color) $554.00. **Pub. Size:** Tabloid. **Wire Svcs.:** CS. **Circ:** 30,000. ***Continues*** *Visitor (Providence, R.I.), 0273-8767.*

US
SAKONNET TIMES. Vol. 1, No. 1 (Oct. 26, 1967)-. Newspaper. English. wk. $17.50 Newport County; $26.00 New England; $30.00 other. Sakonnet Times, 2829 East Main Road, Portsmouth RI 02871. **Tel** (401)683-1000.

US/1040-3337
STANDARD-TIMES (WAKEFIELD, R.I), THE. (THE STANDARD-TIMES.). **VFOAT** Standard Times. 80th Year, No. 31 (Mar. 6, 1969)-. Newspaper. English. sw. Standard Times / Rhode Island, 13 West Main Street, North Kingstown RI 02852. **Tel** (401)294-4576. **ED** Rudi Hempe. **Ad Acc. Circ:** 7,200. ***Continues*** *Standard (North Kingstown, R.I.).*

US
TIMES-GAZETTE. VFOAT Times Gazette; Warren Times-Gazette. Vol. 122, No. 1 (Jan. 6, 1988)-. Newspaper. English. wk. East Bay Newspapers, PO Box 90, Bristol RI 02809-0090. **Tel** (401)253-6000. **ED** Bruce Burdett. **Circ:** 3,137. ***Continues*** *Warren Times-Gazette.*

US/1060-2747
TIMES (PAWTUCKET, R.I.), THE. (THE TIMES.). (19??)-. Newspaper. English. da. $175.50. Times / Pawtucket, 23 Exchange Street, Pawtucket RI 02860. **Tel** (401)722-4000. ***Continues*** *Evening Times (Pawtucket, R.I. : 1978).*

US
WARWICK BEACON. Vol. 1, No. 1 (Nov. 19, 1953)-. Newspaper. English. sw. $30.00. Warwick Beacon, 1944 Warwick Avenue, Warwick RI 02889. **Tel** (401)732-3100, FAX (401)732-3110. **ED** John Howell (Editor-in-Chief) and Marcia O'Brien (Managing Editor). **Bk Rev. Photos. Ad Acc, Adv Mgr:** Alice Stanelun. Full Page (B&W) $1,290.00. Half Page (B&W) $645.00. Full Page (Color) $1,415.00. Half Page (Color) $770.00. **Pub. Size:** Standard. available in microform.

US/1065-1209
WESTERLY SUN, THE. VFOAT Sun. Began with August 7, 1893 issue. Newspaper. English. da (except Saturday). $100.00. Utter Company, 56 Main Street, Westerly RI 02891. **Tel** (401)596-7791 or, (203)433-3307, FAX (401)348-5080. **ED** Charles W Utter, Donald P Lewis and David D Smith. **LC** 7002. **Bk Rev. Ad Acc. Circ:** 13,000. available on microfilm from Graphic Microfilm Division. ***Continues*** *Westerly Narragansett Weekly.*

SOUTH CAROLINA

US
ADVERTIZER-HERALD, THE. Vol. 6, No. 50 (Dec. 14, 1972)-. Newspaper. English. wk. Kilgus Publishing, PO Box 929, Bamberg SC 29003-0929. **Tel** (803)245-5204, FAX (803)245-3900. **ED** Carl Kilgus. **Ad Acc, Adv Mgr:** Cindy Wise. **Circ:** 4,350. ***Formed by the union of*** *Bamberg Herald* ***and*** *Advertizer.*

US/0893-2557
AIKEN STANDARD. Vol. 1, No. 1 (1867?)-. Newspaper. English. da (260 days per year). $7.75 per month. Aiken Standard, PO Box 456, Aiken SC 29801. **Tel** (803)649-5315, FAX (803)648-6052. **ED** Scott Hunter, Jeff Wallace (Managing Editor). **Photos. Ad Acc, Adv Mgr:** Charles O. Grice. Full Page (B&W) $1363.32. Half Page (B&W) $681.66. **Pub. Size:** Broadsheet. **Wire Svcs.:** KR, AP. ***Continues*** *Aiken Standard and Review.*

US
ANDERSON INDEPENDENT-MAIL. Vol. 82, No. 365 (Sept. 30, 1981)-. Newspaper. English. da. $129.00 Georgia & South Carolina; $180.00 other. Anderson Independent Mail, PO Box 2507, Anderson SC 29621. **Tel** (803)224-4321. ***Formed by the union of*** *Anderson Daily Mail* ***and*** *Anderson Independent (Anderson, S.C. : 1944).*

US
BARNWELL PEOPLE-SENTINEL, THE. Vol. 48, No. 40 (June 4, 1925)-. Newspaper. English. wk (52 issues). $30.00 residents of Barnwell County; $36.00 South Carolina; $38.00 other. Barnwell People Sentinel, PO Drawer 1255, Barnwell SC 29812. **Tel** (803)259-3501. ***Formed by the union of*** *Barnwell People* ***and*** *Barnwell Sentinel;* ***Absorbed*** *Williston Way.*

US
BEAUFORT GAZETTE, THE. (1897)-. Newspaper. English. da (Mon. thru Fri.). $88.00. Beaufort Gazette, PO Box 399, Beaufort SC 29901. **Tel** (803)524-3183, FAX (803)524-8728. **ED** Jim Cate. **Photos. Ad Acc, Adv Mgr:** Patsey Parker. **Pub. Size:** Broadsheet. **Wire Svcs.:** AP, SH, NY. **Circ:** 11,000. available on microfilm.

US
BLACK NEWS. (19??)-. Newspaper. English. wk. $25.00. SC Black Media Group, PO Box 11128, Columbia SC 29211. **Tel** (803)799-5252, FAX (803)799-7709.

US/0889-0617
CHERAW CHRONICLE. (1896)-. Newspaper. English. wk. $15.00 in county; $25.00 others. Cheraw Chronicle, 114 Front Street, PO Box 191, Cheraw SC 29520. **Tel** (803)537-5261. **ED** Marty Jackson. **Photos. Ad Acc, Adv Mgr:** Sandy Garris. Full Page (B&W) $603.72. Half Page (B&W) $301.86. Full Page (Color) $688.72. Half Page (Color) $386.86. **Pub. Size:** Broadsheet. available in microform.

US/0889-2334
CHESTERFIELD ADVERTISER, THE. ***Ceased.*** (1???)-(19??). Newspaper. English. wk. Chesterfield Advertiser, PO Box 389, Chesterfield SC 29709.

US/0746-1429
CHRONICLE (CHARLESTON, S.C.), THE. (THE CHRONICLE.). (19??)-. Newspaper. English. wk. $25.00. Chronicle Newspaper, PO Box 20548, Charleston SC 29413. **Tel** (803)723-2785. **ED** Jim French. **Photos. Ad Acc, Adv Mgr:** Nanette Smalls. Full Page (B&W) $1,260.00. Half Page (B&W) $630.00. Full Page (Color) $150.00 per color. Half Page (Color) $150.00 per color. **Pub. Size:** Standard. ***Continues*** *Charleston Chronicle (Charleston, S.C.).*

US
CHRONICLE-INDEPENDENT. Vol. 1, No. 1 (May 11, 1981)-. Newspaper. English. tw. Camden Chronicle Independent, 909 West De Kalb Street, PO Box 1137, Camden SC 29020-4226. **Tel** (803)432-6157. ***Formed by the union of*** *Camden Chronicle* ***and*** *Camden Independent.*

US
CITIZEN NEWS. English. wk. $12.00. Citizen News, Post Office Box 448, Edgefield SC 29832. **Tel** (803) 637-5306.

US/0893-035X
CLINTON CHRONICLE (CLINTON, S.C.), THE. (THE CLINTON CHRONICLE.). (1901)-. Newspaper. English. wk. $19.00 residents of Clinton, Laurens, Mountville, Crosshill, Joanna, Kinards, Graycourt, Waterloo and Fountain Inn counties; $34.00 other. Clinton Chronicle, Box 180, Clinton SC 29325. **Tel** (803)833-1900, FAX (803)833-1902. **ED** Rick Hendricks. **Photos. Ad Acc, Adv Mgr:** Larry Franklin. Full Page (B&W) $709.50. Half Page (B&W) $354.75. Full Page (Color) $774.50. Half Page (Color) $419.75. **Pub. Size:** Broadsheet. **Circ:** 5,650. ***Absorbed*** *Whitmire News (Whitmire, S.C. : 1949).*

US
CLOVER HERALD. (1928)-. Newspaper. English. wk. $12.00 in county; $15.00 others. Clover Herald, PO Box 30, Clover SC 29710-0038. **Tel** (803)684-9903, FAX (803)628-0300. **ED** Mike Faulkenberry. **Photos. Ad Acc, Adv Mgr:** Angie Ferguson. Full Page (B&W) $477.30. Half Page (B&W) $244.20. **Pub. Size:** Standard. **Circ:** 3,000.

US/8750-3425
COASTAL OBSERVER (PAWLEYS ISLAND, S.C.). (COASTAL OBSERVER.). (1982)-. Newspaper. English. wk. $14.00 (one year) Georgetown and Horry Counties; $17.00 (one year) other counties, South Carolina; $23.00 (one year) other. Southeastern Publishing Company, Midway Offices, Commerce Drive Waccamaw Park, PO Box 1170, Pawleys Island SC 29585. **Tel** (803)237-8438. **ED** Charles Swenson. **Bk Rev**, (Qty: 6-8 per year). **Photos. Ad Acc, Adv Mgr:** Squeaky Swenson. Full Page (B&W) $346.50. Half Page (B&W) $189.00. **Pub. Size:** Standard. **Circ:** 4,000.

US
COASTAL TIMES, THE. Vol. 1, No. 1 (July 6, 1983)-. Newspaper. English. wk. $15.00. Coastal Times, BTC Box 1407, 701 East Bay Street, Charleston SC 29403. **Tel** (803)723-5318.

US
DILLON HERALD, THE. (1894)-. Newspaper. English. sw (Tues. & Thurs.). $24.00. Dillon Herald, PO Box 1288, Dillon SC 29536. **Tel** (803)774-3311, FAX (803)841-1930. **ED** Paul Jones. **Photos. Ad Acc, Adv Mgr:** Johnnie Daniels. Full Page (B&W) $585.66. Half Page (B&W) $295.41. Full Page (Color) $660.00. Half Page (Color) $370.41.

US
DISPATCH-NEWS, THE. **VFOAT** Dispatch News. Began in 1920. Newspaper. English. wk. $23.00. Dispatch-News, PO Box 1317, Lexington SC 29072. **Tel** (803)359-3195. **ED** Jerry Bellune. **Bk Rev. Ad Acc. Circ:** 7,000. ***Continues*** *Lexington Dispatch.*
Desc: Covers community news.

US
DORCHESTER EAGLE-RECORD. (1934)-. Newspaper. English. wk. Dorchester Eagle Record, PO Box 278, St. George SC 29477. **Tel** (803)563-3121, FAX (803)563-5355. **ED** William Owens. **Ad Acc. Circ:** 3,100. ***Formed by the union of*** *Dorchester Eagle* ***and*** *Dorchester County Record.*

US
EASLEY PROGRESS, THE. Vol. 76, No. 1 (July 5, 1978)-. Newspaper. English. wk. Easley Progress, PO Box 708, Easley SC 29641. ***Continues*** *Progress (Easley, S.C.).*

US
EDGEFIELD ADVERTISER. (Feb. 11, 1836)-. Newspaper. English. wk. $5.00. Edgefield Advertiser, PO Box 628, Edgefield SC 29824. **Tel** (803)637-3540. **ED** W. W. Mims. **LC** 9694-X. available on microfilm from University Microfilms International (UMI). ***Continues*** *Carolinian (Edgefield, S.C.).*
Desc: Covers 150 years of continuous publication of the "oldest newspaper in SC " by Concurrent Resolutions for SC House and Senate.

US
FLORENCE MORNING NEWS. Vol. 22, No. 592 (Dec. 2, 1945)-. Newspaper. English. da. $126.06 residents of Florence, Effingham, Lake City, Scranton, Kingstree, Turbeville, Marion, Darlington, Bennettsville, Latta, Lakeview, Centenary, Olanta, McBee, Society Hill, Coward, Timmonsville, Pamplico, Johnsonville, Hemingway, Lamar, Hartsville, Dillon, Mullins, Nichols, Sellers, Gresham, Lynchburg, Lydia South Carolina; $147.06 other. Florence Morning News, PO Box 100528, Florence SC 29501. **Tel** (803)669-1771 ext. 268, FAX (803)661-6588. **ED** Frank Sayles Jr. **Ad Acc. Circ:** 34,000 (ctrl). available on microfiche. Documents available from UMI Article Clearinghouse. ***Continues*** *Morning News (Florence, S.C.).*
Ind/Abst Bus. Dateline (Dec. 22, 1991-) [Full Txt.].

US
FORT MILL TIMES. (1892)-. Newspaper. English. wk. $15.00. Fort Mill Times, PO Box 250, Fort Mill SC 29715. **Tel** (803)547-2353. **ED** John Mantle (Editor in Chief) and Jerry McGuire (Managing Editor). **Bk Rev**, (Qty: 12). **Photos. Ad Acc, Adv Mgr:** Carol Rose Mantle. Full Page (B&W) $774.00. Half Page (B&W) $387.00. **Pub. Size:** Broadsheet. **Circ:** 5,500. available in microform. ***Continues*** *Fort Mill News.*

US/0748-934X
GAFFNEY LEDGER, THE. (Nov. 26, 1907)-. Newspaper. English. tw (Sunday, Wednesday, Friday). $33.00 Gaffney County, South Carolina; $55.00 other. Gaffney Ledger, PO Box 670, 1604 Baker Boulevard, Gaffney SC 29342. **Tel** (803)489-1131. **ED** Cody Sossamon, Klonie Jorday (Managing Editor). **Bk Rev. Photos. Ad Acc, Adv Mgr:** Robert Martin. Full Page (B&W) $741.75. Half Page (B&W) $370.88. **Pub. Size:** Standard. **Wire Svcs.:** AP. **Circ:** 9,000. available on microfilm from the publisher. ***Continues*** *Ledger (Gaffney, S.C.).*

US/0746-5734
GEORGETOWN TIMES, THE. Vol. 126, no. 39 (Sept. 9, 1921) -. Newspaper. English. sw. $20.00 Goergeown, Williamsburg, Horry, and Charleston, $40.000 other. Georgetown Times, 615 Front Street, Drawer G, Georgetown SC 29442. **Tel** (803)527-4030. ***Continues*** *Georgetown Times-Index.*

US
GOOSE CREEK GAZETTE. (1979)-. Newspaper. English. wk. Goose Creek Gazette, PO Box 304, Goose Creek SC 29445. **Tel** (803)572-0511, FAX (803)572-0312. **ED** John Vernelson. **Ad Acc. Circ:** 4,500.

US
GREENVILLE NEWS, THE. **VFOAT** Greenville Daily News. (1920)-. Newspaper. English. da. $55.00 daily by carrier; $132.00 daily and Sunday by carrier; $185.00 (US), $370.00 (other) daily and Sunday by mail; $126.00 (US), $252.00 (other) daily; $61.00 Sunday only. Greenville News-Piedmont Company, Box 1688, Greenville SC 29602. **Tel** (803)298-4100, (800)800-5116, FAX (803)298-4023. **ED** John S Pittman. **Circ:** 87,995. available on microfilm from University Microfilms International (UMI).
Ind/Abst PROMT.

US
GREENVILLE PIEDMONT, THE. **Added/Corp** Greenville News-Piedmont Company (S.C.). Vol. 92, No. 52 (Mar. 12, 1927)-. Newspaper. English. da. $54.55. Greenville News-Piedmont Company, Box 1688, Greenville SC 29602. **Tel** (803)298-4100, (800)800-5116, FAX (803)298-4023. **ED** John Pittman, Ann Clark (Managing Editor). **Photos. Ad Acc, Adv Mgr:** Mark Johnston. Full Page (B&W) $5329.80. Half Page (B&W) $2664.90. Full Page (Color) $5904.80. Half Page (Color) $3239.90. **Pub. Size:** Broadsheet. **Wire Svcs.:** AP. **Circ:** 28,500. ***Continues*** *Piedmont.*

US
GREER CITIZEN, THE. (1917)-. Newspaper. English. wk. Greer Citizen, 105 Victoria, Greer SC 29652. **Tel** (803)877-2076, FAX (803)877-3563. **ED** Leland Burch. **Ad Acc. Circ:** 11,000.

US
HAMPTON COUNTY GUARDIAN. (1879)-. Newspaper. English. wk. $20.00 Hampton County; $25.00 South Carolina; $27.00 other. Hampton County Guardian, PO Box 625, Hampton SC 29924. **Tel** (803)943-4645. **ED** Laura McKenzie. **Ad Acc.** ***Continues*** *Ninety Six Guardian;* ***Absorbed*** *Jasper County Record (Ridgeland, S.C.).*

US/8750-3972
HARTSVILLE MESSENGER, THE. (HARTSVILLE MESSENGER.). (Jan. 1908)-. Newspaper. English. sw (104 per year). $20.00 Darlington, Lee and Chesterfield Counties; $30.00 other. Hartsville Messenger, 207 East Carolina Avenue Box 1865, Hartsville SC 29550. **Tel** (803)332-6545. **ED** Dennie Truesdale. **Ad Acc.** ***Continues*** *County Messenger.*

US
HERALD, THE. (Jan. 11, 1986)-. Newspaper. English. da. $108.00. Rock Hill Evening Herald, PO Box 11707, Rock Hill SC 29730. **Tel** (803)329-4000. ***Continues*** *Evening Herald (Rock Hill, S.C.).*

US
HORRY INDEPENDENT, THE. Vol. 1, No. 1 (March 25, 1980)-. Newspaper. English. wk. Horry Independent, 2510 Main Street, Conway SC 29526-4342. **Tel** (803)248-6671, FAX (803)248-6024. **ED** Kathy Ropp. **Ad Acc. Circ:** 6,000.

US/0747-0231
INDEX-JOURNAL, THE. **VFOAT** Index Journal. Vol. 1, No. 1 (Feb. 6, 1919)-. Newspaper. English. da. $93.60. Index-Journal, PO Box 1018, Greenwood SC 29648. **Tel** (803)223-1411, FAX (803)223-7331. **ED** William A. Collins, Jim Joyce (Managing Editor). **Photos. Ad Acc, Adv Mgr:** Harry L. Garrett. Full Page (B&W) $1367.40. Half Page (B&W) $683.70. Full Page (Color) $1457.40. Half Page (Color) $773.70. **Pub. Size:** Standard. **Wire Svcs.:** AP. available on microfilm from University Microfilms International (UMI). ***Formed by the union of*** *Greenwood Daily Journal (Greenwood, S.C.)* ***and*** *Evening Index (Greenwood, S.C.).*

US/0746-4886
ISLAND PACKET, THE. (July 9, 1970)-. Newspaper. English. tw. $76.00 South Carolina and Georgia; $83.00 other US. Island Packet, PO Box 5727, Hilton Head SC 29938. **Tel** (803)785-4293, FAX (803)686-3407. **ED** Fran Smith. **Bk Rev. Ad Acc, Adv Mgr:** Phil Porter.

US/1055-3215
ISLAND TIMES (HILTON HEAD ISLAND, S.C.). (ISLAND TIMES.). (1991)-. Newspaper. English. wk. Island Times, 39 New Orleans Road, Hilton Head Island SC 29928.

US
ITEM, THE. (1987)-. Newspaper. English. da. $132.00 mailed, $91.80 home delivery. Osteen Publishing Company, PO Box 1677, 20 North Magnolia Street, Sumter SC 29151. **Tel** (803)775-6331, FAX (803)775-1024. **ED** Graham Osteen. **Bk Rev**, (Qty: 12). **Photos. Ad Acc, Adv Mgr:** C. F Olavania. Full Page (B&W) $1,354.50. Half Page (B&W) $677.25. Full Page (Color) $1,539.50. Half Page (Color) $862.25. **Pub. Size:** Broadsheet. **Wire Svcs.:** AP. **Circ:** 21,000 (ctrl). available in microform from University Microfilms International (UMI). ***Continues*** *Sumter Daily Item.*

US
JOURNAL, THE. (1955)-. Newspaper. English. wk. $15.00. Williamston Journal, PO Box 369, Williamston SC 29697-1404. **Tel** (803)847-7361, FAX (803)847-9879. **ED** Sharon Crout. **Photos. Ad Acc, Adv Mgr:** David C. Meade. Full Page (B&W) $694.26. Half Page (B&W) $347.13. Full Page (Color) $769.26. Half Page (Color) $422.13. **Pub. Size:** Broadsheet. **Wire Svcs.:** EI. **Circ:** 6,000.

US
JOURNAL/TRIBUNE, THE. 82nd Year, No. 63 (Oct. 21, 1985)-. Newspaper. English. sw. Journal and Tribune, PO Box 547, Seneca SC 29678. ***Continues*** *Journal and Tribune (Seneca, S.C.).*

US
KEOWEE COURIER. Began in 1849. Newspaper. English. wk. Keowee Courier, 111 Short Street, Walhalla SC 29691.

US/0745-7421
LANCASTER NEWS, THE. (1907)-. Newspaper. English. sw. $22.00. Lancaster News, PO Box 640, Lancaster SC 29720. **Tel** 800 283-1133. **ED** Richard M. Gannaway. **Circ:** 12,175. ***Formed by the union of*** *Lancaster Ledger.*

US
LAURENS COUNTY ADVERTISER, THE. Vol. 88, No. 81 (Apr. 18, 1973)-. Newspaper. English. sw. $29.00 Laurens County; $35.00 other. Laurens County Advertiser, PO Box 490, 218 West Laurens Street, Laurens SC 29360. ***Continues*** *Laurens Advertiser.*

US
LEE COUNTY OBSERVER. Vol. 1, No. 1 (Apr. 28, 1977)-. Newspaper. English. wk. Lee County Observer, 218 North Main Street, Bishopville SC 29010-1416. **Tel** (803)484-9431, FAX (803)484-5055. **ED** Carpenter King. **Ad Acc. Circ:** 4,000. ***Absorbed*** *Lee County Messenger.*

US
MANNING TIMES, THE. (1884)-. Newspaper. English. wk. $15.00 (senior citizens); $19.00 in counties; $23.00 others. Manning Times, 4 South Brooks Street, PO Box 576, Manning SC 29102. **Tel** (803)435-8422, FAX (803)435-4189. **ED** Al Young. **Bk Rev**, (Qty: 5). **Photos**. **Ad Acc**, **Adv Mgr:** Sheila Touchberry. Half Page (B&W) $274.13. Full Page (Color) $553.10. Half Page (Color) $324.13. **Pub. Size:** Standard. **Circ:** 3,400. available in microform.
Desc: Community weekly newspaper.

US
MARION STAR AND MULLINS ENTERPRISE. Vol. 143, No. 6 (Mar. 14, 1990)-. Newspaper. English. Fifty-two times a year. $15.00 Marion County; $25.00 other. The Marion Star, PO Box 880, Marion SC 29571. **Tel** (803)423-2050. ***Formed by the union of*** *Marion Star (Marion, S.C. : 1871)* ***and*** *Mullins Enterprise.*

US
MARLBORO HERALD-ADVOCATE. Vol. 66, No. 21 (Sept. 4, 1951) -. Newspaper. English. sw. $25.00 Marlboro and adjoining counties; $30.00 other. Marlboro Herald Advocate, PO Box 656, Bennetsville SC 29512. **Tel** (803)479-3816, (803)479-3815, FAX (803)479-7671. **ED** W.L. Kinney Jr. **Bk Rev**. **Photos**. **Ad Acc**, **Adv Mgr:** Linda Wilson. Full Page (B&W) $580.50. Half Page (B&W) $283.50. Full Page (Color) $655.50. Half Page (Color) $358.50. **Pub. Size:** Standard. **Circ:** 6,800 (paid) (ctrl). ***Formed by the union of*** *Marlboro County Herald* ***and*** *Pee Dee Advocate.*

US
MCCORMICK MESSENGER. (May 1902)-. Newspaper. English. wk (Published on Thursdays). $18.00 McCormick County, SC; $22.00 other. McCormick Messenger, PO Box 98, McCormick SC 29835. **Tel** (803)465-3311. **ED** Janelle Beamer. **Bk Rev**. (Qty: 50). **Ad Acc**. **Circ:** 2,300 (ctrl).

US
NEWBERRY OBSERVER AND HERALD AND NEWS, THE. Newspaper. English. sw. 1716 Main Street, Newberry SC 29108. ***Formed by the union of*** *Newberry Observer* ***and*** *Newberry Herald and News.*

US
NEWS AND PRESS (DARLINGTON, S.C.). (THE NEWS AND PRESS.). Began in 1903. Newspaper. English. wk. News and Press, PO Box 513, Darlington SC 29532.

US
NEWS AND REPORTER. Vol. 102, No. 35 (Sept. 1, 1971)-. Newspaper. English. sw. $30.00 North & South Carolina; $38.00 other. Chester News and Reporter, PO Box 250, Chester SC 29706. **Tel** (803)385-3177, FAX (803)581-2518. **ED** L.D. McKeown. **Ad Acc**. **Circ:** 7,650. ***Formed by the union of*** *Chester News* ***and*** *Chester Reporter.*

US/1063-8415
PAGELAND PROGRESSIVE JOURNAL, THE. Vol. 1, No. 1 (June 30, 1981)-. Newspaper. English. wk. $10.00 Chesterfield County; $15.00 other. Pageland Progressive Journal, PO Box 218, Pageland SC 29729. **Tel** (803)672-2358, FAX (803)672-5593. **ED** Brian Hough. **Photos**. **Ad Acc**, **Adv Mgr:** Jane Hough. Full Page (B&W) $322.50. Half Page (B&W) $161.25. Full Page (Color) $392.50. Half Page (Color) $231.25. **Pub. Size:** Standard. **Circ:** 4,000 paid weekly (ctrl). ***Formed by the union of*** *Pageland Journal* ***and*** *Pageland Progressive.*

US/1061-5105
POST AND COURIER, THE. Vol. 189, No. 196 (Oct. 1, 1991)-. Newspaper. English. da. Evening Post Publishing Co., 134 Columbus Street, Charleston SC 29403. ***Formed by the union of*** *News and Courier (Charleston, S.C. : Daily), 0896-1999* ***and*** *Evening Post (Charleston, S.C. : Daily), 0746-0910.*

US
PRESS AND STANDARD (WALTERBORO, S.C.). ***Title Change.*** (THE PRESS AND STANDARD.). (1890)-?. Newspaper. English. wk. Press and Standard, 113 Washington Street, Walterboro SC 29488. **LC** 9694-X. available on microfilm from Arcata Microfilm Corporation. ***Formed by the union of*** *Collecton Press.* ***Absorbed by*** *Collecton Standard.*

US/0740-4743
SPARTANBURG HERALD-JOURNAL. VFOAT Spartanburg Herald Journal. Vol. 52, No. 83 (Oct. 1, 1982)-. Newspaper. English. da. $109.20 (daily and Sunday/carrier or motor route), $204.00 (daily and Sunday/by mail), $75.00 (daily/carrier or motor route) $132.00 (daily/by mail). Spartanburg Herald-Journal, Circulation Department, PO Box 1657, Spartanburg SC 29304. **Tel** (803)582-4511. **ED** Rudy Rivers. **Circ:** 49,771 daily, 53,922 Sunday. available on an online database (file 635/Full-Text) from DIALOG. Documents available from UMI Article Clearinghouse. ***Continues*** *Spartanburg Herald; Spartanburg Journal (Spartanburg, S.C. : 1949).*
Ind/Abst Bus. Dateline (Dec. 8, 1991-) [Full Txt.].

US
STATE (COLUMBIA, S.C. : 1891 : DAILY). (THE STATE.). **VFOAT** State, The Columbia Record. Vol. 1, No. 1 (Feb. 18, 1891)-. Newspaper. English. ds. $267.65. The State Record Company Inc., PO Box 1333, Columbia SC 29202. **Tel** (803)771-6161. **ED** William E. Rone Jr. and Thomas N. McLean. **Bk Rev**. **Ad Acc**. **Circ:** 137,000 daily, 157,000 Sunday. available on microfilm from University Microfilms International (UMI); available on an online database from VU-TEXT.
Desc: General circulation newspaper.

US
TIMES AND DEMOCRAT, THE. (1869)-. Newspaper. English. tw. $130.00 Orangeburg County; $166.00 other. Times and Democrat, PO Drawer 1766, Orangeburg SC 29115. ***Formed by the union of*** *Orangeburg Times (Orangeburg, S.C. : 1877)* ***and*** *Orangeburg Democrat.*

US/0747-1165
TRIBUNE-TIMES. VFOAT Tribune Times. (1964)-. Newspaper. English. wk. $15.00. Tribune-Times, PO Box 1179, Simpsonville SC 29681. **Tel** (803)967-9580, FAX (803)967-9585. **ED** Pete Martin. **Photos**. **Ad Acc**, **Adv Mgr:** Marsha Justice. Full Page (B&W) $661.50. Half Page (B&W) $355.95. Full Page (Color) $761.50. Half Page (Color) $465.95. **Pub. Size:** Tabloid. **Wire Svcs.:** AP. **Circ:** 8,000 (ctrl). ***Formed by the union of*** *Fountain Inn Tribune* ***and*** *Simpsonville Times.*
Desc: Weekly newspaper serving the suburban Greenville, South Carolina market.

US
UNION DAILY TIMES, THE. VFOAT Union Times. (1920)-. Newspaper. English. da. Union Times Company Inc, PO Box 749, Union SC 29379. **LC** 9741. available on microfilm from Arcata Microfilm Corporation. ***Continues*** *Weekly Union Times.*

US
YORKVILLE ENQUIRER. (Jan. 1855)-. Newspaper. English. wk. $12.00 in county; $15.00 others. Yorkville Enquirer, PO Box 38, York SC 29710. **Tel** (803)684-9903, FAX (803)624-0300. **ED** Gene Graham. **LC** 9742. **Photos**. **Ad Acc**, **Adv Mgr:** Angie Hoccomb. **Pub. Size:** Standard. **Circ:** 3,300. available on microfilm from University Microfilms International (UMI).

SOUTH DAKOTA

US/1074-7117
ABERDEEN AMERICAN-NEWS. VFOAT Aberdeen American News. Vol. 36, No. 173 (June 19, 1940)-. Newspaper. English. da. Aberdeen American News, PO Box 4430, Aberdeen SD 57402. **Tel** (605)225-4100. **ED** Cindy Eikamp. **Ad Acc**. **Circ:** 20,000 (ctrl). available on microfilm from The Library of Congress Photoduplication Service. ***Formed by the union of*** *Aberdeen Morning American* ***and*** *Aberdeen Daily News.*

US
ADVOCATE-LEADER, THE. VFOAT Advocate Leader. Began in 1925. Newspaper. English. wk. Advocate-Leader, PO Box 325, Kennebec SD 57544. ***Formed by the union of*** *Lyman County Argus-Leader* ***and*** *Lyman County Advocate.*

US
ALEXANDRIA HERALD (ALEXANDRIA, S.D.). (THE ALEXANDRIA HERALD.). (18??)-. Newspaper. English. wk. $14.00 South Dakota; $16.00 other. Alexandria Herald, PO Box 450, Alexandria SD 57311. **Tel** (605)239-4521. **ED** David L. Stoltz. **LC** 9744. **Photos**. **Ad Acc**. Full Page (B&W) $277.20. Half Page (B&W) $138.60. **Pub. Size:** Standard. **Circ:** 685. available in microform. ***Continues*** *Valley Pioneer.*

US
ARGUS-LEADER. VFOAT Argus Leader; Sunday Argus Leader. Vol. 92, No. 316 (Nov. 1977)-. Newspaper. English. da. Sioux Falls Argus-Leader, 200 South Minnesota Avenue, PO Box 5034, Sioux Falls SD 57117. **Tel** (605)331-2200, (800)952-0127. **ED** Richard N. Thien. **Circ:** 42,573 daily, 60,483 Sunday. available on microfilm from University Microfilms International (UMI). ***Continues*** *Sioux Falls Argus-Leader.*

US/8750-2488
ARMOUR CHRONICLE, THE. VFOAT Armour, S.D. Chronicle; Armour, SD Chronicle. Newspaper. English. wk. $22.50 North America; $26.50 other $14.00 out of state. The Armour Chronicle, Box 129, Armour SD 57313. **Tel** (605)724-2747. **ED** Kris Bordewyk. **Ad Acc**. **Circ:** 670 (ctrl). ***Continues*** *Chronicle (Armour, S.D.).*
Desc: Local news and feature stories of Armour.

US/1061-6179
BLACK HILLS PIONEER (1989), THE. (THE BLACK HILLS PIONEER.). Vol. 1, No. 1 (Oct. 21, 1989)-. English. wk. Billy T Masterson Jr, PO Box 7, Spearfish SD 57783. **Tel** (605)642-2761, FAX (605)642-8179. ***Continues*** *Weekly Pioneer (Deadwood, S.D.);* ***Absorbed*** *Spearfish Daily, Queen City Mail, 0886-8824* ***and*** *Lead Daily Call.*

US
BOWDLE PIONEER, THE. (1886)-. Newspaper. English. wk. $15.00 in county; $18.00 South Dakota; $20.00 US. Bowdle Pioneer, PO Box 368, Bowdle SD 57428. **Tel** (605)285-6101, FAX (605)285-6520. **ED** Mary Lou Gauer. **LC** 9746. **Photos**. **Ad Acc**. Full Page (B&W) $201.60. Half Page (B&W) $100.80. **Pub. Size:** Tabloid. **Circ:** 750 paid. available in microform.

US/0746-8261
BRANDON VALLEY CHALLENGER. VFOAT Challenger. (1983)-. Newspaper. English. wk. $20.00. Prairie Publications, PO Box 99, Dell Rapids SD 57022. **Tel** (605)582-6025, FAX (605)428-5992. **ED** Alica P. Thiele. **Photos**. **Ad Acc**, **Adv Mgr:** June Ketcham. Full Page (B&W) $300.00. Half Page (B&W) $150.00. Full Page (Color) $390.00. Half Page (Color) $240.00. **Pub. Size:** Tabloid. **Circ:** 1,000 (paid).

US
BROOKINGS REGISTER, THE. (1890)-. Newspaper. English. da. Brookings Register, 312 5th Street, Brookings SD 57006. **LC** 9749. ***Absorbed*** *Brookings County Sentinel; Brookings County Press.*

US/0893-5564
CAPITAL JOURNAL (PIERRE, S.D.). (CAPITAL JOURNAL.). Vol. 104, No. 68 (Apr. 6, 1987)-. Newspaper. English. da (Mon.-Fri.). $72.00 (mail), $60.00 (delivery). Capital Journal, PO Box 878, Pierre SD 57501. **Tel** (605)224-7301, FAX (605)224-9210. **ED** Terry Hipple and Dana Hess (Managing Editor). **Photos**. **Ad Acc**, **Adv Mgr:** Terry Hipple. Full Page (B&W) $606.30. Half Page (B&W) $296.10. Full Page (Color) $651.30. Half Page (Color) $341.10. **Pub. Size:** Standard. **Wire Svcs.:** AP. **Circ:** 4,753 (daily). available on microfilm. ***Continues*** *Daily Capital Journal.*

US
CHAMBERLAIN REGISTER, THE. Began in 1950. Newspaper. English. wk. Chamberlain Register, 218 North Main Street, Chamberlain SD 57325. ***Continues*** *Chamberlain Register-Leader.*

US
CLEAR LAKE COURIER. VFOAT Clear Lake (S.D.) Courier. Began in 1949. Newspaper. English. wk. Clear Lake Courier, Clear Lake SD 57226. ***Continues*** *Clear Lake Courier-Advocate.*

US
DE SMET NEWS, THE. (1898)-. Newspaper. English. wk. $20.00 South Dakota; $25.00 others. Blegen Publishing Inc, PO Box 69, De Smet SD 57231. **ED** Dale Bleger. **LC** 9756. **Photos**. **Ad Acc**. Full Page (B&W) $439.00. Half Page (B&W) $219.50. **Pub. Size:** Broadsheet. ***Continues*** *News and Leader.*

US
EAGLE BUTTE NEWS. (Dec. 8, 1910)-. Newspaper. English. wk. Eagle Butte News, PO Box 210, Eagle Butte SD 57625. **LC** 9758.

US/0899-966X
ELKTON RECORD, THE. Began in 1884. Newspaper. English. wk. RFD News Group Inc, PO Box 8, Volga SD 57071. **ED** Emilie Moore. **Ad Acc**. **Circ:** 900 (ctrl).

US
EMERY ENTERPRISE. (1890)-. Newspaper. English. wk. $14.00 South Dakota; $16.00 other. Emery Enterprise, PO Box 244, Emery SD 57332. **ED** David L. Stoltz. **LC** 9760. **Photos**. **Ad Acc**. Full Page (B&W) $277.20. Half Page (B&W) $138.60. **Pub. Size:** Standard. available in microform.

US
GRANT COUNTY REVIEW (MILBANK, S.D.). (GRANT COUNTY REVIEW.). (Aug. 19, 1880)-. Newspaper. English. wk. $22.00 local; $28.00 other. Grant County Review, PO Box 390, Milbank SD 57252. **ED** Phyllis Justice. **Photos**. **Ad Acc**, **Adv Mgr:** Holli Seehafer. Full Page (B&W) $607.59. Half Page (B&W) $310.86. Full Page (Color) $700.00. Half Page (Color) $400.00. available in microform.

US/8750-7714
HARTFORD "AREA" NEWS, THE. Vol. 1, No. 1 (Jan. 24, 1985)-. Newspaper. English. wk (Published on Thursdays). $7.00 (in state), $9.00 (out-of-state). Hartford Area News, PO Box 128, Canistota SD 57012. **Tel** (605)296-3181, FAX (605)296-3289.

US
HECLA INDEPENDENT. Newspaper. English. wk. Hecla Independent, PO Box 557, Frederick SD 57441.

US
HURON DAILY PLAINSMAN. Newspaper. English. da. Huron Daily Plainsman, Huron SD 57350. ***Continues*** *Daily Plainsman.*

South Dakota

●US/1066-5501
INDIAN COUNTRY TODAY. [Indian ctry. today]. Vol. 12, Iss. 15 (Oct. 8, 1992)-. Newspaper. English. wk. $48.00. Native American Publishing Inc, PO Box 2180, Rapid City SD 57709. **Tel** (605)341-0011. **Photos. Ad Acc, Adv Mgr:** John Painter. **Pub. Size:** Broadsheet. **Continues** Lakota Times, 0744-2238.

US/0744-2238
LAKOTA TIMES, THE. Title Change. (1981)-Vol. 12 Issue 14 (Sept. 30, 1992). Newspaper. English. wk. Lakota Times, PO Box T, Martin SD 57551. **Tel** (605)685-6420. **ED** Tim Giago. **LC** E78.S63; L34. **Bk Rev. Ad Acc. Circ:** 8,000. **Continued by** Indian Country Today, 1066-5501.
Desc: The largest weekly Indian owned newspaper in the United States. Offers up to date news and a contemporary view of and for the Native American.

US
LANGFORD BUGLE, THE. Began in June 1886. Newspaper. English. wk. Langford Bugle, 107 Main Street, Langford SD 57454.

US/8750-3352
LAWRENCE COUNTY CENTENNIAL. (LAWRENCE COUNTY CENTENNIAL : LCC.). **VFOAT** Centennial; LCC; L.C.C. (19??)-. Newspaper. English. wk. $10.00 in county, $11.00 other. LCC, 67 Sherman Street, Deadwood SD 57732. **Continues** Whitewood Centennial.

US
LEAD DAILY CALL. Title Change. (Aug. 12, 1894)-(1993). Newspaper. English. da. Lead Daily Call, 7 South Main Street, Lead SD 57754. **Absorbed by** Black Hills Pioneer (Lead, S.D. : 1989), 1061-6179.

US
MADISON DAILY LEADER. Newspaper. English. da (260 issues per year). $58.00 Lake Minor, Moody, Kingsbury, Minnehaha, McCook, and Brookings counties; $65.00 others in South Dakota, North Dakota, Minnesota, Iowa & Nebraska; $79.00 others in US & Canada. Madison Daily Leader, PO Box 348, Madison SD 57042. **Tel** (605)256-4555.

US
MARION RECORD (MARION, S.D.). (THE MARION RECORD.). Began with April 26, 1900 issue. Newspaper. English. wk. Marion Record, PO Box 298, Marion SD 57043.

US
MILBANK HERALD ADVANCE. Began in April 1890. Newspaper. English. wk. Milbank Herald Advance, 319 South Main Street, Milbank SD 57252. **Formed by the union of** Advance (Milbank, S.D.) **and** Herald (Milbank, S.D.).

US
MILLER PRESS, THE. Newspaper. English. wk. Miller Press, PO Box 196, Miller SD 57362. **Continues** Pioneer Press (Miller, S.D.); **Absorbed** Hand County News; Miller Sun; **Continues** Miller Gazette.

US
MINER COUNTY PIONEER. Began with April 5, 1918 issue. Newspaper. English. wk. Miner County Pioneer, PO Box P, Howard SD 57349. **Continues** Miner County Democrat; **Absorbed** Howard Press; Miner County Messenger.

US
MITCHELL DAILY REPUBLIC. Newspaper. English. ir (Published 6 days a week except Jan. 1, Memorial Day, July 4, Labor day). $84.00 South Dakota $99.00 other. Mitchell Daily Republic, PO Box 1288, Mitchell SD 57301. **Tel** (605)996-5516.

US
MOODY COUNTY ENTERPRISE (FLANDREAU, S.D. : 1938). (MOODY COUNTY ENTERPRISE.). Began in 1938. Newspaper. English. wk. $16.00 local, $20.00 other. RFD News Group Inc, PO Box 8, Volga SD 57071. **ED** Charles F Cecil. **Ad Acc. Circ:** 2,800 (ctrl). **Continues** Moody County Enterprise and Flandreau Herald.

US
NEW ERA (PARKER, S.D.). (THE NEW ERA.). (Oct. 28, 1875)-. Newspaper. English. wk. New Era, 225 North Main Street, Parker SD 57053.

US/0897-3873
PENNINGTON COUNTY NEWS. VFOAT Pennington County News & the Rushmore Press; County News. (19??)-. Newspaper. English. wk (Published on Wednesdays). $13.00 Pennington County, SD; $18.00 other. Tri State Publishing, PO Box 266, Hill City SD 57745. **Tel** (605)574-2538. **Continues** Rushmore Press.

US
RAPID CITY JOURNAL, THE. (19??)-. Newspaper. English. da. $160.00 South Dakota, Wyoming, Nebraska, Montana & North Dakota; $210.00 other; $104.00 (Sunday only). Rapid City Journal, PO Box 450, 507 Main Street, Rapid City SD 57701. **Tel** (605)342-0280, (800)843-2300. **ED** Joe Karius (phone: (605)394-8401). **Ad Acc, Adv Mgr:** Brad Slater. **Circ:** 31,357 (daily), 34,317 (Sunday). **Continues** Rapid City Daily Journal.

US
REDFIELD PRESS, THE. Began with Nov. 21, 1884 issue. Newspaper. English. wk. Redfield Press, 16 East 17th Avenue, Redfield SD 57469. **Absorbed** Redfield Journal-Observer.

US
REPORTER AND FARMER AND THE WEBSTER JOURNAL. VFOAT Reporter and Farmer. Began in 1946?. Newspaper. English. wk. Day County Printing Company, PO Box 30, Webster SD 57274. **Formed by the union of** Webster Journal **and** Webster Reporter and Farmer.

US
SISSETON COURIER, THE. Began in 1915. Newspaper. English. wk. Sisseton Courier, 117 East Oak Street, Sisseton SD 57262. **Absorbed** Sisseton Weekly Standard; Sisseton Journal-Press; Sisseton Ambassador.

US/0886-8824
SPEARFISH DAILY, QUEEN CITY MAIL. Title Change. VFOAT Queen City Mail. (19??)-(1993). Newspaper. English. da. Billy T Masterson Jr, PO Box 7, Spearfish SD 57783. **Tel** (605)642-2761, **FAX** (605)642-8179. Index available. cum. index. **Bk Rev. Ad Acc. Circ:** 6,000 (ctrl). **Continues** Queen City, Spearfish Mail. **Absorbed by** Black Hills Pioneer (Lead, S.D. : 1989), 1061-6179.

US
STICKNEY ARGUS, THE. Began with July 26, 1922 issue. Newspaper. English. wk. Stickney Argus, PO Box 37, Stickney SD 57375. **Continues** Aurora County Argus.

US
TODD COUNTY TRIBUNE. (19??)-. Newspaper. English. wk. $20.00 local, $25.00 other. Figert Printing Inc, PO Box 229, Mission SD 57555. **Tel** (605)856-4469, **FAX** (605)856-2428. **ED** Margaret Figert. **Ad Acc, Adv Mgr:** Ervin Figert, **Tel** (605)856-4469. Full Page (B&W) $516.00. Half Page (B&W) $258.00. Full Page (Color) $576.00. Half Page (Color) $318.00. **Pub. Size:** Broadsheet. **Wire Svcs.:** NF. **Circ:** 2,500.
Desc: American Indian News from the Rosebud Reservation.

US/0899-9635
TORONTO HERALD, THE. Began in 1897. Newspaper. English. wk. RFD News Group Inc, PO Box 8, Volga SD 57071. **ED** Lori Wilber. **Ad Acc. Circ:** 400 (ctrl).

US/0163-6154
VOLGA TRIBUNE, THE. Newspaper. English. wk. $8.00. RFD News Group Inc, PO Box 8, Volga SD 57071. **ED** Kathi Granum. **Ad Acc. Circ:** 1,300 (ctrl).

US/1054-3449
WAKONDA TIMES. VFOAT Vermillion Plain Talk; Vermillion Plain Talk/Wakonda Times. (1988)-. Newspaper. English. wk. Wakonda Times Observer, PO Box 773, Yankton SD 57078. **Continues** Wakonda Times Observer, 0747-3257.

US
WATERTOWN PUBLIC OPINION. (1887)-. Newspaper. English. da (308 issues per year). $87.00 Delivery; $76.00 mail. Watertown Public Opinion, 120 3rd Ave Northwest, Box 10, Watertown SD 57201. **Tel** (605)886-6901. **ED** Gordon R. Garnos. **Photos. Ad Acc, Adv Mgr:** Almon W. Johnson, **Tel** (605)886-6901. Full Page (B&W) $1,750.53. Half Page (B&W) $875.27. Full Page (Color) $1874.53. Half Page (Color) $999.27. **Pub. Size:** Broadsheet. **Wire Svcs.:** AP. **Circ:** 16,173. available on microfilm and microfiche.

US/0899-9805
WHITE LEADER, THE. Began in 1900. Newspaper. English. wk. RFD News Group Inc, PO Box 8, Volga SD 57071. **ED** Lori Wilber. **Ad Acc. Circ:** 800 (ctrl).

US
WILMOT ENTERPRISE, THE. (1917)-. Newspaper. English. wk. $19.00 local; $23.00 other. Wilmot Enterprise, PO Box 37, Wilmot SD 57279. **Tel** (605)938-4683. **ED** Cheryl Rondeau-Bassett. **LC** 9787. **Photos. Ad Acc.** Full Page (B&W) $322.10. Half Page (B&W) $161.05. Full Page (Color) $450.00. **Pub. Size:** Broadsheet. **Circ:** 950. available in microform.

US
YANKTON DAILY PRESS & DAKOTAN. VFOAT Yankton Daily Press and Dakotan. (1??)-. Newspaper. English. wk (Published within 100 miles of Yankton, SD); $91.00 rest of US. Yankton Press & Dakotan Daily, 319 Walnut Street, Yankton SD 57078. **Tel** (605)665-7811, **FAX** (605)665-1721. **ED** Milo Daily. **LC** 9789. **Ad Acc. Circ:** 10,200. available on microfilm. **Continues** Daily Press and Dakotian.

TENNESSEE

US
ADVANCE-SENTINEL, THE. VFOAT Advance Sentinel. (19??)-. Newspaper. English. wk. La Follette Press Publications, PO Box 1261, La Follette TN 37766-1261. **Tel** (615)562-8468, **FAX** (615)566-7060. **ED** Linda Thurston. **Ad Acc, Adv Mgr:** Larry Dilbeck. **Circ:** 663. **Continues** Jellico Advance-Sentinel.

US/0893-3839
BROWNSVILLE STATES-GRAPHIC. VFOAT States-Graphic; States Graphic. (19??)-. Newspaper. English. wk. $16.50 Haywood County; $20.50 others in Tennessee; $28.50 others. Brownsville States-Graphic, PO Box 178, Brownsville TN 38012. **Tel** (901)772-1172. **ED** C. T. Smith. **Photos. Ad Acc, Adv Mgr:** M. Arwood. Full Page (B&W) $441.00. Half Page (B&W) $220.50. Full Page (Color) $516.00. Half Page (Color) $295.50. **Pub. Size:** Standard. **Circ:** 5,250. available in microform. **Continues** States-Graphic.

US
CARTHAGE COURIER. (19??)-. Newspaper. English. wk. $12.00 Smith County, $14.00 other Tennessee, $17.00 other. Carthage Courier, 504 Main Street, PO Box 239, Carthage TN 37030. **Tel** (615)735-1110.

●US
CHATTANOOGA FREE PRESS. (1993)-. English. da. $144.00. Chattanooga Publishing Company, 400 East 11th Street, Chattanooga TN 37401. **Tel** (615)756-6900. **ED** Lee Anderson. **Bk Rev. Photos. Ad Acc, Adv Mgr:** Dan Mausley, **Tel** (615)757-6370. Full Page (B&W) $2,373.21. Half Page (B&W) $1,186.61. **Pub. Size:** Broadsheet. **Wire Svcs.:** AP. **Continues** Chattanooga News-Free Press.

US
CHATTANOOGA NEWS-FREE PRESS. Title Change. VFOAT Chattanooga News Free Press. (Jan. 21, 1940)-(1993). Newspaper. English. da. Chattanooga Publishing Company, 400 East 11th Street, Chattanooga TN 37401. **Tel** (615)756-6900. **ED** Lee Anderson. **Circ:** 56,353 daily, 109,317 Sunday. available on microfilm from University Microfilms International (UMI); and University Microfilms International (UMI). **Formed by the union of** Chattanooga Free Press **and** Chattanooga News. **Continued by** Chattanooga Free Press.

US
CHATTANOOGA TIMES, THE. Vol. 96. No. 113 (Apr. 7, 1965)-. Newspaper. English. da. $144.00. Chattanooga Publishing Company, 400 East 11th Street, Chattanooga TN 37401. **Tel** (615)756-6900. **ED** Michael Loftin. **Circ:** 46,835. available on microfilm from University Microfilms International (UMI); and University Microfilms International (UMI). **Continues** Chattanooga Daily Times.

US/0746-7745
CITIZEN-STATESMAN. VFOAT Citizen Statesman. Vol. 1, No. 1 (Thurs., Dec. 8, 1983)-. Newspaper. English. wk. $13.00 (local), $19.00 (in state), $22.00 (out of state). Citizen-Statesman, PO Box F, Celina TN 38551. **Tel** (615)243-2235, **FAX** (615)243-2232. **ED** Vaughn Owens. **Photos. Ad Acc, Adv Mgr:** Michelle Denton. Full Page (B&W) $378.00. Half Page (B&W) $215.00. Full Page (Color) additional $75.00 per color. Half Page (Color) additional $75.00 per color. **Circ:** 2,400 weekly. **Formed by the union of** Clay Statesman, 0745-5410 **and** Clay Citizen.

US
CITIZEN TRIBUNE. Newspaper. English. ds. $85.00. Citizen Tribune, PO Box 625, Morristown TN 37814. **Tel** (615)581-5630.

US
CLAIBORNE PROGRESS. Began with Oct. 5, 1887 issue. Newspaper. English. wk. Claiborne Progress, PO Box B, Tazewell TN 37879.

US
CLEVELAND DAILY BANNER. (1922)-. Newspaper. English. da. Price varies within Tennessee; $100.00 other. Cleveland Banner, 1505 25th Street Northwest, Box 3600, Cleveland TN 37320. **Tel** (615)472-5041. **Continues** Cleveland Banner (Cleveland, Tenn. : 1918).

US
COLLIERVILLE HERALD, THE. Vol. 1, No. 1 (Mar. 1, 1929)-. Newspaper. English. wk. Collierville Herald, PO Box 427, Collierville TN 38027-0427. **Tel** (901)853-2241. **ED** Van Pritchartt. **Ad Acc. Circ:** 5,700.

US/0745-4856
COMMERCIAL APPEAL, THE. VFOAT Memphis Commercial Appeal. Vol. 10 (July 1, 1894)-. Newspaper. English. da. $234.07 (daily and Sunday editions)-by mail; $167.40 (daily and Sunday editions)-by

carrier; $96.28 (Sunday edition only)-by mail; $137.79 (daily edition only)-by mail; $102.00 (daily edition only)-by carrier. Memphis Publishing Company, PO Box 1730, Memphis TN 38101. **Tel** (901)529-2659, (901)529-2606. **ED** David W. Brown. **LC** 9838. **Bk Rev. Ad Acc. Circ:** 226,675 daily, 295,831 Sunday. available on microfilm from University Microfilms International (UMI). ***Formed by the union of*** *Appeal-Avalanche* ***and*** *Memphis Commercial.*
Ind/Abst PROMT.

US
COVINGTON LEADER, THE. (-8??)-. Newspaper. English. wk (Published on Wednesdays). $14.00 Tipton County, Tennessee; $20.00 other. Covington Leader Newspaper, 2001 Highway 51 South, Box 529, Covington TN 38019. **Tel** (901)476-7116, FAX (901)476-0373. **ED** George T. Whitley. **Bk Rev**, (Qty: 8). **Ad Acc, Adv Mgr:** Larry Whitley. **Circ:** 8,400 (ctrl).

US/0746-0309
CROCKETT CO. SENTINEL, TRI-CO. NEWS, CROCKETT TIMES, THE. VFOAT Crockett Co. Sentinel; Tri-Co. News; Crockett Times; Crockett Times, Crockett Co. Sentinel, Tri-County News. (19??)-. Newspaper. English. wk. Crockett Times, 128 West Main Street, Alamo TN 38001.

US
CROSSVILLE CHRONICLE. (1894)-. Newspaper. English. ir (3 times per week). $33.50 Cumberland Co., Tennessee; $35.50 other Tennessee; $40.00 other. Crossville Chronicle, PO Box 449, Crossville TN 38555. **Tel** (615)484-5145, FAX (615)456-7683. **ED** Mike Moser. **LC** 7002. **Ad Acc, Adv Mgr:** Becky Gilley. **Circ:** 6,500 (paid), 17,000 (Tues.). available on microfilm from Tennessee State Library and Archives. ***Continues*** *Crossville Sentinel.*

US
DAILY HERALD, THE. Vol. 1, No. 1 (Oct. 3, 1899)-. Newspaper. English. da (except Saturday). $75.00 Middle County; $85.00 other. Columbia Publishing Company Inc., PO Box 1425, Columbia TN 38402. **Tel** (615)388-6464.

US/0745-5534
DAILY MESSENGER (UNION CITY, TENN.). (DAILY MESSENGER.). **VFOAT** Union City Daily Messenger. (19??)-. Newspaper. English. da (Mon.-Fri.). $50.00 Tennessee; $70.00 other. Union City Daily Messenger, PO Box 430, Union City TN 38261. **Tel** (901)885-0744. **ED** David G. Critchlow and David Bartholomew. **Bk Rev. Ad Acc. Circ:** 9,000 (ctrl). ***Continues*** *Union City Daily Messenger.*
Desc: General circulation newspaper reporting on Union City, Tennessee.

US/0745-2683
DAILY NEWS JOURNAL (MURFREESBORO, TENN.), THE. (THE DAILY NEWS JOURNAL.). (18??)-. Newspaper. English. da (except Sat.). $72.00. Murfreesboro Daily News, PO Box 68, Murfreesboro TN 37130. **Tel** (615)893-5860. **ED** Michael L. Pirtle. **Circ:** 14,878 daily, 16,690 Sunday.

US
DEMOCRAT-UNION, THE. VFOAT Democrat Union. (1???)-. Newspaper. English. sw. $21.00. Democrat Union / Tennessee, PO Box 685, Lawrenceburg TN 38464. **Tel** (615)762-2222.

US/0747-041X
DICKSON HERALD, THE. (19??)-. Newspaper. English. sw. $15.00. Dickson Herald, 104 Church Street, Dickson TN 37055. **Tel** (615)446-2811. ***Continues*** *Dickson County Herald.*

US/8750-7528
DISPATCH (COOKEVILLE, TENN.). (THE DISPATCH.). Newspaper. English. tw. The Dispatch, 1065 East 10th Street, Cookeville TN 38502.

US
DRESDEN ENTERPRISE AND SHARON TRIBUNE. (18??)-. Newspaper. English. wk. Dresden Enterprise, 113 Wilson, Dresden TN 38225. **Tel** (901)364-2234, FAX (901)364-5774. **ED** Ramona Washburn. **Bk Rev. Ad Acc. Circ:** 5,700.

US
EAST TENNESSEE'S WEEKEND JOURNAL. English. wk. Knoxville News, PO Box 377, Knoxville TN 37901. **Tel** (615)523-3131, (615)521-8181. ***Continues*** *Knoxville Journal.*

US/0747-3761
ELK VALLEY TIMES OBSERVER AND NEWS, THE. VFOAT Elk Valley Times. Newspaper. English. wk. Lakewood Publishers, 418 North Elk Avenue, Fayetteville TN 37334. **Tel** (615)433-6151. **ED** Jim Leonnirth. **Circ:** 8,000.

US/0889-2830
ENTERPRISE (SPRING CITY, TN). ***Ceased.*** (THE ENTERPRISE.). Ceased (Nov. 1988). Newspaper. English. wk. The Enterprise / Tennessee, PO Box 9, Spring City TN 37381. **Tel** (615)365-9200. ***Continues*** *Spring City Enterprise, 0746-3189.*

US
ERWIN RECORD, THE. VFOAT Erwin Record (Combined with Unicoi County Progress). Vol. 1, No. 12 (Jan. 27, 1928)-. Newspaper. English. da. $10.00 Erwin, Tennessee; $15.00 other. Erwin Record, PO Drawer 700, Erwin TN 37650. **Tel** (615)743-4112. ***Absorbed*** *Unicoi County Progress.*

US
FAYETTE FALCON, THE. Newspaper. English. wk. $8.75 in county; $12.75 other. Fayette Falcon Newspaper, 101 W. Court Square, Somerville TN 38068. **Tel** (901)465-3567, FAX (901)465-3568. **ED** Robert T. Koenig. **Bk Rev**, (Qty: 10-12/yr). **Ad Acc. Circ:** 3400.

US/1060-1171
HALLS GRAPHIC, THE. (189?)-. Newspaper. English. wk. Lauderdale County Enterprise, PO Box 289, Ripley TN 38063-0289. **Tel** (901)635-1771, FAX (901)635-2111. **ED** William A. Klutts. **Circ:** 437.

US/0891-169X
HARTSVILLE VIDETTE, THE. (19??)-. Newspaper. English. wk. $7.00 Trousdale county; $15.00 other. The Hartsville Vidette, Box 47, Marlene Street, Hartsville TN 37074. **Tel** (615)374-3556. **ED** Sam Hatcher (Editor-in-Chief) and Angelene Anderson (Managing Editor). **Photos. Ad Acc, Adv Mgr:** Rosemary Denham. Full Page (B&W) $322.50. Half Page (B&W) $165.00. **Pub. Size:** Standard. **Circ:** 2,300.
Desc: General community information.

US/0193-5143
HENDERSONVILLE STAR NEWS. VFOAT Star News. (19??)-. Newspaper. English. Fifty-two times a year. $33.00. Hendersonville Star News, PO Box 68, Hendersonville TN 37075. **Tel** (615)824-8480, FAX (615)824-3126. **ED** Mike McClanahan. **Photos. Ad Acc, Adv Mgr:** Judi McMinn. Full Page (B&W) $912.03. Half Page (B&W) $456.02. Full Page (Color) $1,002.03. Half Page (Color) $546.02. **Pub. Size:** Broadsheet. **Wire Svcs.:** AP.

US
HERALD AND TRIBUNE (JONESBORO, TENN. : 1869). (HERALD AND TRIBUNE.). (August 26, 1869)-. Newspaper. English. wk. $15.00 over 100-mile radius; $10.00 regular; $8.00 senior citizens. Herald and Tribune, PO Box 277, Jonesboro TN 37659. **Tel** (615)753-3136, FAX (615)753-6528. **ED** Kelly S. Arnold. **LC** 9793-X. **Bk Rev**, (Qty: 5). **Photos. Ad Acc, Adv Mgr:** Lois D. Hicks. Full Page (B&W) $464.40. Half Page (B&W) $237.60. Full Page (Color) $563.40. Half Page (Color) $337.60. **Pub. Size:** Broadsheet. available on microfilm from Tennessee State Library and Archives.

US/0893-3707
HERALD-CHRONICLE (WINCHESTER, TENN.), THE. (THE HERALD-CHRONICLE.). **VFOAT** Herald Chronicle. (19??)-. Newspaper. English. Twice a week. $22.00 (in county), $32.00 (out of county). The Winchester Herald, 906 Dinah Shore Boulevard, Winchester TN 37398. **Tel** (615)967-2272. **ED** Eddie Medley. **Bk Rev**, (Qty: 12). **Photos. Ad Acc, Adv Mgr:** Rebekah Moorehead. Full Page (B&W) $728.85. Half Page (B&W) $377.33. **Pub. Size:** Standard. available in microform. ***Formed by the union of*** *Winchester Chronicle* ***and*** *Winchester Herald-Times.*

US/8750-5541
HERALD-CITIZEN (COOKEVILLE, TENN.). (HERALD-CITIZEN.). **VFOAT** Herald Citizen. (1???)-. Newspaper. English. da. $63.00. Herald-Citizen / Cookeville, TN, 124 South Dixie, PO Box 2729, Cookeville TN 38502. **Tel** (615)526-9715, FAX (615)526-1209. **ED** Sam Thompson Jr., Charles Denning (Executive Editor). **Bk Rev**, (Qty: 50). **Photos. Ad Acc, Adv Mgr:** Allen Profant. Full Page (B&W) $1029.42. Half Page (B&W) $514.71. Full Page (Color) $1299.42. Half Page (Color) $784.71. **Pub. Size:** Standard. **Wire Svcs.:** AP. **Circ:** 10,652 evening and Sunday, 12,604 ABC paid.

US/0744-1711
INDEPENDENT HERALD (ONEIDA, TENN.). (INDEPENDENT HERALD.). (19??)-. Newspaper. English. wk. Independent Herald, PO Box 581, Oneida TN 37841.

US/0890-9938
JACKSON SUN (JACKSON, TENN. 1895), THE. (THE JACKSON SUN.). (1985)-. Newspaper. English. da. $126.00 one-year carrier; $141.00 one-year mail. The Jackson Sun, PO Box 1059, 245 West Lafayette, Jackson TN 38301. **Tel** (901)427-3333. **ED** Michael Craft. **LC** 9806. **Circ:** 34,868. available on microfilm from Tennessee State Library and Archives. ***Continues*** *Jackson Daily Sun.*

US
JASPER JOURNAL, THE. (193?)-. Newspaper. English. wk. Jasper Journal, 926 East Main Street, Jasper TN 37347. **Tel** (615)942-2433, FAX (615)942-8835. **ED** Jim Webster. **Bk Rev. Ad Acc, Adv Mgr:** Sue Lond. **Circ:** 4,600.

US
KNOXVILLE JOURNAL (KNOXVILLE, TENN. : 1925). ***Title Change.*** (THE KNOXVILLE JOURNAL.). **VFOAT** Knoxville Sunday Journal. Vol. 38, No. 96 (Feb. 10, 1925)-(19??). Newspaper. English. da. Journal and Tribune Company, PO Box 911, Knoxville TN 37901. **Tel** (615)522-4141. **ED** Ronald D McMahan. **LC** 7002. **Circ:** 41,768. available on microfilm from University Microfilms International (UMI). Documents available from UMI Article Clearinghouse. ***Continues*** *Knoxville Journal and Tribune.* ***Continued by*** *East Tennessee's Weekend Journal.*
Ind/Abst Bus. Dateline.

US
KNOXVILLE NEWS-SENTINEL, THE. VFOAT Knoxville News Sentinel. (Nov. 22, 1926)-. Newspaper. English. da. $90.60 (daily), $171.60 (daily & Sun.) carrier; $86.40 (Sun.), $108.60 (daily), $195.00 (daily & Sun.) mail. Knoxville News, PO Box 377, Knoxville TN 37901. **Tel** (615)523-3131, (615)521-8181. **ED** Harry Moskos. **Circ:** 102,340 daily, 163,108 Sunday. available on microfilm from University Microfilms International (UMI). ***Formed by the union of*** *Knoxville News* ***and*** *Knoxville Sentinel.*

US/0883-6531
LAWRENCE COUNTY ADVOCATE. VFOAT Advocate. Vol. 1, No. 2 (March 13, 1985)-. Newspaper. English. bw. $26.00 Tennessee; $34.00 other. Lawrence County Advocate, PO Box 308, Lawrenceburg TN 38462. **Tel** (615)762-1726, FAX (615)762-7874. **ED** Nancy Brewer (Editor-in-Chief) and Bill Haxton (Managing Editor). **Bk Rev**, (Qty: 20). **Photos. Ad Acc, Adv Mgr:** Kathy Burroughs. Full Page (B&W) $365.00. Half Page (B&W) $380.00. Full Page (Color) $408.00. Half Page (Color) $465.00. **Pub. Size:** Broadsheet. **Circ:** 15,100 (Sunday), 15,900 (Wednesday). available in microform. ***Continues*** *Lawrence County News.*

US/0745-7367
LEAF-CHRONICLE, THE. Newspaper. English. da. $72.80 Montgomery & adjoining counties, $85.80 elsewhere. Leaf-Chronicle, 200 Commerce Street, Clarksville TN 37040.

US
LEBANON DEMOCRAT AND WILSON COUNTY NEWS, THE. (18??)-. Newspaper. English. wk. $30.00 Wilson County, Tennessee; $40.00 other. Lebanon Democrat, 402 North Cumberland, Lebanon TN 37087. **Tel** (615)444-3952.

US
LEWISBURG TRIBUNE. (18??)-. Newspaper. English. wk. Lewisburg Tribune, 116 East Ewing Street, PO Box 407, Lewisburg TN 37091. **Tel** (615)359-1526.

US
LEXINGTON PROGRESS, THE. (18??)-. Newspaper. English. wk. Price varies in Tennessee; $12.00 other. Lexington Progress, 23 North Broad Street, Lexington TN 38351. **Tel** (901)968-6397.

US
LIVINGSTON ENTERPRISE. (191?)-. Newspaper. English. wk. Livingston Enterprise / Tennessee, PO Box 129, Livingston TN 38570. **Tel** (615)823-1274, FAX (615)268-9125. **ED** Richard F. Knight. **Ad Acc. Circ:** 5,300. ***Continues*** *Enterprise (Livingston, Tenn.);* ***Absorbed*** *Clay County Courier.*

US/0745-5976
MACON COUNTY TIMES. (19??)-. Newspaper. English. wk. $15.00. Macon County Times, PO Box 69, Lafayette TN 37083. **Tel** (615)666-2440, FAX (615)666-4909. **ED** Truett Langston. **Photos. Ad Acc, Adv Mgr:** Linda McDonald. Full Page (B&W) $387.00. Half Page (B&W) $193.50. Full Page (Color) $437.00. Half Page (Color) $243.50. **Pub. Size:** Standard. **Circ:** 6,100 (ctrl). available in microform.

US
MARYVILLE-ALCOA DAILY TIMES. VFOAT Maryville Alcoa Daily Times. (1944)-. Newspaper. English. da. Maryville-Alcoa Daily Times, PO Box 568, Maryville TN 37801. available on microfilm from Tennessee State Library and Archives. ***Continues*** *Maryville Times.*

US
MEMPHIS PRESS-SCIMITAR. VFOAT Memphis Press Scimitar. (1926)-. Newspaper. English. ir. Memphis Publishing Company, PO Box 1730, Memphis TN 38101. **Tel** (901)529-2659, (901)529-2606. **LC** 7002. available on microfilm from University Microfilms International (UMI). ***Formed by the union of*** *Memphis Press* ***and*** *Memphis News-Scimitar.*

US/0894-2218
MOUNTAIN PRESS (SEVIERVILLE, TENN.), THE. (THE MOUNTAIN PRESS.). **VFOAT** Daily Mountain Press. (1986)-. Newspaper. English. da. Mountain Press, PO Box 4810, Sevierville TN 37864. **Tel** (615)428-0746. ***Formed by the union of*** *Mountain Press (News-Record Edition), 0746-9098* ***and*** *Mountain Press (Gatlinburg Press Edition).*

US
NASHVILLE BANNER. **VFOAT** Nashville Evening Banner. (Apr. 10, 1876)-. Newspaper. English. da. Newspaper Printing Corporation / Tennessee, 1100 Broadway, Nashville TN 37203. **Tel** (615)259-8300. **LC** 9793-X. available on microfilm.

US/0890-6009
OAK RIDGER, THE. Vol. 1, No. 1 (Jan. 20, 1949)-. Newspaper. English. da (Published Sunday-Friday & no Saturday). $139.00. Oak Ridger, PO Box 3446, Oak Ridge TN 37831. **Tel** (615)482-1021. available on microfilm from University Microfilms International (UMI).

US/0893-3669
PARIS POST-INTELLIGENCER, THE. **VFOAT** Paris Post Intelligencer. (1884)-. Newspaper. English. da (Monday-Friday). $73.50. Paris Post-Intelligencer, PO Box 310, Paris TN 38242-0310. **Tel** (901)642-1162, FAX (901)642-1165. **ED** Michael Williams. **Bk Rev**. **Photos**. **Ad Acc, Adv Mgr:** Brenda Stubblefield. Full Page (B&W) $719.82. Half Page (B&W) $359.91. Full Page (Color) $809.82. Half Page (Color) $449.91. **Pub. Size:** Broadsheet. **Wire Svcs.:** AP. **Circ:** 8,342 (daily). available in microform. ***Formed by the union of*** *Paris Post (Paris, Tenn.)* ***and*** *Weekly Intelligencer (Paris Tenn. : 1866).*

US
PULASKI CITIZEN (PULASKI, TENN. : 1866). (THE PULASKI CITIZEN.). **VFOAT** Citizen and Press. (Jan. 5, 1866)-. Newspaper. English. wk. $24.00. Pulaski Citizen, PO Drawer E, Pulaski TN 38478. **ED** Joe Collins, Phil Willis (Managing Editor). **Photos**. **Ad Acc, Adv Mgr:** Juanita Hoover, **Tel** (615)363-3544. Full Page (B&W) $740.88. Half Page (B&W) $370.44. Full Page (Color) $840.88. Half Page (Color) $470.44. **Pub. Size:** Broadsheet. **Circ:** 8,200. ***Continues*** *Independent Citizen (Pulaski, Tenn.).*

US
RECORD (MEMPHIS, TN). (THE RECORD.). Vol. 3, No. 6 (Jan. 15, 1981)-. Periodical. English. mo. University of Tennessee Health Science Center, 62 South Dunlap/Suite 513, Memphis TN 38163. **Tel** (901)528-5516. **ED** Claire Lowry. **Circ:** 4,500 (ctrl). ***Continues*** *UTCHS Record.*

US
SAVANNAH COURIER. Vol. 1, No. 1 (Sept. 17, 1885)-. Newspaper. English. wk. Price varies in Tennessee; $24.00 other US; $35.00 other. The Courier / Tennessee, PO Box 339, Savannah TN 38372. **Tel** (901)925-6397.

US
SHELBYVILLE TIMES-GAZETTE. **VFOAT** Shelbyville Times Gazette. Began with Feb. 2, 1948 issue. Newspaper. English. da. Shelbyville Times-Gazette, 323 East Depot Street, Shelbyville TN 37160. available on microfilm from Tennessee State Library and Archives. ***Formed by the union of*** *Bedford County Times* ***and*** *Shelbyville Gazette.*

US
SOUTH PITTSBURG HUSTLER. (1899)-. Newspaper. English. wk. $17.00. South Pittsburg Hustler, PO Box 269, South Pittsburg TN 37380. **Tel** (615)837-6312, FAX (615)837-8715. **ED** Jim Shanks, and Mike O'Hagan (Managing Editor). **Photos**. **Ad Acc, Adv Mgr:** Jim Shanks. Full Page (B&W) $516.00. Half Page (B&W) $264.00. Full Page (Color) $566.00. Half Page (Color) $304.00. **Pub. Size:** Broadsheet. **Circ:** 13,600.

US
SOUTHERN STANDARD (MCMINNVILLE, TENN.). (SOUTHERN STANDARD.). Began in 1879?. Newspaper. English. tw. Southern Standard / Tennessee, PO Box 150, McMinnville TN 37110. **Tel** (615)473-2191.

US/1053-6590
TENNESSEAN (1972), THE. (THE TENNESSEAN.). Vol. 67, No. 39 (June 6, 1972)-. Newspaper. English. da. $124.80 (daily), $241.80 (daily and Sunday). Newspaper Printing Corporation / Tennessee, 1100 Broadway, Nashville TN 37203. **Tel** (615)259-8300. **ED** John Seigenthaler. **Circ:** 119,120 daily, 255,318 Sunday. available on microfilm from University Microfilms International (UMI); and University Microfilms International (UMI). ***Continues*** *Nashville Tennessean.*
Ind/Abst PROMT.

US/1041-1569
TENNESSEE REGISTER, THE. **Added/Corp** Catholic Church. Diocese of Nashville (Tenn.). Vol. 33, No. 2 (Jan. 4, 1957)-. Periodical. English. Twenty-six times a year. $15.00. Tennessee Register, 2400 21st Ave South, Nashville TN 37212. **Tel** (615)383-6393, FAX (615)292-8411. **ED** Anthony J. Spence. **Bk Rev**, (Qty: 10). **Photos**. **Ad Acc, Adv Mgr:** Marilyn Rubin. Full Page (B&W) $735.00. Half Page (B&W) $368.00. **Pub. Size:** Standard. **Wire Svcs.:** CS. **Pr Rev. Circ:** 14,500. available in microform. ***Continues*** *Register.*
Desc: Newspaper serving the Catholic community of Middle Tennessee.

US
TENNESSEE REPUBLICAN. Began in 1870. Newspaper. English. wk. Tennessee Republican, 108 2nd Avenue North, Huntingdon TN 38344.

US
TRI-CITY REPORTER, THE. **VFOAT** Tri City Reporter. (193?)-. Newspaper. English. wk. Dyer Tri-City Reporter, 101 North Main Street, Dyer TN 38330. **Tel** (901)692-3506, FAX (901)692-4844. **ED** Robert Barbour. **Bk Rev**. **Ad Acc. Circ:** 3,500 (evening). ***Continues*** *Dyer Reporter.*

TEXAS

US/0895-4291
ABERNATHY WEEKLY REVIEW, THE. (1921)-. Newspaper. English. Fifty-two times a year (Published on Thurs.). $17.00. Abernathy Weekly Review, Drawer 160, 916 Avenue D, Abernathy TX 79311. **Tel** (806)298-2033. **ED** Scott Luce. **Ad Acc, Adv Mgr:** Judy Luce. Full Page (B&W) $399.90. Half Page (B&W) $199.95. Full Page (Color) $439.90. Half Page (Color) $239.95. **Pub. Size:** Standard.

US/0199-3267
ABILENE REPORTER-NEWS. **VFOAT** Abilene Reporter News. (1937)-. Newspaper. English. da. Abilene Reporter News, PO Box 3863, Abilene TX 79604. **Tel** (915)673-4271. **ED** Glenn Dromgoole. **Circ:** 35,351 daily, 57,231 Sunday. available on microfilm from University Microfilms International (UMI). ***Formed by the union of*** *Abilene Morning News* ***and*** *Abilene Daily Reporter.*

US
ADDISON TODAY. Newspaper. English. wk. Addison Today, 1712 Beltline, Carrollton TX 75006. ***Continues*** *Addison-North Dallas Today.*

●US/1069-8205
AFRICAN HERALD, THE. (Sept. 1992)-. Newspaper. English. Twelve times a year. $12.00 (individuals), $15.00 (institutions) US; $16.00 others. African Herald, PO Box 2394, Dallas TX 75221. **Tel** (214)823-7666. **ED** Dr. Richard N. Wachukner. **Bk Rev**, (Qty: 4). **Ad Acc.** ctrl circ. ***Continues*** *Good Hope News.*

US
ALBANY NEWS (ALBANY, TEX.). (THE ALBANY NEWS.). **VFOAT** Albany Weekly News. Began in 1884?. Newspaper. English. wk. $18.00. Albany News, PO Box 278, Albany TX 76430. **Tel** (915)762-2201. **ED** Donnie A Lucas. **Ad Acc. Circ:** 2,100 (ctrl). available on microfilm. ***Formed by the union of*** *Albany Echo (Albany, Tex. : 1883)* ***and*** *Albany Start (Albany, Tex. : 1882).*

US
ALICE ECHO-NEWS. **VFOAT** Alice Echo News. Vol. 74, No. 234 (May 9, l969)-. Newspaper. English. da. $54.66 Texas; $52.00 other. Alice Daily Echo News, PO Box 1610, Alice TX 78333. **Tel** (512)664-6588. ***Continues*** *Alice Daily Echo and Alice News.*

US
ALLEN AMERICAN, THE. Began in 1970?. Newspaper. English. wk. Allen American, PO Box 27, Allen TX 75074.

US
ALPINE AVALANCHE. (1889)-. Newspaper. English. wk. $20.00 local; $24.00 Texas; $28.00 US. Alpine Avalanche Inc, Box 719, 112 North 5th Street, Alpine TX 79831-0719. **Tel** (915)837-3334, FAX (915)837-7181. **ED** Dean Williamson. **Bk Rev**, (Qty: 40). **Photos**. **Ad Acc, Adv Mgr:** Lauren Spear. Full Page (B&W) $428.40. Half Page (B&W) $239.40. Full Page (Color) $528.40. Half Page (Color) $339.40. **Pub. Size:** Standard. **Circ:** 4,228 weekly.

US
ALVARADO POST. (19??)-. Newspaper. English. Fifty times a year (Wed.). $14.50 Johnson County; $16.50 others in Texas; $17.00 others. Alvarado Post, PO Box 1150, Alvarado TX 76009. **Tel** (817)783-8717. **ED** Loree Lewis, (editor's address: 2005 Parkway, Alavarado, TX 76009, phone: (817)790-8717). **Photos**. **Ad Acc. Pub. Size:** Standard. **Circ:** 2,600 (ctrl).

US/8750-1902
ALVIN SUN, THE. Began in 1890. Newspaper. English. wk. Alvin Sun, 201 East House Street, Alvin TX 77511.

US
ALVORD NEWS, THE. Began in 1910?. Newspaper. English. wk. Alvord News, PO Box 65, Alvord TX 76225.

US
AMARILLO DAILY NEWS (AMARILLO, TEX. : 1909). (AMARILLO DAILY NEWS.). **VFOAT** Amarillo Sunday News-Globe. (Nov. 4, 1909)-. Newspaper. English. da. $112.00 (zone 1 & 2), $124.00 (zone 3 & 4 & 5), $139.00 (zone 6 & 7 & 8) one year, daily; $133.00 (zone 1 & 2), $145.00 (zone 3 & 4 & 5), $166.00 (zone 6 & 7 & 8) one year, daily & Sunday; $85.00 (zone 1 & 2), $88.00 (zone 3 & 4 & 5), $94.00 (zone 6 & 7 & 8) one year, Sunday. Amarillo Daily News/Globe Time, PO Box 2091, Amarillo TX 79166. **Tel** (806)376-4488. **ED** Cathy Martindale (phone: (806)376-4488 Ext. 365). **Circ:** 43,321. available on microfilm from Microfilm Center, Inc. ***Absorbed*** *Amarillo Daily Tribune; Daily Panhandle (Amarillo, Tex.: 1906).*

US
AMARILLO GLOBE-TIMES, THE. **VFOAT** Amarillo Globe Times. 28th Year, No. 206 (Dec. 3, 1951)-. Newspaper. English. da. $123.00 (zone 1 & 2), $135.00 (zone 3 & 4 & 5), $156.00 (zone 6 & 7 & 8) one year, (daily & Sunday); $102.00 (zone 1 & 2), $114.00 (zone 3 & 4 & 5), $129.00 (zone 6 & 7 & 8) one year, (daily); $75.00 (zone 1 & 2), $78.00 (zone 3 & 4 & 5), $84.00 (zone 6 & 7 & 8) one year, (Sunday). Amarillo Daily News/Globe Time, PO Box 2091, Amarillo TX 79166. **Tel** (806)376-4488. **ED** Cathy Martindale (phone: (806)376-4488 Ext. 365). **Circ:** 26,906. ***Formed by the union of*** *Amarillo Globe* ***and*** *Amarillo Times.*

US
ANDREWS COUNTY NEWS, THE. (1935)-. Newspaper. English. sw (published Thursday and Sunday). $14.90 Andrews county; $18.80 Texas; $22.50 US; $37.50 other. Andrews County News, 210 East Broadway, Andrews TX 79714. **Tel** (915)523-2085.

US
ANGLETON TIMES, THE. (1893)-. Newspaper. English. da. $48.00 Brazoria county Texas; $53.40 other. Angleton Times, 700 Western Avenue, PO Box 936, Angleton TX 77515. **Tel** (713)849-8581. **ED** Marie Beth Jones. **Circ:** 13,008.

US
ARLINGTON CITIZEN JOURNAL. Vol. 76, No. 79 (April 17, 1973)-. Newspaper. English. sw. Arlington Citizen Journal, 1111 West Abram, Arlington TX 76010. ***Continues*** *Citizen Journal.*

US/1044-1174
ARLINGTON NEWS (1989). (ARLINGTON NEWS.). (1989)-. Newspaper. English. da (Published Sunday thru Friday). $72.00 Texas; $84.00 others. Suburban Newspapers / Texas, 1000 East Avenue H, Arlington TX 76011. **Tel** (817)695-0365. ***Continues*** *Arlington Daily News, 0746-6420.*

US/1040-6522
ATHENS DAILY REVIEW. (1900)-. Newspaper. English. da (except Sat.). $80.00 Henderson County, Texas; $85.00 Texas; $90.00 other. Athens Daily Review / Texas, PO Box 32, Athens TX 75751. **Tel** (214)675-5626. **ED** Jim Goodson. **Ad Acc. Circ:** 7,502.

US
ATHENS WEEKLY REVIEW. Newspaper. English. wk. Athens Weekly Review, 201 South Prairieville Street, Athens TX 75751. ***Continues*** *Athens Review.*

US
AUSTIN AMERICAN-STATESMAN. **VFOAT** Austin American Statesman. Vol. 116, No. 223 (March 5, 1987)-. Newspaper. English. da. $217.57. Austin American-Statesman, PO Box 670, Austin TX 78767. **Tel** (512)445-3500, FAX (512)445-4047. ***Formed by the union of*** *Austin American-Statesman (Morning Ed. : 1973)* ***and*** *Austin American-Statesman (Evening Ed. : 1973).*

US/0740-4581
AUSTIN CHRONICLE (SCOTTSBURG, IND.), THE. (THE AUSTIN CHRONICLE.). (1???)-. Newspaper. English. Fifty-one times per year (Friday). $120.00. Austin Chronicle, PO Box 49066, Austin TX 78765. **Tel** (512)454-5766. **ED** Louis Black (editor's phone: (512)454-5766). **Bk Rev**. **Photos**. **Ad Acc, Adv Mgr:** Jerald Corder. Full Page (B&W) $2040.00. Half Page (B&W) $1125.00. Full Page (Color) $2040.00 plus $160.00 per color. Half Page (Color) $1125.00 plus $160.00 per color. **Pub. Size:** Tabloid. **Circ:** 80,000.
Desc: Weekly arts, entertainment and political coverage, with particular focus on local music, films and politics.

US
AUSTIN LIGHT, THE. (198?)-. Newspaper. English. wk. $18.00. Austin Light, 606 Oltorf, Austin TX 78704. **Tel** (512)462-9933.

US
AZLE NEWS ADVERTISER. Vol. 22, No. 14 (Apr. 1, 1976)-. Newspaper. English. Fifty-two times a year (Thurs.). $19.76 Tarrent and Parker counties; $26.00 other. Azle News Advertiser, PO Box 1409, Azle TX 76020. **Tel** (817)237-1184. **ED** Bob Buckel. **Photos**. **Ad Acc, Adv Mgr:** Marie Maxfield. Full Page (B&W) $630.00. Half Page (B&W) $315.00. Full Page (Color) $720.00. Half Page (Color) $405.00. **Pub. Size:** Standard. **Circ:** 4,500. ***Continues*** *Azle News.*

Texas

US
BALLINGER LEDGER, THE. Vol. 53, No. 4 (Oct. 5, 1933)-. Newspaper. English. wk. Ballinger Ledger, PO Box 111, Ballinger TX 76821. *Continues Ballinger Semi-Weekly Ledger.*

US
BANDERA BULLETIN, THE. Bulletin. English. wk. Bandera Bulletin, PO Box 666, Bandera TX 78003.

US/8750-5800
BANNER-PRESS, THE. VFOAT Banner Press; Brenham Banner Press; Brenham Banner-Press. Vol. 110, No. 129 (July 4, 1976)-. Newspaper. English. da. $46.00. Banner-Press, 2000 Stringer Street, Brenham TX 77833. *Continues Brenham Banner-Press.*

US/0891-1118
BANNER PRESS NEWSPAPER, THE. VFOAT Banner Press. (19??)-. Newspaper. English. wk. $19.00 in county; $22.00 others in Texas; $25.00 others. Banner Press Newspaper, PO Box 490, Columbus TX 78934-0490. **Tel** (409)732-6243, FAX (409)732-6245. **ED** Chad Ferguson. **Photos. Ad Acc, Adv Mgr:** Chad Ferguson. Full Page (B&W) $470.40. Half Page (B&W) $246.23. Full Page (Color) $595.40. Half Page (Color) $371.23. **Pub. Size:** Standard. **Circ:** 5,200.

US
BASTROP ADVERTISER AND COUNTY NEWS, THE. No. 44 (July 31, 1980)-. Newspaper. English. sw. $28.50 in county; $30.50 others. The Bastrop Advertiser and County News, 908 Water Street, Bastrop TX 78602. **Tel** (512)321-2557, FAX (512)321-1680. **ED** Steve Taylor. **Photos. Ad Acc, Adv Mgr:** Steve Taylor. Full Page (B&W) $774.90. Half Page (B&W) $387.45. Full Page (Color) $824.90. Half Page (Color) $437.45. **Pub. Size:** Broadsheet. *Continues Bastrop Advertiser.*

US
BAYLOR COUNTY BANNER, THE. (1895)-. Newspaper. English. wk. $15.00. Banner Publishing Company / Texas, PO Box 912, Seymour TX 76380. **Tel** (817)888-2616, FAX (817)898-3610. **ED** Earl Gwinn. **Bk Rev. Photos. Ad Acc, Adv Mgr:** Earl Gwinn. Full Page (B&W) $207.90. Half Page (B&W) $103.95. Full Page (Color) $282.95. Half Page (Color) $178.95. **Pub. Size:** Standard. **Circ:** 2,900. (ctrl). available on microfilm from Southwest Micropublishing International.

US
BAYSHORE SUN, THE. (19??)-. Newspaper. English. wk (Wed. & Sun.). $31.50 Harris County; $35.00 others. Bayshore Sun Newspapers, PO Box 1414, La Porte TX 77571. **Tel** (713)471-1234. *Continues LaPorte-Bayshore Sun.*

US
BAYTOWN SUN, THE. (1920)-. Newspaper. English. da (Except Saturday). $91.00 (carrier); $108.00 (mail). Baytown Sun, 1301 Memorial Drive, Baytown TX 77520. **Tel** (713)422-8302.

US
BEAUMONT ENTERPRISE. VFOAT Daily Enterprise; Sunday Enterprise; Beaumont Sunday Enterprise Journal; Beaumont Enterprise Journal. (1897)-. Newspaper. English. da. Beaumont Enterprise / Mail Subscription Department, PO Box 2991, Beaumont TX 77704. **Tel** (409)833-3311. **ED** Ben Hansen. **Circ:** 69,569 daily, 79,640 Sunday. available on microfilm.

US/0889-8618
BEEVILLE BEE-PICAYUNE. VFOAT Beeville Bee Picayune. Vol. 58, No. 13 (July 29, 1943)-. Newspaper. English. sw. $36.60. Beeville Bee-Picayune, PO Box 10, Beeville TX 78102. **Tel** (512)358-2550, FAX (512)358-5323. **ED** Chip Latcham, Jeff Latcham. **Photos. Ad Acc, Adv Mgr:** Dick Carter. Full Page (B&W) $4.50 per column inch. Half Page (B&W) $4.68 per column inch. **Pub. Size:** Standard. available in microform. *Continues Bee-Picayune.*

US
BELLAIRE TEXAN, THE. Newspaper. English. wk. Bellaire Texan, PO Box 999, Bellaire TX 77401.

US
BELLVILLE TIMES (BELLVILLE, TEX.). (THE BELLVILLE TIMES.). VFOAT Bellville Times. (1894)-. Newspaper. English. wk. Bellville Times, PO Box 98, Bellville TX 77418. *Continues Times-Standard.*

US/1053-9131
BELTON JOURNAL (BELTON, TEX. : 1923). (THE BELTON JOURNAL.). (19??)-. Newspaper. English. wk. $32.00. Belton Journal Publishing Co., 314 East Central Street, Belton TX 76513. *Continues Belton Journal and Bell County Democrat.*

US
BENBROOK NEWS, THE. (19??)-. Newspaper. English. wk (Published on Thursday). $30.00. Suburban Newspapers Inc, 7820 Wyatt Drive, Fort Worth TX 76108. **Tel** (817)246-2473. **ED** Janice Underwood, Charlsea Littlefield (Managing Editor). **Photos. Ad Acc.** Full Page (B&W) $546.00. Half Page (B&W) $273.00. Full Page (Color) $581.00. Half Page (Color) $308.00. **Pub. Size:** Tabloid. **Circ:** 6,000 (ctrl).
Desc: Tabloid paper covering local news and advertising.

US
BIG LAKE WILDCAT, THE. (1925)-. Newspaper. English. wk. $16.50 Big Lake; $18.50 other in Texas; $20.50 others. The Big Lake Wildcat, 309 2nd Street, PC Box 946, Big Lake TX 76932. **Tel** (915)884-2215, FAX (915)884-5771. **ED** David Werst. **Photos. Ad Acc, Adv Mgr:** David Werst. Full Page (B&W) $419.25. Half Page (B&W) $209.63. Full Page (Color) $494.25. Half Page (Color) $284.63. **Pub. Size:** Standard. *Absorbed Big Lake News and Oil Review.*

US/0745-0702
BIG SANDY & HAWKINS JOURNAL AND TRI-AREA NEWS, THE. VFOAT Big Sandy and Hawkins Journal and Tri-Area News. Newspaper. English. wk. $10.00 Upshur, Wood, Smith & Gregg counties, $13.00 elsewhere in Texas, $15.00 general. Cartwright Communications, PO Box 927, Big Sandy TX 75755.

US/0746-6811
BIG SPRING HERALD. (THE BIG SPRING HERALD.). VFOAT Big Spring (Texas) Herald. (1904)-. Newspaper. English. da. $137.16. Big Spring Herald Newspaper, PO Box 1431, Big Spring TX 79720. **Tel** (915)263-7331. **ED** D.D. Turner. **Bk Rev. Photos. Ad Acc, Adv Mgr:** Ken Dulaney. Full Page (B&W) $1408.68. Half Page (B&W) $687.96. Full Page (Color) $1525.68. Half Page (Color) $804.96. **Pub. Size:** Broadsheet. **Wire Svcs.:** AP. **Circ:** 8,230 daily, 8,797 Sunday. *Continues Big Spring Daily Herald.*

US/1049-2216
BLANCO COUNTY NEWS. [Blanco Cty. news]. Began in 1927?. Newspaper. English. wk. Blanco County News, PO Box 429, Blanco TX 78606. DD 071.

US
BONHAM DAILY FAVORITE, THE. Vol. 12, No. 209 (May 2, 1910)-. Newspaper. English. da. $36.00 Sannin County Texas; $27.00 other. Bonham Daily Favorite, PO Box 550, Bonham TX 75418. **Tel** (903)583-2124, FAX (903)583-8521. *Continues Daily Favorite.*

US
BOOKER NEWS, THE. Began in 1925?. Newspaper. English. wk. Booker News, 204 South Main Street, Booker TX 79005.

US
BORGER NEWS-HERALD. VFOAT Borger News Herald. Began in 1926?. Newspaper. English. da. Panhandle Publishing Company, 209 North Main Street, Borger TX 79007. *Continues Borger Daily Hearld.*

US
BOWIE NEWS, THE. (June 1, 1936)-. Newspaper. English. wk. Bowie News, 216 West Tarrant Street, Bowie TX 76230. *Continues Bowie Booster.*

US
BRADY HERALD, THE. Began in 1942?. Newspaper. English. wk. Brady Herald, 201 South Bridge Street, Brady TX 76825.

US
BRAZORIA COUNTY NEWS, THE. Vol. 1, No. 1 (Oct. 10, 1962)-. Newspaper. English. wk. Brazoria County News, 113 East Bernard Street, West Columbia TX 77486. **Bk Rev. Ad Acc.** ctrl circ.

US
BRAZORIAN NEWS, THE. Vol. 29, No. 24 (Jan. 10, 1963)-. Newspaper. English. wk. Brazorian News, PO Box 34, Lake Jackson TX 77566. *Continues Lake Jackson News.*

US/1065-7886
BRAZOSPORT FACTS, THE. (19??)-. Newspaper. English. da. $120.00. Brazosport Facts, PO Box 547, Clute TX 77531. **Tel** (409)265-7411. **ED** Rob Luwig, (editor's address: 720 South Main, Clute, TX 77531, phone: (409)265-7411). **Ad Acc. Circ:** 21,000 (ctrl). *Continues Freeport Facts.*

US
BRECKENRIDGE AMERICAN. (June 18, 1920)-. Newspaper. English. sw. $20.00. Breckenridge American, 114 East Elm, PO Box 871, Breckenridge TX 76424. **Tel** (817)559-5412, FAX (817)559-3491. **ED** Herrel Hallmark. **Photos. Ad Acc, Adv Mgr:** David Hall. Full Page (B&W) $504.00. Half Page (B&W) $267.75. Full Page (Color) $574.00. Half Page (Color) $337.75. **Pub. Size:** Broadsheet. **Circ:** 3,875 (paid).

US
BREMOND PRESS, THE. Began in 1922?. Newspaper. English. wk. Bremond Press, PO Box 490, Bremond TX 76629.

US
BRIDGEPORT INDEX, THE. (1916)-. Newspaper. English. wk. $15.00. Bridwell Publishing, PO Box 1150, Bridgeport TX 76426. **Tel** (817)683-4021. **ED** Joann Pritchard. **Photos. Ad Acc, Adv Mgr:** Keith Bridwell. Full Page (B&W) $504.00. Half Page (B&W) $252.00. Full Page (Color) $574.00. Half Page (Color) $322.00. **Pub. Size:** Broadsheet. **Circ:** 2,333. *Continues Wise County Index.*

US/0746-0678
BROOKSHIRE BANNER. (19??)-. Newspaper. English. wk. Brookshire Banner, PO Box 718, Brookshire TX 77423. *Continues Brookshire Royal Banner.*

US
BROWNFIELD NEWS AND TERRY COUNTY HERALD, THE. VFOAT News-Herald; Brownfield News Herald. Vol. 17, No. 45 (Nov. 5, 1954)-. Newspaper. English. sw. $26.80. Brownfield News & Terry Herald, PO Box 1272, Brownfield TX 79316. **Tel** (806)637-4535. *Formed by the union of Brownfield News and Terry County Herald.*

US/0894-2064
BROWNSVILLE HERALD (BROWNSVILLE, TEX. : 1910). (BROWNSVILLE HERALD.). VFOAT Valley Sunday Star-Monitor-Herald; Valley Sunday Star Monitor Herald; Brownsville Daily Herald; Brownsville Evening Herald. Vol. 18, No. 279 (Oct. 10, 1910)-. Newspaper. English. da. $144.00. Brownsville Herald, PO Box 351, 1135 East Van Buren, Brownsville TX 78520. **Tel** (512)542-4301. **ED** Lavice Laney. **Photos. Ad Acc, Adv Mgr:** Julie Moreno, **Tel** (210)982-6636. Full Page (B&W) $1,008.00. Half Page (B&W) $510.30. Full Page (Color) $1,173.00. Half Page (Color) $675.30. **Pub. Size:** Broadsheet. **Wire Svcs.:** AP. **Circ:** 18,062 (daily), 20,388 (Sunday). *Continues Brownsville Daily Herald (Brownsville, Tex. : 1897).*

US/0746-6412
BROWNSVILLE TIMES, THE. (1967)-. Newspaper. English. wk. $10.00 in county, $15.00 other. Brownsville Times, 1225 North Expressway, Brownsville TX 78520.

US
BROWNWOOD BULLETIN. (19??)-. Newspaper. English. da. $132.00. Brownwood Bulletin, PO Box 1188, Carnegie Boulevard, Brownwood TX 76801. **Tel** (915)646-2541. *Continues Daily Bulletin (Brownwood, Tex.).*

US/0739-8727
BRYAN-COLLEGE STATION EAGLE. VFOAT Eagle. VAT Bryan, College Station Eagle. Vol. 105, No. 133 (June 8, 1981)-. Newspaper. English. da. $136.00 Texas; $190.00 other. Bryan-College Station Eagle, PO Box 3000, Bryan TX 77805. **Tel** (409)776-4444. *Continues Eagle.*

US
BURKBURNETT INFORMER STAR. Vol. 62, No. 5 (Aug. 28, 1969)-. Newspaper. English. wk. Burkburnett Informer Star, 417 Avenue C, Burkburnett TX 76354. *Continues Burkburnett Star.*

US
BURLESON COUNTY CITIZEN-TRIBUNE AND THE CALDWELL NEWS. VFOAT Burleson County Citizen Tribune and The Caldwell News. Vol. 86, No. 3 (Sept. 17, 1970)-. Newspaper. English. wk. $19.50 in county; $23.50 Texas; $25.00 US. Burleson County Publishing Co., Inc., 205 West Buck Street, Caldwell TX 77836. **ED** Michael Marshall. **Photos. Ad Acc, Adv Mgr:** Charlotte Strong. Full Page (B&W) $409.50. Half Page (B&W) $233.10. **Pub. Size:** Standard. **Circ:** 3,995. *Continues Burleson County Citizen and The Caldwell News.*

US
BURNET BULLETIN. Began in 1873. Bulletin. English. wk. Burnet Bulletin, PO Box 160, Burnet TX 78611.

US
CALLAHAN COUNTY STAR. Vol. 85, No. 14 (Apr. 4, 1969)-. Newspaper. English. wk. Callahan County Star, 101 Market Street, Baird TX 79504. **Tel** (915)854-1008. **ED** Carol Smith. **Bk Rev. Photos. Ad Acc, Adv Mgr:** Carol Smith. Full Page (B&W) $336.00. Half Page (B&W) $168.00. **Pub. Size:** Standard. *Formed by the union of Baird Star and Clyde News.*

US/8750-202X
CAMERON CHRONICLE. (198?)-. Newspaper. English. wk. Cameron Chronicle, 114 Fannin, Cameron TX 76530. DD 071.

US
CAMERON HERALD (CAMERON, TEX.). (THE CAMERON HERALD.). VFOAT Cameron Herald and Centinel. (1882)-. Newspaper. English. sw. $20.45 North America; $25.45 other. Cameron Herald, 108 East 1st Street, Cameron TX 76502. **Tel** (817)697-6671. **(Subscription address:** Cameron Herald, PO Drawer 1230, Cameron TX 76520-1230.) **ED** Frank M Luecke and Mike Peck. **Bk Rev. Ad Acc. Circ:** 7,000 (ctrl). available on microfilm.

US
CANADIAN RECORD, THE. (1893)-. Newspaper. English. wk. $20.00 local; $25.00 other.

Texas

Canadian Record, 211 Main Street, Canadian TX 79014. **Tel** (806)323-6461, (806)323-5321, FAX (806)323-6102. **ED** Nancy M. Ezzell. **Photos. Ad Acc, Adv Mgr:** Tina Stock. Full Page (B&W) $175.00. Half Page (B&W) $87.50. Full Page (Color) $175.00 plus $70.00 per color. Half Page (Color) $87.50 plus $70.00 per color. **Pub. Size:** Tabloid. **Circ:** 2,000.

US/0894-2560
CANTON HERALD (CANTON, TEX.). (CANTON HERALD.). Began in 1882?. Newspaper. English. wk. Canton Herald, PO Box 577, Canton TX 75103. *Continues Van Zandt Enterprises.*

US
CANYON NEWS (CANYON, TEX. : 1926). (THE CANYON NEWS.). Vol. 30, No. 28 (Oct. 7, 1926)-. Newspaper. English. wk. $21.50 local; $31.50 other. Canyon News, PO Box 779, Canyon TX 79015. **ED** Brad Tooley, Kimberly Burk (Managing Editor). **Bk Rev**, (Qty: 5). **Photos. Ad Acc.** Full Page (B&W) $459.20. Half Page (B&W) $252.00. **Pub. Size:** Broadsheet. **Circ:** 3,900 paid, 4,300 total. available in microform. *Continues Randall County News.*

US/0746-3294
CAPITOL REVIEW, THE. Vol 1, No. 1 (Sept. 6, 1983)-. Newspaper. English. wk. $10.00 US; $15.00 other. Capitol Review, Box 1, Allison TX 79003. **Tel** (806)375-2425. **ED** Edwin P Nall. **Ad Acc.**

US
CARROLLTON CHRONICLE. Began in 1904?. Newspaper. English. wk. Carrollton Chronicle, 1712 Beltline, Carrollton TX 75006.

US
CASS COUNTY SUN (1897). (THE CASS COUNTY SUN.). (1897)-. Newspaper. English. wk. $17.50 in county; $22.25 Texas; $27.25 other. Cass County Sun, PO Box 604, Linden TX 75563. **Tel** (903)756-7396, FAX (903)756-3038. **ED** Barbara Carroll. **Photos. Ad Acc, Adv Mgr:** Betty Rhyne. Full Page (B&W) $408.96. Half Page (B&W) $225.11. **Pub. Size:** Standard. **Circ:** 1,000. *Continues Alliance Standard.*

US/1046-8633
CEDAR CREEK PILOT. (1971)-. Newspaper. English. Twice a week. $22.00. Cedar Creek Pilot, 184 Highway 334, Seven Points TX 75143. **Tel** (903)432-3132, FAX (903)432-2002. **ED** Chip Sovza. **Photos. Ad Acc, Adv Mgr:** Kathi Nailling. Full Page (B&W) $528.90. Half Page (B&W) $271.55. **Pub. Size:** Standard. **Circ:** 6,300 Thursday, 6,800 Sunday.

US
CHICO TEXAN, THE. (19??)-. Newspaper. English. wk. $12.50. Chico Texan, PO Box 1150, Bridgeport TX 76426. **Tel** (817)683-4021. **ED** Joann Pritchard (Editor-in-Chief) and Brenda Marlett (Managing Editor). **Photos. Ad Acc, Adv Mgr:** Keith Bridwell. Full Page (B&W) $378.00. Half Page (B&W) $189.00. Full Page (Color) $448.00. Half Page (Color) $259.00. **Pub. Size:** Broadsheet. **Circ:** 600.

US
CHILDRESS INDEX, THE. Began in 1888. Newspaper. English. da. Childress Index, 224 Main Street, Childress TX 79201.

US
CHRONICLE. HOUSTON, TX. (HOUSTON CHRONICLE.). Periodical. English. da. $352.00. Chronicle / Houston, PO Box 4560, Houston TX 77210. available on microfilm from University Microfilms International (UMI).

US
CISCO PRESS, THE. Vol. 35, No. 57 (March 1, 1955)-. Newspaper. English. tw. $18.00 in county; $23.00 adjoining counties; $25.00 Texas; $35.00 others. Cisco Press, PO Drawer 470, Cisco TX 76437. **Tel** (817)442-2244, FAX (817)629-2092. **ED** Richard Kurklin. **Photos. Ad Acc, Adv Mgr:** Bill Sanders, **Tel** (817)629-1707. **Pub. Size:** Standard. **Circ:** 1,575. *Continues Cisco Daily Press.*

US
CITIZENS JOURNAL (ATLANTA, TEX.). (THE CITIZENS JOURNAL.). (March 1879)-. Newspaper. English. sw. Citizens Journal, PO Box 1188, Atlanta TX 75551-1188.

US/1048-8170
CLARENDON NEWS (1990), THE. (THE CLARENDON NEWS.). (January 1990)-. Newspaper. English. wk. $18.50 (in county), $22.50 (out of county). Clarendon Press, PO Box 1110, Clarendon TX 79226. **Tel** (806)874-2259, FAX (806)874-3124. **ED** Bob Williams, Cassie Row (Managing Editor). **Photos. Ad Acc.** Full Page (B&W) $453.60. Half Page (B&W) $226.80. Full Page (Color) $553.60. Half Page (Color) $326.80. **Pub. Size:** Standard. **Circ:** 1,400. *Continues Clarendon Press.*

US/1040-2489
CLARKSVILLE TIMES, THE. (Jan. 18, 1873)-. Newspaper. English. sw. $15.00 in county; $24.00 others. Clarksville Times Press, PO Box 1018, Clarksville TX 75426. **Tel** (214)427-5616, FAX (214)427-5617. **ED** Ben Black. **Bk Rev**, (Qty: 6). **Photos. Ad Acc, Adv Mgr:** Barbara Mitchell. Full Page (B&W) $420.00. Half Page (B&W) $210.00. **Pub. Size:** Standard. available in microform.

US
CLAY COUNTY LEADER, THE. Began in 1932?. Newspaper. English. wk. Clay County Leader, PO Drawer 10, Henrietta TX 76365.

US
CLEBURNE TIMES-REVIEW. VFOAT Cleburne Times Review. Vol. 24, No. 263 (Oct. 1, 1928)-. Newspaper. English. da. Cleburne Times Review, PO Box 1620, Cleburne TX 76031. **Tel** (817)645-2441. *Formed by the union of Cleburne Daily Times and Cleburne Morning Review.*

US/0746-7125
CLEVELAND ADVOCATE (CLEVELAND, TEX.), THE. (THE CLEVELAND ADVOCATE.). Began in 1917?. Newspaper. English. wk. $5.80. Cleveland Advocate, PO Box 1628, Cleveland TX 77327. **Tel** (713)592-2626. **ED** Mike Wheeler. Index available. **Bk Rev. Ad Acc. Circ:** 3,000.
Desc: Local, community, city, county and state news.

US
CLIFTON RECORD, THE. VFOAT Record. (1896)-. Newspaper. English. wk. $22.00 Clifton, Texas; $26.00 other. Progressive Media Communications Inc, PO Box 353, 310 West 5th Street, Clifton TX 76634. **Tel** (817)765-3336. **ED** W. Leon Smith. **Photos. Ad Acc, Adv Mgr:** James W. Smith. Full Page (B&W) $4.85 per column inch. Half Page (B&W) $4.85 per column inch. Full Page (Color) $4.85 per column inch plus $100.00. Half Page (Color) $4.85 per column inch plus $100.00. **Pub. Size:** Broadsheet. **Circ:** 3,300 (ctrl). available on microfilm.

US
CLYDE JOURNAL. Vol. 1, No. 1 (Oct. 31, 1974)-. Newspaper. English. wk. Clyde Journal, PO Drawer W, Clyde TX 79510.

US
COLEMAN COUNTY CHRONICLE. Vol. 1, No. 1 (Jan. 19, 1933)-. Newspaper. English. sw. $21.95 Coleman County; $34.95 others. Coleman Chronicle of Democrat - Voice, PO Box 840, Coleman TX 76834-0840. **Tel** (915)625-4128, FAX (915)625-4129. **ED** Stan Brudney. **Bk Rev**, (Qty: 2). **Photos. Ad Acc, Adv Mgr:** Stan Brudney. Full Page (B&W) $361.20. Half Page (B&W) $180.60. Full Page (Color) $436.20. Half Page (Color) $255.60. **Pub. Size:** Standard. **Circ:** 3,318. available in microform.

US/0745-5909
COLLIN COUNTY COMMERCIAL RECORD. VFOAT Commercial Record. (19??)-. Newspaper. English. wk. $300.00. Daily Commercial Record Inc, 202 West Louisiana/Suite 207, McKinney TX 75069. **LC** K3; .O3438. **DD** 340/.05.

US
COLORADO CITY RECORD. Began in 1906?. Newspaper. English. sw. Colorado City Record, PO Box 92, Colorado City TX 79512.

US
COLORADO COUNTY CITIZEN, THE. Began in 1927?. Newspaper. English. wk. Colorado County Citizen, PO Box 548, Columbus TX 78934. *Continues Colorado Citizen.*

US
COMANCHE CHIEF, THE. (June 1920)-. Newspaper. English. wk. $15.00 Comanche County; $16.50 Texas; $18.00 other. Comanche Chief, 203 West Grand, PO Box 749, Comanche TX 76442. **Tel** (915)356-2636. *Continues Comanche Chief and Pioneer Exponent; Absorbed Comanche Enterprise.*

US
COMMERCE JOURNAL (COMMERCE, TEX.). (THE COMMERCE JOURNAL.). VFOAT Weekly Journal. (1889)-. Newspaper. English. wk. Commerce Journal, 2548 Mangum, Commerce TX 75428.

US
CONCHO HERALD, THE. Began in 1890. Newspaper. English. wk. Concho Herald, PO Box 307, Miles TX 76861.

US
CONROE DAILY COURIER. Vol. 1, No. 1 (Nov. 13, 1955)-. Newspaper. English. da. $99.00 (home delivery), $120.00 (mail). Conroe Daily Courier, PO Box 609, Conroe TX 77301. **Tel** (409)756-6671, FAX (419)756-6676. **ED** Dan Turner. **Photos. Ad Acc, Adv Mgr:** Brenda Roy. Full Page (B&W) $1380.30. Half Page (B&W) $720.47. Full Page (Color) $1455.30. Half Page (Color) $795.47. **Pub. Size:** Broadsheet. **Circ:** 13,500 (ctrl). available on microfilm from Southwest Micropublishing International.

US
COOPER REVIEW. VFOAT Cooper Weekly Review. (190?)-. Newspaper. English. wk. $9.00 Delta County, TX; $10.00 surrounding counties, Texas; $11.00 other Texas; $12.00 other. Cooper Review, PO Box 430, Cooper TX 75432. **Tel** (214)395-2175. **Ad Acc. Circ:** 2,550 (ctrl). *Continues Cooper Weekly Review.*

US/0894-5365
CORPUS CHRISTI CALLER-TIMES. VFOAT Corpus Christi Caller Times. Vol. 105, No. 152 (June 1, 1987)-. Newspaper. English. da. $143.40 (daily and Sun.), $111.00 (Mon.-Sat., daily), $102.00 (Sunday only) Nueces and San Patricio County, TX residents; $155.00 (daily and Sun.), $120.00 (Mon.-Sat., daily) other US; $310.80 (daily and Sun.), $240.00 (Mon.-Sat., daily) $204.00 (Sun.) other (by mail). Corpus Christi Caller-Times, PO Box 9136, Corpus Christi TX 78469. **Tel** (512)884-2011. **ED** Larry Rose. cum. index. **Bk Rev. Ad Acc, Adv Mgr:** Barry Box. **Circ:** 68,000 daily, 94,000 sunday (ctrl). Documents available from UMI Article Clearinghouse. *Formed by the union of Corpus Christi Caller (Corpus Christi, Tex. 1918), 0889-812X and Corpus Christi Times (Corpus Christi, Tex. : 1911), 0747-4474.*
Ind/Abst Bus. Dateline (Dec. 22, 1991-) [Full Txt.].

US/8750-2518
CORSICANA DAILY SUN. (1896)-. Newspaper. English. da. Corsicana Daily Sun, PO Box 622, Corsicana TX 75110. **Tel** (214)872-3931. **ED** Joe Cox. **Circ:** 10,444.

US
COURIER-GAZETTE (MCKINNEY, TEX.). (THE COURIER-GAZETTE.). VFOAT Courier Gazette. Vol. 86, No. 73 (March 27, 1983)-. Newspaper. English. da. McKinney Courier-Gazette, PO Box 400, McKinney TX 75069. **Tel** (214)542-2631. *Continues McKinney Courier Gazette.*

US
CRANE NEWS (CRANE, TEX. : 1945)-. (THE CRANE NEWS.). (1945)-. Newspaper. English. wk. $21.00. Crane News, 401 South Gaston, Crane TX 79731. **Tel** (915)558-3541, FAX (915)558-2676. **ED** Skip Nichols. **Bk Rev**, (Qty: 12). **Photos. Ad Acc, Adv Mgr:** Skip Nichols. **Pub. Size:** Broadsheet. **Circ:** 1,700. *Absorbed McCamey Tri-County Record; McCamey Leader.*

US
CROSBY COUNTY NEWS AND THE CROSBYTON REVIEW. (July 3, 1986)-. Newspaper. English. wk. $18.50. Crosby County News and the Crosbyton Review, 109 West Aspen, Crosbyton TX 79322. **ED** Burnis Lawrence. **Ad Acc. Circ:** 1,800.

US
CROSBYTON REVIEW, THE. Vol. 1, No. 1 (Jan. 14, 1909)-. Newspaper. English. wk. $14.50. The Crosby County News & Chronicle, 109 West Aspen, Crosbyton TX 79322-2501. **Tel** (806)675-2881. **ED** Ben M. Gillespie. **Bk Rev**, (Qty: varies). **Photos. Ad Acc, Adv Mgr:** Donna Gillespie. Full Page (B&W) $289.80. Half Page (B&W) $170.10. Full Page (Color) $399.80. Half Page (Color) $280.10. **Pub. Size:** Standard. **Circ:** 1,437. available in microform from Empire Microfilms.

US
CROSS PLAINS REVIEW (CROSS PLAINS, TEX.). (THE CROSS PLAINS REVIEW.). Began in 1910. Newspaper. English. wk. Cross Plains Review, 155 East 8th Street, Cross Plains TX 76443.

US/1062-1202
CUERO RECORD, THE. Vol. 70, No 80, Apr. 4 (1929)-. Newspaper. English. wk. Cuero Record, 119 East Main Street, Cuero TX 77954. *Formed by the union of Cuero Daily Record and Cuero Weekly Record.*

US/0889-2431
DAILY COMMERCIAL RECORD. (1??)-. Periodical. English. da. Daily Commercial Record, 706 Main Street, Dallas TX 75202. **Tel** (214)741-6366.

US/8750-734X
DAILY COMMERCIAL RECORDER, THE. VFOAT Commercial Recorder. English. da. $106.75. The Daily Commercial Recorder, 414 Dolorosa Street, San

Texas

Antonio TX 78204. **Tel** (512)227-5558. **ED** Michael Cary. **Ad Acc. Circ:** 1,500.
Desc: Covers legal and business news.

US
DAILY FAVORITE, THE. VFOAT Bonham Daily Favorite. (1899)-. Newspaper. English. da. $5.00 (per month). Bonham Daily Favorite, PO Box 550, Bonham TX 75418. **Tel** (903)583-2124, FAX (903)583-8521. **ED** John Frair. **LC** 9888. **Photos. Ad Acc, Adv Mgr:** Elaine Ashlock. Full Page (B&W) $451.50. Half Page (B&W) $252.00. **Wire Svcs.:** AP. available on microfilm from Microfilm Center, Inc.

US/0896-3320
DAILY PASADENA CITIZEN, THE. *Title Change.* VFOAT Citizen. Newspaper. English. da. Daily Pasadena Citizen, PO Box 6192, Pasadena TX 77506. *Continues* Pasadena Citizen. *Continued by* Pasadena Citizen (Pasadena, Tex. : 1990), 1050-3773.

US
DAILY SENTINEL (NACOGDOCHES, TEX.: 1900). (THE DAILY SENTINEL.). Vol. 1, No. 149 (Jan. 15, 1900)-. Newspaper. English. da. Daily Sentinel, PO Box 68, Nacogdoches TX 75951. *Continues* Daily Phone.

US
DAILY TEXAN, THE. VFOAT Texan; Summer Texan. Vol. 14, No. 1 (Sept. 24, 1913)-. Newspaper. English. da. $30.00 (one semester), $55.00 (two semesters); $75.00 (three semesters). Daily Texan and Summer Texan, PO Box D, Austin TX 78713-8904. **Tel** (512)471-5422. **ED** Mary Hopkins (Editor-in-Chief) and Abraham Levy (Managing Editor). **Photos. Ad Acc, Adv Mgr:** Jim Barger, **Tel** (512)471-1951. Full Page (B&W) $1,787.00. Half Page (B&W) $914.00. Full Page (Color) $1,947.00. Half Page (Color) $1,074.00. **Wire Svcs.:** AP. **Circ:** 30,000. available on microfilm. *Continues* Texan.

US
DAILY TRIBUNE (BAY CITY, TEX.). (THE DAILY TRIBUNE.). (1904)-. Newspaper. English. da (Tues.- Fri., Sunday). $5.75. Daily Tribune / Bay City, PO Box 2450, Bay City TX 77404. **Tel** (409)245-5555, FAX (409)244-5908. **ED** Russell E. Maroney and Curt Vincent (Managing Editor). **Photos. Ad Acc, Adv Mgr:** Buzz Crainer. Full Page (B&W) $667.00. Half Page (B&W) $333.00. Full Page (Color) $100.00 per color. Half Page (Color) $100.00 per color. **Pub. Size:** Standard. **Wire Svcs.:** AP. **Circ:** 6,800. available in microform.

US
DAILY TRIBUNE (MT. PLEASANT, TEX.). (THE DAILY TRIBUNE.). Newspaper. English. da. Daily Tribune / Mount Pleasant, PO Box 1177, Mount Pleasant TX 75455.

US
DALHART DAILY TEXAN, THE. Vol. 63, No. 262 (March 6, 1964)-. Newspaper. English. da. Dalhart Daily Texan, 410 Denrock, Dalhart TX 79022. *Continues* Dalhart Texan.

US
DALLAS MORNING NEWS, THE. VFOAT Morning News. Vol. 1, No. 1 (Oct. 1, 1885)-. Newspaper. English. da. $324.00 (daily & Sunday), $276.00 (daily), $252.00 (Saturday & Sunday), $228.00 (Sunday only). Communications Center, PO Box 655237, Dallas TX 75265. **Tel** (214)977-8222, (800)431-0010. **ED** Burl Osborne. **Circ:** 390,987 daily, 531,417 Sunday. available on microfilm. *Absorbed* Dallas Herald; Dallas Times Herald.
Ind/Abst PROMT.

US/0746-7303
DALLAS POST TRIBUNE, THE. Vol. 28, No. 20 (May 17, 1975)-. Newspaper. English. Fifty-two times a year. Dallas Post Tribune, PO Box 763939, Dallas TX 75376-3939. **Tel** (214)946-7678. **ED** T. R. Lee. **Bk Rev. Ad Acc. Pr Rev. Circ:** 30,000 (ctrl). *Continues* Post Tribune (Dallas, Tex.).

US/0885-1271
DALLAS WEEKLY, THE. (19??)-. Newspaper. English. Fifty-two times a year (Thursdays). $60.00. Dallas Weekly, 3101 Martin Luther King, Jr. Boulevard, Dallas TX 75215. **Tel** (214)428-8958, FAX (214)428-2807. **ED** Yolanda Adams (Associate). **Bk Rev. Ad Acc, Adv Mgr:** Andrea Allen. **Circ:** 20,300 (ctrl).

US
DEER PARK BROADCASTER. Vol. 1, No. 1 (May 13, 1981)-. Newspaper. English. Twice a week. $30.00. Broadcaster Publications Inc., PO Box 369, 102 West Pasadena Boulevard, Deer Park TX 77536. **ED** Mary Ellen Wilson. **Bk Rev,** (Qty: 2/year). **Photos. Ad Acc, Adv Mgr:** Randy Wilson, **Tel** (713)479-2760. Full Page (B&W) $1154.55. Half Page (B&W) $577.28. Full Page (Color) $1264.55. Half Page (Color) $687.28. **Pub. Size:** Standard.

US
DEL RIO NEWS-HERALD. VFOAT Del Rio News Herald. Newspaper. English. da. Del Rio News-Herald, 321 South Main Street, Del Rio TX 78840. *Formed by the union of* Del Rio Evening News *and* Val Verde Herald.

US
DENISON HERALD (DENISON, TEX.). (THE DENISON HERALD.). VFOAT Denison Daily Herald. Newspaper. English. da. Denison Herald, 331 West Woodard, Denison TX 75020. *Continues* Denison Daily Herald.

US
DENTON RECORD-CHRONICLE. VFOAT Denton Record Chronicle. (1915)-. Newspaper. English. da. $192.00 (mail), $96.00 (carrier). Denton Record-Chronicle, PO Box 369, Denton TX 76202. **Tel** (817)387-3811. **ED** Chris Cobler. **Bk Rev. Ad Acc, Adv Mgr:** Ron Ray, **Tel** (817)381-9515. **Circ:** 18,000 daily, 20,500 Sun. available on microfilm from Southwest Micropublishing International.

US
DEPORT TIMES, THE. (1909)-. Newspaper. English. wk. $13.00 Red River and Lamar counties, Texas; $16.00 other. Deport Times, PO Box 98, Deport TX 75435. **Tel** (903)652-4205.

US/0747-0428
DESOTO NEWS-ADVERTISER. VFOAT Desoto News Advertiser. (19??)-. Newspaper. English. wk. Desoto News-Advertiser, PO Box L, Desoto TX 75115.

US
DEVIL'S RIVER NEWS. Began in 1890. Newspaper. English. wk. Devil's River News, 220 Northeast Main Street, Sonora TX 76950.

US
DEVINE NEWS, THE. VFOAT News. Began in 1897?. Newspaper. English. wk. Devine News, 216 South Bright Street, Devine TX 78016. **ED** Charlie Pat DuBose. **Circ:** 3,200.

US/0746-603X
DRIPPING SPRINGS DISPATCH, THE. Vol. 1, No. 1 (Apr. 20, 1983)-. Newspaper. English. wk. 415.00. Dripping Springs Dispatch, PO Box 550, Dripping Springs TX 78620. **Tel** (512)858-7893, FAX (512)858-4828. **ED** Dale Roberson. **Bk Rev. Photos. Ad Acc, Adv Mgr:** Dale Roberson. Full Page (B&W) $240.00. Half Page (B&W) $140.00. Full Page (Color) $365.00. Half Page (Color) $265.00. **Pub. Size:** Tabloid. **Circ:** 1,500.

US
DUBLIN PROGRESS (DUBLIN, TEX.: 1923). (THE DUBLIN PROGRESS.). Began in 1923?. Newspaper. English. wk. Dublin Progress, PO Box 958, Stephenville TX 76401. *Continues* Dublin Progress and Telephone.

US/0888-1960
DUNCANVILLE SUBURBAN. Vol. 15, No. 1 (Nov. 1, 1973)-. Newspaper. English. Fifty-two times a year (Thurs.). $21.00. Today Newspapers, 1701 North Hampton Road, Suite A, Desoto TX 75115. **Tel** (214)298-4211, FAX (214)298-6369. **ED** Phil Major. **Photos. Ad Acc, Adv Mgr:** Leslie Nasche. Full Page (B&W) $1,033.20. Half Page (B&W) $516.00. Full Page (Color) $1,383.20. Half Page (Color) $866.60. **Pub. Size:** Broadsheet. **Circ:** 5,944.

US
EAGLE LAKE HEADLIGHT. Began in March 1903?. Newspaper. English. wk. Eagle Lake Headlight, 220 East Main Street, Eagle Lake TX 77434. *Absorbed* Eagle Lake Advertiser.

US
EAGLE PASS NEWS-GUIDE. VFOAT Eagle Pass News Guide. 60th Yr., No. 11 (Mar. 11, 1948)-. Newspaper. English. wk. $9.50 Maverick County; $12.50 Texas; $15.00 US; $32.00 other. Guide Publishing / Eagle Pass, PO Box 764, Eagle Pass TX 78852. **Tel** (512)773-2309. *Continues* International News Guide.

US
EAST TEXAS BANNER. (19??)-. Newspaper. English. wk. East Texas Banner, PO Drawer B, Kirbyville TX 75956. **Tel** (409)423-2696, FAX (409)423-4793. **ED** Joe Herndon. **Bk Rev,** (Qty: 4). **Photos. Ad Acc, Adv Mgr:** Lacole Mitchell. Full Page (B&W) $555.66. Half Page (B&W) $277.83. Full Page (Color) $630.66. Half Page (Color) $315.32. **Pub. Size:** Standard. **Circ:** 3,300. *Continues* Kirbyville Banner.

US
EASTLAND TELEGRAM (EASTLAND, TEX.: 1953). (EASTLAND TELEGRAM.). Vol. 25 (Oct. 6, 1953)-. Newspaper. English. Twice a week. $18.00. Eastland Telegram, PO Box 29, Eastland TX 76448-0029. **Tel** (817)629-1707. **ED** H.V. O'Brien. **Bk Rev,** (Qty: 12 per year). **Photos. Ad Acc.** Full Page (B&W) $1680.00. Half Page (B&W) $840.00. Full Page (Color) $1760.00. Half Page (Color) $920.00. **Pub. Size:** Standard. **Circ:** 2,950. *Continues* Eastland Telegram and Weekly Chronicle.

US/0746-7184
ECHO (HUMBLE, TEX.). (THE ECHO.). Newspaper. English. wk. Houston Community Newspapers, 1136 Sheldon Road, Channelview TX 77530.

US
EDEN ECHO, THE. Began in 1906?. Newspaper. English. wk. Eden Echo, PO Drawer V, Eden TX 76837.

US
EDGEWOOD ENTERPRISE. Began in 1909?. Newspaper. English. wk. Edgewood Enterprise, 111 Front Street, Edgewood TX 75117.

US
EDITOR, EL. (197?)-. Periodical. English (Spanish). wk. $40.00. Amigo Publications, PO Box 11250, Lubbock TX 79408. **Tel** (806)763-3841, FAX (806)741-1110. **ED** Bidal Aguero, Olga Riajas-Aguero (Managing Editor). **Bk Rev. Photos. Ad Acc.** Full Page (B&W) $2016.00. Half Page (B&W) $1008.00. Full Page (Color) $2256.00. Half Page (Color) $1128.00. **Pub. Size:** Broadsheet. **Wire Svcs.:** LA. **Circ:** 15,000 (ctrl).
Desc: Covering news, editorials, and comments focussing on issues that affect the Hispanic community.

US/0746-360X
EL PASO HERALD-POST. VFOAT El Paso Herald Post. (Apr. 15, 1931)-. Newspaper. English. ds. $246.00. Newspaper Printing Corporation, PO Box 20, El Paso TX 79999. **Tel** (800)351-1677, (915)546-6100. **ED** R.W. Lee. **Circ:** 31,483. *Continues* El Paso Herald El Paso Evening Post.

US
EL PASO SUN. Newspaper. English. wk. El Paso Sun, 900 Magoffin, El Paso TX 79998.

US
EL PASO TIMES (EL PASO, TEX.: 1921). (EL PASO TIMES.). Vol. 41, No. 132 (Jan. 1921)-. Newspaper. English. ds. $246.00. Newspaper Printing Corporation, PO Box 20, El Paso TX 79999. **Tel** (800)351-1677, (915)546-6100. *Continues* El Paso Morning Times.

US/8755-9056
ENNIS DAILY NEWS, THE. (1897)-. Newspaper. English. da. Ennis Daily News, 213 North Dallas Street, Ennis TX 75119. **Tel** (214)875-3801. **ED** Charles E. Gentry. **Bk Rev. Ad Acc. Circ:** 4,850 (ctrl). *Absorbed* Ennis Evening Meteor.

US
ENNIS WEEKLY LOCAL, THE. VFOAT Ennis Local. Began in 1887?. Newspaper. English. wk. Ennis Weekly Local, 213-215 North Dallas Street, Ennis TX 75119. *Absorbed* Ennis Saturday Review.

US/0745-547X
EVENING JOURNAL (LUBBOCK, TEX.). (EVENING JOURNAL.). Vol. 1, No. 1 (Jan. 31, 1983)-. Newspaper. English. da (except weekends and holidays). $186.00. Avalanche-Journal Publishing Company, 710 Avenue J, Lubbock TX 79408. **Tel** (806)762-8844. **ED** Thomas Jay Harris. **Bk Rev. Ad Acc. Circ:** 70,926 (ctrl). *Continues* Lubbock Avalanche-Journal.

US
EVERMAN TIMES. (19??)-. Newspaper. English. wk. $12.00 Tarrant County; $17.00 other. B & B Publishing Inc., PO Box 40230, Everman TX 76140. **Tel** (817)478-4661. **ED** Gene S. Blessing. **Ad Acc, Adv Mgr:** Jedd Blessing. Full Page (B&W) $554.40. Half Page (B&W) $277.20. Full Page (Color) $629.40. Half Page (Color) $352.20. **Pub. Size:** Broadsheet. ctrl circ.
Desc: Local news for Tarrant County, Texas.

US
FALFURRIAS FACTS. (1906)-. Newspaper. English (Spanish). wk. $20.00 local; $22.00 other. Falfurrias Publishing Company, 219 East Rice Street, PO Box 619, Falfurrias TX 78355. **Tel** (512)325-2200. **ED** Marcelo Silva. **Photos. Ad Acc, Adv Mgr:** San Juanita Olivarez. Full Page (B&W) $245.10. Half Page (B&W) $135.45. Full Page (Color) $405.10. Half Page (Color) $295.45. **Pub. Size:** Standard. **Circ:** 2,250. available in microform.

US
FAMILIAR (MCALLEN, TEX.), EL. (EL FAMILIAR.). Periodical. English. bm. American GI Forum of Texas, PO Box 4379, McAllen TX 78501.

US/8750-9199
FARMERS BRANCH TIMES. VFOAT Times-Chronicle-Today. Newspaper. English. wk. $30.00. Farmers Branch Times, 1712 Beltline, Carrollton TX 75006.

US
FAYETTE COUNTY RECORD (LA GRANGE, TEX.: 1922). (THE FAYETTE COUNTY RECORD.). (1922)-. Newspaper. English. Three times a year. Fayette County Record, 127 South Washington Street, La Grange TX 78945.

Texas

US
FLATONIA ARGUS, THE. Began in 1877?. Newspaper. English. wk. Flatonia Argus, 214 South Penn Street, Flatonia TX 78941.

US
FLORESVILLE CHRONICLE-JOURNAL. VFOAT Floresville Chronicle Journal. (1912)-. Newspaper. English. wk. $20.00 Texas; $22.00 others. Floresville Chronicle-Journal, 1433 3rd Street, PO Box 820, Floresville TX 78114. **Tel** (210)393-2111, FAX (210)393-9012. **ED** Joe H. Fietsam (Editor-in-Chief) and James J. Fietsam (Managing Editor). **Photos. Ad Acc, Adv Mgr:** James J. Fietsam. Full Page (B&W) $441.00. Half Page (B&W) $220.50. Full Page (Color) $531.00. Half Page (Color) $310.50. **Pub. Size:** Standard. *Formed by the union of Floresville Chronicle and Wilson County Journal.*

US
FLOYD COUNTY HESPERIAN, THE. (1896)-. Newspaper. English. wk. $25.00 Floyd County, Texas; $27.00 Texas; $28.00 other. Floyd County Hesperian, 111 East Missouri, Floydada TX 79235. **Tel** (806)983-3737. *Continues Hesperian.*

US
FOARD COUNTY NEWS AND CROWELL INDEX. VFOAT Foard County News. Began in 1910. Newspaper. English. wk. PO Box 489, Crowell TX 79227. *Formed by the union of Foard County News (Crowell, Tex.: 1891) and Crowell Index.*

US
FORNEY MESSENGER. VFOAT Forney Messenger and News. (1896)-. Newspaper. English. wk. $15.00 (Forney, Texas), $20.00 (other). Forney Messenger, PO Box 936, Forney TX 75126. **Tel** (214)564-3121, FAX (214)552-3599. **ED** Cary L. Griffin. **Photos. Ad Acc, Adv Mgr:** Judy P. Griffin. Full Page (B&W) $400.00. Half Page (B&W) $200.00. Full Page (Color) $500.00. Half Page (Color) $300.00. **Pub. Size:** Broadsheet. **Circ:** 1,800. available in microform from Southwest Micropublishing International. *Absorbed Forney News.*

US
FORT STOCKTON PIONEER, THE. (1908)-. Newspaper. English. wk. $28.00 Fort Stockton and Pecos counties, Texas; $35.00 other Texas; $40.00 other. Fort Stockton Pioneer, PO Box 1528, Fort Stockton TX 79735. **Tel** (915)336-2281.

US/0889-0013
FORT WORTH STAR-TELEGRAM. [Fort Worth star-telegr.]. VFOAT Fort Worth Star Telegram; Fort Worth Star-Telegram and Sunday Record. (Jan. 1, 1909)-. Newspaper. English. da. $119.40 (daily and Sunday by carrier), $107.40 (daily by carrier), $300.00 (daily and Sunday by mail), $240.00 (daily by mail), $204.00 (Sunday only by mail). Fort Worth Star-Telegram, PO Box 1870, Fort Worth TX 76101. **Tel** (817)390-7400, FAX (817)551-2266. **ED** Mike Blackman. **DD** 071. **Circ:** 130,309 daily, 306,548 Sunday. available on microfilm from University Microfilms International (UMI). *Formed by the union of Fort Worth Star and Fort Worth Telegram; Absorbed Fort Worth Record.* **Ind/Abst** PROMT.

US
FRANKSTON CITIZEN, THE. Began in 1912?. Newspaper. English. wk. Frankston Citizen, PO Box 188, Frankston TX 75763-0188.

US/8755-9331
FREDERICKSBURG STANDARD RADIO POST. VFOAT Fredericksburg Standard/Radio Post. 78th Year. No. 17 (Nov. 7, 1984)-. Newspaper. English. wk. Fredericksburg Publishing Company, PO Box 473, 108 East Main Street, Fredericksburg TX 78624. **Tel** (512)997-2155. **ED** Terrill D Collier. **Circ:** 8,500. *Formed by the union of Fredericksburg Standard and Radio Post (Fredericksburg, Tex.: 1922).*

US
FREE PRESS (DIBOLL, TEX.). (THE FREE PRESS.). Newspaper. English. wk. Free Press / Texas, PO Drawer M, Diboll TX 75941. *Continues Diboll New-Bulletin; Huntington Press.*

US
FREER PRESS, THE. (19??)-. Newspaper. English (Spanish). wk. $12.00 (in county), $15.00 (out of county). Freer Press, 309 East Hahl, Box 567, Freer TX 78357. **Tel** (512)394-7402. **ED** Lataine Wright Dillard, Mell Gandy (Managing Editor). Index available. **Bk Rev. Photos. Ad Acc.** Full Page (B&W) $374.10. Half Page (B&W) $187.05. Full Page (Color) $434.10. Half Page (Color) $227.05. **Circ:** 984.

US
FRIONA STAR. Vol. 1, No. 1 (July 21, 1925)-. Newspaper. English. wk. $18.00. Friona Star, PO Box 789, Friona TX 79035. **ED** Bill Ellis. **Ad Acc. Circ:** 2,500.

US
GAINES COUNTY NEWS. Began in 1922?. Newspaper. English. wk. Gaines County News, PO Box 815, Seagraves TX 79359. *Continues Seagraves Signal.*

US
GAINESVILLE DAILY REGISTER (GAINESVILLE, TEX.: 1975). (GAINESVILLE DAILY REGISTER.). VFOAT Gainesville Sunday Rregister. Vol. 85, No. 171 (March 19, 1975)-. Newspaper. English. da (312 issues per year). Price varies within Texas; $88.00 other. Register Publishing Company, 306 E California Street, Gainesville TX 76240. **Tel** (817)665-5511.

US/0738-8047
GALVESTON DAILY NEWS (HOUSTON, TEX.: 1865). (THE GALVESTON DAILY NEWS.). VFOAT Galveston News Tribune; Galveston News. (Feb. 21, 1865)-. Newspaper. English. da (daily & Sunday). Galveston Daily News, PO Box 628, Galveston TX 77553. **Tel** (409)744-3611, FAX (409)744-6228. **ED** Dolph Tillotson. **Ad Acc. Circ:** 28,184 (ctrl). available on microfilm from The Library of Congress Photoduplication Service; available on microfiche. *Absorbed Galveston Tribune.*

US/1045-3997
GARLAND NEWS (1989), THE. (GARLAND NEWS.). (1989)-. Newspaper. English. da (Publishes on Thurs., Fri., & Sun.). $72.00 Texas; $84.00 others. Suburban Newspapers / Texas, 1000 East Avenue H, Arlington TX 76011. **Tel** (817)695-0365. *Continues Garland Daily News, 0745-8142.*

US/0894-4954
GATESVILLE MESSENGER AND STAR-FORUM. VFOAT Gatesville Messenger and Star Forum. Began in Sept. 1907. Newspaper. English. wk. PO Box 799, Gatesville TX 76528. *Formed by the union of Gatesville Messenger and Gatesville Star-Forum.*

US
GIDDINGS TIMES AND NEWS. Newspaper. English. Giddings Times and News, 170 North Knox Avenue, Giddings TX 78942. *Formed by the union of Lee County News and Giddings Times.*

US/8750-0884
GILMER MIRROR, THE. Newspaper. English. wk. Greenway Enterprises, Box 250, Gilmer TX 75644.

US
GLEN ROSE REPORTER, THE. VFOAT Reporter. (1???)-. Newspaper. English. wk. Glen Rose Reporter, PO Box 2009, Glen Rose TX 76043. **Tel** (817)897-2282.

US
GORMAN PROGRESS, THE. Began in 1900?. Newspaper. English. wk. Gorman Progress, PO Box 68, Gorman TX 76454. **ED** J W Cockrill.

US
GRAHAM LEADER (GRAHAM, TEX.: 1975). (THE GRAHAM LEADER.). (1975)-. Newspaper. English. sw (104 issues per year). $34.00 Young County, Texas; $40.00 other Texas; $50.00 other. Graham Leader, 620 Oak Street, PO Box 600, Graham TX 76450. **Tel** (817)549-7800. *Continues Graham Leader-Reporter.*

US/0746-2131
GRANBURY TABLET, THE. Newspaper. English. wk. Granbury Tablet, 108 West Pearl Street, Granbury TX 76048.

US/1044-0097
GRAND PRAIRIE NEWS (GRAND PRAIRIE, TEX.). (GRAND PRAIRIE NEWS.). (198?)-. Newspaper. English. da (Publishes on Thurs., Fri., & Sun.). $72.00 Texas; $84.00 others. Suburban Newspapers / Texas, 1000 East Avenue H, Arlington TX 76011. **Tel** (817)695-0365. *Continues Grand Prairie Daily News, 0746-7524.*

US
GRAND SALINE SUN, THE. Began July 14, 1892. Newspaper. English. wk. Grand Saline Sun, 116 North Main Street, Grand Saline TX 75140. *Absorbed Grand Saline Post.*

US
GRAPELAND MESSENGER, THE. (1898)-. Newspaper. English. wk. $15.00. Grapeland Messenger, PO Box 99, Grapeland TX 75844. **Tel** (409)687-2424. **ED** Weldon Berry. **Photos. Ad Acc.** Full Page (B&W) $307.02. Half Page (B&W) $153.51. **Pub. Size:** Standard.

US/1042-3710
GREENVILLE HERALD-BANNER. VFOAT Greenville Herald Banner; Herald Banner; Herald-Banner. Vol. 63, No. 206 (Oct. 21, 1956)-. Newspaper. English. ds. $96.00. Greenville Herald-Banner, PO Box 6000, Greenville TX 75401. **Tel** (214)445-4220, FAX (214)455-6281. **ED** Melva Geyer. **Photos. Ad Acc, Adv Mgr:** Terri McCreary. Full Page (B&W) $643.71. Full Page (Color) $1387.42. Half Page (B&W) $321.85. Half Page (Color) $743.71. **Pub. Size:** Standard. **Wire Svcs.:** AP. **Circ:** 11,732. available in microform. *Formed by the union of Greenville Morning Herald and Greenville Evening Banner.*

US
GROESBECK JOURNAL. (1892)-. Newspaper. English. wk. $14.00. Groesbeck Journal, PO Box 440, 115 North Ellis, Groesbeck TX 76642. **Tel** (817)125-5103. **ED** Tom Hawkins. **Photos. Ad Acc.** Full Page (B&W) $504.00. Half Page (B&W) $252.00. **Pub. Size:** Standard. available in microform. *Absorbed Thornton Hustler and Kosse Cyclone.*

US
GRUVER STATESMAN. Began in 1972. Newspaper. English. wk. $13.95, $8.95 (inside county). Gruver Statesman, PO Box 796, Gruver TX 79040. **Tel** (806)659-3434. **Ad Acc. Circ:** 600.

US
GULF COAST RECORD, THE. Began in 1908?. Newspaper. English. Gulf Coast Record, PO Box 951, Kingsville TX 78363.

US
GULF COAST TRIBUNE. (19??)-. Newspaper. English. wk. Gulf Coast Tribune, PO Box 388, Needville TX 77461.

US
HAMLIN HERALD (HAMLIN, TEX.: 1906). (THE HAMLIN HERALD.). Began in 1906?. Newspaper. English. wk. Hamlin Herald, PO Box 339, Hamlin TX 79520.

US/0744-5520
HANGUK ILBO (HOUSTON, TEX.). (HANGUK ILBO, HUSUTON / THE KOREA TIMES HOUSTON EDITION.). VFOAT Minju Hanguk; The Korea Times; Korea Times. (19??)-. Newspaper. Korean. sw (except Sundays, Jan. 2-4 & Holidays). Hankook Ilbo, 1803 Antoine, Houston TX 77055-1801.

US
HANSFORD PLAINSMAN, THE. Began in 1959?. Newspaper. English. wk. $24.95, $19.95 (inside county). Hansford Plainsman, PO Box 458, Spearman TX 79081. **Tel** (806)659-3434. **Ad Acc. Circ:** 1,200.

US/1040-6514
HARPER HERALD (HARPER, TEX. 1917), THE. (THE HARPER HERALD.). (1917)-. Newspaper. English. wk. Harper Herald, PO Box 425, Harper TX 78631.

US/0892-239X
HART BEAT, THE. Vol. 1, No. 1 (July 19, 1962)-. Newspaper. English. Fifty-two times a year. $25.00 Castro County; $28.00 others in Texas; $35.00 others. Wall Publications, PO Box 350, Hart TX 79043. **Tel** (8060938-2640. **ED** Neoma Wall. **Ad Acc. Circ:** 500.

US
HASKELL FREE PRESS, THE. Vol. 3, No. 46 (Dec. 1, 1888)-. Newspaper. English. wk. Haskell Free Press, PO Box 1058, Haskell TX 79521-1058. *Continues Haskell City Free Press.*

US/1058-4471
HAYS COUNTY FREE PRESS. VFOAT Free Press. Vol. 15, No. 12 (April 4, 1991)-. Newspaper. English. wk. Hays County Free Press, PO Box 339, Buda TX 78610. *Continues Onion Creek Free Press.*

US
HEARNE DEMOCRAT, THE. Began in 1889?. Newspaper. English. wk. $20.00. Hearne Democrat, 112 3rd Street, Hearne TX 77859. **Tel** (409)279-3411. (**Subscription address:** Box 433, Hearne, TX 77859) **ED** Gracia Thibodeaux. **Circ:** 4,500. available on microfiche.

US
HENDERSON DAILY NEWS. Vol. 1, No. 1 (March 20, 1931)-. Newspaper. English. da. Henderson Daily News, PO Box 30, Henderson TX 75653-0030.

US
HERALD-COASTER, THE. VFOAT Herald Coaster. (1958)-. Newspaper. English. da (except Sat.). $67.80. Herald-Coaster / Department of Circulation, PO Box 1088, Rosenberg TX 77471. **Tel** (713)342-4474. **ED** Clyde King (Editor-in-Chief) and Bob Haenel (Managing Editor). **Bk Rev. Photos. Ad Acc, Adv Mgr:** Debra Anthony. Full Page (B&W) $945.00. Half Page (B&W) $472.50. Full Page (Color) $1,045.00. Half Page (Color) $572.50. **Pub. Size:** Broadsheet. **Wire Svcs.:** AP. available on microfilm from Southwest Micropublishing International. *Formed by the union of Rosenberg Herald and Texas Coaster; Absorbed Fort Bend Reporter.*

US/1055-5005
HERALD (ROCKPORT, TEX. 1990), THE. (THE HERALD.). (1990)-. Newspaper. English. wk. The Herald / Texas, PO Drawer 1448, 2307 North Raht, Rockport TX 78382. *Continues Carrier News Herald, 1051-9750.*

US
HEREFORD BRAND, THE. VFOAT Brand. Began in 1901. Newspaper. English. wk. Hereford Brand, PO Box 673, Hereford TX 79045.

Texas

US
HIGHLANDER, THE. Vol. 28, No. 39 (March 19, 1987)-. Newspaper. English. wk. Highlander, PO Drawer 1000, Marble Falls TX 78654. **Tel** (210)693-4367, FAX (210)693-3650. **Bk Rev. Photos. Ad Acc.** Full Page (B&W) $1,161.00. Half Page (B&W) $585.00. Full Page (Color) $1,311.00. Half Page (Color) $735.00. **Pub. Size:** Standard. **Circ:** 10,100. *Continues Burnet Highlander.*

US
HIGHLANDS STAR, THE. *Title Change.* Vol. 1, No. 1 (June 9, 1955)-(19??). Newspaper. English. wk. Crosby Courier, PO Box 485, Highlands TX 77562. **Tel** (713)328-9605, FAX (713)977-1188. *Continued by The Star-Courier.*

US
HILL COUNTRY NEWS (CEDAR PARK, TEX. : 1978). (HILL COUNTRY NEWS.). **VFOAT** Hill Country News and the Libertarian. Vol. 10, No. 33 (Sept. 7, 1978)-. Newspaper. English. wk. Hill Country News, PO Box 1777, Cedar Park TX 78613. **Tel** (512)258-4127. *Continues Hill Country News and The Libertarian; Absorbed Libertarian.*

US
HONDO ANVIL HERALD, THE. Newspaper. English. wk. $25.00, $15.00 (inside Texas). Hondo Anvil Herald, PO Box 400, Hondo TX 78861. **Tel** (512)426-3346. **ED** W E Berger. **Ad Acc. Circ:** 3,500. available on microfilm. *Continues Anvil Herald.*

US
HOOD COUNTY NEWS. **VFOAT** Hood County Informer-News. Vol. 84, No. 8 (Nov. 5, 1970)-. Newspaper. English. sw. $26.00 (Hood Cty residents); $39.00 (others in TX); $52.00 (all others). Hood County News, PO Box 879, Granbury TX 76048. **Tel** (817) 573-7066. *Continues Hood County Informer-News.*

US
HOPKINS COUNTY ECHO, THE. (1876)-. Newspaper. English. wk. Hopkins County Echo, 401 Church Street, Sulphur Springs TX 75482. *Absorbed Sulphur Springs Gazette.*

US/1074-7109
HOUSTON CHRONICLE (1912). (THE HOUSTON CHRONICLE.). **VFOAT** Houston Chronicle and Herald. Vol. 12, No. 50 (Dec. 3, 1912)-. Newspaper. English. ds $418.00 (daily & Sunday by mail). Houston Chronicle, PO Box 4260, Houston TX 77210. **Tel** (713)220-7211, (800)735-3811. **(Subscription address:** Houston Chronicle, PO Box 2066, Houston, TX 77252) **ED** Phil Warner. **Circ:** 439,044 daily, 518,679 Sunday. available on microfilm from University Microfilms International (UMI). *Continues Houston Chronicle and Herald.*
Ind/Abst Infobank (Jan. 1969-); PROMT.

US
HOUSTON FORWARD TIMES. Vol. 18, No. 38 (Oct. 1, 1977)-. Newspaper. English. wk. $13.50. Houston Forward Times, 4411 Almeda Road, Houston TX 77004. **Tel** (913)026-4727. **ED** Lenora Carter. **Circ:** 9,985. *Continues Forward Times.*

US
HOUSTON INFORMER AND TEXAS FREEMAN, THE. **VFOAT** Informer. Vol. 47, No. 30 (June 14, 1941)-. Newspaper. English. Fifty-two times a year (Published on Tues.). $32.00 one year. The Informer, PO Box 3086, Houston TX 77001. **Tel** (713)527-8261. **LC** 9882-X. available on microfilm from University Microfilms International (UMI). *Continues Informer (Houston, Tex.).*

US/1060-3484
HOUSTON POST (1932). (THE HOUSTON POST.). Vol. 47, No. 303, Feb. 1 (1932)-. Newspaper. English. ds. $300.00 Texas; $318.00 other US; $1302.00 other. The Houston Post, PO Box 4747, Houston TX 77210. **Tel** (713)840-6790, (800)877-1887. **ED** Peter O'Sullivan. **Circ:** 314,581 daily, 365,946 Sunday. available on microfilm from University Microfilms International (UMI); available on an online database (file 639/Full-Text) from DIALOG. Documents available from UMI Article Clearinghouse. *Continues Houston Post-Dispatch.*
Ind/Abst Newsp. Abstr.

US/1071-2941
HOUSTON SUN, THE. (198?)-. Newspaper. English. wk (Published on Mondays). $37.18 Texas; $45.00 other. Houston Sun, PO Box 600603, Houston TX 77260. **Tel** (713)524-4474. **ED** Doris Ellis. **Bk Rev. Ad Acc, Adv Mgr:** Lonal Robinson. **Circ:** 25,000 (ctrl)

US
HOUSTONIAN (HUNTSVILLE, TEX.). (THE HOUSTONIAN.). (1914)-. Newspaper. English. sw. $15.00. Sam Houston State University, PO Box 2178, Huntsville TX 77341. **Tel** (409)294-1495, FAX (409)294-1504. **ED** Jenn Cansler and Jenna Jackson (Managing Editor). **Bk Rev. Photos. Ad Acc, Adv Mgr:** Keri Toma. Half Page (B&W) $405.72. Half Page (Color) $866.44. Half Page (Color) $443.22. **Pub. Size:** Standard. **Wire Svcs.:** AP. **Circ:** 61,000 (morning). available in microform.

US
HOWE ENTERPRISE, THE. Vol. 1, No. 1 (June 27, 1963)-. Newspaper. English. wk. $12.00. Howe Enterprise, 106 East Haning Avenue, PO Box 488, Howe TX 75459-0488. **Tel** (903)532-6012. **ED** Lana Rideout. **Bk Rev,** (Qty: varies). **Photos. Ad Acc, Adv Mgr:** Lana Rideout. Full Page (B&W) $330.00. Half Page (B&W) $175.00. **Pub. Size:** Standard. **Circ:** 600-650 (ctrl). **Desc:** Features school and city news.

US
HUDSPETH COUNTY HERALD AND DELL VALLEY RREVIEW. Vol. 8 No. 52 (Aug. 21 1964)-. Newspaper. English. wk. PO Box 659, Dell City TX 79837. *Formed by the union of Hudspeth County Herald and Dell Valley Review.*

US
HUMBLE ECHO, THE. *Title Change.* (19??)-(1993). Newspaper. English. wk. Houston Community Newspapers, 1136 Sheldon Road, Channelview TX 77530. *Continued by Humble Sun.*

US/0888-4145
HUNTSVILLE ITEM, THE. **VFOAT** Item. (1850)-. Newspaper. English. ir (313 issues per year). $108.00 Texas; $120.00 other. Huntsville Item, PO Box 539, Huntsville TX 77342. **Tel** (409)295-5407. **LC** 9917. available on microfilm from University Microfilms International (UMI).

US
INGLESIDE INDEX, THE. (1952)-. Newspaper. English. wk (52 issues). $22.20 in county; $26.00 other. The Ingleside Index, PO Box 550, Ingleside TX 78362-0550. **Tel** (512)776-7824. **ED** Dick Richards, Mary Cole (Managing Editor). **Bk Rev. Photos. Ad Acc, Adv Mgr:** Patsy Dicken, **Tel** (512)758-5391. Full Page (B&W) $529.20. Half Page (B&W) $289.80. Full Page (Color) $629.20. Half Page (Color) $389.80. **Pub. Size:** Standard.

US
IOWA PARK LEADER, THE. Vol. 1, No. 1 (Sept. 17, 1969)-. Newspaper. English. wk. Iowa Park Leader, PO Box 430, Iowa Park TX 76367.

US
IRVING NEWS. Newspaper. English. da (Publishes on Thurs., Fri., & Sun.) $72.00 Texas; $84.00 others. Suburban Newspapers / Texas, 1000 East Avenue H, Arlington TX 76011. **Tel** (817)695-0365.

US
JACK COUNTY HERALD, THE. (19??)-. Newspaper. English. wk. $16.00 Jack County; $24.00 other. Jack County Herald, PO Drawer 70, Jacksboro TX 76458.

US
JACKSBORO GAZETTE-NEWS. **VFOAT** Jacksboro Gazette-News. Newspaper. English. wk. Jacksboro Gazette-News, PO Box 70, Jacksboro TX 76056. *Formed by the union of Jacksboro Gazette and Jacksboro News.*

US/0746-2824
JASPER NEWS-BOY, THE. **VFOAT** Jasper News Boy. Newspaper. English. wk. Jasper News-Boy, 302 North Wheeler, Jasper TX 75951. *Continues Weekly News-Boy (Jasper, Tex.).*

US/1060-3476
JEFFERSON JIMPLECUTE. **VFOAT** Weekly Jimplecute. Newspaper. English. wk. $18.50. Jefferson Jimplecute, PO Box J, Jefferson TX 75657. **Tel** (214)665-2462. **ED** Lou Anne Suber. **Ad Acc. Circ:** 2,500. available on microfilm. *Continues Jefferson Journal; Jefferson Daily Jimplecute (Jefferson, Tex.: 1937).*

US
JIM HOGG COUNTY ENTERPRISE. Began May 5, 1926. Newspaper. English (Spanish). wk. Jim Hogg County Enterprise, PO Box 759, Hebbronville TX 78361.

US
JUNCTION EAGLE, THE. **VFOAT** Eagle. Vol. 1, No. 1 (1883)-. Newspaper. English. wk. $15.00 local; $18.00 out of state. Junction Eagle, PO Box 226, Junction TX 76849. **Tel** (915)446-2610, FAX (915)446-4025. **ED** Roy Cooper. **Photos. Ad Acc.** Full Page (B&W) $504.00. Half Page (B&W) $252.00. **Pub. Size:** Standard. **Circ:** 2,200 weekly.

US
KARNES CITATION (KARNES CITY, TEX. : 1978). (THE KARNES CITATION.). Vol. 80, No. 35 (Aug. 3, 1978)-. Newspaper. English. wk. Karnes Citation, 110 South Market Street, Karnes City TX 78118. *Continues Karnes City Citation.*

US
KERRVILLE MOUNTAIN SUN. Vol. 43, No. 29 (July 1, 1926)-. Newspaper. English. sw. Kerrville Mountain Sun, PO Box 1249, Kerrville TX 78028. *Continues Kerrville Mountain Sun and Advance.*

US
KERRVILLE TIMES, THE. Began in 1925?. Newspaper. English. da. Kerrville Times, PO Box 1428, Kerrville TX 78029. *Formed by the union of Center Point News.*

US
KILGORE NEWS HERALD, THE. Began in 1931?. Newspaper. English. da. Kilgore News Herald, 610 East Main Street, Kilgore TX 75662.

US
KILLEEN DAILY HERALD. Vol. 1, No. 1 (Jan. 5, 1953)-. Newspaper. English. da. $8.00 per month. Killeen Daily Herald, PO Box 1300, Killeen TX 76540. **Tel** (817)634-2125. **ED** Gerlad Skidmore. **Photos. Ad Acc, Adv Mgr:** Thad Byars. Full Page (B&W) $1564.10. Half Page (B&W) $823.05. Full Page (Color) $1994.10. Half Page (Color) $1162.05. **Pub. Size:** Broadsheet. **Wire Svcs.:** AP. **Circ:** 19,700 daily, 23,500 Sunday. available in microform. *Continues Killeen Herald and Messenger.*

US
KIRBYVILLE BANNER. *Title Change.* (19??)-(19??). Newspaper. English. wk. East Texas Banner, PO Drawer B, Kirbyville TX 75956. **Tel** (409)423-2696, FAX (409)423-4793. *Continued by East Texas Banner.*

US
KNOX COUNTY NEWS, THE. Vol. 1, No. 1 (Oct. 21, 1971)-. Newspaper. English. wk. Knox County News, 107 North 2nd Street, Knox City TX 79529.

US
LA FERIA NEWS, THE. Vol. 1, No. 1 (Dec. 7, 1923)-. Newspaper. English. wk. $15.00 Cameron County, Texas; $17.50 other. La Feria News, PO Box 308, La Feria TX 78559. **Tel** (512)797-1813. **ED** Vincent Bodiford. **Bk Rev,** (Qty: 12). **Ad Acc. Circ:** 4,500.

US
LA MARQUE TIMES, THE. *Title Change.* Vol. 7, No. 16 (Oct. 29, 1953)-. Newspaper. English. wk. La Marque Times, PO Box 158, La Marque TX 77568. *Continues Mainland Times. Continued by Wednesday Times.*

US
LAKE CITIES SUN, THE. Vol. 1, No. 1 (Oct. 16, 1974)-. Newspaper. English. wk. $16.00 Denton County, Texas; $20.00 other. Lake Cities Sun, PO Box 877, Lake Dallas TX 75065. **Tel** (817)497-4141. **Bk Rev. Ad Acc. Circ:** 3,000 (ctrl).

US
LAMB COUNTY LEADER-NEWS. **VFOAT** Lamb County Leader News. Vol. 45, No. 42 (Feb. 13, 1969)-. Newspaper. English. wk. Lamb County Leader-News, PO Box 72, Littlefield TX 79339. *Formed by the union of Lamb County Leader and County Wide News.*

US
LAMESA PRESS-REPORTER. **VFOAT** Lamesa Press Reporter. Vol. 1, No. 1 (March 7, 1968)-. Newspaper. English. Twice a week. $25.25. Lamesa Press-Reporter, 523 North 1st Street, Lamesa TX 79331. **Tel** (806)872-2177, FAX (806)827-2623. **ED** Russel Skiles. **Photos. Ad Acc, Adv Mgr:** Dee Ann McCormick. Full Page (B&W) $409.50. Half Page (B&W) $204.75. Full Page (Color) $619.50. Half Page (Color) $414.75. **Pub. Size:** Broadsheet. **Circ:** 4,300. *Formed by the union of Dawson County Free Press and Lamesa Reporter.*

US/8750-1759
LAMPASAS DISPATCH RECORD. Vol. 78, No. 1 (July 2, 1984)-. Newspaper. English. wk. $36.00. Lampasas Dispatch Record, 416 South Live Oak, Lampasas TX 76550. **Tel** (512)556-6262, FAX (512)556-3278. **ED** Jim Lowe. **Bk Rev. Ad Acc. Circ:** 4,500. *Formed by the union of Lampasas Dispatch and Lampasas Record.*

US
LANTERN (BAYTOWN, TEX.). (THE LANTERN.). Newspaper. English. Lee College, PO Box 818, Baytown TX 77522-0818.

US/0740-5227
LAREDO MORNING TIMES. Vol. 101, No. 16 (June 29, 1982)-. Newspaper. English. da. $125.00 one year. Laredo Morning Times, PO Box 2129, Laredo TX 78040. **Tel** (512)723-2901. *Continues Laredo Times.*

US
LEVELLAND AND HOCKLEY COUNTY NEWS-PRESS. **VFOAT** Levelland and Hockley County News Press. Began in 1979?. Newspaper. English. wk. $30.00. PO Drawer H, Levelland TX 79336-1628. **Tel** (806)894-3121. **ED** Stephen A Henry. **Ad Acc.** ctrl circ. available on microfilm.

US/0746-8334
LEVELLAND LEADER. Newspaper. English. wk. Levelland Leader, PO Box 1575, Levelland TX 79336.

Texas

US/0745-6174
LEWISVILLE DAILY LEADER. VFOAT Leader. Vol. 88, No. 250 (Feb. 6, 1983)-. Newspaper. English. da (Wed. & Sun.). $82.00. Lewisville Leader, PO Box 308, Profes Building, Suite 100, Lewisville TX 75067. **Tel** (214)436-3566. **ED** Wayne Epperson. **Ad Acc. Circ:** 4,510 (ctrl). *Continues Daily Leader.*

US
LEWISVILLE NEWS, THE. Vol. 12, No. 138 (Feb. 20, 1983)-. Newspaper. English. tw. Lewisville News, PO Box 369, Lewisville TX 76202. *Continues Lewisville News-Advertiser.*

US
LIBERTY GAZETTE (LIBERTY, TEX.). (THE LIBERTY GAZETTE.). (19??)-. Newspaper. English. wk. Liberty Gazette, PO Box 1908, Liberty TX 77575. **Tel** (409)336-6416, FAX (409)336-9400. **ED** Edith Smith. **Bk Rev,** (Qty: 4/year). **Photos. Ad Acc, Adv Mgr:** Lawrence Kuslich. Full Page (B&W) $342.72. Half Page (B&W) $189.00. **Pub. Size:** Broadsheet. **Circ:** 8,800.

US/0746-4142
LIGHT CHAMPION. No. 40 (Sept. 30, 1983)-. Newspaper. English. sw. Shelby Newspapers Inc, 205 Austin Street, Center TX 75935. *Formed by the union of East Texas Light and Champion.*

US
LLANO NEWS (LLANO, TEX.). (THE LLANO NEWS.). Newspaper. English. wk. Llano News, PO Box 187, Llano TX 78643-0187. **ED** Will D Cowan.

US
LOCKHART POST-REGISTER. VFOAT Lockhart Post Register. Vol. 37, No. 38 (Feb. 10, 1916)-. Newspaper. English. wk. Lockhart Post-Register, 111 South Church Street, Lockhart TX 78644. *Continues Lockhart Post (Lockhart, Tex. : 1908).*

US
LOCKNEY BEACON, THE. Began in 1903?. Newspaper. English. wk. Lockney Beacon, PO Box 187, Lockney TX 79241.

US
LOGOS, THE. Vol. 1, No. 1 (Oct. 1935)-. Newspaper. English. mo. Incarnate Word College, 4301 Broadway, San Antonio TX 78209.

US
LONGVIEW SUNDAY NEWS-JOURNAL, THE. Began in 1947?. Newspaper. English. wk. Longview Newspapers Inc, 310-316 Methvin Street, Longview TX 75601. **Tel** (214)757-3311. **ED** Jim Giametta. **Circ:** 42,291.

US
LUBBOCK AVALANCHE-JOURNAL. VFOAT Lubbock Avalanche Journal. Vol. 14, No. 22 (Jan. 28, 1940)-. Newspaper. English. wk. $138.00 (morning Saturday and Sunday by mail) $105.00 (morning Saturday and Sunday by carrier), $120.00 (morning only by mail), $69.00 (morning only by carrier), $126.00 (Sunday by mail). Lubbock Avalanche-Journal, PO Box 491, Lubbock TX 79408. **Tel** (806)762-8855. Documents available from UMI Article Clearinghouse. *Continues Sunday Avalanche Journal.*
Ind/Abst Bus. Dateline (Dec. 29, 1991-) [Full Txt.].

US
LUBBOCK AVALANCHE-JOURNAL (LUBBOCK, TEX. : 1959 : MORNING ED.). Ceased. (LUBBOCK AVALANCHE-JOURNAL.). 27th Year, No. 207 (June 29, 1959)-?. Newspaper. English. da. Lubbock Avalanche-Journal, PO Box 491, Lubbock TX 79408. **Tel** (806)762-8855. *Continues Lubbock Morning Avalanche.*

US
LUFKIN DAILY NEWS, THE. Vol. 76, No. 104 (Feb. 28, 1982)-. Newspaper. English. da. Lufkin Daily News, PO Box 1089, Lufkin TX 75901. **Tel** (409)632-6631. *Continues Lufkin News.*

US/0746-3847
MANSFIELD NEWS-MIRROR. VFOAT Mansfield News Mirror. (1883)-. Newspaper. English. bw. $25.95 (in county), $29.95 (out of state). Mansfield News-Mirror, PO Box 337, Mansfield TX 76063-0337. **Tel** (817)473-4451, FAX (817)473-0730. **ED** Jerry T. Ebensberger. **Photos. Ad Acc.** Full Page (B&W) $645.00. Half Page (B&W) $330.00. **Pub. Size:** Broadsheet. **Circ:** 3,989 paid. available on microfilm.

US/0747-119X
MARFA INDEPENDENT AND THE BIG BEND SENTINEL, THE. VFOAT Marfa Independent, The Big Bend Sentinel; Marfa Independent; Big Bend Sentinel. (19??)-. Newspaper. English. wk. $18.00 Texas; $24.00 others. Marfa Independent and The Big Bend Sentinel, PO Box P, Marfa TX 79843. **Tel** (915)729-4342, FAX (915)729-4601. **ED** Robert Halpern and Rosario Halpern (Managing Editor). **Bk Rev**

Photos. Ad Acc, Adv Mgr: Rosario Halpern. **Pub. Size:** Standard. **Circ:** 2,400. available in microform. *Continues Big Bend Sentinel.*

US/1046-1752
MARLIN DEMOCRAT (1989). (MARLIN DEMOCRAT.). 98th Year, No. 133 (Aug. 5-6, 1989)-. Newspaper. English. sw. Marlin Daily Democrat, 211 Fortune Street, Marlin TX 76661. *Continues Marlin Daily Democrat, 0745-9580.*

US/1046-5502
MARSHALL NEWS MESSENGER. Title Change. (1928)-?. Newspaper. English. wk. Marshall News Messenger, PO Box 730, Marshall TX 75670. **Tel** (214)935-7914. *Absorbed Marshall Morning News; Marshall Evening Messenger. Continued by News Messenger (Marshall, Tex.), 1053-5705.*

US/0885-5102
MARTIN COUNTY NEWS. Vol. 1, No. 1 (July 20, 1984)-. Newspaper. English. wk. Community Publishing, 105 West Broadway, Stanton TX 79782.

US
MASON COUNTY NEWS. Began in 1883?. Newspaper. English. wk. $16.00. Mason County News, PO Box Q, Mason TX 76856. **Tel** (915)347-5757. **Ad Acc. Circ:** 2,700 (ctrl). *Absorbed Mason County Star; Fredonia Kicker; Mason Herald; Mason Maverick; Formed by the union of Item (1877) and Register (1883).*

US/1044-0348
MCGREGOR MIRROR AND THE CRAWFORD SUN, THE. Began in 1969?. Newspaper. English. wk. 311 South Main Street, McGregor TX 76657. *Formed by the union of McGregor Mirror and Crawford Sun.*

US
MENARD NEWS AND MESSENGER, THE. Vol. 5, No. 40 (Aug. 7, 1941)-. Newspaper. English. wk. $15.00 in county; $18.00 Texas; $25.00 US. Menard News and Messenger, PO Box 248, Menard TX 76859. **Tel** (915)396-2243. **ED** Dan Feather, Dorothy Kerns (Managing Editor). **Photos. Ad Acc.** Full Page (B&W) $225.00. Half Page (B&W) $141.75. Full Page (Color) $285.00. Half Page (Color) $201.75. **Pub. Size:** Standard. available in microform. *Formed by the union of Menard News and Menard Messenger.*

US/0746-4126
MESQUITE NEWS, THE. (19??)-. Newspaper. English. Fifty-two times a year. Mesquite News, PO Box 850136, Mesquite TX 75185. **Tel** (214)285-6301.

US/8750-5606
METROCREST NEWS, THE. Newspaper. English. wk. News-Texan Inc, 1450 Valwood Parkway, Carrollton TX 75006.

US
MEXIA DAILY NEWS, THE. (Feb. 9, 1923)-. Newspaper. English. sw (104 issues per year). $65.30 Texas; $67.90 other. Mexia Daily News, PO Box 431, Mexia TX 76667. **Tel** (817)562-2868. *Continues Mexia Evening News.*

US/0746-0082
MIAMI CHIEF (CANADIAN, TEX.). (THE MIAMI CHIEF.). Vol. 1, No. 1 (May 19, 1993)-. Newspaper. English. wk. $15.00, $14.00 (within Roberts county). Miami Chief, PO Box 187, Canadian TX 79014. **Tel** (806)323-5263. **ED** Bob Wilburn. **Ad Acc. Circ:** 600.

US/1044-0089
MID-CITIES NEWS, THE. VFOAT Mid Cities News. (198?)-. Newspaper. English. da. $72.00 Texas; $84.00 others. Suburban Newspapers / Texas, 1000 East Avenue H, Arlington TX 76011. **Tel** (817)695-0365. *Continues Mid-Cities Daily News, 8750-6440.*

US/0890-5932
MIDLAND REPORTER-TELEGRAM, THE. VFOAT Midland Reporter Telegram; Reporter-Telegram. Vol. 9, No. 36 (April 20, 1937)-. Newspaper. English. da. $190.00 Texas and Mexico; $370.00 other. The Midland Reporter-Telegram, 201 East Illinois, PO Box 1650, Midland TX 79702. **Tel** (915)682-5311. **ED** James E. Servatius. **Circ:** 24,495 daily, 28,814 Sunday. *Continues Reporter-Telegram (Midland, Tex.: 1929).*

US
MIDLOTHIAN MIRROR, THE. Vol. 1, No. 1 (Dec. 17, 1943)-. Newspaper. English. wk. $12.00 in county; $14.00 others in Texas; $17.00 others. Midlothian Mirror, 214 West Avenue F, PO Box 70, Midlothian TX 76065. **Tel** (214)775-3322. **ED** Barham Alderdice. **Photos. Ad Acc, Adv Mgr:** Debbie Garvin. Full Page (B&W) $504.00. Half Page (B&W) $252.00. Full Page (Color) $569.00. Half Page (Color) $317.00. **Pub. Size:** Standard. *Continues Midlothian News & Midlothian Argus.*

US/0746-6668
MILES MESSENGER. Vol. 35, No. 25 (June 7, 1935)-. Newspaper. English. wk. Miles Messenger, PO Box 307, Miles TX 76861. *Continues The Messenger (Miles, Tex.).*

US
MINERAL WELLS INDEX. (May 5, 1900)-. Newspaper. English. da (260 issues per year). $70.00 Palo Pinto County, Texas; $78.25 other Texas; $83.75 other. Mineral Wells Index, PO Box 370, Mineral Wells TX 76067. **Tel** (817)325-4466. *Continues Daily Index.*

US
MONAHANS NEWS (MONAHANS, TEX. : 1931). (THE MONAHANS NEWS.). (1931)-. Newspaper. English (Spanish). Fifty-four issues per year (Thurs.). $20.00. Monahans News, PO Box 767, Monahans TX 79756. **ED** Pearson Cooper. **Bk Rev. Photos. Ad Acc, Adv Mgr:** David McCaffity, **Tel** (915)943-4313. Full Page (B&W) $516.00. Half Page (B&W) $258.00. Full Page (Color) $596.00. Half Page (Color) $298.00. **Pub. Size:** Broadsheet. **Circ:** 4,100 (ctrl). available in microform from Southwest Micropublishing International. *Absorbed Monahans American.*

US/8750-524X
MONITOR (MCALLEN, TEX.), THE. (THE MONITOR.). Vol. 58, No. 292 (June 9, 1968)-. Newspaper. English. da (365 per year). $144.00. The Monitor, PO Box 760, McAllen TX 78505. **Tel** (512)686-4343. *Continues Valley Evening Monitor.*

US
MOODY COURIER, THE. (1890)-. Newspaper. English. wk. $12.00 in county; $14.00 others. Moody Courier, PO Box 38, Moody TX 76557-0038. **ED** Anna Belle Madson. **Bk Rev,** (Qty: 10). **Photos. Ad Acc.** Full Page (B&W) $352.00. Half Page (B&W) $126.00. Full Page (Color) $417.00. Half Page (Color) $191.00. **Pub. Size:** Standard. **Wire Svcs.:** CH. available in microform.

US
MOORE COUNTY NEWS-PRESS, THE. VFOAT Moore County News Press. Vol. 45, No. 9 (Aug. 22, 1971)-. Newspaper. English. sw. Moore County News-Press, PO Box 757, Dumas TX 79029.

US
MORTON TRIBUNE. (1939)-. Newspaper. English. wk. $15.00. Morton Tribune, PO Box 1016, Morton TX 79346. **Tel** (806)266-5576. **ED** Sherrill Sahlin. **Bk Rev,** (Qty: 10). **Photos. Ad Acc.** Full Page (B&W) $371.70. Half Page (B&W) $192.15. **Pub. Size:** Standard. **Circ:** 1,200 paid.

US
MT. VERNON OPTIC-HERALD. VFOAT Mt. Vernon Optic Herald. (1894)-. Newspaper. English. wk. $15.50. Optic-Herald, PO Drawer H, Mount Vernon TX 75457. **ED** Bob Wright (Editor-in-Chief) and Pat Wright (Managing Editor). **Photos. Ad Acc.** Full Page (B&W) $477.30. Half Page (B&W) $233.10. Full Page (Color) $532.30. **Pub. Size:** Standard. **Circ:** 3,100. *Formed by the union of Optic and Herald.*

US
MULESHOE JOURNAL, THE. Began in 1924?. Newspaper. English. wk. Muleshoe Journal, PO Box 449, Muleshoe TX 79347.

US/8750-6750
MUNDAY COURIER, THE. Vol. 1, No. 1 (Oct. 21, 1971)-. Newspaper. English. wk. $17.50. The Munday Courier, PO Box 130, Munday TX 76371. **Tel** (817)422-4314. **ED** Elaine Michels. **Ad Acc. Circ:** 1,550. **Desc:** News of local interest only. Mainly school activities and agriculture.

US
NAPLES MONITOR, THE. Began in 1886?. Newspaper. English. wk. Naples Monitor, PO Box 39, Naples TX 75568-0039.

US
NEW ULM ENTERPRISE. Began in 1910?. Newspaper. English. sw. New Ulm Enterprise, PO Box 128, New Ulm TX 78950.

US
NEWS, THE. Vol. 76, No. 54 (Feb. 23, 1973)-. Newspaper. English. da. $90.00 (carrier), $132.00 (mail). Port Arthur News / Texas, 549 4th Street, Port Arthur TX 77640. **Tel** (409)985-5541. **ED** W. A. Brown. *Continues Port Arthur News (Port Arthur, Tex. : 1922).*

US/0747-1750
NEWS (LAREDO, TEX.), THE. (THE NEWS.). (19??)-. Newspaper. English. da. Laredo News, 2301 Saunders Avenue, Laredo TX 78041.

US/1053-5705
NEWS MESSENGER (MARSHALL, TEX.). (NEWS MESSENGER.). (19??)-. Newspaper. English. da. Marshall News Messenger, PO Box 730, Marshall TX 75670. **Tel** (214)935-7914. *Continues Marshall News Messenger, 1046-5502.*

Texas

US
NIXON NEWS, THE. Newspaper. English. wk. Nixon News, 217 North Nixon Avenue, Nixon TX 78140. *Continues Nixon Weekly News.*

US
NOCONA NEWS, THE. Began in 1905?. Newspaper. English. wk. Nocona News, PO Box 539, Nocona TX 76225. *Absorbed Nocona Chief.*

US
NORTH SAN ANTONIO TIMES, THE. Vol. 1, No. 1 (March 11, 1971)-. Newspaper. English. wk. $17.95. North San Antonio Times, PO Box 17947, San Antonio TX 78217. **Tel** (210)828-3321, FAX (210)828-3787. **ED** Bill Towery, Steve Henry (Managing Editor). **Bk Rev. Ad Acc, Adv Mgr:** Jim Kennedy. Full Page (B&W) $1512.00. Half Page (B&W) $756.00. Full Page (Color) $1612.00. Half Page (Color) $856.00. **Pub. Size:** Standard. **Circ:** 8,900.

US
NORTH TEXAS DAILY, THE. Vol. 53, No. 29 (Feb. 6, 1970)-. Newspaper. English. da. North Texas State University, PO Box 5427, Denton TX 76201. **Tel** (817)565-3442. *Continues Campus Chat.*

US
ODESSA AMERICAN, THE. **VFOAT** American. (1940)-. Newspaper. English. da. $136.50 (Sunday, mail), $166.40 (daily and Sunday, regular mail), $113.75 (daily and Sunday, carrier), $138.00 (weekend, mail). Odessa American, Box 2952, Odessa TX 79760. **Tel** (915)362-0370. **ED** Jim Welsh. **Circ:** 29,887 daily, 38,756 Sunday. *Continues Odessa News-Times.*

US
OLNEY ENTERPRISE, THE. **VFOAT** The Olney Enterprise - 100 Percent American. (1910)-. Newspaper. English. wk. $11.00 Olney county. $14.00 Texas; $16.00 others. Olney Enterprise, 213 East Main Street, Olney TX 76374. **ED** David H. Penn. **Photos. Ad Acc, Adv Mgr:** David Penn, **Tel** (817)564-5558. Full Page (B&W) $352.80. Half Page (B&W) $176.40. Full Page (Color) $120.00 (each color). Half Page (Color) $120.00 (each color). **Pub. Size:** Standard. **Circ:** 2,522. available in microform.

US
OLTON ENTERPRISE (OLTON, TEX. : 1926). (THE OLTON ENTERPRISE.). Vol. 1, No. 1 (Feb. 18, 1926)-. Newspaper. English. wk. $15.00 (in county), $17.50 (other). Olton Enterprise, PO Box E, Olton TX 79064. **Tel** (806)285-2631. **ED** Sue Cannon. **Photos. Ad Acc.** Full Page (B&W) $346.50. Half Page (B&W) $173.50. Full Page (Color) $421.50. Half Page (Color) $248.50. **Pub. Size:** Broadsheet.

US
ONION CREEK FREE PRESS. *Title Change.* **VFOAT** Free Press. Vol. 4, No. 38 (Oct. 6, 1978)-(19??). Newspaper. English. wk. Onion Creek Free Press, PO Box 339, Buda TX 78610. *Continues River City Sun. Continued by Hays County Free Press, 1058-4471.*

US
OPPORTUNITY VALLEY NEWS. (19??)-. Newspaper. English. wk. Opportunity Valley News, PO Box 1028, Orange TX 77630. **ED** Belinda Gaudet. **Photos. Ad Acc, Adv Mgr:** Jan Bromley, **Tel** (409)883-3571. **Pub. Size:** Tabloid. **Circ:** 23,500 unpaid (ctrl).

US/0885-8047
ORANGE LEADER (ORANGE, TEX.). (THE ORANGE LEADER.). **VFOAT** Orange Leader and Tribune. (Nov. 19, 1926)-. Newspaper. English. ds. $7.00 per month. Orange Leader, PO Box 1028, Orange TX 77630. **Tel** (409)883-3571, FAX (409)883-6342. **ED** Belind Gaudet. **Bk Rev. Photos. Ad Acc, Adv Mgr:** Jan Bromley. Full Page (B&W) $1265.49. Half Page (B&W) $657.80. Full Page (Color) $1368.49. Half Page (Color) $760.80. **Wire Svcs.:** AP. **Circ:** 12,000 paid. available in microform. *Continues Orange Daily Leader.*

US
OZONA STOCKMAN, THE. Began in April 1914. Newspaper. English. wk. Ozona Stockman, 1000 Avenue E, Ozona TX 76943.

US
PADUCAH POST, THE. Began in 1906. Newspaper. English. wk. Paducah Post, PO Box E Paducah TX 79248.

US/1053-5748
PALESTINE HERALD-PRESS. **VFOAT** Palestine Herald Press. Vol. 43, No. 51 (Aug. 1, 1949)-. Newspaper. English. da. Palestine Herald-Press, 519 Elm Street, Palestine TX 75801. *Formed by the union of Palestine Daily Herald and Palestine Press.*

US
PALMER RUSTLER, THE. Began in 1902?. Newspaper. English. wk. Palmer Rustler, 213-215 North Dallas Street, Ennis TX 75119.

US
PAMPA NEWS (PAMPA, TEX. : 1976)-. (THE PAMPA NEWS.). Vol. 70, No. 308 (April 1, 1976)-. Newspaper. English. da. Pampa News, 403 West Atchison, PO Box 2198, Pampa TX 79006. **Tel** (806)669-2525. *Continues Pampa Daily News (Pampa, Tex. : 1945).*

US/8756-2464
PANHANDLE HERALD, THE. (July 22, 1887)-. Newspaper. English. wk. $16.00 Carson County; $18.00 US. Panhandle Herald, PO Box 429, Panhandle TX 79068. **Tel** (806)537-3634. **ED** Betty Biggs. **Photos. Ad Acc.** Full Page (B&W) $246.00. Half Page (B&W) $123.00. **Pub. Size:** Tabloid. ctrl circ.

US
PANOLA WATCHMAN (CARTHAGE, TEX. : 1873). (THE PANOLA WATCHMAN.). Vol. 1, No. 1 (July 2, 1873)-. Newspaper. English. bw. $32.00. Panola Watchman, 109 West Panola, Carthage TX 75633. **Tel** (903)693-7888, FAX (903)693-5857. **ED** Ted Leach. **Bk Rev. Photos. Ad Acc, Adv Mgr:** Bill Holder. Full Page (B&W) $754.65. Half Page (B&W) $368.55. Full Page (Color) $844.65. Half Page (Color) $458.52. **Pub. Size:** Standard. available in microform.

US/8756-2081
PARIS NEWS, THE. Vol. 76, No. 12 (July 31, 1944)-. Newspaper. English. da. $105.00 (by mail). Paris News, PO Box 1078, Paris TX 75460. **Tel** (903)785-8744, FAX (903)785-1263. **ED** Bill Hankins. **Bk Rev. Photos. Ad Acc, Adv Mgr:** Larry Reynolds. Full Page (B&W) $1186.80. Half Page (B&W) $593.40. Full Page (Color) $1291.80. Half Page (Color) $698.40. **Pub. Size:** Standard. **Wire Svcs.:** AP. *Continues Paris News (and the Dinner Horn).*

US
PARK CITIES NEWS, THE. (19??)-. Newspaper. English. wk. $18.00. Park Cities News, 6060 North Central Expressway #134, Dallas TX 75206. **Tel** (214)369-7570. **ED** Marjorie B. Waters and Peter H. Waters. **Ad Acc. Circ:** 8,000 (ctrl).

US/1050-3773
PASADENA CITIZEN (1990). (PASADENA CITIZEN.). Began in 1990-. Newspaper. English. da. Daily Pasadena Citizen, PO Box 6192, Pasadena TX 77506. *Continues Daily Pasadena Citizen, 0896-3320.*

US
PEARLAND JOURNAL, THE. Vol. 1, No. 1 (June 24, 1971)-. Newspaper. English. sw. Pearland Journal, PO Box 1830, Pearland TX 77588. **Tel** (713)485-2785.

US
PECOS FREE PRESS AND ENTERPRISE. (1970)-. Newspaper. English. da. $78.00. Pecos Free Press and Enterprise, 324 South Cedar Street, Pecos TX 79772. **Tel** (915)445-5475. **ED** Mac McKinnon (editor); Jan Fullbright (managing editor). **Photos. Ad Acc, Adv Mgr:** Cristina Bitolas. Full Page (B&W) $5.67. Half Page (B&W) $5.84. Full Page (Color) $65.76. Half Page (Color) $65.84. **Wire Svcs.:** AP. **Circ:** evening 2,500, Sunday 4,500. available on microfilm from Southwest Micropublishing International.

US
PERRYTON HERALD, THE. **VFOAT** Sunday Herald. Vol. 52, No. 1 (Jan. 2, 1969)-. Newspaper. English. wk. Perryton Herald, 401 South Amherst, Perryton TX 79070. *Continues Ochiltree County Herald.*

US/1056-5167
PFLUGERVILLE PRESS, THE. Vol. 1, No. 1 (Jan. 16, 1991)-. Newspaper. English. wk. $20.00. Pflugerville Press, PO Box 986, Pflugerville TX 78660.

US
PINE LOG, THE. Vol. 1, No. 1 (May 31, 1924)-. Newspaper. English. wk (Mon. & Thurs.). $15.00 (per semester); $20.00 (per academic year). Stephen F. Austin State University, Box 13049, SFA Station, Nacogdoches TX 75962. **Tel** (409)468-4703, FAX (409)468-1016. **Bk Rev. Photos. Ad Acc, Adv Mgr:** Emmeline Aguirre. Full Page (B&W) $440.00. Half Page (B&W) $225.00. **Pub. Size:** Standard. **Circ:** 6,500.00 (Spring), 7,000 (Fall).

US
PLAINVIEW DAILY HERALD (PLAINVIEW, TEX. : 1956). (PLAINVIEW DAILY HERALD.). Vol. 54, No. 163 (July 8, 1956)-. Newspaper. English. da. Plainview Daily Herald, 820 Broadway, Plainview TX 79072.

US/0895-4305
PLANO STAR COURIER (1986). (PLANO STAR COURIER.). (1986)-. Newspaper. English. da (except Sat.). $96.40 in county; $130.60 other Texas; $125.80 other US. Plano Star Courier, PO Box 86248, Plano TX 75086. **Tel** (214)424-6565. *Continues Plano Daily Star Courier.*

US
PLEASANTON EXPRESS, THE. Began in 1910. Newspaper. English. wk. Pleasanton Express, 114 Goodwin Street, Pleasanton TX 78064. *Continues Pleasanton Monitor.*

US/8750-3964
PLUS (LONGVIEW, TEX.). (PLUS : +.). **VFOAT** +. V. 1, No. 1 (Oct. 10, 1984)-. Newspaper. English. wk. Longview Newspapers Inc, 310-316 Methvin Street, Longview TX 75601. **Tel** (214)757-3311. *Continues Community News (Longview, Tex.).*

US
POLK COUNTY ENTERPRISE. Began in 1903?. Newspaper. English. wk. Polk County Enterprise, PO Box 1276, Livingston TX 77351.

US
PORT ISABEL SOUTH PADRE ISLAND PRESS. **Added/Corp** News Publishing Co., Inc. (1974)-. Newspaper. English. sw (Mon. and Thurs.). $28.00. Port Isabel / South Padre Press, PO Box 308, Port Isabel TX 78578. **Tel** (210)943-5545. **ED** Tim McKeown. **Ad Acc. Circ:** 4,860 (ctrl). available on microfilm. *Continues Port Isabel Press.*

US/1062-1199
PORT LAVACA WAVE, THE. (190?)-. Newspaper. English. da. Port Lavaca Wave, 301 South Colorado, PO Box 88, Port Lavaca TX 77979.

US
POST DISPATCH, THE. (1926)-. Newspaper. English. wk. $15.00 in county; $18.00 Texas; $24.00 US. Post Publishing Company, 123 East Main Street, Post TX 79356. **ED** Dee Pittman. **Photos. Ad Acc, Adv Mgr:** Lillie Hart. Full Page (B&W) $459.00. Half Page (B&W) $236.25. Full Page (Color) $504.90. Half Page (Color) $281.25. **Pub. Size:** Standard. **Circ:** 1,650.

US/0747-4253
POTTSBORO PRESS. (1984)-. Newspaper. English. wk. $19.00. Pottsboro Press, 305 Highway 120 East, Pottsboro TX 75076. **Tel** (214)786-4051. **ED** John W. Crawford. **Ad Acc. Circ:** 1,500 (ctrl).

US
PRAIRIE (CANYON, TEX.). (THE PRAIRIE.). Vol. 1, No. 1 (Oct. 20, 1919)-. Newspaper. English. sw (during school session). $4.00. Prairie / West Texas State University, Canyon TX 79105. **Tel** (806)656-3887.

US
PRENSA (SAN ANTONIO, TEX. : WEEKLY). (LA PRENSA.). Vol. 1, No. 1 (Feb. 13, 1913)-. Newspaper. Spanish (English). Fifty-two times a year (Published on Fri.). $40.00. La Prensa / San Antonio, TX, 301 South Frio, Suite 105, San Antonio TX 78207. **Tel** (210)270-4590.

US/0890-2666
PROGRESS TIMES. **VFOAT** Progress-Times. Vol. 12, No. 26 (Feb. 1, 1984)-. Newspaper. English. Fifty-two times a year (Wednesday). $18.00. Progress Times, 1217 North Conway, Mission TX 78572. **Tel** (210)585-4893, FAX (210)585-2304. **ED** June K. Braun. **Photos. Ad Acc, Adv Mgr:** Anna Carrillo. Full Page (B&W) $1161.00. Half Page (B&W) $594.00. Full Page (Color) $1286.00. Half Page (Color) $719.00. **Pub. Size:** Broadsheet. *Continues Upper Valley Progress.*

US
QUANAH TRIBUNE-CHIEF. **VFOAT** Quanah Tribune Chief. (June 3, 1897)-. Newspaper. English. wk. $17.90 Texas; $31.25 others. Quanah Tribune-Chief, 310 Mercer, Quanah TX 79252. **Tel** (817)663-5333. **ED** Carol Ann Whitmire. **Photos. Ad Acc, Adv Mgr:** Judy Nelson. Full Page (B&W) $315.00. Half Page (B&W) $157.50. Full Page (Color) $400.00. Half Page (Color) $242.50. **Pub. Size:** Standard. **Circ:** 1,500. available in microform. *Formed by the union of Quanah Tribune and Quanah Chief.*

US
RAINS COUNTY LEADER. (June 10, 1887)-. Newspaper. English. wk. $14.25 Texas; $16.50 others. Rains County Leader, PO Box 127, Emory TX 75440. **Tel** (903)473-2653. **ED** Kathleen Becknell. **Photos. Ad Acc.** Full Page (B&W) $441.00. Half Page (B&W) $220.50. **Pub. Size:** Broadsheet. **Circ:** 2,050. available in microform.

US
RAM PAGE, THE. Newspaper. English. wk. Angelo State University, Department of Journalism, San Angelo TX 76909.

US
RECORD-COURIER (JOHNSON CITY, TEX. : 1981). (RECORD-COURIER.). **VFOAT** Record Courier. Began in 1981?. Newspaper. English. wk. Bluebonnet Media Inc, PO Box 205, Johnson City TX 78636. *Continues Ranchland Post Dispatch.*

US
REPORTER, THE. (19??)-. Newspaper. English. wk (Monday and Thursday). $22.00 (Hill County, Texas), $32.00 (other than Hill County, Texas). Hillsboro

Texas

Reporter, PO Box 569, Hillsboro TX 76645. **Tel** (817)582-3431, FAX (817)582-3800. **ED** Rick Bailey. **Ad Acc. Circ:** 6,000 (ctrl).

US/1045-4004
RICHARDSON NEWS. (Apr. 1989)-. Newspaper. English. da (Thurs. & Sun.). $84.00. Richardson Daily News, PO Box 830630, Richardson TX 75083-0630. **Tel** (214)234-3198. **Continues** Richardson Daily News, 0745-9068.

US
RIESEL RUSTLER, THE. Began in 1898?. Newspaper. English. wk. Riesel Rustler, PO Box 100, Riesel TX 76682.

US
RISING STAR (RISING STAR, TEX.: 1965). (THE RISING STAR.). Vol. 76, No. 1 (Oct. 21, 1965)-. Newspaper. English. wk. $10.00 in county; $15.00 other Texas; $20.00 other. Rising Star, Box 129, Rising Star TX 76471. **Tel** (817)643-4141, FAX (817)629-2092. **ED** H.V. O'Brien and Delana Steubing (Managing Editor). **Bk Rev. Photos. Ad Acc.** Full Page (B&W) $3.75 (per column inch). Half Page (B&W) $3.75 (per column inch). **Pub. Size:** Standard. **Continues** Rising Star Record.

US
ROCKDALE REPORTER AND MESSENGER, THE. (1908)-. Newspaper. English. wk. Rockdale Reporter and Messenger, 221-225 East Cameron Avenue, Rockdale TX 76567. **Formed by the union of** Rockdale Messenger **and** Rockdale Reporter.

US
ROCKPORT PILOT, THE. Began in 1931. Newspaper. English. wk. Rockport Pilot, 1002 Wharf Street, Rockport TX 78382. **Continues** Register-Pilot.

US/1048-8227
ROCKWALL COUNTY JOURNAL-SUCCESS. VFOAT Journal-Success. Newspaper. English. sw. Rockwall Texas Success, PO Box 127, Rockwall TX 75087. **Continues** Rockwall Texas Success, 0882-4940.

US
ROCKWALL COUNTY JOURNAL-SUCCESS. Rockwall County Journal-Success, POB 127, Rockwall TX 75087.

US/0882-4940
ROCKWALL TEXAS SUCCESS, THE. Title Change. Newspaper. English. wk. Rockwall Texas Success, PO Box 127, Rockwall TX 75087. **Continued by** Rockwall County Journal-Success, 1048-8227.

US
ROSEBUD NEWS, THE. Began in 1894?. Newspaper. English. wk. Rosebud News, PO Box 516, Rosebud TX 76570.

US/0164-9124
ROUND ROCK LEADER. (1896)-. Newspaper. English. sw. $25.00. Round Rock Leader, PO Box 428, Round Rock TX 78680. **Tel** (512)255-5827. **ED** Ken Long (Editor-in-Chief) and Will Hampton (Managing Editor). Index available. **Bk Rev. Photos. Ad Acc, Adv Mgr:** Bobby Seijerman, **Tel** (512)255-5827. Full Page (B&W) $595.98. Half Page (B&W) $314.37. Full Page (Color) $720.98. Half Page (Color) $439.37. **Pub. Size:** Broadsheet. **Circ:** 5,950 (ctrl). available on microfilm. **Continues** Round Rock Searchlight.

US
ROWENA PRESS, THE. Newspaper. English. wk. Rowena Press, PO Box 307, Miles TX 76861.

US/0886-3733
ROWLETT RECORD AMERICAN. Vol. 11, No. 74 (Friday, Oct. 25, 1985)-. Newspaper. English. wk. Rowlett Record American, PO Box 400, Rowlett TX 75088. **Continues** Lakeside Record American, 0746-4150.

US
RUSK CHEROKEEAN, THE. (19??)-. Newspaper. English. wk. The Rusk Cherokeean, PO Box 475, Rusk TX 75785. **Absorbed** The Alto Herald.

US
SAINT JO TRIBUNE, THE. Vol. 1, No. 1 (1889)-. Newspaper. English. wk. $14.00 in county; $16.00 others. Saint Jo Tribune, PO Drawer 160, Saint Jo TX 76265. **Tel** (819)995-2586, FAX (819)995-2007. **ED** C. E. Cole (Editor-in-Chief) and Dee Cole (Managing Editor). **Photos. Ad Acc, Adv Mgr:** Rebecca Smith. Full Page (B&W) $228.00. Half Page (B&W) $116.00. **Pub. Size:** Tabloid.

US/0890-5924
SAM KINCH'S TEXAS WEEKLY. [Sam Kinch's Tex. wkly.]. VFOAT Texas Weekly. (198?)-. Newspaper. English. Fifty times a year. $160.00. Sam Kinchs Texas Weekly, PO Box 5306, Austin TX 78763. **Tel** (512)322-9332. **DD** 320.

US
SAN ANGELO STANDARD-TIMES. VFOAT San Angelo Standard Times. Began in 1928?. Newspaper. English. da. $145.80. San Angelo Standard Times, 34 West Harris Avenue, San Angelo TX 76902. **Tel** (915)653-1221. **ED** Dennis Ellsworth. **Bk Rev. Ad Acc. Circ:** 33,624 daily, 39,327 Sunday. **Continues** San Angelo Standard (San Angelo, Tex. : 1884).

US/1065-7908
SAN ANTONIO EXPRESS-NEWS. VFOAT San Antonio Express News. (19??)-. Newspaper. English. da. $144.00 Texas; $170.00 US. San Antonio Express News, PO Box 2171, San Antonio TX 78297. **Tel** (210)225-7411, (800)456-7411, FAX (210)225-2553. **ED** Jim Moss, Bob Rivard (Managing Editor). **Photos. Ad Acc, Adv Mgr:** Bruce Ford, **Tel** (210)351-7413. Full Page (B&W) $19200.00. Half Page (B&W) $9600.00. Full Page (Color) $20008.00. Half Page (Color) $10408.00. **Pub. Size:** Broadsheet. **Wire Svcs.:** AP, LA, SH. **Circ:** 239,416 Mon.-Thurs., 301,605 Fri., 295,195 Sat., 406,927 Sun. **Continues** Express-News (San Antonio, Tex.), 8750-3115. **Ind/Abst** PROMT.

US
SAN ANTONIO LIGHT (SAN ANTONIO, TEX.: 1911). Ceased. (SAN ANTONIO LIGHT.). VFOAT San Antonio Sunday Light. Vol. 32, No. 70 (Apr. 1, 1911)-(1993). Newspaper. English. da. The Light Publications Company, 420 22 Broadway at McCullough, San Antonio TX 78291. **Tel** (512)271-2700. **ED** Ted Warmbold. **Circ:** 138,125 daily, 208,465 Sunday. available on microfilm; available on an online database (file 635/Full-Text) from DIALOG. Documents available from UMI Article Clearinghouse. **Continues** San Antonio Light and Gazette. **Ind/Abst** Bus. Dateline (Dec. 11, 1991-) [Full Txt.].

US
SAN AUGUSTINE TRIBUNE. Began in 1909?. Newspaper. English. wk. San Augustine Tribune, PO Box M, San Augustine TX 75972.

US/0746-8156
SAN MARCOS NEWS. Newspaper. English. wk. San Marcos News, PO Box 2209, San Marcos TX 78666.

US
SAN MARCOS RECORD, THE. Began Sept. 20, 1912. Newspaper. English. wk. San Marcos Record, PO Box 1109, San Marcos TX 78666.

US
SAN PATRICIO COUNTY NEWS. Began in 1908. Newspaper. English. wk. San Patricio County News, PO Drawer B, Sinton TX 78387.

US
SAN SABA NEWS AND STAR, THE. Vol. 94, No. 12 (March 24, 1966)-. Newspaper. English. wk. San Saba News and Star, PO Box 815, San Saba TX 76877. **Continues** San Saba News; San Saba Star.

US
SANDERSON TIMES. Began in 1909?. Newspaper. English. wk. Sanderson Times, PO Box 748, Sanderson TX 79848.

US/0895-4275
SCHULENBURG STICKER, THE. VFOAT Sticker. Began in 1899. Newspaper. English. wk. Schulenburg Sticker, PO Box 160, Schulenburg TX 78956. **Continues** Sticker.

US
SEALY NEWS (SEALY, TEX. : 1915). (THE SEALY NEWS.). VFOAT News. (1915)-. Newspaper. English. wk. $21.00 in county; $25.00 others in Texas; $35.00 others. Sealy News, PO Drawer 480, Sealy TX 77474. **Tel** (409)885-3562. **ED** Wilma Petrunsek. **Photos. Ad Acc, Adv Mgr:** Jim Grimes. Full Page (B&W) $541.80. Half Page (B&W) $270.90. Full Page (Color) $641.80. Half Page (Color) $370.90. **Pub. Size:** Broadsheet. **Circ:** 4,800. **Continues** Sealy Semi-Weekly News.

US
SHAMROCK TEXAN, THE. Vol. 23, No. 33 (Dec. 16, 1926)-. Newspaper. English. wk. $16.00. Shamrock Texan, PO Box 589, Shamrock TX 79079. **Tel** (806)256-2131. **ED** Kip Pezse. **Bk Rev. Ad Acc. Circ:** 1,900 (ctrl). **Continues** Wheeler County Texan.

US
SHERMAN DEMOCRAT (SHERMAN, TEX.). (SHERMAN DEMOCRAT.). Vol. 69, No. 92 (Nov. 30, 1947)-. Newspaper. English. da. $72.00 daily & Sunday by carrier, $75.00 daily and Sunday. Sherman Democrat, PO Box 1128, Attention Sam Fowler, Sherman TX 75090. **Tel** (214)893-8181. **Continues** Sherman Daily Democrat.

US/0887-5634
SHIJIE RIBAO (HOUSTON, TEX.). (SHIH CHIEH JIH PAO). VFOAT World Journal; World Journal of Texas. (1985)-. Newspaper. Chinese. da. World Journal of Texas, 9104-A Bellaire Boulevard, Houston TX 77036. **Tel** (713)771-4363. **Continues** Shih Chieh Jih Pao (Monterey Park, Calif.), 0740-1108.

US
SHINER GAZETTE. VFOAT The Gazette. Began in 1892. Newspaper. English. wk. Shiner Gazette, PO Box 727, Shiner TX 77984.

US
SILSBEE BEE, THE. (1919)-. Newspaper. English. wk. $12.00. Silsbee Bee, PO Drawer 547, Silsbee TX 77656. **Tel** (409)385-5278. **ED** Danny Reneau. **Ad Acc.** Full Page (B&W) $503.37. Half Page (B&W) $251.68. Full Page (Color) Add $50.00 for color. Half Page (Color) Add $150.00 for color. **Pub. Size:** Broadsheet. **Circ:** 6,000. available in microform.

US
SLATON SLATONITE, THE. Vol. 3, No. 21 (Jan. 23, 1914)-. Newspaper. English. wk. Slaton Slatonite, 139 South 9th Street, Slaton TX 79364. **Continues** Slatonite; **Absorbed** Slaton Times.

US
SNYDER DAILY NEWS, THE. Vol. 1, No. 1 (May 1, 1950)-. Newspaper. English. da. $85.00. Snyder Daily News, PO Box 949, Snyder TX 79549. **Tel** (915)573-5486, FAX (915)573-0044. **ED** Bill McChellan. **Photos. Ad Acc, Adv Mgr:** Wayne Burney. Full Page (B&W) $554.40. Half Page (B&W) $280.20. Full Page (Color) $639.40. Half Page (Color) $362.20. **Pub. Size:** Standard. **Wire Svcs.:** AP. **Circ:** 6,500. **Continues** Scurry County Times.

US
SOL DE TEXAS, EL. Vol. 1, No. 1 (Sept. 30, 1966)-. Newspaper. Spanish. wk. $30.00. Organizacion Editorial Hispana, PO Box 803402, Dallas TX 75380. **Tel** (214)386-9120. **ED** Rolando Romero. **Bk Rev.** (Qty: 6). **Photos. Ad Acc, Adv Mgr:** Jaime Montano. Full Page (B&W) $1512.00. Half Page (B&W) $756.00. Full Page (Color) additional $150.00 per color. Half Page (Color) additional $150.00 per color. **Pub. Size:** Broadsheet. **Wire Svcs.:** UPI.

US/0891-818X
SOL (HOUSTON, TEX.), EL. (EL SOL). VFOAT Houston Sun. (19??)-. Newspaper. Spanish (English). wk. El Sol / Texas, PO Box 3795, Houston TX 77001. **Tel** (713)224-0616. **ED** James L. Novarro. **Bk Rev. Circ:** 37,000 (ctrl). **Desc:** Cultural development; linguistic bridge of communication; local, national, international information and bridge of goodwill.

US
SOUTHWEST DIGEST. Vol. 4, No. 2 (Oct. 7-13, 1982)-. Newspaper. English. wk. $20.00. Southwest Digest, 510 East 23rd Street, Lubbock TX 79404. **Tel** (806)762-3612. **ED** Eddie P. Richardson. **Bk Rev.** (Qty: 45). **Photos. Ad Acc.** Full Page (B&W) $1512.00. Half Page (B&W) $756.00. Full Page (Color) $1597.00. Half Page (Color) $841.00. **Pub. Size:** Standard. **Wire Svcs.:** NP. **Continues** Lubbock Digest.

US
SPEARMAN REPORTER, THE. Title Change. Vol. 12, No. 2 (Dec. 1919)-?. Newspaper. English. wk. Spearman Reporter, PO Box 458, Spearman TX 79081. **ED** Mike Hulett. **Ad Acc. Continues** Hansford Headlight. **Continued by** Hansford Headlight.

US
STAMFORD AMERICAN (STAMFORD, TEX. : 1965). (July 15, 1965)-. Newspaper. English. wk. $13.00 local counties; $15.00 Texas; $18.00 US. Stamford American, PO Box 1207, Stamford TX 79553. **Tel** (915)773-3621, FAX (915)773-3622. **ED** Michelle Sanchez, Timmy Sanchez (Managing Editor). **Bk Rev.** (Qty: 10). **Photos. Ad Acc, Adv Mgr:** Chandra Mathis. Full Page (B&W) $332.00. Half Page (B&W) $166.00. Full Page (Color) $422.00. Half Page (Color) $256.00. available on microfilm. **Continues** Stamford American and The Stamford Leader.

US
STAR-COURIER, THE. (19??)-. Newspaper. English. wk. $20.00. Crosby Courier, PO Box 485, Highlands TX 77562. **Tel** (713)328-9605, FAX (713)977-1188. **ED** Gilbert Hoffman (editor's phone: (713)977-2555). **Bk Rev.** (Qty: 26 per year). **Photos. Ad Acc.** Full Page (B&W) $480.00. Half Page (B&W) $240.00. **Pub. Size:** Standard. **Circ:** 4,500. **Continues** The Highlands Star.

US
STATE LINE TRIBUNE, THE. Began in 1911?. Newspaper. English. wk. State Line Tribune, PO Box 255, Farwell TX 79325.

US
STERLING CITY NEWS-RECORD. VFOAT Sterling City News Record. Began in 1902?. Newspaper. English. wk. Sterling City News-Record, PO Box 608, Sterling City TX 76951. **Formed by the union of** Sterling City News **and** Sterling City Record.

Texas

US
STRATFORD STAR, THE. Began in 1901?. Newspaper. English. wk. Stratford Star, 215 North Main Street, Stratford TX 79084.

US/1063-0392
SUBURBAN TRIBUNE, THE. Began Feb. 26 (1953). Newspaper. English. wk. Suburban Tribune, 8017 Lake June Road/Suite B, Dallas TX 75217. *Formed by the union of Suburban News (Dallas, Tex.) and Dallas County Tribune.*

US/0745-6425
SULPHUR SPRINGS NEWS-TELEGRAM. VFOAT News-Telegram. VAT Sulphur Springs News Telegram. (19??)-. Newspaper. English. da. $76.00. Sulphur Springs News-Telegram, PO Box 598, Sulphur Springs TX 75482. **Tel** (214)885-8663. **ED** Dave Hillsamer. **Ad Acc. Circ:** 6,983. available or microfilm. *Continues Daily News-Telegram.*

US
SWEETWATER REPORTER (SWEETWATER, TEX.: 1911). (SWEETWATER REPORTER.). VFOAT Sweetwater Daily Reporter. Began Feb. 14, 1911. Newspaper. English. da. Sweetwater Reporter, PO Box 750, Sweetwater TX 79556.

US
TEMPLE DAILY TELEGRAM. Vol. 1, No. 1 (Nov. 19, 1907)-. Newspaper. English. da. Temple Daily Telegram, 10 South 3rd Street, PO Box 6114, Temple TX 76501. **Tel** (817)778-4444. Documents available from UMI Article Clearinghouse. *Absorbed Temple Daily Tribune.*
Ind/Abst Bus. Dateline (Jan. 26, 1992-) [Full Txt.].

US
TERRELL TRIBUNE, THE. Newspaper. English. da. Terrell Tribune, PO Box 669, Terrell TX 75160. *Continues Terrell Daily Tribune.*

US
TEXAS CITY SUN. (19??)-. Newspaper. English. da. Texas City Sun, 7800 Emmett F. Lowry Expressway, Texas City TX 77591. **Tel** (409)945-3441, FAX (409)935-0428. **ED** Les Daughtry, Jr., John Simsen (Managing Editor). **Bk Rev. Photos. Ad Acc, Adv Mgr:** Larry Cooke. Full Page (B&W) $1225.50. Half Page (Color) $612.75. Full Page (Color) $1350.50. Half Page (Color) $737.75. **Pub. Size:** Broadsheet. **Wire Svcs.:** AP. **Circ:** 10,700. available in microform.

US/0040-439X
TEXAS JEWISH POST, THE. Vol. 1, No. 1 (Jan. 9, 1947)-. Newspaper. English. Fifty-two times a year. $32.00 Texas; $39.00 others in Texas; $70.00 others. Texas Jewish Post, 11333 North Central Expressway, Suite 213, Dallas TX 75243. **Tel** (817)429-0840, (214)692-7283, FAX (817)692-7285. **ED** Jimmy Wiseh. **Bk Rev. Ad Acc.** ctrl circ.

US
TEXAS MOHAIR WEEKLY (ROCKSPRINGS, TEX.). (THE TEXAS MOHAIR WEEKLY.). Vol. 53, No. 40 (Oct. 13, 1961)-. Newspaper. English. wk. Texas Mohair Weekly, PO Box 287, Rocksprings TX 78880. *Continues Texas Mohair Weekly and Rocksprings Record.*

US
TEXAS OBSERVER, THE. (1906)-. Newspaper. English. Twenty-five times a year. Texas Observer, 307 West 7th Street, Austin TX 78701-2917. **Tel** (512)477-0746. **ED** Louis DuBose. Index available. cum. index. **Bk Rev. Ad Acc. Circ:** 12,000. available on microfilm and microfiche from University Microfilms International (UMI). *Absorbed State Observer; East Texas Democrat.*
Desc: Coverage of regional political and cultural news with a liberal slant, some national and international reporting.
Ind/Abst Access (1975-); Chicano Index; Index Period. Artic. Relat. Law.

US
THROCKMORTON TRIBUNE. Began July 1, 1886?. Newspaper. English. wk. Throckmorton Tribune, PO Box 847, Throckmorton TX 76083.

US
TIMES (KATY, TEX.). (THE TIMES.). Newspaper. English. wk. Tri-County Newspapers Inc, PO Box 678, Katy TX 77449.

US/0895-6138
TIMES RECORD NEWS. VFOAT Wichita Falls Times Record News. Vol. 81, No. 94 (Tuesday, Sept. 1, 1987)-. Newspaper. English. da. $121.00 Texas and Oklahoma; $144.00 other. Times Publishing Company of Wichita Falls, 1301 Lamar, Wichita Falls TX 76301. **Tel** (817)767-8341, (800)627-1646. **(Subscription address:** Times Publishing Co. of Wichita Falls, PO Box 120, Wichita Falls, TX 76307**) ED** Don James, (817)767-8346. **Ad Acc. Circ:** 50,000 (ctrl). Documents available from UMI Article Clearinghouse. *Formed by the union of Wichita Falls Record News, 0739-1293 and Wichita Falls Times, 0739-1285.*
Ind/Abst Bus. Dateline (Dec. 29, 1991-) [Full Txt.].

US/1065-2876
TODAY CEDAR HILL. (199?)-. Newspaper. English. wk. $21.00. Today Newspapers, 1701 North Hampton Road, Suite A, Desoto TX 75115. **Tel** (214)298-4211, FAX (214)298-6369. **ED** Phil Major. **Photos. Ad Acc, Adv Mgr:** Leslie Nasche. Full Page (B&W) $844.20. Half Page (B&W) $422.10. Full Page (Color) $1,194.20. Half Page (Color) $772.10. **Pub. Size:** Broadsheet. **Circ:** 3,024. *Continues Cedar Hill Chronicle, 1049-3433.*

●**US/1065-0644**
TODAY LANCASTER. VFOAT Lancaster Today. (1992)-. Newspaper. English. wk. $21.00. Today Newspapers, 1701 North Hampton Road, Suite A, Desoto TX 75115. **Tel** (214)298-4211, FAX (214)298-6369. **ED** Phil Major. **Photos. Ad Acc, Adv Mgr:** Leslie Nasche. Full Page (B&W) $844.20. Half Page (B&W) $422.10. Full Page (Color) $1,194.20. Half Page (Color) $772.10. **Pub. Size:** Broadsheet. **Circ:** 2,700. *Continues Lancaster News (Lancaster, Tex.), 1049-3441.*

US/8750-619X
TOMBALL SUN, THE. (198?)-. Newspaper. English. wk. Free. Tomball Sun, 990 Village Square/Suite Q, Tomball TX 77375-4260. **Tel** (713)351-7218. **ED** Paul Hyde. **Photos. Ad Acc, Adv Mgr:** Lindsay Lewis. Full Page (B&W) $962.00. Half Page (B&W) $521.00. Full Page (Color) $1162.00. Half Page (Color) $721.00. **Pub. Size:** Broadsheet. available in microform.

US
TRINITY STANDARD, THE. VFOAT Trinity Standard-Lovelady Star. Began in July 1938?. Newspaper. English. wk. Trinity Standard, PO Box 712, Trinity TX 75862. *Continues Trinity Standard The Lovelady Star.*

US
TULIA HERALD, THE. Began in 1910?. Newspaper. English. wk (Thursdays). $15.00 Swisher County; $18.00 other. Tulia Herald, PO Drawer 87, Tulia TX 79088. **Tel** (806)995-3535.

US
TYLER COURIER-TIMES, THE. VFOAT Tyler Courier Times; Sunday Courier-Times-Telegraph. Vol. 58, (Mar. 3, 1936)-. Newspaper. English. da. TB Butler Publishing Company, PO Box 2030, Tyler TX 75702. **Tel** (214)597-8111. *Continues Tyler Daily Courier Times.*

US
TYLER COURIER-TIMES-TELEGRAPH. VFOAT Tyler Courier Times Telegraph. (1931)-. Newspaper. English. wk. Price varies from $69.00 to $129.00 (according to zip code). TB Butler Publishing Company, PO Box 2030, Tyler TX 75702. **Tel** (214)597-8111. **ED** Nelson Clyde. **Circ:** 48,825.

US
TYLER MORNING TELEGRAPH. VFOAT Tyler Telegraph. Began in 1877?. Newspaper. English. da. Tyler Morning Telegraph, PO Box 2030, Tyler TX 75710.

US
TYLER WEEKLY COURIER-TIMES. VFOAT Tyler Weekly Courier-Times. (1877)-. Newspaper. English. wk. TB Butler Publishing Company, PO Box 2030, Tyler TX 75702. **Tel** (903)597-8111.

US
UNIVERSITY DAILY, THE. Vol. 42, No. 1 (Sept. 20, 1966)-. Newspaper. English. da. $48.00. Texas Tech University / Texas, Box 43081, Lubbock TX 79409. **Tel** (806)742-3388, FAX (806)742-2434. **ED** Kristi Davis, Michelle Elizardo (Managing Editor). **Bk Rev. Photos. Ad Acc, Adv Mgr:** Susan Peterson. Full Page (B&W) $1600.20. Half Page (B&W) $800.10. **Pub. Size:** Broadsheet. **Wire Svcs.:** AP. **Circ:** 17,000 (ctrl). *Continues Daily Toreador.*

US
UVALDE LEADER-NEWS. VFOAT Uvalde Leader News. Began in 1901. Newspaper. English. wk. Uvalde Leader-News, PO Box 740, Uvalde TX 78801. *Formed by the union of Uvalde News and Uvalde Leader.*

US
VALLEY MORNING STAR. VFOAT Valley Sunday Star-Monitor-Herald. (1929)-. Newspaper. English. da. $78.00 (Monday through Sturday), $69.00 (Monday through Friday), $90.00 (Daily and Sunday). Freedom Communications, 1310 South Commerce St, Box 511, Harlingen TX 78550. **Tel** (210)423-5511. Each issue contains an index to its own contents (no volume index)--loose.

US
VALLEY TRIBUNE, THE. Vol. 9, No. 1 (June 13, 1968)-. Newspaper. English. wk. $17.00. Valley Tribune, PO Box 478, Quitaque TX 79255. **ED** Eunice McFull. **Photos. Ad Acc, Adv Mgr:** Eunice McFull, **Tel** (806)455-1101. Full Page (B&W) $246.50. Half Page (B&W) $173.25. **Circ:** 900.

US
VAN HORN ADVOCATE. (19??)-. Newspaper. English. Fifty-two times a year. $20.00. Van Horn Advocate, PO Box 8, Van Horn TX 79855. **Tel** (915)283-2003. **ED** Larry Simpson, Dawn Simpson (Managing Editor). **Photos. Ad Acc.** Full Page (B&W) $300.00. Half Page (B&W) $178.35. Full Page (Color) $385.00. Half Page (Color) $263.35. **Pub. Size:** Standard. **Circ:** 1,000. available in microform from Southwest Micropublishing International.

US
VICTORIA ADVOCATE (VICTORIA, TEX. : DAILY). (VICTORIA ADVOCATE.). (1897)-. Newspaper. English. da. $102.00 (daily & Sunday by mail). Victoria Advocate, PO Box 2393, Victoria TX 77901. **Tel** (512)575-1451. **ED** James W. Rech and Vince Reedy. **Bk Rev. Ad Acc. Circ:** 36,000 (ctrl). available on microfilm. Documents available from UMI Article Clearinghouse. *Continues Daily Advocate (Victoria, Tex. : 1897).*
Ind/Abst Bus. Dateline (Dec. 20, 1991-) [Full Txt.].

US/0746-6838
VINDICATOR (LIBERTY, TEX.). (THE VINDICATOR.). (19??)-. Newspaper. English. sw. The Vindicator / Department of Circulation, PO Box 9189, Liberty TX 77575. **Tel** (409)336-3611. **ED** Ernie E. Zieschang. **Ad Acc. Circ:** 6,000. *Continues Liberty Vindicator.*

US/0733-1460
VISION (SAN ANTONIO, TEX.). (VISION.). Periodical. English (Spanish). Three times a year. PO Box 28185, San Antonio TX 78228.

US
VOZ DE HOUSTON, LA. (1980)-. Newspaper. Spanish. Fifty-two times a year. $25.00. La Voz de Houston, 7819 Easton Street, Houston TX 77017. **Tel** (713)644-7449, FAX (713)644-9790. **Ad Acc, Adv Mgr:** Jorge Duarte, **Tel** (713)644-7449. **Circ:** 50,000 (ctrl).

US
WACO CITIZEN, THE. VFOAT Waco Citizen and The Lavega Citizen. (1934)-. Newspaper. English. sw. $24.00. Waco Citizen, 1020 North 25th Street, Waco TX 76707. **Tel** (817)754-3511, FAX (817)754-3541. **ED** Andrea Saade. **Bk Rev,** (Qty: 104). **Photos. Ad Acc, Adv Mgr:** Sharon Witcowski. Full Page (B&W) $512.00. Half Page (B&W) $324.00. Full Page (Color) $602.00. Half Page (Color) $384.00. **Wire Svcs.:** KF. available in microform. *Absorbed Texas Citizen and Waco News-Citizen.*

US
WACO MESSENGER, THE. Newspaper. English. wk. Waco Messenger, PO Box 2087, Waco TX 76703.

US
WACO TRIBUNE-HERALD. VFOAT Waco Tribune Herald. Vol. 21, No. 19 (Dec. 26, 1948)-. Newspaper. English. da. $162.29 (daily & Sunday), $108.74 (Saturday & Sunday), $120.88 (daily through Friday). Waco Tribune-Herald, PO Box 2588, Waco TX 76702. **Tel** (817)757-5757. **ED** Robert V. Lott. **Bk Rev. Ad Acc, Adv Mgr:** Bob Nay. **Circ:** 45,312 daily, 61,107 Sunday. available on microfilm. Documents available from UMI Article Clearinghouse. *Continues Waco Sunday Tribune-Herald; Absorbed Waco News-Tribune; Waco Times-Herald.*
Ind/Abst Bus. Dateline (Jan. 12, 1992-) [Full Txt.].

US/0896-0291
WAXAHACHIE DAILY LIGHT, THE. VFOAT Daily Light. Began in 1894?. Newspaper. English. da. Waxahachie Daily Light, 200 West Marvin, Waxahachie TX 75165.

US
WEATHERFORD DEMOCRAT (WEATHERFORD, TX). (WEATHERFORD DEMOCRAT.). Newspaper. English. da. Weatherford Democrat, 512 Palo Pinto Street, Weatherford TX 76086. **Tel** (817)594-7447. **ED** Tim Wood. **Circ:** 6,891 daily, 7,131 Sunday. *Continues Plain Texan and Weatherford Democrat.*

US
WEEKLY MESSENGER (JEWETT, TEX.). (THE WEEKLY MESSENGER.). VFOAT Messenger. Began in 1885?. Newspaper. English. wk. Weekly Messenger, PO Box 155, Jewett TX 75846.

US
WEEKLY MINEOLA MONITOR, THE. *Title Change.* VFOAT Mineola Weekly Monitor. (1877?)-?. Newspaper. English. wk. Weekly Mineola Monitor, PO Box 210, Mineola TX 75773. *Formed by the union of Mineola Hawkeye. Continued by Mineola Monitor.*

Texas

US
WELLINGTON LEADER (WELLINGTON, TEX.). (THE WELLINGTON LEADER.). Began in 1909?. Newspaper. English. wk. Wellington Leader, 913 West Avenue, Wellington TX 79095.

US
WEST NEWS, THE. Began in 1890?. Newspaper. English. wk. West News, 214 West Oak, West TX 76691.

US
WESTERN OBSERVER (ANSON, TEX.: 1945). (THE WESTERN OBSERVER.). Vol. 62, No. 1 (March 29, 1945)-. Newspaper. English. wk. $28.20. Western Observer, PO Box 792, Anson TX 79501. **Tel** (915)823-3253. *Formed by the union of Jones County Observer and Western-Enterprise.*

US/1076-7266
WHARTON JOURNAL-SPECTATOR, THE. VFOAT Wharton Journal Spectator. Vol. 85, No. 1 (May 12, 1974)-. Newspaper. English. sw. $26.00 in county; $42.00 others. Wharton Journal-Spectator, 115 West Burleson, Wharton TX 77488. **Tel** (409)532-8840, FAX (409)532-8845. **ED** Larry C. Jackson (Editor-in-Chief) and Ronald K. Sanders (Managing Editor). **Photos. Ad Acc, Adv Mgr:** Missy Justice. Full Page (B&W) $677.25. Half Page (B&W) $330.75. Full Page (Color) $977.25. Half Page (Color) $630.75. **Pub. Size:** Broadsheet. **Circ:** 4,695. *Formed by the union of Wharton Journal and Wharton Spectator.*

US
WHEELER TIMES, THE. Vol. 1, No. 1 (Dec. 21, 1933)-. Newspaper. English. wk. Wheeler Times, PO Box 1080, Wheeler TX 79096.

US/1049-3387
WHITE ROCKER (1990), THE. (THE WHITE ROCKER.). (1990)-. Newspaper. English. Fifty times a year. $15.00 one year; $25.00 two years; $35.00 three years. White Rocker, PO Box 180698, Dallas TX 75218. **Tel** (214)327-9335. **ED** Retta Hanie. **Bk Rev. Ad Acc, Adv Mgr:** Frances, **Tel** (214)327-9336. **Circ:** 5,000. *Continues White Rocker News.*

US
WHITESBORO NEWS-RECORD. VFOAT Whitesboro News Record. (19??)-. Newspaper. English. wk. $15.00. Whitesboro News-Record, PO Box 68, Whitesboro TX 76273. **Tel** (903)564-3565, FAX (903)564-9655. **ED** Jim Davison, Xina Davison (Managing Editor). **Photos. Ad Acc.** Full Page (B&W) $504.00. Half Page (B&W) $252.00. Full Page (Color) $589.00. Half Page (Color) $337.00. **Pub. Size:** Standard. **Circ:** 2,900. available in microform. *Formed by the union of Whitesboro News and Whitesboro Record.*

US
WHITEWRIGHT SUN, THE. VFOAT Sun. (1??)-. Newspaper. English. wk. $15.00. The Whitewright Sun, PO Box 218, 121 Grand Avenue, Whitewright TX 75491. **ED** Clarc Combs. **Bk Rev** (Qty: 12). **Photos. Ad Acc, Adv Mgr:** Clara Combs, **Tel** (903)364-2276. Full Page (B&W) $250.00. Half Page (B&W) $150.00. Full Page (Color) $350.00. Half Page (Color) $250.00. **Pub. Size:** Standard. **Circ:** 1,000. available in microform.

US
WHITNEY MESSENGER, THE. (1983)-. Newspaper. English. wk. $10.00 Hill County; $13.00 Texas; $15.00 US. Whitney Messenger, PO Box 1195, Whitney TX 76692. **Tel** (817)694-3713, FAX (817)694-3522.

US
WILLIAMSON COUNTY SUN, THE. VFOAT Sunday Sun. Vol. 1, No. 1 (May 19, 1877)-. Newspaper. English. sw (104 per year - published Wed. and Sun.). $28.00 Williamson County; $43.00 other. Williamson County Sun, PO Box 39, Georgetown TX 78627-0039. **Tel** (512)930-4824, FAX (512)863-2474. **ED** Brian Pearson. **Bk Rev, (Qty: 5). Photos. Ad Acc, Adv Mgr:** Mike Winton. Full Page (B&W) $617.40. Half Page (B&W) $349.65. Full Page (Color) $842.40. Half Page (Color) $482.40. **Pub. Size:** Broadsheet. **Circ:** 7,000. available in microform.

US
WINK BULLETIN. Began in 1935?. Bulletin. English. wk. Wink Bulletin, PO Box 697, Wink TX 79789.

US/1048-2997
WINKLER COUNTY NEWS, THE. Began in 1936?. Newspaper. English. wk. Winkler County News, 109 South Poplar Street, Kermit TX 79745.

US/8755-948X
WINNSBORO NEWS (WINNSBORO, TEX. : 1908). (THE WINNSBORO NEWS.). Began with Sept. 24, 1908 issue. Newspaper. English. wk. Winnsboro News, PO Box 87, Winnsboro TX 75494. *Absorbed Winnsboro Wide-Awake; Winnsboro Free Press.*

US
WINTERS ENTERPRISE, THE. Began in 1904?. Newspaper. English. wk. Winters Enterprise, PO Box 37, Winters TX 79567.

US/0746-8679
WISE COUNTY MESSENGER. (1880)-. Newspaper. English. sw. Wise County Messenger, PO Box 149, Decatur TX 76234. **Tel** (817)627-5987. *Continues Paradise Messenger; Absorbed Decatur News (Decatur, Tex. : 1881).*

US/0746-536X
WOLFE CITY MIRROR, THE. (19??)-. Newspaper. English. wk. Wolfe City Mirror, PO Drawer F, Wolfe City TX 75496.

US
WOODSMAN. Vol. 1, No. 1 (April 24, 1980). Newspaper. English. wk. Woodsman, PO Box 339, Woodville TX 75979.

US
WYLIE NEWS, THE. (1948)-. Newspaper. English. wk. Wylie News, PO Box 369, Wylie TX 75098.

US/0883-3133 **Y**
WEEKLY, THE. VFOAT Yweekly. Vol. 1, No. 1 (Sept. 21, 1983)-. Newspaper. English. wk. $15.00 Hays and Travis County, Texas; $18.00 other. The Y Weekly, 5321 Industrial Oaks Boulevard/#126, Austin TX 73735-3324. **Tel** (512)892-5250. **ED** Maryanne Mariotti. **Ad Acc. Circ:** 2,000 (ctrl). **Desc:** Community newspaper serving the Southwest Metropolitan area of Austin, Texas. Government, business, school and general news coverage.

US
ZAVALA COUNTY SENTINEL (LA PRYOR, TEX. : 1913). (ZAVALA COUNTY SENTINEL.). Began in 1913. Newspaper. English. wk. $15.50. Zavala County Sentinel, PO Drawer G, Crystal City TX 78839. **Tel** (512)374-3465. **ED** M Dale Barker. **Bk Rev. Ad Acc. Circ:** 2,300 (ctrl). available on microfilm.

UTAH

US/0896-3312
BEAVER COUNTY NEWS (MILFORD, UTAH : 1956). (THE BEAVER COUNTY NEWS.). Began in 1956. Newspaper. English. wk. Beaver County News, PO Box 369, Milford UT 84751. *Continues Milford News.*

US
BEAVER PRESS, THE. Vol. 24, No. 29 (June 8, 1928)-. Newspaper. English. wk. $14.00 Beaver County; $17.00 US. AC Saunders, PO Box 351, 40 East Center Street, Beaver UT 84713. **Tel** (801)438-2891. *Continues Beaver City Press.*

US/0892-225X
BOX ELDER NEWS JOURNAL (1986). (BOX ELDER NEWS JOURNAL.). Vol. 79, No. 36 (Sept. 3, 1986)-. Newspaper. English. wk (Wed. & Sat.). Box Elder News & Journal, PO Box 370, Brigham City UT 84302. **Tel** (801)723-3471. *Formed by the union of Box Elder News (Brigham City, Utah : 1949) and Box Elder Journal (Brigham City, Utah : 1949).*

US/8750-4677
CITIZEN (AMERICAN FORK, UTAH). (CITIZEN.). Vol. 1, No. 23 (June 21, 1979)-. Newspaper. English. wk (published on Wednesdays). $24.00 Utah County; $30.00 other US; $36.00 other. Newtah News Group, PO Box 7, American Fork UT 84003. **Tel** (801)756-7669, FAX (801)756-5274. **ED** Marc Haddock. **Ad Acc, Adv Mgr:** Brett Brezzant. **Circ:** 4,600. *Continues American Fork Citizen.*

US/0891-2777
DAILY HERALD (PROVO, UTAH. 1939), THE. (THE DAILY HERALD.). VFOAT Sunday Herald. 53rd Year, No. 224 (May 22, 1939)-. Newspaper. English. da. $144.00. Provo Herald, c/o Kirk Parkinson, 1555 No. Freedom Blvd., Box 717, Provo UT 84603. **Tel** (801)373-5050, FAX (801)377-2408. **ED** Paul Richards. **Bk Rev, (Qty: 10-20). Photos. Ad Acc, Adv Mgr:** Mike Stausfield. Full Page (B&W) $2093.67. Half Page (B&W) $1046.84. Full Page (Color) $2383.67. Half Page (Color) $1336.84. **Pub. Size:** Broadsheet. **Wire Svcs.:** KR, AP. **Circ:** 32,395 paid evenings, 33,607 Sunday (ctrl). available on microfilm. *Continues Evening Herald (Provo, Utah); Absorbed Sunday Herald (Provo, Utah).* **Desc:** News, advertising and features.

US/0747-0010
DAILY SPECTRUM (CEDAR CITY, UTAH), THE. (THE DAILY SPECTRUM.). VFOAT Daily Spectrum, Iron County Record; Spectrum; Iron County Record. Vol. 3, No. 259 (Mar. 27, 1983)-. Newspaper. English. da. $120.00 Utah; $144.00 other. Daily Spectrum, PO Box 1630, St. George UT 84771. **Tel** (801)673-3511. *Continues Cedar City Spectrum.*

US/0745-6611
DAILY SPECTRUM (SAINT GEORGE, UTAH), THE. (THE DAILY SPECTRUM.). VFOAT Spectrum. Vol. 21, No. 53 (March 27, 1983)-. Newspaper. English. da. $120.00 Utah; $144.00 other. Daily Spectrum, PO Box 1630, St. George UT 84771. **Tel** (801)673-3511. *Continues Spectrum (Saint George, Utah), 0890-8877.*

US
DAVIS COUNTY CLIPPER. V. 2, No. 9 (April 29, 1892)-. Newspaper. English. sw. Davis County Clipper, PO Box 267, Bountiful UT 84010. *Continues Little Clipper.*

US/0745-4724
DESERET NEWS (SALT LAKE CITY, UTAH : 1964). (DESERET NEWS.). VFOAT Sunday Deseret News. Vol. 362, No. 32 (August 6, 1964)-. Newspaper. English. da. Newspaper Agency Corporation, 143 South Main Street, Salt Lake City UT 84110. **Tel** (801)237-2950, FAX (801)237-2121. **ED** Don Woodward. **Bk Rev. Photos. Ad Acc, Adv Mgr:** Ed McCaffrey, **Tel** (801)237-2712. **Pub. Size:** Broadsheet. **Wire Svcs.:** RN, NY, AP. *Continues Deseret News. Salt Lake Telegram.*

US
EAGLE NEWSPAPERS. (19??)-. Newspaper. English. wk. $25.00. Eagle Newspapers Inc., PO Box 57187, Murray UT 84157. **Tel** (801)262-6682. *Continues Green Sheet.*

US/0747-2129
EMERY COUNTY PROGRESS (1977). (EMERY COUNTY PROGRESS.). Vol. 78, No. 39 (Sept. 29, 1977)-. Newspaper. English. wk. Emery County Progress, PO Box 589, Castle Dale UT 84513. *Continues Emery County Progress-Leader.*

US
EPHRAIM ENTERPRISE (EPHRAIM, UTAH : 1981). (THE EPHRAIM ENTERPRISE.). VFOAT Messenger-Enterprise. Vol. 89, No. 21 (Feb. 19, 1981)-. Newspaper. English. wk. PO Box 4-12, Ephraim UT 84627. **Tel** (801)835-4241. **ED** Max E Call. **Circ:** 800. *Continues Enterprise (Ephraim, Utah).*

US
EUREKA REPORTER, THE. Vol. 4, No. 3 (Nov. 20, 1903)-. Newspaper. English. wk. $12.00 Juab County; $15.50 other. Reporter Publishing Co, PO Box 150, Eureka UT 84628. **Tel** (801)489-5651. *Continues Eureka Weekly Reporter.*

US/1064-7309
GARFIELD COUNTY NEWS (TROPIC, UTAH). (GARFIELD COUNTY NEWS.). (April 16, 1920)-. Newspaper. English. Fifty-two times a year. $16.00 Utah, $21.00 other. Garfield County News, PO Box 127, Tropic UT 84776. **Tel** (801)679-8730, FAX (801)679-8847. **ED** Nancy Twitchell. **Ad Acc. Circ:** 2,000.

US/8750-7684
GRANTSVILLE GAZETTE. VFOAT Gazette. Vol. 1, No. 1 (Oct. 5, 1983)-. Newspaper. English. wk. $18.00. Grantsville Gazette, PO Box 800, Grantsville UT 84029. **Tel** (801)884-6224. **ED** Mary S Thornton. **Ad Acc. Circ:** 1,000. **Desc:** Covers community news.

US
GUNNISON VALLEY NEWS, THE. Vol. 20, No. 29 (May 2, 1919)-. Newspaper. English. wk. $15.00 Utah; $18.00 other. Gunnison Valley News, PO Box 187, Gunnison UT 84634. **Tel** (801)528-3111. *Continues Gunnison Gazette.*

US
HERALD-JOURNAL, THE. VFOAT Herald Journal. Vol. 22, No. 182 (Aug. 5, 1931)-. Newspaper. English. da (Except Sat.). Herald-Journal / Utah, PO Box 487, Logan UT 84321. **Tel** (801)752-2121. *Continues Daily Herald and Journal.*

US/0747-1416
LEADER (TREMONTON, UTAH), THE. (THE LEADER.). VFOAT Leader-Garland Times; Leader-The Garland Times. Vol. 63, No. 6 (Dec. 7, 1983)-. Newspaper. English. Fifty-two times a year (Wed.). The Leader Publishing Company, PO Box 127, Tremonton UT 84337. **Tel** (801)257-5182. *Continues Leader, The Garland Times.*

US/8750-4669
LEHI FREE PRESS. VFOAT Lehi Free Press and the Lehi Sun; Free Press. Vol. 8, No. 19 (Aug. 25, 1932)-. Newspaper. English. Fifty-two times a year (Wed.). American Fork / Lehi Free Press, PO Box 7, American Fork UT 84003. **Tel** (801)756-7669. *Continues Myton Free Press; Absorbed Lehi Sun.*

US
MAGNA TIMES (MAGNA, UTAH : 1982). (THE MAGNA TIMES.). Vol. 68, No. 9 (Jan. 21, 1982)-. Newspaper. English. wk. Magna Times, Magna UT 84044. *Continues West Mountain Times.*

US
MANTI MESSENGER (MANTI, UTAH : 1981). (THE MANTI MESSENGER.). **VFOAT** Messenger-Enterprise. Vol. 95, No. 34 (Feb. 19, 1981)-. Newspaper. English. wk. $16.00 (1 year) Manti, UT; $19.00 (1 year), $35.00 (2 year), $53.00 (3 year) other. Manti Messenger, 35 South Main Street, Manti UT 84642. **Tel** (801)835-4241, FAX (801)835-1493. **ED** Max Call. **Ad Acc. Circ:** 900 (ctrl). ***Continues*** *Messenger (Manti, Utah : 1978).*

US/8750-3093
MILLARD COUNTY CHRONICLE PROGRESS. VFOAT Millard County Chronicle-Progress; Chronicle Progress. Vol. 75, No. 9 (Sept. 6, 1984)-. Newspaper. English (Spanish). wk (52 issues). $30.00 (Millard County), $30.00 other. Duwil Publishers, PO Box 249, Delta UT 84624. **Tel** (801)864-2400. **ED** Susan B. Dutson. **Ad Acc. Circ:** 5,000. ***Formed by the union of*** *Millard County Chronicle* ***and*** *Millard County Progress (Fillmore, Utah : 1982).*
Desc: Information of general interest to residents of Millard County Utah.

US
MILLARD COUNTY GAZETTE, THE. VFOAT Gazette. (1978)-. Newspaper. English. wk. $88.00. Millard County Gazette, PO Box 908, Fillmore UT 84631. **Tel** (801)743-6983.

US
MORGAN COUNTY NEWS. (Oct. 26, 1923)-. Newspaper. English. wk. $20.00 Utah; $25.00 other. Morgan County News, PO Box 190, Morgan UT 84050. **Tel** (801)829-3451.

US
MURRAY EAGLE. VFOAT Eagle. Vol. 37, No. 32 (Jan. 26, 1928)-. Newspaper. English. wk. Murray Eagle, PO Box 7187, Murray UT 84107. ***Continues*** *Murray Eagle and Midvale Journal.*

US
OREM-GENEVA TIMES. VFOAT Orem Geneva Times. (1932)-. Newspaper. English. wk. $10.00 Utah; $18.00 other. Orem Geneva Times, PO Box 65, Orem UT 84057. **Tel** (801)225-1340.

US/0745-9483
PARK RECORD (1964), THE. (THE PARK RECORD.). (July 9, 1964)-. Newspaper. English. Fifty-two times a year (Thursdays). $18.00 Summit County Utah; $33.00 other. Park Record, PO Box 3688, Park City UT 84060. **Tel** (801)649-9014. **ED** Teri Orr (phone: (801)649-9014). **Bk Rev. Ad Acc, Adv Mgr:** Pamela Hamsworth, **Tel** (801)649-9014. ctrl circ. ***Continues in part*** *Summit County Bee and Park Record;* ***Absorbed*** *Newspaper (Park City, Utah).*

US/8755-9072
PLEASANT GROVE REVIEW. VFOAT Review. (1912)-. Newspaper. English. wk (Published on Wednesdays). $24.00 Utah County; $30.00 other US; $36.00 other. Newtah News Group, PO Box 7, American Fork UT 84003. **Tel** (801)756-7669, FAX (801756-5274. **ED** Marc Haddock. **Ad Acc, Adv Mgr:** Brett Brezzant. **Circ:** 2,300.

US
PYRAMID (MOUNT PLEASANT, UTAH). (THE PYRAMID.). Vol. 86, No. 43 (Oct. 26, 1978)-. Newspaper. English. Fifty-two times a year. $18.00 Sanpete County; $21.00 other. The Pyramid, 90 West Main, Mount Pleasant UT 84647. **Tel** (801)489-5651. **ED** Penny Hamilton (49 West Main, Mt. Pleasant, UT 84647; telephone: (801)462-2134). **Ad Acc. Circ:** 2,500. ***Continues*** *Mt. Pleasant Pyramid.*

US/0746-6730
RICHFIELD REAPER, THE. Vol. 12, No. 19 (Mar. 22, 1899)-. Newspaper. English. Fifty-two times a year (Wed.). $20.00 Sevier, Wayne, Piute and South Sanpete counties in Utah; $27.00 other. The Richfield Reaper, PO Box 730, Richfield UT 84701. **Tel** (801)896-5476. **ED** Hal Edwards. **Bk Rev. Ad Acc, Adv Mgr Tel** same as publisher. **Circ:** 5,700. ***Continues*** *Richfield Advocate;* ***Absorbed*** *Sevier Sun; Piute County News.*

US
SALINA SUN (SALINA, UTAH : 1918). (THE SALINA SUN.). (1918)-. Newspaper. English. wk. Salina Sun, 60 East Main Street, Salina UT 84654.

US/0746-3502
SALT LAKE TRIBUNE (SALT LAKE CITY, UTAH : 1890). (THE SALT LAKE TRIBUNE.). Vol. 38, No. 115 (Feb. 25, 1890)-. Newspaper. English. da. $112.36 (daily and Sunday by carrier), $80.12 (daily by carrier); $96.00 (daily), $144.00 (daily and Sunday) $90.00 (Sunday) Utah, Idaho, Nevada and Wyoming; $180.00 (daily), $276.00 (daily and Sunday), $108.00 (Sunday) other. The Salt Lake Tribune, 143 South Main, Salt Lake City UT 84111. **Tel** (801)237-2800. **ED** Will Fehr. **Bk Rev. Ad Acc. Circ:** 111,730, 141,422 (Sunday) (ctrl). ***Continues*** *Salt Lake Daily Tribune.*
Ind/Abst PROMT.

US/0894-3273
SAN JUAN RECORD (1953), THE. (THE SAN JUAN RECORD.). **VFOAT** San Juan Record and Dove Creek Press. Vol. 37, No. 9 (April 2, 1953)-. Newspaper. English. wk. $11.00 in county; $12.00 others. San Juan Record, 937 East Highway 666, PO Box 879, Monticello UT 84535. **Tel** (801)587-2277. **ED** Joyce A. Martin and Bill Boyle (Managing Editor). **Bk Rev,** (Qty: 3 or 4). **Photos. Ad Acc, Adv Mgr:** Bill Boyle. Full Page (B&W) $268.80. Half Page (B&W) $134.40. Full Page (Color) $368.80. Half Page (Color) $234.40. **Pub. Size:** Tabloid. **Circ:** 2,400 (ctrl). ***Continues in part*** *Dove Creek Press and San Juan Record.*

US/0049-1659
SOUTHERN UTAH NEWS. Vol. 22, No. 2 (Nov. 5, 1953)-. Newspaper. English. wk. $22.00. Southern Utah News, 40 East Center Street, Kanab UT 84741. **ED** Dixie Brunner. **Bk Rev. Ad Acc. Circ:** 1,900. ***Continues*** *Kane County Standard.*

US/0892-435X
SPANISH FORK PRESS, THE. VFOAT Press. Vol. 1, No. 1 (Jan. 23, 1902)-. Newspaper. English. wk. $15.00 residents of Spanish Fork; $18.00 other. Spanish Fork Press, 280 North Main Street, PO Box 365, Spanish Fork UT 84660. **Tel** (801)798-2100.

US
SPRINGVILLE HERALD (SPRINGVILLE, UTAH). (THE SPRINGVILLE HERALD.). **VFOAT** Springville Herald and the Springville Beacon. Vol. 35 No. 35 (Feb. 29, 1924)-. Newspaper. English. Fifty-two times a year. $18.00 Utah County; $21.00 others. Springville Herald, 161 South Main Street, Springville UT 84663. **Tel** (801)489-5651, FAX (801)489-7021. **ED** Pat Conover (Editor-in-Chief) and Martin Conover (Managing Editor). **Bk Rev. Photos. Ad Acc, Adv Mgr:** Martin Conover. Full Page (B&W) $150.00. Full Page (Color) $250.00. **Pub. Size:** Standard. available in microform. ***Continues*** *Springville Herald-Beacon.*

US
STANDARD-EXAMINER, THE. VFOAT Ogden Standard Examiner; Standard-Examiner. 50th Year, No. 82 (Apr. 5, 1920)-. Newspaper. English. da. $9.85. Ogden Publishing Corporation, PO Box 951, Ogden UT 84404. **Tel** (801)625-4200, FAX (801)625-4508. **ED** Ron Thornburg. **LC** 9940. **Ad Acc, Adv Mgr:** Brad Roghaar, **Tel** (801)625-4310. Full Page (B&W) $3551.37. Half Page (B&W) $1775.69. Full Page (Color) $3896.37. Half Page (Color) $2120.69. **Pub. Size:** Broadsheet. **Wire Svcs.:** AP, SH. **Circ:** 51,889 daily, 54,227 Sunday. available on an online database (file 635/Full-Text) from DIALOG; available in microform from Western Micrographics. Documents available from UMI Article Clearinghouse. ***Formed by the union of*** *Ogden Standard (Ogden, Utah : 1913)* ***and*** *Ogden Examiner.*
Ind/Abst Bus. Dateline (Dec. 13, 1991-) [Full Txt.].

US
SUMMIT COUNTY BEE (COALVILLE, UTAH : 1964). (SUMMIT COUNTY BEE.). Vol. 31, No. 28 (July 9, 1964)-. Newspaper. English. wk. Summit County Bee, PO Box 7, Coalville UT 84017. ***Continues in part*** *Summit County Bee and Park Record.*

US
SUN-ADVOCATE, THE. VFOAT Sun Advocate. Vol. 37, No. 49 (Dec. 8, 1932)-. Newspaper. English. Twice a week. $32.00. Sun-Advocate, PO Box 870, Price UT 84501. **ED** Lynnda Johnson. **Photos. Ad Acc, Adv Mgr:** Bonnie Johnson. **Pub. Size:** Broadsheet. ***Formed by the union of*** *Sun (Price, Utah)* ***and*** *News-Advocate (Price, Utah);* ***Absorbed*** *Sun Journal (Price, Utah).*

US
TOOELE TRANSCRIPT-BULLETIN. VFOAT Tooele Transcript Bulletin; Transcript-Bulletin. 91st Year, No. 7 (July 9, 1985)-. Newspaper. English. ir (104 issues, published on Tues. and Thurs.). $34.00. Tooele Transcript Bulletin, 58 North Main, Tooele UT 84074. **Tel** (801)355-6525, FAX (801)882-6123. **ED** David Bern. **Ad Acc, Adv Mgr:** Clayton Dunn, **Tel** (801)882-0050. ***Formed by the union of*** *Tooele Bulletin (Tooele, Utah : 1957)* ***and*** *Tooele Transcript (Tooele, Utah : 1957).*

US
UINTAH BASIN STANDARD, THE. Vol. 1, No. 1 (Jan. 3, 1957)-. Newspaper. English. wk. Uintah Basin Standard, PO Box 370, Roosevelt UT 84066. ***Formed by the union of*** *Roosevelt Standard* ***and*** *Uintah Basin Record.*

US
UTAH COUNTY JOURNAL. (19??)-. Newspaper. English. sw. Oldham Associates, 500 W 1200 Street, Orem UT 84058. **Tel** (801)226-1983.

US/0892-1091
VERNAL EXPRESS. VFOAT Vernal Express/Advertiser; Vernal Express Advertiser. Vol. 1, No. 1 (Feb. 11, 1892)-. Newspaper. English. Fifty-two times a year (Wed.). Vernal Express, 54 North Vernal Avenue, PO Box 1000, Vernal UT 84078. **Tel** (801)879-3511. **LC** 9951. ***Continues*** *Uintah Papoose.*

US
WASATCH WAVE, THE. Vol. 1, No. 1 (Mar. 23, 1889)-. Newspaper. English. wk. $31.00. Wasatch Area Voices Express, PO Box 1673, Ogden UT 84402. **Tel** (801)621-7926. **ED** R. W. Hicken. **Circ:** 2,950.
Desc: A newspaper for Weber State University and the Ogden community.

VERMONT

US/0894-8844
BURLINGTON FREE PRESS (1923), THE. (THE BURLINGTON FREE PRESS.). **VFOAT** Burlington Daily Free Press; Burlington Free Press and Times; Burlington (Vt.) Free Press. Vol. 89, No. 129 (May 30, 1923)-. Newspaper. English. da. $234.00 (daily & Sunday), $156.00 (daily), $78.00 (Sunday only) Vermont; $286.00 (daily & Sunday), $192.00 (daily), $94.00 (Sunday only) others. Burlington Free Press, 191 College Street, PO Box 10, Burlington VT 05402-0010. **Tel** (802)863-3441. **ED** Ronald L. Thornberg. **Circ:** 56,971 daily, 63,067 Sunday. available on microfilm from Graphic Microfilm Division. ***Continues*** *Burlington Daily Free Press.*

US/1054-3716
CALEDONIAN-RECORD (SAINT JOHNSBURY, VT.). (THE CALEDONIAN-RECORD.). **VFOAT** Caledonian Record; Evening Caledonian; Newport Record; Evening Caledonian and Newport Record; Evening Caledonian-Record. (June 28, 1920)-. Newspaper. English. da (312 issues per year). $128.00. Caledonian Record, PO Box 8, 35 Federal Streeet, St Johnsbury VT 05819. **Tel** (802)748-8121. **ED** Ellie Dixon. **Photos. Ad Acc, Adv Mgr:** George Wollpath. Full Page (B&W) $806.25. Half Page (B&W) $403.13. Full Page (Color) $886.25. Half Page (Color) $483.13. **Pub. Size:** Broadsheet. **Wire Svcs.:** AP, GN. **Circ:** 11,022. ***Continues*** *Evening Caledonian.*

US/0746-438X
CHRONICLE (BARTON, VT.). (THE CHRONICLE.). (19??)-. Newspaper. English. Fifty-one times per year (Except last week of Dec.). $17.00. The Chronicle / Vermont, PO Box O, Barton VT 05822. **Tel** (802)754-2054 or 525-3531. **ED** Chris Braithwaite. **Bk Rev,** (Qty: 6). **Photos. Ad Acc, Adv Mgr:** Ned Andrews. Full Page (B&W) $322.00. Half Page (B&W) $165.60. Full Page (Color) $382.00. Half Page (Color) $225.60. **Pub. Size:** Tabloid. **Circ:** 8,039.

US/0744-5512
HARDWICK GAZETTE, THE. (19??)-. Newspaper. English. wk (Wednesday). $21.00 Vermont; $24.00 others. Hardwick Gazette, PO Box 367, Hardwick VT 05843. **Tel** (802)472-6521. **ED** Ross Connelly. **Bk Rev. Photos. Ad Acc, Adv Mgr:** Susan Javzyna. Full Page (B&W) $661.50. Half Page (B&W) $330.75. **Pub. Size:** Broadsheet. **Pr Rev. Circ:** 3,300. available on microfilm. ***Continues*** *Green Mountain Gazette.*
Desc: Has served Hardwick and the surrounding area since 1889. Recipient of numerous press awards.

US/0746-1674
JOURNAL-OPINION. VFOAT Journal Opinion. Vol. 113 No. 3 (Jan. 18, 1978)-. Newspaper. English. wk. $15.00. Journal Opinion, PO Box 378, Bradford VT 05033. **Tel** (802)222-5281, FAX (802)222-5438. **ED** Robert Huminski, Charles Glazer (Managing Editor). **Bk Rev,** (Qty: 12). **Photos. Ad Acc, Adv Mgr:** James Jung. **Pub. Size:** Broadsheet. **Circ:** 4,500 weekly paid. ***Formed by the union of*** *Journal (Woodsville, N.H.)* ***and*** *United Opinion (Bradford, Vt.).*

US
NEWS & CITIZEN. English. wk. $15.00 (one year). News & Citizen Inc., PO Box 369, Brooklyn Street, Morrisville VT 05661.

US
RUTLAND DAILY HERALD (RUTLAND, VT. : 1885). (RUTLAND DAILY HERALD.). **VFOAT** Rutland Herald. (1885)-. Newspaper. English. da. $201.60. Rutland Herald, 27 Wales Street, PO Box 668, Rutland VT 05701. **Tel** (802)747-6121, FAX (802)775-2423. **Ad Acc.** available on microfilm from University Microfilms International (UMI). ***Continues*** *Rutland Daily Herald and Globe.*

US
ST. ALBANS MESSENGER. VFOAT Saint Albans Messenger. (19??)-. Newspaper. English. da (312 issues per year). $130.00. St Albans Messenger, PO Box 1250, St Albans VT 05478. **Tel** (802)524-9771. ***Continues*** *St. Albans Daily Messenger.*

US
TIMES ARGUS (BARRE, VT.). (THE TIMES ARGUS.). **VFOAT** Barre-Montpelier Times-Argus; Times-Argus; Barre Times-Argus; Sunday Rutland Herald and the Sunday Times Argus. (Aug. 31, 1959)-. Newspaper. English. da. Times Argus, PO Box 707, Barre

VT 05641. available on microfilm from Vermont Public Records Library. ***Formed by the union of*** *Montpelier Evening Argus **and** Barre Daily Times.*

US/0192-5261
VERMONT NEWS GUIDE. (19??)-. Newspaper. English. wk. Vermont News Guide, PO Box 1265, Manchester Center VT 05255.

US
VERMONT STANDARD, THE. Began in 1857?. Newspaper. English. wk. Vermont Standard, PO Box 88, Woodstock VT 05091. available on microfilm from Vermont Public Records Library. ***Continues*** *Vermont Temperance Standard.*

US/0746-2336
WINDSOR CHRONICLE, THE. Newspaper. English. wk. $19.00 in state, $10.50 out of state. Windsor Chronicle, PO Box 8, Windsor VT 05089.

VIRGINIA

US/8750-4987
ALEXANDRIA GAZETTE, THE. ***Title Change.*** Newspaper. English. da. Alexandria Gazette, PO Box 19, Alexandria VA 22314. ***Continued by*** *Alexandria Gazette Packet, 1050-7620.*

US/1050-7620
ALEXANDRIA GAZETTE PACKET. ***Title Change.*** **VFOAT** Gazette Packet. (1987)-(199?). Newspaper. English. wk. Alexandria Gazette, PO Box 19, Alexandria VA 22314. ***Formed by the union of*** *Alexandria Gazette, 8750-4987 **and** Alexandria Packet.* ***Continued by*** *Alexandria Port Gazette Packet, 1066-6273.*

US/0273-639X
ALEXANDRIA JOURNAL (ALEXANDRIA. 1980), THE. (THE ALEXANDRIA JOURNAL.). (1980)-. Newspaper. English. da. $42.00 (one year) $75.00 (two year). Journal Newspapers, 2720 Prosperity Avenue, Springfield VA 22159. **Tel** (703)560-4000. ***Continues*** *Alexandria Journal and Globe, 0199-056X.*

US/1066-6273
ALEXANDRIA PORT GAZETTE PACKET. **VFOAT** Gazette Packet. (199?)-. Newspaper. English. wk. $25.00. Dominion Newspapers, 717 North St. Asaph Street, Alexandria VA 22314-1911. **Tel** (703)549-0004, FAX (703)548-2228. **ED** Christa Walters, Sheila Hill (Managing Editor). **Photos**. **Ad Acc**, **Adv Mgr:** Chrissy Wick, **Tel** (703)838-0302. Full Page (B&W) $1240.00. Half Page (B&W) $625.00. Full Page (Color) $1240.00 plus 20% of ad cost. Half Page (Color) $625.00 plus 20% of ad cost. **Pub. Size:** Tabloid. **Circ:** 20,200. available in microform. ***Formed by the union of*** *Alexandria Gazette Packet, 1050-7620.*

US/8750-0582
ALLEGHANY HIGHLANDER, THE. Newspaper. English. wk. Alleghany Highlander, 505 Loop Street, Clifton Forge VA 24422.

US/0746-1798
AMELIA BULLETIN MONITOR, THE. Bulletin. English. wk. Amelia Bulletin Monitor, PO Box 123, Amelia VA 23002.

US/0273-6381
ARLINGTON JOURNAL (ALEXANDRIA. 1980), THE. (THE ARLINGTON JOURNAL.). (1980)-. Newspaper. English. da. $39.00. Journal Newspapers, 2720 Prosperity Avenue, Springfield VA 22159. **Tel** (703)560-4000. **ED** Richard Starnes. **Circ:** 10,204. ***Continues*** *Arlington Journal and Globe, 0199-0551.*

US/8750-1570
BEDFORD BULLETIN (1984). (BEDFORD BULLETIN.). Vol. 26, No. 22 (Aug. 1, 1984)-. Bulletin. English. wk. $10.00 (county), #12.00 (outside county area). Bedford Bulletin, PO Box 331, Bedford VA 24523-0331. **Tel** (703)586-8612, FAX (703)586-0834. **ED** Rebecca Clause. **Ad Acc**. **Circ:** 8,600. ***Continues*** *Bedford Bulletin-Democrat.*

US/0890-0809
BEE (DANVILLE, VA.). (THE BEE.). Began with Jan. 25, 1899 issue. Newspaper. English. da. The Bee, 700 Monument Street, Danville VA 24541. available on microfilm from University Microfilms International (UMI).

US/8750-6505
BRISTOL HERALD COURIER, BRISTOL VIRGINIA-TENNESSEAN. **VFOAT** Bristol Herald Courier; Bristol Virginia Tennessean. (Jan. 7, 1985)-. Newspaper. English. da. $126.00 (one year) Sunday only; $168.00 (one year) daily & Sunday. Bristol Newspapers Inc., PO Box 609, Bristol VA 24203. **Tel** (703)628-6632. **ED** John Molley. **Ad Acc**, **Adv Mgr:** Bill Cummings, **Tel** (703)669-2181. **Circ:** 45,000 (ctrl). available on microfilm from University Microfilms International (UMI).

US/0882-9322
CHARLOTTESVILLE ALBEMARLE OBSERVER. **VFOAT** Charlottesville/Albemarle Observer. Newspaper. English. wk. $25.00. Charlottesville, Albemarle Observer Inc, PO Box 617, Charlottesville VA 22901. **Tel** (804)295-0124, FAX (804)293-4047. **ED** John Howland Jr. **Bk Rev**. **Ad Acc**. **Circ:** 4,763. ***Continues*** *Charlottesville Observer.*

US
CLARKE COURIER (BERRYVILLE, VA.). (CLARKE COURIER.). Began with Feb. 19, 1869 issue. Newspaper. English. wk. Clarke Courier, 16 North Buckmarsh Street, Berryville VA 22611. ***Continues*** *Clarke Journal.*

US/8750-1171
CLINCH VALLEY NEWS, THE. (1???)-. Newspaper. English. wk. $38.00. Clinch Valley News, PO Box 977, Tazewell VA 24651. **Tel** (703)988-4770. **ED** Charles Beethe (Editor-in-Chief) and Jim Talburt (Managing Editor). **Photos**. **Ad Acc**, **Adv Mgr:** Audria Liffel. **Circ:** 4,100. available in microform.

US
CLINCH VALLEY TIMES. (19??)-. Newspaper. English. Fifty-two times a year (Thursdays). $14.75 Wise and Russell Counties; $18.20 other. Clinch Valley Times, PO Box 817 / Russell Street, St. Paul VA 24283. **Tel** (703)762-7671. **ED** Ann Y. Gregory. **Photos**. **Ad Acc**, **Adv Mgr:** Allen Gregory. Full Page (B&W) $509.55. Half Page (B&W) $254.78. Full Page (Color) $629.55. Half Page (Color) $374.78. **Pub. Size:** Standard. **Circ:** 2,700. available in microform.

US/0889-3330
COALFIELD PROGRESS, THE. (1912)-. Newspaper. English. sw (104 issues per year). $30.00 Norton and Wise County residents; $46.00 market area; $54.00 other. The Coalfield Progress, PO Box 380, Norton VA 24273. **Tel** (703)679-1101, FAX (703)679-5922. **ED** Jenay Tate. **Bk Rev**. **Photos**. **Ad Acc**. **Wire Svcs.:** AP. available in microform.

US/8755-9463
CREWE, BURKEVILLE JOURNAL, THE. **VFOAT** Crewe-Barkeville Journal. (19??)-. Newspaper. English. wk (51 issues). $12.50 in county; $15.00 others in Virginia; $19.00 others. Crewe Burkeville Journal, 107 West Carolina Avenue, Crewe VA 23930. **Tel** (804)645-7534, (804)645-7550, FAX (804)645-1848. **ED** Jim Eanes. **Bk Rev**. **Photos**. **Ad Acc**. Full Page (B&W) $504.00. Half Page (B&W) $252.00. Full Page (Color) $604.00. Half Page (Color) $352.00. **Pub. Size:** Standard. **Circ:** 6,250. available in microform.

US/0899-4803
CULPEPER STAR-EXPONENT (1988). (CULPEPER STAR-EXPONENT.). (1988)-. Newspaper. English. da. Star-Exponent, Carter Glass Newspapers Inc, PO Box 111, Culpeper VA 22701. **Tel** (703)825-0771. ***Continues*** *Star-Exponent, 0746-7923.*

US/0747-2501
DAILY NEWS LEADER, THE. (19??)-. Newspaper. English. da. $109.20. Leader Publishing Company / News Leader, 11 17 North Central Avenue, PO Box 59, Staunton VA 24401. **Tel** (703)885-7281, FAX (703)885-1904. **ED** Evarts W. Opie Jr. **Bk Rev**. **Ad Acc**. **Circ:** 18,000.

US
DAILY PRESS (NEWPORT NEWS, VA.). (DAILY PRESS.). (1896)-. Newspaper. English. da. $258.60 daily & Sun., $83.00 Sunday (by mail); $65.00 daily, $132.00 daily & Sun. (by carrier). The Daily Press Inc, 7505 Warwick Boulevard, PO Box 746, Newport News VA 23607. **Tel** (804)247-4600. **ED** Jack Davis Jr. (phone: (804)247-4629). **Ad Acc**, **Adv Mgr:** G. McDaniel, **Tel** (804)247-4665. **Circ:** 102,000 daily, 125.000 Sunday.

US/0746-0430
DAILY PROGRESS (CHARLOTTESVILLE, VA.), THE. (THE DAILY PROGRESS.). (1880)-. Newspaper. English. da. $164.00 (daily and Sunday), $84.00 (Sunday). Charlottesville Daily Progress, PO Box 9030, Charlottesville VA 22906. **Tel** (804)978-7200, (800)275-8828. **ED** Lawson H Marshall. **Circ:** 31,783 daily, 33,072 Sunday.
Ind/Abst Text. Technol. Dig. (19??-199?).

US/0744-3242
DANVILLE REGISTER, THE. **VFOAT** Sunday Register. (1896)-. Newspaper. English. da (except Sunday). $85.00. Register Publishing Company Inc., Department of Circulation, Danville VA 24541. **Tel** (804)793-2311. **ED** Bonnie Cooper (Editor-in-Chief) and Arnold Hendrix (Managing Editor). **LC** 7002. **Bk Rev**, (Qty: 52). **Photos**. **Ad Acc**, **Adv Mgr:** George Robinette, **Tel** (804)793-2311 ext. 3032. Full Page (B&W) $2,064.00. Half Page (B&W) $1,032.00. Full Page (Color) $2,412.00. Half Page (Color) $1,380.00. **Pub. Size:** Broadsheet. **Wire Svcs.:** AP. **Circ:** 28,000. available on microfilm from University Microfilms International (UMI). ***Continues*** *Danville Daily Register.*
Desc: A newspaper featuring local and national news and advertisements.

US/1064-4172
DECLARATION (INDEPENDENCE, VA.), THE. (THE DECLARATION.). (Aug. 7, 1980)-. Newspaper. English. wk. $17.00 Grayson & Alleghany Counties in North Carolina; $22.00 Ashe, Surrey Counties in North Carolina, Johnson County in Tennessee, Washinton, Smyth, Wythe and Carroll Counties in Virginia; $25.00 US; $100.00 other. Declaration, 106 West Main Street, Independence VA 24348. **Tel** (703)773-2222.

US/0746-584X
DICKENSON STAR, THE. Newspaper. English. wk. $12.00. Dickenson County Publishing Company, PO Box 398, Clinchco VA 24226. **Tel** (703)835-8625. **ED** Howard C Owen. **Bk Rev**. **Ad Acc**. **Circ:** 3,600 (ctrl).
Desc: County newspaper.

US/0885-1255
DIEN AN TH O. ***Ceased.*** (DIEN DAN THU DO.). **VFOAT** Capital Tribune. (1985)-(19??). Newspaper. Vietnamese. bw. The Capital Tribune, PO Box 5055, Springfield VA 22150. **Tel** (703)866-9784. **ED** Nguyen Ban So, Vu Ha, Do Khoa Luat and Nguyen Gia Tam. **Ad Acc**. **Circ:** 3,000.

US/0273-6403
FAIRFAX JOURNAL (SPRINGFIELD. 1980), THE. (THE FAIRFAX JOURNAL.). (1980)-. Newspaper. English. da. $65.00. Journal Newspapers Inc., 2720 Prosperity Avenue, Fairfax VA 22034. **Tel** (703)560-4000. **ED** Ken Iglehart (Editor-in-Chief) and Jane Touzalin (Managing Editor). **Bk Rev**. **Photos**. **Ad Acc**, **Adv Mgr:** Bob Saupp, **Tel** (703)846-8380. **Pub. Size:** Broadsheet. **Wire Svcs.:** AP. **Circ:** 59,718. ***Continues*** *Fairfax Journal and Globe, 0199-0543.*

US
FARMVILLE HERALD. English. tw (Mondays, Wednesdays, Fridays). $24.00 Prince Edward, Buckingham, Cumberland, Amelia, Appomattax, Charlotte, Nottoway, and Powhatan counties Virginia; $35.00 Virginia; $38.00 other. Farmville Herald, PO Box 307, Farmville VA 23901. **Tel** (804)392-4151, FAX (804)392-6298. **ED** W B Wall. **Ad Acc**. **Circ:** 8,500.

US/1050-7655
FAUQUIER TIMES-DEMOCRAT. **VFOAT** Fauquier Times Democrat. 173rd Year No. 1 (Jan. 4, 1990)-. Newspaper. English. wk. $29.95 in county; $39.95 others. Fauquier Times Democrat, 39 Culpeper Street, Warrenton VA 22186. **Tel** (703)347-4222, FAX (703)349-8676. **ED** Louis M. Hatter. **Bk Rev**. **Photos**. **Ad Acc**, **Adv Mgr:** John T. Toler. Full Page (B&W) $1,461.60. Half Page (B&W) $730.80. Full Page (Color) $1,611.60. Half Page (Color) $880.80. **Pub. Size:** Broadsheet. **Circ:** 548 (unpaid), 14,922 (paid). available in microform. ***Continues*** *Fauquier Democrat.*

US/8750-7323
FINCASTLE HERALD, THE. (187?)-. Newspaper. English. wk. Fincastle Herald, PO Box 127, Fincastle VA 24090. **ED** Edwin L. McCoy. **Bk Rev**. **Photos**. **Ad Acc**, **Adv Mgr:** Joan Bowles. **Pub. Size:** Broadsheet. ***Continues*** *Virginia Herald (Fincastle, Va.).*

US
FREE LANCE STAR, THE. (19??)-. English. da (published daily except Sunday and Christmas). $130.00. Free Lance Star, 616 Amelia Street, Fredericksburg VA 22401. **Tel** (703)374-5000, 800-877-0500, FAX (703)373-8450. **ED** Charles S. Rowe, Edward Jones (Managing Editor). **Bk Rev**, (Qty: 52). **Photos**. **Ad Acc**, **Adv Mgr:** C. Murphy Street, **Tel** (703)374-5470. Full Page (B&W) $2193.00. Half Page (B&W) $1096.50. Full Page (Color) $2563.00. Half Page (Color) $1466.50. **Pub. Size:** Broadsheet. **Wire Svcs.:** AP. **Circ:** 43,500 daily, 47,000 Sunday. available in microform from University Microfilms International (UMI).

US/0739-0106
GAZETTE, GOOCHLAND, THE. (19??)-. Newspaper. English. wk. $13.50 in county, $15.00 elsewhere. The Gazette Inc., PO Box 290, Manakin Sabot VA 23103. **Tel** (804)784-3315.

US/8750-5738
GAZETTE (HURT, VA.), THE. (THE GAZETTE.). Newspaper. English. wk. The Gazette, PO Box 11, Chatham VA 24531-0111. **Tel** (804)324-7283. **ED** Laurie Shelton. **Circ:** 5,500.

US/0745-8614
GAZETTE, POWHATAN, THE. **VFOAT** Powhatan Gazette. Newspaper. English. wk. The Gazette Inc., PO Box 290, Manakin Sabot VA 23103. **Tel** (804)784-3315.

US
HARRISONBURG DAILY NEWS RECORD. (19??)-. Newspaper. English. da (except Sun.). $65.00. Harrisonburg Daily News Record, PO Box 193, Harrisonburg VA 22801. **Tel** (703)433-2702. **ED** Richard Morin (Editor-in-Chief) and Ken Mink (Managing Editor). **Bk Rev**, (Qty: 40). **Photos**. **Ad Acc**, **Adv Mgr:** Linda Wsecker. Full Page (B&W) $2,102.70. Half Page (B&W) $1,051.35. Full Page (Color) $2,352.70. Half Page (Color) $1,301.35. **Pub. Size:** Broadsheet. **Wire Svcs.:** AP. available in microform.

US/0746-794X
INDEPENDENT-MESSENGER. **VFOAT** Independent Messenger. (19??)-. Newspaper. English. wk. Emporia Publishing Company, 157 Baker Street, Emporia VA 23847.

US/1064-4431
INDEPENDENT NEWSPAPER FROM RUSSIA. (INDEPENDENT NEWSPAPER FROM RUSSIA / NEZAVISIMAIA.). [Indep. newsp. Russ.]. **VFOAT** Independent Newspaper; Nezavisimaya Gazeta; Nezavisimaia. Vol. 1, Issue 21 (Feb. 1991)-. Newspaper. English (translations available in Russian). ir (every 3 weeks). $38.00 bulk mail; $58.00 first class mail; $75.00 both editions first class; $126.50 international edition airmail. Independent Newspaper Russia, 7738 Dartford Drive, Suite #9, Mclean VA 22102. **Tel** (703)827-8923, FAX (703)827-8923. **ED** Vitali Tretyakov (Moscow), Cynthia Neu (USA). **DD** 077. **Photos. Ad Acc, Adv Mgr:** Cynthia Neu, **Tel** (703)827-0414. Full Page (B&W) $800.00. Half Page (B&W) $400.00. **Pub. Size:** Tabloid. available in microform from Southwest Micropublishing International. ***Continues*** *Literary Gazette International, 1064-8488.*
Desc: Stories are about politics, the environment, social life, business, crime, culture, literature, outer space, military, education, religion, and sometimes love. The newspaper is written, edited, translated, designed, and photographed in its entirety in Russia by Russian journalists.
Ind/Abst PAIS Int. Print.

US
JOURNAL AND GUIDE, THE. ***Title Change.*** Began in (1901)-(19??). Newspaper. English. wk. Journal & Guide, 3535 F Tidewater Drive, Norfolk VA 23500. **Tel** (804)625-3686. Documents available from UMI Article Clearinghouse. ***Continued by*** *Norfolk Journal and Guide (Norfolk, Va. : 1921).*
Ind/Abst Newsp. Abstr.

US
JOURNAL AND GUIDE (NORFOLK, VA : 1977). ***Title Change.*** (JOURNAL AND GUIDE.). **VFOAT** Journal & Guide. Vol. 78, No. 14 (Apr. 2, 1977)-(19??). Newspaper. English. wk. Journal & Guide, 3535 F Tidewater Drive, Norfolk VA 23500. **Tel** (804)625-3686. available on microfilm from University Microfilms International (UMI). ***Continues*** *New Journal and Guide.* ***Continued by*** *New Journal and Guide.*

US/8750-2275
JOURNAL (KING GEORGE, VA.), THE. (THE JOURNAL.). Vol. 2, No. 35 (Aug. 7, 1984)-. Newspaper. English. wk. $8.50. The Journal / King George, PO Box 408, King George VA 22485. ***Continues*** *King George Journal.*

US/0745-6859
JOURNAL MESSENGER, THE. (1952)-. Newspaper. English. da. Prince William Publishing Company, 9009 Church Street, PO Drawer 431, Manassas VA 22110. **Tel** (703)368-3101. **ED** Bennie Scarton Jr. **Circ:** 12,696. available on microfilm from University Microfilms International (UMI). ***Formed by the union of*** *Messenger (Manassas, VA.)* ***and*** *Manassas Journal.*

US/0889-6135
LEDGER-STAR. **VFOAT** Ledger Star. (195?)-. Newspaper. English. da. $290.00. Virginian Pilot and Ledger Star, PO Box 2160, 150 West Brambleton, Norfolk VA 23510. **Tel** (804)446-2000. **ED** Sandra Rowe. **Circ:** 80,961. available on an online database (file 635/Full-Text) from DIALOG. Documents available from UMI Article Clearinghouse. ***Formed by the union of*** *Ledger-Dispatch (Norfolk, VA.)* ***and*** *Portsmouth Star.*
Ind/Abst Bus. Dateline (Dec. 19, 1991-) [Full Txt.].

US/0740-4034
LOUDOUN TIMES-MIRROR. **VAT** Loudoun Times Mirror. (19??)-. Newspaper. English. Fifty-two times a year. $29.95 Loudoun County; $49.95 other. Loudoun Times-Messenger, 9 East Market Street, PO Box 359, Leesburg VA 22075. **Tel** (703)777-1111.

US
MCLEAN PROVIDENCE JOURNAL AND FAIRFAX HERALD, THE. (1944)-. Newspaper. English. wk (Thursdays). $20.00. McLean Providence Journal, PO Box 580, McLean VA 22101. **Tel** (703)356-3320, FAX (703)556-0825. **ED** R. Cort Kirkwood. **Bk Rev**, (Qty: 5). **Photos. Ad Acc, Adv Mgr:** Chris Brockway, **Tel** (703)356-3181. Full Page (B&W) $664.00. Half Page (B&W) $372.00. **Pub. Size:** Tabloid. available on microfilm.

US/0162-2080
MONTGOMERY JOURNAL, THE. Vol. 34, No. 36 (Sept. 6, 1973)-. Newspaper. English. sw. Journal Newspapers, 2720 Prosperity Avenue, Springfield VA 22159. **Tel** (703)560-4000. ***Formed by the union of*** *Journal (Bethesda/Chevy Chase/Potomac Ed.)* ***and*** *Journal (Silver Spring-Wheaton Ed.).*

US/0028-1670
NAVY NEWS. (19??)-. Periodical. English. wk. $29.95. Navy News, 2429 Bowland Parkway, Suite 115, Virginia Beach VA 23454. **Tel** (804)486-8000. **ED** R.J. Tucker. **Bk Rev. Ad Acc. Circ:** 100,000 (ctrl).
Desc: Contains articles on Naval topics.

US
NEW CASTLE RECORD, THE. **VFOAT** Newcastle Record. Began in 1885. Newspaper. English. wk. New Castle Record, PO Box 116, New Castle VA 24127.

US
NEWS & DAILY ADVANCE. (19??)-. Newspaper. English. ds. $124.95. Worrell Enterprises Inc. / Virginia, PO Box 10129, Lynchburg VA 24506. **Tel** (804)385-5400.

US/0747-2862
NEWS & RECORD. **VFOAT** News and Record. (1???)-. Newspaper. English. sw. $24.00. News & Record, PO Drawer 100, South Boston VA 24592. **ED** Sylvia O. McLaughlin (Editor-in-Chief) and Tom McLaughlin (Managing Editor). **Bk Rev**, (Qty: 100). **Photos. Ad Acc, Adv Mgr:** Tucker McLaughlin Jr., **Tel** (804)572-2928. Full Page (B&W) $477.30. Half Page (B&W) $238.65. Full Page (Color) $537.30. Half Page (Color) $298.65. **Pub. Size:** Broadsheet. **Wire Svcs.:** AP. available in microform.

US/0164-9086
NEWS MESSENGER, THE. (19??)-. Newspaper. English. da. News Messenger, PO Box 419, Christiansburg VA 24073. ***Absorbed*** *Blacksburg Sun;* ***Continues*** *Montgomery Messenger.*

US/8750-7862
NEWS-VIRGINIAN, THE. **VFOAT** News Virginian. (1???)-. Newspaper. English. da. $42.00. The News-Virginian, Box 1027, Waynesboro VA 22980. **Tel** (703)949-8213. **ED** Edward P Berlin Jr. **Circ:** 12,579.

US/1065-1632
NORTHERN VIRGINIA SUN. (19??)-. Newspaper. English. Twice a week. $24.00. Northern Virginia Sun, PO Box 2410, Merrifield VA 22116. **Tel** (703)204-2800, FAX (703)204-3455. **ED** Scott McCaffrey. **Photos. Ad Acc, Adv Mgr:** David Blakeslee. Full Page (B&W) $100.00. Half Page (B&W) $58.00. Full Page (Color) $200.00. Half Page (Color) $158.00. **Pub. Size:** Tabloid. **Circ:** 1,400 (ctrl).
Desc: Newspaper covering local news, features and sports in Northern Virginia.

US/1063-8466
OBSERVER (HERNDON, VA.), THE. (THE OBSERVER.). (19??)-. Newspaper. English. wk. Free in Herndon; $24.00 other. Herndon Observer, PO Box 109, Herndon VA 22070. **Tel** (703)437-5886.

US
ORANGE REVIEW, THE. Newspaper. English. wk. Orange Review, PO Box 589, Orange VA 22960.

US
PAGE NEWS AND COURIER. **VFOAT** 65th Anniversary and Progress Edition. (May 20, 1911)-. Newspaper. English. wk. $15.00. Page News & Courier, PO Box 707, Luray VA 22835. **Tel** (703)743-5123. ***Formed by the union of*** *Page News (Luray, Va. : 1892)* ***and*** *Page Courier.*

US/0162-2099
PRINCE GEORGE'S JOURNAL, THE. Vol. 1, No. 1 (Jan. 2, 1975)-. Newspaper. English. da (Mon.-Fri.). Journal Newspapers, 2720 Prosperity Avenue, Springfield VA 22159. **Tel** (703)560-4000. **ED** Linda Searling. **Circ:** 36,759.

US
PROGRESS-INDEX, THE. **VFOAT** Progress Index. Began in 1924. Newspaper. English. da. Progress-Index, 15 Franklin Street, Petersburg VA 23803. available on microfilm from University Microfilms International (UMI). ***Continues*** *Progress and Index-Appeal.*

US/0888-9473
RECORDER (MONTEREY, VA.). (THE RECORDER.). (1???)-. Newspaper. English. wk. The Recorder / Monterey, PO Box 10, Monterey VA 24465. **Tel** (703)468-2147. ***Continues*** *Highland Recorder.*

US
RICHLANDS NEWS PRESS. (19??)-. Newspaper. English. Fifty-two times a year (Wed.). $36.00 Russell, Tazewell, Buchanan counties in VA; $41.00 Kentucky, Virginia, West Virginia, Tennessee, North Carolina, Washington DC, Maryland, APO & FPO; $42.00 Maine, New Hampshire, Vermont, Massachusetts, Connecticutt, Delaware, New York, Pennsylvania, Ohio, Indiana, Michigan, Illinois, Wisconsin, Minnesota, Iowa, Missouri, Arkansas, Louisiana, Mississippi, Alabama, Rhode Island, Georgia, South Carolina, Florida & New Jersey; $43.00 North & South Dakota, Nebraska, Kansas, Oklahoma, Texas, New Mexico, Colorado, Wyoming, & Montana; $44.00 Alaska, Arizona, California, Utah, Nevada, Idaho, & Oregon. Richlands News Press, PO Box 818, Richlands VA 24641. **Tel** (703)963-1081.

US
RICHMOND NEWS-LEADER, THE. ***Ceased.*** **VFOAT** Richmond News Leader. (Jan. 10, 1925)-(19??). Newspaper. English. da. Richmond Newspapers Inc, PO Box 26551, Richmond VA 23291. **Tel** (804)649-4181 or, 800 468-3382. **Circ:** 108,812. available on microfilm from University Microfilms International (UMI); and University Microfilms International (UMI); available on an online database (file 635/Full-Text) from DIALOG. Documents available from UMI Article Clearinghouse. ***Continues*** *The News Leader.*
Ind/Abst Bus. Dateline (Dec. 23, 1991-199?) [Full Txt.].

US
RICHMOND TIMES-DISPATCH. **VFOAT** Richmond Times Dispatch. Vol. 64 No. 19 (Nov. 1914)-. Newspaper. English. da. $90.00 (Sunday/mail), $225.00 (morning and Sunday/mail), $135.00 (morning only/mail), $128.20 (morning and Sunday/foot route), $135.20 (morning and Sunday/motor route). Richmond Newspapers Inc, PO Box 26551, Richmond VA 23291. **Tel** (804)649-4181 or, 800 468-3382. **Circ:** 137,801 daily, 238,543 Sunday. available on microfilm and microfiche from University Microfilms International (UMI); available on microfilm from University Microfilms International (UMI); available on an online database (files 635,709/Full-Text) from DIALOG. Documents available from UMI Article Clearinghouse. ***Continues*** *Times Dispatch (Richmond, VA.).*
Ind/Abst Bus. Dateline (Dec. 18, 1991-) [Full Txt.]; PROMT; Text. Technol. Dig. (19??-199?).

US
ROANOKE TIMES & WORLD-NEWS. **VFOAT** Roanoke Times and World News. Vol. 181, No. 66 (April 2, 1977)-. Newspaper. English. da. $91.00 Sunday edition (mail); $143.00 daily edition; $49.40 Monday-Friday editions (carrier); $182.00 daily and Sunday editions (mail). Times World Corporation, PO Box 2491, c/o Karen Walrond, Roanoke VA 24010. **Tel** (703)981-3100 or, 800 627-2767, FAX (703)981-3365. **ED** Gene Owens and Forrest M. Landon. **Bk Rev. Ad Acc. Circ:** 78,149 daily, 126,182 Sunday. available on microfilm from University Microfilms International (UMI); available on an online database from VU-TEXT. ***Absorbed*** *World-News; Roanoke Times.*

●US/1064-7740
ROCKBRIDGE DAILY PRESS. Vol. 1, No. 1 (May 13, 1992)-. Newspaper. English. da. Rockbridge Newspapers Co., PO Box 1491, Lexington VA 24450.

US/8750-3832
SCOTT COUNTY VIRGINIA STAR. **VFOAT** Star; Virginia Star. Vol. 80, No. 45 (Oct. 17, 1984)-. Newspaper. English. wk. Scott County Virginia Star, PO Box 218, Gate City VA 24251. **Tel** (703)386-7027. **ED** Jack R Lawrence. **Circ:** 6,123. ***Formed by the union of*** *Scott County Herald Virginian* ***and*** *Scott County Press.*

US/0746-6846
SHENANDOAH HERALD, SHENANDOAH VALLEY, THE. **VFOAT** Shenandoah Herald; Shenandoah Valley-Herald; Shenandoah Valley Herald. (19??)-. Newspaper. English. Fifty-two times a year (Wed.). $12.00 Shenandoah & Rockingham counties, $18.00 other. Shenandoah Valley Herald, PO Box 507, Woodstock VA 22664. **Tel** (703)459-4078. **ED** C. L. Earehart. **Ad Acc, Adv Mgr:** Carol Holmes. **Circ:** 6,300 (ctrl). ***Continues*** *Shenandoah Herald.*

US/0744-0766
SMYTH COUNTY NEWS. (19??)-. Newspaper. English. sw. Smyth County News, PO Box 640, Marion VA 24354-0640. **Tel** (703)783-5121, FAX (703)783-9713. **ED** Linda White. **Ad Acc. Circ:** 8,000.

US/0746-6676
SOUTH HILL ENTERPRISE, THE. Newspaper. English. wk. South Hill Enterprise, 914 West Danville Street, South Hill VA 23970.

US
SOUTHWEST VIRGINIA ENTERPRISE. English. sw. $25.00 (Wythe County), $26.00 (Virginia - outside Wythe County), $28.00 other. Southwest Virginia Enterprise, PO Box 547, Wytheville VA 24382. **Tel** (703)228-6611. **ED** Stephanie Porter, 460 West Main Street, Wytheville Va 24383 (phone: (703)228-6611). **Bk Rev. Ad Acc, Adv Mgr:** Suelyn Arnold, **Tel** (703)228-6611.

US/8750-9598
SUFFOLK NEWS-HERALD. **VFOAT** Suffolk News Herald. **VAT** Suffolk (Virginia) News Herald. Newspaper. English. da. $65.00. Suffolk News-Herald, PO Box 1220, Suffolk VA 23434.

US/0745-9467
SUSSEX-SURRY DISPATCH. **VAT** Sussex, Surry Dispatch. (1???)-. Newspaper. English. Fifty-two times a year. $14.00 Sussex Surrey & Southampton & Prince George counties; $17.00 others. Atlantic Publications Inc., Accomac VA 23301. **Tel** (804)787-7070. **ED** Roy E. Spears. **Ad Acc. Circ:** 2,800.

Virginia

US/0744-7116
TIDEWATER ADVANTAGE. NEWPORT NEWS EDITION, THE. (THE TIDEWATER ADVANTAGE.). Newspaper. English. wk. Advantage Publications / Virginia, PO Box 731, Surry VA 23883.

US
TIMES-REGISTER, THE. **VFOAT** Times Register. (18??)-. Newspaper. English. wk. $18.00. Salem Publishing Co, PO Box 590, Salem VA 24153. **Tel** (703)389-9355.

US
TIMES (SMITHFIELD, VA). (TIMES.). (19??)-. Newspaper. English. wk. $20.00. The Smithfield Times, PO Box 366, Smithfield VA 23431. **Tel** (804)357-3288, FAX (804)357-0404. **ED** John B. Edwards. **Photos. Ad Acc, Adv Mgr:** Lona Ellis. Full Page (B&W) $554.70. Half Page (B&W) $277.35. Full Page (Color) $664.70. Half Page (Color) $387.35. **Pub. Size:** Broadsheet. **Wire Svcs.:** AP. **Circ:** 4,800. available in microform from Bell & Howell.

US/8750-7919
VINTON MESSENGER, THE. (19??)-. Newspaper. English. wk. $10.00 Vinton and Roanoke counties; $14.00 other. The Vinton Messenger, PO Box 508, Vinton VA 24179. **Tel** (703)343-0720. **ED** Daniel Smith.

US/0049-6480
VIRGINIA GAZETTE (1930). (THE VIRGINIA GAZETTE.). Vol. 1, No. 1 (Jan. 10, 1930)-. Newspaper. English. sw. $19.00. Virginia Gazette, PO Box 419, Williamsburg VA 23185. **Tel** (804)220-1736. **ED** W. C. O'Donovan. **Bk Rev. Ad Acc. Circ:** 13,000. available on microfilm from University Microfilms International (UMI).
Desc: Community newspaper serving Williamsburg, James City county and York County.

US
VIRGINIA GAZETTE (VIRGINIA, ILL.). (THE VIRGINIA GAZETTE.). Began in 1872. Newspaper. English. wk. Virginia Gazette, PO Box 419, Williamsburg VA 23185. **Tel** (804)220-1736.

US/0889-6127
VIRGINIAN-PILOT, THE. **VFOAT** Virginian Pilot; Virginian-Pilot and the Ledger-Star; Virginian-Pilot and the Portsmouth Star. Vol.215, No. 39 (May 9, 1955)-. Newspaper. English. da (Monday-Friday, except holidays). $69.95. Virginian Pilot and Ledger Star, PO Box 2160, 150 West Brambleton, Norfolk VA 23510. **Tel** (804)446-2000. **ED** Sandra Rowe. **Circ:** 144,809 daily, 227,330 Sunday. available on microfilm from University Microfilms International (UMI). Documents available from UMI Article Clearinghouse. **Continues** Norfolk Virginian-Pilot.
Ind/Abst Bus. Dateline (Dec. 16, 1991-) [Full Txt.]; PROMT.

US/1064-0665
WINCHESTER STAR (WINCHESTER, VA.). (THE WINCHESTER STAR.). (19??)-. Newspaper. English. da. $58.00 Virginia, Washington DC, Maryland, West Virginia; $68.00 other. Winchester Star, 2 North Kent Street, Winchester VA 22601. **Tel** (703)667-3200, FAX (703)667-0012. **ED** Ron Morris. **Ad Acc, Adv Mgr:** Jerry Howard, **Tel** (800)296-8639. **Circ:** 23,000 daily. **Continues** Winchester Evening Star.

WASHINGTON

US
ANACORTES AMERICAN. **VFOAT** Weekly American. Vol. 1, No. 1 (May 15, 1890)-. Newspaper. English. wk. $25.00. Anacortes American, PO Box 39, Anacortes WA 98221. **Tel** (206)293-3122, FAX (206)293-5000. **ED** Duncan Frazier (Editor in Chief) and Mark Carlson (Managing Editor). **Photos. Ad Acc, Adv Mgr:** James Dean. Full Page (B&W) $910.00. Half Page (B&W) $455.00. Full Page (Color) $1170.00. Half Page (Color) $715.00. **Pub. Size:** Broadsheet.

US
ARLINGTON TIMES, THE. (1897)-. Newspaper. English. Fifty-two times a year. $24.00 (in county); $36.00 (other). Arlington Times, 426 North Olympic, Arlington WA 98223. **Tel** (206)435-5757, FAX (206)435-0999. **Continues** Haller City Times.

US/1048-5309
ASOTIN COUNTY AMERICAN. Ceased. Vol. 3 [i.e. 11], Issue 31 (Aug. 8, 1989)-(19??). Newspaper. English. Fifty-two times a year (Thurs.). American Publishing Company / Washington, 724 6th Street, Clarkston WA 99403. **Tel** (509)758-9797. **Continues** Valley American.

US
ASOTIN COUNTY SENTINEL. (1899)-. Newspaper. English. wk. Tribune Newspapers Inc, PO Box 579, Clarkston WA 99403-0579. **Continues** Sentinel (Asotin, Wash.).

US
BALLARD NEWS-TRIBUNE (SEATTLE, WASH. : 1976). (BALLARD NEWS-TRIBUNE.). **VAT** Ballard News Tribune. Vol. 87, No. 21 (May 19, 1976)-. Newspaper. English. wk. $25.00. Ballard News-Tribune, 2208 Northwest Market, Seattle WA 98107. **Tel** (206)783-1244, FAX (206)789-2455. **ED** Randal Anderson. **Photos. Ad Acc, Adv Mgr:** Lani Doely. Full Page (B&W) $1360.80. Half Page (B&W) $680.40. Full Page (Color) $1660.80. Half Page (Color) $980.40. **Pub. Size:** Broadsheet. **Continues** Ballard News Tribune Today.

US
BEACON HILL NEWS (SEATTLE, WASH.). (BEACON HILL NEWS.). **VFOAT** South District Journal. Began in 1924. Newspaper. English. wk. Beacon Hill News, 2720 Hanford Street, Seattle WA 98144.

US
BELLINGHAM HERALD, THE. (1890)-. Newspaper. English. Fifty-two times a year. Bellingham Herald, PO Box 1277, Bellingham WA 98227. **Tel** (206)676-2600. available on microfilm from University Microfilms International (UMI). **Absorbed** Bellingham Reveille (Bellingham, Wash. : 1927); **Formed by the union of** Evening Herald (Fairhaven, Wash.).

US
CAMAS-WASHOUGAL POST RECORD & BUYER'S BONUS, THE. **VFOAT** Camas-Washougal Post Record and Buyers' Bonus. Vol. 75, No. 2 (Jan. 10, 1984)-. Newspaper. English. wk. PO Box 1013, Camas WA 98607. **Continues** Camas and Washougal Post Record and Shoppers' Guide.

US
CAPITOL HILL TIMES. (1927)-. Newspaper. English. wk. Capitol Hill Times, 2720 South Hanford Street, Seattle WA 98144.

US
CHENEY FREE PRESS. **VFOAT** Medical Lake Press. (1896)-. Newspaper. English. wk. Cheney Free Press, PO Box 218, Cheney WA 99004.

US
CHEWELAH INDEPENDENT, THE. Began in 1903. Newspaper. English. wk. Chewelah Independent, PO Box 5, Chewelah WA 99109.

US/0739-9200
CHINOOK OBSERVER. (1900)-. Newspaper. English. wk. $10.00 in Pacific county, $11.00 out of Pacific county. Chinook Observer, PO Box 427, Long Beach WA 98631.

US
CHRONICLE, THE. 101st Year, 72nd Issue (June 9, 1990)-. Newspaper. English. da. $78.00 Centralia; $104.00 Washington & Oregon. Centralia Chronicle, 321 North Pearl, Centralia WA 98531. **Tel** (206)736-3311. **Continues** Daily Chronicle (Centralia, Wash.).

US/0045-7051
CIVIL LIBERTIES. Added/Corp American Civil Liberties Union of Washington. (19??)-. Periodical. English. Five times a year (Feb., Apr., June, Sept., Nov.). $20.00. American Civil Liberties Union of Washington, 705 2nd Avenue, Suite 300, Seattle WA 98104. **Tel** (206)624-2180. **ED** Public Education Director, (phone: (206)624-2184).
Desc: Reports activities of the ACLU of Washington State.

US
CLARKSTON HERALD (CLARKSTON, WASH. : 1973). (CLARKSTON HERALD.). Vol. 73, No. 1 (Jan. 4, 1973)-. Newspaper. English. wk. Tribune Newspapers Inc, PO Box 579, Clarkston WA 99403-0579. **Continues** Valley Herald News (Clarkston, Wash. : 1964).

US
COLLEGE PLACER, THE. Vol. 1, No. 1 (Mar. 29, 1968)-. Newspaper. English. wk. Tribune Newspapers Inc, PO Box 579, Clarkston WA 99403-0579.

US/1041-1658
COLUMBIA BASIN HERALD. **VFOAT** CBH. 46th Year, No. 113 (Jan. 11, 1988)-. Newspaper. English. da. Columbia Basin Daily Herald, PO Box 910, Moses Lake WA 98837. **Continues** Columbia Basin Daily Herald.

US
COLUMBIA BASIN NEWS. Vol. 5, No. 55 (March 10, 1955)-. Newspaper. English. wk. Tribune Newspapers Inc, PO Box 579, Clarkston WA 99403-0579. **Formed by the union of** Richland Villager and Pasco News (Pasco, Wash. : 1949).

US/1043-4151
COLUMBIAN (VANCOUVER, WASH.). (THE COLUMBIAN.). Vol. 28, No. 155 (April 19, 1937)-. Newspaper. English. da. $9.00 (a month). The Columbian Publishing Company / Scott Campbell, 701 West 8th Street, PO Box 180, Vancouver WA 98666-4014. **Tel** (206)694-3391, FAX (206)737-4014. **ED** Tom Koenninger. **Photos. Ad Acc, Adv Mgr:** Susan Hirtzel. Full Page (B&W) $3,983.52. Half Page (B&W) $1,991.76. Full Page (Color) $4,903.52. Half Page (Color) $2,911.76. **Pub. Size:** Broadsheet. **Wire Svcs.:** AP, LA, WP. **Continues** Vancouver Evening Columbian.
Ind/Abst Am. Hist. Life (1960-1972).

US
CONCRETE HERALD, THE. (1901)-. Newspaper. English. wk. Concrete Herald, 137 Main Street, Concrete WA 98237. **Continues** Hamilton Herald.

US/0889-0005
DAILY NEWS (LONGVIEW, WASH.), THE. (THE DAILY NEWS.). (Jan. 26, 1923)-. Newspaper. English. da (Publish except Sunday). $24.00 weekly edition; $126.00 Cowlitz Wahkiakum, & Pacific Clark & Vancouver Counties in Washington and Columbia County in Oregon; $156.00 other. Daily News / Longview, PO Box 189, Longview WA 98632. **Tel** (206)577-2500. **DD** 071.

US/0883-5748
DAILY NEWS (PULLMAN, WASH.). (DAILY NEWS.). **VFOAT** Idahonian/Daily News. (198?)-. Newspaper. English. da. Daily News / Pullman, 205 East Main Street, Pullman WA 99163.

US
DAILY OF THE UNIVERSITY OF WASHINGTON, THE. Added/Corp University of Washington. Board of Student Publications. **VFOAT** Daily of the University of Washington; Summer Daily of the University of Washington. (Sept. 27, 1976)-. Newspaper. English. ir (When published, published Mon.-Fri. during school year, Wed. throughout summer.). $45.00. Daily of University of Washington, 144 Communications/DS-20, Seattle WA 98195. **Tel** (206)543-7666. **ED** Drake Witham. **DD** 378.79777/05. **Photos. Ad Acc, Adv Mgr:** Stephanie Pure. Full Page (B&W) $550.00. Half Page (B&W) $290.00. Full Page (Color) $675.00. Half Page (Color) $415.00. **Pub. Size:** Tabloid. **Wire Svcs.:** LA, WP. **Circ:** 18,000. **Continues** University of Washington daily.

US
DAILY RECORD (ELLENSBURG, WASH.). (DAILY RECORD.). **VFOAT** Ellensburg Daily Record. Vol. 30, No. 100 (April 23, 1938)-. Newspaper. English. da. Ellensburg Daily Record, PO Box 248, Ellensburg WA 98926. **Tel** (509)925-1414. **Continues** Evening Record (Ellensburg, Wash.).

US/1046-1612
DAILY SUN-NEWS. **VFOAT** Daily Sun News; Sunnyside Daily Sun-News. Vol. 1, No. 1 (Oct. 15, 1986)-. Newspaper. English. da. Daily Sun News, PO Box 878, Sunnyside WA 98944-0878. **Tel** (509)837-4500, FAX (509)837-6397. **ED** Olaf Elze. **Ad Acc, Adv Mgr:** Jim Applegate. **Circ:** 3,747. **Formed by the union of** Sunnyside Sun and Sunnyside Daily News.

US/0740-3135
DAILY WORLD (ABERDEEN, WASH.). (THE DAILY WORLD.). 80th year, No. 182 (March 2, 1969)-. Newspaper. English. da. $160.00 (daily & Sunday, by mail), $97.00 (daily & Sunday, by carrier), $106.00 (daily & Sunday, by motor route). Daily World / Aberdeen, 315 South Michigan, PO Box 269, Aberdeen WA 98520. **Tel** (206)532-4000. **Continues** Aberdeen Daily World.

US
ENTERPRISE (WHITE SALMON, WASH.). (THE ENTERPRISE.). Vol. 39, No. 4 (April 25, 1941)-. Newspaper. English. wk. $8.00, $7.00 (Skamania, Klickitat and Hood River counties). D Nafsinger, PO Box 218, 220 East Jewett Boulevard, White Salmon WA 98672. **Continues** White Salmon Enterprise; **Absorbed** Mt. Adams Sun.

US
ENUMCLAW COURIER-HERALD. **VFOAT** Enumclaw Courier-Herald combined with Buckley News-Banner. 33rd Year, No. 1, (Oct. 6, 1933)-. Newspaper. English. wk. Enumclaw Courier-Herald, 1627 Cole Street, Enumclaw WA 98022. **Formed by the union of** Enumclaw Herald and Enumclaw Courier; **Absorbed** Buckley News-Banner.

US/0427-8879
FACTS (SEATTLE, WASH. : 1962). (THE FACTS.). **VFOAT** Northwest Facts. Vol. 1, No. 1 (July 5, 1962)-. Newspaper. English. Fifty-two times a year (Wed.). The Facts / Washington, 2765 East Cherry, PO Box 22015, Seattle WA 98122. **Tel** (206)324-0552. **ED** Fitzgerald Beaver. **Bk Rev. Ad Acc. Circ:** 40,000.
Desc: Serving Seattle's minority community, with local news about churches and social service organizations and many more.

US
FEDERAL WAY NEWS. **VFOAT** Federal Way-Mid-Cities News Advertiser; Federal Way News Combined with Mid-Cities Advertiser; Federal Way, Fife

News Advertiser; Federal Way Milton, Fife News Advertiser. (1958)-. Newspaper. English. tw. $42.00; $150.00 (mail). Times Community Newspapers Inc., 1634 South 312th Street, Federal Way WA 98063. **Tel** (206)839-0700, FAX (206)941-2641. **ED** Brad Broberg, Sharon Vandecarr (Managing Editor). **Photos**. **Ad Acc**, **Adv Mgr:** Pam Schairbaum. Full Page (B&W) $1935.00. Half Page (B&W) $967.50. Full Page (Color) $2210.00. Half Page (Color) $1242.50. **Pub. Size:** Brcadsheet. ***Continues*** *Greater Federal Way News-Review;* ***Absorbed*** *Mid-Cities Advertiser.*

US
FORKS FORUM-PENINSULA HERALD. June 12, 1975-. Newspaper. English. wk. PO Box 300, Forks WA 98331. ***Continues*** *Forks Forum;* ***Absorbed*** *Clallam Bay's Peninsula Herald.*

US
FRANKLIN COUNTY ENTERPRISE. (19??)-. Newspaper. English. wk. Tribune Newspapers Inc, PO Box 579, Clarkston WA 99403-0579.

US
FRANKLIN COUNTY GRAPHIC. (1954)-. Newspaper. English. wk. $26.00. Franklin County Graphic, PO Box 160, Connell WA 99326. **Tel** (509)234-3181. **ED** Duane Ruser. **Photos**. **Ad Acc**, **Adv Mgr:** Debbie Rochester. Full Page (B&W) $515.00. Half Page (B&W) $258.00. Full Page (Color) $586.00. Half Page (Color) $328.00. **Pub. Size:** Broadsheet.

US
GOLDENDALE SENTINEL, THE. (1884)-. Newspaper. English. wk (published Thursday). $18.00 Goldendale, Washington; $28.00 other. Goldendale Sentinel, 301 South Washington, Goldendale WA 98620. **Tel** (509)773-3777, FAX (509)773-4737. **ED** Brent De LaPaz, Michele Vowell (Managing Editor). **Pub. Size:** Standard. ***Formed by the union of*** *Klickitat Sentinel; Goldendale Gazette.*

US
GRANDVIEW HERALD. Began in 1909. Newspaper. English. wk. Grandview Herald, 107 Division Street, Grandview WA 98930.

US
GRANT COUNTY JOURNAL. Vol. 54, No. 131 (Feb. 20, 1964)-. Newspaper. English. sw. Grant County Journal, PO Box 998, Ephrata WA 98823. **Tel** (509)754-4636, FAX (509)754-5112. **ED** Joe Dennis. **Ad Acc**. **Circ:** 3,100. ***Continues*** *Grant County Daily Journal.*

●US/1064-4806
GRAYS HARBOR BEACON. (1992)-. Newspaper. English. Fifty-two times a year (Wed.). Grays Harbor Beacon, PO Box 1207, Ocean Shores WA 98551. **Tel** (206)289-3359. ***Continues*** *North Beach Beacon.*

US/0888-2290
HANGUK ILBO, SOBUNGMI. **VFOAT** Hanguk Ilbo; Korea Times Northwest Edition. Newspaper. Korean. da. Korea Times / Seattle, WA, 426 Yale Avenue North, Seattle WA 98109. ***Continues*** *Hanguk Ilbo, Siattul, 8750-6564.*

US
HERALD (EVERETT, WASH.), THE. (THE HERALD.). (April 6, 1981)-. Newspaper. English. da. $82.00 (Sunday only by mail); $157.00 US, $108.00 Snohomish County in Washington & Military, $148.00 Island King & Skagit County in Washington, $337.00 others (daily & Sunday by mail); $118.00 Snohomish County, $130.00 Island County (daily & Sunday by carrier); $73.00 (Sunday only by carrier). The Herald Everett Washington, PO Box 930, Everett WA 98206. **Tel** (206)339-3200. **ED** Joann Byrd. **Circ:** 55,570 daily, 57,454 Sunday. ***Continues*** *Everett Herald.*

US
HIGHLINE TIMES. (19??)-. Newspaper. English. Twice a week. $32.00; $97.00 (by mail). Times Community Newspapers Inc., 1634 South 312th Street, Federal Way WA 98063. **Tel** (206)839-0700, FAX (206)941-2641. **ED** Robert Smith. **Photos**. **Ad Acc**, **Adv Mgr:** Carla Royter. Full Page (B&W) $1935.00. Half Page (B&W) $967.50. Full Page (Color) $2210.00. Half Page (Color) $1242.50. **Pub. Size:** Broadsheet. ***Continues*** *Glendale-Highline Gazette.*

US/8756-6451
HOKUBEI HOCHI. [Hokubei hochi]. **VFOAT** North American Post. (19??)-. Newspaper. Japanese. tw. $87.00. North American Post Inc, PO Box 3173, Seattle WA 98114. **Tel** (206)623-0100, FAX (206)625-1424. **ED** Akiko Kusunose. **DD** 071. **Bk Rev**, (Qty: 60). **Ad Acc**, **Adv Mgr:** Reiko Henry. Full Page (B&W) $960.00. Half Page (B&W) $405.00. **Pub. Size:** Tabloid. **Circ:** 3,000 paid.

US
ISSAQUAH PRESS, THE. (1916)-. Newspaper. English. wk. $18.00. Issaquah Press / Deborah Berto, PO Box 1328, Issaquah WA 98027. **Tel** (206)392-6434. **ED** Andrew McKean. **Photos**. **Ad Acc**, **Adv Mgr:** Brian Bretland. Full Page (B&W) $1,638.00. Half Page (B&W) $819.00. Full Page (Color) $1,738.00. Half Page (Color) $919.00. **Pub. Size:** Broadsheet. **Circ:** 8,400 (paid), 11,000 (free). ***Continues*** *Issaquah Independent.*

US/0744-947X
JOURNAL-AMERICAN. **VAT** Journal American. (19??)-. Newspaper. English. ds. From $132.00-$165.00 according to US zip code; $202.00 outside US. Daily Journal-American, PO Box 310, Bellevue WA 98009. **Tel** (206)455-2222.

US/0734-3809
JOURNAL OF THE SAN JUAN ISLANDS. Vol. 76, No. 3 (Sept. 1981)-. Newspaper. English. wk. $30.00 North America; $75.00 other. Director of Theatre Training Programs, PO Box 519, Friday Harbor WA 98250. **Tel** (206)378-4191. **ED** Frank Leeming. **Bk Rev**. **Ad Acc**. **Circ:** 7,000 (ctrl). ***Continues*** *Friday Harbor Journal.*

US
LAKE CHELAN MIRROR. Vol. 91, No. 20 (Feb. 20, 1991)-. Newspaper. English. wk. Chelan Valley Mirror, 315 East Woodin Avenue, Chelan WA 98816. ***Continues*** *Chelan Valley Mirror.*

US
LAKE STEVENS JOURNAL. Vol. 4, No. 2 (Jan. 16, 1964)-. Newspaper. English. wk. $20.00 (one year), $34.00 (two year). Lake Stevens Journal, PO Box 896, Lake Stevens WA 98258. **Tel** (206)334-9252, FAX (206)334-9239. **ED** Darrell Gray. **Photos**. **Ad Acc**, **Adv Mgr:** D. Cahoon. Full Page (B&W) $950.63. Half Page (B&W) $468.00. Full Page (Color) $1,125.63. Half Page (Color) $643.00. **Pub. Size:** Tabloid. **Circ:** 15,000 (ctrl). ***Continues*** *Lake Stevens Shopper.*

US
LEAVENWORTH ECHO, THE. (1904)-. Newspaper. English. wk. Leavenworth Echo, PO Box 39, Leavenworth WA 98826.

US
LIND LEADER (LIND, WASH. : 1946). ***Title Change.*** (LIND LEADER.). (1946)-(19??). Newspaper. English. wk. Tribune Newspapers Inc, PO Box 579, Clarkston WA 99403-0579. ***Continued by*** *Adams County Leader.*

US
LYNDEN TRIBUNE, THE. Vol. 1, No. 1 (July 9, 1908)-. Newspaper. English. wk. Lynden Tribune, 113 North 6th Street, Lynden WA 98264-1912. **Tel** (206)354-4444, FAX (206)734-0575. **ED** Dave Brumbaugh. **Ad Acc**. **Circ:** 6,179.

US
MABTON PRESS, THE. (19??)-. Newspaper. English. wk. Tribune Newspapers Inc, PO Box 579, Clarkston WA 99403-0579.

US
MERCER ISLAND REPORTER. (1954)-. Newspaper. English. wk. $36.00. Mercer Island Reporter, PO Box 38, Mercer Island WA 98040. **ED** Jane Meyer. **Ad Acc**. **Pub. Size:** Broadsheet.

US
METHOW VALLEY NEWS. July 10, 1903-. Newspaper. English. wk. Methow Valley News, 201 Glover, Twisp WA 98856.

US/0890-2879
MONROE MONITOR/VALLEY NEWS. **VFOAT** Monroe Monitor Valley News. Vol. 95, No. 40 (Oct. 2, 1985)-. Newspaper. English. Fifty-two times a year (Wed.). Monroe Monitor Valley News, PO Box 399, Monroe WA 98272. **Tel** (206)794-7116. **ED** Howard Voland. **Ad Acc**. **Circ:** 3,500. ***Formed by the union of*** *Monroe Monitor (Monroe, Wash. : 1917)* ***and*** *Valley News (Sultan, Wash.).*

US/0745-7383
MONTESANO GRAYS HARBOR COUNTY VIDETTE, THE. **VFOAT** Vidette. V. 91, No. 14 (April 5, 1973)-. Newspaper. English. wk. $10.00 Grays Harbor county, $12.00 elsewhere in US; $22.00 others. PO Box 671, Montesano WA 98563. ***Continues*** *Montesano Vidette.*

US/1042-3621
MORNING NEWS TRIBUNE. **VFOAT** Sunday News Tribune; News Tribune. 104th Year, No. 364 (Apr. 6, 1987)-. Newspaper. English. da. The Morning News Tribune, PO Box 11000, Tacoma WA 98411. **Tel** (206)597-8511. **ED** John D. Komen. Index available. cum. index. **Bk Rev**. **Ad Acc**. **Circ:** 115,596 (daily), 126,362 (Sunday) (ctrl). available on microfilm. ***Continues*** *Tacoma News Tribune.*

US
MORTON JOURNAL (MORTON, WASH. : 1988). (THE MORTON JOURNAL.). Vol. 44, No. 1 (Jan. 6, 1988)-. Newspaper. English. wk. $16.00 US; $26.00 other. PO Drawer M, Morton WA 98356-0044. **Tel** (206)496-5993. **ED** Frank DeVaul. **Ad Acc**. **Circ:** 3,000 (ctrl). ***Continues*** *Journal (Morton, Wash.).* **Desc:** General interest in Lewis county.

US/0892-6239
NEWPORT MINER, THE. **VFOAT** Miner. (1899)-. Newspaper. English. Fifty-two times a year. $27.00 Oreille County; $36.00 other. Newport Miner, PO Box 349, Newport WA 99156. **Tel** (509)447-2433, 447-2434, FAX (509)447-9222. **ED** Fred J. Billenbrock II. **Ad Acc**. **Circ:** 6,000 (ctrl). available on microfiche. ***Absorbed*** *Newport Pilot.*

US
NEWS REVIEW (SUMNER, WASH.). ***Ceased.*** (THE NEWS REVIEW.). Vol. 72, No. 31 (August 2, 1972)-Ceased Vol. 90, No. 10 (March 1990). Newspaper. English. wk. News Review, PO Box 428, Sumner WA 98390. ***Continues*** *Sumner News Review.*

●US
NEWS TRIBUNE, THE. (1993)-. Newspaper. English. da. $168.00 (daily by mail). $78.00 (Sunday by mail), $210.00 (daily & Sunday by mail) Washington, Oregon, Idaho & APO; $222.00 (daily by mail), $98.80 (Sunday by mail), $240.00 (daily & Sunday by mail) US. Tacoma News Tribune, PO Box 11000, Tacoma WA 98411. **Tel** (206)597-8711. ***Continues*** *Morning News Tribune, 1042-3621.*

US
NISQUALLY VALLEY NEWS, THE. (1922)-. Newspaper. English. wk. Nisqually Valley News, PO Box 597, Yelm WA 98597. **Tel** (206)458-2681. **ED** Donald Miller. **Ad Acc**. **Circ:** 11,400.

US/1057-3771
NORTHSHORE CITIZEN (1990). (NORTHSHORE CITIZEN.). Vol. 87, No. 38 (Mar. 7, 1990)-. Newspaper. English. wk. $24.00. Northshore Citizen, PO Box 647, Bothell WA 98041. **Tel** (206)486-1231, FAX (206)483-3286. **ED** John Merrill. **Bk Rev**, (Qty: 2-3). **Photos**. **Ad Acc**, **Adv Mgr:** Kim VanderKooy. Full Page (B&W) $1638.00. Half Page (B&W) $819.00. Full Page (Color) $1806.00. Half Page (Color) $984.00. **Pub. Size:** Broadsheet. **Circ:** 25,000. ***Continues*** *Citizen (Bothell, Wash.), 0897-9146.*

US/1062-2934
ODESSA RECORD, THE. Vol. 1, No. 1, May 10 (1901)-. Newspaper. English. wk. $18.00, $14.00 (Washington). Odessa Record, PO Box 458, Odessa WA 99159. **Tel** (509)982-2632. **ED** Tom Bertsch. **Bk Rev**. **Ad Acc**. **Circ:** 1,300. available on microfiche (from Washington State University Library).

US/0746-7575
OLYMPIAN (OLYMPIA, WASH.). (THE OLYMPIAN.). Vol. 91, No. 336 (Feb. 1, 1982)-. Newspaper. English. da. $182.00. The Olympian, PO Box 407, Olympia WA 98507. **Tel** (206)754-5400. available on microfilm from University Microfilms International (UMI). ***Continues*** *Daily Olympian (Olympia, Wash.: 1938).*

US/1064-2617
OMAK-OKANOGAN COUNTY CHRONICLE, THE. **VFOAT** Chronicle; Omak Okanogan County Chronicle; Chronicle (Omak, WA). Vol. 63, No. 25 (Feb. 1, 1973)-. Newspaper. English. wk. $16.00 (in county), $25.00 (in state), $30.00 (out of state). Omak Chronicle, PO Box 553, Omak WA 98841. **Tel** (509)826-1110, FAX (509)826-5819. **ED** John E. Andrist and Mary Koch (Managing Editor). **Photos**. **Ad Acc**, **Adv Mgr:** Marilyn Ries. Full Page (B&W) $1,245.00. Half Page (B&W) $637.50. Full Page (Color) $1,305.00. Half Page (Color) $697.50. **Pub. Size:** Broadsheet. **Wire Svcs.:** AP. **Circ:** 6,000. ***Continues*** *Omak Chronicle.*

US/1056-8328
OUTLOOK (OTHELLO, WASH.), THE. (THE OUTLOOK.). **VFOAT** Othello Outlook. Vol. 28, No. 25 (June 23, 1977)-. Newspaper. English. wk. $18.00 Adams County; $23.00 others. The Outlook / Othello, PO Drawer O, Othello WA 99344. **ED** Nadine Baldridge. **Photos**. **Ad Acc**, **Adv Mgr:** Dick Rex, **Tel** (509)488-3342. Full Page (B&W) $625.65. Half Page (B&W) $310.40. **Pub. Size:** Standard. **Circ:** 4,279. ***Continues*** *Othello Outlook (DLC)sn 88087240.*

US/1050-7000
PENINSULA DAILY NEWS. March 22, 1987-. Newspaper. English. da. Peninsula Daily News, PO Box 1330, Port Angeles WA 98362.

US/1066-2065
PENINSULA GATEWAY, THE. (Aug. 24, 1923)-. Newspaper. English. wk. $17.00. Gig Harbor Peninsula Gateway, PO Box 407, Gig Harbor WA 98335. **ED** Tony Hazovian. **Photos**. **Ad Acc**, **Adv Mgr:** Tom Taylor, **Tel** (206)851-9921. **Pub. Size:** Broadsheet. **Wire Svcs.:** AP. **Circ:** 24,000. available in microform. ***Continues*** *Bay Island News.*

US
PIERCE COUNTY BUSINESS EXAMINER. (1985)-. Newspaper. English. bw. $21.00 1year; $30.00 2 year. Pierce County Business Examiner, 5007 Pacific Hwy East, Tacoma WA 98424. **Tel** (206)922-1522.

US/0192-1401
PIERCE COUNTY HERALD (PUYALLUP, WASH.). (PIERCE COUNTY HERALD.). (Dec. 25, 1974)-. Newspaper. English. ir (Published Tues., Thurs., & Sat.). $25.00. Pierce County Herald, PO Box 517,

Puyallup WA 98371. **Tel** (206)841-2481. **ED** Gordon Koestler. **Circ:** 18,200. ***Continues*** *Pierce County Herald and Puyallup Valley Tribune.*

US
PORT ORCHARD INDEPENDENT. (188?)-. Newspaper. English. wk. $25.00. Port Orchard Independent, PO Box 27, Port Orchard WA 98366. **Tel** (206)876-4414. **ED** Dan Ivanis. **Photos. Ad Acc, Adv Mgr:** Doug Weese. Full Page (B&W) $948.70. Half Page (B&W) $471.50. Full Page (Color) $948.70 plus $130.00 per color. Half Page (Color) $471.50 plus $130.00 per color. **Pub. Size:** Tabloid. ***Continues*** *Sidney Independent.*

US/1050-1460
PORT TOWNSEND JEFFERSON COUNTY LEADER, THE. Vol. 99, No. 41 (Oct. 14, 1987)-. Newspaper. English. Fifty-two times a year. $30.00. Port Townsend Leader, 226 Adams Street, PO Box 552, Port Townsend WA 98368. **Tel** (206)385-2900. **ED** Scott Wilson. **Bk Rev**, (Qty: 10). **Photos. Ad Acc, Adv Mgr:** Dan Huntingford. Full Page (B&W) $919.80. Half Page (B&W) $478.80. Full Page (Color) $1,189.80. Half Page (Color) $768.80. **Pub. Size:** Broadsheet. **Circ:** 9,260. available in microform. ***Continues*** *Port Townsend Leader (1927).*

US
PROSSER RECORD-BULLETIN. July 1, 1920-. Bulletin. English. wk. Prosser Record-Bulletin, PO Box 750, Prosser WA 99350. ***Continues*** *Independent-Record (Prosser, Wash.);* ***Absorbed*** *Republican-Bulletin (Prosser, Wash.).*

US
PULLMAN HERALD. Vol. 1, No. 1 (Nov. 3, 1888)-. Newspaper. English. wk. Pullman Herald, 410 Grand Avenue, Pullman WA 99163.

US
QUAD-CITY HERALD. Vol. 75, No. 40 (Apr. 1, 1976)-. Newspaper. English. wk. $16.00 Brewster, WA; $20.00 Washington State; $25.00 other. Quad-City Herald, PO Box 37, Brewster WA 98812. **Tel** (509)689-2507. **ED** Ivan Vallance. **Ad Acc. Circ:** 2,500. ***Continues*** *Herald-Reporter (Brewster, Wash. : 1974).*

US
QUINCY VALLEY POST-REGISTER, THE. Newspaper. English. wk. $14.00. Quincy Valley Post-Register, PO Box 217, Quincy WA 98848. **Tel** (509)787-4511. **ED** Don Lindberg. **Ad Acc. Circ:** 1,850.

US/0192-8171
RANGER, THE. Periodical. English. wk. The Ranger, PO Box 98801, Tacoma WA 98499.

US/0277-7819
RESOURCE REVIEW. [Resour. rev.]. Periodical. English. wk. $26.00 US; $40.00 other. Resource Review, Inc., Box 18560, Spokane WA 99208.

US/1053-2889
REVIEW (WINSLOW, WASH.), THE. (THE REVIEW.). **VFOAT** Bainbridge Island Review. (19??)-. Newspaper. English. wk. $25.00. Kitsap Newspaper Group, 221 Winslow Way West, Bainbridge Island WA 98110. **Tel** (206)842-6613, FAX (206)842-5867. **ED** Becky Fox Marshall. **Photos. Ad Acc, Adv Mgr:** Chris Allen. Half Page (B&W) $488.75. Half Page (Color) $638.75. **Pub. Size:** Tabloid. **Circ:** 5,961 paid. ***Continues*** *Bainbridge Island Review (Bainbridge Island, Wash. : 1988).*

US
RICHLAND REVIEW. (1968)-. Newspaper. English. wk. Tribune Newspapers Inc, PO Box 579, Clarkston WA 99403-0579.

US
RITZVILLE ADAMS COUNTY JOURNAL, THE. Vol. 74, No. 27 (July 5, 1973)-. Newspaper. English. wk. Ritzville Adams County Journal, Ritzville WA 99169. ***Continues*** *Ritzville Journal-Times.*

US
ROOSEVELT RECORD. (Sept. 14, 1965)-. Newspaper. English. wk. Tribune Newspapers Inc, PO Box 579, Clarkston WA 99403-0579.

US
SAMMAMISH VALLEY NEWS. Established 1946?. Newspaper. English. wk. $13.00. Sammamish Valley News, PO Box 716, Redmond WA 98052. **Tel** (206)883-7187, FAX (206)869-7999. **ED** Tim Chovanak. **Bk Rev. Ad Acc. Circ:** 18,000 (ctrl).

US
SEATTLE DAILY JOURNAL OF COMMERCE. Vol. 96, No. 9 (Jan. 12, 1989)-. Newspaper. English. da. $160.00. Daily Journal of Commerce, PO Box 11050, Seattle WA 98111. **Tel** (206)622-8272, FAX (206)622-8416. **ED** Phil Brown. **Photos.** Full Page (B&W) $1,911.00. Half Page (B&W) $1,029.00. Full Page (Color) $2,111.00. Half Page (Color) $1,229.00. **Pub. Size:** Broadsheet. **Wire Svcs.:** AP. ***Continues*** *Seattle Daily Journal of Commerce and Northwest Construction Record.*

US/0746-5394
SEATTLE MEDIUM, THE. (19??)-. Newspaper. English. Fifty-two times a year (Wed.). The Medium News, PO Box 22047, Seattle WA 98122. ***Continues*** *Medium.*

US/0745-970X
SEATTLE POST-INTELLIGENCER (1921). (SEATTLE POST-INTELLIGENCER.). **VFOAT** Seattle Post Intelligencer; Seattle Times Seattle Post Intelligencer. Vol. 79, No. 155 (Apr. 18, 1921)-. Newspaper. English. da (312 per year). $382.00 Washington, Oregon, Idaho, Montana, & APO FPO Seattle; $394.00 US; $598.00 Canada; $646.00 other. Seattle Times, PO Box 84647, Seattle WA 98124. **Tel** (206)464-2121. **ED** Virgil Fassio. **Circ:** 206,851 daily, 493,916 Sunday. available on microfilm from University Microfilms International (UMI); available on an online database (file 736/Full-Text) from DIALOG. ***Continues*** *Post-Intelligencer, 0746-6307.*

US/0745-9696
SEATTLE TIMES, THE. **VFOAT** Seattle Sunday Times; Seattle Times Seattle Post Intelligencer. Vol. 89, No. 73 (Mar. 14, 1966)-. Newspaper. English. ds. $490.00 Washington, Oregon, Idaho, Montana, & APO FPO Seattle; $514.00 US; $838.00 Canada; $898.00 other. Seattle Times, PO Box 84647, Seattle WA 98124. **Tel** (206)464-2121. **ED** Michael R. Fancher. **Bk Rev. Ad Acc. Circ:** 233,855. available on microfilm from University Microfilms International (UMI); available on an online database (files 493,635,707/Full-Text) from DIALOG; NEXIS; VU-TEXT; and DATATIMES. Documents available from UMI Article Clearinghouse. ***Continues*** *Seattle Daily Times (Seattle, Wash. : 1896).*
Ind/Abst Bus. Dateline; Infobank (Jan. 1969-); PROMT.

US/0898-0845
SEATTLE WEEKLY. **VFOAT** Weekly. Vol. 13, No. 5 (Feb. 3, 1988)-. Newspaper. English. wk. $19.95 Washington; $44.95 other. Sasquatch Publishing Company, 1931 2nd Avenue, Seattle WA 98101. **Tel** (206)441-5555. ***Continues*** *Weekly, 0279-6406.*

US
SHELTON-MASON COUNTY JOURNAL, THE. Vol. 41, No. 14 (March 8, 1927)-. Newspaper. English. wk. $20.00 Mason County; $28.00 Washington; $35.00 other. Shelton Mason County Journal, 227-A Cota Street, PO Box 430, Shelton WA 98534. **Tel** (206)426-4412. **ED** Henry G. Gay and Charlie Gay (Managing Editor). **Photos. Ad Acc, Adv Mgr:** Michael Politz. Full Page (B&W) $867.30. Half Page (B&W) $433.65. Full Page (Color) $932.30. Half Page (Color) $498.65. **Pub. Size:** Broadsheet. **Circ:** 9,874. available in microform. ***Continues*** *Mason County Journal (Shelton, Wash.);* ***Absorbed*** *Shelton Independent; Huckleberry Herald.*

US/1071-197X
SKAGIT VALLEY HERALD. 34th Year, No. 68 (Jan. 3, 1956)-. Newspaper. English. da (Mon.-Sat.). $144.00 (by mail). Skagit Valley Publishing, PO Box 578, Mount Vernon WA 98273. **Tel** (206)424-3251, FAX (206)424-5300. **ED** Nancy G. Erickson. **Bk Rev**, (Qty: 12). **Photos. Ad Acc, Adv Mgr:** Paul Wood. Full Page (B&W) $1,719.57. Full Page (Color) $2,151.57. **Pub. Size:** Broadsheet. **Wire Svcs.:** AP. **Circ:** 20,600 (ctrl). available on microfilm. ***Continues*** *Mount Vernon Daily Herald;* ***Absorbed*** *American Bulletin.*
Desc: Local and regional news with some national and international news.

US
SNOHOMISH COUNTY TRIBUNE. (1889)-. Newspaper. English. wk (publ Weds.). $20.00 Snohomish County, $28.00 others. Snohomish County Tribune, Mach Publishing Co Inc, PO Box 499, Snohomish WA 98291-0499. **Tel** (206)568-4121. **ED** Leslie Hynes. **Photos. Ad Acc, Adv Mgr:** Becky Reed. Full Page (B&W) $660.00. Half Page (B&W) $357.00. Full Page (Color) $860.00. Half Page (Color) $462.00. **Pub. Size:** Standard. ctrl circ. available in microform. ***Absorbed*** *Lake Stevens, Granite Falls News-Press.*
Desc: Covers local news and community events.

US
SNOQUALMIE NORTH BEND VALLEY RECORD. Vol. 57, No. 51 (July 8, 1971)-. Newspaper. English. wk. $15.00 King county; $22.00 other. Falls Printing Co., PO Box 300, Snoqualmie WA 98065. **Tel** (206)888-2311, FAX (206)888-2427. **ED** Brian Kelly. ***Continues*** *Snoqualmie Valley Record.*

US/1063-7567
SNOQUALMIE VALLEY REPORTER. Vol. 1, Issue 1 (Dec. 5, 1990)-. Newspaper. English. wk. $15.00. Snoqualmie Valley Reporter, PO Box 1954, Snoqualmie WA 98065.

US
SOUTH DISTRICT JOURNAL (SEATTLE, WASH. : 1930). (THE SOUTH DISTRICT JOURNAL.). **VFOAT** Beacon Hill News/South District Journal. Began in 1930. Newspaper. English. wk. South District Journal, 2720 Hanford Street, Seattle WA 98144.

US
SOUTH PIERCE COUNTY DISPATCH, THE. Vol. 93, No. 46, (Nov. 12, 1986)-. Newspaper. English. wk. $18.00 Pierce County, WA; $21.00 other WA; $30.00 other. Eatonville Dispatch, PO Box 248, Eatonville WA 98328. **Tel** (206)832-4411. **ED** Jamie Martin-Almy. cum. index. **Bk Rev. Ad Acc. Pr Rev. Circ:** 5,500 (ctrl). ***Continues*** *Dispatch (Eatonville, Wash.).*
Desc: Weekly rural newspaper.

US/1064-0622
SOUTH WHIDBEY RECORD. Vol. 57, No. 11 (Oct. 20, 1981)-. Newspaper. English. Fifty-two times a year (Published on Tues.). $36.00. Whidbey Press, PO Box 387, Langley WA 98260. **Tel** (206)221-5300, FAX (206)221-6474. **ED** Jim Larsen. **Bk Rev**, (Qty: 6-8). **Photos. Ad Acc, Adv Mgr:** Kayla Conner. **Pub. Size:** Standard. **Circ:** 5,000 paid. ***Continues*** *Whidbey Island Record.*
Desc: Weekly newspaper serving South Whidbey Island, Washington.

US
SPOKANE CHRONICLE. **VFOAT** Spokane-Review/Spokane Chronicle; Spokane Review Spokane Chronicle. Vol. 96, No. 96 (Jan. 11, 1982)-. Newspaper. English. da. Cowles Publishing, PO Box 2160, Spokane WA 99210. **Tel** (509)459-5187. Documents available from UMI Article Clearinghouse. ***Continues*** *Spokane Daily Chronicle.*
Ind/Abst Bus. Dateline (Dec. 17, 1991-) [Full Txt.].

US/1064-7317
SPOKESMAN-REVIEW (1894), THE. (THE SPOKESMAN-REVIEW.). **VFOAT** Spokesman Review; Spokesman Review Spokane Chronicle. Vol. 11, No. 53 (June 29, 1894)-. Newspaper. English. da (365 issues). $96.00 US; $190.00 other. Cowles Publishing, PO Box 2160, Spokane WA 99210. **Tel** (509)459-5187. **ED** Christopher Peck. **Bk Rev. Ad Acc. Circ:** 83,941 daily, 137,046 Sunday. available on microfilm from University Microfilms International (UMI); available on an online database (file 635/Full-Text) from DIALOG. Documents available from UMI Article Clearinghouse. ***Continues*** *Spokane Review;* ***Absorbed*** *Spokane Daily Times.*
Ind/Abst Bus. Dateline (Dec. 22, 1991-) [Full Txt.].

US
STARBUCK STAR, THE. (19??)-. Newspaper. English. wk. Tribune Newspapers Inc, PO Box 579, Clarkston WA 99403-0579.

US
STATESMAN-EXAMINER (COLVILLE, WASH.). (STATESMAN-EXAMINER.). **VFOAT** Statesman Examiner. (May 7, 1948)-. Newspaper. English. wk. Statesman-Examiner, 220 South Main Street, Colville WA 99114. ***Formed by the union of*** *Colville Examiner* ***and*** *Statesman-Index (Colville, Wash. : 1927).*

US/1050-3692
SUN (BREMERTON, WASH.), THE. (THE SUN.). Vol. 85, No. 48 (June 1, 1984)-. Newspaper. English. da. $216.00 (daily & Sunday) by mail; $108.00 (daily & Sunday) by carrier; $72.00 (Sunday only) by mail. John P. Scripps Newspapers Corp., PO Box 259, 545 5th Street, Bremerton WA 98310. **Tel** (206)377-3711, FAX (206)377-9237. **ED** Mike Phillips, Marty Bohvechio (Managing Editor). **Bk Rev**, (Qty: 45). **Photos. Ad Acc, Adv Mgr:** Steve Howes. Full Page (B&W) $1746.66. Half Page (B&W) $873.33. Full Page (Color) $1946.66. Half Page (Color) $1073.33. **Pub. Size:** Broadsheet. **Wire Svcs.:** SH, AP. **Circ:** 40,120 daily, 42,267 Sunday. Documents available from UMI Article Clearinghouse. ***Continues*** *Bremerton Sun.*
Ind/Abst Bus. Dateline (Dec. 20, 1991-) [Full Txt.].

US
TENINO INDEPENDENT (TENINO, WASH. : 1968). (THE TENINO INDEPENDENT.). Vol. 44, No. 5 (June 5, 1968)-. Newspaper. English. wk. Tenino Independent, PO Box D, Tenino WA 98589. ***Continues*** *Thurston County Independent;* ***Absorbed*** *South County Sun.*

US
TIMES (WAITSBURG, WASH.). (THE TIMES.). Newspaper. English. wk. Tom Baker, Box 97, Waitsburg WA 99361-0097. ***Continues*** *Waitsburg Times.*

US
TRI-CITY HERALD. (Nov. 13, 1947)-. Newspaper. English. da. $276.00 (daily and Sunday). Tri-City Herald, PO Box 2608, Pasco WA 99302. **Tel** (509)582-1500. **ED** Ken Robertson. **Bk Rev. Ad Acc. Circ:** 40,000 (daily) (ctrl). available on an online database (file 635/Full-Text) from DIALOG. Documents available from UMI Article Clearinghouse. ***Continues*** *Pasco Herald.*
Ind/Abst Bus. Dateline (Dec. 24, 1991-) [Full Txt.].

US
UNIVERSITY HERALD (SEATTLE, WASH.). (UNIVERSITY HERALD.). Vol. 87, No. 21 (May 19, 1976)-. Newspaper. English. wk. Seattle Suburban Publications, 2720 South Hanford Street, Seattle WA 98144. ***Continues*** *University Herald Today.*

West Virginia

US
VALLEY DAILY NEWS. Vol. 102, No. 157 (July 2, 1990)-. Newspaper. English. wk. $75.00 local; $81.00 other. Valley Newspapers Inc., PO Box 130, Kent WA 98032. **Tel** (206)872-6600. *Formed by the union of Valley Daily News (Kent News Journal Ed.); Valley Daily News (Auburn Globe News Ed.) and Valley Daily News (Renton Record Chronicle Ed.)*

US
WAHKIAKUM COUNTY EAGLE. (Apr. 25 or May 2, 1963)-. Newspaper. English. wk. $27.00. Washkiakum County Eagle, PO Box 368, Cathlamet WA 98612. **ED** Rick Nelson and Bob Nelson (Managing Editor). **Bk Rev. Photos. Ad Acc, Adv Mgr Tel** 795-3391. Full Page (B&W) $403.20. Half Page (B&W) $204.80. **Pub. Size:** Standard. *Continues Lower Columbia Eagle.*

US
WALLA WALLA UNION-BULLETIN. **VFOAT** Walla Walla Union Bulletin. Vol. 69, No. 233 (Jan. 16, 1938)-. Bulletin. English. da. Walla Walla Union-Bulletin, First Avenue & Poplar Streets, Walla Walla WA 99362. *Formed by the union of Walla Walla Union (Walla Walla, Wash. : 1911) and Walla Walla Daily Bulletin.*

US
WAPATO INDEPENDENT. Began in 1905. Newspaper. English. wk. Jim Flint, PO Box 67, Wapato WA 98951.

US
WASHTUCNA WORLD. (1962)-. Newspaper. English. wk. Tribune Newspapers Inc, PO Box 579, Clarkston WA 99403-0579.

US
WENATCHEE WORLD, THE. (May 28, 1971)-. Newspaper. English. da. $120.00 Washington; $144.00 other (daily & Sunday by mail). World Publishing Company / Wenatchee, PO Box 1511, Wenatchee WA 98801. **Tel** (509)663-5161. available on microfilm from Bell & Howell. Documents available from UMI Article Clearinghouse. *Continues Wenatchee Daily World.* **Ind/Abst** Bus. Dateline (Dec. 23, 1991-) [Full Txt.].

US
WEST RICHLANDER, THE. (1968)-. Newspaper. English. wk. Tribune Newspapers Inc, PO Box 579, Clarkston WA 99403-0579.

US
WEST SEATTLE HERALD. Began in 1923. Newspaper. English. wk. West Seattle Herald, PO Box 16069, Seattle WA 98116.

US/0043-3748
WESTERN FRONT. Newspaper. English. Western Washington University, College Hall/11, Bellingham WA 98225.

US
WESTERN WALLA WALLA COUNTY ARGUS. (1960)-. Newspaper. English. wk. Tribune Newspapers Inc, PO Box 579, Clarkston WA 99403-0579.

US
WESTSIDE RECORD-JOURNAL. Vol. 1, No. 1 (Nov. 8, 1972)-. Newspaper. English. wk. Westside Record-Journal, 2008 Main Street, Ferndale WA 98248. *Formed by the union of Record (Ferndale, Wash.) and Blaine Journal.*

US/1060-7161
WHIDBEY NEWS-TIMES. **VFOAT** Whidbey News Times. (1959)-. Newspaper. English. ir (Published on Wed. and Sat.). $32.00 Island County Washington (by carrier); $42.00 Island County Washington (by mail); $60.00 US; $100.00 others. Whidbey News-Times, PO Box 10, Oak Harbor WA 98277. **Tel** (206)675-6611, FAX (206)679-2695. **ED** Fred Obee. **Ad Acc, Adv Mgr:** M. Smith. **Circ:** 9,500. *Formed by the union of Oak Harbor News and Island County Times.*

US
WILBUR REGISTER, THE. (1889)-. Newspaper. English. wk. $16.50. Newspaper, Box 186, 110 SE Main, Wilbur WA 99185. **Tel** (509)647-5551, FAX (509)647-5552. **ED** Frank Stepman. **Bk Rev. Photos. Ad Acc, Adv Mgr:** Karen Tilson. Full Page (B&W) $567.00. Half Page (B&W) $283.50. Full Page (Color) $637.00. Half Page (Color) $358.50. **Pub. Size:** Broadsheet.

US/1065-3805
WILLAPA HARBOR HERALD, THE. **VFOAT** Harbor Herald. Vol. 1, No. 1 (Apr. 1, 1981)-. Newspaper. English. Fifty-two times a year. $16.00 Pacific County; $20.00 other. Willapa Harbor Herald, PO Box 706, Raymond WA 98577. **Tel** (206)942-3466. **ED** Meredith Nicholson. **Ad Acc.** ctrl circ. *Formed by the union of South Bend Journal & Harbor Pilot and Raymond Herald (Raymond, Wash. : 1972).*

US
YAKIMA HERALD-REPUBLIC. **VFOAT** Herald-Republic. (April 1, 1968)-. Newspaper. English. da. $9.50 per month. Yakima Herald-Republic Inc., c/o James E. Barnhill, PO Box 9668, Yakima WA 98909. **Tel** (509)248-1251, FAX (509)577-7767 news, (509)577-7766 advertising. **ED** L. Dan Coleman, Tom Fluharty & Kathleen Gilligan (Managing Editors). **Photos. Ad Acc, Adv Mgr:** Brian Vaillancourt, **Tel** (509)577-7732. Full Page (B&W) $2554.20. Half Page (B&W) $1287.00. Full Page (Color) $2739.20. Half Page (Color) $1472.00. **Pub. Size:** Standard. **Wire Svcs.:** AP, KR. **Circ:** 41,115 daily, 43,985 Sunday. available in microform from University Microfilms International (UMI). Documents available from UMI Article Clearinghouse. *Formed by the union of Yakima Morning Herald and Yakima Daily Republic.* **Ind/Abst** Bus. Dateline (Dec. 22, 1991-) [Full Txt.].

US/0745-2322
YIHUA BAO. (HSI HUA PAO.). **VFOAT** Seattle Chinese Post. (Jan. 20, 1982)-. Newspaper. Chinese. wk (Thursdays). $15.00. Seattle Chinese Post, 414 8th Avenue South, Seattle WA 98104. **Tel** (206)223-0623, FAX (206)223-0626. **Bk Rev. Photos. Ad Acc, Adv Mgr:** Mark Shriner. Full Page (B&W) $500.00. Half Page (B&W) $250.00. **Pub. Size:** Standard. **Wire Svcs.:** CTN.

WEST VIRGINIA

US
BARBOUR DEMOCRAT, THE. Vol. 1, No. 1 (July 6, 1893)-. Newspaper. English. wk. Barbour Publishing Company, 113 Church Street, Box 455, Philippi WV 26416. *Absorbed Belington News.*

US
BERKELEY COUNTY HISTORICAL SOCIETY NEWSLETTER. Newsletter. English. Four times a year. $15.00 (individuals), $25.00 (institutions) Comes with Berkeley County Historical Society Membership. Berkeley County Historical Society, PO Box 1624, Martinsburg WV 25401. **Tel** (304)229-3775.

US
BLUEFIELD DAILY TELEGRAPH. **VFOAT** New Daily Telegraph. (1893)-. Newspaper. English. da. $126.00. Daily Telegraph Printing Company, 928 Bluefield Avenue, PO Box 1599, Bluefield WV 24701. **Tel** (304)327-2811, FAX (304)325-6176. **ED** Tom Colley, Melody Kinser (Managing Editor). **LC** 7002. **Bk Rev. Photos. Ad Acc, Adv Mgr:** Donna Clayton, **Tel** (304)327-2816. Full Page (B&W) $1687.32. Half Page (B&W) $1093.92. Full Page (Color) $1982.32. Half Page (Color) $1388.92. **Pub. Size:** Standard. **Wire Svcs.:** AP. **Circ:** 23,534 daily, 25,411 Sunday.

US
BRAXTON CITIZEN'S NEWS. (Feb. 9, 1976)-. Newspaper. English. wk. $16.50. Edward R. Given, 501 Main Street, Sutton WV 26601. **Tel** (304)765-5193. **ED** Edward R. Given (Managing Editor) and Del Thayer (Editor-in-Chief). **Bk Rev. Photos. Ad Acc, Adv Mgr:** Jeanine Given. Full Page (B&W) $223.00. Half Page (B&W) $140.00. Full Page (Color) $288.00. Half Page (Color) $205.00. **Pub. Size:** Broadsheet. **Circ:** 6,500 (ctrl).

US
BRAXTON DEMOCRAT-CENTRAL, THE. **VFOAT** Braxton Democrat Central. Vol. 99, No. 25 (Oct. 8, 1982)-. Newspaper. English. wk. Craig A Smith, Box 427, Sutton WV 26601. **ED** Robert Pullen. *Formed by the union of Braxton Central and Braxton Democrat.*

US
BROOKE COUNTY REVIEW. (19??)-. Newspaper. English. wk. $10.50. Brooke Publishing Inc., 319 Charles Street, PO Box 591, Wellsburg WV 26070. **Tel** (304)737-0946, FAX (304)737-1852. **ED** J. W. George Wallace. **Photos. Ad Acc, Adv Mgr:** Mary Ann Wilson, **Tel** (304)737-0946. Full Page (B&W) $325.00. Half Page (B&W) $195.00. **Pub. Size:** Broadsheet. **Circ:** 1,400. *Continues Brooke News.*

US
BROOKE NEWS. *Title Change.* (1937)-(19??). Newspaper. English. wk. Brooke Publishing Inc., 319 Charles Street, PO Box 591, Wellsburg WV 26070. **Tel** (304)737-0946, FAX (304)737-1852. **ED** J. W. George Wallace. **LC** 7002. **Photos. Ad Acc, Adv Mgr:** Mary Ann Wilson, **Tel** (304)737-0946. Full Page (B&W) $325.00. Half Page (B&W) $195.00. **Pub. Size:** Broadsheet. **Circ:** 1,400. *Continued by Brooke County Review.*

US/1041-2255
CABELL RECORD. (1898)-. Newspaper. English. wk. Cabell Record, PO Box 8, Milton WV 25541. **Tel** (304)538-2342, FAX (304)538-7294. **ED** Page Burdette. **Ad Acc. Circ:** 4,000.

US/1040-399X
CALHOUN CHRONICLE AND THE GRANTSVILLE NEWS, THE. No. 5017 (July 5, 1984)-. Newspaper. English. wk. Carl Morris, PO Box 400, Grantsville WV 26147. **ED** Meryl Pollack. *Formed by the union of Calhoun Chronicle and Grantsville News.*

US
CHARLESTON DAILY MAIL (CHARLESTON, W.VA. : 1920). (THE CHARLESTON DAILY MAIL.). Vol. 74 (Apr. 5, 1920)-. Newspaper. English. da. $106.00 (Mon.-Sat.), $156.00 (Mon.-Sun.) US; other prices available on request. The Charleston Daily Mail, 10001 Virginia Street East, Charleston WV 25330. **Tel** (304)348-5151. **ED** David Greenfield. **Bk Rev. Ad Acc. Circ:** 53,000. *Continues Charleston Mail.*

US
CHARLESTON GAZETTE (CHARLESTON, W. VA. : 1907). (THE CHARLESTON GAZETTE.). Vol. 20, No. 226 (Jan. 29, 1907)-. Newspaper. English. da (except Sunday). Charleston Gazette, PO Box 2993, East Charleston WV 25330. **Tel** 800 888-5140 or, (304)348-5151. **LC** 10189. available on microfilm from University Microfilms International (UMI). *Continues Charleston Daily Gazette.*

US
CHARLESTON NEWSPAPER INDEX. V. 1-1973-. English. an. West Virginia Library Committee, Charleston WV 25306. **LC** A121.C43; C48. **DD** 071/.54/38.

US
CLARKSBURG EXPONENT, THE. **VFOAT** Culpeper Exponent. (May 23 1910)-. Newspaper. English. da. The Clarksburg Publishing Company, PO Box 586, 324-326 Hewes Avenue, Clarksburg WV 26301. **Tel** (304)624-6411.

US
CLARKSBURG TELEGRAM (CLARSKBURG, W.VA. : DAILY). (CLARKSBURG TELEGRAM.). **VFOAT** Daily Telegram. Vol. 1, (1926)-. Newspaper. English. da. The Clarksburg Publishing Company, PO Box 586, 324-326 Hewes Avenue, Clarksburg WV 26301. **Tel** (304)624-6411. **LC** 7002. *Continues Daily Telegram (Clarksburg, W. Va.).*

US
CLAY COUNTY FREE PRESS. **VFOAT** Free Press. Began July 5, 1905?. Newspaper. English. wk. $18.00. Clinton Nichols, PO Box 180, Clay WV 25043-0180. **Tel** (304)587-4250. **ED** Clinton Nichals. **Bk Rev. Ad Acc. Circ:** 5,200 (ctrl). available on microfilm; available on diskette.

US/0745-7111
COAL VALLEY NEWS. (Jan. 24, 1925)-. Newspaper. English. wk. Coal Valley News, PO Box 508, Madison WV 25130-0508. **Tel** (304)369-1165, FAX (304)369-1166. **ED** Dorothea Cooke. **Ad Acc. Circ:** 6,000.

US
DOMINION POST. (July 26, 1973)-. Newspaper. English. da. $152.08. West Virginia Newspaper Publishing Co., 1251 Earl L. Core Road, Morgantown WV 26505. **Tel** (304)292-6301, FAX (304)291-2326. **ED** Ralph Brem. **Photos. Ad Acc, Adv Mgr:** Titus Workman. **Pub. Size:** Broadsheet. **Wire Svcs.:** AP. **Circ:** 20,150 (daily). available in microform from University Microfilms International (UMI). *Formed by the union of Dominion-News and Morgantown Post (Daily).*

US
EVENING JOURNAL, THE. Vol. 71, No. 196 (Jan. 2, 1978)-. Newspaper. English. da. Journal / Martinsburg, 207 West King Street, Martinsburg WV 25401-3211. **Tel** (304)263-8931, FAX (304)263-8058. **ED** William Doolittle. **Ad Acc, Adv Mgr:** James Connors. **Circ:** 19,100. *Continues Martinsburg Journal.*

US
FAYETTE TRIBUNE, THE. Vol. 26, No. 16 (March 5, 1924)-. Newspaper. English. sw. George W Williams, 417 Main Street, Box 139, Oak Hill WV 25901. *Absorbed Fayette Tribune and Free Press; Fayette Journal; Fayette Democrat (Fayetteville, W. Va. : 1914); Montgomery News (Montgomery, W. Va.); Fayette News (Oak Hill, W. Va.).*

US/0746-5890
GLENVILLE DEMOCRAT, THE. Began in 1904?. Newspaper. English. wk. Glenville Democrat Publishing Company, PO Box 430, Glenville WV 26351.

US/0746-5882
GLENVILLE PATHFINDER, THE. Newspaper. English. wk. Glenville Democrat Publishing Company, PO Box 430, Glenville WV 26351.

US
GRANT COUNTY PRESS. (1896)-. Newspaper. English. wk. $14.84 West Virginia; $18.00 others. Grant County Press, PO Box 39, Petersburg WV 26847. **Tel** (304)257-1844, FAX (304)257-1691. **ED** William Fouch (Editor-in-Chief) and Tom Hencke (Managing Editor). **Photos. Ad Acc, Adv Mgr:** Jodi Fouch. Full Page (B&W) $403.20. Half Page (B&W) $201.60. Full Page (Color) $503.20. Half Page (Color) $301.60. **Pub. Size:** Standard. available on microfilm from West Virginia University.

West Virginia

US/0736-5497
HAMPSHIRE REVIEW AND THE SOUTH BRANCH INTELLIGENCER, THE. VFOAT Hampshire Review. Vol. 68, No. 36 (August 6, 1952)-. Newspaper. English. wk. $15.75 (West Virginia); $15.00 all other. Hampshire Review, PO Box 1036, Romney WV 26757. Tel (304)822-3871. *Continues* South Branch Intelligencer.

US
HANCOCK COUNTY COURIER (NEW CUMBERLAND, W. VA. : 1943). (HANCOCK COUNTY COURIER.). Vol. 74, No. 2 (Jan. 14, 1943)-. Newspaper. English. wk. $9.00 West Virginia; $11.00 others. Hugh C. Tage & Joyce Frain, PO Box 547, New Cumberland WV 26047. **ED** Hugh Tate and Joyce Frain. **Bk Rev**, (Qty: 24). **Photos**. **Ad Acc, Adv Mgr:** Hugh Taylor. Full Page (B&W) $321.60. Half Page (B&W) $160.80. **Circ:** 2,200. *Continues* Hancock Courier.

US
HERALD-DISPATCH (HUNTINGTON, W. VA.). (THE HERALD-DISPATCH.). VFOAT Herald Dispatch; Huntington Herald-Dispatch; Herald-Advertiser; Herald Advertiser. (Jan. 17, 1909)-. Newspaper. English. da. Huntington Publishing Company, 946 Fifth Avenue, Huntington WV 25720. **ED** F A McDonald. **LC** 7002. *Formed by the union of Huntington Herald (Huntington, W. Va.) and Huntington Dispatch.*

US
HERALD RECORD (WEST UNION, W. VA.). (THE HERALD RECORD.). Vol. 100, No. 33 (Aug. 16, 1977)-. Newspaper. English. wk. $10.60 in county; $11.66 others in West Virginia; $12.00 others. Virginia Nicholson, 202 East Main Street, West Union WV 26456. **ED** Virginia Nicholson. **Photos**. **Ad Acc, Adv Mgr:** Virginia Nicholson. Full Page (B&W) $252.00. Half Page (B&W) $126.00. **Pub. Size:** Standard. *Formed by the union of Salem Herald (Salem, W.Va. : 1924) and West Union Record.*

US
HINTON NEWS. 76th Yr., No. 254 (June 20, 1978)-. Newspaper. English. wk. $16.00. Hinton News, PO Box 1000, Hinton WV 25951. Tel (304)466-2444. *Continues* Hinton Daily News (Hinton, W.Va. : 1922).

US
HURRICANE BREEZE. Began in 1900?. Newspaper. English. wk. Norman Forth, PO Box 336, Hurricane WV 25526.

US
INDEPENDENT-HERALD (PINEVILLE, W.VA.). (THE INDEPENDENT-HERALD.). VFOAT New Independent Herald; Wyoming Recorder; Independent Herald. Began in 1912. Newspaper. English. wk. Independent-Herald Publishing Company, Box 100, Pineville WV 24874-0100. **ED** Jack Shipman. *Continues* Wyoming Tribune.

US
INDUSTRIAL NEWS (IAEGER, W.VA.). (THE INDUSTRIAL NEWS.). (1923)-. Newspaper. English. wk. $6.36 (Iaeger, West Virginia), $14.84 (other). William A. Johnson, PO Box 180, Iaeger WV 24844. **Tel** (304)938-2142, FAX (304)436-3146. **ED** W. A. Johnson (Editor-in-Chief) and Ruby McCoy (Managing Editor). **Bk Rev**, (Qty: 20). **Photos**. **Ad Acc, Adv Mgr:** Ruby McCoy. Full Page (B&W) $245.10. Half Page (B&W) $122.55. Full Page (Color) $275.10. Half Page (Color) $152.55. **Pub. Size:** Standard. **Circ:** 1,700 (paid) (ctrl). **Desc:** Covers local and state topics.

US
INTELLIGENCER (WHEELING, W.VA.). (THE INTELLIGENCER.). Vol. 109, No. 262 (June 30, 1961)-. Newspaper. English. da. $112.36 West Virginia; $106.00 other. Ogden Newspaper, 1500 Main Street, Wheeling WV 26004. Tel (304)233-0100. **ED** Robert Kelly. **Bk Rev**, (Qty: 150-200). **Ad Acc, Adv Mgr:** Robert Diehl. **Circ:** 24,000. available on microfilm from University Microfilms International (UMI). *Continues* Wheeling Intelligencer.
Desc: General news of East Ohio and northern panhandle of West Virginia; general national and world news.

US
INTER-MOUNTAIN (ELKINS, W.VA. : DAILY). (THE INTER-MOUNTAIN.). VFOAT Inter Mountain. Vol. 58, No. 246 (July 20, 1970)-. Newspaper. English. da. Charles R Olson, 520 Railroad Avenue, PO Box 1339, Elkins WV 26241. Documents available from UMI Article Clearinghouse. *Continues* Elkins Inter-Mountain (Daily).
Ind/Abst Bus. Dateline (Jan. 4, 1992-) [Full Txt.].

US
JACKSON HERALD (RIPLEY, W.VA.). (JACKSON HERALD.). Began in 1876?. Newspaper. English. wk. Richard Simmons, PO Box 31, Ripley WV 25271. **ED** George W Biggs. *Continues* Jackson Democrat.

US/0746-0570
LOGAN BANNER (LOGAN, W. VA. : DAILY). (THE LOGAN BANNER.). Vol. 26, No. 8 (Aug. 21, 1914)-. Newspaper. English. da (312 issues). $121.00. Logan Banner, PO Box 720, Logan WV 25601. Tel (304)752-6950. *Continues* Logan Banner and the Logan Republican.

US
MEADOW RIVER POST. Sept. 15, 1966-. Newspaper. English. wk. Worrell Newspapers of West Virginia Inc, Box 747, 22 Main Street, Rainelle WV 25962.

US
MONROE WATCHMAN, THE. Vol. 25, No. 7 (March 18, 1897)-. Newspaper. English. wk. The Monroe Watchman Inc, Box 179, Union WV 24983. *Continues* Monroe County Watchman.

US
MONTGOMERY HERALD, THE. (Aug. 9, 1940)-. Newspaper. English. wk. $18.00. Montgomery Herald, 406 Lee Street, PO Box 240, Montgomery WV 25961. Tel (304)442-4156, FAX (304)442-8753. **ED** Dave Pollard. **Photos**. **Ad Acc, Adv Mgr:** Nancy Shelton, Tel (304)469-3373. Full Page (B&W) $659.19. Half Page (B&W) $378.95. Full Page (Color) $759.19. Half Page (Color) $478.95. **Pub. Size:** Broadsheet.

US/0740-2651
MOOREFIELD EXAMINER AND HARDY COUNTY NEWS, THE. VFOAT Moorefield Examiner. Vol. 60, No. 12 (March 20, 1957)-. Newspaper. English. sw. $11.00. Moorefield Examiner, 132 South Main Street, Moorefield WV 26836-0380. Tel (304)538-2342. *Continues* Moorefield Examiner.

US/0895-1594
MORGAN MESSENGER (BERKELEY SPRINGS, W. VA.). (THE MORGAN MESSENGER.). Vol. 1, No. 1 (Nov. 16, 1893)-. Newspaper. English. wk. $15.90 (Morgan Cty) $16.96 (WV); $19.00 (PN, VA & MD); $21.00 (other). The Morgan Messenger, 104 Montgomery Street, Berkeley Springs WV 25411-0567. **Tel** (304) 258-1800. *Continues* Morgan Mercury.

US
MOUNDSVILLE DAILY ECHO, THE. (Mar. 17, 1896)-. Newspaper. English. da. Moundsville Daily Echo, 715 Lafayette Avenue, Moundsville WV 26041-2143. Tel (304)845-2660, FAX (304)845-2661. **ED** Samuel Shaw. **Ad Acc**. **Circ:** 4,831.

US/0745-1334
MOUNTAIN STATESMAN (GRAFTON, W. VA.). (THE MOUNTAIN STATESMAN.). Vol. 1, No. 1 (Sept. 11, 1975). Newspaper. English. da. The Mountain Statesman Inc, 914 West Main Street, Grafton WV 26354.

US/1064-6132
MULLENS ADVOCATE, THE. (1913)-. Newspaper. English. wk (52 issues). $15.00. Mullen Advocate, Box 907, Mullens WV 25882. **Tel** (304)294-4144. **ED** Eva Smith. **Bk Rev**, (Qty: 6). **Photos**. **Ad Acc, Adv Mgr:** Eva Smith. Full Page (B&W) $303.15. Half Page (B&W) $155.10. Full Page (Color) $403.15. Half Page (Color) $255.10. **Pub. Size:** Standard. **Circ:** 3,500.

US
NEWS LEADER. Vol. 38, No. 2 (June 20, 1984)-. Newspaper. English. wk. $17.80 West Virginia; $21.00 other. Leader Publishing Co Inc / West Virginia, PO Box 591, Richwood WV 26261. **Tel** (304)846-2666, FAX (304)846-4972. **ED** Jim Comstock. **Photos**. **Ad Acc, Adv Mgr:** Diana. Full Page (B&W) $315.00. Half Page (B&W) $204.75. Full Page (Color) $390.00. Half Page (Color) $279.75. **Pub. Size:** Standard. **Circ:** 4,200. *Continues* Nicholas County News Leader.

US
NICHOLAS CHRONICLE, THE. VFOAT Chronicle. Began in August 1880?. Newspaper. English. wk. Betty Dilley, 603 Church Street, Summerville WV 26651. **ED** Howard Templeton.

US
PANHANDLE PRESS (CHESTER, W. VA.). (PANHANDLE PRESS.). VFOAT The Chester-Newell; Chester Newell. Vol. 1, No. 1 (July 23, 1969)-. Newspaper. English. Fifty-two times a year. $22.00 (one year); $29.00 (two years); $34.00 (three years). Panhandle Press WV, 180 Carolina Avenue, Circulation Department, Chester WV 26034. **Tel** (304)387-1835. **ED** Shirley Allen.

US
PARKERSBURG SENTINEL (PARKESBURG, W.VA. : 1893). (PARKERSBURG SENTINEL.). Vol. 5, No. 30 (Nov. 25, 1893)-. Newspaper. English. da. Parkersburg News, PO Box 1787, Parkersburg WV 26101. Documents available from UMI Article Clearinghouse. *Continues* Parkersburg Daily Sentinel.
Ind/Abst Bus. Dateline (Dec. 24, 1991-) [Full Txt.].

US/8750-3956
PARKERSBURGH NEWS (1916). (THE PARKERSBURG NEWS.). (1915)-. Newspaper. English. da. Parkersburg News, PO Box 1787, Parkersburg WV 26101. **LC** 7002. available on an online database (file 635/Full-Text) from DIALOG. Documents available from UMI Article Clearinghouse. *Continues* Parkersburg Dispatch-News.
Ind/Abst Bus. Dateline (Dec. 24, 1991-) [Full Txt.].

US/0747-3303
PARSONS ADVOCATE. Vol. 5, No. 18 (March 6, 1901)-. Newspaper. English. wk. $15.00 Tucker County; $17.00 others in West Virginia; $22.00 others. The Parsons Advocate, 212 Main Street, Parsons WV 26287. **Tel** (304)478-3533, FAX (304)478-4658. **ED** Mariwyn Smith. **Photos**. **Ad Acc, Adv Mgr:** Gail Jones. Full Page (B&W) $409.50. Half Page (B&W) $204.75. Full Page (Color) $484.50. Half Page (Color) $279.75. **Pub. Size:** Standard. **Circ:** 4,100. available in microform. *Continues* Parsons City Advocate; *Absorbed in part* Tucker Democrat (Parsons, W. Va. : 194U).

US
PENDLETON TIMES (PENDLETON, IND.). (THE PENDLETON TIMES.). (1904)-. Newspaper. English. Fifty-two times a year (Published on Thurs.). $7.50 (one year). William McCoy Jr., Franklin WV 26807. **Tel** (304)358-2304.

US
PENNSBORO NEWS, THE. (1893)-. Newspaper. English. wk. $5.30 in county; $10.60 others in West Virginia; $19.00 others. Roy G. Owens / West Virginia, PO Box 368, Pennsboro WV 26415. **ED** J. McGoldrick (Editor-in-Chief) and Randa Gregg (Managing Editor). **Photos**. **Ad Acc, Adv Mgr:** Randa Gregg. Full Page (B&W) $330.00. Half Page (B&W) $165.00. Full Page (Color) $390.00. Half Page (Color) $225.00. **Pub. Size:** Standard. **Circ:** 5,100. *Continues* Lever.

US
PIEDMONT HERALD (PIEDMONT, W. VA.). (THE PIEDMONT HERALD.). (1882)-. Newspaper. English. wk (52 issues). $27.00. Piedmont Herald, 34 Railroad Lane, Piedmont WV 26750. **Tel** (304)355-2381.

US
PLEASANTS COUNTY LEADER. Vol. 1, No. 20 (Sept. 30, 1898)-. Newspaper. English. wk. $20.79. J. McGoldrick, Box 27, Saint Marys WV 26170. **Tel** (304)684-2424, FAX (304)684-2426. **ED** J. McGoldrick (Editor-in-Chief) and C. Mason (Manging Editor). **Photos**. **Ad Acc, Adv Mgr:** Vermice Simonton. Full Page (B&W) $546.00. Full Page (Color) $621.00. **Pub. Size:** Standard. **Circ:** 2,100. available on microfilm. *Continues* St. Marys Independent.

US/0738-8373
POCAHONTAS TIMES. (May 10, 1883)-. Newspaper. English. Fifty-one times per year (Except Dec.). $10.00 West Virginia; $11.00 others. Pocahontas Times Inc, 810 Second Avenue, Marlinton WV 24954. **Tel** (304)799-4973.

US
POINT PLEASANT REGISTER (DAILY : 1942). (POINT PLEASANT REGISTER.). Vol. 12, No. 29 (August 25, 1942)-. Newspaper. English. da. Point Pleasant Register Company, Point Pleasant WV 25550. **ED** Edward Swint. *Continues* Point Pleasant Daily Register.

US
PRESTON COUNTY NEWS, THE. Vol. 1, No. 1 (April 17, 1952)-. Newspaper. English. wk. Robert G Teets, 805 East State Street, Box 10, Terra Alta WV 26764.

US
PRINCETON TIMES (PRINCETON, W.VA. : WEEKLY). (THE PRINCETON TIMES.). Vol. 4, No. 10 (Aug. 13, 1964)-. Newspaper. English. wk. Ray Brasted, 1101 Mercer Street, PO Box 1199, Princeton WV 24740. *Continues* Princeton Daily Times.

US
PUTNAM DEMOCRAT (WINFIELD, W. VA.). (PUTNAM DEMOCRAT.). (187?)-. Newspaper. English. wk. $10.50 local; $12.00 West Virginia; $15.00 US. William O. Robinson, PO Box 179, Winfield WV 25213. **Tel** (304)586-2451. **ED** William O. Robinson, Shelby Young (Managing Editor). **LC** 10185-X. **Bk Rev**, (Qty: 12). **Photos**. **Ad Acc, Adv Mgr:** Fritzi Whitney. Full Page (B&W) $554.40. Half Page (B&W) $277.20. Full Page (Color) $654.40. Half Page (Color) $377.20. **Pub. Size:** Broadsheet. *Continues* Putnam County Democrat.

US
RAVENSWOOD NEWS, THE. Vol. 11, No. 42 (Aug. 21, 1879)-. Newspaper. English. wk. Phil Fourney, 410 Race Street, PO Box 10, Ravenswood WV 26164. *Continues* Jackson County News.

US
RECORD DELTA, THE. 107th Yr., No. 21 (March 14, 1977)-. Newspaper. English. ir (156 issues).

$64.00 West Virginia, US; $70.00 other. Mountaineer Newspapers Inc., 7 North Locust Street, Buskannon WV 26201. **Tel** (304)472-2800. ***Formed by the union of*** *Republican-Delta* ***and*** *Buckhannon Record.*

US
RITCHIE GAZETTE AND THE CAIRO STANDARD. Vol. 54 (Jan. 5, 1950)-. Newspaper. English. wk. Delores J Smith, 112 116 East Main Street, Box 215, Harrisville WV 26362-0215. **ED** Delores Smith and Judy Newbrough. **Photos. Ad Acc, Adv Mgr:** Judy Newbrough, **Tel** (304)643-2221. Full Page (B&W) $317.50. Half Page (B&W) $167.70. Full Page (Color) $397.50. Half Page (Color) $247.70. **Pub. Size:** Standard. **Circ:** 3,800. ***Formed by the union of*** *Gazette (Harrisville, W.Va.)* ***and*** *Cairo Standard.*

US
ROANE COUNTY REPORTER. Vol. 1, No. 1 (Jan. 15, 1915). Newspaper. English. wk. Spencer Newspapers Inc, 341 Main Street, PO Box 20, Spencer WV 25276. ***Continues*** *Weekly Bulletin (Spencer, W.Va.).*

US
SPIRIT OF JEFFERSON FARMERS ADVOCATE. Vol. 84, No. 9 (March 4, 1948)-. Newspaper. English. wk (Thursday). $18.00. Jefferson Publishing Company Inc, North George Street, PO Box 966, Charles Town WV 25414-0966. **Tel** (304)725-2046. **ED** Edward W. Dockeney Jr. **Photos. Ad Acc, Adv Mgr:** Meade Dorsey. Full Page (B&W) $774.00. Half Page (B&W) $387.00. Full Page (Color) $924.00. **Pub. Size:** Standard. **Circ:** 4,894 (ctrl). ***Formed by the union of*** *Spirit of Jefferson* ***and*** *Farmers Advocate.*
Desc: Local news, sports, features, advertisements, serving Jefferson County, WV. only paper published in the county.

US
SUNDAY EXPONENT-TELEGRAM (CLARKSBURG, W.VA.). (SUNDAY EXPONENT-TELEGRAM.). **VFOAT** Sunday Exponent Telegram. (1927)-. Newspaper. English. wk. The Clarksburg Publishing Company, PO Box 586, 324-326 Hewes Avenue, Clarksburg WV 26301. **Tel** (304)624-6411.

US
SUNDAY GAZETTE-MAIL. VFOAT Sunday Gazette Mail. March 2, 1958-. Newspaper. English. wk. Charleston Gazette, PO Box 2993, East Charleston WV 25330. **Tel** 800 888-5140 or, (304)348-5151. available on microfilm from University Microfilms International (UMI).

US
TIMES-RECORD (SPENCER, W.VA.). (THE TIMES-RECORD.). **VFOAT** Times Record; Spencer Times-Record. Vol. 1, No. 1 (Sept. 4, 1913)-. Newspaper. English. wk. Spencer Newspapers Inc, 341 Main Street, PO Box 20, Spencer WV 25276. **ED** S A Simmons. ***Formed by the union of*** *Roane County Record* ***and*** *Spencer Times.*

US
TIMES-WEST VIRGINIAN (FAIRMONT, W.VA. : DAILY). (TIMES-WEST VIRGINIAN.). **VFOAT** Times West Virginian. Vol. 1, No. 1 (Nov. 29, 1976)-. Newspaper. English. da. Fairmont Newspaper Publishing Company, Ogden and Quincy, Fairmont WV 26554. ***Continues*** *Fairmont Times and West Virginian.*

US
WAYNE COUNTY NEWS (WAYNE, W.VA.). (WAYNE COUNTY NEWS.). Vol. 46, No. 48 (Sept. 11, 1919)-. Newspaper. English. Fifty-two times a year (Published on Wed.). $19.08 Wayne County; $21.20 others in West Virginia; $24.00 others. Wayne County News Inc, 310 Central Avenue, Wayne WV 25570. **Tel** (304)272-3433. ***Continues*** *Wayne News.*

US
WEBSTER REPUBLICAN, THE. Began in 1904?. Newspaper. English. wk. Edna F Dotson, Box 749, Webster Springs WV 26288.

US
WEIRTON DAILY TIMES, THE. (1928)-. Newspaper. English. da. Glenn M Zarfos, 114 Lee Avenue, Weirton WV 26062. ***Continues*** *Weirton Leader-News.*

US/0891-9240
WEST VIRGINIA ADVOCATE, THE. (Apr. 1982)-. Newspaper. English. mo. $5.40 (one year), $10.80 (two year), $14.80 (three year). West Virginia Advocate, PO Box 171, Capon Bridge WV 26711. **Tel** (304)856-3651. **ED** Warren E. Duliere. **Bk Rev. Ad Acc. Circ:** 14,500.

US
WEST VIRGINIA DAILY NEWS, THE. Vol. 70, No. 27 (Feb. 20, 1967)-. Newspaper. English. da. $47.25 West Virginia; $45.00 other. West Virginia Daily News, PO Box 471, Lewisburg WV 24901. **Tel** (304)645-1206. ***Continues*** *West Virginia News.*

US/0888-0409
WEST VIRGINIA HILLBILLY (RICHWOOD, W.VA. : 1986). (THE WEST VIRGINIA HILLBILLY.). (198?)-. Newspaper. English. wk. $35.00. The West Virginia Hillbilly, Box 430, Richwood WV 26261. **Tel** (304)846-2666, FAX (304)846-6292. **ED** James Comstock. **Bk Rev. Ad Acc.** ***Continues*** *West Virginia Then and Now, 0887-4743.*
Desc: History of the state of education.

US
WESTON DEMOCRAT, THE. VFOAT Democrat. (187?)-. Newspaper. English. wk. $14.00 West Virginia; $18.00 others. Weston Democrat Inc, Box 968, Weston WV 26452. **Tel** (304)269-1600, FAX (304)269-4035. **ED** George Whelan. **LC** 10185-X. **Bk Rev. Photos. Ad Acc, Adv Mgr:** Julia Spelsberg. Full Page (B&W) $246.50. Half Page (B&W) $173.25. Full Page (Color) $386.50. Half Page (Color) $213.25. **Pub. Size:** Standard. **Circ:** 8,118. available on microfilm from University Microfilms International (UMI). ***Continues*** *Democrat (Weston, W. Va.);* ***Absorbed in part*** *Weston Sentinel (Weston, W. Va. : 1898).*

US
WETZEL CHRONICLE. Vol. 1, No. 1 (July 5, 1979)-. Newspaper. English. wk. Wetzel Publishing Company, Box 289, New Martinsville WV 26155. ***Formed by the union of*** *Wetzel Democrat* ***and*** *Wetzel Republican.*

US
WHEELING NEWS-REGISTER. VFOAT Wheeling News Register; Sunday News-Register. Vol. 45, No. 337 (Aug. 27, 1935)-. Newspaper. English. ir (Sunday only). $46.64 West Virginia (includes sales tax); $44.00 other. Ogden Newspaper, 1500 Main Street, Wheeling WV 26004. **Tel** (304)233-0100. **ED** J. Michael Myer. **LC** 7002. **Bk Rev**, (Qty: 150-200/year). **Ad Acc, Adv Mgr:** Robert Diehl. **Circ:** 56,000. available on an online database (file 635/Full-Text) from DIALOG. Documents available from UMI Article Clearinghouse. ***Formed by the union of*** *Wheeling Daily News* ***and*** *Wheeling Register.*
Desc: General news of east Ohio and northern panhandle of West Virginia. Also contains general, national and world news.
Ind/Abst Bus. Dateline (Jan. 10, 1992-) [Full Txt.].

US/0883-1602
WILLIAMSON DAILY NEWS. Vol. 1, No. 2 (Jan. 9, 1913)-. Newspaper. English. da. $75.00. Louis P Harvath III, PO Box 1660, Williamson WV 25661. ***Absorbed*** *Progressive West Virginian.*

WISCONSIN

US
ADVANCE (RANDOLPH, WIS. : 1976). (THE ADVANCE.). Vol. 83, No. 47 (Nov. 18, 1976)-. Newspaper. English. Fifty-two times a year (Wed.). Advance / Wisconsin, 115 Williams Street, Randolph WI 53956. **Tel** (414)326-5151. ***Continues*** *Randolph Advance.*

US
ALBANY HERALD. Vol. 43, No. 1 (Jan. 1, 1925)-. Newspaper. English. wk. Albany Herald / Wisconsin, 200 Oak Street, Albany WI 53502. **Tel** (608)862-3224. **ED** George Martin. **Ad Acc, Adv Mgr:** Geneva Thompson. **Circ:** 2,400. ***Continues*** *Albany Vindicator.*

US
ALGOMA RECORD-HERALD. VFOAT Algoma Record Herald; Record Herald. Vol. 45, No. 38 (Feb. 8, 1918)-. Newspaper. English. Fifty-two times a year (Thurs.). $20.00 Wisconsin; $25.00 other. Record Herald / Wisconsin, 401 3rd Street, Algoma WI 54201. **Tel** (414)487-2222. **ED** Dave Ehrhardt. **Ad Acc. Circ:** 4,000. ***Formed by the union of*** *Algoma Herald* ***and*** *Algoma Record.*

US/0748-6898
AMERY FREE PRESS. VFOAT Free Press. (1891)-. Newspaper. English. Fifty-two times a year. $22.00 Wisconsin; $25.00 other. Amery Free Press, 215 South Keller Avenue, PO Box 338, Amery WI 54001. **Tel** (715)268-8101.

US
ARCADIA NEWS-LEADER, THE. VFOAT Arcadia News Leader; News-Leader. Vol. 68, No. 12 (Nov. 2, 1939)-. Newspaper. English. wk. Charles Blaschko, 625 South Dettloff Drive, PO Box 225, Arcadia WI 54612. **ED** B Pavlicin. available on microfilm from The State Historical Society of Wisconsin. ***Continues*** *Leader (Arcadia, Wis. : 1890).*

US/0749-7083
AUGUSTA AREA TIMES. Ninetieth Year, No. 1 (Jan. 1, 1964)-. Newspaper. English. wk. $10.00 Wisconsin. Michael D Jensen, 1721 Omaha Street, Osseo WI 54758. **Tel** (715)597-3313. **Ad Acc.** ctrl circ. available on microfilm from The State Historical Society of Wisconsin. ***Continues*** *Union (Augusta, Wis.).*

US
BANNER-JOURNAL. VFOAT Banner Journal. Vol. 70, No. 11 (March 10, 1926)-. Newspaper. English. Fifty-two times a year (Wed.). News Publishing Company Inc., PO Box 129, 409 East Main Street, Black River Falls WI 54615. ***Formed by the union of*** *Badger State Banner* ***and*** *Jackson County Journal;* ***Absorbed*** *Wisconsin Leader.*

US
BARABOO NEWS REPUBLIC. VFOAT News-Republic. 116th year, No. 32 (Feb. 8, 1971)-. Newspaper. English. da. Baraboo News Republic, 219 First Street, PO Box 9, Baraboo WI 53913. **Tel** (608)356-4808. ***Continues*** *Baraboo News-Republic.*

US/0895-2817
BAY VIEWER, THE. (1976)-. Newspaper. English. wk. $13.75 Oak Creek; $25.65 Wisconsin, Minnesota, Illinois, Michigan, Iowa; $31.85 other. Community Newspapers / Wisconsin, PO Box 7, Oak Creek WI 53154. **Tel** (414)768-5800.

US
BEE, THE. Vol. 79, No. 19 (Dec. 1, 1962)-. Newspaper. English. wk. Bee / Phillips, 115 North Lake Avenue, Phillips WI 54555-1220. **Tel** (715)339-3036. **ED** R. Rivard. **Ad Acc. Circ:** 5,000. ***Continues*** *Bee and the Phillips Times.*

US
BELOIT DAILY NEWS. VFOAT Daily News. Vol. 5, No. 42 (Oct. 4, 1892)-. Newspaper. English. da. William D Behling, 149 State Street, Beloit WI 53511. ***Continues*** *Beloit Daily Grit.*

US/8755-4003
BERLIN JOURNAL, THE. Vol. 61, No. 15 (April 12, 1942)-. Newspaper. English. wk. $20.00 Berlin, Wisconsin; $35.00 other in Wisconsin; $50.00 other. Berlin Journal Company, PO Box 10, Berlin WI 54923. **Tel** (414)361-1515. **ED** Jim Woiff. **Photos. Ad Acc, Adv Mgr:** Betty Van Sistine. Full Page (B&W) $368.00. Half Page (B&W) $184.00. Full Page (Color) $418.00. Half Page (Color) $234.00. **Pub. Size:** Tabloid. **Circ:** 3,500. available on microfilm from The State Historical Society of Wisconsin. ***Continues*** *Berlin Evening Journal.*

US
BLADE-ATLAS, THE. VFOAT Blade Atlas. Vol. 80, No. 40 (May 23, 1968)-. Newspaper. English. wk. $15.00 Wisconsin; $18.00 other. J. Patrick Reilly and T. Michael Reilly, PO Box 116, Blanchardville WI 53516. **Tel** (608)523-4284, FAX (608)523-1019. **ED** Gary McKenzie. **Photos. Ad Acc, Adv Mgr:** Becky Siedenburg, **Tel** (608)935-2331. Full Page (B&W) $308.00. Half Page (B&W) $154.00. **Pub. Size:** Standard. **Circ:** 1,200. available on microfilm from The State Historical Society of Wisconsin. ***Formed by the union of*** *Argyle Atlas* ***and*** *Blanchardville Blade.*

US
BLAIR PRESS, THE. VFOAT Ettrick Advance. (1896)-. Newspaper. English. wk. $18.00 Wisconsin; $24.00 other. Gerald Hjornevik, 109 Gilbert Street, Box 187, Blair WI 54616. **Tel** (608)989-2531, FAX (608)989-2531. **ED** Gerald Hjornevik. **Photos. Ad Acc, Adv Mgr:** Liz Hjornevik. Full Page (B&W) $860.00. Half Page (B&W) $450.00. Full Page (Color) $940.00. Half Page (Color) $530.00. **Pub. Size:** Broadsheet. **Circ:** 2,150. available on microfilm from The State Historical Society of Wisconsin. ***Absorbed*** *Ettrick Advance.*

US/0749-7210
BRILLION NEWS, THE. VFOAT Forest Junction Community News. (1874)-. Newspaper. English. wk. $16.00. Zane C Zander, 425 West Ryan Street, Brillion WI 54110. **Tel** (414)756-2222, FAX (414)756-2107. **ED** Zane C. Zander and Aaron Mollbrook (Managing Editor). **Photos. Ad Acc. Pub. Size:** Tabloid. ***Absorbed*** *Reedsville Banner.*

US
BROOKFIELD NEWS, THE. Vol. 1, No. 1 (Aug. 18, 1955)-. Newspaper. English. wk. $15.95 Oak Creek, Wisconsin; $25.65 other Wisconsin, Minnesota, Illinois, Michigan, Iowa; $31.85 other. Community Newspapers / Wisconsin, PO Box 7, Oak Creek WI 53154. **Tel** (414)768-5800. **ED** J. Cory. available on microfilm from The State Historical Society of Wisconsin.

US
BROWN DEER HERALD. Newspaper. English. wk. $15.95 Oak Creek, Wisconsin; $25.65 other Wisconsin, Illinois, Michigan, Minnesota, Iowa; $31.85 other. Community Newspapers / Wisconsin, PO Box 7, Oak Creek WI 53154. **Tel** (414)768-5800.

US/0749-7261
BURLINGTON STANDARD-PRESS. VFOAT Mini Burlington Standard Press; Mini Standard Press; Standard-Press; Standard Press. Vol. 92, No. 47 (June 2, 1955)-. Newspaper. English. Fifty-two times a year (Thurs.). $15.95. Zimmermann & Sons Inc., 140 Commerce Street, PO Box 437, Burlington WI 53105-0437. **Tel** (414)763-3511. **ED** Carol Marcella. **Photos. Ad Acc, Adv Mgr:** David Wright. Full Page

(B&W) $661.50. Half Page (B&W) $726.50. Full Page (Color) $396.00. Half Page (Color) $461.00. **Pub. Size:** Broadsheet. **Circ:** 6,500 (Wednesday), 14,000 (Sunday). available in microform. ***Formed by the union of*** *Standard Democrat (Burlington, Wis.)* ***and*** *Burlington Free Press (Burlington, Wis.).*

US
BURNETT COUNTY SENTINEL (GRANTSBURG, WIS. : 1962). (BURNETT COUNTY SENTINEL.). Vol. 1, No. 1 (Nov. 22, 1962)-. Newspaper. English. wk. Marjorie G Nelson, 114 Madison Avenue, Box 397, Grantsburg WI 54840-0397.

US/0885-0798
CADOTT SENTINEL, THE. VFOAT Sentinel; Courier-Sentinel. (1914)-. Newspaper. English. wk. Trygg J. Hansen, Box 76, Cadott WI 54727. available on microfilm from The State Historical Society of Wisconsin. ***Continues*** *Cadott Blade.*

US/0749-7202
CAMBRIDGE NEWS (CAMBRIDGE, WIS.). (THE CAMBRIDGE NEWS.). Newspaper. English. wk. $10.00, $9.00 (in-state). Dennis Hawkes, 322 North Main Street, Lake Mills WI 53551.

US/0749-4068
CAPITAL TIMES, THE. Vol. 1, No. 1 (Dec. 13, 1917)-. Newspaper. English. da (except Sunday and major holidays). $163.80 (daily & Sunday), $95.95 (daily only), $84.25 (weekend), $67.90 (Sunday only) in Wisconsin by carrier or mail delivery; $260.00 (daily & Sunday), $156.00 (daily only), $130.00 (weekend), $104.00 (Sunday only) out of state by mail delivery. Madison Newspaper Inc, PO Box 8056, Madison WI 53708. **Tel** (608)252-6400, (800)362-8333. **ED** David Zweifel. **Bk Rev. Ad Acc. Circ:** 30,000. available on microfilm from University Microfilms International (UMI). Documents available from UMI Article Clearinghouse.
Desc: Local, national and international news and columnists.
Ind/Abst Bus. Dateline (Nov. 20, 1991-) [Full Txt.].

US
CASHTON RECORD. Began in August 1896-. Newspaper. English. wk. $18.00. Gerald Eddy, PO Box 100, Cashton WI 54619. **ED** Rose Eddy. **Bk Rev. Ad Acc. Circ:** 1,500 (ctrl). available on microfilm from The State Historical Society of Wisconsin.
Desc: A newspaper covering local news.

US
CENTRAL ST. CROIX NEWS. VFOAT Central Saint Croix News. Began in 1974?. Newspaper. English. wk. Barbara Gardner, 815B Davis Street, Box 215, Hammond WI 54015. **ED** B Gardner. available on microfilm from The State Historical Society of Wisconsin.

US
CHETEK ALERT, THE. VFOAT Alert. Vol. 1, No. 1 (Sept. 15, 1882)-. Newspaper. English. wk. Paul H Lange, PO Box 5, Chetek WI 54728-0005.

US
CHILTON TIMES-JOURNAL. VFOAT Times-Journal. Vol. 76, No. 23 (March 2, 1933)-. Newspaper. English. wk. $14.00. Gary Vercauteren, 19 East Main Street, Chilton WI 53014. **Tel** (414)849-4651. **ED** Jill Ruppert. **Ad Acc. Circ:** 5,210. available on microfilm from The State Historical Society of Wisconsin. ***Formed by the union of*** *Chilton Times* ***and*** *Independent Times (Chilton, Wis.).*

US/8756-2960
CHIPPEWA HERALD-TELEGRAM. VFOAT Chippewa Herald Telegram. 38th Year (Dec. 6, 1926)-. Newspaper. English. da. $60.00. Herald-Telegram Publishing Company, 321 Frenette Drive, Chippewa Falls WI 54729. ***Formed by the union of*** *Chippewa Herald (1894)* ***and*** *Chippewa Telegram.*

US
CLARK COUNTY PRESS (NEILLSVILLE, WIS. : 1938). (THE CLARK COUNTY PRESS.). **VFOAT** Little Clark County Press. 70th year, No. 40 (Oct. 6, 1938)-. Newspaper. English. wk. Ron Zachow, PO Box 149, Neillsville WI 54456. available on microfilm from The State Historical Society of Wisconsin. ***Continues*** *Neillsville Press.*

US
CLINTON TOPPER, THE. Vol. 1, No. 1 (April 28, 1938)-. Newspaper. English. wk. Frederic N Wagner, 400 B Front Street, Box T, Clinton WI 53525. available on microfilm from The State Historical Society of Wisconsin.

US/0749-7024
CLINTONVILLE TRIBUNE-GAZETTE. VFOAT Clintonville Tribune Gazette Clintonville Tribune-Gazette. Vol. 59, No. 52 (July 18, 1940)-. Newspaper. English. wk. $20.00, $12.00 (in-county), $15.00 (others in Wisconsin). Clintonville Publishing, PO Box 270, 13 Eleventh Street, Clintonville WI 54929. available on microfilm from The State Historical Society of Wisconsin. ***Formed by the union of*** *Clintonville Tribune (Clintonville, Wis. : 1891)* ***and*** *Dairyman-Gazette.*

US
COLFAX MESSENGER, THE. VFOAT Colfax Weekly Messenger. Vol. 1, No. 1 (April 30, 1897)-. Newspaper. English. wk. Lyle A Christianson, Box 517, Colfax WI 54730. available on microfilm from The State Historical Society of Wisconsin.

US
COLUMBUS JOURNAL-REPUBLICAN (COLUMBUS, WIS. : 1971). (COLUMBUS JOURNAL-REPUBLICAN.). **VFOAT** Columbus Journal Republican. Vol. 115, No. 22 (Feb. 25, 1971)-. Newspaper. English. wk. $15.00. Marshall Bernhagen / Columbus WI, 145 E James, PO BOx 188, Columbus WI 53925. **Tel** (414)623-3344. **ED** Holly Gregg. Index available. **Ad Acc.** ctrl circ. available on microfilm from The State Historical Society of Wisconsin. ***Continues*** *Journal-Republican (Columbus, Wis. : 1971);* ***Absorbed*** *Rio Journal.*

US/0745-6646
COMMUNITY HERALD (MONONA, WIS.), THE. (THE COMMUNITY HERALD.). V. 15, No. 32 (March 9, 1983)-. Newspaper. English. wk. $16.00. Community Herald, 6041 Monona Drive, Monona WI 53716. **Tel** (608)221-1544. **ED** Steve Gasser. **Bk Rev. Ad Acc. Circ:** 2,500. available on microfilm from The State Historical Society of Wisconsin. ***Continues*** *Monona Community Herald.*
Desc: News of current events for Monona, Monona Grove Schools, Cottage Grove, LaFollette High School.

US/0885-078X
CORNELL AND LAKE HOLCOMBE COURIER, THE. VFOAT Cornell Courier; Courier; Cornell, Lake Holcombe Courier; Courier-Sentinel; Sentinel-Courier. 56th year, No. 24 (Sept. 16, 1971)-. Newspaper. English. wk. $18.00. Trygg J. Hansen, Box 76, Cadott WI 54727. **ED** Trygg Hansen, Mark Counderman (Managing Editor). **Photos. Ad Acc.** Full Page (B&W) $441.00. Half Page (B&W) $220.00. Full Page (Color) $516.00. Half Page (Color) $295.00. **Pub. Size:** Broadsheet. ***Continues*** *Cornell Courier.*

US/0742-4566
COUNTRY CHRONICLE, THE. Vol. 44, No. 3 (April 14, 1982)-. Newspaper. English. wk. $12.00. Frank Wood Jr, 138 Main Street, PO Box 278, Denmark WI 54208. **ED** M. J. Sibilsky. available on microfilm from The State Historical Society of Wisconsin. ***Continues*** *New Farmer's Friend and Rural Reporter.*

US/0192-9658
COUNTRY TODAY, THE. (19??)-. Newspaper. English. wk. $21.00 (one year), $35.00 (two year) US; $50.00 (one year), $64.00 (two year) other. The Country Today, PO Box 570, Eau Claire WI 54702. **Tel** (715)833-9270. **ED** Arnie Hoffman and Jim Massey. **Photos. Ad Acc, Adv Mgr:** Mike Straud. Full Page (B&W) $2,193.00. Half Page (B&W) $1,122.00. Full Page (Color) $2,453.00. Half Page (Color) $1,382.00. **Pub. Size:** Broadsheet. **Pr Rev. Circ:** 38,000. available on microfilm from Crest Information Technologies.
Desc: Rural, agricultural news, and outdoor news.

US/0749-7237
COUNTY LEDGER-PRESS, THE. VFOAT County Ledger Press; Standard Press; Enterprise Press. Vol. 87, No. 41 (April 26, 1984)-. Newspaper. English. wk. $20.00, $13.00 (in-county), $16.00 (Wisconsin and Minnesota). Ledger Publications, 105 Main Street, Balsam Lake WI 54810-0156. ***Continues*** *Polk County Ledger & The Standard-Press.*

US
COURIER-PRESS. VFOAT Courier Press. Vol. 103, No. 1 (Jan. 4, 1956)-. Newspaper. English. sw. E B Howe, 132 South Beaumont, PO Box 149, Prairie du Chien WI 53821. available on microfilm from The State Historical Society of Wisconsin. ***Continues*** *Courier (Prairie du Chien, Wis.);* ***Absorbed in part*** *Kickapoo Papoose.*

US
COURIER-WEDGE, THE. VFOAT Courier Wedge; Entering Wedge; Entering Wedge and the Pepin Co. Courier. No. 1 (July 11, 1918)-. Newspaper. English. wk. Valley Publications / Wisconsin, PO Box 40, Cochrane WI 54622-0027. **Tel** (608)248-2451, FAX (608)248-2422. **ED** Lyle McFarlin. **Ad Acc. Circ:** 4,300. ***Continues*** *Entering Wedge and the Pepin Co. Courier;* ***Absorbed*** *Pepin Herald.*

US
CRAWFORD COUNTY INDEPENDENT AND THE KICKAPOO SCOUT. VFOAT Crawford County Independent-Scout. Vol. 75, No. 20 (Sept. 20. 1979)-. Newspaper. English. wk. Ralph D Goldsmith, Box 188, Gays Mills WI 54631. available on microfilm from The State Historical Society of Wisconsin. ***Continues*** *Crawford County Independent;* ***Absorbed*** *Kickapoo Scout.*

US
CUDAHY REMINDER-ENTERPRISE (CUDAHY, WIS. : 1984). (CUDAHY REMINDER-ENTERPRISE.). **VFOAT** Cudahy Reminder Enterprise. Vol. 75, No. 7 (Feb. 16, 1984)-. Newspaper. English. Fifty-two times a year (Thurs.). Community Newspapers, PO Box 7, Oak Creek WI 53154. **Tel** (414)768-5800. **ED** M. L. Stover. available on microfilm from The State Historical Society of Wisconsin. ***Continues*** *Reminder-Enterprise (Cudahy, Wis. : 1980).*

US/0748-965X
CUMBERLAND ADVOCATE. VFOAT Advocate; Farm Advocate; Morgan's Farm Advocate; Organized Farmer. Vol. 1, No. 1 (April 2, 1885)-. Newspaper. English. wk. $17.50 Barron Burnett Polk and Washburn in Wisconsin; $19.50 others in Wisconsin; $25.00 others. Cumberland Advocate, 1375 Second Avenue, Cumberland WI 54829. **Tel** (715)822-4469. **ED** Craig Bucher. **Ad Acc. Circ:** 3,200. ***Continues*** *Cumberland Herald.*

US/0749-1379
DAILY CITIZEN (BEAVER DAM, WIS. : 1971). (DAILY CITIZEN.). Vol. 61, No. 184 (Sept. 27, 1971)-. Periodical. English. da (except Sunday). Daily Citizen / Beaver Dam, 805 Park Avenue, Beaver Dam WI 53916. **Tel** (414)887-0321. ***Continues*** *Beaver Dam Daily Citizen (Beaver Dam, Wis. : 1930).*

US
DAILY JEFFERSON COUNTY UNION (FORT ATKINSON, WIS. : 1969). (DAILY JEFFERSON COUNTY UNION.). Vol. 99, No. 186 (Sept. 23, 1969)-. Newspaper. English. da. Brian Knox, 28 Milwaukee Avenue, Fort Atkinson WI 53538. **ED** R L Angus. available on microfilm from University Microfilms International (UMI). ***Continues*** *Daily Jefferson County Union and Fort Daily News.*

US/0746-5866
DAILY NEWS (RHINELANDER, WIS. : 1968), THE. (THE DAILY NEWS.). **VFOAT** Rhinelander Daily News. Newspaper. English. da (except Sat.). Northern Lakes Publishing Company, 314 Courtney Street, Rhinelander WI 54501. ***Continues*** *Rhinelander Daily News (Rhinelander, Wis. : 1968).*

US/1050-4095
DAILY PRESS (ASHLAND, WIS.), THE. (THE DAILY PRESS.). **VFOAT** Ashland Daily Press. Vol. 93, No. 298 (May 2, 1966)-. Newspaper. English. da. $69.00 Ashland Area; $89.00 others. Ashland Publishing Corporation, 122 West 3rd Street, Ashland WI 54806. **Tel** (715)682-2313. **ED** Evan Sasman. Index available. cum. index. **Ad Acc, Adv Mgr:** J. Swiston, **Tel** (715)682-2313. **Circ:** 8,500 (ctrl). ***Continues*** *Ashland Daily Press.*

US/0747-2927
DAILY REGISTER (PORTAGE, WIS.). (THE DAILY REGISTER.). Vol. 98, No. 104 (May 3, 1982)-. Newspaper. English. da. $84.00. Daily Register / Wisconsin, PO Box 470, Portage WI 53901. **Tel** (608)742-2111. **ED** Tracy Moeller. **Bk Rev**, (Qty: 12). **Photos. Ad Acc, Adv Mgr:** David Holgate. Full Page (B&W) $874.26. Half Page (B&W) $440.70. Full Page (Color) $939.26. Half Page (Color) $505.70. **Pub. Size:** Broadsheet. **Wire Svcs.:** AP, CH. **Circ:** 5,450 am. ***Continues*** *Portage Daily Register (Portage, Wis. : 1960).*

US/0749-7113
DAILY REPORTER (MILWAUKEE, WIS.), THE. (THE DAILY REPORTER.). (1898)-. Newspaper. English. da (Publishes daily except Sat., Sun. & holidays). $90.00. Daily Reporter / Wisconsin, 207 East Michigan Street, Suite 420, Milwaukee WI 53202. **Tel** (414)276-0273, FAX (414)276-8057. **ED** Eric Spiegler. **Photos. Ad Acc.** Full Page (B&W) $1083.00. Half Page (B&W) $585.00. **Circ:** 2,300 (ctrl).
Desc: News of general circulation devoted to commerce, construction, purchasing, real estate and law.

US
DAILY TELEGRAM, THE. (19??)-. Newspaper. English. da. $91.00 in county, $101.00 out of county. Evening Telegram, 1226 Ogden Avenue, Superior WI 54880. **Tel** (715)394-4411. **ED** Michael Payton. **Bk Rev. Photos. Ad Acc, Adv Mgr:** Betty Porter. Full Page (B&W) $1,115.85. Half Page (B&W) $544.95. Full Page (Color) $1,190.85. Half Page (Color) $619.95. **Pub. Size:** Broadsheet. **Wire Svcs.:** AP. available on microfilm from Dakota Microfilm Service. ***Continues*** *The Evening Telegram.*

US
DAILY TRIBUNE (WISCONSIN RAPIDS, WIS.). (THE DAILY TRIBUNE.). 52nd year, No. 15 (May 15, 1966)-. Newspaper. English. da. Ralph Castelum, 220 First Avenue South, Wisconsin Rapids WI 54494. ***Continues*** *Wisconsin Rapids Daily Tribune.*

US/0748-6219
DE PERE JOURNAL. Vol. 48, No. 11 (June 16, 1966)-. Newspaper. English. Fifty-two times a year (Thurs.). $14.00 (in county). Journal Publishing Company / Wisconsin, 126 South Broadway, PO Box 188, De Pere WI 54115. **Tel** (414)336-4221. **ED** Marie S. Creviere. **Bk Rev**, (Qty: 1-2). **Photos. Ad Acc, Adv Mgr:** P. J. Creviere, Jr. Full Page (B&W) $1070.16. Half Page (B&W) $535.08. Full Page (Color) $1070.16 ($110.00 extra per color). Half Page (Color) $535.08 ($110.00 extra

per color). **Pub. Size:** Broadsheet. **Circ:** 3,721. available on microfilm from The State Historical Society of Wisconsin. ***Continues*** *De Pere Journal-Democrat.*

US/8755-8971
DEFOREST TIMES-TRIBUNE. (DE FOREST TIMES-TRIBUNE.). **VFOAT** DeForest Times-Tribune; De Forest Times Tribune; DeForest Times Tribune. Vol. 54, No. 10 (Nov. 5, 1948)-. Newspaper. English. wk. $10.00. De Forest Times Tribune, 108 Market Street, De Forest WI 53532-1598. **Tel** (608)846-5576, FAX (608)846-5757. **ED** Molly Emerson. **Circ:** 2,500. ***Formed by the union of*** *De Forest Times* ***and*** *Morrisonville Tribune.*

US/1064-4539
DELAVAN ENTERPRISE (1992), THE. (THE DELAVAN ENTERPRISE.). (199?)-. Newspaper. English. wk. $17.50 Walworth County; $20.50 Wisconsin; $25.50 Illinois; $25.50 other. Delavan Enterprise, 1436 Mound Road, Delavan WI 53115. **Tel** (414)728-3411. **ED** Tom Sheehan. **Ad Acc. Circ:** 4,300. ***Continues*** *Delavan Enterprise and the Delavan Republican, 0899-7616.*

US/0899-7616
DELAVAN ENTERPRISE AND THE DELAVAN REPUBLICAN, THE. ***Title Change.*** **VFOAT** Enterprise. No. 18 (May 7, 1959)-(19??). Newspaper. English. sw. A L Petermann, 1436 Mound Road, Delavan WI 53115. ***Formed by the union of*** *Delavan Enterprise (Delavan, Wis. : 1900)* ***and*** *Delavan Republican.* ***Continued by*** *Delavan Enterprise (Delavan, Wisc. : 1992), 1064-4539.*

US
DEMOCRAT-TRIBUNE (MINERAL POINT, WIS.). (THE DEMOCRAT-TRIBUNE.). **VFOAT** Democrat Tribune. (April 8, 1958)-. Newspaper. English. wk. $10.00 Wisconsin; $12.00 US. Democrat Tribune, 334 High Street, Mineral Point WI 53565. **ED** Patrick Reilly, Mike Reilly, Jeanie Lewis (Managing Editor). **Photos. Ad Acc, Adv Mgr:** Sherry Byous, **Tel** (608)987-2141. Full Page (B&W) $288.75. Half Page (B&W) $144.38. Full Page (Color) $368.75. **Pub. Size:** Tabloid. **Circ:** 1,328 paid. available in microform. ***Continues*** *Iowa County Democrat and the Mineral Point Tribune.*

US
DENMARK PRESS (DENMARK, WIS. : 1953). (THE DENMARK PRESS.). Vol. 39, No. 34 (Nov. 5, 1953)-. Newspaper. English. wk. Frank Wood Jr, 138 Main Street, PO Box 278, Denmark WI 54208. available on microfilm from The State Historical Society of Wisconsin. ***Continues*** *Denmark Press and The Dairyland Review.*

US
DODGE COUNTY INDEPENDENT-NEWS, THE. **VFOAT** Dodge County Independent News; Independent-News. Vol. 1, No. 1 (Sept. 6, 1962)-. Newspaper. English. Fifty-two times a year. Dodge County Independent News, 350 East Oak Street, Juneau WI 53039. **Tel** (608)837-5161 ext. 230. ***Formed by the union of*** *Independent (Juneau, Wis.), Hustisford News* ***and*** *Reeseville Review.*

US/0749-7180
DOOR COUNTY ADVOCATE. Vol. 57 No. 19 (Aug. 2 1918)-. Newspaper. English. sw (Tues. & Thurs.). $35.00 (in county). Brown County Publishing, PO Box 130, Sturgeon Bay WI 54235. **Tel** (414)743-3321, FAX (414)743-5817. **Photos. Ad Acc, Adv Mgr:** James Petersen. Full Page (B&W) $800.00. Half Page (B&W) $425.00. Full Page (Color) $870.00. Half Page (Color) $495.00. **Pub. Size:** Broadsheet. ***Formed by the union of*** *Sturgeon Bay Advocate* ***and*** *Door County Democrat.*

US
DUNN COUNTY NEWS, THE. Vol. 1, No. 1 (April 7 1866)-. Newspaper. English. bw (Sunday & Wednesday). $53.00. Menomonie Dunn County News, 710 Main Street, PO Box 40, Menomonie WI 54751. **Tel** (715)235-3411, FAX (715)235-0936. **ED** Peg Zaemisch. **Photos Ad Acc, Adv Mgr:** Denny Bodoh. Full Page (B&W) $883.65. Half Page (B&W) $441.83. Full Page (Color) $983.65. Half Page (Color) $541.83. **Pub. Size:** Broadsheet. **Circ:** 4,050 Sunday, 4,305 Wednesday, 20,554 free. ***Continues*** *Dunn County Lumberman.*

US/0749-5943
EAST TROY NEWS, THE. (1893)-. Newspaper. English. wk (Wednesdays). $13.50. East Troy News, PO Box 47, East Troy WI 53120. **Tel** (414)642-7451, FAX (414)642-5934. **ED** Carol Marcella (Editor-in-Chief) and Richard Berg (Managing Editor). **Photos. Ad Acc, Adv Mgr:** David Wright, **Tel** (414)763-3511. Full Page (B&W) $285.00. Half Page (B&W) $350.00. Full Page (Color) $148.50. Half Page (Color) $213.50. **Pub. Size:** Tabloid. **Circ:** 2,350. available on microfilm from The State Historical Society of Wisconsin.

US
EDGERTON REPORTER, THE. Vol. 78, No 1 (Oct. 19, 1950)-. Newspaper. English. wk. The Reporter Company Inc, 21 North Henry Street, Edgerton WI 53534. ***Continues*** *Wisconsin Tobacco Reporter.*

US
ELKHORN INDEPENDENT (ELKHORN, WIS. : 1892). (THE ELKHORN INDEPENDENT.). **VFOAT** Independent. Vol. 38, No. 37 (Feb. 4, 1892)-. Newspaper. English. wk (Published on Thursdays). $16.00 Walworth County, WI; $18.00 others in Wisconsin; $28.00 others. Elkhorn Independent, 11 West Walworth Street, PO Box 200, Elkhorn WI 53121. **Tel** (414)723-2250, FAX (414)723-7424. **ED** Tim Franklin. **Bk Rev. Ad Acc, Adv Mgr:** R. Johnson. **Circ:** 33,500 (ctrl). available on microfilm. ***Continues*** *Walworth County Independent (Elkhorn, Wis. : 1868).*
Desc: Contains news that pertains to the Elkhorn-Lauderdale Lakes area.

US
ELM GROVE ELM LEAVES. **VFOAT** Elm Leaves. Vol. 34, No. 2 (Jan. 24, 1980)-. Newspaper. English. Fifty-two times a year. $29.95 Milwaukee metro area; $52.25 Wisconsin, Iowa, Illinois, Michigan & Minnesota; $72.75 others. Community Newspapers, PO Box 7, Oak Creek WI 53154. **Tel** (414)768-5800. **ED** C. Jensen. available on microfilm from The State Historical Society of Wisconsin. ***Continues*** *Elm Leaves.*

US
ELMWOOD ARGUS, THE. **VFOAT** Argus. (Dec. 8, 1921)-. Newspaper. English. wk. $9.00 Pierce County, Wisconsin; $12.50 other. Elmwood Argus, South 216 McKay Avenue, Spring Valley WI 54767. **Tel** (715)778-4395. **ED** Duane Kelley. **Photos. Ad Acc.** Full Page (B&W) $193.50. Half Page (B&W) $96.75. ctrl circ. available on microfilm.

US
EVENING TELEGRAM (SUPERIOR, WIS. : 1922). ***Title Change.*** (THE EVENING TELEGRAM.). Vol. 37, No. 184 (Nov. 21, 1922)-(19??). Newspaper. English. da. Evening Telegram, 1226 Ogden Avenue, Superior WI 54880. **Tel** (715)394-4411. **ED** Michael Payton. **LC** 7002. **Ad Acc, Adv Mgr:** Betty Porter. ctrl circ. ***Continues*** *Superior Telegram.* ***Continued by*** *Daily Telegram.*

US/8755-3694
FENNIMORE TIMES. Vol. 13, No. 14 (Dec. 12, 1900)-. Newspaper. English. wk. $11.00 (in-county), $13.00 (elsewhere, in-state), $16.00 (elsewhere). Fennimore Times, PO Box 177, Fennimore WI 53809. **Tel** (608)822-3912. **ED** Matt Johnson. **LC** 10216-X. **Circ:** 2,000. ***Continues*** *Times Review (Fennimore, Wis.).*

US
FITCHBURG STAR. Vol. 1, No. 1 (Jan. 30, 1975)-. Newspaper. English. wk. Community Herald, 6041 Monona Drive, Monona WI 53716. available on microfilm from The State Historical Society of Wisconsin.

US
FLORENCE MINING NEWS, THE. **VFOAT** Mining News. Vol. 1, No. 1 (Jan. 1, 1881)-. Newspaper. English. wk. Ned Cochrane, 140 Florence Avenue, PO Box 79, Florence WI 54121-0079. **ED** N Cochrane. available on microfilm from The State Historical Society of Wisconsin.

US/0747-4415
FOND DU LAC CLARION, THE. **VFOAT** Clarion. English. mo. The Fond du Lac Clarion, PO Box 347, Fond Du Lac WI 54935-0347. ***Continues*** *Diocese of Fond du Lac.*

US
FOREST REPUBLICAN, THE. No. 43 (April 26, 1928)-. Newspaper. English. wk. $8.00 Forest County; $10.00 Wisconsin; $20.00 other. Forest Republican, PO Box 216, Crandon WI 54520. **Tel** (715)478-3315. available on microfilm. ***Continues*** *Forest Republican, Wabeno-Soperton Advertiser;* ***Absorbed*** *Northern Wisconsin News and Forest County Tribune.*

US
FOX POINT-BAYSIDE-RIVER HILLS HERALD. **VFOAT** Fox Point Bayside River Hills Herald; Fox Point-Bayside-River Hills Glendale Brown Deer Shorewood; Tefish Bay Herald; Fox Point Bayside River Hills Glendale Brown Deer Shorewood; Tefish Bay Herald; Bayside Fox Point River Hills Herald. Vol. 7, No. 42 (Nov. 18, 1965)-Vol. 22, No. 38 (Sept. 22, 1977). Newspaper. English. wk. $15.95 Oak Creek, Wisconsin; $25.65 other Wisconsin, Michigan, Illinois, Minnesota, Iowa; $31.85 other. Community Newspapers / Wisconsin, PO Box 7, Oak Creek WI 53154. **Tel** (414)768-5800. available on microfilm from The State Historical Society of Wisconsin. ***Continues*** *Fox Point-Bayside Herald (Shorewood, Wis. : 1963).*

US
FRANKLIN-HALES CORNERS HUB. **VFOAT** Franklin Hales Corners Hub. No. 381 (Dec. 4, 1969)-No. 489 (Dec. 30, 1971). Newspaper. English. wk. $15.95 Oak Creek, Wisconsin; $25.65 other Wisconsin, Minnesota, Illinois, Michigan, Iowa; $31.85 other. Community Newspapers / Wisconsin, PO Box 7, Oak Creek WI 53154. **Tel** (414)768-5800. ***Continues*** *Tri-Town Hub (Hales Corners, Wis. : 1967 : Franklin-Hales Corners Ed.).*

●US/1062-9041
FREEMAN (WAUKESHA, WIS.), THE. (THE FREEMAN.). Vol. 134, no. 1 (Mar. 30, 1992)-. Newspaper. English. da. $97.40. The Freeman, PO Box 7, Waukesha WI 53187. ***Continues*** *Waukesha County Freeman, 0895-6391.*

US
FRIENDSHIP REPORTER. **VFOAT** Adams County Times and Friendship Reporter. Vol. 7, No. 34 (Aug. 27, 1908)-. Newspaper. English. wk. Richard A Hannagan, Friendship WI 53934. ***Continues*** *Dells Reporter.*

US
GALESVILLE REPUBLICAN. Vol. 1, No. 1 (Sept. 30, 1897)-. Newspaper. English. wk. Galesville Republican, 139 South Davis, Galesville WI 54630. **Tel** (608)582-2330, FAX (608)582-2455. **ED** John Graf. **Ad Acc. Circ:** 1,850. available on microfilm. ***Absorbed*** *Galesville Independent.*

US
GLIDDEN ENTERPRISE, THE. **VFOAT** Enterprise. Vol. 1, No. 1 (June 10, 1904)-. Newspaper. English. Fifty-two times a year (Wed.). Hart Publishing Company, PO Box 128, Glidden WI 54527. **Tel** (715)264-3481. available on microfilm from The State Historical Society of Wisconsin.

US
GOOD NEWS. Vol. 1, No. 1 (Feb. 9, 1982)-. Newspaper. English. wk. Good News / Wisconsin, 6041 Monona Drive, Monona WI 53716. **Tel** (608)221-1544. **ED** Diann Laufenberg. **Ad Acc. Circ:** 15,000. available on microfilm. ***Continues*** *Tri-M.*

US
GRANT COUNTY HERALD INDEPENDENT. **VFOAT** Grant County Independent. Vol. 125, No. 26 (July 4, 1968)-. Newspaper. English. wk. $32.00 Grant County, Wisconsin; $36.00 other Wisconsin; $45.00 other. Lancaster Newspaper Inc., PO Box 310, Lancaster WI 53813. **Tel** (608)723-2151, FAX (608)723-7272. **ED** John Ingehritsen. **Photos. Ad Acc, Adv Mgr:** Kevin Kelly. Full Page (B&W) $580.60. Half Page (B&W) $322.50. Full Page (Color) $752.60. Half Page (Color) $408.50. **Pub. Size:** Broadsheet. **Circ:** 4,200. available in microform. ***Formed by the union of*** *Grant County Herald (Lancaster, Wis. : 1850)* ***and*** *Grant County Independent;* ***Absorbed*** *Bloomington Record; Cassville American.*

US
GREEN BAY NEWS-CHRONICLE, THE. **VFOAT** News-Chronicle; Green Bay News Chronicle. Vol. 4, No. 127 (April 12, 1976)-. Newspaper. English. da. $102.00. Green Bay News Chronicle, Box 2467, Green Bay WI 54303. **Tel** (414)432-2941. **ED** Ron Poppenhagen. **Ad Acc, Adv Mgr:** Al Rasmussen. Full Page (B&W) $419.25. Half Page (B&W) $209.62. Full Page (Color) $519.25 (1 color). Half Page (Color) $309.62 (1 color). **Pub. Size:** Tabloid. **Wire Svcs.:** UPI, NY. ***Formed by the union of*** *Brown County Chronicle* ***and*** *Daily News (Green Bay, Wis.).*

US
GREEN BAY PRESS-GAZETTE. **VFOAT** Green Bay Press Gazette. (June 29, 1915)-. Newspaper. English. da. Green Bay Press Gazette, PO Box 19430, Green Bay WI 54307. **Tel** (414)435-4411. available on microfilm from The State Historical Society of Wisconsin. ***Formed by the union of*** *Free Press (Green Bay, Wis.)* ***and*** *Green Bay Gazette.*

US/8755-3988
GREEN LAKE COUNTY REPORTER (GREEN LAKE, WIS. : 1983). (GREEN LAKE COUNTY REPORTER.). **VFOAT** Green Lake County Reporter & Markesan Regional Reporter; Green Lake Reporter. Vol. 83, No. 19 (May 12, 1983)-. Newspaper. English. wk. $20.00 (one year); $35.00 (two years); $50.00 others. Berlin Journal Company, PO Box 10, Berlin WI 54923. **Tel** (414)361-1515. **ED** Jim Wolff. **Photos. Ad Acc, Adv Mgr:** Betty Van Sistine. Full Page (B&W) $368.00. Half Page (B&W) $184.00. Full Page (Color) $418.00. Half Page (Color) $234.00. **Pub. Size:** Tabloid. **Circ:** 1,600. available on microfilm from The State Historical Society of Wisconsin. ***Continues*** *Green Lake County Reporter & Markesan Regional Reporter.*

US
GREENDALE VILLAGE LIFE, THE. **VFOAT** Greenfield Observer; Village Life. No. 1 (Oct. 21, 1960)-. Newspaper. English. Fifty-two times a year (Thurs.). Community Newspapers, PO Box 7, Oak Creek WI 53154. **Tel** (414)768-5800. **ED** D. Dunham. available on microfilm from The State Historical Society of Wisconsin.

US/1050-1185
GREENFIELD OBSERVER (1984). (GREENFIELD OBSERVER.). Vol. 22, No. 7 (Feb. 6, 1984)-. Newspaper. English. Fifty-two times a year (Thurs.). Community Newspapers, PO Box 7, Oak Creek WI 53154. **Tel** (414)768-5800. **ED** J. Bartell. available on microfilm from The State Historical Society of Wisconsin. ***Continues*** *Observer (Greenfield, Wis.).*

US/0740-5944
GWIAZDA POLARNA. (Oct. 23, 1908)-. Newspaper. Polish (English). wk. $40.00 US; $48.00 Canada; $60.00 other. Point Publications, 2619 Post Road, Stevens Point WI 54481. **Tel** (715)345-0744, FAX (715)345-1913. **ED** Malgorzata Terentiew. **LC** 10292. **Bk Rev**, (Qty: 25). **Ad Acc**, **Adv Mgr:** Barbara Bublitz. ctrl circ.
Desc: General interest news and feature stories. Heritage, community, family news along with news on recent developments in Poland and Europe.

US
HERALD (BROWN DEER, GLENDALE, WIS. ED.). (HERALD.). 56th year, No. 7 (Feb. 16, 1984)-. Newspaper. English. wk. Community Newspapers, PO Box 7, Oak Creek WI 53154. **Tel** (414)768-5800. ***Continues*** *Brown Deer/Glendale Herald.*

US
HERALD (WHITEFISH BAY, WIS. ED.). (HERALD.). Vol. 21 (Sept. 15, 1977)-. Newspaper. English. wk. $15.00 Wisconsin; $25.65 Michigan, Minnesota, Illinois, Iowa; $31.85 other. Community Newspapers / Wisconsin, PO Box 7, Oak Creek WI 53154. **Tel** (414)768-5800. ***Continues*** *Whitefish Bay Herald.*

US/0749-7016
HILLSBORO SENTRY-ENTERPRISE. **VFOAT** Hillsboro Sentry Enterprise; Sentry-Enterprise. Vol. 1, No. 14 (June 17, 1902)-. Newspaper. English. wk. $20.00. Hillsboro Sentry Enterprise, 839 Water Avenue, Hillsboro WI 54634. **Tel** (608)489-2264, FAX (608)489-2348. **ED** Jack Knowles. **Photos**. **Ad Acc**, **Adv Mgr:** Scott Hughes. Full Page (B&W) $275.00. Half Page (B&W) $160.00. Full Page (Color) $300.00. Half Page (Color) $200.00. **Pub. Size:** Tabloid. **Wire Svcs.:** NU, KF. **Circ:** 2,300. available on microfilm. ***Formed by the union of*** *Hillsboro Sentry* ***and*** *Hillsboro Enterprise.*

US
HORICON REPORTER. ***Title Change.*** Newspaper. English. wk. Marolla Press, 116 South Vine Street, PO Box 148, Horicon WI 53032-0148. ***Continues*** *Dodge County Reporter.* ***Continued by*** *Reporter (Horicon, Wis.), 1053-9972.*

US/0749-7008
HUDSON STAR-OBSERVER. **VFOAT** Hudson Star Observer. Vol. 54, No. 43 (Feb. 18, 1909)-. Newspaper. English. wk. $13.00 (inside the county), $15.00 Wisconsin and Minnesota, $23.00 all other. Steven A Keller, 112 Walnut Street, PO Box 147, Hudson WI 54016. ***Formed by the union of*** *Hudson Star-Times* ***and*** *St. Croix Observer.*

US
INDEPENDENT (DEERFIELD, WIS.). (THE INDEPENDENT.). 86th year, No. 28 (July 8, 1971)-. Newspaper. English. wk. Richard L Royle, 1 South Main Street, PO Box 27, Deerfield WI 53531. **ED** M.L. Pohlman. available on microfilm from The State Historical Society of Wisconsin. ***Continues*** *Deerfield Independent.*

US
INDEPENDENT-REGISTER, THE. **VFOAT** Independent Register. Vol. 26, No. 37 (July 21, 1909)-Vol. 28, No. 1 (Nov. 9, 1910). Newspaper. English. wk. Richard G Markham, 922 Exchange Street, Brodhead WI 53520. available on microfilm from The State Historical Society of Wisconsin. ***Formed by the union of*** *Brodhead Register* ***and*** *Brodhead Independent (Brodhead, Wis. : 1881);* ***Absorbed*** *Brodhead News; Juda Community News.*

US/8750-9091
INTER-COUNTY LEADER (FREDERIC, WIS.). (THE INTER-COUNTY LEADER.). **VFOAT** Inter County Leader. Vol. 21, No. 37 (July 14, 1954)-. Newspaper. English. wk. $14.00, $11.00 (Polk, Burnett counties), $12.00 (Barron, Washburn, St. Croix, and Chicago counties). Frank Gursky, 303 North Wisconsin Avenue, Frederic WI 54837. ***Continues*** *Inter-County Leader and the Frederic Star;* ***Absorbed*** *Burnett County Leader.*

US/0886-8360
IOLA HERALD, THE. (Nov. 1891)-. Newspaper. English. wk. $18.00 local; $22.00 other. Trey Foerster Ink, Inc., 165 North Main Street, Box 235, Iola WI 54945-0235. **Tel** (715)445-3415, FAX (715)445-3988. **Bk Rev**. **Photos**. **Ad Acc**, **Adv Mgr:** Trey Foerster. Full Page (B&W) $187.00. Half Page (B&W) $100.00. Full Page (Color) $237.00. Half Page (Color) $150.00. **Pub. Size:** Tabloid. **Circ:** 1,300 paid. available on microfilm from The State Historical Society of Wisconsin.

US
IRON COUNTY MINER. 65th year, No. 27 (April 7, 1950)-. Newspaper. English. wk. H W Moore, 216 Copper Street, Hurley WI 54534. available on microfilm from The State Historical Society of Wisconsin. ***Formed by the union of*** *Montreal River Miner (Hurley, Wis. : 1940)* ***and*** *Iron County News.*

US
JANESVILLE GAZETTE (JANESVILLE, WIS. : 1969 : DAILY). (THE JANESVILLE GAZETTE.). **VFOAT** Sunday Gazette. 124th year, No. 228 (May 12, 1969)-. Newspaper. English. da. $140.79. Janesville Gazette, 1 South Parker Drive, Janesville WI 53545. **Tel** (608)754-3311. ***Continues*** *Janesville Daily Gazette (Janesville, Wis. : 1901).*

US/0746-2867
JOURNAL TIMES, THE. Vol. 42, No. 33 (Sept. 10, 1972)-. Newspaper. English. da. $195.00. The Journal Times, 212 4th Street, Racine WI 53403. **Tel** (414)634-3322. ***Continues*** *Racine Journal-Time.*

US
KAUKAUNA TIMES. Vol. 1, No. 1 (Sept. 16, 1880)-. Newspaper. English. sw (Tues. and Thurs.). $22.00. Kaukauna Times, PO Box 109, Kaukauna WI 54130. **Tel** (414)766-4651, FAX (414)766-4736. **ED** Joyce Schubring. **Photos**. **Ad Acc**, **Adv Mgr:** George Kailhofer. Full Page (B&W) $645.00. Half Page (B&W) $354.75. Full Page (Color) $80.00 each color. Half Page (Color) $80.00 each color. **Pub. Size:** Broadsheet. **Circ:** 7,000 morning. available in microform. ***Absorbed*** *Kaukauna Sun.*

US/0749-713X
KENOSHA NEWS. Vol. 68, No. 161 (April 30, 1962)-. Newspaper. English. da. $108.50 (daily by mail); $160.80 (daily & Sunday by carrier); $176.80 (daily & Sunday by mail). Kenosha News Publishing Corporation, 715 58th Street, Kenosha WI 53141. **Tel** (414)657-1000. available on an online database (file 635/Full-Text) from DIALOG. Documents available from UMI Article Clearinghouse. ***Continues*** *Kenosha Evening News.* **Ind/Abst** Bus. Dateline (Dec. 21, 1991-) [Full Txt.].

US
KEWASKUM STATESMAN. Vol. 1, No. 1 (Oct. 5, 1895)-. Newspaper. English (German). wk. William & Marcella Harbeck, 250 Main Street, Kewaskum WI 53040. available on microfilm from The State Historical Society of Wisconsin.

US
KEWAUNEE ENTERPRISE. **VFOAT** Enterprise. Vol. 10, No. 30 (Jan. 13, 1869)-. Newspaper. English. Fifty-two times a year (Wed.). Kewaunee Enterprise, PO Box 86, Kewaunee WI 54216. **Tel** (414)388-3175. available on microfilm from The State Historical Society of Wisconsin. ***Continues*** *Kewaunee County Enterprise.*

US
KEWAUNEE STAR, THE. Newspaper. English. wk. Jackie Svoboda, 214 Harrison Street, Kewaunee WI 54216-0235.

US
KIEL TRI COUNTY RECORD. **VFOAT** Kiel Record. Vol. 58 No. 20 (June 1 1950)-. Newspaper. English. wk (Thurs.). $17.00 Tri-County areas, WI; $25.00 other WI; $35.00 other. Delta Publications / Wisconsin, PO Box 7, Kiel WI 53042. **Tel** (414)894-2828, FAX (414)894-2161. **ED** Michael Mathes. **Photos**. **Ad Acc**, **Adv Mgr:** Joe Mathes. **Pub. Size:** Tabloid. **Circ:** 2,700 (ctrl). available on microfilm. ***Continues*** *Tri-County Record.*

US
LA CROSSE COUNTY COUNTRYMAN. **VFOAT** Countryman; Onalaska Spectrum; Spectrum. No. 48 (July 30, 1970)-. Newspaper. English. Fifty-two times a year. La Crosse County Countryman, PO Box 847, West Salem WI 54669. **Tel** (608)786-1950. **ED** R. Humbel. available on microfilm from The State Historical Society of Wisconsin. ***Formed by the union of*** *Bangor Independent* ***and*** *West Salem Journal.*

US/0745-9793
LA CROSSE TRIBUNE. **VFOAT** LaCrosse Tribune; La Crosse Sunday Tribune. (1944)-. Newspaper. English. da. $175.00 within 75 mile radius of La Crosse, WI; $181.50 other. La Crosse Tribune, PO Box 865C, La Crosse WI 54601. **Tel** (608)782-9710. **ED** David Fuselier. **LC** 7002. **Ad Acc**. **Circ:** 36,500. available on microfilm from University Microfilms International (UMI). Documents available from UMI Article Clearinghouse. ***Continues*** *La Crosse Tribune and Leader-Press.* **Ind/Abst** Bus. Dateline (Dec. 18, 1991-) [Full Txt.].

US/0749-7059
LADYSMITH NEWS (LADYSMITH, WIS. : 1927). (LADYSMITH NEWS.). 33rd year, No. 1 (April 15, 1927)-. Newspaper. English. wk. $18.00, $11.00 (in-county). Thomas Bell, PO Box 189, Ladysmith WI 54848. available on microfilm from The State Historical Society of Wisconsin. ***Continues*** *Ladysmith News-Budget and Rusk County Journal.*

US
LAKE COUNTRY REPORTER. Vol. 1, No. 17 (Jan. 17, 1954)-. Newspaper. English. Twice a week. $24.85. Lake Country Reporter, PO Box 200, Hartland WI 53029. **Tel** (414)367-3272, FAX (414)367-7414. **ED** Scott Peterson. **Photos**. **Ad Acc**, **Adv Mgr:** Gary Jasiek. Full Page (B&W) $566.40. Half Page (B&W) $283.20. Full Page (Color) $641.40. Half Page (Color) $320.70. **Pub. Size:** Tabloid. **Circ:** 7,532 paid. available on microfilm from The State Historical Society of Wisconsin. ***Formed by the union of*** *Hartland News; Delafield Gazette* ***and*** *Pewaukee Post.*

US
LAKE GENEVA REGIONAL NEWS, THE. Vol. 55, No. 12 (March 19, 1936)-. Newspaper. English. Fifty-two times a year (Thurs.). Home News Publishing Company, 315 Broad Street, Lake Geneva WI 53147. **Tel** (414)248-4444. ***Continues*** *Regional News (Lake Geneva, Wis.).*

US
LAKE MILLS HEADER. **VFOAT** Leader. Vol. 4, No. 48 (Oct. 5, 1882)-. Newspaper. English. wk. Dennis Hawkes, 322 North Main Street, Lake Mills WI 53551. ***Continues*** *Lake Mills Spike;* ***Absorbed*** *Rock Lake Journal, Johnson Creek News.*

US/0746-4274
LAKELAND TIMES. **VFOAT** Northern Wisconsin Lakeland Times. Forty-Eighth Year, No. 46 (May 12, 1939)-. Newspaper. English. sw. $38.00. Donald P. Walker, Box 790, Minocqua WI 54548. **ED** Dean Showers. **Ad Acc**, **Adv Mgr:** John Benton. Full Page (B&W) $369.00. Half Page (B&W) $184.00. **Pub. Size:** Tabloid. available in microform. ***Continues*** *Minocqua Times.*

US
LAKESHORE CHRONICLE. Vol. 7, No. 18 (Sept. 30, 1984)-. Newspaper. English. sw. Lakeshore Chronicle, 909 S 29th Street, Manitowoc WI 54220. **Tel** (414)682-5231, FAX (414)682-1804. **ED** Debra Horn. **Ad Acc**. **Circ:** 31,500 (ctrl). available on microfilm from The State Historical Society of Wisconsin. ***Formed by the union of*** *Sunday Lakeshore Chronicle* ***and*** *Midweek Lakeshore Chronicle.*
Desc: General news and community interest.

US/0891-0227
LEADER-TELEGRAM. **VFOAT** Leader Telegram; Leader-Telegram Hilites. Vol. 9, No. 103 (Oct. 7, 1978)-. Newspaper. English. da. $136.40 one year. Leader Telegram, PO Box 570, Eau Claire WI 54702. **Tel** (715)833-9254, FAX (715)833-9244. **ED** Eugene Ringhand (editor's phone: (715)833-9216), Don Huebscher (Managing Editor). **Bk Rev**, (Qty: 150). **Photos**. **Ad Acc**, **Adv Mgr:** Lori Peterson, **Tel** (715)833-9238. Full Page (B&W) $2765.76. Half Page (B&W) $1382.88. Full Page (Color) $2970.76. Half Page (Color) $1587.88. **Pub. Size:** Broadsheet. **Wire Svcs.:** AP, NY. **Pr Rev. Circ:** 31,520 Mon-Fri., 36,925 Sat., 41,220 Sun. available on microfilm from University Microfilms International (UMI); available on an online database (file 635/Full-Text) from DIALOG. ***Continues*** *Eau Claire Leader-Telegram.*

US
LODI ENTERPRISE, THE. **VFOAT** Enterprise. Vol. 1, No. 1 (Feb. 16, 1894)-. Newspaper. English. wk. $34.00 Columbia and Dane County, WI; $40.00 other. Lodi Enterprise, PO Box 16, Lodi WI 53555. **Tel** (608)592-3261.

US
LUXEMBURG NEWS. **VFOAT** News. No. 1 (Feb. 26, 1909)-. Newspaper. English. Fifty-two times a year (Thurs.). $30.00 Wisconsin; $35.00 others. Luxemburg News, PO Box 130, Luxemburg WI 54217. **Tel** (414)845-2525.

US
MARINETTE EAGLE-STAR, THE. **VFOAT** Marinette Eagle Star; Eagle-Star. Vol. 22, No. 97 (August 27, 1913)-. Newspaper. English. da (Mon.-Fri.). $130.50. Eagle Printing Company / Wisconsin, PO Box 77, Marinette WI 54143. **Tel** (715)735-6611. **Ad Acc**. ***Continues*** *Daily Eagle-Star.*

US
MARION ADVERTISER, THE. **VFOAT** Split Rock Record. Vol. 1, No. 1 (April 12, 1895)-. Newspaper. English. wk. Daniel Brandenburg, Box 268, Marion WI 54950. ***Absorbed*** *Tigerton Chronicle.*

US
MARKESAN HERALD. ***Title Change.*** (1981)-?. Newspaper. English. wk. Donald V and Dana E Evans, 51 West Water Street, Markesan WI 53946. ***Continued by*** *Herald (Markesan, Wis.).*

US
MARQUETTE COUNTY TRIBUNE, THE. Vol. 105, No. 18 (May 5, 1960)-. Newspaper. English. wk. $17.00 Wisconsin; $21.00 others. Daniel & Curtis Witte / Montello, PO Box 188, Montello WI 53949. **Tel** (608)297-2424, FAX (608)297-9293. **ED** Mary Faltz. **Photos**. **Ad Acc**. Full Page (B&W) $392.80. Half Page (B&W) $196.40. Full Page (Color) $452.80. Half Page (Color) $256.40. **Pub. Size:** Standard. **Circ:** 4,505. ***Continues*** *Montello Tribune;* ***Absorbed*** *Central Union.*

US/0025-3995
MARQUETTE TRIBUNE (MILWAUKEE), THE. (THE MARQUETTE TRIBUNE.). **Added/Corp** Marquette University. **VFOAT** Marquette University Summer Tribune. (19??)-. Newspaper. English. sw.

$40.00. Marquette University Publications 1131 West Wisconsin Avenue, Milwaukee WI 53233. **Tel** (414)288-7000, (414)288-7190. **ED** Heather J. Gascoigne (Editor-in-Chief) and S. Chris Strout (Managing Editor). **Photos**. **Ad Acc**, **Adv Mgr:** A. Scott DeVouton, **Tel** (414)288-1739. Full Page (B&W) $480.00. Half Page (B&W) $240.00. Full Page (Color) $605.00. Half Page (Color) $365.00. **Pub. Size:** Tabloid. **Wire Svcs.:** AP.

US
MARSHFIELD NEWS-HERALD. VFOAT Marshfield News Herald. Vol. 7, No. 131 (August 8, 1927)-. Newspaper. English. da. Ben Lewis, 111 West 3rd Street, PO Box 70, Marshfield WI 54449-0070. Documents available from UMI Article Clearinghouse. ***Formed by the union of*** *Marshfield Daily News* ***and*** *Marshfield Herald.*
Ind/Abst Bus. Dateline (Dec. 26, 1991-) [Full Txt.].

US/0749-7105
MAYVILLE NEWS, THE. Vol. 1, No. 1 (Feb. 10, 1892)-. Newspaper. English. wk. $8.00 in-state, $10.00 out-of-state. Mayville News Inc, 126 Bridge Street, PO Box 271, Mayville WI 53050.

US/0883-6566
MCFARLAND COMMUNITY LIFE. VFOAT Community Life. V. 1, No. 1 (Aug. 18, 1966)-. Newspaper. English. wk. $16.00. McFarland Community Life, 6041 Monona Drive, Monona WI 53716. **Tel** (608)221-1544. **ED** Peg Zaemisch. **Bk Rev**. **Ad Acc**. **Circ:** 1,500. available on microfilm from The State Historical Society of Wisconsin.
Desc: Current events for McFarland, Wisconsin Town of Dunn, McFarland School district.

US
MENOMONEE FALLS NEWS, THE. VFOAT News. (1889)-. Newspaper. English. wk. $15.95 Oak Creek, Wisconsin; $25.65 other Wisconsin, Michigan, Illinois, Minnesota, Iowa; $31.85 other. Community Newspapers / Wisconsin, PO Box 7, Oak Creek WI 53154. **Tel** (414)768-5800.

US/0749-8519
MID-COUNTY TIMES, THE. VFOAT Midcounty Times. Vol. 62, No. 1 (Jan. 5, 1950)-. Newspaper. English. wk. $10.00, $7.00 (in-county), $8.50 (in-state). Steven D Madsen, 142 North Main Street, Pardeeville WI 53954. available on microfilm from The State Historical Society of Wisconsin. ***Continues*** *Pardeeville-Wyocena Times and the Cambria News.*

US
MILTON COURIER, THE. Vol. 87, No. 14 (April 6, 1967)-. Newspaper. English. wk. $17.00. Doug Welch, PO Box 69, Milton WI 53563. **Tel** (608)868-2442 FAX (608)868-4664. **ED** Doug Welch. **Photos**. **Ad Acc**. Full Page (B&W) $222.00. Half Page (B&W) $130.05. Full Page (Color) $222.00. Half Page (Color) $130.05. **Pub. Size:** Tabloid. **Circ:** 3,100 (weekly). ***Continues*** *Milton and Milton Junction Courier.*

US/0026-4350
MILWAUKEE COURIER. Vol. 1, No. 1 (June 27, 1964)-. Newspaper. English. Fifty-two times a year (Thurs.). $25.00. Milwaukee Courier, 2431 West Hopkins Street, Milwaukee WI 53206. **Tel** (414)449-4860. **ED** Walter Jones. **Bk Rev**, (Qty: 52). **Photos**. **Ad Acc**, **Adv Mgr:** Faithe Colas, **Tel** (414)449-4863. Full Page (B&W) $1,317.96. Half Page (B&W) $658.98. Full Page (Color) $1,467.96. Half Page (Color) $808.98. **Pub. Size:** Broadsheet. **Circ:** 15,000. available on microfilm from University Microfilms International (UMI).

US/1052-4452
MILWAUKEE JOURNAL, THE. VFOAT Daily Journal; Milwaukee Daily Journal. Eighth Year, No. 174 (June 9, 1890)-. Newspaper. English. da (except holidays). $74.40 (daily, by carrier), $84.00 (daily, by motor route), $86.40 (Mon.-Sat. by carrier), $96.00 (Mon-Sat., by motor route), $67.60 (Sun. by carrier) $72.80 (Sun. by motor route), $136.80 (daily & Sun. by carrier). $151.20 (daily & Sun. by motor route); $135.00 (daily by mail for Wisconsin & Upper Michigan), $165.50 (daily by mail for US, Canada, and possessions), $305.91 (daily by mail other) city edition; $97.50 (daily by mail for Wisconsin & Upper Michigan), $125.00 (daily by mail for US, Canada & possessions), $308.88 (daily by mail for other); $207.50 (daily & Sun. by mail for Wisconsin & Upper Michigan), $263.25 (daily & Sun. by mail for US, Canada. and possessions), $487.91 (daily & Sun. by mail for other) city edition; $72.50 (Sunday by mail for Wisconsin & Upper Michigan), $97.75 (Sunday by mail for US, Canada, and possessions), $182.00 (Sunday by mail for other. city edition. Journal Sentinel Inc., 333 West State Street, Milwaukee WI 53201. **Tel** (414)224-2254, FAX (414)224-2045. **ED** Sig Gissler. **Ad Acc**. **Circ:** 828,900. available on microfilm from University Microfilms International (UMI). ***Continues*** *Milwaukee Daily Journal.*
Desc: Daily and Sunday newspapers.
Ind/Abst PROMT.

US/1052-4479
MILWAUKEE SENTINEL (1883), THE. (THE MILWAUKEE SENTINEL.). **VFOAT** Sentinel; Milwaukee Sunday Sentinel; Sunday Sentinel; Sunday Sentinel and Milwaukee Telegram; Milwaukee Sunday News-Sentinel; Milwaukee Sentinel, Milwaukee News. Whole No. 12,571 (Jan. 1, 1883)-. Newspaper. English da. Journal Sentinel Inc., 333 West State Street, Milwaukee WI 53201. **Tel** (414)224-2254, FAX (414)224-2045. **ED** Robert Wills. **Ad Acc**. **Circ:** 185,000. available on microfilm from University Microfilms International (UMI); and University Microfilms International (UMI). ***Continues*** *Daily Republican-Sentinel;* ***Absorbed*** *Sunday Milwaukee Telegraph; Milwaukee News (Milwaukee, Wis. : 1937).*

US
MILWAUKEE STAR (MILWAUKEE, WIS. : 1976). (THE MILWAUKEE STAR.). **VFOAT** Star. Vol. 17, No. 4 (Oct. 7, 1976)-. Newspaper. English. wk. Carole Geary, 3815 North Teutonia, Milwaukee WI 53206. **Circ:** 7,000. ***Continues*** *Milwaukee Star-Times.*

US
MONDOVI HERALD-NEWS, THE. VFOAT Mondovi Herald News. Vol. 50, No. 2 (Jan. 2, 1926)-. Newspaper. English. wk. Mondovi Herald-News, 123 West Main, PO Box 67, Mondovi WI 54755. ***Continues*** *Mondovi Herald and the Buffalo County News.*

US
MONROE COUNTY DEMOCRAT (SPARTA, WIS. : 1895). (MONROE COUNTY DEMOCRAT.). Vol. 34, No. 26 (June 21, 1895)-. Newspaper. English. wk. Fred P Heffling, 114 West Oak Street, Sparta WI 54656. available on microfilm from The State Historical Society of Wisconsin. ***Continues*** *Sparta Democrat (Sparta, Wis. : 1885).*

US/1068-5820
MONROE EVENING TIMES (MONROE, WIS. 1898). (MONROE EVENING TIMES.). (Oct. 13, 1898)-. Newspaper. English. da. $124.00. Larry E. Lund, PO Box 230, Monroe WI 53566. **ED** Judie Hintzman, Mary Jane Bestor (Managing Editor). **LC** 7002. **Bk Rev**, (Qty: 12). **Photos**. **Ad Acc**, **Adv Mgr:** Gary Guralski, **Tel** (608)328-4202. Full Page (B&W) $1073.28. Half Page (B&W) $536.64. Full Page (Color) $1158.28. Half Page (Color) $621.64. **Pub. Size:** Broadsheet. **Wire Svcs.:** AP. **Circ:** 7,600. available in microform.

US/0748-8297
MOSINEE TIMES, THE. Vol. 1, No. 1 (Dec. 27, 1895)-. Newspaper. English. wk. Mosinee River Publishing Company, 407 Third Street, Mosinee WI 54455-1495.

US/0749-7091
MOUNT HOREB MAIL. VFOAT Mail; Mt. Horeb Mail. Began with Nov. 13, 1901 issue. Newspaper. English. wk. $11.00. D & C Witte, 219 East Main Street, Mount Horeb WI 53572. available on microfilm from The State Historical Society of Wisconsin.

US
MUKWONAGO CHIEF, THE. Vol. 1, No. 2 (Jan. 9, 1889)-. Newspaper. English. Fifty-two times a year (publ Weds.). $20.00 Waukesha County, Wisconsin; $23.00 others in Wisconsin; $27.00 other. Chief Publications, PO Box 204, Mukwonago WI 53149. **Tel** (414)363-4045. **ED** James Flahrety (editor's address: 110 Main Street, Mukwonago WI 53149). **Ad Acc**, **Adv Mgr:** Terri Blazek. **Circ:** 4,500 (ctrl). ***Continues*** *Mukwonago Chief and Mail.*
Desc: Local news and sports for Mukwonago and the surrounding communities.

US
MUSKEGO SUN. VFOAT Sun. 53rd Year, No. 46 (Nov. 13, 1980)-. Newspaper. English. Fifty-two times a year (Thurs.). Community Newspapers, PO Box 7, Oak Creek WI 53154. **Tel** (414)768-5800. ***Continues*** *Sun (Hales Corners, Wis.).*

US
NEW BERLIN CITIZEN, THE. Vol. 1, No. 1 (Dec. 10, 1958)-. Newspaper. English. Fifty-two times a year (Thurs.). Community Newspapers, PO Box 7, Oak Creek WI 53154. **Tel** (414)768-5800. available on microfilm from The State Historical Society of Wisconsin.

US/1062-4856
NEW BERLIN ENTERPRISE. Began with: Vol. 1, No. 1 (June 1, 1973)-. Newspaper. English. wk. $10.00 New Berlin residents; $75.00 other. Enterprise Publishing / Wisconsin, 1112 South 60th Street, West Allis WI 53214. **Tel** (414)778-1666, FAX (414)778-1773.

US/0749-6982
NEW HOLSTEIN REPORTER. (Oct. 1919)-. Newspaper. English. Fifty-two times a year (Thurs.). $17.00 local; $25.00 Wisconsin; $35.00 US. New Holstein Reporter, 2118 Wisconsin Avenue, PO Box 177, New Holstein WI 53061. **Tel** (414)898-4276, FAX (414)894-2161. **ED** Mark Sherry. **Bk Rev**. **Photos**. **Ad Acc**, **Adv Mgr:** Joe Mathes. Full Page (B&W) $288.00. Half Page (B&W) $153.00. Full Page (Color) $388.00. Half Page (Color) $253.00. **Pub. Size:** Tabloid. **Circ:** 2,400 (ctrl). available on microfilm. ***Continues*** *Calumet County Reporter.*
Desc: News, sports, feature stories, opinion articles and photos.

US
NEWS (NEW RICHMOND, WIS.). (THE NEWS.). Vol. 109, No. 23 (Feb. 9, 1978)-. Newspaper. English. wk. Robert Bradford, PO Box 98, New Richmond WI 54017. **ED** M R Jensen. available on microfilm from The State Historical Society of Wisconsin. ***Continues*** *New Richmond News (New Richmond, Wis. : 1924).*

US/0749-7253
NIAGARA JOURNAL, THE. (THE NIAGARA JOURNAL, FRANKLIN STOVE.). **VFOAT** Niagara Journal, Franklin's Stove. Vol. 51, Issue 29 (July 8, 1981)-. Newspaper. English. wk. $11.00, $9.00 (Marinette county). Karen Klenke, 1111 Roosevelt Road, Niagara WI 54151. **ED** J J Klenke. available on microfilm from The State Historical Society of Wisconsin. ***Continues*** *Niagara Journal & Franklin's Stove (Niagara, Wis. : 1981).*

US
OAK CREEK PICTORIAL (OAK CREEK, WIS. : 1982). (OAK CREEK PICTORIAL.). **VFOAT** Pictorial. 26th Year, No. 11 (March 18, 1982)-. Newspaper. English. Fifty-two times a year (Thurs.). Community Newspapers, PO Box 7, Oak Creek WI 53154. **Tel** (414)768-5800. **ED** M. L. Stover. available on microfilm from The State Historical Society of Wisconsin. ***Continues*** *Pictorial (Oak Creek, Wis. : 1980 : Oak Creek Ed.).*

US
OCONOMOWOC ENTERPRISE, THE. Vol. 12, No. 34 (March 8, 1901)-. Newspaper. English. Fifty-two times a year (Wed.). $20.00. Oconomowoc Enterprise, PO Box B, Oconomowoc WI 53066. **Tel** (414)567-5511, FAX (414)567-4422. **ED** Robert Van Enkervoort. **Bk Rev**, (Qty: 30-35). **Photos**. **Ad Acc**, **Adv Mgr:** Jan Gust. Full Page (B&W) $10.71 (PCI). Full Page (Color) $90.00. **Pub. Size:** Broadsheet. available on microfilm from The State Historical Society of Wisconsin. ***Continues*** *Enterprise (Oconomowoc, Wis.).*

US
OCONTO COUNTY TIMES-HERALD. VFOAT Oconto County Times Herald; Times-Herald. Vol. 53, No. 41 (Jan. 3, 1952)-. Newspaper. English. wk. Robert Shellman, Box 128, Oconto Falls WI 54154. **ED** E J Shellman. available on microfilm from The State Historical Society of Wisconsin. ***Formed by the union of*** *Gillett Times* ***and*** *Oconto Falls Herald (Oconto Falls, Wis. : 1920).*

US/8755-3961
OMRO HERALD, THE. Vol. 1, No. 1 (May 11, 1894)-. Newspaper. English. wk. $20.00 (one year); $35.00 (two years); $50.00 others. Berlin Journal Company, PO Box 10, Berlin WI 54923. **Tel** (414)361-1515. **ED** Jim Woiff. **Photos**. **Ad Acc**, **Adv Mgr:** Betty Van Sistine. Full Page (B&W) $360.00. Half Page (B&W) $184.00. Full Page (Color) $418.00. Half Page (Color) $234.00. **Pub. Size:** Tabloid. **Circ:** 1,000. available in microform from The State Historical Society of Wisconsin.

US/1053-6906
ONALASKA COMMUNITY LIFE. (Aug. 17, 1989)-. Newspaper. English. Fifty-two times a year (Thurs.). $19.00 La Crosse County, Wisconsin; $25.00 others. Onalaska Community Life, 205 Green Street, PO Box 367, Onalaska WI 54650. **Tel** (608)526-3213, FAX (608)526-4853. **ED** David Skoloda, (editor's address: PO Box 66, Holmen, WI 54636). **Bk Rev**, (Qty: 48). **Ad Acc**. **Circ:** 1,200 (ctrl).

US
ORFORDVILLE JOURNAL AND FOOTVILLE NEWS. Vol. 72, No. 38 (May 29, 1974)-. Newspaper. English. wk. George Stewart, 124 East Spring Street, Orfordville WI 53576-0248. **ED** R M Stewart. available on microfilm from The State Historical Society of Wisconsin. ***Continues*** *Orfordville Journal.*

US
OSCEOLA SUN (OSCEOLA, WIS.). (THE OSCEOLA SUN.). **VFOAT** Dresser Junction Gazette; Dresser Junction News. Vol. 1, No. 1 (Oct. 6, 1897)-. Newspaper. English. wk. Thomas Larson, 108 Cascade Street, Osceola WI 54020. available on microfilm from The State Historical Society of Wisconsin.

US/0300-676X
OSHKOSH ADVANCE-TITAN. Added/Corp University of Wisconsin--Oshkosh. (1894)-. English. wk. $20.00. Rebecca Averbeck, Advance - Titan, University of Oshkosh, Oshkosh WI 54901. **Tel** (414)424-3048, FAX (414)424-7317. **ED** Rebecca Averbeck. **Bk Rev**, (Qty: 7). **Photos**. **Ad Acc**, **Adv Mgr:** Barb Lvedtke, **Tel** (414)424-3049. Full Page (B&W) $647.13. Half Page (B&W) $334.00. **Pub. Size:** Tabloid. **Wire Svcs.:** AP. **Circ:** 11,000.

US
OSHKOSH NORTHWESTERN (OSHKOSH, WIS. : 1979 : DAILY). (THE OSHKOSH NORTHWESTERN.). **VFOAT** Weekend Northwestern. Oct. 29, 1979-. Newspaper. English. da. Oshkosh Northwestern Company, PO Box 2926, 224 State Street, Oshkosh WI 54901. ***Continues*** *Oshkosh Daily Northwestern (Oshkosh, Wis. : 1939).*

US/0194-1712
OUR TOWN. Newspaper. English. wk. Don Harris, 24 West Rives, Rhinelander WI 54501.

US
OZAUKEE COUNTY GUIDE (GRAFTON, WIS.). (OZAUKEE COUNTY GUIDE.). Vol. 26, No. 49 (August 15, 1984)-. Newspaper. English. wk. Steven Karides, 1930 Wisconsin Avenue, Grafton WI 53024. available on microfilm from The State Historical Society of Wisconsin. ***Continues*** *Guide (Port Washington, Wis.).*

US/1056-9006
OZAUKEE COUNTY NEWS GRAPHIC. **VFOAT** News Graphic. (19??)-. Newspaper. English. bw. $28.97 Wisconsin; $33.97 US. Lakeshore Newspapers, PO Box 47, Cedarburg WI 53012. **Tel** (414)375-5115, FAX (414)375-5107. **ED** Phil Paige, Mark Jaeger (Managing Editor). **Photos. Ad Acc, Adv Mgr:** Monika Hughes. Full Page (B&W) $477.00. Half Page (B&W) $238.50. **Pub. Size:** Tabloid. **Circ:** 10,000 paid. ***Continues*** *News Graphic Pilot, 0749-7199.*

US/0749-7164
OZAUKEE PRESS (PORT WASHINGTON, WIS. : 1969). (THE OZAUKEE PRESS.). Vol. 30, No. 11 (Oct. 23, 1969)-. Newspaper. English. Fifty-two times a year. Port Publications Inc., 125 East Main Street, PO Box 249, Port Washington WI 53074. **Tel** (414)284-3494. available on microfilm from The State Historical Society of Wisconsin. ***Continues*** *Press (Port Washington, Wis.).*

US/8755-0539
PALMYRA ENTERPRISE. **VFOAT** Eagle Quill. Vol. 1, No. 1 (March 25, 1874- April 12,1893. Newspaper. English. wk. $5.00 in advance, $8.00 out of state. Poe Printers and Publishers, Mains Street, Palmyra WI 53156.

US
PARK FALLS HERALD, THE. **VFOAT** Butternut News. Vol. 1, No. 1 (Sept. 21 1900)-. Newspaper. English. wk. T Kempkes, PO Box 410, Park Falls WI 54552-0325.

US
PESHTIGO TIMES (PESHTIGO, WIS. : 1949). (PESHTIGO TIMES.). Vol. 62, No. 11 (March 17, 1949)-. Newspaper. English. Fifty-two times a year. Leo J. Jesch Publisher, 130 West Foront Street, Peshtigo WI 54157. available on microfilm from The State Historical Society of Wisconsin. ***Continues*** *Peshtigo Times and Coleman Beacon.*

US/8755-3244
PIERCE COUNTY HERALD (ELLSWORTH, WIS.). (PIERCE COUNTY HERALD.). Vol. 1, No. 1 (Jan. 16, 1868)-. Newspaper. English. wk. $14.00, $10.00 (Pierce county). Steven Dzubay, 122 N 3rd Street, River Falls WI 54022. available on microfilm from The State Historical Society of Wisconsin. ***Absorbed*** *Prescott Journal.*

US
PLATTEVILLE JOURNAL (PLATTEVILLE, WIS. : 1966). (THE PLATTEVILLE JOURNAL.). No. 32 (August 18, 1966)-. Newspaper. English. mo. $36.50. Richard Brockman, 115 West Main, Platteville WI 53818-0266. **Tel** (608)348-3006. available on microfilm from The State Historical Society of Wisconsin. ***Continues*** *Platteville Journal and Grant County News.*

US
POST CRESCENT (APPLETON, WIS.). (THE POST-CRESCENT.). **VFOAT** Saturday Post Crescent. Vol. 78, No. 71 (Jan. 4, 1965)-. Newspaper. English. da. Donald Kampfer, 306 West Washington Street, PO Box 59, Appleton WI 54912. ***Continues*** *Appleton Post-Crescent.*

US
POYNETTE PRESS, THE. Vol. 1, No. 1 (April 17, 1884)-. Newspaper. English. wk. Richard Emerson, PO Box 37, Poynette WI 53955-0037. available on microfilm from The State Historical Society of Wisconsin.

US
PRESCOTT JOURNAL (PRESCOTT, WIS. : 1930). (THE PRESCOTT JOURNAL.). Newspaper. English. wk. $25.00. Gary B Rawn, 121 Orange Street, Prescott WI 54021. **Tel** (715)262-5454, FAX (715)262-5474. **ED** Gary B Rawn. Index available. cum. index. **Bk Rev. Ad Acc. Circ:** 6,000. available on microfilm from The State Historical Society of Wisconsin. ***Continues*** *Prescott Tribune.*

US
PRESS-STAR (NEW LONDON, WIS. : 1979). (PRESS-STAR.). **VFOAT** Press Star. Vol. 93, No. 32 (May 3, 1979)-. Newspaper. English. wk. Vern Otto, PO Box 283, New London WI 54961. available on microfilm from The State Historical Society of Wisconsin. ***Continues*** *Thursday Press-Star.*

US/8755-397X
PRINCETON TIMES-REPUBLIC. **VFOAT** Princeton Times Republic. Vol. 71, No. 17 (June 3, 1937)-. Newspaper. English. wk. $20.00 (one year); $35.00 (two years); $50.00 others. Princeton Times-Republic, PO Box 10, Berlin WI 54923. **ED** Jim Woiff. **Photos. Ad Acc, Adv Mgr:** Betty Van Sistine. Full Page (B&W) $360.00. Half Page (B&W) $184.00. Full Page (Color) $418.00. Half Page (Color) $234.00. **Pub. Size:** Tabloid. **Circ:** 1,500. available on microfilm from The State Historical Society of Wisconsin. ***Formed by the union of*** *Princeton Times* ***and*** *Princeton Republic.*

US
PULASKI NEWS. **VFOAT** Pulaski Hi News. (Aug. 1942)-. Newspaper. English. bw (Every two weeks). $10.00. Pulaski High School, 911 South St. Augustine Street, Pulaski WI 54162. **Tel** (414)822-4263, FAX (414)822-4120. **ED** Kathy Gerds. **Photos. Ad Acc, Adv Mgr:** Mary Lepak. Full Page (B&W) $320.00. Half Page (B&W) $160.00. **Pub. Size:** Broadsheet. ctrl circ. available in microform.
Desc: School and community newspaper written by the students.

US
RECORD-REVIEW. **VFOAT** Record Review. Vol. 1, No. 1 (Feb. 4, 1965)-. Newspaper. English. wk. $20.00 Wisconsin; $27.00 US. TP Printing, 103 West Spruce Street, Abbotsford WI 54405-9734. **Tel** (715)223-2342, FAX (715)223-3505. **ED** Peter Weinschenk. **Photos. Ad Acc, Adv Mgr:** Carol O'Leary. Full Page (B&W) $310.80. Half Page (B&W) $155.40. Full Page (Color) $310.80 plus $100.00 per color. Half Page (Color) $155.40 plus $100.00 per color. **Pub. Size:** Tabloid. **Circ:** 1,900. ***Formed by the union of*** *Edgar Weekly Review* ***and*** *Athens Record.*

US/1053-9972
REPORTER. **VFOAT** Free Press Reporter. Newspaper. English. wk. Marolla Press, 116 South Vine Street, PO Box 148, Horicon WI 53032-0148. ***Continues*** *Horicon Reporter.*

US/0749-7172
REPORTER (FOND DU LAC, WIS.), THE. (THE REPORTER.). (1977)-. Newspaper. English. da (except Sat. and major holidays). $136.00. Reporter / Wisconsin, 33 West Second Street, Fond du Lac WI 54935. **Tel** (414)922-4600. **ED** Stan Gores. **Bk Rev. Ad Acc.**

US/8755-4011
REPRESENTATIVE, FOX LAKE, WISCONSIN, THE. (THE REPRESENTATIVE.). Vol. 113, No. 39 (Sept. 24, 1981)-. Newspaper. English. wk. $20.00 (one year); $35.00 (two years); $50.00 others. Berlin Journal Company, PO Box 10, Berlin WI 54923. **Tel** (414)361-1515. **ED** Jim Woiff. **Photos. Ad Acc, Adv Mgr:** Betty Van Sistine. Full Page (B&W) $360.00. Half Page (B&W) $184.00. Full Page (Color) $418.00. Half Page (Color) $234.00. **Pub. Size:** Tabloid. **Circ:** 750. available on microfilm from The State Historical Society of Wisconsin. ***Continues*** *Fox Lake Representative (Fox Lake, Wis. : 1969).*

US
REPUBLICAN JOURNAL, BELMONT SUCCESS, THE OLD SETTLER, SCHULLSBURG PICK AND GAD. **VFOAT** Republican Journal; Belmont Success; Old Settler; Schullsburg Pick and Gad. Newspaper. English. wk. Brian A Lund, 316 South Main Street, Darlington WI 53530-0020. **ED** E Neuwirth. available on microfilm from The State Historical Society of Wisconsin. ***Continues*** *Republican Journal, Belmont Success, Schullsbug Pic and Gad (Darlington, Wis. : 1982).*

US
REVIEW (PLYMOUTH, WIS.). (REVIEW.). Vol. 99, No. 70 (Sept. 2, 1965)-. Newspaper. English. sw. M C Johanson, 113 East Mill Street, Box 306, Plymouth WI 53073-1776. **ED** R S Johansen. available on microfilm from The State Historical Society of Wisconsin. ***Continues*** *Plymouth Review (Plymouth, Wis. : 1960).*

US
RICHLAND OBSERVER (RICHLAND CENTER, WIS.). (THE RICHLAND OBSERVER.). Vol. 1, No. 1 (April 5, 1962)-. Newspaper. English. Fifty-two times a year (Thurs.). Richland County Publishers, PO Box 31, Richland Center WI 53581-0031. **Tel** (608)647-6149. **ED** J. E. Olson. available on microfilm from The State Historical Society of Wisconsin. ***Formed by the union of*** *Richland Democrat (Richland Center, Wis. : 1892)* ***and*** *Republican Observer.*

US/0748-6863
RIPON COMMONWEALTH-PRESS, THE. **VFOAT** Ripon Commonwealth Press. 93rd year, No. 16 (May 2, 1957)-. Newspaper. English. wk. Doug Lyke, PO Box 6, Ripon WI 54971. available on microfilm from The State Historical Society of Wisconsin. ***Continues*** *Ripon Commonwealth and Ripon Weekly Press.*

US
RIVER FALLS JOURNAL (RIVER FALLS, WIS. : 1872). (RIVER FALLS JOURNAL.). (1872)-. Newspaper. English. wk. $52.00. River Falls Journal / Western Wisconsin Buyer's Guide, PO Box 25, River Falls WI 54022. **Tel** (715)425-1561, FAX (715)425-5660. **ED** Phil Pfuehler (Editor-in-Chief) and Judy Wiff (Managing Editor). **Photos. Ad Acc, Adv Mgr:** Paul Charbonneau. Full Page (B&W) $813.01. Half Page (B&W) $441.83. Full Page (Color) $918.01. Half Page (Color) $546.83. **Pub. Size:** Standard. **Wire Svcs.:** AP, NF. **Circ:** 4,650 (paid), 10,100 (unpaid). available on microfilm from The State Historical Society of Wisconsin. ***Absorbed*** *River Falls Times; River Falls Sentinel.*

US
SAUK-PRAIRIE STAR, THE. **VFOAT** Sauk Prairie Star; Star. (1953)-. Newspaper. English. wk. Daniel & Curtis Witte / Sauk City, 801 Water Street, Box 606, Sauk City WI 53583. ***Formed by the union of*** *Sauk City Star* ***and*** *Sauk County News. The Pioneer Press;* ***Absorbed*** *Sauk-Prairie News.*

US
SHARON REPORTER, THE. **VFOAT** Times, The Reporter. Vol. 1, No. 1 (Aug. 29, 1878)-. Newspaper. English. wk. $14.95 in county; $20.00 others. The Times / Wisconsin, 325 Kenosha Street, PO Box 129, Walworth WI 53184. **Tel** (414)736-4380, FAX (414)275-5259. **ED** Mabel Jackson (Editor-in-Chief) and Dan Snow (Managing Editor). **Photos. Ad Acc, Adv Mgr:** Mabel Jackson. Full Page (B&W) $594.00. Half Page (B&W) $297.60. **Pub. Size:** Broadsheet. available on microfilm from The State Historical Society of Wisconsin.

US/0749-7148
SHAWANO EVENING LEADER. **VFOAT** Evening Leader. Vol. 53, No. 34 (August, 22, 1934)-. Newspaper. English. da. Shawano Evening Leader, 1464 East Green Bay Street, Shawano WI 54166. **Tel** (715)526-2121. ***Continues*** *Leader-Advocate;* ***Formed by the union of*** *Shawano County Journal.*

US/0897-4543
SHEBOYGAN FALLS NEWS, THE. Vol. 1, No. 1 (Sept. 16, 1971)-. Newspaper. English. wk. Barry S & M Christine Johanson, 504 Broadway, Sheboygan WI 53085. available on microfilm from The State Historical Society of Wisconsin.

US/0749-7121
SHEBOYGAN PRESS (SHEBOYGAN, WIS. : 1924). (THE SHEBOYGAN PRESS.). Vol. 17, No. 1 (Dec. 17, 1924)-. Newspaper. English. da (except Sunday). $66.00. Sheboygan Press, 626 Center Avenue, Sheboygan WI 53081. **LC** 10289. available on an online database (file 635/Full-Text) from DIALOG. Documents available from UMI Article Clearinghouse. ***Continues*** *Sheboygan Press-Telegram.*
Ind/Abst Bus. Dateline (Dec. 22, 1991-) [Full Txt.].

US/1071-5185
SHEPHERD EXPRESS. Vol. 7, No. 11 (Oct. 2, 1987)-. Newspaper. English. wk. $30.00. Alternative Publications Inc., 1123 North Water Street, Milwaukee WI 53202. **Tel** (414)276-2222. **ED** Doug Hissom. **Bk Rev,** (Qty: 40). **Ad Acc, Adv Mgr:** Mary Henschel. Full Page (B&W) $1000.00. Half Page (B&W) $550.00. Full Page (Color) $1375.00. Half Page (Color) $925.00. **Pub. Size:** Tabloid. **Wire Svcs.:** AL. **Circ:** 45,000 (ctrl). ***Continues*** *Milwaukee Shepherd.*
Desc: Milwaukee's only alternative newsweekly. Provides news, information, entertainment and humor.

US/0749-7156
SHORELINE LEADER, THE. (SHORELINE LEADER.). **VFOAT** Racine Shoreline Leader!. Vol. 1, No. 1 (March 25, 1965)-. Newspaper. English. wk. $8.00 in county; $9.00 Wisconsin; $10.00 other. Shoreline Leader, 214 State Street, Racine WI 53403. **Tel** (414)637-6771.

US/8755-3686
SOUNDER (RANDOM LAKE, WIS.). (THE SOUNDER.). Vol. 62, No. 8 (June 7, 1979)-. Newspaper. English. wk. $12.00, $7.50 (in-county), $9.75 (in-state). Times Publishing Company Inc, 405 Second Street, PO Box 346, Random Lake WI 53075-0346. **ED** G J Feider. available on microfilm from The State Historical Society of Wisconsin. ***Continues*** *Sounder of Random Lake.*

US
SOUTH MILWAUKEE VOICE GRAPHIC. 95th year, No. 31 (August 6, 1987)-. Newspaper. English. wk. Voice Journal, 723 Milwaukee Avenue, South Milwaukee WI 53172. ***Formed by the union of*** *South Milwaukee Voice Journal* ***and*** *South Milwaukee News Graphic.*

US
SPARTA HERALD (SPARTA, WIS. : 1869). (SPARTA HERALD.). New series Vol. 1, No. 1 (April 13, 1869)-Vol. 54, No. 152 (Feb. 19, 1925)-. Newspaper. English. wk. Sparta Herald, 114 West Oak Street, Sparta WI 54656. **ED** Editors: J.W. Spradling & B.R. McCoy, Sept. 18, 1924-Dec. 16, 1926; T.C. Radde, May 19, 1932-May 26, 1947; D.P. Radde, June 2, 1947-Feb. 21, 1966; C. Masters, Sept. 17, 1973-April 27, 1981; W.V. Gleiss, May 4, 1981-. **LC** 7002. available on microfilm from The State Historical Society of Wisconsin. ***Continues*** *Sparta Democrat (Sparta, Wis. : 1867).*

US/8755-6995
SPOONER ADVOCATE, THE. Vol. 1, No. 1 (June 28, 1901)-. Newspaper. English. wk. $12.00. Keith M Hansen, 515 Front Street, Spooner WI 54801. ***Absorbed*** *Spooner Register.*

US
SPRING VALLEY SUN (SPRING VALLEY, WIS. : 1952). (THE SPRING VALLEY SUN.). Vol. 60, No. 36 (Sept. 4, 1952)-. Newspaper. English. wk. $12.00. Duane Kelley, PO Box 69, Spring Valley WI 54767. **ED** Duane Kelley. **Photos. Ad Acc.** Full Page (B&W) $219.30. Half Page (B&W) $109.65. available on microfilm from The State Historical Society of Wisconsin. ***Continues*** *Sun (Spring Valley, Wis.).*

US/1053-539X
ST. CROIX COUNTY STAR. **VFOAT** Saint Croix County Star. Vol. 22, No. 25 (Sept. 6, 1990)-. Newspaper. English. wk. $12.00 (in county), $18.00 (outside county). Francis Harper, PO Box 167, Somerset WI 54025. ***Continues*** *Somerset Star.*

US
STAR COUNTRYMAN. **VFOAT** Countryman. No. 52 (Nov. 23, 1961)-. Newspaper. English. wk. Richard L Royle, 1 South Main Street, PO Box 27, Deerfield WI 53531. **ED** D Hecke. available on microfilm from The State Historical Society of Wisconsin. ***Continues*** *Sun Prairie Star-Countryman.*

US
STAR NEWS (MEDFORD, WIS.). (THE STAR NEWS.). Vol. 69, No. 37 (Dec. 14, 1944)-. Newspaper. English. wk. Price varies within Wisconsin; $43.00 other US. Star News, PO Box 180, Medford WI 54451. **Tel** (715)748-2626. ***Continues*** *Taylor County Star News.*

US/0748-6332
STEVENS POINT JOURNAL (STEVENS POINT, WIS. : 1981 : DAILY). (STEVENS POINT JOURNAL.). (Jan. 5, 1981)-. Newspaper. English. da (except Sunday). $74.50 (carrier) local; (Mail) $95.00 Portage, Wood, Waushara, Marathon, Waupaca Counties, $117.00 other Wisconsin, $128.00 other US; $160.00 other. Stevens Point Journal, 1200 Third Court, Stevens Point WI 54481. **Tel** (715)344-6100. ***Continues*** *Stevens Point Daily Journal.*

US/1049-0655
STOUGHTON COURIER HUB (STOUGHTON, WIS. : 1981). (THE STOUGHTON COURIER HUB.). **VFOAT** Hub. Vol. 103, No. 14 (July 11, 1981)-. Newspaper. English. wk. $23.75. John Lebeck, 301 West Main Street, PO Box 577, Stoughton WI 53589-0577. **Tel** (608)873-6671. **ED** Eric Neuwirth. **Ad Acc. Circ:** 4,100. available on microfilm from The State Historical Society of Wisconsin. ***Continues*** *Courier Hub.*

US
STRATFORD JOURNAL (STRATFORD, WIS.). (THE STRATFORD JOURNAL.). (Nov. 14, 1913)-. Newspaper. English. wk. $12.50. P W Hale, Box 5, Stratford WI 54484. **Tel** (715)687-4112. **ED** P.W. Hale. **Photos. Ad Acc.** Full Page (B&W) $5.75 per column inch. Full Page (Color) $5.75 per column inch plus an additional $100.00. **Pub. Size:** Tabloid. **Circ:** 750 paid weekly (ctrl).

US/0885-2375
THORP COURIER, THE. Vol. 12, No. 28 (May 30, 1895)-. Newspaper. English. wk. John J La Gasse, Box 487, Thorp WI 54771. ***Continues*** *Courier (Thorp, Wis.).*

US
TIMES PRESS HARTFORD PUBLICATIONS. Periodical. English. Fifty-two times a year (Published on Wednesdays). $16.00 1 year, $29.00 2 year Washington and Dodge Counties; $20.00 1 year, $34.50 2 year other Wisconsin; $25.00 1 year other. Hartford Publications, 225 N Main Street, PO Box 222, Hartford WI 53027. **Tel** (414)673-3500. **ED** Kevin Michalowski. **Ad Acc, Adv Mgr:** Jackie Michalowski. ctrl circ.

US
TIMES PRESS (SEYMOUR, WIS. : 1978). (TIMES PRESS.). **VFOAT** Times-Press. Vol. 93, No. 23 (Dec. 6, 1978)-. Newspaper. English. Fifty-two times a year (Thurs.). $16.00 in county; $20.00 others in Wisconsin; $23.00 others. Seymour Times Press / Wisconsin, 205 North Main Street, PO Box 128, Seymour WI 54165-0128. **Tel** (414)833-2517, FAX (414)833-2454. **ED** Bettyann Kowalski. **Photos. Ad Acc, Adv Mgr:** Ken Hodgden. Full Page (B&W) $464.00. Half Page (B&W) $243.20. Full Page (Color) $564.00. Half Page (Color) $343.20. **Pub. Size:** Tabloid. **Circ:** 2,234. available on microfilm from The State Historical Society of Wisconsin. ***Continues*** *Seymour/Black Creek, Bonduel/Cecil Times Press.*

US
TIMES (WALWORTH, WIS.). (THE TIMES.). **VFOAT** Walworth Times; Times, The Reporter; Times, The Sharon Reporter; Christmas Times. Vol. 53, No. 35 (May 16, 1957)-. Newspaper. English. wk. $14.95. Walworth Newspapers Inc., 325 Kenosha Street, Box 129, Walworth WI 53184. **Tel** (414)275-2166, FAX (414)275-5259. **ED** Kent Johnson (Editor-in-Chief) and Daniel Snow (Managing Editor). **Photos. Ad Acc, Adv Mgr:** Marge Moore. Full Page (B&W) $525.00. Half Page (B&W) $297.60. **Pub. Size:** Broadsheet. available on microfilm from The State Historical Society of Wisconsin. ***Continues*** *Walworth Times.*

US/0749-7040
TRI-COUNTY NEWS (OSSEO, WIS.), THE. (THE TRI-COUNTY NEWS.). **VFOAT** Tricounty News; Tri-County News, Augusta Area Times. Vol. 75, No. 26 (Aug. 19, 1965)-. Newspaper. English. wk. $11.00 Wisconsin. Michael D Jensen, 1721 Omaha Street, Osseo WI 54758. **Tel** (715)597-3313. **Ad Acc. Circ:** 3,700 (ctrl). available on microfilm from The State Historical Society of Wisconsin. ***Formed by the union of*** *Tri-County News (Eleva, Wis. : Eleva Ed.); Tri-County News (Osseo, Wis. : Osseo, Ed.)* ***and*** *Tri-County News (Strum, Wis. : Strum, Ed.).*

US
TRI-COUNTY PRESS. **VFOAT** Tri County Press. Vol. 65, No. 29 (April 2, 1959)-. Newspaper. English. wk. Tri-County Press Publishing Company, 301 South Main, Cuba City WI 53807. **ED** R Goldthorpe. available on microfilm from The State Historical Society of Wisconsin. ***Absorbed*** *Cuba City News; Benton Advocate; Cuba City News-Herald and the Hazel Green Tribune-Reporter.*

US
TRIBUNE-PHONOGRAPH. **VFOAT** Tribune Phonograph. Vol. 1, No. 1 (Feb. 7, 1963)-. Newspaper. English. wk. $20.00 Wisconsin; $27.00 US. TP Printing, 103 West Spruce Street, Abbotsford WI 54405-9734. **Tel** (715)223-2342, FAX (715)223-3505. **ED** Charles Runnue. **Photos. Ad Acc, Adv Mgr:** Carol O'Leary. Full Page (B&W) $310.80. Half Page (B&W) $155.40. Full Page (Color) $310.80 plus $100.00 per color. Half Page (Color) $155.40 plus $100.00 per color. **Pub. Size:** Tabloid. **Circ:** 2,600. ***Formed by the union of*** *Abbotsford Tribune* ***and*** *Colby Phonograph.*

US
TRIBUNE PRESS REPORTER. Vol. 95, No. 52 (July 12, 1984)-. Newspaper. English. wk. $15.00 Wisconsin; $20.00 US; $50.00 other. Carlton De Witt, 215 East Oak Street, Glenwood City WI 54013. **Tel** (715)265-4646, FAX (715)265-7486. **ED** Carlton DeWitt. **Bk Rev. Photos. Ad Acc, Adv Mgr:** Shawn DeWitt. Full Page (B&W) $514.50. Half Page (B&W) $262.50. Full Page (Color) $514.50 plus $100.00 per color. Half Page (Color) $262.50 plus $100.00 per color. **Pub. Size:** Broadsheet. **Circ:** 3,000. ***Formed by the union of*** *Boyceville Press-Reporter* ***and*** *Glenwood City Tribune.*

US
TRIBUNE RECORD-GLEANER, THE. **VFOAT** Tribune-Record-Gleaner. Vol. 84, No. 20 (May 17, 1978)-. Newspaper. English. wk. $22.00. Robert E. Berglund, 318 North Main, Loyal WI 54446. **Tel** (715)255-8531, FAX (715)255-8357. **ED** Dean Lesar (Managing Editor). **Photos. Ad Acc, Adv Mgr:** Nancy Meyer. Full Page (B&W) $825.60. Half Page (B&W) $412.80. Full Page (Color) $935.60. Half Page (Color) $422.80. **Pub. Size:** Standard. available in microform. ***Continues*** *Tribune Record Gleaner.*

US
VALDERS JOURNAL, THE. Vol. 1, No. 1 (Aug. 22, 1940)-. Newspaper. English. wk. $16.00. M F Brockman, 204 N Liberty Street, Valders WI 54245-0400. **Tel** (414)775-4431. **ED** Brian D. Thomsen. **Ad Acc. Circ:** 2,000.
Desc: General community news.

US
VERNON COUNTY BROADCASTER. (19??)-. Newspaper. English. wk. $21.00 local; $30.00 other. Mary Bormann Hollister & Petter Hollister, PO Box 472, Viroqua WI 54665. **Tel** (608)637-3137, FAX (608)637-8557. **ED** Mary Bormann Hollister. **Bk Rev. Photos. Ad Acc, Adv Mgr:** Peter Hollister. Full Page (B&W) $576.00. Half Page (B&W) $300.00. Full Page (Color) $676.00. Half Page (Color) $400.00. **Pub. Size:** Broadsheet. **Circ:** 6,000. ***Continues*** *Vernon County Broadcaster-Censor.*

US
VERNON COUNTY BROADCASTER-CENSOR. ***Title Change.*** **VFOAT** Vernon County Broadcaster Censor; Broadcaster-Censor. Vol. 36, No. 10 (March 8, 1956)-(19??). Newspaper. English. wk. Mary Bormann Hollister & Petter Hollister, PO Box 472, Viroqua WI 54665. **Tel** (608)637-3137, FAX (608)637-8557. available on microfilm from The State Historical Society of Wisconsin. ***Continues*** *Vernon County Broadcaster and Vernon County Censor.* ***Continued by*** *Vernon County Broadcaster.*

US
VERONA PRESS, THE. Vol. 1, No. 1 (May 27, 1965)-. Newspaper. English. wk. $24.00. Community Herald, 6041 Monona Drive, Monona WI 53716. **ED** Henry Schroeder. **Photos. Ad Acc, Adv Mgr:** Terry Leonard, **Tel** (608)845-9559. **Pub. Size:** Tabloid. available on microfilm from The State Historical Society of Wisconsin.

US
VILAS COUNTY NEWS-REVIEW. **VFOAT** Vilas County News Review. Vol. 101, No. 1 (Apr. 24, 1985)-. Newspaper. English. wk (Published on Wed.). $28.00 (one year) Vilas & Oneida Counties in Wisconsin; $32.00 (one year) others in Wisconsin; $39.00 (one year) US & others. Eagle River Publications, PO Box 1929, Eagle River WI 54521. **Tel** (715)479-4421, FAX (715)479-6242. **ED** Kurt Kreuger. **Photos. Ad Acc, Adv Mgr:** Byron McNutt. **Pub. Size:** Broadsheet. **Circ:** 10,500 (ctrl). available on microfilm. ***Continues*** *Vilas County News-Review and Three Lakes News.*

US/8755-0520
WASHBURN COUNTY REGISTER (SHELL LAKE, WIS. : 1928). (WASHBURN COUNTY REGISTER.). (Sept. 22, 1928)-. Newspaper. English. wk. $22.00. Washburn County Register, PO Box 455, Shell Lake WI 54871. **Tel** (715)468-2314, FAX (715)468-2314. **ED** Marc E. Parenteau. **Photos. Ad Acc.** Full Page (B&W) $296.00. Half Page (B&W) $148.00. **Pub. Size:** Tabloid. **Circ:** 1,948. available in microform. ***Continues*** *Washburn County Register and Shell Lake Watchman.*

US
WASHINGTON ISLAND OBSERVER. Vol. 11, No. 1 (Jan. 10 & 17, 1991)-. Newspaper. English. ir (32 issues). $26.00. Washington Island Observer, Inc., Box 24, Washington Island WI 54246. **ED** Gail Larson Toerpe. **Bk Rev,** (Qty: 32). **Photos. Ad Acc, Adv Mgr:** G. L. Toerpe, **Tel** (414)847-2661. Full Page (B&W) $150.00. Half Page (B&W) $75.00. **Pub. Size:** Standard. ***Continues*** *Island Exchange of News & Ads.*

US/0885-680X
WATERTOWN DAILY TIMES (WATERTOWN, WIS.). (WATERTOWN DAILY TIMES.). Began with Nov. 23, 1895 issue. Newspaper. English. da. $70.20 (in city), $67.60 (outside city), $72.80 (motor by route), $62.45 (by mail). John D Clifford, 113 West Main Street, Watertown WI 53094. ***Absorbed*** *Watertown Daily Leader (Watertown, Wis. : 1916).*

US/0895-6391
WAUKESHA COUNTY FREEMAN, THE. ***Title Change.*** **VFOAT** Waukesha County Free Man; Waukesha Free Man; Freeman; Free Man. (19??)-(19??). Newspaper. English. da. Hugh D Hollister, 200 Park Place, Waukesha WI 53187. ***Continues*** *Waukesha Freeman (Waukesha, Wis. : Daily).* ***Continued by*** *Freeman (Waukesha, Wis. : Daily), 1062-9041.*

US
WAUPACA COUNTY POST. Vol. 1, No. 1 (June 7, 1917)- Vol. 9, No. 20 (Sept. 5, 1935)-. Newspaper. English. wk. $16.00. Waupaca County Publishing Company, PO Box 152/717 10th Street, Waupaca WI 54981. **Tel** (715)258-5546, FAX (715)258-8162. **ED** Lonen Spenny. **Photos. Ad Acc, Adv Mgr:** Tim Williams. Full Page (B&W) $504.00. Half Page (B&W) $252.00. **Pub. Size:** Tabloid. ***Formed by the union of*** *Waupaca Record-Leader* ***and*** *Waupaca Republican-Post.*

US
WAUPUN LEADER-NEWS, THE. **VFOAT** Waupun Leader News; Leader News. Vol. 63, No. 32 (Feb. 7, 1929)-. Newspaper. English. wk. Marshall Bernhagen / Waupun WI, PO Box 111, Waupun WI 53963. available on microfilm from The State Historical Society of Wisconsin. ***Formed by the union of*** *Waupun News* ***and*** *Waupun Leader.*

US/0887-4271
WAUSAU DAILY HERALD. **VFOAT** Daily Herald; Wausau Sunday Herald. Vol. 77, No. 89 (March 17, 1985)-. Newspaper. English. da. $137.80. Wausau Daily Herald, PO Box 1286, 800 Scott Street, Wausau WI 54402. **Tel** (715)842-2101 ext. 209, FAX (715)848-9360. **ED** Jim Herman. **Photos. Ad Acc, Adv Mgr:** Vic Brakinder, **Tel** (715)845-0622. **Wire Svcs.:** AP, GN. available on an online database (file 635/Full-Text) from DIALOG; available in microform. Documents available from UMI Article Clearinghouse. ***Continues*** *Daily Herald (Wausau-Merrill, Wis.), 8750-6521.*
Ind/Abst Bus. Dateline (Dec. 11, 1991-) [Full Txt.].

US
WAUSHARA ARGUS, THE. **VFOAT** Argus; Neshkoro News; Wild Rose News. Vol. 5, No. 1 (March 31, 1863)-. Newspaper. English. wk. Mary Kunasch, PO Box 838, Wautoma WI 54982. ***Continues*** *Waushara County Argus;* ***Absorbed*** *Sun-News Press.*

US
WAUWATOSA NEWS-TIMES. **VFOAT** Wauwatosa News Times; News Times. 50th year, No. 11 (April 8, 1948)-. Newspaper. English. wk. Community Newspapers, PO Box 7, Oak Creek WI 53154. **Tel** (414)768-5800. available on microfilm from The State Historical Society of Wisconsin. ***Formed by the union of*** *Wauwatosa Times* ***and*** *Wauwatosa News.*

US/1062-4902
WEST ALLIS ENTERPRISE (WEST ALLIS, WIS. 1967). (WEST ALLIS ENTERPRISE.). Vol. 1, No. 1 (July 27, 1967)-. Newspaper. English. wk. $22.50 (West Allis residents), $65.00 (mailed subscriptions). Enterprise Publishing / Wisconsin, 1112 South 60th Street, West Allis WI 53214. **Tel** (414)778-1666, FAX (414)778-1773.

●US/1067-1862
WEST ALLIS POST (1992), THE. (THE WEST ALLIS POST.). (1992)-. Newspaper. English. wk. $18.00. Post Newspaper Publishers, PO Box 14126, West Allis WI 53214. **Tel** (414)475-7474. ***Continues*** *West Allis Post-Enterprise, 1062-483X.*

US/1062-483X
WEST ALLIS POST-ENTERPRISE, THE. ***Title Change.*** **VFOAT** West Allis Post Enterprise; West Allis Enterprise. Vol. 1, No. 1 (Apr. 11, 1992)-(1992). Newspaper. English. wk. Enterprise Newspapers, 1112 South 60th Street, West Allis WI 53214-3315. ***Continues*** *West Allis Post/Star.* ***Continued by*** *West Allis Post (1992), 1067-1862.*

US
WEST ALLIS STAR. (19??)-. English. Fifty-two times a year. $19.95 one year; $36.00 two years; $51.25 three years. West Allis Star, PO Box 7, 640 East Ryan Road, Oak Creek WI 53134. **Tel** (414)768-5832. **Ad Acc.** ***Continues*** *West Allis Post-Star.*

US/0899-2444
WEST BEND DAILY NEWS. **VFOAT** Daily News. (198?)-. Newspaper. English. da. West Bend Daily News, 100 South Sixth Avenue, PO Box 478, West Bend WI 53095. **Tel** (414)338-0622. ***Continues*** *West Bend News (West Bend, Wis. : 1979).*

US/0749-6990
WESTINE REPORT. (Jan. 5, 1978)-. Newspaper. English. wk. $13.50. William E. Branen, Box 54, Union Grove WI 53182. **ED** Carol Marcella (Editor-in-Chief) and Rose Calek (Managing Editor). **Photos. Ad Acc, Adv Mgr:** David Wright, **Tel** (414)763-3511. Full Page (B&W) $285.00. Half Page (B&W) $350.00. Full Page (Color) $148.50. Half Page (Color) $213.50. **Pub. Size:** Tabloid. **Circ:** 2,100. available on microfilm from The State Historical Society of Wisconsin. ***Continues*** *Westine and NDC Report.*

US/0192-9356
WESTOSHA REPORT. (June 6, 1973)-. Newspaper. English. Fifty-two times a year (Mon.). $15.95. Zimmermann & Sons Inc., 140 Commerce Street, PO Box 437, Burlington WI 53105-0437. **Tel** (414)763-3511. **ED** Diane Jahnke. **Photos. Ad Acc, Adv Mgr:** David Wright. Full Page (B&W) $396.00. Half Page (B&W) $211.50. Full Page (Color) $461.00. Half Page (Color) $276.50. **Pub. Size:** Tabloid. **Circ:** 13,620. ***Continues*** *Westosha Report Incorporated with the Burlington Circle.*

US
WHITEHALL TIMES (WHITEHALL, WIS. : 1924). (THE WHITEHALL TIMES.). No. 45 (Jan. 24, 1924)-. Newspaper. English. wk. Robert O Gauger, 1410 Main Street, Whitehall WI 54773-0095. available on microfilm from The State Historical Society of Wisconsin. ***Continues*** *Whitehall Times-Banner.*

US
WINNECONNE NEWS, THE. Vol. 1, No. 1 (Dec. 13, 1928)-. Newspaper. English. wk. John A Rogers, 140 West Main, Winneconne WI 54986. available on microfilm from The State Historical Society of Wisconsin.

US/0749-405X
WISCONSIN STATE JOURNAL (MADISON, WIS. : 1862). (WISCONSIN STATE JOURNAL.). **VFOAT** Sunday State Journal; State Journal. Vol. 10, No. 278 (Aug. 8, 1862)-. Newspaper. English. da (except New Year's, Memorial Day, July 4th, and Labor Day). $163.80 (daily and Sunday), $95.95 (daily), $84.25 (weekend), $67.90 (Sunday only) in Wisconsin by carrier or mail delivery; $260.00 (daily and Sunday), $156.00 (daily only), $130.00 (weekend), $104.00 (Sunday only) out of state mail delivery. Madison Newspaper Inc, PO Box 8056, Madison WI 53708. **Tel** (608)252-6400, (800)362-8333. **LC** 10254. available on microfilm from University Microfilms International (UMI). Documents available from UMI Article Clearinghouse. ***Continues*** *Wisconsin Daily State Journal;* ***Absorbed*** *Madison Democrat.*
Ind/Abst Bus. Dateline (Dec. 13, 1991-) [Full Txt.].

US/0885-081X
WITTENBERG ENTERPRISE AND BIRNAMWOOD NEWS (WITTENBERG, WIS. : 1982). (WITTENBERG ENTERPRISE AND BIRNAMWOOD NEWS.). **VFOAT** Enterprise-News. No. 3 (April 29, 1982)-. Newspaper. English. wk. Wittenberg Press Inc, Vinal Street, Wittenberg WI 54499. **ED** G Boldig. available on microfilm from The State Historical Society of Wisconsin. ***Continues*** *Enterprise News (Wittenberg, Wis.).*

US/0748-6812
WOODVILLE LEADER AND DUNN COUNTY PICTORIAL MESSENGER, THE. **VFOAT** Woodville Leader. (19??)-. Newspaper. English. wk. $15.00 in county; $18.00 others. The Woodville Leader and Dunn County Pictorial Messenger, 130 South Main, Woodville WI 54028. **ED** Sue Heim. **Bk Rev**, (Qty: 6). **Photos. Ad Acc, Adv Mgr:** Sue Heim, **Tel** (715)698-2401. Full Page (B&W) $259.00. Half Page (B&W) $189.00. Full Page (Color) $320.00. Half Page (Color) $220.00. **Pub. Size:** Broadsheet.

WYOMING

US
BUFFALO BULLETIN, THE. Vol. 1, No. 1 (Oct. 9, 1890)-. Newspaper. English. Fifty-two times a year. $18.00 Wyoming; $26.00 other. Buffalo Bulletin, 58 South Lobban Stret, PO Box 730, Buffalo WY 82834. **Tel** (307)684-2223, FAX (307)684-7380. **ED** Jim Hicks. **Bk Rev**, (Qty: 6-12). **Ad Acc. Circ:** 4,300 (ctrl). ***Continues in part*** *Buffalo Echo.*

US
CASPER STAR-TRIBUNE. **VFOAT** Casper Star Tribune; Sunday Star-Tribune; Sunday Star Tribune. Vol. 74, No. 152 (June 27, 1965)-. Newspaper. English. da. $158.00 Wyoming; $188.00 other (daily and Sunday); $98.00 Wyoming; $108.00 other (Sunday only). Casper Star Tribune, PO Box 80, Casper WY 82602. **Tel** (307)266-0550. ***Formed by the union of*** *Casper Morning Star* ***and*** *Casper Tribune-Herald.*

US/0747-2498
CODY ENTERPRISE, THE. **VFOAT** Cody Enterprise and the Meeteetse News; Cody Enterprise Combined with the Cody Times. Vol. 27, No. 21 (Jan. 4, 1928)-. Newspaper. English. sw. $26.00. Cody Enterprise, PO Box 1090, Cody WY 82414. **Tel** (307)587-2231. **ED** Bruce McCormack. **Bk Rev**, (Qty: 2). **Ad Acc, Adv Mgr:** John T. Malmberg. Full Page (B&W) $882.00. Half Page (B&W) $441.00. Full Page (Color) $957.00. Half Page (Color) $516.00. **Pub. Size:** Broadsheet. **Circ:** 6,025. available in microform. ***Continues*** *Cody Enterprise and the Park County Herald;* ***Absorbed*** *Meeteetse News; Cody Times.*

US
DAILY TIMES, THE. Vol. 73, No. 155 (Aug. 5, 1961)-. Newspaper. English. da. $59.50. Daily Times / Rawlins, PO Box 370, 6th & Buffalo, Rawlins WY 82301. **Tel** (307)324-3411, FAX (307)324-2797. **ED** Sean M. McMahon and Charles Bowlus (Managing Editor). **Bk Rev. Photos. Ad Acc, Adv Mgr:** Ed Walker. **Pub. Size:** Tabloid. **Wire Svcs.:** AP. **Circ:** 3,800 (morning). available in microform. ***Continues*** *Rawlins Daily Times.*

US/1061-1789
GUERNSEY GAZETTE, THE. **VFOAT** Guide; Lingle Guide and the Guernsey Gazette; Guide/Gazette; Lingle Guide, the Guernsey Gazette; Guernsey Gazette, Lingle Guide. (1905)-. Newspaper. English. wk. $16.00 (in county), $20.00 (out of county). Wyoming Newspapers Inc, 2025 Main Street, Torrington WY 82240-2708. **Tel** (307)532-2184, FAX (307)532-2283. **ED** Mary Anne Shields. **Photos. Ad Acc, Adv Mgr:** Cheri Fegler. Full Page (B&W) $348.60. Half Page (B&W) $174.30. Full Page (Color) $398.60. Half Page (Color) $224.30. **Pub. Size:** Tabloid. **Circ:** 600. available in microform. ***Continues*** *Guernsey Iron Gazette.*

US
JACKSON HOLE GUIDE, THE. Vol. 1, No. 1 (July 17, 1952)-. Newspaper. English. wk. $28.00. Jackson Hole Guide, PO Box 648, Jackson WY 83001. **Tel** (307)733-2430, FAX (307)733-7841. **ED** Linda Fantin (Managing Editor). **Bk Rev**, (Qty: 6). **Photos. Ad Acc, Adv Mgr:** Monty Nethercott. Full Page (B&W) $576.00. Half Page (B&W) $289.00. Full Page (Color) $1152.00. Half Page (Color) $576.00. **Pub. Size:** Tabloid. **Wire Svcs.:** AP. **Circ:** 7,000 (paid). available in microform.

US
JACKSON HOLE NEWS. Vol. 1, No. 1 (Apr. 17, 1970)-. Newspaper. English. wk (Published on Wednesdays). Jackson Hole News, 215 South Scott, Jackson WY 83001. **Tel** (307)733-2047, FAX (307)733-2138. **ED** Angus Thuermer & Mark Huffman.

US
KEMMERER GAZETTE, THE. **VFOAT** Gazette. (1924)-. Newspaper. English. wk. $22.50. Kemmerer Gazette, Box 30, Kemmerer WY 83101. **Tel** (307)877-3347. **ED** Don Kominsky. **Photos. Ad Acc.** Full Page (B&W) $378.00. Half Page (B&W) $189.00. **Pub. Size:** Broadsheet. **Circ:** 2,050 (ctrl). available in microform. ***Formed by the union of*** *Kemmerer Camera* ***and*** *Kemmerer Republican.*

US
LANDER WYOMING STATE JOURNAL. **VFOAT** Lander Wyo. State Journal; Wyoming State Journal; Lander Journal; Lander State Journal. Vol. 97, No. 58 (July 22, 1982)-. Newspaper. English. sw (Published on Mondays & Wednesdays). Wyoming State Journal, PO Box 900, Lander WY 82520-0100. **Tel** (307)332-2323, FAX (307)332-9332. **ED** Tom Reed. **Circ:** 5,200. ***Continues*** *Wyoming State Journal (Lander, Wyo.).*

US
LARAMIE DAILY BOOMERANG (LARAMIE, WYO. : 1957). (THE LARAMIE DAILY BOOMERANG.). **VFOAT** Laramie Sunday Boomerang. Vol. 77, No. 36 (April 30, 1957)-. Newspaper. English. da. $84.00 (in county), $120.00 (out of county). Laramie Boomerang, 314 South Fourth Street, Laramie WY 82070. **Tel** (307)742-8153, FAX (307)721-2973. **ED** Robert Wilson. **Bk Rev. Photos. Ad Acc, Adv Mgr:** Sheryn Pulse, **Tel** (307)742-2176. **Pub. Size:** Broadsheet. **Wire Svcs.:** AP. **Circ:** 7,500 paid (ctrl). available in microform. ***Formed by the union of*** *Laramie Republican* ***and*** *Boomerang* ***and*** *Laramie Daily Bulletin.*

US/0739-4926
NEWS-RECORD (GILLETTE, WYO.), THE. (THE NEWS-RECORD.). **VFOAT** News Record. Vol. 11, No. 33 (Apr. 30, 1925)-. Newspaper. English. da (except Saturday). $7.50 per month. News Record / Department of Circulation, PO Box 3006, Gillette WY 82717. **Tel** (307)682-9306. **ED** Ron Franscell. **Photos. Ad Acc, Adv Mgr:** Paul Treide, Jr. Full Page (B&W) $945.00. Half Page (B&W) $472.50. Full Page (Color) $995.00. Half Page (Color) $522.50. **Pub. Size:** Broadsheet. **Wire Svcs.:** AP. ***Formed by the union of*** *Gillette News* ***and*** *Campbell County Record (Gillette, Wyo.);* ***Absorbed*** *Gillette Bulletin.*

US
NORTHERN WYOMING DAILY NEWS, THE. **VFOAT** Northern Wyoming Daily News, Worland Grit, Wyoming News. Vol. 34, No. 22 (June 1, 1939)-. Newspaper. English. da. Northern Wyoming Daily News, PO Box 508, 201 North 8th Street, Worland WY 82401. **Tel** (307)347-3241, FAX (307)347-4267. **ED** Lee Lockhart. ***Continues*** *Worland Grit, the Wyoming News;* ***Absorbed*** *Washakie Signal Fire.*

US
PLATTE COUNTY RECORD-TIMES, THE. **VFOAT** Platte County Record Times. Vol. 34, No. 34 (Jan. 1, 1960)-. Newspaper. English. ir (64 issues). $44.00. Platte County Record Times, PO Box 969, Wheatland WY 82201-0969. **Tel** (307)322-2627, FAX (307)322-9612. **ED** Dee Huls. **Circ:** 4,400. ***Formed by the union of*** *Platte County Record* ***and*** *Wheatland Times (Wheatland, Wyo. : 1937).*

US/0740-1078
POWELL TRIBUNE, THE. Vol. 1, No. 1 (Mar. 13, 1909)-Vol. 11, No. 9 (May 14, 1920); 11th Year, No. 10 (May 21, 1920)-. Newspaper. English. sw. $32.00. Powell Tribune, 128 South Bent, Box 70, Powell WY 82435. **Tel** (307)754-2222. **ED** Dave Bonner (Editor-in-Chief) and Dennis Davis (Managing Editor). **Bk Rev**, (Qty: 2). **Photos. Ad Acc, Adv Mgr:** Diane E. Bonner, **Tel** (307)754-2221. Full Page (B&W) $680.00. Half Page (B&W) $270.44. Full Page (Color) $767.00. Half Page (Color) $457.44. **Pub. Size:** Broadsheet. **Wire Svcs.:** AP. **Circ:** 3,90 (ctrl). available on microfiche; available on microfilm. ***Absorbed*** *Powell Outlook; Powell Leader.*

US
RIVERTON RANGER, THE. Vol. 46, No. 1 (Mar. 5, 1953)-. Newspaper. English. da. $50.00. Riverton Ranger, 421 East Main Street, PO Box 993, Riverton WY 82501. **Tel** (307)856-2244, FAX (307)856-0189. **ED** Dave Perry, Chad Baldwin (Managing Editor). **Bk Rev. Photos. Ad Acc, Adv Mgr:** Anita Ellis. Full Page (B&W) $928.80. Half Page (B&W) $464.40. Full Page (Color) $1028.80. Half Page (Color) $564.40. **Wire Svcs.:** AP. **Circ:** 6,945. ***Formed by the union of*** *Riverton Times* ***and*** *Riverton Review (Riverton, Wyo. : 1937).*

US/0893-3650
ROCK SPRINGS DAILY ROCKET-MINER. **VFOAT** Rock Springs Daily Rocket Miner; Rocket-Miner; Rocket Miner; Rock Springs (Wyo.) Daily Rocket-Miner. Vol. 57, No. 112 (June 5, 1965)-. Newspaper. English. da. $30.30 (6 months), $58.60 (1 year) Wyoming & Daggett County, Utah; $32.40 (6 months), $62.80 (1 year) other. Rock Springs Newspaper, PO Box 98, Rock Springs WY 82901. **Tel** (307)362-3736. ***Continues*** *Rock Springs Miner and Rock Springs Rocket.*

US/0740-4948
SARATOGA SUN (SARATOGA, WYO.), THE. (THE SARATOGA SUN.). **VFOAT** Sun. Vol. 1, No. 1 (July 14, 1891)-. Newspaper. English. Fifty-two times a year. $23.00 Carbon County; $26.50 other. Saratoga Sun, Box 489, Saratoga WY 82331. **Tel** (307)326-8311. ***Absorbed*** *Platte Valley Lyre.*

Wyoming

US/1074-682X
SHERIDAN PRESS (SHERIDAN, WYO.), THE. (THE SHERIDAN PRESS.). 44th Year, No. 1 (Nov. 9, 1930)-. Newspaper. English. da (307 per year). $84.50. The Sheridan Press, Box 2006, Sheridan WY 82801. **Tel** (307)672-2431. **ED** Keith D. Kemper. **Bk Rev. Ad Acc.** ctrl circ. *Formed by the union of Sheridan Journal and Sheridan Post-Enterprise.*

US
STAR VALLEY INDEPENDENT. VFOAT Independent. Vol. 3, No. 1 (Sept. 9, 1904)-. Newspaper. English. wk. $22.00 lincoln county, $24.00 other. Star Valley Independent, 50 East 4th Avenue, Box 158, Afton WY 83110-0158. **Tel** (307)886-5727. *Continues Star Valley Pioneer.*

US/8750-0809
SUNDAY WYOMING TRIBUNE-EAGLE. *Title Change.* VFOAT Sunday Wyoming Tribune Eagle; Wyoming Tribune Eagle; Wyoming Tribune-Eagle. Vol. 1, No. 1 (Sept. 8, 1968)-Vol. 26, No. 27 (Apr. 3, 1994). Newspaper. English. wk. Cheyenne Newspapers Inc., 702 West Lincoln Way, Cheyenne WY 82001. **Tel** (307)634-3361. *Merged with Wyoming State Tribune (Cheyenne, Wyo. : 1937); Wyoming Eagle to form Wyoming Tribune-Eagle.*

US
THERMOPOLIS INDEPENDENT RECORD. VFOAT Thermopolis Independent-Record; Independent-Record. Vol. 45, No. 28 (July 12, 1945)-. Newspaper. English. Fifty-two times a year. $13.00 (local). Thermopolis Independent Record, PO Box 31, Thermopolis WY 82443. **Tel** (307)864-2328, **FAX** (307)864-5711. **ED** Patrick Schmidt (Editor's address: 431 Broadway, Thermopolis, WY 82443). **Photos. Ad Acc, Adv Mgr:** Patrick Schmidt. Full Page (B&W) $648.90. Half Page (B&W) $324.45. **Pub. Size:** Standard. *Continues Thermopolis Independent Record and Journal.*

US
TORRINGTON TELEGRAM. VFOAT Torrington Telegram and the Goshen County Journal. 23rd Year, No. 43 (July 10, 1930)-. Newspaper. English. sw (Published on Wednesdays & Fridays). Wyoming Newspapers Inc, 2025 Main Street, Torrington WY 82240-2708. **Tel** (307)532-2184, **FAX** (307)532-2283. **ED** Cary Berry. **Ad Acc, Adv Mgr:** Bill Hanson. **Circ:** 6,020. *Continues Torrington Telegram and Goshen County Journal; Absorbed Torrington News.*

US
UINTA COUNTY HERALD. VFOAT Uinta County Herald Consolidated with the Wyoming Times; Uinta County Herald Consolidated with the Wyoming Press; Herald-Press. Vol. 1, No. 1 (Aug. 12, 1937)-. Newspaper. English. sw. Esta R Baldwin, PO Box 210, Evanston WY 82931-0210. *Formed by the union of Bridger Valley Enterprise and Evanston Booster; Absorbed Wyoming Times (Evanston, Wyo.) and Wyoming Press.*

US
WIND RIVER NEWS. Vol. 1, No. 1 (Apr. 7, 1983)-. Newspaper. English. wk. $18.75. Wind River News, PO Box J, Lander WY 82520. **Tel** (307)332-2323. *Absorbed Jeffrey City News.*

US/8750-0825
WYOMING EAGLE, THE. *Title Change.* Vol. 1, No. 1 (May 28, 1925)-Vol. 69, No. 223 (Apr. 1, 1994). Newspaper. English. da. Cheyenne Newspapers Inc., 702 West Lincoln Way, Cheyenne WY 82001. **Tel** (307)634-3361. *Merged with Wyoming State Tribune (Cheyenne, Wyo. : 1937); Sunday Wyoming Tribune-Eagle to form Wyoming Tribune-Eagle.*

US/8750-0817
WYOMING STATE TRIBUNE (CHEYENNE, WYO. : 1937). *Title Change.* (WYOMING STATE TRIBUNE.). Vol. 70, No. 137 (Feb. 2, 1937)-Vol. 127, No. 140 (Apr. 1, 1994). Newspaper. English. da. Cheyenne Newspapers Inc., 702 West Lincoln Way, Cheyenne WY 82001. **Tel** (307)634-3361. **LC** 10300. available on microfilm. *Continues Wyoming State Tribune, Cheyenne State Leader, Cheyenne Daily Sun. Merged with Wyoming Eagle; Sunday Wyoming Tribune-Eagle to form Wyoming Tribune-Eagle.*

●US
WYOMING TRIBUNE-EAGLE. VFOAT Wyoming Tribune Eagle. Vol. 26, No. 29 (Apr. 4, 1994)-. Newspaper. English. da. $96.00 Wyoming; $108.00 other. Cheyenne Newspapers Inc., 702 West Lincoln Way, Cheyenne WY 82001. **Tel** (307)634-3361. *Formed by the union of Wyoming State Tribune (Cheyenne, Wyo. : 1937); Wyoming Eagle and Sunday Wyoming Tribune-Eagle.*

●US
WYOMING TRIBUNE-EAGLE. VFOAT Wyoming Tribune Eagle. Vol. 26, No. 29 (Apr. 4, 1994)-. Newspaper. English. da. $96.00 Wyoming; $108.00 other. Cheyenne Newspapers Inc., 702 West Lincoln Way, Cheyenne WY 82001. **Tel** (307)634-3361. *Formed by the union of Wyoming State Tribune (Cheyenne, Wyo. : 1937); Wyoming Eagle and Sunday Wyoming Tribune-Eagle.*

International Newspapers

The following section lists all newspapers in the directory that originated in any country other than the United States. These are arranged by country then alphabetically by title within each country. Following the International Newspaper section are all titles with a major or minor subject of Newspapers, that are considered to be Abstracting, Indexing or Statistical publications.

AFGHANISTAN

AF
KABUL NEW TIMES. (19??)-. Newspaper. English. da. Kabul New Times, PO Box 983, Ansari Wat, Kabul Afghanistan. **ED** Seddiq Rahpoe. **Circ:** 5,000. *Continues* Kabul Times.

ALBANIA

AA
DRITA. Added/Corp Lidhja se Shkrimtareve dhe Artisteve te Shqiperise. (1961)-. Newspaper. Albanian. wk. $15.76. Book Distribution Enterprise, Rruga Kavajes, Tirana, Albania. **Tel** 011 355 42 27246.
Ind/Abst BHA : Biblio. Hist. Art.

ALGERIA

AE/1111-0171
ALGERIE - ACTUALITE. [Alger. - actual.]. (1964)-. Newspaper. French. wk. Algerie Actualite, 2 rue Jacques Cartier, 16000 Algiers Algeria. **Tel** 2 63 54 20, telex 66475. **UDC** 070.431. **Circ:** 250,000.

AMERICAN SAMOA

AS
SAMOA NEWS. 1st Year, No. 1 (Aug. 6, 1969)-. Newspaper. English (Samoan). da (five days per week). $250.00. Samoa News, PO Box 909, Pago Pago, American Samoa. **Tel** (684)633-5599, FAX (684)433-4864. **ED** Lewis Wolman. **Circ:** 5,000.

ANGOLA

AO
JORNAL DE ANGOLA, O. (19??)-. Newspaper. Portuguese. da. O Jornal de Angola, CP 1312, Luanda Angola. **Tel** 331623, telex 3341. **Circ:** 41,000.

ARGENTINA

AG
BUENOS AIRES HERALD. VFOAT Buenos Aires Herald and Times. 21st Year, No. 223 (June 11, 1897)-. Newspaper. English. da. $410.00 Bolivia, Brazil, Chile, Paraguay, Uruguay & Peru, $630.00 US, Canada & Latin America, $735.00 Europe, $905.00 others (daily & Sunday); $70.00 Bolivia, Brazil, Chile, Paraguay, Uruguay, & Peru, $100.00 US, Cananda & Latin America, $119.00 Europe, $145.00 others (Sunday). Buenos Aires Herald Ltd. Azopardo 455, 1107 Buenos Aires Argentina. **Tel** 011 54 1 3428476, FAX 011 54 1 3347917. **Circ:** 30,000. *Continues* Buenos Aires Herald. *Absorbed in part by* Times of Argentina.

AG
CLARIN, BUENOS AIRES. INDICE. (Sept. 1973)-. Spanish. mo. $1.00. Arta Grafico Edi Argentino SA, Piedras 1743, Buenos Aires 1285 Argentina. **Tel** 011 54 1 213661. **LC** AI21.C52; C55.

AG
MARKET OF VEGETABLE OILS AND OILSEED MEALS. Added/Corp J. J. Hinrichsen, S.a. No. 34/91 (Aug. 30th, 1991)-. Newspaper. English. wk. *Continues* Mercado de Aceites Vegetales y Subproductos Oleaginosis.

AG
NACION, LA. Vol. 1 (1964)-. Newspaper. Spanish. wk. $110.55 (Sunday), $624.96 (daily) surface mail; Daily by airmail: $756.00 Chile, Peru, Paraguay,Bolivia, Brazil & Uruguay; $2116.80 Europe; $1753.92 The Americas; $2721.60 other. SA la Nacion, Casilla de Correo 773, 1000 Buenos Aires Argentina. **Tel** 011 54 1 3131003, 011 54 1 3131453, telex 2192. **Ad Acc. Circ:** 250,000 (ctrl).

AG
PRENSA, LA. (18??)-. Newspaper. Spanish. da. $577.00. La Prensa / Buenos Aires, Azopardo 715, 1107 Buenos Aires Argentina. **Tel** 011 54 1 3491000 - 09.

ARMENIA

AI
GOLOS ARMENII : ORGAN TSENTRALNOGO KOMITETA KOMMUNISTICHESKOI PARTII ARMENII. Added/Corp Hayastani Komunistakan Kusaktsutyun. Kentronakan Komite. **VFOAT** Hayastani Dzayn. No. 188 (1990)-. Newspaper. Russian. da. Golos Armenii, Arachunyats Ave 2, 375023 Yerevan Armenia. **ED** B.M. Mkrtchyan. **CODEN** GOAREH. *Continues* Kommunist (Yerevan, Armenian S.S.R.).

AUSTRALIA

AT
ADVERTISER (ADELAIDE, AUSTRALIA). (THE ADVERTISER.). (1???)-. Newspaper. English. da.

AT
AGE, THE. (Oct. 17, 1854)-. Newspaper. English. da. 3740.00Aus$ (full copy airmail). David Symes & Co. Ltd., PO Box 257C, Melbourne, Victoria, 3001 Australia. **Tel** 011 61 3 6012005. **(Subscription address:** TNT Newsfast International, PO Box 351, Mascot NSW 2020 Australia.) available on microfilm.
Ind/Abst Child. Lit. Abstr. (19??-).

AT/0004-8437
AUSTRALASIAN POST. [Australas. post]. (1946)-. Periodical. English. wk. 104.00Aus$ Australia; 140.40Aus$ other. Pacific Publications Pty Ltd, 32 Walsh Street, Melbourne VIC 3000 Australia. **Tel** 011 61 3 3207000. **DD** 052.

AT
EL TELEGRAPH. (19??)-. Newspaper. English. 260.00Aus$. Linkbar Pty Ltd., 310 Marrickville Road, 1st Floor, Marrickville NSW 2204 Australia. **Tel** 011 81 2 560 1066, FAX 011 81 2 569 3087.
Desc: Lebanese and Arab World national newspaper in Australia.

AT
GREEK HERALD. (19??)-. Newspaper. Greek, Modern. da. 105.24Aus$. Foreign Language Publications, PO Box 146, Broadway, Sydney, New South Wales 2007 Australia. **Tel** 011 61 2 660 2033, FAX 011 61 2 692 0649, telex AA122141. **ED** Mr. Mystakidis and Ikards Kyriakou. **Ad Acc. Circ:** 24,000.
Desc: Local and international news relating to Greek and Australian news events.

AT
INVERELL TIMES, THE. Newspaper. English. wk. Nornews Ltd, 37 Vivian Street, Inverell New South Wales 2360 Australia. *Absorbed* Inverell Argus.

AT
KOORI MAIL. (19??)-. English. bw. 45.00Aus$. Koori Mail, PO Box 117, Lismore, New South Wales, 2480 Australia. **Tel** 011 44 66 222666, FAX 011 44 66 222600. **ED** Dona Graham.

AT
LAND, THE. English. wk. 52.00Aus$. Land Newspaper Ltd, PO Box 299 Australia. **Tel** (045) 70 4444, FAX (045) 71 1759, telex 24621. **ED** Peter Austin and Deputy Vern Graham. **Circ:** 75,000.

AT
LOT'S WIFE (MICROFICHE). (LOT'S WIFE.). (19??)-. Newspaper. English. ir (25 (print) per year). Monash University, Monash Assoc Students Publ Com, Clayton Victoria 3168 Australia. **Tel** 5653184, FAX 5434061, telex LOT'S WIFE 32691. **ED** Jenny Munz and Shane Lucas. **Bk Rev. Ad Acc. Circ:** 7,000. available in print.

AT/0817-6922
NEUE HEIMAT UND WELT. [Neue Heim. Welt]. (1985)-. Newspaper. German. bm. 28.00Aus$. Neue Heimat und Welt, 453 Upper Heidelberg Road, Hedelberg Victoria, 3081 Australia. **Tel** 011 61 3 4593571, FAX 011 61 3 2336379. **ED** Nick Schekolin. **DD** 079.94. **Ad Acc. Circ:** 7,600. *Continues* German Times, 0729-3798.

AT
NEW LIFE. (19??)-. Newspaper. English. wk (48 issues). 35.00Aus$. New Life Australia Ltd, PO Box 267, Blacktown VIC 3130 Australia. **Tel** 03 8774833. **ED** Rev. C.R. Thomas. **Bk Rev. Ad Acc. Adv Mgr:** W. Zegelis. **Circ:** 5,900.
Desc: Australia's weekly Christian newspaper.

AT/0030-2333
ON DIT. Added/Corp University of Adelaide. Students Representative Council. Vol. 1 (April 15, 1932)-. Newspaper. English. sm. Student Association / University of Adelaide, North Terrace, Adelaide South Australia 5000 Australia.

AT
PASTORAL TIMES. (18??)-. Newspaper. English. wk. 88.24Aus$. Deniliquin Publications Pty Ltd., 255 Cressy Street, Deniliquin New South Wales 2710 Australia. **Tel** 011 61 058 812322.

AT/1031-3796
RESOURCE RICHMOND. (RESOURCE AUSTRALIA). [Resource Richmond]. (1988)-. Periodical. English. Four times a year (Mar., May, Aug., Dec.). 12.00Aus$ (individuals); 30.00Aus$ (institutions). FKA Mulicultural Resource Centre, 9-11 Stewart Street, First Floor, Richmond VIC 3121 Australia. **Tel** 03 428-4471, FAX 03 429-9252. **DD** 370.19609945. **Bk Rev. Ad Acc. Circ:** 500. *Continues* Newsletter - Multicultural Resource Centre, Free Kindergarten Association of Victoria, 1031-3788.
Desc: An newsletter of an multicultural resource. Articles are explored by some of these issues with bilingual staff and early childhood professionals.

AT
RIVERINE GRAZIER, THE. (18??)-. Newspaper. English. wk. The Riverine Grazier Partnership, 387 Moore Street, Hay New South Wales 2711 Australia. **Tel** 069 931002, FAX 069 931386. **ED** Gavin Johnston. **Bk Rev,** (Qty: 6). **Ad Acc. Circ:** 2,100.
Desc: Local news with emphasis on rural section.

AT
SYDNEY MORNING HERALD, THE. Vol. 14, No. 1623 (Aug. 1, 1842)-. Newspaper. English. Fifty-two times a year. 110.00Aus$. John Fairfax & Sons Ltd, GPO Box 506, Sydney NSW 2001 Australia. **Tel** 011 61 2 2822833, FAX 011 61 2 2822424, telex 23425. available on microfilm. *Continues* Sydney Herald; *Absorbed* Australian Free Press.
Ind/Abst Annu. Bibliogr. Engl. Lang. Lit.

AT
WOCHE IN AUSTRALIEN, DIE. Newspaper. German. Fifty-two times a year (Tuesdays). 100.00Aus$ Australia; 175.00Aus$ Europe; 210.00Aus$ other. Euro-Media Pty Ltd., PO Box 36 / 3 Seddon Street, Bankstown NSW 2200 Australia. **Tel** 011 61 2 7074999, FAX 011 61 2 7086025. **ED** Ludger Heidelbach. **Ad Acc.** Full Page (B&W) $1600.00. Half Page (B&W) $800.00. **Circ:** 30,000.
Desc: A German-Australian independent newspaper.

AUSTRIA

AU
6-UHR-ABENDBLATT. VFOAT Sech-Uhr-Abendblatt; Sechs Uhr Abendblatt. (19??)-. Newspaper. German. da. Hohere Bundeslehr Versuchsanstalt Wein Obstbau, Weinerstr 74, A3400 Klosterneuburg Austria. **Tel** 011 43 2243 2159. **LC** 191.

AU
12 UHR BLATT. VFOAT Twelve Uhr Blatt. (19??)-. Newspaper. German. da. Hohere Bundeslehr Versuchsanstalt Wein Obstbau, Weinerstr 74, A3400 Klosterneuburg Austria. **Tel** 011 43 2243 2159. **LC** 100-X.

AU
ABEND (VIENNA, AUSTRIA : 1918). (DER ABEND.). Vol. 1, No. 122 (Oct. 31, 1918)-. Newspaper. German. da. **LC** 154. *Continues* Neue Abend.

AU
ADLER (VIENNA, AUSTRIA). (DER ADLER.). Vol. 1, No. 1 (July 7, 1933)-. Newspaper. German. da. **LC** 100-X.

AU
ALPENLANDISCHE RUNDSCHAW. (1923)-. Newspaper. German. wk. **LC** 100-X.

AU
AZ. (Dec. 1989)-. Newspaper. German. da. S8.00 (single issue). AZ, Windmuhlgasse 26, 1061 Vienna Austria. available on microfilm. *Continues* Neue AZ.

AU
DEMOKRATISHCHES VOLKSBLATT. (194?)-. Newspaper. German. da. Landesverkehrsamt Salzburg, Mozartplatz 1, 5010 Salzburg Austria. **LC** 146.

Austria

AU
DEUTSCHES VOLKSBLATT (VIENNA, AUSTRIA : WEEKLY). (DEUTSCHES VOLKSBLATT.). Vol. 1, No. 1 (Feb. 2, 1935)-. Newspaper. German. wk.

AU
DEUTSCHOSTERREICHISCHE TAGES-ZEITUNG. VFOAT Deutschosterreichische Tages Zeitung. Vol. 31, No. 89 (April 1 1921)-. Newspaper. German. da. Springer-Verlag Wien, Sachsenplatz 4 6, PO Box 89, A-1201 Vienna Austria. **Tel** 011 43 1 3302415. **(Subscription address:** Springer Verlag New York Inc. / for North America, 44 Hartz Way, Secaucus NJ 07096.) LC 165. **Continues** Deutsche Tageszeitung.

AU
DONAUZEITUNG. (July 15, 1941)-. Newspaper. German. da. **LC** 106. available on microfilm from British Museum Microfilm Service.

AU
HOLLABRUNNER ZEITUNG. (193?)-. Newspaper. English. wk. LC 100-X.

AU
INNSBRUCKER NACHRICHTEN. (1853)-. Newspaper. German. da. LC 114.

AU
KLEINE ZEITUNG. (1903)-. Newspaper. German. da. Stadt Graz, Stadtarchiv, Hans-Sachs-Gasse 1, A-8010 Graz, Austria. LC 107.

AU
KOROSKI SLOVENEC. (19??)-. Newspaper. Slovak. wk.

AU
LINZER-ABENDBOTE. VFOAT Linzer Abendbote. (18??)-. Newspaper. German. da. **LC** 131.

AU
LINZER MITTAGSPOST. (19??)-. Newspaper. German. da. Archiv der Stadt Linz, Linz Austria. **Tel** 0732/2393-2972. LC 100-X.

AU
LINZER VOLKSBLATT. (1869)-. Newspaper. German. da. LC 132.

AU
MONTAG-FRUHBLATT WIENER NEUESTE NACHRICHTEN. (18??)-. Newspaper. German. wk. LC 100-X.

AU
MONTAGSPRESSE. Vol. 1, No. 1 (Nov. 27, 1933)-. Newspaper. German. wk. available on microfilm from The Library of Congress Photoduplication Service.

AU
MUHTVIERTLER BOTE. (Feb. 1946)-. Newspaper. German. tw. LC 134.

AU
NEUE STEIRISCHE ZEITUNG. (May 25, 1945)-. Newspaper. German. da. LC 108.

AU
NEUE ZEIT (LINZ, AUSTRIA : 1935). (DIE NEUE ZEIT.). (1935)-. Newspaper. German. da. Archiv der Stadt Linz, Linz Austria. **Tel** 0732/2393-2972. LC 135.

AU
NEUESTE ZEITUNG. (19??)-. Newspaper. German. da. University of Innsbruck, Faculty of Theology, Innsbruck Austria. **Tel** 05222 5078501, FAX 05222 579799. LC 115.

AU
OBERSTEIRISCHE RUNDSCHAU. Vol. 1 No. 1 (Nov. 24, 1945)-. Newspaper. German. wk. LC 126.

AU
OGNI (SALZBURG, AUSTRIA). (OGNI.). Newspaper. Russian (Russian). wk.

AU/0032-7832
PRESSE, DIE. (1946)-. Periodical. German. da. S2700.00 (Austria); S4400.00 (other). Die Presse, Parking 12A Postfach 6, A1015 Vienna Austria. **Tel** 11 43 222 51414, FAX 011 43 222 51414 251, telex 847 114110 or 01 1250 Mocow A.
Ind/Abst Infomat Int. Bus.; PROMT.

AU
PROMIN. Newspaper. Ukrainian (Ukrainian). wk. Ukrainian Women Association of Canada, A25 10024 82 Avenue, Edmonton Alberta T6G 0T2 Canada.

AU
STEIRERBLATT, DAS. (Oct. 1945)-. Newspaper. German. da.

AU
STIMME (VIENNA, AUSTRIA). (DIE STIMME.). (192?)-. Newspaper. German. wk. LC 100-X.

AU
STUNDE (VIENNA, AUSTRIA). (DIE STUNDE.). (1923)-. Newspaper. German. da. LC 100-X.

AU
WIEN KURIER. (19??)-. Newspaper. German. ds. S4717.26. Mediaprint Zeitungsvertriebges, Lindengasse 52, A 1072 Vienna Austria. **Tel** 011 43 1 521302974.

AU
WIENER ABENDPOST. No. 1 (Jan. 2, 1911)-. Newspaper. German. da. LC 200.

AU
WIENER TAG, DER. (19??)-. Newspaper. German. da. LC 100-X. **Continues** Tag (Vienna, Austria).

AU
WIENER WIRTSCHAFTS-WOCHE. VFOAT Wiener Writschafts Woche. Vol. 1, No. 1 (April 16, 1932)-. Newspaper. German. wk. available on microfilm from The Library of Congress Photoduplication Service.

AU
WOCHEN PRESSE, DIE. Vol. 9, No. 14 (April 2, 1955)-. Newspaper. German. wk. Jupiter Verlagsgesellschaft, Postfach 86, Robertgasse 2, A-1021 Vienna Austria. **Tel** 214-22-94. LC 188. **Continues** Presse (Vienna, Austria : 1946 : Weekly).

AZERBAIJAN

AJ
KHALG GAZETI. VFOAT Xalq Gazeti. (199?)-. Newspaper. Azerbaijani. wk. $299.95. **(Subscription address:** East View Publications Inc., 3020 Harbor Lane North, Suite 110, Minneapolis MN 55447.)

BAHAMAS

BF
NASSAU GUARDIAN, THE. VFOAT Weekend Guardian. (1949)-. Newspaper. English. da. $466.62. Nassau Guardian 1844 Ltd., PO Box N3011, Nassau NP Bahamas. **Continues** Nassau Guardian and Bahama Islands Advocate and Intelligencer.

BAHRAIN

BA
GULF DAILY NEWS. (1978)-. Newspaper. English. $215.00. Al Hilal Corporation, PO Box 224, Manama Bahrain. **ED** George Williams. **Circ:** 11,500.

BANGLADESH

BG
BANGLADESH OBSERVER, THE. 23rd Year, No. 274 (Dec. 23, 1971)-. Newspaper. English. da. $254.00 Asian countries; $325.00 European & African countries; $425.00 other. Bangladesh Observer, Observer House, Notijheel Dacca 2 Bangladesh. **Tel** 11 880 2 2351059, FAX 11 880 2 833565. **ED** Professor K. M. A. Munim. **Bk Rev. Ad Acc. Circ:** 80,000. available on microfilm. **Continues** Observer (Dacca, Bangladesh).
Desc: Entire area of publications including editorials. Contains ideal thoughts, continental developments, current topics, population control home and abroad.

BARBADOS

BB/1019-5076
CARIBBEAN WEEK. [Caribb. week]. (198?)-. Periodical. English. bw. $20.00. Caribbean Communications, Lefferts Place, River Road, St. Michael, Barbados, West Indies. **Tel** 809-436-1902, FAX 809-436-1904. **(Subscription address:** Caribbean Communications, 800 Rene Levesque, Suite 2795, Montreal Quebec H3B 1X9 Canada) **ED** John Gilmore. **Ad Acc, Adv Mgr:** P Starr. ctrl circ.
Desc: The regional newspaper of the Caribbean.

BELGIUM

BE/0771-2510
ARGUS BELGE, L'. (1983)-. Periodical. French. Eleven times a year (July/Aug. issue combined). 1850.00F Belgium; 2700.00F Europe; 3200.00F other. L'Argus Belge, 114 Avenue Louise, PO Box 29, 1050 Brussels Belgium. **Tel** 322 640 7589. Index available.

BE/0770-9021
COURRIER DE GAND, LE. (1977)-. Newspaper. French. wk. 1800F Belgium; 2300F other. EREL, St Sebastiaanstraat 16, 8400 Ostende Belgium. **Tel** 32 059701308, FAX 32 059803451. **ED** Monique Lanoye. **UDC** 39. Index available. **Bk Rev. Ad Acc. Circ:** 21,000.

BE
FEVE NEWS. English (French and German). mo (published monthly except Dec.). 5500.00F. Feve, Avenue Louise 89, B-1050 Brussels Belgium. **Tel** 011 32 2 5393434, FAX 011 32 2 5393752.

BE/0770-4720
INTERFACE OPPREBOIS. [InterfaceOpprebois]. (1981)-. Newspaper. French. qt. Promotion Bibl & Informatique, Rue de l'Abbaye 11, B 5198 Denee Belgium. **Tel** 38 82 699647. **UDC** 22:681.3. **Ind/Abst** Linguist. Lang. Behav. Abstr. (1986-) [Full Cov.]; Soc. Plann. Policy Dev. Abstr.

BE
LIBRE BELGIQUE, LA. (1883)-. Newspaper. French. da. 16945F. La Libre Belgique, Boulevard Emile Jacqmain 127, B-1000 Brussels Belgium. **Tel** 011 32 2 2112777.

BE/0921-9986
WALL STREET JOURNAL (EUROPE). (THE WALL STREET JOURNAL.). [Wall Street j., Europe]. (1983)-. Newspaper. English. da (except Sat., Sun., and legal holidays). $725.00 (one year), $1305.00 (two year). Dow Jones and Company Inc, 200 Burnett Road, Chicopee MA 01021. **Tel** (413)592-7761, (800)568-7625. **(Subscription address:** Dow Jones Publishing Company Europe Inc., In de Cramer 37, NL 6411 RS Heerlen Netherlands.) **ED** Robert Keatley. Index available. **Bk Rev. Ad Acc. Circ:** 47,800. available on microfilm.
Desc: International business newspaper serving any executive with interests in business dealings outside their own country, particularly strong coverage of North American markets.
Ind/Abst Abstr. BioCommer.; F&S Index Plus Text, Int. [Select. Cov.]; Infomat Int. Bus.; Predicasts; Print. Abstr.; PROMT.

BELIZE

BH
BELIZE TIMES, THE. (19??)-. Newspaper. English. wk. Belize Times, 3 Queen Street, PO Box 506, Belize City Belize. **Tel** 2 45757, FAX 2 31940. **ED** Polo Velasquez. **Circ:** 6,000. available on microfilm.

BENIN

DM
NATION, LA. (19??)-. Newspaper. French. da. La Nation, BP 1210, Cotonou Bennin. **Tel** 30 08 75.

BERMUDA ISLANDS

BM
ROYAL GAZETTE, THE. Vol. 57, No. 114 (May 16, 1977)-. Newspaper. English. da. $103.40. Royal Gazette Ltd., PO Box 1025, Hamilton 5 Bermuda. available on microfilm. **Continues** Royal Gazette and Official Government Gazette.

BOLIVIA

BO
PRESENCIA. (Mar. 28, 1952)-. Newspaper. Spanish. da. $380.00 North America; $440.00 Europe; $320.00 Central America; $250.00 South America; $500.00 other. Presencia, Avda Mariscal Santa Cruz 1295, Casilla 3276, La Paz Bolivia. **Tel** 011 591 2 372344, FAX 011 591 2 391040, telex 2659. **LC** 297. **Circ:** 90,000. available on microfilm.

BOSNIA AND HERCEGOVINA

BN/0352-261X
VECERNJE NOVINE (1983). [Vec. nov. 1983]. (1983)-. Newspaper. Serbo-Croatian (Roman). da. Vecernje Novine, Pavla Goranina 13, 71000 Sarajevo Bosnia and Hercegovina. **Tel** 71 518497, FAX 71 271879, telex 41732. **ED** Sergije Princip. **UDC** 32. **Circ:** 61,000. *Continues Sarajevske Novine, 0350-560X.*

BOTSWANA

BS
DIKGANG TSA GOMPIENO. VFOAT Botswana Daily News. (1964)-. Newspaper. Setswana (English). da. Dikgang tsa Gompieno, Private Bag 0060, Gaborone Botswana. **Circ:** 40,000.

BRAZIL

BL
ESTADO DE SAO PAULO. (1875)-. Newspaper. Portuguese. ds. $750.00. Estado de Sao Paulo, Caixa Postal 8005, Sao Paulo Brazil. **Tel** 011 55 11 8562538, 8562541.

BL
JORNAL DO BRASIL. (Apr. 9, 1891)-. Newspaper. Portuguese. da. $1,650.20. Jornal Brasil SA/DPT Assinaturas, Sao Cristouao Avda Brasil 500, 20940 Rio de Janeiro Brazil. **Tel** 011 55 21 5854422. **Ad Acc.** ctr. circ.
 Desc: Paper on various matters: economics, financing, world, country, and city politics, opinions, sports, culture and pleasure.

BRUNEI

BX
BORNEO BULLETIN. (19??)-. Bulletin. English wk. Borneo Bulletin, 74 Jalan Sungei, PO Box 69, Kuala Belait 600C Brunei. **ED** Charles Rex de Silva.

BULGARIA

BU
DEMOKRATSIIA. Added/Corp SDS--Liberali (Political Party). (1991)-. Newspaper. Bulgarian. da. DM203.00. **(Subscription address:** Kubon & Sagner, ABT Zeitschriftenimport, D 80328 Munich Germany.**)**

BU/0861-2153
LITERATUREN FORUM. [Lit. forum]. (1990)-. Newspaper. Bulgarian. wk. DM157.00. **(Subscription address:** Kubon & Sagner, ABT Zeitschriftenimport, D 80328 Munich Germany.**)** **UDC** 886.7. *Continues Literaturen Front, 0205-1028.*
Ind/Abst Annu. Bibliogr. Engl. Lang. Lit. (1990-).

BU
NATSIONALNA BIBLIOGRAFIIA NA REPUBLIKA BULGARIIA. SERIIA 6, LETOPIS NA STATIITE OT BULGARSKITE VESTNITSI. Added/Corp Narodna Biblioteka "Sv. sv. Kiril i Metodii.". **VFOAT** Letopis na Statiite ot Bulgarskite Vestnitsi; Bulgarian National Bibliography. Articles from Bulgarian Neuspapers [sic]. No. 1 (1991)-. Periodical. Bulgarian. mo. **(Subscription address:** Hemus Foreign Trade Organization, 6 Tzar Osvoboditel Boulevard, 1000 Sofia Bulgaria.**)** *Continues Natsionalna Bibliografiia na NR Bulgariia. Seriia 6, Letopis na Statiite ot Bulgarskite Vestnitsi, 0324-0347.*

BU
OTECHESTVEN VESTNIK. Added/Corp Otechestven Suiuz. (1990)-. Newspaper. Bulgarian. da. DM240.00. Izd. na Otechestvenniia Suiuz, Sofia Bulgaria. **(Subscription address:** Kubon & Sagner, ABT Zeitschriftenimport, D 80328 Munich Germany.**)** *Continues Otechestven Front (Sofia, Bulgaria : 1944).*

BURKINA FASO

UV/1013-655X
SIDWAYA. [Sidwaya]. (1984)-. Newspaper. French. da. Sidwaya, 5 rue de Marche, 01 BP 507, Ouagadougou Burkina Faso. **ED** Yamba Yameogo. **UDC** 008(662.5). **Circ:** 5,000.

BURMA

BR
WORKING PEOPLE'S DAILY MICROFORM, THE. (19??)-. Newspaper. English. da. Working Peoples Daily, PO Box 43, 212 Theinbyu Street, Rangoon Burma.

BURUNDI

BD
UBUMWE. (March 31, 1972)-. Newspaper. French (French). wk. Ubumwe, BP 1400, Bujumbura Burundi. **LC** AP27; .U272. **DD** 054.1. *Continues in part Ubumwe (French & Rundi Ed.).*

BYELARUS

BW
NARODNAIA HAZETA : ORHAN VIARKHOUNAHA SAVETA BELARUSKAI SSR. Added/Corp Byelorussian S.S.R. Viarkouny Savet. (19??)-. Newspaper. Byelorussian (Russian). wk. $309.95. **(Subscription address:** East View Publications Inc., 3020 Harbor Lane North, Suite 110, Minneapolis MN 55447.**)** **ED** Iosif P. Siaredzich. **Circ:** 401,000.

CAMBODIA

CB
PRACHEACHON. (19??)-. Newspaper. Pracheachon, 101 Boulevard Tou Samouth, Phnom-Penh Cambodia. **ED** Som Kimsour.

CAMEROON

CM
CAMEROON TRIBUNE. (1974)-. Newspaper. French. da. Cameroon Tribune, BP 1218, Yaounde Cameroon. **Tel** 30 40 12, FAX 30 43 62, telex 8311. **ED** Ebokem Fomenky. **Circ:** 20,000. *Continues Presse du Cameroun.*

CANADA

CN/0710-5541
2 RIVES, LES. [2 rives]. **VAT** Deux Rives. Vol. 1, No. 1 (Sept 1978)-. Newspaper. French. wk. $15.00. Publ S P G, Les 2 Rives, 57 rue Georges, Sorel Quebec J3P 1B9 Canada. **DD** 071/.1451.

CN/0700-303X
7/15, LE JOURNAL DES JEUNES. No. 1 (May 1976)-. Periodical. French. $5.00. Journal 7/15, CP 457 Succursale Beaubien, Montreal Quebec H2B 3E2 Canada. **DD** 070.4/832/05.

CN/0843-0403
100 MILE HOUSE FREE PRESS. [100 Mile House free press]. **VFOAT** Hundred Mile House Free Press. Vol. 9, No. 6 (Feb. 7, 1968)-. Newspaper. English. Fifty-two times a year. 30.00Can$ (within 60km radius of Canada); 35.00Can$ (within 65km radius of Canada); 80.00Can$ others. 100 Mile House Free Press, 100 Mile House, Box 459, 100 Mile House V0K 2E0 Canada. **Tel** (604)395-2219. **ED** Curtis Pollack. **DD** 071/.112. **Ad Acc, Adv Mgr:** Terry Gibbons, **Tel** (604)395-2219. **Circ:** 5,000. *Continues 100 Mile Free Press.*
 Desc: An community newspaper.

CN/0824-4561
1441. [1441]. **VFOAT** Fourteen Forty-One. **VAT** Quatorze Quarante et Un. Vol. 1, No. 1 (April 1979)-. Newspaper. English (French). mo. YMCA Montreal Downtown Branch, 1441 Drummond Street, Montreal Quebec H3G 1W5 Canada. **DD** 071/.14281.

CN/0824-1481
A LA PAGE (STE-MARIE). (A LA PAGE.). [A page]. Vol. 1, No, 1 (27 April 1984)-. Newspaper. French. wk. Boutique Pierre Gregoire, CP 1195, 55 Nord, Rue Notre-Dame, Ste-Marie Beauce, Quebec G6E 3C3 Canada. **DD** 071/.1471.

CN/0705-7490
ABITIBI-PRICE. Added/Corp Abitibi Paper Company. Harrison Price Company. (197?)-. Newspaper. English. Abitibi Paper Company, Public Relations Department, Toronto-Dominion Centre, Toronto Ontario M5K 1B3 Canada. **DD** 338.7/63/49.

CN/0705-839X
ACHIMOWIN. V. 3, No. 25- Aug. 25, 1975-. English. wk. Achimowin, c/o A. Guiboche, 1 Public Road, Thompson, Manitoba R8N 0M3 Canada. **DD** 071/.127/2. *Continues Achimowin Weekly, 0705-839X.*

CN/1191-0690
ACTION REGIONALE, L'. [Action reg.]. Vol. 1, No 1 (April 22 1991)-. Newspaper. French. wk. 60.00Can$ per year. Presses du Grand-Sault, CP 2438, Grand-Sault, New Brunswick E0J 1M0 Canada. **DD** 071/.15/53.

CN
ACTON FREE PRESS. Newspaper. English. wk. 49.49Can$ Acton; 74.75Can$ other. Acton Free Press, 211 Armstrong Avenue, Georgetown Ontario L7G 4X5 Canada. **Tel** (416)873-0301. **ED** Robin Inscoe. **Ad Acc, Adv Mgr:** S. Dorsey. **Circ:** 4,650 (ctrl).

CN/0824-6610
ADVANCE (ZURICH). (THE ADVANCE.). [Advance]. Newspaper. English. wk. 10.00Can$ Canada; $45.00 US. The Advance, PO Box 190, Zurich Ontario N0M 2T0 Canada. **Tel** (519)236-4312. **ED** Herb Turkheim. **DD** 071/.1322. **Ad Acc. Circ:** 3,124 (ctrl). available on microfiche (from Oakville, Ont. : Ontario Community Newspapers Association).

CN/1194-1103
ADVOCATE NEWSPAPER. (THE ADVOCATE NEWSPAPER [MICROFORM].). **VFOAT** Byron Advocate. Issue No. 62 (Oct. 1, 1979)-. English. Information Graphics, Box 1843, Station A, London, Ontario N6A 5H9 Canada. **DD** 071/.1326. *Continues Advocate (London, Ont. : 1978)., 1194-109X.*

●CN/1189-5055
AFRICAN ORACLE, THE. [Afr. oracle]. Vol 1 (Mar. 31 1992)-. Newspaper. English. mo. $1.00 per issue. The African Oracle, 994A St. Clair Avenue West, Toronto Ontario M6C 1C8 Canada. **DD** 960/.05.

CN/0834-5783
AGINCOURT NEWS. (AGINCOURT NEWS [MICROFORM].). [Agincourt News]. (1951)-. Newspaper. English. wk (published on Wednesday). 15.00Can$. Watson Publishing Company, 150 Milner Avenue, Unit 35, Sacrborough, Ontario, M1S 3R3 Canada. **Tel** (416)291-2583. **DD** 071/.13541.

CN
AIRDRIE ECHO. Newspaper. English. wk. 27.00Can$ Canada; 46.00Can$ other. Airdrie Echo, Box 3820, Airdrie, Alberta, T4B 2B9 Canada. **Tel** (403)948-7280, FAX (403)233-7226.

Canada

CN/0319-5414
ALBERTAN'S NORTH SIDE MIRROR, THE. VFOAT North Side Mirror. Began with March 18, 1975 issue. Newspaper. English. wk. The Albertan, 830-10th Avenue SW, Calgary Alberta T2R 0B1 Canada. **DD** 071/.123/3.

CN/0704-707X
ALGONQUIN IMPACT. Began with Jan. 29, 1976 issue?. Newspaper. English (French). wk. Free. Algonquin College of Applied Arts and Technology, Students Union, 1385 Woodroffe Avenue, Ottawa Ontario K2G 1V8 Canada. **DD** 378.713/84. ctrl circ. *Supersedes Arrow.*

CN/0845-8464
ALLIANCE (NATIVE ALLIANCE OF QUEBEC). (ALLIANCE.). [Alliance - Alliance autoch. Que.]. Vol. 11, No. 4 (Oct. 15, 1984). Newspaper. English (French). mo. $5.00 (individuals), $10.00 (institutions). Native Alliance of Quebec, 21 Brodeur Street, Hull Quebec J8Y 2P6 Canada. **DD** 971.4/00497/005. *Continues Alliance Journal, 0845-8456.*

CN/1185-1864
ALTERNATIVE VOICE, THE. [Altern. voice]. (Dec. 13, 1990)-. Newspaper. English. wk. Dave Patterson, Rural Route 1, Winsloe, Prince Edward Island C0A 2H0 Canada. **ED** Dave Patterson. **DD** 071/.175.

CN/0229-799X
ANTIGONISH SPECTATOR, THE. [Antigonish spect.]. Vol. 1, No. 1 (Dec. 8, 1976)-. Newspaper. English. bw. $0.25 per no. L. Chisholm, PO Box 1542 Antigonish, NS B2G 2L8. **DD** 071/.1614.

CN/0382-9251
APAGAY (MONTREAL). (ABAGAY. ABAKA.). [Apagay]. Added/Corp Tekeyan Armenian Cultural Association. Tekeyan Publication Center. VFOAT Abaka. Vol. 1, (Sept. 13, 1975)-. Newspaper. English (French and Armenian). Fifty times a year (Except two weeks in July). 55.00Can$ Canada; $75.00 (Pan America); $105.00 other. Abaka, 825 Rue Manoogian St Laurent, Quebec Quebec H4N 1Z5 Canada. **Tel** (514)747-6680, FAX (514)747-6162. **ED** Arsene Mamourian. **DD** 071/.14/281. **Bk Rev**, (Qty: varies): **Ad Acc. Circ:** 1,200 (ctrl).
Desc: Community and Canadian news, reviews of Armenian life in the diaspora, editorials, articles dealing with Armenian, as well as political issues, book reviews and literary profiles.

CN/0824-5568
APNA WATAN (MONTREAL, QUEBEC). (APNA WATAN.). [Apna watan]. Newspaper. English (Urdu). mo. Free. APNA Watan, 1675 Grenet Street/Suite 16, Saint-Laurent, Quebec H4L 2R6 Canada. **DD** 954/.005.

CN/0710-1120
ARCADIAN RECORDER. (THE ARCADIAN RECORDER.). [Arcadian rec.]. VFOAT Recorder. VAT Recorder (Halifax). (1980)-. Newspaper. English. $6.50. Arcadian Recorder, PO Box 2437 Station M, Halifax Nova Scotia B3J 3E4 Canada. **DD** 071/.1622.

CN/0714-5705
ARN MESSAGER. [ARN messager]. Newspaper. French. Free. ARN Messager, Local C-207/90 Vincent d'Indy, Montreal Quebec H2V 2S9 Canada. **DD** 378.714/281.

CN/0319-5589
ARROWSMITH STAR, THE. Vol. 1 (March 4, 1975)-. Newspaper. English. wk. Free. The Arrowsmith Star, PO Box 1300, Parksville British Columbia V0R 2S0 Canada. **DD** 071/.11/34.

CN
ASHCROFT CACHE CREEK JOURNAL. English. wk (published Tuesdays). 33.00Can$ Canada; 100.00Can$ other. Ashcroft Cache Creek Journal, Box 190, Ashcoft, British Columbia, V0K 1A0 Canada. **Tel** (604)453-2261, FAX (604)453-9625. **ED** Barry Tait. **Ad Acc, Adv Mgr:** J. Van Allen. **Circ:** 1,700 (ctrl).

CN/1186-3064
ASSINIBOIA TODAY. (ASSINIBOIA TODAY [MICROFORM].). Vol. 1, No. 1 (Jan. 22, 1990)-. English. Preston Microfilming Services, 2215 Queen Street East, Toronto Ontario M4E 1E8 Canada. **Tel** (416)699-7154. **DD** 071/.1244.

CN/0711-1975
ASSU NEWS. (ASSU NEWS : ARTS AND SCIENCE STUDENTS' UNION NEWSLETTER.). [ASSU news]. VAT Arts and Science Students' Union News. Newsletter. English. Arts and Science Students' Union, University of Toronto, Room 1068/100 Saint George Street, Toronto Ontario M5S 1A1 Canada. **DD** 378.713/541.

CN
ATIKOKAN PROGRESS. (19??)-. Newspaper. English. Fifty-one times per year (Published on Monday & except Christmas). 45.00Can$. Atikokan Progress, Box 220, Atikokan Ontario P0T 1C0 Canada. **Tel** (807)597-2731. **ED** Mike McKinnon. **Ad Acc, Adv Mgr:** Eve Shine. **Circ:** 1,800 (ctrl).

CN/0226-6296
ATLIN NUGGET, THE. [Atlin nugget]. V. 1- Nov. 1978-. Newspaper. English. mo. $6.00 Canada; $12.00 US; $15.00 other. The Atlin Nugget, PO Box 227, Atlin BC V0W 1A0. **DD** 071/.111.

CN/0711-3900
AVA-YI IRAN. [Ava-yi Iran]. VFOAT The Voice of Iran; Voice of Iran; Ava-Yi Iran; Ava-Ye Iran (The Voice of Iran). 1981-. Newspaper. Persian. mo. $8.00 Canada; $12.00 other. Voice of Iran, PO Box 580, Station B, Ottawa Ontario K1P 6C3 Canada. **DD** 955/.054/05.

CN/1197-1193
AVANT-POSTE (AMQUI). (L'AVANT-POSTE.). [Avant-poste]. (1991)-. Newspaper. French. Fifty-two times a year. 32.00Can$ Canada; 52.00Can$ other. Group Bellavance, 73, St-Germain Est., Rimouski Quebec G5L 7C4 Canada. **Tel** (418)723-4800. **DD** 071/.14775. *Continues L'Avant-Poste Gaspesien., 1181-3598.*

CN/0714-427X
AVENIR DU NORD (SAINT-JEROME, QUEBEC : 1981). (L'AVENIR DU NORD.). [Avenir nord]. Vol. 1, No. 1, (Aug. 26, 1981)-. Newspaper. French. wk. Free. L'Avenir du Nord, 335 rue Labelle, CP 21, Sainte-Jerome Quebec J7Z 5T7 Canada. **DD** 071/.1424.

CN/0821-1477
AVIRON (ED QUEBECOISE). (L'AVIRON.). [Aviron]. 15 Dec. 1982-. Newspaper. French. wk. 22.00Can$ Canada; $34.00 US. L'Aviron, CP 129, New Richmond Quebec G0C 2B0 Canada. **Tel** (418)392-5083. **ED** Guy Lavoie. **DD** 071/.1478. **Ad Acc. Circ:** 14,535 (ctrl).
Desc: General information in our community, sports, etc. **Ind/Abst** SportSearch (May 1987-).

CN/0715-4135
AWAZ (TORONTO). (AWAZ.). [Awaz]. VFOAT Aawaz; Monthly Aawaz. Vol. 1, No. 1 (April 1980)-. Newspaper. Urdu. mo. 25.00Can$. Awaz, PO Box 2114 Station B, Scarborough Ontario M1N 2E5 Canada. **Tel** (416)283-7255. **ED** Sohail Akhtar. **DD** 071/.13541. Index available. **Bk Rev. Ad Acc. Circ:** 3,000.

CN/0710-5401
AYLMER BULLETIN. [Aylmer bull.]. No. 1, 1st Year (May 21, 1981)-. Bulletin. English. wk. $0.25. per no., $10.00 per. year. Aylmer Bulletin, 478 de Bruyne Crescent, Aylmer Quebec J9H 5N7 Canada. **DD** 071/.14221. available on microfilm.

CN/0714-9107
BABILLARD DE R.D.P. (LE BABILLARD DE R.D.P.). [Babillard R.D.P.]. Added/Corp Regroupement des Organismes Communautaires de la Rivieres des Prairies. VAT Babillard de Riviere des Prairies. Vol. 1, No. 1 (Sept. 1982)-. Newspaper. French. mo. Free to residents. Babillard de R.D.P., 12755 42E Avenue, Montreal Quebec H1E 2G2 Canada. **DD** 071/.14281.

CN/0709-0358
BALITA. Vol. 1, No. 11 (Jan. 16/31, 1979)-. Newspaper. English (Tagalog; summaries and/or abstracts in Tagalog). sm. 4.00Can$. Kalayaan Media Balita, PO Box 392 Station A, Toronto Ontario M5W 1C2 Canada. **DD** 071/.13/541. *Continues Balita Natin, 0709-034X.*

CN/0710-1236
BANKUBA SHINPO. [Bankuba shinpo]. VFOAT Vancouver Shimpo. Newspaper. Japanese. wk. Vancouver Shimpo, PO Box 69780 Station K, Vancouver British Columbia V5K 4 Canada. **DD** 071/.1133.

CN/0846-0396
BARRHAVEN INDEPENDENT. [Barrhaven indep.]. Vol. 1, No. 1 (Mar. 20, 19??)-. Periodical. English. wk. Limited free distribution. Morris Newspaper Group, 806 Greenbank Road, Nepean, Ontario K2J 1A2 Canada. **DD** 071/.1383.

CN/0226-6377
BATTLEFORD TELEGRAPH. [Battleford telegr.]. VFOAT Telegraph; Battleford's Advertiser-Post. VAT Telegraph (Battleford). Vol. 1 (Apr. 20, 1978)-. Newspaper. English. ir. 35.00Can$ Canada; 80.00Can$ others. Turner Warwick Publishing Inc., PO Box 1029, North Battleford Saskatchewan, S9A 3E6 Canada. **Tel** (306)445-7261, FAX (306)445-3223. **ED** L. Susan Sandberg, Lois Walsh and Mark Kotchorek. **DD** 071/.1242. **Ad Acc. Circ:** 23,813 (Mon.), 5,000 (Wed. & Fri.). available on microfilm from Saskatchewan Archives Board.
Desc: Includes national and international wire news in addition to local and regional news and sports.

CN/0712-4988
BEACON (GLACE BAY). (THE BEACON.). [Beacon]. (1981)-. Periodical. English. wk. Free. The Beacon / Nova Scotia, c/o Citizen Publishing, 17 Prince Street, Sydney Nova Scotia B1P 5J4 Canada. **DD** 071/.1695.

CN/0229-6802
BEACON (PARRY SOUND). (THE BEACON.). [Beacon]. VFOAT Parry Sound Beacon. Vol. 1, No. 1 (May 15, 1980)-. Newspaper. English. wk. 52.81Can$ (combined subscription with Parry Sound North Star). Parry Sound Beacon Star, 67 James Street, Parry Sound Ontario P2A 2X4 Canada. **Tel** (705)746-4228. **DD** 071/.1315.

CN/0703-2102
BEACON TIMES. (THE BEACON TIMES.). Vol. 1, (Dec. 4, 1975)-. Newspaper. English. wk (Wednesday). 26.75Can$ (within 40 mile radius of Port Elgin); 37.45Can$ (Canada); 50.00Can$ (other). Beacon Times, Box 580, Port Elgin Ontario N0H 2C0 Canada. **Tel** (519)832-9001, FAX (519)389-4793. **DD** 071/.13/21. **Circ:** 4,228. available on microfiche (from Oakville, Ont. : Ontario Community Newpapers). *Formed by the union of Port Elgin Times, 1194-1294 and Beacon Times (Port Elgin, Ont.), 0703-2102.*

CN/0712-3027
BEACONSFIELD REPORTER. [Beaconsfield report.]. **Main/Corp** Beaconsfield (Quebec). Vol. 1, No. 1 (Oct. 1969)-. Newspaper. English (French). ir. Free. Reporter / Beaconsfield, 303 Beaconsfield Boulevard, Beaconsfield Quebec H9W 4A7 Canada. **DD** 352.0714/28.

CN/0711-3420
BEAUCE MEDIA. [Beauce media]. Vol. 1, No. 1 (Aug. 19, 1980)-. Newspaper. French. wk. $27.09. Beauce Media, 164 Notre Dame South Street, St-Marie de Beauce, Beauceville Quebec G0S 2Y0 Canada. **Tel** (418)387-8000. **DD** 071/.1471.

CN/0844-2665
BEAUCE NOUVELLE. *Title Change.* (BEAUCE NOUVELLE. MICROFORME.). [Beauce nouv.]. Vol. 1, No. 1 (March 1968)-(19??). French. Societe Canadienne du Microfilm, Bureua 10, 464 rue Saint Jean, Montreal Quebec H24 2S1 Canada. **Tel** (514)288-5404, (514)288-5591. **DD** 071/.1471. *Continued by Eclaireur Progres; Eclaireur Progres, Beauce Nouvelle.*

CN/0834-5643
BELLE RIVER NORTH ESSEX NEWS. (BELLE RIVER NORTH ESSEX NEWS / MICROFORM.). [Belle River North Essex news]. (1???)-. English. wk (published Wednesday). 23.38Can$ Belle River; 29.63Can$ Canada; 52.00Can$ other. North Essex News, PO Box 429, Belle River Ontario, N0R 1A0 Canada. **Tel** (519)728-1028, FAX (519)728-4551. **ED** Kelly Finnerty and Andrew Sinclair. **DD** 071/.1331.

CN/0832-2937
BENGOUGH BULLETIN. (BENGOUGH BULLETIN MICROFORM.). (Dec. 1983)-. Bulletin. English. Saskatchewan Archives Board, University of Saskatchewan, Murray Building, Saskatchewan S7N 0W0 Canada. **Tel** (306)933-8326, FAX (306)933-7305. **DD** 071/.1244.

CN/0316-0270
BENITO STANDARD. V. 1- Dec. 21, 1973-. Newspaper. English. $2.00 within 40 miles of Benito area, $3.00 elsewhere in Canada. Benito Standard, PO Box 424, Benito Manitoba R0L 0C0 Canada. **DD** 071/127/2.

CN/0382-7577
BIG COUNTRY VOICE, THE. V. 1- Oct. 2, 1975-. Newspaper. English. wk. $8.00. Big Country Voice, PO Box 70, Hafford Saskatchewan S0J 1A0 Canada. **DD** 071/.124/2.

CN/1184-7794
BLAINE LAKE JOURNAL. [Blaine Lake j.]. Vol. 1, No. 1 (June 6, 1990)-. Newspaper. English. wk. $0.40 (single issue). Blaine Lake Journal, PO Box 493, Blaine Lake, Saskatchewan S0J 0J0 Canada. **DD** 071/.1242.

CN/1180-6761
BOITE A NOUVELLES. (LA BOITE A NOUVELLES [MICROFORME].). (198?)-. Newspaper. French. Fifty-two times a year (Wednesday). 27.00Can$ US & Canada; 75.00Can$ others. Boite A Nouvelles, Case Postale 1268, Iroquois Falls POK 1G0 Canada. **Tel** (705)232-5222, FAX (705)232-7755. **ED** Yvonne Bissonnette, (editor's address: 30 Main Street, Iroquois Falls, POK 1G0 Canada). **DD** 071/.13142. **Bk Rev. Ad Acc, Adv Mgr:** Suzanne Lacroix, **Tel** (705)232-5222. **Circ:** 1,400. available on microfilm.

CN/0383-7866
BONJOUR CHEZ-NOUS. [Bonjour chez-nous]. No. 1- March 1976-. Newspaper. French. $11.61. Bonjour Chex Nous, 2-2-1 Laurier CP 1149, Rockland Ontario Canada. **Tel** (613)446-5196. **ED** Pierre Cremer. **DD** 071/.13/85. **Bk Rev. Ad Acc. Circ:** 2,600. available on microfiche (from Oakville, Ont. : Ontario Community Newspapers Association).
Desc: Community news and information.

CN/0821-6177
BORDERLAND REPORTER. [Borderl. report.]. Vol. 1, No. 1 (July 22, 1982)-. Newspaper. English. wk. Don McCahill, PO Box 569, Coronach Sask. S0H 0B0. **DD** 071/.1244.

CN/0834-5686
BOTHWELL TIMES. (BOTHWELL TIMES [MICROFORM].). [Bothwell times]. (Mar. 24, 1874)-. Newspaper. English. wk (Published on Wednesdays). 22.00Can$ Ontario; 35.00Can$ other Canadian provinces; 57.00Can$ other. Bothwell Times, PO Box 40, Bothwell Ontario, N0P 1C0 Canada. **Tel** (519) 692-3105. **DD** 071/.1333.

CN/0226-8663
BOUEILLE, LA. [Boueille]. Published since July 1975?. Newspaper. French. wk. $10.00. Editions Du Sud, CP 329 Cap-pele, NB E0A 1J0 Canada. **DD** 071/.15.

CN/0822-8671
BOUNDARY CREEK TIMES, THE. [Bound. Creek times]. Apr. 15, 1983-. Newspaper. English. wk. 13.00Can$ Canada; 30.00Can$ other. Boundary Creek Times, 318 Cooper Street, PO Box 107, Greenwood City British Columbia V0H 1J0 Canada. **Tel** (604)445-2233. **ED** Edward E Trainer. **DD** 071.1142. **Ad Acc. Circ:** 800.

CN/0316-697X
BOW VALLEY VIEWS. V. 1, No. 3- Oct. 11, 1974-. English. Bow Valley Views, PO Box 831, Canmore Alta T0L 0M0 Canada. **DD** 071/.123/3. ***Continues*** *Valley Views, 0316-6961.*

CN/0704-0490
BOWDEN EYE OPENER, THE. [Bowden eye opener]. Vol. 1 No. 1 (Oct. 6, 1976)-. Newspaper. English. wk. Bowden Printers, Box 70, Bowden Alberta T0M 0K0 Canada. **DD** 071/.1233.

CN/0704-0210
BRACEBRIDGE EXAMINER. [Bracebridge exam.]. Vol. 1 (May 19, 1977)-. Newspaper. English. Fifty-two times a year (Wed.). 32.13Can$. Bracebridge Examiner, PO Box 1049, Bracebridge Ontario P0B 1C0 Canada. **DD** 071/.131/6.

CN/0707-7998
BRANT NEWS. [Brant news]. V. 1- Feb. 1, 1978-. Newspaper. English. wk. $21.67. The Brant News, PO Box 2079, Brantford Ontario N3T 5Y6 Canada. **Tel** (519)759-5550. **ED** Dave Harrison. **DD** 071/.13/47. cum. index. **Ad Acc. Circ:** 38,000 (ctrl). available on microfiche (from Oakville, Ont. : Ontario Community Newspapers Association). ***Supersedes*** *Brant Shopping News.*
Desc: Covers community news.

CN
BRIDGE RIVER LILLOOET NEWS. Newspaper. English. wk. 29.90Can$. Bridge River Lillooet News, PO Box 709, Lillooet Canada. **Tel** (604)256-4322. **ED** Christi Roshard (604)256-4219. **Bk Rev**, (Qty: 1). **Ad Acc, Adv Mgr:** J. Wright. **Circ:** 2,300 (ctrl).

CN/0834-5899
BRIGHTON INDEPENDENT, THE. [Brighton indep.]. Vol. 13, No. 8; Feb. 20, 1985-. English. Brighton Independent, Box 1030 Ontario K0K 1H0 Canada. **DD** 071/.1357. ***Continues*** *Independent (Brighton, Ont.), 0829-6731.*

CN/07?3-620X
BROSSARD ECLAIR. [Brossard eclair]. **VFOAT** Eclair. **VAT** Eclair (Brossard). Vol. 1, No. 1 (Oct. 21, 1980)-. Newspaper. French. wk. 78.13Can$. Brossard Eclair, 7900 Boulevard Tachereau Loc A 105, Brossard Quebec J4X 1C2 Canada. **Tel** (514)466-3344. **DD** 071/.1434.

CN/0823-9681
CALEDON CITIZEN. [Caledon citiz.]. (1977)-. Newspaper. English. wk. 20.00Can$. Caledon Citizen, 25 Queen Street North, Bolton Ontario L7E 1A0 Canada. **DD** 071/.13535. available on microfiche.

CN/0715-5778
CALENDAR (WINFIELD). (THE CALENDAR.). [Calendar]. Vol. 1 I.E. 28, No. 1 (Oct. 1, 1979)-. Newspaper. English. wk. The Calendar, PO Box 54, Winfield British Columbia V0H 2C0 Canada. **DD** 071/.1142. ***Continues*** *Winfield Calendar.*

CN/0711-3684
CALGARY CITY SCENE. [Calgary city scene]. **VFOAT** City Scene. **VAT** City Scene (1981). Vol. 1 (June 17/25, 1981)-. Newspaper. English. wk. $0.25 per number. Calgary City Scene, North Hill News Ltd, Box 3160 Station B, 4000-19th Street North East, Calgary Alberta T2M 4L7 Canada. **DD** 790/.097123/3. ***Continues*** *City Scene.*

CN/0828-1815
CALGARY HERALD. [Calg. her.]. (19??)-. Newspaper. English. da. 547.94Can$ Canada, 875.00Can$ others (Seven days per week); 417.76Can$ Canada, 825.00Can$ others (Mon - Sat.); 252.34Can$ Canada, 420.00Can$ others (tri-weekly); 144.86Can$ Canada, 240.00Can$ others (Sat. only); 93.46Can$ Canada, 180.00Can$ others (Sunday only). Southam Inc. / Attention: Mail Subscriptions, Box 2400 Station M, Calgary Alberta T2P 0W8 Canada. **Tel** (403)235-7100, (403)235-0121, FAX (403)235-8675. **DD** 071.1233. available on an online database (file 635/Full-Text) from DIALOG.
Ind/Abst Can. Lit. Index (1985-1986); Can. News Index.

CN
CALGARY SUN. English. ds. 130.00Can$. Calgary Sun, 2615 12th Street Northeast, Calgary, Alberta, T2E 7W9 Canada. **Tel** (403)250-4186. **ED** Robert Poole (403)250-4200. **Ad Acc, Adv Mgr:** G. Norrie. **Circ:** 70,000 daily, 96,000 Sunday (ctrl).

CN/0318-9538
CAMPBELL RIVER UPPER ISLANDER, THE. Began publication in 1967?. Newspaper. English. wk. 85.00Can$ Canada; $26.00 other. The Campbell River Upper Islander, Box 310, Campbell River British Columbia V9W 5B5 Canada. **Tel** (604)287-7464. **ED** George LeMasurier. **DD** 071/.11/34. **Bk Rev. Ad Acc. Circ:** 8,000 (ctrl).
Desc: General interest newspaper covering northern Van Covven Island.

CN/0008-2775
CANADAN UUTISET. (CANADAN UUTISET [MICROFORM].). [Can. uut.]. **VFOAT** Canada News. Vol. 1, No. 1 (Mar 11, 1915)-. Finnish (English and Multiple languages). Fifty times a year (Published on Wed.). 51.00Can$ Canada; 80.00Can$ US; 100.00Can$ others. Canadan Utiset Canada News, 218 Wilson Street, Thunder Bay ONT P7B 1M8 Canada. **Tel** (807)344-1611, FAX (807)344-1879. **DD** 071/.1312. **Ad Acc, Adv Mgr:** Helena Itkonen, **Tel** 344-1611. **Circ:** 2,100.

CN/0834-6925
CANADIAN CHAMPION. (THE CANADIAN CHAMPION [MICROFORM].). [Can. champion]. **VFOAT** Milton Canadian Champion. (198?)-. English. Fifty-two times a year. 26.00Can$ Canada; 85.00Can$ others. Canadian Champion, 191 Main Street, Milton ONT L9T 1N7 Canada. **Tel** (417)878-2341, FAX (417)878-4943. **DD** 071/.13533.

●CN/1192-4160
CANADIAN INDEX (TORONTO). (CANADIAN INDEX.). [Can. index]. Vol. 1, No. 1 (Jan. 1993)-. Abstracting/Indexing Service. English. mo. Micromedia Limited, 20 Victoria Street, Toronto Ontario M5C 2N8 Canada. **Tel** (416)362-5211, (800)387-2689, FAX (416)362-6161, telex 06524668. **DD** 011/.34. ***Formed by the union of*** *Canadian Business Index, 0227-8669* ***and*** *Canadian News Index, 0225-7459 Canadian Magazine Index (Toronto, Ont.), 0829-8777.*

CN/0225-7459
CANADIAN NEWS INDEX TORONTO. ***Title Change.*** (CANADIAN NEWS INDEX.). [Can. news index]. (1980)-(1992). Abstracting/Indexing Service. English. mo. Micromedia Limited, 20 Victoria Street, Toronto Ontario M5C 2N8 Canada. **Tel** (416)362-5211, (800)387-2689, FAX (416)362-6161, telex 06524668. **LC** AI3; .C2414. **DD** 071/.1; 011/.34/0971. ***Continues*** *Canadian Newspaper Index, 0384-983X.* ***Merged with*** *Canadian Business Index, 0227-8669* ***and*** *Canadian Magazine Index (Toronto, Ont.), 0829-8777* ***to form*** *Canadian Index (Toronto, Ont.), 1192-4160.*

CN/0225-7459
CANADIAN NEWS INDEX (TORONTO). (CANADIAN NEWS INDEX : ANNUAL CUMULATION.). [Can. news index]. Vol. 4, No. 1-12 (Jan.-Dec. 1980)-. English. an. Micromedia Limited, 20 Victoria Street, Toronto Ontario M5C 2N8 Canada. **Tel** (416)362-5211, (800)387-2689, FAX (416)362-6161, telex 06524668. **ED** Luci Lemieux. **LC** AI3; .C2414. **DD** 071/.1. **Bk Rev. Ad Acc.** ctrl circ. ***Continues*** *Canadian Newspaper Index (Annual Cumulation), 0384-983X.*
Desc: A key reference tool designed to provide bibliographic access to Canada's daily newspapers.

CN/1043-7495
CANADIAN NEWSPAPER CIRCULATION FACTBOOK. [Can. newsp. circ. factbook]. **Added/Corp** Audit Bureau of Circulations. (1988)-. English. Audit Bureau of Circulations, 151 Bloor Street West, Toronto Ontario M5S 1S4 Canada. **Tel** (312)885-0910, FAX (416)962-5844. **DD** 071. ***Continues*** *ABC Canadian Daily/Weekly Newspaper Circulation Factbook, 0278-162X.*

CN/0824-3646
CANMORE LEADER. [Canmore lead.]. (1983)-. Newspaper. English. wk. 38.13Can$ Canmore Banss and Cochrane in Canada; 48.13Can$ Canada; 78.13Can$ other. Black Tusk Holdings, PO Box 1320, Canmore Alberta T0L 0M0 Canada. **Tel** (403)678-2365, FAX 6782996. **ED** Bob Warwick. **DD** 071/.1233. **Bk Rev. Ad Acc. Circ:** 2,600.
Desc: Community newspaper that also publishes two tourist guide publications, and printing of all types.

CN/0713-0139
CANTONS. (LES CANTONS / ASSOCIATION CULTURELLE ET TOURISTIQUE DES CANTONS.). [Cantons]. **VFOAT** Journal les Cantons; Progres de Magog. Vol. 1, No. 1 June 15 1981-. Newspaper. French. mo. Journal les Cantons, c/o Progres de Magog, 287 Ouest rue Principale, Magog Quebec J1X 2A8 Canada. **DD** 917.14/6044.

CN/0227-1192
CARDSTON CHRONICLE, THE. [Cardston chron.]. Vol. 1 (Jan. 15, 1980)-. Newspaper. English. Fifty-two times a year (Tues.). 28.13Can$ Cardston; 43.13Can$ Canada; 83.13Can$ others. Cardston Chronicle, Box 8, Cardston Alberta T0K 0K0 Canada. **Tel** (403)653-3607. **DD** 071.123/4. ***Supersedes*** *Westwind News, 0319-1664.*
Ind/Abst Bibliogr. Carto.

CN/0704-0792
CARIBOU, LE. V. 1- March 28, 1977-. Newspaper. French. wk. Free. Le Caribou, 131 Rue D'Auteuil, Thetford-Mines, Quebec G6B 2N3. **DD** 071/.14/575.

CN/0823-7557
CARSTAIRS COURIER, THE. [Carstairs cour.]. V. 1, No. 1 (Nov. 30, 1982)-. Newspaper. English. wk. Free to residents. Carstairs Courier, PO Box 40, Irricana Alberta T0M 0B0 Canada. **DD** 071/.1233.

CN/0820-7402
CASAULT FOL. (LE CASAULT FOL : JOURNAL DES ETUDIANTS EN JOURNALISME DE L'UNIVERSITE LAVAL.). [Casault fol]. Vol. 1, No. 1 (March 1981)-. Newspaper. French. Three times a year. 20.00Can$ (individuals), 24.00Can$ (institutions), 14.00Can$ (students). Casault Fol, a/s Pavillon Casault, Local 5453, Quebec Quebec G1K 7P4 Canada. **Tel** (418)656-7588. **ED** Roger de la Garde. **DD** 378.714/471. Index available. cum. index. **Bk Rev. Circ:** 500.
Desc: Scientific, university-based journal covering theory of communication, media studies, journalism and journalistic practices. Contains articles, book reviews and research notes.

CN/1185-1899
CASTLEGAR SUN, THE. [Castlegar sun]. (Nov. 28, 1990)-. Newspaper. English. wk. 53.50Can$. Castlegar Sun, 465 Columbia Avenue, Castlegar, British Columbia V1N 1G8 Canada. **Tel** (604)365-5266. **DD** 071/.1162. **Ad Acc.**

CN/0707-4956
CASTOR REVIEW. V. 1- Oct. 1977-. Newspaper. English. mo. $3.00. Sailboat and Sailing Journal, PO Box 21176, San Jose CA 95151. **DD** 071/.13/85.

CN/0705-9124
CELTA SOCIAL. Began publication in 1976 or 1977. Newspaper. Spanish. $10.00. Centro Gellego de Toronto, 973 College Street, Toronto Ontario M6H 1A6 Canada. **DD** 071/.13/541. ***Supersedes*** *Celta, 0705-9116.*

CN/0701-0842
CENTRAL BUTTE STAR, THE. V. 1- Oct. 20, 1976-. English. wk. $5.00. H. Friedel, Box 460, Central Butte, Sask S0H 0t0 Canada. **DD** 071/.124/3.

CN/0832-2414
CHAPLEAU SENTINEL. (THE CHAPLEAU SENTINEL [MICROFORM].). [Chapleau sentin.]. (Nov. 19, 1964)-. English. Fifty-one times per year. 30.00Can$ Canada; 46.00Can$ US. Chapleau Sentinel, PO Box 158, 17 Young Street, Chapleau ONT P0M 1K0 Canada. **Tel** (705)864-0640, FAX (705)864-2317. **ED** Rene C. Decosse. **DD** 071/.13133. **Ad Acc, Adv Mgr:** Michelle, **Tel** (705)864-0640. **Circ:** 1,400 (ctrl).

CN/1185-5614
CHATHAM THIS WEEK. [Chatham this week]. Vol. 1, No. 1 (Feb. 20, 1991)-. Newspaper. English. wk. Limited free distribution. Chatham This Week, 234 Queen Street, Chatham Ontario N7M 2H1 Canada. **DD** 071/.1333.

CN/1185-5614
CHATHAM THIS WEEK. (CHATHAM THIS WEEK [MICROFORM].). [Chatham this week]. Vol. 1, No. 1 (Feb. 20, 1991)-. English. Ontario Community Newspapers Association, PO Box 451, 1184 Speers Road, Oakville Ontario L6J 5A8. **DD** 071/.1333.

CN/0702-7982
CHATSWORTH RECORD AND THE QUEEN'S BUSH QUILL, THE. Began publication in 1974. Newspaper. English. The Chatsworth Record, Box 128, Chatsworth Ontario N0H 1G0. **DD** 071/.13/18.

CN/0225-7017
CHELSEY OVERVIEW. **VFOAT** Overview. V. 1- June 1979-. Newspaper. English. wk. $7.00. Chesley Overview, PO Box 560, Chesley Ontario N0G 1L0 Canada. **DD** 071/.1318.

CN
CHEVRON, THE. (1960)-. Newspaper. English. ir. University of Waterloo Federation of Students, Waterloo Ontario Canada.

Canada

CN/0821-7696
CHIEFTAIN (IROQUOIS). (THE CHIEFTAIN.). [Chieftain]. Vol. 1, No. 1 (June 9, 1982)-. Newspaper. English. wk (Weds.). 23.00Can$ (Iroquis County), 33.00Can$ (in 60 mile radius), 42.00Can$ (others) Canada; 96.00Can$ others. The Chieftain, PO Box 529 Shopping Plaza, Iroquois Ontario K0E 1K0 Canada. **Tel** (613)652-4395. **ED** Shelley Cumberland (phone: (613)652-4576). **DD** 071/.1375. Index available. cum. index. **Bk Rev. Ad Acc, Adv Mgr:** Sharron Bolte. **Circ:** 2,100. *Continues Iroquois Post.*

CN/0707-3860
CHINOOK REPORTER. Vol. 1 (March 20, 1978)_. Newspaper. English. wk. Lethbridge Herald, PO Box 670, Lethbridge Alberta T1J 3Z7 Canada. **DD** 071/.123/4.

CN/0828-1807
CHRONICLE-HERALD, THE. [Chron.-Her.]. (1949)-. Periodical. English. da. 117.00Can$ US; 65.00Can$ Canada (Saturday by mail), 105.00Can$ (6 days a week by carrier), 387.50Can$ Canada; 697.00Can$ US (6 days a week by surface mail). Halifax Herald Ltd, 1650 Argyle Street, PO Box 610, Halifax Nova Scotia B3J 2T2 Canada. **Tel** (902)426-2811. **DD** 071.1622.

CN/0712-7464
CHRONIQUE (LAC BEAUPORT). (LA CHRONIQUE.). [Chronique]. Vol. 1, No. 1 (Sept. 1980)-. Newspaper. French. mo. $2.00. La Municipalite de Beauport la Chronique, c/o La Mairie, CP 159, 5 Chemin la Tour du Lac, Lac Beauport Quebec G0A 2C0 Canada. **DD** 071/.1447. *Continues Passe-Montagne.*

CN/0704-7282
CISILUTE. (LA CISILUTE.). **Added/Corp** Fogolars Federation of Canada. (May 1973)-. Newspaper. Italian (summaries and/or abstracts in English). ir. Free to Friulans across Canada. La Cisilute, PO Box 427, Rexdale Ontario M9W 5L4 Canada. **DD** 071/.1.

CN/0319-5198
CITES NOUVELLES. (March 1974)-. Newspaper. French (English). Fifty-one times per year. 75.00Can$ Canada; 90.00Can$ other. Cites Nouvelles, 15716 Gouin Boulevard, Ste Genevieve H9H 1C4 Canada. **Tel** (514)620-0781, FAX (514)620-3705. **ED** Publications Demont (editor's address: 9216 Boivin LaSalle, Quebec, Canada (363-3106). **DD** 071/.1427. cum. index. **Bk Rev. Ad Acc, Adv Mgr:** Marc Forge, **Tel** (514)6200781. **Circ:** 57,000.

CN/0712-1075
CITIZEN. CAPITAL IDEAS, THE. [Citiz., Cap. ideas]. **VFOAT** Capital Ideas. No. 1 (June 7, 1978)-. Newspaper. English. da. $131.56. Citizen / Canada, 1101 Baxter Road, Box 5020, Ottawa Ontario K2C 3M4 Canada. **Tel** (613)596-1950. **DD** 071/.1384.

CN/0829-9269
CITIZEN (SAINT JOHN, N.B.). (THE CITIZEN.). [Citizen]. Vol. 1, No. 1 (March 1985)-. Newspaper. English. wk. Free. The Citizen / Canada, PO Box 6190 Station A, Saint John New Brunswick, E2L 4RL Canada. **Tel** (506)632-4388. **DD** 071/.1532. available on microfiche (from Oakville, Ont. : Ontario Community Newspapers Association).

CN/0822-8957
CITOYEN (COWANSVILLE). (LE CITOYEN.). [Citoyen]. Newspaper. French. wk. Free. Les Publications Le Citoyen, 238 1st Avenue, Box 208, Asbestos Quebec G1T 1Y4 Canada. **Tel** (819)879-5409. **DD** 071.14/62.

CN/0229-3943
CITOYEN (NORMETAL). (LE CITOYEN : JOURNAL INTERMUNICIPAL, SECTEUR NORD.). [Citoyen]. Newspaper. French. mo. $0.25 per no. Le Citoyen, CP 368, Normetal Quebec J02 3A0 Canada. **DD** 071/.1417.

CN/0316-0211
CLARION (CAPREOL). (THE CLARION.). Began publication June 15, 1972. Newspaper. English. wk. 15.00Can$ per no. T and E Poole, PO Box 1027, Capreol Ontario P0M 1H0 Canada. **DD** 071/13/133.

CN/0834-6151
CLINTON NEWS-RECORD. MICROFORM. [Clint. news-rec.]. **VFOAT** Clinton News Advertiser; Clinton Record News. English. Clinton News-Record, PO Box 39 Canada. **DD** 071/.1322.

CN/0707-6916
COASTAL COURIER. (THE COASTAL COURIER.). (Sept. 14, 1977)-. Newspaper. English. Fifty-two times a year. 41.00Can$ Canada; 51.50Can$ other. Bay Publishing Company, PO Box 369, Grace Bay Nova Scotia B1A 5V5 Canada. **Tel** (902)849-1830. **DD** 071/.16/95.

CN/0707-2325
COASTER, THE. V. 1- Sept. 9, 1978-. Newspaper. English. bw. $20.00 Canada; $30.00 other. Bebb Publishing, Box 623, Grand Falls Newfoundland A2A 2K2. **DD** 071/.18.

CN/0319-745X
COCHRANE TIMES. V. 1- May 15, 1974-. Newspaper. English. wk. Cochrane Times, PO Box 776, Cochrane Alberta T0L 0W0 Canada. **Tel** (403)932-2055. **ED** M Maxie. **DD** 071/.123/3. **Bk Rev. Ad Acc. Circ:** 2,300 (ctrl).
Desc: Weekly community newspaper. Covers all general news in area surrounding Cochrane Alberta.

CN/0711-2181
COLDWATER JOURNAL, THE. [Coldwater j.]. Vol. 1, No. 1 (July 18, 1979)-. Newspaper. English. wk. Free. The Coldwater Journal, Box 280, Coldwater Ontario L0K 1E0. **DD** 071/.1317.

CN/1182-9095
COLLINGWOOD CONNECTION, THE. [Collingwood connect.]. Vol. 1, Ed. 1 (July 15, 1990)-. Newspaper. English. wk. Limited free distribution. James E. Baker, 150 St. Paul Street, Collingwood, Ontario L9Y 3P2 Canada. **DD** 071/.1317.

CN/0710-0078
COLLINGWOOD TIMES, THE. [Collingwood times]. **VFOAT** Times. **VAT** Times (Collingwood). (1980)-. Newspaper. English. wk. 11.00Can$. Collingwood Times, Box 339, Elmvale Ontario L0L 1PQ Canada. **Tel** (705)322-1871. **DD** 071/.1317. available on microfiche (from Oakville, Ont. : Ontario Community Newspapers Association).

CN/0824-5800
COMERCIO (TORONTO. 1982). (EL COMERCIO.). [Comercio]. Vol. 1 No. 1 (April 15 1982)-. Newspaper. Spanish. bw. $12.00. J Fernandez, PO Box 592, Station U, Toronto Ontario M8Z 5Y9. **DD** 980/.005.

CN/0710-0086
COMMUNITY REFLECTION. [Community reflect.]. Newspaper. English. wk. $10.40. Community Reflections, 299 Lawrence Avenue, Kitchener Ontario N2M 1Y5 Canada. **DD** 071/.1345.

CN/0382-8794
COMUNIDADE (HULL). (COMUNIDADE.). [Comunidada]. Yearly V. 1- Jan. 1974-. Portuguese. 0.25Can$ per no. Comunidade, 140 Wright Street, Hull Quebec J8X 2G9 Canada. **DD** 071/.13/83.

CN/0228-0515
CONFLUENCE (FORT SIMPSON). (CONFLUENCE.). V. 1- March 1977-. Newspaper. English. wk. 0.25Can$ per no. MacKenzie News, Confluence, PO Box 346, Fort Simpson Northwest Territories X03 0N0 Canada. **DD** 071/.193.

CN/0317-381X
CONSUMER GUIDES (KAPUSKASING). (THE CONSUMER GUIDES.). V. 1- Nov. 10, 1971-. Newspaper. English. wk. Free. King's Printing and Stationery Ltd, 9-11 O'Brien Avenue, Kapuskasing Ontario P5N 1X4 Canada. **DD** 071/.13/132.

CN/0226-9074
CONTACT WEST ISLAND. [Contact West Island]. Vol. 1, Ed. 1 (Nov. 21, 1979)-. Newspaper. English (French). wk. Free. Contact West Island, 88 Donegani, Pointe-Claire Quebec H9R 2V4 Canada. **DD** 071/.1428.

CN/0226-6385
CONTINUUM (MONTREAL). (CONTINUUM.). [Continuum]. V. 1- Sept. 6, 1977-. Newspaper. French. wk. Continuum / Canada, Federation des Associations Etudiantes du Campus de l'Universte de Montreal, Local 1267, 3200 rue Jean Brillant, Montreal Quebec H3T 1N8 Canada. **Tel** (514)343-5988. **ED** Staphane Kelly and Yves Jubinville. **DD** 378.714/281. **Ad Acc. Circ:** 15,000 (ctrl).
Desc: Informs student's on Montreal's University affairs and generally on social, cultural and world events.

CN
CORNER BROOK WESTERN STAR. Newspaper. English. da. 202.14Can$ Newfoundland & Labrador; 254.95Can$ Corner Brook; 225.23Can$ others in Canada; 310.74Can$ others. Corner Brook Western Star, PO Drawer 460, Corner Brook Newfoundland, A2H 6E7 Canada. **Tel** (709)634-4348. **ED** Richard Williams. **Ad Acc, Adv Mgr:** Dan Johnson, **Tel** (709)634-4348. ctrl circ.

CN/0836-4915
COTEAU REVIEW. *Ceased.* [Coteau rev.]. Vol. 1 (July 1, 1986)-(19??). Newspaper. English. wk. Country View Publishing, Box 151, Beechy Saskatchewan S0L 0C0 Canada. **Tel** (306)809-2050. **DD** 071/.1243.

CN/1182-9974
COUNTRY CONNECTION (NORTH BATTLEFORD). (COUNTRY CONNECTION.). [Ctry. connect.]. (1990)-. Newspaper. English. wk. $17.00. Country Connection, Number 201-1106, 101st Street, North Battleford, Saskatchewan S9A 0Z6 Canada. **DD** 051.

CN/0715-545X
COUNTY NEIGHBOURS. (THE COUNTY NEIGHBOURS.). [Cty. neighb.]. (1978)-. Newspaper. English. wk. Free. County Neighbours, c/o Beacon Herald, 108 Ontario Street, Stratford Ontario N5A 6T6 Canada. **DD** 071/.1323.

CN/0710-3786
COUP D'OEIL (NAPIERVILLE). (COUP D'OEIL.). [Coup d'oeil]. Vol. 1, No. 1; Oct. 25, 1978-. Newspaper. French. wk. Free. Journal Coup d'Oeil, 412 Saint Jacques, Napierville Quebec J0J 1L0 Canada. **DD** 071/.1438.

CN/0045-8872
COURIER (CANADA. CANADIAN FORCES BASE (COLD LAKE, ALTA.)). (COURIER / CANADIAN FORCES BASE COLD LAKE.). [Cour. - Can. Forces Base Cold Lake]. **Added/Corp** Canada. Canadian Forces Base (Cold Lake, Alta.). **VFOAT** Canadian Forces Base Cold Lake Courier. (1967)-. Newspaper. English. Twenty-two times a year. Free to residents of Cold Lake; 20.00Can$ Canada; 25.00Can$ other. Cold Lake Courier, PO Box 2350, Medley Alberta T0A 2M0 Canada. **Tel** (403)594-5206. **ED** Fran Iverson. **DD** 358.4/17/0971233. **Bk Rev. Ad Acc. Circ:** 3,100 (ctrl).

CN/0316-0262
COURIER (ORLEANS). (THE COURIER.). V. 1- Nov. 16, 1973-. Newspaper. English. mo. Wynnmur Publications, PO Box 709, Orleans Ontario K0A 2V0. **DD** 071/.13/83.

CN/0707-4905
COURIER WEEKEND. Vol. 1 (Mar. 4, 1978)-. Newspaper. English. wk (Friday). $45.26 Charlotte County, Nebraska; $51.26 Washington County, Maine; $65.26 other US; $88.26 other. St Croix Printing & Publishing Company, PO Box 250, St. Stephen New Brunswick E3L 2X2 Canada. **Tel** (506)466-3220, FAX (506)466-4718. **ED** Laura Haley. **DD** 071/.15/33. **Ad Acc. Circ:** 4,743. available on microfilm.
Desc: An international community newspaper covering local international issues.

CN/0228-6645
COURRIER DE GRAND'MERE, LE. [Courr. Grand'Mere]. **VFOAT** Courrier. Newspaper. French. wk. $6.00. Publi-Page, 578 8E Rue, Grand-Mere, Quebec G9T 4K5 Canada. **DD** 071/.14465. *Continues Metropolitain.*

CN/0226-9139
COURRIER DE LOTBINIERE, LE. [Courr. Lotbiniere]. 13 June 1978-. Newspaper. French. wk. Free. Editions De Niolet, 1000, Rue St. Joseph, Laurier-Station Quebec G0S 1N0. **DD** 017/.1458. ctrl circ.

CN/0228-6297
COURRIER DE PORTNEUF, LE. [Courr. Portneuf]. **VFOAT** Courrier. **VAT** Courrier (Donnacona). Vol. 1, No. 1 (Nov. 8, 1977)-. Periodical. French. wk. 78.26Can$. Le Courrier de Portneuf, CP 1030, Donnacona Quebec G0A 1T0 Canada. **Tel** 011 418 285-0211. **DD** 071/.14466.

CN
COURRIER DE ST. HYACINTHE, LE. Newspaper. Fifty-two times a year (Wednesdays). 46.68Can$. Le Courrier de St. Hyacinthe, 655 Avenue Ste. Anne, St. Hyacinthe J2S 5G4 Canada. **Tel** (514)773-6028, FAX (514)773-3115. available on microfilm.

CN/0710-4561
COURRIER DU SURVENANT, LE. Vol. 1, No. 1 (Sept. 21 1981)-. Newspaper. French. wk. Free. Courrier Du Survenant, 645 Route Marie-Victorin, Tracy Quebec J3R 1K9 Canada. **DD** 071/.1451.

CN/0710-9938
COURRIER EXPRESS DE VAUDREUIL-SOULANGES, LE. [Courr. express Vaudreuil-Soulanges]. **VFOAT** Courrier Express. **VAT** Courrier Express (Dorion). V. 1, No. 1, (June 11, 1980)-. Newspaper. French. wk. Free. Le Courrier Express, CP 37, Dorion Quebec J7V 5V8 Canada. **DD** 071/.1426.

CN/0704-0474
COURRIER FRONTENAC. **VFOAT** Courrier de Frontenac. (Mar. 1977)-. Newspaper. French. wk. 235.00Can$. Courrier de Frontenac, PO Box 789, Thetford Mines Quebec G6G 5V3, Canada. **Tel** (418)338-5181, FAX (418)338-5482. **DD** 071/.4/57. **Bk Rev. Ad Acc. Circ:** 18,746 (ctrl).
Desc: Regional news (in general).

CN/0829-2442
COURRIER LAURENTIDES (EDITION EST). (COURRIER LAURENTIDES.). [Courr. Laurent.]. Vol. 40, No. 2 (29 Feb. 1984)-. Newspaper. French. wk. 103.26Can$. Les Hebdos du Bloc Nord, 17 Rue Montmorency, Laval Rapids Quebec, H7N1X1 Canada. **Tel** (514)667-1500. **DD** 071/.1425. **Ad Acc.** *Continues in part Courrier Laurentides.*

CN/0712-6794
COURRIER SAINT-HUBERT. [Courr. Saint-Hubert]. Vol. 1, No. 1 (24 Mar. '82)-. Newspaper. French. wk. Free. Courrier Saint-Hubert, 1136 Rue Victoria, Ville Lemoyne, Quebec Canada. **DD** 071/.1437.

CN/0703-9220
COWICHAN NEWS. Began publication in 1976. Newspaper. English. wk. Free. Cowichan Valley News, 101A-2255 Canada Avenue, Duncan BC V9L 1T6. **DD** 071/.11/34.

CN/0708-0239
CRANBROOK'S RESPONSE. V. 1- July 4, 1978-. Newspaper. English. sw. $10.00. Cranbrook's Response, 915 Baker Street, Cranbrook British Columbia V1C 1A4 Canada. **DD** 071/.11/45.

CN/0842-5205
CROSS-COUNTRY CONNECTION, THE. ***Ceased.*** [Cross-ctry. connect.]. Vol. 1, No. 1 (Aug. 2, 1988)-(1992). Newspaper. English. wk. The Cross-Country Connection, POB 580, Bengough Saskatchewan S0C 0K0 Canada. **DD** 071/.1244.

CN/0822-8299
CROSSFIELD CHRONICLE. [Crossfield chron.]. (May 18, 1982)-. Newspaper. English. wk. Airdrie & District Echo Publishing Company, PO Box 580, Airdrie Alberta T0M 0B0 Canada. **DD** 071/.1233.

CN
CROSSROADS (SHOAL LAKE, MAN.). (CROSSROADS.). Vol. 1, No. 1 (Apr. 22, 1982)-. Newspaper. English. wk. 15.00Can$ Canada; 35.50Can$ US. Crossroads / Manitoba, PO Box 160, Shoal Lake Manitoba R0J 1Z0 Canada. **Tel** (204)759-2644, FAX (204)759-2521. **ED** Gregory Nesbitt. **DD** 071/.1273. **Bk Rev. Ad Acc. Circ:** 6,200 (ctrl).
Desc: General news, sports and advertising.

CN/0822-6261
D.O.T.C. NEWS (1983). (D.O.T.C. NEWS / DAKOTA OJIBWAY TRIBAL COUNCIL.). [D.O.T.C. news]. **Added/Corp** Dakota Ojibway Tribal Council. **VAT** Dakota Ojibway Tribal Council News (1982); DOTC News (1982). Vol. 8, No. 3 (Mar. 1982)-. Newspaper. English. mo. 8.00Can$ Canada; $10.00 US. Dakota Ojibway Tribal Council, PO Box 31148, 702 Douglas Street, Brandon Manitoba R7A 5Z2 Canada. **Tel** (204)725-3560. **ED** Janice Daniels. **DD** 971.27/00497. **Ad Acc. Circ:** 1,500 (ctrl). ***Continues*** *Dakota Ojibway Tribal Council News, 0822-6253.*
Desc: Published for the eight DOTC reserves. It's contents include happenings from each reserve, school activities, and items of native interest. These items must not be politically oriented.

CN
DAILY GLEANER. (1???)-. Periodical. English. da. 210.00Can$ Canada, 300.00Can$ others (daily by mail); 63.15Can$ Canada, 62.70Can$ others (Saturday by mail). Daily Gleaner, Box 3370, Fredericton NB E3B 5A2 Canada. **Tel** (506)452-6671.

CN/0832-4298
DAILY GRAPHIC (PORTAGE LA PRAIRIE. 1954). (THE DAILY GRAPHIC [MICROFORM].). [Dly. graph.]. (1954)-. English. da. 101.65Can$. Bowes Publishers Limited, Box 130 Portage la Prairie, Manitoba R1N 3B4 Canada. **Tel** (204)857-3427, FAX (204)239-1270. **ED** Simon Blake. **DD** 071/.1273. **Ad Acc, Adv Mgr:** Barry Clayton. **Circ:** 5,000 (ctrl). ***Continues*** *The Portage la Prairie Daily Graphic, 0832-428X.*

CN
DAILY MINER & NEWS. Newspaper. English. da. 104.00Can$ Canada; 240.00Can$ others. Bowes Publishers, PO Box 7400 Station E, London Ontario N5Y 4X3 Canada. **Tel** (519)472-7601, FAX (519)473-2256. **ED** Ross Porter, (phone: (519)568-5555). **Ad Acc.**

CN/0715-4321
DAILY NEWS HALIFAX-DARTMOUTH EDITION. (THE DAILY NEWS.). [Dly. news]. (1981)-. Newspaper. English. da. 242.06Can$ Canada, 368.26Can$ others (Monday thru Saturday by mail); 200.46Can$ Canada, 465.66Can$ other (Halifax NS daily). Daily News / Halifax, PO Box 8330, Station A, Halifax Nova Scotia B3K 5M1 Canada. **Tel** (902)465-1222. **ED** Lyndon Watkins. **DD** 071/.1622. **Bk Rev. Ad Acc. Circ:** 22,000 (ctrl). available on microfilm.
Desc: General interest pertaining to Halifax, Dartmouth, Nova Scotia, Canada.

CN/0225-7025
DALMENY REVIEW. [Dalmeny rev.]. V. 1- Sept. 15, 1977-. Newspaper. English. bw. $4.00 Saskatchewan, $5.00 Canada, and $6.00 other countries. G Grimsdale, Dalmeny Review, PO Box 249, Dalmeny Saskatchewan S0K 1E0 Canada. **DD** 071/.1242.

CN/0833-3831
DAN SHA. ***Ceased.*** [Dan sha]. **Added/Corp** Ye Sa To Communications Society. **VFOAT** Native Sun. Vol. 13, No. 1 (Jan. 10, 1986)-(19??). Newspaper. English. Twelve times a year. Ye Sa to Communications Society, 22 Nisutlin Drive, Whitehorse Yukon Y1A 3S5 Canada. **Tel** (403)667-2775, (403)667-6923. **ED** Eric Huggard. **DD** 971.9/100497. **Ad Acc**. ctrl circ. ***Continues*** *Yukon Indian News, 0382-7305.*

CN/0826-273X
DEFI (OTTAWA). (LE DEFI.). [Defi]. Vol. 1, No. 1 (17 Jan. 1984)-. Newspaper. French. wk. Defi / Universite d'Ottawa, Local 348/85 rue Hastey, Ottawa Ontario K1N 6N5 Canada. **DD** 378.713/84.

CN
DELHI NEWS RECORD. English. wk. 23.36Can$ Canada; 95.00Can$ US; 120.00Can$ other. NCC Publishing, 222 Argyle Avenue, Delhi Ontario N4B 2Y2 Canada. **Tel** (519)582-2513, FAX (519)582-4040.

CN/0710-1422
DELTA OPTIMIST, THE. [Delta optimist]. Newspaper. English. tw (Tues., Fri., and Sun.). $70.00. Ernest Bexley Publisher, PO Box 40, Delta British Columbia V4K 3N5 Canada. **Tel** (604)946-4451, FAX (604)946-5680. **DD** 071/.1133. **Bk Rev. Ad Acc. Circ:** 13,000 (ctrl).

CN/0839-2676
DEUTSCHE PRESSE (TORONTO. GERMAN ED.). (DEUTSCHE PRESSE : THE LARGEST GERMAN NEWSPAPER PRINTED IN TORONTO / WOECHENTLICHES ORGAN DER DEUTSCHSPRACHIGEN BEVOELKERUNG IN KANADA.). [Dtsch. Presse]. **VFOAT** German Press. Vol. 4, No. 14 (Apr. 1982)-. Newspaper. German. wk. 77.85Can$ Canada; 132.85Can$ other. Deutsche Presse, 455 Spadina Avenue Suite 303, Toronto Ontario Canada. **Tel** (416)595-9714. **DD** 971/.00431/05. ***Continues*** *Oesterreicher (Toronto, Ont.), 0712-6395.*

CN
DEVOIR (MONTREAL, QUEBEC). (LE DEVOIR.). (1910)-. Newspaper. French. da. 141.55Can$ daily Mon-Fri by carrier; $900.72 US, $1,013.01 others daily & Sat. (airmail); 205.95Can$ Canada, 699.17Can$ others daily & Sat. (surface mail); $196.70 US, $260.42 others Sat. (airmail); 67.00Can$ Canada, 225.94Can$ other Sat. (surface mail); $704.01 US, $752.59 others daily Mon-Fri (airmail); 155.95Can$ Canada, 494.23Can$ others daily Mon-Fri (surface mail). Le Devoir, 2050 de Bleury 9E Etage, Montreal Quebec H3A 3M9 Canada. **Tel** (514)985-3355.

CN/0710-5495
DEVON DISPATCH, THE. [Devon dispatch]. Vol. 1, No. 1 (May 27, 1976)-. Newspaper. English. wk. 23.16Can$ (within forty mile radius to Devon), 27.16Can$ other. Devon Dispatch, Box 479, Devon Alberta T0C 1E0 Canada. **Tel** (403)987-2222. **ED** Hugh Johnston. **DD** 071/.1233. **Ad Acc. Circ:** 1,546 (ctrl).

CN/0316-683X
DIDSBURY BOOSTER AND MOUNTAIN VIEW COUNTY NEWS. Vol. 13, No. 2 (Jan. 8, 1974)-. Newspaper. English. Fifty times a year. 24.00Can$ Canada; 37.50Can$ other. Didsbury Review, PO Box 760, Didsbury Alberta T0M 0W0 Canada. **Tel** (403)335-3301, FAX (403)335-8143. **ED** Janice Harington. **DD** 071/.123/3. **Ad Acc, Adv Mgr:** Alison Wright. **Circ:** 2,100 (ctrl). ***Formed by the union of*** *Didsbury Booster, 0316-6848;* ***Didsbury Pioneer and*** *Mountain View County News.*

CN/0710-1619
DOWNTOWNER (TORONTO). (THE DOWNTOWNER.). [Downtowner]. Vol. 1, No. 1 (Nov. 7, 1979)-. Newspaper. English. wk. Free. The Downtowner, 33 Britain Street, Toronto Ontario M5A 3Z3 Canada. **DD** 071/.13541. ctrl circ.

CN/0714-637X
DRUMHELLER MAIL. (1911)-. Newspaper. English. wk. 22.00Can$ within 40 miles of Drumheller; 26.00Can$ Canada. Drumheller Mail Ltd, PO Box 1629, Drumheller Alberta T0J 0Y0, Canada. **Tel** (403)823-2580. ***Absorbed*** *Drumheller Review, 0714-6388.*

CN/0709-0595
DRUMHELLER SUN, THE. Vol. 12, No. 16 (Aug. 16, 1978)-. Newspaper. English. wk. $7.00 Canada; $8.00 other. The Drumheller Sun, PO Box 1480, Drumheller Alberta T0J 0Y0 Canada. **DD** 071/.123/3. ***Continues*** *Big Country News.*

CN/0821-5847
DURHAM SPECTRUM AND RECREATION. [Durham spectr. recreat.]. Newspaper. English. mo. $0.15 per number. Durham Spectrum and Recreation, 1730 McPherson Ct, Pickering Ontario L1W 3E6 Canada. **DD** 790/.09713/56.

CN/0713-8539
E AKROPOLIS. [Akropolis]. **VFOAT** Acropolis Newspaper. **VAT** Acropolis (Vancouver). (1956)-. Newspaper. Greek, Modern. mo. Akropolis, Suite 215/222 Ash Street, New Westminster British Columbia V3M 3M4 Canada. **DD** 071/.1133.

CN/0821-2171
EAGLEVIEW POST, THE. [Eagleview post]. Vol. 1, No. 1 (Sept. 15, 1981)-. Newspaper. English. wk. Free. The Eagleview Post, PO Box 771, Turner Valley Alberta T0L 2A0 Canada. **DD** 071/.1234. ctrl circ.

CN/0702-9020
EAR FALLS ECHO, THE. Began publication in July 1975. Newspaper. English. wk. 0.20Can$ per no. Ear Falls Echo, Box 54, Ear Falls Ontario P0V 1T0. **DD** 071/.13/112.

CN/0226-5117
EASTERN NEWS (MISSISSAUGA). (EASTERN NEWS.). [East. news]. **VFOAT** Sada-Yi Mashriq. (Aug. 1979)-. Newspaper. Urdu (English). bw. $30.00 Canada; $45.00 other. Eastern News, PO Box 1061 Station B, Mississauga Ontario L4Y 2E0 Canada. **Tel** (416)858-7525. **ED** Masood Khan. **DD** 971.3/54100491412. **Circ:** 5,000.

CN/0707-6908
EASTERN SHORE ECHO. V. 1- Feb. 1977-. Newspaper. English. sm. $.25. Eastern Marine Arts Technology and Crafts Heritage Society, PO Box 186, Sheet Harbour Nova Scotia B0J 3B0 Canada. **DD** 071/.16/22.

CN/0046-1016
EAU VIVE, L'. [Eau vive]. **Added/Corp** Association Culturelle Franco-Canadienne de la Saskatchewan. (1971)-. Periodical. French. Forty-seven times a year. 28.04Can$ (one year), 51.41Can$ (two year). L'Eau Vive, 2606 rue Centrale, Regina Saskatchewan S4N 2N9 Canada. **Tel** (306)347-0481, FAX (306)565-3450. **ED** Francis Potie. **DD** 971.24/004/114. **Bk Rev**, (Qty: 40). **Ad Acc. Circ:** 1,400 (ctrl).
Desc: Community newspaper serving the French people in Saskatchewan.

CN/1182-3100
ECHO. (DAS ECHO.). [Echo]. **VFOAT** Echo Communautaire du Canadien-Allemand; Echo of the German-Canadian Community; Echo der Deutschkanadischen Gemeinschaft. Vol. 10, No. 94 (Dec. 1988)-. Newspaper. German. mo. Das Echo, 20 Boulevard Cremazie West, Montreal Quebec H2P 1C8 Canada. **DD** 053/.1. ***Continues*** *Echo der Deutschkanadischen Gemeinschaft, 0715-5670.*

CN/0844-0905
ECHO ABITIBIEN. (L'ECHO ABITIBIEN [MICROFORME].). [Echo abitib.]. Vol. 1, No. 1 (Jan. 18, 1950)-. French. Five times a year. $67.69 Canada, $85.00 other. Societe Canadienne Microfilm, 464 rue Street Gean, Montreal H24 2S1 Canada. **Tel** (514)288-5404 or (514)288-5591. **DD** 071/.1413. ***Absorbed*** *Gazette du Nord, 0832-462X.*

CN/0823-5503
ECHO DES FRONTIERES, L'. [Echo front.]. Vol. 1, No. 1 (24 May 1983)-. French. wk. Free to citizens. L'Echo des Frontieres, 420, 2E Avenue, Iberville Quebec J2X 2X8. **DD** 071/.1461.

CN/0319-1710
ECLOSION, L'. 27 Nov. 1972-. Newspaper. French. wk. Directeur de l'Eclosion, c/o Services Collectifs Inc, 2410 Chemin, Ste Foy Quebec G1V 1T3 Canada. **DD** 378.714/471.

CN/0710-1708
ECLUSE, L'. [Ecluse]. **VFOAT** Journal l'Ecluse. Vol. 1, No. 1 (28 Jan. 1981)-. Newspaper. French. wk. $20.00. Whellar Print, 810 Rue East Main, Welland Ontario L3B 3Y5, Canada. **DD** 071/.1338.

CN/0383-803X
EDITION SPECIALE. Vol. 1 No. 14 (Jan. 1976)-. Newspaper. French. Fifty-two times a year. 135.00Can$ Comes with Canada Gazette. Canada Communication Group Publishers, Order Processing, Ottawa Ontario K1A 0S9 Canada. **Tel** (819)956-4800, (819)956-4802. **DD** 071/.14/36.

●CN/1189-3281
EDMONTON JEWISH LIFE. [Edmont. Jew. life]. **VFOAT** Jewish Life. (Jan. 10, 1992)-. Newspaper. English. Limited free distribution. N.R. Loomer, 10135-100 Street, Lower Mall-Westin Hotel, Edmonton Alta T5J 0N7. **DD** 071/.123/34088296.

CN
EDMONTON JOURNAL. (Oct. 2, 1911)-. Newspaper. English. da. 675.00Can$ (seven days per week), 145.00Can$ (Saturday only), 135.00Can$ (one day per week Sun.-Fri.) Canada; 1,300 (seven days per week), 210.00 Can$ (Saturday only), 197.00Can$ (one day per week Sun.-Fri.) other. Edmonton Journal, PO Box 2421, Circulation Department, Edmonton Alberta T5J 2S6 Canada. **Tel** (403)498-5500. available on microfilm. ***Continues*** *Evening Journal (Edmonton, Alta.).* **Ind/Abst** PROMT.

CN/0705-405X
EDMONTON SUN, THE. No. 1 (Nov. 12, 1977)-. Newspaper. English. ir (Sun.-Fri.). 195.16Can$ Canada;

494.16Can$ other. Edmonton Sun, 250-4990 92 Avet, Edmonton Alberta T6B 3A1 Canada. **Tel** (403)468-0100. **DD** 071/.123/3.

CN/0710-0272
EGATIKA NEA. (ERGATIKA NEA.). [Ergatika nea]. Newspaper. Greek, Modern. mo. Free. Ergatika Nea, 5359 Park Avenue Canada. **DD** 331.6/2/4950714. ctrl circ.

CN/0704-0229
ELK ISLAND TRIANGLE, THE. Vol. 1 (Aug. 17, 1977)-. Newspaper. English. Fifty-two times a year. 30.16Can$ Canada; 53.16Can$ others. Elk Island Triangle, PO Box 173, Lamont Alberta T0B 2R0 Canada. **Tel** (403)895-2838. **DD** 071/.123/3.

CN/0828-7759
ELK POINT LAKELAND REVIEW. [Elk Point Lakeland rev.]. **VFOAT** Lakeland Review. **VAT** Lakeland Review (1984). (1984)-. Newspaper. English. wk. 18.16Can$ Elk Point, Alberta, Canada; 19.16Can$ other Canada. Elk Point Lakeland Review, PO Box 309, Elk Point Alberta T0A 1A0 Canada. **Tel** (403)724-4087. **ED** Vici Brooker. **DD** 071/.1233. **Ad Acc. Circ:** 2,500 (ctrl). ***Continues*** *Lakeland Review, 0828-7740.*

CN/0226-6350
ELK POINT REFLECTIONS. [Elk Point reflect.]. V. 1- Apr. 10, 1979-. Newspaper. English. wk. $5.00 Canada; $10.00 other. Mannville Reflections, Elk Point Reflections, PO Box 668, Elk Point Alberta T0A 1A0 Canada. **DD** 071/.1233.

CN/0226-6369
ELK POINT SENTINEL. [Elk Point sentinel]. **VFOAT** Sentinel. **VAT** Sentinel (Elk Point). V. 1- Sept. 26, 1979-. Newspaper. English. wk. Elk Point Sentinel, PO Box 608 Canada. **DD** 071/.1233.

CN/0821-7270
ELLENIKA NEA (LONDON, ONT.). (TA ELLENIKA NEA.). [Ell. nea]. **VFOAT** The Hellenic News; Hellenic News. Greek, Modern (English). mo. 10.00Can$ Canada; $15.00 US; $20.00 other. Ta Ellenika Nea, c/o G Drossos, The Hellenic News, 37 Hillsmount Road, London Ontario N6K 1W1 Canada. **Tel** (519)472-4807. **ED** G N Drossos. **DD** 071/.1326. Index available. **Bk Rev. Ad Acc. Circ:** 5,000. available on microfilm.
Desc: A review magazine with news and articles on education, finance, art, literary news, philosophy, science, travel, classified, etc.

CN/0820-7801
ELLENOKANADIKA CHRONIKA. [Ell.kan. chron.]. **VFOAT** Chronika; Hellenic-Canadian Chronicles. (May 20, 1981)-. Newspaper. Greek, Modern (English). wk. 40.00Can$ Canada; $50.00 US. Hellenic Canadian Chronicles, Suite 201/370 Danforth Avenue, Toronto Ontario M4K 1N8 Canada. **Tel** (416)465-4628, FAX 462-0051. **ED** Costis Hadjicostis and Tasos Milionis. **DD** 071/.13541. Index available. **Bk Rev. Ad Acc. Circ:** 6,000 (ctrl).

CN/0046-6387
ELLENOKANADIKON VEMA. [Ellenokan. bema]. **VFOAT** Greek Canadian Tribune. Began in 1963?. Newspaper. Greek, Modern. ir. Ellinokanadika Vima, 5619 Park Avenue, Montreal Quebec 152 Canada. **Tel** (514)272-6873. **DD** 071/.14/281.

●CN/1194-1030
ELMIRA INDEPENDENT. [Elmira indep.]. **VFOAT** Independent. (Sept. 21, 1992)-. Newspaper. English. wk. 26.00Can$ Ontario; 37.00Can$ other Canada; 60.00Can$ other (includes national edition). North Waterloo Publishing Ltd., 15 King Street, Elmira Ontario N3B 2R1 Canada. **Tel** (519)669-5155, FAX (519)669-5928. **ED** Bob Verdun. **DD** 071/.1344. **Ad Acc, Adv Mgr:** Kathy Beisel. **Circ:** 6,800 (ctrl). available on microfiche from OCNA. ***Continues*** *Independent (Elmira, Ont. : Local Ed.), 0834-6720.*
Desc: A community newspaper covering the Elmira and it's trading area in Waterloo, Wellington and Perth counties. Focusing on municipal government, community organizations and youth sports.

CN/1184-1060
ELORA SENTINEL, THE. [Elora sentinel]. Vol. 1, No. 1 (Aug. 21, 1990)-. Newspaper. English. wk. North Waterloo Publishing, 157 Geddes Street, Elora, Ontario N0B 1S0 Canada. **DD** 071/.1342.

CN/0711-4567
ENTRAIDE SOCIALE, L'. Vol. 1 (Sept./Oct. 1981)-. Newspaper. French. mo. $20.00 per issue. Entraide Sociale, Suite 104, 72 Laval, Hull Quebec J8X 3H3. **DD** 361/.97142.

CN/0225-3569
ENTREMETTEUR. (L'ENTREMETTEUR : JOURNAL DE LA COMMUNAUTI ETUDIANTE DU COLLIGE DE L'OUTAOUAIS.). [Entremetteur]. Vol. 1, No. 1 (1 Oct. 1979)-. Newspaper. French. bw. Free. L'Entremetteur, College de L'Outaouais, 333 Boulevard CITE Des Jeunes, Hull Quebec J8y 6M5 Canada. **Tel** 778-6631. **DD** 378.714/221. **Ad Acc. Circ:** 2,500 (ctrl).

CN/0821-0403
ESQUIMALT STAR, THE. [Esquimalt star]. Newspaper. English. Free to residents. Esquimalt Star, 1534 Monterey Avenue, Victoria BC V8R 5V4. **DD** 071/.11/34.

CN
ESSEX FREE PRESS. English. wk. $25.00 (one year). Essex Free Press, 16 Centre Street, Essex Ontario, N8M 1N9 Canada. **Tel** (519) 776-8511.

CN
ESTEVAN MERCURY. Newspaper. English. wk. 23.51Can$. Estevan Mercury, PO Box 730, Estevan Saskatchewan S4A 2A6 Canada. **Tel** (306)634-2654, FAX (306)634-3934. **ED** Jonas Weinrauch. **Ad Acc. Circ:** 4,900 (ctrl).

CN/0711-4761
ETCHEMIN DE ST-ROMUALD, L'. [Etchemin de St-Romuald]. Vol. 1, No. 1 (Nov. 1980)-. Newspaper. French. mo. Free to citizens of St-Romuald. Etchemin De St. Romuald, CP 2180, St. Romuald Quebec G6W 5V5. **DD** 071/.1459.

CN/0712-2624
ETHELBERT ECHO. [Ethelbert echo]. Newspaper. English. Ethelbert Echo, Box 102, Pine River Manitoba R0L 1M6 Canada. **DD** 071/.1272.

CN/0319-4124
ETOILE DE L'OUTAOUAIS-ST-LAURENT, L'. V. 1- 16 Sept. 1968-. Newspaper. French. wk. L'Etoile de l'Outaouais-St-Laurent, 111 rue Dumont, Doroin Quebec J7V 1W9 Canada. **DD** 071.14/26.

CN/0384-7845
EVEIL (SAINT-EUSTACHE). (L'EVEIL.). First issue in 1972?. Newspaper. French. wk. Editions Deux-Montagnes, CP 23 Saint-Eustache Quebec J7R 4K5 Canada. **DD** 071/.14/25.

CN
EVENING PATRIOT. Newspaper. English. ir. 132.60Can$ Prince Edward Islands; 148.60Can$ Canada; 322.00Can$ other. Guardian Patriot, PO Box 760, Charlottetown Prince Edward Islands, C1A 4R7 Canada. **Tel** (902)894-8506.

CN/0839-4164
EXAMINER (BARRIE). (THE EXAMINER [MICROFORM].). [Examiner]. 113th Year, No. 73 (Mar. 28, 1977)-. English. da (Published Mon.-Sat.). $238.60 Within 25 mile radius of Barrie; $504.60 others. Barrie Examiner, PO Box 70, Barrie ONT L4M 4T6 Canada. **Tel** (705)726-6537. **ED** Mike Beaudin. **DD** 071/.1317. **Ad Acc, Adv Mgr:** Chuck McCaren, **Tel** (705)726-6539. **Circ:** 14,750 (ctrl). ***Continues*** *Barrie Examiner,, 0839-4156.*

CN/0823-1915
EXCALIBUR (DOWNSVIEW, ONT.). (EXCALIBUR.). [Excalibur]. Began publication with V. 1, No. 1 (Oct. 7, 1966). Newspaper. English. wk. free. Excalibur Publications, Room 111/Central Square Ross Building, York University, 4700 Keele Street, Downsview Ontario M3J 1P3 Canada. **Tel** (416)736-5238. **ED** Jeannine Amber and Douglas Saunders. **DD** 378.713/541. **Bk Rev. Ad Acc. Circ:** 16,000 (ctrl). available on microfilm; available on microfiche; available in microform.
Desc: York University Community News and Metropolitan Toronto News and Arts coverage. Features student issues, contemporary politics and culture.

CN
EXETER TIMES-ADVOCATE. English. wk. 30.00Can$ residents within 40 mile radius of Exeter in Canada; 60.00Can$ Residents outside 40 mile radius; 99.00Can$ other. Exeter Times-Advocate, PO Box 850, Exeter Ontario Canada. **Tel** (519)235-1331, FAX (519)235-0766. **ED** Adrian Harte. **Ad Acc.** ctrl circ.

CN/0713-5483
EXPRESS (DRUMMONDVILLE). (L'EXPRESS.). [Express]. May 73-. Newspaper. French. wk. 90.00Can$ Canada; 100.00Can$ US. Graphi-Cite, 393 Rue Heriot, Drummondville Quebec J2B 2B1. **ED** Romeo Clement. **DD** 071/.14563. **Ad Acc. Circ:** 32,000 (ctrl).

CN/1183-4323
EXPRESS PLUS. [Express plus]. Vol. 1, No 1 (Mar 1991)-. Newspaper. French. wk. Express Plus, 905 Despres, St-Hyacinthe, Quebec J2S 6L4 Canada. **DD** 071/.14523.

CN/1187-0664
EXTRA! EXTRA! NEWSPAPERS ACROSS CANADA. [Extra! extra! newspap. across Can.]. 1st Print. (1991)-. English. be. $16.50 per volume. H & M Enterprises, Box 29563, Valley Fair Postal Outlet, Maple Ridge, British Columbia V2X 0V2 Canada. **DD** 071/.1/025.

CN/0229-5520
EYE OPENER (YORKTON). (THE EYE OPENER.). [Eye opener]. Newspaper. English. wk. Free. Eye Opener, PO Box 520, Yorkton Saskatchewan S3N 2W4 Canada. **DD** 071/.242.
Ind/Abst Can. Index.

CN/0316-5639
FALCON FLYER. (THE FALCON FLYER.). (Jan. 1973)-. Newspaper. English. mo. $3.60. Garry Lacey, PO Box 217, Falconbridge Ontario P0M 1S0 Canada. **DD** 071/.13/133.

CN/0714-8135
FERGUS-ELORA PHOENIX. **VFOAT** Phoenix. Vol. 1, Issue 1 May 13, 1981. Newspaper. English. wk. $8.00 per year. Phoenix Publishing, 122 St. Andrew Street West, Fergus Ontario N1M 1N5 Canada. **DD** 071/.1342.

CN/0710-5339
FLAMBOROUGH NEWS. ***Ceased.*** [Flamborough news]. Vol. 1, No. 1 (April 29, 1981)-(19??). Newspaper. English. wk. Flamborough News, c/o Brabant Newspapers, 333 Arvin Avenue, Stoney Creek Ontario Canada L8E 2M6. **Tel** (416)561-1090, FAX (416)664-3102. **ED** Dave Butler and Martha Jette. **DD** 071/.1352. Index available. **Ad Acc. Pr Rev. Circ:** 9,300 (ctrl). available on microfiche (from Oakville, Ont. : Ontario Community Newpapers Association).
Desc: Weekly community newspaper.

CN/0715-464X
FOREST HILL VILLAGER. [For. Hill villager]. **VFOAT** Forest Hill Village. Vol. 1, No. 1 (May 26, 1981)-. Newspaper. English. mo. Free. Town Crier Inc., 3 Massey Square, Toronto Ontario M4C 5L5. **DD** 071/.13541. ctrl circ.

CN
FORT FRANCES TIMES. (19??)-. Newspaper. English. wk (published on Wednesday). 28.00Can$ Fort Frances; 42.50Can$ Canada; 130.00Can$ other. Fort Frances Times Ltd, 116 1st Street East, Box 339, Fort Frances Ontario, P9A 3M7 Canada. **Tel** (807)274-5373. **ED** Mike Behan. **Ad Acc, Adv Mgr:** Debbie Logan. ctrl circ. available on microfiche.

CN/0715-4925
FORT MCMURRAY EXPRESS. [Fort McMurray express]. Vol. 1, No. 1 (June 21, 1979)-. Newspaper. English. $0.50 per number. Fort McMurray Express Northstar Communications, 8323 Fraser Avenue, Fort McMurray Alberta T9H 1W9 Canada. **DD** 071/.1232.

CN/0316-7542
FORT MCMURRAY TODAY. [Fort McMurray today]. Vol. 1, (Oct. 8, 1974)-. Newspaper. English. da (Monday-Friday). 48.67Can$ Canada, 123.44Can$ others (Friday only); 208.16Can$ Canada, 248.16Can$ US, 498.16Can$ other (first class mail); 101.95Can$ Canada, 293.53Can$ US, 638.39Can$ others (second class mail). Fort McMurray Today, 8550 Franklin Avenue, PO Bag 4008, Fort McMurray ALB T9H 3G1 Canada. **Tel** (403)743-8186, FAX 790-1006. **ED** Darrell Skidnuk and Mike Beaudinc. **DD** 071/.123/2. Index available. **Bk Rev. Ad Acc. Circ:** 8,300 (ctrl). available on microfilm.
Desc: Contents includes local, national, international news and sports features.

CN/0712-6387
FOUR-TOWN JOURNAL. (THE FOUR-TOWN JOURNAL.). [Four-town j.]. Vol. 1, No. 1 (Oct. 7, 1981)-. Newspaper. English. Forty-nine times a year. 22.80Can$ Canada; $45.00Can$ other. Four-Town Journal, PO Box 68, Langenburg Saskatchewan, SOA 2A0 Canada. **Tel** (306)743-2299. **ED** William Johnston. **DD** 071/.1244. **Ad Acc. Circ:** 1,900 (ctrl). available on microfilm from Saskatchewan Archives Board.

CN/0715-5131
FREE PRESS (SPARWOOD). (THE FREE PRESS.). [Free press]. Vol. 1, No. 1 (Nov. 13, 1981)-. Newspaper. English. sw. 42.00Can$. Free Press / Canada, c/o Fernie Free Press, 342 Second Avenue, Box 1320, Fernie British Columbia V0B 1M0 Canada. **Tel** (604)423-4666. **ED** W Johnson. **DD** 071/.114. **Ad Acc. Circ:** 4,000 (ctrl).

CN/0706-7224
FREELANCER (MAYERTHORPE). (THE FREELANCER.). Vol 1, Apr. 5, (1978)-. Newspaper. English. wk (52 issues). 68.16Can$. Lynard Publishers Ltd, PO Box 785, Mayerthorpe Alberta T0E 1N0 Canada. **Tel** (403)786-2602. **DD** 071/.123/3.

CN/0820-5280
FREIGHTER, THE. [Freighter]. Vol. 1, Issue 1 (Nov. 1983)-. Newspaper. English. wk. 39.00Can$. Norhub Publications Ltd, 550 Lamminen, Timmins Ontario P4N 4R3 Canada. **Tel** (705)268-4282, FAX (705)268-4427. **DD** 071/.13142. **Bk Rev,** (Qty: 6). **Ad Acc, Adv Mgr:** Lou Thibault. **Circ:** 1,000. available on microfiche.

CN/0711-4451
FRIDAY CITIZEN, THE. [Friday citiz.]. Newspaper. English. wk. Free. The Friday Citizen, PO Box 609, Midland Ontario L4R 4L3 Canada. **DD** 071/.1317. ctrl circ.

CN/0707-543X
FRIDAY TIMES. (THE FRIDAY TIMES.). Vol. 1 (May 4, 1977)-. Newspaper. English. wk. Free. Markle Community Newspapers, PO Box 609, Midland Ontario L4R 4L3 Canada. **DD** 071/.13/17. ctrl circ.

CN/0700-9410
FT. GARRY PIONEER. V. 1- Aug. 18, 1976-. English. wk. Reliance Press, 1397 Erin Street, Winnipeg Manitoba R3E 2S9 Canada. **Tel** 694-0173. **DD** 071/.127/4.

CN/1187-0702
GABRIOLA SOUNDER, THE. [Gabriola sound.]. Vol. 1, No. 8 (May 1991)-. Newspaper. English. mo. Limited free distribution. Gabriola Sounder, PO Box 217, Gabriola British Columbia V0R 1X0 Canada. **DD** 071/.112. ***Continues*** *Sounder (Gabriola, B.C.), 1187-0699.*

CN/0703-7198
GAZETTE DE MALARTIC, LA. V. 1- May 1975-. Newspaper. French. mo. 0.25Can$ per no. Gazette De Malartic, CP 1092, Malartic Quebec J0Y 1Z0 Canada. **DD** 071/.14/212.

CN/0227-1206
GAZETTE DU C. L. S. C, LA. [Gaz. C.L.S.C.]. **Main/Corp** Centre Local de Services Communautaires Saint-Hubert. **VAT** Gazette du Centre Local de Services Communautaires St-Hubert. V. 1- July 1977-. Periodical. French. Free. Centre Local de Services Communautaires Saint-Huber, Bureau 225/5245 Boulevard Cousineau, St-Huber Quebec J3Y 6J8 Canada. **DD** 071/.1437. ctrl circ.

CN/0228-9164
GAZETTE (GRAND FALLS). (LA GAZETTE.). [Gazette]. **VFOAT** The Gazette. Newspaper. English (French). wk. 0.25Can$ per number. Henely Publishing, 165 Broadway, Grand Falls NB E0J 1M0. **DD** 071/.1553.

CN/0384-1294
GAZETTE (MONTREAL). (THE GAZETTE.). [Gazette]. (19??)-. Newspaper. English. ds. $832.03 Quebec; $770.40 Canada; $1130.00 US; $1260.00 other. Montreal Gazette, 250 St Antoine Quest West, Montreal Quebec H2Y 3R7 Canada. **Tel** (514)987-2282 ext. 8475. ***Continues*** *The Montreal Gazette.* **Ind/Abst** PROMT.

CN/0834-6518
GEORGETOWN INDEPENDENT. (THE GEORGETOWN INDEPENDENT.). [Georget. indep.]. Vol. 13, Issue 4 (Nov. 6, 1985)-. English. wk. 49.49Can$ Canada; 74.75Can$ other. Georgetown Independent, 211 Armstrong Avenue, Georgetown Ontario L7G 4X5 Canada. **Tel** (416)873-0301. **ED** Robin Inscoe. **DD** 071/.13533. **Ad Acc, Adv Mgr:** S Dorsey. **Circ:** 11,750 (ctrl). ***Continues*** *The Independent Georgetown, 0834-650X.*

CN/0381-9566
GEORGIAN (STEPHENVILLE). (THE GEORGIAN.). (Nov. 5, 1970)-. Newspaper. English (French; summaries and/or abstracts in French). Fifty-two times a year. 80.00Can$ Canada; 150.00Can$ others. Robinson-Blackmore Publishing Ltd, PO Box 129, Grand Falls Newfoundland A2A 2J4 Canada. **Tel** (709)489-2162, FAX (709)489-4817. **DD** 071/.18.

CN/1182-5804
GEORGIAN SUN. [Georgian sun]. **VFOAT** Sun. (1990)-. Newspaper. English. wk. Limited free distribution. Telemedia Community Newspapers, PO Box 609, Midland Ontario L4R 4L3 Canada. **DD** 071/.1317.

CN/1182-5804
GEORGIAN SUN. (GEORGIAN SUN [MICROFORM].). [Georgian sun]. (1990)-. English. Ontario Community Newspapers Association, PO Box 451, 1184 Speers Road, Oakville Ontario L6J 5A8. **DD** 071/.1317.

CN/0834-6275
GERALDTON-LONGLAC TIMES STAR. Vol. 34, No. 17 (Mar. 25, 1981)-. English (French). wk. $27.00 Canada-airmail; $39.00 US and overseas-airmail. Times Star Publishing, Box 490, Geraldton Ontario P0T 1M0 Canada. **Tel** (807)854-1919. **ED** Doug Brydges. **DD** 071/.1312. **Ad Acc, Adv Mgr:** Donna, **Tel** (807)854-1919. **Circ:** 1,900 (ctrl). ***Continues*** *Geraldton Times Star, 1181-4993.*

CN/1187-3388
GERMAN PRESS (TORONTO. 1991). (GERMAN PRESS.). [Germ. press]. Jun-Sept 4 (1991)-. Newspaper. English. mo. $49.35 per year. English Edition of the Deutsche Presse, Suite 303, 455 Spadina Avenue, Toronto Ontario M5S 2G8 Canada. **DD** 971/.00431/05. ***Continues*** *The English Edition to the Deutsche Presse., 1185-3549.*

CN/0702-7796
GLEBE REPORT. V. 1- June, 1973-. Newspaper. English. mo. Free to residents of Glebe area. Pike, 276 Second Avenue, Ottawa Ontario K1S 2H8 Canada. **DD** 071/.13/84. ***Supersedes*** *Glebe News, 0702-780X.*

CN/0704-0202
GLOBAL NEWS. V. 1- June 17, 1977-. Newspaper. English. wk. $21.00 Canada; $21.00 US. Global News, 70 Snidercroft Road Concord, Toronto Ontario L4K 1B1 Canada. **DD** 071/.13/541.

CN/0319-0714
GLOBE AND MAIL, THE. [Globe mail]. (Nov. 23, 1936)-. Newspaper. English. da. 533.18Can$ Canada; 613.18Can$ US; 2254.38Can$ Far East; 1754.14Can$ other. Globe & Mail, 444 Front Street West, Toronto Ontario M5V 2S9 Canada. **Tel** (416)585-5000, FAX (416)585-5249. **[CCC].** available on CD-ROM. ***Formed by the union of*** *Globe* ***and*** *Mail and Empire.* **Ind/Abst** F&S Index Plus Text, Int. [Select. Cov.]; Infomat Int. Bus.; PROMT.

CN/0319-0714
GLOBE AND MAIL. (THE GLOBE AND MAIL [MICROFORM].). [Globe mail]. Vol. 93, No. 27,120 (Nov. 23, 1936)-. English. Twenty-four times a year. 1450.00Can$ positive 35mm vesicular film; 1780.00Can$ positive or negative silver halide film. Globe & Mail, 444 Front Street West, Toronto Ontario M5V 2S9 Canada. **Tel** (416)585-5000, FAX (416)585-5249. **DD** 071/.13541. **[CCC].** ***Formed by the union of*** *Globe (Toronto, Ont. : Daily), 0839-3680.*

CN/0849-8288
GOLDBELT GAZETTE. [Goldbelt gaz.]. Vol. 1, No. 1 (May 24, 1989)-. Newspaper. English. wk. $30.00 (local), $37.00 North America; $100.00 other. Goldbelt Gazette, PO Box 900, Creighton Saskatchewan S0P 0A0 Canada. **Tel** (306)688-3999, FAX (306)688-3919. **ED** Eric Shaw. **DD** 071/.1242. **Ad Acc. Pr Rev. Circ:** 2,000 (ctrl). **Desc:** Community news.

CN/0383-1213
GOLDSTREAM GAZETTE. (Mar. 17, 1976)-. Newspaper. English. Fifty-two times a year. 38.15Can$ Canada; 53.16Can$ US. Goldstream Gazette Weekly, 839 Goldstream Avenue, Victoria British Columbia V9B 2X8 Canada. **Tel** (604)478-9552. **DD** 71/.11/34.

CN/0316-6635
GOULBOURN MIRROR. Vol. 3, No. 1 (Sept. 5, 1974)-. Newspaper. English. wk. $3.50 within 40 miles of Goulbourn township, $4.50 others. Goulbourn Mirror, PO Box 400, Stittsville Ontario K0A 3G0 Canada. **DD** 071/.13/83. ***Formed by the union of*** *Stittsville Review, 0316-6651* ***and*** *Richmond Review, 0316-6643.*

CN/0227-3470
GRAND BEND SUN. (THE GRAND BEND SUN.). [Grand Bend sun]. Vol. 6, No. 26 (June 28, 1979)-. Newspaper. English. Eighteen times a year. 8.00Can$ Canada; 16.00Can$ other. Leader Publications / Canada, Box 490, Dresden Ontario N0P 1M0 Canada. **Tel** (519)882-1270, (519)683-4485. **DD** 071/.1327. ***Continues*** *North Lambton Sun, 0319-5430.*

CN/0833-1014
GRAND FALLS ADVERTISER. (THE GRAND FALLS ADVERTISER H.[MICROFORM].). [Gd. Falls advert.]. Vol. 1, No. 1 (Apr. 8, 1936)-. English. sw. 95.00Can$ Canada; 150.00Can$ other. Robinson-Blackmore Publishing Ltd, PO Box 129, Grand Falls Newfoundland A2A 2J4 Canada. **Tel** (709)489-2162, FAX (709)489-4817. **ED** Kimberly Brett, (phone: 489-2162). **DD** 071/.18. **Ad Acc, Adv Mgr:** B. Andrews. **Circ:** 12,100 (ctrl). **Desc:** This is a community newspaper.

CN
GRAND FORKS GAZETTE. Newspaper. English. wk (Published every Wednesday). 40.00Can$ Canada; 80.00Can$ other. Grand Forks, PO Box 700, 7330 2nd Street, British Columbia, V0H 1H0 Canada. **Tel** (604)442-2191, FAX (604)442-3336. **ED** Alec Tully. **Ad Acc, Adv Mgr:** Sandra Huffner.

CN/0226-6415
GRAND TRUNK POPLAR PRESS, THE. [Grand Trunk poplar press]. **VFOAT** Poplar Press. Vol. 1 (Aug. 22, 1979)-. Newspaper. English. wk. 28.16Can$. Bowes Publishing, 6960 Dreyton Valley, Wildwood Alberta T0E 0M0 Canada. **Tel** (403)542-4379. **DD** 071/.1233. ctrl circ.

CN/0834-616X
GRAND VALLEY STAR AND VIDETTE. (THE GRAND VALLEY STAR AND VIDETTE [MICROFORM].). [Gd. Val. star vidette]. **VFOAT** Star and Vidette. (198?)-. English. Fifty-two times a year (Published on Wednesdays). 22.00Can$ (within 40 mile radius of Grand Valley) Canada; 30.00Can$ others in Canada. Grand Valley Star and Vidette, PO Box 119, 18 Main Street, Grand Valley ONT LON1GO Canada. **Tel** (519)928-2822. **ED** Sheila Duncan (phone: (519)941-2230). **DD** 071/.1341. **Bk Rev. Ad Acc, Adv Mgr:** Shirley Gade, **Tel** (519)941-2230. **Circ:** 1,100. ***Continues*** *Star and Vidette (Grand Valley, Ont.), 1180-6044.*

CN/0715-4488
GRAVELBOURG GAZETTE. [Gravelbourg gaz.]. Vol. 1, No. 1 (Sept. 30, 1981)-. Newspaper. English. wk. 12.00Can$. Gravelbourg Gazette, PO Box 863, Gravelbourg Saskatchewan S0H 1X0 Canada. **DD** 071/.1243.

CN/0710-1082
GRAVENHURST LEADER, THE. [Gravenhurst lead.]. **VFOAT** Leader. V. 1, No. 1 (Jan. 28, 1981)-. Newspaper. English. wk. $10.00 within 40 miles of Gravenhurst, $12.00 elsewhere in Canada. Elinwill Holdings, 160 Muskoka Road South, Gravenhurst Ontario P0C 1G0 Canada. **DD** 071/.1316.

CN/1186-4303
GREENBORO HUNT CLUB PARK NEWS [MICROFORM]. Vol. 1, Issue 1 (Mar. 7, 1991)-. English. Ontario Community Newspapers Association, PO Box 451, 1184 Speers Road, Oakville Ontario L6J 5A8. **DD** 071/.1384.

CN/0821-3038
GREENFIELD PARK JOURNAL. [Greenfield Park j.]. **VFOAT** Greenfield Park Bulletin; Journal of Greenfield Park. Vol. 1, No. 1 (Sept. 23, 1982)-. Newspaper. English (French). wk (published weekly except last two weeks in July). 21.42Can$. Greenfield Park Journal, 574 Victoria Street, Lambert, Quebec, Quebec J4P 2J5 Canada. **Tel** (514)671-0014. **DD** 071/.1437.

CN/0710-5649
GRIFFON (DRUMMONDVILLE). (LE GRIFFON.). [Griffon]. No. 1 Oct 1978-. Newspaper. French. $0.50 per no. Le Griffon, CP 892, Drummondville Quebec J2B 6X1 Canada. **DD** 071/.14563.

CN/0834-6623
GRIMSBY INDEPENDENT. (THE GRIMSBY INDEPENDENT [MICROFORM].). [Grimsby indep.]. Vol. 100, No. 38 (Sept. 18, 1985)-. English. wk. 25.00Can$. Grimsby Independent, PO Box 310, 19 Adelaide Street, Grimsby Ontario L3M 4G5 Canada. **Tel** (905)945-8192, FAX (905)945-0540. **ED** Julie Hendriks. **DD** 071/.1339. **Ad Acc, Adv Mgr:** Robert Van Wyngaarden, **Tel** (905)563-5393. **Circ:** 4,500. available on microfiche. ***Continues*** *Independent (Grimsby, Ont.), 0834-6615.*

CN/0318-1650
GROVE EXAMINER, THE. V. 1- April 2, 1974-. Newspaper. English. wk. 18.00Can$ Canada; 50.00Can$ other. Lynard Publishers Ltd, PO Box 785, Mayerthorpe Alberta T0E 1N0 Canada. **Tel** (403)786-2602. **ED** Heather Bell. **DD** 071/.123/3. **Ad Acc. Circ:** 6,000 (ctrl). **Desc:** Serving community of Spruce Grove with local news and advertising.

CN
GUARDIAN. English. ir. 133.00Can$ Price Edward Islands; 168.00Can$ Canada; 322.00Can$ other. Guardian Patriot, PO Box 760, Charlottetown Prince Edward Islands, C1A 4R7 Canada. **Tel** (902)894-8506.

CN/0700-7167
GUARDIAN (WINDSOR). (THE GUARDIAN.). Began publication in 1953. English. 1855 Turner Road, Windsor Ontario N8W 3K2 Canada.

CN/0229-6799
GUELPH EXAMINER, THE. [Guelph exam.]. **VFOAT** Examiner. **VAT** Examiner (Guelph). V. 1, Issue 1 (Oct. 3, 1979)-. Newspaper. English. wk. $0.25 per no. 69 Wyndham Street North, Guelph Ontario N1H 4E7 Canada. **DD** 071/.1343.

CN/0226-6326
GUELPH THIS WEEK. [Guelph this week]. V. 1- April 11, 1979-. Newspaper. English. wk. Free. Guelph This Week, 17-219 Silvercreek Parkway, Guelph Ontario N1H 7K4. **DD** 790/.09713/43.

CN/0227-5368
GUIDE (HAWKESBURY). (LE GUIDE.). [Guide]. **VFOAT** The Guide. V. 1, Publ. 1 (Sept. 20, 1977). Newspaper. French (English). wk. Free. Le Guide, C.P. 569, Hawkesbury Ontario K6A 2Y2. **DD** 071/.1385.

CN/0833-1065
GULF NEWS. [Gulf news]. (?975)-. Newspaper. English. Fifty-two times a year. 80.00Can$ Canada; 150.00Can$ other. Robinson-Blackmore Publishing Ltd, PO Box 129, Grand Falls Newfoundland A2A 2J4 Canada. **Tel** (709)489-2162, FAX (709)489-4817. **ED** Ken Simmons, (phone: (709)695-3671). **DD** 071.18. **Ad Acc. Circ:** 4,100 (ctrl). **Desc:** This is the community newspaper.

CN/0715-4143
HA-SHILTH-SA. [Ha-Shilth-Sa]. **Added/Corp** West Coast District Council of Indian Chiefs. Vol. 1, No. 3 (March 11, 1974)-. Newspaper. English. mo. 10.00Can$ Canada; $12.00 other. Ha-Shilth-Sa, PO Box 1383, Port Alberni, British Columbia V9Y 7M2 Canada. **Tel** (604)724-5757, FAX (604)723-0463. **ED** Bob Soderlund. **DD** 971.1/00497. **UDC** 971.1; 908.711. **Bk Rev. Ad Acc. Circ:** 2,000 (ctrl). ***Continues*** *Your Paper Needs a Name, 0715-4143.* **Desc:** A native Indian publication concentrating on native issues on the west coast of Vancouver islands. Includes politics, culture, social events, sports and human interest.

Canada

CN/0705-081X
HAMILTON EXPRESS, LE. V. 1- Nov. 1976-. Newspaper. French. wk. Le Hamilton Express, PO Box 127 Station F, Toronto Ontario M4Y 2L4 Canada. **DD** 071/.13/.52.

CN/0839-0185
HAMILTON SPECTATOR (DAILY : 1984). (THE HAMILTON SPECTATOR. MICROFORM.). [Hamilt. spect.]. Nov. 5, 1984-. English. Hamilton Spectator, 44 Frid Street, Hamilton Ontario L8N 3G3 Canada. **Tel** (416)526-3315. **DD** 071/.1352. **Continues** Spectator (Hamilton, Ont. : 1969), 0839-0177.

CN/0714-8844
HAMPSTEAD JOURNAL. [Hampstead j.]. Vol. 1, No. 1 (July 2, 1981)-. Newspaper. English. qt. Free to Hampstead residents, $9.00 others. Hampstead Journal, 1928 Centre Street, Montreal Quebec H3K 1H9 Canada. **DD** 071/.1428.

CN/0847-8988
HANOVER POST POSTSCRIPTS, THE. [Hanover post postscr.]. **VFOAT** Hanover Post; Postscripts; Post Scripts. Vol. 1 (Mar. 3, 1989)-. Newspaper. English. wk. 28.60Can$ within 40 miles of Hanover & district; 45.00Can$ Canada; 66.00Can$ other. Hanover Post, 413 18th Avenue, Hanover Ontario N4N 3S5 Canada. **Tel** (519)364-2001, FAX (519)364-6950. **ED** Mike Turner. **DD** 071/.1318. **Ad Acc**, **Adv Mgr:** Marie David. **Circ:** 4,800 (ctrl).

CN/0381-0283
HARRISTON REVIEW, THE. Vol. 1 (June 20, 1895)-. Periodical. English. wk (except first week in Aug. and Christmas week). 30.11Can$ Harriston, Ontario; 55.11Can$ over 40 miles from Harriston, Ontario; 62.11Can$ US. Harriston Review, 44 Arthur Street East Box 370, Harriston ONT N0G 1Z0 Canada. **Tel** (519)338-2341. **ED** C.B. Williams. **Ad Acc**, **Adv Mgr:** B. Newman. **Circ:** 1,161 (ctrl).

CN/0382-0017
HAVELOCK CITIZEN. (July 9, 1975)-. Newspaper. English. wk (published on Wednesdays). 18.16Can$ Canada; 38.15Can$ other. Havelock Citizen, Box 250, Marmora Ontario, K0K 2M0 Canada. **Tel** (613)472-2431. **DD** 071/.13/.67.

CN/0226-6407
HAVRE (CHANDLER). (LE HAVRE.). [Havre]. V. 1- 12 Oct. 1977-. Newspaper. French. wk. $12.50 Canada; $15.60 other. Le Havre, C P 910, Chandler Quebec G0C 1K0 Canada. **DD** 071.1479.

CN/0226-6318
HAWKESBURY EXPRESS. [Hawkesbury express]. **VAT** Express (Hawkesbury). Vol. 1 (March 2, 1979)-. Newspaper. English (French). wk. 100.00Can$. Hawkesbury Express (Le Moniteur and The Echo), 88 Main Street East, Hawkesbury Ontario K6A 1A3 Canada. **Tel** (613)632-0191, FAX (613)632-6383. **ED** Andre Cayer. **DD** 071/.1385.

CN/0714-4784
HEBDO DE BELLECHASSE (DORCHESTER), L'. [Hebdo Bellechasse, Dorchester]. Vol. 1, No. 1 (1 Sept. 1981)-. Newspaper. French. wk. Free. Hebdo de Bellechasse, 164 Sud rue Notre-Dame, Ste-Marie Beauce Quebec G0S 2X0 Canada. **DD** 071/.14733.

CN/0711-8074
HEBDO DE LA ROUGE, L'. [Hebdo Rouge]. V. 1, No. 1, (Feb. 3, 1981)-. Newspaper. French. wk. $0.35 per issue. Publilaur Inc., CP 365, 248 Rue Isabelle, L'Annonciation, Quebec J0T 1T0 Canada. **DD** 071/.14225.

CN/0822-7535
HEBDO DE LAVAL, L'. [Hebdo Laval]. Vol. 1, No. 1 (23 Mar. 1983)-. Newspaper. French (English). wk. $100.00. Hebdo de Laval, 245 Boulevard des Laurentides, Laval Quebec H7G 2T7 Canada. **Tel** (514)668-8004. **ED** Pierre Francoeur. **DD** 071/.14271. **Ad Acc. Circ:** 72,000 (ctrl).
Desc: Contains local news, specialized sections, and news of the community.

CN/0229-9887
HEBDO JOURNAL. No. 1, (1981)-. Newspaper. French. Fifty-two times a year. Free. Publi Hebdos Inc., 44 de la Fonderie, CAP Madeleine G8T 2E8 Canada. **Tel** (819)379-1490. **DD** 971.4/04.

CN/1184-2814
HEBDO PENINSULE. [Hebdo penins.]. Vol. 1, No 1 (sept. 12, 1990)-. Newspaper. French. wk. Les Editions de l'Acadie Nouvelle, CP 1100, Caraquet, New Brunswick E0B 1K0 Canada. **DD** 071/.1512.

CN/0705-1336
HELLENOKANADIKI HEBDOMADA. [Ellenokan, ebd.]. **VFOAT** Greek Canadian Weekly. Began with Oct. 15, 1976 issue. Newspaper. Greek, Modern. wk. 0.50Can$ per no. Greek Canadian Weekly, 59 Cambridge Avenue, Toronto Ontario M4K 2L2 Canada. **DD** 071/.13/.541.

CN/0318-1863
HERALD (MACKENZIE). (THE HERALD.). V. 1- April 24, 1974-. Newspaper. English. wk. The Herald / Mackenzie, PO Box 609, MacKenzie British Columbia V0J 2C0 Canada. **Tel** (604)997-6675. **DD** 071/.11/.1.

CN
HIGH LEVEL ECHO. English. 20.00Can$ High Level and surrounding areas; 25.95Can$ Canada; 80.00Can$ other. High Level Echo, Box 240, High Level, Alberta T0H 1Z0 Canada. **Tel** (403)926-2000.

CN/0316-7534
HIGH PRAIRIE REPORTER. V. 1- Feb. 27, 1974-. English. wk. $45.50. High Prairie Reporter, PO Box 1194, High Prairie Alberta T0G 1E0 Canada. **DD** 071/.123/.1.

CN/0821-4824
HIGHWAY 12 WEEKENDER. **VFOAT** Stettler Independent; Weekender. Vol. 1, No. 1 (Oct. 16, 1981)-. Newspaper. English. wk. 30.00Can$. Stettler Independent, PO Box 310, Stettler Alberta T0C 2L0 Canada. **Tel** (403)742-2395, FAX (403)742-8050. **ED** R W Willis. **DD** 071/.1233. **Ad Acc. Circ:** 4,932 (ctrl).

CN/0704-0458
HIGHWAY 43 LEADER. **VFOAT** Leader. **VAT** Highway Forty Three Leader. Aug. 23, 1977-. Newspaper. English. wk. Free to rate payers of Lac Ste Anne County. Barrhead Printers and Stationers, Highway 43 Leader 0E0 Canada. **DD** 071/.123/.3.

CN/0712-6476
HOMESTEAD (KENTVILLE). (HOMESTEAD.). [Homestead]. Newspaper. English. wk. Free. Keutville Publishing, PO Box 430, Kentville Nova Scotia B4N 3X2 Canada. **Tel** (902)678-2121. **ED** H L Woodman. **DD** 071/.1633. **Bk Rev. Ad Acc. Circ:** 31,000 (ctrl).
Desc: Tabloid-entertainment section, three local weeklies; lifestyle and television section. Books and records reviewed. Stamp column.

CN/0229-768X
HOODOOS HIGHLANDER, THE. [Hoodoos highl.]. Newspaper. English. wk. $6.50. Hoodoos Highlander, PO Box 657, Canmore Alta. T0L 0M0. **DD** 071/.1233.

CN/1195-0390
HOSPITAL MANAGEMENT SMARTS. Ceased. (19??)-(Dec. 1994). Newsletter. English. Twelve times a year. Griffin Communications, 30 Relroy Court, Agincourt Ontario M1W 2Y7 Canada. **Tel** (416)498-4996, FAX (416)498-4996. **ED** Brandon Jones.
Desc: Providing tips on hospital management, fund raising, cutting down on cost and better efficiency techniques.

CN
HUDSON BAY POST REVIEW. Newspaper. English. 18.00Can$ Saskatchewan; 30.00Can$ Canada; 50.00Can$ other. Hudson Bay Post Review, Box 10, Hudson Bay Saskatchewan 30E 0Y0 Canada. **Tel** (306)865-2771.

CN/0715-5352
IGNACE COURIER. [Ignace cour.]. **VAT** Ignace Courier Weekly News. Newspaper. English. wk. $5.00. Guide Publishing & Print, PO Box 510, Ignace Ontario P0T 1T0. **DD** 071/.13112.

CN/0226-7233
ILE LETTREE, L'. V. 1- Dec. 1979-. Newspaper. French. mo. College Marguerite-Bourgeoys, 4873 Avenue Westmount, Westmount Quebec H3Y 1X9 Canada. **DD** 378.714/281. **Supersedes** Camelot.

CN/0821-543X
ILLISIBLE. (L'ILLISIBLE : JOURNAL DES ETUDIANTES/TS DU CEGEP DE SAINT-LAURENT.). [Illisible]. Newspaper. French. Free. Association Etudiante du CEGEP Saint-Laurent, 625 Boulevard Ste-Croix, Saint-Laurent Quebec H4L 3X7 Canada. **DD** 378.714/.28.

CN/0227-5430
IMAGE DE LA RIVE SUD, L'. [Image rive sud]. **VFOAT** South Shore Image. Vol. 1, No. 1 (8 March 1978)-. Newspaper. French (English). wk. $0.15 each no. Image De La Rive Sud, 460 Ouest, Rue St-Charles, Longueuil Quebec J4H 1G4 Canada. **DD** 071/.1437.

CN/0228-9830
IMPRESSION (VALLEYFIELD). (L'IMPRESSION : JOURNAL DES ETUDIANTS DU CEGEP DE VALLEYFIELD.). [Impression]. Vol. 1, No 1-. Newspaper. French. Cegep de Valleyfield, Local B-203, 169 Champlain, Valleyfield Quebec J6T 1X6 Canada. **DD** 378.714/.32.

CN/0833-8019
INDEPENDENT (ELMIRA). (THE INDEPENDENT.). [Independent]. Vol. 1 No. 1 (Mar. 4, 1986)-. Newspaper. English. Twelve times a year. 15.00Can$. North Waterloo Publishing Ltd., 15 King Street, Elmira Ontario N3B 2R1 Canada. **Tel** (519)669-5155, FAX (519)669-5928. **ED** Bob Verdun. **DD** 071/.1344. **Bk Rev**, (Qty: varies). **Circ:** 8,000 (ctrl)

available on microfiche from OCNA.
Desc: Editorial contents on world affairs and featuring views on the Canadian governments.

CN/0712-4953
INDEPENDENT (PORT HOPE). (THE INDEPENDENT.). [Independent]. **VFOAT** Port Hope Independent. Vol. 1, Issue 1 (May 6, 1981)-. Periodical. English. Free. Port Hope Independent, 8 Queen Street, Port Hope Ontario L1A 2Y7 Canada. **DD** 071/.1356.

CN/0838-0449
INDEX DE L'ACTUALITE, L'. [Index actual.]. (Jan. 1988)-. Periodical. French. Twelve times a year. 485.00Can$ (former subscribers to Index des Affaires); 685.00Can$ (regular subscribers). Documensa, 801 rue Sherbrooke Estate, Suite 615, Montreal Quebec H2L 1K7 Canada. **Tel** (514)524-7722. **DD** 071/.14. Index available. cum. index. **Continues** Index de l'Actualite a A Travers la Presse Ecrite, 0836-3099.

CN/0708-949X
INDO-CANADIAN TIMES. [Indo Can. times]. **VFOAT** Indo Canadian times. (March 24, 1978)-. Newspaper. Panjabi. wk. 65.42Can$ (second class), 186.92Can$ (first class) (1 year) Canada; $80.00 (second class), $220.00 (first class) (1 year) US; 350.00Can$ (1 year) other. Indo-Canadian Times, PO Box 2296, Vancouver BC V6B 3W5 Canada. **Tel** (604)599-5408, FAX (604)599-5415. **ED** Tara Singh Hayer. **DD** 071/.11/.33. **Ad Acc. Circ:** 15,200.
Desc: Covers news, political essays, short stories, poems, sports, letters, and editorial.

CN/0229-2068
INFOMANE. (L'INFOMANE : JOURNAL DES ETUDIANTS DU CEGEP BOIS-DE-BOULOGNE.). [Infomane]. Newspaper. French. wk. Free. Journal l'Infomane, 10500 Av Bois-de-Boulogne, Montreal Quebec H4N 1L3 Canada. **DD** 378.714/281. ctrl circ.

CN/0700-9062
INFORMATION (SAINTE-JULIE). (L'INFORMATION; JOURNAL DE SAINTE-JULIE, DE SAINT-AMABLE ET DE LA REGION.). Vol. 1 (Nov. 1975)-. Newspaper. French. ir. l'Information Sainte Julie, 500 rue Jules Choquet, Sainte Julie Que G3E1W6 Canada. **Tel** (514)649-0719. **DD** 071/.4/36.

CN/0227-7999
INFORMER, THE. [Inf.]. (Oct. 1977)-. Newspaper. English. bw. $5.00. The Informer / Canada, PO Box 204, Tiverton Ontario N0G 1T0 Canada. **DD** 071/.1321.

CN/0225-1604
INNISFIL SCOPE, THE. [Innisfil scope]. (Aug. 1978)-. Newspaper. English. Fifty-two times a year. 24.65Can$. Simcoe York Printing, PO Box 310, Beeton ONT L0G 1A0 Canada. **Tel** (416)729-2287. **ED** Lorna Davis (phone: (705)458-4434). **DD** 071/.1317. **Ad Acc, Adv Mgr:** John, **Tel** (416)729-2287. **Circ:** 2,850. available on microfiche (from Oakville, Ont., Ontario Community Newpapers Association).
Desc: General and community news.

CN/1184-7786
INTERLAKE LEADER. [Interlake lead.]. (1990)-. Newspaper. English. mo. Limited free distribution. Interlake Leader, PO Box 20, Arborg, Manitoba R0C 0A0 Canada. **DD** 071/.1272.

CN/0824-149X
INTERLAKE'S REGIONAL NEWS, THE. [Interlake's reg. news]. Vol. 1, Issue 1 (July 26, 1978)-. Newspaper. English. bw. M. Macfarlane, 322 Manitoba Avenue, Selkirk Manitoba R1A 0Y7 Canada. **DD** 071/.1272.

CN/0832-2007
IRANIYAN (TORONTO). (IRANIYAN / IRANIANS : ETHNIC NEWSPAPER.). [Iraniyan]. **VFOAT** Iranians. (Sept. 1985)-. Newspaper. Persian (English). mo. 75.00Can$ Canada. Iranians Community Newspaper, 39 Kimberlock Court #507, Scarborough ONT M1S 5B5 Canada. **Tel** (416)297-7680, FAX (416)348-9082. **ED** M. H. Yazdanfar. **DD** 071/.13541. **Bk Rev**, (Qty: 12). **Ad Acc. Circ:** 9,000.
Desc: 60 percent Canadian, 20 percent world, 20 percent home country news and events, including social, economic, cultural, arts and business.

CN/0318-207X
ISLAND STAR. Vol. 1 No. 49 (Oct. 9 1974)-. Newspaper. English. wk. $6.00. Island Star Press, 863 Eighth Street, Courtenay BC V9N 1N9. **DD** 071/.11/.34. **Continues** Comox Valley Star, 0318-2061.

CN
JAMAICAN WEEKLY GLEANER, THE. (1951)-. Newspaper. English. wk. 61.00Can$ US; 118.00Can$ other. Jamaican Weekly Gleaner, 1390 Elington Avenue W, Toronto, Ontario, M6C 2E4 Canada. **Tel** (416)784-3002.

CN/0836-6063
JEWISH POST & NEWS, THE. [Jew. post news]. **VAT** Jewish Post and News. Vol. 1, No. 1 (Aug. 6, 1987)-. Periodical. English (summaries and/or abstracts

in Hebrew and Yiddish). wk. 70.00Can$ Canada; 140.00Can$ other. Jewish Post / Canada, 117 Hutchings Street, Winnipeg Manitoba R2X 2V4 Canada. **Tel** (204)694-3332. **DD** 971.2/004924. ***Formed by the union of*** *Jewish Post., 0839-4687* ***and*** *The Western Jewish News., 0839-4679.*

CN/0228-2283
JEWISH STAR (CALGARY). (THE JEWISH STAR.). [Jew. star]. **VAT** Jewish Star. Calgary Edition. Vol. 1, No. 1 (Aug. 22/Sept. 4, 1980)-. Newspaper. English. sm. 16.50Can$ Canada; $22.00 other. Jewish Star Newspaper Ltd., 2315 98th Avenue Southwest, Calgary Alberta T2V 4S7 Canada. **ED** Douglas L Wertheimer. **DD** 305.8/924/071233. Index available. cum. index. **Bk Rev. Ad Acc. Circ:** 1,800 (ctrl).
Desc: Jewish community newspaper, a member of the American Jewish Press Association.

CN/0228-6017
JEWISH STAR (EDMONTON EDITION). (THE JEWISH STAR.). [Jew. star, Edmont. ed.]. Vol. 1, No. 1 (Dec. 1980)-. Newspaper. English. mo. 16.50Can$ (one year), 27.50Can$ (two year). Jewish Star Newspaper Ltd., 2315 98th Avenue Southwest, Calgary Alberta T2V 4S7 Canada. **ED** Douglas L Wertheimer. **DD** 305.8/924/071233. **Bk Rev. Ad Acc. Circ:** 1,400 (ctrl).
Desc: A Jewish community newspaper, member of the American Jewish Press Association.

CN/0021-6879
JEWISH WESTERN BULLETIN. [Jew. west. bull.]. **Added/Corp** Vancouver Jewish Administrative Council. Vancouver Jewish Community Council. Vol. 1, No. 31- (Oct. 9, 1930)-. Bulletin. English. ir. 39.60Can$ Canada; 39.75Can$ US; 41.00Can$ other. Jewish Western Bulletin, 3268 Heather Street, Vancouver British Columbia V5Z 3K5 Canada. **Tel** (604)879-6575. **ED** Samuel Kaplan. **Bk Rev. Ad Acc, Adv Mgr:** R Freedman. **Circ:** 3,000 (ctrl). ***Continues*** *Jewish Centre News.*
Desc: News and features on Jewish themes, religious as well as secular, book reviews, cultural and educational, Israel-Diaspora communities' news.

CN/0711-6705
JIAJING HUABAO. (CHIA CHING HUA PAO. THE CAPITAL CHINESE NEWS.). [Jia jing hua bao]. **VFOAT** Capital Chinese News; Ottawa Chinese Community Newsletter; National Capital Chinese Community Newsletter. **VAT** Capital Chinese News. Vol. 1 (July 1977)-. Newspaper. Chinese (English). Twelve times a year. 10.00Can$. Capital Chinese News, 695 Somerset Street West, Ottawa Ontario K1R 6P5 Canada. **Tel** (613)837-3564. **DD** 071/.13/84.

CN/0703-699X
JOUR (MONTREAL. 1977). (LE JOUR.). [Jour]. V. 1- Feb. 4, 1977-. Newspaper. French. wk. $50.00 Canada; $60.00 other. Journal Le Jour Inc., Bureau 801, 1435 rue De Bleury, Montreal Quebec H3A 2H7. **DD** 071/.14.

CN/0228-6289
JOURNAL ACTON REGIONAL. [J. Acton reg.]. **VFOAT** Journal Acton. Vol. 1, No. 1 (10 Oct. 1979)-. Newspaper. French. wk. $12.00. Journal Acton Regional, C P 1138, Acton Vale Quebec J0H 1A0 Canada. **DD** 071/.14525.

CN/0824-6394
JOURNAL (ASHCROFT). (THE JOURNAL.). [Journal]. **VFOAT** Logan Lake Leader. Newspaper. English. wk. $0.25 per no. Journal Publishing, PO Box 190, Ashcroft British Columbia V0K 1A0 Canada. **DD** 071/.1141.

CN/0318-2134
JOURNAL CHALEUR. (LE JOURNAL CHALEUR.). [J. chal.]. **VFOAT** Chaleur. (March 19, 1975)-. Newspaper. French. Fifty-two times a year. 45.00Can$ Canada; 85.00Can$. Group Bellavance, 73, St-Germain Est., Rimouski Quebec G5L 7C4 Canada. **Tel** (418)723-4800. **DD** 071/.14/78.

CN/0822-0794
JOURNAL COTE-DES-NEIGES. [J. Cote-des-Neiges]. Vol. 1, No. 1 (May 83)-. Periodical. English (French). mo. Free. Cote-Des-Neiges, Suite 204, 3600 Van Horne, Montreal Quebec H3S 1R6 Canada. **DD** 071/.14281. **Ad Acc. Circ:** 15,000.
Desc: Community newspaper interested in local activities and local actuality. Principal subjects includes youth, community groups, education, ethics, crime prevention and housing.

CN/0704-0660
JOURNAL DE CORNWALL, LE. [J. Corn.]. Vol. 1 (Aug. 26, 1977)-. Newspaper. French. wk. 12.50Can$ Canada; $25.00 other. Le Journal de Cornwall, 113 Chemin Montreal, Cornwall Ontario K6H 1B2 Canada. **Tel** (613)938-1433. **ED** Roger Duplantie. **DD** 071/.13/76. **Bk Rev. Ad Acc. Circ:** 1,100 (ctrl). available on microfiche (from Oakville, Ont. : Ontario Community Newspapers Association). ***Continues*** *Francor, 0712-9270.*
Desc: Local newspaper (French). Municipal coverage, school boards, other activities.

CN/0227-2911
JOURNAL DE LA COTE. [J. Cote]. **VFOAT** Cote. Published since 1976. Newspaper. French. bw. Publications Bernard Cleary, 2873 Chemin Ste Foy, CP 9694, Ste Foy Quebec G1V 4C2 Canada. **DD** 071/.1448.

CN/0822-6938
JOURNAL DE ST-DOMINIQUE. [J. St-Dominique]. (1978)-. Newspaper. French. mo. Journal de St-Dominique, St-Damase, Quebec J0H 1S0 Canada. **DD** 352.0714/525. ***Continues*** *Information Regionale, St-Damase, St-Pie, St-Cesaire, 0822-692X.*

CN/0821-5081
JOURNAL DE VILLERAY, LE. [J. Villeray]. Vol. 1, No. 1 (8 Sept. 1982)-. Newspaper. French. wk. Free to citizens. Journal de Villeray, 1008 Est rue Fleury, Montreal Quebec H2C 1P7 Canada. **DD** 071/.14281.

CN/0707-7858
JOURNAL DES TRAVAILLEURS D'HOPITAUX. V. 1- March 1978-. Newspaper. French. mo. $4.00. L'Association Ouvriere Canadienne, C P 666 Succursale C, Montreal Quebec H2L 4L5 Canada. **DD** 331.2/041/362110971.

CN/0380-2051
JOURNAL DU NORD-OUEST, LE. V. 1- Oct. 7, 1974-. Newspaper. French. da. $1.50 per week. La Frontiere, 167 Dallaire, CP 490, Rouyn Quebec J9X 4T3 Canada. **DD** 071/.14/13.

CN/0229-981X
JOURNAL DU SAMEDI, LE. V. 2, No. 1 (April 5-11 1981)-. Newspaper. French. wk. $37.00 Canada; $50.00 other. Publications Quebecor, 225 East rue Roy, Montreal Quebec H2W 2N6 Canada. **DD** 071/.14.

CN/0228-2569
JOURNAL LA MITIS. [J. Mitis]. **VFOAT** Mitis. V. 1, No. 1- Oct. 4, 1978-. Newspaper. French. wk. $15.60 Canada, $20.00 others. Journal La Mitis, CP 10, 16000 Boul., Jacques Cartier, Mont-Joli Quebec G5H 3K8 Canada. **DD** 071/.14771.

CN/0226-3580
JOURNAL LA REPUBLIQUE. [J. repub.]. **VFOAT** Republique. **VAT** Republique (Edmunston). V. 1, No. 1- Aug. 30, 1978. Newspaper. French. wk. $15.60 Canada, $20.00 others. Journal La Republique, CP 606, 173, Rue Victoria, Edmunston, NB E3V 3L2. **DD** 071/.1554.

CN/0227-1249
JOURNAL (LACHUTE). (JOURNAL.). [Journal]. V. 1- 20 Sept. 1978-. Newspaper. English (French). wk. Free. A. Vigeant, PO Box 564, 387 Principale Street, Lachute Quebec J8H 1Y1 Canada. **DD** 071/.1423. ctrl circ.

CN/0228-278X
JOURNAL LE NORD. [J. nord]. **VFOAT** Nord. **VAT** Le Nord (Annonciation). Published since March 1977?. Newspaper. French. wk. $8.00. Journal le Nord, CP 820, L'Annonciation Quebec J0T 1T0 Canada. **DD** 071/.14225.

CN/0227-1222
JOURNAL LE ST-FRANCOIS. [J. St-Francois]. **VFOAT** Le St-Francois. V. 1- Dec. 7, 1977-. Newspaper. French. **DD** 071/.1432.

CN/0713-6420
JOURNAL L'INFORMATION DU NORD. [J. inf. nord.]. **VFOAT** Information du Nord. Vol. 1, No. 1 (Nov. 2, 1981)-. Newspaper. French. wk. Free. Journal l'Information du Nord, CP 1480, St-Jovite Quebec J0T 2H0 Canada. **DD** 071/.1424.

CN/0711-4745
JOURNAL MASKOUTAIN, LE. [J. maskoutain]. Vol. 1, No. 1 March 18 1981-. Newspaper. French. wk. Free to citizens of St-Hyacinthe. J G Asselin, Journal Maskoutain, CP 700, St-Hyacinthe Quebec J2S 7C2 Canada. **DD** 071/.14523.

CN/1184-5139
JOURNAL (PENETANGUISHENE). (JOURNAL [MICROFORM].). Vol. 1, No. 1 (Feb. 12, 1991)-. English. Ontario Community Newspapers Association, PO Box 451, 1184 Speers Road, Oakville Ontario L6J 5A8. **DD** 071/.1317.

CN/0706-3318
JOURNAL REGIONAL (QUEBEC). (LE JOURNAL REGIONAL.). V. 1- Aug. 29, 1978-. Newspaper. French. wk. $20.00 Canada; $25.00 other. Le Journal Regional, 1310, Rue Principale, Saint-Roch De, Quebec J0K 3H0. **DD** 071/.14416.

CN/0821-414X
JOURNAL REGIONAL (SAINT-JEAN). (LE JOURNAL REGIONAL.). [J. reg.]. **VFOAT** Regional. **VAT** Regional (Saint-Jean). Newspaper. French. Publicite Boris, 169 Boul. Du Seminaire, St-Jean Quebec J3B 5K4 Canada. **DD** 071/.1438.

CN/0710-2186
JOURNAL ST-LOUIS. [J. St-Louis]. **VAT** St Louis Journal (1977); Ephemerida Saint-Loui. Vol. 4, No. 2 (July 1977)-. Newspaper. English (French, Greek and Modern, Portuguese). mo. Free. **DD** 362.8/4/009714281. ctrl circ. ***Continues*** *St-Louis Journal, 0710-2178.*

CN/0229-7817
JOURNAL WEST (DUNDAS). (JOURNAL WEST.). [J. west]. Vol. 2, No. 1 (Sept. 16, 1976)-. Newspaper. English. wk. $7.50. Preston Publishing, 36 King Street East, Dundas, Ontario L9H 1B8. **DD** 071/.1352.

CN/0707-7157
KAMOURASKA (LA POCATIERE). (LE KAMOURASKA.). [Kamouraska]. (Feb. 1978)-. Newspaper. French. Fifty-two times a year. 65.16Can$ Canada; 73.16Can$ other. Le Kamouraska, 401 91eme rue CP 1418, Lapocatiere Quebec G0R 1Z0 Canada. **Tel** (418)856-4531. **ED** Claude Bellavance. **DD** 071/.14/75. ctrl circ.
Desc: Local and regional news.

CN/0712-8878
KANADA KURIER (ALBERTA AUSG.). (KANADA KURIER.). [Kan. Kur.]. Vol. 91, No. 38 (18 Sept. 1980)-. Newspaper. German. wk. (Thursday). 64.00Can$ Canada; 156.51Can$ US; 123.78Can$ other (published in eight editions). Courier Press Ltd, PO Box 1054, 955 Alexander Avenue, Winnipeg Manitoba R3C 2X8 Canada. **Tel** (204)774-1883, FAX (204)783-5740, telex 07-55470. **ED** E J Priebe. **DD** 071/.123. **Bk Rev. Ad Acc.** ctrl circ. ***Continues*** *Alberta Courier, 0837-0990.*
Desc: National and international news, fashions, travel and sports.

CN/0712-8886
KANADA KURIER (AUSGABE FUER BRITISH COLUMBIA). (KANADA KURIER.). [Kan. Kur., Ausg. B.C.]. **VFOAT** Ausg. fur British Columbia. (1980)-. Newspaper. German. wk. 64.00Can$ Canada; 156.51Can$ US; 123.78Can$ other (published in eight editions). Courier Press Ltd, PO Box 1054, 955 Alexander Avenue, Winnipeg Manitoba R3C 2X8 Canada. **Tel** (204)774-1883, FAX (204)783-5740, telex 07-55470. **ED** E J Priebe. **DD** 071/.11. **Bk Rev. Ad Acc.** ctrl circ. ***Continues*** *British Columbia Courier.*
Desc: National and international news, fashions, travel and sports.

CN/0712-8894
KANADA KURIER (MANITOBA AUSG.). (KANADA KURIER.). [Kan. Kur.]. Vol. 91, No. 38 (Sept. 18, 1980)-. Newspaper. German. wk (Thursday). 64.00Can$ Canada; 156.51Can$ US; 250.14Can$ other (published in eight editions). Courier Press Ltd, PO Box 1054, 955 Alexander Avenue, Winnipeg Manitoba R3C 2X8 Canada. **Tel** (204)774-1883, FAX (204)783-5740, telex 07-55470. **ED** Ralf Neuendorff. **DD** 071/.127. **Bk Rev. Ad Acc.** ctrl circ. ***Continues*** *Manitoba Courier, 0837-0982.*
Desc: National and international news, fashions, travel and sports.

CN/0712-8908
KANADA KURIER (MONTREAL AUSG.). (KANADA KURIER.). [Kan. Kur.]. Vol. 91, No. 38 (Sept. 18, 1980)-. Newspaper. German. wk (Thursday). 64.00Can$ Canada; 156.51Can$ US; 123.78Can$ other (published in eight editions). Courier Press Ltd, PO Box 1054, 955 Alexander Avenue, Winnipeg Manitoba R3C 2X8 Canada. **Tel** (204)774-1883, FAX (204)783-5740, telex 07-55470. **ED** E J Priebe. **DD** 071/.14281. **Bk Rev. Ad Acc.** ctrl circ. ***Continues*** *Montreal Courier, 0837-1032;* ***Absorbed*** *Montrealer Zeitung, 0837-0834.*
Desc: National and international news, fashions, travel, and sports.

CN/0712-8916
KANADA KURIER (ONTARIO AUSGABE). (KANADA KURIER.). [Kan. Kur., Ont. Ausg.]. Vol. 91, No 38 (18 Sept. 1980)-. Newspaper. German. wk. 64.00Can$ Canada; 156.51Can$ US; 123.78Can$ other (published in eight editions). Courier Press Ltd, PO Box 1054, 955 Alexander Avenue, Winnipeg Manitoba R3C 2X8 Canada. **Tel** (204)774-1883, FAX (204)783-5740, telex 07-55470. **ED** E J Priebe. **DD** 071/.13. **Bk Rev. Ad Acc.** ctrl circ. ***Continues*** *Ontario Courier.*
Desc: National and international news, fashions, travel, and sports.

CN/0712-8924
KANADA KURIER (OTTAWA AUSG.). (KANADA KURIER.). [Kan. Kur.]. Vol. 91, No. 38 (18 Sept. 1980)-. Newspaper. German. wk. 64.00Can$ Canada; 156.51Can$ US; 123.78Can$ other (published in eight editions). Courier Press Ltd, PO Box 1054, 955 Alexander Avenue, Winnipeg Manitoba R3C 2X8 Canada. **Tel** (204)774-1883, FAX (204)783-5740, telex 07-55470. **ED** E J Priebe. **DD** 071/.1384. **Bk Rev. Ad Acc.** ctrl circ. ***Continues*** *Ottawa Courier, 0227-2563.*
Desc: National and international news, fashions, travel, and sports.

CN/0712-8932
KANADA KURIER (SASKATCHEWAN AUSG.). (KANADA KURIER.). [Kan. Kur.]. Vol. 91, No. 38 (18 Sept. 1980)-. Newspaper. German. wk (Thursday).

64.00Can$ Canada; 156.51Can$ US; 123.78Can$ other (published in eight editions). Courier Press Ltd, PO Box 1054, 955 Alexander Avenue, Winnipeg Manitoba R3C 2X8 Canada. **Tel** (204)774-1883, FAX (204)783-5740, telex 07-55470. **ED** E J Priebe. **DD** 071/.124. **Bk Rev. Ad Acc.** ctrl circ. ***Continues*** *Saskatchewan Courier (Winnipeg, Man.), 0837-1008.*
Desc: National and international news, fashions, travel, and sports.

CN/0712-8940
KANADA KURIER (TORONTO AUSGABE). (KANADA KURIER.). [Kan. Kur.]. Vol. 91, No. 38 (Sept. 18, 1980)-. Newspaper. German. wk (Thursday). 64.00Can$ Canada; 156.51Can$ US; 123.78Can$ other (published in eight editions). Courier Press Ltd, PO Box 1054, 955 Alexander Avenue, Winnipeg Manitoba R3C 2X8 Canada. **Tel** (204)774-1883, FAX (204)783-5740, telex 07-55470. **ED** E J Priebe. **DD** 071/.13541. **Bk Rev. Ad Acc.** ctrl circ. ***Continues*** *Toronto Courier.*
Desc: National and international news, fashions, travel, and sports.

CN/0449-7368
KANADSKE LISTY (TORONTO. 1973). (KANADSKE LISTY.). [Kan. listy]. **Added/Corp** Klub Novych. (Jan. 1973)-. Czech (Slovak). mo. 19.00Can$. Czechoslovak Newcomers Club, 388 Atwater Avenue, Mississauga ONT L5G 2A3 Canada. **Tel** (416)278-4116. **ED** Mirko Janecek. **LC** F1035.C9; H5. **DD** 971/.004/9186. **Bk Rev. Ad Acc. Circ:** 2,500. available with illustrations. ***Continues*** *HLAS Novych.*

CN/0228-0221
KANATA SOSIG. **VFOAT** Korean-Canadian Time. SIC. Feb. 26, 1980-. Newspaper. Korean. sm. $20.00. Korean-Canadian Times, Suite 3303/132 A Avenue, Edmonton Alberta T5A 3K4 Canada. **DD** 971.23/004957. **UDC** 971.2(=957).

CN/0227-3489
KELOWNA TODAY. [Kelowna today]. V. 1- Aug. 26, 1976-. Newspaper. English. wk. 0.20Can$ per no. Kelowna Today, 561 Lawrence Avenue, Kelowna BC V1Y 6L8. **DD** 071/.1142.

CN/0228-7897
KENNEBECASIS VALLEY POST. [Kennebecasis Val. post]. **VFOAT** Valley Post. Vol. 1, No. 1 (Dec. 12, 1979)-. Newspaper. English. wk. Society of American Foresters, 5400 Grosvenor Lane, Bethesda MD 20814-2198. **Tel** (301)897-8720, FAX (301)897-3690, telex 9102501089 SAFFOREST UQ. **DD** 071/.1541.

CN/0715-5360
KETTLE RIVER ECHO, THE. [Kettle River echo]. Newspaper. English. bw. $4.50. Kettle River Echo, Box 65/Rock Creek, British Columbia V0H 1Y0 Canada. **DD** 071/.1141.

CN/0846-3913
KEY (CALGARY). (THE KEY.). [Key]. **Added/Corp** Falconridge/Castleridge Community Association. Whitehorn Community Association. **VFOAT** Key Community News. Vol. 1, No.1 (Aug. 1991)-. Periodical. English. mo. Limited free distribution. **DD** 071/.12338.

CN
KIMBERLY DAILY BULLETIN. (19??)-. Newspaper. English. ir (250 per year). 105.32Can$ Canada; 334.00Can$ other. Kimberly Daily Bulletin, % C Murray, 335 Spokane Street, Kimberly BC ViA 1Y9, Canada. **Tel** (604) 427-5333, (604) 426-5201, FAX (604) 427-5336, (604) 426-5003.

CN/0834-6674
KINCARDINE INDEPENDENT, THE. [Kincardine indep.]. (198?)-. Newspaper. English. wk. 21.03Can$ local Kincardine; 45.00Can$ Canada; 60.00Can$ other. Independent / Kincardine Canada, Box 1240, Kincardine Ontario N2Z 2Z4 Canada. **Tel** (519)396-3111. **ED** Eric Howald. **DD** 071/.1321. **Bk Rev. Ad Acc. Circ:** 3,300. ***Continues*** *The Independant, 0319-1400.*

CN/0824-2402
KINEDIT. [Kinedit]. V. 1, No. 1 (Feb. 1981)-. Newspaper. French. Kinedit, Universite de Montreal, CP 6128/Succursale A, Montreal Quebec H3C 3J7 Canada. **DD** 613.7/1/05.

CN/0380-3686
KING TOWNSHIP WEEKLY, THE. Vol. 1, No. 25, (Nov. 20, 1974)-. Newspaper. English. wk. The King Township Weekly, PO Box 331, Woodbridge Ontario L4L 1B2 Canada. **DD** 071/.13/54. ***Continues*** *King Township & Nobleton Advertiser, 0380-3678.*

CN/0712-9068
KINGSTON THIS WEEK. [Kingst. this week]. Newspaper. English. wk. Free. Kingston This Week, 677 Gardiners Road, Kingston Ontario K7M 3Y4 Canada. **Tel** (613)389-6908. **ED** Dan Donohue and Michael Crofton. **DD** 071/.13/72. **Bk Rev. Ad Acc. Circ:** 36,000 (ctrl). available on microfiche (from Oakville, Ont. : Ontario Community Newspapers Association). ***Continues*** *Kingston Shoppers News, 0228-0507.*
Desc: Covers news, features, sports, real estate and automobiles.

CN
KINISTINO POST [MICROFORM], THE. (Dec. 1945)-. English. wk. 12.50Can$ within 40 mile radius of Kinistino, Canada; 16.00Can$ other Canada (print). Kinistino Post, Box 340, Kinistino SASK S0J 1H0 Canada. **Tel** (306)864-2266. **ED** Ron Phillips. **DD** 071/.1242. **Bk Rev. Ad Acc.** ctrl circ.

CN/0824-5150
KITCHENER-WATERLOO RECORD. (KITCHENER-WATERLOO RECORD MICROFORM.). [Kitchener-Waterloo rec.]. **VFOAT** Kitchener-Waterloo. Jan. 1948-. Newspaper. English. $107.00 (carrier); $388.00 (mail) Canada; $537.00 (mail) other. Kitchener-Waterloo Record, 225 Fairway Road S, Kitchener Ontario N2G 4E5 Canada. **Tel** (519)579-2231, telex (519)894-3912. **DD** 071/.1345. ***Continues*** *Kitchener Daily Record.*

CN/0715-4593
KOOTENAY GRAPEVINE, THE. [Kootenay grapevine]. Vol. 1, No. 1 (Jan. 13, 1981)-. Newspaper. English. wk. Free. Kootenay Marketing, 501D Vernon Street, Nelson BC V1L 3E9. **DD** 071/.1144.

CN/0712-1733
KOREA TIMES. TORONTO EDITION. (THE KOREA TIMES.). **VFOAT** Hankukilbo; Hankookilbo. **VAT** Hankookilbo (Toronto); Hankukilbo (Toronto). No. 528 (June 1, 1981)-. Newspaper. Korean. da. $90.00. Lower Thames Valley Conservation Authority, 41 Fourth Street, Chatham Ontario N7M 2G3. **DD** 071/.13541. ***Continues*** *Canada News, 0319-2962.*

CN
L UNION VICTORIAVILLE CANADA. French. wk. 30.00$Can; 75.00$Can other. L Union Victoriaville Canada, CP 130, Victoriaville G6P 6S8 Canada. **Tel** (819)357-2065. **ED** Richard Lacoursiere. **Ad Acc.** ctrl circ. available on microfiche.

CN/0715-4941
LABRADORIAN, THE. [Labradorian]. (197?)-. Newspaper. English. Fifty-two times a year. 48.16Can$ Canada; 93.16Can$ other. The Labradorian, PO Box 39 Station A, H Valley Labrad A0P 1EP Canada. **Tel** (706)896-3341. **DD** 071/.182.

CN/0821-4816
LAKEFIELD, THE CHRONICLE. [Lakefield chron.]. **VFOAT** Lakefield Chronicle. Vol. 1, No. 1 (Oct. 6, 1982)-. Newspaper. English. wk. $10.00 Canada; $25.00 other. Lakefield Chronicle, PO Box 250, Marmora Ontario K0K 2M0 Canada. **DD** 071/.1367. available on microfiche (from Oakville, Ont. : Ontario Community Newspapers Association).

CN
LAKES DISTRICT NEWS. Newspaper. English. Fifty-two times a year (Wednesdays). 33.60Can$ local; 44.00Can$ other. Cariboo Press / Lakes District News, 23-3rd Avenue, Box 309, Burns Lake BC V0J 1E0 Canada. **Tel** (604)692-7526. **ED** Grant Stephens. **Ad Acc.**

CN/0821-3372
LAKESIDE LEADER. [Lakesside lead.]. (1975)-. Newspaper. English. Fifty-one times per year. 32.96Can$ Canada (within 40 mile radius); 44.81Can$ others (outside a 40 miles radius); 105.11Can$ others. Lakeside Leader, PO Box 849, Slave Lake Alberta T0G 2A0 Canada. **Tel** (403)849-4380. **ED** Roderick D. Brooks. **DD** 071/.1231. **Ad Acc. Circ:** 2,509 (ctrl). ***Continues*** *Northland Free Press, 0821-3380.*
Desc: A community newspaper serving the province's North Central oil and timber district.

CN/0383-8080
LAMBTON COUNTY GAZETTE, THE. V. 1- April 1, 1976-. Newspaper. English. wk. Free. Sarnia Gazette Publishing Company Ltd, 287 Front Street North, PO Box 99, Sarnia Ontario N7T 5S6 Canada. **DD** 071/.13/27.

CN/0380-4607
LANGFORD TO COLWOOD TELEGRAM. **VFOAT** Telegram. V. 1- Jan. 29, 1975-. Newspaper. English. wk. Community News / Victoria, 506 David Street, Victoria British Columbia V8T 2C8 Canada. **DD** 071/.11/34.

CN/0711-7450
LANGLEY TIMES. [Langley times]. Vol. 1, No. 1 (Feb. 18, 1981)-. Newspaper. English. wk. Free. Langley Times Publishing Company Ltd, 20525 Fraser Highway, Langley British Columbia V3A 4S1 Canada. **DD** 071/.1133. ctrl circ.

CN
LANIGAN ADVISOR. Newspaper. English. wk. 14.25Can$ Lanigan; 18.00Can$ Canada; 30.00Can$ US; 56.00Can$ other. Lanigan Advisor, Box 1029, Lanigan Saskatchewan, S0K 2M0 Canada. **Tel** (306)365-2010, FAX (306)3653388. **Ad Acc, Adv Mgr:** Karen. ctrl circ.

CN/0710-5487
LANTZVILLE LOG, THE. [Lantzville log]. Newspaper. English. mo. Free to residents; 7.50Can$ other. Lantzville Log, Box 114, Lantzville British Columbia V0R 2H0 Canada. **Tel** (604)390-4471. **ED** Lynn Reeve. **DD** 071/.1134. **Bk Rev. Ad Acc. Circ:** 2,350 (ctrl). ***Continues*** *Lantzville Newsletter.*
Desc: Local news and views with virtually all copy locally generated.

CN/1182-8323
LAURENTIAN SUN. [Laurent. sun]. **VFOAT** Laurentian. Vol. 1, No. 1 (Oct. 1990)-. Newspaper. English. mo. Limited free distribution. Laurentian Sun, 43 Filion Street, Sain-Sauveur-des-Monts, Quebec J0R 1R0 Canada. **DD** 071/.1424.

CN/0834-6666
LEADER (MORRISBURG). (THE LEADER [MICROFORM].). **VFOAT** Morrisburg Leader; Morrisburg Review. (198?)-. Newspaper. English. wk (published Wednesday). 19.00Can$ Canada with 0 as second letter in postal code, 21.00Can$ Canada outside 40 mile radius with 0 as second letter in postal code, 41.00Can$ Canada with the numeral 1-9 as second letter in postal code; 70.00Can$ other. Morrisburg Leader, Box 891, Morrisburg, Ontario, K0C 1X0 Canada. **Tel** (613)543-2981. **ED** A. B. Laurin (613)543-2987. **DD** 071/.1375. **Ad Acc. Circ:** 2,850.

CN/0715-4631
LEASIDE VILLAGER, THE. [Leaside villager]. Vol. 1, No. 1 (Sept. 16, 1981)-. Newspaper. English. mo. Free. Town Crier Inc., 3 Massey Square, Toronto Ontario M4C 5L5. **DD** 071/.13541. ctrl circ.

CN/0824-2712
LELIRE ET L'ECRIRE. (LELIRE --- ET L'ECRIRE : JOURNAL DES ETUDIANTS-ES DE L'UQTR.). **VFOAT** Lelire. Jan. 1983-. Newspaper. French. mo. Lelire, CP 500, Trois-Rivieres Quebec G9A 5H7 Canada. **DD** 378.714/45. ***Continues*** *Relance (Trois-Rivieres, Quebec), 0714-332X.*

CN/0839-4938
LETHBRIDGE HERALD MICROFORM, THE. [Lethbridge her.]. Newspaper. English. Commonwealth Microfilm Library, 3395 American Drive, Unit 11, Mississauga, Ontario, L4V 1T5 Canada. **Tel** (905)671-4173. **DD** 071/.1233.

CN/0713-7974
LIFELINE - CANADIAN MEMORIAL CHIROPRACTICE COLLEGE. (LIFELINE.). [Lifeline - Can. Meml. Chiropr. Coll.]. Vol. 1, No. 1 (Feb. 1978)-. Newspaper. English. bm. Free. Lifeline, c/o Students' Administration Council Canadian Memorial Chiropractic College, 1900 Bayview Avenue, Toronto Ontario M4G 3E6 Canada. **DD** 378.713/541. ctrl circ.

CN/0707-7939
LIGHT TRUCK EQUIPMENT NEWS. V. 1- July 10, 1978-. Newspaper. English. ir. $5.00. Warren Publishing, 1730 Amico Blvd., Mississauga Ontario L4W 1Y3 Canada. **DD** 629.22/3/05.

CN/0228-0566
LINDSAY THIS WEEK. [Lindsay this week]. Vol. 1 (Sept. 13, 1978)-. Newspaper. English. ir. 14.00Can$. Lindsay This Week, 10 York Street North, Lindsay Ontario K9V 3Z9 Canada. **DD** 071/.1364. available on microfiche (from Oakville, Ont. : Ontario Community Newspapers Association).

CN/0833-3858
LISAN AL-ARAB. (LISAN AL-ARAB / THE ARAB COMMUNITY CENTRE OF TORONTO.). Newspaper. English (Arabic). bm. Free. Arab Community Centre of Toronto, 5298 Dundas Street West, Toronto Ontario M9B 1B2 Canada. **Tel** (416)231-7746. **DD** 971.3/541004927. **Bk Rev. Ad Acc. Circ:** 2,000 (ctrl). ***Continues*** *The Arab Community Centre News, 0824-5983.*
Desc: Publishes articles, news and reports of interest primarily to Arabs in Toronto and Canada. It's a non-religious, non-racial, non-political paper.

CN/0316-6902
LITTLE BEND. V. 1- Sept., 1974-. Newspaper. English. bm. 15.00Can$ per no. Westco Enterprises Ltd, PO Box 250, Petitcodiac New Brunswick E0A 2H0 Canada. **DD** 071/.15/23.

CN/0839-0681
LONDON FREE PRESS (MORNING : 1907). (THE LONDON FREE PRESS. MICROFORM.). [Lond. free press]. Oct. 31, 1907-. Newspaper. English. London Free Press, PO Box 2280, London Ontario N6A 4G1 Canada. **Tel** (519)679-1111. **DD** 071/.1326. ***Continues*** *Free Press (London, Ont. : Morning : 1873), 0839-0673.*

CN/1194-0387
LONDON NEWS (LONDON. EAST ED.). ***Ceased.*** (LONDON NEWS [MICROFORM].). Issue 76 (Mar. 31, 1976)-(19??). English. **DD** 071/.1326. ***Continues*** *East London News,, 0316-6511.*

CN/0710-281X
LONDON TRIBUNE. [Lond. trib.]. Vol. 1 No. 1 (Sept. 4, 1980)-. Newspaper. English. wk. $0.25 per number. London Tribune, 364 Richmond Street, London Ontario N6A 3C3 Canada. **DD** 071/.1326.

CN/0383-8102
LOOKOUT (SIOUX LOOKOUT). (THE LOOKOUT.). V. 1- Sept. 1, 1976-. Periodical. English. wk. $12.00. The Lookout, PO Box 1359, Sioux Lookout Ontario P0V 2T0 Canada. **DD** 071/.13/112

CN/0715-4569
LUMBY REVIEW. [Lumby rev.]. Vol. 1, No. 1 (Mar. 26, 1981)-. Newspaper. English. wk. $0.15 per no. Lumby Review, Box 160, Lumby British Columbia Canada. **DD** 071/.1142.

CN/0707-5324
LUSITANO (CAMBRIDGE). (O LUSITANO.). [Lusitano]. No. 1- July 21, 1978-. Newspaper. Portuguese. bw. $4.00. O Lusitano, 1236 Valentine Drive, Cambridge Ontario N3H 2N8 Canada. **DD** 071/.13/44.

CN/0228-0558
MACKENZIE DRIFT. [Mackenzie drift]. V. 1- Apr. 3, 1979-. Newspaper. English. bw. 10.00Can$ NWT and Yukon, 12.50Can$ Southern Canada, 18.00Can$ all other countries. Rosmar Publications, PO Box 2600, Inuvik Northwest Territories X0E 0T0 Canada. **DD** 071/.196.

CN/0706-7240
MACKLIN MIRROR. Vol. 1 (Nov. 10, 1977)-. Newspaper. English. Fifty-two times a year. 35.10Can$. Macklin Mirror, Box 100, Macklin Saskatchewan S0L 2C0 Canada. **Tel** (306)753-2424, FAX (306)753-2424. **ED** Robert Brost. **DD** 071/.124/2. **Ad Acc. Circ:** 873 (ctrl). available on microfilm.

CN/0706-7011
MADOC NEWS, THE. V. 1- Apr. 5, 1978-. Newspaper. English. The Madoc News, Box 655, Madoc Ontario K0K 2K0 Canada. **DD** 071/.13/585.

CN/1182-0691
MAGAZINES AND NEWSPAPERS - CALGARY PUBLIC LIBRARY. (MAGAZINES AND NEWSPAPERS.). [Mag. newsp. - Calg. Public Libr.]. **Main/Corp** Calgary Public Library. (1990)-. English. Calgary Public Library, 616 MacLeod Trail South East, Calgary Alberta T2G 2M2 Canada. **DD** 018/.134. ***Continues** Periodicals & Newspapers., 0714-3591.*

CN/0833-0883
MAGYAR ELET. (MAGYAR ELET [MICROFORM].). [M. elet]. **VFOAT** Hungarian Life. (1948)-. Hungarian. Fifty times a year. $35.00. Reform Hungaria Publishing Service Inc., 21 Vaughan Road, Suite 201, Toronto ONT M6G 2N2 Canada. **Tel** (416)652-6370, FAX (416)652-6370. **ED** Gabuella Schree. **DD** 071/.1. **Ad Acc. Circ:** 7,000.

CN/0700-8082
MALTON PILOT, THE. Newspaper. English. wk. Offset Publications, 7205 Goreway Drive, Mississauga Ontario L4T 2T9. **DD** 071/.13/535.

CN/0708-9457
MANITOBA CHINESE POST. Vol. 1 (Nov. 1978)-. Newspaper. Chinese (summaries and/or abstracts in English). mo. Free on request. Manitoba Chinese Post, PO Box 58, Winnipeg Manitoba R3C 3K3 Canada. **Tel** (204)452-6491. **DD** 071/.127/4.

CN/0025-2239
MANITOBA CO-OPERATOR. [Manit. co-op.]. **Added/Corp** Manitoba Pool Elevators. Vol. 1 (July 1, 1943)-. Periodical. English. Fifty-one times per year. 25.00Can$ Canada & Manitoba; 60.00Can$ US; 70.00Can$ other. Manitoba Co-Operator, PO Box 9800, Winnipeg Manitoba 4C3 3K7 Canada. **Tel** (204)934-0401, FAX (204)934-0480. **ED** John Morris (phone: (204)934-0408). **Ad Acc, Adv Mgr:** Champ Rossenholt, **Tel** (204)934-0416. **Circ:** 30,000 (ctrl). **Ind/Abst** AGRICOLA.

CN
MANITOBAN. (1913)-. Newspaper. English. wk (except Monthly in Summer). 35.00Can$. Students Union / University of Manitoba, University of Manitoba, University Centre, Winnipeg R3T 2N2 Manitoba CN. **Tel** (204)474-6535, FAX (204)474-1299. **(Subscription address:** The Manitoban, Room 118 University Centre, Winnipeg Manitoba R3T 2N2 Canada) **ED** Alayne Armstrong. **Bk Rev. Ad Acc. Circ:** 16,000. **Desc:** Student newspaper of University of Manitoba, publishing campus and city news affecting students, entertainment reviews and sports and leisure articles.

CN/0834-6682
MANITOULIN EXPOSITOR. (THE MANITOULIN EXPOSITOR [MICROFORM].). (May 24, 1879)-. Newspaper. English. wk. 25.00Can$ Manitoulin; 50Can$ other Canada and US; 85.00Can$ other. Manitoulin Publishing Company, Box 369f Little Current, Ontario P0P 1K0 Canada. **Tel** (705)368-2744, FAX (705)368-3822. **ED** Jane Story & Ross Muir. **DD** 071/.13135. **Bk Rev**, (Qty: 10-15). **Ad Acc, Adv Mgr:** Ruth Mohammed. **Circ:** 6,900 (ctrl). **Desc:** A newspaper serving a community made up equally of Native Americans and European descendents.

CN/0228-054X
MANNVILLE REFLECTIONS. [Mannville reflect.]. V. 1- July 18, 1978-. Newspaper. English. wk. $5.00 local, $7.00 other parts of Canada, $10.00 other countries. Vermilion-Mannville Reflections Ltd, PO Box 2167, Vermilion Alberta T0B 2W0 Canada. **DD** 071/.1233.

CN/0700-8058
MANOTICK NEWS, THE. (19??)-. Periodical. English. wk. $6.00. J Curry, PO Box 610, Stittsville Ontario K0A 3G0 Canada. **DD** 071./13/83.

CN
MARMORA HERALD. English. wk. 30.00Can$ (Canada); 65.00Can$ (other). Marmora Herald, PO Box 250, Marmora Ontario, K0K 2M0 Canada. **Tel** (613) 472-2431, FAX (613) 472-5026.

CN/0834-6828
MATTAWA RECORDER [MICROFORM], THE. (May 10, 1972). English. wk. $28.00 (print). Mattawa Recorder, PO Box 67, 341 McConnell Street, Mattawa ONT P0H 1V0 Canada. **Tel** (705)744-5361. **DD** 071/.13147.

CN/0820-7984
MCMASTER COURIER, THE. [McMaster cour.]. **VFOAT** Courier. **VAT** Courier - McMaster University. Vol. 1, No. 1 (Feb. 5, 1982)-. Newspaper. English. bw. Department of Information and Publications, McMaster University, 1280 Main Street West, Hamilton Ontario L8S 4L9 Canada. **DD** 378.713/52. ***Continues** Contact (Hamilton, Ont.).*

CN
MEADOW LAKE PROGRESS. Newspaper. English. wk (52 issues per year - Published on Wednesdays). 17.00Can$ within 65 kilometers of Saskatchewan; 15.00Can$ others in Canada; 85.00Can$ other. Meadow Lake Progress, PO Box 879, Meadow Lake Saskatchewan, S0M 1V0 Canada. **Tel** (306)236-5265. ctrl circ.

CN/0319-1672
MEAFORD CENTENNIAL, THE. V. 1- June 6, 1974-. Newspaper. English. wk. $6.00, $4.00 (senior citizens) Canada; $8.00 other. The Meaford Centennial, PO Box 1509, 39 Sykes Street, Meaford Ontario N0H 1Y0 Canada. **DD** 071/.13/18.

CN/0047-665X
MEIE ELU OUR LIFE. (1???)-. Newspaper. Estonian. wk (Publish on Wednesday). $80.00 Canada; $92.00 other. Estonian Publishing Company Toronto Ltd, 958 Broadview Avenue, Toronto Ontario M4K 2R6 Canada. **Tel** (416)466-0951, FAX (416)461-0448. **ED** Dr. Tonv Parminl, (phone: (416)466-8404). **Bk Rev**, (Qty: 10). **Ad Acc, Adv Mgr:** Astrid Vaikla, **Tel** (416)466-0951. **Circ:** 2,500 (ctrl). **Desc:** "Meie Elu" is the oldest Estonian language periodical publication in Canada. It is been judged the highest quality Estonian Newspaper outside Estonia. Content is redominantley Estonian.

CN
MELVILLE ADVANCE. (19??)-. Newspaper. English. wk (Wednesday). 17.00Can$ local; 30.00Can$ Canada; 100.00Can$ other. Melville Advance, Box 1420, Melville Sask. S0A 2P0 Canada. **Tel** (306)728-5448, FAX (306)728-4004. **ED** Lin Orosz. **Ad Acc, Adv Mgr:** Mark Orosz. **Circ:** 4,300 (ctrl).

CN/0380-0121
MENNONITE REPORTER. Vol. 2, No. 1 (Jan. 10, 1972)-. Periodical. English. Twenty-five times a year (Except every three weeks in July and August). 26.17Can$ Canada; 43.00Can$ other. Mennonite Publishing Service Inc, 3-312 Marsland Drive, Waterloo Ontario N2J 3Z1 Canada. **Tel** (519)884-3810, FAX (519)884-3331. **ED** Ron Rempel. Index available (Bound in last iss. per year). **Bk Rev**, (Qty: 20-30). **Ad Acc. Circ:** 11,000. available on microfilm from Micromedia Limited. ***Continues** Canadian Mennonite Reporter, 0380-013X.* **Desc:** News and comment about the Mennonites in Canada. Commentary on wider church and world issues from Anabaptist-Mennonite perspective. **Ind/Abst** Can. Index.

CN/0824-9040
MENSUEL DE LACHUTE, LE. [Mens. Lachute]. **VFOAT** Journal le Mensuel de Lachute Enr. V. 1, No. 1, (Dec. 1983)-. Newspaper. French. mo. Free to citizens of Lachute and its surroundings. Journal le Mensuel de Lachute, Enr 1117 rue Gilles Vigneault, Blainville Quebec J7C 2X8 Canada. **DD** 071/.1423.

CN/0823-6941
MENSUEL DE STE-DOROTHEE, LE. [Mens. Ste-Dorothee]. Newspaper. French. mo. Free to citizens. Mensuel de Ste-Dorothee, C P 123 Succursale Ste-Dorothee, Laval Quebec H7X 2T5 Canada. **DD** 071/.14271.

CN/0710-3794
MERCREDI SOIR, LE. Newspaper. French. wk. Free. Editions Le Mercredi Soir, CP 4070, Val-Belair G0A 1G0 Canada. **DD** 071/.1447.

CN/0713-6862
MESSAGER DE LA MINGANIE, LE. [Messager Minganie]. Vol. 1, No. 1 (3 Sept. 1980)-. Newspaper. French. wk. Free. Le Messager de la Minganie, 74 rue Lemaire, Sept-Iles Quebec G4S 1A3 Canada. **DD** 071/.1417.

CN/0821-4174
MESSAGER DORVAL, LE. [Messager Dorval]. **VFOAT** Dorval Messenger. Newspaper. English (French). bw. $20.00. Dorval Messenger, 1015 Notre-Dame, Lachine Quebec H8S 2C3 Canada. **DD** 071/.1428.

CN/0228-2828
MESSENGER (SCARBOROUGH). (THE MESSENGER.). [Messenger]. **VFOAT** Pighambar; Fortnightly Messenger. **VAT** Fortnightly Messenger (Scarborough). V. 1- Mar. 3 1978-. Newspaper. Urdu (English). bw. 20.00Can$ Canada; $16.00 US; $20.00 other. The Messenger / Canada, 2 Middleport Cres, Scarborough Ontario M1B 4L5 Canada. **Tel** (416)283-7255. **ED** Sohail Akhtar. **DD** 971.3/00491412. **UDC** 971.3. Index available. **Bk Rev. Ad Acc. Circ:** 3,000.

CN/0709-4663
METRO MATIN. V. 1, No. 44 (Jan. 15, 1979)-. Newspaper. French. da. 0.25Can$ each number. Les Publications P G M, 8401 Boulevard Ray-Lawson, Ville d'Anjou Quebec H1J 1K6 Canada. **DD** 071/.14/27. ***Continues** Metro P.M., 0709-4655.*

CN/0381-5080
METRO-SUD. ***Title Change.*** First issue in 1966. Newspaper. French. wk. Metro-Sud, 937 Boul. Taschereau, Longueil Quebec J4K 2X2 Canada. **DD** 071/.14/37. ***Continued by** Echo Expression.*

CN/1184-6402
MICMAC MALISEET NATION NEWS. [Micmac Maliseet Nation news]. **Added/Corp** Confederacy of Mainland Micmacs. Vol. 2, No. 1 (Jan. 1991)-. Newspaper. English. mo. $12.00 per year. Confederacy of Mainland Micmacs, PO Box 1590, Truro, Nova Scotia B2N 5V3 Canada. **DD** 971.5/004973. ***Continues** Micmac Nation News, 1184-6399.*

CN/0845-2555
MICMAC NEWS. ***Suspended.*** [Micmac news]. **VFOAT** Mic Mac News; Micmac News from Around the Island. (1965)-(19??). Newspaper. English. mo. Native Communication Society of Nova Scotia, PO Box 344, Sydney, Nova Scotia B1P 6H2 Canada. **Tel** (902)539-0045. **DD** 971.00497.

CN/0227-3853
MID-NORTH MONITOR, THE. [Mid-north monit.]. **VFOAT** Monitor. Vol. 1 (Oct. 11, 1978)-. Newspaper. English (French). Fifty-two times a year. 17.00Can$ Local to Espanola; 35.00Can$ Canada; 75.00Can$ other. Mid-North Monitor, Box 1126, Espanola Ontario P0P 1C0 Canada. **Tel** (705)869-2860, FAX (705)869-5140. **ED** Robert J. Gordon. **DD** 071/.13/133. **Bk Rev. Ad Acc. Pr Rev. Circ:** 3,500 (ctrl). available on microfiche (from Oakville, Ont. : Ontario Community Newspapers Asssociation). ***Supersedes** Mid-North Weekly, 0228-0000.* **Desc:** Includes local council news, correspondent-originated social news, and local hard news feature articles.

CN/0710-5363
MID-TOWN/MT. PLEASANT REVUE. (REVUE, MID-TOWN/MT. PLEASANT.). [Mid-town/Mt. Pleasant rev.]. (1979)-. Newspaper. English. The Revue, 5171 Victoria Drive V5P 3V1 Canada. **DD** 071/.1133.

CN/0228-037X
MILE ZERO NEWS. (THE MILE ZERO NEWS.). [Mile zero news]. Vol. 1 (Jan. 31 1979)-. Newspaper. English. wk. 15.00Can$. MacKenzie Highway News/Mile Zero News, PO Box 1010, Grimshaw Alberta T0H 1W0 Canada. **DD** 071/.1231.

CN/0706-683X
MILTON WEEKLY TRIBUNE. V. 1 (Sept. 20, 1978)-. Newspaper. English. wk. 0.20Can$ each number. L Fairbanks, Milton Weekly Tribune, 158 Main Street East, Milton Ontario L9T 1N6 Canada. **DD** 071/.13533. ***Supersedes** Milton Month, 0707-4921.*

CN/0225-1205
MINCHUNG SINMUN. (MINCHUNG SINMUN. MINJOONG SHINMOON.). [Minchung sinmun]. **VFOAT** Minjoong Shinmoon. No. 1 (Feb. 23, 1979)-. Newspaper. Korean (English; summaries and/or abstracts in English). sw. 70.00Can$. Minjoong-Shinmoon Ltd, 802 Bloor Street West, Toronto Ontario M6G 1L9 Canada. **Tel** (416)537-3473. **DD** 071/.13541. available on microfilm.

CN/0316-9103
MIRABEL, LE. V. 1- 22 May 1974-. French. wk. Le Mirabel, CP 276, 300 rue Labelle/Suite 100, St Jerome Quebec J7Z 5L1 Canada. **Tel** (514)436-8200. **DD** 071/.14/24.

Canada

CN/0711-3781
MIRABEL (SAINT-EUSTACHE). (LE MIRABEL.). **VFOAT** Journal le Mirabel; Mirabel St-Eustache. Vol. 1, No. 1 (March 3, 1981)-. Newspaper. French. wk. 53.10Can$ Canada; 68.10Can$ other. Le Mirabel, CP 276, 300 rue Labelle/Suite 100, St Jerome Quebec J7Z 5L1 Canada. **Tel** (514)436-8200. **DD** 071/.1425. ctrl circ.

CN/0712-1105
MIRROR (DAWSON CREEK). (THE MIRROR.). [Mirror]. **VFOAT** Dawson Creek Mirror. Vol. 1, No. 1 (May 8, 1980)-. Newspaper. English. sw. $80.00 U.S. The Mirror, 1-10224 10th Street, Dawson Creek British Columbia V1G 1P5 Canada. **Tel** (604)782-9424. **ED** Marilyn Croutch. **DD** 071/.111. **Bk Rev**. **Ad Acc**. **Circ:** 10,200 (ctrl).
Desc: A community newspaper featuring local content primarily and some news that would be of general interest to the community.

CN/1196-071X
MIRROR-EXAMINER. (THE MIRROR - EXAMINER.). [Mirror-exam.]. (Mar. 19, 1986)-. Newspaper. English. wk. $58.00 Canada; $85.00 other. **ED** Andy Gillis. **DD** 071/.1632. **Ad Acc**. **Circ:** 4,500 (ctrl). *Formed by the union of Examiner (Middleton, N.S.), 1196-0701 and Valley Mirror.*
Desc: Community news.

CN
MISSISSAUGA NEWS. English. ir. 166.92Can$. Mississauga News, 3125 Wolfdale Road, Mississauga, Ontario, L5C 3A9 Canada. **Tel** (416)273-8236. **ED** Judy Hughes. **Ad Acc**. **Circ:** 104,000 (ctrl).

CN/0225-0969
MON JOURNAL LAURIER DES LAURENTIDES. [Mon. j. Laurier Laurentides]. V. 1- Aug. 1979-. Newspaper. French. bm. Free to Laurentides. Mon Journal Laurier des Laurentides, 390 Chemin Gauthier, La Plaine Quebec J0N 1B0 Canada. **DD** 071/.144. *Supersedes Mon Journal des Laurentides, 0225-0950.*

CN/0703-1513
MONITOR (CHARLOTTETOWN). (MONITOR.). (1975)-. Newspaper. English. wk. $7.50. Monitor Publishing / Prince Edward Island, 102A Queen Street, Charlottetown Prince Edward Island, C1N 3N8 Canada. **DD** 071/.17/5.

CN/1183-9473
MONITOR (TORONTO). *Title Change.* (THE MONITOR.). [Monitor]. Vol. 1, No. 1 (Sept. 1991)-(1992). Periodical. English. qt. Monitor, Suite 700, 30 St. Clair Avenue West, Toronto Ontario M4V 3A1 Canada. **DD** 071. *Continued by Class Monitor, 1191-8845.*

CN/1186-2165
MONTREAL TRIBUNE (1990). (THE MONTREAL TRIBUNE.). [Montr. trib.]. Vol. 1, No. 1 (Dec. 1990)-. Newspaper. English. mo. 54.00Can$. Montreal Tribune, PO Box 91, Station B, Montreal, Quebec H3B 3J5 Canada. **Tel** (514)279-0615. **DD** 338.4.

CN
MOOSE JAW TIMES-HERALD. Newspaper. English. ir. 104.00Can$ in Moose Jaw; 116.75Can$ in Saskatchewan; 132.50Can$ in rest of Canada; 357.00Can$ other. Moose Jaw Times Herald, 44 Fairford Street West, Moose Jaw Saskatchewan, S6H 6E4 Canada. **Tel** (306)692-6441, FAX (306)692-2101.

CN/0711-3811
MORINVILLE MIRROR. [Morinville mirror]. Vol. 1, No. 1 (Sept. 26, 1979)-. Newspaper. English. wk. $22.00 Canada; $30.00 US. Morinville Mirror, PO Box 1649, Morinville Alberta T0G 1P0 Canada. **Tel** (403)939-2133. **DD** 071/.1233.

CN/0316-0254
MOUNT BRYDGES BULLETIN, THE. Began publication in Aug. 1973?. Bulletin. English. wk. $4.00 Canada; $5.00 US. Neighborly News Publishing, 17 Adelaide Street South, Mount Brydges Ontario N0L 1W0 Canada. **DD** 071/.13/25.

CN/0826-2748
MOUTON NOIR. (LE MOUTON NOIR : JOURNAL ETUDIANT CEGEP DE DRUMMONDVILLE.). [Mouton noir]. **Main/Corp** Cegep de Drummondville. Newspaper. French. mo. Free to Students. Mouton Noir, 960 Saint-Georges Canada. **DD** 378.714/563.

CN/0701-1199
MUSKOKA FREE PRESS. V. 1- June 30, 1976-. Periodical. English. wk. 8.00Can$. F T Botham Publications, 53 Main Street, Huntsville Ontario P0A 1K0 Canada. **DD** 071/.13/76.

CN/0225-0594
NEA PATRIDA. [Nea patrida]. No. 1- Oct. 15, 1978-. Newspaper. Greek, Modern (English). bw. 0.50Can$ per issue. Nea Patrida Publications, 1089 West Broadway, Vancouver BC V6H 1E5. **DD** 071/.1133.

CN/0715-4410
NEA TOY HAMILTON. [Nea toy Hamilt.]. **VFOAT** Hellenic Hamilton News. No. 1 (July 1980)-. Newspaper. Greek, Modern. mo. 7.00Can$ Canada; $7.00 US; 15.00Can$ Greece. Nea Toy Hamilton, 8 Morris Avenue, Hamilton Ontario L8L 1X7 Canada. **Tel** 549-9208. **ED** Panos Andronipis. **DD** 071/.1352. **Ad Acc**. **Circ:** 1,000.
Desc: Editorial about Greece, Canada, international and Greek community subjects.

CN/0823-3934
NEW BRUNSWICK COURIER. (NEW BRUNSWICK COURIER [MICROFORM] / CANADIAN LIBRARY ASSOCIATION NEWSPAPER MICROFILMING PROJECT.). [N.B. courier]. **Added/Corp** Canadian Library Association. Newspaper Microfilming Project. **VAT** Courier (Saint John). (19??)-. Newspaper. English. Canadian Library Association, 200 Elgin Street, Suite 602, Ottawa Ontario K2P 1L5 Canada. **Tel** (613)232-9625. **DD** 071/.15.

CN/0703-9042
NEW EDINBURGH NEWS. Began publication in 1976. Newspaper. English. Free. E Dunn, 34 Dufferin Road, Ottawa Ontario K1M 2A8 Canada. **DD** 071/.13/84.

CN/0227-8030
NEW ERA (LANARK). (THE NEW ERA.). [New era]. V. 1- Nov. 15, 1979-. Newspaper. English. wk. $12.00. New Era/Canada, 106 Main Street, Melita Manitoba R0M 1L0 Canada. **Tel** (204)522-3491. **ED** A W Lenz. **DD** 071/.1382. **Ad Acc**. **Circ:** 2,500.

CN/0713-4789
NEW MARITIMES. [New Marit.]. **Added/Corp** New Maritimes Editorial Council. Vol. 1, No. 1 (Sept. 1982)-. Newspaper. English. bm. 17.00Can$ individuals; 25.00Can$ other. New Maritimes, PO Box 31269, Halifax Nova Scotia B3K 5Y5 Canada. **Tel** (902)425-6622. **ED** Scott Milsom. **DD** 331/.09715. **Bk Rev**. **Ad Acc**. **Circ:** 1,900. available on microfilm.
Desc: Features on issues of interest to Maritimers: regional politics, environment, labor, culture and history. Features regular columns on regional media, books and third-world issues.
Ind/Abst Altern. Press Index; Can. Index; Can. Period. Index.

CN/0710-0116
NEWCASTLE INDEPENDENT (1977). (THE NEWCASTLE INDEPENDENT.). [Newcastle indep.]. **VFOAT** Independent. Newspaper. English. wk. Free to residents of Newcastle. Newcastle Independent, 62-66 King Street West, Bowmanville Ontario L1M 3K9 Canada. **DD** 071/.1356.

CN/0317-2309
NEWFOUNDLAND SIGNAL, THE. V. 1- Nov. 6, 1974-. Newspaper. English. wk. Hibbs'-Power Communication, Apt 214, 396 Avenue Road, Toronto Ontario M4V 2H5. **DD** 971.8/005.

CN
NEWS ADVERTISER (AJAX CANADA). (NEWS ADVERTISER.). (19??)-. English. sw (published Fri. and Sun.). 70.00Can$. News Advertiser, 130 Commercial Avenue, Ajax Ontario L1S 2M5 Canada. **Tel** (416)683-5100, FAX (416)683-7363. **ED** Greg Coates. **Ad Acc**, **Adv Mgr:** Bruce Dunford, **Tel** same as publisher. **Circ:** 35,000 (ctrl).

CN/0316-0238
NEWS ADVERTISER (KITIMAT). (THE NEWS ADVERTISER.). Began with Nov. 7, 1972 issue. Newspaper. English. Free distribution in Kitimat, Terrace, Thornhill. Northern Sentinel Press, 626 Enterprise Avenue, Kitimat British Columbia V8C 2E4 Canada. **DD** 071/.11/32.

CN/0317-9885
NEWS BURLINGTON. V. 1, No. 35- Aug. 30, 1973-. Newspaper. English. wk. Box 807, Burlington Ontario Canada. **DD** 071/.13/533. *Continues Sports Burlington, 0317-9877.*

CN/0227-2598
NEWS (MAPLE RIDGE). (THE NEWS : THE VOICE OF THE NORTH FRASER VALLEY.). [News]. Vol. 2, No. 21 (Oct. 10, 1979)-. Newspaper. English. wk. 0.15Can$ per no. Janor Publications, 22757 Selkirk Avenue, Maple Ridge British Columbia V2X 2Y1 Canada. **DD** 071/.1133. *Continues Meadow Ridge News.*

CN/0828-1521
NEWS/NORTH. [News/north]. **VFOAT** News North. (June 20, 1980)-. Newspaper. English. wk. 69.23Can$ Canada; 87.93Can$ other. Northern News Services, PO Box 2820, Yellowknife Northwest Territories, 1XA 2R1 Canada. **Tel** (403)873-4031. *Continues News of the North.*

CN/0229-7752
NEWS (ROBLIN). *Title Change.* (THE NEWS.). [News]. Vol. 1, No. 1 (Mar. 16, 1977)-. Newspaper. English. wk. **DD** 071/.1272. *Continued by Roblin News, 0229-7760.*

CN/0709-6119
NEWS, SOUTHERN AFRICA. V. 1- June 1978-. Periodical. English. Manitoba Anti-Apartheid Coalition, Box 55, Station C, Winipeg Manitoba R3M 3S3 Canada. **DD** 968/.005. *Supersedes South Africa Newsclippings, 0381-5420.*

CN/0711-1762
NEWSFILE (TORONTO). (NEWSFILE.). [Newsfile]. Vol. 1, Issue 1 (Sept. 1981)-. Periodical. English. sm. $35.00. Newsfile, c/o Moore & Moore Design, 284 Avenue Road, Toronto Ontario M4V 2G7 Canada. **DD** 016.07.

CN/0823-132X
NEWSPAPER GEOG. LIST - CARLETON UNIVERSITY. (NEWSPAPER GEOG. LIST MICROFORM / CARLETON UNIVERSITY.). [Newsp. geog. list - Carleton Univ.]. **Main/Corp** Carleton University. Library. **VFOAT** Newspaper Index. Periodical. English. 1.00Can$. Carleton University Library, Ottawa Ontario K1S 5B6 Canada. **Tel** (613)564-6647. **DD** 018/.135.
Desc: Catalogue of all newspapers in Carleton University library, organized by country, and provincial breakdown for Canadian items.

CN/0227-7409
NEWSPAPER (TORONTO). (THE NEWSPAPER.). [Newspaper]. V. 1- Sept. 6, 1978-. Newspaper. English. wk. Free, University of Toronto Campus. $15.00 others. Planet Publications, The Newspaper, Room 121/10 Saint George Street, University of Toronto, Toronto Ontario M5S 1A1 Canada. **DD** 071/.13541.

CN/0839-1572
NIAGARA FALLS REVIEW. (NIAGARA FALLS REVIEW [MICROFORM].). [Niagara F. rev.]. (May 4, 1970)-. English. da. 430.00Can$ one year; 443.00Can$ other. Niagara Falls Review, 4801 Valley Way, Niagara Falls L2E 6T6 Canada. **ED** Michael Brown (phone: (416)358-5711 Ext. 120). **DD** 071/.1339. **Ad Acc**, **Adv Mgr:** Tony Bove, **Tel** (416)358-5711 Ext.181. ctrl circ. *Continues Niagara Falls Evening Review, 0844-9481.*

CN/0226-2002
NIKKA TAIMUSU. (NIKKA TAIMUSU. THE NIKKA TIMES.). [Nikka taimusu]. **VFOAT** Nikka Times. (Oct. 17, 1979)-. Newspaper. Japanese. Fifty times a year. 30.00Can$. The Nikka Times, 720 Spabina Avenue/Suite 420, Toronto Ontario M5S 2T9 Canada. **Tel** (416)923-2819. **DD** 071/.13451.

CN/1187-4953
NORD-EST PLUS. [Nord-Est plus]. Vol. 1, No 1 (Oct. 9 1991)-. Newspaper. French. wk. Free Limited Distribution. Nord-Est Plus, 365 Boulevard Laure, Sept-Iles Quebec G4R 1X2 Canada. **DD** 071/.1417.

CN/0382-8883
NORD (HEARST). (LE NORD.). [Nord]. Vol. 1, (March 24, 1976)-. Newspaper. French. wk (Published on Wednesdays). 25.00Can$ Canada; 50.00Can$ other. Le Nord, 905 rue Georges, Case Postale 2320, Hearst Ontario P0L 1N0 Canada. **Tel** (705)372-1233, FAX (705)362-5954. **ED** Omer Cantin. **DD** 071/.13/142. **Bk Rev**. **Ad Acc**. **Circ:** 3,900 (ctrl). available on microfiche (from Oakville, Ont. : Ontario Community Newspapers Association).
Desc: Covers local and regional news.

CN/0704-0245
NORFOLK GAZETTE, THE. Vol. 1, (Jan. 19, 1977)-. Newspaper. English. wk. The Norfolk Gazette, Ad-Rite Associates Ltd, PO Box 418, Cayuga Ontario N0A 1E0 Canada. **DD** 071/.13/36.

CN
NORTH BATTLEFORD NEWS OPTIMIST. Newspaper. English. Twice a week (published on Monday and Thursday). 48.20Can$. North Battleford News Optimist, Box 430, North Battleford, Saskatchewan, Canada. **Tel** (306)445-4401, FAX (306)445-1977. **ED** Lorne Cooper. **Ad Acc**. ctrl circ. available on microfiche.

CN/0316-0203
NORTH DELTA SENTINEL. Began with Nov. 1973 issue. Newspaper. English. mo. Delta Publications / Canada, 9345-120th Street, North Delta BC Canada. **DD** 071/.11/33.

CN/0703-9034
NORTH-EAST REGION COMMUNITY BOOSTER, THE. [North-east reg. community booster]. V. 1- Mar. 1972-. Newspaper. English. ir. 0.25Can$ per no. Community Printers Ltd, Box 2014, Nipawin Saskatchewan S0E 1E0 Canada. **DD** 071/.124/2.

CN/0700-950X
NORTH FRONTENAC NEWS. Began publication with Dec. 1970 issue. Newspaper. English. wk. Free to residents of Northern Frontenac, Lanark, and Lennox-Addington Counties, $40.00 Canada; $50.00 North America; $96.00 UK. North Frontenac News, PO Box 250, Sharbot Lake Ontario K0H 2P0 Canada. **Tel**

(613)279-3150. **ED** Mauveen Bush. **DD** 071/.13/71. **Ad Acc. Circ:** 4,100 winter, 4,500 summer (ctrl).
Desc: A community newspaper which the main purpose is to report the happenings in the eight northern townships of Frontenac County, and parts of Lennox-Addington and Lanark Counties.

CN/1182-6126
NORTH INTERLAKE ECHO. [North Interlake echo]. Vol. 1, No. 1 (Jan. 22, 1990)-. Newspaper. English. mo. Limited free distribution. Nordheim Printing & Graphics, TBJ Mall, Ashern Manitoba R0C 0E0 Canada. **DD** 071/.1272. ***Continues*** *Our Backyard., 1182-6118.*

CN/0823-7387
NORTH KAWARTHA TIMES. [North Kawartha times]. No. 1 (March 2, 1983)-. Newspaper. English. wk. 12.00Can$ (local seniors), 14.00Can$ (regular) Canada; $25.00 US. North Kawartha Times, 44 Colborne Street, Box 717, Fenelon Falls Ontario K0M 1N0 Canada. **Tel** (705)887-5151, FAX (705)887-4037. **ED** Patti Cragg. **DD** 071/.1364. **Ad Acc. Circ:** 2,000, 7,500 (May-Sept.) (ctrl). available on microfiche (from Oakville, Ont. : Ontario Community Newspapers Association).
Desc: A community newspaper dealing with people and events in the Northern part of Victoria County.

CN/0821-2376
NORTH LANCE. [North lance]. (1977)-. Newspaper. English. wk. North Lance, 620 Dakota Street Canada. **DD** 071/.1274.

CN/0712-5348
NORTH SHORE NEWS. [North shore news]. (Jan. 7, 1976)-. Newspaper. English. wk. $72.00. North Shore News, 1139 Longsdale, North Vancouver British Columbia V7M 2H4 Canada. **Tel** (604)985-2131. **DD** 071/.1133. ctrl circ. ***Continues*** *North Shore Shopper (1972).*

CN/0715-5786
NORTH SHORE SENTINEL. [North shore sentinel]. **VFOAT** Sentinel. **VAT** Sentinel (Bruce Mines). (1965)-. Newspaper. English. Fifty-two times a year. 23.97Can$ North Shore & Algoma; 46.27Can$ US; 38.31Can$ others. The North Shore Sentinel, 9 Huron Street West, PO Box 670, Thessalon Ontario P0R 1L0 Canada. **Tel** (705)842-2504. **ED** Hank Babbitt. **DD** 071/.13132. **Bk Rev. Ad Acc. Circ:** 3,500 (ctrl). available on microfiche (from Oakville, Ont. : Ontario Community Newspapers Association).
Desc: Community newspaper.

CN/0701-0761
NORTH SHORE TIMES (STE-THERESE). (THE NORTH SHORE TIMES.). Vol. 1 (Nov. 3, 1976)-. Periodical. English. Les Editions, JMC 15 rue de l Eglise, Ste-Therese Quebec J7E 3K Canada. **DD** 071/.14/24.

CN/0225-2082
NORTH YORK CONSUMER, THE. [North York consum.]. **VFOAT** Consumer. **VAT** Consumer (Don Mills). V. 1- Sept. 14, 1977-. Newspaper. English. ir. $37.14. Metro Mirror Publishers, 10 Tempo Avenue, Willowdale Ontario M2H 2N8 Canada. **DD** 640.73/09713/541.

CN/0841-2707
NORTH YORK NEWS (1970?). (NORTH YORK NEWS [MICROFORM].). [North York News]. (1970?)-. Newspaper. English. wk. 15.00Can$. Watson Publishing Company, 150 Milner Avenue, Unit 35, Sacrborough, Ontario, M1S 3R3 Canada. **Tel** (416)291-2583. **DD** 071/.13541.

CN/0715-514X
NORTHERN JOURNAL, THE. [North. j.]. Vol. 1, No. 1 (July 8, 1981)-. Newspaper. English. wk. $0.30 per issue. Whisky Jack Enterprises, PO Box 1829, La Ronge Sask S0J 1L0 Canada. **DD** 071/.1241.

CN/0700-527X
NORTHERN LIFE (SUDBURY). (NORTHERN LIFE.). [North. life]. Vol. 1 (April 11, 1973)-. Newspaper. English. wk. 90.00Can$ Canada; 174.00Can$ other. Laurentian Publishing Company, 158 Elgin Street South, Sudbury Ontario P3E 3N5 Canada. **Tel** (705)673-5667, FAX (705)673-4652. **ED** Carol Mulligan. **DD** 071/.13/133. **Bk Rev**, (Qty: less than 10). **Ad Acc, Adv Mgr:** K. Johansson. **Circ:** 49,066. available on microfiche (from Oakville, Ont. : Ontario Community Newspapers Association).

CN/0384-0840
NORTHERN MOSAIC (THUNDER BAY). ***Suspended.*** (NORTHERN MOSAIC.). **Added/Corp** Thunder Bay Council of Ethnic Organizations. Vol. 1 (Aug. 1975)-(19??). Periodical. English. qt. $3.86. Thunder Bay Multicultural Association, 17 North Court Street, Thunder Bay Ontario P7A 4T4 Canada. **Tel** (807)345-0551. **ED** Frank Obljubek. **DD** 971.3/12/004. **Bk Rev. Ad Acc. Circ:** 2,000.
Desc: A newspaper promoting and publicizing the concept of multiculturalism to create an awareness and appreciation of the cultural diversity of our area.

CN/0229-0391
NORTHERN PEN. (THE NORTHERN PEN.). [North. pen]. (1980)-. Newspaper. English. wk. 45.00Can$ (Canada); 150.00Can$ (other). The Northern Pen, c/o Bern Bromley, PO Box 520, St Anthony Newfoundland, Canada. **Tel** (709)454-2191, FAX (709)454-3718. **ED** Allan Bock. **DD** 017/.18. **Ad Acc, Adv Mgr:** Sharon Warren. **Circ:** 6,500 (ctrl).
Desc: News and sports from the local area, TV listings and features on local people.

CN/0383-1221
NORTHERN PIONEER, THE. Vol. 1, (Feb. 5, 1976)-. Newspaper. English. Fifty-one times per year. 33.16Can$ Canada; 48.16Can$ other. The Northern Pioneer, Box 427 Fort Vermillion, Fort Vermillion La Crete Canada. **Tel** (403)927-3731. **DD** 071/.123/1.

CN/0227-2512
NORTHERN TIMES (WHITEHORSE). (THE NORTHERN TIMES.). [North. times]. (1978)-. Newspaper. English. wk. $24.00. Yukon News / Northern Times, PO Box 5149, Whitehorse Yukon Territory Y1A 4S3 Canada. **Tel** (705)335-2283. **ED** Wayne Major. **DD** 071/.191. **Ad Acc. Circ:** 5,500.

CN/0228-0531
NORTHUMBERLAND NEWS. ***Ceased.*** [Northumberl. news]. Vol. 1 (May 30, 1979)-?. Newspaper. English. wk. Northumberland News, PO Box 517, Chatham New Brunswick E1N 3A8 Canada. **Tel** (506)773-9431. **ED** Lois F Martin. **DD** 071/.1521. **Bk Rev. Ad Acc. Circ:** 5,087 (ctrl).
Desc: A newspaper which covers highlights of events which occur in Northumberland county as well as opinions, sports and features on people, past and present.

●CN/1186-5601
NORTHUMBERLAND PUBLISHERS' WEEKENDER. (NORTHUMBERLAND PUBLISHERS' WEEKENDER [MICROFORM].). **VFOAT** Weekender; Northumberland Weekender. (Feb. 22, 1992)-. English. Ontario Community Newspapers Association, PO Box 451, 1184 Speers Road, Oakville Ontario L6J 5A8. **DD** 071/.1357.

CN/0712-5089
NORTHWEST EXPLORER (SIOUX LOOKOUT). ***Ceased.*** (NORTHWEST EXPLORER.). [Northwest explor.]. **VFOAT** Explorer. **VAT** Explorer (Sioux Lookout). Vol. 1, No. 1 (Oct. 17, 1979)-(19??). Newspaper. English. wk. Northwest Explorer, c/o F Smith, PO Box 989, Sioux Lookout Ontario P0V 2T0 Canada. **DD** 071/.13112.

CN
NORWOOD REGISTER. (19??)-. English. Fifty-two times a year. 40.00Can$ Canada; 75.00Can$ other. Cembal Publications Ltd., PO Box 250, Marmora Ontario, K0K 2M0 Canada. **Tel** (613)472-2431, FAX (613)472-5026.

CN/0710-1740
NOTTAWASAGA/SUNNIDALE NEWS, THE. [Nottawasaga/Sunnidale news]. **VFOAT** News. **VAT** News (Nottawasaga/Sunnidale). Vol. 1, No 1 (Jan. 28, 1981)-. Newspaper. English. wk. Wasaga Publications, PO Box 254, Wasaga Beach Ontario L0L 2P0 Canada. **DD** 071/.1317.

CN/0712-2489
NOUVEAU JOURNAL DE ST-MICHEL, LE. [Nouv. j. St-Michel]. **VFOAT** Journal de St-Michel. Vol. 1, No. 1 (17 Oct. 1979)-. Newspaper. French. wk. Free. Le Nouveau Journal de St-Michel/Suite 1, Montreal Quebec H1Z 3E1 Canada. **DD** 071/.14281. ctrl circ.

CN/0821-7378
NOUVEL-EST. [Nouvel-est]. 30 Sept. 1980-. Newspaper. French. wk. $15.00. Nouvel-Est, 148 rue de la Cathedrale, Rimouski Quebec G5L 5H8 Canada. **DD** 071/.147.

CN/0827-2085
NOUVELLE (BEAUMONT). (LA NOUVELLE : BEAUMONT.). [Nouvelle]. Vol. 1, No. 1 (Jan. 9, 1984)-. Newspaper. English. wk. 23.16Can$. La Nouvelle, PO Box 1209, Beaumont Alberta T0C 0H0 Canada. **Tel** (403)929-5552. **ED** Hugh Johnston. **DD** 071/.1233. **Ad Acc. Circ:** 1,459 (ctrl).
Desc: Community newspaper for the town of Beaumont and surrounding area.

CN/0227-8472
NOUVELLES D'OUTREMENT. [Nouv. Outrement]. **VFOAT** Outrement News. V. 1- Apr. 25, 1979-. Newspaper. English (French). wk. **DD** 071/.14281.

CN/0316-019X
NOVA (MIDDLETON). (NOVA.). V. 1- Apr. 9, 1974-. Newspaper. English. wk. 5.00Can$ Annapolis & Kings counties, 6.50Can$ elsewhere in Canada, 8.00Can$ other. Nova, PO Box 1027, Middleton Nova Scotia B0S 1P0 Canada. **DD** 071/16/33.

CN/0029-5310
NOVIJ SLAH. (NOVYI SHLIAKH.). [Nov. slah]. **Added/Corp** Ukrainian National Federation. **VFOAT** New Pathway; Nouveau Chemin. (Oct. 30, 1930)-. Newspaper. Ukrainian (English). wk. 45.00Can$. New Pathway Publ Ltd., 297 College Street, Toronto Ontario M5T 1S2 Canada. **Tel** (416)960-3424. **ED** J. Karmanin. **Bk Rev. Ad Acc. Circ:** 5,000.

CN/0822-8035
NOVO MUNDO (TORONTO). (NOVO MUNDO.). [Novo mundo]. Yearly V. 3, Ed. 128 (August 24, 1983)-. Newspaper. Portuguese. wk. $.50 per no. Novo Mundo, 803 Dundas Street West, Toronto Ontario M6J 1V2. **DD** 071/.13541. ***Continues*** *Mundo (Toronto, Ont.), 0229-1118.*

CN/0702-7915
NUNATSIAQ NEWS. [Nunatsiaq news]. **VFOAT** Nunatsiark. Vol. 4, No. 23 (July 7, 1976)-. Newspaper. English (Eskimo). wk. 45.00Can$ US; 60.00Can$ other. Nunatext Publishing Corporation, Iqaluit Northwest Territories, Canada X0A 0H0. **Tel** (819)979-5357, FAX (819)979-4763. **ED** Todd Phillips and Jim Bell. **DD** 071/.19/5. **Ad Acc. Circ:** 6,012. available on microfiche (from the Ontario Community Newspapers Association of Oakville, Ontario). ***Continues*** *Inuksuk, 0702-7923.*
Desc: Community Newspaper.

CN/0227-2121
NUNS' ISLAND JOURNAL. [Nuns' Isl. j.]. **VFOAT** Journal Ile des Soeurs. Began publication in Apr. 1978. Newspaper. English (French). wk. Free to residents of Nuns' Island. D Leonardo, PO Box 67, Deux-Montagnes, Quebec J7R 4K1 Canada. **DD** 971.4/28/005. **UDC** 325.2(09) (78/79).

CN/0821-6525
NUOVO MONDO (EDMONTON). (IL NUOVO MONDO : L'UNICO GIORNALE ITALIANO DELL' ALBERTA.). Newspaper. Italian. mo. $5.00, Alberta residents, $6.00 Canada. Interprovincial Advertising, 4545-118 Avenue, Edmonton Alta T5W 1A8 Canada. **DD** 071/.1233.

CN/0229-7892
O ELLEN AGGELIAPHOROS. [Ell. aggeliafor.]. **VFOAT** Greek Messenger. Vol. 1, No. 1 (Mar. 1976)-. Newspaper. Greek, Modern. sm. $0.35 each no. O Ellen Aggeliaphoros, 457 Ontario Street, London Ontario N5W 3X1 Canada. **DD** 071/.1326.

CN/0380-4542
OAK BAY STAR. Began publication in 1974?. Newspaper. English. Community News / Victoria, 506 David Street, Victoria British Columbia V8T 2C8 Canada. **DD** 071/.11/34.

CN/0702-763X
OAK LAKE TOWN AND COUNTRY NEWS. Newspaper. English. sm. $5.00. Oak Lake Town & Country, Newspaper Board, Oak Lake Manitoba R0M 1P0 Canada. **DD** 071/.127/3.

CN/1185-6351
OBSERVATEUR (TORONTO). (L'OBSERVATEUR.). [Observateur]. Vol. 1, No 1 (Jul 2 1991)-. Newspaper. French. wk. Free Limited Distribution. Observateur, 11 Avenue Carlow, Toronto Ontario M4M 2R6 Canada. **DD** 071/.13541.

CN/0712-4929
OGGI CANADA. **VFOAT** Canada Today. **VAT** Canada Today (Downsview). First Year, No. 1 (14/20 March 1980)-. Newspaper. Italian. wk. $0.50 each number. OGGI Canada Pub, Unite 13 101 di Toro Road, Downsview Ontario M3J 2Z1 Canada. **DD** 071/.13541.

CN/0712-3345
OMELLETTE, L'. [Omellette]. V. 1, No. 1, (Aug. 25, 1980)-. Newspaper. French. Free. Association des Etudiants du Cegep de Matane, College de Matane, 616 Avenue, St Redempteur, Matane Quebec G4W 3H6 Canada. **DD** 378.714/775. ctrl circ.

CN/0708-000X
OMINECA ADVERTISER, THE. V. 1- June 7, 1978-. Newspaper. English. wk. Free. Omineca Advertiser Ltd, PO Box 1007, Vanderhoof British Columbia V0J 3A0 Canada. **DD** 071/.11/2. ctrl circ.

CN/0823-7131
ONOWAY TRIBUNE. (THE ONOWAY TRIBUNE.). [Onoway trib.]. (1980)-. Newspaper. English. wk. $0.25 each number. The Onoway Tribune, PO Box 570, Onoway Alta, T0E 1V0. **DD** 071/.1233. ***Continues*** *Tribune (Onoway, Alta.).*

CN/0707-5448
OPASQUIA TIMES. Vol. 1, (Mar. 17, 1978)-. Newspaper. English. wk. 55.00Can$ (one year) Canada; 177.00Can$ (two years) other. Opasquia Times, Box 750, The Pas Manitoba R9A 1K8 Canada. **Tel** (204)623-3435. **DD** 071/.127/2. **Ad Acc. Circ:** 3,648 (ctrl).
Desc: Includes community and provincial news, sports, crafts, home improvement, law, politics, health, medicine, education, family care and entertainment.

CN/0383-1949
OR BLANC. (L'OR BLANC.). Vol. 1 (Aug. 12 1975)-. Newspaper. French. wk. 0.25Can$ per no. Editions De L'Amiante, 131 D'Auteuil, C.P. 516 Thetford Mines, Quebec G6G 2N3. **DD** 071/.17/14575.

Canada

CN/0319-180X
ORANGEVILLE CITIZEN, THE. V. 1- Sept. 18, 1974-. Newspaper. English. wk. 18.00Can$. The Orangeville Citizen, 81 Broadway, Orangeville Ontario L9W 1K1 Canada. **Tel** 941-9316. **ED** Art Selletier. **DD** 071/.13/41. **Bk Rev. Ad Acc. Circ:** 8,600 (ctrl). available on microfiche (from Oakville, Ont. : Ontario Community Newspapers Association).

CN/0823-6763
ORILLIA SUN. [Orillia sun]. Oct. 27, 1982-. Newspaper. English. wk. Champlain Press, 517806 Ontario, Orillia. **DD** 071/.1317. available on microfiche (from Oakville, Ont. : Ontario Community Newspapers Association).

CN/1186-4893
ORILLIA TODAY [MICROFORM]. (June 4, 1991)-. English. Ontario Community Newspapers Association, PO Box 451, 1184 Speers Road, Oakville Ontario L6J 5A8. **DD** 071/.1317.

CN/1186-4265
ORO-VESPRA INDEPENDENT [MICROFORM]. (May 2, 1991)-. English. Ontario Community Newspapers Association, PO Box 451, 1184 Speers Road, Oakville Ontario L6J 5A8. **DD** 071/.1317. *Continues* Independent (Barrie, Ont.), 1181-3474.

CN/0710-5460
OROMOCTO POST, THE. [Oromocto post]. Newspaper. English. wk. Free. $15.00. Oromocto Post, 101 Hersey Street, Oromocto New Brunswick Canada. **Tel** (506)357-9813. **ED** J Ross Ingram. **DD** 071/.1543. **Bk Rev. Ad Acc. Circ:** 4,800 (ctrl).
 Desc: A weekly community newspaper.

CN/0715-5476
OSCAR : OTTAWA SOUTH COMMUNITY ASSOCIATION REVIEW. [OSCAR, Ottawa South Community Assoc. rev.]. **VFOAT** Ottawa South Community Association Review. Newspaper. English. mo. Free to Ottawa South homes and business. Ottawa South Community Association, 260 Sunnyside Avenue, Ottawa Ontario K1S 0R7 Canada. **DD** 071/.1384.

CN/0229-7744
OSHAWA THIS WEEKEND. Newspaper. English. wk. Inland Publishing Company, 54 Main Street, Stouffville Ontario Canada. **DD** 071/.1356.

CN/0839-3222
OTTAWA CITIZEN. MICROFORM, THE. [Ott. citiz.]. (Oct. 4, 1986)-. English. ir. $139.59 (daily and Sunday); $373.70 Canada; $926.22 other. Commonwealth Microfilm Library, 3395 American Drive, Unit 11, Mississauga, Ontario, L4V 1T5 Canada. **Tel** (905)671-4173. **DD** 071/.1384. *Continues Citizen (Ottawa, Ont.: 1973), 0839-3214.*

CN/0715-3325
OTTAWA REPORTER, THE. [Ottawa report.]. Vol. 1, No. 1 (Apr. 15, 1981)-. Newspaper. English. mo. Ottawa Reporter, 403 Catherine Street, Ottawa Ontario K1A 5T6 Canada. **DD** 071/.1384.

CN/0843-2570
OTTAWA SUN, THE. [Ott. sun]. **VFOAT** Ottawa Sunday Sun. Vol. 1, No. 1 (Nov. 7, 1988)-. Newspaper. English. da (Monday - Fridays & Sundays). 228.00Can$ Canada, 700.00Can$ other, (by mail; 104.15Can$ Other & Carleton, 115.70Can$ other, (by carrier); 67.95Can$ Canada, 194.21Can$ other, (Sunday - Friday, 78 issues); 49.76Can$ Canada, 146.06Can$ other, (Monday - Friday, 65 issues); 18.19Can$ Canada, 48.15 Can$ other, (Sunday only, 13 issues). The Ottawa Sun, 380 Hunt Club Road, Ottawa Ontario K1G 5H7 Canada. **Tel** (613)739-7200, FAX (613)739-8043. **ED** Mr. R. Van Sickle, (phone: (613)739-7000). **DD** 071/.1384. **Bk Rev**, (Qty: 24). **Ad Acc. Adv Mgr:** L. Desgrosilliers. **Circ:** 55,000 (ctrl). available on microfilm. *Continues Ottawa Sunday Sun, 0841-7733.*
 Desc: With coverage of the sports, news, business, and entertainment.

CN/0704-0237
OWEN SOUND LIFE. Vol. 1 (Feb. 1977)-. Newspaper. English. wk. Free. Owen Sound Life, Box 218, Owen Sound Ontario N4K 5P3. **DD** 071/.13/.18.

CN
OWEN SOUND SUN TIMES. English. Six issues per week (Mor.-Sat.). 135.00Can$; 415.00Can$ other. The Sun Times, 290 9th Street East, PO Box 200, Owen Sound, Ontario, N4K 5P2 Canada. **Tel** (519)376-2250, FAX (519)376-7190. **ED** Jim Merrimam. **Ad Acc. Adv Mgr:** Warren Elder. **Circ:** 23,500.

CN
PACIFIC TRIBUNE (VANCOUVER, B.C.). (PACIFIC TRIBUNE.). Began Feb. 15, 1946. Newspaper. English. wk. 3.00Can$ (introduction rate), 10.00Can$ (6 months), 16.00Can$ Canada; 25.00Can$ other. Tribune Publishing Company Ltd, 2681 East Hastings Street V5K 1Z5 Canada. **Tel** (604)251-1186. **ED** Sean Griffin. **Bk Rev. Ad Acc. Circ:** 5,000 (ctrl).
 Desc: B.C.'s only weekly labor newspaper. News and analysis from a working class perspective. Trade union, unemployed, peace, solidarity reports.

CN/0317-7033
PALACHUV HLASATEL. VFOAT The Palach Herald; Palach Herald. Periodical. Czech. ir. Palach Herald, 245 Dunn Avenue/Apartment 910, Toronto Ontario M6K 1S6 Canada.

CN/0715-4801
PANJABI ESHEEA TAEEMZ (MARCH, 1975). (PANJABI ESHEEA TAEEMZ.). [Panjabi Esheea taeemz]. **VFOAT** Panjabi Asia Times. March 1975-. Periodical. Panjabi (English). wk. $35.00 Canada; $45.00 other. Asia Publications, 1433 Bloor Street West, Toronto Ontario M6P 3L6 Canada. **Tel** (416)533-8243. **ED** M Safri and T Gill. **DD** 954/.005. *Continues Punjabi Asia Times, 0319-8707.*
 Desc: News and views from South Asia, especially Panjabi, Canada and other Panjabi speaking residents around the world.

CN/0712-2977
PAPERASSE. (LA PAPERASSE : JOURNAL ETUDIANT DE L'ECOLE SECONDAIRE JEAN DE-LA-MENNAIS.). [Paperasse]. Vol. 1, No. 1 (25 Nov. 1981)-. Newspaper. French. $0.25 per number. La Paperasse, c/o Comite du Journal la Paperasse, 870 Chemin de Saint Jean, La Prairie Quebec J5R 2L5 Canada. **DD** 373.714/.34.

CN/0700-947X
PAROIKIAKA NEA. [Paroik. nea]. **VFOAT** Parikiaka Nea. Began publication in 1973?. Newspaper. Greek, Modern. 0.25Can$ per no. Paroikiaka Nea, 7, Cote Street, Catherine Road, Montreal Quebec H2V 1Z9. **DD** 071/.14/281.

CN/0229-4702
PAS GRAPHIC, THE. [Pas graph.]. V. 1, No. 1 (Wed., Aug. 15, 1979)-. Newspaper. English. wk. $6.00 Nor-Man Graphics, PO Box 1738, The Pas Manitoba R9A 1L5 Canada. **DD** 071/.1272.

CN/0380-4135
PASS PROMOTER, THE. V. 1- Feb. 14, 1973-. Newspaper. English. wk. 16.50Can$. The Pass Promoter, Box 1019, Blairmore Alberta T0L 0E0 Canada. **Tel** (403)562-8884. **ED** Edward H Moser. **DD** 071/.123/4. **Ad Acc. Circ:** 3,500 (ctrl).
 Desc: Focuses on local news and sports events and local columnists, professionally presented.

CN/0715-5913
PATRIS (VANCOUVER). (PATRIS.). [Patris]. **VFOAT** Fatherland : Weekly Greek News Paper; Fatherland. No. 1 (Nov. 26, 1976)-. Newspaper. Greek, Modern. wk. $.35. Patris, 2856 West Broadway, Vancouver British Columbia V6K 2G7 Canada. **DD** 071/.1133.

CN/0048-3095
PAZIFISCHE RUNDSCHAU. VFOAT Pacific Review. **VAT** Pacific Review (Vancouver). Vol. 6, No. 67 (Jan. 10, 1970)-. Newspaper. German. Twenty-four times a year. $15.00 US & Canada, $30.00 others (surface mail), $30.00 US & Canada, $60.00 others (airmail). Pazifische Rundschau, PO Box 94325, Richmond British Columbia V6Y 2A6 Canada. **Tel** (604)270-2923, FAX (604)273-9563. **(Subscription address:** Ackermann's Adv. & New Service, PO Box 0 1, Blanie WA 98230.) **ED** Baldwin Ackermann. **DD** 071/.1133. **Bk Rev. Ad Acc. Circ:** 15,000 (ctrl). *Continues Dies und Das, 0715-5239.*
 Desc: Anything that might interest the German speaking population in Canada and the USA.

CN/0821-5251
PEACE ARCH NEWS WEEKENDER, THE. [Peace Arch news weekender]. Vol. 1, No. 1 (Sept. 12, 1982)-. Newspaper. English. wk. Free. The Peace Arch News Weekender, PO Box 131, White Rock British Columbia V4B 4Z7 Canada. **DD** 071/.1133. ctrl circ.

CN/0834-7042
PELHAM HERALD. (PELHAM HERALD MICROFORM.). [Pelham her.]. Began publication in 1957. English. Ontario Community Newspapers Association, PO Box 451, 1184 Speers Road, Oakville Ontario L6J 5A8. **DD** 071/.1338.

CN/0715-5735
PENSE PROGRESS. [Pense prog.]. Newspaper. English. mo. 5.00Can$. Pense Progress, Box 282, Pense Saskatchewan S0G 3W0 Canada. **Tel** (306)345-2235. **ED** Brenda Wilson. **DD** 071/.1244. **Ad Acc. Circ:** 260. *Continues Pense Paper.*
 Desc: Local news and interests announcements and reports.

CN/0826-2276
PENSEE DE BAGOT. (LA PENSEE DE BAGOT.). [Pensee Bagot]. (1981)-. Newspaper. French. wk. 63.16Can$. Pensee de Bagot, C P 190, Acton Vale Quebec, H0H 1A0 Canada. **Tel** (514)546-3271. **DD** 071/.14525.

CN/0708-9503
PERDESI PANJAB. (PARADESI PANJAB. PERDESI PANJAB.). **VFOAT** Perdesi Panjab. Vol. 1 (Mar. 10 1977)-. Newspaper. Panjabi. Fifty-two times a year. $35.00. Pardesi Panjab, 2749 Dundas St West, Toronto Ontario M6P 1E1 Canada. **Tel** (416)767-2726. **ED** Gurdip Chauhan. **DD** 071/.13/.541. **Ad Acc. Circ:** 5,000.

CN
PETERBOROUGH EXAMINER. Newspaper. English. ds. 248.19Can$ Canada; 363.19Can$ other. Peterborough Examiner Company Ltd, PO Box 389, 400 Water Street, Peterborough, Ontario, K9J 6Z4 Canada. **Tel** (705)745-4641. **ED** Ed Arnold. **Ad Acc, Adv Mgr:** B. Barthorpe, **Tel** 745-4641. **Circ:** 28,000 (ctrl).

CN/0839-0878
PETERBOROUGH EXAMINER (DAILY ED.). (THE PETERBOROUGH EXAMINER [MICROFORM].). [Peterb. exam.]. (19??)-. Newspaper. English. da. 245.00Can$ Canada; 360.00Can$ other. Peterborough Examiner Company Ltd, PO Box 389, 400 Water Street, Peterborough, Ontario, K9J 6Z4 Canada. **Tel** (705)745-4641. **ED** Ed Arnold. **DD** 071/.1368. **Ad Acc, Adv Mgr:** B. Barthorpe, **Tel** 745-4644. **Circ:** 28,000 (ctrl). *Continues Daily Examiner (Peterborough, Ont. : 1891)., 0839-086X.*

CN/0225-2066
PETIT PROMENEUR, LE. [Petit promeneur]. No. 2, (April 30, 1979)-. Newspaper. French. ir. Journal le Petit Promeneur, CP 493, Ste-Marthe-sue-le-Lac Quebec J0N 1P0 Canada. **DD** 071/.14/25. *Continues Promeneur-Matin, 0225-2058.*

CN/0712-2705
PETITE CAISSE. (LA PETITE CAISSE : JOURNAL ETUDIANT DES SCIENCES ECONOMIQUES ET ADMINISTRATIVES DE L'UQAC.). [Petite caisse]. Vol. 1, No. 1 Jan. 14 1980-. Newspaper. French. bw. 8.16Can$ U.S. La Petite Caisse, Universite du Quebec A Chicoutimi, 555 Blu Universite, Chicoutimi Quebec G7H 2B1 Canada. **Tel** (418)545-5584. **DD** 658/.007/1171416. **Circ:** 6,000.

CN/0228-9954
PETITE NATION, LA. Newspaper. French. wk. 0.39Can$ Canada; $52.00 US. La Petite Nation, CP 240, Saint-Andre-Avellin Quebec J0V 1W0 Canada. **Tel** (819)983-2725. **ED** Serge Lamarche. **DD** 071/.14227. **Ad Acc. Circ:** 7,489 (ctrl). *Continues Revue de la Petite Nation; Vallee de la Petite Nation.*

CN/0229-7701
PETROLIA-ENNISKILLEN GAZETTE, THE. [Petrolia-Enniskillen gaz.]. **VFOAT** Gazette. Vol. 1, No. 1 (Mar. 15, 1979)-. Newspaper. English. wk. The Petrolia-Enniskillen Gazette, PO Box 99, Sarnia Ontario N7T 7H8 Canada. **DD** 071/.1327.

CN/0713-679X
PEUPLE/COURRIER DE LA COTE-DU-SUD. [Peuple/courr. Cote-du-Sud]. Ser. D, V. 1, No. 1 Jan. 4/11, 1973-. Newspaper. French. Peuple/Courrier de la Cote-du-Sud, 55 Avenue de la Fabrique, Montmagny Quebec G5V 2J3 Canada. **DD** 071/.1473. *Formed by the union of Peuple (Montmagny, Quebec) and Courrier (Montmagny, Quebec).*

CN/0228-703X
PEUPLE DE LA CHAUDIERE. (LE PEUPLE DE LA CHAUDIERE : L'HEBDO DES CHUTES.). [Peuple Chaudiere]. Vol. 1, No. 1 (3 Sept. 1980)-. Newspaper. French. wk. $15.00. **DD** 071/.1459.

CN/0228-5703
PEUPLE (ST-AGAPIT). (LE PEUPLE : HEBDO DE LOTBINIERE.). [Peuple, Hebdo lotbiniere]. **VFOAT** Hebdo de Lotiniere; Peuple de Lotbiniere. Vol. 1, No 1 (June 21, 1978)-. Newspaper. French. wk. 22.00Can$ Canada; 87.00Can$ other. Peuple Hebdo de Lotbiniere, PO Box 130, 167 Boulevard Laurier, Laurier Station Quebec G0S 1N0 Canada. **Tel** (418)728-2131, FAX (418)728-4819. **DD** 071/.1458. **Circ:** 10,500 (ctrl).

CN/0383-7572
PEUPLE-TRIBUNE. *Title Change.* Vol. 1 (Aug. 6, 1975)-?. Newspaper. French. wk. Publications le Peuple, 2 Route Trans-Canada #48, Levis Quebec G6V 6W8 Canada. **Tel** (418)833-9398. **DD** 071/.14/7. **Ad Acc. Circ:** 20,814 (ctrl). *Absorbed by Peuple de la Rive-Sud, 0227-6003; Continued by Tribune de Levis-Metro.*
 Desc: General news, local and surrounding areas, sports news, local and regional.

CN/0318-9317
PHENIX (ST-FULGENCE). (LE PHENIX.). (1973)-. French. Le Phenix, Hotel de Ville St-Fulgence, St-Fulgence Quebec Canada. **DD** 071/.14/16.

Canada

CN/0711-4753
PIERRE-BRILLANT. (LE PIERRE-BRILLANT.).
[Pierre-brillant]. Vol. 1, No. 1 (June 18, 1980)-.
Newspaper. French. mo. $5.00. Pierre-Brillant, c/o
Journal de Val-Brillant, 9A St-Pierre Ouest, Val-Brillant
Quebec G0J 3L0 Canada. **DD** 071/.14775.

CN/0228-0523
PIONEER (CHETWYND). (THE PIONEER.).
[Pioneer]. V. 1- Dec. 6, 1979-. Newspaper. English. wk.
13.00Can$ Canada; 30.00Can$ other. R Torgerson, PO
Box 600, Chetwynd British Columbia V0C 1J0 Canada.
Tel (604)788-3255. **ED** Ruth Torgerson. **DD** 071/.111.
Ad Acc. Circ: 1,500.
Desc: Community news.

CN/0710-5428
PIONEER (COCHRANE). (THE PIONEER.).
[Pioneer]. Vol. 1, No. 1 (Sept. 3, 1980)-. Newspaper.
English. sm. Free. Cochrane Times, PO Box 776,
Cochrane Alberta T0L 0W0 Canada. **Tel** (403)932-2055.
DD 071/.1234.

CN/0701-0877
PLAIN DEALER (FREDERICTON). (THE
PLAIN DEALER.). V. 1- June 1976-. Newspaper. English.
da. $137.80. Plain Dealer, PO Box 6730 T, Cleveland OH
44101. **Tel** (216)344-4600, FAX (216)694-6369. **DD**
071/.15/51.

CN/0317-0683
PLEIN-JOUR SUR CHARLEVOIX. VFOAT
Plein-Jour. V. 1- 24 July. 1974-. French. wk. 15.00Can$
per no. Plein-Jour sur Charlevoix, CP 760, Forestville
Quebec G0T 1E0 Canada. **DD** 071/.14/49.

CN/1184-972X
**PLEIN-JOUR SUR LA MANICOUAGAN,
LE.** [Plein-jour Manicouagan]. Vol 26, No 8 (March 27
1991)-. Newspaper. French. sw. 0.50Can$ per issue.
Plein-Jour sur la Manicouagan, 896 Rue de Puyjalon,
Baie-Comeau, Quebec G5C 1N1 Canada. **DD** 071/.1417.
Continues Promo-Services., 1180-7644.

CN/0228-9199
POINT (ALEXANDRIA). (LE POINT.). [Point]. V.
1, No. 1, (Aug. 5, 1980)-. Newspaper. French. wk. $0.25
per no. Le Point / Bathurst, 140 rue de Rennes, CP 878,
75280 Paris Cedex 06 France. **Tel** 011 33 1 45443900.
DD 071/.1377.

CN/0227-2288
POINT (BATHURST). (LE POINT.). [Point]. Vol. 1,
(April 12, 1978)-. Newspaper. French. wk. $9.28. Le Point
/ Bathurst, 140 rue de Rennes, CP 878, 75280 Paris
Cedex 06 France. **Tel** 011 33 1 45443900. **DD** 071/.1512.

CN/0710-2364
POINT COMMUN, LE. [Point commun].
Newspaper. French. Free. Institut Teccart, 3155 rue
Hochelaga, Montreal Quebec H1W 1G4 Canada. **DD**
378.714/281. ctrl circ.

CN/0229-3277
POINT DE VUE (SENNETERRE). (LE POINT
DE VUE.). [Point vue]. **Added/Corp** Senneterre
(Quebec). (1979)-. Periodical. French. mo. $0.40 per no.
Imprimerie Senneterre, CP 1830, Senneterre Quebec J0Y
2M0 Canada. **DD** 071/.1413. **Continues** Senneterre,
0229-3269.

CN/0382-6309
POINT (DOLBEAU). (LE POINT.). V. 1- 19 Nov.
1975-. Newspaper. French. wk. Les Publications Dolbeau
Inc, 1945 Provencher, Bolbeau Quebec Canada. **DD**
071/.14/14.

CN/0319-5805
POINT (LASALLE). (LE POINT.). V. 1- Aug. 27,
1975-. Newspaper. French (English). wk. Free to citizens
of LaSalle and St-Pie, $10.00 others. Journal Le Point,
2107 Lapierre Street, Lasalle Quebec Canada. **DD**
071/.14/28.

CN/0227-2296
PONT, LE. [Pont]. Vol 1 (June 20, 1979)-.
Newspaper. French. wk. $10.00 Canada; $15.00 other.
Le Pont, CP 55, Grand-Mere Quebec G9T 5K7 Canada.
DD 071/.14465.

CN/1182-9044
PORCUPINE PRESS. [Porcup. Press]. Vol. 1, No.
1 (Sept. 5, 1990)-. Newspaper. English. wk. **DD**
071/.1242.

CN/0834-7166
PORT DOVER MAPLE LEAF. (PORT DOVER
MAPLE LEAF [MICROFORM].). VFOAT Maple Leaf.
(190?)-. English. Fifty-two times a year. 30.00Can$
Canada; 65.00Can$ other. Port Dover Maple Leaf, PO
Box 70, Port Dover ONT N0A 1N0 Canada. **Tel**
(519)583-0112. **ED** Stan Morris. **DD** 071/.1337. **Bk Rev**,
(Qty: 6). **Ad Acc. Circ:** 5,000.

CN/0228-6262
PORTAGE (RIVIERE-DU-LOUP). (LE
PORTAGE.). [Portage]. (1979)-. Newspaper. French.
Fifty-two times a year. 39.49Can$ Quebec; 65.81Can$
others. La Maison de la Presse, 16 rue la Domaine, Rivier
Loop Quebec G5R 2P5 Canada. **Tel** (418)862-1774. **DD**
071/.1476.

CN/0229-320X
POSTILLON DE CHAMPLAIN. (LE
POSTILLON DE CHAMPLAIN : AU FIL DU CHEMIN DU
ROY.). [Postillon Champlain]. V. 1, No. 1, (Dec. 1980)-.
Newspaper. French. Three times a year. Le Postillon, a/s
Gaetain Duchaine Inc, 2830 Ave St-Charles, Point-du-Lac
Quebec G0X 1Z0 Canada. **DD** 971.4/465.

CN/0032-664X
PRAIRIE MESSENGER. (1???)-. English.
Forty-seven times a year (Published on Mondays).
20.09Can$ Canada; 46.73Can$ other; 70.00Can$
Canada, 120.00Can$ other, airmail. Prairie Messenger,
Box 190, Muenster Saskatchewan S0K 2Y0 Canada. **Tel**
(306)682-5245. **ED** Andrew M. Britz or Marian Noll
(phone: (306)682-5215). **Bk Rev**, **Ad Acc**, **Adv Mgr:**
Rose Marie Strueby. **Circ:** 8,900 (ctrl). available on
microfilm.
Desc: Strong ecumenical and social justice deals with
issues that is militarism, uranium mining and distribution.

CN/0712-2640
PRESENT (MATANE). (LE PRESENT.).
[Present]. Vol. 1, No. 1 Sept. 8 1981-. Newspaper.
French. wk. Free. Le Present, 195 du Phare O, CP 244,
Matane Quebec G4W 1V8 Canada. **DD** 071/.14775.

CN
PRESSE (MONTREAL). (LA PRESSE.). (1???)-.
Newspaper. French. da. 507.35Can$ Canada;
920.40Can$ other. La Presse, CP 6041, 7 rue St.
Jacques, Montreal Quebec H3C 3E3 Canada. **Tel**
(514)285-6886. **Ad Acc.**

CN/0714-8534
PRINCE ALBERT SUN. [Prince Albert sun].
VFOAT Sun. VAT Sun (Prince Albert). Newspaper.
English. wk. $16.70. Prince Albert Sun, 135 River Street
West, Prince Albert Sask S6V 3K6. **DD** 071/.1242.

CN
PRINCE RUPERT DAILY NEWS. (19??)-.
Newspaper. English. da. 178.83Can$ Canada;
363.83Can$ other. Sterling Publishers Ltd., 801 2nd
Avenue West, Prince Rupert, BC V8J 1H6 Canada. **Tel**
(604)624-6781. **Ad Acc.**

CN/0713-5521
PRISME (QUEBEC. 1964). (LE PRISME /
PETIT SEMINAIRE DE QUEBEC.). [Prisme]. V. 1, No. 1,
(Dec. 1964)-. Newspaper. French. Free. Le Prisme, c/o
Direction des Etudiants, Section Secondaire Petit
Seminaire de Quebec, 1 rue de la Fabrique, CP 460,
Quebec Quebec G1R 4R7 Canada. **DD** 373.714/471. ctrl
circ.

CN/0822-563X
PROGRES DU NORD, AHUNTSIC. Title
Change. VAT Progres du Nord
(1981). No. 29, (Aug. 4, 1981)-. Newspaper. French. wk.
DD 071/.1428. **Continues** Progres du Nord. Continued
by Progres Ahuntsic.

CN/0839-3311
PROVINCE. (THE PROVINCE. MICROFORM.).
[Province]. 59th Year, No. 66 (June 12, 1956)-. English.
Province, 2250 Granville Street, Vancouver British
Columbia V6H 3G2 Canada. **Tel** (604)732-2605. **DD**
071/.1133. **Continues** Vancouver Province, 0839-3303.

CN/0316-5922
**PUBLICATION SERIES - TRANSPORT
GROUP. DEPARTMENT OF CIVIL
ENGINEERING. UNIVERSITY OF
WATERLOO.** (PUBLICATION SERIES -
UNIVERSITY OF WATERLOO, DEPARTMENT OF CIVIL
ENGINEERING, TRANSPORT GROUP.). **Main/Corp**
University of Waterloo. Transport Group. Newspaper.
English. Transport Group, University of Waterloo,
Waterloo Ontario N26 3G1 Canada. **DD** 380.5.

CN
QUEBEC CHRONICLE-TELEGRAPH.
(19??)-. Newspaper. English. Fifty times a week.
26.57Can$ Canada; 50.00Can$ other. Quebec
Chronicle-Telegraph, 3484 Chemin Ste-Foy, Quebec
GLX 1S8 Canada. **Tel** (418)650-1764. **Bk Rev**, (Qty: 40).
Ad Acc. Circ: 3,500 (ctrl). available on microfilm and
microfiche.

CN/0820-7216
QUEBEC DIMANCHE. [Que. dimanche]. Vol 1
(Dec. 12, 1982)-. Newspaper. French. wk. $0.75 (per
issue). Quebec Dimanche, 157 Ouest rue des Chenes,
Quebec Quebec G1L 1G8 Canada. **DD** 071/.14.

CN/0707-7572
QUEBEC SUD-OUEST. V. 1- 17 Aug. 1977-.
Newspaper. French. wk. Productions Sud-Ouest, 18B
Montee Du Lac, Ste-Barbe Quebec J0S 1P0 Canada. **DD**
071/14/31.

CN/0710-5797
**QUEBECOIS LIBRE D'OUTREMONT,
LE.** Vol. 1, No. 1 (Oct. 1973)-. Newspaper. French. Parti
Quebecois D'Outremont, 700, Av. Mceachran, Outremont
Quebec H2V 3C7 Canada. **DD** 971.4/04.

CN
**QUEEN CHARLOTTE ISLANDS
OBSERVER.** (19??)-. Newspaper. English. wk.
29.91Can$ Queen Charlotte Island; 40.19Can$ Canada;
76.00Can$ US; 85.00Can$ other. Observer Publishing
Co. Ltd. / Canada, Box 205, Queen Charlotte BC V0T
1S0 Canada. **Tel** (604)559-4680, FAX (604)559-8433.
ED W. J. King. **Ad Acc. Circ:** 1,800.

CN/1195-5023
QUESNEL CARIBOO OBSERVER.
[Quesnel Cariboo obs.]. VFOAT Cariboo Observer. (May
7, 1968)-. Newspaper. English. Twice a week. 41.00Can$
Quesnel; 54.00Can$ other Canada; 100.00Can$ other.
Cariboo Observer, #4 62 Reid Street, Quesnel BC V2J
2M6 Canada. **Tel** (604)992-2121. **ED** Jerry MacDonald.
DD 071/.1175. **Ad Acc, Adv Mgr:** Dave Sales. **Circ:**
4,800 (ctrl). **Continues** The Cariboo Observer.
Desc: Community newspaper with local news, sports,
and happenings.

CN/0712-2810
RACONTEUR (TIMMINS). (LE RACONTEUR.).
[Raconteur]. Newspaper. French. wk. $13.00 Timmins
and Iroquois Falls, $15.00 others. Raconteur / Canada,
70 Avenue 6 East, Timmins Ontario P4N 5L9 Canada. **DD**
071/.13142.

CN/0715-3910
RANJIT. [Ranjit]. VFOAT Ranjeet. Newspaper.
Panjabi (summaries and/or abstracts in English). sm
(irregular). Ranjeet, PO Box 67516 Station O, Vancouver
British Columbia V5W 3T9 Canada. **DD** 071/.1133.

CN/0701-0079
REDCLIFF REVIEW. V. 1- Oct. 6, 1976-.
Newspaper. English. $6.00. Redcliff Publications, 120
Broadway East, Redcliff Alta. T0J 2P0 Canada. **DD**
071/.123/4.

CN/0707-5529
REFLET D'AMOS, LE. V. 1- 5 July. 1978-.
Newspaper. French. wk. $10.00. Reflet d'Amos, 25 1ERE
Avenue EST, Amos Quebec J9T 1H2. **DD** 071/.14/13.

CN/0229-3560
REFLET DE MON MILIEU. Vol. 1 (Oct. 1976)-.
Newspaper. French. mo. Free. Reflet de Mon Milieu, 809
Boulevard des Chutes, Beauport Quebec Canada. **DD**
071/.1447. ctrl circ.

CN/1186-2025
REFLET TEMISCAMIEN, LE. [Reflet
temiscamien]. (1991)-. Newspaper. French. wk. Free for
residents. Reflet Tescamien, CP 877, Ville-Marie Quebec
J0Z 3W0 Canada. **DD** 071/.1413.

CN/0823-6631
REGARD NOUVEAU. (REGARD NOUVEAU :
JOURNAL ETUDIANT DU CEGEP
FRANCOIS-XAVIER-GARNEAU.). [Regard nouv.]. Vol. 1,
No 1 (9 Nov. 79)-. Newspaper. French. bw. Free.
Association Etudiante du CEGEP
Francois-Xavier-Garneau, 1660 Boul de l'Entente,
Sainte-Foy Quebec G1T 2S5 Canada. **DD** 378.714/47.

CN/0704-7053
REGENT PARK COMMUNITY NEWS.
Began publication with Feb. 1972 issue. Newspaper.
English. mo. Free. Regent Park Community Improvement
Association, 44 Blevins Place, Toronto Ontario M5A 3M4
Canada. **DD** 071/.13/541. ctrl circ.

CN/1185-1872
REGENT PARK T.O.! [Regent Park T.O.!].
Added/Corp Parachute Community Employment Centre.
VAT Regent Park Toronto. Vol. 1, No 1 (Apr. 26, 1990)-.
Newspaper. English. bw. Free. Parachute Community
Employment Centre, 44 Blevin's Place, Toronto, Ontario
M5A 3M6 Canada. **DD** 071/.13541.

CN/0711-4834
REGIONAL DE DRUMMONDVILLE. (LE
REGIONAL DE DRUMMONDVILLE : CAHIER
AGRICOLE.). [Reg. Drummondville]. Sept. 16, 1980-.
Newspaper. French. wk. Free. La Parole, 1159 Boulevard
St-Joseph, Drummondville Quebec J2C 2C8 Canada. **DD**
071/.14563. ctrl circ.

CN/0319-1656
REGIONAL ECHO, THE. Began publication in
1973?. Newspaper. English. T Wyatt, PO Box 38,
Makefing Manitoba R0L 1B0 Canada. **DD** 071/.127/2.

Canada

CN/0704-0261
REGIONAL NEWS (CAYUGA). (THE REGIONAL NEWS.). V. 1- Nov. 10, 1976-. Newspaper. English. wk. Free to households and businesses in the Haldimand region; $7.50 US and Canada; $10.00 other. The Regional News, PO Box 418, Cayuga Ontario N0A 1E0 Canada. **DD** 071/.13/37.

CN/0712-1083
REGIONAL NEWSPAPER, THE. [Reg. Newsp.]. May 12, 1981-. Newspaper. English. sm. $7.00. Parkland Communications, 38-1st Avenue NW, Dauphin Man. R7N 1G7. **DD** 071/.1272.

CN/0317-5847
REGIONAL TELEGRAPH, THE. Began with Jan. 15, 1975 issue. English. wk. $2.50 Canada; $4.00 other. Regional Telegraph, PO Box 340, Cayuga Ontario N0A 1E0 Canada. **DD** 071/.13/37.

CN/0710-0949
REPORTER (ALLISTON). (THE REPORTER.). [Reporter]. Newspaper. English. wk. $0.20 each number. Rolling Hills Publishing, PO Box 998, Alliston Ontario L0M 1A0 Canada. **DD** 071/.1317. *Continues Alliston & Cookstown Reporter, 0707-5502.*

CN/0828-6248
REPORTER (LONDON). (THE REPORTER.). [Reporter]. **Added/Corp** University of Western Ontario. School of Journalism. (1983)-. Newspaper. English. bw. Free. Reporter / Ontario, c/o A MacFarlane School of Journalism, Middlesex College, University of Western Ontario, London Ontario N6H 5B7 Canada. **DD** 071/.1326.

CN/0380-8874
REPORTER (PORT ELGIN). (THE REPORTER.). V. 1 (Oct. 1, 1975)-. Newspaper. English. wk. $8.00. Norman-Watson Enterprises, PO Box 1079, Port Elgin Ontario N0H 2C0 Canada. **DD** 071/.13/21.

CN/0228-6653
REVEIL A CHICOUTIMI, LE. *Title Change.* [Reveil Chicoutimi]. **VAT** Reveil (Chicoutimi). (May 1978)-(1987?). Newspaper. French. wk. Le Reveil a Jonquiere, 3386 Boul St Francois, Jonquiere Quebec G7X 7W4 Canada. **Tel** (418)695-2601. **DD** 071/.1416. *Continued by Chicoutimi le Reveil, 1193-3526.*

CN/0228-636X
REVEIL A JONQUIERE, LE. [Reveil Jonquiere]. **VFOAT** Reveil. **VAT** Reveil (Jonquiere). (1978)-. Newspaper. French. Fifty-two times a year. 100.00Can$ Quebec; 105.00Can$ others in Canada; 110.00Can$ others. Le Reveil a Jonquiere, 3386 Boul St Francois, Jonquiere Quebec G7X 7W4 Canada. **Tel** (418)695-2601. **DD** 071/.1416. *Continues Reveil.*

CN/0228-6661
REVEIL A LA BAIE, LE. [Reveil Baie]. **VAT** Reveil (Ville de la Baie). Newspaper. French. wk. $15.00. Le Reveil a Jonquiere, 3386 Boul St Francois, Jonquiere Quebec G7X 7W4 Canada. **Tel** (418)695-2601. **DD** 071/.1416.

CN/0229-0936
REVEIL DU PONTIAC, LE. [Reveil Pontiac]. (1976)-. Newspaper. French (English; summaries and/or abstracts in English). mo. Le Reveil Du Pontiac, CP 766 Fort-Coulonge, Quebec J0X 1V0. **DD** 071/.14215.

CN
REVELSTOKE TIMES. *Title Change.* English. wk. Crazy Creek Publishing, PO Box 120, Revelstoke British Columbia V0E 2S0 Canada. **Tel** (604)837-4667, FAX (604)837-5050. **ED** Penny Graham. **Ad Acc. Circ:** 3,500 (ctrl). *Continued by Revelstoke Front Row Centre.* **Desc:** Community news.

CN/0226-9945
REVUE DE PAPINEAU, LA. [Rev. Papineau]. Newspaper. French. wk. 0.37Can$. La Revue de la Pte Nation, 418 Avenue du Golf, Gatineau Quebec J8P 6K2 Canada. **Tel** (819)663-7736. **ED** M Michel St Louis. **DD** 071/.14227.

CN/0316-5442
REXDALE TIMES REVIEW. VFOAT Times Review. Began publication Aug. 29, 1974. Newspaper. English. wk. 0.10Can$ per no. Times Review, PO Box 2053 Station B, Rexcale Ontario M9V 2G2 Canada. **DD** 071/.13/541.

CN
RIMBEY RECORD. Newspaper. English. Fifty-two times a year. 15.00Can$ Rimbey and local area; 30.00Can$ other Canada; 85.00Can$ other. Rimbey Record, Box 380, Rimbey Alberta T0C 2J0 Canada. **Tel** (403)843-2231, FAX (403)843-2990. **ED** John Roberts. **Ad Acc. Circ:** 2,060.

CN/0823-7573
RIVERVIEW GAZETTE, THE. [Riverview gaz.]. Vol. 1, No. 1 (Feb. 1, 1983)-. Newspaper. English. wk. Riverview Gazette, PO Box 354, Canada. **DD** 071/.1611.

CN/0381-6613
ROCK FLUFF. Began with June 1968 issue. Newspaper. English. ir. Box 2703, Whitehorse Yukon Territory Y1A 2C6 Canada. **DD** 071/.19/1.

CN/0821-7262
ROCKY VIEW FIVE VILLAGE WEEKLY. *Title Change.* [Rocky View five village wkly.]. (1982)-?. Newspaper. English. wk. Rocky View Five Village Weekly, T0M 1B0 Canada. **DD** 071/.1233. *Absorbed by Rocky View Weekly., 0823-6054; Five Village Weekly., 0701-0907.*

CN/0715-4992
ROCKY VIEW TIMES, THE. [Rocky View times]. Newspaper. English. wk. $0.20 per no. Rocky View Times, PO Box 580, Airdrie Alberta T0M 0B0 Canada. **DD** 071/.1233.

CN/0383-8153
ROSSLAND AND DISTRICT WEEKLY, THE. V. 1- March 24, 1976-. Newspaper. English. wk. $9.90. Ourtowne Publications, PO Box 1198, Rossland BC V0G 1Y0. **DD** 071/.11/44.

CN/0715-5271
RURAL ROUTE (WALLACEBURG, ONT.). (RURAL ROUTE.). [Rural route]. Newspaper. English. wk. Free. Wallaceburg News, 222 Wellington Street, Wallaceburg Ontario N8A 4L5 Canada. **DD** 338.1/09713. ctrl circ.

CN/0821-6428
SAWT AL-URUBAH (TURANTU). (SAWT AL-URUBAH.). **VFOAT** Arabs' Voice; Arab's I.E. Arabs' Voice. **VAT** Arabs' Voice (Toronto); Arab Voice (Toronto). V. 1, No. 1 (November 1981)-. Newspaper. Arabic. mo. $12.00. M. Barsum, Suite 205, 11 Eccleston Drive, Toronto Ontario M4A 1K2 Canada. **DD** 071/.13541.

CN/0225-2074
SCARBORO CONSUMER. [Scarboro consum.]. **VFOAT** Mirror Consumer. V. 1- Aug. 24, 1977-. Newspaper. English. wk. Free. Metrospan Community Newspapers, 44 Lesmill Road, Don Mills Ontario M3B 2T5. **DD** 640.73/09713/541. ctrl circ.

CN/0834-7131
SCARBOROUGH NEWS. (SCARBOROUGH NEWS [MICROFORM].). [Scarb. news]. (198?)-. Newspaper. English. wk (published on Wednesday). 15.00Can$. Watson Publishing Company, 150 Milner Avenue, Unit 35, Sacrborough, Ontario, M1S 3R3 Canada. **Tel** (416)291-2583. **DD** 071/.713541.

CN/0229-6071
SCHOMBERG-NOBLETON NEWS. [Schomberg-Nobleton news]. **VFOAT** News. Vol. 1, No. 1 (Oct. 3, 1979)-. Newspaper. English. wk. $9.50. PBK Publishing, 9 Mill Street East, PO Box 70, Tottenham Ontario Canada. **DD** 071/.13547.

CN/0707-2333
SCRATCHING RIVER POST, THE. [Scratch. River post]. V. 1- Jan. 16, 1978-. Newspaper. English. wk. 20.00Can$ Canada; $35.00 US. The Scratching River Post, Box 160, Morris Manitoba R0G 1K0 Canada. **Tel** (204)746-2823. **ED** Doug Penner, Sandra Penner, and Christina Lambert. **DD** 071/.127/4. **Ad Acc. Circ:** 9,400 (ctrl).

CN/1186-4907
SCUGOG CITIZEN [MICROFORM]. (1991)-. English. Ontario Community Newspapers Association, PO Box 451, 1184 Speers Road, Oakville Ontario L6J 5A8. **DD** 071/.1356.

CN/0704-0431
SEVERN-WASHAGO MIRROR. V. 1, No. 17- Aug. 1, 1977-. Newspaper. English. bw. 5.50Can$. Stewart Smith, Box 291, Washago Ontario L0K 2B0 Canada. **DD** 071/.13/16. *Continues Severn-Washago Newspaper.*

CN/0711-0774
SEXTANT (SEPT-ILES). (LE SEXTANT / COMMISSION SCOLAIRE DU LITTORAL.). [Sextant]. **VFOAT** Journal le Sextant; The Sextant. Newspaper. English (French). mo. Free. The Sextant, c/o D Mauger, Chevery Quebec G0G 1G0 Canada. **DD** 379.1/531/0971417.

CN/0709-4647
SHARE (TORONTO). (SHARE.). Vol. 1 (Apr. 8, 1978)-. Newspaper. English. Fifty-two times a year. 221.00Can$ Korea; 135.00Can$ US & Canada. Share Communications of Toronto, 1554A Eglinton Avenue West, Toronto Ontario M6E 2G8 Canada. **Tel** (416)789-0691, FAX (416)789-0696. **DD** 971.3/541/00496. **Bk Rev. Ad Acc. Circ:** 30,000 (ctrl). **Desc:** Community newspaper.

CN/0710-6564
SHELF LISTING - MIDWESTERN REGIONAL LIBRARY SYSTEM. (SHELF LISTING MICROFORM.). [Shelf listing - Midwest. Reg. Libr. Syst.]. **Main/Corp** Midwestern Regional Library System (Ont.). **VFOAT** Shelf Listing of Adult Books.

English. an. Midwestern Regional Library System, 637 Victoria Street North, Kitchener Ontario N2H 5G4 Canada. **DD** 017/.13.

CN
SHOAL LAKE STAR. (19??)-. English. wk. 18.69Can$ Shoal Lake, Manitoba; 60.00Can$ other. Shoal Lake Star, Box 160, Shoal Lake Manitoba R0J 1Z0 Canada. **Tel** (204)759-2644, FAX (204)759-2521. **ED** Greg Nesbitt. **Bk Rev**, (Qty: 4). **Ad Acc, Adv Mgr Tel** same as publisher.

CN/0383-8161
SHOESTRING PRESS. June 1975-. Newspaper. English (French and Italian). mo. Free. Shoestring Press / Canada, 787 1/2 Somerset Street West, Ottawa K1R 6R3. **DD** 071/.13/84.

CN/0712-1296
SIGNAL (RYCROFT). (THE SIGNAL.). [Signal]. **VFOAT** Central Peace Signal. Vol. 1, No. 1 (May 14, 1980)-. Newspaper. English. wk. 22.00Can$ Canada and US; 33.00Can$ other. Schierbeck Printing and Publishing, PO Box 250, Rycroft Alberta T0H 3A0 Canada. **Tel** (403)765-3604, FAX (403)765-2188. **ED** Philip Breeze. **DD** 071/.1231. **Ad Acc. Circ:** 2,750 (ctrl). **Desc:** Local community news publication.

CN/0712-5569
SIMCOE MIRROR, THE. [Simcoe mirror]. Vol. 1, No. 1 (Oct. 27, 1981)-. Newspaper. English. wk. Free. Nanticoke Publications, PO Box 1024, Simcoe Ontario N3Y 5B3 Canada. **DD** 071/.1336. ctrl circ.

CN/0707-4964
SLAVE RIVER JOURNAL. Vol. 1 (June 2, 1977)-. Newspaper. English. wk (Published on Wednesday). 30.00Can$ Fort Smith & North West Territory; 35.00Can$ Canada. Slave River Journal, PO Box 990, Fort Smith, North West Territory X0E 0P0 Canada. **Tel** (403)872-2784, FAX (403)872-2744. **DD** 071/.19/3. **Bk Rev. Ad Acc, Adv Mgr:** Tony Dowler, **Tel** (403)872-2764. **Circ:** 2,200 (ctrl). **Desc:** Serving the community and the area from Ft. Chipewyan to Ft. Resolution with a view to the current issues in the South Mackenzie and the Northwest Territories.

CN/0381-8365
SMITHS FALLS STAR. V. 1- July 15, 1975-. Newspaper. English. wk. $5.00. Smiths Falls Star, PO Box 784, Smiths Falls Ontario K7A 4W6 Canada. **DD** 071/.1/382.

CN/0229-7949
SMOKY LAKE SIGNAL. [Smoky Lake signal]. (1978)-. Newspaper. English. wk. 23.10Can$ local; 29.10Can$ other. Smoky Lake Signal, PO Box 328, Smoky Lake Alberta T0A 3C0 Canada. **Tel** (403)656-4114. **DD** 071/.1233.

CN/0227-9304
SMOKY RIVER NEWS, THE. [Smoky River news]. **VFOAT** Falher Courier and Smoky River; Falher, Alta., Smoky River News. Vol. 1, No. 38 (June 1, 1953)-. Newspaper. English. wk. $2.00. Smoky River Express, Box 644 Falker Alberta, T0H 1M0 Canada. **DD** 071/.1231. *Continues Courier (Edmonton, Alta. : 1952), 0227-9290.*

CN/0826-2241
SNOW LAKE NEWS. [Snow Lake news]. Vol. 1, No. 1 (Mar. 10, 1983)-. Newspaper. English. Fifty-two times a year. 73.10Can$. Forsyth Agency, PO Box 550, Snow Lake Manitoba R0B 1M0 Canada. **Tel** (204)358-2649. **DD** 071/.1272.

●CN/1194-7098
SOLEIL DE COLOMBIE-BRITANNIQUE. (LE SOLEIL DE COLOMBIE-BRITANNIQUE.). [Soleil C.-B.]. (1993). Newspaper. French. wk. 25.00Can$ Canada; 30.00Can$ other. Le Soleil de Colombie, 1645 West Fifth Avenue, Vancouver BC V6J 1N5 Canada. **Tel** (604)730-9575. **DD** 071/.1133. *Continues Le Soleil de Colombie., 1181-4292.*

CN/1182-9966
SOOKE STANDARD, THE. [Sooke stand.]. (1990)-. Newspaper. English. wk. Limited free distribution. The Sooke Standard, 2-6726 West Coast Road, Box 1112, Sooke, British Columbia V0S 1N0 Canada. **DD** 071/.1128.

CN/0714-3303
S'ORGANISER. (S'ORGANISER : JOURNAL DES ETUDIANTS-TES DU CEGEP DE SOREL-TRACY.). [S'organiser]. Vol. 1, No. 1 (Oct. 1980)-. Newspaper. French. Free. Association Generale Des Ste-Anne, Sorel, Quebec J3P 1J6 Canada. **DD** 378.714/51. *Continues Tire-Bouchon.*

CN
SOURCE, THE. VFOAT Mawrid. Newspaper. Multiple languages (English and Arabic). bw. $10.00. The Source, PO Box 992, Edmonton Alberta Canada.

CN/0707-2295
SOUTH CENTRAL BANNER. Vol. 1 (Jan. 17, 1978)-. Newspaper. English. wk. $5.00. Earl Barron Publ Inc, Box 143, Crystal City, Manitoba R0K 0N0. **DD** 071/.127/4.

CN/0384-7934
SOUTH EAST LANCE. V. 1- May 19, 1976-. Newspaper. English. wk. Lance Publishing Company, 620 Dakota Street, Winnipeg Manitoba R2M 3K2 Canada. **DD** 071/.127/4. ***Formed by the union of*** *St. Boniface Courier, 0384-7926* ***and*** *St. Vital Lance, 0383-7254.*

CN/0710-0213
SOUTH SHORE NEWS. [South Shore news]. Vol. 1, No. 1 (June 4, 1980)-. Newspaper. English. wk. Free. South Shore News, 120 Dufferin Street, Bridgewater Nova Scotia, B4V 2G5 Canada. **DD** 071/.1623. ctrl circ.

CN/0821-0187
SOUTH VANCOUVER REVUE. [South Vanc. rev.]. **VFOAT** Revue. (1973)-. Newspaper. English. Twenty-four times a year. 38.00Can$. Raglin Publishing, 4968 Victoria Drive, Vancouver British Columbia, V5P 3T6 Canada. **Tel** (604)327-0221. **ED** Rod Raglin. **DD** 071/.1133. **Ad Acc, Adv Mgr:** R. Raglin. **Circ:** 15,000 (ctrl). ***Absorbed*** *Marpole Revue; Revue, Mid-town/Mt.Pleasant, 0710-5363; South Burnaby Revue.* ***Continued in part by*** *Marpole Revue (1988), 0845-8634.*
Desc: General interest community newspaper.

CN/0824-6726
SOUTH VOICE, THE. [South voice]. Newspaper. English. wk. Free to citizens of Fort Carry, St Norbert, River Heights, and Tuxedo Manitoba, $18.00 others. Active Communications, 105-1383 Pembina Highway, Winnipeg Man. R3T 2B9. **DD** 071/.1274.

CN/0319-6224
SOUTHERN GAZETTE. Vol. 1 (May 29, 1975)-. Newspaper. English. Fifty-two times a year. 80.00Can$ Canada; 150.00Can$ others. Robinson-Blackmore Publishing Ltd., PO Box 8660, St. Johns Newfoundland A1B 3T7 Canada. **Tel** (709)579-1312. **DD** 071/.18.

CN/0226-9120
SPEC (NEW CARLISLE). (SPEC.). [Spec]. Vol. 1, No. 1 (May 15, 1975)-. Newspaper. English. wk. 20.00Can$ Canada; $30.00 US. Spec, PO Box 99, New Carlisle Quebec G0C 1Z0 Canada. **Tel** (418)752-5400. **DD** 071/.1477. **Bk Rev**. **Ad Acc. Circ:** 3,000 (ctrl). available on microfilm from Bibliotheque National du Quebec.
Desc: Newspaper (in English) of Eastern Quebec.

CN/0715-5921
SRBIJA (WINONA). (SRBIJA : GLAS SRPSKIH BORACA.). [Srbija]. **VFOAT** Serbia : Voice of Serbian Fighters for Freedom. **VAT** Srbija (Fruitland); Serbia (Fruitland); Serbia (Winona). Newspaper. Serbo-Croatian (Cyrillic). mo. $10.00. Serbia, PO Box 70, Fruitland Ontario L0R 1L0 Canada. **DD** 320.9497.

CN/0826-4295
ST. LAMBERT JOURNAL. **VFOAT** Journal St-Lambert. (1982)-. Newspaper. English (French). Fifty times a year. 73.16Can$. St. Lambert Journal, 574 Victoria Street, St. Lambert Quebec J4P 2JP Canada. **Tel** (514)671-0014. **DD** 071/.1437.

CN/1194-076X
ST. THOMAS COURIER. (THE ST. THOMAS COURIER [MICROFORM].). Vol. 3, No. 4 (Aug. 17, 1977)-. English. Information Graphics, Box 1843, Station A, London, Ontario N6A 5H9 Canada. **DD** 071/.1335. ***Continues*** *Courier (St. Thomas, Ont.)., 0319-7026.*

CN/0700-9518
ST. VITAL LEADER. V. 1- Aug. 18, 1976-. Newspaper. English. wk. Reliance Press, 1397 Erin Street, Winnipeg Manitoba R3E 2S9 Canada. **Tel** 694-0173. **DD** 071/.127/4.

CN/0827-6609
STANDARD (ELLIOT LAKE). (THE STANDARD.). [Standard]. (1955)-. Newspaper. English. wk. $41.12 Elliot Lake; $54.60 other Canada; $87.37 other. Elliot Lake Standard, PO Box 86, Elliot Lake Ontario, P5A 2X1 Canada. **Tel** (705)848-7195. **ED** Bill Stevenson. **DD** 071/.13132. **Ad Acc, Adv Mgr:** Sandra Dudeck. **Circ:** 5,500 (ctrl). available on microfilm.

CN/0702-7893
STANDARD (SWAN RIVER). (STANDARD.). Began publication between July-Oct. 1976. Newspaper. English. $2.00. Standard, PO Box 1629, Swan River Manitoba R0L 1Z0 Canada. **DD** 071/.127/2. ***Supersedes*** *Parkland Standard, 0702-7907.*

CN/0832-4174
STAR-PHOENIX (SASKATOON, SASK.). (STAR-PHOENIX. MICROFORM.). [Star-phoenix]. 65th Year, No. 190 (May 31, 1967)-. English. Star-Phoenix, 204-5 Avenue North, Saskatoon Saskatchewan S7K 2P1 Canada. **Tel** (306)664-8223. **DD** 071/.1242. ***Continues*** *Saskatoon Star-Phoenix, 0832-4182.*

CN/0824-7501
STAR (VICTORIA). (THE STAR.). [Star]. **VFOAT** City-Wide Star. Vol. 1, No. 1 (Aug. 31, 1983)-. Newspaper. English. wk. Limited free distribution. The Star, 1157 Newport Avenue, Victoria British Columbia V8S 5E6 Canada. **DD** 071/.1134. ctrl circ.

CN
STAYNER SUN. Newspaper. $20.00 within a forty mile radius of style; $30.00 other in Canada; $40.00 other. The Stayner Sun, Box 80, Stayner Ont L0M 1S0 Canada. **Tel** (705)428-2638, FAX (705)428-6909.

CN/0834-7425
STAYNER SUN [MICROFORM], THE. (Aug. 28, 1877)-. English. wk (Wednesday). 25.00Can$ within 40 mile radius of Stayner, Ont.; 35.00Can$ other Canada; 60.00Can$ other (print). The Stayner Sun, Box 80, Stayner Ont L0M 1S0 Canada. **Tel** (705)428-2638, FAX (705)428-6909. **ED** Alicia Savage. **DD** 071/.1317. **Ad Acc, Adv Mgr:** Sue Nicholson. ctrl circ. available on microfiche (Simcoe County Archives).

CN
STIRLING NEWS-ARGUS. (19??)-. English. wk (51 per year). 30.00Can$ Canada; 65.00Can$ other. Cembal Publications Ltd., PO Box 250, Marmora Ontario, K0K 2M0 Canada. **Tel** (613)472-2431, FAX (613)472-5026.

CN/0821-0225
STOUFFVILLE SUN. [Stouffv. sun]. Vol. 1, No. 1 (Oct. 27, 1982)-. Newspaper. English. wk. $20.00 Canada; $45.00 other. Stouffville Sun, 11 Main Street West, Stouffville Ontario L0H 1L0 Canada. **DD** 071/.1354.

CN/0710-4537
STRAND. (THE STRAND / VICTORIA COLLEGE.). [Strand]. Newspaper. English. Free. The Strand, c/o Vusac Offices, 150 Charles Street West, Toronto Ontario M5S 1K9 Canada. **DD** 378.713/541.

CN/0229-6519
STRATHCLAIR & DISTRICT REVIEW. [Strathclair & dist. rev.]. Vol. 1, Issue 1 (Jan. 12, 1978)-. Newspaper. English. wk. $6.00. Strathclair & District Review, PO Box 244, Strathclair Manitoba R0J 2C0 Canada. **DD** 071/.1273.

CN/0712-7944
STUDENT TIMES (MONTREAL). ***Title Change.*** (THE STUDENT TIMES.). [Stud. times]. Vol. 1, No. 1 (Mar. 1981)-. Newspaper. English (French). mo. Student Times, c/o Raeu, Bureau 412, 3480 McTavish Street, Montreal Quebec H3A 1X9 Canada. **Tel** (514)392-8971. **ED** Ian Brodie. **DD** 371.8/1/09714. **Ad Acc.** ***Continued by*** *Student Express.*
Desc: A monthly review of issues facing university students in Quebec.

CN/0229-2998
SUBURBAN. COTE DES NEIGES EDITION. (THE SUBURBAN.). [Suburban, Cote des Neiges ed.]. Newspaper. English (French). wk. 105.00Can$ (add 7% tax). Michael Publishers, 8170 Walnell Road, Cote-Saint-Luc Quebec H4W 1M3 Canada. **Tel** (514)484-1107, FAX (514)484-7284. **ED** Christy McCormick. **DD** 071/.14281. **Bk Rev**. **Ad Acc. Circ:** 101,000 (ctrl).
Desc: Community newspaper serving Montreal's upwardly mobile suburbs with regionalized editions.

CN/0226-9686
SUBURBAN (COTE-SAINT-LUC ED.). (THE SUBURBAN.). [Suburban]. (1963)-. Newspaper. English (summaries and/or abstracts in French). wk. 198.10Can$. Michael Publishers, 8170 Walnell Road, Cote-Saint-Luc Quebec H4W 1M3 Canada. **Tel** (514)484-1107, FAX (514)484-7284. **ED** Martin Stone. **DD** 071/.1428. **Bk Rev**. **Ad Acc. Circ:** 19,000 (ctrl). available on microfiche.
Desc: Community newspaper serving Montreal's predominantly English-speaking, upwardly mobile suburbs, with regionalized editions. Quebec's largest English language weekly and Montreal's second largest anglophone publication.

CN/0229-298X
SUBURBAN. DOLLARD DES ORMEAUX EDITION. (THE SUBURBAN.). [Suburban, Dollard des Ormeaux ed.]. (197?)-. Newspaper. English (French; summaries and/or abstracts in French). wk. 198.10Can$. Michael Publishers, 8170 Walnell Road, Cote-Saint-Luc Quebec H4W 1M3 Canada. **Tel** (514)484-1107, FAX (514)484-7284. **ED** Michael A. Wollock. **DD** 071/.1428. **Bk Rev**. **Ad Acc. Pub. Size:** Tabloid. **Circ:** 101,000 (ctrl).

CN/0704-7363
SUBURBAN MIRROR, THE. **VAT** Mirror (St. John's). V. 1- Nov. 2, 1977-. Newspaper. English. wk. $17.00 Canada; $20.00 other. The Suburban Mirror, 18 O'Leary Avenue, St John's Newfoundland A1B 2C7 Canada. **DD** 071/.18.

CN/0229-3013
SUBURBAN. NEW BORDEAUX, CARTIERVILLE EDITION. (THE SUBURBAN.). [Surburban, New Bordeaux, Cartierville ed.]. Newspaper. English (French). wk. $105.00. Michael Publishers, 8170 Walnell Road, Cote-Saint-Luc Quebec H4W 1M3 Canada. **Tel** (514)484-1107, FAX (514)484-7284. **ED** Christy McCormick. **DD** 071/.14281. **Bk Rev**. **Ad Acc. Circ:** 101,000 (ctrl). ***Continues*** *Suburban (Nouveau-Bordeaux Edition), 0712-7316.*

CN/0229-2971
SUBURBAN. NOTRE DAME DE GRACE EDITION. (THE SUBURBAN.). [Suburban, Notre dame de Grace ed.]. Newspaper. English (French). wk. 65.00Can$ Canada; $85.00 US. Michael Publishers, 8170 Walnell Road, Cote-Saint-Luc Quebec H4W 1M3 Canada. **Tel** (514)484-1107, FAX (514)484-7284. **ED** Martin Stone. **DD** 071/.14281. **Bk Rev**. **Ad Acc. Circ:** 9,206 (ctrl).
Desc: Community newspaper serving Montreal's upwardly mobile suburbs with regionalized editions.

CN/0229-303X
SUBURBAN. ST. LAURENT EDITION. (THE SUBURBAN.). [Suburban, St. Laurent ed.]. Newspaper. English (French). wk. 105.00Can$ (add 7% tax). Michael Publishers, 8170 Walnell Road, Cote-Saint-Luc Quebec H4W 1M3 Canada. **Tel** (514)484-1107, FAX (514)484-7284. **ED** Christy McCormick. **DD** 071/.1428. **Bk Rev**. **Ad Acc. Circ:** 101,000 (ctrl).
Desc: Community newspaper serving Montreal's predominantly English-speaking, upwardly mobile suburbs, with regionalized editions. Quebec's largest English language weekly and Montreal's second largest Anglophone publication.

CN/0229-3021
SUBURBAN. TOWN OF MOUNT ROYAL EDITION. (THE SUBURBAN.). Newspaper. English (French). wk. Free. Michael Publishers, 8170 Walnell Road, Cote-Saint-Luc Quebec H4W 1M3 Canada. **Tel** (514)484-1107, FAX (514)484-7284. **DD** 071/.14281. ctrl circ.

CN/0229-3005
SUBURBAN (WESTMOUNT EDITION). (THE SUBURBAN.). [Suburban, Westmount ed.]. Newspaper. English (French). wk. 65.00Can$ Canada; $85.00 US. Michael Publishers, 8170 Walnell Road, Cote-Saint-Luc Quebec H4W 1M3 Canada. **Tel** (514)484-1107, FAX (514)484-7284. **ED** Martin Stone. **DD** 071/.14281. **Bk Rev**. **Ad Acc. Circ:** 3,000 (ctrl).
Desc: Newspaper serving Montreal's predominantly upwardly mobile suburbs, with regionalized editions.

CN/0705-4033
SUN (FREDERICTON). (THE SUN.). V. 1- Feb. 1, 1978-. Newspaper. English (French). wk. $8.00. **DD** 071/.15/51.

CN/0710-0019
SUN (GRAND CENTRE). (SUN.). [Sun]. **VFOAT** Grand Centre-Cold Lake Sun; Grand Centre-Cold Lake-Bonnyville Sun. (1977)-. Newspaper. English. wk. 42.06Can$ Canada; 90.00Can$ other. Grande Centre Cold Lake, Box 268, Grande Center Alberta T0A 1T0 Canada. **Tel** (403)594-5881. **ED** Jim Bentein. **DD** 071/.1233. **Ad Acc. Circ:** 6,742.
Desc: Weekly community newspaper.

CN/0380-8912
SUN (LEAMINGTON). (THE SUN.). V. 1- Aug. 13, 1975-. Monographic series. English. wk. Price varies per volume. Sunparlour Publishing Company, 33 John Street, Leamington Ontario N8H 1H3. **DD** 071/.13/31.

CN/0711-2149
SUNDAY GAZETTE. [Sunday gaz.]. **VFOAT** Sunday Gazette/Herald. Newspaper. English. wk. $.15 each number. WE Dunning Publishing Company, 22610 Dewdney Trunk Road, Maple Ridge BC V2X 3H6 Canada. **DD** 071/.1133.

CN/0712-1113
SURREY/NORTH DELTA TODAY. (SURREY / N. DELTA TODAY.). [Surrey/N. Delta today]. **VFOAT** Surrey, North Delta Today. Vol. 1, No. 1 (Sept. 15, 1980)-. Newspaper. English. wk. Free. Columbian Company, N. Delta Today, #2, 13634 104th Avenue, Surrey BC V3T 1W2. **DD** 071/.1133.

CN/0229-6861
SURREY TIMES. (THE SURREY TIMES.). [Surrey times]. Vol. 1, No. 1 (Feb. 28, 1979)-. Newspaper. English. wk. $0.20 each number. The Surrey Times, Office D, Suite 14673/108th Avenue, Surrey British Columbia Canada. **DD** 071/.1133.

CN/0383-7343
TAHSIS INLET OUTLET, THE. V. 1- July 11, 1974-. Newspaper. English. bw. $5.00. C la Flam, RR #7, Duncan British Columbia V9L 4W4, Canada. **DD** 071/.11/34.

CN/0710-1112
TAMARAW TIMES. (THE TAMARAW.). [Tamaraw times]. **VFOAT** Maliwanag ang Katotohanan. Vol. 1, No. 1

(Apr./May 1980)-. Newspaper. English. ir. Free. Tamaraw Times, PO Box 1623 Station B, Montreal Quebec H3B 3L3 Canada. **DD** 971.4/270049921. **UDC** 971.4. ctrl circ.

CN/0382-0653
TEMISCAMIEN (1976). (LE TEMISCAMIEN.). [Temiscamien]. (1976)-. Newspaper. French. wk (52 issues per year). 30.00Can$. Le Temiscamien/Temoin de la Vie Temiscamienne, CP 219, Ville-Marie Quebec J0Z 3W0 Canada. **Tel** (819)629-2618. **DD** 071/.14212. **Ad Acc. Circ:** 4,000 (ctrl). ***Continues*** *Journal Temiscamien, 0821-3178.*

CN/0229-6594
THAMES VALLEY TIMES. [Thames Val. times]. Vol. 1, No. 1 (1979)-. Newspaper. English. mo. Natural Dynamics, PO Box 640, Jarvis Ontario N0A 1J0. **DD** 640.

CN/0707-4794
THAMESFORD TOWN CRIER. VFOAT Town Crier. **VAT** Town Crier (Thamesford). V. 1- Nov. 24, 1977-. Newspaper. English. wk. $7.50. Thamesford Town Crier, Box 399 Canada. **DD** 071/.13/46.

CN/0821-2333
THIS WEEK (HARROW). (THIS WEEK : HARROW AND COLCHESTER SOUTH.). [This week]. **VFOAT** Harrow and Colchester South This Week. Newspaper. English. wk. $0.15Can$ each number. c/o T Hunter, PO Box 310, Harrow Ontario N0R 1G0 Canada. **DD** 071/.1331. available on microfiche (from Oakville, Ont : Ontario Community Newspapers).

CN/0713-0562
TIDE (LEWISPORTE). (THE TIDE.). [Tide]. Vol. 1, No. 1 (Apr. 12/25)-. Newspaper. English. sm. $0.20 each number. Tide Publishing Company, 166 Main Street, Lewisporte Newfoundland, A0G 3A0. **DD** 071/.18.

CN
TILBURY TIMES. (19??)-. English. wk. 53.28Can$ US. Tilbury Times, Box 490 Tilbury Ontario N0P 2L0 Canada. **Tel** (519)682-0411, FAX (519)682-3633. **ED** Gerry Harvieux. Index available. cum. index. **Ad Acc, Adv Mgr:** Victoria Charron. **Circ:** 3,300.

CN/0834-7344
TILBURY TIMES. (THE TILBURY TIMES [MICROFORM].). (1884)-. English. Tilbury Times, Box 490, Tilbury Ontario N0P 2L0 Canada. **Tel** (519)682-0411, FAX (519)682-3633. **DD** 071/.1333. **Ad Acc. Circ:** 3,300.

CN/0839-427X
TIMES COLONIST (VICTORIA). (TIMES COLONIST [MICROFORM].). [Times colon.]. (Sept. 2, 1980)-. Newspaper. English. ds. 334.00Can$ Vancouver Island; 353.00Can$ Canada; 532.00Can$ other. Victoria Times Colonist, 2621 Douglas Street, Victoria, British Columbia, V8W 2N4 Canada. **Tel** (604)380-5211, FAX (604)380-5255. **DD** 071/.1134. ***Formed by the union of*** *Victoria Times (Victoria, B.C. : Daily)., 0839-4318.*

CN/0380-4569
TIMES OF NORTH AND WEST VANCOUVER, THE. Began with Dec. 30, 1971 issue. Newspaper. English. wk. 0.15Can$ each copy. The Times of North and West Vancouver, 1442 Pemberton Avenue North, Vancouver British Columbia V7P 2R8 Canada. **DD** 071/.11/33. ***Continues*** *Lions Gate Times.*

CN/1185-1880
TIMES OF SRI LANKA, THE. [Times of Sri Lanka]. Vol. 1, No. 1 (Aug. 1990)-. Newspaper. English. mo. North American Publications, Unit 36, 80 Nashdene Road, Scarborough, Ontario M1V 5E4 Canada. **DD** 071/.13541.

CN/0821-2473
TIMES (WINNIPEG). (THE TIMES.). [Times]. Vol. 1, No. 1 (Oct. 22, 1980)-. Newspaper. English. wk. $7.00 Canada; $8.00 US. Reliance Press, 1397 Erin Street, Winnipeg Manitoba R3E 2S9 Canada. **Tel** 694-0173. **DD** 071/.1274.

CN/0316-6872
TIMMINS PORCUPINE NEWS. V. 1- Nov. 6, 1974-. Newspaper. English. wk. 10.50Can$ Canada; 12.50Can$ other. Timmins Porcupine News, 815 Pine Street South, Timmins Ontario P4N 2M2 Canada. **DD** 071/.14/142.

CN/1191-0771
TIMMINS TIMES, THE. [Timmins times]. Vol. 1, No. 1 (Mar. 17, 1991)-. Newspaper. English. wk. 58.00Can$ Canada; 70.00Can$ other. Ontario Inc., 81 Balsam Street South, Timmins Ontario P4N 2C9 Canada. **Tel** (705)268-6252, FAX (705)268-2252. **ED** Kevin Vincent. **DD** 071/.13142. **Ad Acc, Adv Mgr:** J.Lapraik, **Tel** (705)268-6252. **Circ:** 19,000 (ctrl). available on microfilm.

CN/1187-0672
TOM TAC, LE REGIONAL. [Tom tac reg.]. Vol. 3, No 8 (Feb 1991)-. Newspaper. French (summaries and/or abstracts in English). wk. Limited Free Distribution. Tom Tac, Le Regional, CP 83, Ste-Martine Quebec J0S 1V0 Canada. **DD** 071/.143. ***Continues*** *Tom Tac., 1187-0680.*

CN/0229-3196
TORONTO CLARION. [Tor. clarion]. **VFOAT** Clarion. Vol. 1, No. 1 (Oct. 15, 1976)-. Newspaper. English. mo. $23.21. Western Gap Communication Coop, Ontario M5B 1G7 Canada. **Tel** (416)363-4404. **DD** 071/.13541.

CN/0319-0781
TORONTO STAR. [Tor. star]. (1971)-. Newspaper. English. ds. 708.21Can$ Canada; 2392.18Can$ Western Hemisphere; 4425.38Can$ Europe; 5304.18Can$ Asia & Africa; 5668.18Can$ Pacific Rim. Toronto Star Newspapers Ltd., 1 Yonge Street, Toronto Ontario M5E 1E6 Canada. **Tel** (416)367-2138. **(Subscription address:** International Media Service, 3330 Pacific Avenue Suite 404, Virginia Beach VA 23451.**)** available on CD-ROM from Optim Corporation; available on an online database (file 635/Full-Text) from DIALOG. ***Continues*** *Toronto Daily Star.*
Ind/Abst Can. Lit. Index (1985-1986); Can. News Index.

CN/0837-3175
TORONTO SUN. MICROFORM, THE. [Tor. sun]. **VFOAT** Saturday Sun; Sunday Sun. (Nov. 1, 1971)-. English. mo. 2236.80Can$ Canada; 2272.80Can$ US; 2383.20Can$ other. Toronto Sun, 333 King Street East, Toronto Ontario M5A 3X5 Canada. **Tel** (416)868-2257. **(Subscription address:** CD-ROM Vendor: Innotech Inc., 110 Silver Star Boulevard, Unit 107, Scarborough Ontario M1V 5A2 Canada**) DD** 071/.13541. available on CD-ROM from Innotech Inc.

CN/0712-3299
TOULADI. (LE TOULADI.). [Touladi]. Vol. 1 No. 1 (Oct. 3 1979)-. Newspaper. French. Fifty-two times a year (Sundays). 48.10Can$ Canada; 58.10Can$ others. Touladi, Box 430, Cabano Quebec G0L R0I Canada. **Tel** (418)854-2766. **ED** Jn Claude Pelletier. **DD** 071/.1476. **Ad Acc. Circ:** 9,500 (ctrl).

CN/1183-1936
TOUR DES PONTS, LE. [Tour ponts]. Vol. 1, No 1 (Jan. 1991)-. Newspaper. French. mo. 15.00Can$. Editions a la Lettre, CP 74, Saint-Anselme, Quebec G0R 2N0 Canada. **DD** 071/.1472.

CN/0710-541X
TOWN CRIER (COCHRANE). (THE TOWN CRIER.). [Town crier]. Vol. 1, No. 1 (Oct. 8, 1980)-. Newspaper. English. Free. Cochrane Times, PO Box 776, Cochrane Alberta T0L 0W0 Canada. **Tel** (403)932-2055. **DD** 071/.1233.

CN/0834-700X
TOWN OF MOUNT ROYAL WEEKLY POST. (TOWN OF MOUNT ROYAL WEEKLY POST [MICROFORM].). [Town Mt. R. wkly. post]. **VFOAT** Mount Royal Weekly Post. (1940)-. English (summaries and/or abstracts in French). wk. 22.43Can$ (1 year), 40.19Can$ (2 year), 54.21Can$ (3 year) Canada; 25.92Can$ (1 year), 45.44Can$ (2 year), 62.64Can$ (3 year) other (print). Town of Mount Royal Weekly Post, 233 Dunbar Avenue, Room 301, Mount Royal Quebec H3P 2H4 Canada. **Tel** (514)739-3302. **DD** 071/.1428.

CN/0380-3694
TOWN OF VAUGHAN WEEKLY, THE. V. 1- June 6, 1974-. Newspaper. English. wk. The Town of Vaughan Weekly, PO Box 331, Woodbridge Ontario L4L 1B2 Canada. **DD** 071/.13/54.

CN/0316-022X
TOWNSHIPS SUN, THE. (1974)-. Newspaper. English. mo. 15.00Can$ Canada; 20.00Can$ US. The Townships Sun, Box 28, Lennoxville QUE J1M 1Z3 Canada. **Tel** (819)566-7424. **DD** 071/14/6. **Bk Rev**, (Qty: 12). **Ad Acc, Adv Mgr:** Patricia Ball, **Tel** (819_566-7424. **Circ:** 1,400 (ctrl).
Desc: Stories and pictures are of general interest, but focus upon life in the Eastern Township.

CN/0713-5726
TRACT (CHICOUTIMI). (LE TRACT / COLLEGE DE CHICOUTIMI.). [Tract]. Newspaper. French. wk. Free. Le Tract, College de Chicoutimi, 534 East rue Jacques-Cartier, Chicoutimi Quebec G7H 1Z6 Canada. **DD** 378.714/16. ctrl circ.

CN
TRAIL DAILY TIMES. (19??)-. Newspaper. English. da. 112.35Can$ (includes GST) Canada; 165.00Can$ other. Trail Times Ltd., 1163 Cedar Avenue, Trail BC V1R 4B8 Canada. **Tel** (604)368-8551, FAX (604)368-3818.

CN/0227-5562
TRAIT D'UNION (MASCOUCHE). (LE TRAIT D'UNION.). [Trait union]. Vol. 1, No. 1, (Sept. 1976)-. Newspaper. French. Fifty-two times a year (Monday). 113.10Can$. Le Trait D'Union, 2522 rue Ste Marie, Mascouche Quebec J7K 1M5 Canada. **Tel** (514)474-2488. **DD** 071/.14416.

CN/0710-0221
TRI-LAKE RECORDER, THE. [Tri-lake rec.]. **VFOAT** Recorder. **VAT** Recorder (Penticton). Vol. 1, No. 1 (Jan. 29, 1979)-. Newspaper. English. wk. Free in Penticton. The Recorder / Canada, 2375 Government Street, Penticton British Columbia V2A 6J7 Canada. **DD** 071/.1142.

CN/0823-6925
TRIANGLE NEWS (CORONACH). (TRIANGLE NEWS.). [Triangle news]. Vol. 1, No. 1 (Apr. 13, 1983)-. Newspaper. English. Fifty-two times a year (Tues.). 15.00Can$ Coronach; 18.00Can$ Saskatchewan; 20.00Can$ others provinces in Canada. Triangle News, PO Box 689, Coronach Saskatchewan S0H 0Z0 Canada. **Tel** (306)267-3381, FAX (306)267-3381. **ED** Randall Burns. **DD** 071/.1244.

●CN
TRIBUNE, THE. ***Suspended.*** 70th year, No. 2781 (May 4, 1992)-(199?). Newspaper. English. wk. Tribune / Toronto Canada, 290A Danforth Avenue, Toronto Ontario M4K 1L5 Canada. ***Formed by the union of*** *Canadian Tribune (Toronto, Ont.)* ***and*** *Pacific Tribune (Vancouver, B.C.).*

CN/0829-6650
TRIBUNE (GRAVELBOURG). (TRIBUNE.). [Tribune]. Vol. 1, No. 1 (Nov. 14, 1984)-. Newspaper. English (French). wk. 18.00Can$ (one year), 32.00Can$ (two year). Gravel Subscriptions Ltd, Po Box 1017, Gravelbourg Saskatchewan, S0H 1X0 Canada. **Tel** (306)648-3479 or, 625-3386, FAX (306)648-2520. **ED** Paul Boisvert. **DD** 071/.1243.

CN
TRIBUNE (SHERBROOKE QUEBEC), LA. (LA TRIBUNE.). (19??)-. French. da. 179.12Can$ (retail trading zone) Sherbrooke & surrounding areas, 242.68Can$ others in Canada, 600.00Can$ others (by mail); 181.00Can$ (by motor route & carrier). Tribune / Sherbrooke Canada, 1950 rue Roy, Sherbrooke Quebec J1K 9Z9 Canada. **Tel** (819)564-5466.

CN/0319-7956
TRUE NORTH. V. 1- Oct. 1974-. Newspaper. English. mo. $4.50. True North Communications, Box 4, Site 36, R.R. 2, Sudbury Ontario P3E 4N3. **DD** 071/.13/133.

CN/0229-7957
TWO MOUNTAINS JOURNAL. [Two Mt. j.]. **VFOAT** Journal Deux-Montagnes. Vol. 1, No. 1-. Newspaper. English (French). bm. D Leonardo, PO Box 67, Deux-Montagnes, Quebec J7R 4K1 Canada. **DD** 071/.1425.

●CN/1193-2813
UKRAINIAN CANADIAN HERALD. [Ukr. Can. her.]. **VFOAT** Ukrains Ko-Kanadskyi Visnyk. (1992)-. Newspaper. English (Ukrainian). ir. $27.00 per year. Kobzar Publishing Company Ltd, 962 Bloor Street West, Toronto Ontario M6J 1L6 Canada. **Tel** 534-8662. **DD** 071/.1/08991791.

CN/0041-6002
UKRAINSKI VISTI (EDMONTON). (UKRAINIAN NEWS :UKRAINSKI VISTI.). [Ukr. visti]. **VFOAT** Ukrainski Visti. No. 25 (June 15, 1988)-. Newspaper. English (Ukrainian). mo. 20.00Can$. Ukrainski Visti / Ukrainian News, 1. 12227 - 107 Avenue, Edmonton Alberta, T5M 1Y9 Canada. **Tel** (403)488-3693, FAX (403)488-3859. **ED** Marco Levytsky. **DD** 971.23/3400491791. **Ad Acc, Adv Mgr:** Richard Sheps. **Circ:** 6,271 (ctrl). ***Continues*** *Ukrainski Visty (Edmonton, Alta.)., 0041-6002.*

CN/0834-7336
UXBRIDGE TIMES-JOURNAL. (UXBRIDGE TIMES-JOURNAL [MICROFORM].). **VFOAT** Uxbridge Times Herald; Uxbridge Times. (1???)-. English. wk. $28.00 Canada; $75.00 other. Uxbridge Times Journal, PO Box 339 Uxbridge, Ontario L9P 1M9 Canada. **Tel** (416)852-9141, FAX (416)852-9341. **ED** Jeff Hurst. **DD** 071/.1356. **Ad Acc. Circ:** 5000 (ctrl).

CN/0841-6419
VALLEY COURIER (PORT ALBERNI, B.C. : 1988). (THE VALLEY COURIER.). [Val. cour.]. Vol. 1, No. 1; March 23, 1980-. Newspaper. English. wk. Free to residents in Alberni Valley. Valley Courier, 4961 Argyle Street, Port Alberni British Columbia V9Y 1V6 Canada. **DD** 071/.1134.

CN/0715-4887
VALLEY NEWS (MONTEBELLO). (VALLEY NEWS.). [Val. news]. Newspaper. English (French). ir. Free. Sedbergh School Association, Montebello Quebec J0V 1L0 Canada. **Tel** (819)423-5523. **DD** 378.714/23. **Bk Rev. Circ:** 2,000 (ctrl).

CN/0715-321X
VALLEY REPORTER. [Val. report.]. Newspaper. English. Valley Reporter, PO Box 129, Salmo British Columbia V0G 1Z0 Canada. **DD** 071/.1144.

CN/0711-4427
VALLEY REVIEW (PEMBROKE). (VALLEY REVIEW.). [Val. rev.]. Newspaper. English. wk. 0.15Can$ per no. Valley Review, PO Box 983, Pembroke Ontario K8A 7M5 Canada. **DD** 071/.1381.

Canada

CN/0845-4183
VALLEY SENTINEL (VALEMOUNT). (VALLEY SENTINEL.). [Val. sentinel]. Vol. 3, Issue 24 (June 15, 1988)-. Newspaper. English. wk. 25.00Can$ Canada; 50.00Can$ other. Valley Sentinel, PO Box 688, Valemount British Columbia V0E 2Z0 Canada. **Tel** (604)566-4425, FAX (604)566-4528. **ED** Maureen Brownlee. **DD** 071/.112. **Ad Acc**. **Circ:** 1,200 (ctrl). **Continues** Valemount Sentinel, 0845-4140.
Desc: Community newspaper serving the Robson/Canoe Valley which includes Valemount, McBride, Tete Jaune Cache, Blue River, Dome Creek, Crescent Spur, and Mount Robson.

CN/1186-7698
VANCOUVER EAST NEWS. Ceased. [Vanc. east news]. (Jan. 2, 1991)-(December 1991). Newspaper. English. wk. West Ender/East Ender Publications Ltd., 1035 Davie Street, Vancouver British Columbia V6E 1M5 Canada. **DD** 071/.1133. **Continues** The Metro Vancouver News., 1186-7671.

CN/0227-3772
VANCOUVER EXPRESS. [Vanc. express]. Vol. 1 (Feb. 21, 1970)-. Newspaper. English. tw (Monday, Wednesday, Friday). 78.00Can$ Canada; 101.40Can$ other. Vancouver Express, 554 East 15th Avenue, Vancouver British Columbia V5T 2R5 Canada. **DD** 071/.1133. available on microfilm.

CN/0715-4895
VANCOUVER NEWS (VANCOUVER, 1977). (THE VANCOUVER NEWS.). [Vanc. news]. (1977)-. Newspaper. English. sm. Free to residents of East Vancouver. Foremost Publishing Company, 3 East Broadway/Suite 2033, Vancouver British Columbia V5T 1V5 Canada. **DD** 071/.1133.

CN/1186-768X
VANCOUVER SOUTH NEWS (1991). (VANCOUVER SOUTH NEWS.). [Vanc. south news]. (Jan. 16, 1991)-. Newspaper. English. wk. Limited free distribution. West Ender/East Ender Publications Ltd., 1035 Davie Street, Vancouver British Columbia V6E 1M5 Canada. **DD** 071/.1133.

CN/0832-1299
VANCOUVER SUN (1986). (THE VANCOUVER SUN.). [Vanc. sun]. Vol. 99, No. 402 (March 4, 1986)-. Periodical. English. ir (308 per year). 616.82Can$ Canada; 1170.00Can$ US; 1836.00Can$ other. Division of Pacific Press, 2250 Granville Street, Vancouver British Columbia V6H 3G2 Canada. **Tel** (604)732-2944. **DD** 071/.1133. **Continues** Sun (Vancouver, B.C. : 1983), 0828-1793.
Ind/Abst Can. News Index.

CN/0710-0191
VAUGHAN COURIER, THE. [Vaughan cour.]. **VFOAT** Courier. Newspaper. English. wk. $0.10 per no. Vaughan Courier, PO Box 462, Kleinburg Ontario Canada. **DD** 071/.13547.

CN/0706-7550
VAUXHALL ADVANCE, THE. VFOAT Advance. **VAT** Advance (Vauxhall). Vol. 1 (Oct. 26, 1978)-. Newspaper. English. wk. 12.00Can$. Taber Times, PO Box 2020, Taber Alberta T0K 2G0 Canada. **Tel** (403)223-2266. **DD** 071/.123/.4.

CN/0703-8747
VICTORIA COUNTY RECORD. V. 1- Oct. 1976-. Newspaper. English. wk. 26.00Can$ Canada; $36.00 other. The Victoria County Record, PO Box 928, Perth-Andover New Brunswick E0J 1V0 Canada. **Tel** (506)273-2285. **ED** Mark Richard. **DD** 071/.15/.53. **Ad Acc**. **Circ:** 4,500 (ctrl).
Desc: Covering events throughout Victoria County. Offices in Perth-Andover and Grand-Falls.

CN
VICTORIA TIMES COLONIST. Newspaper. English. wk. 151.50Can$ Canada; 182.00Can$ other. Victoria Times Colonist, 2621 Douglas Street, Victoria, British Columbia, V8W 2N4 Canada. **Tel** (604)380-5211, FAX (604)380-5255.

CN
VICTORIA TIMES COLONIST / BY CARRIER. Newspaper. English. wk. $153.40. Victoria Times Colonist, 2621 Douglas Street, Victoria, British Columbia, V8W 2N4 Canada. **Tel** (604)380-5211, FAX (604)380-5255.

CN/1186-1525
VILLAGE OF YORKVILLE VOICE, THE. [Village Yorkv. voice]. **VFOAT** Voice. Vol. 1, No. 1 (Spring 1990)-. Periodical. English. qt. $2.00 per issue. Amber York Marketing, 83 Scollard Street, Toronto, Ontario M5R 1G4 Canada. **DD** 071/.3541.

CN/0711-3439
VILLAGEOIS, LE. [Villageois]. Vol. 1, No. 1 (July, 1979)-. Newspaper. French. mo. $5.00 per issue. Le Villageois, CP 269 St-Jean Baptiste, Quebec J0L 2B0 Canada. **DD** 071/.1453.

CN/0226-5907
VILLAGER (MISSISSAUGA). (THE VILLAGER.). [Villager]. (Apr. 1980)-. Newspaper. English. mo (plus special issue in Dec.). Village Publications Ltd., 2259 Bloor Street West, Toronto Ontario M6S 1N8 Canada. **Tel** (416)767-3644. **ED** Verner Kure. **DD** 071/.13535. **Bk Rev**. **Ad Acc**. **Circ:** 39,500 (ctrl).
Desc: Community newspaper serving the west Toronto area.

CN/0834-745X
VILLAGER (TORONTO. 1982). (VILLAGER.). [Villager]. (1982)-. Newspaper. English. mo. $0.25 per no. Villager, 2259 Bloor St. W., Toronto Ontario M65 1V8 Canada. **DD** 071/.13541. **Continues** Bloor West Villager, 0703-1912.

CN/0714-3230
VISITANDIN, LE. [Visitandin]. Vol. 1, No. 1 (31 Mar. 1981)-. Newspaper. French. ir $5.00. Le Visitandin, 116 rue St-Joseph, La Visitation Quebec J0G 1C0 Canada. **DD** 071/.1454.

CN/0842-9715
VOCE DEGLI ITALO CANADESI. (LA VOCE DEGLI ITALO CANADESI : QUINDICINALE APOLITICO AL SERVIZIO DEGLIO IMMAGRATI IN CANADA.). [Voce Italo Can.]. Vol. 1, No. 1 (Jan. 15, 1989)-. Newspaper. Italian (English). bw. $0.25 per no. Voce Degli Italo Canadesi, 6737 Monk Blvd., Montreal Quebec H4E 3J1 Canada. **DD** 971/.00451/05.

CN/0822-7896
VOICE (VANCOUVER. 1983). (VOICE / VANCOUVER COMMUNITY COLLEGE.). [Voice]. **Added/Corp** Vancouver Community College. Vol. 1 No. 1 (Sept. 16, 1983)-. Newspaper. English. wk. Free to students. Journalism Department, Langara Campus, Vancouver Community College, 100 West 49th Avenue, Vancouver British Columbia V5Y 2Z6 Canada. **DD** 378.711/33. **Continues** VCC Voice., 0821-5871.

CN
WADENA NEWS [MICROFORM], THE. **Added/Corp** Saskatchewan Archives Board. **VFOAT** Quill Lake Record; Margo Times and Wadena News. (June 19, 1929)-. English. Forty-nine times a year. $18.00 Saskatchewan; $25.00 others; $35.00 letters carriers. The Wadena News, PO Box 100, Wadena Sask S0A 4J0 Canada. **Tel** (306)338-2231, FAX (306)338-2266. **ED** James R. Headington (phone: (306)338-3776). **DD** 071/.1242. **Ad Acc**, **Adv Mgr:** Headington. **Circ:** 4,500. **Continues** Wadena Herald.
Desc: Local news, events, community coverage, and advertising.

CN/0712-1865
WANGAR. [Wangar]. Vol. 1, No. 1 Oct./Nov. 1976. Newspaper. English. bm. 20.00Can$ Canada and US; 25.00Can$ other. Wangar, PO Box 69646 Station K V5K 4W7 Canada. **Tel** (604)420-2972. **ED** Hari P Sharma. **DD** 071/.1133. **Bk Rev**. **Circ:** 1,500 (ctrl).
Desc: News and analysis on developments in India.

CN/0704-4895
WASAGA BEACH NEWS (1979). (WASAGA BEACH NEWS.). V. 2 (May 1979)-. Newspaper. English. wk. 0.15Can$ each number. Wasaga Publications, PO Box 254, Wasaga Beach Ontario L0L 2P0 Canada. **DD** 071/.1317. **Continues** Wasaga Beach News Magazine, 0704-4887.

CN/1185-4901
WASAGA STAR TIMES. (WASAGA STAR TIMES [MICROFORM].). [Wasaga star times]. (Feb. 14, 1991)-. English. Ontario Community Newspapers Association, PO Box 451, 1184 Speers Road, Oakville Ontario L6J 5A8. **DD** 071/.1317. **Continues** Wasaga Times, 0834-4620.

CN/0382-8379
WASCANA WITNESS. (June 17, 1975)-. Newspaper. English. wk. Wascana Witness, Box 3053, Regina Saskatchewan S4P 3G7 Canada. **DD** 071/.124/.4.

CN
WATERLOO CHRONICLE. (19??)-. Newspaper. English. Fifty-two times a year (Wednesdays). 45.00Can$ Canada; 90.00Can$ other. Waterloo Chronicle, 75 King Street South, 2nd Floor, Waterloo ONT N2J 1P2 Canada. **Tel** (519)886-2830. **ED** Melodee Martinuk. **Bk Rev**. **Ad Acc**, **Adv Mgr:** Bill Karges. **Circ:** 24,500 (ctrl).

CN
WEEKEND MAGAZINE INDEX CARDS MICROFORM. Reel No. 1-. Newspaper. English. Preston Microfilming Services, 2215 Queen Street East, Toronto Ontario M4E 1E8 Canada. **Tel** (416)699-7154. **DD** 051.

CN/1184-0374
WEEKLY HERALD (MONTREAL). (THE WEEKLY HERALD.). [Wkly. her.]. **VFOAT** Cote St. Luc, Hampstead, Westmount, T.M.R. Weekly Herald. Vol. 1, Issue No. 39 (Jan. 16/22, 1990)-. Newspaper. English. wk. $48.00 per year, Canada. Weekly Herald / Canada, Suite 341, 6900 Decarie Boulevard, Montreal Quebec H3X 2T8 Canada. **DD** 071/.1428. **Continues** Hampstead Herald., 1184-0382.

CN/0712-3043
WEEKLY NEWS (STRATFORD). (THE WEEKLY NEWS.). [Wkly. news]. Vol. 1, No. 14 (Jan. 16TH, 1980)-. Newspaper. English. wk. Free. Family Publications, 123 Ontario Street, Stratford Ontario N5A 3H1 Canada. **DD** 071/.1323. **Continues** Advertisers News, 0712-3051.

CN/0710-0175
WEEKLY REVIEW (VIKING). (THE WEEKLY REVIEW.). [Wkly. rev.]. Vol. 1, No. 1 (Feb. 14, 1978)-. Newspaper. English. wk. $7.74. The Weekly Review / Canada, Box 240, Viking Alberta T0B 4N0 Canada. **DD** 071/.1233.

CN/0712-1806
WELLAND NEWS MAGAZINE. [Welland news mag.]. **VAT** Welland Consumer News (1981). Vol. 3, No. 16 (4/21/81)-. Newspaper. English. wk. $0.25 each number. Otter Publishing, PO Box 458, Welland Ontario L3B 5R2. **DD** 071/.1338. **Continues** Welland Consumer News, 0712-1792.

CN/0229-6713
WEST CARLETON BANNER. [West Carleton banner]. **VFOAT** Banner. **VAT** Banner (Carp). Vol. 1, No. 1 (Apr. 10, 1979)-. Newspaper. English. wk. $10.00 Carp, $14.00 elsewhere in Canada, $25.00 others. West Careltron Banner, PO Box 279, Carp Ontario K0A 1L0 Canada. **DD** 071/.1383.

CN/0707-509X
WEST EDMONTON EXAMINER. VFOAT Examiner. **VAT** Examiner (West Edmonton). V. 1- Nov. 9, 1977-. Newspaper. English. wk. Free. Grove Publishing, 9509-156 Street, Edmonton Alta T5P 4J5. **DD** 071/.123/3. ctrl circ.

CN/0229-6012
WEST ENDER. [West ender]. Vol. 1, No. 1 (July 12, 1979)-. Newspaper. English. wk. 153.29Can$; $121.23. Westender, 1035 Davie Street, Vancouver British Columbia V6E 1M5 Canada. **Tel** (604)682-0686. **ED** Ted Townsend. **DD** 071/.1133. **Ad Acc**, **Adv Mgr:** Heidi Franke. **Circ:** 28,500 (ctrl).
Desc: Community news for Vancouver's downtown and west end community.

CN/0841-2588
WEST HILL NEWS. (WEST HILL NEWS [MICROFORM].). [West Hill News]. (1966)-. Newspaper. English. wk (published on Wednesday). 15.00Can$. Back of the Yards Journal, 4625 South Ashland Avenue, Chicago IL 60609. **Tel** (312)927-7203. **DD** 071/.13541.

CN/0710-6416
WEST PRINCE GRAPHIC. [West Prince graph.]. Vol. 1, No. 1 (Oct. 22, 1980)-. Newspaper. English. wk (published on Wed.). 27.82Can$ Prince Edward Island (excluding Charlottetown and Summerside); 44.94Can$ other Canada; 90.00Can$ other. The West Prince Graphic, PO Box 339, Alberton Prince Edward Island C0B 1B0 Canada. **Tel** (902)853-3320, FAX (902)853-3071. **DD** 071/.171.

CN/0821-5197
WEST TORONTO NEWS-EXPRESS, THE. [West Tor. news-express]. Newspaper. English. mo. Free. Enviro News Express, 1264 College Street, Toronto Ontario M6H 1C2. **DD** 071/.13541. ctrl circ. **Continues** Enviro-News Express.

CN
WEYBURN REVIEW [MICROFORM]. (1909)-. Newspaper. English. wk. 23.00Can$ City of Weyburn (by carrier); 30.00Can$ other Saskatchewan (by mail); 42.00Can$ other Canada (by mail); 80.00Can$ other. Weyburn Review, Box 400, Weyburn Saskatchewan, S4H 2K4 Canada. **Tel** (306)842-7487, FAX (306)842-0282. **DD** 071/.1244.

CN/0383-820X
WHISTLER QUESTION. (THE WHISTLER QUESTION.). Vol. 1 (April 14, 1976)-. Newspaper. English. wk. 36.47Can$ Whistler, Pemberton, and Squamish. 50.49Can$ other Canada; 78.10Can$ US; 128.10Can$ other. Whistler Printing and Publishing, PO Box 126, Whistler British Columbia, V0N 1B0 Canada. **Tel** (604)932-5131, (604)681-4986. **ED** Mike Youds. **DD** 071/.11/.33. **Bk Rev**. **Ad Acc**. **Circ:** 4,000.
Desc: A community newspaper.

CN/0844-398X
WHITBY FREE PRESS. (WHITBY FREE PRESS [MICROFORM].). [Whitby free press]. (June 30, 1971)-. English. wk. $32.00. Whitby Free Press, PO Box 206, 131 Brock Street North, Whitby ONT L1N 5S1 Canada. **Tel** (416)668-6111. **DD** 071/.1356. **Ad Acc**. **Circ:** 26,000 (ctrl).

CN/0844-398X
WHITBY FREE PRESS. (WHITBY FREE PRESS [MICROFORM].). [Whitby free press]. (June 30, 1971)-. English. wk. $32.00. Whitby Free Press, PO Box 206, 131 Brock Street North, Whitby ONT L1N 5S1 Canada. **Tel** (416)668-6111. **DD** 071/.1356. **Ad Acc**. ctrl circ.

Canada

CN/0821-5553
WHITECOURT FREE PRESS, THE.
[Whitecourt free press]. Vol. 1, No. 1 (Oct. 13, 1982)-. Newspaper. English. wk. $0.25 each number. W & E Cowley Publishing, PO Box 336, Whitecourt Alta. T0E 2L0 Canada. **DD** 071/.1233.

CN/0847-8597
WHITECOURT STAR. (WHITECOURT STAR. MICROFORM.). [Whitecourt star]. (June 8, 1962)-. Newspaper. English. wk (Published on Wednesdays). 32.87Can$. Whitecourt Star, PO Box 630, Whitecourt Alberta, T0E 2L0 Canada. **Tel** (403)778-3977. **ED** Randy Provencal. **DD** 071/.1233. **Ad Acc.** ctrl circ.
 Desc: Community news.

CN/0706-5094
WILD ROSE CHRONICLE. V. 1- Jan. 1978-. Newspaper. English. mo. $7.00. Wild Rose Chronicle, PO Box 1654, Vermilion Alta T0B 4M0 Canada. **DD** 071/.123/3.

CN/0712-6417
WINDMILL HERALD. (THE WINDMILL HERALD : GOED NIEUWS.). [Windmill her.]. **VAT** Goed Nieuws (1972). Vol. 14, No. 189 (Jan. 21, 1972)-. Newspaper. Dutch (English). sm. $17.50 US. Vanderheide Publishing Company, PO Box 9033, Surrey British Columbia V3T 4X3 Canada. **Tel** (604)597-2144. **ED** A A van der Heide. **DD** 071/.1133. **Bk Rev. Ad Acc. Circ:** 12,000. **Continues** Goed Nieuwus, 0712-6409; Hollandia News, 0319-8537.
 Desc: News is provided from the Netherlands and from Dutch immigrant communities across North America.

CN/0837-3299
WINDMILL HERALD (CENTRAL-EASTERN CANADA ED.). (THE WINDMILL HERALD : YOUR DUTCH LANGUAGE NEWSPAPER.). [Windmill her.]. **VFOAT** Windmill Post. Issue No. 570 (Aug. 1986)-. Newspaper. Dutch (summaries and/or abstracts in English). sm. 19.07Can$ North America; 60.07Can$ other. Vanderheide Publishing Company, PO Box 9033, Surrey British Columbia V3T 4X3 Canada. **Tel** (604)597-2144. **DD** 971/.0043931. **Continues** Hollandia News, 0319-8537.

CN/0839-2277
WINDSOR STAR MICROFORM, THE. [Windsor star]. Reel 694 (Feb. 10/27, 1960)-. Newspaper. English. da. 360.19Can$ Canada; 1143.74Can$ other. Windsor Star Ltd, 167 Ferry Street, Windsor Ontario N9A 4M5 Canada. **Tel** (519)255-5774, **FAX** (519)255-5515. **DD** 071/.1332. **Bk Rev.** available on an online database. **Continues** Windsor Daily Star.

CN/0834-177X
WINDSPEAKER. [Windspeaker]. **Added/Corp** Aboriginal Multi-Media Society of Alberta. Vol. 4, No. 1 (March 14, 1986)-. Newspaper. English (Eskimo). bw. 28.00Can$. Aboriginal Multi-Media Soc Alb, 15001 112 Avenue, Edmonton Alberta T5M 2V6 Canada. **Tel** (403)455-2700, **FAX** (403)452-1428. **ED** Linda Caldwell. **DD** 971.23/00497/005. Index available. cum. index. **Bk Rev**, (Qty: 1-2/yr). **Ad Acc, Adv Mgr:** Cliff. **Circ:** 15,000. available in microform. **Continues** AMMSA, 0822-6245.
 Ind/Abst Can. Index; Can. Period. Index (19??-); Ethnoarts Index.

CN/0828-1785
WINNIPEG FREE PRESS. [Winn. free press]. (Jan. 1932)-. Newspaper. English. ds. 533.13Can$ Canada; 1293.13Can$ other. Winnipeg Free Press Company Ltd., 1355 Mountain Avenue, Winnipeg Manitoba R2X 3B6 Canada. **Tel** (204)697-7075. **ED** M. Burt. **Ad Acc. Circ:** 179,000. available on microfilm. **Continues** Manitoba Free Press, (OCoLC) 7881137.
 Desc: Local and international news coverage.

CN/0703-5292
WINNIPEG GUIDE, THE. (197?)-. Newspaper. English. bw. Central Manitoba Publishing, Suite 1/590 Roseberry Street, Winnipeg Manitoba R3H 0T1 Canada. **DD** 071/.127/4.

CN/0711-3773
WINNIPEG SUN (1980). (THE WINNIPEG SUN.). [Winn. sun.]. Vol. 1, No. 1 (Nov. 5, 1980)-. Newspaper. English. Six times a year. $208.75 Canada; $450.70 other. Winnipeg Sun, 1700 Church Avenue, Winnipeg Manitoba R2X 3A2 Canada. **Tel** (204)697-0759, FAX 697-0759. **ED** John Bertrand. **DD** 071/.1274. Index available. **Bk Rev. Ad Acc. Pr Rev. Circ:** 50,000 (ctrl). available on microfiche (from Calgary : Commonwealth Microfilm Library).
 Desc: Covers all aspects of news, business, and sports.

CN
WINNIPEG TRIBUNE. Newspaper. English. Winnipeg Tribune, PO Box 7000, Winnipeg Manitoba R3C 3B2 Canada. **Tel** (204)985-4600.

CN/0842-084X
WOLSLEY BULLETIN, THE. [Wolseley bull.]. Vol. 1, Ed. 1 (Dec. 4, 1987)-. Newspaper. English. Fifty-two times a year (Fri.). 26.17Can$ Canada; 39.00Can$ others. Wolseley Bulletin, PO Box 89, Wolsley Saskatchewan S0G 5H0 Canada. **Tel** (306)698-2271,

FAX (306)698-2808. **ED** Eleanor Dahlman. **DD** 071/.1244. **Ad Acc, Adv Mgr:** E. Dahlman. **Circ:** 1,000 (ctrl).

CN/0319-0994
WOMEN CAN. *Title Change.* Began with Mar. 1974 issue. Newspaper. English. Women Can, 6854 Inverness, Vancouver British Columbia V5X 4G2 Canada. **DD** 301.41/2/0971133. **Continues** Pedestal, 0016-5476. **Continued by** Pedestal, 0319-1001.

CN/1182-6096
YELLOWHEAD STAR. [Yellowhead star]. (Apr. 30, 1990)-. Newspaper. English. te. Limited free distribution. Yellowhead Star, PO Box 1020, Barriere British Columbia V0E 1E0 Canada. **DD** 071/.1172. **Continues** Advertiser (Barriere, B.C.).

CN/0710-2011
YORK REGIONAL TOPIC, THE. [York reg. top.]. **VAT** Topic (Bradford). Newspaper. English. wk. $30.95. Bradford Paper Group, PO Box 1090, Bradford Ontario L0G 1C0 Canada. **DD** 071/.13547.

CN/1186-429X
YORKTON THIS WEEK & ENTERPRISE. (1990)-. Newspaper. English. sw (104 per year). 30.00Can$ Saskatchewan; 45.00Can$ other Canada; 150.00Can$ other. Yorkton This Week & Enterprise, PO Box 1300, Yorkton Saskatchewan S3N 2X3 Canada. **Tel** (306)782-2465. *Formed by the union of* Yorkton This Week, 0380-2833 and Enterprise (Yorkton), 0842-0254.

CN/0833-2908
YOUR NEWS. [Your news]. (1985)-. Periodical. English. Ten times a year (monthly except July and Aug.). 12.15Can$. Your News, PO Box 563, Sta Cote St Luc, Montreal Quebec, H4Z 2Z2 Canada. **ED** Frances Phelan (editor's Address: 131 Percival, Montreal West Quebec H4X 1T7 Canada; editor's Phone: (514)487-5797). **DD** 071/.14281. **Bk Rev**, (Qty: 4-5). **Circ:** 7,500.
 Desc: A teaching newspaper used in the classroom to teach language arts, ESL, literacy, special education or regular curriculum middle school.

CN/0318-1952
YUKON NEWS (1972). (YUKON NEWS.). (July 21, 1972)-. Newspaper. English. wk (Wednesday and Friday). 110.00Can$ Canada; 245.00Can$. Yukon News Ltd., 211 Wood Street, Whitehorse Yukon Y1A 2E4 Canada. **Tel** (403)667-6285, **FAX** (403)668-3755. **ED** Patricia Living. **DD** 071/.19/1. **Bk Rev. Ad Acc. Circ:** 8,600. **Continues** Yukon Daily News.
 Desc: Community newspaper covering all of Yukon, Canada.

CN
ZEIT, DIE. (19??)-. Newspaper. German. Fifty-two times a year. $54.00 US; $79.50 other. Team Publications, 29 Coldwater Road, Toronto ONT M3B 1Y8 Canada. **Tel** (416)391-4196. **ED** Haug V. Kuenheim. **Circ:** 8,500 (ctrl).

CN/0824-6017
ZHUJI. (TSU CHI.). [Zhu ji]. **VFOAT** Footprint; The Footprint : Official Publication of the Joint Committee of Chinese Students' Association of University of Toronto. Newspaper. Chinese. (English). Joint Publication Board, Box 595 Station P, Toronto Ontario M5S 2T1 Canada. **DD** 378.713/54.

CN
ZWIAZKOWIEC. No. 1 (1984)-. Newspaper. Polish. tw (Mon., Weds., Fri.). 70.00Can$ Canada; 120.00Can$ other. Polish Alliance Press Ltd., 1638 Bloor Street West, Toronto Ontario M6P 4A8 Canada. **Tel** (416)531-2491. **ED** Robert Dlugoborski. **Ad Acc. Circ:** 8,500.

CHILE

CL
FORTIN MAPOCHO DIARIO. Edicion No. 580 (Oct. 20 1987)-. Newspaper. Spanish. da. Agustinas, 1161 40 Piso, Casilla 9493 Santiago Chile. **Tel** 726219, telex 645458 CUCOM CT. **Continues** Fortin Mapocho.

CL
MERCURIO, EL. (1???)-. Periodical. Spanish. da. $2,860.00 US; $3,150.00 others. Empresa El Mercurio Sap Co, 1214 Casilla 13-D, Santiago Chile. **Tel** 011 562 2287048.

CL
SOUTH PACIFIC MAIL, THE. (Nov. 6, 1909)-. Newspaper. English. Twelve times a year. $550.00. South Pacific Mail, Casilla 4068, Santiago Chile. **Tel** 011 56 2 6322796, **FAX** (562)225-8922. **ED** Nicholas Asheshov. available on microfilm from The Library of Congress Photoduplication Service.

CHINA

CC
CHINA COURIER, THE. (1926)-. Newspaper. English. da. China National Publishing Company, 380 Bei Su Zhou Lu, Shanghai, People's Republic of China. **LC** 606.
 Ind/Abst Hum. Rights Intern. Rep.

CC/0253-9543
CHINA DAILY (INTERNATIONAL EDITION). (CHINA DAILY.). [China dly.]. **VFOAT** Chung-Kuo Jih Pao. Vol. 1, No. 1 (June 1, 1981)-. Academic Scholarly Publication. English (Chinese). da. $140.00 North America; $360.00 Europe; $350.00 others. China Daily, 15 Huixin Dongjie Chaoyang, Beijing, People's Republic of China. **Tel** 011 86 4224488, 011 86 4219308. **(Subscription address:** China Daily Distribution Company, 15 Mercer Street, Suite 401, New York NY 10013.) **ED** Chen Li. **CODEN** CHDADN. **Ad Acc. Circ:** 5,000. Documents available from CASDDS.
 Desc: Providing an impartial coverage of Chinese and international events.
 Ind/Abst Chem. Abstr. (1981-1983).

CC
CHING CHI JIH PAO. **VFOAT** Economic Daily. No. 574 (Jan. 1, 1983)-. Newspaper. Chinese. da. $76.80. **(Subscription address:** China International Book Trading Corporation, PO Box 399, Library Service Department, Beijing 100044 People's Republic of China.) **Continues** Chung-Kuo Tsai Mao Pao.

CC
CHUNG-KUO SHAO NIEN PAO. **VFOAT** Zhongguo Shaonian Bao. Chinese. da. $5.76. Science Press, 16 Donghuangchenggen North Street, Beijing 100707, People's Republic of China. **Tel** 011 86 1 4019821, 011 86 1 4010642, **FAX** 011 86 1 4012180, 011 86 1 4019810, telex 210147.

CC
JEN MIN JIH PAO. **VFOAT** Renmin Ribao; People's Daily. (19??)-. Newspaper. Chinese. da. $445.60 institutions. **(Subscription address:** China Books & Periodicals Inc., 2929 24th Street, San Francisco CA 94110.)

CC
JEN MIN JIH PAO SO YIN. (19??)-. Chinese. mo. $36.00. China National Publishing Company, 380 Bei Su Zhou Lu, Shanghai, People's Republic of China. **LC** AI21.J45; .J47. **DD** 079/.51156. **Bk Rev. Ad Acc.** ctrl circ.
 Desc: A microprinted collection of People's Daily, a newspaper in China belonging to the Central Committee of Communist Party.

CC
JEN MIN JIH PAO SO YIN HO TING PEN (MICROFORM). **VFOAT** Renmin Ribao. 1981.1-. Newspaper. Chinese. mo. $43.20. China National Publishing Import & Export Corporation, 16 Gongti E Rd., Chaoyang Dist., Beijing 100704, People's Republic of China. **Tel** 011 8601 50630169, 5066688, **FAX** 011 8601 5063101, 5063010, telex 22313. **Continues** Jen Min Jih Pao Ho Ting Pen.

CC
JIEFANG RIBAO. **VFOAT** Liberation Daily. Chinese. da (365 issues). $278.16. **(Subscription address:** China International Book Trading Corporation, PO Box 399, Library Service Department, Beijing 100044 People's Republic of China.)

CHINA (Republic: 1949)

CH
CHUNG YANG JIH PAO / CENTRAL DAILY NEWS. **VFOAT** Central Daily News. (195?)-. Newspaper. Chinese. da. $124.00. Central Daily News, 260 Patch Road, SEC 2 Stone Shih, Taipei 10401 Taiwan. **Tel** 02 771 6992.

CH
FREE CHINA JOURNAL, THE. **VFOAT** Tzu Yu Chung-Kuo Chi Shih Pao. Vol. 1, No. 1 (Jan. 1, 1984)-. Newspaper. English. wk. NT$350.00 Taiwan; $12.00 US. Kwang Hwa Publishing Company, PO Box 337, Taipei Taiwan. **Tel** (02)331-6753, telex 11636. **ED** Tang Wang. **Bk Rev. Ad Acc. Circ:** 25,000 (ctrl). available on microfilm and microfiche from University Microfilms International (UMI). **Continues** Free China Weekly.
 Desc: To keep friends overseas informed about news, views and developments in the Republic of China.

CH
HSIN HSIN WEN CHOU KAN. **VFOAT** Hsin Hsin Wen; Journalist. (March 12, 1987)-. Periodical. Chinese. wk. Culture Books, PO Box 1439, Monterey Park CA 91754. **Tel** (818)300-9028. **LC** AP95.C4; H731415. **DD** 951.05/05.

CH
UNITED DAILY NEWS. (19??)-. Newspaper. Chinese. ds. $191.44. United Daily News, 55 Chunghsiao East Road, Sec 4, Taipei 105 Taiwan. **Tel** 011 2 7681234 ext. 2530. **Ad Acc.** ctrl circ.
 Desc: A general news report in Chinese.

COLOMBIA

CK/0120-5331
CIFRAS. [Cifras]. (1982)-. Periodical. Spanish. mo. 15.00Col$. Camara de Comercio de Medellin, Apartado Aereo No. 1894, Medellin Colombia. **Tel** 5116111, FAX 2318648, telex 66768. **DD** 330. Index available. cum. index. **Bk Rev. Pr Rev. Circ:** 2,000 (ctrl). **Continues** Boletin Bibliografico - Camara de Comercio de Medellin, 0120-3711; Indicadores Economicos - Camara de Comercio de Medellin, 0120-3657.
 Desc: Articles related to business, economics, international trade, and commercial law.

CK
REPUBLICA, LA. (1953)-. Newspaper. Spanish. da. La Republica, Calle 15 No 4-96, Bogata Columbia. available on microfilm from University of Chicago Library; and The Library of Congress Photoduplication Service.

CK
TIEMPO, EL. Periodical. Spanish. da. El Tiempo, Av Elderado 59, 70 Apartado 3633, Bogota Colombia.

CONGO (Brazzaville)

CF
MWETI. (19??)-. Newspaper. da. Mweti, BP 991, 991 Brazzaville Congo. **Tel** 81 10 87. **ED** Hubert Madouaba. **Circ:** 8,000.

COSTA RICA

CR
TICO TIMES, THE. (1956)-. Newspaper. English. wk. $45.00 The Americas; $70.00 Europe & Middle East; $80.00 Africa, Asia & Far East. Tico Times, Apartado 4632, San Jose Costa Rica. **Tel** 011 506 228952. available on microfilm.

CROATIA

CI/0017-0771
GLAS ISTRE. [Glas Istre]. (1944)-. Newspaper. Serbo-Croatian (Roman). da. Glas Istre, Obala Marsala Tita br. 10, 52000 Pula Croatia. **Tel** 011 385 52 23577, FAX 011 385 52 41434, telex 25248. **UDC** 32. **Circ:** 25,000.

CI/0350-3968
GLAS SLAVONIJE. [Glas Slavon.]. (1943)-. Newspaper. Serbo-Croatian (Roman). da. Glas Slavonije, Prolaz Vitomira Sukica 2, Osijek Croatia. **Tel** 011 385 54 126722, FAX 011 385 54 26751, telex 28276. **ED** Drago Hedl. **UDC** 32. **Circ:** 21,735.

CI
NEDJELJNA DALMACIJA. (19??)-. Periodical. Serbo-Croatian (Roman). da. Slobodna Dalmacija, Splitskog Odreda 4, Split Croatia. **ED** Dusko Mazibrada. **LC** AP56; .N4. **Circ:** 55,000.

CI/0350-4301
NOVI LIST. [Novi list]. (1947)-. Newspaper. Serbo-Croatian (Roman). da. Novi List, bul. Marksa i Englesa 20, PO Box 130, Rijeka Croatia. **Tel** 011 385 51 32122, telex 24236. **UDC** 32. **Circ:** 59,000.

CI
NOVI VJESNIK. **Title Change.** **VFOAT** Vjesnik. (1992)-(1993). Newspaper. Serbo-Croatian (Roman). da. Novi Vjesnik, Slavonska Avenija 4, 41000 Zagreb Croatia. **Tel** 011 385 41 333333, FAX 011 385 41 341650, telex 21121. **Continues** Vjesnik Socialisticog Saveza Radnog Naroda Hrvatske. **Continued by** Vjesnik (Zagreb, Croatia : 1993).

CI/0350-4662
SLOBODNA DALMACIJA. [Slob. Dalm.]. (1943)-. Newspaper. Serbo-Croatian (Roman). da. Slobodna Dalmacija, Splitskog Odreda 4, Split Croatia. **UDC** 32. **Circ:** 140,000.

CI/0350-5006
VECERNJI LIST. [Vec. list]. (1957)-. Newspaper. Serbo-Croatian (Roman). da. Vecernji List, Av. Bratstva i Jedinstva 4, 41000 Zagreb Croatia. **Tel** 011 385 41 342780, FAX 011 385 41 341850, telex 21121. **ED** Ivo Lajtman. **UDC** 32. **Circ:** 290,850.

●CI
VJESNIK. **VFOAT** Nedjeljni Vjesnik. (1993)-. Newspaper. Serbo-Croatian (Roman). da. $449.64. Novi Vjesnik, Slavonska Avenija 4, 41000 Zagreb Croatia. **Tel** 011 385 41 333333, FAX 011 385 41 341650, telex 21121. **(Subscription address:** Jugoslovenska Knjiga, PO Box 36, YU 11001 Belgrade Yugoslovia.**) Continues** Novi Vjesnik.

CUBA

CU/0017-3223
GRANMA (DAILY EDITION, SPANISH). (GRANMA.). **Added/Corp** Partido Comunista de Cuba. Comite Central. Vol. 1 (Oct. 4, 1965)-. Newspaper. Spanish. da (311 issues per year). $60.00. Ediciones Cubanas, Obispo 527, Altos ESQ Bernaza, CP 10100 Havana Cuba. **Tel** 011 632980, 631942, FAX 011 631011, telex 512337, 6540. **Bk Rev**. **Ad Acc, Adv Mgr:** Jose Polo. **Tel** 707290. **Circ:** 300,000 (ctrl). available on microfilm from University Microfilms International (UMI). **Absorbed** Mundo (Havana, Cuba); **Formed by the union of** Revolucion (Havana, Cuba) **and** Hoy (Havana, Cuba).
 Desc: Articles and editorials that reflect the opinion of the Communist Party of Cuba on various topics. Political, economic, social and cultural information, as well as articles on international politics.

CU/0864-4616
GRANMA INTERNACIONAL. Vol. 26, No. 11 (Mar 17, 1991)-. Newspaper. Spanish. wk. Ediciones Cubanas, Obispo 527, Altos ESQ Bernaza, CP 10100 Havana Cuba. **Tel** 011 632980, 631942, FAX 011 631011, telex 512337, 6540. **Continues** Granma Weekly Review. Spanish. Granma. Resumen Semanal.

CU/0864-4624
GRANMA INTERNATIONAL. Vol. 26, No. 11 (Mar. 17, 1991)-. Newspaper. English (French, Spanish and Portuguese). wk. 40.00Can$. Ediciones Cubanas, Obispo 527, Altos ESQ Bernaza, CP 10100 Havana Cuba. **Tel** 011 632980, 631942, FAX 011 631011, telex 512337, 6540. **ED** Jose Polo. **Bk Rev. Ad Acc. Pr Rev. Circ:** 45,000 (ctrl). **Continues** Granma Weekly Review.

CU
JR; JUVENTUD REBELDE. July 12, 1968-. Newspaper. Spanish. Ediciones Cubanas, Obispo 527, Altos ESQ Bernaza, CP 10100 Havana Cuba. **Tel** 011 632980, 631942, FAX 011 631011, telex 512337, 6540. **Continues** Juventud Rebelde.

CU
TRABAJADORES. Periodical. Spanish. da. $60.00 US. Ediciones Cubanas, Obispo 527, Altos ESQ Bernaza, CP 10100 Havana Cuba. **Tel** 011 632980, 631942, FAX 011 631011, telex 512337, 6540. **Bk Rev. Ad Acc. Circ:** 150,000.
 Desc: Articles that reflect the development achieved by the Cuban working class including information on economics, politics, culture, social matters and work.

CYPRUS

CY
SIMERINI. (19??)-. Newspaper. Greek, Modern. da. Simerini, PO Box 1836, 31 Archangelos Avenue, Strovolos Nicosia Cyprus. **Tel** telex 3826. **ED** Savvas Iakovides. **Circ:** 13,000.

CZECH REPUBLIC

XR
CESKY DENIK. Volume 1 (1991)-. Newspaper. Czech. da.

●XR
EXPRES. Roc. 3, Cis. 58 (1992)-. Newspaper. Czech. da. **Continues** Cesky Expres.

XR
KNIHY. (1991)-. Newspaper. Czech. wk.

XR
KULTURA (PRAGUE, CZECHOSLOVAKIA). (KULTURA.). (19??)-. Newspaper. Czech. wk. **LC** AP52; .K83.

XR
LABYRINT. Vol. 1 (1991)-. Newspaper. Czech. mo.

XR/0862-5921
LIDOVE NOVINY. (1988)-. Newspaper. Czech. da. $355.00. Lidove Novine Corporation, Narodni 11, 111 21 Prague 1, Czech Republic. **ED** Libor Sevcik and Michal Klima. **Photos**. **Ad Acc, Adv Mgr:** Iva Sladka. Full Page (B&W) 98000 Kc. **Pub. Size:** Tabloid. **Wire Svcs.:** RN. **Circ:** 50,000. available on microfilm.
 Desc: An independent daily newspaper including commentaries and 4 supplements: sports, economic, cultural and weekend.

XR
PRAGUE POST. Vol. 1, No. 1 (Oct. 1-7, 1991)-. Newspaper. English. wk. $170.00 (1 year), $325.00 (2 year) Czechoslovakia; $130.00 (1 year), $230.00 (2 year) other. Prague Post, Politickych Veznu 9, 110 00 Prague 1 Czech Republic. **Tel** 011 42 2 267177, FAX 011 42 2 265186. **Circ:** 14,000.

XR
PROGNOSIS. Vol. 1, Issue 1 (1991)-. Newspaper. English. wk. $8.00. Prognosis, Arabska 683, 160 00 Prague 6, Czech Republic. **Tel** 011 422 316-7007, 011 422 316-7827, FAX 011 422 316-7805. **ED** Charles Hornberger (Editor in Chief). **LC** AP4; .P769. **Ad Acc, Adv Mgr:** Anne Harvey.

XR
RUDE PRAVO. **Added/Corp** Komunisticka Strana Ceskoslovenska. Ustredni Vybor. Vol. 1 (Sept. 21, 1920)-. Newspaper. Czech. da. $364.50. Borgis Akciova Spolecnost, PO Box 197, 11121 Prague 1 Czech Republic. **Tel** 011 42 2 267487, 821111. **Absorbed** Pravo Lidu.

XR
TYDENIK OBCHODU A PODNIKANI. **VFOAT** TOP. (1990)-. Newspaper. Czech. wk. **Ind/Abst** PROMT.

DENMARK

DK
BERLINGSKE TIDENDE. **VFOAT** Berlingske Sndag. (June 1935)-. Newspaper. Danish. Fifty-two times a year. kr1257.12. Berlingske Tidende, Pilestraded 34, 1147 Copenhagen K Denmark. **Tel** 011 45 33 75753375. **ED** Hans Dam. Index available. **Ad Acc.** **Circ:** 135,000 (ctrl). **Continues** Berlingske Politiske og Avertissements-Tidende (Copenhagen, Denmark : Morning).

DK/0109-1182
JYLLANDS-POSTEN. [Jyllands-posten]. **VFOAT** Morgenavisen Jyllands-Posten. (1871)-. Newspaper. Danish. **DD** 078.9.
 Ind/Abst PROMT.

DK
POLITIKEN. English. wk. kr788.93. Politiken, Radhuspladsen 37, DK 1585 Copenhagen v Denmark. **Tel** 011 45 3 3118511.

DJIBOUTI

FT
NATION DJIBOUTI, LA. (June 1980)-. Newspaper. French. wk. La Nation Djibouti, Place du 27 Juin, BP 32, Djibouti. **Tel** 352201. available on microfilm. **Continues** Reveil de Djibouti.

DOMINICAN REPUBLIC

DR
SANTO DOMINGO NEWS. (19??)-. Newspaper. English. wk. $35.00 US & Canada; $40.00

Dominican Republic

Europe, Asia, South America. The Santo Domingo News, PO Box 106-2, Santo Domingo Dominican Republic. **Tel** (809)532-1333.

ECUADOR

EC
COMERCIO, EL. (1906)-. Newspaper. Spanish. da. $800.00 The Americas; $1400.00 other. El Comercio, Av Pedro Vicente, Maldonado 11515 y el Tablon, Quito Ecuador. **Tel** 011 593 2 260020. available on microfilm.

EC
VISTAZO. (June 1957)-. Newspaper. Spanish. Twenty-four times a year. $75.00 Central and South America; $90.00 US and Canada; $95.00 Europe; $140.00 Asia. Editores Nacionales, Box 1239, Guayaquil Ecuador. **Tel** 011 593 4 328505. **ED** Patricia de Burbano. **LC** AP63; .V575. Index available. cum. index. **Bk Rev**. **Ad Acc**, **Adv Mgr**: Roberto Comacho. **Circ**: 80,000.
 Desc: Covers politics, economics, cinema, medicine, law, science, literature, arts, theater, education, business, religion, and travel.

EGYPT

UA
AL AHRAM. (19??)-. Newspaper. Arabic. da. $610.00 Asia, Africa, Japan & Australia; $310.00 others. Al Ahram, Al Ahram Building, Al Galaa Street, Cairo ARE Egypt. **Tel** 011 20 2 755500, 011 20 2 745666. **(Subscription address:** Al Ahram Newspaper, 405 Lexington Avenue, Chrysler Building, New York NY 10174.**)**

UA
AL-AHRAM WEEKLY. **VFOAT** Ahram Weekly. No. 1 (Feb. 28, 1991)-. Newspaper. English. wk. Al Ahram, Al Ahram Building, A Galaa Street, Cairo ARE Egypt. **Tel** 011 20 2 755500, 011 20 2 745666.

UA
EGYPTIAN GAZETTE, THE. No. 1 1880-. Newspaper. English. da. $105.00. United Distribution Company, 21 Kasr El Nil Street, Cairo Egypt. available on microfilm from The Library of Congress Photoduplication Service; available on an online database (files 772,799/Full-Text) from DIALOG.

EL SALVADOR

ES
DIARIO DE HOY. REPERTORIO, EL. (Oct. 25, 1942)-. Newspaper. Spanish. da. $50.00 US; $92.00 surface mail; $478.00 airmail. El Diario de Hoy, c/o Fabricio Altamirano, 11 C. Ote #271, San Salvador El Salvador. **Tel** 503 2710100. **Ad Acc**, **Adv Mgr**: Fabricio Altamirano, **Tel** 503 2710122. Full Page (B&W) $1344.00. Half Page (B&W) $672.00. **Circ**: 108,000 daily paid.
 Desc: A mass-market, general interest daily.

ES
DIARIO LATINO. (Nov. 7, 1903)-. Newspaper. Spanish. da. Diario Latino, 23A Avda Sur 225, Apartado 96, San Salvador El Salvacor. **ED** Miguel Angel Pinto. **LC** 3286. **Circ**: 20,000. **Continues** Latino Americano (San Salvador, El Salvador).

ESTONIA

ER/1019-7286
BALTIC INDEPENDENT, THE. No. 62 (June 6-12, 1991)-. Periodical. English. wk. $96.00 (institutions), $75.00 (individuals). Baltic Independent, PO Box 45, EE0090 Tallinn Estonia. **Tel** 011 372 2 683074. **ED** Tarmu Tammerk. **LC** DK502.3; .E876. **Circ**: 8,500. **Continues** Estonian Independent.

ETHIOPIA

ET
ETHIOPIAN HERALD, THE. Vol. 1, No. 1 (July 3, 1943)-. Newspaper. English. da. Ethiopian Herald, PO Box 30701, Addis Ababa Ethiopia. **ED** Kiflom Hadgoi. **LC** 933. available on microfilm.

FIJI

FJ
FIJI REPUBLIC GAZETTE. Newspaper. English. wk. $105.00. Fiji Government Printing & Statistics Department, PO Box 98, Suva Fiji Islands. **Tel** 011 679 385999. **Bk Rev**. ctrl circ.

FJ
FIJI SUN. (1974)-. Newspaper. English. da. available on microfilm from The Library of Congress Photoduplication Service.

FJ
FIJI TIMES, THE. Vol. 1, No. 1 (April 30, 1956)-. Newspaper. English. da. 495.00Fij$ Fiji; $350.00US. Fiji Times & Herald Ltd., GPO Box 1167, Suva Fiji Islands. **Tel** 011 679 304111, FAX 011 679 301521, telex FJ 2124. **ED** Vijendra Kumar. Index available. **Bk Rev**. **Ad Acc**. **Circ**: 30,500 (ctrl). available on microfilm from The Library of Congress Photoduplication Service. **Continues** Fiji Times and Herald.
 Desc: Fiji's most respected and responsible newspaper.

FINLAND

FI/0355-2047
HELSINGIN SANOMAT. [Hels. san.]. (1904)-. Newspaper. Finnish. da. Fmk110.00 sunday, Fmk418.00 daily, US; Fmk78.00 sunday, Fmk278.00 daily, Europe; Fmk150.00 daily, Fmk53.00 sunday, Scandinavia;. Helsingin Sanomat, Tilaajapalvelupl 10, SF-01771 Vantaa Finland. **Tel** 011 358 0 1222941, FAX 011 358 0 1222957. **Bk Rev**. **Ad Acc**. **Circ**: 480.866 daily, 571.866 sundays (ctrl). **Continues** Paivalehti (Helsinki, Finland).

FI/0356-0724
HUFVUDSTADSBLADET. [Hufvudstadsbladet]. (1864)-. Newspaper. Swedish. da. Fmk1547.20 Scandinavian countries; Fmk2263.60 other Europe; Fmk2542.00 other. Hufvudstadsbladet Maud, Maud Koskinen, Mannerheimvagen 18, 00100 Helsingfors Finland. **Tel** 011 358 0 1253267. **UDC** 07.

FI
KAUPPALEHTI. Finnish. da. Fmk3651.90. Uusi Suomi Oy, PO Box 139, SF 00101 Helsinki Finland. **Tel** 011 358 0 50771.

FRANCE

FR
ACTUEL. (Oct. 1970)-. Newspaper. French. Twelve times a year. 225.27F France; 325.00F others. Actuel, 13 rue du Faubourg, St. Antoine, 75011 Paris France. **Tel** 011 33 1 43475004. **(Subscription address:** Actuel, 4 rue du Andre Boulle, 94942 Creteil Cedex 9 France.**)** available on microfilm from Bell & Howell's Underground Newspaper Collection.

FR
AGRA EUROPE. (FRENCH EDITION). (19??)-. Newspaper. French. Fifty-two times a year. 7110.67F France; 7180.00F French overseas departments; 7600.00F other. Agra Presse, 29 rue du General Foy, 75008 Paris France. **Tel** 011 33 1 43871589.

FR
ARDENNAIS, L'. Began with Sept. 4, 1944 issue. Newspaper. French. da. Ardennais, Boite Postale 220, 08102 Charleville Mezieres France. **Tel** 24 33 91 51. **LC** 992.

FR
BIEN PUBLIC, LE. Newspaper. French. tw. Bien Public, 7 BVD Chanoine Kir, BP550, 21015 Dijon Cedex France.

FR
BRETAGNE, REVUE POLITIQUE, MARITIME ET LITTERAIRE, LA. (1843)-. Newspaper. French. wk.

FR
CHARENTAIS, LE. (18??)-. Newspaper. French. sw. **LC** 5682.

FR/0750-0424
COTE DESFOSSES. *Title Change.* [Cote Desfosses]. (1920)-(1992). Newspaper. French. da. Cote Desfosses, 42 rue Notre Dame des Victoire, 75002 Paris France. **Tel** 42 33 21 30. **UDC** 336.76. *Absorbed by* La Tribune (Paris. 1992), 1168-6944.

FR
DAUPHINE LIBERE, LE. Began with Sept. 7, (1945) Issue-. Newspaper. French. da. Dauphine Libere Centre Presse, Les Iles Cordees, 38113 Veurey Voroize France. **LC** 974X.

FR/0181-7981
DEPECHE DU MIDI TOULOUSE, LA. **VFOAT** Depeche du Dimanche (Toulouse). (1947)-. Newspaper. French. da. La Depeche du Midi, Avenue Jean Baylet, 31095 Toulouse Cedex France. **Tel** 011 33 61 411149, FAX 011 33 61 447474. **UDC** 070.2(1-3)(448.6). **Circ**: 228,000. *Continues* La Democratie (Toulouse), 1155-6196.

FR
DEUTSCHE VOLKS-ZEITUNG. **VFOAT** Deutsche Volks Zeitung. (1934)-. Newspaper. German (German). wk.

FR
FIGARO, LE. (1826)-. Newspaper. French. da. Socpresse le Figaro, 37 rue du Louvre, 75081 Paris Cedex 02 France. **Tel** 011 33 1 42213445.

FR
FRANCE-SOIR. **VFOAT** France Soir. Nov. 8, 1944-. Newspaper. French. da. France-Soir, 100 rue Reaumur, 75060 Paris Cedex 01 France. *Continues* Defense de la France (Paris, France); *Absorbed* Paris-Press-l'Intransigeant-France-Soir.

FR
GAZETTE DE METZ ET DE LORRAINE. (18??)-. Newspaper. French. tw. **LC** 5682.

FR
IMPARTIAL DE LA MEURTHE ET DES VOSGES, L'. (18??)-. Newspaper. French. **LC** 5682.

FR
INDUSTRIEL DE VAUCLUSE, L'. (184?)-. Newspaper. French. wk. **LC** 5682.

FR/0294-8052
INTERNATIONAL HERALD TRIBUNE. [Int. her. trib.]. No. 26,236 (May 22, 1967)-. Newspaper. English. da (except Sunday). $357.00 New York; $390.00 Canada; $377.00 US. International Herald Tribune, 181 Avenue Charles de Gaulle, 92521 Neuilly Cedex France. **Tel** 011 33 1 46379361. **(Subscription address:** International Herald Tribune / US, 850 Third Avenue, New York NY 10022.**) CODEN** IHTREH. available on microfilm from University Microfilms International (UMI). *Continues* New York Herald Tribune International, The Washington Post.
 Ind/Abst Curr. Mil. Pol. Lit.; Infomat Int. Bus.; Sage Race Relat. Abstr.

FR
IVME REPUBLIQUE, LA. (Oct. 1943)-. Newspaper. French. da. **LC** 974.

FR
MARSEILLAISE, LA. (1943)-. Newspaper. French. da. available on microfilm from The Library of Congress Photoduplication Service.

FR
MERIDIONAL-LA FRANCE, LE. **VFOAT** Meridional la France. Vol. 10, No. 2611 (Feb 2, 1953)-. Newspaper. French. da. *Formed by the union of* Meridional *and* France de Marseille et du Sud-Est.

FR
METZER ZEITUNG (METZ, FRANCE : 1916). (METZER ZEITUNG.). (1916)-. Newspaper. German (German). da.

FR/0395-2037
MONDE, LE. [Monde]. Vol. 1, No. 1 (Dec. 19, 1944)-. Newspaper. French. da (312 issues). $895.00. Le Monde / Immeuble Sirius, 1 Place Hubert Beuve Mery, 94852 Ivry-sur-Seine CX France. **Tel** 011 33 1 49603000, 011 33 1 49603290. available on microfilm from Research Publications. *Continues* Temps (Paris, France : 1861).
 Ind/Abst Infobank (Jan. 1969-); Point Repere (19??-19??); Predicasts.

FR/0395-2037
MONDE, LE. (1944)-. Newspaper. French. ir. Le Monde / Immeuble Sirius, 1 Place Hubert Beuve Mery, 94852 Ivry-sur-Seine CX France. **Tel** 011 33 1 49603000, 011 33 1 49603290. *Continues* Temps.

FR/0153-789X
MONDE. REIMPRESSION EN MINIFORMAT, LE. (LE MONDE.). [Monde, Reimpress. miniformat]. Dec. 19, 1944-. Newspaper. French. $126.91 US. Le Monde Immeuble Sirius, 1 Place Hubert Beuve Mery, 94852 Ivry Sur Seine France. **Tel** 011 33 1 49603000, 011 33 1 49603290.
 Ind/Abst F&S Index Plus Text, Int. [Select. Cov.]; Predicasts F&S Index, U. S. Annu. Ed.

FR/0026-9360
MONDE. SELECTION HEBDOMADAIRE, LE. [Monde. Sel. hebd.]. VFOAT Selection Hebdomadaire du Journal le Monde. Vol. 1, No. 1 (Oct. 1948)-. Newspaper. French. wk. $145.00. Le Monde / Immeuble Sirius, 1 Place Hubert Beuve Mery, 94852 Ivry-sur-Seine CX France. **Tel** 011 33 1 49603000, 011 33 1 49603290. **[CCC]**.
 Ind/Abst Point Repere (1988-).

FR
NEZAVISIMAYA GAZETA. FRENCH EDITION. French. da. 1586.94F France; 1619.03F other. Courrier International, 4 rue Raoul Du'y, 75980 Paris Cedex 20 France. **Tel** 33 1 43584949, **FAX** 33 1 43584900.

FR/0153-3762
NHAN BAN. (1977)-. Periodical. Vietnamese. mo. 150.00F France; 230.00F other. Assn Generale des Etudiants Vietnamiens de Paris, 185 187 rue Chateau Rentiers, 75013 Paris France. **Tel** 011 33 1 45833865. UDC 32. **Ad Acc.** ctrl circ.
 Desc: News, Vietnamese activities in the world, poems, short stories and analysis.

FR
NICE MATIN. French. da. 950.00F. Nice Matin, 214 Route de Grenoble, 06029 Nice Cedex France. **Tel** 011 33 83 91 91.

FR
NOUVELLE REPUBLIQUE DE BORDEAUX ET DU SUD-OUEST, LA. VFOAT Nouvelle Republique de Bordeaux et du Sud Ouest. Newspaper. French. da. La Nouvelle Republique Centre Quest, 4A 18 rue Prefecture, 37048 Tours Cedex France. available on microfilm from The Library of Congress Photoduplication Service. **Continues** Nouvelle Republique.

FR
OUEST FRANCE. (19??)-. Newspaper. French. da (304 per year). 1175.32F France; 2790.00F other. Ouest France, 10 rue du Breil, 35051 Rennes Cedex France. **Tel** 011 33 99 326357, FAX 011 33 99 326025

FR
PETIT COURRIER DE BAR-SUR-SEINE, LE. VFOAT Petit Courrier de Bar sur Seine; Petit Courrier. (18??)-. Newspaper. French. wk. **LC** 5682.

FR
PETIT MEUNIER. French. sm. 600.00F. Le Petit Meunier, 30 rue de Turbigo, 75003 Paris France. **Tel** 011 33 1 42746543.

FR
PROGRES, LE. (1859)-. Newspaper. French. da. available on microfilm from The Library of Congress Photoduplication Service.

FR
PROVENCAL, LE. No. 1 (1944)-. Newspaper. French. da. available on microfilm from The Library of Congress Photoduplication Service.

FR
QUOTIDIEN DE PARIS. (19??)-. Newspaper. French. da. 1077.38F France. SEQP / Societe Edn. Quotidien Paris, 140 rue Jules Guesde, 92593 Levallois Perret, France. **Tel** 011 33 1 47307800. **Ad Acc**

FR/0336-0067
QUOTIDIEN DU MEDECIN. French. da 1037.38F France; 2200.00F other. SESC Soc Edm Scoi Culturelle, 2 rue Jules Guesde, 92593 Levallois Perret France. **Tel** 011 33 1 47307500.

FR
RUSSKAIA MYSL. VFOAT Pensee Russe. (1947)-. Newspaper. Russian. wk. 400.00F France; 600.00F other. La Pensee Russe, 217 rue du Faubourg St Honore, 75008 Paris France. **Tel** 011 33 1 42255794, FAX 011 33 1 40740497, telex 649813. **ED** Irina Ilovaisky Alberti.

FR
SUD-QUEST. VFOAT Sud Ouest. (1944)-. Newspaper. French. da. available on microfilm from The Library of Congress Photoduplication Service.

FRENCH POLYNESIA

FP
TAHITI SUN PRESS. Vol. 1, No. 1 (July 17, 1980)-. Newspaper. English. wk. $50.00 North America; $56.00 South America; $58.00 Europe; $57.00 Southeast Asia; $44.00 Pacific Islands. Tahiti Sun Press, BP 887, Papeete Tahiti French Polynesia. **Tel** 011 689 426850.

GABON

GO
UNION, L'. (19??)-. Newspaper. French. da. 50.00CFAF (single issue). L'Union / Gabon, BP 3849, Libreville Gabon. **Circ:** 15,000.

GAMBIA

GM/0046-5380
GAMBIA WEEKLY, THE. **Added/Corp** Gambia Information Services. No. 1 (24th Mar. 1989)-. Newspaper. English. wk. Gambia Weekly, 14 Hagan Street, Banjul Gambia. **ED** A. F. Sagnia. **Circ:** 500.
Continues Gambia News Bulletin.

GEORGIA (Republic)

GS
SVOBODNAIA GRUZIIA : ORGAN VERKHOVNOGO SOVETA RESPUBLIKI GRUZIIA. **Added/Corp** Georgian S.S.R. Verkhovnyi Sovet. No. 56 (Apr. 10 1991)-. Newspaper. Russian. da. **CODEN** SVGREO. **Continues** Vestnik Gruzin.

GERMANY

GW
AACHENER NACHRICHTEN. Vol. 1, No. 1 (Jan. 1945)-. Newspaper. German. tw. Aachener Nachrichten, Dresdner Strasse 3, 5100 Aachen Germany. **Tel** 011 49 241 5101 0, telex 832365. **LC** 1270.

GW
AACHENER VOLKSZEITUNG. (1946)-. Newspaper. German. tw. Aachener Nachrichten, Dresdner Strasse 3, 5100 Aachen Germany. **Tel** 011 49 241 5101 0, telex 832365. **ED** Ottmar Braun. **LC** 1271. **Circ:** 106,000.

GW
BAYERNKURIER. (19??)-. Newspaper. German. wk. Bayernkurier, Nymphenburger Str. 64, 8000 Munchen 19 Germany. **Tel** 011 49 89 120110. **ED** W. Scharnagl. **LC** AP30; .B26. **DD** 059/.43. **Circ:** 161,802.

GW
BILDZEITUNG. German. da. DM280.00. Axel Springer Verlag Ag, Brieffach 2460, D 20350 Hamburg Germany. **Tel** 011 49 40 34724503. **(Subscription address:** German Language Publ Inc., 153 South Deanstreet, Englewood, NJ 07631)

GW/0406-4224
BLICK DURCH DIE WIRTSCHAFT. [Blick Wirtsch.]. (1958)-. Newspaper. German. da. DM384.00. Frankfurter Allgemeine Zeitung, Postfach Auslandsvertrieb, D 60267 Frankfurt Germany. **Tel** 011 49 69 75911637.
 Ind/Abst Informat Int. Bus.; PROMT.

GW
BONNER RUNDSCHAU. (19??)-. Newspaper. German. da. Bonner Rundschau, Thomas-Mann Str. 51-53, Postfach 1248, 5300 Bonn Germany. **Tel** 011 49 228 7211, telex 886702. **LC** 1270-X. **Circ:** 24,300.

GW/0343-7728
BORSEN-ZEITUNG 1972. (1972)-. Periodical. German. da (Tues.-Sat.). DM1902.00 Germany; DM1902.60 other Europe; DM2750.41 US; DM2370.60 other. Boersen Zeitung/Wertpapier, Postfach 110932, D-60044 Frankfurt Germany. **Tel** 011 49 69 2732187. **UDC** 336.76. **CODEN** 332.

GW
BRAUNSCHWEIGER ZEITUNG. Vol. 1 No. 1 (Jan. 1946)-. Newspaper. German. da. Braunschweiger Zeitung, Hamburger Str. 277, 3300 Braunschweig Germany. **Tel** 011 49 531 39000, telex 952722. **ED** Arnold Rabbow. **LC** 1423. **Circ:** 184,270. **Continues** Braunschweiger Neue Presse.

GW
DARMSTADTER ECHO. Vol. 1, No. 1 (Nov. 1945)-. Newspaper. German. da. Darmstadter Echo, Holzhofallee 25-31, Postfach 110269, 6100 Darmstadt Germany. **Tel** 011 49 6151 3871, FAX 011 49 6151 387307, telex 419363. **ED** Roland Hof. **LC** 1441. **Circ:** 120,000.

GW
DARMSTADTER ZEITUNG. (1848)-. Newspaper. German. **LC** 1270-X.

GW/0012-088X
DEUTSCHE UNIVERSITATSZEITUNG VEREINIGT MIT HOCHSCHUL-DIENST BONN, DIE. Vol. 1 (1969)-. Periodical. German. sm. Dr Josef Raabe Verlags GMBH, Rotebuhlstr 51, D 70178 Stuttgart Germany. **Tel** 011 49 711 6290043, telex 722232. **Formed by the union of** Deutsche Universitatszeitung and Hochschul-Dienst (German Ed.).

GW
DEUTSCHES ALLGEMEINES SONNTAGSBLATT. VAT Deutsches Allgemeines Sonntags Blatt. V. 20, No. 40, Oct. 1, 1967-. Newspaper. German. wk. DM160.00 Germany; $115.00 US. Hansisches Druck, Verlagshaus 2, Hamburg 13 Germany. **Tel** 40 414190. **ED** Gunter Geschke, Dietrich Sattles. **Bk Rev.** **Ad Acc.** **Circ:** 125,000 (ctrl). **Continues** Sonntagsblatt.
 Desc: Review of important political, financial and cultural trends, religious subjects, travel section, book review.

GW
DUSSELDORFER NACHRICHTEN. Newspaper. German. da. Verlag W Giradet, Postfach 101365, Girardetstrasse 2, W-4300 Essen 1 Germany.

GW
DZIMTENES BALSS. Newspaper. Latvian (Latvian). wk. available on microfilm from The Library of Congress Photoduplication Service.

GW/0174-4909
FRANKFURTER ALLGEMEINE. [Frankf. Allg.]. (Nov. 1, 1949)-. Newspaper. German. Six issues per week. $460.00 US; DM477.60 Germany; DM744.00 other. Frankfurter Allgemeine Zeitung, Postfach Auslandsvertrieb, D 60267 Frankfurt Germany. **Tel** 011 49 69 75911637. **(Subscription address:** US: German Language Publishers Inc., 153 South Deanstreet, Englewood, NJ 07631) Phone: (201)871-1010) **Bk Rev. Ad Acc. Circ:** 348,000 Mon-Fri, 426,000 Sat.
 Ind/Abst Coal Abstr.; Energy Res. Abstr. (April 1976-); F&S Index Plus Text, Int. [Select. Cov.]; Informat Int. Bus.; PROMT.

GW
FRANKFURTER RUNDSCHAU. Vol. 1 No. 1 (Aug. 1, 1945)-. Newspaper. German. da. DM604.00. Druck Verlagshaus / Frankfurt, Am Main Gmbh, D 60266 Frankfurt Germany. **Tel** 011 49 69 2199478. **LC** 1497. available on microfilm.

GW
FREIHEIT (BERLIN, GERMANY). (FREIHEIT.). Vol. 1, No. 1 (Nov. 15, 1918)-. Newspaper. German. da. available on microfilm.

GW
GUARDIAN. (GUARDIAN (BERLIN EDITION).). English. da. DM1083.48. Gebrueder Petermann, Kurfuerstenstr 111, W-1000 Berlin 30 Germany. **Tel** 49 30 219920.

GW/0175-6346
KANADIER. (DER KANADIER : THE NEWSPAPER OF THE CANADIAN FORCES IN EUROPE.). [Kanadier]. VFOAT L'Hebdomadaire des Forces Canadiennes en Europe. Newspaper. English (French). wk. Free. Canadian Armed Forces, CFPO 5000, 7630 Lahr Federal Republic of Germany. **DD** 355.1/0971. ctrl circ.

GW/0178-3556
MANIPULATOR, THE. [Manipulator]. (198?)-. Periodical. English (French, German and Italian). qt. $56.00. Moser & Colby GMBH, Duisburger Str 44, 40477 Dusseldorf Germany. **Tel** 011 49 211 4982068. **ED** Wilhelm Moser and David Colby. **Ad Acc. Circ:** 20,000.

GW
MORGEN, DER. Vol. 1, No. 1 (Aug. 3, 1945)-. Newspaper. German. da. LKG Leipziger Kommissions & Grossbuchhandel, Leninstrasse 16, Postfach 520, D 04005 Leipzig, Germany. **Tel** 011 49 341 71310. **LC** 1362. available in microform (from Mikropress, GMBH, and the Library of Congress, Photoduplication Service).

GW/0028-3347
NEUE RUNDSCHAU. (DIE NEUE RUNDSCHAU.). [Neue Rundsch.]. Vol. 15, No. 1 (Jan. 1904)-. Periodical. German. qt. S Fischer Verlag Gmbh, Postfach 700355, D 60553 Frankfurt Germany. **Tel** 011 49 69 60620. **LC** AP30; .N5. cum. index. Documents available from The Genuine Article. **Continues** Neue Deutsche Rundschau.

Germany

Ind/Abst Arts Humanit. Citation Index (19??-19??) [Full Cov.]; Curr. Contents Arts Humanit.; MLA Int. Bibl. Books Artic. Mod. Lang. Lit.; Res. Alert [Full Cov.]; Soc. Sci. Cit. Index [Select. Cov.].

GW
NEUE ZEIT. Vol. 1, No. 1 (July 22, 1945)-. Newspaper. German. da. **(Subscription address:** Victor Kamkin, 4956 Boiling Brook Parkway, Rockville MD 20852.) **LC** 1368. available on microfilm from The Library of Congress Photoduplication Service.

GW
NEUES DEUTSCHLAND / ZENTRALORGAN DER SOZIALISTISCHEN EINHEITSPARTEI DEUTSCHLANDS. Added/Corp Sozialistische Einheitspartei Deutschlands. Sozialistische Einheitspartei Deutschlands. Zentralkomitee. Vol. 1 No. 145 (Oct. 11, 1946)-. Newspaper. German. da. DM696.00. Verlag Neues Deutschland, Franz Mehring Platz 1, D 10243 Berlin Germany. **Tel** 011 49 30 58312275. available on microfilm from Stanford University; Mikropress; Infoserv; and The Library of Congress Photoduplication Service. **Continues in part** Neues Deutschland (Berlin, Germany).
Ind/Abst Potato Abstr.

GW
NOVOE SLOVO (BERLIN, GERMANY). (NOVOE SLOVO.). **VFOAT** Neue Wort. Newspaper. Russian (German). sw.

GW
RHEINISCHE POST. (Mar. 2, 1946)-. Newspaper. German. da. Rheinische Post, Zulpicherstr. 10, Postfach 101135, 4000 Dusseldorf Germany. **Tel** 011 49 211 5050, FAX 011 49 211 5047562, telex 8581901. **ED** Joachim Sobotta. **LC** 1465. **Circ:** 390,000. available on microfilm.

GW
SCHWARZWAELDER BOTE. Newspaper. German. da. DM352.80. Schearzwaelder Bote Gmbh & Co., Postfach 1380, W 7238 Oberndorf F R Germany. **Tel** 011 49 7423 780, FAX 011 49 7423 7873.

GW/0341-7093
STAMM LEITFADEN DURCH PRESSE UND WERBUNG. [Stamm-Leitf. Presse Werb.]. **VFOAT** Leitfaden Durch Presse und Werbung; Presse- und Medien-Handbuch; Annual Directory Through Press and Advertising. Aug. 29 (1976)-. German (English, French and German). an. DM182.75 Germany; DM184.00 other. Stamm Verlag GmbH, Goldammerweg 16, D 45134 Essen Germany. **Tel** 011 49 201 41757. **ED** W. Stamm. **LC** Z6956.G3; L4; PN5208. **DD** 073. **NLM** Z 6956.G3 L718. **Ad Acc. Circ:** 8,500. **Continues** Stamm Leitfaden fur Presse und Werbung, 0341-7093.
Desc: Bibliography and description of newspapers and periodicals in Germany as well as of the most important abroad.

GW
SUDKURIER. No. 1 (Sept. 8, 1945)-. Newspaper. German. ir. Suedkurier GmbH, Postfach 4300, W-7750 Konstanz Germany. **LC** 1440.

GW/0174-4917
SUEDDEUTSCHE ZEITUNG. [SEuddtsch. Ztg.]. (Oct. 6, 1945)-. Newspaper. German. da. $460.00 US; $790.00 Canada and Mexico; DM784.80 other. Sueddeutscher Verlag GmbH, PF 202220, D 80289 Munich Germany. **Tel** 011 49 89 2183644. **(Subscription address:** German Language Publishing Inc., 153 South Deanstreet, Englewood, NJ 07631) available on microfilm. **Continues** Munchner Neueste Nachrichten und Handels-Zeitung, Alpine und Sports-Zeitung, Theater- und Kunst-Chronik.
Ind/Abst F&S Index Plus Text, Int. [Select. Cov.]; Infomat Int. Bus.; PROMT.

GW
TAGESSPIEGEL, DER. Vol. 1, No. 1 (Sept. 1945)-. Newspaper. German. da. DM322.80 Germany; DM466.80 Europe; DM1402.80 other. Der Tagesspiegel, Postfach 304330, D 10723 Berlin Germany. **Tel** 011 49 30 26009241. **LC** 1385. available on microfilm.

GW
WELT, DIE. (19??)-. Newspaper. German. da. $390.00 US; $650.00 Canada & Mexico. Axel Springer Verlag Ag, Brieffach 2460, D 20350 Hamburg Germany. **Tel** 011 49 40 34724503. **(Subscription address:** German Language Publications Inc., 153 South Deanstreet, Englewood, NJ 07631)

GW/0340-0107
ZEITUNGS-INDEX. Vol. 1 (Jan./March 1974)-. German. qt (4 issues). DM498.00 (includes handbook). K.G. Saur Verlag KG, A Reed Reference Publishing Company, Part of Reed International PLC, Ortlerstrasse 8, D 81373 Munich Germany. **Tel** 011 49 89 769020, FAX 011 49 89 76902150, telex 5212067-SAUR-D.
(Subscription address: K G Saur Inc., 245 West 17th Street, New York NY 10011.) **ED** Willi Gorzny. **LC** AI9; .Z44. **DD** 016.073. **[CCC]. Bk Rev.** ctrl circ. available on CD-ROM.

GHANA

●GH
DAILY GRAPHIC. No. 13402 (Jan. 1, 1994)-. Newspaper. English. da. Daily Graphic, Graphic Road, PO Box 742, Accra Ghana. **Tel** 21 228911. **ED** Sam Clegg. **Continues** People's Daily Graphic.

GREECE

GR
TA NEA. (1931)-. Newspaper. Greek, Modern. da. $197.00. Lambrakis Press SA, 3 Christou Lada, 102 37 Athens Greece. **Tel** 011 30 1 3237283, 011 30 1 3230221. **Ad Acc. Pr Rev.**

GR
TO VIMA. Greek, Modern. da. $47.00 Sunday only. Lambrakis Press SA, 3 Christou Lada, 102 37 Athens Greece. **Tel** 011 30 1 3237283, 011 30 1 3230221. **Ad Acc. Pr Rev. Circ:** 200000.

GRENADA

GD
GRIOT, THE. Vol. 1, No. 1 (1987)-. Periodical. English. bm. The Griot, Hillsborough Street, PO Box 313, St. George's Grenada. **ED** Alvin Clouden.

GUAM

GU/0196-2485
PACIFIC DAILY NEWS. VFOAT Pacific Sunday News; Sunday News. Vol. 1, No. 1 (Feb. 2, 1970)-. Newspaper. English. da. $279.50 (second class), $566.60 (priority mail) daily & Sunday; $80.40 (second class), $153.00 (priority mail) Sunday. Pacific Media Inc, PO Box DN, Agana Guam 96910. **Tel** 011 671 4779711. **Continues** Guam Daily News.

GU
PACIFICA. VFOAT Pacifica Newsmagazine. Vol. 1, No. 1 (April 1984)-. Newspaper. English. mo. $16.00 US and Micronesia. Pacifica Publications Company, PO Box 2143, Saipan Guam. **LC** DU1; .P175. **DD** 990/.05.
Ind/Abst Am. Bibliogr. Slavic East Europ. Stud.

GUATEMALA

GT/0536-5708
IMPARCIAL [MICROFORM], EL. (June 16, 1922)-. Newspaper. Spanish. da. $54.00. El Imparcial, 7A Calle 10-54 Zona 1, Guatemala City Guatemala.

GUYANA

GY
LIST OF CURRENT GUYANESE PERIODICALS AND NEWSPAPERS. Main/Corp University of Guyana. Library. English.

GY
OPEN WORD. (198?)-. Periodical. English. wk.
Ind/Abst Hum. Rights Intern. Rep.

HAITI

HT
UNION, L'. (19??)-. Newspaper. French. da. L'Union / Haiti, 11 Avenue Pie XII, Port-Au-Prince Haiti.

HONDURAS

HO
HERALDO, EL. (19??)-. Newspaper. Spanish. da. El Heraldo, Avda los Proceres, Frente Instituto del Torax, Tegucigalpa Honduras. **Circ:** 45,000.

HONG KONG

HK
SOUTH CHINA MORNING POST. VFOAT South China Sunday Post; South China Sunday Post-Herald; Sunday Post-Herald; South China Sunday Morning Post. Vol. 2, No. 745 (October 1, 1946)-. Newspaper. English. ds. $812.30. South China Morning Post Ltd., PO Box 47, Tong Chong St., Hong Kong Hong Kong. **Tel** 011 852 5652472, FAX 011 852 5658961. **LC** 597. available on microfilm; available on an online database (files 726,771,772,799/Full-Text) from DIALOG. **Continues in part** South China Morning Post & the Hongkong Telegraph.

HK/0039-8675
TA-KUNG-PAO. - . Newspaper. Chinese. wk. HK$1,440.00 Hong Kong & China & Taiwan; HK$2,460.00 others. Ta Kung Pao She, 342 Hennessy Road, Hong Kong.

HUNGARY

HU/0133-0306
DAILY NEWS BUDAPEST. VFOAT Neueste Nachrichten. (1967)-. Newspaper. Multiple languages. da. Daily News / Budapest, Naphegy ter 8, 1016 Budapest Hungary. **Tel** 011 36 1 175-6928, FAX 011 36 1 118-8384. **ED** Sandor Korospataki Kiss. **UDC** 32. **CODEN** 908. **Circ:** 10,000.

HU/0865-9109
HEVES MEGYEI HIRLAP. [Heves m. hirl.]. (1990)-. Newspaper. Hungarian. da. Heves Megyei Hirlap, Barkoczy u. 7, 3301 Eger Hungary. **ED** Levente Kaposi. **UDC** 070. **Continues** Heves Megyei Nepujsag, 0865-6878.

HU/0133-1906
MAGYAR HIRLAP. (1967)-. Newspaper. Hungarian. da. $320.00 Austria, Croatia, Czech Republic, Slovakia, Romania, Yugoslavia, Slovenia & Ukraine; $402.00 other. Magyar Hirlap, Kerepesi ut 29B, 1087 Budapest Hungary. **Tel** 011 36 1 134-3330, telex 22-4268. **(Subscription address:** Kultura, PO Box 149, H 1389 Budapest 62 Hungary) **ED** Peter Nemeth. **LC** AN82.B92; M2125. **Circ:** 75,000.

HU/0133-185X
MAGYAR NEMZET. Added/Corp Fuggetlen Kisgazda Part. Hazafias Nepfront Part. (1942)-. Newspaper. Hungarian. ir (305 issues per year). $197.00. Athenaeum, Buddhapest, Hungary. **(Subscription address:** Kultura, PO Box 149, H 1389 Budapest 62 Hungary (011 36 1 359370))

HU/0239-0639
MAI NAP. [Mai nap]. (1989)-. Newspaper. Hungarian. da. Mai Nap, Konyves Kalman Building 76, 1087 Budapest Hungary. **Tel** 011 36 1 113-0284, FAX 011 36 1 133-9153, telex 22-3634. **ED** Istvan Horvath. **UDC** 070. **Circ:** 104,000.

HU/0133-1752
NEPSZABADSAG. Added/Corp Magyar Szocialista Munkaspart. (1956)-. Newspaper. Hungarian. da. $233.00. **(Subscription address:** Kultura, PO Box 149, H 1389 Budapest 62 Hungary) **Continues** Szabad Nep.

ICELAND

IC/1021-8459
TIMINN REYKJAVIK. (1917)-. Newspaper. Icelandic. da. Timinn, Lynghalsi 9, Box 370, Reykjavik Iceland. **ED** Ingvar Gislason. **Circ:** 15,000.

INDIA

II
ANNUAIRE DE LA PRESSE ET DE LA PUBLICITE. Vol. 1 Ed. 1880-. French. an. Agence Diffusion & Publicite, 24 Place du Gal-Catroux, 75017 Paris France. *Continues La Publicite en France.*

II
BLITZ. (1???)-. Newspaper. English. Fifty-two times a year. Rs150.00 India; Rs168.00 Bangladesh; Rs280.00 Pakistan; Rs384.00 Australia & China & Korea & Indonesia & Japan & Laso Malaysia & New Zealand & Phillippines & Papua & Singapore & Maldives Naura & Thailand & Sri Lanka; Rs410.00 others. Blitz Publication Private Ltd, Canada Building Dr D. N. Road, Bombay 4000 001 India. **Tel** 011 91 22 2047022.

II
FINANCIAL EXPRESS. (Mar. 17, 1961)-. Newspaper. English. da. Indian Express Newspapers Ltd, Express Towers, PB No 867, Nariman Point Bombay 1 India. **Tel** 294838-8. available on microfilm. **Ind/Abst** PROMT.

II
HINDU (MADRAS, INDIA : DAILY). (THE HINDU.). (Sept. 20, 1878)-. Newspaper. English. Fifty-two times a year. $24.00 Bhutan & Nepal, $32.00 Bangladesh, $46.00 others (international edition); $212.00 (surface mail); $150.00 Bhutan & Nepal, $190.00 Bangladesh, $570.00 others (airmail). Kasturi & Sons Ltd., Kasturi Buildings, 859 860 Annasal, Madras 600 002 India. **Tel** 011 91 44 835067. **(Subscription address:** Hindu, 4701 Willard Avenue, Apt. 1531, Chevy Chase MD 20815.) **ED** R. Chakrapani. Index available. **Bk Rev. Ad Acc. Circ:** 500,000. available on microfilm.

II
HINDUSTAN TIMES. **VFOAT** Hindustan Times Weekly. (1923)-. Newspaper. English. da. $112.00 (surface mail), $262.00 (airmail) Daily; $26.00 (surface mail), $100.55 (airmail) Sunday;. Hindustan Times Ltd, 18-20 Kasturba Gandhi Marg, New Delhi 110031 India. **Tel** 011 91 11 3318201. available on microfilm

II/0019-2430
ILLUSTRATED WEEKLY OF INDIA, THE. (1880)-. Newspaper. English. wk. $66.00. Illustrated Weekly of India, Bombay, India. **(Subscription address:** Prints India, 11 Darya Ganj, New Delhi, 110002 India, (Phone: 011 91 11 3268645)) **LC** AP8; .I25.

II/0304-162X
INDEX TO THE TIMES OF INDIA. (THE TIMES OF INDIA, BOMBAY. INDEX.). Jan./Apr. 1973-. English. Rs303.00. Times of India, Reference Department, Bombay 400 001 India. **LC** AI21.T65; T55. **DD** 079/.54/.792.

II
INDIAN EXPRESS. **VFOAT** Sunday Standard. Vol. 21, No. 230 (July 1, 1953)-. Newspaper. English. da. $850.00 (air mail). Indian Express Newspapers Ltd, Express Towers, PB No 867, Nariman Point Bombay 1 India. **Tel** 294838-8. **(Subscription address:** Prints India, 11 Darya Ganj, New Delhi, 110002 India, (Phone: 011 91 11 3268645)) *Absorbed Delhi Express.*

II
INDIAN NATION, THE. **VFOAT** Sunday Indian Nation. (1930)-. Newspaper. English. da. Newspapers & Publications Ltd, Mazharol Haque Path, Patna 800001 India. **Tel** 22136. available on microfilm from The Library of Congress Photoduplication Service.

II
INDIAN NEWSPAPER SOCIETY PRESS HANDBOOK. **Added/Corp** Indian Newspaper Society. **VFOAT** INS Press Handbook; Indian and Eastern Newspaper Society Press Handbook. (1988)-. English. IENS Buildings, Rafi Marg 110001, New Delhi Incia. **LC** Z6958.I4; I46a. *Continues Indian & Eastern Newspaper Society Press Handbook.*

II/0019-6177
INDIAN PRESS INDEX. (INDIAN PRESS INDEX / DELHI LIBRARY ASSOCIATION). **Added/Corp** Delhi Library Association. Vol. 1, No. 1 (Apr. 1968)-. Periodical. English. mo. $80.00. Delhi Library Association, PO Box 1270 Queens Garden, Delhi 6 India. **Tel** 7112721. **(Subscription address:** Prints India, 11 Darya Ganj, New Delhi 110002 India.) **LC** AI3; .I75. **DD** 079/.54.

II
JANG. Newspaper. Urdu. da. Rs850.00 Pakistan; $400.00 US. Daily Jang of Karachi, PO Box 52, Off LL Chundrigar, Karachi 1 Pakistan. **Tel** 210710, telex 2748 JANG PK. **ED** Khalil-ur-Rahman, Javed Rahman, Skakil-ur-Rahman, Javed Rahman, Sarkar Ahmed, Ashraf Qazi. **Bk Rev. Ad Acc. Circ:** 750,000.

Desc: An independent newspaper offering most comprehensive and widest news coverage in Pakistan supplemented with colour magazine pages nearly every day.

II
NEW AGE WEEKLY. Vol. 1 (Oct. 4, 1953)-. Periodical. English. wk. $40.00. **(Subscription address:** Prints India, 11 Darya Ganj, New Delhi 110002 India.) **LC** AP8; .N35.

II
STATESMAN. Newspaper. English. da. Rs580.00 India, Rs1,400.00 others (surface mail). Statesman Ltd, 4 Chowringhee Square, PO Box 272, Calcutta 700 001 India. **Tel** 011 91 33 271000.

II
TIMES OF INDIA. (18??)-. Newspaper. English. da. $850.00 (air mail). Bennett Coleman & Co., Dr D N Road, Bombay 400 001 India. **Tel** 011 91 22 2620271. **(Subscription address:** Prints India, 11 Darya Ganj, New Delhi 110002 India.) available on microfilm.

INDONESIA

IO
INDEKS BERITA DAN ARTIKEL SURAT KABAR BIDANG ILMU-ILMU SOSIAL DAN KEMANUSIAAN. Indonesian. sa. Departemen P Dan K, Pusat Pembinaan Perpustakan, Jl Merdeka Selatan 11, Jakarta Indonesia. **LC** AI19.I55; I54.

IO
INDONESIAN OBSERVER. Newspaper. English. da. $65.00. Indonesian Observer Ltd, Djalan M Sangadji, Djakarta Indonesia.

IO
JAKARTA POST, THE. Vol. 1, No. 1 (Apr. 25, 1983)-. Newspaper. English. da. $489.00. PT Gramedia/Export Department, JL Gajah Mada 104/ PO Box 615, Jakarta 11140 Indonesia. **Tel** 011 62 21 6297809 Ext. 4610, FAX 011 62 21 6498475, telex 41216. available on microfilm.

IO/0452-3970
KOMPAS. No. 1 (1951)-. Newspaper. Indonesian. da. $561.00 Asia; $1101.00 Australia and Japan; $1305.00 Saudi Arabia and Europe; $1821.00 other. PT Gramedia/Export Department, JL Gajah Mada 104/ PO Box 615, Jakarta 11140 Indonesia. **Tel** 011 62 21 6297809 Ext. 4610, FAX 011 62 21 6498475, telex 41216. **Desc:** National general interest newspaper.

IO
MERDEKA. Oct. 1, 1945-. Newspaper. English. da. Merdeka Press, Jl M Sangadji 11, Jakarta Indonesia.

IO
PRESS-INDEX BIDANG ILMU-ILMU SOSIAL DAN KEMANUSIAAN. No. 1 (Jan./March 1973)-. Indonesian. Perpustakaan Sejarah Politik dan Sosial, Jl Merdeka Selatan 11, Jakarta Indonesia. **LC** AI19.I55; P74 . *Continues Press Index.*

IRAN

IR
DIRECTORY OF IRANIAN NEWSPAPERS. (1969)-. Directory. English (Persian). an. 400.00IR. National Library of Iran, 30 Tir St, 11364 Tehran, Iran. **Tel** 0098-21-673315, FAX 0098-21-662040. **ED** Kobra Khodaparast. **DD** 070. **Circ:** 1,000.

IR
ETTELAAT. Newspaper. Persian. ir (295 issues per year). $600.00 US, Canada, China; $700.00 European Countries; $500.00 Japan & India; $170.00 France, Turkey & Arabian Countries; $670.00 other. Ettala At Publications, PO Box 11365 9365A, Tehran 11144 Iran. **Tel** 328265. **ED** J. Rafee. **Bk Rev. Ad Acc. Circ:** 200,000. **Desc:** Newspaper for Iran. Covers foreign news and international news in the fields of politics economics, sports etc.

IR
KAYHAN-I HAV. (19??)-. Newspaper. Persian. wk. $109.00 (Middle East); $116.00 (Europe); $130.00 (other). Kayhan Publications Institute, Martyr Shahcheraghi Avenue, Tehran, Iran. **Tel** 3110251-60, telex 212467.

●IR
KAYHAN URDU. **VFOAT** Urdu Kayhan. (1992)-. Newspaper. Urdu.

IRAQ

IQ
AL-THAWRAH AL-USBUI. **VFOAT** Ath-Thawra Weekly. Arabic. wk. 0.02ID single issue. Dar Al-Thawrah Lil-Sihafah Wa-Al-Nashr Sahat Aqabat IBN Nafi Tariq Muaskar Al-Rashid, S B 2009, Baghdad Iraq.

IRELAND

IE
ALLIANCE. Vol. 1 (Feb. 1971)-. Periodical. English. mo. £15.00 Ireland; £25.00 other. Alliance Party of Northern Ireland, 88 University Street, Belfast GT7 1HE Northern Ireland. **Tel** 0232-324274, FAX 0232-333147. **ED** Eileen Bell. **Bk Rev. Ad Acc.** ctrl circ. *Supersedes Alliance Bulletin.*

IE/0021-0951
IRELAND'S OWN. [Irel. own]. (1902)-. Periodical. English. wk (Plus one special Christmas issue annually). $46.00. People Newspapers Ltd, North Main Street, Wexford Ireland. **Tel** 011 053 22155. **DD** 052.

IE
IRISH INDEPENDENT. Vol. 14, No. 1 (Jan. 2, 1905)-. Newspaper. English. da. Independent Newspapers Ltd, 90 Middle Abbey Street, Dublin 1 Ireland. **Tel** 731666. **LC** 2383. *Continues Irish Daily Independent and Daily Nation; Absorbed Freeman's Journal.* **Ind/Abst** Infomat Int. Bus.

IE
IRISH NEWS AND BELFAST MORNING NEWS, THE. (Aug. 29, 1982)-. Newspaper. English. da. £70.00 UK; £274.35 other. Irish News Ltd, 113-117 Donegall Street, Belfast Ireland BT1 2GE 0232-322226 England. **ED** Jim Fitzpatrick. **Bk Rev. Ad Acc. Circ:** 43,000 (ctrl). available on microfiche. *Continues Irish News.* **Desc:** Goal is to articulate at the highest level of professional journalism, the applications of constitutional nationalism.

IE
IRISH PRESS, THE. Vol. 1, No. 1 (1931)-. Newspaper. English. da. Irish Press Ltd., Burgh Quay, Dublin 2 Ireland. **Tel** 011 353 1 713333. **LC** 2385. **DD** 072.917.

IE
IRISH TIMES ANNUAL REVIEW. (1966)-. English. an. $1,013 (airmail), $588.00 (surface mail). Irish Times Ltd, PO Box 74, 11-15 d'Olier Street, Dublin 2 Ireland. **Tel** 792022, telex 25167. **Circ:** 90,000. *Continues Irish Review and Annual.*

IE
KERRYMAN. (19??)-. English. wk. 28.60p. Kerryman Newspapers, Clash Industrial Estate, Tralee Co Kerry Ireland. **Tel** 066 21666.

IE
PHOBLACHT, AN. **VFOAT** Republican News. (19??)-. English (Irish). wk (50 issues). 35p Ireland; £35.00 Britain; $90.00 US; 100.00Can$ Canada; 150.00Aus$ other; £50.00 other. An Phoblact Republican News, 58 Parnell Square, Dublin 1 Ireland. **Tel** 011 353 1 733611, 011 353 1 733839, FAX 8733074. **ED** Mehail MacDonnacha. **Bk Rev. Circ:** 42,000. **Desc:** Contains Irish political news.

IE/0791-2617
SUNDAY BUSINESS POST, THE. [Sunday bus. post]. (1989)-. Newspaper. English. Fifty times a year. 61.53p Eire; 96.53p Europe; 206.53p others. Sunday Business Post, Merchants House, 27 30 Merch Quay, Dublin 8 Eire Ireland. **Tel** 011 353 16799777. **DD** 072.915. **Ind/Abst** Infomat Int. Bus.

IE/0039-5218
SUNDAY INDEPENDENT. (19??)-. English. wk. 9.88p Ireland; 17.55p other (3 months, surface mail). Independent Newspapers Ltd, 90 Middle Abbey Street, Dublin 1 Ireland. **Tel** 731666.

ISRAEL

IS
HA'ARETZ. (19??)-. Newspaper. Hebrew. da. $849.00 (one year), $648.00 (six year) daily edition, $239.00 (one year), $175.50 (six year) weekend edition airmail, $629.00 (one year), $489.00 (six year) daily edition surface mail, $130.00 (one year), $95.00 (six year) weekend edition surface mail. Israel Communications Inc, 350 5th Avenue/Room 1902, New York NY 10118. **Tel** (212)947-8375, FAX (212)967-1724. **ED** G Schoken. **Bk Rev. Ad Acc. Circ:** 100,000 (ctrl). available on microfilm from University Microfilms International (UMI).
Desc: The oldest, independent newspaper in Israel.

IS
JERUSALEM POST, THE. Vol. 26, No. 7237 (Apr. 23, 1950)-. Newspaper. English. da. $410.00 (surface mail); $470.00 Europe & UK, $630.00 North America, Africa, & Far East, $740.00 South America & Australia (airmail). Jerusalem Post, PO Box 81, Jerusalem 91000 Israel. **Tel** 011 972 2 551616. available on microfilm from InterDocumentation. **Continues** Palestine Post.
Ind/Abst Infomat Int. Bus.; PROMT.

IS
JERUSALEM POST [MICROFORM], THE. VFOAT Jerusalem Post Weekly. (19??)-. Newspaper. English. Fl750.00. Inter Documentation Company, PO Box 11205, 2301 EE Leiden Netherlands. **Tel** 011 31 71 142700, 141941, FAX 011 31 71 131721, telex 39308, 868819.

IS
MAARIV. (19??)-. Newspaper. Hebrew. da. $1,098.00 US & Canada & Mexico, $1,101.00 others (daily); $158.00 (nine months), $190.00 (one year) youth weekly for US & Canada; $211.00 (nine months), $282.00 (one year) weekend & one weekday edition for US & Canada. Maariv Promotions Ltd. / New York, 60 East 42nd Street, New York NY 10165. **Tel** (212)687-1632, FAX (212)687-2156. **ED** Avi Alcalay and Amnon Beirav (phone: 972 3 563 2111). **Ad Acc, Adv Mgr:** Tali Sever, **Tel** (212)687-1632. **Circ:** 200,000 daily, 250,000 Friday (ctrl).
Desc: An independent newspaper.

ITALY

IT
ADIGE. (19??)-. Italian. da. L360000. Giornale l'Adige, Via Missioni Africane 17, 38100 Trento Italy. **Tel** 011 39 461 886111.

IT
AGENZIA GIORNALISTICA REPUBBLICA. (19??)-. Italian. ir. L800000.00. Agenzia Giornalistica Repubblica, Via in Arcione 98, 00187 Rome Italy. **Tel** 011 39 6 6789305.

IT
AGENZIA QUOTIDIANA INFORMAZIONI. (19??)-. Italian. da. Agenzia Parlamento Italiano, Viale Vaticano 84, 00165 Rome Italy. **Tel** 011 39 6 39720806.

IT
ALTO ADIGE. (19??)-. Italian. da. L360000. Seta Spa, LGO Talvera S Quirino 26, 39100 Bolzano Italy. **Tel** 011 39 471 904111.

IT
ARENA DI VERONA. Societa Athesis Spa, Viale Del Lavoro 11, 37036 S Martino B Alber Italy.

IT/0391-6685
AVANTI. [Avanti]. (1897)-. Periodical. Italian. ir. Nuova Editrice Avanti Spa, Via Tomacelli 146, 00186 Rome Italy. **Tel** 011 39 6 6860418. **UDC** 07.

IT/1120-6020
AVVENIRE. [Avvenire]. (1968)-. Periodical. Italian. da (312 issues). L318000.00 Italy; L665000.00 other. Nuova Editoriale Italiana Spa, Via M Macchi 61, 20124 Milan Italy. **Tel** 011 39 2 67801. **UDC** 07.

IT
BERGAMO OGGI. Italian. da. L320000.00. Investeditor Spa, Via L Palazzolo 89, 24100 Bergamo Italy. **Tel** 011 39 35 359111, FAX 035/219146.

IT
BRESCIAOGGI NUOVO. (19??)-. Italian. da. L350000.00 Italy. Edizioni Brescia Spa, Via Eritrea 20, 25122 Brescia Italy. **Tel** 011 39 30 22941.

IT
CORRIERE ADRIATICO. (19??)-. Newspaper. Italian. ds. L360000. Corriere Adriatico, Via Berti 20, 60126 Ancona Italy. **Tel** 011 39 71 42985.

IT
CORRIERE DEL GIORNO PUGLIA E LUCANIA. (19??)-. Newspaper. Italian. da. L260000. Cooperativa 19 Luglio, Piazza Dante 5, 74100 Taranto Italy. **Tel** 011 39 99 323152.

IT
CORRIERE DELLA SERA. VFOAT Corriere della Sera del Lunedi. Vol. 84, No. 111 (1959)-. Newspaper. Italian. da. $1144.00. RCS Editoriale Quotidiani, via Solferino 28, 20120 Milan Italy. **Tel** 011 39 2 6339. **(Subscription address:** Speedimpex USA, Inc., 35 02 48th Avenue, Long Island City NY 11101.) available on microfilm. **Continues** Nuovo Corriere della Sera.

IT
CORRIERE DELLA VALLE D'AOSTA. Italian. ir. L32000. Corriere Valle Aosta, C So Padre Lorenzo 5, 11100 Aosta Italy. **Tel** 011 39 165 34605.

IT
CORRIERE DI NOVARA. (19??)-. Italian. sw. L100000.00. Corriere Di Novara, Via Merula 1, 28100 Novara Italy. **Tel** 011 39 321 393296.

IT
ECO DI BERGAMO. (19??)-. Italian. da. L370000.00 Italy; L800000.00 other. Eco Di Bergamo, Ufficio Abbona, Viale Papa Giovanni 118, 24100 Bergamo Italy. **Tel** 011 39 35 212344.

IT
ECO DI BIELLA. L Eco Biella, Via Volpi 2, 13051 Biella Italy.

IT
ESPRESSO SERA. Espresso Sera, Amministrazione 95126 Catania Italy.

IT/0391-6405
FIORINO. [Fiorino]. (1969)-. Periodical. Italian. da. L145000 Italy; L280000 other. Societa Editrice Esedra Srl, Via Parigi 11, 00185 Rome Italy. **Tel** 011 39 6 474901, FAX 011 39 6 488-3435. **UDC** 33.

IT
GAZZETTA DEL MEZZOGIORNO. (19??)-. Italian. Edisut Spa, V Le Scipione l'Africano 264, 70124 Bari Italy.

IT
GAZZETTA DEL SUD. (19??)-. Italian. da. L350000 Italy; L800000 Europe. SES / Societa Editrice Siciliana, Via Taormina 15 C, 98124 Messina Italy. **Tel** 011 39 90 2936359.

IT/1120-5067
GAZZETTA DELLO SPORT, LA. [Gazz. sport Milano. 1897]. (1897)-. Newspaper. Italian. da. RCS Editoriale Quotidiani, via Solferino 28, 20120 Milan Italy. **Tel** 011 39 2 6339. **UDC** 070.446.

IT
GAZZETTA DI AREZZO, LA. (19??)-. Italian. da. L325000 Italy; L650000 other. Edizioni Locali Srl, Via Spadoni 19, 60020 Candia An Italy. **Tel** 011 39 71 28691, FAX 011 39 71 8046103.

IT
GAZZETTA DI FIRENZE. Suspended. (19??)-Suspended June 1992. Periodical. Italian. Edizioni Locali SRL, Via Locchi 35/R, 50141 Florence Italy.

IT
GAZZETTA DI PARMA. (19??)-. Italian. da. L350000.00 Italy; L520000.00 other. Gazzetta di Parma, Via E Casa 5/A, 43100 Parma Italy. **Tel** 011 39 521 2159.

IT
GAZZETTA DI REGGIO : 6 DAYS A WEEK. Editoriale le Gazzetta SRL, Galleria Mortara 2, 46100 Mantova Italy.

IT
GAZZETTA UFFICIALE DELLA REPUBBLICA ITALIANA. SUPPLEMENTO ORDINARIO. Main/Corp Italy. Italian. da. $48.71. Inst Poligrafico dello Stato, Piazza Verdi 10, 00198 Rome Italy.

IT
GIORNALE DI BRESCIA. (19??)-. Italian. da. L340000 (daily & Sunday). Editoriale Bresciana Spa, Via Solferino 22, Uff Abbon, 25121 Brescia Italy. **Tel** 011 39 30 2004212.

IT
GIORNALE DI MONCALIERI. (19??)-. Italian. wk. L45000.00. SEP, Piazza Martiri Dell Liberta 13, 10024 Moncalieri Italy. **Tel** 011 39 6407438.

IT
GIORNALE DI NAPOLI. Offset Meridionale SRL, Via Diocleziano 109, 80125 Naples Italy.

IT
GIORNALE DI VICENZA. (19??)-. Newspaper. Italian. da L374000. Athesis Spa, Viale San Lazzaro 89, 36100 Vicenza Italy. **Tel** 011 39 444 564533.

IT
GIORNALE D'ITALIA. (19??)-. Italian. da. L124000.00. Societa Editrice Esedra Srl, Via Parigi 11, 00185 Rome Italy. **Tel** 011 39 6 474901, FAX 011 39 6 488-3435.

IT
GIORNO, IL. (19??)-. Italian. L343000.00 Italy; L773800.00 other (daily & Sunday). Segisa ED, Piazza Cavour 2, 20121 Milan Italy. **Tel** 011 39 2 7768224.

IT
ITALIA OGGI. Vol. 1, No. 1,(Nov. 19, 1986)-. Newspaper. Italian. da. available on an online database (files 771,772,799/Full-Text) from DIALOG.

IT
LIBERTA, LA. Tito Brandsma, Via Garibaldi 26, 42016 Guastalla Italy.

IT/0025-2158
MANIFESTO. [Manifesto]. (1971)-. Periodical. Italian. da. L310000 Itlay; L684000 Europe; L1012000 other. Il Manifesto, Via Tomacelli 146, 00186 Rome Italy. **Tel** 011 39 6 6878487, 011 39 6 3227311. **CODEN** 32. available on microfilm from University Microfilms International (UMI).

IT
MATTINO DI PADOVA. (19??)-. Italian. da. L195000 (3 months), L405000 (6 months). Editoriale Quotidiani Veneti, Via Pellizzo 3, 35128 Padua Italy. **Tel** 011 39 49 8292604.

IT
MATTINO (NAPLES, ITALY : 1950). (IL MATTINO.). (April 5, 1950)-. Newspaper. Italian. da. Editrice Edime Spa, Via Chiatamone 65, 80121 Naples Italy. **Continues** Risorgimento.

IT
MESSAGGERO DI LUCCA, IL. Periodical. Italian. da. L325000 Italy; L1837000 Americas & Asia; L1117000 Mediterranean Countries; L1027000 Europe; L1657000 Africa; L2467000 other. Il Messaggero, Via del Tritone 152, 00187 Rome Italy. **Tel** 011 39 6 47201.

IT/1120-608X
MESSAGGERO VENETO. [Messagg. Veneto]. (1946)-. Periodical. Italian. da. L350000. Messaggero Veneto, Viale Palmanova 290, 33100 Udine Italy. **Tel** 011 39 432 513100. **UDC** 07.

IT/0391-6863
NAZIONE. [Nazione]. (1953)-. Periodical. Italian. da. L270000 Italy, L530000 others (Monday - Friday); L320000 Italy, L628000 others (Monday - Saturday); L370000 Italy, L730000 others (daily & Sunday). Poligrafici Editoriale Spa, Via F Paolieri 2, 50121 Florence Italy. **Tel** 011 39 55 24851, telex 570271. **UDC** 07 (450).

IT
NOVESE, IL. (19??)-. Newspaper. Italian. wk. L35000. Il Novese, Piazza XXVII Aprile 5, 15067 Novi Ligure Al Italy. **Tel** 011 39 143 2127.

IT
NUOVA SARDEGNA, LA. Italian. da. L144000 (six months). Editoriale Nuova Sardegna Spa, Via Porcellana 9, 07100 Sassari Italy. **Tel** 79/222400, FAX 79/236293.

IT
NUOVA VENEZIA. Italian. da. L344000. Editoriale Quotidiani Veneti, Via Pellizzo 3, 35128 Padua Italy. **Tel** 011 39 49 8292604.

IT
NUOVA VICENZA. Ceased. (19??)-(1992). Italian. da. Edizioni Vicentine Srl, Via Dei Montecchi 15, 36100 Vicenza Italy.

IT
ORA, L'. (19??)-. Italian. da. L255000 (Thursday through Saturday). Nuova Editrice Meridionale Srl, Piazza F Napoli 5, 90141 Palermo Italy. **Tel** 011 91 581733.

IT
ORE 12. (19??)-. Italian. ir. L200000 Italy; L1820000 other. Societa Editrice Ore 12, Via Alfana 39, 00191 Rome Italy. **Tel** 011 39 6 3331418.

IT
PROVINCIA CREMONA. (19??)-. Newspaper. Italian. da (312 issues). L320000 Italy. Giornale Quotidiano Provincia, Piazza Comune 9, 26100 Cremona, Italy. **Tel** 011 39 372 462800. **Ad Acc.**

IT
PROVINCIA GRANDA. L36.000. Provincia Granda, C So Statuto 21, 12086 Mondovi Italy.
Desc: News and local press.

IT
PUGLIA. Societa Coop Olimpico, Via Melo 195, 70121 Bari Italy.

IT
QUOTIDIANO DI LECCE, IL. Edisalento Srl, Viale Degli Studenti, 73100 Lecce Italy.

IT
REPUBBLICA (ROME, ITALY). (LA REPUBBLICA.). (1976)-. Newspaper. Italian. da. L147500.00 Italy; L260000.00 others. La Repubblica Editoriale SPA, Piazza Indipendenza 11B, 00185 Rome Italy. **Tel** 011 39 6 49823247. **ED** Eugenio Scalfari. available on microfilm from The Library of Congress Photoduplication Service.

IT
RESTO DEL CARLINO. (19??)-. Newspaper. Italian. da (360 issues). L400000 Italy. Poligrafici Editoriale, Via Mattei 106, 40138 Bologna, Italy. **Tel** 011 39 51 536111. **Ad Acc.**

IT
SICILIA. (19??)-. Periodical. Italian (summaries and/or abstracts in English, French, German and Spanish). Domenico Sanfilippo Editore, Vle Odorico Da Pordenone 50, 95126 Catania Italy. **LC** DG861; .S563.

IT/0391-786X
SOLE 24 ORE. VFOAT Sole Ventiquattro Ore. (1966)-. Periodical. Italian. da. L450000.00 Italy; L880000.00 other. Editrice Il Sole 24 Ore Spa, Via Busto Arsizio 36, 20151 Milan Italy. **Tel** 011 39 2 31031. **UDC** 05.
 Ind/Abst F&S Index Plus Text, Int. [Select. Cov.]; Infomat Int. Bus.; PROMT.

IT
STAMPA, LA. wk. $120.00. La Stampa, Via Marenco 32, 10126 Turin Italy. **Tel** 011 39 11 65681.

IT
TEMPO. English. da. L295000. Editrice Romana Srl, Piazza Colonna 366, 00186 Rome Italy. **Tel** 011 39 6 65041.

IT
TRIBUNA DI TREVISO, LA. (19??)-. Italian. da. L370000. Editoriale Quotidiani Veneti, Via Pellizzo 3, 35128 Padua Italy. **Tel** 011 39 49 8292604.

IT
UNIONE SARDA, L'. (19??)-. Newspaper. Italian. ds. L315000 Italy. Unione Sarda, Viale Regina Elena 14, 09100 Cagliari, Italy. **Tel** 011 39 70 60131.

IT
UNITA (MICROFICHE), L'. (L'UNITA.). Feb. 12, 1924-. Newspaper. Italian. L'Unita, Via Vulvio Testi 75, 20162 Milan Italy.

IVORY COAST

IV
FRATERNITE MATIN (MICROFICHE). (FRATERNITE MATIN.). Newspaper. French. Soc Presse Edition Cote Ivoire 01, Abidjan 01 Ivory Coast.

JAMAICA

JM/0259-0336
GLEANER INDEX / NATIONAL LIBRARY OF JAMAICA, THE. Added/Corp National Library of Jamaica. Vol. 1, No. 1 (Jan.-Mar. 1986)-. Periodical. English. qt. National Library of Jamaica, Institute of Jamaica, PO Box 823, 12-16 East Street, Kingston Jamaica. **Tel** (809)922-0620, FAX (809)922-5567, telex NALIBJAM. **ED** Charmaine McKenzie. **LC** AI21; .G62. **DD** 079/.7292. cum. index. **Bk Rev. Ad Acc.** ctrl circ.
Continues AIRS, Index to the Daily Gleaner of Jamaica.
 Desc: Index to the Daily Gleaner and Sunday Gleaner covering local and regional contents.

JM
JAMAICA HERALD. (183?)-. Newspaper. English. da. Jamaica Herald, 29 Molynes Road, Kingston 10 Jamaica. **Tel** 968-7721, FAX 968-7722. **ED** Franklin McKnight.

JAPAN

JA/0025-2816
ASAHI EVENING NEWS. (Jan. 20, 1954)-. Newspaper. English. da. Overseas Courier Service Company Ltd., 9 Shibaura 2-Chome Minato-Ku, Tokyo 108 Japan. **Tel** 011 81 3 3453 8311. **(Subscription address:** Overseas Courier Service of America Inc., 5 East 44th Street, New York NY 10017.**) LC** 2546. **Ad Acc. Circ:** 30,280. **Continues** Tokyo Evening News.
 Desc: English edition of Asahi newspaper with articles on current events.

JA
ASAHI SHINBUN. VFOAT Asahi Shimbun. (1940)-. Newspaper. Japanese. da. $1250.00. **(Subscription address:** Japan Publications Trading Company, Ltd., PO Box 5030, Tokyo International, Tokyo 100-31 Japan.**)** available on microfilm. **Formed by the union of** Osaka Asahi Shiumbun; Nagoya Asahi Shimbun; Kyushu Asahi Shimbun **and** Tokyo Asahi Shimbun.

JA
DAILY YOMIURI. Japanese. da. $780.00. **(Subscription address:** Overseas Courier Services of America, Inc., 5 East 44th Street, New York, NY 10017**)**

JA
DEMPA SHIMBUN. (19??)-. Newspaper. Japanese. da. Dempa Publications Inc., 1 11 15 Higashi Gotanda, Shinagawa Ku Tokyo 141 Japan. **Tel** 011 81 3 34456111.

JA/0447-5763
JAPAN TIMES (OVERSEAS ED.), THE. (THE JAPAN TIMES.). VFOAT Japan Times Weekly International Edition. Vol. 30, No. 5 (Feb. 5-11, 1990)-. Newspaper. English. wk. $105.00 US and Japan; $135.00 other. The Japan Times Ltd, CPO Box 144, Tokyo 100-91 Japan. **(Subscription address:** The Japan Times, 445 South Figueroa Street, Suite 2900, Los Angeles, CA 90071**)** available on microfilm from University Microfilms International (UMI). **Continues** Japan Times (Tokyo, Japan : 1987 : Weekly Overseas ed.), 0447-5763.

JA/0289-1956
JAPAN TIMES (TOKYO. 1956), THE. (THE JAPAN TIMES.). [Japan times]. No. 20, (July 1, 1956)-. Newspaper. English (English). da. $1,758.00 US & Central America & Oceania & Middle East; $1,904.00 Europe & South America & Africa; $1,490.00 others. **(Subscription address:** Japan Publications Trading Company, Ltd., PO Box 5030, Tokyo International, Tokyo 100-31 Japan.**)** available on microfilm. Documents available from Documents on Demand. **Continues** Nippon Times.
 Ind/Abst Environ. Abstr.

JA
JAPANESE PRESS, THE. Began in 1950?. English. an. ¥2000 Japan; $20.00 other. Nihon Shinbun Kyokai, Press Center Building/7th Floor, 2-1 Uchisaiwaicho 2-chome, Chiyoda-ku Tokyo 100 Japan. **Tel** (03)591-4401, FAX (03)591-6149, telex J27504 NSK JAPAN. **ED** Manji Gonda. Index available. **Bk Rev. Ad Acc. Circ:** 3,000. **Continues** Japanese Press, Past and Present.
 Desc: A year-book describing trends and giving statistical facts about the newspaper industry in Japan. Also lists Japanese newspaper, Japanese correspondents overseas, etc.

JA
KENSEI KANKEI SHIMBUN KIJI KIRINUKI SAKUIN. (1972)-. Newspaper. Japanese. qt. Okinawa Kengikai Jimukyoku, 2-14 Senzaki 1, Naha Japan. **LC** Z7165.J3; K44.

JA
MAINICHI DAILY NEWS. (May 10, 1960)-. Newspaper. English (English). da. **(Subscription address:** Overseas Courier Services America, 5 East 44th Street, New York, NY 10017**)** available on microfilm from University Microfilms International (UMI). **Continues** Mainichi.
 Ind/Abst Numis. Lit.

JA
MAINICHI SHINBUN. (1872)-. Newspaper. Japanese. da. $1180.00. **(Subscription address:** Japan Publications Trading Company, Ltd., PO Box 5030, Tokyo International, Tokyo 100-31 Japan.**)**

JA
NIKKEI SANGYO SHIMBUN. Newspaper. Japanese. da (except Sunday). ¥2600 (per month) Japan; ¥3500 (per month) US. Nihon Keizai Shimbun Inc., 9-5 Otemachi 1 Chome, Chiyoda-Ku Tokyo 100 Japan. **Tel** 011 81 3 32700251. **ED** Goh Higuchi. **LC** HC462.9; .N5339. Index available. **Ad Acc. Circ:** 250,000. available on an online database (files 772,799/Full-Text) from DIALOG.
 Ind/Abst Infomat Int. Bus.

JA
NIKKEI SATELLITE EDITION. Newspaper. Japanese. da. $1080.00. **(Subscription address:** Overseas Courier Service of America, 5 East 44th Street, New York, 10017**)**

JA
PACIFIC STARS AND STRIPES. **Added/Corp** United States. Far East Command. Troop Information and Education Section. VFOAT Stars and Stripes. Vol. 1, No. 1 (Oct. 3, 1945)-. Newspaper. English. da (daily except for Jan. 2). $163.00. Stars and Stripes, Unit 45002 Attn: Sub Department, APO AP 96337. **Tel** 011-81-33-4018912, FAX 011-81-33-4088936. **LC** AP8; .P25. **DD** 078.52.

JA/0031-5036
PEOPLE'S KOREA, THE. No. 1 (1961)-. Newspaper. English (French, Spanish, Korean and Japanese). wk. $52.00. Choson Sinbo Company, Tsukudo-Hachiman-cho, Shinjuku-ku, Tokyo 162 Japan. **Tel** 011 81 3 32605881. **ED** Song Jae Ryong. **DD** 951.93/005. **Ad Acc. Circ:** 30,000.
 Desc: Korean affairs.

JA
SHUKAN TOCHO. VFOAT Tocho. Newspaper. Japanese. wk. ¥190. Tokyo-to Tomin Shiryoshitsu, 5-1 Marunouchi 3 Chiyoda-ku, Tokyo 100 Japan.

JA
ZASSHI SHINBUN SOKATAROGU. PERIODICALS IN PRINT. VFOAT Periodicals in Print. No. 1 (1979)-. Japanese. an. Media Research Center Inc, Irimajir Building 6-40 Shin-Ogawa, Hinjuku-ku Tokyo 160 Japan. **Tel** 81-03-267-6551, FAX 81-03-267-550. **ED** Chow Li-Chun. **LC** Z6958.J3; Z37; PN5407.P4. available on CD-ROM.

JA
ZENKOKU SHIMBUN MAIKUROFIRUMU SEISAKU SHOZO ICHIRAN. Added/Corp Kokuritsu Kokkai Toshokan (Japan). Etsuranbu. VFOAT List of Japanese Newspapers on Microfilm in Japan. (1970)-. Periodical. Japanese. Kohuristu Kokkai Toshokan, 1-10-1 Nagatacho Chiyoda-ku, Tokyo Japan. **LC** Z6958.J3; Z45.

JORDAN

JO
RAY. VFOAT Rai. (19??)-. Newspaper. Arabic. da. $555.00. Alrai Jordan Press Foundation, PO Box 6710, Amman, Jordan. **Tel** 011 962 6 667171.

KAZAKHSTAN

KZ
KAZAKHSTANSKAIA PRAVDA : ORGAN TSENTRALNOGO KOMITETA KOMMUNISTICHESKOI PARTII KAZAKHSTANA. Added/Corp Qazaqstan KP Ortalyq Komiteti. Kazakh S.S.R. Zhogharghy Soveti. Kazakh S.S.R. Ministrler Soveti. (1921)-. Newspaper. Russian. da. $349.95. **(Subscription address:** East View Publications Inc., 3020 Harbor Lane North, Suite 110, Minneapolis MN 55447.**)**

KENYA

KE
STANDARD (NAIROBI, KENYA). (THE STANDARD.). VFOAT Sunday Standard. No. 18703 (July 1, 1974)-. Newspaper. English. da. Sh7644.62 (surface mail); Sh38985.02 America & Australia & Far East; Sh31559.42 Europe & Asia Zone; Sh27846.62 Africa & East Africa (airmail) daily. Standard Limited, PO Box 30080, Nairobi Kenya. **Tel** 011 254 2 540280. available on microfilm from University Microfilms International (UMI); and The Library of Congress Photoduplication Service. **Continues** East African Standard (Nairobi, Kenya : Daily); Leader, and the Mombasa Times.

KOREA (South)

KO
CHINDAN HAKPO. Added/Corp Chindan Hakhoe. VFOAT Chin-Tan Hakpo. (1934)-. Periodical. Korean. qt. **LC** DS904; .C463.
 Ind/Abst Am. Hist. Life (1955-1966, 1974-1982).

KO
KOREA HERALD, THE. VFOAT Korio Heraldu. Vol. 13, No. 1 (Aug. 15, 1965)-. Newspaper. English. da (except Monday). $362.40 North America. The Korea Herald Inc, 150 West 51st Street/Suite 1426, New York NY 10019. **Tel** FAX (212)582-5205(914) 472-1195. **(Subscription address:** Korea Herald Subscriber Inc, PO Box 312, Hartsdale, NY 10530) **ED** Cook-chin Ahn. **Bk Rev. Ad Acc. Circ:** 15,000 (ctrl). available on

Korea (South)

microfilm from University Microfilms International (UMI). **Continues** *Korean Republic.*
Desc: Only English newspaper published daily covering developments in Korea. Edited in New York for the American reader, presenting the latest news of business, culture, or politics in Korea.

KUWAIT

KU
KUWAIT TIMES. (19??)-. Newspaper. English. da. Kuwait Times, PO Box 1301, Safat Kuwait City Kuwait. **ED** Yousuf Alyyan. **Circ:** 30,000.

KYRGYZSTAN

KG
SLOVO KYRGYZSTANA : ORGAN TSENTRALNOGO KOMITETA KOMPARTII KYRGYZSTANA, VERKHOVNOGO SOVETA I KABINETA MINISTROV RESPUBLIKI KYRGYZSTAN. Added/Corp Kyrgystan KP BK. Kirghiz S.S.R. Zhogorku Sovet. Kirghiz S.S.R. Ministrler Soveti. **VFOAT** V Kontse Nedeli. No. 48 (Feb 26 1991)-. Newspaper. Russian. tw. Izdatelstvo TSK Kompartii Kyrgyzstana, Bishkek Kyrgyzstan. **CODEN** SLKYET. **Continues** *Sovetskaia Kirgiziia.*

LATVIA

●LV
BALTIC OBSERVER : NEWS FROM ESTONIA, LATVIA, AND LITHUANIA, THE. (1992)-. Periodical. English. Fifty-two times a year (Thurs.). $85.00 (one year); $145.00 (two year). Baltic News Ltd., Balasta Dambis 3, Riga LV 1081 Latvia. **Tel** 011 371 2 462119, FAX 011 371 2 463387. **ED** Karlis Freibergs. **LC** DK502.3; .B36. **DD** 320.947/4. **Bk Rev. Ad Acc, Adv Mgr:** Einars Vitols, **Tel** 371-2-462119. available on microfilm from the publisher.
Desc: News coverage about Estonia, Latvia, and Lithuania.

●LV
LATVIIAS LAIKS. (1992)-. Newspaper. Russian. wk.

LEBANON

LE
FATEH. Newspaper. English. sm. Fateh, PO Box 5427, Beirut Lebanon.

LESOTHO

LO
MIRROR. Vol. 1, No. 1 (July 1988)-. Periodical. English. wk. **ED** Mike Pitso. **Circ:** 4,000.

LIBERIA

LB
LIBERIA HERALD, THE. (1930)-. Newspaper. English. wk. **ED** Annie Broderick. available on microfilm.

LITHUANIA

●LI
LITHUANIAN WEEKLY. Vol. 1, No 1 (Feb. 5-12, 1992)-. Newspaper. English. wk. $38.00 Europe; $40.00 other. Lithuanian Weekly, PO Box 533, 2024 Vilnius 24 Lithuania.

MALAWI

MW
DAILY TIMES. (Jan. 1, 1973)-. Newspaper. English. da. Malawi Daily Times, PB 39, Ginnery Corner Blantyre Malawi. **ED** Poulton Ntenje. **Continues** *Times (Blantyre, Malawi).*

MALAYSIA

MY
BUSINESS TIMES [MICROFORM]. (1976)-. Newspaper. English. da. 223.20Mal$ (Malaysia); 272.80Mal$ (Sarawok); 297.60Mal$ (Sabah); 1032.90Mal$ (other). New Straits Times Press, Balai Berita 31 Jalan Riong, 59100 Kuala Lumpur Malaysia. **Tel** 011 60 3 2823131, 011 60 3 2823322, FAX 011 60 3 2825502.

MY
NEW STRAITS TIMES. VFOAT New Sunday Times, (Aug. 31, 1974)-. Newspaper. English. da. 432.37Mal$ Malaysia; 1647.23Mal$ other. New Straits Times Press, Balai Berita 31 Jalan Riong, 59100 Kuala Lumpur Malaysia. **Tel** 011 60 3 2823131, 011 60 3 2823322, FAX 011 60 3 2825502. **Continues** *Straits Times (Kuala Lumpur, Malaysia).*

MY
NEW SUNDAY TIMES, MALAYSIA. (19??)-. Newspaper. English. wk. 88.27Mal$ Malaysia; 305.87Mal$ other. New Straits Times Press, Balai Berita 31 Jalan Riong, 59100 Kuala Lumpur Malaysia. **Tel** 011 60 3 2823131, 011 60 3 2823322, FAX 011 60 3 2825502. **Continues** *Sunday Times, Malaysia.*

MALTA

MM/1017-2106
IN-NAZZJON TAGHNA HAMRUN. Newspaper. Maltese. da. In-Nazzjon Taghna, Stamperija Indipendenza, Herbert Ganado Street Pieta, PO Box 37, Hamrun Malta. **Tel** 243641, FAX 242886, telex 1941. **ED** Maria Schiavone. **UDC** 070.2(1-4). **Circ:** 20,000.

MARSHALL ISLANDS

XE/0892-2098
MARSHALL ISLANDS JOURNAL (1980). (MARSHALL ISLANDS JOURNAL.). (1980)-. Newspaper. English (Marshall). wk (Fri.). $81.00 Marshall Islands; $211.00 other. Marshall Islands Journal, PO Box 14 Majuro, Majuro, Marshall Islands HI 96960. **Tel** (692)625-3251, FAX (692)625-3132. **ED** Giff Johnson. **Bk Rev. Ad Acc. Circ:** 11,000. **Continues** *Micronesian Independent.*
Desc: Community news/comment on the Marshall Islands.

MEXICO

MX
EXCELSIOR. (Mar. 18 1917)-. Newspaper. Spanish. da. $1090.00. Excelsior Cia Editorial Scl, Paseo Reforma 10, Subscripciones, Mexico 1 DF Mexico. **Tel** 11 52 5 7054444, 5669360. available on microfilm.

MX/0185-2973
INFORMACION SISTEMATICA. Ceased. Ceased (1985). Periodical. Spanish. mo. Informacion Sistematica, Valencia 84 Apt Postal 19-308, Mexico 19 D F Mexico. **Tel** 598-6043 OR 598-6325. **ED** Bernardo Aualos. cum. index. **Bk Rev. Ad Acc. Circ:** 2,000 (ctrl). available on microfilm.
Desc: 3,000 abstracts a month of 13 major Mexican newspapers included in publication permit access to 15,000 clippings systematically structured. Published each month since 1976.

MX
JORNADA (MEXICO CITY, MEXICO). (LA JORNADA.). No. 1 (1985)-. Periodical. Spanish. da. Balderas No 68 Centro, Mexico 06050 DF Mexico.

MX
NORTE (MICROFICHE), EL. (EL NORTE.). Periodical. Spanish. da. $300.00. Editora el Sol SA, Apt PO 186, Wshngtn Oriente 62929, Monterrey NL Mexico. **Tel** 52 455100.

MX
UNIVERSAL, EL. (1916)-. Newspaper. Spanish. da. $1442.00. El Universal Comapny Periodista Nac, Bucareli 8, Department Subscripciones, 06040 Mexico DF Mexico. **Tel** 011 52 5 7091313.

MOLDOVA

●MV
NEZAVISIMAIA MOLDOVA : ORGAN PARLAMENTA I PRAVITELSTVA RESPUBLIKI MOLDOVA. Added/Corp Moldova. Parlament. (Oct. 1991)-. Newspaper. Russian. $299.95. Nezavisimaia Moldova, 277612 Chisinau str., Pushkin 22 Moldova. **Tel** 3732 23 36 05. **(Subscription address:** East View Publications Inc., 3020 Harbor Lane North, Suite 110, Minneapolis MN 55447.) **ED** Yelena Zamura. **CODEN** NEMOE7. **Circ:** 27,645. **Continues** *Sovetskaia Moldova.*

NAMIBIA

SX
NAMIBIAN, THE. English. wk. R174.06 South Africa; R634.06 North America. Namibian, PO Box 20783, Windhoek 9000 Namibia. **Tel** 011 27 61 36970 2 3 4, FAX (061)33980.

NETHERLANDS

NE
ALGEMEEN DAGBLAD. Dutch. da. Fl286.08. Nederlandse Dagbladunie BV, Postbus 945, 3000 AX Rotterdam Netherlands. **Tel** 011 31 10 4067211.
Ind/Abst Child. Lit. Abstr. (19??-).

NE
BRUG, DE. Mar. 1978-. Dutch. wk. Fl39.00 Netherlands; Fl78.00 other. Abdij Van Berne, Abdijstraat 53, NL 5473 AC Heeswijk-Dinther Netherlands. **Tel** 04139-1330. **ED** L H A Becht. **Bk Rev. Ad Acc. Circ:** 50 (ctrl).
Desc: A newspaper for nearly ten villages in a radius of 25 KM.

NE/0166-0470
BULLETIN - KNOB. [Bull.- KNOB]. (1974)-. Periodical. Dutch. Six times a year. Fl65.00. Koninklijke Nederlandse OUD BN, Achter de Sint Pieter 21, 3512 HR Utrecht Netherlands. **Tel** 011 31 30 321756. **UDC** 7.02. **Continues** *Bulletin van de Nederlandsche Oudheidkundige Bond.*
Ind/Abst BHA : Biblio. Hist. Art.

NE
FINANCIEN BERICHT-PERSBERICHT FINANCIEN. Dutch. wk. Min V Financien, Tav Centrale Dir Vakbladpers Postbus 20201. **Tel** 011 31 703427540.

NE
HANDBOEK VAN DE NEDERLANDSE PERS EN PUBLICITEIT. Vol. 42 (Sept. 1974)-. Periodical. Dutch. sa. Nijgh Periodicken BV, Postbus 122, 3100 AC Schiedam Netherlands. **Tel** 011 31 10 4274174. **Continues** *Handboek Van de Nederlandse Pers.*

NE
MISSETS DISTRIFOOD NIEUWSBLAD. Dutch. wk. Uitgeversmaatschappij Misset, Postbus 40, 7000 BA Doetinchem Netherlands. **Tel** 011 31 08340 49911.

NE
NRC HANDELSBLAD. (1970)-. Newspaper. Dutch. da (305 per year). Fl433.19 Netherlands; Fl1043.19 Belgium; Fl1530.19 other. Nederlandse Dagbladunie NV, Marten Meesweg 35, c/o Mr C. Trakzel, 3068 AV Rotterdam Netherlands. **Tel** 011 31 10 4067211. **Ad Acc. Circ:** 242,000. available with illustrations.
Ind/Abst Child. Lit. Abstr. (19??-); Infomat Int. Bus.

NE
RUSLAND MONITOR. (March 1989)-. Periodical. Dutch. bm. Fl38.50 (students), Fl48.50 (general), Fl58.50 (institutions). **LC** DK276; .R85. **Formed by the union of** *Ruslandbulletin,* 0166-1582 **and** *Sovjet Monitor.*

NE
TROUW. DAGBLAD. Dutch. da. Fl347.60. Ochtenblad Trouw, Postbus 2104, 1000 CC Amsterdam Netherlands. **Tel** 011 31 20 6681300.

NE
VOLKSKRANT, DE. (1919)-. Newspaper. Dutch. da (260 issues). Fl352.04 Netherlands; Fl535.91 Belgium; Fl1204.87 Europe; Fl1619.96 others. De Vo kskrant, Wibautstraat 150, 1091 GR Amsterdam Netherlands. **Tel** 011 31 020 5622685. **(Subscription address:** Prescombinatie NV, Postbus 2104, 1000 CC Amsterdam Netherlands.**)** available on microfilm.

NEW ZEALAND

NZ/0112-8787
NEW ZEALAND HERALD, THE. (Nov. 13, 1863)-. Newspaper. English. da. 1424.80Aus$ (daily), 286.00Aus$ (Saturday only) Australia and South Pacific; 2828.80Aus$ (daily), 624.00Aus$ (Saturday only) other. Wilson & Horton Ltd, PO Box 32, Auckland New Zealand. **Tel** 011/64/9/795050, FAX 011/64/9/3660146. available on an online database (files 771,772,799/Full-Text) from DIALOG.

NZ
OTAGO DAILY TIMES, THE. (Nov. 15, 1861)-. Newspaper. English. da. 927.00NZ$ (surface mail, daily ed.), 2472.00NZ$ (air mail, daily ed.), 156.00NZ$ (surface mail, Sat. ed.), 416.00NZ$ (air mail, Sat. ed.) Australasia and Asia; 2472.00NZ$ (surface mail, daily ed.) 4326.00NZ$ (air mail, daily ed.), 416.00NZ$ (surface mail, Sat. ed.) 728.00NZ$ (air mail, Sat. ed.) Europe and Americas. Allied Press Limited, PO Box 517, Lower Stuart Street, Dunedin New Zealand. **Tel** 774760, FAX 778616, telex 5692.

NZ/0112-9910
SOUTHLAND TIMES. [Southl. times]. (?866)-. Periodical. English. da. 358.00NZ$ New Zealand; 579.00NZ$ other. Southland Times Ltd, PO Box 805, 67 Esk Street, Invercargill New Zealand. **Tel** 011 64 21 81909, FAX 03 218 4349. **ED** Clive Lind (phone: 03 218-1909). **DD** 052. **Bk Rev**. **Ad Acc, Adv Mgr:** A. R. Wills, **Tel** (03)218 1909. **Circ:** 33,500 (ctrl). **Desc:** General news and information.

NZ
WAITOMO NEWS. Newspaper. English. bw (published on Tuesday and Thursday). 88.20NZ$. Waitomo News Ltd, 38 Taupiri Street, Tekuiti, New Zealand. **Tel** 011 64 081 388005, FAX 011 64 08¹ 388006. **ED** Steve Brightwell (editor's address: PO Box 269, Tekuiti, New Zealand 2500; phone: 07 878 8005 Ext. 15). **Ad Acc, Adv Mgr:** F. Rawling, **Tel** (07)878 8005 Ext. 13. **Circ:** 6,300 (ctrl).

NIGERIA

NR
DAILY TIMES. Jan. 3, 1949-. Newspaper. English. da. $1362.34. Daily Times of Nigeria Ltd, Publications Division, New Isheri Road Agidingbi, PMB 21340 Ikeja West Africa. **Tel** 900850-900859. **ED** Farouk Umar Muhammed. **Bk Rev**. **Ad Acc**. **Circ:** 250,000 (ctrl). *Continues Nigerian Daily Times.*
Desc: An independent newspaper: fearless and vocal. The choice of readers. With up to date information on economic, social and government activities.

NR
GASKIYA TA FI KWABO. (Jan. 1939)-. Newspaper. Hausa. Fifty-two times a year. New Nigerian Newspaper Ltd, Ahmadu Bello Way, PO Box 254, Kaduna Nigeria. **Tel** 011 234 62 201420. **ED** Muhammad Sabanzara Hassan. **Bk Rev**. **Ad Acc**. **Circ:** 66,000.
Desc: The paper publishes news both, local and foreign. It also covers other areas like religion, agriculture, sports, health and features on various topics.

NR
NEW NIGERIAN. Began publication in 1966?. Newspaper. English. da. New Nigerian Newspaper Ltd, Ahmadu Bello Way, PO Box 254, Kaduna Nigeria. **Tel** 011 234 62 201420.

NR/0331-2569
SUNDAY TRIBUNE. [Sunday trib.]. (1978)-. Newspaper. English. wk. $277.00. Distrinews, PO Box 61, 1040 Etterbeek 1 Belgium.

NORWAY

NO
AFTENPOSTEN. (1860)-. Newspaper. Norwegian. da. Kr2544.41 Sweden, Denmark, Greenland, Finland, Iceland and the Faroe Islands; Kr7560.41 Europe; Kr11496.41 other. Aftenposten, Postboks 1178 Sentrum, 0107 Oslo 1 Norway. **Tel** 011 47 2 863000. available on an online database (file 16/Full-Text) from DIALOG.
Ind/Abst Energy Res. Abstr. (Sept. 1980-); F&S Index Plus Text, Int. [Select. Cov.]; Infomat Int. Bus.; PROMT [Full Txt.].

NO
DAGENS NRINGSLIV [MICROFORM]. (1987)-. Newspaper. Norwegian. da. Kr2580.00 Scandinavia; Kr4400.00 Europe; Kr5350.00 other. Dagens Naeringsliv, PO Box 1182, Sentrum 0107 Oslo 1 Norway. **Tel** 011 47 2 178300 OR 178317. *Continues Norges Handels og Sjfartstidende.*
Ind/Abst F&S Index Plus Text, Int. [Select. Cov.]; Infomat Int. Bus.; PROMT.

NO/0029-1870
NORSK BOKFORTEGNELSE. [Nor. bokfort.]. **Added/Corp** Norske Bokhandlerforening. Universitetsbiblioteket i Oslo. Norske Avdeling. **VFOAT** Norwegian National Bibliography; Arskatalog Over Norsk Litteratur; Arskatalog. (1847)-. Newspaper. Norwegian. Eleven times a year. Kr380.00. Norwegian Booksellers Association, Ovre Vollgate 15, 0158 Oslo 1 Norway. **Tel** 011 47 2 410 760. **(Subscription address:** Wennergren Cappelen A S, Postboks 738 Sentrum, 0105 Oslo 1 Norway.**)** *Continued in part by Norsk Bokfortegnelse. Musikktrykk.*
Ind/Abst Annu. Bibliogr. Engl. Lang. Lit.

NO/0029-2257
NORSK UKEBLAD. (19??)-. Newspaper. Norwegian. wk. Nor Data, Postboks 2233, 7001 Trondheim Norway. [CCC].

NO
NYTT FRA NORGE. No. 1 (1954)-. Norwegian. wk. Nytt Fra Norge Inc, PO Box 241 Sentrum, 0103 Oslo 1 Norway.

OMAN

MK
TIMES OF OMAN. (19??)-. Newspaper. English. da. $336.00. Times of Oman, PO Box 3770, Muscat Sultanate of Oman. **Tel** 011 968 701953, FAX 011 968 799153, telex 3362. **ED** Arif Ali. **Bk Rev**. **Ad Acc**. **Circ:** 15,000.

PAKISTAN

PK
ERU PRESS INDEX. **VFOAT** E.R.U. Press Index. **VAT** Economist Research Unit Press Index. Jan. 1983-. Periodical. English. mo. Economist Research Unit, PO Box 10449, Karachi 4 Pakistan. **LC** Z3193; .E78; DS376.9. **DD** 079/.5491.

PK
PAKISTAN TIMES. (1947)-. Newspaper. English. da. $279.00. Progressive Papers Limited, Opp Mayo Hospital, Lahore 7 Pakistan. **Tel** 226721, telex 44811. available on microfilm.

PK
PAKISTAN TIMES MICROFORM. V. 1 (1947)-. Newspaper. English. da. $222.38. Progressive Papers Limited, Opp Mayo Hospital, Lahore 7 Pakistan. **Tel** 226721, telex 44811.

PANAMA

PN
ESTRELLA DE PANAMA, LA. (1849)-. Newspaper. Spanish. da. $880.00. Ercina SA, Apartado Q, Panama 4 Panama. available on microfilm.

PERU

PE
PERU, CARTA MINERA. **Added/Corp** Andean Air Mail & Peruvian Times. **VFOAT** Carta Minera. (1982)-. Periodical. Spanish. wk. $290.00. Peru/Carta Minera, Apartado Postal 531, Lima 100 Peru. **Tel** 469-120, telex PE PB 25202.

PHILIPPINES

PH
MANILA BULLETIN. (1986)-. Newspaper. English. da. $216.24. Manila Bulletin Publishing Corporation, PO Box 769, Manila Philippines. **Tel** 011 63 2 471551. available on microfilm. *Continues Bulletin Today.*

PH
MANILA CHRONICLE, THE. Vol. 1, No. 161 (Nov. 11, 1991)-. Newspaper. English. da. Manila Chronicle Publishing Co., 371 Bonifacio Drive Port Area, Manila Philippines. available on microfilm. *Continues Chronicle (Manila, Philippines : 1991).*

PH/0116-0443
PHILIPPINE INQUIRER. [Philipp. inq.]. (1985)-. Newspaper. English. wk. **DD** 320.
Ind/Abst Hum. Rights Intern. Rep.

POLAND

PL/0867-0374
CZAS KRAKOWSKI. (1990)-. Newspaper. Polish. da. $130.00. **(Subscription address:** ARS Polona, PO Box 1001, 00068 Warsaw Poland.**)** **UDC** 323(438). **CODEN** 304(438).

PL/0137-9062
DZIENNIK BALTYCKI. (1945)-. Newspaper. Polish. da (312 issues). $156.00. **(Subscription address:** ARS Polona, PO Box 1001, 00068 Warsaw Poland.**)** **UDC** 323(438). **CODEN** 327.

PL/0208-7707
DZIENNIK LODZKI 1980. (DZIENNIK LODZKI.). **VFOAT** D. Dziennik Lodzki. (1980)-. Newspaper. Polish. da (312 issues). $156.00. **(Subscription address:** ARS Polona, PO Box 1001, 00068 Warsaw Poland.**)** **UDC** 323(438). **CODEN** 327.

PL/0867-5090
DZIENNIK LUBELSKI. (1990)-. Newspaper. Polish. da (260 issues). $130.00. **(Subscription address:** ARS Polona, PO Box 1001, 00068 Warsaw Poland.**)** **UDC** 323(438). **CODEN** 327.

PL/0137-9089
DZIENNIK POLSKI. (1945)-. Newspaper. Polish. da (312 issues). $156.00. **(Subscription address:** ARS Polona, PO Box 1001, 00068 Warsaw Poland.**)** **UDC** 323(438). **CODEN** 327.

PL
DZIENNIK URZEDOWY WOJEWODZTWA SZCZECINSKIEGO.
Main/Corp Szczecin (Poland : Voivodeship). **Added/Corp** Urzad Wojewodzki w Szczecinie. Polish. **LC** KKP2935.S97; A14.

PL/0137-9046
DZIENNIK WIECZORNY. (1959)-. Newspaper. Polish. da. $130.00. **(Subscription address:** ARS Polona, PO Box 1001, 00068 Warsaw Poland.**)** **UDC** 323(438). **CODEN** 327.

PL/0137-9038
DZIENNIK ZACHODNI. (1945)-. Newspaper. Polish. da. $156.00. **(Subscription address:** ARS Polona, PO Box 1001, 00068 Warsaw Poland.**)** **UDC** 323(438)/. **CODEN** 327.

PL/0137-902X
ECHO DNIA. (1971)-. Newspaper. Polish. da. $130.00. **(Subscription address:** ARS Polona, PO Box 1001, 00068 Warsaw Poland.**)** **UDC** 323(438). **CODEN** 327.

PL/0137-9011
ECHO KRAKOWA. (1946)-. Newspaper. Polish. da. $130.00. **(Subscription address:** ARS Polona, PO Box 1001, 00068 Warsaw Poland.**)** **UDC** 323(438). **CODEN** 327.

Poland

PL/0137-9100
EP. EXPRESS POZNANSKI. VFOAT Express Poznanski. (1946)-. Newspaper. Polish. da. $130.00. **(Subscription address:** ARS Polona, PO Box 1001, 00068 Warsaw Poland.**)** UDC 323(438). CODEN 327.

PL/0137-9097
EXPRESS ILUSTROWANY. (1923)-. Newspaper. Polish. da. $130.00. **(Subscription address:** ARS Polona, PO Box 1001, 00068 Warsaw Poland.**)** UDC 323(438). CODEN 327.

PL
EXPRESS WIECZORNY. VFOAT Express Wieczorny Kulisy; Kulisy. (May 20, 1946)-. Newspaper. Polish. da. $130.00. **(Subscription address:** ARS Polona, PO Box 1001, 00068 Warsaw Poland.**)**

PL
FOLKS-SHTIME. Ceased. Added/Corp Towarzystwo Spoeczno-Kulturalne Zydow w Polsce. VFOAT Foks-Sztyme; Gos ludu. (19??)-(19??). Periodical. Yiddish (Polish). wk. **(Subscription address:** ARS Polona, PO Box 1001, 00068 Warsaw Poland.**)**

PL/0208-7693
GAZETA KRAKOWSKA 1980. (GAZETA KRAKOWSKA.). (1980)-. Newspaper. Polish. da. $156.00. **(Subscription address:** ARS Polona, PO Box 1001, 00068 Warsaw Poland **)** UDC 323(438). CODEN 327.

PL/0137-9518
GAZETA LUBUSKA 1975. (GAZETA LUBUSKA.). (1975)-. Newspaper. Polish. da. $156.00. **(Subscription address:** ARS Polona, PO Box 1001, 00068 Warsaw Poland.**)** UDC 323(438). CODEN 327.

PL/0137-9127
GAZETA OLSZTYNSKA. (1970)-. Newspaper. Polish. da. $130.00. **(Subscription address:** ARS Polona, PO Box 1001, 00068 Warsaw Poland.**)** UDC 323(438). CODEN 327.

PL/0208-8746
GAZETA POZNANSKA 1981. (GAZETA POZNANSKA.). (1981)-. Newspaper. Polish. da. $156.00. **(Subscription address:** ARS Polona, PO Box 1001, 00068 Warsaw Poland.**)** UDC 323(438). CODEN 327.

PL/0137-9143
GAZETA ROBOTNICZA. (1948)-. Newspaper. Polish. da. $156.00. **(Subscription address:** ARS Polona, PO Box 1001, 00068 Warsaw Poland.**)** UDC 323(438). CODEN 327.

PL/0137-9488
GAZETA WSPOCZESNA. (1975)-. Newspaper. Polish. da. $130.00. **(Subscription address:** ARS Polona, PO Box 1001, 00068 Warsaw Poland.**)** UDC 323(438). CODEN 327.

PL/0860-908X
GAZETA WYBORCZA. VFOAT Gazeta Swiateczna. (1989)-. Newspaper. Polish. da. $156.00. Gazeta Wyborcza, 00-732 Warsaw, Czerska 8/10 Poland. **Tel** 011 48 22 6285231, **FAX** 011 48 22 6284929. **(Subscription address:** ARS Polona, PO Box 1001, 00068 Warsaw Poland.**) ED** Adam Michnik. **Circ:** 540,000 (daily), 780,000 (weekend).

PL/0137-9526
GOS POMORZA. (1975)-. Newspaper. Polish. da. $156.00. **(Subscription address:** ARS Polona, PO Box 1001, 00068 Warsaw Poland.**)** UDC 323(438). CODEN 327.

PL/0867-4590
GOS PORANNY. (1990)-. Newspaper. Polish. da. $156.00. **(Subscription address:** ARS Polona, PO Box 1001, 00068 Warsaw Poland.**)** UDC 323(438). CODEN 327.

PL/0137-9178
GOS SZCZECINSKI. (1949)-. Newspaper. Polish. da. $156.00. **(Subscription address:** ARS Polona, PO Box 1001, 00068 Warsaw Poland.**)** UDC 323(438). CODEN 327.

PL/0137-9186
GOS WIELKOPOLSKI. (1945)-. Newspaper. Polish. da. $156.00. **(Subscription address:** ARS Polona, PO Box 1001, 00068 Warsaw Poland.**)** UDC 323(438). CODEN 327.

PL/0137-9194
GOS WYBRZEZA. (1946)-. Newspaper. Polish. da. $156.00. **(Subscription address:** ARS Polona, PO Box 1001, 00068 Warsaw Poland.**)** UDC 323(438). CODEN 327.

PL/0137-9224
KURIER LUBELSKI. (1957)-. Newspaper. Polish. da. ca94. **(Subscription address:** ARS Polona, PO Box 1001, 00068 Warsaw Poland.**)** UDC 323(438). CODEN 327.

PL/0137-9240
KURIER SZCZECINSKI. (1945)-. Newspaper. Polish. da. $130.00. **(Subscription address:** ARS Polona, PO Box 1001, 00068 Warsaw Poland.**)** UDC 323(438). CODEN 327.

●PL
NOWE PODKARPACIE. (1993)-. Newspaper. Polish. wk. $52.00. **(Subscription address:** ARS Polona, PO Box 1001, 00068 Warsaw Poland.**)** Continues Podkarpacie.

PL/0137-9534
NOWINY. (NOWINY : DZIENNIK POLSKIEJ ZJEDNOCZONEJ PARTII ROBOTNICZEJ.). **Added/Corp** Polska Zjednoczona Partia Robotnicza. (19??)-. Newspaper. Polish. da. $130.00. **(Subscription address:** ARS Polona, PO Box 1001, 00068 Warsaw Poland.**)**

PL/0137-9259
NOWOSCI TORUN. (NOWOSCI.). (1967)-. Newspaper. Polish. da. $130.00. **(Subscription address:** ARS Polona, PO Box 1001, 00068 Warsaw Poland.**)** UDC 323(438). CODEN 327.

PL
NOWY TYDZIEN. Vol.2, No. 24 (June 16 1991)-. Newspaper. Polish. wk. Continues Wokanda.

PL
POLSKA ZBROJNA. Added/Corp Poland. Ministerstwo Obrony Narodowej. Vol. 1, No. 1 (1990)-. Newspaper. Polish. da. $130.00. Polska Zbrojna, ul. Grzybowska 77, 00-950 Warsaw Poland. **Tel** 011 48 22 204293, **FAX** 011 48 22 202127. **(Subscription address:** ARS Polona, PO Box 1001, 00068 Warsaw Poland.**) ED** Antoni Bartkiewicz. **Circ:** 50,000. Continues Zolnierz Rzeczypospolitej.

PL/0208-9130
RZECZPOSPOLITA WARSZAWA. (RZECZPOSPOLITA.). (1982)-. Newspaper. Polish. da. $156.00. **(Subscription address:** ARS Polona, PO Box 1001, 00068 Warsaw Poland.**)** UDC 32. CODEN 008.

PL/0137-9275
SOWO LUDU. (1949)-. Newspaper. Polish. da. $156.00. **(Subscription address:** ARS Polona, PO Box 1001, 00068 Warsaw Poland.**)** UDC 323(438). CODEN 327.

PL/0137-9291
SOWO POLSKIE. (1946)-. Newspaper. Polish. da. $156.00. **(Subscription address:** ARS Polona, PO Box 1001, 00068 Warsaw Poland.**)** UDC 323(438). CODEN 327.

PL/0867-8723
SUPER EXPRESS. (1991)-. Newspaper. Polish. da. $130.00. **(Subscription address:** ARS Polona, PO Box 1001, 00068 Warsaw Poland.**)** UDC 304(438). CODEN 338(438).

PL
TRYBUNA. Vol. 1, No. 1 (Dec 2, 1990)-. Newspaper. Polish. da. $156.00. **(Subscription address:** ARS Polona, PO Box 1001, 00068 Warsaw Poland.**)** Continues Trybuna Kongresowa, 0137-9348.

PL/0867-4507
TRYBUNA SLASKA 1990. (TRYBUNA SLASKA.). (1990)-. Newspaper. Polish. da. $156.00. **(Subscription address:** ARS Polona, PO Box 1001, 00068 Warsaw Poland.**)** UDC 323(438). CODEN 327.

PL
TYGODNIK POWSZECHNY. (March 24, 1945)-. Newspaper. Polish. wk. $104.00. **(Subscription address:** ARS Polona, PO Box 1001, 00068 Warsaw Poland.**)**
Ind/Abst Annu. Bibliogr. Engl. Lang. Lit.

PL/0208-8045
TYGODNIK SOLIDARNOSC. [Tyg. Solidarnosc]. **Added/Corp** NSZZ "Solidarnosc" (Labor Organization). Krajowa Komisja Porozumiewawcza. NSZZ "Solidarnosc" (Labor Organization). VFOAT Solidarnosc; Solidarnosc, Tygodnik. Vol. 1 (1981)-Vol. 37 (1981); Vol. 2, No. 1 (1989)-. Periodical. Polish. wk. $78.00. Tygodnik Solidarnosc, Czackiejo 15-17, 00950 Warsaw Poland. **(Subscription address:** ARS Polona, PO Box 1001, 00068 Warsaw Poland.**) LC** DK4448; .T94.

PL/0860-7591
WARSAW VOICE, THE. [Wars. voice]. (Oct. 1988)-. Newspaper. English. wk. $156.00 North America; £93.60 UK. Warsaw Voice Inc., PO Box 28, 00 950 Warsaw 1 Poland. **Tel** 011 48 22 366329, 3711995. **(Subscription address:** Warsaw Voice Inc. / for North, South and Central America, 413 B Logan Boulevard, Lakemont, Altoona PA 16602.**) LC** WMLC 93/4769. **Ad Acc. Circ:** 15,000.
Desc: English-language weekly published through a joint Polish-American venture. Reports news with a range of social, political, economic, and financial information regarding Poland and other East European countries such as the former Soviet Union, Hungary, the Czech Republic and Slovakia.
Ind/Abst Infomat Int. Bus.

PL/0137-9364
WIECZOR KATOWICE. (WIECZOR.). (1957)-. Newspaper. Polish. da. $130.00. **(Subscription address:** ARS Polona, PO Box 1001, 00068 Warsaw Poland.**)** UDC 323(438). CODEN 327.

PL/0137-9372
WIECZOR WROCAWIA. VFOAT WW. Wieczor Wrocawia. (1967)-. Newspaper. Polish. da. $130.00. **(Subscription address:** ARS Polona, PO Box 1001, 00068 Warsaw Poland.**)** UDC 323(438). CODEN 327.

PL/0137-9380
WIECZOR WYBRZEZA. (1957)-. Newspaper. Polish. da. $130.00. **(Subscription address:** ARS Polona, PO Box 1001, 00068 Warsaw Poland.**)** UDC 323(438). CODEN 327.

PL/0208-7421
ZIEMIA KALISKA. (1957)-. Polish. wk. $52.00. **(Subscription address:** ARS Polona, PO Box 1001, 00068 Warsaw Poland.**)** UDC 304(438). CODEN 943.8.

PL/0137-9410
ZYCIE CZESTOCHOWY. (1947)-. Newspaper. Polish. da. $156.00. **(Subscription address:** ARS Polona, PO Box 1001, 00068 Warsaw Poland.**)** UDC 323(438). CODEN 327.

PL
ZYCIE WARSZAWY. (1944)-. Newspaper. Polish. da (312 issues). $156.00. **(Subscription address:** ARS Polona, PO Box 1001, 00068 Warsaw Poland.**)**

PORTUGAL

PO
DIARIO DE NOTICIAS (LISBON, PORTUGAL). (DIARIO DE NOTICIAS.). (Dec. 29, 1864)-. Newspaper. Portuguese. da. 37200$00. Empresa Nacional de Publicidad, Avenida da Liberdade, 266 Lisbon 2 Portugal. **Tel** 011 351 1 3561151.
Ind/Abst F&S Index Plus Text, Int. [Select. Cov.]; Infomat Int. Bus.; PROMT.

PO
JORNAL NOVO. Newspaper. Portuguese. 400$00 single issue. Novimprensa, Distribuidora Dig Portugal.

PO
TEMPO. (19??)-. Newspaper. Portuguese. wk. 680.00. Imprenova, Travessa das Chagas 4 - 1, Lisbon Portugal.

PUERTO RICO

PR
DEBATE, EL. Ceased. (1911)-(19??). Newspaper. Spanish. sw.

PR/8750-5428
INTERAMERICANA (RIO PIEDRAS, P.R.). (INTERAMERICANA : EL PERIODICO OFICIAL DE LA UNIVERSIDAD INTERAMERICANA.). [Interamericana]. Vol. 1, No. 1 (Oct. 1979)-. Newspaper. Spanish. ir (seven issues yearly). $3.00. Public Relations Office, Inter American University of Puerto Rico, GPO Box 3255, San Juan, Puerto Rico 00936. **Tel** (809)766-1912. **ED** Ela Betancourt. **DD** 378. **Bk Rev. Circ:** 12,000 (ctrl).
Desc: Official newspaper for an Institution-IAU. Oriented toward alumni, students and academic community.

PR
PITIRRE, EL. Ceased. (1975)-(19??). Newspaper. Spanish. mo.

PR/8750-6122
SAN JUAN STAR, THE. (Nov. 2, 1959)-. Newspaper. English. da. $96.00 (Sunday regular mail), $230.00 (daily regular mail), $360.00 (daily and Sunday regular mail). Star Publishing Corporation / The San Juan Star, GPO Box 364187, San Juan, Puerto Rico 00936. **Tel** (809)782-4200. **ED** Andrew T. Viglucci. **Bk Rev. Ad Acc. Circ:** 36,027 daily, 38,687 Sunday (ctrl).

ROMANIA

RM
SCINTEIA. Ceased. **Added/Corp** Partidul Comunist Roman. Comitetul Central. (19??)-(19??). Newspaper. Romanian. da. **(Subscription address:** Rompresfilatelia, PO Box 12 201, Bucharest Romania.**)**

RM
TIMES OF BUCHAREST. Romanian. wk (52 issues per year). $91.00 Europe; $124.00 North America & Asia; $148.00 other. **(Subscription address:** Orion Press SRL, SPL Independentei 202-A, Bucharest 6 Romania (telephone 011 40 1 3122425)**)**

RUSSIA (Republic)

●**RU**
BUSINESS MN. VFOAT Biznes MN. No. 1 (1992)-. Periodical. Russian. wk. $119.95. **(Subscription address:** East View Publications Inc., 3020 Harbor Lane North, Suite 110, Minneapolis MN 55447.**)** LC HF3621; .B87.

RU
CHAS PIK. Added/Corp Soiuz Zhurnalistov SSSR. Leningradskaia Organizatsiia. Leningradskii Soiuz Zhrunalistov. (Feb. 26, 1990)-. Newspaper. Russian. wk. $229.95. **(Subscription address:** East View Publications Inc., 3020 Harbor Lane North, Suite 110, Minneapolis MN 55447.**)**
Ind/Abst Curr. Dig. Post Sov. Press.

RU
DELOVOI MIR. VFOAT Business World. (1990)-. Newspaper. Russian. ir (260 issues per year). $344.95. **(Subscription address:** East View Publications Inc., 3020 Harbor Lane North, Suite 110, Minneapolis MN 55447.**)**
Ind/Abst F&S Index Plus Text, Int. [Select. Cov.]; PROMT.

RU
DOMOSTROI. (19??)-. Periodical. Russian. wk. $103.95. **(Subscription address:** East View Publications Inc., 3020 Harbor Lane North, Suite 110, Minneapolis MN 55447.**)** LC AP50; .D65.

RU
GLASNOST. Added/Corp TSK KPSS. (199?)-. Newspaper. Russian. wk. $99.95. **(Subscription address:** East View Publications Inc., 3020 Harbor Lane North, Suite 110, Minneapolis MN 55447.**)**

RU
GOLOS RODINY. Added/Corp Sovetskoe Obshchestvo po Kulturnym Sviaziam s Sootechestvennikami za Rubezhom. (19??)-. Newspaper. Russian. wk. $99.95. **(Subscription address:** East View Publications Inc., 3020 Harbor Lane North, Suite 110, Minneapolis MN 55447.**)**

RU
GUDOK. Added/Corp Russia (1923-U.S.S.R.). Narodnyi Komissariat Putei Soobshcheniia. Russia (1923-U.S.S.R.). Ministerstvo Putei Soobshcheniia. Professionalnyi Soiuz Rabochikh Zheleznodorozhnogo Transporta. Tsentralnyi Komitet. (Dec. 1917)-. Newspaper. Russian. ir. $199.95. **(Subscription address:** East View Publications Inc., 3020 Harbor Lane North, Suite 110, Minneapolis MN 55447.**)** LC Microfilm S-521TF; TF4.
Ind/Abst Curr. Dig. Post Sov. Press.

●**RU**
GUDOK. (1993)-. Russian. ir. $199.95. **(Subscription address:** East View Publications Inc., 3020 Harbor Lane North, Suite 110, Minneapolis MN 55447.**)**
Ind/Abst Curr. Dig. Post Sov. Press.

RU
IZVESTIA. (19??)-. Newspaper. Russian. da. Librairie du Globe/Sce Abonmts, 43 Rue Amelot, F 75011 Paris France. Tel 011 33 1 43265499.

RU/0023-2378
KNIZHNOE OBOZRENIE. Added/Corp Russia (1923-U.S.S.R.) Gosudarstvennyi Komitet po Pechati. (1966)-. Periodical. Russian. wk. $119.95. Izdatelstvo Kniga, 50 Gorky Ulitsa, 125047 Moscow Russia. **(Subscription address:** East View Publications Inc., 3020 Harbor Lane North, Suite 110, Minneapolis MN 55447.**)** LC Z372; .A32. available in microform. *Continues* Novye Knigi.
Ind/Abst Curr. Dig. Post Sov. Press.

●**RU**
KOMMERSANT DAILY. (1992)-. Newspaper. Russian. ir (260 issues per year). $574.95. **(Subscription address:** East View Publications Inc., 3020 Harbor Lane North, Suite 110, Minneapolis MN 55447.**)**
Ind/Abst F&S Index Plus Text, Int. [Select. Cov.]; PROMT.

RU
KOMSOMOLSKAIA PRAVDA : ORGAN TSENTRALNOGO KOMITETA VLKSM. Added/Corp Vsesoiuznyi Leninskii Kommunisticheskii Soiuz Molodezhi. Tsentralnyi Komitet. (May 1925)-. Newspaper. Russian. da (260 issues per year). $229.95. **(Subscription address:** East View Publications Inc., 3020 Harbor Lane North, Suite 110, Minneapolis MN 55447.**)**

RU
KURANTY. (1983)-. Newspaper. Russian. ir (260 issues per year). $252.95. **(Subscription address:** East View Publications Inc., 3020 Harbor Lane North, Suite 110, Minneapolis MN 55447.**)**

RU/0024-1172
LETOPIS' GAZETNYKH STATEI. Added/Corp Vsesoiuznaia Knizhnaia Palata. (1936)-. Russian. wk. $249.95. Izdatelstvo Kniga, 50 Gorky Ulitsa, 125047 Moscow Russia. **(Subscription address:** East View Publications Inc., 3020 Harbor Lane North, Suite 110, Minneapolis MN 55447.**)** LC AI15; .L35. NLM ZAI 15 L646. Circ: 3,000.

RU/0868-5827
MEGAPOLIS EXPRESS. VFOAT Megapolis Ekspress. (19??)-. Newspaper. Russian. wk. $119.95. **(Subscription address:** East View Publications Inc., 3020 Harbor Lane North, Suite 110, Minneapolis MN 55447.**)**
Ind/Abst Curr. Dig. Post Sov. Press.

RU/0027-1306
MOSCOW NEWS. (1930)-. Newspaper. English (French, Spanish, Arabic, Russian and German). wk. $112.50. Moscow News, 16-2 Tverckaya Ulitsa, Moscow Russia. Tel 7095-209-1984, FAX 7095-209-0267. **(Subscription address:** East View Publications Inc., 3020 Harbor Lane North, Suite 110, Minneapolis MN 55447.**)** Bk Rev. Ad Acc. available in microform; available on an online database from DIALOG. Documents available from UMI Article Clearinghouse.
Desc: Newspaper printing materials about Post-Soviet life and activity on the international scene, as well as documents adopted by the government.
Ind/Abst Expand. Acad. Index (1992-); Newsp. Period. Abstr. (1992-); Curr. Dig. Post Sov. Press.

RU
MOSKOVSKIE NOVOSTI MICROFORM : MN : EZHENEDELNAIA GAZETA SOIUZA SOVETSKIKH OBSHCHESTV DRUZHBY I KULTURNOI SVIAZI S ZARUBEZHNYMI STRANAMI I AGENTSTVO PECHATI NOVOSTI. Added/Corp Soiuz Sovetskikh Obshchestv Druzhby i Kulturnoi Sviazi s Zarubezhnymi Stranami. Agentstvo Pechati "Novosti.". VFOAT MN. (19??)-. Newspaper. Russian.
Ind/Abst F&S Index Plus Text, Int. [Select. Cov.]; PROMT.

RU
MOSKOVSKIE NOVOSTI : MN : EZHENEDELNAIA GAZETA SOIUZA SOVETSKIKH OBSHCHESTV DRUZHBY I KULTURNOI SVIAZI S ZARUBEZHNYMI STRANAMI I AGENTSTVA PECHATI NOVOSTI. Added/Corp Soiuz Sovetskikh Obshchestv Druzhby i Kulturnoi Sviazi s Zarubezhnymi Stranami. Agentstvo Pechati "Novosti.". VFOAT MN. (19??)-. Periodical. Russian. wk. $150.00. **(Subscription address:** East View Publications Inc., 3020 Harbor Lane North, Suite 110, Minneapolis MN 55447.**)** LC PN5279.M63; M666.

RU
NEDELIA. (19??)-. Newspaper. Russian. wk. $129.95. **(Subscription address:** East View Publications Inc., 3020 Harbor Lane North, Suite 110, Minneapolis MN 55447.**)** LC AP50; .N38.

RU
NEVSKII PROSPEKT. Added/Corp Kuibyshevskii Raionnyi Sovet Narodnykh Deputatov. No. 1 (1990)-. Newspaper. Russian. mo. $43.00. **(Subscription address:** Victor Kamkin, 4956 Boiling Brook Pkwy., Rockville, MD 20852; Telephone: (301)881-5973) LC DK543; .N48.

RU
NEZAVISIMAIA GAZETA. Added/Corp Moskovskii Gorodskoi Sovet Narodnykh Deputatov. VFOAT Nezavisimaia; Russian Indep. (1990)-. Newspaper. Russian. da. $316.00. **(Subscription address:** Victor Kamkin, 4956 Boiling Brook Parkway, Rockville MD 20850.**)** CODEN NEZGEE. Pub. Size: Standard.

RU
PATRIOT. (1991)-. Newspaper. Russian. wk. $99.95. **(Subscription address:** East View Publications Inc., 3020 Harbor Lane North, Suite 110, Minneapolis MN 55447.**)**

RU
POZITSIIA. (1988)-. Newspaper. Russian. Twelve times a year. $99.95. **(Subscription address:** East View Publications Inc., 3020 Harbor Lane North, Suite 110, Minneapolis MN 55447.**)** ED Editor: 1988- V.G. Bondarenko.

RU
PRAVDA. Added/Corp Rossiiskaia Sotsial-Demokraticheskaia Rabochaia Partiia (Bolshevikov) Rossiiskaia Kommunisticheskaia Partiia (Bolshevikov) Vsesoiuznaia Kommunisticheskaia Artiia (Bolshevikov) Kommunisticheskaia Partiia Sovetskogo Soiuza. (1917)-. Newspaper. Russian. da (156 issues per year). $264.95. Librairie du Globe/Sce Abonmts, 43 Rue Amelot, F 75011 Paris France. Tel 011 33 1 43265499. **(Subscription address:** East View Publications Inc., 3020 Harbor Lane North, Suite 110, Minneapolis MN 55447.**)** available on microfilm. *Continues* Rabochii Put; *Absorbed* Sotsial-Demokrat (Moscow, R.S.F.S.R. : 1917).

RU
RABOCHAIA TRIBUNA. Added/Corp TSK KPSS. No. 1 (Jan. 1990)-. Newspaper. Russian. ir (260 issues per year). $229.95. **(Subscription address:** East View Publications Inc., 3020 Harbor Lane North, Suite 110, Minneapolis MN 55447.**)** CODEN RATREX. *Formed by the union of* Sotsialisticheskaia Industriia *and* Stroitelnaia Gazeta.

RU
RADIKAL. (1990)-. Newspaper. Russian. ir. $99.95. **(Subscription address:** East View Publications Inc., 3020 Harbor Lane North, Suite 110, Minneapolis MN 55447.**)** CODEN RADKEY.

RU
ROSSIISKIE VESTI : EZHENEDELNAIA GAZETA PRAVITELSTVA ROSSIISKOI FEDERATSII. Added/Corp Russian S.F.S.R. Verkhovnyi Sovet. (Apr. 1991)-. Newspaper. Russian. da. $349.95. **(Subscription address:** East View Publications Inc., 3020 Harbor Lane North, Suite 110, Minneapolis MN 55447.**)** CODEN ROVEEY.

RU
SANKT-PETERBURGSKIE VEDOMOSTI. (Sept. 1991)-. Newspaper. Russian. ir (312 issues per year). $259.95. *Continues* Leningradskaia Pravda.

RU
SELSKAIA ZHIZN. Added/Corp TSK KPSS. (Apr. 17, 1960)-. Newspaper. Russian. ir (156 issues per year). $229.95. **(Subscription address:** East View Publications Inc., 3020 Harbor Lane North, Suite 110, Minneapolis MN 55447.**)** *Continues* Selskoe Khoziaistvo.

RU
SIBIRSKAIA GAZETA. (18??)-. Newspaper. Russian. wk. $109.95. **(Subscription address:** East View Publications Inc., 3020 Harbor Lane North, Suite 110, Minneapolis MN 55447.**)** LC WMLC L 83/5122.

RU
SITUATSIIA. Added/Corp Soviet Union. Ministerstvo Vnutrennykh Del. (Feb. 1990)-. Newspaper. Russian. wk. $99.95. **(Subscription address:** East View Publications Inc., 3020 Harbor Lane North, Suite 110, Minneapolis MN 55447.**)**

RU
SLAVIANE. (1991)-. Newspaper. Russian (Bulgarian, Czech, English, Polish, Serbian and Slovak). wk. $109.95. **(Subscription address:** East View Publications Inc., 3020 Harbor Lane North, Suite 110, Minneapolis MN 55447.**)**

RU
TORGOVAIA GAZETA. Added/Corp Soviet Union. Ministerstvo Torgovli. Tsentrosoiuz (Soviet Union) Vsesoiuznaia Federatsiia Organizatsii Professionalnogo Soiuza Rabotnikov Torgovli, Obshchestvennogo Pitaniia, i Potrebitelskoi Kooperatsii. Sovet. (Nov. 1990)-. Newspaper. Russian. tw (156 issues per year). $126.95. **(Subscription address:** East View Publications Inc., 3020 Harbor Lane North, Suite 110, Minneapolis MN 55447.**)** *Continues* Sovetskaia Torgovlia.

RU
TRUD. Added/Corp Vsesoiuznyi Tsentralnyi Sovet Professionalnykh Soiuzov. (Feb. 1921)-. Newspaper. Russian. ir (260 issues per year). $229.95. **(Subscription address:** East View Publications Inc., 3020 Harbor Lane North, Suite 110, Minneapolis MN 55447.**)**

RU
UCHITELSKAIA GAZETA. (Oct. 1924)-. Newspaper. Russian. wk. $105.00. **(Subscription address:** East View Publications Inc., 3020 Harbor Lane North, Suite 110, Minneapolis MN 55447.**)**
Ind/Abst Curr. Dig. Post Sov. Press.

SAUDI ARABIA

SU/0254-833X
ARAB NEWS. [Arab news]. Vol. 1 (1976)-. Newspaper. English. da. $275.00. Arab Press House / Saudi Research & Marketing, 182-184 High Holborn, London WC1V 7AP England. Tel 011 44 071 831 8181,

Saudi Arabia

FAX 011 44 071 831 2310, telex 889272. **(Subscription address:** Attache International, 3050 Broadway, Suite 300, Boulder CO 80304.) **ED** Khalid Al-Maeena. **Ad Acc. Circ:** 41,408.
  Desc: Saudi Arabia's foremost English-language newspaper provides firsthand information about Saudi business activities, local and international news and cultural activities.

SU
SAUDI GAZETTE. (April 1976)-. Newspaper. English. ds. $234.45 Saudia Arabia; $300.00 other. Okaz Organization Press Publishers, PO Box 5576, Saud Islam, Jeddah Saudi Arabia. available on an online database (files 771,772,799/Full-Text) from DIALOG.
  Desc: National and international correspondents; covers worldwide social, economic and political news with a concentration on Western participation in industrial and technological development in Saudi Arabia.

SINGAPORE

SI
BUSINESS TIMES SINGAPORE. Newspaper. English. da. 964.47Sing$. Appalachian State University Department of English, Boone NC 28608. **Tel** (704)262-2000.

SI
LIANHE WANBAO. (19??)-. Chinese. da. Singapore Press Holdings Ltd, 82 Genting Lane Level 2, Singapore 1334 Singapore. **Tel** 011 65 7438800, FAX 011 65 7444875, 011 65 7461925, telex 55959. **ED** Chen Cheng 740-1418. **Ad Acc, Adv Mgr:** Lawrence Loh, **Tel** 740-2038. **Circ:** 115,000.
  Desc: Local news, international news, Malaysia news, business news, sports, racing, arts & engertainment

SI
LIANHE ZAO BOA. Chinese. da. 199.10Sing$ Singapore; 1,466.10Sing$. Singapore Press Holdings Ltd, 82 Genting Lane Level 2, Singapore 1334 Singapore. **Tel** 011 65 7438800, FAX 011 65 7444875, 011 65 7461925, telex 55959. **ED** Loy Teck Juan 740-1405/1406. **Bk Rev**, (Qty: 520 /year). **Ad Acc, Adv Mgr:** Lawrence Loh, **Tel** 740-2038. **Circ:** 200,000.
  Desc: Local news, Malaysia news, commentary/forum, China/Taiwan/Hong Kong news, business news, sports, racing, international news, entertainment, arts and news from Asean.

SI
STRAITS TIMES, THE. VFOAT Sunday Times. (1845)-. Newspaper. English. da. 156.00Sing$ Singapore; 1,248.00Sing$ (surface mail) other. Singapore Press Holdings Ltd, 82 Genting Lane Level 2, Singapore 1334 Singapore. **Tel** 011 65 7438800, FAX 011 65 7444875, 011 65 7461925, telex 55959. **ED** Cheong Yip Seng. **Bk Rev. Ad Acc. Circ:** 260,000. **Continues** Straits Times and Singapore Journal of Commerce.

SI
SUNDAY TIMES. English. wk. 28.60Sing$ Singapore; 211.00Sing$ other. Singapore Press Holdings Ltd, 82 Genting Lane Level 2, Singapore 1334 Singapore. **Tel** 011 65 7438800, FAX 011 65 7444875, 011 65 7461925, telex 55959.

SLOVAKIA

XO/0018-2869
HLAS L'UDU. [Hlas l'udu]. (1944)-. Newspaper. Slovak. wk. Hlas l'Udu, Sliacska 1, 830 08 Bratislava Slovakia. **Tel** 011 42 7 251 383, FAX 011 42 7 251 268. **ED** Pavol Dinka. **UDC** 32. **Circ:** 28,800.

XO
KNIZNA REVUE. (1991)-. Newspaper. Slovak. bw.

XO
NARODNA OBRODA. (1990)-. Newspaper. Slovak. da. Narodna Obroda, Trnavska Cesta 112, PO Box 63, 830 00 Bratislava Slovakia. **Tel** 011 42 7 220 433, FAX 011 42 7 296 281, telex 92738.

XO/1210-2059
NOVY SLOVAK. [Novy Slovak]. (1990)-. Newspaper. Slovak. da. Novy Slovak, Teslova 26, PO Box 254, 814 99 Bratislava Slovakia. **Tel** 011 42 7 672 39, FAX 011 42 7 670 42. **ED** Peter Skultety. **UDC** 07. **Circ:** 18,000.

XO
PRAVDA. Vol. 1, No. 1 (Oct. 1991)-. Newspaper. Slovak. da. **Continues** Pravda (Bratislava, Czechoslovakia).

XO
PRAVDA (PRAGUE, CZECHOSLOVAKIA). (PRAVDA.). Periodical. Czech. da. kcs118.00. Pravda Czech, Sturova 6, Bratislava Slovakia.

XO
SLOVENSKY DENNIK. (1990)-. Newspaper. Slovak. da. Slovensky Dennik, Zabotova 2, 811 04 Bratislava Slovakia. **Tel** 011 42 7 491 137. **ED** Robert Rom. **Circ:** 27,000.

SLOVENIA

XV/0353-8184
NEODVISNI DNEVNIK. [Neodv. dnev.]. (1990)-. Newspaper. Slovenian. da. Neodvisni Dnevnik, Kopitarjeva 2, 61000 Ljubljana Slovenia. **Tel** 011 38 61 325261, FAX 011 38 61 312775, telex 31177. **ED** Zlatko Setinc. **UDC** 32. **Circ:** 74,000. **Continues** Dnevnik (Ljubljana), 0350-753X.

XV/0354-1088
SLOVENSKE NOVICE. [Slov. nov.]. (1991)-. Newspaper. Slovenian. da. Slovenske Novice, Dunajska 5, 61000 Ljubljana Slovenia. **Tel** 011 38 61 115315, FAX 011 38 61 318193. **ED** Marjan Bauer. **UDC** 32"52". **Absorbed** Delo Plus, 0353-7331.

SOUTH AFRICA

SA
ARGUS (MICROFICHE). (THE ARGUS.). VFOAT Cape Argus. Jan. 3, 1857-. Newspaper. English. da. $158.38. Argus Printing & Publishing Co Ltd, PO Box 56, 122 Saint Georges Street, Cape Town 8000 South Africa. **Tel** 011 27 21 2084911. **ED** Andrew Drysaacc. **Bk Rev. Ad Acc. Circ:** 90,000.
  Desc: Largest English daily.
  Ind/Abst Point Repere.

SA
BUSINESS DAY. (May 1, 1985)-. Newspaper. English. da. R507.00. Times Media Ltd., PO Box 1138, Johannesburg 2000 South Africa. **Tel** 011 27 11 4972602.
  Ind/Abst Infomat Int. Bus.

SA
CAPE TIMES (MICROFICHE). (CAPE TIMES.). Established 1876. Newspaper. English. da. $45.10. Cape Times Cape Town, PO Box 492, Salt River 7925 South Africa.

SA
HUISGENOOT, DIE. VFOAT Huis Genoot. (1916)-. Periodical. Afrikaans. wk. R232.02 (all except South Africa, Namibia, and Homelands), R161.10 (South Africa), R149.86 (Namibia), R170.46 (Homelands). Nasionale Tydskrite, PO Box 1802, Cape Town 8000 South Africa. **Tel** 011-27-21-254850 ext.2360-61-2, FAX 011-27-21-252128, telex 521125. **LC** AP17; .H85.

SA
NEW NATION, THE. Added/Corp Catholic Church. South African Catholic Bishops' Conference. Vol. 1, No. 1 (Jan. 16-29, 1986)-. Newspaper. English. wk. R84.00 South Africa, Namibia & Homelands; R150.00 neighboring state; R220.00 Africa; £104.00 Britain & Western Europe; $180.00 US, Canada & Australia. New Nation / South Africa, PO Box 10674, Johannesburg 2000 South Africa. available on microfilm.

SA
STAR, THE. (1887)-. Newspaper. English. da. R1090.08 (S Africa & Nat. States); R1879.44 (other). Star / South Africa, PO Box 1014, 47 Sauer Street, Johannesburg 2000, South Africa. **Tel** 11 27 11 6339111, 4923914. **LC** 3557. available on microfilm.

SA
STAR (JOHANNESBURG, SOUTH AFRICA). (THE STAR.). VFOAT Johannesburg Star. (19??)-. Newspaper. English. R206.08 (weekly), R1345.92 (daily & Sunday) S Africa & Nat. States; R337.64 (weekly), R2266.84 (daily & Sunday) other. Star / South Africa, PO Box 1014, 47 Sauer Street, Johannesburg 2000, South Africa. **Tel** 11 27 11 6339111, 4923420.

SA
SUNDAY TIMES (MICROFICHE). (SUNDAY TIMES.). March 4, 1906-. Newspaper. English. $30.07. S A Associated Newspapers Ltd, PO Box 1138, Johannesburg 2000 South Africa.

SA
WEEKLY MAIL (JOHANNESBURG, SOUTH AFRICA). (THE WEEKLY MAIL.). (June 14, 1985)-. Newspaper. English. Fifty-two times a year (Fri.). R136.46 South Africa; R277.78 Africa; R1000.00 others. Wm Publications Pty. Ltd., PO Box 31141, Braamfontein 2017 South Africa. **Tel** 011 27 11 7268267. **(Subscription address:** National Circulation Services, PO Box 91080, Auckland Park 2006 South Africa.**)**

SPAIN

SP
ABC. (1905)-. Newspaper. Spanish. da. 27573ptas Ceuta, Melilla, Canaries, and Andorra; 28400ptas others. Prensa Espanola Sa, Juan Ignacio, Luca de Tena 7, 28027 Madrid Spain. **Tel** 011 34 1 3399011.

SP
ABC DOMINICAL. English. wk. 9160.00ptas Spain; 8893.00ptas Ceuta Melilla, Canaries & Andorra; 15235.00ptas Gibraltar, Portugal, Azores, Madeira, Philippines, Macoa & Port Timor; 16070.00ptas other. Prensa Espanola Sa, Juan Ignacio, Luca de Tena 7, 28027 Madrid Spain. **Tel** 011 34 1 3399011.

SP
ABC (EDICION INTERNACIONAL). (ABC.). VFOAT ABC International. (1905)-. Periodical. Spanish. wk. 8350.00ptas. Prensa Espanola Sa, Juan Ignacio, Luca de Tena 7, 28027 Madrid Spain. **Tel** 011 34 1 3399011. **Continues** ABC (Madrid, Spain : Edicion Semanal Aerea).

SP
AVUI. (19??)-. Newspaper. Catalan. da. 38200ptas (Spain); 58900ptas (Europe); 152060ptas (other). Premsa Catalana SA, C Consell Cent 425, 08013 Barcelona Spain. **Tel** 011 34 1 932656000.

SP
CINCO DIAS. Spanish. da. 62700.00ptas. Estructura SA Grupo Estudios Economicos, Gran Via 32, 28013 Madrid Spain. **Tel** 011 34 1 5210164.
  Ind/Abst F&S Index Plus Text, Int. [Select. Cov.]; Infomat Int. Bus.; PROMT.

SP
DIARI OFICIAL DE LA GENERALITAT DE CATALUNYA. Main/Corp Catalonia (Spain). **Added/Corp** Catalonia (Spain). Servei Central de Publicacions. (19??)-. Newspaper. Catalan. ir (Mon., Wed., Fri.). 17000ptas Spain; 16490ptas others. Diari Oficial de la Generalitat de Catalunya, Casa dels Canon C del Bisbe 6, 08002 Barcelona Spain. **Tel** 011 34 3 4121014. **DD** 349.46/7/05; 344.67005.

SP
EXPANSION. Spanish. wk. 112112.68ptas America & Africa; 41112.68ptas Portugal & Spain; 49112.68ptas Canary Islands; 81012.68ptas Europe; 158812.68ptas other. Editorial Expansion, C Recoletos 3-1A Planta, 28001 Madrid Spain. **Tel** 011 34 1 3373220.

SP
GACETA DE LOS NEGOCIOS, LA. Spanish. da. 37500.00ptas Spain; 50300.00ptas Europe; 76000.00ptas other. Grupo Zeta, C O Donnell 12, 28009 Madrid Spain. **Tel** 011 34 1 5863300.

SP
PAIS, EL. Vol. 1, No. 1 (May 4, 1976)-. Newspaper. Spanish. da. 30,000.00ptas Spain; 52,000.00ptas other (daily & Sunday surface mail). Diario el Pais SA, Miguel Yuste 40, 28037 Madrid Spain. **Tel** 011 34 1 3378363, 011 34 1 3378341. available on microfilm.

SP
PAIS (MADRID, SPAIN : EDICION INTERNACIONAL). (EL PAIS.). Vol. 1, No. 1 (May 30, 1983)-. Periodical. Spanish. wk. $100.00 US & Canada; $120.00 Eastern Asia and Oceania; $90.00 other. Diario el Pais SA, Miguel Yuste 40, 28037 Madrid Spain. **Tel** 011 34 1 3378363, 011 34 1 3378341. Index available. cum. index. **Ad Acc.** ctrl circ.
  Ind/Abst F&S Index Plus Text, Int. [Select. Cov.]; Infomat Int. Bus.; PROMT.

SP/0211-2744
REVISTA JURIDICA ESPANOLA LA LEY. [Rev. jurid. esp. Ley]. VFOAT Ley. (1980)-. Periodical. Spanish. da. 75600.00ptas Spain; 90720.00ptas Europe; 98280.00ptas; $1092.75 other. Distribuciones la Ley, Monterry 1 LA Coruna KM 17200, 282030 Las Rozas Madrid Spain. **Tel** 011 34 1 6342200. **UDC** 34/35.

SP
TIEMPO, EL. Spanish. wk. 20500.00ptas. Ediciones Tiempo Sa, O'Donnell 12 4A Planta, 28009 Madrid Spain. **Tel** 011 34 1 5781572.

SP
VANGUARDIA, LA. Spanish. da. 104658ptas. La Vanguardia, Departamento de Sus Pelayo 28, Barcelona 1 Spain. **Tel** 011 34 3 3015454. **Continues** La Vanguardia Espanola.
 Ind/Abst F&S Index Plus Text, Int. [Select. Cov.]; Infomat Int. Bus.; PROMT.

SP
YA SPAIN. (19??)-. Newspaper. Spanish. da (310 issues). 18300ptas Madrid; 16800ptas Spain; 31650ptas other. La Editorial Catolica SA, Mateo Inurria 15, Apartado 466, Madrid 16 Spain.

SWAZILAND

SQ
SWAZILAND GOVERNMENT GAZETTE. English. wk. E204.05. Swaziland Printing and Publishing, PO Box 28, Mbabane Swaziland. **Tel** 011 268 42716, FAX 42710 (Swaziland). **ED** V.R. Steinberg. **Circ:** 1,000 (ctrl).

SWEDEN

SW
DAGENS NYHETER. (1???)-. Newspaper. Swedish. wk. Kr936.00 Europe; Kr520.00 other. Dagens Nyheter, Box 138, 10515 Stockholm Sweden. **Tel** 011 87381725.

SW
SVENSKA DAGBLADET. (1884)-. Swedish. da. Kr2106.00 Denmark, Iceland, Finland & Norway; Kr4086.00 (surface mail) Non-Nordic countries; Kr5346.00 (airmail) Europe; Kr6246.00 other. Svenska Dagbladet, Ralambsvaegen 7, S-10517 Stockholm Sweden. **Tel** 011 46 8 1350000, FAX 011 46 8 135801.

SW
VECKO REVYN. wk. Kr637.00 Scandinavia; Kr739.00 other. Pressdata, Box 3263, 103 65 Stockholm Sweden. **Tel** 011 46 8 7996200.

SWITZERLAND

SZ/0252-5119
IDEAS FORUM. [Ideas forum]. (1978)-. Newspaper. English. tq.
 Ind/Abst Hum. Rights Intern. Rep.

SZ
JOURNAL DE GENEVE. (1826)-. French. da. Journal de Geneve, 12 rue de Hesse, 1211 Geneve 11 Switzerland. available in microform.

SZ/1021-1721
JOURNAL DE GENEVE ET GAZETTE DE LAUSANNE. [J. Geneve gaz. Lausanne]. (1991)-. Newspaper. French. da. **UDC** 07. **Formed by the union of** Journal de Geneve, 1010-2108 **and** Gazette de Lausanne et Journal Suisse, 1010-206X.
 Ind/Abst Infomat Int. Bus.; PROMT.

SZ
NEUE ZURCHER ZEITUNG UND SCHWEIZERISCHES HANDELSBLATT. **VFOAT** Schweizerisches Handelsblatt; NZZ; Neue Zurcher Zeitung. Vol. 51. (1871)-. Newspaper. German. da. Neue Zuercher Zeitung, Auslandvertrieb, Postfach 660, CH-8021 Zuerich Switzerland. **Tel** 011 41 1 2581111, telex 816 570 NZZV. available on microfilm. **Continues** Neue Zurcher Zeitung.

SZ
TAGES ANZEIGER. (19??)-. German. wk (52 issues). 126.05F. Tages Anzeiger, Vertrieb Werdstr 21 Postfach, CH-8021 Zuerich Switzerland. **Tel** 011 41 1 2484111.

TANZANIA

TZ
UHURU (DAR ES SALAAM, TANZANIA). (UHURU.). 1961-. Newspaper. Swahili. da. available on microfilm from The Library of Congress Photoduplication Service.

THAILAND

TH
BANGKOK POST, THE. Vol. 1, No. 1 (Aug. 1, 1946)-. Newspaper. English. da. $1531.70 US and Canada; $1575.05 other. Post Publishing Company Ltd., 136 Na Ranong Road, Klong Toey 10110 Bangkok, Thailand. **Tel** 011 66 2 2403700. **ED** Micheal J. Gorman. **Ad Acc.** ctrl circ. available on an online database (files 771,772,799/Full-Text) from DIALOG.

TH
BANGKOK WORLD. Ceased. (1957)-?. Newspaper. English. da. Allied Newspaper Ltd, 968 Rama IV Road, Bangkok Thailand.

TH
NATION. Newspaper. English. da. $320.00 Asia & Australia; $435.00 other. Nation Publishing Group, 44 MOO 10, Bangna-Taad Road, Prakhanong Acct, Bangkok 10260 Thailand. **Tel** 011 66 2 3171366. Documents available from UMI Article Clearinghouse.
 Ind/Abst Mag. Express (1986-) [Full Txt.]; Resource/One Ondisc.

TRINIDAD AND TOBAGO

TR
TRINIDAD GUARDIAN. **VFOAT** Sunday Guardian. (Sept. 2, 1917)-. Newspaper. English. da. TT$1366.35. Trinidad Publishing Co. Ltd., PO Box 122 Abercromby Street, Port of Spain Trinidad. **Tel** (809)623-8870. available on microfilm.

TURKEY

TU
CUMHURIYET. (1974)-. Turkish. da. $360.00. Yeni Gun Haber Ajansi Basin VE, Yayincilik AS PO Box 246, Istanbul Turkey. **Tel** 011 90 1 5120505, telex 22246. **ED** Hasan Cemal. **Bk Rev.** **Ad Acc.** **Circ:** 150,000.
 Desc: Social Democrat newspaper; includes a weekend magazine, a science and technology magazine and a sports magazine.

TURKMENISTAN

TK
TURKMENSKAIA ISKRA : ORGAN TSENTALNOGO KOMITETA KOMMUNISTICHESKOI PARTII TURKMENISTANA. **Added/Corp** TKP MK. (1924)-. Newspaper. Russian. da.

UKRAINE

UN
DEMOKRATYCHNA UKRAINA. (1991)-. Newspaper. Ukrainian. da. **Continues** Radianska Ukraina (Kiev, Ukraine : 1943).

UN
KOZA. (1991)-. Newspaper. Russian. da. **Continues** Komsomolskoe Znamia.

UN
NEWS FROM UKRAINE. **Added/Corp** Tovarystvo Kulturnykh Zviazkiv z Ukraintsiamy za Kordonom URSR. (196?)-. Periodical. English. wk. $149.95. Association for Cultural Relations with Ukrainians Abroad, Odessa, Ukraine. **(Subscription address:** East View Publications Inc., 3020 Harbor Lane North, Suite 110, Minneapolis MN 55447.**)** available on microfilm from The Library of Congress Photoduplication Service.
 Desc: Newspaper carrying the latest news concerning the economy, culture, education, science and sport in the Ukraine.

UN
PRAVDA UKRAINY : ORGAN TSENTRALNOGO KOMITETA KOMMUNISTICHESKOI PARTII UKRAINY, VERKHOVNOGO SOVETA I SOVETA MINISTROV UKRAINSKOI SSR. **Added/Corp** Komunistychna Partiia Ukrainy. Tsentralnyi Komitet. Ukraine. Verkhovna Rada. Ukraine. Rada Ministriv. (Jan. 11, 1944)-. Newspaper. Russian. ir (260 issues per year). $259.95. **(Subscription address:** East View Publications Inc., 3020 Harbor Lane North, Suite 110, Minneapolis MN 55447.**)** **Continues** Sovetskaia Ukraina.

UNITED KINGDOM

UK
AMERICAN. English. bw. £20.00. British American Newspapers Ltd, 114-115 West Street, Farnham Surrey GU9 7HL England. **Continues** American & The American Traveller.

UK/0265-5772
AS-SARQ AL-AWSAT. (AL-SHARQ AL-AWSAT.). [as-Sarq al-Awsat]. **VFOAT** Asharq Al Awsat. (1978)-. Newspaper. Arabic. da. $300.00. Attache International, 3050 Broadway, Suite 300, Boulder CO 80304. **Tel** (303)442-8900, FAX (303)442-7979. **Bk Rev.** **Ad Acc.** **Circ:** 2,000,000.
 Ind/Abst Numis. Lit.

UK/0307-5664
BELFAST TELEGRAPH. (Apr. 19, 1918)-. Newspaper. English. da. $1314.40 US and Canada; $1351.60 other. Belfast Telegraph Newspapers Ltd., 124 Royal Ave, Belfast BT1 1EB Northern Ireland. **Tel** 011 44 321242, telex BELFAST 74269. **LC** 2007. available on microfilm. **Continues** Belfast Evening Telegraph.

UK/0307-5664
BELFAST TELEGRAPH [MICROFORM]. (Apr. 19, 1918)-. Newspaper. English. da. $254.87. Belfast Telegraph Newspapers Ltd., 124 Royal Ave, Belfast BT1 1EB Northern Ireland. **Tel** 011 44 321242, telex BELFAST 74269. **ED** Roy Lilley. Index available. cum. index. **Bk Rev.** **Ad Acc.** **Circ:** 144,237. available on microfilm; available on an online database (files 771,772/Full-Text) from DIALOG. **Continues** Belfast Evening Telegraph.

UK/0962-1539
BOLTON EVENING NEWS. (1867)-. Newspaper. English. da. Reed Northern Newspapers, Newspaper House, Churchgate Bolton BL1 1DE England.

UK
BRITISH NEWSPAPERS : HISTORY AND GUIDE FOR COLLECTORS. English. £12.00. Richard Joseph Publishers Ltd, Unit 2 Monks Walk, Farnham, Surrey GU9 8HT England. **Tel** 11 44 252 734347, FAX 11 44 252 734307. **LC** PN5114. **DD** 072.

UK
BRITISH PRESS, THE. Newspaper. English. da.

UK/0963-4029
CAMBRIDGE EVENING NEWS. (1888)-. Newspaper. English. da. £275.20. Cambridge Newspapers Ltd., 51 Newmarket Road, Cambridge CD5 8EJ England. **Tel** 011 44 224 358877.

UK/0952-9950
CLOVER NEWSPAPER INDEX. [Clover newsp. index]. (198?)-. Periodical. English. Forty-Four times a year. £172.00 UK, £295.00 other. Clover Publications, 32 Ickwell Road Northhill, Beds SG18 9AB England. **Tel** 011 44 767 627363.

UK
CLYDEBANK POST. English. wk. Craig M Jeffrey Ltd, 15 Colquhoun Square, Helenburgh Dunbartonshire G84 8SE Scotland. **Tel** 041-952-1345, FAX 041-952-7267. **(Subscription address:** 88 Dumgarton Road, Clydebank, Dunbartonshire G81 1UG Scotland**)** **ED** Paul Jain. **Circ:** 9,000.
 Desc: Local news, sports and advertising.

UK
DAILY EXPRESS (LONDON, ENGLAND). (DAILY EXPRESS.). (April 24, 1900)-. Newspaper. English. da (except Sunday). £376.00 Europe; £680.00 South East Asia & Oceania; £524.00 Middle East & North Africa; £608.00 other. Express Newspapers PlC, Ludgate House, 245 Blackfriars Road, London SE1 9UX United Kingdom. **Tel** 011 44 71 9288000. **(Subscription address:** Spectrum International Mailing, Unit 18, Central Trading Estate, Staines Middlesex TW18 4XE United Kingdom.**)** available on microfilm from University Microfilms International (UMI); The Library of Congress Photoduplication Service; and British Museum Microfilm Service.
 Ind/Abst Infomat Int. Bus.

UK
DAILY MAIL (LONDON, ENGLAND). (DAILY MAIL.). Began with May 4, 1896 issue. Newspaper. English. da. Mail Newspapers, Carmelite House, London EC4Y 0JA England. available on microfilm from The Library of Congress Photoduplication Service; available on an online database (files 771,772,799/Full-Text) from DIALOG. ***Absorbed*** *News Chronicle and Daily Dispatch.*
Ind/Abst Infomat Int. Bus.

UK
DAILY MIRROR (LONDON, ENGLAND). (LONDON DAILY MIRROR.). **VFOAT** Daily Illustrated Mirror. (Nov. 2, 1903)-. Newspaper. English. da. £262.08 UK, £321.36 Europe, £333.84 others (surface mail); £371.28 (airmail). Mirror Group Newspapers Ltd, 33 Holborn Circus, London EC1P 1DQ England. **Tel** 011 44 71 353 0246, FAX 011 44 71 8223405, telex 27286. available on microfilm.

UK
DAILY POST (LIVERPOOL, ENG. : 1978). (DAILY POST.). (Sept. 9, 1978)-. Newspaper. English. da. The Liverpool Daily Post and Echo Ltd, PO Box 48 Old Hall Street, Liverpool L69 3EB England. available on microfilm from The Library of Congress Photoduplication Service; available on an online database (files 771,772,799/Full-Text) from DIALOG. ***Continues*** *Liverpool Daily Post (Liverpool, Eng. : 1935).*

UK
DAILY TELEGRAPH (LONDON, ENGLAND : 1969). (THE DAILY TELEGRAPH.). **VFOAT** London Daily Telegraph. No. 35608 (Oct. 21, 1969)-. Periodical. English. da. Daily Telegraph Ltd, 135 Fleet Street, London EC4P 4BL England. **Tel** (212)582-2626. cum. index. available on microfilm. ***Continues*** *Daily Telegraph and Morning Post.*
Ind/Abst Infomat Int. Bus.; PROMT.

UK
DERBY EVENING TELEGRAPH. (Aug. 15, 1933)-. Newspaper. English. da. £225.68. Derby Daily Telegraph Ltd, Northcliffe House, Meadow Road, Derby DE1 2DW England. **Tel** 011 44 332 291111. **LC** 1868-X. ***Continues*** *Derby Evening Telegraph and Derby Daily Express.*

UK/0307-0956
EASTERN DAILY PRESS. [East. dly. press]. (1871)-. Newspaper. English. da. £287.56. Eastern Counties Newspapers Ltd., Prospect House, Rouen Road, Norwich Norfolk NR1 1RE England. **Tel** 011 44 603 628311, FAX 011 44 603 612930. **ED** Peter Franzen. **Bk Rev**, (Qty: 400). **Ad Acc, Adv Mgr:** Marie Barnes, **Tel** same as publisher. **Circ:** 81,236. Documents available from BLDSC. ***Continues*** *Eastern Counties Daily Press.*

UK
EESTI HAAL. **VFOAT** Estonian News. Vol. 1, No. 1 (Dec. 20, 1947)-. Newspaper. Estonian (Estonian). sm. £12.00 England; £13.00 other. Estonian News, Estonian House, 18 Cheptow Villas, London W11 2RB England. **Tel** 01 780 1242. **ED** Angus Lembra, An Hebbema. **Bk Rev. Ad Acc. Circ:** 650 (ctrl). available on microfilm from The Library of Congress Photoduplication Service.

UK/0968-3623
EVENING CHRONICLE (OLDHAM). (1880)-. Newspaper. English. da (Mon.-Fri.). £26.00. Hirst Kidd & Rennie Ltd., Union Street, Oldham OL1 1EQ England. **Tel** 011 44 61 633 2121, FAX 011 44 61 627 0905. **ED** Philip Hirst. **Bk Rev**, (Qty: 250+). **Ad Acc, Adv Mgr:** Jim Whittingham, **Tel** same as publisher. **Acid Free. Circ:** 37,110. Documents available from BLDSC.
Desc: Local daily newspaper.

UK/0964-4946
EVENING NEWS (NORWICH. 1991). (1991)-. Newspaper. English. da. Eastern Counties Newspapers Ltd., Prospect House, Rouen Road, Norwich Norfolk NR1 1RE England. **Tel** 011 44 603 628311, FAX 011 44 603 612930. **ED** Peter Ware. **Bk Rev. Ad Acc. Circ:** 42,181. Documents available from BLDSC.

UK/0965-9269
EXCHANGE & MART NORTH/MIDLAND ED. [Exch. mart North/Midl. ed.]. **VFOAT** Exchange and Mart (North/Midland ed.); Exchange & Mart (N/M). (1970)-. Newspaper. English. wk. £116.00 Europe; £46.00 UK; £203.00 other. Link House / Exchange and Mart, West Street, Poole BH16 1LL England. **Tel** 011 44 202 445000, FAX 011 44 202 445189. ***Continues*** *Exchange & Mart, 0014-4460.*

UK/0307-1766
FINANCIAL TIMES (LONDON ED.). (THE FINANCIAL TIMES.). [Financ. times]. New Ser., No. 1 (Feb. 13, 1888)-. Newspaper. English. da (Monday-Saturday). $1144.80 US and Canada; $1177.20 other. The Financial Times, 1 Southwark Bridge, London SE1 9HL England. **Tel** 011 44 71 873 3000, FAX 01 236 9764. **ED** Geoffrey Owen. **LC** 1932. Index available. **Bk Rev. Ad Acc. Circ:** 306,857. available on microfilm. ***Absorbed*** *Bullionist; Financier and Bullionist; Financial News.*
Ind/Abst Abstr. BioCommer.; Chem. Bus. Bull.; Chem. Bus. NewsBase (1985-); Chem. Bus. Update; Coal Abstr.; Eng. Mater. Abstr.; GeoRef; Index Bus. Reports; Infobank (Jan. 1969-); Int. Packag. Abstr.; Manage. Market. Abstr.; Print. Abstr.; PROMT.

UK
GARDENERS' CHRONICLE NEWSPAPER, THE. June 23, 1855-. Newspaper. English. wk.

UK
GLOBE AND TRAVELLER (LONDON, ENGLAND : 1907). (THE GLOBE AND TRAVELLER.). Newspaper. English. wk.

UK/0261-3077
GUARDIAN (LONDON). (THE GUARDIAN.). [Guardian]. No. 35, 192 (Aug. 24, 1959)-. Newspaper. English. da. £388.00 UK; £478.00 other. The Guardian, 164 Deansgate, Manchester M60 2RR England. **Tel** 011 44 61 8327200. **ED** Peter J. Preston. Index available. cum. index. **Bk Rev. Ad Acc. Circ:** 450,000 (ctrl). available on microfilm; available on diskette; available on an online database. ***Continues*** *Manchester Guardian (Manchester, England : 1828), 0307-756X.*
Ind/Abst Appl. Soc. Sci. Index Abstr.; Br. Humanit. Index; Infobank (Jan. 1969-); Infomat Int. Bus.; PROMT; Sage Race Relat. Abstr.

UK
GUERNSEY EVENING PRESS AND STAR. English. da. The Guernsey Press Co Ltd, Braye Road/Industrial Estate, Vale Guernsey Channel Islands United Kingdom. **Tel** 0481 745866, FAX 0481 748972. **ED** D Prigent. **Bk Rev. Ad Acc. Circ:** 17,600.
Desc: Covers local news and features.

UK
HARTLEPOOL MAIL. English. Six issues per week. £24.00. Sunderland & Hartlepool Publishing & Printing Ltd, Westhouse, Clarence Road, Hartlepool TS24 8BU England. **Tel** 0429 274441. **ED** AC Smith; FAX 0429 869024. **Bk Rev. Ad Acc. Circ:** 28,600.
Desc: Local and national news, general features, TV and radio guide, pop page, gardening, country matters, letters page and children's page.

UK
INDEPENDENT (LONDON, ENGLAND). (THE INDEPENDENT.). (1986)-. Newspaper. English. da (Monday-Saturday). £224.30 England; £298.72 (surface mail), £419.14 (airmail) North America; £298.72 (surface mail), £592.82 (airmail) other. Newspaper Publishing PLC, 40 City Road, London EC1Y 2DB England. **Tel** 011 44 71 9561689, 011 44 71 2531222. **ED** Andreas Whittam-Smith. **Bk Rev. Ad Acc. Circ:** 414,120 (ctrl). available on microfilm; available on CD-ROM.
Desc: National quality newspaper.
Ind/Abst Br. Humanit. Index; Child. Lit. Abstr. (19??-); Index Bus. Reports; Infomat Int. Bus.; Int. Packag. Abstr.; Manage. Market. Abstr.; Print. Abstr.; PROMT; Sage Race Relat. Abstr.

UK
INDEPENDENT ON SUNDAY, THE. (Jan. 28, 1990)-. Newspaper. English. Fifty-two times a year. £150.80 UK, £168.48 others (surface mail); $307.32 US, Canada, South America, Africa, India, North Africa, Iran, Israel, Aden, £163.28 Europe, Cyprus, Malta, Gibraltar, £354.12 others (airmail). Newspaper Publishing PLC, 40 City Road, London EC1Y 2DB England. **Tel** 011 44 71 9561689, 011 44 71 2531222. **(Subscription address:** Johnston International News Ltd., A3 Lantern Court, Mill Harbour London E14 9TU England.**) CODEN** INDSEG. cum. index.
Ind/Abst Infomat Int. Bus.

UK
JERSEY EVENING POST. Jersey Evening Post Ltd, Braye Road, Vale Guernsey Channel Islands United Kingdom.

UK
LIVERPOOL ECHO. (Oct. 27, 1879)-. Newspaper. English. da. The Liverpool Daily Post and Echo Ltd, PO Box 48 Old Hall Street, Liverpool L69 3EB England. available on an online database (files 771,772/Full-Text) from DIALOG.

UK
LONDON GAZETTE, THE. **Main/Corp** Great Britain. (1665)-. Newspaper. English. da. £360.00. Her Majesty's Stationery Office, 51 Nine Elms Lane, London SW8 5DR England. **Tel** 011 44 71 873 8459, 011 44 71 873 8499, FAX 011 44 71 873 8499, 011 44 71 873 8456, telex 297138. **(Subscription address:** Her Majestys Stationery Offic, PO Box 276 Public Centre, London SW8 5DT England**) LC** J7; .G6. available on microfilm.

UK/0305-1765
LOUGHTON REVIEW. [Lought. rev.]. (1969)-. Newspaper. English. mo. Free. Monkswood Press, Caxton House, Old Station Road, Loughton, Essex IG10 4PE England.

UK/0263-8878
MAIL ON SUNDAY. [Mail Sunday]. (1982)-. Newspaper. English. wk. £65.52 UK; £88.92 Europe; £92.04 other. Hart Mailing Services, 18 Hillside Avenue, Purley, Surrey CR8 2DP England. **Tel** 011 44 81 7630140. **DD** 072.1. available on an online database from DIALOG.

UK/0025-200X
MANCHESTER GUARDIAN WEEKLY. **VFOAT** Guardian Weekly; Guardian. Newspaper. English. wk. $98.00. Guardian, 164 Deansgate, Manchester M60 2RR England. **Tel** 011 44 61 8327200. **(Subscription address:** Manchester Guardian, 20 E 53rd Street, New York, NY 10022**)** ***Absorbed*** *Monde. English Edition.*

UK/0959-3608
MANCHESTER GUARDIAN WEEKLY (1985). (THE MANCHESTER GUARDIAN WEEKLY.). [Manch. guard. wkly.]. **VFOAT** Guardian Weekly. Vol. 132, No. 1 (Jan. 6 1985)-. Newspaper. English. wk. $78.00 one year; $150.00 two years. The Guardian, 164 Deansgate, Manchester M60 2RR England. **Tel** 011 44 61 8327200. **(Subscription address:** Manchester Guardian / for US, 19 West 44th Street, Suite 1613, New York NY 10036.**)** available on microfilm from University Microfilms International (UMI). ***Continues*** *Guardian Weekly (Manchester, England).*
Ind/Abst Book Rev. Index; NEXIS (Jan. 4, 1981-).

UK
MORNING ADVERTISER. (Feb. 8, 1794)-. Newspaper. English. da. £208.53. Morning Advertiser, Elvian House, Nixey Chose, Slough SL1 1NQ England. **Tel** 011 44 753 811911. **LC** 1949. available on an online database (files 771,772,799/Full-Text) from DIALOG.
Ind/Abst Infomat Int. Bus.

UK/1186-5393
MORNING CHRONICLE (HALIFAX. TRI-WEEKLY ED.). ***Ceased.*** (THE MORNING CHRONICLE [MICROFORM].). (Jan. 24, 1844)-(1992). English. British Library, Great Russell Street, London WC1B 3DG England. **DD** 071/.1622.

UK
MORNING STAR, THE. (Jan. 1894)-. Periodical. English. da. £152.88. Morning Star, 75 Farringdon Road, London EC1M 3JX England. **Tel** 01 405 9242. **ED** Tony Chater. Index available in last issue of volume--attached. **Bk Rev. Ad Acc. Circ:** 28,500. ***Supersedes*** *Excellent Things.*
Desc: Newspaper of the left owned by its readers in co-operative society.

UK
MORNING STAR (LONDON, ENGLAND). (MORNING STAR.). No. 1/10746 (April 25, 1966)-. Newspaper. English. da. Morning Star, 75 Farringdon Road, London EC1M 3JX England. **Tel** 01 405 9242. available on microfilm from The Library of Congress Photoduplication Service. ***Continues*** *Daily Worker (London, England).*

UK
NEW DIPLOMAT. (March 19, 1948)-. Newspaper. English (Russian). wk. **LC** 1956.

UK/0028-6362
NEW MUSICAL EXPRESS. MICROFORM, THE. **VFOAT** NME. No. 269 (March 7, 1952)-. Newspaper. English. wk. $125.00. IPC Magazines Ltd., Perrymount Road, Haywards Heath, West Sussex RH16 3DH England. **Tel** 011 44 444 440421. **[CCC].** ***Continues*** *Musical Express (London, England).*

UK
NEW ZEALAND JOURNAL, THE. No. 1 (Feb. 8, 1840)-. Newspaper. English. bw.

UK/0028-8500
NEW ZEALAND NEWS UK. **VFOAT** New Zealand News U.K. (1927)-. Periodical. English. Fifty-two times a year. £28.00 UK; £38.50 Europe; £57.75 other. New Zealand News UK, PO Box 10, Berwick-Upon-Tweed, Northumberland TD15 1BW England. **ED** Kevin McMenamin; 11 44 286 306677. **LC** DU400; .N454. **DD** 993.1/005. **Bk Rev. Ad Acc, Adv Mgr:** Ana Hensley, **Tel** 11 44 71 9306451. **Circ:** 15,500.
Desc: The closest link to home for thousands of New Zealanders either travelling or living overseas.

UK
NEWS OF THE WORLD, THE. **VFOAT** News of the World & Empire News. (Oct. 1, 1843)-. Newspaper. English. wk (Published on Sundays). £49.00 UK and North Ireland; £69.00 other. News International Newspapers Ltd., PO Box 495 Virginia Street, London E1 9XU England. **Tel** 011 44 71 7823000. **LC** 1959. available on microfilm.

UK/0957-9125
NEWSPAPER FOCUS. [Newsp. focus]. (1988)-. Newspaper. English. mo (12 issues). £30.00 UK; £40.00 Eire & Europe; £52.00 America, Middle East, Africa & India; £60.00 Australia, New Zealand & Japan; £52.00 other. Haymarket Publishing Ltd., 12 14 Ansdell Street, London W8 5TR England. **Tel** 011 44 483 733800, FAX 011 44 483 776573. **(Subscription address:** Haymarket

UK

NEWSTIME (LONDON, ENGLAND).
Ceased. (NEWSTIME.). ( )-(Sept. 1988). Periodical. English. mo. Newspaper Society, 6 Carmelite Street, London EC4Y 0BL England. **Tel** 01 583 3311, FAX 01 353 7179, telex 265 871 MONREF Q. **ED** Gary Cullum. **LC** PN4701; .N43. **DD** 070/.05. **Bk Rev**. **Ad Acc**. **Circ**: 2,500 (ctrl).
Desc: Journal of the Newspaper Society; covers matters concerning newspaper publishing and management, law, technology, sales and advertising.
Ind/Abst Print. Abstr.

UK/0029-7712
OBSERVER (LONDON). (THE OBSERVER.). [Observer]. (Dec. 4, 1791)-. Newspaper. English. wk (Sunday). £290.00 Australasia, Far East & Pacific; £160.00 US & Canada; £105.00 UK; £150.00 Europe; £240.00 other. The Guardian, 164 Deansgate, Manchester M60 2RR England. **Tel** 011 44 61 8327200. **ED** Donald Trelford. **Bk Rev**. **Ad Acc**. **Circ**: 700,000. available on microfilm.
Ind/Abst Annu. Bibliogr. Engl. Lang. Lit.; Book Rev. Index; Br. Humanit. Index; Child. Lit. Abstr. (19??-); Infobank (Jan. 1969-); Infomat Int. Bus.

UK

OVERSEAS NEWSPAPERS AND PERIODICALS GUIDE BOOK. English. New Product Newsletter Ltd, 1A Chesterfield Street, London W1 England.

UK

PUBLIC LEDGER, THE. (July 3, 1837)-. Newspaper. English. da. £330.00 UK; £380.00 Europe; £410.00 other. UK Publications, 10 Little College Street, London SW1P 35H England. **Tel** 011 44 71 976 7772, FAX 011 44 71 976 0861. **LC** 1967. **Ad Acc**. **Continues** Constitutional and Public Ledger.

UK

SCOTSMAN, THE. (Jan. 1 1860)-. Newspaper. English. da (Mon.-Sat.). £254.50 UK; £369.42 Europe; £534.26 North & South America and Arab countries; £736.54 others. Scotsman Publishing Ltd, 20 North Bridge, Edinburgh EH1 1YT Scotland. **Tel** 011 44 31 255 2468. **LC** 2013. **Continues** Daily Scotsman.
Ind/Abst Infomat Int. Bus.

UK/0955-7024
SCOTTISH WORLD. Vol. 1, No. 1 (April 1989)-. Newspaper. English. mo. Scottish World, POB 1, Oban Argyll PA34 5PY Scotland.

UK

SUN (LONDON, ENGLAND). (SUN.). No. 1 (Sept. 15, 1964)-. Newspaper. English. da. Sun, 30 Boriverie Street, London EC4Y 8DE England. available on microfilm from University of Chicago Library.
Continues Daily Herald (London, England).

UK

SUNDAY EXPRESS (LONDON, ENGLAND). (SUNDAY EXPRESS.). (Dec. 29, 1918)-. Newspaper. English. wk. £84.00 Europe; £128.00 Southeast Asia and Oceania; £108.00 Middle East and North Africa; £120.00 other. Express Newspapers PlC, Ludgate House, 245 Blackfriars Road, London SE1 9UX United Kingdom. **Tel** 011 44 71 9288000. (**Subscription address**: Spectrum International Mailing, Unit 18, Central Trading Estate, Staines Middlesex TW18 4XE United Kingdom.) **LC** 1868-X.

UK

SUNDAY TELEGRAPH (LONDON, ENGLAND). (THE SUNDAY TELEGRAPH.). No. 1 (Feb. 5, 1961)-. Newspaper. English. Fifty-two times a year. £100.83 UK; £146.14 others. Johnsons International Media Services, 43 Millharbour, London E14 9TR England. **Tel** 011 44 71 538 8288. available on microfilm from The Library of Congress Photoduplication Service; available on an online database (files 771,772,799/Full-Text) from DIALOG.
Ind/Abst Child. Lit. Abstr. (19??-); Infomat Int. Bus.

UK

SUNDAY TIMES, THE. (Oct. 20, 1822)-. Newspaper. English. ir. $667.80 US and Canada; $686.70 other. News International Newspapers Ltd., PO Box 495 Virginia Street, London E1 9XU England. **Tel** 011 44 71 7823000. (**Subscription address**: Research Publications Inc. / Microfilm, 12 Lunar Drive Drawer AB, Woodbridge CT 06525.)

UK

SUNDAY TIMES (LONDON, ENGLAND : 1931). (SUNDAY TIMES.). No. 5622 (Jan. 11, 1931)-. Newspaper. English. Fifty-two times a year. $238.00 North America. News International Newspapers Ltd., PO Box 495 Virginia Street, London E1 9XU England. **Tel** 011 44 71 7823000. **ED** Andrew Neil. **Bk Rev**. **Ad Acc**. **Circ**: 1,250,000. available on microfilm from Research Publications. **Continues** Sunday Times and Sunday Special.

UK/0260-0668
TIMES INDEX, THE. (Jan./Mar. 1973)-. Periodical. English. Thirteen times a year. £561.00. Research Publications Ltd., PO Box 45, Reading RG1 8HF England. **Tel** 011 44 734 583247, 011 44 734 583248, FAX 011 44 734 591325, telex 848336 RPLG. **LC** AI21; .T46. **DD** 072/.1. **Continues** Index to the Times, 0046-8924.

UK

TIMES (LONDON, ENGLAND), THE. Times Newspapers Ltd / London, POB 496, Virginia Street, London E2 9XT England.
Ind/Abst Index Bus. Reports; Manage. Market. Abstr.

UK/0140-0460
TIMES (LONDON, ENGLAND: 1788). (THE TIMES.). **VFOAT** London Times; Times of London. No. 1023 (Mar. 18, 1788)-. Newspaper. English. da. $530.00. News International Newspapers Ltd., PO Box 495 Virginia Street, London E1 9XU England. **Tel** 011 44 71 7823000. available on CD-ROM from Chadwyck-Healey, Inc.; available on microfilm. **Continues** Times, or, Daily Universal Register.
Ind/Abst Br. Humanit. Index (1962-); Infobank (Jan. 1969-); Infomat Int. Bus.; PROMT.

UK/0041-2821
TRIBUNE. No. 1 (Jan. 1937)-. Periodical. English. wk (52 issues). £40.00 UK; £55.00 other. Tribune Publishing Company / UK, 308 Gray's Inn Road, London WC1X 8DY England. **Tel** 011 44 1 278 0911. **ED** Phil Kelly. **Bk Rev**. **Ad Acc**.
Desc: Newspaper covering political and current affairs.
Ind/Abst Sage Race Relat. Abstr.

UK/0041-8226
UNIVERSE MANCHESTER. (THE UNIVERSE.). [Universe Manch.]. (1860)-. Newspaper. English. wk. £36.00 UK; £44.00 EIRE and Europe; £48.00 other. Gabriel Communications Ltd, 1st Floor, St. James Building, Oxford M1 8PS England. **Tel** 011 44 71 278 7321. **ED** A. Knowles (editor's phone: 011 44 61 236 8856). Index available (bound in all issues). **Ad Acc**.

UK

WORD IN ACTION. Added/Corp British and Foreign Bible Society. (1972)-. Newspaper. English. tq. Free. British and Foreign Bible Society, Stonehill Green, Westlea Swindon, Wilts. SN5 7DC England. **Tel** 011 44 793 513713, FAX 011 44 793 512539. **ED** Joy Alred. **Pub**. **Size**: Tabloid. **Circ**: 170,000. **Supersedes** Bible in the World.

UZBEKISTAN

UZ/0013-3051
EKONOMIKA I ZHIZN. Added/Corp Uzbek S.S.R. Gosudarstvennaia Planovaia Komissiia. Uzbek S.S.R. Sovet Narodnogo Khoziaistva. (1959)-. Russian. wk. $149.95. **LC** HC487.U9; A3.
Ind/Abst Infomat Int. Bus.; PROMT; Curr. Dig. Post Sov. Press.

UZ

UZBEKISTON ADABIETI VA SANATI (TASHKENT, S.S.R. : 1956). (UZBEKISTON ADABIETI VA SANATI.). **VFOAT** Literatura i Iskusstvo Uzbekistana. (Jan. 4, 1956)-. Newspaper. Uzbek. wk. $149.95. Izdatelstvo Tsk Kompartii Uzbekistana, Ulitsa Pravdy Vostoka 26, Tashkent Uzbekistan. (**Subscription address**: East View Publications Inc., 3020 Harbor Lane North, Suite 110, Minneapolis MN 55447.)

VATICAN CITY

VC/0030-6312
OSSERVATORE ROMANO, L'. Newspaper. Italian (English, French, Spanish, German, Portuguese and Polish). da (Italy; W). L48000 (surface mail) Italy; $54.00 (airmail) Europe and the Mediterranean area; $66.00 (airmail) North America; $48.00 (airmail) Central and South America; $54.00 (airmail) Africa; $60.00 (airmail) Asia; $66.00 (airmail) Oceania; $48.00 (airmail) other. L'Osservatore Romano, Vatican City 00120 Italy. **Tel** 011 39 6 6983494. **ED** John Muthig. Index available. **Bk Rev**. **Ad Acc**. ctrl circ. available on microfilm from University Microfilms International (UMI).
Desc: Contains all the speeches and documents of the Holy Father, documents issued by the Holy See, and news of the Church and of the world.
Ind/Abst Bibliogr. Mission.; Abr. Cathol. Period. Lit. Index; Cathol. Period. Lit. Index.

VENEZUELA

VE

NACIONAL (CARACAS, VENEZUELA). (EL NACIONAL.). No. 1 (August 1943)-. Newspaper. Spanish. da. Press Agencias SA, Apartado 209, Caracas Venezuela. **Tel** 011 58 2 4083294, 011 58 2 4083295.

VIETNAM

VM/0574-8070
CUU QUOC (MICROFICHE). (CUU QUOC.). Newspaper. Vietnamese. ir. Xunhasaba Exports and Imports, 7 Nguyen Thi Minh Khai Str, Dit 1 Ho Chi Minh City Vietnam. **Tel** 011 84 8 294893, telex 278 XUNHASABA.

VM

HSIN YUEH HUA PAO. Added/Corp Yueh-Nan Hua Chiao Lien Ho Tsung Hui. **VFOAT** Bao Tan Viet Hoa. (19??)-. Newspaper. Chinese.

VIRGIN ISLANDS (U.S.)

VI

ST. CROIX AVIS. **VFOAT** Avis. V. 1, No. 1, (Jan. 1, 1844)-. Newspaper. English. ir. St Croix Avis, Brodhurst Printery, St Croix Virgin Islands. **Continues** Dansk Vestindisk Regierings Avis (Saint Croix, V.I. : 1815).

VI/0895-0970
TRADEWINDS (SAINT JOHN, V.I.). (TRADEWINDS.). **VFOAT** Trade Winds; Saint John's Tradewinds Newspaper; St. John's Tradewinds Newspaper; Tradewinds Newspaper. Vol. 1 No. 1 (Feb. 1977)-. Newspaper. English. mo. Trade Wind Charters, PO Box 500, Cruz Bay US Virgin Islands 00830. **ED** Forrest Fisher. **Continues** St. John Drum.
Ind/Abst Text. Technol. Dig. (19??-199?).

VI

VIRGIN ISLANDS DAILY NEWS, THE. **VFOAT** Daily News. 48th year, No. 12044 (May 18, 1978)-. Newspaper. English. da. $226.25. Daily News / Virgin Islands, PO Box 7760, St. Thomas Virgin Islands 00801. **ED** Ariel Melchior, Jr. **Continues** Daily News of the Virgin Islands.

YUGOSLAVIA

YU/0352-7220
CATALOGUE OF YUGOSLAV PERIODICALS AND NEWSPAPERS. English. (**Subscription address**: Jugoslovenska Knjiga, PO Box 36, YU 11001 Belgrade Yugoslavia.) **LC** Z6956.Y9; C37; PN5355.Y8. **DD** 015.497034.

YU/0023-2416
KNJIZEVNE NOVINE : ORGAN SAVEZA KNJIZEVNIKA JUGOSLAVIJE. Added/Corp Savez Knjizevnika Jugoslavije. Udruzenje Knjizevnika Srbije. Vol. 1, No. 1 (Feb. 17, 1948)-. Periodical. Serbo-Croatian (Cyrillic). sm. **LC** AP56; .K615.
Ind/Abst MLA Int. Bibl. Books Artic. Mod. Lang. Lit.

ZAMBIA

ZA

TIMES OF ZAMBIA, THE. (1964)-. Newspaper. English. da. $1,095.00 (one year). Newspaper Distributors Ltd., PO Box 70069, Ndola Zambia. **Tel** 011 260 26 4065 3641.
Desc: Reels for 1972 include the Sunday edition: The Sunday times of Zambia.

Zambia

ZA
ZAMBIA DAILY MAIL MICROFORM. Began with Aug. 13, 1965 issue. Newspaper. English. Zambia Publishing Company, Box 1421, Lusaka Zambia. *Continues* Zambia Mail.

ABSTRACTING, BIBLIOGRAPHIES AND STATISTICS

US/1059-8154
ALTERNATIVE INDEX. [Altern. index]. **VFOAT** Frankfort's Alternative Index. (1991)-. Newspaper. English. wk. Alternative Index, PO Box 326, Westmoreland KS 66549-0326. **DD** 070. available on microfilm. *Continues* Frankfort's Alternative Index.

US/0893-2727
BOSTON GLOBE INDEX (1987), THE. (THE BOSTON GLOBE INDEX.). [Boston globe index]. **Added/Corp** University Microfilms International. (Jan. 1987)-. Abstracting/Indexing Service. English. an. $860.00. University Microfilms International, 300 North Zeeb Road, Ann Arbor MI 48106-1346. **Tel** (313)761-4700, (800)521-0600 Exts. 2490, 2491, FAX (313)973-1540. **ED** Andrew Horvay. **DD** 071. *Continues* Bell & Howell Newspaper Index to the Boston Globe, 0741-5281.

●CN/1192-4160
CANADIAN INDEX (TORONTO). (CANADIAN INDEX.). [Can. index]. Vol. 1, No. 1 (Jan. 1993)-. Abstracting/Indexing Service. English. mo. Micromedia Limited, 20 Victoria Street, Toronto Ontario M5C 2N8 Canada. **Tel** (416)362-5211, (800)387-2689, FAX (416)362-6161, telex 06524668. **DD** 011/.34. *Formed by the union of* Canadian Business Index, 0227-8669 *and* Canadian News Index, 0225-7459 Canadian Magazine Index (Toronto, Ont.), 0829-8777.

CN/0225-7459
CANADIAN NEWS INDEX (TORONTO). (CANADIAN NEWS INDEX : ANNUAL CUMULATION.). [Can. news index]. Vol. 4, No. 1-12 (Jan.-Dec. 1980)-. English. an. Micromedia Limited, 20 Victoria Street, Toronto Ontario M5C 2N8 Canada. **Tel** (416)362-5211, (800)387-2689, FAX (416)362-6161, telex 06524668. **ED** Luci Lemieux. **LC** AI3; .C2414. **DD** 071/.1. **Bk Rev**. **Ad Acc**. ctrl circ. *Continues* Canadian Newspaper Index (Annual Cumulation), 0384-983X.
Desc: A key reference tool designed to provide bibliographic access to Canada's daily newspapers.

YU/0352-7220
CATALOGUE OF YUGOSLAV PERIODICALS AND NEWSPAPERS. English. **(Subscription address:** Jugoslovenska Knjiga, PO Box 36, YU 11001 Belgrade Yugoslavia.**) LC** Z6956.Y9; C37; PN5355.Y8. **DD** 015.497034.

US/0731-9045
CHICAGO TRIBUNE INDEX. [Chicago tribune index]. Vol. 1, No. 1 (Jan. 1982)-. English. mo. **LC** AI21.C45; C47. **DD** 071/.73/11. available in microform from University Microfilms International (UMI); available on CD-ROM from University Microfilms International (UMI); available on an online database. *Continues* Bell & Howell Newspaper Index to the Chicago Tribune, 0195-6353.

AG
CLARIN, BUENOS AIRES. INDICE. (Sept. 1973)-. Spanish. mo. $1.00. Arta Grafico Edi Argentino SA, Piedras 1743, Buenos Aires 1285 Argentina. **Tel** 011 54 1 213661. **LC** AI21.C52; C55.

US/0893-2433
DETROIT NEWS INDEX, THE. [Detroit news index]. **Added/Corp** University Microfilms International. (Jan. 1987)-. English. mo (with quarterly and annual cumulations). $680.00. University Microfilms International, 300 North Zeeb Road, Ann Arbor MI 48106-1346. **Tel** (313)761-4700, (800)521-0600 Exts. 2490, 2491, FAX (313)973-1540. **ED** Andrew Horvay. **LC** AI21.D46; B44. **DD** 071. *Continues* Bell & Howell Newspaper Index to the Detroit News, 0195-637X.
Desc: Comprehensive subject index; includes access by personal and corporate name headings; informative abstracts.

IR
DIRECTORY OF IRANIAN NEWSPAPERS. (1969)-. Directory. English (Persian). an. 400.00IR. National Library of Iran, 30 Tir St, 11364 Tehran, Iran. **Tel** 0098-21-673315, FAX 0098-21-662040. **ED** Kobra Khodaparast. **DD** 070. **Circ:** 1,000.

US/0738-8411
FORUM INDEX, THE. (THE FORUM INDEX : AN INDEX TO THE DAILY NEWSPAPER, THE FORUM.). **Added/Corp** North Dakota State University. Library. Reference Dept. (1982)-. Newspaper. English. an. $25.00. North Dakota State University Library, Reference Department, Fargo ND 58105. **Tel** (701)237-8886. **LC** AI21.F67; F57. **DD** 071/.84/13. *Continues* Five Year Index to the Daily Newspaper the Forum, 0732-4367.
Desc: Indexes news items pertaining to the Red River Valley, North Dakota, and western Minnesota. Obituaries have been indexed beginning with 1985.

US/0098-6062
INDEX TO ST. LOUIS NEWSPAPERS. English. St Louis Public Library, 1301 Olive Street, St Louis MO 63103. **Tel** (314)241-2288. **LC** AI3; .I64. **DD** 016.071/78/66.

US
INTERNATIONAL MEDIA GUIDE. NEWSPAPERS WORLDWIDE : IMG. **Added/Corp** Directories International, Inc. International Media Enterprises. **VFOAT** Newspapers Worldwide. (198?)-. English. $157.50. IMG Inc., 85 Perimeter Road, Nashua NH 03063. **Tel** (603)882-9576, FAX (603)595-0437. *Continues* International Media Guide. Edition, Newspapers Worldwide, (OCoLC)9656645.

US/0190-7468
JOURNAL INDEX TO THE ALBUQUERQUE JOURNAL. (JOURNAL INDEX TO THE ALBUQUERQUE JOURNAL / COMPILED AND EDITED BY MARY S. RASK.). **VFOAT** Journal Index. (1979)-. English. Four times a year. $180.00. Raindance Enterprises, 3232 San Mateo Northeast, Suite 205, Albuquerque NM 87110. **Tel** (505)266-8098. **LC** AI21.A45; J68. **DD** 071/.89/61.

US/0273-3676
NATIONAL NEWSPAPER INDEX. (NATIONAL NEWSPAPER INDEX [MICROFORM].). [Natl. newsp. index]. **VFOAT** IAC National Newspaper Index; I.A.C. National Newspaper Index. **VAT** Information Access Corporation National Newspaper Index. (1979)-. Abstracting/Indexing Service. English. Twelve times a year. $1632.00. Information Access Company, 362 Lakeside Drive, Foster City CA 94404. **Tel** (800)227-8431. **(Subscription address:** Information Access Company, PO Box 61000, Department 1851, San Francisco CA 84161.**) DD** 071. available on an online database from DIALOG; available on microfiche; available on CD-ROM.
Desc: Provides comprehensive index coverage of five nationally distributed newspapers. Provides information to verify dates, create a chronology of events, track business news, follow election campaigns and legislative activities, locate editorials and speech transcripts, monitor public opinion, follow company announcements, and find biographies, interviews and obituaries.

US
NATIONAL NEWSPAPER INDEX (MONTHLY). (NATIONAL NEWSPAPER INDEX [COMPUTER FILE].). **Added/Corp** Information Access Company. (1988)-. Periodical. English. Twelve times a year. Information Access Company, 362 Lakeside Drive, Foster City CA 94404. **Tel** (800)227-8431. available on microfilm and microfiche; available on an online database.

US/0147-538X
NEW YORK TIMES INDEX, THE. **VFOAT** New York Times Index for the Published News. Vol. 1 (Jan./Mar. 1913)-. English. ir. The New York Times, 229 West 43rd Street, New York NY 10036. **Tel** (800)631-2580, (212)556-1234, FAX (212)556-4603. **LC** AI21; .N45. **DD** 071/.47/1. **NLM** ZAI 21 N44. *Supersedes* New York Times Index. Prior Series.

US/0095-5663
NEW YORK TIMES SCHOOL MICROFILM COLLECTION INDEX BY REELS, THE. English. Microfilming Corporation of America, 21 Harristown Road, Glen Rock NJ 07452. **LC** AI21.N44; N48. **DD** 071.

US
NEWSPAPER ABSTRACTS. (NEWSPAPER ABSTRACTS [ONLINE DATABASE].). Abstracting/Indexing Service. English. University Microfilms International, 300 North Zeeb Road, Ann Arbor MI 48106-1346. **Tel** (313)761-4700, (800)521-0600 Exts. 2490, 2491, FAX (313)973-1540. available on magnetic tape and CD-ROM from OCLC.
Desc: Part of the Newspaper & Periodical Abstracts Database, this portion features abstracting and indexing to significant articles from 27 regional and national newspapers.

US/1064-993X
NEWSPAPER ABSTRACTS ONDISC. (NEWSPAPER ABSTRACTS ONDISC : [COMPUTER FILE].). [Newsp. abstr. ondisc]. **Added/Corp** University Microfilms International. **VFOAT** Newspaper Abstracts on Disc; NA Ondisc. (19??)-. Abstracting/Indexing Service. English. mo. $2,950.00 (except the Americas) complete set; price varies for individual newspaper selections. University Microfilms International, 300 North Zeeb Road, Ann Arbor MI 48106-1346. **Tel** (313)761-4700, (800)521-0600 Exts. 2490, 2491, FAX (313)973-1540. **LC** AI1. **DD** 070. available on magnetic tape and an online database from OCLC EPIC; available in microform.
Desc: Cover-to-cover indexing to articles from eight of the nation's best newspapers. Coverage from 1985 forward for most newspapers. All subscriptions automatically include The New York Times, and all indexing is fully cross-referenced.

US
NEWSPAPER & PERIODICAL ABSTRACTS [ONLINE DATABASE]. Abstracting/Indexing Service. English. an. University Microfilms International, 300 North Zeeb Road, Ann Arbor MI 48106-1346. **Tel** (313)761-4700, (800)521-0600 Exts. 2490, 2491, FAX (313)973-1540. available on magnetic tape and CD-ROM from OCLC; and DIALOG.
Desc: Online service containing concise abstracts and thorough indexing for information from 1600 periodicals, 26 major newspapers and transcripts from nearly seventy television programs. Coverage dates from 1986. Transcripts available from: Journal Graphics, 1535 Grant Street, Denver, CO 80203; Telephone: (800)TALK-SHO.

US/0893-2425
SAN FRANCISCO CHRONICLE INDEX. [San Franc. chron. index]. **Added/Corp** University Microfilms International. (Jan. 1987)-. English. mo (with quarterly and annual cumulations). $680.00. University Microfilms International, 300 North Zeeb Road, Ann Arbor MI 48106-1346. **Tel** (313)761-4700, (800)521-0600 Exts. 2490, 2491, FAX (313)973-1540. **ED** Andrew Horvay. **LC** AI21.S25; S26. cum. index. *Continues* Bell & Howell Newspaper Index to the San Francisco Chronicle, 0195-6396.
Desc: Comprehensive subject index; includes access by personal and corporate name headings; informative abstracts.

GW/0341-7093
STAMM LEITFADEN DURCH PRESSE UND WERBUNG. [Stamm-Leitf. Presse Werb.]. **VFOAT** Leitfaden Durch Presse und Werbung; Presse- und Medien-Handbuch; Annual Directory Through Press and Advertising. Aug. 29 (1976)-. German (English, French and German). an. DM182.75 Germany; DM184.00 other. Stamm Verlag GmbH, Goldammerweg 16, D 45134 Essen Germany. **Tel** 011 49 201 41757. **ED** W. Stamm. **LC** Z6956.G3; L4; PN5208. **DD** 073. **NLM** Z 6956.G3 L718. **Ad Acc**. **Circ:** 8,500. *Continues* Stamm Leitfaden fur Presse und Werbung, 0341-7093.
Desc: Bibliography and description of newspapers and periodicals in Germany as well as of the most important abroad.

Alphabetical Title Index

The following index lists every primary title (Key Title/Title Statement) in the Directory, in alphabetical order. Main Entries are given with a "see" note to the primary title. Preceding entries are given with a "see" note to the primary title if the primary title has a CONSER publication start date (field 008/7-10) later than 1992. Country of publication and ISSN, when available, follow the primary title, as well as the CONSER control number in enclosed brackets. Page numbers printed in bold are the pages upon which the serial listing appears. Page numbers following the CONSER control number guide you to related subjects.

10.5155.20 : ART CONTEMPORAIN (CN/0714-6906) [09340492] **335**

● .22 RIMFIRE (US/1066-6834) [27028746] **4881**

1+1 (CN/0316-5051) [02247354] **2784**

1/1 (SAN FRANCISCO, CALIF.) (US/8756-7717) [11652544] 5315, **4098**

● 1-2-3 FOR MACINTOSH REPORT, THE (US/1058-6954) [24358477] **1283**

1-2-3 FOR WINDOWS REPORT, THE (US/1057-2333) [23983780] **1169**

● 1-2-3 SOFTWARE CONNECTION (US/1065-0768) [26515464] **1283**

1/2 DE CAMBIO (PE) [09879539] **1544**

● 1:87 SCALE (US/1055-6311) [23245629] **5375**

1:250,000 GEOLOGICAL SERIES. EXPLANATORY NOTES (AT) [01759969] **1364**

1:250,000 GEOLOGICAL SERIES EXPLANATORY NOTES. AUSTRALIAN NATIONAL GRID SHEET (AT) [01518690] **1364**

01 INFORMATIQUE (FR/0398-1185) [I03981185] **1169**

01 INFORMATIQUE. ANNUAIRE (FR/0299-5948) [15250759] **1169**

01 INFORMATIQUE (HEBDOMADAIRE) (FR/0298-2285) [14978816] **1246**

01 REFERENCES (PARIS) (FR/0997-654X) [21980561] **2484**

1 SOFT DECISION NEWS (US/0896-033X) [16892860] **1283**

1 TO ONE (MARKHAM, ONT.) (UK) [20136061] 1059, **5013**

1. [I.E. ERSTE] OSTERREICHISCHER MUSIK-EXPRESS (AU) [01789410] **4098**

● 1ST PLACE MARKETING (US/1062-2462) [25558158] **920**

1ST READING (SACRAMENTO, CALIF.) (US/0744-6748) [08490745] 3775, **2926**

2 D DRAMA, DANCE (UK/0261-6939) [08501011] 1310, **383**

2 MONDES (CN/1188-2506) [25796380] **5361**

2 RIVES, LES (CN/0710-5541) [08716770] **5779**

2 TO 22 DAYS AROUND THE GREAT LAKES (US/1058-6113) [23752110] **5458**

● 2 TO 22 DAYS IN ASIA (US/1062-4325) [25167663] **5458**

● 2 TO 22 DAYS IN AUSTRALIA (US/1062-4333) [25208043] **5458**

● 2 TO 22 DAYS IN EUROPE / RICK STEVES (US/1059-2946) [24536800] **5458**

● 2 TO 22 DAYS IN FLORIDA (US/1062-4341) [25222147] **5458**

2 TO 22 DAYS IN FRANCE (US/1059-8278) [24151018] **5458**

● 2 TO 22 DAYS IN GERMANY, AUSTRIA, AND SWITZERLAND (US/1058-6059) [24339028] **5458**

2 TO 22 DAYS IN GREAT BRITAIN (US/1058-6105) [24339576] 2513, **5458**

● 2 TO 22 DAYS IN HAWAII (US/1062-435X) [25167493] **5459**

● 2 TO 22 DAYS IN ITALY (US/1064-9328) [26464041] **5459**

2 TO 22 DAYS IN NEW ENGLAND / ANNE E. WRIGHT (US/1059-2962) [24150845] **5459**

2 TO 22 DAYS IN NEW ZEALAND (US/1062-4473) [24961782] **5459**

2 TO 22 DAYS IN NORWAY, SWEDEN, AND DENMARK (US/1058-6091) [24150993] **5459**

● 2 TO 22 DAYS IN SPAIN AND PORTUGAL (US/1058-6067) [24339133] **5459**

● 2 TO 22 DAYS IN THAILAND (US/1062-4570) [25624840] **5459**

● 2 TO 22 DAYS IN THE AMERICAN SOUTHWEST (US/1058-6075) [24339284] **5459**

2 TO 22 DAYS IN THE PACIFIC NORTHWEST (US/1059-2954) [24146441] **5459**

● 2 TO 22 DAYS IN THE ROCKIES (US/1058-6083) [24339498] **5459**

2 X 4 (CN/0824-0868) [13448643] **633**

2E WERELD (NE/0923-6198) [22514501] **4503**

2ND TIER, THE (CN/1183-6024) [24690811] **3543**

3-2-1 CONTACT (US/0195-4105) [05468966] 1720, **1059**

3/16 SCALE RAILROADING (US/1046-2147) [20365956] **5429**

3 & 4 WHEEL ACTION (US/0884-7126) [12414634] **4881**

3-D DATA (US/1044-7350) [17166851] **2436**

● 3-DIMENSIONAL ILLUSTRATORS AWARDS ANNUAL (US/1065-1276) [25904284] **376**

3 R, ROHRE, ROHRLEITUNGSBAU, ROHRLEITUNGSTRANSPORT (GW/0340-3386) [04295556] **2096**

3 R'S (FREDERICTON, N.B.) (CN/0710-7722) [08858322] **1720**

3. WELT MAGAZIN (GW/0002-0362) [04750512] **4514**

3D ARTIST (US/1058-9503) [24439537] **376**

3D LONDON ***SUSPENDED***. (UK/0953-2331) [I09532331] **1169**

3TECH (SANTA CLARA, CALIF.) (US/1051-9637) [22160502] **1240**

● 3W REGISTER OF CHINESE BUSINESS (US/1063-0503) [25516112] **1596**

3X/400 INFORMATION MANAGEMENT ***CEASED***. (US/1053-7015) [22611075] **858**

3X/400 SYSTEMS MANAGEMENT (US/1070-6097) [28438520] **1169**

4 FOR 20 (CN/0229-3684) [07970458] **4881**

4-H HAPPINESS (US) [06778889] **1059**

4-H NORTHERN NEWS (CN/1182-9796) [23659181] **42**

4-H SOUNDER (US/0740-848X) [08963810] **1059**

4E JOUR (CN/0820-8778) [09631075] **4931**

4SIGHT (US/0746-9837) [10446308] **4366**

4TH MEDIA JOURNAL ***See*** INTERACTIVE WORLD **1113**

4X4 MAGAZINE (FR/0247-6886) [I02476886] **4848**

● 5.0 MUSTANG (US/1073-4740) [29410906] **5403**

● 5-STAR INVESTOR (US/1065-3414) [26577080] **890**

5-YEAR CUMULATED BIBLIOGRAPHY OF ORTHOPAEDIC SURGERY (US/0146-5066) [02935043] **3654**

6-UHR-ABENDBLATT (AU) [20449742] **5777**

7/15, LE JOURNAL DES JEUNES (CN/0700-303X) [03279260] **5779**

7 DAYS (LONDON, ENGLAND) (UK) [14509311] **4539**

8-TRACK MIND MAGAZINE (US) **2770**

9-1-1 MAGAZINE (US/1040-7316) [18504989] 2287, **1103**

9H (UK/0144-7726) [09581230] **286**

11TH CIRCUIT LAW LETTER ***CEASED***. (US/0892-7308) [15248581] **2926**

12 UHR BLATT (AU) [20360968] **5777**

13TH MOON (US/0094-3320) [02587697] **3357**

13TH STREET JOURNAL, THE (US/1041-3111) [18759692] **311**

15-21 (TI) [09737363] **5041**

16 MAGAZINE (US/0270-899X) [05001590] **1059**

16 MM FILM CATALOGUE - RED RIVER COMMUNITY COLLEGE, LEARNING RESOURCES CENTRE (CN/0820-9545) [09654046] **4062**

16 MM. SOUND FREE LOAN FILMS, SALES AND RENTAL SUBJECTS ***See*** FREE LOAN FILMS **4071**

16 (NEW YORK, N.Y.) (US/1075-3109) [30017282] **1059**

16MM FILM ADDENDUM - MIDWESTERN REGIONAL LIBRARY SYSTEM (CN/0821-1116) [09770583] **4062**

16MM FILMS AVAILABLE FROM THE PUBLIC LIBRARIES OF METROPOLITAN TORONTO (CN/0315-7326) [02441924] **4062**

17 - 18 (FR/0291-3798) [11200239] **3357**

18 ALMANAC (US/0163-1640) [03276543] **1088**

18 KARATI (IT) [10990062] 2595, **4881**

19TH CENTURY MUSIC (US/0148-2076) [03280195] **4098**

20/20 (US/0192-1304) [04964595] **4214**

20/20 (US/1046-1566) [20340654] **821**

Alphabetical Title Index

20 / 20 EUROPE (US) **4214**

20/20'S ... ANNUAL REPORT OF THE OPTICAL INDUSTRY AND DISPENSING PROFESSIONS (US) [09239665] **4214**

20/20'S VISIONMONDAY (US/0891-1770) [14639843] **1596**

20 ANS (FR) **5550**

20 CENTURY BRITISH HISTORY (UK/0955-2359) [22481516] **2671**

20 DE MAYO (US/0164-5234) [04588367] 2253, **5631**

21.C (AT/1035-6754) [I10356754] **2609**

21MO : SECOLO SCIENZA E TECNOLOGIA (IT) **5078**

●21ST CENTURY AFRO REVIEW (US/1074-9144) [29875805] **2253**

21ST CENTURY CHRISTIAN MAGAZINE (US/1048-4124) [20962902] **4931**

●21ST CENTURY FUELS (US/1075-038X) [29924819] **4248**

21ST CENTURY POLICY REVIEW (US/1055-3630) [23159943] **2253**

21ST CENTURY SCIENCE & TECHNOLOGY (US/0895-6820) [16736129] **5078**

21ST GENERATION, THE (CN/0381-145X) [04129419] **2436**

22 DAYS AROUND THE WORLD (US/1062-4317) [21892797] **5459**

22 DAYS IN ASIA *See* 2 TO 22 DAYS IN ASIA **5458**

22 DAYS IN AUSTRALIA *See* 2 TO 22 DAYS IN AUSTRALIA **5458**

22 DAYS IN EUROPE *See* 2 TO 22 DAYS IN EUROPE / RICK STEVES **5458**

22 DAYS IN FLORIDA *See* 2 TO 22 DAYS IN FLORIDA **5458**

22 DAYS IN GERMANY, AUSTRIA, AND SWITZERLAND *See* 2 TO 22 DAYS IN GERMANY, AUSTRIA, AND SWITZERLAND **5458**

22 DAYS IN HAWAII *See* 2 TO 22 DAYS IN HAWAII **5459**

22 DAYS IN SPAIN AND PORTUGAL *See* 2 TO 22 DAYS IN SPAIN AND PORTUGAL **5459**

22 DAYS IN THAILAND *See* 2 TO 22 DAYS IN THAILAND **5459**

22 DAYS IN THE ROCKIES *See* 2 TO 22 DAYS IN THE ROCKIES **5459**

24 IMAGES (CN/0707-9389) [05841389] **4062**

24HOURS (SANTA MONICA, CALIF.) (US/1047-451X) [20696934] **2526**

25-1-1 (CN/0707-8544) [05257136] **2671**

25 I.E. VINTE E CINCO DE SETEMBRO (PO) [05542676] **4461**

29ER, THE (US/0494-3384) [06078403] **5632**

"30" (CN/0384-9325) [03402936] **2917**

30 I.E. TRENTE JOURS D'EUROPE *CEASED.* (FR) [01792124] **1544**

30 JOURS DANS L'EGLISE ET DANS LE MONDE (FR) [19402562] **5022**

30 MILLIONS D'AMIS, LA VIE DES BETES (FR/0246-2591) [I02462591] **1059**

30 MILLIONS D'AMIS PARIS. 1987 (FR/0984-4708) [I09844708] **5572**

33 METAL PRODUCING (US/0149-1210) [03451809] **1596**

35/70 : JOURNAL OF THE FEATURE FILM INDUSTRY (UK) [06307409] **4062**

36 CITIES : REAL ESTATE FORECAST AND REVIEW (US) [16965779] **4833**

49-50-51 FORD OWNERS NEWSLETTER *See* 1949-50-51 FORD/MERCURY OWNERS MAGAZINE **5403**

50 PLUS (DURHAM, ONT.) (CN/0840-5395) [19647490] **5177**

50-STATE LEGISLATIVE DIRECTORY (US) [20084645] **4461**

64'ER (GW/0176-8824) [I01768824] **1169**

65 A L'HEURE (CN) [01792193] **5269**

68 MICRO JOURNAL *CEASED.* (US/0194-5025) [04785369] **1265**

73 AMATEUR RADIO TODAY (US/1052-2522) [22239204] **1125**

80 I.E. DELAPAN PULUH, BUKU PUISI (IO) [02653407] **3459**

99 NEWS, THE (US/0273-608X) [06749114] **3**

100 A1 (UK/0266-8971) [04904425] **5447**

100 COMPANIES RECEIVING THE LARGEST DOLLAR VOLUME OF PRIME CONTRACT AWARDS / ISSUED BY DEPARTMENT OF DEFENSE, WASHINGTON HEADQUARTERS SERVICES, DIRECTORATE FOR INFORMATION OPERATIONS AND REPORTS (US) [08246742] **1596**

●100 DESIGNERS' FAVORITE ROOMS (US/1064-9948) [26479034] **2898**

100 HIGHEST YIELDS (US/0885-4777) [12642225] 890, **768**

100 MILE HOUSE FREE PRESS (CN/0843-0403) [19465390] **5779**

100 MODERN REAGENTS (UK) [20944838] **958**

100'S OF BAKING AND DESSERT IDEAS (US) [07864293] **2788**

100S OF IDEAS *CEASED.* (US/0278-8330) [07118404] **369**

100'S OF NEEDLEWORK & CRAFT IDEAS (US/0278-7504) [05898839] **5182**

123 USER'S JOURNAL (US/0891-5121) [14085292] **1283**

200 GROUPES FRANCAIS D'AFRIQUE NOIRE : A28 (FR) **5237**

200 PREMIERES BANQUES DU MONDE ARABE : A34 (FR) **768**

200TH HIGHEST HOUR TRAFFIC VOLUMES, TENNESSEE / PREPARED BY THE TENNESSEE DEPARTMENT OF TRANSPORTATION, BUREAU OF PLANNING AND DEVELOPMENT, PLANNING DIVISION, MAPPING AND STATISTICS OFFICE, TRAFFIC AND SAFETY PLANNING, IN COOPERATION WITH THE U.S. DEPARTMENT OF TRANSPORTATION, FEDERAL HIGHWAY ADMINISTRATION (US) [08674155] **5438**

201 (US/0730-7330) [08049217] **3357**

204 REPORTER (CN/0824-3573) [10386408] **1642**

303 (FR/0762-3291) [16912218] **335**

305(B) TECHNICAL REPORT FOR OKLAHOMA (US/0740-9923) [09923385] 5528, **2222**

370/390 DATA BASE MANAGEMENT (US/1056-974X) [23905904] **1252**

401 (K) REPORTER, THE (US/0884-7657) [12493251] **890**

483 VALIDATION MONITOR FOR STERILE, NON-STERILE AND MEDICAL DEVICES (US) [11050566] 4288, **3543**

500 CONTRACTORS RECEIVING THE LARGEST DOLLAR VOLUME OF PRIME CONTRACT AWARDS FOR RESEARCH, DEVELOPMENT, TEST, AND EVALUATION (US/0884-1314) [09878607] **4033**

501 (C)OMPUTING NEWS : AN INFORMATION NEWSLETTER SERVING THE 501(C) NON-PROFIT COMMUNITY (US/1056-2222) [23600308] **1169**

501(C)(3) MONTHLY LETTER (US/0897-5736) [15051739] **636**

596 (CN/0822-4331) [10381562] **4366**

800 900 REVIEW (US) **1148**

800 ITALIANO (IT) [25837424] **335**

0898 BRIEFING *See* AUDIOTEX BRIEFING **1149**

1,000 LARGEST GOVERNMENTS, THE (US/0883-413X) [12151215] **4623**

1000 LARGEST SAVINGS & LOANS / SHESHUNOFF (US) [11040345] **768**

1000 LARGEST U.S. BANKS (US/0361-4727) [02170003] **768**

1000 UND 1 BUCH (AU) **1059**

1001 & 1 BUCH (AU) **3186**

1001 CRAFT IDEAS (US/0276-9069) [07445167] **369**

1001 HOME IDEAS *SUSPENDED.* (US/0278-0844) [07701658] 369, **2898**

1033 BETTER WAYS TO DO IT *See* BETTER WAYS TO DO IT **370**

1040 PREPARATION (US/0363-2997) [02438994] **4708**

1040NR FORMS AND INSTRUCTIONS (US) [25769057] **4708**

1199 DRUG & HOSPITAL NEWS *See* 1199 NEWS **1642**

1199 NEWS (US/0012-6535) [04625424] 3775, **1642**

1199 NEWS / LOCAL 1199 DRUG, HOSPITAL AND HEALTHCARE EMPLOYEES UNION (US) [24930805] **1642**

1441 (CN/0824-4561) [10615573] **5779**

1590 BROADCASTER (US/0192-8597) [05119839] **5707**

●1650-1850 (NEW YORK, N.Y.) (US/1065-3112) [26569919] 335, **4339**

1810 OVERTURE (US/0093-0288) [01791050] **4098**

1851 CENSUS INDEX SERIES (UK/0263-5712) [13211856] **2436**

1869 TIMES (US/0363-6542) [02487396] **2784**

●1949-50-51 FORD/MERCURY OWNERS MAGAZINE (US/1068-1256) [27447545] **5403**

1990 CENSUS PROFILE (US) [24100662] **2812**

●1991 CENSUS OF CANADA, INFORMATION RELEASE (CN/1193-2732) [26776095] **4549**

1992 AND AFTER (UK) [20079449] **2513**

1992 AND BEYOND *CEASED.* (US/1049-6645) [21274451] **1632**

●1992 DIRECTORY OF AGING RESOURCES (US/1061-3056) [25236752] 3748, **5269**

1992 LECTURE SERIES WORKING PAPERS (US/1046-1671) [20340791] **2717**

1992 M & A MONTHLY *See* TRANSLINK'S 1992 M & A MONTHLY **716**

1992, THE EXTERNAL IMPACT OF EUROPEAN UNIFICATION (US/1043-4380) [19477440] **1632**

1999 (GW/0930-9977) [17153470] **4539**

1999 NOW / A EUROPEAN REVIEW PUBLISHED QUATERLY BY IBM EUROPE (FR) [24168645] **1632**

2000 AD PRESENTS (US/1043-3635) [19409246] **1059**

2000, AN (CN/0227-261X) [08503294] **4856**

2000-YON (KO) [10248884] **2501**

2001 DOIS MIL E UM (BL) [01787527] **2551**

2600 (US/0749-3851) [11124041] **1225**

AP3SCEP2SWP (HOUSTON, TEX.) (US/1053-4288) [22529303] **1642**

A-95 CLEARINGHOUSE REPORT (US/0148-2289) [03253029] **2812**

A.A.G. BYDRAGEN (NE/0511-0726) [03191516] **42**

A.A. GRAPEVINE, THE (US) [04307135] **1338**

A A R N NEWSLETTER (CN/0001-0197) [03317750] **3849**

A. A.'S FAR EAST BUSINESSMAN'S DIRECTORY (HK/0532-9175) [01784505] **821**

A & V, MONOGRAFIAS DE ARQUITECTURA Y VIVIENDA (SP/0213-487X) [16630487] **286**

A & W BASICS IN MEDICINE SERIES (US/1057-9575) [24171366] **3543**

A (BROOKLYN, N.Y.) (US/0732-4650) [07061279] **3357**

A.C.A. INDUSTRY GUIDE TO HEARING AIDS. INTERNATIONAL EDITION (US/0095-3474) [01796573] **4382**

A.C. BRABY (PTY) LTD *See* BRABY'S CAPE PROVINCE DIRECTORY **5500**

A. C. C. L. UNION LIST OF SERIALS (CN/0226-7195) [06562318] **3136**

A/C FLYER, THE (US/0194-8652) [05062494] **3**

A.C. NIELSEN COMPANY *See* NIELSEN REPORT ON TELEVISION / NIELSEN MEDIA RESEARCH **1135**

A C P D Q BULLETIN (CN/0384-5915) [03248442] 3912, **1314**

A C P NEWSLETTER (CN/0700-3579) [03304200] **4811**

A C P NOTEBOOK (CN/0705-6621) [04097925] **4811**

A.C.T. PAPERS ON EDUCATION (AT/0726-6553) [I07266553] 1799, **1720**

A.C.T. PAPERS ON EDUCATION : A PUBLICATION OF THE SCHOOL OF TEACHER EDUCATION, CANBERRA COLLEGE OF ADVANCED EDUCATION (AT) [07515729] **1720**

A-D AN INTIMATE JOURNAL FOR ART DIRECTORS, PRODUCTION MANAGERS, AND THEIR ASSOCIATES (US) [01922070] **753**

A.D.P.H.S.O (FR/0339-8854) [I03398854] **3775**

A DEBRECENI AGRARTUDOMANYI EGYETEM TUDOMANYOS KOZLEMENYEI (HU) [07485982] **42**

A.E.A. DIRECTORY OF TRACTORS AND AGRICULTURAL MACHINERY (UK) [01938730] **158**

A-E BUSINESS REVIEW (US) 1963, **286**

A-E-C AUTOMATION NEWSLETTER (US/0277-1659) [07516099] 597, 2108, **286**

A/E/C SYSTEMS COMPUTER SOLUTIONS (US/1061-7663) [25454623] **1246**

A.E. LEGAL NEWSLETTER (US/0090-2411) [01784870] 1963, **286**

A/E MARKETING JOURNAL (US/0732-7943) [08435389] 286, **920**

A.E. RES (US/0545-4441) [C4176685] 1459, **42**

A.F.P. SCIENCES (FR/0397-829X) [I0397829X] **5079**

A.G.R (US/0095-2486) [04198294] **42**

A.G.R.A. FRANCE (FR/0183-7656) [I01837656] **42**

Alphabetical Title Index — AAEC

A.G.T. DOKUMENTATION (GW) [08250338] **2034**

A GRANJA : UMA REVISTA RURAL AO SERVICO DO RIO GRANDE DO SUL (BL) [09798753] **42**

A.H. AUMONERIES DES HOPITAUX (FR/0241-5089) [I02415089] 2248, **3543**

A.H.E.A. ACTION (US/0194-7176) [02253977] **2788**

A.H.M.H. INC. : ASSOCIATION DU HOCKEY MINEUR DE HULL INC (CN/0826-2314) [10926576] **4881**

A.I.D. BIBLIOGRAPHY SERIES : DEVELOPMENT ADMINISTRATION (US/0362-644X) [02314279] **1528**

A.I.D. ECONOMIC DATA BOOK. AFRICA (US) [03339496] **1459**

A.I.D. ECONOMIC DATA BOOK, EAST ASIA (US) [03342751] **1459**

A.I.D. ECONOMIC DATA BOOK, LATIN AMERICA (US) [03339524] **1459**

A.I.D. ECONOMIC DATA BOOK, NEAR EAST AND SOUTH ASIA (US/0503-4922) [03342810] 2907, **2913**

A.I.D. EVALUATION SPECIAL STUDY (US/0735-1488) [08576244] **5079**

A. I. D. MEMORY DOCUMENTS (US/0091-2840) [01786847] 1459, **1528**

A.I.D. REFERENCE CENTER *See* A. I. D. MEMORY DOCUMENTS **1528**

A.I.D. RESEARCH AND DEVELOPMENT ABSTRACTS (US/0096-1507) [01798797] 2907, **2913**

A.I.I. JOURNAL (AT/0314-8580) [I03148580] **2872**

A.I.M (US) [06742368] 5269, **5177**

A I M L S SELF ASSESSMENT PROGRAMMES SERIES (AT) **3891**

A.I.P. CANADA (ENGLISH ED.) (CN/0825-5229) [10884335] **3**

A.I.P.P.I. : JOURNAL OF THE JAPANESE GROUP OF AIPPI (JA) [07742802] **1300**

A.I.R. DIRECTORY OF RADIO PROGRAMMING (US/0278-4467) [07782916] **1125**

A IDEIA (PO) [10133643] **4539**

A.L.B.A. BOWLS (US/0001-1754) [03970778] **4881**

A LA PAGE (STE-MARIE) (CN/0824-1481) [11847643] **5779**

A L'AUTRE, UNE *CEASED.* (CN/0824-8230) [11245751] **3755**

A.M. AMMINISTRAZIONE & MANAGEMENT (IT/1121-0788) [I11210788] 858, **4623**

A.M. BEST COMPANY *See* BEST'S EXECUTIVE DATA SERVICE. REPORT A7-, FIVE YEAR EXPERIENCE BY STATE **2875**

A.M. BEST COMPANY *See* BEST'S RETIREMENT INCOME GUIDE **2876**

A.M. BEST COMPANY *See* BEST'S UNDERWRITING GUIDE FOR COMMERCIAL LINES **2876**

A.M. BEST COMPANY *See* BEST'S EXECUTIVE DATA SERVICE. REPORT A 4 - HIGH RISK AUTO STUDY **2875**

A.M. BEST COMPANY *See* BEST'S INSURANCE SECURITIES RESEARCH SERVICE **2876**

A.M. BEST COMPANY *See* BEST'S EXECUTIVE DATA SERVICE: LIFE-HEALTH INDUSTRY MARKETING RESULTS **2875**

A.M. BEST COMPANY *See* BEST'S EXECUTIVE DATA SERVICE. REPORT A6- COMPARATIVE EXPERIENCE BY STATE (STATE LEADERS) **2875**

A.M.C. MAINE MOUNTAIN GUIDE, THE (US/0514-9738) [01143790] **4868**

A.M.E. CHURCH REVIEW, THE (US/0360-3725) [01856226] **4931**

A.M.E. ZION QUARTERLY REVIEW, THE (US/0360-3717) [07050414] **5054**

A. MAGAZINE (US/1070-9401) [26920970] **2253**

"A" MAGAZINE (US) [03288808] **286**

A MAGYAR TALALKOZO KRONIKAJA (US/0580-4760) [01789477] **2671**

A.N.A. AUDIOLOGIA PROTESICA *CEASED.* (SP) **3885**

A.N.C.O.L.D. BULLETIN (AT/0045-0731) [I00450731] **1963**

A.N.CH.A. AGENCIA NOTICIOSA CHILENA ANTIFASCISTA (EDICION INGLESA) (CN/0229-1347) [08010314] **4539**

A P C O PUBLIC SAFETY COMMUNICATIONS (US) [02251061] 1103, **4763**

A.P.C. REVIEW (AT/0313-380X) [I0313380X] **1720**

A.P.E.P. (ENGLISH EDITION) (CN) [08507307] **4461**

A.P.L.I.C. SPECIAL PUBLICATION (US/0883-7376) [06577125] **3186**

A PRIORI (OTTAWA) (CN/0838-5009) [19032698] **1859**

A PROPOS - AMERICAN CENTER OF UNIMA (US/0275-9195) [07144048] **388**

A PROPOS (MONTREAL) (CN/1183-2096) [24368694] **3630**

A/R/C, ARCHITECTURE, RESEARCH, CRITICISM *SUSPENDED.* (CN/1180-0933) [22470944] **286**

A.R.P.S. YEAR BOOK & STEAM PRESERVATION GUIDE (UK) [01784673] **5429**

A.R. PRESS BOLETIN (AG) **2484**

A.R.S. S. AGRICULTURAL RESEARCH SERVICE. SOUTHERN REGION (US/0092-1939) [01787553] **42**

A RAYONS OUVERTS (CN/0835-8672) [17556593] **3186**

A.S.A. ARTISAN (US/0892-3582) [15175732] **335**

A + S AKTUELL (GW/0178-0999) [I01780999] **4763**

A.S.F. DOCUMENTATION (FR) [02382781] **2671**

A S T I S CURRENT AWARENESS BULLETIN (CN/0705-8454) [04589574] **406**

A SINISTRA (IT) **4461**

A + T (AT) [24118293] **335**

A.T.A. JOURNAL (HK/1015-8138) [I10158138] **5347**

A T A MAGAZINE (CN/0380-9102) [03317788] **1887**

A T A NEWS (CN/0001-267X) [03317824] **1887**

A.T.A. NEWS BULLETIN *See* TRANSPORT TOPICS **5396**

A T E N S CONFERENCE REPORT (CN/0705-8586) [04249987] 1887, **3357**

● A TO Z (US/1059-5112) [24608808] **2185**

A TO Z OF WHO IS WHO IN AUSTRALIA'S HISTORY, THE (AT) [19976534] **2668**

A TRAVERSO (IT) [18251794] **2484**

A + U (JA/0389-9160) [03010408] 2812, **286**

A.U.A. TODAY (US/1046-1051) [20333533] **3987**

A.U.M.L.A (AT/0001-2793) [01518636] 3337, **3260**

A.V. GUIDE (US/0091-360X) [01096985] **1887**

A-V ONLINE [COMPUTER FILE] (US) [17626253] **1887**

A.W. MELLON LECTURES IN THE FINE ARTS (US/0065-0129) [01981579] **311**

A.W.R. BULLETIN (AU/0001-2947) [01951106] **5269**

A-Z BUSINESS INFORMATION SOURCES (UK) **636**

A-Z OF EUROPEAN BUSINESS INFORMATION SOURCES (UK) **636**

A-Z OF UK MARKETING DATA, THE (UK) [08355954] **920**

A2-CENTRAL (US/0885-4017) [19224078] **1170**

A3 (CN/0824-5576) [11240741] 335, **287**

A3 TIMES (UK) [21309600] **287**

AA CAMPING AND CARAVANNING IN BRITAIN (UK) [09387629] 5403, **4868**

AA EVENTS (UK) **287**

AA FILES (UK/0261-6823) [09116240] **287**

AA GUIDE TO CAMPING AND CARAVANNING (UK) [03981344] 4868, **5500**

AA HANDBOOK (ZA) [01792165] **5403**

AAA, ARBEITEN AUS ANGLISTIK UND AMERIKANISTIK (AU/0171-5410) [03593710] 3357, **3260**

AAA GUIDE (US) [20708945] **227**

AAA TRAVELER. MUSKINGUM AAA EDITION, THE (US/0744-6535) [08483205] 5459, **5403**

AAA WORLD (ALASKA, ED.) *See* AAA WORLD (ALASKA, HAWAII ED.) **5459**

AAA WORLD (ALASKA, HAWAII ED.) (US/1063-3863) [25993420] 5403, **5459**

AAA WORLD. HAWAII (US/0731-8723) [08267035] 5403, **5459**

AAA WORLD (HAWAII, ED.) *See* AAA WORLD (ALASKA, HAWAII ED.) **5459**

AAA WORLD (LOUISIANA) (US/0743-0736) [10502151] 5403, **5459**

AAA WORLD (LOUISIANA ED.) *See* AAA WORLD (LOUISIANA, MISSISSIPPI ED.) **5459**

AAA WORLD (LOUISIANA, MISSISSIPPI ED.) (US/1063-3871) [25994634] 5403, **5459**

AAA WORLD. MASSACHUSETTS (US/0277-1039) [07502576] 5403, **5459**

AAA WORLD (MASSACHUSETTS, ED.) *See* AAA WORLD (MASSACHUSETTS, NEW HAMPSHIRE ED.) **5459**

AAA WORLD (MASSACHUSETTS, NEW HAMPSHIRE ED.) (US/1063-388X) [25995659] 5403, **5459**

AAA WORLD (MISSISSIPPI ED.) *See* AAA WORLD (LOUISIANA, MISSISSIPPI ED.) **5459**

AAA WORLD (MISSISSIPPI EDITION) (US/0743-0663) [10502190] 5403, **5459**

AAA WORLD. NEW HAMPSHIRE (US/0277-1012) [07502524] 5403, **5459**

AAA WORLD (NEW HAMPSHIRE, ED.) *See* AAA WORLD (MASSACHUSETTS, NEW HAMPSHIRE ED.) **5459**

AAA WORLD (NEW MEXICO ED.) *See* AAA WORLD (TEXAS, NEW MEXICO, OKLAHOMA ED.) **5459**

AAA WORLD (OKLAHOMA ED.) *See* AAA WORLD (TEXAS, NEW MEXICO, OKLAHOMA ED.) **5459**

AAA WORLD. POTOMAC (US/0279-0270) [07502491] 5403, **5459**

AAA WORLD (TEXAS ED.) *See* AAA WORLD (TEXAS, NEW MEXICO, OKLAHOMA ED.) **5459**

AAA WORLD (TEXAS, NEW MEXICO, OKLAHOMA ED.) (US/1063-3898) [25997628] 5403, **5459**

AAA WORLD (VIRGINIA ED.) (US/1058-5052) [24322881] 5403, **5459**

AAA WORLD. WISCONSIN (US/0277-1411) [07509023] 5403, **5459**

AAAA ROSTER AND ORGANIZATION (US/0569-2407) [01698121] **753**

AAACE MEMBERSHIP DIRECTORY (US) [10293090] **1799**

AAAD BULLETIN, THE (US/1071-1414) [14766875] **4881**

AAAS HANDBOOK (US/1062-2195) [22135827] **5079**

● AAAS PROGRAM/ABSTRACTS / AMERICAN ASSOCIATION FOR THE ADVANCEMENT OF SCIENCE (US) [26883177] **5079**

AAAS PUBLICATION (US/0271-2229) [01479348] **5079**

AAAS SCIENCE AND TECHNOLOGY POLICY YEARBOOK (US) [24575485] **5079**

AAAS SELECTED SYMPOSIA SERIES *CEASED.* (US/0164-0429) [04562105] **5079**

AAASA NEWSLETTER (ET) [03674341] **42**

AAASS NEWSLETTER (US/0883-9549) [02160522] **2671**

AABB NEWS BRIEFS (US/8756-6095) [11615225] **3769**

AABB NEWSLETTER (UK) **439**

AABC NEWSLETTER (US/0094-260X) [01793468] **1806**

AACAR BULLETIN OF THE ASSOCIATION FOR THE ADVANCEMENT OF CENTRAL ASIAN RESEARCH (US/0898-6827) [17881653] **2644**

AACCLA OUTLOOK (US) [09468249] **817**

AACCLA REPORT (US) [01783718] **817**

AACD LEGAL SERIES, THE (US/1053-9549) [22699636] **2926**

AACG NEWSLETTER (US/0896-1654) [16942460] **1031**

AACHEN. TECHNISCHE HOCHSCHULE. INSTITUT FUR BAUFORSCHUNG *See* IBAC MITTEILUNGEN **616**

AACHENER GESCHICHTSVEREIN *See* ZEITSCHRIFT DES AACHENER GESCHICHTSVEREINS **2716**

AACHENER KUNSTBLATTER (DUMONT BUCHVERLAG) (GW/0515-0612) [00949859] **335**

AACHENER NACHRICHTEN (GW) [11975560] **5801**

AACHENER VOLKSZEITUNG (GW) [11975553] **5801**

AACJC MEMBERSHIP DIRECTORY (US) [16142296] **1806**

AACN CLINICAL ISSUES IN CRITICAL CARE NURSING (US/1046-7467) [20502221] **3849**

AACN NURSING SCAN IN CRITICAL CARE (US/1055-8349) [23352533] **3849**

AACP NEWS / AMERICAN ASSOCIATION OF COLLEGES OF PHARMACY (US) [07582928] **4288**

AACSB NEWSLINE (US/0360-697X) [01738521] 636, **1806**

AACTE DIRECTORY / AMERICAN ASSOCIATION OF COLLEGES FOR TEACHER EDUCATION (US/0516-9313) [24014192] **1859**

AADE EDITORS' JOURNAL (US/0160-6999) [03700923] **4811**

AAEA NEWSLETTER (AMES, IOWA) (US/0888-9651) [04649148] **42**

AAEC NUCLEAR NEWS (AT) [10186182] **1930**

AAEL NEWS BULLETIN (US/0883-0827) [12041414] **768**

AAEP REPORT (US) [20425020] **5501**

AAFDBI FITPRINTS *See* AFB ACTION **4763**

AAFP REPORTER (US/0896-6877) [01820305] **3736**

AAG-AAG (US/8756-7636) [11657290] **3459**

AAG NEWSLETTER (US/0275-3995) [04746297] **2553**

AAH EXAMINER : THE NEWSLETTER OF AFRICAN AMERICANS FOR HUMANISM (US) [25492270] 2253, **4339**

AAHE BULLETIN (US/0162-7910) [04232945] **1806**

AAHPERD UPDATE *See* ALLIANCE UPDATE **1854**

AAHS JOURNAL (US/0882-9365) [06430189] **3**

AAHS NEWSLETTER (US/0300-6875) [01421148] **3**

AAICJ NEWSLETTER (US/0893-0724) [11467319] **4503**

AAII JOURNAL, THE (US/0192-3315) [05015010] **890**

AALAS BULLETIN *See* CONTEMPORARY TOPICS IN LABORATORY ANIMAL SCIENCE **5508**

AALC REPORTER (US/0001-009X) [02171940] **1642**

AALL PUBLICATION SERIES (US) [01479378] **2926**

AALT TECHNICIAN (CN/0703-5276) [03781886] **3186**

AAMA APPAREL SALES COMPENSATION SURVEY *See* APPAREL SALES/MARKETING COMPENSATION SURVEY **921**

AAMA PERSONNEL POLICIES AND BENEFITS SURVEY (US/0161-4401) [03922333] 1642, **938**

AAMC CURRICULUM DIRECTORY (US/0092-0371) [01796755] 3543, **1806**

AAMC DIRECTORY *See* AAMC DIRECTORY OF AMERICAN MEDICAL EDUCATION **1806**

AAMC DIRECTORY OF AMERICAN MEDICAL EDUCATION (US/0360-7437) [01842359] 3543, **1806**

AAMC REPORTER (US) [24840023] **3543**

AAMI MEMBERSHIP DIRECTORY (US/0883-4172) [11940912] **3543**

AAMI NEWS (US/0739-0270) [09701038] **3543**

AAMI STANDARDS AND RECOMMENDED PRACTICES (US) [16417788] **3685**

AAMOA REPORTS (US/0360-7178) [01850606] 2253, **4098**

AAMVA BULLETIN / AMERICAN ASSOCIATION OF MOTOR VEHICLE ADMINISTRATORS (US/0001-0154) [01479386] 5403, **5399**

AAN ANNUAL CONVENTION REPORT (US/0098-5228) [02240113] **2416**

AANA JOURNAL (US/0094-6354) [01020703] 3680, **3849**

AANA NEWSBULLETIN (US/0199-2554) [04157072] 3680, **3849**

A&B COMPUTING (UK) **1170**

AANDRIJFTECHNIEK (NE/0165-5108) [I01655108] **2108**

AANSPRAAK AMSTERDAM (NE/0922-2928) [I09222928] **938**

AANVULLINGEN OP WARENWET (NE) **2325**

AANWINSTENLIJST : LIJST VAN AANWINSTEN DER BIBLIOTHEKEN VAN DE RPD EN HET HIROV (NE) [19769411] **2812**

AAOHN JOURNAL (US/0891-0162) [13035605] **3849**

AAOHN NEWS / AMERICAN ASSOCIATION OF OCCUPATIONAL HEALTH NURSES, INC (US/0746-620X) [10165044] **3850**

AAOMS DIRECTORY / AMERICAN ASSOCIATION OF ORAL AND MAXILLOFACIAL SURGEONS (US/0738-2375) [08855899] **1314**

AAP-AUPS UNIVERSITY PRESS STATISTICS (US/0094-7970) [01794987] **5320**

AAP PEDIATRIC UPDATE (US) **3899**

AAPG BULLETIN (US/0149-1423) [03569079] **4248**

AAPG CONTINUING EDUCATION COURSE NOTE SERIES (US/0270-8043) [03683563] **4248**

AAPG EXPLORER (US/0195-2986) [05523813] 4248, **1364**

AAPG MEMOIR (US/0271-8529) [06694528] **1364**

AAPG REPRINT SERIES (US/0272-1511) [03347541] 4248, **1364**

AAPG STUDIES IN GEOLOGY (US/0271-8510) [05983374] **4248**

AAPG TREATISE OF PETROLEUM GEOLOGY. ATLAS OF OIL AND GAS FIELDS (US/1043-6103) [19496282] **4248**

AAPMA RULES FOR SAFE TRANSPORT HANDLING & STORAGE OF DANGEROUS SUBSTANCES & OILS PORT AREAS (AT) **2222**

AAPPO JOURNAL (US/1054-5913) [22920052] **3775**

AAR RAILROAD COST INDEXES (US/0899-2029) [14440268] **5429**

AAR STUDIES IN RELIGION (US/0145-2789) [03247777] **4931**

AARBGER FOR NORDISK OLDKYNDIGHED OG HISTORIE / UDGIVNE AF DET KONGELIGE NORDISKE OLDSKRIFT-SELSKAB (DK) [01670110] 253, **2671**

AARBOG / KOEBSTADMUSEET "DEN GAMLE BY" (DK/0105-9254) [10187828] **2671**

AARBOK FOR UNIVERSITETET I BERGEN., MATEMATISK-NATURVITENSKAPELIG SERIE (NO/0522-9189) [02755527] **5079**

AARCTIMES (US/0893-8520) [15176922] **3947**

AARDAPPELWERELD (NE/0165-6031) [14472056] **161**

AARDE & I.E. EN KOSMOS (NE/0166-4786) [01799260] **5079**

AARDKUNDIGE MEDEDELINGEN (BE/0250-7803) [07494587] **1364**

AARDRIJKSKUNDE, DE (BE) [04810858] **2553**

AARHUS, DENMARK. UNIVERSITET. MATEMATISK INSTITUT *See* LECTURE NOTES SERIES - AARHUS, DENMARK. UNIVERSITET. MATEMATISK INSTITUT **3516**

AARHUS FRIMRKEHANDEL *See* AFA OSTEUROPA FRIMARKEHANDEL **2784**

AARHUS FRIMRKEHANDEL *See* AFA VESTEUROPA FRIMRKEKATALOG **2784**

AARHUS UNIVERSITET *See* AARSBERETNING **1806**

AARHUS UNIVERSITET *See* ACTA JUTLANDICA; AARSKRIFT ... HUMANISTISK SERIE **2841**

AARHUS UNIVERSITET. FYSISK INSTITUT *See* ANNUAL REPORT / INSTITUTE OF PHYSICS, AARHUS UNIVERSITY **4397**

AARHUS UNIVERSITET. GEOLOGISK INSTITUT *See* ARSBERETNING - AARHUS UNIVERSITET. GEOLOGISK INSTITUT **1366**

AARHUS UNIVERSITET. MATEMATISK INSTITUT *See* VARIOUS PUBLICATIONS SERIES - AARHUS UNIVERSITET. MATEMATISK INSTITUT **3540**

AARNA PULSE: ALBERTA ASSOCIATION OF REGISTERED NURSING ASSISTANTS *See* CHCG PULSE **3853**

AAROGRAM (CN/0833-4390) [16206139] **4248**

AARON BURR ASSOCIATION *See* CHRONICLE OF THE AARON BURR ASSOCIATION, THE **2728**

AAROT NEWSLETTER *See* PERSPECTIVES / ALBERTA ASSOCIATION OF REGISTERED OCCUPATIONAL THERAPISTS **3932**

AARP BULLETIN (US/1044-1123) [19685775] **5177**

AARSBERETNING (NO) [01460512] **1806**

AAS HISTORY SERIES (US/0730-3564) [03610810] **3**

AAS MICROFICHE SERIES (US/0065-7417) **3**

AAS MILAVNEWS *CEASED.* (UK) [02180203] **4033**

AASA EXECUTIVE HANDBOOK SERIES (US) [05236448] **1859**

AASA PROFESSOR, THE (US/0898-252X) [08808288] **1859**

AASHTO JOURNAL (US) **5375**

AASHTO QUARTERLY (US/0147-4847) [02716268] 597, **5375**

AASP NEWSLETTER (US/0732-6041) [07024990] **1364**

AASTARAAMAT (ER) [05038152] 4083, **227**

AATCC TECHNICAL MANUAL (US/0734-8894) [05277026] **5347**

AATF NATIONAL BULLETIN (US/0883-6795) [12192989] 1887, **3260**

AATSEEL'S NEWSLETTER / AMERICAN ASSOCIATION OF TEACHERS OF SLAVIC AND EAST EUROPEAN LANGUAGES (US) [04165938] 3260, **1720**

AATSP PORTUGUESE NATIONAL NEWSLETTER (US) [05423064] **3260**

AAU REPORTS / BOTANICAL INSTITUTE AARHUS UNIVERSITY (DK/0904-6453) [18934329] **496**

AAUG MONOGRAPH SERIES (US) [03380805] **4514**

AAUP BOOK SHOW CATALOGUE (US/0161-0988) [03822029] **4563**

AAVSO CIRCULAR (US/0197-2979) [04902039] **391**

AAVSO MONOGRAPH (US/0892-4244) [14115945] **391**

●AAVSO PHOTOELECTRIC PHOTOMETRY NEWSLETTER (US) **4432**

AAWH QUARTERLY (US) **2595**

AAZPA ... ANNUAL CONFERENCE PROCEEDINGS (US/0731-0390) [08077794] **5572**

AAZPA ANNUAL REPORT ON CONSERVATION AND SCIENCE (US/1061-9135) [24636787] **2185**

AAZPA REGIONAL CONFERENCE PROCEEDINGS (US/0731-0439) [08077599] **5572**

AB, ARHITEKTOV BILTIN (XV/0352-1982) [24531792] **287**

AB : ARQUITETURA BRASILEIRA *See* ARQUITETURA DO BRASIL : AB **292**

AB BOOKMAN'S WEEKLY (US/0001-0340) [02337289] **4822**

AB BOOKMAN'S YEARBOOK (US/0065-0005) [00924321] **4822**

AB (BRESCIA) (IT/0393-3369) [16274448] **2159**

AB TOUCH (US) **5054**

ABA BANK COMPLIANCE (US/0887-0187) [13704774] **768**

ABA BANKERS WEEKLY *See* BANKERS NEWS **776**

ABA BANKERS WEEKLY (US/0889-7662) [14056253] **768**

ABA BANKING JOURNAL (US/0194-5947) [04868109] **768**

ABA/BNA LAWYERS' MANUAL ON PROFESSIONAL CONDUCT. CURRENT REPORTS (US/0740-4050) [09935493] 2248, **2926**

ABA JOURNAL (US/0747-0088) [10269097] **2926**

ABA JOURNAL OF AFFORDABLE HOUSING & COMMUNITY DEVELOPMENT LAW (US/1061-4354) [25308952] 2926, **2812**

ABA JUVENILE & CHILD WELFARE LAW REPORTER (US/0887-896X) [13321981] 5269, **3119**

ABA NEWSWIRE (US) [04012618] **4822**

ABA SECTION OF TAXATION ANNUAL ADVANCED STUDY SESSIONS, ADVANCED TAX PLANNING FOR CLOSELY HELD BUSINESS : ALI-ABA COURSE OF STUDY, MATERIALS (US) [08406095] **3094**

ABA SECTION OF TAXATION ANNUAL ADVANCED STUDY SESSIONS. SELECTED PROBLEMS AND TECHNIQUES IN ESTATE PLANNING (US/0732-8184) [08423862] **3117**

ABA SOFTWARE REVIEW (US/0883-4695) [12157578] 1283, **2926**

ABAA NEWSLETTER, THE (US/1070-700X) [24151783] **4311**

ABACO (SP/0213-6252) [18514087] **5189**

ABACO (MADRID, SPAIN) (SP/0572-3000) [01460522] **3357**

ABACUS (MILAN, ITALY) (IT) [15563781] **287**

ABACUS (SYDNEY) (AT/0001-3072) [01460523] **735**

ABAP ANUARIO (BL) [08737611] **753**

●ABARE RESEARCH REPORT (AT/1037-8286) [26873208] **42**

ABATEMENT AND POLLUTION CONTROL TRAINING AND EDUCATIONAL PROGRAMS PRESENTED BY THE UNITED STATES ENVIRONMENTAL PROTECTION AGENCY (US/0093-1616) [01791551] **2222**

ABB REVIEW (SZ/1013-3119) [18439137] **2109**

ABBAY (ET/0244-8327) [06825901] **2636**

ABBEVILLE HERALD (US) [12599832] **5629**

ABBEVILLE MERIDIONAL (US) [17614629] **5683**

ABBEY (US) [02735612] **3357**

ABBEY CHRONICLE (UK/0957-1248) [I09571248] **3457**

ABBEY LETTER (US) [06009156] **4931**

ABBEY NEWSLETTER, THE (US/0276-8291) [04447717] **2478**

ABBIA *CEASED.* (CM/0001-3102) [01607717] **5267**

Alphabetical Title Index

ABBOTSFORD-CLEARBROOK DIRECTORY (BUSINESS EDITION) (CN/0380-5301) [02443246] **2553**

ABBOTT, LANGER & ASSOCIATES *See* INTER-CITY WAGE & SALARY DIFFERENTIALS **1680**

ABBOTT, LANGER & ASSOCIATES *See* SALARIES & BENEFITS IN BOAT MANUFACTURING **1709**

ABBOTT, LANGER & ASSOCIATES *See* COLLEGE RECRUITING REPORT **1660**

ABBOTT, LANGER & ASSOCIATES *See* SALARIES AND RELATED MATTERS IN THE SERVICE DEPARTMENT **1709**

ABBREVIATED ANNUAL REPORT / U.S. DEPARTMENT OF HEALTH AND HUMAN SERVICES, OFFICE OF INSPECTOR GENERAL (US) [10351872] **4623**

ABBWA JOURNAL (US/8756-0267) [11454782] 2253, **3357**

ABC (PE) [04425972] **2717**

ABC (SP) [01460447] **5810**

ABC (FR) [09089156] **2898**

ABC AIR CARGO GUIDE (UK) [26737781] 3, **5459**

ABC AIR TRAVEL ATLAS (UK) [07219974] 3, **5459**

ABC AIRWAYS MAP OF THE WORLD (FR) 3, **5459**

ABC AND D. ARCHITECT BUILDER CONTRACTOR AND DEVELOPER (UK/0966-9647) [I09669647] 597, **287**

ABC CRUISE AND FERRY GUIDE (UK) 3, **5459**

ABC DE LAS AMERICAS (US) [01792761] **2526**

ABC DER DEUTSCHEN WIRTSCHAFT. CD-ROM (GW) **1596**

ABC DER DEUTSCHEN WIRTSCHAFT. ORTSLEXIKON FUER WIRTSCHAFT UND VERKEHR (GW) [04259432] **1459**

ABC DER DEUTSCHEN WIRTSCHAFT. QUELLENWERK FUER EINKAUF-VERKAUF (GW) [04204534] **1459**

ABC DETAILS (US) **439**

ABC DOMINICAL (SP) **5810**

ABC (EDICION INTERNACIONAL) (SP) [10851855] **5810**

ABC EDITION, EUROP PRODUCTION *See* EUROP PRODUCTION **1634**

ABC EXECUTIVE FLIGHT PLANNER. ASIA, PACIFIC (UK/0959-2911) [I09592911] 636, **5459**

ABC EXECUTIVE FLIGHT PLANNER EUROPE MID EAST & AFRICA/ SEMIANNUAL FOR BENELUX/ FORMERLY ABC AIR EUROPE (UK) 3, **5459**

ABC EXECUTIVE FLIGHT PLANNER EUROPE, MIDDLE EAST, AFRICA (UK/0959-1389) [I09591389] 636, **5459**

ABC FILM REVIEW (UK/0001-0413) **4062**

ABC GUIDE TO INTERNATIONAL TRAVEL (UK/0141-6278) [I01416278] 3, **5459**

ABC INTERNATIONAL'S EXECUTIVE FLIGHT PLANNER *See* EXECUTIVE FLIGHT PLANNER. AMERICAS **5469**

ABC (MADRID, SPAIN : EDICION SEMANAL AEREA) *See* ABC (EDICION INTERNACIONAL) **5810**

ABC NEWS INDEX (US/0891-8775) [15049670] **1125**

ABC OF SOCIAL AND POLITICAL KNOWLEDGE (RU) [13320804] 4461, **5189**

ABC PASSENGER SHIPPING GUIDE (UK/0001-0480) [13474327] **5447**

ABC POL SCI. ADVANCE BIBLIOGRAPHY OF CONTENTS: POLITICAL SCIENCE & GOVERNMENT (US/0001-0456) [00809405] 4461, **4501**

ABC RAIL GUIDE (UK/0001-0472) [I00010472] 3, **5460**

●ABC TODAY (US/1062-3698) [25403622] **597**

ABC TRAVEL DIRECTORY (UK) **5460**

ABC TRAVEL GUIDES LTD *See* ABC AIR TRAVEL ATLAS **5459**

ABC WORLD AIRWAYS GUIDE, THE (UK) [08693838] 3, **5460**

ABC WORLDWIDE HOTEL GUIDE (UK) [13984748] **2803**

ABCS OF THE CALIFORNIA BOATING LAW (US) [02239434] **591**

ABD (US/0001-0502) [02161406] **3**

ABD. ASIAN/PACIFIC BOOK DEVELOPMENT (JA/0916-7838) [I09167838] **4822**

●ABDOMINAL IMAGING (US/0942-8925) [27261530] **3938**

ABECOR COUNTRY REPORT. BOLIVIA, PARAGUAY, AND URUGUAY (UK) [20784874] **1544**

ABECOR COUNTRY REPORTS (UK) **1459**

ABEGWEIT REVIEW (CN/0382-4632) [02627832] **2253**

ABEILLE (CN/0821-5111) [09606622] **5572**

ABEILLE DE FRANCE ET L'APICULTEUR, L' (FR/0373-4625) [01460529] **5573**

ABEILLE DE FRANCE ET L'APICULTEUR, L' (FR/0373-4625) [08250490] **42**

ABEND (VIENNA, AUSTRIA : 1918) (AU) [20255531] **5777**

●ABERATIONS (WALNUT CREEK, CALIF.) (US/1058-2509) [24250074] **3357**

ABERDEEN AMERICAN-NEWS (US/1074-7117) [12893827] **5743**

ABERDEEN EXAMINER (ABERDEEN, MISS.: 1866) (US/1055-3061) [10079680] **5704**

ABERDEEN PETROLEUM QUARTERLY (UK/0956-6333) [I09566333] **4248**

ABERDEEN PETROLEUM REPORT (UK/0263-5054) [I02635054] **4249**

ABERDEEN TIMES, THE (US) [18409502] **5674**

ABERDEEN UNIVERSITY AFRICAN STUDIES GROUP *See* BULLETIN OF THE ABERDEEN UNIVERSITY AFRICAN STUDIES GROUP **2638**

ABERDEEN UNIVERSITY REVIEW (UK/0001-320X) [01460538] **1088**

ABERDEEN'S CONCRETE CONSTRUCTION (US/1051-5526) [21986073] **597**

ABERDEEN'S CONCRETE TRADER (US/1055-0356) [23063335] **597**

ABERDEEN'S CONSTRUCTION MARKETING TODAY (US/1051-483X) [21977813] 920, **597**

ABERDEEN'S MAGAZINE OF MASONRY CONSTRUCTION (US/1055-4408) [22584221] **597**

ABERDEEN'S PARKING AREA MAINTENANCE & INTERNATIONAL SWEEPER (US/1051-4856) [21977806] **2222**

ABERDEEN'S PAVEMENT MAINTENANCE (US/1051-4848) [21977809] **5438**

ABERDEEN'S PAVEMENT MAINTENANCE TRADER (US/1053-2870) [22502190] **5438**

ABERNATHY WEEKLY REVIEW, THE (US/0895-4291) [13826661] **5746**

ABFALLWIRTSCHAFT IN FORSCHUNG UND PRAXIS (GW) [14105862] **2222**

ABG *CEASED.* (GW) [02359706] **5189**

ABHA. ANNUAL BIBLIOGRAPHY OF THE HISTORY OF THE PRINTED BOOK AND LIBRARIES (NE/0303-5964) [01791729] 3186, **3257**

ABHANDLUNGEN (GW) [02365553] **3337**

ABHANDLUNGEN AUS DEM GEBIETE DER AUGENHEILKUNDE (GW/0567-4921) [07354638] **3871**

ABHANDLUNGEN AUS DEM INDUSTRIESEMINAR DER UNIVERSITAT ZU KOLN (GW/0531-0350) [03211705] **1806**

ABHANDLUNGEN AUS DEM LANDESMUSEUM FUR NATURKUNDE ZU MUNSTER IN WESTFALEN (GW) [02487628] 4161, **4083**

ABHANDLUNGEN AUS DEM MATHEMATISCHEN SEMINAR DER HAMBURGISCHEN UNIVERSITAT (GW/0025-5858) [01913576] **3490**

ABHANDLUNGEN - BAYERISCHE AKADEMIE DER WISSENSCHAFTEN, PHILOSOPHISCH-HISTORISCHE KLASSE (GW) [01478730] **1073**

ABHANDLUNGEN DER AKADEMIE DER WISSENSCHAFTEN DER DDR (GW/0302-8054) [01792807] **5079**

ABHANDLUNGEN DER AKADEMIE DER WISSENSCHAFTEN IN GOTTINGEN. MATHEMATISCH-PHYSIKALISCHE KLASSE (GW/0341-9843) [02884114] 1806, 4395, **3490**

ABHANDLUNGEN DER AKADEMIE DER WISSENSCHAFTEN IN GOTTINGEN. PHILOLOGISCH-HISTORISCHE KLASSE (GW/0930-4304) [19833767] **1073**

ABHANDLUNGEN DER BRAUNSCHWEIGISCHEN WISSENSCHAFTLICHEN GESELLSCHAFT (GW/0068-0737) [02812072] **5079**

ABHANDLUNGEN DER DEUTSCHEN ORIENT-GESELLSCHAFT (GW/0417-2442) [05014172] 1806, **253**

ABHANDLUNGEN DER GEISTES- UND SOZIALWISSENSCHAFTLICHEN KLASSE / AKADEMIE DER WISSENSCHAFTEN UND DER LITERATUR (GW/0002-2977) [01478740] **5189**

ABHANDLUNGEN DER GEOLOGISCHEN BUNDESANSTALT (AU/0378-0864) [08492152] 1806, **1364**

ABHANDLUNGEN DER HEIDELBERGER AKADEMIE DER WISSENSCHAFTEN, PHILOSOPHISCH-HISTORISCHE KLASSE (GW/0017-9574) [01751944] 2609, **4339**

ABHANDLUNGEN DER KAISERLICH-KONIGLICHEN GEOLOGISCHEN REICHSANSTALT *See* ABHANDLUNGEN DER GEOLOGISCHEN BUNDESANSTALT **1364**

ABHANDLUNGEN DER KLASSE DER LITERATUR / AKADEMIE DER WISSENSCHAFTEN UND DER LITERATUR (GW/0002-2985) [01478741] **3357**

ABHANDLUNGEN DER MATHEMATISCH-NATURWISSENSCH AFTLICHEN KLASSE - AKADEMIE DER WISSENSCHAFTEN UND DER LITERATUR (GW/0002-2993) [01478742] 3490, 3543, **5079**

●ABHANDLUNGEN DER NORDRHEIN-WESTFAELISCHEN AKADEMIE DER WISSENSCHAFTEN. SONDERREIHE PAPYROLOGICA COLONIENSIA (GW) [30559815] **5079**

ABHANDLUNGEN DER RHEINISCH-WESTFAELISCHEN AKADEMIE DER WISSENSCHAFTEN. SONDERREIHE PAPYROLOGICA COLONIENSIA (GW/0078-9410) [10478495] **5079**

ABHANDLUNGEN DER SACHSISCHEN AKADEMIE DER WISSENSCHAFTEN ZU LEIPZIG. MATHEMATISCH-NATURWISSENSCHAFTLICHE KLASSE (GW/0365-6470) [06506144] **5079**

ABHANDLUNGEN DER SACHSISCHEN AKADEMIE DER WISSENSCHAFTEN ZU LEIPZIG, PHILOLOGISCH-HISTORISCHE KLASSE (GW/0080-5297) [01764732] **2671**

ABHANDLUNGEN DER SENCKENBERGISCHEN NATURFORSCHENDEN GESELLSCHAFT (GW/0365-7000) [06569735] **4161**

ABHANDLUNGEN DES METEOROLOGISCHEN DIENSTES DER DEUTSCHEN DEMOKRATISCHEN REPUBLIK *CEASED.* (GW/0138-5658) [02611656] 1806, **1419**

ABHANDLUNGEN FUER DIE KUNDE DES MORGENLANDES / HRSG. VON DER DEUTSCHEN MORGENLANDISCHEN GESELLSCHAFT (LH/0567-4980) [08995490] 3357, **3260**

ABHANDLUNGEN. ISLAMISCHE REIHE (GW/0418-9728) [05181409] **253**

ABHANDLUNGEN. KOPTISCHE REIHE (GW/0417-3341) [05037386] **253**

ABHANDLUNGEN UND BERICHTE DES NATURKUNDEMUSEUMS GORLITZ (GW/0373-7586) [03325199] **4161**

ABHANDLUNGEN UND BERICHTE DES STAATLICHEN MUSEUMS FUER VOLKERKUNDE, DRESDEN (GW/0070-7295) [01687676] **4083**

ABHANDLUNGEN UND MATERIALIEN ZUR PUBLIZISTIK (GW/0065-0323) [02757964] **2609**

ABHANDLUNGEN ZUR HANDELS-UND SOZIALGESCHICHTE (GE) [08359775] **5189**

ABHANDLUNGEN ZUR KARST- UND HOHLENKUNDE. REIHE A. SPELAOLOGIE (GW) [07849733] **1402**

ABHANDLUNGEN ZUR KARST- UND HOHLENKUNDE. REIHE F : GESCHICHTE DER SPELAEOLOGIE, BIOGRAPHIEN, VOLKSKUNDE (GW/0176-2540) [06537431] **1402**

ABHANDLUNGEN ZUR KUNST-, MUSIK- UND LITERATURWISSENSCHAFT (GW/0567-4999) [01460552] 4098, 3357, **311**

ABHANDLUNGEN ZUR SPRACHE UND LITERATUR (GW/0178-8515) [01788515] 3260, **3357**

ABHANDLUNGEN ZUR THEOLOGIE DES ALTEN UND NEUEN TESTAMENTS (SZ) [01460555] **5013**

ABHATH (MR) [11901563] **5189**

ABHATH ARABIYAH (FR) [05213785] **2644**

ABHIGYAN : THE JOURNAL OF FOUNDATION OF ORGANISATIONAL RESEARCH (II) [12704234] **858**

ABHINAYA (II) [03435699] 5361, **3357**

ABHIRUCI (NEW DELHI, INDIA) (II) [08619711] **3357**

ABI/INFORM GLOBAL EDITION [COMPUTER FILE] (US) 636, **725**

ABI/INFORM ONDISC (US/1062-5127) [19615230] 636, **725**

ABI/INFORM ONDISC: EXPRESS EDITION [COMPUTER FILE] (US) 636, **725**

ABI-TECHNIK (GW/0720-6763) [09346082] **3186**

ABIDJAN — Alphabetical Title Index

ABIDJAN, IVORY COAST. UNIVERSITE See CIRES, CAHIERS IVOIRIENS DE RECHERCHE ECONOMIQUE ET SOCIALE **1551**

ABIDJAN, IVORY COAST. UNIVERSITE See ANNALES DE L'UNIVERSITE D'ABIDJAN. SERIE G : GEOGRAPHIE **2554**

ABIDJAN, IVORY COAST. UNIVERSITE See ANNALES DE L'UNIVERSITE D'ABIDJAN. SERIE I : HISTOIRE **2637**

ABILENE REFLECTOR-CHRONICLE (US/0890-345X) [11098331] **5668**

ABILENE REPORTER-NEWS (US/0199-3267) [03967993] **5746**

ABILITIES (CALGARY) (CN/0845-4469) [19900744] **4382**

ABILITY AND ENTERPRISE (CN/0832-7890) [15609255] **5269**

● ABILITY MAGAZINE (IRVINE, CALIF.) (US/1062-5321) [25649522] **2484**

● ABILITY NETWORK (CN/1192-1188) [27898479] **4503**

ABINGDON CLERGY INCOME TAX GUIDE (US/0163-1241) [03887517] **4708**

ABINGDON CLERGY TAX RECORD BOOK (US/0734-8606) [08879320] **4708**

ABINGDON PREACHER'S ANNUAL (US/1047-5486) [20709677] **4931**

ABINGTON JOURNAL (CLARKS SUMMIT, PA.) (US) [16314432] **5734**

ABIRA DIGEST (US/0196-0652) [05729339] **429**

ABITARE (IT/0001-3218) [01460559] 2898, **287**

ABITARE CON ARTE (IT/1120-6772) [11206772] **2898**

ABITIBI-PRICE (CN/0705-7490) [04233455] **5779**

ABLATIVE (AT/0814-5180) [I08145180] **636**

ABM (AT) **636**

ABMD DIRECTORY OF CERTIFIED EMERGENCY PHYSICIANS (US/0742-0366) [10236263] **3723**

ABMS COMPENDIUM OF CERTIFIED MEDICAL SPECIALISTS See OFFICIAL AMERICAN BOARD OF MEDICAL SPECIALTIES (ABMS) DIRECTORY OF BOARD CERTIFIED MEDICAL SPECIALISTS, THE **3623**

ABMS DIRECTORY OF CERTIFIED ALLERGY AND IMMUNOLOGY PHYSICIANS (US/0883-2994) [12100616] 3912, **3662**

ABMS DIRECTORY OF CERTIFIED ANESTHESIOLOGISTS (US/0883-122X) [12064943] 3912, **3680**

ABMS DIRECTORY OF CERTIFIED COLON AND RECTAL SURGEONS (US/0884-1470) [12208089] 3912, **3957**

ABMS DIRECTORY OF CERTIFIED DERMATOLOGISTS (US/0884-1489) [12264737] 3912, **3717**

ABMS DIRECTORY OF CERTIFIED FAMILY PHYSICIANS (US/0884-643X) [12401697] 3912, **3736**

ABMS DIRECTORY OF CERTIFIED INTERNISTS (US/0884-6448) [12401645] 3912, **3794**

ABMS DIRECTORY OF CERTIFIED NEUROLOGICAL SURGEONS (US/0882-2832) [10874761] 3912, **3957**

ABMS DIRECTORY OF CERTIFIED NEUROLOGISTS (US/0884-1500) [12319295] 3912, **3825**

ABMS DIRECTORY OF CERTIFIED NUCLEAR MEDICINE SPECIALISTS See OFFICIAL AMERICAN BOARD OF MEDICAL SPECIALTIES (ABMS) DIRECTORY OF BOARD CERTIFIED NUCLEAR MEDICINE SPECIALISTS, THE **3849**

ABMS DIRECTORY OF CERTIFIED OBSTETRICIANS AND GYNECOLOGISTS (US/0884-1535) [12319443] 3912, **3755**

ABMS DIRECTORY OF CERTIFIED OPHTHALMOLOGISTS (US/8756-9175) [10897572] 3912, **3871**

ABMS DIRECTORY OF CERTIFIED ORTHOPAEDIC SURGEONS (US/0883-1211) [12064843] 3912, **3880**

ABMS DIRECTORY OF CERTIFIED OTOLARYNGOLOGISTS (US/0883-3001) [12100885] **3912**

ABMS DIRECTORY OF CERTIFIED PATHOLOGISTS (US/0883-1203) [12065044] 3912, **3892**

ABMS DIRECTORY OF CERTIFIED PEDIATRICIANS (US/0884-1497) [12319214] 3912, **3899**

ABMS DIRECTORY OF CERTIFIED PHYSICAL MEDICINE AND REHABILITATION PHYSICIANS (US/0883-2986) [12100559] 3912, **3543**

ABMS DIRECTORY OF CERTIFIED PLASTIC SURGEONS (US/0749-839X) [10874738] 3912, **3957**

ABMS DIRECTORY OF CERTIFIED PREVENTIVE MEDICINE PHYSICIANS (US/0883-2978) [12100474] 3912, **3543**

ABMS DIRECTORY OF CERTIFIED PSYCHIATRISTS (US/0884-1519) [12323417] 3912, **3918**

ABMS DIRECTORY OF CERTIFIED RADIOLOGISTS See ABMS ... DIRECTORY OF CERTIFIED RADIOLOGISTS AND RADIOLOGICAL PHYSICISTS **3938**

ABMS ... DIRECTORY OF CERTIFIED RADIOLOGISTS AND RADIOLOGICAL PHYSICISTS (US) [25012886] 3912, **3938**

ABMS DIRECTORY OF CERTIFIED SURGEONS (US/0884-1527) [12319780] 3912, **3957**

ABMS DIRECTORY OF CERTIFIED THORACIC SURGEONS (US/0884-1462) [10874746] 3912, **3957**

ABMS DIRECTORY OF CERTIFIED UROLOGISTS (US/0742-0374) [10236218] 3912, **3987**

● ABMS RECORD (US) [25842679] 3912, **3543**

ABN CORRESPONDENCE (GW/0001-0545) [01718908] **4514**

ABN ECONOMIC REVIEW (NE/0169-5363) [10936314] **768**

ABN NEWS / NATIONAL LIBRARY OF AUSTRALIA, AUSTRALIAN BIBLIOGRAPHIC NETWORK (AT/0726-0644) [12388011] **3186**

ABNF JOURNAL, THE (US/1046-7041) [20496528] 2253, **3850**

ABO AKADEMI See ACTA ACADEMIAE ABOENSIS. SER. A. HUMANIORA **2841**

ABOGADA INTERNACIONAL. THE INTERNATIONAL WOMAN LAWYER, LA (US/0567-5111) [02254904] 5550, **3122**

ABORIGINAL BUSINESS COURIER (CN/1186-9291) [23665501] **2526**

ABORIGINAL CHILD AT SCHOOL, THE (AT) [05762304] 2253, **1874**

ABORIGINAL HISTORY (AT/0314-8769) [05739081] **227**

ABORIGINAL HOSTELS LIMITED See ANNUAL REPORT / ABORIGINAL HOSTELS LIMITED **5461**

● ABORIGINAL JUSTICE BULLETIN (CN/1193-3100) [26776150] **2926**

ABORIGINAL LAW BULLETIN (AT) [07818868] **2926**

ABORIGINAL NEWS (CANBERRA) (AT/0310-723X) [02245950] 227, **2253**

ABORIGINAL SCIENCE FICTION (US/0895-3198) [16568156] **3357**

ABORIGINAL VOICE, THE (CN/0848-9033) [21486852] **2609**

ABORTION AND FAMILY PLANNING BIBLIOGRAPHY CEASED. (US/1055-5935) [22660002] **587**

ABORTION RESEARCH NOTES CEASED. (US/0361-1116) [02014387] **587**

ABORTION REVIEW (UK/0262-7299) [I02627299] **3755**

ABORTION STATISTICS. ENGLAND & WALES (UK/0140-5314) [03644784] 587, **591**

ABORTION SURVEILLANCE (US/0094-0933) [01793509] **587**

ABOUT (CN/0712-8606) [09046718] **2526**

ABOUT ALFORDS (US/0883-1173) [12067085] **2436**

ABOUT COWS. (CD-ROM) (US) **204**

"ABOUT JAPAN" SERIES (JA) [04989364] **2501**

ABOUT OUR SCHOOLS (US) **1887**

ABOUT THE HOUSE CEASED. (UK/0001-3242) [06754203] **4098**

ABOUT ... TIME (US/1060-3905) [04663841] **2526**

ABOUT WOMEN ON CAMPUS (US/1061-768X) [25454442] 5550, **1720**

ABOVE & BEYOND (CN/0843-7815) [20977874] **2553**

ABOVE THE BRIDGE MAGAZINE (US) [13412526] **3459**

ABOVEGROUND STORAGE TANK GUIDE SERVICE (US) **4033**

● ABOVEGROUND TANK STATE REGULATORY GUIDE (US/1064-1289) [26210442] **2926**

ABOVEGROUND TANK UPDATE (US/1059-6615) [24661199] **4033**

ABOYEUR, L' (CN/0710-1694) [08415760] **2788**

ABR-NAHRAIN (NE/0065-0382) [01460568] 3260, **5013**

ABRAJUNA / TUSDIRUHA SHARIKAT QATAR LIL-ASMIDAH AL-KIMAWIYAH QAFKU (QA) [10235858] 42, **1596**

ABRAKADABRA (SW/0280-2414) [I02802414] **3357**

ABRASAX (CORPUS CHRISTI, TEX.) (US/1066-5455) [26994689] **4240**

ABRASIVE ENGINEERING SOCIETY See ABRASIVE ENGINEERING SOCIETY MAGAZINE **2109**

ABRASIVE ENGINEERING SOCIETY MAGAZINE (US/0195-0932) [05274131] **2109**

ABRASIVE ENGINEERING SOCIETY (U.S.). CONFERENCE/EXHIBITION See PROCEEDINGS - ABRASIVE ENGINEERING SOCIETY (U.S.) CONFERENCE/EXHIBITION **4016**

ABRASIVES (US) **2109**

ABRATES (BL) [03024221] **3357**

ABRAVA See REVISTA DO FRIO **2608**

ABRAXAS (HOLLYWOOD, LOS ANGELES, CALIF.) (US/8755-1780) [11201377] **5041**

ABRAXAS (MADISON) (US/0361-1663) [01952622] 3337, **3459**

ABRENTE (SP/0212-6117) [I02126117] **311**

ABRICOT PARIS (FR/0994-2653) [I09942653] **2325**

ABRIDGED CATHOLIC PERIODICAL AND LITERATURE INDEX, THE (US/0737-3457) [09351757] 5022, **5012**

ABRIDGED FINAL REPORT - WORLD METEOROLOGICAL ORGANIZATION. COMMISSION FOR AGRICULTURAL METEOROLOGY (SZ/0510-9078) [01721740] **1419**

ABRIDGED INDEX MEDICUS (US/0001-3331) [01752727] 3543, **3654**

ABRIDGED READERS' GUIDE TO PERIODICAL LITERATURE (US/0001-334X) [02253357] 2484, **2496**

ABRIDGED TRADE STATISTICS FOR TANZANIA, UGANDA, AND KENYA (KE/0304-5919) [02243977] 821, **725**

ABRUZZI (ITALY) See BOLLETTINO UFFICIALE **4465**

ABS NEWSTATS (CN/0709-9541) [05843205] **5320**

ABSATZWIRTSCHAFT, DIE (GW/0567-5235) [07383649] **920**

ABSATZWIRTSCHAFT DUSSELDORF. 1969 (GW/0001-3374) [I00013374] **920**

ABSCHLUSSBERICHT UBER DIE BESONDERE ERNTEERMITTLUNG BEI GETREIDE UND KARTOFFELN / C.BUNDESMINISTERIUM FUR ERNAHRUNG, LANDWIRTSCHAFT UND FORSTEN, ABTEILUNG VI, WIRTSCHAFTSBEOBACHTUNG, VERBRAUCHERANGELEGENHEITEN, REFERAT VI A 2 (GW) [04530836] **42**

ABSEES (UK/0044-5622) [01460575] **2671**

ABSOLUTE REFERENCE SUSPENDED. (US/0741-997X) [10265937] **1283**

ABSOLUTE SOUND, THE (US/0097-1138) [01798742] **5315**

ABSORPTION SPECTRA IN THE INFRARED REGION (UK) [02243853] 1012, **4432**

ABSTRACT ACCOUNT - CENTRAL FUND (IRELAND) (IE) [04978915] **4708**

ABSTRACT BULLETIN OF THE INSTITUTE OF PAPER CHEMISTRY (US) [02447671] 4232, **4240**

ABSTRACT BULLETIN OF THE INSTITUTE OF PAPER CHEMISTRY. KEYWORD INDEX CEASED. (US) [05467668] **4232**

ABSTRACT BULLETIN OF THE INSTITUTE OF PAPER CHEMISTRY. KEYWORD SUPPLEMENT See ABSTRACT BULLETIN OF THE INSTITUTE OF PAPER CHEMISTRY. KEYWORD INDEX **4232**

ABSTRACT BULLETIN OF THE INSTITUTE OF PAPER SCIENCE AND TECHNOLOGY (US/1047-2083) [20639999] 4232, **4240**

ABSTRACT CARDIO PARIS (FR/0763-7446) [I07637446] **3697**

ABSTRACT DERMATO PARIS (FR/0763-7454) [I07637454] **3717**

ABSTRACT GYNECO PARIS (FR/0296-9947) [I02969947] **3755**

ABSTRACT JOURNAL IN EARTHQUAKE ENGINEERING (US/0363-5732) [01719080] 2018, **2002**

ABSTRACT ME (US/1058-9538) [24439706] **3357**

ABSTRACT NEURO ET PSY PARIS (FR/0296-9955) [I02969955] 4570, **3825**

ABSTRACT OF STATISTICS - BARBADOS. STATISTICAL SERVICE (BB/0522-3725) [01143171] **5320**

ABSTRACT OF STATISTICS ON AGRICULTURE, FORESTRY AND FISHERIES, JAPAN (JA) [01134098] 42, **149**

ABSTRACT OF STATISTICS (PAPUA NEW GUINEA. NATIONAL STATISTICAL OFFICE) (PP) [09502035] **5320**

ABSTRACT PEDIATRIE PARIS (FR/0297-8156) [I02978156] **3899**

Alphabetical Title Index **ACADEMIA**

ABSTRACT REVIEW IN SCIENCE EXTENSION (HU/0238-6178) [I02386178] **5079**

ABSTRACT RHUMATO PARIS (FR/0295-2556) [I02952556] **3802**

ABSTRACTA BOTANICA (HU/0133-6215) [07051067] **496**

ABSTRACTA IRANICA (IR/0240-8910) [06644394] **406**

ABSTRACTS (CN) [01979297] **1412**

ABSTRACTS - ALBERTA. BUREAU OF STATISTICS (CN/0848-659X) [23264551] **5320**

ABSTRACTS / AMERICAN ACADEMY OF RELIGION (US/0164-1816) [04578750] **4931**

ABSTRACTS (AMERICAN SOCIETY OF AGRONOMY) *See* AGRONOMY ABSTRACTS (MADISON, WIS.) **56**

ABSTRACTS - AMERICAN SOCIETY OF ANIMAL SCIENCE (US/0198-9863) [06242995] **5501**

ABSTRACTS, ANNUAL MEETING - AMERICAN SOCIETY FOR ARTIFICIAL INTERNAL ORGANS (US/0099-250X) [01712559] **3957**

ABSTRACTS, ANNUAL MEETING - ASSOCIATION OF AMERICAN GEOGRAPHERS (US/0197-1700) [05972261] **2553**

ABSTRACTS - FLOUR MILLING AND BAKING RESEARCH ASSOCIATION (UK/0430-7941) [01569479] **2325**

ABSTRACTS FOR THE SOCIETY OF MAGNETIC RESONANCE IMAGING (US) **3938**

ABSTRACTS (GRAPHIC ARTS TECHNICAL FOUNDATION) (US) [13313751] **4570**

ABSTRACTS IN ANTHROPOLOGY (US/0001-3455) [01460581] **227, 248**

ABSTRACTS IN ARTIFICIAL INTELLIGENCE / THE TURING INSTITUTE *CEASED.* (UK/0269-8862) [15604231] **1210**

ABSTRACTS IN BIOCOMMERCE (UK/0263-6778) [08841973] **3685, 3654**

ABSTRACTS IN GERMANY ANTHROPOLOGY *CEASED.* (GW/0173-2986) [07562980] **227**

ABSTRACTS IN HUMAN-COMPUTER INTERACTION *SUSPENDED.* (US/1042-0193) [18905455] **1210, 1227, 1208**

ABSTRACTS IN INFECTIOUS DISEASE (US/1054-9218) [23021492] **3711**

ABSTRACTS IN MARYLAND ARCHEOLOGY (US/0743-4251) [10574287] **253**

ABSTRACTS IN SOCIAL GERONTOLOGY (US/1047-4862) [20701297] **3748, 3654**

ABSTRACTS - INTERNATIONAL FERTILITY RESEARCH PROGRAM (US/0147-3948) [03147442] **587**

ABSTRACTS, MEETING OF THE WEED SCIENCE SOCIETY OF AMERICA (US) [01769538] **161**

ABSTRACTS OF AIT REPORTS AND PUBLICATIONS ON ENERGY (TH/0857-6181) [18504070] **1930, 1961**

ABSTRACTS OF ARI RESEARCH PUBLICATIONS (US) [08414782] **5189**

ABSTRACTS OF BULGARIAN SCIENTIFIC LITERATURE. CULTURE / BULGARIAN ACADEMY OF SCIENCES, SCIENTIFIC INFORMATION CENTRE (BU/0205-3799) [21256721] **335**

ABSTRACTS OF BULGARIAN SCIENTIFIC LITERATURE. INDUSTRY, BUILDING AND TRANSPORT. STATE COMMITTEE FOR SCIENCE AND TECHNICAL PROGRESS, CENTRAL INSTITUTE FOR SCIENTIFIC AND TECHNICAL INFORMATION (BU/0204-577X) [06821876] **1963**

ABSTRACTS OF BULGARIAN SCIENTIFIC MEDICAL LITERATURE (BU/0001-3536) [01779043] **3543**

ABSTRACTS OF BULLETIN OF JCES (JA) [10615891] **1721**

ABSTRACTS OF CHINESE MEDICINES : ACME (HK/1010-0091) [16733579] **3543**

ABSTRACTS OF CLINICAL CARE GUIDELINES (US/1042-4423) [19050582] **3543, 3654**

ABSTRACTS OF CONTRIBUTED PAPERS - MEDICAL CARE SECTION (US/0363-3837) [02385330] **4763, 3543**

ABSTRACTS OF ENGLISH STUDIES *SUSPENDED.* (US/0001-3560) [01460584] **3337, 3356**

ABSTRACTS OF ENTOMOLOGY (US/0001-3579) [00978199] **5604**

ABSTRACTS OF FIELD BEANS (PHASEOLUS VULGARIS L.) *CEASED.* (CK) [05213893] **42**

ABSTRACTS OF FISHERY RESEARCH REPORTS (US/0094-3630) [01792667] **2293**

ABSTRACTS OF MARDI PUBLICATIONS (MY) [07514937] **42**

ABSTRACTS OF MILITARY BIBLIOGRAPHY *CEASED.* (AG) [03487811] **4033, 4061**

ABSTRACTS OF MYCOLOGY (US/0001-3617) [01460590] **574, 476**

ABSTRACTS OF NATIVE STUDIES (CN/0831-3180) [15732381] **2276**

ABSTRACTS OF PAPERS - AMERICAN CHEMICAL SOCIETY (US/0065-7727) [01123848] **958**

ABSTRACTS OF PAPERS - BYZANTINE STUDIES CONFERENCE (US/0147-3387) [03144468] **2671**

ABSTRACTS OF PAPERS PRESENTED AT ... MEETINGS - LABORATORY OF QUNATITATIVE BIOLOGY (US/0084-8824) [01770725] **439**

ABSTRACTS OF PAPERS PRESENTED AT THE ... ANNUAL MEETING OF THE CONFERENCE OF RESEARCH WORKERS IN ANIMAL DISEASE (US) [09546419] **5501**

ABSTRACTS OF PAPERS PRESENTED AT THE ... ANNUAL MEETING ... / THE AMERICAN INSTITUTE FOR CONSERVATION OF HISTORIC AND ARTISTIC WORKS (US) [21237809] **4822, 335**

ABSTRACTS OF PAPERS PRESENTED AT THE ... TOBACCO ROOT GEOLOGICAL SOCIETY CONFERENCE (US/8755-1942) [11257566] **1364**

ABSTRACTS OF PAPERS PRESENTED AT THE ... WORLD CONGRESS OF THE INTERNATIONAL POLITICAL SCIENCE ASSOCIATION (CN/0709-6895) [06653169] **4514**

ABSTRACTS OF PAPERS PRESENTED TO THE AMERICAN MATHEMATICAL SOCIETY (US/0192-5857) [05149137] **3490**

ABSTRACTS OF PAPERS READ AT THE ... ANNUAL MEETING OF THE AMERICAN MUSICOLOGICAL SOCIETY (US/0893-1305) [04649200] **4098**

ABSTRACTS OF PAPERS READ AT THE ... INTERNATIONAL SYMPOSIUM OF ODONATOLOGY (NE) [09096834] **5573**

ABSTRACTS OF PUBLICATIONS - NATIONAL SCIENCE FOUNDATION U.S (US) [03173780] **5079**

ABSTRACTS OF PUBLISHED PAPERS / CSIRO, INSTITUTE OF ENERGY AND EARTH RESOURCES, DIVISION OF GEOMECHANICS (AT) [11648060] **1351**

ABSTRACTS OF REFINING LITERATURE (US/0003-0422) [03602445] **4249, 4283**

ABSTRACTS OF RESEARCH IN PASTORAL CARE AND COUNSELING (US/0733-2599) [06451672] **4570, 5012**

ABSTRACTS OF ROMANIAN SCIENTIFIC AND TECHNICAL LITERATURE (RM/0365-6330) [01387525] **5079**

ABSTRACTS OF SCIENCE AND TECHNOLOGY IN JAPAN. ELECTRONICS AND COMMUNICATION *CEASED.* (JA) [14389022] **2034, 2002**

ABSTRACTS OF SCIENCE AND TECHNOLOGY IN JAPAN: ENERGY TECHNOLOGY *CEASED.* (JA/0912-2311) [I09122311] **5173**

ABSTRACTS OF SOVIET AND EAST EUROPEAN EMIGRE PERIODICAL LITERATURE (US/0738-2707) [08397329] **2513**

ABSTRACTS OF STAFF REPORTS (US/0749-3193) [10755242] **42**

ABSTRACTS OF THE ANNUAL MEETING - AMERICAN ANTHROPOLOGICAL ASSOCIATION (US/0160-1873) [03634585] **227**

ABSTRACTS OF THE CANADIAN SOCIETY OF MICROBIOLOGY (CN) **558**

ABSTRACTS OF THE ... GENERAL MEETING OF THE AMERICAN SOCIETY FOR MICROBIOLOGY (US/1060-2011) [24063454] **558, 476**

ABSTRACTS OF THE THESES ACCEPTED FOR THE PH D. DEGREE OF BANARAS HINDU UNIVERSITY (II/0522-0750) [03246523] **1806**

ABSTRACTS OF THESES AND DISSERTATIONS (BOWLING GREEN, OHIO) (US/0473-9507) [01761107] **1806**

ABSTRACTS OF UPPSALA DISSERTATIONS FROM THE FACULTY OF SCIENCE (SW) [03251266] **5079**

ABSTRACTS OF WORKING PAPERS IN ECONOMICS : THE OFFICIAL JOURNAL OF THE AWPE DATABASE (US/0951-0079) [15459912] **1459**

ABSTRACTS ON CASSAVA (MANIHOT ESCULENTA CRANTZ) *CEASED.* (CK/0120-288X) [04794765] **161**

ABSTRACTS ON HYGIENE AND COMMUNICABLE DISEASES (UK/0260-5511) [07140771] **4763, 3711, 4809**

ABSTRACTS ON MANAGEMENT & ADMINISTRATION OF PHARMACY (US/0197-6176) [06045781] **4288**

ABSTRACTS ON RURAL DEVELOPMENT IN THE TROPICS *CEASED.* (NE/0169-605X) [13245834] **5189**

ABSTRACTS ON SUSTAINABLE AGRICULTURE : ABSTRECO (NE) [25118001] **42**

ABSTRACTS ON TROPICAL AGRICULTURE (NE/0304-5951) [02241004] **42, 149**

●ABSTRACTS, RUSSIAN AND EAST EUROPEAN SERIES : ABREES (US) [28203114] **2671**

ABSTRACTS - SOCIETY FOR NEUROSCIENCE (US/0190-5295) [04337305] **3825**

ABSTRACTS. STATE APPALACHIAN DEVELOPMENT PLANS AND INVESTMENT PROGRAMS (US/0272-7978) [04458196] **2813**

ABSTRACTS, STRENGTHENING RESEARCH LIBRARY RESOURCES PROGRAM (US) [08247449] **3186**

ABSTRACTS. SYMPOSIA PAPERS PRESENTED BEFORE THE APHA ACADEMY OF PHARMACEUTICAL SCIENCES AT THE ANNUAL MEETING OF THE AMERICAN PHARMACEUTICAL ASSOCIATION (US/0098-6437) [01123877] **4288**

ABSTRACTS - SYMPOSIUM ON MOLECULAR SPECTROSCOPY (US/0192-5652) [05024182] **4432**

ABSTRACTS - SYMPOSIUM ON RECENT ADVANCES IN THE ANALYTICAL CHEMISTRY OF POLLUTANTS (AU/0379-6914) [04521445] **2222, 1012**

ABSTRACTS WITH PROGRAMS - GEOLOGICAL SOCIETY OF AMERICA (US/0016-7592) [00853306] **1364**

ABSTRAK MINYAK DAN GAS BUMI DALAM NEGERI (IO) [02914378] **2132**

ABSTRAK SKRIPSI SARJANA & KARYA TULIS KEAHLIAN UNIVERSITAS INDONESIA (IO) [07211434] **1806**

ABTEE (AT/0810-6118) [I08106118] **1125**

ABU MAGAZINE (NE) **1642, 4201**

ABU TECHNICAL REVIEW (MY/0126-6209) [03348172] **1148, 1125**

ABU ZABY. WIZARAT AL-TARBIYAH *See* AL-TAQRIR AL-SANAWI - HUKUMAT ABU ZABI, WIZARAT AL-TARBIYAH **1723**

ABUH PHYSIO : THE JOURNAL OF THE PHYSIOTHERAPY DEPT. OF THE INSTITUTE OF HEALTH, AHMADU BELLO UNIVERSITY, ZARIA (NR/0331-9113) [12031102] **4378**

ABUI NETWORK NEWS *See* ENTREPRISE NETWORKING **672**

ABUI NETWORK NEWS (US/1061-5547) [25355331] **636**

ABUJA BUSINESS DIRECTORY (NR) [25481412] **636**

ABV (BU/0205-0838) [25294082] **4822**

ABWASSERTECHNIK 1983 (GW/0932-3708) [I09233708] **2222**

ABWASSERTECHNISCHE VEREINIGUNG *See* BERICHTE DER ABWASSERTECHNISCHEN VEREINIGUNG **2225**

●ABYA YALA NEWS (US/1071-3182) [28532127] **2253**

AC. THE ADCRAFTER (US/0001-8066) [03949342] **753**

AC/UNU NEWSLETTER / THE AMERICAN COUNCIL FOR THE UNITED NATIONS UNIVERSITY (US) [08680641] **1806**

ACA BULLETIN (CN/0709-4604) [05540519] **2478**

ACA BULLETIN - ASSOCIATION FOR COMMUNICATION ADMINISTRATION (US/0360-0939) [02171786] **1103**

●ACA JOURNAL / AMERICAN COMPENSATION ASSOCIATION (US/1068-0918) [27373299] **1642, 938**

ACA JOURNAL OF CHIROPRACTIC, THE (US/0044-7609) [03943359] **3543**

ACA JOURNAL, THE *SUSPENDED.* (US/0888-5567) [13659190] **1338**

ACA NEWS (EDMONTON) (CN/0826-497X) [11377365] **5177**

ACAATO HANDBOOK (CN/0822-5710) [10157009] **1806**

ACADEME (WASHINGTON. 1979) (US/0190-2946) [04688683] **1806**

ACADEMIA ANTIOQUENA DE HISTORIA, MEDELLIN, COLOMBIA *See* REPERTORIO HISTORICO **2757**

ACADEMIA ARGENTINA DE LETRAS *See* BOLETIN DE LA ACADEMIA ARGENTINA DE LETRAS **3368**

ACADEMIA CHILENA DE LA HISTORIA *See* BOLETIN DE LA ACADEMIA CHILENA DE LA HISTORIA **2723**

ACADEMIA CHILENA, SANTIAGO DE CHILE *See* BOLETIN DE LA ACADEMIA CHILENA CORRESPONDIENTE DE LA REAL ACADEMIA ESPANOLA **3368**

ACADEMIA — Alphabetical Title Index

ACADEMIA COLOMBIANA See BOLETIN DE LA ACADEMIA COLOMBIANA **2513**

ACADEMIA COLOMBIANA DE HISTORIA ECLESIASTICA See REVISTA DE LA ACADEMIA COLOMBIANA DE HISTORIA ECLESIASTICA **2758**

ACADEMIA DAS CIENCIAS DE LISBOA. CLASSE DE LETRAS See MEMORIAS DA ACADEMIA DAS CIENCIAS DE LISBOA. CLASSE DE LETRAS **5233**

ACADEMIA DE BUENAS LETRAS DE BARCELONA See BOLETIN DE LA REAL ACADEMIA DE BUENAS LETRAS DE BARCELONA **2843**

ACADEMIA DE CIENCIAS EXACTAS, FISICO-QUIMICAS Y NATURALES DE ZARAGOZA See REVISTA DE LA ACADEMIA DE CIENCIAS EXACTAS, FISICO-QUIMICAS Y NATURALES DE ZARAGOZA **5148**

ACADEMIA DE FARMACIA, MADRID See ANALES **4290**

ACADEMIA DE GEOGRAFIA E HISTORIA DE GUATEMALA See ANALES DE LA ACADEMIA DE GEOGRAFIA E HISTORIA DE GUATEMALA **228**

ACADEMIA DE HISTORIA DEL VALLE DEL CAUCA See BOLETIN DE LA ACADEMIA DE HISTORIA DEL VALLE DEL CAUCA **2723**

ACADEMIA DE STIINTE AGRICOLE SI SILVICE See BULLETIN DE L'ACADEMIE DES SCIENCES AGRICOLES ET FORESTIERES **69**

ACADEMIA GOIANA DE LETRAS See REVISTA DA ACADEMIA GOIANA DE LETRAS **3430**

ACADEMIA MEXICANA DE LA HISTORIA See MEMORIAS DE LA ACADEMIA MEXICANA DE LA HISTORIA **2746**

ACADEMIA NACIONAL DE BELLAS ARTES, BUENOS AIRES See ANUARIO - ACADEMIA NACIONAL DE BELLAS ARTES **337**

ACADEMIA NACIONAL DE CIENCIAS (ARGENTINA) See BOLETIN DE LA ACADEMIA NACIONAL DE CIENCIAS **5089**

ACADEMIA NACIONAL DE CIENCIAS EXACTAS, FISICAS Y NATURALES (ARGENTINA) See ANALES DE L'ACADEMIA NACIONAL DE CIENCIAS EXACTAS, FISICAS Y NATURALES, BUENOS AIRES **5082**

ACADEMIA NACIONAL DE CIENCIAS MORALES Y POLITICAS See ANALES - ACADEMIA NACIONAL DE CIENCIAS MORALES Y POLITICAS **5190**

ACADEMIA NACIONAL DE ECONOMIA (URUGUAY) See RESENA DE LA ACTIVIDAD DURANTE EL EJERCICIO **1581**

ACADEMIA NACIONAL DE LA HISTORIA (ARGENTINA) See BOLETIN DE LA ACADEMIA NACIONAL DE LA HISTORIA **2723**

ACADEMIA NACIONAL DE LA HISTORIA, CARACAS. DEPARTAMENTO DE INVESTIGACIONES See COLLECCION BIBLIOGRAFICA - ACADEMIA NACIONAL DE LA HISTORIA, DEPARTAMENTO DE INVESTIGACIONES **2635**

ACADEMIA NACIONAL DE LA HISTORIA (VENEZUELA) See BOLETIN DE LA ACADEMIA NACIONAL DE LA HISTORIA (CARACAS) **2723**

ACADEMIA NORTEAMERICANA DE LA LENGUA ESPANOLA See BOLETIN - ACADEMIA NORTEAMERICANA DE LA LENGUA ESPANOLA **3269**

ACADEMIA PAULISTA DE LETRAS (SAO PAULO, BRAZIL) See REVISTA DA ACADEMIA PAULISTA DE LETRAS **2853**

ACADEMIA PERNAMBUCANA DE LETRAS See REVISTA DA ACADEMIA PERNAMBUCANA DE LETRAS **3430**

ACADEMIA PORTUGUESA DA HISTORIA See ANAIS - ACADEMIA PORTUGUESA DA HISTORIA **2673**

ACADEMIA PUERTORRIQUENA DE LA HISTORIA See BOLETIN DE LA ACADEMIA PUERTORRIQUENA DE LA HISTORIA **2723**

ACADEMIA (REAL ACADEMIA DE BELLAS ARTES DE SAN FERNANDO) (SP/0567-560X) [01635608] **311**

ACADEMIA REPUBLICII POPULARE ROMINE. STUDII SI CERCETARI DE ANTROPOLOGIE See STUDII SI CERCETARI DE ANTROPOLOGIE **246**

ACADEMIA REPUBLICII SOCIALISTE ROMANIA. INSTITUTUL DE ISTORIE SI ARHEOLOGIE A. D. XENOPOL See ANUARUL INSTITUTULUI DE ISTORIE SI ARHEOLOGIE A. D. XENOPOL **256**

ACADEMIA : REVUE INTERNATIONALE DE LA FORMATION DANS L'ENSEIGNEMENT SUPERIEUR (CN) **1806**

ACADEMIA SOBRALENSE DE ESTUDOS E LETRAS See REVISTA DA ACADEMIA SOBRALENSE DE ESTUDOS E LETRAS **2757**

ACADEMIC ABSTRACTS (US/1056-7496) [23716169] 2484, **2496**

ACADEMIC ABSTRACTS FULL TEXT ELITE (US/1060-6750) [25058332] 2484, **2496**

ACADEMIC ABSTRACTS FULL TEXT SELECT *CEASED*. (US/1058-0662) [24190512] **2484**

ACADEMIC AND CLINICAL REPORTS - INSTITUTE OF LARYNGOLOGY AND OTOLOGY ASSOCIATED WITH THE ROYAL NATIONAL THROAT, NOSE AND EAR HOSPITAL (UK/0309-698X) [02785977] **3885**

ACADEMIC AND LIBRARY COMPUTING (US/1055-4769) [23188929] 1274, 3186, **1265**

●ACADEMIC EMERGENCY MEDICINE (US/1069-6563) [28131897] **3723**

ACADEMIC FINANCIER *CEASED*. (US/0889-3292) [13907578] **1806**

ACADEMIC HONDURENA DE LA LENGUA See BOLETIN DE LA ACADEMIE HONDURENA DE LA LENGUA **3269**

ACADEMIC INDEX. [COMPUTER FILE] (US) 2484, **2496**

ACADEMIC INFORMATION SERVICE, INC See TAX GUIDE FOR COLLEGE TEACHERS AND OTHER COLLEGE PERSONNEL **4752**

ACADEMIC JOURNAL (NEWTOWN, CONN.), THE (US/0740-5960) [01645224] **1721**

ACADEMIC LEADER (US/8750-7730) [11747079] 1859, **1806**

ACADEMIC LIBRARY BOOK REVIEW (US/0894-993X) [16397676] 3186, **4822**

ACADEMIC MEDICINE (US/1040-2446) [18356569] 3543, **1806**

ACADEMIC NURSE, THE (US/1062-0249) [23347086] 3850, **4201**

ACADEMIC PROGRESS OF THE UNIVERSITY; REPORT TO THE BOARD OF GOVERNORS, THE (IS) [01784352] **1807**

ACADEMIC PSYCHIATRY (US/1042-9670) [19260322] **3918**

ACADEMIC QUESTIONS (US/0895-4852) [16657327] **1807**

ACADEMIC REVIEWER, THE (US/0567-6487) [01460634] 4823, **1807**

ACADEMIC SEARCH (US/1071-2720) [28599912] 2484, **2496**

ACADEMIC STUDIES SERIES / JOINT KOREA-U.S. ACADEMIC SYMPOSIUM (US/1054-6944) [22939694] **1544**

ACADEMIC TALENT (US/0882-5866) [11885448] **1721**

ACADEMIC YEAR ABROAD (US/1047-2576) [17883310] **1721**

ACADEMIC YEAR ABROAD IN EUROPE-AFRICA-AUSTRALIA (US/0098-6356) [02241609] **1721**

ACADEMIC YEAR & SUMMER PROGRAMS ABROAD (US/0278-3584) [04259404] **1721**

ACADEMICA : REVISTA DE STIINTA, CULTURA SI ARTA / ACADEMIA ROMANA (RM) [25264158] **312**

ACADEMICREVIEW (PH) [09801155] **2644**

ACADEMIE D'AIX: LISTE DESCRIPTIVE DES ETABLISSEMENTS PUBLICS D'ENSEIGNEMENT DE SECOND DEGRE DISPENSANT UN ENSEIGNEMENT PROFESSIONNEL DE CYCLE COURT OU DE CYCLE LONG See ACADEMIE D'AIX-MARSEILLE : LISTE DESCRIPTIVE DES ETABLISSEMENTS PUBLICS D'ENSEIGNEMENT DE SECOND DEGRE DISPENSANT UN ENSEIGNEMENT PROFESSIONNEL DE CYCLE COURT OU DE CYCLE LONG **1909**

ACADEMIE D'AIX-MARSEILLE : LISTE DESCRIPTIVE DES ETABLISSEMENTS PUBLICS D'ENSEIGNEMENT DE SECOND DEGRE (FR) [02441221] **1721**

ACADEMIE D'AIX-MARSEILLE : LISTE DESCRIPTIVE DES ETABLISSEMENTS PUBLICS D'ENSEIGNEMENT DE SECOND DEGRE DISPENSANT UN ENSEIGNEMENT PROFESSIONNEL DE CYCLE COURT OU DE CYCLE LONG (FR) [02441201] **1909**

ACADEMIE D'ARCHITECTURE (FR/0001-3994) **287**

ACADEMIE DE BESANCON : LISTE DESCRIPTIVE DES ETABLISSEMENTS PUBLICS D'ENSEIGNEMENT DE SECOND DEGRE DISPENSANT UN ENSEIGNEMENT PROFESSIONNEL DE CYCLE COURT OU DE CYCLE LONG (FR) [02441199] **1909**

ACADEMIE DE BORDEAUX: LISTE DESCRIPTIVE DES ETABLISSEMENTS PUBLICS D'ENSEIGNEMENT DE SECOND DEGRE (FR) [01783487] **1721**

ACADEMIE DE CAEN : LISTE DESCRIPTIVE DES ETABLISSEMENTS PUBLIC D'ENSEIGNEMENT DE SECOND DEGRE (FR) [01797994] **1721**

ACADEMIE DE CAEN : LISTE DESCRIPTIVE DES ETABLISSEMENTS PUBLICS D'ENSEIGNEMENT DE SECOND DEGRE DISPENSANT UN ENSEIGNEMENT PROFESSIONNEL DE CYCLE COURT OU DE CYCLE LONG (FR) [02441202] **1909**

ACADEMIE DE CLERMONT-FERRAND : LISTE DESCRIPTIVE DES ETABLISSEMENTS PUBLIC D'ENSEIGNEMENT DE SECOND DEGRE (FR) [01800004] **1721**

ACADEMIE DE CLERMONT-FERRAND: LISTE DESCRIPTIVE DES ETABLISSEMENTS PUBLICS D'ENSEIGNEMENT DE SECOND DEGRE DISPENSANT UN ENSEIGNEMENT PROFESSIONNEL DE CYCLE COURT OU DE CYCLE LONG (FR) [02246303] **1909**

ACADEMIE DE CRETEIL: LISTE DESCRIPTIVE DES ETABLISSEMENTS PUBLICS D'ENSEIGNEMENT DE SECOND DEGRE (FR) [02245776] **1721**

ACADEMIE DE CRETEIL : LISTE DESCRIPTIVE DES ETABLISSEMENTS PUBLICS D'ENSEIGNEMENT DE SECOND DEGRE DISPENSANT UN ENSEIGNEMENT PROFESSIONNEL DE CYCLE COURT OU DE CYCLE LONG (FR) [02246831] **1909**

ACADEMIE DE DIJON : LISTE DESCRIPTIVE DES ETABLISSEMENTS PUBLICS D'ENSEIGNEMENT DE SECOND DEGRE DISPENSANT UN ENSEIGNEMENT PROFESSIONNEL DE CYCLE COURT OU DE CYCLE LONG *CEASED*. (FR) [02246832] **1909**

ACADEMIE DE DIJON: LISTE GENERALE DES ETABLISSEMENTS D'ENSEIGNEMENT DE SECOND DEGRE (FR) [01783569] **1721**

ACADEMIE DE GRENOBLE : LISTE DESCRIPTIVE DES ETABLISSEMENTS PUBLICS D'ENSEIGNEMENT DE SECOND DEGRE (FR) [02246388] **1721**

ACADEMIE DE LILLE : LISTE DESCRIPTIVE DES ETABLISSEMENTS PUBLICS D'ENSEIGNEMENT DE SECOND DEGRE (FR) [02441218] **1721**

ACADEMIE DE LIMOGES : LISTE DESCRIPTIVE DES ETABLISSEMENTS PUBLICS D'ENSEIGNEMENT DE SECOND DEGRE (FR) [02441217] **1721**

ACADEMIE DE LIMOGES: LISTE DESCRIPTIVE DES ETABLISSEMENTS PUBLICS D'ENSEIGNEMENT DE SECOND DEGRE DISPENSANT UN ENSIGNEMENT PROFESSIONNEL DE CYCLE COURT OU DE CYCLE LONG (FR) [01800099] **1909**

ACADEMIE DE LYON, L' (FR) [01795140] **1721**

ACADEMIE DE LYON : LISTE DESCRIPTIVE DES ETABLISSEMENTS PUBLICS D'ENSEIGNEMENT DE SECOND DEGRE (FR) [02246364] **1721**

ACADEMIE DE MACON. SOCIETE DES ARTS, SCIENCES, BELLES-LETTRES, ET AGRICULTURE DE SAONE-ET-LOIRE See ANNALES DE L'ACADEMIE DE MACON / SOCIETE DES ARTS, SCIENCES, BELLES-LETTRES, ET AGRICULTURE DE SAONE-ET-LOIRE **2841**

ACADEMIE DE MONTPELLIER : LISTE DESCRIPTIVE DES ETABLISSEMENTS PUBLICS D'ENSEIGNEMENT DE SECOND DEGRE *CEASED*. (FR) [02246865] **1721**

ACADEMIE DE NANCY: LISTE DESCRIPTIVE DES ETABLISSEMENTS PUBLICS D'ENSEIGNEMENT DE SECOND DEGRE DISPENSANT UN ENSIGNEMENT PROFESSIONNEL DE CYCLE COURT OU DE CYCLE LONG (FR) [01790935] **1721**

ACADEMIE DE NANTES: LISTE DESCRIPTIVE DES ETABLISSEMENTS PUBLICS D'ENSEIGNEMENT DE SECOND DEGRE (FR) [02358421] **1721**

ACADEMIE DE NANTES : LISTE DESCRIPTIVE DES ETABLISSEMENTS PUBLICS D'ENSEIGNEMENT DE SECOND DEGRE DISPENSANT UN ENSEIGNEMENT PROFESSIONNEL DE CYCLE COURT OU DE CYCLE LONG (FR) [02246866] **1909**

ACADEMIE DE NICE: LISTE DESCRIPTIVE DES ETABLISSEMENTS PUBLICS D'ENSEIGNEMENT DE SECOND DEGRE (FR) [01800102] **1721**

ACADEMIE DE NICE: LISTE DESCRIPTIVE DES ETABLISSEMENTS PUBLICS D'ENSEIGNEMENT DE SECOND DEGRE DISPENSANT UN ENSEIGNEMENT PROFESSIONNEL DE CYCLE COURT OU DE CYCLE LONG (FR) [02369997] **1909**

ACADEMIE DE PARIS : LISTE DESCRIPTIVE DES ETABLISSEMENTS PUBLICS D'ENSEIGNEMENT DE SECOND DEGRE (FR) [02358007] **1721**

ACADEMIE DE PARIS: LISTE DESCRIPTIVE DES ETABLISSEMENTS PUBLICS D'ENSEIGNEMENT DE SECOND DEGRE DISPENSANT UN ENSEIGNEMENT PROFESSIONNEL DE CYCLE COURT OU DE CYCLE LONG (FR) [02246868] **1909**

ACADEMIE DE POITIERS: LISTE DESCRIPTIVE DES ETABLISSEMENTS PUBLICS D'ENSEIGNEMENT DE SECOND DEGRE (FR) [01790941] **1721**

ACADEMIE DE POITIERS : LISTE DESCRIPTIVE DES ETABLISSEMENTS PUBLICS D'ENSEIGNEMENT DE SECOND DEGRE DISPENSANT UN ENSEIGNEMENT PROFESSIONNEL DE CYCLE COURT OU DE CYCLE LONG (FR) [02246360] **1909**

ACADEMIE DE REIMS : LISTE DESCRIPTIVE DES ETABLISSEMENTS PUBLICS D'ENSEIGNEMENT DE SECOND DEGRE DISPENSANT UN ENSEIGNEMENT PROFESSIONNEL DE CYCLE COURT OU DE CYCLE LONG (FR) [02246889] **1909**

ACADEMIE DE RENNES : LISTE DESCRIPTIVE DES ETABLISSEMENTS PUBLICS D'ENSEIGNEMENT DE SECOND DEGRE DISPENSANT UN ENSEIGNEMENT PROFESSIONNEL DE CYCLE COURT OU DE CYCLE LONG (FR) [02246863] **1909**

ACADEMIE DE ROUEN : LISTE DESCRIPTIVE DES ETABLISSEMENTS PUBLICS D'ENSEIGNEMENT DE SECOND DEGRE (FR) [02246842] **1721**

ACADEMIE DE ROUEN : LISTE DESCRIPTIVE DES ETABLISSEMENTS PUBLICS D'ENSEIGNEMENT DE SECOND DEGRE DISPENSANT UN ENSEIGNEMENT PROFESSIONNEL DE CYCLE COURT OU DE CYCLE LONG (FR) [02246879] **1909**

ACADEMIE DE STRASBOURG : LISTE DESCRIPTIVE DES ETABLISSEMENTS PUBLICS D'ENSEIGNEMENT DE SECOND DEGRE (FR) [02358090] **1721**

ACADEMIE DE STRASBOURG : LISTE DESCRIPTIVE DES ETABLISSEMENTS PUBLICS D'ENSEIGNEMENT DE SECOND DEGRE DISPENSANT UN ENSEIGNEMENT PROFESSIONNEL DE CYCLE COURT OU DE CYCLE LONG (FR) [02246362] **1909**

ACADEMIE DE TOULOUSE : LISTE DESCRIPTIVE DES ETABLISSEMENTS PUBLICS D'ENSEIGNEMENT DE SECOND DEGRE (FR) [02246840] **1721**

ACADEMIE DE VERSAILLES : LISTE DESCRIPTIVE DES ETABLISSEMENTS PUBLICS D'ENSEIGNEMENT DE SECOND DEGRE (FR) [02246839] **1721**

ACADEMIE DE VERSAILLES : LISTE DESCRIPTIVE DES ETABLISSEMENTS PUBLICS D'ENSEIGNEMENT DE SECOND DEGRE DISPENSANT UN ENSEIGNEMENT PROFESSIONNEL DE CYCLE COURT OU DE CYCLE LONG (FR) [02246369] **1909**

ACADEMIE DENTAIRE See BULLETIN DE L'ACADEMIE DENTAIRE **1318**

ACADEMIE DES INSCRIPTIONS & BELLES-LETTRES (FRANCE) See COMPTES RENDUS DES SEANCES - ACADEMIE DES INSCRIPTIONS & BELLES-LETTRES **2844**

ACADEMIE DES INSCRIPTIONS ET BELLES-LETTRES (FRANCE) See RECUEIL DES HISTORIENS DE LA FRANCE. OBITUAIRES **434**

ACADEMIE DES INSCRIPTIONS ET BELLES-LETTRES, PARIS See RECUEIL DES HISTORIENS DE LA FRANCE. POUILLES **5035**

ACADEMIE DES INSCRIPTIONS ET BELLES-LETTRES, PARIS See RECUEIL DES HISTORIENS DE LA FRANCE. DOCUMENTS FINANCIERS **2705**

ACADEMIE DES SCIENCES, BELLES-LETTRES ET ARTS DE ROUEN See PRECIS ANALYTIQUE DES TRAVAUX DE L'ACADEMIE DES SCIENCES, BELLES-LETTRES ET ARTS DE ROUEN **2852**

ACADEMIE DES SCIENCES, BELLES-LETTRES ET ARTS DE SAVOIE See MEMOIRES **2850**

ACADEMIE DES SCIENCES ET LETTRES DE MONTPELLIER See BULLETIN DE L'ACADEMIE DES SCIENCES ET LETTRES DE MONTPELLIER **2843**

ACADEMIE DES SCIENCES (FRANCE) See ANNUAIRE - ACADEMIE DES SCIENCES **5083**

ACADEMIE DES SCIENCES (FRANCE) See NOUVELLES DE L'ACADEMIE / ACADEMIE DES SCIENCES, LES **5135**

ACADEMIE DES SCIENCES, INSCRIPTIONS ET BELLES-LETTRES DE TOULOUSE See MEMOIRES DE L'ACADEMIE DES SCIENCES, INSCRIPTIONS ET BELLES-LETTRES DE TOULOUSE **2850**

ACADEMIE D'ORLEANS: LISTE DESCRIPTIVE DES ETABLISSEMENTS PUBLICS D'ENSEIGNEMENT DE SECOND DEGRE (FR) [01783568] **1721**

ACADEMIE D'ORLEANS-TOURS : LISTE DESCRIPTIVE DES ETABLISSEMENTS PUBLICS D'ENSEIGNEMENT DE SECOND DEGRE (FR) [05146080] **1722**

ACADEMIE INTERNATIONALE D'HISTOIRE DES SCIENCES See COLLECTION DE TRAVAUX DE L'ACADEMIE INTERNATIONALE D'HISTOIRE DES SCIENCES **5095**

ACADEMIE ROYALE DES SCIENCES, DES LETTRES DES BEAUX-ARTS DE BELGIQUE. CLASSE DES BEAUX-ARTS See BULLETIN DE LA CLASSE DE BEAUX-ARTS ACADEMIE ROYALE DE BELGIQUE **316**

ACADEMIE ROYALE DES SCIENCES, DES LETTRES ET DES BEAUX-ARTS DE BELGIQUE See BIOGRAPHIE NATIONALE **430**

ACADEMIE ROYALE DES SCIENCES, DES LETTRES ET DES BEAUX-ARTS DE BELGIQUE, BRUSSELS. CLASSE DES LETTRES ET DES SCIENCES MORALES ET POLITIQUES See BULLETIN DE LA CLASSE DES LETTRES ET DES SCIENCES MORALES ET POLITIQUES **3339**

ACADEMIE ROYALE DES SCIENCES D'OUTRE-MER See BULLETIN DES SEANCES - ACADEMIE ROYALE DES SCIENCES D'OUTRE-MER **5091**

ACADEMIE ROYALE DES SCIENCES D'OUTRE-MER See MEDEDELINGEN DER ZITTINGEN - KONINKLIJKE ACADEMIE VOOR OVERZEESE WETTENSCHAPEN **5127**

ACADEMIE ROYALE DES SCIENCES D'OUTRE-MER. CLASSE DES SCIENCES TECHNIQUES See ACADEMIE ROYALE DES SCIENCES D'OUTRE-MER. CLASSE DES SCIENCES TECHNIQUES **1722**

ACADEMIE ROYALE DES SCIENCES D'OUTRE-MER. CLASSE DES SCIENCES TECHNIQUES (BE/0373-7063) [03095971] 5079, **1722**

ACADEMIE SPECTRUM (GW/0940-225X) [25475116] **5079**

ACADEMIE VOOR WETENSCHAPPEN, LETTEREN EN SCHONE KUNSTEN VAN BELGIE. KLASSE DER WETENSCHAPPEN See VERHANDELINGEN VAN DE KONINKLIJKE ACADEMIE VOOR WETENSCHAPPEN, LETTEREN EN SCHONE KUNSTEN VAN BELGIE, KLASSE DER WETENSCHAPPEN **5168**

ACADEMY ACCENTS (US/1071-376X) [11818769] **4931**

ACADEMY BOOKMAN, THE (US/0001-4249) [01460705] **3654**

ACADEMY FORUM (NEW YORK), THE (US/0192-1088) [04774291] **3918**

ACADEMY NEWS! (CN/0711-3471) [08478806] **4098**

ACADEMY NEWSLETTER, THE (US/0897-5523) [15673786] **5079**

ACADEMY OF ACCOUNTING HISTORIANS See DIRECTORY - ACADEMY OF ACCOUNTING HISTORIANS **742**

ACADEMY OF FLORIDA TRIAL LAWYERS See JOURNAL OF THE ACADEMY OF FLORIDA TRIAL LAWYERS **2989**

ACADEMY OF MANAGEMENT See ACADEMY OF MANAGEMENT REVIEW, THE **859**

ACADEMY OF MANAGEMENT See ACADEMY OF MANAGEMENT NEWS, THE **859**

ACADEMY OF MANAGEMENT See ACADEMY OF MANAGEMENT JOURNAL **858**

ACADEMY OF MANAGEMENT See BEST PAPERS PROCEEDINGS / ACADEMY OF MANAGEMENT **861**

ACADEMY OF MANAGEMENT JOURNAL (US/0001-4273) [01460711] **858**

ACADEMY OF MANAGEMENT NEWS, THE (US) [22226984] **859**

ACADEMY OF MANAGEMENT REVIEW, THE (US/0363-7425) [02060965] **859**

ACADEMY OF MARKETING SCIENCE See DEVELOPMENTS IN MARKETING SCIENCE **923**

ACADEMY OF MARKETING SCIENCE See JOURNAL OF THE ACADEMY OF MARKETING SCIENCE **929**

ACADEMY OF MEDICINE, TORONTO, ONT See BULLETIN OF THE ACADEMY OF MEDICINE, TORONTO **3560**

ACADEMY OF MOTION PICTURE ARTS AND SCIENCES See WRITING AWARDS : REMINDER LIST OF ELIGIBLE RELEASES **4080**

ACADEMY OF NATURAL SCIENCES OF PHILADELPHIA See NOTULAE NATURAE OF THE ACADEMY NATURAL SCIENCES OF PHILADELPHIA **5134**

ACADEMY OF NATURAL SCIENCES OF PHILADELPHIA See PROCEEDINGS OF THE ACADEMY OF NATURAL SCIENCES OF PHILADELPHIA **4170**

ACADEMY OF NATURAL SCIENCES OF PHILADELPHIA See MONOGRAPHS - ACADEMY OF NATURAL SCIENCES OF PHILADELPHIA **4168**

ACADEMY OF NURSING OF THE PHILIPPINES See ANPHI PAPERS, THE **3851**

ACADEMY OF RELIGION AND PSYCHICAL RESEARCH. ACADEMIC CONFERENCE See PROCEEDINGS OF THE ACADEMY OF RELIGION AND PSYCHICAL RESEARCH ... ANNUAL ACADEMIC CONFERENCE **4242**

ACADEMY PLAYERS DIRECTORY (US) [08117752] 4062, **4080**

ACADEMY REPORTER (WASHINGTON) (US/0199-6037) [06046748] **4288**

ACADIA See ACADIA QUARTERLY / ASSOCIATION FOR COMPUTER-AIDED DESIGN IN ARCHITECTURE **1231**

●ACADIA QUARTERLY / ASSOCIATION FOR COMPUTER-AIDED DESIGN IN ARCHITECTURE (US) [25900919] 287, **1231**

ACADIAN ENTOMOLOGICAL SOCIETY. MEETING See PROCEEDINGS OF THE ... ANNUAL MEETING / ACADIAN ENTOMOLOGICAL SOCIETY **5595**

ACADIAN GENEALOGY EXCHANGE (US/0199-9591) [05536600] **2436**

ACADIAN LETTERS (CN/0705-5560) [04097917] **958**

ACADIANA PROFILE (US/0001-4397) [03775533] **2254**

ACADIENSIS (FREDERICTON) (CN/0044-5851) [01670823] **2717**

ACADS QUARTERLY See TECHNICAL COMPUTING (ALEXANDRIA) **1204**

ACAECER (AG/0325-3902) [08248942] **42**

ACAFADE / ASOCIACION CENTROAMERICANA DE FAMILIARES DE DETENIDOS-DESAPARECIDOS (CR) [19496157] **4033**

ACAFO (AG) **4366**

ACANTHUS (FI) [23525981] **287**

ACAP NEWS (CN/1188-0392) [25796660] **2185**

●ACAPA SERIAL (US/1061-2920) [25228329] **1632**

ACARI INDEX, THE (US/0736-5330) [08701189] **4461**

ACAROLOGIA (FR/0044-586X) [01641830] **5573**

ACAROLOGIE (GW/0567-672X) [06125513] **439**

ACAT MICROBIOLOGICA HUNGARICA See ACTA MICROBIOLOGICA ET IMMUNOLOGICA HUNGARICA **558**

ACC BASKETBALL (US/0193-7960) [05243435] **4881**

ACC BASKETBALL HANDBOOK (US/0733-0448) [08515901] **4881**

●ACC CURRENT JOURNAL REVIEW (US/1062-1458) [25532666] **3697**

ACC INJURY STATISTICS. WORK (NZ) [26384496] **2858**

ACCA DOCKET (US/0895-9544) [14713345] **3094**

ACCADEMIA DELLE SCIENZE DELL'ISTITUTO DI BOLOGNA See ANNUARIO DELLA ACCADEMIA DELLE SCIENZE DELL'INSTITUTO DI BOLOGNA : CLASSE DI SCIENZE FISICHE **4397**

ACCADEMIA DELLE SCIENZE DI TORINO. CLASSE DI SCIENZE MORALI, STORICHE E FILOLOGICHE See ATTI **5192**

ACCADEMIA NAZIONALE DE RAGIONERIA See PAPERS ON BUSINESS ADMINISTRATION **881**

ACCADEMIA NAZIONALE DEI LINCEI See NOTIZIE DEGLI SCAVI DI ANTICHITA / ACCADEMIA NAZIONALE DEI LINCEI **276**

ACCADEMIA NAZIONALE DEI LINCEI. CLASSE DI SCIENZE FISICHE, MATEMATICHE E NATURALI See MEMORIE / CLASSE DI SCIENZE FISICHE, MATEMATICHE E NATURALI **5128**

ACCADEMIA NAZIONALE DEI LINCEI, ROME. BIBLIOTECA See INDICI E SUSSIDI BIBLIOGRAFICI **417**

ACCADEMIA NAZIONALE DEI LINCEO, ROMA. CENTRO LINCEO INTERDISCIPLINARE DI SCIENZE MATEMATICHE E LORO APPLICAZIONI See CONTRIBUTI DEL CENTRO LINCEO INTERDISCIPLINARE DI SCIENZE E LORO APPLICAZIONI **3502**

ACCADEMIA PONTANIANA (1825) See ATTI DELLA ACCADEMIA PONTANIANA **1074**

ACCADEMIA ROVERETANA DEGLI AGIATI See ATTI DELLA ACCADEMIA ROVERETANA DEGLI AGIATI **1074**

ACCADEMIE E BIBLIOTECHE D'ITALIA (IT/0001-4451) [02256885] **3186**

ACCART NEWS (AT/1032-3945) [21253262] **5501**

ACCC COMMUNITY (CN/0839-0088) [18608922] **1807**

ACCEL (US) [01779056] **3697**

ACCEL. SUPPLEMENT (US) [01779057] **3697**

ACCELERATION AND PASSING ABILITY (US/0360-6090) [02244048] 4763, **5375**

ACCELERATOR (SASKATOON. 1988) (CN/1193-7114) [27203170] **1887**

ACCELERATORS AND STORAGE RINGS (SZ/0272-5088) [05878531] **5403**

ACCENT (US/0192-7507) [05103904] 2916, **2913**

ACCENT (US/0162-1955) [02250634] **4931**

●ACCENT (MARLBORO, MASS.) (US/1064-6981) [26458575] 2609, **2254**

ACCENT
Alphabetical Title Index

ACCENT ON ARTS (CN/0821-0209) [09670540] **5054**

ACCENT ON MUSIC (US/0730-8906) [08054579] **4098**

ACCENT ON WORSHIP **SUSPENDED.** (US/0276-2358) [07325843] **4931**

ACCENT/REVIEWS (US/0277-9102) [07667298] **4931**

ACCENTS (NEW BRUNSWICK TEACHERS' ASSOCIATION. MUSIC EDUCATION COUNCIL) (CN/0710-6335) [08371791] 1722, **4098**

ACCEPTABLE METHODS, TECHNIQUES, AND PRACTICES. AIRCRAFT ALTERATIONS (US) [02786264] **3**

●ACCEPTABLE RISK (US/1073-2012) [29350915] **636**

ACCEPTED MEAT AND POULTRY EQUIPMENT (US/1057-7793) [02569758] **158**

ACCES A L'INFORMATION EXPRESS (CN/1183-2363) [24296594] **406**

●ACCESS ADVISOR (US/1066-7253) [27033850] **1283**

ACCESS / ARNN, ASSOCIATION OF REGISTERED NURSES OF NEWFOUNDLAND (CN/1182-8897) [23599048] **3850**

ACCESS BY DESIGN (UK/0959-1591) [24799967] **287**

ACCESS (CHICAGO, ILL.) (US/1050-0758) [21389248] **1315**

ACCESS CONTROL (US/1042-2617) [18979117] **2034**

ACCESS EPA (US) [24771439] **2159**

ACCESS (GLOUCESTER) (CN/1183-3149) [24368555] **4383**

ACCESS GUIDE TO GOVERNMENT RECORDS AND INFORMATION (CN/1187-4317) [25351950] **4623**

ACCESS (HALIFAX) (CN/0227-1435) [06516255] **4383**

ACCESS (LANSING, MICH.) (US/1051-0818) [21800454] **3186**

ACCESS (LONDON, ONT.) (CN/0710-0132) [08555886] 4033, **3186**

●ACCESS MAGAZINE (VANCOUVER) (CN/1195-0889) [30377434] **1460**

●ACCESS MEXICO (US/1064-928X) [26461545] **920**

ACCESS (MILWAUKEE, WIS.) (US/0883-0916) [11996734] **636**

ACCESS (NEW YORK, N.Y. : 1983) (US/0890-4537) [12833066] **1722**

ACCESS NIPPON (JA/0915-4841) [21968652] **890**

ACCESS REPORTS (US/0364-7625) [08138682] **4461**

ACCESS REPORTS, PRIVACY (US/0191-6688) [04951614] **2926**

ACCESS REPORTS REFERENCE FILE (US/0191-6696) [02353830] **2926**

ACCESS (RESEARCH TRIANGLE PARK, N.C.) **CEASED.** (US/0733-8074) [08619902] **1265**

ACCESS (SYRACUSE) (US/0095-5698) [01328670] 2484, **2496**

ACCESS TO ENERGY (US/0890-8265) [03506260] **1930**

ACCESS TO WANG (US/1052-6366) [18650428] **1264**

ACCESS USA NEWS (US/1069-6784) [28130615] **4383**

ACCESS (VANCOUVER) (CN/0317-039X) [02247586] **3186**

ACCESS (VICTORIA, AUSTRALIA) (AT/1030-0155) [18396332] 3186, **1802**

●ACCESSASIA (SEATTLE, WASH.) (US/1069-4374) [25651335] **4623**

ACCESSION LIST - NATIONAL INDIAN BROTHERHOOD, LIBRARY (CN/0316-4837) [02603514] **2254**

ACCESSIONS BULLETIN / TROPICAL DEVELOPMENT AND RESEARCH INSTITUTE, LIBRARY (UK) [10730980] **3186**

ACCESSIONS BULLETIN - TROPICAL PRODUCTS INSTITUTE, LIBRARY (UK) [04398965] **42**

ACCESSIONS LIST, BRAZIL AND URUGUAY (BL/1041-1763) [18678777] **406**

ACCESSIONS LIST, BRAZIL. CUMULATIVE LIST OF SERIALS / LIBRARY OF CONGRESS (BL/0731-4515) [08187325] **406**

ACCESSIONS LIST, EASTERN AFRICA (KE/0090-371X) [02403577] **406**

ACCESSIONS LIST, EASTERN AFRICA. ANNUAL SERIAL SUPPLEMENT (KE/0192-7388) [05061785] **406**

●ACCESSIONS LIST, EASTERN AND SOUTHERN AFRICA (KE/1070-2717) [28310688] **406**

ACCESSIONS LIST - EXTERNAL AFFAIRS AND INTERNATIONAL TRADE CANADA. LIBRARY (CN/0848-4856) [23247573] **3186**

ACCESSIONS LIST, MIDDLE EAST (UA/0041-7769) [05918016] **406**

ACCESSIONS LIST / MINISTRY OF HOME AFFAIRS AND NATIONAL HERITAGE, DEPARTMENT OF KENYA NATIONAL ARCHIVES, NATIONAL DOCUMENTATION AND INFORMATION RETRIEVAL SERVICES (KE) [24341285] **2478**

ACCESSIONS LIST, SOUTH ASIA (II/0271-6445) [06674270] **406**

ACCESSIONS LIST, SOUTHEAST ASIA (PK/0096-2341) [02088682] **406**

ACCESSIONS LIST, SOUTHEAST ASIA. CUMULATIVE LIST OF INDONESIAN SERIALS (IO/0163-4054) [03424398] **406**

ACCESSIONS LIST, SOUTHEAST ASIA. CUMULATIVE LIST OF MALAYSIA, SINGAPORE AND BRUNEI SERIALS (IO/0163-4046) [03585217] **406**

ACCESSIONS LIST, SOUTHEAST ASIA. CUMULATIVE LIST OF SERIALS, BURMA, THAILAND AND LAOS (IO/0732-7374) [08415994] **406**

ACCESSIONS - PUBLIC ARCHIVES CANADA (CN/0835-1945) [17544493] **406**

ACCESSIONSKATALOG - DENMARK. RIGSBIBLIOTEKAREMBEDET (DK/0084-9715) [01566180] **3187**

ACCESSIONSKATALOG FOR DRAMATISK BIBLIOTEK (DK) [04459976] **3187**

ACCESSORIES (US/8750-2453) [11175181] **1081**

ACCESSORIES TODAY (US) [27715934] **2898**

ACCI NEWSLETTER / AMERICAN COUNCIL ON CONSUMER INTERESTS (US/0010-9975) [20547760] **1293**

ACCIAIO **CEASED.** (IT) [05699792] **4461**

ACCIAIO INOSSIDABILE, L' (IT/0515-2291) [07593673] **3996**

ACCIDENT ANALYSIS AND PREVENTION (UK/0001-4575) [01460775] **4763**

●ACCIDENT AND EMERGENCY NURSING (UK/0965-2302) [28310049] **3850**

ACCIDENT AND HEALTH BUSINESS (US) [05107559] 2872, **4763**

ACCIDENT AND SAFETY ADVISORY : ASA **CEASED.** (US/0895-7142) [16781996] **4763**

ACCIDENT AND VIOLATION ANALYSIS FOR LICENSED OREGON DRIVERS (US/0360-9847) [02245143] **5438**

ACCIDENT COMPENSATION. VICTORIA (AT) **2872**

ACCIDENT CONTROL REPORT (US/0364-4693) [02658049] **2185**

ACCIDENT FACTS (CHICAGO) (US/0148-6039) [01460776] **4763**

ACCIDENT FATALITIES, CANADA (CN/0316-7283) [02247824] **4763**

ACCIDENT/INCIDENT BULLETIN (US/0163-4674) [04124987] 5429, **4763**

ACCIDENT/INCIDENT REPORTING ADREP (CN/1014-4498) [I10144498] **3**

ACCIDENT PREVENTION (CN/0044-5878) [02293931] **2858**

ACCIDENT PREVENTION (ARLINGTON, VA.) (US/1057-5561) [24059092] 4763, **3**

ACCIDENT PREVENTION MAGAZINE (CN) **2858**

ACCIDENT PREVENTION MANUAL FOR BUSINESS & INDUSTRY (US) [01191951] **2858**

ACCIDENT RECONSTRUCTION JOURNAL (US/1057-8153) [20782681] 5438, **5403**

ACCIDENTAL POISONING IN WISCONSIN (US/0094-5927) [01789828] **4763**

ACCIDENTS DE LA CIRCULATION SUR LA VOIE PUBLIQUE AVEC TUES OU BLESSES (BE/0770-237X) [04305011] **5438**

ACCIDENTS IN NORTH AMERICAN MOUNTAINEERING (US/0065-082X) [02476376] 4763, **4868**

ACCION (PY) [02782468] **5189**

ACCION CIVICA (NQ) [03415459] **4033**

ACCION CRITICA (PE/0258-2678) [03829878] **5269**

ACCION (EL PASO, TEX.) (US/0731-2687) [08147128] **5054**

ACCION EMPRESARIAL (SP/0044-5894) [I00445894] 636, **1460**

ACCION PARLAMENTARIA (AG) [12006042] **4623**

ACCIS NEWSLETTER (SZ/0254-3133) [14164138] **1170**

ACCIS (ORGANIZATION) **See** MEMBERSHIP DIRECTORY / ACCIS **1835**

ACCOKEEK FOUNDATION **See** BIENNIAL REPORT - THE ACCOKEEK FOUNDATION **4163**

ACCOMPLISHMENTS FOR RESEARCH, EXTENSION, AND HIGHER EDUCATION / JOINT COUNCIL ON FOOD AND AGRICULTURAL SCIENCES (US/0743-555X) [10393329] **42**

ACCOMPLISHMENTS OF FISCAL YEAR - NORTHEASTERN AREA, STATE AND PRIVATE FORESTRY (US/0271-1532) [04966317] **2373**

ACCOMPLISHMENTS OF THE COMMITTEE ON INTERIOR AND INSULAR AFFAIRS OF THE HOUSE OF REPRESENTATIVES DURING THE ... CONGRESS (US) [01240539] **4461**

ACCORD (US) [07237277] **4098**

ACCORD (CALGARY) (CN/0226-7845) [09145730] **2254**

ACCORD (NEW YORK, N.Y.) (US/0883-8933) [12175693] **5054**

ACCORDIA RESEARCH PAPERS : THE JOURNAL OF THE ACCORDIA RESEARCH CENTRE (UK) [27312101] **335**

ACCOUNTABILITY IN RESEARCH (US/0898-9621) [17959730] **5079**

●ACCOUNTABILITY NEWS FOR HEALTH CARE MANAGERS (US/1076-8432) [30620926] **859**

ACCOUNTABILITY REPORT, AND ... STATE PLAN FOR THE ADMINISTRATION OF VOCATIONAL EDUCATION IN THE STATE OF OKLAHOMA (US) [11893320] **1909**

ACCOUNTABILITY REPORT FOR VOCATIONAL EDUCATION IN MICHIGAN / MICHIGAN STATE BOARD OF EDUCATION (US) [07268607] **1909**

ACCOUNTABILITY REPORT FOR VOCATIONAL-TECHNICAL EDUCATION / STATE OF VERMONT (US) [08368407] **1909**

ACCOUNTANCY AGE (UK/0001-4672) [03319285] **735**

ACCOUNTANCY IRELAND (IE/0001-4699) [05783408] **735**

ACCOUNTANCY (LONDON) (UK/0001-4664) [01460778] **735**

ACCOUNTANCY SA (SA/0258-7254) [10217383] **735**

ACCOUNTANT (AMSTERDAM) (NE/0001-4729) [02064544] **735**

ACCOUNTANT (LONDON) (UK/0001-4710) [02444302] **735**

ACCOUNTANT (NAIROBI), THE (KE/1010-4135) [11980374] **735**

ACCOUNTANTS DIGEST (LONDON, ENGLAND) (UK/0307-0336) [12406006] **735**

ACCOUNTANTS' INDEX. SUPPLEMENT **See** ACCOUNTING AND TAX INDEX **725**

ACCOUNTANTS' JOURNAL (PH/0001-4753) [01460784] **735**

ACCOUNTANTS' JOURNAL (WELLINGTON) (NZ/0001-4745) [01460785] **735**

ACCOUNTANTS' LIABILITY (US/8756-4262) [08921963] 2926, **736**

ACCOUNTANT'S MAGAZINE, THE (UK/0001-4761) [01460786] **736**

ACCOUNTANT'S TAX WEEKLY (US/1059-7654) [24727984] **736**

ACCOUNTANT'S WEEKLY TAX REPORT (US/1049-1139) [21136681] **736**

ACCOUNTER (CALGARY) (CN/0702-5300) [03956703] **736**

ACCOUNTING & ASC COMPLIANCE (AT/1037-1869) [I10371869] **736**

ACCOUNTING AND AUDITING DISCLOSURE MANUAL (US/0737-3325) [09313651] **736**

ACCOUNTING & AUDITING UPDATE SERVICE (US/1045-1447) [12213324] **736**

ACCOUNTING AND BUSINESS RESEARCH (UK/0001-4788) [01460787] **736**

ACCOUNTING AND BUSINESS REVIEW (SI/0218-5563) **736**

ACCOUNTING AND FINANCE (AT/0110-5159) [06483230] **736**

ACCOUNTING AND FINANCE PARKVILLE (AT/0810-5391) [I08105391] **736**

●ACCOUNTING AND TAX DATABASE [ONLINE DATABASE] (US) 736, **725**

●ACCOUNTING AND TAX INDEX (US/1063-0287) [25843446] 736, **725**

ACCOUNTING ARTICLES (US) [02259587] 736, **725**

ACCOUNTING, AUDITING & ACCOUNTABILITY JOURNAL (UK/0951-3574) [21278378] **736**

ACCOUNTING BUSINESS AND FINANCIAL HISTORY (UK/0958-5206) [23805016] **736**

5824

Alphabetical Title Index ACM

ACCOUNTING CORPORATION OF AMERICA *See* BAROMETER OF SMALL BUSINESS **642**

ACCOUNTING + DATA PROCESSING ABSTRACTS (UK/0001-4796) [02620304] 736, 1255, **725**

ACCOUNTING DEPARTMENT MANAGEMENT & ADMINISTRATION REPORT (US/1042-928X) [19252450] **736**

●ACCOUNTING EDUCATION (UK/0963-9284) [25741263] **736**

ACCOUNTING EDUCATION NEWS (US/0882-956X) [07828978] **736**

ACCOUNTING EDUCATORS' JOURNAL, THE (US/1041-0392) [18436230] **736**

ACCOUNTING ENQUIRIES (CN/1183-904X) [25066633] **736**

ACCOUNTING FOR LAW FIRMS (US/0898-8102) [17665307] **736**

ACCOUNTING FOR LAWYERS (US/0730-7721) [05630173] 2926, **737**

ACCOUNTING FORUM (ADELAIDE, S. AUST.) (AT/0155-9982) [11744007] **737**

ACCOUNTING HISTORIANS JOURNAL, THE (US/0148-4184) [03228548] **737**

ACCOUNTING HISTORIANS NOTEBOOK, THE (US/1075-1416) [06564337] **737**

ACCOUNTING HORIZONS (US/0888-7993) [13721422] **737**

ACCOUNTING JOURNAL (NEW YORK), THE (US/0198-7283) [04202739] **737**

ACCOUNTING JOURNAL, THE (MY/0126-625X) [01784306] **737**

ACCOUNTING, MANAGEMENT, AND INFORMATION TECHNOLOGIES (US/0959-8022) [24900243] **737**

ACCOUNTING OFFICE MANAGEMENT & ADMINISTRATION REPORT (US/0749-2928) [11101652] 859, **737**

ACCOUNTING, ORGANIZATIONS AND SOCIETY (UK/0361-3682) [02336682] **737**

ACCOUNTING PRINCIPLES AND PRACTICES IN CANADA AND THE UNITED STATES OF AMERICA (CN/0824-300X) [10334984] **737**

ACCOUNTING RESEARCH JOURNAL (AT) [I10309616] **737**

ACCOUNTING RESEARCH MONOGRAPH (US/0146-9800) [03063267] **737**

ACCOUNTING REVIEW, THE (US/0001-4826) [01460791] **737**

ACCOUNTING SERVICES CONFERENCE (US) [17734895] **737**

ACCOUNTING STANDARDS BOARD AND INTERNATIONAL ACCOUNTING STANDARDS (UK) **737**

ACCOUNTING STANDARDS BOARD PAPERS (UK) **737**

ACCOUNTING STANDARDS. CURRENT TEXT (US/0745-886X) [08833908] **737**

ACCOUNTING STANDARDS. CURRENT TEXT AS OF JUNE 1 ... / FINANCIAL ACCOUNTING STANDARDS BOARD (US/0745-886X) [10491044] **737**

ACCOUNTING STANDARDS. GUIDELINES AND EXPOSURE DRAFTS (UK) **737**

●ACCOUNTING TECHNOLOGY (US/1068-6452) [27722505] **738**

ACCOUNTING TODAY (US/1044-5714) [18968151] **738**

ACCOUNTING TRENDS & TECHNIQUES (US) [03262368] **738**

ACCOUNTING WORLD (UK/0953-2579) [I09532579] **738**

ACCOUNTS (UK) [18302334] **5347**

ACCOUNTS FOR THE YEAR ENDED 31ST DECEMBER ... : AUDITOR-GENERAL'S REPORT / REPUBLIC OF ZAMBIA, THE COUNCIL OF LEGAL EDUCATION (ZA) [10768263] 2926, **4708**

ACCOUNTS - NEW HEBRIDES CONDOMINIUM. COMPTES - CONDOMINIUM DES NOUVELLES-HEBRIDES (NN) [03475653] **4708**

ACCOUNTS OF CHEMICAL RESEARCH (US/0001-4842) [01460793] **958**

ACCOUNTS OF HONG KONG AND ANNUAL REPORT OF THE ACCOUNTANT GENERAL (HK) [02539169] **4708**

ACCOUNTS OF THE NORTHERN IRELAND HOUSING EXECUTIVE (IE/0306-9907) [01795983] **2813**

ACCOUNTS, TREASURER'S AND AUDITORS' REPORTS / AMNESTY INTERNATIONAL (UK) [09563828] **4461**

●ACCRA COST OF LIVING INDEX (US/1070-9169) [27283072] **1460**

ACCREDITATION (US/0099-0256) [01646696] **1807**

ACCREDITATION BOARD FOR ENGINEERING & TECHNOLOGY U.S.) *See* ANNUAL REPORT YEAR ENDING SEPT. 30 ... / ACCREDITATION BOARD FOR ENGINEERING AND TECHNOLOGY **5084**

●ACCREDITATION MANUAL FOR AMBULATORY HEALTH CARE : AMAHC (US) [25895275] **3543**

●ACCREDITATION MANUAL FOR HEALTH CARE NETWORKS. VOL. 1, STANDARDS (US/1078-0076) [30952561] **3775**

●ACCREDITATION MANUAL FOR HEALTH CARE NETWORKS. VOL. 2, SCORING GUIDELINES (US/1077-9817) [30938553] **3775**

ACCREDITATION MANUAL FOR HOSPITALS / THE JOINT COMMISSION (US/1059-7409) [18900335] **3775**

ACCREDITATION MANUAL FOR LONG TERM CARE (US) **3775**

ACCREDITED INSTITUTIONS OF POSTSECONDARY EDUCATION, PROGRAMS, CANDIDATES (US/0270-1715) [03145291] **1807**

ACCREDITED POSTSECONDARY INSTITUTIONS AND PROGRAMS (US) [01647926] **1807**

ACCREDITED RESIDENT MANAGER NEWS / INSTITUTE OF REAL ESTATE MANAGEMENT OF THE NATIONAL ASSOCIATION OF REALTORS (US/0746-2751) [09910569] 4833, **859**

ACCT TRUSTEE QUARTERLY (US/0271-9746) [04960602] **1807**

ACCURACY IN MEDIA, INC *See* AIM REPORT **2917**

ACE. ASSOCIATION OF CULTURAL EXECUTIVES (CN/0833-451X) [16219338] **312**

ACE BULLETIN (LONDON, ENGLAND) (UK) [11410238] **1722**

ACE INTERNATIONAL. ENGLISH EDITION (US/0148-8856) [03383724] **5315**

ACE (NEW YORK, N.Y.) (US/0733-043X) [08505209] **4881**

ACE NEWS (AT/0727-6796) [I07276796] **1722**

ACEC REVIEW (BE/0001-0669) [08157700] **2034**

ACEID NEWSLETTER (TH) [03571338] **1722**

ACER NEWSLETTER (AT) [04547120] **1722**

ACERIAS PAZ DEL RIO, S.A *See* INFORME - ACERIAS PAZ DEL RIO, S.A **1612**

ACERO Y ENERGIA (SP/0001-4850) [02444304] **3996**

ACERVO : REVISTA DO ARQUIVO NACIONAL (BL) [17554175] **2478**

ACFA BULLETIN (US/0744-9631) [08682454] **4285**

ACFO INFO (CN/0315-1697) [01678898] **2526**

ACFOA NEWS (AT/0811-4692) [08114692] **4514**

ACGIH TRANSACTIONS (US/0882-4274) [09535196] **2858**

ACH, MODELS IN CHEMISTRY (HU/1217-8969) [12178969] **959**

ACHAB ROMA (IT/1120-849X) [I1120849X] **3357**

ACHADEMIA LEONARDI VINCI (IT/0394-8501) [19520357] **4222**

ACHATS ET ENTREPRISE PARIS (FR/1161-7748) [I11617748] **948**

ACHATS ET ENTRETIEN DU MATERIEL INDUSTRIEL (FR) [16819755] **1963**

ACHEMA JAHRBUCH (GW) [01460797] **959**

ACHIEVEMENT (LONDON. 1969) (UK/0001-4907) [01460798] **1596**

ACHIEVEMENTS OF ESA SCIENTIFIC SATELLITES, THE (NE) **3**

ACHIEVEMENTS (WASHINGTON) (US/0270-7578) [05863775] **4701**

ACHIMOWIN (CN/0705-839X) [04249974] **5779**

ACHPER NATIONAL JOURNAL, THE (AT) [09806613] **2595**

ACHPER NATIONAL JOURNAL [MICROFORM], THE (US/0813-2283) [16885749] **2595**

ACHTZEHNTE JAHRHUNDERT, DAS (GW) [05622136] **2672**

ACI DIRECTORY (US/0363-2296) [01726988] **2018**

ACI MANUAL OF CONCRETE PRACTICE (US/0065-7875) [03935812] **598**

ACI MATERIALS JOURNAL (US/0889-325X) [13846872] 598, **2018**

ACI STANDARDS / AMERICAN CONCRETE INSTITUTE (US/0569-4027) [03834874] **2018**

ACI STRUCTURAL JOURNAL (US/0889-3241) [13846957] 598, **2018**

ACIAR FOOD LEGUME NEWSLETTER (AT/0814-4133) [I08144133] **42**

ACIAR MONOGRAPH SERIES (AT) [I10318194] **42**

ACIAR PROCEEDINGS (AT/1038-6920) [I10386920] **43**

ACIAR TECHNICAL REPORTS (AT) [18386044] **43**

ACIAR TECHNICAL REPORTS SERIES (AT/0816-7923) [I08167923] **43**

ACIAR WORKING PAPER (AT/0819-7857) [I08197857] **43**

ACID MAGAZINE (SW/0282-0196) [11327902] **2222**

ACID NEWS STOCKHOLM (SW/0281-5087) [I02815087] **2223**

ACID PRECIPITATION (US/0741-5230) [10167573] **2223**

ACID PRECIPITATION DIGEST *CEASED.* (US/0740-2252) [09265957] **2223**

ACID RAIN (SW/0281-5087) [17937365] **2185**

ACID RAIN ESSENTIALS (US/0883-3435) [12123607] **2223**

ACID RAIN NOTES (CN/0824-5096) [10615639] **2223**

ACIDIC PRECIPITATION IN ONTARIO STUDY (CN/0824-880X) [I0824880X] **2223**

ACIDIFICATION RESEARCH IN SWEDEN *CEASED.* (SW) [11292614] **4029**

ACIER ARABE (AE) [02371428] **1596**

ACIER POUR CONSTRUIRE, L' (FR/0153-5471) [I01535471] **598**

ACIP: REVUE DE L'ASSOCIATION DES CADRES DE L'INDUSTRIE PHARMACEUTIQUE (FR) **4288**

ACIS : JOURNAL OF THE ASSOCIATION FOR CONTEMPORARY IBERIAN STUDIES (UK/0955-4270) [22463144] 2553, 2672, **3260**

ACJ (PLATTE CITY, MO.) (US/1068-8021) [27819311] 5501, **204**

ACKERMAN WAREHOUSING FORUM (US/1060-3182) [24931502] **636**

ACKNOWLEDGE : THE WINDOW LETTER (US/1043-0768) [19295680] **1283**

ACKNOWLEDGE WINDOWS LETTER *See* WINDOWS LETTER **1292**

●ACLA BULLETIN (US) [29766661] **3357**

ACLA NEWSLETTER (US/0891-3277) [14755883] **3357**

ACLALS BULLETIN *CEASED.* (II/0157-6283) [08023829] 3261, **3357**

ACLD NEWSBRIEFS (US/0739-909X) [08775231] **1874**

ACLIS NEWS (AT/1032-0431) [I10320431] **3187**

ACLS ALERT (US/1041-7974) [18853776] **3697**

ACLS OCCASIONAL PAPER (US/1041-536X) [17613722] 1887, **2841**

ACLU NEWS (US) [09396372] **4503**

●ACM ADA LETTERS : A BIMONTHLY PUBLICATION OF SIGADA, THE ACM SPECIAL INTEREST GROUP ON ADA (US) [28480866] **1277**

ACM COMPUTING SURVEYS (US/0360-0300) [01731026] **1170**

ACM GUIDE TO COMPUTING LITERATURE (US/0149-1199) [04111189] 1255, **1208**

●ACM LETTERS ON PROGRAMMING LANGUAGES AND SYSTEMS (US/1057-4514) [24037443] **1277**

ACM MONOGRAPH SERIES *CEASED.* (US/0572-4252) [04057538] **1170**

ACM NO-NONSENSE GUIDE TO COMPUTING CAREERS (US) 1170, **4201**

ACM SIGPLAN NOTICES : A MONTHLY PUBLICATION OF THE SPECIAL INTEREST GROUP ON PROGRAMMING LANGUAGES (US) [25073822] **1278**

ACM SPECIAL INTEREST GROUP FOR AUTOMATA AND COMPUTABILITY THEORY *See* SIGACT NEWS **1202**

ACM TRANSACTIONS ON COMPUTER SYSTEMS (US/0734-2071) [08707114] 1231, **1246**

ACM TRANSACTIONS ON DATABASE SYSTEMS (US/0362-5915) [02303032] **1252**

ACM TRANSACTIONS ON GRAPHICS (US/0730-0301) [07941481] **1231**

ACM TRANSACTIONS ON INFORMATION SYSTEMS : PUBLICATION OF THE ASSOCIATION FOR COMPUTING MACHINERY (US/1046-8188) [20309308] **1255**

ACM TRANSACTIONS ON MATHEMATICAL SOFTWARE (US/0098-3500) [01748060] 3490, **1283**

ACM TRANSACTIONS ON MODELING AND COMPUTER SIMULATION : A PUBLICATION OF THE ASSOCIATION FOR COMPUTING MACHINERY (US/1049-3301) [21207232] 3490, **1282**

ACM TRANSACTIONS ON PROGRAMMING LANGUAGES AND SYSTEMS (US/0164-0925) [04574696] **1278**

●ACM TRANSACTIONS ON SOFTWARE ENGINEERING AND METHODOLOGY (US/1049-331X) [21207269] 1283, **1227**

ACME (IT/0001-494X) [01964842] **2841**

ACOA ACTION NEWS (US/0743-8834) [10690515] **4503**

ACOFAR : REVISTA DEL MUNDO FARMACEUTICO (SP) [19369422] **4288**

ACOG CURRENT JOURNAL REVIEW (US/0897-1471) [17418905] **3755**

ACOG NEWSLETTER (US/0400-048X) [06269174] **3755**

ACOG TECHNICAL BULLETIN (US/1074-8628) [06658583] **3756**

ACOG UPDATE (AUDIO CASSETTE) (US) **3756**

ACOLAM NEWSLETTER / STANDING CONFERENCE OF NATIONAL AND UNIVERSITY LIBRARIES, ADVISORY COMMITTEE ON LATIN AMERICAN MATERIALS (UK/0263-6824) [19411160] **3187**

ACONCAGUA (VADUZ) (LH/0001-4958) [02256894] **4288**

ACONEX (CL) [19566617] **43**

ACONTECER MIGRATORIO (VE) [06987468] **1642**

ACOPEL (CK) [01786467] **3261**

ACOPS YEARBOOK / ADVISORY COMMITTEE ON POLLUTION OF THE SEA, LONDON *CEASED.* (UK/1012-4411) [18095819] **2223**

ACORDO DE CLASSIFICACAO NO ESTADO DE MATO GROSSO *See* DADOS ESTATISTICOS : PRODUTOS AGRO PECUARIOS SAIDOS DE MATO GROSSO **152**

ACORN JOURNAL (AT/1031-1017) [10311017] **3850**

ACORN JOURNAL : OFFICIAL JOURNAL OF THE AUSTRALIAN CONFEDERATION OF OPERATING ROOM NURSES (AT/0156-3491) [23297668] **3850**

ACORN (PLATTEVILLE), THE (US/0274-8762) [06669452] **1887**

ACORN (SANDWICH, MASS.) (US) [09093690] **2585**

ACORN : STORIES, POEMS, ESSAYS, REVIEWS / ENTIRELY WRITTEN AND EDITED BY YOUNG WRITERS (US) [02735638] 1059, **3357**

ACORN STORYTELLER (US) **1887**

ACORN, THE ARCHITECTURAL CONSERVANCY OF ONTARIO R NEWSLETTER (CN/0704-0083) [05018409] **287**

ACORNS TO OAKS (US) **2436**

A'COURT'S BUSINESS HANDBOOK NEW ZEALAND EDITION (NZ) [11706112] **2927**

ACOUSTIC CORPORATION OF AMERICA *See* A.C.A. INDUSTRY GUIDE TO HEARING AIDS. INTERNATIONAL EDITION **4382**

ACOUSTIC GUITAR (US/1049-9261) [21354637] **4098**

ACOUSTIC PERFORMER *CEASED.* (US/1054-0717) [22753665] **4098**

ACOUSTICAL IMAGING (US/0270-5117) [08264158] **4451**

●ACOUSTICAL PHYSICS (US/1063-7710) [26142019] **4452**

ACOUSTICS ABSTRACTS (UK/0001-4974) [00881846] 4452, **4426**

ACOUSTICS AUSTRALIA / AUSTRALIAN ACOUSTICAL SOCIETY (AT/0814-6039) [12570425] **4452**

ACOUSTICS BULLETIN (UK/0308-437X) [I0308437X] **4452**

ACOUSTICS LETTERS (UK/0140-1599) [03879361] **4452**

ACP BASIC STATISTICS (LU/1015-213X) [09403070] 1460, **1528**

ACP HEALTH LIBRARY *CEASED.* (US/1043-6251) [19498971] 3187, **3543**

ACP JOURNAL CLUB (US/1056-8751) [23085040] **3794**

ACPA *SUSPENDED.* (CU/0138-6247) [09772190] **204**

ACPM NEWS (US/1044-4211) [19784042] **3544**

ACQ INFORME (CN/0712-2535) [08808134] **43**

ACQUA ARIA (1977) (IT/0391-5557) [04455817] **2159**

ACQUE SOTTERRANEE; RICERCHE, SFRUTTAMENTO, CONSERVAZIONE (IT) [20177253] **5528**

ACQUERELLO ITALIANO (AUDIOCASSETTE) (US) **2513**

ACQUIRED IMMUNE DEFICIENCY SYNDROME NEWSLETTER (US/1041-4487) [18603947] 3711, **3662**

ACQUIRED IMMUNE DEFICIENCY SYNDROME ... (REPORTED COSTS) (US) [14387931] **4763**

ACQUISA (GW/0938-7927) [I09387927] **952**

ACQUISITION, BIBLIOGRAPHY, CATALOGUING NEWS / NATIONAL LIBRARY OF AUSTRALIA (AT/0725-0037) [08269440] **3187**

ACQUISITION/DIVESTITURE WEEKLY REPORT (US/0279-4160) [06856786] **636**

ACQUISITION FINANCIAL STATUS / AFSC COMPTROLLER (US) [23808496] **3**

ACQUISITION ISSUES (US/1052-1674) [22200947] 2927, **4708**

ACQUISITION LIST / UNIVERSITY OF HAWAII LIBRARY, HAWAIIAN COLLECTION (US) [13998757] **407**

ACQUISITIONS AND MERGERS IN A TROUBLED ENVIRONMENT (US/0883-4407) [07361286] **3094**

ACQUISITIONS AND MERGERS IN A TROUBLED ENVIRONMENT (US) [24766796] **636**

ACQUISITIONS - ARCHIVES PUBLIQUES CANADA (CN/0835-1937) [17544483] **407**

ACQUISITIONS - CANADIAN HOUSING INFORMATION CENTRE (CN/0711-9674) [08871340] **2813**

ACQUISITIONS LIBRARIAN, THE (US/0896-3576) [17009807] **3187**

●ACQUISITIONS LIST - CANADIAN HOUSING INFORMATION CENTRE (CN/1197-7485) [30097716] **2813**

ACQUISITIONS LIST - CANADIAN MUSEUM OF NATURE. LIBRARY SERVICES (CN/1180-3592) [23247561] **3187**

ACQUISITIONS LIST - CENTRE OF CRIMINOLOGY LIBRARY, UNIVERSITY OF TORONTO (CN/0701-0524) [03400178] **3078**

ACQUISITIONS LIST / MANITOBA, DEPT. OF EDUCATION, LIBRARY (CN/0228-3867) [08963934] **1792**

ACQUISITIONS MEDICALES RECENTES (FR/0075-4463) [01337940] **3544**

ACQUISITIONS, MERGERS, SPIN-OFFS, AND OTHER RESTRUCTURINGS (US/1070-907X) [28489908] **636**

ACQUISITIONS / METROPOLITAN TORONTO LIBRARY, GENERAL REFERENCE DEPARTMENT (CN/0226-2509) [07857874] **3187**

ACQUISITIONS - METROPOLITAN TORONTO LIBRARY, MUSIC DEPARTMENT (CN/0226-2541) [07822763] **4098**

ACQUISITIONS / METROPOLITAN TORONTO LIBRARY, SOCIAL SCIENCES DEPARTMENT (CN/0226-2568) [07822690] **5189**

ACQUISITIONS MONTHLY (UK) [18759787] **636**

ACQUISITIONS NEWSLETTER *CEASED.* (AT) [02383597] **3187**

ACQUISITIONS ULTIMO (AT/0815-0494) [I08150494] 2478, **3187**

ACQUISIZIONI FUSIONI CONCORRENZA (IT) **1596**

ACQUISTION BIBLIOGRAHPY CATALOGUING NEWS *See* NLA GATEWAYS **3237**

ACR BULLETIN (US/0098-6070) [01123814] **3938**

ACREAGE MARKETING GUIDES. SPRING VEGETABLES AND MELONS (US/0565-1905) [03877190] **2407**

ACREAGE-MARKETING GUIDES, WINTER VEGETABLES AND POTATOES (US/0565-1921) [03164207] **2325**

ACRES, U.S.A (US) [02796002] **43**

ACRL PUBLICATIONS IN LIBRARIANSHIP (US/0193-1784) [01432032] 1807, **3187**

ACROD NEWSLETTER (AT/0729-8463) [I07298463] **4383**

ACRONYMS (US/0163-6774) [04439996] **1170**

ACRONYMS, INITIALISMS & ABBREVIATIONS DICTIONARY (US/0270-4404) [02516185] **3261**

ACROSS ARCHITECTURE *CEASED.* (UK) [11008826] **287**

ACROSS THE BOARD (US/0147-1554) [02600355] **636**

ACROSS THE BORDER (BLOOMINGTON, MINN.) (US/1053-0614) [21955355] **2436**

ACROSS THE TABLE (US/0362-8493) [02361649] **3143**

ACS MONOGRAPH (US) [01780002] **959**

ACS NEWSLETTER / ASSOCIATION FOR CANADIAN STUDIES (CN/0714-2579) [09387052] **2526**

ACS SERVICE REPORT (US/0277-8025) [07623843] **1541**

ACS SINGLE ARTICLE ANNOUNCEMENT *CEASED.* (US/0044-7587) [02489852] **959**

ACS SYMPOSIUM SERIES (US/0097-6156) [01421658] **959**

AC'S TECH FOR THE COMMODORE AMIGA (US/1053-7929) [22646766] **1170**

ACSI-ON (CN/0821-5049) [09816229] **3187**

ACSJC OCCASIONAL PAPERS (AT/1032-2205) [I10322205] **4503**

ACSM / ASPRS CONVENTION PROCEEDINGS (US) **2580**

ACSM BULLETIN (US/0747-9417) [09781501] **2580**

●ACSM MEMBERSHIP DIRECTORY/ AMERICAN COLLEGE OF SPORTS MEDICINE (US) [25454941] **3953**

●ACSM TECHNICAL PAPERS / ACSM/ASPRS ANNUAL CONVENTION & EXPOSITION (US) [29371121] **2580**

ACSUS. CANADIAN STUDIES UPDATE (US/0734-4546) [08755394] **2717**

ACSUS MEMBERSHIP DIRECTORY (US/0892-7111) [11703507] **2717**

ACT 511 TAXES (US) [06568306] **1859**

ACT. ADVERTISING/COMMUNICATIONS TIMES (US/0193-4457) [05205475] **753**

ACT DIGEST (UK/0305-9286) [I03059286] 1722, **4931**

ACT (NEW YORK, N.Y.), THE *SUSPENDED.* (US/0885-6702) [12869471] **335**

ACT NEWSLETTER (SIMSBURY, CONN.) (US/0742-7751) [08405717] **1887**

ACT NEWSLETTER - SOCIETY FOR COMPUTERS AND THE LAW, A.C.T (AT/0813-6270) [I08136270] 1170, **2927**

ACT PAPERS IN ADULT EDUCATION AND TRAINING (AT/1030-858X) [I1030858X] **1799**

ACT SCIENCE TEACHER (AT/0818-2019) [I08182019] **1887**

ACT TAFE COURSE GUIDE (AT) **4201**

ACT TEACHER JOURNAL (AT) **1887**

ACT (WHITING) (US/0001-5083) [01774759] 2276, **4931**

ACTA ACADEMIAE ABOENSIS. SER. A. HUMANIORA (FI/0355-578X) [01767859] **2841**

ACTA ACADEMIAE ABOENSIS. SERIES: B, MATHEMATICA ET PHYSICA (FI/0001-5105) [09529861] 4395, **3490**

ACTA ACADEMIAE AGRICULTURAE AC TECHNICAE OLSTENENSIS (PL) [15501952] **43**

ACTA ACADEMIAE AGRICULTURAE AC TECHNICAE OLSTENENSIS. AEDIFICATIO ET MECHANICA (PL/0860-2956) [I08602956] **43**

ACTA ACADEMIAE AGRICULTURAE AC TECHNICAE OLSTENENSIS. AGRICULTURA (PL/0860-2832) [14199491] **43**

ACTA ACADEMIAE AGRICULTURAE AC TECHNICAE OLSTENENSIS. OECONOMICA (PL/0860-2948) [I08602948] **43**

ACTA ACADEMIAE AGRICULTURAE AC TECHNICAE OLSTENENSIS. PROTECTIO AQUARUM ET PISCATORIA (PL/0860-2611) [14536391] **43**

ACTA ACADEMIAE AGRICULTURAE AC TECHNICAE OLSTENENSIS. TECHNOLOGIA ALIMENTORUM (PL/0860-2859) [I08602859] **43**

ACTA ACADEMIAE AGRICULTURAE AC TECHNICAE OLSTENENSIS. VETERINARIA (PL/0860-2840) [14918420] **5501**

ACTA ACADEMIAE AGRICULTURAE AC TECHNICAE OLSTENENSIS. ZOOTECHNICA (PL/0860-2603) [14536517] **5573**

ACTA ACUSTICA (FR) **4395**

ACTA AD ARCHAEOLOGIAM ET ARTIUM HISTORIAM PERTINENTIA (IT/0065-0900) [01193300] 253, **335**

ACTA ADRIATICA (CI/0001-5113) [01179290] **552**

ACTA AGRARIA ET SILVESTRIA. SERIES AGRARIA (PL/0065-0919) [10075456] **43**

ACTA AGRARIA ET SILVESTRIA. SERIES SILVESTRIS (PL/0065-0927) [09799238] **2373**

ACTA AGRARIA ET SILVESTRIA. SERIES ZOOTECHNICA (PL/0065-0935) [01460811] **204**

ACTA AGRICULTUR SCANDINAVICA *See* ACTA AGRICULTUR SCANDINAVICA. SECTION B, SOIL AND PLANT SCIENCE **43**

Alphabetical Title Index — ACTA

ACTA AGRICULTUR SCANDINAVICA See ACTA AGRICULTUR SCANDINAVICA. SECTION A, ANIMAL SCIENCE **43**

●ACTA AGRICULTUR SCANDINAVICA. SECTION A, ANIMAL SCIENCE (DK/0906-4702) [25613760] 5501, **43**

●ACTA AGRICULTUR SCANDINAVICA. SECTION B, SOIL AND PLANT SCIENCE (DK/0906-4710) [25615392] 161, **43**

ACTA AGRICULTURAE SCANDINAVICA. SUPPLEMENTUM (SW/0065-0943) [01460815] **43**

ACTA AGROBOTANICA (PL/0065-0951) [01460817] **496**

ACTA AGRONOMICA HUNGARICA (HU/0238-0161) [16440312] **43**

ACTA AGRONOMICA (PALMIRA) (CK/0044-5959) [01460819] **43**

ACTA AGRONOMICA (UNIVERSIDAD NACIONAL DE COLOMBIA. FACULTAD DE CIENCIAS AGROPECUARIAS) (CK/0120-2812) [09710105] **43**

ACTA ALIMENTARIA (BUDAPEST) (HU/0139-3006) [04551208] **2325**

ACTA ALIMENTARIA POLONICA See POLISH JOURNAL OF FOOD AND NUTRITION SCIENCES / POLISH ACADEMY OF SCIENCES **2353**

ACTA AMAZONICA (BL/0044-5967) [03495363] **439**

ACTA AMAZONICA. SUPLEMENTO (BL) [04365368] **439**

ACTA ANAESTHESIOLOGICA BELGICA (BE/0001-5164) [01460822] **3680**

ACTA ANAESTHESIOLOGICA ITALICA (IT/0374-4965) [01779060] **3680**

ACTA ANAESTHESIOLOGICA SCANDINAVICA (DK/0001-5172) [01180097] **3680**

ACTA ANAESTHESIOLOGICA SCANDINAVICA. SUPPLEMENT (DK/0515-2720) [01586171] **3680**

●ACTA ANAESTHESIOLOGICA SINICA (CC) [30542926] **3680**

ACTA ANATOMICA (SZ/0001-5180) [01460824] 531, 541, **3678**

ACTA ANTHROPOGENETICA (II/0258-0357) [03727707] 541, **227**

ACTA ANTIQUA ACADEMIAE SCIENTIARUM HUNGARICAE (HU/0044-5975) [01460827] 1073, **3261**

ACTA APOSTOLICA SEDIS, COMMENTARIUM OFFICIALE (VC/0001-5199) [01460828] 2927, **5022**

ACTA APPLICANDAE MATHEMATICAE (NE/0167-8019) [09710183] **3490**

ACTA ARACHNOLOGICA (JA/0001-5202) [01460829] **5573**

ACTA ARCHAEOLOGICA (DK/0065-101X) [01460830] **253**

ACTA ARCHAEOLOGICA ACADEMIAE SCIENTIARUM HUNGARICAE (HU/0001-5210) [01460831] **253**

ACTA ARCHAEOLOGICA CARPATHICA (PL/0001-5229) [01652389] **253**

ACTA ARCHAEOLOGICA LODZIENSIA (PL/0065-0986) [05198308] **253**

ACTA ARCHAEOLOGICA LOVANIENSIA (BE/0776-2984) [07762984] **253**

ACTA ARITHMETICA (PL/0065-1036) [01460834] **3490**

ACTA ASIATICA (JA/0567-7254) [01460835] **2644**

ACTA ASTRONAUTICA (UK/0094-5765) [01794490] **3**

ACTA ASTRONOMICA (PL/0001-5237) [01460837] **391**

ACTA AUTOMATICA SINICA / INSTRUMENT SOCIETY OF AMERICA (US) [07051538] **2109**

ACTA BALTICA (GW/0567-7289) [01460838] **2672**

ACTA BALTICO-SLAVICA (PL/0065-1044) [01460839] **2672**

ACTA BELGICA HISTORIAE MEDICINAE : OFFICIAL JOURNAL OF THE BELGIAN ASSOCIATION FOR THE HISTORY OF MEDICINE (BE) [18713392] **3544**

ACTA BIO-MEDICA DE L'ATENEO PARMENSE (IT/0392-4203) [07849198] **3544**

ACTA BIOCHIMICA ET BIOPHYSICA HUNGARICA (HU/0237-6261) [14695450] 494, **479**

ACTA BIOCHIMICA POLONICA (PL/0001-527X) [01460841] **479**

ACTA BIOLOGIAE ET MEDICINAE EXPERIMENTALIS (YU/0350-5901) [05369742] 3544, **439**

ACTA BIOLOGIAE EXPERIMENTALIS SINICA (CC) [01460843] **439**

ACTA BIOLOGICA (PL) [06899241] **439**

ACTA BIOLOGICA BENRODIS (GW/0177-9214) [21194287] 5573, **4161**

ACTA BIOLOGICA CRACOVIENSIA. SERIES: BOTANICA (PL/0001-5296) [05454203] **496**

ACTA BIOLOGICA CRACOVIENSIA. SERIES: ZOOLOGIA (PL/0001-530X) [01460847] **5573**

ACTA BIOLOGICA HUNGARICA (HU/0236-5383) [10705062] **439**

ACTA BIOLOGICA LEOPOLDENSIA (BL/0101-5354) [06999481] 541, **531**

ACTA BIOLOGICA PARANAENSE (BL/0301-2123) [02638779] **439**

ACTA BIOLOGICA SILESIANA (PL) [15207119] **439**

ACTA BIOLOGICA (SZEGED. 1955) (HU/0563-0592) [02065178] **440**

ACTA BIOLOGICA VENEZUELICA (VE/0001-5326) [01460850] **440**

ACTA BIOQUIMICA CLINICA LATINOAMERICANA (AG/0325-2957) [03181975] **479**

ACTA BIOTECHNOLOGICA (GW/0138-4988) [08180665] **3685**

ACTA BIOTHEORETICA (NE/0001-5342) [01460851] 4339, **440**

ACTA BOREALIA (NO/0800-3831) [13807801] **1351**

ACTA BOTANICA BARCINONENSIA (SP) [04533507] **496**

ACTA BOTANICA CROATICA (CI/0365-0588) [02914398] **496**

ACTA BOTANICA FENNICA (FI/0001-5369) [01460855] **496**

●ACTA BOTANICA GALLICA : BULLETIN DE LA SOCIETE BOTANIQUE DE FRANCE (FR) [28347469] **496**

ACTA BOTANICA HUNGARICA (HU/0236-6495) [10923133] **496**

ACTA BOTANICA INDICA (II/0379-508X) [01797750] **497**

ACTA BOTANICA ISLANDICA (IC/0374-5066) [01795802] **497**

ACTA BOTANICA MALACITANA (SP/0210-9506) [06618451] 2210, **497**

ACTA BOTANICA MEXICANA (MX/0187-7151) [18182443] **497**

ACTA BOTANICA NEERLANDICA (NE/0044-5983) [01460856] **497**

ACTA BOTANICA SINICA (US/0095-4195) [01796176] **497**

ACTA - BRATISLAVA. UNIVERZITA. FAKULTA TELESNEJ VYCHOVY A SPORTU (XO) [03257064] **4881**

ACTA - BRESLAU. POLITEKNIKA (PL) [05377958] **407**

ACTA CAMPANOLOGICA (DK/0105-6255) [I01056255] 3871, **3544**

ACTA CARDIOLOGICA (BE/0001-5385) [01460857] **3697**

ACTA CARDIOLOGICA MEDITERRANEA (IT/0392-9698) [16920754] **3697**

ACTA CARDIOLOGICA. SUPPLEMENTUM (BE/0373-7934) [01779062] **3697**

ACTA - CENTER FOR MEDIEVAL AND EARLY RENAISSANCE STUDIES, STATE UNIVERSITY OF NEW YORK AT BINGHAMTON (US/0361-7491) [02116326] **2672**

ACTA CHEMICA SCANDINAVICA (COPENHAGEN, DENMARK : 1989) (DK/0904-213X) [19257462] **1049**

ACTA CHIMICA HUNGARICA (HU/0231-3146) [09678193] **959**

ACTA CHIRURGIAE ORTHOPAEDICAE ET TRAUMATOLOGIAE CECHOSLOVACA (XR/0001-5415) [06522609] **3880**

ACTA CHIRURGICA AUSTRIACA (AU/0001-544X) [06363513] **3957**

ACTA CHIRURGICA BELGICA (BE/0001-5458) [01460863] **3957**

ACTA CHIRURGICA CATALONIAE (SP/0211-660X) [I0211660X] **3957**

ACTA CHIRURGICA HUNGARICA (HU/0231-4614) [10333640] **3957**

ACTA CHIRURGICA ITALICA (IT/0001-5466) [01681344] **3957**

ACTA CHIRURGICA IUGOSLAVICA (CI/0001-5474) [01623946] **3957**

EUROPEAN JOURNAL OF SURGERY, THE **3964**
ACTA CIENCIA INDICA. CHEMISTRY (II/0253-7338) [06438542] **959**

ACTA CIENCIA INDICA. MATHEMATICS (II/0970-0455) [06438743] **3490**

ACTA CIENCIA INDICA. PHYSICS (II/0253-732X) [06438451] **4395**

ACTA CIENTIFICA VENEZOLANA (VE/0001-5504) [02109510] **5080**

ACTA CLASSICA (SA/0065-1141) [01967547] **1073**

ACTA CLINICA BELGICA (BE/0001-5512) [01460865] **3544**

ACTA CLINICA BELGICA. SUPPLEMENTUM (BE/0567-7386) [01781259] **3544**

ACTA CLINICA ODONTOLOGICA (CK/0120-9906) [12036794] **1315**

ACTA COMENIANA (CS/0232-0878) [01713849] **1722**

ACTA COMENIANA (XR) [01645447] **1722**

ACTA CRYSTALLOGRAPHICA. SECTION A, FOUNDATIONS OF CRYSTALLOGRAPHY See ACTA CRYSTALLOGRAPHICA. SECTION A, FUNDAMENTALS OF CRYSTALLOGRAPHY **1031**

●ACTA CRYSTALLOGRAPHICA. SECTION A, FUNDAMENTALS OF CRYSTALLOGRAPHY (DK) [29973423] **1031**

ACTA CRYSTALLOGRAPHICA. SECTION B, STRUCTURAL SCIENCE (DK/0108-7681) [09375674] **1031**

ACTA CRYSTALLOGRAPHICA. SECTION C, CRYSTAL STRUCTURE COMMUNICATIONS (DK/0108-2701) [09210431] **1031**

●ACTA CRYSTALLOGRAPHICA. SECTION D, BIOLOGICAL CRYSTALLOGRAPHY (DK/0907-4449) [27327092] **1031**

ACTA CYBERNETICA (HU/0324-721X) [01788323] **1250**

ACTA CYTOBIOLOGICA ET MORPHOLOGICA (BU/0861-0509) [24878424] **531**

ACTA CYTOLOGICA (US/0001-5547) [01417018] **531**

ACTA DE ODONTOLOGIA PEDIATRICA SUSPENDED. (DR/0252-1032) [08260294] **1315**

ACTA DEMOGRAPHICA / DEUTSCHE GESELLSCHAFT FUER BEVOLKERUNGSWISSENSCHAFT (GW/0937-907X) [25138791] **1589**

ACTA DENDROBIOLOGICA (XO/0231-5335) [06954252] **497**

ACTA DERMATO-VENEREOLOGICA (SW/0001-5555) [01460871] **3717**

ACTA DERMATO-VENEREOLOGICA. SUPPLEMENTUM (FI/0365-8341) [04649366] **3717**

ACTA DERMATOLOGICA (JA/0065-1176) [01779064] **3717**

ACTA DIABETOLOGICA (GW/0940-5429) [25007351] **3726**

ACTA DIRECTORY (CN/0848-2497) [20777845] **5460**

ACTA ECCLESIASTICA SLOVENIAE (XV/0351-2789) [11309021] **2672**

ACTA EMBRYOLOGIAE ET MORPHOLOGIAE EXPERIMENTALIS ("HALOCYNTHIA" ASSOCIATION) See ANIMAL BIOLOGY **5502**

ACTA ENDOCRINOLOGICA (COPENHAGEN) (DK/0001-5598) [01460873] **3726**

ACTA ENDOCRINOLOGICA. SUPPLEMENTUM (DK/0300-9750) [01779065] **3726**

ACTA ENTOMOLOGICA BOHEMOSLOVACA (CS/0001-5601) [04952288] **5604**

ACTA ENTOMOLOGICA BOHEMOSLOVACA See EUROPEAN JOURNAL OF ENTOMOLOGY **5608**

ACTA ENTOMOLOGICA CHILENA (CL/0716-5072) [18101594] **5604**

ACTA ENTOMOLOGICA JUGOSLAVICA (CI/0350-5510) [01716962] **5573**

ACTA ENTOMOLOGICA LITUANICA (LI) [03511351] **5573**

ACTA ESTOMATOLOGICA VALENCIANA (SP/0214-6568) [I02146568] **3544**

ACTA ESTRABOLOGICA (SP/0210-4695) [I02104695] **3871**

ACTA ETHNOGRAPHICA ACADEMIAE SCIENTIARUM HUNGARICAE See ACTA ETHNOGRAPHICA HUNGARICA **227**

●ACTA ETHNOGRAPHICA HUNGARICA (HU/1216-9803) [30457655] **227**

ACTA EUROPAEA FERTILITATIS (IT/0587-2421) [01604057] **3544**

ACTA FACULTATIS FORESTALIS, ZVOLEN (XO/0231-5785) [16164180] **2373**

ACTA FACULTATIS MEDICAE FLUMENENSIS (CI/0065-1206) [02943685] **3544**

ACTA FACULTATIS PHARMACEUTICAE UNIVERSITATIS COMENIANAE (XO/0301-2298) [08630081] **4288**

ACTA FACULTATIS RERUM NATURALIUM UNIVERSITATIS COMENIANAE (XO/0231-715X) [07063574] **2553**

ACTA FACULTATIS RERUM NATURALIUM UNIVERSITATIS COMENIANAE. BOTANICA (XO/0524-2371) [02676468] **497**

ACTA FACULTATIS RERUM NATURALIUM UNIVERSITATIS COMENIANAE. GENETICA ET BIOLOGIA MOLECULARIS (XO) [26940550] **541**

ACTA — Alphabetical Title Index

ACTA FACULTATIS RERUM NATURALIUM UNIVERSITATIS COMENIANAE. PHYSIOLOGIA PLANTARUM (XO/0373-8205) [02253047] **497**

ACTA FACULTATIS RERUM NATURALIUM UNIVERSITATIS COMENIANAE. ZOOLOGIA (XO/0524-2363) [02623987] **5573**

ACTA FARMACEUTICA BONAERENSE (AG/0326-2383) [09823376] **4288**

ACTA FORESTALIA FENNICA (FI/0001-5636) [01460882] **2373**

ACTA FYTOTECHNICA (XO/0567-7432) [03435525] 43, **2407**

ACTA GASTRO-ENTEROLOGICA BELGICA (BE/0001-5644) [01460883] **3743**

ACTA GASTROENTEROLOGICA BOLIVIANA (BO/0253-5513) [07867112] **3743**

ACTA GASTROENTEROLOGICA LATINOAMERICANA (AG/0300-9033) [01695922] **3794**

ACTA GENETICAE MEDICAE ET GEMELLOLOGIAE (IT/0001-5660) [01460885] **541**

ACTA GEODAETICA, GEOPHYSICA ET MONTANISTICA HUNGARICA (HU/0236-5758) [11240581] **1402**

ACTA GEOGRAPHICA AC GEOLOGICA ET METEOROLOGICA DEBRECINA (HU/0209-9004) [08813301] **1351**

ACTA GEOGRAPHICA LODZIENSIS (PL/0065-1249) [07147525] **2553**

ACTA GEOGRAPHICA LOVANIENSIA (BE/0065-1257) [03833815] **2553**

ACTA GEOGRAPHICA (PARIS) (FR/0001-5687) [01460888] **2553**

ACTA GEOGRAPHICA SINICA (CC/0375-5444) [01767466] **2553**

ACTA GEOLOGICA (CI/0448-0155) [03918736] **1364**

ACTA GEOLOGICA ET GEOGRAPHICA UNIVERSITATIS COMENIANAE. GEOLOGICA (XO/0567-7491) [02444323] **1364**

ACTA GEOLOGICA HUNGARICA (HU/0236-5278) [10918131] **1364**

ACTA GEOLOGICA LEOPOLDENSIA (BL/0102-1249) [04072747] **1364**

ACTA GEOLOGICA LILLOANA (AG/0567-7513) [01460891] **1364**

ACTA GEOLOGICA POLONICA (PL/0001-5709) [02256912] **1364**

ACTA GEOLOGICA SINICA *CEASED*. (US/0361-6886) [02441323] **1364**

ACTA GEOLOGICA SINICA : JOURNAL OF THE GEOLOGICAL SOCIETY OF CHINA (CC/1000-9515) [18183147] **1364**

ACTA GEOLOGICA TAIWANICA (CH/0065-1265) [01460892] **1364**

ACTA GEOPHYSICA POLONICA (PL/0001-5725) [03189773] **1402**

ACTA GEOPHYSICA SINICA (US) [02246890] **1402**

ACTA GERMANICA (SZ/0065-1273) [01795810] **3261**

ACTA GERONTOLOGICA JAPONICA (JA/0001-5768) [01900028] **3748**

ACTA GINECOLOGICA (SP/0001-5776) [I00015776] **3756**

ACTA. GYMNICA (XR) [06638929] **1854**

ACTA HAEMATOLOGICA (SZ/0001-5792) [01460896] **3769**

ACTA HAEMATOLOGICA POLONICA (PL/0001-5814) [11465943] **3794**

ACTA HISTOCHEMICA (GW/0065-1281) [01460898] **531**

ACTA HISTOCHEMICA ET CYTOCHEMICA (JA/0044-5991) [02256915] 959, **531**

ACTA HISTOCHEMICA. SUPPLEMENTBAND *CEASED*. (GW/0567-7556) [01718031] 531, **479**

ACTA. HISTORIA UNIVERSITATIS CAROLINAE PRAGENSIS (XR) [06639055] **1807**

ACTA HISTORIAE ARTIUM ACADEMIAE SCIENTARIUM HUNGARICAE (HU/0001-5830) [01460899] **335**

ACTA HISTORIAE RERUM NATURALIUM NECNON TECHNICARUM. SPECIAL ISSUE (XR/0231-6005) [05461733] **5080**

ACTA HISTORICA ACADEMIAE SCIENTIARUM HUNGARICAE (HU/0001-5849) [01460901] **2672**

ACTA HISTORICA ET ARCHAEOLOGICA MEDIAEVALIA (SP) [08608932] **253**

ACTA HISTORICA LEOPOLDINA (GW/0001-5857) [01460902] **5080**

ACTA HISTORICA SCIENTIARUM NATURALIUM ET MEDICINALIUM (DK/0065-1311) [01460903] **5080**

ACTA HISTORICO-OECONOMICA IUGOSLAVIAE (CI/0350-3631) [04343614] **1544**

ACTA HORTICULTURAE (NE/0567-7572) [01772773] **2407**

ACTA HOSPITALIA (BE/0044-6009) [05377749] **3775**

ACTA HUMBOLDTIANA (GW/0567-7580) [04761965] **2609**

ACTA HYDROBIOLOGICA (PL/0065-132X) [02068227] **552**

ACTA HYDROBIOLOGICA SINICA (CC/0559-9385) [06313088] **552**

ACTA HYDROCHIMICA ET HYDROBIOLOGICA (GW/0323-4320) **1412**

ACTA HYDROENTOMOLOGICA LATVICA / SOCIETAS ENTOMOLOGICA LATVICA, SOCIETAS INTERNATIONALIS ODONATOLOGICA (LV) [25758199] **5573**

ACTA HYDROPHYSICA (BERLIN) *CEASED*. (SZ/0065-1338) [01978702] **1412**

ACTA ICHTHYOLOGICA ET PISCATORIA (PL/0137-1592) [03526989] **2293**

ACTA INFORMATICA (GW/0001-5903) [00949362] **1255**

ACTA IRANICA. DEUXIEME SERIE. HOMMAGES ET OPERA MINORA (IR/0378-4215) [03784215] **2767**

ACTA JURIDICA (CAPE TOWN) (SA/0065-1346) [01460910] **2927**

ACTA JURIDICA HUNGARICA / HUNGARIAN JOURNAL OF LEGAL STUDIES (HU) [27930215] **3122**

ACTA JUTLANDICA; AARSKRIFT ... HUMANISTISK SERIE (DK) [03106623] **2841**

ACTA JUTLANDICA : AARSSKRIFT FOR UNIVERSITETSUNDERVISNINGEN I JYLLAND (DK/0065-1354) [01633824] **1807**

ACTA LEPROLOGICA (SZ/0001-5938) [09520875] **3544**

ACTA LINGUISTICA HAFNIENSIA / PUBLISHED UNDER THE AUSPICES OF THE LINGUISTIC CIRCLE OF COPENHAGEN (DK/0374-0463) [05338775] **3261**

ACTA LINGUISTICA HUNGARICA (HU/1216-8076) [29034758] **3261**

ACTA LITERARIA (CL/0716-0909) [03959569] **3337**

ACTA MANILANA (PH) [16630817] **5080**

ACTA MATHEMATICA (SW/0001-5962) [01460915] **3490**

ACTA MATHEMATICA HUNGARICA (HU/0236-5294) [09938525] **3490**

ACTA MATHEMATICA SINICA. NEW SERIES (CC/1000-9574) [14053994] **3490**

ACTA MATHEMATICA VIETNAMICA (VM/0251-4184) [04243095] **3490**

ACTA MATHEMATICAE APPLICATAE SINICA (CH/0168-9673) [12727137] **3490**

ACTA MECHANICA (AU/0001-5970) [01460916] **2109**

ACTA MECHANICA SINICA (CC/0567-7718) [16847671] **4427**

ACTA MECHANICA SOLIDA SINICA (CC/0894-9166) [16310305] **5080**

ACTA MEDICA AUSTRIACA (AU/0303-8173) [01204415] **3794**

ACTA MEDICA AUSTRIACA. SUPPLEMENT (AU/0303-8181) [01219501] **3794**

ACTA MEDICA AUXOLOGICA (IT/0001-6004) [02477218] **3544**

ACTA MEDICA COSTARRICENSE (CR/0001-6012) [03758395] **3544**

ACTA MEDICA CROATICA : CASOPIS HRVATSKE AKADEMIJE MEDICINSKIH ZNANOSTI (CI/1330-0164) [25864342] **3544**

ACTA MEDICA DEL VALLE *See* COLOMBIA MEDICA : CM **3567**

ACTA MEDICA DOMINICANA : REVISTA CIENTIFICA PARA MEDICOS (DR/0379-4857) [24034909] **3544**

ACTA MEDICA ET BIOLOGICA (JA/0567-7734) [01779072] 440, **3544**

ACTA MEDICA HUNGARICA (HU/0236-5286) [10486862] **3544**

ACTA MEDICA IRANICA (IR/0044-6025) [01460918] **3544**

ACTA MEDICA ITALICA DI MEDICINA TROPICALE E SUBTROPICALE E DI GASTROENTEROLOGIA (IT) [07343112] **3544**

ACTA MEDICA KINKI UNIVERSITY (JA/0386-6092) [04556955] **3544**

ACTA MEDICA (MEXICO) (MX/0001-5997) [01779071] **3544**

ACTA MEDICA NAGASAKIENSIA (JA/0001-6055) [03524672] **3544**

ACTA MEDICA OKAYAMA (JA/0386-300X) [01640916] **3544**

ACTA MEDICA PHILIPPINA (PH/0001-6071) [01460920] **3544**

ACTA MEDICA POLONA (PL/0001-608X) [01460921] **3545**

ACTA MEDICA PORTUGUESA (PO/0253-0562) [05728567] **3545**

ACTA MEDICA ROMANA (IT/0001-6098) [01779076] **3545**

ACTA MEDICA VETERINARIA (IT/0001-6136) [01460923] **5501**

ACTA MEDICAE HISTORIAE PATAVINA *CEASED*. (IT/0065-1389) [01651832] **3545**

ACTA MEDICINAE LEGALIS ET SOCIALIS *See* PROCEEDINGS / CONGRESS OF THE INTERNATIONAL ACADEMY OF FORENSIC AND SOCIAL MEDICINE **3742**

ACTA MEDICOTECHNICA (1979) (GW/0172-6099) [06564336] **3545**

ACTA MEDITERRANEA DI PATOLOGIA INFETTIVA E TROPICALE (IT/0392-9515) [11231970] **3985**

ACTA METALLURGICA ET MATERIALIA (US/0956-7151) [21019048] **3996**

ACTA METALLURGICA SINICA. SERIES B, PROCESS METALLURGY & MISCELLANEOUS *CEASED*. (CC/1000-9450) [22893144] **3997**

ACTA MEXICANA DE CIENCIA Y TECNOLOGIA *SUSPENDED*. (MX/0567-7785) [01727022] **5080**

ACTA MICROBIOLOGICA BULGARICA (BU/0204-8809) [04851645] **558**

●ACTA MICROBIOLOGICA ET IMMUNOLOGICA HUNGARICA (HU/1217-8950) [30775931] **558**

ACTA MICROBIOLOGICA HUNGARICA (HU/0231-4622) [10168403] **558**

ACTA MICROBIOLOGICA POLONICA (PL/0001-6195) [01460928] **558**

ACTA MICROBIOLOGICA SINICA (US/0098-9150) [02242884] **558**

ACTA MINERALOGICA-PETROGRAPHICA (SZEGED) (HU/0365-8066) [06998098] **1437**

ACTA MONTANA (XR/0365-1398) [01786871] **2132**

ACTA MORPHOLOGICA HUNGARICA (HU/0236-5391) [10001088] **3545**

ACTA MOZARTIANA (GW/0001-6233) [01979216] **4098**

ACTA MUSEI NAPOCENSIS (RM/0578-5391) [03562237] **2672**

ACTA MUSEI REGINAEHRADECENSIS. SERIE B, SCIENTIAE SOCIALES (XR/0232-0487) [08595800] **5189**

ACTA MUSICOLOGICA (GW/0001-6241) [04978216] **4098**

ACTA MYCOLOGIA SINICA (CH) [09648478] **497**

ACTA MYCOLOGICA (PL/0001-625X) [01414800] **574**

ACTA NATURALIA DE L'ATENEO PARMENSE (IT/0392-419X) [09949637] 1364, **5080**

ACTA NATURALIA ISLANDICA (IC/0365-4850) [01386750] 497, **4161**

ACTA NEOPHILOLOGICA (XV/0567-784X) [01653936] **3357**

ACTA NEURO PSYCHIATRICA (NE) 3918, **3825**

ACTA NEUROBIOLOGIAE EXPERIMENTALIS (PL/0065-1400) [01460936] 440, **3825**

ACTA NEUROCHIRURGICA (AU/0001-6268) [01460937] 3825, **3957**

ACTA NEUROCHIRURGICA : SUPPLEMENTUM (AU/0065-1419) [01779078] **3957**

ACTA NEUROLOGICA *CEASED*. (IT/0001-6276) [01589431] **3825**

ACTA NEUROLOGICA BELGICA (BE/0300-9009) [01460938] **3825**

ACTA NEUROLOGICA SCANDINAVICA (DK/0001-6314) [01460941] **3825**

ACTA NEUROLOGICA SCANDINAVICA. SUPPLEMENTUM (DK/0065-1427) [01645879] **3825**

ACTA NEUROPATHOLOGICA (GW/0001-6322) [01460942] 3825, **3892**

ACTA NEUROPSYCHIATRICA (NE/0924-2708) [I09242708] **3826**

●ACTA NUMERICA (UK/0962-4929) [25756019] **3490**

ACTA NUMISMATICA (SP) [01653954] **2779**

ACTA NUNTIATURAE GALLICAE (IT/0065-1443) [01775615] **5022**

ACTA OBSTETRICA Y GINECOLOGICA HISPANO-LUSITANA (SP/0210-9832) [I02109832] **3756**

ACTA OBSTETRICIA ET GYNECOLOGICA SCANDINAVICA (SW/0001-6349) [01460945] **3756**

ACTA OBSTETRICIA ET GYNECOLOGICA SCANDINAVICA. SUPPLEMENTUM (SW/0300-8835) [01588084] **3756**

ACTA OCEANOGRAPHICA TAIWANICA (CH/0379-7481) [03431689] **1445**

ACTA ODONTOLOGICA LATINOAMERICANA (AG/0326-4815) [12092277] **1315**

ACTA ODONTOLOGICA SCANDINAVICA (NO/0001-6357) [01460946] **1315**

ACTA OECOLOGICA (MONTROUGE) (FR/1146-609X) [22217138] **2210**

ACTA OECONOMICA (HU/0001-6373) [01079329] **1460**

ACTA ONCOLOGICA (SP/0001-6381) [I00016381] **3808**

ACTA ONCOLOGICA BRASILEIRA (BL/0100-3127) [03702799] **3808**

ACTA ONCOLOGICA PADOVA (IT/0393-7542) [I03937542] **3808**

ACTA ONCOLOGICA (STOCKHOLM, SWEDEN) (SW/0284-186X) [16273336] **3808**

ACTA OPHTHALMOLOGICA (DK/0001-639X) [01460948] **3871**, **3545**

ACTA ORDINIS FRATRUM MINORUM (IT/0001-6411) [01652365] **5022**

ACTA ORGANOLOGICA (GW/0567-7874) [01789765] **4098**

ACTA ORIENTALIA ACADEMIAE SCIENTIARUM HUNGARICAE (HU/0001-6446) [01460949] **2644**

ACTA ORIENTALIA (KBENHAVN) (DK/0001-6438) [01460950] **3261**

ACTA ORNITHOLOGICA (PL/0001-6454) [01477030] **5614**

ACTA ORNITHOLOGICA LITUANICA / AKADEMIIA NAUK LITOVSKOI SSR, INSTITUT ZOOLOGII I PARAZITOLOGII [AND] LITOVSKOE ORNITOLOGICHESKOE OBSHCHESTVO--OTDELENIE VSESOIUZNOGO ORNITOLOGICHESKOGO OBSHCHESTVA (LI/0135-3861) [22633368] **5614**

ACTA ORTHOPAEDICA BELGICA (BE/0001-6462) [01779082] **3880**

ACTA ORTHOPAEDICA SCANDINAVICA (DK/0001-6470) [01460952] **3880**

ACTA ORTHOPAEDICA SCANDINAVICA. SUPPLEMENTUM (DK/0300-8827) [01714960] **3880**

ACTA OTO-LARYNGOLOGICA. SUPPLEMENT (SW/0365-5237) [01779083] **3885**

ACTA OTO-RHINO-LARYNGOLOGICA BELGICA (BE/0001-6497) [01604841] **3885**

ACTA OTORHINO-LARYNGOLOGICA ITALICA (IT/0392-100X) [08741608] **3885**

ACTA OTORRINOLARINGOLOGICA ESPANOLA (SP/0001-6519) [07431003] **3885**

ACTA PAEDIATRICA HUNGARICA (HU/0231-441X) [09949749] **3899**

ACTA PAEDIATRICA JAPONICA. OVERSEAS EDITION (JA/0374-5600) [01779084] **3899**

ACTA PAEDIATRICA LATINA (IT/0365-5504) [01779085] **3899**

●ACTA PAEDIATRICA (OSLO) (NO/0803-5253) [25266094] **3899**

ACTA PAEDIATRICA SCANDINAVICA See ACTA PAEDIATRICA (OSLO) **3899**

ACTA PAEDIATRICA SCANDINAVICA ED. ESPANOLA *CEASED.* (SP/0213-0580) [I02130580] **3899**

ACTA PAEDIATRICA SCANDINAVICA. SUPPLEMENT (SW/0300-8843) [01779086] **3899**

●ACTA PAEDIATRICA. SUPPLEMENT (NO/0803-5326) [25806859] **3899**

ACTA PAEDOLOGICA (US/0737-5166) [09405998] **4570**

ACTA PAEDOPSYCHIATRICA *CEASED.* (SZ/0001-6586) [01460958] **3899, 3918**

ACTA PALAEOBOTANICA (PL/0001-6594) [01460953] **497**

ACTA PALAEONTOLOGICA POLONICA (PL/0567-7920) [02051833] **4226**

ACTA PALYNOLOGICA : AP *CEASED.* (FR/0998-4364) [20406828] **5080**

ACTA PARASITOLOGICA LITUANICA (LI/0567-7939) [10417954] **5573**

ACTA PARASITOLOGICA POLONICA See ACTA PARASITOLOGICA / WITOLD STEFANSKI INSTITUTE OF PARASITOLOGY **4243**

●ACTA PARASITOLOGICA / WITOLD STEFANSKI INSTITUTE OF PARASITOLOGY (PL) [26496009] **558, 4243**

ACTA PATHOLOGICA JAPONICA (JA/0001-6632) [01460965] **3892**

ACTA PDIATRICA SCANDINAVICA. SUPPLEMENT See ACTA PAEDIATRICA. SUPPLEMENT **3899**

ACTA PEDIATRICA ESPANOLA (SP) [I00016640] **3899**

ACTA PHARMACEUTICA (IO/0125-9407) [06234379] **4288**

●ACTA PHARMACEUTICA : A QUARTERLY JOURNAL OF CROATIAN PHARMACEUTICAL SOCIETY AND SLOVENIAN PHARMACEUTICAL SOCIETY, DEALING WITH ALL BRANCHES OF PHARMACY AND ALLIED SCIENCES (CI) [26901107] **4288**

ACTA PHARMACEUTICA FENNICA (FI/0356-3456) [03219834] **4288**

ACTA PHARMACEUTICA HUNGARICA (BUDAPEST. 1953) (HU/0001-6659) [05347929] **4288**

ACTA PHARMACEUTICA INDONESIA (IO/0216-616X) [11602958] **4289**

ACTA PHARMACEUTICA INTERNATIONALIA (DK/0400-4116) [I04004116] **4289**

ACTA PHARMACEUTICA JUGOSLAVICA See ACTA PHARMACEUTICA : A QUARTERLY JOURNAL OF CROATIAN PHARMACEUTICAL SOCIETY AND SLOVENIAN PHARMACEUTICAL SOCIETY, DEALING WITH ALL BRANCHES OF PHARMACY AND ALLIED SCIENCES **4288**

ACTA PHARMACEUTICA NORDICA (SW/1100-1801) [19865220] **4289**

ACTA PHARMACEUTICA TURCICA (TU/1010-0849) [11272012] **4289**

ACTA PHILOLOGICA (PL/0065-1524) [01653905] **3261**

ACTA PHILOSOPHICA FENNICA (FI/0355-1792) [01460971] **4339**

ACTA PHILOSOPHICA GOTHOBURGENSIA (SW/0283-2380) [I02832380] **4339**

●ACTA PHILOSOPHICA ROMA (IT/1121-2179) [I11212179] **4339**

ACTA PHONIATRICA LATINA (IT/0392-3088) [I03923088] **3885**

ACTA PHYSICA ET CHIMICA DEBRECINA (HU/0567-7947) [04404229] **959, 4395**

ACTA PHYSICA HUNGARICA (HU/0231-4428) [10138356] **4395**

ACTA PHYSICA POLONICA, A (PL/0587-4246) [01780723] **4395**

ACTA PHYSICA POLONICA, B (PL/0587-4254) [00819038] **4445**

ACTA PHYSICA SINICA *CEASED.* (US/1044-8357) [19916896] **4395**

ACTA PHYSICA SLOVACA (XO/0323-0465) [01790999] **4395**

ACTA PHYSICA UNIVERSITATIS COMENIANAE (XO/0231-889X) [10759988] **4395**

ACTA PHYSIOLOGIAE PLANTARUM (PL/0137-5881) [08355072] **497**

ACTA PHYSIOLOGICA ET PHARMACOLOGICA BULGARICA (BU/0323-9950) [01277079] **4289, 577**

ACTA PHYSIOLOGICA HUNGARICA (HU/0231-424X) [09998729] **577**

ACTA PHYSIOLOGICA, PHARMACOLOGICA ET THERAPEUTICA LATINOAMERICANA : ORGANO DE LA ASOCIACION LATINOAMERICANA DE CIENCIAS FISIOLOGICAS Y [DE] LA ASOCIACION LATINOAMERICANA DE FARMACOLOGIA (AG) [24761409] **4289, 577**

ACTA PHYSIOLOGICA SCANDINAVICA (UK/0001-6772) [01644339] **577**

ACTA PHYSIOLOGICA SCANDINAVICA. SUPPLEMENTUM (UK/0302-2994) [01460981] **577**

ACTA PHYTOGEOGRAPHICA SUECICA (SW/0084-5914) [01642883] **497**

ACTA PHYTOMEDICA (GW/0065-1567) [02149695] **497**

ACTA PHYTOPATHOLOGICA ET ENTOMOLOGICA HUNGARICA (HU/0238-1249) [15800441] **5604, 497**

ACTA PHYTOTAXONOMICA ET GEOBOTANICA. SHOKUBUTSU BUNRUI CHIRI (JA/0001-6799) [01460984] **497**

ACTA POLITICA (NE/0001-6810) [01652356] **4461**

ACTA POLONIAE HISTORICA (PL/0001-6829) [01460986] **2672**

ACTA POLONIAE PHARMACEUTICA (PL/0001-6837) [03851141] **4289**

ACTA POLYMERICA (GW/0323-7648) [05087612] **1020, 5347**

ACTA POLYTECHNICA. III, PRACE CVUT V PRAZE / CESKE VYSOKE UCENI TECHNICKE V PRAZE (XR/0374-2474) [14767310] **2034**

ACTA POLYTECHNICA SCANDINAVICA. APPLIED PHYSICS SERIES PH (FI/0355-2721) [02958350] **4395**

ACTA POLYTECHNICA SCANDINAVICA. CHEMICAL TECHNOLOGY AND METALLURGY SERIES (FI/0001-6853) [10713149] **1963**

ACTA POLYTECHNICA SCANDINAVICA. CHEMICAL TECHNOLOGY AND METALLURGY SERIES (FI/0781-2698) [10700734] **3997, 2007**

ACTA POLYTECHNICA SCANDINAVICA. CIVIL ENGINEERING AND BUILDING CONSTRUCTION SERIES. CI (FI/0355-2705) [06462143] **598, 2018**

ACTA POLYTECHNICA SCANDINAVICA. ELECTRICAL ENGINEERING SERIES (FI/0001-6845) [02444340] **2034**

ACTA POLYTECHNICA SCANDINAVICA. MATHEMATICS AND COMPUTER SCIENCE SERIES. MA (FI/0355-2713) [03144846] **1170, 3490**

ACTA POLYTECHNICA SCANDINAVICA. MECHANICAL ENGINEERING SERIES (FI/0001-687X) [06453768] **2109**

ACTA POLYTECHNICAE WRATISLAVIENSIS (PL) [02356915] **5080**

ACTA PRAEHISTORICA ET ARCHAEOLOGICA (GW) [01075521] **253**

ACTA PROTOZOOLOGICA (PL/0065-1583) [01157006] **5573**

ACTA PRUHONICIANA (CS) [03431617] **43**

ACTA PSIQUIATRICA Y PSICOLOGICA DE AMERICA LATINA (AG/0001-6896) [01779087] **4570, 3918**

ACTA PSYCHIATRICA BELGICA (BE/0300-8967) [01460996] **3919**

ACTA PSYCHIATRICA SCANDINAVICA (DK/0001-690X) [00825431] **3919**

ACTA PSYCHIATRICA SCANDINAVICA. SUPPLEMENTUM (DK/0065-1591) [01715350] **3919**

ACTA PSYCHOLOGICA (NE/0001-6918) [01447968] **4570**

ACTA RADIOBOTANICA ET GENETICA. BULLETIN OF THE INSTITUTE OF RADIATION BREEDING (JA/0065-1621) [01604981] **4432**

ACTA RADIOLOGICA (STOCKHOLM, SWEDEN : 1987) (SW/0284-1851) [15802741] **3938**

ACTA RADIOLOGICA. SUPPLEMENTUM (SW/0365-5954) [01461001] **3938**

ACTA REGIAE SOCIETATIS SCIENTIARUM ET LITTERARUM GOTHOBURGENSIS. BIOMEDICA (SW/1101-8429) [27195965] **3871**

ACTA ROMANICA (SZEGED) (HU/0567-8099) [07083143] **3261**

ACTA SAGITTARIANA (GW/0001-6942) [03744875] **4098**

ACTA SALMANTICENSIA, FILOSOFIA Y LETRAS (SP) [01461008] **2841**

ACTA SCIENTIARUM MATHEMATICARUM (HU/0001-6969) [01714225] **3490**

ACTA SEISMOLOGICA SINICA *CEASED.* (US/1000-9116) [17211693] **1402**

ACTA SEMIOTICA ET LINGUISTICA (BL/0102-4264) [04043060] **3261**

ACTA SLAVICA IAPONICA (JA/0288-3503) [09777388] **2672**

ACTA SOCIETATIS BOTANICORUM POLONIAE (PL/0001-6977) [01461011] **497**

ACTA SOCIETATIS ZOOLOGICAE BOHEMOSLOVACAE (XR/0862-5247) [21540239] **5573**

ACTA SOCIOLOGICA (DK/0001-6993) [01461013] **5237**

ACTA STEREOLOGICA (XV/0351-580X) [09911157] **3491**

ACTA STOMATOLOGICA BELGICA (BE/0001-7000) [01461014] **1315**

ACTA STOMATOLOGICA CROATICA (CI/0001-7019) [07435276] **3545**

ACTA SUMEROLOGICA (JA/0387-8082) [05737855] **3261**

ACTA TECHNICA / ACADEMIAE SCIENTIARUM HUNGARICAE (HU/0001-7035) [01461016] **5080**

ACTA TECHNICA CSAV (XR/0001-7043) [03349327] **5080**

ACTA TECHNOLOGIAE ET LEGIS MEDICAMENTI (IT/1121-2098) [I11212098] **3545**

ACTA THEOLOGICA DANICA (NE/0065-1672) [01908375] **4931**

ACTA THERAPEUTICA (BE/0378-0619) [02716001] **4289**

ACTA THERIOLOGICA (PL/0001-7051) [01411901] **204**

ACTA THERMOGRAPHICA. SUPPLEMENT (IT/0392-0712) [04890147] **3938**

ACTA TOXICOLOGICA ET THERAPEUTICA (IT/0393-635X) [15469915] **3978**

ACTA TROPICA (SZ/0001-706X) [02256933] **3985**

ACTA — Alphabetical Title Index

ACTA TROPICA. SUPPLEMENTUM (SZ/0365-1541) [01779092] **3985**

ACTA UNIVERSITATIS AGRICULTURAE FACULTAS AGROECONOMICA (XR) [01537502] **43**

ACTA UNIVERSITATIS AGRICULTURAE. FACULTAS AGRONOMICA (XR/0524-7403) [05746552] **44**

ACTA UNIVERSITATIS AGRICULTURAE FACULTAS SILVICULTURAE (XR/0524-7438) [01780569] **2373**

ACTA UNIVERSITATIS CAROLINAE. BIOLOGICA (XR/0001-7124) [01461020] **440**

ACTA UNIVERSITATIS CAROLINAE. GEOGRAPHICA (XR/0300-5402) [01657255] **2553**

ACTA UNIVERSITATIS CAROLINAE. GEOLOGICA (XR/0001-7132) [04517742] **1364**

ACTA UNIVERSITATIS CAROLINAE. IURIDICA. MONOGRAPHIA *SUSPENDED.* (XR/0567-8242) [06430764] **2927**

ACTA UNIVERSITATIS CAROLINAE. MATHEMATICA ET PHYSICA (XR/0001-7140) [05585477] 4395, **3491**

ACTA UNIVERSITATIS CAROLINAE. MEDICA (XR/0001-7116) [01779096] **3545**

ACTA UNIVERSITATIS CAROLINAE. MEDICA. MONOGRAPHIA (XR/0567-8250) [01680940] **3545**

ACTA UNIVERSITATIS CAROLINAE. PHILOLOGICA (XR/0567-8269) [01461022] **3261**

ACTA UNIVERSITATIS CAROLINAE. PHILOSOPHICA ET HISTORICA (XR/0567-8293) [01461023] 2609, **4339**

ACTA UNIVERSITATIS CAROLINAE. PHILOSOPHICA ET HISTORICA. MONOGRAPHIA (XR/0567-8307) [01461024] 4339, **2609**

ACTA UNIVERSITATIS LODZIENSIS. FOLIA ARCHAEOLOGICA (PL/0208-6034) [07393626] **253**

ACTA UNIVERSITATIS LODZIENSIS. FOLIA CHIMICA / UNIWERSYTET ODZKI (PL) [10650103] **959**

ACTA UNIVERSITATIS LODZ ENSIS. FOLIA GEOGRAPHICA (PL) [C8970458] **2553**

ACTA UNIVERSITATIS LODZIENSIS. FOLIA IURIDICA (PL/0208-6069) [07393879] **2927**

ACTA UNIVERSITATIS LODZIENSIS. FOLIA SOCIOLOGICA (PL/0208-600X) [08125367] **5238**

ACTA UNIVERSITATIS NICOLAI COPERNICI. NAUKI HUMANISTYCZNO-SPOECZNE. ARCHEOLOGIA (PL/0137-6616) [I01376616] **253**

ACTA UNIVERSITATIS OULUENSIS. SER. D, MEDICA (FI/0355-3221) [02065396] **3545**

ACTA UNIVERSITATIS PALACKIANAE OLOMUCENSIS. FACULTAS PHILOSOPHICA. HISTORICA (XR/0472-8947) [02691888] **2672**

ACTA UNIVERSITATIS PALACKIANAE OLOMUCENSIS FACULTATIS MEDICAE (XR/0301-2514) [06313271] **3545**

ACTA UNIVERSITATIS PALACKIANAE OLOMUCENSIS FACULTATIS MEDICAE SUPPLEMENTUM (XR/0472-8998) [01338004] **3545**

ACTA UNIVERSITATIS PALACKIANAE OLOMUCENSIS. SUPPLEMENTUM *See* ACTA UNIVERSITATIS PALACKIANAE OLOMUCENSIS FACULTATIS MEDICAE SUPPLEMENTUM **3545**

ACTA UNIVERSITATIS STOCKHOLMIENSIS. STOCKHOLM SLAVIC STUDIES (SW/0585-3575) [01766563] **3357**

ACTA UNIVERSITATIS SZEGEDIENSIS (HU/0324-6523) [I03246523] 3357, **2609**

ACTA UNIVERSITATIS SZEGEDIENSIS. ACTA MINERALOGICA-PETROGRAPHICA (HU/0565-8066) [06011752] 1458, **1437**

ACTA UNIVERSITATIS SZEGEDIENSIS DE ATTILA JOZSEF NOMINATAE ACTA HISTORICA (HU/0324-6965) [07588359] **2672**

ACTA UNIVERSITATIS TAMPERENSIS. SER. A (FI) [16285219] 3261, **3358**

ACTA UNIVERSITATIS UMENSIS (SW/0345-0147) [08230921] **2841**

ACTA UNIVERSITATIS UPSALIENSIS (SW/0347-1314) [13131270] **1722**

ACTA UNIVERSITATIS UPSALIENSIS. COMPREHENSIVE SUMMARIES OF UPPSALA DISSERTATIONS FROM THE FACULTY OF MEDICINE (SW/0282-7476) [24074055] **3545**

ACTA UNIVERSITATIS WRATISLAVIENSIS (PL/0239-6661) [02353702] **2841**

ACTA UNIVERSITATIS WRATISLAVIENSIS. BIBLIOTEKOZNAWSTWO (PL) [11080703] **3187**

ACTA UNIVERSITATIS WRATISLAVIENSIS. MATEMATYKA, FIZYKA, ASTRONOMIA (PL/0084-2966) [11082110] 4395, **3491**

ACTA UNIVERSITATIS WRATISLAVIENSIS. STUDIA LINGUISTICA (PL/0137-1169) [03053835] **3261**

ACTA UROLOGICA BELGICA (BE/0001-7183) [02835146] **3987**

ACTA VENEZOLANA (VE) [02256935] **227**

ACTA VETERINARIA (BEOGRAD) (YU/0567-8315) [01461027] **5501**

ACTA VETERINARIA (BRNO, CZECHOSLOVAKIA) (CS/0001-7213) [05796828] **1020**

ACTA VETERINARIA HUNGARICA (BUDAPEST. 1983) (HU/0236-6290) [10717461] **5501**

ACTA VETERINARIA JAPONICA (JA/0001-7221) [01461029] **5501**

ACTA VETERINARIA SCANDINAVICA (DK/0044-605X) [01461030] **5501**

ACTA VETERINARIA SCANDINAVICA. SUPPLEMENTUM (DK/0065-1699) [01779099] **5501**

ACTA VIROLOGICA (ANGLICKA VERZE) (XR/0001-723X) [01461031] **3545**

ACTA ZOOLOGICA BULGARICA (BU/0324-0770) [02243121] **5573**

ACTA ZOOLOGICA CRACOVIENSIA (PL/0065-1710) [01427289] **5573**

ACTA ZOOLOGICA ET PATHOLOGICA ANTVERPIENSIA *CEASED.* (BE/0001-7280) [01461035] **5573**

ACTA ZOOLOGICA FENNICA (FI/0001-7299) [01386652] **5573**

ACTA ZOOLOGICA HUNGARICA *SUSPENDED.* (HU/0236-7130) [11027961] **5573**

ACTA ZOOLOGICA LILLOANA (AG/0065-1729) [01461037] **5573**

ACTA ZOOLOGICA MEXICANA (MX/0065-1737) [01461038] **5573**

ACTA ZOOLOGICA (STOCKHOLM) (SW/0001-7272) [01461033] **5574**

ACTA ZOOTECHNICA (XO/0567-8331) [01461039] **5574**

ACTAC (AT) 1059, **1125**

ACTAS CLINICAS DELFOS (SP/0212-8608) [I02128608] **3545**

ACTAS DE CULTURA Y ENSAYOS FOTOGRAFICOS F/8 (SP) [08309208] **4366**

ACTAS DE LA 1.- REUNION ANUAL DE MATEMATICOS ESPANOLES (SP) [20919923] **3491**

ACTAS DE LA FACULTAD DE MEDICINA, UNIVERSIDAD AUTONOMA DE GUADALAJARA (MX/0185-2167) [08531276] **3545**

ACTAS DE LA FUNDACION PUIGVERT : UROLOGIA, NEFROLOGIA, ANDROLOGIA / INSTITUTO DE UROLOGIA, NEFROLOGIA, ANDROLOGIA, HOSPITAL DE LA SANTA CRUZ Y SAN PABLO (SP/0213-2885) [25199999] **3987**

ACTAS DEL CONGRESO GEOLOGICO ARGENTINO (AG/0325-2620) [02253469] 1437, **1365**

ACTAS DERMO-SIFILOGRAFICAS (SP/0001-7310) [06435526] **3717**

ACTAS / II SEMINARIO INTERNACIONAL DE HISTORIA INDO-PORTUGUESA (PO) [16305251] **2644**

ACTAS LUSO-ESPANOLAS DE NEUROLOGIA, PSIQUIATRIA Y CIENCIAS AFINES (SP/0300-5062) [07533539] 3919, **3826**

ACTAS PROCESALES DEL DERECHO VIVO (VE/0254-072X) [03367792] **2927**

ACTAS UROLOGICAS ESPANOLAS (SP/0210-4806) [03257796] **3988**

ACTAS Y TRABAJOS DEL ... ENCUENTRO VENEZOLANO DE ENTOMOLOGIA (VE) [10900562] **5574**

ACTEME. ACTUALIZACION DE TEMAS MEDICOS (SP/0214-3925) [I02143925] **3545**

ACTES *CEASED.* (FR) [01605129] **5080**

ACTES. / ASSOCIATION CANADIENNE DE LINGUISTIQUE APPLIQUEE (CN) [05194587] **3261**

ACTES - COLLOQUE INTERNATIONAL D'HISTOIRE MARITIME (FR/0531-0067) [03196676] **4174**

ACTES DE COLLOQUES (BREST) (FR/0761-3962) [14092733] 552, **1445**

ACTES DE LA RECHERCHE EN SCIENCES SOCIALES (FR/0335-5322) [02262884] **5189**

ACTES DE LECTURE, LES (FR/0758-1475) [07581475] **1722**

ACTES DE L'INSTITUT AGRONOMIQUE ET VETERINAIRE HASSAN II (MR/0851-0466) [19965150] 5501, **44**

ACTES DU ... COLLOQUE INTERNATIONAL D'ETUDES GAULOISES, CELTIQUES ET PROTOCELTIQUES (FR/0531-0059) [03196652] **2609**

ACTES DU CONGRES / ASSOCIATION CANADIENNE DES PROFESSEURS D'IMMERSION (CN/0825-513X) [11180176] **1722**

ACTES DU ... CONGRES NATIONAL DES SOCIETES SAVANTES. SECTION DES SCIENCES (FR/0300-8010) [16777776] **5080**

ACTES ET COMMUNICATIONS / INSTITUT NATIONAL DE LA RECHERCHE AGRONOMIQUE, DEPARTEMENT D'ECONOMIE ET SOCIOLOGIE RURALES (FR) [18926205] 1460, 5238, **44**

ACTES - INTERNATIONAL CONGRESS ON PHOSPHORUS COMPOUNDS (FR) [04607944] **959**

ACTES (UNIVERSITE PAUL VALERY. CENTRE D'ETUDES ET DE RECHERCHES SOCIOCRITIQUES) (FR) [19223945] **3358**

ACTEURS/AUTEURS *CEASED.* (FR) [18900734] **5361**

ACTFL FOREIGN LANGUAGE EDUCATION SERIES, THE (US/0147-1236) [03110590] 1887, **3261**

ACTIEN BOERSE (GW) **5361**

ACTINOMYCETES (1982), THE (IT/0732-0574) [08313100] **558**

ACTION (UK) [05123606] 1103, **4932**

ACTION (ALBANY) (US/0001-7396) [03949298] **1338**

ACTION ALERT (WASHINGTON, D.C. 1980) (US/1053-4083) [22197708] **5550**

ACTION AND REACTION (US/0745-5615) [04508960] **4514**

ACTION AUTOMOBILE ET TOURISTIQUE, L' (FR/0001-7418) [I00017418] **5403**

ACTION CANADA FRANCE (CN/0318-7306) [03235645] **817**

ACTION - CANADIAN ASSOCIATION FOR THE ADVANCEMENT OF WOMEN IN SPORT AND PHYSICAL ACTIVITY (CN/0849-0759) [24368108] **4881**

ACTION (CENTRAL ILLINOIS CONFERENCE EDITION) (US/0363-731X) [01908321] **4932**

ACTION COMICS (US/0899-2843) **4856**

ACTION COMICS WEEKLY (US/0899-2843) [18060710] **4856**

ACTION COMMERCIALE, MANUELS (FR/1142-7086) [I11427086] **920**

ACTION COMMITTEE AGAINST NARCOTICS *See* NARCOTICS PROGRESS REPORT **1347**

ACTION, CULTURE, REFLECTION (UV) [05724450] **1722**

ACTION ERA VEHICLE, THE (US/0044-6092) [05735346] **5403**

ACTION FAMILIALE ET SCOLAIRE (FR/0152-1977) [I01521977] **1722**

ACTION FOR CANADA'S CHILDREN (CN/0229-2653) [08070836] **1059**

ACTION FOR LIBRARIES (US/0363-0250) [02352007] **3187**

ACTION FRANCAISE HEBDO, L' (FR/1166-3286) [28901960] **4461**

ACTION (GREENWOOD, IND.) (US/0744-0375) [08027479] **4623**

ACTION GUNS (FR/0292-5370) [I02925370] **4881**

ACTION IN KENTUCKY *See* KENTUCKY JOURNAL OF COMMERCE AND INDUSTRY, THE **843**

ACTION IN TEACHER EDUCATION (US/0162-6620) [04115808] **1887**

ACTION INFORMATION (US) [04107001] **4932**

ACTION INFORMATIQUE *CEASED.* (CN/0844-0883) [19461251] **1235**

ACTION JURIDIQUE CFDT (FR) **2927**

ACTION KIT FOR HOSPITAL LAW (US) [02024017] 3775, **2927**

ACTION (LIMIILOU) (CN/0227-2040) [06688566] **4932**

ACTION LINE (BALTIMORE) (US/0001-7442) [04580360] **1722**

ACTION (LITTLE ROCK), THE (US/0363-4337) [02457113] **1544**

ACTION MISSIONNAIRE PARIS (FR/0184-6345) [I01846345] **4932**

ACTION - NATIONAL ACTION COMMITTEE ON THE STATUS OF WOMEN (CN/0820-5728) [16861072] **5550**

ACTION NATIONALE (CN/0001-7469) [01971439] **2526**

ACTION NETWORK (AT/1032-9005) [I10329005] **5178**

ACTION NEWS DIGEST (US) [03455786] **1460**

ACTION NOW (SAN JUAN CAPISTRANO, CALIF.) *CEASED.* (US/0279-8689) [07325639] **4848**

ACTION PAYROLL INSERTS (US) **738**

Alphabetical Title Index — ACTUALITE

ACTION POETIQUE (FR) [01983364] **3459**

ACTION PREVENTION (SAINTE-FOY) (CN/1183-9201) [25066319] **3156**

ACTION PURSUIT GAMES (US/0893-9489) [15792470] **4856**

ACTION (REDONDO BEACH, CALIF.) (US/8750-1333) [11008742] **4932**

ACTION (REGINA) (CN/0824-3468) [10386401] **2526**

ACTION REGIONALE, L' (CN/1191-0690) [25883008] **5779**

ACTION REPORT / MEDICAL BOARD OF CALIFORNIA (US) [24306310] **3912**

ACTION-SANTE (TORONTO) (CN/1180-1050) [23242834] **3545**

ACTION SOCIALE DES CAISSES D'ALLOCATIONS FAMILIALES, L' (FR) [01799303] **5269**

ACTION SPORTS RETAILER (1993) (US/1072-9291) [29240677] 4881, **952**

ACTION SPORTS (SOUTH LAGUNA, CALIF.) (US/1068-2619) [27519931] **4881**

ACTION SPORTS (SOUTH LAGUNA, CALIF.) See ACTION SPORTS RETAILER (1993) **952**

ACTION (TORONTO. 1970) (CN/0315-6036) [02227694] **4932**

ACTION UPDATE (US/0892-1768) [15144862] **1596**

ACTION VETERINAIRE, L' (FR/0001-7523) [02209204] **5501**

ACTION (WINDSOR) (CN/0700-5067) [03406129] **4240**

ACTION (WINNIPEG) (CN/0701-1547) [03406536] **5550**

ACTIONLINE (SOUTHFIELD, MICH.) (US/0898-2538) [17762797] **5403**

ACTIONS OF THE BOARD, APPLICATIONS AND REPORTS RECEIVED DURING THE WEEK ENDING ... : ANNOUNCEMENT / BY BOARD OF GOVERNORS OF THE FEDERAL RESERVE SYSTEM (US) [03458716] **768**

ACTIVATION ANALYSIS ABSTRACTS (UK/0307-9945) [02241113] **1012**

ACTIVATION AND METABOLISM OF CARCINOGENS (US) [03457717] **3808**

ACTIVE AND HEALTHY QUARTERLY (AT/1321-1609) **4763**

ACTIVE AND PASSIVE ELECTRONIC COMPONENTS (US/0882-7516) [11961236] **2034**

ACTIVE (BELCONNEN) (AT/1031-282X) [I1031282X] 5550, **4881**

●ACTIVE LIVING (TORONTO) (CN/1188-620X) [26497809] **2595**

ACTIVE NAMES OF BUREAU PROJECTS AND MAJOR STRUCTURES (US/0099-1856) [02243210] **2087**

ACTIVE RESEARCH TASKS REPORT (CINCINNATI) (US/0092-9891) [01789815] **2159**

ACTIVE SOLAR INSTALLATIONS SURVEY (US/0738-4882) [09122688] **1930**

ACTIVIDAD ECONOMICA (MX) [05887060] **1460**

ACTIVIDAD MINERA (AG/0326-6672) [I03266672] 1930, **2132**

ACTIVIDADES (SP) [12617926] **4366**

ACTIVIDADES EN TURRIALBA / CATIE **CEASED.** (CR/0304-2529) [11992306] **44**

ACTIVIN & INHIBIN (UK/1351-5268) 479, **3545**

ACTIVITE CINEMATOGRAPHIQUE FRANCAISE . / CNC, CENTRE NATIONAL DE LA CINEMATOGRAPHIE, L' (FR/0397-8435) [15547698] **4062**

ACTIVITE DES ABATTOIRS EN ... / REPUBLIQUE FRANCAISE, MINISTERE DE L'AGRICULTURE, DIRECTION GENERALE DE L'ADMINISTRATION ET DU FINANCEMENT, SERVICE DES ENQUETES ET ETUDES STATISTIQUES (FR/0243-6566) [10544387] **204**

ACTIVITE DES COURS ET TRIBUNAUX. STATISTIQUES DIVERSES (BE) [09878478] 2927, **3078**

ACTIVITE PHILOSOPHIQUE ET SOCIALE, SCIENTIFIQUE, MEDICALE ET LITTERAIRE, L' (FR/1140-6011) [I1406011] **2841**

ACTIVITE SCIENTIFIQUE DU CENTRE DE SOCIOLOGIE URBAINE, L' (FR) [10321154] **5238**

ACTIVITES - ASSOCIATION POUR LES ETUDES D'AMENAGEMENT ET D'URBANISME DE LA REUNION (FR) [09987330] **2813**

ACTIVITES (CHAMBRE DE COMMERCE ET D'INDUSTRIE DE NICE ET DES ALPES-MARITIMES) (FR/0150-5726) [11798982] **4623**

ACTIVITES - COMITE D'EXPANSION DE LA METROPOLE NORD (FR) [01788967] **2813**

ACTIVITES DE L'INSTITUT DE RECHERCHE DES TRANSPORTS (FR) [03055234] **5375**

ACTIVITES DU CQRI (CN/0382-8468) [02378295] **4514**

ACTIVITES : LES BANQUES A CHARTE DU CANADA (CN/0319-5112) [04879751] **768**

ACTIVITES SCIENTIFIQUES ET TECHNIQUES - COMMISSARIAT A L'ENERGIE ATOMIQUE (FR) [01795749] **2153**

ACTIVITIES See YOUR CHICAGO EXPRESS **2897**

ACTIVITIES, ADAPTATION & AGING (US/0192-4788) [05038658] 5178, **3748**

ACTIVITIES AND PROGRAMS - OFFICE OF TELECOMMUNICATIONS POLICY (US/0363-8103) [02386141] **1148**

ACTIVITIES AND SUMMARY REPORT OF THE COMMITTEE ON THE DISTRICT OF COLUMBIA, HOUSE OF REPRESENTATIVES (US/0277-1845) [02902711] **4623**

ACTIVITIES / BUREAU DE RECHERCHES ET DE PARTICIPATIONS MINIERES (MR) [07313268] **2132**

ACTIVITIES / CHEMICAL INDUSTRY INSTITUTE OF TOXICOLOGY (US/8755-4259) [11284582] **3978**

ACTIVITIES DIGEST **CEASED.** (AT/0725-3249) [07253249] 4383, **3748**

ACTIVITIES / FLORIDA SOLAR ENERGY CENTER (US) [09209163] **1930**

ACTIVITIES OF DAILY LIVING UPDATE (US/0893-0538) [15337002] **2526**

ACTIVITIES OF THE COMMITTEE ON THE DISTRICT OF COLUMBIA, HOUSE OF REPRESENTATIVES (US) [27820303] **4623**

ACTIVITIES OF THE FEDERAL COUNCIL FOR SCIENCE AND TECHNOLOGY AND THE FEDERAL COORDINATING COUNCIL FOR SCIENCE, ENGINEERING AND TECHNOLOGY (US/0149-2829) [03173243] **5080**

ACTIVITIES OF THE HOUSE COMMITTEE ON GOVERNMENT OPERATIONS (US/0739-3288) [01588757] **4623**

ACTIVITIES OF THE LUSAKA CITY LIBRARIES (ZA) [06166539] **3187**

ACTIVITIES RECHERCHE - ECOLE NATIONALE SUPERIEURE DE TECHNIQUES AVANCEES See RAPPORT D'ACTIVITES SUR LES RECHERCHES A L'ENSTA **5144**

ACTIVITIES REPORT - ALABAMA DEPT. OF PUBLIC HEALTH See ANNUAL REPORT OF THE ACTIVITIES OF THE ALABAMA DEPT. OF PUBLIC HEALTH **4766**

ACTIVITIES REPORT - COLORADO. CIVIL RIGHTS COMMISSION (US) [01564139] **4503**

ACTIVITIES REPORT OF THE R & D ASSOCIATES (US/0198-0181) [06177206] **2326**

ACTIVITIES REPORT - U.S. NATIONAL COMMITTEE FOR THE INTERNATIONAL INSTITUTE OF REFRIGERATION (US/0360-0793) [02242360] **2602**

ACTIVITIES - THE TENNESSEE STATE PLANNING OFFICE (US/0361-9753) [02441491] **2813**

ACTIVITIES TO MAINTAIN AND STRENGTHEN STATEWIDE SECONDARY VOCATIONAL STUDENT ORGANIZATIONS (US) [08745165] **1910**

ACTIVITY (US/0065-7859) [01479687] **1807**

ACTIVITY DIRECTOR'S GUIDE (US) [02251546] **5178**

ACTIVITY OF THE POLISH INSTITUTE OF INTERNATIONAL AFFAIRS (PL) [02717915] 4514, **4461**

ACTIVITY PROGRAMMERS SOURCEBOOK (US/0362-5923) [02303130] 4856, **1722**

ACTIVITY REPORT - KOREA THEOLOGICAL STUDY INSTITUTE (KO) [02694386] **4932**

ACTIVITY REPORT OF THE VIRGINIA STATE APPLE COMMISSION (US/0092-8348) [01791194] **2407**

ACTIVITY REPORT / OKLAHOMA AERONAUTICS COMMISSION (US) [27647737] **3**

ACTIVITY REPORT - PUBLIC LEGAL EDUCATION AND INFORMATION SERVICE OF NEW BRUNSWICK (CN/0846-3980) [25127977] 2927, **4623**

ACTIVITY REPORT - PUBLIC LEGAL EDUCATION AND INFORMATION SERVICE OF NEW BRUNSWICK (CN/0846-3980) [25127978] **4624**

ACTIVITY SUMMARY DRUG AND NARCOTIC CASES (US/0097-8973) [01799519] **1338**

ACTON FREE PRESS (CN) **5779**

ACTS AND FACTS (US) [09857350] **4932**

ACTS AND JOINT RESOLUTIONS OF THE GENERAL ASSEMBLY OF THE STATE OF SOUTH CAROLINA (US) [01766095] **4624**

ACTS AND PROCEEDINGS OF THE GENERAL ASSEMBLY OF THE PRESBYTERIAN CHURCH IN CANADA (CN/0079-4996) [02247718] **5054**

ACTS FACTS (US/1070-9274) [19616406] 383, 5361, **2858**

ACTS FOR THE YEAR ... / ST. VINCENT & THE GRENADINES (XM) [11041873] **2927**

ACTS IN ACTION (CN/1183-4153) [24690581] **4932**

ACTS OF PARLIAMENT (II/0445-6319) [02692187] **4624**

ACTS OF THE GENERAL ASSEMBLY OF THE COMMONWEALTH OF KENTUCKY (US) [07634291] **4624**

ACTUA (MONTREAL) (CN/0381-193X) [03782134] **1854**

ACTUACIONS INDUSTRIALS / INSTITUT CATALA DEL SOL, GENERALITAT DE CATALUNYA, DEPARTMENT DE POLITICA TERRITORIAL I OBRES PUBLIQUES (SP) [20409203] **1596**

ACTUACIONS RESIDENCIALS / INSTITUT CATALA DEL SOL, GENERALITAT DE CATALUNYA, DEPARTAMENT DE POLITICA TERRITORIAL I OBRES PUBLIQUES (SP) [20409169] **2813**

ACTUALIDAD ADMINISTRATIVA MADRID (SP/1130-9946) [I11309946] **2927**

ACTUALIDAD BIBLIOGRAFICA DE FILOSOFIA Y TEOLOGIA (SP/0211-4143) [10361053] 4932, **4339**

ACTUALIDAD CIVIL (SP/0213-7100) [I02137100] **3088**

ACTUALIDAD CIVIL. LEGISLACION (SP/1130-7390) [I11307390] **3088**

ACTUALIDAD DERMATOLOGICA (SP/0210-279X) [I0210279X] **3717**

ACTUALIDAD ECONOMICA (SP/0001-7655) [05434091] **1544**

ACTUALIDAD ECONOMICA DEL PERU (CENTRO DE ASESORIA LABORAL (LIMA, PERU)) (PE/03989184] **1544**

ACTUALIDAD ECONOMICA : REVISTA BIMESTRAL DEL INSTITUTO DE ECONOMIA Y FINANZAS (AG/0327-585X) [26165872] **1460**

ACTUALIDAD ELECTRONICA (SP/0210-6302) [I02106302] **2034**

ACTUALIDAD... EN EL LABORATORICO CLINICO F. SUNER CASADEVALL, LA (SP/0213-9693) [I02139693] **5080**

ACTUALIDAD FINANCIERA (SP/0213-6929) [I02136929] **2927**

ACTUALIDAD LABORAL (SP/0213-7097) [I02137097] **2927**

ACTUALIDAD LABORAL LEGISLACION (SP) **2927**

ACTUALIDAD MEDICA (SP/0365-7965) [I03657965] **3545**

ACTUALIDAD OBSTETRICO GINECOLOGICA MADRID (SP/1132-029X) [I1132029X] **3756**

ACTUALIDAD PANADERA DE CATALUNA (SP) 1642, **2326**

ACTUALIDAD PASTORAL (AG) [01793447] **5022**

ACTUALIDAD PENAL (SP/0213-6562) [I02136562] **2927**

ACTUALIDAD PESQUERA (PE) [08672652] **2293**

ACTUALIDAD TABAQUERA (SP) **44**

ACTUALIDAD TRIBUTARIA (SP) **2927**

ACTUALIDAD TRIBUTARIA LEGISLACION (SP) **2927**

ACTUALIDAD Y DERECHO (SP) **2927**

ACTUALIDADES - CENTRO DE ESTUDIOS LATINOAMERICANOS ROMULO GALLEGOS (VE/0252-905X) [03057780] **3358**

ACTUALIDADES DE LA INFORMACION CIENTIFICA Y TECNICA (CU/0138-7324) [02243882] **3187**

ACTUALITE - ALLIANCE DE LA FONCTION PUBLIQUE DU CANADA. ELEMENT NATIONAL (CN/1184-9800) [24690745] **1642**

ACTUALITE CANADA (CN/0823-9096) [11847672] **2526**

ACTUALITE CHIMIQUE, L' (FR/0151-9093) [01649981] **959**

ACTUALITE DE LA FORMATION PERMANENTE. REPERTOIRE D'ADRESSES UTILES (FR/0153-2448) [I01532448] **1807**

ACTUALITE DES ARTS PLASTIQUES (FR/0293-9789) [I02939789] **335**

ACTUALITE — Alphabetical Title Index

ACTUALITE DIOCESAINE (CN/0823-552X) [10440795] **4932**

ACTUALITE DU DIRIGEANT (FR) **821**

ACTUALITE ECONOMIQUE (CN/0001-771X) [01983457] **1589**

● ACTUALITE ET DOSSIER EN SANTE PUBLIQUE (FR/1243-275X) [I1243275X] **4763**

ACTUALITE FIDUCIAIRE, L' (FR/0044-6157) [I00446157] **2927**

ACTUALITE GOUVERNEMENTALE / COMMUNICATION-QUEBEC, BAS-SAINT-LAURENT, L' (CN/1188-1542) [25468265] **4624**

ACTUALITE IMMOBILIERE (CN/0701-0516) [03406125] **4833**

ACTUALITE JOLIETTAINE, L' (CN/0319-3926) [02442881] **2526**

ACTUALITE JUIVE (CN/0711-2092) [08674349] **5045**

ACTUALITE JURIDIQUE *See* ACTUALITE JURIDIQUE : DROIT ADMINISTRATIF, L' **2927**

ACTUALITE JURIDIQUE : DROIT ADMINISTRATIF, L' (FR) [07758629] **2927**

ACTUALITE JURIDIQUE. PROPRIETE IMMOBILIERE, L' (FR/0001-7736) [09432575] **2927**

ACTUALITE / LE MENSUEL DE L'ACTUALITE ECONOMIQUE & SOCIALE (FR) **1460**

ACTUALITE LEGISLATIVE DALLOZ (FR/0753-874X) [09377654] **2927**

ACTUALITE MEDICAL BELGE (BE) **3545**

ACTUALITE MEDICALE, L' (CN/0229-9429) [08099399] **3912**

ACTUALITE (MONTREAL. 1976) (CN/0383-8714) [05116581] **2513**

ACTUALITE PHARMACEUTIQUE, L' (CN) **4289**

ACTUALITE POLICIERE 1975 L' (FR/0339-7858) [I03397858] **3156**

ACTUALITE RELIGIEUSE DANS LE MONDE (1983) (FR/0757-3529) [09718610] **4932**

ACTUALITE-SEMENCE (CN/0715-4844) [09332355] **161**

ACTUALITE TERMINOLOGIQUE (CN/0001-7779) [03421366] **3261**

ACTUALITE VIE (CN/0714-8828) [09099643] **4503**, **2248**

ACTUALITES BIBLIQUES (CN/1184-7204) [24266847] **5013**

ACTUALITES BIOLOGIQUES (FR/0753-3918) [I07533918] **440**

ACTUALITES CHIRURGICALES (FR/0376-6276) [01598101] **3957**

ACTUALITES COMMUNAUTAIRES (FR/1011-923X) [I1011923X] **3122**

ACTUALITES D'ANGEIOLOGIE (FR) [I02458659] **3697**

ACTUALITES DE CHIMIE ANALYTIQUE, ORGANIQUE, PHARMACEUTIQUE ET BROMATOLOGIQUE (BE/0373-9805) [04408987] **4289**, **959**

ACTUALITES DE CHIMIE THERAPEUTIQUE (FR/0338-8999) [03702631] **4289**

ACTUALITES DU DROIT : REVUE DE LA FACULTE DE DROIT DE LIEGE (BE) [24253019] **2927**

ACTUALITES ECONOMIQUES DE LA REUNION (RE/0335-3400) [I03353400] **1460**

ACTUALITES EN ANALYSE TRANSACTIONNELLE (BE) **1544**

ACTUALITES EN MEDECINE DU SPORT (FR/0223-2928) [18581847] **3953**

ACTUALITES EXPATRIATION PARIS (FR/0989-7445) [I09897445] **1918**

ACTUALITES GYNECOLOGIQUES (PARIS. 1971) (FR/0223-4661) [13206088] **3756**

ACTUALITES JURIDIQUES PHARMACEUTIQUES (BE/1370-0464) **4289**

ACTUALITES MEDICALES INTERNATIONALES EN ANGIOLOGIE (FR) **3545**

ACTUALITES MEDICALES INTERNATIONALES PSYCHIATRIE (FR/0766-3897) [07663897] **3919**

ACTUALITES NEPHROLOGIQUES DE L'HOPITAL NECKER (FR/0567-8811) [06363667] **3988**

ACTUALITES ODONTO-STOMATOLOGIQUES (FR/0001-7817) [01461063] **1315**

ACTUALITES (PARIS) *SUSPENDED*. (FR/0183-5017) [08269069] **821**

ACTUALITES PHARMACEUTIQUES (FR/0515-3700) [I05153700] **4289**

ACTUALITES PHARMACOLOGIQUES (FR/0567-8854) [05514199] **4289**

ACTUALITES PREVENTION (CN/0711-169X) [08770667] **4763**

ACTUALITES PSYCHIATRIQUES (FR/0300-8274) [I03008274] **3919**

ACTUALITES SCIENTIFIQUES ET AGRONOMIQUES DE L'I.N.R.A (FR/0181-0979) [09163497] **44**

ACTUALITES SCIENTIFIQUES ET INDUSTRIELLES (FR/0365-6861) [11486891] **5080**

ACTUALITES SCIENTIFIQUES ET TECHNIQUES DANS LES INDUSTRIES AGRO-ALIMENTAIRES (FR/0764-8650) [I07648650] **44**

ACTUALITES SDM (CN/0842-1854) [19586098] **1103**

ACTUALITES SOCIALES HEBDOMADAIRES (FR/1145-8690) [11458690] **5269**

ACTUALITES SOVIETIQUES PARIS (FR/0398-2882) [03982882] **4539**

ACTUALITES SPORT ET MEDECINE ROYAN (FR/1151-3195) [I11513195] **3953**

ACTUALITIES HEMATOLOGIQUES (FR/0567-8757) [01605603] **3794**

ACTUALITES MEDICALES INTERNATIONALES. HYPERTENSION (FR/0997-7287) [21591699] **3697**

ACTUALIZACION POLITICA (AG/0327-6058) [25880476] **4461**

ACTUALIZACIONES EN INFECTOLOGIA (UY) [20939898] **3711**

ACTUALIZACIONES TERAPEUTICAS EN CARDIOLOGIA (SP) **3697**

ACTUALQUARTO GERPINNES (BE/0776-4677) [07764677] **2276**

ACTUARIAL DIGEST, THE (US) [09837115] 3491, **2872**

ACTUARIAL REPORT FOR STATE FISCAL YEAR ENDING ..., AND SYSTEM PLAN YEAR BEGINNING ... / SCHOOL RETIREMENT SYSTEM OF THE STATE OF NEBRASKA (US) [28437604] 1887, **1642**

ACTUARIAL REPORT, NEBRASKA STATE PATROLMEN'S RETIREMENT SYSTEM *See* ACTUARIAL VALUATION, NEBRASKA STATE PATROLMEN'S RETIREMENT SYSTEM **2872**

ACTUARIAL REPORTS ON THE SOUTH AUSTRALIAN SUPERANNUATION FUND AS AT ... (AT) [11897521] **1642**

ACTUARIAL RESEARCH CLEARING HOUSE (US/0732-5428) [08371704] **2872**

ACTUARIAL REVIEW, THE (US/1046-5081) [11003312] **2872**

ACTUARIAL SOCIETY OF AMERICA. YEAR BOOK *See* YEAR BOOK / SOCIETY OF ACTUARIES **2896**

ACTUARIAL STUDY (UNITED STATES. SOCIAL SECURITY ADMINISTRATION. OFFICE OF THE ACTUARY) (US) [01743354] **5269**

ACTUARIAL TABLES EFFECTIVE FOR TERMINATIONS (US/0148-3145) [03226526] **2872**

ACTUARIAL VALUATION, NEBRASKA STATE PATROLMEN'S RETIREMENT SYSTEM (US/0363-9274) [02593856] **2872**

ACTUARY (US/0001-7825) [02734385] **2872**

ACTUEL (FR) [02256948] **5800**

ACTUEL CIDJ (FR/0337-9566) [I03379566] **2484**

ACTUEL MARX (FR) [17976404] **4539**

ACTUM LUCE (IT/0391-9994) [05114584] **2672**

ACUCAA BULLETIN (US) [06828501] **383**

ACUHO INTERNATIONAL NEWS (US/0744-1029) [08039774] **1807**

ACUMEN MAGAZINE (UK) [15725310] **3459**

ACUPUNCTURE & ELECTRO-THERAPEUTICS RESEARCH (UK/0360-1293) [02367938] **3545**

ACUPUNCTURE LETTER, THE (US/0163-1314) [04275794] **3546**

ACUPUNCTURE (LOS ANGELES) (US/0092-5047) [01790984] **3546**

ACUPUNCTURE TODAY (CN/0706-9812) [04589222] **3546**

ACUSTICA (GW/0001-7884) [01461065] **4452**

ACUTE CARE *CEASED*. (SZ/0254-0819) [11259702] 3775, **3850**

ACUTE CARE MEDICINE *CEASED*. (US/0742-1567) [10268237] **3546**

ACUTE CARE THERAPEUTICS (US/0898-2783) [14275772] **3546**

ACUTE TOXICITY DATA *CEASED*. (US/1044-2049) [19721720] **3978**

ACWORTH NEIGHBOR, THE (US/0191-7269) [04960799] **5651**

AD 2000 (AT/1031-8453) [I10318453] **4932**

AD / ARCHITECTURAL DIGEST (IT) **287**

AD ASTRA (WASHINGTON, D.C.) (US/1041-102X) [18631742] 391, **3**

AD BUSINESS REPORT (US/1061-1371) [25188524] **753**

AD CHANGE; THE STANDARD DIRECTORY OF ADVERTISERS BULLETIN *CEASED*. (US) [01461066] **753**

AD CYCLE NEWSLETTER (AT) **1170**

AD-EXPRESS AND DAILY IOWEGIAN AND CITIZEN (US/0746-1119) [09764291] **5656**

AD NEWS HANDBOOK (AT) **753**

AD NEWS SURRY HILLS (AT/0814-6942) [108146942] **753**

AD : REVISTA INTERNACIONAL DE DECORACION, DISENO Y ARQUITECTURA (SP) **2898**

AD/SOLUTIONS REPORT (US/1054-3953) [22876409] **1170**

AD $ SUMMARY (US/0190-7166) [02657604] **753**

AD VALOREM PROPERTY TAX LEVEY REPORT (US) [12264616] **4833**

AD VANTAGE (CANOGA PARK, CALIF.) (US/0886-6813) [12984033] **753**

AD VERBUM (AG) [01789558] **4383**

ADA BUFFET. CD-ROM (US) **1170**

ADA COMPLIANCE GUIDE (US/1054-5948) [22904781] **4383**

ADA IC NEWSLETTER (US/1064-1505) [26226152] **1278**

ADA JOURNEYMAN (US) **1170**

ADA LETTERS (US/0736-721X) [07897919] **1278**

ADA LETTERS *See* ACM ADA LETTERS : A BIMONTHLY PUBLICATION OF SIGADA, THE ACM SPECIAL INTEREST GROUP ON ADA **1277**

ADA NEWSLETTER (EDMONTON) (CN/0849-5866) [21353564] **1315**

ADA POLICY & LAW *CEASED*. (US/1067-4713) [27241777] **4383**, **2927**

ADA STRATEGIES (US/0893-0570) [15345369] **1255**

ADA TODAY (US/0896-3134) [12776527] **4461**

ADA USER (NE/0268-652X) [24565686] **1278**

● ADA WATCH *SUSPENDED*. (US/1062-0176) [25505539] **4383**

ADA WHITESANDS. CD-ROM (US) **1170**

ADAB AL-GHAD (UA) [12004416] **3358**

ADAB (JAMIAT AL-KHARTUM. KULLIYAT AL-ADAB) (SJ) [09138508] **3261**

ADAB WA-NAQD (UA) [11742109] **3358**

ADABI MUJALLAH (II) [11862365] **3358**

ADABI PROSES / AZARBAIJAN SSR ELMLAR AKADEMIIASY, NIZAMI ADYNA KHALGLAR DOSTLUGHU ORDENLI ADABIIIAT INSTITUTU (AJ) [18677052] **3358**

ADAC NEWS : DETENTION ACTION COMMITTEE NEWSLETTER (SA) [19058043] **3156**

● ADAC REPORT (US/1065-7037) [26684873] **4383**

ADADATA (US/8756-0577) [10366927] **1283**

ADAIR COUNTY FREE PRESS (GREENFIELD, IOWA : 1984) (US) [12935814] **5668**

ADAIR COUNTY REVIEW (US/1063-9926) [20810385] **2436**

ADAIR NEWS (WITH THE CASEY VINDICATOR), THE (US) [12796418] **5668**

ADALBERT STIFTER-INSTITUT DES LANDES OBEROSTERREICH *See* VIERTELJAHRESSCHRIFT **3451**

ADALET DERGISI (TU/1011-730X) [I1011730X] **2927**

ADALIA (FR/0980-0611) [I09800611] **44**

ADAM FILM WORLD GUIDE. ADAM FILM WORLD DIRECTORY OF ADULT FILMS (US) [10621205] **4062**

ADAM INTERNATIONAL REVIEW (UK/0001-8015) [01965286] 1089, **3187**

ADAMHA ADVISORY COMMITTEES (US) [24257153] **4763**

ADAMHA DATA BOOK (US/0891-3897) [03920719] **1338**

ADAMHA NEWS (1990) (US/1057-6215) [22247905] **1338**

ADAMHA NEWS ON ALCOHOL, DRUG ABUSE, AND MENTAL HEALTH (US) [19068700] **1338**

ADAMHA NEWS (ROCKVILLE, MD. : 1990) *See* SAMHSA NEWS / SUBSTANCE ABUSE AND MENTAL HEALTH SERVICES ADMINISTRATION **1349**

ADAMHA PUBLIC ADVISORY COMMITTEES (US) [17782001] **1338**

Alphabetical Title Index — ADMINISTRATION

ADAMHA PUBLIC ADVISORY COMMITTEES *See* ADAMHA ADVISORY COMMITTEES **4763**

ADAMIS ANNUAL REPORT (US) [10715393] **5270**

ADAMS ADDENDA (US/0739-0076) [03999667] **2436**

ADAMS CHRONICLE, THE (US/1040-4449) [18419718] **1300**

ADAMS COUNTY LEGAL JOURNAL (US) [01461069] **3138**

●ADAMS JOBS ALMANAC, THE (US/1072-592X) [29042316] **4201**

ADAMS, ROY J. COMPARATIVE IR NEWSLETTER *See* COMPARATIVE INDUSTRIAL RELATIONS NEWSLETTER **1660**

ADAPTED PHYSICAL ACTIVITY QUARTERLY (US/0736-5829) [09159651] **1854**

●ADAPTIVE BEHAVIOR (US/1059-7123) [24681430] **4571**

ADB BUSINESS OPPORTUNITIES (PH) **636**

ADB BUSINESS OPPORTUNITIES : PROPOSED PROJECTS, PROCUREMENT NOTICES AND CONTRACT AWARDS / ASIAN DEVELOPMENT BANK (PH/0015-6209) [21284286] **768**

ADB QUARTERLY REVIEW (PH/0115-074X) [02287317] **768**

●ADB REVIEW / ASIAN DEVELOPMENT BANK (PH) [31125842] **768**

ADBRIEF (AT/0311-2225) [I03112225] **754**

ADBRIEF REGISTER (AT/0819-6648) [I08196648] **754**

ADBUSTERS (VANCOUVER) (CN/0847-9097) [20676928] **754**

ADC DU CREDIT (CN/0226-5575) [06315894] **768**

ADC TIMES (US/0749-2642) [11111053] **2254**

ADCA, AMERICAN DIRECTORY OF COLLECTION AGENCIES *See* ADCA, AMERICAN DIRECTORY OF COLLECTION AGENCIES AND ATTORNEYS **768**

ADCA, AMERICAN DIRECTORY OF COLLECTION AGENCIES AND ATTORNEYS (US/0148-5350) [02986796] **768**

ADCOM (BOSTON, MASS.) (US/1061-3242) [25252260] **754**

●ADDICTION (UK/0965-2140) [27367194] **1338**

ADDICTION ABSTRACTS (UK/0968-7610) **1338**

ADDICTION & RECOVERY (US/1052-4614) [22291456] **1338**

ADDICTION LETTER, THE (US/8756-405X) [11558322] **1338**

ADDICTION NURSING NETWORK (US/0899-9112) [18264014] **3850**

●ADDICTION RESEARCH (US/1058-6989) [24358604] **1338**

ADDICTION RESEARCH FOUNDATION OF ONTARIO *See* JOURNAL - ADDICTION RESEARCH FOUNDATION, THE **4786**

ADDICTION THERAPIST, THE (CN/0702-8008) [03412256] **1338**

●ADDICTIONS NURSING (US/1073-886X) [29541809] **3850**

ADDICTIONS NURSING NETWORK *See* ADDICTIONS NURSING **3850**

ADDICTIVE BEHAVIORS (UK/0306-4603) [01343464] **1338**

ADDISON-NORTH DALLAS TODAY *See* ADDISON TODAY **5746**

ADDISON TODAY (US) [16515869] **5746**

ADDISON-WESLEY BOOK OF ATARI SOFTWARE, THE ***CEASED.*** (US/0739-5485) [09748582] **1283**

ADDITIONS TO GENERATING CAPACITY ... FOR THE CONTIGUOUS UNITED STATES / AS PROJECTED BY THE REGIONAL ELECTRIC RELIABILITY COUNCILS IN THEIR ... LONG-RANGE COORDINATED PLANNING REPORTS TO THE DEPARTMENT OF ENERGY (US) [06496105] **1930**

ADDITIONS TO STATE MENTAL HEALTH FACILITIES, FISCAL YEAR ... (US) [07480373] **4763**

ADDITIVES FOR POLYMERS (UK/0306-3747) [I03063747] **1038**

ADDLIS NEWS (AT/0811-9392) [I08119392] 3187, **1338**

ADDRESS BOOK FOR FAMILY HISTORY SEARCHERS AND HISTORIANS / WHOLLY COMPILED BY JAMES MCCLELLAND RESEARCH (AT) [08413226] **2436**

ADDRESS DIRECTORY / SOCIETY OF VERTEBRATE PALEONTOLOGY (US/0276-444X) [06994596] **4226**

ADDRESS LIST / NATIONAL CLEARINGHOUSE FOR CENSUS DATA SERVICES (US/0744-1010) [07920797] **5320**

ADDRESS LIST, REGIONAL AND SUBREGIONAL LIBRARIES FOR THE BLIND AND PHYSICALLY HANDICAPPED (US/0163-3805) [04351507] 4383, **3187**

ADDRESSES (CN) [22923775] 2526, **1103**

ADDRESSES AND DISCUSSIONS PRESENTED AT THE ... ANNUAL READING CONFERENCE / CONDUCTED BY THE SCHOOL OF EDUCATION, UNIVERSITY OF SOUTH CAROLINA (US) [04450857] 1887, **3261**

ADDRESSES AND RESOLUTIONS / CENTRAL ADVISORY BOARD OF EDUCATION (II) [12882489] **1722**

ADDRESSES DELIVERED TO THE MEMBERS DURING THE SESSIONS OF . *See* ADDRESSES **1103**

ADDVANTAGE (US/0149-4082) [03472482] **4881**

ADE. ALCOHOL AND DRUG EDUCATION (CN/0705-6389) [04098144] 1722, **1338**

ADE BULLETIN (US/0001-0898) [01804271] 1807, **3261**

ADEL NEWS TRIBUNE (US/0746-0716) [09722937] **5651**

ADELAIDE LAW REVIEW, THE (AT/0065-1915) [01461082] **2927**

ADELAIDE REVIEW (AT/0815-5992) [I08155992] 3358, **312**

ADELANTE (EL PASO, TX.) (US/0731-2733) [08148798] **5054**

ADELPHI PAPERS (UK/0567-932X) [01447950] **4514**

ADELPHIA LAW JOURNAL (US/8756-3630) [08791446] **2927**

ADEM (BE/0001-8171) [06873509] **4098**

ADENA (US/0191-8664) [04923037] **2717**

ADEPT REPORT, THE (US/1053-2668) [22496452] **1315**

ADESIONE (IT) **5080**

ADETEM MARKETING DEMAIN (FR) **920**

ADF NEWS (CN/0835-2305) [17366331] **44**

ADFL BULLETIN (US/0148-7639) [03366503] 1887, **3261**

ADFO DIRECT MAGAZINE (NE) **920**

ADFOMEDIA HANDBOEK (NE/0925-2932) [25221877] **1103**

ADGEZIA RASPLAVOV I PAJHA MATERIALOV (RU/0136-1732) [03568833] **4026**

ADHA ACCESS *See* ACCESS (CHICAGO, ILL.) **1315**

ADHAESION *See* KLEBEN UND DICHTEN **1055**

ADHAESION (GW/0001-8198) [08414149] **1049**

ADHD NEWSLETTER (US) **4571**

●ADHD REPORT, THE (US/1065-8025) [26739345] **1874**

ADHESION (LONDON) (UK/0260-4450) [04098973] **1049**

ADHESIVE & SEALANT COUNCIL *See* JOURNAL OF THE ADHESIVE AND SEALANT COUNCIL, THE **1026**

ADHESIVES ABSTRACTS (UK/0891-7760) [14989008] **1049**

ADHESIVES AGE (US/0001-821X) [01461090] **2007**

●ADHESIVES & SEALANTS INDUSTRY (US/1070-9592) [28521142] **1020**

ADHESIVES & SEALANTS NEWSLETTER (US/0890-0884) [08459045] **1049**

ADHESIVES & SEALANTS YEARBOOK AND DIRECTORY /BASA, BRITISH ADHESIVES AND SEALANTS ASSOCIATION (UK) [20625910] **3997**

ADHESIVES DIRECTORY; A DIRECTORY FOR THE INDUSTRIAL USER OF ADHESIVES (UK) [04619118] **1049**

ADHESIVES EURO-GUIDE (UK) **1049**

ADHYAYANAMALA (IT) [02240209] **2644**

ADICCIONES PALMA DE MALLORCA (SP/0214-4840) [I02144840] **1338**

ADIGE (IT) **5804**

ADIL (KUALA LUMPUR, MALAYSIA) (IO) [08449345] **2927**

ADIQ (MONTREAL) (CN/1186-124X) [24267118] **1596**

ADIRONDAC (US/0001-8236) [05431595] **4868**

ADIRONDACK DAILY ENTERPRISE (US) [13511539] **5707**

ADIRONDACK ECHO (US/0745-7332) [09421366] **5713**

ADIRONDACK LIFE (US/0001-8252) [01983651] **2526**

ADIRONDACK MOUNTAIN CLUB : [NEWSLETTER], THE (US/1056-2370) [23591580] 5460, **4868**

ADIRONDACK MOUNTAIN TIMES (US/0746-8075) [12388785] **2527**

ADISTA : AGENZIA D'INFORMAZIONE STAMPA (IT) 4932, **4461**

ADIX (US/0191-4278) [04901536] **1103**

ADJUDICATION/ARBITRATION HIGHLIGHTS (CN/1185-1724) [24257214] **1642**

●ADJUNCT INFO (US/1063-861X) [26178174] **1089**

ADJUNCT MENTOR *See* TEACHING FOR SUCCESS **1850**

ADJUNCT MENTOR, THE (US/1043-0857) [19294904] **1807**

ADL ON THE FRONTLINE (US/1061-5202) [24637226] 5045, **2254**

ADLA ***CEASED.*** (US/0887-4514) [13233837] **335**

ADLER MUSEUM BULLETIN (SA) [06173954] 3546, **4083**

ADLER (VIENNA, AUSTRIA) (AU) [20349412] **5777**

ADLER (WIEN) (AU/0001-8260) [04575433] **2436**

ADLI TP DERGISI (TU/1018-5275) [I10185275] **3739**

ADLIB UPDATE (US/8755-9846) [11452236] **3187**

ADMAP : THE JOURNAL OF ADVERTISING MEDIA ANALYSIS AND PLANNING (UK) [08790627] **754**

ADMIN REVIEW (AT/0814-1231) [I08141231] **4624**

ADMINISTRACAO DO PORTO DE SAO FRANCISCO DO SUL *See* BOLETIM ESTATISTICO / ESTADO DE SANTA CATARINA, SECRETARIA DOS TRANSPORTES E OBRAS, ADMINISTRACAO DO PORTO DE SAO FRANCISCO DO SUL **5400**

ADMINISTRACAO DO PORTO DO RECIFE *See* BOLETIM ESTATISTICO - ADMINISTRACAO DO PORTO DO RECIFE **5400**

ADMINISTRACAO DO PORTO DO RECIFE. SUB-SETOR DE CONTROLE E ESTATISTICA *See* ESTATISTICA / EMPRESA DE PORTOS DO BRASIL S/A, PORTOBRAS, ADMINISTRACAO DO PORTO DO RECIFE, SETOR COMERCIAL, SUB-SETOR DE CONTROLE E ESTATISTICA **5400**

ADMINISTRACAO GERAL DO ACUCAR E DO ALCOOL *See* BOLETIM - ADMINISTRACAO GERAL DO ACUCAR E DO ALCOOL **1599**

ADMINISTRACION MILITAR Y LOGISTICA (AG) [16115774] **4033**

ADMINISTRACION PUBLICA (PE) [04479360] **4624**

ADMINISTRACION Y DESARROLLO (1981) (CK) [10692193] **4624**

ADMINISTRATEUR DU CREDIT AGRICOLE, L' (FR/0988-9183) [I09889183] 1460, **44**

ADMINISTRATEUR SCOLAIRE PROFESSIONNEL, L' (CN/0701-2861) [03412058] **1859**

ADMINISTRATION & MANAGEMENT ***CEASED.*** (US/0364-7986) [05694757] **4624**

ADMINISTRATION & MANAGEMENT SPECIAL INTEREST SECTION NEWSLETTER (US/8756-629X) [11614900] **859**

ADMINISTRATION AND POLICY IN MENTAL HEALTH (US/0894-587X) [16149653] 4763, **5270**

ADMINISTRATION & SOCIETY (US/0095-3997) [01796118] **4624**

ADMINISTRATION AND SUPPLEMENTARY INFORMATION : CATALOG - UNIVERSITY OF ALABAMA (US/0361-0780) [02349953] **1859**

ADMINISTRATION (DUBLIN) (IE/0001-8325) [01461096] 4461, **4624**

ADMINISTRATION ET GESTION (CN/0704-9765) [04236711] **4624**

ADMINISTRATION FEDERALE DU CANADA, L' (CN/0576-1409) [02329800] **4624**

ADMINISTRATION FOR DEVELOPMENT (PP/0304-6028) [01795024] **4624**

ADMINISTRATION IN SOCIAL WORK (US/0364-3107) [03113247] **5270**

ADMINISTRATION LAW JUDGE DECISIONS REPORT (US/0742-616X) [08289214] **3143**

ADMINISTRATION OF JUSTICE MEMORANDA (US/0147-3603) [03145694] **2927**

ADMINISTRATION OF JUSTICE STATISTICS ... ESTIMATES (UK/0264-6552) [10661543] **3078**

ADMINISTRATION OF PUBLIC LAWS 81-874 & 81-815 (US/0272-538X) [06593722] **1859**

ADMINISTRATION — Alphabetical Title Index

ADMINISTRATION OF THE MARINE MAMMAL PROTECTION ACT OF 1972. (UNITED STATES. FISH AND WILDLIFE SERVICE) (US/0194-1488) [04397239] **2185**

ADMINISTRATION PARIS. 1962 (FR/0223-5439) [I02235439] **4461**

ADMINISTRATION PUBLIQUE (BE) [04376933] **3091**

ADMINISTRATION REPORT - KARNATAKA STATE ROAD TRANSPORT CORPORATION (II) [02377962] **5375**

ADMINISTRATION REPORT OF THE ANIMAL HUSBANDRY DEPARTMENT FOR THE YEAR ... (II) [04412986] **44**

ADMINISTRATION REPORT OF THE CIVIL COURTS STATISTICS FOR THE YEAR ... (II) [17417702] **3078**

ADMINISTRATION REPORT - PORT OF SPAIN, TRINIDAD AND TOBAGO. PUBLIC HEALTH DEPT (TR) [01782701] 4624, **4763**

ADMINISTRATION REPORTS ON THE WORKING OF CO-OPERATIVE SOCIETIES IN TAMIL NADU / CO-OPERATION DEPARTMENT (II) [11420075] **1541**

ADMINISTRATIONSDEPARTEMENTET : ARSBERETNING (DK) [19346819] **4461**

ADMINISTRATIVE ACTION (US/0892-0923) [15078868] **1807**

ADMINISTRATIVE AFFAIRS IN BANGLADESH (BG) [07706121] **4624**

ADMINISTRATIVE AND ACCOUNTING GUIDE FOR DEFENSE CONTRACTS *See* ADMINISTRATIVE AND ACCOUNTING GUIDE FOR GOVERNMENT CONTRACTS **738**

ADMINISTRATIVE AND ACCOUNTING GUIDE FOR GOVERNMENT CONTRACTS *CEASED.* (US/0888-5400) [13661121] **738**

ADMINISTRATIVE AND TECHNICAL SALARY SURVEY (US/0098-3578) [02241419] **1642**

ADMINISTRATIVE APPEALS REPORTS (AT/0813-779X) [13519731] **4624**

●ADMINISTRATIVE ASSISTANT'S UPDATE (CN/1191-7881) [27391240] **859**

ADMINISTRATIVE BRIEFS (US/0147-524X) [03171350] **3775**

ADMINISTRATIVE CHANGE (II) [01790587] **4624**

ADMINISTRATIVE CODE COMMITTEE BIENNIAL REPORT TO THE ... LEGISLATURE (US) [07698832] **4461**

ADMINISTRATIVE CONFERENCE OF THE UNITED STATES *See* RECOMMENDATIONS AND REPORTS / ADMINISTRATIVE CONFERENCE OF THE UNITED STATES **4678**

ADMINISTRATIVE CONFERENCE OF THE UNITED STATES *See* ANNUAL REPORT / ADMINISTRATIVE CONFERENCE OF THE UNITED STATES **4626**

ADMINISTRATIVE DIRECTIVE - DEPARTMENT OF SOCIAL SERVICES (US) [02865924] **5270**

ADMINISTRATIVE DIRECTORY OF THE IMPERIAL ETHIOPIAN GOVERNMENT *See* ADMINISTRATIVE DIRECTORY OF THE PROVISIONAL MILITARY GOVERNMENT OF SOCIALIST ETHIOPIA **4624**

ADMINISTRATIVE DIRECTORY OF THE PROVISIONAL MILITARY GOVERNMENT OF SOCIALIST ETHIOPIA (ET) [04183668] **4624**

ADMINISTRATIVE FOCUS (US/1056-1293) [23469505] **1859**

ADMINISTRATIVE HANDBOOK (AT) **1722**

ADMINISTRATIVE INFORMATION REPORT / NASSP (US) [10463514] **1859**

ADMINISTRATIVE, INSTRUCTIONAL AND NON-INSTRUCTIONAL SALARIES IN OHIO *See* SALARY STUDY / DIVISION OF COMPUTER SERVICES AND STATISTICAL REPORTS **1870**

ADMINISTRATIVE JUDICIARY NEWS AND JOURNAL, THE (US/1064-394X) [20949633] **3138**

ADMINISTRATIVE LAW BULLETIN (US) 4624, **2927**

ADMINISTRATIVE LAW DECISIONS (AT/0726-5816) [07265816] **2927**

ADMINISTRATIVE LAW (GARDENA) (US/0149-3272) [03467409] **3091**

●ADMINISTRATIVE LAW JOURNAL OF THE AMERICAN UNIVERSITY, THE (US) [26019507] **2927**

ADMINISTRATIVE LAW JOURNAL (WASHINGTON, D.C.) *See* ADMINISTRATIVE LAW JOURNAL OF THE AMERICAN UNIVERSITY, THE **2927**

ADMINISTRATIVE LAW JOURNAL (WASHINGTON, D.C.), THE (US/1052-2913) [17693129] **3091**

ADMINISTRATIVE LAW NEWS (AMERICAN BAR ASSOCIATION. SECTION OF ADMINISTRATIVE LAW : 1974) (US/0567-9494) [01461099] **3091**

ADMINISTRATIVE LAW NOTES / SECTION ON ADMINISTRATIVE LAW, FEDERAL BAR ASSOCIATION (US/0742-9673) [10493007] **3091**

ADMINISTRATIVE LAW REPORTS (UK/0957-9710) [I09579710] **2927**

ADMINISTRATIVE LAW REPORTS (TORONTO) (CN/0824-2615) [10638742] **3091**

ADMINISTRATIVE LAW REVIEW (US/0001-8368) [01461100] **3092**

ADMINISTRATIVE LAW, THIRD SERIES (US) [20024606] 4624, **2927**

ADMINISTRATIVE LAW TREATISE (US) [09484855] **3092**

ADMINISTRATIVE OFFICE OF PENNSYLVANIA COURTS *See* REPORT - ADMINISTRATIVE OFFICE OF PENNSYLVANIA COURTS **3142**

●ADMINISTRATIVE OPHTHALMOLOGY (US/1060-5991) [25043402] **3871**

ADMINISTRATIVE RADIOLOGY (US/0738-6974) [09659440] **3938**

ADMINISTRATIVE REGISTER OF KENTUCKY (US/0096-1493) [01796780] **2928**

ADMINISTRATIVE REVIEW COUNCIL (AUSTRALIA) *See* ANNUAL REPORT / ADMINISTRATIVE REVIEW COUNCIL **2934**

ADMINISTRATIVE SCIENCE QUARTERLY (US/0001-8392) [01461102] **4624**

ADMINISTRATIVE SCIENCE REVIEW (BG/0001-8406) [01461103] **4624**

ADMINISTRATIVE SUPPORT MANUAL (US) [05153817] **1144**

ADMINISTRATIVE SURVEY OF FISCAL YEAR ... ADULT BASIC EDUCATION PROGRAMS IN THE COMMONWEALTH OF PENNSYLVANIA / PLANNING STUDIES IN CONTINUING EDUCATION, THE PENNSYLVANIA STATE UNIVERSITY (US) [07645262] **1799**

ADMINISTRATOR (LONDON, ENGLAND) (UK) [09505763] **3094**

ADMINISTRATOR (MADISON, WIS.) (US/0744-7078) [08508491] **1859**

ADMINISTRATORS BULLETIN (AT/0048-6418) [I00486418] **1859**

ADMINISTRATOR'S NOTEBOOK (US/0001-8430) [01461108] **1859**

ADMIRALTY LIST OF RADIO SIGNALS DIAGRAMS RELATING TO RADIOBEACONS (UK) [09163991] 1125, **4174**

ADMIRALTY TIDE TABLES (UK) [20144609] **4174**

ADMISSION REQUIREMENTS OF U.S. AND CANADIAN DENTAL SCHOOLS (US/0091-729X) [01795510] 1807, **1315**

ADMISSIONS DECISIONS STUDY - FLORIDA. UNIVERSITY, GAINESVILLE. GRADUATE SCHOOL (US/0148-9097) [01407469] **1792**

ADMISSIONS MARKETING REPORT (US/0884-7398) [12489666] **1807**

ADMISSIONS TO JUVENILE INSTITUTIONS (US) [04663239] **3156**

ADNEWS (OCT. 13, 1981) *CEASED.* (CN/0712-9041) [08734041] **754**

ADOBE NEWS (1988) (US/0896-8403) [17304755] **598**

ADOLESCENCE (US/0001-8449) [01788916] 5189, **1059**

●ADOLESCENCE MAGAZINE (US) [26514505] 4571, **1338**

ADOLESCENCE (PARIS, FRANCE) (FR/0751-7696) [16521105] **4571**

ADOLESCENT AND PEDIATRIC GYNECOLOGY (US/0932-8610) [17768522] 3899, **3756**

ADOLESCENT COUNSELOR (US/1042-7589) [19133388] **4571**

ADOLESCENT MEDICINE (GLENVIEW) (US/0044-6335) [01461111] **3899**

ADOLESCENT MEDICINE (NEW YORK) (US/0160-8231) [03506304] **3899**

ADOLESCENT MEDICINE (PHILADELPHIA, PA.) (US/1041-3499) [18729684] **3546**

ADOLESCENT PREGNANCY PREVENTION AND SERVICES PROGRAM, ANNUAL REPORT / PREPARED BY THE NEW YORK STATE DEPARTMENT OF SOCIAL SERVICES (US) [25816793] 587, **5270**

ADOLESCENT PREGNANCY PREVENTION CLEARINGHOUSE (US/0899-5591) [18138176] 2276, **5270**

ADOLESCENT PSYCHIATRY (US/0065-2008) [02256965] 3919, **3899**

ADOLESCENZA (IT/1120-3714) [I112003714] 4571, **1059**

ADONIS CD-ROM (NE) **3685**

ADONIS NEWS (NE) [24000755] **3187**

ADOPTED BUDGET - CITY OF NEW YORK (US) [07031270] 4708, **4624**

ADOPTED CHILD (US/0745-3167) [09062590] **2276**

ADOPTED TEXTS / STANDING CONFERENCE OF LOCAL AND REGIONAL AUTHORITIES OF EUROPE / TEXTES ADOPTES / CONFERENCE PERMANENTE DES POUVOIRS LOCAUX ET REGIONAUX DE L'EUROPE (FR) [24852607] **4624**

ADOPTION (US/1046-3569) [20388516] **2276**

ADOPTION & FOSTERING (UK/0308-5759) [02573393] **5270**

ADOPTION DIRECTORY, THE (US) [19718478] **2276**

ADOPTION HELPER (CN/1181-845X) [23004404] **5270**

ADOPTION THERAPIST (US/1055-6109) [23239745] **5270**

ADOPTIONS IN CALIFORNIA, AGENCY, INDEPENDENT, INTERCOUNTRY. ANNUAL STATISTICAL REPORT (US) [25910987] **5270**

ADOPTIONS - STATE OF VERMONT, DEPARTMENT OF SOCIAL AND REHABILITATION SERVICES (US) [01794285] **5270**

●ADOPTIVE FAMILIES (US/1076-1020) [30404654] 2276, **5270**

ADOPTIVE FAMILIES TOGETHER : AFT (US/1058-9155) [24426737] **2276**

ADP AND TELECOMMUNICATION STANDARDS INDEX *See* FEDERAL ADP AND TELECOMMUNICATIONS STANDARDS INDEX **1185**

ADP AND TELECOMMUNICATION STANDARDS INDEX / OFFICE OF INFORMATION RESOURCES MANAGEMENT, U.S. GENERAL SERVICES ADMINISTRATION (US) [10640871] 1148, **1255**

ADP PREVENTION HIGHLIGHTS / DEPARTMENT OF ALCOHOL AND DRUG PROGRAMS, DIVISION OF ALCOHOL PROGRAMS (US) [25264969] **1339**

ADPA. AUTOMATIC DATA PROCESSING AND ARCHIVES *CEASED.* (CN/0382-9197) [02172383] **2478**

ADRENAL MEDULLA, THE (US/0704-4917) [06018438] **3546**

ADRESBOEKJE VAN DE AMSTERDAMSE GENEESKUNDIGEN (NE) **3775**

ADRESSBUCH DER GOLDSTADT PFORZHEIM, DER GROSSEN KREISSTADT MUHLACKER, SOWIE STADTEN UND GEMEINDEN DES ENZKREISES (GW) [03262813] **2672**

ADRESSBUCH DER STADT FURTH (GW) [03787791] **2672**

ADRESSBUCH DER STADT HANAU (GW) [05912374] **2672**

ADRESSBUCH DES DEUTSCHSPRACHIGEN BUCHHANDEL (GW/0065-2032) [03635076] **4823**

ADRESSBUCH PFORZHEIM UND UMGEBUNG (GW) [02240687] **2672**

ADRESSBUCH STADT UND KREIS ESSLINGEN (GW) [01784758] **2672**

ADRICHALUT YISRAELIT (IS) **287**

ADRIFT (US/0736-4970) [09143100] **3358**

ADRIKHALUT *See* ARKHITEKTURAH **291**

ADRIS NEWSLETTER *SUSPENDED.* (US/0300-7022) [01427074] **4932**

●ADS INTERNATIONAL (UK/1350-1402) [13501402] **754**

ADS : NOTIZIARIO SETTIMANALE ASSICURATIVO ECONOMICO FINANZIARIO (IT) **2872**

ADS NOTIZIE (IT) **2484**

ADSORBCIJA I ADSORBENTY (UN/0320-7218) [10768982] 959, **4396**

ADSORPTION (NE/0929-5607) **959**

ADSORPTION AND ADSORBENTS (US/0092-8089) [01784395] **1049**

ADSORPTION SCIENCE & TECHNOLOGY (UK/0263-6174) [10444052] 2096, **2007**

ADTALK (CN/0225-6991) [06272411] **754**

ADUK, ADRESAR UKRAINTSIV U VILNOMU SVITI (FR) [02245733] **2672**

ADULESCENS (IT) **1722**

ADULIS (FR/0760-9736) [18790660] **2636**

ADULT AND CONTINUING EDUCATION TODAY (US/0001-8473) [01461116] **1799**

ADULT BASIC AND SECONDARY EDUCATION (US/0731-3268) [07729820] **1799**

ADULT BASIC EDUCATION (US) [04485098] **1799**

ADULT BASIC EDUCATION (ATHENS, GA.) (US/1052-231X) [22218755] **1799**

Alphabetical Title Index

ADVANCES

ADULT BIBLE STUDIES (US/0149-8347) [03565067] **5014**

ADULT CINEMA REVIEW (US/0277-2914) [07528740] **4062**

ADULT CONTEMPORARY MUSIC RESEARCH LETTER, THE (US/1063-7494) [26145276] **4098**

ADULT CONTINUING EDUCATION YEAR BOOK (UK) [28283147] **1799**

ADULT CORRECTIONAL SERVICES IN CANADA (CN/0715-2973) [09869582] 3156, **3078**

ADULT DAY CARE LETTER (US/0885-4572) [12645511] **5270**

ADULT EDUCATION (US) [06910505] **1799**

ADULT EDUCATION AND DEVELOPMENT. EDUCATION DES ADULTES ET DEVELOPPEMENT. EDUCACION DE ADULTOS Y DESARROLLO (GW) [04447111] **1799**

ADULT EDUCATION IN FINLAND (FI/0001-8503) [04303159] **1799**

ADULT EDUCATION QUARTERLY (AMERICAN ASSOCIATION FOR ADULT AND CONTINUING EDUCATION) (US/0741-7136) [09406042] **1799**

ADULT FAITH RESOURCES NETWORKER (US/0898-9729) [17965353] **4932**

ADULT LEARNING (US/1045-1595) [20025291] **1799**

ADULT LIFE AND WORK LESSON ANNUAL (US/0732-3573) [08331863] **4932**

●ADULT LIFE AND WORK STUDY GUIDE (US/1071-4383) [28648178] **5054**

ADULT MIGRANT EDUCATION PROGRAM (AT) [18759663] **1799**

ADULT PROBATION ADMISSIONS (US/0095-4004) [04043940] **3156**

ADULT PROSECUTION: REFERENCE TABLES (US) [07098229] **3156**

ADULT SABBATH SCHOOL LESSONS (EASY ENGLISH ED.) (US/0747-1564) [10595999] **5054**

ADULT STUDENT *See* ADULT STUDENT GUIDE **4932**

●ADULT STUDENT GUIDE (US/1059-3225) [24564859] 1722, **4932**

ADULT TEACHER *See* ADULT TEACHER GUIDE **4932**

●ADULT TEACHER GUIDE (US/1059-3233) [24565272] **4932**

ADULT TEACHER'S GUIDE (US/0162-9212) [04261254] **1887**

ADULT VIDEO NEWS (US/0883-7090) [12197226] **4366**

ADULTOS EN LA ESCUELA DOMINICAL *See* INTERPRETE ALUMNOS, EL **1102**

ADULTS LEARNING (UK/0955-2308) [20104150] **1799**

ADVANCE (US) [09989937] **3546**

●ADVANCE ACS ABSTRACTS (US/1068-8382) [27825426] **959**

ADVANCE ANNOTATION SERVICE TO THE CODE OF ALABAMA 1975 (US/0747-6612) [08071603] **2928**

ADVANCE BUDGETING. A REPORT TO THE CONGRESS (US/0147-1945) [03113557] 4708, **4624**

ADVANCE DATA FROM VITAL AND HEALTH STATISTICS OF THE NATIONAL CENTER FOR HEALTH STATISTICS (US/0147-3956) [02778178] **4809**

ADVANCE DATA SERVICE / INTERNATIONAL LEAD AND ZINC STUDY GROUP (UK) **3997**

ADVANCE (DES MOINES, IOWA) (US/0889-8170) [05690116] **1125**

ADVANCE DRILLING DATA *See* GULF OF MEXICO DRILLING REPORT **1608**

ADVANCE FOR HEALTH INFORMATION PROFESSIONALS (US/1061-3269) [25250569] **4210**

ADVANCE FORECAST REPORT TO THE MINNESOTA ENVIRONMENTAL QUALITY BOARD ... (US/0742-9282) [09342405] **2034**

ADVANCE-LEADER (LIGONIER, IND.) (US) [15966350] **5662**

ADVANCE LEADER, THE (US) [17681843] **5734**

ADVANCE (MILBANK, S.D.) *See* MILBANK HERALD ADVANCE **5744**

ADVANCE-MONTICELLONIAN (US) [22228348] **5628**

ADVANCE NOTICE (PRINCETON, N.J.) *SUSPENDED.* (US/1060-6645) [23852637] 2436, **3187**

ADVANCE OF BUCKS COUNTY, THE (US) [20569005] **5734**

ADVANCE PROGRAM (US) [01801556] 5528, **2034**

ADVANCE (RANDOLPH, WIS. : 1976) (US) [13058411] **5763**

ADVANCE RELEASE OF DATA FOR THE ... STATISTICAL YEARBOOK OF THE ELECTRIC UTILITY INDUSTRY (US/0894-5020) [08849891] **4759**

ADVANCE REPORT ON DURABLE GOODS MANUFACTURERS' SHIPMENTS AND ORDERS (US) [06418062] **3475**

ADVANCE REPORTER, THE (US/0747-3338) [10743453] **5722**

ADVANCE-SENTINEL, THE (US) [19085801] **5744**

ADVANCE (SPRINGFIELD) (US/0001-8589) [03790194] **5054**

ADVANCE STATISTICS OF EDUCATION (CN/0575-786X) [02442363] 1722, **1793**

ADVANCE STUDIES IN LIFELONG EDUCATION (UK) [05461145] **1722**

ADVANCE (WASHINGTON, D.C. 1986) *CEASED.* (US/0886-778X) [12985965] **1460**

ADVANCE-YEOMAN (US) [12412281] **5679**

ADVANCE (ZURICH) (CN/0824-6610) [10862190] **5779**

ADVANCED ANTITRUST WORKSHOP *See* ANNUAL ADVANCED ANTITRUST WORKSHOP **3095**

ADVANCED ASSET MANAGEMENT CREDIT UNION DIRECTORY (US) [14476001] **768**

ADVANCED BATTERY TECHNOLOGY (US/0001-8627) [07845966] **2034**

●ADVANCED CEMENT-BASED MATERIALS (US/1065-7355) [26714237] 1020, 2018, **598**

ADVANCED CERAMICS REPORT (NE/0268-9847) [16243811] **2585**

ADVANCED COATINGS & SURFACE TECHNOLOGY (US/0896-422X) [17156963] **1020**

ADVANCED COMPOSITE MATERIALS : THE OFFICIAL JOURNAL OF THE JAPAN SOCIETY OF COMPOSITE MATERIALS (JA/0924-3046) [24704610] **2100**

ADVANCED COMPOSITES *CEASED.* (US/0895-0407) [15746620] **2100**

ADVANCED COMPOSITES BULLETIN (UK) [21251469] **4453**

ADVANCED COMPOSITES LETTERS (UK/0963-6935) [I09636935] **2100**

ADVANCED CRIMINAL TRIAL TACTICS FOR PROSECUTION AND DEFENSE / PRACTISING LAW INSTUTUTE (US) [06928201] **3104**

ADVANCED DEVELOPMENT (US/1042-2021) [18968738] **1874**

ADVANCED DRUG DELIVERY REVIEWS (NE/0169-409X) [13190647] **4289**

ADVANCED ENGINEERING MATERIALS RESEARCH PROFILE DIRECTORY (US) **2100**

ADVANCED EXERCISES IN DIAGNOSTIC RADIOLOGY *CEASED.* (US/0160-1636) [02766340] **3938**

ADVANCED FOSSIL ENERGY TECHNOLOGIES (US/0896-520X) [17197580] **1930**

ADVANCED GERIATRIC MEDICINE (UK/0261-2763) [08230324] **3748**

ADVANCED HOSPITAL TECHNOLOGY (UK) **5080**

ADVANCED IMAGING (WOODBURY, N.Y.) (US/1042-0711) [18929091] **1276**

ADVANCED IMMIGRATION WORKSHOP (US/8756-873X) [11167406] 1918, **2928**

●ADVANCED INTELLIGENT NETWORK NEWS (US/1072-0030) [28826683] **1240**

ADVANCED INTELLIGENT NETWORKS REPORT (US/1056-7119) [23819443] **1240**

ADVANCED LABANOTATION (SZ/1053-4261) [22529224] **1310**

ADVANCED LIGHTER THAN AIR REVIEW *SUSPENDED.* (US/0149-5747) [03522552] **1103**

ADVANCED MANUFACTURING TECHNOLOGY (US/0885-5684) [12086349] 5080, **1217**

ADVANCED MATERIALS & PROCESSES (US/0882-7958) [11981589] **2100**

ADVANCED MATERIALS & TECHNOLOGY (FR) **2100**

●ADVANCED MATERIALS FOR OPTICS AND ELECTRONICS (UK/1057-9257) [24223016] **5080**

ADVANCED MATERIALS IN AEROSPACE APPLICATIONS (US/1055-9418) [23071656] **3**

ADVANCED MATERIALS (METUCHEN, N.J.) (US/0734-7146) [08273007] **2100**

ADVANCED MATERIALS TECHNOLOGY *CEASED.* (UK/0957-4778) **5080**

ADVANCED MATERIALS (WEINHEIM) (US/0935-9648) [21104347] **2100**

ADVANCED METALLIZATION FOR ULSI APPLICATIONS (US) **2100**

ADVANCED METALS TECHNOLOGY *CEASED.* (UK/0957-9729) **3997**

ADVANCED MICRO DEVICES ... ANNUAL PROCEEDINGS (US/0883-1262) [12074845] **1265**

ADVANCED MILITARY COMPUTING (US/0884-9471) [12532641] 4033, **1210**

ADVANCED MUNICIPAL BONDS WORKSHOP (US/1043-755X) [17995635] **2928**

ADVANCED OFFICE TECHNOLOGIES REPORT (US/1054-1462) [22773560] **1170**

ADVANCED OIL AND GAS RECOVERY TECHNOLOGIES (US/0896-5188) [17197557] **1930**

●ADVANCED PACKAGING (US/1065-0555) [26493484] **2034**

ADVANCED PERFORMANCE MATERIALS (NE/0929-1881) **2100**

ADVANCED PLANNING / VIZITERV, INSTITUTE FOR HYDRAULIC PLANNING (HU) [10992934] **2087**

ADVANCED POWDER TECHNOLOGY (NE/0921-8831) [I09218831] **5080**

ADVANCED REAL ESTATE LAW COURSE (US/0198-9448) [06257131] 4833, **2928**

ADVANCED RECOVERY WEEK (US/1050-1347) [21187483] **4249**

ADVANCED ROBOTICS (NE/0169-1864) [14883000] 1227, **1210**

ADVANCED RUSSIAN TECHNOLOGIES (UK) **5081**

ADVANCED SALES REFERENCE SERVICE (US/0163-8939) [04523223] **2872**

ADVANCED SEARCHER (UK/0960-3247) [I09603247] **3187**

ADVANCED SERIES IN AGRICULTURAL SCIENCES (US/0172-4207) [01711854] **44**

ADVANCED SERIES IN MANAGEMENT (NE) [10265983] **859**

ADVANCED SERIES IN MATHEMATICAL PHYSICS (SI) [19657467] 3491, **4396**

ADVANCED SERIES ON COMPLEX SYSTEMS (SI) [17700188] **440**

ADVANCED STUDIES IN CONTEMPORARY MATHEMATICS (US/0884-0016) [12568431] **3491**

ADVANCED STUDIES IN PURE MATHEMATICS (TOKYO, JAPAN) (JA) [02251549] **3491**

ADVANCED STUDIES IN THEORETICAL AND APPLIED ECONOMETRICS (NE) [09815587] **5320**

●ADVANCED SYSTEMS (US/1074-9306) [29812921] **1265**

ADVANCED TECHNOLOGY IN THE PACIFIC NORTHWEST (US/8755-7258) [11401018] **5081**

ADVANCED TECHNOLOGY IN WASHINGTON STATE (US/0749-4874) [09770090] **5081**

ADVANCED TECHNOLOGY LIBRARIES (US/0044-636X) [01669939] **3187**

ADVANCED TEXTBOOKS IN ECONOMICS (NE/0169-5568) [10004029] **1460**

ADVANCED TWO-PHASE FLOW INSTRUMENTATION PROGRAM QUARTERLY PROGRESS REPORT FOR ... (US) [08496249] **2153**

ADVANCED UNDERWRITING SERVICE (US) 2872, 2928, **4708**

ADVANCED WILL DRAFTING (US/0732-7579) [05084554] **3117**

ADVANCED WIRELESS COMMUNICATIONS (US/1058-7713) [24383257] **1103**

ADVANCES (US/0741-9783) [10240637] **3546**

ADVANCES AND TECHNICAL STANDARDS IN NEUROSURGERY (US/0095-4829) [01160320] 3826, **3957**

ADVANCES FOR MEDICINE (US) [06654058] **3546**

ADVANCES FOR PUBLIC WORKS PLANNING PROGRAM (US) [05293166] **2813**

ADVANCES IN ACCOUNTING (US/0882-6110) [11297487] **738**

●ADVANCES IN ACCOUNTING INFORMATION SYSTEMS (US) [25286796] **738**

ADVANCES IN ADOLESCENT MENTAL HEALTH (US/0891-9879) [13657896] **4571**

ADVANCES IN AGRICULTURAL BIOTECHNOLOGY (NE/0169-0566) [13212000] **44**

ADVANCES IN AGRICULTURAL TECHNOLOGY (NORTH CENTRAL SERIES) (US/0193-3701) [04934660] **44**

ADVANCES IN AGRICULTURAL TECHNOLOGY (SOUTHERN SERIES) (US/0193-3728) [04977899] **44**

ADVANCES — Alphabetical Title Index

ADVANCES IN AGRICULTURAL TECHNOLOGY (WESTERN SERIES) (US/0193-3736) [04719744] **44**

ADVANCES IN AGRONOMY (US/0065-2113) [01461140] **44**

ADVANCES IN ALS/MND (UK/0965-1802) [I09651802] **3826**

ADVANCES IN ANALYSIS OF BEHAVIOUR (UK/0271-9738) [06771473] **4571**

●ADVANCES IN ANALYTICAL GEOCHEMISTRY (US) [29884040] 1365, **959**

ADVANCES IN ANALYTICAL TOXICOLOGY *CEASED.* (US/0749-7431) [10602443] **3978**

●ADVANCES IN ANATOMIC PATHOLOGY (US/1072-4109) [28941339] **3892**

ADVANCES IN ANATOMY, EMBRYOLOGY AND CELL BIOLOGY (GW/0301-5556) [01787967] 531, 541, **3678**

ADVANCES IN ANESTHESIA (US/0737-6146) [09417566] **3680**

ADVANCES IN ANTIVIRAL AGENT DESIGN (US) **959**

ADVANCES IN APPLIED BIOTECHNOLOGY SERIES (US/1053-4490) [21076997] **3685**

ADVANCES IN APPLIED BUSINESS STRATEGY (US/0749-6826) [11058728] **859**

●ADVANCES IN APPLIED LIPID RESEARCH (UK) [26076061] **440**

ADVANCES IN APPLIED MATHEMATICS (US/0196-8858) [05913757] **3491**

ADVANCES IN APPLIED MECHANICS (US/0065-2156) [01461143] **2109**

ADVANCES IN APPLIED MICROBIOLOGY (US/0065-2164) [01461144] **558**

ADVANCES IN APPLIED MICROECONOMICS (US/0278-0984) [07701781] **1460**

ADVANCES IN APPLIED NEUROLOGICAL SCIENCES (GW/0935-0195) [12291460] **3826**

ADVANCES IN APPLIED PROBABILITY (UK/0001-8678) [01461145] **3491**

ADVANCES IN APPLIED SOCIAL PSYCHOLOGY (US/0883-3656) [07111455] 5238, **4571**

ADVANCES IN ARTIFICIAL INTELLIGENCE IN ECONOMICS, FINANCE, AND MANAGEMENT (US) 1210, **636**

ADVANCES IN ASTHMA ALLERGY & PULMONARY DISEASES *SUSPENDED.* (US/0164-7075) [04391287] **3947**

ADVANCES IN ASTHMA & ALLERGY (US/0163-1578) [03059391] **3948**

ADVANCES IN ATMOSPHERIC SCIENCES / EDITED BY CHINESE COMMITTEE OF METEOROLOGY AND ATMOSPHERIC PHYSICS AND INSTITUTE OF ATMOSPHERIC PHYSICS, ACADEMIA SINICA (CC/0256-1530) [12795886] **1419**

ADVANCES IN ATOMIC, MOLECULAR, AND OPTICAL PHYSICS (US/1049-250X) [20844402] **959**

ADVANCES IN AUDIOLOGY (SZ/0254-8747) [10715888] **4383**

ADVANCES IN AUSTRIAN ECONOMICS (US) **1460**

ADVANCES IN AUTOMATION AND ROBOTICS (US) [13422328] **1210**

ADVANCES IN BEHAVIORAL ASSESSMENT OF CHILDREN AND FAMILIES (US/0893-6110) [14232054] **4571**

ADVANCES IN BEHAVIORAL BIOLOGY (US/0099-6246) [01906330] 4571, **440**

ADVANCES IN BEHAVIORAL ECONOMICS (US/0890-0159) [14122830] **1460**

ADVANCES IN BEHAVIORAL MEDICINE (US/0885-0836) [12356527] **4571**

ADVANCES IN BEHAVIORAL PHARMACOLOGY *CEASED.* (US/0147-071X) [03126126] **4571**

ADVANCES IN BEHAVIOUR RESEARCH AND THERAPY (UK/0146-6402) [03453960] **4571**

ADVANCES IN BEHAVIOURAL MEDICINE (AT) [09224691] **3546**

ADVANCES IN BIOCHEMICAL ENGINEERING/BIOTECHNOLOGY (GW/0724-6145) [09397594] **2007**

ADVANCES IN BIOCHEMICAL PSYCHOPHARMACOLOGY (US/0065-2229) [01461149] 4289, **3826**

ADVANCES IN BIOENGINEERING (US/0360-9960) [02245725] 3685, **1963**

ADVANCES IN BIOLOGICAL PSYCHIATRY (SZ/0378-7354) [04798019] **3919**

ADVANCES IN BIOLOGICAL RESEARCH (II) [11640603] **440**

ADVANCES IN BIOMATERIALS (UK/0272-3840) [06832932] **3546**

ADVANCES IN BIOMATERIALS (LANCASTER, PA.) (US/1043-3252) [15809389] **3546**

ADVANCES IN BIOPHYSICAL CHEMISTRY (US/1057-8943) [23106647] 494, 1049, **479**

ADVANCES IN BIOPHYSICS (IE/0065-227X) [01461154] **494**

ADVANCES IN BIOSCIENCES (II/0970-0315) [19585035] **440**

ADVANCES IN BIOSENSORS (UK/1061-8945) [24014375] 2034, **440**

ADVANCES IN BIOTECHNOLOGICAL PROCESSES (US/0736-2293) [09090999] **3685**

ADVANCES IN BOTANICAL RESEARCH (UK/0065-2296) [01461155] **497**

ADVANCES IN BRYOLOGY (GW/0253-6226) [08442943] **498**

ADVANCES IN BUSINESS MANAGEMENT AND FORECASTING (US) **1460**

ADVANCES IN BUSINESS MARKETING *See* ADVANCES IN BUSINESS MARKETING AND PURCHASING **920**

●ADVANCES IN BUSINESS MARKETING AND PURCHASING (US/1069-0964) [27030708] **920**

ADVANCES IN CANCER CHEMOTHERAPY (US/0190-4817) [04719759] **3808**

ADVANCES IN CANCER RESEARCH (US/0065-230X) [01461156] **3808**

ADVANCES IN CARBENE CHEMISTRY (US) **959**

ADVANCES IN CARBOCATION CHEMISTRY (US/1047-3645) [20661422] **1038**

ADVANCES IN CARBOHYDRATE ANALYSIS (UK/1062-0044) [25001912] **959**

ADVANCES IN CARBOHYDRATE CHEMISTRY AND BIOCHEMISTRY (US/0065-2318) [01793761] **479**

ADVANCES IN CARDIAC SURGERY (US/0889-5074) [13912750] 3697, **3957**

ADVANCES IN CARDIOLOGY (SZ/0065-2326) [03490010] **3697**

ADVANCES IN CARDIOVASCULAR PHYSICS (SZ/0378-6900) [05878509] 3698, **494**

ADVANCES IN CATALYSIS (US/0360-0564) [01636053] **1049**

●ADVANCES IN CELL AND MOLECULAR BIOLOGY OF MEMBRANES (US/1074-7567) [28698744] **440**

ADVANCES IN CELL BIOLOGY (GREENWICH, CONN.) *See* ADVANCES IN MOLECULAR AND CELL BIOLOGY **531**

ADVANCES IN CEMENT RESEARCH (UK/0951-7197) [17389021] **598**

ADVANCES IN CERAMICS (US/0730-9546) [08090653] **2585**

ADVANCES IN CEREAL SCIENCE AND TECHNOLOGY *CEASED.* (US/0362-1634) [02196724] **2326**

ADVANCES IN CHEMICAL ENGINEERING (US/0065-2377) [01461163] **2007**

ADVANCES IN CHEMICAL PHYSICS (US/0065-2385) [00928160] **1049**

ADVANCES IN CHEMISTRY SERIES (US/0065-2393) [01269845] **959**

ADVANCES IN CHILD BEHAVIORAL ANALYSIS AND THERAPY (US/0739-7313) [07769621] **4571**

ADVANCES IN CHILD DEVELOPMENT AND BEHAVIOR (US/0065-2407) [01461167] **4571**

●ADVANCES IN CHILD NEUROPSYCHOLOGY (US/0940-8606) [25380287] 3826, **4571**

ADVANCES IN CHROMATOGRAPHY (HOUSTON) (US/0270-773X) [06507512] **1020**

ADVANCES IN CHROMATOGRAPHY (NEW YORK, N.Y.) (US/0065-2415) [01373446] **1038**

ADVANCES IN CLADISTICS : PROCEEDINGS OF THE ... MEETING OF THE WILLI HENNIG SOCIETY *CEASED.* (US/0740-9028) [09820449] **440**

●ADVANCES IN CLASSICAL TRAJECTORY METHODS (US/1066-5005) [26265812] **1049**

ADVANCES IN CLINICAL CARDIOLOGY *CEASED.* (US/0272-9237) [06973419] **3698**

ADVANCES IN CLINICAL CHEMISTRY (US/0065-2423) [01461169] 959, **3892**

ADVANCES IN CLINICAL CHILD PSYCHOLOGY (US/0149-4732) [03490015] 3899, **4571**

ADVANCES IN CLINICAL NEUROPSYCHOLOGY (US/0748-4410) [10205703] 4571, **3826**

●ADVANCES IN CLINICAL OPHTHALMOLOGY (US/1070-5384) [28402186] **3871**

ADVANCES IN CNS DRUG-RECEPTOR INTERACTIONS (US) [24359902] 3826, **4289**

●ADVANCES IN COGNITION AND EDUCATIONAL PRACTICE (US) [26596876] 1722, **4571**

ADVANCES IN COLLOID AND INTERFACE SCIENCE (NE/0001-8686) [01164308] **1049**

ADVANCES IN COMPARATIVE AND ENVIRONMENTAL PHYSIOLOGY (GW/0938-2763) [18690473] **577**

●ADVANCES IN COMPUTATIONAL MATHEMATICS (NE/1019-7168) [28473015] **3491**

ADVANCES IN COMPUTER-AIDED ENGINEERING DESIGN (US/0892-4260) [12985361] **1231**

ADVANCES IN COMPUTER CHESS (UK) [03470804] **1230**

ADVANCES IN COMPUTER GRAPHICS HARDWARE (GW) [19925630] **1231**

ADVANCES IN COMPUTER SECURITY MANAGEMENT *CEASED.* (US/0197-1514) [05970255] **1225**

ADVANCES IN COMPUTERS (US/0065-2458) [01461174] **1255**

ADVANCES IN COMPUTING RESEARCH (US/0741-9341) [10222174] **1170**

ADVANCES IN CONNECTIONIST AND NEURAL COMPUTATION THEORY (US/1060-2410) [23920278] **1210**

●ADVANCES IN CONSCIOUSNESS RESEARCH (NE) **3261**

ADVANCES IN CONSUMER RESEARCH (US/0098-9258) [02239683] **1293**

ADVANCES IN CONTRACEPTION (UK/0267-4874) [12139626] **587**

ADVANCES IN CONTRACEPTIVE DELIVERY SYSTEMS (US/1012-8689) [12246869] **587**

ADVANCES IN CONTROL SYSTEMS AND SIGNAL PROCESSING (GW) [08235090] **1963**

ADVANCES IN CRIMINOLOGICAL THEORY (US/0894-2366) [15876755] **3156**

ADVANCES IN CRYOGENIC ENGINEERING (US/0065-2482) [01461177] 4430, **1963**

ADVANCES IN CRYOGENIC ENGINEERING MATERIALS (US/0886-1587) [07766271] 4430, **1964**

ADVANCES IN CYCLOADDITION (US/1052-2077) [18125795] **1038**

ADVANCES IN DATA BASE MANAGEMENT *CEASED.* (US/0196-8718) [05910520] **1252**

ADVANCES IN DATA BASE THEORY (US) [07399682] 1255, **1252**

ADVANCES IN DATA COMMUNICATIONS MANAGEMENT (US/0197-1476) [05970322] **1255**

ADVANCES IN DATA PROCESSING MANAGEMENT (US/0196-8696) [05910604] **1255**

ADVANCES IN DENDRITIC MACROMOLECULES (US) **959**

ADVANCES IN DENTAL RESEARCH (US/0895-9374) [16857667] **1315**

ADVANCES IN DERMATOLOGY (US/0882-0880) [11748285] **3717**

ADVANCES IN DESCRIPTIVE PSYCHOLOGY (US/0276-9913) [07340159] **4571**

ADVANCES IN DESERT AND ARID LAND TECHNOLOGY AND DEVELOPMENT (SZ/0142-5889) [05766909] **5081**

ADVANCES IN DETAILED REACTION MECHANISMS (US/1063-0619) [25426049] 1049, **1038**

ADVANCES IN DEVELOPMENTAL AND BEHAVIORAL PEDIATRICS (US/0737-7452) [09355793] 4571, **3899**

●ADVANCES IN DEVELOPMENTAL BIOCHEMISTRY (US/1064-2722) [25825960] **479**

●ADVANCES IN DEVELOPMENTAL BIOLOGY (US) [25406939] **541**

ADVANCES IN DEVELOPMENTAL POLICY STUDIES (US) **2907**

ADVANCES IN DEVELOPMENTAL PSYCHOLOGY *CEASED.* (US/0275-3049) [07113759] **4571**

ADVANCES IN DISCOURSE PROCESSES (US/0896-470X) [05821490] **3261**

ADVANCES IN DISEASE PREVENTION *CEASED.* (US/0277-0687) [07492806] **3546**

ADVANCES IN DISEASE VECTOR RESEARCH (US/0934-6112) [18694097] **5604**

ADVANCES IN DISTRIBUTED PROCESSING MANAGEMENT (US/0197-1433) [05969845] **1255**

●ADVANCES IN DISTRIBUTION CHANNEL RESEARCH (US/1071-9679) [27439411] **920**

ADVANCES

●ADVANCES IN DNA SEQUENCE SPECIFIC AGENTS (US/1067-568X) [26521941] **1012**

ADVANCES IN DRUG RESEARCH (UK/0065-2490) [03938076] **4289**

ADVANCES IN DRYING *CEASED*. (US/0272-4790) [06871592] **2096**

ADVANCES IN EARLY EDUCATION AND DAY CARE (US/0270-4021) [06318179] **1802**

ADVANCES IN EATING DISORDERS (US/1052-0465) [17209100] 3794, **3919**

ADVANCES IN ECHO-CONTRAST (UK/0925-5206) [24245984] **3938**

ADVANCES IN ECOLOGICAL RESEARCH (UK/0065-2504) [01220531] **2210**

ADVANCES IN ECONOMETRICS (US/0731-9053) [08136598] **1460**

ADVANCES IN ECONOMIC BOTANY (US/0741-8280) [10209699] **498**

ADVANCES IN EDUCATIONAL ADMINISTRATION (US) [22155974] **1859**

ADVANCES IN EDUCATIONAL PRODUCTIVITY (US) [22157105] **1887**

ADVANCES IN EDUCATIONAL RESEARCH : SUBSTANTIVE FINDINGS, METHODOLOGICAL DEVELOPMENTS (US) [24098578] **1722**

ADVANCES IN ELECTROCHEMICAL SCIENCE AND ENGINEERING (GW/0938-5193) [21913498] **1033**

ADVANCES IN ELECTRON TRANSFER CHEMISTRY (US/1061-8937) [24220118] **1038**

ADVANCES IN ELECTRONICS AND ELECTRON PHYSICS (US/0065-2539) [01461183] **2034**

ADVANCES IN ELECTRONICS AND ELECTRON PHYSICS. SUPPLEMENT (US/0065-2547) [01461184] **2034**

ADVANCES IN ELECTROPHORESIS (GW/0932-3031) [18167814] **2034**

ADVANCES IN ENDOCRINOLOGY AND METABOLISM (US/1049-6734) [21276472] **3726**

ADVANCES IN ENGINEERING (US/0065-2555) [02477314] **1964**

●ADVANCES IN ENGINEERING SOFTWARE (1992) (UK/0965-9978) [25958496] **1964**

ADVANCES IN ENGINEERING SOFTWARE AND WORKSTATIONS *See* ADVANCES IN ENGINEERING SOFTWARE (1992) **1964**

ADVANCES IN ENGINEERING SOFTWARE & WORKSTATIONS (UK) **1284**

●ADVANCES IN ENTREPRENEURSHIP, FIRM EMERGENCE, AND GROWTH (US) [28638989] **636**

ADVANCES IN ENVIRONMENT, BEHAVIOR, AND DESIGN (US/1040-4309) [16619968] **2159**

ADVANCES IN ENVIRONMENTAL SCIENCE AND TECHNOLOGY (US/0065-2563) [01793749] **2223**

ADVANCES IN ENZYME REGULATION (UK/0065-2571) [01461187] **531**

ADVANCES IN ENZYMOLOGY AND RELATED SUBJECTS (US/0065-258X) [02444367] **479**

ADVANCES IN EPILEPTOLOGY (US/0892-726X) [04623600] **3826**

ADVANCES IN ETHOLOGY (1987) (GW/0931-4202) [17283077] **4571**

ADVANCES IN EXPERIENTIAL SOCIAL PROCESSES *CEASED*. (UK/0192-4346) [04092534] 1103, **5189**

ADVANCES IN EXPERIMENTAL MEDICINE AND BIOLOGY (US/0065-2598) [01461189] 440, **3546**

ADVANCES IN EXPERIMENTAL SOCIAL PSYCHOLOGY (US/0065-2601) [01283539] 5238, **4571**

●ADVANCES IN EXPERT SYSTEMS FOR MANAGEMENT (US/1074-7532) [28861654] 859, **1210**

ADVANCES IN EXPLORATION IN GEOPHYSICS (NE) [18154128] 4396, **1365**

ADVANCES IN EXTRACTIVE METALLURGY (UK) [05754615] **3997**

ADVANCES IN FAMILY INTERVENTION, ASSESSMENT AND THEORY (US/0270-9228) [06456990] **3919**

ADVANCES IN FAMILY PSYCHIATRY (US/0887-4298) [06575068] **3919**

ADVANCES IN FEED TECHNOLOGY (GW/0936-2975) [I09362975] **199**

ADVANCES IN FINANCIAL PLANNING AND FORECASTING (US) [12800099] **768**

ADVANCES IN FIRE RETARDANTS (US/0094-3932) [01783687] **2287**

ADVANCES IN FOOD AND NUTRITION RESEARCH (US/1043-4526) [19499025] **4186**

ADVANCES IN FORENSIC HAEMOGENETICS (GW/0930-9535) [16075514] 3739, **3770**

ADVANCES IN FORENSIC PSYCHOLOGY AND PSYCHIATRY (US/0747-6353) [10764439] 3919, 3739, **4571**

ADVANCES IN FORESTRY RESEARCH IN INDIA (II) [19340182] **2373**

ADVANCES IN FUTURES AND OPTIONS RESEARCH (US/1048-1559) [15637146] 1460, **636**

ADVANCES IN GAS CHROMATOGRAPHY *See* ADVANCES IN CHROMATOGRAPHY (HOUSTON) **1020**

ADVANCES IN GASTROINTESTINAL RADIOLOGY (US/1055-808X) [23347361] **3794**

ADVANCES IN GENE TECHNOLOGY (UK) [23158500] **3685**

ADVANCES IN GENETICS (US/0065-2660) [01461194] **542**

●ADVANCES IN GENOME BIOLOGY (US/1067-5701) [26293981] **440**

●ADVANCES IN GEO ECOLOGY (GW) **1351**

ADVANCES IN GEOPHYSICAL DATA PROCESSING (US/0882-6129) [11828328] **1402**

ADVANCES IN GEOPHYSICAL RESEARCH (CC/0962-3647) [21931338] **1402**

ADVANCES IN GEOPHYSICS (US/0065-2687) [01259814] **1402**

ADVANCES IN GEOPHYSICS. SUPPLEMENT (US/0065-2695) [04350794] **1402**

●ADVANCES IN GLOBAL HIGH-TECHNOLOGY MANAGEMENT (US) [26639535] 5081, **859**

ADVANCES IN GROUP PROCESSES (US/0882-6145) [11537584] **5238**

ADVANCES IN GYNAECOLOGICAL ONCOLOGY (II) **3756**

ADVANCES IN GYNECOLOGICAL AND OBSTETRIC RESEARCH SERIES (UK) [23835822] **3756**

ADVANCES IN HEALTH ECONOMICS AND HEALTH SERVICES RESEARCH (US/0731-2199) [07973131] **4763**

ADVANCES IN HEALTH ECONOMICS AND HEALTH SERVICES RESEARCH. SUPPLEMENT (US/1054-1888) [21468242] 1460, **3546**

ADVANCES IN HEALTH EDUCATION (US/0890-4073) [14221617] **4763**

ADVANCES IN HEALTH EDUCATION AND PROMOTION (US/0896-1255) [13283791] 1722, **4763**

ADVANCES IN HEAT TRANSFER (US/0065-2717) [01461197] **4430**

ADVANCES IN HETEROCYCLIC CHEMISTRY (US/0065-2725) [01461198] **1038**

ADVANCES IN HETEROCYCLIC NATURAL PRODUCT SYNTHESIS (US/1067-571X) [23278952] **1038**

ADVANCES IN HIGH-TECH MATERIALS *CEASED*. (US/0890-2771) [14191469] **5081**

ADVANCES IN HORTICULTURAL SCIENCE (IT/0394-6169) [18903149] **2407**

ADVANCES IN HORTICULTURE AND FORESTRY (II/0971-0507) [I09710507] 2373, **2407**

ADVANCES IN HUMAN-COMPUTER INTERACTION (US/0748-8602) [11018329] **1217**

●ADVANCES IN HUMAN ECOLOGY (US/1069-0573) [26076065] **5238**

ADVANCES IN HUMAN FACTORS / ERGONOMICS (NE/0921-2647) [12123036] **2109**

ADVANCES IN HUMAN GENETICS (US/0065-275X) [01461201] **542**

ADVANCES IN HUMAN NUTRITION (US/0891-7396) [12739927] **4186**

ADVANCES IN HUMAN PSYCHOPHARMACOLOGY (US/0272-068X) [06728969] 4571, **4289**

ADVANCES IN HYDROGEN ENERGY (UK/0276-2412) [07340839] **1931**

●ADVANCES IN HYPERTENSION (US/1056-618X) [23748050] **3698**

ADVANCES IN IMMUNITY AND CANCER THERAPY (US/0178-2134) [12546663] **3662**

ADVANCES IN IMMUNOLOGY (US/0065-2776) [00981306] **3662**

ADVANCES IN IMMUNOPHARMACOLOGY : PROCEEDINGS OF THE INTERNATIONAL CONFERENCE ON IMMUNOPHARMACOLOGY (UK) [14275767] **3662**

ADVANCES IN INDUSTRIAL AND LABOR RELATIONS (US/0742-6186) [10235929] **1642**

ADVANCES IN INFANCY RESEARCH (US/0732-9598) [07863811] **4571**

ADVANCES IN INFLAMMATION RESEARCH (US/0197-8322) [05348769] **3546**

ADVANCES IN INFORMATION PROCESSING IN ORGANIZATIONS *See* ADVANCES IN MANAGERIAL COGNITION AND ORGANIZATIONAL INFORMATION PROCESSING **1255**

ADVANCES IN INFORMATION STORAGE SYSTEMS (US/1053-184X) [22469353] **1170**

ADVANCES IN INORGANIC BIOCHEMISTRY *CEASED*. (US/0190-0218) [04632922] 1035, **479**

ADVANCES IN INORGANIC CHEMISTRY (US/0898-8838) [15901259] **1035**

ADVANCES IN INSECT PHYSIOLOGY (UK/0065-2806) [01461206] 577, **5604**

ADVANCES IN INSTRUCTIONAL PSYCHOLOGY (US/0163-5379) [04396488] **4572**

ADVANCES IN INSTRUMENTATION AND CONTROL (US/1054-0032) [20834426] 1964, **5081**

●ADVANCES IN INSTRUMENTATION AND CONTROL (US/1054-0032) [30478855] 1964, **5081**

ADVANCES IN INTERNAL MEDICINE (US/0065-2822) [01461208] **3794**

ADVANCES IN INTERNATIONAL ACCOUNTING (US/0897-3660) [16651655] **738**

ADVANCES IN INTERNATIONAL COMPARATIVE MANAGEMENT (US/0747-7929) [10448245] **859**

ADVANCES IN INTERNATIONAL MARKETING (US) [13960643] **920**

ADVANCES IN INTERPENETRATING POLYMER NETWORKS (US/1068-3550) [23056219] **959**

ADVANCES IN INVERTEBRATE REPRODUCTION : PROCEEDINGS OF THE ... INTERNATIONAL CONGRESS OF INVERTEBRATE REPRODUCTION *CEASED*. (NE) [24426895] **5574**

ADVANCES IN INVESTMENT ANALYSIS & PORTFOLIO MANAGEMENT (UK) **890**

ADVANCES IN INVESTMENTS ANALYSIS AND PORTFOLIO MANAGEMENT (US) [24499942] **890**

ADVANCES IN LABORATORY AUTOMATION ROBOTICS (US) [12698695] **3546**

ADVANCES IN LASER SPECTROSCOPY (LONDON, ENG.) (UK/0264-8423) [08925030] **4432**

ADVANCES IN LAW AND CHILD DEVELOPMENT *CEASED*. (US/0732-3565) [08142728] 4572, **3119**

ADVANCES IN LEARNING AND BEHAVIORAL DISABILITIES (US/0735-004X) [08823030] **1874**

ADVANCES IN LECTIN RESEARCH (GW) [19061072] **498**

ADVANCES IN LIBRARIANSHIP (US/0065-2830) [01461209] **3187**

ADVANCES IN LIBRARY ADMINISTRATION AND ORGANIZATION (US/0732-0671) [08172642] **3187**

ADVANCES IN LIBRARY INFORMATION TECHNOLOGY (US/0899-1227) [17996652] **3188**

ADVANCES IN LIBRARY RESOURCE SHARING (US/1052-262X) [22231772] **3188**

ADVANCES IN LIPID RESEARCH (US/0065-2849) [01345947] **479**

ADVANCES IN LONG-TERM CARE (US/1053-0606) [22444522] **5270**

ADVANCES IN LOW-TEMPERATURE BIOLOGY (US) **440**

●ADVANCES IN LOW-TEMPERATURE BIOLOGY (UK) [26393296] **440**

ADVANCES IN LOW-TEMPERATURE PLASMA CHEMISTRY, TECHNOLOGY, APPLICATIONS (US/0887-6193) [12649291] **3770**

ADVANCES IN MAGNETIC AND OPTICAL RESONANCE (US/1057-2732) [22741438] 1049, **4443**

ADVANCES IN MAGNETIC RESONANCE IMAGING (US) **3938**

ADVANCES IN MAGNETIC RESONANCE. SUPPLEMENT (US/1043-707X) [03165382] 1049, **4443**

ADVANCES IN MAN-MACHINE SYSTEMS RESEARCH *CEASED*. (US/0882-6137) [10698002] **2034**

●ADVANCES IN MANAGEMENT ACCOUNTING (US) [26835837] **738**

●ADVANCES IN MANAGERIAL COGNITION AND ORGANIZATIONAL INFORMATION PROCESSING (US) [30924308] 1103, **1255**

ADVANCES IN MARINE BIOLOGY (UK/0065-2881) [01308600] **552**

ADVANCES IN MARKETING AND PUBLIC POLICY (US/1048-1540) [17534025] **920**

ADVANCES IN MASS SPECTROMETRY (1985) (UK/0887-2430) [13168297] **4432**

ADVANCES IN MASS SPECTROMETRY IN BIOCHEMISTRY AND MEDICINE (US/0145-4811) [02739623] 479, **960**

ADVANCES IN MATHEMATICAL PROGRAMMING AND FINANCIAL PLANNING (US/1048-4760) [15563477] **859**

● ADVANCES IN MATHEMATICAL SCIENCES AND APPLICATIONS (JA) [28306367] **3491**

ADVANCES IN MATHEMATICS (NEW YORK, 1965) (US/0001-8708) [01588740] **3491**

ADVANCES IN MATHEMATICS : SUPPLEMENTARY STUDIES *CEASED*. (US) [05044376] **3491**

ADVANCES IN MEDICAL SOCIAL SCIENCE (US/0275-5742) [07164824] 3546, **5238**

ADVANCES IN MEDICAL SOCIOLOGY (US/1057-6290) [22743023] 3546, **5238**

● ADVANCES IN MEDICINAL CHEMISTRY (US/1067-5698) [26237858] **1039**

ADVANCES IN MEMBRANE FLUIDITY (US/1042-4156) [18582180] **440**

ADVANCES IN MENTAL HANDICAP RESEARCH *CEASED*. (UK/0271-9266) [06771428] **3919**

ADVANCES IN MENTAL RETARDATION AND DEVELOPMENTAL DISABILITIES (US/0742-6313) [10116929] **3919**

● ADVANCES IN METAL AND SEMICONDUCTOR CLUSTERS (US/1075-1629) [28287312] 4396, **1035**

ADVANCES IN METAL-ORGANIC CHEMISTRY (US/1045-0688) [19822292] **1039**

ADVANCES IN METALS IN MEDICINE (US) **3546**

ADVANCES IN MICROBIAL ECOLOGY (US/0147-4863) [03175360] **2211**

ADVANCES IN MICROBIAL PHYSIOLOGY (UK/0065-2911) [01461218] 577, **558**

ADVANCES IN MICROCIRCULATION *CEASED*. (SZ/0065-2938) [01461220] **3698**

ADVANCES IN MODELLING & SIMULATION (FR/0761-2494) [l07612494] **2109**

ADVANCES IN MODERN ENVIRONMENTAL TOXICOLOGY (US/0276-5063) [07368707] 3978, **2858**

● ADVANCES IN MOLECULAR AND CELL BIOLOGY (US) [26710674] **531**

ADVANCES IN MOLECULAR AND CELLULAR IMMUNOLOGY (US) [29966917] **3662**

ADVANCES IN MOLECULAR ELECTRONIC STRUCTURE THEORY (US/1057-8951) [23225560] **1039**

ADVANCES IN MOLECULAR MODELING (US/1054-0954) [18149384] **440**

ADVANCES IN MOLECULAR VIBRATIONS AND COLLISION DYNAMICS (US/1063-5467) [25454023] **1049**

ADVANCES IN MOLTEN SALT CHEMISTRY (US/0065-2954) [01461225] **1035**

ADVANCES IN MOTIVATION AND ACHIEVEMENT: A RESEARCH ANNUAL (US/0749-7423) [10821901] **1807**

ADVANCES IN MOTOR DEVELOPMENT RESEARCH (US/0888-9287) [13751260] **4572**

ADVANCES IN MRI CONTRAST (US/0925-9848) **3938**

ADVANCES IN MULTI-PHOTON PROCESSES AND SPECTROSCOPY (SI) [12383434] **1012**

ADVANCES IN MULTIDIMENSIONAL LUMINESCENCE (US/1058-4382) [23436508] **1012**

ADVANCES IN NEAR-INFRARED MEASUREMENT (US) **960**

ADVANCES IN NEPHROLOGY FROM THE NECKER HOSPITAL (US/0084-5957) [02256982] **3988**

ADVANCES IN NEURAL AND BEHAVIORAL DEVELOPMENT *CEASED*. (US/8755-0032) [11241583] 4572, **3826**

ADVANCES IN NEURAL INFORMATION PROCESSINGS SYSTEMS (US/1049-5258) [19891678] **1210**

ADVANCES IN NEURAL SCIENCE (US/1074-7575) [29178547] 440, **3826**

ADVANCES IN NEUROCHEMISTRY (US/0098-6089) [01484214] **3826**

ADVANCES IN NEUROGERONTOLOGY (US/0272-0787) [06758549] **3826**

ADVANCES IN NEUROIMMUNOLOGY (UK/0960-5428) [23968555] 3662, **3826**

ADVANCES IN NEUROLOGY (US/0091-3952) [01779104] **3826**

ADVANCES IN NEUROPSYCHIATRY AND PSYCHOPHARMACOLOGY (US) [23664197] 3919, **3826**

ADVANCES IN NEUROPSYCHOLOGY AND BEHAVIORAL NEUROLOGY (US/0741-8957) [08855873] 4572, **3826**

ADVANCES IN NEUROSCIENCE (US/1059-1540) [23133570] **3826**

ADVANCES IN NEUROSURGERY (GW/0302-2366) [01780742] **3957**

ADVANCES IN NONPROFIT MARKETING (US/0892-9556) [12637028] **920**

ADVANCES IN NUCLEAR QUADRUPOLE RESONANCE *CEASED*. (UK/0143-7178) [04337538] **4445**

ADVANCES IN NUCLEAR SCIENCE AND TECHNOLOGY (US/0065-2989) [01461228] 4445, **2153**

ADVANCES IN NUMERICAL COMPUTATION SERIES (IE/0332-3196) [12178384] **3491**

ADVANCES IN NUMERICAL METHODS FOR LARGE SPARSE SETS OF LINEAR EQUATIONS (JA) [17696888] **3491**

ADVANCES IN NURSING SCIENCE (US/0161-9268) [04064666] **3850**

ADVANCES IN NUTRITIONAL RESEARCH (US/0149-9483) [03582055] **4186**

● ADVANCES IN OBSTETRICS AND GYNECOLOGY (ST. LOUIS, MO.) (US/1070-5392) [28402265] **3756**

ADVANCES IN ODONTOLOGY : PROCEEDINGS OF THE ... INTERNATIONAL SYMPOSIUM OF ODONTOLOGY (NE) [09706358] **5574**

ADVANCES IN OPHTHALMIC PLASTIC AND RECONSTRUCTIVE SURGERY (US/0276-3508) [07343152] 3871, **3958**

ADVANCES IN OPTICAL AND ELECTRON MICROSCOPY (UK/0065-3012) [01461231] 4433, **572**

ADVANCES IN ORGANOMETALLIC CHEMISTRY (US/0065-3055) [01330679] **1039**

ADVANCES IN ORTHOPAEDIC SURGERY (US/0738-2278) [09544191] **3958**

ADVANCES IN ORTHOPEDICS (US) **3880**

ADVANCES IN OTO-RHINO-LARYNGOLOGY (SZ/0065-3071) [01461235] **3885**

ADVANCES IN OTOLARYNGOLOGY--HEAD AND NECK SURGERY (US/0887-6916) [13346744] **3958**

ADVANCES IN OXYGENATED PROCESSES (US/1044-4696) [19250687] **440**

ADVANCES IN PAIN RESEARCH AND THERAPY (US/0146-0722) [02847703] **3826**

ADVANCES IN PARALLEL COMPUTING (GREENWICH, CONN.) *CEASED*. (US/1057-3461) [23987048] **1170**

ADVANCES IN PARASITOLOGY (UK/0065-308X) [01325467] **440**

ADVANCES IN PARENTERAL SCIENCES (US/1041-004X) [12115769] **4289**

ADVANCES IN PATHOBIOLOGY (US/0099-1147) [01163598] 3892, **440**

ADVANCES IN PATHOLOGY AND LABORATORY MEDICINE (US/1057-1256) [23958530] **3892**

ADVANCES IN PEDIATRIC INFECTIOUS DISEASES (US/0884-9404) [12532678] 3711, **3899**

ADVANCES IN PEDIATRICS (US/0065-3101) [01461237] **3899**

ADVANCES IN PERINATAL MEDICINE (US/0731-1400) [07290775] **3756**

ADVANCES IN PERITONEAL DIALYSIS (CN/1197-8554) [23465202] **3546**

ADVANCES IN PERSONALITY ASSESSMENT (US/0278-2367) [07753955] **4572**

ADVANCES IN PHARMACEUTICAL SCIENCES (UK/0065-3136) [01461240] **4289**

ADVANCES IN PHARMACOLOGY (US/1054-3589) [22409643] **4289**

ADVANCES IN PHOTOCHEMISTRY (US/0065-3152) [01461242] **1049**

ADVANCES IN PHYSICAL GEOCHEMISTRY (US/0722-3269) [07786406] 1351, **960**

ADVANCES IN PHYSICAL ORGANIC CHEMISTRY (UK/0065-3160) [01461243] 1039, **1049**

ADVANCES IN PHYSICS (UK/0001-8732) [01461245] **4396**

ADVANCES IN PHYSIOLOGY (US) [20050128] **577**

ADVANCES IN PHYSIOLOGY EDUCATION (US/1043-4046) [19451287] **577**

ADVANCES IN PINEAL RESEARCH (UK/0269-0071) [14690880] 3678, **440**

ADVANCES IN PLANNED PARENTHOOD (NE/0065-3179) [01426955] **587**

ADVANCES IN PLANT PATHOLOGY (UK/0736-4539) [08861704] **498**

ADVANCES IN PLANT SCIENCES (MUZAFFARNAGAR, INDIA) (II/0970-3586) [18675855] **498**

ADVANCES IN PLANT SCIENCES SERIES (US/1052-5432) [18882254] **498**

ADVANCES IN PLASTIC AND RECONSTRUCTIVE SURGERY (US/0748-5212) [10961953] **3958**

ADVANCES IN POLLEN-SPORE RESEARCH (II/0376-480X) [02129004] **498**

ADVANCES IN POLYMER BLENDS AND ALLOYS TECHNOLOGY (US/1058-7489) [18391240] **4453**

ADVANCES IN POLYMER SCIENCE (GW/0065-3195) [02256985] **1039**

ADVANCES IN POLYMER TECHNOLOGY (US/0730-6679) [08030467] **4453**

ADVANCES IN POROUS MEDIA (NE) [25603022] **1103**

ADVANCES IN POWDER METALLURGY *See* ADVANCES IN POWDER METALLURGY & PARTICULATE MATERIALS **3997**

● ADVANCES IN POWDER METALLURGY & PARTICULATE MATERIALS (US/1065-5824) [26638789] **3997**

● ADVANCES IN PRESERVATION AND ACCESS (US/1063-2263) [25931151] **3188**

ADVANCES IN PRIMATOLOGY (US) [01461247] **5574**

ADVANCES IN PRINTING SCIENCE AND TECHNOLOGY : PROCEEDINGS OF THE ... INTERNATIONAL CONFERENCE OF PRINTING RESEARCH INSTITUTES (UK) [11827334] **4563**

ADVANCES IN PROBABILITY AND RELATED TOPICS *CEASED*. (US/0065-3217) [01461248] **3491**

ADVANCES IN PROGRAM EVALUATION (US) [23687023] **1887**

ADVANCES IN PROSTAGLANDIN, THROMBOXANE, AND LEUKOTRIENE RESEARCH (US/0732-8141) [08432542] **3726**

ADVANCES IN PROTEIN CHEMISTRY (US/0065-3233) [01461249] **1039**

ADVANCES IN PROTEIN PHOSPHATASES (BE/0775-051X) [15351707] **577**

● ADVANCES IN PSYCHIATRIC TREATMENT (UK) **3919**

ADVANCES IN PSYCHOLOGICAL ASSESSMENT *CEASED*. (US/0065-325X) [01461250] **4572**

ADVANCES IN PSYCHOLOGY (NE/0166-4115) [05253350] **4572**

ADVANCES IN PSYCHOPHYSIOLOGY (UK/0892-7901) [13491273] 4572, **577**

ADVANCES IN PSYCHOSOMATIC MEDICINE (SZ/0065-3268) [01461251] 440, **4572**

ADVANCES IN PUBLIC INTEREST ACCOUNTING (US/1041-7060) [12821877] **738**

ADVANCES IN QUANTITATIVE ANALYSIS OF FINANCE AND ACCOUNTING (US/1061-8910) [23892612] **738**

ADVANCES IN QUANTUM CHEMISTRY (US/0065-3276) [01461252] **1049**

ADVANCES IN RADIATION BIOLOGY (US/0065-3292) [01461254] 3938, **440**

ADVANCES IN RAMAN SPECTROSCOPY (UK/0309-2534) [01624011] **4396**

ADVANCES IN R&D (US/0890-2763) [14191528] **5081**

ADVANCES IN READING/LANGUAGE RESEARCH (US/0735-0171) [08822975] **1887**

ADVANCES IN RESEARCH AND THEORIES OF SCHOOL MANAGEMENT AND EDUCATIONAL POLICY (US) [22410599] **1859**

ADVANCES IN RESEARCH ON TEACHING (US) [21250116] **1887**

ADVANCES IN RISK ANALYSIS (US) [11054434] 4763, **4809**

ADVANCES IN ROBOTICS (US/0749-1603) [11079900] **1210**

ADVANCES IN SCHOOL PSYCHOLOGY *CEASED*. (US/0270-3920) [06400197] 1722, **4572**

ADVANCES IN SECOND MESSENGER AND PHOSPHOPROTEIN RESEARCH (US/1040-7952) [18178973] **577**

ADVANCES IN SERIALS MANAGEMENT (US/1040-4384) [15068907] **3188**

● ADVANCES IN SERVICES MARKETING AND MANAGEMENT (US/1067-5671) [26207068] **920**

ADVANCES IN SILICON CHEMISTRY (US/1059-4256) [23807556] **1035**

ADVANCES IN SMALL ANIMAL MEDICINE AND SURGERY (US/1041-7826) [18897033] **5501**

ADVANCES IN SMALL ANIMAL PRACTICE (OXFORD, ENGLAND : 1988) (UK) [19010609] **5501**

ADVANCES IN SOCIAL COGNITION (US/0898-2007) [17740157] **5238**

ADVANCES IN SOCIAL SCIENCE AND COMPUTERS (US/1047-2010) [20612207] 1265, **5189**

ADVANCES IN SOCIAL SCIENCE METHODOLOGY (US/1047-2002) [20612302] **5238**

ADVANCES IN SOFTWARE SCIENCE AND TECHNOLOGY (US/1044-7997) [19909978] **1284**

ADVANCES IN SOIL SCIENCE (NEW YORK) (US/0176-9340) [11181860] **161**

ADVANCES IN SOLAR ENERGY (US/0731-8618) [08260864] **1931**

ADVANCES IN SOLID-STATE CHEMISTRY (US/1046-5723) [19958039] **1049**

ADVANCES IN SONOCHEMISTRY (UK) [22408452] **1050**

ADVANCES IN SOVIET MATHEMATICS (US/1051-8037) [22123385] **3491**

ADVANCES IN SPACE BIOLOGY AND MEDICINE (US) [25126789] 3546, **441**

ADVANCES IN SPACE RESEARCH (UK/0273-1177) [07004415] **3**

ADVANCES IN SPECIAL EDUCATION (US/0270-4013) [06347067] **1874**

ADVANCES IN SPECIAL ELECTROMETALLURGY (UK/0267-4009) [12278769] **3997**

ADVANCES IN SPECTROSCOPY (1986) (UK/0892-2888) [15110888] **4433**

ADVANCES IN SPEECH, HEARING, AND LANGUAGE PROCESSING (US/0963-5580) [23077641] **3261**

ADVANCES IN STATISTICAL ANALYSIS AND STATISTICAL COMPUTING (US/1045-6821) [14179113] **5320**

ADVANCES IN STATISTICAL SIGNAL PROCESSING (US/1058-8957) [17959362] **1170**

ADVANCES IN STEREOENCEPHALOTOMY (SZ) [04651431] **3826**

ADVANCES IN STRAIN IN ORGANIC CHEMISTRY (UK/1061-8902) [24835062] **1039**

ADVANCES IN STRATEGIC MANAGEMENT (US/0742-3322) [10091173] **859**

ADVANCES IN STRAWBERRY PRODUCTION *See* ADVANCES IN STRAWBERRY RESEARCH **44**

●ADVANCES IN STRAWBERRY RESEARCH (US/1068-4883) [27007243] 5081, **44**

ADVANCES IN STRUCTURAL BIOLOGY (US/1064-6000) [26068146] **479**

ADVANCES IN SUBSTANCE ABUSE, BEHAVIORAL AND BIOLOGICAL RESEARCH (US/0272-1740) [06688866] 4572, **1339**

ADVANCES IN SUICIDOLOGY (NE/0922-3061) [20615458] **3919**

ADVANCES IN SUPRAMOLECULAR CHEMISTRY (US/1068-7459) [23160411] **1039**

ADVANCES IN SURGERY (CHICAGO) (US/0065-3411) [01461263] **3958**

ADVANCES IN SYSTEM ANALYSIS (GW/0932-593X) [15621462] **1964**

ADVANCES IN TAXATION (US/1058-7497) [17625578] **4708**

ADVANCES IN TEACHER EDUCATION (US/0748-0067) [10858234] **1887**

ADVANCES IN TELECOMMUNICATIONS MANAGEMENT (US/1050-9291) [21656009] **1148**

ADVANCES IN TELEMATICS (US/1050-9496) [21719218] **1148**

ADVANCES IN TEST ANXIETY RESEARCH (NE/0923-019X) [09135225] 1722, **4572**

ADVANCES IN THANATOLOGY (US/0196-1934) [03940018] **4572**

ADVANCES IN THE ASTRONAUTICAL SCIENCES (US/0065-3438) [01461266] **3**

ADVANCES IN THE BIOLOGY OF DISEASE (US/0743-5592) [10608528] **3892**

ADVANCES IN THE BIOSCIENCES *CEASED.* (UK/0065-3446) [00985948] **441**

ADVANCES IN THE ECONOMIC ANALYSIS OF PARTICIPATORY AND LABOR-MANAGED FIRMS (US/0885-3339) [12531998] 938, **1642**

ADVANCES IN THE ECONOMICS OF ENERGY AND RESOURCES (US/0192-558X) [04855458] 2185, **1931**

ADVANCES IN THE IMPLEMENTATION AND IMPACT OF COMPUTER SYSTEMS *CEASED.* (US/1061-8929) [24079986] **1246**

ADVANCES IN THE MANAGEMENT OF CLINICAL HEART DISEASE (US/0146-8790) [02846261] **3698**

ADVANCES IN THE MECHANICS AND PHYSICS OF SURFACES (SW/0272-0434) [06743516] **2100**

ADVANCES IN THE PSYCHOLOGY OF HUMAN INTELLIGENCE *CEASED.* (US/0278-2359) [07759675] 1722, **4572**

ADVANCES IN THE STUDY OF BEHAVIOR (US/0065-3454) [01461267] **4572**

ADVANCES IN THE STUDY OF COMMUNICATION AND AFFECT (US/0190-9703) [04027836] 1103, **4572**

ADVANCES IN THE STUDY OF ENTREPRENEURSHIP, INNOVATION, AND ECONOMIC GROWTH (US/1048-4736) [15477159] **1460**

ADVANCES IN THE SYNTHESIS AND REACTIVITY OF SOLIDS (US) [24057569] **960**

ADVANCES IN THEORETICALLY INTERESTING MOLECULES (US/1046-5766) [20425782] **1039**

ADVANCES IN THERAPY (US/0741-238X) [10113075] **3546**

ADVANCES IN THERMAL ENGINEERING (US/0192-2734) [04986276] **1964**

ADVANCES IN TRANSPORT PROCESSES *CEASED.* (US/0271-2334) [06584352] **4430**

ADVANCES IN TRAUMA AND CRITICAL CARE (US) [24600455] **3546**

ADVANCES IN TUMOUR PREVENTION, DETECTION AND CHARACTERIZATION (US) [07084291] **3808**

ADVANCES IN ULTRAHARD MATERIALS APPLICATION TECHNOLOGY (UK/0267-680X) [14229359] **5081**

ADVANCES IN UNDERWATER TECHNOLOGY, OCEAN SCIENCE, AND OFFSHORE ENGINEERING / SOCIETY FOR UNDERWATER TECHNOLOGY (UK) [17451635] **2087**

ADVANCES IN URETHANE SCIENCE AND TECHNOLOGY (US/0044-6378) [07931935] **5081**

ADVANCES IN UROLOGY (US/0894-4385) [16077676] **3988**

●ADVANCES IN VASCULAR BIOLOGY (SZ/1072-0618) [28855781] **441**

●ADVANCES IN VASCULAR SURGERY (US/1069-7292) [28145143] **3958**

ADVANCES IN VEGETATION SCIENCE (NE/0168-8022) [07841121] **498**

ADVANCES IN VETERINARY SCIENCE AND COMPARATIVE MEDICINE (US/0065-3519) [01461271] **5501**

ADVANCES IN VIRAL ONCOLOGY (US/0735-0104) [08617111] **3808**

ADVANCES IN VIRUS RESEARCH (US/0065-3527) [01461272] **558**

ADVANCES IN VLSI AND COMPUTER SYSTEM SERIES *CEASED.* (US/0888-224X) [13503314] **1246**

ADVANCES IN VLSI SERIES (US/1040-5852) [18455531] **4396**

ADVANCES IN WATER RESOURCES (UK/0309-1708) [03502701] **5528**

ADVANCES IN WORKING CAPITAL MANAGEMENT (US/1041-6749) [18716104] 1460, **636**

●ADVANCES IN WOUND CARE (US/1076-2191) [29810648] **3546**

ADVANCES IN X-RAY ANALYSIS (US/0376-0308) [01461274] **3938**

ADVANCES IN X-RAY CONTRAST (NE/0928-1509) **3938**

ADVANCES. THE JOURNAL OF MIND BODY HEALTH (US) **3546**

ADVANCING CONVERTING AND PACKAGING TECHNOLOGIES (US/0882-5777) [11893924] **4217**

ADVANCING PHILANTHROPY (US) **754**

ADVANCING THE CONSUMER INTEREST (US/1044-7385) [19880349] **1293**

ADVENT CHRISTIAN WITNESS (1983), THE (US/0741-4307) [09746131] **5054**

ADVENT, THE (II) [01587084] **4823**

ADVENTIST HERITAGE (US/0360-389X) [02245718] **5054**

ADVENTIST REVIEW (MONTHLY, INTER-AMERICAN EDITION) (US/0163-8866) [04526479] **5054**

ADVENTIST REVIEW (WEEKLY) (US/0161-1119) [03828373] **5054**

ADVENTIST REVIEW (WEEKLY, SOUTHWESTERN EDITION) (US/0745-6441) [09319989] **5054**

ADVENTIST THEOLOGICAL SOCIETY MONOGRAPHS (US/1059-7905) [24766193] **4932**

●ADVENTURE FLORIDA (US/1062-7545) [25732472] **5460**

ADVENTURE GAMES FOR MICROCOMPUTERS (US/1056-2451) [23596939] **1230**

ADVENTURE HOLIDAYS (UK/0143-389X) [07085448] **5460**

ADVENTURE. MEDIA KIT (US/0736-9379) [09106656] **1103**

ADVENTURE (NASHVILLE) (US/0001-8783) [04167535] **4932**

ADVENTURE TRAVEL (EMMAUS, PA.) (US/1041-9314) [18885879] **5460**

●ADVENTURE WEST (US) [28755893] **4868**

ADVENTURES IN TOTAL DEVELOPMENT (US/0883-5659) [12173587] **4572**

ADVENTURES OF SUPERMAN, THE (US/0893-4428) [14641696] **4856**

ADVENTURES OF THE INCREDIBLE LIBRARIAN (US) **3188**

ADVENTURES (SILVER SPRING, MD) (US/1049-5045) [21244879] **754**

ADVENTURING IN CONSERVATION (CN/0225-6533) [08770599] 2373, **2185**

ADVERSE DRUG REACTION BULLETIN (UK/0044-6394) [01461282] **3978**

ADVERSE DRUG REACTIONS AND TOXICOLOGICAL REVIEWS (UK/0964-198X) [23951747] 4289, **3978**

●ADVERSE EFFECTS OF HERBAL DRUGS (GW) [25807296] **4289**

ADVERTENTIEBLAD VAN DE REPUBLIEK SURINAME (SR) [05719416] **4461**

ADVERTISER (ADELAIDE, AUSTRALIA) (AT) [16964802] **5777**

ADVERTISER-GLEAM, THE (US) [11832342] **5625**

ADVERTISER (NEW MILFORD, CONN.) (US/0746-7605) [10258981] **5644**

ADVERTISER, THE (US) [17249518] **5734**

ADVERTISER-TRIBUNE, THE (US) [11987448] **5726**

ADVERTISER'S WEEKLY *See* ADWEEK **754**

ADVERTISING AGE (US/0001-8899) [01461285] **754**

ADVERTISING AGE. 100 LEADING NATIONAL ADVERTISERS (US) [09663474] **754**

ADVERTISING AGENCY REVIEW (UK) **754**

ADVERTISING AGES BUSINESS MARKETING (US) **920**

ADVERTISING CAREER DIRECTORY (US/0882-8253) [12004226] **754**

ADVERTISING COMPLIANCE SERVICE (US/0277-9943) [07677059] **754**

ADVERTISING CREATIVITY NEWSLETTER (US) **754**

ADVERTISING DIGEST. CLASSIFIED EDITION (US/0161-6889) [04013979] **754**

ADVERTISING EXPENDITURE IN MAIN MEDIA (AT/0313-2382) [I03132382] **1103**

ADVERTISING FORECAST, THE (UK/0263-8118) [I02638118] **754**

ADVERTISING LAW & PRACTICE (UK/0267-0763) [12891085] 754, **2928**

ADVERTISING LAW ANTHOLOGY (US/0093-1985) [01784470] 754, **2928**

ADVERTISING OPTIONS PLUS : SRDS DIRECTORY OF OUT-OF-HOME MEDIA (US/1058-2592) [22879352] **754**

ADVERTISING RATIOS AND BUDGETS (US) [19087408] **754**

ADVERTISING RESEARCH DIRECTORY (US/1046-3755) [12951365] **754**

ADVERTISING RESEARCH FOUNDATION *See* ADVERTISING RESEARCH DIRECTORY **754**

ADVERTISING SPECIALTY REGISTER (1983) (US/0740-2716) [09885914] **754**

ADVERTIZER-HERALD, THE (US) [27866356] **5741**

ADVIESBRIEVEN EN- NOTA'S VAN DE EMANCIPATIERAAD (NE) [12005144] **4503**

ADVISER (WOLVERHAMPTON) (UK/0950-5458) [I09505458] **1293**

ADVISING QUARTERLY, THE (US/0895-1101) [16531077] **1722**

ADVISOR (CHAMPAIGN, ILL.), THE (US/0736-0436) [09069781] **1722**

ADVISOR NEWSPAPER. UTICA-SHELBY EDITION, THE (US/0191-7064) [04922425] **5685**

ADVISOR (NOROTON, CONN.) (US/0892-3892) [15347308] **754**

ADVISOR, THE (US) [14238833] **5734**

ADVISORY BULLETIN (AT/1036-0867) [24905558] **44**

ADVISORY — Alphabetical Title Index

ADVISORY BULLETIN - OFFICE OF PIPELINE SAFETY OPERATIONS (US) [03457396] **5375**

ADVISORY COMMISSION ON INTERGOVERNMENTAL RELATIONS PUBLICATIONS (US) **4461**

ADVISORY COUNCIL FOR TECHNICAL-VOCATIONAL EDUCATION IN TEXAS *See* ANNUAL REPORT FOR THE ADVISORY COUNCIL FOR TECHNICAL-VOCATIONAL EDUCATION IN TEXAS **1910**

ADVISORY OPINIONS OF THE STATE OF SOUTH CAROLINA STATE ETHICS COMMISSION (US) [05345792] **2248**

ADVISORY PANEL ON ALZHEIMER'S DISEASE (U.S.) *See* REPORT OF THE ADVISORY PANEL ON ALZHEIMER'S DISEASE **3844**

ADVISORY REPORT - UNIVERSITY OF WISCONSIN SEA GRANT COLLEGE PROGRAM (US/0270-7195) [05257833] **1807**

ADVOCACIA DINAMICA : ADV (BL) [08965250] **2928**

ADVOCACIA DINAMICA, SELECOES JURIDICAS : ADV (SP) [08962471] **2928**

ADVOCACY FOR SENIOR CITIZENS PRACTICE MANUAL (US) **5178**

ADVOCATE (US) [20518048] **1722**

ADVOCATE (US) [13070883] **1887**

ADVOCATE (US) **1089**

●ADVOCATE (BATON ROUGE, LA.), THE (US/1061-3978) [25151288] **5683**

ADVOCATE (BOISE, IDAHO), THE (US/0515-4987) [01461295] **2928**

ADVOCATE (BOSTON, MASS.) (US/0568-0425) [02254909] **2928**

ADVOCATE / BRONX COUNTY BAR ASSOCIATION, THE (US) [24465034] **2928**

ADVOCATE (DENVER, COLO.) (US/1040-2225) [10493235] **4285**

ADVOCATE (EDMONTON) (CN/0847-2890) [21540378] **5270**

ADVOCATE (INDIANAPOLIS, IND. : 1984) (US) [10844018] **4503**

ADVOCATE-LEADER, THE (US) [12814203] **5743**

ADVOCATE (LOS ANGELES, CALIF.), THE (US/0001-8996) [02256995] **2793**

ADVOCATE (LOS ANGELES TRIAL LAWYERS ASSOCIATION) (US/0199-1876) [05717400] **2928**

ADVOCATE MEN (US/0742-4701) [10353145] **5186**

ADVOCATE-MESSENGER, THE (US/0889-0056) [13765074] **5679**

ADVOCATE - MINNESOTA EDUCATION ASSOCIATION (US/1053-3362) [22518048] **1860**

ADVOCATE (MUNCIE, IND.), THE (US/0279-7097) [07244823] **5228**

ADVOCATE (NEW YORK, N.Y.), THE *CEASED.* (US/0001-9003) [03349728] **2254**

ADVOCATE (NEWARK, OHIO), THE (US/0740-2120) [09898663] **5726**

ADVOCATE NEWSPAPER (CN/1194-1103) [27391053] **5779**

ADVOCATE (STAMFORD, CONN.), THE (US/0279-5167) [07935516] **5644**

ADVOCATE, THE (US) [18899374] **5656**

ADVOCATE, THE (CN/0382-456X) [02479145] **2928**

ADVOCATE, THE (US) [24445674] **5658**

ADVOCATE (TORONTO. 1976) *CEASED.* (CN/0229-5407) [08730701] **4383**

ADVOCATE (VANCOUVER) (CN/0044-6416) [01461296] **2928**

ADVOCATENBLAD (NE) [08617226] **2928**

ADVOCATE'S ADVOCATE *CEASED.* (US) **2928**

ADVOCATES' QUARTERLY (CN/0704-0288) [03761916] **3088**

ADVOCATES' SOCIETY JOURNAL, THE (CN/0824-3344) [10446015] **2928**

ADVOGADO, O (BL) [03409564] **2928**

ADVOKATEN (STOCKHOLM) (SW/0281-3505) [10033363] **2928**

ADWEEK (UK) [01788385] **754**

ADWEEK AGENCY DIRECTORY (US) [15128464] **754**

ADWEEK AGENCY DIRECTORY (EASTERN ED. 1986) (US/0898-2228) [15128307] **754**

ADWEEK AGENCY DIRECTORY (MIDWESTERN EDITION) (US/1054-0555) [15128378] **754**

ADWEEK AGENCY DIRECTORY (NATIONAL ED.) (US/1055-8950) [16948963] **755**

ADWEEK AGENCY DIRECTORY NATIONAL EDITION SOUTHWEST (US) **755**

ADWEEK AGENCY DIRECTORY (SOUTHWESTERN ED.) (US/1046-5146) [15128511] **755**

ADWEEK CLIENT/BRAND DIRECTORY (US) [21270874] **755**

ADWEEK CLIENT/BRAND DIRECTORY (NATIONAL ED.) (US/1049-7064) [21275511] **755**

ADWEEK (EASTERN ED.) (US/0199-2864) [05757293] **755**

ADWEEK (MIDWEST ED.) (US/0276-6612) [07391322] **755**

ADWEEK (NEW ENGLAND ED.) (US/0888-0840) [13407251] **755**

ADWEEK (SOUTHEAST EDITION) (US/8756-6389) [11626364] **755**

ADWEEK (SOUTHWEST ED.) (US/0746-892X) [09170436] **755**

ADWEEK SPECIAL REPORT (US/0895-3848) [16634883] **755**

ADWEEK. WESTERN ADVERTISING NEWS (US/0199-4743) [05906739] **755**

ADWEEK'S GUIDE TO NEW ENGLAND ADVERTISING & PUBLIC RELATIONS AGENCIES *See* ADWEEK'S GUIDE TO NEW ENGLAND ADVERTISING, DIRECT MARKETING & PUBLIC RELATIONS AGENCIES **755**

●ADWEEK'S GUIDE TO NEW ENGLAND ADVERTISING, DIRECT MARKETING & PUBLIC RELATIONS AGENCIES (US) [25157867] **755**

ADWEEK'S GUIDE TO NEW ENGLAND MARKETS & MEDIA (US/1055-2022) [22982635] **920**

ADWEEK'S MARKETING WEEK (US/0892-8274) [14220423] **755**

ADY FARANY (MG) [01787373] **4539**

ADYAR LIBRARY BULLETIN, THE (II/0001-902X) [07779709] **5041**

AE (SOUTH CAROLINA CROP AND LIVESTOCK REPORTING SERVICE) (US/0561-0095) [02892026] **44**

AE (UNIVERSITY OF ILLINOIS AT URBANA-CHAMPAIGN. DEPT. OF AGRICULTURAL ECONOMICS) (US) [11008471] 1460, **44**

AEA ADVOCATE (US/0194-8849) [05072740] **1860**

AEB, AGRICULTURAL ECONOMICS AND BUSINESS (CN/0832-8773) [20936483] **44**

AEB, ANALYTICAL & ENUMERATIVE BIBLIOGRAPHY (US/0161-0376) [03110313] 407, **3457**

AECQ STRATEGY (CN/0225-5162) [06264712] **598**

AED (LONDON, ENGLAND) (UK/0144-8234) [06903096] 636, **1544**

AEE DIRECTORY OF ENERGY PROFESSIONALS, THE (US/0164-0917) [04574867] **2109**

AEG NEWS (US/0899-5788) [17605815] **2018**

AEGEAN JOURNAL OF LANGUAGE AND LITERATURE (TU) [20325154] 3358, **3261**

AEGEAN MEDICAL JOURNAL (TU/0304-4939) [03388155] **3546**

AEGEAN REVIEW *SUSPENDED.* (US/0891-7213) [15004129] **3358**

AEGIS INTERNATIONAL *CEASED.* (GW) [09973916] **1072**

AEGIS, THE (US) [20304891] **5690**

AEGIS (WASHINGTON, D.C.) *SUSPENDED.* (US/0883-0029) [04649349] 5550, **4503**

AEGYON UI OL (KO) [09156932] **4285**

AEGYPTUS (IT/0001-9046) [01461304] **253**

●AEI. AUTOMAZIONE ENEGIA INFORMAZIONE (IT/1122-2824) [I11222824] **2034**

AEI PUBLICATIONS / AMERICAN ENTERPRISE INSTITUTE (US) [06717877] **4625**

AEI STUDIES (US) [04225563] **1931**

AEIC JOURNAL (US) [08082485] **4932**

AEJMC NEWS (US/0747-8909) [10179124] 1807, **2917**

AEQUATIONES MATHEMATICAE (SZ/0001-9054) [01461306] **3491**

AERA MONOGRAPH SERIES ON CURRICULUM EVALUATION *CEASED.* (US/0077-0590) [04320706] **1887**

AERIAL APPLICATOR, FARM, FOREST AND FIRE (US) [01461310] 2287, **158**

AERIAL ARCHAEOLOGY (UK/0140-9220) [05915830] **253**

AERO (BL) [02244768] **3**

AERO ARMOR-SERIES (US/0276-6760) [07370035] **4033**

AERO INDEX *SUSPENDED.* (US/0279-7119) [07238973] **4**

AERO MODELLER, THE (UK/0001-9232) [07902344] **4**

AERO REVUE (SZ/0001-9186) [04255274] **4**

AERO SUN-TIMES (US/1046-0993) [07930207] **1931**

AEROBICS NEWS, THE *CEASED.* (US/0890-7668) [13740692] **2595**

AEROBIOLOGIA (IT/0393-5965) [I03935965] **441**

AEROCOMERCIAL (AG/0326-1360) [I03261360] **4**

AERODINE'S FLY-IN RESTAURANT GUIDE (US/1049-782X) [21252355] **5070**

AERODROMES; INTERNATIONAL STANDARDS AND RECOMMENDED PRACTICES. ANNEX 14 TO THE CONVENTION ON INTERNATIONAL CIVIL AVIATION (CN) [01753440] **4**

AEROESPACIO (BUENOS AIRES, ARGENTINA) (AG) [07918677] **4**

AEROKURIER (GW/0341-1281) [04916717] **4**

AEROMED WEEK *CEASED.* (US/0893-6587) [15614417] **5270**

AEROMEDICAL REVIEW (US/0065-3683) [10899620] 3546, **4**

AERONAUTICA & DIFESA (IT/0394-820X) [I0394820X] **4**

AERONAUTICAL CHART CATALOGUE / CATALOGUE DES CARTES AERONAUTIQUES / CATALOGO DE CARTAS AERONAUTICAS / KATALOG AERONAVIGATSIONNIKH KART (CN) [06272809] **4**

AERONAUTICAL CHARTS; INTERNATIONAL STANDARDS AND RECOMMENDED PRACTICES. ANNEX 4 TO THE CONVENTION ON INTERNATIONAL CIVIL AVIATION (CN) [01643480] **4**

AERONAUTICAL ENGINEERING (WASHINGTON, DC.) (US/0163-4941) [01664053] **4**

AERONAUTICAL INFORMATION PUBLICATION (GW) **4**

AERONAUTICAL INFORMATION SERVICES; INTERNATIONAL STANDARDS AND RECOMMENDED PRACTICES. ANNEX 15 TO THE CONVENTION ON INTERNATIONAL CIVIL AVIATION (CN) [01753441] **4**

AERONAUTICAL INFORMATION SERVICES PROVIDED BY STATES / SERVICES D'INFORMATION AERONAUTIQUE ASSURES PAR LES ETATS / SERVICIOS DE INFORMACION AERONAUTICA SUMINISTRADOS POR LOS ESTADOS (CN) [06271849] **4**

AERONAUTICAL JOURNAL, THE (UK/0001-9240) [02244599] **4**

AERONAUTICAL NOTE (CN) [09858553] **4**

AERONAUTICAL REPORT LR (CN/0077-5541) [10446004] **4**

AERONAUTICAL SOCIETY OF INDIA *See* JOURNAL OF THE AERONAUTICAL SOCIETY OF INDIA, THE **26**

AERONAUTICAL TELECOMMUNICATIONS, INTERNATIONAL STANDARDS AND RECOMMENDED PRACTICES. ANNEX 10 TO THE CONVENTION ON INTERNATIONAL CIVIL AVIATION (CN) [01753442] **4**

AERONAUTICS AND SPACE REPORT OF THE PRESIDENT *See* AERONAUTICS AND SPACE REPORT OF THE PRESIDENT. ACTIVITIES **4**

AERONAUTICS AND SPACE REPORT OF THE PRESIDENT. ACTIVITIES (US/0277-6499) [05924866] **4**

AERONAUTIQUE ET L'ASTRONAUTIQUE, L' (FR/0001-9275) [01709009] **4**

AERONOMICA ACTA. A (BE/0572-3159) [02834475] **5**

AERONOMY REPORT (US/0568-0581) [03973983] **5**

AEROPHILE EXTRA (US/0148-6691) [04292712] 2770, **5**

AEROPHILE (SAN ANTONIO) *CEASED.* (US/0147-7668) [03225230] 2770, **5**

AEROPLANT MONTHLY (UK/0143-7240) [03415460] **5**

AEROPORT DE PARIS. DEPARTEMENT INFORMATIQUE. STATISTIQUES *See* VENTILATION DU TRAFIC COMMERCIAL **39**

AEROPORT DE PARIS. SECTION ETUDES STATISTIQUES *See* TRAFIC INTERNATIONAL DU FRET **38**

AEROPORT DE PARIS. SERVICE STATISTIQUE *See* STATISTIQUES DE TRAFIC : GRANDS AEROPORTS DE L'OUEST DE L'EUROPE **42**

AEROPORTS MAGAZINE (FR/0336-626X) [I0336626X] **5**

AEROSOL AND PRESSURIZED PRODUCTS SURVEY (US/0360-4446) [01698254] **1020**

Alphabetical Title Index — AFL-CIO

AEROSOL RELEASE AND TRANSPORT PROGRAM QUARTERLY PROGRESS REPORT / PREPARED FOR THE U.S. NUCLEAR REGULATORY COMMISSION, OFFICE OF NUCLEAR REGULATORY RESEARCH; PREPARED BY THE OAK RIDGE NATIONAL LABORATORY (US) [09420916] 3475, **4217**

AEROSOL REVIEW (UK/0568-062X) [01461331] 3475, **4217**

AEROSOL SCIENCE AND TECHNOLOGY (US/0278-6826) [07870727] **1020**

AEROSOL SPRAY REPORT : INTERNATIONAL PERIODICAL FOR THE AEROSOL AND SPRAY INDUSTRY (GW/0941-0295) [26034878] **1020**

AEROSPACE AMERICA (US/0740-722X) [09991520] **5**

AEROSPACE & DEFENSE SCIENCE *CEASED.* (US/1051-9793) [21721392] 4033, **5**

AEROSPACE BIBLIOGRAPHY / COMPILED FOR NATIONAL AERONAUTICS AND SPACE ADMINISTRATION BY JEAN F. BLASHFIELD (US) [06544421] **41**

AEROSPACE CENTER (U.S.) *See* DMA AERONAUTICAL CHART UPDATING MANUAL, CHUM **18**

AEROSPACE COMPOSITES & MATERIALS (UK/0954-5832) [20652526] **5**

AEROSPACE CONSULTANTS DIRECTORY (US/0747-8151) [10808440] **5**

AEROSPACE DAILY (US/0193-4546) [05266757] **5**

AEROSPACE DAILY'S AEROGRAM (US/1057-1191) [23958381] **5**

AEROSPACE DAILY'S WEEKLY BRIEFING (US/1057-333X) [24014204] **5**

AEROSPACE DESIGN & COMPONENTS (UK) [20150235] **5**

AEROSPACE ENGINEERING (WARRENDALE, PA.) (US/0736-2536) [09090151] **5**

AEROSPACE EUROPE (UK/0143-1145) [18775377] **5**

AEROSPACE FACTS AND FIGURES (US) [01461335] **41**

AEROSPACE FINANCIAL NEWS (US/1057-0950) [23948784] **5**

AEROSPACE INFORMATION REPORT (US/0883-0096) [10170069] **5**

AEROSPACE INTELLIGENCE *CEASED.* (US/1041-7419) [11888935] **5**

AEROSPACE (LONDON, 1974) (UK/0305-0831) [07501833] **5**

AEROSPACE MATERIAL SPECIFICATIONS (US) [04404494] **5**

AEROSPACE MATERIALS *CEASED.* (UK) **5**

AEROSPACE MEDICINE AND BIOLOGY (US/0001-9410) [01832161] 5, **3547**

●AEROSPACE NEWS (US) [27253803] **5**

AEROSPACE NEWS AND REVIEW (US) 4033, **5**

AEROSPACE PRODUCTS *CEASED.* (US/1054-7045) [18634373] **5**

AEROSPACE PROPULSION (WASHINGTON, D.C. 1990) (US/1050-5245) [21516177] **5**

AEROSPACE SINGAPORE (SI/0129-1815) [I01291815] **5**

AEROSPACE WORLD (FR) **5**

AEROSPACE WORLD : BUSINESS & TECHNOLOGY (SZ/0983-1592) [22997014] **5**

AEROSPACO (BL) [01788388] **6**

AEROSTATION (ALEXANDRIA, VA.) (US/0741-5974) [05213520] **6**

AEROTECNICA MISSILI E SPAZIO, L' (IT/0365-7442) [05468676] **6**

AERR *CEASED.* (US/0090-4503) [03133617] **44**

AERZTEBLATT THUERINGEN (GW/0863-5412) **3547**

AES : JOURNAL OF THE AUDIO ENGINEERING SOCIETY, AUDIO/ACOUSTICS/APPLICATIONS (US) [14118308] 4452, **5315**

AES (SERIES) (US/1071-6947) [13145259] 2109, **1931**

AES WORKING PAPER (AT/0725-6272) [I07256272] **2159**

AESAN HAKPO (KO) [09209047] **2644**

●AESCLEPIUS (MARTINEZ, CALIF.) (US/1067-8646) [27360671] 3547, **287**

AESE BLUELINE (US/0846-7390) [07803842] **1351**

AESIS QUARTERLY (AT/0313-704x) [04563085] 1351, **1361**

AESSE : AZIONE SOCIALE (IT) **4461**

AESTHETE, THE (CN/0381-6656) [02624920] **3358**

AESTHETIC PLASTIC SURGERY (US/0364-216X) [02575058] **3958**

AESTHETICA. PRE-PRINT (IT/0393-8522) [I03938522] **335**

AETEI JOURNAL (II) **4932**

AETHERIUS SOCIETY NEWSLETTER (HOLLYWOOD, CALIF. : 1962) *See* AETHERIUS SOCIETY NEWSLETTER, THE **4932**

●AETHERIUS SOCIETY NEWSLETTER, THE (US/1063-0937) [25863507] **4932**

AETHLON (SAN DIEGO, CALIF.) (US/1048-3756) [18952049] 3358, **4882**

AETS YEARBOOK (US) [04428416] **5081**

AEU. ARCHIV. FUER ELEKTRONIK UND UBERTRAGUNGSTECHNIK (GW/0001-1096) [01481946] 2034, **1148**

AEU : JOURNAL OF ASIA ELECTRONICS UNION (JA/0385-0447) [04854795] **2034**

AEU (LONDON, ENGLAND) (UK) [15642515] **1964**

AEVUM (IT/0001-9593) [02003485] **3262**

AEVUM ANTIQUUM / ISTITUTO DI FILOLOGIA CLASSICA E DI PAPIROLOGIA (IT) [20399092] **3358**

AF, ARTE FOTOGRAFICO (SP/0514-9193) [05308866] **4366**

AFA BULLETIN *See* BULLETIN - AMERICAN FEDERATION OF ASTROLOGERS **390**

AFA OSTEUROPA FRIMARKEHANDEL (DK) [02297765] **2784**

AFA VESTEUROPA FRIMRKEKATALOG (DK) [02325943] **2784**

AFA WATCHBIRD, THE (US/0199-543X) [03506992] 5502, **4285**

AFANAF (CN/0317-1507) [02247837] **1807**

AF&R, ALBERTA FARM & RANCH MAGAZINE (CN/0845-5007) [20367132] **44**

AFAQ (LE) [03488591] **2644**

AFAQ AMNIYAH (BA) [10330414] **3156**

AFAQ ARABIYAH (IQ) [02533148] 2841, **312**

AFAQ SIHHIYAH / AL-MUNAZZAMAH AL-RIYADIYAH WA-AL-THAQAFIYAH LIL-MUAQIN (TI) [07844901] **4378**

AFAS QUARTERLY OF THE AUTOMOTIVE FINE ARTS SOCIETY (US/0899-9171) [18265917] 2770, **5403**

AFA'S RESOURCE HOTLINE : THE COMMUNICATION NETWORK OF THE AMERICAN FORESTRY ASSOCIATION (US) [13163351] **2373**

AFB ACTION (US/0891-7450) [15069609] 636, **4763**

AFCPE NEWSLETTER (US/1076-464X) [26508420] **768**

AFDC UPDATE : NEWS OF THE ALTERNATIVE FUELS DATA CENTER (US) [24772050] **1931**

AFER (KE/0250-4650) [02162501] **4932**

AFERS INTERNACIONALS (SP/0212-1786) [26319374] **4461**

AFF (TOKYO, JAPAN) *See* NORIN SUISANSHO KOHO **114**

AFFAIRE DE COEUR (US/0739-3881) [09725209] **5073**

AFFAIRES 500, LES (CN) **636**

AFFAIRES, LES (FR/0001-9615) [01799584] **1544**

AFFAIRES (MONTREAL. 1981) (CN/0229-3404) [07970501] **636**

AFFAIRES TRIMESTRIEL, LES (CN) **636**

AFFARI E FINANZA (IT) **768**

AFFARI ESTERI (IT/0001-964x) [01662162] **4514**

AFFARI SOCIALI INTERNAZIONALI (IT/0390-1181) [01795757] **5189**

AFFARSVARLDEN (1974) (SW/0345-3766) [01799141] **1544**

AFFICHE PARIS (FR/0989-0165) [I09890165] **335**

AFFICHES DE NORMANDIE, LES (FR/1145-8488) [I11458488] **755**

AFFILIA (US/0886-1099) [12871850] 5550, **5270**

AFFILIATE ARTISTS, INC *See* NEWS - AFFILIATE ARTISTS **326**

AFFILIATE, THE (US/0360-5485) [02244772] **2928**

AFFIRMATION (RICHMOND, VA.) (US/0001-9674) [19648408] **4932**

AFFIRMATIONS (US/0162-8038) [02648757] 5550, **4932**

AFFIRMATIVE ACTION COMPLIANCE MANUAL FOR FEDERAL CONTRACTORS (US/0148-8147) [03382114] **1642**

●AFFIRMATIVE ACTION FORUM (SASKATOON) (CN/1187-8924) [26621259] **1642**

AFFIRMATIVE ACTION INFORMATION (US/0099-1910) [02243565] **1642**

AFFIRMATIVE ACTION INFORMATION. COLUMBIA BASIN LABOR AREAS (US) [18032484] **1642**

AFFIRMATIVE ACTION INFORMATION. LABOR AREAS IN NORTHEAST WASHINGTON (US) [29657377] **1642**

AFFIRMATIVE ACTION INFORMATION. OLYMPIA MSA, METROPOLITAN STATISTICAL AREA (THURSTON COUNTY) (US) [11177224] 1642, **1528**

AFFIRMATIVE ACTION NEWS *See* AFFIRMATIVE ACTION FORUM (SASKATOON) **1642**

AFFIRMATIVE ACTION PLAN / ALASKA DEPARTMENT OF FISH AND GAME (US) [10379690] **2293**

AFFIRMATIVE ACTION PLAN FOR EQUAL EMPLOYMENT OPPORTUNITY (US/0148-4885) [03304891] **1807**

AFFIRMATIVE ACTION PLAN - MAINE. DEPT. OF MENTAL HEALTH AND CORRECTIONS (US/0731-3446) [08146931] **4763**

AFFIRMATIVE ACTION PLAN / OKLAHOMA HEALTH PLANNING COMMISSION (US) [09958636] **4763**

AFFIRMATIVE ACTION PLAN. PART 1, POLICIES & PROCEDURES / ALASKA DEPT. OF COMMUNITY & REGIONAL AFFAIRS (US) [10410306] **4625**

AFFIRMATIVE ACTION PLAN - THOMAS JEFFERSON UNIVERSITY (US) [05225677] **4503**

AFFIRMATIVE ACTION PROGRAM - ILLINOIS DEPT. OF MENTAL HEALTH AND DEVELOPMENTAL DISABILITIES (US) [02972984] **4763**

AFFIRMATIVE ACTION REGISTER (US/0146-2113) [02273613] **938**

AFFIRMATIVE ACTION REPORT - TEXAS. EQUAL EMPLOYMENT OPPORTUNITY OFFICE (US/0361-9036) [02246701] **4701**

AFFIRMATIVE ACTION/STATUS OF WOMEN (CN/0849-987X) [22135179] 5550, **4503**

AFFLUENT MARKETS ALERT (US/1041-7508) [18839352] **859**

●AFFORDABLE CARIBBEAN, THE (US/1062-9084) [25805770] **5460**

AFGE GOVERNMENT STANDARD (US/1041-5335) [13516620] **4701**

AFGHAN HOUND REVIEW, THE (US/8750-9776) [11982199] **4285**

AFGHAN REALITIES (FR/0291-2708) [I02912708] 2254, **4503**

AFGHANICA : THE AFGHANISTAN STUDIES NEWSLETTER (UK) [19910012] **2841**

AFGHANISTAN EN LUTTE (FR/0244-9676) [10353118] 4462, **2644**

AFGHANISTAN FORUM (US/0889-2148) [11355997] **2484**

AFGHANISTAN (KABUL) (AF/0001-9682) [01461361] **2644**

AFGHANISTAN, PAKISTAN : ENERGIEWIRTSCHAFT (GW) [05224848] **1931**

AFGHANISTAN REPORT *CEASED.* (PK) [12682558] **4514**

AFGHANISTAN STUDIES JOURNAL (US/1046-9834) [18565354] 2644, **2501**

AFINIDAD (SP/0001-9704) [04419054] **960**

AFIP LETTER (US/0498-3564) [04539066] **3892**

AFKAR (UA) [06575104] **3337**

AFKAR (PK/0515-5649) [05320458] **3358**

AFKAR INQUIRY *SUSPENDED.* (UK/0267-842X) [12000870] **4932**

AFL-CIO *See* AFL-CIO INTERNAL DISPUTES PLAN, THE **1642**

AFL-CIO *See* POLICY RESOLUTIONS ADOPTED BY THE CONSTITUTIONAL CONVENTION **1702**

AFL-CIO *See* PUBLICATION - AMERICAN FEDERATION OF LABOR AND CONGRESS OF INDUSTRIAL ORGANIZATIONS **1704**

AFL-CIO *See* PROCEEDINGS OF THE CONSTITUTIONAL CONVENTION OF THE AFL-CIO **1703**

AFL-CIO *See* AFL-CIO NEWS **1642**

AFL-CIO. CONSTITUTIONAL CONVENTION *See* PROCEEDINGS OF THE ... CONSTITUTIONAL CONVENTION OF THE AFL-CIO **1703**

AFL-CIO CONVENTION PROCEEDINGS (US) **1642**

AFL-CIO. INDUSTRIAL UNION DEPT *See* PROCEEDINGS, CONSTITUTIONAL CONVENTION OF THE INDUSTRIAL UNION DEPARTMENT, AFL-CIO **1703**

AFL-CIO INTERNAL DISPUTES PLAN, THE (US/0735-214X) [01399494] **1642**

AFL-CIO LEGISLATIVE ALERT! (US/0883-8275) [12243395] 1460, **1642**

AFL-CIO NEWS (US/0001-1185) [01913622] **1642**

AFOSR TECHNICAL REPORT SUMMARIES / PREPARED BY: ... CHIEF, TECHNICAL DOCUMENTS SECTION (US) [11585800] **5081**

AFP ANNUAL REPORT (PH) [10515980] **4033**

AFPC POLICY ISSUES PAPER / AGRICULTURAL AND FOOD POLICY CENTER, DEPTARTMENT OF AGRICULTURAL ECONOMICS, TEXAS AGRICULTURAL EXPERIMENT STATION, TEXAS AGRICULTURAL EXTENSION SERVICE, TEXAS A&M UNIVERSITY (US) [22527963] **44**

AFPC POLICY RESEARCH REPORT (US) [22528043] **45**

AFPC POLICY WORKING PAPER (US/1053-1653) [21422948] **45**

AFR INVESTOR (AT/1034-2338) [I10342338] **636**

AFRAID (ANAHEIM, CALIF.) (US/1050-0448) [21382959] **1596**

AFRC NEWS (UK/0267-8489) [20742343] **45**

AFRIBIBLIOS (NR/0378-7990) [06232036] **407**

AFRICA (IT/0001-9747) [01657957] **2254**

AFRICA (US/0065-3802) [02257007] **2636**

AFRICA (PO) [05301583] **3358**

AFRICA : A DOCUMENTATION LIST (II/0012-4664) [01799471] **407**

AFRICA AGRICULTURE (UK) [07511016] **45**

AFRICA ANALYSIS (UK/0950-902X) [16652216] **1460**

AFRICA, ASIA, & EUROPE DIRECTORY (UA) [06516361] **821**

AFRICA BIBLIOGRAPHY (UK/0266-6731) [12928641] **407**

AFRICA BUSINESS & ECONOMIC REVIEW *CEASED.* (US/0197-8012) [06121913] **1632**

AFRICA CALLS (RH) [20175619] **5574**

AFRICA COMMUNICATIONS (US/1053-2897) [22502845] **1103**

AFRICA CONFIDENTIAL (UK/0044-6483) [01461369] **4514**

AFRICA CONSTRUCTION (UK) [08681440] **598**

AFRICA CONTEMPORARY RECORD (US/0065-3845) [01461370] **2636**

AFRICA DEVELOPMENT (SG/0378-3006) [03338003] **1544**

AFRICA ENERGY & MINING (FR/0994-0235) [I09940235] 2132, **1931**

AFRICA ENTERPRISE UPDATE (SA) 2497, **2254**

AFRICA EVENTS *CEASED.* (UK/0267-6362) [13023825] **2497**

AFRICA FORUM (UK/0961-1142) [23825539] **2501**

AFRICA; FOUILLES, MONUMENTS ET COLLECTIONS ARCHEOLOGIQUES EN TUNISIE (TI/0568-1057) [05376072] **2636**

AFRICA GAZETTE (UK) [05376056] **4625**

AFRICA HEALTH (UK/0141-9536) [05199837] **3547**

AFRICA HEALTH MARKETLETTER (UK) [17651334] **4763**

AFRICA INLAND MISSION, CANADA (CN/0824-3166) [10195299] **4932**

AFRICA INSIDER (US/0748-4356) [10941324] 4514, **4462**

AFRICA INSIGHT (SA/0256-2804) [06746011] 2841, **5189**

AFRICA INSTITUTE *See* OCCASIONAL PAPERS **2851**

AFRICA INSTITUTE OF SOUTH AFRICA *See* CHAIRMAN'S REPORT - AFRICA INSTITUTE OF SOUTH AFRICA **2638**

AFRICA INTERNATIONAL (US/8755-0067) [11242086] **2636**

AFRICA INTERNATIONAL (DAKAR, SENEGAL) (FR) [13523949] **2636**

AFRICA INTERNATIONAL PERSPECTIVE (LB) [02236276] **2636**

AFRICA INVESTMENT MONITOR (US/1053-8763) [22683876] **890**

AFRICA ISMAILI (KE) [01792411] **5041**

AFRICA JOURNAL OF EVANGELICAL THEOLOGY (KE) [22748210] **4932**

AFRICA (LEVIS) (CN/0706-8581) [04589143] **4932**

AFRICA (LONDON. 1928) (UK/0001-9720) [01461367] **3262**

AFRICA MARKETS MONITOR (SZ) [18691227] **1632**

AFRICA MEDIA REVIEW (KE/0258-4913) [17688229] **1103**

AFRICA-MIDDLE EAST BUSINESS DIGEST (LE) [02602103] **637**

AFRICA MUSIC (UK) [10686784] **4098**

AFRICA NEWS (DURHAM) *CEASED.* (US/0191-6521) [03725999] **4514**

AFRICA NEWSFILE (UK/0952-4290) [17669645] **1544**

AFRICA NOW *CEASED.* (UK) [08957563] **2497**

AFRICA PERSPECTIVE (SA/1012-9391) [04873413] **2636**

AFRICA QUARTERLY (II/0001-9828) [01461375] **2636**

AFRICA RECOVERY (US/1014-0255) [17212631] **1596**

AFRICA REPORT (US/0001-9836) [01461376] **2636**

AFRICA RESEARCH BULLETIN : ECONOMIC, FINANCIAL AND TECHNICAL SERIES (UK/0001-9852) [01461377] **1632**

AFRICA RESEARCH BULLETIN : ECONOMIC SERIES (UK) [12032734] **1460**

AFRICA RESEARCH BULLETIN. POLITICAL SERIES *See* AFRICA RESEARCH BULLETIN. POLITICAL, SOCIAL, AND CULTURAL SERIES **5238**

●AFRICA RESEARCH BULLETIN. POLITICAL, SOCIAL, AND CULTURAL SERIES (UK/0001-9844) [25734117] 4462, **5238**

AFRICA REVIEW (UK) [12129897] **4462**

AFRICA (ROME, ITALY) (IT/0001-9747) [10993612] **2636**

AFRICA SOUTH OF THE SAHARA (UK/0065-3896) [01087495] **1923**

AFRICA SUD (SA) [02858113] **2672**

AFRICA TELECOMMUNICATIONS REPORT (US/0890-5657) [14267528] **1148**

AFRICA-TERVUREN (BE) [06991007] **2497**

AFRICA THEOLOGICAL JOURNAL (TZ/0253-9322) [01776348] **4933**

AFRICA TODAY (US/0001-9887) [01461380] 5238, **4462**

AFRICA TODAY (LONDON, ENGLAND) (UK/0261-1562) [08040297] **2497**

●AFRICA TODAY (NEW YORK, N.Y.) (US/1062-8584) [25771832] **4462**

AFRICA (TUNIS) (TI) [02003608] **335**

AFRICA (WASHINGTON, D.C.) (US/0084-2281) [01625885] **2636**

AFRICA WHO'S WHO (UK/0261-1570) [08042726] **429**

AFRICAN ADMINISTRATIVE STUDIES (MR/0007-9588) [02323734] **4625**

AFRICAN AFFAIRS (LONDON) (UK/0001-9909) [05330671] **4462**

●AFRICAN-AMERICAN ALMANAC, THE (US/1071-8710) [28744934] **2254**

AFRICAN-AMERICAN ARCHAEOLOGY (US/1060-0671) [24056681] **253**

●AFRICAN-AMERICAN BUSINESS (US/1065-0180) [26483242] 2254, **637**

AFRICAN/AMERICAN DIRECTORY (US/0275-2875) [07113775] **637**

AFRICAN-AMERICAN FAMILY HISTORY ASSOCIATION *See* NEWSLETTER - AFRICAN-AMERICAN FAMILY HISTORY ASSOCIATION **2463**

AFRICAN AMERICAN JOURNAL (US/1057-9001) [24150515] **2254**

AFRICAN-AMERICAN JOURNAL OF CHIROPRACTIC (US/1050-6071) [21550813] **2254**

AFRICAN-AMERICAN LABOR CENTER *See* AALC REPORTER **1642**

●AFRICAN AMERICAN REVIEW (US/1062-4783) [25636550] **3358**

●AFRICAN-AMERICAN SITES & INSIGHTS (US/1072-4052) [28939229] **5460**

AFRICAN-AMERICAN TRAVELER, THE (US/0895-6235) [16707322] 5460, **2553**

AFRICAN AND AFRO-AMERICAN STUDIES AND RESEARCH CENTER REPRINTS (US/0198-9278) [06268565] **2636**

●AFRICAN ANVIL AND BUSINESS NEWS, THE (US/1055-0127) [23055829] **637**

AFRICAN ARCHAEOLOGICAL REVIEW, THE (UK/0263-0338) [10397789] **253**

AFRICAN ARTS (US/0001-9933) [01461383] **312**

AFRICAN BIBLIOGRAPHY SERIES (US) [03280644] **407**

AFRICAN BOOK PUBLISHING RECORD, THE (UK/0306-0322) [02242481] **4811**

AFRICAN BOOK WORLD & PRESS: DIRECTORY, THE (UK) [03583984] **4823**

AFRICAN BOOKS IN PRINT (UK/0306-9516) [01826529] **407**

AFRICAN BUSINESS (UK/0141-3929) [04163567] **637**

AFRICAN BUSINESS & CHAMBER OF COMMERCE REVIEW (SA/0250-0817) [12248164] **817**

AFRICAN CHALLENGE (NR/0001-9968) [01590417] **4933**

AFRICAN CHRISTIAN STUDIES (KE/1013-171X) [I1013171X] 5012, **4933**

AFRICAN CHRISTIAN STUDIES: THE JOURNAL OF THE FACULTY OF THEOLOGY OF THE CATHOLIC HIGHER INSTITUTE OF EASTERN AFRICA, NAIROBI (KE) [14694676] **4933**

●AFRICAN CHRONICLE, THE (US/1054-9781) [23041547] **2636**

AFRICAN COMMENTARY *CEASED.* (US/1045-2303) [20049644] **2497**

AFRICAN COMMUNIST (UK/0001-9976) [01461387] **4539**

AFRICAN CONCORD *SUSPENDED.* (UK/0951-0966) [12994068] **2636**

AFRICAN CONTINENT NEWS (US) [29603487] **2497**

AFRICAN CRUSADER (NR) [05167537] **2636**

AFRICAN DENTAL JOURNAL : OFFICIAL PUBLICATION OF THE FEDERATION OF AFRICAN DENTAL ASSOCIATIONS (NR/0794-7348) [19346225] **1315**

AFRICAN DEVELOPMENT PERSPECTIVES YEARBOOK (GW) [23129648] **2907**

AFRICAN DEVELOPMENT REPORT (IV) [22211635] **1544**

AFRICAN DEVELOPMENT REVIEW (IV/1017-6772) [21202052] **768**

AFRICAN DIRECTIONS (US/0149-4724) [03490140] **2636**

AFRICAN DIRECTORY OF STATISTICIANS *See* DIRECTORY OF AFRICAN STATISTICIANS / ECONOMIC COMMISSION FOR AFRICA **5326**

AFRICAN ECHO (US/8756-4653) [11565520] **2636**

AFRICAN ECONOMIC HISTORY (US/0145-2258) [02673339] **1544**

●AFRICAN ENTOMOLOGY (SA/1021-3589) [28296720] **5605**

AFRICAN ENVIRONMENT (SG/1010-5522) [02472271] 2211, **2159**

AFRICAN FARMER (ENGLISH ED.) (US/1053-8623) [18806220] **45**

AFRICAN FARMING AND FOOD PROCESSING (UK) [12150642] 2326, **45**

AFRICAN FREEDOM ANNUAL (SA) [03878086] **2636**

AFRICAN GEOLOGICAL SURVEYS *See* BULLETIN D'INFORMATION ET DE LIAISON - ASSOCIATION DES SERVICES GEOLOGIQUES AFRICAINS **1369**

●AFRICAN HERALD, THE (US/1069-8205) [26849024] **5746**

AFRICAN HISTORICAL DICTIONARIES (US) [03313649] **2636**

AFRICAN INSTITUTE FOR ECONOMIC AND SOCIAL DEVELOPMENT *See* RAPPORT D'ACTIVITE - INSTITUT AFRICAIN POUR LE DEVELOPPEMENT ECONOMIQUE ET SOCIAL **1515**

AFRICAN INTELLIGENCE DIGEST (US/8755-5565) [10447538] **2636**

AFRICAN INTERNATIONAL ORGANIZATION DIRECTORY, AND AFRICAN PARTICIPATION IN OTHER INTERNATIONAL ORGANIZATIONS (GW) [11889138] **3122**

AFRICAN JOURNAL OF ACADEMIC LIBRARIANSHIP (NR/0189-6709) [12353929] **3188**

AFRICAN JOURNAL OF AGRICULTURAL SCIENCES (ET/0253-5955) [06434813] **45**

AFRICAN JOURNAL OF CLINICAL AND EXPERIMENTAL IMMUNOLOGY *CEASED.* (SA/0253-052X) [06416965] **3985**

AFRICAN JOURNAL OF ECOLOGY (UK/0141-6707) [05022522] 5574, **2211**

AFRICAN JOURNAL OF INTERNATIONAL AND COMPARATIVE LAW (UK/0954-8890) [20297647] **3122**

AFRICAN JOURNAL OF INTERNATIONAL LAW, THE (UK/1011-663X) [18150680] **3122**

AFRICAN JOURNAL OF LIBRARY, ARCHIVES & INFORMATION SCIENCE (NR/0795-4778) [25585308] **3188**

AFRICAN JOURNAL OF NEUROLOGICAL SCIENCES : OFFICIAL ORGAN OF THE PAN AFRICAN ASSOCIATION OF NEUROLOGICAL SCIENCES, THE (KE) [18838415] **3826**

AFRICAN JOURNAL OF PHARMACY AND THE PHARMACEUTICAL SCIENCES (NR) [01695198] **4289**

AFRICAN JOURNAL OF PSYCHIATRY, THE (NR/0331-0175) [04220588] **3919**

Alphabetical Title Index — AFROTECH

AFRICAN JOURNAL OF RANGE AND FORAGE SCIENCE (SA) **45**

AFRICAN JOURNAL OF SOCIOLOGY (KE/1010-4127) [08150363] **5238**

AFRICAN LANGUAGES AND CULTURES (UK/0954-416X) [19224256] 227, **3262**

AFRICAN LANGUAGES / LANGUES AFRICAINES (UK) [02592709] **3262**

AFRICAN LAW BIBLIOGRAPHY (BE) **2928**

AFRICAN LAW BIBLIOGRAPHY. SUPPLEMENT (BE) [09268306] **2928**

AFRICAN LAW DIGEST *SUSPENDED.* (ET/0002-0052) [01461393] **2928**

AFRICAN LETTER, THE (CN/0827-8040) [18117473] 2636, **2254**

AFRICAN LITERATURE ASSOCIATION *See* ALA BULLETIN : A PUBLICATION OF THE AFRICAN LITERATURE ASSOCIATION **3359**

AFRICAN LITERATURE TODAY (UK/0065-4000) [01264557] **3358**

AFRICAN METHODIST EPISCOPAL ZION CHURCH *See* A.M.E. ZION QUARTERLY REVIEW, THE **5054**

AFRICAN MIRROR (WASHINGTON, D.C.), THE (US/1056-0483) [23452856] **2637**

AFRICAN MUSIC (SA/0065-4019) [01036109] **4098**

AFRICAN MUSICOLOGY / INSTITUTE OF AFRICAN STUDIES, UNIVERSITY OF NAIROBI *SUSPENDED.* (KE) [11191158] **4098**

AFRICAN NEWS SHEET / INTERNATIONAL SOCIAL SECURITY ASSOCIATION (TG/0379-7074) [07864505] **5270**

AFRICAN NEWSPAPER INDEX, THE (US/0278-6605) [07855382] **5685**

AFRICAN NOTES (NR/0002-0087) [00968132] **2254**

●AFRICAN ORACLE, THE (CN/1189-5055) [26757915] **5779**

AFRICAN POPULATION NEWSLETTER (ET) [03565356] **4549**

●AFRICAN PUBLISHERS NETWORKING DIRECTORY AND NAMES & NUMBERS (UK) [29217874] **4811**

AFRICAN RECORDER (II/0002-0125) [01461403] **2497**

AFRICAN RED FAMILY (UK) [01789712] **4539**

AFRICAN REFUGEES (ET) [17939786] **1918**

AFRICAN RESEARCH & DOCUMENTATION (UK/0305-862X) [02914514] **3188**

AFRICAN REVIEW (DAR ES SALAAM, TANZANIA) (TZ/0002-0117) [01461406] **5189**

AFRICAN REVIEW OF BUSINESS AND TECHNOLOGY (UK/0954-6782) [18528132] **5081**

●AFRICAN RURAL AND URBAN STUDIES (US/1073-4600) [29407692] **2813**

AFRICAN SMALL MAMMAL NEWSLETTER (BE/0763-6776) [07636776] **5574**

AFRICAN SOCIAL RESEARCH *SUSPENDED.* (ZA/0002-0168) [01205105] **5189**

AFRICAN SOCIAL SECURITY DOCUMENTATION (SZ) [06804214] **5270**

AFRICAN SOCIAL STUDIES FORUM (KE) [16073929] **5189**

AFRICAN SPECIAL BIBLIOGRAPHIC SERIES (US/0749-2308) [11094567] **407**

AFRICAN SPOTLIGHT (KE) [04585394] **2637**

AFRICAN STATISTICAL YEARBOOK. ANNUAIRE STATISTIQUE POUR L'AFRIQUE (ET) [02278564] **5320**

AFRICAN STOCK MARKETS (US/1061-8880) [25100147] **890**

●AFRICAN STUDIES ABSTRACTS : THE ABSTRACTS JOURNAL OF THE AFRICAN STUDIES CENTRE, LEIDEN (UK/1352-2175) [30372754] 5189, 2841, **5226**

AFRICAN STUDIES ASSOCIATION *See* PAPERS PRESENTED AT THE ANNUAL MEETING OF THE AFRICAN STUDIES ASSOCIATION **2500**

AFRICAN STUDIES BY SOVIET SCHOLARS (RU) [06715491] **4539**

AFRICAN STUDIES (JOHANNESBURG) (SA/0002-0184) [01461408] 2637, **227**

AFRICAN STUDIES JOURNAL (GH) [04372201] **2637**

AFRICAN STUDIES REVIEW (US/0002-0206) [01461411] **2498**

AFRICAN STUDIES SERIES (UK/0065-406X) [01461412] **2637**

AFRICAN STUDY MONOGRAPHS (JA/0285-1601) [08137689] **2498**

AFRICAN STUDY MONOGRAPHS. SUPPLEMENTARY ISSUE (JA/0286-9667) [08815821] **2498**

AFRICAN TAX SYSTEMS (NE) [05393507] **4708**

AFRICAN TECHNOLOGY FORUM (US/1050-0014) [21366051] **5081**

AFRICAN TEXTILES (UK/0144-7521) [09917183] **5347**

AFRICAN, THE (MW/0300-4651) [02177785] **2497**

AFRICAN TIMES (LONDON, ENGLAND : 1984) (UK) [14399310] **2484**

AFRICAN URBAN QUARTERLY (US/0747-6108) [10756552] **2813**

AFRICAN URBAN STUDIES (EAST LANSING, MICH.) *CEASED.* (US/0736-6760) [04108503] **2813**

AFRICAN URBAN STUDIES (MICHIGAN STATE UNIVERSITY. AFRICAN STUDIES CENTER) *See* AFRICAN RURAL AND URBAN STUDIES **2813**

AFRICAN VIOLET MAGAZINE (US/0002-0265) [02444405] **2408**

AFRICAN WILDLIFE (SA/0002-0273) [03511379] **2185**

AFRICAN WILDLIFE UPDATE (US/1058-9805) [24450739] **4868**

AFRICAN WOMAN (UK/0953-9816) [20815365] **5550**

AFRICAN WORLD NEWS, THE *SUSPENDED.* (US/0747-8879) [10830309] **2498**

AFRICAN WRITERS SERIES (UK/0065-4108) [03265465] **3358**

AFRICANA *SUSPENDED.* (KE/0002-0281) [01775522] 2185, **5574**

AFRICANA. AFRIKANSKII ETNOGRAFICHESKII SBORNIK (RU) [07012017] **227**

AFRICANA ANNUAL (US) [18649685] 2254, **3188**

AFRICANA BULLETIN (PL/0002-029X) [02013410] **2637**

AFRICANA DIRECTIONS (US/0277-1373) [07506540] **1923**

AFRICANA JOURNAL *See* AFRICANA ANNUAL **3188**

AFRICANA LIBRARIES NEWSLETTER (URBANA, ILL.) (US/0148-7868) [09977658] **3188**

AFRICANA LINGUISTICA (BE) [02905168] **3262**

AFRICANA MARBURGENSIA (GW/0002-0311) [03268933] **2637**

AFRICANA NOTES AND NEWS *SUSPENDED.* (SA/0002-032X) [02013528] **2498**

AFRICANA (PORTO, PORTUGAL) (PO) [17945171] **2609**

AFRICANA RESEARCH BULLETIN (SL/0259-9651) [01661163] **5189**

AFRICANA-SAMMLUNG IN DER STADTBIBLIOTHEK WINTERTHUR *See* AFRICANA-SAMMLUNG UND AFRICANA-KATALOG IN DER STADTBIBLIOTHEK WINTERTHUR **3262**

AFRICANA-SAMMLUNG UND AFRICANA-KATALOG IN DER STADTBIBLIOTHEK WINTERTHUR (SZ) [11351483] **3262**

AFRICANA SOCIETY OF PRETORIA *See* YEARBOOK - AFRICANA SOCIETY OF PRETORIA **2644**

AFRICANIST NEWS AND VIEWS / ISSUED BY THE PAN AFRICANIST CONGRESS OF AZANIA (SOUTH AFRICA) (UA) [08541914] **2498**

AFRICANISTIQUE (LUBUMBASHI, ZAIRE) *See* LINGUISTIQUE ET SCIENCES HUMAINES **3299**

AFRICANUS (SA) [05640715] 4515, **4462**

AFRICASCOPE (FR) [19524599] **3262**

AFRICENTRIC MONITOR, THE (US/1058-6156) [24343114] **2637**

AFRICUS *SUSPENDED.* (US/0733-1533) [08514634] **821**

●AFRIKA 2001 (SA) [27195374] **5081**

AFRIKA BULLETIN (DK) [03218194] **2637**

AFRIKA. ENGLISH EDITION (GW/0340-5788) [14783457] **4515**

AFRIKA FOCUS : TIJDSCHRIFT VAN DE AVRUG (BE/0772-084X) [16714895] **2498**

AFRIKA, HANDEL MIT DER BUNDESREPUBLIK DEUTSCHLAND / BUNDESSTELLE FUR AUSSENHANDELSINFORMATION (GW) [09962398] **821**

AFRIKA INFORMASJON (NO/0332-6241) [06336276] **2637**

AFRIKA JAHRBUCH (GW) [19093344] 5189, **4462**

AFRIKA MATHEMATICA (CM/1012-9405) [07720397] **3491**

●AFRIKA MIX (US/1061-3730) [25277488] **1125**

AFRIKA-POST (GW/0002-0389) [10568857] **4515**

AFRIKA-STUDIEN (GW/0568-1715) [03262909] **2637**

AFRIKA UND DIE DEUTSCHEN : JAHRBUCH DER DEUTSCHEN AFRIKA-STIFTUNG (GW/0721-3107) [09364052] **2637**

AFRIKA UND UBERSEE (GW/0002-0427) [04429146] **3262**

AFRIKA ZAMANI (CM) [02242701] **2637**

AFRIKAANS-DUITSE KULTUURUNIE *See* NUUSBRIEF - AFRIKAANS-DUITSE KULTUURUNIE **2642**

AFRIKAANS HANDELS-INDEKS *See* NATIONAL TRADE-INDEX OF SOUTH AFRICA **847**

AFRIKANISTISCHE ARBEITSPAPIERE (GW/0178-725X) [13356412] **3262**

AFRIKASPECTRUM (GW/0002-0397) [01661172] **5189**

AFRIQUE *CEASED.* (UK) [06893534] **2637**

AFRIQUE AGRICULTURE (FR/0337-9515) [02379851] **45**

AFRIQUE CONTEMPORAINE (FR/0002-0478) [02014937] **4515**

AFRIQUE ENTREPRISE (FR/0221-5772) [17857982] **1544**

AFRIQUE ET L'ASIE MODERNES, L' *CEASED.* (FR/0399-0370) [02015289] 2644, **2637**

AFRIQUE ET PHILOSOPHIE (CG) [04762564] **4339**

AFRIQUE EXPANSION (FR/0396-6046) [l03966046] **2498**

AFRIQUE HISTOIRE U.S *SUSPENDED.* (US/0741-2592) [09115589] **2637**

AFRIQUE LITTERAIRE, L' *SUSPENDED.* (FR/0245-8160) [06632718] **3358**

AFRIQUE MAGAZINE (FR) [19372687] **2484**

AFRIQUE MEDECINE ET SANTE *CEASED.* (FR) [17725408] **4763**

AFRIQUE MEDICALE (SG/0002-0516) [06363765] **3892**

AFRIQUE NOIRE POLITIQUE ET ECONOMIQUE, L' (FR) [05591265] **1460**

AFRIQUE NOUVELLE *CEASED.* (SG/0002-0532) [02257024] **2498**

AFRISCOPE (NR/0044-667X) [01585840] **2907**

AFRO-AMERICAN (BALTIMORE, MD. : NATIONAL ED.) (US) [12049092] **5685**

AFRO-AMERICAN CULTURE SOCIETY MONOGRAPH SERIES (US/0882-5297) [11886920] **2717**

AFRO-AMERICAN HISTORICAL AND GENEALOGICAL SOCIETY (WASHINGTON, D.C.) *See* JOURNAL OF THE AFRO-AMERICAN HISTORICAL AND GENEALOGICAL SOCIETY **2455**

●AFRO-AMERICAN HISTORY KIT (7TH GRADE AND ABOVE ED.) (US/1055-7385) [23285144] 2254, **2717**

AFRO-AMERICAN HISTORY KIT (K-6 ED.) *CEASED.* (US/1055-7393) [23285007] 2717, **2637**

AFRO-AMERICAN HISTORY KIT (WASHINGTON, D.C. : 1987) *See* AFRO-AMERICAN HISTORY KIT (7TH GRADE AND ABOVE ED.) **2717**

AFRO-AMERICAN MUSIC OPPORTUNITIES ASSOCIATION, INC *See* AAMOA REPORTS **4098**

AFRO-AMERICANS IN NEW YORK LIFE AND HISTORY (US/0364-2437) [02800381] **2254**

AFRO-ASIA (BL/0002-0591) [01478473] 2644, **2637**

AFRO-ASIAN ECONOMIC REVIEW *SUSPENDED.* (UA/02444411) **1544**

AFRO-ASIAN JOURNAL OF NEMATOLOGY (UK/0963-6420) [l09636420] 498, **5574**

AFRO-ASIAN JOURNAL OF OPHTHALMOLOGY (II/0254-0517) [08941625] **3871**

AFRO CANADIAN (CN) **2717**

AFRO-HISPANIC REVIEW (US/0278-8969) [07903215] 3358, **3262**

AFRO IMAGE (NR) [01791612] **2637**

AFRO SCHOLAR NEWSLETTER (US/0894-0762) [08602186] **5189**

AFRO TECHNICAL PAPERS (CF/0250-8621) [06174161] **4764**

AFRO TIMES (BROOKLYN, N.Y.) (US/1044-7199) [18878353] **5713**

AFROASIATIC DIALECTS (US/0732-6416) [03262852] **3262**

AFROASIATIC LINGUISTICS *SUSPENDED.* (US/0362-3637) [02223022] **3262**

●AFROCENTRIC SCHOLAR, THE (US/1056-8689) [23887039] **2254**

●AFROTECH ENVIRONMENTALIST (US/1066-3053) [26917264] 2254, **2159**

AFRRI — Alphabetical Title Index

AFRRI REPORTS (US/0894-1106) [14056410] **441**

AFS WORLD (US/1063-0902) [25059564] **1722**

AFSIC NOTES / ALTERNATIVE FARMING SYSTEMS INFORMATION CENTER, NATIONAL AGRICULTURAL LIBRARY (US) [25813240] **45**

AFSM INTERNATIONAL (US/1049-2135) [19581094] **1235**

AFT : SEMESTRALE DELL'ARCHIVIO FOTOGRAFICO TOSCANO (IT) [18430436] **4366**

AFTENPOSTEN (NO) [01478476] **5807**

AFTER 8? (CN/0709-9185) [06860886] **1723**

AFTER-SCHOOL AND WEEKEND OPPORTUNITIES FOR GIFTED AND TALENTED STUDENTS (US) [10660079] **1874**

●AFTER SCHOOL MAGAZINE (US/1073-1555) [29347203] **1807**

AFTERIMAGE (US/0300-7472) [01335227] **4366**

AFTERIMAGE (LONDON, ENGLAND) (UK/0261-4472) [01685279] **4062**

AFTERLOSS (RANCHO MIRAGE, CALIF.) (US/1044-0534) [19657810] **4572**

AFTERMARKET BUSINESS (US/0892-1121) [13866774] **637**

AFTERMARKET EXECUTIVE (US/0162-6604) [04335696] **5403**

AFTERMARKET STATISTICAL YEARBOOK (US/0740-8676) [10037365] **5400**

AFTERMATH (US/0737-1381) [09314816] **4856**

AFTERNOON TV (US/0164-6508) [04468962] **1125**

AFTERWORDS (US/8756-3010) [11617257] **5270**

AFTON STAR-ENTERPRISE, THE (US) [13956791] **5668**

AFTRA (US/0044-7676) [03999656] **1148**

AFVA BULLETIN / AMERICAN FILM AND VIDEO ASSOCIATION (US) [17988051] 1723, **4062**

AFVA EVALUATIONS **CEASED.** (US/1051-5925) [18311202] 3188, **4062**

AFYA (NAIROBI) (KE/0378-4851) [03855641] 4764, **3547**

AFZ. ALLGEMEINE FISCHWIRTSCHAFTSZEITUNG (GW/0001-1258) [01696353] **2293**

AFZ : ALLGEMEINE FORST ZEITSCHRIFT FUER WALDWIRTSCHAFT UND UMWELTVORSORGE (GW) [19789786] **2373**

AG ALERT (US/0161-5408) [03974252] **45**

AG-ALERT (LONDON, ONT.) (CN) [29592975] **45**

●AG CHEM NEW COMPOUND REVIEW (US/1072-7361) [25911473] **45**

AG CHEM NEW PRODUCT REVIEW (US) [21480060] **45**

AG CONSULTANT (US/0894-7155) [15319695] **45**

AG IMPACT (US/0196-0857) [03428418] **45**

AG. MARKET CHARTS (US/0744-1452) [08065716] **45**

AG-NEWS See ILLINOIS AGRI-NEWS **94**

AG PILOT INTERNATIONAL (US/0740-1434) [09940361] **6**

●AG RETAILER (US/1072-9267) [29238533] **45**

AG. REVIEW (PUTNAM, CONN.) (US/0194-6625) [04922062] **45**

AG-TELEFUNKEN. FACHBEREICH HALBLEITER See DIODEN **2042**

AG UPDATE / (US/0279-9014) [07349024] 204, **191**

AGACCESS (US/8756-7733) [11652864] 2408, **45**

AGADA (US/0740-2392) [07863645] **5045**

AGAIN MAGAZINE (US/0885-9795) [09230848] **4933**

AGAINST THE CURRENT (US/0739-4853) [09201501] **4462**

AGAINST THE GRAIN (CHARLESTON, S.C.) (US/1043-2094) [19378899] 4811, **3188**

AGALIA : REVISTA DA ASSOCIACOM GALEGA DA LINGUA (SP) [19739167] 3358, **3262**

AGAPE MAGAZINE (BE) **4933**

AGARD CONFERENCE PROCEEDINGS (UK/0549-7191) [02922388] **6**

AGARD HIGHLIGHTS (FR/0302-5020) [01793527] **6**

AGARD LECTURE SERIES (FR/0549-7213) [01695358] **6**

AGARDOGRAPH (FR/0365-2467) [01387296] **6**

AGARNA OCH MAKTEN I SVERIGES BORSFORETAG (SW) [17719961] **637**

AGATE. ALBERTA GIFTED AND TALENTED EDUCATION (CN/0833-0603) [17311370] **1874**

AGB REPORTS (US/0044-961X) [08341400] **1807**

AGBIOBUSINESS See IMPACT AGBIOINDUSTRY **3693**

AGBIOTECH NEWS AND INFORMATION (UK/0954-9897) [19359355] 45, 3685, **149**

AGBIOTECH STOCK LETTER (US/1066-0569) [10660569] 45, **3685**

AGBIOTECHNOLOGY NEWS (US/0899-3998) [16171623] 45, **3685**

AGCHEMPRICE (US/8756-243X) [11501029] **45**

AGD DENTAL UPDATE **CEASED.** (US) **1315**

AGE (US/0884-6669) [11994963] **2436**

AGE AND AGEING (UK/0002-0729) [01715551] **3748**

AGE & NUTRITION (FR) [24538281] **4186**

AGE DIGEST See AGE REFDEX **5081**

AGE DISCRIMINATION IN EMPLOYMENT ACT OF 1967 (US/0193-063X) [00924385] **1642**

AGE D'OR, L' (FR/0294-1155) [10115649] **4933**

AGE OF ATHEISM, THE (II) [03573757] **4339**

AGE OF JOHNSON, THE (US/0884-5816) [12406843] 429, **3358**

AGE OF REVOLUTION AND ROMANTICISM, THE (US/1045-4497) [20113103] **5073**

AGE (OMAHA) (US/0161-9152) [03486826] **3748**

AGE REFDEX (TH) [15161684] **5081**

AGE, THE (AT) [09662590] **5777**

AGECOP LIAISON (FR/0336-2086) [03977085] **5238**

AGED CARE & SERVICES REVIEW (US/0161-1151) [03863485] 5178, **5270**

AGEING AND SOCIETY (UK/0144-686P) [07963198] **3748**

AGEING INTERNATIONAL (US/0163-5158) [03654146] **5270**

AGENCE CAMBODGE - LAOS (FR/0983-737X) [I0983737X] **4462**

AGENCE DE COOPERATION CULTURELLE ET TECHNIQUE See AGECOP LIAISON **5238**

AGENCE DE PRESSE LIBRE DU QUEBEC See BULLETIN - AGENCE DE PRESSE LIBRE DU QUEBEC **2917**

AGENCE DE PROMOTION DES INVESTISSEMENTS See RAPPORT ANNUEL - AGENCE DE PROMOTION DES INVESTISSEMENTS **1623**

AGENCE ECONOMIQUE ET FINANCIERE (FR/0755-1940) [I07551940] 1460, **768**

AGENCE MAURITANIENNE DE PRESSE See BULLETIN DOCUMENTAIRE MENSUEL - AGENCE MAURITANIENNE DE PRESSE **2638**

AGENCIES & ORGANIZATIONS REPRESENTED IN AAPOR MEMBERSHIP See BLUE BOOK OF THE ASSOCIATION FOR PUBLIC OPINION RESEARCH, WORLD ASSOCIATION FOR PUBLIC OPINION RESEARCH : AGENCIES & ORGANIZATIONS REPRESENTED IN AAPOR/WAPOR MEMBERSHIP, THE **5240**

AGENCY ACCOUNTABILITY SURVEY (US/0091-3812) [01787120] 5550, **1642**

●AGENCY BUDGET DETAIL (US) [24315033] **4708**

AGENCY DIRECTORY - AMERICAN HUMANE (US/0147-4383) [03162790] 2249, **5270**

AGENCY EXAMINER, THE (US/1051-7332) [22102063] **1460**

AGENCY FOR INSTRUCTIONAL TELEVISION See CATALOG OF TELEVISION AND AUDIOVISUAL MATERIALS **1130**

AGENCY INSIGHT (CN/0843-4700) [20996443] **4764**

AGENCY LIST, GEOGRAPHIC (US/0270-2797) [06372356] **5460**

AGENCY LIST NUMERIC SEQUENCE (US) [05089957] **5460**

AGENCY NEWS **CEASED.** (US) [05159198] **637**

AGENCY OF INDUSTRIAL SCIENCE AND TECHNOLOGY : AIST (JA) [08035486] **5081**

AGENCY SALES (US/0749-2332) [07972471] **921**

AGENDA (US) 5550, **2917**

AGENDA DES FESTIVALS AUDIOVISUELS EN EUROPE, L' (BE/0777-6268) [I07776268] **5315**

●AGENDA DES JURISTES, L' (CN/1189-5136) [26758155] **2928**

AGENDA DES PROFESSIONS JUDICIAIRES ET JURIDIQUES (FR) [02477078] **3138**

●AGENDA, JEWISH EDUCATION (US/1072-1150) [28774782] 2254, **1723**

AGENDA, L' (IT) **3547**

AGENDA (LONDON) (UK/0002-0796) [00927880] **3459**

AGENDA NEW YORK (US/1045-4969) [20149435] **5271**

AGENDA (NEW YORK, N.Y. 1991) (US/1055-1247) [23086237] **1723**

AGENDA - OBRA SINDICAL EDUCACION Y DESCANSO, BARCELONA (SP) [01788249] **2672**

AGENDA OF REGULATIONS (US/1044-9876) [20020812] **2153**

AGENDA - ONTARIO HOSPITAL ASSOCIATION **CEASED.** (CN/0847-1495) [21493424] **3775**

AGENDA (OTTAWA) (CN/0706-2613) [04448909] **5081**

AGENDA PARKVILLE (AT/1033-1115) [I10331115] **312**

AGENDA (SCHOLASTIC INC.) See AMERICA'S AGENDA **1724**

AGENDA SYNOPSIS (US) **2813**

AGENDA / THE NIAGARA INSTITUTE (CN/0711-494X) [08652007] **859**

AGENDEN / AKTIVITATEN 90/91 (AU) **4625**

AGENOR (BE/0002-080X) [01478485] **4515**

AGENT AMERICA (CN) **5460**

AGENT & MANAGER (US/1065-5921) [26641958] **859**

AGENT CANADA (CN/0834-0471) [16292243] **5460**

AGENT DE VOYAGES, L' See LETTRE TOURISTIQUE PARIS, LA **5483**

AGENT, THE (US) [07958479] **5347**

AGENTS AND ACTIONS (SZ/0065-4299) [01478487] **4289**

AGENTS AND ACTIONS. SUPPLEMENTS (SZ/0379-0363) [03696259] **3978**

AGENTS & BUYERS MARKET SERVICE See SHORTCUT2 **2893**

AGENTS ECONOMIQUES DU ZAIRE : ANNUAIRE (CG) [03236713] **1148**

AGENT'S HOTEL GAZETTEER : TOURIST CITIES OF EUROPE, THE (UK) [02240920] **2803**

AGENTS OF FOREIGN CORPORATIONS - LOUISIANA. DEPT. OF STATE (US) [01782533] **1596**

AGENZIA ECONOMICA FINANZIARIA (IT) **1460**

AGENZIA GIORNALISTICA REPUBBLICA (IT) **5804**

AGENZIA OMNIA PRESS (IT) **1460**

AGENZIA QUOTIDIANA INFORMAZIONI (IT) **5804**

AGENZIA VIAGGI (IT) **5460**

AGESCS (US) [06050802] **45**

AGEVOLAZIONI FINANZIARIE TESTO UNICO (IT) **768**

AGEXPORTER (WASHINGTON, D.C.) (US/1047-4781) [19069534] **45**

AGFACTS / DEPARTMENT OF AGRICULTURE, NEW SOUTH WALES (AT/0725-7759) [10573892] **45**

AGFOCUS (MIDDLETOWN, N.Y.) (US/0899-7535) [18204097] **45**

AGGIORNAMENTI CODICI A SCHEDA PEM (IT) **1460**

AGGIORNAMENTI DI TERAPIA OFTALMOLOGICA (IT/0002-0915) [01696283] **3871**

AGGIORNAMENTI IN CHIRURGIA GENERALE **CEASED.** (IT/0393-3873) [05622411] **3958**

AGGIORNAMENTI SOCIALI (IT/0002-094X) [03331792] 5189, **4933**

AGGIORNAMENTI SULLE TOSSICODIPENDENZE (IT) **3978**

AGGIORNAMENTO DEL MEDICO (IT/0392-3002) [I03923002] **3547**

AGGIORNAMENTO PEDIATRICO (IT/0002-0958) [01478489] **3899**

AGGRESSION AND ANTI-SOCIAL BEHAVIOR IN CHILDHOOD AND ADOLESCENCE (US) [06080590] **4572**

AGGRESSIVE BEHAVIOR (US/0096-140X) [01225717] **4572**

AGGS NEWS VIEWS (US/1040-449X) [18422220] **4811**

AGHAM (PH/0115-5679) [07228174] **5081**

Alphabetical Title Index **AGRI-FOOD**

AGHAM-TAO (PH) [10675441] **227**

AGHE EXCHANGE (US/0890-278X) [14337259] **3748**

AGIA NEWSLETTER (AT/0313-1696) [I03131696] **1351**

AGID NEWS (TH) [03702055] **1351**

AGIFORS (SOCIETY). SYMPOSIUM *See* ANNUAL SYMPOSIUM PROCEEDINGS / AGIFORS **12**

AGINCOURT NEWS (CN/0834-5783) [16074672] **5779**

AGING (UK/0268-1544) **3749**

AGING *CEASED.* (US/0002-0966) [01478490] **5178, 3749**

AGING ACTION ALERT (US/1050-3188) [12743923] **5271**

AGING ALERT (US/0892-5372) [14998871] **5182, 5178**

AGING AND AGING DISORDERS *CEASED.* (UK/0959-1346) [22304999] **3749**

AGING AND COGNITION (NE/0928-9917) **4572**

AGING & LEISURE LIVING (US/0194-455X) [04674556] **3749**

●AGING & NEUROSCIENCE (US/1061-6306) [25381790] **577**

AGING AND SENSORY CHANGE : AN ANNOTATED BIBLIOGRAPHY (US) **3749**

AGING (BOCA RATON) (US/0273-2467) [05696256] **5178**

AGING (GUILFORD, CONN.) (US/0272-3808) [06536965] **3749**

AGING, IMMUNOLOGY AND INFECTIOUS DISEASE (US/0892-8762) [15276867] **3662**

AGING (MILAN, ITALY) (IT/0394-9532) [23176357] **3749**

AGING NETWORK NEWS (US/0742-3438) [13940517] **5178**

AGING (NEW YORK, N.Y.) (US/0160-2721) [03165396] **3749**

●AGING NEWS ALERT : THE SENIOR SERVICES & FUNDING REPORT (US) [26273670] **5178**

AGING PROGRAM LETTER *See* AGING NETWORK NEWS **5178**

AGING RESEARCH & TRAINING NEWS (US/0888-6830) [13074398] **3749**

AGIR (MONTREAL) (CN/0847-9798) [20873567] **3123**

AGIS : ATTORNEY-GENERAL'S INFORMATION SERVICE (AT/0312-4592) [11347340] **2928**

AGITATION (SZ) [01787980] **4539**

AGITATOR TADZHIKISTANA (TA) [03218663] **4625**

AGLOW *CEASED.* (US/0748-6677) [07868528] **4933**

AGLOW NEWSLETTER (MELVILLE) (CN/0823-0315) [09809112] **5054**

AGMA DIRECTORY (US/0572-502X) [02239854] **2109**

AGMAZINE (US) [06614109] **4098**

AGNI (BOSTON, MASS.) (US/1046-218X) [18338115] **3358**

AGNOTE (AU/0157-8243) [21370252] **2293**

AGO NEWS *CEASED.* (CN/0829-4437) [13924837] **335**

AGO NEWS *See* JOURNAL - ART GALLERY OF ONTARIO **4090**

AGO TIMES, The (US/0362-5907) [02302991] **4099**

AGON (UY) [07443054] **3358**

AGORA MELBOURNE (AT/0044-6726) [I00446726] **2609, 1887**

AGORA NORWOOD (AT/0812-8383) [I08128383] **3188**

AGORA, PAPELES DE FILOSOFIA (SP) **4339**

AGORA PARIS. 1986 (FR/0984-4783) [I09844783] **2249**

AGORA (PHILADELPHIA, PA.) (US/0899-1146) [17993241] **2672**

AGORA (POTSDAM) *SUSPENDED.* (US/0002-1016) [02094304] **2841**

AGORA (RALEIGH, N.C.) *SUSPENDED.* (US/0891-3293) [14709494] **1089**

AGORA (TOKYO JAPAN : 1972) (JA) [09914100] **5550**

AGRA ALIMENTATION (FR/0339-4409) [I03394409] **45**

AGRA-BRIEFING (UK/0266-3570) [I02663570] **46**

AGRA EUROPE (BRITISH EDITION) (UK/0002-1024) [03946113] **1460, 46**

AGRA EUROPE. (FRENCH EDITION) (FR) **5800**

AGRA EUROPE. MILK PRODUCTS (UK/0950-3730) [I09503730] **191**

AGRA EUROPE. POTATO MARKETS (UK/0141-2221) [I01412221] **46**

AGRA EUROPE. PRESERVED MILK (UK/0141-223X) [I0141223X] **191**

AGRA EUROPE SPECIAL REPORT (UK/0142-422X) [I0142422X] **46**

AGRA PRESS (IT) **46**

AGRA UNIVERSITY *See* AGRA UNIVERSITY JOURNAL OF RESEARCH. LETTERS **46**

AGRA UNIVERSITY *See* AGRA UNIVERSITY JOURNAL OF RESEARCH. SCIENCE **5081**

AGRA UNIVERSITY JOURNAL OF RESEARCH. LETTERS (II/0568-2339) [01478495] **46**

AGRA UNIVERSITY JOURNAL OF RESEARCH. SCIENCE (II/0002-1082) [01478494] **5081**

AGRAFILE (UK) **46**

AGRAFILE. GRAIN & OILSEEDS (UK/0950-494X) [I0950494X] **161**

AGRAFILE. LIVESTOCK & MEAT (UK/0950-4958) [I09504958] **2326, 46**

AGRAFOOD ASIA (UK/1354-4128) **46**

AGRAR- UND UMWELTFORSCHUNG IN BADEN-WURTTEMBERG (GW) [10866986] **46**

AGRARBERICHTERSTATTUNG. HEFT 4, VIEHHALTUNG (GW) [10452517] **204, 149**

AGRARBERICHTERSTATTUNG NORDRHEIN-WESTFALEN. VIEHHALTUNG UND BODENNUTZUNG DER LANDWIRTSCHAFTLICHEN BETRIEBE (GW) [19612787] **46**

AGRARFORSCHUNG BERN (SZ/1022-663X) [I1022663X] **46**

AGRARIAN HISTORY OF ENGLAND & WALES (UK) **2672**

AGRARISCH RECHT (NE/0167-4242) [08819547] **46, 2928**

AGRARISCH WEEKOVERZICHT (NE/0002-1075) [03947353] **46**

AGRARISCHE BUITENLANDSE HANDEL VAN POLEN, DE (NE) [04338447] **2326**

AGRARISCHE RUNDSCHAU (AU/0002-0710) [03947399] **46**

AGRARMARKTE BR DEUTSCHLAND, EWG UND WELTMARKT, DIE (GW) [02239489] **821**

AGRARMARKTE BR DEUTSCHLAND, EWG UND WELTMARKT : EIER UND GEFLUGEL, DIE (GW) [01788904] **204**

AGRARMARKTE BR DEUTSCHLAND, EWG UND WELTMARKT. MILCH UND MILCHERZEUGNISSE, DIE (GW) [04571714] **191**

AGRARMARKTE BR DEUTSCHLAND, EWG UND WELTMARKT. VIEH UND FLEISCH, DIE (GW) [01707673] **204**

AGRARMARKTE IN DER BUNDESREPUBLIK *See* AGRARMARKTE BR DEUTSCHLAND, EWG UND WELTMARKT, DIE **821**

AGRAROKOLOGIE (GW) [25844811] **46**

AGRARRECHT (GW/0340-840X) [01785792] **46, 2928**

AGRARSPECTRUM / DACHVERBAND WISSENSCHAFTLICHER GESELLSCHAFTEN DER AGRAR-, FORST-, ERNAHRUNGS-, VETERINAR-, UND UMWELTFORSCHUNG (GW) [09726679] **46**

AGRARTECHNIK INTERNATIONAL (GW) [04573237] **158**

AGRARTUDOMANYI EGYETEM, KESZTHELY. MOSONMAGYAROVARI MEZOGAZDASAGTUDOMANYI KAR *See* MOSONMAGYAROVARI MEZOGAZDASAGTUDOMANYI KAR KOZLEMENYEI, A **110**

AGRARWIRTSCHAFT (GW/0002-1121) [01478499] **46, 637**

AGRARWIRTSCHAFT. SONDERHEFT (GW/0515-6866) [01478498] **46**

AGRARWIRTSCHAFT UND AGRARSOZIOLOGIE (SZ) [23996106] **46**

AGRARWIRTSCHAFTLICHE STUDIEN (SZ/0256-6303) [I02566303] **1460**

AGREKON (SA/0303-1853) [01478500] **46**

AGRESSOLOGIE (FR/0002-1148) [01478501] **4572**

AGRESTE. ANALYSES & ETUDES (FR/0998-4186) [I09984186] **46**

AGRESTE. ANALYSES & ETUDES, CAHIERS (FR/0998-4178) [I09984178] **46**

AGRESTE. ANALYSES & ETUDES, COUP D'OEIL SUR RHONE-ALPES (FR/1150-1987) [I11501987] **46**

AGRESTE. ANALYSES & ETUDES, TRAJECTOIRES BRETAGNE (FR/1167-4563) [I11674563] **46**

AGRESTE. CONJONCTURE, BULLETIN REGIONAL CHAMPAGNE-ARDENNE (FR/1150-224X) [I1150224X] **46, 149**

AGRESTE. CONJONCTURE, CONJONCTURE GENERALE (FR/0998-416X) [26513454] **46**

AGRESTE. CONJONCTURE, FRUITS (FR/1148-5639) [I11485639] **161**

AGRESTE. CONJONCTURE, GRANDES CULTURES (FR/1148-5620) [I11485620] **46**

AGRESTE. CONJONCTURE. INFOS RAPIDES HAUTE ET BASSE-NORMANDIE (FR) **46**

AGRESTE. CONJONCTURE, LAIT ET PRODUITS LAITIERS (FR/1148-5647) [I11485647] **191**

AGRESTE. CONJONCTURE, LEGUMES (FR/1148-5655) [I11485655] **161**

AGRESTE CONJONCTURE NORD-PAS-DE-CALAIS (FR/1167-1416) [I11671416] **46**

AGRESTE. CONJONCTURE, NOTE DE CONJONCTURE AGRICOLE MIDI-PYRENEES (FR/1150-1707) [I11501707] **46**

AGRESTE. CONJONCTURE, POITOU-CHARENTES (FR/1150-1693) [I11501693] **47**

AGRESTE. CONJONCTURE, PRODUCTIONS ANIMALES (FR/1148-5612) [I11485612] **204**

AGRESTE. CONJONCTURE, PROVENCE ALPES COTE D'AZUR (FR/1148-5167) [I11485167] **47**

AGRESTE. CONJONCTURE, REGION ILE-DE-FRANCE (FR/1157-3554) [I11573554] **47**

AGRESTE. CONJONCTURE, RHONE-ALPES (FR/1148-5671) [I11485671] **47**

AGRESTE. CONJONCTURE, VITICULTURE (FR/1148-5663) [I11485663] **161**

AGRESTE. DONNEES, BULLETIN BOURGOGNE (FR/1150-1898) [I11501898] **47, 149**

AGRESTE. DONNEES, BULLETIN DE STATISTIQUE AGRICOLE D'AQUITAINE (FR/1150-1901) [I11501901] **47, 150**

AGRESTE. DONNEES, BULLETIN DE STATISTIQUE AGRICOLE GUADELOUPE (GP/1155-4037) [I11554037] **47, 150**

AGRESTE. DONNEES, BULLETIN DE STATISTIQUE AGRICOLE HAUTE ET BASSE-NORMANDIE (FR/1150-1723) [I11501723] **47, 150**

AGRESTE. DONNEES, BULLETIN DE STATISTIQUE AGRICOLE MARTINIQUE (MQ/1155-4479) [I11554479] **47, 150**

AGRESTE. DONNEES, BULLETIN DE STATISTIQUE AGRICOLE REUNION (RE/1150-1448) [I11501448] **47, 150**

AGRESTE, SER. BULL (FR/1142-3218) [26513418] **47**

AGRESTE. SERIES, ANIMAUX HEBDO (FR/1155-4487) [I11554487] **204**

AGRESTE. SERIES, AVICULTURE (FR/1150-1529) [I11501529] **204**

AGRESTE. SERIES, BULLETIN ALSACE (FR/1150-2037) [I11502037] **47**

AGRESTE. SERIES, BULLETIN BIMESTRIEL DE STATISTIQUE AGRICOLE DES PAYS DE LA LOIRE (FR/1146-5751) [I11465751] **47, 150**

AGRESTE. SERIES, BULLETIN DE STATISTIQUE AGRICOLE ILE DE FRANCE (FR/1157-3546) [I11573546] **47, 150**

AGRESTE. SERIES, BULLETIN DE STATISTIQUE AGRICOLE REGION MIDI-PYRENEES (FR/1150-1731) [I11501731] **47, 150**

AGRESTE. SERIES, BULLETIN MENSUEL LANGUEDOC-ROUSSILLON (FR/1148-5558) [I11485558] **47**

AGRESTE. SERIES, COMMERCE EXTERIEUR BOIS ET DERIVES (FR/1155-4495) [I11554495] **821, 2399**

AGRESTE. SERIES, LE BULLETIN DE FRANCHE-COMTE (FR/1148-5361) [I11485361] **47**

AGRESTE. SERIES, LE BULLETIN POITOU-CHARENTES (FR/1155-4088) [I11554088] **47**

AGRESTE. SERIES, LE BULLETIN TRIMESTRIEL LIMOUSIN (FR/1150-1537) [I11501537] **47**

AGRI-BOOK MAGAZINE (CN/0705-3878) [03739753] **47**

AGRI-BOOK MAGAZINE. TOP CROP MANAGER (CN) **47**

AGRI-EQUIPMENT & CHEMICAL (US) [14911999] **158**

AGRI FINANCE (US/0002-1164) [04948950] **47, 768**

●AGRI-FOOD AND FISHERIES PROJECT, THE (CN/0849-2360) [22928293] **2293, 47**

AGRI-FOOD BUSINESS IN P.E.I (CN/1182-9133) [23248980] **2326, 47**

●AGRI-FOOD PERSPECTIVES (CN/1193-8277) [26174643] **47**

AGRI-FOOD — Alphabetical Title Index

● AGRI-FOOD RESEARCH IN ONTARIO (CN/1192-7704) [27751289] **47**

AGRI-HOLLAND (NE) [03713404] **47**

AGRI HORTIQUE GENETICA (SW/0002-1172) [01478504] **2408**

AGRI MARKETING (US/0002-1180) [02251069] **47**

AGRI-NATURALIST (US/0882-9292) [11565446] **47**

AGRI NEWS (US/0745-3450) [03309543] **5694**

AGRI-NEWS (BILLINGS, MONT.) (US) [13378459] **5702**

AGRI-PLASTICS REPORT, THE (US/1073-1776) [14639323] 4454, **47**

AGRI-PRACTICE (US/0745-452X) [09181636] **47**

AGRI-PULSE (US/0884-7606) [12428726] **47**

AGRI-SERVICE INTERNATIONAL (BE/1021-4240) [I10214240] **47**

AGRI/STATS I. CD-ROM (US) 48, **150**

AGRI-TIMES NORTHWEST (US/0887-2910) [13173597] **48**

AGRI-TOPICS (BELTSVILLE, MD.) (US/1052-2255) [22218252] **48**

AGRI VIEW (US) **48**

AGRI-VIEW (US/1053-9603) [09599418] 48, **150**

AGRI-VIEW FARM WEEKLY (US) **48**

AGRIASIA / PRODUCED BY AGRICULTURAL INFORMATION BANK FOR ASIA (PH/0115-2440) [04218719] **48**

AGRIBIOLOGICAL RESEARCH (GW/0938-0337) [22254307] **48**

AGRIBUSINESS DECISION (AT/0311-0370) [03306838] 637, **48**

AGRIBUSINESS (NEW YORK, N.Y.) (US/0742-4477) [10340394] 637, **48**

AGRIBUSINESS NEWS FOR KENTUCKY (US/0899-1294) [18000443] 637, **48**

AGRIBUSINESS WORLDWIDE (US) [12411550] **48**

AGRIBUSINESS WORLDWIDE (US/0199-1671) [05689260] **48**

AGRICELL REPORT (US/0738-145X) [09530223] **48**

AGRICHEMICAL BRIEFING *CEASED.* (US/0743-8400) [10681987] 1020, **48**

AGRICOLA (US/1050-6810) [22296080] 48, **150**

AGRICOLA ; CRIS *CEASED.* (US/0897-3237) [21025347] **48**

AGRICOLA VERGEJ (SP) **48**

AGRICOLTURA 2000 *SUSPENDED.* (IT) **48**

AGRICOLTURA DELL VENEZIE (IT/0400-776X) [I0400776X] **48**

AGRICOLTURA E INNOVAZIONE (IT/0394-2805) [I03942805] **48**

AGRICOLTURA MEDITERRANEA (OSPEDALETTO) (IT/0394-0438) [17292101] **48**

AGRICOLTURA RICERCA *SUSPENDED.* (IT/0392-5609) [I03925609] **48**

AGRICOLTURE DELLE VENEZIE : ORGANO MENSILE DELLA CONSULTA REGIONALE PER L'AGRICOLTURA E LE FORESTE DELLE VENEZIE... (IT) [04579728] **48**

AGRICOMP (US) [10451966] 1170, **48**

AGRICONTACT ED. FRANCAISE (BE/0770-285X) [I0770285X] **48**

AGRICOTURA BIOLOGICA (IT) **48**

AGRICULTOR VENEZOLANO, EL (VE) [01478508] **48**

AGRICULTURA & COOPERATIVISMO (BL) [03644424] **48**

AGRICULTURA DE LAS AMERICAS (OVERLAND PARK, KANS.) (US/0002-1350) [11075257] **48**

AGRICULTURA EM SAO PAULO (BL/0044-6793) [02253035] **48**

AGRICULTURA (MADRID, SPAIN) (SP/0002-1334) [04589023] **49**

AGRICULTURA : PERSPECTIVAS - BRAZIL. COMISSAO DE FINANCIAMENTO DA PRODUCAO (BL) [03594022] **49**

AGRICULTURA SOCIALISTA *CEASED.* (RM) [04589131] **49**

AGRICULTURA TECNICA (CL/0365-2807) [05139410] **49**

AGRICULTURA TECNICA EN MEXICO (MX/0568-2517) [01478514] **49**

AGRICULTURA TROPICA ET SUBTROPICA (XR) [05841519] **49**

AGRICULTURA Y GANADERIA (CK) [05146845] **49**

AGRICULTURAL ABSTRACTS *CEASED.* (UK) [03297660] **49**

AGRICULTURAL AID TO DEVELOPING COUNTRIES (CN/0713-0465) [07990018] **2907**

AGRICULTURAL AND BIOLOGICAL CHEMISTRY *See* BIOSCIENCE, BIOTECHNOLOGY, AND BIOCHEMISTRY **3687**

● AGRICULTURAL & ENVIRONMENTAL BIOTECHNOLOGY ABSTRACTS (US/1063-1151) [25866542] 49, 3685, **150**

AGRICULTURAL AND FOREST METEOROLOGY (NE/0168-1923) [10550627] 49, 2373, **1419**

● AGRICULTURAL AND RESOURCE ECONOMICS REVIEW (USUS/1068-2805) [27556272] 1460, **49**

AGRICULTURAL AND VETERINARY CHEMICALS (UK/0567-431X) [01460501] 49, 5502, **960**

AGRICULTURAL & VETERINARY CHEMICALS ASSOCIATION OF AUSTRALIA *See* AVCA DIRECTORY : MEMBERS, OFFICERS, ACTIVITIES, AND SECRETARIAT **1021**

AGRICULTURAL AVIATION (WASHINGTON, D.C.) (US/0745-4864) [09140554] 49, **6**

AGRICULTURAL BANK OF TASMANIA. BOARD OF MANAGEMENT *See* ANNUAL REPORTS OF THE BOARD OF MANAGEMENT AND OF THE CLOSER SETTLEMENT BOARD FOR THE YEAR ENDED 30TH JUNE ... TO WHICH ARE APPENDED FINANCIAL STATEMENTS AND OTHER INFORMATION / THE AGRICULTURAL BANK OF TASMANIA **772**

AGRICULTURAL BANKER (II) [04968601] 49, **769**

AGRICULTURAL BOOKS AND INFORMATION (US) 2408, **49**

AGRICULTURAL BUILDING COST GUIDE (1987) (US/1046-7947) [15730527] **598**

AGRICULTURAL CENSUS (II) [06947596] 49, **150**

AGRICULTURAL COMMUNICATORS IN EDUCATION (U.S.) *See* DIRECTORY - AGRICULTURAL COMMUNICATORS IN EDUCATION (U.S.) **79**

AGRICULTURAL COOPERATIVE DEVELOPMENT INTERNATIONAL *See* ANNUAL REPORT / AGRICULTURAL COOPERATIVE DEVELOPMENT INTERNATIONAL **1541**

AGRICULTURAL CREDIT BIBLIOGRAPHY (IT) [06292270] **150**

AGRICULTURAL CREDIT CONDITIONS SURVEY (US/0737-948X) [03647394] 769, **49**

AGRICULTURAL CREDIT INDICATORS (PK) [25663920] 49, **769**

AGRICULTURAL CREDIT LETTER *See* WEBSTER AGRICULTURAL LETTER, THE **145**

AGRICULTURAL CREDIT LETTER, THE (US/0887-7521) [13377765] 49, **1460**

AGRICULTURAL DATA BOOK FOR THE FAR EAST AND OCEANIA, THE (US/0568-2606) [04124836] **49**

AGRICULTURAL ECONOMIC REPORT (WASHINGTON, D.C.) (US/0083-0445) [01188329] **49**

AGRICULTURAL ECONOMICS (NE/0169-5150) [13163627] 1460, **49**

AGRICULTURAL ECONOMICS AND MARKETS REPORT (RH) [07817760] **49**

AGRICULTURAL ECONOMICS BULLETIN (ARMIDALE, N.S.W.) (AT/0313-377X) [11279167] **49**

AGRICULTURAL ECONOMICS BULLETIN (SYDNEY) (AT/0811-4447) [11411321] **49**

AGRICULTURAL ECONOMICS DISCUSSION PAPER (AT) [09421323] 1460, **49**

AGRICULTURAL ECONOMICS REPORT (AT) [06114907] **49**

AGRICULTURAL ECONOMICS REPORT. AGRICULTURAL RESEARCH INSTITUTE (NICOSIA) (CY/0379-0827) [03431674] **49**

AGRICULTURAL ECONOMICS REPORT (MICHIGAN STATE UNIVERSITY. DEPT. OF AGRICULTURAL ECONOMICS) (US/0065-4442) [01681187] 1460, **49**

AGRICULTURAL ECONOMICS REPORT (NORTH DAKOTA AGRICULTURAL EXPERIMENT STATIONS (FARGO)) (US/0549-8295) [02252363] 1461, **49**

AGRICULTURAL ECONOMICS RESEARCH REPORT (MISSISSIPPI AGRICULTURAL AND FORESTRY EXPERIMENT STATION) (US) [11964833] 1461, **50**

AGRICULTURAL ECONOMICS STAFF PAPER SERIES (UNIVERSITY OF WISCONSIN--EXTENSION) (US) [11964897] 1461, **50**

AGRICULTURAL ECONOMICS STATISTICAL SERIES (US/0148-2920) [03282796] 50, **150**

AGRICULTURAL ECONOMICS TECHNICAL PUBLICATION (US/0883-0088) [09511265] 1461, **50**

AGRICULTURAL EDUCATION MAGAZINE, THE (US/0732-4677) [06108243] 1723, **50**

AGRICULTURAL ENGINEER, THE (UK/0308-5732) [03506458] 1964, **50**

AGRICULTURAL ENGINEERING (US/0002-1458) [01478533] 50, **1964**

AGRICULTURAL ENGINEERING ABSTRACTS (UK/0308-8863) [02563501] 50, 1964, **150**

AGRICULTURAL ENGINEERING AUSTRALIA (AT/0044-6807) [11901268] 1964, **50**

AGRICULTURAL ENGINEERING INDEX (US/0733-1770) [08564598] 50, **150**

AGRICULTURAL ENGINEERING SOCIETY (AUSTRALIA). NEWSLETTER *See* AGRICULTURAL ENGINEERING AUSTRALIA **50**

AGRICULTURAL ENGINEERING TODAY (II) [06411077] **1964**

AGRICULTURAL ENGINEERS ASSOCIATION *See* A.E.A. DIRECTORY OF TRACTORS AND AGRICULTURAL MACHINERY **158**

AGRICULTURAL FINANCE DATABOOK (WASHINGTON, D.C. 1989) (US/1070-6755) [27088910] **50**

AGRICULTURAL FINANCE REVIEW (US/0002-1466) [01478536] 50, **769**

AGRICULTURAL FINANCE STATISTICS (US/0091-3502) [01786630] 769, **726**

AGRICULTURAL GAZETTE OF TASMANIA (AT) [01478538] **50**

AGRICULTURAL HISTORY (US/0002-1482) [01478539] **50**

AGRICULTURAL HISTORY REVIEW, THE (UK/0002-1490) [01478540] **50**

AGRICULTURAL INFORMATION BULLETIN / PRODUCTION AND MARKETING INTELLIGENCE SERVICE, ANTIGUA & BARBUDA (AQ) [19805760] **50**

AGRICULTURAL INPUT PRICE INDEX DUBLIN (IE/0791-3346) [I07913346] **50**

AGRICULTURAL INPUT PRICES, PRICE INDICES AND AVAILABILITY IN ALBERTA (CN) [05930246] **50**

AGRICULTURAL ISSUES OVERVIEW / NATIONAL AGRICULTURAL LIBRARY, UNITED STATES DEPARTMENT OF AGRICULTURE (US) [10343951] **50**

AGRICULTURAL LAND RESERVE STATISTICS (CN/0713-1631) [07744072] 50, **150**

AGRICULTURAL LAND USE AND SELECTED INPUTS, WESTERN AUSTRALIA *See* SUMMARY OF CROPS, WESTERN AUSTRALIA **157**

AGRICULTURAL LARGEHOLDINGS (PRELIMINARY) (PP) [09822708] **50**

AGRICULTURAL LAW DIGEST (US/1051-2780) [21248634] 2928, **50**

AGRICULTURAL LIBRARIES INFORMATION NOTES (US/0095-2699) [01197824] **3188**

AGRICULTURAL LIBRARIES INFORMATION NOTES. SUPPLEMENT (US) [03882489] **3188**

AGRICULTURAL MANAGEMENT AND ECONOMICS (US) **50**

AGRICULTURAL MARKETING (II/0002-1555) [03431630] **161**

● AGRICULTURAL NEWS (HAMDEN, N.Y.) (US/1075-3354) [30018676] **50**

AGRICULTURAL NEWS LETTER (SRINAGAR, INDIA) (II) [10306728] **50**

AGRICULTURAL NEWSLETTER (SUDBURY) (CN/0228-2038) [06777756] **50**

AGRICULTURAL OUTLOOK (WASHINGTON, D.C. : 1975) (US/0099-1066) [02243568] 1461, **51**

AGRICULTURAL OUTPUT PRICE INDEX DUBLIN (IE/0791-3354) [I07913354] **51**

AGRICULTURAL POLICIES, MARKETS, AND TRADE (FR/1015-1540) [18540110] **51**

AGRICULTURAL POLICY AND ECONOMIC ISSUES (US/0895-9781) [14127325] **51**

AGRICULTURAL POLICY DISCUSSION PAPER (NZ/0112-0603) [I01120603] **51**

AGRICULTURAL POLICY PROCEEDINGS (NZ/0111-6339) [I01116339] **51**

AGRICULTURAL POLICY REPORTS (SERIES) (FR) [01761437] **51**

AGRICULTURAL PRICES ... SUMMARY / UNITED STATES DEPARTMENT OF AGRICULTURE, STATISTICAL REPORTING SERVICE, CROP REPORTING BOARD (US) [10941080] **51**

AGRICULTURAL PRICES (WASHINGTON, D.C.) (US/0002-1601) [02554222] **51**

AGRICULTURAL PROGRESS (UK/0065-4493) [03531839] **51**

Alphabetical Title Index — AGROFORESTERIA

AGRICULTURAL REAL ESTATE VALUES IN ALBERTA (CN/0701-7502) [03979729] 51, **4833**

AGRICULTURAL REFINANCE AND DEVELOPMENT CORPORATION *See* CIRCULARS OF THE AGRICULTURAL REFINANCE AND DEVELOPMENT CORPORATION FROM ... **75**

AGRICULTURAL REFINANCE AND DEVELOPMENT CORPORATION *See* ARDC NEWS **62**

AGRICULTURAL RESEARCH AND ADVISORY STATION, CONDOBOLIN *See* BIENNIAL REPORT / AGRICULTURAL RESEARCH AND ADVISORY STATION, CONDOBOLIN **66**

AGRICULTURAL RESEARCH AND ADVISORY STATION, GRAFTON *See* BIENNIAL RESEARCH REPORT / AGRICULTURAL RESEARCH AND ADVISORY STATION, GRAFTON **66**

AGRICULTURAL RESEARCH CENTRES (UK) [10335117] **51**

AGRICULTURAL RESEARCH COUNCIL OF NIGERIA *See* ANNUAL REPORT OF AGRICULTURAL RESEARCH COUNCIL OF NIGERIA **61**

AGRICULTURAL RESEARCH IN KANSAS (US/0749-2197) [08466520] **51**

AGRICULTURAL RESEARCH INSTITUTE OF ONTARIO *See* REPORT OF THE AGRICULTURAL RESEARCH INSTITUTE OF ONTARIO **126**

AGRICULTURAL RESEARCH INSTITUTE (U.S.) *See* PROCEEDINGS AND MINUTES, ANNUAL MEETING OF THE AGRICULTURAL RESEARCH INSTITUTE **121**

AGRICULTURAL RESEARCH JOURNAL OF KERALA (II/0002-1628) [01713600] **51**

AGRICULTURAL RESEARCH NEWS LETTER (II) [03531809] **51**

AGRICULTURAL RESEARCH ORGANIZATION. VOLCANI CENTER. DIVISION OF SCIENTIFIC PUBLICATIONS *See* SPECIAL PUBLICATION - AGRICULTURAL RESEARCH ORGANIZATION, THE VOLCANI CENTER **137**

AGRICULTURAL RESEARCH RESULTS. (SOUTHERN SERIES) (US/0193-2853) [08055741] **51**

AGRICULTURAL RESEARCH REVIEW (UA/0374-5252) [02386952] **51**

AGRICULTURAL RESEARCH (WASHINGTON) (US/0002-161X) [01478561] **51**

AGRICULTURAL REVIEW FOR EUROPE (US) [13167209] **51**

AGRICULTURAL REVIEWS (II/0253-1496) [08521486] **51**

AGRICULTURAL REVIEWS AND MANUALS (NORTHEASTERN SERIES) (US/0193-3752) [05186524] **52**

AGRICULTURAL REVIEWS AND MANUALS. WESTERN SERIES (US/0193-3760) [04588115] **52**

AGRICULTURAL SCIENCE DIGEST (AGRICULTURAL RESEARCH COMMUNICATION CENTER.) (II/0253-150X) [08472451] **161**

●AGRICULTURAL SCIENCE IN FINLAND (FI/0789-600X) [25742064] **52**

AGRICULTURAL SCIENCE IN THE NETHERLANDS (NE) [06519410] **52**

AGRICULTURAL SCIENCE. MELBOURNE (AT/1030-4614) [26279609] **52**

AGRICULTURAL SITUATION AND OUTLOOK (US) [02368022] **52**

AGRICULTURAL SITUATION IN INDIA (II/0002-1679) [01478575] **52**

AGRICULTURAL SITUATION IN THE COMMUNITY; REPORT, THE (BE) [04452980] **52**

AGRICULTURAL SITUATION IN THE PEOPLE'S REPUBLIC OF CHINA AND OTHER COMMUNIST ASIAN COUNTRIES, THE (US/0360-3393) [02441091] **52**

AGRICULTURAL SITUATION IN THE SOVIET UNION, THE (US/0360-4098) [02244316] **52**

AGRICULTURAL SOCIETIES NEWSLETTER (CN/0228-1090) [06777649] **52**

AGRICULTURAL SOCIETY OF TRINIDAD & TOBAGO *See* JOURNAL OF THE AGRICULTURAL SOCIETY OF TRINIDAD & TOBAGO **101**

AGRICULTURAL STATISTICA (DES MOINES, IOWA) (US) [14126014] **52**

AGRICULTURAL STATISTICAL BULLETIN (TZ) [25679818] **52**

AGRICULTURAL STATISTICS (LU) [02326065] 52, **150**

AGRICULTURAL STATISTICS AND REVIEW OF AGRICULTURE (CN/0715-1438) [03265043] 52, **150**

AGRICULTURAL STATISTICS FOR ARKANSAS (US) [03733038] 52, **150**

AGRICULTURAL STATISTICS FOR ONTARIO (CN/0568-2894) [03424681] 52, **150**

AGRICULTURAL STATISTICS, JUNE ..., LAND UTILISATION AND NUMBERS OF LIVESTOCK, REGIONAL ANALYSIS (IE/0791-3524) [107913524] **52**

AGRICULTURAL STATISTICS OF SABAH (MY) [01783775] **150**

AGRICULTURAL STATISTICS (WASHINGTON, D.C.) (US/0082-9714) [01773189] **150**

AGRICULTURAL SUPPLY INDUSTRY (UK/0140-4822) [04697007] **158**

AGRICULTURAL SYSTEMS (UK/0308-521X) [02191472] **52**

AGRICULTURAL TRADE HIGHLIGHTS (US) [18824048] 52, **821**

AGRICULTURAL TRENDS (BRISBANE, QLD.) (AT/0705-8101) [14407211] **52**

AGRICULTURAL WATER MANAGEMENT (NE/0378-3774) [02953868] **52**

AGRICULTURAL WORK FORCE OF ... (US) [22939334] 1642, **53**

AGRICULTURAL ZOOLOGY REVIEWS (UK/0269-0543) [15074804] 5574, **53**

AGRICULTURE ACROSS MICHIGAN (US/0194-4452) [04656026] **53**

AGRICULTURE AFRICAINE, L' (FR) [07009959] **53**

AGRICULTURE ALGERIENNE. A64 (FR) **53**

AGRICULTURE AND AGRO-INDUSTRIES JOURNAL (II/0002-1725) [01478578] **53**

●AGRICULTURE & EQUIPMENT INTERNATIONAL (UK) [27924219] **53**

AGRICULTURE & FOOD (US/0364-7994) [02254016] 2326, **53**

AGRICULTURE AND FORESTRY BULLETIN *SUSPENDED.* (CN/0705-3983) [03268883] 2373, **53**

AGRICULTURE & HUMAN RESOURCE SERIES AGRICULTURE. CD-ROM (US) **53**

AGRICULTURE AND HUMAN VALUES (US/0889-048X) [10794933] **53**

AGRICULTURE AND RESOURCES QUARTERLY *See* AUSTRALIAN COMMODITIES **64**

AGRICULTURE & RESOURCES QUARTERLY (AT/1032-9722) [19836027] 2185, **53**

AGRICULTURE CANADA ANNUAL REPORT (CN/1200-1627) [24914758] **53**

AGRICULTURE DE L'AVENIR, L' (CN/0821-2732) [09822919] **53**

AGRICULTURE DECISIONS (US/0002-1741) [01768305] **53**

AGRICULTURE ECONOMIC STATISTICS (CN/0833-6210) [16517478] **53**

AGRICULTURE, ECOSYSTEMS & ENVIRONMENT (NE/0167-8809) [09506512] **53**

AGRICULTURE ET COOPERATION *CEASED.* (FR/1181-955X) **53**

AGRICULTURE ET DEVELOPPEMENT (FR) **53**

AGRICULTURE, FISHERIES, FOOD (UK) [02723518] 2293, 2326, **53**

AGRICULTURE, FORESTRY, AND FISHERIES FINANCE CORPORATION : REPORT (JA) [08340725] 2373, **54**

AGRICULTURE HANDBOOK (UNITED STATES. DEPT. OF AGRICULTURE) (US/0065-4612) [01573294] **53**

AGRICULTURE IN IDAHO (US/0279-1412) [07586499] **54**

AGRICULTURE IN NORTHERN IRELAND (1986) (IE) [15116062] **54**

AGRICULTURE INFORMATION BULLETIN (US/0065-4639) [01576392] **54**

AGRICULTURE INTERNATIONAL (UK/0269-2457) [13097849] **54**

AGRICULTURE, KENTUCKY'S PRIDE (US/0898-9303) [17955690] **54**

AGRICULTURE MATERIALS IN LIBRARIES (US/0895-5506) [16670084] 54, **3188**

AGRICULTURE (MONTREAL) (CN/0002-1687) [02231246] **54**

AGRICULTURE NORTH (CN/0712-7375) [09502119] **54**

AGRICULTURE (PARIS) *See* AGRO MAGAZINE PARIS **54**

AGRICULTURE PARIS (FR/0002-1709) [100021709] **54**

AGRICULTURE RESEARCH DIGEST (US) [24788454] **54**

AGRICULTURE REVIEW (LEXINGTON, MASS.) (US/0733-1517) [08512364] **54**

AGRICULTURE (SAINT LOUIS, MO.) (US) [10042748] **54**

AGRICULTURE STATISTICS. CD-ROM (US) **54**

AGRICULTURE TEACHERS DIRECTORY (US) [03562602] 1723, **54**

AGRICULTURE TODAY (US/0895-2442) [16520155] **54**

AGRICULTURE, WESTERN AUSTRALIA (AT) [08188729] **54**

AGRICULTURES ACTUALITE (FR/0995-5178) [21664513] **161**

AGRIDATA NETWORK REVIEW (US/0888-1804) [13546994] **54**

AGRIGIORNALE DEL COMMERCIO (IT/0394-5537) [03945537] **54**

AGRILOPER WAGENINGEN *CEASED.* (NE/0925-2762) [109252762] **54**

AGRINDEX (IT/0254-8801) [02240017] 54, **150**

AGRIPROMO ABIDJAN (IV/1018-8568) [I10188568] **2813**

AGRIS [CD-ROM] (US) [22211729] **54**

AGRISCIENCE (OTTAWA) (CN/0840-8289) [20114042] **54**

AGRISCIENTIA (AG) [27636725] **54**

AGRISCOPE : REGARDS SUR L'AGRICULTURE *SUSPENDED.* (FR/0751-7378) [12026331] **54**

AGRISEARCH (CARBONDALE, ILL.) (US) [10453572] **54**

●AGRISEARCH [COMPUTER FILE] : CRIS, SIS-SPAAR, ICAR, ARRIP, AGREP (US) [27098164] **54**

AGRITALK (AT) 54, **1887**

AGRITRADE (UK) [04054116] **54**

AGRITROP [ENGLSIH ED.] (FR) [03666299] **54**

AGRIVITA (IO/0126-0537) [07377600] **55**

AGRIWEEK (CN/0228-5584) [08368419] **199**

AGRO BONUS (AU) **2373**

AGRO-CHEMICALS NEWS IN BRIEF (TH) [15026049] 4243, **55**

AGRO-CIENCIA / FACULTAD DE CIENCIAS AGROPECUARIAS Y FORESTALES, UNIVERSIDAD DE CONCEPCION (CL/0716-1689) [17854223] **55**

AGRO-ENVIRONMENTAL PROTECTION (CH/1000-0267) [24341104] 2159, **55**

AGRO-INDUSTRY HI-TECH (IT/1120-6012) [25651015] 3685, **55**

AGRO MAGAZINE PARIS (FR/1166-7729) [I11667729] 1461, **55**

AGRO PERFORMANCES (FR/0989-2648) [I09892648] **55**

AGRO-SINTESIS (MX) [02759656] **55**

AGRO SUR (CL/0304-8802) [02824680] **55**

AGROANALYSIS (BL/0100-4298) [01004298] **55**

AGROARD, GITUTYUN EV ARTADRUTYUN (AI) [19654409] **55**

AGROBOREALIS (US/0002-1822) [02251071] **55**

AGROBOTANIKAI INTEZET *See* INDEX SEMINUM **513**

AGROCHEMIA (PL/0002-1849) [03974498] **55**

AGROCHEMIA (BRATISLAVA) (XO/0002-1830) [03759913] **55**

AGROCHEMICAL SERVICE (UK) 960, **55**

AGROCHEMICALS HANDBOOK (UK) 55, **960**

AGROCHEMICALS HANDBOOK, THE *See* PESTICIDE MANUAL, THE **119**

AGROCHEMICALS JAPAN (JA) **162**

AGROCHIMICA (IT/0002-1857) [01478588] 960, **55**

AGROCIENCIA (MX/0568-3025) [01478589] **55**

AGROCIENCIA. SERIE CIENCIA ANIMAL (MX/0188-3038) [I01883038] **55**

AGROCIENCIA. SERIE FITOCIENCIA (MX/0188-302X) [I0188302X] 498, **55**

AGROCIENCIA. SERIE MATEMATICAS APLICADAS, ESTADISTICA Y COMPUTACION (MX/0188-3054) [I01883054] **3491**

AGROCIENCIA. SERIE PROTECCION VEGETAL (MX/0188-3046) [I01883046] **55**

AGROCIENCIA. SERIE RECURSOS NATURALES RENOVABLES (MX/0188-3062) [I01883062] **55**

AGROCIENCIA. SERIE SOCIOECONOMIA (MX/0188-3070) [I01883070] **1461**

AGROCIENCIA. SERIE SUELO, AGUA Y CLIMA (MX/0188-3089) [I01883089] **55**

●AGROEKONOMIKA (XO) [26605988] **55**

AGROEUROPA (SP) **55**

AGROFORESTERIA (TURRIALBA) (CR/1019-1984) [26152400] **55**

AGROFORESTRY — Alphabetical Title Index

AGROFORESTRY ABSTRACTS (UK/0952-1453) [19358855] 55, 2373, **2398**

AGROFORESTRY SYSTEMS (NE/0167-4366) [08841716] 55, 225, **2211**

AGROFORESTRY TODAY (KE/0255-8173) [20004604] 2373, **55**

AGROHEMIJA (YU/0002-1865) [03760387] **56**

AGROHIMIJA (RU/0002-1881) [01606871] 960, **56**

AGROKEMIA ES TALAJTAN (HU/0002-1873) [04770050] 960, **56**

AGRONOMIA COLOMBIANA (CK/0120-9965) [16778318] **56**

AGRONOMIA COSTARRICENSE (CR/0377-9424) [03408090] **56**

AGRONOMIA LUSITANA (PO/0002-1911) [03511341] **56**

AGRONOMIA SULRIOGRANDENSE (BL/0400-8111) [04771969] **56**

AGRONOMIA TROPICAL (VE/0002-192X) [01478596] **56**

AGRONOMIE (FR/0249-5627) [07472823] **56**

AGRONOMIE TROPICALE, L' *CEASED.* (FR/0002-1946) [02257046] **162**

AGRONOMIST, THE (US) [11081691] **56**

AGRONOMY (US/0065-4663) [01478599] **56**

AGRONOMY ABSTRACTS (MADISON, WIS.) (US/0375-5495) [01644021] **56**

AGRONOMY AND SOILS DEPARTMENTAL SERIES (US) [08102214] 162, **56**

AGRONOMY DEPARTMENT SERIES (US/0886-4381) [07217280] **56**

AGRONOMY JOURNAL (US/0002-1962) [01578829] **162**

AGRONOMY NEWS (US/0568-3106) [01777624] **162**

AGRONOMY NEWS LETTER (II) [11869284] **56**

AGRONOMY NOTES / UNIVERSITY OF KENTUCKY, COLLEGE OF AGRICULTURE, DEPARTMENT OF AGRONOMY (US/1057-1698) [14372009] **162**

AGRONOMY RESEARCH REPORT (US/0886-4403) [02810394] **56**

AGRONOMY RESEARCH REPORT AG (US/0886-4373) [02628257] **56**

AGRONOMY SOCIETY OF NEW ZEALAND See PROCEEDINGS ... ANNUAL CONFERENCE / AGRONOMY SOCIETY OF NEW ZEALAND **121**

AGROPECUARIA CATARINENSE (BL/0103-0779) [18378010] **56**

AGROPECUARIA : PRECOS, MEDIOS E INDICES DE ARRENDAMENTOS, VENDAS DE TERRAS, SALARIOS, SERVICOS (BL) [03590566] **56**

AGROPLANTAE (SA) [08445861] 2408, **56**

AGROPROMYSHLENNYI KOMPLEKS KAZAKHSTANA (KZ/0235-2958) [17021430] 56, **2326**

AGROPUR NOUVELLES (CN/1182-2015) [22391607] **56**

AGROSELEKT. REIHE 1, LANDTECHNIK *CEASED.* (GE/0233-2655) [12227813] **56**

AGROSELEKT. REIHE 3, TIERPRODUKTION *CEASED.* (GW/0233-2752) [12207685] **204**

AGROSELEKT. REIHE 4, VETERINARMEDIZIN *CEASED.* (GW/0233-2809) [12740414] **5502**

AGROTECHNOLOGY TRANSFER (US/0883-8631) [12247809] **57**

AGROTECNIA DE CUBA (CU/0568-3114) [01478604] **57**

AGROTIKE (ATHENS, GREECE, : 1983) (GR) [10837723] **57**

AGROTIKE TRAPEZA See AGROTIKE (ATHENS, GREECE, : 1983) **57**

AGROTROPICA (BL/0103-3816) [23117454] **57**

AGROW (UK/0268-313X) [21286930] **57**

AGRUPACION SINDICAL NACIONAL DE EMPRESAS DE FINANCIACION See CENSO - AGRUPACION SINDICAL NACIONAL DE EMPRESAS DE FINANCIACION **782**

AGSA NEWSLETTER (AT/1033-8624) [I0338624] **542**

AGSCENE (US/0279-666X) [03937539] **57**

●AGSO JOURNAL OF AUSTRALIAN GEOLOGY & GEOPHYSICS (AT/1320-1271) [28472332] 1402, **1365**

AGTE QADAMU PABULIKESHANI (PK) [02239403] **4625**

AGUA - TECNOLOGIA Y TRATAMIENTO (AG) [04947933] **5529**

AGUDAH HA-YISREELIT LE-MADAE HA-GARIN See TRANSACTIONS - THE ISRAEL NUCLEAR SOCIETY, THE ISRAEL HEALTH PHYSICS SOCIETY, RADIATION RESEARCH SOCIETY OF ISRAEL, THE ISRAEL SOCIETY OF MEDICAL PHYSICS, THE ISRAEL SOCIETY OF NUCLEAR MEDICINE **4451**

AGUPTEM : ENERGIEWIRTSCHAFT (GW) [05764219] **1931**

AGVENTURE (US/0887-9133) [13450759] **57**

AGWEEK (US/0884-6162) [12401135] **57**

AGYPTEN, FORSCHUNGSPOLITIK UND FORSCHUNGSPRAXIS / BUNDESSTELLE FUER AUSSENHANDELSINFORMATION (GW) [11508299] **4462**

AGYPTEN, WIRTSCHAFTLICHE ENTWICKLUNG / BUNDESSTELLE FUER AUSSENHANDELSINFORMATION (GW) [11580601] **1461**

AGYPTEN, WIRTSCHAFTSDATEN UND WIRTSCHAFTSDOKUMENTATION / BUNDESSTELLE FUR AUSSENHANDELSINFORMATION (GW) [09962132] **1461**

AGYPTISCHE URKUNDEN AUS DEN STAATLICHEN MUSEEN BERLIN: GRIECHISCHE URKUNDEN (GW) [04032020] **253**

AHA (US/8755-500X) [10782857] **312**

'AHA' ILONO (US/0098-9738) [02239902] **3138**

AHA NEWS (CHICAGO, ILL.) (US/0891-6608) [14948216] **3775**

AHA PAMPHLETS (US/0065-857X) [03346537] **2717**

AHA!!!--THE PREACHER'S RESEARCH ASSISTANT (CN/1183-2118) [25066674] **4933**

AHEPAN (US/0746-133X) [09787799] **1723**

AHFAD JOURNAL, THE (SJ/0255-4070) [12747640] **5550**

AHFS DRUG INFORMATION (US/1063-8792) [19752302] **4290**

AHI QUARTERLY (US) [23438004] **5502**

AHMADIYYA GAZETTE (CN/0229-5644) [08405143] **5041**

AHMADU BELLO UNIVERSITY. DEPT. OF GEOLOGY See BULLETIN - DEPARTMENT OF GEOLOGY, AHMADU BELLO UNIVERSITY **1369**

AHMADU BELLO UNIVERSITY. POST GRADUATE SCHOOL See POSTGRADUATE PROSPECTUS / POST GRADUATE SCHOOL, AHMADU BELLO UNIVERSITY **1842**

AHMADU BELLO UNIVERSITY, ZARIA, NIGERIA. INSTITUTE FOR AGRICULTURAL RESEARCH AND SPECIAL SERVICES See REPORT TO THE BOARD OF GOVERNORS ON THE INSTITUTE'S WORK **184**

AHMEDABAD TEXTILE INDUSTRY'S RESEARCH ASSOCIATION See PROCEEDINGS OF THE TECHNOLOGICAL CONFERENCE **5355**

AHMEDABAD TEXTILE MILLS' ASSOCIATION See ANNUAL REPORT - AHMEDABAD TEXTILE MILL'S ASSOCIATION **5347**

AHORA (UK/0961-8481) [24457426] **3262**

AHORA (EL PASO, TEX.) (US/0731-2679) [08147404] **5054**

AHORRO (SP) [06472565] **769**

AHOY! (NEW YORK, N.Y.) *CEASED.* (US/8750-4383) [11395055] **1170**

AI ALERT *CEASED.* (US/0887-6592) [13388246] **1210**

AI & SOCIETY (GW/0951-5666) [14769084] **1210**

AI APPLICATIONS (US/1051-8266) [22135311] **1210**

AI COMMUNICATIONS (NE/0921-7126) [23379025] **1210**

AI CORPORATE DIRECTORY (US) **1210**

AI DIRECTORY (US/1050-7965) [21177472] **1210**

AI EXPERT (US/0888-3785) [13552690] **1210**

AI HOC VA TRUNG HOC CHUYEN NGHIEP (VM) [02240637] **1723**

AI MAGAZINE (US/0738-4602) [08838993] **1211**

AI REVIEW OF PRODUCTS, SERVICES, AND RESEARCH (US/1054-8645) [20715411] **1964**

AI SOURCEBOOK: THE AI TRENDS ANNUAL REPORT (US) 1227, 1250, **1211**

AI TODAY (US/0893-6552) [15626335] **1211**

AI TRENDS (MONTHLY) (US/8756-7687) [11652018] **1211**

AI WATCH (UK/1354-2001) **1211**

AIA BULLETIN (UK/0309-0051) [13219137] **253**

AIA DIRECTORY OF HELIPORTS & HELISTOPS IN THE UNITED STATES, CANADA, PUERTO RICO, AND DIRECTORY OF HOSPITAL HELIPORTS & HELISTOPS (US/0882-3367) [11361583] **6**

AIAA JOURNAL (US/0001-1452) [00809393] **6**

AIAA PAPER (US/0146-3705) [02924186] **6**

AIAA ROSTER (US/0065-8693) [01480016] **6**

AIAA STUDENT JOURNAL (US/0001-1460) [00807527] **6**

AIARCHITECT (US) **287**

AIAS OCCASIONAL PUBLICATION (AT/0728-859X) [I0728859X] **57**

AIBC BULLETIN (US/1040-6018) [18474576] **1419**

AIBDA ACTUALIDADES (CR) [08587615] 57, **3188**

AIC INVESTMENT BULLETIN / AIC INVESTMENT ADVISORS, INC (US) [13305392] **890**

AIC NEWS : NEWSLETTER OF THE AMERICAN INSTITUTE FOR CONSERVATION OF HISTORIC AND ARTISTIC WORKS (US/1060-3247) [24926703] **335**

AIC SERIES (US/1051-9963) [22166726] **2293**

AICARC (SZ) [12098952] **335**

AICARC BULLETIN (SW/0347-4240) [02304033] **335**

AICCM BULLETIN (AT) **2841**

AICHE APPLICATIONS SOFTWARE SURVEY FOR PERSONAL COMPUTERS *CEASED.* (US/0743-0183) [10491232] 2007, **1284**

AICHE EQUIPMENT TESTING PROCEDURE (US/0569-5473) [03466052] **2007**

AICHE JOURNAL (US/0001-1541) [01460435] **2007**

AICHE MONOGRAPH SERIES (US/0065-8804) [01480042] **2007**

AICHE SYMPOSIUM SERIES (US/0065-8812) [01480041] **2007**

AICHE WORKSHOP SERIES (US/0569-5457) [02181209] **2007**

AICHI-GAKUIN DAIGAKU SHIGAKKAI-SHI (JA/0044-6912) [01124019] **1315**

AICHI IKA DAIGAKU IGAKKAI See AICHI IKA DAIGAKU IGAKKAI ZASSHI **3547**

AICHI IKA DAIGAKU IGAKKAI ZASSHI (JA/0301-0902) [05849948] **3547**

AICHI, JAPAN. DAI 3-JI CHINO KEIKAKU KENKYUJO (JAPAN) See AICHI REPOTO **1544**

AICHI, JAPAN. RODOBU See AICHI-KEN RODO KEIZAI NO BUNSEKI **1642**

AICHI-KEN CHIIKI BOSAI KEIKAKU. FUZOKU SHIRYO (JA) [10920563] **5271**

AICHI-KEN EISEI KENKYUSHOHO (JA/0515-7803) [I05157803] **4764**

AICHI-KEN (JAPAN). RODO KEIZAI CHOSASHITSU See CHUSHO KIGYO NO CHINGIN JIJO **1659**

AICHI-KEN KOGAI CHOSA SENTA See AICHI-KEN KOGAI CHOSA SENTA SHOHO **2223**

AICHI-KEN KOGAI CHOSA SENTA SHOHO (JA) [01797140] **2223**

AICHI-KEN KOGYO GIJUTSU SENTA HOKOKU (JA/0286-262X) [10295246] **5081**

AICHI-KEN KYODO SHIRYO SOGO MOKUROKU (JA) [01790121] **407**

AICHI-KEN NOGYO SOGO SHIKENJO KEKNYU HOKOKU (JA/0388-7995) [09965564] **57**

AICHI-KEN RODO KEIZAI NO BUNSEKI (JA) [02667441] **1642**

AICHI-KEN TOKONAME YOGYO GIJUTSU SENTA HOKOKU (JA/0385-6860) [10244216] **2585**

AICHI KENRITSU DAIGAKU. BUNGAKUBU. KOKUBUNGAKUKA See AICHI KENRITSU DAIGAKU BUNGAKUBU RON SHU : KOKUBUNGAKUKA HEN **3358**

AICHI KENRITSU DAIGAKU BUNGAKUBU RON SHU : KOKUBUNGAKUKA HEN (JA) [01790196] **3358**

AICHI KENRITSU KANGO TANKI DAIGAKU See AICHI KENRITSU KANGO TANKI DAIGAKU ZASSHI **3850**

AICHI KENRITSU KANGO TANKI DAIGAKU ZASSHI (JA) [01790321] **3850**

AICHI KOGYO DAIGAKU KENKYU HOKOKU, B, SENMON KANKEI RONBUNSHU (JA/0387-0812) [10238502] **5081**

AICHI KYOIKU DAIGAKU KENKYU HOKOKU. GEIJUTSU, HOKEN TAIIKU, KASEI, GIJUTSU KAGAKU (JA/0388-7367) [10863034] **5081**

AICHI KYOIKU DAIGAKU KENKYU HOKOKU. SOSAKU HEN (JA/0289-0569) [10858028] **312**

AICHI KYOIKU DAIGAKU KYOKA KYOIKU SENTA KENKYU HOKOKU (JA) [10074644] **1723**

AICHI REPOTO (JA) [02242991] **1544**

AICPA PROFESSIONAL STANDARDS (US) [02576717] **738**

AICPA TECHNICAL PRACTICE AIDS (US) [04357015] **738**

AICPA'S UNIFORM CPA EXAM, THE (US/1047-5079) [18654184] **738**

AID BULLETIN (KENT, OHIO) *CEASED.* (US/0275-6692) [07193857] **5238**

AID-FINANCED UNIVERSITY CONTRACTS *See* AID-FINANCED UNIVERSITY CONTRACTS AND GRANTS ACTIVE DURING THE PERIOD ... **1807**

AID-FINANCED UNIVERSITY CONTRACTS AND GRANTS ACTIVE DURING THE PERIOD ... (US) [12388467] **1807**

AID FOR EDUCATION REPORT (US/1058-1324) [24225420] **1723**

AID RESEARCH AND DEVELOPMENT ABSTRACTS ARDA (US) 2913, **2907**

AID TO FAMILIES WITH DEPENDENT CHILDREN (US) [04946609] **5271**

AIDA PARKER NEWSLETTER (SA) **4515**

AIDE A L'IMPLANTATION MONASTIQUE *See* BULLETIN DE L'A.I.M **4940**

●AIDE-SOIGNANTE, L' (FR) [27073744] **3850**

AIDJEX BULLETIN (US/0091-3480) [02629277] **1412**

AIDS (GW) [13554972] **3663**

AIDS *CEASED.* (US/0894-931X) [15815344] **3663**

●AIDS ABSTRACTS (ATLANTA, GA.) (US/1066-1107) [26863227] 3663, 3711, **3654**

●AIDS ABSTRACTS : INTERNATIONAL LITERATURE ON ACQUIRED IMMUNODEFICIENCY SYNDROME AND RELATED RETROVIRUSES (UK/0968-5480) [27447840] **3663**

AIDS ACTION (UK/0953-0096) [17826594] **3663**

AIDS ALERT *CEASED.* (US/0887-0292) [13013286] 3711, **3663**

AIDS ANALYSIS AFRICA (SA/1016-4731) [24014685] **3663**

AIDS & PUBLIC POLICY JOURNAL (US/0887-3852) [13205125] 4764, **3663**

AIDS AND RESEARCH TOOLS IN ANCIENT NEAR EASTERN STUDIES (US/0732-6505) [05967969] **2767**

AIDS & SOCIETY (US/1055-0380) [23024971] 3711, **3663**

AIDS & TB ABSTRACTS FROM CONFERENCE PROCEEDINGS *See* AIDS & TB WEEKLY ABSTRACTS FROM CONFERENCE PROCEEDINGS **3663**

AIDS & TB ARTICLE SUMMARIES (US) 3711, **3663**

AIDS & TB WEEKLY ABSTRACTS FROM CONFERENCE PROCEEDINGS (US) 3711, **3663**

●AIDS & TB WEEKLY ARTICLE SUMMARIES (US/1074-2883) [29665964] **3547**

●AIDS & TB WEEKLY ARTICLE SUMMARIES (US) 3711, **3663**

AIDS ARTICLE SUMMARIES (US/1068-6282) [27732429] 3711, **3663**

AIDS BIBLIOGRAPHY (US/1052-0287) [18035434] **3654**

AIDS BULLETIN TYGERBERG (SA/1019-8334) [I10198334] **3711**

AIDS CABISCO NEWS (US/0895-9765) [16878814] **3663**

AIDS CARE (UK/0954-0121) [19937310] **3663**

AIDS CASES, STATE OF NEW JERSEY, AS OF ... (US) [14972133] **3663**

AIDS CLINICAL CARE (US/1043-1543) [19329833] 3663, **3711**

AIDS CLINICAL DIGEST *CEASED.* (US/0899-0263) [17974370] **3663**

AIDS CLINICAL REVIEW (US/1045-2877) [19528174] **3663**

AIDS CRISIS, THE (US/0893-7613) [15639548] 4764, **3663**

●AIDS DIRECTORY, THE (US/1065-6162) [26649674] 3711, **3663**

AIDS EDUCATION (US/0895-8882) [16851408] 4764, **3663**

AIDS EDUCATION AND PREVENTION (US/0899-9546) [18277211] **4764**

AIDS EPIDEMIOLOGICAL AND CLINICAL STUDIES (US) 3733, **3711**

AIDS-FORSCHUNG (GW/0179-3098) [14380098] **3663**

AIDS HEALTH PROMOTION, EXCHANGE (NE/1013-7785) [18727504] 4764, 3711, **3663**

AIDS/HIV RECORD *CEASED.* (US/0899-742X) [18202551] 3711, **3663**

AIDS/HIV TREATMENT DIRECTORY (US/1057-5065) [22066451] **3663**

AIDS INFORMATION (UK/0953-1580) [18127867] **3664**

AIDS INFORMATION EXCHANGE (US/0891-7426) [13104386] **4764**

AIDS INFORMATION SOURCEBOOK *CEASED.* (US/1044-2138) [20101141] **3664**

AIDS LAW AND LITIGATION REPORTER (US) 2928, **3664**

AIDS LAW REPORTER, THE *CEASED.* (US/0896-6370) [16841308] 3664, **2928**

AIDS LETTER, THE (UK/0952-7427) [16689374] **3664**

AIDS LITERATURE & NEWS REVIEW (US/0893-1526) [15365898] 4764, **3664**

AIDS LITIGATION REPORTER (US/0899-1464) [17663992] 3664, **3739**

AIDS (LONDON) (UK/0269-9370) [16016361] **3664**

AIDS NEWS REPORTER, THE (US/0899-6733) [18180844] **3664**

AIDS NEWSLETTER (LONDON, ENGLAND) (UK/0268-8360) [16806858] 3711, **3664**

AIDS PATIENT CARE (US/0893-5068) [15565535] **3664**

AIDS (PHOENIX, ARIZ.) *CEASED.* (US/0899-9449) [18271464] **3664**

AIDS POLICY & LAW (US/0887-1493) [13108642] 3664, **2928**

AIDS READER, THE (US/1053-0894) [22448511] 3711, **3664**

AIDS REFERENCE AND RESEARCH COLLECTION (US) 4764, **3664**

AIDS REPORT (WESTPORT, CONN.) (US/0893-5084) [15554595] **3664**

AIDS RESEARCH AND HUMAN RETROVIRUSES (US/0889-2229) [13812822] **3664**

AIDS RESEARCH REVIEWS (US/1056-1080) [23466927] 3711, **3664**

AIDS SCAN *CEASED.* (US/1040-6778) [20213250] **3664**

AIDS SURVEILLANCE QUARTERLY UPDATE FOR CASES REPORTED THROUGH... (US) [24061850] **4764**

●AIDS TARGETED INFORMATION (US/1067-0718) [27129009] **3664**

AIDS TARGETED INFORMATION NEWSLETTER (US/0892-0125) [15060276] **3664**

AIDS THERAPIES (US) **3664**

AIDS TO NAVIGATION BULLETIN / DEPARTMENT OF TRANSPORTATION, COAST GUARD (US) [04573295] **4174**

AIDS TREATMENT NEWS (US/1052-4207) [15869175] 3711, **3664**

AIDS UPDATE (ALBANY, N.Y.) *CEASED.* (US/1053-9093) [17449873] 4764, **3664**

AIDS UPDATE (RESTON, VA.) *CEASED.* (US/1042-4784) [18115014] **3665**

AIDS UPDATES (US/1040-6247) [18473802] 3711, **3665**

AIDS WATCH (US) 3665, **3711**

AIDS WATCH *CEASED.* (UK) [17759038] **3665**

AIDS WEEKLY (US/1069-1456) [23259675] 3711, **3665**

AIDS WIESBADEN *CEASED.* (GW/0934-1129) [I09341129] 3712, **3665**

AIDS (WYLIE, TEX.) (US) [18804641] **3665**

AIDSMONTHLY (BUSINESS AND FINANCE ED.) (US/1059-8847) [24801268] 4764, **5271**

AIDSMONTHLY (EDUCATION ED.) (US/1059-8839) [24801284] **1723**

AIDSMONTHLY (GOVERNMENT ED.) (US/1059-8855) [24801303] 3712, **3665**

AIDSMONTHLY (HEALTHCARE ED.) (US/1059-8820) [24801239] 3712, **3665**

AIDSMONTHLY (INTERNATIONAL ED.) (US/1059-8901) [24801477] 3712, **3665**

AIDSMONTHLY (JOURNAL ED.) (US/1059-8812) [24801192] 3712, **3665**

AIDSMONTHLY (LEGAL ED.) *CEASED.* (US/1059-8871) [24801390] 2929, 3712, **3665**

AIDSMONTHLY (PSYCHOSOCIAL ED.) (US/1059-8863) [24801355] 3712, **3665**

AIDSMONTHLY (RESEARCH ED.) (US/1059-8898) [24801451] 3712, **3665**

AIDSMONTHLY (SERVICE ORGANIZATION ED.) (US/1059-891X) [24801511] 3712, **3665**

AIDSMONTHLY (TREATMENT ED.) (US/1059-8804) [24801123] 3712, **3665**

AIDSMONTHLY (WORKPLACE ED.) (US/1059-888X) [24801418] 3712, **3665**

AIFLD BRIEFS *See* AIFLD OUTLOOK : A PUBLICATION OF THE AMERICAN INSTITUTE FOR FREE LABOR DEVELOPMENT **1643**

●AIFLD OUTLOOK : A PUBLICATION OF THE AMERICAN INSTITUTE FOR FREE LABOR DEVELOPMENT (US) [26972234] **1643**

AIFS ACADEMIC YEAR & SUMMER PROGRAMS (US) [12322940] **1723**

AIGA JOURNAL OF GRAPHIC DESIGN (US/0736-5322) [08962753] **376**

AIIM BUYING GUIDE : THE OFFICIAL REGISTRY OF INFORMATION AND IMAGE MANAGEMENT PRODUCTS AND SERVICES / ASSOCIATION FOR INFORMATION AND IMAGE MANAGEMENT (US) [11892384] 1170, **3188**

AIKAKAUSKIRJA (FI) [02012223] **253**

AIKEN STANDARD (US/0893-2557) [08264461] **5741**

AIKI NEWS ENGLISH ED (JA/0915-9517) [I09159517] **2595**

AILA MONTHLY MAILING (US/0898-1663) [17735081] **3123**

AILLEURS PARIS (FR/0180-3468) [I01803468] **3358**

AIM (UK/0142-887X) [I0142887X] **4083**

AIM : AMERICAS INTERCULTURAL MAGAZINE (US) 2254, **5238**

AIM. AUTOMOTIVE INDUSTRY MATTERS (AT/0044-5681) [I00445681] **5403**

AIM FOR RACIAL HARMONY & PEACE (US/0194-2069) [05250236] 2254, **5238**

AIM (GLENDALE, CALIF.) (US/1050-3471) [21469997] **2609**

AIM INTERNATIONAL (US/0884-6316) [09599989] **4933**

AIM : RACIAL HARMONY & PEACE *See* AIM : AMERICAS INTERCULTURAL MAGAZINE **5238**

AIM REPORT (US/0738-7792) [02795994] **2917**

AIMER ET SERVIR *CEASED.* (FR) [17771802] **3547**

AIMR NEWSLETTER (US) **890**

AIMS NEWSLETTER (US/0895-3155) [16570601] **5081**

AIN REPORT *See* ADVANCED INTELLIGENT NETWORK NEWS **1240**

AINSWORTH STAR-JOURNAL (US/0746-6439) [10195931] **5726**

AIOLIKA GRAMMATA (GR/1010-4569) [01792077] **3358**

AION : ANNALI DEL SEMINARIO DI STUDI DEL MONDO CLASSICO, SEZIONE LINGUISTICA (IT) [08543942] **3262**

●AION. SLAVISTICA : ANNALI DELL'ISTITUTO UNIVERSITARIO ORIENTALE DI NAPOLI / DIPARTIMENTO DI STUDI DELL'EUROPA ORIENTALE, SEZIONE SLAVISTICA (IT/1122-195X) [30868365] **3262**

AIP CONFERENCE PROCEEDINGS (US/0094-243X) [01480073] **4396**

AIP INFORMACAO (PO/0870-287X) [I0870287X] **637**

AIPE FACILITIES (US/1054-7541) [22965809] 859, **1964**

AIPE FACILITIES MANAGEMENT, OPERATIONS & ENGINEERING *See* AIPE FACILITIES **1964**

AIPE NEWSLINE (US/8750-2046) [11101192] **1964**

AIPLA BULLETIN / AMERICAN INTELLECTUAL PROPERTY LAW ASSOCIATION, INC (US) [10718336] **1301**

AIPLA QUARTERLY JOURNAL (US/0883-6078) [10686580] **1301**

AIR ACTION (FR/0992-065X) [I0992065X] **6**

AIR ACTUALITES PARIS (FR/0002-2152) [I00022152] 6, **4033**

AIR ALMANAC (1953), THE (US/0400-8456) [02257061] **6**

AIR AND BUSINESS TRAVEL NEWS TRAVEL INDUSTRY DIRECTORY (UK) **5460**

AIR & COSMOS *See* AEROSPACE WORLD **5**

●AIR AND SPACE LAW (NE) [25390925] 2929, **6**

AIR AND SPACE LAWYER: FORUM COMMITTEE ON AIR AND SPACE LAW. AMERICAN BAR ASSOCIATION, THE (US/0747-7449) [10354685] 6, **2929**

AIR & SPACE SMITHSONIAN (US/0886-2257) [12849809] **6**

AIR — Alphabetical Title Index

● AIR & WASTE : JOURNAL OF THE AIR & WASTE MANAGEMENT ASSOCIATION (US) [27335008] **2223**

AIR AND WASTE MANAGEMENT ASSOCIATION *See* NEWS & VIEWS (PITTSBURGH, PA.) **5298**

AIR & WASTE MANAGEMENT ASSOCIATION *See* PROCEEDINGS, A&WMA ANNUAL MEETING **2239**

AIR & WASTE MANAGEMENT ASSOCIATION. MEETING *See* PROCEEDINGS / A & WMA ANNUAL MEETING **2180**

AIR & WATER POLLUTION CONTROL (US/0890-0396) [14152589] **2223**

AIR CANADA *See* ANNUAL REPORT - AIR CANADA **11**

AIR CARGO WORLD (US/0745-5100) [09200355] **6, 5375**

AIR CARRIER INDUSTRY SCHEDULED SERVICE TRAFFIC STATISTICS QUARTERLY (US/0896-0577) [13295778] **6**

AIR CARRIER OPERATIONS IN CANADA (CN/0008-2570) [02443635] **7**

AIR CARRIER TRAFFIC AT CANADIAN AIRPORTS (QUARTERLY EDITION) (CN/0701-7928) [03566928] **7**

AIR CHARTER GUIDE, THE (US/0890-2925) [14195950] **7, 5375**

AIR CHARTER STATISTICS / STATISTICS CANADA, TRANSPORTATION DIVISION, AVIATION STATISTICS CENTRE (CN/0828-8208) [15020971] **7**

AIR CLASSICS (US/0002-2241) [03949983] **7**

AIR COMBAT (US/0044-6955) [05390013] **7**

AIR CONDITIONING & REFRIGERATION NEWS (UK/0266-6871) [I02666871] **2602**

AIR CONDITIONING, HEATING & REFRIGERATION NEWS (US/0002-2276) [05436578] **2602**

AIR CONDITIONING, HEATING & REFRIGERATION NEWS : DIRECTORY SECTIONS (US) [02032083] **2602**

AIR CONSERVATION (PL) [01476491] **2185**

AIR COOLED NEWS (US) [07972538] **5403**

AIR DEFENSE ARTILLERY (US/0740-803X) [09482828] **4033**

AIR DISTANCES MANUAL (UK) [07039778] **7**

AIR ENTHUSIAST (UK/0143-5450) [01786359] **7**

AIR EXTRA (UK/0307-7411) [02240917] **7**

AIR FACTS (US/0002-2322) [03165400] **7**

AIR FAN (FR/0223-0038) [I02230038] **4033**

AIR FORCE COMPTROLLER, THE (US/0002-2365) [01696318] **4033**

AIR FORCE JOURNAL OF LOGISTICS (US/0270-403X) [05948130] **4033**

AIR FORCE LAW REVIEW, THE (US/0094-8381) [01794266] **3182**

AIR FORCE MAGAZINE (US/0730-6784) [05169825] **4034**

AIR FORCE OFFICER'S GUIDE, THE (US/0739-635X) [02666473] **4034**

AIR FORCE REPORT (US/0273-4370) [06703593] **4034**

AIR FORCE SYSTEMS COMMAND *See* YEAR IN REVIEW / AIR FORCE SYSTEMS COMMAND, THE **4061**

AIR FORCE TIMES (US/0002-2403) [02251554] **4034**

AIR FORCES MONTHLY (UK) **7**

AIR FRANCE *See* AIR FRANCE EN **7**

AIR FRANCE EN (FR) [09476820] **7**

AIR FREIGHT DIRECTORY (US/0092-2870) [01789151] **5375**

AIR FREIGHT DIRECTORY OF POINTS IN THE UNITED STATES SERVED DIRECTLY BY AIR AND BY PICK-UP AND DELIVERY SERVICE AND BY CONNECTING MOTOR CARRIERS *See* AIR FREIGHT DIRECTORY **5375**

AIR FREIGHT LOSS & DAMAGE CLAIMS. ANNUAL SUMMARIES (US) [04157754] **7**

AIR/GROUND SKY-WAVE PROPAGATION CHARTS FOR SELECTED WORLD WIDE STATIONS (US/0090-1008) [01784697] **7**

AIR GUN (US/0164-2863) [04598397] **4882**

AIR INTERNATIONAL (UK/0306-5634) [01794989] **7**

AIR INTERNATIONAL (BOUND VOLUMES) (UK) [19831234] **4034, 7**

AIR JOBS DIGEST (US/1056-5051) [23034609] **7**

AIR LAW *See* AIR AND SPACE LAW **6**

AIR LINE EMPLOYEE, THE (US/0002-2411) [03950970] **7, 1643**

AIR LINE PILOT (US/0002-242X) [02251072] **7**

AIR MAIL (UK) [07956186] **4034**

AIR MAIL MAGAZINE (UK) [04304866] **2784**

● AIR MEDICAL JOURNAL (US/1067-991X) [27403750] **7, 3547**

AIR NAVIGATION PLAN, CARRIBBEAN AND SOUTH AMERICAN REGIONS / PLAN DE NAVIGATION AERIENNE, REGIONS CARAIBES ET AMERIQUE DU SUD. PLAN DE NAVEGACION AEREA, REGIONES DEL CARIBE Y DE SUDAMERICA (CN) [04350857] **7**

AIR NAVIGATION PLAN, EUROPEAN REGION (CN/0304-7652) [02242669] **7**

AIR NAVIGATION PLAN : MIDDLE EAST AND SOUTH EAST ASIA REGIONS / PLAN DE NAVIGATION AERIENNE : REGIONS MOYEN-ORIENT ET ASIE DU SUD-EST / PLAN DE NAVEGACION AEREA : REGIONES DEL ORIENTE MEDIO Y DEL ASIA SUDORIENTAL (CN) [06324627] **7**

AIR NAVIGATION - THE ORDER AND REGULATIONS (UK) **7**

AIR OFFICER'S GUIDE *See* AIR FORCE OFFICER'S GUIDE, THE **4034**

AIR PASSENGER ORIGIN AND DESTINATION. CANADA-UNITED STATES (CN/0705-4343) [02442439] **7**

AIR PASSENGER ORIGIN AND DESTINATION. DOMESTIC REPORT (CN/0703-2692) [02442441] **8**

AIR PICTORIAL (UK/0002-2462) [01658058] **8**

AIR PICTORIAL (ASCOT) *See* AIR PICTORIAL INTERNATIONAL **8**

AIR PICTORIAL INTERNATIONAL (UK/0965-1896) [I09651896] **41, 8**

AIR POLLUTION CONSULTANT, THE (US/1058-6628) [24350659] **2223**

AIR POLLUTION CONTROL (US/0161-3901) [03909737] **2223**

AIR POLLUTION CONTROL ASSOCIATION *See* CUMULATIVE INDEX OF THE JOURNAL OF THE AIR POLLUTION CONTROL ASSOCIATION **2227**

AIR POLLUTION CONTROL ASSOCIATION *See* APCA DIRECTORY AND RESOURCE BOOK **2224**

AIR POLLUTION CONTROL HANDBOOK (CN) **2223**

AIR POLLUTION TITLES *CEASED.* (US/0002-2497) [01478635] **2223, 2183**

AIR POWER (UK) [08255657] **8**

AIR POWER HISTORY (US/1044-016X) [19417850] **8**

AIR PROFESSIONAL FILE, THE (US/8756-6168) [11611816] **1807**

AIR PROGRESS (US/0002-2500) [01478636] **8**

AIR PROGRESS MILITARY AIRPOWER *CEASED.* (US/0886-3857) [12898389] **8, 4034**

AIR PROGRESS WARBIRDS INTERNATIONAL (US/0885-2502) [12600020] **4034, 8**

AIR QUALITY ABSTRACTS (US/0094-5293) [01794674] **2223**

AIR QUALITY CONTROL DIGEST (US) [01478637] **2223**

AIR QUALITY CONTROL FOR ARIZONA (US/8755-6243) [10355294] **2223**

AIR QUALITY DATA (US/0093-8165) [01793109] **2223**

AIR QUALITY DATA FROM THE NATIONAL AIR SURVEILLANCE NETWORKS AND CONTRIBUTING STATE AND LOCAL NETWORKS *See* AIR QUALITY DATA - STATISTICS **2183**

AIR QUALITY DATA - STATISTICS (US) [03244423] **2223, 2183**

AIR QUALITY DIGEST *See* AQMD ADVISOR **2224**

AIR QUALITY IN HONG KONG (HK) [19078026] **2159**

AIR QUALITY IN MINNESOTA (US/0361-5650) [02246757] **2223**

AIR QUALITY IN SELECTED URBAN AREAS (SZ/1013-5480) [04612328] **2223**

AIR QUALITY MONOGRAPHS (US/0568-3653) [03552165] **2223**

AIR QUALITY, NORTHWESTERN ONTARIO : ANNUAL REPORT ... (CN/0713-9330) [08964067] **2223**

AIR QUALITY WEEK (US) **2223**

AIR REGULATIONS AND AERONAUTICS ACT (CN) [03754041] **8**

AIR RESEARCH SUMMARY (US/0094-8160) [05754051] **2223**

AIR SAFETY WEEK (US/1044-727X) [19876423] **8**

AIR TAXI CHARTER & RENTAL DIRECTORY OF NORTH AMERICA (US/0270-5079) [02244295] **8**

AIR TOXICS REPORT *CEASED.* (US/1048-4485) [18111417] **2223**

AIR TRAFFIC CONFERENCE OF AMERICA. DATA SERVICES DIVISION *See* AGENCY LIST, GEOGRAPHIC **5460**

AIR TRAFFIC CONFERENCE OF AMERICA. PUBLICATIONS SERVICES DIVISION *See* AGENCY LIST NUMERIC SEQUENCE **5460**

AIR TRAFFIC CONTROL (US) [02786698] **8**

AIR TRAFFIC CONTROL ASSOCIATION *See* PROCEEDINGS OF THE ANNUAL AIR TRAFFIC CONTROL ASSOCIATION FALL CONFERENCE **32**

● AIR TRAFFIC CONTROL QUARTERLY (US/1064-3818) [26296216] **1964, 8**

● AIR TRAFFIC MANAGEMENT (UK/0969-6725) [I09696725] **8**

AIR TRAFFIC RESEARCH QUARTERLY (US) **1964**

AIR TRAFFIC SERVICES, AIR TRAFFIC CONTROL SERVICE, FLIGHT INFORMATION SERVICE, ALERTING SERVICE; INTERNATIONAL STANDARDS AND RECOMMENDED PRACTICES. ANNEX 11 TO THE CONVENTION OF INTERNATIONAL CIVIL AVIATION (CN) [01639955] **8**

AIR TRANSPORT ASSOCIATION OF AMERICA *See* AIR TRANSPORT (WASHINGTON) **8**

AIR TRANSPORT SAFETY (US) [04298935] **8**

AIR TRANSPORT STATISTICS. FLIGHT CREW LICENCES (AT/0727-2774) [07029350] **41**

AIR TRANSPORT (WASHINGTON) (US/0190-552X) [01478642] **5375, 8**

AIR TRANSPORT WORLD (US/0002-2543) [02018610] **8**

AIR TRAVEL BARGAINS / BY JIM WOODMAN (US/0065-4868) [11275626] **5460, 8**

AIR TRAVEL RESERVE FUND AGENCY *See* REPORT AND ACCOUNTS - AIR TRAVEL RESERVE FUND AGENCY **33**

AIR UNIVERSITY ABSTRACTS OF RESEARCH REPORTS *SUSPENDED.* (US/0503-5368) [04101348] **8**

AIR UNIVERSITY LIBRARY INDEX TO MILITARY PERIODICALS (US/0002-2586) [02500050] **4034, 4061**

AIR UNIVERSITY (U.S.). LIBRARY *See* AIR UNIVERSITY ABSTRACTS OF RESEARCH REPORTS **8**

AIR (VANCOUVER) (CN/0044-6947) [02735695] **3459**

AIR/WATER POLLUTION REPORT (US/0002-2608) [01780747] **2159**

AIR WAVES (US) [06584506] **2223**

AIR ZIMBABWE ... ANNUAL REPORT (RH) [08438229] **8**

AIR ZIMBABWE CORPORATION *See* AIR ZIMBABWE ... ANNUAL REPORT **8**

AIRBORNE ELECTRONICS FORECAST (US) **4034**

AIRBORNE MAGAZINE (AT/1030-0090) [I10300090] **8**

AIRBORNE RETROFIT & MODERNIZATION SYSTEMS FORECAST (US) **4034**

AIRBRUSH ACTION (US/1040-8509) [15044933] **369**

AIRBRUSH DIGEST *CEASED.* (US/0276-7597) [07423502] **376**

AIRBRUSH TECHNIQUES (US/0883-668X) [12184012] **369**

AIRCARGO NEWS INTERNATIONAL (UK/0951-7782) [I09517782] **5375**

AIRCLAIMS INFORMATION DIGEST *See* BLUE PRINT **14**

AIRCRAFT ACCIDENT DIGEST *SUSPENDED.* (CN) [05916172] **8**

AIRCRAFT ACCIDENT INQUIRY; INTERNATIONAL STANDARDS AND PRACTICES. ANNEX 13 TO THE CONVENTION ON INTERNATIONAL CIVIL AVIATION (CN) [01753443] **8**

AIRCRAFT ACCIDENT REPORTS. BRIEF FORMAT, U.S. CIVIL AND FOREIGN AVIATION / NATIONAL TRANSPORTATION SAFETY BOARD (US) [11110376] **8**

AIRCRAFT & AEROSPACE (AT/1032-9366) [19644471] **9**

AIRCRAFT BLUEBOOK MARKETLINE (US/1043-9382) [19609953] **9**

AIRCRAFT BLUEBOOK-PRICE DIGEST (US/1043-3767) [12397746] **9**

AIRCRAFT CERTIFICATION DIRECTORY (US/0747-5586) [10737361] **9**

AIRCRAFT COST EVALUATOR / HELICOPTERS (US) **9**

AIRCRAFT COST EVALUATOR / JETS (US) **9**

AIRCRAFT COST EVALUATOR / TURBOPROPS (US) **9**

AIRCRAFT ECONOMICS (UK) **9**

Alphabetical Title Index — AKADAMIIA

AIRCRAFT ENGINEERING AND AEROSPACE TECHNOLOGY (UK) [14249804] **9**

AIRCRAFT FORECAST (US/0194-469X) [04692977] **9**

AIRCRAFT ILLUSTRATED (UK/0002-2675) [13586295] **9**

AIRCRAFT ILLUSTRATED ANNUAL (UK) [11561724] **9**

AIRCRAFT INDEX MAGAZINE (US/0147-1244) [03111453] **9**

AIRCRAFT MAINTENANCE INTERNATIONAL (UK/0955-8063) [I09558063] **9**

●AIRCRAFT MAINTENANCE TECHNOLOGY (US/1072-3145) [28910016] **9**

AIRCRAFT NATIONALITY AND REGISTRATION MARKS; INTERNATIONAL STANDARDS. ANNEX 7 TO THE CONVENTION ON INTERNATIONAL CIVIL AVIATION (CN) [01753444] **9**

AIRCRAFT NOISE; INTERNATIONAL STANDARDS AND RECOMMENDED PRACTICES. ANNEX 16 TO THE CONVENTION ON INTERNATIONAL CIVIL AVIATION (CN) [01623719] **9**

AIRCRAFT OWNERS AND PILOTS ASSOCIATION *See* AOPA PILOT, THE **12**

AIRCRAFT PRODUCTION USA (SZ) [10830522] **9**

AIRCRAFT PROPELLERS (US/0275-4983) [03056908] **9**

AIRCRAFT REMOTE SENSING OF SOIL MOISTURE AND HYDROLOGIC PARAMETERS, CHICKASHA, OKLA., ... DATA REPORT (US/0743-5479) [10592027] **162**

AIRCRAFT REMOTE SENSING OF SOIL MOISTURE AND HYDROLOGIC PARAMETERS, TAYLOR CREEK, FLA., AND LITTLE RIVER, GA. DATA REPORT (US/0731-8405) [08225865] **1412**

AIRCRAFT TECHNICIAN (US/1044-8012) [19910078] **9**

●AIRCRAFT TECHNOLOGY ENGINEERING & MAINTENANCE (UK/0967-439X) [I0967439X] **1964**

AIRCRAFT TYPE CERTIFICATE DATA SHEETS AND SPECIFICATION. VOLUME I, SINGLE-ENGINE AIRPLANES (US) [07629065] **9**

AIRCRAFT TYPE DESIGNATORS (INT/1014-0107) [I10140107] **9**

●AIRCRAFT VALUE NEWSLETTER (US/1065-8688) [26784004] **9**

AIRDRIE ECHO (CN) **5779**

AIRFAIR (US/0044-7005) [03776186] **5460**

AIRFARE DISCOUNT BULLETIN (US/0733-5407) [08623766] **9**

AIRFINANCE ANNUAL (UK/0266-2132) [11746052] **9**

AIRFINANCE JOURNAL (UK/0143-2257) [10474091] **769, 9**

AIRFORCE (CN/0704-6804) [03790766] **9**

AIRING EDINBURGH (UK/0953-6000) [I09536000] **1211**

AIRLIFT (SCOTT AIR FORCE BASE, ILL.) *See* MAC FORUM: THE JOURNAL OF THE MILITARY AIRLIFT COMMAND, THE **4049**

AIRLINE BUSINESS (UK/0268-7615) [I02687615] **9**

AIRLINE CODING DIRECTORY (CN/1013-4050) [19037710] **9**

AIRLINE DELAY TRENDS / PREPARED FOR U.S. DEPARTMENT OF TRANSPORTATION, FEDERAL AVIATION ADMINISTRATION, OFFICE OF SYSTEMS ENGINEERING MANAGEMENT (US) [04448405] **9**

AIRLINE FINANCIAL NEWS (US/1040-5410) [14644439] **10**

AIRLINE HANDBOOK (US/0095-4683) [01796567] **5460**

AIRLINE INDUSTRY DIRECTORY (US/0194-0961) [05174281] **10**

●AIRLINE MARKETING NEWS (US/1071-1325) [28555749] **10**

AIRLINE NEWSLETTER (US) [01478650] **10**

AIRLINE PASSENGER TARIFF (SW) **10**

AIRLINE QUARTERLY, THE (US) [20663327] **10**

AIRLINE SEATING GUIDE (POCKET ED.) (US/0884-1624) [11690780] **10**

AIRLINE, SHIP & CATERING ONBOARD SERVICES MAGAZINE (US/0892-4236) [15188989] **2326**

AIRLINE TARIFF PUBLISHING COMPANY *See* ATPCO PASSENGER TARIFF SET **12**

●AIRLINER / BOEING CUSTOMER SERVICES DIVISION (US) [26640308] **10**

AIRLINER PRICE GUIDE OF COMMERCIAL-REGIONAL & COMMUTER AIRCRAFT, THE (US) [13620054] **10**

AIRLINER PRODUCTION LIST *CEASED.* (UK/0952-2131) [I09522131] **10**

AIRLINERS INTERNATIONAL *CEASED.* (US/0090-8770) [01786132] **10**

AIRLINERS (MIAMI, FLA.) (US/0896-6575) [17241224] **10, 5460**

AIRMAN, THE (US/0002-2756) [01478651] **10, 4034**

AIRMAN'S INFORMATION MANUAL (US) [01794009] **10**

AIRMAN'S INFORMATION MANUAL. BASIC FLIGHT INFORMATION AND ATC PROCEDURES (US/1057-963X) [04122864] **10**

AIRMAN'S INFORMATION MANUAL (FALLBROOK, CALIF.) (US/0094-047X) [02246581] **10**

AIRMAN'S INFORMATION MANUAL. PT. 3. OPERATIONAL DATA (US) [02784451] **10**

AIRONE (IT) **4161**

AIRONE JUNIOR (IT) **2211**

AIRPORT ALERT (UK) **10**

AIRPORT AND ROUTE FACILITIES : FINANCIAL DATA AND SUMMARY TRAFFIC DATA / INSTALLATIONS ET SERVICES D'AEROPORT ET DE ROUTE : DONNEES FINANCIERES ET STATISTIQUES DE TRAFIC SOMMAIRES (CN) [12039142] **10**

●AIRPORT BUSINESS (US/1072-1797) [28884698] **10, 637**

AIRPORT DIRECTORY (US) [07052400] **10**

AIRPORT DIRECTORY OF THE STATE OF COLORADO (US/0145-4633) [02733521] **10**

AIRPORT EXECUTIVES (US/0742-7379) [10407912] **10**

AIRPORT FBO DIRECTORY (US) **10**

AIRPORT FORUM (GW/0002-2802) [01606795] **10**

AIRPORT FORUM NEWS *See* MOMBERGER AIRPORT INFORMATION **29**

AIRPORT HANDLING MANUAL (CN/0256-3193) [10889708] **10**

AIRPORT HIGHLIGHTS (US) **10**

AIRPORT MAGAZINE (US/1048-2091) [20850120] **10**

AIRPORT MANAGEMENT *CEASED.* (US/1061-3145) [25243454] **859, 10**

AIRPORT MANAGEMENT : THE ROLE OF PERFORMANCE INDICATORS *CEASED.* (UK) **10**

AIRPORT NOISE REPORT (US/1041-8318) [18859970] **10**

AIRPORT OPERATIONS (US/1057-5537) [24056952] **5375, 10**

AIRPORT POCKET GUIDE (DOMESTIC ED.) (US/0894-1513) [15807228] **5460**

AIRPORT SERVICES *See* AIRPORT MANAGEMENT **10**

AIRPORT SERVICES *See* AIRPORT BUSINESS **637**

AIRPORT STATISTICS, STATEWIDE AIRPORT SYSTEM (US) [09459445] **41**

AIRPORT SUPPORT (UK) [25293450] **10**

AIRPORTS INTERNATIONAL (UK/0002-2853) [06072282] **11**

AIRPORTS OF MEXICO AND CENTRAL AMERICA (US/0275-2077) [07083664] **11**

AIRPORTS (WASHINGTON, D.C.) (US/1044-9469) [15034562] **11**

AIRPOST JOURNAL, THE (US/0739-0939) [06476104] **1144**

AIRPOWER (GRANADA HILLS, LOS ANGELES, CALIF.) (US/1067-1048) [06262382] **11**

AIRPOWER JOURNAL (US/0897-0823) [16481534] **11, 4034**

AIRSTREAM, INC *See* AIRSTREAM SERVICE MANUAL **5403**

AIRSTREAM SERVICE MANUAL (US/0160-3019) [03658609] **5403**

AIRTRADE (UK/0306-0349) [08334500] **821**

AIRTRAN NEWS (US/0193-4538) [05266727] **11**

AIRWAVES (US/0278-9639) [07939827] **1125**

AIRWORTHINESS DIRECTIVE SUMMARY (US) [15004808] **11**

AIRWORTHINESS NOTICES (UK) **11**

AIRWORTHINESS OF AIRCRAFT; INTERNATIONAL STANDARDS. ANNEX 8 TO THE CONVENTION ON INTERNATIONAL CIVIL AVIATION (CN) [01753445] **11**

AISA GUIDE TO SHIPPING COOPERATIVES (US) [09332795] **5447, 1541**

AISB QUARTERLY (UK/0268-4179) [11155751] **1211**

AISC NEWS (US) [26949440] **598**

AISLE VIEW : THE NEWSLETTER OF TIPS, TACTICS AND HOW-TO'S FOR SMALL EXHIBITORS (US) **921**

AISM-IALA *See* BULLETIN (INTERNATIONAL ASSOCIATION OF LIGHTHOUSE AUTHORITIES) **4175**

AISPICH CHAKWAN (CN/0824-4715) [10513294] **5271**

AISPLAYBACK (CN/0824-6505) [11050388] **3188**

AISTHESIS (CL/0568-3939) [02257075] **2841**

AISYIYAH (ASSOCIATION) *See* SUARA AISYIYAH **5566**

AIT. ARCHITEKTUR, INNENARCHITEKTUR, TECHNISCHER AUSBAU (GW/0173-8046) [06351416] **2898, 287**

AITIA (US/0731-5880) [03976846] **2841, 4339**

AITIM : BOLETIN DE INFORMACION TECNICA / ASOCIACION DE INVESTIGACION TECHNICA DE LAS INDUSTRIAS DE LA MADERNA Y CORCHO (PO) [04202245] **2374**

AITKIN INDEPENDENT AGE (US) [01478657] **5694**

AITSUGU SABETSU JIKEN (JA) [07044392] **4503**

AIXA : REVISTA ANUAL DE LA GABELLA, MUSEU ETNOLOGIC DEL MONTSENY (SP) [19751412] **4099**

AIZ. ALLGEMEINE IMMOBILIEN-ZEITUNG (GW/0001-1673) [I00011673] **4833**

AJ FOCUS (UK/0951-5380) [19210689] **287**

AJAKALA (II) [01657149] **2501**

AJAKIRI (CN/0384-8469) [03250947] **2254**

AJAR (CN/0229-463X) [08036464] **3358**

AJASTAN KENSABANAKAN ANDES (AI/0002-2918) [05841888] **441**

AJATUS; SUOMEN FILOSOFISEN YHDISTYKSEN VUOSIKIRJA (FI/0355-1725) [01540329] **4339**

AJCU HIGHER EDUCATION REPORT (US/1053-8933) [08287112] **1807**

AJIA-AFURIKA BUNKA KENKYUJO KENKYU NEMPO (JA) [04524146] **2645**

AJIA CHUTO DOKO NENPO (JA) [09185039] **2645**

AJIA KEIZAI (JA/0002-2942) [01390716] **5189, 1461**

AJIA KEIZAI KENKYUJO, TOKYO KEIZAI SEICHO CHOSABU *See* HATTEN TOJOKOKU KEIZAI TOKEI YORAN **1565**

AJIA KEIZAI SHIRYO GEPPO (JA/0020-2827) [05313867] **3188**

AJIA KENKYU (AJIA SEIKEI GAKKAI) (JA/0044-9237) [01820485] **2645**

AJIA SHOKOKU YORAN (JA) [03411741] **5320**

AJIKEN NYUSU (JA/0389-0007) [11931423] **1461**

AJKAL (PK) [02245807] **3358**

AJL NEWSLETTER (US/0747-6175) [06231855] **5045, 3188**

AJL NEWSLINE (US/0279-6929) [07216062] **5271**

AJME NEWS / AMERICANS FOR JUSTICE IN THE MIDDLE EAST (LE) [04816977] **4515**

AJN CAREER GUIDE FOR ... (US) [27307342] **3850**

AJN GUIDE TO NURSING CAREER OPPORTUNITIES *See* AJN CAREER GUIDE FOR ... **3850**

AJN GUIDE TO NURSING CAREER OPPORTUNITIES, THE (US) [17781342] **3850**

AJN/MOSBY ... NURSING BOARDS REVIEW FOR THE NCLEX-RN EXAMINATION (US) [23963266] **3850**

AJR INFORMATION (UK) [07858331] **4515**

AJS BULLETIN (SZ) [25612947] **5045**

AJS REVIEW (US/0364-0094) [02552686] **5045**

AJURIS (BL) [01796466] **2929**

AK JOURNAL (AU/1012-9421) [11248997] **3547**

AKABRI (IO) [03082339] **4034**

AKAD DIRECTORY OF BUSINESSES, TRADES, AND THE PROFESSIONS (NR) [07320819] **637**

AKADAMIIA NAUK URSR, KIEV. BOTANICHNA SEKTSIIA *See* UKRAINSKII BOTANICHNII ZHURNAL **529**

AKADEMIA — Alphabetical Title Index

AKADEMIA ATHENON *See* ANNUAIRE - ACADEMIE D'ATHENES **1808**

AKADEMIA GORNICZP-HUTNICZA IM. STANISLAWA STASZICA. ZESZYTY NAUKOWE: CERAMIKA (PL/0075-7012) [I00757012] **3997**

AKADEMIA ROLNICZA W KRAKOWIE *See* ZESZYTY NAUKOWE. AKADEMIA ROLNICZA W KRAKOWIE, ZOOTECHNIKA **224**

AKADEMIA ROLNICZA W POZNANIU. WYDZIA ZOOTECHNICZNY *See* ROCZNIKI AKADEMII ROLNICZEJ W POZNANIU - WYDZIA ZOOTECHNICZNY **220**

AKADEMIA ROLNICZA W SZCZECINIE *See* ROZPRAWY - AKADEMIA ROLNICZA W SZCZECINIE **131**

AKADEMIA ROLNICZA W SZCZECINIE *See* ZESZYTY NAUKOWE - AKADEMIA ROLNICZA W SZCZECINIE **149**

AKADEMIA ROLNICZA W WARSZAWIE *See* SERIA HISTORYCZNA **133**

AKADEMIA ROLNICZA WE WROCAWIU *See* ZESZYTY NAUKOWE. WETERYNARIA **5528**

AKADEMIA WYCHOWANIA FIZYCZNEGO W POZNANIU *See* ROCZNIKI NAUKOWE **2601**

AKADEMIAJ STUDOJ (CN/0824-3050) [10105495] **3262**

AKADEMIE DER WISSENSCHAFTEN, BERLIN. JAHRBUCH *See* JAHRBUCH DER AKADEMIE DER WISSENSCHAFTEN DER DDR **5232**

AKADEMIE DER WISSENSCHAFTEN DER DDR *See* ABHANDLUNGEN DER AKADEMIE DER WISSENSCHAFTEN DER DDR **5079**

AKADEMIE DER WISSENSCHAFTEN DER DDR *See* JAHRBUCH DER AKADEMIE DER WISSENSCHAFTEN DER DDR **5232**

AKADEMIE DER WISSENSCHAFTEN DER DDR. INSTITUT FUR WIRKSTOFFORSCHUNG *See* VERZEICHNIS WISSENSCHAFTLICHER PUBLIKATIONEN **4332**

AKADEMIE DER WISSENSCHAFTEN DER DDR. ZENTRALINSTITUT FUR GESCHICHT *See* SCHRIFTEN **2708**

AKADEMIE DER WISSENSCHAFTEN IN GOTTINGEN *See* ABHANDLUNGEN DER AKADEMIE DER WISSENSCHAFTEN IN GOTTINGEN. MATHEMATISCH-PHYSIKALISCHE KLASSE **3490**

AKADEMIE DER WISSENSCHAFTEN IN GOTTINGEN *See* JAHRBUCH DER AKADEMIE DER WISSENSCHAFTEN IN GOTTINGEN **322**

AKADEMIE DER WISSENSCHAFTEN, MUNICH. KOMMISSION FUR DIE HERAUSGABE UNGEDRUCKTER TEXTE AUS DER MITTELALTERLICHEN GEISTESWELT *See* VEROFFENTLICHUNGEN **1080**

AKADEMIE DER WISSENSCHAFTEN, MUNICH. PHILOSOPHISCH-HISTORISCHE KLA *See* ABHANDLUNGEN - BAYERISCHE AKADEMIE DER WISSENSCHAFTEN, PHILOSOPHISCH-HISTORISCHE KLASSE **1073**

AKADEMIE DER WISSENSCHAFTEN UND DER LITERATUR, (GERMANY) *See* ABHANDLUNGEN DER MATHEMATISCH-NATURWISSENSCH AFTLICHEN KLASSE - AKADEMIE DER WISSENSCHAFTEN UND DER LITERATUR **5079**

AKADEMIE DER WISSENSCHAFTEN, VIENNA. MATHEMATISCH-NATURWISSENSCH AFTEN KLASSE *See* SITZUNGBERICHTE **5236**

AKADEMIE FUR RAUMFORSCHUNG UND LANDESPLANUNG (HANNOVER, GERMANY) *See* FORSCHUNGS- UND SITZUNGSBERICHTE **2823**

AKADEMII A NAUK SSSR *See* DOKLADY. BOTANICAL SCIENCES **508**

AKADEMIIA FANHOI RSS TOJIKISTON. SHUBAI FANHOI BIOLOGI *See* IZVESTIJA AKADEMII SSR. OTDELENIE BIOLOGICESKIH NAUK **460**

AKADEMIIA NA SELSKOSTOPANSKITE NAUKI *See* DOKLADY **80**

AKADEMIIA NAUK GRUZINSKOI SSR *See* IZVESTIIA AKADEMII NAUK GRUZINSKOI SSR : SERIIA KHIMICHESKAIA **979**

AKADEMIIA NAUK SSSR *See* DOKLADY. PHYSICAL CHEMISTRY **1051**

AKADEMIIA NAUK SSSR *See* DOKLADY. CHEMISTRY **974**

AKADEMIIA NAUK SSSR *See* DOKLADY. BIOLOGICAL SCIENCES **454**

AKADEMIIA NAUK SSSR *See* IZVESTIIA. SERIIA KHIMICHESKAIA **979**

AKADEMIIA NAUK SSSR *See* IZVESTIYA. ATMOSPHERIC AND OCEANIC PHYSICS **1407**

AKADEMIIA NAUK SSSR *See* DOKLADY AKADEMII NAUK SSSR **1354**

AKADEMIIA NAUK SSSR *See* DOKLADY AKADEMII NAUK **1024**

AKADEMIIA NAUK SSSR *See* IZVESTIIA. SERIIA FIZICHESKAIA **4407**

AKADEMIIA NAUK SSSR *See* PROCEEDINGS OF THE ACADEMY OF SCIENCES OF THE USSR. APPLIED PHYSICS SECTIONS **4418**

AKADEMIIA NAUK SSSR *See* IZVESTIIA AKADEMII NAUK SSSR. SERIIA BIOLOGICHESKAIA **459**

AKADEMIIA NAUK SSSR *See* POWER ENGINEERING (NEW YORK) **2124**

AKADEMIIA NAUK SSSR *See* IZVESTIJA. AKADEMIIA NAUK SSSR. NEORGANICESKIE MATERIALY **1036**

AKADEMIIA NAUK SSSR *See* DOKLADY. BIOCHEMISTRY **486**

AKADEMIIA NAUK SSSR *See* MECHANICS OF SOLIDS **4412**

AKADEMIIA NAUK SSSR *See* DOKLADY. BIOPHYSICS **495**

AKADEMIIA NAUK SSSR *See* IZVESTIIA : MEKHANIKA TVERDOGO TELA **2117**

AKADEMIIA NAUK SSSR *See* VESTNIK AKADEMII NAUK SSSR **5168**

AKADEMIIA NAUK SSSR *See* DOKLADY AKADEMII NAUK **1024**

AKADEMIIA NAUK SSSR. BIBLIOTEKA *See* BIBLIOGRAFIIA IZDANII AKADEMII NAUK SSSR; EZHEGODNIK. BIBLIOGRAPHY OF PUBLICATIONS OF THE ACADEMY OF SCIENCES OF THE USSR; A YEAR-BOOK **409**

AKADEMIIA NAUK SSSR. GELMINTOLOGICHESKAIA LABORATORIIA *See* TRUDY GELMINTOLOGICHESKOI LABORATORII **5599**

AKADEMIIA NAUK SSSR. IAKUTSKII FILIAL. INSTITUT BIOLOGII *See* TRUDY **475**

AKADEMIIA NAUK SSSR. INSTITUT ARKHEOLOGII *See* KRATKIE SOOBSHCHENIIA - AKADEMIIA NAUK SSSR, INSTITUT ARKHEOLOGII **272**

AKADEMIIA NAUK SSSR. IZVESTIIA AKADEMII NAUK SSSR. SERIIA BIOLOGICHESKAIA. ENGLISH *See* BIOLOGY BULLETIN OF THE RUSSIAN ACADEMY OF SCIENCES **446**

AKADEMIIA NAUK SSSR. LABORATORIIA TEORII PROTSESSOV PERENOSA *See* CISLENNYE METODY V DINAMIKE RAZREZENNYH GAZOV **4427**

AKADEMIIA NAUK SSSR. MATEMATICHESKII INSTITUT IM. V. A. STEKLOVA *See* TRUDY **3539**

AKADEMIIA NAUK SSSR. NAUCHNYI SOVET PO KOMPLEKSNOI PROBLEMA KIBERNETIKA *See* INFORMATSIONNYE MATERIALY ; KIBERNETIKA **1251**

AKADEMIIA NAUK SSSR. PUSHKINSKAI A KOMISSIIA *See* VREMENNIK PUSHKINSKOI KOMISSII / AKADEMIA NAUK SSSR, OTDELENIE LITERATURY I IAZYKA PUCHKINSKAIA KOMMISSIIA **3451**

AKADEMIIA NAUK SSSR. SIBIRSKOE OTDELENIE *See* IZVESTIIA SIBIRSKOGO OTDELENIIA AKADEMII NAUK SSSR. SERIIA BIOLOGICHESKIKH NAUK **460**

AKADEMIIA NAUK SSSR. VESTNIK AKADEMII NAUK SSSR *See* VESTNIK ROSSIISKOI AKADEMII NAUK **5169**

AKADEMIIA NAUK SSSR. VYCHISLITELNYI TSENTR *See* OBRABOTKA SIMVOLNOI INFORMATSII **3307**

AKADEMIIA NAUK URSR, KIEV. INSTYTUT GEOLOGICHNYKH NAUK *See* TRUDY. MEMOIRS **1400**

AKADEMIIA NAVUK BELARUSKAI SSR *See* IZVESTIIA AKADEMII NAUK BELARUSI. SERIIA FIZIKO-MATEMATISCHEKIKH NAUK **3510**

AKADEMIJA NAUKA I UMJETNOSTI BOSNE I HERCEGOVINE *See* RADOVI ODJELJENJE DRUSTVENIH NAUKA **1843**

AKADEMIKA (SALA, INDONESIA) (IO/0216-8219) [08945918] **1544**

AKADEMISKA DZIVE (US/0516-3145) [01695683] **1918**

AKARUKU TADASHII SENKYO NAGOYA-SHI SUISHIN KYOGIKAI *See* WATASHITACHI NO SENKYO; SENKYO HAKUSHO UNDO NO TAIKEN KIROKU **4500**

AKASHI KOGYO KOTO SEMMON GAKKO *See* KENKYU KIYO - AKASHI KOGYO KOTO SEMMON GAKKO **5123**

AKASHVANI (NEW DELHI) (II/0970-4809) [06638985] **1126**

AKCENT : A (PL/0208-6220) [08102178] **312**

AKHBAR AL-AKADIMIYAH / TUSDIRUHA AKADIMIYAT AL-BAHTH AL-ILMI WA-AL-TIKNULUJIYA (UA) [08013425] **5081**

AKHBAR AL-TURATH AL-ARABI (KUWAIT) (KU) [09658898] **407**

AKHBAR DUBAYY (TS) [03335846] **2645**

AKHBAR TALABAT AL-ALAM (XR) [09850963] **1887**

AKHBOROTI AKADEMIAI FANHOI RSS TOJIKISTON. SHUBAI FANHOI FIZIKAIU MATEMATIKA, KHIMIIA VA GEOLOGIII (TA/0002-3485) [09491527] **5081**

AKHBOROTI AKADEMIIAI FANHOI RSS TOJIKISTON. SERIIAI SHARQSHINOSI TARIKH FILOLOGIIA (TA/0235-0041) [15541450] **3262**

AKHIR SAAH (UA) [05304903] **2498**

AKIKI, THE (US/0091-1607) [01786127] **2436**

AKITA DAIGAKU KOZAN GAKUBU KENKYU HOKOKU (JA/0389-8040) [09472521] **2132**

AKITA DAIGAKU KOZAN GAKUBU SHIGEN CHIGAKU KENKYU SHISETSU HOKOKU (JA/0913-9907) [22779638] **2185**

AKITA IGAKU (JA/0386-6160) [08742651] **3547**

AKITA, JAPAN, AKITA FRUIT-TREE EXPERIMENT STATION *See* AKITA-KEN KAJU SHIKENJUO KENKYUU HUOKOKU **2408**

AKITA-KEN KAJU SHIKENJUO KENKYUU HUOKOKU (JA/0385-3152) [06607609] 2326, **2408**

AKKADICA (BE) [03295049] **2672**

AKKERBOUW (NE) [02381072] **57**

AKRON BEACON JOURNAL, THE (US) [09666962] **5726**

AKRON BUGLE (US) [16003093] **5713**

AKRON BUSINESS AND ECONOMIC REVIEW *CEASED.* (US/0044-7048) [04941615] 1461, **637**

AKRON BUSINESS REPORTER (US/0886-5183) [12902403] **637**

AKRON LAW REVIEW (US/0002-371X) [01478876] **2929**

AKRON MENTONE NEWS, THE (US) [15118251] **5662**

AKRON, OHIO. DEPT. OF FINANCE *See* ANNUAL REPORT, BOND PAYMENT FUND **4710**

AKRON TAX JOURNAL (US/1044-4130) [10126628] **4708**

AKROS (UK/0002-3728) [02055017] **3459**

AKTA TOWARZYSTWA HISTORYCZNO-LITERACKIEGO W PARYZU (PL) [24079677] **3358**

AKTEN ZUR DEUTSCHEN AUSWARTIGEN POLITIK, 1918-1945. SER. E : 1941-1945 (GW) [05358298] **2609**

AKTIENGESELLSCHAFT, DIE (GW/0002-3752) [05151549] **1596**

AKTIVITETEN I SYGEHUSVSENET / SUNDHEDSSTYRELSEN (DK) [09632057] **3775**

AKTIVNOST MESNIH ZAJEDNICA (YU) [01799398] **4696**

AKTIVNYE SISTEMY / ORDENA LENINA INSTITUT PROBLEM UPRAVLENIIA (RU) [20368335] **1217**

AKTUALNE PROBLEMY INFORMACJI I DOKUMENTACJI (PL/0002-3787) [09543769] **1923**

AKTUALNYE PROBLEMY ISTORII FILOSOFII NARODOV SSSR (RU) [05653209] **4340**

AKTUALNYE PROBLEMY LEKSIKOLOGII I SLOVOOBRAZOVANIIA (RU) [05467461] 3358, **3262**

AKTUALNYE PROBLEMY REVMATOLOGII (RU) [06855223] **3547**

AKTUALNYE VOPROSY BIBLIOTECHNOI RABOTY / GOSUDARSTVENNAIA BIBLIOTEKA SSSR IMENI V.I. LENINA (RU/0203-4972) [08678822] **3188**

AKTUAL'NYE VOPROSY EPIDEMIOLOGII (UN/0365-3803) [01139793] **3733**

AKTUALNYE VOPROSY TRAVMATOLOGII I ORTOPEDII (RU) [05369866] **3880**

AKTUELL (UK/0959-5740) [24457471] **3262**

AKTUELL (GW) [01785944] **2609**

AKTUELL AUF DEUTSCH (UK/0954-1063) [22192986] **2513**

AKTUELLE AUGENHEILKUNDE (GW/0942-5276) [I09425276] **498**

AKTUELLE AUGENHEILKUNDE (GW/0942-5276) [31422107] **3871**

AKTUELLE BEITRAGE DER STAATS- UND RECHTSWISSENSCHAFT (GW/0568-7551) [05356197] **2929**

AKTUELLE CHIRURGIE (GW/0001-785X) [07544241] **3958**

AKTUELLE DERMATOLOGIE (GW/0340-2541) [01535468] **3717**

AKTUELLE ENDOKRINOLOGIE *CEASED.* (GW/0943-1837) [I09431837] **3726**

AKTUELLE ENDOKRINOLOGIE UND STOFFWECHSEL (GW/0172-4606) [06564486] **3726**

AKTUELLE ERNAHRUNGSMEDIZIN (GW/0341-0501) [04643710] **4186**

AKTUELLE FRAGEN DER PSYCHIATRIE UND NEUROLOGIE (SZ/0082-4917) [02580825] **3826**, **3919**

AKTUELLE NEUROLOGIE (GW/0302-4350) [06464132] **3826**

AKTUELLE PROBLEME DER INTENSIVMEDIZIN (LEIPZIG) (GW/0323-651X) [11320054] **3547**

AKTUELLE PROBLEME DER NEUROPATHOLOGIE (AU/0253-5297) [09388008] **3892**

AKTUELLE PROBLEME IN CHIRURGIE UND ORTHOPADIE (SZ/0378-8504) [03291112] **3880**, **3958**

AKTUELLE RADIOLOGIE (GW/0939-267X) [23268032] **3938**

AKTUELLE RHEUMATOLOGIE (GW/0341-051X) [02948565] **3802**

AKTUELLE SKATTETALL (NO/0332-8422) [01784579] **4708**

AKTUELLE TRAUMATOLOGIE (GW/0044-6173) [06363854] **3547**

AKTUELLE UROLOGIE (GW/0001-7868) [06455072] **3988**

AKTUELLER INFORMATIONSDIENST AFRIKA. BEIHEFT / INSTITUT FUER AFRIKA-KUNDE, DOKUMENTATIONS-LEITSTELLE AFRIKA (GW/0720-5139) [11336834] **2498**

●AKTUELLES BAUEN (SZ) [25572129] **598**, **287**

AKTUELLT OM HISTORIA (SW/0348-503X) [I0348503X] **2609**

AKTUELNI PROBLEMI PRIVREDNIH KRETANJA I EKONOMSKE POLITIKE JUGOSLAVIJE (CI) [07548912] **4462**, **1461**

AKTUIL (IO/0568-7683) [01795125] **2501**

AKUPUNKTUR / DEUTSCHE ARZTEGESELLSCHAFT FUER AKUPUNKTUR E.V. ... [ET AL.] (GW/0340-3130) [24538425] **3547**

AKUPUNKTURARZT, AURIKULOTHERAPEUT, DER (GW/0172-9322) [27143469] **3547**

AKUROSU (JA) [10772681] **1544**

AKUSERSTVO I GINEKOLOGIJA (MOSKVA) (RU/0002-3906) [01326356] **3756**

AKUSHERSTVO I GINEKOLOGIIA (BU/0324-0959) [01326437] **3756**

AKUSTICESKIJ ZURNAL (RU/0320-7919) [01850672] **4452**

AKUSTIKA I ULTRAZVUKOVAJA TEHNIKA (KIEV) (UN/0321-477X) [10768501] **5082**

AKVARIUM A TERARIUM *See* AKVARIUM, TERARIUM **4285**

AKVARIUM, TERARIUM (XR) [09276462] **4285**

●AKWE:KON JOURNAL (US) [25937395] **2717**

AKWESASNE NOTES *SUSPENDED.* (US/0002-3949) [02257108] **2254**, **5268**

AKZENTE (MUNCHEN) (GW/0002-3957) [01478886] **3358**

AL-AALAM (UK) [11104924] **2501**

AL-ABHATH (LE/0002-3973) [01460557] **2841**

AL-ADAB AL-AJNABIYAH (SY) [06258162] **3358**

AL-ADIB AL-MUASIR (IQ) [02802616] **3358**

AL AHRAM (UA) [01478606] **5800**

AL-AHRAM WEEKLY (UA) [24987878] **5800**

AL-AJNIHAH (JO) [05589891] **11**

AL-AKADIMIYAH AL-ARABIYAH LIL-NAQL AL-BAHARI (EGYPT) *See* MAJALLAT AL-AKADEMIYAH AL-ARABIYAH LIL-NAQL AL-BAHARI **4178**

AL-AKHILLA (TI) [11901271] **3358**

AL-ALAM AL-THALITH (UA) [25423724] **1544**

AL-AMAL FI KHIDMAT LUBNAN (LE) [03956608] **4625**

AL-AMAL; IJTIMAIYAH, UMMALIYAH, SHAHRIYAH (TI) [06834790] **1643**

AL-AMIL (KU) [06010421] **1643**

AL-AMN (TS) [08228181] **3156**

AL-AMN WA-AL-HAYAH (SU) [11150610] **3156**

AL-ANBA (LE) [04471279] **4515**

AL-ANON FAMILY GROUP HEADQUARTERS, INC *See* WORLD DIRECTORY OF AL-ANON FAMILY GROUPS AND ALATEENS **1350**

AL-ARAB (SU) [03348344] **2645**

AL-ARABIYYA (US/0889-8731) [03954834] **3358**, **3262**

AL-ARD (SY) [02441234] **2767**

AL-ARD (US) [06345800] **4515**

AL-ARD AL-IQTISADI WA-AL-MALI (SU) [03616018] **5320**

AL-ASAS (MR) [06587378] **2767**

AL-ASWAQ AL-ARABIYAH WA-AL-ALAMIYAH (UA) [10125717] **1461**

AL-ATASH (PK) [05199322] **5041**

AL AWAMIA (MR/0572-2721) [01518951] **57**

AL-BAHITH (FR) [05389842] **2645**

AL-BAHITH AL-ARABI (UK) [11592057] **2767**

AL-BALAGH (PK) [02245935] **2767**

AL-BALAGH (KU) [05719902] **5041**

AL-BANK AL-MARKAZI-AL-TUNISI *See* STATISTIQUES FINANCIERES **734**

AL-BARLAMAN (SJ) [10941527] **4539**

AL-BARNEAMAJ AL-SANAWI / AL-MARKAZ AL-QAWMI LIL-TANMIYAH WA-AL-TADRIB AL-TAAWUNI (SJ) [11063068] **1643**

AL-BASHIR (PK) [02239396] **5041**

AL-BAYADIR AL-SIYASI (IS) [09330730] **2525**

AL-BAYAN (SJ) [02998351] **5041**

AL-BAYRAQ (BA) [03502515] **4034**

AL-BAYT (LY) [05671337] **2498**

AL-BIAH / TUSDIRUHA AMANAT AL-LAJNAH AL-QAWMIYAH LIL-BIAH, AL-MAJLIS AL-QAWMI LIL-BUHUTH (SJ) [07658488] **2211**

AL-BIBLIYUGHRAFIYA AL-WATANIYAH AL-URDUNIYAH / TUSDIRUHA JAMIYAT AL-MAKTABAT AL-URDUNIYAH (JO) [08119917] **407**

AL-BINA (SU) [08070494] **287**

AL-BUHUTH (SJ) [05047442] **5189**

AL-DALIL AL-HADITH LIL-HAYAT WA-AL-MUASSASAT WA-AL-SHARIKAT (TS) [02603779] **1596**

AL-DALIL AL-SINAI AL-SURI (SY) [06564633] **1544**

AL-DALIL AL-TIJARI (UA) [04150536] **822**

AL-DARAH (SU) [03194590] **2645**

AL-DAWAH (UA) [04678849] **5041**

AL-DAWHAH (QA) [03424327] **2767**

AL-DIBLUMASI (UA) [07617571] **4462**

AL-DIFA AL-ARABI. ARAB DEFENCE JOURNAL (UK) [05769687] **4034**

AL-DIRASAT AL-ILAMIYAH LIL-SUKKAN WA-AL-TANMIYAH WA-AL-TAMIR (UA) [03487848] **2767**

AL-DIRASAT AL-ISLAMIYAH (PK/0002-399X) [01566669] **5041**

AL-FAJR (SU) [02454237] **2525**

AL-FAJR AL-IQTISADI (JO) [03790573] **1544**

AL-FAJR : JERUSALEM PALESTINIAN WEEKLY *SUSPENDED.* (US/1066-3479) [19688718] **2254**

AL-FAYSAL AL-TIBBIYAH (SU) [10297126] **3547**

AL-FIHRIST (LE) [08227795] **407**

AL-FIKR AL-ARABI AL-MUASIR (LE) [07378602] **2525**

AL-FIKR AL-ISTIRATIJI AL-ARABI (LE) [08353226] **4034**

AL-FIKR AL-JADID (UA) [04100489] **2637**

AL-FUNUN (YE) [07639581] **312**

AL-FURSAN AL-FIKRI WA-AL-SIYASI (SY) [09424253] **2767**

AL-FUSUL AL-ARBAAH (LY) [05842116] **2498**

AL-FUSUL AL-LUBNANIYAH (LE) [07320154] **2525**

AL-GEZIRA (SP/0213-2966) [I02132966] **2553**, **2609**

AL-GHURFAH (MK) [06899803] **1544**

AL-HAFT WA-AL-TAAWUN AL-ARABI (KU) [03910530] **4249**

AL HAKEEM (SJ/0253-9691) [04719677] **3547**

AL-HIKMAH (LY) [05887315] **4340**

AL-HIKMAH (YE) [03383699] **3358**

AL-HILAL (CN) [01639361] **2767**

AL-HUDA AL-JADIDAH (US/0300-5453) [03442459] **5713**

AL-HUKM AL-SHABI AL-MAHALLI (SJ) [01794129] **4462**

AL-IDARI (LE) [04151462] **1596**

AL-IHSAAT AL-IQTISADIYAH AL-QAWMIYAH. AL-WADAI WA-AL-ITIMAN AL-MASRIFI / AL-JIHAZ AL-MARKAZI LIL-TABIAH AL-AMMAH WA-AL-IHSA (UA) [09294653] **769**

AL-ILM (UA) [07260960] **5082**

AL-ILM WA-AL-IMAN (TI) [03790490] **5041**

AL-'ILM WA-AL-TIKNULUGIYA (LE/1013-2392) [I10132392] **5082**

AL-INSAN WA-AL-TATAWWUR / TUSDIRUHA JAMIYAT AL-TIBB AL-NAFSI AL-TATAWWURI (UA) [07507304] **4572**

AL-IQTISAD (SY) [02418898] **1461**

AL-IQTISAD WA-AL-TIJARAH (LY) [03228072] **822**

AL-IQTISADI AL-KUWAYTI (KU) [03941098] **1544**, **1528**

AL-IRSHAD (MR) [05255442] **5041**

AL-ISHTIRAKI (SJ) [01790802] **4539**

AL-ISKANDARIYAH (UA) [10172013] **2637**

AL ISLAM (MY) [02245665] **5041**

AL-ISTIKHLASAT AL-TARBAWIYAH / YUSDIRUHA QISM AL-TAWTHIQ AL-TARBAWI (SU) [10235825] **1723**

AL-ITISAM (UA) [04710008] **5041**

AL-JAMAHIRIYAH FI USB (UK) [09246171] **2637**

AL-JAMIAH (SJ) [03468182] **1808**

AL-JAMIAH / TUSDIRUHA JAMIAT AL-MALIK FAYSAL BI-AL-MINTAQAH AL-SHARQIYAH (SU) [10378277] **5228**

AL-JAMIYAH AL-ILMIYAH AL-TULLABIYAH-TIBB AL-AZHAR (UA) [07656133] **3547**

AL-JARIDAH AL-RASMIYAH LIL-MAMLAKAH AL-URDUNIYAH AL-HASHIMIYAH (JO) [02241505] **2929**

AL-JAWHARAH (QA) [05230631] **5550**

AL-JAZAIRIYAH (AE) [06565154] **5550**

AL-JIL (SJ) [03188367] **2498**

AL-KAHHAL (SY) [07564919] **3871**

AL-KARMIL (IS) [11823831] **3358**

AL-KHAFJI (SU) [08069709] **2525**

AL-KITAB AL-MAGHRIBI / TUSDIRUHA AL-JAMIYAH AL-MAGHRIBIYAH LIL-TALIF WA-AL-TARJAMAH WA-AL-NASHR (MR) [10536652] **407**

AL-KJHALI AL-IQTISADI (KU) [08392643] **637**

AL-KUWAYT AL-YAWM (KU) [03511654] **2929**

AL-MADAR (RU) [09877448] **2672**

AL-MAGALLA AL-MISRIYYA LI-L-MAHASIL (UA/0379-3575) [03143016] **162**

AL-MAGALLA AL-MISRIYYA LI-N-NABAT (UA/0375-9237) [03115207] **498**

AL-MAGALLA AL-TIBBIYYA AL-URDUNIYYA (JO/0446-9283) [03098748] **3547**

AL-MAHAD AL-QAWMI AL-ILMI WA-AL-FANNI LIL-UQYANUS WA-AL-SAYD *See* BULLETIN DE L'INSTITUT NATIONAL SCIENTIFIQUE ET TECHNIQUE D'OCEANOGRAPHIE ET DE PECHE **553**

AL-MAHAD AL QQWMI LIL-IHSA *See* BULLETIN MENSUEL DE STATISTIQUE - INSTITUT NATIONAL DE LA STATISTIQUE (AL-MAHAD) **5324**

AL-MAHAD AL-WATANI LIL-ASAR *See* PRIX INFORMATION (ALGER) **1594**

AL-MAHD LIL-THQAFAH WA-AL-FUNUN (JO) [11858139] **3358**

AL-MAJALLAH AL-ARABIYAH LIL-BUHUTH AL-TARBAWIYAH (TI) [08251189] **1723**

AL-MAJALLAH AL-ARABIYAH LIL-DIRASAT AL-LUGHAWIYAH (SJ) [09494931] **3262**

AL-MAJALLAH AL-ARABIYAH LIL-TARBIYAH (TI) [08251225] **1723**

AL-MAJALLAH AL-MUSIQIYAH (UA) [01790799] **4099**

AL-MAJALLAH AL-THAQAFIYAH / TASDURU AN AL-JAMIAH AL-URDUNIYAH (JO) [11040061] **5228**

AL-MAJALLAH AL-TIBBIYAH AL-SAUDIYAH (SA) [10259337] **3547**

AL-MAJALLAH AL-TUNISIYAH LI-ULUM AL-TARBIYAH (TI) [05765226] **1723**

AL-MAL WA-AL-ALAM (LE) [07848928] **822**

AL-MAL WA-AL-TIJARAH (UA) [01790798] **1544**

AL-MALAYIN AL MALAYEEN (LE) [10288622] **2788**

AL-MANSURAH (UA) [11115137] **2637**

AL-MARAH — Alphabetical Title Index

AL-MARAH AL-JADIDAH (SJ) [02953813] **5550**

AL-MARAHIL (BL) [07881937] **2717**

AL-MARJI AL-TIJARI LIL-ALAM AL-ARABI WA-DUWAL AL-SHARQ AL-AWSAT (UA) [01797939] **822**

AL-MASAQ (UK/0950-3110) [19253730] **5189**

AL-MASHAL (US) [05978333] **5054**

AL-MASIR AL-DIMUQRATI (LE) [07863941] **2609**

AL-MASKUKAT (IQ) [01089733] **2779**

AL-MATHURAT AL-SHABIYAH (QA) [13113047] **2321**

AL-MAWAKIB (IS) [12076008] **2525**

AL-MAWAQIF (BA) [02436419] **2525**

AL-MAWQIF AL-ADABI (SY) [01791895] **3358**

AL-MIHRAJAN (MR) [10053592] **2498**

AL-MILAFF (CY/0258-7947) [11000206] **4515**

AL-MITHAQ AL-WATANI AL-USBUI (MR) [06155372] **2637**

AL MITZPE HAHINUCH (CN/0316-5256) [02247478] 1723, **5045**

AL MOMIN (KE) [10940007] **5041**

AL-MUARRIKH AL-ARABI : MAJALLAH FASLIYAH TARIKHIYAH MUHAKKAMAH TUNI BI-SHUUN AL-TURATH WA-AL-TARIKH AL-ARABI WA-AL-ALAMI (IQ) [15524741] **2609**

AL-MUJTAMA (KU) [03619438] **2767**

● AL-MUJTAMA AL-MADANI WA-AL-TAHAWWUL AL-DIMUQRATI FI AL-WATAN AL-ARABI (UA) [26134588] **4625**

AL-MUNAZZAMAH AL-ARABIYAH LIL-TARBIYAH WA-AL-THAQAFAH WA-AL-ULUM *See* TADRIS AL-ULUM WA-AL-RIYADIYAT **5161**

AL-MUNTALAQ (LE) [06564758] **5041**

AL-MUSAFIR AL-ARABI (UK/0267-0194) [11862203] **5460**

AL-MUSAWWAR (UA) [05180702] **2498**

AL-MUSAWWAR AL-JADID (LE) [02441508] **2767**

AL-MUSIQA WA-AL-MASRAH (SU) [08392938] **383**

AL-MUSLIH (PK) [02240259] **5041**

AL-MUSLIM AL-MUASIR (LE) [03040176] **5041**

AL-MUSTAHLIK (JO) [11860004] 2788, **1293**

AL-MUSTAQBAL *CEASED.* (US/0153-3401) [03734279] **2525**

AL-MUSTAQBAL (SJ) [04509439] **2637**

AL-MUSTAQBAL AL-ARABI (LE) [05521867] **2767**

AL-NAFT WA-AL-ALAM (IQ) [02951474] **4249**

AL-NAFT WA-AL-TANMIYAH (IQ) [04152136] **4249**

AL-NAHAR. AL-KITAB AL-SANAWI (UA) [02441434] **4462**

AL-NAHDAH (KU) [03718463] **2525**

AL-NAHDAH (MY/0127-2284) [09661773] **5041**

AL-NASHIR AL-ARABI (LY) [10513488] **4811**

AL-NASHRAH AL-FASLIYAH LI-ASAR AL-JUMLAH (KU) [16163414] **1461**

AL-NASHRAH AL-IKHBARIIYAH / TASDURU AN WAHDAT AL-MALUMAT AL-TABIAH LIL-NADWAH AL-ALAMIYAH LIL-ANSHITAH AL-ILMIYAH AL-ISLAMIYAH (KU) [09986456] **2525**

AL-NASHRAH AL-IQTISADIYAH AL-ARABIYAH (FR) [11083650] **1544**

AL-NASHRAH AL-SANAWIYAH LIL-MILAHAH WA-AL-NAQL AL-BAHRI / AL-JIHAZ AL-MARKAZI LIL-TABIAH AL-AMMAH WA-AL-IHSA (UA) [08353991] **5447**

AL-NASHRAH AL-SHAHRIYAH LIL-IHSA - IDARAT AL-IHSAAT WA-AL-DIRASAT AL-IQTISADIYAH (MU) [01794021] **5320**

AL-NASHRAH AL-TARBAWIYAH LIL-TALIM AL-IBTIDAI WA-LIL-TALIM AL-THANAWI (TI) [01798342] **1887**

AL-NASHRAH AL-WABAIYAH LI-IQLIM SHARQ AL-BAHR AL-MUTAWASSIT (UA/1014-2347) [19349695] 3734, **3712**

AL-NASIRIYAH (UK) [09246246] **2767**

AL-NASRA AS-SAYDALIYYA AL-MISRIYYA (UA/0013-2438) [01335749] **4290**

AL-NASRAT AL-TIBIYYA AL-ARABIYYAT (SJ/1013-1930) [11472372] **3547**

AL-NAZEER (US/0749-7415) [11135734] **4462**

AL-NIQABI AL-ARABI (UA) [04161335] **1643**

AL-QANTARA (MADRID) (SP/0211-3589) [08086900] **2672**

AL-QAWMI AL-ARABI (LE) [09850850] **2767**

AL-QISSAH (UA) [02556300] **3262**

AL-QUDS (LE) [07425666] **2767**

AL-QUWAH (BA) [05153998] **4034**

AL-RAID / YUSDIRUHA AL-MARKAZ AL-ISLAMI FI AKHIN (MASJID BILAL) WA-ITTIHAD AL-TALABAH AL-MUSLIMIN FI URUBBA (GW) [07860316] **5041**

AL-RAIDAH (LE) [05324096] **5550**

AL-RAYYAN / YUSDIRUHA MATHAF QATAR AL-WATANI BI-AL-DAWHAH (QA) [11176319] **2767**

AL-RIM (JO) [09329711] **2185**

AL-RISALAH AL-ISLAMIYAH (LE) [03731418] **5041**

AL-RISALAH AL-ISLAMIYAH / TASDURUAN WIZARAT AL-AWQAF WA-AL-SHUUN AL-DINIYAH (IQ) [07243402] **5041**

AL-RISALAH AL-TARBAWIYAH / AL-MAMLAKAH AL-MAGHRIBIYAH, WIZARAT AL-TARBIYAH AL-WATANIYAH (MR) [10000732] **1723**

AL-RIYADAH WA-AL-SHABAB (TS) [09832376] 1059, **4882**

AL-RUYA / YUSDIRUHA ITTIHAD AL-KUTTAB AL-JAZAIRIYIN (AE) [12003733] **3359**

AL-SABAH AL-JADID / LISAN HAL AL-HIZB AL-ITTIHADI AL-DIMUQRATI WA-JABHAT AL-MUARADAH AL-WATANIYAH AL-DIMUQRATIYAH AL-SUDANIYAH (UK) [07997114] **2637**

AL-SALAM; MAJALLAH SHAHRIYAH SIYASIYAH THAQAFIYAH JAMIAH (UA) [06567389] **2637**

AL-SAQR (QA) [05319030] **4882**

AL-SHABAB (IQ) [06566458] **2525**

AL-SHABAB WA-ULUM AL-MUSTAQBAL (UA) [06575699] 5082, **1059**

AL-SHARQ (SU) [05323974] **2767**

AL-SHARQIYAH (FR) [05849770] **5550**

AL-SHASHAH AL-SAGHIRAH (UA) [07235964] **312**

AL-SHIRA (IS) [05337618] **2525**

AL-SINAAH WA-AL-IQTISAD (UA) [12121101] **1544**

AL-SINAAH WA-AL-TANMIYAH (SJ) [01799572] **1596**

AL-SINAI (IQ) [05502877] **1461**

AL-SINAI AL-ARABI (UA) [09511931] **1544**

AL-SINIMA AL-ARABIYAH (UA) [07511725] **4063**

AL-SINIMA WA-AL-MASRAH (UA) [03399265] 5361, **4063**

AL-SINIMA WA-AL-NAS (UA) [06588701] **4063**

AL-SIYASAH AL-DAWLIYAH (UA/0583-4597) [02166058] **4462**

AL-SIYASAH WA-AL-ISTRATIJIYAH (SJ) [10106499] **4462**

AL-SUAL (MR) [11596571] **2767**

AL-SULB AL-ARABI (SJ/0253-9659) [03262550] 3997, **1596**

AL-SUNDUQ AL-ARABI LIL-INMA AL-IQTISADI WA-AL-IJTIMAI *See* AL-TAQRIR AL-SANAWI - AL-SUNDUQ AL-ARABI LIL-INMA AL-IQTISADI WA-AL-IJTIMAI **1544**

AL-TAAWUN (SJ) [04028076] **1596**

AL-TAAWUN AL-SINAI FI AL-KHALIJ AL-ARABI (QA) [10283325] **1544**

AL-TAHADDI (MR) [09788058] **2637**

AL-TAKAMUL (UA) [09493367] **2637**

AL-TALIAH (KU) [03268348] **2767**

AL-TALIAH AL-ADABIYAH (IQ) [03188475] **3359**

AL-TALIAH; SIYASIYAH USBUIYAH (IS) [07856682] **4462**

AL-TAMWIL WA-AL-TANMIYAH (US/0250-7455) [08525932] **4708**

AL-TANMIYAH (JO) [04208396] **1544**

AL-TANMIYAH WA-AL-TIJARAH (UA) [09723803] **1544**

AL-TAQRIR AL-ISLAMI (LE) [06782503] **5041**

AL-TAQRIR AL-SANAWI (SU) [08819110] **769**

AL-TAQRIR AL-SANAWI - AL-SUNDUQ AL-ARABI LIL-INMA AL-IQTISADI WA-AL-IJTIMAI (KU) [02608636] **1544**

AL-TAQRIR AL-SANAWI - BANK AL-NILAYN (SJ) [03225378] **769**

AL-TAQRIR AL-SANAWI - HUKUMAT ABU ZABI, WIZARAT AL-TARBIYAH (TS) [01798872] **1723**

AL-TAQRIR AL-SANAWI - MAJLIS AL-NAQD (TS) [04450414] **769**

AL-TAQRIR AL-SANAWI WA-AL-BAYANT AL-HISABIYAH AL-KHITAMIY AH LIL-SANAH AL-MUNTAHIYAH FI ... / SUNDUQ AL-NAQD AL-SANAWI (TS) [09396066] **769**

AL-TAQYIS : NASHRAT AL-MUNAZZAMAH AL-ARABIYAH LIL-MUWASAFAT WA-AL-MAQAYIS (JO) [07919259] **4029**

AL-TARBIYAH AL-ISLAMIYAH (LE) [03409722] **5041**

AL-TARBIYAH AL-JADIDAH (LE) [03024414] **1723**

AL-TASAWWUF AL-ISLAMI : SHARIAH WA-TARIQAH WA-HAQIQAH (UA) [06566900] **5042**

AL-TAWHID (UA) [05193286] **5042**

AL-TAWTHIQ AL-ILAMI / TASDURU AN MARKAZ AL-TAWTHIQ AL-ILAMI LI-DUWAL AL-KHALIJ AL-ARABI (IQ) [09660101] **3188**

AL-THAQAFAH (SY) [03258038] **3359**

AL-THAQAFAH (IQ) [01796628] **2525**

AL-THAQAFAH AL-AJNABIYAH (IQ) [11078967] 312, **3359**

AL-THAQAFAH AL-ALAMIYAH (KU) [08001404] **2525**

AL-THAQAFAH AL-THAWRIYAH (FR) [05369084] **312**

AL-THAQAFAH AL-USBUIYAH (SY) [05194227] **5238**

AL-THAQAFAH AL-USBUIYAH (UA) [02245670] **2498**

AL-THAWRAH (LE) [05385978] **2637**

AL-THAWRAH AL-USBUI (IQ) [07299583] **5803**

AL-TIJARAH (TS) [03258103] **1545**

AL-TURATH AL-ILMI AL-ARABI (IQ) [06567142] **5082**

AL-UDISSIH (LE) [11628124] **3459**

AL-URUBAH. AL-OUROBA (QA) [03282973] **2525**

AL-USBU AL-ARABI (LE) [06254201] **2525**

AL-USBU AL-JADID (IS) [09877371] **2526**

AL-VIDYU AL-ARABI (UK) [10025213] **4366**

AL VOCANTE (SP) **2872**

AL-WAHDAH AL-ARABIYAH (LY) [03180233] **2645**

AL-YAMAMAH (SU) [03427532] **2645**

AL-YAMANI (YE) [09159527] **2767**

AL-YARMUK (JO) [08748981] **2484**

AL-ZAFRAH (TS) [03790536] **2767**

AL-ZAMAN AL-MAGHRIBI (MR) [09331505] **2637**

AL-ZIMAM WA-AL-MISAHAT AL-MUNZARIAH FI JUMHURIYAT MISR AL-ARABIYAH / AL-JIHAZ AL-MARKAZI LIL-TABIAH AL-AMMAH WA-AL-IHSA (UA) [08819194] **1461**

ALA-ARTS (US/0146-9398) [03077977] **312**

ALA BLACK CAUCUS. BLACK CAUCUS NEWSLETTER *See* BLACK CAUCUS OF ALA NEWSLETTER / ALA BLACK CAUCUS **3196**

ALA BRIEF (US/0162-2986) [04128527] **2929**

ALA BULLETIN : A PUBLICATION OF THE AFRICAN LITERATURE ASSOCIATION (CN/0146-4965) [08331767] **3359**

ALA DIMENSIONS *See* LATVIAN DIMENSIONS **2267**

ALA HANDBOOK OF ORGANIZATION (US/0084-6406) [01415962] **3188**

ALA HANDBOOK OF ORGANIZATION AND MEMBERSHIP DIRECTORY (US/0273-4605) [07048214] **3188**

ALA NEWS (VERNON HILLS, ILL.) (US/1045-1153) [11925837] **2929**

ALA SIGHTS TO SEE BOOK (US/0090-8614) [01786037] **5403**

ALA SURVEY OF LIBRARIAN SALARIES (US/0747-7201) [10774031] 3188, **1643**

ALA TOO (KG/0320-7390) [06847717] **3359**

ALA WASHINGTON NEWSLETTER (US/0001-1746) [06553285] **3188**

ALA WHERE TO STAY BOOK, EAST (US/0731-3152) [08134976] **2803**

ALA WHERE TO STAY BOOK, WEST (US/8755-9242) [09495769] **2803**

ALA ... WORLDWIDE DIRECTORY & FACT BOOK (US/0741-076X) [10066587] **4034**

ALABAMA ADMINISTRATIVE MONTHLY (US) [10125151] **2929**

ALABAMA. ADMINISTRATIVE OFFICE OF COURTS *See* ANNUAL REPORT, ALABAMA JUDICIAL SYSTEM **3138**

ALABAMA AGRIBUSINESS (US/0516-3854) [04799930] **57**

Alphabetical Title Index — ALASKA

ALABAMA. AGRICULTURAL AND MECHANICAL UNIVERSITY. SCHOOL OF AGRICULTURE AND ENVIRONMENTAL SCIENCE See RESEARCH BULLETIN - ALABAMA AGRICULTURAL AND MECHANICAL UNIVERSITY, SCHOOL OF AGRICULTURE AND ENVIRONMENTAL SCIENCE **127**

ALABAMA. AGRICULTURAL EXPERIMENT STATION. DEPT. OF AGRONOMY AND SOILS See DEPARTMENTAL SERIES - DEPARTMENT OF AGRONOMY AND SOILS, AGRICULTURAL EXPERIMENT STATION, AUBURN UNIVERSITY **78**

ALABAMA AGRICULTURAL STATISTICS (US/0270-2436) [03686371] **57, 151**

ALABAMA. ALCOHOLIC BEVERAGE CONTROL BOARD See ANNUAL BEER REPORT / ALABAMA ALCOHOLIC BEVERAGE CONTROL BOARD **2363**

ALABAMA ANNUAL PROGRAM PLAN, FY ... FOR PART B OF THE EDUCATION OF THE HANDICAPPED ACT AS AMENDED BY PUBLIC LAW 94-142 (US) [09107343] **1874**

ALABAMA ARCHITECTURE (US) [10044612] **287**

ALABAMA. ATTORNEY GENERAL'S OFFICE See QUARTERLY REPORT OF THE ATTORNEY GENERAL OF ALABAMA **3142**

● ALABAMA AUTOMOTIVE REPORT (US/1061-8295) [25474250] **5403**

ALABAMA BAPTIST HISTORIAN, THE (US/0002-4147) [06954905] **5054**

ALABAMA BAPTIST, THE (US/0738-7741) [09664239] **5625**

ALABAMA BIRDLIFE (US/0516-3870) [07866584] **5614**

ALABAMA. BUREAU OF CREDIT UNIONS See REPORT OF THE CREDIT UNION SUPERVISOR **808**

ALABAMA BUSINESS & ECONOMIC INDICATORS (US/1055-4645) [21924974] **637**

ALABAMA CATTLEMAN (US/0516-3889) [04800240] **204**

ALABAMA CONSERVATION (US/0002-4171) [08732198] **2185**

ALABAMA COUNTY DATA BOOK (US/0892-9084) [03921132] **4625**

ALABAMA. COURTS See ALABAMA RULES OF COURTS **3138**

ALABAMA CPA NEWSLETTER (US) **738**

ALABAMA. DEPARTMENT OF MENTAL HEALTH AND MENTAL RETARDATION See ANNUAL REPORT / ALABAMA DEPARTMENT OF MENTAL HEALTH AND MENTAL RETARDATION **5272**

ALABAMA. DEPT. OF CONSERVATION AND NATURAL RESOURCES See FY ... ANNUAL REPORT / ALABAMA DEPARTMENT OF CONSERVATION AND NATURAL RESOURCES **2194**

ALABAMA. DEPT. OF DEPARTMENT OF CONSERVATION AND NATURAL RESOURCES See FY ... ANNUAL REPORT / ALABAMA DEPARTMENT OF CONSERVATION AND NATURAL RESOURCES **2194**

ALABAMA. DEPT. OF INDUSTRIAL RELATIONS. DIVISION OF SAFETY AND INSPECTION See ANNUAL REPORT - ALABAMA. DEPT. OF INDUSTRIAL RELATIONS. DIVISION OF SAFETY AND INSPECTION **2859**

ALABAMA. DEPT. OF PUBLIC HEALTH See ANNUAL REPORT / ALABAMA DEPARTMENT OF PUBLIC HEALTH **4765**

ALABAMA. DEPT. OF PUBLIC HEALTH See ANNUAL REPORT OF THE ACTIVITIES OF THE ALABAMA DEPT. OF PUBLIC HEALTH **4766**

ALABAMA. DEPT. OF VETERANS AFFAIRS See ANNUAL REPORT / DEPARTMENT OF VETERANS AFFAIRS, ALABAMA **4035**

ALABAMA DEVELOPMENT NEWS (US/0889-7468) [05589527] **1545**

ALABAMA DEVELOPMENT OFFICE See NEW AND EXPANDED INDUSTRIES ANNOUNCED IN ALABAMA **1619**

ALABAMA DIRECTORY SUSPENDED. (US) [04156391] **4625**

ALABAMA ECHOES (US/0745-6786) [03792870] **4933**

ALABAMA ECONOMIC OUTLOOK / DEVELOPED BY CENTER FOR BUSINESS AND ECONOMIC RESEARCH, UNIVERSITY OF ALABAMA (US) [04721986] **1545**

ALABAMA EMPLOYMENT LAW LETTER (US/1049-9369) [21356944] **3143**

ALABAMA ENGINEER, THE (US/0401-1457) [10332977] **1964**

● ALABAMA ENVIRONMENTAL COMPLIANCE UPDATE (US/1066-1131) [26860636] **3109**

ALABAMA FACTS (US/1056-2168) [23587099] **2717**

ALABAMA FAMILY HISTORY AND GENEALOGY NEWS (1984) (US) [16848413] **2436**

ALABAMA FARMER (US) [15112253] **57**

ALABAMA FORESTS (US/0275-6625) [05113007] **2374**

ALABAMA GAME & FISH (US/0279-6783) [07164485] **4868**

ALABAMA GENEALOGICAL REGISTER / BY BETTY WOOD THOMAS, THE (US/0516-396X) [04859971] **2436**

ALABAMA GENEALOGICAL SOCIETY See MAGAZINE - ALABAMA GENEALOGICAL SOCIETY, INC **2459**

ALABAMA. GOVERNOR See EXECUTIVE BUDGET : EDUCATIONAL FUNDS - ALABAMA **1746**

ALABAMA GUEST GUIDE; A TOUR THROUGH THE HEART OF DIXIE (US) [04878624] **5460**

● ALABAMA HEALTH CARE IN PERSPECTIVE (US/1065-4038) [26604513] **4764**

ALABAMA HERITAGE (US/0887-493X) [13257082] **2717**

ALABAMA HISTORICAL COMMISSION See ANNUAL REPORT - ALABAMA HISTORICAL COMMISSION **4626**

ALABAMA IN PERSPECTIVE (US/1065-5301) [26627248] **5320**

ALABAMA INDUSTRIAL DIRECTORY (US/1061-9585) [23991385] **2133**

ALABAMA JOURNAL, THE CEASED. (US/0745-323X) [02666111] **5625**

ALABAMA JUNIOR & COMMUNITY COLLEGE CONFERENCE BASEBALL NEWS BUREAU (US) **4882**

ALABAMA JUNIOR & COMMUNITY COLLEGE CONFERENCE WOMEN'S BASKETBALL NEWS BUREAU (US) **4882**

ALABAMA LANDINGS, ANNUAL SUMMARY (US/0360-7992) [02244495] **2293**

ALABAMA LAW INSTITUTE See HANDBOOK - ALABAMA LAW INSTITUTE **2976**

ALABAMA LAW OF DAMAGES (US) **2929**

ALABAMA LAW REVIEW (US/0002-4279) [01478936] **2929**

ALABAMA LAWYER, THE (US/0002-4287) [01478937] **2929**

ALABAMA LEGAL DIRECTORY, THE (US/0145-4390) [02737430] **2929**

ALABAMA LIBRARIAN, THE (US/0002-4295) [01478938] **3188**

ALABAMA LITERARY REVIEW (US/0890-1554) [14160454] **3359**

ALABAMA LIVING (MONTGOMERY, ALA.) (US/1047-031X) [19753003] **2527**

ALABAMA LOCAL GOVERNMENT JOURNAL See ALABAMA MUNICIPAL JOURNAL, THE **4625**

ALABAMA MAGAZINE (US/1040-2349) [10666313] **2527**

ALABAMA MANUFACTURERS REGISTER (US/1045-2664) [20059005] **3475**

ALABAMA MEDICAID (US) [09035826] **3547, 2872**

ALABAMA MEDICAID AGENCY See ANNUAL REPORT / THE ALABAMA MEDICAID AGENCY **3551**

ALABAMA MEDICINE (US/0738-4947) [09607797] **3547**

ALABAMA MESSENGER, THE (US/0273-9593) [05333083] **5625**

ALABAMA-MESSENGER, THE (US) [15744406] **2929, 5625**

ALABAMA MUNICIPAL JOURNAL, THE (US/0002-4309) [05458905] **4625**

ALABAMA NURSE, THE (US/0002-4317) [05507977] **3850**

ALABAMA OFFICIAL DIRECTORY See ALABAMA DIRECTORY **4625**

ALABAMA PEACE OFFICERS' JOURNAL (US/0279-5175) [07935998] **3156**

ALABAMA PLANNING RESOURCE CHECKLIST : COUNTY/REGIONAL SERIES (US/0147-8419) [03232366] **2813**

ALABAMA POLICE JOURNAL (US/0274-7448) [06549588] **3156**

ALABAMA. PROGRAM FOR EXCEPTIONAL CHILDREN AND YOUTH See ALABAMA ANNUAL PROGRAM PLAN, FY ... FOR PART B OF THE EDUCATION OF THE HANDICAPPED ACT AS AMENDED BY PUBLIC LAW 94-142 **1874**

ALABAMA PUBLIC LIBRARY SERVICE See ALABAMA PUBLIC LIBRARY SERVICE ANNUAL REPORT **3189**

ALABAMA PUBLIC LIBRARY SERVICE See BASIC STATE PLAN AND ANNUAL PROGRAM **3193**

ALABAMA PUBLIC LIBRARY SERVICE See LIBRARY DIRECTORY AND ... STATISTICAL REPORT **3225**

ALABAMA PUBLIC LIBRARY SERVICE ANNUAL REPORT (US) [03890563] **3189**

ALABAMA PURCHASOR (US/0002-4325) [04264230] **948**

ALABAMA REVIEW, THE (US/0002-4341) [01478944] **2718**

ALABAMA RULES ANNOTATED (US/0747-6620) [10715725] **2929**

ALABAMA RULES OF COURTS (US/0198-0319) [06157779] **3138**

ALABAMA SCHOOL BOARDS (US/1065-1861) [06024184] **1723**

ALABAMA SCHOOL JOURNAL (US/0002-435X) [02272714] **1860**

ALABAMA SHPA MONTHLY REVIEW (US/0891-1665) [14687433] **4764**

ALABAMA. STATE BOARD OF REGISTRATION FOR FORESTERS See ROSTER OF REGISTERED FORESTERS : STATE OF ALABAMA **2394**

ALABAMA. STATE BOARD OF REGISTRATION FOR PROFESSIONAL ENGINEERS AND LAND SURVEYORS See BIENNIAL ROSTER OF REGISTERED PROFESSIONAL ENGINEERS AND LAND SURVEYORS AND ALABAMA LAW REGULATING PRACTICE OF ENGINEERING AND LAND SURVEYING **1966**

ALABAMA STATE NURSES' ASSOCIATION. BULLETIN See ALABAMA NURSE, THE **3850**

ALABAMA THOROUGHBRED JOURNAL (US) [14937237] **2796**

ALABAMA TRUCKER CEASED. (US/0002-4384) [09611720] **5375**

ALABAMA. WATER IMPROVEMENT COMMISSION See REPORT TO THE HONORABLE ... GOVERNOR OF THE STATE OF ALABAMA AND MEMBERS OF THE ALABAMA LEGISLATURE, A **2242**

ALABAMA WILDLIFE (US/0894-8356) [16265877] **4868**

ALABAMA'S HEALTH (US/0145-6857) [01478946] **4764**

ALABAMA'S VITAL EVENTS (US/0095-3431) [01796394] **5320**

ALADDIN'S WINDOW (US/1070-6836) [28451981] **3994**

ALAFUA AGRICULTURAL BULLETIN (WS/1015-8499) [10158499] **57**

ALAKANANDA (II) [02239611] **3359**

ALALITCOM, THE (US/0887-0209) [07208497] **3359**

ALALUZ (US/0044-7064) [02460854] **3359**

ALAM AL-BINA (UA) [10716104] **287**

ALAM AL-FIKR (KU) [05204688] **5190**

ALAM AL-ISTITHMAR AL-ARABI. ARAB BUSINESS REPORT (NE) [05428244] **4515, 1545**

ALAM AL-KUTUB (SU) [06871685] **4823**

ALAM AL-MIYAH AL-ARABI (LE) [11304682] **5529**

ALAM AL-NAFT (LE) [03256531] **4249**

ALAM AL-QISSAH / YUSDIRUHA NADI AL-QISSAH BI-AL-ISKANDARIYAH (UA) [06827608] **3359**

ALAM AL-SINAAH (SU) [10378704] **1461**

ALAM SEKITAR (MY/0126-7280) [05077940] **2223**

ALAM TUB AL-ASSNAN (GW) **1315**

ALAMANCE GENEALOGIST (US) **2436**

ALAMANCE NEWS, THE (US) [13118364] **5706**

ALAMBICCO DELL ANCHID (IT) **1012**

ALAMBRE (GW/0002-4406) [03096511] **3475**

ALAMEDA TIMES STAR (US) [28700318] **5632**

● ALAMO AREA SQUARE AND ROUND DANCE ASSOCIATION NEWSLETTER (US/1063-8024) [26139778] **1310**

ALAMOGORDO DAILY NEWS (US) [10674593] **5712**

ALAN REVIEW, THE (US/0882-2840) [05217304] **3359**

ALARMES, PROTECTION, SECURITE (FR/0290-0106) [I02900106] **2858**

ALASKA ADMINISTRATIVE CODE : CONTAINING THE PERMANENT AND EMERGENCY REGULATIONS OF THE STATE OF ALASKA, ANNOTATED / PUBLISHED BY THE LIEUTENANT GOVERNOR'S OFFICE [WITH THE STAFFS OF THE ALASKA LEGISLATIVE COUNCIL AND THE LEGISLATIVE AFFAIRS AGENCY]; ANNOTATED, INDEXED AND PRINTED BY THE BOOK PUBLISHING COMPANY (US) [09485075] **4625**

ALASKA — Alphabetical Title Index

ALASKA. ADULT AND CONTINUING EDUCATION *See* ANNUAL REPORT - ADULT AND CONTINUING EDUCATION (ALASKA) **1799**

ALASKA AGRICULTURAL STATISTICS (US) [01473591] 57, **151**

ALASKA AIRLINES MAGAZINE (US) [12743736] **2527**

●ALASKA ALMANAC : FACTS ABOUT ALASKA, THE (US) [29421162] **2527**

ALASKA (ANCHORAGE, ALASKA) (US/0002-4562) [02246735] **4868**

ALASKA BAPTIST MESSENGER (US/0194-7834) [01776350] **5054**

ALASKA BAR RAG, THE (US/0276-1025) [07289734] **2929**

ALASKA BASIN OUTLOOK REPORT (US) 1419, **5529**

ALASKA BUDGET IN BRIEF (US/0733-2912) [08466525] **4709**

ALASKA BUSINESS DIRECTORY (US/1048-7069) [21011952] **637**

ALASKA BUSINESS MONTHLY (US/8756-4092) [11698090] **637**

ALASKA CATCH AND PRODUCTION, COMMERCIAL FISHERIES STATISTICS (US) [06287542] **2293**

ALASKA. CETA DIVISION *See* COMPREHENSIVE EMPLOYMENT AND TRAINING PLAN, ANNUAL PLAN. BALANCE OF STATE / STATE OF ALASKA, CETA DIVISION **1660**

ALASKA COMMERCIAL SALMON CATCHES / DIVISION OF COMMERCIAL FISHERIES, ALASKA DEPARTMENT OF FISH AND GAME (US) [09520387] **2293**

ALASKA. COMMISSION ON JUDICIAL CONDUCT *See* ANNUAL REPORT / STATE OF ALASKA, COMMISSION ON JUDICIAL CONDUCT **3139**

ALASKA COMMISSION ON POSTSECONDARY EDUCATION *See* STUDENT FINANCIAL AID PROGRAMS, ANNUAL REPORT **1848**

ALASKA CONTRACTOR : A PUBLICATION OF THE ASSOCIATED GENERAL CONTRACTORS OF ALASKA, THE (CN/0846-3247) [25066276] **598**

ALASKA COURT RULES, STATE AND FEDERAL (US) [22736496] **2929**

ALASKA COURT SYSTEM NEWSLETTER (US) [07560270] **3138**

ALASKA DATA INVENTORY CATALOG (US) [05870802] **4462**

ALASKA. DEPT. OF ADMINISTRATION *See* CAPITAL BUDGET AND SIX YEAR IMPROVEMENT PROGRAM **4716**

ALASKA. DEPT. OF ADMINISTRATION. DIVISION OF DATA PROCESSING *See* DATA PROCESSING IN ALASKA **1257**

ALASKA. DEPT. OF COMMERCE AND ECONOMIC DEVELOPMENT *See* ANNUAL REPORT - DEPARTMENT OF COMMERCE AND ECONOMIC DEVELOPMENT **822**

ALASKA. DEPT. OF COMMERCE AND ECONOMIC DEVELOPMENT *See* DIRECTORY OF PERMITS, STATE OF ALASKA **4644**

ALASKA. DEPT. OF COMMUNITY AND REGIONAL AFFAIRS *See* AFFIRMATIVE ACTION PLAN. PART 1, POLICIES & PROCEDURES / ALASKA DEPT. OF COMMUNITY & REGIONAL AFFAIRS **4625**

ALASKA. DEPT. OF EDUCATION *See* ANNUAL REPORT - DEPARTMENT OF EDUCATION **1725**

ALASKA. DEPT. OF EDUCATION *See* TITLE III ESEA MINI-GRANT PROJECT ABSTRACTS **1788**

ALASKA. DEPT. OF FISH AND GAME *See* AFFIRMATIVE ACTION PLAN / ALASKA DEPARTMENT OF FISH AND GAME **2293**

ALASKA. DEPT. OF FISH AND GAME *See* COMMERCIAL OPERATORS **2299**

ALASKA. DEPT. OF HEALTH AND SOCIAL SERVICES *See* PROPOSED COMPREHENSIVE ANNUAL SOCIAL SERVICES PLAN **5302**

ALASKA. DEPT. OF HEALTH AND SOCIAL SERVICES *See* DEPARTMENT OF HEALTH AND SOCIAL SERVICES QUARTERLY MAGAZINE **5281**

ALASKA. DEPT. OF HEALTH AND SOCIAL SERVICES. HSS QUARTERLY *See* DEPARTMENT OF HEALTH AND SOCIAL SERVICES QUARTERLY MAGAZINE **5281**

ALASKA. DEPT. OF HEALTH AND SOCIAL SERVICES. OFFICE OF INFORMATION SYSTEMS *See* PUBLIC ASSISTANCE RECIPIENT AND EXPENDITURE STUDY **5303**

ALASKA. DEPT. OF LABOR. RESEARCH AND ANALYSIS SECTION *See* ALASKA STATISTICAL QUARTERLY **1528**

ALASKA. DEPT. OF LABOR. RESEARCH AND ANALYSIS SECTION *See* LABOR MARKET INFORMATION DIRECTORY **1683**

ALASKA. DEPT. OF REVENUE. RESEARCH & ANALYSIS SECTION *See* REVENUE NEWS **4747**

ALASKA. DEPT. OF TRANSPORTATION AND PUBLIC FACILITIES *See* ANNUAL REPORT - DEPT. OF TRANSPORTATION AND PUBLIC FACILITIES **5376**

ALASKA. DEPT. OF TRANSPORTATION AND PUBLIC FACILITIES *See* SIX-YEAR CAPITAL IMPROVEMENT PROGRAM, THE **5393**

ALASKA. DEPT. OF TRANSPORTATION AND PUBLIC FACILITIES *See* CAPITAL IMPROVEMENT PROGRAM **5379**

ALASKA. DEPT. OF TRANSPORTATION AND PUBLIC FACILITIES. RESEARCH SECTION *See* ANNUAL REPORT TO DIRECTOR ... / RESEARCH SECTION, DIVISION OF PLANNING AND PROGRAMMING, DEPT. OF TRANSPORTATION (ALASKA) **5377**

ALASKA DIRECTORY OF ATTORNEYS (US/0275-1895) [07066690] **2929**

ALASKA. DIVISION OF ALCOHOLISM AND DRUG ABUSE *See* STATE OF ALASKA ALCOHOLISM AND DRUG ABUSE PLAN **1349**

ALASKA. DIVISION OF BUDGET & MANAGEMENT *See* ALASKA BUDGET IN BRIEF **4709**

ALASKA. DIVISION OF COMMUNITY AND RURAL DEVELOPMENT *See* LEGISLATIVE SUMMARY - DEPARTMENT OF COMMUNITY AND REGIONAL AFFAIRS, DIVISION OF COMMUNITY AND RURAL DEVELOPMENT **3002**

ALASKA. DIVISION OF ECONOMIC ENTERPRISE *See* COMMUNITY MATRIX FOR DEVELOPMENT PROJECTS **2818**

ALASKA. DIVISION OF FISHERIES REHABILITATION, ENHANCEMENT, AND DEVELOPMENT *See* FRED ... ANNUAL REPORT TO THE ALASKA STATE LEGISLATURE **2304**

ALASKA. DIVISION OF GAME *See* ANNUAL REPORT OF SURVEY-INVENTORY ACTIVITIES **4869**

ALASKA. DIVISION OF GEOLOGICAL AND GEOPHYSICAL SURVEYS *See* INFORMATION CIRCULAR - ALASKA. DIVISION OF GEOLOGICAL AND GEOPHYSICAL SURVEYS **1356**

ALASKA. DIVISION OF GEOLOGICAL AND GEOPHYSICAL SURVEYS *See* SPECIAL REPORT - ALASKA. DIVISION OF GEOLOGICAL AND GEOPHYSICAL SURVEYS **1398**

ALASKA. DIVISION OF OCCUPATIONAL SAFETY AND HEALTH *See* REPORT TO THE ALASKA LEGISLATURE - DIVISION OF OCCUPATIONAL SAFETY AND HEALTH **2869**

ALASKA ECONOMIC REPORT, THE (US) [01409653] **1461**

ALASKA ECONOMIC TRENDS (US/0160-3345) [01478967] **1461**

ALASKA EDUCATION DIRECTORY (US/0733-236X) [07506085] **1723**

ALASKA EDUCATION NEWS *CEASED.* (US/0516-4842) [08041338] **1723**

ALASKA (EL CAJON, CALIF.) (US/0739-3792) [09714014] **5460**

ALASKA. EMPLOYMENT SECURITY DIVISION. RESEARCH AND ANALYSIS SECTION *See* ALASKA LABOR FORCE ESTIMATES BY INDUSTRY & AREA **1643**

ALASKA FEDERAL-STATE-PRIVATE COOPERATIVE SNOW SURVEYS BASIN OUTLOOK REPORTS (US) [22342249] **5529**

ALASKA FEST (US/0199-0586) [05542986] **5460**

ALASKA FISHERMAN'S JOURNAL (US/0164-8330) [04315587] **2293**

ALASKA FISHERY RESEARCH BULLETIN (US) **2293**

ALASKA FISHING GUIDE (US/0361-3984) [02058945] **2293**

ALASKA GEOGRAPHIC (US/0361-1353) [01148967] **2553**

●ALASKA HEALTH CARE IN PERSPECTIVE (US/1065-4046) [26604579] **4764**

ALASKA HIGH SCHOOL SENIORS SURVEY REPORT (US) [09534572] **1723**

ALASKA HISTORY (CN/0828-1858) [07985920] **2718**

ALASKA HISTORY (ANCHORAGE, ALASKA) (US/0890-6149) [12073473] **2718**

ALASKA HUNTING GUIDE (US/0095-5760) [02246621] **4868**

ALASKA IN PERSPECTIVE (LAWRENCE, KAN.) (US/1065-531X) [26627282] **5320**

ALASKA JOURNAL (JUNEAU, ALASKA : 1971) *CEASED.* (US/0002-4503) [01268531] **2527**

ALASKA JOURNAL OF COMMERCE (US) [23280590] **822**

ALASKA JOURNAL OF COMMERCE & PACIFIC RIM REPORTER (US/0271-3276) [06606387] **822**

ALASKA LABOR FORCE ESTIMATES BY INDUSTRY & AREA (US/0362-4196) [02338289] **1643**

ALASKA LAND & HOME MAGAZINE (US) **2484**

ALASKA LAW REVIEW (US/0883-0568) [10767319] **2929**

ALASKA. LEGISLATURE. AUDIT COMMITTEE. ANNUAL REPORT *See* ANNUAL REPORT - STATE OF ALASKA, LEGISLATIVE BUDGET AND AUDIT COMMITTEE **4710**

ALASKA. LEGISLATURE. BUDGET AND AUDIT COMMITTEE *See* ANNUAL REPORT - STATE OF ALASKA, LEGISLATIVE BUDGET AND AUDIT COMMITTEE **4710**

ALASKA LIBRARY DIRECTORY (US/0146-1028) [02852996] **3189**

ALASKA. LIEUTENANT GOVERNOR'S OFFICE *See* ALASKA ADMINISTRATIVE CODE : CONTAINING THE PERMANENT AND EMERGENCY REGULATIONS OF THE STATE OF ALASKA, ANNOTATED / PUBLISHED BY THE LIEUTENANT GOVERNOR'S OFFICE [WITH THE STAFFS OF THE ALASKA LEGISLATIVE COUNCIL AND THE LEGISLATIVE AFFAIRS AGENCY]; ANNOTATED, INDEXED AND PRINTED BY THE BOOK PUBLISHING COMPANY **4625**

ALASKA MARINE RADIO DIRECTORY (US/8755-3422) [11254423] **1148**

ALASKA MARINE RESOURCE QUARTERLY (US/1060-2895) [17684078] 2294, **1446**

ALASKA MEDICAL FACILITY AUTHORITY *See* ANNUAL REPORT AND FINANCIAL STATEMENTS / ALASKA MEDICAL FACILITY AUTHORITY **3776**

ALASKA MEDICINE (US/0002-4538) [01696094] **3547**

ALASKA MINES & GEOLOGY *CEASED.* (US/0278-368X) [07499121] **1365**

ALASKA MISSION OUTREACH (US) [08615383] **4933**

ALASKA MUNICIPAL BOND BANK *See* ANNUAL REPORT AND FINANCIAL STATEMENTS - ALASKA MUNICIPAL BOND BANK **891**

ALASKA MUNICIPAL OFFICIALS DIRECTORY (US/0363-4167) [02455881] **4625**

ALASKA NATIVE HUMAN RESOURCES DEVELOPMENT PROGRAM *See* ANNUAL REPORT - ALASKA NATIVE HUMAN RESOURCES DEVELOPMENT PROGRAM **1648**

ALASKA NATIVE HUMAN RESOURCES DEVELOPMENT PROGRAM. FISCAL YEAR REPORT *See* ANNUAL REPORT - ALASKA NATIVE HUMAN RESOURCES DEVELOPMENT PROGRAM **1648**

ALASKA NATIVE LANGUAGE CENTER RESEARCH PAPERS (US/0883-8526) [07848419] 2254, 2527, **3262**

ALASKA NATIVE MEDICAL CENTER *See* ANNUAL REPORT - ALASKA NATIVE MEDICAL CENTER **3776**

ALASKA. NORTHERN OPERATIONS OF RAIL TRANSPORTATION AND HIGHWAYS COMMISSION *See* ANNUAL REPORT OF THE NORTH COMMISSION (ALASKA) **5429**

ALASKA NURSE, THE (US/0002-4546) [04814627] **3850**

ALASKA. OCCUPATIONAL SAFETY AND HEALTH REVIEW BOARD *See* DECISIONS OF THE OCCUPATIONAL SAFETY AND HEALTH REVIEW BOARD **2959**

ALASKA OCSEAP NEWSLETTER *CEASED.* (US/0734-4155) [08408439] **2185**

ALASKA. OFFICE OF ALCOHOLISM *See* ANNUAL UPDATE TO THE ALASKA STATE PLAN FOR THE REDUCTION OF ALCOHOLISM AND ALCOHOL ABUSE **1341**

ALASKA. OFFICE OF ALCOHOLISM *See* REPORT - OFFICE OF ALCOHOLISM, DEPARTMENT OF HEALTH AND SOCIAL SERVICES, STATE OF ALASKA **1348**

ALASKA. OFFICE OF THE GOVERNOR *See* GOVERNOR'S MANPOWER PLAN (JUNEAU) **1676**

ALASKA OIL AND GAS CONSERVATION COMMISSION *See* BULLETIN - STATE OF ALASKA, ALASKA OIL AND GAS CONSERVATION COMMISSION **2189**

ALASKA OIL & INDUSTRY NEWS (US/0889-7352) [14066335] **4249**

ALASKA OIL SPILL REPORTER (US/1045-7070) [20214397] **4249**

Alphabetical Title Index — ALBERTA

ALASKA OPEN-FILE REPORT (US/0196-0776) [03466113] 1402, **1365**

ALASKA PERSONAL LINES STATISTICAL ANALYSIS, PRIVATE PASSENGER AUTOMOBILE INSURANCE, HOMEOWNERS INSURANCE / DIVISION OF INSURANCE, DEPARTMENT OF COMMERCE AND ECONOMIC DEVELOPMENT, STATE OF ALASKA (US) [09317375] 2872, **2897**

ALASKA PETROLEUM & INDUSTRIAL DIRECTORY *CEASED.* (US/0065-5813) [01150743] **4249**

ALASKA PHARMACIST (US/0735-519X) [08615373] **4290**

ALASKA PUBLIC AFFAIRS JOURNAL, THE *SUSPENDED.* (US/1048-8952) [21075504] **1461**

ALASKA PUBLIC EMPLOYEE / APEA, FEDERATION OF STATE EMPLOYEES, AFT, AFL-CIO, THE (US) [23297332] **1643**

ALASKA QUARTERLY REVIEW (US/0737-268X) [09310389] **3359**

ALASKA REGION REPORT (US/0737-3961) [06073710] **2374**

ALASKA REVIEW OF SOCIAL AND ECONOMIC CONDITIONS (US/0162-5403) [04008249] **1545**

ALASKA SEA GRANT COLLEGE PROGRAM *See* ANNUAL REPORT / ALASKA SEA GRANT COLLEGE PROGRAM **2294**

ALASKA SHIPPERS GUIDE (US/0271-8987) [06699728] **5447**

ALASKA SNOW SURVEY REPORT / UNITED STATES DEPARTMENT OF AGRICULTURE, SOIL CONSERVATION SERVICE (US) [29657097] **5529**

ALASKA SNOW SURVEYS AND FEDERAL-STATE-PRIVATE COOPERATIVE SNOW SURVEYS (US) [14581782] 1412, **5529**

ALASKA STATE DRUG ABUSE PLAN. REVISED UPDATE (US) [05963463] **1339**

ALASKA. STATE MANPOWER SERVICES COUNCIL *See* COMPREHENSIVE EMPLOYMENT & TRAINING PROGRAMS IN ALASKA **1660**

ALASKA. STATE OFFICE OF ALCOHOLISM AND DRUG ABUSE *See* ALASKA STATE DRUG ABUSE PLAN. REVISED UPDATE **1339**

ALASKA STATE PLAN FOR THE REDUCTION OF ALCOHOLISM AND ALCOHOL ABUSE, THE (US) **1339**

ALASKA STATISTICAL QUARTERLY (US/0401-1961) [07039608] 1643, **1528**

ALASKA TODAY *CEASED.* (US/0191-328X) [04872283] 1126, **2917**

ALASKA TRANSPORTER : THE OFFICIAL PUBLICATION OF THE ALASKA TRUCKING ASSOCIATION, INC (CN/1186-7558) [24368578] **5375**

ALASKA. UNIVERSITY. INSTITUTE OF SOCIAL, ECONOMIC AND GOVERNMENT RESEARCH *See* ISEGR REPORT **1568**

ALASKA WORKFORCE ESTIMATES BY INDUSTRY AND AREA *See* ALASKA LABOR FORCE ESTIMATES BY INDUSTRY & AREA **1643**

ALASKAMEN USA (US/1055-2227) [23115559] **5550**

ALASKAN EPIPHANY (US/0742-7735) [06631878] **5054**

ALASKA'S INSIDE PASSAGE TRAVELER : SEE MORE, SPEND LESS! (US/1046-5871) [15719895] **5460**

ALASKA'S MINERAL INDUSTRY (US/0741-5168) [10137823] **1437**

ALASKA'S RESOURCES (US/0164-9558) [04252099] **2186**

ALASKA'S WILDLIFE *CEASED.* (US/1052-2727) [22233295] **4868**

ALATEEN TALK (US/1054-1411) [22762227] **1339**

ALAUDA (FR/0002-4619) [01478999] **5614**

ALAZET : REVISTA DE FILOLOGIA (SP/0214-7602) [21465110] **3262**

ALBA DE AMERICA (US/0888-3181) [12795639] **3359**

ALBA POMPEIA (IT/0394-9427) [l03949427] **335**

ALBA : REVISTA DE POESIA (SP) **3459**

ALBANIA REPORT *CEASED.* (US/0002-4651) [03022783] **4462**

ALBANIA TODAY *CEASED.* (AA/0044-7072) [01661316] **4462**

ALBANIAN CATHOLIC BULLETIN (US/0272-7250) [06901004] **5022**

ALBANY DAILY HERALD (ALBANY, GA.) (US) [15229624] **5652**

ALBANY EAGLE, THE *CEASED.* (US) [17383303] **5713**

ALBANY HERALD (US) [11361051] **5765**

ALBANY HERALD (US) [19744220] **5652**

ALBANY JOURNAL (ALBANY, GA.) *See* JOURNAL, THE **5654**

ALBANY LAW JOURNAL OF SCIENCE & TECHNOLOGY (US/1059-4280) [23860428] 5082, **2929**

ALBANY LAW REVIEW (US/0002-4678) [01479006] **2929**

ALBANY LAW SCHOOL *See* ALUMNI DIRECTORY / ALBANY LAW SCHOOL OF UNION UNIVERSITY **1097**

ALBANY NEWS (ALBANY, TEX.) (US) [13882330] **5746**

ALBANY PRESERVATION REPORT (US/1040-6964) [14261274] **2718**

ALBANY STATE COLLEGE *See* ALUMNI DIRECTORY - ALBANY STATE COLLEGE **1097**

ALBANY STATE COLLEGE. DIVISION OF ARTS AND SCIENCES *See* ALBANY STATE COLLEGE JOURNAL OF ARTS AND SCIENCES **1808**

ALBANY STATE COLLEGE JOURNAL OF ARTS AND SCIENCES (US/0199-9826) [06289065] **1808**

ALBANY : THE UNIVERSITY AT ALBANY MAGAZINE WITH THE CARILLON (US) [25564412] **1089**

ALBEMARLE MAGAZINE, THE (US/0273-7841) [06752911] **2527**

... ALBERT LEA TRIBUNE, THE (US/1051-7421) [20607968] **5694**

ALBERTA *See* STATUTES OF ALBERTA **3059**

ALBERTA *See* ALBERTA GAZETTE **4625**

ALBERTA *See* ESTIMATES OF EXPENDITURE : INCOME ACCOUNT **4721**

ALBERTA *See* ESTIMATES OF EXPENDITURE : CAPITAL ACCOUNT AND SUMMARY OF AMOUNTS TO BE VOTED (ALBERTA) **4721**

ALBERTA *See* GOVERNMENT ESTIMATES **4728**

ALBERTA ADVISORY COUNCIL ON WOMEN'S ISSUES (CN/1182-7718) [23257554] **5550**

ALBERTA AGENCY FOR INTERNATIONAL DEVELOPMENT *See* ANNUAL REVIEW / ALBERTA AGENCY FOR INTERNATIONAL DEVELOPMENT **2907**

ALBERTA AGRICULTURAL DEVELOPMENT CORPORATION *See* ANNUAL REPORT - ALBERTA AGRICULTURAL DEVELOPMENT CORPORATION **60**

ALBERTA. ALBERTA AGRICULTURE. RESOURCE ECONOMICS BRANCH *See* AGRICULTURAL REAL ESTATE VALUES IN ALBERTA **4833**

ALBERTA. ALBERTA CONSUMER AND CORPORATE AFFAIRS *See* PUBLIC CONTRIBUTIONS ACT ... ANNUAL REPORT ..., THE **5303**

ALBERTA. ALBERTA CULTURE AND MULTICULTURALISM *See* ANNUAL REPORT / ALBERTA CULTURE AND MULTICULTURALISM **2528**

ALBERTA. ALBERTA EDUCATION *See* ANNUAL REVIEW, ALBERTA EDUCATION **1725**

ALBERTA. ALBERTA ENVIRONMENT *See* ANNUAL REPORT - ALBERTA ENVIRONMENT **2160**

ALBERTA. ALBERTA FAMILY AND SOCIAL SERVICES. STAFF DEVELOPMENT *See* STAFF DEVELOPMENT CALENDAR - ALBERTA. ALBERTA FAMILY AND SOCIAL SERVICES. STAFF DEVELOPMENT **5311**

ALBERTA. ALBERTA FORESTRY, LANDS AND WILDLIFE *See* ANNUAL REPORT / ALBERTA FORESTRY, LANDS AND WILDLIFE **2374**

ALBERTA. ALBERTA HEALTH *See* ANNUAL REPORT / ALBERTA HEALTH **4765**

ALBERTA. ALBERTA HEALTH *See* HEALTH VISION **4782**

ALBERTA. ALBERTA LABOUR *See* ANNUAL REPORT - ALBERTA LABOUR **1648**

ALBERTA. ALBERTA TOURISM *See* ANNUAL REPORT / DEPARTMENT OF TOURISM **5461**

ALBERTA. ALBERTA TRANSPORTATION AND UTILITIES *See* ANNUAL REPORT - ALBERTA TRANSPORTATION AND UTILITIES **5376**

ALBERTA. ALBERTA TREASURY *See* FINANCIAL SUMMARY AND BUDGETARY REVIEW **4726**

ALBERTA. ALBERTA TREASURY *See* PUBLIC SERVICE MANAGEMENT PENSION PLAN, ANNUAL REPORT **4677**

ALBERTA & BRITISH COLUMBIA GOLF GUIDE (CN/0848-838X) [21320664] **4882**

ALBERTA ARCHAEOLOGICAL REVIEW, THE (CN/0701-1776) [03409618] **253**

ALBERTA. ASSESSMENT EQUALIZATION BOARD *See* LAND ASSESSMENT/SALES RATIO STUDY AND EQUALIZED ASSESSMENTS **4660**

ALBERTA ASSOCIATION OF ARCHITECTS *See* REGISTER AND FIRM INDEX / THE ALBERTA ASSOCIATION OF ARCHITECTS **307**

ALBERTA ASSOCIATION OF LIBRARY TECHNICIANS *See* AALT TECHNICIAN **3186**

ALBERTA ASSOCIATION OF REGISTERED NURSES *See* A A R N NEWSLETTER **3849**

ALBERTA. ATMOSPHERIC ENVIRONMENT SERVICE *See* CLIMATE OF ALBERTA WITH DATA FOR YUKON AND NORTHWEST TERRITORIES, REPORT **1422**

ALBERTA BADMINTON ASSOCIATION *See* HANDBOOK - ALBERTA BADMINTON ASSOCIATION **4898**

ALBERTA BEEF (1991) (CN/1187-0761) [25066852] **205**

ALBERTA BILLS (CN) **4625**

ALBERTA. BUREAU OF STATISTICS *See* ABSTRACTS - ALBERTA. BUREAU OF STATISTICS **5320**

ALBERTA. BUREAU OF STATISTICS *See* ABS NEWSTATS **5320**

ALBERTA BUSINESS (CALGARY) (CN/0827-2603) [11762405] **637**

ALBERTA BUSINESS WHO'S WHO & DIRECTORY (CN/0827-5750) [13924793] 637, **429**

ALBERTA CATHOLIC DIRECTORY (CN/0316-473X) [02578339] **5022**

ALBERTA CATTLEMAN, THE (CN/0226-6075) [06472477] **205**

ALBERTA. CHIEF ELECTORAL OFFICER *See* ANNUAL REPORT OF THE CHIEF ELECTORAL OFFICER ADMINISTERING THE ELECTION FINANCES AND CONTRIBUTIONS DISCLOSURE ACT **4628**

ALBERTA. CHIEF ELECTORAL OFFICER *See* REPORT OF THE CHIEF ELECTORAL OFFICER ON THE ... GENERAL ENUMERATION **4680**

ALBERTA COAL INDUSTRY ANNUAL STATISTICS (CN/0380-4321) [02443987] 1931, **1961**

ALBERTA COLLEGE OF ART. GALLERY *See* ANNUAL WILD WEST SHOW **337**

ALBERTA CONSTRUCTION (CN/0709-2431) [05375524] **598**

ALBERTA CONSTRUCTION & RESOURCE INDUSTRIES DIRECTORY/PURCHASING GUIDE (CN/0713-4045) [09026014] **598**

ALBERTA COORDINATED HOME CARE PROGRAM *See* ALBERTA COORDINATED HOME CARE PROGRAM DIRECTORY **4764**

ALBERTA COORDINATED HOME CARE PROGRAM DIRECTORY (CN/1182-4867) [23259484] **4764**

ALBERTA. CORPORATE TAX ADMINISTRATION *See* INTERPRETATION BULLETIN / ALBERTA TREASURY, CORPORATE TAX ADMINISTRATION **3100**

ALBERTA COUNCIL OF COLLEGE LIBRARIANS *See* A. C. C. L. UNION LIST OF SERIALS **3186**

ALBERTA COUNCIL ON ADMISSIONS AND TRANSFER *See* ALBERTA TRANSFER GUIDE **1808**

ALBERTA COUNSELLETTER (CN/0381-5951) [02294852] **1723**

ALBERTA COURT CALENDAR (CN/0226-4196) [06689119] **3138**

ALBERTA CRAFT MAGAZINE (CN/0834-910X) [16753639] **369**

●ALBERTA DAIRYMAN (CN/1194-9589) [28954868] **191**

ALBERTA DECISIONS, CIVIL AND CRIMINAL CASES (CN/0319-7980) [02627310] **2929**

ALBERTA DEMOCRAT, THE (CN/1187-3396) [25589924] **4462**

ALBERTA. DEPT. OF BUSINESS DEVELOPMENT AND TOURISM *See* INDUSTRY & RESOURCES **1611**

ALBERTA. DEPT. OF HOUSING *See* ANNUAL REPORT - ALBERTA DEPARTMENT OF HOUSING **2814**

ALBERTA. DISTANCE LEARNING *See* HANDBOOK FOR CLASSROOM STUDENTS/ ALBERTA DISTANCE LEARNING CENTRE **1749**

ALBERTA. DISTANCE LEARNING *See* HANDBOOK FOR NON-CLASSROOM STUDENTS / ALBERTA DISTANCE LEARNING CENTRE **1749**

ALBERTA DOCTORS' DIGEST, THE (CN/0833-8477) [15128013] **3547**

ALBERTA
Alphabetical Title Index

ALBERTA DRILLING PROGRESS AND PIPELINE RECEIPTS WEEKLY REPORT (CN/0227-3357) [06635503] **4249**

ALBERTA ECHO (CN/0319-1737) [02442222] **2718**

ALBERTA (EDMONTON) *CEASED.* (CN/0843-9931) [20781791] 5190, **312**

ALBERTA ELECTRIC INDUSTRY. ANNUAL STATISTICS (CN/0706-1420) [05590352] 1931, **1961**

ALBERTA ENERGY RESOURCE INDUSTRIES, MONTHLY STATISTICS (CN/0710-6874) [09273093] 1931, **1961**

ALBERTA. ENERGY RESOURCES CONSERVATION BOARD *See* RESERVES OF COAL, PROVINCE OF ALBERTA **1955**

ALBERTA. ENERGY RESOURCES CONSERVATION BOARD *See* RESERVOIR PERFORMANCE CHARTS: OIL POOLS **4276**

ALBERTA. ENERGY RESOURCES CONSERVATION BOARD *See* MONTHLY STATISTICS. ALBERTA COAL INDUSTRY **1963**

ALBERTA. ENERGY RESOURCES CONSERVATION BOARD *See* RESERVOIR PERFORMANCE CHARTS: GAS POOLS **4276**

ALBERTA. ENERGY RESOURCES CONSERVATION BOARD *See* MONTHLY STATISTICS. ALBERTA ELECTRIC ENERGY INDUSTRY **1950**

ALBERTA. ENERGY RESOURCES CONSERVATION BOARD *See* SUMMARY OF ORDERS AND APPROVALS - ENERGY RESOURCES CONSERVATION BOARD **1958**

ALBERTA. ENERGY RESOURCES CONSERVATION BOARD *See* ALBERTA COAL INDUSTRY ANNUAL STATISTICS **1961**

ALBERTA. ENERGY RESOURCES CONSERVATION BOARD *See* ALBERTA DRILLING PROGRESS AND PIPELINE RECEIPTS WEEKLY REPORT **4249**

ALBERTA. ENGINEERING AND HOME DESIGN BRANCH *See* AGRICULTURAL INPUT PRICES, PRICE INDICES AND AVAILABILITY IN ALBERTA **50**

ALBERTA ENGLISH (CN/0382-5191) [02297987] 1888, **3262**

ALBERTA ENVIRONMENTAL RESEARCH TRUST *See* ALERT (CALGARY) **2159**

ALBERTA FACT SHEET (CN/0704-4488) [05711296] **5178**

ALBERTA FAMILY HISTORIES SOCIETY QUARTERLY (CN/0228-9288) [07822620] **2436**

ALBERTA FARM & RANCH (CN/0823-6720) [09985999] **57**

ALBERTA FARM & RANCH, FARM DIRECTORY (CN/0832-4867) [17311457] **57**

ALBERTA FIELD/POOL PRODUCTION AND INJECTION MONTHLY SUPPLEMENT (CN/1183-7004) [25351945] **4249**

ALBERTA FIRE NEWS (1990) (CN/0848-6794) [23455448] **2287**

ALBERTA FISHING GUIDE (CN/0318-4943) [02442059] **2294**

ALBERTA FOUNDATION FOR THE PERFORMING ARTS *See* ANNUAL REPORT - THE ALBERTA FOUNDATION FOR THE PERFORMING ARTS **383**

ALBERTA GAME WARDEN, THE (CN/1184-2687) [24265635] **4868**

ALBERTA GAZETTE (CN/0002-4775) [02249539] **4625**

ALBERTA GENEALOGICAL SOCIETY *See* ANCESTOR INDEX **2437**

ALBERTA GOVERNMENT LIBRARIES' NEWSLETTER (CN/0707-0306) [04634879] **3189**

ALBERTA GOVERNMENT PUBLICATIONS (CN/0840-4976) [19284859] **407**

ALBERTA GOVERNMENT PUBLICATIONS QUARTERLY LIST (CN/1184-9851) [24860777] **407**

ALBERTA GREENHOUSE NOTES (CN) [17222168] **2408**

ALBERTA GUIDE TO SPORTFISHING (CN/1185-2836) [24623937] **4868**

ALBERTA HAIL AND CROP INSURANCE CORPORATION *See* ANNUAL REPORT - ALBERTA HAIL AND CROP INSURANCE CORPORATION **2873**

ALBERTA HANSARD (CN/0383-3623) [02242488] **4625**

ALBERTA HEALTH AND SOCIAL SERVICE EDUCATION PROGRAMS INVENTORY (CN/0848-399X) [22569889] 4764, **5271**

ALBERTA HEALTH AND SOCIAL SERVICES DISCIPLINES COMMITTEE *See* ANNUAL REPORT - ALBERTA HEALTH AND SOCIAL SERVICES DISCIPLINES COMMITTEE **3913**

ALBERTA HEALTH DISCIPLINES BOARD *See* ANNUAL REPORT OF THE ALBERTA HEALTH DISCIPLINES BOARD FOR THE PERIOD OF JANUARY 1 ... TO DECEMBER 31 **4766**

ALBERTA HEALTH FACILITIES REVIEW COMMITTEE *See* ANNUAL REPORT ... OF ALBERTA HEALTH FACILITIES REVIEW COMMITTEE **3776**

ALBERTA HERITAGE FOUNDATION FOR MEDICAL RESEARCH *See* NEWSLETTER / ALBERTA HERITAGE FOUNDATION FOR MEDICAL RESEARCH **3621**

ALBERTA HISTORY (CN/0316-1552) [02244503] **2718**

ALBERTA INSURANCE DIRECTORY (CN/0712-9343) [08977463] **2873**

ALBERTA JOURNAL OF EDUCATIONAL RESEARCH (CN/0002-4805) [01773746] **1723**

ALBERTA. LAND-RELATED INFORMATION SERVICES BRANCH *See* LRIS NEWSLETTER **2387**

ALBERTA LAW REFORM INSTITUTE *See* ANNUAL REPORT / ALBERTA LAW REFORM INSTITUTE **2934**

ALBERTA LAW REPORTS (CN/0703-3117) [02703442] **2929**

ALBERTA LAW REVIEW (CN/0002-4821) [01479040] **2929**

ALBERTA LEARNING RESOURCES JOURNAL (CN/0380-1306) [02731704] **1888**

ALBERTA LEGAL TELEPHONE DIRECTORY (CN/0823-2350) [10436243] **3138**

ALBERTA. LEGISLATIVE ASSEMBLY *See* LEGISLATIVE ASSEMBLY OF ALBERTA **4661**

ALBERTA. LEGISLATIVE ASSEMBLY *See* ALBERTA HANSARD **4625**

ALBERTA LIBRARY BOARD *See* ALBERTA LIBRARY BOARD REPORT **3189**

ALBERTA LIBRARY BOARD REPORT (CN/0715-1640) [07389829] **3189**

ALBERTA LIBRARY NEWS *CEASED.* (CN/0705-6087) [04101040] **3189**

ALBERTA LIST (CN/0568-9163) [02441594] **4625**

ALBERTA MANUFACTURERS INDEX (CN/0823-4450) [09833945] **3475**

ALBERTA MODERN LANGUAGE JOURNAL (CN/0318-5176) [02442143] **3263**

ALBERTA MORTGAGE AND HOUSING CORPORATION *See* ANNUAL REPORT / AMHC, ALBERTA MORTGAGE AND HOUSING CORPORATION **2814**

ALBERTA MUSEUMS REVIEW (CN/0380-3279) [02442934] **4083**

ALBERTA NATIVE NEWS (CN/0829-4135) [15997700] **2254**

ALBERTA. OFFICE OF THE AUDITOR GENERAL *See* REPORT OF THE AUDITOR GENERAL (EDMONTON) **4745**

ALBERTA. OFFICE OF THE FARMERS' ADVOCATE *See* ANNUAL REPORT - OFFICE OF THE FARMERS' ADVOCATE (ALBERTA) **2935**

ALBERTA OIL & FORESTRY REVIEW QUARTERLY (CN/0840-6146) [20286791] 2374, **4249**

ALBERTA PARLIAMENTARY DIGEST (CN/0830-9760) [13647613] **2929**

ALBERTA PAST (CN) **2718**

ALBERTA PERSPECTIVE *SUSPENDED.* (CN/0713-8067) [09088984] **5271**

●ALBERTA PETROLEUM EQUIPMENT & SERVICES DIRECTORY (CN/1193-3097) [26776169] **4249**

ALBERTA PHYSICIANS AND SURGEONS, PROVINCE OF ALBERTA (CN/0319-5031) [02442236] **3913**

ALBERTA POPULATION GROWTH (CN/0848-2845) [15796746] **4549**

ALBERTA. PRIVATE COLLEGES ACCREDITATION BOARD *See* MANAGEMENT PLAN / PRIVATE COLLEGES ACCREDITATION BOARD **1866**

ALBERTA. PROVINCIAL FILM LIBRARY *See* PROVINCIAL FILM LIBRARY RESOURCE CATALOGUE **3242**

ALBERTA PROVINCIAL PARKS USER STATISTICS (CN/0821-0683) [09578618] **4856**

ALBERTA. PUBLIC AFFAIRS BUREAU *See* LIST OF ALBERTA PUBLICATIONS AND LEGISLATION **4662**

ALBERTA. PUBLIC AFFAIRS. TABLE OF ALBERTA LEGISLATION (CN) **2929**

ALBERTA PUBLIC SAFETY SERVICES *See* ANNUAL REPORT - PUBLIC SAFETY SERVICES (ALBERTA) **4766**

ALBERTA. RECREATION, PARKS AND WILDLIFE FOUNDATION *See* ANNUAL REPORT / RECREATION, PARKS AND WILDLIFE FOUNDATION **4706**

ALBERTA REGISTERED DIETITIANS ASSOCIATION *See* MEMBERSHIP ROSTER / ALBERTA REGISTERED DIETITIANS ASSOCIATION **4194**

ALBERTA REPORT (CN/0225-0519) [06054578] **2527**

ALBERTA REPORTS (FREDERICTON, N.B. : BOUND CUMULATION) (CN/0703-3109) [09157079] **3180**

ALBERTA RESEARCH COUNCIL *See* ANNUAL REPORT / ALBERTA RESEARCH COUNCIL **2096**

ALBERTA RESTAURANT NEWS *CEASED.* (CN/0848-631X) [22768705] **5070**

ALBERTA RURAL DEVELOPMENT STUDIES (CN/0707-9818) [04955197] **57**

ALBERTA RURAL MONTH (CN/0823-0218) [09801035] **57**

ALBERTA SASKATCHEWAN MANITOBA CRIMINAL DECISIONS (CN/0715-3155) [09113404] **3104**

ALBERTA SCIENCE EDUCATION JOURNAL (CN/0701-1024) [03402767] 1888, **5082**

ALBERTA SCIENCE TEACHER, THE (CN/0229-3099) [07869869] **5082**

ALBERTA SECURITIES COMMISSION *See* ANNUAL REPORT - SECURITIES COMMISSION (EDMONTON) **4629**

ALBERTA SECURITIES COMMISSION *See* SUMMARY - ALBERTA SECURITIES COMMISSION **3060**

ALBERTA SOCIETY OF ARTISTS *See* OFFICERS / ALBERTA SOCIETY OF ARTISTS **361**

ALBERTA STABLE DIRECTORY (CN/1184-163X) [23263682] **2796**

ALBERTA STATISTICAL REVIEW (ANNUAL ED.) (CN/0317-3917) [01796290] **5320**

ALBERTA. SUPERINTENDENT OF INSURANCE *See* ANNUAL REPORT / SUPERINTENDENT OF INSURANCE **2873**

ALBERTA TEACHERS' ASSOCIATION *See* A T A NEWS **1887**

ALBERTA TEACHERS' ASSOCIATION *See* MEMBERS' HANDBOOK - THE ALBERTA TEACHERS' ASSOCIATION **1866**

ALBERTA TEACHERS' ASSOCIATION *See* A T A MAGAZINE **1887**

ALBERTA TEACHERS' ASSOCIATION. CONSEIL FRANCAIS *See* NEWSLETTER - ALBERTA TEACHERS' ASSOCIATION **1867**

ALBERTA TEACHERS' ASSOCIATION. INDUSTRIAL EDUCATION COUNCIL *See* INDEC COMMUNICATOR, THE **1751**

ALBERTA TEACHERS' ASSOCIATION. INDUSTRIAL EDUCATION COUNCIL *See* NEWS 'N' NOTES - INDUSTRIAL EDUCATION COUNCIL OF THE ALBERTA TEACHERS' ASSOCIATION **1867**

ALBERTA TEACHERS' ASSOCIATION. LEARNING RESOURCES COUNCIL *See* NEWSLETTER - LEARNING RESOURCES COUNCIL OF THE ALBERTA TEACHERS' ASSOCIATION **1867**

ALBERTA TEACHERS' ASSOCIATION. SPECIAL EDUCATION COUNCIL *See* NEWSLETTER - SPECIAL EDUCATION COUNCIL OF THE ALBERTA TEACHERS' ASSOCIATION **1882**

ALBERTA TRAFFIC COLLISION FACTS (CN/0825-5709) [10351788] **5438**

ALBERTA TRANSFER GUIDE (CN/0848-4244) [22569902] **1808**

ALBERTA TRANSPORTATION (CALGARY) (CN/0821-7718) [09859939] **5375**

ALBERTA. TREASURY DEPT *See* PUBLIC ACCOUNTS: ALBERTA **4743**

ALBERTA. TREASURY DEPT *See* ESTIMATES OF EXPENDITURE (ALBERTA. TREASURY DEPT.) **4721**

ALBERTA. TREASURY DEPT *See* ESTIMATES OF EXPENDITURE. SUPPLEMENTARY INFORMATION. RECONCILIATION OF HISTORICAL DATA **4722**

ALBERTA. VISUAL ARTS *See* REPORT - VISUAL ARTS (EDMONTON) **363**

ALBERTA. VITAL STATISTICS DIVISION *See* VITAL STATISTICS ANNUAL REVIEW **4807**

ALBERTA WASTE MATERIALS EXCHANGE (CN/1182-2376) [22436350] **2223**

ALBERTA WEEKLY LAW DIGEST (CN/0713-892X) [09113379] **2930**

ALBERTA WILD ROSE QUARTER HORSE JOURNAL (CN/0227-0579) [08028222] **2796**

ALBERTAN'S NORTH SIDE MIRROR, THE (CN/0319-5414) [02443092] **5780**

ALBERTA'S ENERGY RESOURCES (CN/0706-1412) [02955384] 4249, **1931**

Alphabetical Title Index — ALGERIA

ALBERTA'S FISHING & HUNTING MAGAZINE **CEASED.** (CN/0833-0867) [16439752] **2294**

ALBERTA'S RECLAMATION RESEARCH PROGRAM (CN/0713-1224) [08250800] **162**

ALBERTA'S RESERVES OF CRUDE OIL, OIL SANDS, GAS, NATURAL GAS LIQUIDS, AND SULPHUR (CN/0837-9750) [11413757] **4249**

ALBERTA'S RESERVES OF GAS (CN/0229-8546) [08099163] **4249**

ALBERTOA (BL) [14696795] **498**

ALBERTSEN'S (INTERNATIONAL ED.) (US/1052-522X) [22294950] **407**

ALBERTSEN'S SINGLES DIRECTORY (US/1058-5826) [24334512] **5550, 3994**

ALBIA UNION-REPUBLICAN, THE (US) [15217726] **5668**

ALBION (UK) [05721382] **4811, 4563**

ALBION (BOONE) (US/0095-1390) [01479044] **2672**

ALBION NEW ERA, THE (US/8750-6513) [11048214] **5662**

ALBION NEWS, THE (US) [15259038] **5734**

ALBRIGHT JOURNAL, THE (US/0146-4043) [02934843] **391**

ALBUM (SP) **2841**

ALBUM DE ORO (US) [10269126] **429**

ALBUM (MADRID, SPAIN) (SP) [16274368] **335**

ALBUM NETWORK, THE (US/0739-1641) [09716260] **4099**

ALBUQUERQUE BI-WEEKLY REPORT, THE (US/0888-8396) [13735981] **921**

ALBUQUERQUE JOURNAL (ALBUQUERQUE, N.M. : 1926) (US) [09392114] **5712**

ALBUQUERQUE MONTHLY (US/1040-4279) [18410589] **2527**

ALBUQUERQUE TRIBUNE, THE (US) [09392099] **5712**

ALCALDE See TEXAS ALCALDE **1103**

ALCES (CN/0835-5851) [11806361] **2211, 4868, 2186**

● ALCHEMIST JOURNAL, THE (US/1065-8033) [26739395] **960**

ALCHEMIST (LASALLE) (CN/0384-8523) [03248475] **3359**

ALCHERINGA (SYDNEY) (AT/0311-5518) [02177918] **4226**

ALCOHOL AND ALCOHOLISM (OXFORD) (UK/0735-0414) [08856275] **1339**

ALCOHOL AND ALCOHOLISM. SUPPLEMENT (UK) [18329098] **1339**

ALCOHOL & DRUG ABUSE See GRANT$ FOR ALCOHOL AND DRUG ABUSE **4336**

ALCOHOL AND DRUG ABUSE RESOURCE DIRECTORY (US) [23931893] **1339**

ALCOHOL AND DRUG ABUSE SERVICES IN THE STATE OF MAINE (US) [08585052] **1339**

ALCOHOL AND DRUG ABUSE YEARBOOK/DIRECTORY, THE (US/0193-3981) [05206645] **1339**

ALCOHOL, DRUG ABUSE, MENTAL HEALTH, RESEARCH GRANT AWARDS (US/0096-1485) [02648927] **1339**

ALCOHOL, DRUGS, AND AGING. USAGE AND PROBLEMS (US/0278-5129) [07787475] **1339**

ALCOHOL, DRUGS AND DRIVING (US/0891-7086) [12402870] **1339**

ALCOHOL, DRUGS, AND TRAFFIC SAFETY : CURRENT RESEARCH LITERATURE (SW/0280-7645) [09187390] **5375, 1339**

ALCOHOL (FAYETTEVILLE, N.Y.) (US/0741-8329) [10222257] **1339**

ALCOHOL FUELS PROGRAM TECHNICAL REVIEW (US) [08216482] **1931**

ALCOHOL HEALTH AND RESEARCH WORLD (US/0090-838X) [01785965] **1339**

ALCOHOL ISSUES INSIGHTS (US/1067-3105) [21457918] **2363**

ALCOHOL OUTLOOK (US/1072-8767) [29231396] **4249**

ALCOHOL RESEARCH REVIEW SERIES (US/0731-8049) [08252361] **1339**

ALCOHOL SERVER LIABILITY : A COMPILATION OF DRAM SHOP AND RELATED STATUTES AND JUDICIAL RULINGS (US) [14985300] **3104**

ALCOHOL STUDIES, RETROSPECTIVE BIBLIOGRAPHIES (US) [07985280] **1350**

ALCOHOL TECHNICAL REPORTS (US/0146-8332) [03039276] **1339**

ALCOHOL WEEK See NEW FUELS REPORT **4266**

ALCOHOLFABRIEKEN EN DISTILLEERDERIJEN, BIERBROUWERIJEN EN MOUTERIJEN, FRISDRANKENINDUSTRIE PRODUKTIESTATISTIEKEN (NE) [05589100] **2363**

ALCOHOLIC BEVERAGE EXECUTIVES' NEWSLETTER See ALCOHOLIC BEVERAGE EXECUTIVES' NEWSLETTER INTERNATIONAL **2363**

ALCOHOLIC BEVERAGE EXECUTIVES' NEWSLETTER INTERNATIONAL (US/0889-3519) [13409546] **2363**

ALCOHOLISM & ADDICTION & RECOVERY LIFE See BEHAVIORAL HEALTH MANAGEMENT **1341**

ALCOHOLISM AND DRUG ABUSE FACILITIES IN THE STATE OF SOUTH DAKOTA (US/0161-9926) [04064455] **1339**

ALCOHOLISM & DRUG ABUSE WEEK (US/1042-1394) [18946138] **1340**

ALCOHOLISM AND DRUG ABUSE WEEK See ALCOHOLISM AND DRUG ABUSE WEEKLY **1340**

ALCOHOLISM AND DRUG ABUSE WEEKLY (US) **1340**

● ALCOHOLISM BRIEFS (US) **1340**

ALCOHOLISM : CLINICAL AND EXPERIMENTAL RESEARCH (US/0145-6008) [02777940] **1340**

ALCOHOLISM DIGEST ANNUAL, THE (US/0093-3279) [01793691] **1340**

ALCOHOLISM REPORT, THE (US/0276-3613) [01717065] **1340**

ALCOHOLISM TREATMENT QUARTERLY (US/0734-7324) [08794863] **1340**

ALCOHOLISM (ZAGREB) (CI/0002-502X) [02257145] **1340**

ALCOLOGIA (IT/0394-9826) [I03949826] **1340**

ALCONA COUNTY REVIEW (US/0746-8172) [10310465] **5690**

ALCOOL OU SANTE PARIS (FR/0002-5054) [I00025054] **1340**

ALCOOLIQUES ANONYMES See VIGNE A A, LA **1350**

ALCOOLOGIE (PARIS) (FR/1142-1983) [I11421983] **2363**

ALCTS NEWSLETTER (US/1047-949X) [20820888] **3189**

ALCUIN (UK) [03197631] **5055**

ALCUIN CLUB See ALCUIN **5055**

ALCUIN/GROW LITURGICAL STUDY (UK/0951-2667) [I09512667] **4933**

ALDEN ADVANCE (US/0898-526X) [01479057] **5694**

ALDEN'S CONCISE TORONTO GUIDE (CN/0827-3162) [11807728] **5460**

ALDERSGATE COLLEGE See ALDERSGATE NEWS **4933**

ALDERSGATE NEWS (CN/0711-2769) [08469797] **1808, 4933**

ALDHU : BOLETIN INFORMATIVO DE LA ASOCIACION LATINOAMERICANA PARA LOS DERECHOS HUMANOS (EC) [12982237] **4503**

ALDRICH CHEMICAL COMPANY See ALDRICHIMICA ACTA **960**

ALDRICHIMICA ACTA (US/0002-5100) [02305947] **960**

ALDRING OG ELDRE (NO/0801-9991) [I08019991] **5178**

ALDUS MAGAZINE (US/1046-0616) [20315165] **1284**

ALE SEFER (IS) [02399665] **3359, 5045**

ALE-SIAH (TEL-AVIV, ISRAEL : 1974) (IS) [07402490] **3359**

ALEF (IS/0736-8518) [09264358] **5045, 2254**

ALEPH (MANIZALES, COLOMBIA) (CK/0120-0216) [05179503] **4340, 3359**

ALERGIA (MEXICO) (MX/0002-5151) [01777795] **3665**

ALERT (US) **637**

ALERT (US) [05518366] **1643**

ALERT (CALGARY) (CN/1185-0388) [23659457] **2159**

ALERT : MEDICAL DEVICES (CN/0706-5493) [04590190] **3547**

ALERT (MERION, PA.) (US) [07856339] **2672**

ALERT! (NEW YORK, N.Y. 1984) **CEASED.** (US/0887-7106) [11896716] **2718**

ALERT / REDACTIONELE VERANTWOORDELIJKHEID VAN HET MINISTERIE VAN BINNENLANDSE ZAKEN (NE/0920-3168) [16721626] **1072**

ALERT (SACRAMENTO, CALIF.) (US/0882-0929) [11752029] **817**

ALERTA INFORMATIVA. SERIA A: QUIMICA INDUSTRIAL **SUSPENDED.** (SP) [05932219] **960**

● ALERTA (TORONTO) (CN/1188-875X) [25881556] **4503**

ALERTE (STE-PETRONILLE. 1976) (CN/0383-896X) [03248423] **4933**

ALEXANDER CITY OUTLOOK, THE (US/0738-5110) [09612603] **5625**

ALEXANDER LECTURES, THE (US/0065-616X) [02046839] **3359**

ALEXANDER PARIS REPORT, THE (US/0747-7813) [10808044] **1461, 890**

ALEXANDRIA (ALDERSHOT) (UK/0955-7490) [20626567] **3189**

ALEXANDRIA DAILY TOWN TALK, THE (US) [09267737] **5683**

ALEXANDRIA ECHO PRESS (US) **5694**

ALEXANDRIA GAZETTE PACKET (US/1050-7620) [21587663] **5758**

ALEXANDRIA GAZETTE, THE (US/8750-4987) [11484264] **5757**

ALEXANDRIA HERALD (ALEXANDRIA, S.D.) (US) [12800740] **5743**

ALEXANDRIA, IN. TIMES-TRIBUNE See ALEXANDRIA TIMES-TRIBUNE (1992), THE **5662**

ALEXANDRIA JOURNAL (ALEXANDRIA. 1980), THE (US/0273-639X) [06780277] **5758**

ALEXANDRIA JOURNAL OF AGRICULTURAL RESEARCH **CEASED.** (PL/0044-7250) [01479075] **57**

ALEXANDRIA NEWS WEEKLY (US) [18887798] **5683**

ALEXANDRIA PORT GAZETTE PACKET (US/1066-6273) [27017703] **5758**

ALEXANDRIA SCIENCE EXCHANGE (EG/1010-1098) [13258798] **5082**

● ALEXANDRIA TIMES-TRIBUNE (1992), THE (US/1063-553X) [26061144] **5662**

ALEXANOR (FR/0002-5208) [03739431] **441, 5574**

ALF **CEASED.** (US/1044-6745) [17352989] **4856**

ALF NEWS / ASSOCIATION OF LIBERTARIAN FEMINISTS (US) [22376139] **5550**

ALFA (BL/0002-5216) [01609843] **3263, 3359**

ALFA OWNER (US/0364-930X) [02659336] **5403**

ALFABETISMO E CULTURA SCRITTA **CEASED.** (IT) [23722584] **3263**

ALFABETYCZNY KATALOG SKADOWY (PL) [01789604] **407**

ALFOLD (HU/0401-3174) [05161912] **3359**

ALFRED BENZON SYMPOSIUM (DK/0105-3639) [08273644] **3547**

ALFRED DEAKIN LECTURE, THE (AT) [03299910] **4625**

ALFRED HITCHCOCK'S MYSTERY MAGAZINE (US/0002-5224) [01479088] **5074**

ALFRED P. SLOAN FOUNDATION See REPORT - ALFRED P. SLOAN FOUNDATION **1516**

ALFRED SUN, THE (US) [11107723] **5713**

ALGAE ABSTRACTS (US/0094-6362) [01021908] **5529**

ALGEBRA AND LOGIC (US/0002-5232) [01479091] **3491**

ALGEBRA-BERICHTE (GW) [02250947] **3491**

ALGEBRA I ANALIZ (RU/0234-0852) [20368411] **3491**

ALGEBRA I ANALIZ. ENGLISH. LENINGRAD MATHEMATICAL JOURNAL See ST. PETERSBURG MATHEMATICAL JOURNAL **3536**

ALGEBRA, LOGIC AND APPLICATIONS (US/1041-5394) [18798596] **3491**

ALGEBRA UNIVERSALIS (CN/0002-5240) [01479092] **3491**

ALGEBRAS, GROUPS, AND GEOMETRIES (US/0741-9937) [10240449] **3492**

ALGEMEEN DAGBLAD (NE) **5806**

ALGEMEEN DOOPSGEZIND WEEKBLAD (NE) [07725720] **5055**

ALGEMEEN NEDERLANDS TIJDSCHRIFT VOOR WIJSBEGEERTE (NE/0002-5275) [03286340] **4340**

ALGEMEEN POLITIEBLAD VAN HET KONINKRIJK DER NEDERLANDEN (NE) [08394798] **3156**

ALGEMEEN WERKLOOSHEIDSFONDS See JAARVERSLAG / ALGEMEEN WERKLOOSHEIDSFONDS **2885**

ALGEMEINER JOURNAL, DER (US) [17860857] **5713**

ALGEMENE MILIEUSTATISTIEK / CENTRAAL BUREAU VOOR DE STATISTIEK (NE) [02784731] **2224, 2183**

ALGERBRA I LOGIKA (RU/0373-9252) [10094708] **3492**

ALGERIA See JOURNAL OFFICIEL DE LA REPUBLIQUE ALGERIENNE DEMOCRATIQUE ET POPULAIRE **2990**

ALGERIA

ALGERIA. MUDIRIYAT AL-IHSAAT WA-AL-MUHASABAH AL-WATANIYA *See* BULLETIN TRIMESTRIEL DE STATISTIQUES - DIRECTION DES STATISTIQUES ET DE LA COMPTABILITE NATIONALE **5324**

ALGERIE - ACTUALITE (AE/1111-0171) [I11110171] **5777**

ALGERIEN ELEKTRIZITATSWIRTSCHAFT / BUNDESSTELLE FUER AUSSENHANDELSINFORMATION (GW) [07368976] **4625**

ALGERIEN : WIRTSCHAFTSDATEN UND WIRTSCHAFTSDOKUMENTATION (GW) [06465536] **1545**

ALGERIEN WIRTSCHAFTSSTRUKTUR / BUNDESSTELLE FUER AUSSENHANDELSINFORMATION (GW) [07333362] **1545**

ALGO 2000 (SP/0214-0381) [I02140381] **2513**

ALGOMA RECORD-HERALD (US) [12984585] **5765**

ALGONA UPPER DES MOINES, THE (US) [16128458] **5668**

ALGONQUIAN AND IROQUOIAN LINGUISTICS (CN/0711-382X) [07081291] 227, **3263**

ALGONQUIAN LINGUISTICS *See* ALGONQUIAN AND IROQUOIAN LINGUISTICS **3263**

ALGONQUIN COLLEGE. RESOURCE CENTRE *See* ALGONQUIN PERIODICALS, UNION LISTING / ALGONQUIN RESOURCE CENTRE, STUDENT SERVICES DIVISION **3189**

ALGONQUIN COLLEGE. RESOURCE CENTRE. STUDENT SERVICES DIVISION *See* ALGONQUIN PERIODICALS, UNION LISTING / ALGONQUIN RESOURCE CENTRE, STUDENT SERVICES DIVISION **3189**

ALGONQUIN COUNTRYSIDE (US/0744-527X) [08334684] **5658**

ALGONQUIN IMPACT (CN/0704-707X) [03797349] **5780**

●ALGONQUIN PERIODICALS, UNION LISTING / ALGONQUIN RESOURCE CENTRE, STUDENT SERVICES DIVISION (CN/1193-1426) [26757917] **3189**

ALGORISMUS (GW) [19406290] 5082, **3492**

ALGORITHM, THE PERSONAL PROGRAMMING NEWSLETTER *CEASED.* (CN/0843-9753) [21102355] **1265**

ALGORITHMICA (US/0178-4617) [13320393] **1170**

ALGORITHMS AND COMBINATORICS (GW) [15638246] **3492**

ALGORITMY I PROGRAMMY (RU) [02359775] **1278**

ALI-ABA CLE REVIEW (US/0044-7560) [02083016] **1808**

ALI-ABA CONFERENCE. CONFERENCE ON FEDERAL INCOME TAX SIMPLIFICATION: PAPERS (US/0191-3689) [04848959] 4709, **2930**

ALI-ABA COURSE MATERIALS JOURNAL (US/0145-6342) [02765069] **2930**

ALI-ABA COURSE OF STUDY : ABA SECTION OF TAXATION, ADVANCED STUDY SESSIONS, ADVANCED ESTATE PLANNING TECHNIQUES : MATERIALS (US/0191-412X) [04849273] **3117**

ALI-ABA COURSE OF STUDY. ABA SECTION OF TAXATION, ADVANCED STUDY SESSIONS, ESTATE AND INCOME TAX PLANNING FOR EXECUTIVES AND SMALL BUSINESS OWNERS : MATERIALS (US/0191-8249) [04915767] 4709, **3117**

ALI-ABA COURSE OF STUDY : ABA SECTION OF TAXATION, ANNUAL ADVANCED STUDY SESSIONS, BUSINESS AND ESTATE PLANNING WITH LIFE AND DISABILITY INSURANCE : MATERIALS (US/0271-3578) [06597531] 2873, **3117**

ALI-ABA COURSE OF STUDY. ABA SECTION OF TAXATION, ANNUAL OF TAXATION, ANNUAL ADVANCED STUDY SESSIONS, ADVANCED TAX PLANNING FOR REAL ESTATE TRANSACTIONS: MATERIALS (US/0277-3252) [07528996] 4833, **2930**

ALI-ABA COURSE OF STUDY. ADVANCED BUSINESS TAX PLANNING : MATERIALS (US/0191-1651) [04791609] **3094**

ALI-ABA COURSE OF STUDY. ADVANCED TAX PLANNING FOR THE CLOSELY HELD BUSINESS : MATERIALS (US) [06511277] 4709, **3094**

ALI-ABA COURSE OF STUDY. ALI-ABA CONFERENCE ON ERISA : MATERIALS (US/0192-821X) [05070433] 1643, **2930**

ALI-ABA COURSE OF STUDY. ATOMIC ENERGY LICENSING AND REGULATION : MATERIALS (US/0190-9673) [04753686] **2153**

ALI-ABA COURSE OF STUDY : BANK DEFENSE OF NEGOTIABLE INSTRUMENT CASES : MATERIALS (US/0191-0280) [04752856] **3084**

ALI-ABA COURSE OF STUDY. BANKING AND COMMERCIAL LENDING LAW : MATERIALS (US/0271-356X) [06597894] **3084**

ALI-ABA COURSE OF STUDY. BASIC ESTATE AND GIFT TAXATION: MATERIALS (US/0271-3551) [06598706] **3117**

ALI-ABA COURSE OF STUDY. BASIC LAW OF PENSIONS AND DEFERRED COMPENSATION: MATERIALS (US/0191-0272) [04752649] **2930**

ALI-ABA COURSE OF STUDY. BROKER-DEALER REGULATION: MATERIALS (US/0271-3535) [06597776] 890, **2930**

ALI-ABA COURSE OF STUDY. BUSINESS TAX PLANNING : MATERIALS (US/0193-6905) [05228737] **3094**

ALI-ABA COURSE OF STUDY: BUSINESS WORKOUTS *See* ALI-ABA COURSE OF STUDY. BUSINESS WORKOUTS: MATERIALS **3094**

ALI-ABA COURSE OF STUDY. BUSINESS WORKOUTS: MATERIALS (US/0190-9665) [04753094] **3094**

ALI-ABA COURSE OF STUDY. CLASS AND DERIVATIVE ACTIONS AND OTHER MULTIPARTY COMPLEX LITIGATION : MATERIALS (US/0191-2011) [04795033] **3088**

ALI-ABA COURSE OF STUDY. CONDOMINIUM CONVERSIONS: MATERIALS (US/0191-202X) [04800462] 598, **2930**

ALI-ABA COURSE OF STUDY. DOMESTIC TAXATION OF HARD MINERALS : MATERIALS (US/0191-2623) [04814506] 4709, **2930**

ALI-ABA COURSE OF STUDY. EMINENT DOMAIN : MATERIALS (US/0190-9339) [04753639] **2930**

ALI-ABA COURSE OF STUDY : ENERGY AND THE LAW, PROBLEMS AND CHALLENGES OF THE LATE 70'S : MATERIALS (US/0191-2585) [04818970] 1931, **2930**

ALI-ABA COURSE OF STUDY. ENERGY LAW : MATERIALS (US/0272-8990) [06949448] 1931, **2930**

ALI-ABA COURSE OF STUDY. ENVIRONMENTAL LAW: MATERIALS (US/0192-0820) [04947089] **3109**

ALI-ABA COURSE OF STUDY. ENVIRONMENTAL LITIGATION : MATERIALS (US/0191-166X) [04790498] **3109**

ALI-ABA COURSE OF STUDY. ERISA AND THE FEDERAL SECURITIES LAWS : MATERIALS (US/0191-2224) [04790974] 890, 1643, **2930**

ALI-ABA COURSE OF STUDY. ERISA-PHASE II : MATERIALS (US/0191-4308) [04868554] 1643, **2930**

ALI-ABA COURSE OF STUDY. ESTATE PLANNING FOR RETIRING OR DYING CLIENTS : MATERIALS (US/0270-7594) [06466164] **3117**

ALI-ABA COURSE OF STUDY. ESTATE PLANNING FOR THE CLOSELY HELD BUSINESS : MATERIALS (US/0271-3543) [06598609] **3117**

ALI-ABA COURSE OF STUDY. ESTATE PLANNING IN DEPTH : MATERIALS (US/0191-8656) [04922681] **3117**

ALI-ABA COURSE OF STUDY. ESTATE PLANNING : MATERIALS (US/0270-9694) [06512535] **3117**

ALI-ABA COURSE OF STUDY : ESTATE PLANNING UNDER THE NEW ESTATE AND GIFT TAX LAW : MATERIALS (US/0190-9584) [04753250] **3117**

ALI-ABA COURSE OF STUDY. FEDERAL ELECTION LAW: MATERIALS (US/0191-2372) [04814143] **2930**

ALI-ABA COURSE OF STUDY. FEDERAL RULES OF EVIDENCE : MATERIALS (US/0191-3859) [04849114] **2930**

ALI-ABA COURSE OF STUDY. FOREIGN INVESTMENT IN U.S. REAL ESTATE : MATERIALS (US/0270-9708) [06512442] **4833**

ALI-ABA COURSE OF STUDY. FRAUD, INSIDE INFORMATION, AND FIDUCIARY DUTY UNDER RULE 10B-5 : MATERIALS (US/0191-2178) [04794969] **3094**

ALI-ABA COURSE OF STUDY. INVESTMENT ADVISER REGULATION : MATERIALS (US/0270-9686) [06510803] 890, **2930**

ALI-ABA COURSE OF STUDY. LABOR RELATIONS AND EMPLOYMENT LAW FOR THE CORPORATE COUNSEL AND THE GENERAL PRACTITIONER: MATERIALS (US/0272-9393) [06958224] **3143**

ALI-ABA COURSE OF STUDY. LAND PLANNING AND REGULATION OF DEVELOPMENT : MATERIALS (US/0191-8125) [04915209] 2813, **2930**

ALI-ABA COURSE OF STUDY. LAND USE LITIGATION, CRITICAL ISSUES FOR ATTORNEYS, DEVELOPERS, AND PUBLIC OFFICIALS : MATERIALS (US/0190-9592) [04753189] **2930**

ALI-ABA COURSE OF STUDY : LEGAL ASPECTS OF MUSEUM OPERATIONS : MATERIALS (US/0191-1945) [04795015] 4083, **2930**

ALI-ABA COURSE OF STUDY. LEGAL ISSUES IN THE COAL INDUSTRY : MATERIALS (US/0191-1589) [04791451] 2133, **2931**

ALI-ABA COURSE OF STUDY : LEGAL PROBLEMS OF MUSEUM ADMINISTRATION : MATERIALS (US/0191-3069) [04826804] 4083, **2931**

ALI-ABA COURSE OF STUDY. LITIGATION UNDER THE FEDERAL SECURITIES LAWS : MATERIALS (US/0191-2046) [04799810] **2931**

ALI-ABA COURSE OF STUDY MATERIALS. CONSTRUCTION CONTRACTING IN THE MIDDLE EAST: PROBLEMS AND SOLUTIONS (US/0190-387X) [04679668] 598, **2931**

ALI-ABA COURSE OF STUDY MATERIALS. PRACTICE AND PROCEDURE IN FEDERAL TAX CONTROVERSIES: TAX COURT AND ELSEWHERE (US/0190-3888) [04679605] 4709, **2931**

ALI-ABA COURSE OF STUDY: MODERN REAL ESTATE TRANSACTIONS *See* ALI-ABA COURSE OF STUDY : MODERN REAL ESTATE TRANSACTIONS: MATERIALS **2931**

ALI-ABA COURSE OF STUDY : MODERN REAL ESTATE TRANSACTIONS : MATERIALS (US/0191-2003) [04791392] 4833, **2931**

ALI-ABA COURSE OF STUDY : OIL SPILLS AND THE LAW : MATERIALS (US/0191-2038) [04799468] **3109**

ALI-ABA COURSE OF STUDY : PENSION, PROFIT SHARING, AND OTHER DEFERRED COMPENSATION PLANS *See* PENSION, PROFIT-SHARING, WELFARE, AND OTHER COMPENSATION PLANS **3153**

ALI-ABA COURSE OF STUDY. POSTGRADUATE COURSE IN FEDERAL SECURITIES LAW: MATERIALS (US/0191-1570) [04790435] **3084**

ALI-ABA COURSE OF STUDY. PRODUCTS LIABILITY : PREVENTION, LITIGATION, AND LAW REFORM : MATERIALS (US/0272-8982) [06949594] **2931**

ALI-ABA COURSE OF STUDY. QUALIFIED PLANS, INSURANCE, AND PROFESSIONAL CORPORATIONS : MATERIALS (US/0271-1370) [06534457] **3094**

ALI-ABA COURSE OF STUDY. REAL ESTATE CONDOMINIUMS AND PUDS : MATERIALS (US/0190-9347) [04753589] 4834, **2931**

ALI-ABA COURSE OF STUDY. REAL ESTATE SYNDICATIONS. MATERIALS (US/0730-4722) [07990639] 4834, **2931**

ALI-ABA COURSE OF STUDY : SECTION 8 HUD-SUBSIDIZED HOUSING, NEW TAX-EXEMPT FINANCING TECHNIQUES : MATERIALS (US/0191-2240) [04801765] 2813, **2931**

ALI-ABA COURSE OF STUDY. SELECTED PROBLEMS IN TAX PLANNING FOR AGRICULTURE : MATERIALS (US/0190-9657) [04753744] 57, **2931**

ALI-ABA COURSE OF STUDY : STATE AND LOCAL TAXATION AND FINANCE : MATERIALS (US/0191-2380) [04814584] 4709, **2931**

ALI-ABA COURSE OF STUDY. TAX AND BUSINESS PLANNING FOR THE SMALL BUT GROWING BUSINESS : MATERIALS (US/0190-9355) [04753165] **3095**

ALI-ABA COURSE OF STUDY. TAX PLANNING FOR AGRICULTURE : MATERIALS (US/0272-8133) [06922599] 57, **2931**

ALI-ABA COURSE OF STUDY. THE COPYRIGHT ACT OF 1976 : MATERIALS (US/0191-3077) [04826361] **1301**

ALI-ABA COURSE OF STUDY. THE ECONOMICS OF ANTITRUST : MATERIALS (US/0191-2399) [04801801] **3095**

ALI-ABA COURSE OF STUDY: THE SUPREME COURT AND THE FEDERAL SECURITIES LAWS: IMPLICATIONS FOR LIABILITIES *See* ALI-ABA COURSE OF STUDY. THE SUPREME COURT AND THE FEDERAL SECURITIES LAWS, IMPLICATIONS FOR LIABILITIES : MATERIALS **2931**

ALI-ABA COURSE OF STUDY. THE SUPREME COURT AND THE FEDERAL SECURITIES LAWS, IMPLICATIONS FOR LIABILITIES : MATERIALS (US/0190-9975) [04753696] **2931**

ALI-ABA COURSE OF STUDY. TRIAL EVIDENCE IN FEDERAL AND STATE COURTS, A CLINICAL STUDY OF RECENT DEVELOPMENTS: MATERIALS (US/0271-2504) [06546082] **2931**

Alphabetical Title Index — ALLEN

ALI-ABA COURSE OF STUDY. WATER AND AIR POLLUTION: MATERIALS (US/0191-4073) [04849187] **3109**

ALI-ABA REAL ESTATE COURSE MATERIALS JOURNAL (US/1055-2472) [23126234] **4834**

ALI-ABA SYMPOSIUM. REGIONAL SYMPOSIUM ON THE STRUCTURE AND GOVERNANCE OF CORPORATIONS : MATERIALS (US/0191-3697) [04848201] **3095**

ALI-ABA TAX COURSE MATERIALS JOURNAL (US/1055-2480) [23126275] **4709**

ALI ANTICHE (IT/0394-6185) [I03946185] **11**

ALI REPORTER, THE (US/0164-5757) [04551446] **2931**

ALICE ECHO-NEWS (US) [12854263] **5746**

ALICIA PATTERSON FOUNDATION *See* APF REPORTER **2917**

ALIEN LEGION, THE (US/0894-3397) [12737701] **4856**

ALIF (TI) [01798733] **2498**

ALIF (CAIRO, EGYPT) (UA) [08342641] **3359**

ALIGARH BULLETIN OF MATHEMATICS, THE (II) [08584803] **3492**

ALIGARH CRITICAL MISCELLANY, THE (II) [19478533] **3359**

ALIGARH JOURNAL OF ENGLISH STUDIES, THE (II/0258-0365) [03218081] **3359**

ALIGARH JOURNAL OF STATISTICS, THE (II) [12251337] **3542**

ALIGHIERI, L' (IT/0516-6551) [02029489] **3359**

ALIGNMENT TECH/TALK (US/1058-9082) [24425099] **5403**

ALIMARKET MONTHLY (SP) **57**

ALIMENTA (SZ/0002-5402) [02861550] **2326**

ALIMENTACAO (SAO PAULO) (BL/0100-9397) [08438343] **2326**

ALIMENTACION, EQUIPOS Y TECNOLOGIA (SP/0212-1689) [10541317] **4187**

ALIMENTALEX (MADRID) (SP/0214-803X) [24169230] 2931, **2326**

ALIMENTARIA (SP/0300-5755) [02144357] **4764**

ALIMENTARISTA, L' (IT/0394-8404) [I03948404] **2326**

ALIMENTARY PHARMACOLOGY & THERAPEUTICS (UK/0269-2813) [15808072] **4290**

ALIMENTARY PHARMACOLOGY & THERAPEUTICS SUPPLEMENT (UK/0953-0673) [I09530673] **4290**

ALIMENTATION (MONTREAL) (CN/0834-2431) [16349156] **2326**

ALIMENTATION QUEBEC, FISHERIES (CN/0844-9031) [20316379] **2294**

ALIMENTAZIONE, NUTRIZIONE, METABOLISMO (1979) (IT/0392-7512) [06509537] **4187**

ALIMENTOLOGUE (CN/0823-9355) [11453887] **2326**

● ALIMENTOS BALANCEADOS PARA ANIMALES (US/1075-0487) [29926426] **205**

ALIMENTOS E NUTRICAO / UNIVERSIDADE ESTADUAL PAULISTA (BL/0103-4235) [24056638] **4187**

ALIMENTOS PROCESADOS (US/0744-625X) [08441310] **2326**

ALINORM (IT/0304-8918) [01650325] **2326**

ALIOIKEUKSISSA VIREILLEPANNUT JA LOPPUUNKASITELLY KONKURSSIT (FI) [06785560] **769**

ALIRAN MONTHLY (MY/0127-5127) [12766121] **5190**

ALISA. AUSTRALIAN LIBRARY AND INFORMATION SCIENCE ABSTRACTS (AT/0810-9265) [I08109265] 3189, **3257**

ALISCOPE *CEASED.* (FR) [I07637853] 4187, **225**

ALISEI (IT/1120-3277) [I11203277] **11**

ALISO (US/0065-6275) [01479108] **498**

ALIVE (II) [19683715] **3337**

ALIVE (ALTRINCHAM, CHESHIRE) *See* VEGETARIAN (ALTRINCHAM, CHESHIRE : 1980) **4200**

ALIVE NOW! (US/0891-8767) [06600552] **4933**

ALIVE (VANCOUVER) (CN/0228-586X) [08458491] 3547, **4187**

ALIZES LATINO-AMERICANISTE : BULLETIN D'INFORMATION / GRECO 26 [AND] AFSSAL (FR) [16960160] **2551**

ALKALINE PAPER ADVOCATE (US/0897-2524) [17371604] **4232**

ALKALINE PULPING CONFERENCE (US/0364-2763) [02582856] **4232**

ALKALMAZOTT MATEMATIKAI LAPEK (HU/0133-3399) [02549413] **3492**

ALKALOIDS. CHEMISTRY AND PHARMACOLOGY, THE (US/0099-9598) [10245182] **1039**

ALKI (US/8756-4173) [11558092] **3189**

ALKOHOL OCH NARKOTIKA (SW/0345-0732) [I03450732] **1340**

ALKOHOL- OG NARKOTIKAMISBRUGET KBENHAVN. 1988 (DK/0904-4450) [I09044450] **1340**

ALKOHOLIKIRJALLISUUS SUOMESSA *CEASED.* (FI) [19610417] **1340**

ALKOHOLIPOLITIIKKA (FI/0355-9750) [I03559750] **1340**

ALKOHOLITILASTOLLINEN VUOSIKIRJA / ALKOHOLSTATISTISK AARSBOK / ALCOHOL STATISTICAL YEARBOOK (FI/0783-1374) [17754366] **1340**

ALKOHOLSTATISTIK (SW) [06235511] 1340, **1350**

ALL ABOUT ARIZONA : THE HEALTHFUL STATE (US) [05274810] **5460**

ALL ABOUT BEER (US/0898-9001) [17946183] **2363**

ALL ABOUT BLOWOUT (NO) [17891913] **4249**

ALL ABOUT BUSINESS IN HAWAII (US/1046-5480) [04770745] **637**

ALL ABOUT HAWAII (US) [05671873] **2527**

ALL ABOUT HOMES (CN/0703-9743) [04589250] **4834**

ALL ABOUT ISSUES (US/0733-1231) [08538442] **4933**

ALL ABOUT MEDICAID *CEASED.* (US/0735-2883) [08899271] 3547, **2873**

ALL ABOUT MEDICARE *CEASED.* (US/0735-2891) [08899224] 3548, **2873**

ALL AFRICA CONFERENCE OF CHURCHES. REFUGEE DEPT *See* SERVICE TO REFUGEES; PROGRESS REPORT **4996**

ALL-AROUND, THE (US/1047-546X) [20709225] 205, **4882**

ALL ASIA REVIEW (HK) [22787355] **4823**

ALL-CANADA WEEKLY SUMMARIES (CN/0705-1360) [03963455] **3088**

ALL CHEVY (US/0898-8986) [17943976] **5403**

ALL ENGLAND LAW REPORTS ANNUAL REVIEW, THE (UK) [10094295] **2931**

ALL ENGLAND LAW REPORTS (INCORPORATING THE LAW TIMES REPORTS AND THE LAW JOURNAL REPORTS) OF CASES DECIDED IN THE HOUSE OF LORDS, THE PRIVY COUNCIL, ALL DIVISIONS OF THE SUPREME COURT, AND COURTS OF SPECIAL JURISDICTION, THE (UK) [01472201] **2931**

ALL ENGLAND LAW REPORTS, THE (UK) [05691083] **2931**

ALL HANDS (ALEXANDRIA, VA.) (US/0002-5577) [02555618] **4174**

ALL IN COMMUNICATIONS (US/1058-126X) [24237075] **1103**

ALL-IN-ONE BUSINESS CONTACTBOOK (US/1049-8257) [21319512] **637**

ALL INDIA CRIMINAL LAW REPORTER (II) [10832824] **3104**

ALL INDIA INSTITUTE OF SPEECH AND HEARING *See* JOURNAL OF THE ALL INDIA INSTITUTE OF SPEECH AND HEARING, THE **3889**

ALL INDIA OPERATIVE REVIEW *See* INDIAN COOPERATIVE REVIEW **1542**

ALL INDIA PREVENTION OF FOOD ADULTERATION CASES (II) [01784083] 2326, **2931**

ALL INDIA REPORTER (II/0002-5593) [01479119] **2501**

ALL-IRELAND HERITAGE, THE *SUSPENDED.* (US/0742-5910) [10372859] **2436**

ALL LOW-RENT PUBLIC HOUSING PROGRAMS, REGION 1: BOSTON (US/0091-2352) [01786855] **2813**

ALL LOW-RENT PUBLIC HOUSING PROGRAMS, REGION 2: NEW YORK (US/0091-2433) [01786856] **2813**

ALL LOW-RENT PUBLIC HOUSING PROGRAMS, REGION 3: PHILADELPHIA (US/0091-2514) [01786875] **2813**

ALL LOW-RENT PUBLIC HOUSING PROGRAMS, REGION 4: ATLANTA (US/0091-2522) [01786876] **2813**

ALL LOW-RENT PUBLIC HOUSING PROGRAMS, REGION 5: CHICAGO (US/0091-4770) [01786860] **2813**

ALL LOW-RENT PUBLIC HOUSING PROGRAMS, REGION 6: FORT WORTH (US/0091-245X) [01786866] **2813**

ALL LOW-RENT PUBLIC HOUSING PROGRAMS, REGION 7: KANSAS CITY (US/0091-2530) [01786878] **2813**

ALL LOW-RENT PUBLIC HOUSING PROGRAMS, REGION 8: DENVER (US) [01794848] **2813**

ALL LOW-RENT PUBLIC HOUSING PROGRAMS, REGION 9: SAN FRANCISCO (US/0091-2441) [01786865] **2813**

ALL LOW-RENT PUBLIC HOUSING PROGRAMS, REGION 10: SEATTLE (US/0091-2344) [01786877] **2813**

ALL MOSCOW (RU) [22963333] **2672**

ALL NEWSLETTER / ACADEMIC LAW LIBRARIES SPECIAL INTEREST SECTION, AMERICAN ASSOCIATION OF LAW LIBRARIES (US) [08250184] 2931, **3189**

ALL OF MEXICO AT LOW COST (US) [01783755] **5460**

ALL PAKISTAN TEXTILE MILLS ASSOCIATION *See* APTMA DIRECTORY OF MEMBERS - ALL PAKISTAN TEXTILE MILLS ASSOCIATION **5347**

ALL POINTS BULLETIN (CN/0834-0102) [15586782] **5375**

ALL STATES TAX HANDBOOK (US/0148-9976) [03410101] **4709**

ALL THE WORLD. [A QUARTERLY REVIEW OF THE WORLD-WIDE WORK OF THE SALVATION ARMY] (UK/0002-2680) [02012680] 4933, **5271**

ALL TV PUBLICITY OUTLETS, NATIONWIDE (US/0889-2717) [13342790] **755**

ALL-UNIVERSITY GERONTOLOGY CENTER PUBLIC POLICY SERIES (US/1059-3799) [24579001] 4625, **5178**

ALLAHABAD LAW JOURNAL (II) [01479129] **2931**

ALLAHABAD MATHEMATICAL SOCIETY LECTURE NOTE SERIES (II) [25226635] **3492**

ALLAM- ES JOGTUDOMANY (HU/0002-564X) [01663756] 4462, **2931**

ALLAMAKEE JOURNAL AND LANSING MIRROR (US) [15744247] **5668**

ALLAMI GAZDASAG (HU/0587-4815) [02335634] **57**

ALLAN HANCOCK MONOGRAPHS IN MARINE BIOLOGY (US/0065-6364) [01479132] **552**

ALLATTANI KOEZLEMENYEK (HU/0002-5658) [02739915] **5574**

ALLATTENYESZTES ES TARKARMANYOZAS (HU/0230-1814) [08817783] **205**

ALLE HENS (NE/0002-5674) [01793996] **4174**

ALLE KVINNER; MAGAZINE FOR WOMEN (NO) [01479133] **5550**

ALLEE'S ALL AROUND (US/0883-5926) [12120557] **2436**

ALLEGANY AGRICULTURE (US/1052-7540) [20307936] **57**

ALLEGHANY HIGHLANDER, THE (US/8750-0582) [10957577] **5758**

ALLEGHENY BUSINESS NEWS (US) **637**

ALLEGHENY CO., PA. COUNTY CONTROLLER *See* COUNTY OF ALLEGHENY BUDGET FOR OPERATING DEPARTMENTS, THE **4719**

ALLEGHENY COLLEGE, MEADVILLE, PA. LIBRARY *See* REPORT OF THE LIBRARIAN TO THE PRESIDENT - ALLEGHENY COLLEGE, MEADVILLE, PA **3245**

ALLEGHENY LUDLUM HORIZONS (US/0149-1997) [03434162] **3997**

ALLEGHENY LUDLUM INDUSTRIES. A L METALS GROUP *See* ALLEGHENY LUDLUM HORIZONS **3997**

ALLEGHENY REVIEW, THE (US/0742-096X) [10282120] **1089**

ALLEGHENY TIMES (US) [15259130] **5734**

ALLEGORIA *CEASED.* (IT) [20413166] **3359**

ALLEGORICA (US/0363-2377) [02438836] **3359**

ALLEGRO (NEW YORK, N.Y.) (US/0002-5704) [03952697] **4099**

ALLEMAGNE D'AUJOURD'HUI (FR/0002-5712) [02196898] **2513**

ALLEMEINE ENZYKLOPADIE DER WISSENSCHAFTEN UND KUNSTE (AU) [01579949] **1923**

ALLEN AMERICAN, THE (US) [17392591] **5746**

ALLEN & HILARY WEINER, FIRM, NEW YORK *See* CATALOG OF FINE ANTIQUE CAMERAS & PHOTOGRAPHIC IMAGES **250**

ALLEN COUNTY-FORT WAYNE HISTORICAL SOCIETY BULLETIN (US/1041-9381) [17717500] 2436, **2718**

ALLEN COUNTY LINES (US) [11337627] **2436**

ALLEN — Alphabetical Title Index

ALLEN UNIVERSITY *See* ALUMNI DIRECTORY / ALLEN UNIVERSITY **1097**

ALLEN'S TRADEMARK DIGEST (US/0899-191X) [16907319] **1301**

ALLENSBACHER JAHRBUCH DER DEMOSKOPIE (AU) [02512791] **5238**

ALLER SIMPLE (FR/0240-883X) [09703773] **312**

ALLERGIC DISEASE AND THERAPY (US/1053-1092) [21232311] **3665**

ALLERGIE ET IMMUNOLOGIE PARIS (FR/0397-9148) [I03979148] **3665**

ALLERGIE UND IMMUNOLOGIE *CEASED.* (GW/0323-4398) [01479140] **3665**

ALLERGOLOGIA ET IMMUNOPATHOLOGIA (SP/0301-0546) [03161256] **3665**

ALLERGOLOGIE (GW/0344-5062) [05755553] **3665**

ALLERGY ALERT (CN/0824-1333) [11807942] **3665**

ALLERGY & CLINICAL IMMUNOLOGY NEWS (CN/0838-1925) [20350873] **3665**

ALLERGY CONNECTIONS (US/1059-4205) [24584103] **3665**

ALLERGY PROCEEDINGS (US/1046-9354) [18952712] **3666**

ALLERGY SUPPLEMENTUM (DK/0108-1675) [15212900] **3666**

ALLERTON PARK INSTITUTE *See* PAPERS PRESENTED AT THE ALLERTON PARK INSTITUTE **3240**

ALLERTONIA (US/0735-8032) [03530517] **498**

ALLES UBER WEIN (GW/0175-8314) [I01758314] 5460, **2363**

ALLESTIRE (IT) **287**

ALLGEMEINBILDENDE SCHULEN IN NORDRHEIN-WESTFALEN (GW/0723-8207) [19771539] **1723**

ALLGEMEINE FLEISCHER ZEITUNG (GW) [03978207] **2326**

ALLGEMEINE FORST UND JAGDZEITUNG (GW/0002-5852) [01479149] **2374**

ALLGEMEINE HOTEL- UND GASTSTATTEN-ZEITUNG (GW/0002-5895) [I00025895] 5070, **2803**

ALLGEMEINE ORTSKRANKENKASSE, BERLIN *See* GESCHAFTSBERICHT - ALLGEMEINE ORTSKRANKENKASSE BERLIN **1676**

ALLGEMEINE SCHWEIZERISCHE MILITARZEITSCHRIFT (SZ) [07926958] **4034**

ALLGEMEINE VERMESSUNGS-NACHRICHTEN (1985) (GW) [13267887] 1964, **2553**

ALLGEMEINE ZEITSCHRIFT FUER PHILOSOPHIE (GW) [02882658] **4340**

ALLGEMEINES MINISTERIALBLATT DER BAYERISCHEN STAATSREGIERUNG, DES BAYERISCHEN MINISTERPRASIDENTEN, DER BAYERISCHEN STAATSKANZLEI, DES BAYERISCHEN STAATSMINISTERIUMS DER INNERN (GW) [18619412] **4462**

ALLGEMEINES STATISTISCHES ARCHIV (GW/0002-6018) [01479164] **5320**

ALLIANCE (IE) [05218089] **5803**

ALLIANCE ALERT. CHEMICALS/MATERIALS/AGRICULTURE (US/1053-0673) [22445598] **1020**

ALLIANCE ALERT. COMMUNICATIONS (US/1053-0657) [22445560] **1104**

ALLIANCE ALERT. ELECTRONICS/COMPUTER HARDWARE/INDUSTRIAL AUTOMATION (US/1050-0367) [21379557] **1235**

ALLIANCE ALERT. MEDICAL/HEALTH (US/1053-0649) [22444353] 4290, **3775**

ALLIANCE ALERT. SOFTWARE/INFORMATION SERVICES (US/1053-0665) [22445555] **1235**

ALLIANCE CHORALE ALBERTA *See* INFO-COMPTOIR MUSICAL **4122**

ALLIANCE DE LA FONCTION PUBLIQUE DU CANADA. SECTION DES GRIEFS ET DE L'ARBITRAGE *See* RAPPORTS DE LA SECTION DES GRIEFS ET DE L'ARBITRAGE **3034**

ALLIANCE FOR PROGRESS : REPORT ON THE PROGRESS OF ECONOMIC AND SOCIAL DEVELOPMENT IN LATIN AMERICA AND PROSPECTS FOR THE FUTURE, THE (US) [06619439] **1545**

ALLIANCE LETTER (US/1052-9381) [16170940] **2718**

ALLIANCE LIFE (US/1040-6794) [15731951] **4933**

ALLIANCE (MONTREAL. 1969) (CN/0711-6829) [09157052] **1860**

ALLIANCE (NATIVE ALLIANCE OF QUEBEC) (CN/0845-8464) [20444593] **5780**

ALLIANCE (NORWOOD, N.J.) (US/0734-2837) [08753052] **637**

ALLIANCE OF CANADIAN TRAVEL ASSOCIATIONS *See* ACTA DIRECTORY **5460**

ALLIANCE (OTTAWA. ENGLISH ED.) (CN/0838-7990) [18243119] **1643**

ALLIANCE PLUS (US/1056-621X) [23763155] **3189**

ALLIANCE REPORT (CN/0838-6579) [18115947] **2527**

ALLIANCE REVIEW (ALLIANCE, OHIO : 1924) (US) [11129646] **5726**

ALLIANCE UPDATE (US/0273-8023) [06952986] **1854**

ALLIANCE (WHITE ROCK) (CN/1185-8591) [25423222] **2294**

ALLIANCE WORLD (CAMP HILL, PA.), THE (US/0270-9678) [06542408] **4933**

ALLIANCELETTER : MONTHLY NEWSLETTER OF THE BOSTON PRESERVATION ALLIANCE (US) [06702802] **2718**

●ALLIANZ REPORT (GW/0943-4569) **2109**

ALLIED DUNBAR TAX GUIDE / BY W.I. SINCLAIR (UK) [13351471] **4709**

ALLIED HEALTH EDUCATION DIRECTORY (US/0194-3766) [04379063] 3548, **1923**

ALLIED HEALTH EDUCATION NEWSLETTER *CEASED.* (US) [04326108] 1723, **3548**

ALLIED HEALTH EDUCATION PROGRAMS IN JUNIOR AND SENIOR COLLEGES. HEALTH PLANNERS EDITION (US/0148-5067) [03243626] 1808, **4764**

ALLIED HEALTH TRENDS (US/0275-7699) [05459083] **4764**

ALLIED INDUSTRIAL WORKER (US/0002-6107) [02382310] **1643**

ALLIED LANDSCAPE INDUSTRY MEMBER DIRECTORY (US/0098-793X) [02240111] **2408**

ALLIED NEWS (US) [19226729] **5734**

ALLIONIA (IT/0065-6429) [08521964] **498**

ALLMAN MANADSSTATISTIK (SW/0039-7253) [01766983] **5320**

ALLMENDE (GW/0720-3098) [10335415] **3359**

ALLO POLICE (1986) (CN/0834-230X) [16221188] **3156**

ALLONS (UK/0957-6215) [24457518] **1723**

ALLOY DIGEST (US/0002-614X) [04850826] **3997**

ALLOYS INDEX (US/0094-8233) [01795508] **3997**

ALLPANCHIS (PE/0252-8835) [11012830] **5022**

ALLPOINTS (WILLOWDALE) (CN/1186-0057) [24265847] **859**

ALLPRISER (CN) **2603**

ALLSTATE MOTOR CLUB AMERICA'S FAVORITE NATIONAL PARKS (US/1043-5832) [19501372] **5460**

ALLSTATE MOTOR CLUB GREAT CAMPING VACATIONS, NORTHWEST (US/1044-0771) [19681528] **5460**

ALLSTATE MOTOR CLUB GREAT NATIONAL PARK VACATIONS (US/1043-9021) [19597151] **5460**

ALLSTATE MOTOR CLUB RV SALES, RENTAL & SERVICE DIRECTORY (US/1043-5824) [19487664] **5375**

ALLT I HEMMET 1987 (SW/0284-1754) [I02841754] **1293**

ALLT OM BOCKER (SW) [19470845] 3359, **4823**

ALLTAG, DER (SZ) [05845357] **2513**

●ALLTON-ALTON-AULTON ASSOCIATION FAMILY NEWSLETTER (US/1059-7719) [24728264] **2436**

ALLUMINIO E LEGHE (IT) **3997**

ALLURE (NEW YORK, N.Y. 1985) (US/0883-5349) [12148296] **402**

ALMA (FR/0154-5868) [06686676] **3263**

ALMA MATER (US/0065-6445) [02257185] **1315**

ALMA MATER (RU) [24031712] **1723**

ALMA ROMA (IT/0391-724X) [I0391724X] **335**

ALMA TIMES-STATESMAN (US/0745-7898) [09458177] **5652**

ALMAGESTE (CN/0226-7160) [06515414] **391**

ALMAMATER (IO/0569-0803) [01790685] **57**

ALMANAC FOR FARMERS & CITY FOLK, THE (US/0739-6961) [09801698] **2527**

ALMANAC (MCMURRAY), THE (US/0193-581X) [05232251] **5734**

ALMANAC OF AMERICAN POLITICS, THE (US/0362-076X) [02456882] **4462**

ALMANAC OF BUSINESS AND INDUSTRIAL FINANCIAL RATIOS (US/0747-9107) [01587875] **637**

ALMANAC OF FAMOUS PEOPLE (US/1040-127X) [18330762] **429**

ALMANAC OF FEDERAL PACS (US/0886-2567) [12876866] **4462**

ALMANAC OF HIGHER EDUCATION, THE (US/1044-3096) [19745425] **1808**

ALMANAC OF SEAPOWER, THE (US/0736-3559) [09104779] **4174**

ALMANAC OF THE 50 STATES (US/0887-0519) [12181378] **1923**

ALMANAC OF THE CANNING, FREEZING, PRESERVING INDUSTRIES, THE (US/0887-4999) [04280479] **2362**

ALMANAC OF THE FEDERAL JUDICIARY (US) **3138**

ALMANAC OF VIRGINIA POLITICS, THE (US/0276-9980) [03856762] **4462**

ALMANACCO DI FOTOGRAFARE (IT/0393-9758) [I03939758] **4366**

ALMANACCO (MILAN, ITALY) (IT) [08979798] **2513**

ALMANACCO MUSICA (IT) [06570388] **4099**

ALMANACCO PIEMONTESE (IT) [02480165] **2672**

ALMANACH DE KUYPER DE CHASSE ET PECHE, L' (CN/0381-8233) [02588124] **4868**

ALMANACH DE LA FEMME (CN/0710-0884) [08099407] **5550**

ALMANACH DE L'AUTO (MONTREAL) (CN/0821-7505) [09818987] **5403**

ALMANACH DU BAS-DU-FLEUVE (CN/0228-1422) [06859863] **2527**

ALMANACH DU PEUPLE (CN/0065-650X) [02247990] **2527**

ALMANACH-GRAPHIQUE - CENTRE DE QUEBEC, SOCIETE ROYALE D'ASTRONOMIE DU CANADA (CN/0384-7691) [03348822] **391**

ALMANACH JULES VERNE *CEASED.* (FR) **3359**

ALMANACH - K.K.L. STRASBOURG (FR) [06880658] **2609**

ALMANACH MODERNE *CEASED.* (CN/0315-2898) [02247673] **2484**

ALMANACH - OSTERREICHISCHE AKADEMIE DER WISSENSCHAFTEN (AU/0378-8644) [01478732] **2513**

ALMANACH POLONII (PL) [01791983] **2513**

ALMANACH POPULAIRE CATHOLIQUE (CN/0821-4034) [09457167] **5023**

ALMANACK FOR THE YEAR OF OUR LORD ... (LONDON, ENGLAND) (UK/0083-9256) [01128041] **1923**

ALMANACK - INSTITUTE OF ELECTRICAL AND ELECTRONICS ENGINEERS, INC. PHILADELPHIA SECTION (US/0163-4496) [04086592] **2034**

ALMANAK ANTARA (IO) [06306404] **2501**

ALMANAK EKUIN (IO) [11012344] **822**

ALMANAK (INDONESIA. BADAN METEOROLOGI DAN GEOFISIKA) (IO) [08440644] **1419**

ALMANAK INSA (IO) [08150543] **5447**

ALMANAK KEPOLISIAN REPUBLIK INDONESIA (IO) [09428149] **3156**

ALMANAK MUHAMMADIJAH *See* ALMANAK MUHAMMADIYAH **5042**

ALMANAK MUHAMMADIYAH (IO) [02244806] **5042**

ALMANAK PERHUBUNGAN DAN PARIWISATA INDONESIA (IO) [08455526] **5375**

ALMANAKH GOMONU UKRAJINY (CN/0441-1196) [02575466] **2513**

ALMANAKH (NIU - IORK. 1980) (US) [07368294] **3359**

ALMANAKH PANORAMA (US/0889-0730) [07415133] **5632**

ALMANAKH UKRAINSKOHO NARODNOHO SOIUZU (US/0883-7368) [04171752] **1923**

AL'MANAKH VYDAVNYTSTVA "TRYZUB" (CN/0824-5908) [11197209] **4812**

ALMANAQUE ABRIL (BL) [04307182] **1923**

ALMANAQUE DA PARAIBA (BL) [02243219] **2551**

ALMANAQUE MINO (BL) [02511644] **2513**

ALMANAQUE MUNDIAL (US) [05177949] **1923**

ALMANAQUE NAUTICO (SP) [04375690] **391**

Alphabetical Title Index — ALUMINIUM

ALMANAQUE PUERTORRIQUENO (PR) [04050905] **2527**

ALMANSOR (PO/0870-0249) [12385097] **2672**

ALMBAUER, DER (GW) [03988287] **57**

ALMENA PLAINDEALER (ALMENA, KAN. : 1905) (US) [12332583] **5674**

ALMENARA (MADRID) *CEASED.* (SP/0211-2310) [02589947] **2645**

ALMOGAREN (AU) [01964782] **253**

ALMOND FACTS (US/0886-4365) [02762730] **2408**

ALMOST FREE RECIPES AND COOKBOOKS UPDATES (US/0736-170X) [09091652] **2788**

ALN; AUTO LAUNDRY NEWS *See* AUTO LAUNDRY NEWS **5404**

ALO, 160 (BU/0204-8531) [24102519] **2287**

ALOCANA (II/0569-1176) [04094931] **3263**

ALOE (SA) [04816328] **498**

ALOFT (US/0742-3624) [10310853] **2527**

ALOHA (HONOLULU) (US/0147-5436) [03451653] **5460**

ALOITTANEET JA LOPETTANEET YRITYKSET (FI/0785-546X) [19415321] **637**

ALON HA-NOTEA (IS/0333-8886) [11189423] **162**

ALON HA-ONATI - NEOT QEDUMIM, HA- (IS/0303-1500) [01793304] **5014**

ALOR NOVISIMO *CEASED.* (SP) [12171104] **3359**

ALPEN (SZ) [05963271] **2513**

ALPENA NEWS (US) **5690**

ALPENLANDISCHE RUNDSCHAW (AU) [20154689] **5777**

ALPES, LES (SZ) [03313337] **5461**

ALPES (QUARTERLY) (SZ) [03313393] **4868**

ALPES : SAVOIE, DAUPHINE (FR) [03499931] **2672**

ALPHA ACTION REPORTER (CN/0227-0897) [08364260] **4383**

ALPHA BEAT SOUP (CN/0838-391X) [17869745] **3359**

ALPHA DELTA KAPPAN (US/0002-6387) [05344383] **5228**

ALPHA DELTA PHI LITERARY JOURNAL, THE (CN/0712-4589) [09088967] **1089**

ALPHA FLIGHT (US/8750-0558) [10957332] **4856**

●ALPHA FORUM (US/1062-5895) [25677706] **1252**

ALPHA GAMMA DELTA *See* ALUMNAE DIRECTORY / ALPHA GAMMA DELTA **5228**

ALPHA (MEMPHIS) (US/0162-5918) [04181311] **1808**

ALPHA OMEGA ALPHA *See* PHAROS OF ALPHA OMEGA ALPHA-HONOR MEDICAL SOCIETY, THE **3627**

ALPHA OMEGAN (US/0002-6417) [02257192] **1315**

ALPHA (WELLINGTON, N.Z.) (NZ/0111-1957) [12297141] **5082**

ALPHA (WOLFEVILLE) (CN/0701-0656) [03406503] **3359**

ALPHABET : THE JOURNAL OF THE FRIENDS OF CALLIGRAPHY (US) [21213915] **369**

ALPHABETIC LIST OF LENDERS (US/0192-3455) [04739620] **1723**

ALPHABETICAL CATALOG OF THE BOOKS AND PAMPHLETS OF THE INTERNATIONAL INSTITUTE OF SOCIAL HISTORY, AMSTERDAM. SUPPLEMENT (US/0099-0779) [02242675] **407**

ALPHABETICAL DIRECTORY OF ATTORNEYS IN NEW YORK STATE (US/0738-8152) [09183148] **2932**

ALPHABETICAL INDEX OF CONSTITUENT PARTICULARS OF TRADE MARKS (AT/0312-3278) [01796008] **1301**

ALPHABETICAL LIST OF ENGLISH LANGUAGE BOOK TITLES AVAILABLE FROM CANADIAN SOURCES MICROFORM (CN/0824-3352) [10386379] **407**

ALPHABETICAL LIST OF THE FOREIGN EMBASSIES AND LEGATIONS IN LONDON *See* LONDON DIPLOMATIC LIST / FOREIGN OFFICE, THE **3132**

ALPHABETICAL ROSTER, PROFESSIONAL ENGINEERS AND PROFESSIONAL LAND SURVEYORS (US) [21254052] **1964**

ALPHABETISCHER KATALOG. NACHTRAGSBAND (US) [04694264] **2609**

ALPHABETIZED DIRECTORY OF AMERICAN JOURNALISTS (US/0149-5186) [03493675] **2917**

ALPHANUMERIC REPORTS PUBLICATIONS INDEX (UK/0964-3400) [l09643400] **3189**

ALPHARETTA NEIGHBOR, THE (US/0191-8494) [04968743] **5652**

ALPINE AVALANCHE (US) [05026564] **5746**

ALPINE JOURNAL, THE (UK/0065-6569) [01479201] **4868**

ALPINE SKIING COMPETITION GUIDE. EASTERN/CENTRAL EDITION (US/0733-9356) [08660709] **4882**

ALPINE SKIING COMPETITION GUIDE. ROCKY MOUNTAIN EDITION (US/0278-2960) [08650303] **4882**

ALPINE SKIING COMPETITION GUIDE. WESTERN/ROCKY EDITION (US/0733-9348) [08660651] **4882**

ALPINE SUN (US/8750-8257) [11822668] **5633**

ALPIRANDO (FR/0759-2167) [l07592167] 4868, **4882**

ALS NEWS (CN/0715-3139) [09099675] **3802**

ALSA SWIMMERS' GUIDE (US/1067-4535) [27252109] 2595, **4882**

ALSACE LE PAYS (FR) **2553**

ALSC NEWSLETTER (US/0162-6612) [04199869] **3189**

ALSHP NEWSLETTER (US) **4290**

ALT-HILDESHEIM (GW/0344-1873) [01795237] **2672**

ALT-THURINGEN (GW/0065-6585) [01479202] 253, **2673**

ALTA DIRECCION (SP/0002-6549) [02257194] **1596**

ALTA FIDELIDAD EN AUDIO Y EN VIDEO (SP/1130-4855) [l11304855] 5315, **1126**

ALTA FREQUENZA. RIVISTA DI ELETTRONICA (IT/1120-1908) [22000919] **2034**

ALTA NEWSLETTER (US/0734-8991) [08822638] **3189**

ALTADENA REVIEW, THE *CEASED.* (US/0162-8208) [04248660] **3337**

ALTALANOS NYELVESZETI TANULMANYOK (HU/0569-1338) [02033297] **3263**

ALTAMIRA (SP/0211-4003) [06670584] **2673**

ALTAMONT ENTERPRISE (1983), THE (US/0890-6025) [14354034] **5713**

ALTAMONT NEWS, THE (US/1047-9317) [09347291] **5658**

ALTAMURA (IT/0569-1346) [l05691346] **335**

ALTANLAGEN-REPORT (GW) [07590612] **2224**

ALTDEUTSCHE TEXTBIBLIOTHEK (GW) [01479205] **3360**

ALTDEUTSCHE TEXTE IN KRITISCHEN AUSGABEN (GW) [06657791] **3337**

ALTE KUNST (GW) [06295852] **335**

ALTE STADT, DIE (GW/0170-9364) [03926314] **2673**

ALTE UHREN UND MODERNE ZEITMESSUNG *See* UHREN 1992 **367**

ALTE UHREN UND MODERNE ZEITMESSUNG (GW/0932-2655) [l09322655] **335**

ALTE UND NEUE KUNST (GW/0344-1822) [l03441822] **312**

ALTENBURGER NATURWISSENSCHAFTLICHE FORSCHUNGEN (GE/0065-6631) [09445696] **4161**

ALTER ORIENT UND ALTES TESTAMENT (GW) [03296706] **5014**

ALTERNATE ENERGY SOURCES (US/0732-7099) [08416526] **1931**

ALTERNATE ROUTES (CN/0702-8865) [03439392] **5238**

ALTERNATE SOURCE, THE (US/0277-2418) [07525294] **1264**

ALTERNATIV ODLING (SW/1100-116X) [22142385] **57**

ALTERNATIVE AGRICULTURE NEWS (US/8755-4941) [09886469] **58**

●ALTERNATIVE AND COMPLEMENTARY THERAPIES (US/1076-2809) [30446084] **3548**

ALTERNATIVE AQUACULTURE NETWORK (US/8755-7894) [11402239] **552**

ALTERNATIVE CHILD CARE PROGRAMS (US) [05039301] **5271**

ALTERNATIVE DESIGNS (US/0747-9263) [10836440] **4764**

ALTERNATIVE ENERGY (BEVERLY HILLS, CALIF.) (US/0886-828X) [12001251] **1931**

ALTERNATIVE ENERGY DIGESTS (US/1050-3145) [21456790] 1964, **1931**

ALTERNATIVE ENERGY RETAILER (US/0273-8163) [06954584] **1931**

ALTERNATIVE FUELS DATA CENTER (NATIONAL RENEWABLE ENERGY LABORATORY) *See* AFDC UPDATE : NEWS OF THE ALTERNATIVE FUELS DATA CENTER **1931**

ALTERNATIVE INDEX (US/1059-8154) [24648418] **5814**

ALTERNATIVE LAW FORUM (PH/0117-1577) [l01171577] **2932**

●ALTERNATIVE LAW JOURNAL (AT/1037-969X) [25566937] **3179**

ALTERNATIVE LIBRARY LITERATURE (US/0749-6885) [11124077] **3189**

ALTERNATIVE MEDIA *CEASED.* (US/0730-1766) [07963594] 2917, **4463**

ALTERNATIVE MEDICINE *CEASED.* (NE/0168-8448) [12761851] **3548**

ALTERNATIVE METHODS IN TOXICOLOGY (US/0737-402X) [09364567] **3978**

ALTERNATIVE (MONTREAL, QUEBEC) *CEASED.* (CN/0843-0586) [20125675] 4463, **1643**

ALTERNATIVE ORANGE, THE (US/1066-3452) [26936300] **1089**

ALTERNATIVE PRESS (CLEVELAND, OHIO) (US/1065-1667) [23380417] **4099**

ALTERNATIVE PRESS INDEX (US/0002-662X) [01479213] 4185, **4186**

ALTERNATIVE REVENUE SOURCES FOR YELLOW PAGES PUBLISHERS (US) [23078692] **921**

ALTERNATIVE VOICE, THE (CN/1185-1864) [24257149] **5780**

ALTERNATIVES (AMSTERDAM) (US/0304-3754) [02579435] **1545**

ALTERNATIVES ECONOMIQUES DIJON (FR/0247-3739) [l02473739] **1589**

ALTERNATIVES (INGRAM, TEX.) (US/0893-5025) [15560462] **2595**

ALTERNATIVES (NEW MARKET) (US/0270-2924) [06363941] **2527**

ALTERNATIVES NEWSLETTER (AT) **5023**

ALTERNATIVES (PETERBOROUGH) (CN/0002-6638) [01777636] **2159**

ALTERNATIVES REPORT, THE (US/1044-0100) [19644342] **5502**

ALTERNATIVES THEATREALES (BE) [10037979] **383**

ALTERNATIVES TO THE HIGH COST OF LITIGATION (US/0736-3613) [09126312] **3095**

●ALTERNATIVES (WASHINGTON, D.C.) (US/1070-3047) [28315699] **4625**

ALTERTUM, DAS (GW/0002-6646) [01479215] **2673**

ALTES HANDWERK (GW) [04675161] **369**

ALTMAN & WEIL PUBLICATIONS, INC *See* ALTMAN WEIL PENSA REPORT TO LEGAL MANAGEMENT, THE **2932**

ALTMAN WEIL PENSA REPORT TO LEGAL MANAGEMENT, THE (US/0191-863X) [04917440] 859, **2932**

ALTO ADIGE (IT) **5804**

ALTO HERALD, THE *See* RUSK CHEROKEEAN, THE **5754**

ALTONAER MUSEUM IN HAMBURG *See* JAHRBUCH - ALTONAER MUSEUM IN HAMBURG **4089**

ALTOONA HERALD-MITCHELLVILLE INDEX, THE (US) [15709896] **5668**

ALTOONA MIRROR (US) [12617826] **5734**

ALTRA EUROPA / CENTRO RUSSIA CRISTIANA, L' (IT/1120-0685) [15712010] **4933**

ALTRA EUROPE *See* NUOVA EUROPA, LA **4983**

ALTREITALIE (IT/1120-0413) [20324882] **1918**

ALTRI TERMINI (II) [01794803] **3360**

ALTRIMEDIA (IT/0392-5692) [l03925692] **1104**

ALTRO POLO (AT/0727-0046) [05585877] 2254, **2673**

ALTROCONSUMO (IT/0392-5722) [l03925722] **2211**

ALTSCHUL SYMPOSIA SERIES (US) [25962641] **3698**

ALTSPRACHLICHE UNTERRICHT, DER (GW/0002-6670) [01663608] **3263**

ALTUS TIMES, THE (US) [18032614] **5731**

ALUMI-NEWS (CN/0705-4157) [03956623] **598**

ALUMINIUM (DK) [01786867] **3997**

ALUMINIUM (DUSSELDORF) (GW/0002-6689) [03718142] **3997**

ALUMINIUM ENGLISH (GW/0343-7442) [10378925] **3997**

ALUMINIUM

ALUMINIUM INDUSTRY (UK/0268-5280) [02685280] **3997**

● ALUMINIUM INDUSTRY ABSTRACTS (US/1066-0623) [25213087] **3997**, **4025**

ALUMINIUM TODAY (UK/0955-8209) [24171475] **3997**, **2100**

ALUMINUM STATISTICAL REVIEW (US/0065-6666) [01479222] **4025**

ALUMNAE DIRECTORY / ALPHA GAMMA DELTA (US) [13695854] **5228**

ALUMNAE DIRECTORY - BENNETT COLLEGE (GREENSBORO, N.C.) (US/0731-4140) [08159770] **1096**

ALUMNAE DIRECTORY - COLUMBIA COLLEGE (COLUMBIA, S.C.) (US/0731-9584) [08243760] **1096**

ALUMNAE DIRECTORY / DELTA ZETA SORORITY (US) [15705535] **1096**

ALUMNAE DIRECTORY / MOUNT VERNON COLLEGE (US) [08556107] **1096**

ALUMNAE DIRECTORY OF SWEET BRIAR COLLEGE (US) [12987371] **1096**

ALUMNAE DIRECTORY - QUEENS COLLEGE (CHARLOTTE, N.C.) (US/0731-9010) [08252699] **1096**

ALUMNAE DIRECTORY / RANDOLPH-MACON WOMAN'S COLLEGE (US) [08244032] **1096**

ALUMNAE DIRECTORY / SIGMA SIGMA SIGMA (US) [25365441] **1096**

ALUMNAE DIRECTORY / STEPHENS COLLEGE (US/0738-6842) [09627523] **1096**

ALUMNAE DIRECTORY / THE BREARLEY SCHOOL (US/0742-5007) [10353208] **1096**

ALUMNAE DIRECTORY / ZETA PHI BETA SORORITY, INC (US/8756-677X) [11578641] **1808**

ALUMNAE DIRECTORY / ZETA TAU ALPHA FRATERNITY (US) [15078928] **1808**

ALUMNAE/I DIRECTORY / BOSTON UNIVERSITY, COLLEGE OF ENGINEERING (US) [25385982] 1964, **1096**

ALUMNAE/I DIRECTORY / LAKE ERIE COLLEGE (US/0738-2510) [09534751] **1097**

ALUMNAE/I DIRECTORY - RUTGERS LAW SCHOOL (NEWARK, N.J.) (US/0738-6672) [09623292] 2932, **1097**

ALUMNAE MAGAZINE - SWEET BRIAR COLLEGE (US/0039-7342) [03937312] **1808**

ALUMNAE REGISTER / MOUNT HOLYOKE COLLEGE (US/0742-0218) [10235949] **1097**

ALUMNEWS (NORFOLK, VA.) (US/0892-7839) [07765990] **1097**

ALUMNI/AE DIRECTORY / ARCHBISHOP CARROLL HIGH SCHOOL (US) [24204338] **1097**

● ALUMNI/AE DIRECTORY / HARVARD DIVINITY SCHOOL (US) [26322841] **1097**

ALUMNI AND ALUMNAE DIRECTORY (US) [18174072] **1097**

ALUMNI AND ALUMNAE DIRECTORY / HOBART AND WILLIAM SMITH COLLEGES (US/0738-6796) [09615587] **1097**

ALUMNI BULLETIN *See* BULLETIN - U.S. COAST GUARD ACADEMY ALUMNI ASSOCIATION **1101**

● ALUMNI DIRECTORY (US) [25606181] **1097**

ALUMNI DIRECTORY (US) [25781908] **1097**

● ALUMNI DIRECTORY (US) [26331163] **1097**

ALUMNI DIRECTORY / ALBANY LAW SCHOOL OF UNION UNIVERSITY (US) [07896458] 2932, **1097**

ALUMNI DIRECTORY - ALBANY STATE COLLEGE (US/0740-1620) [09868426] **1097**

● ALUMNI DIRECTORY / ALLEN UNIVERSITY (US) [26329760] **1097**

ALUMNI DIRECTORY (AMHERST, MASS.) (US/0278-887X) [07859163] **1097**

ALUMNI DIRECTORY AND NEWSLETTER - UNIVERSITY OF NORTH CAROLINA AT CHAPEL HILL. DEPT. OF GEOLOGY (US) [11828830] **1097**

ALUMNI DIRECTORY / ANTIOCH COLLEGE (US) [18053835] **1097**

ALUMNI DIRECTORY / BELMONT ABBEY COLLEGE (US/0740-1752) [09878764] **1097**

ALUMNI DIRECTORY - BETHEL COLLEGE (MCKENZIE, TENN.) (US/0731-4159) [08159669] **1097**

● ALUMNI DIRECTORY / BLACK HILLS STATE UNIVERSITY (US) [25384198] **1097**

ALUMNI DIRECTORY / BOSTON UNIVERSITY, COLLEGE OF BASIC STUDIES (US) [25385987] **1097**

ALUMNI DIRECTORY / BOSTON UNIVERSITY, GENERAL EDUCATION (US) [25385993] **1097**

ALUMNI DIRECTORY - BOSTON UNIVERSITY. SCHOOL OF MEDICINE. ALUMNI ASSOCIATION (US/0743-5533) [10596492] **3548**

ALUMNI DIRECTORY / BRIGHAM YOUNG UNIVERSITY, COLLEGE OF ENGINEERING AND TECHNOLOGY (US) [24369201] **1097**

ALUMNI DIRECTORY / BRYANT COLLEGE (US/0738-1158) [09504897] **1097**

ALUMNI DIRECTORY / BUENA VISTA COLLEGE (US) [08329134] **1097**

ALUMNI DIRECTORY - CALIFORNIA COLLEGE OF ARTS AND CRAFTS (OAKLAND, CALIF.) (US/0731-8928) [08243943] **1097**

ALUMNI DIRECTORY / CALIFORNIA STATE UNIVERSITY, NORTHRIDGE (US/0736-6426) [09167735] **1097**

ALUMNI DIRECTORY / CANISIUS COLLEGE (US) [09186601] **1097**

ALUMNI DIRECTORY / CAPITAL UNIVERSITY LAW AND GRADUATE CENTER (US) [21947558] **1097**

ALUMNI DIRECTORY / CARROLL COLLEGE (US) [24524131] **1097**

ALUMNI DIRECTORY / CATAWBA COLLEGE (US/0732-345X) [08319995] **1097**

ALUMNI DIRECTORY / CHOATE ROSEMARY HALL (US/0738-680X) [09627074] **1097**

ALUMNI DIRECTORY - CHRISTIAN BROTHERS COLLEGE (MEMPHIS, TENN.) (US/0740-1779) [09878555] **1098**

ALUMNI DIRECTORY / COKER COLLEGE (US) [08329061] **1098**

● ALUMNI DIRECTORY / COLLEGE OF BUSINESS ADMINISTRATION (US) [26709898] **1098**

ALUMNI DIRECTORY / COLLEGE OF ENGINEERING, UNIVERSITY OF MASSACHUSETTS AT AMHERST (US) [18713350] 1964, **1098**

ALUMNI DIRECTORY / COLLEGE OF LETTERS, ARTS AND SCIENCES, UNIVERSITY OF SOUTHERN CALIFORNIA (US) [24258622] **1098**

● ALUMNI DIRECTORY / COLLEGE OF LIBERAL ARTS, THE UNIVERSITY OF TEXAS AT AUSTIN (US) [26710833] **1098**

Alphabetical Title Index

ALUMNI DIRECTORY - COLUMBIA COLLEGE (COLUMBIA UNIVERSITY) (US/0738-9817) [09658863] **1098**

ALUMNI DIRECTORY - CORNELL COLLEGE (MOUNT VERNON, IOWA) (US/0731-891X) [08243360] **1098**

ALUMNI DIRECTORY / CREIGHTON PREPARATORY SCHOOL (US/0740-1787) [09879220] **1098**

ALUMNI DIRECTORY - CULINARY INSTITUTE OF AMERICA (US/0738-1557) [09510000] **1098**

ALUMNI DIRECTORY - CUSHING ACADEMY (US/0738-6664) [09626972] **1098**

● ALUMNI DIRECTORY / DANIEL WEBSTER COLLEGE, NEAI (US) [26657062] **1098**

ALUMNI DIRECTORY / DICKINSON COLLEGE (US/1071-6777) [28603094] **1098**

ALUMNI DIRECTORY / DUKE, THE FUQUA SCHOOL OF BUSINESS (US) [25310353] **1098**

ALUMNI DIRECTORY / EMORY & HENRY COLLEGE (US/0738-3738) [09559482] **1098**

● ALUMNI DIRECTORY / FERRIS STATE UNIVERSITY, COLLEGE OF ALLIED HEALTH SCIENCES (US) [26753723] **1098**

ALUMNI DIRECTORY - FLORIDA SOUTHERN COLLEGE (US) [07858487] **1098**

ALUMNI DIRECTORY / GLENVILLE STATE COLLEGE (US/0732-040X) [08276472] **1098**

● ALUMNI DIRECTORY / GOLDEN GATE BAPTIST THEOLOGICAL SEMINARY (US) [26324264] **1098**

ALUMNI DIRECTORY / GRAMBLING STATE UNIVERSITY (US/0738-6818) [09615590] **1098**

ALUMNI DIRECTORY / GROVE CITY COLLEGE (US/0743-4405) [10564390] **1098**

ALUMNI DIRECTORY / HAWKEN SCHOOL (US) [08681061] **1098**

ALUMNI DIRECTORY / HOLMES COMMUNITY COLLEGE (US) [24366046] **1098**

ALUMNI DIRECTORY / INTERLOCHEN CENTER FOR THE ARTS (US) [24529337] **1098**

ALUMNI DIRECTORY / JOHNSON C. SMITH UNIVERSITY (US/0738-2006) [09521433] **1098**

ALUMNI DIRECTORY / LIVINGSTON UNIVERSITY ; COMPILED AND PUBLISHED BY COLLEGE & UNIVERSITY PRESS (US) [08398006] **1098**

ALUMNI DIRECTORY - LOOMIS CHAFFEE SCHOOL (US/0738-5897) [09615892] **1098**

● ALUMNI DIRECTORY / LUTHERAN SCHOOL OF THEOLOGY AT CHICAGO (US) [26335279] **1098**

ALUMNI DIRECTORY / MARSHALL UNIVERSITY (US) [08316116] **1098**

● ALUMNI DIRECTORY / MERCY COLLEGE (US) [26651755] **1098**

ALUMNI DIRECTORY / MICHIGAN STATE UNIVERSITY, COLLEGE OF AGRICULTURE AND NATURAL RESOURCES (US/0739-6147) [09762786] **1098**

ALUMNI DIRECTORY / MINNEAPOLIS COLLEGE OF ART AND DESIGN (US) [23905657] **1098**

● ALUMNI DIRECTORY / MONTANA STATE UNIVERSITY (US) [26648967] **1098**

ALUMNI DIRECTORY / NEW MEXICO HIGHLANDS UNIVERSITY (US) [25640362] **1099**

ALUMNI DIRECTORY / NEW MEXICO MILITARY INSTITUTE (US/0738-8160) [08968719] **1099**

ALUMNI DIRECTORY / NEW YORK MILITARY ACADEMY (US/8755-6952) [11351903] **1099**

ALUMNI DIRECTORY - NICHOLS SCHOOL (BUFFALO, N.Y.) (US/0732-0388) [08262241] **1099**

ALUMNI DIRECTORY / NORTHWEST COLLEGE (US) [25843647] **1099**

ALUMNI DIRECTORY / NORTHWESTERN (US) [24369208] **1099**

ALUMNI DIRECTORY / NOVA SCOTIA AGRICULTURAL COLLEGE (CN) [24186237] **1099**

ALUMNI DIRECTORY / PENNSTATE COLLEGE OF EARTH AND MINERAL SCIENCES (US) [24778766] **1099**

ALUMNI DIRECTORY / POPULATION COUNCIL (US) [06720487] 4549, **1099**

ALUMNI DIRECTORY - QUEENS COLLEGE (NEW YORK, N.Y.) (US/0738-5196) [09600494] **1099**

ALUMNI DIRECTORY / SAINT LEO COLLEGE (US) [24489066] **1099**

ALUMNI DIRECTORY / SAINT MARGARET'S-MCTERNAN (US) [08371998] **1099**

ALUMNI DIRECTORY / SCHOOL OF MUSIC, UNIVERSITY OF SOUTHERN CALIFORNIA (US) [25597262] 4099, **1099**

ALUMNI DIRECTORY / SHAW UNIVERSITY (US/0740-9362) [10028184] **1099**

ALUMNI DIRECTORY / SIENA COLLEGE (US/0738-8179) [09633787] **1099**

ALUMNI DIRECTORY / SOUTHERN METHODIST UNIVERSITY (US/0738-1174) [08147969] **1099**

ALUMNI DIRECTORY / SOUTHERN UNIVERSITY AT NEW ORLEANS (US) [18602123] **1099**

ALUMNI DIRECTORY - SPRINGFIELD COLLEGE (US) [07821189] **1099**

ALUMNI DIRECTORY / STATE UNIVERSITY OF NEW YORK AT ALBANY (US/0733-1541) [08515477] **1099**

● ALUMNI DIRECTORY / STOCKTON STATE COLLEGE (US/1065-5166) [26616431] **1099**

ALUMNI DIRECTORY / TEIKYO WESTMAR UNIVERSITY (US) [23281007] **1099**

ALUMNI DIRECTORY / TEXAS A & I UNIVERSITY (US/0738-2219) [09534926] **1099**

ALUMNI DIRECTORY - TEXAS CHRISTIAN UNIVERSITY, THE (US/0147-4898) [03175146] **1099**

ALUMNI DIRECTORY / THE ALUMNI ASSOCIATION OF THE UNIVERSITY OF VIRGINIA (US/0738-0852) [09493685] **1099**

● ALUMNI DIRECTORY / THE CALIFORNIA CULINARY ACADEMY (US) [26735162] **1099**

● ALUMNI DIRECTORY / THE STATE UNIVERSITY OF NEW YORK COLLEGE AT BROCKPORT (US) [26662184] **1099**

ALUMNI DIRECTORY - THE UNIVERSITY OF CHICAGO LAW SCHOOL (US/0162-0371) [01554121] 2932, **1099**

ALUMNI DIRECTORY / THE UNIVERSITY OF HEALTH SCIENCES, COLLEGE OF OSTEOPATHIC MEDICINE (US) [24778701] **1099**

ALUMNI DIRECTORY / THE UNIVERSITY OF MICHIGAN, SCHOOL OF INFORMATION AND LIBRARY STUDIES (US) [25642682] 3189, **1099**

Alphabetical Title Index — AMATEUR

ALUMNI DIRECTORY / THE UNIVERSITY OF NORTH CAROLINA AT CHARLOTTE (US) [18308281] **1099**

ALUMNI DIRECTORY / THOMAS COLLEGE, WATERVILLE, MAINE (US) [25266853] **1099**

ALUMNI DIRECTORY / TRI-STATE UNIVERSITY (US) [08401680] **1099**

ALUMNI DIRECTORY - TRINITY COLLEGE (HARTFORD, CONN.) (US/0740-1671) [09868510] **1099**

ALUMNI DIRECTORY - UNIVERSITY OF CALIFORNIA, BERKELEY. GRADUATE SCHOOL OF BUSINESS ADMINISTRATION (US/0742-4353) [10329427] 638, **1099**

ALUMNI DIRECTORY / UNIVERSITY OF CALIFORNIA, DAVIS (US/0742-4345) [10331052] **1100**

ALUMNI DIRECTORY - UNIVERSITY OF CALIFORNIA, LOS ANGELES. GRADUATE SCHOOL OF MANAGEMENT (US/0738-1182) [09507071] **1100**

ALUMNI DIRECTORY / UNIVERSITY OF COLORADO, BOULDER, COLLEGE OF BUSINESS AND ADMINISTRATION (US) [09504802] **1100**

ALUMNI DIRECTORY / UNIVERSITY OF DENVER (US/0738-3630) [09564065] **1100**

ALUMNI DIRECTORY / UNIVERSITY OF EVANSVILLE (US/0738-078X) [09494651] **1100**

ALUMNI DIRECTORY / UNIVERSITY OF GUELPH (CN/1182-9877) [23598372] **1100**

●ALUMNI DIRECTORY / UNIVERSITY OF ILLINOIS, COLLEGE OF VETERINARY MEDICINE (US) [26656875] 5502, **1100**

ALUMNI DIRECTORY / UNIVERSITY OF MINNESOTA MEDICAL SCHOOL (US/0739-6899) [09788692] 3548, **1100**

ALUMNI DIRECTORY / UNIVERSITY OF NEBRASKA-LINCOLN ALUMNI ASSOCIATION (US) [23939592] **1100**

ALUMNI DIRECTORY / UNIVERSITY OF NORTH CAROLINA AT CHAPEL HILL (US/0146-7433) [03019043] **1100**

ALUMNI DIRECTORY / UNIVERSITY OF REDLANDS (US/0739-1366) [09663590] **1100**

ALUMNI DIRECTORY - UNIVERSITY OF ROCHESTER. SCHOOL OF MEDICINE AND DENTISTRY (US/0736-6671) [09313189] 3548, **1100**

ALUMNI DIRECTORY - UNIVERSITY OF TORONTO (CN/0225-2333) [06131571] **1100**

ALUMNI DIRECTORY / UNIVERSITY OF TORONTO, UNITED STATES ALUMNI (US) [25743972] **1100**

ALUMNI DIRECTORY - UNIVERSITY OF VIRGINIA. ALUMNI ASSOCIATION (US/0738-3762) [09559542] **1100**

ALUMNI DIRECTORY / UNIVERSITY OF WESTERN ONTARIO (CN) [24529352] **1100**

ALUMNI DIRECTORY / VIRGINIA INTERMONT COLLEGE (US/0738-5250) [09599138] **1100**

ALUMNI DIRECTORY - VIRGINIA UNION UNIVERSITY (RICHMOND, VA.) (US/0740-1795) [09879269] **1100**

ALUMNI DIRECTORY - WEST GEORGIA COLLEGE (US/0278-8845) [07889465] **1100**

ALUMNI DIRECTORY / WEST LIBRARY STATE COLLEGE (US/0732-0450) [08275554] **1100**

ALUMNI DIRECTORY / WESTBROOK COLLEGE (US) [23280997] **1100**

●ALUMNI DIRECTORY / WESTCHESTER COMMUNITY COLLEGE (US) [26649761] **1100**

ALUMNI DIRECTORY / WESTFIELD STATE COLLEGE (US) [25427955] **1100**

ALUMNI DIRECTORY / WHEELOCK COLLEGE (US) [17721325] **1100**

●ALUMNI DIRECTORY / WILLIAM E. SIMON GRADUATE SCHOOL OF BUSINESS ADMINISTRATION, UNIVERSITY OF ROCHESTER (US) [26517447] 638, **1100**

ALUMNI DIRECTORY / WILLIAMS COLLEGE (US/0738-3517) [09543945] **1100**

ALUMNI FAKULTAS PERTANIAN UNIVERSITAS SUMATERA UTARA (IO) [04455421] 58, **1100**

ALUMNI MAGAZINE - ALUMNI ASSOCIATION OF THE JOHNS HOPKINS HOSPITAL SCHOOL OF NURSING, THE (US/0149-2608) [03443864] 3850, **1100**

ALUMNI MAGAZINE / COLUMBIA UNIVERSITY-PRESBYTERIAN HOSPITAL SCHOOL OF NURSING ALUMNI ASSOCIATION, INC (US/0898-4093) [12194608] **3850**

ALUMNI MAGAZINE (MORGANTOWN, W. VA.) (US) [06497885] **1100**

ALUMNI NEWSLETTER / UNIVERSITY OF CALIFORNIA, LOS ANGELES, DEPARTMENT OF EARTH & SPACE SCIENCES (US) [22302604] 1100, **1351**

ALUMNI UPDATE : PHILADELPHIA COLLEGE OF TEXTILES AND SCIENCE (US) **1101**

ALUMNINEWS - CARLETON UNIVERSITY (CN/0226-5389) [06959948] **1101**

ALUMNUS, THE See WESLEYAN (MIDDLETOWN) **1103**

ALURAMA *CEASED.* (NE) [I03499863] 2109, **287**

ALVA REVIEW-COURIER, THE (US) [27953827] **5731**

ALVARADO POST (US) **5746**

ALVIN SUN, THE (US/8750-1902) [11098054] **5746**

ALVORD NEWS, THE (US) [13864353] **5746**

ALWAN (AE) [02483578] **2637**

ALWAYS JUKIN' (US/0896-9345) [17338323] **4099**

ALXEBRA (SP/0211-5239) [I02115239] **3492**

ALYAH See ANNUAL REPORT - ALIA **11**

ALYTES (FR/0753-4973) [10129292] **5574**

ALZEYER GESCHICHTSBLATTER (GW/0569-1613) [03304579] **2673**

ALZHEIMER ACTUALITES (FR/0299-2507) [I02992507] 3919, **3826**

●ALZHEIMER'S CARE GUIDE (US/1070-5112) [28395342] **5271**

AM : AUTO MOTORI (IT) **2109**

AM-FM FACILITIES CHANGES ADDENDA (US/0193-3671) [05215121] **1148**

AM-FM RADIO GUIDE NEW YORK (US/0160-8150) [03767205] **1126**

AM NEWS *CEASED.* (SA/0001-1932) [I00011932] **1126**

AM NEWS BOX HILL (AT/1037-6445) [I10376445] **859**

AM-POL EAGLE (US/0276-1904) [04255227] **5713**

AMA, AGRICULTURAL MECHANIZATION IN ASIA (JA) [02471822] **158**

AMA. AGRICULTURAL MECHANIZATION IN ASIA, AFRICA AND LATIN AMERICA (JA/0084-5841) [08646961] **158**

AMA FREIDA (US/1049-5282) [21247779] **3548**

AMA GUIDE TO MANAGEMENT DEVELOPMENT & TRAINING COURSES / AMERICAN MANAGEMENT ASSOCIATION, THE (US) [14157175] **859**

AMA MANAGEMENT BRIEFING (US) [07396544] **859**

AMA NEWSLETTER (CN/0827-0074) [13297706] **2478**

AMA SURVEY REPORT, AN (US) [02444708] **859**

AMA WINTER EDUCATORS' CONFERENCE (US/1054-0806) [16002287] **921**

AMAA NEWS See MUSEUM NATIONAL **4092**

AMACOM See NEW BOOK ANNOUNCEMENTS. ANNUAL BOOK CATALOG **4830**

AMADEUS : IL MENSILE DELLA GRANDE MUSICA (IT) [22547850] **4099**

AMADOR LEDGER DISPATCH (US/1045-8336) [20273815] **5633**

●AMAHC : ACCREDITATION MANUAL FOR AMBULATORY HEALTH CARE (US) [26061574] **3775**

AMANAH (JAKARTA, INDONESIA) (IO/0215-255X) [14868093] **4933**

AMANDLA (NE) [07715034] **4503**

AMANECER (ENGLISH ED.) *CEASED.* (US/1055-7008) [18735536] **4933**

AMANTE : CINE, EL (AG) [27805454] **4063**

AMANUENSIS (US/0044-7412) [03772967] **3360**

AMAR CHITRA KATHA (II) [08623231] **1059**

AMARANTH TODAY (US/0883-0142) [12033322] **162**

AMARILLO DAILY NEWS (AMARILLO, TEX. : 1909) (US) [03968146] **5746**

AMARILLO GLOBE-TIMES, THE (US) [13830894] **5746**

AMARO LAV (XR) [24818024] **2254**

AMATEUR ARCHAEOLOGIST (US/0363-969X) [02563861] **253**

AMATEUR ATHLETIC UNION OF THE UNITED STATES See OFFICIAL AAU PHYSIQUE HANDBOOK : OFFICIAL RULES **2600**

AMATEUR ATHLETIC UNION OF THE UNITED STATES See OFFICIAL A.A.U. BASKETBALL HANDBOOK **4908**

AMATEUR ATHLETIC UNION OF THE UNITED STATES See INFOAAU **2598**

AMATEUR ATHLETIC UNION OF THE UNITED STATES See BATON TWIRLING RULES AND REGULATIONS **383**

AMATEUR ATHLETIC UNION OF THE UNITED STATES See OFFICIAL AAU TRAMPOLINE AND TUMBLING HANDBOOK **4909**

AMATEUR ATHLETIC UNION OF THE UNITED STATES See OFFICIAL RULES FOR COMPETITIVE SWIMMING **4910**

AMATEUR ATHLETIC UNION OF THE UNITED STATES See OFFICIAL AAU SYNCHRONIZED SWIMMING HANDBOOK **4908**

AMATEUR ATHLETIC UNION OF THE UNITED STATES See DIRECTORY / AMATEUR ATHLETIC UNION OF THE UNITED STATES **4892**

AMATEUR ATHLETIC UNION OF THE UNITED STATES See OFFICIAL AAU TAE KWON DO RULES **2600**

AMATEUR ATHLETIC UNION OF THE UNITED STATES See OFFICIAL HANDBOOK OF THE AAU CODE **4909**

AMATEUR ATHLETIC UNION OF THE UNITED STATES See OFFICIAL AAU CODE AND DIRECTORY **4908**

AMATEUR ATHLETIC UNION OF THE UNITED STATES See OFFICIAL AAU TRACK AND FIELD HANDBOOK **4908**

AMATEUR ATHLETIC UNION OF THE UNITED STATES See OFFICIAL CODE/DIRECTORY / AMATEUR ATHLETIC UNION OF THE UNITED STATES, INC **4909**

AMATEUR ATHLETIC UNION OF THE UNITED STATES. A.A.U. OFFICIAL TRACK AND FIELD HANDBOOK See OFFICIAL AAU TRACK AND FIELD HANDBOOK **4908**

AMATEUR BASEBALL NEWS (US/0002-6816) [03953262] **4882**

AMATEUR CALL BOOK, THE (US/0278-1379) [07710672] **1148**

AMATEUR CHAMBER MUSIC PLAYERS See NORTH & CENTRAL AMERICAN DIRECTORY **4142**

AMATEUR COLLECTOR'S STAMP CATALOGUE OF SWITZERLAND, THE (UK) [07366661] **2784**

AMATEUR D'ART, L' (FR/0002-6824) [02025701] **335**

AMATEUR DE BORDEAUX, L' (FR) **2363**

AMATEUR ENOLOGIST, THE (CN/0316-6317) [02247650] **2363**

AMATEUR ENTOMOLOGIST : THE JOURNAL OF THE AMATEUR ENTOMOLOGISTS' SOCIETY, THE (UK) [12485579] **5605**

AMATEUR ENTOMOLOGISTS' SOCIETY (GREAT BRITAIN) See BULLETIN OF THE AMATEUR ENTOMOLOGISTS' SOCIETY, THE **5606**

AMATEUR GARDENING (UK) [03988477] **2408**

AMATEUR MUSICIEN (1980) (CN/0227-4310) [29205965] **4099**

AMATEUR MUSICIEN (1980) (CN/0227-4310) [29205967] **4099**

AMATEUR PHOTOGRAPHER (UK/0002-6840) [03989867] **4366**

AMATEUR RADIO (BICESTER) (UK/0264-2557) [24578645] **1126**

AMATEUR RADIO CALL DIRECTORY. UNITED STATES LISTINGS. GEOGRAPHICAL INDEX (US/0737-7185) [09373930] **1126**

AMATEUR ROWING ASSOCIATION (GREAT BRITAIN) See BRITISH ROWING ALMANACK AND ARA YEAR BOOK **4849**

AMATEUR SATELLITE REPORT (US/0889-6089) [13944537] **1148**

AMATEUR SPORT NEWS (CN/0824-4049) [10392331] **4882**

AMATEUR SPORT NEWS (BRITISH COLUMBIA ED.) (CN/0824-4014) [10392361] **4882**

AMATEUR SPORT NEWS (CENTRAL ALBERTA ED.) (CN/0824-4065) [10392342] **4882**

AMATEUR SPORT NEWS (EDMONTON ED.) (CN/0824-4057) [10392345] **4882**

AMATEUR SPORT NEWS (NORTHERN BRITISH COLUMBIA ED.) (CN/0824-4006) [10392436] **4882**

AMATEUR SPORT NEWS (NORTHERN SASKATCHEWAN ED.) (CN/0824-4030) [10392338] **4882**

AMATEUR SPORT NEWS (SOUTHERN ALBERTA ED.) (CN/0822-8280) [10441388] **4882**

AMATEUR SPORT NEWS (SOUTHERN BRITISH COLUMBIA ED.) (CN/0823-3999) [10392444] **4882**

AMATEUR SPORT NEWS (SOUTHERN SASKATCHEWAN ED.) (CN/0824-4022) [10392356] **4882**

AMATEUR STAGE (UK) **5361**

AMATEUR

AMATEUR TELEVISION QUARTERLY (US/1042-198X) [18968714] **1148**

AMATEUR WINE MAKER (UK/0002-6883) [03302794] **2363**

AMATEUR WRESTLING NEWS (US/0569-1796) [02444567] **4882**

AMATEURFUNK-MAGAZIN (GW) [01787070] **1126**

'AMATL (MX/0187-6112) [I01876112] 4232, **1089**

AMATYC REVIEW, THE (US/0740-8404) [07919217] **3492**

AMAZIGH (MR) [10932184] **2637**

AMAZIND BULLETIN (SZ) [02162725] **2718**

AMAZING CINEMA (US) [08078174] **4063**

AMAZING COMPUTING (US/0886-9480) [13081353] **1264**

AMAZING COMPUTING FOR THE COMMODORE AMIGA (US/1053-4547) [22600825] **1264**

AMAZING HEROES **SUSPENDED.** (US/0745-6506) [07616065] **1059**

AMAZING MOBY. CD-ROM (US) **1284**

AMAZING SPIDER-MAN, THE (US/0274-5232) [04863653] **4856**

AMAZING STORIES (1986) (US/1058-0751) [19078942] **3360**

AMAZONIA (BL) [02958021] **1545**

AMAZONIA INDIGENA / COPAL, SOLIDARIDAD CON LOS GRUPOS NATIVOS (PE) [09000462] **227**

AMAZONIA PERUANA (PE/0252-886X) [04023218] **227**, **2718**

AMAZONIANA (GW/0065-6755) [05045745] **552**

AMBASSADOR REPORT (US/0882-2123) [11891591] **4933**

AMBASSADOR, THE (PH/0044-7439) [01786358] **4515**

AMBASSADOR (WASHINGTON, D.C.) (US) [19739117] **2254**

AMBC NEWS (US/1064-1599) [09037292] **205**

AMBC NEWS See AMERICAN LIVESTOCK BREEDS CONSERVANCY NEWS **58**

AMBER (DARTMOUTH) (CN/0318-5753) [01691528] **3459**

AMBIANCE (US/0148-9135) [03504035] 402, **1081**

AMBIENTE (IT) **2211**

AMBIENTE CUCINA, L' (IT/0392-5730) [I03925730] **2898**

AMBIENTE E SICUREZZA SUL LAVORO (IT/0393-7054) [I03937054] **2858**

AMBIENTE MEDICO : REVISTA DEL HOSPITAL J.A. FERNANDEZ (AG/0326-0674) [24034638] **3775**

AMBIENTE (OFFENBURG, GERMANY) (GW) [09184887] **2898**

AMBIENTE RISORSE SALUTE (IT/0393-0521) [I03930521] **2160**

AMBIENTE SALUTE TERRITORIO (IT) **2211**

AMBIENTE Y RECURSOS NATURALES : REVISTA DE DERECHO, POLITICA Y ADMINISTRACION (AG/0326-422X) [10773963] **3109**

AMBIO (SW/0044-7447) [01074032] **2160**

AMBIT (UK/0002-6972) [01845808] **3459**

AMBITO FINANCIERO (AG) [19044569] 4463, **638**

AMBIX (UK/0002-6980) [01479234] **960**

AMBLER GAZETTE, THE (US) [13448090] **5734**

AMBOY NEWS, THE (US) [27160379] **5658**

AMBULANCE MANAGEMENT INTERNATIONAL (UK/0952-3758) [I09523758] **3723**

AMBULANCE WORLD (1986) (AT/0817-4474) [I08174474] **3723**

AMBULANT OPERIEREN (GW/0944-5943) **3548**

AMBULATORY CARE (US/0894-3672) [13292811] **3775**

AMBULATORY HEALTH CARE STANDARDS MANUAL (US/0898-7351) [11280616] **3775**

AMBULATORY MEDICINE LETTER See PRIMARY CARE LETTER **3629**

AMBULATORY MEDICINE LETTER, THE (US/0897-554X) [17543373] **3548**

AMBULATORY RECORD MONITOR (US/1057-753X) [24116419] **3776**

●AMBULATORY SURGERY (UK/0966-6532) [I09666532] **3958**

AMC. ACTA MEDICA COLOMBIANA (CK/0120-2448) [07470722] **3794**

AMC. AMERICAN MARITIME CASES (US/0160-6786) [03737842] **3180**

AMC JOURNAL (US/0891-6209) [14509700] **2133**

AMC NEWSLETTER **SUSPENDED.** (US) [06462172] **4099**

●AMC OUTDOORS (US/1067-5604) [27257617] **4868**

AMCA NEWSLETTER (US/0195-4180) [05466293] **2160**

AMCHAM ARGENTINA See AMERICAN BUSINESS IN ARGENTINA ... DIRECTORY **638**

AMCHAM BUSINESS JOURNAL (PH) [25494139] **818**

AMCHAM : THE MAGAZINE OF THE AMERICAN CHAMBER OF COMMERCE IN BELGIUM (BE/0778-2624) [23763698] **818**

AMD (NEW YORK, N.Y.) (US/0160-8835) [03782947] **2109**

AMDEL NEWS **CEASED.** (AT/0810-8056) [I08108056] **3997**

AME ET LA CORDE, L' (FR/0294-4782) [09694479] **4099**

AME JOURNAL (US) **11**

AMEGHINIANA (AG/0002-7014) [01794678] **4226**

AMELIA (US/0743-2755) [10584649] **3360**

AMELIA BULLETIN MONITOR, THE (US/0746-1798) [09833618] **5758**

AMENAGEMENT DE L'ESPACE ET DU TEMPS ET DEVELOPPEMENT DU TOURISME : ACTES DU CONSEIL SUPERIEUR DU TOURISME (FR) [09843963] **5461**

AMENAGEMENT ET NATURE (FR/0044-7463) [10163822] **2186**

AMENAGEMENT HYDROELECTRIQUE D'EASTMAN 1, L' (CN/1186-6918) [24402175] **1931**

AMENDED ANNUAL PROGRAM PLAN FOR FY ... UNDER P.L. 94-142, PART B, EDUCATION FOR ALL HANDICAPPED CHILDREN ACT (US) [07886754] **1874**

AMENDED ANNUAL PROGRAM PLAN, PART B, EDUCATION OF THE HANDICAPPED ACT AS AMENDED BY PUBLIC LAW 94-142 (US) [04620996] **1874**

AMENITY MANAGEMENT (UK/0957-8870) [I09578870] **4848**

AMERASIA JOURNAL (US/0044-7471) [01666962] 2645, **2254**

AMERICA (IT) **755**

AMERICA AT LARGE **SUSPENDED.** (US/1056-4322) [23711274] **2527**

AMERICA, BUSINESS TODAY (US/1071-9105) [28762996] **638**

AMERICA FAMILY, THE See YOUTH POLICY **5314**

AMERICA, HISTORY AND LIFE. FIVE YEAR INDEX (US) [04339444] **2718**

AMERICA, HISTORY AND LIFE ON DISC. COMPUTER FILE (US/0002-7065) [25024407] **2718**

AMERICA : HISTORY AND LIFE. PART A : ARTICLE ABSTRACTS AND CITATIONS (US) [01781761] **2718**

AMERICA, HISTORY AND LIFE (SANTA BARBARA, CALIF. : 1989) (US/0002-7065) [19247941] 2609, **2634**

AMERICA, HISTORY AND LIFE. SUPPLEMENT (US) [06800911] **2718**

AMERICA INDIGENA (MX/0185-1179) [01479245] 2718, **227**

AMERICA LATINA **CEASED.** (RU) [01353680] **2718**

AMERICA LATINA 2001 I.E. DOS MIL UNO (CK) [02659389] **5082**

AMERICA LATINA INTERNACIONAL (AG) **2718**

AMERICA LATINA (MEXICO CITY, MEXICO : 1979) (MX) [06100611] **2718**

AMERICA MERIDIONAL : REVISTA DE LA SOCIEDAD REGIONAL DE CIENCIAS HUMANAS (UY) [09976634] **5190**

AMERICA (NEW YORK, N.Y. 1909) (US/0002-7049) [01479242] **5023**

AMERICA OGGI (US/1042-6965) [19109105] **5709**

AMERICA UKRAINIAN CATHOLIC DAILY (US/0279-6201) [07120828] 5023, **2254**

AMERICA VOTES (US/0065-678X) [01240412] **4463**

AMERICAN (UK) **5811**

AMERICAN ACADEMY AND INSTITUTE OF ARTS AND LETTERS See PROCEEDINGS OF THE AMERICAN ACADEMY AND INSTITUTE OF ARTS AND LETTERS **328**

AMERICAN ACADEMY AND INSTITUTE OF ARTS AND LETTERS. PROCEEDINGS OF THE AMERICAN ACADEMY AND INSTITUTE OF ARTS AND LETTERS See PROCEEDINGS OF THE AMERICAN ACADEMY OF ARTS AND LETTERS **328**

AMERICAN ACADEMY AND INSTITUTE OF ARTS AND LETTERS. REPORT OF ACTIVITIES (US) [06978252] **312**

AMERICAN ACADEMY IN ROME See MEMOIRS OF THE AMERICAN ACADEMY IN ROME **1078**

AMERICAN ACADEMY IN ROME See PAPERS AND MONOGRAPHS - AMERICAN ACADEMY IN ROME **305**

AMERICAN ACADEMY OF ACTUARIES See YEAR BOOK - AMERICAN ACADEMY OF ACTUARIES **2896**

AMERICAN ACADEMY OF ADVERTISING. CONFERENCE See PROCEEDINGS OF THE CONFERENCE OF THE AMERICAN ACADEMY OF ADVERTISING (1985) **764**

AMERICAN ACADEMY OF ARTS AND LETTERS (1993-) See PROCEEDINGS OF THE AMERICAN ACADEMY OF ARTS AND LETTERS **328**

AMERICAN ACADEMY OF ARTS AND LETTERS. REPORT OF ACTIVITIES See AMERICAN ACADEMY AND INSTITUTE OF ARTS AND LETTERS. REPORT OF ACTIVITIES **312**

AMERICAN ACADEMY OF ARTS AND SCIENCES See BULLETIN - AMERICAN ACADEMY OF ARTS AND SCIENCES **316**

AMERICAN ACADEMY OF ARTS AND SCIENCES See RECORDS OF THE ACADEMY **329**

AMERICAN ACADEMY OF CHILD PSYCHIATRY See MONOGRAPHS OF THE JOURNAL OF THE AMERICAN ACADEMY OF CHILD PSYCHIATRY **3906**

AMERICAN ACADEMY OF DERMATOLOGY See JOURNAL OF THE AMERICAN ACADEMY OF DERMATOLOGY **3721**

AMERICAN ACADEMY OF DERMATOLOGY See DIRECTORY - AMERICAN ACADEMY OF DERMATOLOGY **3720**

AMERICAN ACADEMY OF DERMATOLOGY. ROSTER: BYLAWS, OFFICERS, COMMITTEES See DIRECTORY - AMERICAN ACADEMY OF DERMATOLOGY **3720**

AMERICAN ACADEMY OF INSTITUTE OF ARTS AND LETTERS See PUBLICATION - AMERICAN ACADEMY AND INSTITUTE OF ARTS AND LETTERS **328**

AMERICAN ACADEMY OF ORTHOPAEDIC SURGEONS See INSTRUCTIONAL COURSE LECTURES **3966**

AMERICAN ACADEMY OF PEDIATRICS See BIOGRAPHICAL DIRECTORY OF THE AMERICAN ACADEMY OF PEDIATRICS **3655**

AMERICAN ACADEMY OF PEDIATRICS. COMMITTEE ON INFECTIOUS DISEASES See REPORT OF THE COMMITTEE ON INFECTIOUS DISEASES **3715**

AMERICAN ACADEMY OF PHYSICAL EDUCATION. MEETING See AMERICAN ACADEMY OF PHYSICAL EDUCATION PAPERS **1854**

AMERICAN ACADEMY OF PHYSICAL EDUCATION PAPERS (US/0741-4633) [10204205] **1854**

AMERICAN ACADEMY OF PODIATRIC SPORTS MEDICINE NEWSLETTER (US) [13098975] **3953**

AMERICAN ACADEMY OF PSYCHIATRY AND NEUROLOGY See JOURNAL OF THE AMERICAN ACADEMY OF PSYCHIATRY AND NEUROLOGY **3930**

AMERICAN ACADEMY OF PSYCHIATRY AND THE LAW See BULLETIN OF THE AMERICAN ACADEMY OF PSYCHIATRY AND THE LAW **3922**

AMERICAN ACADEMY OF PSYCHOANALYSIS See MEMBERSHIP ROSTER - AMERICAN ACADEMY OF PSYCHOANALYSIS **4603**

AMERICAN ACADEMY OF RELIGION See AAR STUDIES IN RELIGION **4931**

AMERICAN ACADEMY OF RELIGION See JOURNAL OF THE AMERICAN ACADEMY OF RELIGION **4970**

AMERICAN ACADEMY OF RELIGION See ABSTRACTS / AMERICAN ACADEMY OF RELIGION **4931**

AMERICAN ACADEMY OF RELIGION ACADEMY SERIES (US/0277-1071) [07511253] **4933**

AMERICAN ACADEMY OF RELIGION. AFRO-AMERICAN RELIGIOUS HISTORY GROUP See NEWSLETTER OF THE AFRO-AMERICAN RELIGIOUS HISTORY GROUP OF THE AMERICAN ACADEMY OF RELIGION **2750**

AMERICAN ACADEMY OF RELIGION. PHILOSOPHY OF RELIGION AND THEOLOGY SECTION See PHILOSOPHY OF RELIGION AND THEOLOGY : PROCEEDINGS **4986**

AMERICAN AERONAUT (US/0279-7968) [06260337] **1643**

AMERICAN AGENT & BROKER (US/0002-7200) [01786126] **2873**

AMERICAN AGRICULTURAL ECONOMICS ASSOCIATION See AAEA NEWSLETTER (AMES, IOWA) **42**

AMERICAN AGRICULTURE NEWS (US/0745-001X) [06205370] **58**

Alphabetical Title Index — AMERICAN

AMERICAN AGRICULTURIST (1976) (US/0161-8237) [03954633] **58**

AMERICAN AIREDALE, THE (US/1059-4477) [24595087] **4285**

AMERICAN ALMANAC OF JOBS AND SALARIES, THE (US) [15229583] **4201**

AMERICAN ALPINE JOURNAL, THE (US/0065-6925) [01479278] **4868**

AMERICAN AMATEUR JOURNALIST, THE (US/1046-0470) [20315409] **2770**

AMERICAN ANALGESIA SOCIETY See JOURNAL OF THE AMERICAN ANALGESIA SOCIETY **3597**

AMERICAN & THE AMERICAN TRAVELLER See AMERICAN **5811**

AMERICAN & WORLD INTELLECTUAL PROPERTY REPORT (CN/0835-7560) [17748627] **1301**

AMERICAN ANGLER (INTERVALE, N.H.) (US/1055-6737) [23261374] **2294**

AMERICAN ANIMAL HOSPITAL ASSOCIATION See BULLETIN - AMERICAN ANIMAL HOSPITAL ASSOCIATION **5506**

AMERICAN ANIMAL HOSPITAL ASSOCIATION See DIRECTORY OF MEMBERSHIP OF THE AMERICAN ANIMAL HOSPITAL ASSOCIATION **5509**

AMERICAN ANIMAL HOSPITAL ASSOCIATION See SCIENTIFIC PRESENTATIONS OF THE ANNUAL MEETING - AMERICAN ANIMAL HOSPITAL ASSOCIATION **5521**

AMERICAN ANIMAL HOSPITAL ASSOCIATION See JOURNAL OF THE AMERICAN ANIMAL HOSPITAL ASSOCIATION, THE **5513**

AMERICAN ANNALS OF THE DEAF (WASHINGTON, D.C. 1886) (US/0002-726X) [05695496] **4383**

AMERICAN ANTHROPOLOGICAL ASSOCIATION See AAA GUIDE **227**

AMERICAN ANTHROPOLOGICAL ASSOCIATION See SPECIAL PUBLICATION OF THE AMERICAN ANTHROPOLOGICAL ASSOCIATION, A **245**

AMERICAN ANTHROPOLOGICAL ASSOCIATION See ABSTRACTS OF THE ANNUAL MEETING - AMERICAN ANTHROPOLOGICAL ASSOCIATION **227**

AMERICAN ANTHROPOLOGIST (US/0002-7294) [01479294] **227**

AMERICAN ANTHROPOLOGIST [MICROFORM] (US/0002-7294) [08074192] **227**

AMERICAN ANTIQUARIAN SOCIETY See NEWS-LETTER OF THE AMERICAN ANTIQUARIAN SOCIETY **4831**

AMERICAN ANTIQUARIAN SOCIETY See PROCEEDINGS OF THE AMERICAN ANTIQUARIAN SOCIETY **2755**

AMERICAN ANTIQUITY; A QUARTERLY REVIEW OF AMERICAN ARCHAEOLOGY (US/0002-7316) [01479302] **253**

AMERICAN APPAREL MANUFACTURERS ASSOCIATION See DIRECTORY, MEMBERS AND ASSOCIATE MEMBERS - AMERICAN APPAREL MANUFACTURERS ASSOCIATION (1983) **1083**

AMERICAN APPAREL MANUFACTURERS ASSOCIATION. PERSONNEL RELATIONS COMMITTEE See AAMA PERSONNEL POLICIES AND BENEFITS SURVEY **938**

AMERICAN-ARAB AFFAIRS (US/0731-6763) [08230947] **4515**

AMERICAN ARACHNOLOGY (US/0364-9504) [02693344] **5574**

AMERICAN ARBITRATION ASSOCIATION See ANNUAL REPORT / AMERICAN ARBITRATION ASSOCIATION **2934**

AMERICAN ARBITRATION ASSOCIATION See SUMMARY OF LABOR ARBITRATION AWARDS **1712**

AMERICAN ARBITRATION ASSOCIATION. OFFICE OF THE GENERAL COUNSEL See ARBITRATION & THE LAW **2936**

AMERICAN ARCHEOLOGIST, THE (US) [02489710] **254**

AMERICAN ARCHEOLOGY **SUSPENDED.** (US/0740-8358) [10028512] **254**

AMERICAN ARCHIVIST, THE (US/0360-9081) [01479314] **2478**

AMERICAN ART DIRECTORY (US/0065-6968) [01479316] **335**

AMERICAN ART DIRECTORY (US/0065-6968) [01259642] **333**

AMERICAN ART JOURNAL, THE (US/0002-7359) [01000070] **336**

AMERICAN ART / NATIONAL MUSEUM OF AMERICAN ART, SMITHSONIAN INSTITUTION (US) [24162804] **336**

AMERICAN ART REVIEW (US/0092-1327) [01789238] **336**

AMERICAN ART THERAPY ASSOCIATION NEWSLETTER (US/1066-4076) [12071812] 3548, **4572**

AMERICAN ARTIST (US/0002-7375) [03005862] **336**

AMERICAN ARTIST DIRECTORY OF ART SCHOOLS AND WORKSHOPS (US/0146-9606) [03064450] **312**

AMERICAN ARTISTS OF RENOWN (US/0276-5691) [07391331] **336**

AMERICAN ASIAN REVIEW, THE (US/0737-6650) [09444259] **2645**

AMERICAN ASSEMBLY OF COLLEGIATE SCHOOLS OF BUSINESS See MEMBERSHIP DIRECTORY / AACSB **1835**

AMERICAN ASSEMBLY OF COLLEGIATE SCHOOLS OF BUSINESS See AACSB NEWSLINE **1806**

AMERICAN ASSOCIATION FOR ADULT AND CONTINUING EDUCATION See AAACE MEMBERSHIP DIRECTORY **1799**

AMERICAN ASSOCIATION FOR CANCER RESEARCH See DIRECTORY OF MEMBERS / AMERICAN ASSOCIATION FOR CANCER RESEARCH **3816**

AMERICAN ASSOCIATION FOR CANCER RESEARCH See ANNUAL MEETING OF THE AMERICAN ASSOCIATION FOR CANCER RESEARCH PROCEEDINGS **3808**

AMERICAN ASSOCIATION FOR GERIATRIC PSYCHIATRY NEWSLETTER (US/0734-6026) [08813521] 3749, **3919**

AMERICAN ASSOCIATION FOR HIGHER EDUCATION See AAHE BULLETIN **1806**

AMERICAN ASSOCIATION FOR TEXTILE TECHNOLOGY See TECHNICAL REVIEW & REGISTER **5356**

AMERICAN ASSOCIATION FOR THE ADVANCEMENT OF SCIENCE See DIRECTORY OF AAAS FELLOWS **5100**

AMERICAN ASSOCIATION FOR THE ADVANCEMENT OF SCIENCE See AAAS HANDBOOK **5079**

AMERICAN ASSOCIATION FOR THE ADVANCEMENT OF SLAVIC STUDIES See NEWSLETTER - AMERICAN ASSOCIATION FOR THE ADVANCEMENT OF SLAVIC STUDIES **2700**

AMERICAN ASSOCIATION FOR THE ADVANCEMENT OF SLAVIC STUDIES See AAASS NEWSLETTER **2671**

AMERICAN ASSOCIATION FOR THE ADVANCEMENT OF SLAVIC STUDIES See NEWSNET (STANFORD, CALIF.) **2700**

AMERICAN ASSOCIATION FOR THE ADVANCEMENT OF SLAVIC STUDIES. AAASS NEWSLETTER See NEWSNET (STANFORD, CALIF.) **2700**

AMERICAN ASSOCIATION FOR THE ADVANCEMENT OF TENSION CONTROL See TENSION CONTROL **4620**

AMERICAN ASSOCIATION OF ADVERTISING AGENCIES See AAAA ROSTER AND ORGANIZATION **753**

AMERICAN ASSOCIATION OF BOVINE PRACTITIONERS. CONFERENCE. AMERICAN ASSOCIATION OF BOVINE PRACTITIONERS CONFERENCE: [PROCEEDINGS] (US) [28554226] **205**

AMERICAN ASSOCIATION OF BOVINE PRACTITIONERS. CONVENTION See PROCEEDINGS OF THE ANNUAL CONVENTION - AMERICAN ASSOCIATION OF BOVINE PRACTITIONERS. CONVENTION **5519**

AMERICAN ASSOCIATION OF CEREAL CHEMISTS See APPROVED METHODS OF THE AMERICAN ASSOCIATION OF CEREAL CHEMISTS **961**

AMERICAN ASSOCIATION OF CEREAL CHEMISTS See MONOGRAPH SERIES - AMERICAN ASSOCIATION OF CEREAL CHEMISTS **2350**

AMERICAN ASSOCIATION OF CHRISTIAN COUNSELORS See AMERICAN ASSOCIATION OF CHRISTIAN COUNSELORS MEMBERSHIP REGISTRY **4933**

AMERICAN ASSOCIATION OF CHRISTIAN COUNSELORS MEMBERSHIP REGISTRY (US/1055-873X) [23104542] **4933**

AMERICAN ASSOCIATION OF COLLEGES FOR TEACHER EDUCATION See AACTE DIRECTORY / AMERICAN ASSOCIATION OF COLLEGES FOR TEACHER EDUCATION **1859**

AMERICAN ASSOCIATION OF COLLEGES FOR TEACHER EDUCATION See DIRECTORY OF MEMBERS / AMERICAN ASSOCIATION OF COLLEGES FOR TEACHER EDUCATION **1862**

AMERICAN ASSOCIATION OF COLLEGES FOR TEACHER EDUCATION. AACTE DIRECTORY (1991) See DIRECTORY OF MEMBERS / AMERICAN ASSOCIATION OF COLLEGES FOR TEACHER EDUCATION **1862**

AMERICAN ASSOCIATION OF COLLEGES OF PHARMACY See ROSTER OF TEACHING PERSONNEL IN COLLEGES OF PHARMACY **4328**

AMERICAN ASSOCIATION OF COLLEGES OF PHARMACY. OFFICE STUDENT AFFAIRS See PHARMACY SCHOOL ADMISSION REQUIREMENTS **4323**

AMERICAN ASSOCIATION OF COMMUNITY AND JUNIOR COLLEGES See AACJC MEMBERSHIP DIRECTORY **1806**

AMERICAN ASSOCIATION OF COST ENGINEERS. MEETING See TRANSACTIONS OF THE AMERICAN ASSOCIATION OF COST ENGINEERS **2100**

AMERICAN ASSOCIATION OF DENTAL SCHOOLS See ADMISSION REQUIREMENTS OF U.S. AND CANADIAN DENTAL SCHOOLS **1315**

AMERICAN ASSOCIATION OF DENTAL SCHOOLS See FACULTY SALARY SURVEY **1669**

AMERICAN ASSOCIATION OF DENTAL SCHOOLS See GUIDEBOOK OF U.S. & CANADIAN POSTDOCTORAL DENTAL PROGRAMS **1324**

AMERICAN ASSOCIATION OF EQUINE PRACTITIONERS See PROCEEDINGS OF THE ANNUAL CONVENTION OF THE AMERICAN ASSOCIATION OF EQUINE PRACTITIONERS **2801**

AMERICAN ASSOCIATION OF EQUINE PRACTITIONERS See MEMBERSHIP DIRECTORY - AMERICAN ASSOCIATION OF EQUINE PRACTITIONERS **5516**

AMERICAN ASSOCIATION OF EXPORTERS AND IMPORTERS See MEMBERSHIP DIRECTORY / AMERICAN ASSOCIATION OF EXPORTERS AND IMPORTERS **845**

AMERICAN ASSOCIATION OF FEED MICROSCOPISTS See OFFICIAL PROCEEDINGS, ANNUAL MEETING - AMERICAN ASSOCIATION OF FEED MICROSCOPISTS **116**

AMERICAN ASSOCIATION OF HOMES FOR THE AGING See DIRECTORY OF MEMBERS / AMERICAN ASSOCIATION OF HOMES FOR THE AGING **5283**

AMERICAN ASSOCIATION OF LAW LIBRARIES See AALL PUBLICATION SERIES **2926**

AMERICAN ASSOCIATION OF LAW LIBRARIES. CONTEMPORARY SOCIAL PROBLEMS SPECIAL INTEREST SECTION See CONTEMPORARY SOCIAL PROBLEMS **5196**

AMERICAN ASSOCIATION OF LAW LIBRARIES NEWSLETTER (US/0572-4953) [19690310] 2932, **3189**

AMERICAN ASSOCIATION OF LAW LIBRARIES. STATE, COURT, AND COUNTY LAW LIBRARIES SECTION See NEWSLETTER-STATE, COURT, AND COUNTY LAW LIBRARIES SECTION **3236**

AMERICAN ASSOCIATION OF NURSE ANESTHETISTS See AANA NEWSBULLETIN **3849**

AMERICAN ASSOCIATION OF NURSERYMEN See AAN ANNUAL CONVENTION REPORT **2416**

AMERICAN ASSOCIATION OF NURSERYMEN. ANNUAL MEETING See AAN ANNUAL CONVENTION REPORT **2416**

AMERICAN ASSOCIATION OF ORAL AND MAXILLOFACIAL SURGEONS See AAOMS DIRECTORY / AMERICAN ASSOCIATION OF ORAL AND MAXILLOFACIAL SURGEONS **1314**

AMERICAN ASSOCIATION OF PETROLEUM GEOLOGISTS See AAPG CONTINUING EDUCATION COURSE NOTE SERIES **4248**

AMERICAN ASSOCIATION OF PETROLEUM GEOLOGISTS See AAPG EXPLORER **1364**

AMERICAN ASSOCIATION OF PETROLEUM GEOLOGISTS See AAPG REPRINT SERIES **1364**

AMERICAN ASSOCIATION OF PETROLEUM GEOLOGISTS See COMPREHENSIVE INDEX OF PUBLICATIONS OF THE AMERICAN ASSOCIATION OF PETROLEUM GEOLOGISTS **4253**

AMERICAN ASSOCIATION OF PETROLEUM GEOLOGISTS. PACIFIC SECTION See MISCELLANEOUS PUBLICATION **1388**

AMERICAN ASSOCIATION OF PETROLEUM GEOLOGISTS. PACIFIC SECTION See GUIDEBOOK (AMERICAN ASSOCIATION OF PETROLEUM GEOLOGISTS **1381**

AMERICAN ASSOCIATION OF PETROLEUM LANDMEN See LANDMEN'S DIRECTORY **4263**

AMERICAN ASSOCIATION OF PHYSICS TEACHERS See ANNOUNCER (COLLEGE PARK, MD.) **4397**

AMERICAN — Alphabetical Title Index

AMERICAN ASSOCIATION OF PSYCHIATRIC SERVICES FOR CHILDREN *See* NEWSLETTER OF THE A.A.P.S.C **3907**

AMERICAN ASSOCIATION OF RAILROAD SUPERINTENDENTS *See* PROCEEDINGS OF THE ANNUAL MEETING AND REGIONAL MEETING - AMERICAN ASSOCIATION OF RAILROAD SUPERINTENDENTS **5434**

AMERICAN ASSOCIATION OF SCHOOL ADMINISTRATORS *See* AASA EXECUTIVE HANDBOOK SERIES **1859**

AMERICAN ASSOCIATION OF STATE COLLEGES AND UNIVERSITIES *See* MEMO: TO THE PRESIDENT **1835**

AMERICAN ASSOCIATION OF STATE HIGHWAY AND TRANSPORTATION OFFICIALS *See* STANDARD SPECIFICATIONS FOR HIGHWAY BRIDGES **2031**

AMERICAN ASSOCIATION OF STATE HIGHWAY AND TRANSPORTATION OFFICIALS *See* STANDARD SPECIFICATIONS FOR TRANSPORTATION MATERIALS AND METHODS OF SAMPLING AND TESTING **2031**

AMERICAN ASSOCIATION OF STATE HIGHWAY AND TRANSPORTATION OFFICIALS *See* AASHTO QUARTERLY **5375**

AMERICAN ASSOCIATION OF STATE HIGHWAY OFFICIALS COMMITTEE ON COMPUTER TECHNOLOGY *See* PROCEEDINGS - COMMITTEE ON COMPUTER TECHNOLOGY **5442**

AMERICAN ASSOCIATION OF STATE HIGHWAY OFFICIALS PROCEEDINGS (US) **5375**

AMERICAN ASSOCIATION OF STRATIGRAPHIC PALYNOLOGISTS *See* AASP NEWSLETTER **1364**

AMERICAN ASSOCIATION OF STRATIGRAPHIC PALYNOLOGISTS *See* CONTRIBUTIONS SERIES - AMERICAN ASSOCIATION OF STRATIGRAPHIC PALYNOLOGISTS **1372**

AMERICAN ASSOCIATION OF STRATIGRAPHIC PALYNOLOGISTS *See* PALYNOLOGY **1390**

AMERICAN ASSOCIATION OF TEACHERS OF ESPERANTO *See* QUARTERLY BULLETIN OF THE AMERICAN ASSOCIATION OF TEACHERS OF ESPERANTO **3313**

AMERICAN ASSOCIATION OF TEACHERS OF SLAVIC AND EAST EUROPEAN LANGUAGES *See* AATSEEL'S NEWSLETTER / AMERICAN ASSOCIATION OF TEACHERS OF SLAVIC AND EAST EUROPEAN LANGUAGES **1720**

AMERICAN ASSOCIATION OF TEACHERS OF SPANISH AND PORTUGUESE *See* AATSP PORTUGUESE NATIONAL NEWSLETTER **3260**

AMERICAN ASSOCIATION OF TEXTILE CHEMISTS AND COLORISTS *See* BUYER'S GUIDE - AMERICAN ASSOCIATION OF TEXTILE CHEMISTS AND COLORISTS **5348**

AMERICAN ASSOCIATION OF TEXTILE CHEMISTS AND COLORISTS *See* BOOK OF PAPERS - AMERICAN ASSOCIATION OF TEXTILE CHEMISTS AND COLORISTS. INTERNATIONAL CONFERENCE & EXHIBITION **5348**

AMERICAN ASSOCIATION OF THEOLOGICAL SCHOOLS *See* MONTHLY NEWSLETTER - AMERICAN ASSOCIATION OF THEOLOGICAL SCHOOLS **4979**

AMERICAN ASSOCIATION OF TISSUE BANKS *See* NEWSLETTER - AMERICAN ASSOCIATION OF TISSUE BANKS **3621**

AMERICAN ASSOCIATION OF UNIVERSITY PROFESSORS. NEW YORK CONFERENCE *See* NEW YORK **1837**

AMERICAN ASSOCIATION OF UNIVERSITY WOMEN *See* OUTLOOK (WASHINGTON, D.C. 1989) **5564**

AMERICAN ASSOCIATION OF UNIVERSITY WOMEN. SEATTLE BRANCH *See* SEATTLE BRANCH NEWSLETTER / AMERICAN ASSOCIATION OF UNIVERSITY WOMEN **1847**

AMERICAN ASSOCIATION OF UNIVERSITY WOMEN. SEATTLE BRANCH *See* SEATTLE BRANCH NEWSLETTER / AMERICAN ASSOCIATION OF UNIVERSITY WOMEN **1847**

AMERICAN ASSOCIATION OF VARIABLE STAR OBSERVERS *See* AAVSO CIRCULAR **391**

AMERICAN ASSOCIATION OF VARIABLE STAR OBSERVERS *See* BULLETIN - THE AMERICAN ASSOCIATION OF VARIABLE STAR OBSERVERS **394**

AMERICAN ASSOCIATION OF VETERINARY LABORATORY DIAGNOSTICIANS. MEETING *See* PROCEEDINGS OF ... ANNUAL MEETING - AMERICAN ASSOCIATION OF VETERINARY LABORATORY DIAGNOSTICIANS **5519**

AMERICAN ASSOCIATION OF ZOOLOGICAL PARKS AND AQUARIUMS *See* AAZPA REGIONAL CONFERENCE PROCEEDINGS **5572**

AMERICAN ASSOCIATION OF ZOOLOGICAL PARKS AND AQUARIUMS *See* AAZPA ... ANNUAL CONFERENCE PROCEEDINGS **5572**

AMERICAN ASSOCIATION OF ZOOLOGICAL PARKS AND AQUARIUMS *See* PROCEEDINGS; ANNUAL AAZPA CONFERENCE **5595**

AMERICAN ASTROLOGY (US/0002-7529) [11105519] **389**

AMERICAN ASTRONAUTICAL SOCIETY *See* AAS HISTORY SERIES **3**

AMERICAN ASTRONOMICAL SOCIETY *See* BULLETIN - AMERICAN ASTRONOMICAL SOCIETY **402**

AMERICAN ASTRONOMICAL SOCIETY *See* MEMBERSHIP DIRECTORY - AMERICAN ASTRONOMICAL SOCIETY (1984) **397**

AMERICAN ATHEIST, THE *SUSPENDED.* (US/0516-9623) [03160253] 4340, **4933**

AMERICAN ATHLETICS ANNUAL (US) [08697873] **4882**

AMERICAN AUTOMATIC MERCHANDISER *See* AUTOMATIC MERCHANDISER **2328**

AMERICAN AUTOMOBILE ASSOCIATION *See* TOUR BOOK: NEW YORK **5493**

AMERICAN AUTOMOBILE ASSOCIATION *See* DIGEST OF MOTOR LAWS **2961**

AMERICAN AUTOMOBILE ASSOCIATION *See* TOUR BOOK: ILLINOIS, INDIANA, OHIO **5492**

AMERICAN AUTOMOBILE ASSOCIATION *See* TOUR BOOK: MAINE, NEW HAMPSHIRE, VERMONT **5492**

AMERICAN AUTOMOBILE ASSOCIATION *See* TOUR BOOK : ARKANSAS, KANSAS, MISSOURI, OKLAHOMA **5492**

AMERICAN AUTOMOBILE ASSOCIATION *See* TOURBOOK: COLORADO, UTAH **5493**

AMERICAN AUTOMOBILE ASSOCIATION *See* TOUR BOOK: NEW JERSEY, PENNSYLVANIA **5493**

AMERICAN AUTOMOBILE ASSOCIATION *See* TOURBOOK : MID-ATLANTIC **5493**

AMERICAN AUTOMOBILE ASSOCIATION *See* TOUR BOOK: CONNECTICUT, MASSACHUSETTS, RHODE ISLAND **5492**

AMERICAN AUTOMOBILE ASSOCIATION *See* EASTERN CANADA CAMPING **4871**

AMERICAN AUTOMOBILE ASSOCIATION *See* TOUR BOOK: MICHIGAN, WISCONSIN **5493**

AMERICAN AUTOMOBILE ASSOCIATION *See* TOUR BOOK: TEXAS **5493**

AMERICAN AUTOMOBILE ASSOCIATION *See* TOUR BOOK: ATLANTIC PROVINCES AND QUEBEC **5492**

AMERICAN AVIATION HISTORICAL SOCIETY *See* AAHS JOURNAL **3**

AMERICAN AVIATION HISTORICAL SOCIETY *See* AAHS NEWSLETTER **3**

AMERICAN AVIATION WORLD WIDE DIRECTORY *See* WORLD AVIATION DIRECTORY **40**

AMERICAN BABY (US/0044-7544) [01479443] **2276**

AMERICAN BABY'S CHILDBIRTH EDUCATOR *CEASED.* (US/0279-490X) [07910117] **3756**

AMERICAN BABY'S HEALTHY KIDS. BIRTH-3 *See* HEALTHY KIDS. BIRTH-3 **2598**

AMERICAN BANK ATTORNEYS (US) [01479446] **3084**

AMERICAN BANK DIRECTORY (US/0569-292X) [03510845] **769**

AMERICAN BANK DIRECTORY. SINGLE STATE EDITION (US) **769**

AMERICAN BANK DIRECTORY. US EDITION (US) **769**

AMERICAN BANK LAWYER, THE (US/1059-2474) [24516968] 769, **2932**

AMERICAN BANKER (US/0002-7561) [03954795] **769**

AMERICAN BANKER. CONSUMER SURVEY (US/1055-1077) [22498243] **769**

AMERICAN BANKER CORPORATE SURVEY *CEASED.* (US/1043-724X) [18553143] **769**

AMERICAN BANKER INDEX (ANN ARBOR, MICH.) (US/0893-2468) [15476381] **769**

AMERICAN BANKER TECHNOLOGY SURVEY (US) [22226779] **769**

AMERICAN BANKERS ASSOCIATION *See* GOVERNMENT RELATIONS STATUS REPORT **3087**

AMERICAN BANKERS ASSOCIATION *See* ABA BANKING JOURNAL **768**

AMERICAN BANKERS ASSOCIATION *See* BANKING LEGISLATION IN THE CONGRESS **3085**

AMERICAN BANKERS ASSOCIATION BANKING LITERATURE INDEX (US/0736-5659) [08966229] **3084**

AMERICAN BANKERS ASSOCIATION. COMMITTEE ON UNIFORM SECURITY IDENTIFICATION PROCEDURES *See* C.U.S.I.P. DIRECTORY **893**

AMERICAN BANKERS ASSOCIATION. COMMITTEE ON UNIFORM SECURITY IDENTIFICATION PROCEDURES *See* C.U.S.I.P. DIRECTORY. CORPORATE DIRECTORY **893**

AMERICAN BANKERS ASSOCIATION. FEDERAL LEGISLATIVE COMMITTEE *See* BANKING LEGISLATION IN THE ... SESSION, ... CONGRESS **3085**

AMERICAN BANKERS ASSOCIATION. PROTECTIVE BULLETIN; ISSUED BY THE PROTECTIVE DEPARTMENT OF THE AMERICAN BANKERS ASSOCIATION *See* BANK PROTECTION BULLETIN **775**

AMERICAN BANKER'S WASHINGTON WATCH (US) **769**

● AMERICAN BANKRUPTCY INSTITUTE LAW REVIEW, THE (US/1068-0861) [27423817] **2932**

AMERICAN BANKRUPTCY LAW JOURNAL, THE (US/0027-9048) [01479451] **3084**

AMERICAN BAPTIST *See* AMERICAN BAPTISTS IN MISSION **5055**

AMERICAN BAPTIST CHURCHES IN THE U.S.A *See* DIRECTORY OF THE AMERICAN BAPTIST CHURCHES IN THE U.S.A **5059**

AMERICAN BAPTIST CHURCHES IN THE U.S.A *See* SUPPLEMENTARY DIRECTORY OF THE AMERICAN BAPTIST CHURCHES IN THE U.S.A **5068**

AMERICAN BAPTIST CHURCHES IN THE U.S.A *See* YEARBOOK OF THE AMERICAN BAPTIST CHURCHES IN THE U.S.A **5069**

AMERICAN BAPTIST CHURCHES IN THE U.S.A. DIVISION OF COMMUNICATION. AB INPUT *See* AMERICAN BAPTISTS IN MISSION **5055**

AMERICAN BAPTIST QUARTERLY (US/0745-3698) [08960423] **5055**

AMERICAN BAPTIST, THE (US/0002-757X) [01798554] **5055**

AMERICAN BAPTIST WOMAN, THE (US/0191-0183) [01624319] 5550, **5055**

● AMERICAN BAPTISTS IN MISSION (US) [27846010] **5055**

AMERICAN BAR ASSOCIATION *See* LAW DAY U.S.A. PLANNING GUIDE AND PROGRAM MANUAL **2995**

AMERICAN BAR ASSOCIATION *See* POLICY AND PROCEDURES HANDBOOK **3029**

AMERICAN BAR ASSOCIATION *See* DIRECTORY / AMERICAN BAR ASSOCIATION **2961**

AMERICAN BAR ASSOCIATION. DIVISION OF BAR SERVICES *See* DIRECTORY OF BAR ACTIVITIES **2961**

AMERICAN BAR ASSOCIATION. FORUM COMMITTEE ON COMMUNICATIONS LAW *See* DIRECTORY / FORUM COMMITTEE ON COMMUNICATIONS LAW **2961**

AMERICAN BAR ASSOCIATION. FORUM COMMITTEE ON FRANCHISING *See* DIRECTORY - FORUM COMMITTEE ON FRANCHISING **3099**

AMERICAN BAR ASSOCIATION. FORUM COMMITTEE ON FRANCHISING. ANNUAL FORUM *See* ANNUAL FORUM - AMERICAN BAR ASSOCIATION. FORUM COMMITTEE ON FRANCHISING. ANNUAL FORUM **3095**

AMERICAN BAR ASSOCIATION. FORUM COMMITTEE ON HEALTH LAW *See* DIRECTORY - FORUM COMMITTEE ON HEALTH LAW, AMERICAN BAR ASSOCIATION **2961**

AMERICAN BAR ASSOCIATION. FORUM COMMITTEE ON THE CONSTRUCTION INDUSTRY *See* DIRECTORY - FORUM COMMITTEE ON THE CONSTRUCTION INDUSTRY, AMERICAN BAR ASSOCIATION **2961**

AMERICAN BAR ASSOCIATION. FORUM COMMITTEE ON THE ENTERTAINMENT AND SPORTS INDUSTRIES *See* DIRECTORY - FORUM COMMITTEE ON THE ENTERTAINMENT AND SPORTS INDUSTRIES **2961**

AMERICAN BAR ASSOCIATION. HOUSE OF DELEGATES *See* SUMMARY OF ACTION **3060**

AMERICAN BAR ASSOCIATION. HOUSE OF DELEGATES *See* SUMMARY OF ACTION TAKEN BY THE HOUSE OF DELEGATES OF THE AMERICAN BAR ASSOCIATION **3060**

Alphabetical Title Index — AMERICAN

AMERICAN BAR ASSOCIATION. SECTION OF ADMINISTRATIVE LAW *See* SECTION OF ADMINISTRATIVE LAW DIRECTORY **3094**

AMERICAN BAR ASSOCIATION. SECTION OF ADMINISTRATIVE LAW. DIRECTORY *See* SECTION OF ADMINISTRATIVE LAW DIRECTORY **3094**

AMERICAN BAR ASSOCIATION. SECTION OF GENERAL PRACTICE *See* GENERAL PRACTICE SECTION DIRECTORY AND OPERATING MANUAL **2973**

AMERICAN BAR ASSOCIATION. SECTION OF INSURANCE, NEGLIGENCE AND COMPENSATION LAW *See* PROCEEDINGS - AMERICAN BAR ASSOCIATION. SECTION OF INSURANCE, NEGLIGENCE AND COMPENSATION LAW **3031**

AMERICAN BAR ASSOCIATION. SECTION OF LEGAL EDUCATION AND ADMISSIONS TO THE BAR *See* REVIEW OF LEGAL EDUCATION IN THE UNITED STATES, A **3040**

AMERICAN BAR ASSOCIATION. SECTION OF LITIGATION *See* MONOGRAPH SERIES **3011**

AMERICAN BAR ASSOCIATION. SECTION OF LITIGATION. FALL MEETING *See* ANNUAL FALL MEETING / SECTION OF LITIGATION, AMERICAN BAR ASSOCIATION **2934**

AMERICAN BAR ASSOCIATION. SECTION OF LOCAL GOVERNMENT LAW *See* COMMITTEE REPORTS - LOCAL GOVERNMENT LAW SECTION OF THE AMERICAN BAR ASSOCIATION **2953**

AMERICAN BAR ASSOCIATION. SECTION OF PUBLIC UTILITY, COMMUNICATIONS AND TRANSPORTATION LAW *See* ANNUAL REPORT, SECTION OF PUBLIC UTILITY, COMMUNICATIONS AND TRANSPORTATION LAW **4759**

AMERICAN BAR ASSOCIATION. SECTION OF PUBLIC UTILITY LAW. ANNUAL REPORT *See* ANNUAL REPORT, SECTION OF PUBLIC UTILITY, COMMUNICATIONS AND TRANSPORTATION LAW **4759**

AMERICAN BAR ASSOCIATION. SECTION OF REAL PROPERTY, PROBATE AND TRUST LAW *See* DIRECTORY OF OFFICERS, COUNCIL, AND COMMITTEES **2962**

AMERICAN BAR ASSOCIATION. SECTION OF REAL PROPERTY, PROBATE, AND TRUST LAW. MEMBERSHIP DIRECTORY, OFFICERS AND COMMITTEES *See* DIRECTORY OF OFFICERS, COUNCIL, AND COMMITTEES **2962**

AMERICAN BAR ASSOCIATION. STANDING COMMITTEE ON ENVIRONMENTAL LAW *See* QUARTERLY NEWSLETTER - STANDING COMMITTEE ON ENVIRONMENTAL LAW **3115**

AMERICAN BAR ASSOCIATION. STANDING COMMITTEE ON ETHICS AND PROFESSIONAL RESPONSIBILITY *See* RECENT ETHICS OPINIONS **2253**

AMERICAN BAR ASSOCIATION. TORT AND INSURANCE PRACTICE SECTION *See* DIRECTORY / SECTION OF TORT AND INSURANCE PRACTICE **2962**

AMERICAN BAR ASSOCIATION. YOUNG LAWYERS DIVISION *See* DIRECTORY / THE YOUNG LAWYERS DIVISION OF THE AMERICAN BAR ASSOCIATION **2962**

AMERICAN BAR FOUNDATION *See* REPORT OF AMERICAN BAR FOUNDATION, THE **3038**

AMERICAN BAR REFERENCE HANDBOOK, THE (US/0094-3584) [01793911] **2932**

AMERICAN BAR, THE (US/1046-5197) [08308264] **2932**

AMERICAN BAR, THE CANADIAN BAR, THE INTERNATIONAL BAR, THE (US) [01479460] **3123**

AMERICAN BEE JOURNAL (US/0002-7626) [01479576] **58**

AMERICAN BEHAVIORAL SCIENTIST (BEVERLY HILLS) (US/0002-7642) [01332710] **5190**

AMERICAN BELL ASSOCIATION *See* MEMBERSHIP DIRECTORY / THE AMERICAN BELL ASSOCIATION **4130**

AMERICAN BELL ASSOCIATION. DIRECTORY *See* MEMBERSHIP DIRECTORY / THE AMERICAN BELL ASSOCIATION **4130**

AMERICAN BENCH, THE (US/0160-2578) [03470774] **3138**

AMERICAN BENEDICTINE ACADEMY *See* AMERICAN BENEDICTINE ACADEMY NEWSLETTER, THE **5023**

AMERICAN BENEDICTINE ACADEMY NEWSLETTER, THE (US) [08562056] **5023**

AMERICAN BENEDICTINE REVIEW, THE (US/0002-7650) [01479581] **5023**

AMERICAN BIBLE SOCIETY *See* AMERICAN BIBLE SOCIETY RECORD **5014**

AMERICAN BIBLE SOCIETY *See* ANNUAL REPORT OF THE AMERICAN BIBLE SOCIETY **5014**

AMERICAN BIBLE SOCIETY RECORD (US/0006-0801) [01608168] **5014**

AMERICAN BIBLIOGRAPHY OF SLAVIC AND EAST EUROPEAN STUDIES (US/0094-3770) [01783626] 2645, 2673, **2634**

AMERICAN BICYCLIST AND MOTORCYCLIST (US/0002-7677) [05256318] **427**

AMERICAN BICYCLIST MAGAZINE (US/1074-4983) [29717657] **427**

AMERICAN BIOGRAPHICAL INSTITUTE RESEARCH ASSOCIATION *See* ABIRA DIGEST **429**

AMERICAN BIOLOGY TEACHER, THE (US/0002-7685) [01479589] 1888, **441**

AMERICAN BIOTECHNOLOGY LABORATORY (US/0749-3223) [10900538] **3685**

AMERICAN BIRDS (US/0004-7686) [01090547] **5614**

AMERICAN BLACK DIRECTORY (US/0364-0833) [02583935] **638**

AMERICAN (BLACKDUCK, MINN.), THE (US/0747-0363) [10509249] **5694**

AMERICAN BMXER. MEMBERSHIP ED (US/8750-5827) [11556614] **427**

AMERICAN BMXER (NEWSSTAND EDITION) (US/8756-5358) [11613435] **428**

AMERICAN BOARD OF ORTHOPAEDIC SURGERY, THE *See* DIRECTORY OF DIPLOMATES **3881**

AMERICAN BOOK COLLECTOR (1980) (US/0196-5654) [05841186] 4823, **2770**

AMERICAN BOOK PRICES CURRENT (US/0091-9357) [01782211] **4823**

AMERICAN BOOK PUBLISHING RECORD (US/0002-7707) [12443523] **4812**

AMERICAN BOOK PUBLISHING RECORD (US/0002-7707) [01479600] **4812**

AMERICAN BOOK REVIEW, THE (US/0149-9408) [03919942] **3337**

AMERICAN BOOK TRADE DIRECTORY (US/0065-759X) [01479602] **4821**

AMERICAN BOOKSELLER (NEW YORK. 1977) (US/0148-5903) [03451218] **4823**

AMERICAN BOOKSELLERS ASSOCIATION *See* ABA NEWSWIRE **4822**

AMERICAN BOOKSELLERS ASSOCIATION *See* WHO'S WHO AT THE ABA **436**

AMERICAN BOTTOM ARCHAEOLOGY : FAI-270 SITE REPORTS (US) [10319176] **254**

AMERICAN BREWER (HAYWARD, CALIF.) (US/1055-470X) [23006791] **2363**

AMERICAN BREWERIANA JOURNAL (US/0748-8343) [11013143] **2363**

AMERICAN BROADCASTING COMPANIES *See* AMERICAN BROADCASTING COMPANIES ANNUAL REPORT **1126**

AMERICAN BROADCASTING COMPANIES ANNUAL REPORT (US/0271-7263) [05806185] **1126**

AMERICAN BRONCHO-ESOPHAGOLOGICAL ASSOCIATION. MEETING *See* TRANSACTIONS - AMERICAN BRONCHO-ESOPHAGOLOGICAL ASSOCIATION. MEETING **3952**

AMERICAN BUDDHIST NEWSLETTER, THE (US/0747-900X) [10821164] **5020**

AMERICAN BUILDING CONTRACTOR, THE (US/0740-3607) [09956049] **598**

AMERICAN BUILDING SUPPLIES (US/0002-7731) [02962972] **598**

AMERICAN BULLETIN, THE (US/0517-032X) [01479611] **2718**

AMERICAN BULLMASTIFF, THE (US/0002-774X) [02722227] **4285**

AMERICAN BUNGALOW (US/1055-0674) [23067690] **598**

AMERICAN BUREAU FOR MEDICAL ADVANCEMENT IN CHINA *See* NEWS FROM ABMAC **3621**

AMERICAN BUREAU FOR MEDICAL ADVANCEMENT IN CHINA *See* ANNUAL REPORT - AMERICAN BUREAU FOR MEDICAL ADVANCEMENT IN CHINA, INC **3550**

AMERICAN BUREAU OF SHIPPING *See* ANNUAL REPORT / AMERICAN BUREAU OF SHIPPING **5447**

AMERICAN BUREAU OF SHIPPING *See* APPROVED WELDING ELECTRODE WIRE-FLUX AND WIRE-GAS COMBINATIONS **4026**

AMERICAN BUREAU OF SHIPPING *See* RECORD OF THE AMERICAN BUREAU OF SHIPPING **5455**

AMERICAN BUREAU OF SHIPPING *See* RULES FOR CERTIFICATION OF CARGO CONTAINERS **4221**

AMERICAN BUSINESS (US/0363-566X) [02548426] **638**

AMERICAN BUSINESS CLIMATE AND ECONOMIC PROFILES (US) **638**

AMERICAN BUSINESS COMMUNITY IN IRAN (IR) [02482979] **822**

AMERICAN BUSINESS DISK, THE (US/1062-5119) [25335269] **638**

AMERICAN BUSINESS IN ARGENTINA ... DIRECTORY (AG) [11860879] **638**

AMERICAN BUSINESS IN BRITAIN (UK/0140-5799) [03926160] **638**

AMERICAN BUSINESS LAW JOURNAL (US/0002-7766) [01479620] **3095**

AMERICAN BUSINESS REVIEW (US/0743-2348) [10571029] 769, **859**

AMERICAN BUSINESS TREND SYNOPSIS, THE (US/8756-3053) [11617338] **638**

AMERICAN CAGE-BIRD MAGAZINE (US/0002-7782) [03955311] 5614, **4285**

AMERICAN CAMELLIA YEARBOOK, THE (US/0065-762X) [03511229] **2408**

AMERICAN-CANADIAN GENEALOGIST (US/1076-3902) [24596764] **2436**

AMERICAN CATHOLIC PHILOSOPHICAL ASSOCIATION *See* PROCEEDINGS OF THE AMERICAN CATHOLIC PHILOSOPHICAL ASSOCIATION **4357**

AMERICAN CATHOLIC PHILOSOPHICAL QUARTERLY (US/1051-3558) [21936453] **4340**

AMERICAN CATHOLIC STUDIES NEWSLETTER (US) [07472811] **5023**

AMERICAN CAUCUS *CEASED.* (US/1061-8570) [25480592] **4463**

AMERICAN CEMENT DIRECTORY, THE (US) [05417846] **598**

AMERICAN CEMETERY, THE (US/0002-7804) [03955369] **2406**

● AMERICAN CENTER FOR DESIGN JOURNAL (US/1062-0966) [25523337] **287**

AMERICAN CERAMIC CIRCLE JOURNAL (US/0899-806X) [18229842] **2586**

AMERICAN CERAMIC SOCIETY *See* JOURNAL OF THE AMERICAN CERAMIC SOCIETY **2591**

AMERICAN CERAMIC SOCIETY BULLETIN (US/0002-7812) [01479637] **2586**

AMERICAN CERAMICS (US/0278-9507) [07938825] **2586**

AMERICAN CHAMBER OF COMMERCE FOR BRAZIL. RIO DE JANEIRO CHAMBER *See* ANNUAL DIRECTORY / AMERICAN CHAMBER OF COMMERCE FOR BRAZIL, RIO DE JANEIRO - SALVADOR **818**

AMERICAN CHAMBER OF COMMERCE FOR BRAZIL. RIO DE JANEIRO CHAMBER. MEMBERSHIP DIRECTORY *See* ANNUAL DIRECTORY / AMERICAN CHAMBER OF COMMERCE FOR BRAZIL, RIO DE JANEIRO - SALVADOR **818**

AMERICAN CHAMBER OF COMMERCE FOR BRAZIL, SAO PAULO *See* REPORT ON ACTIVITIES OF THE AMERICAN CHAMBER OF COMMERCE FOR BRAZIL-SAO PAULO IN ... FOR PRESENTATION AT THE ... ANNUAL GENERAL MEETING **821**

AMERICAN CHAMBER OF COMMERCE IN EGYPT *See* MEMBERSHIP DIRECTORY - AMERICAN CHAMBER OF COMMERCE IN EGYPT **820**

AMERICAN CHAMBER OF COMMERCE IN FRANCE *See* DIRECTORY / THE AMERICAN CHAMBER OF COMMERCE IN FRANCE **819**

AMERICAN CHAMBER OF COMMERCE IN HONG KONG *See* AMERICAN CHAMBER OF COMMERCE IN HONG KONG : DIRECTORY, THE **818**

AMERICAN CHAMBER OF COMMERCE IN HONG KONG : DIRECTORY, THE (HK) [09134706] **818**

AMERICAN CHAMBER OF COMMERCE IN ITALY *See* DIRECTORY / AMERICAN CHAMBER OF COMMERCE IN ITALY **819**

AMERICAN CHAMBER OF COMMERCE IN SPAIN. MEMBERSHIP DIRECTORY *See* DIRECTORIO DE SOCIOS / CAMARA DE COMERCIO AMERICANA EN ESPANA **819**

AMERICAN CHAMBER OF COMMERCE OF GUATEMALA *See* MEMBERSHIP DIRECTORY - AMERICAN CHAMBER OF COMMERCE OF GUATEMALA **820**

AMERICAN CHAMBER OF COMMERCE SPAIN *See* DIRECTORIO DE SOCIOS / CAMARA DE COMERCIO AMERICANA EN ESPANA **819**

AMERICAN CHARACTER, THE (US/1059-4515) [24595488] **2249**

AMERICAN CHEMICAL SOCIETY *See* ACS SINGLE ARTICLE ANNOUNCEMENT **959**

AMERICAN — Alphabetical Title Index

AMERICAN CHEMICAL SOCIETY *See* REPORTS ON RESEARCH ASSISTED BY THE PETROLEUM RESEARCH FUND **1029**

AMERICAN CHEMICAL SOCIETY *See* JOURNAL OF THE AMERICAN CHEMICAL SOCIETY **982**

AMERICAN CHEMICAL SOCIETY *See* ACS SYMPOSIUM SERIES **959**

AMERICAN CHEMICAL SOCIETY *See* ACS MONOGRAPH **959**

AMERICAN CHEMICAL SOCIETY. CHEMICAL ABSTRACTS SERVICE *See* CAS REPORT (COLUMBUS) **966**

AMERICAN CHEMICAL SOCIETY. CHEMICAL ABSTRACTS SERVICE *See* CHEMICAL ABSTRACTS SERVICE SOURCE INDEX **1011**

AMERICAN CHEMICAL SOCIETY COMMITTEE ON ANALYTICAL REAGENTS *See* REAGENT CHEMICALS : AMERICAN CHEMICAL SOCIETY SPECIFICATIONS **990**

AMERICAN CHEMICAL SOCIETY. DELAWARE SECTION *See* DEL-CHEM BULLETIN, THE **974**

AMERICAN CHEMICAL SOCIETY. DIVISION OF ENVIRONMENTAL CHEMISTRY *See* NATIONAL MEETING - AMERICAN CHEMICAL SOCIETY, DIVISION OF ENVIRONMENTAL CHEMISTRY **987**

AMERICAN CHEMICAL SOCIETY. DIVISION OF ENVIRONMENTAL CHEMISTRY *See* PREPRINT EXTENDED ABSTRACT - AMERICAN CHEMICAL SOCIETY. DIVISION OF ENVIRONMENTAL CHEMISTRY **989**

AMERICAN CHEMICAL SOCIETY. DIVISION OF ENVIRONMENTAL CHEMISTRY. PREPRINTS OF PAPERS *See* PREPRINT EXTENDED ABSTRACT - AMERICAN CHEMICAL SOCIETY. DIVISION OF ENVIRONMENTAL CHEMISTRY **989**

AMERICAN CHEMICAL SOCIETY. DIVISION OF FUEL CHEMISTRY *See* PREPRINTS OF PAPERS PRESENTED - AMERICAN CHEMICAL SOCIETY. DIVISION OF FUEL CHEMISTRY **989**

AMERICAN CHEMICAL SOCIETY. DIVISION OF PETROLEUM CHEMISTRY *See* PREPRINTS - AMERICAN CHEMICAL SOCIETY. DIVISION OF PETROLEUM CHEMISTRY **1028**

AMERICAN CHEMICAL SOCIETY. DIVISION OF POLYMER CHEMISTRY *See* PAPERS PRESENTED AT THE MEETING **1045**

AMERICAN CHEMICAL SOCIETY. FLORIDA SECTION. NEWS *See* FLACS **975**

AMERICAN CHEMICAL SOCIETY. OFFICE OF MANPOWER STUDIES *See* PROFESSIONALS IN CHEMISTRY **990**

●AMERICAN CHESS JOURNAL (CAMBRIDGE, MASS.) (US/1066-8292) [27056825] **4856**

AMERICAN CHIANINA JOURNAL (US/0198-8816) [03816953] **205**

AMERICAN CHIROPRACTIC ASSOCIATION *See* MEMBERSHIP DIRECTORY / AMERICAN CHIROPRACTIC ASSOCIATION **3615**

AMERICAN CHIROPRACTIC ASSOCIATION *See* ACA JOURNAL OF CHIROPRACTIC, THE **3543**

AMERICAN CHIROPRACTOR, THE (US/0194-6536) [04914192] **4379**

AMERICAN CHOW CHOW INC, THE *See* AMERICAN CHOW CHOW INC, THE **4285**

AMERICAN CHOW CHOW INC, THE (US/0194-5173) [04786467] **4285**

AMERICAN CHRISTMAS TREE GROWERS' JOURNAL *See* AMERICAN CHRISTMAS TREE JOURNAL **58**

AMERICAN CHRISTMAS TREE JOURNAL (US/0569-3845) [01792712] 2374, **58**

AMERICAN CINEMATOGRAPHER (US/0002-7928) [01479664] **4063**

AMERICAN CITIZEN, THE (US/0279-3555) [07785992] **2527**

●AMERICAN CITIZENS REVIEW (US/1065-7622) [26725763] **2527**

AMERICAN CITY & COUNTY, THE (US/0149-337X) [02243821] **5238**

AMERICAN CIVIL LIBERTIES UNION *See* POLICY GUIDE OF THE AMERICAN CIVIL LIBERTIES UNION **4511**

AMERICAN CIVIL LIBERTIES UNION *See* AMERICAN CIVIL LIBERTIES UNION RECORDS AND PUBLICATIONS UPDATE, THE **2932**

AMERICAN CIVIL LIBERTIES UNION *See* ANNUAL REPORT - AMERICAN CIVIL LIBERTIES UNION **4504**

AMERICAN CIVIL LIBERTIES UNION RECORDS AND PUBLICATIONS UPDATE, THE (US/0197-8195) [06120030] **2932**

AMERICAN CLASSICAL LEAGUE NEWSLETTER (US/0196-2086) [04700960] **2527**

AMERICAN CLASSICAL REVIEW *SUSPENDED.* (US/0044-7633) [01479670] **1081**

AMERICAN CLASSICAL STUDIES (US/0278-5943) [06728344] **1073**

AMERICAN CLAY EXCHANGE *SUSPENDED.* (US/0739-6546) [09787420] **2586**

AMERICAN CLEAN CAR (US/0095-1811) [01786790] 5403, **638**

AMERICAN CLEFT PALATE-CRANIOFACIAL ASSOCIATION *See* MEMBERSHIP-TEAM DIRECTORY **3970**

AMERICAN CLINICAL AND CLIMATOLOGICAL ASSOCIATION *See* TRANSACTIONS OF THE AMERICAN CLINICAL AND CLIMATOLOGICAL ASSOCIATION **3647**

AMERICAN CLINICAL LABORATORY (US/1041-3235) [18719659] **3548**

AMERICAN COIN-OP (US/0092-2811) [01789413] **5347**

AMERICAN COLLECTOR'S JOURNAL, THE (US/0164-7008) [04419117] 2770, **248**

AMERICAN COLLEGE (BRYN MAWR, PA.) *See* ANNUAL REPORT - AMERICAN COLLEGE **2873**

AMERICAN COLLEGE OF DENTISTS *See* JOURNAL OF THE AMERICAN COLLEGE OF DENTISTS, THE **1328**

AMERICAN COLLEGE OF HEALTHCARE EXECUTIVES *See* DIRECTORY / AMERICAN COLLEGE OF HEALTHCARE EXECUTIVES **3779**

AMERICAN COLLEGE OF OCCUPATIONAL AND ENVIRONMENTAL MEDICINE *See* MEMBERSHIP DIRECTORY / AMERICAN COLLEGE OF OCCUPATIONAL AND ENVIRONMENTAL MEDICINE **3615**

AMERICAN COLLEGE OF OCCUPATIONAL MEDICINE *See* MEMBERSHIP DIRECTORY / AMERICAN COLLEGE OF OCCUPATIONAL MEDICINE **3615**

AMERICAN COLLEGE OF OCCUPATIONAL MEDICINE. MEMBERSHIP DIRECTORY *See* MEMBERSHIP DIRECTORY / AMERICAN COLLEGE OF OCCUPATIONAL AND ENVIRONMENTAL MEDICINE **3615**

AMERICAN COLLEGE OF PHYSICIANS *See* MEMBERSHIP DIRECTORY / AMERICAN COLLEGE OF PHYSICIANS **1927**

AMERICAN COLLEGE OF PHYSICIANS. DIRECTORY (1949) *See* MEMBERSHIP DIRECTORY / AMERICAN COLLEGE OF PHYSICIANS **1927**

AMERICAN COLLEGE OF PREVENTIVE MEDICINE *See* DIRECTORY OF PREVENTIVE MEDICINE RESIDENCY PROGRAMS IN THE UNITED STATES AND CANADA **3572**

AMERICAN COLLEGE OF SPORTS MEDICINE *See* ACSM MEMBERSHIP DIRECTORY / AMERICAN COLLEGE OF SPORTS MEDICINE **3953**

AMERICAN COLLEGE OF SURGEONS *See* SURGICAL FORUM **3976**

AMERICAN COLLEGE OF SURGEONS *See* BULLETIN OF THE AMERICAN COLLEGE OF SURGEONS **3961**

AMERICAN COLLEGE OF VETERINARY INTERNAL MEDICINE *See* SCIENTIFIC PROCEEDINGS / AMERICAN COLLEGE OF VETERINARY INTERNAL MEDICINE **5521**

AMERICAN COLLEGE TESTING PROGRAM *See* ACTIVITY **1807**

AMERICAN COLLEGE TESTING PROGRAM *See* COLLEGE PLANNING/SEARCH BOOK **1817**

AMERICAN COLLEGE TESTING PROGRAM *See* HANDBOOK FOR FINANCIAL AID ADMINISTRATORS **1827**

AMERICAN COLLEGE TESTING PROGRAM. RESEARCH AND DEVELOPMENT DIVISION *See* YOUR COLLEGE-BOUND STUDENTS **1854**

AMERICAN COMMITTEE ON AFRICA *See* ANNUAL REPORT / THE AMERICAN COMMITTEE ON AFRICA **4464**

AMERICAN COMMUNITIES TOMORROW (US/0192-5903) [05066007] **5190**

AMERICAN COMMUNITY, TECHNICAL, AND JUNIOR COLLEGES (US/0749-2650) [11111453] **1910**

AMERICAN COMPARATIVE LITERATURE ASSOCIATION *See* ACLA NEWSLETTER **3357**

AMERICAN COMPARATIVE LITERATURE ASSOCIATION. ACLA NEWSLETTER *See* ACLA BULLETIN **3357**

AMERICAN COMPENSATION ASSOCIATION *See* MEMBERSHIP DIRECTORY - AMERICAN COMPENSATION ASSOCIATION **944**

AMERICAN COMPUTER LAW DIGEST (US/8755-1675) [11191244] 1225, **2932**

AMERICAN CONCHOLOGIST (US/1072-2440) [24653648] **5574**

AMERICAN CONCRETE INSTITUTE *See* ACI DIRECTORY **2018**

AMERICAN CONCRETE INSTITUTE *See* PUBLICATION SP **625**

AMERICAN CONCRETE INSTITUTE *See* ACI STANDARDS / AMERICAN CONCRETE INSTITUTE **2018**

AMERICAN CONCRETE PIPE ASSOCIATION *See* CONCRETE PIPE INDUSTRY STATISTICS **632**

AMERICAN CONFERENCE OF GOVERNMENTAL INDUSTRIAL HYGIENISTS *See* ACGIH TRANSACTIONS **2858**

AMERICAN CONSERVATORY OF MUSIC *See* NEWSBRIEF / AMERICAN CONSERVATORY OF MUSIC **4140**

AMERICAN CONSTRUCTION INDUSTRY DIRECTORY (US/0195-9484) [05732409] **598**

AMERICAN CONTRACT BRIDGE LEAGUE. BULLETIN *See* CONTRACT BRIDGE BULLETIN, THE **4859**

AMERICAN COONER (US/0002-807X) [03955528] **4882**

AMERICAN COOPERATION (US/0065-793X) [01480046] **1541**

●AMERICAN COST OF LIVING SURVEY (US/1071-099X) [28552008] **638**

AMERICAN COUNCIL FOR JUDAISM *See* SPECIAL INTEREST REPORT / THE AMERICAN COUNCIL FOR JUDAISM **5053**

AMERICAN COUNCIL FOR NATIONALITIES SERVICE *See* INTERPRETER RELEASES **2984**

AMERICAN COUNCIL FOR THE UNITED NATIONS UNIVERSITY *See* AC/UNU NEWSLETTER / THE AMERICAN COUNCIL FOR THE UNITED NATIONS UNIVERSITY **1806**

AMERICAN COUNCIL OF INDEPENDENT LABORATORIES *See* DIRECTORY / AMERICAN COUNCIL OF INDEPENDENT LABORATORIES, INC **5100**

AMERICAN COUNCIL OF LIFE INSURANCE *See* MAP, MONITORING ATTITUDES OF THE PUBLIC **2887**

AMERICAN COUNCIL OF LIFE INSURANCE. LEGAL SECTION. MEETING *See* LEGAL SECTION PROCEEDINGS / THE ... ANNUAL MEETING OF THE LEGAL SECTION OF THE AMERICAN COUNCIL OF LIFE INSURANCE **2886**

AMERICAN COUNCIL OF LIFE INSURANCE. MEDICAL SECTION. MEETING *See* MEDICAL SECTION PROCEEDINGS : THE ... ANNUAL MEETING OF THE MEDICAL SECTION OF THE AMERICAN COUNCIL OF LIFE INSURANCE **2888**

AMERICAN COUNCIL OF LIFE INSURANCE. STATISTICAL SERVICES *See* LIFE INSURANCE BUYING **2886**

AMERICAN COUNCIL ON CONSUMER INTERESTS. CONFERENCE *See* PROCEEDINGS ... ANNUAL CONFERENCE OF THE AMERICAN COUNCIL ON CONSUMER INTERESTS **1299**

AMERICAN COUNCIL ON EDUCATION *See* GUIDE TO THE EVALUATION OF EDUCATIONAL EXPERIENCES IN THE ARMED SERVICES **1827**

AMERICAN COUNCIL ON THE TEACHING OF FOREIGN LANGUAGES *See* ACTFL FOREIGN LANGUAGE EDUCATION SERIES, THE **3261**

●AMERICAN COUNSELOR *SUSPENDED.* (US/1059-3497) [24572292] **4572**

AMERICAN COUNTRY (US/0892-6492) [15246723] **2788**

AMERICAN COUNTRY CHRISTMAS (US/1044-4904) [19816063] **369**

AMERICAN COUNTRY COLLECTIBLES (US) [25252709] **2770**

AMERICAN COUNTRY LIFE ASSOCIATION *See* PROCEEDINGS OF THE CONFERENCE OF THE AMERICAN COUNTRY LIFE ASSOCIATION, INC **5254**

AMERICAN COWBOY (US/0738-9795) [09648696] **4882**

AMERICAN COWBOY MAGAZINE *See* AMERICAN COWBOY **4882**

AMERICAN CRAFT (US/0194-8008) [05024322] **369**

AMERICAN CRAFT ENTERPRISES *See* BUYERS BOOK OF AMERICAN CRAFTS, THE **370**

AMERICAN CRIMINAL LAW REVIEW, THE (US/0164-0364) [01479741] **3105**

AMERICAN CRYSTALLOGRAPHIC ASSOCIATION *See* C A MONOGRAPHS, A **1031**

AMERICAN CRYSTALLOGRAPHIC ASSOCIATION *See* TRANSACTIONS - AMERICAN CRYSTALLOGRAPHIC ASSOCIATION **1033**

Alphabetical Title Index — AMERICAN

AMERICAN CULTURAL HERITAGE SERIES (US) [08601751] **2718**

AMERICAN CURRENTS (US/1070-7352) [03804030] **2294**

AMERICAN CURRENTS (WASHINGTON, D.C.) (US/1056-2605) [23606171] **2718**

AMERICAN DAHLIA SOCIETY *See* BULLETIN OF THE AMERICAN DAHLIA SOCIETY, INC **2411**

AMERICAN DAIRY SCIENCE ASSOCIATION. MEETING *See* PROGRAM - AMERICAN DAIRY SCIENCE ASSOCIATION. MEETING **198**

AMERICAN DANCE DIRECTORY (US/0197-6869) [05766854] **1310**

AMERICAN DANCE GUILD *See* AMERICAN DANCE GUILD NEWSLETTER **1310**

AMERICAN DANCE GUILD NEWSLETTER (US/0300-7448) [01328735] **1310**

AMERICAN DANCE THERAPY ASSOCIATION *See* MONOGRAPH - AMERICAN DANCE THERAPY ASSOCIATION **1882**

AMERICAN DEFENSE ANNUAL (US/0882-1038) [11751103] **4034**

AMERICAN DEFENSE PREPAREDNESS ASSOCIATION *See* ANNUAL DIRECTORY AND REPORT - AMERICAN DEFENSE PREPAREDNESS ASSOCIATION **4034**

AMERICAN DELI-BAKERY NEWS (US/0891-3331) [14710310] **2326**

AMERICAN DEMOGRAPHICS (US/0163-4089) [04369249] **4549**

AMERICAN DENTAL ASSOCIATION *See* JOURNAL OF THE AMERICAN DENTAL ASSOCIATION (USA ED.), THE **1328**

AMERICAN DENTAL ASSOCIATION *See* ANNUAL REPORTS AND RESOLUTIONS - AMERICAN DENTAL ASSOCIATION **1316**

AMERICAN DENTAL ASSOCIATION. BUREAU OF ECONOMIC RESEARCH AND STATISTICS *See* SURVEY OF DENTAL PRACTICE **1336**

AMERICAN DENTAL ASSOCIATION NEWS (US/0895-2930) [15285924] **1315**

AMERICAN DENTAL DIRECTORY (US/0065-8073) [01479765] **1315**

AMERICAN DIALECT SOCIETY *See* NEWSLETTER OF THE AMERICAN DIALECT SOCIETY **3306**

AMERICAN DIETETIC ASSOCIATION *See* JOURNAL OF THE AMERICAN DIETETIC ASSOCIATION **4194**

AMERICAN DIRECTORY OF OBSTETRICIANS AND GYNECOLOGISTS (US) [05636007] **3756**

AMERICAN DOCTORAL DISSERTATIONS (US/0065-809X) [01479778] **1808**

AMERICAN DOWSER (US/0093-089X) [01789200] **4240**

AMERICAN DRAMA (US/1061-0057) [24998330] **5361**

AMERICAN DREAM CARS, 1946-1972 *CEASED.* (US/1055-9833) [23446578] **5403**

AMERICAN DROP-SHIPPERS DIRECTORY (US/0065-8103) [07011678] **822**

AMERICAN DRUG INDEX (US/0065-8111) [01479781] **4290**

AMERICAN DRUGGIST (1974) (US/0190-5279) [01777826] **4290**

AMERICAN DRY CLEANER (US/0002-8258) [01796652] **1596**

AMERICAN DRYCLEANER (US/0002-8258) [09223475] **5347**

AMERICAN DYESTUFF REPORTER (US/0002-8266) [01479786] 1020, **5347**

AMERICAN EAGLE (ESTERO, FLA.), THE (US/0742-8197) [02923877] **2609**

AMERICAN ECONOMIC REVIEW, THE (US/0002-8282) [01075058] **1461**

AMERICAN ECONOMIST (NEW YORK, N.Y. 1960), THE (US/0569-4345) [05667043] **1461**

AMERICAN EDUCATIONAL RESEARCH ASSOCIATION *See* AERA MONOGRAPH SERIES ON CURRICULUM EVALUATION **1887**

AMERICAN EDUCATIONAL RESEARCH JOURNAL (US/0002-8312) [01479801] **1723**

AMERICAN EDUCATOR (US/0148-432X) [02866801] **1723**

AMERICAN ELECTRONICS ASSOCIATION *See* EXECUTIVE COMPENSATION IN THE HIGH-TECHNOLOGY INDUSTRIES **1668**

AMERICAN ELECTRONICS ASSOCIATION *See* DIRECTORY - AMERICAN ELECTRONICS ASSOCIATION **2042**

AMERICAN ELECTRONICS ASSOCIATION *See* SALARY SURVEY OF SUPERVISORY AND NON-SUPERVISORY PROFESSIONAL ENGINEERS **1709**

AMERICAN ELECTROPLATERS AND SURFACE FINISHERS SOCIETY *See* PROCEEDINGS OF THE AESF ANNUAL TECHNICAL CONFERENCE, THE **2076**

AMERICAN ELM, THE (US/0736-9794) [08147867] **2436**

AMERICAN ENTERPRISE INSTITUTE FOR PUBLIC POLICY RESEARCH *See* AEI PUBLICATIONS / AMERICAN ENTERPRISE INSTITUTE **4625**

AMERICAN ENTERPRISE (WASHINGTON, D.C.), THE (US/1047-3572) [20677006] **638**

AMERICAN ENTOMOLOGICAL INSTITUTE *See* MEMOIRS OF THE AMERICAN ENTOMOLOGICAL INSTITUTE **5611**

AMERICAN ENTOMOLOGICAL INSTITUTE *See* CONTRIBUTIONS OF THE AMERICAN ENTOMOLOGICAL INSTITUTE **5607**

AMERICAN ENTOMOLOGICAL SOCIETY *See* TRANSACTIONS OF THE AMERICAN ENTOMOLOGICAL SOCIETY (1890) **5614**

AMERICAN ENTOMOLOGICAL SOCIETY *See* MEMOIRS OF THE AMERICAN ENTOMOLOGICAL SOCIETY **5611**

AMERICAN ENTOMOLOGIST (LANHAM, MD.) (US/1046-2821) [20371794] **5605**

AMERICAN ENTREPRENEUR (US) **638**

AMERICAN ENVIRONMENTAL LABORATORY (US/1051-2306) [20859845] **2160**

AMERICAN ETHNOLOGIST (US/0094-0496) [01793717] **228**

AMERICAN EXAMINER (EAST LANSING, MICH.) (US/0736-9948) [09250630] **2718**

AMERICAN EXECUTIVE TRAVEL COMPANION (US/0363-535X) [02475472] **5461**

AMERICAN EXPLORATION AND TRAVEL SERIES (US/0065-8219) [01479828] **2718**

AMERICAN EXPORT MARKETER, THE *CEASED.* (US/0732-8877) [08464347] **822**

AMERICAN EXPORT REGISTER (US/0272-1163) [06701555] **822**

AMERICAN EXPRESS INTERNATIONAL INDEX *See* DATAMEX. WESTERN HEMISPHERE **5468**

AMERICAN EXPRESS SKY GUIDE (US/0744-091X) [08027052] **11**

AMERICAN EXPRESS ... SURVEY OF BUSINESS TRAVEL, THE (US) [11734225] **5461**

AMERICAN FABRICS AND FASHIONS (1984) *CEASED.* (US) [10932765] 1081, **5347**

AMERICAN FAMILY PHYSICIAN (1970) (US/0002-838X) [01777828] **3736**

AMERICAN FAMILY PHYSICIAN. [CD-ROM] (US) **3736**

AMERICAN FAMILY (WASHINGTON), THE (US/0161-1178) [03856372] **2276**

AMERICAN FARM & HOME ALMANAC, THE (US/0065-8278) [04859920] **2527**

AMERICAN FARM BUREAU FEDERATION *See* FARM BUREAU NEWS (WASHINGTON) **84**

AMERICAN FARRIERS' JOURNAL (US/0274-6565) [01998833] **2796**

AMERICAN FASTENER JOURNAL (US/1064-3834) [25122688] **1596**

AMERICAN FEDERAL TAX REPORTS (US) [01479844] **4709**

AMERICAN FEDERATION OF ARTS *See* PROGRAM CATALOGUE **362**

AMERICAN FEDERATION OF AVICULTURE *See* AFA WATCHBIRD, THE **4285**

AMERICAN FEDERATION OF CLINICAL ONCOLOGIC SOCIETIES *See* DIRECTORY OF MEMBERS - AMERICAN FEDERATION OF CLINICAL ONCOLOGIC SOCIETIES **3816**

AMERICAN FEDERATION OF LABOR AND CONGRESS OF INDUSTRIAL ORGANIZATIONS. LOUISIANA. POLITICAL INFORMATION COMMITTEE *See* POLITICS (BATON ROUGE) **4491**

AMERICAN FENCING (US/0002-8436) [03283335] **4882**

AMERICAN FERN JOURNAL (US/0002-8444) [01479862] **498**

●AMERICAN FESTIVAL MAGAZINE (US/1053-1327) [22459612] **312**

AMERICAN FIELD (US/0002-8452) [08657587] **4868**

AMERICAN FILM *CEASED.* (US/0361-4751) [02246336] **4063**

AMERICAN FILM AND VIDEO FESTIVAL (US) [13996276] **4366**

AMERICAN FILM INSTITUTE VIDEO FESTIVAL : CATALOG (US) [20002822] **4063**

AMERICAN FINANCIAL DIRECTORY (US/1047-9759) [20286396] **769**

AMERICAN FIRE JOURNAL (US/0739-3709) [09718507] **2287**

AMERICAN FIREWORKS NEWS (US/8755-3163) [11267272] **2007**

AMERICAN FISHERIES DIRECTORY & REFERENCE BOOK, THE (US/0162-6728) [08016151] **2294**

AMERICAN FISHERIES SOCIETY *See* MONOGRAPH - AMERICAN FISHERIES SOCIETY **2308**

AMERICAN FISHERIES SOCIETY *See* TRANSACTIONS OF THE AMERICAN FISHERIES SOCIETY (1900) **2315**

AMERICAN FISHERIES SOCIETY SYMPOSIUM (US/0892-2284) [15124675] **2294**

AMERICAN FITNESS (US/0893-5238) [15559873] **2595**

AMERICAN FITNESS QUARTERLY (US/0889-2121) [13831539] **2596**

AMERICAN FLINT (US/0002-8525) [03956009] **1643**

AMERICAN FLY FISHER, THE (US/0884-3562) [03810433] **2294**

AMERICAN FOLK MUSIC AND FOLKLORE RECORDINGS (US/0748-5905) [10980167] 2318, **4099**

AMERICAN FOLKLIFE (US/0092-5519) [01790973] **2318**

●AMERICAN FOLKLORE SOCIETY NEWS (US) [29551163] **2318**

AMERICAN FOLKLORE SOCIETY NEWSLETTER, THE (US/0745-5178) [09262905] **2318**

AMERICAN FOOD AND AG EXPORTER (US/1065-3775) [24460028] **2326**

AMERICAN FOOTWEAR INDUSTRIES ASSOCIATION. STATISTICAL DEPT *See* FACTS AND FIGURES ON FOOTWEAR **1084**

AMERICAN FOREIGN LANGUAGE TEACHER *SUSPENDED.* (US/0044-5665) [01721246] 1888, **3263**

AMERICAN FOREIGN POLICY CURRENT DOCUMENTS (WASHINGTON, D.C. : 1984) (US/0501-9877) [11577599] **4515**

AMERICAN FORESTS (US/0002-8541) [01479884] **2374**

AMERICAN FOUNDATION FOR THE BLIND *See* WASHINGTON REPORT **5314**

AMERICAN FRANCHISE & BUSINESS OPPORTUNITY DIRECTORY (US/0098-7328) [02241703] **638**

AMERICAN FRESHMAN: NATIONAL NORMS, THE (US/0278-6990) [02254068] **1808**

AMERICAN FROZEN FOOD INSTITUTE *See* FROZEN FOOD PACK STATISTICS **2362**

AMERICAN FROZEN FOOD INSTITUTE *See* MEMBERSHIP DIRECTORY AND BUYERS' GUIDE - AMERICAN FROZEN FOOD INSTITUTE **2350**

AMERICAN FROZEN FOOD INSTITUTE. DIRECTORY *See* MEMBERSHIP DIRECTORY AND BUYERS' GUIDE - AMERICAN FROZEN FOOD INSTITUTE **2350**

AMERICAN FRUIT GROWER (WILLOUGHBY, OHIO : 1931) (US/0002-8568) [05691157] **2408**

AMERICAN FUCHSIA SOCIETY *See* AMERICAN FUCHSIA SOCIETY BULLETIN **2408**

AMERICAN FUCHSIA SOCIETY BULLETIN (US/0194-3456) [05383529] **2408**

AMERICAN FUNERAL DIRECTOR (US/0002-8576) [01479897] **2406**

●AMERICAN FURNITURE (US/1069-4188) [28033728] **2904**

AMERICAN GAS (US/1043-0652) [19038135] **4249**

AMERICAN GAS ASSOCIATION *See* RESEARCH AND DEVELOPMENT - AMERICAN GAS ASSOCIATION **4276**

AMERICAN GAS ASSOCIATION *See* INFORMATION SERVICE / AMERICAN GAS ASSOCIATION **4260**

AMERICAN GAS ASSOCIATION *See* MONTHLY GAS UTILITY STATISTICAL REPORT **4698**

AMERICAN GAS ASSOCIATION. DEPT. OF STATISTICS *See* GAS FACTS **4283**

AMERICAN GAS ASSOCIATION. OPERATING SECTION *See* OPERATING SECTION PROCEEDINGS **4271**

AMERICAN GEAR MANUFACTURERS ASSOCIATION *See* AGMA DIRECTORY **2109**

AMERICAN — Alphabetical Title Index

AMERICAN GENEALOGICAL-BIOGRAPHICAL INDEX (US) **2478**

AMERICAN GENEALOGIST (DES MOINES) (US/0002-8592) [02444644] **2437**

AMERICAN GENEALOGY MAGAZINE (US/1049-6696) [21276071] **2437**

AMERICAN GERIATRICS SOCIETY *See* NEWSLETTER **3754**

AMERICAN GINSENG TRENDS (US/1047-7527) [20770619] **1596**

●AMERICAN GIRL (MIDDLETON, WIS.) (US/1062-7812) [25739296] **1060**

AMERICAN GLASS REVIEW (US/0002-8649) [08218018] **2586**

AMERICAN GO ASSOCIATION *See* AMERICAN GO JOURNAL, THE **4856**

AMERICAN GO JOURNAL, THE (US/0148-0243) [03256551] 2583, **4856**

AMERICAN GOAT SOCIETY *See* YEARBOOK / AMERICAN GOAT SOCIETY **224**

AMERICAN GOLD NEWS & WESTERN PROSPECTOR *SUSPENDED.* (US/0894-2706) [16122643] 2133, **1437**

AMERICAN GOSPEL MAGAZINE *SUSPENDED.* (US/1056-7380) [23841321] 4933, **4099**

AMERICAN GOVERNANCE (US/1045-3865) [20086217] **4625**

AMERICAN GOVERNMENT (US/0891-3390) [06696647] **4463**

AMERICAN GOVERNMENT : TEXT (US/0090-547X) [01783681] 4625, **4463**

AMERICAN GROUP PRACTICE ASSOCIATION *See* DIRECTORY - AMERICAN GROUP PRACTICE ASSOCIATION **3779**

AMERICAN GROUP PSYCHOTHERAPY ASSOCIATION *See* DIRECTORY / AMERICAN GROUP PSYCHOTHERAPY ASSOCIATION **3924**

AMERICAN GUIDE TO U.S. COINS *SUSPENDED.* (US/0884-5670) [04408336] **2779**

AMERICAN GUILD OF MUSICAL ARTISTS *See* AGMAZINE **4098**

AMERICAN GUILD OF ORGANISTS. NEW YORK CITY CHAPTER *See* AGO TIMES, THE **4099**

AMERICAN GYNECOLOGICAL AND OBSTETRICAL SOCIETY *See* TRANSACTIONS OF THE AMERICAN GYNECOLOGICAL AND OBSTETRICAL SOCIETY **3769**

AMERICAN HANDGUNNER, THE (US/0145-4250) [02735456] **4882**

AMERICAN HARMONICA ASSOCIATES NEWSLETTER (US/1050-7493) [21583443] **4099**

AMERICAN HARP JOURNAL, THE (US/0002-869X) [02444646] **4099**

●AMERICAN HARPOON, THE (US/1064-7139) [26379372] **2527**

AMERICAN HAWKWATCHER (US/0748-8319) [11014079] **5614**

AMERICAN HEALTH (NEW YORK, N.Y.) (US/0730-7004) [08049660] **2596**

AMERICAN HEART JOURNAL, THE (US/0002-8703) [01479953] **3698**

AMERICAN HELICOPTER SOCIETY *See* ANNUAL FORUM PROCEEDINGS - AMERICAN HELICOPTER SOCIETY **11**

AMERICAN HELICOPTER SOCIETY *See* JOURNAL OF THE AMERICAN HELICOPTER SOCIETY **26**

AMERICAN HEREFORD JOURNAL (US/0002-872X) [01479962] **205**

AMERICAN HERITAGE (US/0002-8738) [01479963] **2718**

AMERICAN HERITAGE OF INVENTION & TECHNOLOGY (US/8756-7296) [11638224] **5082**

AMERICAN HIGH SCHOOL ATHLETE / COMPILED BY ATHLETIC PUBLISHING GROUP, INC (US) [08541835] **4882**

AMERICAN HIKER (US/0279-9472) [07369281] **4868**

AMERICAN HISTORICAL ASSOCIATION *See* ANNUAL REPORT OF THE AMERICAN HISTORICAL ASSOCIATION **2610**

AMERICAN HISTORICAL ASSOCIATION *See* AHA PAMPHLETS **2717**

AMERICAN HISTORICAL ASSOCIATION. PUBLICATION *See* AHA PAMPHLETS **2717**

AMERICAN HISTORICAL PRINT COLLECTORS SOCIETY *See* MEMBER DIRECTORY - AMERICAN HISTORICAL PRINT COLLECTORS SOCIETY **358**

AMERICAN HISTORICAL REVIEW (US/0002-8762) [01830326] **2609**

AMERICAN HISTORICAL SOCIETY OF GERMANS FROM RUSSIA *See* JOURNAL OF THE AMERICAN HISTORICAL SOCIETY OF GERMANS FROM RUSSIA **2695**

AMERICAN HISTORICAL SOCIETY OF GERMANS FROM RUSSIA *See* NEWSLETTER - AMERICAN HISTORICAL SOCIETY OF GERMANS FROM RUSSIA **2463**

AMERICAN HISTORY (US) **2719**

AMERICAN HISTORY (US/0733-3560) [08231094] **2719**

●AMERICAN HISTORY (US/1076-8866) [30148811] **2719**

AMERICAN HISTORY ILLUSTRATED (US/0002-8770) [01479976] **2719**

AMERICAN HISTORY (WESTPORT, CONN.) *CEASED.* (US/0748-6731) [11000891] **2719**

AMERICAN HOCKEY MAGAZINE (US/8756-3789) [11528538] **4882**

AMERICAN HOLIDAY & LIFE (US/1055-9191) [23379210] **5268**

AMERICAN HOLINESS JOURNAL (US) [01588034] **4933**

AMERICAN HOLISTIC MEDICAL ASSOCIATION *See* DIRECTORY / AMERICAN HOLISTIC MEDICAL ASSOCIATION AND FOUNDATION **3913**

AMERICAN HOME *See* REDBOOK **5565**

AMERICAN HOME ECONOMICS ASSOCIATION *See* AMERICAN HOME ECONOMICS ASSOCIATION ACTION **2788**

AMERICAN HOME ECONOMICS ASSOCIATION *See* A.H.E.A. ACTION **2788**

●AMERICAN HOME ECONOMICS ASSOCIATION ACTION (US/0194-7176) [29754976] **2788**

AMERICAN HOME ECONOMICS ASSOCIATION. HOME ECONOMISTS IN BUSINESS SECTION *See* DIRECTORY - HOME ECONOMISTS IN BUSINESS, SECTION OF THE AMERICAN HOME ECONOMICS ASSOCIATION **2789**

AMERICAN HOMEOPATHY (1984) (US/0747-606X) [10756482] **3774**

AMERICAN HOME'S BEST PROJECTS (US/0147-5169) [03181443] **369**

AMERICAN HOME'S TREASURY OF AMERICANA (US/0161-5203) [03946853] **248**

AMERICAN HORSES IN SPORT (US/0897-1498) [17417195] **2796**

AMERICAN HORTICULTURIST (ALEXANDRIA) (US/0096-4417) [01190579] **2408**

AMERICAN HORTICULTURIST NEWS (US) [07477951] **2408**

AMERICAN HOSPITAL ASSOCIATION *See* PUBLICATIONS CATALOG - AMERICAN HOSPITAL ASSOCIATION **3791**

AMERICAN HOSPITAL ASSOCIATION GUIDE TO THE HEALTH CARE FIELD (US/0094-8969) [01070558] **3548**

AMERICAN HOSPITAL ASSOCIATION HOSPITAL STATISTICS (US) [29879416] 3776, **3654**

AMERICAN HUMANE ASSOCIATION *See* AGENCY DIRECTORY - AMERICAN HUMANE **5270**

AMERICAN HUMANITIES INDEX, THE (US/0361-0144) [01739910] 2841, **2857**

AMERICAN HUNTER, THE (US/0092-1068) [01789140] **4868**

AMERICAN ILLUSTRATION SHOWCASE (US/0278-8128) [07912734] **376**

AMERICAN IMAGO (US/0065-860X) [01479999] **4572**

AMERICAN IMMIGRATION AND CITIZENSHIP CONFERENCE *See* NEWS - AMERICAN IMMIGRATION AND CITIZENSHIP CONFERENCE **1920**

AMERICAN INDIAN AND ALASKA NATIVE MENTAL HEALTH RESEARCH (US/0893-5394) [15565658] **5271**

AMERICAN INDIAN ART MAGAZINE (US/0192-9968) [04343382] **336**

AMERICAN INDIAN ARTIFACT PRICE GUIDE (US/0362-9767) [02397200] **336**

AMERICAN INDIAN CALENDAR (US) [03214596] **2719**

AMERICAN INDIAN COLLEGE STUDENTS IN NEW YORK STATE : NEW YORK STATE AMERICAN INDIAN AID FOR POSTSECONDARY EDUCATION (US) [23865583] 1808, **2254**

AMERICAN INDIAN CULTURE AND RESEARCH JOURNAL (US/0161-6463) [01781938] **2254**

AMERICAN INDIAN EARLY CHILDHOOD EDUCATION (US/0145-9910) [03124943] 2255, **1802**

AMERICAN INDIAN JOURNAL (US/0145-7993) [02256009] **2932**

AMERICAN INDIAN LAW NEWSLETTER *CEASED.* (US/0002-8886) [01480008] **2932**

AMERICAN INDIAN LAW REVIEW (US/0094-002X) [01793421] 2255, **2932**

AMERICAN INDIAN LIBRARIES NEWSLETTER (US/0193-8207) [03633821] **3189**

AMERICAN INDIAN MAP BOOK SERIES (US) [01130796] **2255**

AMERICAN INDIAN QUARTERLY (US/0095-182X) [01795987] **2255**

AMERICAN INDIAN REGISTRY FOR THE PERFORMING ARTS, THE (US/0882-4487) [11837725] **383**

●AMERICAN INDIAN RELIGIONS (US/1065-8068) [26749026] **4933**

AMERICAN INDIAN REPORT (US/0894-4040) [13058212] **2719**

●AMERICAN INDIAN STUDIES (US/1058-563X) [24329658] 2719, **2255**

AMERICAN INDIAN TALENT DIRECTORY (US/0882-4495) [11837924] **383**

AMERICAN INDONESIAN CHAMBER OF COMMERCE *See* INFORMATION BULLETIN - AMERICAN INDONESIAN CHAMBER OF COMMERCE, INC **820**

AMERICAN INDUSTRIAL DEVELOPMENT COUNCIL *See* CONFERENCE NOTES - AMERICAN INDUSTRIAL DEVELOPMENT COUNCIL, INC **1602**

AMERICAN INDUSTRIAL HYGIENE ASSOCIATION JOURNAL (US/0002-8894) [01579808] **2858**

AMERICAN INDUSTRY (US/0002-8908) [13807754] 1596, **859**

AMERICAN INKMAKER (US/0002-8916) [08660030] **4563**

AMERICAN INSTITUTE COUNSELORS *See* INVESTMENT BULLETIN **902**

AMERICAN INSTITUTE FOR CONSERVATION OF HISTORIC AND ARTISTIC WORKS *See* ABSTRACTS OF PAPERS PRESENTED AT THE ... ANNUAL MEETING ... / THE AMERICAN INSTITUTE FOR CONSERVATION OF HISTORIC AND ARTISTIC WORKS **335**

AMERICAN INSTITUTE FOR CONSERVATION OF HISTORIC AND ARTISTIC WORKS *See* JOURNAL OF THE AMERICAN INSTITUTE FOR CONSERVATION **323**

AMERICAN INSTITUTE FOR DECISION SCIENCES. WESTERN REGIONAL CONFERENCE *See* PROCEEDINGS AND ABSTRACTS, AMERICAN INSTITUTE FOR DECISION SCIENCES, ANNUAL MEETING, WESTERN REGIONAL CONFERENCE **4608**

AMERICAN INSTITUTE FOR ECONOMIC RESEARCH *See* RESEARCH REPORTS: AMERICAN INSTITUTE FOR ECONOMIC RESEARCH **1517**

AMERICAN INSTITUTE FOR ECONOMIC RESEARCH *See* ANNUITIES FROM THE BUYER'S POINT OF VIEW **2874**

AMERICAN INSTITUTE FOR ECONOMIC RESEARCH. LIFE INSURANCE AND ANNUITIES FROM THE BUYER'S POINT OF VIEW *See* ANNUITIES FROM THE BUYER'S POINT OF VIEW **2874**

AMERICAN INSTITUTE FOR FOREIGN STUDY *See* AIFS ACADEMIC YEAR & SUMMER PROGRAMS **1723**

AMERICAN INSTITUTE FOR FOREIGN STUDY *See* ACADEMIC YEAR & SUMMER PROGRAMS ABROAD **1721**

AMERICAN INSTITUTE FOR FREE LABOR DEVELOPMENT. AIFLD REPORT *See* AIFLD OUTLOOK : A PUBLICATION OF THE AMERICAN INSTITUTE FOR FREE LABOR DEVELOPMENT **1643**

AMERICAN INSTITUTE OF ACTUARIES. YEAR BOOK *See* YEAR BOOK / SOCIETY OF ACTUARIES **2896**

AMERICAN INSTITUTE OF AERONAUTICS AND ASTRONAUTICS *See* AIAA PAPER **6**

AMERICAN INSTITUTE OF AERONAUTICS AND ASTRONAUTICS *See* MONOGRAPHS **29**

AMERICAN INSTITUTE OF AERONAUTICS AND ASTRONAUTICS *See* AIAA ROSTER **6**

AMERICAN INSTITUTE OF AERONAUTICS AND ASTRONAUTICS *See* AIAA JOURNAL **6**

AMERICAN INSTITUTE OF AERONAUTICS AND ASTRONAUTICS *See* AIAA STUDENT JOURNAL **6**

AMERICAN INSTITUTE OF ARCHITECTS *See* PRO FILE: THE OFFICIAL DIRECTORY OF THE AMERICAN INSTITUTE OF ARCHITECTS **306**

AMERICAN INSTITUTE OF ARCHITECTS *See* AMERICAN INSTITUTE OF ARCHITECTS MEMBERSHIP DIRECTORY **287**

AMERICAN INSTITUTE OF ARCHITECTS *See* MEMO - AMERICAN INSTITUTE OF ARCHITECTS (1971) **303**

AMERICAN INSTITUTE OF ARCHITECTS *See* DIRECTORY OF INSTITUTE/COMPONENT OFFICERS **297**

Alphabetical Title Index — AMERICAN

AMERICAN INSTITUTE OF ARCHITECTS MEMBERSHIP DIRECTORY (US/0276-668X) [04546386] **287**

AMERICAN INSTITUTE OF ARCHITECTS. SEATTLE CHAPTER *See* HONOR AWARDS PROGRAM / SEATTLE CHAPTER, AMERICAN INSTITUTE OF ARCHITECTS **300**

AMERICAN INSTITUTE OF BANKING *See* REPORT OF AIB CHAPTER PROGRAMS & ... ACTIVITIES **807**

AMERICAN INSTITUTE OF CERTIFIED PLANNERS *See* ROSTER - AMERICAN INSTITUTE OF CERTIFIED PLANNERS **1582**

AMERICAN INSTITUTE OF CERTIFIED PUBLIC ACCOUNTANTS *See* RULES OF CONDUCT. BYLAWS AND IMPLEMENTING RESOLUTIONS OF COUNCIL **751**

AMERICAN INSTITUTE OF CERTIFIED PUBLIC ACCOUNTANTS *See* COMMITTEE HANDBOOK - AICPA **741**

AMERICAN INSTITUTE OF CERTIFIED PUBLIC ACCOUNTANTS *See* AICPA'S UNIFORM CPA EXAM, THE **738**

AMERICAN INSTITUTE OF CERTIFIED PUBLIC ACCOUNTANTS. ACCOUNTING STANDARDS DIVISION *See* STATEMENTS OF POSITION OF THE ACCOUNTING STANDARDS DIVISION AS OF JANUARY 1 ... **751**

AMERICAN INSTITUTE OF CHEMICAL ENGINEERS *See* AICHE EQUIPMENT TESTING PROCEDURE **2007**

AMERICAN INSTITUTE OF CHEMICAL ENGINEERS *See* MEETING PAPERS ON MICROFICHE **2015**

AMERICAN INSTITUTE OF CHEMICAL ENGINEERS *See* ANNUAL MEETING - AMERICAN INSTITUTE OF CHEMICAL ENGINEERS **2007**

AMERICAN INSTITUTE OF CHEMICAL ENGINEERS *See* AICHE WORKSHOP **2007**

AMERICAN INSTITUTE OF CHEMICAL ENGINEERS *See* NATIONAL MEETING; PROGRAM **2015**

AMERICAN INSTITUTE OF CHEMICAL ENGINEERS *See* AICHE JOURNAL **2007**

AMERICAN INSTITUTE OF CHEMISTS *See* PROFESSIONAL DIRECTORY / THE AMERICAN INSTITUTE OF CHEMISTS **990**

AMERICAN INSTITUTE OF COOPERATION *See* AMERICAN COOPERATION **1541**

AMERICAN INSTITUTE OF GRAPHIC ARTS *See* COMMUNICATION GRAPHICS **377**

AMERICAN INSTITUTE OF INDIAN STUDIES *See* ANNUAL REPORT - AMERICAN INSTITUTE OF INDIAN STUDIES **2255**

AMERICAN INSTITUTE OF INDIAN STUDIES *See* BIENNIAL REPORT - AMERICAN INSTITUTE OF INDIAN STUDIES **2647**

AMERICAN INSTITUTE OF INDIAN STUDIES. AIIS ANNUAL REPORT *See* BIENNIAL REPORT - AMERICAN INSTITUTE OF INDIAN STUDIES **2647**

AMERICAN INSTITUTE OF ISLAMIC STUDIES *See* BIBLIOGRAPHIC SERIES **5012**

AMERICAN INSTITUTE OF MINING, METALLURGICAL, AND PETROLEUM ENGINEERS *See* TRANSACTIONS OF THE AMERICAN INSTITUTE OF MINING, METALLURGICAL AND PETROLEUM ENGINEERS **1999**

AMERICAN INSTITUTE OF MINING, METALLURGICAL, AND PETROLEUM ENGINEERS *See* LIGHT METALS (NEW YORK) **4007**

AMERICAN INSTITUTE OF PHYSICS *See* PHYSICS MANPOWER, EDUCATION AND EMPLOYMENT STUDIES **4427**

AMERICAN INSTITUTE OF PHYSICS. PHYSICS: EDUCATION, EMPLOYMENT, FINANCIAL SUPPORT; A STATISTICAL HANDBOOK *See* PHYSICS MANPOWER, EDUCATION AND EMPLOYMENT STUDIES **4427**

AMERICAN INSTITUTE OF PLANT ENGINEERS *See* AIPE NEWSLINE **1964**

AMERICAN INSTITUTE OF PROFESSIONAL GEOLOGISTS *See* MEMBERSHIP DIRECTORY / AMERICAN INSTITUTE OF PROFESSIONAL GEOLOGISTS **1387**

AMERICAN INSTITUTE OF REAL ESTATE APPRAISERS *See* DIRECTORY OF MEMBERS / THE INSTITUTE **4836**

AMERICAN INSTITUTE OF STEEL CONSTRUCTION. ANNUAL REPORT *See* AISC NEWS **598**

AMERICAN INSTITUTE OF ULTRASOUND IN MEDICINE *See* ULTRASOUND IN MEDICINE **3648**

AMERICAN INSURANCE ASSOCIATION *See* SALARY SURVEY (NEW YORK) **1709**

AMERICAN INTELLECTUAL PROPERTY LAW ASSOCIATION *See* AIPLA BULLETIN / AMERICAN INTELLECTUAL PROPERTY LAW ASSOCIATION, INC **1301**

AMERICAN INTELLIGENCE JOURNAL (US/0883-072X) [09449816] **4034**

AMERICAN INTERNATIONAL INVESTMENT CORPORATION, SAN FRANCISCO *See* WORLD CURRENCY CHARTS **920**

AMERICAN INVENTOR (BLOOMINGTON, IND.) (US/1042-1890) [18966461] **5082**

AMERICAN INVESTOR (RESEARCH TRIANGLE PARK, N.C.) (US/1061-8872) [25323558] **890**

AMERICAN IRIS SOCIETY *See* BULLETIN OF THE AMERICAN IRIS SOCIETY **2411**

AMERICAN IRIS SOCIETY. REGION 4 *See* NEWS CAST - AMERICAN IRIS SOCIETY. REGION 4 **2425**

AMERICAN IRIS SOCIETY. REGION 4. NEWSLETTER *See* NEWS CAST - AMERICAN IRIS SOCIETY. REGION 4 **2425**

AMERICAN IRISH NEWSLETTER, THE (US/0897-2109) [16002530] **2609**

AMERICAN IRON AND STEEL INSTITUTE *See* SHIPMENTS OF STEEL PRODUCTS: ALL GRADES INCLUDING CARBON, ALLOY AND STAINLESS **4019**

AMERICAN IRON AND STEEL INSTITUTE *See* ANNUAL STATISTICAL REPORT - AMERICAN IRON AND STEEL INSTITUTE **4025**

AMERICAN IRON AND STEEL INSTITUTE *See* CHARTING STEEL'S PROGRESS **1601**

AMERICAN IRON & STEEL INSTITUTE BASIC STEEL OPERATION STATISTICS. AIS 7, 10 & 16 (US) 3997, **4025**

AMERICAN IRON & STEEL INSTITUTE FOREIGN TRADE STATISTICS. APPARENT STEEL SUPPLY REPORT (US) 3997, **4025**

AMERICAN IRON & STEEL INSTITUTE FOREIGN TRADE STATISTICS. IMPORTS 3 & IMPORTS 4 (US) 3997, **4025**

AMERICAN IRON & STEEL INSTITUTE FOREIGN TRADE STATISTICS. INDIVIDUAL IMPORT & EXPORT REPORTS (US) 3997, **4025**

AMERICAN IRON & STEEL INSTITUTE MONTHLY PACKAGE (US) **3997**

AMERICAN IRON & STEEL INSTITUTE QUARTERLY AIS PACKAGE (US) **3997**

AMERICAN ISSUE (DES MOINES), THE **SUSPENDED.** (US/0195-1556) [01776792] **1340**

AMERICAN JAILS (US/1056-0319) [16677874] **3156**

AMERICAN JEWELRY MANUFACTURER (US/0193-0931) [08228919] **2913**

AMERICAN JEWISH ARCHIVES (US/0002-905X) [01480108] 4934, **2255**

AMERICAN JEWISH COMMITTEE. INSTITUTE OF HUMAN RELATIONS. BLAUSTEIN LIBRARY *See* ARTICLES OF INTEREST IN CURRENT PERIODICALS **408**

AMERICAN JEWISH CONGRESS *See* GUIDE TO JEWISH CHICAGO, AND YEARBOOK **2262**

AMERICAN JEWISH HISTORY (US/0164-0178) [04304304] 5045, **2255**

... AMERICAN-JEWISH MEDIA DIRECTORY, THE (US/1041-0139) [18610177] **755**

AMERICAN JEWISH WORLD, THE (US/0002-9084) [01480115] **5045**

AMERICAN JEWISH YEAR BOOK (US/0065-8987) [01480116] **5045**

AMERICAN JOURNAL (NEW YORK) (US/0092-119X) [01787068] **2527**

AMERICAN JOURNAL OF ACUPUNCTURE (US/0091-3960) [01605501] **3548**

●AMERICAN JOURNAL OF ADOPTION REFORM (US/1065-3457) [26584493] **5271**

AMERICAN JOURNAL OF AGRICULTURAL ECONOMICS (US/0002-9092) [02240143] 1461, **58**

AMERICAN JOURNAL OF ALTERNATIVE AGRICULTURE (US/0889-1893) [12903367] **58**

AMERICAN JOURNAL OF ALZHEIMER'S CARE AND RELATED DISORDERS & RESEARCH (US/0895-5336) [16687145] **3827**

AMERICAN JOURNAL OF ANATOMY *See* DEVELOPMENTAL DYNAMICS **3679**

AMERICAN JOURNAL OF ANCIENT HISTORY (US/0362-8914) [02379315] **1073**

●AMERICAN JOURNAL OF ANESTHESIOLOGY, THE (US/1078-4500) [31091563] **3680**

AMERICAN JOURNAL OF ARCHAEOLOGY, THE (US/0002-9114) [05696010] **254**

AMERICAN JOURNAL OF ART THERAPY (US/0007-4764) [01798034] 3919, **336**

AMERICAN JOURNAL OF ASTHMA & ALLERGY FOR PEDIATRICIANS, THE (US/0899-7411) [18202520] 3899, **3948**

AMERICAN JOURNAL OF AUDIOLOGY (US/1059-0889) [24477823] **4383**

AMERICAN JOURNAL OF BOTANY (US/0002-9122) [01480121] **498**

AMERICAN JOURNAL OF CARDIAC IMAGING (US/0887-7971) [13351454] 3938, **3698**

AMERICAN JOURNAL OF CARDIOLOGY, THE (US/0002-9149) [00850121] **3698**

AMERICAN JOURNAL OF CARDIOVASCULAR PATHOLOGY, THE (US/0887-8005) [13352913] **3698**

AMERICAN JOURNAL OF CASE MANAGEMENT, THE (US/1051-8967) [22146620] **5190**

AMERICAN JOURNAL OF CHINESE MEDICINE, THE (US/0192-415X) [04655940] **3548**

AMERICAN JOURNAL OF CLINICAL HYPNOSIS, THE (US/0002-9157) [01480126] **2857**

AMERICAN JOURNAL OF CLINICAL NUTRITION, THE (US/0002-9165) [01480127] **4187**

AMERICAN JOURNAL OF CLINICAL ONCOLOGY (US/0277-3732) [07580250] **3808**

AMERICAN JOURNAL OF CLINICAL PATHOLOGY (US/0002-9173) [01480128] **3892**

AMERICAN JOURNAL OF COMMUNITY PSYCHOLOGY (US/0091-0562) [01798402] 5238, **4573**

AMERICAN JOURNAL OF COMPARATIVE LAW, THE (US/0002-919X) [00844194] **3123**

AMERICAN JOURNAL OF CONTACT DERMATITIS (US/1046-199X) [20348451] **3717**

AMERICAN JOURNAL OF COSMETIC SURGERY, THE (US/0748-8068) [11012910] **3958**

AMERICAN JOURNAL OF CRIMINAL JUSTICE : AJCJ (US/1066-2316) [13148437] **3156**

AMERICAN JOURNAL OF CRIMINAL LAW (US/0092-2315) [01774780] **3105**

●AMERICAN JOURNAL OF CRITICAL CARE (US/1062-3264) [25588350] **3850**

AMERICAN JOURNAL OF DANCE THERAPY (US/0146-3721) [03098586] 1310, **4573**

AMERICAN JOURNAL OF DENTISTRY (US/0894-8275) [16264374] **1315**

AMERICAN JOURNAL OF DERMATOPATHOLOGY, THE (US/0193-1091) [05058734] **3717**

AMERICAN JOURNAL OF DISEASES OF CHILDREN (1960) *See* ARCHIVES OF PEDIATRICS & ADOLESCENT MEDICINE **3900**

AMERICAN JOURNAL OF DISEASES OF CHILDREN (1960) (US/0002-922X) [01480134] **3899**

AMERICAN JOURNAL OF DISTANCE EDUCATION, THE (US/0892-3647) [15170029] **1724**

AMERICAN JOURNAL OF DRUG AND ALCOHOL ABUSE, THE (US/0095-2990) [01796465] **1340**

AMERICAN JOURNAL OF ECONOMICS AND SOCIOLOGY, THE (US/0002-9246) [01480136] **5190**

AMERICAN JOURNAL OF EDUCATION (CHICAGO) (US/0195-6744) [05585126] **1724**

AMERICAN JOURNAL OF EEG TECHNOLOGY, THE (US/0002-9238) [01480135] **3827**

AMERICAN JOURNAL OF EMERGENCY MEDICINE, THE (US/0735-6757) [08996781] **3723**

AMERICAN JOURNAL OF ENOLOGY AND VITICULTURE (US/0002-9254) [04919664] **2363**

AMERICAN JOURNAL OF EPIDEMIOLOGY (US/0002-9262) [01480139] 4764, **3734**

AMERICAN JOURNAL OF FAMILY LAW (US/0891-6330) [14938334] **3119**

AMERICAN JOURNAL OF FAMILY THERAPY, THE (US/0192-6187) [04941265] 2276, **4573**

AMERICAN JOURNAL OF FORENSIC MEDICINE AND PATHOLOGY, THE (US/0195-7910) [05664235] 3892, **3739**

AMERICAN JOURNAL OF FORENSIC PSYCHIATRY, THE (US/0163-1942) [04314035] **3919**

AMERICAN JOURNAL OF FORENSIC PSYCHOLOGY, THE (US/0733-1290) [08516904] 2932, 4573, **3739**

AMERICAN — Alphabetical Title Index

AMERICAN JOURNAL OF GASTROENTEROLOGY, THE (US/0002-9270) [01480140] **3743**

AMERICAN JOURNAL OF GERIATRIC CARDIOLOGY, THE (US) [26855248] **3698**

AMERICAN JOURNAL OF GERIATRIC PSYCHIATRY, THE (US/1064-7481) [26387933] 3919, **3749**

AMERICAN JOURNAL OF GERMANIC LINGUISTICS AND LITERATURES (US/1040-8207) [18541879] **3263**

AMERICAN JOURNAL OF GYNECOLOGIC HEALTH, THE **CEASED.** (US/0895-3643) [16572860] **3756**

AMERICAN JOURNAL OF HEALTH PROMOTION (US/0890-1171) [13830677] **4764**

AMERICAN JOURNAL OF HEMATOLOGY (US/0361-8609) [02144014] **3770**

AMERICAN JOURNAL OF HOSPICE AND PALLIATIVE CARE, THE (US/1049-9091) [21269606] **5271**

AMERICAN JOURNAL OF HOSPITAL PHARMACY (US/0002-9289) [01480144] 3776, **4290**

AMERICAN JOURNAL OF HUMAN BIOLOGY (US/1042-0533) [18924802] **441**

AMERICAN JOURNAL OF HUMAN GENETICS (US/0002-9297) [01480145] **542**

AMERICAN JOURNAL OF HYPERTENSION (US/0895-7061) [16748912] **3698**

AMERICAN JOURNAL OF INDUSTRIAL MEDICINE (US/0271-3586) [06624472] **3548**

AMERICAN JOURNAL OF INFECTION CONTROL (US/0196-6553) [05861167] **3734**

AMERICAN JOURNAL OF INTERNATIONAL LAW, THE (US/0002-9300) [01480149] **3123**

AMERICAN JOURNAL OF ISLAMIC SOCIAL SCIENCES, THE (US/0887-7653) [12534110] 5042, **5190**

AMERICAN JOURNAL OF JURISPRUDENCE (NOTRE DAME), THE (US/0065-8995) [01480151] **2932**

AMERICAN JOURNAL OF KIDNEY DISEASES (US/0272-6386) [06887399] **3988**

AMERICAN JOURNAL OF KNEE SURGERY, THE (US/0899-7403) [17886578] **3958**

AMERICAN JOURNAL OF LAW & MEDICINE (US/0098-8588) [02242483] 3739, **2932**

AMERICAN JOURNAL OF LEGAL HISTORY, THE (US/0002-9319) [01480152] **2932**

●AMERICAN JOURNAL OF MANAGEMENT DEVELOPMENT (UK/1354-5787) **859**

AMERICAN JOURNAL OF MATHEMATICAL AND MANAGEMENT SCIENCES (US/0196-6324) [05874087] **3492**

AMERICAN JOURNAL OF MATHEMATICS (US/0002-9327) [01480153] **3492**

AMERICAN JOURNAL OF MEDICAL GENETICS (US/0148-7299) [03372843] **542**

●AMERICAN JOURNAL OF MEDICAL QUALITY (US/1062-8606) [25797414] **3776**

AMERICAN JOURNAL OF MEDICINE. EDICION ESPANOLA (SP/0210-5713) [l02105713] **3548**

AMERICAN JOURNAL OF MEDICINE, THE (US/0002-9343) [01480156] **3548**

AMERICAN JOURNAL OF MENTAL RETARDATION (US/0895-8017) [16799715] **4383**

AMERICAN JOURNAL OF NEPHROLOGY (SZ/0250-8095) [07963279] **3988**

AMERICAN JOURNAL OF NEURORADIOLOGY (US/0195-6108) [05527029] 3938, **3827**

AMERICAN JOURNAL OF NONINVASIVE CARDIOLOGY (SZ/0258-4425) [14817317] **3698**

AMERICAN JOURNAL OF NUMISMATICS (1989) (US/1053-8356) [22332895] **2779**

AMERICAN JOURNAL OF NURSING, THE (US/0002-936X) [01743347] **3850**

AMERICAN JOURNAL OF OBSTETRICS AND GYNECOLOGY (US/0002-9378) [01480163] **3756**

AMERICAN JOURNAL OF OCCUPATIONAL THERAPY, THE (US/0272-9490) [01480164] **1874**

AMERICAN JOURNAL OF OPHTHALMOLOGY (US/0002-9394) [01480165] **3871**

AMERICAN JOURNAL OF ORTHODONTICS AND DENTOFACIAL ORTHOPEDICS (US/0889-5406) [13922942] **1315**

●AMERICAN JOURNAL OF ORTHOPEDICS, THE (US/1078-4519) [31091622] **3880**

AMERICAN JOURNAL OF ORTHOPSYCHIATRY (US/0002-9432) [01480170] **3919**

AMERICAN JOURNAL OF OTOLARYNGOLOGY (US/0196-0709) [05752902] **3885**

AMERICAN JOURNAL OF OTOLOGY (NEW YORK, N.Y.), THE (US/0192-9763) [05139947] **3886**

AMERICAN JOURNAL OF PAIN MANAGEMENT (US/1059-1494) [24486718] **3548**

AMERICAN JOURNAL OF PATHOLOGY, THE (US/0002-9440) [01479398] **3892**

AMERICAN JOURNAL OF PEDIATRIC HEMATOLOGY/ONCOLOGY, THE (US/0192-8562) [05089126] 3808, **3900**

AMERICAN JOURNAL OF PERINATOLOGY (US/0735-1631) [08875325] **3756**

AMERICAN JOURNAL OF PHARMACEUTICAL EDUCATION (US/0002-9459) [01480171] **4290**

AMERICAN JOURNAL OF PHARMACY AND THE SCIENCES SUPPORTING PUBLIC HEALTH (1981) (US/0730-7780) [08070280] **4290**

AMERICAN JOURNAL OF PHILOLOGY (US/0002-9475) [01480174] 3263, **1073**

AMERICAN JOURNAL OF PHYSICAL ANTHROPOLOGY (US/0002-9483) [01480176] 441, **228**

AMERICAN JOURNAL OF PHYSICAL MEDICINE & REHABILITATION (US/0894-9115) [16308327] **4379**

AMERICAN JOURNAL OF PHYSICS (US/0002-9505) [01480178] **4396**

AMERICAN JOURNAL OF PHYSIOLOGIC IMAGING **CEASED.** (US/0885-8276) [12738591] **577**

AMERICAN JOURNAL OF PHYSIOLOGY (US/0002-9513) [01480180] **577**

AMERICAN JOURNAL OF PHYSIOLOGY : CELL PHYSIOLOGY (US/0363-6143) [02954084] **577**

AMERICAN JOURNAL OF PHYSIOLOGY : ENDOCRINOLOGY AND METABOLISM (US/0193-1849) [05160965] 3726, **577**

AMERICAN JOURNAL OF PHYSIOLOGY : GASTROINTESTINAL AND LIVER PHYSIOLOGY (US/0193-1857) [05160963] **578**

AMERICAN JOURNAL OF PHYSIOLOGY : HEART AND CIRCULATORY PHYSIOLOGY (US/0363-6135) [02960615] 3698, **578**

AMERICAN JOURNAL OF PHYSIOLOGY. LUNG CELLULAR AND MOLECULAR PHYSIOLOGY (US/1040-0605) [18304294] **3948**

AMERICAN JOURNAL OF PHYSIOLOGY : REGULATORY, INTEGRATIVE AND COMPARATIVE PHYSIOLOGY (US/0363-6119) [03022253] **578**

AMERICAN JOURNAL OF PHYSIOLOGY RENAL, FLUID AND ELECTROLYTE PHYSIOLOGY (US/0363-6127) [02960350] **578**

AMERICAN JOURNAL OF POLICE (US/0735-8547) [08406651] **3156**

AMERICAN JOURNAL OF POLITICAL SCIENCE (US/0092-5853) [01789847] **4463**

AMERICAN JOURNAL OF PREVENTIVE MEDICINE (US/0749-3797) [11120856] **3549**

AMERICAN JOURNAL OF PRIMATOLOGY (US/0275-2565) [07113717] **5574**

AMERICAN JOURNAL OF PRIMATOLOGY. SUPPLEMENT (US/0736-7880) [09161337] **441**

AMERICAN JOURNAL OF PSYCHIATRY, THE (US/0002-953X) [01480183] **3920**

AMERICAN JOURNAL OF PSYCHOANALYSIS (US/0002-9548) [01355186] **3920**

AMERICAN JOURNAL OF PSYCHOLOGY, THE (US/0002-9556) [01408768] **4573**

AMERICAN JOURNAL OF PSYCHOTHERAPY (US/0002-9564) [01480186] **3920**

AMERICAN JOURNAL OF PUBLIC HEALTH (1971) (US/0090-0036) [01642844] **4764**

AMERICAN JOURNAL OF REPRODUCTIVE IMMUNOLOGY : AJRI (DK/1046-7408) [19900119] **3666**

●AMERICAN JOURNAL OF RESPIRATORY AND CRITICAL CARE MEDICINE (US/1073-449X) [29407978] **3948**

AMERICAN JOURNAL OF RESPIRATORY CELL AND MOLECULAR BIOLOGY (US/1044-1549) [19699650] **3948**

AMERICAN JOURNAL OF RHINOLOGY (US/1050-6586) [18325507] 3666, **3886**

AMERICAN JOURNAL OF ROENTGENOLOGY (1976) (US/0361-803X) [02471317] **3938**

AMERICAN JOURNAL OF SCIENCE (1880) (US/0002-9599) [05694945] **5082**

AMERICAN JOURNAL OF SEMIOTICS (US/0277-7126) [07632823] **3263**

AMERICAN JOURNAL OF SOCIAL PSYCHIATRY, THE **CEASED.** (US/0277-8173) [07627688] **3920**

AMERICAN JOURNAL OF SOCIOLOGY (US/0002-9602) [01831931] **5238**

AMERICAN JOURNAL OF SPEECH-LANGUAGE PATHOLOGY (US/1058-0360) [24201505] **4383**

AMERICAN JOURNAL OF SPORTS MEDICINE, THE (US/0363-5465) [02314681] **3953**

AMERICAN JOURNAL OF SURGERY, THE (US/0002-9610) [01480194] **3958**

AMERICAN JOURNAL OF SURGICAL PATHOLOGY, THE (US/0147-5185) [03181447] 3958, **3892**

AMERICAN JOURNAL OF TAX POLICY, THE (US/0739-7569) [08724835] **4709**

AMERICAN JOURNAL OF THE MEDICAL SCIENCES, THE (US/0002-9629) [01480197] **3549**

AMERICAN JOURNAL OF THEOLOGY & PHILOSOPHY (US/0194-3448) [05395184] **4340**

●AMERICAN JOURNAL OF THERAPEUTICS (UK/1075-2765) **3549**

AMERICAN JOURNAL OF TRIAL ADVOCACY, THE (US/0160-0281) [03486243] **2932**

AMERICAN JOURNAL OF TROPICAL MEDICINE AND HYGIENE, THE (US/0002-9637) [01724826] **3985**

AMERICAN JOURNAL OF VETERINARY RESEARCH (US/0002-9645) [01480202] **5502**

●AMERICAN JOURNAL ON ADDICTIONS, THE (US/1055-0496) [23065277] 3920, **1340**

AMERICAN JOURNALISM (US/0882-1127) [11008462] **2917**

●AMERICAN JOURNALISM REVIEW (US/1067-8654) [27363765] **2917**

AMERICAN JURISPRUDENCE PLEADING AND PRACTICE FORMS ANNOTATED (US) [01649747] **3088**

AMERICAN KENNEL CLUB AWARDS (US/0888-627X) [13682170] **4285**

AMERICAN KENNEL CLUB STUD BOOK REGISTER (US/0162-2013) [03679255] 5502, **4285**

AMERICAN KITE (US/1045-3598) [20080634] **4882**

AMERICAN LABOR BEACON (US/0744-6454) [08467260] **1643**

AMERICAN LABOR (WASHINGTON, D.C.) **CEASED.** (US/0889-0609) [07483318] **1643**

AMERICAN LABORATORY (FAIRFIELD) (US/0044-7749) [01051418] 441, **960**

AMERICAN LANGUAGE JOURNAL, THE (US/0734-7545) [08799083] **3263**

AMERICAN LAUNDRY DIGEST (US/0002-9718) [01772779] **5347**

AMERICAN LAW INSTITUTE **See** RESTATEMENT OF THE LAW SECOND: TRUSTS / SUBMITTED TO THE MEMBERS BY THE COUNCIL **3039**

AMERICAN LAW INSTITUTE **See** ALI REPORTER, THE **2931**

AMERICAN LAW INSTITUTE **See** PROCEEDINGS / AMERICAN LAW INSTITUTE **3031**

AMERICAN LAW INSTITUTE-AMERICAN BAR ASSOCIATION COMMITTEE ON CONTINUING PROFESSIONAL EDUCATION See ALI-ABA CLE REVIEW **1808**

AMERICAN LAW INSTITUTE-AMERICAN BAR ASSOCIATION COMMITTEE ON CONTINUING PROFESSIONAL EDUCATION **See** ANNUAL REPORTS **2935**

AMERICAN LAW INSTITUTE. COUNCIL. EXECUTIVE COMMITTEE **See** MINUTES OF THE MEETING OF THE EXECUTIVE COMMITTEE OF THE COUNCIL - AMERICAN LAW INSTITUTE **695**

AMERICAN LAW OF MINING (US) [01715488] 2133, **2932**

AMERICAN LAW REPORTS. ALR 4TH: CASES AND ANNOTATIONS **See** AMERICAN LAW REPORTS. ALR 5TH, ANNOTATIONS AND CASES **2932**

●AMERICAN LAW REPORTS. ALR 5TH, ANNOTATIONS AND CASES (US/1062-2446) [25142281] **2932**

AMERICAN

AMERICAN LAW REPORTS. ALR FEDERAL: CASES AND ANNOTATIONS (US) [01480246] **2932**

AMERICAN LAW REVIEW (DALLAS, TEX.), THE (US/8750-8214) [11696054] **2932**

AMERICAN LAWN BOWLS ASSOCIATION *See* A.L.B.A. BOWLS **4881**

AMERICAN LAWYER GUIDE TO LEADING LAW FIRMS, THE *SUSPENDED.* (US/8755-4461) [09341679] **2932**

AMERICAN LAWYER MANAGEMENT SERVICE, THE (US) **2932**

AMERICAN LAWYER (NEW YORK. 1979), THE (US/0162-3397) [04153838] **2933**

AMERICAN LEAGUE REDBOOK (US/0736-0444) [07830565] **4882**

AMERICAN LEATHER CHEMISTS ASSOCIATION *See* JOURNAL OF THE AMERICAN LEATHER CHEMISTS ASSOCIATION, THE **3184**

AMERICAN LEGION *See* AMERICAN LEGION FIRING LINE, THE **4539**

AMERICAN LEGION. AUXILIARY *See* NATIONAL NEWS - AMERICAN LEGION AUXILIARY **5234**

AMERICAN LEGION FIRING LINE, THE (US) [08656181] **4539**

AMERICAN LEGION. NATIONAL CONVENTION *See* PROCEEDINGS OF ... NATIONAL CONVENTION OF THE AMERICAN LEGION **4054**

AMERICAN LEGION, THE (US/0886-1234) [09009612] **4034**

AMERICAN LETTERS & COMMENTARY (US/1049-7153) [20549200] **3360**

AMERICAN LIBRARIES (CHICAGO, ILL.) (US/0002-9769) [00854299] **3189**

AMERICAN LIBRARY ASSOCIATION *See* ALA HANDBOOK OF ORGANIZATION **3188**

AMERICAN LIBRARY ASSOCIATION *See* ALA HANDBOOK OF ORGANIZATION AND MEMBERSHIP DIRECTORY **3188**

AMERICAN LIBRARY ASSOCIATION *See* COGNOTES **3202**

AMERICAN LIBRARY ASSOCIATION. OFFICE FOR INTELLECTUAL FREEDOM *See* MEMORANDUM - AMERICAN LIBRARY ASSOCIATION. OFFICE FOR INTELLECTUAL FREEDOM **1306**

AMERICAN LIBRARY ASSOCIATION. REFERENCE AND ADULT SERVICES DIVISION *See* RASD UPDATE **3244**

AMERICAN LIBRARY ASSOCIATION. YOUNG ADULT SERVICES DIVISION *See* BEST BOOKS FOR YOUNG ADULTS **4824**

AMERICAN LIBRARY DIRECTORY (US/0065-910X) [02441557] **3257**

AMERICAN LIBRARY LAWS *CEASED.* (US) [02253662] **3189**

AMERICAN LIBRARY TRUSTEE ASSOCIATION *See* ALTA NEWSLETTER **3189**

AMERICAN LISZT SOCIETY *See* JOURNAL OF THE AMERICAN LISZT SOCIETY **4126**

●AMERICAN LISZT SOCIETY STUDIES SERIES (US/1062-4031) [25099466] **4099**

AMERICAN LITERARY HISTORY (US/0896-7148) [17275100] **3360**

AMERICAN LITERARY REALISM, 1870-1910 (US/0002-9823) [01480318] **3337**

AMERICAN LITERARY REVIEW (US/1051-5062) [21984784] **3360**

AMERICAN LITERARY SCHOLARSHIP (US/0065-9142) [01480319] **3360**

AMERICAN LITERATURE (US/0002-9831) [01480320] **3360**

AMERICAN LITERATURE REVIEW (US/0899-1448) [18005732] **3360**

●AMERICAN LIVESTOCK BREEDS CONSERVANCY NEWS (US) [28948344] **58**

AMERICAN LOBBYISTS DIRECTORY (US/1045-3679) [20113462] **4463**

AMERICAN LOGISTICS ASSOCIATION *See* ALA ... WORLDWIDE DIRECTORY & FACT BOOK **4034**

AMERICAN LUNG ASSOCIATION *See* BULLETIN - AMERICAN LUNG ASSOCIATION **3948**

AMERICAN LUTHERIE (US/1041-7176) [17941073] **4099**

AMERICAN MACHINIST (1988) (US/1041-7958) [18392315] 3997, **2109**

AMERICAN MACHINIST MANUFACTURING COST ESTIMATING GUIDE (US/0731-5368) [08201479] 3997, **3475**

AMERICAN MAGAZINE AND HISTORICAL CHRONICLE, THE *SUSPENDED.* (US/0882-5351) [11884212] **2719**

AMERICAN MALACOLOGICAL BULLETIN (US/0740-2783) [09753438] **5574**

AMERICAN MANAGEMENT ASSOCIATION *See* AMA SURVEY REPORT, AN **859**

AMERICAN MANAGEMENT ASSOCIATION. EXECUTIVE COMPENSATION SERVICE *See* HOSPITAL AND HEALTH CARE REPORT **3783**

AMERICAN MANAGEMENT ASSOCIATION. EXECUTIVE COMPENSATION SERVICE *See* REPORTS ON INTERNATIONAL COMPENSATION : BRAZIL **1707**

AMERICAN MANAGEMENT ASSOCIATION. EXECUTIVE COMPENSATION SERVICE *See* REPORTS ON INTERNATIONAL COMPENSATION : ARGENTINA **1707**

AMERICAN MANAGEMENT ASSOCIATION. EXECUTIVE COMPENSATION SERVICE *See* REPORT ON EXECUTIVE PREREQUISITES **1707**

●AMERICAN MANUFACTURERS DIRECTORY (US/1061-219X) [25215424] **3475**

AMERICAN MARINE ENGINEER *See* MARINE OFFICER **4049**

AMERICAN MARINE ENGINEER, THE (US/0002-9866) [02444709] **4174**

AMERICAN MARINE REGISTER (US/0091-5491) [01787614] **5447**

AMERICAN MARITIME LIBRARY, THE (US/0065-9207) [03304507] **4174**

AMERICAN MARKETING ASSOCIATION *See* ... MARKETING NEWS INTERNATIONAL DIRECTORY OF THE AMERICAN MARKETING ASSOCIATION AND MARKETING SERVICES GUIDE, THE **931**

AMERICAN MARKETING ASSOCIATION *See* AMERICAN MARKETING ASSOCIATION INTERNATIONAL MEMBERSHIP DIRECTORY AND MARKETING SERVICES GUIDE **921**

AMERICAN MARKETING ASSOCIATION *See* ... MARKETING NEWS INTERNATIONAL DIRECTORY OF THE AMERICAN MARKETING ASSOCIATION AND THE MARKETING YELLOW PAGES, THE **931**

AMERICAN MARKETING ASSOCIATION INTERNATIONAL MEMBERSHIP DIRECTORY AND MARKETING SERVICES GUIDE (US) [16386669] **921**

AMERICAN MARKETING ASSOCIATION. MARKETING NEWS INTERNATIONAL DIRECTORY OF THE AMERICAN MARKETING ASSOCIATION AND MARKETING SERVICES GUIDE *See* ... MARKETING NEWS INTERNATIONAL DIRECTORY OF THE AMERICAN MARKETING ASSOCIATION AND THE MARKETING YELLOW PAGES, THE **931**

AMERICAN MARKETPLACE (US/0276-2900) [13990906] **1293**

AMERICAN MARKSMAN *See* NRA TOURNAMENT NEWS **4908**

AMERICAN MARKSMAN, THE (US/0199-6770) [06078691] **4883**

AMERICAN MATHEMATICAL MONTHLY, THE (US/0002-9890) [01480361] **3492**

AMERICAN MATHEMATICAL SOCIETY *See* TRANSACTIONS OF THE AMERICAN MATHEMATICAL SOCIETY **3539**

AMERICAN MATHEMATICAL SOCIETY *See* TRANSLATIONS - AMERICAN MATHEMATICAL SOCIETY **3539**

AMERICAN MATHEMATICAL SOCIETY *See* ABSTRACTS OF PAPERS PRESENTED TO THE AMERICAN MATHEMATICAL SOCIETY **3490**

AMERICAN MATHEMATICAL SOCIETY *See* PROCEEDINGS OF THE AMERICAN MATHEMATICAL SOCIETY **3528**

AMERICAN MATHEMATICAL SOCIETY *See* MEMOIRS OF THE AMERICAN MATHEMATICAL SOCIETY **3522**

AMERICAN MATHEMATICAL SOCIETY *See* NOTICES OF THE AMERICAN MATHEMATICAL SOCIETY **3525**

AMERICAN MCD *See* AMERICAN MOTOR CARRIER DIRECTORY (NORTH AMERICAN EDITION) **5375**

AMERICAN MCD. NEW ENGLAND EDITION (US/0146-0811) [02857982] **5375**

AMERICAN MCD. PACIFIC STATES EDITION (US/0146-082X) [02858103] **5375**

AMERICAN MEDICAL ASSOCIATION *See* DIRECTORY OF OFFICIALS AND STAFF / AMERICAN MEDICAL ASSOCIATION **1925**

AMERICAN MEDICAL DIRECTORY *See* DIRECTORY OF PHYSICIANS IN THE UNITED STATES / AMERICAN MEDICAL ASSOCIATION **1925**

AMERICAN MEDICAL DIRECTORY UPDATE / AMERICAN MEDICAL ASSOCIATION (US) [07717807] **3913**

AMERICAN MEDICAL NEWS (US/0001-1843) [01480406] **3549**

AMERICAN MEDICAL WOMEN'S ASSOCIATION *See* MEMBERSHIP DIRECTORY **3915**

AMERICAN MEDICAL WOMEN'S ASSOCIATION *See* JOURNAL OF THE AMERICAN MEDICAL WOMEN'S ASSOCIATION (1972) **3597**

AMERICAN MEDICAL WRITERS ASSOCIATION *See* MEMBERSHIP DIRECTORY / AMERICAN MEDICAL WRITERS ASSOCIATION **5233**

AMERICAN MEDICAL WRITERS ASSOCIATION *See* AMWA FREELANCE DIRECTORY, THE **2917**

AMERICAN MEDICAL WRITERS ASSOCIATION *See* FREELANCE DIRECTORY **2920**

AMERICAN MEDICAL WRITERS ASSOCIATION AMWA JOURNAL (US) [15239050] 2917, **3549**

AMERICAN MEN & WOMEN OF SCIENCE (US/0000-1287) [19407934] **5173**

AMERICAN MEN AND WOMEN OF SCIENCE: BIOLOGY (US/0146-0048) [03280237] **5173**

AMERICAN MEN AND WOMEN OF SCIENCE: CHEMISTRY (US/0146-0056) [03281702] **5173**

AMERICAN MEN AND WOMEN OF SCIENCE: CONSULTANTS (US/0146-0064) [03355269] **5173**

AMERICAN MEN AND WOMEN OF SCIENCE: ECONOMICS (US/0094-5315) [01794731] **5173**

AMERICAN MEN AND WOMEN OF SCIENCE: MEDICAL AND HEALTH SCIENCES (US/0145-9996) [03263454] **5173**

AMERICAN MEN AND WOMEN OF SCIENCE: PHYSICS, ASTRONOMY, MATHEMATICS, STATISTICS, AND COMPUTER SCIENCE (US/0146-003X) [03280223] **5173**

AMERICAN MENSA LIMITED *See* MEMBERSHIP LIST - AMERICAN MENSA LIMITED **5233**

AMERICAN MENSA LIMITED *See* AMERICAN MENSA REGISTER **5228**

AMERICAN MENSA REGISTER (US/0738-5218) [09603054] **5228**

AMERICAN MERCURY (1951), THE (US/0002-998X) [04712467] **2527**

AMERICAN METAL MARKET (US) [18501439] **3997**

AMERICAN METEOROLOGICAL SOCIETY *See* BULLETIN OF THE AMERICAN METEOROLOGICAL SOCIETY **1421**

AMERICAN METEOROLOGICAL SOCIETY *See* CURRICULA IN THE ATMOSPHERIC AND OCEANOGRAPHIC SCIENCES **1424**

AMERICAN METEOROLOGICAL SOCIETY *See* AMS NEWSLETTER (BOSTON, MASS.) **1419**

AMERICAN METRIC JOURNAL *CEASED.* (US/0094-3096) [01794182] **4029**

AMERICAN MIDDLE SCHOOL EDUCATION *SUSPENDED.* (US/0889-552X) [07475359] **1860**

AMERICAN MIDLAND NATURALIST, THE (US/0003-0031) [05731039] 441, **4161**

AMERICAN MILITARY INSTITUTE *See* AMERICAN MILITARY INSTITUTE DIRECTORY OF MEMBERS **4034**

AMERICAN MILITARY INSTITUTE DIRECTORY OF MEMBERS (US/0272-4480) [06824608] **4034**

AMERICAN MILKING SHORTHORN SOCIETY *See* MILKING SHORTHORN YEAR BOOK **197**

AMERICAN MINERALOGIST, THE (US/0003-004X) [01480430] **1437**

AMERICAN MINES HANDBOOK (CN/0840-8610) [19501382] **2133**

AMERICAN MINING CONGRESS *See* AMERICAN MINING CONGRESS LEGISLATIVE BULLETIN **2133**

AMERICAN MINING CONGRESS LEGISLATIVE BULLETIN (US/0276-4547) [02444716] **2133**

●AMERICAN MODELER (RALEIGH, N.C.) (US/1061-9399) [25489400] **2771**

AMERICAN MOSQUITO CONTROL ASSOCIATION *See* AMCA NEWSLETTER **2160**

AMERICAN MOTOR CARRIER (US/0003-0066) [03960079] 4625, **5375**

AMERICAN MOTOR CARRIER DIRECTORY (NORTH AMERICAN EDITION) (US/0897-0807) [07430491] **5375**

AMERICAN MOTORCYCLIST (US/0277-9358) [07658474] **4080**

AMERICAN MOVER (US/0886-9707) [13058950] **638**

AMERICAN MUSEUM NOVITATES (US/0003-0082) [01480459] 4226, **5574**

AMERICAN

AMERICAN MUSIC (CHAMPAIGN, ILL.) (US/0734-4392) [08741667] **4099**

● AMERICAN MUSIC RESEARCH CENTER JOURNAL, THE (US/1058-3572) [24307564] **4099**

AMERICAN MUSIC TEACHER, THE (US/0003-0112) [01480467] **4099**

AMERICAN MUSICAL INSTRUMENT SOCIETY *See* MEMBERSHIP DIRECTORY **4130**

AMERICAN MUSICAL INSTRUMENT SOCIETY *See* JOURNAL OF THE AMERICAN MUSICAL INSTRUMENT SOCIETY **4126**

AMERICAN MUSICAL INSTRUMENT SOCIETY *See* NEWSLETTER - AMERICAN MUSICAL INSTRUMENT SOCIETY **4140**

AMERICAN MUSICOLOGICAL SOCIETY *See* DIRECTORY / AMERICAN MUSICOLOGICAL SOCIETY **4114**

AMERICAN MUSICOLOGICAL SOCIETY *See* STUDIES AND DOCUMENTS **4155**

AMERICAN MUSICOLOGICAL SOCIETY *See* JOURNAL OF THE AMERICAN MUSICOLOGICAL SOCIETY **4126**

AMERICAN MUSICOLOGICAL SOCIETY. MEETING *See* ABSTRACTS OF PAPERS READ AT THE ... ANNUAL MEETING OF THE AMERICAN MUSICOLOGICAL SOCIETY **4098**

AMERICAN NATIONAL METRIC COUNCIL *See* REPORT TO THE NATION ON THE MANAGEMENT OF METRIC IMPLEMENTATION. A **4032**

AMERICAN NATIONAL STANDARDS CATALOG (US/1075-6809) [27910265] **4029**

AMERICAN NATIONAL STANDARDS FOR INFORMATION SCIENCES (US/8756-0860) [11482199] **3189**

AMERICAN NATIONAL STANDARDS INSTITUTE *See* CATALOG OF AMERICAN NATIONAL STANDARDS **4030**

AMERICAN NATIONAL STANDARDS INSTITUTE *See* AMERICAN NATIONAL STANDARDS FOR INFORMATION SCIENCES **3189**

AMERICAN NATIONAL STANDARDS INSTITUTE *See* ANSI REPORTER **4029**

AMERICAN NATIONAL STANDARDS INSTITUTE. NATIONAL ELECTRICAL SAFETY CODE COMMITTEE *See* INTERIM COLLECTION OF THE NATIONAL ELECTRICAL SAFETY CODE INTERPRETATIONS / NATIONAL ELECTRICAL SAFETY CODE COMMITTEE, ANSI C2 **2066**

AMERICAN NATIVE PRESS (US/0882-2522) [10204716] **5631**

AMERICAN NATURALIST, THE (US/0003-0147) [01480477] **4161**

AMERICAN NEAR EAST REFUGEE AID *See* ANERA NEWSLETTER **1918**

AMERICAN NEPTUNE, THE (US/0003-0155) [01480480] **4174**

AMERICAN NEWSPAPER PUBLISHERS ASSOCIATION *See* MEMORANDUM - AMERICAN NEWSPAPER PUBLISHERS ASSOCIATION **4816**

AMERICAN NURSE, THE (US/0098-1486) [01386575] **3850**

AMERICAN NURSERYMAN (US/0003-0198) [05695980] **2408**

AMERICAN NURSES ASSOCIATION *See* CAPITAL UPDATE **3853**

AMERICAN NURSES' ASSOCIATION *See* DIRECTORY OF CERTIFIED NURSES **3855**

AMERICAN NURSES' ASSOCIATION *See* CLINICAL AND SCIENTIFIC SESSIONS **3853**

AMERICAN NURSES' ASSOCIATION *See* HOUSE OF DELEGATES REPORTS (1966) **3856**

AMERICAN NURSES' ASSOCIATION. CONVENTION *See* SUMMARY OF PROCEEDINGS / AMERICAN NURSES' ASSOCIATION ... CONVENTION **3870**

AMERICAN NURSES' ASSOCIATION. COUNCIL OF SPECIALISTS IN PSYCHIATRIC AND MENTAL HEALTH NURSING *See* DIRECTORY - COUNCIL OF SPECIALISTS IN PSYCHIATRIC AND MENTAL HEALTH NURSING **3855**

AMERICAN OFFICE DEALER (US/1046-6096) [20479702] **4210**

AMERICAN OIL & GAS REPORTER, THE (US/0145-9198) [02801059] **4249**

AMERICAN OLD TIME FIDDLERS' NEWS (US/0003-0228) [01788481] **4099**

AMERICAN OPHTHALMOLOGICAL SOCIETY *See* TRANSACTIONS OF THE AMERICAN OPHTHALMOLOGICAL SOCIETY ANNUAL MEETING **3879**

● AMERICAN OPTICIAN (CN) [26501533] **4214**

AMERICAN OPTOMETRIC ASSOCIATION *See* JOURNAL OF THE AMERICAN OPTOMETRIC ASSOCIATION **4216**

AMERICAN OPTOMETRIC ASSOCIATION *See* DIRECTORY OF THE AMERICAN OPTOMETRIC ASSOCIATION **4215**

AMERICAN OPTOMETRIC ASSOCIATION NEWS (US/0094-9620) [01075145] **4215**

AMERICAN ORCHID SOCIETY *See* AMERICAN ORCHID SOCIETY BULLETIN **2408**

AMERICAN ORCHID SOCIETY *See* BULLETIN - AMERICAN ORCHID SOCIETY **2411**

AMERICAN ORCHID SOCIETY *See* AWARDS QUARTERLY **501**

AMERICAN ORCHID SOCIETY BULLETIN (US/0003-0252) [01480503] **2408**

AMERICAN ORGANIST (1979), THE (US/0164-3150) [04598878] **4099**

AMERICAN ORIENTAL SERIES, ESSAY (US/0065-9541) [01480508] **2645**

AMERICAN ORIENTAL SOCIETY *See* JOURNAL OF THE AMERICAN ORIENTAL SOCIETY **3292**

AMERICAN ORIENTAL SOCIETY *See* AMERICAN ORIENTAL SERIES, ESSAY **2645**

AMERICAN ORTHODONTIC SOCIETY NEWSLETTER *See* WIRELINE (DALLAS, TEX.) **1337**

AMERICAN ORTHOPTIC JOURNAL (US/0065-955X) [01480514] **3871**

AMERICAN OSTEOPATHIC ASSOCIATION *See* DO, THE **3573**

AMERICAN OTOLOGICAL SOCIETY *See* TRANSACTIONS OF THE AMERICAN OTOLOGICAL SOCIETY **3891**

AMERICAN OVERSEAS BOOK COMPANY *See* TITLE MASTER **426**

AMERICAN/OVERSEAS INVESTOR, THE (US/1057-0020) [23906427] **890**

AMERICAN OXONIAN, THE (US/0003-0295) [01480518] **1808**

AMERICAN PAINT & COATINGS JOURNAL (US/0098-5430) [02240363] **4222**

AMERICAN PAINT & COATINGS JOURNAL. CONVENTION DAILY (US/0097-4749) [01798124] **4222**

AMERICAN PAINTING CONTRACTOR (US/0003-0325) [01480520] **4222**

AMERICAN PAPER INSTITUTE. PRINTING-WRITING PAPER DIVISION *See* ANNUAL STATISTICAL SUMMARY **4240**

AMERICAN PAPER INSTITUTE. PULP, FIBER AND RAW MATERIALS GROUP *See* WOOD PULP AND FIBER STATISTICS **4240**

AMERICAN PAPERMAKER (1991) (US/1056-4772) [23722397] **4232**

AMERICAN PEANUT RESEARCH AND EDUCATION SOCIETY *See* PROCEEDINGS OF AMERICAN PEANUT RESEARCH AND EDUCATION SOCIETY, INC **183**

AMERICAN PEN, THE (US/0003-0376) [01480530] **5228**, **3360**

AMERICAN PENSTEMON SOCIETY *See* BULLETIN OF THE AMERICAN PENSTEMON SOCIETY **2411**

AMERICAN PEONY SOCIETY *See* AMERICAN PEONY SOCIETY BULLETIN, THE **2408**

AMERICAN PEONY SOCIETY BULLETIN, THE (US) [08252461] **2408**

AMERICAN PERIODICALS : A JOURNAL OF HISTORY, CRITICISM, AND BIBLIOGRAPHY (US/1054-7479) [22964230] **4812**

AMERICAN PETROLEUM INSTITUTE *See* API INDEXES : INDEX TERM USE STATISTICS **4250**

AMERICAN PETROLEUM INSTITUTE. CENTRAL ABSTRACTING AND INDEXING SERVICE *See* THESAURUS - AMERICAN PETROLEUM INSTITUTE **3253**

AMERICAN PETROLEUM INSTITUTE. PRODUCTION DEPARTMENT *See* ANNUAL MEETING PAPERS - AMERICAN PETROLEUM INSTITUTE. PRODUCTION DEPT **4249**

AMERICAN PETROLEUM INSTITUTE. REFINING DEPT *See* PROCEEDINGS - REFINING DEPARTMENT **4275**

AMERICAN PETROLEUM INSTITUTE. STATISTICS DEPT *See* MONTHLY STATISTICAL REPORT - AMERICAN PETROLEUM INSTITUTE. STATISTICS DEPT **4284**

AMERICAN PHARMACEUTICAL ASSOCIATION *See* EVALUATIONS OF DRUG INTERACTIONS **4303**

AMERICAN PHARMACY (US/0160-3450) [03665041] **4290**

AMERICAN PHARMACY TECHNICIAN JOURNAL, THE *CEASED*. (US/1060-5576) [25035676] **4290**

AMERICAN PHILATELIST, THE (US/0003-0473) [01480549] **2784**

AMERICAN PHILOLOGICAL ASSOCIATION *See* TRANSACTIONS OF THE AMERICAN PHILOLOGICAL ASSOCIATION (1974) **3329**

AMERICAN PHILOLOGICAL ASSOCIATION *See* DIRECTORY OF MEMBERS - AMERICAN PHILOLOGICAL ASSOCIATION **3277**

AMERICAN PHILOSOPHICAL ASSOCIATION *See* PROCEEDINGS AND ADDRESSES OF THE AMERICAN PHILOSOPHICAL ASSOCIATION **4357**

AMERICAN PHILOSOPHICAL QUARTERLY (OXFORD) (UK/0003-0481) [01591067] **4340**

AMERICAN PHILOSOPHICAL SOCIETY *See* MEMOIRS OF THE AMERICAN PHILOSOPHICAL SOCIETY HELD AT PHILADELPHIA FOR PROMOTING USEFUL KNOWLEDGE **4352**

AMERICAN PHILOSOPHICAL SOCIETY *See* YEAR BOOK - THE AMERICAN PHILOSOPHICAL SOCIETY **4365**

AMERICAN PHONOGRAPH JOURNAL (US/0162-0312) [04082693] **5315**

AMERICAN PHOTO (US/1046-8986) [20553467] **4366**

AMERICAN PHOTOGRAPHY (US) **4366**

AMERICAN PHOTOGRAPHY SHOWCASE (US/0278-8314) [07936161] **4366**

AMERICAN PHYSICAL SOCIETY *See* BULLETIN OF THE AMERICAN PHYSICAL SOCIETY **4399**

AMERICAN PHYSICAL SOCIETY *See* APSNEWS **4398**

AMERICAN PHYSICAL SOCIETY. BULLETIN OF THE AMERICAN PHYSICAL SOCIETY *See* APSNEWS **4398**

AMERICAN PHYSICAL THERAPY ASSOCIATION (1921-) *See* PROGRESS REPORT - AMERICAN PHYSICAL THERAPY ASSOCIATION **4382**

AMERICAN PIGEON JOURNAL (US/0003-0511) [01480571] **5574**

AMERICAN PLANNING ASSOCIATION *See* JOURNAL OF THE AMERICAN PLANNING ASSOCIATION **2826**

AMERICAN PLANNING ASSOCIATION. TEXAS CHAPTER *See* NEWSLETTER - AMERICAN PLANNING ASSOCIATION, TEXAS CHAPTER **2829**

AMERICAN PLYWOOD ASSOCIATION *See* MANAGEMENT REPORT **2402**

AMERICAN PODIATRIC MEDICAL ASSOCIATION *See* DESK REFERENCE **3917**

AMERICAN PODIATRY ASSOCIATION *See* BIOGRAPHICAL DIRECTORY OF THE AMERICAN PODIATRY ASSOCIATION **3655**

AMERICAN POETRY REVIEW, THE (US/0360-3709) [01674393] **3337**, **3460**

AMERICAN POETRY REPORT, THE (US/8755-562X) [09947499] **4463**

AMERICAN POLITICAL SCIENCE ASSOCIATION *See* APSA DEPARTMENTAL SERVICES PROGRAM, SURVEY OF DEPARTMENTS **4464**

AMERICAN POLITICAL SCIENCE ASSOCIATION *See* APSA DIRECTORY OF MEMBERS - AMERICAN POLITICAL SCIENCE ASSOCIATION **4464**

AMERICAN POLITICAL SCIENCE ASSOCIATION *See* BIOGRAPHICAL DIRECTORY / AMERICAN POLITICAL SCIENCE ASSOCIATION **430**

AMERICAN POLITICAL SCIENCE ASSOCIATION *See* APSA DIRECTORY OF DEPARTMENT CHAIRPERSONS **4464**

AMERICAN POLITICAL SCIENCE ASSOCIATION *See* DIRECTORY OF MEMBERS / AMERICAN POLITICAL SCIENCE ASSOCIATION **4472**

AMERICAN POLITICAL SCIENCE REVIEW, THE (US/0003-0554) [01480588] **4463**

AMERICAN POLITICS QUARTERLY (US/0044-7803) [01784726] **4463**

AMERICAN POLITICS (WASHINGTON, D.C. : 1983) (US/0741-1111) [10085634] **4463**

AMERICAN POOL PLAYER (US/0732-8176) [08436578] **4883**

AMERICAN POPULAR CULTURE (US/0193-6859) [05251719] **2527**, **5268**

AMERICAN PORTUGUESE SOCIETY *See* JOURNAL OF THE AMERICAN PORTUGUESE SOCIETY, THE **2695**

AMERICAN POSTAL WORKER, THE (US/0044-7811) [02257389] **1144**, **1643**

AMERICAN POSTCARD JOURNAL (US/0145-3920) [02731111] **1144**

AMERICAN POTATO JOURNAL (US/0003-0589) [07633741] **162**

AMERICAN POWDER METALLURGY INSTITUTE. MEMBERSHIP DIRECTORY AND YEARBOOK *See* WHO'S WHO IN P/M **437**

AMERICAN POWER BOAT ASSOCIATION *See* RULES FOR OUTBOARD PERFORMANCE, CRAFT AND DRAG RACING **595**

Alphabetical Title Index — AMERICAN

AMERICAN POWER BOAT ASSOCIATION *See* AMERICAN POWER BOAT ASSOCIATION ROSTER **591**

AMERICAN POWER BOAT ASSOCIATION *See* RULES FOR STOCK OUTBOARD, PRO OUTBOARD, MODIFIED OUTBOARD **595**

AMERICAN POWER BOAT ASSOCIATION *See* RULES FOR INBOARD, INBOARD ENDURANCE, UNLIMITED RACING **595**

AMERICAN POWER BOAT ASSOCIATION ROSTER (US/0278-7040) [07860007] **591**

AMERICAN PRACTICE ADVISOR (US) **2596**

AMERICAN PREMIERE (US/0279-0041) [07420478] 638, **4063**

AMERICAN PRESBYTERIANS (US/0886-5159) [12900413] **5055**

AMERICAN PRESERVATION (US/0148-3668) [03450866] **2719**

AMERICAN PRINTER (1982) (US/0744-6616) [08162333] **4563**

AMERICAN PRINTMAKERS (US/0094-7490) [01796813] **4563**

AMERICAN PROFESSIONAL CONSTRUCTOR, THE (US/0146-7557) [03025388] **2018**

AMERICAN PROGRAMMER (US/1048-5600) [17747843] **1284**

AMERICAN PSYCHIATRIC ASSOCIATION *See* BIOGRAPHICAL DIRECTORY OF THE FELLOWS & MEMBERS OF THE AMERICAN PSYCHIATRIC ASSOCIATION **3655**

AMERICAN PSYCHIATRIC ASSOCIATION *See* BIOGRAPHICAL DIRECTORY - AMERICAN PSYCHIATRIC ASSOCIATION **430**

AMERICAN PSYCHOANALYST, THE (US/1052-7958) [22843123] **4573**

AMERICAN PSYCHOANALYTIC ASSOCIATION *See* JOURNAL OF THE AMERICAN PSYCHOANALYTIC ASSOCIATION. MONOGRAPH SERIES **4601**

AMERICAN PSYCHOANALYTIC ASSOCIATION *See* JOURNAL OF THE AMERICAN PSYCHOANALYTIC ASSOCIATION **4601**

AMERICAN PSYCHOLOGICAL ASSOCIATION *See* APA MEMBERSHIP REGISTER **4574**

AMERICAN PSYCHOLOGICAL ASSOCIATION *See* APA MONITOR **4574**

AMERICAN PSYCHOLOGICAL ASSOCIATION *See* DIRECTORY OF THE AMERICAN PSYCHOLOGICAL ASSOCIATION (1978) **1925**

AMERICAN PSYCHOLOGICAL SOCIETY *See* MEMBERSHIP DIRECTORY OF THE AMERICAN PSYCHOLOGICAL SOCIETY **4603**

AMERICAN PSYCHOLOGIST, THE (US/0003-066X) [01435230] **4573**

AMERICAN PUBLIC HEALTH ASSOCIATION *See* BIOGRAPHICAL DIRECTORY OF THE AMERICAN PUBLIC HEALTH ASSOCIATION **4809**

AMERICAN PUBLIC HEALTH ASSOCIATION *See* STANDARD METHODS FOR THE EXAMINATION OF DAIRY PRODUCTS (1967) **4803**

AMERICAN PUBLIC OPINION DATA (US/0885-6893) [11416644] **5238**

AMERICAN PUBLIC OPINION INDEX (US/0740-8978) [10012333] **5238**

AMERICAN PUBLIC TRANSIT ASSOCIATION. STATISTICAL DEPT *See* TRANSIT OPERATING REPORT **5395**

AMERICAN PUBLIC WAREHOUSE REGISTER (US) **1597**

AMERICAN PUBLIC WORKS ASSOCIATION *See* SPECIAL REPORT - AMERICAN PUBLIC WORKS ASSOCIATION **4686**

AMERICAN PUBLIC WORKS ASSOCIATION *See* DIRECTORY - AMERICAN PUBLIC WORKS ASSOCIATION **4760**

AMERICAN PUBLIC WORKS ASSOCIATION *See* REPORTER - AMERICAN PUBLIC WORKS ASSOCIATION **4682**

AMERICAN PURPOSE (US/0891-446X) [14780545] **4515**

AMERICAN QUARTERLY (US/0003-0678) [01480637] **2719**

AMERICAN QUILTER (US/8756-6591) [11617403] **5182**

AMERICAN RABBI (CANOGA PARK, LOS ANGELES, CALIF.), THE (US/0164-3916) [04703435] **5045**

●AMERICAN RACING CLASSICS (US/1069-1693) [27943045] **4883**

AMERICAN RACING MANUAL, THE (US) [04101803] **2796**

AMERICAN RACING PIGEON NEWS, THE (US/0003-0686) [01604691] 5502, 58

AMERICAN RACING PIGEON NEWS, THE (US/0003-0686) [08251768] 5614, 225

AMERICAN RADIO RELAY LEAGUE *See* ARRL REPEATER DIRECTORY **1126**

AMERICAN RADIO REPORT (US/0738-8675) [03811705] **1126**

AMERICAN RAG, THE **SUSPENDED.** (US/0163-8211) [04479919] **3360**

AMERICAN RAILS (US/8750-5762) [11540795] **5429**

AMERICAN RAILWAY BRIDGE AND BUILDING ASSOCIATION. CONVENTION *See* PROCEEDINGS OF THE ... ANNUAL CONVENTION OF THE AMERICAN RAILWAY BRIDGE AND BUILDING ASSOCIATION **2029**

AMERICAN RAILWAY ENGINEERING ASSOCIATION *See* BULLETIN - AMERICAN RAILWAY ENGINEERING ASSOCIATION **5430**

AMERICAN RAILWAY ENGINEERING ASSOCIATION *See* PROCEEDINGS OF THE AMERICAN RAILWAY ENGINEERING ASSOCIATION **5434**

AMERICAN RAILWAY ENGINEERING ASSOCIATION *See* MANUAL OF THE AMERICAN RAILWAY ENGINEERING ASSOCIATION **5432**

AMERICAN RAILWAY ENGINEERING ASSOCIATION *See* PROCEEDINGS OF THE ANNUAL CONVENTION - AMERICAN RAILWAY ENGINEERING ASSOCIATION **5434**

AMERICAN RATIONALIST, THE (US/0003-0708) [03966585] **4340**

AMERICAN READING FORUM. ANNUAL CONFERENCE *See* YEARBOOK OF THE AMERICAN READING FORUM **3334**

AMERICAN RECORD GUIDE (US/0003-0716) [03437879] 4099, **5315**

AMERICAN RECORDER SOCIETY *See* NEWSLETTER. AMERICAN RECORDER SOCIETY **4140**

AMERICAN RECORDER, THE (US/0003-0724) [01480655] 383, **4099**

AMERICAN RECOVERY ASSOCIATION *See* DIRECTORY - AMERICAN RECOVERY ASSOCIATION, INC **666**

AMERICAN RECYCLING MARKET ... DIRECTORY/REFERENCE MANUAL : ARM (US) [22943940] **2224**

AMERICAN RED ANGUS (US/0886-4357) [04282463] **205**

AMERICAN REFERENCE BOOKS ANNUAL (US/0065-9959) [01028287] **1923**

AMERICAN REGISTER OF PRINTING AND GRAPHIC ARTS SERVICES, THE **CEASED.** (US/0276-5519) [07363181] 376, **4563**

AMERICAN REHABILITATION (US/0362-4048) [02087085] **5271**

AMERICAN RESEARCH CENTER IN EGYPT *See* NEWSLETTER - AMERICAN RESEARCH CENTER IN EGYPT **276**

AMERICAN RESEARCH CENTER IN EGYPT *See* JOURNAL OF THE AMERICAN RESEARCH CENTER IN EGYPT **2641**

AMERICAN REVENUER, THE (US/0163-1608) [04307580] **2784**

AMERICAN REVIEW OF ART AND SCIENCE **SUSPENDED.** (US/0569-7344) [01788154] 5190, **336**

AMERICAN REVIEW OF CANADIAN STUDIES, THE (US/0272-2011) [03364885] **2719**

AMERICAN REVIEW OF DIAGNOSTICS (US/0735-1283) [08869097] **3698**

AMERICAN REVIEW OF INTERNATIONAL ARBITRATION, THE (US/1050-4109) [20604368] **2933**

AMERICAN REVIEW OF POLITICS (US) **4463**

AMERICAN REVIEW OF PUBLIC ADMINISTRATION (US/0275-0740) [07075486] **4625**

AMERICAN REVIEW OF RESPIRATORY DISEASE *See* AMERICAN JOURNAL OF RESPIRATORY AND CRITICAL CARE MEDICINE **3948**

AMERICAN REVIEW OF RESPIRATORY DISEASE, THE (US/0003-0805) [01480677] **3948**

●AMERICAN RIDER (US/1072-4893) [28987398] **5375**

AMERICAN RIFLEMAN (US/0003-083X) [05667316] 4869, **4883**

AMERICAN RIVERS (US/0888-899X) [13754697] **2186**

AMERICAN RODDER (US/1041-3138) [18759894] **5403**

AMERICAN ROSE ANNUAL / AMERICAN ROSE SOCIETY, THE (US/0066-0000) [01480692] **2408**

AMERICAN ROSE MAGAZINE, THE (US) [24570833] **2408**

AMERICAN ROSE REGISTRY (US/1042-3427) [19000626] **2408**

AMERICAN ROWING (US/0888-1154) [13339708] **4883**

AMERICAN SAILOR (US/0279-9553) [07387385] **591**

AMERICAN SALARIES AND WAGES SURVEY (US/1055-7628) [23293286] **1643**

AMERICAN SALESMAN, THE (US/0003-0902) [01480696] **859**

AMERICAN SALON: OFFICIAL PUBLICATION OF THE NHCA (US/0741-5737) [10176526] **402**

AMERICAN SALON'S GREEN BOOK (US/1044-8705) [18102529] **402**

AMERICAN SAMOA *See* SESSION LAWS AND DIGEST **3048**

AMERICAN SAMOA. LAWS, STATUES, ETC *See* REVISED CODE OF AMERICAN SAMOA. CUMULATIVE SUPPLEMENT **3040**

AMERICAN SAVINGS DIRECTORY (US) [08228467] **769**

AMERICAN SCHLESWIG-HOLSTEIN HERITAGE SOCIETY NEWSLETTER (US/1045-9960) [19498193] **2437**

AMERICAN SCHOLAR, THE (US/0003-0937) [01480704] **2484**

AMERICAN SCHOOL & UNIVERSITY (US/0003-0945) [01480705] **1860**

AMERICAN SCHOOL BOARD JOURNAL, THE (US/0003-0953) [01480706] **1860**

AMERICAN SCHOOL OF CLASSICAL STUDIES AT ATHENS *See* CORINTH : RESULTS OF EXCAVATIONS CONDUCTED BY THE AMERICAN SCHOOL OF CLASSICAL STUDIES AT ATHENS **1076**

AMERICAN SCHOOLS OF ORIENTAL RESEARCH *See* ANNUAL OF THE AMERICAN SCHOOLS OF ORIENTAL RESEARCH, THE **255**

AMERICAN SCHOOLS OF ORIENTAL RESEARCH *See* BULLETIN OF THE AMERICAN SCHOOLS OF ORIENTAL RESEARCH **264**

AMERICAN SCHOOLS OF ORIENTAL RESEARCH *See* NEWSLETTER - AMERICAN SCHOOLS OF ORIENTAL RESEARCH **1768**

AMERICAN SCIENTIST (US/0003-0996) [01480717] **5082**

AMERICAN SEAFOOD INSTITUTE REPORT (US/1050-0839) [21389532] **2294**

AMERICAN SECONDARY EDUCATION (US/0003-1003) [00852486] **1724**

AMERICAN SELF-PROTECTION ASSOCIATION *See* WORLD OF ASP **4808**

●AMERICAN SENIOR, THE (US/1055-8306) [23352411] **5178**

AMERICAN SENTINEL (WASHINGTON, D.C.) *See* PINK SHEET ON THE LEFT (1993), THE **4487**

AMERICAN SENTINEL (WASHINGTON, D.C.), THE (US/0278-0585) [07695318] **4463**

AMERICAN SEPHARDI, THE **CEASED.** (US/0003-102X) [02285754] **5045**

AMERICAN SERIES IN MATHEMATICAL AND MANAGEMENT SCIENCES (US/0883-6221) [09116809] 860, **3492**

AMERICAN SERIES OF FOREIGN PENAL CODES (US) [01480723] 3156, **3105**

AMERICAN SHIPPER (1991) (US/1074-8350) [26252975] **822**

AMERICAN SHIPPER INTERNATIONAL (US) [23304704] **5447**

AMERICAN SHOEMAKING (US/0003-1038) [03967901] **3183**

AMERICAN SHOEMAKING DIRECTORY OF SHOE MANUFACTURERS (US/0146-6437) [01738560] **1081**

AMERICAN SHORE AND BEACH PRESERVATION ASSOCIATION *See* NEWSLETTER - AMERICAN SHORE AND BEACH PRESERVATION ASSOCIATION **2200**

AMERICAN SHORT FICTION (US/1051-4813) [21979675] **3360**

AMERICAN SHORTWAVE LISTENERS CLUB *See* ASWLC **1126**

AMERICAN SHOTGUNNER, THE (US/0162-153X) [04112449] 4869, **4883**

AMERICAN SHOWCASE *See* AMERICAN ILLUSTRATION SHOWCASE **376**

AMERICAN SHOWCASE. ILLUSTRATION (US) [23531422] **376**

AMERICAN SHOWCASE OF ILLUSTRATION AND PHOTOGRAPHY (US/0278-8683) [07912784] 755, **4366**

AMERICAN SHOWMAN, THE (US/0194-1534) [05355629] **860**

AMERICAN SINGLES MAGAZINE (US/1059-4701) [24600720] 5550, **3994**

AMERICAN

AMERICAN SKATING WORLD (US/0744-1363) [08041421] **4883**

AMERICAN SKI COACH (US) **4883**

AMERICAN SKIER (US/1055-0615) [23067279] **4883**

● AMERICAN SMALL FARM MAGAZINE (US/1064-7473) [26387871] **58**

AMERICAN SOCIETY FOR CLINICAL PHARMACOLOGY AND THERAPEUTICS *See* DIRECTORY - AMERICAN SOCIETY FOR CLINICAL PHARMACOLOGY AND THERAPEUTICS **4299**

AMERICAN SOCIETY FOR CONSERVATION ARCHAEOLOGY *See* PROCEEDINGS / AMERICAN SOCIETY FOR CONSERVATION ARCHAEOLOGY **279**

AMERICAN SOCIETY FOR HORTICULTURAL SCIENCE *See* JOURNAL OF THE AMERICAN SOCIETY FOR HORTICULTURAL SCIENCE **2421**

AMERICAN SOCIETY FOR INFORMATION SCIENCE *See* PROCEEDINGS OF THE ASIS ANNUAL MEETING **3242**

AMERICAN SOCIETY FOR INFORMATION SCIENCE *See* BULLETIN OF THE AMERICAN SOCIETY FOR INFORMATION SCIENCE **3198**

AMERICAN SOCIETY FOR INFORMATION SCIENCE *See* ASIS ... HANDBOOK AND DIRECTORY **3192**

AMERICAN SOCIETY FOR INFORMATION SCIENCE *See* PROCEEDINGS OF THE ASIS MID-YEAR MEETING **3242**

AMERICAN SOCIETY FOR INFORMATION SCIENCE *See* JOURNAL OF THE AMERICAN SOCIETY FOR INFORMATION SCIENCE **3220**

AMERICAN SOCIETY FOR INFORMATION SCIENCE. SPECIAL INTEREST GROUP ON THE AUTOMATED OFFICE OF THE FUTURE (SIG/AOF) *See* SIG NEWSLETTER **3249**

AMERICAN SOCIETY FOR MICROBIOLOGY *See* DIRECTORY OF MEMBERS - AMERICAN SOCIETY FOR MICROBIOLOGY **562**

AMERICAN SOCIETY FOR MICROBIOLOGY *See* ASM NEWS **560**

AMERICAN SOCIETY FOR MICROBIOLOGY. GENERAL MEETING *See* ABSTRACTS OF THE ... GENERAL MEETING OF THE AMERICAN SOCIETY FOR MICROBIOLOGY **476**

AMERICAN SOCIETY FOR NEUROCHEMISTRY *See* TRANSACTIONS OF THE AMERICAN SOCIETY FOR NEUROCHEMISTRY **3847**

AMERICAN SOCIETY FOR NONDESTRUCTIVE TESTING *See* PAPER SUMMARIES - AMERICAN SOCIETY FOR NONDESTRUCTIVE TESTING **1990**

AMERICAN SOCIETY FOR PREVENTIVE DENTISTRY *See* JOURNAL OF THE AMERICAN SOCIETY FOR PREVENTIVE DENTISTRY **1328**

AMERICAN SOCIETY FOR PSYCHOPROPHYLAXIS IN OBSTETRICS *See* ASPO/LAMAZE MEMBERSHIP DIRECTORY **3757**

AMERICAN SOCIETY FOR PUBLIC ADMINISTRATION. NATIONAL CAPITAL AREA CHAPTER *See* MEMBERSHIP DIRECTORY - AMERICAN SOCIETY FOR PUBLIC ADMINISTRATION, NATIONAL CAPITAL AREA CHAPTER **4664**

AMERICAN SOCIETY FOR QUALITY CONTROL *See* ANNUAL QUALITY CONGRESS TRANSACTIONS **5083**

AMERICAN SOCIETY FOR TESTING AND MATERIALS *See* FIVE-YEAR INDEX TO ASTM TECHNICAL PAPERS AND REPORTS **2102**

AMERICAN SOCIETY FOR TESTING AND MATERIALS *See* ASTM STANDARDS IN BUILDING CODES **599**

AMERICAN SOCIETY FOR TESTING AND MATERIALS *See* POWDER DIFFRACTION FILE **1037**

AMERICAN SOCIETY FOR TESTING AND MATERIALS *See* ANNUAL BOOK OF ASTM STANDARDS **2100**

AMERICAN SOCIETY FOR TESTING AND MATERIALS *See* ASTM DIRECTORY **2100**

AMERICAN SOCIETY FOR TESTING AND MATERIALS *See* ASTM YEAR BOOK **2101**

AMERICAN SOCIETY FOR THE ADVANCEMENT OF ANESTHESIA IN DENTISTRY *See* PROCEEDINGS - AMERICAN SOCIETY FOR THE ADVANCEMENT ANESTHESIA IN DENTISTRY **3684**

AMERICAN SOCIETY FOR THEATRE RESEARCH *See* ASTR, AMERICAN SOCIETY FOR THEATRE RESEARCH NEWSLETTER **5361**

AMERICAN SOCIETY OF AGRICULTURAL ENGINEERS *See* ASAE PUBLICATION **1965**

AMERICAN SOCIETY OF AGRICULTURAL ENGINEERS *See* TRANSACTIONS OF THE ASAE **1999**

AMERICAN SOCIETY OF AGRICULTURAL ENGINEERS *See* PAPER - AMERICAN SOCIETY OF AGRICULTURAL ENGINEERS **1990**

AMERICAN SOCIETY OF AGRICULTURAL ENGINEERS *See* ASAE STANDARDS **1965**

AMERICAN SOCIETY OF AGRICULTURAL ENGINEERS *See* ASAE DISTINGUISHED LECTURE SERIES; TRACTOR DESIGN **158**

AMERICAN SOCIETY OF ANESTHESIOLOGISTS *See* DIRECTORY OF MEMBERS **3964**

AMERICAN SOCIETY OF ANESTHESIOLOGISTS *See* ASA NEWSLETTER (PARK RIDGE) **3682**

AMERICAN SOCIETY OF ANIMAL SCIENCE. WESTERN SECTION. MEETING *See* PROCEEDINGS / WESTERN SECTION, AMERICAN SOCIETY OF ANIMAL SCIENCE **219**

AMERICAN SOCIETY OF ASSOCIATION EXECUTIVES *See* ASSOCIATION EXECUTIVE COMPENSATION STUDY **640**

AMERICAN SOCIETY OF ASSOCIATION EXECUTIVES *See* WHO'S WHO IN ASSOCIATION MANAGEMENT **436**

AMERICAN SOCIETY OF BAKERY ENGINEERS *See* PROCEEDINGS OF THE ... ANNUAL MEETING / AMERICAN SOCIETY OF BAKERY ENGINEERS **2354**

AMERICAN SOCIETY OF BREWING CHEMISTS *See* JOURNAL OF THE AMERICAN SOCIETY OF BREWING CHEMISTS **982**

AMERICAN SOCIETY OF BREWING CHEMISTS *See* NEWSLETTER - AMERICAN SOCIETY OF BREWING CHEMISTS **987**

AMERICAN SOCIETY OF CIVIL ENGINEERS *See* OFFICIAL REGISTER - AMERICAN SOCIETY OF CIVIL ENGINEERS **2028**

AMERICAN SOCIETY OF CIVIL ENGINEERS *See* ASCE NEWS **2018**

AMERICAN SOCIETY OF CIVIL ENGINEERS *See* TRANSACTIONS OF THE AMERICAN SOCIETY OF CIVIL ENGINEERS **2007**

AMERICAN SOCIETY OF CIVIL ENGINEERS *See* MEMBERSHIP DIRECTORY / AMERICAN SOCIETY OF CIVIL ENGINEERS **2027**

AMERICAN SOCIETY OF CIVIL ENGINEERS *See* ASCE ANNUAL COMBINED INDEX **2002**

AMERICAN SOCIETY OF CLINICAL ONCOLOGY. MEETING *See* PROGRAM/ PROCEEDINGS / AMERICAN SOCIETY OF CLINICAL ONCOLOGY **3822**

AMERICAN SOCIETY OF COMPOSERS, AUTHORS AND PUBLISHERS, *See* ASCAP IN ACTION **4101**

AMERICAN SOCIETY OF CORPORATE SECRETARIES *See* REPORT ON SHAREHOLDER PROPOSALS **1624**

AMERICAN SOCIETY OF CORPORATE SECRETARIES *See* MEMBER'S YEAR BOOK - AMERICAN SOCIETY OF CORPORATE SECRETARIES **879**

AMERICAN SOCIETY OF CORPORATE SECRETARIES. YEAR BOOK *See* MEMBER'S YEAR BOOK - AMERICAN SOCIETY OF CORPORATE SECRETARIES **879**

AMERICAN SOCIETY OF FARM MANAGERS AND RURAL APPRAISERS *See* JOURNAL OF THE AMERICAN SOCIETY OF FARM MANAGERS AND RURAL APPRAISERS **101**

AMERICAN SOCIETY OF HOSPITAL PHARMACISTS *See* ASHP NEWSLETTER **4293**

AMERICAN SOCIETY OF HUMAN GENETICS *See* JOINT MEMBERSHIP DIRECTORY - AMERICAN SOCIETY OF HUMAN GENETICS **548**

AMERICAN SOCIETY OF HYPERTENSION SYMPOSIUM SERIES (US/0898-672X) [16998340] **3794**

AMERICAN SOCIETY OF INDEXERS *See* NEWSLETTER / AMERICAN SOCIETY OF INDEXERS **3234**

AMERICAN SOCIETY OF INTERNATIONAL LAW *See* PROCEEDINGS OF THE ANNUAL MEETING - AMERICAN SOCIETY OF INTERNATIONAL LAW **3134**

AMERICAN SOCIETY OF JOURNALISTS AND AUTHORS *See* DIRECTORY / AMERICAN SOCIETY OF JOURNALISTS AND AUTHORS **2919**

AMERICAN SOCIETY OF JOURNALISTS AND AUTHORS. DIRECTORY OF PROFESSIONAL WRITERS *See* DIRECTORY / AMERICAN SOCIETY OF JOURNALISTS AND AUTHORS **2919**

AMERICAN SOCIETY OF LANDSCAPE ARCHITECTS *See* ASLA MEMBERS' HANDBOOK **2409**

AMERICAN SOCIETY OF MECHANICAL ENGINEERS *See* TRANSACTIONS OF THE AMERICAN SOCIETY OF MECHANICAL ENGINEERS **2130**

AMERICAN SOCIETY OF MECHANICAL ENGINEERS *See* ASME GUIDE FOR GAS TRANSMISSION AND DISTRIBUTION PIPING SYSTEMS **2110**

AMERICAN SOCIETY OF MECHANICAL ENGINEERS *See* REPORT ON DIESEL AND GAS ENGINES POWER COSTS **2128**

AMERICAN SOCIETY OF MECHANICAL ENGINEERS *See* COMPANIES HOLDING NUCLEAR CERTIFICATES OF AUTHORIZATION **2154**

AMERICAN SOCIETY OF MECHANICAL ENGINEERS *See* ASME NEWS (1981) **2110**

AMERICAN SOCIETY OF MECHANICAL ENGINEERS *See* WEAR OF MATERIALS **2132**

AMERICAN SOCIETY OF MECHANICAL ENGINEERS *See* PAPERS - AMERICAN SOCIETY OF MECHANICAL ENGINEERS **2124**

AMERICAN SOCIETY OF MECHANICAL ENGINEERS. APPLIED MECHANICS DIVISION *See* AMD (NEW YORK, N.Y.) **2109**

AMERICAN SOCIETY OF MECHANICAL ENGINEERS. BOILER AND PRESSURE VESSEL COMMITTEE *See* COMPANIES HOLDING BOILER AND PRESSURE VESSEL CERTIFICATES OF AUTHORIZATION FOR USE OF CODE SYMBOL STAMPS **2112**

AMERICAN SOCIETY OF MECHANICAL ENGINEERS. BOILER AND PRESSURE VESSEL COMMITTEE *See* ASME BOILER AND PRESSURE VESSEL CODE **2110**

AMERICAN SOCIETY OF MECHANICAL ENGINEERS. SUBGROUP ON CARE AND OPERATION OF HEATING BOILERS *See* RECOMMENDED RULES FOR THE CARE AND OPERATION OF HEATING BOILERS **2127**

AMERICAN SOCIETY OF MECHANICAL ENGINEERS. SUBGROUP ON CARE OF POWER BOILERS *See* RECOMMENDED RULES FOR CARE OF POWER BOILERS **2127**

AMERICAN SOCIETY OF MEXICO (FOUNDED 1942) *See* BULLETIN **2257**

AMERICAN SOCIETY OF NEWSPAPER EDITORS *See* BULLETIN OF THE AMERICAN SOCIETY OF NEWSPAPER EDITORS, THE **2917**

AMERICAN SOCIETY OF NEWSPAPER EDITORS. CONVENTION *See* ASNE : PROCEEDINGS OF THE ... CONVENTION OF THE AMERICAN SOCIETY OF NEWSPAPER EDITORS **2917**

AMERICAN SOCIETY OF PAPYROLOGISTS *See* BULLETIN OF THE AMERICAN SOCIETY OF PAPYROLOGISTS, THE **264**

AMERICAN SOCIETY OF PENSION ACTUARIES *See* YEARBOOK - AMERICAN SOCIETY OF PENSION ACTUARIES **1720**

AMERICAN SOCIETY OF PENSION ACTUARIES *See* TRANSCRIBINGS, ANNUAL CONFERENCE - AMERICAN SOCIETY OF PENSION ACTUARIES **1715**

AMERICAN SOCIETY OF PLANT PHYSIOLOGISTS *See* DIRECTORY OF THE AMERICAN SOCIETY OF PLANT PHYSIOLOGISTS **508**

AMERICAN SOCIETY OF PLANT PHYSIOLOGISTS *See* BULLETIN - AMERICAN SOCIETY OF PLANT PHYSIOLOGISTS **504**

● AMERICAN SOCIETY OF POST ANESTHESIA NURSES (ASPAN) (US/1066-8977) [27088893] **3680, 3851**

AMERICAN SOCIETY OF RADIOLOGIC TECHNOLOGISTS *See* ASRT SCANNER **3939**

AMERICAN SOCIETY OF SAFETY ENGINEERS *See* ASSE SOCIETY UPDATE **1965**

AMERICAN SOCIETY OF SANITARY ENGINEERING *See* YEARBOOK - AMERICAN SOCIETY OF SANITARY ENGINEERING **2248**

AMERICAN SOCIETY OF SUGAR CANE TECHNOLOGISTS. FLORIDA DIVISION *See* JOURNAL - AMERICAN SOCIETY OF SUGAR CANE TECHNOLOGISTS. FLORIDA DIVISIONS **175**

AMERICAN SOCIETY OF TRAVEL AGENTS *See* MEMBERSHIP ROSTER - AMERICAN SOCIETY OF TRAVEL AGENTS INC **5484**

AMERICAN SOCIETY OF TRAVEL AGENTS. LISTS OF MEMBERS *See* MEMBERSHIP ROSTER - AMERICAN SOCIETY OF TRAVEL AGENTS INC **5484**

AMERICAN SOCIETY OF UNIVERSITY COMPOSERS *See* PROCEEDINGS OF THE ANNUAL CONFERENCE - AMERICAN SOCIETY OF UNIVERSITY COMPOSERS **4147**

AMERICAN

AMERICAN SOCIOLOGICAL ASSOCIATION See ANNUAL PROCEEDINGS - AMERICAN SOCIOLOGICAL ASSOCIATION **5239**

AMERICAN SOCIOLOGICAL ASSOCIATION See EMPLOYMENT BULLETIN (AMERICAN SOCIOLOGICAL ASSOCIATION : 197€) **4204**

AMERICAN SOCIOLOGICAL ASSOCIATION See DIRECTORY OF MEMBERS / THE AMERICAN SOCIOLOGICAL ASSOCIATION **5244**

AMERICAN SOCIOLOGICAL ASSOCIATION. BIOGRAPHICAL DIRECTORY OF MEMBERS See DIRECTORY OF MEMBERS / THE AMERICAN SOCIOLOGICAL ASSOCIATION **5244**

AMERICAN SOCIOLOGICAL REVIEW (US/0003-1224) [01480848] **5238**

AMERICAN SOCIOLOGIST, THE (US/0003-1232) [01411199] **5239**

AMERICAN SONGWRITER (US/0896-8993) [17342741] **4099**

AMERICAN SPACEMODELING See SPORT ROCKETRY **2778**

AMERICAN SPACEMODELLING (US/0883-0991) [11007239] 11, **2771**

AMERICAN SPEAKER (US) **1104**

AMERICAN SPECTATOR (ARLINGTON, VA.), THE (US/0148-8414) [03398190] **3337**

AMERICAN SPEECH (US/0003-1283) [01480854] **3263**

AMERICAN SPEECH-LANGUAGE-HEARING ASSOCIATION See ASHA MEMBERSHIP DIRECTORY **3886**

AMERICAN SPEECH-LANGUAGE-HEARING ASSOCIATION See DIRECTORY OF BILINGUAL SPEECH-LANGUAGE PATHOLOGISTS AND AUDIOLOGISTS **4386**

AMERICAN SPEECH LANGUAGE HEARING ASSOCIATION See ASHA (ROCKVILLE, MD.) **1875**

●AMERICAN SPIRIT / TAKE PRIDE IN AMERICA (US) [26678970] **2186**

AMERICAN SQUARE DANCE (US/0091-3383) [01786794] **1310**

AMERICAN STAMP NEWS (CN/0384-6679) [02653568] **2784**

AMERICAN STATISTICAL ASSOCIATION See AMSTAT NEWS **5320**

AMERICAN STATISTICAL ASSOCIATION See DIRECTORY OF MEMBERS - AMERICAN STATISTICAL ASSOCIATION; BIOMETRIC SOCIETY. EASTERN NORTH AMERICAN REGION. BIOMETRIC SOCIETY. WESTERN NORTH AMERICAN REGION **5326**

AMERICAN STATISTICAL ASSOCIATION. BUSINESS AND ECONOMIC STATISTICS SECTION See PROCEEDINGS OF THE BUSINESS AND ECONOMIC STATISTICS SECTION **1537**

AMERICAN STATISTICAL ASSOCIATION. GOVERNMENT STATISTICS SECTION See PROCEEDINGS OF THE GOVERNMENT STATISTICS SECTION / AMERICAN STATISTICAL ASSOCIATION **4492**

AMERICAN STATISTICAL ASSOCIATION. MEETING See AMERICAN STATISTICAL ASSOCIATION PROCEEDINGS OF THE BIOPHARMACEUTICAL SECTION **4334**

AMERICAN STATISTICAL ASSOCIATION PROCEEDINGS OF THE BIOPHARMACEUTICAL SECTION (US/0898-4654) [11049406] **4334**

AMERICAN STATISTICAL ASSOCIATION. SECTION ON STATISTICAL EDUCATION See PROCEEDINGS OF THE SECTION ON STATISTICAL EDUCATION - AMERICAN STATISTICAL ASSOCIATION. SECTION ON STATISTICAL EDUCATION **5336**

AMERICAN STATISTICAL ASSOCIATION. SECTION ON STATISTICAL GRAPHICS See PROCEEDINGS OF THE SECTION ON STATISTICAL GRAPHICS **5336**

AMERICAN STATISTICAL ASSOCIATION. SECTION ON STATISTICS AND THE ENVIRONMENT See PROCEEDINGS OF THE SECTION ON STATISTICS AND THE ENVIRONMENT / AMERICAN STATISTICAL ASSOCIATION **2180**

AMERICAN STATISTICAL ASSOCIATION. SOCIAL STATISTICS SECTION See PROCEEDINGS OF THE SOCIAL STATISTICS SECTION (WASHINGTON) **5336**

AMERICAN STATISTICAL ASSOCIATION. STATISTICAL COMPUTING SECTION See PROCEEDINGS OF THE STATISTICAL COMPUTING SECTION **3528**

AMERICAN STATISTICAL ASSOCIATION. SURVEY RESEARCH METHODS SECTION See PROCEEDINGS OF THE SECTION ON SURVEY RESEARCH METHODS **3542**

AMERICAN STATISTICIAN, THE (US/0003-1305) [01480867] **5320**

AMERICAN STATISTICS INDEX (US/0091-1658) [01784446] 4625, **4696**

AMERICAN STEEPLECHASING (US/0162-0568) [04082597] **2796**

AMERICAN STOCK EXCHANGE See AMEX DATABOOK **890**

AMERICAN STOCK EXCHANGE See STOCKS & BONDS **916**

AMERICAN STRING TEACHER (US/0003-1313) [00849560] **4100**

AMERICAN STUDIES ASSOCIATION OF TEXAS See JOURNAL OF THE AMERICAN STUDIES ASSOCIATION OF TEXAS **2742**

AMERICAN STUDIES IN PAPYROLOGY (US/0569-8642) [01480876] **1074**

AMERICAN STUDIES IN SCANDINAVIA (NO/0044-8060) [01480877] **2719**

AMERICAN STUDIES INTERNATIONAL (US/0883-105X) [02077111] 4340, 3360, **2719**

AMERICAN STUDIES INTERNATIONAL NEWSLETTER (US/0883-1068) [09354750] **2719**

AMERICAN STUDIES (LAWRENCE) (US/0026-3079) [00818197] 312, **2719**

AMERICAN STUDIES LIBRARY NEWSLETTER (UK/0265-3389) [11078094] **3189**

AMERICAN STUDIES (MUNICH, GERMANY) (GW/0178-1987) [10571958] **5190**

AMERICAN STUDIES / THE WILLIAM L. BRYANT FOUNDATION (US) [01769891] **2719**

AMERICAN SURGEON, THE (US/0003-1348) [01480881] **3958**

AMERICAN SURGICAL ASSOCIATION See TRANSACTIONS OF THE MEETING OF THE AMERICAN SURGICAL ASSOCIATION **3976**

AMERICAN SURVIVAL GUIDE (US/8750-5878) [11587310] **2527**

AMERICAN SUZUKI JOURNAL (US/0193-5372) [04761944] **4100**

AMERICAN SWIMMING : A PUBLICATION OF THE AMERICAN SWIMMING COACHES ASSOCIATION (US/0747-6000) [25300153] **4883**

AMERICAN SWIMMING COACHES ASSOCIATION WORLD CLINIC YEARBOOK (US/0747-5853) [03331671] **4883**

AMERICAN TAXIDERMIST MAGAZINE (US) [08722129] **2771**

AMERICAN TEACHER (US/0003-1380) [02133339] **1888**

AMERICAN TELEPHONE AND TELEGRAPH COMPANY. ECONOMIC ANALYSIS SECTION See BUSINESS CONDITIONS (NEW YORK) **646**

AMERICAN THEATRE (US/8750-3255) [10594175] **5361**

AMERICAN THEOLOGIÇAL LIBRARY ASSOCIATION See ATLA BIBLIOGRAPHY SERIES **5012**

AMERICAN THEOLOGICAL LIBRARY ASSOCIATION See SUMMARY OF PROCEEDINGS. ANNUAL CONFERENCE / AMERICAN THEOLOGICAL LIBRARY ASSOCIATION **3251**

AMERICAN THEOLOGICAL LIBRARY ASSOCIATION See NEWSLETTER - AMERICAN THEOLOGICAL LIBRARY ASSOCIATION **3235**

AMERICAN THEOLOGICAL LIBRARY ASSOCIATION See ATLA MONOGRAPH SERIES **3192**

AMERICAN THEOSOPHIST, THE (US/0003-1402) [03967981] **4934**

AMERICAN TOOL, DIE & STAMPING NEWS (US/0192-5709) [05082832] 3997, **3475**

AMERICAN TOPICAL ASSOCIATION See DIRECTORY OF ATA MEMBERS **2785**

AMERICAN TOWMAN, THE (US/0274-8215) [06629089] **5403**

AMERICAN TRADE SCHOOLS DIRECTORY (US/0517-564X) [01480915] **1910**

AMERICAN TRAIL SERIES (US/0066-0884) [01587340] **2719**

AMERICAN TRAILS SERIES. NEW YORK (US) [01775012] **2719**

AMERICAN TRAKEHNER, THE (US/0730-2975) [07985274] **2796**

AMERICAN TRANSLATORS ASSOCIATION See TRANSLATION SERVICES DIRECTORY **3329**

AMERICAN TRANSLATORS ASSOCIATION SCHOLARLY MONOGRAPH SERIES (US/0890-4111) [14222288] **3263**

AMERICAN TRAPPER (US/1050-4036) [21477897] **2186**

AMERICAN TRAVELER (US/0747-0843) [10534173] **5461**

AMERICAN TRUCKING ASSOCIATIONS See MOTOR CARRIER ANNUAL REPORTS **5387**

AMERICAN TRUCKING ASSOCIATIONS. DIVISION OF RESEARCH AND ECONOMICS See MOTOR CARRIER STATISTICAL SUMMARY **5401**

AMERICAN TRUCKING ASSOCIATIONS. F & OS See EXECUTIVE AND OWNERSHIP REPORT. CLASS I & II MOTOR CARRIERS OF PROPERTY **673**

AMERICAN TRUCKING TRENDS (US) [01480923] **5403**

AMERICAN TURF MONTHLY (US/0003-1445) [03968020] **2796**

AMERICAN TYPE CULTURE COLLECTION See CATALOGUE OF CELL LINES AND HYBRIDOMAS / AMERICAN TYPE CULTURE COLLECTION **561**

AMERICAN TYPE CULTURE COLLECTION See CATALOGUE OF YEASTS **506**

AMERICAN TYPE CULTURE COLLECTION See CATALOGUE OF FILAMENTOUS FUNGI / AMERICAN TYPE CULTURE COLLECTION **451**

AMERICAN UNIVERSITIES AND COLLEGES (US/0066-0922) [01239901] **1808**

AMERICAN UNIVERSITIES FIELD STAFF See POPULATION : PERSPECTIVE **4557**

AMERICAN UNIVERSITIES FIELD STAFF See REPORTS **1845**

AMERICAN UNIVERSITY JOURNAL OF INTERNATIONAL LAW AND POLICY, THE (US/0888-630X) [13392259] **3123**

AMERICAN UNIVERSITY LAW REVIEW, THE (US/0003-1453) [01480950] **2933**

AMERICAN UNIVERSITY STUDIES. SERIES I, GERMANIC LANGUAGES AND LITERATURES (US/0721-1392) [10038156] 3360, **3263**

AMERICAN UNIVERSITY STUDIES. SERIES II, ROMANCE LANGUAGES AND LITERATURE (US/0740-9257) [10093860] 3360, **3263**

AMERICAN UNIVERSITY STUDIES. SERIES IV, ENGLISH LANGUAGE AND LITERATURE (US/0741-0700) [10085262] 3360, **3263**

AMERICAN UNIVERSITY STUDIES. SERIES VI, FOREIGN LANGUAGE INSTRUCTION (US/0739-6406) [09801043] **3263**

AMERICAN UNIVERSITY STUDIES. SERIES VII, THEOLOGY AND RELIGION (US/0740-0446) [09866094] **4934**

AMERICAN UNIVERSITY STUDIES. SERIES XII, SLAVIC LANGUAGES AND LITERATURE (US/0740-0497) [09885679] 3263, **3360**

AMERICAN UNIVERSITY STUDIES. SERIES XIII, LINGUISTICS (US/0740-4557) [09961121] **3263**

AMERICAN UNIVERSITY STUDIES. SERIES XIV, EDUCATION (US/0740-4565) [09961161] **1808**

AMERICAN UNIVERSITY STUDIES. SERIES XIX, .GENERAL LITERATURE (US/0743-6645) [10635617] **3360**

AMERICAN UNIVERSITY STUDIES. SERIES XV, COMMUNICATIONS (US/0740-5111) [09960164] **1104**

AMERICAN UNIVERSITY STUDIES. SERIES XVIII, AFRICAN LITERATURE (US/0742-1923) [10495045] **3360**

AMERICAN UNIVERSITY STUDIES. SERIES XX, FINE ARTS (US/0890-412X) [14222391] **312**

AMERICAN UNIVERSITY STUDIES. SERIES XXI, REGIONAL STUDIES (US/0895-0482) [16415101] **2609**

AMERICAN UNIVERSITY STUDIES. SERIES XXII, LATIN AMERICAN STUDIES (US/0895-0490) [16415151] **2719**

AMERICAN UNIVERSITY STUDIES. SERIES XXIV, AMERICAN LITERATURE (US/0895-0512) [16415216] **3360**

AMERICAN UNIVERSITY STUDIES. SERIES XXVI, THEATER ARTS (US/0899-9880) [18283285] **383**

AMERICAN UNIVERSITY STUDIES. SERIES XXVII, FEMINIST STUDIES (US/1042-5985) [19090092] **5550**

AMERICAN UNIVERSITY, WASHINGTON, D.C. CENTER FOR RESEARCH IN SOCIAL SYSTEMS See CINFAC BIBLIOGRAPHIC REVIEW. SUPPLEMENT **4061**

AMERICAN URBAN GUIDENOTES : THE NEWSLETTER OF GUIDEBOOKS (US) [06562266] **5461**

AMERICAN VACUUM SOCIETY See DIRECTORY OF MEMBERS, OFFICERS, COMMITTEES - AMERICAN VACUUM SOCIETY **2113**

AMERICAN

AMERICAN VEGETABLE GROWER (1983) (US/0741-9848) [09490433] **162**

AMERICAN VETERINARY MEDICAL ASSOCIATION *See* JOURNAL OF THE AMERICAN VETERINARY MEDICAL ASSOCIATION **5513**

AMERICAN VETERINARY MEDICAL ASSOCIATION. DIVISION OF MEMBERSHIP AND FIELD SERVICES *See* AVMA DIRECTORY **5505**

AMERICAN VIET PRESS (US/0896-1433) [16918902] **2484**

AMERICAN VISIONS (US/0884-9390) [12532797] **2720**

AMERICAN VOICE (LOUISVILLE, KY.), THE (US/0884-4356) [12412332] **3360**

AMERICAN VOLLEYBALL (US/1045-7186) [20189814] **4883**

AMERICAN WAR MOTHER, THE (US/0199-8072) [01480973] **2720**

AMERICAN WAR MOTHERS *See* AMERICAN WAR MOTHER, THE **2720**

AMERICAN WATER WORKS ASSOCIATION. CONFERENCE *See* PROCEEDINGS AWWA ANNUAL CONFERENCE **4761**

AMERICAN WATER WORKS ASSOCIATION. ONTARIO SECTION *See* DIRECTORY - AMERICAN WATER WORKS ASSOCIATION, ONTARIO SECTION **5532**

AMERICAN WAY (DALLAS, TEX.) (US/0003-1518) [12008572] 5461, **11**

AMERICAN WEATHER OBSERVER (US/8755-9552) [11456625] **1419**

AMERICAN WHITEWATER (US/0300-7626) [01331864] **4883**

● AMERICAN WHOLESALERS AND DISTRIBUTORS DIRECTORY (US/1061-2114) [25214894] **1597**

AMERICAN WILDLIFE REGION SERIES *CEASED*. (US) [05784466] **2186**

AMERICAN WIND ENERGY ASSOCIATION WIND ENERGY WEEKLY, THE (US/0747-5500) [10744814] **1931**

AMERICAN WINE SOCIETY *See* JOURNAL - AMERICAN WINE SOCIETY **2368**

AMERICAN WINE SOCIETY MANUAL, THE (US/0149-676X) [03893579] **2363**

AMERICAN WOMAN (NEW YORK, N.Y.: 1987) (US) [16324366] **5550**

AMERICAN WOMAN (NEW YORK, N.Y. 1991) (US/1054-9595) [23034359] **5550**

AMERICAN WOOD-PRESERVERS' ASSOCIATION *See* PROCEEDINGS, ... ANNUAL MEETING OF THE AMERICAN WOOD-PRESERVERS' ASSOCIATION **2403**

AMERICAN WOOD PRESERVERS' ASSOCIATION *See* PROCEEDINGS, ANNUAL MEETING OF THE AMERICAN WOOD-PRESERVERS' ASSOCIATION **2403**

AMERICAN WOODTURNER (US/0895-9005) [16850550] **822**

AMERICAN WOODWORKER *See* RODALE'S AMERICAN WOODWORKER **635**

AMERICAN WOODWORKER, THE (US/8750-9318) [11924850] **633**

AMERICAN WORKER, THE (US/1047-7136) [20778115] **1643**

AMERICAN WRITING (PHILADELPHIA, PA.) (US/1049-815X) [21315901] 3337, **312**

AMERICAN YOUTH (US/0003-1542) [02251091] **1060**

AMERICAN ZIONIST, THE *SUSPENDED*. (US/0003-1550) [02885757] **2645**

AMERICAN ZOOLOGIST (US/0003-1569) [01480990] **5574**

AMERICANA *CEASED*. (US/0090-9114) [04938125] **2527**

AMERICANA ANNUAL, THE (US/0196-0180) [01480992] **1923**

AMERICANA (BRAUNSCHWEIG, GERMANY) (GW) [08967125] **4869**

AMERICANS BEFORE COLUMBUS (US/0066-121X) [01480995] **2720**

AMERICANS FOR EFFECTIVE LAW ENFORCEMENT *See* LIABILITY REPORTER **3169**

AMERICANS TALK ISSUES (US/1061-8198) [24310378] **5239**

● AMERICANS TRAVELING ABROAD (US/1070-3365) [28318221] **5461**

AMERICAR AUSTRALIA (AT/1032-6499) [I10326499] **5403**

AMERICA'S AGENDA (US/1064-8984) [26289677] **1724**

AMERICA'S BEST MONEY MANAGERS (US/1061-7051) [25422412] **890**

● AMERICA'S BEST QUILTING PROJECTS (US/1064-1718) [26243001] 370, **5183**

AMERICAS (BONN, GERMANY) (GW/0933-8853) [19287479] 2551, **2527**

AMERICA'S CENSORED NEWSLETTER *CEASED*. (US/1061-4230) [25306013] **2917**

AMERICA'S CIVIL WAR (US/1046-2899) [18111753] **2720**

AMERICAS COMMON MARKET NEWS, THE (US/1056-6287) [23752596] **822**

AMERICA'S CORPORATE FAMILIES (US/0890-6645) [07918138] **638**

AMERICA'S CORPORATE FAMILIES AND INTERNATIONAL AFFILIATES (US/0740-4018) [09814554] **638**

AMERICA'S CORPORATE FINANCE DIRECTORY (US) 638, **769**

AMERICAS (ENGLISH EDITION) (US/0379-0940) [01481000] **2551**

AMERICA'S FASTEST GROWING COMPANIES (1985) *CEASED*. (US/0883-7953) [12218634] **638**

AMERICA'S FINEST COMPANIES (US/1057-5642) [24059315] **638**

AMERICA'S FUTURE FOOD TRENDS (US) **2326**

AMERICA'S FUTURE (NEW ROCHELLE, N.Y.) (US/0003-1593) [01481002] **4463**

AMERICA'S GREAT OUTDOORS : NEWSLETTER FOR THE NATIONAL RECREATION STRATEGY (US) [24165060] 4705, **2374**

AMERICA'S HEALTH *CEASED*. (US) [04535577] **4765**

AMERICA'S INVENTOR / OFFICIAL NEWSLETTER OF THE NATIONAL CONGRESS OF INVENTOR ORGANIZATIONS (US) [25057857] **1301**

AMERICA'S NEW FOUNDATIONS (US/1048-4965) [20977711] **5271**

AMERICA'S OUTSTANDING NAMES AND FACES (US/0196-3465) [05019037] **429**

AMERICAS REVIEW (HOUSTON, TEX.) (US/1042-6213) [14118295] **3360**

AMERICAS REVIEW / WORLD OF INFORMATION, THE (UK) [21995202] **1923**

AMERICA'S TEXTILES INTERNATIONAL (US/0890-9970) [14558603] 3475, **5347**

● AMERICAS TRADE & FINANCE (US/1062-8118) [25762046] 822, **769**

AMERICAS (WASHINGTON. 1944), THE (US/0003-1615) [01481001] **2720**

AMERICAS WATCH (US/1068-8919) [27313684] **4503**

AMERICAS WATCH (NEWSLETTER) *See* HUMAN RIGHTS WATCH/AMERICAS **4509**

AMERICA'S WONDERFUL LITTLE HOTELS & INNS. MIDWEST, THE ROCKY MOUNTAINS AND THE SOUTHWEST *See* AMERICA'S WONDERFUL LITTLE HOTELS & INNS. THE ROCKY MOUNTAINS AND THE SOUTHWEST **2804**

AMERICA'S WONDERFUL LITTLE HOTELS & INNS. MIDWEST, THE ROCKY MOUNTAINS, AND THE SOUTHWEST *See* AMERICA'S WONDERFUL LITTLE HOTELS & INNS. THE MIDWEST **2803**

● AMERICA'S WONDERFUL LITTLE HOTELS & INNS. THE MIDWEST (US/1063-0007) [25279289] 5461, **2803**

AMERICA'S WONDERFUL LITTLE HOTELS & INNS : THE MIDWEST, THE ROCKY MOUNTAINS, AND THE SOUTHWEST (US) [24575495] **2803**

● AMERICA'S WONDERFUL LITTLE HOTELS & INNS. THE ROCKY MOUNTAINS AND THE SOUTHWEST (US/1062-9998) [25071013] **2804**

AMERICUS TIMES-RECORDER (US) [21134729] **5652**

AMERIKA GAKKAI (JAPAN) *See* AMERIKA-GAKUKAI KAIHO **2720**

AMERIKA-GAKUKAI KAIHO (JA) [06124912] **2720**

AMERIKA KENKYU (TOKYO. 1967) (JA/0387-2815) [05080302] **3337**

AMERIKA WOCHE (US/0745-6557) [09328374] **5658**

● AMERIKAI MAGYAR LEVELESTAR (US/1054-4607) [22895276] **2673**

AMERIKAI MAGYAR SZO (US/0194-7990) [02257473] **5713**

AMERIKAN UUTISET (US/0745-9971) [01480959] **5647**

AMERIKANSKI SLOVENEC (CHICAGO, ILL.) (US/0745-5453) [09273347] **5658**

AMERIKANSKII EZHEGODNIK (RU/1010-5557) [01841084] **2527**

AMERIKASTUDIEN (GW/0340-2827) [01795328] **2720**

AMERIKASTUDIEN. SCHRIFTENREIHE. AMERICAN STUDIES (GW) [07217817] **2720**

AMERINDIA (FR/0221-8852) [04199210] **3263**

AMERISKA DOMOVINA (US/0164-680X) [04409084] **5726**

AMERITECH INDUSTRIAL PURCHASING GUIDE. EASTERN PENNSYLVANIA/SOUTHERN NEW JERSEY/DELAWARE (US) [24089714] **948**

AMERITECH INDUSTRIAL PURCHASING GUIDE. FLORIDA (US/1060-2399) [24579158] **948**

AMERITECH INDUSTRIAL PURCHASING GUIDE. GEORGIA/ALABAMA/EASTERN & CENTRAL TENNESSEE (US/1059-6909) [24491919] **948**

AMERITECH INDUSTRIAL PURCHASING GUIDE. INDIANA (US) [23259468] **948**

AMERITECH INDUSTRIAL PURCHASING GUIDE. MARYLAND/VIRGINIA/DISTRICT OF COLUMBIA (US) [23936322] **948**

AMERITECH INDUSTRIAL PURCHASING GUIDE. MICHIGAN (US) [24570737] **948**

AMERITECH INDUSTRIAL PURCHASING GUIDE. NEW YORK, WESTERN PENNSYLVANIA (US/1063-9993) [24887743] 1597, **948**

AMERITECH INDUSTRIAL PURCHASING GUIDE. OHIO (US) [24584170] 1597, **948**

● AMERITECH INDUSTRIAL PURCHASING GUIDE. UPSTATE NEW YORK, WESTERN PENNSYLVANIA (US/1071-0302) [27153996] 1597, **949**

AMERITECH INDUSTRIAL YELLOW PAGES. ILLINOIS/WISCONSIN REGION (US) [16991999] **1597**

AMERITECH INDUSTRIAL YELLOW PAGES. INDIANA REGION (US) [13304600] **1597**

AMERITECH INDUSTRIAL YELLOW PAGES PURCHASING GUIDE. WESTERN PENNSYLVANIA, WEST/CENTRAL NEW YORK *See* AMERITECH INDUSTRIAL PURCHASING GUIDE. NEW YORK, WESTERN PENNSYLVANIA **948**

AMERRIKUA! (SCHUYLER FALLS, N.Y.) *CEASED*. (US/1043-7029) [19537415] **2255**

AMERY FREE PRESS (US/0748-6898) [11002690] **5765**

AMES FORESTER (US) [01481014] 1089, **2374**

AMES HIGH ALUMNI NEWSLETTER (US/1055-5196) [23197753] **1101**

AMES LABORATORY *See* ANNUAL SUMMARY REPORT. PROGRESS AND PLANS - AMES LABORATORY, U.S.A.E.C **2154**

AMESBURY NEWS (US/0192-8910) [05139542] **5684**

AMETHYST (ATLANTA, GA.) (US/0893-7958) [15646398] **2793**

AMETHYST MATTERS : NEWSLETTER OF AMETHYST WOMEN'S ADDICTION CENTRE (CN/0844-5761) [20279037] **5271**

AMEX DATABOOK (US/0550-6557) [01781764] **890**

AMFITEATRU : REVISTA LITERARA SI ARTISTICA EDITATA DE UNIUNEA ASOCIATIILOR STUDENTILOR COMUNISTI DIN ROMANIA (RM) [09692871] **312**

AMH : ACCREDITATION MANUAL FOR HOSPITALS / THE JOINT MISSION (US) [24472775] **3776**

AMHERST BEE, THE (US) [12957674] **5713**

AMI COOP LIMOGES, L' (FR/0003-1771) [I00031771] **1081**

AMI DES BETES, L' (CN/0824-8494) [10680872] **4285**

AMI DES JARDINS ET DE LA MAISON, L' (FR/0044-8095) [I00448095] **2408**

AMI (MISSISSAUGA, ONT.) (CN/0830-8586) [13490182] **383**

● AMIA NEWSLETTER (US/1075-6477) [28525975] **4063**

AMICA (IT/1120-432X) [I1120432X] **5550**

AMICA NEWS BULLETIN, THE (US/1043-5379) [19453230] **4100**

AMICI DEL BURUNDI (IT) [05167341] **4934**

AMICIZIA PALERMO (IT/1120-5768) [I11205768] **2484**

AMICUS CURIAE (CORAL GABLES, FLA.) (US/8756-3428) [11542723] **2933**

AMICUS CURIARUM (US/0145-8574) [02791518] **3138**

AMICUS JOURNAL, THE (US/0276-7201) [06567953] **2186**

AMICUS JURIS (US/0161-0783) [03822459] **2933**

AMIE (US/0198-9391) [06285315] **2484**

AMIGA (BL) [04951248] **1126**

AMIGA USER INTERNATIONAL (UK/0955-1077) [I09551077] **1264**

AMIGA USER, THE (US/0889-5783) [13923907] **1264**

AMIGA WORLD (US/0883-2390) [12094310] **1264**

AMIGAWORLD TECH JOURNAL, THE **CEASED.** (US/1054-4631) [22901260] **1264**

AMIGO DEL HOGAR (DR) **4934**

AMIGO (MONTREAL) (CN/0318-5729) [01691458] **4934**

AMINA (FR) [01791445] **5550**

AMINO ACIDS (AU/0939-4451) [25007247] **960**

AMINO ACIDS AND PEPTIDES *See* AMINO ACIDS, PEPTIDES, AND PROTEINS. (CAMBRIDGE, ENGLAND) **960**

●AMINO ACIDS, PEPTIDES, AND PROTEINS. (CAMBRIDGE, ENGLAND) (UK) [30851377] **960**

AMIRA ... ANNUAL REPORT / AUSTRALIAN MINERAL INDUSTRIES RESEARCH ASSOCIATION LIMITED (AT) [10954286] **2133**

AMIS DE JESUS, LES (CN/0823-6178) [10420577] **4934**

AMIS DE LA BANQUE D'YEUX DU QUEBEC (CN/0710-1368) [08144024] **3872**

AMIS DES ROSES, LES (FR/0003-1844) [04826418] **2408**

AMISOL (CN/0318-5737) [01691493] **1060**

AMITIE CHARLES PEGUY *See* CAHIERS **3370**

●AMITIE SP : BULLETIN DE L'ASSOCIATION QUEBECOISE DES AMIS DE LA SCLEROSE EN PLAQUES (CN/1193-2805) [26715092] **3920**

AMITIES ACADIENNES (FR/0220-4592) [24690842] **2255**

AMITYVILLE RECORD, THE (US) [25104387] **5713**

AMJ, AIRPORT MANAGEMENT JOURNAL **CEASED.** (US/0362-5001) [02294099] 860, **11**

AMJ NEWSLETTER **CEASED.** (JA/0388-1423) [I03881423] **1217**

AMMATILLISET OPPILAITOKSET (FINLAND. AMMATTIKASVATUSHALLITUS) (FI) [19892633] **1874**

AMMATILLISET OPPILAITOKSET. YRKESUTBILDNINGSANSTALTERNA (FI) [05806969] **1910**

AMMATILLISIIN OPPILAITOKSIIN JA KANSANOPISTOIHIN PYRKINEET JA OTETUT (FI) [05238671] **1724**

AMMATILLISIIN OPPILAITOKSIIN SEKA KANSANKORKEAKOULUTHIN KANSANKORKEAKOULUTHIN PYUKINEET JAOTETUT (FI) [03352558] 4549, **1910**

AMMATILLISISSA OPPILAITOKSISSA VUONNA ... SUORITETUT TUTKINNOT (FI) [10569123] **1910**

AMMATILLISTEN OPPILAITOSTEN OPPILASMAARA (FI) [07052123] **1910**

AMMATILLISTEN OPPILAITOSTEN SEKA KANSANOPISTOJEN JA-KORKEAKOULUJEN OPPILASMAARA (FI) [03939709] **1724**

AMMINISTRARE : RIVISTA QUADRIMESTRALE DELL'ISTITUTO PER LA SCIENZA DELL'AMMINISTRAZIONE PUBBLICA (IT) [05704508] **4625**

AMMINISTRAZIONE & FINANZA (IT) **769**

AMMINISTRAZIONE & FINANZA ORO (IT/1121-2438) [I11212438] **769**

AMMINISTRAZIONE E POLITICA (IT/0392-579X) [I0392579X] **4463**

AMMINISTRAZIONE ITALIANA (IT/0303-9722) [I03039722] **4625**

AMMO (US/0161-9810) [04080889] **1643**

AMMONIA PLANT SAFETY (AND RELATED FACILITIES) (US/0360-7011) [02573417] **2007**

AMMONITE (UK/0951-2500) [17978434] **3360**

AMMONITE GILLINGHAM, DORSET (UK/0951-2500) [I09512500] **2318**

AMN (SAUDI ARABIA. IDARAH AL-AMMAH LIL-THAQAFAH WA-AL-TAWJIH) (SU) [09139044] **3156**

AMNESTY ACTION / AI, USA (US) [02252664] **4503**

AMNESTY EDUCATION NEWSLETTER / AMNESTY EDUCATION OFFICE, CHANCELLOR'S OFFICE, CALIFORNIA COMMUNITY COLLEGES (US) [23251732] **1808**

AMNESTY INTERNATIONAL *See* AMNESTY INTERNATIONAL NEWSLETTER **4503**

AMNESTY INTERNATIONAL *See* AMNESTY INTERNATIONAL REPORT, THE **4504**

AMNESTY INTERNATIONAL *See* ACCOUNTS, TREASURER'S AND AUDITORS' REPORTS / AMNESTY INTERNATIONAL **4461**

AMNESTY INTERNATIONAL CANADA *See* COMMUNICATIONS - AMNISTIE INTERNATIONALE, SECTION CANADIENNE **3126**

AMNESTY INTERNATIONAL NEWSLETTER (UK/0308-6887) [03323685] **4503**

AMNESTY INTERNATIONAL REPORT, THE (UK) [04540266] **4504**

AMOCO TRAVELER (US/0275-5564) [07151367] **5461**

AMOEBA AMSTERDAM. 1976 (NE/0926-3543) [I09263543] **4161**

AMON HEN (UK) [02436107] 429, **3360**

AMONG THE COLES (US/0743-2801) [10526556] **2437**

AMORTIZATION AND INSURANCE PREMIUM TABLES FOR HOME MORTGAGES AND LOANS TO BE INSURED UNDER THE NATIONAL HOUSING ACT *See* AMORTIZATION, INSURANCE PREMIUM AND OUTSTANDING PRINCIPAL BALANCE TABLES FOR HOME MORTGAGES AND LOANS INSURED UNDER THE NATIONAL HOUSING ACT **769**

AMORTIZATION, INSURANCE PREMIUM AND OUTSTANDING PRINCIPAL BALANCE TABLES FOR HOME MORTGAGES AND LOANS INSURED UNDER THE NATIONAL HOUSING ACT (US/0095-3520) [01795945] 2873, **769**

AMORY ADVERTISER (1957), THE (US/0899-0085) [11652515] **5699**

AMPERSAND (SAN FRANCISCO, CALIF.), THE (US/0740-5804) [09006655] **4563**

AMPHIBIA-REPTILIA (GW/0173-5373) [06984908] **5575**

AMPHIBIOUS WARFARE REVIEW (US/0886-344X) [10179574] **4034**

AMPHORA (CN/0003-200X) [02225811] **4823**

AMPHORA BRAINE-L'ALLEUD (BE/0778-4287) [I07784287] **254**

AMPI MEDICAL PHYSICS BULLETIN (II/0250-5002) [06895791] **4396**

AMPLEFORTH JOURNAL, THE (UK/0003-2018) [01774792] **5023**

AMPO (JA) [01481026] **4463**

AMR REPORT (US) **860**

AMR REPORT ON MES *See* AMR REPORT

AMREP RESOURCE POLITICS (AT/1033-2774) [I10332774] **2133**

AMRO (UK) [19483057] **3549**

AMR'S CIM STRATEGIES (US) **3475**

AMRTAYANA (II) [11789361] **3360**

●AMS ANCIENT AND CLASSICAL STUDIES (US/1058-238X) [24243551] **1074**

AMS ARS POETICA (US/0734-7618) [08808159] **3360**

AMS FLEXIBLE WORK SURVEY **CEASED.** (US) [13770621] **1643**

AMS FOOD PURCHASES. WEEKLY SUMMARY / UNITED STATES DEPARTMENT OF AGRICULTURE, AGRICULTURAL MARKETING SERVICE (US) [09993016] **2326**

●AMS INTERNATIONAL STUDIES (US/1058-2371) [24243493] **3360**

AMS ... MANAGEMENT SALARIES REPORT **CEASED.** (US/1048-6135) [18434188] **860**

AMS NEWSLETTER (BOSTON, MASS.) (US/0730-2029) [06056098] **1419**

AMS OFFICE, PROFESSIONAL & DATA PROCESSING SALARIES REPORT **CEASED.** (US/1053-8402) [22196529] **1643**

●AMS STUDIES IN 19TH CENTURY LITERATURE AND CULTURE (US/1059-5406) [24622907] **3360**

AMS STUDIES IN ANTHROPOLOGY (US/0738-064X) [09500873] **228**

AMS STUDIES IN CRIMINAL JUSTICE (US/0270-2991) [06384597] **3156**

●AMS STUDIES IN CULTURAL HISTORY (US/1058-2398) [24243587] **2609**

AMS STUDIES IN EDUCATION (US/0882-438X) [11836045] **1724**

AMS STUDIES IN GERMAN LITERATURE AND CULTURE (US/1045-6023) [20155341] **3361**

AMS STUDIES IN LIBRARY AND INFORMATION SCIENCE (US/1040-5631) [18453601] **3189**

AMS STUDIES IN MODERN LITERATURE (US/0270-2983) [06384571] **3361**

AMS STUDIES IN MODERN SOCIETY (US/0275-8407) [07243923] **5190**

●AMS STUDIES IN RELIGIOUS TRADITION (US/1059-7255) [24689034] **4934**

AMS STUDIES IN SOCIAL HISTORY (US/0270-6253) [06459206] **2610**

AMS STUDIES IN THE EIGHTEENTH CENTURY (US/0196-6561) [05876333] **3361**

AMS STUDIES IN THE EMBLEM (US/0892-4201) [15187867] **4563**

AMS STUDIES IN THE MIDDLE AGES (US/0270-6261) [06459224] **2673**

AMS STUDIES IN THE NINETEENTH CENTURY (US/0196-657X) [05875942] **3361**

AMS STUDIES IN THE RENAISSANCE (US/0195-8011) [05688325] **2673**

AMS STUDIES IN THE SEVENTEENTH CENTURY (US/0731-2342) [08139854] **2673**

AMSA HANDBOOK (AT) [06460448] 1446, **552**

AMSSEE NEWS (UK/0143-361X) [I0143361X] **4083**

AMSTAT NEWS (US/0163-9617) [01613888] **5320**

AMSTERDAM (NETHERLANDS). GEMEENTEARCHIEF *See* JAAROVERZICHT / GEMEENTEARCHIEF AMSTERDAM **2482**

AMSTERDAM (NETHERLANDS). GEMEENTEARCHIEF *See* JAARVERSLAG / GEMEENTEARCHIEF AMSTERDAM **2482**

AMSTERDAM. STEDELIJK MUSEUM *See* ATELIER **4222**

AMSTERDAM STUDIES IN THE THEORY AND HISTORY OF LINGUISTIC SCIENCE. SERIES 1, AMSTERDAM CLASSICS IN LINGUISTICS, 1800-1925 (NE/0304-0712) [08079088] **3264**

AMSTERDAM STUDIES IN THE THEORY AND HISTORY OF LINGUISTIC SCIENCE. SERIES 2. CLASSICS IN PSYCHOLINGUISTICS (NE/0165-716X) [I0165716X] **3263**

AMSTERDAM STUDIES IN THE THEORY AND HISTORY OF LINGUISTIC SCIENCE. SERIES III, STUDIES IN THE HISTORY OF THE LANGUAGE SCIENCES (NE/0304-0720) [17154105] **3263**

AMSTERDAM STUDIES IN THE THEORY AND HISTORY OF LINGUISTIC SCIENCE. SERIES IV, CURRENT ISSUES IN LINGUISTIC THEORY (NE/0304-0763) [03335760] **3264**

AMSTERDAM STUDIES IN THE THEORY AND HISTORY OF LINGUISTIC SCIENCE. SERIES V, LIBRARY AND INFORMATION SOURCES IN LINGUISTICS (NE/0165-7267) [04767920] **3264**

AMSTERDAM STUDIES IN THE THEORY AND HISTORY OF THE LINGUISTIC SCIENCE. SERIES 3: STUDIES IN THE HISTORY OF LINGUISTICS *See* AMSTERDAM STUDIES IN THE THEORY AND HISTORY OF LINGUISTIC SCIENCE. SERIES 1, AMSTERDAM CLASSICS IN LINGUISTICS, 1800-1925 **3264**

AMSTERDAMER BEITRAEGE ZUR ALTEREN GERMANISTIK (NE) [01481033] **3264**

AMSTERDAMER BEITRAEGE ZUR NEUEREN GERMANISTIK (NE/0304-6257) [01786488] **3361**

AMSTERDAMER PUBLIKATIONEN ZUR SPRACHE UND LITERATUR (NE/0169-0221) [03315948] **3361**

AMSTERDAMS SOCIOLOGISCH TIJDSCHRIFT 1988 (NE/0921-4933) [I09214933] **5239**

AMTLICHE MITTEILUNGEN DER BUNDESANSTALT FUER ARBEITSSCHUTZ (GW/0177-3062) [18403174] **2858**

AMTLICHE NACHRICHTEN DER BUNDESANSTALT FUER ARBEIT (GW/0007-585X) [I0007585X] 638, **1799**

AMTLICHE NACHRICHTEN DER BUNDESANSTALT FUER ARBEIT. ARBEITSSTATISTIK ... JAHRESZAHLEN (GW/0170-2696) [11387745] **5320**

AMTLICHE PFLANZENSCHUTZBESTIMMUNGEN (GW) [02383583] **2408**

AMTLICHE SAMMLUNG DES BUNDESRECHTS (SZ) [18175874] **2933**

AMTLICHE SCHRIFTTUM DER BUNDESREPUBLIK, DAS (GW/0433-7867) [01468857] **407**

AMTLICHES BULLETIN DER BUNDESVERSAMMLUNG (SZ) [03392862] **4463**

AMTLICHES GEMEINDEVERZEICHNIS FUER NIEDERSACHSEN *See* GEMEINDEVERZEICHNIS FUER NIEDERSACHSEN **2823**

AMTLICHES KURSBUCH *See* KURSBUCH - DEUTSCHE BUNDESBAHN **5432**

AMTLICHES OSTERREICHISCHES KURSBUCH *See* FAHRPLANE **5382**

AMTLICHES STENOGRAPHISCHES BULLETIN *See* AMTLICHES BULLETIN DER BUNDESVERSAMMLUNG **4463**

AMTLICHES — Alphabetical Title Index

AMTLICHES VERZEICHNIS DER TEILNEHMER AM FERNSCHREIVWAHLVERKEHR (TELEXVERKEHT) See AMTLICHES VERZICHNISUDER FERNSCHREIBTEILNEHMER (TELEX-VERZEICHNIS) **1148**

AMTLICHES VERZEICHNIS DER TEILNEHMER DES OFFENTLICHEN BILDUBERTRAGUNGSNETZES (GW) [03946427] **1148**

AMTLICHES VERZICHNISUDER FERNSCHREIBTEILNEHMER (TELEX-VERZEICHNIS) (AU) [03620831] **1148**

AMTRAK See SUMMARY OF C-D TRIPS (ALL TRAINS) **5437**

AMTRAK MATRIX SYSTEM ANNUAL ORIGIN/DESTINATION PASSENGER COUNT (US) [04141472] **5429**

AMTRAK'S INVENTORY AND PROPERTY CONTROLS NEED STRENGTHENING (US/0275-9829) [07236575] **5429**

AMTRI LIBRARY BULLETIN (JK) **3475**

AMTS- UND MITTEILUNGSBLATT / BAM, BUNDESANSTALT FUER MATERIALFORSCHUNG UND -PRUFUNG (GW/0340-7551) [18632103] **1964**

AMTSBLATT DER PHYSIKALISCH-TECHNISCHEN BUNDESANSTALT See MITTEILUNGEN - PTB **5129**

AMTSBLATT DER STADT WIEN (AU) [02244350] **4625**

AMTSBLATT DES BAYERISCHEN STAATSMINISTERIUMS DER FINANZEN (GW) [04388488] **4709**

AMTSBLATT DES BAYERISCHEN STAATSMINISTERIUMS FUER ARBEIT UND SOZIALORDNUNG (GW/0340-1790) [01795335] **3144**

AMTSBLATT DES EUROPAISCHEN PATENTAMTS (GW/0170-9291) [I01709291] **1301**

AMTSBLATT DES HESSISCHEN KULTUSMINISTERS (GW) [10944193] **2841**

AMTSBLATT FUER DAS VERMESSUNGSWESEN (AU) [06721749] **2018**

AMTSTATIGKEIT DER ARBEITSINSPEKTORATE M JAHRE, DIE (AU) [19959874] **1643**

AMUKA (CG) [04562061] **2498**

AMUSE USA (US/1058-1669) [24233921] **4856**

AMUSEMENT BUSINESS (US/0003-2344) [01481035] **4856**

AMUSEMENT-INDUSTRIE (GW/0171-7243) [I01717243] 5461, **4848**

AMUSEMENT INDUSTRY BUYERS GUIDE (US/1044-8268) [14956805] **4856**

AMUSEMENT JEUNESSE (CN/0709-2415) [05375760] **4856**

AMUSEMENT PARK GUIDEBOOK (US) [15709051] **4848**

AMUSEMENT PARK JOURNAL CEASED. (US/0271-7999) [06672530] **4857**

AMWA FREELANCE DIRECTORY, THE (US/0194-004X) [05255066] **2917**

AMYGDALA (SAN CRISTOBAL, N.M.) (US/1048-1680) [20881629] **3492**

AMYLOID: THE INTERNATIONAL JOURNAL OF EXPERIMENTAL AND CLINICAL INVESTIGATION (UK/1350-6129) **3549**

AN-ALFABETEN, DIE (GW/0934-9219) [I09349219] **1060**

AN COSANTOIR (IE) [08392924] **4040**

AN-HUI SHIH FAN TA HSUEH HSUEH PAO See AN-HUI SHIH TA HSUEH PAO **2841**

AN-HUI SHIH TA HSUEH PAO (CC) [07859194] **2841**

AN-HUI WEN HSUEH (CC) [18604857] **3361**

AN-NA-PAO T'UNG HSUN (US) [01827274] **2501**

ANA CLINICAL SESSIONS (US/0065-9495) [01524794] **3851**

● ANABAPTIST TIMES, THE (US/1065-6812) [26677746] **4934**

ANABOLIC REFERENCE UPDATE See MUSCLE MEDIA 2000 **2600**

ANACONDA LEADER, THE (US) [10256321] **5705**

ANACORTES AMERICAN (US) [17347854] **5758**

ANACOSTIA GRAPE VINE, THE (US/1062-2985) [25573846] **5647**

ANACRUSIS (CN/0826-7464) [11868864] **4100**

ANADARKO DAILY NEWS, THE (US/0744-1398) [08042582] **5731**

ANADOLU. ANATOLIA (TU) [01481036] **5461**

ANAELE UNIVERSITATII DIN GALATI. FASCICULA VIII (RM) **1964**

● ANAEROBE (LONDON, ENGLAND) (UK/1075-9964) [30350986] **441**

ANAESTHESIA (UK/0003-2409) [01481037] **3680**

ANAESTHESIA AND INTENSIVE CARE (AT/0310-057X) [01695566] **3680**

ANAESTHESIA (EDINBURGH) (UK/0263-1512) [10541987] **3680**

ANAESTHESIOLOGIA ES INTENSIV THERAPIA (HU/0133-5405) [02841013] **3680**

ANAESTHESIOLOGICA (OULU) (FI/0358-4836) [04813934] **3680**

ANAESTHESIOLOGIE UND INTENSIVMEDIZIN (ERLANGEN) (GW/0170-5334) [06899345] **3680**

ANAESTHESIOLOGIE UND REANIMATION (GW/0323-4983) [02550478] **3680**

ANAESTHESIOLOGY (CN/0824-7412) [11559835] **3680**

ANAESTHESIST, DER (GW/0003-2417) [01481038] **3681**

● ANAESTHETIC PHARMACOLOGY REVIEW (UK) [28358500] 4290, **3681**

ANAHEIM ... BUSINESS AND INDUSTRIAL DIRECTORY (US/0742-7298) [10381704] 1597, **638**

ANAHUTA (II) [06467019] **3361**

ANAIS - ACADEMIA PORTUGUESA DA HISTORIA (PO/0870-077X) [01635522] **2673**

ANAIS AZEVEDOS (PO/0003-2425) [I00032425] **4290**

ANAIS BRASILEIROS DE DERMATOLOGIA (BL/0365-0596) [01778554] **3717**

ANAIS - COLOQUIO DE ESTUDOS LUSO-BRASILEIROS (JA/0069-598X) [03765729] **2720**

ANAIS DA ACADEMIA BRASILEIRA DE CIENCIAS (BL/0001-3765) [01143768] **5082**

ANAIS DA ACADEMIA MINEIRA DE MEDICINA (BL/0301-4487) [01081146] **3549**

ANAIS DA BIBLIOTECA NACIONAL (BL) [01716786] **3457**

ANAIS DA CONFERENCIA NACIONAL DE SAUDE (BL) [05746263] **4765**

ANAIS DA ESCOLA SUPERIOR DE AGRICULTURA LUIZ DE QUEIROZ (BL/0071-1276) [02418271] **4161**

ANAIS DA FACULDADE DE CIENCIAS (PO) [02673418] **5082**

ANAIS DA FACULDADE DE MEDICINA VETERINARIA / UNIVERSIDADE TECNICA DE LISBOA (PO) [24685024] **5502**

ANAIS DA ... REUNIAO / SOCIEDADE BRASILEIRA DE PESQUISA HISTORICA, SBPH (BL) [09860232] **2720**

ANAIS DA SOCIEDADE ENTOMOLOGICA DO BRASIL (BL/0301-8059) [01792281] **5605**

ANAIS DA UTAD (PO/0871-0635) [I08710635] **58**

ANAIS DAS ESCOLAS DE AGRONOMIA E DE VETERINARIA : ORGAO OFICIAL DAS ESCOLAS DE AGRONOMIA E VETERINARIA, UNIVERSIDADE FEDERAL DE GOIAS (BL) [28052762] 5502, **58**

ANAIS DE FARMACIA E QUIMICA DE SAO PAULO (BL/0003-2441) [02257483] **4290**

ANAIS DO CBEN (BL/0102-2334) [07078440] **3851**

ANAIS DO ... CONGRESSO LATINO-AMERICANO DE MICROGRAFICA (PO) [08119472] **4563**

ANAIS DO CONPAT (BL) [04148798] **2858**

ANAIS DO INSTITUTO DE HIGIENE E MEDICINA TROPICAL (PO/0303-7762) [01142313] **3549**

ANAIS DO MUSEU DE ANTROPOLOGIA (BL/0101-451X) [11465110] **228**

ANAIS DO MUSEU HISTORICO NACIONAL (BL/0225-1823) [02251823] **2720**

ANAIS DO MUSEU PAULISTA (BL) [02915147] **2720**

ANAIS FORENSES DO ESTADO DE MATO GROSSO (BL/0251-0675) [02510675] **2933**

ANAIS HIDROGRAFICOS (BL) [07239477] **5529**

ANAIS (LOS ANGELES, CALIF.) (US/8755-3910) [10487610] **3361**

ANALE DE ISTORIE (RM/1010-5506) [02244150] **4625**

ANALECTA ANSELMIANA. UNTERSUCHUNG UBER PERSON U. WERK ANSELMUS VON CANTERBURY (GW) [01777403] **4934**

ANALECTA AUGUSTINIANA (IT) [01705332] **5023**

ANALECTA BIBLICA (IT) **5014**

ANALECTA BOLLANDIANA (BE/0003-2468) [01481044] **4934**

ANALECTA CALASANCTIANA (SP/0569-9789) [02055839] **5023**

ANALECTA CARTUSIANA (AU/0253-1593) [03320183] **4934**

ANALECTA CISTERCIENSIA (IT/0003-2476) [06098807] **5023**

ANALECTA CISTERCIENSIA (IT/0003-2476) [01705281] 2610, **4934**

ANALECTA GEOLOGICA (DK/0569-9797) [04129771] **1365**

ANALECTA GREGORIANA (IT/0066-1376) [01481045] **4934**

ANALECTA MALACITANA (SP/0211-9358) [05258347] **3264**

ANALECTA MUSICOLOGICA (GW/0569-9827) [01481047] **4100**

ANALECTA ORIENTALIA (IT) [01481048] **2610**

ANALECTA PRAEHISTORICA LEIDENSIA (NE/0169-7447) [01708883] **2610**

ANALECTA PRAEMONSTRATENSIA (BE) [02029694] 429, **2610**

ANALECTA ROMANA INSTITUTI DANICI (DK/0066-1392) [01708903] 287, **254**

ANALECTA ROMANA INSTITUTI DANICI. SUPPLEMENTUM (DK/0066-1406) [03322430] 287, **254**

ANALECTA ROMANICA (GW/0569-986X) [02063589] **3264**

ANALECTA SACRA TARRACONENSIA (SP/0304-4300) [01707607] **4934**

ANALECTA SLAVICA (GW) [03755033] **2841**

ANALECTA TERTII ORDINIS REGULARIS SANCTI FRANCISCI (IT) [12227916] **5023**

ANALECTA VETERINARIA (AG/0365-5148) [01481054] **5502**

ANALELE INSTITUTULUI DE BIOLOGIE SI NUTRITIE ANIMALA BALOTESTI (RM) [21284039] 205, **5502**

ANALELE INSTITUTULUI DE CERCETARI PENTRU CEREALE SI PLANTE TEHNICE, FUNDULEA (RM/0253-1682) [03622117] **58**

ANALELE INSTITUTULUI DE CERCETARI PENTRU PEDOLOGIE SI AGROCHIMIE (RM/0258-6959) [05214851] **162**

ANALELE - INSTITUTULUI DE CERCETARI PENTRU PROTECTIA PLANTELOR, ACADEMIA DE STIINTE AGRICOLE SI SILVICE (RM/0365-575X) [02460572] **498**

ANALELE INSTITUTULUI DE GEODEZIE, FOTOGRAMMETRIE, CARTOGRAFIE SI ORGANIZAREA TERITORIULUI (RM/0253-1232) [07378968] **1351**

ANALELE STIINTIFICE ALE UNIVERSITATII "AL. I. CUZA" DIN IASI. SERIE NOUA. SECTIUNEA 1A, MATEMATICA (RM/0041-9109) [04230953] **3492**

ANALELE STIINTIFICE ALE UNIVERSITATII "AL. I. CUZA" DIN IASI. SERIE NOUA. SECTIUNEA IIA, BIOLOGIE (RM/0041-9133) [11363516] **441**

ANALELE STIINTIFICE ALE UNIVERSITATII "AL. I. CUZA" DIN IASI. SERIE NOUA. SECTIUNEA III E, LINGVISTICA (RM/0379-7880) [09698846] **3264**

ANALELE STIINTIFICE ALE UNIVERSITATII "AL. I. CUZA" DIN IASI. SERIE NOUA. SECTIUNEA III F, LITERATURA (RM/0379-7899) [09698833] **3361**

ANALELE UNIVERSITABII DIN GALATI. FASCICULA IX, METALURGIE SI COCSERIE (RM) [15367100] **3997**

ANALELE UNIVERSITATII DIN GALATI. FASCICULA II - MATEMATICA, FIZICA, MECANICA TEORETICA (RM) 4396, **3492**

ANALELE UNIVERSITATII BUCURESTI : BIOLOGIE (RM/0378-8989) [06325238] **441**

ANALELE UNIVERSITATII BUCURESTI. DREPT (RM) [04339248] **2933**

ANALELE UNIVERSITATII BUCURESTI : FILOSOFIE (RM) [04843852] **4340**

ANALELE UNIVERSITATII BUCURESTI. FIZICA (1977) (RM/0254-8895) [03633193] **4396**

ANALELE UNIVERSITATII BUCURESTI. GEOLOGIE (RM/0068-3183) [05796390] **1365**

ANALELE UNIVERSITATII BUCURESTI : ISTORIE (RM/0068-3205) [05705706] **2673**

ANALELE UNIVERSITATII BUCURESTI. LIMBA SI LITERATURA ROMANA (RM/0068-3256) [02724556] **3361**

ANALELE UNIVERSITATII BUCURESTI : LIMBI SI LITERATURI STRAINE (RM) [04174512] **3264**

ANALELE UNIVERSITATII BUCURESTI : LITERATURA UNIVERSALA SI COMPARATA (RM/0068-3264) [02721460] **3361**

Alphabetical Title Index — ANALES

ANALELE UNIVERSITATII BUCURESTI. MATEMATICA (RM/1010-5433) [03567305] 1170, **3492**

ANALELE UNIVERSITATII BUCURESTI: PSIHOLOGIE (RM) [05665943] **4573**

ANALELE UNIVERSITATII BUCURESTI: SOCIOLOGIE (RM/0068-3302) [05665955] **5239**

ANALELE UNIVERSITATII DIN CRAIOVA. MATHEMATICA, FIZICA-CHIMIE (RM/0253-1860) [07436578] 4396, **3492**

ANALELE UNIVERSITATII DIN CRAIOVA. MECANICA, ELECTROTEHNICA (RM) [09483499] **2034**

ANALELE UNIVERSITATII DIN CRAIOVA: SERIA ISTORIE, GEOGRAFIE, FILOLOGIE (RM) [01798533] 2553, **2673**

ANALELE UNIVERSITATII DIN CRAIOVA. SERIA: STIINTE ECONOMICE SI GEOGRAFIE (RM) [06896845] **1461**

ANALELE UNIVERSITATII DIN CRAIOVA : STIINTE FILOLOGICE (RM) [05181466] **3264**

ANALELE UNIVERSITATII DIN GAGATI. FASCICULA III (RM) **2035**

ANALELE UNIVERSITATII DIN GALATI. FASCICULA I, STIINTE SOCIALE SI UMANISTE (RM/1015-9606) [I10159606] **5190**

ANALELE UNIVERSITATII DIN GALATI. FASCICULA III (RM) 1170, **2035**

ANALELE UNIVERSITATII DIN GALATI. FASCICULA IV (RM) **1964**

ANALELE UNIVERSITATII DIN GALATI. FASCICULA VI, TEHNOLOGIA SI CHIMIA PRODUSELOR ALIMENTARE (RM/1011-4025) [15367425] 960, **5082**

ANALELE UNIVERSITATII DIN GALATI.FASCICULA VII, TEHNICA PISCICOLA (RM) [25905556] **2294**

ANALELE UNIVERSITATII DIN GALATI. FASCICULA X (RM) **2109**

ANALELE UNIVERSITATII DIN GALATI. FASCICULA XI (RM) **5447**

ANALELE UNIVERSITATII DIN GALATI. FASCICULA XII (RM) **4026**

ANALELE UNIVERSITATII DIN GALATI. FASCICULA XIII (RM) 3264, **3361**

ANALELE UNIVERSITATII DIN TIMISOARA. SERIA STINTE FIZICE-CHIMICE (RM/0082-4453) [03341778] 960, **4396**

ANALELE UNIVERSITATII DIN TIMISOARA. STIINTE FILOLOGICE (RM) [20461883] **3264**

ANALELE UNIVERSITATII DIN TIMISOARA. STIINTE MATEMATICE (RM) [12848805] **3492**

ANALELE UNIVERSITATII DIN TIMISOARA. STIINTE SOCIALE SI ECONOMICE (RM) [11340016] **5190**

ANALELE UNIVERSITATII. FASCICULA V (RM) **2109**

ANALES (AG) [06414054] **558**

ANALES (SP/0034-0618) [03561511] **4290**

ANALES / ACADEMIA DE GEOGRAFIA E HISTORIA DE COSTA RICA (CR/0567-6509) [05514339] 2553, **2720**

ANALES - ACADEMIA NACIONAL DE CIENCIAS MORALES Y POLITICAS (AG) [02591783] **5190**

ANALES ANTROPOLOGICOS / FACULTAD DE ANTROPOLOGIA DE LA UNIVERSIDAD VERACRUZANA (MX) [26176103] **228**

ANALES CERVANTINOS (SP/0569-9878) [01695318] **3361**

ANALES - CIDEPINT (AG/0325-4186) [I03254186] **5082**

ANALES CIENTIFICOS - UNIVERSIDAD NACIONAL DEL CENTRO DEL PERU (PE) [01785931] **5082**

ANALES DE ANATOMIA (SP/0569-9894) [01481057] **3678**

ANALES DE ANTROPOLOGIA / INSTITUTO DE INVESTIGACIONES ANTROPOLOGICAS (MX/0185-1225) [15242242] **228**

ANALES DE ARQUEOLOGIA Y ETNOLOGIA / UNIVERSIDAD NACIONAL DE CUYO, FACULTAD DE FILOSOFIA Y LETRAS (AG/0325-0288) [06405487] 228, **254**

ANALES DE ARQUITECTURA : REVISTA DEL DEPARTAMENTO DE TEORIA DE LA ARQUITECTURA Y PROYECTOS ARQUITECTONICOS, ESCUELA TECNICA SUPERIOR DE ARQUITECTURA DE VALLADOLID (SP/0214-4727) [25119896] **287**

ANALES DE BIOLOGIA (SP) [19279970] **441**

ANALES DE BIOLOGIA. SECCION BIOLOGIA AMBIENTAL (SP/0213-4004) [13763689] 441, **2211**

ANALES DE BROMATOLOGIA (SP/0003-2492) [04836076] **4187**

ANALES DE CIENCIAS HUMANAS (PN) [05778375] **1461**

ANALES DE CIENCIAS - UNIVERSIDAD DE MURCIA (SP/0213-5469) [14768688] 2007, 3492, **960**

ANALES DE CIRUGIA (AG/0066-1465) [01481059] **3958**

ANALES DE DERECHO (SP) [05268753] **2933**

ANALES DE FILOLOGIA HISPANICA / UNIVERSIDAD DE MURCIA *SUSPENDED.* (SP/0213-4365) [16988761] **3264**

● ANALES DE FISICA (SP/1133-0376) [29164947] **4396**

ANALES DE FISICA. SERIE A, FENOMENOS E INTERACCIONES (SP/0211-6243) [08047533] **4396**

ANALES DE FISICA. SERIE A: FENOMENOS E INTERACCIONES *See* ANALES DE FISICA **4396**

ANALES DE FISICA. SERIE B: APLICACIONES, METODOS E INSTRUMENTOS *See* ANALES DE FISICA **4396**

ANALES DE GEOGRAFIA (MX) [04322895] **2553**

ANALES DE GEOGRAFIA DE LA UNIVERSIDAD COMPLUTENSE / SECCION DE GEOGRAFIA (SP/0211-9803) [09780179] **2553**

ANALES DE HISTORIA CONTEMPORANEA (SP) [10370135] **2673**

ANALES DE INGENIERIA (CK) [05284407] **1964**

ANALES DE INVESTIGACION HISTORICA (PR) [08394256] **2720**

ANALES DE JURISPRUDENCIA (MX) [01481061] **2933**

ANALES DE LA ACADEMIA DE GEOGRAFIA E HISTORIA DE GUATEMALA (GT/0252-337X) [08623842] **228**

ANALES DE LA ACADEMIA NACIONAL DE CIENCIAS. CUADERNO 2 : SERIE CIENCIAS DE LA NATURALEZA (BO/0567-5911) [01081191] **441**

ANALES DE LA ASOCIACION DE PALINOLOGOS DE LENGUA ESPAfNOLA (SP/0213-1811) [I02131811] **3264**

ANALES DE LA ASOCIACION QUIMICA ARGENTINA (AG/0365-0375) [06018473] **960**

ANALES DE LA CATEDRA DE TISIONEUMONOLOGIA (AG/0326-5412) [09027685] **3948**

ANALES DE LA CATEDRA FRANCISCO SUAREZ (SP/0008-7750) [01454694] 2933, **4340**

ANALES DE LA ESCUELA NACIONAL DE CIENCIAS BIOLOGICAS (MEXICO) (MX/0365-1932) [02448594] **441**

ANALES DE LA ESTACION EXPERIMENTAL DE AULA DEI (SP/0365-1800) [02407142] **58**

ANALES DE LA FACULTAD DE VETERINARIA DE LEON (SP/0373-1170) [01394479] **5502**

ANALES DE LA FUNDACION JUAN MARCH (SP/0532-8500) [06243157] **4334**

ANALES DE LA FUNDACION PUIGVERT (SP/0303-4690) [01041792] **3988**

ANALES DE LA LITERATURA ESPANOLA CONTEMPORANEA (US/0272-1635) [06796841] **3361**

ANALES DE LA REAL ACADEMIA DE MEDICINA Y CIRUGIA DE CADIZ (SP/0210-7058) [I02107058] **3958**

ANALES DE LA REAL ACADEMIA DE MEDICINA Y CIRUGIA DE VALLADOLID (SP/0210-6523) [I02106523] **3958**

ANALES DE LA REAL ACADEMIA NACIONAL DE MEDICINA, MADRID (SP/0034-0634) [01081375] **3549**

ANALES DE LA SOCIEDAD CIENTIFICA ARGENTINA (AG/0037-8437) [01765722] **5082**

ANALES DE LA SOCIEDAD ERGOFTALMOLOGICA ESPANOLA (SP/0210-0681) [I02100681] **3872**

ANALES DE LA UNIVERSIDAD CATOLICA DE VALPARAISO (CL/0504-9903) [01466809] **1808**

ANALES DE LA UNIVERSIDAD DE ALICANTE. HISTORIA CONTEMPORANEA (SP) [11628972] **2673**

ANALES DE LA UNIVERSIDAD DE CADIZ (SP) [13085733] **1089**

ANALES DE LA UNIVERSIDAD DE CHILE *SUSPENDED.* (CL/0365-7779) [01554269] **1724**

ANALES DE LA UNIVERSIDAD DE MURCIA: CIENCIAS *See* ANALES DE CIENCIAS - UNIVERSIDAD DE MURCIA **960**

ANALES DE LA UNIVERSIDAD DE MURCIA. LETRAS (SP) [09473723] **1808**

ANALES DE L'ACADEMIA NACIONAL DE CIENCIAS EXACTAS, FISICAS Y NATURALES, BUENOS AIRES (AG/0365-1185) [03680944] **5082**

ANALES DE LITERATURA HISPANOAMERICANA (SP) [01789589] **3361**

ANALES DE MECANICA Y ELECTRICIDAD (SP/0003-2506) [09845503] **2035**

ANALES DE MEDICINA (PE) [05166427] **3549**

ANALES DE MEDICINA INTERNA : ORGANO OFICIAL DE LA SOCIEDAD ESPANOLA DE MEDICINA INTERNA (SP/0212-7199) [24538303] **3794**

ANALES DE OTORRINOLARINGOLOGIA (SP) **3886**

ANALES DE PEDAGOGIA (SP/0212-8322) [I02128322] **1724**

ANALES DE PREHISTORIA Y ARQUEOLOGIA (SP/0213-5663) [19792437] **254**

ANALES DE PSIQUIATRIA (SP/0213-0599) [24913885] **3920**

ANALES DE QUIMICA (MADRID. 1990) (SP/1130-2283) [22217852] **960**

ANALES DE QUIMICA. SERIE A, QUIMICA FISICA Y QUIMICA TECNICA (SP) [06729003] **4396**

ANALES DE VETERINARIA DE MURCIA (SP/0213-5434) [20335873] **5502**

ANALES DEL CARIBE (CU/1017-8937) [I10178937] 3361, **2841**

ANALES DEL DESARROLLO (SP/0569-9908) [20787675] **441**

ANALES DEL FORO (UY) [10060583] **2933**

ANALES DEL HOSPITAL DE LA SANTA CRUZ Y SAN PABLO *See* SANT PAU **3638**

ANALES DEL INSTITUTO BARRAQUER (SP/0020-3645) [01394506] **3872**

ANALES DEL INSTITUTO BELGRANIANO CENTRAL (AG) [07486400] **2720**

ANALES DEL INSTITUTO DE BIOLOGIA. SERIE BOTANICA (MX/0185-254X) [I0185254X] **498**

ANALES DEL INSTITUTO DE BIOLOGIA. SERIE ZOOLOGIA (MX/0185-2590) [I01852590] **5502**

ANALES DEL INSTITUTO DE BIOLOGIA, UNIVERSIDAD NACIONAL AUTONOMA DE MEXICO. SERIE BOTANICA (MX/0374-5511) [01589807] **498**

ANALES DEL INSTITUTO DE BIOLOGIA, UNIVERSIDAD NACIONAL AUTONOMA DE MEXICO. SERIE ZOOLOGIA (MX/0368-8720) [01589861] **5575**

ANALES DEL INSTITUTO DE CIENCIAS DEL MAR Y LIMNOLOGIA, UNIVERSIDAD NACIONAL AUTONOMA DE MEXICO (MX/0185-3287) [09005796] **552**

ANALES DEL INSTITUTO DE ESTUDIOS GERUNDENSES (SP/0211-2329) [03812329] **2673**

ANALES DEL INSTITUTO DE ESTUDIOS MADRILENOS (SP/0584-6374) [01779968] **2673**

ANALES DEL INSTITUTO DE INVESTIGACIONES ESTETICAS (MX/0185-1276) [01628173] 2841, **336**

ANALES DEL INSTITUTO DE INVESTIGACIONES MARINAS DE PUNTA DE BETIN (CK/0120-3959) [04456851] **552**

ANALES DEL INSTITUTO DE INVESTIGACIONES VETERINARIAS (SP/0365-3536) [01756415] **5502**

ANALES DEL INSTITUTO DE LA PATAGONIA. SERIE CIENCIAS NATURALES (CL/0716-6486) [18146248] **4161**

ANALES DEL INSTITUTO DE LA PATAGONIA. SERIE CIENCIAS SOCIALES (CL/0716-6478) [18146180] **5190**

ANALES DEL INSTITUTO DE MATEMATICAS (MX/0185-0644) [01757266] **3492**

ANALES DEL JARDIN BOTANICO DE MADRID (1979) (SP/0211-1322) [06712079] **499**

ANALES DEL MUSEO DE HISTORIA NATURAL DE VALPARAISO (CL) [03885261] **4161**

ANALES DEL MUSEO NACIONAL "DAVID J. GUZMAN." (ES/0374-5546) [05291228] **1724**

ANALES DEL SEMINARIO DE HISTORIA DE LA FILOSOFIA (SP) [08379640] **4340**

ANALES DEL SEMINARIO DE METAFISICA (SP/0580-8650) [05544215] **4340**

ANALES ESPANOLES DE PEDIATRIA (SP/0302-4342) [10262162] **3900**

ANALES ESPANOLES DE PEDIATRIA. SUPLEMENTO (SP/0213-9146) [I02139146] **3900**

ANALES GALDOSIANOS (US/0569-9924) [01481067] **3337**

ANALES — Alphabetical Title Index

ANALES - INSTITUTO MEDICO BENEFICENCIA (SP/0210-5403) [I02105403] **3549**

ANALES - MUSEO NACIONAL DE HISTORIA NATURAL (URUGUAY) (UY) [01787218] **4161**

ANALES OTORRINOLARINGOLOGICOS IBERO-AMERICANOS (SP/0303-8874) [01197252] **3886**

ANALES PARLAMENTARIOS / REPUBLICA ORIENTAL DEL URUGUAY, PALACIO LEGISLATIVO - BIBLIOTECA (UY) [05041536] **4625**

ANALES - SALA PROVINCIA (SP) [01791900] **336**

ANALES TOLEDANOS (SP/0538-1983) [01775660] **2673**

ANALES VALENTINOS (SP/0210-0460) [02436820] **4934**

ANALGESIA COMPUTERFILE (US/1057-4131) [24032180] **3958**

●ANALGESIA (ELMSFORD, N.Y.) (US/1071-569X) [28679004] **3681**

●ANALGESIAFILE (SAN ANTONIO, TEXAS) (US/1057-2260) [23980363] **3549**

ANALI GAZI HASREV-BEGOVE BIBLIOTHEKE (BN/0350-1418) [03615272] **2673**

ANALISE (BL) [02517302] **1545**

ANALISE CONJUNTURAL DO EMPREGO (BL) [07228228] **1643**

ANALISE DAS INFORMACOES SOCIO-EDUCACIONAIS DOS CANDIDATOS AOS CONCURSOS VESTIBULARES *See* ANALISE E INTERPRETACAO PARCIAL DAS INFORMACOES SOCIO-EDUCACIONAIS DOS CANDIDATOS AOS CONCURSOS VESTIBULARES **1808**

ANALISE DO SETOR AGROPECUARIO DE SERGIPE (BL) [02241282] **58**

ANALISE E INTERPRETACAO PARCIAL DAS INFORMACOES SOCIO-EDUCACIONAIS DOS CANDIDATOS AOS CONCURSOS VESTIBULARES (BL) [10006974] **1808**

ANALISE PSICOLOGICA (PO/0870-8231) [04219202] **4573**

ANALISE SOCIAL (PO/0003-2573) [04803604] **5239**

ANALISI E DOCUMENTI (IT) [01785512] **407**

ANALISI FINANZIARIA (IT) **770**

ANALISIS (CL) [06843838] **5055**

ANALISIS (PE) [03604001] **5190**

ANALISIS CLINICOS (SP/0212-4572) [I02124572] **3549**

ANALISIS-CONFIRMADO (US) [01785496] **2551**

ANALISIS CSIS (IO/0126-222X) [20448070] **4515**

ANALISIS DE LA AGRICULTURA SINALOENSE *CEASED.* (MX) [04902063] **58**

ANALISIS E INVESTIGACIONES CULTURALES (SP) [07684046] **2673**

ANALISIS ESTADISTICO, URUGUAY: IMPORTACION - EXPORTACION (UY) [03720086] **822**

ANALISIS FILOSOFICO (AG/0326-1301) [12714166] **4340**

ANALISIS FINANCIERO (SP) 890, **770**

ANALISIS LATINOAMERICANO (US/0195-9328) [05740479] **4515**

ANALISIS (PANAMA, PANAMA) (PN) [15150441] **2527**

ANALISIS PENDIDIKAN (IO) [08102313] **1724**

ANALISIS (SAN JUAN, P.R.) (PR) [09223844] **5271**

ANALISIS Y MODIFICACION DE CONDUCTA (SP/0211-7339) [I02117339] **4573**

ANALIZ NA PROBLEMNYKH SETIAKH / AKADEMIIA NAUK SSSR, INSTITUT MIROVOI EKONOMIKI I MEZHDUNARODNYKH OTNOSHENII (RU/0130-9412) [09930406] **3493**

ANALIZ STILEI ZARUBEZHNOI KHUDOZHESTVENNOI I NAUCHNOI LITERATURY (RU/0202-2435) [05525975] 3361, **3264**

ANALOG ANNUAL (US/0362-7403) [02315942] **3361**

ANALOG DEVICES, INC *See* DATA-ACQUISITION DATABOOK **2040**

ANALOG INTEGRATED CIRCUITS AND SIGNAL PROCESSING (US/0925-1030) [25106273] **2035**

ANALOG SCIENCE FICTION & FACT (US/1059-2113) [24509427] **3361**

ANALOG SOUNDS (US/0097-6482) [01799269] **4100**

ANALUSIS (FR/0365-4877) [01814765] **1012**

ANALYSE (NE/0166-7688) 1643, **3549**

ANALYSE & KRITIK (GW/0171-5860) [07985313] **5190**

ANALYSE CHIMIQUE ET CARACTERISATION (BE) **960**

ANALYSE DE LA CAMPAGNE / CENTRAIDE CANADA (CN/0228-6610) [07857968] **5271**

ANALYSE DE L'INDUSTRIE DE LA CONSTRUCTION AU QUEBEC (CN/0317-5901) [06101822] **598**

ANALYSE FINANCIERE (FR/0153-9841) [I01539841] **770**

ANALYSE MUSICALE *SUSPENDED.* (FR/0295-3722) [16913906] **4100**

ANALYSE NUMERIQUE ET LA THEORIE DE L'APPROXIMATION, L' (RM/1010-3376) [03773030] **3493**

ANALYSEN UND BERICHTE AUS GESELLSCHAFTSWISSENSCHAFTEN *See* ABG **5189**

ANALYSES COMPARATIVES - COMMISSION BANCAIRE PARIS (FR/1167-5128) [I11675128] **770**

ANALYSES DE LA S.E.D.E.I.S (FR/0399-1245) [03746230] **1461**

ANALYSES OF HAZARDOUS SUBSTANCES IN BIOLOGICAL MATERIALS (GW/0179-7247) [13151343] 441, **2224**

ANALYSES OF NATURAL GASES (US) [04173196] **4249**

ANALYSES OF NEW JERSEY PUBLIC LIBRARY STATISTICS FOR ... (US) [10609004] 3189, **3257**

ANALYSES OF PROPOSED CONSTITUTIONAL AMENDMENTS FOR ELECTION ... (US) [08769768] **2933**

ANALYSES OF THE ... ILLINOIS PUBLIC LIBRARY STATISTICS (US/0736-5616) [03808399] 3189, **3257**

ANALYSES OF TIPPLE AND DELIVERED SAMPLES OF COAL (US) [02536259] **1931**

ANALYSES, THEORIE *CEASED.* (FR/0181-7205) [10055360] **3264**

ANALYSIS (GW) [10812320] **3493**

ANALYSIS AND FORECASTS (BE) [08690503] **5375**

ANALYSIS AND SUMMARY OF CONDITION AND PERFORMANCE OF THE FARM CREDIT BANKS AND ASSOCIATIONS (US) [25603038] 58, **770**

ANALYSIS MATHEMATICA (BUDAPEST) (HU/0133-3852) [02244325] **3493**

ANALYSIS (NEW YORK (N.Y.) (US/0003-2638) [05719059] **4340**

ANALYSIS OF ANNUAL REPORTS OF LICENSEES (US/0093-979X) [01793314] **770**

ANALYSIS OF BICYCLE/MOTOR VEHICLE COLLISIONS REPORTED IN MANITOBA, JANUARY 1,-DECEMBER 31 ..., AN (CN/0711-9453) [03592878] **5376**

ANALYSIS OF BUDGETED EXPENDITURE ON EDUCATION (II) [11500966] **1860**

ANALYSIS OF CLASS 1 RAILROADS (US) [09631910] **5400**

ANALYSIS OF DRUGS AND METABOLITES BY GAS CHROMATOGRAPHY-MASS SPECTROMETRY (US/0164-0453) [04553210] **1012**

ANALYSIS OF FACTORS RELATED TO THE OPERATION OF THE COLLEGES AND THE SCHOOLS AND THE INSTRUCTIONAL DEPARTMENTS OF THE FLORIDA STATE UNIVERSITY, AN (US/0428-6715) [01342577] **1808**

ANALYSIS OF FEDERAL AND STATE CAMPAIGN FINANCE LAW (US) [02363335] **2933**

ANALYSIS OF FEDERAL AND STATE CAMPAIGN FINANCE LAW, SUMMARIES, AND QUICK-REFERENCE CHARTS *See* CAMPAIGN FINANCE LAW **2947**

ANALYSIS OF FEDERAL R&D FUNDING BY FUNCTION, AN (US) [02368400] **4625**

ANALYSIS OF GOVERNOR'S RECOMMENDED ... BUDGET (US) [19053280] **4709**

... ANALYSIS OF IMPULSE SNACK BAR OPERATIONS : A STUDY PRESENTED TO THE GOLD MEDAL PRODUCTS COMPANY OF CINCINNATI, OHIO / BY WENDELL G. EARLE AND GEORGE S. HAYWARD, THE (US) [07980534] **5070**

ANALYSIS OF KEY SEC NO-ACTION LETTERS (US/0887-1337) [12784467] **3095**

ANALYSIS OF MARYLAND SALES AND USE TAX ... REVENUES COLLECTED IN MONTGOMERY COUNTY / MONTGOMERY COUNTY GOVERNMENT, DEPARTMENT OF FINANCE (US/0739-3059) [09701025] **4709**

ANALYSIS OF MICHIGAN PUBLIC SCHOOL REVENUES AND EXPENDITURES / MICHIGAN STATE BOARD OF EDUCATION (US) [08077673] **1724**

ANALYSIS OF MOTOR CARRIER ACCIDENTS INVOLVING VEHICLE DEFECTS OR MECHANICAL FAILURE (US) [05930157] **5376**

ANALYSIS OF OFFICIAL PESTICIDE SAMPLES (US/0099-1929) [02242222] **4243**

ANALYSIS OF PROVISIONS IN SELECTED ARTICLES OF AGREEMENTS (US/0190-0579) [04374584] **1860**

ANALYSIS OF RAW, POTABLE AND WASTE WATERS *See* METHODS FOR THE EXAMINATION OF WATERS AND ASSOCIATED MATERIALS **2236**

ANALYSIS OF RESEARCH PUBLICATIONS SUPPORTED BY NIH AND NHLBI (US) [08964962] **4765**

ANALYSIS OF RESEARCH PUBLICATIONS SUPPORTED BY NIH AND NIAID (US) [08965016] **4765**

ANALYSIS OF REVISIONS OF THE UNIFORM BUILDING CODE, U.B.C. STANDARDS ... (US/0896-9752) [06611604] 598, **2933**

ANALYSIS OF SINGLE EMPLOYER DEFINED BENEFIT PLAN TERMINATIONS (US/0197-1581) [04517796] **1643**

ANALYSIS OF THE ... GOVERNOR'S BUDGET : A STAFF REPORT TO THE CALIFORNIA POSTSECONDARY EDUCATION COMMISSION (US) [23300956] **1808**

ANALYSIS OF THE PRESIDENT'S BUDGETARY PROPOSALS, AN *CEASED.* (US/0747-5187) [04863837] **4709**

ANALYSIS OF VERBAL BEHAVIOR, THE (US/0889-9401) [13592629] **4573**

ANALYSIS OF WORKMEN'S COMPENSATION LAWS (US/0191-118X) [04327212] **3144**

ANALYSIS - TEXAS. COMPTROLLER'S OFFICE (US/0147-6637) [03214998] **4709**

●ANALYST DIRECTORY. LISTED BY COMPANY (US/1073-6301) [29507647] **890**

ANALYST (LONDON) (UK/0003-2654) [01481074] **1012**

ANALYST WATCH (US/1071-2364) [28576986] 1462, **890**

ANALYSTE (MONTREAL, QUEBEC) *CEASED.* (CN/0715-7649) [09796299] **2527**

ANALYST'S HANDBOOK (US/0884-6936) [01717076] **890**

ANALYTIC TEACHING (US/0890-5118) [10813994] 1888, **4340**

ANALYTICA *SUSPENDED.* (FR/0246-2826) [08582978] **4573**

ANALYTICA (GW) **4340**

ANALYTICA CHIMICA ACTA (NE/0003-2670) [01716731] **1012**

ANALYTICAL ABSTRACTS (UK/0003-2689) [01481076] 1013, **996**

ANALYTICAL AND QUANTITATIVE CYTOLOGY AND HISTOLOGY (US/0884-6812) [12009962] **531**

ANALYTICAL BIOCHEMISTRY (US/0003-2697) [01481077] **479**

ANALYTICAL CELLULAR PATHOLOGY (NE/0921-8912) [20103459] **532**

ANALYTICAL CHEMISTRY SYMPOSIA SERIES (NE/0167-6350) [06398838] **1013**

ANALYTICAL CHEMISTRY (WASHINGTON) (US/0003-2700) [01481078] **1013**

ANALYTICAL CONSUMER (US/1052-3065) [22248286] **1293**

ANALYTICAL ELECTRON MICROSCOPY (US/0738-2014) [09511742] **572**

ANALYTICAL INSTRUMENT INDUSTRY REPORT (UK/0265-3435) [22331949] **1597**

ANALYTICAL INSTRUMENTATION (US/0743-5797) [10613127] **3549**

ANALYTICAL LETTERS (US/0003-2719) [01481079] **1013**

●ANALYTICAL METHODS AND INSTRUMENTATION (UK/1063-5246) [26057219] **1020**

ANALYTICAL METHODS FOR RESIDUES OF PESTICIDES IN FOODSTUFFS (NE) **4244**

ANALYTICAL MICROBIOLOGY (US/0090-2284) [01783008] **558**

ANALYTICAL PROCEEDINGS (UK/0144-557X) [06056313] **1013**

ANALYTICAL PROFILES OF DRUG SUBSTANCES (US/0099-5428) [03715669] 4290, **1050**

●ANALYTICAL PROFILES OF DRUG SUBSTANCES AND EXCIPIENTS (US) [27052258] **4290**

ANALYTICAL SCIENCES : THE INTERNATIONAL JOURNAL OF THE JAPAN SOCIETY FOR ANALYTICAL CHEMISTRY (JA/0910-6340) [12754332] **1013**

ANALYTICAL SPECTROSCOPY LIBRARY (NE/0926-4345) [22472827] **4433**

ANALYTICAL STUDIES FOR THE U.S. ENVIRONMENTAL PROTECTION AGENCY (US/0270-0697) [05175855] **2160**

ANALYTISCHE PSYCHOLOGIE (SZ/0301-3006) [07708711] **4573**

ANAMBRA STATE (NIGERIA) *See* APPROVED ESTIMATES OF ANAMBRA STATE OF NIGERIA **4711**

ANAMNESES VILLEJUIF *CEASED.* (FR/1166-9829) [11669829] **2610**

ANAMOSA JOURNAL-EUREKA, THE (US) [12306657] **5668**

ANANDA PATRIKA (II) [11808818] **3361**

ANANDA SANDESA (II) [02239373] **5040**

ANAP (CU) [01785937] **58**

ANAP (ORGANIZATION) *See* ANAP **58**

ANAPERIKON VEMA (GR) [05131222] **5271**

ANAPORC (SP) **205**

ANARCHIST ENCYCLOPAEDIA (UK/0267-6141) [15925934] **4539**

●ANARCHIST STUDIES (UK/0967-3393) [28277565] **4539**

ANARCHY (UK/0003-2751) [01704184] **4539**

ANARCHY (COLUMBIA, MO.) (US/1044-1387) [11733794] **4539**

ANARE NEWS (AUSTRALIAN NATIONAL ANTARCTIC RESEARCH EXPEDITIONS) (AT) [13846038] **5082**

ANARE RESEARCH NOTES (AT/0729-6533) [10235272] **1365**

ANARE SCIENTIFIC REPORTS. SERIES A (3), GEOLOGY (AT) [09533581] **5082**

ANARE SCIENTIFIC REPORTS. SERIES B (1), ZOOLOGY (AT) [09533588] **5083**

ANARISUTO GAIDO / ANALYSTS' GUIDE (JA) [07003097] **890**

ANASTHESIOLOGIE, INTENSIVMEDIZIN, NOTFALLMEDIZIN, SCHMERZTHERAPIE : AINS (GW/0939-2661) [24148773] 3723, **3681**

ANASTHESIOLOGIE UND INTENSIVMEDIZIN (BERLIN, WEST) (GW/0171-1814) [04558909] **3681**

ANATOLIAN STUDIES (UK/0066-1546) [01481085] **254**

ANATOLICA (NE/0066-1554) [01681302] 5042, **3264**

ANATOMIA, HISTOLOGIA, EMBRYOLOGIA (GW/0340-2096) [01372304] **5502**

ANATOMIA HUMANA (SP) [08091970] **3678**

ANATOMICA, PATHOLOGICA, MICROBIOLOGICA (FI/0358-4895) [04818344] 558, 3892, **3678**

ANATOMICAL BOARD OF THE STATE OF TEXAS *See* ANNUAL FINANCIAL STATEMENT / ANATOMICAL BOARD OF THE STATE OF TEXAS **3678**

ANATOMICAL BOARD OF THE STATE OF TEXAS *See* ANNUAL MEETING OF THE BOARD, ... MINUTES / ANATOMICAL BOARD OF THE STATE OF TEXAS **3678**

ANATOMICAL RECORD. SUPPLEMENT, THE (US/0749-3002) [10503181] **3678**

ANATOMICAL RECORD, THE (US/0003-276X) [01481086] **3678**

ANATOMICAL SOCIETY OF INDIA *See* JOURNAL OF THE ANATOMICAL SOCIETY OF INDIA **3679**

ANATOMISCHE GESELLSCHAFT *See* VERHANDLUNGEN DER ANATOMISCHEN GESELLSCHAFT **3680**

ANATOMISCHER ANZEIGER (GW/0003-2786) [01481090] **3678**

ANATOMY AND EMBRYOLOGY (GW/0340-2061) [01342716] 541, **3678**

ANB MUNAZZAMAT AL-AMAL AL-ARABIYAH (UA) [03058359] **1643**

ANBAR ACCOUNTING & FINANCE ABSTRACTS (UK/0961-2742) [24491903] 738, **726**

ANBAR MANAGEMENT OF QUALITY ABSTRACTS (UK) **860**

ANBAR MARKETING & DISTRIBUTION ABSTRACTS (UK/0305-0661) [28188503] 921, **726**

ANBAR TOP MANAGEMENT ABSTRACTS (UK) [23244290] 860, **726**

ANBAR YEARBOOK (UK/0307-0409) [01786026] **638**

ANCESTOR (AT/0044-8222) [03346481] **2437**

ANCESTOR CHARTS (US/0742-7212) [10411194] **2437**

ANCESTOR HUNT (US/0736-9115) [06219511] **2437**

ANCESTOR INDEX (CN/0704-6618) [03963629] **2437**

... ANCESTOR SURNAME DIRECTORY, THE (US) [17989439] **2437**

●ANCESTOR UPDATE (US/1064-0738) [26204645] **2437**

ANCESTORING (US/0272-0426) [06724517] **2437**

ANCESTORS UNLIMITED EDITION (COLLEGE PARK, GA. : 1982) *See* ANCESTOR UPDATE **2437**

ANCESTORS UNLIMITED (MCCOOK, NEB.) (US/0888-5273) [08148018] **2437**

ANCESTORS WEST (US/0734-4988) [08744728] **2437**

ANCESTRAL PURSUIT *CEASED.* (US/0894-8895) [16286471] **2437**

ANCESTREE / LOGAN COUNTY GENEALOGICAL SOCIETY (US) [13022846] **2437**

ANCESTRY (US) [07933808] **2437**

ANCESTRY NEWSLETTER (US/0749-5927) [11148794] **2437**

●ANCESTRY (SALT LAKE CITY, UTAH) (US/1075-475X) [29990034] **2437**

ANCESTRY TRAILS (US/1054-2310) [14145286] **2437**

ANCETRE (QUEBEC) (CN/0316-0513) [02247396] **2437**

ANCHOR BIBLE, THE (US) [04326648] **5014**

ANCHOR (LOMITA, CALIF.) (US/0732-4340) [08353924] **4934**

ANCHOR NEWS (US) [08740915] **3180**

ANCHOR POINT (US/0895-366X) [16573559] **3264**

ANCHORAGE GENEALOGICAL SOCIETY QUARTERLY (US) **2437**

ANCHORAGE TIMES *CEASED.* (US) [09527134] **5628**

ANCI NOTIZIE (IT/0393-3962) [I03933962] **4626**

ANCI RIVISTA (IT/0393-3938) [I03933938] **4626**

●ANCIENNE USINE A GAZ DE LA RUE VERDUN A QUEBEC, L' (CN/1191-4025) [26498135] **960**

ANCIENT AND MEDIEVAL PHILOSOPHY. SERIES 2 (BE) [06754744] **4340**

ANCIENT CHRISTIAN WRITERS : THE WORKS OF THE FATHERS IN TRANSLATION (US/0066-1597) [01481096] **4934**

ANCIENT CITY GENEALOGIST, THE (US/1072-8953) [28698653] **2437**

●ANCIENT CIVILIZATIONS FROM SCYTHIA TO SIBERIA (NE/0929-077X) 2645, **2673**

ANCIENT CONTROVERSY (US/1042-2471) [18976908] **4515**

ANCIENT HISTORY BULLETIN (CN/0835-3638) [16886032] **1074**

ANCIENT HISTORY: RESOURCES FOR TEACHERS (AT/0310-5814) [19831697] **2610**

ANCIENT INDIA (II) [01481098] **2645**

ANCIENT INTERFACE, THE (US/0097-8442) [02246601] **591**

ANCIENT MESOAMERICA (US/0956-5361) [21544811] **254**

ANCIENT MESOAMERICA (UK) [08546892] **254**

ANCIENT MONUMENTS SOCIETY *See* TRANSACTIONS OF THE ANCIENT MONUMENTS SOCIETY **366**

ANCIENT MYSTERIES (UK/0308-5406) [07664374] **4240**

ANCIENT ORDER OF UNITED WORKMEN. SUPREME LODGE *See* REPORTS OF OFFICERS AND PROCEEDINGS OF THE SUPREME LODGE OF THE ANCIENT ORDER OF UNITED WORKMEN **5236**

ANCIENT PAKISTAN (PK/0066-1600) [01604632] **2645**

ANCIENT PHILOSOPHY (PITTSBURGH, PA.) (US/0740-2007) [07531090] **4340**

ANCIENT SCIENCE OF LIFE (II/0257-7941) [09640913] **499**

ANCIENT SOCIETY (BE/0066-1619) [01481100] **2610**

ANCIENT TIMES (US/0091-7176) [01787914] **4100**

ANCIENT TL (UK/0735-1348) [08872085] **254**

ANCIENT WISDOM FOR MODERN LIVING *CEASED.* (US/1060-8052) [25067945] **4340**

ANCIENT WORLD, THE (US/0160-9645) [03901303] 1074, **254**

●ANCILLARY PROFITS (US/1065-8769) [26790300] **1597**

ANCLA (EL PASO, TEX.) (US/0279-7216) [06302833] **4934**

ANCORA (IT) **3337**

AND. JOURNAL OF ART AND ART EDUCATION (UK/0266-6057) [I02666057] **336**

ANDA (IO) [04709837] **4573**

ANDALUCIA COOPERATIVA (SP/0214-9923) [I02149923] **1541**

ANDALUCIA ECONOMICA (SP/1130-4413) [11304413] **1462**

ANDALUSIA STAR-NEWS, THE (US/0746-2115) [09865133] **5625**

ANDEAN AIR MAIL & PERUVIAN TIMES *See* PERUVIAN TIMES **1578**

ANDEAN NEWSLETTER / ANDEAN COMMISSION OF JURISTS (PE) [16950026] **4504**

ANDEAN PAST (US/1055-8756) [17282868] **254**

ANDEAN PERSPECTIVE NEWSLETTER *CEASED.* (US) [05283799] **228**

ANDEAN REPORT, THE (PE/0251-2491) [02459458] **1545**

ANDERE SINEMA (BE/0773-5855) [07952519] **4063**

ANDERSEN : IL MONDO DELL INFANZIA (IT) **1060**

ANDERSON FAMILY COURIER (US/8756-7571) [11658339] **2437**

ANDERSON HERALD-BULLETIN (US/0893-908X) [15503834] **5662**

ANDERSON INDEPENDENT-MAIL (US) [27841227] **5741**

ANDERSON PLANNER, THE (US) 3749, **4857**

ANDERSON REPORT, THE (US/0197-7040) [05283636] **1231**

ANDERSON'S CAMPGROUND DIRECTORY (US/0163-268X) [04324690] **4869**

ANDERSON'S OHIO CASE LOCATOR (US/1059-518X) [24611205] **2933**

ANDES : ANTROPOLOGIA E HISTORIA (AG/0327-1676) [23852194] **2720**

ANDES (ROME, ITALY) *SUSPENDED.* (IT) [19526094] 5239, **4463**

ANDHRA AGRICULTURAL JOURNAL, THE (II/0003-2956) [01481118] **58**

ANDHRA LAW TIMES. SUPPLEMENT (II) [09168036] **2933**

ANDHRA PRADESH AKADEMI OF SCIENCES *See* JOURNAL - ANDHRA PRADESH AKADEMI OF SCIENCES **5118**

ANDHRA PRADESH AKADEMI OF SCIENCES *See* YEAR BOOK - ANDHRA PRADESH AKADEMI OF SCIENCES **5171**

ANDHRA PRADESH BUDGET IN BRIEF (II/0570-0329) [01704208] **4709**

ANDHRA PRADESH (INDIA) *See* DETAILED IRRIGATION BUDGET **4720**

ANDHRA PRADESH (INDIA) *See* ANDHRA PRADESH BUDGET IN BRIEF **4709**

ANDHRA PRADESH (INDIA). BUREAU OF ECONOMICS AND STATISTICS *See* ECONOMIC & STATISTICAL BULLETIN **1532**

ANDHRA PRADESH (INDIA). DEPT. OF FISHERIES *See* PERFORMANCE BUDGET - DEPARTMENT OF FISHERIES **2310**

ANDHRA PRADESH (INDIA). DEPT. OF WOMAN AND CHILD WELFARE *See* PERFORMANCE BUDGET - DEPARTMENT OF WOMAN AND CHILD WELFARE **5301**

ANDHRA PRADESH (INDIA). DIRECTORATE OF EMPLOYMENT & TRAINING *See* ANNUAL EMPLOYMENT REVIEW (INDIA) **1645**

ANDHRA PRADESH, INDIA. LEGISLATURE. LEGISLATIVE ASSEMBLY. COMMITTEE ON PUBLIC UNDERTAKINGS *See* REPORT ON ANDHRA PRADESH MINING CORPORATION **1624**

ANDHRA PRADESH (INDIA). LEGISLATURE. LEGISLATIVE ASSEMBLY. ESTIMATES COMMITTEE *See* REPORT - ANDHRA PRADESH (INDIA). LEGISLATURE. ESTIMATES COMMITTEE **4744**

ANDHRA PRADESH, INDIA LEGISLATURE. LEGISLATIVE COUNCIL *See* JOURNAL - ANDHRA PRADESH, INDIA. LEGISLATURE. LEGISLATIVE COUNCIL **4478**

ANDHRA PRADESH, INDIA. LEGISLATURE. LEGISLATIVE COUNCIL *See* REVIEW - ANDHRA PRADESH, INDIA. LEGISLATURE. LEGISLATIVE COUNCIL **4683**

ANDHRA PRADESH JOURNAL OF ARCHAEOLOGY, THE (II/0258-0373) [06670216] **254**

ANDHRA PRADESH ORIYANTAL RISARC JARNAL (II) [24648690] **3190**

ANDHRA PRADESH STATE FINANCIAL CORPORATION See REPORT AND ACCOUNTS - ANDHRA PRADESH STATE FINANCIAL CORPORATION **807**

ANDHRA PRADESH STATE FINANCIAL CORPORATION. REPORT See REPORT AND ACCOUNTS - ANDHRA PRADESH STATE FINANCIAL CORPORATION **807**

ANDORRA See BUTLLETI OFICIAL DEL PRINCIPAT D'ANDORRA **2945**

ANDORRA 7 (AN) [09444856] **2673**

ANDOVER ADVOCATE, THE (US/0746-6447) [09809948] **5674**

ANDOVER NEWTON REVIEW *CEASED.* (US) **4934**

ANDOVER REVIEW, THE (US/0362-6075) [02255214] **1888**

ANDOVER TOWNSMAN, THE (US) [12042138] **5687**

ANDRADE : REVISTA TRIMESTRAL DE POESIA (SP) **3361**

ANDRE GAYOT'S TASTES, WITH THE BEST OF GAULT MILLAU (US/1052-1666) [22200886] **2326**

ANDREJ BELYJ SOCIETY NEWSLETTER, THE (US/0743-2410) [10380697] 3361, **3457**

●ANDREW SEYBOLD'S OUTLOOK ON MOBILE COMPUTING (US/1066-8845) [27076556] **1170**

ANDREW SEYBOLD'S REPORT ON MOBILE EMERGENCY COMMUNICATIONS (US/0270-241X) [06385768] **1104**

ANDREWS COUNTY NEWS, THE (US) [15123411] **5746**

ANDREWS' PROFESSIONAL LIABILITY LITIGATION REPORTER (US/1059-3969) [24509425] 3095, **3084**

ANDREWS SCHOOL ASBESTOS ALERT *CEASED.* (US/0887-7866) [11145530] **598**

●ANDREWS' TOXIC TORTS ANNUAL (US/1067-6996) [27321547] **2933**

ANDREWS UNIVERSITY SEMINARY STUDIES (US/0003-2980) [01780045] **4934**

ANDREWS UNIVERSITY. SEVENTH-DAY ADVENTIST THEOLOGICAL SEMINARY See ANDREWS UNIVERSITY SEMINARY STUDIES **4934**

ANDREWSREPORT (INDIANAPOLIS, IND.) *CEASED.* (US/0892-0850) [15079223] **4834**

ANDROLOGIA (BERLIN, WEST) (GW/0303-4569) [00944824] **3549**

ANDVARI (IC) [01723913] **3361**

... ANDY AWARDS ANNUAL, THE (US) [13082486] **336**

ANECDOTA SCOWAH (US) [03165601] **4857**

ANEJOS DE ESTUDIOS FILOLOGICOS (CL/0071-1721) [01978219] **3264**

ANEJOS DEL BOLETIN DE LA DIRECCION GENERAL DE ARCHIVOS Y BIBLIOTECAS (SP) [01640754] **2479**

ANEKA EKONOMI (IO) [02741250] **1462**

ANEKS *CEASED.* (UK/0345-0295) [01795651] **2673**

ANELLO CHE NON TIENE, L' (US/0899-5273) [18123864] **3361**

ANEP. ANNUAIRE EUROPEEN DE PETROLE (GW/0342-6947) [05970623] **4249**

ANERA NEWSLETTER (US/1066-3584) [01589905] **1918**

ANESTESIA E RIANIMAZIONE (IT/0570-0760) [09838466] **3681**

ANESTESIOLOGIA CLINICA (IT) **3681**

ANESTEZIOLOGIJA I REANIMATOLOGIJA (RU/0201-7563) [04059509] **3681**

ANESTEZJA, REANIMACJA, INTENSYWNA TERAPIA (PL/0324-8216) [01906940] **3681**

ANESTHESIA AND ANALGESIA (US/0003-2999) [01481131] **3681**

ANESTHESIA & PAIN CONTROL IN DENTISTRY (US/1055-7601) [23293265] 3681, **1316**

ANESTHESIA MALPRACTICE PROTECTOR (US/1050-8775) [21664015] **3681**

ANESTHESIA PROGRESS (US/0003-3006) [04240121] 3681, **1316**

ANESTHESIAFILE (US/0740-1914) [09926595] **3681**

ANESTHESIE REANIMATION PRATIQUE PARIS (FR/0996-8296) [09968296] **3681**

ANESTHESIOLOGIST'S CLINICAL UPDATE *CEASED.* (US/1050-6470) [21567913] **3681**

ANESTHESIOLOGY BIBLIOGRAPHY *CEASED.* (US/0090-1385) [01681385] **3654**

ANESTHESIOLOGY CLINICS OF NORTH AMERICA (US/0889-8537) [14091814] **3681**

ANESTHESIOLOGY (GLENDALE, CALIF.) (US/0271-1265) [01778665] 1888, **3681**

ANESTHESIOLOGY NEWS (US/0747-4679) [10897089] **3958**

ANESTHESIOLOGY (PHILADELPHIA) (US/0003-3022) [01481133] **3681**

ANESTHESIOLOGY RESIDENT, THE *CEASED.* (US/1063-8571) [26150173] **3681**

ANESTHESIOLOGY REVIEW (US/0093-4437) [01793189] **3681**

ANFIONE ZETO (IT) [22299513] **287**

ANFORA (BUENOS AIRES, ARGENTINA) (AG) [17854187] **3460**

ANG NEWS / AUSTRALIAN NATIONAL GALLERY (AT) [08160750] **4083**

ANGEIOLOGIE *CEASED.* (FR/0003-3049) [02257509] **3549**

ANGEL EXHAUST (UK/0143-8050) [07598020] **3460**

ANGELES & SOUTHERN CALIFORNIA PROMPTER, LOS See LOS ANGELES **2537**

ANGELES COUNTY MUSEUM OF ART, LOS See AT THE MUSEUM **343**

ANGELES COUNTY MUSEUM OF ART. MEMBERS' CALENDAR, LOS See AT THE MUSEUM **343**

ANGELES MESA WAVE (US) [10535359] **5633**

ANGELES MURAL CONSERVANCY JOURNAL, LOS See MURAL CONSERVANCY OF LOS ANGELES JOURNAL **359**

ANGELICUM (IT/0003-3081) [05663388] 4934, **4340**

ANGELINA COUNTY COURT DIGEST (US) [03940215] **2933**

ANGELOS (HALIFAX) (CN/0710-0612) [08569908] **4934**

ANGESTELLTEN MAGAZIN (GW/0341-017X) [05062747] **1643**

ANGESTELLTEN-VERSICHERUNG, DIE (GW) [08445781] **5271**

ANGEWANDTE BOTANIK (GW/0066-1759) [01481136] **499**

ANGEWANDTE CHEMIE. INTERNATIONAL EDITION IN ENGLISH (GW/0570-0833) [01481137] **960**

ANGEWANDTE CHEMIE (WEINHEIM AN DER BERGSTRASSE, GERMANY) (GW/0044-8249) [05845277] **961**

ANGEWANDTE MAKROMOLEKULARE CHEMIE (SZ/0003-3146) [01481139] **4454**

ANGEWANDTE PARASITOLOGIE (GW/0003-3162) [01481141] **5575**

ANGEWANDTE SOZIALFORSCHUNG (GW) **5190**

ANGEWANDTE STATISTIK UND OKONOMETRIE (GW/0720-8227) [07050516] **1528**

ANGGARAN HASIL DAN PERBELANJAAN BAGI TAHUN ... (MICROFORM) (SZ) [10840923] **4709**

ANGIER INDEPENDENT, THE (US/8750-0221) [10916370] **5722**

ANGIO : ZEITSCHRIFT DER DEUTSCHEN GESELLSCHAFT FUER GEFASSCHIRURGIE (GW/0721-9318) [24844831] **3698**

ANGIOLOGIA (SP/0003-3170) [01608034] **3698**

ANGIOLOGY (US/0003-3197) [01481144] **3794**

ANGLE DROIT PARIS (FR/1156-4148) [11564148] 1104, **2933**

ANGLE ORTHODONTIST, THE (US/0003-3219) [01481145] **1316**

ANGLER & HUNTER (PETERBOROUGH, ONT.) *CEASED.* (CN/0828-7341) [12326511] **4869**

ANGLERS' NEWS *CEASED.* (US/0739-019X) [09689615] **2294**

ANGLES ON THE ENGLISH SPEAKING WORLD (DK) [18453725] **3264**

ANGLES (VANCOUVER) (CN/0824-2100) [10845159] **2793**

ANGLESEY ANTIQUARIAN SOCIETY See TRANSACTIONS - ANGLESEY ANTIQUARIAN SOCIETY AND FIELD CLUB **2713**

ANGLETON TIMES, THE (US) [13912414] **5746**

ANGLIA : ZEITSCHRIFT FUER ENGLISCHE PHILOLOGIE (GW) [08488510] **3264**

ANGLICA ET AMERICANA (DK/0105-9963) [I01059963] 3361, **3264**

ANGLICAN AND EPISCOPAL HISTORY (US/0896-8039) [15349617] **5055**

ANGLICAN CHURCH DIRECTORY / THE ANGLICAN CHURCH OF CANADA (CN/1193-9737) [27750563] **4934**

ANGLICAN CHURCH OF AUSTRALIA. GENERAL SYNOD See PROCEEDINGS OF THE ... GENERAL SYNOD, OFFICIAL REPORT / ANGLICAN CHURCH OF AUSTRALIA **4988**

ANGLICAN CHURCH OF CANADA See MCCAUSLAND'S ORDER OF DIVINE SERVICE **4976**

ANGLICAN CHURCH OF CANADA See ANGLICAN CHURCH DIRECTORY / THE ANGLICAN CHURCH OF CANADA **4934**

ANGLICAN CHURCH OF CANADA. DIOCESE OF OTTAWA. SYNOD See CONVENING CIRCULAR AND SYNOD JOURNAL FOR THE ... SESSION OF SYNOD **4950**

ANGLICAN CHURCH OF CANADA. GENERAL SYNOD See JOURNAL OF THE ... GENERAL SYNOD / ANGLICAN CHURCH OF CANADA **5062**

ANGLICAN DIGEST, THE (US/0003-3278) [01589123] **5055**

ANGLICAN JOURNAL (CN/0847-978X) [20873433] **4934**

ANGLICAN MESSENGER (EDMONTON) (CN/0823-8308) [11607578] **5055**

ANGLICAN NEWS (COBOURG) (CN/0710-1139) [08144014] **5023**

ANGLICAN OPINION (US) [14972487] **4934**

ANGLICAN, THE (CN/0517-7731) [02992045] **5055**

ANGLICAN THEOLOGICAL REVIEW (US/0003-3286) [01481151] **4934**

ANGLICAN THEOLOGICAL REVIEW. SUPPLEMENTARY SERIES (US/0097-4951) [01332758] **4934**

ANGLICAN YEAR BOOK (CN/0317-8765) [02248239] **4934**

ANGLISTICA (DK/0066-1805) [01481153] **3264**

ANGLISTIK & ENGLISCHUNTERRICHT (GW/0344-8266) [09205751] **3264**

ANGLISTISCHE FORSCHUNGEN (GW/0179-1389) [01481155] 3361, **3264**

ANGLO-AMERICAN DIRECTORY OF MEXICO (MX) [01481159] **2528**

ANGLO AMERICAN FORUM (SZ) **3337**

ANGLO-AMERICAN LAW REVIEW, THE (UK/0308-6569) [01481160] **2933**

ANGLO AMERICAN STUDIES *SUSPENDED.* (SP/0211-7215) [09595698] **2610**

ANGLO AMERICAN TRADE DIRECTORY (UK/0066-1813) [02050296] **822**

ANGLO JAPANESE JOURNAL (UK/0955-5129) [20002519] **1632**

ANGLO NORMAN DICTIONARY *CEASED.* (UK) **2841**

ANGLO-NORMAN STUDIES ... : PROCEEDINGS OF THE BATTLE CONFERENCE (UK/0954-9927) [11319864] **2673**

ANGLO-NORMAN TEXT SOCIETY See ANGLO-NORMAN TEXTS **2673**

ANGLO-NORMAN TEXTS (UK/0066-183X) [01481168] **2673**

ANGLO-SAXON ENGLAND (UK/0263-6751) [01716466] **2673**

ANGLO-SAXON STUDIES IN ARCHAEOLOGY AND HISTORY (UK/0264-5254) [06523006] 2673, **254**

ANGLO-SOVIET JOURNAL, THE (UK/0044-8265) [02174068] **2673**

ANGLOFILE (US) **2484**

ANGOLA. DIRECAO PROVINCIAL DOS SERVICOS DE ESTATISTICA See BOLETIM MENSAL DE ESTATISTICA **5323**

ANGOLA. DIRECCAO PROVINCIAL DOS SERVICOS DE GEOLOGIA E MINAS See ESTATISTICA DA ACTIVIDADE MINEIRA NO ESTADO DE ANGOLA **2004**

ANGOLA, ENERGIEWIRTSCHAFT / BUNDESSTELLE FUR AUSSENHANDELSINFORMATION (GW) [09963154] **1931**

ANGOLA UPDATE *CEASED.* (US/1051-8134) [19231948] **1104**

ANGOLITE (US/0402-4249) [04674128] **3156**

ANGORABOT & SYBOTHAAR -BLAD (SA/0003-3464) [05653616] **205**

ANGUILLA See LAWS OF ANGUILLA **2997**

ANGUILLA See NATIONAL ACCOUNTS STATISTICS **1536**

ANGUILLA. ACCOUNTANT GENERAL See REPORT AND STATEMENTS OF ACCOUNTS OF THE ACCOUNTANT GENERAL FOR THE YEAR ENDED 31ST DECEMBER ... **4744**

ANGUILLA CONSOLIDATED INDEX OF STATUTES AND SUBSIDIARY LEGISLATION TO ... (BB) [13871843] **3123**

ANGUS JOURNAL (US/0194-9543) [05158743] **205**

ANGUS TIMES *CEASED.* (CN/0849-6188) [21352916] **205**

ANGUS TOPICS (US/0402-4265) [04580161] **205**

●ANH / THE AUSTRALIAN MUSEUM TRUST (AT) [26882824] 4161, **4083**

ANHUI CHIAO YU HSUEH YUAN HSUEH PAO / JOURNAL OF ANHUI INSTITUTE OF EDUCATION (CC/1001-5116) [24588625] **1724**

ANIE PUBBLICAZIONI (IT) **1643**

ANIMA (BL) [02673220] **2551**

ANIMA (CHAMBERSBURG) (US/0097-1146) [01798894] **4185**

ANIMAG (CN/0709-4116) [05694477] **4285**

ANIMAL AGRICULTURE UPDATE NEWSLETTER / COOPERATIVE EXTENSION SERVICE, UNIVERSITY OF MARYLAND SYSTEM, DEPARTMENT OF ANIMAL SCIENCES (US/1057-2120) [21475392] **58**

ANIMAL AND ANIMAL PRODUCTS; OUTLOOK (CN) [01796092] **205**

ANIMAL AND GRASSLAND RESEARCH INSTITUTE (HURLEY, BERKSHIRE) *See* ANNUAL REPORT / ANIMAL AND GRASSLAND RESEARCH INSTITUTE **205**

ANIMAL BEHAVIOR ABSTRACTS (US/0301-8695) [08529163] 5575, **5604**

ANIMAL BEHAVIOR CONSULTANT NEWSLETTER (US) **225**

ANIMAL BEHAVIOUR (UK/0003-3472) [04699737] **5575**

●ANIMAL BIOLOGY (IT/1121-1431) [26558887] 441, **5502**

ANIMAL BIOTECHNOLOGY (US/1049-5398) [21248361] 3685, **5502**

ANIMAL BREEDING ABSTRACTS (UK/0003-3499) [01481177] 205, **151**

ANIMAL DAMAGE CONTROL (US/1057-2457) [12773251] **58**

ANIMAL DEFENCE LEAGUE OF CANADA *See* NEWS BULLETIN - ANIMAL DEFENCE LEAGUE OF CANADA **226**

ANIMAL FEED SCIENCE AND TECHNOLOGY (NE/0377-8401) [02352576] **199**

ANIMAL FEED SERVICE BULLETIN (PH/0115-5784) [I01155784] **200**

ANIMAL FINDERS' GUIDE (US) [18623506] 205, **4285**

ANIMAL GENETIC RESOURCES INFORMATION (IT/1014-2339) [I10142339] **542**

ANIMAL GENETICS (UK/0268-9146) [13459823] **542**

ANIMAL HEALTH & NUTRITION SERVICE (UK) **5502**

ANIMAL HEALTH NEWSLETTER (US/0884-092X) [09418267] **5502**

ANIMAL HEALTH TRUST *See* ANNUAL REPORT OF THE ANIMAL HEALTH TRUST **5503**

ANIMAL HEALTH (WEST LAFAYETTE, IND.) *CEASED.* (US/0894-8437) [13733275] **205**

ANIMAL HEALTH YEARBOOK (IT) [01999050] **5502**

ANIMAL HUSBANDRY AND AGRICULTURAL JOURNAL (PH) [03343063] **58**

ANIMAL HUSBANDRY & VETERINARY MEDICINE (CC) [26274627] **5502**

ANIMAL IMPROVEMENT PROGRAMS LABORATORY *See* REPORT OF RANDOM SAMPLE EGG PRODUCTION TESTS, UNITED STATES AND CANADA **126**

ANIMAL KEEPERS' FORUM (US/0164-9531) [03509056] **5575**

ANIMAL LAW NEWSLETTER / ANIMAL PROTECTION COMMITTEE, YOUNG LAWYER'S DIVISION, AMERICAN BAR ASSOCIATION (US) [29857535] **2933**

ANIMAL LAW REPORT *See* ANIMAL LAW NEWSLETTER / ANIMAL PROTECTION COMMITTEE, YOUNG LAWYER'S DIVISION, AMERICAN BAR ASSOCIATION **2933**

ANIMAL LEARNING & BEHAVIOR (US/0090-4996) [01787764] 4573, **5575**

ANIMAL LIBERATION ACTION (AT/0816-486X) [I0816486X] **225**

ANIMAL MAGAZINE, L' (CN/0710-9148) [08655525] **4285**

ANIMAL MODELS OF HUMAN DISEASE (US) [07058131] **3892**

ANIMAL MODELS OF PSYCHIATRIC DISORDERS *CEASED.* (SZ/1011-6982) [19079164] **3920**

ANIMAL NUTRITION RESEARCH HIGHLIGHTS (US) **58**

ANIMAL ORGANIZATIONS & SERVICES DIRECTORY *CEASED.* (US/0748-5069) [10940705] **225**

●ANIMAL PEOPLE (US/1071-0035) [28391400] **225**

ANIMAL PEOPLE'S DIRECTORY, THE (US/0733-4710) [08561876] **225**

ANIMAL PHARM (UK/0262-2238) [10908520] **5502**

ANIMAL PRODUCTION (LU) [17896315] **151**

ANIMAL PRODUCTION (UK/0003-3561) [01481185] **205**

ANIMAL QUARANTINE *CEASED.* (AT) [03579414] **4765**

ANIMAL REPRODUCTION SCIENCE (NE/0378-4320) [04122595] **5503**

ANIMAL RESEARCH AND DEVELOPMENT (GW/0340-3165) [02622436] **5575**

ANIMAL RIGHTS LAW REPORTER (US/0730-6792) [06176536] 225, **2933**

ANIMAL SCIENCE (UK) **205**

ANIMAL SCIENCE AND TECHNOLOGY (US) **5575**

ANIMAL SCIENCE PAPERS AND REPORTS / POLISH ACADEMY OF SCIENCES INSTITUTE OF GENETICS AND ANIMAL BREEDING, JASTRZEBIEC (PL/0860-4037) [15319809] 5503, **59**

ANIMAL SCIENCE RESEARCH REPORT (US) [07865760] 205, **5503**

ANIMAL SCIENCE RESEARCH REPORT (BLACKSBURG, VA.) (US/0899-3920) [08127851] **205**

ANIMAL TECHNOLOGY (UK/0264-4754) [09666005] **5503**

ANIMAL WELFARE (UK) [02561325] **225**

●ANIMAL WELFARE (UK/0962-7286) [26105301] **225**

ANIMAL WELFARE INFORMATION CENTER NEWSLETTER (US/1050-561X) [21538961] **225**

ANIMAL WELFARE INSTITUTE QUARTERLY *See* AWI QUARTERLY **226**

ANIMAL WELFARE INSTITUTE QUARTERLY, THE (US/0743-0841) [08266312] **225**

ANIMAL WELFARE. LIST OF LICENSED EXHIBITORS (US/0747-5128) [10510013] **225**

ANIMAL WELFARE. LIST OF REGISTERED CARRIERS AND INTERMEDIATE HANDLERS (US/0747-5136) [10510383] **225**

ANIMAL WELFARE. LIST OF REGISTERED RESEARCH FACILITIES (US/0747-5144) [10510338] **225**

ANIMAL WORLD HORSHAM (UK/0968-2147) [09682147] **225**

ANIMALAND (US/0019-3127) [02606852] **5575**

ANIMALIA (BARCELONA) (SP/0214-3151) [21223516] **4285**

ANIMALIS FAMILIARIS BRUSSEL (BE/0775-6992) [07756992] **5503**

ANIMALS AGENDA (US/0892-8819) [11816969] **225**

ANIMALS (BOSTON) (US/0030-6835) [02241237] **225**

ANIMALS FOR RESEARCH *CEASED.* (US/0547-8626) [05540634] **5503**

ANIMALS INTERNATIONAL (UK/0254-3923) [18410322] **5503**

ANIMALS' VOICE (CN/0700-8392) [02994818] **225**

ANIMALS' VOICE (CHICO, CALIF.), THE (US/0889-6712) [13990046] **225**

ANIMALS' VOICE MAGAZINE, THE (US/1062-2942) [19278361] **225**

ANIMATEUR D'ENTRAINEMENT PHYSIQUE DANS LE MONDE MODERNE, L' (FR/0753-5058) [I07535058] **2596**

ANIMATION HANNOVER (GW/0172-9721) [I01729721] **2596**

●ANIMATION JOURNAL (US/1061-0308) [25161230] 336, 376, **4063**

ANIMATION MAGAZINE (US/1041-617X) [18794679] **4063**

ANIMATIONS (UK/0140-7740) [I01407740] **5361**

ANIMATO! (CAMBRIDGE, MASS.) (US/1042-539X) [19081197] **4063**

ANIMATOR ST. ALBANS (UK/0964-5586) [I09645586] **4063**

ANIMATRIX (LOS ANGELES, CALIF.) (US/1069-2088) [17470216] **4063**

ANIMAZIONE ED ESPRESSIONE (IT) **383**

ANIMAZIONE SOCIALE (IT/0392-5870) [I03925870] **5271**

ANISHINAABE GIIGIDOWIN (US/0195-3400) [04319799] **3264**

ANISHINABEK NEWS (CN/1182-3178) [23598087] **2720**

ANITAF DIRECTORY (PO) [08440629] **5347**

ANITAF (ORGANIZATION) *See* ANITAF DIRECTORY **5347**

ANJOU (ANJOU, QUEBEC) (CN/0713-6803) [08924103] **4626**

ANKARA. ORTA DOGU TEKNIK UNIVERSITESI. IDARI ILIMLER FAKULTESI *See* ODTU : GELISME DERGISI **1509**

ANKARA UNIVERSITESI ECZACILIK FAKULTESI DERGISI (TU/1015-3918) [I10153918] **4290**

ANKARA. UNIVERSITESI. SIYASAL BILGILER FAKULTESI *See* SIYASAL BILGILER FAKULTESI DERGISI **4496**

ANKENY PRESS CITIZEN (US) [15744331] **5668**

ANKETA O OSTVARIVANJU PRAVA RADNIKA IZ RADNOG ODNOSA (YU) [01789032] 1643, **1528**

ANKETA O PORODICNIM BUDZETIMA RADNICKIH DOMACINSTAVA (YU/0300-2543) [01784846] **5321**

ANKETA O PRIHODIMA, RASHEDIMA I POTRESNJI DOMACINSTAVA (YU) [02241546] 1462, **1528**

ANKETA O SEOSKIM DOMACINSTVIMA (YU) [01789031] **5321**

ANL-HEP-CP (ARGONNE NATIONAL LABORATORY, HIGH ENERGY PHYSICS DIVISION) (US/0195-7236) [05579164] **4396**

ANLA BULLETIN / ASSOCIATION OF NEWFOUNDLAND AND LABRADOR ARCHIVISTS (CN/0821-7157) [10763973] **2479**

ANLAGEPRAXIS (GW/0172-7419) [I01727419] **770**

ANLAIDS NOTIZIE (IT) **3712**

ANN ARBOR LABOR MARKET REVIEW *See* ANN ARBOR'S LABOR MARKET NEWS **1643**

ANN ARBOR NEWS, THE (US) [09497417] **5690**

ANN ARBOR OBSERVER (US/0192-5717) [05082849] **2484**

●ANN ARBOR'S LABOR MARKET NEWS (US) [25949877] **1643**

ANNA : BURDA KNITTING & NEEDLECRAFTS (GW) [17016176] **370**

ANNA JOURNAL (US/8750-0779) [10960316] 3988, **3851**

ANNABEL (UK) [08391364] **5550**

ANNALAS DALA SOCIETAD RHAETO-ROMANSCHA. NSS (SZ) [05868106] 3264, **2674**

ANNALE (ISTITUTO REGIONALE PER LA STORIA DELLA RESISTENZA E DELLA GUERRA DI LIBERAZIONE IN EMILIA ROMAGNA) (IT) [07601104] **2674**

ANNALEN DER METEOROLOGIE (GW/0072-4122) [01481211] **1419**

ANNALEN DER PHYSIK (GW/0003-3804) [05854993] **4396**

ANNALEN DES HISTORISCHEN VEREINS FUER DEN NIEDERRHEIN, INSBESONDERE DAS ALTE ERZBISTUM KOLN (GW/0341-289X) [11358439] **2674**

ANNALEN DES NATURHISTORISCHEN MUSEUMS IN WIEN. SERIE B, FUER BOTANIK UND ZOOLOGIE (AU/0255-0105) [10363522] 5575, **499**

ANNALEN - KONINKLIJKE MUSEUM VOOR MIDDEN-AFRIKA ECONOMISCHE WETENSCHAPPEN (BE/0773-4123) [07734123] **1462**

ANNALEN VAN DE BELGISCHE VERENIGING VOOR STRALINGSBESCHERMING (BE/0250-5010) [06058360] **4433**

ANNALEN VAN DE KONINKLIJKE OUDHEIDKUNDIGE KRING VAN HET LAND VAN WAAS (BE/0775-7506) [07757506] **2674**

ANNALES (FR) **4340**

ANNALES (TI) [06877570] 1462, **59**

ANNALES ACADEMIAE MEDICAE GEDANENSIS (PL/0303-4135) [01645436] **3549**

ANNALES ACADEMIAE MEDICAE SILESIENSIS (PL/0208-5607) [10049038] **3550**

ANNALES ACADEMIAE SCIENTIARUM FENNICAE. DISSERTATIONES HUMANARUM LITTERARUM (FI/0355-113X) [08528675] **2841**

ANNALES ACADEMIAE SCIENTIARUM FENNICAE. SER. A5: MEDICA (FI/0066-1996) [02039880] **3550**

ANNALES ACADEMIAE SCIENTIARUM FENNICAE. SERIES A. I, MATHEMATICA DISSERTATIONES (FI/0355-0087) [04175934] **3493**

ANNALES ACADEMIAE SCIENTIARUM FENNICAE. SERIES A. I, MATHEMATICA (HELSINKI, FINLAND : 1975) (FI/0066-1953) [02116506] **3493**

ANNALES ACADEMIAE SCIENTIARUM FENNICAE. SERIES A. III : GEOLOGICA-GEOGRAPHICA (FI/0066-197X) [01716827] **5083**

ANNALES — Alphabetical Title Index

ANNALES ACADEMIAE SCIENTIARUM FENNICAE. SERIES A. VI: PHYSICA *CEASED.* (FI/0066-2003) [01641244] **4396**

ANNALES ACADEMIAE SCIENTIARUM FENNICAE. SERIES A2: CHEMICA (FI/0066-1961) [01766817] **961**

ANNALES ACADEMIAE SCIENTIARUM FENNICAE. SERIES A4: BIOLOGICA (FI/0066-1988) [07590325] **441**

ANNALES ACADEMIAE SCIENTIARUM FENNICAE. SERIES B (FI/0066-2011) [01766818] **254**

ANNALES AEQUATORIA (CG/0254-4296) [07334315] **228**

ANNALES AFRICAINES (FR/0066-202X) [01481222] **2933**

ANNALES AGRICULTURE FENNIAE *See* AGRICULTURAL SCIENCE IN FINLAND **52**

ANNALES ARCHEOLOGIQUES ARABES SYRIENNES (SY/0570-1554) [02990689] **254**

ANNALES BENJAMIN CONSTANT (SZ/0263-7383) [09308525] 2674, **3361**

ANNALES BIOLOGIE ANIMALE (FR/0069-4681) [03162050] **205**

ANNALES BOGORIENSES (IO/0517-8452) [01481229] **499**

ANNALES BOTANICI FENNICI (FI/0003-3847) [01481230] **499**

ANNALES CHIRURGIAE ET GYNAECOLOGIAE (FI/0355-9521) [02433259] **3756**

ANNALES CHIRURGIAE ET GYNAECOLOGIAE. SUPPLEMENTUM (FI/0355-9874) [03048473] **3757**

ANNALES DE BIOCHIMIE CLINIQUE DU QUEBEC (CN/0709-8502) [06473665] **480**

ANNALES DE BIOLOGIE CLINIQUE (PARIS) (FR/0003-3898) [01481238] **3892**

ANNALES DE BOURGOGNE (FR/0003-3901) [02026698] **2674**

ANNALES DE BRETAGNE ET DES PAYS DE L'OUEST (FR/0399-0826) [02858144] **2674**

ANNALES DE CARDIOLOGIE ET D'ANGEIOLOGIE (FR/0003-3928) [06364189] **3698**

ANNALES DE CHIMIE (PARIS. 1914) (FR/0151-9107) [03821364] **961**

ANNALES DE CHIRURGIE (FR/0003-3944) [01481243] **3958**

ANNALES DE CHIRURGIE DE LA MAIN ET DU MEMBRE SUPERIEUR (FR/1153-2424) [22178113] **3958**

ANNALES DE CHIRURGIE PLASTIQUE ET ESTHETIQUE (FR/0003-3960) [09715857] **3959**

ANNALES DE CHIRURGIE THORACIQUE ET CARDIOVASCULAIRE (FR/0066-2054) [01481246] **3959**

ANNALES DE CHIRURGIE VASCULAIRE (FR/0299-2213) [02992213] **3959**

ANNALES DE DEMOGRAPHIE HISTORIQUE (FR/0066-2062) [01709098] **4549**

ANNALES DE DERMATOLOGIE ET DE VENEREOLOGIE (FR/0151-9638) [02937625] **3717**

ANNALES DE DROIT DE LOUVAIN (BE/0770-6472) [09766992] **2933**

ANNALES DE GASTROENTEROLOGIE ET D'HEPATOLOGIE (FR/0066-2070) [01481251] **3743**

ANNALES DE GEMBLOUX (BE/0303-9099) [09844520] **59**

ANNALES DE GENETIQUE (FR/0003-3995) [01481253] **542**

ANNALES DE GEOGRAPHIE (FR/0003-4010) [03341949] **2553**

ANNALES DE GEOGRAPHIE (BEIRUT, LEBANON) (LE/0250-7668) [10219947] **2553**

ANNALES DE HAUTE-PROVENCE (FR/0240-4672) [I02404672] **2674**

ANNALES DE KINESITHERAPIE (FR/0309-427X) [06464207] **4379**

ANNALES DE L'A C F A S (CN/0066-8842) [02441725] **5083**

ANNALES DE LA FACULTE DE DROIT (CG) [01796146] **2933**

ANNALES DE LA FACULTE DES LETTRES ET SCIENCES HUMAINES SERIE LETTRES / UNIVERSITE DE YAOUNDE (CM) [18696194] **3361**

ANNALES DE LA FACULTE DES LETTRES ET SCIENCES HUMAINES SERIE SCIENCES HUMAINES / UNIVERSITE DE YAOUNDE (CM) [15350555] **2841**

ANNALES DE LA FACULTE DES SCIENCES DE TOULOUSE (FR/0240-2963) [06290157] **3493**

ANNALES DE LA FACULTE DES SCIENCES: SECTION MATHEMATIQUE-PHYSIQUE (CG) [04223155] **3493**

ANNALES DE LA FACULTE DES SCIENCES. SERIE III, BIOLOGIE-BIOCHIMIE : AFS / UNIVERSITE DE YAOUNDE (CM/1012-1773) [15466772] **480**

ANNALES DE LA FACULTE DES SCIENCES, UNIVERSITE DE DAKAR (SG/0418-2952) [01559962] **5083**

ANNALES DE LA FONDATION LOUIS DE BROGLIE (FR/0182-4295) [04952322] **4396**

ANNALES DE LA FOUNDATION FYSSEN (FR/0980-157X) [19968948] 4226, **228**

ANNALES DE LA PROPRIETE INDUSTRIELLE, ARTISTIQUE ET LITTERAIRE (FR) [05869553] **1301**

ANNALES DE LA RECHERCHE URBAINE, LES (FR/0180-930X) [05856529] **5239**

ANNALES DE LA SOCIETE ARCHEOLOGIQUE DE NAMUR (BE) [09096204] 255, **2674**

ANNALES DE LA SOCIETE BELGE DE MEDECINE TROPICALE (BE/0365-6527) [01732255] **3985**

ANNALES DE LA SOCIETE BELGE D'HISTOIRE DES HOPITAUX (BE/0583-8142) [01943898] **3776**

ANNALES DE LA SOCIETE DES SCIENCES NATURELLES ET D'ARCHEOLOGIE DE TOULON ET DU VAR (FR/0373-7039) [103737039] 4161, **255**

ANNALES DE LA SOCIETE D'HORTICULTURE ET D'HISTOIRE NATURELLE DE L'HERAULT (FR/0373-8701) [05768544] **2408**

ANNALES DE LA SOCIETE ENTOMOLOGIQUE DE FRANCE (FR/0037-9271) [01765810] **5575**

ANNALES DE LA SOCIETE GEOLOGIQUE DE BELGIQUE (BE/0037-9395) [01765826] **1365**

ANNALES DE LA SOCIETE GEOLOGIQUE DU NORD (FR/0767-7367) [01642285] 4226, **1365**

ANNALES DE LA SOCIETE JEAN-JACQUES ROUSSEAU (SZ/0259-6563) [02596563] **3361**

ANNALES DE LA SOCIETE ROYALE D'ARCHEOLOGIE DE BRUXELLES (BE) [01777559] **255**

ANNALES DE LA SOCIETE SCIENTIFIQUE ET LITTERAIRE DE CANNES ET DE L'ARRONDISSEMENT DE GRASSE (FR/0995-9181) [I09959181] **4161**

ANNALES DE L'ACADEMIE DE MACON / SOCIÉTÉ DES ARTS, SCIENCES, BELLES-LETTRES, ET AGRICULTURE DE SAONE-ET-LOIRE (FR) [01775603] **2841**

ANNALES DE L'ECONOMIE PUBLIQUE, SOCIALE ET COOPERATIVE, LES (FR/0379-3699) [07066000] **1462**

ANNALES DE L'EST (FR/0365-2017) [07185519] **2674**

ANNALES DE L'EST; MEMOIRE (FR/0373-7462) [03321810] **2674**

ANNALES DE L'EXAMEN FINAL UNIFORME / ORDRES DES COMPTABLES AGREES DU CANADA ET DES BERMUDES (CN/0820-0386) [09375325] **738**

ANNALES DE L'I.H.P. PHYSIQUE THEORIQUE (FR/0246-0211) [09811706] **4396**

ANNALES DE L'I.H.P. PROBABILITES ET STATISTIQUES (FR/0246-0203) [09867017] **3493**

ANNALES DE LIMNOLOGIE (FR/0003-4088) [01481271] **1412**

ANNALES DE L'INSTITUT ARCHEOLOGIQUE DU LUXEMBOURG (BE/0776-1244) [I07761244] **255**

ANNALES DE L'INSTITUT BELGE DU PETROLE (BE/0020-2185) [02852870] **4249**

ANNALES DE L'INSTITUT DE PHILOSOPHIE ET DE PHILOSOPHIE ET DE SCIENCES MORALES (BE) [08236525] **4340**

ANNALES DE L'INSTITUT D'ETUDES OCCITANES (FR/0180-4200) [02670537] **3264**

ANNALES DE L'INSTITUT FOURIER (FR/0373-0956) [01751588] **3493**

ANNALES DE L'INSTITUT HENRI POINCARE. ANALYSE NON LINEAIRE (FR/0294-1449) [10974421] **3493**

ANNALES DE L'INSTITUT MICHEL PACHA (FR/0073-8565) [08264465] 578, **552**

ANNALES DE L'INSTITUT NATIONAL AGRONOMIQUE (FR/0373-0816) [04845741] **59**

ANNALES DE L'INSTITUT NATIONAL DE LA RECHERCHE AGRONOMIQUE DE TUNISIE (TI/0365-4761) [09677140] 499, **59**

ANNALES DE L'INSTITUT PASTEUR ACTUALITES (FR/0924-4204) [I09244204] **5083**

ANNALES DE L'INSTITUT PHYTOPATHOLOGIQUE BENAKI (GR/0365-5814) [01755149] **499**

ANNALES DE L'INSTITUT TECHNIQUE DU BATIMENT ET DES TRAVAUX PUBLICS (FR/0020-2568) [02253819] **598**

ANNALES DE L'IRETIJ MONTPELLIER, LES (FR/1150-3637) [I11503637] **2933**

ANNALES DE L'UNIVERSITE D'ABIDJAN. SERIE F: ETHNOSOCIOLOGIE (IV/0587-4149) [01654559] **228**

ANNALES DE L'UNIVERSITE D'ABIDJAN. SERIE G : GEOGRAPHIE (IV/0302-0924) [01654217] **2554**

ANNALES DE L'UNIVERSITE D'ABIDJAN. SERIE I : HISTOIRE (IV) [01653826] **2637**

ANNALES DE L'UNIVERSITE D'ABIDJAN. SERIES K, SCIENCES ECONOMIQUES (IV) [05270632] **1462**

ANNALES DE L'UNIVERSITE DE MADAGASCAR. BIOLOGIE, CLINIQUE, SANTE PUBLIQUE (MG/0253-6390) [06119235] 3550, 4765, **441**

ANNALES DE L'UNIVERSITE DES SCIENCES SOCIALES DE TOULOUSE (FR/0563-9727) [I05639727] **5190**

ANNALES DE MEDECINE INTERNE (FR/0003-410X) [01481274] **3794**

ANNALES DE MEDECINE VETERINAIRE (BE/0003-4118) [01481275] **5503**

ANNALES DE MEDICINA (SP) [02550580] **3550**

ANNALES DE NORMANDIE (FR/0003-4134) [01481276] 255, **2674**

ANNALES DE PALEONTOLOGIE (1982) (FR/0753-3969) [08770809] **4226**

ANNALES DE PARASITOLOGIE HUMAINE ET COMPAREE (FR/0003-4150) [01481278] 5575, **441**

ANNALES DE PATHOLOGIE (FR/0242-6498) [07632951] **3893**

ANNALES DE PEDIATRIE (PARIS) (FR/0066-2097) [01481279] **3900**

ANNALES DE PHILOSOPHIE (LE/0250-8036) [10683069] **4340**

ANNALES DE PHYSIQUE. COLLOQUE (FR) [14114194] **4397**

ANNALES DE PHYSIQUE (PARIS) (FR/0003-4169) [01481283] **4397**

ANNALES DE PSYCHIATRIE (FR/0768-7559) [I07687559] **3920**

ANNALES DE PSYCHOTHERAPIE (FR/0338-9375) [103389375] 4573, **3920**

ANNALES DE RADIOLOGIE (FR/0003-4185) [01481287] **3938**

ANNALES DE READAPTATION ET DE MEDECINE PHYSIQUE : REVUE SCIENTIFIQUE DE LA SOCIETE FRANCAISE DE REEDUCATION FONCTIONNELLE DE READAPTATION ET DE MEDECINE PHYSIQUE (FR/0402-4621) [15285813] **4379**

ANNALES DE RECHERCHES SYLVICOLES (FR/0398-494X) [03745361] **2374**

ANNALES DE RECHERCHES VETERINAIRES (FR/0003-4193) [01481288] **5503**

ANNALES DE SPELEOLOGIE *SUSPENDED.* (FR/0003-4215) [02129325] **1402**

ANNALES DE ZOOTECHNIE (FR/0003-424X) [04384455] **5575**

ANNALES D'ECONOMIE ET DE STATISTIQUE (FR/0769-489X) [15360252] **1462**

ANNALES D'ENDOCRINOLOGIE (FR/0003-4266) [01481293] **3726**

ANNALES DES FALSIFICATIONS, DE L'EXPERTISE CHIMIQUE ET TOXICOLOGIQUE (FR/0242-6110) [06995236] **3978**

ANNALES DES MINES DE BELGIQUE *CEASED.* (BE/0003-4290) [02444831] 1931, **2133**

ANNALES DES PAYS NIVERNAIS (FR/0153-7121) [I01537121] **2674**

ANNALES DES PONTS ET CHAUSSEES (FR/0152-9668) [01780762] **2018**

ANNALES DES SCIENCES FORESTIERES (FR/0003-4312) [03153376] **2374**

ANNALES DES SCIENCES MATHEMATIQUES DU QUEBEC (CN/0707-9109) [05528954] **3493**

ANNALES DES SCIENCES NATURELLES *CEASED.* (FR/0003-4320) [05887102] **499**

ANNALES DES SCIENCES NATURELLES. ZOOLOGIE ET BIOLOGIE ANIMALE (FR/0003-4339) [01481305] 441, **5575**

ANNALES DES TELECOMMUNICATIONS (FR/0003-4347) [02129391] **1148**

ANNALES DES TRAVAUX PUBLICS DE BELGIQUE *CEASED.* (BE/0373-0891) [04353501] **1964**

ANNALES D'HISTOIRE DE L'ART ET D'ARCHEOLOGIE (BE/0771-2723) [11349752] 255, **336**

ANNALI

ANNALES D'HISTOIRE DES ENSEIGNEMENTS AGRICOLES (FR/0298-7929) [16804555] **59**

ANNALES D'HISTOIRE ET D'ARCHEOLOGIE / UNIVERSITE SAINT-JOSEPH, FACULTE DES LETTRES ET DES SCIENCES HUMAINES (LE) [10235248] 255, **2645**

ANNALES D'HISTOIRE ET DE SCIENCE SOCIALE (FR) **2674**

ANNALES D'ORL (FR) **3886**

ANNALES D'OTO-LARYNGOLOGIE ET DE CHIRURGIE CERVICO FACIALE : BULLETIN DE LA SOCIETE D'OTO-LARYNGOLOGIE DES HOPITAUX DE PARIS (FR/0003-438X) [17631080] **3886**

ANNALES DU CENTRE DE RECHERCHES SUR L'AMERIQUE ANGLOPHONE (FR/0399-0443) [05247290] 2255, **3362**

ANNALES DU CENTRE UNIVERSITAIRE MEDITERRANEEN (FR/0399-0389) [04022091] **1089**

ANNALES DU CERCLE ARCHEOLOGIQUE DE MONS (BE/0776-135X) [0776135X] **255**

ANNALES DU CERCLE ARCHEOLOGIQUE D'ENGHIEN (BE/0776-1252) [07761252] **255**

ANNALES DU GROUPE NUMISMATIQUE DU COMTAT ET DE PROVENCE (FR/0997-055X) [0997055X] **2779**

ANNALES DU MIDI (FR/0003-4398) [01481318] **255**

ANNALES DU SERVICE DES ANTIQUITES DE L'EGYPTE (UA) [02302175] **255**

ANNALES DU TABAC. SECTION 1, RECHERCHE ET DEVELOPPEMENT (FR/0399-0206) [10152845] **5372**

ANNALES DU TABAC. SECTION 1, RECHERCHE ET INGEGNIERIE *See* ANNALES DU TABAC. SECTION 1, RECHERCHE ET DEVELOPPEMENT **5372**

ANNALES DU TABAC. SECTION 2 (FR/0399-0354) [07496541] **5372**

ANNALES D'UROLOGIE (FR/0003-4401) [01481319] **3988**

ANNALES; ECONOMIES, SOCIETES, CIVILISATIONS (FR) [01481221] **5190**

ANNALES FRANCAISES D'ANESTHESIE ET DE REANIMATION (FR/0750-7658) [08659996] **3682**

ANNALES FRANCAISES DES MICROTECHNIQUES ET DE CHRONOMETRIE (FR/0294-1228) [10575854] 2096, **4397**

ANNALES FRIBOURGEOISES (SZ/1013-3534) [03338605] **2674**

ANNALES GEOLOGIQUES DES PAYS HELLENIQUES (GR/0402-4664) [01710851] **1365**

ANNALES GEOPHYSICAE (1988) (FR/0992-7689) [16770354] **1402**

ANNALES HISTORICO-NATURALES MUSEI NATIONALIS HUNGARICI (BUDAPEST, HUNGARY : 1965) (HU) [05785100] **4161**

ANNALES HISTORIQUES DE LA REVOLUTION FRANCAISE (FR/0003-4436) [01481323] **2674**

ANNALES HYDROGRAPHIQUES (FR/0373-3629) [01791728] 1446, **1412**

ANNALES INTERNATIONALES DE CRIMINOLOGIE (FR/0003-4452) [01481324] **3156**

ANNALES ISLAMOLOGIQUES (UA) [08693711] **5042**

ANNALES LITTERAIRES (FR/0547-2016) [01643846] **3362**

ANNALES MEDICALES DE NANCY ET DE L'EST (FR/0221-3796) [05527925] **3550**

ANNALES MEDICO PSYCHOLOGIQUES (FR/0003-4487) [01481330] **4573**

ANNALES MONEGASQUES (MC/0257-960X) [04067784] **2674**

ANNALES MUSEI GOULANDRIS (GR/0302-1033) [01793293] 2186, **4161**

ANNALES MUSICOLOGIQUES, MOYEN-AGE ET RENAISSANCE (FR/0583-8363) [02004066] **4100**

ANNALES NESTLE (SZ/0517-8606) [10462866] **4187**

ANNALES ORTHOPEDIQUES DE L'OUEST (FR) [03568842] **3880**

ANNALES PADEREWSKI (SZ) [07188924] **4100**

ANNALES (PARIS, FRANCE : 1946) (FR/0395-2649) [01481220] **2513**

ANNALES PARLEMENTAIRES. PARLEMENTAIRE HANDELINGEN (BE) [07988270] **4463**

ANNALES PHARMACEUTICI (PL/0365-5539) [I03655539] **4291**

ANNALES PHARMACEUTIQUES BELGES (BE) [09844303] **4291**

ANNALES PHARMACEUTIQUES FRANCAISES (FR/0003-4509) [01481335] **4291**

ANNALES POLONICI MATHEMATICI (PL/0066-2216) [01481338] **3493**

ANNALES PUBLIEES PAR L'UNIVERSITE DE TOULOUSE - LE MIRAIL (FR/0182-855X) [01080839] 2841, **1808**

ANNALES. RECHTS- UND WIRTSCHAFTSWISSENSCHAFTLICHE ABTEILUNG (GW) [01764714] **2933**

ANNALES SCIENTIFIQUES DE L'ECOLE NORMALE SUPERIEURE (FR/0012-9593) [02449439] **3493**

ANNALES SCIENTIFIQUES DE L'UNIVERSITE DE FRANCHE-COMTE-BESANCON. MEDECINE ET PHARMACIE (FR/0224-5264) [05858400] 3550, **4291**

ANNALES SCIENTIFIQUES DE L'UNIVERSITE DE FRANCHE-COMTE. BIOLOGIE-ECOLOGIE (FR/1142-2998) [23913841] 2211, **441**

ANNALES SILESIAE (PL/0066-2224) [01708783] **2674**

ANNALES SOCIETATIS DOCTRINAE STUDENTIUM ACADEMIAE MEDICAE SILESIENSIS (PL) [04187176] **3550**

ANNALES SOCIETATIS GEOLOGORUM POLONIAE (PL/0208-9068) [I02089068] **1365**

ANNALES SOCIETATIS MATHEMATICAE POLONAE. COMMENTATIONES MATHEMATICAE (PL/0373-8299) [01796535] **3493**

ANNALES SOCIETATIS MATHEMATICAE POLONAE. SERIES IV, FUNDAMENTA INFORMATICAE *See* FUNDAMENTA INFORMATICAE **1185**

ANNALES - SOCIETE D'ARCHEOLOGIE D'HISTOIRE ET DE FOLKLORE DE NIVELLES ET DU BRABANT WALLON (BE) [02241193] **2674**

ANNALES STATISTIQUES DE TRANSPORT / CONFERENCE EUROPEENNE DES MINISTRES DES TRANSPORTS (FR) [13316277] **5376**

ANNALES TECTONIC : AT (IT/0394-5596) [17372170] **1365**

ANNALES THEOLOGICI (IT/0394-8226) [03948226] **4934**

ANNALES UNIVERSITATIS MARIAE CURIE-SKLODOWSKA. SECTION I: PHILOSOPHIA-SOCIOLOGIA (PL/0066-2240) [04851383] **4340**

ANNALES UNIVERSITATIS MARIAE CURIE-SKODOWSKA. SECTIO A. MATHEMATICA (PL/0365-1029) [01773951] **3493**

ANNALES UNIVERSITATIS MARIAE CURIE-SKODOWSKA. SECTIO AA, CHEMIA (PL/0137-6853) [06796995] **961**

ANNALES UNIVERSITATIS MARIAE CURIE-SKODOWSKA. SECTIO AAA: PHYSICA (PL/0137-6861) [05378022] **4397**

ANNALES UNIVERSITATIS MARIAE CURIE-SKODOWSKA. SECTIO C. BIOLOGIA (PL/0066-2232) [02251022] **442**

ANNALES UNIVERSITATIS MARIAE CURIE-SKODOWSKA. SECTIO D, MEDICINA (PL/0066-2240) [01778886] **3550**

ANNALES UNIVERSITATIS MARIAE CURIE-SKODOWSKA. SECTIO DD, MEDICINA VETERINARIA (PL/0301-7737) [05328183] **5503**

ANNALES UNIVERSITATIS MARIAE CURIE-SKODOWSKA. SECTIO E AGRICULTURA (PL/0365-1118) [01756255] **59**

ANNALES UNIVERSITATIS MARIAE CURIE-SKODOWSKA. SECTIO EE, ZOOTECHNICA (PL/0239-4243) [13415748] **5575**

ANNALES UNIVERSITATIS MARIAE CURIE-SKODOWSKA. SECTIO H OECONOMIA (PL/0459-9586) [02663116] **1462**

ANNALES UNIVERSITATIS SARAVIENSIS. MEDICINAE. SUPPLEMENT (GW/0931-9913) [08447082] **3550**

ANNALES UNIVERSITATIS SARAVIENSIS. REIHE : MATHEMATISCH-NATURWISSENSCHAFTLICHE FAKULTAT (GW/0080-5165) [03173047] 3493, **4162**

ANNALES UNIVERSITATIS SARAVIENSIS. SERIES MATHEMATICAE (SW) [18707110] **3493**

ANNALES UNIVERSITATIS SCIENTIARUM BUDAPENTINENSIS DE ROLANDO EOTVOS NOMINATAE. SECTIO PHILOLOGICA MODERNA (HU) [03019398] **3264**

ANNALES UNIVERSITATIS SCIENTIARUM BUDAPESTINENSIS DE ROLANDO EOTVOS NOMINATAE. SECTIO COMPUTATORICA (HU/0138-9491) [08155132] **3493**

ANNALES UNIVERSITATIS SCIENTIARUM BUDAPESTINENSIS DE ROLANDO EOTVOS NOMINATAE. SECTIO GEOGRAPHICA (HU/0524-8965) [02710656] **2554**

ANNALES UNIVERSITATIS SCIENTIARUM BUDAPESTINENSIS DE ROLANDO EOTVOS NOMINATAE. SECTIO HISTORICA (HU/0524-8981) [02710758] **2841**

ANNALES UNIVERSITATIS SCIENTIARUM BUDAPESTINENSIS DE ROLANDO EOTVOS NOMINATAE. SECTIO IURIDICA (HU/0524-899X) [01537561] **2933**

ANNALES UNIVERSITATIS SCIENTIARUM BUDAPESTINENSIS DE ROLANDO EOTVOS NOMINATAE. SECTIO LINGUISTICA (HU/0572-7251) [03019351] **3265**

ANNALES UNIVERSITATIS SCIENTIARUM BUDAPESTINENSIS DE ROLANDO EOTVOS NOMINATAE. SECTIO MATHEMATICA (HU/0524-9007) [02710891] **3493**

ANNALES UNIVERSITATIS SCIENTIARUM BUDAPESTINENSIS DE ROLANDO EOTVOS NOMINATAE. SECTIO PHILOSOPHICA ET SOCIOLOGICA (HU/0524-9023) [03019375] 5239, **4341**

ANNALES / UNIVERSITE FRANCOPHONE D'ETE SAINTONGE-QUEBEC (FR) [09439135] **1808**

ANNALES VALAISANNES (SZ/1013-3488) [01712025] **2674**

ANNALES ZOOLOGICI (PL/0003-4541) [01443837] **5575**

ANNALI DEL DIPARTIMENTO DI FILOSOFIA / UNIVERSITA DE FIRENZE (IT) [13740255] **4341**

ANNALI DEL DIPARTIMENTO DI STUDI DELLEUROPA ORIENTALE (US) [20368059] **2813**

ANNALI DEL DIPARTIMENTO DI STUDI DELL'EUROPA ORIENTALE. SEZIONE LETTERARIO-ARTISTICA *See* AION. SLAVISTICA : ANNALI DELL'ISTITUTO UNIVERSITARIO ORIENTALE DI NAPOLI / DIPARTIMENTO DI STUDI DELL'EUROPA ORIENTALE, SEZIONE SLAVISTICA **3262**

ANNALI DEL DIPARTIMENTO DI STUDI DELL'EUROPA ORIENTALE. SEZIONE LINGUISTICO-FILOLOGICA *See* AION. SLAVISTICA : ANNALI DELL'ISTITUTO UNIVERSITARIO ORIENTALE DI NAPOLI / DIPARTIMENTO DI STUDI DELL'EUROPA ORIENTALE, SEZIONE SLAVISTICA **3262**

ANNALI DEL DIPARTIMENTO DI STUDI DELL'EUROPA ORIENTALE. SEZIONE STORICO-POLITICO-SOCIALE *See* AION. SLAVISTICA : ANNALI DELL'ISTITUTO UNIVERSITARIO ORIENTALE DI NAPOLI / DIPARTIMENTO DI STUDI DELL'EUROPA ORIENTALE, SEZIONE SLAVISTICA **3262**

ANNALI DEL MUSEO CIVICO DI STORIA NATURALE GIACOMO DORIA (IT/0365-4389) [15566555] **4162**

ANNALI DEL SEMINARIO GIURIDICO (IT) **2933**

ANNALI DELL ISTITUTO SPERIMENTALE PER LA CEREALICOLTURA *CEASED.* (IT) **200**

ANNALI DELL' ISTITUTO SPERIMENTALE PER L'OLIVICOLTURA (IT/0304-0534) [I03040534] **59**

ANNALI DELLA BIBLIOTECA STATALE E LIBRERIA CIVICA DI CREMONA (IT) [01785480] **3190**

ANNALI DELLA FACOLTA DI AGRARIA UNIVERSITA CATTOLICA DEL SACRO CUORE MILANO (IT/0540-049X) [04771903] **59**

ANNALI DELLA FACOLTA DI AGRARIA. UNIVERSITA DEGLI STUDI DI PERUGIA (IT/0373-2673) [I03732673] **59**

ANNALI DELLA FACOLTA DI AGRARIA UNIVERSITA PERUGIA (IT/0374-4981) [04853480] **59**

ANNALI DELLA FACOLTA DI GIURISPRUDENZA DI GENOVA (IT) **2933**

ANNALI DELLA FACOLTA DI LETTERE E FILOSOFIA (IT) [06804623] **2842**

ANNALI DELLA FACOLTA DI LETTERE E FILOSOFIA (IT) [01519194] **4341**

ANNALI DELLA FACOLTA DI LETTERE E FILOSOFIA DELL'UNIVERSITA DI NAPOLI (IT/0469-5461) [I04695461] **4341**

ANNALI DELLA FACOLTA DI MEDICINA VETERINARIA DI PISA (IT/0365-4729) [01639228] **5503**

ANNALI DELLA FACOLTA DI MEDICINA VETERINARIA DI TORINO (IT/0496-4748) [03276443] **5503**

ANNALI DELLA FACOLTA DI MEDICINA VETERINARIA. UNIVERSITA DI PARMA (IT/0393-4802) [I03934802] **5503**

ANNALI DELLA FACOLTA DI SCIENZE AGRARIE DELLA UNIVERSITA DEGLI STUDI DI NAPOLI, PORTICI (IT/0365-799X) [10319956] **59**

ANNALI DELLA FACOLTA DI SCIENZE AGRARIE DELLA UNIVERSITA DEGLI STUDI DI TORINO (IT/0082-6871) [02609648] 442, **59**

ANNALI DELLA FONDAZIONE GIULIO PASTORE (IT) [17343076] **1644**

ANNALI — Alphabetical Title Index

ANNALI DELLA FONDAZIONE LUIGI EINAUDI (IT/0531-9870) [01320686] 1462, **5190**

ANNALI DELLA PUBBLICA ISTRUZIONE (IT) [01785507] **1724**

ANNALI DELLA SANITA PUBBLICA (IT) [02257535] **4765**

ANNALI DELLA SCUOLA NORMALE SUPERIORE DI PISA, CLASSE DI LETTERE E FILOSOFIA (IT/0392-095X) [10200506] 4341, **3362**

ANNALI DELLA SCUOLA NORMALE SUPERIORE DI PISA, CLASSE DI SCIENZE (IT/0391-173X) [02679124] **3493**

ANNALI DELLA SOCIETA ITALIANA DI STUDI SUL SECOLO XVIII (IT) [12842108] **2610**

ANNALI DELL'INSTITUTO SPERIMENTALE PER LA MECCANIZZAZIONE AGRICOLA (IT) [03372095] **59**

ANNALI DELL'ISTITUTO "ALCIDE CERVI" (IT) [07139441] **5190**

ANNALI DELL'ISTITUTO CARLO FORLANINI (1981) (IT) [19346103] **3948**

ANNALI DELL'ISTITUTO DI LINGUE E LETTERATURE GERMANICHE *SUSPENDED.* (IT/0390-0576) [05939133] **3362**

ANNALI DELL'ISTITUTO ITALIANO PER GLI STUDI STORICI (IT) [03399938] **2610**

ANNALI DELL'ISTITUTO SPERIMENTALE AGRONCMICO (IT/0304-0615) [01779815] **59**

ANNALI DELL'ISTITUTO SPERIMENTALE PER IL TABACCO (IT/0391-4836) [03959736] **5372**

ANNALI DELL'ISTITUTO SPERIMENTALE PER LA FLORICOLTURA (IT/0304-0550) [03409418] **2408**

ANNALI DELL'ISTITUTO SPERIMENTALE PER LA FRUTTICOLTURA (IT/0304-0569) [03380627] **2326**

ANNALI DELL'ISTITUTO SPERIMENTALE PER LA NUTRIZIONE DELLE PIANTE (IT/0365-7043) [01795807] **59**

ANNALI DELL'ISTITUTO SPERIMENTALE PER LA PATOLOGIA VEGETALE (IT/0304-0585) [24190621] **2408**

ANNALI DELL'ISTITUTO SPERIMENTALE PER LA SELVICOLTURA (IT/0390-0010) [02240475] **2374**

ANNALI DELL'ISTITUTO SPERIMENTALE PER LA VALLORIZZAZIONE TECNOLOGICA DEI PRODOTTI AGRICCLI (IT/0304-0577) [03399664] **2326**

ANNALI DELL'ISTITUTO SPERIMENTALE PER LA ZOOTECNIA (IT/0365-3498) [01771756] **5575**

ANNALI DELL'ISTITUTC SPERIMENTALE PER L'AGRUMICOLTURA (IT) [02670249] 162, **59**

ANNALI DELL'ISTITUTO STORIA (IT) [06834557] **2674**

ANNALI DELL'ISTITUTO STORICO ITALO GERMANICO (IT) [11273922] **2674**

ANNALI DELL'ISTITUTO STORICO ITALO-GERMANICO IN TRENTO. JAHRBUCH DES ITALIENISCH-DEUTSCHEN HISTORISCHEN INSTITUTS IN TRIENT (IT) [04546670] **2610**

ANNALI DELL'ISTITUTO SUPERIORE DI SANITA (IT/0021-2571) [01394558] **4765**

ANNALI DELL'ISTITUTO UNIVERSITARIO ORIENTALE DI NAPOLI, SEMINARIO DI STUDI DEL MONDO CLASSICO, SEZIONE FILOLOGICO-LETTERARIA (IT) [15479776] 3362, **3265**

ANNALI DELL'OSPEDALE MARIA VITTORIA DI TORINO (IT/0390-5454) [01712660] **3550**

ANNALI DELL'OSPEDALE PSICHIATRICO DI PERUGIA *See* ANNALI DI NEUROLOGIA E PSICHIATRIA **3920**

ANNALI DELL'UNIVERSITA DI FERRARA. SEZIONE 7 : SCIENZE MATEMATICHE (IT/0430-3202) [02438314] **3494**

ANNALI DI ARCHITETTURA (IT) [21986013] **287**

ANNALI DI CA' FOSCARI (IT) [01498018] **3362**

ANNALI DI CHIMICA (IT/0003-4592) [02207353] **961**

ANNALI DI IGIENE : MEDICINA PREVENTIVA E DI COMUNITA (IT) [21230332] **3550**

ANNALI DI MATEMATICA PURA ED APPLICATA (IT/0373-3114) [01481351] **3494**

ANNALI DI MEDICINA NAVALE (IT/0003-4630) [01778584] **3550**

ANNALI DI MICROBIOLOGIA ED ENZIMOLOGIA (IT/0003-4649) [07579410] **558**

ANNALI DI NEUROLOGIA E PSICHIATRIA (IT) [19346088] **3920**

ANNALI DI OSTETRICIA, GINECOLOGIA, MEDICINA PERINATALE (IT/0300-0087) [05212588] **3757**

ANNALI DI OTTALMOLOGIA E CLINICA OCULISTICA (IT/0003-4665) [03208175] **3872**

ANNALI DI SOCIOLOGIA (IT/0066-2275) [06585720] **5239**

ANNALI D'ITALIANISTICA (US/0741-7527) [10201805] **3362**

ANNALI / FONDAZIONE DI STUDI DI STORIA DELL'ARTE ROBERTO LONGHI, FIRENZE (IT/0394-1744) [16077950] **336**

ANNALI - FONDAZIONE GIANGIACOMO FELTRINELLI (IT/0393-3954) [03087545] **4539**

ANNALI / FONDAZIONE LELIO E LISLI BASSO-ISSOCO (IT) [02641943] **2610**

ANNALI - INSTITUTO UNIVERSITARIO ORIENTALE, SEZIONE GERMANICA. ANGLISTICA (IT/0391-5956) [03243833] **3265**

ANNALI / ISTITUTO ITALIANO DI NUMISMATICA (IT/0578-9923) [02774620] **2779**

ANNALI (ISTITUTO UNIVERSITARIO ORIENTALE (NAPLES, ITALY)) (IT) [01758987] **3265**

ANNALI ITALIANI DI CHIRURGIA (IT/0003-469X) [01778585] **3959**

ANNALI ITALIANI DI DERMATOLOGIA CLINICA E SPERIMENTALE (IT/0365-169X) [0365169X] 3666, **3717**

ANNALI ITALIANI DI MEDICINA INTERNA : ORGANO UFFICIALE DELLA SOCIETA ITALIANA DI MEDICINA INTERNA (IT/0393-9340) [15499239] **3794**

ANNALI, NUOVA SERIE : SEZIONE 3, BIOLOGIA ANIMALE. SUPPLEMENTO (IT) [03220250] **5576**

ANNALI SCIENTIFICI (IT) **5083**

ANNALI SCLAVO *CEASED.* (IT/0003-472X) [03574040] **558**

ANNALI SCLAVO. COLLANA MONOGRAFICA (IT/0003-472X) [15285839] **3666**

ANNALI. SEZIONE GERMANICA (IT) [27930926] **3362**

ANNALI - SEZIONE ROMANZA (IT/0547-2121) [02264527] **3265**

ANNALI SOTIC (IT) **3550**

ANNALS - ASSOCIATION FOR ASIAN STUDIES. SOUTHEAST CONFERENCE (US/0883-8909) [09224125] **2645**

ANNALS - INSTITUTE OF CHILD HEALTH (II) [01784258] **3900**

ANNALS - JAPAN ASSOCIATION FOR PHILOSOPHY OF SCIENCE (JA) [06159562] **5083**

ANNALS OF AGRICULTURAL RESEARCH (II/0970-3179) [10257817] **59**

ANNALS OF AGRICULTURAL SCIENCE (UA) [01481362] **59**

ANNALS OF AGRICULTURAL SCIENCE (UA/0570-1783) [05701783] **59**

ANNALS OF AGRICULTURAL SCIENCE, MOSHTOHOR (UA/0570-1791) [02195728] **59**

ANNALS OF AIR AND SPACE LAW (CN/0701-158X) [03183621] 11, **3123**

ANNALS OF ALLERGY (US/0003-4738) [01481364] **3666**

● ANNALS OF ANATOMY (GW/0940-9602) [25775346] **3678**

ANNALS OF APPLIED BIOLOGY (UK/0003-4746) [01481367] **442**

ANNALS OF APPLIED PROBABILITY, THE (US/1050-5164) [21526818] **3494**

ANNALS OF ARID ZONE (II/0570-1791) [01481369] **162**

ANNALS OF BALLOON HISTORY AND MUSEOLOGY (US) [25357246] **11**

ANNALS OF BEHAVIORAL MEDICINE (US/0883-6612) [12181616] 4573, 3550, **3654**

ANNALS OF BIOLOGY (LUDHIANA) (II/0970-0153) [14707540] **442**

ANNALS OF BIOMEDICAL ENGINEERING (US/0090-6964) [01707364] **3685**

ANNALS OF BOTANY (UK/0305-7364) [01481373] **499**

ANNALS OF CHILD DEVELOPMENT (UK/0747-7902) [10755543] **4573**

ANNALS OF CLINICAL AND LABORATORY SCIENCE (US/0091-7370) [02864670] **3893**

ANNALS OF CLINICAL BIOCHEMISTRY (UK/0004-5632) [01481376] **480**

ANNALS OF CLINICAL PSYCHIATRY (US/1040-1237) [18330797] **3920**

ANNALS OF DENTISTRY (US/0003-4770) [01481380] **1316**

ANNALS OF DERMATOLOGY (KO/1013-9087) [20566477] **3717**

ANNALS OF DIFFERENTIAL EQUATIONS. WEI FEN FANG CHENG NIEN KAN (CC/1002-0942) [19898354] **3494**

ANNALS OF DISCRETE MATHEMATICS (NE/0167-5060) [04277334] **3494**

ANNALS OF DYSLEXIA (US/0736-9387) [08872116] **1874**

ANNALS OF EARTH (US/1070-9983) [28528421] **1351**

ANNALS OF EMERGENCY MEDICINE (US/0196-0644) [05729547] **3723**

ANNALS OF ENTOMOLOGY (II) [15250681] **5576**

ANNALS OF EPIDEMIOLOGY (US/1047-2797) [20649595] **3734**

ANNALS OF GLACIOLOGY (UK/0260-3055) [07343093] **1412**

ANNALS OF GLOBAL ANALYSIS AND GEOMETRY (GW/0232-704X) [11165201] **3494**

ANNALS OF HEMATOLOGY (GW/0939-5555) [23289683] **3770**

ANNALS OF HUMAN BIOLOGY (UK/0301-4460) [03101135] **442**

ANNALS OF HUMAN GENETICS (UK/0003-4800) [01481384] **542**

ANNALS OF INTERNAL MEDICINE (US/0003-4819) [01481385] **3794**

ANNALS OF INTERNAL MEDICINE. CD-ROM (US) **3795**

ANNALS OF IOWA (US/0003-4827) [01481386] **2720**

ANNALS OF ITALIAN OPERA (US) [23359069] 4100, **383**

ANNALS OF LIBRARY SCIENCE AND DOCUMENTATION (II/0003-4835) [04814159] **3190**

ANNALS OF MATHEMATICS (US/0003-486X) [01481391] **3494**

ANNALS OF MATHEMATICS AND OF ARTIFICIAL INTELLIGENCE (NE/1012-2443) [23345571] 3494, **1211**

ANNALS OF MATHEMATICS STUDIES (US/0066-2313) [01481392] **3494**

ANNALS OF MEDICINE (HELSINKI) (FI/0785-3890) [19550892] **3550**

ANNALS OF NEUROLOGY (US/0364-5134) [02802351] **3827**

ANNALS OF NUCLEAR ENERGY (UK/0306-4549) [02243298] **2153**

ANNALS OF NUCLEAR MEDICINE (JA) [19683500] **3938**

ANNALS OF NUMERICAL MATHEMATICS (NE) **3494**

ANNALS OF NUTRITION & METABOLISM (SZ/0250-6807) [07520506] **4187**

ANNALS OF OCCUPATIONAL HYGIENE, THE (UK/0003-4878) [01481394] **2858**

ANNALS OF ONCOLOGY : OFFICIAL JOURNAL OF THE EUROPEAN SOCIETY FOR MEDICAL ONCOLOGY (NE/0923-7534) [21289099] **3808**

ANNALS OF OPERATIONS RESEARCH (NE/0254-5330) [11521382] **5083**

ANNALS OF OPHTHALMOLOGY (BIRMINGHAM) (US/0003-4886) [01481395] **3872**

ANNALS OF ORIENTAL RESEARCH / UNIVERSITY OF MADRAS (II) [10074173] **2645**

ANNALS OF OTOLOGY, RHINOLOGY & LARYNGOLOGY. SUPPLEMENT, THE (US/0096-8056) [01379560] **3886**

ANNALS OF OTOLOGY, RHINOLOGY & LARYNGOLOGY, THE (US/0003-4894) [01481398] **3886**

ANNALS OF PAEDIATRIC SURGERY (II/0970-2121) [12085358] 3959, **3900**

● ANNALS OF PHARMACOTHERAPY, THE (US/1060-0280) [24850495] **4291**

ANNALS OF PHYSICS (US/0003-4916) [01481402] **4397**

ANNALS OF PHYSIOLOGICAL ANTHROPOLOGY, THE (JA/0287-8429) [11161403] **228**

ANNALS OF PLANT PHYSIOLOGY AKOLA (II/0970-9924) [109709924] **2408**

ANNALS OF PLASTIC SURGERY (US/0148-7043) [03451617] **3959**

ANNALS OF PROBABILITY, THE (US/0091-1798) [01786664] **3494**

ANNALS OF PUBLIC AND CO-OPERATIVE ECONOMY (BE/0770-8548) [05784802] **1545**

ANNALS OF PUBLIC AND COOPERATIVE ECONOMY (BE) [01481403] **1462**

ANNALS OF PURE AND APPLIED LOGIC (NE/0168-0072) [09792318] **3494**

ANNALS OF REGIONAL SCIENCE, THE (GW/0570-1864) [01036033] **2814**

ANNALS OF SAINT ANNE DE BEAUPRE (1974) (CN/0318-434X) [02442023] **4934**

ANNALS OF SAUDI MEDICINE (SU/0256-4947) [12388567] **3550**

ANNALS OF SCHOLARSHIP (US/0192-2858) [04985429] **2842**

ANNALS OF SCIENCE (UK/0003-3790) [01481407] **5083**

ANNALS OF SEX RESEARCH (CN/0843-4611) [20284364] 4574, **5186**

ANNALS OF SOFTWARE ENGINEERING (NE) **1227**

ANNALS OF STATISTICS, THE (US/0090-5364) [01785358] **5321**

ANNALS OF SURGERY (US/0003-4932) [01481411] **3959**

●ANNALS OF SURGICAL ONCOLOGY (US/1068-9265) [27859406] **3959**

ANNALS OF THE ACADEMY OF MEDICINE, SINGAPORE (SI/0304-4602) [01145745] **3550**

ANNALS OF THE AMERICAN ACADEMY OF POLITICAL AND SOCIAL SCIENCE (US/0002-7162) [01479265] 4463, **5190**

ANNALS OF THE ASSOCIATION OF AMERICAN GEOGRAPHERS (US/0004-5608) [01514553] **2554**

ANNALS OF THE BHANDARKAR ORIENTAL RESEARCH INSTITUTE (II/0378-1143) [01774249] 3337, **3265**

ANNALS OF THE CAPE PROVINCIAL MUSEUMS. HUMAN SCIENCES (SA) [05852717] 255, **4083**

ANNALS OF THE CAPE PROVINCIAL MUSEUMS. NATURAL HISTORY (SA/0570-1880) [08981217] **4162**

ANNALS OF THE CARNEGIE MUSEUM (US/0097-4463) [01261514] **4162**

ANNALS OF THE CHINESE HISTORICAL SOCIETY OF THE PACIFIC NORTHWEST / MEI-KUO HSI PEI HUA JEN LI SHIH HSUEH HUI, THE (US/0740-8536) [09755490] **2255**

ANNALS OF THE ENTOMOLOGICAL SOCIETY OF AMERICA (US/0013-8746) [01145791] **5605**

ANNALS OF THE GEOLOGICAL SURVEY OF EGYPT (UA/0365-2777) [03909324] **1365**

ANNALS OF THE HISTORY OF COMPUTING *See* IEEE ANNALS OF THE HISTORY OF COMPUTING **1187**

ANNALS OF THE ICRP (UK/0146-6453) [03313204] **3938**

ANNALS OF THE INSTITUTE FOR ORGONOMIC SCIENCE (US/8755-3252) [11285168] **4291**

ANNALS OF THE INSTITUTE OF SOCIAL SCIENCE (JA/0563-8054) [03138191] 5226, **5191**

ANNALS OF THE INSTITUTE OF STATISTICAL MATHEMATICS (JA/0020-3157) [02141895] **3542**

ANNALS OF THE ISRAEL PHYSICAL SOCIETY (UK/0309-8710) [03885382] **5228**

ANNALS OF THE MISSOURI BOTANICAL GARDEN (US/0026-6493) [01764787] **499**

ANNALS OF THE NATAL MUSEUM, PIETERMARITZBURG (SA/0304-0798) [01590722] **4162**

ANNALS OF THE NATIONAL ACADEMY OF MEDICAL SCIENCES (INDIA) (II/0379-038X) [04276236] **3550**

ANNALS OF THE NATIONAL ASSOCIATION OF GEOGRAPHERS, INDIA (II/0970-972X) [09107649] **2554**

ANNALS OF THE NEW YORK ACADEMY OF SCIENCES (US/0077-8923) [01306678] 3550, **5083**

ANNALS OF THE NYINGMA LINEAGE IN AMERICA (US/0147-4839) [03175911] **5020**

ANNALS OF THE RHEUMATIC DISEASES (UK/0003-4967) [08771855] **3802**

ANNALS OF THE ROYAL AUSTRALASIAN COLLEGE OF DENTAL SURGEONS (AT/0158-1570) [06564568] **1316**

ANNALS OF THE ROYAL COLLEGE OF PHYSICIANS AND SURGEONS OF CANADA (CN/0035-8800) [09533695] **3913**

ANNALS OF THE ROYAL COLLEGE OF SURGEONS OF ENGLAND (UK/0035-8843) [02832178] **3959**

ANNALS OF THE SCHOOL OF BUSINESS ADMINISTRATION, KOBE UNIVERSITY, THE (JA/0085-2570) [01755196] **638**

ANNALS OF THE SOUTH AFRICAN MUSEUM (SA/0303-2515) [01647291] 5083, **4083**

ANNALS OF THE TRANSVAAL MUSEUM (SA/0041-1752) [01714046] **4162**

ANNALS OF THE UKRAINIAN ACADEMY OF ARTS AND SCIENCES IN THE UNITED STATES (US/0503-1001) [02130982] **2842**

ANNALS OF THEORETICAL PSYCHOLOGY (US/0747-5241) [10635268] **4574**

ANNALS OF THORACIC SURGERY, THE (US/0003-4975) [01481414] **3959**

ANNALS OF TOURISM RESEARCH (US/0160-7383) [02724733] 5461, **5191**

ANNALS OF TROPICAL MEDICINE AND PARASITOLOGY (UK/0003-4983) [01481415] **3985**

ANNALS OF TROPICAL PAEDIATRICS (UK/0272-4936) [06855069] **3985**

ANNALS OF TROPICAL RESEARCH (PH/0116-0710) [05305890] **5083**

ANNALS OF VASCULAR SURGERY (US/0890-5096) [13283685] **3959**

ANNALS OF WARSAW AGRICULTURAL UNIVERSITY, SGGW--AR. AGRICULTURE (PL/0208-5712) [16896508] **59**

ANNALS OF WARSAW AGRICULTURAL UNIVERSITY, SGGW-AR. ANIMAL SCIENCE (PL/0208-5739) [12263643] **205**

ANNALS OF WARSAW AGRICULTURAL UNIVERSITY - SGGW-AR. FORESTRY AND WOOD TECHNOLOGY (PL/0208-5704) [10953277] **2374**

ANNALS OF WARSAW AGRICULTURAL UNIVERSITY, SGGW-AR. HORTICULTURE (PL/0208-5747) [13924404] **2409**

ANNALS OF WARSAW AGRICULTURAL UNIVERSITY SGGW-AR. LAND RECLAMATION (PL/0208-5771) [10953271] **59**

ANNALS OF WARSAW AGRICULTURAL UNIVERSITY, SGGW-AR. VETERINARY MEDICINE (PL/0208-5763) [09399580] **5503**

ANNALS OF WYOMING (US/0003-4991) [01481417] **2720**

ANNALS (SOCIETY OF LOGISTICS ENGINEERS) *SUSPENDED.* (US/0885-3916) [12629258] **1964**

ANNALS / UNIVERSITAT CATALANA D'ESTIU (SP) [11351709] **1808**

ANNAPOLITAN (ANNAPOLIS, MD.) *CEASED.* (US/0899-2320) [18040292] **2528**

ANNE BURNETT TANDY LECTURES IN AMERICAN CIVILIZATION, THE (US) [07854629] **2720**

ANNEE AFRICAINE *CEASED.* (FR/0570-1937) [01481422] **2637**

ANNEE BALZACIENNE, L' (FR/0084-6473) [01226547] **3362**

ANNEE BATEAUX (ENGLISH ED.) (FR) [09078448] **591**

ANNEE BIOLOGIQUE, L' (SZ/0003-5017) [01481424] **442**

ANNEE CANONIQUE, L' (FR/0570-1953) [01711195] 4935, **2933**

ANNEE DE LA RECHERCHE EN SCIENCES DE L'EDUCATION (FR) 5083, **1724**

ANNEE ... DE LA SCIENCE-FICTION ET DU FANTASTIQUE, L' (FR/0183-9950) [05529237] **3362**

ANNEE DU MEDECIN, L' (FR/0399-3914) [03299894] **3550**

ANNEE DU ROCK, L' (FR) [10819200] **4100**

ANNEE DU TENNIS, L' (FR) [09821707] **4883**

ANNEE EPIGRAPHIQUE, L' (FR/0066-2348) [01196530] **1074**

ANNEE PHILOLOGIQUE; BIBLIOGRAPHIE CRITIQUE ET ANALYTIQUE DE L'ANTIQUITE GRECO-LATINE, L' (FR) [01481432] **3265**

ANNEE PHILOLOGIQUE (PARIS), L' (FR/0184-6949) [01846949] **1081**

ANNEE PLANCHE A VOILE, L' (FR) [07352481] **4883**

ANNEE PSYCHOLOGIQUE, L' (FR/0003-5033) [01437340] **4574**

ANNEE SAINTE AVEC PAUL VI (CN/0319-7166) [02443242] **4935**

ANNEE SOCIALE / INSTITUT DE SOCIOLOGIE, UNIVERSITE LIBRE DE BRUXELLES, L' (BE/0066-2380) [01709135] **5191**

ANNEE SOCIOLOGIQUE (1940/48) (FR/0066-2399) [07635912] **5239**

ANNEE TECHNOLOGIQUE : SECTEUR PAR SECTEUR, LE POINT SUR L'EVOLUTION DES MOYENS DE PRODUCTION, UNE SELECTION DE PLUS DE 700 PRODUITS INDUSTRIELS NOUVEAUX, L' (FR) [18371653] **1597**

ANNEES. DOCUMENTS CLEIRPPA (FR/0184-6531) [I01846531] **3749**

ANNEES. DOCUMENTS CLEIRPPA *See* CLEIRPPA INFOS PARIS **3750**

ANNEX COMPUTER REPORT (US/0738-419X) [09595258] **1170**

ANNIE'S CROCHET NEWSLETTER (US/0745-6360) [09318646] **5183**

ANNIE'S PATTERN CLUB NEWSLETTER *See* ANNIE'S QUICK & EASY PATTERN CLUB **5347**

ANNIE'S QUICK & EASY PATTERN CLUB (US/1051-3337) [21928381] 1081, **5347**

ANNISTON STAR, THE (US) [12961379] **5625**

ANNIVERSARY REPORT (US) [15354238] **3092**

ANNIVERSARY REPORT - HARVARD COLLEGE, CLASS OF 1971 (US/0363-4019) [02439097] **1808**

ANNLAS DE L'INSTITUT D'ESTUDIS GIRONINS (SP/0213-6228) [I02136228] **2674**

ANNOTATED BIBLIOGRAPHIES FOR ANTHROPOLOGISTS (US) [25724574] **228**

ANNOTATED BIBLIOGRAPHY OF BIBLIOGRAPHIES ON SELECTED GOVERNMENT PUBLICATIONS AND SUPPLEMENTARY GUIDES TO THE SUPERINTENDENT OF DOCUMENTS CLASSIFICATION SYSTEM. SUPPLEMENT *CEASED.* (US/0198-6996) [04801949] **407**

ANNOTATED BIBLIOGRAPHY OF DRUG ABUSE RESEARCH REPORTS AND EVALUATIONS (US) [05986176] **1350**

ANNOTATED BIBLIOGRAPHY OF NEW PUBLICATIONS IN PERFORMING ARTS *CEASED.* (US/0360-6538) [01711123] **333**

ANNOTATED BIBLIOGRAPHY OF STATISTICAL METHODOLOGY (US/0278-9221) [06559483] **5321**

ANNOTATED BIBLIOGRAPHY. SERIES B - COMMONWEALTH BUREAU OF AGRICULTURAL ECONOMICS (UK) [03316575] **151**

ANNOTATED BIBLIOGRAPHY / THE COMMONWEALTH BUREAU OF ANIMAL HEALTH (UK) [03793041] **5528**

ANNOTATED BIBLIOGRAPHY (WEED RESEARCH ORGANIZATION) (UK/0305-2443) [10012467] **2409**

ANNOTATED CATALOGUE OF BOOKS PUBLISHED IN JAPAN (JA) [04403335] **4823**

ANNOTATED DIRECTORY OF SELF-PUBLISHED TEXTILE BOOKS (US/0162-7651) [04215573] **5347**

ANNOTATED GUIDE TO WOMEN'S PERIODICALS IN THE U.S. & CANADA, THE (US/0741-9899) [10265798] **5550**

ANNOTATED LEGISLATION SERVICE (UK) [12250199] **4626**

ANNOTATED MANUAL OF STATUTES AND REGULATIONS (US) [02786138] **3084**

ANNOTATED ONTARIO RULES OF CRIMINAL PRACTICE (CN/1197-8538) [30013313] **3105**

ANNOTATED SECONDARY BIBLIOGRAPHY SERIES ON ENGLISH LITERATURE IN TRANSITION (US) [03347713] **407**

ANNOTATED STUDENT AFFAIRS BIBLIOGRAPHY (US/0732-4545) [08339870] **3654**

ANNOTATED TREMEEAR'S CRIMINAL CODE (CN/1184-0293) [22603179] **3105**

ANNOTATION (US/0160-8460) [02045943] **2720**

ANNOTATIONES ZOOLOGICAE ET BOTANICAE (XO/0570-202X) [03642420] **5576**

ANNOUNCEMENT OF PROGRAMS / JAPAN-UNITED STATES FRIENDSHIP COMMISSION (US) [05350711] **4515**

ANNOUNCEMENTS ... RECORD - CLEMSON UNIVERSITY (US) [04223930] **1808**

ANNOUNCER (COLLEGE PARK, MD.) (US/1042-0851) [18939160] 1888, **4397**

ANNUAIRE (FR) [01792506] **4445**

ANNUAIRE - 4 SOCIETES D'HISTOIRE DE LA VALLEE DE LA WEISS (FR/0765-1252) [I07651252] **2674**

ANNUAIRE ABREGE DE STATISTIQUES AGRICOLES, REGION RHONE-ALPES (FR) [02239452] 5321, **151**

ANNUAIRE - ACADEMIE D'ATHENES (GR/0302-6868) [01793652] **1808**

ANNUAIRE - ACADEMIE DES SCIENCES (FR/0065-0552) [01460659] **5083**

ANNUAIRE ADMINISTRATIF DU QUEBEC (CN) [01794542] **4626**

ANNUAIRE — Alphabetical Title Index

ANNUAIRE ADMINISTRATIF ET JUDICIAIRE DE BELGIQUE. ADMINISTRATIEF EN GERECHTELIJK JAARBOEK VOOR BELGIE (BE/0066-2461) [06071292] 2934, **4626**

ANNUAIRE - ARCHIDIOCESE DE SHERBROOKE (1977) (CN/0706-9774) [04590148] **5023**

ANNUAIRE - ASSOCIATION D'ALSACE POUR LA CONSERVATION DES MONUMENTS NAPOLEONIENS (FR/0986-9042) [l09869042] **2674**

ANNUAIRE - ASSOCIATION DES CAMPS DU QUEBEC (CN/0226-5877) [09414438] **4869**

ANNUAIRE - ASSOCIATION DES COLLEGES DU QUEBEC (1979) (CN/0228-7730) [07821097] **1808**

ANNUAIRE - ASSOCIATION DES INSTITUTIONS DE NIVEAUX PRESCOLAIRE ET ELEMENTAIRE DU QUEBEC (CN/0315-8764) [02443153] **1724**

ANNUAIRE - ASSOCIATION DES INSTITUTIONS D'ENSEIGNEMENT SECONDAIRE (CN/0066-8990) [02441670] **1724**

ANNUAIRE - ASSOCIATION DES ROUTES ET TRANSPORTS DU CANADA (CN/0701-1636) [C3409814] **5376**

ANNUAIRE / ASSOCIATION GENERALE DES HUGIENISTES ET TECHNICIENS MUNICIPAL X (FR) [10032199] **4765**

ANNUAIRE ASTRONOMIQUE (MONTREAL, QUEBEC) (CN/0825-9984) [12877363] **391**

ANNUAIRE-BULLETIN DE LA SOCIETE DE L'HISTOIRE DE FRANCE (FR/0399-1350) [01772471] **2674**

ANNUAIRE (CANADIAN UNIVERSITY MUSIC SOCIETY) (CN/0710-5398) [08559467] 1888, **4100**

ANNUAIRE CATHOLIQUE DE FRANCE (FR/0066-2488) [03351958] **5023**

ANNUAIRE - CEGEP DE LA GASPESIE ET DES ILES (CN/0842-5361) [19763257] **1809**

ANNUAIRE : CHIMIE (FR) [03053899] **961**

ANNUAIRE CNRS SCIENCES DE L'HOMME ET DE LA SOCIETE (FR/0245-9930) [23148093] **5239**

ANNUAIRE / COMMISSION SCOLAIRE REGIONALE LOIS-FRECHETTE (CN/0823-566X) [10440772] **1724**

ANNUAIRE - CONFERENCE DES EVEQUES CATHOLIQUES DU CANADA (CN/0702-7737) [03436691] **5023**

ANNUAIRE (CONSEIL DE LA COOPERATION DE LA SASKATCHEWAN) (CN/0822-9368) [10805517] **822**

ANNUAIRE / CORPORATION PROFESSIONNELLE DES URBANISTES DU QUEBEC (CN/0824-1430) [11816168] **2814**

ANNUAIRE DE DROIT MARITIME ET AERO-SPATIAL (FR) [17576233] 11, **3180**

ANNUAIRE DE HULL, GATINEAU, AYLMER, QUEBEC (CN/0711-4982) [08537620] **2554**

ANNUAIRE DE JURISPRUDENCE ET DE DOCTRINE DU QUEBEC (CN/1180-9434) [23455424] **2934**

ANNUAIRE DE LA COUR DE CASSATION (FR) [20373853] **3138**

ANNUAIRE DE LA FRANCE PROTESTANTE (FR) [10210796] **5055**

ANNUAIRE DE LA MAREE ET DE LAQUACULTURE (FR) [19227430] **2294**

ANNUAIRE DE LA MEDIATIQUE (FR) **3920**

ANNUAIRE DE LA PRESSE ET DE LA PUBLICITE **CEASED.** (FR) [02244633] **755**

ANNUAIRE DE LA PRESSE ET DE LA PUBLICITE (II) [01481449] **5803**

ANNUAIRE DE LA RECHERCHE / UNIVERSITE DE PARIS 1 PANTHEON-SORBONNE (FR) [10600141] **2842**

ANNUAIRE DE LA SOCIETE DES AMIS DU PALAIS DES PAPES ET DES MONUMENTS D'AVIGNON (FR/0997-0568) [l09970568] **2610**

ANNUAIRE DE LA SOCIETE DES AMIS DU VIEUX STRASBOURG (FR/0986-2684) [l09862684] **2674**

ANNUAIRE DE LA SOCIETE D'HISTOIRE DES QUATRE CANTONS (FR/0761-8654) [l07618654] **2674**

ANNUAIRE DE LA SOCIETE D'HISTOIRE DES REGIONS DE THANN - GUEBWILLER (FR/1146-7371) [24692083] **2674**

ANNUAIRE DE LA SOCIETE D'HISTOIRE DU VAL DE VILLE (FR/0399-2330) [l03992330] **2674**

ANNUAIRE DE LA SOCIETE D'HISTOIRE DU VAL ET DE LA VILLE DE MUNSTER (FR/1146-7363) [01943924] **2674**

ANNUAIRE DE LA SOCIETE D'HISTOIRE ET D'ARCHEOLOGIE DE DAMBACH-LA-VILLE, BARR, OBERNAI (FR/0990-2473) [02998045] 255, **2674**

ANNUAIRE DE LA SOCIETE D'HISTOIRE SUNDGAUVIENNE (FR) [22725205] **2674**

ANNUAIRE DE L'ADMINISTRATION DES DIRECTIONS REGIONALES DE L'INDUSTRIE ET DE LA RECHERCHE (FR/1140-7123) [l11407123] **2133**

ANNUAIRE DE L'ADMINISTRATION DES MINES (FR) [09554109] **2133**

ANNUAIRE DE L'ADMINISTRATION ET DU CORPS DES MINES *See* ANNUAIRE DE L'ADMINISTRATION DES MINES **2133**

ANNUAIRE DE L'ADMINISTRATION LOCALE (FR) [07417731] **4626**

ANNUAIRE DE L'AFRIQUE DU NORD (FR/0066-2607) [01481450] **2498**

ANNUAIRE DE L'ARMEMENT A LA PECHE (FR/0066-2623) [02010599] **2294**

ANNUAIRE DE L'ART INTERNATIONAL (FR) [11542998] **312**

ANNUAIRE DE L'ARTISANAT AFRICAIN (BE) [10636841] **370**

ANNUAIRE ... DE L'ASSOCIATION CANADIENNE DES PERIODIQUES CATHOLIQUES (CN/0828-5462) [12035518] **407**

ANNUAIRE DE L'AUDIOVISUEL DE LA COMMUNAUTE FRANCAISE (BE) [16714681] **1148**

ANNUAIRE DE L'AUTO, L' *See* MAGAZINE CARGUIDE **5418**

ANNUAIRE DE L'AVIATION CIVILE ET DE LA METEOROLOGIE (FR) [03554586] **1419**

ANNUAIRE DE LEGISLATION FRANCAISE ET ETRANGERE / PUBLIE PAR LE CENTRE FRANCAIS DE DROIT COMPAREE **CEASED.** (FR/0066-2658) [01481453] **3123**

ANNUAIRE DE L'EGLISE CATHOLIQUE AU CANADA (CN/0821-9885) [10003751] **5023**

ANNUAIRE DE L'EGLISE CATHOLIQUE AU CANADA (CN/0821-9885) [10003755] **5023**

ANNUAIRE DE L'EGLISE DU QUEBEC (CN/0706-8328) [04433059] **5023**

ANNUAIRE DE L'INDUSTRIE ET DU COMMERCE DE LA REPUBLIQUE UNIE DU CAMEROUN (CM) [03495143] **1545**

ANNUAIRE DE L'INDUSTRIE PHARMACEUTIQUE EN FRANCE (FR/0997-0509) [l09970509] **4291**

ANNUAIRE DE L'INSTITUT DE DROIT INTERNATIONAL (FR) [01753234] **3123**

ANNUAIRE DE L'INSTITUT DE PHILOLOGIE ET D'HISTOIRE ORIENTALES ET SLAVES. SUPPLEMENT (BE) [11675270] **3265**

ANNUAIRE DE STATISTIQUE AGRICOLE (FRANCE. SERVICE REGIONAL DE STATISTIQUE AGRICOLE, POITOU-CHARENTES) (FR/0243-6507) [10685271] 60, **151**

ANNUAIRE DENTAIRE (FR) [07605808] **1316**

ANNUAIRE DENTAIRE / ORDRE DES DENTISTES DU QUEBEC (CN/0826-2233) [10399648] **1316**

ANNUAIRE DEPARTEMENTAL PRIVE : ILE DE LA REUNION (FR) [02244147] **4626**

ANNUAIRE DES ABONNES AU SERVICE TELEX / REPUBLIQUE POPULAIRE DE BULGARIE, MINISTERE DES POSTES ET TELECOMMUNICATIONS (BU) [08012333] **1148**

ANNUAIRE DES BIBLIOTHECAIRES-CONSEILS DU QUEBEC (CN/0825-3927) [11431374] **3190**

ANNUAIRE DES COLLECTIVITES LOCALES / C.N.R.S., G.R.A.L (FR/0248-0573) [08966412] **4626**

ANNUAIRE DES COMMISSIONS SCOLAIRES (CN/1187-2136) [25351995] **1724**

ANNUAIRE DES COMMUNAUTES EUROPEENNES ET DES AUTRES ORGANISATIONS EUROPEENNES (BE/0771-7962) [05238483] **4515**

ANNUAIRE DES EDITEURS (CN/0844-465X) [19900086] **4812**

ANNUAIRE DES ENTREPRISES D'OUTRE-MER (FR) [03350126] **1462**

ANNUAIRE DES ENTREPRISES DU GABON (GO) [03423616] **638**

ANNUAIRE DES ENTREPRISES EXPORTATRICES ET EXPEDITRICES (MQ) [18804525] **822**

ANNUAIRE DES FEMMES DE MONTREAL, L' (CN/0823-0188) [09801046] 5550, **5271**

ANNUAIRE DES GEOGRAPHES DE LA FRANCE ET DE L'AFRIQUE FRANCOPHONE (FR) [02370355] **2554**

ANNUAIRE DES LOISIRS SCIENTIFIQUES (CN/0229-6616) [08070744] **5083**

ANNUAIRE DES MEMBRES DE L'ASSOCIATION DES BIBLIOTHECAIRES FRANCAIS (FR) [02242786] **3190**

ANNUAIRE DES MEMBRES ... ET MANUEL DE REFERENCE / ABQ, ASSOCIATION BETON QUEBEC (CN/1186-6012) [24368253] **598**

ANNUAIRE DES MUSEES ROYAUX DES BEAUX-ARTS DE BELGIQUE (BE) [03252808] **4083**

ANNUAIRE DES ORGANISMES COOPERATIFS, REGION RHONE-ALPES (FR) [02242933] 60, **1541**

ANNUAIRE DES ORGANISMES DENSEIGNEMENT PRIMAIRE ET SECONDAIRE PUBLIC (CN/0844-6377) [19978065] **1724**

ANNUAIRE DES PAYS DE L'OCEAN INDIEN (FR/0247-400X) [04511432] **2637**

ANNUAIRE DES PETITES ET MOYENNES ENTREPRISES (CG) [02243363] **638**

ANNUAIRE DES PRODUCTEURS ET EXPORTATEURS DU ZAIRE (CG) [05277421] **1597**

ANNUAIRE DES PROFESSIONS JUDICIAIRES ET JURIDIQUES (FR) [03520421] **3138**

ANNUAIRE DES RESSOURCES COMMUNAUTAIRES DE LILE DE MONTREAL (CN/0835-3360) [17500424] **5271**

ANNUAIRE DES SOCIETES ET DES ADMINISTRATEURS (FR) [08585449] **4626**

ANNUAIRE DES STATISTIQUES DU COMMERCE EXTERIEUR DU TOGO (TG) [01799486] 822, **726**

ANNUAIRE DES STATISTIQUES DU COMMERCE EXTERIEUR (KINSHASA) (CG/0304-5692) [01786410] **5321**

ANNUAIRE DES STATISTIQUES DU TOURISME (SP) [16196253] **5461**

ANNUAIRE DESFOSSES (FR) [07087018] 1462, **638**

ANNUAIRE DU CANADA (CN) [01784898] **1923**

ANNUAIRE DU CENTENAIRE / CERCLE BELGE DE LA LIBRAIRIE (BE) [12823429] **4823**

ANNUAIRE DU CINEMA QUEBECOIS (CN/0849-5726) [21320916] **4063**

ANNUAIRE DU COLLEGE DE FRANCE (FR/0069-5580) [02705914] **1809**

ANNUAIRE DU MARKETING (FR) [08514491] **921**

ANNUAIRE DU MUSEUM NATIONAL D'HISTOIRE NATURELLE POUR L'ANNEE (FR) [04867887] **4162**

ANNUAIRE DU PAPIER, L' (FR/0337-4971) [08823717] **4232**

ANNUAIRE DU SECRETARIAT GENERAL A L'AVIATION CIVILE *See* ANNUAIRE DE L'AVIATION CIVILE ET DE LA METEOROLOGIE **1419**

ANNUAIRE DU SPORT UNIVERSITAIRE QUEBECOIS ET CALENDRIERS DES ACTIVITES (CN/0228-7005) [07966585] **4883**

ANNUAIRE DU TRAVAIL (CN/0831-0513) [13647629] **1644**

ANNUAIRE ECONOMIQUE DE LA TUNISIE (TI) [06221042] **1545**

ANNUAIRE EGYPTIEN DES ENTREPRISES, DES SERVICES, DE L'INDUSTRIE ET DU COMMERCE EXTERIEUR (UA) [09419837] **822**

ANNUAIRE ET RAPPORT D'ACTIVITES - DEPARTEMENT DE DEMOGRAPHIE, UNIVERSITE DE MONTREAL (CN/0225-2716) [06183746] **4549**

ANNUAIRE / ETABLISSEMENT PUBLIC REGIONAL DE BRETAGNE (FR) [10660715] **4626**

ANNUAIRE EUROPEEN D'ADMINISTRATION PUBLIQUE (FR) [06075476] **4626**

ANNUAIRE EUROPEEN DE DEFENSE (FR/0298-895X) [21016081] 4515, **4034**

ANNUAIRE FRANCAIS DE DROIT INTERNATIONAL (FR/0066-3085) [01481462] **3123**

ANNUAIRE (FRANCE. MINISTERE DE LA JEUNESSE, DES SPORTS ET DES LOISIRS. DIVISION DES ETUDES ET DE LA STATISTIQUE) (FR) [09529453] 1854, **4883**

ANNUAIRE / FRERES PRECHEURS, PROVINCE SAINT-DOMINIQUE DU CANADA (CN/0826-5119) [11377363] **4935**

ANNUAIRE GENERAL - FRANCE. MINISTERE DE L'ECONOMIE ET DES FINANCES (FR) [01790048] **1462**

ANNUAIRE GENERALE - COMMISSION SCOLAIRE REGIONALE DE L'ESTRIE (CN/0381-713X) [02862110] **1860**

ANNUAIRE HISTORIQUE DE LA VILLE DE MULHOUSE (FR/0996-5750) [19739204] **2674**

Alphabetical Title Index — ANNUAL

ANNUAIRE HYDROMETRIQUE / DEPARTEMENT DE LA REUNION, DIRECTION DEPARTEMENTALE DE L'AGRICULTURE, REGIE DEPARTEMENTALE DES TRAVAUX AGRICOLES ET RURAUX, SECTION HYDROLOGIE (FR) [09819405] **1412**

ANNUAIRE INFORMATIQUE-PHYSIQUE (FR) [02675976] **4397**

ANNUAIRE - INSTITUT ROYAL METEOROLOGIQUE DE BELGIQUE. MAGNETISME TERRESTRE (BE/0770-4569) [I0770 4569] 1419, **1365**

ANNUAIRE INTERNATIONAL DE JUSTICE CONSTITUTIONNELLE / GROUPEMENT D'ETUDES ET DE RECHERCHES SUR LA JUSTICE CONSTITUTIONNELLE (FR) [19409139] **3092**

ANNUAIRE INTERNATIONAL DES FOIRES-EXPOSITIONS & I.E. ET SALONS SPECIALISES, L' (FR) [02240096] **5083**

ANNUAIRE INTERNATIONAL DES VENTES (FR) [01635640] **336**

ANNUAIRE - INTERNATIONAL ELECTROTECHNICAL COMMISSION (SZ) [01792352] **2035**

ANNUAIRE JEUNE AFRIQUE, L' (FR) [23994399] **2634**

ANNUAIRE : L'EGLISE DE MONTREAL (CN/0826-0338) [10805591] **5023**

ANNUAIRE - LES AMIS DE LA BIBLIOTHEQUE HUMANISTE DE SELESTAT (FR/0182-6557) [04781770] **3190**

ANNUAIRE LP (FR) [15344957] **2934**

ANNUAIRE LP CEE (FR) **2934**

ANNUAIRE: MAGNETISME TERRESTRE. JAARBOEK: AARDMAGNETISME (BE) [03139096] **4443**

ANNUAIRE MARITIME NATIONAL / CONSEIL NATIONAL DES CHARGEURS DU CAMEROUN (CM) [10682361] **5447**

ANNUAIRE MINEMET (FR) [06049753] **2133**

ANNUAIRE MUNICIPAL DE SAINT DENIS (FR) [05213837] **5023**

ANNUAIRE NATIONAL DE LA CONSERVE (FR) [08985339] **2326**

ANNUAIRE NATIONAL DE LA REPUBLIQUE GABONAISE (GO) [07954743] **2637**

ANNUAIRE NATIONAL OFFICIEL DE LA REPUBLIQUE GABONAISE (GO) [01789859] **4626**

ANNUAIRE NAVIS (FR/0077-6270) **5083**

ANNUAIRE OFFICIEL DES ASSURANCES AFRICAINES (CG) [04721650] **2873**

ANNUAIRE OFFICIEL TELEX DU ZAIRE (CG) [04934846] **1148**

ANNUAIRE POLK DE BAIE-COMEAU (CN/0316-8271) [02247168] **2554**

ANNUAIRE POLK DE GRANBY QUEBEC (CN/0317-1515) [02578813] **2554**

ANNUAIRE POLK DE HULL (CN/0316-7992) [02247871] **2554**

ANNUAIRE POLK DE RIMOUSKI ET MONT-JOLI QUEBEC (CN/0380-3961) [02443056] **2554**

ANNUAIRE POLK DE SEPT-ILES (CN/0380-3775) [02443103] **2554**

ANNUAIRE POLK DE SOREL TRACY ET ST-JOSEPH (CN/0700-7272) [02804432] **2554**

ANNUAIRE. QUALITE DES EAUX (CN/0388-557X) [01787214] 2224, **5529**

ANNUAIRE; RAYONNEMENT SOLAIRE. JAARBOEK: ZONNESTRALING (BE) [05672285] **1419**

ANNUAIRE REGIONAL DE STATISTIQUE AGRICOLE (FR) [02534752] 60, **151**

ANNUAIRE REGIONAL - SERVICE CENTRAL DES ENQUETES ET ETUDES STATISTIQUES, REGION DE PROGRAMME BOURGOGNE (FR) [02240133] 5321, **151**

ANNUAIRE REGIONAL: STATISTIQUE AGRICOLE (FR) [01794942] 60, **151**

ANNUAIRE RHONE-ALPES (FR) [03536751] **5321**

ANNUAIRE ROUMAIN D'ANTHROPOLOGIE (RM/0570-2259) [02158021] **228**

ANNUAIRE / SOCIETE D'HISTOIRE DE MUTZIG ET ENVIRONS (FR) [19999564] **2610**

ANNUAIRE - SOCIETE D'HISTOIRE ET D'ARCHEOLOGIE DE COLMAR (FR/0766-5911) [03027910] 255, **2675**

ANNUAIRE / SOCIETE D'HISTOIRE ET D'ARCHEOLOGIE DE MOLSHEIM ET ENVIRONS (FR) [17573065] 255, **2675**

ANNUAIRE STATISTIQUE (HT) [17939923] **1860**

ANNUAIRE STATISTIQUE (CHAMBRE DE COMMERCE ET D'INDUSTRIE DE LA MARTINIQUE. DIRECTION DE L'INFORMATION ET DES RELATIONS CONSULAIRES) (MQ) [19034565] **638**

ANNUAIRE STATISTIQUE DE DJIBOUTI / REPUBLIQUE DE DJIBOUTI, MINISTERE DU COMMERCE, DES TRANSPORTS ET DU TOURISME, DIRECTION NATIONALE DE LA STATISTIQUE (FT) [11314067] **5321**

ANNUAIRE STATISTIQUE DE LA BELGIQUE (BE/0066-3646) [01844034] **5321**

ANNUAIRE STATISTIQUE DE LA FRANCE (FR/0066-3654) [01135427] 1462, **1528**

ANNUAIRE STATISTIQUE DE LA JUSTICE (FR) [08268667] 2934, **3078**

ANNUAIRE STATISTIQUE DE LA SECURITE SOCIALE *See* ANNUAIRE STATISTIQUE DE LA SECURITE SOCIALE (BRUSSELS, BELGIUM : 1981) **5271**

ANNUAIRE STATISTIQUE DE LA SECURITE SOCIALE (BRUSSELS, BELGIUM : 1981) (BE) [12333519] **5271**

ANNUAIRE STATISTIQUE DE L'ALGERIE (AE) [02868590] **5321**

ANNUAIRE STATISTIQUE DE L'ENSEIGNEMENT (GO) [04836620] 1724, **1793**

ANNUAIRE STATISTIQUE DE POCHE - INSTITUT NATIONAL DE STATISTIQUE (BE/0067-5431) [01076061] **5321**

ANNUAIRE STATISTIQUE DES TELECOMMUNICATIONS DU SECTEUR PUBLIC (GENEVA, SWITZERLAND: 1980) (SZ) [20496468] **1149**

ANNUAIRE STATISTIQUE DU BURUNDI *See* ANNUAIRE STATISTIQUE / INSTITUT DE STATISTIQUES ET D'ETUDES ECONOMIQUES DU BURUNDI **1528**

ANNUAIRE STATISTIQUE DU MAROC (RABAT, MOROCCO : 1982) (MR) [11874695] **5321**

ANNUAIRE STATISTIQUE DU TOGO (TG) [01786062] **5321**

ANNUAIRE STATISTIQUE / INSTITUT DE STATISTIQUES ET D'ETUDES ECONOMIQUES DU BURUNDI (BD) [30488759] **1528**

ANNUAIRE STATISTIQUE (INSTITUT NATIONAL DE LA STATISTIQUE ET DE L'ANALYSE ECONOMIQUE) (DM) [07507754] **5321**

ANNUAIRE SUISSE DU FOLK : MUSICIENS. SCHWEIZER FOLK-KALENDAR : MUSIKER (SZ) [07096652] **4100**

ANNUAIRE SUISSE DU FOLK: ORGANISATEURS. SCHWEIZER FOLK-KALENDER: VERANSTALTER (SZ) [06164437] **4100**

ANNUAIRE SUISSE DU MONDE ET DES AFFAIRES (SZ) [01789469] **429**

ANNUAIRE SUISSE FOLK & CHANSON. MUSICIENS, ORGANISATEURS (SZ) [10819864] **4100**

ANNUAIRE SUISSE-TIERS MONDE (SZ) [08942178] **1632**

ANNUAIRE TELEPHONIQUE - CENTRE DE CULTURE DIALOGUE ORIENTAL (CN/0703-2153) [03951181] **5239**

ANNUAIRE TELEPHONIQUE DES ORGANISMES SCOLAIRES DE LA MONTEREGIE (CN/0848-6697) [23264477] **1724**

ANNUAIRE TELEPHONIQUE JUDICIAIRE DU QUEBEC (CN/0316-6120) [02247656] **2934**

ANNUAIRE THEATRAL, L' (CN/0827-0198) [13925115] **5361**

ANNUAIRE - UNION DES ECRIVAINES ET ECRIVAINS QUEBECOIS (CN/0849-3928) [23242463] 3362, **2917**

ANNUAIRE - UNIVERSITE D'OTTAWA *CEASED.* (CN/0317-6142) [02441683] **1809**

ANNUAIRE - UNIVERSITE PARIS 7 (FR) [02678745] **1809**

ANNUAL 4-H YOUTH DEVELOPMENT ENROLLMENT REPORT (US) [22141880] **5228**

ANNUAL ABSTRACT OF GREATER LONDON STATISTICS (UK/0533-2117) [02255578] **5321**

ANNUAL ABSTRACT OF STATISTICS (UK/0072-5730) [02252977] **5321**

ANNUAL ABSTRACT OF STATISTICS - NIGERIA. FEDERAL OFFICE OF STATISTICS (NR/0078-0626) [01147691] **5321**

ANNUAL ABSTRACTS OF STATISTICS - CENTRAL OFFICE OF STATISTICS (VALLETTA) (MM/0256-8047) [01785757] **5321**

ANNUAL ACTION PROGRAMS - MONTANA. BOARD OF CRIME COUNCIL (US) [05259812] **3156**

ANNUAL ADAPSO INDUSTRY REPORT (US/0098-8324) [02163703] **1235**

ANNUAL ADMINISTRATION REPORT - FOOD AND DRUG ADMINISTRATION, MAHARASHTRA STATE (II/0376-5563) [01797805] 4291, **4626**

ANNUAL ADMINISTRATION REPORT FOR THE YEAR ... / GOVERNMENT OF TAMIL NADU, AGRICULTURE DEPARTMENT (II) [11965340] **60**

ANNUAL ADMINISTRATION REPORT FOR THE YEAR ... / TEA BOARD (INDIA) (II) [07591871] 1597, **4626**

ANNUAL ADMINISTRATION REPORT ON SCHEDULED AREAS IN GUJARAT STATE (II/0533-5752) [05328055] **2814**

ANNUAL ADMINISTRATION REPORT ON THE PROGRESS OF EDUCATION IN ORISSA FOR THE YEAR ... (II) [09678597] **1724**

ANNUAL ADVANCED ANTITRUST WORKSHOP (US/0194-1127) [04975268] **3095**

ANNUAL ADVANCED FAMILY LAW COURSE (US/0190-7395) [04732910] **3119**

ANNUAL AGENCY PLAN (US) [20789233] **2160**

ANNUAL AIR QUALITY DATA SUMMARY FOR MONTANA *See* MONTANA AIR QUALITY DATA AND INFORMATION SUMMARY FOR ... **2236**

ANNUAL AMENDMENT - NUMBER 13 TO THE NEBRASKA STATE PLAN FOR TITLE 1A OF THE HIGHER EDUCATION ACT OF 1965 (US) [04084884] **1809**

ANNUAL AND FIVE YEAR UTAH STATE PLAN ... FOR THE ADMINISTRATION OF VOCATIONAL EDUCATION UNDER THE VOCATIONAL EDUCATION AMENDMENTS OF 1976, PUBLIC LAW 94-482 / UTAH STATE BOARD FOR VOCATIONAL EDUCATION (US) [10787140] **1910**

ANNUAL AND QUARTERLY ENERGY PRICE AND TAX STATISTICS (FR) **5321**

ANNUAL AREA LABOR REVIEW (US/0149-3779) [03472185] **1644**

ANNUAL - ASSOCIATION OF TRACK AND FIELD STATISTICIANS *CEASED.* (US/0361-8048) [02247129] 4883, **4856**

ANNUAL AUDIT - ARIZONA STATE PARKS BOARD (US/0095-6643) [01798251] 2186, **738**

ANNUAL AUDIT PLAN (US) [06032323] **2814**

ANNUAL AUSTRALIAN NOTICES TO MARINERS IN FORCE ON 1ST JANUARY (AT/1035-6878) [I10356878] **4174**

ANNUAL AUTOMATION REPORT TO THE ARIZONA LEGISLATURE / DATA PROCESSING DIVISION, DEPARTMENT OF ADMINISTRATION, STATE OF ARIZONA (US) [05097507] **4626**

ANNUAL AVERAGES, LABOR FORCE AND NONAGRICULTURAL EMPLOYMENT ESTIMATES (US) [24111954] **1644**

ANNUAL AVERAGES, ... MISSISSIPPI BY COUNTIES (US) [07657700] **1644**

ANNUAL AWARDS CEREMONY / U.S. DEPARTMENT OF HOUSING AND URBAN DEVELOPMENT (US) [08369429] **2814**

ANNUAL - BALTIMORE MUSEUM OF ART (US/0067-3080) [01519073] **336**

ANNUAL BANKRUPTCY LITIGATION INSTITUTE (US) [09491651] **3084**

ANNUAL BEER REPORT / ALABAMA ALCOHOLIC BEVERAGE CONTROL BOARD (US) [09139626] **2363**

ANNUAL BENZENE & DERIVATIVES (US/1042-8364) [19120559] **4249**

ANNUAL BIBLIOGRAPHY / AUSTRALIAN INSTITUTE OF ABORIGINAL AND TORRES STRAIT ISLANDER STUDIES (AT) [25006528] 2668, **2276**

ANNUAL BIBLIOGRAPHY OF BRITISH AND IRISH HISTORY. PUBLICATIONS OF ... / ROYAL HISTORICAL SOCIETY (UK/0308-4558) [02813271] **2634**

ANNUAL BIBLIOGRAPHY OF CHRISTIANITY IN INDIA (II) [10810852] 2645, **4935**

ANNUAL BIBLIOGRAPHY OF COMPUTER-ORIENTED BOOKS *CEASED.* (US) [04440379] **1208**

ANNUAL BIBLIOGRAPHY OF ENGLISH LANGUAGE AND LITERATURE (UK/0066-3786) [05918934] 3265, 3362, **3457**

ANNUAL BIBLIOGRAPHY OF MODERN ART / THE MUSEUM OF MODERN ART LIBRARY, NEW YORK (US/0898-7300) [16828111] **333**

ANNUAL BIBLIOGRAPHY OF ORTHOPAEDIC SURGERY (US/0090-1393) [01643439] **3880**

ANNUAL BIBLIOGRAPHY OF THE HISTORY OF NATURAL HISTORY *CEASED.* (UK/0268-9936) [12880343] 4162, **4174**

ANNUAL BIBLIOGRAPHY OF THE HISTORY OF NATURAL HISTORY (UK) [12707834] 4162, **429**

ANNUAL BIBLIOGRAPHY OF VICTORIAN STUDIES (CN/0227-1400) [07140046] **3356**

ANNUAL BLACK CONSUMER BUYING SURVEY, FOOD SALES (US/0270-4366) [06387003] **1462**

ANNUAL — Alphabetical Title Index

ANNUAL BOOK OF ASTM STANDARDS (US/0192-2998) [02187052] **2100**

ANNUAL BOOKLET - MINNESOTA, DIVISION OF VOCATIONAL REHABILITATION, DEPARTMENT OF EDUCATION (US/0098-3993) [02241297] **1644**

ANNUAL BRIEF SUBMITTED BY THE QUEBEC ASSOCIATION FOR THE MENTALLY RETARDED TO THE GOVERNMENT OF QUEBEC (CN/0713-8555) [09086754] **5271**

ANNUAL BUDGET/ CITY OF PALO ALTO *See* TWO YEAR BUDGET/ CITY OF PALO ALTO **4757**

ANNUAL BUDGET STATEMENT OF PAKISTAN RAILWAYS (PK) [03256500] 4709, **5429**

ANNUAL BUDGET TO CONTINUE CURRENT PROGRAMS (US/0360-5647) [02244655] **4709**

ANNUAL BULLETIN - BRITISH SOCIETY FOR PLANT GROWTH REGULATION (UK/0963-6749) [l09636749] **499**

ANNUAL BULLETIN OF COAL STATISTICS FOR EUROPE (US/0066-3808) [01261776] **1961**

ANNUAL BULLETIN OF ELECTRIC ENERGY STATISTICS FOR EUROPE (US/0066-3816) [01483422] **2035**

●ANNUAL BULLETIN OF ELECTRIC ENERGY STATISTICS FOR EUROPE AND NORTH AMERICA / BULLETIN ANNUEL DE STATISTIQUES DE L'ENERGIE ELECTRIQUE POUR L'EUROPE ET L'AMERIQUE DU NORD / EZHEGODNYI BIULLETEN' STATISTIKI ELEKTROENERGII DLIA EVROPY I SEVERNOI AMERIKI (US) [31034765] **2035**

ANNUAL BULLETIN OF GAS STATISTICS FOR EUROPE (US/0066-3824) [01183778] **4283**

ANNUAL BULLETIN OF GENERAL ENERGY STATISTICS FOR EUROPE / ECONOMIC COMMISSION FOR EUROPE (US) [01715131] **1961**

ANNUAL BULLETIN OF HISTORICAL LITERATURE (UK/0066-3832) [01752119] **2610**

ANNUAL BULLETIN OF HOUSING AND BUILDING STATISTICS FOR EUROPE (US/0066-3840) [01261977] **2839**

ANNUAL BULLETIN OF STATISTICS (UK/0305-2370) [02808194] 2363, **2362**

ANNUAL BULLETIN OF STATISTICS ON COCOA, COFFEE & TEA (NR) [07471055] 2363, **2362**

ANNUAL BULLETIN OF STATISTICS, SABAH *See* SIARAN PERANGKAAN TAHUNAN, SABAH. ANNUAL BULLETIN OF STATISTICS, SABAH **5338**

ANNUAL BULLETIN OF STEEL STATISTICS FOR EUROPE (US) [01486664] **4025**

ANNUAL BULLETIN OF THE MODERN HUMANITIES RESEARCH ASSOCIATION (UK) [08180144] **2842**

ANNUAL BULLETIN OF TRADE IN CHEMICAL PRODUCTS. BULLETIN ANNUEL DU COMMERCE DES PRODUITS CHIMIQUES. EZHEGODNYI BIULLETEN EVROPEISKOI TORGOVLI KHIMICHESKMI PRODUKTAMI (US) [02863541] 1020, **1597**

ANNUAL BULLETIN OF TRANSPORT STATISTICS FOR EUROPE. BULLETIN ANNUEL DE STATISTIQUES DE TRANSPORTS POUR L'EUROPE. EZHEGODNYI BIULLETEN' EVROPEISKOI STATISTIKI TRANSPORTA (US/0066-3859) [01768055] **5376**

ANNUAL BULLETIN / RESEARCH INSTITUTE OF LOGOPEDICS AND PHONIATRICS, FACULTY OF MEDICINE, UNIVERSITY OF TOKYO (JA/0564-7630) [02396689] **3886**

ANNUAL BULLETIN - SOCIETE JERSIAISE (UK/0141-1942) [I01411942] **2675**

ANNUAL BULLETIN - UNITED STATES AIR FORCE ACADEMY (US) [06558330] 11, **4034**

ANNUAL - CANADIAN GLADIOLUS SOCIETY (CN/0319-1915) [02443035] **2409**

ANNUAL CAPITAL INVESTMENT BUDGET - COLORADO. OFFICE OF STATE PLANNING AND BUDGETING (US) [08558840] 4709, **890**

ANNUAL CASH REPORT / TEXAS COMPTROLLER OF PUBLIC ACCOUNTS (US) [20779494] **4709**

ANNUAL CATALOGUE OF ART CALENDARS ... (US) [05850122] **336**

ANNUAL CATALOGUE OF COMMONWEALTH PUBLICATIONS (AT/0725-1130) [09098700] **407**

ANNUAL CAUSES & CONDITIONS OF POVERTY IN SOUTH DAKOTA (US/0091-0724) [01786254] **5272**

ANNUAL CBAC SURVEY OF PERFORMING ARTS ORGANIZATIONS (CN/0229-3153) [07869989] **383**

ANNUAL CETA REPORT FOR ... - ILLINOIS. DEPT. OF COMMERCE AND COMMUNITY AFFAIRS (US) [08173411] **1644**

ANNUAL CHAPTER 1 EDUCATION REPORT PROGRAM INFORMATION / CALIFORNIA HEALTH AND WELFARE AGENCY, STATE DEPARTMENT OF DEVELOPMENTAL SERVICES (US) [18090606] **1724**

ANNUAL CHARITIES DIGEST *See* CHARITIES DIGEST **5277**

ANNUAL CHECKLIST OF PUBLICATIONS OF THE STATE OF ARIZONA (US/0570-9326) [02441123] **3190**

ANNUAL COLLECTION AND STORAGE OF SOLAR ENERGY FOR THE HEATING OF BUILDINGS (US/0270-7586) [06466374] **1931**

ANNUAL COMPANIES HANDBOOK / THE KUALA LUMPUR STOCK EXCHANGE (MY/0127-2462) [15528343] **890**

ANNUAL COMPUTER LAW INSTITUTE (US/1052-8350) [18663940] 1170, **2934**

ANNUAL CONFERENCE. CONFERENCE SUMMARIES - CANADIAN NUCLEAR SOCIETY (CN/0227-0129) [08569819] **2153**

ANNUAL CONFERENCE - COUNCIL OF LOGISTICS MANAGEMENT (U.S.) (US/0898-6614) [15026505] **860**

ANNUAL CONFERENCE / NATIONAL ASSOCIATION OF CHURCH BUSINESS ADMINISTRATORS (US/0730-1561) [07950294] 860, **4935**

ANNUAL CONFERENCE OF STATE MEDICAID DIRECTORS. CONFERENCE REPORT (US/0192-8643) [05024328] **2873**

ANNUAL CONFERENCE OF THE ATLANTIC CANADA ECONOMICS ASSOCIATION (CN/0319-003X) [02441971] **1462**

ANNUAL CONFERENCE ON CATV RELIABILITY (US/0198-0270) [03833432] **1126**

ANNUAL CONFERENCE ON FIRE RESEARCH (US/0278-1050) [04879516] **2287**

ANNUAL CONFERENCE. PROCEEDINGS - CANADIAN NUCLEAR SOCIETY (CN/0227-1907) [09071371] **2154**

ANNUAL CONFERENCE, PROCEEDINGS - ELECTRON MICROSCOPY SOCIETY OF SOUTHERN AFRICA (SA/0250-0418) [I02500418] **572**

ANNUAL CONFERENCE PROCEEDINGS - INSTITUTE OF TRANSPORTATION ENGINEERS, CANADA (CN/0705-677X) [04097800] **5376**

ANNUAL CONFERENCE PROCEEDINGS - NATIONAL COUNCIL ON FAMILY RELATIONS (US/1059-4469) [24594992] **2276**

ANNUAL CONFERENCE PROCEEDINGS - STANDARDS ENGINEERING SOCIETY. CONFERENCE (US/0732-6173) [08401798] **1965**

ANNUAL CONFERENCE REPORT ON COTTON INSECT RESEARCH AND CONTROL (US/0098-0196) [05294241] **4244**

ANNUAL CONFERENCE / THE ONTARIO PETROLEUM INSTITUTE (CN/0078-5040) [09513000] **4249**

ANNUAL CONFERENCE / TRAVEL AND TOURISM RESEARCH ASSOCIATION (US/0276-8968) [14234808] **5461**

ANNUAL CONTRACTOR EVALUATION REPORT FOR BLUE CROSS/BLUE SHIELD OF MICHIGAN. PART B CARRIER (US/0736-9026) [09231227] 2873, **1644**

ANNUAL CONTRACTORS' CONFERENCE : PROGRAM (US) [03296985] **3988**

ANNUAL CONVENTION - CANADIAN NUMISMATIC ASSOCIATION (CN/0318-4951) [02442056] **2779**

ANNUAL CONVENTION - NEWFOUNDLAND AND LABRADOR FEDERATION OF LABOUR (CN/0319-0153) [02442018] **1644**

ANNUAL CONVENTION OF THE HUDSON BAY ROUTE ASSOCIATION (CN) [02370883] **5447**

ANNUAL CONVENTION REFERENCE MATERIALS (US/0747-8135) [04891087] **2934**

ANNUAL CRAFT FAIRS IN ONTARIO (CN/1184-0307) [23302851] **370**

●ANNUAL CRAFT SHOWS IN ONTARIO / CRAFT RESOURCE CENTRE (CN/1189-4555) [26715064] **370**

ANNUAL CREDIT UNION CALL REPORT / THE COMMONWEALTH OF MASSACHUSETTS, OFFICE OF THE COMMISSIONER OF BANKS (US) [10859523] **770**

ANNUAL CROP SUMMARY / IOWA CROP AND LIVESTOCK REPORTING SERVICE (US) [05985891] **162**

ANNUAL DATA PLAN / PENNSYLVANIA DEPARTMENT OF EDUCATION (US) [10682143] **1724**

ANNUAL DEGARMO LECTURE (US/0882-7133) [11965552] **1724**

ANNUAL DEMOGRAPHIC DATA FOR MIGRANT FAMILY HOUSING CENTERS (US) [08622164] 2814, **4549**

ANNUAL DEMOGRAPHIC INFORMATION. SERVICE DELIVERY AREA I, CLALLAM, JEFFERSON, AND KITSAP COUNTIES : A LABOR MARKET INFORMATION REPORT OF THE RESEARCH AND ANALYSIS BRANCH, WASHINGTON STATE EMPLOYMENT SECURITY DEPARTMENT / PREPARED IN COOPERATION WITH THE EMPLOYMENT AND TRAINING ADMINISTRATION, U.S. DEPARTMENT OF LABOR (US) [10864519] **1644**

ANNUAL DEMOGRAPHIC INFORMATION. SERVICE DELIVERY AREA II, GRAYS HARBOR, LEWIS, MASON, PACIFIC, AND THURSTON COUNTIES : A LABOR MARKET INFORMATION REPORT OF THE RESEARCH AND ANALYSIS BRANCH, WASHINGTON STATE EMPLOYMENT SECURITY DEPARTMENT / PREPARED IN COOPERATION WITH THE EMPLOYMENT AND TRAINING ADMINISTRATION, U.S. DEPARTMENT OF LABOR (US) [11857956] **1644**

ANNUAL DEMOGRAPHIC INFORMATION. SERVICE DELIVERY AREA III, ISLAND, SAN JUAN, SKAGIT, AND WHATCOM COUNTIES : A LABOR MARKET INFORMATION REPORT OF THE RESEARCH AND ANALYSIS BRANCH, WASHINGTON STATE EMPLOYMENT SECURITY DEPARTMENT / PREPARED IN COOPERATION WITH THE EMPLOYMENT AND TRAINING ADMINISTRATION, U.S. DEPARTMENT OF LABOR (US) [11855663] **1644**

ANNUAL DEMOGRAPHIC INFORMATION. SERVICE DELIVERY AREA IX, KITTITAS, KLICKITAT, AND YAKIMA COUNTIES : A LABOR MARKET INFORMATION REPORT OF THE RESEARCH AND ANALYSIS BRANCH, WASHINGTON STATE EMPLOYMENT SECURITY DEPARTMENT / PREPARED IN COOPERATION WITH THE EMPLOYMENT AND TRAINING ADMINISTRATION, U.S. DEPARTMENT OF LABOR (US) [10864410] **1644**

ANNUAL DEMOGRAPHIC INFORMATION. SERVICE DELIVERY AREA VIII, ADAMS, CHELAN, DOUGLAS, GRANT, AND OKANOGAN COUNTIES : A LABOR MARKET INFORMATION REPORT OF THE RESEARCH AND ANALYSIS BRANCH, WASHINGTON STATE EMPLOYMENT SECURITY DEPARTMENT / PREPARED IN COOPERATION WITH THE EMPLOYMENT AND TRAINING ADMINISTRATION, U.S. DEPARTMENT OF LABOR (US) [11855594] **1644**

ANNUAL DEMOGRAPHIC INFORMATION. SERVICE DELIVERY AREA X, ASOTIN, COLUMBIA, FERRY, GARFIELD, LINCOLN, PEND OREILLE, STEVENS, AND WHITMAN COUNTIES : A LABOR MARKET INFORMATION REPORT OF THE RESEARCH AND ANALYSIS BRANCH, WASHINGTON STATE EMPLOYMENT SECURITY DEPARTMENT / PREPARED IN COOPERATION WITH THE EMPLOYMENT AND TRAINING ADMINISTRATION, U.S. DEPARTMENT OF LABOR (US) [10864583] **1644**

ANNUAL DEMOGRAPHIC INFORMATION. SERVICE DELIVERY AREA XI, BENTON, FRANKLIN, AND WALLA WALLA COUNTIES : A LABOR MARKET INFORMATION REPORT OF THE RESEARCH AND ANALYSIS BRANCH, WASHINGTON STATE EMPLOYMENT SECURITY DEPARTMENT / PREPARED IN COOPERATION WITH THE EMPLOYMENT AND TRAINING ADMINISTRATION, U.S. DEPARTMENT OF LABOR (US) [10860765] **1644**

ANNUAL DEMOGRAPHIC INFORMATION. SERVICE DELIVERY AREA XII, SPOKANE COUNTY : A LABOR MARKET INFORMATION REPORT OF THE RESEARCH AND ANALYSIS BRANCH, WASHINGTON STATE EMPLOYMENT SECURITY DEPARTMENT / PREPARED IN COOPERATION WITH THE EMPLOYMENT AND TRAINING ADMINISTRATION, U.S. DEPARTMENT OF LABOR (US) [11804194] **1644**

ANNUAL DEPARTMENTAL REPORT BY THE COMMISSIONER OF PRISONS (HK) [05146762] **3156**

ANNUAL DESCRIPTIVE REPORT OF PROGRAM ACTIVITIES FOR VOCATIONAL EDUCATION (US/0091-5882) [01786868] **1910**

ANNUAL DESCRIPTIVE REPORT: VOCATIONAL TECHNICAL EDUCATION IN PENNSYLVANIA (US/0146-8618) [03046857] **1910**

... ANNUAL, DEVELOPING HUMAN RESOURCES, THE (US/1046-333X) [10311162] **938**

ANNUAL DEVELOPMENT PLAN FOR ... / PRODUCED BY THE MINISTRY OF FINANCE, ECONOMIC AFFAIRS AND PLANNING (TZ) [19256736] **1545**

ANNUAL DIGEST OF PUBLIC UTILITIES REPORTS (US/0895-1713) [07270433] **4760**

Alphabetical Title Index — ANNUAL

ANNUAL DIRECTORY / AMERICAN CHAMBER OF COMMERCE FOR BRAZIL, RIO DE JANEIRO - SALVADOR (BL) [07207774] **818**

ANNUAL DIRECTORY AND REPORT - AMERICAN DEFENSE PREPAREDNESS ASSOCIATION (US/0092-7422) [01791225] **4034**

ANNUAL DIRECTORY - DEPARTMENT OF NATURAL RESOURCES. GEOLOGICAL SURVEY DIVISION (LANSING) (US/0085-3372) [02341623] **1365**

ANNUAL DIRECTORY / HAWAII STATE BAR ASSOCIATION (US/0277-0520) [07468199] **2934**

ANNUAL DIRECTORY OF MICHIGAN MUNICIPAL OFFICIALS *See* DIRECTORY OF MICHIGAN MUNICIPAL OFFICIALS **4643**

ANNUAL DIRECTORY OF OKLAHOMA LIBRARIES *See* ROSTER AND STATISTICS OF OKLAHOMA PUBLIC AND INSTITUTIONAL LIBRARIES **3247**

ANNUAL DIRECTORY OF WORLD LEADERS *CEASED.* (US/1044-825X) [19900552] **4626**

ANNUAL DIRECTORY / TEXAS RETAIL GROCERS ASSOCIATION (US/0276-4458) [07348791] **2327**

ANNUAL DIVIDEND RECORD (CN/1198-1180) [29684746] **639**

ANNUAL DIVIDEND RECORD / STANDARD AND POOR'S CORPORATION (US) [07587528] **890**

ANNUAL DRUG DATA REPORT (SP/0379-4121) [12813426] **4291**

ANNUAL DRUG DATA REPORT (SP) [20298937] **4291**

ANNUAL ECE/FAO PRICE REVIEW (SZ/0251-3986) [I02513986] **2327**

ANNUAL ECONOMIC REPORT ... DESCHUTES COUNTY (US) [09221694] **1545**

ANNUAL ECONOMIC REPORT ... DOUGLAS COUNTY (US) [09221475] **1545**

ANNUAL ECONOMIC REPORT ... GRANT COUNTY (US) [09221583] **1545**

ANNUAL ECONOMIC REPORT ... JACKSON COUNTY (US) [09314464] **1545**

ANNUAL ECONOMIC REPORT ... JEFFERSON COUNTY (US) [09473586] **1545**

ANNUAL ECONOMIC REPORT ... NORTH COAST AREA : CLATSOP COUNTY, COLUMBIA COUNTY, TILLAMOOK COUNTY (US) [09742120] **1545**

ANNUAL ECONOMIC REPORT OF AIRFREIGHT FORWARDERS; REPORTING MORE THEN $10,000,000 TRANSPORTATION REVENUES (US) [04157879] **11**

ANNUAL ECONOMIC REPORT / SOUTH AFRICAN RESERVE BANK (SA/0081-2528) [01949791] **770**

ANNUAL ECONOMIC REPORT / STATISTICAL, ECONOMIC AND SOCIAL RESEARCH AND TRAINING CENTRE FOR ISLAMIC COUNTRIES, ORGANIZATION OF THE ISLAMIC CONFERENCE (TU) [17802250] **1545**

ANNUAL ECONOMIC REPORT ... WALLOWA COUNTY (US) [09473646] **1545**

ANNUAL ECONOMIC REPORT - WISCONSIN DEPARTMENT OF REVENUE (US/0095-3016) [01796408] **4709**

ANNUAL ECONOMIC REVIEW (HONOLULU) (US/0067-3633) [01189190] **1545**

ANNUAL ECONOMIC SURVEY (PORT OF SPAIN, TRINIDAD AND TOBAGO) (TR/1011-6311) [17158975] **1545**

ANNUAL ECONOMIC SURVEY (ZOMBA, MALAWI) (MW) [11629794] **1462**

ANNUAL EDITION: NOTICES TO MARINERS (CN) [03202174] **4174**

ANNUAL EDITIONS. DRUGS, SOCIETY, AND BEHAVIOR (US) [13118427] **1340**

ANNUAL EDITIONS : READINGS IN BUSINESS (US/0090-4309) [01783692] **639**

ANNUAL EDITIONS. READINGS IN SOCIAL PROBLEMS *See* SOCIAL PROBLEMS (GUILFORD) **5259**

ANNUAL EDITIONS. READINGS IN SOCIAL PSYCHOLOGY *See* SOCIAL PSYCHOLOGY (GUILFORD, CONN.) **4618**

ANNUAL EDITIONS. READINGS IN SOCIOLOGY *See* SOCIOLOGY (GUILFORD, CONN.) **5262**

ANNUAL EDUCATIONAL SUMMARY NEW YORK STATE (US/0085-4077) [03676973] **1724**

ANNUAL EGYPTOLOGICAL BIBLIOGRAPHY (NE) [01607404] **286**

ANNUAL ELECTRICITY STATISTICS (FR) **1931**

ANNUAL EMPLOYMENT AND TRAINING REPORT TO THE MAYOR, DISTRICT OF COLUMBIA / EMPLOYMENT AND TRAINING SERVICES ADVISORY COUNCIL (US) [10582509] **1645**

ANNUAL EMPLOYMENT REVIEW (INDIA) (II) [05120848] **1645**

ANNUAL ENERGY BALANCE (U.S.) (US/0278-5951) [07831510] **1931**

ANNUAL ENERGY LITIGATION INSTITUTE : EFFECTIVE STRATEGIES & TECHNIQUES (US/0273-7000) [06659592] 1931, 4249, **2934**

ANNUAL ENERGY OUTLOOK (US/0740-4190) [09587622] **1931**

ANNUAL ENERGY REVIEW (WASHINGTON, D.C.) (US/0740-3909) [09563095] **1932**

ANNUAL ENERGY SUMMARY (US/0736-4997) [08598524] **1932**

ANNUAL - ENTE AUTONOMO PER LE FIERE DI BOLOGNA (IT) [06473847] **312**

ANNUAL ENVIRONMENTAL MONITORING REPORT. MOUND FACILITY (US) [06098797] **2160**

ANNUAL EQUAL POSTSECONDARY EDUCATIONAL OPPORTUNITY STATUS REPORT FOR THE PERIOD ... (MARYLAND) (US) [10084346] **1809**

ANNUAL ESTABLISHMENT ENQUIRY (PK) [19926910] **1645**

ANNUAL ESTIMATE OF POPULATION FOR THE STATE OF GEORGIA (US/0361-6053) [02247054] **4549**

ANNUAL EVALUATION - NEW MEXICO. ENVIRONMENTAL IMPROVEMENT DIVISION (US/0742-8022) [10427338] **2160**

ANNUAL EVALUATION OF THE NEW YORK STATE UNEMPLOYMENT INSURANCE FUND (US/0093-8017) [01793135] 2873, **1645**

ANNUAL EVALUATION OF VOCATIONAL EDUCATION IN KANSAS (US) [06113859] **1910**

ANNUAL EVALUATION REPORT - LOUISIANA. MIGRANT EDUCATION PROGRAM (US) [06387747] **1725**

ANNUAL EVALUATION REPORT / MINNESOTA STATE ADVISORY COUNCIL FOR VOCATIONAL EDUCATION (US) [11835868] **1910**

ANNUAL EVALUATION REPORT OF TRANSITIONAL BILINGUAL EDUCATION PROGRAMS (US) [09353528] **1874**

ANNUAL EXHIBITION - NATIONAL SCULPTURE SOCIETY (US/0098-4817) [02240322] **336**

ANNUAL EXHIBITION OF OLD MASTER PAINTINGS (UK) [06987303] **336**

ANNUAL EXHIBITION OF THE CANADIAN SOCIETY OF PAINTERS IN WATER COLOUR (CN/0318-4978) [02442039] **336**

ANNUAL FAA AVIATION FORECAST CONFERENCE PROCEEDINGS (US/1046-8838) [18763029] **11**

ANNUAL FALL FIELD CONFERENCE - BIG RIVERS AREA GEOLOGICAL SOCIETY (US/0271-4973) [03875318] **1365**

ANNUAL FALL MEETING / SECTION OF LITIGATION, AMERICAN BAR ASSOCIATION (US/0731-4493) [06967518] **2934**

... ANNUAL FEEDER'S DAY REPORT, THE (CN) [04873967] **205**

ANNUAL FERTILIZER REPORT (US) [06271146] **60**

ANNUAL FESTIVAL OF DRAMA AND ANNUAL FESTIVAL OF MUSIC *See* STRAFFORD FESTIVAL **388**

ANNUAL FINANCIAL ANALYSIS FOR PENNSYLVANIA SCHOOLS (US/0149-4988) [03490054] **1860**

ANNUAL FINANCIAL REPORT (US) [19032568] **60**

ANNUAL FINANCIAL REPORT AND REPORT OF OPERATIONS / PUBLIC EMPLOYEES' RETIREMENT SYSTEM, STATE OF CALIFORNIA (US/0732-4618) [09837528] **4626**

ANNUAL FINANCIAL REPORT / EXECUTIVE DEPARTMENT (US) [11836079] **4626**

ANNUAL FINANCIAL REPORT FOR THE CALENDAR YEAR ENDED DECEMBER 31 ... - PUBLIC EMPLOYEES RETIREMENT SYSTEM OF OHIO (US) [10248669] **4626**

ANNUAL FINANCIAL REPORT FOR THE FISCAL YEAR ENDING AUGUST 31 ... - TEXAS. STATE DEPT. OF HIGHWAYS AND PUBLIC TRANSPORTATION (US) [07944052] **5376**

ANNUAL FINANCIAL REPORT FOR YEAR ENDING AUG. 31 ... - TEXAS. ATTORNEY-GENERAL'S OFFICE (US) [07583368] **4709**

ANNUAL FINANCIAL REPORT OF CALIFORNIA SCHOOLS (K-12) : REPORT TO THE CALIFORNIA STATE LEGISLATURE FOR THE FISCAL YEAR / STATE OF CALIFORNIA, OFFICE OF THE CONTROLLER (US) [25742993] **1725**

ANNUAL FINANCIAL REPORT OF THE DIRECTOR OF ADMINISTRATIVE SERVICES (US/0361-1019) [02245124] **4709**

ANNUAL FINANCIAL REPORT OF THE EXECUTIVE DEPARTMENT, STATE OF TEXAS *See* ANNUAL FINANCIAL REPORT / EXECUTIVE DEPARTMENT **4626**

ANNUAL FINANCIAL REPORT OF THE TEXAS PARKS & WILDLIFE DEPARTMENT (US/0731-0226) [08065912] **2186**

ANNUAL FINANCIAL REPORT - SOUTH DAKOTA DEPARTMENT OF GAME, FISH AND PARKS *See* ANNUAL FINANCIAL REPORT - SOUTH DAKOTA DEPARTMENT OF WILDLIFE, PARKS AND FORESTRY **4869**

ANNUAL FINANCIAL REPORT - SOUTH DAKOTA DEPARTMENT OF WILDLIFE, PARKS AND FORESTRY (US) [05815379] 2374, **4869**

ANNUAL FINANCIAL REPORT, STATE OWNED TOLL BRIDGES (US) [10379973] 4709, **5376**

ANNUAL FINANCIAL REPORT / TEXAS ANIMAL HEALTH COMMISSION (US) [06394085] 5503, **4709**

ANNUAL FINANCIAL REPORT / TEXAS DEPARTMENT OF HEALTH (US) [09047438] 4709, **4765**

ANNUAL FINANCIAL REPORT - TEXAS HEALTH FACILITIES COMMISSION (US) [06433836] **3776**

ANNUAL FINANCIAL REPORT TO THE RETIREMENT BOARD, PUBLIC EMPLOYEES RETIREMENT SYSTEM OF OHIO FOR THE CALENDAR YEAR ENDED DECEMBER 31 . *See* ANNUAL FINANCIAL REPORT FOR THE CALENDAR YEAR ENDED DECEMBER 31 ... - PUBLIC EMPLOYEES RETIREMENT SYSTEM OF OHIO **4626**

ANNUAL FINANCIAL REVIEW - FOOD MARKETING INSTITUTE (US/0192-379X) [03761274] **2327**

ANNUAL FINANCIAL REVIEW - SUPER MARKET INSTITUTE (US) [03154153] **2327**

ANNUAL FINANCIAL STATEMENT / ANATOMICAL BOARD OF THE STATE OF TEXAS (US) [05905986] **3678**

ANNUAL FINANCIAL STATEMENT AND EXPLANATORY MEMORANDUM ON THE BUDGET OF THE PUNJAB GOVERNMENT (II/0304-6516) [01784232] 4626, **4709**

ANNUAL FINANCIAL STATEMENT (BUDGET) OF THE GOVERNMENT OF GUJARAT FOR THE YEAR ... (II) [16833991] **4709**

ANNUAL FIRE REPORT (WASHINGTON) (US) [01436753] **2288**

ANNUAL FISCAL REPORT (CASH BASIS) STATE OF NEBRASKA *See* ANNUAL FISCAL REPORT YEAR ENDING JUNE 30 ... / STATE OF NEBRASKA **4709**

ANNUAL FISCAL REPORT YEAR ENDING JUNE 30 ... / STATE OF NEBRASKA (US) [07542980] **4709**

ANNUAL FOLIO LITERARY DINNER & DEBATE (UK) [17496254] **3362**

ANNUAL FORECAST OF ALBERTA SCHOOL ENROLMENTS, ... (CN/0714-9301) [07842258] **1860**

ANNUAL FOREIGN TRADE STATISTICS BY COMMODITIES. SERIES C (FR) **1632**

ANNUAL FOREIGN TRADE STATISTICS TURKEY (TU) 822, **726**

ANNUAL FORUM - AMERICAN BAR ASSOCIATION. FORUM COMMITTEE ON FRANCHISING. ANNUAL FORUM (US/0739-1323) [09668506] **3095**

ANNUAL FORUM PROCEEDINGS - AMERICAN HELICOPTER SOCIETY (US/0733-4249) [07315648] **11**

ANNUAL GAMING CONFERENCE (US/0272-0736) [06738924] **3156**

ANNUAL GENERAL MEETING / DEVON AND CORNWALL RECORD SOCIETY (UK) [12607232] **5228**

ANNUAL GRAZING STATISTICAL REPORT (US/0091-438X) [02641526] 2374, **2398**

ANNUAL GUIDE TO PUBLIC POLICY EXPERTS, THE (US/0731-339X) [08161894] **5191**

ANNUAL GUIDE TO SYNCHRONIZED SWIMMING (CN/1180-4491) [23242819] **4883**

ANNUAL HANDBOOK (UK) [01786911] **4883**

ANNUAL HEALTH MANPOWER CONFERENCE (US/0094-8942) [01792445] **3913**

ANNUAL HIGHLIGHTS OF THE ENERGY TECHNOLOGY PROGRAMS (US) [06025219] **1932**

ANNUAL HOSPITAL REPORT (US/0277-9579) [07654309] **3776**

ANNUAL   Alphabetical Title Index

ANNUAL HOUSE MARKET REPORT : THE STATE OF THE HOUSING MARKET (US) [14813390] **2814**

ANNUAL HOUSING SURVEY (US) [02237058] **2814**

ANNUAL IMMIGRATION AND NATURALIZATION INSTITUTE (US/0147-1309) [03124833] 1918, **2934**

ANNUAL IMMIGRATION AND NATURALIZATION INSTITUTE. PROCEEDINGS (US) [05218833] 1918, **2934**

ANNUAL IMPLEMENTATION PLAN FOR NORTHERN INDIANA, AN (US) [06638656] **4765**

ANNUAL IMPLEMENTATION PLAN / HEALTH POLICY COUNCIL (US) [22735882] **4765**

ANNUAL IMPLEMENTATION PLAN (WATERBURY) (US/0273-2203) [07009480] **4765**

ANNUAL IMPORT PAYMENTS (BG) [02245027] **822**

ANNUAL IN THERAPEUTIC RECREATION (US) [21566812] 4848, **4379**

ANNUAL INDEX OF FOUNDATION REPORTS / OFFICES OF THE ATTORNEY GENERAL (US) [12037585] **4334**

ANNUAL INDEX OF THE REPORTS ON PLANT CHEMISTRY (JA/0570-2496) [01481476] 499, **476**

ANNUAL INDEX TO MOTION PICTURE CREDITS (US/0163-5123) [04402113] **4063**

ANNUAL INDEX TO THE CURRENT DIGEST OF THE SOVIET PRESS (US/1049-4197) [07063320] **407**

ANNUAL INDEX TO THE FINANCIAL TIMES (UK) [08726062] **4709**

ANNUAL INSTITUTE FOR CORPORATE COUNSEL (US/0195-3680) [05391421] **3095**

ANNUAL INSTITUTE OF EMPLOYMENT LAW (US/0743-4146) [09768950] **3144**

ANNUAL INSTITUTE ON ACQUISITIONS & TAKEOVERS : [PROCEEDINGS] (US) [15674292] **3095**

ANNUAL INSTITUTE ON MINERAL LAW (US/0273-5253) [02139406] 4249, **2934**

ANNUAL INSTITUTE ON SECURITIES REGULATION (US/0195-5756) [02128727] **890**

ANNUAL INSTITUTE ON SECURITIES REGULATION (US) [05896495] **2934**

ANNUAL INSTITUTE, SECURITIES ACTIVITIES OF BANKS (US/1051-1539) [17870439] **3084**

ANNUAL INTERNATIONAL CONFERENCE / CANADIAN NUCLEAR ASSOCIATION (CN/0706-1293) [06316100] 1932, **2154**

ANNUAL JOURNAL / PETER W. RODINO INSTITUTE OF CRIMINAL JUSTICE (US/0276-8151) [06647851] **3156**

ANNUAL JOURNAL - SINGAPORE POLYTECHNIC BUILDING SOCIETY (SI/0376-6322) [01790694] **598**

ANNUAL - KAJAKS TRACK AND FIELD CLUB (CN/0229-0618) [07869861] **4883**

ANNUAL LABOR & EMPLOYMENT LAW INSTITUTE (US) **3144**

ANNUAL LABOR AREA REPORT. NEW YORK STATE (US) [11625217] **1645**

ANNUAL LABOR MARKET REVIEW. HACKENSACK LABOR AREA #5600, NEW JERSEY (US/0742-6283) [08804464] **1645**

ANNUAL LABOR MARKET REVIEW. JERSEY CITY LABOR AREA #3640, NEW JERSEY (US) [08780466] **1645**

ANNUAL LABOR MARKET REVIEW. NEW BRUNSWICK, PERTH AMBOY, SAYREVILLE LABOR AREA #5460, NEW JERSEY / STATE OF NEW JERSEY, DEPARTMENT OF LABOR, DIVISION OF PLANNING AND RESEARCH AFFILIATED WITH THE EMPLOYMENT AND TRAINING ADMINISTRATION, U.S. DEPARTMENT OF LABOR (US) [09148038] **1645**

ANNUAL LABOR MARKET REVIEW. NEWARK LABOR AREA #5640, NEW JERSEY / PREPARED BY ANDREW M. SMAKULA (US) [08577213] **1645**

ANNUAL LABOR MARKET REVIEW. PATERSON-CLIFTON-PASSAIC LABOR AREA #6040, NEW JERSEY / STATE OF NEW JERSEY, DEPARTMENT OF LABOR, DIVISION OF PLANNING AND RESEARCH (US) [08804608] **1645**

ANNUAL LABOR MARKET REVIEW. VINELAND-MILLVILLE-BRIDGETON LABOR AREA / STATE OF NEW JERSEY, DEPARTMENT OF LABOR, DIVISION OF PLANNING AND RESEARCH (US) [09680861] **1645**

ANNUAL LANDINGS SUMMARY (US) [25781077] **2294**

ANNUAL LAW SCHOOL SUMMER SCHOOL PROGRAMS AT HOME AND ABROAD (US) 1809, **2934**

ANNUAL LECTURE SERIES (GERMAN HISTORICAL INSTITUTE (WASHINGTON, D.C.)) (UK) [19338947] **2675**

ANNUAL LETTER (PR) [03012671] **2374**

ANNUAL LICENSING LAW AND BUSINESS INSTITUTE (US/0271-3489) [06597774] **3095**

ANNUAL LIST OF PUBLICATIONS - DEPARTMENT OF THE ENVIRONMENT. DEPARTMENT OF TRANSPORT. LIBRARY SERVICES (UK/0141-2604) [03466178] **2160**

ANNUAL MAGAZINE / WESTERN AUSTRALIAN SCHOOL OF MINES (AT) [22427028] **2133**

ANNUAL MAJOR EXHIBIT HALL DIRECTORY *See* TRADESHOW WEEK'S MAJOR EXHIBIT HALL DIRECTORY **767**

ANNUAL MANAGEMENT COMPENSATION STUDY (US/0192-611X) [03957192] **1645**

ANNUAL MANPOWER PLANNING REPORT. CHICAGO STANDARD METROPOLITAN STATISTICAL AREA (US/0091-4908) [02243692] **1645**

ANNUAL MCGRAW-HILL SURVEY : BUSINESS' SPENDING PLANS FOR PLANTS AND EQUIPMENT (US/0272-6696) [04607314] **1546**

ANNUAL MEETING - AMERICAN INSTITUTE OF CHEMICAL ENGINEERS (US/0196-7282) [02251080] **2007**

ANNUAL MEETING - AMERICAN INSTITUTE OF ORAL BIOLOGY (US/0098-6119) [01124325] 442, **1316**

ANNUAL MEETING & INTERNATIONAL CONFERENCE ON NUCLEAR ENERGY (US) **1932**

ANNUAL MEETING - INTERNATIONAL OIL SCOUTS ASSOCIATION (US/0731-9800) [01787668] **4249**

ANNUAL MEETING - NATIONAL MASTITIS COUNCIL, INC (US/0271-9967) [04871964] **191**

ANNUAL MEETING - NATIONAL UNION OF STUDENTS (CN/0708-157X) [05071883] **1809**

ANNUAL MEETING OF NORDISK NEUROKIRURGISK FORENING, THE (US) [05947821] **3959**

ANNUAL MEETING OF THE AMERICAN ASSOCIATION FOR CANCER RESEARCH PROCEEDINGS (US/0197-016X) [05937684] **3808**

ANNUAL MEETING OF THE BOARD, ... MINUTES / ANATOMICAL BOARD OF THE STATE OF TEXAS (US) [07359125] **3678**

ANNUAL MEETING OF THE MINNESOTA SECTION, AIME AND ANNUAL MINING SYMPOSIUM (US/0270-7837) [07313681] **2133**

● ANNUAL MEETING OF THE SOCIETY FOR ORGANIC PETROLOGY. ABSTRACTS AND PROGRAM (US/1060-7250) [25060376] **1458**

ANNUAL MEETING PAPERS - AMERICAN PETROLEUM INSTITUTE. PRODUCTION DEPT *CEASED*. (US/0275-6323) [04767490] **4249**

ANNUAL MEETING PROCEEDINGS (CN) [10929864] **60**

ANNUAL MEETING. PROCEEDINGS. CANADIAN URBAN TRANSIT ASSOCIATION (CN/0316-7933) [01791865] **5376**

ANNUAL MEETING PROCEEDINGS - COLLEGE ENTRANCE EXAMINATION BOARD (US/0588-277X) [01794006] **1809**

ANNUAL MEETING PROCEEDINGS - INTERNATIONAL INSTITUTE OF SYNTHETIC RUBBER PRODUCERS, INC (US/0146-3977) [01753550] **5075**

ANNUAL MEETING, TECHNICAL COMMITTEE REPORTS (US/0149-354X) [03460941] **2288**

ANNUAL MEMBERSHIP DIRECTORY - NATIONAL ASSOCIATION OF ADVISORS FOR THE HEALTH PROFESSIONS (US/1075-6507) [30100570] 1910, **3913**

ANNUAL MEMENTO / INTERNATIONAL DAIRY FEDERATION (BE/0538-7078) [03389494] **191**

ANNUAL METEOROLOGICAL SUMMARY, TORONTO, ONTARIO, WITH COMPARATIVE DATA (CN) [02249134] **1420**

ANNUAL NATIONAL VEHICLE POPULATION PROFILE : IMPORT CARS (US/0148-6861) [03349054] **5403**

ANNUAL NATIONAL VEHICLE POPULATION PROFILE : LIGHT TRUCKS (US/0148-6276) [03337972] **5403**

ANNUAL NEVADA STREET AND HIGHWAY CONFERENCE (US/0550-7898) [05152337] **5438**

ANNUAL NEWSPRINT SUPPLEMENT - CANADIAN PULP AND PAPER ASSOCIATION (CN/0316-4241) [01795016] **4232**

ANNUAL NORTHERN EXPENDITURE PLAN (CN/0382-2486) [14928016] **4709**

ANNUAL NOTRE DAME ESTATE PLANNING INSTITUTE (US/0732-8850) [08380737] **3117**

ANNUAL NUMBER / NATIONAL ACADEMY OF SCIENCES, INDIA (II/0469-6786) [08706683] **5083**

ANNUAL NURSING HOME SURVEY / SOUTH DAKOTA DEPARTMENT OF HEALTH, STATE CENTER FOR HEALTH STATISTICS (US) [07658138] **3776**

ANNUAL OBITUARY, THE *CEASED*. (US/0278-1573) [07592213] **429**

ANNUAL OF ARMENIAN LINGUISTICS (US/0271-9800) [06465995] **3265**

ANNUAL OF CARDIAC SURGERY (UK/0952-0562) [23031551] 3698, **3959**

ANNUAL OF DISPLAY & COMMERCIAL SPACE DESIGNS IN JAPAN (JA) [09471876] **639**

● ANNUAL OF DRUG THERAPY (US/1068-3178) [27644856] **4291**

ANNUAL OF GASTROINTESTINAL ENDOSCOPY (UK/0952-6293) [20763360] **3743**

ANNUAL OF INDUSTRIAL PROPERTY LAW (UK) [02246461] **2934**

ANNUAL OF NEW ART AND ARTISTS, AN (US/0092-7929) [01791367] **336**

ANNUAL OF POWER AND CONFLICT (UK) [01709182] **4463**

ANNUAL OF PSYCHOANALYSIS, THE *CEASED*. (US/0092-5055) [00924392] **3920**

ANNUAL OF THE AMERICAN SCHOOLS OF ORIENTAL RESEARCH, THE (US/0066-0035) [05768891] 2645, **255**

ANNUAL OF THE BRITISH SCHOOL AT ATHENS, THE (UK/0068-2454) [01537363] **2675**

ANNUAL OF THE DEPARTMENT OF ANTIQUITIES (JO/0449-1564) [01782611] **2645**

ANNUAL OF THE INTERNATIONAL FISCAL ASSOCIATION *See* YEARBOOK - IFA **4759**

ANNUAL OF THE JAPANESE BIBLICAL INSTITUTE (JA/0912-9243) [02411972] **5014**

ANNUAL OF THE SOCIETY FOR THE STUDY OF CAUCASIA, THE (US/1073-6255) [21405127] **3265**

ANNUAL OF THE SOCIETY OF CHRISTIAN ETHICS, THE (US/0732-4928) [08230855] 2249, **4935**

... ANNUAL OFFICIAL VOLLEYBALL REFERENCE GUIDE OF THE UNITED STATES VOLLEYBALL ASSOCIATION, THE (US) [06008954] **4883**

ANNUAL OIL MARKET REPORT *CEASED*. (FR) [10735592] **4250**

ANNUAL OPERATING PLAN, WESTERN DIVISION, MISSOURI RIVER BASIN (US/0565-0585) [02239732] **2087**

ANNUAL OPERATIONS SURVEY *See* ANNUAL PERFORMANCE STUDY - WINE AND SPIRITS WHOLESALERS OF AMERICA **2363**

ANNUAL PEAK DISCHARGES FROM SMALL DRAINAGE AREAS IN MONTANA THROUGH ... / UNITED STATES DEPARTMENT OF THE INTERIOR, GEOLOGICAL SURVEY (US/0566-8174) [04183451] **1365**

ANNUAL PERFORMANCE STUDY - WINE AND SPIRITS WHOLESALERS OF AMERICA (US/0360-3075) [02243919] **2363**

ANNUAL PERSONNEL AND BUDGET STUDY OF OREGON LAW ENFORCEMENT AGENCIES (US) [06739913] **3156**

ANNUAL PETROLEUM REVIEW (US/0747-5594) [07764536] **4250**

ANNUAL PHI ZETA RESEARCH DAY OF THE ZETA CHAPTER (US) [22100660] **5503**

ANNUAL PHILATELIC EXHIBITION / BRITISH VIRGIN ISLANDS PHILATELIC SOCIETY (VB) [23181871] **2784**

ANNUAL PLAN FOR FISCAL YEAR ... / NATIONAL TOXICOLOGY PROGRAM (US) [07604428] **3978**

ANNUAL PLAN FOR THE GOVERNOR'S SPECIAL GRANT / STATE COMPREHENSIVE EMPLOYMENT & TRAINING OFFICE (US) [08076966] 4626, **1645**

ANNUAL PLAN FOR VOCATIONAL EDUCATION AND ... ACCOUNTABILITY REPORT (IDAHO) (US) [10735631] **1910**

ANNUAL PLAN - GOVERNMENT OF KARNATAKA, PLANNING DEPARTMENT (II) [06182293] 4626, **1546**

ANNUAL PLAN ... OF THE ILLINOIS DEPARTMENT OF MENTAL HEALTH AND DEVELOPMENTAL DISABILITIES (US/0276-6922) [06811303] **4765**

Alphabetical Title Index — ANNUAL

ANNUAL PLAN REVIEW: AREA I (US) [05005152] **2814**

ANNUAL PLAN REVIEW: AREA II (US) [07228193] **2814**

ANNUAL PLAN REVIEW: AREA III (US) [05005176] **2814**

ANNUAL PLAN REVIEW: AREA IV (US) [06287827] **2814**

ANNUAL PLAN REVIEW - OFFICE OF COMPREHENSIVE PLANNING (VIRGINIA) (US) [03786815] **2814**

● ANNUAL PLAN UPDATING THE NEW YORK STATE COMPREHENSIVE HOUSING AFFORDABILITY HOUSING ACT (US) [26834310] **2814**

ANNUAL PLANNING INFORMATION (US) [15300657] **1645**

ANNUAL PLANNING INFORMATION (US) [20322313] **1645**

ANNUAL PLANNING INFORMATION, BELKNAP COUNTY (US) [05953596] **1645**

ANNUAL PLANNING INFORMATION. BRIDGEPORT-NORWALK-STAMFORD-VALLEY SERVICE DELIVERY AREA (US) [17103816] **4626**

ANNUAL PLANNING INFORMATION, BURLINGTON, IOWA LABOR AREA, DES MOINES COUNTY (US) [06832452] **1645**

ANNUAL PLANNING INFORMATION. BUTTE COUNTY (US) [05761334] **1645**

ANNUAL PLANNING INFORMATION, CALIFORNIA (US) [05206797] **1645**

ANNUAL PLANNING INFORMATION. CHARLESTON, WEST VIRGINIA STANDARD METROPOLITAN STATISTICAL AREA (US) [16464697] **5321**

ANNUAL PLANNING INFORMATION, CITY OF SUNNYVALE (US) [07103259] **1645**

ANNUAL PLANNING INFORMATION. CLAREMONT, NEW HAMPSHIRE, LABOR MARKET AREA / ECONOMIC ANALYSIS AND REPORTS SECTION (US) [12096499] **1645**

ANNUAL PLANNING INFORMATION. COLUMBUS, GEORGIA, STANDARD METROPOLITAN STATISTICAL AREAS, COLUMBUS CONSORTIUM (US/0737-4275) [09340601] **1645**

ANNUAL PLANNING INFORMATION. COLUSA COUNTY (US) [11851124] **1646**

ANNUAL PLANNING INFORMATION. CONCORD, NEW HAMPSHIRE, LABOR MARKET AREA / ECONOMIC ANALYSIS AND REPORTS SECTION (US) [12096571] **1646**

ANNUAL PLANNING INFORMATION, DAVENPORT, IOWA LABOR AREA FOR FISCAL YEAR ... (US) [06832631] **1646**

ANNUAL PLANNING INFORMATION. DEL NORTE COUNTY (1985) (US) [13202541] **1646**

ANNUAL PLANNING INFORMATION, DUBUQUE COUNTY FOR FISCAL YEAR ... (US) [06859563] **1646**

ANNUAL PLANNING INFORMATION, FISCAL YEAR ... - MICHIGAN EMPLOYMENT SECURITY COMMISSION, BUREAU OF RESEARCH AND STATISTICS (US) [10451422] **1646, 1528**

ANNUAL PLANNING INFORMATION FOR AROOSTOOK COUNTY (US) [06150039] **1646**

ANNUAL PLANNING INFORMATION FOR BRISTOL-NEW BRITAIN SERVICE DELIVERY AREA, PLANNING YEAR ... (US) [11528253] **1646**

ANNUAL PLANNING INFORMATION FOR COLUMBIA SMSA (US) [08601785] **1646, 1528**

ANNUAL PLANNING INFORMATION FOR CUMBERLAND COUNTY (US) [06025542] **1646**

ANNUAL PLANNING INFORMATION FOR FISCAL YEAR ..., CEDAR RAPIDS, IOWA LABOR AREA (LINN COUNTY) (US) [06832602] **1646**

ANNUAL PLANNING INFORMATION FOR FISCAL YEAR ... / LABOR MARKET INFORMATION SERVICES SECTION, UTAH DEPARTMENT OF EMPLOYMENT SECURITY (US) [07873257] **1646**

ANNUAL PLANNING INFORMATION FOR MISSOURI (US) [07670096] **1646**

ANNUAL PLANNING INFORMATION FOR MONTANA, RURAL CEP AREA, BALANCE-OF-THE-STATE, BILLINGS SMSA, GREAT FALLS SMSA (US) [04877371] **1646**

ANNUAL PLANNING INFORMATION FOR NEW HAVEN LABOR MARKET AREA (US) [08800200] **1646**

ANNUAL PLANNING INFORMATION FOR PENOBSCOT CONSORTIUM (US) [06025279] **1646**

ANNUAL PLANNING INFORMATION FOR SMSA'S IN ARKANSAS (US) [07590570] **1646**

ANNUAL PLANNING INFORMATION FOR SPRINGFIELD SMSA (US) [08616176] **1646**

ANNUAL PLANNING INFORMATION FOR STAMFORD LABOR MARKET AREA (US) [07397834] **1646**

ANNUAL PLANNING INFORMATION FOR STATE OF MAINE (US) [06514591] **1646**

ANNUAL PLANNING INFORMATION FOR YORK COUNTY (US) [04564949] **1646**

ANNUAL PLANNING INFORMATION : HILLSBOROUGH COUNTY (US) [06435685] **1646**

ANNUAL PLANNING INFORMATION. HUMBOLDT COUNTY (US/0736-6787) [09169636] **1646**

ANNUAL PLANNING INFORMATION. HUNTINGTON-ASHLAND-IRONTON STANDARD METROPOLITAN STATISTICAL AREA / PREPARED BY LABOR & ECONOMIC RESEARCH SECTION (US) [08617386] **1646, 1529**

ANNUAL PLANNING INFORMATION. INYO/MONO COUNTIES / STATE OF CALIFORNIA, HEALTH AND WELFARE AGENCY, EMPLOYMENT DEVELOPMENT DEPARTMENT, SOUTHERN CALIFORNIA EMPLOYMENT DATA AND RESEARCH (US) [11220370] **1646**

ANNUAL PLANNING INFORMATION. KEENE, NEW HAMPSHIRE, LABOR MARKET AREA / ECONOMIC ANALYSIS AND REPORTS SECTION (US) [12096663] **1646**

ANNUAL PLANNING INFORMATION. LABOR AREA, WATERLOO-CEDAR FALLS SMSA, CETA PRIME SPONSOR JURISDICTION, BLACK HAWK COUNTY (US) [07763175] **1646, 1529**

ANNUAL PLANNING INFORMATION. LACONIA, NEW HAMPSHIRE, LABOR MARKET AREA / ECONOMIC ANALYSIS AND REPORTS SECTION (US) [12096598] **1646**

ANNUAL PLANNING INFORMATION. MANCHESTER, NEW HAMPSHIRE, LABOR MARKET AREA / ECONOMIC ANALYSIS AND REPORTS SECTION (US) [12096702] **1646**

ANNUAL PLANNING INFORMATION. MARIN COUNTY (US) [11164347] **1647**

ANNUAL PLANNING INFORMATION. MERCED COUNTY (US/0883-301X) [06740462] **1647**

ANNUAL PLANNING INFORMATION. MERIDEN-MIDDLESEX SERVICE DELIVERY AREA (US) [16271447] **1647**

ANNUAL PLANNING INFORMATION. NASHUA, NEW HAMPSHIRE, LABOR MARKET AREA / ECONOMIC ANALYSIS AND REPORTS SECTION (US) [12096629] **1647**

ANNUAL PLANNING INFORMATION, NEW HAMPSHIRE (US) [04299949] **1647**

ANNUAL PLANNING INFORMATION. NORTHEAST SERVICE DELIVERY AREA (US) [17018886] **1647**

ANNUAL PLANNING INFORMATION. OTTUMWA, IOWA LABOR AREA, WAPELLO COUNTY (US) [06859604] **1647**

ANNUAL PLANNING INFORMATION. PARKERSBURG-MARIETTA STANDARD METROPOLITAN STATISTICAL AREA (US) [08616452] **1647, 1529**

ANNUAL PLANNING INFORMATION. PORTSMOUTH, NEW HAMPSHIRE, LABOR MARKET AREA / ECONOMIC ANALYSIS AND REPORTS SECTION (US) [12096540] **1647**

ANNUAL PLANNING INFORMATION REPORT : BEAUMONT-PORT ARTHUR-ORANGE SMSA (US) [04947177] **1647, 1529**

ANNUAL PLANNING INFORMATION REPORT. COLORADO (US/0749-7857) [09941210] **1647**

ANNUAL PLANNING INFORMATION REPORT: DALLAS-FORT WORTH SMSA (US) [04657089] **1647, 1529**

ANNUAL PLANNING INFORMATION REPORT, FISCAL YEAR ... BOSTON, MASSACHUSETTS STANDARD METROPOLITAN STATISTICAL AREA / PREPARED BY EDWARD F. KAZONCHA, LABOR MARKET ECONOMIST (DIVISION OF EMPLOYMENT SECURITY, JOB MARKET RESEARCH, LABOR AREA RESEARCH) (US) [08648479] **1647**

ANNUAL PLANNING INFORMATION REPORT FOR FISCAL YEAR ... ATLANTA STANDARD METROPOLITAN STATISTICAL AREA (US) [09340564] **1647**

ANNUAL PLANNING INFORMATION REPORT FOR FISCAL YEAR ... AUGUSTA, GEORGIA AREA, RICHMOND AND COLUMBIA COUNTIES, GEORGIA AND AIKEN COUNTY, SOUTH CAROLINA AND THE CENTRAL SAVANNAH RIVER AREA (US) [09340537] **1647**

ANNUAL PLANNING INFORMATION REPORT FOR FISCAL YEAR ... SAVANNAH SMSA SAVANNAH/CHATHAM CONSORTIUM (US) [09340780] **1647, 1529**

ANNUAL PLANNING INFORMATION REPORT ... MIAMI SMSA AND SOUTH FLORIDA CETA CONSORTIUM (US) [08648301] **1647**

ANNUAL PLANNING INFORMATION REPORT. ORLANDO SMSA AND ORANGE COUNTY, ORLANDO CITY, SEMINOLE COUNTY CETA PRIME SPONSOR AREAS (US) [08648429] **1647, 1529**

ANNUAL PLANNING INFORMATION REPORT ... PENSACOLA SMSA AND OKALOOSA COUNTY (US) [08648351] **1647, 1529**

ANNUAL PLANNING INFORMATION REPORT. PITTSBURGH PRIMARY METROPOLITAN STATISTICAL AREA, LABOR MARKET AREA NO. 6280 (US) **1529**

ANNUAL PLANNING INFORMATION REPORT ... TALLAHASSEE SMSA AND LEON-GADSDEN CETA CONSORTIUM (US) [08612331] **1647**

ANNUAL PLANNING INFORMATION REPORT: WACO SMSA (US) [04656985] **1647**

ANNUAL PLANNING INFORMATION. SALEM, NEW HAMPSHIRE, LABOR MARKET AREA / ECONOMIC ANALYSIS AND REPORTS SECTION (US) [12096655] **1647**

ANNUAL PLANNING INFORMATION. SAN FRANCISCO CITY AND COUNTY (US) [11169169] **1647**

ANNUAL PLANNING INFORMATION: SAN FRANCISCO-OAKLAND STANDARD METROPOLITAN STATISTICAL AREA, CITY OF BERKELEY (US/0272-6815) [06879348] **1647**

ANNUAL PLANNING INFORMATION : SAN FRANCISCO-OAKLAND STANDARD METROPOLITAN STATISTICAL AREA, CITY OF OAKLAND (US) [06064237] **1647**

ANNUAL PLANNING INFORMATION. SAN FRANCISCO-OAKLAND STANDARD METROPOLITAN STATISTICAL AREA, CITY OF RICHMOND (US/0272-703X) [06884522] **1647**

ANNUAL PLANNING INFORMATION : SAN FRANCISCO-OAKLAND STANDARD METROPOLITAN STATISTICAL AREA, CONTRA COSTA COUNTY, EXCLUDING THE CITY OF RICHMOND (US/0198-8662) [06226323] **1647**

ANNUAL PLANNING INFORMATION. SARASOTA SMSA (US) [09428296] **1648**

ANNUAL PLANNING INFORMATION, SIOUX CITY SMSA / PREPARED BY JEFFREY C. HARCUM [FOR] IOWA DEPARTMENT OF JOB SERVICE (US) [06887047] **1648, 1529**

ANNUAL PLANNING INFORMATION. SOUTH EAST SERVICE DELIVERY AREA (US) [14964245] **1648**

ANNUAL PLANNING INFORMATION, STATE OF FLORIDA (US) [07954554] **1648**

ANNUAL PLANNING INFORMATION / STATE OF MAINE (US) [08609567] **1648**

ANNUAL PLANNING INFORMATION, STATE OF WEST VIRGINIA (US) [08630615] **1648, 1529**

ANNUAL PLANNING INFORMATION : VALLEJO-FAIRFIELD-NAPA STANDARD METROPOLITAN STATISTICAL AREA, NAPA COUNTY (US) [06934360] **1648**

ANNUAL PLANNING INFORMATION, WATERLOO-CEDER FALLS SMSA, CETA PRIME SPONSOR JURISDICTION, BLACK HAWK COUNTY *See* ANNUAL PLANNING INFORMATION. LABOR AREA, WATERLOO-CEDAR FALLS SMSA, CETA PRIME SPONSOR JURISDICTION, BLACK HAWK COUNTY **1529**

ANNUAL PLANNING INFORMATION. WHEELING-BRIDGEPORT STANDARD METROPOLITAN STATISTICAL AREA (US) [08612811] **1648, 1529**

ANNUAL PLANNING REPORT ... ADA COUNTY / PRODUCED BY THE IDAHO DEPARTMENT OF EMPLOYMENT, BUREAU OF PLANNING, RESEARCH, AND EVALUATION (US) [07214998] **1648**

ANNUAL PLANNING REPORT, CITY OF PHOENIX (US) [05770364] **1648**

ANNUAL PLANNING REPORT, DISTRICT OF COLUMBIA (US) [06605745] **1648**

ANNUAL PLANNING REPORT (EMPLOYMENT SECURITY COMMISSION OF WYOMING. RESEARCH AND ANALYSIS SECTION) *See* WYOMING ANNUAL PLANNING REPORT **1720**

ANNUAL PLANNING REPORT : FALL RIVER, MASSACHUSETTS-RHODE ISLAND LABOR MARKET AREA (US/0148-5075) [03315162] **1648**

ANNUAL — Alphabetical Title Index

ANNUAL PLANNING REPORT, FISCAL YEAR ... CHAMPAIGN SMSA (US) [04407425] 1648, **1529**

ANNUAL PLANNING REPORT FOR CUMBERLAND COUNTY FEATURING THE PORTLAND SMSA *See* ANNUAL PLANNING INFORMATION FOR CUMBERLAND COUNTY **1646**

ANNUAL PLANNING REPORT FOR THE PENOBSCOT CONSORTIUM FEATURING THE BANGOR-BREWER LABOR MARKET AREA *See* ANNUAL PLANNING INFORMATION FOR PENOBSCOT CONSORTIUM **1646**

ANNUAL PLANNING REPORT: MAINE, BALANCE OF STATE (US) [04403478] **1648**

ANNUAL PLANNING REPORT - NEBRASKA DEPARTMENT OF LABOR, DIVISION OF EMPLOYMENT (US) [04818839] **1648**

ANNUAL PLANNING REPORT. OLYMPIA SMSA (US) [08999186] 1648, **1529**

ANNUAL PLANNING REPORT: ROCHESTER LABOR AREA (US) [04373237] **1648**

ANNUAL PLANNING REPORT : SAN FRANCISCO-OAKLAND STANDARD METROPOLITAN STATISTICAL AREA, BALANCE OF ALAMEDA COUNTY, ALAMEDA COUNTY EXCEPT CITIES OF OAKLAND AND BERKELEY (US/0160-0451) [03596578] **1648**

ANNUAL PLANNING REPORT. SAN FRANCISCO-OAKLAND STANDARD METROPOLITAN STATISTICAL AREA, CITY OF BERKELEY *See* ANNUAL PLANNING INFORMATION: SAN FRANCISCO-OAKLAND STANDARD METROPOLITAN STATISTICAL AREA, CITY OF BERKELEY **1647**

ANNUAL PLANNING REPORT. SAN FRANCISCO-OAKLAND STANDARD METROPOLITAN STATISTICAL AREA, CITY OF OAKLAND *See* ANNUAL PLANNING INFORMATION : SAN FRANCISCO-OAKLAND STANDARD METROPOLITAN STATISTICAL AREA, CITY OF OAKLAND **1647**

ANNUAL PLANNING REPORT. SAN FRANCISCO-OAKLAND STANDARD METROPOLITAN STATISTICAL AREA, RICHMOND OF RICHMOND *See* ANNUAL PLANNING INFORMATION : SAN FRANCISCO-OAKLAND STANDARD METROPOLITAN STATISTICAL AREA, CITY OF RICHMOND **1647**

ANNUAL PLANNING REPORT : SEATTLE-EVERETT, WASHINGTON AREA (US/0145-7187) [02776364] **1648**

ANNUAL PLANNING REPORT - STATE OF FLORIDA, DEPARTMENT OF COMMERCE, DIVISION OF EMPLOYMENT SECURITY (US/0147-4901) [03175268] **1648**

ANNUAL PLANNING REPORT, STATE OF WYOMING (US) [04238425] **1648**

ANNUAL PLANNING REPORT : VALLEJO-FAIRFIELD-NAPA STANDARD METROPOLITAN STATISTICAL AREA, NAPA COUNTY (US/0160-0494) [03596744] **1648**

ANNUAL POWDER METALLURGY CONFERENCE PROCEEDINGS (US/0079-6719) [13791148] **3998**

ANNUAL PRESERVATION PROGRAM - MINNESOTA HISTORICAL SOCIETY. STATE HISTORIC PRESERVATION OFFICE, THE (US) [04168194] **2720**

ANNUAL PRESERVATION PROGRAM, THE (US/0148-2521) [03276901] **2186**

ANNUAL PRICE REVIEW (US/0270-4188) [06416086] **60**

ANNUAL PRICE SURVEY: FAMILY BUDGET COSTS (US/0069-7818) [01564516] **1462**

ANNUAL PRIVACY AND SECURITY AUDIT REPORT ON THE PROCEDURES, POLICIES, AND PRACTICES OF THE DEPARTMENT OF LAW ENFORCEMENT FOR MAINTAINING CRIMINAL HISTORY RECORD INFORMATION FOR THE PERIOD ENDING ... / ILLINOIS CRIMINAL JUSTICE INFORMATION COUNCIL (US) [06512624] **3156**

ANNUAL PROCEEDINGS - AMERICAN SOCIOLOGICAL ASSOCIATION (US) [04476211] **5239**

ANNUAL PROCEEDINGS / DUBLIN SEMINAR FOR NEW ENGLAND FOLKLIFE (US/0888-3165) [03728047] 2720, **255**

ANNUAL PROCEEDINGS OF THE PHYTOCHEMICAL SOCIETY OF EUROPE (UK/0197-8969) [05301209] **480**

ANNUAL PROCEEDINGS, PRE-CONVENTION REPORT - LOCOMOTIVE MAINTENANCE OFFICERS ASSOCIATION (U.S.) (US/0883-6035) [11953278] **5429**

ANNUAL PROCEEDINGS, RELIABILITY PHYSICS SYMPOSIUM (US/0099-9512) [I00999512] **4397**

ANNUAL PROCEEDINGS / THE ASSOCIATED SCIENTIFIC AND TECHNICAL SOCIETIES OF SOUTH AFRICA, THE (SA/0373-4250) [04877749] **5083**

ANNUAL PROCEEDINGS. WATER SYMPOSIUM / ARIZONA WATER SYMPOSIUM (US/0731-874X) [07895231] 2186, **5529**

ANNUAL PROCUREMENT AND FEDERAL ASSISTANCE REPORT (US/0748-6278) [10960739] **4626**

ANNUAL PROCUREMENT REPORT (US) [04103054] **11**

ANNUAL PRODUCTION BY ACTIVE FIELDS, OIL AND GAS DIVISION (US/0098-4043) [02241121] **4250**

ANNUAL PROGRAM INFORMATION NOTICE (US/0277-478X) [06796166] **1932**

ANNUAL PROGRAM; LIBRARY SERVICES AND CONSTRUCTION ACT - SOUTH CAROLINA. STATE LIBRARY, COLUMBIA (US/0364-7803) [02653470] **3190**

ANNUAL PROGRAM PLAN AMENDMENT FOR PART B OF THE EDUCATION OF THE HANDICAPPED ACT AS AMENDED BY PUBLIC LAW 94-142 (US) [05002772] **1875**

ANNUAL PROGRAM PLAN AMENDMENT FOR PART B OF THE EDUCATION OF THE HANDICAPPED ACT AS AMENDED BY PUBLIC LAW 94-142 (US) [03722361] **1875**

ANNUAL PROGRAM PLAN AMENDMENT FOR PART B (P.L. 94-142) (US) [07037555] **1725**

ANNUAL PROGRAM PLAN FOR FISCAL YEAR ... / U.S. DEPARTMENT OF JUSTICE, NATIONAL INSTITUTE OF CORRECTIONS (US) [23248949] **3156**

ANNUAL PROGRAM PLAN FOR FISCAL YEARS - KANSAS. STATE DEPT. OF EDUCATION (US) [05392694] **1725**

ANNUAL PROGRAM PLAN FOR VOCATIONAL EDUCATION FOR FISCAL YEAR ... AND ACCOUNTABILITY REPORT FOR FISCAL YEAR ... (TEXAS) (US) [07010742] **1910**

ANNUAL PROGRAM PLAN FOR VOCATIONAL EDUCATION IN ILLINOIS (US) [05057305] **1910**

ANNUAL PROGRAM PLAN : TITLE I, ESEA - KANSAS. STATE DEPT. OF EDUCATION (US) [05182920] **1875**

ANNUAL PROGRAM PLAN TITLE IV ESEA (US) [04756800] **1725**

ANNUAL PROGRAM PLAN / WASHINGTON STATE, COMMISSION FOR VOCATIONAL EDUCATION (US) [08561927] **1910**

ANNUAL PROGRESS IN CHILD PSYCHIATRY AND CHILD DEVELOPMENT (US/0066-4030) [01481485] 3920, **3900**

ANNUAL PROGRESS REPORT, CHILKAT RIVER COOPERATIVE BALD EAGLE STUDY (US/8755-4690) [11303578] 2186, **5576**

ANNUAL PROGRESS REPORT - DIVISION OF GAME AND FRESHWATER FISHERIES (US) [02944427] **2294**

ANNUAL PROGRESS REPORT / ECONOMIC RESEARCH BUREAU, UNIVERSITY OF DAR ES SALAAM (TZ) [11383264] **1589**

ANNUAL PROGRESS REPORT ... / GOVERNOR'S OFFICE OF INTERGOVERNMENTAL PERSONNEL (MISSISSIPPI) (US) [06718395] **4701**

ANNUAL PROGRESS REPORT - MICHIGAN DEPARTMENT OF TRANSPORTATION (US) [06968125] **5376**

ANNUAL PROGRESS REPORT OF THE NEW YORK STATE NEWSPAPER RECYCLING TASK FORCE MONITORING COMMITTEE / PREPARED BY NEW YORK NEWSPAPER PUBLISHERS ASSOCIATION, NEW YORK PRESS ASSOCIATION, NEW YORK STATE DEPARTMENT OF ECONOMIC DEVELOPMENT, NEW YORK STATE DEPARTMENT OF ENVIRONMENTAL CONSERVATION (US) [25560075] **2224**

ANNUAL PROGRESS REPORT - SOUTHEAST LOUISIANA DAIRY AND PASTURE EXPERIMENT STATION (US) [02293075] **191**

ANNUAL PROGRESS REPORT / SOUTHEAST RESEARCH STATION, LOUISIANA AGRICULTURAL EXPERIMENT STATION (US/1057-3216) [18486057] **205**

ANNUAL PROGRESS REPORT TO THE GOVERNOR AND TO THE JOINT COMMITTEE ON HUMAN SERVICES OF THE ... CONNECTICUT GENERAL ASSEMBLY FROM OFFICE AND BOARD OF PROTECTION AND ADVOCACY FOR HANDICAPPED AND DEVELOPMENTALLY DISABLED PERSONS (US) [17979838] **4383**

ANNUAL PROGRESS REPORT TO THE INTERNATIONAL JOINT COMMISSION FROM THE INTERNATIONAL REFERENCE GROUP ON GREAT LAKES POLLUTION FROM LAND USE ACTIVITIES (PLUARG) (CN/0842-3733) [04019243] **2224**

ANNUAL PROGRESS REPORT, TRACT C-A (US/8756-0518) [08634427] **5083**

ANNUAL PROGRESS REPORT - UNIVERSITY OF CALIFORNIA, LABORATORY OF NUCLEAR MEDICINE AND RADIATION BIOLOGY (US/0193-5224) [05186495] 3939, **3847**

ANNUAL PROGRESS REPORT / WALTER REED ARMY INSTITUTE OF RESEARCH (US) [09887685] **3550**

ANNUAL PROGRESS REPORT - WATER MANAGEMENT RESEARCH PROJECT (US/0198-1994) [06126063] 2087, **5529**

ANNUAL PROJECT HISTORY : MANN CREEK PROJECT (US) [01555221] **2087**

ANNUAL PROJECT HISTORY : PACIFIC NORTHWEST-PACIFIC SOUTHWEST INTERTIE, ARIZONA, CALIFORNIA, NEVADA (US) [01597749] **2035**

ANNUAL PUBLIC DEFENDERS' WORKSHOP (US/0093-8653) [05725309] **3105**

ANNUAL QUALITY CONGRESS TRANSACTIONS (US/1067-7267) [07906568] **5083**

ANNUAL RECORD OF OPERATIONS - ATMOSPHERIC ENVIRONMENT SERVICE (CN/0317-669X) [02246715] **1420**

ANNUAL RECORD OF TRADE MARKS OFFICE PROCEEDINGS (AT) [12111031] **1301**

ANNUAL REGISTER, CERTIFIED PUBLIC ACCOUNTANTS (US) [08503883] **738**

ANNUAL REGISTER (LONDON, ENGLAND : 1964) (UK/0066-4057) [08988874] **2610**

ANNUAL REGISTER OF BOOK VALUES. EARLY PRINTED BOOKS (UK/0968-7513) [28492600] **4821**

●ANNUAL REGISTER OF BOOK VALUES. MODERN FIRST EDITIONS (UK/0968-7521) [28490031] **4823**

●ANNUAL REGISTER OF BOOK VALUES. VOYAGES, TRAVEL & EXPLORATION (UK/0968-7548) [28490656] **407**

ANNUAL REGISTER OF CERTIFIED PUBLIC ACCOUNTANTS AND PUBLIC ACCOUNTANTS (SOUTH DAKOTA. STATE BOARD OF ACCOUNTANCY) (US) [07956169] **738**

ANNUAL REGISTER OF CERTIFIED PUBLIC ACCOUNTANTS, PUBLIC ACCOUNTANTS, ACCOUNTING PRACTITIONERS / IOWA BOARD OF ACCOUNTANCY (US) [05437684] **738**

ANNUAL REGISTER OF GRANT SUPPORT (US/0066-4049) [01123776] **1809**

ANNUAL REGISTER OF INDIAN POLITICAL PARTIES, THE (II) [01790593] **4464**

ANNUAL REGISTER OF MERCHANTS' PREMISES (UK/0267-999X) [I0267999X] **60**

ANNUAL REGISTER OF PRACTITIONERS OF ACCOUNTANCY *See* ANNUAL REGISTER OF CERTIFIED PUBLIC ACCOUNTANTS AND PUBLIC ACCOUNTANTS (SOUTH DAKOTA. STATE BOARD OF ACCOUNTANCY) **738**

ANNUAL REPORT (ABBREVIATED). TECHNISCHE UNIVERSITAT BERLIN. INSTITUT FUR SOZIALOKONOMIE DER AGRARENTWICKLUNG.-- (GW) [08301250] **1809**

ANNUAL REPORT / ABORIGINAL HOSTELS LIMITED (AT) [20427751] **5461**

ANNUAL REPORT / ADMINISTRATIVE CONFERENCE OF THE UNITED STATES (US/0898-3100) [11728823] **4626**

ANNUAL REPORT / ADMINISTRATIVE REVIEW COUNCIL (AT/0155-025X) [06782525] **2934**

ANNUAL REPORT - ADULT AND CONTINUING EDUCATION (ALASKA) (US) [07777543] **1799**

ANNUAL REPORT - ADULT DEVELOPMENT AND AGING RESEARCH COMMITTEE, NATIONAL INSTITUTES OF HEALTH (US) [04024641] **3749**

ANNUAL REPORT - ADVISORY COMMISSION ON INTERGOVERNMENTAL RELATIONS (US/0082-8610) [01236164] **4626**

ANNUAL REPORT / ADVISORY COMMITTEE ON PESTICIDES (UK) [15799294] **4244**

ANNUAL REPORT - ADVISORY COMMITTEE ON THE LAW OF THE SEA (US/0360-0750) [02243750] **3180**

ANNUAL REPORT - ADVISORY COUNCIL ON INTERGOVERNMENTAL RELATIONS (US) [04420289] **4709**

ANNUAL REPORT / AGRICULTURAL & VETERINARY CHEMICALS ASSOCIATION OF AUSTRALIA (AT) [24587855] 205, **5503**

Alphabetical Title Index — ANNUAL

ANNUAL REPORT / AGRICULTURAL COOPERATIVE DEVELOPMENT INTERNATIONAL (US/0741-2568) [02215079] **1541**

ANNUAL REPORT (AGRICULTURAL FINANCE CORPORATION) (RH) [07186760] **60**

ANNUAL REPORT - AGRICULTURAL RESEARCH DEPARTMENT, PHILIPPINE COCONUT AUTHORITY (PH) [02240633] **60**

ANNUAL REPORT - AHMEDABAD TEXTILE MILL'S ASSOCIATION (II) [10129766] **5347**

ANNUAL REPORT - AIR CANADA (CN/0568-3424) [01793829] **11**

ANNUAL REPORT / ALABAMA DEPARTMENT OF MENTAL HEALTH AND MENTAL RETARDATION (US) [12301493] **5272**

ANNUAL REPORT / ALABAMA DEPARTMENT OF PUBLIC HEALTH (US) [08294284] **4765**

ANNUAL REPORT - ALABAMA. DEPT. OF INDUSTRIAL RELATIONS. DIVISION OF SAFETY AND INSPECTION (US) [06609091] **2859**

ANNUAL REPORT - ALABAMA HISTORICAL COMMISSION (US) [08620716] **4626**

ANNUAL REPORT, ALABAMA JUDICIAL SYSTEM (US) [08744403] **3138**

ANNUAL REPORT - ALASKA NATIVE HUMAN RESOURCES DEVELOPMENT PROGRAM (US) [09269896] **1648**

ANNUAL REPORT - ALASKA NATIVE MEDICAL CENTER (US/0362-6849) [02315990] **3776**

ANNUAL REPORT / ALASKA SEA GRANT COLLEGE PROGRAM (US) [12090777] **2294**

ANNUAL REPORT - ALBERTA AGRICULTURAL DEVELOPMENT CORPORATION *CEASED.* (CN/0380-3120) [02246976] **60**

ANNUAL REPORT / ALBERTA CULTURE AND MULTICULTURALISM (CN/0848-2128) [20323617] **2528**

ANNUAL REPORT - ALBERTA DEPARTMENT OF HOUSING (CN/0822-4382) [11640146] **2814**

ANNUAL REPORT - ALBERTA ENVIRONMENT (CN/0383-3739) [02243245] **2160**

ANNUAL REPORT / ALBERTA FORESTRY, LANDS AND WILDLIFE (CN/0832-6916) [17371871] **2374**

ANNUAL REPORT - ALBERTA HAIL AND CROP INSURANCE CORPORATION (CN/0319-3535) [02244659] **2873**

ANNUAL REPORT / ALBERTA HEALTH (CN/1185-2984) [24860833] **4765**

ANNUAL REPORT - ALBERTA HEALTH AND SOCIAL SERVICES DISCIPLINES COMMITTEE (CN/0707-1434) [05640034] **3913**

ANNUAL REPORT - ALBERTA LABOUR (CN/0702-9667) [04450638] **1648**

ANNUAL REPORT / ALBERTA LAW REFORM INSTITUTE (CN) [20409811] **2934**

ANNUAL REPORT - ALBERTA PUBLIC UTILITIES BOARD (CN/0383-3690) [02241559] **4626**

ANNUAL REPORT / ALBERTA RESEARCH COUNCIL (CN/0701-5151) [04880134] **2096**

ANNUAL REPORT - ALBERTA TRANSPORTATION AND UTILITIES (CN/0836-1509) [18101752] 4759, **5376**

ANNUAL REPORT - ALIA (JO/0376-5520) [01794319] **11**

ANNUAL REPORT - AMDEL (AT/0155-3437) [01695999] **3998**

ANNUAL REPORT / AMERICAN ARBITRATION ASSOCIATION (US) [05451832] **2934**

ANNUAL REPORT - AMERICAN BUREAU FOR MEDICAL ADVANCEMENT IN CHINA, INC (US/0197-0909) [05925639] **3550**

ANNUAL REPORT / AMERICAN BUREAU OF SHIPPING (US/0569-3578) [03897606] **5447**

ANNUAL REPORT - AMERICAN CIVIL LIBERTIES UNION (US/0197-1239) [01479667] 3092, **4504**

ANNUAL REPORT - AMERICAN COLLEGE (US) [05536635] **2873**

ANNUAL REPORT - AMERICAN INSTITUTE OF INDIAN STUDIES (US/0360-3687) [01670061] **2255**

ANNUAL REPORT / AMHC, ALBERTA MORTGAGE AND HOUSING CORPORATION (CN/0837-6816) [14077027] **2814**

ANNUAL REPORT AND ACCOUNTS - BHARAT PUMPS & COMPRESSORS LIMITED (II) [01797687] **2109**

ANNUAL REPORT AND ACCOUNTS / BRITISH GAS (UK) [19828103] **1597**

ANNUAL REPORT AND ACCOUNTS - BRITISH TRUST FOR ORNITHOLOGY (UK) [06257259] **5614**

ANNUAL REPORT AND ACCOUNTS FOR ... / KENYA RAILWAYS CORPORATION *See* ANNUAL REPORT / KENYA RAILWAYS **4627**

ANNUAL REPORT AND ACCOUNTS FOR ... / ROYAL MUSICAL ASSOCIATION (UK) [08330997] **4100**

ANNUAL REPORT AND ACCOUNTS FOR THE YEAR ENDED 31ST MARCH ... - RURAL DEVELOPMENT CORPORATION OF ZAMBIA (ZA) [09698548] **60**

ANNUAL REPORT AND ACCOUNTS FOR THE YEAR ENDED DECEMBER 31ST, ... / THE COCONUT INDUSTRY BOARD, JAMAICA, WEST INDIES (JM) [03683345] **2327**

ANNUAL REPORT AND ACCOUNTS - GUJARAT SMALL INDUSTRIES CORPORATION (II) [01797680] **1597**

ANNUAL REPORT & ACCOUNTS - GUYANA NATIONAL CO-OPERATIVE BANK (GY) [04162806] **770**

ANNUAL REPORT AND ACCOUNTS - HOWARD FLOREY INSTITUTE OF EXPERIMENTAL PHYSIOLOGY AND MEDICINE (AT/1031-4709) [15199851] **3726**

ANNUAL REPORT AND ACCOUNTS / INDEFUND LIMITED (MW) [11607827] **770**

ANNUAL REPORT AND ACCOUNTS - INDUSTRIAL DEVELOPMENT BANK LIMITED (KE/0304-6486) [02242941] **770**

ANNUAL REPORT AND ACCOUNTS - KARNATAKA STATE FINANCIAL CORPORATION (II/0304-6710) [02240221] **770**

ANNUAL REPORT AND ACCOUNTS - NATIONAL INSTITUTE FOR PRODUCTIVITY (TZ) [04011809] **1597**

ANNUAL REPORT AND ACCOUNTS - NATIONAL WATER COUNCIL (UK) [02610376] **5529**

ANNUAL REPORT AND ACCOUNTS - NORTHERN IRELAND ELECTRICITY SERVICE (UK) [06409568] **2035**

ANNUAL REPORT AND ACCOUNTS OF THE FORESTRY COMMISSION (UK) [01428916] **2374**

ANNUAL REPORT AND ACCOUNTS / TANZANIA INDUSTRIAL RESEARCH AND DEVELOPMENT ORGANIZATION (TZ) [10665305] **5083**

ANNUAL REPORT AND ACCOUNTS / THE RAINER FOUNDATION (UK) [20709378] **3157**

ANNUAL REPORT & ACCOUNTS / THE TEA BOARD OF KENYA (KE) [24298366] **60**

ANNUAL REPORT AND ACCOUNTS / THE WHITSUN FOUNDATION (RH) [07599135] **1546**

ANNUAL REPORT AND ACCOUNTS / TISCO (TZ) [08608961] **1597**

ANNUAL REPORT & ACCOUNTS / WAIKATO DAIRY CO-OPERATIVE LIMITED (NZ) [19575339] **191**

ANNUAL REPORT AND ACCOUNTS - WATER RESEARCH CENTRE (UK/0144-9370) [06287192] 5529, **2224**

ANNUAL REPORT AND ACCOUNTS / WESTERN AUSTRALIAN POTATO MARKETING BOARD (AT) [15648608] **162**

ANNUAL REPORT AND AGRICULTURAL STATISTICS / STATE OF OHIO DEPARTMENT OF AGRICULTURE (US) [27398410] **60**

ANNUAL REPORT AND AUDITED FINANCIAL STATEMENTS AS OF ... (US) [08215378] **4709**

ANNUAL REPORT AND AUDITED FINANCIAL STATEMENTS / NORTHEAST MARYLAND WASTE DISPOSAL AUTHORITY (US) [11957398] **2224**

ANNUAL REPORT AND BALANCE SHEET AND REVENUE AND EXPENDITURE ACCOUNT (RH) [03590506] **312**

ANNUAL REPORT AND CARGO STATISTICS *See* ANNUAL REPORT / MACKAY PORT AUTHORITY **5447**

ANNUAL REPORT AND DIRECTORY OF MINES / STATE OF WEST VIRGINIA, DIVISION OF ENERGY, HEALTH SAFETY AND TRAINING, MINES AND MINERALS (US) [23248217] **2133**

ANNUAL REPORT AND FINANCIAL STATEMENTS / ALASKA MEDICAL FACILITY AUTHORITY (US/0737-0601) [09275187] **3776**

ANNUAL REPORT AND FINANCIAL STATEMENTS - ALASKA MUNICIPAL BOND BANK (US/0270-6326) [06449570] **891**

ANNUAL REPORT AND FINANCIAL STATEMENTS FOR THE YEAR ENDED ... (TS) [08447766] **770**

ANNUAL REPORT AND GUIDE TO PROGRAMS / IDAHO DEPARTMENT OF HEALTH AND WELFARE (US) [27751027] 4626, **4765**

ANNUAL REPORT ... AND ... HANDBOOK / INSTITUTE OF DEVELOPMENT STUDIES (UK) [07102378] **1462**

ANNUAL REPORT AND MINUTES OF THE ANNUAL MEETING - CANADIAN SEED GROWERS' ASSOCIATION (CN/0700-6691) [02792453] **162**

ANNUAL REPORT AND NOTICE OF ORDINARY GENERAL MEETING / BANK OF NEW SOUTH WALES (AT) [08252537] **770**

ANNUAL REPORT AND PROCEEDINGS OF THE ANNUAL ENCAMPMENT (LANSING) (US/0094-596X) [01794267] **4034**

ANNUAL REPORT AND REPORT OF ... TRAINING PROGRAMME - EASTERN AND SOUTHERN AFRICAN MANAGEMENT INSTITUTE (TZ) [08543680] **5550**

ANNUAL REPORT AND REVIEW OF ACTIVITIES FOR THE YEAR / THE EMPLOYERS' CONSULTATIVE ASSOCIATION OF MALAWI (MW) [15462934] **938**

ANNUAL REPORT AND STATEMENT OF ACCOUNTS (BF) [01791300] **770**

ANNUAL REPORT AND STATEMENT OF ACCOUNTS - BANCA NAZIONALE SOMALA (SO) [04840408] **770**

ANNUAL REPORT & STATEMENT OF ACCOUNTS / BARBADOS NATIONAL BANK (BB) [11302731] **770**

ANNUAL REPORT AND STATEMENT OF ACCOUNTS - CENTRAL BANK OF MALTA (MM) [05253146] **770**

ANNUAL REPORT AND STATEMENT OF ACCOUNTS FOR THE YEAR ENDED 30TH JUNE ... / NATIONAL COMMERCIAL BANK OF DOMINICA (DQ) [20785212] **770**

ANNUAL REPORT AND STATEMENT OF ACCOUNTS FOR THE YEAR ENDED ... / ELECTRICITY SUPPLY COMMISSION OF MALAWI (MW) [11585044] **2035**

ANNUAL REPORT AND STATEMENT OF ACCOUNTS / KENYA TEA DEVELOPMENT AUTHORITY (KE) [08674245] **822**

ANNUAL REPORT AND STATEMENT OF ACCOUNTS - RURAL RECONSTRUCTION BOARD (HOBART) (AT/0310-4559) [01786301] **2814**

ANNUAL REPORT AND STATEMENTS OF ACCOUNT. AUSTRALIAN INSTITUTE OF PETROLEUM (AT/0314-3171) [I03143171] **4250**

ANNUAL REPORT AND STATISTICAL DATA - DIVISION OF INSURANCE (MISSOURI) (US) [01795644] 2873, **2897**

ANNUAL REPORT AND SUMMARY OF ANNUAL STATEMENTS BY THE DIRECTOR OF INSURANCE TO ... GOVERNOR, FOR YEAR ENDING DECEMBER 31 ... INCLUDING FISCAL REPORT FOR YEAR ENDING JUNE 30 ... (US) [10217950] **2873**

ANNUAL REPORT / ANIMAL AND GRASSLAND RESEARCH INSTITUTE (UK/0951-0257) [17720669] **205**

ANNUAL REPORT ... ANNUAL MEETING / OREGON HORTICULTURAL SOCIETY (US/0885-7849) [05587985] **2409**

ANNUAL REPORT ... / ARIZONA COUNCIL FOR THE DEAF (US) [08416485] 1104, **4383**

ANNUAL REPORT / ARIZONA DEPARTMENT OF WATER RESOURCES (US/0743-5134) [08619773] **5529**

ANNUAL REPORT, ARIZONA FRUITS AND VEGETABLES (US) [03764961] **162**

ANNUAL REPORT - ARIZONA GAME & FISH DEPARTMENT (US) [01517117] **2294**

ANNUAL REPORT - ARIZONA. OFFICE OF THE STATE CLIMATOLOGIST (US/0883-3303) [11981815] **1420**

ANNUAL REPORT - ARIZONA STATE ECONOMIC OPPORTUNITY OFFICE (US/0090-6182) [01785615] **1546**

ANNUAL REPORT / ARKANSAS ARTS COUNCIL (US) [09448964] **312**

ANNUAL REPORT - ARKANSAS DEPARTMENT OF LABOR (US) [03990550] **1648**

ANNUAL REPORT - ARKANSAS ENVIRONMENTAL PRESERVATION COMMISSION (US/0095-2206) [01795985] **2186**

ANNUAL REPORT / ARKANSAS FORESTRY COMMISSION (US/8756-8292) [11587608] **2374**

ANNUAL REPORT - ARKANSAS-WHITE-RED BASINS INTER-AGENCY COMMITTEE (US/0278-1484) [01211359] **2087**

ANNUAL REPORT - ARTERIOSCLEROSIS AND HYPERTENSION ADVISORY COMMITTEE, NATIONAL INSTITUTES OF HEALTH (US) [04536460] **3698**

ANNUAL REPORT - ASIAN DEVELOPMENT BANK (PH/0066-8370) [01514431] **770**

ANNUAL — Alphabetical Title Index

ANNUAL REPORT - ASIAN PRODUCTIVITY ORGANIZATION (JA/0066-846X) [06129194] 60, **1597**

ANNUAL REPORT / ASSOCIATION OF AMERICAN PUBLISHERS (US/0276-5349) [07268245] **4812**

ANNUAL REPORT / AUCKLAND INSTITUTE AND MUSEUM (NZ) [08179267] **5083**

ANNUAL REPORT - AUDITOR OF STATE (US) [03258123] **4710**

ANNUAL REPORT - AUSTRALIA COUNCIL (AT) [03211134] **312**

ANNUAL REPORT - AUSTRALIAN ACADEMY OF TECHNOLOGICAL SCIENCES (AT/0313-6736) [IC3136736] **5083**

ANNUAL REPORT - AUSTRALIAN ARBITRATION INSPECTORATE (AT/0310-5148) [01793342] **1648**

ANNUAL REPORT - AUSTRALIAN BROADCASTING TRIBUNAL (AT/0728-8883) [06994603] **1126**

ANNUAL REPORT / AUSTRALIAN CHAMBER OF SHIPPING (AT) [12010056] **5447**

ANNUAL REPORT / AUSTRALIAN COAL INDUSTRY RESEARCH LABORATORIES (AT/0067-1762) [05063902] **2133**

ANNUAL REPORT - AUSTRALIAN COUNCIL OF LIBRARIES AND INFORMATION SERVICES (AT/1034-1854) [I10341854] **3190**

ANNUAL REPORT / AUSTRALIAN COUNCIL OF SOCIAL SERVICE (AT) [21010494] **5272**

ANNUAL REPORT / AUSTRALIAN DAIRY CORPORATION (AT) [05624628] **191**

ANNUAL REPORT / AUSTRALIAN DEFENCE FORCE ACADEMY (AT) [19534394] **4034**

ANNUAL REPORT - AUSTRALIAN INSTITUTE OF MARINE SCIENCE 1987 (AT/1037-3314) [I10373314] **1351**

ANNUAL REPORT - AUSTRALIAN LAND INFORMATION COUNCIL (AT/1037-4973) [I10374973] **2554**

ANNUAL REPORT / AUSTRALIAN MANUFACTURING COUNCIL (AT) [08429567] **3475**

ANNUAL REPORT - AUSTRALIAN NATIONAL DAIRY COMMITTEE (AT) [04049753] **191**

ANNUAL REPORT / AUSTRALIAN NATIONAL GALLERY (AT/0314-9919) [20432880] **4083**

ANNUAL REPORT / AUSTRALIAN NATIONAL RAILWAYS COMMISSION (AT) [09266062] **5429**

ANNUAL REPORT / AUSTRALIAN NATIONAL UNIVERSITY RESEARCH SCHOOL OF EARTH SCIENCES (AT/0155-2112) [05143565] **1351**

ANNUAL REPORT / AUSTRALIAN NUCLEAR SCIENCE AND TECHNOLOGY ORGANISATION (AT) [19091752] **2154**

ANNUAL REPORT - AUSTRALIAN ROAD RESEARCH BOARD (AT/0313-6833) [I03136833] **5376**

ANNUAL REPORT ... / BAHAMAS DEVELOPMENT BANK (BF) [07260270] **770**

ANNUAL REPORT / BALTIMORE REGIONAL COUNCIL OF GOVERNMENTS (US) **4627**

ANNUAL REPORT - BANGLADESH BANK (BG) [02441312] **770**

ANNUAL REPORT - BANK EKSPOR IMPOR INDONESIA (IO/0302-6795) [01790734] **770**

ANNUAL REPORT - BANK FOR INTERNATIONAL SETTLEMENTS (SZ/0067-3560) [01519125] **770**

ANNUAL REPORT / BANQUE INTERNATIONALE A LUXEMBOURG (LU) [11880040] **770**

ANNUAL REPORT - BANTU MINING CORPORATION (SA) [01799090] **2133**

ANNUAL REPORT / BATTELLE MEMORIAL INSTITUTE (US/0736-6159) [08393307] **5084**

ANNUAL REPORT / BCSC, BRITISH COLUMBIA SYSTEMS CORPORATION (CN) [07515550] **1597**

ANNUAL REPORT - BIBLIOGRAPHICAL CENTER FOR RESEARCH (US/0191-4316) [04429841] **3190**

ANNUAL REPORT / BINGHAM PUBLIC LIBRARY, CIRENCESTER (UK) [08558650] **3190**

ANNUAL REPORT - BIOLOGICAL FIELD STATION, COOPERSTOWN, NEW YORK (US/0364-9512) [02693103] **442**

ANNUAL REPORT - BIOMEDICAL LIBRARY REVIEW COMMITTEE, NATIONAL LIBRARY OF MEDICINE, NATIONAL INSTITUTES OF HEALTH (US) [04073575] **3190**

ANNUAL REPORT - BLACK RESETTLEMENT BOARD (SA) [07378283] **4627**

ANNUAL REPORT / BLUE DIAMOND (US) [20493810] **162**

ANNUAL REPORT / BOARD OF MANAGEMENT, AUSTRALIAN INSTITUTE OF FAMILY STUDIES (AT) [19883717] **2276**

ANNUAL REPORT - BOARD OF NURSE REGISTRATION AND NURSING EDUCATION (US/0360-4624) [02243038] **3851**

ANNUAL REPORT, BOND PAYMENT FUND (US/0360-6627) [01682362] **4710**

ANNUAL REPORT / BONNEVILLE POWER ADMINISTRATION (US/0898-3917) [16503576] **2035**

ANNUAL REPORT / BOPHUTHATSWANA, DEPARTMENT OF HEALTH AND SOCIAL SERVICES (SA) [20688973] **4765**

ANNUAL REPORT / BOTSWANA AGRICULTURAL MARKETING BOARD (BS) [03225806] **60**

ANNUAL REPORT / BRITISH COLUMBIA ACID MINE DRAINAGE TASK FORCE (CN/1181-9294) [23598065] **2133**

ANNUAL REPORT - BRITISH COLUMBIA BOARD OF PAROLE (CN/0710-7412) [10189860] **3157**

ANNUAL REPORT / BRITISH COLUMBIA, INDUSTRIAL RELATIONS COUNCIL (CN/0838-0899) [18021819] **1597**

ANNUAL REPORT / BRITISH COLUMBIA. MINISTRY OF ENVIRONMENT (1989) (CN/1181-8336) [23659399] **2160**

ANNUAL REPORT / BRITISH COLUMBIA PLACE LTD (CN/0828-3117) [10718484] **4834**

ANNUAL REPORT - BRITISH COLUMBIA TRADE DEVELOPMENT CORPORATION (CN/1182-3348) [23265284] **822**

ANNUAL REPORT - BRITISH LIBRARY (UK/0305-7887) [02243451] **3190**

ANNUAL REPORT / BROOKLYN BOTANIC GARDEN (US) [05111571] **499**

ANNUAL REPORT - BUCKNELL UNIVERSITY (US/0099-1198) [02243300] **1809**

ANNUAL REPORT - BUREAU DE RECHERCHES GEOLOGIQUES ET MINIERES (FR) [04091834] **1365**

ANNUAL REPORT - BUREAU OF ECONOMIC GEOLOGY, THE UNIVERSITY OF TEXAS AT AUSTIN (US/0082-3287) [01135582] **1365**

ANNUAL REPORT / BUREAU OF FRUIT, VEGETABLE, AND PEANUT MARKETING SERVICES (US) [08595491] **2327**

ANNUAL REPORT - BUREAU OF POLLUTION CONTROL. STATE OF NEW JERSEY. DEPARTMENT OF ENVIRONMENTAL PROTECTION (US/0090-5429) [01785210] **2224**

ANNUAL REPORT / BURLINGTON INDUSTRIES INC *CEASED.* (US) [10489295] **1597**

ANNUAL REPORT BY THE BOARD OF REGENTS TO THE GOVERNOR AND LEGISLATURE ON STATE STUDENT FINANCIAL AID PROGRAMS (US) [24391302] **1809**

ANNUAL REPORT BY THE INSPECTOR-GENERAL IN BANKRUPTCY ON THE OPERATION OF THE BANKRUPTCY ACT 1966 (AT/0811-4498) [29888232] 770, **3138**

ANNUAL REPORT - CAISSE CENTRALE DE COOPERATION ECONOMIQUE (FR) [05123133] **2907**

ANNUAL REPORT - CAISSE DE DEPOT ET PLACEMENT DU QUEBEC (CN) [03453413] **770**

ANNUAL REPORT, CAL-VET INSURANCE PLANS (US) [07616649] **2873**

ANNUAL REPORT - CALIFORNIA. COMMISSION FOR ECONOMIC DEVELOPMENT (US/0097-9236) [01796333] **1462**

ANNUAL REPORT / CALIFORNIA DEPARTMENT OF FAIR EMPLOYMENT AND HOUSING (US) [16961132] **1648**

ANNUAL REPORT - CALIFORNIA. DEPT. OF FAIR EMPLOYMENT AND HOUSING. OFFICE OF PUBLIC INFORMATION AND EDUCATION (US) [11266362] **4627**

ANNUAL REPORT - CALIFORNIA. DEPT. OF FORESTRY (US/0882-8326) [09659802] **2374**

ANNUAL REPORT - CALIFORNIA JOB DEVELOPMENT CORPORATION LAW EXECUTIVE BOARD (US/0092-4253) [01789463] **639**

ANNUAL REPORT / CALIFORNIA OFFICE OF EMERGENCY SERVICES (US) [07968451] **5272**

ANNUAL REPORT - CAMP FIRE, INC (US/0884-1381) [12221826] **5228**

ANNUAL REPORT - CANADA-ALBERTA SOIL CONSERVATION INITIATIVE (CN/1184-2075) [23454853] **162**

ANNUAL REPORT - CANADA. GOVERNMENT TELECOMMUNICATIONS AGENCY (CN/1189-3125) [24690986] **1149**

ANNUAL REPORT - CANADA. GOVERNMENT TELECOMMUNICATIONS AGENCY (CN/1189-3125) [24690981] **1149**

ANNUAL REPORT - CANADIAN BAR ASSOCIATION. ALBERTA BRANCH (CN) [10987344] **2934**

ANNUAL REPORT / CANADIAN BROADCASTING CORPORATION (CN/0708-9392) [02244975] **1126**

ANNUAL REPORT / CANADIAN CENTRE FOR MANAGEMENT DEVELOPMENT (CN/1187-2160) [25314229] **4627**

ANNUAL REPORT - CANADIAN CENTRE FOR MANAGEMENT DEVELOPMENT (CN/1187-2160) [25314233] **860**

ANNUAL REPORT - CANADIAN COUNCIL OF MINISTERS OF THE ENVIRONMENT (CN/1185-9660) [25467971] **5272**

ANNUAL REPORT - CANADIAN COUNCIL OF MINISTERS OF THE ENVIRONMENT (CN/1185-9660) [25467965] **2160**

ANNUAL REPORT - CANADIAN COUNCIL ON SOCIAL DEVELOPMENT *CEASED.* (CN) [04981234] **5239**

ANNUAL REPORT - CANADIAN GRAIN COMMISSION (CN/0706-2575) [04236450] **60**

ANNUAL REPORT - CANADIAN HUMAN RIGHTS COMMISSION (CN/0708-5516) [05374541] **4504**

ANNUAL REPORT / CANADIAN NATIONAL (CN/0824-8265) [09553433] 1104, **5376**

ANNUAL REPORT / CANADIAN NATIONAL RAILWAYS *See* RAPPORT ANNUEL / CANADIAN NATIONAL **5390**

ANNUAL REPORT / CANMET (CN/0846-5029) [20779692] 1932, **1437**

ANNUAL REPORT / CAPE BRETON DEVELOPMENT CORPORATION (CN/0228-4723) [03230015] **4627**

ANNUAL REPORT - CAPE OF GOOD HOPE. CAPE SCHOOL BOARD (SA) [01785832] **1860**

ANNUAL REPORT - CAPITAL AREA PLANNING COUNCIL (US/0091-3510) [01785408] **2814**

ANNUAL REPORT - CARDIOVASCULAR AND PULMONARY STUDY SECTION, NATIONAL INSTITUTES OF HEALTH (US) [04097058] **3699**

ANNUAL REPORT - CARNEGIE CORPORATION OF NEW YORK (US/0069-0635) [01266813] **4334**

ANNUAL REPORT / CEA, FRENCH ATOMIC ENERGY COMMISSION (FR) [23897578] **1932**

ANNUAL REPORT ... / CEDEFOP (GW) [08480993] **1910**

ANNUAL REPORT ... CENTER FOR ANALYTICAL CHEMISTRY (US) [09383715] **1013**

ANNUAL REPORT - CENTER FOR LAW AND HEALTH SCIENCES (US/0162-9417) [04214046] **3739**

ANNUAL REPORT - CENTER FOR MATERIALS SCIENCE (NATIONAL MEASUREMENT LABORATORY) (US/0883-2862) [10240921] **4029**

ANNUAL REPORT - CENTER FOR RESEARCH IN WATER RESOURCES, THE UNIVERSITY OF TEXAS AT AUSTIN (US/0276-0177) [02658048] **5529**

ANNUAL REPORT - CENTRAL BANK OF BARBADOS (BB/0304-6796) [02240954] 770, **1546**

ANNUAL REPORT - CENTRAL BANK OF EGYPT (UA) [03799915] **770**

ANNUAL REPORT ... / CENTRAL BANK OF LESOTHO (LO) [11684313] **1546**

ANNUAL REPORT / CENTRAL BANK OF SEYCHELLES (SE) [11080155] **771**

ANNUAL REPORT / CENTRAL BANK OF THE PHILIPPINES (PH/0069-1585) [02693424] **771**

ANNUAL REPORT / CENTRAL BANK OF TRINIDAD AND TOBAGO (TR/0069-1593) [02241552] **1546**

ANNUAL REPORT / CENTRAL COUNCIL FOR RESEARCH IN UNANI MEDICINE (II/0255-8726) [09100828] **3550**

ANNUAL REPORT - CENTRAL INSTITUTE OF FISHERIES NAUTICAL & ENGINEERING TRAINING (INDIA) (II) [11830766] **2294**

ANNUAL REPORT / CENTRAL LAND COUNCIL (AT) [21097924] **4627**

ANNUAL REPORT / CENTRAL MINNESOTA ARTS COUNCIL (US) [12184118] **312**

ANNUAL REPORT - CENTRE FOR ENVIRONMENTAL STUDIES (UK) [03047196] **2160**

ANNUAL REPORT - CENTRE FOR POLICY ON AGING (LONDON, ENGLAND) (UK) [12130004] **5178**

ANNUAL REPORT / CHAMBER OF MINES OF SOUTH AFRICA (SA/0379-4520) [02210794] **2133**

ANNUAL REPORT / CHAMBRE OF MINES, ZIMBABWE (RH) [21051357] **2133**

ANNUAL REPORT - CHESAPEAKE BAY FOUNDATION (US/0742-5066) [10344513] **4162**

ANNUAL REPORT - CHILD WELFARE LEAGUE OF AMERICA, INC (US/0412-1058) [05174184] **5272**

ANNUAL REPORT - CINCINNATI CITY PLANNING COMMISSION (US/0091-1577) [01786283] **2814**

ANNUAL REPORT - CITIZENS ADVISORY COUNCIL (HARRISBURG) (US/0092-7937) [01789967] **2160**

ANNUAL REPORT - CITY OF CHICAGO/HSA (US/0271-339X) [04869012] **4765**

ANNUAL REPORT - CITY OF DETROIT, HUMAN RIGHTS DEPT (US) [04062779] **4504**

ANNUAL REPORT - CITY OF NEW YORK, MAYOR'S OFFICE OF MODEL CITIES (US) [04921885] **2814**

ANNUAL REPORT - CLINICAL APPLICATIONS AND PREVENTION ADVISORY COMMITTEE, NATIONAL INSTITUTES OF HEALTH (US) [04071424] **3550**

ANNUAL REPORT CMA/ACRI (US) [04977883] **2327**

ANNUAL REPORT ... / COCONUT BOARD (FIJI) (FJ) [11922966] **1597**

ANNUAL REPORT / COLD SPRING HARBOR LABORATORY (US) [04362151] **442**

ANNUAL REPORT - COLD SPRING HARBOR, NEW YORK. LABORATORY OF QUANTITATIVE BIOLOGY (US/0069-5009) [01555031] **442**

ANNUAL REPORT / COLLEGE OF AGRICULTURAL & ENVIRONMENTAL SCIENCES (US) [26000984] **60**

ANNUAL REPORT / COLLEGE RELATIONS COMMISSION (CN/0824-989X) [10664435] **1809**

ANNUAL REPORT (COLONIAL WILLIAMSBURG FOUNDATION) (US/1049-3085) [14340677] **2528**

ANNUAL REPORT / COLORADO DEPARTMENT OF CORRECTIONS (US) [10816627] **3157**

ANNUAL REPORT - COLORADO. DEPT. OF HIGHWAYS (US/1051-0850) [21579125] **5438**

ANNUAL REPORT - COMMISSION ON THE STATUS OF WOMEN OF SOUTH DAKOTA (US/0362-9252) [02381046] **5550**

ANNUAL REPORT / COMMISSIONER FOR EQUAL OPPORTUNITY (AT) [17756263] **1648**

ANNUAL REPORT / COMMISSIONER FOR MAIN ROADS (AT/0155-7084) [10879649] **5438**

ANNUAL REPORT / COMMISSIONER OF INTERNAL REVENUE AND THE CHIEF COUNSEL FOR THE INTERNAL REVENUE SERVICE (US) [08261550] **4710**

ANNUAL REPORT - COMMISSIONER OF OFFICIAL LANGUAGES (CN/0382-1161) [01148142] **3265**

ANNUAL REPORT - COMMITTEE OF HEADS OF EDUCATION *CEASED.* (SA) [01798149] **1860**

ANNUAL REPORT / COMMODITY FUTURES TRADING COMMISSION (US/0148-9283) [03392640] **891**

ANNUAL REPORT / COMMONWEALTH OF MASSACHUSETTS, DEPARTMENT OF REVENUE (US) [09150713] **4710**

ANNUAL REPORT / COMMONWEALTH OF MASSACHUSETTS, OFFICE FOR CHILDREN (US/0360-0076) [02243507] **4627**

ANNUAL REPORT / COMMONWEALTH OF VIRGINIA, DEPARTMENT OF MILITARY AFFAIRS (US) [06212364] **4035**

ANNUAL REPORT / COMMONWEALTH OF VIRGINIA, DES, DEPARTMENT OF EMERGENCY SERVICES (US) [15117377] **4765**

ANNUAL REPORT - COMMONWEALTH TEACHING SERVICE (AT) [02240061] 1888, **1649**

ANNUAL REPORT - COMMUNITY RECREATION COUNCIL OF WESTERN AUSTRALIA (AT) [02244345] **4848**

ANNUAL REPORT / COMPAGNIE GENERALE D'ELECTRICITE (FR) [11366924] **1597**

ANNUAL REPORT - CONGRESSIONAL AWARD FOUNDATION (U.S.) (US/0882-0341) [11685545] **4627**

ANNUAL REPORT - CONNECTICUT JUSTICE COMMISSION (US) [04458105] **3157**

ANNUAL REPORT - CONNECTICUT OFFICE OF LABOR RELATIONS (US) [04265192] **1649**

ANNUAL REPORT / CORPORATE AFFAIRS DEPARTMENT, WESTERN AUSTRALIA (AT) [16572231] **4627**

ANNUAL REPORT / COUNCIL FOR MINERAL TECHNOLOGY (SA) [08605787] **2133**

ANNUAL REPORT / COUNCIL FOR NATIONAL ACADEMIC AWARDS *CEASED.* (UK) [10672633] **1725**

ANNUAL REPORT - COUNCIL OF BETTER BUSINESS BUREAUS (US/0094-8853) [01794377] **1293**

ANNUAL REPORT - COUNCIL OF MARITIME PREMIERS (CN/0380-0768) [01787031] **4515**

ANNUAL REPORT - COUNCIL OF MINISTERS OF EDUCATION, CANADA (CN/0706-9502) [04519127] **1725**

ANNUAL REPORT - COUNCIL ON FOREIGN RELATIONS, INC (US/0192-236X) [01565298] **4515**

ANNUAL REPORT / CREDIT COMMERCIAL DE FRANCE (FR) [10289018] **771**

ANNUAL REPORT / CRIME VICTIMS BOARD (US) [09461213] **3157**

ANNUAL REPORT - CRIMINAL COURT OF THE CITY OF NEW YORK (US/0098-1834) [03135969] **3078**

ANNUAL REPORT - CRIMINAL JUSTICE TRAINING AND STANDARDS COUNCIL (US/0095-179X) [01794589] **3157**

ANNUAL REPORT - CSIRO. COAL AND ENERGY TECHNOLOGY (AT/1036-1367) [10361367] **1932**

ANNUAL REPORT - CSIRO DIVISION OF SOILS (1987) (AT/1032-5441) [18759979] **162**

ANNUAL REPORT / CSIRONET (AT) [15733522] **1170**

ANNUAL REPORT / CURTIN UNIVERSITY OF TECHNOLOGY (AT/1031-1378) [20256892] **5084**

ANNUAL REPORT - CYPRUS ORNITHOLOGICAL SOCIETY (CY/0590-4935) [04511011] **5614**

ANNUAL REPORT - CYPRUS PORTS AUTHORITY (CY) [05840839] **5447**

ANNUAL REPORT / D.C. WATER RESOURCES RESEARCH CENTER (US) [08057102] **5529**

ANNUAL REPORT - DEFENCE CONSTRUCTION (1951) LIMITED (CN/0317-4077) [02239900] **4035**

ANNUAL REPORT / DELAWARE RIVER BASIN COMMISSION (US/0418-5455) [02200553] **5529**

ANNUAL REPORT - DELEK, THE ISRAEL FUEL CORPORATION (IS) [02441337] **4250**

ANNUAL REPORT / DEN NORSKE CREDITBANK (NO) [10116753] **771**

ANNUAL REPORT - DENMARK. STATENS REGNSKABSDIREKTORAT (DK) [19452467] **4710**

ANNUAL REPORT - DENNISON MANUFACTURING COMPANY (US) [05181607] **3475**

ANNUAL REPORT; DENTAL EDUCATION (US/0147-0256) [03049948] 1809, **1316**

ANNUAL REPORT / DEPARTMENT OF AGRICULTURE (US/1062-4929) [21416652] **60**

ANNUAL REPORT - DEPARTMENT OF BANTU EDUCATION (SA) [03484628] **1725**

ANNUAL REPORT - DEPARTMENT OF COMMERCE AND ECONOMIC DEVELOPMENT (US/0149-4864) [03302761] 1462, **822**

ANNUAL REPORT - DEPARTMENT OF COMMISSIONERS OF THE LAND OFFICE (OKLAHOMA CITY) (US/0093-6367) [01123737] **4627**

ANNUAL REPORT / DEPARTMENT OF COMMUNITY SERVICES (AT) [19547993] **5272**

ANNUAL REPORT / DEPARTMENT OF CONSERVATION AND LAND MANAGEMENT (AT) [16568846] **2186**

ANNUAL REPORT / DEPARTMENT OF DEFENCE, DEFENCE SCIENCE AND TECHNOLOGY ORGANISATION, WEAPONS SYSTEMS RESERCH LABORATORY (AT) [07522553] **4035**

ANNUAL REPORT / DEPARTMENT OF EDUCATION (SA) [08832996] **1725**

ANNUAL REPORT / DEPARTMENT OF EDUCATION (US) [04507379] **1725**

ANNUAL REPORT - DEPARTMENT OF ENVIRONMENTAL CONSERVATION (US) [02244731] **2186**

ANNUAL REPORT / DEPARTMENT OF FISHERIES (AT) [11219887] **2294**

ANNUAL REPORT / DEPARTMENT OF FISHERIES AND OCEANS (CN/0711-0782) [07781084] **2294**

ANNUAL REPORT / DEPARTMENT OF FOREIGN AFFAIRS AND TRADE (AT/1032-2019) [20970619] **822**

ANNUAL REPORT - DEPARTMENT OF HEALTH AND SOCIAL SERVICES (CHARLOTTETOWN) (CN/0820-9979) [08834771] **4765**

ANNUAL REPORT - DEPARTMENT OF HEALTH & WELFARE (US) [04372420] **5272**

ANNUAL REPORT - DEPARTMENT OF HOUSING & COMMUNITY DEVELOPMENT (US/0363-4183) [02456072] **2814**

ANNUAL REPORT / DEPARTMENT OF INDUSTRY, TECHNOLOGY AND COMMERCE (AT/0816-3073) [15245850] **4627**

ANNUAL REPORT / DEPARTMENT OF JUSTICE, QUEENSLAND GOVERNMENT (AT) [19548136] **2934**

ANNUAL REPORT / DEPARTMENT OF LANDS ADMINISTRATION (AT) [20004039] **4627**

ANNUAL REPORT / DEPARTMENT OF MANUFACTURING AND INDUSTRY DEVELOPMENT, VICTORIA, AUSTRALIA (AT) [25523800] **2133**

ANNUAL REPORT / DEPARTMENT OF MENTAL HEALTH (US) [08304234] **4765**

ANNUAL REPORT - DEPARTMENT OF MINES AND ENERGY, NORTHERN TERRITORY (AT/0725-9727) [I07259727] 1932, **2133**

ANNUAL REPORT / DEPARTMENT OF OCCUPATIONAL HEALTH, SAFETY & WELFARE (AT) [16574685] **2859**

ANNUAL REPORT / DEPARTMENT OF OCEANOGRAPHY. UNIVERSITY OF BRITISH COLUMBIA (CN/0828-1939) [08143848] **1446**

ANNUAL REPORT / DEPARTMENT OF PLANNING AND HOUSING (AT/1037-5171) [27986124] **2814**

ANNUAL REPORT - DEPARTMENT OF PRIMARY INDUSTRIES, QUEENSLAND (AT/0480-9696) [03335728] **60**

ANNUAL REPORT - DEPARTMENT OF PROFESSIONAL REGULATION (FLORIDA) (US) [11666859] **1649**

ANNUAL REPORT - DEPARTMENT OF PUBLIC HEALTH (PP/0377-9203) [01606374] **4765**

ANNUAL REPORT / DEPARTMENT OF RESOURCES DEVELOPMENT (AT) [19527570] **2186**

ANNUAL REPORT - DEPARTMENT OF REVENUE AND TAXATION. AD VALOREM TAX DIVISION (CHEYENNE) (US/0093-7207) [01793017] **4710**

ANNUAL REPORT - DEPARTMENT OF SAFETY (US/0095-1994) [01795972] **5438**

ANNUAL REPORT - DEPARTMENT OF SOCIAL SERVICES, DIVISION OF DATA PROCESSING (MISSOURI) (US) [07051750] **5272**

ANNUAL REPORT - DEPARTMENT OF SOCIAL SERVICES (HALIFAX) (CN/0383-4808) [02241198] **5272**

ANNUAL REPORT - DEPARTMENT OF SPACE. GOVERNMENT OF INDIA (II/0376-5466) [05803366] **11**

ANNUAL REPORT - DEPARTMENT OF THE ENVIRONMENT (NORTHERN IRELAND) (UK) [03504862] **2160**

ANNUAL REPORT - DEPARTMENT OF THE INTERIOR (SA/0304-694X) [02241182] **4627**

ANNUAL REPORT / DEPARTMENT OF TOURISM (CN/0837-4171) [16656218] **5461**

ANNUAL REPORT / DEPARTMENT OF TRADE AND INDUSTRY (PH) [22464094] 1597, **822**

ANNUAL REPORT / DEPARTMENT OF TRADE & RESOURCES (AT/0158-040X) [I0158040X] **822**

ANNUAL REPORT / DEPARTMENT OF TRANSPORT AND COMMUNICATIONS (AT/1032-1896) [19299965] **5376**

ANNUAL REPORT / DEPARTMENT OF VETERANS AFFAIRS, ALABAMA (US) [08811671] **4035**

ANNUAL REPORT - DEPARTMENT OF WATER RESOURCES (AT) [20161176] **5529**

ANNUAL REPORT - DEPARTMENT ON AGING (CONNECTICUT) (US) [06967762] **5272**

ANNUAL REPORT / DEPT. OF EMPLOYMENT, VOCATIONAL EDUCATION, TRAINING, AND INDUSTRIAL RELATIONS (AT) [24037871] **1649**

● ANNUAL REPORT / DEPT. OF SOCIAL WELFARE, NEW ZEALAND (NZ) [28951945] **5272**

ANNUAL REPORT - DEPT. OF TRANSPORTATION AND PUBLIC FACILITIES (US) [04148044] **5376**

ANNUAL REPORT - DESERT BOTANICAL GARDEN (US) [23351008] 2409, **499**

ANNUAL — Alphabetical Title Index

ANNUAL REPORT / DET NORSKE VERITAS (NO) [08957080] 4250, **5447**

ANNUAL REPORT / DEVELOPMENT BANK OF SEYCHELLES (SE) [10367964] **771**

ANNUAL REPORT - DIAGNOSTIC RESEARCH ADVISORY GROUP, NATIONAL INSTITUTES OF HEALTH (US) [04277983] **3808**

ANNUAL REPORT: DIRECTORS' REPORT, BALANCE SHEET AND ACCOUNTS (II/0304-6966) [01797708] **2873**

ANNUAL REPORT - DIVISION OF CANCER CONTROL AND REHABILITATION (US) [03519068] **3808**

ANNUAL REPORT - DIVISION OF FORESTRY, FISHERIES, AND WILDLIFE DEVELOPMENT, TENNESSEE VALLEY AUTHORITY (US/0094-5021) [01793775] 2294, **2374**

ANNUAL REPORT - DIVISION OF LABOR AND INDUSTRY (MARYLAND) (US/0363-4485) [02466422] **1649**

ANNUAL REPORT / DIVISION OF LIBRARY DEVELOPMENT AND SERVICES (US) [21533435] **3190**

ANNUAL REPORT - DIVISION OF LONG-TERM CARE (US/0149-1539) [03319703] **5272**

ANNUAL REPORT / DIVISION OF MATERIALS SCIENCE AND TECHNOLOGY, CSIRO AUSTRALIA (AT) [23000695] 2096, **2100**

ANNUAL REPORT - DIVISION OF MENTAL HYGIENE AND MENTAL RETARDATION (US) [04519627] **4765**

ANNUAL REPORT / DIVISION OF PLANT INDUSTRY (US) [03453395] **2409**

ANNUAL REPORT - DIVISION OF REHABILITATION *See* BIENNIAL REPORT - STAFF SERVICES SECTION, DIVISION OF VOCATIONAL REHABILITATION **1911**

ANNUAL REPORT - DIVISION OF TUBERCULOSIS CONTROL (LEDGERS) (CN/0702-9306) [03981978] **3948**

ANNUAL REPORT - DIVISION OF VETERAN'S AFFAIRS (FLORIDA) (US) [04598328] **4035**

ANNUAL REPORT / DIVISION, SAVINGS AND LOAN ASSOCIATIONS AND SAVINGS BANKS (US) [25855662] **771**

ANNUAL REPORT / DRIED FRUITS RESEARCH COUNCIL (AT) [19548148] **2327**

ANNUAL REPORT - EARTH RESOURCES FOUNDATION. UNIVERSITY OF SYDNEY (AT/0156-0204) [I01560204] **2186**

ANNUAL REPORT / EAST-CENTRAL STATE OF NIGERIA, MINISTRY OF CO-OPERATIVES (NR) [08007821] **1541**

ANNUAL REPORT - EAST-WEST POPULATION INSTITUTE (US/0097-6032) [01798960] **4549**

ANNUAL REPORT / EASTERN HEALTH AND SOCIAL SERVICES BOARD, NORTHERN IRELAND (UK/0144-7084) [09295510] **4765**

ANNUAL REPORT - ECONOMIC AND SOCIAL COMMISSION FOR ASIA AND THE PACIFIC (US) [02246732] **5191**

ANNUAL REPORT / EDUCATION FACT FINDING COMMISSION, STATE OF NORTH DAKOTA, THE (US) [07513935] **1725**

ANNUAL REPORT - EDUCATIONAL COMMISSION FOR FOREIGN MEDICAL GRADUATES (US/0145-2037) [02705925] 1809, **3550**

ANNUAL REPORT / ELECTED OFFICIALS' RETIREMENT SYSTEM, STATE OF ARIZONA (US) [10167631] **4627**

ANNUAL REPORT - ELECTRICITY TRUST OF SOUTH AUSTRALIA (AT/0728-8069) [I07288069] **2035**

ANNUAL REPORT - EMPLOYEES' RETIREMENT SYSTEM (US/0435-4842) [01795245] **1649**

ANNUAL REPORT / EMPLOYMENT DEPARTMENT GROUP, TRAINING COMMISSION (UK) [20975612] **1649**

ANNUAL REPORT - EMPLOYMENT DIVISION (US/0099-1260) [02242280] **1649**

ANNUAL REPORT / ENAMI, EMPRESA NACIONAL DE MINERIA (CL) [08755156] **2133**

ANNUAL REPORT - ENGINEERING AND WATER SUPPLY DEPARTMENT ADELAIDE (AT/0728-7879) [I07287879] **2087**

ANNUAL REPORT - ENGLISH TOURIST BOARD (UK) [02790724] **5461**

ANNUAL REPORT - ENVIRONMENT CANADA (1980) (CN/0711-1320) [08003437] **2160**

ANNUAL REPORT - ENVIRONMENT PROTECTION AUTHORITY MELBOURNE (AT/0310-4796) [I03104796] **2160**

ANNUAL REPORT / ENVIRONMENTAL APPEAL BOARD (CN/1188-021X) [25423308] **3109**

ANNUAL REPORT - ENVIRONMENTAL CONTROL COUNCIL (CN/0317-3526) [01798539] **3109**

ANNUAL REPORT - ENVIRONMENTAL DEFENSE FUND (US/0091-9837) [01788497] **2160**

ANNUAL REPORT - ENVIRONMENTAL QUALITY COUNCIL (US/0091-0457) [01786324] **2160**

ANNUAL REPORT - EPIDEMIOLOGY & DISEASE CONTROL STUDY SECTION, NATIONAL INSTITUTES OF HEALTH (US) [04096430] 4765, **3734**

ANNUAL REPORT / EPILEPSY ADVISORY COMMITTEE, NATIONAL INSTITUTES OF HEALTH (US) [04023521] **3827**

ANNUAL REPORT / EQUAL OPPORTUNITIES COMMISSION (UK) [07888947] **4504**

ANNUAL REPORT - ETHIOPIA. YAERSA MINISTER. EXTENSION AND PROJECT IMPLEMENTATION DEPT (ET) [01792376] **60**

ANNUAL REPORT - ETHIOPIAN CHAMBER OF COMMERCE (ET/0376-544X) [01796277] **818**

ANNUAL REPORT / ETHNOGRAPHICAL MUSEUM (HU) [10861211] **228**

ANNUAL REPORT / EUROPEAN FOUNDATION FOR THE IMPROVEMENT OF LIVING AND WORKING CONDITIONS (LU) [14922982] **1649**

ANNUAL REPORT - EUROPEAN INVESTMENT BANK (BE/0071-2868) [01568453] 771, **891**

ANNUAL REPORT / EUROPEAN SCIENCE FOUNDATION (FR) [10616540] **5084**

ANNUAL REPORT - EXPORT DEVELOPMENT CORPORATION (CN/0709-1605) [01318869] **822**

ANNUAL REPORT - EXPORT PAYMENTS INSURANCE CORPORATION (AT/0311-953X) [01794758] **2873**

ANNUAL REPORT / EXTERNAL AFFAIRS AND INTERNATIONAL TRADE CANADA (CN/0848-4554) [22145648] **4515**

ANNUAL REPORT - FAMILY GUIDANCE ASSOCIATION OF ETHIOPIA (ET) [02477430] **588**

ANNUAL REPORT - FAMILY PLANNING ASSOCIATION OF KENYA (KE) [02244132] **588**

ANNUAL REPORT - FARM CREDIT CORPORATION (CN/0382-1501) [03013612] **771**

ANNUAL REPORT / FEDERAL AVIATION ADMINISTRATION (US) [30900168] **11**

ANNUAL REPORT / FEDERAL COMMUNICATIONS COMMISSION (US/0083-0585) [01249089] **1104**

ANNUAL REPORT / FEDERAL ENFORCEMENT TRAINING CENTER (US/0740-3038) [07768324] **3157**

ANNUAL REPORT / FEDERAL FINANCIAL INSTITUTIONS EXAMINATION COUNCIL (U.S.) (US) [08002533] **771**

ANNUAL REPORT / FEDERAL JUDICIAL CENTER (US/0096-8854) [01798567] **2934**

ANNUAL REPORT - FEDERAL POWER COMMISSION (US) [02532547] **1932**

ANNUAL REPORT - FEDERAL RESERVE BANK OF CLEVELAND (US/0361-798X) [01332214] **771**

ANNUAL REPORT - FIELD FOUNDATION OF ILLINOIS (US/0743-5118) [10582672] **5239**

ANNUAL REPORT / FINANCE AUTHORITY OF MAINE (US) [10706919] 1597, **771**

ANNUAL REPORT / FINANCIAL ACCOUNTING STANDARDS BOARD (US) [10771244] **738**

●ANNUAL REPORT / FINANCIAL INSTITUTIONS COMMISSION (CN/1192-0254) [26776231] 2873, **771**

ANNUAL REPORT / FIRST INTERSTATE BANCORP (US) [08340497] **639**

ANNUAL REPORT - FIRST NATIONAL STORES INC (US/0361-8706) [02687465] **2327**

ANNUAL REPORT, FISCAL YEAR ENDED JUNE 30 ... / STATE OF OKLAHOMA, STATE AUDITOR AND INSPECTOR (US) [11670181] **4710**

ANNUAL REPORT, FISCAL YEAR ... / STATE OF CONNECTICUT, SUPERIOR COURT, FAMILY DIVISION (US) [09490523] **3119**

ANNUAL REPORT, FISCAL YEAR ... VOCATIONAL EDUCATION IN ILLINOIS (US) [08165872] **1910**

ANNUAL REPORT - FISHERIES RESEARCH BOARD OF CANADA (CN/0068-7499) [01280422] **2294**

ANNUAL REPORT - FISHING INDUSTRY RESEARCH COMMITTEE (AT/0311-8959) [01794138] **2294**

ANNUAL REPORT - FLORIDA COOPERATIVE EXTENSION SERVICE (US/0890-2038) [04073979] **60**

ANNUAL REPORT FOR FISCAL YEAR ... / BUREAU OF LIBRARIES, MUSEUMS, AND ARCHAEOLOGICAL SERVICES (VI) [12198236] 4083, **3190**

ANNUAL REPORT FOR FISCAL YEAR ... / COMMODITY CREDIT CORPORATION (US) [20925804] **60**

ANNUAL REPORT FOR FISCAL YEAR ... / VERMONT STATE HOSPITAL (US) [03949245] 3920, **3776**

ANNUAL REPORT FOR ... / LEUMI MORTGAGE BANK LTD (IS) [08842209] **771**

ANNUAL REPORT FOR MAGNETIC OBSERVATORIES AND REPEAT STATIONS (CN) [17001420] **4443**

ANNUAL REPORT FOR NEBRASKA LAW ENFORCEMENT TRAINING CENTER *See* ANNUAL REPORT - NEBRASKA COMMISSION ON LAW ENFORCEMENT AND CRIMINAL JUSTICE **3157**

ANNUAL REPORT FOR ... / NEW YORK POWER AUTHORITY (US) [21959007] **4759**

ANNUAL REPORT FOR PERIOD ... / DEVELOPMENT AND SERVICES BOARD (NATAL) (SA) [10613904] **4765**

ANNUAL REPORT FOR ... SEASON (FIJI. SUGAR BOARD) (FJ) [07889772] **60**

ANNUAL REPORT FOR THE ADVISORY COUNCIL FOR TECHNICAL-VOCATIONAL EDUCATION IN TEXAS (US/0090-2799) [01784857] **1910**

ANNUAL REPORT FOR ... / THE AUSTRALIAN NATIONAL UNIVERSITY, DEPARTMENT OF ECONOMICS, RESEARCH SCHOOL OF PACIFIC STUDIES (AT) [16996670] **1462**

ANNUAL REPORT FOR THE ... FINANCIAL YEAR ... TO BE SUBMITTED AT THE GENERAL MEETING OF SHAREHOLDERS ON . *See* ANNUAL REPORT KLM ROYAL DUTCH AIRLINES **11**

ANNUAL REPORT FOR THE ... FISCAL YEAR / BANCO DE LA REPUBLICA ORIENTAL DEL URUGUAY (UY) [07793371] **771**

●ANNUAL REPORT FOR THE FISCAL YEAR ENDING ... / NOVA SCOTIA PROVINCIAL HEALTH COUNCIL (CN/1193-3003) [26776110] **4765**

ANNUAL REPORT FOR THE FISCAL YEAR JULY 1 ... TO JUNE 30 ... / THE METROPOLITAN WATER DISTRICT OF SOUTHERN CALIFORNIA (US) [08182068] **5529**

ANNUAL REPORT FOR THE FISCAL YEAR ... / SOUTH CAROLINA STATE BOARD OF EXAMINERS FOR NURSING HOME ADMINISTRATORS (US) [07841044] **3776**

ANNUAL REPORT FOR THE FISCAL YEAR ... TO THE GOVERNOR AND LEGISLATURE OF THE STATE OF WASHINGTON (US) [15033593] **4710**

ANNUAL REPORT FOR THE PERIOD ... / CANCER FOUNDATION OF WESTERN AUSTRALIA INC (AT/0819-8756) [11981277] **3808**

ANNUAL REPORT FOR THE PERIOD ... / QUEEN'S UNIVERSITY, CENTRE FOR RESOURCE STUDIES (CN) [07844970] **2186**

ANNUAL REPORT FOR THE YEAR ... / COMMISSIONER FOR CORPORATE AFFAIRS (AT) [12009680] **3095**

ANNUAL REPORT FOR THE YEAR ENDED 30 JUNE ... (AT) [17641788] **3190**

ANNUAL REPORT FOR THE YEAR ENDED 30TH JUNE ... / ABORIGINAL AFFAIRS PLANNING AUTHORITY (AT) [02438904] **4627**

ANNUAL REPORT FOR THE YEAR ENDED 30TH JUNE ... / AUSTRALIAN WINE AND BRANDY CORPORATION (AT) [09289028] **2363**

ANNUAL REPORT FOR THE YEAR ENDED 31 DECEMBER (IE) [23065518] **1462**

ANNUAL REPORT FOR THE YEAR ENDED AUGUST 31 ... / CENTRAL OFFICE (US) [08580233] **5272**

ANNUAL REPORT FOR THE YEAR ENDED ... / DAIRY CONTROL BOARD (SOUTH AFRICA) (SA) [10607959] **191**

ANNUAL REPORT FOR THE YEAR ENDED ... / EMPLOYMENT APPEALS TRIBUNAL (IE) [07523318] **3144**

ANNUAL REPORT FOR THE YEAR ENDED MARCH 31 ... / RESTRICTIVE TRADE PRACTICES COMMISSION (CANADA) (CN) [07969731] **3095**

Alphabetical Title Index — ANNUAL

ANNUAL REPORT FOR THE YEAR ENDED ... / MEXIA STATE SCHOOL (US) [07246159] **3550**

ANNUAL REPORT ... FOR THE YEAR ENDED NOVEMBER 30 ... / SANYO DENKI KABUSHIKI KAISHA (JA) [16539620] **2035**

ANNUAL REPORT FOR THE YEAR ENDED - ZIMBABWE. DIVISION OF LIVESTOCK AND PASTURES (RH) [07501729] **205**

ANNUAL REPORT FOR THE YEAR ENDING 30TH JUNE ... / GREAT SOUTHERN DEVELOPMENT AUTHORITY (AT) [20386387] **4627**

ANNUAL REPORT FOR THE YEAR ENDING 31ST DECEMBER ... / BANK OF SUDAN (SJ) [08146602] **771**

ANNUAL REPORT FOR THE YEAR ENDING JUNE 30 ... OF THE WORKERS' COMPENSATION AND REHABILITATION COMMISSION (AT) [17566861] **1649**

ANNUAL REPORT FOR THE YEAR ENDING JUNE 30 ... / SOUTH CAROLINA, STATE BOARD OF COSMETIC ART EXAMINERS (US) [03741207] **402**

ANNUAL REPORT FOR THE YEAR ENDING JUNE 30 ... / STATE OF MICHIGAN, DEPARTMENT OF COMMERCE (US) [06125435] **823**

ANNUAL REPORT FOR THE YEAR ENDING JUNE 30TH ... (AT) [09419431] **2133**

ANNUAL REPORT FOR THE YEAR ENDING MARCH 31 ... / SASKATCHEWAN HEALTH (CN) [07989890] **4765**

ANNUAL REPORT FOR THE YEAR ENDING ... / SKIPJACK SURVEY AND ASSESSMENT PROGRAMME (NL) [05048558] **2294**

ANNUAL REPORT FOR THE YEAR JULY 1 ...-JUNE 30 ... / STATE OF TENNESSEE, ALCOHOLIC BEVERAGE COMMISSION (US) [21005944] **1340**

ANNUAL REPORT FOR THE YEAR ... / REPUBLIC OF ZAMBIA, MINISTRY OF HOME AFFAIRS (ZA/0514-5562) [01474019] **4627**

ANNUAL REPORT FOR THE YEAR ... / STATE OF ARKANSAS, EMPLOYMENT SECURITY DIVISION, DEPARTMENT OF LABOR (US) [08705951] **2873, 1649**

ANNUAL REPORT FOR THE YEAR ... / TEA RESEARCH FOUNDATION OF KENYA (KE/0258-4476) [09816328] **163**

ANNUAL REPORT FOR THE YEARS ... / REPUBLIC OF ZAMBIA, MINISTRY OF LEGAL AFFAIRS (ZA) [07902830] **4627**

ANNUAL REPORT FOR ... / WESTERN AUSTRALIA, LEGISLATIVE ASSEMBLY, PUBLIC ACCOUNTS AND EXPENDITURE REVIEW COMMITTEE (AT) [19816931] **4710**

ANNUAL REPORT FOR YEAR ENDED 30 JUNE ... / QUEENSLAND RAILWAYS (AT) [11219950] **5429**

ANNUAL REPORT FOR YEAR ENDING 30 JUNE ... CONSERVATION COMMISSION OF THE NORTHERN TERRITORY (AT) [08334594] 4705, **2186**

ANNUAL REPORT / FORENSIC PSYCHIATRIC SERVICES COMMISSION OF BRITISH COLUMBIA (CN/1180-5463) [23265239] **3920**

ANNUAL REPORT - FOREST RESEARCH COUNCIL OF BRITISH COLUMBIA (CN/0826-1725) [10864474] **2374**

ANNUAL REPORT / FORESTRY COMMISSION OF TASMANIA (AT/1031-7740) [23271145] **2375**

ANNUAL REPORT / FOSTER CARE REVIEW BOARD (US) [10961821] **5272**

ANNUAL REPORT FROM THE SECRETARY OF THE DEPARTMENT OF HEALTH AND HUMAN SERVICES TO THE PRESIDENT AND CONGRESS OF THE UNITED STATES : DRUG ABUSE PREVENTION, TREATMENT, AND REHABILITATION (US/0739-246X) [08665319] **1341**

ANNUAL REPORT / GARDA SIOCHANA COMPLAINTS BOARD (IE) [20079428] **4627**

ANNUAL REPORT - GENERAL CLINICAL RESEARCH CENTERS COMMITTEE, NATIONAL INSTITUTES OF HEALTH (US) [04121969] **3776**

ANNUAL REPORT - GEORGETOWN SHIPYARD INC (CN/0704-8343) [03673993] **4174**

ANNUAL REPORT / GEORGIA DEPARTMENT OF TRANSPORTATION (US) [14562074] **5376**

ANNUAL REPORT - GEORGIA ORGANIZED CRIME PREVENTION COUNCIL (US/0362-9996) [02399012] **3157**

ANNUAL REPORT / GIRLS CLUBS OF AMERICA (US) [08734255] **1060**

ANNUAL REPORT / GOVERNMENT OF INDIA, DEPARTMENT OF NON-CONVENTIONAL ENERGY SOURCES, MINISTRY OF ENERGY (II) [10880718] **1932**

ANNUAL REPORT / GOVERNMENT OF INDIA, MINISTRY OF PETROLEUM AND CHEMICALS, DEPARTMENT OF CHEMICALS & PETROCHEMICALS (II) [23363995] 1020, **4250**

ANNUAL REPORT / GOVERNMENT OF WESTERN AUSTRALIA, DEPARTMENT OF COMPUTING & INFORMATION TECHNOLOGY (AT) [15996329] **4627**

ANNUAL REPORT - GOVERNOR'S COMMITTEE ON CRIME, DELINQUENCY AND CORRECTIONS (CHARLESTON) (US/0094-4238) [01794348] **3157**

ANNUAL REPORT - GOVERNOR'S COUNCIL ON DRUG AND ALCOHOL ABUSE (US/0149-7596) [03534985] **1341**

ANNUAL REPORT - GRADUATE DEPARTMENT OF LIBRARY SCIENCE, THE CATHOLIC UNIVERSITY OF AMERICA *See* ANNUAL REPORT - GRADUATE DEPT. OF LIBRARY AND INFORMATION SCIENCE, THE CATHOLIC UNIVERSITY OF AMERICA **3190**

ANNUAL REPORT - GRADUATE DEPT. OF LIBRARY AND INFORMATION SCIENCE, THE CATHOLIC UNIVERSITY OF AMERICA (US/0272-9385) [06191256] **3190**

ANNUAL REPORT - GREAT LAKES FISHERY COMMISSION (US/0072-7296) [01516101] **2294**

ANNUAL REPORT - GREATER LONDON COUNCIL. DEPT. OF PUBLIC HEALTH ENGINEERING (UK) [01792153] 1965, **4765**

ANNUAL REPORT / GROUP OF THIRTY (US/0735-2034) [08421228] 1632, **771**

ANNUAL REPORT - HARVARD UNIVERSITY. MUSEUM OF COMPARATIVE ZOOLOGY (US/1046-3143) [07137355] **5576**

ANNUAL REPORT / HAWAII COASTAL ZONE MANAGEMENT PROGRAM (US/0743-1767) [10502668] **2814**

ANNUAL REPORT / HAZELNUT MARKETING BOARD (US) [16927226] **163**

ANNUAL REPORT - HEALTH AND COMMUNITY SERVICES. NEW BRUNSWICK (CN/0838-3693) [18993328] **4765**

ANNUAL REPORT - HERITAGE CONSERVATION AND RECREATION SERVICE, MID-CONTINENT REGION (US) [04993107] **2186**

ANNUAL REPORT / HEWLETT-PACKARD COMPANY (US) [07532092] **639**

ANNUAL REPORT, HIGHWAY SAFETY IMPROVEMENT PROGRAMS IN VIRGINIA / PREPARED BY THE DIVISION OF TRAFFIC AND SAFETY FOR THE VIRGINIA DEPARTMENT OF HIGHWAYS AND TRANSPORTATION (US) [08697353] **4766**

ANNUAL REPORT - HISTORICAL SOCIETY OF YORK COUNTY (PA.) (US/0882-035X) [11654549] **2720**

ANNUAL REPORT - HOLLINGER MINES LIMITED (CN/0382-0734) [02275193] **2133**

ANNUAL REPORT / HOME DEVELOPMENT MUTUAL FUND (PHILIPPINES) (PH) [12016009] **2814**

ANNUAL REPORT, HORSE RACING, HARNESS RACING (US) [21569078] **2797**

ANNUAL REPORT / HORTICULTURE RESEARCH INTERNATIONAL (UK/0963-3235) [25835229] **2409**

ANNUAL REPORT - HOSPITALS AND HEALTH SERVICES COMMISSION (AT) [02246918] **3776**

ANNUAL REPORT / HOUSING AND BUILDING RESEARCH INSTITUTE, DACCA (BG) [07351924] **598**

ANNUAL REPORT / HOWARD UNIVERSITY COLLEGE OF MEDICINE (US/0278-5137) [07787552] 3550, **1809**

ANNUAL REPORT - HUNTINGTON LIBRARY, ART GALLERY, BOTANICAL GARDENS (US/0363-3306) [01639805] 4083, **3190**

ANNUAL REPORT / HYDRAULICS RESEARCH STATION (UK) [07082811] **2087**

ANNUAL REPORT / IEA COAL RESEARCH (UK) [13027698] **2133**

ANNUAL REPORT / IETE (II) [11900842] **2035**

ANNUAL REPORT - ILLINOIS DEPARTMENT OF BUSINESS AND ECONOMIC DEVELOPMENT (US/0090-1016) [01784692] **1546**

ANNUAL REPORT / ILLINOIS ENVIRONMENTAL FACILITIES FINANCING AUTHORITY (US) [07872491] **2160**

ANNUAL REPORT - ILLINOIS. GENERAL ASSEMBLY. LEGISLATIVE INVESTIGATING COMMITTEE (US/0276-9468) [04645966] **4627**

ANNUAL REPORT / ILLINOIS GUARDIANSHIP AND ADVOCACY COMMISSION *CEASED.* (US) [08173392] **2934**

ANNUAL REPORT - ILLINOIS HEALTH FACILITIES AUTHORITY (US) [04484057] **3776**

ANNUAL REPORT / ILLINOIS HEALTH FINANCE AUTHORITY (US) [06435919] **3776**

ANNUAL REPORT - ILLINOIS INSTITUTE FOR ENVIRONMENTAL QUALITY (US/0090-8967) [01786129] **2160**

ANNUAL REPORT INCLUDING ... OBJECTIVES AND ACTION PLANS - EQUAL OPPORTUNITIES FOR WOMEN (CN/0823-5864) [05895832] 4627, **5551**

ANNUAL REPORT / INDEPENDENT BROADCASTING AUTHORITY (UK) [20512208] **1126**

ANNUAL REPORT. INDIA. DEPT. OF RURAL DEVELOPMENT (II) [15482865] **1546**

ANNUAL REPORT - INDIA. NATIONAL REMOTE SENSING AGENCY (II) [10747943] **2554**

ANNUAL REPORT - INDIAN INSTITUTE OF FOREIGN TRADE (II/0073-6473) [01645495] **823**

ANNUAL REPORT - INDIAN NATIONAL SCIENTIFIC DOCUMENTATION CENTRE (II) [10786386] **3190**

ANNUAL REPORT - INDIANA ARTS COMMISSION (US/0098-2040) [02240836] **312**

ANNUAL REPORT / INDIANA STATE ADVISORY COUNCIL ON VOCATIONAL EDUCATION (US/0735-9764) [08530968] **1910**

ANNUAL REPORT - INDONESIAN NATIONAL SCIENTIFIC DOCUMENTATION CENTER (IO) [02906058] **5084**

ANNUAL REPORT / INDUSTRIAL BANK OF KOREA (KO) [22529108] **771**

ANNUAL REPORT - INDUSTRIAL ENVIRONMENTAL RESEARCH LABORATORY (US/0364-3964) [02628402] **2160**

ANNUAL REPORT / INDUSTRIAL TECHNOLOGY APPLICATION PROGRAM (UA) [12111345] **2096**

ANNUAL REPORT - INDUSTRIAL TRAINING COMMISSION OF VICTORIA (AT) [03318726] **370**

ANNUAL REPORT / INDUSTRY RESEARCH AND DEVELOPMENT BOARD (AT/1030-3316) [20475340] **1597**

ANNUAL REPORT, INFORMATION COMMISSIONER (CN/0826-9904) [11146360] **4627**

ANNUAL REPORT / INH (SP) [12607399] **4250**

ANNUAL REPORT - INSTITUTE FOR CONTEMPORARY HISTORY, UNIVERSITY OF THE ORANGE FREE STATE (SA) [03635021] **2610**

ANNUAL REPORT - INSTITUTE FOR NUCLEAR STUDY, UNIVERSITY OF TOKYO (JA) [02148770] **4445**

ANNUAL REPORT / INSTITUTE OF ATMOSPHERIC PHYSICS, ACADEMIA SINICA (CC) [13674057] **1420**

ANNUAL REPORT / INSTITUTE OF BIOLOGICAL RESOURCES (AT/0158-7404) [07263250] 442, **2186**

ANNUAL REPORT / INSTITUTE OF DEVELOPMENT STUDIES AT THE UNIVERSITY OF SUSSEX (UK) [01242861] **5191**

ANNUAL REPORT / INSTITUTE OF MANPOWER STUDIES (UK) [20030707] **1649**

ANNUAL REPORT / INSTITUTE OF OCCUPATIONAL HEALTH (FI) [07702335] **2859**

ANNUAL REPORT (INSTITUTE OF PHYSICAL SCIENCES (COMMONWEALTH SCIENTIFIC AND INDUSTRIAL RESEARCH ORGANIZATION)) (AT/0158-7439) [10999476] **4397**

ANNUAL REPORT / INSTITUTE OF PHYSICS, AARHUS UNIVERSITY (DK) [28475955] **4397**

ANNUAL REPORT / INSTITUTE OF RESOURCE ASSESSMENT (TZ/0856-2369) [20329685] **1597**

ANNUAL REPORT - INSURANCE CORPORATION OF BRITISH COLUMBIA (CN/0317-7947) [01796698] **2873**

ANNUAL REPORT : INTER-AMERICAN COMMISSION ON HUMAN RIGHTS (US) [03532508] **4504**

ANNUAL REPORT / INTER-AMERICAN DEVELOPMENT BANK (US/0074-087X) [02003688] **1462**

ANNUAL REPORT - INTERAGENCY COMMITTEE ON EMERGENCY MEDICAL SERVICES, HEALTH SERVICES ADMINISTRATION (US) [03998370] **3723**

ANNUAL REPORT - INTERIM COMPLIANCE PANEL (WASHINGTON) (US/0093-2396) [01788828] 2133, **2934**

ANNUAL — Alphabetical Title Index

ANNUAL REPORT. INTERNATIONAL BUREAU OF FISCAL DOCUMENTATION (NE) [05462930] **4710**

ANNUAL REPORT / INTERNATIONAL CENTER FOR THE DISABLED (US/0732-8826) [08444103] **3880, 4383**

ANNUAL REPORT / INTERNATIONAL CENTER OF PHOTOGRAPHY (US) [20102646] **4366**

ANNUAL REPORT - INTERNATIONAL CENTRE FOR DIARRHOEAL DISEASE RESEARCH (BG/0253-5386) [07914814] **3743**

ANNUAL REPORT / INTERNATIONAL CENTRE FOR RESEARCH IN AGROFORESTRY (KE) [26987695] **2375**

ANNUAL REPORT - INTERNATIONAL CENTRE FOR THEORETICAL PHYSICS (IT/0304-7091) [01792393] **4397**

ANNUAL REPORT - INTERNATIONAL COMMITTEE OF THE RED CROSS (SZ) [02513942] **5272**

ANNUAL REPORT / INTERNATIONAL FERTILIZER DEVELOPMENT CENTER (US/0748-5875) [10972393] **163**

ANNUAL REPORT - INTERNATIONAL INSTITUTE FOR LAND RECLAMATION AND IMPROVEMENT (NE/0155-1803) [01730673] **4627**

ANNUAL REPORT - INTERNATIONAL METEOROLOGICAL INSTITUTE IN STOCKHOLM (SW/0349-0068) [01793922] **1420**

ANNUAL REPORT - INTERNATIONAL PACIFIC HALIBUT COMMISSION (US/0074-7238) [01753664] **2294**

ANNUAL REPORT - INTERNATIONAL PLANNED PARENTHOOD FEDERATION (UK/0307-6857) [02339974] **2276**

ANNUAL REPORT / INTERNATIONAL PLANNED PARENTHOOD FEDERATION (UK) [17806950] **4549**

ANNUAL REPORT - INTERNATIONAL TIN COUNCIL **CEASED.** (UK/0074-9125) [02381087] **3998**

ANNUAL REPORT / INVESTMENT CANADA (CN/0839-9506) [15181417] **891**

ANNUAL REPORT - IONOSPHERE PREDICTION SERVICE (CANBERRA) (AT/0311-0877) [01795938] **1420**

ANNUAL REPORT - IOWA DEPARTMENT FOR THE BLIND (US) [19565807] **4383**

ANNUAL REPORT - IOWA DEPARTMENT OF ELDER AFFAIRS (US) [17524897] **3749**

ANNUAL REPORT - IOWA DEPARTMENT OF PUBLIC SAFETY (US) [06318988] **4766**

ANNUAL REPORT / IOWA DEPARTMENT OF WATER, AIR, AND WASTE MANAGEMENT (US) [11456175] **2224**

ANNUAL REPORT, IOWA'S IMPLEMENTATION OF THE CAREER EDUCATION INCENTIVE ACT PUBLIC LAW 95-207 (US) [09907548] **1725**

ANNUAL REPORT - IRISH SEA FISHERIES BOARD (IE/0578-736X) [01973150] **2294**

ANNUAL REPORT : ISLAMIC DEVELOPMENT BANK (SU) [03373747] **771**

ANNUAL REPORT / JOHN TYLER COMMUNITY COLLEGE (US) [11957234] **1809**

ANNUAL REPORT - JOINT FEDERAL-STATE LAND USE PLANNING COMMISSION FOR ALASKA (US/0094-9515) [01794590] **4627**

ANNUAL REPORT. JUDGES OF THE PROVINCIAL COURT SUPERANNUATION FUND (CN/0711-2807) [08462231] **3139**

ANNUAL REPORT - JUSTICE DEVELOPMENT COMMISSION (BRITISH COLUMBIA) (CN/0706-3806) [04441888] **2934**

ANNUAL REPORT - JUSTICE INSTITUTE OF BRITISH COLUMBIA (CN/0709-9983) [06032624] **2934**

ANNUAL REPORT / JUSTICE SOCIETY (UK) [01638885] **2934**

ANNUAL REPORT / KANSAS ADVISORY COUNCIL ON AGING (US/0743-0981) [08359792] **3749**

ANNUAL REPORT / KAWASAKI HEAVY INDUSTRIES, LTD (JA/0287-1793) [10427453] **1597**

ANNUAL REPORT / KEELE UNIVERSITY (UK) [19651409] **1809**

ANNUAL REPORT - KENTUCKY MANPOWER DEVELOPMENT, INC (US/0095-5574) [01796506] **3913**

ANNUAL REPORT / KENYA AGRICULTURAL RESEARCH INSTITUTE, VETERINARY RESEARCH DEPARTMENT (KE) [13647485] **60, 5503**

ANNUAL REPORT - KENYA. MINISTRY OF LABOUR (KE/0075-5893) [01784039] **1649**

ANNUAL REPORT / KENYA RAILWAYS (KE) [17844839] **5429, 4627**

ANNUAL REPORT / KENYA TUBERCULOSIS AND RESPIRATORY DISEASES RESEARCH CENTRE (KE/1015-0072) [11055589] **3948**

ANNUAL REPORT - KILOMBERO SUGAR COMPANY (TZ) [03525697] **2327**

ANNUAL REPORT KLM ROYAL DUTCH AIRLINES (NE) [06646403] **11**

ANNUAL REPORT - KREDIETBANK, N. V., BRUSSELS (BE) [01783572] **771**

ANNUAL REPORT - KUCHING WATER BOARD (MY) [01783609] **5529, 4759**

ANNUAL REPORT / KUWAIT PETROLEUM CORPORATION (KU) [09726304] **4250**

ANNUAL REPORT / LAND AUTHORITY FOR WALES (UK) [07515591] **4627**

ANNUAL REPORT - LAND BANK OF THE PHILIPPINES (PH) [03139270] **771**

ANNUAL REPORT - LAND RESOURCE SCIENCE. UNIVERSITY OF GUELPH (CN/0820-3997) [13980981] **163**

ANNUAL REPORT / LATIN AMERICAN RESERVE FUND (CK) [25496294] **771**

ANNUAL REPORT / LAW LIBRARY, SUPREME COURT OF WESTERN AUSTRALIA (AT) [11063123] **2934, 3190**

ANNUAL REPORT - LAW REFORM COMMISSION OF CANADA (CN/0382-1463) [02885904] **2934**

ANNUAL REPORT / LEGISLATIVE AUDIT COMMITTEE. (COLORADO) (US/0588-4519) [04173434] **4710**

ANNUAL REPORT / LEGISLATIVE SERVICE OFFICE - WYOMING (US) [05588638] **4627**

ANNUAL REPORT / LIBRARY COUNCIL OF NEW SOUTH WALES (AT/0155-4204) [19413447] **3190**

ANNUAL REPORT - LIPID METABOLISM ADVISORY COMMITTEE, NATIONAL INSTITUTES OF HEALTH (US) [04050043] **4766**

ANNUAL REPORT - LIQUEFIED PETROLEUM GAS DIVISION OF THE RAILROAD COMMISSION OF TEXAS (US/0492-8717) [01227590] **4250**

ANNUAL REPORT - LLOYD'S REGISTER OF SHIPPING (UK) [04483934] **771**

ANNUAL REPORT - LOS ANGELES COUNTY AREA AGENCY ON AGING, ADVISORY COUNCIL (US) [06430144] **5272**

ANNUAL REPORT / LOS ANGELES OLYMPIC ORGANIZING COMMITTEE (US/0884-1276) [12207469] **4883**

ANNUAL REPORT / LOS ANGELES POLICE DEPARTMENT (US/0275-0872) [01586017] **3157**

ANNUAL REPORT - LOUISIANA STATE BAR ASSOCIATION (US/0882-9845) [11925823] **2934**

ANNUAL REPORT - LOWER COLORADO RIVER AUTHORITY (US/0162-0320) [04082081] **2087**

ANNUAL REPORT / MACAULAY LAND USE RESEARCH INSTITUTE (UK/0954-7010) [19400321] **163**

ANNUAL REPORT / MACKAY PORT AUTHORITY (AT) [17636030] **5447**

● ANNUAL REPORT / MAINE AGRICULTURAL AND FOREST EXPERIMENT STATION, UNIVERSITY OF MAINE (US) [30836646] **60**

ANNUAL REPORT / MAINE DEPARTMENT OF TRANSPORTATION, BRIDGE DESIGN SECTION (US) [22631605] **5438**

ANNUAL REPORT - MAINE. DEPT. OF MARINE RESOURCES (US/0742-9061) [10443704] **442**

ANNUAL REPORT - MALAWI DEVELOPMENT CORPORATION (MW) [03526186] **1597**

ANNUAL REPORT - MALAYAN AGRICULTURAL PRODUCERS ASSOCIATION (MY/0580-5120) [01790682] **60**

ANNUAL REPORT / MANAGEMENT SERVICES AND RESEARCH UNIT, DEPARTMENT OF HEALTH (NEW ZEALAND) (NZ) [10718094] **4766**

ANNUAL REPORT / MANITOBA CROP INSURANCE CORPORATION (CN/0542-5395) [03219303] **60, 2873**

ANNUAL REPORT / MANITOBA DATA SERVICES (CN/0715-6758) [09362940] **1235**

ANNUAL REPORT - MANITOBA ENVIRONMENT AND WORKPLACE SAFETY AND HEALTH (CN/0845-9606) [13570799] **2224, 2160**

ANNUAL REPORT - MANITOBA ENVIRONMENTAL COUNCIL (CN/0380-9803) [02239748] **2160**

ANNUAL REPORT - MANITOBA HEALTH RESEARCH COUNCIL (US/0844-9430) [11087303] **3550**

ANNUAL REPORT / MANITOBA LOTTERIES FOUNDATION (CN/0837-6840) [14219516] **4627**

ANNUAL REPORT - MANITOBA NATURAL RESOURCES (CN/0837-6786) [17863583] **2133**

ANNUAL REPORT / MANITOBA RESEARCH COUNCIL (CN/0837-6425) [17863857] **4464**

ANNUAL REPORT / MARCH OF DIMES BIRTH DEFECTS FOUNDATION (US/0730-1286) [07318851] **4766, 3551**

ANNUAL REPORT - MARKET DEVELOPMENT CENTRE (CN) [01788485] **921**

ANNUAL REPORT - MARYLAND. ADVISORY COUNCIL ON ALCOHOLISM CONTROL (US/0883-3249) [12038542] **1341**

ANNUAL REPORT - MARYLAND AGRICULTURAL EXPERIMENT STATION (US/0096-8676) [06262320] **61**

ANNUAL REPORT / MARYLAND COMMISSION ON HEREDITARY DISORDERS (US/0882-8997) [11858065] **542**

ANNUAL REPORT - MARYLAND HIGH BLOOD PRESSURE COMMISSION (US/8755-707X) [11364103] **3699**

ANNUAL REPORT - MARYLAND HISTORICAL TRUST (US/0098-3403) [02240696] **2720**

ANNUAL REPORT / MARYLAND HOUSING FUND (US) [11383112] **2873**

ANNUAL REPORT - MASSACHUSETTS ADVOCACY CENTER (US/0362-1383) [02303918] **2934**

ANNUAL REPORT / MASSACHUSETTS DEPARTMENT OF SOCIAL SERVICES (US) [11940399] **5272**

ANNUAL REPORT - MASSACHUSETTS HOME MORTGAGE FINANCE AGENCY (US/0271-1621) [05953148] **771**

ANNUAL REPORT - MASSACHUSETTS INDUSTRIAL FINANCE AGENCY (US) [06557876] **771**

ANNUAL REPORT - MASSACHUSETTS LABOR RELATIONS COMMISSION (US/0147-6475) [03208139] **3144**

ANNUAL REPORT / MASSACHUSETTS TECHNOLOGY DEVELOPMENT CORPORATION (US/0275-1917) [07083541] **5084**

ANNUAL REPORT - MEDICAL DEVICES APPLICATIONS COMMITTEE, NATIONAL INSTITUTES OF HEALTH (US) [04049625] **3551**

ANNUAL REPORT - (MEDIEVAL SETTLEMENT RESEARCH GROUP) (UK) [17474228] **2675**

ANNUAL REPORT - MEDIUM INDUSTRY BANK (KO) [03765708] **771**

ANNUAL REPORT - MEGHALAYA INDUSTRIAL DEVELOPMENT CORPORATION LIMITED (II) [01797722] **1597**

ANNUAL REPORT / MENTAL HEALTH COMMISSION OF NEW BRUNSWICK (CN/1183-997X) [25127853] **5272, 4766**

ANNUAL REPORT / MENTAL HEALTH COMMISSION OF NEW BRUNSWICK (CN/1183-997X) [25127848] **4766**

ANNUAL REPORT - MENTAL HEALTH COMMISSION OF NEW BRUNSWICK. REGION II (CN/1187-7243) [25608107] **3920**

ANNUAL REPORT - MENTAL HYGIENE ADMINISTRATION (US/0270-3300) [06366713] **4766**

ANNUAL REPORT - METROPOLITAN TRANSIT COMMISSION (US/0082-710X) [01794106] **5376**

ANNUAL REPORT - METROPOLITAN WATER BOARD (AT) [01786685] **4759, 5529**

ANNUAL REPORT - MICHIGAN DEPARTMENT OF CIVIL SERVICE (US) [06350466] **4701**

ANNUAL REPORT / MICHIGAN DEPARTMENT OF MENTAL HEALTH, RECIPIENT RIGHTS COMMITTEE (US) [23158512] **3920**

ANNUAL REPORT - MICHIGAN STATE BOARD OF EDUCATION (US) [06875436] **1725**

ANNUAL REPORT, MICHIGAN TRANSPORTATION FUND (US) [11227333] **5376**

ANNUAL REPORT - MICHIGAN VETERANS TRUST FUND. BOARD OF TRUSTEES (US) [10952518] **4035**

ANNUAL REPORT - MIDWEST REGION LIBRARY NETWORK (US) [06547047] **3190**

● ANNUAL REPORT. MIKROELEKTRONIK CENTRET (DK) **2035**

ANNUAL REPORT - MILWAUKEE COUNTY TRANSIT BOARD (US) [04442637] **5376**

ANNUAL REPORT - MINDOLO ECUMENICAL FOUNDATION (RH) [03956083] **4935**

Alphabetical Title Index — **ANNUAL**

ANNUAL REPORT / MINERALS AND ENERGY RESEARCH INSTITUTE OF WESTERN AUSTRALIA (AT/1032-111X) [22202531] **1932**

ANNUAL REPORT / MINISTRY OF CITIZENSHIP (CN/0840-7185) [20020108] **4627**

ANNUAL REPORT - MINISTRY OF CULTURE AND COMMUNICATIONS (TORONTO) (CN/0840-7193) [20349402] **1149**

ANNUAL REPORT - MINISTRY OF GOVERNMENT SERVICES (CN/0317-6827) [01796003] **4627**

ANNUAL REPORT - MINISTRY OF HEALTH (VICTORIA) (CN/0706-4810) [04631542] **4766**

ANNUAL REPORT - MINISTRY OF HOUSING (TORONTO. 1986) (CN/0835-0213) [16395729] **2814**

ANNUAL REPORT - MINISTRY OF LABOUR AND CONSUMER SERVICES (VICTORIA) (CN/0836-1126) [17680765] **1649**

ANNUAL REPORT - MINISTRY OF PARKS (VICTORIA) (CN/0847-4516) [22443764] **4705**

ANNUAL REPORT - MINISTRY OF THE ATTORNEY GENERAL (TORONTO) (CN/0382-1803) [02534685] **3139**

ANNUAL REPORT - MINISTRY OF TOURISM AND RECREATION (TORONTO) (CN/0824-8915) [10992358] **5461**

ANNUAL REPORT, MINNESOTA BOARD ON JUDICIAL STANDARDS FOR THE CALENDAR YEAR ... / MINNESOTA BOARD ON JUDICIAL STANDARDS (US) [06247880] **3139**

ANNUAL REPORT / MINNESOTA DEPARTMENT OF JOBS AND TRAINING (US) [13530137] **1649**

ANNUAL REPORT / MINNESOTA. LIVESTOCK SANITARY BOARD *See* MINNESOTA. LIVESTOCK SANITARY BOARD. ANNUAL REPORT **5516**

ANNUAL REPORT ... / MINNESOTA PROGRAM FOR VICTIMS OF SEXUAL ASSAULT, MINNESOTA DEPARTMENT OF CORRECTIONS (US) [09329255] **5272**

ANNUAL REPORT - MISSISSIPPI AIR AND WATER POLLUTION CONTROL COMMISSION (US/0193-158X) [05120992] **2224**

ANNUAL REPORT - MISSISSIPPI ARTS COMMISSION (US/0360-1099) [02243528] **312**

ANNUAL REPORT - MISSISSIPPI. DEPT. OF WILDLIFE CONSERVATION (US/0733-2017) [08514642] **2186**

ANNUAL REPORT - MISSISSIPPI HEALTH CARE COMMISSION *CEASED.* (US) [07320677] **4766**

ANNUAL REPORT - MISSISSIPPI MARINE RESOURCES COUNCIL (US/0095-6783) [01798490] **1446**

ANNUAL REPORT / MISSISSIPPI SCHOOL FOR THE BLIND (US) [17946506] 1875, **4383**

ANNUAL REPORT / MISSISSIPPI, STATE DEPARTMENT OF HEALTH (US) [12158021] **4766**

ANNUAL REPORT - MISSOURI. DEPT. OF LABOR AND INDUSTRIAL RELATIONS (US) [01589957] **1649**

ANNUAL REPORT - MISSOURI ELECTIONS COMMISSION (US/0149-2403) [03057151] **4628**

ANNUAL REPORT / MISSOURI HIGHWAY & TRANSPORTATION COMMISSION (US) [11987662] **5438**

ANNUAL REPORT - MONTANA. BOARD OF MILK CONTROL (US) [01784903] **192**

ANNUAL REPORT - MONTANA. FIRE MARSHAL BUREAU (US/0732-9148) [08462522] **5272**

ANNUAL REPORT - MONTGOMERY COUNTY, MD *See* REPORT ON ACTIVITIES OF THE COUNTY GOVERNMENT DURING THE FISCAL YEAR, A **4681**

ANNUAL REPORT ... - MSU-DOE PLANT RESEARCH LABORATORY (US/0893-1674) [10128805] **499**

ANNUAL REPORT, MUNICIPAL EDUCATION DEPARTMENT, FOR THE YEAR ... (KE) [10522996] **1725**

ANNUAL REPORT / N.V. KONINKLIJKE NEDERLANDS VLIEGTUIGENFABRIEK FOKKER (NE) [10305043] **1597**

ANNUAL REPORT - NATAL PROVINCIAL LIBRARY SERVICE AND MUSEUM SERVICES (SA) [03295468] **3190**

ANNUAL REPORT - NATIONAL ADVISORY ENVIRONMENTAL HEALTH SCIENCES COUNCIL, NATIONAL INSTITUTES OF HEALTH (US) [03997025] **2161**

ANNUAL REPORT - NATIONAL ASSOCIATION OF INDEPENDENT SCHOOLS (US/0090-6239) [01785477] **1725**

ANNUAL REPORT / NATIONAL AUSTRALIA BANK LIMITED (AT) [20053685] **771**

ANNUAL REPORT / NATIONAL BANK OF ETHIOPIA (ET) [06527161] **771**

ANNUAL REPORT / NATIONAL BANK OF HUNGARY (HU) [11210036] **771**

ANNUAL REPORT - NATIONAL BLOOD RESOURCE PROGRAM ADVISORY COMMITTEE, NATIONAL INSTITUTES OF HEALTH (US) [03998252] **4766**

ANNUAL REPORT - NATIONAL BOARD OF MEDICAL EXAMINERS (US/0146-1524) [02824889] **3913**

ANNUAL REPORT - NATIONAL BUREAU OF ECONOMIC RESEARCH (US) [03066075] **1462**

ANNUAL REPORT - NATIONAL CANCER INSTITUTE, DIVISION OF CANCER BIOLOGY AND DIAGNOSIS (US/0148-8333) [03381330] **3808**

ANNUAL REPORT - NATIONAL CANCER INSTITUTE, DIVISION OF CANCER TREATMENT (US) [03509481] **3808**

ANNUAL REPORT - NATIONAL CANCER INSTITUTE (U.S.). DIVISION OF CANCER PREVENTION AND CONTROL (US/0883-3176) [12076241] **3808**

ANNUAL REPORT - NATIONAL CANCER INSTITUTE (U.S.). DIVISION OF EXTRAMURAL ACTIVITIES (US/0738-0372) [09480197] **3808**

ANNUAL REPORT - NATIONAL CANCER INSTITUTE (U.S.). FIELD STUDIES AND STATISTICS PROGRAM (US/0730-6911) [08030429] **3808**

ANNUAL REPORT - NATIONAL CENTER FOR RESOURCE RECOVERY (US) [03014347] **2224**

ANNUAL REPORT - NATIONAL CENTER FOR STATE COURTS (US/0196-5433) [03858867] **3139**

ANNUAL REPORT - NATIONAL COMMERCIAL FINANCE ASSOCIATION (U.S.) (US/8755-7754) [11383365] **771**

ANNUAL REPORT / NATIONAL COMMISSION ON LIBRARIES AND INFORMATION SCIENCE (US/1045-4837) [08986809] **3190**

ANNUAL REPORT - NATIONAL COUNCIL FOR EDUCATIONAL TECHNOLOGY (UK/0956-1242) [20278322] **1725**

ANNUAL REPORT - NATIONAL COUNCIL, NICRO (SA) [05686298] **3157**

ANNUAL REPORT - NATIONAL ENDOWMENT FOR THE ARTS/NATIONAL COUNCIL ON THE ARTS (US/0083-2103) [02533080] **313**

ANNUAL REPORT - NATIONAL ENERGY ADVISORY COMMITTEE CANBERRA (AT/0725-0827) [07250827] **1932**

ANNUAL REPORT / NATIONAL EYE INSTITUTE (US/0161-7699) [03993857] **3872**

ANNUAL REPORT - NATIONAL FARM PRODUCTS MARKETING COUNCIL (CN/0383-414X) [03827831] **61**

ANNUAL REPORT - NATIONAL FOUNDATION FOR ADVANCEMENT IN THE ARTS (U.S.) (US/0882-245X) [09310117] **313**

ANNUAL REPORT - NATIONAL GALLERY OF ART (U.S.) (US/0091-7222) [03225099] 4083, **336**

ANNUAL REPORT / NATIONAL GAS CONSUMERS' COUNCIL (GREAT BRITAIN) (UK) [10677074] **4628**

ANNUAL REPORT / NATIONAL HEART, LUNG, AND BLOOD INSTITUTE (US/0278-0577) [07661865] **3699**

ANNUAL REPORT - NATIONAL HYDATIDS COUNCIL (NZ/0110-9901) [04798006] **5503**

ANNUAL REPORT / NATIONAL INSTITUTE FOR COAL RESEARCH (SA/0250-2348) [12263581] **2133**

ANNUAL REPORT / NATIONAL INSTITUTE FOR GLOBAL ENVIRONMENTAL CHANGE (US) [24614450] **2161**

ANNUAL REPORT - NATIONAL INSTITUTE OF DENTAL RESEARCH (U.S.) (US/8756-6885) [11546686] **1316**

ANNUAL REPORT / NATIONAL INSTITUTE OF GENERAL MEDICAL SCIENCES (US/0565-775X) [03885183] **442**

ANNUAL REPORT / NATIONAL INSTITUTE OF GENETICS (JA) [05157524] **542**

ANNUAL REPORT - NATIONAL INSTITUTE OF HEALTH (U.S.). DIVISION OF RESEARCH SERVICES (US/0735-1992) [08030768] 5503, **3551**

ANNUAL REPORT - NATIONAL INSTITUTE OF HYGIENE (PL/0208-595X) [06366839] **4766**

ANNUAL REPORT - NATIONAL INSTITUTE OF MENTAL HEALTH (U.S.). DIVISION OF INTRAMURAL RESEARCH PROGRAMS (US/0747-6531) [10757754] **3920**

ANNUAL REPORT / NATIONAL INSTITUTE OF RURAL DEVELOPMENT (II) [09910073] **2814**

ANNUAL REPORT - NATIONAL INSTITUTES OF HEALTH (U.S.). BIOMEDICAL ENGINEERING AND INSTRUMENTATION BRANCH (US/8756-8144) [11641185] **3685**

ANNUAL REPORT - NATIONAL LIBRARY OF AUSTRALIA (AT) [02401117] **3190**

ANNUAL REPORT / NATIONAL LIBRARY OF CANADA / RAPPORT ANNUEL / BIBLIOTHEQUE NATIONALE DU CANADA (CN/0830-0089) [25590095] **3190**

ANNUAL REPORT / NATIONAL MANPOWER COMMISSION (SA) [23027288] **1649**

ANNUAL REPORT / NATIONAL MULTIPLE SCLEROSIS SOCIETY (US) [04267898] **3827**

ANNUAL REPORT - NATIONAL MUSEUM OF SCIENCE AND TECHNOLOGY (OTTAWA) (CN/1187-3728) [25796647] 5084, **4083**

ANNUAL REPORT - NATIONAL PARKS AND WILDLIFE SERVICE (ZAMBIA) (ZA) [03313051] **2186**

ANNUAL REPORT - NATIONAL PROFESSIONAL STANDARDS REVIEW COUNCIL *CEASED.* (US/0361-9052) [02246745] **3551**

ANNUAL REPORT - NATIONAL PSORIASIS FOUNDATION (U.S.) (US/8756-2243) [11481592] **3717**

ANNUAL REPORT - NATIONAL SCIENCE FOUNDATION (US/0083-2332) [01252438] **5084**

ANNUAL REPORT / NATIONAL SEVERE STORMS LABORATORY (US) [09246721] **1420**

ANNUAL REPORT / NATIONAL SOFT DRINK ASSOCIATION (US/0742-0390) [10231868] **2363**

ANNUAL REPORT / NATIONAL TRUST FOR HISTORIC PRESERVATION (US/0091-5467) [01785782] **2720**

ANNUAL REPORT / NATIONAL TRUST FOR SCOTLAND (UK) [12886070] **2675**

ANNUAL REPORT - NATIONAL TRUST OF AUSTRALIA, W.A (AT) [04972950] **4628**

ANNUAL REPORT - NATIONAL VEGETABLE RESEARCH STATION (UK/0510-002X) [02754886] **163**

ANNUAL REPORT - NAVY PERSONNEL RESEARCH AND DEVELOPMENT CENTER (U.S.) (US/0882-2417) [11760133] **4035**

ANNUAL REPORT - NEBRASKA COMMISSION ON LAW ENFORCEMENT AND CRIMINAL JUSTICE (US/0360-0483) [02243503] **3157**

ANNUAL REPORT ... / NEBRASKA WHEAT COMMITTEE (US) [07636960] **1597**

ANNUAL REPORT - NEW BRUNSWICK ARTS BOARD (CN/1187-2454) [24986873] **313**

ANNUAL REPORT / NEW BRUNSWICK ARTS BOARD (CN/1187-2454) [24986866] **313**

ANNUAL REPORT - NEW BRUNSWICK. DEPT. OF INTERGOVERNMENTAL AFFAIRS (CN/1183-2614) [23686741] **4628**

ANNUAL REPORT - NEW CASTLE STATE HOSPITAL (US/0145-773X) [02781558] **3776**

ANNUAL REPORT - NEW JERSEY CASINO CONTROL COMMISSION (US) [06471744] **3157**

ANNUAL REPORT / NEW JERSEY JUDICIARY (US) [07802263] **3139**

ANNUAL REPORT - NEW JERSEY NETWORK (FIRM) (US/0737-0733) [09289765] **1149**

ANNUAL REPORT / NEW JERSEY, PINELANDS COMMISSION (US) [12499435] **1462**

ANNUAL REPORT - NEW JERSEY STATE AGENCY FOR OLD AGE AND SURVIVORS' INSURANCE SERVICE *See* ANNUAL REPORT - NEW JERSEY. STATE AGENCY FOR SOCIAL SECURITY **5272**

ANNUAL REPORT - NEW JERSEY. STATE AGENCY FOR SOCIAL SECURITY (US) [01793400] 2873, **5272**

ANNUAL REPORT / NEW JERSEY WATER SUPPLY AUTHORITY (US) [09355114] **5529**

ANNUAL REPORT - NEW MEXICO DEPARTMENT OF GAME AND FISH (US) [01511328] **2294**

ANNUAL REPORT / NEW MEXICO, GOVERNOR'S COMMITTEE ON CONCERNS OF THE HANDICAPPED (US) [10201043] **5272**

ANNUAL REPORT - NEW MEXICO. REAL ESTATE COMMISSION (US/0092-413X) [01789829] **4834**

ANNUAL REPORT / NEW MEXICO RESEARCH AND DEVELOPMENT INSTITUTE (US) [15641576] **1932**

ANNUAL REPORT / NEW MEXICO STATE LAND OFFICE (US) [11393383] **4628**

ANNUAL   Alphabetical Title Index

ANNUAL REPORT ... NEW YORK, NEW JERSEY / PALISADES INTERSTATE PARK COMMISSION (US) [14922278] **4628**

ANNUAL REPORT / NEW YORK STATE ASSEMBLY, COMMITTEE ON CHILDREN & FAMILIES (US) [11781321] **3119**

ANNUAL REPORT / NEW YORK STATE ASSEMBLY, COMMITTEE ON CONSUMER AFFAIRS & PROTECTION (US) [11226946] **1293**

ANNUAL REPORT / NEW YORK STATE ASSEMBLY, COMMITTEE ON EDUCATION (US) [11788802] **1725**

ANNUAL REPORT / NEW YORK STATE ASSEMBLY, COMMITTEE ON VETERANS' AFFAIRS (US) [12128766] **4035**

ANNUAL REPORT / NEW YORK STATE ASSEMBLY, STANDING COMMITTEE ON GOVERNMENTAL OPERATIONS (US) [05254518] **4628**

ANNUAL REPORT - NEW YORK STATE DEPARTMENT OF COMMERCE (US/0731-0560) [05060145] **823**

ANNUAL REPORT - NEW YORK (STATE). DEPT. OF LABOR (US) [10953831] **1649**

ANNUAL REPORT - NEW YORK STATE HOUSING FINANCE AGENCY (US/0545-6533) [04715928] **2814**

ANNUAL REPORT - NEW YORK STATE MEDICAL CARE FACILITIES FINANCE AGENCY (US/0361-4018) [02246483] **3776**

ANNUAL REPORT / NEW YORK STATE, OFFICE OF ADVOCATE FOR THE DISABLED (US) [11707228] **4628**

ANNUAL REPORT / NEW YORK'S LOTTERY (US) [16903558] **4628**

ANNUAL REPORT - NEW ZEALAND COUNCIL FOR EDUCATIONAL RESEARCH (NZ/0545-7564) [02586361] **1725**

ANNUAL REPORT - NEWARK MUSEUM (US/8755-1411) [10370365] **4083**

ANNUAL REPORT / NEWFOUNDLAND FARM PRODUCTS CORPORATION (CN/1185-0418) [23659438] **61**

ANNUAL REPORT / NORFOLK SOUTHERN (US/0748-8750) [09571369] **5429**

ANNUAL REPORT / NORTH AMERICAN ELECTRIC RELIABILITY COUNCIL (US/1048-4744) [08873975] **2035**

ANNUAL REPORT - NORTH CAROLINA HUMAN RELATIONS COMMISSION (US/0093-5085) [01792290] **5191**

ANNUAL REPORT - NORTH DAKOTA STATE BOARD OF PHARMACY (US) [02253515] **4291**

ANNUAL REPORT - NORTHERN INDIANA HEALTH SYSTEMS AGENCY (US) [06638580] **4766**

ANNUAL REPORT - NORTHERN TERRITORY. DEPARTMENT OF PRIMARY INDUSTRY AND FISHERIES (AT/1034-7356) [22617013] **2294**

ANNUAL REPORT / NORTHWEST ATLANTIC FISHERIES ORGANIZATION (CN/0704-4798) [06680278] **2294**

ANNUAL REPORT - NOVA SCOTIA DEPARTMENT OF CONSUMER AFFAIRS (CN/0713-715X) [08620938] **1293**

ANNUAL REPORT - NURSING HOME OMBUDSMEN OFFICE (US) [04618445] **3776**

ANNUAL REPORT - NYS PROJECT FINANCE AGENCY (US/0275-3162) [05091788] **4628**

ANNUAL REPORT / OAK RIDGE ASSOCIATED UNIVERSITIES (US/0078-2904) [07600049] **4446**

ANNUAL REPORT, OCCUPATIONAL AND PROFESSIONAL LICENSING BOARDS / PREPARED BY THE STATE REORGANIZATION COMMISSION AND THE LEGISLATIVE AUDIT COUNCIL IN COOPERATION WITH THE BUDGET AND CONTROL BOARD (US) [07508074] **4201**

ANNUAL REPORT OF ACTIVITIES (US/0730-8914) [08055303] **4035**

ANNUAL REPORT OF ACTIVITIES / THE LEONARD DAVIS INSTITUTE FOR INTERNATIONAL RELATIONS (IS) [21709309] **4515**

ANNUAL REPORT OF AD HOC COMMITTEE ON GEODYNAMICS TO THE FEDERAL COUNCIL FOR SCIENCE AND TECHNOLOGY (US) [02955066] **5084**

ANNUAL REPORT OF AGRICULTURAL RESEARCH COUNCIL OF NIGERIA (NR) [03278161] **61**

ANNUAL REPORT ... OF ALBERTA HEALTH FACILITIES REVIEW COMMITTEE (CN/0713-1887) [06856805] **3776**

ANNUAL REPORT OF BOARD OF MEDICAL EXAMINERS (US/0734-337X) [08720607] **3913**

ANNUAL REPORT OF ... / BY THE ILLINOIS LEGISLATIVE INVESTIGATING COMMISSION (US) [08839562] **4628**

ANNUAL REPORT OF CANCER INCIDENCE IN MASSACHUSETTS (US/0888-7713) [11041206] **3808**

ANNUAL REPORT OF COMMISSIONER OF LABOR ... ON THE ECONOMY, WORKFORCE AND TRAINING NEEDS IN CONNECTICUT (US) [22356473] **1649**

ANNUAL REPORT OF COUNCIL AND ACCOUNTS - CHEMICAL SOCIETY (UK/0306-4875) [01795784] **961**

ANNUAL REPORT OF DEPARTMENT OF FISHERIES (HALIFAX) (CN/0550-1717) [02444038] **2295**

ANNUAL REPORT OF DEPARTMENT OF LABOR OF THE STATE OF ARKANSAS See ANNUAL REPORT - ARKANSAS DEPARTMENT OF LABOR **1648**

ANNUAL REPORT OF ECONOMIC SECURITY NEEDS AND RESOURCES (US) [04025701] **1649**

ANNUAL REPORT OF FEDERAL PREVAILING RATE ADVISORY COMMITTEE (US/0098-2296) [02240499] **4628**

ANNUAL REPORT OF ILLINOIS CREDIT UNIONS See ANNUAL REPORT OF ILLINOIS STATE CHARTERED CREDIT UNIONS **771**

ANNUAL REPORT OF ILLINOIS STATE CHARTERED CREDIT UNIONS (US) [04144702] **771**

ANNUAL REPORT OF INDIAN EDUCATION IN EASTERN OKLAHOMA (US) [08287043] 2255, **1725**

ANNUAL REPORT OF INTRAMURAL ACTIVITIES - NATIONAL INSTITUTE OF ALLERGY AND INFECTIOUS DISEASES (U.S.) (US/0882-2239) [11673796] 3666, **3712**

ANNUAL REPORT OF MUNICIPAL STATISTICS (CN) [02937458] **4696**

ANNUAL REPORT OF OHIONET (US/0270-0107) [06325139] **3190**

ANNUAL REPORT OF OKLAHOMA LIBRARIES / COMPILED BY THE OKLAHOMA DEPARTMENT OF LIBRARIES (US) [11952506] **3191**

ANNUAL REPORT OF OPERATIONS AND FOREST PEST CONDITIONS (US/0362-6482) [02309392] **2375**

ANNUAL REPORT OF OPERATIONS UNDER THE MEAT IMPORT ACT (CN/0837-2535) [18121227] **206**

ANNUAL REPORT OF OSAKA PREFECTURAL RADIATION RESEARCH INSTITUTE (JA) [20745057] **4433**

ANNUAL REPORT OF PROGRAMS AND EVALUATIONS OF THE CONNECTICUT STATE BOARD OF EDUCATION (US) [04069337] **1725**

ANNUAL REPORT OF RAILROAD ACCIDENTS OCCURRING IN CALIFORNIA AND REPORTED UNDER GENERAL ORDER 22-B AND ... / CALIFORNIA PUBLIC UTILITIES COMMISSION, TRANSPORTATION DIVISION, RAILROAD OPERATIONS AND SAFETY BRANCH (US) [06564176] **5429**

ANNUAL REPORT OF RAILROAD ACCIDENTS REPORTED UNDER GENERAL ORDER NO. 22-B FOR YEAR . See ANNUAL REPORT OF RAILROAD ACCIDENTS OCCURRING IN CALIFORNIA AND REPORTED UNDER GENERAL ORDER 22-B AND ... / CALIFORNIA PUBLIC UTILITIES COMMISSION, TRANSPORTATION DIVISION, RAILROAD OPERATIONS AND SAFETY BRANCH **5429**

ANNUAL REPORT OF SOUTH CAROLINA DEPARTMENT OF VETERANS AFFAIRS (US/0362-6229) [02328955] **4035**

ANNUAL REPORT OF STUDIES IN ANIMAL NUTRITION AND ALLIED SCIENCES CEASED. (UK/0307-8035) [02418089] **206**

ANNUAL REPORT OF SURVEY-INVENTORY ACTIVITIES (US/0362-6962) [02319911] **4869**

ANNUAL REPORT OF THE ACTIVITIES OF THE ALABAMA DEPT. OF PUBLIC HEALTH (US) [02241664] **4766**

ANNUAL REPORT OF THE AIR SURVEY DIVISION (TZ/0494-6367) [01241998] **2554**

ANNUAL REPORT OF THE ALBERTA HEALTH DISCIPLINES BOARD FOR THE PERIOD OF JANUARY 1 ... TO DECEMBER 31 (CN) [13442025] **4766**

ANNUAL REPORT OF THE ALCOHOLISM CONTROL ADMINISTRATION FOR ... - MARYLAND (US) [11329575] **1341**

ANNUAL REPORT OF THE AMERICAN BIBLE SOCIETY (US/0740-6401) [01479583] **5014**

ANNUAL REPORT OF THE AMERICAN HISTORICAL ASSOCIATION (US/0065-8561) [01150082] **2610**

ANNUAL REPORT OF THE ANIMAL HEALTH TRUST (UK/0142-6591) [06021374] **5503**

ANNUAL REPORT OF THE ARCHITECT OF THE CAPITOL FOR THE PERIOD ... (US/0738-5870) [05015128] **287**

ANNUAL REPORT OF THE ASSOCIATION OF OFFICIAL SEED CERTIFYING AGENCIES (US) [01772004] **163**

ANNUAL REPORT OF THE ATLANTIC STATES MARINE FISHERIES COMMISSION (US) [01112404] **2295**

ANNUAL REPORT OF THE ATTORNEY GENERAL OF THE UNITED STATES (US/0148-5229) [02394728] **3139**

ANNUAL REPORT OF THE AUDITOR GENERAL OF BRITISH COLUMBIA TO THE LEGISLATIVE ASSEMBLY (CN) [17670979] **4710**

ANNUAL REPORT OF THE AUDITOR GENERAL / STATE OF ARIZONA (US) [09480087] **4710**

ANNUAL REPORT OF THE AUDITOR-GENERAL UPON THE BOOKS AND ACCOUNTS OF THE BRISBANE CITY COUNCIL (AT) [07745445] **4710**

ANNUAL REPORT OF THE BEAN IMPROVEMENT COOPERATIVE (US/0084-7747) [05058840] **163**

ANNUAL REPORT OF THE BOARD OF DIRECTORS OF THE RURAL TELEPHONE BANK (US) [20921372] **1149**

ANNUAL REPORT OF THE BOARD OF EXAMINERS FOR COUNTY HIGHWAY AND CITY STREET SUPERINTENDENTS (US/0098-6364) [02239485] **5438**

ANNUAL REPORT OF THE BOARD OF PHARMACY OF THE STATE OF ARIZONA (US/0899-8612) [05097523] **4291**

ANNUAL REPORT OF THE BOARD OF TRUSTEES FOR THE YEAR - PUBLIC ARCHIVES OF NOVA SCOTIA (CN/0846-7951) [21496236] **2479**

ANNUAL REPORT OF THE BOARD OF VISITORS OF THE BUFFALO PSYCHIATRIC CENTER TO THE DEPARTMENT OF MENTAL HYGIENE (US/0198-8034) [06209827] **3920**

ANNUAL REPORT OF THE BRITISH TOURIST AUTHORITY (UK) [05105436] **5461**

ANNUAL REPORT OF THE BUREAU OF FINANCIAL INSTITUTIONS, STATE CORPORATION COMMISSION, COMMONWEALTH OF VIRGINIA (US) [05541896] **771**

ANNUAL REPORT OF THE CALENDAR YEAR ENDING DECEMBER 31 . See ANNUAL REPORT / VERMONT LOTTERY **4630**

ANNUAL REPORT OF THE CALIFORNIA HORSE RACING BOARD FOR THE PERIOD JULY 1 ... TO JUNE 30 ... (US) [09746181] 4883, **2797**

ANNUAL REPORT OF THE CHAIRMAN OF THE COUNCIL OF THE NATIONAL LIBRARY AND DOCUMENTATION SERVICE FOR THE YEAR ENDED ... (RH) [26986082] **3191**

ANNUAL REPORT OF THE CHIEF ADMINISTRATOR OF THE COURTS - NEW YORK (US) [06833553] **3139**

ANNUAL REPORT OF THE CHIEF ELECTORAL OFFICER ADMINISTERING THE ELECTION FINANCES AND CONTRIBUTIONS DISCLOSURE ACT (CN/0227-8073) [06703847] **4628**

ANNUAL REPORT OF THE COLORADO JUDICIARY (US/0731-3195) [07651749] **3139**

ANNUAL REPORT OF THE COMMISSION OF BANKS RELATING TO CREDIT UNIONS FOR THE YEAR ENDED ... FINANICIAL STATEMENT (US) [20926405] **771**

ANNUAL REPORT OF THE COMMISSION ON FIRE PROTECTION, PERSONNEL STANDARDS, AND EDUCATION (US) [09931093] **2288**

ANNUAL REPORT OF THE COMMISSION ON JUDICIAL DISCIPLINE, STATE OF HAWAII (FOR PERIOD JUNE 1, ... TO JUNE 30, ...) (US) [07260764] **3139**

ANNUAL REPORT OF THE COMMISSIONER FOR CONSUMER AFFAIRS FOR THE YEAR ENDED JUNE 30 ... / GOVERNMENT OF WESTERN AUSTRALIA (AT) [10225774] **1293**

ANNUAL REPORT OF THE COMMISSIONER OF BANKS RELATING TO CREDIT UNIONS FOR THE YEAR ENDED ... OFFICERS (US) [20926372] **771**

ANNUAL REPORT OF THE COMMISSIONER OF LAND TAX ON THE OPERATION OF THE ACTS DURING THE YEAR ... / QUEENSLAND (AT) [16621726] **4628**

ANNUAL REPORT OF THE COMMISSIONER OF THE NORTHWEST TERRITORIES (CN/0549-9879) [01238239] **4628**

Alphabetical Title Index — ANNUAL

ANNUAL REPORT OF THE COMMISSIONER OF TRANSPORTATION TO THE GOVERNOR (US/0363-3330) [02468708] **5376**

ANNUAL REPORT OF THE COMMUNITY RELATIONS SERVICE (US) [10352657] 4504, **4628**

ANNUAL REPORT OF THE CONNECTICUT HISTORICAL SOCIETY, THE (US/0893-9780) [01141457] **2720**

ANNUAL REPORT OF THE CONNECTICUT STATE LIBRARY (US) [11655621] **3191**

ANNUAL REPORT OF THE CONSUMER AFFAIRS COUNCIL UPON THE ACTIVITIES OF THE COUNCIL (AT) [05068310] **1293**

ANNUAL REPORT OF THE CORRECTIONAL INVESTIGATOR (CN/0383-4379) [01799490] **3157**

ANNUAL REPORT OF THE COUNCIL (UK) [20042707] **11**

ANNUAL REPORT OF THE COUNCIL AND INSTITUTE ACCOUNTS (UK) [01787260] **2018**

ANNUAL REPORT OF THE COUNCIL OF THE CHARTERED INSTITUTE OF PATENT AGENTS FOR THE YEAR ENDED ... - (LONDON, ENG.) (UK) [11670260] **1301**

ANNUAL REPORT OF THE COUNCIL OF THE CORPORATION OF FOREIGN BONDHOLDERS (UK) [06391825] **891**

ANNUAL REPORT OF THE COUNCIL ON TRIBUNALS FOR THE PERIOD, THE (UK) [07630989] **4628**

ANNUAL REPORT OF THE CRIMINAL HISTORY SYSTEMS BOARD *See* COMBINED ANNUAL REPORTS FOR FISCAL YEAR ... **3160**

ANNUAL REPORT OF THE DELAWARE RACING COMMISSION TO THE GOVERNOR OF THE STATE OF DELAWARE (US) [04584348] **2797**

ANNUAL REPORT OF THE DELAWARE THOROUGHBRED RACING COMMISSION TO THE GOVERNOR OF THE STATE OF DELAWARE (US) [09014967] **2797**

ANNUAL REPORT OF THE DEPARTMENT FOR YOUTH, SPORT, AND RECREATION / GOVERNMENT OF WESTERN AUSTRALIA (AT) [07523519] **4848**

ANNUAL REPORT OF THE DEPARTMENT OF AGRICULTURE AND MARKETING (HALIFAX) (CN/0703-5977) [06758224] **61**

ANNUAL REPORT OF THE DEPARTMENT OF AGRICULTURE (MONTANA) (US/0092-9786) [01786186] **61**

ANNUAL REPORT OF THE DEPARTMENT OF ANIMAL HUSBANDRY AND VETERINARY SERVICES IN KARNATAKA, INDO-DANISH PROJECT HESSARGHATTA AND BANGALORE DAIRY, BANGALORE *CEASED.* (II) [02246652] 4628, **5503**

ANNUAL REPORT OF THE DEPARTMENT OF ANTIQUITIES FOR THE YEAR ... / REPUBLIC OF CYPRUS, MINISTRY OF COMMUNICATIONS WORKS (CY) [11602160] **255**

ANNUAL REPORT OF THE DEPARTMENT OF BUSINESS REGULATION (HELENA) (US/0093-8246) [01792867] **823**

ANNUAL REPORT OF THE DEPARTMENT OF COMMERCE AND INSURANCE (US) [11641228] 2873, **823**

ANNUAL REPORT OF THE DEPARTMENT OF CONSUMER AFFAIRS OF THE STATE OF SOUTH CAROLINA (US) [07695044] **1293**

ANNUAL REPORT OF THE DEPARTMENT OF INSURANCE OF THE STATE OF INDIANA FOR THE FISCAL YEAR ENDING SEPTEMBER 30 ... (US) [07728504] **2873**

ANNUAL REPORT OF THE DEPARTMENT OF LABOR AND INDUSTRIAL RELATIONS, STATE OF HAWAII (US/0438-7473) [01199915] **1649**

ANNUAL REPORT OF THE DEPARTMENT OF MILITARY AFFAIRS TO THE GOVERNOR OF MONTANA (US/0091-0368) [01785846] **4035**

ANNUAL REPORT OF THE DEPARTMENT OF NATURAL RESOURCES (REGINA) (CN) [01172071] **2186**

ANNUAL REPORT OF THE DEPARTMENT OF POSTAL SERVICES (CYPRUS) (CY/0256-8535) [06685718] **1144**

ANNUAL REPORT OF THE DEPARTMENT OF POSTS *See* ANNUAL REPORT OF THE DEPARTMENT OF POSTAL SERVICES (CYPRUS) **1144**

ANNUAL REPORT OF THE DEPARTMENT OF SOCIAL AND REHABILITATION SERVICES TO THE GOVERNOR OF MONTANA (US/0091-0996) [01786172] **5272**

ANNUAL REPORT OF THE DEPARTMENT OF SPORT AND RECREATION FOR THE YEAR ENDED (AT) [29130999] 4883, **4848**

ANNUAL REPORT OF THE DEPARTMENT OF TOWN AND COUNTRY PLANNING (ZA) [27331800] **2814**

ANNUAL REPORT OF THE DEPARTMENT OF TRANSPORT FOR THE YEAR ENDED JUNE 30 ... (AT) [16824448] **5376**

ANNUAL REPORT OF THE DEPARTMENT OF WATER AND NATURAL RESOURCES ON THE WATER RESOURCES MANAGEMENT SYSTEM (SOUTH DAKOTA) (US) [07663883] **5529**

ANNUAL REPORT OF THE DIGESTIVE DISEASES COORDINATING COMMITTEE TO THE SECRETARY, U.S. DEPARTMENT OF HEALTH AND HUMAN SERVICES (US/0891-8465) [08576668] **3795**

ANNUAL REPORT OF THE DIRECTOR GENERAL, AGRICULTURE AND FISHERIES FOR THE PERIOD 1 APRIL ... TO 31 MARCH / REPUBLIC OF SOUTH AFRICA (SA) [09311486] 2295, **61**

ANNUAL REPORT OF THE DIRECTOR GENERAL, AGRICULTURE FOR THE PERIOD ... / REPUBLIC OF SOUTH AFRICA, DEPARTMENT OF AGRICULTURE (SA) [10227928] **61**

ANNUAL REPORT OF THE DIRECTOR GENERAL OF FAIR TRADING TO THE SECRETARY OF STATE FOR PRICES AND CONSUMER PROTECTION (GREAT BRITAIN) *CEASED.* (UK) [02247037] 1293, **823**

ANNUAL REPORT OF THE DIRECTOR, HOUSING DEVELOPMENT AND MANAGEMENT DEPARTMENT FOR THE YEAR.../CITY COUNCIL OF NAIROBI (KE) [10975257] **2814**

ANNUAL REPORT OF THE DIRECTOR OF SOCIAL SERVICES & HOUSING FOR THE YEAR - MOMBASA KENYA (KE) [16372942] 2814, **5272**

ANNUAL REPORT OF THE DIRECTOR OF THE ARNOLD ARBORETUM TO THE PRESIDENT AND FELLOWS OF HARVARD UNIVERSITY FOR . *See* DIRECTOR'S REPORT FOR THE ARNOLD ARBORETUM, THE **508**

ANNUAL REPORT OF THE DIRECTOR OF WORKS FOR THE YEAR (RH) [19476759] **4628**

ANNUAL REPORT OF THE DIRECTOR - PAN AMERICAN SANITARY BUREAU. BUREAU (US/0085-462X) [06297093] **3712**

ANNUAL REPORT OF THE DIRECTOR TO THE BOARD OF GOVERNORS (UK) [03857986] **4628**

ANNUAL REPORT OF THE DIVISION OF BIOLOGICAL EFFECTS, BUREAU OF RADIOLOGICAL HEALTH / PREPARED BY DIVISION OF BIOLOGICAL EFFECTS STAFF (US) [08288165] **3939**

ANNUAL REPORT OF THE DIVISION OF FISH AND GAME, INDIANA DEPARTMENT OF CONSERVATION (US/0442-7637) [01506555] **2186**

ANNUAL REPORT OF THE DIVISION OF SOCIAL SERVICES OF THE DEPARTMENT OF HEALTH AND SOCIAL SERVICES (US/0090-3051) [01784907] **5272**

ANNUAL REPORT OF THE DUKE ENDOWMENT (US) [01782936] **4334**

ANNUAL REPORT OF THE EASTERN ENVIRONMENTAL RADIATION FACILITY, U. S. ENVIRONMENTAL PROTECTION AGENCY (US/0361-9087) [02385477] **2161**

ANNUAL REPORT OF THE ELECTRICITY DIVISION FOR THE YEAR ... (SEYCHELLES) (SE) [07534059] **4628**

ANNUAL REPORT OF THE EQUAL OPPORTUNITY BOARD (AT) [07036445] **4504**

ANNUAL REPORT OF THE EUROPEAN FREE TRADE ASSOCIATION (SZ/0531-4127) [01234798] **823**

ANNUAL REPORT OF THE EUROPEAN ORGANIZATION FOR NUCLEAR RESEARCH (SZ/0071-2973) [02385761] **4446**

ANNUAL REPORT OF THE EXECUTIVE BOARD - INTERNATIONAL MONETARY FUND (US/0250-7498) [05705422] **1632**

ANNUAL REPORT OF THE EXECUTIVE DIRECTOR *See* ANNUAL REPORTS **2935**

ANNUAL REPORT OF THE FAMILY PLANNING ASSOCIATION OF HONG KONG (CC) [03619118] **588**

ANNUAL REPORT OF THE FARM CREDIT ADMINISTRATION (US/0883-329X) [03107752] **61**

ANNUAL REPORT OF THE FARM CREDIT ADMINISTRATION AND THE COOPERATIVE FARM CREDIT SYSTEM (US) [02707165] **61**

ANNUAL REPORT OF THE FEDERAL LABOR RELATIONS AUTHORITY AND THE FEDERAL SERVICE IMPASSES PANEL FOR THE FISCAL PERIOD ... (US/0275-200X) [07083123] **1649**

ANNUAL REPORT OF THE FEDERAL TRADE COMMISSION (US) [02859166] 1293, **823**

ANNUAL REPORT OF THE FISHERIES DEVELOPMENT AUTHORITY FOR THE YEAR ENDING 30 JUNE ... (TASMANIA) (AT) [07523273] **2295**

ANNUAL REPORT OF THE FORESTRY RESEARCH INSTITUTE OF NIGERIA FOR THE PERIOD ... (NR/0331-3751) [04324207] **2375**

ANNUAL REPORT OF THE GAZANKULU PUBLIC SERVICE COMMISSION, GAZANKULU GOVERNMENT (SA) [17156482] **4701**

ANNUAL REPORT OF THE GEOLOGICAL SURVEY AND MINES DEPARTMENT, SWAZILAND (SQ) [02010522] **1365**

ANNUAL REPORT OF THE GEOLOGICAL SURVEY DEPARTMENT (LUSAKA) (ZA/0084-473X) [02246882] **1365**

ANNUAL REPORT OF THE GEOLOGICAL SURVEY. NEW HEBRIDES CONDOMINIUM (NN/0077-8435) [09145577] **1365**

ANNUAL REPORT OF THE GOVERNMENT OF THE NORTHWEST TERRITORIES (CN/0384-2479) [02885575] **4628**

ANNUAL REPORT OF THE HARNESS RACING COMMISSION TO THE GOVERNOR OF MAINE *See* REPORT OF THE ... RACING SEASON / MAINE STATE HARNESS RACING COMMISSION **4915**

ANNUAL REPORT OF THE IDAHO DEPARTMENT OF LABOR AND INDUSTRIAL SERVICES (US/0362-3912) [02299708] **1649**

ANNUAL REPORT OF THE IDAHO DEPARTMENT OF WATER RESOURCES (US/0362-3289) [02279969] **5529**

ANNUAL REPORT OF THE IMMIGRATION AND NATURALIZATION SERVICE (US) [06975040] **1918**

ANNUAL REPORT OF THE INDIANA DEPARTMENT OF MENTAL HEALTH, THE (US/0098-4205) [02241462] **4766**

ANNUAL REPORT OF THE INHALATION TOXICOLOGY RESEARCH INSTITUTE (US/0149-4392) [03487929] **3979**

ANNUAL REPORT OF THE INSTITUTE OF GEOSCIENCE, THE UNIVERSITY OF TSUKUBA (JA/0285-3175) [04633654] **1351**

ANNUAL REPORT OF THE INSTITUTE OF PHYSICS, ACADEMIA SINICA (CH/0304-5293) [01797580] **4397**

ANNUAL REPORT OF THE INSTITUTE OF SOCIAL SCIENCES, MEIJI UNIVERSITY (JA) [05069908] **5191**

ANNUAL REPORT OF THE INTER-AMERICAN COMMISSION ON HUMAN RIGHTS / ORGANIZATION OF AMERICAN STATES (US) [09450150] **4504**

ANNUAL REPORT OF THE INTER-AMERICAN TROPICAL TUNA COMMISSION (US/0074-1000) [01714978] **2295**

ANNUAL REPORT OF THE INTERNATIONAL COUNCIL FOR RESEARCH IN AGROFORESTRY (KE) [18428939] **2375**

ANNUAL REPORT OF THE JOINT ENERGY COMMITTEE *See* REPORT OF THE JOINT ENERGY COMMITTEE **1955**

ANNUAL REPORT OF THE JUDICIAL COUNCIL OF NEW MEXICO (US/0360-4659) [02242918] **2934**

ANNUAL REPORT OF THE JUDICIAL COUNCIL OF THE STATE OF WASHINGTON (US) [03881854] **3139**

ANNUAL REPORT OF THE JUSTICE SYSTEM IMPROVEMENT ACT AGENCIES / BUREAU OF JUSTICE STATISTICS, LAW ENFORCEMENT ASSISTANCE ADMINISTRATION, NATIONAL INSTITUTE OF JUSTICE, OFFICE OF JUSTICE ASSISTANCE, RESEARCH, AND STATISTICS (US/0278-0526) [07681846] **3157**

ANNUAL REPORT OF THE KANSAS INSURANCE DEPARTMENT (US) [08240875] **2873**

ANNUAL REPORT OF THE LAND DIVISION (TZ/0494-6588) [01243132] **2554**

ANNUAL REPORT OF THE LAND VALUE APPRAISAL COMMISSION (CN/0709-258X) [02380227] **4834**

ANNUAL REPORT OF THE LAW REFORM COMMISSION OF BRITISH COLUMBIA (CN/0381-2510) [01792088] **2935**

ANNUAL — Alphabetical Title Index

ANNUAL REPORT OF THE LEGISLATIVE BUDGET AND FINANCE COMMITTEE FOR THE REGULAR SESSION OF THE GENERAL ASSEMBLY OF THE COMMONWEALTH OF PENNSYLVANIA (US/0147-0507) [03082383] **4710**

ANNUAL REPORT OF THE MALDEN PUBLIC LIBRARY (US/0194-116X) [04590348] **3191**

ANNUAL REPORT OF THE MANAGEMENT SERVICES SECTION FOR THE YEARS ... (ZA) [11608156] **4628**

ANNUAL REPORT OF THE MANITOBA WATER SERVICES BOARD (CN/0318-3912) [02240496] **5529**

ANNUAL REPORT OF THE MARTIN LUTHER KING, JR. FEDERAL HOLIDAY COMMISSION TO FULFILL THE KING LEGACY *See* ANNUAL REPORT PREPARED FOR THE PRESIDENT OF THE UNITED STATES AND THE UNITED STATES CONGRESS **4629**

ANNUAL REPORT OF THE MARYLAND BICENTENNIAL COMMISSION TO THE GOVERNOR, THE GENERAL ASSEMBLY, AND THE SECRETARY, DEPARTMENT OF ECONOMIC AND COMMUNITY DEVELOPMENT (US/0099-1287) [02241079] **2720**

ANNUAL REPORT OF THE MARYLAND BOARD OF PHARMACY (US/0098-0099) [01799336] **4291**

ANNUAL REPORT OF THE MASSACHUSETTS COMMISSION ON JUDICIAL CONDUCT (US) [10704541] **3139**

ANNUAL REPORT OF THE MAURITIUS POLICE FORCE (MF) [02410838] **3157**

ANNUAL REPORT OF THE MENTAL HEALTH DIVISION OF THE DEPARTMENT OF HEALTH OF THE PROVINCE OF ONTARIO (CN) [03635429] **4766**

ANNUAL REPORT OF THE MINISTER FOR AGRICULTURE AND FOOD (IE/0791-0177) [19124147] **61**

ANNUAL REPORT OF THE MINISTER UNDER THE CROP INSURANCE ACT (CN/0711-8198) [07873077] **61**

ANNUAL REPORT OF THE MISSISSIPPI DEPARTMENT OF ARCHIVES AND HISTORY (US/0160-1415) [01645724] **2479**

ANNUAL REPORT OF THE MOTOR ACCIDENTS BOARD FOR THE YEAR ENDED 30 JUNE ... (VICTORIA) (AT) [10501744] **5438**

ANNUAL REPORT OF THE MUSEUMS ASSOCIATION FOR THE YEAR (UK) [19988784] **4084**

ANNUAL REPORT OF THE NATIONAL CREDIT UNION ADMINISTRATION (US/0146-6046) [02990460] **771**

ANNUAL REPORT OF THE NATIONAL INSTITUTES OF HEALTH. PROGRAM BEHAVIORAL NUTRITION RESEARCH AND TRAINING (US/0732-7013) [08339915] **4187**

ANNUAL REPORT OF THE NATIONAL LABOR RELATIONS BOARD (US/0083-2200) [01606614] **1649**

ANNUAL REPORT OF THE NATIONAL WOMEN'S ADVISORY COUNCIL ... (AT) [07268283] **5551**

ANNUAL REPORT OF THE NEBRASKA STATE BOARD OF EXAMINERS FOR PROFESSIONAL ENGINEERS AND ARCHITECTS (US/0275-8008) [02515904] 288, **1965**

ANNUAL REPORT OF THE NEW MEXICO STATE PERMANENT FUND AND SEVERENCE TAX PERMANENT FUND (US) [06392486] **891**

ANNUAL REPORT OF THE NEW YORK STATE SENATE STANDING COMMITTEE ON INSURANCE (US) [18480835] **2873**

ANNUAL REPORT OF THE NEW ZEALAND BIRD BANDING SCHEME (NZ/0549-0162) [01320943] **5614**

ANNUAL REPORT OF THE NORTH COMMISSION (ALASKA) (US) [01179619] **5429**

ANNUAL REPORT OF THE NORTHERN NUT GROWERS ASSOCIATION (US/0099-7838) [10570659] **61**

ANNUAL REPORT OF THE OFFICE OF COMMISSIONER OF BANKING (US/0146-8871) [03066805] **772**

ANNUAL REPORT OF THE OFFICE OF REVENUE SHARING (WASHINGTON) *CEASED.* (US/0093-660X) [01792702] **4710**

ANNUAL REPORT OF THE OFFICE OF THE COMMISSIONER OF BANKING (HK) [19492710] **772**

ANNUAL REPORT OF THE OHIO DEPARTMENT OF TAXATION (US/0196-6103) [01589468] **4710**

ANNUAL REPORT OF THE OIL AND GAS DIVISION (AUSTIN) (US) [01213018] **4250**

ANNUAL REPORT OF THE OILSEED CONTROL BOARD FOR THE PERIOD ... / OILSEED CONTROL BOARD (SA) [05211497] 163, **4628**

ANNUAL REPORT OF THE OKLAHOMA ALCOHOLIC BEVERAGE CONTROL BOARD (US/0093-6243) [01792599] **1341**

ANNUAL REPORT OF THE ONTARIO HIGHWAY TRANSPORT BOARD (CN/0701-9971) [03991467] **5376**

ANNUAL REPORT OF THE ONTARIO HUMAN RIGHTS COMMISSION (CN/0702-0538) [04450721] **4504**

ANNUAL REPORT OF THE OXFORD ORTHOPAEDIC ENGINEERING CENTRE (UK/0263-2535) [11032503] 3880, **3685**

ANNUAL REPORT OF THE PARLIAMENTARY COMMISSIONER. OMBUDSMAN (CN/0708-7217) [06116793] **4628**

ANNUAL REPORT OF THE PARLIAMENTARY LIBRARIAN (CN/0700-2254) [03421436] **3191**

ANNUAL REPORT OF THE PIG MEAT PROMOTION ADVISORY COMMITTEE FOR THE YEAR ENDED 30 JUNE ... / DEPARTMENT OF PRIMARY INDUSTRY (AT) [07878269] **4628**

ANNUAL REPORT OF THE PLANNING CONSULTATIVE COUNCIL FOR THE YEAR ENDED 30 JUNE ... (VICTORIA) (AT) [10156843] **1546**

ANNUAL REPORT OF THE POLICE COMPLAINTS AUTHORITY (UK/0950-9305) [I09509305] **3157**

ANNUAL REPORT OF THE POSTMASTER GENERAL (US) [27029605] **1144**

ANNUAL REPORT OF THE PRESIDENT / BLUE RIDGE COMMUNITY COLLEGE (US) [11002133] **1809**

ANNUAL REPORT OF THE PRESIDENT ON FEDERAL ADVISORY COMMITTEES (US) [17192998] **4628**

ANNUAL REPORT OF THE PRINCE EDWARD ISLAND DEPARTMENT OF COMMUNITY AND CULTURAL AFFAIRS (CN/0827-987X) [11724481] **4628**

ANNUAL REPORT OF THE PRIVACY COMMISSIONER (CN/0825-7361) [12239216] 4464, 4504, **2935**

ANNUAL REPORT OF THE PROSECUTOR COUNCIL (TEXAS) (US) [08273133] **3105**

ANNUAL REPORT OF THE PUBLIC EMPLOYEE RETIREMENT SYSTEM OF IDAHO (US) [05817193] **4629**

ANNUAL REPORT OF THE PUBLIC SERVICE COMMISSION TO THE HONORABLE GOVERNOR OF PUERTO RICO (PR) [01190729] **4629**

ANNUAL REPORT OF THE PUBLIC TRUSTEE OF QUEENSLAND FOR THE FINANCIAL YEAR ENDED 30TH JUNE (AT) [22254855] **4710**

ANNUAL REPORT OF THE PUBLIC WORKS DEPARTMENT (BELIZE) (BH) [01211368] **4629**

ANNUAL REPORT OF THE QUEENSLAND TOURIST & TRAVEL CORPORATION (AT) [07490364] **5461**

ANNUAL REPORT OF THE REAL ESTATE AND BUSINESS AGENTS SUPERVISORY BOARD FOR THE PERIOD 1ST JULY ... TO 30TH JUNE ... (WESTERN AUSTRALIA) (AT) [09242832] **4834**

ANNUAL REPORT OF THE REGISTER OF COPYRIGHTS (US/0090-2845) [07932086] **1301**

ANNUAL REPORT OF THE REGISTRAR OF BANKS AND FINANCIAL INSTITUTIONS FOR THE YEAR ENDED 31ST DEC. ... (ZA) [11769463] **772**

ANNUAL REPORT OF THE REGISTRAR OF BANKS (SOUTH AFRICA) (SA) [03739672] **772**

ANNUAL REPORT OF THE REHABILITATION SERVICES ADMINISTRATION TO THE PRESIDENT AND THE CONGRESS ON FEDERAL ACTIVITIES RELATED TO THE ADMINISTRATION OF THE REHABILITATION ACT OF 1973, AS AMENDED *See* UNITED STATES. REHABILITATION SERVICES ADMINISTRATION. ANNUAL REPORT TO THE PRESIDENT AND CONGRESS, FISCAL YEAR **5313**

ANNUAL REPORT OF THE SASKATCHEWAN AGRICULTURAL RETURNS STABILIZATION FUND *See* ANNUAL REPORT ... SASKATCHEWAN AGRICULTURAL RETURNS STABILIZATION FUND **61**

ANNUAL REPORT OF THE SASKATCHEWAN COMPUTER UTILITY CORPORATION OF THE PROVINCE OF SASKATCHEWAN (CN/0703-4849) [02242544] **1235**

ANNUAL REPORT OF THE SASKATCHEWAN DEVELOPMENT FUND CORPORATION OF THE PROVINCE OF SASKATCHEWAN (CN/0702-3316) [02242542] **772**

ANNUAL REPORT OF THE SASKATCHEWAN PORK PRODUCERS MARKETING BOARD (CN/0837-6875) [17784880] 4629, **2327**

ANNUAL REPORT OF THE SECRETARY FOR EDUCATION *See* ANNUAL REPORT OF THE SECRETARY FOR HIGHER EDUCATION FOR THE YEAR ENDED ... **1809**

ANNUAL REPORT OF THE SECRETARY FOR HIGHER EDUCATION FOR THE YEAR ENDED ... (RH) [23163393] **1809**

ANNUAL REPORT OF THE SECRETARY GENERAL TO THE GENERAL ASSEMBLY (US/0078-6403) [01063605] **3123**

ANNUAL REPORT OF THE SECRETARY OF THE STATE HORTICULTURAL SOCIETY OF MICHIGAN (US/0096-7688) [04984828] **2409**

ANNUAL REPORT OF THE SOUTH CAROLINA DEPARTMENT OF HIGHWAYS AND PUBLIC TRANSPORTATION TO THE GENERAL ASSEMBLY (US) [03885393] **5438**

ANNUAL REPORT OF THE SOUTH CAROLINA EDUCATIONAL TELEVISION COMMISSION (US) [04238424] **1725**

ANNUAL REPORT OF THE STATE BOARD OF EDUCATION TO THE GOVERNOR AND LEGISLATURE OF THE STATE OF NEBRASKA FOR THE FISCAL YEAR COMMENCING JULY 1, AND ENDING JUNE 30 ..., THE (US) [07867182] **1725**

ANNUAL REPORT OF THE STATE BOARD OF FINANCIAL INSTITUTIONS OF THE STATE OF SOUTH CAROLINA (US) [07493757] **772**

ANNUAL REPORT OF THE STATE DEPARTMENT OF HEALTH OF NEW YORK (US) [01760127] **4766**

ANNUAL REPORT OF THE STATE DEPARTMENT OF YOUTH SERVICES FOR THE PERIOD BEGINNING JULY 1 ... AND ENDING JUNE 30 ... (SOUTH CAROLINA) (US) [09530785] **3157**

ANNUAL REPORT OF THE STATE OF CALIFORNIA FOR THE FISCAL YEAR ENDED JUNE 30 ... (US) [08203444] **4710**

ANNUAL REPORT OF THE STATE OIL AND GAS SUPERVISOR (US/0362-1243) [02441457] 4250, **4283**

ANNUAL REPORT OF THE STATE TREASURER FOR THE PERIOD JANUARY 1 ... TO DECEMBER 31 ... / DEPARTMENT OF TREASURY (US) [08642081] **4710**

ANNUAL REPORT OF THE SUPERINTENDENT OF INSURANCE (QUEBEC. 1977) (CN/0225-8579) [08328229] **2873**

ANNUAL REPORT OF THE SURVEY DIVISION (TANZANIA) (TZ) [11858456] **2554**

ANNUAL REPORT OF THE TEXAS DEPARTMENT OF LABOR AND STANDARDS (US) [04029611] **1649**

ANNUAL REPORT OF THE TRAFFIC BOARD FOR THE YEAR ENDING JUNE 30 ... (WESTERN AUSTRALIA) (US) [10203632] **5438**

ANNUAL REPORT OF THE TREASURER (STATE OF NEW HAMPSHIRE) (US/0148-6519) [03346065] **4710**

ANNUAL REPORT OF THE U.S. DEPARTMENT OF HEALTH AND HUMAN SERVICES TO THE CONGRESS OF THE UNITED STATES ON SERVICES PROVIDED TO HANDICAPPED CHILDREN IN PROJECT HEAD START (US/0882-5203) [09104259] **5272**

ANNUAL REPORT OF THE UNDER SECRETARY, DEPARTMENT OF COMMUNITY SERVICES (AT) [16786234] **5272**

ANNUAL REPORT OF THE UNIVERSITY LIBRARIAN (AT) [11948877] **3191**

ANNUAL REPORT OF THE UNIVERSITY LIBRARIAN FOR ... VICTORIA UNIVERSITY OF WELLINGTON, THE LIBRARY (NZ) [12016160] **3191**

ANNUAL REPORT OF THE UTAH LIQUOR CONTROL COMMISSION (US) [05243515] 3157, **4629**

ANNUAL REPORT OF THE VIOLENT CRIMES COMPENSATION BOARD (NEWARK) (US/0092-3079) [01789078] **3157**

ANNUAL REPORT OF THE VIRGINIA WATER COMMISSION TO THE GOVERNOR AND THE GENERAL ASSEMBLY OF VIRGINIA (US) [24996494] **5529**

ANNUAL REPORT OF THE WASHINGTON STATE HOSPITAL COMMISSION (US) [09659019] **3776**

ANNUAL REPORT OF THE WATER DEVELOPMENT AND IRRIGATION DIVISION (DAR ES SALAAM) (TZ/0496-831X) [01189262] **2087**

Alphabetical Title Index — ANNUAL

ANNUAL REPORT OF THE WESTERN AUSTRALIAN POST SECONDARY EDUCATION COMMISSION FOR THE PERIOD ... TO ... (AT) [07696551] **1809**

ANNUAL REPORT OF THE WILDLIFE DIVISION, PARKS AND WILDLIFE DEPARTMENT (US/0495-2928) [01983016] **2186**

ANNUAL REPORT OF THE YEAR ENDING DECEMBER 31 ... / CANADA. IMMIGRATION APPEAL BOARD (CN) [13518775] **1918**

ANNUAL REPORT OF TREASURER OF THE STATE OF COLORADO *See* STATE TREASURER'S ANNUAL REPORT (COLORADO) **4750**

ANNUAL REPORT - OFFICE OF BOATING WATER SAFETY (WASHINGTON (STATE)) (US/0097-7594) [01798644] **591**

ANNUAL REPORT - OFFICE OF DIRECTOR. OREGON DEPARTMENT OF TRANSPORTATION (US/0090-6247) [01785527] **5376**

ANNUAL REPORT - OFFICE OF ENERGY PLANNING ADELAIDE (AT/1037-5945) [I10375945] **1932**

ANNUAL REPORT / OFFICE OF INDUSTRIAL RELATIONS (AT) [20442426] **1597**

ANNUAL REPORT / OFFICE OF OKLAHOMA STATE BOARD OF PHARMACY (US) [08675304] **4291**

ANNUAL REPORT / OFFICE OF THE ATTORNEY GENERAL, DEPARTMENT OF JUSTICE, STATE OF NEW MEXICO (US) [07221692] **3139**

ANNUAL REPORT / OFFICE OF THE COMMISSIONER OF SAVINGS AND RESIDENTIAL FINANCE, STATE OF ILLINOIS (US) [23824765] **772**

ANNUAL REPORT - OFFICE OF THE FARMERS' ADVOCATE (ALBERTA) (CN/0318-5044) [02241661] 61, **2935**

ANNUAL REPORT / OFFICE OF THE GOVERNOR, DIVISION OF MEDICAID (US) [15090078] **2873**

ANNUAL REPORT - OFFICE OF THE SECRETARY OF STATE (US/0160-1520) [03620260] **4629**

ANNUAL REPORT / OHIO ENVIRONMENTAL PROTECTION AGENCY (US) [08190251] **2161**

ANNUAL REPORT / OHIO INDUSTRIAL COMMISSION [AND] OHIO BUREAU OF WORKERS' COMPENSATION (US) [04714623] **1649**

ANNUAL REPORT / OKLAHOMA. AERONAUTICS COMMISSION (US/0092-9980) [01789071] **11**

ANNUAL REPORT - OKLAHOMA. DEPT. OF HUMAN SERVICES (US/0277-8289) [07635579] **5272**

ANNUAL REPORT - OKLAHOMA EDUCATIONAL TELEVISION AUTHORITY (US/0198-988X) [03161397] 1126, **1888**

ANNUAL REPORT - OKLAHOMA POLICE PENSION & RETIREMENT BOARD (US) [08535915] **3157**

ANNUAL REPORT - OKLAHOMA PUBLIC EMPLOYEES RETIREMENT SYSTEM (US) [06350483] **4629**

ANNUAL REPORT, OKLAHOMA PUBLIC LIBRARIES IN COMMUNITIES AND STATE LIBRARIES / PREPARED BY THE DEPT. OF LIBRARIES, PUBLIC INFORMATION OFFICE (US) [22712104] **3191**

ANNUAL REPORT, OKLAHOMA PUBLIC LIBRARY STATISTICS IN COMMUNITIES AND STATE INSTITUTIONS *See* ANNUAL REPORT, OKLAHOMA PUBLIC LIBRARIES IN COMMUNITIES AND STATE LIBRARIES / PREPARED BY THE DEPT. OF LIBRARIES, PUBLIC INFORMATION OFFICE **3191**

ANNUAL REPORT - OKLAHOMA. STATE BOARD OF EXAMINERS OF PSYCHOLOGISTS (US/0733-3609) [03160839] **4574**

ANNUAL REPORT - OKLAHOMA TOURISM AND RECREATION DEPARTMENT (US/0149-8770) [03565123] **5500**

ANNUAL REPORT - OKLAHOMA WATER RESOURCES BOARD (US/0099-1635) [02243586] **5529**

ANNUAL REPORT - OMBUDSMAN. ONTARIO (1984) (CN/0826-7294) [23659504] **4629**

ANNUAL REPORT ... ON ACTIVITIES TO 30 JUNE ... / THE AUSTRALIAN BICENTENNIAL AUTHORITY (AT/0726-9943) [19905056] **4629**

ANNUAL REPORT ON AFRRI RESEARCH (US) [28013191] **494**

ANNUAL REPORT ON ALLIED DENTAL EDUCATION (US) [23905623] **1316**

ANNUAL REPORT ON ARTIFICIAL INSEMINATION IN CANADA, YEAR ENDING DECEMBER 31ST ... (CN) [05277705] **206**

ANNUAL REPORT ON CACAO RESEARCH (TR/0374-5759) [01795322] **163**

ANNUAL REPORT ON CARCINOGENS (US/0272-2836) [06543913] **3808**

ANNUAL REPORT ON CHILD WELFARE, FOR THE ... SESSION OF THE ADVISORY COMMITTEE ON SOCIAL QUESTIONS (SZ) [12498154] **5272**

ANNUAL REPORT ON DEPOSITORY ACTIVITIES, FY ... / OFFICE OF THE DISTRICT OF COLUMBIA AUDITOR (US) [08570178] **4710**

ANNUAL REPORT ON ELECTRONICS RESEARCH AT THE UNIVERSITY OF TEXAS AT AUSTIN (US) [04332762] **2035**

ANNUAL REPORT ON ENGLISH AND AMERICAN STUDIES : AREAS (GW) [26387591] **3265**

ANNUAL REPORT ON EXCHANGE ARRANGEMENTS AND EXCHANGE RESTRICTIONS - INTERNATIONAL MONETARY FUND (US/0250-7366) [20577460] **823**

ANNUAL REPORT ON HAZARDOUS MATERIALS TRANSPORTATION : HAZARDOUS MATERIALS TRANSPORTATION ACT (TITLE I, PUBLIC LAW 93-633) (US) [09129658] 5376, **2935**

ANNUAL REPORT ON INDIAN EPIGRAPHY FOR... / DEPARTMENT OF ARCHAEOLOGY (II/0970-0617) [01605119] **255**

ANNUAL REPORT ON MARKETING, IRRIGATION, PRODUCTION (US/0270-8892) [05217790] **163**

ANNUAL REPORT ON MONITORING AND IMPLEMENTATION OF THE INDIANA PLAN FOR HEALTH *CEASED*. (US) [10660499] **4766**

ANNUAL REPORT ON RADIO FREE EUROPE/RADIO LIBERTY (US) [17597963] **1126**

ANNUAL REPORT ON ST. LUCIA, B.W.I (UK) [04877933] **5461**

ANNUAL REPORT ON THE ACTIVITIES OF THE INDEPENDENT COMMISSION AGAINST CORRUPTION (HK) [02711448] **4629**

ANNUAL REPORT ON THE COMPREHENSIVE WATER RESOURCES PLAN (US/0095-4659) [01795112] **5529**

ANNUAL REPORT ON THE CONDITION OF WISCONSIN CREDIT UNIONS (US) [09545888] **772**

ANNUAL REPORT ON THE CONSUMER PRICE INDEX (HK) [11978483] 1293, **1589**

ANNUAL REPORT ON THE FOOD AND AGRICULTURAL SCIENCES, FROM THE SECRETARY OF AGRICULTURE TO THE PRESIDENT AND THE CONGRESS OF THE UNITED STATES (US/0882-2026) [09901343] **61**

ANNUAL REPORT ON THE GEOTHERMAL RESOURCES ACT OF 1975 (TEXAS) (US/0149-0184) [03406741] **2554**

ANNUAL REPORT ON THE KENYA METEOROLOGICAL DEPARTMENT FOR THE PERIOD 1ST JULY ... TO 30TH JUNE ... (KE) [08925063] **1420**

ANNUAL REPORT ON THE PROVISION OF CHILD WELFARE SERVICES IN NEW YORK STATE (US/0363-9673) [02567567] **5273**

ANNUAL REPORT ON THE QUALITY OF THE AIR IN WASHINGTON, D.C (US/0093-4135) [01792175] **2224**

ANNUAL REPORT ON THE QUALITY OF THE ENVIRONMENT (ST. PAUL) (US/0094-1697) [01793478] **2161**

ANNUAL REPORT ON THE RESULTS OF TREATMENT IN GYNECOLOGICAL CANCER (SW/0348-8799) [06241546] **3809**

ANNUAL REPORT ON THE RONDEVLEI BIRD SANCTUARY BY THE WARDEN *See* WARDEN'S ... ANNUAL REPORT ON THE RONDEVLEI BIRD SANCTUARY FOR THE YEAR ... / RONDEVLEI BIRD SANCTUARY, THE **2208**

ANNUAL REPORT ON THE STATUS OF POVERTY IN CALIFORNIA, AN (US/0749-9337) [09473794] **5273**

ANNUAL REPORT ON THE TERRITORY OF NORFOLK ISLAND (NX/0572-0494) [01238155] **4629**

ANNUAL REPORT ON THE UTAH STATE RETIREMENT SYSTEM, SCHOOL DIVISION TO THE UTAH STATE RETIREMENT BOARD (US/0567-0497) [03046729] 1888, **1649**

ANNUAL REPORT ON THE WORK OF THE GEORGIA COURTS (US/0739-8247) [09801898] **2935**

ANNUAL REPORT ON TITLE I, PUBLIC LAW 89-313 (US) [04453058] **1860**

ANNUAL REPORT ON TOBACCO STATISTICS (1980) (US/0747-5314) [08372894] **5375**

ANNUAL REPORT ON TRAINING RESEARCH / EMPLOYMENT DEPARTMENT (UK) [24525849] **938**

ANNUAL REPORT / ONONDAGA COUNTY PUBLIC LIBRARY (US/0883-3508) [12122736] **3191**

ANNUAL REPORT / ONTARIO ADVISORY COUNCIL ON MULTICULTURALISM AND CITIZENSHIP (CN/0710-8990) [09269283] **2720**

ANNUAL REPORT - ONTARIO ADVISORY COUNCIL ON SENIOR CITIZENS (CN/0704-2663) [02244356] **5178**

ANNUAL REPORT--ONTARIO HERITAGE FOUNDATION (CN/0706-0106) [04880320] **2721**

ANNUAL REPORT / ONTARIO HYDRO (CN/0382-2826) [18127667] 4759, **2035**

ANNUAL REPORT - ONTARIO INSURANCE COMMISSION (CN/1183-9309) [25796715] **2873**

ANNUAL REPORT - ONTARIO INSURANCE COMMISSION (CN/1183-9309) [25796716] **2873**

ANNUAL REPORT / ONTARIO LABOUR RELATIONS BOARD (CN/0711-849X) [08069996] **3144**

ANNUAL REPORT / ONTARIO, MINISTRY OF TRANSPORTATION (CN/0843-4042) [18952649] **5376**

ANNUAL REPORT / ONTARIO SHARE AND DEPOSIT INSURANCE CORPORATION (CN/0227-5864) [08874962] **2873**

ANNUAL REPORT. OPERATION OF THE COLORADO RIVER BASIN. PROJECTED OPERATIONS (US/0363-8383) [02548361] **2087**

ANNUAL REPORT ... OPINIONS / VERMONT LABOR RELATIONS BOARD (US) [11502022] **3144**

ANNUAL REPORT - OREGON. SOLID WASTE DIVISION (US/0883-3222) [12036340] **2224**

ANNUAL REPORT / OREGON VOCATIONAL REHABILITATION DIVISION (US) [07855052] **1649**

ANNUAL REPORT / OUTER CONTINENTAL SHELF OIL AND GAS LEASING AND PRODUCTION PROGRAM (US/8755-2884) [11218825] **4250**

ANNUAL REPORT - OVERSEAS DEVELOPMENT COUNCIL (US/0092-7643) [01791326] **1598**

ANNUAL REPORT - PANAMA CANAL COMPANY, CANAL ZONE GOVERNMENT (US/0475-6126) [01253695] **4629**

ANNUAL REPORT - PARKLAWN COMPUTER CENTER (US/0147-9016) [03245673] **4766**

ANNUAL REPORT - PARLIAMENTARY COMMISSIONER FOR ADMINISTRATION (UK) [03829085] **4629**

ANNUAL REPORT - PENNSYLVANIA. BUREAU OF FORESTRY (US/0734-6565) [08772637] **2375**

ANNUAL REPORT - PINELAND HOSPITAL & TRAINING CENTER (US/0464-5685) [02457329] **3776**

ANNUAL REPORT - PIPELINE AUTHORITY (AT/0311-7197) [I03117197] **4250**

ANNUAL REPORT. PLANNING AND DEVELOPMENT (US/0735-3243) [05299386] **61**

ANNUAL REPORT / POLYMER SCIENCE AND STANDARDS DIVISION (US/0198-9677) [06263146] 2008, **2100**

ANNUAL REPORT / POSTS AND TELECOMMUNICATIONS CORPORATION (RH) [02806595] **1149**

ANNUAL REPORT - PRAIRIE FARM REHABILITATION ADMINISTRATION (CN/0829-1772) [03822713] **61**

●ANNUAL REPORT PREPARED FOR THE PRESIDENT OF THE UNITED STATES AND THE UNITED STATES CONGRESS (US) [30632764] **4629**

ANNUAL REPORT PRESENTED TO THE NEW YORK STATE BOARD OF REGENTS (US) [22751976] **1910**

ANNUAL REPORT / PRESIDENTIAL ADVISORY COMMITTEE ON SMALL AND MINORITY BUSINESS OWNERSHIP *CEASED*. (US/0741-322X) [09840777] **639**

ANNUAL REPORT - PRICES JUSTIFICATION TRIBUNAL (AUSTRALIA) (AT) [02244137] **1590**

ANNUAL REPORT - PRINCE EDWARD ISLAND. DEPT. OF THE ENVIRONMENT (1989) (CN/0848-5844) [23257580] **2187**

ANNUAL REPORT - PRINCE EDWARD ISLAND. ENVIRONMENTAL CONTROL COMMISSION (CN) [01787157] **2161**

ANNUAL REPORT / PRINCE EDWARD ISLAND HOUSING CORPORATION (CN) [11063263] **2815**

ANNUAL REPORT / PRINCE EDWARD ISLAND LENDING AUTHORITY (CN/0824-9873) [01788012] **772**

ANNUAL REPORT - PRISONS DEPARTMENT (INDIA) (II) [05141825] **3157**

ANNUAL — Alphabetical Title Index

ANNUAL REPORT ... PROGRAM INSPECTOR GENERAL (US) [15603070] **4464**

ANNUAL REPORT - PROJECT MODEL (US/0361-9133) [02441438] **1910**

ANNUAL REPORT - PROJECTS & DEVELOPMENT INDIA LTD (II) [11547222] **1598**

ANNUAL REPORT - PROVINCIAL AGRICULTURAL LAND COMMISSION (BRITISH COLUMBIA) (CN/0708-4048) [05324839] **61**

ANNUAL REPORT / PROVINCIAL ELECTRICITY AUTHORITY (TH) [03132889] **4629**

ANNUAL REPORT - PROVISIONAL MILITARY GOVERNMENT OF SOCIALIST ETHIOPIA, LIVESTOCK AND MEAT BOARD (ET) [06257988] **206**

ANNUAL REPORT / PUBLIC AND PRIVATE RIGHTS BOARD (CN/0709-4949) [05721091] **2935**

ANNUAL REPORT - PUBLIC EMPLOYEES' RETIREMENT ASSOCIATION OF NEW MEXICO (US/0196-6685) [05848911] **4529**, **1649**

ANNUAL REPORT / PUBLIC FINANCE FOUNDATION (UK) [20480949] **4710**

ANNUAL REPORT - PUBLIC SAFETY SERVICES (ALBERTA) (CN/0833-7659) [14773037] **5273**, **4766**

ANNUAL REPORT - PUBLIC SERVICE BOARD (AUSTRALIA) *SUSPENDED.* (AT) [05504033] **4701**

ANNUAL REPORT - PUBLIC SERVICE BOARD (PERTH) (AT/0312-5688) [02241725] **4701**

ANNUAL REPORT / PUBLIC SERVICE COMMISSION OF WESTERN AUSTRALIA (AT) [24980124] **4701**

ANNUAL REPORT, PUBLIC WATER SUPPLIES FOR THE STATE OF OKLAHOMA, NORTHWEST DISTRICT (US/0272-4529) [06825793] **4759**, **2224**

ANNUAL REPORT, PUBLIC WATER SUPPLIES FOR THE STATE OF OKLAHOMA, SOUTH CENTRAL DISTRICT (US/0276-4539) [C7351878] **5529**

ANNUAL REPORT / PUERTO RICO INDUSTRIAL DEVELOPMENT COMPANY (PR/0748-5530) [10960153] **891**

ANNUAL REPORT - PULP AND PAPER FOUNDATION (1988) (US/1053-2781) [22459907] **4232**

ANNUAL REPORT - PULP AND PAPER RESEARCH INSTITUTE OF CANADA *CEASED.* (CN/0079-7960) [01641329] **4232**

ANNUAL REPORT - PUNJAB NATIONAL BANK (II/0304-8101) [01799956] **772**

ANNUAL REPORT PURSUANT TO ARTICLE 78F (5) OF THE ECSC TREATY / COURT OF AUDITORS OF THE EUROPEAN COMMUNITIES (UK) [07851853] **1598**

ANNUAL REPORT / PUSAT PENELITIAN UNIVERSITAS KATOLIK INDONESIA ATMA JAYA (IO) [11093985] **1725**

ANNUAL REPORT - QUEBEC PENSION BOARD (CN) [01785522] **1649**

ANNUAL REPORT - QUEENSLAND. DEPARTMENT OF RESOURCE INDUSTRIES (AT/1034-7380) [I10347380] **2133**

ANNUAL REPORT / QUEENSLAND FOREST SERVICE (AT) [23172302] **2375**

ANNUAL REPORT / QUEENSLAND MEAT INDUSTRY ORGANIZATION AND MARKETING AUTHORITY *See* ANNUAL REPORT / THE LIVESTOCK AND MEAT AUTHORITY OF QUEENSLAND **206**

ANNUAL REPORT - RAILROAD RETIREMENT BOARD (US/0891-8066) [02841407] **1650**

ANNUAL REPORT RECEIPTS (BG) [18116476] **823**

ANNUAL REPORT / RECREATION, PARKS AND WILDLIFE FOUNDATION (CN/0711-2815) [07533137] 2187, **4706**

ANNUAL REPORT - REPSOL (FIRM) (SP) [18531383] **4250**

ANNUAL REPORT - REPUBLIC OF ZAMBIA, MINISTRY OF RURAL DEVELOPMENT, DEPARTMENT OF MARKETING AND COOPERATIVES (ZA) [06934530] **1598**

ANNUAL REPORT / REPUBLIC OF ZAMBIA, OFFICE OF THE PRIME MINISTER, PROVINCIAL AND LOCAL GOVERNMENT ADMINISTRATION DIVISION, EASTERN PROVINCE (ZA) [19472940] **4629**

ANNUAL REPORT / RESERVE BANK OF FIJI (FJ) [22570309] **772**

ANNUAL REPORT / RESIDENTIAL UTILITY CONSUMER UNIT, OFFICE OF CONSUMER SERVICES, MINNESOTA DEPARTMENT OF COMMERCE (US) [06168525] **4629**

ANNUAL REPORT - RESOURCES FOR THE FUTURE (US/0486-5561) [01179864] **2187**

ANNUAL REPORT - RESTRICTIVE PRACTICES COMMISSION. (IRELAND) (IE) [02762958] **2935**

ANNUAL REPORT - RHODE ISLAND. DEPT. OF HEALTH (1979) (US/0731-244X) [08093628] **4766**

ANNUAL REPORT - RHODE ISLAND GOVERNOR'S COUNCIL ON MENTAL HEALTH (US/0556-8471) [03243203] **4766**

ANNUAL REPORT - ROYAL BOTANICAL GARDENS (CN/0300-3140) [01784674] **499**

● ANNUAL REPORT / ROYAL COMMISSION ON THE HISTORICAL MONUMENTS OF ENGLAND (UK) [26912897] **2675**

ANNUAL REPORT - ROYAL ONTARIO MUSEUM (CN/0082-5115) [01110968] **4084**

ANNUAL REPORT - ROYAL ONTARIO MUSEUM (CN/0082-5115) [25146600] **4084**

ANNUAL REPORT / RS, REHABILITATION SERVICES, WEST VIRGINIA STATE BOARD OF REHABILITATION (US) [18495725] **5273**

ANNUAL REPORT / RURAL BANK LIMITED (NZ) [25285456] **772**

ANNUAL REPORT - RURAL RECONSTRUCTION AUTHORITY OF WESTERN AUSTRALIA (AT) [01789881] **4629**

ANNUAL REPORT / SAINT LAWRENCE SEAWAY DEVELOPMENT CORPORATION (US/0558-194X) [01914612] **5447**

ANNUAL REPORT / SALAAM. BUREAU OF RESOURCE ASSESSMENT AND LAND USE *See* ANNUAL REPORT / INSTITUTE OF RESOURCE ASSESSMENT **1597**

ANNUAL REPORT - SAMUEL H. KRESS FOUNDATION (US/0581-4766) [01791727] **5273**

ANNUAL REPORT ... SASKATCHEWAN AGRICULTURAL RETURNS STABILIZATION FUND (CN/0715-2965) [08698042] **61**

ANNUAL REPORT - SASKATCHEWAN CENTRE OF THE ARTS (CN/0701-6433) [02242541] **313**

ANNUAL REPORT / SASKATCHEWAN ENVIRONMENT AND PUBLIC SAFETY (CN/0839-8658) [18829841] **4766**

ANNUAL REPORT - SASKATCHEWAN HEALTH, HEARING AID PLAN (CN/0707-963X) [03348634] **4383**

ANNUAL REPORT / SASKATCHEWAN HEALTH RESEARCH BOARD (CN/0715-9714) [07938176] **4766**

ANNUAL REPORT / SASKATCHEWAN HOG MARKETING COMMISSION (CN/0228-6114) [02242543] **206**

ANNUAL REPORT / SASKATCHEWAN HUMAN RIGHTS COMMISSION (CN/0826-953X) [10664574] **4504**

ANNUAL REPORT / SASKATCHEWAN. LABOUR RELATIONS BOARD (CN/1191-033X) [25652443] **1650**

ANNUAL REPORT / SASKATCHEWAN LEGISLATIVE LIBRARY (CN/0837-9823) [15057897] **4629**

ANNUAL REPORT - SASKATCHEWAN. TRIPARTITE BEEF ADMINISTRATION BOARD (CN/1191-0321) [25652442] **206**

ANNUAL REPORT / SASKATCHEWAN WHEAT POOL (CN/0316-4128) [01793407] **163**

ANNUAL REPORT / SASKATOON HEALTH SERVICES AUTHORITY (CN/1191-0313) [25652440] **4766**

ANNUAL REPORT / SAVANNAH VALLEY AUTHORITY (US) [19771355] **5529**

ANNUAL REPORT / SCHOOL OF ORIENTAL AND AFRICAN STUDIES, UNIVERSITY OF LONDON (UK) [23935661] 2637, **2645**

ANNUAL REPORT - SCIENCE COUNCIL OF CANADA (CN/0080-7478) [02248763] **5084**

ANNUAL REPORT - SCOTTISH AGRICULTURAL DEVELOPMENT COUNCIL (UK) [01789704] **61**

ANNUAL REPORT / SCOTTISH CROP RESEARCH INSTITUTE (UK/0263-7200) [09313278] **163**

ANNUAL REPORT / SCOTTISH LAW COMMISSION (UK/0080-7915) [01645628] **2935**

ANNUAL REPORT - SCRIPPS INSTITUTION OF OCEANOGRAPHY (1984) (US/1046-9443) [10525719] **1446**

ANNUAL REPORT / SEA FISH INDUSTRY AUTHORITY (UK) [15649370] **2295**

ANNUAL REPORT / SEATRAD CENTRE (MY) [10916401] **2134**

ANNUAL REPORT - SECRETARY OF STATE, MERIT COMMISSION (US) [05236910] **4701**

ANNUAL REPORT, SECTION OF PUBLIC UTILITY, COMMUNICATIONS AND TRANSPORTATION LAW (US/1064-0959) [26184121] **4759**

ANNUAL REPORT - SECURITIES AND EXCHANGE COMMISSION (PH) [03405919] **891**

ANNUAL REPORT - SECURITIES COMMISSION (EDMONTON) (CN/0702-0724) [03084541] **4629**

ANNUAL REPORT / SECURITIES INDUSTRY ASSOCIATION (US) **891**

ANNUAL REPORT / SETTLEMENT AGENTS SUPERVISORY BOARD (AT) [10545705] **4834**

ANNUAL REPORT - SIEMENS AKTIENGESELLSCHAFT (GW) [20465062] **1598**

ANNUAL REPORT / SINGAPORE INTERNATIONAL CHAMBER OF COMMERCE (SI) [26757836] **818**

ANNUAL REPORT / SMALL BUSINESS ADMINISTRATION (US/0083-3274) [01796303] **639**

ANNUAL REPORT - SOCIAL SCIENCE RESEARCH COUNCIL (NEW YORK) (US/0361-462X) [01167657] **5191**

ANNUAL REPORT / SOIL CONSERVATION SERVICE OF NSW (AT/0817-4245) [20465867] **163**

ANNUAL REPORT - SOIL SURVEY. ENGLAND AND WALES (UK/0141-1675) [02240043] **163**

ANNUAL REPORT / SOLICITOR GENERAL CANADA (CN/0576-4076) [08828331] **3157**

ANNUAL REPORT - SOUTH AFRICAN NATIONAL MUSEUM OF MILITARY HISTORY (SA) [02757932] 4035, **4084**

ANNUAL REPORT - SOUTH AUSTRALIAN CHAMBER OF MINES INCORPORATED (AT/0813-2127) [I08132127] **2134**

ANNUAL REPORT / SOUTH CAROLINA GENERAL ASSEMBLY. STUDY COMMITTEE ON AGING *CEASED.* (US) [17161510] **3749**

ANNUAL REPORT / SOUTH CAROLINA, HUMAN SERVICES COORDINATING COUNCIL (US) [22754358] **938**

ANNUAL REPORT - SOUTH CAROLINA LAND RESOURCES CONSERVATION COMMISSION (US/0364-1619) [02605768] **2187**

ANNUAL REPORT, SOUTH DAKOTA GOVERNOR'S TRAFFIC SAFETY PROGRAM (US) [04550463] 4766, **5438**

ANNUAL REPORT - SOUTH DAKOTA HOUSING DEVELOPMENT AUTHORITY (US/0098-941X) [02246811] **2815**

ANNUAL REPORT - SOUTH WESTERN REGIONAL LIBRARY SYSTEM (ENGLAND) (UK) [11273989] **3191**

ANNUAL REPORT - SOUTHEASTERN LIBRARY NETWORK (US/0099-085X) [02243180] **3191**

ANNUAL REPORT - SOUTHERN RESEARCH INSTITUTE (US/0361-6452) [01969101] **5084**

ANNUAL REPORT / SOUTHERN RHODESIA. DIVISION OF LIVESTOCK AND PASTURES *See* ANNUAL REPORT FOR THE YEAR ENDED - ZIMBABWE. DIVISION OF LIVESTOCK AND PASTURES **205**

ANNUAL REPORT/SOUTHWEST FLORIDA WATER MANAGEMENT DISTRICT (US) [17633963] **5529**

ANNUAL REPORT / STANDING COMMITTEE ON LABOR, NEW YORK STATE ASSEMBLY (US) [09420354] **3144**

ANNUAL REPORT / STANFORD UNIVERSITY LIBRARIES (US) [12708962] **3191**

ANNUAL REPORT - STATE COMPENSATION FUND (ARIZONA) (US/0160-3337) [04168081] **1650**

ANNUAL REPORT - STATE ENVIRONMENTAL IMPROVEMENT AUTHORITY (US/0190-3934) [04691837] **2224**

ANNUAL REPORT / STATE FISHERIES DEVELOPMENT CORPORATION LIMITED (CALCUTTA, INDIA) (II) [11585597] **2295**

ANNUAL REPORT: STATE HOSPITALS FOR THE MENTALLY DISORDERED (US) [03717793] 3921, **3776**

ANNUAL REPORT - STATE INVESTMENT COUNCIL. STATE OF NEBRASKA (US/0091-0686) [01785834] **4710**

ANNUAL REPORT / STATE OF ALASKA, COMMISSION ON JUDICIAL CONDUCT (US) [12226194] **3139**

ANNUAL REPORT - STATE OF ALASKA, LEGISLATIVE BUDGET AND AUDIT COMMITTEE (US/0095-3865) [01796768] **4710**

ANNUAL REPORT - STATE OF ARKANSAS, PUBLIC SERVICE COMMISSION (US/0191-1457) [01514129] **4759**

ANNUAL

Alphabetical Title Index

ANNUAL REPORT - STATE OF CONNECTICUT HEALTH & EDUCATIONAL FACILITIES AUTHORITY (US/0098-4167) [02241680] **3776**

ANNUAL REPORT, STATE OF ILLINOIS ALCOHOLISM PLANS AND PROGRAMS (US/0160-161X) [03617541] **1341**

ANNUAL REPORT - STATE OF ILLINOIS, EDUCATIONAL TELEVISION COMMISSION (US) [04215951] **1809**

ANNUAL REPORT - STATE OF MARYLAND. CRIMINAL INJURIES COMPENSATION BOARD (US/0092-6051) [01788547] **3157**

ANNUAL REPORT - STATE OF NEBRASKA. DEPARTMENT OF HEALTH (US/0090-3795) [01784972] **4767**

ANNUAL REPORT - STATE OF NEVADA, DEPARTMENT OF MOTOR VEHICLES, HIGHWAY PATROL DIVISION (US) [05811732] **3157**

ANNUAL REPORT - STATE OF NEW JERSEY, DEPARTMENT OF BANKING, COMMISSIONER OF BANKING (US) [04595274] **772**

ANNUAL REPORT - STATE OF NEW JERSEY, DEPARTMENT OF INSTITUTIONS AND AGENCIES, DIVISION OF MEDICAL ASSISTANCE AND HEALTH SERVICES-MEDICAID (US/0362-4218) [03139834] **5273, 2873**

ANNUAL REPORT / STATE OF NEW MEXICO, REGULATION & LICENSING DEPARTMENT (US) [18190368] **4629**

ANNUAL REPORT - STATE OF NEW YORK, DEPARTMENT OF MOTOR VEHICLES (US/0196-6723) [01760142] **5403**

ANNUAL REPORT - STATE OF OHIO, LEGISLATIVE BUDGET OFFICE OF THE LEGISLATIVE SERVICE COMMISSION, LEGISLATIVE BUDGET COMMITTEE (US/0099-1627) [02246696] **4710**

ANNUAL REPORT / STATE OF OHIO, STATE PARKING COMMISSION (US) [22746823] **5403**

ANNUAL REPORT - STATE OF OKLAHOMA, DEPARTMENT OF ECONOMIC AND COMMUNITY AFFAIRS (US/0364-8257) [02676854] **1546**

ANNUAL REPORT / STATE OF TENNESSEE, DEPARTMENT OF FINANCIAL INSTITUTIONS (US) [10860806] **772**

ANNUAL REPORT - STATE PARK AND RECREATION COMMISSION (US) [03888157] **4848**

ANNUAL REPORT - STATE PLANNING OFFICE. EXECUTIVE DEPARTMENT. STATE OF MAINE (US/0091-0678) [01786346] **2815**

ANNUAL REPORT / STATE WATER QUALITY ADVISORY COMMITTEE (US) [11994263] **5530**

ANNUAL REPORT, STATISTICAL SUPPLEMENT / NEW YORK STATE DEPARTMENT OF SOCIAL SERVICES (US) [16880727] **5273**

ANNUAL REPORT - STATISTICS CANADA *CEASED.* (CN/0703-2633) [19963463] **5321**

ANNUAL REPORT - STUDSVIK ENERGITEKNIK AB (SW) [11009715] **4446**

ANNUAL REPORT / SUBVERSIVE ACTIVITIES CONTROL BOARD (US/0500-3970) [01585930] **4464**

ANNUAL REPORT - SUGARCANE BREEDING INSTITUTE (II/0530-0371) [03191577] **163**

ANNUAL REPORT. SUPERINTENDENT OF BANKRUPTCY (OTTAWA) (CN/0703-2625) [03980359] **3084**

ANNUAL REPORT / SUPERINTENDENT OF INSURANCE (CN/0229-7108) [22038405] **2873**

ANNUAL REPORT - SUPERVISING SCIENTIST FOR THE ALLIGATOR RIVERS REGION (AT/0158-4030) [l01584030] **5084**

ANNUAL REPORT / SUPPLEMENTAL ANNUITY COLLECTIVE TRUST FUND OF NEW JERSEY (US) [25976861] **4629**

ANNUAL REPORT / SYRACUSE (N.Y.) DEPT. OF AVIATION (US/0735-4606) [07339573] **11**

ANNUAL REPORT - TAIWAN PROVINCIAL INSTITUTE OF FAMILY PLANNING (CH) [02821159] **588**

ANNUAL REPORT / TANZANIA BUREAU OF STANDARDS (TZ) [07745377] **4029**

ANNUAL REPORT - TASKFORCE ON THE CHURCHES AND CORPORATE RESPONSIBILITY (CN/0711-7000) [l07117000] **5239**

ANNUAL REPORT - TAXATION & REVENUE DEPARTMENT, PROPERTY TAX DIVISION (US) [04914705] **4710**

ANNUAL REPORT - TECHNISCH-PHYSISCHE DIENST TNO-TH (NE/0304-8292) [01799426] **4397**

ANNUAL REPORT - TECHNISCHE HOGESCHOOL DELFT (NE) [19550031] **5084**

ANNUAL REPORT / TELEFILM CANADA (CN/0837-2446) [20668948] **4063**

ANNUAL REPORT - TELEVERKET (SW) [02694175] **1149**

ANNUAL REPORT - TENNESSEE ARTS COMMISSION (US/0091-259X) [01786839] **313**

ANNUAL REPORT / TENNESSEE FILM, TAPE, AND MUSIC COMMISSION (US) [09237928] **4366, 4063**

ANNUAL REPORT / TERRELL STATE HOSPITAL (US) [07246070] **3776**

ANNUAL REPORT - TERRITORIAL HOSPITAL INSURANCE SERVICES AND MEDICARE (CN/0715-2647) [08394414] **2874**

ANNUAL REPORT / TEXAS BOARD OF LICENSURE FOR NURSING HOME ADMINISTRATORS (US/0277-0571) [05858671] **3776**

ANNUAL REPORT / TEXAS COASTAL AND MARINE COUNCIL (US/0277-0563) [07243459] **2815**

ANNUAL REPORT. TEXAS DEPT. OF AGRICULTURE *See* ANNUAL FINANCIAL REPORT **60**

ANNUAL REPORT / THE ALABAMA MEDICAID AGENCY (US) [27482613] **3551**

ANNUAL REPORT - THE ALBERTA FOUNDATION FOR THE PERFORMING ARTS (CN/0226-0816) [06270355] **383**

ANNUAL REPORT / THE AMERICAN COMMITTEE ON AFRICA (US/0743-1287) [10502713] **4464**

ANNUAL REPORT / THE ARIZONA BOARD OF MEDICAL EXAMINERS (US) [10153971] **3913**

ANNUAL REPORT / THE ATLANTIC SALMON FEDERATION (CN/0837-1059) [12928428] **2295**

ANNUAL REPORT / THE CANADIAN DAIRY COMMISSION / RAPPORT ANNUEL / LA COMMISSION CANADIENNE DU LAIT (CN/0382-3229) [10314806] **192**

ANNUAL REPORT / THE CANADIAN WHEAT BOARD (CN) [02248738] **200**

ANNUAL REPORT / THE CENTRAL BANK OF CHINA (CH) [09004176] **772**

ANNUAL REPORT-THE COMMONWEALTH OF MASSACHUSETTS, SECURITY AND PRIVACY COUNCIL *See* COMBINED ANNUAL REPORTS FOR FISCAL YEAR ... **3160**

ANNUAL REPORT / THE CONFERENCE BOARD (US/0899-2231) [16962123] **1462**

ANNUAL REPORT / THE COUNCIL OF STATE GOVERNMENTS (US) [11545317] **4629**

ANNUAL REPORT / THE DIVISION OF SAFETY AND HYGIENE, BUREAU OF WORKERS' COMPENSATION (US) [22610971] **2859**

ANNUAL REPORT / THE ELECTRICITY COUNCIL (UK/0307-1146) [02275466] **4759, 4696**

ANNUAL REPORT - THE FRANKLIN MCLEAN MEMORIAL RESEARCH INSTITUTE (US) [02804174] **3847, 3809**

ANNUAL REPORT / THE GRAIN POOL OF W. A (AT) [16583693] **200**

ANNUAL REPORT / THE GREAT BARRIER REEF MARINE PARK AUTHORITY (AT/0155-8072) [14217599] **2187**

ANNUAL REPORT / THE HAKLUYT SOCIETY (UK) [13079341] **5461**

ANNUAL REPORT - THE INSTITUTE FOR CERTIFICATION OF COMPUTER PROFESSIONALS (US/0098-2431) [02241464] **1255**

ANNUAL REPORT / THE JAPAN-UNITED STATES FRIENDSHIP COMMISSION (US/0163-5557) [03884343] **5239**

ANNUAL REPORT / THE LAW COMMISSION, SRI LANKA (CE) [08530636] **2935**

ANNUAL REPORT / THE LIVESTOCK AND MEAT AUTHORITY OF QUEENSLAND (AT/0816-2816) [20070740] **206**

ANNUAL REPORT / THE MANITOBA FARM LANDS OWNERSHIP BOARD (CN/0842-4632) [19542366] **4834, 61**

ANNUAL REPORT - THE MANITOBA HYDRO-ELECTRIC BOARD (CN/0460-9581) [03193233] **4759**

ANNUAL REPORT ... / THE MARYLAND INDUSTRIAL DEVELOPMENT FINANCING AUTHORITY (US) [08470418] **4629**

ANNUAL REPORT / THE MEDICAL AND DENTAL DEFENCE UNION OF SCOTLAND LIMITED (UK) [17588544] **2935, 3551**

ANNUAL REPORT / THE NATIONAL MUSEUM OF AUSTRALIA (AT) [19717341] **4084**

ANNUAL REPORT / THE NETHERLANDS-AMERICA COMMUNITY ASSOCIATION, INC (US) [11218493] **5239**

ANNUAL REPORT / THE NORWEGIAN BANKERS' ASSOCIATION (NO) [20940223] **772**

ANNUAL REPORT / THE OPEC FUND (AU) [07659583] **2907**

ANNUAL REPORT / THE POPULATION COUNCIL (US/0361-7858) [01038396] **588, 4549**

ANNUAL REPORT / THE PREMIER'S DEPARTMENT (AT) [19753864] **4629**

ANNUAL REPORT - THE RAILWAY & LOCOMOTIVE HISTORICAL SOCIETY, INC (US/0483-9005) [01763395] **5429**

ANNUAL REPORT / THE ROASTING PLANT (RH) [19476337] **3998**

ANNUAL REPORT / THE ROWETT RESEARCH INSTITUTE (UK/0952-7222) [20550419] **5503**

ANNUAL REPORT / THE SCOTTISH CIVIC TRUST (UK) [17497345] **2815**

ANNUAL REPORT / THE SOUTH AFRICAN TRANSPORT SERVICES (SA) [08499511] **5376**

ANNUAL REPORT - THE SOUTHERN REGIONAL COUNCIL (US) [06443095] **2721**

ANNUAL REPORT - THE SOUTHWESTERN LEGAL FOUNDATION (US/0561-1784) [01766226] **2935**

ANNUAL REPORT - THE STATE OF OKLAHOMA, OFFICE OF COMMUNITY AFFAIRS AND PLANNING (US/0360-3547) [02243374] **4629**

ANNUAL REPORT / THE STATE UNIVERSITY CONSTRUCTION FUND (US) [10063412] **598**

ANNUAL REPORT. THE STATUS OF WOMEN IN FLORIDA (US/0093-7118) [01792568] **5551**

ANNUAL REPORT / THE TEXTILE INDUSTRY (UK) [17008352] **5347**

ANNUAL REPORT / THE UNIVERSITY OF ADELAIDE (AT/0729-9885) [19760807] **1809**

ANNUAL REPORT / THE UNIVERSITY OF NEWCASTLE N.S.W (AT) [16886346] **1809**

ANNUAL REPORT / THE URBAN INSTITUTE (US/0092-7481) [03885998] **5191**

ANNUAL REPORT - THE WATER QUALITY COUNCIL OF QUEENSLAND (AT/0311-2101) [02241563] **5530**

ANNUAL REPORT TO CALIFORNIA LEGISLATURE / CALIFORNIA TRANSPORTATION COMMISSION (US) [12115777] **5377**

ANNUAL REPORT TO CONGRESS FOR FY ... ELECTRIC AND HYBRID VEHICLE PROGRAM *See* ELECTRIC AND HYBRID VEHICLES PROGRAM **5381**

ANNUAL REPORT TO CONGRESS ON THE FEDERAL EQUAL OPPORTUNITY RECRUITMENT PROGRAM (US) [24478653] **4701**

ANNUAL REPORT TO CONGRESS ON THE IMPLEMENTATION OF PUBLIC LAW 94-413, THE ELECTRIC & HYBRID VEHICLE RESEARCH, DEVELOPMENT & DEMONSTRATION ACT OF 1976 (US/0161-0759) [03818307] **5377**

ANNUAL REPORT TO CONGRESS ON THE POST-VIETNAM ERA VETERANS' EDUCATIONAL ASSISTANCE PROGRAM (US/0747-6795) [10508602] **4035**

ANNUAL REPORT TO CONGRESS ON THE USE OF ALCOHOL IN MOTOR FUELS (US/0271-5341) [06466839] **1020**

ANNUAL REPORT TO CONGRESS ON TRUTH IN LENDING (US) [03692597] **4710**

● ANNUAL REPORT TO CONGRESS / UNITED STATES CONSUMER PRODUCT SAFETY COMMISSION (US/1075-6833) [29394476] **1293**

ANNUAL REPORT TO CONGRESS - URBAN INITIATIVES ANTI-CRIME PROGRAM (US/0272-8974) [06758301] **3157**

ANNUAL REPORT TO DIRECTOR ... / RESEARCH SECTION, DIVISION OF PLANNING AND PROGRAMMING, DEPT. OF TRANSPORTATION (ALASKA) (US) [08642536] **5377**

ANNUAL REPORT TO GOVERNOR ... ON EMPLOYMENT AND TRAINING ACTIVITIES THROUGHOUT NEW MEXICO DURING FISCAL YEAR ... (US) [09449235] **1650**

ANNUAL REPORT TO THE CALIFORNIA LEGISLATURE - CALIFORNIA. HEALTH MANPOWER POLICY COMMISSION (US) [02582329] **3913**

ANNUAL — Alphabetical Title Index

ANNUAL REPORT TO THE CITIZENS' ADVISORY BOARD ON CORRECTIONS (US) [03431513] **3157**

ANNUAL REPORT TO THE CONGRESS BY THE OFFICE OF TECHNOLOGY ASSESSMENT (US/0095-2109) [01795650] **5084**

ANNUAL REPORT TO THE CONGRESS FOR FISCAL YEAR ... / SOCIAL SECURITY (US) [08616615] **5273**

ANNUAL REPORT TO THE CONGRESS OF THE UNITED STATES FROM THE DIRECTORY OF THE SELECTIVE SERVICE SYSTEM (US) [22259006] **4035**

ANNUAL REPORT TO THE GENERAL ASSEMBLY / LEGISLATIVE BUDGET AND FINANCE COMMITTEE (US) [23190193] **4710**

ANNUAL REPORT TO THE GENERAL ASSEMBLY ON THE ABUSE OF DANGEROUS DRUGS IN ILLINOIS (US) [06309967] **1341**

ANNUAL REPORT TO THE GOVERNOR (US) [18138353] 2249, **4464**

ANNUAL REPORT TO THE GOVERNOR AND GENERAL ASSEMELY - STATE OF CONNECTICUT, COMMISSION ON HOSPITALS & HEALTH CARE (US/0146-7077) [03007435] **3776**

ANNUAL REPORT TO THE GOVERNOR AND LEGISLATURE ON PREPAID HEALTH PLANS, PHPS (JS/0145-9171) [02811172] **2874**

ANNUAL REPORT TO THE GOVERNOR AND LEGISLATURE - STATE BOARD OF INDIGENTS' DEFENSE SERVICES (KANSAS) (US) [12047613] **4035**

ANNUAL REPORT TO THE GOVERNOR AND LEGISLATURE / STATE OF FLORIDA, HEALTH CARE COST CONTAINMENT BOARD (US) [20118681] **3776**

ANNUAL REPORT TO THE GOVERNOR AND MEMBERS OF THE GENERAL ASSEMBLY - MISSOURI COMMISSION ON HIGHER EDUCATION (US/0090-9874) [01786245] **1809**

ANNUAL REPORT TO THE GOVERNOR AND THE GENERAL ASSEMBLY OF MARYLAND (US/0149-5402) [03496849] **1809**

ANNUAL REPORT TO THE GOVERNOR / NEW MEXICO STATE BOARD OF PSYCHOLOGIST EXAMINERS (US) [11406959] **4574**

ANNUAL REPORT TO THE GOVERNOR OF THE STATE OF LOUISANA (US) [17801149] **3851**

ANNUAL REPORT TO THE GOVERNOR ON EMPLOYMENT AND TRAINING. MASSACHUSETTS (US) [09100054] **1650**

... ANNUAL REPORT TO THE GOVERNOR ON EMPLOYMENT AND TRAINING, THE (US) [08642731] **1650**

ANNUAL REPORT TO THE GOVERNOR / TEXAS PLANNING COUNCIL FOR DEVELOPMENTAL DISABILITIES (US) [15618697] **5273**

ANNUAL REPORT TO THE GOVERNOR / WEST VIRGINIA BUREAU OF EMPLOYMENT PROGRAMS (US) [25642154] **1650**

ANNUAL REPORT TO THE LEGISLATIVE ASSEMBLY - PROVINCE OF BRITISH COLUMBIA. OMBUDSMAN (CN/0835-5428) [17682160] **4629**

ANNUAL REPORT TO THE LEGISLATURE - CORRECTIONAL ASSOCIATION OF NEW YORK (US) [01565188] **3157**

ANNUAL REPORT TO THE LEGISLATURE / LEGISLATIVE COMMISSION ON EXPENDITURE (US) [18154537] **4711**

ANNUAL REPORT TO THE LEGISLATURE OF THE ALCOHOL AND DRUG COMMISSION (VICTORIA) (CN/0704-2493) [02452746] **1341**

ANNUAL REPORT TO THE MAYOR OF THE DISTRICT OF COLUMBIA (US) [03305465] **1650**

ANNUAL REPORT TO THE MINISTER OF AGRICULTURE (AGRICULTURAL STABILIZATION BOARD) (CN/0527-4664) [02510860] **61**

ANNUAL REPORT TO THE OKLAHOMA TURNPIKE AUTHORITY (US/0748-5077) [10939913] 5438, **4629**

ANNUAL REPORT TO THE PRESIDENT AND THE CONGRESS - NATIONAL ADVISORY COUNCIL ON THE EDUCATION OF DISADVANTAGED CHILDREN (US/0565-7024) [02697418] **1875**

ANNUAL REPORT TO THE PRESIDENT AND THE CONGRESS ON THE STATE ENERGY CONSERVATION PROGRAM (US/0161-1674) [08437455] **1932**

ANNUAL REPORT TO THE PRESIDENT AND THE CONGRESS ON THE WEATHERIZATION ASSISTANCE PROGRAM (US/0195-4806) [05117999] 598, **1932**

ANNUAL REPORT TO THE SECRETARY, DEPARTMENT OF THE INTERIOR (US/0098-745X) [03146007] **1446**

ANNUAL REPORT - TOBACCO WORKING GROUP, NATIONAL INSTITUTES OF HEALTH (US) [04279157] **5372**

ANNUAL REPORT - TOKYO-TO KOGAI KENKYUJO (JA) [01792413] **2224**

ANNUAL REPORT - TOWN AND COUNTRY PLANNING ASSOCIATION (UK/0308-082X) [02244108] **2815**

ANNUAL REPORT - TRADE DEVELOPMENT AUTHORITY (NEW DELHI) (II/0302-4784) [01797681] **823**

ANNUAL REPORT / TRADE PRACTICES COMMISSION (AT/0314-0520) [10154589] **3095**

ANNUAL REPORT - TRANSPORT USERS CONSULTATIVE COMMITTEE FOR WALES (UK) [07034436] **5429**

ANNUAL REPORT: TUBERCULOSIS CONTROL IN THE PROVINCE OF NEW BRUNSWICK (CN) [02980426] **4767**

ANNUAL REPORT - TUBERCULOSIS CONTROL SERVICES, NOVA SCOTIA (CN/0078-2505) [04342084] **3948**

ANNUAL REPORT - TUSKEGEE INSTITUTE. HUMAN RESOURCES DEVELOPMENT CENTER (US/0739-7127) [09790946] **5239**

ANNUAL REPORT - TWENTIETH CENTURY FUND (US/0363-3047) [01606778] **5228**

ANNUAL REPORT / U.S. DEPARTMENT OF EDUCATION (US/0278-5730) [07130229] **1725**

ANNUAL REPORT / U.S. DEPARTMENT OF TRANSPORTATION (US) [01588545] **5377**

ANNUAL REPORT / U.S. NATIONAL HOUSING AGENCY (US) [01471918] **2815**

ANNUAL REPORT / U.S. NAVY'S MILITARY SEALIFT COMMAND (US/0884-9951) [12207257] **4174**

ANNUAL REPORT / U.S. NUCLEAR REGULATORY COMMISSION **SUSPENDED.** (US/0363-7956) [02311319] **2154**

ANNUAL REPORT / UGANDA FRESHWATER FISHERIES RESEARCH ORGANIZATION (UG) [15809954] **2295**

ANNUAL REPORT / UIA, UNITED ISRAEL APPEAL, INC (US) [07119830] **5273**

ANNUAL REPORT UNDER THE BANKING ACT FOR ... (UK) [18457543] **772**

ANNUAL REPORT / UNICEF (US) [11009426] **3123**

ANNUAL REPORT - UNITED CHURCH BOARD FOR WORLD MINISTRIES (US/0145-0824) [01767999] **4935**

ANNUAL REPORT - UNITED NATIONS, ECONOMIC COMMISSION FOR AFRICA (US/0252-2047) [01185850] **1462**

ANNUAL REPORT - UNITED PLANTING ASSOCIATION OF MALAYSIA (MY/0304-8349) [01795231] **61**

ANNUAL REPORT - UNITED STATES DEPARTMENT OF THE INTERIOR, BUREAU OF SPORT FISHERIES AND WILDLIFE, FISH AND WILDLIFE SERVICE (US/0362-6997) [02319661] **2187**

ANNUAL REPORT - UNITED STATES. DEPT. OF AGRICULTURE (US) [06107367] **61**

ANNUAL REPORT - UNITED STATES. DEPT. OF THE TREASURY. OFFICE OF THE INSPECTOR GENERAL (US/0739-6058) [09308109] **4711**

ANNUAL REPORT - UNITED STATES. ECONOMIC DEVELOPMENT ADMINISTRATION (1969) (US/0565-4408) [01179718] **1598**

ANNUAL REPORT - UNITED STATES. FOREIGN CLAIMS SETTLEMENT COMMISSION (US/0739-5353) [09461956] **3123**

ANNUAL REPORT / UNITED STATES INTERNATIONAL TRADE COMMISSION (US/0147-5568) [02704690] **823**

ANNUAL REPORT - UNITED TECHNOLOGIES (US/0149-3965) [03469125] **2096**

ANNUAL REPORT - UNIVERSITY OF JAMMU (II) [01790453] **1809**

ANNUAL REPORT / UNIVERSITY OF LONDON, INSTITUTE OF ADVANCED LEGAL STUDIES (UK) [20577313] **2935**

ANNUAL REPORT / UNIVERSITY OF OREGON. BUREAU OF GOVERNMENTAL RESEARCH AND SERVICE (US) [19904970] **4630**

ANNUAL REPORT / UNIVERSITY OF RHODESIA. INSTITUTE OF MINING RESEARCH *See* ANNUAL REPORT OF THE INTER-AMERICAN COMMISSION ON HUMAN RIGHTS / ORGANIZATION OF AMERICAN STATES **4504**

ANNUAL REPORT - UNIVERSITY OF ZAMBIA. SCHOOL OF HUMANITIES & SOCIAL SCIENCES (ZA) [05001135] 5191, **2842**

ANNUAL REPORT (UNIVERSITY OF ZIMBABWE. INSTITUTE OF MINING RESEARCH). (RH) [13408025] **2134**

ANNUAL REPORT - URBAN AFFAIRS (OTTAWA) (CN) [02241821] 2815, **4630**

ANNUAL REPORT - UTAH. DEPT. OF NATURAL RESOURCES (US/0882-7583) [10495968] **4630**

ANNUAL REPORT / VALIO, FINNISH CO-OPERATIVE DAIRIES' ASSOCIATION (FI) [05206205] **192**

ANNUAL REPORT - VANCOUVER ART GALLERY (CN/0083-5161) [03114605] **336**

ANNUAL REPORT / VERMONT LOTTERY (US) [15555449] **4630**

ANNUAL REPORT - VIA RAIL CANADA INC (CN/0706-5698) [04590211] **5429**

ANNUAL REPORT - VICTORIA, AUSTRALIA. ENVIRONMENT PROTECTION AUTHORITY (AT) [01785899] **3109**

ANNUAL REPORT / VICTORIAN ETHNIC AFFAIRS COMMISSION (AT/0812-566X) [13440203] 2255, **4630**

ANNUAL REPORT / VICTORIAN MINISTRY OF IMMIGRATION & ETHNIC AFFAIRS (AT) [08226243] 2255, **1918**

ANNUAL REPORT / VIRGINIA AGRICULTURAL DEVELOPMENT AUTHORITY (US/0883-0967) [11823148] **61**

ANNUAL REPORT / VIRGINIA AGRICULTURAL FOUNDATION (US/0883-1017) [11848673] **61**

ANNUAL REPORT / VIRGINIA ASSOCIATION OF COMMUNITY SERVICES BOARDS, INC (US) [12125031] **5273**

ANNUAL REPORT - VIRGINIA DEPARTMENT OF PERSONNEL AND TRAINING (US) [06727581] **4701**

ANNUAL REPORT / VIRGINIA ENVIRONMENTAL ENDOWMENT (US/0191-4049) [04853006] 5530, **2161**

ANNUAL REPORT / VIRGINIA STATE APPLE COMMISSION (US) [11613728] **1598**

ANNUAL REPORT - VIRGINIA STATE OFFICE ON VOLUNTEERISM (US) [04690535] **5273**

ANNUAL REPORT - VIRGINIA WATER RESOURCES RESEARCH CENTER ***CEASED.*** (US/0736-3923) [06132596] **5530**

ANNUAL REPORT / VOLKSWAGEN DO BRASIL, S.A (BL) [11765399] **1598**

ANNUAL REPORT - VOLVO (SW) [02243074] **5403**

ANNUAL REPORT / WASHINGTON STATE LOTTERY (US) [11658012] **772**

ANNUAL REPORT / WATER AUTHORITY OF WESTERN AUSTRALIA (AT/1031-5225) [16754204] 4759, **5530**

ANNUAL REPORT / WATER WORKS AND SEWER BOARD OF THE CITY OF BIRMINGHAM (US) [16934547] 4759, **5530**

ANNUAL REPORT - WAYNE COUNTY DEPARTMENT OF SOCIAL SERVICES (US/0093-7665) [01792611] **5273**

ANNUAL REPORT - WEST AFRICA RICE DEVELOPMENT ASSOCIATION (LB) [03171667] **163**

ANNUAL REPORT / WEST JAPAN RAILWAY COMPANY (JA) [26912083] **5429**

ANNUAL REPORT / WEST VIRGINIA BOARD OF REGENTS (US) [22602264] **1809**

ANNUAL REPORT / WEST VIRGINIA DEPARTMENT OF NATURAL RESOURCES (US) [07792942] **2187**

ANNUAL REPORT - WEST VIRGINIA GOVERNOR'S HIGHWAY SAFETY ADMINISTRATION (US/0360-0246) [02243303] 5377, **4630**

ANNUAL REPORT / WEST VIRGINIA STATE ADVISORY COUNCIL ON VOCATIONAL EDUCATION (US) [11000280] **1910**

ANNUAL REPORT - WESTERN AUSTRALIAN COASTAL SHIPPING COMMISSION (AT) [02242091] **5447**

ANNUAL REPORT / WESTERN AUSTRALIAN EGG MARKETING BOARD (AT) [16642778] **2327**

ANNUAL REPORT - WESTERN STATE LIBRARY (NR/0302-4873) [01793614] **3191**

ANNUAL REPORT - WESTERN STATES WATER COUNCIL (US/0511-8182) [01187413] **5530**

ANNUAL REPORT - WILLIAM T. GRANT FOUNDATION (US/0160-7200) [03720928] **5273**

ANNUAL REPORT / WORKERS' COMPENSATION BOARD, NEWFOUNDLAND AND LABRADOR (CN/0225-3291) [06273411] **1650**

ANNUAL REPORT - WORLD BANK (US/0252-2942) [14107247] 772, **2907**

ANNUAL REPORT - WYOMING ENERGY CONSERVATION OFFICE (US/0197-0496) [05935309] **1932**

ANNUAL REPORT - WYOMING STATE BOARD OF NURSING (US/0098-2679) [02240051] **3851**

ANNUAL REPORT, YEAR ENDED 30 JUNE ... / PUBLIC RECORD OFFICE (AT) [08078838] **2479**

ANNUAL REPORT YEAR ENDING SEPT. 30 ... / ACCREDITATION BOARD FOR ENGINEERING AND TECHNOLOGY (US) [07166680] **5084**

ANNUAL REPORT, YEAR TO 31ST MARCH ... / BRITISH-BORNEO PETROLEUM SYNDICATE, P.L.C (UK) [08690883] **4250**

ANNUAL REPORT - YORK GEORGIAN SOCIETY (UK/0959-3640) [02246401] **5228**

ANNUAL REPORT / ZENTRALINSTITUT FUER VERSUCHSTIERZUCHT (GW) [19563871] **5503**

ANNUAL REPORTS (US) [23937313] **2935**

ANNUAL REPORTS AND RESOLUTIONS - AMERICAN DENTAL ASSOCIATION (US/0090-3329) [03521149] **1316**

ANNUAL REPORTS / ENVIRONMENTAL PROTECTION AUTHORITY AND CONSERVATION AND ENVIRONMENT COUNCIL (AT) [10649381] **2161**

ANNUAL REPORTS FOR THE YEARS ... / REPUBLIC OF ZAMBIA, MINISTRY OF LABOUR AND SOCIAL SERVICES, INDUSTRIAL RELATIONS COURT (ZA) [08815301] **3144**

ANNUAL REPORTS FOR ... / UNIVERSITY OF OXFORD, INSTITUTE OF ECONOMICS AND STATISTICS (UK) [08135227] 1650, **1590**

ANNUAL REPORTS IN MEDICINAL CHEMISTRY (US/0065-7743) [01481490] 961, **4291**

ANNUAL REPORTS IN ORGANIC SYNTHESIS (US/0066-409X) [00923988] 480, **1039**

ANNUAL REPORTS - INDIANA STATE HIGHWAY COMMISSION, DIVISION OF ACCOUNTING & CONTROL (US/0363-9312) [02593602] **5438**

ANNUAL REPORTS OF OFFICERS, COMMITTEES, SECTIONS, AND OTHER BAR-RELATED GROUPS *See* BLUE BOOK / ILLINOIS STATE BAR ASSOCIATION **2942**

ANNUAL REPORTS OF PROGRESS - REHABILITATION ENGINEERING CENTER AT RANCHO LOS AMIGOS HOSPITAL (US/0147-0876) [03065148] **3685**

ANNUAL REPORTS OF THE BOARD OF MANAGEMENT AND OF THE CLOSER SETTLEMENT BOARD FOR THE YEAR ENDED 30TH JUNE ... TO WHICH ARE APPENDED FINANCIAL STATEMENTS AND OTHER INFORMATION / THE AGRICULTURAL BANK OF TASMANIA (AT) [05281994] **772**

ANNUAL REPORTS OF THE NATIONAL COLLEGIATE ATHLETIC ASSOCIATION (US/0077-3794) [02244318] **4883**

ANNUAL REPORTS OF THE NORTH CAROLINIANA SOCIETY, INC. AND THE NORTH CAROLINA COLLECTION (US/0270-5303) [05379819] **2721**

ANNUAL REPORTS OF THE RESEARCH REACTOR INSTITUTE, KYOTO UNIVERSITY (JA/0454-9244) [01797969] **4446**

ANNUAL REPORTS OF THE SYNDICATE AND OF THE FRIENDS OF THE FITZWILLIAM FOR THE YEAR ENDING ..., THE (UK) [03498243] **4084**

ANNUAL REPORTS ON NATIONAL LIFE (JA) [06114223] **1546**

ANNUAL REPORTS ON NMR SPECTROSCOPY (UK/0066-4103) [01481492] **4443**

ANNUAL REPORTS ON THE EXCHANGE OF MEDICAL INFORMATION AND SHARING MEDICAL RESOURCES (US/0190-5031) [04163978] **3551**

ANNUAL REPORTS ON THE PROGRESS OF CHEMISTRY. SECTION A, INORGANIC CHEMISTRY (UK/0260-1818) [07093197] **1035**

ANNUAL REPORTS ON THE PROGRESS OF CHEMISTRY. SECTION B, ORGANIC CHEMISTRY (UK/0069-3030) [01645552] **1039**

ANNUAL REPORTS ON THE PROGRESS OF CHEMISTRY. SECTION C, PHYSICAL CHEMISTRY (UK/0260-1826) [07102763] **1050**

ANNUAL REPORTS - OREGON STATE BAR (US/0739-6627) [07908124] **2935**

ANNUAL REPORTS / STATE OF ILLINOIS, DEPARTMENT OF HUMAN RIGHTS [AND] HUMAN RIGHTS COMMISSION (US) [08725937] **4504**

ANNUAL RESEARCH CONFERENCES OF THE BUREAU OF BIOLOGICAL RESEARCH, THE (US/0080-4967) [05329585] **442**

ANNUAL RESEARCH REPORT (NZ) [19077970] **1725**

ANNUAL RESEARCH REPORT / INSTITUTE FOR COMMERCIAL FORESTRY RESEARCH (SA) [25030546] **2375**

ANNUAL RESEARCH REPORT - RED RIVER VALLEY AGRICULTURAL EXPERIMENT STATION (BOSSIER CITY, LA.) (US/0886-4500) [02638823] **163**

ANNUAL RESEARCH REPORT / RICE RESEARCH STATION (US/1054-8300) [19132345] **163**

ANNUAL RESEARCH REVIEW - CALIFORNIA DEPARTMENT OF CORRECTIONS (US/0196-7746) [01552376] **3158**

ANNUAL RETAIL TRADE (CN/0843-557X) [20475523] **952**

ANNUAL REVIEW / ALBERTA AGENCY FOR INTERNATIONAL DEVELOPMENT (CN/0715-240X) [09062748] **2907**

ANNUAL REVIEW, ALBERTA EDUCATION (CN/0319-0617) [01795659] **1725**

ANNUAL REVIEW - ATLANTIC LOTTERY, CANADA (CN/0848-6719) [23264606] **4630**

ANNUAL REVIEW / BRITISH AGENCIES FOR ADOPTION AND FOSTERING (UK) [08333447] **5273**

ANNUAL REVIEW / CHIEF, NATIONAL GUARD BUREAU (US/0192-4559) [03237642] **4035**

ANNUAL REVIEW / DEPARTMENT OF PHYSICAL PLANNING, MINISTRY OF LOCAL GOVERNMENT, RURAL AND URBAN DEVELOPMENT (RH) [19476447] **2815**

ANNUAL REVIEW - ECONOMIC COUNCIL OF CANADA *CEASED*. (CN/0070-8488) [02248816] **1463**

ANNUAL REVIEW - EUROPEAN COMMISSION OF HUMAN RIGHTS (FR) [01786922] **4504**

ANNUAL REVIEW FOR ... / THE GAME CONSERVANCY (UK) [09059738] 5614, **2187**

ANNUAL REVIEW FOR THE YEAR RELATING TO OIL AND GAS (US/0190-3926) [04693421] **4250**

ANNUAL REVIEW / FRESHWATER FISHERIES LABORATORY, PITLOCHRY (UK/0951-3752) [19418210] **2295**

ANNUAL REVIEW IN AUTOMATIC PROGRAMMING (UK/0066-4138) [01275654] **1278**

ANNUAL REVIEW - INTERNATIONAL LEAGUE FOR HUMAN RIGHTS (US) [04094569] **4504**

ANNUAL REVIEW - INTERNATIONAL LEAGUE FOR THE RIGHTS OF MAN *See* ANNUAL REVIEW - INTERNATIONAL LEAGUE FOR HUMAN RIGHTS **4504**

ANNUAL REVIEW - LABOUR CANADA (CN/0225-9923) [06213188] **1650**

ANNUAL REVIEW / MARINE LABORATORY ABERDEEN (UK/0951-3760) [17949697] **1446**

ANNUAL REVIEW - NATIONAL CHILDREN'S BUREAU (UK) [01792442] **5273**

ANNUAL REVIEW - NATIONAL FUTURES ASSOCIATION (U.S.) (US/8756-226X) [11197507] **891**

ANNUAL REVIEW - NEWFOUNDLAND REGION (CN) [09358965] **2295**

ANNUAL REVIEW, NORTH CAROLINA (US/0738-0798) [08876605] **2935**

ANNUAL REVIEW OF ADDICTIONS RESEARCH AND TREATMENT (US/0955-663X) [25880301] **1341**

ANNUAL REVIEW OF AIRCRAFT ACCIDENT DATA. U.S. GENERAL AVIATION / NATIONAL TRANSPORTATION SAFETY BOARD (US) [03998477] **11**

ANNUAL REVIEW OF ANTHROPOLOGY (US/0084-6570) [01783647] **228**

ANNUAL REVIEW OF APPLIED LINGUISTICS (UK/0267-1905) [07873852] **3265**

ANNUAL REVIEW OF ASTRONOMY AND ASTROPHYSICS (US/0066-4146) [01481495] **391**

ANNUAL REVIEW OF BANKING LAW (US/0739-2451) [09158198] **3084**

ANNUAL REVIEW OF BIOCHEMISTRY (US/0066-4154) [01481496] **480**

● ANNUAL REVIEW OF BIOPHYSICS AND BIOMOLECULAR STRUCTURE (US/1056-8700) [23884496] **494**

ANNUAL REVIEW OF BIOPHYSICS AND BIOPHYSICAL CHEMISTRY *See* ANNUAL REVIEW OF BIOPHYSICS AND BIOMOLECULAR STRUCTURE **494**

ANNUAL REVIEW OF CALIFORNIA OIL AND GAS PRODUCTION (US/0197-5641) [02533620] **4250**

ANNUAL REVIEW OF CELL BIOLOGY (US/0743-4634) [10586991] **532**

ANNUAL REVIEW OF CHRONOPHARMACOLOGY (UK/0743-9539) [10728955] **4291**

ANNUAL REVIEW OF COFFEE (TZ) [19058907] **2363**

● ANNUAL REVIEW OF COMMUNICATIONS (US/1073-0885) [27660235] **1149**

ANNUAL REVIEW OF CRIMINAL LAW (CN/0821-7912) [09581970] **3105**

ANNUAL REVIEW OF EARTH AND PLANETARY SCIENCES (US/0084-6597) [01783648] 391, **1351**

ANNUAL REVIEW OF ECOLOGY AND SYSTEMATICS (US/0066-4162) [01404265] **2211**

ANNUAL REVIEW OF ENERGY AND THE ENVIRONMENT (US/1056-3466) [23669325] **1932**

ANNUAL REVIEW OF ENGINEERING INDUSTRIES AND AUTOMATION ... (INT/0255-9293) [02559293] **1965**

ANNUAL REVIEW OF ENGLISH BOOKS ON ASIA (US/0098-7379) [02239672] **4823**

ANNUAL REVIEW OF ENTOMOLOGY (US/0066-4170) [01321134] **5605**

ANNUAL REVIEW OF EUROPEAN EXPORT INDUSTRIES : FURNITURE (GW) [05093306] 823, **2904**

ANNUAL REVIEW OF FAMILY THERAPY *CEASED*. (US/0198-9731) [06288005] **3921**

ANNUAL REVIEW OF FISH DISEASES (US/0959-8030) [23862489] **2295**

ANNUAL REVIEW OF FLUID MECHANICS (US/0066-4189) [01481500] **2087**

ANNUAL REVIEW OF GENETICS (US/0066-4197) [01481501] **542**

ANNUAL REVIEW OF GERONTOLOGY & GERIATRICS (US/0198-8794) [06267560] **3749**

ANNUAL REVIEW OF GOVERNMENT FUNDED R&D / CABINET OFFICE (UK) [12310304] **4630**

ANNUAL REVIEW OF HEAT TRANSFER (US/1049-0787) [21122807] 4430, **4427**

ANNUAL REVIEW OF HONG KONG EXTERNAL TRADE .... (HK) [26918867] **823**

ANNUAL REVIEW OF HYDROCEPHALUS (GW) **3551**

ANNUAL REVIEW OF IMMUNOLOGY (US/0732-0582) [08297364] **3666**

ANNUAL REVIEW OF INFORMATION SCIENCE AND TECHNOLOGY (US/0066-4200) [01481502] **3191**

ANNUAL REVIEW OF IRISH LAW (IE/0791-1084) [18247449] **2935**

ANNUAL REVIEW OF JAZZ STUDIES (US/0731-0641) [08099505] **4100**

ANNUAL REVIEW OF MATERIALS SCIENCE (US/0084-6600) [00944843] **2100**

ANNUAL REVIEW OF MEDICINE (US/0066-4219) [01481504] 442, **3551**

ANNUAL REVIEW OF MILITARY RESEARCH AND DEVELOPMENT (US/0741-9090) [09929935] **4035**

ANNUAL REVIEW OF NEUROSCIENCE (US/0147-006X) [03505758] **3827**

ANNUAL REVIEW OF NICARAGUAN SOCIOLOGY *CEASED*. (US/0899-5370) [18132691] **5239**

ANNUAL REVIEW OF NUCLEAR AND PARTICLE SCIENCE (US/0163-8998) [04447733] **4446**

ANNUAL REVIEW OF NURSING RESEARCH (US/0739-6686) [09801492] **3851**

ANNUAL REVIEW OF NUTRITION (US/0199-9885) [06307740] **4187**

ANNUAL REVIEW OF OCEAN AFFAIRS--LAW & POLICY, MAIN DOCUMENTS (US/1040-824X) [18542825] **3123**

ANNUAL REVIEW OF PHARMACOLOGY AND TOXICOLOGY (US/0362-1642) [02203939] 3979, **4291**

ANNUAL REVIEW OF PHYSICAL CHEMISTRY (US/0066-426X) [01373069] **1050**

ANNUAL REVIEW OF PHYSIOLOGY (US/0066-4278) [01481511] **578**

ANNUAL REVIEW OF PHYTOPATHOLOGY (US/0066-4286) [01481512] **500**

ANNUAL REVIEW OF PLANT PHYSIOLOGY AND PLANT MOLECULAR BIOLOGY (US/1040-2519) [18068169] **500**

ANNUAL REVIEW OF POLITICAL SCIENCE (US/0748-8599) [11018296] **4464**

ANNUAL REVIEW OF POPULATION LAW (US/0364-3417) [02639777] 588, **2935**

ANNUAL — Alphabetical Title Index

ANNUAL REVIEW OF PSYCHOLOGY (US/0066-4308) [01435605] **4574**

ANNUAL REVIEW OF PSYCHOPATHOLOGY (US) [24245997] **4574**

ANNUAL REVIEW OF PUBLIC HEALTH (US/0163-7525) [04471173] **4767**

ANNUAL REVIEW OF RETAIL GROCERY STORE TRENDS (US) [22968830] **2327**

ANNUAL REVIEW OF SEX RESEARCH (US/1053-2528) [22486946] **5186**

ANNUAL REVIEW OF SOCIOLOGY (US/0360-0572) [02244366] **5239**

ANNUAL REVIEW OF THE CHEMICAL INDUSTRY (US) [06715817] **1598**

ANNUAL REVIEW OF THE EMPLOYMENT SITUATION (CANADA) (CN) [03105761] **1650**

... ANNUAL REVIEW OF THE NATIONAL TRANSPORTATION AGENCY OF CANADA, THE (CN/0845-1109) [20382159] **5377**

ANNUAL REVIEW OF THE NEW ZEALAND SHEEP AND BEEF INDUSTRY (NZ/0112-739X) [22636085] **206**

ANNUAL REVIEW OF THE ROYAL INSCRIPTIONS OF MESOPOTAMIA PROJECT *SUSPENDED*. (CN/0822-2525) [10513360] 255, **3265**

ANNUAL REVIEW OF THE SITUATION IN AGRICULTURE (IE) [20322195] **62**

ANNUAL REVIEW OF WOMEN IN WORLD RELIGIONS, THE (US/1056-4578) [23719077] 5551, **4935**

ANNUAL REVIEW PULMONARY AND CRITICAL CARE MEDICINE *CEASED*. (US/0887-8242) [13390625] **3948**

ANNUAL REVIEW - SCIENCE COUNCIL OF CANADA (CN/0228-6246) [08091148] **5084**

ANNUAL REVIEW - TAVISTOCK INSTITUTE OF HUMAN RELATIONS, LONDON (UK) [01783091] **5191**

ANNUAL REVIEW / THE EDINBURGH SCHOOL OF AGRICULTURE (UK/0953-6884) [18036703] **62**

ANNUAL REVIEW - THE JUNIOR CHAMBER OF COMMERCE FOR LONDON (UK/0306-8501) [01795777] **818**

ANNUAL REVIEW ... U.S. ZINC AND CADMIUM INDUSTRY, INCLUDING STATEMENTS FROM OTHER COUNTRIES (US/0730-2711) [06945617] **1598**

ANNUAL ROSTER - TEXAS STATE BOARD OF LANDSCAPE ARCHITECTS (US/0092-3745) [01787119] **2409**

ANNUAL RPEORT OF THE TEXAS MIGRANT PROGRAM, ESEA, TITLE I (US) [04674471] **1725**

ANNUAL RREPORT AND ACCOUNTS / MILK MARKETING BOARD (UK) [03112525] **192**

ANNUAL RREPORT / REPUBLIC OF BOPHUTHATSWANA, DEPARTMENT OF HEALTH AND SOCIAL WELFARE, NURSING DIVISION (SA) [08620044] **3851**

ANNUAL SALARIES, NURSES, MAJOR HOSPITAL AGREEMENTS, CANADA (CN/0825-2815) [12069339] **3851**

ANNUAL SALARY SURVEYS. ADMINISTRATIVE & FINANCE REPORT / KPMG,PEAT MARWICK STEVENSON & KELLOGG, MANAGEMENT CONSULTANTS (CN/1184-9525) [24623793] **1650**

ANNUAL SALARY SURVEYS. EXECUTIVE COMPENSATION REPORT (CN/1185-3565) [24860283] **1650**

ANNUAL SALARY SURVEYS. INFORMATION SYSTEMS REPORT (CN/1184-9517) [24623795] **1650**

ANNUAL SALARY SURVEYS. PRODUCTION & DISTRIBUTION REPORT (CN/1185-3573) [24860252] **1650**

ANNUAL SCIENCE AND TECHNOLOGY REPORT TO THE CONGRESS (US/0734-5526) [07758063] **5084**

ANNUAL SCIENTIFIC REPORT OF THE I.V.R.I. CAMPUS, BANGALORE, FOR THE YEAR ... (II) [11189278] **5504**

ANNUAL SECURITIES SEMINAR COURSE HANDBOOK (US/0160-1555) [03620011] **2935**

ANNUAL SECURITY AND SHRINKAGE STUDY (US/0743-5460) [10591273] 952, **860**

ANNUAL SERVICES PLAN - DEPARTMENT OF SOCIAL SERVICES (US) [03811789] **5273**

ANNUAL SHEEP RETURNS *See* SHEEP RETURNS **221**

ANNUAL SILVER REVIEW AND OUTLOOK (US/0736-2455) [09050462] **3998**

ANNUAL SPEED STUDY, WASHINGTON ... AND CERTIFICATION OF 55 MPH ENFORCEMENT / PREPARED BY THE DEPARTMENT OF HIGHWAYS, HIGHWAY PLANNING DIVISION, IN COOPERATION WITH THE U.S. DEPARTMENT OF TRANSPORTATION, FEDERAL HIGHWAY ADMINISTRATION (US) [08245524] **5438**

ANNUAL STATE AID ENTITLEMENT STATISTICS ... , ILLINOIS PUBLIC SCHOOLS (US/09040671) 1725, **1793**

ANNUAL STATE HISTORIC PRESERVATION PLAN (INDIANA) (US) [03880655] **2721**

ANNUAL STATE HISTORIC PRESERVATION PLAN (WYOMING) (US) [04025967] **2721**

ANNUAL STATE PLAN FOR VOCATIONAL EDUCATION WITHIN CAREER EDUCATION. EXECUTIVE SUMMARY (US) [07039517] **1910**

ANNUAL STATE WATER-DATA REPORTS [COMPUTER FILE] : A DIGITAL REPRESENTATION OF THE HYDROLOGIC RECORDS OF THE UNITED STATES FOR ... (US) [25500414] **1412**

ANNUAL STATEMENT, CONCESSIONS IN THE CALIFORNIA STATE PARK SYSTEM (US/0362-6377) [02314668] **4706**

ANNUAL STATEMENT OF ACCOUNTS - HOUSING BOARD. RAJASTHAN, INDIA (II) [01790485] **2815**

ANNUAL STATEMENT / STATE OF NEW HAMPSHIRE, LIQUOR COMMISSION (US) [27783246] **2363**

ANNUAL STATISTICAL BULLETIN / NATIONAL COUNCIL ON COMPENSATION INSURANCE (US) [08173792] 1650, 2874, **1529**

ANNUAL STATISTICAL BULLETIN (ORGANIZATION OF PETROLEUM EXPORTING COUNTRIES) (AU) [08085834] 4250, **4283**

ANNUAL STATISTICAL BULLETIN. PUBLIC UNIVERSITY LIBRARY STATISTICS (US/0733-0979) [08277658] **5321**

ANNUAL STATISTICAL BULLETIN - SWAZILAND. CENTRAL STATISTICAL OFFICE (SQ/0300-2098) [01784711] **5321**

ANNUAL STATISTICAL BULLETIN - WASHINGTON STATE LIBRARY *See* ANNUAL STATISTICAL BULLETIN. PUBLIC UNIVERSITY LIBRARY STATISTICS **5321**

ANNUAL STATISTICAL DIGEST - BOARD OF GOVERNORS OF THE FEDERAL RESERVE SYSTEM (US/0148-4338) [03308771] **772**

ANNUAL STATISTICAL DIGEST - CENTRAL STATISTICAL OFFICE (PORT-OF-SPAIN) (TR/0564-2604) [01157323] **5321**

ANNUAL STATISTICAL REPORT / AMERICAN ASSOCIATION OF COLLEGES OF OSTEOPATHIC MEDICINE (US/0738-6230) [09445885] 3551, **3654**

ANNUAL STATISTICAL REPORT - AMERICAN IRON AND STEEL INSTITUTE (US) [01480089] 3998, **4025**

ANNUAL STATISTICAL REPORT - DIVISION OF FAMILY SERVICES (US/0093-6715) [01792569] 5273, **5266**

ANNUAL STATISTICAL REPORT / EMILY P. BISSELL HOSPITAL (US) [09163565] 3776, **3654**

ANNUAL STATISTICAL REPORT. MENTAL HEALTH SERVICES. MENTAL RETARDATION SERVICES. VETERANS' HOMES SERVICE (NEBRASKA) (US/0146-2148) [02865731] 5273, **5266**

ANNUAL STATISTICAL REPORT / NORTH CAROLINA DEPARTMENT OF COMMUNITY COLLEGES (US) [22999668] **1809**

ANNUAL STATISTICAL REPORT OF EXPENDITURES MADE IN CONNECTION WITH ELECTIONS, THE (US/0149-1962) [03440220] **4501**

ANNUAL STATISTICAL REPORT OF PENNSYLVANIA COUNTY PRISONS AND JAILS / DIVISION OF PLANNING AND RESEARCH (US) [06801977] 3158, **3078**

ANNUAL STATISTICAL REPORT - SOUTH DAKOTA DEPARTMENT OF SOCIAL SERVICES (US/0147-6467) [03208288] 5273, **5266**

ANNUAL STATISTICAL REVIEW - PROVINCE OF PRINCE EDWARD ISLAND. PLANNING & STATISTICS DIVISION. DEPARTMENT OF FINANCE (CN/0833-5176) [08328032] 1650, **1529**

ANNUAL STATISTICAL SUMMARY (US) [08249390] 4232, **4240**

ANNUAL STATISTICAL SUMMARY OF THE STATE OF MARYLAND FAMILY PLANNING PROGRAM (US/0098-390X) [02241257] **2287**

●ANNUAL STATISTICAL SUPPLEMENT, ... TO THE SOCIAL SECURITY BULLETIN (US) [28328831] 2874, **5273**

ANNUAL STATISTICS / MANITOBA HEALTH SERVICES COMMISSION (CN/0708-7233) [04520912] **4809**

ANNUAL STATISTICS OF ELECTRIC COMPANIES (US) [16274682] **4759**

ANNUAL STATISTICS OF GAS COMPANIES (US) [17250835] 4759, **4696**

ANNUAL STATISTICS OF MEDICAL SCHOOL LIBRARIES IN THE UNITED STATES AND CANADA (US/0196-6448) [04601982] 3191, **3257**

ANNUAL STATUS REPORT. NUCLEAR MEASUREMENTS / COMMISSION OF THE EUROPEAN COMMUNITIES (LU) [11545283] **4446**

ANNUAL STATUS REPORT ON FEMALE AND MALE STUDENTS AND EMPLOYEES IN VOCATIONAL EDUCATION (OKLAHOMA) (US) [10790715] **1910**

ANNUAL STATUS REPORT ON THE INACTIVE URANIUM MILL TAILINGS SITES REMEDIAL ACTION PROGRAM (US/0271-9754) [06694765] **2224**

ANNUAL STATUS REPORT ON THE URANIUM MILL TAILINGS REMEDIAL ACTION PROGRAM (US/0277-0504) [07455721] **2224**

ANNUAL STATUS REPORT. THERMONUCLEAR FUSION TECHNOLOGY / COMMISSION OF THE EUROPEAN COMMUNITIES (LU) [11313864] **2154**

ANNUAL STREET FINANCE REPORT FOR THE INCORPORATED CITIES AND TOWNS OF IOWA *See* STREET FINANCE REPORT FOR IOWA CITIES **5445**

ANNUAL STUDY EXECUTIVE COMPENSATION / PREPARED BY SIBSON & COMPANY, INC (US) [07540499] **1650**

ANNUAL SUMMARY BY THE COMMISSIONER OF RATING AND VALUATION (HONGKONG) (HK) [05185813] **4711**

ANNUAL SUMMARY, CHARACTERISTIC OF THE INSURED UNEMPLOYED (MASSACHUSETTS) (US) [03905469] **1650**

ANNUAL SUMMARY / DIVISION OF SPECIAL EDUCATION (US) [09950253] **1875**

ANNUAL SUMMARY - IOWA. STATE DEPT. OF HEALTH. DIVISION OF DISEASE PREVENTION (US/0730-6814) [08024375] **3712**

ANNUAL SUMMARY OF ACTIVITIES - ARIZONA DEPARTMENT OF ECONOMIC SECURITY (US/0146-891X) [03067459] **1650**

ANNUAL SUMMARY OF AUSTRALIAN NOTICES TO MARINERS (AT/0312-6056) [02243766] **4174**

ANNUAL SUMMARY OF CLASSES AND ENROLLMENT IN COMMUNITY SCHOOLS FOR ADULTS (US) [04418916] **1799**

ANNUAL SUMMARY OF DWELLING UNITS AUTHORIZED BY BUILDING PERMITS (NEW JERSEY) (US) [03791948] **2815**

ANNUAL SUMMARY OF LAWS AND REGULATIONS RELATING TO THE CONTROL OF NARCOTIC DRUGS (US) [01476406] 1341, **3123**

ANNUAL SUMMARY OF PROGRAMS IN ENERGY SCIENCES (US) [06025162] **1932**

ANNUAL SUMMARY OF RECEIPTS AND DISBURSEMENTS / MUNICIPAL BOND COMMISSION OF WEST VIRGINIA (US) [07421508] **891**

ANNUAL SUMMARY OF SPEED LIMIT 55 MONITORING PROGRAM / MINNESOTA, DEPARTMENT OF TRANSPORTATION (US) [09801848] **5377**

ANNUAL SUMMARY OF VITAL STATISTICS, KANSAS (1969) (US/0364-2372) [02620653] **5321**

ANNUAL SUMMARY REPORT. PROGRESS AND PLANS - AMES LABORATORY, U.S.A.E.C (US/0091-875X) [01787499] **2154**

ANNUAL SUPPLEMENT TO HONG KONG TRADE STATISTICS, COUNTRY BY COMMODITY IMPORTS (HK/0304-8489) [02241039] 823, **726**

ANNUAL SURVEY - NATIONAL ASSOCIATION OF STATE SCHOLARSHIP AND GRANT PROGRAMS (US/0731-1206) [07349009] **1809**

ANNUAL SURVEY - NATIONAL CONFERENCE OF CATHOLIC CHARITIES (US/0161-4894) [03939785] **5023**

ANNUAL SURVEY OF AMERICAN LAW (US/0066-4413) [02069008] **2935**

ANNUAL SURVEY OF AUSTRALIAN LAW, AN (AT/0727-4076) [08843743] **2935**

ANNUAL SURVEY OF BANKRUPTCY LAW (US/0270-1464) [06192745] **3084**

ANNUAL SURVEY OF COLLEGES (US/8755-8696) [10853976] 1810, **1793**

ANNUAL SURVEY OF COLORADO LAW (US/0160-5658) [03695387] **2935**

ANNUAL SURVEY OF COMMUNITY PHARMACY OPERATIONS (CN/0829-2078) [16292552] **4291**

ANNUAL SURVEY OF FACULTY SALARIES (US) [07365400] **4291**

ANNUAL SURVEY OF INDIAN LAW (II/0570-2666) [01481523] **2935**

ANNUAL SURVEY OF INDUSTRIES (PONDICHERRY (INDIA : UNION TERRITORY). BUREAU OF ECONOMICS AND STATISTICS) (II) [08164004] **1546**

ANNUAL SURVEY OF MANUFACTURES. MANUFACTURERS' ALTERNATIVE ENERGY CAPABILITIES (US) [04470911] **3475**

ANNUAL SURVEY OF MANUFACTURES. STATISTICS FOR INDUSTRY GROUPS AND INDUSTRIES (INCLUDING CAPITAL EXPENDITURES, INVENTORIES AND SUPPLEMENTAL LABOR, FUEL, AND ELECTRIC ENERGY COSTS) (US) [18517099] **1650**

ANNUAL SURVEY OF MANUFACTURES. STATISTICS FOR STATES, STANDARD METROPOLITAN STATISTICAL AREAS, LARGE INDUSTRIAL COUNTIES, AND SELECTED CITIES (US) [03312925] **3475, 3489**

ANNUAL SURVEY OF MANUFACTURES. VALUE OF MANUFACTURERS' INVENTORIES (US) [03705208] **3475**

ANNUAL SURVEY OF MANUFACTURES. VALUE OF PRODUCT SHIPMENTS : ASM (US) [03313126] **3475**

ANNUAL SURVEY OF MANUFACTURES (WASHINGTON) (US/0082-9307) [00993098] **3475**

ANNUAL SURVEY OF MUSIC LIBRARIES (UK) [15480648] **4100, 3191**

ANNUAL SURVEY OF NON-CASH BENEFITS *See* NON-CASH BENEFITS SIC SURVEY **1695**

●ANNUAL SURVEY OF PRESCRIPTION AND OVER-THE-COUNTER DRUGS (CN/1196-5290) [29920142] **4291**

ANNUAL SURVEY OF SOUTH AFRICAN LAW (SA/0376-4605) [01481526] **2935**

ANNUAL SURVEY OF VICTORIAN PUBLIC LIBRARIES / VICTORIAN MINISTRY FOR THE ARTS (AT/1035-4832) [28186586] **3191**

ANNUAL SYMPOSIUM ON FOUNDATIONS OF COMPUTER SCIENCE (US) [23102428] 3494, **1250**

ANNUAL SYMPOSIUM PROCEEDINGS / AGIFORS (US) [13920766] **12**

ANNUAL SYMPOSIUM PROCEEDINGS / SOCIETY OF FLIGHT TEST ENGINEERS (US/1050-9690) [12213833] **12**

ANNUAL TABLESERVICE RESTAURANT OPERATIONS REPORT ... FOR THE UNITED STATES / NATIONAL RESTAURANT ASSOCIATION (US) [04044730] **5070**

ANNUAL TECHNICAL CONFERENCE (US) [20455911] **5429**

ANNUAL TECHNICAL CONFERENCE TRANSACTIONS - AMERICAN SOCIETY FOR QUALITY CONTROL (US/0360-6929) [01823880] **860**

ANNUAL TECHNICAL REPORT OF THE GEOLOGICAL SURVEY OF SOUTH AFRICA (SA) [20761174] **1365**

ANNUAL TECHNICAL REPORT / UNITED STATES DEPARTMENT OF AGRICULTURE, SOIL CONSERVATION SERVICE, BISMARCK PLANT MATERIALS CENTER (US) [09244137] **5084**

ANNUAL - THEATRE HISTORICAL SOCIETY (U.S.) (US/0885-3940) [05013623] **5361**

ANNUAL TRADITIONAL CRAFT DAYS (US/0273-3838) [07042280] **370**

ANNUAL U.S. ECONOMIC DATA (US/0891-8414) [10816098] **1463**

ANNUAL UPDATE TO THE ALASKA STATE PLAN FOR THE REDUCTION OF ALCOHOLISM AND ALCOHOL ABUSE (US/0146-9053) [03095017] **1341**

ANNUAL UPLAND GAME BIRD REPORT (BOISE) (US/0445-1953) [01999201] **5576**

ANNUAL VOLUME OF PEDIATRICS CLUB BY CONTRIBUTING MEMBERS (US/0197-873X) [06039039] **3900**

ANNUAL VOLUME / THE OLD WATER-COLOUR SOCIETY'S CLUB *CEASED.* (UK/0958-8825) [01773325] **337**

ANNUAL WASTE CONFERENCE PROCEEDINGS : MUNICIPAL AND INDUSTRIAL WASTE (US) **2224**

ANNUAL WATER-RESOURCES REVIEW, WHITE SANDS MISSILE RANGE (US/0731-5120) [04060770] **5530**

ANNUAL WHO'S IN CHARGE HERE YEARBOOK (US/0733-5229) [08594996] **2721**

ANNUAL WILD WEST SHOW (CN/0826-4376) [11193134] **337**

ANNUAL WORK PLAN ... FOR THE OFFICE OF HEALTH PROTECTION, COLORADO DEPARTMENT OF HEALTH (US) [08924297] **4767**

ANNUAL WORK PROGRAM - SOUTHWEST NEW MEXICO COUNCIL OF GOVERNMENTS (US/0095-4810) [01796284] **2815**

ANNUAL WORK PROGRAM - WASHINGTON TRAFFIC SAFETY COMMISSION (US/0095-3385) [01796406] 5438, **4767**

ANNUAL WORKERS' COMPENSATION CONFERENCE, THE (US/1058-6504) [24343495] 2874, **1650**

ANNUAL WORKSHOP ON SPACE OPERATIONS APPLICATIONS AND RESEARCH (SOAR ...) (US) [23173894] **12**

ANNUAL WORLD'S BEST SF, THE (US/1047-8981) [03462013] **3362**

ANNUAL YEAR BOOK - UNITED STATES TROTTING ASSOCIATION, INC (US/0083-3517) [04723503] **2797**

ANNUARIO DE ESTADISTICAS ESTATALES (MX) [13108719] **5322**

ANNUARIO DEGLI ARTISTI VISIVI ITALIANI (IT) [01785298] **337**

ANNUARIO DEL COMMERCIO ESTERO (IT/0304-0364) [01796572] **823**

ANNUARIO DEL GRUPPO IRI (IT) [05118364] **1463**

ANNUARIO DEL RESTAURO O DEI BENI CULTURALI / CON IL PATROCINIO DEL MINISTERO PER I BENI CCULTURALI E AMBIENTALI (IT) [24273491] **337**

ANNUARIO DEL VENETO (IT) [17304686] **2554**

ANNUARIO DELLA ACCADEMIA DELLE SCIENZE DELL'INSTITUTO DI BOLOGNA : CLASSE DI SCIENZE FISICHE (IT/0567-6738) [03006549] **4397**

ANNUARIO DELLA COOPERAZIONE ITALIANA (IT) [19721291] **1546**

ANNUARIO DELLA R. UNIVERSITA DEGLI STUDI DI PADOVA *See* ANNUARIO PER GLI ANNI ACCADEMICI ... / UNIVERSITA DEGLI STUDI DI PADOVA **1074**

ANNUARIO DELLA SCUOLA ARCHEOLOGICA DI ATENE E DELLE MISSIONI ITALIANE IN ORIENTE (IT/0067-0081) [01518524] **255**

ANNUARIO DELL'ABBIGLIAMENTO E DEL TEMPO LIBERO (IT) [05089866] **1081**

ANNUARIO DELL'AGRICOLTURA ITALIANA (IT/0304-0666) [11377152] **62**

ANNUARIO DELL'ALIMENTAZIONE E DELLE ATTIVITA RICETTIVE (IT) [05090000] **2327**

ANNUARIO ... DELLE AUTONOMIE LOCALI (IT) [16633290] **2935**

ANNUARIO DELLE AZIENDE DI CREDITO E FINANZIARE (IT) [08488991] **772**

ANNUARIO DELLE UNIVERSITA DEGLI STUDI IN ITALIA / ISTITUTO NAZIONALE DELL'INFORMAZIONE (IT/0392-8411) [05385835] **1810**

ANNUARIO DELL'EDILIZIA E ARREDAMENTO (IT) [05090110] **598**

ANNUARIO DELL'INDUSTRIA (IT) [05089929] **1598**

ANNUARIO ... DELL'INDUSTRIA ITALIANA DELLA MAGLIERIA E DELLA CALZETTERIA / MAGLIECALZE (IT) [11821447] **5347**

ANNUARIO DELL'ISTITUTO STORICO ITALIANO PER L'ETA MODERNA E CONTEMPORANEA (IT/0391-7010) [08724175] **2675**

ANNUARIO DI DIRITTO COMPARATO E DI STUDI LEGISLATIVI (IT/0003-5149) [01481529] **3123**

ANNUARIO FILOSOFICO (IT/0394-1809) [14274530] **4341**

ANNUARIO - INSTITUTO GIAPPONESE DI CULTURA IN ROMA (IT/0080-391X) [02220186] **2645**

ANNUARIO - ISTITUTO "AGOSTINO GEMELLI" PER LO STUDIO SPERIMENTALE DI PROBLEMI SOCIALI DELL'INFORMAZIONE VISIVA (IT/0544-1358) [02163405] **1104**

ANNUARIO NAZIONALE DELL ENERGIA E DELL AMBIENTE (IT) [18214852] **1932**

ANNUARIO PER GLI ANNI ACCADEMICI ... / UNIVERSITA DEGLI STUDI DI PADOVA (IT) [20478181] **1074**

ANNUARIO PER GLI ANNI ACCADEMICI ... / UNIVERSITA DEGLI STUDI DI ROMA LA SAPIENZA (IT) [20937517] **1725**

ANNUARIO POLITICO (IT) [02399774] **4464**

ANNUARIO PONTIFICIO (VC) [02160642] **5023**

ANNUARIO PONTIFICIO PER L'ANNO ... (IT) [04371310] **5023**

ANNUARIO SEAT. VOL. A, SIDERURGIA E MECCANICA (IT) [11046526] **3998**

ANNUARIO SEAT. VOL. B, ELETTROTECNICA, TERMOTECNICA E ATTREZZATURE INDUSTRIALI (IT) [11385577] **5084**

ANNUARIO SEAT. VOL. C, CHIMICA, MATERIE PLASTICHE, MEDICINA (IT) [11049294] **961**

ANNUARIO SEAT. VOL. D, EDILIZIA (IT) [08547743] **598**

ANNUARIO SEAT. VOL. E, ARREDAMENTO (IT) [10596061] 2904, **2810**

ANNUARIO SEAT. VOL. F, ABBIGLIAMENTO ED ESTETICA (IT) [10596021] 3183, **1081**

ANNUARIO SEAT. VOL. G, P.TURISMO E TEMPO LIBERO (IT) [10595977] 2771, **5461**

ANNUARIO SEAT. VOL. H, AGRICOLTURA ED ALIMENTAZIONE (IT) [11048617] **62**

ANNUARIO SEAT. VOL. I, TRASPORTI, CARTOTECNICA ED EDITORIA (IT) [10597595] **1598**

ANNUARIO SEAT. VOL. L, CREDITO, ASSICURAZIONI E SERVIZI PER LE AZIENDE (IT) [10596257] **772**

ANNUARIO STATISTICO ITALIANO (IT/0066-4545) [01771759] **5322**

ANNUARIO STORICO DELLA VALPOLICELLA (IT) [15650645] **2675**

ANNUARIO - UNIVERSITA CATTOLICA DEL SACRO CUORE (IT) [04578050] **1810**

ANNUARIUM HISTORIAE CONCILIORUM (GW/0003-5157) [02160680] **2610**

ANNUELLES ET LEGUMES. RESULTATS DES CULTURES D'ESSAI (CN/0319-3098) [02583202] **2409**

ANNUITIES FROM THE BUYER'S POINT OF VIEW (US) [02865284] **2874**

ANNUITY & LIFE INSURANCE SHOPPER (US/1071-4510) [26434150] 2874, **891**

ANNUNCIATORE POLIGRAFICO *CEASED.* (IT) **4563**

ANO AUTOMOVIL, EL (SP) [04691412] **4883**

ANO DE LA NAUTICA, EL (SP) [03038959] **4174**

ANO DE LOMATO, EL (SP) [03278562] 4883, **4080**

ANO DEL TRANSPORTE, EL (SP) [02479781] **5377**

ANO PEDAGOGICO (SP/0577-8484) [03105623] **1725**

ANODIC BEHAVIOR OF METALS AND SEMICONDUCTOR SERIES, THE (US/0271-8286) [03047928] **3998**

ANOKA COUNTY UNION, THE (US) [01481536] **5694**

ANON Y ALATEEN NEW ACCION CON SELECCIONES DEL FORUM, AL (US) **1341**

ANOTHER CHICAGO MAGAZINE (US/0272-4359) [06859778] 3460, **3362**

ANPA RESEARCH INSTITUTE *See* R. I. BULLETIN **2923**

ANPHI PAPERS, THE (PH/0065-0676) [02253975] **3851**

ANPI MAGAZINE (BE/0778-7383) [I07787383] 4767, **2288**

ANQ (LEXINGTON, KY.) (US/0895-769X) [16793974] **3362**

ANREGUNGEN FUR PRODUKTION UND ABSATZ (GW) [02015464] **2409**

ANS NEWS (US/0737-6812) [09435390] **2154**

ANSCHLAGE (GW) [05885875] **4100**

ANSCHNITT, DER (GW/0003-5238) [08950770] **2134**

ANSCHRIFTEN DEUTSCHER VERLAGE, BUNDESREPUBLIK DEUTSCHLAND, DDR UND AUS DEM DEUTSCHSPRACHIGEN RAUM OSTERREICH, SCHWEIZ, SOWIE ANSCHRIFTEN WEITERER AUSLANDISCHER VERLAG MIT DEUTSCHEN AUSLIEFERUNGEN (GW/0066-4596) [12305185] **4812**

ANSCHRIFTEN DEUTSCHER VERLAGE UND AUSLEANDISCHE VERLAGE MIT DEUTSCHEN AUSLIEFERUNGEN *See* ANSCHRIFTEN DEUTSCHER VERLAGE, BUNDESREPUBLIK DEUTSCHLAND, DDR UND AUS DEM DEUTSCHSPRACHIGEN RAUM OSTERREICH, SCHWEIZ, SOWIE ANSCHRIFTEN WEITERER AUSLANDISCHER VERLAG MIT DEUTSCHEN AUSLIEFERUNGEN **4812**

ANSEARCHIN' NEWS (US/0003-5246) [04984450] **2437**

ANSI REPORTER (US/0038-9676) [01460482] **4029**

ANSLAGSFRAMSTALLNING FOR BUDGETARET (SW) [06545239] **2154**

ANSLAGSFRAMSTALLNING — Alphabetical Title Index

ANSLAGSFRAMSTALLNING FOR BUDGETARET ... / STATENS RAD FOR BYGGNADSFORSKNING (SW) [10203846] 599, **4711**

ANSTO/E (AT/1030-7745) [I10307745] 2154, **5084**

ANSTO TECHNOLOGY (AT/1031-8216) [I10318216] **4446**

ANSWERS FOR LIFE'S QUESTIONS (US/1056-1994) [23535931] **4935**

ANT. ANTRIEBSTECHN K (1962) (GW/0518-066X) [02444875] **5084**

ANTARA KITA *SUSPENDED.* (US/0275-312X) [05085829] **5191**

ANTARA (NEWS AGENCY) *See* ALMANAK ANTARA **2501**

ANTARA (ORGANIZATION) *See* CURRENT AFFAIRS TRANSLATIONS - ANTARA **2650**

ANTARCTIC (NZ/0003-5327) [01719408] **1351**

ANTARCTIC AND SOUTHERN OCEANS LAW AND POLICY OCCASIONAL PAPERS (AT/1034-361X) [I1034361X] **3123**

ANTARCTIC BIBLIOGRAPHY (US/0066-4626) [01064353] **3457**

ANTARCTIC JOURNAL OF THE UNITED STATES (US/0003-5335) [01481549] **2554**

ANTARCTIC METEORITE NEWSLETTER (US/0270-7179) [05243857] **1420**

ANTARCTIC RESEARCH SERIES (US/0066-4634) [01479925] **1402**

ANTARCTIC SCIENCE (UK/0954-1020) [19566001] **5084**

ANTARES LA VALETTE (FR/0751-7580) [I07517580] **3362**

ANTARIKSHA VIBHAGA KI ANUDANOM KI MANGEM (II) [02411779] **12**

ANTARKTIKA (RU/0570-2844) [03260126] **5084**

ANTARTIDA (BUENOS AIRES) (AG/0302-5691) [01793439] **2554**

ANTELOPE VALLEY PRESS (US/0744-5830) [08403932] **5633**

ANTENA (PL/0208-7782) [I02087782] **1126**

ANTENNA (UK/0140-1890) [03452087] **5576**

ANTENNA NUOVA *See* GTV L'ANTENNA **2056**

ANTENNAS AND PROPAGATION (US/0272-4693) [06878233] **2035**

ANTENNE MARSEILLE, L' (FR/0395-8582) [I03958582] **5377**

ANTENNE (MONTREAL) (CN/0701-1865) [03409795] **3265**

ANTENNES (FR/0396-8995) [I03968995] **860**

ANTENNY (MOSKVA) (RU/0320-9601) [06693999] **2035**

ANTEREM (IT) [18485432] **3362**

ANTHOLOGICA ANNUA (IT) [03784062] **5023**

ANTHOLOGY (JA) [05810239] **3460**

ANTHOLOGY OF MAGAZINE VERSE AND YEARBOOK OF AMERICAN POETRY (1980) *SUSPENDED.* (US/0196-2221) [05782841] **3460**

ANTHONY & BERRYMAN'S MAGISTRATES' COURT GUIDE (UK/0262-3234) [I02623234] **2935**

ANTHONY REPUBLICAN AND THE ANTHONY BULLETIN (ANTHONY, KAN. : 1973) (US) [11531172] **5674**

ANTHOS; GARTEN- UND LANDSCHAFTSGESTALTUNG (SZ/0003-5424) [01811443] **2409**

ANTHROPINES SHESEIS (GR/0302-1122) [01792988] **5191**

ANTHROPOLGISCHE VERKENNINGEN (NE) [I09221174] **228**

ANTHROPOLOGIA (XO/0524-2304) [02676414] **228**

ANTHROPOLOGICA (BARCELONA) (SP/0301-6587) [01792507] **228**

ANTHROPOLOGICA DEL DEPARTAMENTO DE CIENCIAS SOCIALES (PE/0254-9212) [10583158] **228**

ANTHROPOLOGICA (OTTAWA) (CN/0003-5459) [01481555] 2255, **228**

ANTHROPOLOGICAL FIELD STUDIES (US) [09514357] **229**

ANTHROPOLOGICAL FORUM (AT/0066-4677) [01481556] **229**

ANTHROPOLOGICAL INDEX TO CURRENT PERIODICALS IN THE LIBRARY OF THE ROYAL ANTHROPOLOGICAL INSTITUTE (UK/0003-5467) [10070098] 229, **248**

ANTHROPOLOGICAL JOURNAL ON EUROPEAN CULTURES (SZ/0960-0604) [I09600604] **229**

ANTHROPOLOGICAL LINGUISTICS (US/0003-5483) [01481558] 3265, **229**

ANTHROPOLOGICAL LITERATURE (US/0190-3373) [20386569] 229, **248**

ANTHROPOLOGICAL PAPERS (CARSON CITY) (US/0077-7897) [02264813] **229**

ANTHROPOLOGICAL PAPERS OF THE AMERICAN MUSEUM OF NATURAL HISTORY (US/0065-9452) [01116815] **4162**

ANTHROPOLOGICAL PAPERS OF THE UNIVERSITY OF ALASKA (US/0041-9354) [04949087] **229**

ANTHROPOLOGICAL PAPERS OF THE UNIVERSITY OF ARIZONA (US/0066-7501) [01514079] **229**

ANTHROPOLOGICAL PAPERS (UNIVERSITY OF MICHIGAN. MUSEUM OF ANTHROPOLOGY) (US/0076-8367) [01757334] **229**

ANTHROPOLOGICAL PAPERS / UNIVERSITY OF UTAH (US) [06327837] **229**

ANTHROPOLOGICAL QUARTERLY (US/0003-5491) [01481559] **229**

ANTHROPOLOGICAL RESEARCH PAPER (US/0271-0641) [04827638] **229**

●ANTHROPOLOGICAL SCIENCE : JOURNAL OF THE ANTHROPOLOGICAL SOCIETY OF NIPPON (JA/0918-7960) [27973202] **229**

ANTHROPOLOGICAL SERIES / PENNSYLVANIA. HISTORICAL AND MUSEUM COMMISSION (US) [01714656] **229**

ANTHROPOLOGIE ET SOCIETES (CN/0702-8997) [03987692] **229**

ANTHROPOLOGIE : INTERNATIONAL JOURNAL FOR THE SCIENCE OF MAN (SZ/0003-553X) **229**

ANTHROPOLOGIE MARITIME (FR/0758-5683) [17668754] **229**

ANTHROPOLOGIE (PARIS) (FR/0003-5521) [01481566] **229**

ANTHROPOLOGIE VISUELLE (FR/0993-4871) [I09934871] **229**

ANTHROPOLOGISCHE GESELLSCHAFT IN WIEN *See* MITTEILUNGEN DER ANTHROPOLOGISCHEN GESELLSCHAFT IN WIEN **241**

ANTHROPOLOGISCHER ANZEIGER (GW/0003-5548) [01481569] **229**

●ANTHROPOLOGY & ARCHEOLOGY OF EURASIA (US/1061-1959) [25215713] 255, **229**

ANTHROPOLOGY & EDUCATION QUARTERLY (US/0161-7761) [02820781] 1888, **230**

●ANTHROPOLOGY AND HUMANISM (US) [28598923] **230**

ANTHROPOLOGY AND HUMANISM QUARTERLY (US/0193-5615) [02754576] **230**

ANTHROPOLOGY AND RELATED DISCIPLINES / INTERNATIONAL CURRENT AWARENESS SERVICES *CEASED.* (UK/0960-1511) [23855941] **230**

ANTHROPOLOGY GRANTS INDEX : (GRINDEX) (US) [22834746] **230**

ANTHROPOLOGY (GUILFORD, CONN.) (US) [07682603] **230**

ANTHROPOLOGY NEWSLETTER (US/0098-1605) [02240128] **230**

ANTHROPOLOGY OF CONSCIOUSNESS (US/1053-4202) [22528213] **230**

ANTHROPOLOGY OF THE NORTH (CN/0066-4715) [01481571] **230**

ANTHROPOLOGY OF WORK REVIEW (US/0883-024X) [09810295] **230**

ANTHROPOLOGY OF YIDDISH FOLKSONGS (IS) [13437534] 230, **4100**

ANTHROPOLOGY TODAY (UK/0268-540X) [11788665] **230**

ANTHROPOLOGY UCLA (US/0003-5564) [01481572] **230**

ANTHROPOS (GR) [01798363] **230**

ANTHROPOS (BARCELONA, SPAIN) (SP/0211-5611) [08161012] **2842**

ANTHROPOS FRIBOURG (SZ/0257-9774) [I02579774] 3265, **230**

ANTHROPOS INSTITUTE *See* COLLECTANEA INSTITUTI ANTHROPOS **234**

ANTHROPOS (LJUBLJANA) (XV/0587-5161) [03351086] 4341, **4574**

ANTHROPOS (SALZBURG, AUSTRIA) (AU) [01481573] **3265**

ANTHROPOS. SUPLEMENTOS (SP/1130-2089) [I11302089] **2842**

ANTHROPOZOOLOGICA PARIS (FR/0761-3032) [I07613032] **5576**

ANTHROQUEST (US/0749-1751) [09514513] **230**

ANTHROZOOS (US/0892-7936) [15261905] 2211, **5576**

ANTHUS (GW) [01789590] **5576**

ANTI (GR) [09867084] **4515**

ANTI-BOLSHEVIK BLOC OF NATIONS *See* ABN CORRESPONDENCE **4514**

ANTI-CANCER DRUG DESIGN (UK/0266-9536) [12929721] **3809**

ANTI-CANCER DRUGS (UK/0959-4973) [22982535] 4291, **3979**

ANTI-CORROSION METHODS AND MATERIALS (UK/0003-5599) [01736843] 2100, **2008**

ANTI-DRUG FUNDING ALERT (US/1060-4707) [25015309] 4711, **4630**

ANTI-SLAVERY REPORTER (ANTI-SLAVERY SOCIETY FOR THE PROTECTION OF HUMAN RIGHTS) (UK) [10170133] **4504**

ANTI-SUBMARINE WARFARE FORECAST (US) **4035**

ANTI-VIVISECTION COUNCIL OF OTTAWA. MONTHLY BULLETIN *See* NEWS BULLETIN - ANIMAL DEFENCE LEAGUE OF CANADA **226**

ANTIBACTERIAL REVIEW (CN/1182-9648) [23454620] **3551**

ANTIBIOTHERAPIE AUJOURD'HUI (CN/1182-963X) [23454636] **3551**

ANTIBIOTIC GUIDELINES (AT/0729-218X) [I0729218X] **3551**

ANTIBIOTICA (IT/0003-5629) [05802911] **559**

ANTIBIOTICS AND CHEMOTHERAPY (SZ/0066-4758) [01344164] **4291**

ANTIBIOTICS. ANTIBIOTIKI (US) [05108257] **4291**

ANTIBIOTICS (NEW YORK. 1967) *CEASED.* (US/0097-4668) [01276964] **4291**

ANTIBIOTIKI I HIMIOTERAPIA (RU/0235-2990) [17863283] **4291**

ANTIBODY, IMMUNOCONJUGATES, AND RADIOPHARMACEUTICALS (US/0892-7049) [15239334] **3809**

ANTICANCER RESEARCH (GR/0250-7005) [07636918] **3809**

ANTICHITA PISANE (IT/0390-0584) [03337946] **2675**

ANTICHITA VIVA (IT/0003-5645) [02166390] **337**

ANTICHNAIA DREVNOST I SREDNIE VEKA (RU) [02465536] **255**

ANTICHNYI MIR I ARKHEOLOGIIA (RU) [05504750] **255**

ANTICHTHON (AT/0066-4774) [01481592] **1074**

ANTICON (CN/0316-9057) [02247390] **1860**

ANTIC'S AMIGA PLUS *CEASED.* (US/1044-8306) [19913530] **1170**

ANTIEK (NE/0003-5653) [01711939] 248, **337**

ANTIFRICTION BEARINGS *CEASED.* (US/0744-2270) [05807446] **3475**

ANTIFURTO (IT/0391-6227) [I03916227] **5176**

ANTIGONE (FR/0767-2055) [19907611] 3362, **4366**

ANTIGONISH REVIEW, THE (CN/0003-5661) [01785445] **3337**

ANTIGONISH SPECTATOR, THE (CN/0229-799X) [08308065] **5780**

ANTIGUA AND BARBUDA *See* LAWS OF ANTIGUA AND BARBUDA **2997**

ANTIGUA & BARBUDA CONSOLIDATED INDEX TO STATUTES AND SUBSIDIARY LEGISLATION TO ... (BB) [13551480] **3123**

ANTIGUA AND BARBUDA FORUM : JOURNAL OF PUBLIC ISSUES FORUM (AQ) [19027692] **4464**

ANTIGUA AND BARBUDA. MINISTRY OF FINANCE *See* BUDGET ADDRESS **4714**

ANTIGUEDAD Y CRISTIANISMO / UNIVERSIDAD DE MURCIA, CATEDRA DE HISTORIA ANTIGUA, FUNDACION PASTOR DE ESTUDIOS CLASICOS Y UNIVERSIDAD DE ALCALA DE HENARES, CATEDRA DE HISTORIA ANTIGUA (SP) [19092109] **1074**

●ANTIINFECTIVE DRUGS AND CHEMOTHERAPY (GW) **3551**

ANTIINFLAMMATORY ANTIALLERGIC AND GI PATENT FAST-ALERT *CEASED.* (UK) **3551**

ANTIKE KUNST (SZ/0003-5688) [02254516] 337, **255**

ANTIKE KUNST. BEIHEFT (SZ/0066-4782) [01481598] **337**

ANTIKE MUNZEN UND GESCHNITTENE STEINE (US/0420-025X) [01913408] **2779**

ANTIKE PLASTIK (GW/0518-018X) [01624071] 337, **255**

ANTIKE UND ABENDLAND (GW/0003-5696) [01481599] **1074**

ANTIKE WELT (GW/0003-570X) [01712096] **2610**

ANTIKE WELT SONDERNUMMER (GW/1015-9274) [I10159274] 255, **2610**

ANTILLEN REVIEW (NE) [07540537] **2721**

ANTIMICROBIAL AGENTS AND CHEMOTHERAPY (US/0066-4804) [01778594] **559**

ANTIMICROBIAL CHEMOTHERAPY SERIES (UK/0742-3195) [10066888] 961, **3551**

ANTIMICROBIAL NEWSLETTER (NZ/1170-8875) [I11708875] **559**

ANTIMICROBIC NEWSLETTER *See* ANTIMICROBICS AND INFECTIOUS DISEASES NEWSLETTER **559**

ANTIMICROBIC NEWSLETTER, THE (US/0738-1751) [09535293] 3551, **559**

●ANTIMICROBICS AND INFECTIOUS DISEASES NEWSLETTER (US/1069-417X) [28033779] 3551, **559**

ANTIMONY IN ... (US) [03028395] 1437, 2134, **2002**

ANTINCENDIO (1979) (IT/0393-7089) [08714190] **2288**

ANTIOCH ALUMNI DIRECTORY *See* ALUMNI DIRECTORY / ANTIOCH COLLEGE **1097**

ANTIOCH COLLEGE *See* ALUMNI DIRECTORY / ANTIOCH COLLEGE **1097**

ANTIOCH DAILY LEDGER *See* DAILY LEDGER (ANTIOCH, CALIF.) **5634**

ANTIOCH REVIEW, THE (US/0003-5769) [01481603] **3337**

ANTIPODAS : JOURNAL OF HISPANIC STUDIES OF THE UNIVERSITY OF AUCKLAND (NZ/0113-2415) [20814338] **3362**

ANTIPODE (UK/0066-4812) [02754322] **2554**

ANTIPODES (BROOKLYN, NEW YORK, N.Y.) (US/0893-5580) [15585667] **3362**

●ANTIPODES BRUXELLES (BE/1370-009X) [I1370009X] **4464**

ANTIQUA (ARCHEOCLUB D'ITALIA) (IT) [09288253] **255**

ANTIQUA CONSOLIDATED INDEX OF STATUTES AND SUBSIDIARY LEGISLATION TO . *See* ANTIGUA & BARBUDA CONSOLIDATED INDEX TO STATUTES AND SUBSIDIARY LEGISLATION TO ... **3123**

●ANTIQUARIAN BOOK MONTHLY (UK) [27825991] **4823**

ANTIQUARIAN BOOK MONTHLY REVIEW (UK/0306-7475) [03356741] **4823**

ANTIQUARIAN HOROLOGICAL SOCIETY *See* MONOGRAPH / ANTIQUARIAN HOROLOGICAL SOCIETY **2916**

ANTIQUARIAN HOROLOGY AND THE PROCEEDINGS OF THE ANTIQUARIAN HOROLOGICAL SOCIETY (UK/0003-5785) [05203325] **2916**

ANTIQUARIAN TRADE LIST ANNUAL *CEASED.* (US/0197-0364) [07120882] **4823**

ANTIQUARIATO (IT) [26370267] **248**

ANTIQUARIES JOURNAL (UK/0003-5815) [01481608] **255**

ANTIQUARISCHE GESELLSCHAFT IN ZURICH *See* MITTEILUNGEN DER ANTIQUARISCHEN GESELLSCHAFT IN ZURICH **2699**

ANTIQUE AIRPLANE DIGEST (US) [04868008] 248, **12**

ANTIQUE & CLASSIC CARS, TRUCKS, MOTORCYCLES *CEASED.* (US/0747-9786) [10832795] 248, **5404**

ANTIQUE & COLLECTORS FAYRE (UK) [20865527] **248**

●ANTIQUE & COLLECTORS REPRODUCTION NEWS (US/1065-3694) [26594282] 2771, **248**

ANTIQUE AUTOMOBILE CLUB OF OTTAWA *See* MEMBERS & CARS **5418**

ANTIQUE AUTOMOBILE, THE (US/0003-5831) [01481611] 248, **5404**

ANTIQUE BOTTLE & GLASS COLLECTOR (US/8750-1481) [11035963] **248**

ANTIQUE CAR TIMES (US/0164-7237) [04405403] 2771, 5404, **248**

ANTIQUE CLOCKS (UK/0954-593X) [20386702] 249, **2916**

ANTIQUE COLLECTING (UK) [08378269] **249**

ANTIQUE COLLECTING (EPHRATA (PA.) (US) [06636408] **249**

ANTIQUE COLLECTOR, THE (UK/0003-5858) [01481612] **249**

ANTIQUE COLLECTORS' CLUB *See* GUIDE TO THE ANTIQUE SHOPS OF BRITAIN **250**

ANTIQUE DEALER AND COLLECTORS' GUIDE (UK/0003-5866) [03583423] **249**

●ANTIQUE DOLL WORLD (US/1069-5141) [28081399] 2771, **249**

ANTIQUE GAZETTE (US) **249**

ANTIQUE (LONDON) (UK/0951-6913) [22389712] **249**

●ANTIQUE MAP PRICE RECORD & HANDBOOK (US/1070-8421) [28478311] **2580**

ANTIQUE MAPS, SEA CHARTS, CITY VIEWS, CELESTIAL CHARTS & BATTLE PLANS (US/0749-4971) [09864545] 249, **2554**

ANTIQUE MARKET REPORT (US/8750-9024) [11921757] **249**

ANTIQUE MOTORCYCLE CLUB OF AMERICA. QUARTERLY BULLETIN *See* ANTIQUE MOTORCYCLE, THE **4080**

ANTIQUE MOTORCYCLE, THE (US/0364-6963) [02667514] 249, **4080**

ANTIQUE PHONOGRAPH MONTHLY, THE (US/0361-2147) [02246370] 4100, **249**

ANTIQUE POWER MAGAZINE (US/1042-7392) [19121751] **249**

ANTIQUE RECORDS (UK) [01789614] 249, **5315**

ANTIQUE REVIEW (US/0883-833X) [12032267] **249**

ANTIQUE SHOP GUIDE (US/0149-0192) [03403581] **249**

ANTIQUE SHOWCASE (CN/0713-6315) [09000493] **249**

ANTIQUE TOY WORLD (US/0742-0420) [08693543] 249, **2583**

ANTIQUE TRADER *See* ANTIQUE TRADER WEEKLY, THE **249**

ANTIQUE TRADER ANTIQUES & COLLECTIBLES PRICE GUIDE, THE (US/0882-6897) [11350181] 2771, **249**

ANTIQUE TRADER PRICE GUIDE TO ANTIQUES AND COLLECTORS' ITEMS, THE *See* COLLECTOR MAGAZINE & PRICE GUIDE **250**

ANTIQUE TRADER WEEKLY, THE (US/0161-8342) [04030205] 2771, **249**

ANTIQUES (IT) [23862423] **249**

ANTIQUES ACROSS THE WORLD (UK/0260-9606) [13454584] **249**

ANTIQUES & COLLECTIBLES (GREENVALE, N.Y.) (US/0274-6085) [06514424] **249**

ANTIQUES & COLLECTING HOBBIES (US/0884-6294) [12187475] 2771, **249**

ANTIQUES & COLLECTING MAGAZINE (US) [28904979] 2771, **249**

ANTIQUES & FINE ART *CEASED.* (US/0886-7208) [12962314] 337, **249**

ANTIQUES AND THE ARTS WEEKLY (US) [08901208] 313, **249**

ANTIQUES (ORLANDO, FLA.) *CEASED.* (US/0747-6736) [10701766] **249**

ANTIQUEWEEK (US/0888-5451) [13663341] **249**

ANTIQUITAS. REIHE 2. ABHANDLUNGEN AUS DEM GEBIETE DER VOR UND FRUHGESCHICHTE (GW/0066-4847) [01481618] **2610**

ANTIQUITAS. REIHE 4. BEITREAGE ZUR HISTORIA-AUGUSTA-FORSCHUNG (SW/0066-4863) [01481620] **2610**

ANTIQUITAS. REIHE 4, SERIE 3, BEITRAEGE ZUR HISTORIA-AUGUSTA-FORSCHUNG. KOMMENTARE (GW) [23380338] **2675**

ANTIQUITE CLASSIQUE, L' (BE/0770-2817) [01894687] **1074**

ANTIQUITES AFRICAINES (FR/0066-4871) [01481623] **2637**

ANTIQUITES NATIONALES (FR) [09970576] **4084**

ANTIQUITY (UK/0003-598X) [01481624] **255**

ANTIREVOLUTIONAIRE STAATKUNDE *See* AR STAATKUNDE IN CHRISTEN-DEMOCRATISCH PERSPECTIEF **4464**

ANTISENSE RESEARCH & DEVELOPMENT (US/1050-5261) [21526813] **578**

ANTISEPTIC, THE (II/0003-5998) [01481627] **3551**

ANTITHESIS (AT/1030-3839) [20582428] **2842**

ANTITHESIS (MARIETTA, PA.) (US/0732-8923) [08504428] **5074**

ANTITRUST ADVISOR (US) [06055797] **3095**

ANTITRUST & COMMERCE REPORT (US) [09806140] **3095**

ANTITRUST & TRADE REGULATION REPORT (US/0003-6021) [01537823] **3095**

ANTITRUST BULLETIN (US/0003-603X) [01481628] **3095**

ANTITRUST (CHICAGO, ILL.) (US/0162-7996) [14708243] **3095**

ANTITRUST DIVISION MANUAL (US) [05880377] **3095**

ANTITRUST FREEDOM OF INFORMATION LOG (US/0891-8546) [15049623] **3095**

ANTITRUST LAW & ECONOMICS REVIEW (US/0003-6048) [01481629] **3095**

ANTITRUST LAW HANDBOOK (US/0738-5919) [09631781] **3095**

ANTITRUST LAW JOURNAL (US/0003-6056) [01285492] **3096**

ANTITRUST LAWS AND TRADE REGULATION (US) [01769284] **3096**

ANTITRUST REPORT (WASHINGTON, D.C. 1991) (US/1057-8919) [23436114] **3096**

ANTIVIRAL AGENTS BULLETIN (US/0897-9871) [17686161] **3551**

ANTIVIRAL CHEMISTRY & CHEMOTHERAPY (UK/0956-3202) [20073994] **961**

ANTIVIRAL RESEARCH (US/0166-3542) [07603702] **3551**

ANTOLOGIA (AG) [03603211] **3362**

ANTOLOGIA DERMATOLOGICA (SP/0210-1300) [I02101300] **3717**

ANTOLOGIA DI BELLE ARTI (IT/0394-0136) [04083084] **337**

ANTON BRUCKNER GESAMTAUSGABE (AU) **4100**

ANTONIANUM (IT/0003-6064) [01776370] 4341, **4935**

ANTONIE VAN LEEUWENHOEK (NE/0003-6072) [01481634] **559**

ANTRIEBSTECHNIK HANDBUCH (GW) [13201808] **2109**

●ANTRIM COUNTY NEWS (US) **5690**

ANTROPOLOGIA (SP/1131-5814) [25727192] **230**

ANTROPOLOGIA (BO) [05046185] **230**

ANTROPOLOGIA (VE/0503-8413) [01496510] **230**

ANTROPOLOGIA CONTEMPORANEA (IT) [10265588] **230**

ANTROPOLOGIA E HISTORIA DE GUATEMALA (GT/0003-6102) [02444876] **2721**

ANTROPOLOGIA FISICA CHILENA / UNIVERSIDAD DE CHILE, CENTRO DE ESTUDIOS ANTROPOLOGICOS (CL/0518-0678) [02257606] **230**

ANTROPOLOGIA MEDICA : AM (IT/0393-9081) [18505728] **230**

ANTROPOLOGIA (MEXICO CITY, MEXICO) (MX) [12705622] **230**

ANTROPOLOGIA PORTUGUESA (PO/0870-0990) [12048551] **230**

ANTROPOLOGIA Y ETNOLOGIA (SP) [05701612] **230**

ANTROPOLOGIA Y PALEOECOLOGIA HUMANA / LABORATORIO DE ANTROPOLOGIA, UNIVERSIDAD DE GRANADA Y PATRONATO CUEVA DEL AGUA, EXCMA. DIPUTACION PROVINCIAL (SP) [09573507] **231**

ANTROPOLOGIA Y TECNICA (MX/0186-9787) [20288944] **231**

ANTROPOLOGICA (VE/0003-6110) [02257607] **231**

ANTROPOLOGISKA STUDIER (SW/0345-0902) [07914928] **231**

ANTUS *CEASED.* (US/0003-5319) [01481545] **3362**

ANTWERP BEE-ARGUS, THE (US) [09030123] **5726**

ANTWERP (BELGIUM : PROVINCE) *See* BESTUURSMEMORIAAL **4632**

ANTWERP. CHAMBRE DE COMMERCE. BULLETIN *See* BULLETIN - CHAMBRE DE COMMERCE ET D'INDUSTRIE D'ANVERS **1549**

ANTWERP. CHAMBRE D'INDUSTRIE. BULLETIN *See* BULLETIN - CHAMBRE DE COMMERCE ET D'INDUSTRIE D'ANVERS **1549**

ANTWERP FACETS (BE/0777-0626) [I07770626] **2913**

ANTWERP. MUSEE ROYALE DES BEAUX-ARTS. ANNUAIRE *See* JAARBOEK VAN HET KONINKLIJK MUSEUM VOOR SCHONE KUNSTEN **353**

ANTWERP PAPERS IN LINGUISTICS (BE) [18886485] **3265**

ANU HISTORICAL JOURNAL (AT/0001-2068) [01518853] **2610**

ANUAR DE LINGVISTICA SI ISTORIE LITERARA (RM/0066-4987) [05522917] 2842, **3265**

ANUARI DE FILOLOGIA. SECCIO B, ESTUDIS ARABS / UNIVERSITAT DE BARCELONA, FACULTAT DE FILOLOGIA (SP) [24514255] **3265**

ANUARI DE FILOLOGIA. SECCIO C, LLENGUA I LITERATURA CATALANES / UNIVERSITAT DE BARCELONA, FACULTAT DE FILOLOGIA (SP) [24514206] **3265**

ANUARI — Alphabetical Title Index

ANUARI DE FILOLOGIA. SECCIO D, STUDIA GRAECA ET LATINA / UNIVERSITAT DE BARCELONA, FACULTAT DE FILOLOGIA (SP) [24514165] **3265**

ANUARI DE FILOLOGIA. SECCIO E, ESTUDIS HEBREUS I ARAMEUS / UNIVERSITAT DE BARCELONA, FACULTAT DE FILOLOGIA (SP) [25467551] **3265**

ANUARI DE FILOLOGIA. SECCIO F, ESTUDIOS DE LENGUA Y LITERATURA ESPANOLAS / UNIVERSITAT DE BARCELONA, FACULTAT DE FILOLOGIA (SP) [24514137] 3362, **3265**

ANUARI ESTADISTIC DE LA CIUTAT DE BARCELONA (SP) [20478134] **5322**

ANUARIO - ABDIB (BL) [02177280] **5084**

ANUARIO - ACADEMIA NACIONAL DE BELLAS ARTES (AG) [02829986] **337**

ANUARIO ALLAN KARDEC (BL) [02650756] **4240**

ANUARIO ANTROPOLOGICO (BL) [04485665] **231**

ANUARIO BIBLIOGRAFICO COLOMBIANO "RUBEN PEREZ ORTIZ" (CK) [06419517] 3266, **3362**

ANUARIO BIBLIOGRAFICO DE HISTORIA DEL PENSAMIENTO IBERO E IBEROAMERICANO *SUSPENDED.* (US/1044-0623) [19677606] **3362**

ANUARIO BIBLIOGRAFICO PERUANO (PE) [01481639] 3362, **3457**

ANUARIO - BOLSA DE MADRID (SP) [02438280] **891**

ANUARIO BRASILEIRO DE CERAMICA (BL) [07689152] **2586**

ANUARIO BRASILEIRO DE MEDIA *See* ANUARIO BRASILEIRO DE MIDIA **1104**

ANUARIO BRASILEIRO DE MIDIA (BL) [08119292] **1104**

ANUARIO BRASILEIRO DE RECURSOS HUMANOS (BL) [10894241] **938**

ANUARIO BRASILEIRO DE SUPERMERCADOS (BL) [01785322] **639**

ANUARIO BRASILEIRO DE TINTAS & I.E. E VERNIZES (BL) [03375826] **4222**

ANUARIO BRASILEIRO DO FRIO (BL) [01791871] **2603**

ANUARIO - CAMARA VENEZOLANO BRITANICA DE COMERCIO E INDUSTRIA (VE) [02468224] **823**

ANUARIO CASA DOS ARTISTAS (BL) [10712620] **383**

ANUARIO CIENTIFICO (BARRANQUILLA, COLOMBIA) (CK) [12028491] **5084**

ANUARIO COLOMBIANO DE HISTORIA SOCIAL Y DE LA CULTURA (CK/0066-5045) [01586457] **5191**

ANUARIO CONSULTIVO DE TRABAJO (SP/0304-8497) [01794807] **3144**

ANUARIO DA INDUSTRIA BRASILEIRA DE AUTOPECAS (BL) [04799389] **5404**

ANUARIO DA INDUSTRIA ELETRICA E ELETRONICA DO BRASIL (BL) [08286835] **2035**

ANUARIO DA INDUSTRIA ELETRO-ELETRONICA NO BRASIL *See* ANUARIO DA INDUSTRIA ELETRICA E ELETRONICA DO BRASIL **2035**

ANUARIO DAS INDUSTRIAS (BL) [18308141] **1598**

ANUARIO DAS INDUSTRIAS DO ESTADO DO RIO DE JANEIRO (BL) [08146366] **823**

ANUARIO DE BIBLIOTECOLOGIA, ARCHIVOLOGIA E INFORMATICA (MX) [01717724] 2479, **3191**

ANUARIO DE COMERCIO EXTERIOR (BOGOTA) (CK) [01226179] **823**

ANUARIO DE DERECHO ADMINISTRATIVO (CL) [04453395] **3092**

ANUARIO DE DERECHO AMBIENTAL (VE) [05734251] **3109**

ANUARIO DE DERECHO CIVIL (SP) [01481642] **3088**

ANUARIO DE DERECHO INTERNACIONAL *SUSPENDED.* (SP/0212-0747) [02635904] **3124**

ANUARIO DE DERECHO (PANAMA : 1981) (PN/0553-0814) [11544541] **2935**

ANUARIO DE DERECHO PENAL (SP) **3158**

ANUARIO DE DERECHOS HUMANOS *CEASED.* (SP) [13386883] **4504**

ANUARIO DE DIVULGACAO CIENTIFICA (BL) [02244555] **2721**

ANUARIO DE EPIDEMIOLOGIA Y ESTADISTICA VITAL (VE) [04042616] 3712, **3654**

ANUARIO DE ESTADISTICA (EC) [02697699] **5322**

ANUARIO DE ESTADISTICA AGRARIA (SP) [02243816] 5322, **151**

ANUARIO DE ESTADISTICAS HOSPITALARIAS (EC) [01786935] **3776**

ANUARIO DE ESTADISTICAS VITALES. NACIMIENTOS Y DEFUNCIONES (EC) [17993568] **4767**

ANUARIO DE ESTUDIOS AMERICANOS (SP/0210-5810) [01481644] **2721**

ANUARIO DE ESTUDIOS ATLANTICOS (SP/0570-4065) [01481645] **2675**

ANUARIO DE ESTUDIOS CENTROAMERICANOS (CR/0377-7316) [02353803] **5191**

ANUARIO DE ESTUDIOS COOPERATIVOS (SP) [22392555] **1541**

ANUARIO DE ESTUDIOS FILOLOGICOS (SP) [06237776] **3266**

ANUARIO DE ESTUDIOS MEDIEVALES (SP/0066-5061) [01481646] **2675**

ANUARIO DE ESTUDIOS MEDIEVALES. ANEJO (SP) [01640007] **2675**

ANUARIO DE FILOLOGIA (CARACAS) (VE/0066-507X) [05779451] **3266**

ANUARIO DE GEOGRAFIA (MX/0570-4073) [01757259] **2554**

ANUARIO DE HISTORIA CONTEMPORANEA (SP/0210-9603) [10365287] **2675**

ANUARIO DE HISTORIA DEL DERECHO ESPANOL (SP/0304-4319) [01481648] **2935**

ANUARIO DE HISTORIA ECONOMICA Y SOCIAL / SEMINARIO DE HISTORIA SOCIAL Y ECONOMICA, FACULTAD DE FILOSOFIA Y LETRAS DE LA UNIVERSIDAD DE MADRID (SP/0066-5088) [01774802] **1546**

ANUARIO DE INFORMATICA CWB (BL/0101-8477) [19483714] **1170**

ANUARIO DE LA ARQUITECTURA EN COLOMBIA (CK) [01799174] **288**

ANUARIO DE LA FOTOGRAFIA ESPANOLA (SP) [01786796] **4366**

ANUARIO DE LA MINERIA DE CHILE / MINISTERIO DE ECONOMIA, SERVICO NACIONAL DE GEOLOGIA Y MINERIA (CL/0066-5096) [01554266] **2134**

ANUARIO DE LA NIEVE (SP) **4883**

ANUARIO DE LA NOBLEZA DE ESPANA. MICROFORM (US) [19870796] **2513**

ANUARIO DE LA RELOJERIA PARA ESPANA E HISPANOAMERICA (SP) [01786124] **2916**

ANUARIO DE LA RELOJERIA Y ARTE EN METAL PARA ESPANA E HISPANOAMERICA (SP/0066-510X) [I0066510X] **3998**

ANUARIO DE LA UNIVERSIDAD DE BARCELONA (SP) [20230669] **1089**

ANUARIO DE LAS RELACIONES LABORALES EN ESPANA (SP) [02649064] **1650**

ANUARIO DE LETRAS (MEXICO) (MX/0185-1373) [01642215] **3362**

ANUARIO DE LINGUISTICA HISPANICA (SP/0213-053X) [12778065] **3266**

ANUARIO DE POETAS DO BRASIL (BL) [02623839] **3460**

ANUARIO DE PORTOS E NAVIOS (BL) [03720239] **5447**

ANUARIO DE PSICOLOGIA (SP) [01471820] **4574**

ANUARIO DEL ARTE ESPANOL (SP) [01793617] **337**

ANUARIO DEL CENTRO DE ESTUDIOS MARTIANOS (CU) [05688461] **2721**

ANUARIO DEL CINE (AG) [04856509] **4063**

ANUARIO DEL DEPARTAMENTO DE HISTORIA (AG/0589-6924) [02259807] **2610**

ANUARIO DEL EXPORTADOR (MX) [03761027] **823**

ANUARIO DEL MINISTERIO DE JUSTICIA (UY) [08643947] **2935**

ANUARIO DEL PUERTO AUTONOMO DE BARCELONA (SP) [07912576] **5447**

ANUARIO DEL SERVICIO NACIONAL DE PRUEBAS / INSTITUTO COLOMBIANO PARA EL FOMENTO DE LA EDUCACION SUPERIOR (CK) [06980949] **1810**

ANUARIO DELTA (BL) [18775056] **1923**

ANUARIO DENTAL ESPANOL Y PORTUGUES (SP) **1316**

ANUARIO DO INSTITUTO DE ENGENHARIA (BL) [02241283] **1965**

ANUARIO : EMPRESAS JAPONESAS NO BRASIL (BL) [06298521] **772**

ANUARIO ESPANOL DE ACEITES Y GRASAS E INDUSTRIAS AUXILIARES (SP) [01792291] **1598**

ANUARIO ESPANOL DE HOSTELERIA Y COLECTIVIDADES (SP) **2804**

ANUARIO ESPANOL DE JOYERIA Y RELOJERIA (SP) **2913**

ANUARIO ESPANOL DE LAS ARTES GRAFICAS (SP) **4563**

ANUARIO ESPANOL DE PARA-FARMACIA (SP) **4292**

ANUARIO ESPANOL DE SEGUROS (SP/0211-125X) [I0211125X] **891**

ANUARIO ESPANOL Y PORTUGUES DE ANALITICA (SP) **3551**

ANUARIO ESPANOL Y PORTUGUES DE OPTICA Y AUDIOMETRIA (SP) **4215**

ANUARIO ESTADISTICO DE ANTIOQUIA (CK/0120-3495) [02479856] **5322**

ANUARIO ESTADISTICO DE ESPANA (SP) [01205724] **5322**

ANUARIO ESTADISTICO DE LA SIDERURGIA Y MINERIA DEL HIERRO DE AMERICA LATINA / INSTITUTO LATINOAMERICANO DEL FIERRO Y EL ACERO (CL) [05244775] 2134, **2002**

ANUARIO ESTADISTICO DE LAS CUENTAS MONETARIAS (CR) [17887196] **772**

ANUARIO ESTADISTICO DE SEGUROS (SP/0303-4763) [01793953] 2874, **2897**

ANUARIO ESTADISTICO DE TRANSPORTE TERRESTRE (CL) [20242931] **5377**

ANUARIO ESTADISTICO DEL COMERCIO EXTERIOR DE LOS ESTADOS UNIDOS MEXICANOS (MX) [01606261] **5400**

ANUARIO ESTADISTICO - DEPTO ACTUARIAL Y ESTADISTICO *CEASED.* (CR) [02246942] **5273**

ANUARIO ESTADISTICO. ENERGIA ELECTRICA (AG) [01746724] 2035, **2002**

ANUARIO ESTADISTICO (INSTITUTO NACIONAL DE ESTADISTICA Y CENSOS (ARGENTINA)) (AG) [10647906] **5322**

ANUARIO ESTADISTICO / JUNTA MONETARIA, SUPERINTENDENCIA DEL SISTEMA FINANCIERO, ASESORIA ACTUARIAL Y ESTADISTICA (ES/0067-3234) [12541831] 772, **726**

ANUARIO ESTADISTICO (BL) [01786795] 5273, **5266**

ANUARIO ESTADISTICO - COMISSAO DE FINANCIAMENTO DA PRODUCAO, DEPARTAMENTO DE PESQUISAS ECONOMICAS (BL) [02240652] 5322, **151**

ANUARIO ESTADISTICO / CONSIDER, CONSELHO DE NAO-FERROSOS E DE SIDERURGIA / STATISTICAL YEARBOOK / THE IRON, STEEL, AND NONFERROUS METALS COUNCIL (BL) [09603193] 3998, **4025**

ANUARIO ESTATISTICO - CORREIOS E TELECOMUNICACOES DE PORTUGAL (PO) [04451527] 1149, **1124**

ANUARIO ESTATISTICO DAS FERROVIAS DO BRASIL (BL) [03947460] **5400**

ANUARIO ESTATISTICO DE ENERGIA ELECTRICA / COMPANIA ENERGETICA DE SAO PAULO, DIVISAO DE ESTUDOS DO MERCADO DE ENERGIA ELETRICA (BL) [07357098] 1932, **1961**

ANUARIO ESTATISTICO DO AMAPA (BL) [01798059] **5322**

ANUARIO ESTATISTICO DO BRASIL / MINISTERIO DA AGRICULTURA, INDUSTRIA E COMMERCIO, DIRECTORIA GERAL DE ESTATISTICA (BL/0100-1299) [01718475] **5322**

ANUARIO ESTATISTICO DO ESTADO DE SAO PAULO (BL/0100-8730) [07107747] **5322**

ANUARIO ESTATISTICO DO ESTADO DO RIO DE JANEIRO (BL) [05818274] **5322**

ANUARIO ESTATISTICO DOS TRANSPORTES (BL) [01796065] **5400**

ANUARIO ESTATISTICO - SERVICO SOCIAL DO COMERCIO, ADMINISTRACAO REGIONAL EM MINAS GERAIS (BL) [06715642] 5273, **5266**

ANUARIO FILOSOFICO (SP/0066-5215) [01717728] **4341**

ANUARIO FINANCIERO DE MEXICO (MX) [01588426] **772**

ANUARIO FLAMENCO Y GUIA DE FESTIVALES (SP) [20151420] **1310**

ANUARIO GERAL DE PORTUGAL (PO) [05303232] **2675**

ANUARIO GUIA DE SANTA CRUZ DE TENERIFE Y SU PROVINCIA (SP) [02240680] **2675**

ANUARIO HISPANO-LUSO-AMERICANO DE DERECHO INTERNACIONAL (SP/0570-4316) [01481656] **3124**

ANUARIO HORTOFRUTICOLA ESPANOL (SP) [02679716] **2409**

ANUARIO IEHS (AG/0326-9671) [17554685] **2721**

ANUARIO INDIGENISTA (MX/0304-2596) [05855137] 2721, **231**

Alphabetical Title Index — API

ANUARIO (INSTITUTO DE INVESTIGACIONES HISTORICAS DR. JOSE GASPAR RODRIGUEZ DE FRANCIA) (PY) [07303506] **2721**

ANUARIO INTERAMERICANO DE ARCHIVOS (AG/0325-3899) [12701067] **2479**

ANUARIO INTERAMERICANO DE DERECHOS HUMANOS (NE/0920-7775) [01791306] **4504**

ANUARIO JURIDICO (MX/0185-3295) [02250252] **2935**

ANUARIO JURIDICO INTERAMERICANO *SUSPENDED*. (US) [01481658] **3124**

ANUARIO LATINOAMERICANO DE LAS ARTES PLASTICAS (AG) [09114321] **337**

ANUARIO MERCANTIL (SP) [03498859] **1149**

ANUARIO MINERAL BRASILEIRO (BL/0100-9303) [01785907] 1437, **1361**

ANUARIO MUSICAL (SP/0211-3538) [01766297] **4100**

ANUARIO PRENSA ECONOMICA. TENDENCIAS..., ARGENTINA... (AG) [07901542] **1546**

ANUARIO TURISTICO DE PERNAMBUCO (BL) [03603620] **5461**

ANUARIO (UNIVERSIDAD CENTRAL DE VENEZUELA. ESCUELA DE LETRAS) (VE) [08381066] **3266**

ANUARIO VERITAS / UNIVERSIDAD REGIOMONTANA (MX) [08758099] **5228**

ANUARUL INSTITUTULUI DE GEOLOGIE SI GEOFIZICA (RM/0250-2933) [02245102] **1365**

ANUARUL INSTITUTULUI DE ISTORIE SI ARHEOLOGIE A. D. XENOPOL (RM/0074-039X) [01636581] **256**

ANUARUL INSTITUTULUI DE ISTORIE SI ARHEOLOGIE CLUJ-NAPOCA (RM/0253-1550) [I02531550] **2675**

ANUARUL STATISTIC AL ROMANIEI (RM) [23938032] **5322**

ANUDANOM KI MANGEM (II) [01784093] **313**

ANUDANOM KI MANGEM (INDIA. DEPT. OF COMPANY AFFAIRS) (II) [05218597] **4630**

ANUDANOM KI MANGEM (INDIA. DEPT. OF ELECTRONICS) (II) [01784096] **2035**

ANUDANOM KI MANGEM (INDIA. DEPT. OF SCIENCE AND TECHNOLOGY) (II) [01784092] **5084**

ANUDANOM KI MANGEM (INDIA. MINISTRY OF LAW AND JUSTICE) (II) [01784094] **2935**

ANUDANOM KI MANGEM (INDIA. MINISTRY OF WORKS AND HOUSING) (II) [01784097] **2815**

ANUDANOM KI MANGEM, NAGARA VIKASA MANTRALAYA (II) [25755446] **2815**

ANUDANOM KI MANGEM, NAUVAHANA AURA PARIVAHANA MANTRALAYA (II) [25841255] **5447**

ANUDANOM KIMANGEM, SAMAJA KAJANA MANTRALAYA (II) [22466848] **5273**

ANUNCIO (BL) [05160199] **755**

ANUNCIOS MADRID (SP/0214-4905) [I02144905] **921**

ANVESAK (II) [01481662] **1546**

ANVIKSIKI (II) [01790443] **4341**

ANVIL MAGAZINE (US/1059-2997) [24537307] **2797**

ANVIL (NOTTINGHAM, NOTTINGHAMSHIRE) (UK) [10618595] **4935**

ANVIL'S RING, THE (US/0889-177X) [08005079] 3475, **3998**

ANWALTSBLATT (GW) [04459140] **2936**

●ANXIETY (NEW YORK, N.Y.) (US/1070-9797) [28524247] **4574**

ANXIETY RESEARCH *See* ANXIETY, STRESS AND COPING **4574**

●ANXIETY, STRESS AND COPING (SZ/1061-5806) [25364505] **4574**

ANYAGGAZDALKODAS ES RAKTARGAZDALKODAS (HU/0139-1054) [11567597] **1598**

ANYAGMOZGATASI ES CSOMAGOLASI SZAKIRODALMI TAJEKOZTATO (HU/0230-5348) [I02305348] **4217**

ANYAMOZGATAS GEPESITESE A GEPIPARBAN, AZ (HU/0303-2000) [02239810] **1598**

ANZA VALLEY OUTLOOK (US/0883-6124) [12164884] **5633**

ANZEIGER DER ORNITHOLOGISCHE GESELLSCHAFT IN BAYERN (GW/0030-5715) [02449343] **5614**

ANZEIGER DES GERMANISCHEN NATIONALMUSEUMS (GW/0341-8383) [01772302] **337**

ANZEIGER FUER DIE ALTERTUMSWISSENSCHAFT (AU/0003-6293) [01481664] **256**

ANZEIGER FUER DIE SEELSORGE (GW/0721-1937) [I07211937] **4935**

ANZEIGER FUER SCHADLINGSKUNDE, PFLANZENSCHUTZ, UMWELTSCHUTZ (GW/0340-7330) [01664766] **4244**

ANZEIGER FUER SLAVISCHE PHILOLOGIE (AU/0066-5282) [01481668] **3266**

ANZEIGER (OSTERREICHISCHE AKADEMIE DER WISSENSCHAFTEN) (AU/0376-1606) [08471341] **5084**

ANZEIGER / OSTERREICHISCHE AKADEMIE DER WISSENSCHAFTEN, PHILOSOPHISCH-HISTORISCHE KLASSE (AU/0378-8652) [02257080] **2675**

ANZEN KOGAKU (JA/0570-4480) [10295877] **2096**

ANZLIC NEWS (AT/1037-9630) [I10379630] **4630**

AOA OCCASIONAL PAPERS IN GERONTOLOGY (US/0191-7854) [04895853] **3749**

AOCS MONOGRAPH (US/0731-4183) [08343098] **961**

AOE NEWWORK (US) **3551**

AOHA *See* AOHA PROGRESS : A PUBLICATION OF THE AMERICAN OSTEOPATHIC HOSPITAL ASSOCIATION **3777**

AOHA : A PUBLICATION OF THE AMERICAN OSTEOPATHIC HOSPITAL ASSOCIATION (US/1058-6385) [24301589] **3551**

●AOHA PROGRESS : A PUBLICATION OF THE AMERICAN OSTEOPATHIC HOSPITAL ASSOCIATION (US) [26458969] **3777**

AOHA TODAY! (US/1044-1980) [19714745] **3777**

AOMORI-KEN CHIKUSAN SHIKENJO HOKOKU (JA) [07603811] **206**

AOMORI-KEN KOGAI SENTA SHOHO (JA) [02246488] **2224**

AOMORI-KEN NOGYO SHIKENJO KENKYU HOKOKU (JA) [13041471] **62**

AONDE VAMOS? (BL) [03531533] **2645**

●AONE'S LEADERSHIP PROSPECTIVES (US/1072-5067) [28988385] 3777, **3851**

AONTAS NEWSLETTER (IE/1805-1157) [14333297] **1799**

AOPA PILOT, THE (US/0001-2084) [01587549] **12**

AOPA'S AVIATION USA (US) [02117504] **12**

AOR OBSERVER, THE (US/0885-9965) [12812433] **4210**

AOR REPORTER (US/0146-0579) [02851561] **4630**

AORN JOURNAL (US/0001-2092) [01460484] 3959, **3851**

AORN JOURNAL (US/0001-2092) [08384974] **3851**

AORTA (NEW YORK, N.Y.) (US) [08542355] **3699**

AOSTRA JOURNAL OF RESEARCH (CN) [11888326] **4250**

AOYAMA BUSINESS REVIEW (JA) [01737183] **639**

AOYAMA SHAKAI KAGAKU KIYO (JA) [01790182] **5191**

APA MAGAZINE (US/1046-4522) [20407485] **4366**

APA MEMBERSHIP REGISTER (US/0737-1446) [08635769] **4574**

APA MONITOR (US/0001-2114) [01460485] **4574**

●APA NEWSLETTERS ON THE BLACK EXPERIENCE, COMPUTER USE, FEMINISM, LAW, MEDICINE, TEACHING (US/1067-9464) [26345503] 2255, **4341**

APA STRUCTURAL PANEL STATISTICS (US) [14176116] **2399**

APACE (US) [03259631] **12**

APACHE LUTHERAN (US) [01777408] **4935**

APAGAY (MONTREAL) (CN/0382-9251) [03219689] **5780**

APAIS. AUSTRALIAN PUBLIC AFFAIRS INFORMATION SERVICE (AT/0727-8926) [01518859] 4630, **4696**

APALACHEE (US/0736-5357) [01481672] **2721**

APALACHEE QUARTERLY, THE (US/0890-6408) [02753170] **3362**

APARATO LOCOMOTOR (SP/0213-0645) [I02130645] 3959, **3880**

APARTADO (SP/0069-3561) [03105537] **1365**

APARTHEID NON (FR/0369-8262) [19999031] **4504**

APARTMENT ADVISOR, THE (US/1075-4636) [30060151] **772**

APARTMENT AGE (US/0192-0030) [05091557] **2815**

APARTMENT & BUILDING (CN/0318-9651) [02248408] **2815**

APARTMENT & CONDOMINIUM NEWS (US/8756-1387) [11505111] **4834**

APARTMENT CONSTRUCTION NEWS *See* MULTI-HOUSING NEWS **2828**

APARTMENT LETTER *See* APARTMENT ADVISOR, THE **772**

APARTMENT LETTER, THE (US/1067-1498) [27152747] **772**

APARTMENT MANAGEMENT NEWSLETTER (US/0744-9143) [08650361] 860, **4834**

APARTMENT WORLD IN WINNIPEG (CN/0225-9532) [06141470] **2815**

APAVE (FR/0001-2122) [02683080] **2035**

APC NEWSLETTER : JOURNAL OF THE ASSOCIATION OF PROFESSIONAL COMPOSERS (UK) [11001147] **4100**

APC (SASKATCHEWAN. AIR POLLUTION CONTROL BRANCH) (CN/0826-6425) [02862424] **2224**

APCA DIRECTORY *See* APCA DIRECTORY AND RESOURCE BOOK **2224**

APCA DIRECTORY AND RESOURCE BOOK (US/0094-9191) [01791192] **2224**

APCO BULLETIN, THE (US/0001-2165) [05309252] 1072, **4767**

APCO REPORTS (US) **4767**

APDA TOOLS CATALOG. UPDATE (US) [26662940] **1284**

APE, L' (SZ/1010-3619) [04014462] **62**

APEA JOURNAL, THE (AT/0084-7534) [03085732] **4250**

APEC, ANALISE E PERSPECTIVA ECONOMICA (BL/0001-2181) [01110204] **1546**

APEC JOURNAL (US/0893-0457) [13789292] **1965**

APEIRON (CLAYTON) (CN/0003-6390) [17533270] 4341, **1074**

APELLES *CEASED*. (US/0736-5365) [05758183] **313**

APERCU - ASSOCIATION CANADIENNE DE LA CONSTRUCTION (CN/1186-9119) [25313799] **599**

APERCU ECONOMIQUE TRIMESTRIEL (BE/0773-9664) [11041999] **1546**

APERCU, L' (CN/1185-1996) [24257317] **5273**

●APERCU TRIMESTRIEL DE L'ECONOMIE (BE) [28208757] **1463**

APERIODICITY AND ORDER (US/1051-0303) [20227016] **3998**

APERITIF (CN/0711-0944) [08496147] **2327**

APERTURA (PARIS, FRANCE) (FR) [19170061] **3921**

APERTURE (MILLERTON, N.Y.) (US/0003-6420) [01481673] **4366**

APEX *SUSPENDED*. (UK/0003-6439) [04571465] **1316**

APEX (BRUSSELS) (BE/0773-5251) [13981106] **5576**

APEX (KIDDERMINSTER) (UK/0141-2205) [06287357] **5273**

●APEX OF THE M (US/1072-9232) [29238771] **3460**

APF REPORTER (US/0193-4562) [05210443] **2917**

APHA NEWSLETTER : A PUBLICATION OF THE AMERICAN PRINTING HISTORY ASSOCIATION, THE (US) [13154156] **4563**

APHASIA, APRAXIA, AGNOSIA (US/0883-2013) [04754921] **3827**

APHASIOLOGY (UK/0268-7038) [14814735] **3551**

●APHELION (SANTA ANA, CALIF.) (US/1062-502X) [25641797] 1060, **4857**

APHIS 81 (US/0094-3789) [04256104] **2409**

APHIS 82 (US) [01784693] **5504**

APHIS 91 (US/0094-3797) [05637383] **62**

API ABSTRACTS. HEALTH & ENVIRONMENT (US) [14083345] 4250, 2161, **2183**

API ABSTRACTS : OILFIELD CHEMICALS (US) [07289539] 4250, **4283**

API ACCOUNT, THE (US/0883-2102) [09674859] **738**

API. ARCHITECTURAL PERIODICALS INDEX (UK/0266-4380) [01588199] 288, 599, **311**

API INDEXES : INDEX TERM USE STATISTICS (US/0147-9903) [03251674] **4250**

API REPORTS OF AMERICAN SHIPMENTS OF CASING. TUBING, & DRILL PIPE (US) **4250**

API TOXICOLOGICAL REVIEWS (US) [01460487] **3979**

APIACTA (RM/0003-6455) [01481675] **62**

APIBIZ [ONLINE DATABASE] (US) **4250, 4283**

APICOLTORE MODERNO, L' (IT/0518-1259) [04014549] **5605**

APICOLTURA : RIVISTA SCIENTIFICA DI APIDOLOGIA (IT/0393-4241) [12797899] **62**

APICS BIBLIOGRAPHY (US) [16555822] **860**

APICS, THE PERFORMANCE ADVANTAGE (US/1056-0017) [23443266] 1598, **860**

APICULTURA IN ROMANIA (RM/0378-2425) [03098841] **5576**

APICULTURAL ABSTRACTS (UK/0003-648X) [01481679] 5576, **5604**

APIDOLOGIE (FR/0044-8435) [01481682] **5576**

APILIT [ONLINE DATABASE] (US) **4250, 4283**

● APIS, THE (US/0887-7336) [13338516] **226**

APK-EKONOMIKA, UPFAVLENIE / GOSUDARSTVENNYI AGROPROMYSHLENNYI KOMITET SSSR (RU/0235-2443) [18097277] **62**

APL QUOTE QUAD (US/0163-6006) [01998682] **1278**

APL : [CONFERENCE PROCEEDINGS] (US) [05820688] **1278**

APLA BULLETIN (CN/0001-2203) [02672580] **3191**

APLA NEWSLETTER (US) [24621500] 231, **2936**

APLASTIC ANEMIA FOUNDATION OF AMERICAN NEWSLETTER (US) **4767**

APLEC DE TREBALLS - CENTRE D'ESTUDIS DE LA CONCA DE BARBERA (SP) [06893509] **2675**

APLIC BULLETIN (CN/0825-186X) [11895319] **3191**

APLICOMMUNICATOR (US/0891-0847) [14574676] **4549**

APLUS (BE) [03400508] **288**

APMA NEWS (US/8750-2585) [11189194] **3917**

APMIS : ACTA PATHOLOGICA, MICROBIOLOGICA ET IMMUNOLOGICA SCANDINAVICA (DK/0903-4641) [17476618] **3666**

APMIS. ACTA PATHOLOGICA, MICROBIOLOGICA ET IMMUNOLOGICA SCANDINAVICA. SUPPLEMENTUM (DK/0903-465X) [18181317] 559, **3666**

APN. APPAREL PRODUCTION NEWS (JA/0914-7594) [I09147594] **1081**

APNA WATAN (MONTREAL, QUEBEC) (CN/0824-5568) [10680934] **5780**

● APO PRODUCTIVITY JOURNAL (JA/0919-0589) [29732775] **62**

APOCALYPSE (US) [02753188] **4857**

APOLLINARIS; COMMENTARIUS IURIDICO-CANONICUS (IT) [01772209] **2936**

APOLLO (LONDON. 1925) (UK/0003-6536) [01481683] **337**

APOLLO NEWS-RECORD (US) [15079751] **5734**

APOLOGETISCHE BLATTER *See* ORIENTIERUNG (ZURICH) **4984**

APOPTOSIS (UK/1350-4541) 480, **3551**

APORTES (CR) [10428905] **2511**

APORTES MATEMATICOS / UNIVERSIDAD DE TARAPACA, FACULTAD DE CIENCIAS, DEPARTAMENTO DE MATEMATICAS (CL) [16415893] **3494**

APOSTROPHE (SILLERY) (CN/0715-9900) [09863991] **5551**

APOTEKARIS (SP) **3872**

APOTHECARY AND NEW ENGLAND DRUGGIST *See* APOTHECARY (BOSTON), THE **4292**

APOTHECARY (BOSTON), THE (US/0003-6560) [05769368] **4292**

APOTHEEK IN PRAKTIJK *CEASED.* (NE/0924-4107) [I09244107] 4767, **4292**

APOTHEKE HEUTE (GW/0173-1882) [I01731882] **921**

APOTHEKE UND KRANKENHAUS : ZEITSCHRIFT DES VERBANDES DER KRANKENHAUSVERSORGENDEN OFFIZIN-APOTHEKER E.V (GW/0177-9591) [14997586] **4292**

APOTHEKENHELFERIN, DIE (GW) [05305907] **4292**

APOTHEKENHELFERIN HEUTE (GW/0939-3331) [I09393331] **4292**

APOTHEKER-JAHRBUCH (GW/0066-5347) [01481688] **4292**

APOTHEKER UND KUNST *CEASED.* (GW/0341-0110) [05586019] **4292**

APOTHEKER-ZEITUNG STUTTGART (GW/0178-4862) [I01784862] **4292**

APOTHEKERSBLAD, HET (BE/0003-6579) [I00036579] **4292**

APOZITIA (GW) [03008971] **313**

APPA NEWSLETTER (US/0736-7252) [06932902] **1810**

APPALACHIA (BOSTON) (US/0003-6587) [01481692] **4869**

APPALACHIA. BULLETIN ISSUE (US/1052-5319) [04545132] **4869**

APPALACHIA MEDICINE (US/0003-6609) [01701925] **3551**

APPALACHIA (WASHINGTON) (US/0003-6595) [01481691] **1463**

APPALACHIAN ADVANCE (US/0066-5355) [01702009] **1726**

APPALACHIAN FAMILIES (US/1041-8466) [18898249] **2437**

APPALACHIAN HERITAGE (US/0363-2318) [01589342] 2318, **3362**

APPALACHIAN JOURNAL (US/0090-3779) [01784971] **2721**

APPALACHIAN MOUNTAIN CLUB *See* A.M.C. MAINE MOUNTAIN GUIDE, THE **4868**

APPALACHIAN NURSERIES *See* LINING OUT STOCK FOR ... / APPALACHIAN NURSERIES **2424**

APPALACHIAN OUTLOOK (US/0003-6625) [02444887] **407**

APPALACHIAN READER, THE (US/1043-2809) [18329182] **5273**

APPALACHIAN REGIONAL COMMISSION *See* RESEARCH PROGRAM PROSPECTUS / APPALACHIAN REGIONAL COMMISSION **4683**

APPALACHIAN REGIONAL COMMISSION *See* ABSTRACTS. STATE APPALACHIAN DEVELOPMENT PLANS AND INVESTMENT PROGRAMS **2813**

APPALACHIAN ROOTS (US/0888-6814) [11730696] **2437**

APPALACHIAN TRAILWAY NEWS (US/0003-6641) [03229435] 2187, **4869**

APPALACHIAN VOICE, THE (US/0190-3322) [04692918] 4869, **2187**

APPALOOSA JOURNAL (US/0892-385X) [15180616] **2797**

APPARATURA I METODY RENTGENOVSKOGO ANALIZA (RU/0365-4141) [I03654141] **3939**

APPAREL (NZ) [05340973] **1081**

APPAREL DIGEST (US) [11740338] **5347**

APPAREL IMPORT DIGEST (US) [07465016] **1081**

APPAREL INDUSTRY (AT) **1081**

APPAREL INDUSTRY MAGAZINE (US/0192-1878) [05132534] **1081**

APPAREL INTERNATIONAL (UK/0263-1008) [08357847] **1081**

APPAREL NEWS SOUTH (US/0744-6403) [08462695] **1081**

APPAREL OUTLOOK (US/0191-1392) [04781686] **1081**

APPAREL PERSONNEL POLICIES & BENEFITS SURVEY (US/1053-2382) [08852656] **1650**

APPAREL PLANT WAGES SURVEY (US/0275-8873) [07227774] 1081, **1650**

APPAREL (SAINTE-ANNE-DE-BELLEVUE) (CN/1196-2283) [29593004] **1081**

APPAREL SALES/MARKETING COMPENSATION SURVEY (US/0731-3802) [08156834] 1081, **921**

APPAREL STRATEGIST (US) **1081**

APPARENT CONSUMPTION OF FOODSTUFFS AND NUTRIENTS, AUSTRALIA (AT/1031-0533) [I10310533] 2327, **2362**

APPARENT PER CAPITA FOOD CONSUMPTION IN CANADA. PART 1 (CN/0226-823X) [15514743] **2327**

APPARENT PER CAPITA FOOD CONSUMPTION IN CANADA. PART 2 (CN/0226-8248) [15514819] **2327**

APPARENT PLACES OF FUNDAMENTAL STARS (GW/0174-254X) [01722620] **391**

APPARENT USE OF PORTLAND CEMENT BY STATE AND MARKET / MARKET AND ECONOMIC RESEARCH (US) [11886273] 1598, **599**

APPEAL DEMOCRAT, THE (US) [27480879] **5633**

APPEARANCES (US/0884-2213) [12226088] **313**

APPEARANCES OF LEADING CHINESE OFFICIALS (US/0744-1630) [06467703] **4630**

APPEARANCES OF SOVIET LEADERS (US/0145-0700) [01784040] **4630**

APPEL, DE (NE) **755**

APPEL DU SACRE-COEUR, L' (CN/0705-9590) [04060513] **5055**

APPELBAUM/GRISSO REPORT ON LAW AND MENTAL HEALTH, THE *CEASED.* (US/1056-9111) [23893217] 3921, **2810**

APPELES A LA LIBERTE (LEGARDEUR, QUEBEC) (CN/0828-4695) [11873810] **4935**

APPELLATE COURT ADMINISTRATION REVIEW (US/0191-8524) [04320939] **3139**

APPENDICE NUOVISSIMO DIGESTO (IT) **2936**

APPENDIX TO THE DIABETES MELLITUS COORDINATING COMMITTEE ... ANNUAL REPORT TO THE DIRECTOR, NATIONAL INSTITUTES OF HEALTH (US) [08272475] **3726**

APPETITE (UK/0195-6663) [05585150] **4187**

APPI-CRUDE OILS (HK) **4250**

● APPIC DIRECTORY (US/1078-7178) [29243490] **4574**

APPITA JOURNAL : JOURNAL OF THE TECHNICAL ASSOCIATION OF THE AUSTRALIAN AND NEW ZEALAND PULP AND PAPER INDUSTRY (AT) [15564097] **4232**

APPLAUSE/BEST PLAYS THEATER YEARBOOK OF . *See* BEST PLAYS OF ..., THE **5362**

APPLAUSE/BEST PLAYS THEATER YEARBOOK, THE (US/1063-620X) [26085532] 383, **5361**

APPLAUSE THEATRE BOOK REVIEW & CATALOG, THE (US) [20069514] 5361, **383**

APPLE ACCESS (US/0749-5277) [11198681] **1264**

APPLE BITS (US/0882-0406) [11764495] **1171**

APPLE BUSINESS (UK/0953-4474) [I09534474] **1171**

APPLE INDEX, THE (US/0741-2347) [10107524] **1264**

APPLE LIBRARY USERS GROUP NEWSLETTER (US/1057-1159) [23865733] **1171**

APPLE MAGAZINE LES ULIS *CEASED.* (FR/0992-3012) [I09923012] **1171**

APPLE SOFTWARE DIRECTORY (US) [10760961] **1284**

APPLE (SPRINGFIELD) (US/0003-6765) [02246535] **3460**

APPLE UTILISATEUR LES ULIS (FR/0999-5919) [I09995919] **1171**

APPLE-WORKS FORUM (US/0893-4118) [15602535] **1171**

APPLELAND BULLETIN, THE (US/0736-0800) [08148139] **2437**

APPLESAUCE (US) [05705102] **1726**

APPLESEED QUARTERLY (CN/1183-3785) [24267071] **3363**

APPLESOURCE (US/0730-1391) [07955423] **1284**

APPLETON PRESS (US) [01481708] **5694**

APPLEWOOD SEED CO *See* WHOLESALE PRICE AND ORDER SHEET / APPLEWOOD SEED CO **2433**

APPLEWOOD TRANSCRIPT (US) **5641**

APPLEWORKS JOURNAL (US/0898-1183) [16842062] 639, **1278**

APPLIANCE (US/0003-6781) [01481716] **2810**

APPLIANCE MANUFACTURER (US/0003-679X) [02255579] 3475, **2810**

APPLIANCE MANUFACTURER. DIRECTORY (US) [05574921] **2810**

APPLIANCE SERVICE NEWS (US/0003-6803) [03398813] **2810**

APPLIANCES AND RECREATION (US) **2810**

APPLICABLE ALGEBRA IN ENGINEERING, COMMUNICATION AND COMPUTING (GW/0938-1279) [24633838] 1965, **3494**

APPLICABLE ANALYSIS (US/0003-6811) [01481717] **3494**

APPLICANDO (IT) **1171**

APPLICANTS AND OPENINGS / SOUTH CAROLINA EMPLOYMENT SECURITY COMMISSION (US) [08778495] **1651**

APPLICANTS GUIDE, JUVENILE JUSTICE PROGRAMS ..., VICTIMS OF CRIME ACT-VICTIM ASSISTANCE PROGRAM (US) [19346639] **2936**

APPLICATION AND ENROLLMENT PATTERNS OF TRANSFER STUDENTS (ALBANY) (US/0093-4046) [05218463] **1810**

APPLICATION AND INSTRUCTIONS FOR VEHICLE PRORATION (US) [07538647] **5377**

Alphabetical Title Index

APPLIED

APPLICATION DEVELOPMENT STRATEGIES (US) **1171**

APPLICATION DEVELOPMENT TOOLS (US) **1284**

●APPLICATION DEVELOPMENT TRENDS (US) [29569869] 1284, **1227**

APPLICATION OF COMPUTERS AND OPERATIONS RESEARCH IN THE MINERAL INDUSTRY / SPONSORED BY COLORADO SCHOOL OF MINES (US/0741-0603) [10075807] 2134, **1171**

APPLICATION OF FINANCIAL REPORTING STANDARDS (UK) **738**

APPLICATION OF OPTICAL INSTRUMENTATION IN MEDICINE (US/0362-5443) [02438575] **3552**

APPLICATION OF POLYMER EMULSIONS *See* EMULSION POLYMERISATION AND POLYMER EMULSIONS **4223**

APPLICATION STATISTICS (TORONTO) (CN/0382-912X) [01794832] 1810, **1793**

APPLICATION TECHNOLOGY (US) **62**

APPLICATION THROUGH INSURANCE, SINGLE FAMILY, SECTION 203(N) (US) [05281792] **2815**

●APPLICATIONS AND SOLUTIONS (US/1062-3760) [25602598] **5085**

APPLICATIONS IN BASIC MARKETING (US) [22638336] **921**

APPLICATIONS OF ARTIFICIAL INTELLIGENCE *See* APPLICATIONS OF ARTIFICIAL INTELLIGENCE: KNOWLEDGE-BASED SYSTEMS **1211**

●APPLICATIONS OF ARTIFICIAL INTELLIGENCE: KNOWLEDGE-BASED SYSTEMS (US/1019-0716) [25270008] **1211**

APPLICATIONS OF COMPUTER SCIENCE SERIES (US/0888-2231) [13503257] **1171**

APPLICATIONS OF CRYOGENIC TECHNOLOGY (US/0093-8815) [01783333] **5085**

APPLICATIONS OF MANAGEMENT SCIENCE (US/0276-8976) [07301523] **860**

APPLICATIONS OF MATHEMATICS (US/0172-4568) [09151952] **3494**

APPLICATIONS OF MATHEMATICS / CZECHOSLOVAK ACADEMY OF SCIENCES (XR/0862-7940) [24242013] **3494**

APPLICATIONS OF MATHEMATICS (PRAGUE) (XR/0862-7940) [23959594] **3494**

APPLICATIONS PROGRAMS (US/0145-9880) [02827717] **1278**

APPLICATIONS TO THE PROFESSIONAL SCHOOLS AND COLLEGES FOR THE FALL TERM 1948: MEDICINE, DENTISTRY, VETERINARY MEDICINE, PHARMACY, OPTOMETRY, OSTEOPATHY, LAW (US) [01458823] 1810, **3552**

APPLICATOR, THE (US) **599**

APPLIED ACOUSTICS (UK/0003-682X) [01481719] **2097**

●APPLIED AND COMPUTATIONAL HARMONIC ANALYSIS (US/1063-5203) [26049297] **3494**

APPLIED AND ENVIRONMENTAL MICROBIOLOGY (US/0099-2240) [01712042] **559**

●APPLIED & PREVENTIVE PSYCHOLOGY : JOURNAL OF THE AMERICAN ASSOCIATION OF APPLIED AND PREVENTIVE PSYCHOLOGY (US/0962-1849) [25484803] **4574**

APPLIED AND THEORETICAL ELECTROPHORESIS (UK/0954-6642) [19350113] **1013**

APPLIED ANIMAL BEHAVIOUR SCIENCE (NE/0168-1591) [10567613] **5504**

APPLIED ARTIFICIAL INTELLIGENCE (US/0883-9514) [12269568] **1211**

APPLIED ARTS MAGAZINE (CN) [27827290] **376**

APPLIED ARTS QUARTERLY *See* APPLIED ARTS MAGAZINE **376**

●APPLIED BEHAVIORAL SCIENCE REVIEW (US/1068-8595) [27829563] 5239, **4574**

APPLIED BIOCHEMISTRY AND BIOTECHNOLOGY (US) [07033031] **3685**

APPLIED BIOCHEMISTRY AND MICROBIOLOGY (US/0003-6838) [02413358] 559, **480**

APPLIED BOTANY (UK/0309-1791) [02784971] **500**

APPLIED BOTANY ABSTRACTS (II) [07601733] **500**

APPLIED CARDIOPULMONARY PATHOPHYSIOLOGY : ACP (US/0920-5268) [15923355] **3699**

APPLIED CATALYSIS *See* APPLIED CATALYSIS. B : ENVIRONMENTAL **2161**

APPLIED CATALYSIS A : GENERAL (NE/0926-860X) [24979680] **2008**

●APPLIED CATALYSIS. B : ENVIRONMENTAL (NE/0926-3373) [25512114] **2161**

APPLIED CATEGORICAL STRUCTURES (NE/0927-2852) [28726761] **3494**

APPLIED CLAY SCIENCE (NE/0169-1317) [12645477] **5085**

●APPLIED CLINICAL TRIALS (US/1064-8542) [26434881] **4292**

APPLIED COGNITIVE PSYCHOLOGY (UK/0888-4080) [13566982] **4574**

APPLIED COMPOSITE MATERIALS (NE/0929-189X) **2100**

APPLIED COMPUTATIONAL ELECTROMAGNETICS SOCIETY JOURNAL (US/1054-4887) [20476454] **4443**

APPLIED COMPUTER AND COMMUNICATIONS LAW (UK/0267-6621) [11965308] 1225, **2936**

●APPLIED COMPUTING REVIEW : A PUBLICATION OF THE SPECIAL INTEREST GROUP ON APPLIED COMPUTING (US) [28175412] 1278, **1284**

APPLIED CYTOGENETICS (US/1056-5191) [21264881] 532, **542**

APPLIED DATA AND KNOWLEDGE ENGINEERING **SUSPENDED.** (GW/0942-251X) **1965**

APPLIED DEMOGRAPHY (US) **4549**

APPLIED ECONOMICS (UK/0003-6846) [01481720] **1463**

APPLIED ECONOMICS LETTERS (UK/1350-5851) **1463**

APPLIED ENERGY (UK/0306-2619) [02246728] **1932**

●APPLIED ENERGY (US/1068-7181) [27773792] **2109**

APPLIED ENGINEERING IN AGRICULTURE (US/0883-8542) [12258667] 62, **1965**

APPLIED ENTOMOLOGY AND ZOOLOGY (JA/0003-6862) [01481721] **5605**

APPLIED ERGONOMICS (UK/0003-6870) [01702062] **1965**

APPLIED FINANCIAL ECONOMICS (UK/0960-3107) [23964400] **1633**

APPLIED FLUORESCENCE TECHNOLOGY (AU/1018-6247) [I10186247] **4433**

APPLIED GENETICS NEWS (US/0271-7107) [06683380] **542**

APPLIED GEOCHEMISTRY (UK/0883-2927) [12100988] **1366**

APPLIED GEOGRAPHY AND DEVELOPMENT (GW/0173-7619) [06748201] **2554**

APPLIED GEOGRAPHY (SEVENOAKS) (UK/0143-6228) [07622039] **2554**

APPLIED H.R.M. RESEARCH (US/1055-9094) [23467386] **938**

APPLIED HEALTH PHYSICS ABSTRACTS AND NOTES (UK/0305-7615) [05672227] **4433**

●APPLIED HYDROGEOLOGY : INTERNATIONAL JOURNAL FOR HYDROGEOLOGISTS (GW) [25643092] **1366**

●APPLIED IMMUNOHISTOCHEMISTRY (US/1062-3345) [25587383] **480**

APPLIED INTELLIGENCE (NE/0924-669X) [25272842] **1211**

APPLIED LANGUAGE LEARNING (US/1041-679X) [18824112] **3266**

APPLIED LINGUISTICS (UK/0142-6001) [06416547] **3266**

APPLIED LINGUISTICS ASSOCIATION OF AUSTRALIA *See* OCCASIONAL PAPERS - APPLIED LINGUISTICS ASSOCIATION OF AUSTRALIA **3307**

APPLIED MAGNETIC RESONANCE (RU/0937-9347) [23561957] **4397**

APPLIED MANAGEMENT NEWSLETTER (US/0889-8227) [07433158] **938**

APPLIED MATHEMATICAL FINANCE (UK/1350-486X) **3494**

APPLIED MATHEMATICAL MODELLING (UK/0307-904X) [02600908] **3495**

APPLIED MATHEMATICAL SCIENCES (US/0066-5452) [01481724] **3495**

APPLIED MATHEMATICS (US/0888-479X) [13608089] **3495**

APPLIED MATHEMATICS AND COMPUTATION (US/0096-3003) [01798807] 1171, **3495**

APPLIED MATHEMATICS AND ENGINEERING SCIENCE TEXTS (UK/0950-5903) [I09505903] 1965, **3495**

APPLIED MATHEMATICS AND MECHANICS (US) [08802227] **3495**

APPLIED MATHEMATICS AND MECHANICS (HK/0253-4827) [08603125] 2109, **3495**

APPLIED MATHEMATICS AND OPTIMIZATION (US/0095-4616) [01795522] **3495**

APPLIED MATHEMATICS LETTERS (US/0893-9659) [15716169] **3495**

APPLIED MATHEMATICS SERIES (US/1049-4685) [00936279] **3495**

APPLIED MEASUREMENT IN EDUCATION (US/0895-7347) [16767194] **1726**

APPLIED MECHANICS REVIEWS (US/0003-6900) [01064296] 2109, **2002**

APPLIED MICROBIOLOGY AND BIOTECHNOLOGY (GW/0175-7598) [10397249] 3685, **559**

●APPLIED MICROWAVE & WIRELESS (US/1075-0207) [29872930] **4433**

APPLIED MICROWAVE MAGAZINE (US/1061-3528) [25259540] **4433**

APPLIED NEUROPSYCHOLOGY (DK) **4574**

APPLIED NUMERICAL MATHEMATICS : TRANSACTIONS OF IMACS (NE/0168-9274) [12160367] **3495**

APPLIED NURSING RESEARCH : ANR (US/0897-1897) [17429532] **3851**

APPLIED OCCUPATIONAL AND ENVIRONMENTAL HYGIENE (US/1047-322X) [20665448] **2859**

APPLIED OCEAN RESEARCH (UK/0141-1187) [04648153] **1446**

APPLIED OPTICS (US/0003-6935) [01481728] **4433**

APPLIED OPTICS AND OPTICAL ENGINEERING (US/0197-8535) [05881226] **4433**

APPLIED ORGANOMETALLIC CHEMISTRY (UK/0268-2605) [15586837] **961**

●APPLIED PARASITOLOGY (GW/0943-0938) [28082728] **3552**

APPLIED PHYSICS. A, SOLIDS AND SURFACES (GW/0721-7250) [07820569] **4397**

●APPLIED PHYSICS. B, LASERS AND OPTICS (GW) [29901949] **4433**

APPLIED PHYSICS. B, PHOTOPHYSICS AND LASER CHEMISTRY (GW/0721-7269) [07820598] **4433**

APPLIED PHYSICS LETTERS (US/0003-6951) [01580952] **4397**

APPLIED PLANT SCIENCE (SA/0259-5605) [17022576] **163**

APPLIED PROBABILITY (US/0937-3195) [17795421] **3495**

APPLIED PSYCHOLINGUISTICS (UK/0142-7164) [06275910] **3266**

APPLIED PSYCHOLOGICAL MEASUREMENT (US/0146-6216) [02998464] **4574**

APPLIED PSYCHOLOGY (UK/0269-994X) [15228444] **4574**

●APPLIED RADIATION AND ISOTOPES : INCLUDING DATA, INSTRUMENTATION AND METHODS FOR USE IN AGRICULTURE, INDUSTRY AND MEDICINE (UK/0969-8043) [27456684] **4433**

APPLIED RADIOLOGY (1976) (US/0160-9963) [03783853] 3847, **3939**

APPLIED RESEARCH IN COACHING AND ATHLETICS ANNUAL (US) [21577894] **1854**

APPLIED RESEARCH SUMMARY OF AWARDS (US/0275-939X) [06149576] **5085**

APPLIED SCIENCE & TECHNOLOGY INDEX (US/0003-6986) [01581557] 5085, **5173**

APPLIED SCIENCE & TECHNOLOGY INDEX (CD-ROM ED.) (US/1063-8695) [24886088] **5173**

APPLIED SCIENTIFIC RESEARCH (NE/0003-6994) [02243502] 2087, **2109**

APPLIED SIGNAL PROCESSING (UK/0941-0635) **1255**

●APPLIED SOCIAL PROBLEMS AND INTERVENTION STRATEGIES (US/1070-6585) [28444978] **4575**

APPLIED SOCIAL PSYCHOLOGY (US) 5239, **4575**

APPLIED SOCIAL RESEARCH METHODS SERIES (US) [11808357] 5191, **5239**

●APPLIED SOIL ECOLOGY : A SECTION OF AGRICULTURE, ECOSYSTEMS & ENVIRONMENT (NE/0929-1393) [30817283] **163**

APPLIED SOLAR ENERGY (US/0003-701X) [01775013] **1932**

APPLIED SPECTROSCOPY (US/0003-7028) [01577663] **4433**

APPLIED SPECTROSCOPY REVIEWS (SOFTCOVER ED.) (US/0570-4928) [01915254] **1013**

APPLIED STATISTICS (UK/0035-9254) [01685424] **5322**

APPLIED — Alphabetical Title Index

APPLIED STOCHASTIC MODELS AND DATA ANALYSIS (UK/8755-0024) [11241541] **3495**

●APPLIED SUPERCONDUCTIVITY (UK/0964-1807) [26659511] **2035**

APPLIED SURFACE SCIENCE (NE/0169-4332) [12605690] **4397**

APPLIED THERMAL SCIENCES *CEASED.* (US/1042-0959) [18940303] **2097**

APPLIED TIME SERIES ANALYSIS (US) [04578243] **3495**

APPLIED VIROLOGY RESEARCH (US/1041-245X) [18141588] **559**

APPLYING RESEARCH TO THE CLASSROOM (CN/0832-9842) [17759060] **1888**

APPM UPDATE (US) **4292**

APPOINT (JONQUIERE) (CN/1188-2131) [25796369] **1810**

APPRAISAL (US/0003-7052) [01481739] 1060, **5085**

APPRAISAL DIGEST *SUSPENDED.* (US/0003-7060) [04747744] **4834**

APPRAISAL INSTITUTE OF CANADA *See* DIRECTORY OF DESIGNATED MEMBERS - APPRAISAL INSTITUTE OF CANADA **4836**

APPRAISAL INSTITUTE (U.S.) *See* DIRECTORY OF MEMBERS - APPRAISAL INSTITUTE (U.S.) **4836**

APPRAISAL JOURNAL, THE (US/0003-7087) [01625941] **4834**

APPRAISAL REVIEW & MORTGAGE UNDERWRITING JOURNAL (US/1041-1585) [13309319] 2874, **4834**

APPRAISER NEWS (US/1054-5999) [22922199] **4834**

APPRAISERS ASSOCIATION OF AMERICA *See* MEMBERSHIP DIRECTORY - APPRAISERS ASSOCIATION OF AMERICA, NC **4840**

APPRAISERS' INFORMATION EXCHANGE, THE (US/8755-4348) [11313187] **4834**

APPRENTI SORCIER (GATINEAU) (CN/0846-3409) [25066785] **4857**

APPRENTICE (OTTAWA) (CN/0706-7399) [04955209] **4857**

APPRENTISSAGE ET SOCIALISATION (1991) (CN/1189-3958) [26497714] **1875**

APPRISE (US/0883-9336) [12256993] **2721**

APPROACH (NORFOLK) (US/0570-4979) [01643259] **4174**

APPROACH TO PHYSICAL SCIENCES (AT/0518-1623) [06243490] **4398**

APPROACHES TO ANSWERING THE UNIFORM FINAL EXAMINATIONS, PLUS EXAMINERS' COMMENTS (CN/0318-1081) [02248337] **738**

APPROACHES TO SEMIOTICS (GW/0066-5576) [01481744] **3266**

APPROACHES TO SEMIOTICS. PAPERBACK SERIES *CEASED.* (NE/0066-5576) [03354585] **3266**

APPROACHES TO TEACHING WORLD LITERATURE (US/1059-1133) [15051186] **3363**

APPROACHES TO TRANSLATION STUDIES (NE) [03348201] **3363**

APPROCHES (MONTREAL, QUEBEC) (CN/0827-1690) [14937998] **4935**

APPROPRIATE TECHNOLOGY (UK/0305-0920) [01794271] **5085**

APPROPRIATE TECHNOLOGY DOCUMENTATION BULLETIN (II) [02380223] **5085**

APPROPRIATE TECHNOLOGY FOR WATER SUPPLY AND SANITATION (US/0253-4525) [08839067] 5530, **2224**

APPROPRIATE TECHNOLOGY INDEX (AT) [14340343] **5085**

APPROPRIATION ACCOUNTS (IE) [05925591] **4711**

APPROPRIATION ACCOUNTS, GOVERNMENT OF ORISSA (II) [05461937] **4711**

APPROPRIATION ACCOUNTS, REVENUE STATEMENTS, ACCOUNTS OF THE FUNDS AND OTHER PUBLIC ACCOUNTS OF TANZANIA, THE (TZ) [02245755] **4711**

APPROPRIATIONS AND LETTERS OF INTENT FOR ... (US) [07661338] **4630**

APPROPRIATIONS REPORT / COMMITTEE ON STATE FISCAL AFFAIRS (US) [05869614] **4711**

APPROPRIATIONS REPORT / KANSAS LEGISLATIVE RESEARCH DEPARTMENT (US) [06245293] **4711**

APPROPRIATIONS REPORT (MICHIGAN) (US) [12120043] **4630**

APPROVAL OF AWARDS FOR INSTITUTIONS PARTICIPATING IN THE COLLEGE WORK-STUDY PROGRAM (US/0149-3698) [03453917] 1888, **1651**

APPROVED BIOEQUIVALENCY CODES (US) **4292**

APPROVED CROSSWORD PUZZLES (US/0199-5596) [05987178] **4857**

APPROVED DRUG PRODUCTS WITH THERAPEUTIC EQUIVALENCE EVALUATIONS (US/1048-5996) [12771735] **4292**

APPROVED ESTIMATES OF ANAMBRA STATE OF NIGERIA (NR/0331-1619) [05273772] **4711**

APPROVED ESTIMATES OF REVENUE AND EXPENDITURE (BM) [04197473] **4711**

APPROVED METHODS OF THE AMERICAN ASSOCIATION OF CEREAL CHEMISTS (US) [02489816] **961**

APPROVED RESEARCH PROGRAMME - FEDERAL DEPARTMENT OF AGRICULTURAL RESEARCH (NR) [04154171] **62**

APPROVED REVENUE, RECURRENT AND CAPITAL ESTIMATES (NIGERIA) (NR/0189-9023) [09875495] **4711**

APPROVED VARIETY PUZZLES PLUS CROSSROADS (US/1076-9021) [30635478] **4857**

APPROVED WELDING ELECTRODE WIRE-FLUX AND WIRE-GAS COMBINATIONS (US/0148-9380) [03383396] 2036, **4026**

APPROXIMATION & OPTIMIZATION (GW/0937-4051) [l09374051] **3495**

APPROXIMATION THEORY AND ITS APPLICATIONS (CC/1000-9221) [17312439] **3495**

APPUI (CN/0823-8014) [11054355] **2721**

APPUNTI DEL CIRCOLO CULTURALE G GHISLANDI *CEASED.* (IT) **3337**

APR. ALLGEMEINE PAPIER-RUNDSCHAU (1966) (GW/0002-5917) [15496749] **4232**

APR EUROPE (GW/0939-141X) [I0939141X] **4232**

APRA (AUSTRALASIAN PERFORMING RIGHT ASSOCIATION) (AT) [09383676] **4100**

APRA JOURNAL *See* APRA (AUSTRALASIAN PERFORMING RIGHT ASSOCIATION) **4100**

APRES-DEMAIN (FR/0003-7176) [01720949] **4464**

APRG REPORT (AT/1037-051X) [I1037051X] **5439**

APRI JOURNAL (NR) [24483325] **4464**

APRIL 17 (IS) **2767**

APS BULLETIN / AMERICAN PAIN SOCIETY (US/1057-1590) [23959537] 3552, **578**

APS DIPLOMAT (CY) **4630**

●APS JOURNAL (US/1058-9139) [24426049] **3552**

APS MONOGRAPH SERIES (US/1051-1113) [21867146] **500**

APS OBSERVER (US/1050-4672) [20876579] **4575**

APS REVIEW (CY) **1598**

APS REVIEW, THE (US) [04942999] 4630, **4464**

APSA DEPARTMENTAL SERVICES PROGRAM, SURVEY OF DEPARTMENTS (US/0094-7954) [01794921] **4464**

APSA DIRECTORY OF DEPARTMENT CHAIRMEN *See* APSA DIRECTORY OF DEPARTMENT CHAIRPERSONS **4464**

APSA DIRECTORY OF DEPARTMENT CHAIRPERSONS (US/0196-5255) [02171764] **4464**

APSA DIRECTORY OF MEMBERS - AMERICAN POLITICAL SCIENCE ASSOCIATION (US/01794952) **4464**

APSA NEWSLETTER (AT/0725-2390) [l07252390] **4464**

APSI : ACTUALIDAD NACIONAL E INTERNACIONAL (CL) [09421949] **2721**

●APSNEWS (US/1058-8132) [24383764] **4398**

APT BULLETIN (1986) (CN/0848-8525) [15324781] **288**

APT COMMUNIQUE (US/1062-6190) [20787526] **288**

●APT FOR LIBRARIES (US/1062-0664) [25517105] **3191**

APT. REVIEW. EGLINTON EDITION (CN/0226-6040) [06511114] **383**

APT TELECOM JOURNAL : JOURNAL OF THE ASIA PACIFIC TELECOMMUNITY (TH) [25988205] **1149**

APTD (US/0361-2945) [01791503] **2224**

APTIRC BULLETIN (SI/0217-6661) [23981104] 891, **4711**

APTMA DIRECTORY OF MEMBERS - ALL PAKISTAN TEXTILE MILLS ASSOCIATION (PK) [02386015] **5347**

APUA NEWSLETTER (UK) [04225151] **62**

APUA NEWSLETTER / ALLIANCE FOR THE PRUDENT USE OF ANTIBIOTICS (US) [20351410] **4292**

APULUM : ACTA MUSEI APULENSIS (RM) [01786893] **2675**

APUNGO (NP) [02239630] **3363**

APUNTES (PE/0252-1865) [01794971] **5191**

APUNTES (CL) [06429056] 5361, **3363**

APUNTES ARQUEOLOGICOS (GT) [27954903] **256**

APUNTES (DALLAS, TEX.) (US/0279-9804) [07411555] 2255, **4935**

APUNTES DE CARDIOLOGIA (SP/0214-3917) [l02143917] **3699**

APUNTES DE INGENIERIA (CL/0716-0348) [02414052] **1965**

APUNTES PASTORALES (CR) **4935**

APUNTES TRIMESTRALES (PY) [14393644] **2721**

APUNTS (SP) **3552**

APUNTS. MEDICINA DE L'ESPORT (SP/0213-3717) [l02133717] **3953**

APUROCHI. APPROACH (JA/0003-7117) [01843871] **599**

AQ (GW) [04602978] **313**

AQEIC. BOLETIN TECNICO (SP/0365-5873) [l03655873] **961**

AQIS BULLETIN (AT/1033-9280) [22638367] 163, 5504, **2327**

AQMD ADVISOR (US) **2224**

AQUA (DULUTH, MINN.) (US/1041-388X) [18505813] **2810**

AQUA FENNICA (FI/0356-7133) [02255256] **1412**

AQUA-FIELD SPORTSMAN (US/0742-910X) [10446729] 4883, **3475**

AQUA (LONDON) (UK/0003-7214) [02068204] **5530**

AQUA (MILAN, ITALY) (IT) [17304721] **591**

AQUA REVUE (FR/0295-0448) [l02950448] **2295**

AQUA TERRA (EUREKA SPRINGS, ARK.) (US/1048-8111) [21063973] **5530**

AQUACULTURA HUNGARICA (HU/0138-9092) [06169831] **2295**

AQUACULTURAL ENGINEERING (UK/0144-8609) [08378615] **2295**

AQUACULTURE (NE/0044-8486) [01586829] 552, **2295**

AQUACULTURE AND FISHERIES MANAGEMENT (UK/0266-996X) [12386466] **2295**

AQUACULTURE & THE FISH FARMER (US) [01714747] **2295**

AQUACULTURE EUROPE (BE) [22725036] **552**

AQUACULTURE INFORMATION SERIES (UK/0953-2781) [24905281] **2295**

●AQUACULTURE INTERNATIONAL (UK/0967-6120) 442, **2295**

AQUACULTURE IRELAND (IE/0790-0929) [14155111] **2295**

AQUACULTURE MAGAZINE (US/0199-1388) [05622897] **2295**

AQUACULTURE MAGAZINE. BUYER'S GUIDE ... AND INDUSTRY DIRECTORY (US/0898-9540) [15178631] **2296**

●AQUACULTURE NEWS (US) **2296**

AQUACULTURE NUTRITION (UK/1353-5773) **552**

●AQUACULTURE RESEARCH (UK/1355-557X) 2296, **553**

AQUACULTURE SITUATION AND OUTLOOK REPORT (US/1042-6221) [19090398] 62, **5530**

AQUACULTURE TECHNICAL BULLETIN (IE/0332-2475) [12579669] **2296**

AQUACULTURE TODAY *CEASED.* (CN/0842-5914) [19746869] **442**

AQUALERT (UK) **5530**

AQUALINE ABSTRACTS (UK/0263-5534) [10910510] 2087, **2002**

AQUALINK (AT/1032-6189) [l10326189] **4883**

AQUANAUT (UK/0264-259X) [l0264259X] **1351**

AQUAPHYTE (US/0893-7702) [06513906] 2211, **500**

●AQUAPOLIS *SUSPENDED.* (IT) [26386262] **2815**

AQUARAMA (FR/0151-6981) [01791920] **4285**

AQUARAMA (FR/0151-6981) [l01516981] **2771**

AQUAREF (CN) 5530, 2224, **5549**

AQUARIMANTIMA (CK) [02246355] **3460**

AQUARIST AND PONDKEEPER (UK/0003-7273) [03408700] **2296**

AQUARIUM (US) **553**

AQUARIUM DIGEST INTERNATIONAL *CEASED.* (GW) [02122941] **2296**

AQUARIUM FISH MAGAZINE (US/0899-045X) [17978410] **4285**

AQUARIUM MILANO (IT/0392-2863) [l03922863] **5576**

Alphabetical Title Index — ARBEITEN

AQUARIUS (UK/0003-7303) [02752755] **3460**

AQUARIUS (LOGAN) (US/0587-341X) [02257640] **5530**

AQUASPHERE (BOSTON, MASS. : 1985) (US/0889-5775) [13923752] **442**

AQUATIC BOTANY (NE/0304-3770) [02254712] **500**

AQUATIC CONSERVATION (UK/1052-7613) [22367607] **2211**

AQUATIC ENVIRONMENT PROTECTION : ANALYTICAL METHODS (UK/0953-4466) [18310454] **2211**

AQUATIC GEOCHEMISTRY (NE/1380-6165) **961**

AQUATIC INSECTS (NE/0165-0424) [05133489] **5605**

AQUATIC LIVING RESOURCES (MONTROUGE) (FR/0990-7440) [18180839] **2296**

AQUATIC MAMMALS (UK/0167-5427) [01624502] **5504, 5576**

AQUATIC MICROBIOLOGY NEWSLETTER (US/0570-5118) [02191123] **559**

AQUATIC PLANT MANAGEMENT PROGRAM PROPOSALS FOR ... (CN) [07705681] **1446, 2409**

AQUATIC SCIENCES (SZ/1015-1621) [19636793] 5504, **1412**

AQUATIC SCIENCES & FISHERIES ABSTRACTS See AQUATIC SCIENCES AND FISHERIES ABSTRACTS. PART 1 : BIOLOGICAL SCIENCES AND LIVING RESOURCES **2316**

AQUATIC SCIENCES & FISHERIES ABSTRACTS (CD-ROM ED.) (US/1064-0460) [26204829] 2296, **2316**

AQUATIC SCIENCES AND FISHERIES ABSTRACTS. PART 1 : BIOLOGICAL SCIENCES AND LIVING RESOURCES (US/0140-5373) [03924687] 2296, **2316**

AQUATIC SCIENCES AND FISHERIES ABSTRACTS. PART 2 : OCEAN TECHNOLOGY, POLICY AND NON-LIVING RESOURCES (US/0140-5381) [03999218] 2296, **2316**

AQUATIC SCIENCES AND FISHERIES ABSTRACTS. PART 3 : AQUATIC POLLUTION AND ENVIRONMENTAL QUALITY (US/1045-6031) [20156603] 2296, **2317**

AQUATIC SERIES (US/0271-0331) [03673369] 1446, **2187**

●AQUATIC SURVIVAL (CN/1188-553X) [26244881] 2187, **2296**

AQUATIC TOXICOLOGY (AMSTERDAM, NETHERLANDS) (NE/0166-445X) [07505256] **3979**

AQUATIC TOXICOLOGY SERIES (US/0734-1687) [08341586] 3979, **2211**

AQUATICS INTERNATIONAL (US/1058-7039) [24359604] **4883**

AQUEDUCT (LOS ANGELES) (US/0092-0622) [03829124] **5530**

AQUELARRE (VANCOUVER) (CN/0843-7920) [20661625] **5551**

AQUI MAGAZINE (US) **2484**

AQUILA (HU/0374-5708) [01458668] **5614**

AQUILEIA NOSTRA (IT/0391-7304) [04053931] **256**

AQUILO. SER. BOTANICA (FI/0570-5169) [02444902] **500**

AQUILO SER ZOOLOGICA (FI/0570-5177) [03676825] **5576**

AQUILON (YELLOWKNIFE) (CN/0834-1443) [16082536] **3266**

AQUINAS (IT/0003-7362) [01640557] **4341**

AQUINAS JOURNAL (CE) [12498378] 2842, 4935, **5191**

AQUINAS LECTURE (US/0066-5614) [01481756] **4341**

AQUITANIA (FR/0758-9670) [11919420] **2675**

AR (GW) [10195662] **4035**

AR; ARMEE RUNDSCHAU. MICROFORM (GW) [17271767] **4035**

AR DARBA SARKANÂA KAROGA ORDENI APBALVOTAS LATVIJAS LAUKSAIMNIECIBAS AKADEMIJAS RAKSTI See TRUDY LSKHA **142**

AR FALZ (FR/0755-883X) [12206397] **3363**

AR STAATKUNDE IN CHRISTEN-DEMOCRATISCH PERSPECTIEF (NE) [04614971] **4464**

ARA-YAYIN DIZISI / OCCASIONAL PAPER SERIES / M.E.T.U. FACULTY OF ARCHITECTURE. O.D.T.U. MIMARLIK FAKULTESI (TU) [05704481] **288**

ARAB AFFAIRS CEASED. (UK/0950-0731) [14707749] **2610**

ARAB AMERICAN ALMANAC (US/0742-9576) [10479598] **2721**

ARAB AND NEAR EAST PLANT PROTECTION NEWSLETTER (LE/1014-6334) [21206185] **500**

ARAB-ASIAN AFFAIRS (UK/0196-3538) [05793719] **4464**

ARAB BANKER (UK/0261-2925) [11618845] **772**

ARAB BOOK WORLD (US/0890-1341) [07851155] **4823**

ARAB DAWN (1977) (CN/0715-4054) [10334917] **4515**

ARAB ECONOMIST, THE (LE) [02244962] **1633**

ARAB GULF JOURNAL OF SCIENTIFIC RESEARCH (SU/1015-4442) [21015299] **5085**

ARAB HORSE SOCIETY See ARAB HORSE SOCIETY NEWS, THE **2797**

ARAB HORSE SOCIETY NEWS, THE (UK/0402-7493) [20374780] **2797**

ARAB JOURNAL OF EDUCATION (TI) **1726**

ARAB JOURNAL OF MATHEMATICS, THE (IQ) [20387310] **3495**

ARAB JOURNAL OF MEDICINE: MONTHLY INTERNATIONAL MEDICAL JOURNAL OF THE ARAB DOCTORS (FR) **3552**

ARAB JOURNAL OF PLANT PROTECTION (LE/0255-982X) [12896811] **2409**

ARAB JOURNAL OF THE SOCIAL SCIENCES, THE SUSPENDED. (UK/0269-2325) [18796332] **5191**

ARAB LAW QUARTERLY (UK/0268-0556) [12876602] **2936**

ARAB MARKETS CEASED. (US/0191-9032) [04965498] **823**

ARAB MEDICO (GW/0723-5100) 4035, **3552**

ARAB MONETARY FUND See AL-TAQRIR AL-SANAWI WA-AL-BAYANT AL-HISABIYAH AL-KHITAMIY AH LIL-SANAH AL-MUNTAHIYAH FI ... / SUNDUQ AL-NAQD AL-SANAWI **769**

ARAB MONETARY FUND See ANNUAL REPORT AND FINANCIAL STATEMENTS FOR THE YEAR ENDED ... **770**

ARAB MONETARY FUND. ANNUAL REPORT See ANNUAL REPORT AND FINANCIAL STATEMENTS FOR THE YEAR ENDED ... **770**

ARAB MONETARY FUND. ANNUAL REPORT. ARABIC. TAQRIR AL-SANAWI See AL-TAQRIR AL-SANAWI WA-AL-BAYANT AL-HISABIYAH AL-KHITAMIY AH LIL-SANAH AL-MUNTAHIYAH FI ... / SUNDUQ AL-NAQD AL-SANAWI **769**

ARAB NEWS (SU/0254-833X) [04574467] **5809**

ARAB NEWS & REPORTS (FR/0757-648X) [10757648X] **2501**

ARAB OIL AND ECONOMIC REVIEW See ARAB OIL (ARAB OIL PUB. CO. : 1980.) **4250**

ARAB OIL & GAS (FR/0031-6369) [02257647] **4250**

ARAB OIL & GAS DIRECTORY (FR/0304-8551) [02243176] **4250**

ARAB OIL (ARAB OIL PUB. CO. : 1980.) (UK/1013-5464) [07394200] **4250**

ARAB PALESTINIAN RESISTANCE / PALESTINE LIBERATION ARMY--POPULAR LIBERATION FORCES (SY) [02257648] **4515**

ARAB SHIPPING (UK/0141-4151) [03639509] **5447**

ARAB STUDIES QUARTERLY (US/0271-3519) [05050436] **2645**

ARAB TRIBUNE, THE (US) [09717248] **5625**

ARAB WOMEN YEAR 2000 (US/1058-9511) [24448719] **5551**

ARAB WORLD AGRIBUSINESS (BA/0267-0216) [16266845] **62**

ARAB WORLD, THE (KE) [03882706] **2767**

ARABANKS MIDYEAR SURVEY FOR ... (FR) [09171257] **772**

ARABESQUE (NEW YORK, N.Y.) (US/0148-5865) [03323903] 1310, **4100**

ARABIA SAUDITA OGGI CEASED. (IT) [02246977] **2767**

ARABIAN ARCHAEOLOGY AND EPIGRAPHY (DK/0905-7196) [22978181] **256**

ARABIAN BUSINESS COMPUTING (UK/0954-8912) [I09548912] 639, **1171**

ARABIAN COMPUTER NEWS (UK/0950-5075) [I09505075] **1235**

ARABIAN HORSE See ARABIAN HORSE JOURNAL, THE **2797**

ARABIAN HORSE EXPRESS (US/0194-6803) [04413225] **2797**

ARABIAN HORSE JOURNAL, THE (US/0191-2577) [04818539] **2797**

ARABIAN HORSE TIMES, THE (US/0279-8425) [01772783] **2797**

ARABIAN HORSE WORLD (US/0003-7494) [01772784] **2797**

ARABIAN JOURNAL FOR SCIENCE AND ENGINEERING (UK/0377-9211) [04172796] **5085**

ARABIAN SYSTEMS GUIDE (UK) **1171**

ARABIAN TRANSPORT (UK) [11149387] **5377**

ARABIAN TRANSPORT DIRECTORY See ARABIAN TRANSPORT **5377**

ARABIC SCIENCES AND PHILOSOPHY : A HISTORICAL JOURNAL (UK/0957-4239) [23882909] **5085**

ARABICA (NE/0570-5398) [01481762] **2767**

ARABIDOPSIS INFORMATION SERVICE CEASED. (GW/0066-5657) [01794944] 542, **500**

ARABIES (FR/0983-1509) [16799945] **2637**

ARABISCHE REPUBLIK JEMEN, ENERGIEWIRTSCHAFT / BUNDESSTELLE FUR AUSSENHANDELSINFORMATION (GW) [09963213] **1933**

ARABISCHE REPUBLIK JEMEN : WIRTSCHAFTLICHE ENTWICKLUNG (GW) [04451432] **1546**

ARABISCHE REPUBLIK JEMEN, WIRTSCHAFTSDATEN UND WIRTSCHAFTSDOKUMENTATION / BUNDESSTELLE FUR AUSSENHANDELSINFORMATION (GW) [09963989] **1546**

ARABLE FARMING (UK/0269-6797) [01902816] **62**

ARACHNOLOGIA : BULLETIN D'INFORMATION ET DE LIAISON DU CENTRE INTERNATIONAL DE DOCUMENTATION ARACHNOLOGIQUE (FR/0763-1901) [13067520] **5576**

ARAISA (VE) [02487811] **3363**

ARAL MADRID (SP/1130-8109) [I11308109] **2327**

ARALDO DELLA SCIENZA CRISTIANA, L' (US/0145-7519) [03243551] **4935**

ARAM PERIODICAL (UK/0959-4213) [I09594213] **2767**

ARAM PERIODICAL (UK/0959-4213) [20688477] 3363, **3266**

ARAMCO WORLD (1987) (US/1044-1891) [17215633] **2768**

ARANCEL ADUANERO DE CHILE (CL) [06126960] **823**

ARANCEL DE ADUANAS (TARIC) UPDATES (SP) **823**

ARANETA RESEARCH JOURNAL (PH) [01588334] **62**

ARAP ULKELERI EKONOMIK RAPORU (TU) [02240115] **1546**

ARAPAHO LANGUAGE AND CULTURE INSTRUCTIONAL MATERIALS SERIES (US) [08137843] **3266**

ARARAT (NEW YORK) (US/0003-7583) [02029535] **3363**

ARASH (IR) [10172088] **2526**

ARAUCARIA DE CHILE (SP) [04347227] **2721**

ARAUTO DA CIECIA CRISTA, O (US/0145-7489) [03244042] **4935**

ARAUTO DA SANTIDADE, O (US/8750-4723) [08520262] **5055**

ARBA SICULA (US/0271-0730) [06537255] **3363**

ARBEIDERHISTORIE (NO/0801-7778) [17642546] **1651**

ARBEIDERVERN (NO/0332-7124) [01786920] **2859**

ARBEIDSMARKED OG ARBEIDSMARKEDSPOLITIKK I NORDEN. TYOMARKKINAT JA TYOMARKKINAPOLITIIKKA (DK) [06510175] **1651**

●ARBEIDSOMSTANDIGHEDEN (NE/0920-119X) [25586336] **2859**

●ARBEIDSOMSTANDIGHEDEN ACTUEEL (NE) [25586385] **2859**

ARBEIDSRECHT (NE) 2936, **1651**

ARBEIT, BERUF UND ARBEITSLOSENHILFE See ARBEIT UND BERUF **4630**

ARBEIT UND ARBEITSRECHT (GW/0323-4568) [01481765] **1651**

ARBEIT UND BERUF (GW) [02322866] 1651, **4630**

ARBEIT UND RECHT (GW/0003-7648) [06522325] **3144**

ARBEIT UND SOZIALPOLITIK (GW/0340-8434) [06613432] **1651**

ARBEITEN AUS DEM PAUL-EHRLICH-INSTITUT (BUNDESAMT FUER SERA UND IMPFSTOFFE) ZU FRANKFUERT A.M (GW/0936-8671) [24707501] **3666**

ARBEITEN AUS DER KOMMISSION FUER GEOMORPHOLOGIE DER BAYERISCHEN AKADEMIE DER WISSENSCHAFTEN (GW) [03768017] **2555**

ARBEITEN

ARBEITEN ZUR ANGEWANDTEN STATISTIK (GW/0066-5673) [03356160] **3495**

ARBEITEN ZUR GESCHICHTE DES ANTIKEN JUDENTUMS UND DES URCHRISTENTUMS (NE) [01772211] **4935**

ARBEITEN ZUR GESCHICHTE DES PIETISMUS (GW) [03350964] **4935**

ARBEITEN ZUR KIRCHENGESCHICHTE HAMBURGS (GW/0518-2107) [03500811] **4935**

ARBEITEN ZUR KIRCHLICHEN ZEITGESCHICHTE. REIHE B: DARSTELLUNGEN (GW) [04685629] **4935**

ARBEITEN ZUR LITERATUR UND GESCHICHTE DES HELLENISTISCHEN JUDENTUMS (NE) [01481770] **2675**

ARBEITEN ZUR MECHANISIERUNG DER PFLANZEN- UND TIERPRODUKTION (GW/0233-0652) [I02330652] 62, 5504, **2327**

ARBEITEN ZUR RECHTSVERGLEICHUNG (GW/0066-5703) [01481771] **1366**

ARBEITEN ZUR SCHLESISCHEN KIRCHENGESCHICHTE (GW) [18366227] **2675**

ARBEITER IM ANGESTELLTENVERHALTNIS IN DER INDUSTRIE OSTERREICHS (AU) [05810198] **1651**

ARBEITERBEWEGUNG UND PARLAMENTARISMUS (GW) [06213411] **1651**

ARBEITGEBER-AUSSCHUSS NORDRHEIN-WESTFALEN. SAMMLUNG ARBEITSRECHTLICHER ENTSCHEIDUNGEN *See* SAE, SAMMLUNG ARBEITSRECHTLICHER ENTSCHEIDUNGEN **3154**

ARBEITGEBER, DER (GW/0402-7787) [06335809] **1651**

ARBEITGEBER NRW (GW) [07002588] **1651**

ARBEITNEHMER (GW) [03519910] 1463, **1651**

ARBEITS- UND FORSCHUNGSBERICHTE ZUR SACHSISCHEN BODENDENKMALPFLEGE (GE/0402-7817) [03355773] **4084**

ARBEITS UND SOZIALRECHT (GW) 1651, **1598**

ARBEITS- UND SOZIALRECHTLICHE SCHRIFTENREIHE *CEASED.* (AU/0172-4576) [08768899] **3144**

ARBEITS- UND SOZIALSTATISTIK (GW) [02412305] 1651, **1529**

ARBEITS- UND SOZIALSTATISTIK. HAUPTERGEBNISSE / DER BUNDESMINISTER FUR ARBEIT UND SOZIALORDNUNG (GW/0341-7840) [05842186] 5273, **1651**

ARBEITS- UND SOZALSTATISTIKEN (GW) [03745545] 1651, **1529**

ARBEITS- UND SOZIALSTATISTISCHE MITTEILUNGEN *See* ARBEITS- UND SOZIALSTATISTIK **1529**

ARBEITSBERICHT (AKADEMIE FUR RAUMFORSCHUNG UND LANDESPLANUNG (GERMANY)) *See* JAHRESBERICHT (AKADEMIE FUR RAUMFORSCHUNG UND LANDESPLANUNG (GERMANY)) **2825**

ARBEITSBERICHT - ARBEITSSTELLE FUR DAS BIBLIOTHEKSWESEN (GW) [01796703] **3191**

ARBEITSBERICHT DES INSTITUTS FUR MITTELSTANDSFORSCHUNG (GW) [06720048] **639**

ARBEITSBERICHTE DES IBERO-AMERIKA INSTITUT FUER WIRTSCHAFTSFORSCHUNG AN DER UNIVERSITAT GOTTINGEN (GW) [01751291] **1633**

ARBEITSBLATTER FUER RESTAURATOREN (GW/0066-5738) [05165953] 313, **256**

ARBEITSBLATTER / SEMINAR FUER ETHNOLOGIE, UNIVERSITAT BERN (SZ) [21016000] **231**

ARBEITSGEMEINSCHAFT DER DEUTSCHEN WERTPAPIERBOERSEN. ANNUAL REPORT *See* ANNUAL REPORT **891**

ARBEITSGEMEINSCHAFT DER GROSSFORSCHUNGSEINRICHTUNG EN (GERMANY) *See* PROGRAMM-BUDGET **4742**

ARBEITSGEMEINSCHAFT DER GROSSFORSCHUNGSEINRICHTUNG EN (GERMANY) *See* HANDBUCH DER GROSSFORSCHUNG / ARBEITSGEMEINSCHAFT DER GROSSFORSCHUNGSEINRICHTUNG EN (AGR) **5109**

ARBEITSGEMEINSCHAFT DER OFFENTLICH-RECHTLICHEN RUNDFUNKANSTALTEN DER BUNDESREPUBLIK DEUTSCHLAND *See* ARD JAHRBUCH **1149**

ARBEITSGEMEINSCHAFT FUER MITTELRHEINISCHE MUSIKGESCHICHTE *See* MITTEILUNGEN DER ARBEITSGEMEINSCHAFT FUER MITTELRHEINISCHE MUSIKGESCHICHTE **4131**

ARBEITSGEMEINSCHAFT FUR JUGENDHILFE *See* MITTEILUNGEN - ARBEITSGEMEINSCHAFT FUR JUGENDHILFE **5296**

ARBEITSGEMEINSCHAFT FUR JURISTISCHES BIBLIOTHEKS- UND DOKUMENTATIONSWESEN (GERMANY) *See* MITTEILUNGEN - ARBEITSGEMEINSCHAFT FUR JURISTISCHES BIBLIOTHEKS- (GERMANY) **3011**

ARBEITSGEMEINSCHAFT FUR OKOLOGISCHE ENTOMOLOGIE IN GRAZ *See* BERICHTE DER ARBEITSGEMEINSCHAFT FUER OKOLOGISCHE ENTOMOLOGIE IN GRAZ **5605**

ARBEITSGEMEINSCHAFT MEDIA-ANALYSE (GERMANY) *See* MA BERICHTSBAND **5251**

ARBEITSGEMEINSCHAFT TECHNIK UND BAU IN DER TIERHALTUNG *See* INFORMATIONEN **213**

ARBEITSGRUPPE FUR EMPIRISCHE BILDUNGSFORSCHUNG *See* UBERSICHT UBER DIE BISHERIGEN ARBEITEN **1788**

ARBEITSKOSTEN IM HANDEL SOWIE IM BANK- UND VERSICHERUNGSGEWERBE, DIE (GW) [03417866] **1651**

ARBEITSKOSTEN IM PRODUZIERENDEN GEWERBE UND IM DIENSTLEISTUNGSBEREICH (GW/0722-2432) [14639523] 1651, **1529**

ARBEITSKRAEFTE IN DEN LANDWIRTSCHAFTLICHEN BETRIEBEN (GW) [10365460] **62**

ARBEITSKRAFTEERHEBUNG IN DER LANDWIRTSCHAFT (GW) [07035174] 62, **1651**

ARBEITSKREIS DER DEUTSCHEN AFRIKA-FORSCHUNGS- UND DOKUMENTATIONSSTELLEN *See* RUNDBRIEF **2643**

ARBEITSMAPPE SOZIAL- UND WIRTSCHAFTSKUNDE (GW) **4464**

ARBEITSMARKT IN BADEN-WURTTEMBERG; JAHRESBERICHT, DER (GW) [06868428] 1651, **1529**

ARBEITSMARKT IN HESSEN. JAHRESBERICHT, DER (GW/0722-3285) [11632694] **1651**

ARBEITSMARKT IN HESSEN: JAHRESZAHLEN, DER (GW) [07040798] **1651**

ARBEITSMARKT IN HESSEN. STATISTISCHE UBERSICHTEN, DER (GW) [11256035] 1651, **1529**

ARBEITSMARKTSTATISTISCHE ZAHLEN IN ZEITREIHENFORM (GW) [05626871] **1651**

ARBEITSMATERIALIEN ZUR GEISTESGESCHICHTE (GW) [17496213] **2675**

ARBEITSMEDIZIN, SOZIALMEDIZIN, PRAVENTIVMEDIZIN (GW/0300-581X) [01777673] **2859**

ARBEITSMEDIZINISCHE FRAGEN IN DER OPHTHALMOLOGIE (GW) [06398236] **3872**

ARBEITSPAPIERE ZUR LINGUISTIK (GW/0343-8694) [06407108] **3266**

ARBEITSRECHT DER GEGENWART, DAS (GW/0066-586X) [01481781] **3144**

ARBEITSRECHT IN STICHWORTEN (GW/0003-7761) [I00037761] **1651**

ARBEITSSCHUTZ, ARBEITSHYGIENE (GW/0138-1555) [07268389] **2859**

ARBEITSSICHERHEIT (GW) [17666972] **2859**

ARBEITSSTATTEN DES GROSSHANDELS UND DER HANDELSVERMITTLUNG IN RHEINLAND-PFALZ, DIE (GW) [11668220] **5322**

ARBEITSSTELLE FUR ETHNOMEDIZIN *See* MITTEILUNGEN DER ARBEITSSTELLE FUR ETHNOMEDIZIN **3617**

ARBEJDERHISTORIE (DK/0107-8461) [08692555] **1651**

ARBEJDSDIREKTORATETS OG ARBEJDSFORMIDLINGENS ARSSTATISTIK FOR ... (DK/0901-4527) [19372215] **5322**

ARBEJDSMARKEDETS HANDBOG KOEBENHAVN. 1974 (DK/0903-8388) [I09038388] **1651**

ARBEJDSMARKEDSUDDANNELSERN E STATISTIK. TABELMATERIALE VEDRRENDE OMSKOLING OG ERHVERVSINTRODUKTION (DK/0106-9896) [10195354] **1651**

ARBEJDSRETLIGE KENDELSER (DK) [10327314] **3144**

ARBETARHISTORIA : MEDDELANDE FRAN ARBETARRORELSENS ARKIV OCH BIBLIOTEK (SW/0281-7446) [12895714] **1651**

ARBETARRORELSENS ARSBOK (SW/0347-2965) [01642741] **1651**

ARBETSGIVAREN (SW) [01481786] **1651**

ARBETSKARFTSUNDERSOKNINGEN. BEFOLKNINGEN I ALDERN 65-74 AR : AKU (SW) [19961464] **5178**

ARBETSKRAFTSUNDERSOKNINGEN : AKU (SW) [01785206] 1651, **1529**

ARBETSMILJO (SW/0347-7193) [13716268] **2859**

ARBETSMILJON I SIFFROR. MILFOSTATISTISK ARSBOK (SW) [17965037] **2859**

ARBETSRAPPORT / SVERIGES LANTBRUKSUNIVERSITET, INSTITUTIONEN FOR SKOGSEKONOMI (SW/0280-4158) [22781391] **2375**

ARBETSTERAPEUTEN (CN/0345-0988) [I03450988] **3552**

● ARBIDO (SZ) **3191**

ARBIDO B *See* ARBIDO **3191**

ARBIDO R *See* ARBIDO **3191**

ARBITRAGE, POINTS SAILLANTS (CN/1185-1716) [24257210] **1652**

● ARBITRATION AND DISPUTE RESOLUTION LAW JOURNAL, THE (UK/0965-7053) [I09657053] **3124**

ARBITRATION & THE LAW (US/0733-6160) [08567188] **2936**

ARBITRATION AWARDS-- IN NEW BRUNSWICK *See* COLLECTIVE BARGAINING IN NEW BRUNSWICK **1660**

ARBITRATION IN THE SCHOOLS (US/0003-7885) [01481789] **1726**

ARBITRATION INTERNATIONAL (UK/0957-0411) [12645143] **3124**

ARBITRATION JOURNAL *See* DISPUTE RESOLUTION JOURNAL **2963**

ARBITRATION JOURNAL, THE (US/0003-7893) [01481790] **2936**

ARBITRATION (LONDON, ENGLAND) (UK/0003-7877) [10795946] **2936**

ARBITRATION MATERIALS (SZ/1013-7432) [19969459] **2936**

ARBITRATION NEWSLETTER (US) [07234241] **2936**

ARBITRATION REPORTS (AT) [01518754] **2936**

ARBITRATION TIMES (US/8756-5455) [08401941] **2936**

ARBITRATOR BARTON (AT/0729-7904) [I07297904] **2936**

ARBITRIUM : ZEITSCHRIFT FUER REZENSIONEN ZUR GERMANISTISCHEN LITERATURWISSENSCHAFT (GW) [09651021] **3337**

ARBITRON COMPANY *See* ARBITRON TELEVISION POPULATION BOOK **4549**

ARBITRON TELEVISION POPULATION BOOK (US/0731-3721) [05281855] 1126, **4549**

ARBO KNIPSELKRANT (NE) 938, **5273**

ARBOG FOR KVINDESTUDIER VED AUC (DK) [11139239] **5551**

ARBOG - HANDELS- OG SFARTMUSEET PA KRONBORG (DK/0085-1418) [01751972] **823**

ARBOG (HISTORISK-TOPOGRAFISK SELSKAB FOR GLADSAXE KOMMUNE) (DK/0903-2738) [17304736] **2675**

ARBOK - BERGEN, NORWAY. VESTLANDSKE KUNSTINDUSTRIMUSEUM (NO/0405-4474) [03246819] **370**

ARBOK HINS ISLENZKA FORNLEIFAFELAGS (IC/0256-8462) [01645557] **256**

ARBOK LISTASAFNS ISLANDS (IC) [21614673] **337**

ARBOK - NORGES GEOLOGISKE UNDERSKELSE (NO) [06294201] **1366**

ARBOK - UNIVERSITETETS OLDSAKSAMLING (NO) [02716200] **256**

ARBOR (SP/0210-1963) [01481796] **5085**

ARBOR AGE (US/0279-0106) [07441019] **2375**

ARBORESCENCES (PARIS) (FR/0767-337X) [24470106] **2375**

ARBORETUM KORNICKIE (PL/0066-5878) [01481797] **500**

ARBORETUM LEAVES (US/0518-2662) [02444903] 2409, **500**

ARBORICULTURAL ABSTRACTS (US) [06348886] **2409**

ARBORICULTURAL JOURNAL, THE (UK/0307-1375) [01113830] **2375**

ARBORICULTURE (US) [01481798] **2409**

ARBORICULTURE FRUITIERE, L' (FR/0003-794X) [03778276] **163**

ARBORICULTURE RESEARCH NOTE (UK) [05579028] **2375**

ARBRE DE VIE (LOUISEVILLE) (CN/0713-4436) [08898769] **4379**

ARBUTUS (US) [05717752] **1810**

ARBUTUS TIMES (US/0748-5271) [10962825] **2485**

ARC (ARLINGTON, TEX. : MAY 20, 1980) (US/0274-5704) [06413603] **4884**

ARC-EN-CIEL (ROUYN) (CN/0712-3310) [08890911] **313**

ARC (MONTREAL) (CN/0229-2807) [08773931] **5055**

ARC NEWS LETTER (UK) [07902940] **383**

ARC NEWS (REDLANDS, CALIF.) (US/1064-6108) [20316854] 2555, **1284**

ARC (OTTAWA) (CN/0705-6397) [04098039] **3460**

ARC REMARKS (US) [12275639] **1875**

● ARC TODAY, THE (US) [25977487] **5273**

ARCA DEL SUR (AG) [24959996] **5046**

ARCA, L' (IT) [16945470] **288**

ARCADE HERALD (US/0746-102X) [09751998] **5713**

ARCADE (MONTREAL) (CN/0714-5926) [09313110] **3363**

ARCADE (SEATTLE, WASH.) (US) [07911030] **288**

ARCADE STAMP CATALOGUE / AS (SA) [08024640] **2784**

ARCADE STAMP SHOP See ARCADE STAMP CATALOGUE / AS **2784**

ARCADIA (GW/0003-7982) [01481801] **3363**

ARCADIA BIBLIOGRAPHICA VIRORUM ERUDITORUM (GW/0195-7163) [05701756] **407**

ARCADIA NEWS-LEADER, THE (US) [12872939] **5765**

ARCADIA VA AL CINE (CK) [09264411] **4063**

ARCADIAN RECORDER (CN/0710-1120) [08401506] **5780**

ARCATA UNION, THE (US) [26733242] **5633**

ARCH + (GW/0587-3452) [05211240] **288**

ARCH NOTES (CN/0048-1742) [02037352] **256**

ARCHAEO-PHYSIKA (GW) [03778045] **256**

ARCHAEOASTRONOMY (UK/0142-7253) [05425881] 391, **256**

ARCHAEOASTRONOMY & ETHNOASTRONOMY NEWS (US/1062-189X) [24655240] 2610, **391**

ARCHAEOASTRONOMY (COLLEGE PARK) (US/0190-9940) [04770512] 391, **256**

ARCHAEOLOGIA AELIANA (UK/0261-3417) [01481804] **256**

ARCHAEOLOGIA ATLANTICA (GW/0720-2156) [02641124] **256**

ARCHAEOLOGIA AUSTRIACA (AU/0003-8008) [01481805] **256**

ARCHAEOLOGIA CAMBRENSIS (UK/0306-6924) [01641359] **256**

ARCHAEOLOGIA CANTIANA (UK/0066-5894) [01481806] **256**

ARCHAEOLOGIA, OR MISCELLANEOUS TRACTS RELATING TO ANTIQUITY (UK/0261-3409) [01481803] **256**

ARCHAEOLOGIA POLONA / POLSKA AKADEMIA NAUK, INSTYTUT HISTORII KULTURY MATERIALNEJ (PL/0066-5924) [02830486] **256**

ARCHAEOLOGIA ZAMBIANA (ZA) [02710000] **256**

ARCHAEOLOGICA PRAGENSIA : ARCHEOLOGICKY SBORNIK MUZEA HLAVNIHO MESTA PRAHY (XR) [08286282] 2675, **256**

ARCHAEOLOGICAL COMPUTING NEWSLETTER (UK/0952-3332) [19643877] **256**

ARCHAEOLOGICAL DIALOGUES (NE) **256**

ARCHAEOLOGICAL FIELDWORK AND OPPORTUNITIES BULLETIN See ARCHAEOLOGICAL FIELDWORK OPPORTUNITIES BULLETIN **256**

ARCHAEOLOGICAL FIELDWORK OPPORTUNITIES BULLETIN (US/1061-8961) [09599568] **256**

ARCHAEOLOGICAL INSTITUTE OF AMERICA See BULLETIN OF THE ARCHAEOLOGICAL INSTITUTE OF AMERICA **264**

ARCHAEOLOGICAL JOURNAL, THE (UK/0066-5983) [01481817] 288, **256**

ARCHAEOLOGICAL METHOD AND THEORY (US/1043-1691) [19330881] **257**

ARCHAEOLOGICAL NEWS (US/0194-3413) [02566803] **257**

● ARCHAEOLOGICAL PROSPECTION (UK/1075-2196) [29969290] **257**

ARCHAEOLOGICAL RESEARCH REPORT (TORONTO) (CN/0706-1226) [06703812] **257**

ARCHAEOLOGICAL REVIEW FROM CAMBRIDGE (UK/0261-4332) [09856618] **257**

ARCHAEOLOGICAL SERIES (TUCSON) (US/0196-5409) [03779762] **257**

ARCHAEOLOGICAL SOCIETY OF CONNECTICUT See BULLETIN OF THE ARCHAEOLOGICAL SOCIETY OF CONNECTICUT **264**

ARCHAEOLOGICAL SOCIETY OF DELAWARE See BULLETIN OF THE ARCHAEOLOGICAL SOCIETY OF DELAWARE **264**

ARCHAEOLOGICAL SOCIETY OF NEW MEXICO See PAPERS OF THE ARCHAEOLOGICAL SOCIETY OF NEW MEXICO **278**

ARCHAEOLOGICAL STUDIES : CIRCULAR (US/0561-0478) [01399385] **257**

ARCHAEOLOGICAL SURVEY OF EGYPT. MEMOIR (UK/0307-5117) [13453736] **257**

ARCHAEOLOGICAL SURVEY REPORT (SAN ANTONIO, TEX.) (US) [03985202] **257**

ARCHAEOLOGISCHE MITTEILUNGEN AUS IRAN (US/0066-6033) [02878589] **257**

ARCHAEOLOGY (US/0003-8113) [01481828] **257**

ARCHAEOLOGY AND BIBLICAL RESEARCH (US/1071-0507) [17944152] **257**

ARCHAEOLOGY AND ENVIRONMENT (SW/0281-5877) [I02815877] **257**

ARCHAEOLOGY IN GHANA (GH) [06887527] **257**

ARCHAEOLOGY IN MONTANA (US/0044-8591) [02541651] **257**

ARCHAEOLOGY IN NEW ZEALAND (NZ/0113-7832) [18360500] **257**

ARCHAEOLOGY IN NEWFOUNDLAND & LABRADOR (CN/0715-2086) [09273045] **257**

ARCHAEOLOGY IN OCEANIA (AT/0728-4896) [07785113] **257**

ARCHAEOLOGY IN THE BIBLICAL WORLD (US/1058-2673) [24178791] **257**

ARCHAEOLOGY IRELAND (IE/0790-892X) [17448731] **257**

ARCHAEOLOGY JAMAICA (JM) [29552075] **257**

ARCHAEOLOGY MONOGRAPH (CN/0316-1285) [02441780] **257**

ARCHAEOLOGY OF EASTERN NORTH AMERICA (US/0360-1021) [02242805] **257**

ARCHAEOLOGY OF SVENDBORG, DENMARK, THE (DK/0106-0880) [08275204] **257**

ARCHAEOMETRY (UK/0003-813X) [01481830] 231, **257**

ARCHAEONAUTICA (FR) [06108721] **257**

ARCHAEUS (US/0895-1268) [16734048] **4575**

ARCHAIOGNOSIA (GR) [08471494] **1074**

ARCHAIOLOGIA (GR) [09999313] **258**

ARCHAIOLOGIKA ANALEKTA EX ATHENON. ATHENS ANNALS OF ARCHAEOLOGY (GR/0004-6604) [02244116] **258**

ARCHAIOLOGIKE EPHEMERIS : EKDIDOMENE TES ARCHAIOLOGIKES HETAIREIAS (GR/1105-0950) [02257664] **258**

ARCHAIOLOGIKON DELTION (GR) [01481835] **258**

ARCHAOLOGIE DER SCHWEIZ (SZ) [04339670] **258**

ARCHAOLOGISCH-EPIGRAPHISCHE STUDIEN (AU) [19546011] **258**

ARCHAOLOGISCHE AUSGRABUNGEN IN BADEN-WURTTEMBERG (GW/0724-8954) [09416066] **258**

ARCHAOLOGISCHE BERICHTE AUS DEM YEMEN / DEUTSCHES ARCHAOLOGISCHES INSTITUT SANA (GW) [08885554] **258**

ARCHAOLOGISCHE BERICHTE / HERAUSGEGEBEN VON DER DEUTSCHEN GESELLSCHAFT FUER UR- UND FRUHGESCHICHTE (GW) [18366336] 231, **258**

ARCHAOLOGISCHE BIBLIOGRAPHIE (GW) [01924204] **286**

ARCHAOLOGISCHE BIBLIOGRAPHIE (GW/0341-8308) [05857335] **286**

ARCHAOLOGISCHE FORSCHUNGEN (GW) [03357696] **258**

ARCHAOLOGISCHE GESELLSCHAFT ZU BERLIN See WINCKELMANNSPROGRAMM DER ARCHAOLOGISCHEN GESELLSCHAFT ZU BERLIN **368**

ARCHAOLOGISCHE INFORMATIONEN (GW/0341-2873) [04374615] **258**

ARCHAOLOGISCHE JAHR IN BAYERN, DAS (GW/0721-2399) [I07212399] **258**

ARCHAOLOGISCHE MITTEILUNGEN AUS IRAN. ERGANZUNGSBAND (GW/0170-5814) [12040760] **258**

ARCHAOLOGISCHE NACHRICHTEN AUS BADEN (GW/0178-045X) [I0178045X] **258**

ARCHAOLOGISCHER ANZEIGER (GW/0003-8105) [01152684] **258**

ARCHAOLOGISCHES KORRESPONDENZBLATT (GW/0342-734X) [01722596] **258**

ARCHBISHOP CARROLL HIGH SCHOOL See ALUMNI/AE DIRECTORY / ARCHBISHOP CARROLL HIGH SCHOOL **1097**

ARCHBOLD BUCKEYE (US) [09030116] **5726**

ARCHBOLD NEWS (UK/0961-4249) [I09614249] **3105**

ARCHE (1957) (FR/0518-2840) [07144704] **5046**

ARCHEIA OPHTHALMOLOGIKES HETAIREIAS BOREIOU HELLADOS (GR/0471-6981) [06541977] **3872**

ARCHEION EUVOIKON MELETON (GR) [01724143] 258, **2675**

ARCHEION PONTOU (GR/0518-2867) [01720863] **2675**

ARCHEION : THE NEWSLETTER OF THE STATE ARCHIVES (AT/0812-6755) [21010173] **2675**

ARCHEO (IT) [13175140] **258**

ARCHEO-LOG / EDITEE PAR LE GROUPE DIAPRE EN COLLABORATION AVEC LE CENTRE D'INFORMATIQUE DE LA PHILOSOPHIE ET LETTRES (FR) [18365986] **258**

ARCHEOGRAFO TRIESTINO (IT) [01741414] **2675**

ARCHEOLOGIA (FR/0570-6270) [02069763] **258**

ARCHEOLOGIA CLASSICA (IT/0391-8165) [01888093] 1074, **258**

ARCHEOLOGIA CORSA (FR/0154-2656) [15312800] **258**

ARCHEOLOGIA HISTORICA (XR/0231-5823) [I02315823] **258**

ARCHEOLOGIA MEDIEVALE (IT/0390-0592) [02592841] **258**

ARCHEOLOGIA MEDIOEVO (IT) [16187380] **258**

ARCHEOLOGIA POLSKI (PL/0003-8180) [02846475] **258**

ARCHEOLOGIA (ROMA) (IT/0003-8164) [01722159] **258**

ARCHEOLOGIA VENETA (IT/0392-9876) [08683227] **258**

ARCHEOLOGIA VIVA (IT) [10320334] **258**

ARCHEOLOGIA (WARSAW. 1947) (PL/0066-605X) [02844224] **258**

ARCHEOLOGICAL AND HISTORICAL DATA RECOVERY PROGRAM (US/0749-9116) [09450839] **258**

ARCHEOLOGICAL REPORT (US/0526-9938) [01144239] **259**

ARCHEOLOGICAL SOCIETY OF NEW JERSEY See BULLETIN OF THE ARCHAEOLOGICAL SOCIETY OF NEW JERSEY **264**

ARCHEOLOGICAL SOCIETY OF VIRGINIA See QUARTERLY BULLETIN - ARCHEOLOGICAL SOCIETY OF VIRGINIA **280**

ARCHEOLOGICAL SURVEY REPORT (AUSTIN) (US) [01155686] **259**

ARCHEOLOGICKE ROZHLEDY (XR/0044-8605) [02257667] **259**

ARCHEOLOGIE BRUXELLES (BE/0003-8210) [I00038210] **259**

ARCHEOLOGIE DU MIDI MEDIEVAL (FR/0758-7708) [15110012] **259**

ARCHEOLOGIE EN BRETAGNE. SUPPLEMENT (FR/0293-9134) [I02939134] **259**

ARCHEOLOGIE EN LANGUEDOC (FR/0221-4792) [06572207] **259**

ARCHEOLOGIE ET BRETAGNE SUSPENDED. (FR/0335-5233) [03600965] **259**

ARCHEOLOGIE IN VLAANDEREN (BE/0778-2837) [I07782837] **259**

ARCHEOLOGIE ISLAMIQUE (FR/1156-7198) [24294677] **259**

ARCHEOLOGIE MEDIEVALE (FR/0153-9337) [01780065] **259**

ARCHEOMATERIALS (US/0891-2920) [14696978] 231, **259**

ARCHEONUMIS (FR/0339-7890) [I03397890] **259**

ARCHER (CAMAS VALLEY, OR.), THE (US/0003-8237) [02752871] **4884**

ARCHERY ACTION WITH OUTDOOR CONNECTIONS (AT/1037-6720) [I10376720] **4884**

ARCHETYPAL — Alphabetical Title Index

ARCHETYPAL IMAGES IN GREEK RELIGION (UK/0570-6378) [03352783] **4935**

ARCHI FUER MITTELRHEINISCHE KIRCHENGESCHICHTE (GW/0066-6432) [01737640] **4935**

ARCHIBALD CLAN NEWSLETTER (US/0736-7082) [09179683] **2437**

ARCHIE AT RIVERDALE HIGH (US/0746-8660) [10351945] **4857**

ARCHIE COMICS *See* ARCHIE (NEW YORK, N.Y.) **4857**

ARCHIE COMICS DIGEST MAGAZINE (US/8750-0620) [10956910] **4857**

ARCHIE (NEW YORK, N.Y.) (US/0735-6455) [08968347] **4857**

ARCHIE (ST. LAMBERT) (CN) **4857**

ARCHIEF VOOR DE GESCHIEDENIS VAN DE KATHOLIEKE KERK IN NEDERLAND *See* TRAJECTA **5037**

ARCHIE'S PAL JUGHEAD COMICS (US/1069-0999) [27927431] **4857**

ARCHIE'S PALS 'N GALS *CEASED.* (US/0745-7774) [09444484] **4857**

ARCHIFACTS (NZ/0303-7940) [02240119] **2479**

ARCHIGINNASIO, L' (IT/0409-5448) [06989922] **3191**

ARCHIMAG VINCENNES (FR/0769-0975) [I07690975] **2479**

ARCHIMEDE (IT/0003-8369) [03280403] **3495**

ARCHIMEDES WORLD (UK/0961-8414) [I09618414] **1171**

ARCHIPEL (IO) [01783521] **2555**

ARCHIPEL PARIS (FR/0044-8613) [I00448613] **2501**

ARCHIPELAG : A (GW) [12143703] **3363, 4540**

ARCHIPELAGO (PH/0303-8564) [01798301] **2768**

ARCHIPIELAGO (BARCELONA, SPAIN) (SP) [18485527] **2513**

ARCHIS (NE/0921-8041) [13226833] **288**

ARCHITECT (NE/0044-8621) [10193198] **288**

ARCHITECT AND BUILDER (SA/0003-8407) [I00038407] 599, **288**

ARCHITECT AND CONTRACTOR (US/0003-8423) [03076062] **288**

ARCHITECT & SURVEYOR (UK/0308-8596) [16458510] 599, **288**

ARCHITECT AND SURVEYOR *See* BUILDING ENGINEER **603**

ARCHITECT DESIGNED HOUSES (AT/1034-4101) [I10344101] **288**

ARCHITECT (PERTH, W.A.) *See* ARCHITECT, W.A. : THE OFFICIAL JOURNAL OF THE ROYAL AUSTRALIAN INSTITUTE OF ARCHITECTS, W.A. CHAPTER, THE **288**

ARCHITECT. THEMA (NE/0925-6830) [I09256830] **288**

ARCHITECT, W.A. : THE OFFICIAL JOURNAL OF THE ROYAL AUSTRALIAN INSTITUTE OF ARCHITECTS, W.A. CHAPTER, THE (AT/0003-8393) [09424418] **288**

ARCHITECTES, ARCHITECTURE *CEASED.* (FR/0762-5731) [26167937] **288**

ARCHITECTI (PO) [19908570] **288**

ARCHITECTS, CONTRACTORS, ENGINEERS GUIDE TO CONSTRUCTION COSTS (US/0066-6157) [02905713] **599**

ARCHITECTS' EMPLOYMENT CLEARINGHOUSE *CEASED.* (US) [18881802] **288**

ARCHITECTS INDIA (II/0970-6852) [I09706852] **288**

ARCHITECTS' JOURNAL (LONDON) (UK/0003-8466) [04651322] **288**

ARCHITECTS TRADE JOURNAL (II/0304-8594) [01790521] 599, **288**

ARCHITECTURA (GW/0044-863X) [01639523] **288**

ARCHITECTURA (DK/0106-3030) [28178806] **288**

●ARCHITECTURAL & CONSTRUCTION MEDIA SOURCE (US/1071-4634) [28642815] 599, **288**

ARCHITECTURAL ASSOCIATION ANNUAL REVIEW, THE (UK) [05622782] **288**

ARCHITECTURAL ASSOCIATION (GREAT BRITAIN) *See* ARCHITECTURAL ASSOCIATION ANNUAL REVIEW, THE **288**

ARCHITECTURAL CONSERVANCY OF ONTARIO *See* ACORN, THE ARCHITECTURAL CONSERVANCY OF ONTARIO R NEWSLETTER **287**

ARCHITECTURAL DESIGN (UK/0003-8504) [08353757] **288**

ARCHITECTURAL DESIGNS (US/0747-5179) [10718008] **289**

ARCHITECTURAL DIGEST (LOS ANGELES, CALIF.) (US/0003-8520) [01481856] **289**

ARCHITECTURAL DIGEST. THE ... ART AND ANTIQUES ANNUAL (US/0743-5517) [10595589] 249, **289**

ARCHITECTURAL, ENGINEERING AND SCIENTIFIC SERVICES (CN/0846-8583) [12178133] 289, 1965, **5085**

ARCHITECTURAL HERITAGE (FR) [16650672] **259**

ARCHITECTURAL HERITAGE : THE JOURNAL OF THE ARCHITECTURAL HERITAGE SOCIETY OF SCOTLAND (UK) [24232780] **289**

ARCHITECTURAL HISTORY (UK/0066-622X) [01481858] **289**

ARCHITECTURAL INDEX, THE (US/0570-6483) [02204032] **289**

ARCHITECTURAL INSTITUTE OF BRITISH COLUMBIA *See* NEWS, VIEWS AND REVIEWS - ARCHITECTURAL INSTITUTE OF BRITISH COLUMBIA **304**

ARCHITECTURAL JOURNAL (PH) [09593177] **289**

ARCHITECTURAL LIGHTING (US/0894-0436) [15272445] 2036, **289**

ARCHITECTURAL MONOGRAPHS (UK/0141-2191) [04212244] **289**

ARCHITECTURAL PRESERVATION AND NEW DESIGN IN CONSERVATION (UK/0262-219X) [09235593] **289**

ARCHITECTURAL PSYCHOLOGY NEWSLETTER *SUSPENDED.* (UK) [01811394] 289, **4575**

ARCHITECTURAL RECORD (US/0003-858X) [01481864] **289**

ARCHITECTURAL RECORD *See* RECORD HOUSES AND APARTMENTS OF THE YEAR **2903**

ARCHITECTURAL REPORTS OF THE TOHOKU UNIVERSITY, THE (JA) **289**

ARCHITECTURAL REVIEW (LONDON) (UK/0003-861X) [01481867] **289**

ARCHITECTURAL SCHOOLS IN NORTH AMERICA (US/0092-7856) [01791494] 1810, **289**

ARCHITECTURAL SCIENCE REVIEW (AT/0003-8628) [01481868] **289**

●ARCHITECTURAL SPECIFIER (US/1068-8560) [27829628] **289**

ARCHITECTURE & COMPORTEMENT (SZ/0379-8585) [07360243] **289**

●ARCHITECTURE AND DESIGN INSITE (CN/1195-227X) [29323247] **2898**

ARCHITECTURE AND SOCIETY / ARKHITEKTURA I OBSHCHESTVO : AS (BU) [11919448] **289**

ARCHITECTURE AUSTRALIA (AT/0003-8725) [03076514] **289**

ARCHITECTURE CALIFORNIA (US/0738-1131) [09506820] **290**

ARCHITECTURE CONCEPT (CN/0003-8687) [02502051] **290**

ARCHITECTURE D'AUJOURD'HUI, L' (BE/0003-8695) [01481879] **290**

ARCHITECTURE + DESIGN (II) [12175258] **290**

ARCHITECTURE, DOMESTIC *See* HOUSE BEAUTIFUL'S HOUSES AND PLANS **300**

ARCHITECTURE/GEORGIA (US/1059-4434) [23850432] **290**

ARCHITECTURE INTERIEURE-C.R.E.E (FR/0294-8567) [03782050] 2097, **290**

ARCHITECTURE JOURNAL / SCHOOL OF ARCHITECTURE, NATIONAL UNIVERSITY OF SINGAPORE (SI/0129-5829) [11335273] **290**

ARCHITECTURE MEDITERRANEENNE (FR/0761-7909) [18956505] **290**

ARCHITECTURE MINNESOTA (US/0149-9106) [02253666] **290**

ARCHITECTURE. NEW ENGLAND (US/0360-6562) [01811209] **290**

ARCHITECTURE NEW JERSEY *CEASED.* (US/0003-8733) [05094822] **290**

ARCHITECTURE NEW ZEALAND (NZ/0113-4566) [17631762] **290**

ARCHITECTURE : OFFICIAL JOURNAL OF THE ARCHITECTURAL ASSOCIATION OF KENYA (KE) [22348134] **290**

ARCHITECTURE (PARIS 1979) (FR/0220-7591) [I02207591] **290**

ARCHITECTURE PLUS (US/0090-9521) [01786088] **290**

ARCHITECTURE SA (SA/0250-054X) [I0250054X] **290**

ARCHITECTURE SERIES--BIBLIOGRAPHY *CEASED.* (US/0194-1356) [05260794] **311**

ARCHITECTURE TODAY (UK/0958-6407) [21505460] **290**

ARCHITECTURE VERNACULAIRE, L' (FR/0761-7305) [I07617305] **290**

ARCHITECTURE (WASHINGTON, D.C.) (US/0746-0554) [09715411] **290**

ARCHITECTURE WEST MIDLANDS (UK/0308-6747) [103086747] **290**

ARCHITECTURES *CEASED.* (US/0882-2492) [11800976] **290**

ARCHITECTUS (SAINT PAUL, MINN.) (US/1054-4666) [22901299] **290**

ARCHITECTUUR, BONWEN (NE/0169-4421) [I01694421] 599, **290**

ARCHITEKT (STUTTGART), DER (GW/0003-875X) [01723978] **290**

ARCHITEKTONIKA THEMATA (GR/0066-6262) [01481887] **290**

ARCHITEKTUR AKTUELL FACH-JOURNAL (AU/0570-6602) [11847830] **290**

ARCHITEKTUR & BAUFORUM (AU) **291**

ARCHITEKTUR & WOHNEN (GW/0171-7928) [01717928] **291**

ARCHITEKTUR IN DEUTSCHLAND (GW) [18965937] **291**

●ARCHITEKTUR JAHRBUCH (GW) [27856525] **291**

ARCHITEKTUR WETTBEWERBE (GW/0341-2784) [03953936] **291**

ARCHITEKTURA (XR) [26287917] **291**

ARCHITEKTURA A URBANIZMUS (XO/0044-8680) [01811163] **291**

ARCHITEKTURA BUDAPEST. 1966 (HU/0066-6270) [I00666270] **291**

ARCHITEKTURA CSR (CS/0300-5305) [01723931] **291**

ARCHITETTO, L' (IT/0003-8822) [I00038822] **291**

ARCHITETTURA; CRONACHE E STORIA, L' *CEASED.* (IT/0570-6629) [06271016] **291**

ARCHITETTURA, L' (IT/0003-8830) [02054286] **291**

ARCHITETTURA/MATERIALI (IT) [20283433] **291**

ARCHITETTURA, STORIA E DOCUMENTI : RIVISTA SEMESTRALE DI STORIA DELL'ARCHITETTURA DEL CENTRO DI STUDI STORICO-ARCHIVISTICI PER LA STORIA DELL'ARTE E DELL'ARCHITETTURA MEDIOEVALE E MODERNA (IT) [13019353] **291**

ARCHITHESE (1914) (SZ/1010-3600) [01785529] **291**

ARCHITHESE (1980) (SZ/1010-4089) [06221578] **291**

ARCHIV ANATOMII, GISTOLOGII I EMBRIOLOGII *See* MORFOLOGIIA **3679**

ARCHIV DER DEUTSCHEN JUGENDBEWEGUNG *See* JAHRBUCH DES ARCHIVS DER DEUTSCHEN JUGENDBEWEGUNG **5249**

ARCHIV DER GESCHICHTE DER NATURWISSENSCHAFTEN (AU/0253-7400) [07514972] **5085**

ARCHIV DER MATHEMATIK (SW/0003-889X) [01481903] **3495**

ARCHIV DER PHARMAZIE (WEINHEIM) (GW/0365-6233) [01481904] **4292**

ARCHIV DES INSTITUTS FUER BANKHISTORISCHE FORSCHUNG *See* BANKHISTORISCHES ARCHIV **776**

ARCHIV DES OFFENTLICHEN RECHTS (GW/0003-8911) [08996733] **3092**

ARCHIV DES VOLKERRECHTS (GW/0003-892X) [01481910] **3124**

ARCHIV FUER ACKER- UND PFLANZENBAU UND BODENKUNDE (SW/0365-0340) [01714793] **163**

ARCHIV FUER ACKER- UND PFLANZENBAU UND BODENKUNDE *See* KUHN-ARCHIV **177**

ARCHIV FUER BEGRIFFSGESCHICHTE (GW/0003-8946) [01481919] **4341**

ARCHIV FUER DEUTSCHE POSTGESCHICHTE (GW/0003-8989) [01704903] **1144**

ARCHIV FUER DIE CIVILISTISCHE PRAXIS (GW/0003-8997) [01481932] **3088**

ARCHIV FUER DIPLOMATIK : SCHRIFTGESCHICHTE, SIEGEL, UND WAPPENKUNDE (GW/0066-6297) [01481945] **2675**

ARCHIV FUER EISENBAHNTECHNIK; BEIHEFT ZU DER ZEITSCHRIFT EISENBAHN TECHNISCHE RUNDSCHAU (GW/0341-0463) [09221091] **5429**

ARCHIV FUER ELEKTROTECHNIK (BERLIN) (GW/0003-9039) [01481947] **2036**

ARCHIV FUER EXPERIMENTELLE VETERINAERMEDIZIN *CEASED.* (GW/0003-9055) [06274268] **5504**

ARCHIV FUER FISCHEREIWISSENSCHAFT (GW/0003-9063) [03565358] **2296**

ARCHIVES

Alphabetical Title Index

ARCHIV FUER FISCHEREIWISSENSCHAFT UND MEERESFORSCHUNG See ARCHIVE OF FISHERY AND MARINE RESEARCH **2296**

ARCHIV FUER FRANKFUERTS GESCHICHTE UND KUNST (GW/0341-8324) [01481953] **2675**

ARCHIV FUER GEFLUGELKUNDE (GW/0003-9098) [02024285] **206**

ARCHIV FUER GESCHICHTE DER PHILOSOPHIE (GW/0003-9101) [01481957] **4341**

ARCHIV FUER GESCHICHTE DER PHILOSOPHIE (GW/0003-9101) [01611929] **4341**

ARCHIV FUER GESCHICHTE DES BUCHWESENS (GW/0066-6327) [01536638] **4823**

ARCHIV FUER GESCHICHTE VON OBERFRANKEN (GW/0066-6335) [01481959] **2675**

ARCHIV FUER HYDROBIOLOGIE (GW/0003-9136) [02392773] 442, **5530**

ARCHIV FUER HYDROBIOLOGIE. SUPPLEMENTBAND, ALGOLOGICAL STUDIES (GW/0342-1120) [01479102] 1446, **442**

ARCHIV FUER HYDROBIOLOGIE. SUPPLEMENTBAND, MONOGRAPHISCHE BEITRAEGE (GW/0341-2881) [07838591] **553**

ARCHIV FUER JAPANISCHE CHIRURGIE. NIPPON GEKA HOKAN (JA/0003-9152) [01760393] **3959**

ARCHIV FUER KATHOLISCHES KIRCHENRECHT (GW/0003-9160) [01590581] 5023, **2936**

ARCHIV FUER KOMMUNALWISSENSCHAFTEN (GW/0003-9209) [01664279] **4630**

ARCHIV FUER KRIMINOLOGIE (GW/0003-9225) [09115376] **3158**

ARCHIV FUER KULTURGESCHICHTE (GW/0003-9233) [01481973] 2842, **2610**

ARCHIV FUER LAGERSTATTENFORSCHUNG DER GEOLOGISCHEN BUNDESANSTALT (AU/0253-097X) [09671375] **1366**

ARCHIV FUER LEBENSMITTELHYGIENE (GW/0003-925X) [07594780] **2327**

ARCHIV FUER LITERATUR UND VOLKSDICHTUNG (AU) [05579259] **3460**

ARCHIV FUER LITURGIEWISSENSCHAFT (GW/0066-6386) [01731924] **4935**

ARCHIV FUER METEOROLOGIE, GEOPHYSIK UND BIOKLIMATOLOGIE. SER. B: KLIMATOLOGIE, UMWELTMETEOROLOGIE, STRAHLUNGSFORSCHUNG (AU/0374-5449) [02882620] **1351**

ARCHIV FUER MOLLUSKENKUNDE DER SENCKENBERGISCHE NATURFORSCHENDE GESELLSCHAFT (GW/0003-9284) [02444941] **5576**

ARCHIV FUER MUSIKWISSENSCHAFT (GW/0003-9292) [01481987] **4100**

ARCHIV FUER MUSIKWISSENSCHAFT. BEIHEFTE (GW) [06934137] **4100**

ARCHIV FUER NATURSCHUTZ UND LANDSCHAFTSFORSCHUNG (GW/0003-9306) [01481993] **2187**

ARCHIV FUER ORIENTFORSCHUNG (AU/0066-6440) [05758156] **3266**

ARCHIV FUER OSTERREICHISCHE GESCHICHTE (AU/0003-9322) [01481994] **2676**

ARCHIV FUER PAPYRUSFORSCHUNG UND VERWANDTE GEBIETE (GW/0066-6459) [01482000] **3266**

ARCHIV FUER PHYTOPATHOLOGIE UND PFLANZENSCHUTZ (GW/0323-5408) [03764206] **500**

● ARCHIV FUER POST UND TELEKOMMUNIKATION (GW/0943-2337) [I09432337] **1149**

ARCHIV FUER PROTISTENKUNDE (GW/0003-9365) [01482009] **5576**

ARCHIV FUER RECHTS- UND SOZIALPHILOSOPHIE (GW/0001-2343) [01482013] **2936**

ARCHIV FUER REFORMATIONSGESCHICHTE (GW/0003-9381) [01482015] **2676**

ARCHIV FUER REFORMATIONSGESCHICHTE. BEIHEFT, LITERATURBERICHT (GW/0341-8375) [02243878] 4935, **2676**

ARCHIV FUER RELIGIONSPSYCHOLOGIE (GW) [06179694] 4575, **4935**

ARCHIV FUER SCHLESISCHE KIRCHENGESCHICHTE (GW/0066-6491) [01728308] **5055**

ARCHIV FUER SOZIALGESCHICHTE (GW/0066-6505) [01664562] 5191, **2676**

ARCHIV FUER TIERARZTLICHE FORTBILDUNG (GW/0720-1893) [03290809] **5504**

ARCHIV FUER TIERERNAHRUNG (GW/0003-942X) [01482026] **5504**

ARCHIV FUER TIERZUCHT (GW/0003-9438) [01482027] **206**

ARCHIV FUER URHEBER-, FILM-, FUNK- UND THEATERRECHT (GW) [07265688] **5361**

ARCHIV FUER VATERLANDISCHE GESCHICHTE UND TOPOGRAPHIE. HRSG. VON DEM GESCHICHTVEREINE FUER KARNTEN. UNTER VERANTWORTLICHER REDACTION DES VEREINS-AUSSCHUSSES (GW/0003-9462) [01730828] 2555, **2676**

ARCHIV FUER VERGLEICHENDE KULTURWISSENSCHAFT (GW) [01482030] **2842**

ARCHIV FUER VOLKERKUNDE (AU/0066-6513) [01482032] **231**

ARCHIV FUER ZUCHTUNGSFORSCHUNG **CEASED**. (GW/0365-8406) [05313296] **5085**

ARCHIV FUR DAS STUDIUM DER NEUEREN SPRACHEN UND LITERATUREN (1961) (GW/0003-8970) [06748016] 3363, **3266**

ARCHIV FUR FORSTWESEN See BEITRAEGE FUER DIE FORSTWIRTSCHAFT **2375**

ARCHIV FUR KIRCHENGESCHICHTE VON BOHMEN-MAHREN-SCHLESLEN (GW) [01789689] **5023**

ARCHIV FUR SIPPENFORSCHUNG UND ALLE VERWANDTEN GEBIETE (GW/0003-9403) [02257676] **2437**

ARCHIV ORIENTALNI (XR/0044-8699) [01482037] 2645, **3266**

ARCHIVA ZOOTECHNICA (RM/1016-4855) [I10164855] **5576**

ARCHIVAL INFORMER, THE (US/8756-9663) [11777786] **2479**

● ARCHIVAL ISSUES : JOURNAL OF THE MIDWEST ARCHIVES CONFERENCE (US/1067-4993) [27251432] **2479**

● ARCHIVAL OUTLOOK / THE SOCIETY OF AMERICAN ARCHIVISTS (US) [27766001] **2479**

ARCHIVALISCHE ZEITSCHRIFT (GW/0003-9497) [01730747] **2479**

ARCHIVAR, DER (GW/0003-9500) [03778607] **2479**

ARCHIVARIA (CN/0318-6954) [03247908] **2479**

ARCHIVE FOR HISTORY OF EXACT SCIENCES (GW/0003-9519) [01482042] **5085**

ARCHIVE FOR MATHEMATICAL LOGIC (GW/0933-5846) [18237511] **3496**

ARCHIVE FOR RATIONAL MECHANICS AND ANALYSIS (GW/0003-9527) [01482043] **4427**

ARCHIVE OF APPLIED MECHANICS (1991) (US/0939-1533) [23096343] **2109**

ARCHIVE OF AUSTRALIAN JUDAICA HOLDINGS TO ... (AT) [16893554] 2255, **2479**

ARCHIVE OF FISHERY AND MARINE RESEARCH (GW/0944-1921) **2296**

ARCHIVE OF FOLK CULTURE (U.S.) See LC FOLK ARCHIVE FINDING AID **5269**

ARCHIVE SERVICES STATISTICS ... ESTIMATES (UK/0955-1034) [19687833] **2479**

ARCHIVE (TUCSON, ARIZ.), THE (US/0735-5572) [08439306] **4366**

ARCHIVERT (FR/0222-2027) [06778547] **291**

ARCHIVES (FR) **2479**

ARCHIVES (RM/0041-6940) [01587733] **3552**

ARCHIVES AND MANUSCRIPTS (AT/0157-6895) [01482046] **2479**

ARCHIVES & MUSEUM INFORMATICS (US/1042-1467) [18946585] 2479, **1217**

ARCHIVES AND MUSEUM INFORMATICS TECHNICAL REPORT (US/1042-1459) [18946635] **2479**

ARCHIVES AUTHORITY OF NEW SOUTH WALES See ARCHEION : THE NEWSLETTER OF THE STATE ARCHIVES **2479**

ARCHIVES BELGES DE MEDECINE SOCIALE HYGIENE, MEDECINE DU TRAVAIL ET MEDECINE LEGALE (BE/0003-9578) [01482048] **3552**

ARCHIVES CANADA MICROFICHES (CN/0827-018X) [03980307] **2479**

ARCHIVES D'ANATOMIE ET DE CYTOLOGIE PATHOLOGIQUES (FR/0395-501X) [02433324] 532, 3893, **3678**

ARCHIVES DE FOLKLORE, LES (CN/0085-5243) [01482059] **2318**

ARCHIVES DE L'ART FRANCAIS (FR) [01482060] **337**

ARCHIVES DE L'EGLISE D'ALSACE (FR) [03111867] **5023**

ARCHIVES DE L'INSTITUT PASTEUR D'ALGERIE (AE/0020-2460) [01479100] **3552**

ARCHIVES DE L'INSTITUT PASTEUR DE MADAGASCAR (MG/0020-2495) [01394568] **3666**

ARCHIVES DE L'INSTITUT PASTEUR DE TUNIS (TI/0020-2509) [01394570] **3552**

ARCHIVES DE L'INSTITUTE RAZI (IR) [01753209] **5504**

● ARCHIVES DE PEDIATRIE : ORGANE OFFICIEL DE LA SOCIETE FRANCAISE DE PEDIATRIE (FR/0929-693X) [29789429] **3900**

ARCHIVES DE PHILOSOPHIE (FR/0003-9632) [01772219] **4341**

ARCHIVES DE PHILOSOPHIE DU DROIT (FR/0066-6564) [01482069] **2936**

ARCHIVES DE POLITIQUE CRIMINELLE (FR) [03135125] **3105**

ARCHIVES DE PSYCHOLOGIE (SZ/0003-9640) [01440840] **4575**

ARCHIVES DE SCIENCES SOCIALES DES RELIGIONS (FR/0335-5985) [01794707] 5239, **4935**

ARCHIVES DES LETTRES MODERNES (FR/0003-9675) [01908359] **3363**

ARCHIVES DES MALADIES DU COEUR ET DES VAISSEAUX (FR/0003-9683) [05855157] **3699**

ARCHIVES DES MALADIES PROFESSIONNELLES DE MEDECINE DU TRAVAIL ET SECURITE SOCIALE (FR/0003-9691) [01482082] 5273, **3552**

ARCHIVES DES SCIENCES ET COMPTE RENDU DES SEANCES DE LA SOCIETE (SZ/0252-9289) [20411797] 5085, **4162**

ARCHIVES D'HISTOIRE DOCTRINALE ET LITTERAIRE DU MOYEN AGE (FR/0373-5478) [02444948] **4341**

ARCHIVES ET BIBLIOTHEQUES DE BELGIQUE (BE/0003-9748) [02108170] 3191, **2479**

ARCHIVES ET DOCUMENTS, MICRO-EDITION. SCIENCES HUMAINES (FR/0248-3912) [07955231] **2857**

ARCHIVES EUROPEENNES DE SOCIOLOGIE (FR/0003-9756) [00849594] **5240**

ARCHIVES FRANCAISES DE PEDIATRIE (FR/0003-9764) [01482097] **3900**

ARCHIVES FRANCAISES DE PEDIATRIE See ARCHIVES DE PEDIATRIE : ORGANE OFFICIEL DE LA SOCIETE FRANCAISE DE PEDIATRIE **3900**

ARCHIVES HERALDIQUE SUISSES (SZ) **2438**

ARCHIVES HISTORIQUES DU POITOU (FR) [01772220] **2676**

ARCHIVES II RESEARCHER BULLETIN / NATIONAL ARCHIVES AND RECORDS ADMINISTRATION (US) [25695906] **2479**

ARCHIVES INFORMATION BULLETIN (US) [04973171] **2479**

ARCHIVES INFORMATION CIRCULAR (US/0093-9056) [01793396] **2479**

ARCHIVES INTERNATIONALES DE PHARMACODYNAMIE ET DE THERAPIE (BE/0003-9780) [05806034] **4292**

ARCHIVES INTERNATIONALES DE PHYSIOLOGIE, DE BIOCHIMIE ET DE BIOPHYSIQUE (BE/0778-3124) [23978866] 480, 494, **578**

ARCHIVES INTERNATIONALES D'HISTOIRE DES SCIENCES (GW/0003-9810) [01482110] **5085**

ARCHIVES ITALIENNES DE BIOLOGIE (IT/0003-9829) [01482111] **442**

ARCHIVES JUIVES (FR) [01786082] **2676**

ARCHIVES (LONDON) (UK/0003-9535) [01482044] **2479**

ARCHIVES NATIONALES DU CANADA See ORIENTATIONS STRATEGIQUES DES ARCHIVES NATIONALES DU CANADA **2482**

ARCHIVES OF ACOUSTICS (PL/0137-5075) [05004870] **4452**

ARCHIVES OF AIDS RESEARCH See ARCHIVES OF STD/HIV RESEARCH **3666**

ARCHIVES OF ANDROLOGY (UK/0148-5016) [03486750] **3678**

ARCHIVES OF APPALACHIA See ARCHIVES OF APPALACHIA NEWSLETTER / EAST TENNESSEE STATE UNIVERSITY **2318**

ARCHIVES OF APPALACHIA NEWSLETTER / EAST TENNESSEE STATE UNIVERSITY (US) [07136139] 2480, **2318**

ARCHIVES OF APPLIED MECHANICS (GW) **2110**

ARCHIVES OF ASIAN ART (US/0066-6637) [01482119] **337**

ARCHIVES OF BIOCHEMISTRY AND BIOPHYSICS (US/0003-9861) [01482120] 494, **480**

ARCHIVES OF CHILD HEALTH (II/0044-8710) [08855895] **3900**

ARCHIVES — Alphabetical Title Index

● ARCHIVES OF CIVIL ENGINEERING / POLISH ACADEMY OF SCIENCES, INSTITUTE OF FUNDAMENTAL TECHNOLOGICAL RESEARCH [AND] COMMITTEE FOR CIVIL ENGINEERING (PL) [27182821] **2018**

ARCHIVES OF CLINICAL NEUROPSYCHOLOGY (US/0887-6177) [13307299] **3827**

ARCHIVES OF COMPLEX ENVIRONMENTAL STUDIES : ACES (FI/0787-0396) [22178164] **2161**

ARCHIVES OF DERMATOLOGICAL RESEARCH (GW/0340-3696) [03955287] **3717**

ARCHIVES OF DERMATOLOGY (US/0003-987X) [01482124] **3718**

ARCHIVES OF DISEASE IN CHILDHOOD (UK/0003-9888) [01513868] **3900**

ARCHIVES OF EMERGENCY MEDICINE (UK/0264-4924) [10738779] **3723**

ARCHIVES OF ENVIRONMENTAL CONTAMINATION AND TOXICOLOGY (US/0090-4341) [01787012] 3979, **2161**

ARCHIVES OF ENVIRONMENTAL HEALTH (US/0003-9896) [01513869] **4767**

● ARCHIVES OF FAMILY MEDICINE (US/1063-3987) [26001153] **3736**

ARCHIVES OF FAMILY PRACTICE *CEASED.* (US/0270-9074) [06515370] **3736**

ARCHIVES OF GENERAL PSYCHIATRY (US/0003-990X) [01513870] **3921**

ARCHIVES OF GERONTOLOGY AND GERIATRICS (NE/0167-4943) [08634173] **3749**

ARCHIVES OF GERONTOLOGY AND GERIATRICS. SUPPLEMENT (NE/0924-7947) [20103290] **3749**

ARCHIVES OF GYNECOLOGY AND OBSTETRICS (GW/0932-0067) [16522545] **3757**

ARCHIVES OF HISTOLOGY AND CYTOLOGY (JA/0914-9465) [18091878] **532**

ARCHIVES OF INSECT BIOCHEMISTRY AND PHYSIOLOGY (US/0739-4462) [09734825] **5605**

ARCHIVES OF INTERNAL MEDICINE (1960) (US/0003-9926) [01513873] **3795**

ARCHIVES OF MECHANICS (PL/0373-2029) [01787963] **2110**

● ARCHIVES OF MEDICAL RESEARCH (MX/0188-0128) [28473251] **3552**

ARCHIVES OF MICROBIOLOGY (GW/0302-8933) [02239811] **559**

ARCHIVES OF MINING SCIENCES (PL/0860-7001) [08607001] **2134**

ARCHIVES OF NATURAL HISTORY (UK/0260-9541) [07989535] **4162**

ARCHIVES OF NEUROLOGY (CHICAGO) (US/0003-9942) [01513880] **3827**

ARCHIVES OF OPHTHALMOLOGY (US/0003-9950) [01513884] **3872**

ARCHIVES OF OPTHALMOLOGY ED. ESPANOLA. BARCELONA (SP/1130-5134) [I11305134] **3872**

ARCHIVES OF ORAL BIOLOGY (UK/0003-9969) [02484813] **1316**

ARCHIVES OF ORTHOPAEDIC AND TRAUMA SURGERY (GW/0936-8051) [19945004] 3880, **3959**

ARCHIVES OF OTO-RHINO-LARYNGOLOGY. SUPPLEMENT *See* EUROPEAN ARCHIVES OF OTO-RHINO-LARYNGOLOGY. SUPPLEMENT **3888**

ARCHIVES OF OTOLARYNGOLOGY-HEAD & NECK SURGERY (US/0886-4470) [12897795] **3886**

ARCHIVES OF PATHOLOGY & LABORATORY MEDICINE (US/0003-9985) [02300010] **3893**

● ARCHIVES OF PEDIATRICS & ADOLESCENT MEDICINE (US/1072-4710) [28958056] **3900**

ARCHIVES OF PHARMACAL RESEARCH (KO/0253-6269) [06012687] **4292**

ARCHIVES OF PHYSICAL MEDICINE AND REHABILITATION (US/0003-9993) [01513891] **4379**

ARCHIVES OF PODIATRIC MEDICINE AND FOOT SURGERY (US/0092-7651) [01791229] **3917**

ARCHIVES OF PODIATRIC MEDICINE AND FOOT SURGERY. SUPPLEMENT (US/0164-2553) [04588488] **3917**

ARCHIVES OF PSYCHIATRIC NURSING (US/0883-9417) [12257580] **3851**

ARCHIVES OF PUBLIC HEALTH / ARCHIVES BELGES DE SANTE PUBLIQUE (BE) [27008951] **4767**

ARCHIVES OF RESEARCH ON INDUSTRIAL CARCINOGENESIS (US/8756-0585) [11463580] **3552**

ARCHIVES OF SEXUAL BEHAVIOR (US/0004-0002) [01183760] **5186**

● ARCHIVES OF STD/HIV RESEARCH (US/1071-0906) [28034747] 3712, **3666**

ARCHIVES OF SURGERY (CHICAGO. 1960) (US/0004-0010) [01513896] **3959**

ARCHIVES OF THE FOUNDATION OF THANATOLOGY (1976) (US/0160-7081) [03677474] **4341**

ARCHIVES OF THE KOHNO CLINICAL MEDICINE RESEARCH INSTITUTE (JA) [16863608] **3552**

ARCHIVES OF TOXICOLOGY (GW/0340-5761) [01588539] **3979**

ARCHIVES OF TOXICOLOGY. SUPPLEMENT (GW/0171-9750) [04158456] **3979**

ARCHIVES OF VIROLOGY (AU/0304-8608) [02243267] **560**

ARCHIVES PARLEMENTAIRES DE 1787 A 1860 (FR) [01607789] 2676, **2480**

ARCHIVES PERPIGNAN (FR/0985-2395) [I09852395] **4063**

ARCHIVES (PERPIGNAN, FRANCE) (FR) [08350848] **2480**

ARCHIVES PUBLIQUES CANADA *See* ACQUISITIONS - ARCHIVES PUBLIQUES CANADA **407**

ARCHIVES (QUEBEC) (CN/0044-9423) [01639350] **2480**

ARCHIVES REPORT / CALIFORNIA WATER RESOURCES CENTER, UNIVERSITY OF CALIFORNIA (US/1045-8727) [07618501] **5530**

ARCHIVI (IT) [03368027] **337**

ARCHIVI & COMPUTER (IT/1121-2462) [I11212462] **1171**

ARCHIVI E IMPRESSE : BOLLETTINO INFORMAZIONI STUDI E RICERCHE (IT) **1463**

ARCHIVI PER LA STORIA : RIVISTA DELL'ASSOCIAZIONE NAZIONALE ARCHIVISTICA ITALIANA (IT/0394-9044) [19546109] **2480**

ARCHIVIO DEL TEATRO ITALIANO (IT) [06494309] **5361**

ARCHIVIO DELLA CORRISPONDENZA DEGLI SCIENZIATI ITALIANI (IT) [12957477] **5085**

ARCHIVIO DELLA NUOVA PROCEDURA PENALE (IT/1120-687X) [26338845] **2936**

ARCHIVIO DELLA SOCIETA ROMANA DI STORIA PATRIA (1947) (IT/0391-6952) [I03916952] **1074**

ARCHIVIO DELLE LOCAZIONI E DEL CONDOMINIO (IT/0392-615X) [I0392615X] **2815**

ARCHIVIO DI CHIRURGIA TORACICA E CARDIOVASCOLARE (IT/0004-007X) [01588027] **3960**

ARCHIVIO DI FILOSOFIA (IT/0004-0088) [01513907] **4341**

ARCHIVIO DI FISIOLOGIA (IT/0004-0096) [01513908] **578**

ARCHIVIO DI MEDICINA INTERNA PARMA (IT/0004-010X) [I0004010X] **3795**

ARCHIVIO DI MEDICINA LEGALE E DELLE ASSICURAZIONI (IT/0392-5145) [07747203] **3739**

ARCHIVIO DI ORTOPEDIA E REUMATOLOGIA (IT/0390-7368) [01438095] 3880, **3803**

ARCHIVIO DI OSTETRICIA E GINECOLOGIA (IT/0004-0126) [01513909] **3757**

ARCHIVIO DI PSICOLOGIA, NEUROLOGIA E PSICHIATRIA (IT/0004-0150) [01513912] 3921, 3827, **4575**

ARCHIVIO DI SCIENZE DEL LAVORO (IT) [18418719] **2859**

ARCHIVIO DI STORIA DELLA CULTURA (IT) [18854729] **2611**

ARCHIVIO DI STUDI URBANI E REGIONALI (IT/0004-0177) [26043641] **2815**

ARCHIVIO ECONOMICO DELL'UNIFICAZIONE ITALIANA. SERIE I *CEASED.* (IT/0518-3499) [05473189] 2480, **1546**

ARCHIVIO EDILE (IT) **599**

ARCHIVIO GIURIDICO (IT) [01513917] **2936**

ARCHIVIO GIURIDICO DELLA CIRCOLAZIONE E DEI SINISTRI STRADALI (IT) [I05183510] **2936**

ARCHIVIO GIURIDICO DELLE OPERE PUBBLICHE (IT/0393-1374) [I03931374] **2936**

ARCHIVIO GLOTTOLOGICO ITALIANO (IT/0004-0207) [01513918] **3266**

ARCHIVIO ITALIANO DI ANATOMIA E DI EMBRIOLOGIA (IT/0004-0223) [01513921] 541, **3678**

ARCHIVIO ITALIANO DI ANATOMIA E EMBRILOGIA *See* ITALIAN JOURNAL OF ANATOMY & EMBRIOLOGY **3679**

ARCHIVIO ITALIANO DI PATOLOGIA E CLINICA DEI TUMORI (IT/0004-0266) [01778631] **3809**

ARCHIVIO ITALIANO DI SCIENZE MEDICHE TROPICALI E DI PARASSITOLOGIA (IT/0004-0282) [01778632] **3552**

ARCHIVIO ITALIANO DI UROLOGIA ANDROLOGIA (IT) [29185727] **3988**

ARCHIVIO ITALIANO DI UROLOGIA NEFROLOGIA ANDROLOGIA *See* ARCHIVIO UROLOGIA NEFROLOGIA **3988**

ARCHIVIO MONALDI PER LE MALATTIE DEL TORACE (IT/1120-0391) [19464101] **3948**

ARCHIVIO PENALE (IT/0004-0304) [I00040304] **2936**

ARCHIVIO PER L'ALTO ADIGE (IT/0392-1050) [02860716] 3266, 2318, **2255**

ARCHIVIO PER L'ANTROPOLOGIA E LA ETNOLOGIA (IT/0373-3009) [01513926] **231**

ARCHIVIO PIOMBINESE DI STUDI STORICI (IT) [01791018] **2676**

ARCHIVIO PUTTI DI CHIRURGIA DEGLI ORGANI DI MOVIMENTO (IT/0066-670X) [01778635] **3960**

ARCHIVIO SICILIANO DE MEDICINA E CHIRURGIA. 4, ACTA MEDICA MEDITERRANEA (IT/0393-6384) [18466557] **3960**

ARCHIVIO SICILIANO DI MEDICINA E CHIRURGIA. 1, ACTA CHIRURGICA MEDITERRANEA (IT) [19022560] **3960**

ARCHIVIO SICILIANO DI MEDICINA E CHIRURGIA. 5, ACTA PEDIATRICA MEDITERRANEA (IT/0393-6392) [16920784] **3900**

ARCHIVIO STOMATOLOGICO (IT/0004-0320) [01513928] **1316**

ARCHIVIO STORICO BERGAMASCO *SUSPENDED.* (IT) [10484766] **2676**

ARCHIVIO STORICO DELLA DIOCESI DE COMO (IT) [21959897] **5023**

ARCHIVIO STORICO DI BELLUNO, FELTRE E CADORE (IT/0392-2065) [01731962] **2676**

ARCHIVIO STORICO ITALIANO (IT/0391-7770) [01513930] **2480**

ARCHIVIO STORICO ITALIANO *See* BIBLIOTECA DELL'ARCHIVIO STORICO ITALIANO **2480**

ARCHIVIO STORICO LODIGIANO (IT/0004-0347) [I00040347] **2611**

ARCHIVIO STORICO LOMBARDO (IT/0392-0232) [01513931] **2676**

ARCHIVIO STORICO MESSINESE (IT/0392-0240) [01730527] **2676**

ARCHIVIO STORICO PER LA CALABRIA E LA LUCANIA (IT/0004-0355) [02221597] **2676**

ARCHIVIO STORICO PER LA SICILIA ORIENTALE (IT/0004-0363) [01737288] **2676**

ARCHIVIO STORICO PER LE PROVINCE PARMENSI (IT/0392-0283) [01730595] **2676**

ARCHIVIO STORICO PRATESE (IT/0392-0259) [01730702] **2676**

ARCHIVIO STORICO PUGLIESE (IT/0392-0054) [01731872] **2676**

ARCHIVIO STORICO SICILIANO (IT) [04873574] **2676**

ARCHIVIO STORICO SIRACUSANO (IT/0044-8737) [01730724] **2676**

ARCHIVIO UROLOGIA NEFROLOGIA (IT) **3988**

ARCHIVIO VENETO (IT/0392-0291) [01513936] **2676**

ARCHIVIO VENETO, A CURA DELLA R. DEPUTAZIONE DI STORIA PATRIA PER LE VENEZIE (IT) [02865093] **2676**

ARCHIVIO VETERINARIO ITALIANO (IT/0004-0479) [01513937] **5504**

ARCHIVIST, THE (CN/0705-2855) [02437459] **2480**

ARCHIVIUM (GW) **3191**

ARCHIVIUM HIBERNICUM (IE/0044-8745) [01605085] **2480**

ARCHIVMITTEILUNGEN (GW/0004-038X) [01513939] **2480**

ARCHIVNI CASOPIS (XR/0004-0398) [01731830] 3191, **2480**

ARCHIVO DE ARTE VALENCIANO; PUBLICACION DE LA REAL ACADEMIA DE BELLAS ARTES DE SAN CARLOS (SP/0211-5808) [16899387] **337**

ARCHIVO DE PREHISTORIA LEVANTINA (SP/0210-3230) [01196482] **2611**

ARCHIVO DOMINICANO (SP) [08332806] **2480**

ARCHIVO ESPANOL DE ARQUEOLOGIA (SP/0066-6742) [01196500] **259**

ARCHIVO ESPANOL DE ARTE (SP/0004-0428) [01513944] **337**

ARCHIVO GENERAL DE LA PROVINCIA DE SANTA FE *See* BOLETIN - ARCHIVO GENERAL DE LA PROVINCIA DE SANTA FE **2723**

ARCHIVO HISPALENSE (SP/0210-4067) [02024209] **2676**

ARCHIVO HISTORICO DE MIRAFLORES (VENEZUELA) *See* BOLETIN DEL ARCHIVO HISTORICO DE MIRAFLORES **2480**

ARCHIVO HISTORICO DEL GUAYAS *See* REVISTA DEL ARCHIVO HISTORICO DEL GUAYAS **2483**

ARCHIVO IBERO-AMERICANO (SP/0004-0452) [02257705] **2676, 2721**

ARCHIVO STORICO CIVICO (MILAN, ITALY) *See* LIBRI E DOCUMENTI, ARCHIVO STORICO CIVICO E BIBLIOTECA TRIVULZIANA **2622**

ARCHIVO TEOLOGICO GRANADINO (SP/0210-1629) [05575038] **5023**

ARCHIVOS (CL/0577-8557) [03115904] **4575**

ARCHIVOS ARGENTINOS DE DERMATOLOGIA (AG/0066-6750) [01778636] **3718**

ARCHIVOS (BOGOTA) (CK) [01737762] **2480**

ARCHIVOS DE ANATOMIA Y EMBRIOLOGIA (SP) 541, **3679**

ARCHIVOS DE BIOLOGIA ANDINA (PE/0250-5037) [03743135] **442**

ARCHIVOS DE BIOLOGIA Y MEDICINA EXPERIMENTALES (CL/0004-0533) [02255218] 3552, **442**

ARCHIVOS DE BIOQUIMICA, QUIMICA Y FARMACIA, TUCUMAN (AG/0365-0871) [03650871] **480**

ARCHIVOS DE BRONCONEUMOLOGIA (SP/0300-2896) [10260340] **3948**

ARCHIVOS DE CRIMINOLOGIA, NEUROPSIQUIATRIA Y DISCIPLINAS CONEXAS (EC) [01667352] **3158**

ARCHIVOS DE FARMACOLOGIA Y TOXICOLOGIA *CEASED*. (SP/0304-8616) [01917202] 3979, **4292**

ARCHIVOS DE INFORMACION SOBRE EL IDIOMA Y LA CULTURA DE LOS NAHUAS (MX) [04126160] **231**

ARCHIVOS DE INVESTIGACION MEDICA *See* ARCHIVES OF MEDICAL RESEARCH **3552**

ARCHIVOS DE LA FACULTAD DE MEDICINA DE OVIEDO (SP/0210-5527) [25366248] **3552**

ARCHIVOS DE LA FACULTAD DE MEDICINA DE ZARAGOZA (SP/0558-6291) [01145868] **3552**

ARCHIVOS DE LA SOCIEDAD CANARIA DE OFTALMOLOGIA (SP/0211-2698) [05133614] **3872**

ARCHIVOS DE LA SOCIEDAD ESPANOLA DE OFTALMOLOGIA (SP) [20868879] **3872**

ARCHIVOS DE MEDICINA DEL DEPORTE : PUBLICACION DE LA FEDERACION ESPANOLA DE MEDICINA DEL DEPORTE / FEMEDE (SP/0212-8799) [24466608] **3953**

ARCHIVOS DE MEDICINA VETERINARIA (CL/0301-732X) [04798010] **5504**

ARCHIVOS DE NEUROBIOLOGIA (SP/0004-0576) [06455105] **3827**

ARCHIVOS DE ODONTOESTOMATOLOGIA (SP/0213-4144) [15484307] **1316**

ARCHIVOS DE OFTALMOLOGIA DE BUENOS AIRES (AG/0066-6777) [01513953] **3872**

ARCHIVOS DE PEDIATRIA (SP/0402-9054) [21214701] **3900**

ARCHIVOS DE ZOOTECNIA *CEASED*. (SP/0004-0592) [03653474] **206**

ARCHIVOS DEL INSTITUTO DE CARDIOLOGIA DE MEXICO (MX/0020-3785) [03525078] **3699**

ARCHIVOS DOMINICANOS DE PEDIATRIA (DR/0004-0606) [06336802] **3900**

ARCHIVOS ESPANOLES DE UROLOGIA (SP/0004-0614) [01513957] **3988**

ARCHIVOS LATINOAMERICANOS DE NUTRICION (VE/0004-0622) [01513961] **4187**

ARCHIVOS LEONESES (SP/0004-0630) [05454842] **2480**

ARCHIVOS - SOCIEDAD AMERICANA DE OFTALMOLOGIA Y OPTOMETRIA (CK/0037-8364) [01644804] **3872**

ARCHIVOS VENEZOLANOS DE PSIQUIATRIA Y NEUROLOGIA (VE) [06367141] 3827, **3921**

ARCHIVPFLEGE IN WESTFALEN UND LIPPE / IM AUFTRAGE DES LANDSCHAFTSVERBANDES WESTFALEN-LIPPE HERAUSGEGEBEN VOM WESTFALISCHEN LANDESAMT FUR ARCHIVPFLEGE (GW) [09602762] **2480**

ARCHIVS (AT/0570-720X) [02694706] **2255**

ARCHIVUM ARCIS (IT) [22461006] **337**

ARCHIVUM BIBLIOGRAPHICUM CARMELITANUM (IT/0570-7242) [01739792] **408**

ARCHIVUM BOBIENSE : RIVISTA DEGLI ARCHIVI STORICI BOBIENSI (IT/0392-0305) [10378099] **2676**

ARCHIVUM COMBUSTIONIS (PL/0208-4198) [09939325] 2110, **4430**

ARCHIVUM EURASIAE MEDII AEIVI (GW/0724-8822) [02659373] **2676**

ARCHIVUM FRANCISCANUM HISTORICUM (IT/0004-0665) [01513971] **5024**

ARCHIVUM FRATRUM PRAEDICATORUM (IT/0391-7320) [01705177] **5024**

ARCHIVUM HERALDICUM *See* ARCHIVES HERALDIQUE SUISSES **2438**

ARCHIVUM HISTORIAE PONTIFICIAE (IT/0066-6785) [01697126] **4936**

ARCHIVUM HISTORICUM SOCIETATIS IESU (VC/0037-8887) [01513974] **5024**

ARCHIVUM IURIDICUM CRACOVIENSE (PL/0066-6882) [01513976] **2936**

ARCHIVUM MATHEMATICUM (XR/0044-8753) [05538165] **3496**

ARCHIVUM (MUNCHEN) (FR/0066-6793) [01513968] **2480**

ARCHIVUM (OVIEDO) (SP/0570-7218) [01198507] **3266**

● ARCHIVUM VETERINARIUM POLONICUM / POLISH ACADEMY OF SCIENCES, COMMITTEE OF VETERINARY SCIENCES (PL) [28468883] **5504**

ARCHIVY (WINDSOR) (CN/0828-3192) [17661718] **2480**

ARCHIWA BIBLIOTEKI I MUZEA KOSCIELNE (PL/0518-3766) [05627175] **5024**

ARCHIWUM BUDOWY MASZYN (PL/0004-0738) [01725134] **2110**

ARCHIWUM ELEKTROTECHNIKI (PL/0004-0746) [01725170] **2036**

ARCHIWUM ENERGETYKI (PL/0066-684X) [01784829] **2036**

ARCHIWUM GORNICTWA (PL/0004-0754) [05838069] **2134**

ARCHIWUM HISTORII I FILOZOFII MEDYCYNY (PL/0860-1844) [13080139] **3552**

ARCHIWUM HUTNICTWA (PL/0004-0770) [02444961] **3998**

ARCHIWUM HYDROTECHNIKI (PL/0004-0789) [05916103] **2087**

ARCHIWUM INZYNIERII LADOWEJ *See* ARCHIVES OF CIVIL ENGINEERING / POLISH ACADEMY OF SCIENCES, INSTITUTE OF FUNDAMENTAL TECHNOLOGICAL RESEARCH [AND] COMMITTEE FOR CIVIL ENGINEERING **2018**

ARCHIWUM MEDYCYNY SADOWEJ I KRJMINOLOGII (PL/0324-8267) [11450811] **3552**

ARCHIWUM MINERALOGICZNE (PL/0066-6912) [02250642] **1438**

ARCHIWUM NAUKI O MATERIAACH (PL/0138-032X) [07083354] **2100**

ARCHIWUM OCHRONY SRODOWISKA (PL/0324-8461) [02852181] **2161**

ARCHIWUM TERMODYNAMIKI (PL/0208-418X) [08288457] 2110, **4430**

ARCHOLOGIAI ERTESITO (HU/0003-8032) [02829620] **259**

ARCHOZOOLOGIA (FR/0299-3600) [16707725] **259**

ARCHTYPE (TORONTO) (CN/0712-1873) [08790783] 2936, **4383**

ARCO (CK/0570-7293) [01785942] **2842**

ARCO ADVERTISER, THE (US/0890-1511) [13172260] **5656**

ARCO DI GIANO (IT) **4464**

ARCTIC (CN/0004-0843) [01513979] **2555**

ARCTIC AND ALPINE RESEARCH (US/0004-0851) [01197556] 5085, **2555**

ARCTIC & ANTARCTIC REGIONS (US/1043-7479) [19545098] **1351**

ARCTIC ANTHROPOLOGY (US/0066-6939) [00824336] **231**

ARCTIC CIRCLE *CEASED*. (CN/1180-4629) [22391345] **2611**

ARCTIC GAS. BIOLOGICAL REPORT SERIES (CN/0316-9707) [02247548] 4251, **443**

ARCTIC INSTITUTE OF NORTH AMERICA. LIBRARY *See* LIBRARY ACCESSIONS - ARCTIC INSTITUTE OF NORTH AMERICA **3223**

ARCTIC MEDICAL RESEARCH (FI/0782-226X) [13279409] **3552**

ARCTIC NEWS (CN/0518-3839) [01639135] **4936**

ARCTIC NEWS RECORD (NO) [10681901] **2555**

ARCTIC PETROLEUM REVIEW *CEASED*. (CN/0834-2709) [16410197] **4251**

ARCTIC PILOT (UK) [04648878] **4174**

ARCTIC RESEARCH OF THE UNITED STATES (US/1045-4764) [17367136] **2555**

ARCTIC SCIENCE AND TECHNOLOGY INFORMATION SYSTEM *See* ASTIS BIBLIOGRAPHY **5173**

ARCTIC SCIENCE AND TECHNOLOGY INFORMATION SYSTEM *See* A S T I S CURRENT AWARENESS BULLETIN **406**

ARCTIC SOUNDER, THE (US/0897-9502) [17679487] **5628**

ARCTOS (FI/0066-6998) [01730474] **3266**

ARD AL-SALAM (UA) [09520116] **2645**

ARD JAHRBUCH (GW/0066-5746) [05741147] **1149**

ARDC NEWS (II/0257-7992) [03087887] **62**

ARDEA (NE/0373-2266) [01513989] **5614**

ARDECHE ARCHEOLOGIE (FR/0980-7527) [I09807527] **259**

ARDELL WELLNESS REPORT, THE (US/0882-0171) [11788278] **4767**

ARDENNAIS, L' (FR) [12362908] **5800**

ARDENNE AGRICOLE (FR) [I07501536] **62**

ARDEOLA (SP/0570-7358) [03682037] **5615**

ARDI (SP/0214-0055) [I02140055] **2676**

ARDOISE, L' (CN/0705-0690) [03956679] **1810**

ARDOISE (QUEBEC) *CEASED*. (CN/0820-5523) [16796064] 1799, **2815**

AREA BUSINESS DATABANK. PRINT INDEX (US) [12623722] **639**

AREA CODE HANDBOOK (US/1040-032X) [18296050] **1149**

AREA DEVELOPMENT IN JAPAN (JA) [01513991] **2815**

AREA DEVELOPMENT SITES & FACILITY PLANNING (US/1048-6534) [18670950] 599, **4834**

AREA ELECTRICIDAD (CL) [03568381] **2036**

AREA FISICA (CL) [12822852] **4398**

AREA FOOTPRINTS (US/0736-4024) [09106566] **2438**

AREA GEOCIENCIAS (CL/0716-0127) [11093425] **1366**

AREA INGENIERIA QUIMICA (CL) [03580655] **2008**

AREA (LONDON 1969) (UK/0004-0894) [01513990] **2555**

AREA MANPOWER REVIEW : CITY OF BERKELEY (US/0146-2415) [02915747] **1652**

AREA MANPOWER REVIEW: CITY OF OAKLAND (US/0145-7179) [02773870] **1652**

AREA MANPOWER REVIEW : CITY OF RICHMOND (US/0145-6415) [02766335] **1652**

AREA MANPOWER REVIEW : MARIN COUNTY (US/0145-7160) [02774503] **1652**

AREA MANPOWER REVIEW : RICHMOND, VIRGINIA STANDARD METROPOLITAN STATISTICAL AREA (US) [04411232] **1652**

AREA MANPOWER REVIEW : ROANOKE, VIRGINIA AREA (US) [04411033] **1652**

AREA MANPOWER REVIEW : SACRAMENTO STANDARD METROPOLITAN STATISTICAL AREA. PLACER COUNTY SUPPLEMENT (US/0145-7144) [02774941] **1652**

AREA MANPOWER REVIEW : SACRAMENTO-YOLO PLANNING AREA (US/0145-6393) [02767447] **1652**

AREA MANPOWER REVIEW : SAN FRANCISCO CITY AND COUNTY (US/0145-7128) [02774993] **1652**

AREA MANPOWER REVIEW : SAN MATEO COUNTY (US/0145-7101) [02773664] **1652**

AREA MANPOWER REVIEW : SOLANO COUNTY (US/0145-6407) [02766493] **1652**

AREA MANPOWER REVIEW : VALLEJO-FAIRFIELD-NAPA SMSA. NAPA COUNTY SUPPLEMENT (US/0145-708X) [02774656] 1652, **1529**

AREA MATEMATICAS (CL) [03703416] **3496**

AREA METALURGIA (CL) [03568598] **3998**

AREA (MILAN, ITALY) (IT/0394-0055) [09292904] **291**

AREA NEWS, THE (US) [23279749] **5658**

AREA — Alphabetical Title Index

AREA QUIMICA (CL) [03583193] **961**

AREA REPORT SERIES (IO/0377-9793) [01967746] **588**

AREA TRENDS IN EMPLOYMENT AND UNEMPLOYMENT (US/0004-0916) [03761804] **1652**

AREA WAGE SURVEY (US) [22140450] **1652**

AREA WAGE SURVEY (US) [19650618] **1652**

AREA WAGE SURVEY. ALASKA / U.S. DEPARTMENT OF LABOR, BUREAU OF LABOR STATISTICS (US) [08129172] **1652, 1529**

AREA WAGE SURVEY. ATLANTA, GEORGIA, METROPOLITAN AREA *See* OCCUPATIONAL COMPENSATION SURVEY--PAY ONLY. ATLANTA, GEORGIA, METROPOLITAN AREA / U.S. DEPARTMENT OF LABOR, BUREAU OF LABOR STATISTICS **1697**

AREA WAGE SURVEY. AUSTIN, TEX. / U.S. DEPARTMENT OF LABOR, BUREAU OF LABOR STATISTICS (US) [09274775] **1652**

AREA WAGE SURVEY : AUSTIN, TEXAS, METROPOLITAN AREA (US/0091-5009) [01786832] **1652**

AREA WAGE SURVEY : BIRMINGHAM, ALABAMA, METROPOLITAN AREA (US/0197-4424) [02504871] **1652**

AREA WAGE SURVEY. BRUNSWICK, GA *See* OCCUPATIONAL COMPENSATION SURVEY--PAY AND BENEFITS. BRUNSWICK, GA / U.S. DEPARTMENT OF LABOR, BUREAU OF LABOR STATISTICS **1696**

AREA WAGE SURVEY. CHARLESTON-NORTH CHARLESTON-WALTERBORO, SC *See* OCCUPATIONAL COMPENSATION SURVEY--PAY AND BENEFITS. CHARLESTON, SC / U.S. DEPARTMENT OF LABOR, BUREAU OF LABOR STATISTICS **1696**

AREA WAGE SURVEY. CHEYENNE, WYO *See* OCCUPATIONAL COMPENSATION SURVEY--PAY ONLY. CHEYENNE, WY / U.S. DEPARTMENT OF LABOR, BUREAU OF LABOR STATISTICS **1697**

AREA WAGE SURVEY. CINCINNATI, OHIO-KENTUCKY-INDIANA, METROPOLITAN AREA *See* OCCUPATIONAL COMPENSATION SURVEY--PAY AND BENEFITS. CINCINNATI, OHIO-KENTUCKY-INDIANA, METROPOLITAN AREA / U.S. DEPARTMENT OF LABOR, BUREAU OF LABOR STATISTICS **1696**

AREA WAGE SURVEY. CLARKSVILLE-HOPKINSVILLE, TENN.-KY *See* OCCUPATIONAL COMPENSATION SURVEY--PAY AND BENEFITS. CLARKSVILLE-HOPKINSVILLE, TN-KY / U.S. DEPARTMENT OF LABOR, BUREAU OF LABOR STATISTICS **1696**

AREA WAGE SURVEY. DAYTON-SPRINGFIELD, OH *See* OCCUPATIONAL COMPENSATION SURVEY--PAY ONLY. DAYTON-SPRINGFIELD, OHIO, METROPOLITAN AREA / U.S. DEPARTMENT OF LABOR, BUREAU OF LABOR STATISTICS **1697**

AREA WAGE SURVEY. DAYTONA BEACH, FLORIDA, METROPOLITAN AREA (US/0098-020X) [01799443] **1652**

AREA WAGE SURVEY : FORT LAUDERDALE-HOLLYWOOD AND WEST PALM BEACH, FLORIDA, METROPOLITAN AREAS (US/0093-867X) [01792821] **1652**

AREA WAGE SURVEY. FRESNO, CALIFORNIA, METROPOLITAN AREA (US/0361-7386) [02441444] **1652**

AREA WAGE SURVEY. GARY-HAMMOND, INDIANA METROPOLITAN AREA *See* OCCUPATIONAL COMPENSATION SURVEY--PAY AND BENEFITS. GARY-HAMMOND, INDIANA, METROPOLITAN AREA **1696**

AREA WAGE SURVEY. GREEN BAY, WISCONSIN, METROPOLITAN AREA (US) [02720203] **1652**

AREA WAGE SURVEY. GREENSBORO-WINSTON SALEM-HIGH POINT, NC *See* OCCUPATIONAL COMPENSATION SURVEY--PAY AND BENEFITS. GREENSBORO-WINSTON SALEM-HIGH POINT, NC / U.S. DEPARTMENT OF LABOR, BUREAU OF LABOR STATISTICS **1696**

AREA WAGE SURVEY. GREENSBORO-WINSTON-SALEM-HIGH POINT, NORTH CAROLINA, METROPOLITAN AREA (US/0361-1574) [02246368] **1652**

AREA WAGE SURVEY. GREENVILLE-SPARTANBURG, SOUTH CAROLINA, METROPOLITAN AREA (US/0361-655X) [02247097] **1652, 1529**

AREA WAGE SURVEY. HUNTSVILLE, ALABAMA, METROPOLITAN AREA *See* OCCUPATIONAL COMPENSATION SURVEY--PAY AND BENEFITS. HUNTSVILLE, ALABAMA, METROPOLITAN AREA / U.S. DEPARTMENT OF LABOR, BUREAU OF LABOR STATISTICS **1696**

AREA WAGE SURVEY. JACKSON, MISSISSIPPI, METROPOLITAN AREA *See* OCCUPATIONAL COMPENSATION SURVEY--PAY AND BENEFITS. JACKSON, MISSISSIPPI, METROPOLITAN AREA / U.S. DEPARTMENT OF LABOR, BUREAU OF LABOR STATISTICS **1696**

AREA WAGE SURVEY. JACKSONVILLE, FLORIDA, METROPOLITAN AREA (US) [02225692] **1652, 1529**

AREA WAGE SURVEY. KANSAS CITY, MISSOURI-KANSAS, METROPOLITAN AREA *See* OCCUPATIONAL COMPENSATION SURVEY--PAY ONLY. KANSAS CITY, MISSOURI-KANSAS, METROPOLITAN AREA / U.S. DEPARTMENT OF LABOR, BUREAU OF LABOR STATISTICS **1698**

AREA WAGE SURVEY. MACON, GA / U.S. DEPARTMENT OF LABOR, BUREAU OF LABOR STATISTICS (US) [09334657] **1652**

AREA WAGE SURVEY. MANSFIELD, OHIO / U.S. DEPARTMENT OF LABOR, BUREAU OF LABOR STATISTICS (US) [09340909] **1653**

AREA WAGE SURVEY. MELBOURNE-TITUSVILLE-PALM BAY, FL *See* OCCUPATIONAL COMPENSATION SURVEY--PAY AND BENEFITS. MELBOURNE-TITUSVILLE-PALM BAY, FL / U.S. DEPARTMENT OF LABOR, BUREAU OF LABOR STATISTICS **1696**

AREA WAGE SURVEY. MINNEAPOLIS-ST. PAUL, MINNESOTA-WISCONSIN, METROPOLITAN AREA *See* OCCUPATIONAL COMPENSATION SURVEY--PAY ONLY. MINNEAPOLIS-ST. PAUL, MINNESOTA-WISCONSIN, METROPOLITAN AREA / U.S. DEPARTMENT OF LABOR, BUREAU OF LABOR STATISTICS **1698**

AREA WAGE SURVEY. MONTGOMERY, ALA *See* OCCUPATIONAL COMPENSATION SURVEY--PAY AND BENEFITS. MONTGOMERY, AL / U.S. DEPARTMENT OF LABOR, BUREAU OF LABOR STATISTICS **1696**

AREA WAGE SURVEY. MONTGOMERY, ALA. / U.S. DEPARTMENT OF LABOR, BUREAU OF LABOR STATISTICS (US) [08136071] **1653**

AREA WAGE SURVEY. NEW YORK, NEW YORK, METROPOLITAN AREA (US) [21013553] **1653**

AREA WAGE SURVEY. NEW YORK, NEW YORK, METROPOLITAN AREA (WASHINGTON, D.C. : 1989) *See* OCCUPATIONAL COMPENSATION SURVEY--PAY ONLY. NEW YORK, NEW YORK, METROPOLITAN AREA **4014**

AREA WAGE SURVEY. NORFOLK-VIRGINIA BEACH-PORTSMOUTH AND NEWPORT NEWS-HAMPTON, VIRGINIA, METROPOLITAN AREA *See* AREA WAGE SURVEY. NORFOLK-VIRGINIA BEACH-PORTSMOUTH AND NEWPORT NEWS-HAMPTON, VIRGINIA-NORTH CAROLINA METROPOLITAN AREA **1653**

AREA WAGE SURVEY. NORFOLK-VIRGINIA BEACH-PORTSMOUTH AND NEWPORT NEWS-HAMPTON, VIRGINIA-NORTH CAROLINA METROPOLITAN AREA (US/0149-600X) [02720671] **1653**

AREA WAGE SURVEY. NORTHERN NEW YORK / U.S. DEPARTMENT OF LABOR, BUREAU OF LABOR STATISTICS (US) [08129446] **1653**

AREA WAGE SURVEY. OAKLAND, CALIFORNIA, METROPOLITAN AREA *See* OCCUPATIONAL COMPENSATION SURVEY--PAY ONLY. OAKLAND, CALIFORNIA, METROPOLITAN AREA / U.S. DEPARTMENT OF LABOR, BUREAU OF LABOR STATISTICS **1698**

AREA WAGE SURVEY. ORLANDO, FLORIDA, METROPOLITAN AREA (US) [19683771] **1653**

AREA WAGE SURVEY. PATERSON-CLIFTON-PASSAIC, NEW JERSEY METROPOLITAN AREA (US) [02719778] **1653**

AREA WAGE SURVEY. PORTSMOUTH-CHILLICOTHE-GALLIPOLIS, OHIO *See* OCCUPATIONAL COMPENSATION SURVEY-- PAY ONLY. PORTSMOUTH-CHILLICOTHE-GALLIPOLIS, OH / U.S. DEPARTMENT OF LABOR, BUREAU OF LABOR STATISTICS **1698**

AREA WAGE SURVEY. PROVIDENCE, RI *See* OCCUPATIONAL COMPENSATION SURVEY--PAY ONLY. PROVIDENCE, RI / U.S. DEPARTMENT OF LABOR, BUREAU OF LABOR STATISTICS **1698**

AREA WAGE SURVEY. PROVIDENCE-WARWICK-PAWTUCKET, RHODE ISLAND-MASSACHUSETTS, METROPOLITAN AREA (US/0197-4335) [02514802] **1653**

AREA WAGE SURVEY. PUERTO RICO *See* OCCUPATIONAL COMPENSATION SURVEY--PAY ONLY. PUERTO RICO / U.S. DEPARTMENT OF LABOR, BUREAU OF LABOR STATISTICS **1698**

AREA WAGE SURVEY. RALEIGH-DURHAM, N.C. / U.S. DEPARTMENT OF LABOR, BUREAU OF LABOR STATISTICS (US) [08164713] **1653**

AREA WAGE SURVEY. SACRAMENTO, CALIFORNIA, METROPOLITAN AREA *See* OCCUPATIONAL COMPENSATION SURVEY--PAY ONLY. SACRAMENTO, CALIFORNIA, METROPOLITAN AREA **1698**

AREA WAGE SURVEY. SACRAMENTO, CALIFORNIA, METROPOLITAN AREA (US/0099-1899) [02243266] **1653**

AREA WAGE SURVEY. SALINAS-SEASIDE-MONTEREY, CA *See* OCCUPATIONAL COMPENSATION SURVEY--PAY AND BENEFITS. SALINAS-SEASIDE-MONTEREY, CA / U.S. DEPARTMENT OF LABOR, BUREAU OF LABOR STATISTICS **1696**

AREA WAGE SURVEY. SALT LAKE CITY-OGDEN, UTAH, METROPOLITAN AREA *See* OCCUPATIONAL COMPENSATION SURVEY--PAY ONLY. SALT LAKE CITY-OGDEN, UTAH, METROPOLITAN AREA / U.S. DEPARTMENT OF LABOR, BUREAU OF LABOR STATISTICS **1698**

AREA WAGE SURVEY. SAN FRANCISCO, CALIFORNIA, METROPOLITAN AREA *See* OCCUPATIONAL COMPENSATION SURVEY--PAY ONLY. SAN FRANCISCO, CALIFORNIA, METROPOLITAN AREA / U.S. DEPARTMENT OF LABOR, BUREAU OF LABOR STATISTICS **1698**

AREA WAGE SURVEY. SAN JOSE, CALIFORNIA, METROPOLITAN AREA *See* OCCUPATIONAL COMPENSATION SURVEY--PAY ONLY. SAN JOSE, CALIFORNIA, METROPOLITAN AREA **1698**

AREA WAGE SURVEY. SELMA, AL *See* OCCUPATIONAL COMPENSATION SURVEY--PAY AND BENEFITS. SELMA, AL / U.S. DEPARTMENT OF LABOR, BUREAU OF LABOR STATISTICS **1696**

AREA WAGE SURVEY. SOUTH BEND, INDIANA, METROPOLITAN AREA *See* OCCUPATIONAL COMPENSATION SURVEY--PAY AND BENEFITS. SOUTH BEND-MISHAWAKA, INDIANA, METROPOLITAN AREA / U.S. DEPARTMENT OF LABOR, BUREAU OF LABOR STATISTICS **1697**

AREA WAGE SURVEY. ST. LOUIS, MISSOURI-ILLINOIS, METROPOLITAN AREA *See* OCCUPATIONAL COMPENSATION SURVEY--PAY AND BENEFITS. ST. LOUIS, MISSOURI-ILLINOIS, METROPOLITAN AREA / U.S. DEPARTMENT OF LABOR, BUREAU OF LABOR STATISTICS **1697**

AREA WAGE SURVEY : STAMFORD, CONNECTICUT, METROPOLITAN AREA (US/0146-3233) [02720130] **1653**

AREA WAGE SURVEY. STOCKTON, CALIF. / U.S. DEPARTMENT OF LABOR, BUREAU OF LABOR STATISTICS (US) [08136768] **1653**

AREA WAGE SURVEY: THE RALEIGH-DURHAM, NORTH CAROLINA, METROPOLITAN AREA (US/0364-4731) [02657707] **1653**

AREA WAGE SURVEY. TOPEKA, KS *See* OCCUPATIONAL COMPENSATION SURVEY--PAY ONLY. TOPEKA, KS / U.S. DEPARTMENT OF LABOR, BUREAU OF LABOR STATISTICS **1698**

AREA WAGE SURVEY. TUCSON-DOUGLAS, AZ *See* OCCUPATIONAL COMPENSATION SURVEY--PAY AND BENEFITS. TUCSON-DOUGLAS, AZ / U.S. DEPARTMENT OF LABOR, BUREAU OF LABOR STATISTICS **1697**

AREA WAGE SURVEY. TULSA, OKLA. / U.S. DEPARTMENT OF LABOR, BUREAU OF LABOR STATISTICS (US) [08138041] **1653**

AREA WAGE SURVEY. UPPER PENINSULA, MICH *See* OCCUPATIONAL COMPENSATION SURVEY--PAY ONLY. UPPER PENINSULA, MI / U.S. DEPARTMENT OF LABOR, BUREAU OF LABOR STATISTICS **1698**

AREA WAGE SURVEY. UPPER PENINSULA, MICH. / U.S. DEPARTMENT OF LABOR, BUREAU OF LABOR STATISTICS (US) [08127511] **1653**

AREA WAGE SURVEY. VALLEJO-FAIRFIELD-NAPA, CALIF *See* OCCUPATIONAL COMPENSATION SURVEY--PAY AND BENEFITS. VALLEJO-FAIRFIELD-NAPA, CA / U.S. DEPARTMENT OF LABOR, BUREAU OF LABOR STATISTICS **1697**

AREA WAGE SURVEY. VERMONT *See* OCCUPATIONAL COMPENSATION SURVEY--PAY AND BENEFITS. VERMONT / U.S. DEPARTMENT OF LABOR, BUREAU OF LABOR STATISTICS **1697**

AREA WAGE SURVEY. WASHINGTON, D.C.-MD.-VA., METROPOLITAN AREA *See* OCCUPATIONAL COMPENSATION SURVEY--PAY AND BENEFITS. WASHINGTON, D.C.-MARYLAND-VIRGINIA, METROPOLITAN AREA / U.S. DEPARTMENT OF LABOR, BUREAU OF LABOR STATISTICS **1697**

AREA WAGE SURVEY : WESTCHESTER COUNTY, NEW YORK (US/0361-7637) [02287567] **1653**

AREA WAGE SURVEY. WICHITA, KS *See* OCCUPATIONAL COMPENSATION SURVEY--PAY AND BENEFITS. WICHITA, KS / U.S. DEPARTMENT OF LABOR, BUREAU OF LABOR STATISTICS **1697**

AREA WAGE SURVEY. YORK, PENNSYLVANIA, METROPOLITAN AREA (US/0270-5923) [03214147] **1653**

AREA WAGE SURVEYS (US) **1653**

AREA WAGE SURVEYS: SELECTED METROPOLITAN AREAS (US) [01285592] **1653**

AREAS OF CONCERN (US/0044-8788) [02861600] **2197**

AREAS SERVED BY GAS IN CANADA *See* AREAS SERVED BY NATURAL GAS **4759**

● AREAS SERVED BY NATURAL GAS (CN/1199-1801) [30673828] **4251, 4759**

AREAWIDE ACTION PLAN OF THE UPPER CUMBERLAND DEVELOPMENT DISTRICT (US) [06471429] **2815**

AREE. ANNUAL REVIEW OF ENVIRONMENTAL EDUCATION (UK/0953-0428) [I09530428] **2161**

AREEA REPORT, THE (US/1064-1092) [26207813] **4834**

AREITO (US/0360-0467) [02243312] **2255**

ARENA (AT/0004-0932) [03370228] **4464**

ARENA (UK) **4101**

ARENA DI VERONA (IT) **5804**

ARENA JOURNAL (AT) **4540**

● ARENA MAGAZINE (AT/1039-1010) [28040493] **4540**

ARENA (MOSCOW, R.S.F.S.R.) (RU) [18197019] **3363**

ARENA TEKSTIL (IO/0518-4010) [01795560] **5347**

ARENSA SINDICAL (PE) [01792987] **1653**

AREOPAGUS : A LIVING ENCOUNTER WITH TODAY'S RELIGIOUS WORLD (HK) [17247774] **4936**

ARERUGI (JA/0021-4884) [09348527] **3666**

ARES (LYON, FRANCE) (FR/0181-009X) [07749297] **3124**

ARES. SPECIAL ED (US/0737-6545) [09438558] **5074**

ARET RUNT (SW) [01460511] **2485**

ARETE (US/0885-9787) [01534234] **5273**

ARETE (SAN FRANCISCO) (US/0363-2903) [02438186] **5273**

ARETHUSA (US/0004-0975) [01513998] **1074**

ARETS TRYCK (SW/0348-6729) [02239921] **5322**

AREUEA JOURNAL *See* JOURNAL OF THE AMERICAN REAL ESTATE AND URBAN ECONOMICS ASSOCIATION **4839**

ARFFAS VIEWPOINT (AT) **4035**

ARGENSOLA (SP/0518-4088) [04862998] **1351**

ARGENT ET VOUS, L' (CN/0832-8684) [16886649] 891, **772**

ARGENTINA (AG) [04722722] **2721**

ARGENTINA AEREA (AG) [04295872] **12**

ARGENTINA (LONDON, ENGLAND) (UK/0267-9949) [13173534] **639**

ARGENTINA. MINISTERIO DE CULTURA Y EDUCACION *See* EDUCACION EN LA REPUBLICA ARGENTINA, LA **1737**

ARGENTINA. MINISTERIO DE ECONOMIA *See* INFORME ECONOMICO. RESUMEN **1567**

ARGENTINA OUTREACH (US/0194-2832) [04678434] **4504**

ARGENTINE-AMERICAN BUSINESS REVIEW DIRECTORY / ARGENTINE-AMERICAN CHAMBER OF COMMERCE, THE (US) [04740581] **639**

ARGENTINE REPUBLIC *See* DIGESTO NOTARIAL **4720**

ARGENTINE REPUBLIC. ARMADA. BIBLIOTECA CENTRAL *See* BOLETIN BIBLIOGRAFICO - BIBLIOTECA CENTRAL DE LA ARMADA **411**

ARGENTINE REPUBLIC. DIRECCION GENERAL DE NAVEGACION, HIDROGRAFIA, FAROS Y BALIZAS *See* DERROTERO ARGENTINO **4176**

ARGENTINE REPUBLIC. DIRECCION NACIONAL DE ECONOMIA Y SOCIOLOGIA RURAL *See* PUBLICACION ESR **123**

ARGENTINE REPUBLIC. DIRECCION NACIONAL DE LA PROPIEDAD INDUSTRIAL *See* MARCAS DE FABRICA, COMERCIO Y AGRICULTURA **1306**

ARGENTINE REPUBLIC. DIRECCION NACIONAL DE LA PROPIEDAD INDUSTRIAL *See* MODELOS Y DISENOS INDUSTRIALES **1306**

ARGENTINE REPUBLIC. DIRECCION NACIONAL DE PROGRAMACION E INVESTIGACION *See* PRESUPUESTOS PROVINCIALES Y PRESUPUESTO NACIONAL DISTRIBUIDO FOR PROVINCIAS **4741**

ARGENTINE REPUBLIC. INSTITUTO DE SUELOS Y AGROTECNIA. PUBLICACION *See* SUELOS **188**

ARGENTINE REPUBLIC. INSTITUTO NACIONAL DE CIENCIA Y TECNICA HIDRICAS. CENTRO DE TECNOLOGIA DEL AGUA *See* PUBLICACION **1417**

ARGENTINE REPUBLIC. INSTITUTO NACIONAL DE MICROBIOLOGIA *See* ANALES **558**

ARGENTINE REPUBLIC. JUNTA NACIONAL DE CARNES *See* SINTESIS ESTADISTICA - MINISTERIO DI ECONOMIA, JUNTA NACIONAL DE CARNES DE LA REPUBLICA ARGENTINA **156**

ARGENTINE REPUBLIC. MINISTERIO DE CULTURA Y EDUCACION. DEPARTAMENTO DE ESTADISTICA *See* RETENCION Y DESGRANAMIENTO : EDUCACION PRIMARIA, EDAD ESCOLAR **1797**

ARGENTINE REPUBLIC. MINISTERIO DE MARINA *See* BOLETIN DEL CENTRO NAVAL **4175**

ARGENTINE REPUBLIC. OFICINA SECTORIAL DE DESARROLLO DE ENERGIA *See* ANUARIO ESTADISTICO. ENERGIA ELECTRICA **2002**

ARGENTINE REPUBLIC. SECRETARIA DE ESTADO DE COMUNICACIONES *See* BOLETIN DE LA SECRETARIA DE ESTADO DE COMUNICACIONES **1144**

ARGENTINE REPUBLIC. SUBSECRETARIA DE COMUNICACIONES. BOLETIN *See* BOLETIN DE LA SECRETARIA DE ESTADO DE COMUNICACIONES **1144**

ARGENTINIEN, FORSCHUNGSPOLITIK UND FORSCHUNGSPRAXIS / BUNDESSTELLE FUR AUSSENHANDELSINFORMATION (GW) [09962481] **5085**

ARGENTINIEN, LANDWIRTSCHAFT / BUNDESSTELLE FUR AUSSENHANDELSINFORMATION (GW) [09105884] **62**

ARGENTINIEN, LANDWIRTSCHAFT UND AGRARPOLITIK *See* ARGENTINIEN, LANDWIRTSCHAFT / BUNDESSTELLE FUR AUSSENHANDELSINFORMATION **62**

ARGENTINIEN, LANDWIRTSCHAFTLICHE ANBAUPRODUKTE / BUNDESSTELLE FUR AUSSENHANDELSINFORMATION (GW) [09351310] **2327**

ARGENTINIEN WIRTSCHAFTSDATEN / BUNDESSTELLE FUER AUSSENHANDELSINFORMATION (GW) [08705371] **1546**

ARGENTINIEN WIRTSCHAFTSDATEN UND WIRTSCHAFTSDOKUMENTATION / BUNDESSTELLE FUER AUSSENHANDELSINFORMATION (GW) [07414571] **1546**

ARGENTINIEN WIRTSCHAFTSSTRUKTUR / BUNDESSTELLE FUR AUSSENHANDELSINFORMATION (GW) [07414438] **1546**

ARGIEF-JAARBOEK VIR SUID-AFRIKAANSE GESKIEDENIS (SA) [04414646] 2638, **2480**

ARGILE BLEUE, L' (CN/0228-2550) [06959906] **1860**

ARGO (GR) [02242895] **5447**

ARGO / NARODNI MUZEJ V LJUBLJANI (XV/0570-8869) [01743409] 259, **4084**

ARGO NEWS (CN/0704-0822) [03797322] **4884**

ARGOMENTI DI CARDIOLOGIA (IT/1120-8635) [I11208635] **3699**

ARGOMENTI DI GASTROENTEROLOGIA CLINICA (IT/1120-8651) [I11208651] **3743**

ARGOMENTI DI GERONTOLOGIA (IT/1120-6888) [I11206888] **3749**

ARGOMENTI DI NEUROLOGIA (IT/1120-866X) [I1120866X] **3827**

ARGOMENTI DI ONCOLOGIA (IT) **3809**

ARGONAUT (MOSCOW, IDAHO) (US/0896-1409) [16935608] **5656**

ARGONAUTA (POINTE-CLAIRE. 1986) (CN/0842-0866) [19043413] **4174**

ARGONAUTI, GLI (IT) [09631334] **4575**

ARGONNE NATIONAL LABORATORY *See* FUSION POWER PROGRAM QUARTERLY PROGRESS REPORT **1945**

ARGONNE NATIONAL LABORATORY. DIVISION OF BIOLOGICAL AND MEDICAL RESEARCH *See* RESEARCH SUMMARY / DIVISION OF BIOLOGICAL AND MEDICAL RESEARCH, ARGONNE NATIONAL LABORATORY **5147**

ARGONNE NATIONAL LABORATORY. HIGH ENERGY PHYSICS DIVISION *See* ANL-HEP-CP (ARGONNE NATIONAL LABORATORY, HIGH ENERGY PHYSICS DIVISION) **4396**

ARGONNE NEWS : ABOUT THE PEOPLE AND PROGRAMS OF ARGONNE NATIONAL LABORATORY (US) [08069718] **1923**

ARGOS (AG) [04040859] **3266**

ARGOS (FR) **3266**

ARGOS (DK/0900-338X) **1089**

ARGOS LE PERREUX (FR/0995-2187) [I09952187] **3363**

ARGUMENT, DAS (GW/0004-1157) [01743472] 5191, **4341**

ARGUMENT-SONDERBANDE (GW/0341-3039) [13746206] **5240**

ARGUMENTA PALAEOBOTANICA (GW/0587-5404) [05165546] 500, **4226**

ARGUMENTATION (NE/0920-427X) [15646014] **4341**

ARGUMENTATION AND ADVOCACY (US/1051-1431) [18603907] **1104**

ARGUMENTOS (SP) [06832087] **4540**

ARGUMENTS & FACTS INTERNATIONAL *CEASED.* (UK/0957-0020) [23010824] **639**

ARGUMENTY I FAKTY : BIULLETEN ORDENA LENINA VSESOIUZNOGO OBSHCHESTVA "ZNANIE," LEKTORAM, PROPAGANDISTAM, POLITINFORMATORAM, AGITATORAM (RU/0204-0476) [05522385] **2676**

ARGUMENTY (MOSCOW, R.S.F.S.R.) (RU) [08737496] **4540**

ARGUMENTY (WARSAW, POLAND) (PL/0518-5289) [05883542] **4936**

ARGUS BELGE, L' (BE/0771-2510) [I07712510] **5778**

ARGUS-CHAMPION, THE (US) [22220662] **5708**

ARGUS DE L'AUTOGRAPHE & DU MANUSCRIT : REPERTOIRE BIBLIOGRAPHIQUE, L' (FR) [22162536] **4823**

ARGUS DE L'AUTOMOBILE & DES LOCOMOTIONS, L' (FR) **5404**

ARGUS DES METAUX PARIS (FR/0220-3332) [I02203332] **3998**

ARGUS DU LIVRE DE COLLECTION (FR) [30952835] **4823**

ARGUS DU LIVRE DE COLLECTION. REPERTOIRE BIBLIOGRAPHIQUE, L' (FR/0764-8111) [18101413] **408**

ARGUS (EDWARDSBURG, MICH.) (US) [12248852] **5691**

ARGUS ET LA SEMAINE, L' (FR/0150-6854) [I01506854] **2874**

ARGUS ETHNIQUE (CN/1191-1115) [25796594] **5191**

ARGUS EUROPEAN PRODUCTS (UK) **4251**

ARGUS INTERNATIONAL DES CARTES POSTALES DE COLLECTION, L' (FR) [06769670] **376**

ARGUS-LEADER (US) [09769622] **5743**

ARGUS (MICROFICHE) (SA) [03657189] **5810**

ARGUS (MONTREAL) (CN/0315-9930) [07921636] **3191**

ARGUS (MONTREAL) (CN/0315-9930) [02228738] **726**

ARGUS PROMOTIONNEL OFICHIER D'ORDINATEUR (CN/0840-478X) [29533986] **1104**

ARGUS (SAN FRANCISCO) (US/0194-8172) [05037142] **3872**

ARGUS SECTORIEL (CN/0840-4798) [18931085] **3266**

ARGUS-TIMES, THE (US/0746-1623) [09819486] **5731**

ARHAIOLOGIKON DELTION (GR/0570-622X) [I0570622X] **259**

ARHEOGRAFSKI PRILOZI (YU) [06509917] **4823**

ARHEOLOGIA MOLDOVEI (RM/0066-7358) [02444967] **259**

ARHEOLOGICESKIJ SBORNIK (RU/0320-9393) [I03209393] **259**

ARHEOLOGIJA (BU/0324-1203) [01841072] **259**

ARHEOLOGIJA UN ETNOGRAFIJA (LV/0570-6343) [05805773] 231, **259**

ARHEOLOSKI RADOVI I RASPRAVE (CI/0570-8958) [03758295] **259**

ARHEOLOSKI — Alphabetical Title Index

ARHEOLOSKI VESTNIK (XV/0570-8966) [01514041] **259**

ARHITECTURA *SUSPENDED.* (RM/0300-5356) [02144633] **291**

ARHITEKTURA (BU/0324-1254) [I03241254] **291**

ARHITEKTURA (CI/0350-3666) [01748025] **291**

ARHITEKTURA, URBANIZAM (CI/0004-1238) [02257732] **291**

ARHIV PATOLOGIJ (RU/0004-1955) [01778647] **3893**

ARHIV ZA FARMACIJU (YU/0004-1963) [I00041963] **4292**

ARHIV ZA HIGIJENU RADA I TOKSIKOLOGIJU (CR/0004-1254) [02257733] **2859**

ARHIV ZA POLJOPRIVREDNE NAUKE (YU/0004-1262) [01772027] **62**

ARHIV ZA ZASTITU MAJKE I DJETETA (CI/0004-1289) [I00041289] **3757**

ARHIVELE OLTENIEI / ACADEMIA DE STIINTE SOCIALE SI POLITICE A REPUBLICII SOCIALISTE ROMANIA, CENTRUL DE STIINTE SOCIALE, CRAIOVA (RM) [08684562] **2676**

ARHIVI UKRAINI (RU/0320-9466) [I03209466] **259**

ARHIVIST (YU/0350-2856) [03758355] **2480**

ARHIVSKI VJESNIK (CI/0570-9008) [01741281] **2480**

ARHUS HAVN (FIRM) *See* DANSK ILLUSTRERET SKIBSLISTE **5448**

ARI, KANAN (PE) [04013379] **2551**

ARIA NEWS (CN/1187-2705) [25423622] **5315**

ARIADNE : REVUE DER RECLAME (NE) [07233505] **755**

ARIAKE KOGYO KOTO SEMMON GAKKO *See* ARIAKE KOGYO KOTO SEMMON GAKKO KIYO **5086**

ARIAKE KOGYO KOTO SEMMON GAKKO KIYO (JA/0385-6844) [07116214] 1089, **5086**

ARICA (CL) [02464761] **1810**

ARID LANDS NEWSLETTER (US/0277-9455) [05041908] **2187**

ARID SOIL RESEARCH & REHABILITATION (US/0890-3069) [14198075] **163**

ARIEL (CN/0004-1327) [01514044] **3363**

ARIEL (ENGLISH EDITION) (IS/0004-1343) [01514045] 337, **3363**

ARIEL : KETAV ET LI-YEDIAT ERETS-YISRAEL (IS/0334-4916) [14395278] **2611**

ARIEL (LEXINGTON, KY.) (US/0895-8920) [16851741] **3363**

ARIEL : QUADRIMESTRALE DI DRAMMATURGIA DELL'ISTITUTO DI STUDI PIRANDELLIANI E SUL TEATRO ITALIANO CONTEMPORANEO (IT) [15813885] **5361**

ARIES / ASSOCIATION POUR LA RECHERCHE ET L'INFORMATION SUR L'ESOTERISME (FR/0752-2452) [11225294] **4240**

ARIES' BIOTECHNOLOGY CHEMONOMIES REPORT (US/0734-5151) [08759504] **3685**

ARINSANA : REVISTA DE LA COOPERACION INTERNACIONAL EN AREAS INDIGENAS DE AMERICA LATINA (PE) [16998693] **2721**

ARION / BOSTON UNIVERSITY (US) [23118188] 2842, **3363**

ARION (BUDAPEST, HUNGARY) (HU/0572-4082) [01739919] **3460**

ARIRANG (KO) [05084885] **2501**

ARIS (SW/0044-5711) [01811123] **337**

ARIS FUNDING REPORT / BIOMEDICAL SCIENCES (US) **3685**

ARIS FUNDING REPORT. SOCIAL AND NATURAL SCIENCES REPORT (US/0747-9921) [21098601] 5086, **5191**

ARIS FUNDING REPORTS. CREATIVE ARTS AND HUMANITIES REPORT (US) [21097036] 2842, **313**

● ARIS (PITTSBURGH, PA.) (US/1063-1305) [25895153] **291**

ARISE *SUSPENDED.* (US/0160-1792) [03822809] **1875**

ARISTOS (US/0737-0407) [09293173] **313**

● ARISTOS (TACOMA, WASH.) (US/1059-8553) [24804479] **3363**

ARISTOTELEION PANEPISTEMION THESSALONIKES. PHILOSOPHIKE SCHOLE *See* EPISTEMONIKE EPETERIS TES PHILOSOPHIKES SCHOLES **3279**

ARISTOTELES WERKE (GW) **4341**

ARISTOTELIAN SOCIETY (GREAT BRITAIN) *See* PROCEEDINGS OF THE ARISTOTELIAN SOCIETY **4358**

ARITHMETIC TEACHER *See* TEACHING CHILDREN MATHEMATICS **3538**

ARITHMETIC TEACHER, THE (US/0004-136X) [01514052] 1888, **3496**

ARITRA (II) [10513275] **2645**

ARIZONA *See* ANNUAL BUDGET TO CONTINUE CURRENT PROGRAMS **4709**

ARIZONA ADMINISTRATIVE REGISTER (US) [15087347] **4630**

ARIZONA ADVOCATE (US/0004-1386) [02254943] **2936**

ARIZONA ALL-AROUND *See* ALL-AROUND, THE **4882**

ARIZONA AND NEW MEXICO ZIP+4 STATE DIRECTORY (US) [11537186] **1144**

ARIZONA ANTHROPOLOGIST (US/1062-1601) [24121306] **231**

ARIZONA ARCHAEOLOGICAL COUNCIL NEWSLETTER (US/0890-1333) [10192733] **259**

ARIZONA ARCHITECT (US/0004-1416) [01811097] **291**

ARIZONA ASSOCIATION OF COUNTIES SALARY AND BENEFIT SURVEY (US/0096-3399) [01796035] **1653**

ARIZONA ATTORNEY (US/1040-4090) [18397729] **2936**

ARIZONA BAPTIST BEACON (ARIZONA SOUTHERN BAPTIST CONVENTION) (US/1044-0186) [19647459] **4936**

ARIZONA BEVERAGE ANALYST (US/0164-6281) [04442159] **2363**

ARIZONA BEVERAGE GUIDE (US/0746-1151) [09770815] **2363**

ARIZONA BICENTENNIAL REVIEW (US/0149-7987) [03547444] **1653**

ARIZONA BLUE CHIP ECONOMIC FORECAST (US/1042-6787) [19105854] **1463**

ARIZONA BOARD OF MEDICAL EXAMINERS *See* ANNUAL REPORT / THE ARIZONA BOARD OF MEDICAL EXAMINERS **3913**

ARIZONA. BUREAU OF VITAL RECORDS AND INFORMATION SERVICES. RESEARCH AND STATISTICAL ANALYSIS *See* INFORMATION GUIDE - ARIZONA DEPARTMENT OF HEALTH SERVICES **4784**

ARIZONA BUSINESS (US/0093-0717) [01780082] 639, **1463**

ARIZONA BUSINESS AND DEVELOPMENT *See* ARIZONA BUSINESS MAGAZINE **639**

ARIZONA BUSINESS & DEVELOPMENT (US) **639**

ARIZONA BUSINESS GAZETTE (US/0273-6950) [06821199] **639**

ARIZONA BUSINESS/INDUSTRY (US/0193-7480) [05250138] **639**

ARIZONA BUSINESS MAGAZINE (US) **639**

ARIZONA BUSINESS REPORTS (US/0743-9997) [07966979] **639**

ARIZONA CAPITOL TIMES (US/0744-7477) [08509854] **4630**

ARIZONA CATTLELOG (1985) (US/8750-8281) [11852600] **206**

ARIZONA COMPREHENSIVE BEHAVIORAL HEALTH PLAN (US/0162-6922) [04178550] **4767**

ARIZONA CONSUMER, THE (US/0739-3857) [09724203] **1293**

ARIZONA COUNCIL FOR THE DEAF *See* ANNUAL REPORT ... / ARIZONA COUNCIL FOR THE DEAF **4383**

ARIZONA DAILY STAR (US/0888-546X) [02949521] **5629**

ARIZONA DAILY SUN (FLAGSTAFF, ARIZ.) (US/1054-9536) [10668635] **5629**

ARIZONA DENTAL JOURNAL (US/0004-1459) [02257736] **1316**

ARIZONA DEPARTMENT OF WATER RESOURCES BULLETIN (US/0749-1735) [10030182] **5530**

ARIZONA. DEPT. OF ADMINISTRATION. DATA PROCESSING DIVISION *See* ANNUAL AUTOMATION REPORT TO THE ARIZONA LEGISLATURE / DATA PROCESSING DIVISION, DEPARTMENT OF ADMINISTRATION, STATE OF ARIZONA **4626**

ARIZONA. DEPT. OF ADMINISTRATION. FINANCE DIVISION *See* FEDERAL GRANT-IN-AID PROGRAMS (PHOENIX) **4723**

ARIZONA. DEPT. OF ECONOMIC SECURITY *See* ARIZONA LABOR FORCE DATA **1653**

ARIZONA. DEPT. OF ECONOMIC SECURITY *See* ANNUAL SUMMARY OF ACTIVITIES - ARIZONA DEPARTMENT OF ECONOMIC SECURITY **1650**

ARIZONA. DEPT. OF ECONOMIC SECURITY *See* ANNUAL PLANNING REPORT, CITY OF PHOENIX **1648**

ARIZONA. DEPT. OF ECONOMIC SECURITY *See* ANNUAL REPORT OF ECONOMIC SECURITY NEEDS AND RESOURCES **1649**

ARIZONA. DEPT. OF ECONOMIC SECURITY. ANNUAL REPORT *See* ANNUAL REPORT OF ECONOMIC SECURITY NEEDS AND RESOURCES **1649**

ARIZONA. DEPT. OF ECONOMIC SECURITY. BUREAU OF STATISTICAL INFORMATION, RESEARCH AND ANALYSIS *See* PIMA COUNTY EMPLOYER WAGE SURVEY **1702**

ARIZONA. DEPT. OF ECONOMIC SECURITY. BUREAU OF STATISTICAL INFORMATION, RESEARCH AND ANALYSIS *See* ARIZONA BICENTENNIAL REVIEW **1653**

ARIZONA. DEPT. OF ECONOMIC SECURITY. BUREAU OF STATISTICAL INFORMATION, RESEARCH AND ANALYSIS *See* WOMEN IN THE WORKING WORLD **5570**

ARIZONA. DEPT. OF ECONOMIC SECURITY. LABOR MARKET INFORMATION RESEARCH ANALYSIS SECTION *See* MARICOPA COUNTY LABOR MARKET REVIEW **1690**

ARIZONA. DEPT. OF ECONOMIC SECURITY. LABOR MARKET INFORMATION RESEARCH AND ANALYSIS SECTION *See* ARIZONA LABOR MARKET REVIEW **1653**

ARIZONA. DEPT. OF EDUCATION *See* SERVICES HANDBOOK - ARIZONA DEPARTMENT OF EDUCATION **1783**

ARIZONA. DEPT. OF EDUCATION *See* YEAR-ROUND EDUCATION ACTIVITIES IN THE UNITED STATES **1792**

ARIZONA. DEPT. OF EDUCATION *See* REPORT TO THE GOVERNOR - ARIZONA DEPARTMENT OF EDUCATION **1778**

ARIZONA. DEPT. OF EDUCATION *See* READING ACHIEVEMENT TEST REPORT **1903**

ARIZONA. DEPT. OF HEALTH SERVICES. PLANNING AND ANALYSIS MANAGEMENT INFORMATION SYSTEMS *See* ARIZONA SUICIDE STATISTICS **4561**

ARIZONA. DEPT. OF LIBRARY, ARCHIVES & PUBLIC RECORDS *See* CHECKLIST OF OFFICIAL PUBLICATIONS OF THE STATE OF ARIZONA **3201**

ARIZONA. DEPT. OF MINERAL RESOURCES *See* LEAD AND ZINC INDUSTRY **4007**

ARIZONA. DEPT. OF REVENUE *See* DEPARTMENT OF REVENUE ANNUAL REPORT (ARIZONA) **4642**

ARIZONA. DEPT. OF TRANSPORTATION *See* ARIZONA'S FIVE-YEAR TRANSPORTATION CONSTRUCTION PROGRAM **2018**

ARIZONA. DEPT. OF TRANSPORTATION *See* BIENNIAL STATEWIDE TRANSPORTATION NEEDS REPORT TO THE ARIZONA LEGISLATURE **5378**

ARIZONA. DEPT. OF TRANSPORTATION. PLANNING SURVEY GROUP *See* ARIZONA TRAFFIC **5439**

ARIZONA. DEPT. OF WATER RESOURCES *See* ANNUAL REPORT / ARIZONA DEPARTMENT OF WATER RESOURCES **5529**

ARIZONA DIRECTORY OF STATE REGULATORY AGENCIES FOR BUSINESSES AND OCCUPATIONS (US/0098-9746) [02242581] **4630**

ARIZONA. DIVISION OF LIBRARY, ARCHIVES, AND PUBLIC RECORDS *See* ANNUAL CHECKLIST OF PUBLICATIONS OF THE STATE OF ARIZONA **3190**

ARIZONA. DIVISION OF MENTAL HEALTH AND MENTAL RETARDATION *See* ARIZONA STATE PLAN FOR CONSTRUCTION OF MENTAL HEALTH CENTERS **4767**

ARIZONA ECONOMIC INDICATORS (TUCSON, ARIZ. : 1984) (US) [10661503] **1546**

● ARIZONA ECONOMIC TRENDS (US) [26085905] **1653**

ARIZONA EDUCATION ASSOCIATION *See* AEA ADVOCATE **1860**

ARIZONA EDUCATIONAL DIRECTORY (US/0095-005X) [01795692] **1726**

ARIZONA. ELECTED OFFICIALS' RETIREMENT SYSTEM *See* ANNUAL REPORT / ELECTED OFFICIALS' RETIREMENT SYSTEM, STATE OF ARIZONA **4627**

ARIZONA EMPLOYMENT LAW LETTER (US/1075-9611) [30332512] **3144**

ARIZONA ENGLISH BULLETIN (US/0004-1483) [04587003] **3267**

ARIZONA ENVIRONMENTAL LAW LETTER (US/1049-9342) [21356895] 2161, **2936**

ARIZONA EPISCOPALIAN, THE (US/1047-1936) [20508892] **5055**

Alphabetical Title Index — ARKANSAS

ARIZONA EVENTS CALENDAR (US/1054-8963) [23019148] **313**

ARIZONA FACTS (US/1043-1659) [18213941] **2721**

ARIZONA FARM BUREAU FEDERATION *See* ARIZONA FARM BUREAU NEWS **62**

ARIZONA FARM BUREAU NEWS (US/0274-7014) [05340702] **62**

●ARIZONA FARMER (1993) (US/1071-6521) [28492616] **62**

ARIZONA FARMER-STOCKMAN (US/8750-6432) [11625365] **62**

ARIZONA FILM THEATRE & TELEVISION *See* ON THE ARIZONA SET **386**

ARIZONA FILM, THEATRE & TELEVISION : AFT & T (US/0896-0364) [16893919] **383**

ARIZONA FRUIT AND VEGETABLE STANDARDIZATION SERVICE *See* ANNUAL REPORT, ARIZONA FRUITS AND VEGETABLES **162**

ARIZONA. GAME AND FISH COMMISSION. REPORT *See* ANNUAL REPORT - ARIZONA GAME & FISH DEPARTMENT **2294**

ARIZONA. GAME AND FISH DEPT *See* ANNUAL REPORT - ARIZONA GAME & FISH DEPARTMENT **2294**

ARIZONA GEOLOGICAL SOCIETY DIGEST (US/0066-7412) [01514093] **1366**

ARIZONA GEOLOGY (US/1045-4802) [18810151] 2134, **1366**

ARIZONA. GOVERNOR *See* EXECUTIVE BUDGET / STATE OF ARIZONA **4723**

ARIZONA GREAT OUTDOORS (US/1069-0298) [27892529] **4869**

ARIZONA GROCER (US/0004-1505) [05364172] **2327**

●ARIZONA HEALTH CARE IN PERSPECTIVE (US/1065-4054) [26604603] **4767**

ARIZONA HEALTH STATUS AND VITAL STATISTICS (US) [13614784] **4809**

ARIZONA HIGH TECH DIRECTORY (US/1055-0097) [18183483] **2036**

ARIZONA HIGHWAYS (US/0004-1521) [01514094] **5461**

ARIZONA HISTORY *SUSPENDED*. (US) [10835404] **2721**

ARIZONA HUNTER & ANGLER (US/0888-840X) [13735923] 2296, **4884**

ARIZONA IN PERSPECTIVE (US/1065-5328) [26627306] **5322**

ARIZONA INDUSTRIAL DIRECTORY (US/1071-3514) [16796219] 1598, **3475**

ARIZONA JEWISH POST (US/1053-5616) [22576323] **5629**

ARIZONA JOURNAL OF INTERNATIONAL AND COMPARATIVE LAW (US/0743-6963) [09208774] **3124**

ARIZONA LABOR FORCE DATA (US) [02243028] **1653**

ARIZONA LABOR MARKET INFORMATION NEWSLETTER *See* ARIZONA ECONOMIC TRENDS **1653**

ARIZONA LABOR MARKET NEWSLETTER (US/0743-5657) [05304817] **1653**

ARIZONA LABOR MARKET REVIEW (US) [03787649] **1653**

ARIZONA LAND & PEOPLE (US/0744-5474) [08349215] **62**

ARIZONA LAW REVIEW (US/0004-153X) [01514097] **2937**

ARIZONA LEGISLATIVE SERVICE (US/0094-4246) [01794245] **2937**

ARIZONA LIVING *CEASED*. (US/0279-6376) [06997870] **2528**

ARIZONA MOBILE CITIZEN *CEASED*. (US/0004-1564) [11543172] **2815**

ARIZONA MUSIC NEWS (US/0518-6129) [03256902] **4101**

ARIZONA NURSE (US/0004-1599) [02255221] **3851**

ARIZONA. OFFICE OF HIGHWAY SAFETY *See* ARIZONA TRAFFIC ACCIDENT SUMMARY **5439**

ARIZONA. OFFICE OF HIGHWAY SAFETY *See* SAFETY SADISTICS **4801**

ARIZONA. OFFICE OF THE AUDITOR GENERAL *See* ANNUAL REPORT OF THE AUDITOR GENERAL / STATE OF ARIZONA **4710**

ARIZONA. OFFICE OF THE STATE CLIMATOLOGIST *See* ANNUAL REPORT - ARIZONA. OFFICE OF THE STATE CLIMATOLOGIST **1420**

ARIZONA ONLINE USER GROUP (US/0894-9948) [04979162] **1274**

ARIZONA PHARMACIST, THE (US/0004-1602) [02257737] **4292**

ARIZONA PORTFOLIO, THE (US/0882-4932) [11893557] 4366, **337**

ARIZONA POST *See* ARIZONA JEWISH POST **5629**

ARIZONA PROGRESS (US/0197-5412) [01514099] **1546**

ARIZONA PUBLIC SAFETY SURVEY (US) [07514154] **4767**

ARIZONA QUARTERLY, THE (US/0004-1610) [01514101] **3363**

ARIZONA REALTOR DIGEST (US/0199-9206) [06289175] **4834**

ARIZONA REPUBLIC (US/0892-8711) [02609778] **5629**

ARIZONA REVIEW *CEASED*. (US/0004-1629) [01514102] 4630, **639**

ARIZONA. SALES AND USE TAX DIVISION. SUMMARY OF TOTAL REVENUES COLLECTED BY THE SALES AND USE TAX DIVISION *See* SUMMARY OF TOTAL REVENUES COLLECTED BY THE SALES AND USE TAX SECTION FOR THE MONTH OF FISCAL YEAR ... / ARIZONA DEPARTMENT OF REVENUE **4751**

ARIZONA SENIOR WORLD, THE (US/0270-0425) [05760703] 5178, **5629**

ARIZONA SILVER BELT (US) [02702590] **5629**

ARIZONA. STATE BOARD OF ACCOUNTANCY *See* ROSTER - ARIZONA STATE BOARD OF ACCOUNTANCY **751**

ARIZONA. STATE COMPENSATION FUND *See* ANNUAL REPORT - STATE COMPENSATION FUND (ARIZONA) **1650**

ARIZONA. STATE DEPT. OF FINANCE. PLANNING DIVISION *See* REPORT OF THE PLANNING DIVISION, STATE DEPARTMENT OF FINANCE **4681**

ARIZONA. STATE DEPT. OF PUBLIC WELFARE *See* PUBLIC WELFARE ACTIVITIES IN ARIZONA **5303**

ARIZONA. STATE ECONOMIC OPPORTUNITY OFFICE *See* ANNUAL REPORT - ARIZONA STATE ECONOMIC OPPORTUNITY OFFICE **1546**

ARIZONA STATE LAW JOURNAL (US/0164-4297) [01781492] **2937**

ARIZONA STATE PARKS BOARD *See* ANNUAL AUDIT - ARIZONA STATE PARKS BOARD **738**

ARIZONA. STATE PERSONNEL COMMISSION *See* SALARY SURVEY OF STATE GOVERNMENT EMPLOYERS (PHOENIX) **1709**

ARIZONA STATE PLAN FOR CONSTRUCTION OF MENTAL HEALTH CENTERS (US) [06797638] **4767**

ARIZONA STATE UNIVERSITY LAW FORUM (US/0742-0226) [09735443] **2937**

ARIZONA STATESMAN *See* ARIZONA STATESMAN OUTLOOK **1101**

ARIZONA STATESMAN OUTLOOK (US/0279-5183) [07919948] **1101**

ARIZONA STATISTICAL ABSTRACT : A ... DATA HANDBOOK (US/1045-4195) [06185453] **5322**

ARIZONA SUICIDE STATISTICS (US) [04901881] **4561**

ARIZONA THOROUGHBRED, THE (US/0091-4401) [05364354] **2797**

ARIZONA TRAFFIC (US/0360-7720) [02244686] **5439**

ARIZONA TRAFFIC ACCIDENT SUMMARY (US/0096-9796) [03593582] **5439**

ARIZONA TREND AZ (US/1046-476X) [20424537] **2528**

ARIZONA. UNIVERSITY. OPTICAL SCIENCES CENTER *See* OPTICAL SCIENCES CENTER NEWSLETTER **4216**

ARIZONA WILDLIFE NEWS (US/0745-0834) [08798982] **2187**

ARIZONA WILDLIFE VIEWS (US/0882-5572) [11771134] 4869, **2187**

ARIZONA'S ECONOMY (US) [04695992] **1463**

ARIZONA'S FIVE-YEAR TRANSPORTATION CONSTRUCTION PROGRAM (US/0148-5768) [03337585] **2018**

ARK (UK) [04161517] **226**

ARK RIVER REVIEW, THE (US/0044-8885) [02495581] **3363**

ARK (TORONTO) (CN/0849-1410) [23237022] **2187**

ARK VALLEY NEWS, THE (US) [12600428] **5674**

ARKA TECH (US/0004-1882) [03972137] **1089**

ARKANSAS *See* WORKERS' COMPENSATION LAW OF THE STATE OF ARKANSAS **3155**

ARKANSAS ACADEMY OF SCIENCE *See* PROCEEDINGS OF THE ARKANSAS ACADEMY OF SCIENCE **5140**

ARKANSAS AMATEUR, THE (US/0518-6617) [03759863] 231, **259**

ARKANSAS ANIMAL MORBIDITY REPORT (US/0093-142X) [04233481] **5504**

ARKANSAS ARCHAEOLOGIST, THE (US/0004-1718) [04913053] **259**

ARKANSAS ARCHEOLOGICAL SURVEY *See* ARKANSAS ARCHEOLOGICAL SURVEY RESEARCH REPORT **259**

ARKANSAS ARCHEOLOGICAL SURVEY RESEARCH REPORT (US/0277-6308) [04995593] **259**

ARKANSAS ARCHEOLOGICAL SURVEY RESEARCH SERIES (US/0882-5491) [11253693] **259**

ARKANSAS ARCHEOLOGICAL SURVEY TECHNICAL PAPER (US/0882-5483) [11956975] **259**

ARKANSAS ARTS COUNCIL *See* ANNUAL REPORT / ARKANSAS ARTS COUNCIL **312**

ARKANSAS. ATTORNEY GENERAL'S OFFICE *See* DIGEST OF OFFICIAL OPINIONS - ATTORNEY GENERAL (LITTLE ROCK) **3140**

ARKANSAS BANKER, THE (US/0004-1726) [03687360] **773**

ARKANSAS BAPTIST (1987) (US/1040-6506) [18487741] **5055**

ARKANSAS BAR ASSOCIATION *See* NEWS BULLETIN - ARKANSAS BAR ASSOCIATION **3017**

ARKANSAS BUSINESS (US/1053-6582) [11456070] **639**

ARKANSAS BUSINESS AND ECONOMIC REVIEW (US/0004-1742) [01514143] 1463, **639**

ARKANSAS BUSINESS DIRECTORY (US/1048-7190) [18008375] **639**

ARKANSAS CATTLE BUSINESS (US/0004-1750) [03114678] **206**

ARKANSAS CITY TRAVELER (ARKANSAS CITY, KAN. : 1970) (US/0888-8485) [10435589] **5674**

ARKANSAS COMPREHENSIVE MANPOWER PLAN (US/0094-1166) [01793850] **1463**

ARKANSAS DAILY LEGISLATIVE DIGEST (US) **4630**

ARKANSAS DEMOCRAT GAZETTE (US/1060-4332) [24592418] **5631**

ARKANSAS DENTISTRY (US/1056-4764) [23289844] **1316**

ARKANSAS. DEPT. OF EDUCATION. ADMINISTRATIVE SERVICES. SCHOOL CENSUS FOR THE STATE OF ARKANSAS *See* SCHOOL CENSUS FOR THE STATE OF ARKANSAS **1871**

ARKANSAS. DEPT. OF EDUCATION. DIVISION OF ADMINISTRATION SERVICES. RESEARCH AND STATISTICS *See* SCHOOL CENSUS FOR THE STATE OF ARKANSAS **1871**

ARKANSAS. DEPT. OF FINANCE AND ADMINISTRATION. OFFICE OF BUDGET *See* STATE OF ARKANSAS ... BIENNIAL BUDGET **4749**

ARKANSAS. DEPT. OF FINANCE AND ADMINISTRATION. OFFICE OF BUDGET *See* BUDGET PREPARATION MANUAL **4715**

ARKANSAS. DEPT. OF LABOR *See* ANNUAL REPORT - ARKANSAS DEPARTMENT OF LABOR **1648**

ARKANSAS. DEPT. OF PLANNING *See* PROGRAM DIRECTORY - ARKANSAS DEPARTMENT OF PLANNING **4675**

ARKANSAS. DIVISION OF ASSESSMENT COORDINATION *See* INTERIM REPORT OF THE ASSESSMENT COORDINATION DIVISION **4732**

ARKANSAS DOCUMENTS (US/0732-9202) [07484941] **408**

ARKANSAS EDUCATOR (US/0161-7753) [03789724] **1888**

ARKANSAS. EMPLOYMENT SECURITY DIVISION *See* ANNUAL REPORT FOR THE YEAR ... / STATE OF ARKANSAS, EMPLOYMENT SECURITY DIVISION, DEPARTMENT OF LABOR **1649**

ARKANSAS. EMPLOYMENT SECURITY DIVISION. RESEARCH AND ANALYSIS SECTION *See* ANNUAL PLANNING INFORMATION FOR SMSA'S IN ARKANSAS **1646**

ARKANSAS. ENVIRONMENTAL PRESERVATION COMMISSION *See* ANNUAL REPORT - ARKANSAS ENVIRONMENTAL PRESERVATION COMMISSION **2186**

ARKANSAS EPISCOPALIAN, THE (US/0890-5258) [12870565] **5055**

ARKANSAS FAMILY HISTORIAN, THE (US/0571-0472) [03734312] **2438**

ARKANSAS FARM RESEARCH (US/0004-1785) [01514145] **62**

ARKANSAS FORESTRY COMMISSION *See* ANNUAL REPORT / ARKANSAS FORESTRY COMMISSION **2374**

ARKANSAS GAME AND FISH *See* ARKANSAS WILDLIFE **2187**

ARKANSAS GAME AND FISH COMMISSION *See* HUNTER CASUALTY REPORT / ARKANSAS GAME AND FISH COMMISSION **4856**

ARKANSAS
Alphabetical Title Index

ARKANSAS GAZETTE INDEX (US/0273-4001) [07036598] **2528**

ARKANSAS. GENERAL ASSEMBLY. DIVISION OF LEGISLATIVE AUDIT *See* AUDIT REPORT, DEPARTMENT OF ARKANSAS NATURAL AND CULTURAL HERITAGE, ARKANSAS TERRITORIAL CAPITOL RESTORATION COMMISSION **4712**

ARKANSAS. GENERAL ASSEMBLY. DIVISION OF LEGISLATIVE AUDIT *See* AUDIT REPORT, DEPARTMENT OF PARKS AND TOURISM, MONUMENTS AND HISTORICAL SITES DIVISION, ARKANSAS TERRITORIAL CAPITOL RESTORATION **4712**

ARKANSAS GEOLOGICAL COMMISSION *See* INFORMATION CIRCULAR - ARKANSAS GEOLOGICAL COMMISSION **1382**

ARKANSAS GEOLOGICAL COMMISSION *See* LIST OF PUBLICATIONS / ARKANSAS GEOLOGICAL COMMISSION **1363**

ARKANSAS GROCER (US/0004-1815) [03972285] **2327**

●ARKANSAS HEALTH CARE IN PERSPECTIVE (US/1065-4062) [26604639] **4767**

ARKANSAS HEALTH MANPOWER STATISTICS : LICENSED PRACTICAL NURSES (US/0272-586X) [06432415] 1654, 3851, **3654**

ARKANSAS HEALTH MANPOWER STATISTICS : REGISTERED NURSES (US/0272-5878) [06432397] 1654, 3851, **3654**

ARKANSAS HIGHWAY COMMISSION ANNUAL REPORT TO THE GOVERNOR OF ARKANSAS (US) [07192600] **5439**

ARKANSAS HISTORICAL QUARTERLY, THE (US/0004-1823) [01514148] **2721**

ARKANSAS IN PERSPECTIVE (US/1065-5336) [26627326] **5322**

ARKANSAS JOURNAL (LITTLE ROCK, ARK. : 1985) (US/0883-8984) [12195425] **1598**

ARKANSAS LAW NOTES (US/1052-293X) [10001147] **2937**

ARKANSAS LAW REVIEW (US/0004-1831) [01796791] **2937**

ARKANSAS LAWYER (US/0571-0502) [01514151] **2937**

ARKANSAS LEGAL DIRECTORY, THE (US) [07810374] **2937**

ARKANSAS LIBRARIES (US/0004-184X) [01514152] **3191**

ARKANSAS, LOUISIANA AND MISSISSIPPI LEGAL DIRECTORY *See* MISSISSIPPI LEGAL DIRECTORY, THE **3011**

ARKANSAS, LOUISIANA, AND MISSISSIPPI LEGAL DIRECTORY *See* ARKANSAS LEGAL DIRECTORY, THE **2937**

ARKANSAS LP NEWS (US/0044-8893) [03972311] **4251**

ARKANSAS. MANPOWER COUNCIL *See* ARKANSAS COMPREHENSIVE MANPOWER PLAN **1654**

ARKANSAS MENTAL HEALTH SERVICES *See* ARKANSAS MENTAL HEALTH SERVICES [BIENNIAL REPORT] **4767**

ARKANSAS MENTAL HEALTH SERVICES [BIENNIAL REPORT] (US) [04303736] **4767**

ARKANSAS MUSEUM SERVICES *See* GRANTS / ARKANSAS MUSEUM SERVICES **4088**

ARKANSAS NATURAL HERITAGE COMMISSION *See* PROGRESS REPORT - ARKANSAS NATURAL HERITAGE COMMISSION **4171**

ARKANSAS NURSING NEWS (US) **3851**

ARKANSAS. OFFICE OF SECRETARY OF STATE *See* HISTORICAL REPORT OF THE SECRETARY OF STATE, ARKANSAS **4476**

ARKANSAS. OFFICE OF TITLE XX SERVICE *See* COMPREHENSIVE ANNUAL SERVICES PROGRAM PLAN - (ARKANSAS) **5280**

ARKANSAS. OFFICE OF TITLE XX SERVICES *See* PROPOSED TITLE XX COMPREHENSIVE SERVICES PROGRAM PLAN **5302**

ARKANSAS. OFFICE OF TITLE XX SERVICES *See* PROPOSED COMPREHENSIVE ANNUAL SERVICES PROGRAM PLAN **5302**

ARKANSAS OIL AND GAS STATISTICAL BULLETIN *See* STATISTICAL BULLETIN **4279**

ARKANSAS PERSONAL INCOME HANDBOOK (US) [07160172] **4711**

ARKANSAS PHILOLOGICAL ASSOCIATION *See* PUBLICATIONS OF THE ARKANSAS PHILOLOGICAL ASSOCIATION **3312**

ARKANSAS PRESERVATION (US) **2187**

ARKANSAS. PUBLIC SERVICE COMMISSION *See* ANNUAL REPORT - STATE OF ARKANSAS, PUBLIC SERVICE COMMISSION **4759**

ARKANSAS REGISTER, THE (US) [03405272] **4630**

ARKANSAS SOCIAL SERVICES ANNUAL REPORT (US/0092-0215) [01788617] **5273**

ARKANSAS. SOCIAL SERVICES. RESEARCH AND STATISTICS *See* ARKANSAS SOCIAL SERVICES ANNUAL REPORT **5273**

ARKANSAS SOCIAL STUDIES TEACHER, THE (US/0196-8122) [03958094] 1888, **5191**

ARKANSAS SPORTSMAN (US/0744-4184) [08256702] 4884, **4869**

ARKANSAS STATE AGENCIES DIRECTORY (US) [30592601] **4630**

ARKANSAS STATE AND COUNTY ECONOMIC DATA (US) [12832484] **4711**

ARKANSAS STATE DIRECTORY (US) [02933364] **4630**

ARKANSAS STATE HEALTH PLANNING AND DEVELOPMENT AGENCY *See* STATE HEALTH PLAN (LITTLE ROCK, ARK.) **4804**

ARKANSAS. STATE HIGHWAY COMMISSION *See* ARKANSAS HIGHWAY COMMISSION ANNUAL REPORT TO THE GOVERNOR OF ARKANSAS **5439**

ARKANSAS. STATE HIGHWAY DEPT *See* YOUR HIGHWAY DEPARTMENT, ARKANSAS **5446**

ARKANSAS STATE HORTICULTURAL SOCIETY *See* PROCEEDINGS OF THE ANNUAL MEETING / ARKANSAS STATE HORTICULTURAL SOCIETY **2429**

ARKANSAS STATE HOSPITAL. BIENNIAL REPORT OF THE ARKANSAS STATE HOSPITAL FOR THE PERIOD JULY 1 ... TO JUNE . *See* ARKANSAS MENTAL HEALTH SERVICES [BIENNIAL REPORT] **4767**

ARKANSAS STATE LIBRARY *See* INFORMATION FOR DECISION-MAKING, ANNUAL PROGRAM FOR LIBRARY DEVELOPMENT IN ARKANSAS **3215**

ARKANSAS STATE LIBRARY. DOCUMENTS SERVICES *See* ARKANSAS DOCUMENTS **408**

ARKANSAS STATE PRESS (US) [10766826] **2255**

ARKANSAS STATISTICAL ABSTRACT / PREPARED BY THE STATE DATA CENTER, UNIVERSITY OF ARKANSAS AT LITTLE ROCK (US) [15081207] 1463, **2528**

ARKANSAS TECH UNIVERSITY *See* ARKA TECH **1089**

ARKANSAS TECH UNIVERSITY. DEPT. OF HISTORY *See* OCCASIONAL PAPERS - DEPARTMENT OF HISTORY, ARKANSAS TECH UNIVERSITY **2624**

ARKANSAS TIMES (US/0164-6273) [04442064] **3363**

ARKANSAS. TREASURER OF STATE *See* BIENNIAL REPORT OF THE TREASURER OF STATE OF THE STATE OF ARKANSAS FOR THE BIENNIAL PERIOD BEGINNING JULY 1 ... AND ENDING JUNE 30 ... **4713**

ARKANSAS VALLEY JOURNAL (US/0004-1890) [03972843] **63**

ARKANSAS WATER RESOURCES RESEARCH CENTER *See* PUBLICATION / ARKANSAS WATER RESOURCES RESEARCH CENTER **5537**

ARKANSAS. WATERWAYS COMMISSION *See* BIENNIAL REPORT - ARKANSAS WATERWAYS COMMISSION **5447**

ARKANSAS-WHITE-RED BASINS INTER-AGENCY COMMITTEE *See* ANNUAL REPORT - ARKANSAS-WHITE-RED BASINS INTER-AGENCY COMMITTEE **2087**

ARKANSAS-WHITE-RED BASINS INTER-AGENCY COMMITTEE *See* MINUTES OF THE MEETING - ARKANSAS-WHITE-RED BASINS INTER-AGENCY COMMITTEE **5536**

ARKANSAS-WHITE-RED BASINS INTER-AGENCY COMMITTEE. STANDING COMMITTEE ON EXCHANGE OF PROGRAM INFORMATION *See* PREAUTHORIZATION OF PLANNING ACTIVITIES OF THE BUREAU OF RECLAMATION, THE CORPS OF ENGINEERS, AND THE SOIL CONSERVATION SERVICE **5537**

●ARKANSAS WILDLIFE (US/1063-0953) [25685693] 4869, **2187**

ARKEOLOGIA SUOMESSA (FI/0784-235X) [20939740] **260**

ARKEOLOGISKE SKRIFTER (NO) [05321083] **260**

ARKEOLOJI-SANAT TARIHI DERGISI (TU) [16503551] **337**

ARKHEOGRAFICHESKII EZHEGODNIK / AKADEMIIA NAUK SSSR, OTDELENIE ISTORICHESKIKH NAUK, ARKHEOGRAFICHESKAIA KOMISSIIA (RU/0571-0626) [01514155] **260**

ARKHEOLOGICHESKIE ISSLEDOVANIIA V MOLDAVII V ... GG. / AKADEMIIA NAUK MOLDAVSKOI SSR, OTDEL ETNOGRAFII I ISKUSSTVOVEDENIIA (MV) [10522269] **260**

ARKHEOLOGICHESKIE OTKRYTIIA NA NOVOSTROIKAKH (RU) [19862699] **260**

ARKHEOLOHIIA (UN/0235-3490) [20005787] **260**

ARKHIMEDES (FI/0004-1920) [06148296] **3496**

ARKHITEKTURA I STROITELSTVO BELORUSSII (BW) [24860958] **291**

ARKHITEKTURA I STROITELSTVO ROSSII : AS (RU/0235-7259) [19596790] 599, **291**

ARKHITEKTURA UKRAINY (UN) [24493868] **291**

ARKHITEKTURAH (IS) [12860450] **291**

ARKHITEKTURNOE NASLEDSTVO (RU/0320-0841) [01514161] **291**

ARKHITEKTURNOE TVORCHESTVO SSSR (RU) [02341719] **291**

ARKHIV AKADEMII NAUK SSSR (RU) [08158175] **5086**

ARKHIV ANATOMII, GISTOLOGII I EMBRIOLOGII (RU/0004-1947) [01514162] 532, 541, **3679**

●ARKHIV RUSSKOI ISTORII / TSENTRALYI GOSUDARSTVENNYI ARKHIV DREVNYKH AKTOV (RU) [26449970] **2480**

ARKHIYON HA-MERKAZI LE-TOLDOT HA-AM HA-YEHUDI *See* NEWSLETTER - CENTRAL ARCHIVES FOR THE HISTORY OF THE JEWISH PEOPLE **2482**

ARKHIYON HA-TSIYONI HA-MERKAZI (JERUSALEM) *See* SIFRUT HA-TSIYONIT / ZIONIST LITERATURE, HA- **4997**

ARKITEKTEN (DK/0004-198X) [01514166] **291**

ARKITEKTNYTT (NO/0004-1998) [I00041998] **292**

ARKITEKTUR DK (DK/0004-2013) [03958508] **292**

ARKITEKTUR OG SKIPULAG (IC/1016-7293) [19852092] **292**

ARKITEKTUR (STOCKHOLM, SWEDEN : 1959) (SW/0004-2021) [01514168] **292**

ARKITEKTURMUSEET (STOCKHOLM, SWEDEN) *See* ARSBOK / ARKITEKTURMUSEET **292**

ARKIV (DK/0004-203X) [04646541] **2480**

ARKIV (SW) [09992449] **1654**

ARKIV FOR DET FYSISKE SEMINAR I TRONDHEIM (NO/0365-2459) [02082590] **4398**

ARKIV FOR LUFTRETT (NO/0004-2072) [01514172] **2937**

ARKIV FOR NORDISK FILOLOGI (SW/0066-7668) [01514175] **3267**

ARKIV FUER MATEMATIK (SW/0004-2080) [00855484] **3496**

ARKKITEHTI (FI/0004-2129) [01514178] **292**

ARKKITEHTUURIKILPAILUJA (FI/0066-7676) [01514179] **292**

ARKOLOGISKE UDGRAVNINGER I DANMARK / RIGSANTIKVARENS ARKOLOGISKE SEKRETARIAT (DK/0901-0815) [18058491] **260**

ARL (US/1050-6098) [21579815] **3191**

ARL ANNUAL SALARY SURVEY (US/0361-5669) [01962271] **1654**

ARL STATISTICS (US/0147-2135) [02622851] 3192, **3257**

ARLINGTON ADVOCATE (US) [09225840] **5687**

ARLINGTON CATHOLIC HERALD (US/0361-3712) [02246542] **5024**

ARLINGTON CITIZEN JOURNAL (US) [17013426] **5746**

ARLINGTON HEIGHTS HERALD (US) [16769997] **5658**

ARLINGTON HISTORICAL MAGAZINE, THE (US/0066-7684) [01802280] **2721**

ARLINGTON JOURNAL (ALEXANDRIA. 1980), THE (US/0273-6381) [06780364] **5758**

ARLINGTON NEWS (1989) (US/1044-1174) [19687250] **5746**

ARLINGTON TIMES, THE (US) [17359624] **5760**

ARLIS/ANZ NEWS (AT/0157-4043) [10628254] **408**

ARLIS/NA MEMBERSHIP DIRECTORY (US) [02239792] **3192**

ARLIS/NA UPDATE (US/0743-040X) [10527127] 313, **3192**

ARLIS/NORTH AMERICA *See* ARLIS/NA MEMBERSHIP DIRECTORY **3192**

ARMADA INTERNATIONAL (SZ/0252-9793) [05928321] **4035**

ARMADA TIMES (US/0890-3751) [14227138] **5691**

ARMAMENT & DEFENSE SURVEY (US/0195-8232) [05669619] **4035**

ARMARIUM CODICUM INSIGNIUM (BE) [17974721] **2676**

ARMAS E TROFEUS (PO) [07934421] **2438**

ARMAS Y LETRAS - UNIVERSIDAD DE NUEVO LEON (MX/0185-9811) [02257752] **1089**

ARMAZENAGEM (BL) [02580495] **63**

ARMCHAIR DETECTIVE, THE (US) [08556372] **3363**

ARMCHAIR DETECTIVE, THE (US/0004-217X) [01514186] **3363**

ARMCHAIR RESEARCHERS. QUERIES & BOOK REVIEWS, THE (US/8756-6842) [11501980] **2438**

ARMED FORCES (SA) [03411342] **4035**

ARMED FORCES AND SOCIETY (US/0095-327X) [01796471] 5240, **4035**

ARMED FORCES COMPTROLLER, THE (US/0004-2188) [01707011] **4035**

ARMED FORCES INSTITUTE OF PATHOLOGY (U.S.) *See* AFIP LETTER **3892**

ARMED FORCES JOURNAL INTERNATIONAL (US/0196-3597) [03157857] **4035**

ARMED FORCES PERSONNEL AND CIVILIANS IN DEFENCE ESTABLISHMENT BOOK ON SERVICE CONDITIONS (II) [01713690] **4036**

ARMED FORCES RADIOBIOLOGY RESEARCH INSTITUTE (U.S.) *See* ANNUAL REPORT ON AFRRI RESEARCH **494**

ARMEE ET DEFENSE (FR/0004-2242) [08251213] **4036**

ARMEE RUNDSCHAU (FR) **4036**

ARMEES D'AUJOURD'HUI (FR) [03647430] **4036**

ARMEES ET DEFENSE (FR) **4036**

ARMEMENT (FR) **4036**

ARMEMENT : REVUE DE LA DELEGATION GENERALE POUR L'ARMEMENT, L' (FR) [22785001] **4036**

ARMENIA TODAY (RU/0004-2293) [05021177] **2255**

ARMENIAN CAUSE, THE (CN/0826-2667) [11360430] 4516, **2645**

ARMENIAN MIRROR-SPECTATOR, THE (US/0004-234X) [08835210] **5687**

ARMENIAN OBSERVER, THE (US/0044-894X) [03972386] **5633**

ARMENIAN REVIEW, THE (US/0004-2366) [02029471] **2501**

ARMENIAN STUDIES (LE/0304-8624) [01799508] **2645**

ARMENIAN WEEKLY, THE (US/0004-2374) [03291832] **5687**

ARMIIA *CEASED.* (RU) [24472070] **4036**

ARMJANSKIJ HIMICESKIJ ZURNAL (AI/0515-9628) [05365221] **961**

ARMONIA DI VOCI (IT) [05061838] **4101**

ARMOR (US/0004-2420) [04759508] **4036**

ARMOUR CHRONICLE, THE (US/8750-2488) [11173907] **5743**

ARMS AND ARMOR ANNUAL (US/0093-6014) [01784450] **4036**

ARMS COLLECTING (CN/0380-982X) [03202259] **2771**

ARMS CONTROL AND DISARMAMENT AGREEMENTS (US) [06751540] **4036**

ARMS CONTROL, DISARMAMENT AND INTERNATIONAL SECURITY *CEASED.* (US/0899-6547) [18189248] **4036**

●ARMS CONTROL DISCUSSION PAPERS (US/1065-6383) [26661645] **4036**

ARMS CONTROL (LONDON, ENGLAND) (UK/0144-0381) [07622309] **4036**

ARMS CONTROL REPORTER, THE (US/0886-3490) [09160157] **4516**

ARMS CONTROL TODAY (US/0196-125X) [02197658] **3124**

ARMS GAZETTE (US/0197-2863) [04788352] **4036**

ARMS REGISTER (US) **755**

ARMSTRONG CHRONICLES (US/0898-1329) [17700964] **2438**

ARMSTRONG LABORATORY (U.S.). HUMAN RESOURCES DIRECTORATE *See* NEWSLETTER / ARMSTRONG LABORATORY HUMAN RESOURCES DIRECTORATE, HUMAN SYSTEMS DIVISION (AFSC) **4052**

ARMSTRONG OIL DIRECTORIES, LOUISIANA, TEXAS GULF COAST, EAST TEXAS, ARK. AND MISS (US/0273-4931) [06055712] **4251**

ARMSTRONG OIL DIRECTORIES, ROCKY MOUNTAIN AND CENTRAL UNITED STATES (US/0273-5229) [06105264] **4251**

ARMSTRONG OIL DIRECTORIES, TEXAS AND SOUTHEASTERN NEW MEXICO (US/0277-2280) [06104764] **4251**

ARMY, AIR FORCE AND NAVAL AIR STATISTICAL RECORD (UK/0004-2463) 12, **4036**

ARMY AVIATION (US/0004-248X) [09295833] 4036, **12**

ARMY BATTLEFIELD ENVIRONMENT / US ARMY CORPS OF ENGINEERS (US) [25454609] **4036**

●ARMY CHAPLAINCY : PROFESSIONAL BULLETIN OF THE UNIT MINISTRY TEAM, THE (US) [28127164] **4036**

ARMY CLUB SYSTEM ANNUAL REPORT, FISCAL YEAR ... (US/0270-9848) [07606850] **4036**

ARMY COMMUNICATOR, THE (US/0362-5745) [02304247] 2036, **4036**

ARMY HISTORY (US) [21069441] **4036**

ARMY LAWYER, THE (US/0364-1287) [01086688] **3182**

ARMY LOGISTICIAN (US/0004-2528) [01514210] **4036**

ARMY MAN (US/1048-5015) [20959933] **2485**

ARMY MEDICAL SERVICES MAGAZINE (UK) [01645421] 4036, **3552**

ARMY MORALE, WELFARE, AND RECREATION (US/0742-728X) [09432790] **4036**

ARMY MOTORS (US/0195-5632) [05518363] 5377, **4036**

ARMY/NAVY STORE & OUTDOOR MERCHANDISER (US/0160-7278) [03737945] **1081**

ARMY OFFICER'S GUIDE, THE (US/0148-6799) [03354446] **4036**

ARMY QUARTERLY AND DEFENCE JOURNAL, THE (UK/0004-2552) [02338035] **4036**

ARMY RD & A BULLETIN (US/0892-8657) [15274362] **4036**

ARMY RECREATION AND TRAVEL GUIDE (US/0094-9736) [01795464] **4036**

ARMY RESERVE MAGAZINE (US/0004-2579) [06208057] **4036**

ARMY TIMES (US/0004-2595) [01514213] **4037**

ARMY TRAINER (US/0731-3144) [08069800] **4037**

ARMY (WASHINGTON. 1956) (US/0004-2455) [05838019] **4037**

ARN MESSAGER (CN/0714-5705) [09106588] **5780**

ARNEWS ANNUAL REPORT (CN/1188-2891) [25079396] 2187, **2375**

ARNOLD ARBORETUM *See* DIRECTOR'S REPORT FOR THE ARNOLD ARBORETUM, THE **508**

ARNOLD G. RUDOFF'S TAX SHELTER DIRECTORY (US/0732-491X) [08360808] 4711, **891**

ARNOLD SCHOENBERG INSTITUTE *See* JOURNAL OF THE ARNOLD SCHOENBERG INSTITUTE **4126**

ARNOLDIA (JAMAICA PLAIN) (US/0004-2633) [02444988] 500, **2409**

ARNOVA NEWS (US) [26995787] **5274**

AROGYA (II/0253-682X) [09252747] **3552**

AROIDEANA (US/0197-4033) [04247530] **2409**

AROMA-CHOLOGY REVIEW (US) **5086**

AROMATIKKUSU (JA/0365-6187) [02444991] **961**

AROUND EUROPE (BE) **2513**

AROUND THE BEND (RICHMOND, TEX.) (US/0749-517X) [11092749] **2438**

AROUND THE GLOBE (SJ) [06495479] **2611**

ARPEL (IT) [03304897] **3183**

ARPENTEURS & GEOMETRES (CN/0228-6637) [07869877] **2555**

ARPLA LABOUR ADMINISTRATION BULLETIN (TH) [13830984] **1654**

ARQ (CL/0716-0852) [11927072] **292**

ARQ : ARCHITECTURE/QUEBEC (CN/0710-1163) [08332585] **292**

ARQIOVPS DPS TROBIMAOS DE ALCADA : ORGAO OFICIAL DOS TRIBUNAIS DE ALCADA DO ESTADO DO RIO DE JANEIRO (BL) [10579005] **2937**

ARQUEOLOGIA (MX/0187-6074) [19072050] **260**

ARQUEOLOGIA (PORTO) (PO/0870-2306) [08144270] **260**

ARQUIPELAGO. CIENCIAS DA NATUREZA (PO/0870-6581) [22477600] **4162**

ARQUITECTO PERUANO, EL (PE/0004-2676) [04678693] **292**

ARQUITECTOS DE MEXICO (MX) [02793312] **292**

ARQUITECTURA (UY) [01514218] **292**

ARQUITECTURA CUBA (CU/1010-3821) [06020230] **292**

ARQUITECTURA (MADRID, 1959) (SP/0004-2706) [03580083] **292**

ARQUITECTURA/MEXICO *SUSPENDED.* (MX/0004-2684) [01514219] **292**

ARQUITECTURA VIVA (SP/0214-1256) [20575203] **292**

ARQUITECTURA Y DECORACION HOSTELERIA *CEASED.* (SP) **292**

ARQUITECTURA Y DECORACION OFICINAS *CEASED.* (SP) **292**

ARQUITECTURA Y URBANISMO (CU) [09506930] **292**

ARQUITETURA DO BRASIL : AB (BL) [09435947] **292**

ARQUIVIO DE PATOLOGIA (PO/0004-2714) [01514221] **3893**

ARQUIVO BRASILEIRO DE MEDICINA VETERINARIA E ZOOTECNIA (BL/0102-0935) [10139384] **5504**

ARQUIVO COIMBRAO (BOLETIM DA BIBLIOTECA MUNICIPAL) (PO/0871-6102) [03296749] **3192**

ARQUIVO DE BEJA (PO) [06574641] **2480**

ARQUIVOS (BL) [03218035] **2721**

ARQUIVOS (PO/0412-8877) [03178097] **4292**

ARQUIVOS BRASILEIROS DE CARDIOLOGIA (BL/0066-782X) [06410464] **3699**

ARQUIVOS BRASILEIROS DE CIRURGIA DIGESTIVA ABCD: BRAZILIAN ARCHIVES OF DIGESTIVE SURGERY (BL/0102-6720) [18689681] **3960**

ARQUIVOS BRASILEIROS DE ENDOCRINOLOGIA E METABOLOGIA (BL/0004-2730) [01588377] **3726**

ARQUIVOS BRASILEIROS DE MEDICINA (BL/0365-0723) [01587495] **3552**

ARQUIVOS BRASILEIROS DE OFTALMOLOGIA (BL/0004-2749) [09883257] **3872**

ARQUIVOS CATARINENSES DE MEDICINA (BR/0004-2773) [04103898] **3552**

ARQUIVOS DA ESCOLA DE MEDICINA VETERINARIA DA UNIVERSIDADE FEDERAL DA BAHIA (BL/0100-2597) [07107007] **5504**

ARQUIVOS DA MATERNIDADE DR. ALFREDO DA COSTA (PO/0871-4592) [23274555] **3757**

ARQUIVOS DA UNIVERSIDADE FEDERAL RURAL DO RIO DE JANEIRO (BL/0100-2481) [01192209] **63**

ARQUIVOS DE ANGOLA (AO/0004-2781) [02257764] **2638**

ARQUIVOS DE BIOLOGIA E TECNOLOGIA (BL/0365-0979) [01514223] **443**

ARQUIVOS DE GASTROENTEROLOGIA (BL/0004-2803) [02257765] **3743**

ARQUIVOS DE MEDICINA : REVISTA DE CIENCIA E ARTE MEDICAS (PO/0871-3413) [25962525] **3552**

ARQUIVOS DE NEURO-PSIQUIATRIA (BL/0004-282X) [01514228] 3921, **3827**

ARQUIVOS DE REUMATOLOGIA E DOENCAS OSTEO-ARTICU-LARES (PO/0871-4304) [25199559] **3803**

ARQUIVOS DE ZOOLOGIA (BL/0066-7870) [03732240] **5576**

ARQUIVOS DO CENTRO CULTURAL PORTUGUES (FR/0590-966X) [04802236] **2676**

ARQUIVOS DO CENTRO DE ESTUDOS DO CURSO DE ODONTOLOGIA. UNIVERSIDADE FEDERAL DE MINAS GERAIS (BL/0004-2838) [04454936] **1316**

ARQUIVOS DO INSTITUTO BACTERIOLOGICO CAMARA PESTANA (LISBOA) (PO/0365-2998) [01753289] **560**

ARQUIVOS DO INSTITUTO DE DIREITO SOCIAL (BL) [07586798] **2937**

ARQUIVOS DO MINISTERIO DA JUSTICA (BL/0100-1213) [02240029] **2937**

ARQUIVOS DO MUSEU BOCAGE. NOVA SERIE (PO/0871-4843) [17935543] 5576, **4162**

ARQUIVOS DO MUSEU DE HISTORIA NATURAL (BL/0102-4272) [02242796] **4162**

ARQUIVOS DO MUSEU NACIONAL (BL/0365-4508) [01307720] **4084**

ARQUIVOS - FACULDADE DE VETERINARIA, UFRGS (BL) [05883359] **5504**

ARQUIVOS — Alphabetical Title Index

ARQUIVOS FLUMINENSES DE MEDICINA VETERINARIA (BL/0102-7794) [17279248] **5504**

ARQUIVOS PORTUGUESES DE OTORRINOLARINGOLOGIA E DE PATOLOGIA CERVICO-FACIAL (PO) [19022013] **3886**

ARRABONA (HU/0571-1304) [01749618] **337**

ARRB RESEARCH REPORT ARR (AT/0158-071X) [06899576] 5439, **5377**

ARREARAGE TABLES OF AMOUNTS DUE AND UNPAID 90 DAYS OR MORE ON FOREIGN CREDITS OF THE UNITED STATES GOVERNMENT (1979) (US/0884-2221) [08069450] **4711**

ARRECADACAO DOS TRIBUTOS FEDERAIS / MINISTERIO DA FAZENDA, SECRETARIA DA RECEITA FEDERAL, CENTRO DE INFORMACOES ECONOMICO-FISCAIS (BL) [03114562] **4711**

ARREDARE LA TAVOLA (IT) **5551**

ARREDO. TESSILI-COMPLEMENTI (IT/0393-4462) [103934462] **5348**

ARREST LAW BULLETIN (US/8755-8300) [06122960] **3158**

ARRETS DU TRIBUNAL FEDERAL SUISSE. RECUEIL OFFICIEL (SZ) [02256289] **2937**

ARRIBA (COMMITTEE FOR HISPANIC ARTS AND RESEARCH, AUSTIN, TX.) (US) [08105719] **313**

ARRIS (ATLANTA, GA.) (US/1048-5945) [20487064] **292**

ARRL ANTENNA BOOK, THE (US/1048-1699) [03507345] **1126**

ARRL HANDBOOK FOR THE RADIO AMATEUR, THE (US/0890-3565) [11527380] **1126**

ARRL REPEATER DIRECTORY (US/0190-3632) [04710554] **1126**

ARROWSMITH STAR, THE (CN/0319-5589) [02442293] **5780**

ARROYO (TUCSON, ARIZ.) (US/1058-1383) [17547705] **5530**

ARROZ EN LAS AMERICAS (CK/0120-2634) [21253319] **63**

ARROZ / FEDERACION SINDICAL DE AGRICULTORES ARROCEROS DE ESPANA, DEPARTMENTO DE INFORMATION, PRENSA Y PROGAGANDE (SP) [05368388] **164**

ARS (US/1052-5386) [12615991] **63**

ARS (XO/0044-9008) [05627933] **337**

ARS 41 (US/0498-2231) [05786845] **63**

ARS 43 / AGRICULTURAL RESEARCH SERVICE, UNITED STATES DEPARTMENT OF AGRICULTURE (US/0498-224X) [01520496] **63**

ARS AEQUI (NE/0004-2870) [01514240] **2937**

ARS BAVARICA (GW/0341-8480) [04760823] **337**

ARS CERAMICA (US/1043-3317) [12203891] **2586**

ARS COMBINATORIA (CN/0381-7032) [03258528] **3496**

ARS DECORATIVA (HU) [05592606] **370**

ARS DIRECTORY / UNITED STATES DEPARTMENT OF AGRICULTURE, AGRICULTURAL RESEARCH SERVICE (US) [10963852] **63**

ARS-H (US/0098-2946) [02630644] **63**

ARS HUNGARICA (HU/0133-1531) [03577530] **337**

ARS LYRICA (US/1043-3848) [08840887] 4101, **3460**

ARS MEDICI, MONATSSCHRIFT FUER ALLGEMEINMEDIZIN (SZ/0004-2897) [01514242] **3552**

ARS MUSICA DENVER (US/1058-7500) [20078222] **4101**

ARS NOVA (SA) [04718120] **4101**

ARS ORGANI (GW/0004-2919) [03101011] **4101**

ARS ORIENTALIS (US/0571-1371) [01514243] **337**

ARS PHARMACEUTICA (SP/0004-2927) [01514244] **4292**

ARS POPULI (XO/0231-908X) [0231908X] **337**

ARS PRAEHISTORICA (SP) [10370922] **260**

ARS ROSACEAE (US/0747-8976) [10830199] **2409**

ARS TEXTRINA (CN/0824-9091) [11085038] **5348**

ARS VETERINARIA (BL/0102-6380) [15972176] **5504**

ARS VITRARIA (XR/0231-5890) [08881070] **2586**

ARSBERATTELSE - NORDFORSK (SW) [04513153] **5086**

ARSBERATTELSE - SIK-SVENSKA LIVSMEDELSINSTITUTET (SW) [06427773] **2327**

ARSBERETNING (DK) [22145658] **200**

ARSBERETNING (DK) [19483063] **1910**

ARSBERETNING (DK) [19483178] **1546**

ARSBERETNING (DK) [20271042] **5377**

ARSBERETNING (DK/0902-0608) [20027048] **4037**

ARSBERETNING - AARHUS UNIVERSITET. GEOLOGISK INSTITUT (DK/0106-8202) [09031044] **1366**

ARSBERETNING ANGAENDE SUNDHEDSTILSTANDEN I KBENHAVN *See* SUNDHEDSTILSTANDEN I KBENHAVN; STADSLGENS ARSBERETNING **4804**

ARSBERETNING / DANTEST (DK) [10129350] **4029**

ARSBERETNING - DENMARK-AMERIKA FONDET (DK) [03527516] **2721**

ARSBERETNING / FORBRUGERSTYRELSEN (DK) [23878482] **1293**

ARSBERETNING - GEOLOGISK CENTRALINSTITUT (KBENHAVN) (DK/0303-2310) [04324709] **1366**

ARSBERETNING - GRONLANDS GEOLOGISKE UNDERSOGELSE (DK) [02749876] 1366, **860**

ARSBERETNING - JUSTERVSENET (DK) [05739463] **4029**

ARSBERETNING / KBENHAVNS SPORVE *See* BERETNING OG REGNSKAB - KBENHAVNS SPORVEJE **5377**

ARSBERETNING / LABORATORY FOR SEMICONDUCTOR TECHNOLOGY (DK) [11446050] **2036**

ARSBERETNING / NORGES GEOGRAFISKE OPPMALING (NO) [09404527] **2555**

ARSBERETNING - OLJEDIREKTORATET (NO) [03027615] **2134**

ARSBERETNING / ROSKILDE UNIVERSITETSCENTER, INSTITUT FOR GEOGRAFI, SAMFUNDSANALYSE OG DATALOGI (DK/0106-2778) [11119249] **5191**

ARSBERETNING / TROMS MUSEUM (NO/0332-7647) [10149967] **4084**

ARSBERETNING / UNIVERSITETET I TRONDHEIM, VITENSKAPSMUSEET (NO) [19032751] 4084, **4162**

ARSBERETNINGER FRA AFDELINGER, INSTITUTTER OG LABORATORIER VED DEN POLYTEKNISKE LREANSTALT, DANMARKS TEKNISKE HJSKOLE GLDENDE FOR PERIODEN FRA ... / DEN POLYTEKNISKE LREANSTALT, DANMARKS TEKNISKE HJSKOLE (DK) [28828587] **1875**

ARSBOK / ARKITEKTURMUSEET (SW/0280-2686) [20818319] **292**

ARSBOK FOR STATENS KONSTMUSEER (SW/0349-6236) [12905075] **337**

ARSBOK FOR SVERIGES KOMMUNER (SW/0065-020X) [01607186] **4696**

ARSBOK / KUNGL. HUMANISTISKA VETENSKAPS-SAMFUNDET I UPPSALA (SW/0349-0416) [09872000] **2842**

ARSBOK - RIKSSKATTEVERKET (SW) [03049843] **4711**

ARSBOK - VETENSKAPSSOCIETETEN I LUND (SW/0349-053X) [01769045] 3363, **1074**

ARSC JOURNAL (US) [15355304] **5315**

ARSIS (FI/0780-9859) [107809859] **313**

ARSLEDIGHEDEN (DK) [19817130] **1654**

ARSMELDING - NORGES GEOLOGISKE UNDERSKELSE (NO) [02474956] **1366**

ARSMELDING - NORGES VETERINRHGSKOLE (NO/0801-9533) [19690388] **5504**

ARSON REPORTER (US) [09045838] **2288**

ARSRAPPORT (NO/0800-4072) [15864145] **12**

ARSRAPPORT FRA AVDELINGER OG INSTITUTTER / UNIVERSITETET I TRONDHEIM, NORGES TEKNISKE HGSKOLE (NO) [21026471] **5086**

ARSRAPPORT FRA INSTITUTTENE *See* ARSRAPPORT FRA AVDELINGER OG INSTITUTTER / UNIVERSITETET I TRONDHEIM, NORGES TEKNISKE HGSKOLE **5086**

ARSREDOVISNING / NOBELSTIFTELSEN (SW) [10102138] **3144**

ARSREDOVISNING / SJ (SW) [10351602] **5429**

ARSREDOVISNING - TELEVERKET (SW) [02242214] **1149**

ARSSKRIFT / BIRKENES HISTORIELAG (NO) [11081676] **2676**

ARSSKRIFT - CARLSBERGFONDET, FREDERIKSBORGMUSEET, NY CARLSBERGFONDET (DK/0105-9858) [06275968] **1074**

ARSSKRIFT - DANSK GEOLOGISK FORENING (DK) [02380356] **1366**

ARSSKRIFT - LOKALHISTORISK FORENING FOR SONDERHALD KOMMUNE (DK) [06545253] **2676**

ARSSKRIFT - LOLLAND-FALSTERS STIFTSMUSEUM 1983 (DK/0109-2731) [101092731] **4084**

ARSSKRIFT - SYDSVENSKA ORTNAMNSSALLSKAPETS (SW/0302-8348) [01792787] **3267**

ARSTRYCK - GOTEBORGS ETNOGRAFISKA MUSEUM (SW/0436-2020) [01436798] **231**

ART & ACADEME (US/1040-7812) [18527909] **337**

ART & ANTIQUES (US/0195-8208) [10648737] 250, **337**

ART AND ARCHAEOLOGY TECHNICAL ABSTRACTS (US/0004-2994) [01514256] 260, 338, **333**

ART AND ARCHITECTURE BOOK GUIDE (US/0098-2822) [01790838] 292, **338**

ART & AUCTION (NEW YORK, N.Y.) (US/0197-1093) [05966296] 370, **250**

ART AND AUSTRALIA (AT/0004-301X) [04087074] **338**

ART & CRAFT (UK) [05079500] **370**

ART & CRAFTS CATALYST (US) **370**

ART & DECORATION (FR/0004-3168) [01514277] **338**

ART & DESIGN / ARCHITECTURAL DESIGN PUBLICATIONS (UK/0267-3991) [11981997] **338**

ART & DESIGN NEWS (US/1055-2286) [23071886] **376**

ART AND DESIGN NEWSLETTER *CEASED.* (UK/0269-7858) [102697858] **338**

ART & FACT (BE/0774-1863) [11481869] **313**

ART AND MAN *See* SCHOLASTIC ART **364**

ART & OXYGEN (US/8756-7695) [11652231] **338**

ART AND POETRY TODAY (II) [05817473] 3460, **338**

ART & STYLE INTERNATIONAL *CEASED.* (CN/8750-0477) [11777593] **402**

ART & TEXT (AT/0727-1182) [10976893] **338**

ART AND THE ARTIST (II) [01514263] **338**

ART-ANTIQUES INVESTMENT REPORT, THE (US/0161-1232) [03822512] 250, 338, **891**

ART AT AUCTION IN AMERICA (US/1046-4999) [20429984] **338**

ART AUREA (GW) [20769767] 2913, **338**

ART BULLETIN (NEW YORK, N.Y.), THE (US/0004-3079) [05784747] **338**

ART BULLETIN OF VICTORIA (AT/0066-7935) [03384942] **338**

ART BUSINESS NEWS (US/0273-5652) [07079011] 639, **338**

ART BUYER'S HANDBOOK (GW/0932-3333) **338**

ART CALENDAR (GREAT FALLS, VA.) (US/0893-3901) [15538688] 639, **338**

ART CATALOGUES (US) **313**

ART CRITICISM (US/0195-4148) [05518918] **338**

ART CULINAIRE (ATLANTA, GA.) (US/0892-1024) [15079096] **2788**

ART DE BASSE-NORMANDIE (FR/0571-1509) [06694088] **338**

ART, DESIGN, ARCHITECTURE : ADA (SA) [22445200] 292, **338**

ART DIRECTION (US/0004-3109) [05837912] 756, **338**

ART DIRECTORS' INDEX, THE (US) [08966497] **338**

ART DIRECTORS' INDEX TO ILLUSTRATORS (SZ) [15864219] **4366**

ART DIRECTORS' INDEX TO PHOTOGRAPHERS (UK/0587-3576) [02852844] **4366**

ART DOCUMENTATION (US/0730-7187) [08046519] 313, **3192**

ART DU THEATRE (PARIS, FRANCE : 1985) *CEASED.* (FR/0297-2557) [13883375] **5361**

ART E DOSSIER (IT/0394-0179) [14589762] **338**

ART ECONOMIST, THE (US/0736-6809) [09201122] 1463, **338**

ART EDUCATION (RESTON) (US/0004-3125) [01514275] 1888, **338**

ART EDUCATION (SASKATOON) (CN/0708-5354) [05385321] 1726, **338**

Alphabetical Title Index — ARTHUR

ART ET ARCHEOLOGIE EN RHONE ALPES (FR/0764-9673) [15313393] **338**

ART ET ARTISTES (FR/0292-4625) [09014982] **338**

●ART ET CULTURE AU QUEBEC (CN/1188-4282) [27019086] **313**

ART ET METIERS DU LIVRE (FR) [06613082] **338, 4823**

ART ET POESIE (FR) [04423951] **313**

ART ET THERAPIE (FR/0293-4906) [I02934906] **338, 1875**

ART FOCUS (CN) [29396483] **313**

ART GALLERY OF NOVA SCOTIA JOURNAL (CN/0843-9184) [23455467] **313**

ART GALLERY, THE **SUSPENDED.** (US/0004-3184) [00849631] **339**

ART (HAMBURG) (GW/0173-2781) [07057225] **339**

ART HAPPENINGS MAGAZINE (US) [13652977] **339**

ART HAZARDS NEWS (US/0197-7903) [04575060] **383**

ART HERITAGE : CATALOG (II) [11652668] **339**

ART HERITAGE (GALLERY) *See* ART HERITAGE : CATALOG **339**

ART HISTORY (UK/0141-6790) [03952807] **339**

●ART IMAGE MAGAZINE (US/1062-8819) [25780646] **313**

ART IMPRESSIONS (CN/0831-2133) [16938294] **250, 339**

ART IN AMERICA (1939) (US/0004-3214) [01514286] **339**

ART IN AMERICA. ANNUAL GUIDE TO GALLERIES, MUSEUMS, ARTISTS (US/0736-7619) [08694284] **339**

ART INDEX (US/0004-3222) [01514289] **339, 334**

ART INDEX. CD-ROM (US/0004-3222) **334**

ART INSIGHT (US/0194-9071) [05103741] **339**

ART INSTITUTE OF CHICAGO NEWS & EVENTS, THE (US) [17285201] **4084, 339**

ART INTERNATIONAL **SUSPENDED.** (FR) [16958417] **339**

ART INVESTMENT REPORT, THE (US/0090-9211) [01786145] **339, 891**

ART ISSUES (US/1046-8471) [19419400] **339**

ART JOURNAL (NEW YORK. 1960) (US/0004-3249) [01514294] **339**

ART LAW AND ACCOUNTING REPORTER (US/0886-1013) [09665874] **313, 738, 2937**

ART LIBRARIES JOURNAL (UK/0307-4722) [02591913] **339, 3192**

ART LIBRARIES SOCIETY *See* DIRECTORY / ART LIBRARIES SOCIETY **349**

ART LINE (CN/0711-1312) [09086758] **370**

ART LOVERS' ART & CRAFT FAIR BULLETIN (US/0892-1202) [14758880] **370**

ART MAGAZINE, THE (UK) **339**

ART MARKETING LETTER, THE **CEASED.** (US/0740-2198) [09889043] **339**

ART MATERIAL TRADE NEWS (US/0004-3265) [01514295] **339**

●ART MATERIALS TODAY (US/1066-4173) [26944627] **339**

ART MONTHLY (UK/0142-6702) [04547163] **339**

ART MONTHLY AUSTRALIA (AT/1033-40253) [21123850] **339**

ART MURPHY'S ... BOXOFFICE REGISTER (US) [13980331] **4063**

ART MUSCLE (US) [14705565] **313**

ART NEW ENGLAND (US/0274-7073) [06516895] **339**

ART NEW ZEALAND (NZ/0110-1102) [05719053] **339**

ART NEWSPAPER (IT/0960-6556) [23658809] **339**

ART NEXUS (CK) [23854345] **339**

ART NOW GALLERY GUIDE. INTERNATIONAL (US/1059-7689) [22773087] **4084, 340**

ART OF CALIFORNIA (US/1045-8913) [19009782] **313**

ART OF EATING, THE (US/0895-6200) [16707373] **2327**

ART OF HOTEL ADVERTISING, THE (US/0735-9233) [08893358] **756**

ART OF MEDICATION, THE (US/0731-3047) [07963488] **4292**

ART OF NEGOTIATING NEWSLETTER, THE **CEASED.** (US/0270-8388) [06498879] **1654**

ART OF THE AMERICAS BULLETIN (US/0004-329X) [04447948] **340**

ART OF THE WEST (US/1047-4994) [19702314] **340**

●ART ON SCREEN (US/1062-9459) [25813635] **340**

●ART ON SCREEN CLOSE-UPS (US/1062-9467) [25813670] **340**

ART PAPERS (US/0278-1441) [07219444] **340**

ART POST *See* ART FOCUS **313**

ART POST, THE (CN/0829-0784) [10954115] **340**

ART PRESS (PARIS, FRANCE : 1981) (FR/0245-5676) [08102256] **313**

ART READING MATERIAL (AT/1036-2045) [I10362045] **340**

ART REFERENCE COLLECTION (US/0193-6867) [05251656] **313, 334**

●ART REFERENCE SERVICES QUARTERLY (US/1050-2548) [21431329] **292, 340**

ART SALES INDEX (WEYBRIDGE, SURREY : 1985) (UK) [12827444] **340**

ART SCAPE (US/0276-5659) [07382468] **340**

ART SCHOOL DIRECTORY (WASHINGTON (D.C.)) (US) [05135222] **340**

ART SCHOOL MAGAZINE (NE) **376**

ART TALENT *See* NORTH LIGHT **360**

ART-TALK (US/0741-496X) [10015971] **340**

ART THERAPY : JOURNAL OF THE AMERICAN ART THERAPY ASSOCIATION (US/0742-1656) [10294649] **3553, 4575**

ART TIMES (SAUGERTIES, N.Y.) (US/0891-9070) [15045002] **340**

ART TO SCIENCE IN TISSUE CULTURE (US) [16462072] **443**

ART TO ZOO (US/0882-6838) [07181917] **1888**

ART TRIBAL (SZ) [16992508] **340**

ART VIEW VIANEN (NE/0925-1332) [I09251332] **340**

ART VOICES (WEST PALM BEACH, FLA.) (US/0272-2097) [06801418] **340**

ART WORLD (IT) **340**

ART/WORLD (NEW YORK. 1976) **SUSPENDED.** (US/0194-1070) [04736143] **340**

ARTA (BUCURESTI) (RM/0004-3354) [02069830] **340**

ARTBIBLIOGRAPHIES. CURRENT TITLES (UK/0307-9961) [01783670] **340, 334**

ARTBIBLIOGRAPHIES MODERN (UK/0300-466X) [01796113] **340, 334**

ARTE A BOLOGNA : BOLLETTINO DEI MUSEI CIVICI D'ARTE ANTICA (IT) [25837514] **340**

ARTE AL DIA : REVISTA QUINCENAL DE INFORMACIONES DEL MERCADO DE ARTE Y ANTIGUEDADES (AG) [14093426] **250, 340**

ARTE ARGOMENTI (IT) **313**

ARTE BIANCA : LA PANIFICAZIONE ITALIANA, L' (IT) [05378579] **2327**

ARTE CRISTIANA (IT/0004-3400) [01774812] **4936, 340**

ARTE, DE (SA) [05620654] **340**

ARTE DEI GIARDINI (IT) [25226713] **2409**

ARTE DOCUMENTO (IT/1121-0524) [20141850] **340**

ARTE EM REVISTA (BL) [05715735] **313**

ARTE ESPANOL (SP) [03583252] **340**

ARTE FACTUM (ANTWERPEN) (BE/0771-761X) [11481901] **340**

ARTE HOJE (BL) [05189838] **341**

ARTE IN (IT) [20967369] **341**

ARTE IN FRIULI, ARTE A TRIESTE (IT) [10765367] **341**

ARTE LOMBARDA (IT/0004-3443) [01514321] **313**

ARTE MEDIEVALE (IT/0393-7267) [11059169] **341**

ARTE NAIVE (IT/0390-1319) [I03901319] **341**

ARTE ORIENTALE IN ITALIA (IT) [05438759] **341**

ARTE TESSILE : RIVISTA-ANNUARIO DEL CENTRO ITALIANO PER LO STUDIO DELLA STORIA DEL TESSUTO (IT) [23527099] **1081, 5348**

ARTE VENETA : RIVISTA DI STORIA DELL'ARTE (IT/0392-5234) [01514323] **341**

ARTE Y CEMENTO (SP/0212-8578) [I02128578] **599**

ARTE Y JOYA INTERNATIONAL (SP) **2913**

ARTEFACT (MONTREAL) (CN/1181-8441) [24256518] **341**

ARTEFACT, THE (AT/0044-9075) [05136608] **231, 260**

ARTEGUIA (SP/0211-5271) [20602828] **341**

ARTEMIA NEWSLETTER (BE/0775-454X) [I0775454X] **2296**

ARTERE (MONTREAL) (CN/0823-4124) [10517801] **3777**

ARTERES ET VEINES (FR/0293-5090) [I02935090] **3699**

ARTERIOSCLEROSIS AND THROMBOSIS (US/1049-8834) [21341263] **3699**

ARTERY (US/0098-6127) [02245987] **3795**

ARTES (SW/0345-0015) [03600947] **314**

ARTES CONSTRUCTIONUM (FI/0355-3213) [04818583] **599, 2018**

ARTES DE MEXICO (MX/0300-4953) [01514326] **314**

ARTES GRAFICAS (AG) [01784721] **4563, 376**

ARTES GRAFICAS (PORT SAINT LUCIE, FLA.) (US/1048-8219) [21050454] **341**

ARTES PLASTICAS LISBOA (PO/0871-9276) [I08719276] **341**

ARTES PLASTICAS : REVISTA DE LA ESCUELA NACIONAL DE ARTES PLASTICAS, UNIVERSIDAD NACIONAL AUTONOMA DE MEXICO (MX) [16967785] **341**

ARTES TEXTILES (BE/0776-3670) [06934178] **5348**

ARTES VISUALES (PR) [01789057] **341**

ARTESANIA Y FOLKLORE DE VENEZUELA (VE) [04011243] **314**

ARTESANIA Y FOLKLORE DE VENEZUELA (VE/0254-1572) [I02541572] **2318, 341**

ARTESANIAS DE AMERICA (EC) [12077618] **341**

ARTESIA DAILY PRESS (US) [15615995] **5712**

ARTEXTREME (US/0278-3827) [07797897] **341**

ARTFORCE (AT/0312-6765) [I03126765] **341**

ARTFORUM INTERNATIONAL (US) [20458258] **341**

ARTFUL DODGE (US/0196-691X) [05872806] **3363**

ARTHA SUCHI : AN INDEX TO INDIAN ECONOMIC LITERATURE (II) [11428456] **1463**

ARTHA VIJNANA (II/0004-3559) [01587766] **1546**

ARTHA-VIKAS (II/0004-3567) [01802065] **1546**

ARTHANITI (II/0004-3575) [01773631] **1590**

ARTHIKA VARSHA KO KARYAKRAMA VIVARANA (NP) [02239570] **4711**

ARTHRITIS AND RHEUMATISM (US/0004-3591) [01514332] **3803**

ARTHRITIS AND RHEUMATISM (NE/0014-4355) [02682415] **3803**

ARTHRITIS CARE AND RESEARCH (US/0893-7524) [15639071] **3803**

ARTHRITIS FOUNDATION *See* ARTHRITIS FOUNDATION ANNUAL REPORT **3803**

ARTHRITIS FOUNDATION ANNUAL REPORT (US/0191-2836) [04796518] **3803**

ARTHRITIS INTERAGENCY COORDINATING COMMITTEE ANNUAL REPORT TO THE SECRETARY, U.S. DEPARTMENT OF HEALTH, EDUCATION, AND WELFARE (US/0198-7216) [05978975] **3803**

ARTHRITIS NEWS (TORONTO) (CN/0820-9006) [09590489] **3803**

ARTHRITIS, RHEUMATIC DISEASES, AND RELATED DISORDERS (US) [05722744] **3803**

ARTHRITIS TODAY (US/0890-1120) [14153840] **3803**

ARTHRO EXPRESS (CN) **3803**

ARTHROPOD-BORNE VIRUS INFORMATION EXCHANGE (US/0736-7899) [04481369] **443**

●ARTHROPOD MANAGEMENT TESTS (US) **4244**

ARTHROPODS OF FLORIDA AND NEIGHBORING LAND AREAS (US/0066-8036) [01321323] **5576**

ARTHROSCOPY (US/0749-8063) [11198618] **3880**

ARTHROSCOPY: THE JOURNAL OF ARTHROSCOPIC AND RELATED SURGERY (US) **3960**

ARTHROSKOPIE (GW/0933-7946) [21076975] **3880, 3960**

ARTHUR ANDERSEN & CO *See* POCKET GUIDE TO EUROPEAN INDIVIDUAL TAXES **4741**

ARTHUR
Alphabetical Title Index

ARTHUR ANDERSEN & CO *See* CANADIAN TAX AND TRADE BRIEFS **4716**

● ARTHUR ANDERSEN CORPORATE REGISTER, THE (UK/0956-2893) [26926202] **639**

ARTHUR ENTERPRISE, THE (US) [13412869] **5706**

ARTHUR FROMMER'S DOLLARWISE GUIDE TO NEW ENGLAND (US/0271-9827) [06444824] **5461**

ARTHUR FROMMER'S DOLLARWISE GUIDE TO THE SOUTHEAST AND NEW ORLEANS (US/0731-857X) [04272593] **5461**

ARTHUR FROMMER'S GUIDE TO ATHENS (US) [03526547] **5461**

ARTHUR FROMMER'S GUIDE TO IRELAND : DUBLIN/SHANNON (US) [03526642] **5461**

ARTHUR GRAPHIC-CLARION, THE (US) [21767232] **5658**

ARTHUR RIMBAUD (FR) [01792757] **3363**

ARTHURIAN LITERATURE (UK) [08072790] **3364**

ARTHURIAN STUDIES (UK) [08152589] 2677, **3364**

ARTHURIAN YEARBOOK, THE (US/1053-3877) [21544861] **3364**

ARTI E MERCATURE (IT) [06462350] **823**

ARTI MUSICES (CI/0587-5455) [01850544] **4101**

ARTIBUS ASIAE (SZ/0004-3648) [01514339] 260, **341**

ARTIBUS ASIAE. SUPPLEMENTUM (SZ) [01514340] 260, **341**

ARTIBUS ET HISTORIAE (AU/0391-9064) [07377675] 341, **4063**

ARTICHOKE (CALGARY) (CN/0847-3277) [21205862] **341**

ARTICLE 17 (IS) **2767**

ARTICLE II : A GUIDE TO THE NORTH CAROLINA LEGISLATURE / NORTH CAROLINA CENTER FOR PUBLIC POLICY RESEARCH (US) [08813863] **4630**

ARTICLE SUMMARIES (AT) **5504**

ARTICLES ET DOCUMENTS *See* PROBLEMES POLITIQUES ET SOCIAUX **5213**

ARTICLES OF INTEREST IN CURRENT PERIODICALS *CEASED.* (US) [02255572] **408**

ARTICULACAO PESQUISA-EXTENSAO / EMPRESA CAPIXABA DE PESQUISA AGROPECUARIA, EMPRESA DE ASSISTENCIA TECNICA E EXTENSAO RURAL DE ESTADO DE ESPIRITO SANTO (BL/0102-4418) [27157924] **63**

ARTICULATE VOTER *See* MINNESOTA VOTER, THE **4482**

ARTICULATION (US/0275-9675) [06759194] **1810**

ARTICULATOR (COLUMBUS), THE (US/0272-9067) [06907915] **1317**

ARTICULOS EN LINGUISTICA Y CAMPOS AFINES (CK) [02756238] **3267**

ARTIFACT, THE (US/0004-3680) [01707612] **260**

ARTIFACTS (DAYTON) (US/0160-6034) [03699195] **2721**

ARTIFEX (MINNEAPOLIS, MINN.) (US/0895-125X) [16573039] **4575**

● ARTIFICIAL CELLS, BLOOD SUBSTITUTES, AND IMMOBILIZATION BIOTECHNOLOGY (US/1073-1199) [29333477] **3553**

ARTIFICIAL INTELLIGENCE (NE/0004-3702) [01514343] **1211**

ARTIFICIAL INTELLIGENCE (UK) **1211**

ARTIFICIAL INTELLIGENCE ABSTRACTS *CEASED.* (US/0882-1410) [11707495] 1211, **1208**

● ARTIFICIAL INTELLIGENCE AND LAW (NE/0924-8463) [26773112] 2937, **1211**

ARTIFICIAL INTELLIGENCE FOR ENGINEERING DESIGN, ANALYSIS AND MANUFACTURING (UK/0890-0604) [14137848] **1211**

ARTIFICIAL INTELLIGENCE IN ENGINEERING (UK/0954-1810) [20279971] 1965, **1211**

ARTIFICIAL INTELLIGENCE IN MEDICINE (NE/0933-3657) [21516938] **1211**

ARTIFICIAL INTELLIGENCE REVIEW, THE (UK/0269-2821) [15186519] **1211**

ARTIFICIAL INTELLIGENCE SERIES, THE (US/0272-1686) [06794704] **1212**

● ARTIFICIAL LIFE (US/1064-5462) [26326076] **5086**

ARTIFICIAL ORGANS (US/0160-564X) [03695286] **3960**

ARTIFICIAL ORGANS TODAY : THE OFFICIAL INTERNATIONAL JOURNAL OF THE JAPANESE SOCIETY FOR ARTIFICIAL ORGANS (NE/0924-3054) [24245929] **3553**

ARTIFICIAL SATELLITES. PLANETARY GEODESY / POLISH ACADEMY OF SCIENCES, SPACE RESEARCH CENTRE (PL/0208-841X) [13151174] **1402**

ARTILLERI TIDSKRIFT (SW) [09840313] **4037**

ARTILLERI-TIDSKRIFT (SW/0004-3788) [I00043788] **4061**

ARTILLERYMAN, THE (US/0884-4747) [12382348] **4037**

ARTIMES *CEASED.* (US) **314**

ARTINF (AG) [14048677] **341**

ARTINUMBRIA (IT/0393-747X) [I0393747X] **341**

ARTINUMBRIA *See* TITOLO **4833**

ARTIS (GW/0004-3842) [01514348] 250, **370**

ARTIS (KONSTANZ) (SZ/0004-3842) [09551310] **341**

ARTIS KUNST (GW) **314**

ARTISAN MELBOURNE (AT/0812-7158) [I08127158] 2842, **5192**

ARTISAN (OTTAWA. 1976) (CN/0381-5021) [03230459] **370**

ARTIST (CALCUTTA) (II/0304-8640) [02239394] **314**

ARTIST, DER (GW) [09073550] **4101**

ARTIST (LONDON. 1931) (UK/0004-3877) [03290536] **341**

ARTISTA (FLORENCE, ITALY) (IT) [21022427] **341**

ARTISTIC TRAVELER, THE (US/1060-2569) [24923856] **5461**

ARTISTS AND ILLUSTRATORS (UK) **341**

ARTIST'S AND ILLUSTRATOR'S MAGAZINE (UK/0269-4697) [I02694697] **341**

ARTISTS ASSOCIATES *See* A. A.'S FAR EAST BUSINESSMAN'S DIRECTORY **821**

ARTISTS EQUITY ASSOCIATION. NATIONAL NEWSLETTER *See* ARTISTS EQUITY NEWS **341**

ARTISTS EQUITY NEWS (US/0161-6692) [03983798] **341**

ARTISTS IN EDUCATION DIRECTORY / DELAWARE STATE ARTS COUNCIL (US) [11459400] **314**

ARTIST'S MAGAZINE, THE (US/0741-3351) [10131531] **314**

ARTIST'S MARKET (1979) (US/0161-0546) [03818412] 921, **376**

ARTISTS RESOURCE GUIDE TO NEW ENGLAND, THE (US/1053-4156) [19569079] 4084, **341**

ARTISTS USING SCIENCE AND TECHNOLOGY DIRECTORY / YLEM (US) [27765807] **341**

ARTITUDES INTERNATIONAL (FR) [01788419] **314**

ARTIUM QUAESTIONES / UNIWERSYTET IM. ADAMA MICKIEWICZA W POZNANIU (PL/0239-202X) [11766573] **342**

ARTJOB/BANK (SANTA FE, N.M.) (US/1070-8901) [27242543] 1654, **314**

● ARTLANTA (US/1059-7263) [24689097] **342**

ARTLETTER / CROCKER ART MUSEUM (US) [25505289] **342**

ARTLINK (AT/0727-1239) [I07271239] **342**

ARTLOOK (AT) [04634741] **342**

ARTNEWS (US/0004-3273) [02392716] **314**

ARTNEWS INTERNATIONAL DIRECTORY OF CORPORATE ART COLLECTIONS (US/1060-3662) [17495544] **342**

ARTNEWSLETTER, THE (US/0145-7241) [02776465] **342**

ARTPAPER *CEASED.* (US/0739-8646) [09823637] **342**

ARTPARK (US/0164-1298) [03819051] **342**

ARTRACES. BULLETIN (FR/0294-135X) [10282431] **314**

ARTS ADVOCATE WELLINGTON (NZ/1171-8536) [I11718536] **342**

ARTS AND ACTIVITIES (US/0004-3931) [01514367] 1888, **314**

ARTS AND ACTIVITIES YEARBOOK (US/0518-8172) [05810351] **342**

ARTS & BOOKS : CHICAGO'S WEEKLY ARTS AND ENTERTAINMENT MAGAZINE (US) [07667676] **2528**

ARTS AND CRAFTS MAGAZINE (US) **370**

ARTS AND CRAFTS QUARTERLY MAGAZINE (US) **370**

ARTS & CRAFTS RETAILER *CEASED.* (US/1067-1463) [27152624] **314**

ARTS & CULTURE FUNDING REPORT (US/1047-3297) [20666613] **314**

ARTS AND EDUCATION (AT/0813-3425) [I08133425] 342, **1726**

ARTS & HUMANITES SEARCH (US) 2842, **314**

ARTS & HUMANITIES CITATION INDEX. CITATION INDEX, PERMUTERM SUBJECT INDEX (US) [04217379] **2842**

ARTS & HUMANITIES CITATION INDEX (COMPACT DISC ED.) (US/1060-9202) [25108378] 2842, **314**

ARTS & HUMANITIES CITATION INDEX. PERMUTERM SUBJECT INDEX (US/0162-8445) [04564389] **2842**

ARTS & HUMANITIES CITATION INDEX (PRINT ED.) (US/0162-8445) [04122996] 314, 2842, **2857**

ARTS & LETTERS (DAYTON, TENN.) (US/0893-4088) [15537601] **314**

ARTS & METIERS (FR/0004-4008) [07507439] **5086**

ARTS & SCIENCE MONOGRAPHS (CN/0703-8720) [03564630] **314**

ARTS & SCIENCES JOURNAL (PH) [09803552] **314**

ARTS & THE ISLAMIC WORLD (UK) [09639754] **314**

ARTS & WERELD (NE/0165-5299) [06458985] **3553**

ARTS + ARCHITECTURE (US/0730-9481) [07880242] 292, **314**

ARTS ASIATIQUES (PARIS) (FR/0004-3958) [01514371] **342**

ARTS B. C (CN/0706-9731) [03300840] **314**

ARTS BEAT (HAMILTON) (CN/0843-2260) [19769976] **342**

ARTS BULLETIN OF THE CANADIAN CONFERENCE OF THE ARTS (CN/0707-9532) [06054185] **314**

ARTS CALENDAR QUARTERLY, THE (US/0882-8571) [11964410] **314**

ARTS COUNCIL OF GREAT BRITAIN *See* REPORT - ARTS COUNCIL OF GREAT BRITAIN **329**

ARTS D'AFRIQUE NOIRE (FR/0337-1603) [03932587] 231, **314**

ARTS DE L'OUEST (FR/0220-2220) [I02202220] **342**

ARTS DIRECTORY (HAMILTON) (CN/0843-2198) [20113927] **314**

● ARTS EDUCATION POLICY REVIEW (US/1063-2913) [25961467] 1726, **314**

ARTS EDUCATION REVIEW OF BOOKS, THE *SUSPENDED.* (US/0889-2172) [11983675] **315**

ARTS EDUCATION : THE MAGAZINE OF THE NATIONAL FOUNDATION FOR ARTS EDUCATION (UK) 1726, **315**

ARTS, ENTERTAINMENT & SPORTS LAW NEWS (US) [29857538] **2937**

ARTS ET LIVRES (FR/0296-8630) [I02968630] **342**

ARTS ET METIERS MAGAZINE PARIS (FR/0999-4084) [I09994084] **315**

ARTS ET TECHNIQUES GRAPHIQUES (FR/0040-1366) [01846324] **376**

ARTS IN GUELPH, THE (CN/0824-5495) [10680961] **315**

ARTS IN PSYCHOTHERAPY, THE (US/0197-4556) [06035558] 342, **3921**

ARTS IN VIRGINIA *CEASED.* (US/0004-4032) [02954171] **315**

ARTS INDIANA (US/0897-859X) [16723807] **315**

ARTS JOURNAL (ASHEVILLE, N.C.), THE *CEASED.* (US/0739-8662) [05106611] **315**

● ARTS MAGAZINE. INTERNATIONAL DIRECTORY OF EXHIBITION CATALOGUES (US) [26639589] **342**

ARTS MAGAZINE (NEW YORK) *CEASED.* (US/0004-4059) [01514378] **342**

ARTS MAGAZINE (PARIS, FRANCE) (FR) [07365124] **315**

ARTS MANAGEMENT (US/0004-4067) [01514381] **315**

ARTS MARKETING POWER (US) **315**

ARTS (PARIS, FRANCE) (FR) [08092838] **315**

ARTS PATRONAGE SERIES (US/0066-8168) [01514385] 4334, **315**

ARTS QUARTERLY (NEW ORLEANS, LA. 1978) (US/0740-9214) [03702191] 4084, **342**

● ARTS REACH (US/1065-8130) [26750528] **315**

ARTS REVIEW (UK/0004-4091) [01514387] **315**

ARTS REVIEW YEAR BOOK (UK) [08309218] **342**

ARTS / THE ARTS IN RELIGIOUS & THEOLOGICAL STUDIES (US) 4936, **315**

Alphabetical Title Index — ASEAN

ARTS / THE JOURNAL OF THE SYDNEY UNIVERSITY ARTS ASSOCIATION (AT/0066-8095) [06084820] **315**

ARTS TIMES See ARTS ADVOCATE WELLINGTON **342**

ARTSAMERICA FINE ART FILM & VIDEO SOURCE BOOK CEASED. (US) [14937066] **342, 4063**

ARTSATLANTIC (CN/0704-7916) [03945753] **315**

ARTSBOARD (TORONTO) (CN/0823-9746) [12782123] **383**

ARTSCENE (LOS ANGELES, CALIF.) (US/0733-4869) [08380058] **4084, 342**

ARTSCRIBE CEASED. (UK/0954-4178) [21895529] **342**

ARTSEARCH (US/0730-9023) [08006311] **4201, 383**

●ARTSOURCE (RENAISSANCE, CALIF.) (US/1064-6620) [26367563] **315**

ARTSPACE (US) **342**

ARTSPACE CEASED. (US/0193-6956) [03711496] **342**

ARTSPEAK (NEW YORK, N.Y.) (US/1065-1543) [08321251] **342**

ARTSTUDIO SUSPENDED. (FR) [14118344] **342**

ARTVIEW (US/0146-2342) [02890834] **342**

ARTWALK (LETHBRIDGE, ALTA.) See ARTWALK MAGAZINE **315**

●ARTWALK MAGAZINE (CN/1191-4785) [26714909] **315**

ARTWEEK (CASTRO VALLEY, CALIF.) (US/0004-4121) [01385458] **342**

ARTWORK MAGAZINE (AT/1033-0216) [I10330216] **342**

ARTWORLD EUROPE (US/1062-8312) [25558336] **342**

ARTWORLD HOTLINE (US/1057-5413) [24060661] **315**

ARTZAKANK (CN/0046-1040) [03564326] **2722**

ARUBAITO HAKUSHO (JA) [09224353] **1654**

ARUKORU KENKYU TO YAKUBUTSU IZON (JA/0389-4118) [07558888] **1341**

ARUNA (II/0304-8659) [01784134] **2501**

ARUP JOURNAL (UK/0951-0850) [08838510] **292**

ARUSHA CHAMBER OF COMMERCE, AGRICULTURE & INDUSTRY See BULLETIN TO MEMBERS / ARUSHA CHAMBER OF COMMERCE, AGRICULTURE & INDUSTRY **818**

ARUSHA CHAMBER OF COMMERCE AND AGRICULTURE. BULLETIN TO MEMBERS See BULLETIN TO MEMBERS / ARUSHA CHAMBER OF COMMERCE, AGRICULTURE & INDUSTRY **818**

ARV (SW/0066-8176) [01514391] **2318**

ARVADA JEFFERSON SENTINEL, THE (US/1060-5207) [25014890] **5641**

ARVADA SENTINEL See ARVADA JEFFERSON SENTINEL, THE **5641**

ARX (IT/0394-0624) [I03940624] **342**

ARXIU DE TEXTOS CATALANS ANTICS (SP/0211-9811) [09346736] **408**

ARYANA, AFGHANISTAN REPUBLIC (AF) [03803785] **2645**

ARZNEI-TELEGRAMM : FAKTEN UND VERGLEICHE FUR DIE RATIONALE THERAPIE (GW/0066-8192) [25366367] **4292**

ARZNEIMITTEL FORSCHUNG (GW/0004-4172) [01514393] **4292**

ARZNEIMITTELBRIEF (GW) **3553**

ARZNEIMITTELPRAXIS (AU) **3553**

ARZNEIMITTELTHERAPIE (GW/0723-6913) [10551037] **4293**

ARZT IM KRANKENHAUS UND IM GESUNDHEITSWESEN (1981), DER (GW/0175-7814) [09522027] **3553**

ARZT UND PATIENT (BADEN-BADEN) (GW/0173-5764) [07900135] **3553**

ARZTE (SZ/0253-0341) [06310873] **3553**

ARZTE-ZEITUNG (GW/0175-5811) [I01755811] **3553**

ARZTEBLATT BADEN-WURTTEMBERG (GW/0001-947X) [04558949] **3553**

ARZTEZEITSCHRIFT FUER NATURHEILVERFAHREN : ORGAN DES ZENTRALVERBANDES DER ARZTE FUER NATURHEILVERFAHREN E. V (GW/0720-6003) [22808000] **3553**

ARZTLICHE JUGENDKUNDE CEASED. (GW/0001-9518) [06009441] **3553**

ARZTLICHE MONATSHEFTE (GW/0930-1178) [13863728] **3553**

ARZTLICHE PRAXIS (GW/0001-9534) [01643303] **3553**

ARZTRECHT (1977) (GW/0343-5733) [04122751] **3739**

AS. ACTUALITE DE LA SCENOGRAPHIE (FR/0986-1351) [I09861351] **4063**

A'S & B'S OF ACADEMIC SCHOLARSHIPS (1987), THE (US/1052-0201) [17974210] **1810**

AS, ANNUAIRE DU SPECTACLE (FR) [03767948] **383**

AS. MAANDBLAD AKTIVITEITENSEKTOR (NE/0168-2857) [I01682857] **5274**

AS PICTURE PROFESSIONAL (US/1047-5427) [18376236] **4366**

AS-SARQ AL-AWSAT (UK/0265-5772) [04744088] **5811**

AS THE SPIRIT MOVES (CN/0227-499X) [08143807] **4936**

ASA (TH) [01827250] **292**

ASA MONOGRAPHS (US) **5240, 231**

ASA NEWS (LOS ANGELES, CALIF.) (US/0278-2219) [07522531] **2498**

ASA NEWSLETTER - APPLIED SCIENCE AND ANALYSIS, INC, THE (US/1057-9419) [22411161] **2859, 4037**

ASA NEWSLETTER (PARK RIDGE) (US/0270-5877) [03165543] **3682**

ASA SPECIAL PUBLICATION (US/0066-0566) [01480770] **63**

ASA STUDIES (US/0272-0566) [04861181] **231**

ASAE DISTINGUISHED LECTURE SERIES; TRACTOR DESIGN (US/0730-8701) [05871803] **158**

ASAE PUBLICATION (US/0197-1662) [05970530] **63, 1965**

ASAE STANDARDS (US/8755-1187) [10838580] **63, 1965**

ASAG FRAT HAVZAS ... YUZEY ARASTRMALAR (TU) [20668813] **260**

ASAHI EVENING NEWS (JA/0025-2816) [01514397] **5805**

ASAHI GARASU KENKYU HOKOKU (JA/0004-4210) [05001118] **2586, 1021**

ASAHI GARASU ZAIDAN KENKYU HOKOKU (JA/0916-7064) [25287068] **2586**

ASAHI GURAFU BESSATSU (JA) [02245093] **5228**

ASAHI GYARARI NENKAN (JA) [04597124] **342, 4084**

ASAHI JANARU CEASED. (JA/0571-2378) [01514398] **3192**

ASAHI SHIMBUN JAPAN ACCESS SUSPENDED. (JA/0917-0332) [22416103] **2501**

ASAHI SHINBUN (JA) [01514400] **5805**

ASAHIKAWA KOGYO KOTO SENMON GAKKO KENKYU HOBUN (JA/0389-9306) [10239708] **5086**

●ASAIO JOURNAL (1992) (US/1058-2916) [24256275] **3960**

ASAIO TRANSACTIONS See ASAIO JOURNAL (1992) **3960**

ASAO MONOGRAPH (US/0587-1964) [01889960] **231**

ASAP (US) **921**

ASAR (II) [02240261] **2501**

ASB BULLETIN, THE (US/0001-2386) [03093594] **443**

ASBESTOS (US) [06217169] **2134**

ASBESTOS (US/0004-4237) [02445038] **599**

ASBESTOS ABATEMENT REPORT (US/0893-858X) [15679517] **4767**

●ASBESTOS & LEAD ABATEMENT REPORT (US/1068-2643) [27543003] **4767**

ASBESTOS CONTROL REPORT (US/0893-4533) [15559712] **2224**

ASBESTOS LITIGATION REPORTER (US/0273-3048) [07046841] **599, 2937**

ASBESTOS MA VILLE (CN/0711-8031) [08465851] **4630**

ASBESTOS MANAGEMENT SOURCEBOOK (US/1046-0438) [20311545] **2859, 599**

ASBESTOS MDL 875 UPDATE (US/1059-6232) [24521317] **2937**

ASBESTOS PROPERTY LITIGATION REPORTER (US/1041-5130) [18764142] **2937, 599**

ASBESTOS (QUEBEC) See ASBESTOS MA VILLE **4630**

ASBESTOS WATCH (CN/1182-9982) [23598349] **599**

ASBESTOS WORKERS JOURNAL (US/1054-4100) [20305334] **1654**

ASBSD BULLETIN (US/0001-2408) [04157114] **1860**

ASBURY PARK PRESS (US) [16894042] **5709**

ASBURY THEOLOGICAL JOURNAL, THE (US) [14472115] **4936**

ASBURY THEOLOGICAL SEMINARY HERALD, THE (US) [06397340] **4936**

ASC BULLETIN (US) **532**

ASC CYBERNETICS FORUM (US) [07865322] **1250**

ASC DIGEST (AT) **639**

ASC FORUM See ASC CYBERNETICS FORUM **1250**

ASC REPORT (UK) **738**

ASCA NEWSLETTER (FORT LAUDERDALE, FLA.) (US/0747-6000) [10765423] **4884**

ASCAP IN ACTION (US/0197-7849) [05715334] **4101**

ASCATOPICS (US/0730-8574) [04774259] **2528, 2496**

ASCD UPDATE (US/0733-3293) [06692939] **1888**

ASCE ANNUAL COMBINED INDEX (US/0742-1753) [09991894] **2018, 2002**

ASCE NEWS (US/0197-4076) [06025682] **2018**

ASCE PUBLICATIONS INFORMATION (US/0734-1962) [08694400] **2018, 2002**

ASCENT (CN/0707-5588) [05377799] **1933**

ASCENT (KOOTENAY BAY) (CN/0315-8179) [03244953] **4936**

ASCENT TECHNOLOGY MAGAZINE : ATM (AT) [24801506] **5086**

ASCENT (URBANA, ILL.) (US/0098-9363) [02242922] **3364**

ASCHEFFENBURGER JAHRBUCH FUER GESCHICHTE, LANDESKUNDE UND KUNST DES UNTERMAINGEBIETES (GW/0518-8520) [I05188520] **342**

ASCHKENAS (AU) [25003048] **5046**

ASCI JOURNAL OF MANAGEMENT (II/0257-8069) [09690179] **860**

ASCLEPIO : ARCHIVO IBEROAMERICANO DE HISTORIA DE LA MEDICINA Y ANTROPOLOGIA MEDICA (SP/0210-4466) [01777675] **3553**

ASCOM TECHNICAL REVIEW (SZ/1015-5481) [24949408] **5086**

ASCOM TECHNISCHE MITTEILUNGEN (SZ/1015-5473) [I10155473] **1149**

ASCP WASHINGTON REPORT ON NATIONAL AND STATE LABORATORY ISSUES (US/1052-7893) [22378364] **3893**

ASCS COMMODITY FACT SHEET. HONEY / UNITED STATES DEPARTMENT OF AGRICULTURE, AGRICULTURAL STABILIZATION AND CONSERVATION SERVICE (US) [04261266] **63**

ASDA GUIDES TO POSTDOCTORAL PROGRAMS. GENERAL PRACTICE RESIDENCIES AND ADVANCED EDUCATION IN GENERAL DENTISTRY (US) [20821402] **1317**

ASDA GUIDES TO POSTDOCTORAL PROGRAMS. ORAL AND MAXILLOFACIAL SURGERY RESIDENCIES (US) [20821436] **1317**

ASDA GUIDES TO POSTDOCTORAL PROGRAMS. ORAL PATHOLOGY (US) [21069841] **1317**

ASDA HANDBOOK (US/0277-3619) [07580330] **1317**

ASDA NEWS (1981) (US/0277-3627) [07580360] **1317**

ASEA TIDNING (SW/0346-6582) [10443871] **2036**

ASEA YONGU (KO/0021-9126) [01514401] **2645**

ASEAN See ASEAN BRIEFING **1547**

ASEAN See ASEAN BUSINESS QUARTERLY **639**

ASEAN BRIEFING (HK/0251-2521) [I02512521] **2501**

ASEAN BRIEFING (US) [05313211] **1547**

ASEAN BUSINESS QUARTERLY CEASED. (SI/0129-2900) [04573376] **639**

ASEAN ECONOMIC BULLETIN (SI/0217-4472) [11554228] **1463**

ASEAN FOOD JOURNAL (MY/0127-7324) [13637135] **2327**

ASEAN INVESTOR (TH/0125-7382) [09563358] **891**

ASEAN JOURNAL OF CLINICAL SCIENCES (SI/0129-4881) [11352297] **3553**

ASEAN JOURNAL ON SCIENCE & TECHNOLOGY FOR DEVELOPMENT (SI/0217-5460) [I02175460] **5086**

ASEAN LAW JOURNAL (PH) [11156529] **2937**

ASEAN NEWSLETTER / ASSOCIATION OF SOUTHEAST ASIAN NATIONS (IO/0215-1618) [07967588] **2645**

ASEAN PRESS YEARBOOK ... (IO) [07073578] **2917**

ASEAN REVIEW (MY/0126-5245) [03262998] **2645**

ASEE PRISM (US/1056-8077) [23860261] **1965**

ASEMKA (GH/0855-000X) [02241858] **3364**

ASEPSIS (ARLINGTON, TEX.) (US/1062-0281) [15114836] **3553**

ASFA AQUACULTURE ABSTRACTS (US/0739-814X) [09816422] **2296**

ASFA MARINE BIOTECHNOLOGY ABSTRACTS (US/1054-2027) [22716796] 3685, **553**

ASFIS REFERENCE SERIES / AQUATIC SCIENCES AND FISHERIES INFORMATION SYSTEM (IT) [07284908] **2296**

ASG - MATERIALSAMMLUNG / AGRARSOZIALE GESELLSCHAFT (GW/0344-5712) [07418722] **63**

ASGSB BULLETIN (US/0898-4697) [17823012] **12**

ASH AT WORK (US/0886-3148) [04774266] 1598, **2134**

ASH SMOKING AND HEALTH REVIEW (US/1048-907X) [10346624] **4767**

ASHA MEMBERSHIP DIRECTORY (US) [14037142] 4383, **3886**

ASHA MONOGRAPHS (US/0066-071X) [07016009] **4384**

ASHA REPORTS (US/0569-8553) [05777666] **3886**

ASHA (ROCKVILLE, MD.) (US/0001-2475) [05700026] 4384, **1875**

ASHCROFT CACHE CREEK JOURNAL (CN) **5780**

ASHEVILLE CITIZEN (ASHEVILLE, N.C. : 1885) (US) [11384051] **5722**

●ASHEVILLE CITIZEN-TIMES (US/1060-3255) [24097281] **5722**

ASHI TECHNICAL JOURNAL OF HOME INSPECTION AND IN-SERVICE BUILDING COMPONENT FAILURES (US/1061-7035) [25423882] **2815**

ASHINGTONIA (UK/0309-1120) [07350692] 2409, **500**

ASHITA: GEKKAN HAISHI (JA) [03252349] **3364**

ASHLAND THEOLOGICAL JOURNAL (US/1044-6494) [08314719] **4936**

ASHLAR (UK/0143-3717) [I01433717] **292**

ASHLEY COURTENAY'S LET'S HALT AWHILE: ENGLAND, WALES, SCOTLAND, IRELAND See LET'S HALT AWHILE IN GREAT BRITAIN **2807**

ASHLEY NEWS OBSERVER, THE (US) [22151477] **5631**

ASHLEYS OF AMERICA, INC See ASHLEYS OF AMERICA QUARTERLY **2438**

ASHLEYS OF AMERICA QUARTERLY (US/0096-1469) [01798588] **2438**

ASHMOLEAN, THE (UK) [09269543] **4084**

ASHP NEWSLETTER (US/0001-2483) [04066505] **4293**

ASHRAE HANDBOOK (US/1041-2344) [12854039] **2603**

ASHRAE HANDBOOK. EQUIPMENT See ASHRAE HANDBOOK. HEATING, VENTILATING, AND AIR-CONDITIONING SYSTEMS AND EQUIPMENT **2603**

ASHRAE HANDBOOK. HEATING, VENTILATING, AND AIR-CONDITIONING APPLICATIONS (US) [24303304] **2603**

ASHRAE HANDBOOK. HEATING, VENTILATING, AND AIR-CONDITIONING SYSTEMS AND APPLICATIONS See ASHRAE HANDBOOK. HEATING, VENTILATING, AND AIR-CONDITIONING SYSTEMS AND EQUIPMENT **2603**

ASHRAE HANDBOOK. HEATING, VENTILATING, AND AIR-CONDITIONING SYSTEMS AND APPLICATIONS See ASHRAE HANDBOOK. HEATING, VENTILATING, AND AIR-CONDITIONING SYSTEMS AND EQUIPMENT **2603**

●ASHRAE HANDBOOK. HEATING, VENTILATING, AND AIR-CONDITIONING SYSTEMS AND EQUIPMENT (US) [26133763] **2603**

●ASHRAE HANDBOOK. HEATING, VENTILATING, AND AIR-CONDITIONING SYSTEMS AND EQUIPMENT (US/1041-2344) [27143297] **2603**

ASHRAE HANDBOOK. REFRIGERATION SYSTEMS AND APPLICATIONS (US) [13995346] **2603**

ASHRAE INSIGHTS (US/0891-4249) [14770012] **2603**

ASHRAE JOURNAL (US/0001-2491) [01460492] **2603**

ASHRAE TECHNICAL DATA BULLETIN (US/0884-0490) [12298202] **2603**

ASHRAE TRANSACTIONS (US/0001-2505) [07182738] 1965, **2603**

ASHTABULA COUNTY HISTORICAL SOCIETY See QUARTERLY BULLETIN - ASHTABULA COUNTY HISTORICAL SOCIETY **2755**

ASHTON GAZETTE, THE (US) [26679347] **5658**

ASHTREE ECHO (US/0004-4377) [04587976] **2438**

ASI ES MI TIERRA (ES) [10473431] **2722**

ASI JOURNAL LONDON (UK/0956-4241) [I09564241] **292**

ASI LAMB AND WOOL MARKET NEWS (US) **206**

ASIA 2000 (HK) [08360962] **5086**

ASIA & AFRICA MILITARY REVIEW See STRATEGY & DEFENCE **4058**

ASIA AND AFRICA TODAY (RU) [03825150] **2645**

ASIA & AUSTRALASIA. BASIC OIL LAWS AND CONCESSION CONTRACTS, ORIGINAL TEXTS. SUPPLEMENT (PHOTOCOPY) (US/0094-6559) [01788029] **4251**

ASIA AND OTHER SELECTED COUNTRIES QUARTERLY REVIEW (US) [15606450] **1463**

ASIA & PACIFIC REVIEW (UK) [12191440] **4464**

ASIA BUSINESS REPORT (AT) **639**

ASIA CABLE (US/0748-6014) [10974945] **1126**

ASIA CALLING (US/0004-4431) [01514417] **2646**

ASIA COMPUTER WEEKLY (SI/0129-5896) [I01295896] 1246, 1265, **1235**

ASIA FOUNDATION QUARTERLY, THE (US) [14994980] **2842**

ASIA INSURANCE REVIEW (SI/0218-2696) [I02182696] **2874**

ASIA JOURNAL OF THEOLOGY (SI/0218-0812) [16261750] **4936**

ASIA LABOUR MONITOR (HK) [12201268] **1654**

ASIA LAW (HK/1022-0267) [I10220267] **2937**

ASIA LAW AND PRACTICE (HK) [19759507] **2937**

ASIA LETTER, THE (US/0004-4466) [02906012] **1463**

ASIA LINK (HK) **2501**

ASIA LINK (HK) **2646**

ASIA LUTHERAN NEWS : ALN (HK) [08615406] **5055**

ASIA MAGAZINE, THE (HK/0004-4474) [02905995] **2501**

ASIA MAJOR (US/0004-4482) [01514421] **2646**

ASIA ... MEASURES & MAGNITUDES (HK) [06151598] **773**

ASIA MONEY & FINANCE (HK) [25128532] **773**

ASIA (NEW YORK, N.Y. : 1984) (US) [12847674] **5228**

ASIA-OCEANIA JOURNAL OF OBSTETRICS AND GYNAECOLOGY (JA/0389-2328) [07618667] **3757**

ASIA : ORGANO DE DIVULGACION TECNICA E INFORMACION DE LA ASOCIACION SALVADORENA DE INGENIEROS Y ARQUITECTOS (ES) [08740710] **1965**

ASIA-PACIFIC AFRICA-MIDDLE EAST PETROLEUM DIRECTORY (US/0748-4089) [10938105] **4251**

ASIA-PACIFIC AGRIBUSINESS REPORT (US) 640, **63**

●ASIA/PACIFIC AUTOMOTIVE BULLETIN (US) **5404**

ASIA-PACIFIC BROADCASTING UNION See ABU TECHNICAL REVIEW **1125**

ASIA PACIFIC CHEMICALS (UK) **1021**

ASIA PACIFIC CONTRACTOR See ASIAN ARCHITECT AND CONTRACTOR **292**

ASIA-PACIFIC DEFENCE REPORTER (AT) [22162950] **4037**

ASIA-PACIFIC DEFENCE REPORTER ANNUAL REFERENCE EDITION (AT/1037-1435) [I10371435] **4037**

ASIA PACIFIC DUTY-FREE (UK/0957-1817) [I09571817] **823**

ASIA-PACIFIC ENGINEERING JOURNAL. PART A, ELECTRICAL ENGINEERING CEASED. (SI/0129-5411) [25625004] **2036**

ASIA PACIFIC HANDBOOK (UK/0966-0453) [I09660453] **640**

ASIA PACIFIC HRM See ASIA PACIFIC JOURNAL OF HUMAN RESOURCES **938**

ASIA PACIFIC INTERNATIONAL JOURNAL OF BUSINESS LOGISTICS (HK/0952-8067) [18339784] **640**

ASIA PACIFIC INTERNATIONAL JOURNAL OF MARKETING (HK/0954-7517) [20371955] **921**

ASIA PACIFIC INTERNATIONAL MANAGEMENT REVIEW CEASED. (HK/0954-2957) [20647344] **860**

ASIA PACIFIC JOURNAL OF CLINICAL NUTRITION (UK/0964-7058) **4187**

●ASIA PACIFIC JOURNAL OF HUMAN RESOURCES (AT/1038-4111) [25984643] **938**

ASIA PACIFIC JOURNAL OF MANAGEMENT (SI/0217-4561) [10515989] **860**

●ASIA PACIFIC JOURNAL OF MARKETING AND LOGISTICS (UK) [29833739] **921**

ASIA-PACIFIC JOURNAL OF OPERATIONAL RESEARCH (SI/0217-5959) [11878005] **1598**

ASIA PACIFIC JOURNAL OF PHARMACOLOGY (SI/0217-9687) [15808093] **4293**

ASIA-PACIFIC JOURNAL OF PUBLIC HEALTH : ASIA-PACIFIC ACADEMIC CONSORTIUM FOR PUBLIC HEALTH (TH/1010-5395) [16410445] **4767**

●ASIA PACIFIC JOURNAL OF QUALITY MANAGEMENT (HK/0965-3570) [28874251] **860**

ASIA-PACIFIC JOURNAL OF RURAL DEVELOPMENT (BG/1018-5291) [10185291] **1463**

ASIA PACIFIC MANAGEMENT FORUM CEASED. (UK) **860**

ASIA-PACIFIC NEWSLETTER (TH/0857-2062) [I08572062] **2646**

ASIA PACIFIC PAPERMAKER (AT/1320-9787) **4232**

ASIA-PACIFIC POPULATION & POLICY (US/0891-6683) [14986236] **4549**

ASIA-PACIFIC POPULATION JOURNAL (TH/0259-238X) [15288841] 588, **4549**

ASIA PACIFIC PULP & PAPER (AT) **4232**

ASIA-PACIFIC REGIONAL COMPENSATION SURVEY. AUSTRALIA (US/0092-7627) [01797967] **1654**

ASIA PACIFIC REPORT (CN/0834-194X) [16083228] **2501**

ASIA-PACIFIC SATELLITE DIRECTORY (US) **640**

ASIA PACIFIC SOLIDARITY CEASED. (AT) **4504**

ASIA-PACIFIC TAX BULLETIN (NE) 738, **4711**

ASIA PACIFIC TECH MONITOR (II/0256-9957) [I02569957] **5086**

ASIA PACIFIC TRAVEL (US/1045-3881) [20109761] **5461**

ASIA-PACIFIC TRAVEL INDEX CEASED. (SI) [07645457] **5461**

●ASIA PULP & PAPER, TECHNOLOGY MARKETS (JA) [27665612] **4232**

ASIA TEACHERS' BULLETIN (AT/0311-2799) [I03112799] **1726**

ASIA THEOLOGICAL NEWS CEASED. (CH) [04774298] **4936**

ASIA TIMES (LOS GATOS, CALIF.) (US/1040-8231) [18542681] **2501**

ASIA TODAY (AT/0813-2844) [I08132844] **640**

ASIA TODAY INTERNATIONAL (US/1052-987X) [22425961] **2646**

ASIA TODAY (WASHINGTON, D.C.) (US/1045-2230) [20043021] **2646**

ASIA TODAY (WASHINGTON, D.C.) See ASIA TODAY INTERNATIONAL **2646**

ASIA TRAVEL TRADE (HK) [07090645] **5462**

ASIA WORLD (II) [06514694] **2646**

ASIA YEARBOOK (HK) [01748261] **1463**

ASIA YEARBOOK (HK) [01791821] **1547**

●ASIAFAB : ASIA FERTILIZER AND AGROCHEMICALS BULLETIN (UK) [27932174] **164**

ASIAMAC JOURNAL (HK/1015-5023) [I10155023] 860, **2110**

ASIAMONEY (UK/0958-9309) [28563216] **891**

ASIAN ACTION : NEWSLETTER OF THE ASIAN CULTURAL FORUM ON DEVELOPMENT (TH) [09099917] **5192**

ASIAN ADVERTISING & MARKETING CEASED. (HK/0257-893X) [I0257893X] 921, **756**

ASIAN AFFAIRS (BG) [06936543] **4516**

ASIAN AFFAIRS (LONDON) (UK/0306-8374) [01798049] **2646**

ASIAN AFFAIRS (NEW YORK) (US/0092-7678) [01791495] **4516**

ASIAN AIR TRANSPORT (CH/1021-3740) [I10213740] **5377**

ASIAN ALMANAC (SI/0004-4520) [01820150] **2646**

●ASIAN AMERICAN AND PACIFIC ISLANDER JOURNAL OF HEALTH (US/1072-0367) [28861662] **4768**

ASIAN AMERICAN JOURNEY, THE (US/0741-0336) [07828553] **4936**

ASIAN

ASIAN AMERICAN NEWS (HOUSTON, TEX.) (US/1070-3969) [28358136] 4936, **2255**

ASIAN AMERICAN POLICY REVIEW (US/1062-1830) [24524222] 4516, **2255**

●ASIAN AMERICANS INFORMATION DIRECTORY (US/1059-2458) [24517003] **2255**

ASIAN AND AFRICAN LINGUISTIC STUDIES (XR) [15377734] 2646, **3267**

ASIAN AND AFRICAN STUDIES (BRATISLAVA, CZECHOSLOVAKIA) (XO/0571-2742) [01514427] 3364, 2638, **2646**

ASIAN AND AFRICAN STUDIES (JERUSALEM) (IS/0066-8281) [01514428] 2646, **2638**

ASIAN AND PACIFIC ARCHAEOLOGY SERIES (US/0066-829X) [01780093] **260**

ASIAN AND PACIFIC COUNCIL. FOOD & FERTILIZER TECHNOLOGY CENTER *See* TECHNICAL BULLETIN - ASPAC, FOOD & FERTILIZER TECHNOLOGY CENTER **2359**

●ASIAN AND PACIFIC MIGRATION JOURNAL : APMJ (PH) [27347904] **1918**

ASIAN AND PACIFIC POPULATION FORUM *CEASED.* (US/0891-2823) [14694006] **4549**

ASIAN & PACIFIC QUARTERLY OF CULTURAL AND SOCIAL AFFAIRS (KO/0251-3110) [04416908] **2842**

ASIAN AQUACULTURE (PH/0115-4974) [04679745] **2296**

ASIAN ARCHITECT AND CONTRACTOR (HK) [10773689] 599, **292**

ASIAN ARCHIVES OF ANAESTHESIOLOGY & RESUSCITATION (II/0301-0368) [07607934] **3960**

ASIAN ART *See* ASIAN ART & CULTURE **343**

ASIAN ART (US/0894-234X) [15897409] **343**

●ASIAN ART & CULTURE (US/1352-2744) [30043563] 2501, **343**

ASIAN ART NEWS (HK) 343, **2501**

ASIAN-AUSTRALASIAN JOURNAL OF ANIMAL SCIENCES (KO/1011-2367) [19558122] **5504**

ASIAN AUTOTECH REPORT (JA) **5404**

ASIAN AVIATION (SI) [08049578] **12**

●ASIAN AVIATION NEWS (US/1071-0663) [28539375] **12**

ASIAN BOOK DEVELOPMENT NEWSLETTER (JA) [04969642] **4823**

ASIAN BOOKS NEWSLETTER (II/0004-4547) [03420534] **4823**

ASIAN BUILDING & CONSTRUCTION (HK/0264-8164) [07942014] 599, **292**

ASIAN BUSINESS (HK/0254-3729) [06456358] 1463, **640**

ASIAN BUSINESS & INDUSTRY (HK/1013-9958) [01787761] **1598**

ASIAN CENTRE OF EDUCATIONAL INNOVATION FOR DEVELOPMENT *See* ACEID NEWSLETTER **1722**

ASIAN CINEMA (US/1059-440X) [21550552] **4063**

ASIAN COLLISION ESTIMATING GUIDE (US) **5404**

ASIAN COMMUNICATIONS (UK/0952-7516) [109527516] **1149**

ASIAN COMPANY HANDBOOK (JA) [23371344] **640**

ASIAN COMPUTER DIRECTORY (HK) [13211863] **1171**

ASIAN COMPUTER MONTHLY *CEASED.* (HK/0254-217X) [10672679] **1235**

ASIAN CORPORATE LAW *See* ASIA LAW **2937**

ASIAN CULTURAL CENTRE FOR UNESCO *See* ASIAN CULTURAL CENTRE FOR UNESCO, ITS ORGANIZATION AND ACTIVITIES **2646**

ASIAN CULTURAL CENTRE FOR UNESCO *See* WHO'S WHO FOR ACCU, A **436**

ASIAN CULTURAL CENTRE FOR UNESCO, ITS ORGANIZATION AND ACTIVITIES (JA) [01795664] **2646**

ASIAN CULTURE QUARTERLY (CH/0378-8911) [01797593] **2646**

ASIAN DEFENCE JOURNAL (MY/0126-6403) [01790688] **4037**

ASIAN DEVELOPMENT BANK *See* ADB QUARTERLY REVIEW **768**

ASIAN DEVELOPMENT BANK *See* ANNUAL REPORT - ASIAN DEVELOPMENT BANK **770**

ASIAN DEVELOPMENT BANK *See* ADB REVIEW / ASIAN DEVELOPMENT BANK **768**

ASIAN DEVELOPMENT BANK. ADB QUARTERLY REVIEW *See* ADB REVIEW / ASIAN DEVELOPMENT BANK **768**

ASIAN DEVELOPMENT OUTLOOK : ADO (PH/0117-0481) [20328702] **1547**

ASIAN DEVELOPMENT REVIEW (PH/0116-1105) [09526040] **1547**

ASIAN DIGEST (UK/0144-9753) [07510657] **2501**

ASIAN ECONOMIC AND SOCIAL REVIEW, THE (II/0970-6305) [02712848] **1547**

ASIAN ECONOMIC JOURNAL : JOURNAL OF THE EAST ASIAN ECONOMIC ASSOCIATION (HK/1351-3958) [25524827] **1633**

ASIAN ECONOMIC REVIEW, THE (II/0004-4555) [01773633] **1547**

ASIAN ECONOMIES (KO/0304-260X) [01785535] **1547**

ASIAN ELECTRICITY (UK/0264-3340) [I02643340] **2036**

ASIAN ELECTRONIC ENGINEER (HK) **2036**

ASIAN ENVIRONMENT (PH/0116-2993) [11687985] **2161**

ASIAN FINANCE DIRECTORY (US/1044-4718) [19796315] **1463**

ASIAN FISHERIES SCIENCE (PH/0116-6514) [18578340] **2296**

ASIAN FISHING AND SHIPPING MAGAZINE (PH) [02187128] 5447, **2296**

ASIAN FOLKLORE STUDIES (JA/0385-2342) [01514433] **2318**

ASIAN GEOGRAPHER (HK) [08744191] **2555**

ASIAN HOSPITAL (HK/1011-596X) [I1011596X] **3777**

ASIAN HOTEL AND CATERING TIMES (HK) **2804**

ASIAN IC CONNECTION, THE (US/1057-8285) [24124219] **1598**

ASIAN INTELLIGENCE (HK) 1463, **4464**

ASIAN INTERNATIONAL LABORATORY (US) **5086**

ASIAN JEWELRY (HK) **2913**

ASIAN JOURNAL OF CHEMISTRY (II) [19934528] **961**

ASIAN JOURNAL OF CHEMISTRY REVIEWS (II/0971-0523) [22435234] **961**

ASIAN JOURNAL OF DAIRY RESEARCH (II/0253-6595) [09492080] **192**

ASIAN JOURNAL OF ECONOMICS AND SOCIAL STUDIES (II) [15482282] 5192, **1463**

ASIAN JOURNAL OF PHARMACEUTICAL SCIENCES (SI/0129-4172) [06228211] **4293**

ASIAN JOURNAL OF PHARMACY (PH/0066-8419) [02040132] **4293**

ASIAN JOURNAL OF PHILOSOPHY, THE (CC) [21314954] **4341**

ASIAN JOURNAL OF PHYSICAL EDUCATION (CH) [11699181] **1854**

ASIAN JOURNAL OF PLANT SCIENCE (II/0971-2402) [24774255] **500**

ASIAN JOURNAL OF PSYCHOLOGY & EDUCATION, THE (II) [07082572] 1726, **4575**

ASIAN JOURNAL OF PUBLIC ADMINISTRATION / YA-CHOU KUNG KUNG HSING CHENG HSUEH / UNIVERSITY OF HONG KONG, THE (HK) [10116570] **4630**

ASIAN JOURNAL OF SURGERY (HK/1015-9584) [23247525] **3960**

ASIAN LAW AND PRACTICE *See* ASIA LAW **2937**

ASIAN LAW FORUM (US/0145-0220) [02725908] **2937**

ASIAN LEASING JOURNAL, THE *SUSPENDED.* (US/1050-3706) [21469739] **2501**

ASIAN LIBRARIES (TH/1017-6748) [23952000] **3192**

ASIAN LIVESTOCK : MONTHLY PUBLICATION OF THE ANIMAL PRODUCTION AND HEALTH COMMISSION FOR ASIA, THE FAR EAST AND THE SOUTH-WEST PACIFIC (TH) [03644507] 5504, **206**

●ASIAN M&A AND INVESTMENT DATABASE (US/1076-3708) [30396944] **891**

ASIAN MANUFACTURING (HK/0301-7117) [01792464] **3475**

ASIAN MARKETS MONITOR *CEASED.* (HK) [18887318] **891**

ASIAN MEDICAL & BIOTECHNOLOGY NEWS (US/0887-3127) [13207351] **3685**

ASIAN MEDICAL JOURNAL (JA/0004-461X) [07336001] **3553**

ASIAN MEDICINE (US/1053-7813) [22645854] **3553**

ASIAN MIGRANT (PH) [18054578] **1918**

ASIAN MISSION (SI) [20555324] **4175**

ASIAN MISSIONS ADVANCE: BULLETIN OF THE ASIAN MISSIONS ASSOCIATION (KO) [05186640] **4936**

ASIAN MONETARY MONITOR (HK/1010-416X) [06930403] 1463, **640**

ASIAN MUSIC (US/0044-9202) [01748126] 383, **4101**

ASIAN NEWS SHEET (II/0518-8881) [06969031] **5274**

ASIAN OIL & GAS (HK) **4251**

ASIAN OUTLOOK *See* WORLD OUTLOOK / SHIH CHIEH CHAN WANG **4501**

ASIAN PACIFIC BUSINESS MAGAZINE *CEASED.* (US) [15808908] **640**

ASIAN PACIFIC CULTURE : APC : CROSS-CULTURAL MAGAZINE OF THE ASIAN CULTURAL CENTRE FOR UNESCO (JA) [18643329] **2501**

ASIAN-PACIFIC ECONOMIC LITERATURE (UK/0818-9935) [17598701] 1463, **1530**

ASIAN-PACIFIC ENVIRONMENT *SUSPENDED.* (MY/0127-7170) [20589603] **2161**

ASIAN PACIFIC JOURNAL OF ALLERGY AND IMMUNOLOGY (TH/0125-877X) [10409292] **3666**

ASIAN-PACIFIC POPULATION PROGRAMME NEWS *CEASED.* (TH/0125-6718) [04544822] **4549**

●ASIAN PACIFIC QUARTERLY (KO) [29697867] **2842**

ASIAN PERSPECTIVE (KO) [03423775] **4516**

ASIAN PERSPECTIVES (HONOLULU) (US/0066-8435) [01514437] 231, **260**

ASIAN PETROLEUM (MY) **1933**

ASIAN PHILOSOPHICAL STUDIES (US/0066-8443) [06398676] **4341**

ASIAN PHILOSOPY (UK/0955-2367) [23899533] **4341**

ASIAN POPULATION STUDIES SERIES (US/0066-8451) [01514438] **4549**

ASIAN PRESS AND MEDIA DIRECTORY, THE (PH/0115-2254) [01798916] **756**

ASIAN PRESS, THE (KO/0304-8667) [01786596] **2917**

ASIAN PRODUCTIVITY ORGANIZATION *See* ANNUAL REPORT - ASIAN PRODUCTIVITY ORGANIZATION **1597**

ASIAN PROFILE (HK/0304-8675) [01796720] **5192**

ASIAN RECORDER (II/0004-4644) [01703895] **2646**

ASIAN REVIEW OF BUSINESS AND TECHNOLOGY (UK/0956-3784) **640**

ASIAN SECURITY (JA) [06000462] **4516**

ASIAN SHIPPING (HK) [08593082] **5447**

ASIAN SOCIAL SCIENCE BIBLIOGRAPHY WITH ANNOTATIONS AND ABSTRACTS (II/0066-8478) [01833806] **5226**

ASIAN SOURCES COMPUTER PRODUCTS (HK/0254-5586) [10989863] **1235**

ASIAN SOURCES ELECTRONIC COMPONENTS *See* ELECTRONIC COMPONENTS **2047**

ASIAN SOURCES ELECTRONICS (HK/0254-1114) [09718000] 3475, **2036**

ASIAN SOURCES GARMENTS AND ACCESSORIES *See* FASHION ACCESSORIES **1084**

ASIAN SOURCES GIFTS & HOME PRODUCTS *See* GIFTS & HOME PRODUCTS **2906**

ASIAN SOURCES HARDWARES FOR WORLD MARKETS (HK) [15069954] 2810, **1598**

ASIAN SOURCES TIMEPIECES (HK/0254-1173) [13899409] **2916**

ASIAN STUDENT NEWS (HK) **1726**

ASIAN STUDIES (PH/0004-4679) [00850177] **2501**

ASIAN STUDIES AT HAWAII (US/0066-8486) [01514445] **2646**

ASIAN STUDIES (CALCUTTA, INDIA) (II) [10228094] **2501**

ASIAN STUDIES CENTER BACKGROUNDER (US/0749-0062) [10224575] **4516**

ASIAN STUDIES NEWSLETTER (US/0362-4811) [02294382] **2646**

ASIAN STUDIES REVIEW (AT/1035-7823) [22530588] 3364, **2646**

ASIAN STUDIES SERIES (US) [17540335] **2646**

ASIAN SURVEY (US/0004-4687) [01514447] 2646, **5192**

ASIAN TAX AFFAIRS (US) [09697906] **4711**

ASIAN TEXTILE JOURNAL (II/0971-3425) [109713425] **5348**

ASIAN THEATRE JOURNAL (US/0742-5457) [10362505] 5361, **383**

ASIAN THOUGHT & SOCIETY (US/0361-3968) [02566761] **4540**

ASIAN TIMBER (UK) [09720454] **2399**

ASIAN TIMBER (SINGAPORE) (SI/0217-4421) [I02174421] **2375**

ASIAN TIMES (UK/0264-8490) **2485**

ASIAN VENTURE CAPITAL JOURNAL, THE (HK/1012-3334) [19086783] **891**

ASIAN VOICE (US/0195-8097) [05592462] **2722**

ASIAN WALL STREET JOURNAL (HK/0377-9920) [02841673] **640**

ASIAN WALL STREET JOURNAL. WEEKLY, THE (US/0191-0132) [04771470] **1547**

ASIAN WATER & SEWAGE (HK) [I02184559] **2224**

ASIAN WETLAND NEWS (MY/0128-0538) [23041606] 2211, **2187**

ASIAN WOMAN / OFFICIAL PUBLICATION OF THE ASIAN WOMEN'S INSTITUTE (IT) [09709034] **5551**

ASIAN YEARBOOK OF INTERNATIONAL LAW (NE/0928-432X) [27607314] **3124**

ASIANWEEK (US/0195-2056) [05361856] **5633**

ASIAPACIFIC BRIEFING PAPER (US/1055-6095) [23238643] **2646**

ASIA'S 7,500 LARGEST COMPANIES (UK) [12494342] **640**

ASIATHEQUE (CN/0228-4138) [08072163] **2646**

ASIATIC HERPETOLOGICAL RESEARCH (US/1051-3825) [21942935] **5577**

ASIATIC SOCIETY OF BANGLADESH *See* JOURNAL OF THE ASIATIC SOCIETY OF BANGLADESH **5232**

ASIATIC SOCIETY OF BOMBAY *See* JOURNAL OF THE ASIATIC SOCIETY OF BOMBAY **5232**

ASIATISCHE STUDIEN (SZ/0004-4717) [01514460] **2646**

ASIATRADE (AT) 4711, **1633**

ASIAWEEK (HK) [02510196] **2501**

●ASIC & EDA (US/1067-9804) [27399735] **4398**

ASIC TECHNOLOGY & NEWS *See* ASIC & EDA **4398**

ASIDES. ABERDEEN STUDIES IN DEFENCE ECONOMICS (UK/0305-1641) [I03051641] **1464**

ASIE DU SUD-EST ET MONDE INSULINDIEN (FR/0395-2681) [05369835] **2646**

ASIE NOUVELLE, L' (FR/0403-4465) [02905935] 1464, **1633**

ASIEN (GW/0721-5231) [08563454] **2501**

ASIEN, AFRIKA, LATEINAMERIKA (GW) [08561875] **2485**

ASIEN, AFRIKA, LATEINAMERIKA (GW/0066-8508) [01789709] **1547**

ASIEN, PAZIFIK / OSTASIATISCHER VEREIN E.V (GW) [24488441] **2646**

ASIFA. ASSOCIATION INTERNATIONALE DU FILM D'ANIMATION, CANADA (CN/0828-7511) [12227573] **4063**

ASIGNACIONES FAMILIARES (URUGUAY) *See* BOLETIN ESTADISTICO - ASIGNACIONES FAMILIARES **5275**

●ASIMOV'S SCIENCE FICTION (US/1065-2698) [26559528] **3364**

ASINO D'ORO, L' (IT) [24162774] **3364**

ASIRYADA (II/0304-8683) [01784175] **2501**

ASIS ... HANDBOOK AND DIRECTORY (US) [13112937] **3192**

ASISTENCIA RECIPROCA PETROLERA ESTATAL LATINOAMERICANA *See* BOLETIN TECNICO - ARPEL **4252**

ASK (BETHESDA, MD.) *CEASED*. (US/0731-2350) [08139799] **5086**

ASKAR (CD) [03666572] **4037**

ASKOV AMERICAN (US) [01514464] **5694**

ASL (AT/1034-9154) [23714342] **3192**

ASLA MEMBERS' HANDBOOK (US/0192-5067) [05038577] **2409**

●ASLIB BOOK GUIDE / ASLIB (UK) [25364997] **5086**

ASLIB BOOK-LIST *See* ASLIB BOOK GUIDE / ASLIB **5086**

ASLIB INFORMATION (LONDON, ENGLAND : 1973) (UK/0305-0033) [01514470] **3192**

ASLIB PROCEEDINGS (UK/0001-253X) [02059961] **3192**

ASLN *See* ASL **3192**

ASM INTERNATIONAL *See* ASM NEWS (METALS PARK, OHIO) **3998**

ASM NEWS (US/0044-7897) [02936870] **560**

ASM NEWS (METALS PARK, OHIO) (US/0044-7889) [17065945] **3998**

ASM SERIES IN METAL PROCESSING (US) [12577518] **3998**

ASMAL AUSTRALIA TRAVEL (NZ/1171-3631) [I11713631] **5462**

ASMAL NEW ZEALAND TRAVEL (NZ/1171-3690) [I11713690] **5462**

ASMAT SKETCH BOOK, AN (US) [01785693] 2255, **231**

ASME BOILER AND PRESSURE VESSEL CODE (US/0517-5321) [01480822] **2110**

ASME CHEMICAL PLANT & PETROLEUM REFINERY PIPING (US) **2110**

ASME GUIDE FOR GAS TRANSMISSION AND DISTRIBUTION PIPING SYSTEMS (US) [05138210] **2110**

ASME NEWS (1981) (US/0279-9316) [07365000] **2110**

ASMP--THE SOCIETY OF PHOTOGRAPHERS IN COMMUNICATIONS *See* BULLETIN - ASMP--THE SOCIETY OF PHOTOGRAPHERS IN COMMUNICATIONS **4367**

ASNE : PROCEEDINGS OF THE ... CONVENTION OF THE AMERICAN SOCIETY OF NEWSPAPER EDITORS (US) [09060306] **2917**

ASOCIACION ARGENTINA DE ASTRONOMIA *See* BOLETIN / ASOCIACION ARGENTINA DE ASTRONOMIA **393**

ASOCIACION ARGENTINA DE CONSORCIOS REGIONALES DE EXPERIMENTACION AGRICOLA *See* REVISTA DE LOS CREA **129**

ASOCIACION ARGENTINA DE ECONOMIA POLITICA *See* REUNION ANUAL - AAEP **1594**

ASOCIACION BIOQUIMICA ARGENTINA *See* REVISTA DE LA ASOCIACION BIOQUIMICA ARGENTINA **493**

ASOCIACION COLOMBIANA DE PROFESORES DE ESPANOL Y LITERATURA A NIVEL SUPERIOR *See* ACOPEL **3261**

ASOCIACION DE BIBLIOTECARIOS GRADUADOS DE LA REPUBLICA ARGENTINA *See* BOLETIN INFORMATIVO DE LA ASOCIACION DE BIBLIOTECARIOS GRADUADOS DE LA REPUBLICA ARGENTINA **3196**

ASOCIACION DE BIBLIOTECAS UNIVERSITARIAS Y ESPECIALIZADAS DE NICARAGUA *See* BOLETIN - ASOCIACION DE BIBLIOTECAS UNIVERSITARIAS Y ESPECIALIZADAS DE NICARAGUA **3196**

ASOCIACION DE INDUSTRIALES METALURGICOS Y DE MINERIA DE VENEZUELA *See* MEMORIA Y CUENTA DE LA ASOCIACION DE INDUSTRIALES METALURGICOS Y DE MINERIA DE VENEZUELA **4008**

ASOCIACION DE INVESTIGACION DEL TRANSPORTE (SPAIN) *See* REVISTA AIT **5436**

ASOCIACION DE TECNICOS AZUCAREROS DE CUBA *See* ATAC, ASOCIACION DE TECNICOS AZUCAREROS DE CUBA **2328**

ASOCIACION ESPANOLA DE ENTOMOLOGIA *See* BOLETIN DE LA ASOCIACION ESPANOLA DE ENTOMOLOGIA **5606**

ASOCIACION GENERAL DE AUTORES DEL URUGUAY *See* REVISTA OFICIAL DE LA ASOCIACION GENERAL DE AUTORES DEL URUGUAY **3430**

ASOCIACION GENERAL DE AUTORES DEL URUGUAY. BOLETIN *See* REVISTA OFICIAL DE LA ASOCIACION GENERAL DE AUTORES DEL URUGUAY **3430**

ASOCIACION LATINO-AMERICANA DE FILOSOFOS CATOLICOS *See* BOLETIN - ASOC. LATINO-AMERICANA DE FILOSOFOS CAT **4342**

ASOCIACION LATINOAMERICANA DE INSTITUCIONES FINANCIERAS DE DESARROLLO *See* MEMORIA - ALIDE **798**

ASOCIACION LATINOAMERICANA DE LIBRE COMERCIO *See* LISTA NACIONAL DE ARGENTINA **3003**

ASOCIACION LATINOAMERICANA DE LIBRE COMERCIO *See* COMPENDIO TEORICO Y PRACTICO - ALALC **829**

ASOCIACION LATINOAMERICANA DE LIBRE COMERCIO *See* NEWSLETTER - LATIN AMERICAN FREE TRADE ASSOCIATION **847**

ASOCIACION MEDICA DE PUERTO RICO *See* BOLETIN DE LA ASOCIACION MEDICA DE PUERTO RICO **3558**

ASOCIACION MEXICANA DE BIBLIOTECARIOS *See* NOTICIERO DE LA AMBAC **3237**

ASOCIACION MEXICANA DE TECNICOS DE LAS INDUSTRIAS DE LA CELULOSA Y DEL PAPEL *See* ATCP **4232**

ASOCIACION NACIONAL DE BIBLIOTECARIOS, ARCHIVEROS Y ARQUEOLOGOS *See* BOLETIN DE LA A.N.A.B.A **3196**

ASOCIACION NACIONAL DE INDUSTRIALES *See* REVISTA ANDI **1625**

ASOCIACION NACIONAL DE INDUSTRIALES. ANDI, REVISTA BIMESTRAL *See* REVISTA ANDI **1625**

ASOCIACION NACIONAL DE INSTITUCIONES FINANCIERAS *See* CARTA FINANCIERA - ANIF **4717**

ASOCIACION NACIONAL PARA EL FOMENTO DE EXPORTACIONES MEXICANAS *See* BOLETIN INFORMATIVO ANAFEM **825**

ASOCIACION ODONTOLOGICA ARGENTINA *See* REVISTA DE LA ASOCIACION ODONTOLOGICA ARGENTINA **1334**

ASOCIACION QUIMICA ARGENTINA *See* ANALES DE LA ASOCIACION QUIMICA ARGENTINA **960**

ASOCIACION TECNICA ESPANOLA DEL PRETENSADO (SP) **2018**

ASOCIACION VENEZOLANA DE GEOLOGIA, MINERIA Y PETROLEO *See* BOLETIN AVGMP **1367**

ASOMANTE (PR/0004-4903) [01514478] **3364**

●ASORN NEWS (US/1061-4338) [25309195] **3851**

ASOTIN COUNTY AMERICAN *CEASED*. (US/1048-5309) [20514902] **5760**

ASOTIN COUNTY SENTINEL (US) [16992888] **5760**

ASPARAGUS RESEARCH NEWSLETTER (NZ) [11484445] 164, **2409**

ASPAREZ (US/0004-4229) [03973991] **5633**

ASPBAE COURIER (AT/0814-3811) [I08143811] **1799**

ASPE. AGENZIA DI STAMPA SUI PROBLEMI DELL' EMARGINAZIONE (IT/0394-6479) [I03946479] **5240**

ASPECTEN VAN INTERNATIONALE SAMENWERKING. MAANDBLAD VAN HET DIRECTORAAT-GENERAAL INTERNATIONALE SAMENWERKING VAN HET MINISTERIE VAN BUITENLANDSE ZAKEN (NE) [08190288] **2907**

ASPECTS & DOCUMENTS (BE) 3124, **773**

ASPECTS DE LA FRANCE (FR) [05469247] **4464**

ASPECTS OF APPLIED BIOLOGY (UK/0265-1491) [11738889] **443**

ASPECTS OF EDUCATION : JOURNAL OF THE INSTITUTE OF EDUCATION, THE UNIVERSITY OF HULL (UK/0066-8672) [02277505] **1726**

ASPECTS OF EDUCATIONAL AND TRAINING TECHNOLOGY (UK/1350-1933) [20584289] **1888**

ASPECTS OF HOMOGENEOUS CATALYSIS *CEASED*. (NE) [04612081] **1039**

ASPECTS OF MATHEMATICS. D (GW/0179-2148) [I01792148] **3496**

ASPECTS OF MATHEMATICS. E (GW/0179-2156) [08948941] **3496**

ASPECTS OF MODERN LAND SURVEYING (UK/0271-9231) [06772018] **2018**

ASPECTS OF PLANT SCIENCES (II) [02477217] **500**

ASPECTS TECHNIQUES DE LA SECURITE ROUTIERE (BE) [05430448] 4768, **5439**

ASPEN DAILY NEWS (US) [21220195] **5641**

ASPEN INSTITUTE BERLIN *See* REPORT FROM ASPEN INSTITUTE BERLIN **2853**

ASPEN INSTITUTE QUARTERLY (QUEENSTOWN, MD.), THE *CEASED*. (US/1045-5930) [20156414] 4464, **5192**

ASPEN MAGAZINE (US/1043-5085) [19479091] **2528**

ASPEN : THE MAGAZINE IN A BOX (US/0004-4938) [01514482] **2528**

ASPEN TIMES, THE (US) [13179962] **5641**

ASPEN VACATION GUIDE (US/0147-0043) [03061248] **5462**

ASPEN'S ADVISOR FOR NURSE EXECUTIVES *See* ASPEN'S NURSE EXECUTIVE NETWORK **3851**

ASPEN'S ADVISOR FOR NURSE EXECUTIVES (US/0883-9743) [12267817] **3851**

●ASPEN'S NURSE EXECUTIVE NETWORK (US/1064-8119) [26408131] **3851**

ASPESA PAPERS (AT/0818-9757) [I08189757] **1726**

ASPETTI STRUTTURALI DELLE PRINCIPALI COLTIVAZIONI LEGNOSE AGRARIE (IT) [20688870] 63, **2409**

Alphabetical Title Index — ASSOCIATION

ASPHALT AND TAR ROOFING AND SIDING PRODUCTS (US/0744-0340) [03060904] **599**

ASPHALT CONTRACTOR, THE (US/1055-9205) [23379358] **5439**

ASPHALT INSTITUTE See INFORMATION SERIES - ASPHALT INSTITUTE **2024**

ASPHALT PAVING TECHNOLOGY (US/0270-2932) [06382963] **2018**

ASPHALT ROOFING (CN/0380-5786) [02443703] **633**

ASPHALT SALES (US/0197-3703) [04171551] **599**

ASPHALT WEEKLY MONITOR (US) **599**

●ASPIRE INTERNATIONAL NEWSLETTER (US/1065-2566) [26538541] **3553**

●ASPIRE (NASHVILLE, TENN.) (US/1076-5778) [30535545] **2596**

ASPLO NEWSLETTER (CN/0827-2735) [13844050] **3192**

ASPO/LAMAZE MEMBERSHIP DIRECTORY (US) [21168442] **3757**

ASPR NEWSLETTER (US) [04260835] **4240**

ASPRENAS (IT) [05084638] **2677**

ASPRS-ACSM ANNUAL CONVENTION. TECHNICAL PAPERS See ACSM TECHNICAL PAPERS / ACSM/ASPRS ANNUAL CONVENTION & EXPOSITION **2580**

ASR NEWS : AUTOMATIC SPEECH RECOGNITON NEWS (US/1051-4163) [21956592] **1171, 1104**

ASRC REPORT (US/0197-2944) [05377665] **1420**

ASRT SCANNER (US/0161-3863) [03922488] **3939**

ASSAM (INDIA). VETERINARY DEPT See PERFORMANCE BUDGET ON ANIMAL HUSBANDRY & VETERINARY **5518**

ASSAM REVIEW AND TEA NEWS, THE (II) [05379094] **63**

ASSAM SCIENCE SOCIETY See JOURNAL OF THE ASSAM SCIENCE SOCIETY **5120**

ASSAPH. SECTION B. STUDIES IN ART HISTORY (IS/0333-6476) [I03336476] **343**

ASSAPH. SECTION C. STUDIES IN THE THEATRE (IS/0334-5963) [11385209] **5361**

●ASSAULT RIFLES (US/1059-5708) [24638904] **4869, 4037**

ASSE SOCIETY UPDATE (US/0273-4737) [05748568] **1965**

ASSECURANZ-COMPASS (AU) [06227507] **2874**

ASSEMBLAGE (US/0889-3012) [13832217] **292**

ASSEMBLAGES 1981 (FR/0750-1269) [I07501269] **1021**

ASSEMBLIES OF GOD. DEPT. OF EDUCATION See ASSEMBLIES OF GOD EDUCATOR **1726**

ASSEMBLIES OF GOD EDUCATOR (US/0196-9560) [04305632] **1726**

ASSEMBLIES OF GOD. GENERAL COUNCIL See ASSEMBLIES OF GOD HOME MISSIONS **4936**

ASSEMBLIES OF GOD HERITAGE (US/0896-4394) [11014406] **4936**

ASSEMBLIES OF GOD HOME MISSIONS (US/0162-2234) [04124254] **4936**

ASSEMBLING (US/0161-8318) [02763689] **343**

ASSEMBLY (US) [04057851] **5024**

ASSEMBLY AUTOMATION (UK/0144-5154) [07757601] **1217**

ASSEMBLY (CAROL STREAM, ILL.) (US/1050-8171) [21663887] **3475, 2110**

ASSEMBLY DIRECTORY & HANDBOOK See ASSEMBLY ENGINEERING MASTER CATALOG **2110**

ASSEMBLY ENGINEERING MASTER CATALOG CEASED. (US/0066-8702) [02086466] **2110**

ASSEMBLY TECHNOLOGY BUYERS GUIDE (US/8756-5528) [11584399] **1965**

ASSEMBLY (WEST POINT, N.Y.) (US/1041-2581) [07906315] **1101**

ASSERT CEASED. (US/0890-7854) [04886885] **4575**

ASSERTIVE UTILIZATION MANAGEMENT REPORT, THE (US/1064-4962) [26406721] **3553**

ASSESSMENT ACTIVITIES (US) [08258180] **5086**

ASSESSMENT AND EVALUATION IN HIGHER EDUCATION (UK/0260-2938) [07495352] **1810**

ASSESSMENT AND VALUATION LEGAL REPORTER (US/0090-6352) [01785378] **2937, 4711**

ASSESSMENT DIGEST (US/0731-0277) [05290575] **4834, 4711**

ASSESSMENT HIGHLIGHTS. GRADE 3 SCIENCE ACHIEVEMENT TESTING PROGRAM (CN/1189-3478) [25796825] **1726**

ASSESSMENT HIGHLIGHTS. GRADE 9 SOCIAL STUDIES ACHIEVEMENT TESTING PROGRAM (CN/1189-3532) [25796823] **5192, 1726**

●ASSESSMENT IN EDUCATION: PRINCIPLES, POLICY AND PRACTICE (UK/0969-594X) **1726**

●ASSESSMENT JOURNAL (US/1073-8568) [29539667] **4711**

ASSESSMENT OF THE COMMONWEALTH (US) [05365868] **4711**

ASSESSMENT/SALES RATIO STUDY (US) [06106635] **4711**

ASSESSMENT UPDATE (US/1041-6099) [18810264] **1810**

ASSESSOR, O (BL) [03531027] **4711**

ASSET FINANCE & LEASING DIGEST (UK) [13345737] **773**

ASSET INTERNATIONAL (GREENWICH, CONN.) (US/1060-4642) [24998363] **891**

ASSET RATIO REPORT FOR ... (US) [08496676] **773**

ASSET SALES REPORT (US/0894-6175) [16147807] **773**

ASSET (ST. LOUIS, MO.), THE (US/0883-7384) [07510734] **738**

ASSETS (US/0275-5610) [07152332] **640**

ASSETS AND LIABILITIES OF INSURED DOMESTICALLY CHARTERED AND FOREIGN RELATED BANKING INSTITUTIONS (US/0895-1217) [12442496] **773**

ASSETS PROTECTION (US) **1225**

ASSETS PROTECTION SOURCEBOOK (US/0899-0468) [17978474] **891**

ASSIA. APPLIED SOCIAL SCIENCES INDEX & ABSTRACTS (UK/0950-2238) [15307879] **5192, 5226**

ASSIA, JEWISH MEDICAL ETHICS (IS/0334-3871) [18671411] **2937, 3553**

ASSIA PLUS [COMPUTER FILE] (UK) **5192, 5226**

ASSICURAZIONE; QUINDICINALE DI TECHNICA, CRONACA E GIURISPRUDENZA ASSICURATIVA (IT/0004-5098) [04888403] **2874**

ASSICURAZIONI (IT) [06589849] **2874**

ASSICURAZIONI SOCIALI OBBLIGATORIE (IT) **2874**

ASSIG NEWSLETTER (AT/1030-3812) [I10303812] **3192**

ASSIGNATION (UK/0265-2587) [I02652587] **5192**

ASSIGNMENTS IN MANAGEMENT See SUPERVISOR'S NEWSLETTER, THE **947**

ASSINEWS (IT) **2874**

ASSINIBOIA TODAY (CN/1186-3064) [24279937] **5780**

ASSISTANCE LEAGUE OF SOUTHERN CALIFORNIA See NEWS - ASSISTANCE LEAGUE OF SOUTHERN CALIFORNIA **5298**

ASSISTANCE PAYMENTS STATISTICS (US) [09050819] **5274, 5266**

ASSISTANT EDITOR SUSPENDED. (US/1051-3299) [21929573] **3192**

ASSISTANT LIBRARIAN (UK/0004-5152) [01514498] **3192**

ASSISTANTSHIPS AND GRADUATE FELLOWSHIPS IN THE MATHEMATICAL SCIENCES (US/1040-7650) [18518723] **3496, 1810**

ASSISTED REPRODUCTIVE REVIEWS (US/1051-2446) [21898132] **3757**

ASSISTENZ (GW/0722-3587) [I07223587] **2255**

ASSISTENZA SANITARIA, L' (IT/0392-050X) [04647759] **3777**

ASSISTENZA SOCIALE, L' (IT/0392-1026) [06598868] **5274**

ASSISTIVE TECHNOLOGY (US/1040-0435) [18299357] **4384**

ASSIUT JOURNAL OF AGRICULTURAL SCIENCES (UA/0258-3275) [02465822] **63**

ASSIUT VETERINARY MEDICAL JOURNAL (UA/1012-5973) [09475151] **5504**

ASSOCIACAO BRASILEIRA DA INDUSTRIA FARMACEUTICA See RELATORIO ANUAL - ASSOCIACAO BRASILEIRA DA INDUSTRIA FARMACEUTICA **4327**

ASSOCIACAO BRASILEIRA DE ESCOLAS SUPERIORES CATOLICAS See CADERNOS ABESC **4941**

ASSOCIACAO BRASILEIRA DE ORCAMENTO PUBLICO See REVISTA ABOP **4747**

ASSOCIACAO BRASILEIRA DE TRADUTORES See ABRATES **3357**

ASSOCIACAO BRASILEIRA PARA O DESENVOLVIMENTO DAS INDUSTRIAS DE BASE See ANUARIO - ABDIB **5084**

ASSOCIACAO BRASILEIRA PARA O DESENVOLVIMENTO DAS INDUSTRIAS DE BASE See RELATORIO ANUAL DA DIRETORIA - ASSOCIACAO BRASILEIRA PARA O DESENVOLVIMENTO DAS INDUSTRIAS DE BASE **1624**

ASSOCIACAO COMERCIAL DE LOURENCO MARQUES See BOLETIM DA ASSOCIACAO COMERCIAL DE LOURENCO MARQUES **825**

ASSOCIACAO DE DIRIGENTES DE EMPRESAS DO MERCADO IMOBILIARIO (RIO DE JANEIRO, BRAZIL) See REVISTA ADEMI **626**

ASSOCIACAO DOS MAGISTRADOS DO PARANA See REVISTA DA ASSOCIACAO DOS MAGISTRADOS, PARANA **3040**

ASSOCIACAO MEDICA BRASILEIRA. AMB See REVISTA DA ASSOCIACAO MEDICA BRASILEIRA **3635**

ASSOCIATE REFORMED PRESBYTERIAN, THE (US/0362-0816) [01981544] **5055**

ASSOCIATED CHAMBERS OF COMMERCE OF ZIMBABWE See CHAMBERS OF COMMERCE DIRECTORY, ZIMBABWE **819**

ASSOCIATED CHURCH PRESS See DIRECTORY / THE ASSOCIATED CHURCH PRESS **4953**

ASSOCIATED CHURCHES OF CHRIST IN NEW ZEALAND See HANDBOOK, ANNUAL CONFERENCE - ASSOCIATED CHURCHES OF CHRIST IN NEW ZEALAND **4962**

ASSOCIATED EQUIPMENT DISTRIBUTORS See RENTAL RATES COMPILATION **626**

ASSOCIATED GENERAL CONTRACTORS OF AMERICA. CAROLINAS BRANCH See ROSTER - ASSOCIATED GENERAL CONTRACTORS OF AMERICA. CAROLINAS BRANCH **627**

ASSOCIATED HARVARD ALUMNI. DIRECTORY OF OFFICERS See DIRECTORY OF CLUB OFFICERS **1101**

ASSOCIATED LANDSCAPE CONTRACTORS OF AMERICA See WHO'S WHO IN LANDSCAPE CONTRACTING (1979) **2433**

ASSOCIATED LANDSCAPE CONTRACTORS OF AMERICA See GUIDE TO SPECIFICATIONS FOR INTERIOR LANDSCAPING, A **2418**

ASSOCIATED LANDSCAPE CONTRACTORS OF AMERICA. INTERIOR LANDSCAPE DIVISION See WHO'S WHO IN INTERIOR LANDSCAPING **437**

ASSOCIATED LOCKSMITHS OF AMERICA See MEMBERSHIP DIRECTORY / ALOA, ASSOCIATED LOCKSMITHS OF AMERICA, INC **4206**

ASSOCIATED SCHOOL BOARDS OF SOUTH DAKOTA See ASBSD BULLETIN **1860**

ASSOCIATED WRITING PROGRAMS See AWP NEWSLETTER (NORFOLK) **3365**

ASSOCIATION ADVOCATE / STATE OF NEVADA EMPLOYEES ASSOCIATION (US) [22939127] **4701**

ASSOCIATION & SOCIETY MANAGER CEASED. (US/0004-5292) [02957344] **860**

ASSOCIATION BELGE DE RADIOPROTECTION See ANNALEN VAN DE BELGISCHE VERENIGING VOOR STRALINGSBESCHERMING **4433**

ASSOCIATION BETON QUEBEC See ANNUAIRE DES MEMBRES ... ET MANUEL DE REFERENCE / ABQ, ASSOCIATION BETON QUEBEC **598**

ASSOCIATION BRETONNE, SAINT-BRIEUC See COMPTES RENDUS, PROCES-VERBAUX, MEMOIRES - MEMOIRES - ASSOCIATION BRETONNE ET UNION REGIONALISTE BRETONNE **2684**

ASSOCIATION CANADIENNE D'ATHLETISME See REGLEMENTS OFFICIELS / ASSOCIATION CANADIENNE D'ATHLETISME **4914**

ASSOCIATION CANADIENNE DE BADMINTON See MANUEL - ASSOCIATION CANADIENNE DE BADMINTON **4904**

ASSOCIATION CANADIENNE DE DEVELOPPEMENT INDUSTRIEL See REPERTOIRE - ASSOCIATION CANADIENNE DE DEVELOPPEMENT INDUSTRIEL (1987) **1624**

ASSOCIATION CANADIENNE DE FOOTBALL AMATEUR See REGLES DU JEU CANADIENNES POUR LE FOOTBALL AVEC PLAQUE **4914**

ASSOCIATION CANADIENNE DE LA CONSTRUCTION See DIRECTORY OF CORPORATE MEMBER FIRMS AND MEMBER-ASSOCIATIONS / CANADIAN CONSTRUCTION ASSOCIATION **613**

ASSOCIATION Alphabetical Title Index

ASSOCIATION CANADIENNE DE LA CONSTRUCTION See APERCU - ASSOCIATION CANADIENNE DE LA CONSTRUCTION **599**

ASSOCIATION CANADIENNE DES AUTOMOBILISTES See ENONCES DE PRINCIPE - ASSOCIATION CANADIENNE DES AUTOMOBILISTES **5414**

ASSOCIATION CANADIENNE DES PRODUCTEURS DE PATES ET PAPIERS. SECTION TECHNIQUE See PRETIRES, CONFERENCE TECHNOLOGIQUE ESTIVALE **4237**

ASSOCIATION CANADIENNE DES PROFESSEURS D'UNIVERSITE See NOTE DE SERVICE - ASSOCIATION CANADIENNE DES PROFESSEURS D'UNIVERSITE **1838**

ASSOCIATION CANADIENNE DU GAZ See NORME **622**

ASSOCIATION CANADIENNE DU PERSONNEL ADMINISTRATIF UNIVERSITAIRE See DELIBERATIONS DU CONGRES - ASSOCIATION CANADIENNE DU PERSONNEL ADMINISTRATIF UNIVERSITAIRE **1819**

ASSOCIATION CANADIENNE-FRANCAISE DE L'ONTARIO See ACFO INFO **2526**

ASSOCIATION CANADIENNE-FRANCAISE POUR L'AVANCEMENT DES SCIENCES See ANNALES DE L'A C F A S **5083**

ASSOCIATION CATHOLIQUE CANADIENNE DE LA SANTE See REVUE A. C. C. S **3792**

ASSOCIATION D'AMITIE FRANCO-VIETNAMIENNE See BULLETIN D'INFORMATION ET DE DOCUMENTATION **4517**

ASSOCIATION DE LA CONSTRUCTION DE MONTREAL ET DU QUEBEC See BULLETIN JURIDIQUE **2944**

ASSOCIATION DE LA CONSTRUCTION DE MONTREAL ET DU QUEBEC See NOUVELLES. SECURITE. ASSOCIATION DE LA CONSTRUCTION DE MONTREAL ET DU QUEBEC **623**

ASSOCIATION DE LA CONSTRUCTION DE MONTREAL ET DU QUEBEC See SERVICES AUX MEMBRES - ASSOCIATION DE LA CONSTRUCTION DE MONTREAL ET DU QUEBEC **1710**

ASSOCIATION DE LA CONSTRUCTION DE MONTREAL ET DU QUEBEC See NOUVELLES. RELATIONS OUVRIERES. ASSOCIATION DE LA CONSTRUCTION DE MONTREAL ET DU QUEBEC **1695**

ASSOCIATION DE MESSES DES MISSIONNAIRES DES SAINTS-APOTRES, L' (CN/0820-7836) [09457110] **4936**

ASSOCIATION DE PARALYSIE CEREBRALE DU QUEBEC See SERVICE DE LA BIBLIOTHEQUE : SUPPLEMENT AU GUIDE DE L'USAGER **3661**

ASSOCIATION DE PLACEMENT UNIVERSITAIRE ET COLLEGIAL See JOURNAL DE L'APUC (EDITION FRANCAISE) **1832**

ASSOCIATION DE PLANIFICATION FISCALE ET FINANCIERE. CONGRES See CONGRES - ASSOCIATION DE PLANIFICATION FISCALE ET FINANCIERE **3118**

ASSOCIATION DENTAIRE CANADIENNE See DELIBERATIONS DE L'ASSOCIATION DENTAIRE CANADIENNE **1320**

ASSOCIATION DENTAIRE CANADIENNE See DIRECTORY OF CANADIAN DENTAL ASSOCIATION **1322**

ASSOCIATION DES AMIS DE RABELAIS ET DE LA DEVINIERE See BULLETIN - ASSOCIATION DES AMIS DE RABELAIS ET DE LA DEVINIERE **3369**

ASSOCIATION DES ASSUREURS-VIE DE QUEBEC See ASSUREUR VIE A L'ECOUTE **2874**

ASSOCIATION DES BIBLIOTHECAIRES FRANCAIS See BULLETIN DE L'ASSOCIATION DES BIBLIOTHECAIRES FRANCAIS **3198**

ASSOCIATION DES BIBLIOTHECAIRES FRANCAIS See ANNUAIRE DES MEMBRES DE L'ASSOCIATION DES BIBLIOTHECAIRES FRANCAIS **3190**

ASSOCIATION DES BIBLIOTHEQUES DE LA SANTE DU CANADA See C H L A/A B S C NEWSLETTER **3199**

ASSOCIATION DES COLLEGES DU QUEBEC See ANNUAIRE - ASSOCIATION DES COLLEGES DU QUEBEC (1979) **1808**

ASSOCIATION DES COMPTABLES GENERAUX AGREES DU CANADA See NATIONAL DIRECTORY OF PUBLIC PRACTITIONERS / CGA CANADA **748**

ASSOCIATION DES CONSEILLERS EN ORGANISATION ET METHODES DE QUEBEC See BULLETIN - ASSOCIATION DES CONSEILLERS EN ORGANISATION ET METHODES DE QUEBEC, LE **862**

ASSOCIATION DES CONSOMMATEURS DU QUEBEC See JOUETS (MONTREAL. 1976) **2584**

ASSOCIATION DES DIRECTEURS DE CREDIT DE MONTREAL See ADC DU CREDIT **768**

ASSOCIATION DES FAMILLES KIROUAC : BULLETIN, L' (CN/0833-1685) [11050397] **2438**

ASSOCIATION DES GEOLOGUES DU BASSIN DE PARIS See BULLETIN D'INFORMATION DES GEOLOGUES DU BASSIN DE PARIS **1369**

ASSOCIATION DES HOPITAUX DE LA PROVINCE DE QUEBEC See HEBDO A H P Q **3783**

ASSOCIATION DES INGENIEURS ELECTRICIENS SORTIS DE L'INSTITUT ELECTROTECHNIQUE MONTEFIORE See BULLETIN SCIENTIFIQUE DE L'ASSOCIATION DES INGENIEURS ELECTRICIENS SORTIS DE L'INSTITUT ELECTROTECHNIQUE MONTEFIORE **2037**

ASSOCIATION DES INSPECTEURS EN HYGIENE PUBLIQUE DU QUEBEC See JOURNAL DE L'A. I. H. P. Q, LE **4786**

ASSOCIATION DES INSTITUTIONS DE NIVEAUX PRESCOLAIRE ET ELEMENTAIRE DU QUEBEC See ANNUAIRE - ASSOCIATION DES INSTITUTIONS DE NIVEAUX PRESCOLAIRE ET ELEMENTAIRE DU QUEBEC **1724**

ASSOCIATION DES INSTITUTIONS D'ENSEIGNEMENT SECONDAIRE See ANNUAIRE - ASSOCIATION DES INSTITUTIONS D'ENSEIGNEMENT SECONDAIRE **1724**

ASSOCIATION DES MEDECINS DE LANGUE FRANCAISE DU CANADA See BULLETIN - ASSOCIATION DES MEDECINS DE LANGUE FRANCAISE DU CANADA (1977) **3559**

ASSOCIATION DES NATURLISTES DU MALI See BULLETIN DE L'ASSOCIATION DES NATURALISTES DU MALI **4163**

ASSOCIATION DES PASTEURS DE FRANCE See CAHIERS DE L'APF **4941**

ASSOCIATION DES PROFESSEURS DE MATHEMATIQUES DE L'ENSEIGNEMENT PUBLIC, PARIS See BULLETIN DE L'ASSOCIATION DES PROFESSEURS DE MATHEMATIQUES ET L'ENSEIGNEMENT PUBLIC **3498**

ASSOCIATION DES PROFESSEURS D'HISTOIRE LOCALE DU QUEBEC See BULLETIN - ASSOCIATION DES PROFESSEURS D'HISTOIRE LOCALE DU QUEBEC **2724**

ASSOCIATION DES RENCONTRES CULTURELLES AVEC LES DETENUS See INFORMATION - A R C A D **3166**

ASSOCIATION DES SERVICES AUX ETUDIANTS DES COLLEGES ET UNIVERSITES DU CANADA See MEMBERSHIP DIRECTORY - CANADIAN ASSOCIATION OF COLLEGE AND UNIVERSITY STUDENT SERVICES **1835**

ASSOCIATION DES STOMISES DES BASSES LAURENTIDES (CN/0820-9995) [10392596] **3777**

ASSOCIATION DES TRADUCTEURS ANGLOPHONES DU QUEBEC See T A Q JOURNAL, A **3327**

ASSOCIATION DES TRADUCTEURS ET INTERPRETES DE L'ONTARIO See DIRECTORY OF MEMBERS OF THE ASSOCIATION OF TRANSLATORS AND INTERPRETERS OF ONTARIO **3277**

ASSOCIATION DES TRADUCTEURS ET INTERPRETES DE L'ONTARIO. REPERTOIRE See DIRECTORY OF MEMBERS OF THE ASSOCIATION OF TRANSLATORS AND INTERPRETERS OF ONTARIO **3277**

ASSOCIATION DES UNIVERSITES ET COLLEGES DU CANADA See INFO DE L'A U C C **1830**

ASSOCIATION DES UNIVERSITES PARTIELLEMENT OU ENTIEREMENT DE LANGUE FRANCAISE See REPERTOIRE DES ENSEIGNANTS ET CHERCHEURS DES INSTITUTIONS D'ENSEIGNEMENT SUPERIEUR MEMBRES DE L'AUPELF-UREF (AFRIQUE, CARAIBE, OCEAN INDIEN) **1844**

ASSOCIATION DES UNIVERSITES PARTIELLEMENT OU ENTIEREMENT DE LANGUE FRANCAISE See REPERTOIRE DES ETABLISSEMENTS D'ENSEIGNEMENT SUPERIEUR MEMBRES DE L'AUPELF-UREF **1844**

ASSOCIATION DES UNIVERSITES PARTIELLEMENT OU ENTIEREMENT DE LANGUE FRANCAISE See REPERTOIRE INTERNATIONAL DES DEPARTMENTS ET DES CENTRES D'ETUDES FRANCAISES **3315**

ASSOCIATION D'HISTOIRE COMPARATIVE DES INSTITUTIONS ET DU DROIT DE LA REPUBLIQUE SOCIALISTE DE ROUMANIE See RECHERCHES SUR L'HISTOIRE DES INSTITUTIONS ET DU DROIT **3134**

ASSOCIATION DU BARREAU CANADIEN See ... YEARBOOK OF THE CANADIAN BAR ASSOCIATION AND THE MINUTES OF PROCEEDINGS OF THE ... ANNUAL MEETING, THE **3077**

ASSOCIATION DU TRANSPORT AERIEN INTERNATIONAL See REGLEMENTATION POUR LE TRANSPORT DES MARCHANDISES DANGEREUSES **2180**

ASSOCIATION EXECUTIVE COMPENSATION STUDY (US/0273-0367) [06984268] **640**

ASSOCIATION FOR APPLIED PSYCHOPHYSIOLOGY AND BIOFEEDBACK See MEMBERSHIP DIRECTORY **4603**

ASSOCIATION FOR APPLIED PSYCHOPHYSIOLOGY AND BIOFEEDBACK. MEETING See PROCEEDINGS / ANNUAL MEETING. ASSOCIATION FOR APPLIED PSYCHOPHYSIOLOGY **4608**

ASSOCIATION FOR ASIAN STUDIES See MONOGRAPHS OF THE ASSOCIATION FOR ASIAN STUDIES **2659**

ASSOCIATION FOR ASIAN STUDIES. COMMITTEE ON EAST ASIA LIBRARIES See COMMITTEE ON EAST ASIAN LIBRARIES BULLETIN **3203**

ASSOCIATION FOR ASIAN STUDIES. COMMITTEE ON EAST ASIAN LIBRARIES See CEAL DIRECTORY **2648**

ASSOCIATION FOR ASIAN STUDIES. COMMITTEE ON EAST ASIAN LIBRARIES See COMMITTEE ON EAST ASIAN LIBRARIES DIRECTORY **2613**

ASSOCIATION FOR ASIAN STUDIES. COMMITTEE ON EAST ASIAN LIBRARIES. CEAL DIRECTORY See COMMITTEE ON EAST ASIAN LIBRARIES DIRECTORY **2613**

ASSOCIATION FOR ASIAN STUDIES. COMMITTEE ON EAST ASIAN LIBRARIES. DIRECTORY OF EAST ASIAN COLLECTIONS IN NORTH AMERICAN LIBRARIES See CEAL DIRECTORY **2648**

ASSOCIATION FOR ASIAN STUDIES. SOUTHEAST CONFERENCE See ANNALS - ASSOCIATION FOR ASIAN STUDIES. SOUTHEAST CONFERENCE **2645**

ASSOCIATION FOR BUSINESS SIMULATION AND EXPERIENTIAL LEARNING. CONFERENCE See PROCEEDINGS OF THE ... ANNUAL CONFERENCE OF THE ASSOCIATION FOR BUSINESS SIMULATION AND EXPERIENTIAL LEARNING **704**

ASSOCIATION FOR CANADIAN STUDIES IN THE UNITED STATES See ACSUS MEMBERSHIP DIRECTORY **2717**

ASSOCIATION FOR CANADIAN THEATRE RESEARCH See NEWSLETTER / ASSOCIATION FOR CANADIAN THEATRE RESEARCH **5366**

ASSOCIATION FOR COMMUNICATION ADMINISTRATION See ACA BULLETIN - ASSOCIATION FOR COMMUNICATION ADMINISTRATION **1103**

ASSOCIATION FOR COMMUNICATION ADMINISTRATION. ACA BULLETIN See JACA : JOURNAL OF THE ASSOCIATION FOR COMMUNICATION ADMINISTRATION **1114**

ASSOCIATION FOR COMPUTATIONAL LINGUISTICS. MEETING See PROCEEDINGS OF THE CONFERENCE - ASSOCIATION FOR COMPUTATIONAL LINGUISTICS. MEETING **3312**

ASSOCIATION FOR COMPUTING MACHINERY See ACM TRANSACTIONS ON MATHEMATICAL SOFTWARE **1283**

ASSOCIATION FOR COMPUTING MACHINERY See COLLECTED ALGORITHMS FROM ACM. SUPPLEMENT **1175**

ASSOCIATION FOR COMPUTING MACHINERY See ACM TRANSACTIONS ON DATABASE SYSTEMS **1252**

ASSOCIATION FOR COMPUTING MACHINERY See JOURNAL OF THE ASSOCIATION FOR COMPUTING MACHINERY **1192**

ASSOCIATION FOR COMPUTING MACHINERY See ACM TRANSACTIONS ON PROGRAMMING LANGUAGES AND SYSTEMS **1278**

ASSOCIATION FOR COMPUTING MACHINERY See ROSTER OF MEMBERS **1209**

ASSOCIATION FOR COMPUTING MACHINERY See ACM COMPUTING SURVEYS **1170**

ASSOCIATION FOR COMPUTING MACHINERY See ACM MONOGRAPH SERIES **1170**

ASSOCIATION FOR COMPUTING MACHINERY See ACM GUIDE TO COMPUTING LITERATURE **1208**

ASSOCIATION FOR COMPUTING MACHINERY. SPECIAL INTEREST COMMITTEE ON COMPUTER GRAPHICS See SICGRAPH NEWSLETTER **1235**

ASSOCIATION FOR COMPUTING MACHINERY. SPECIAL INTEREST GROUP ON BIOMEDICAL COMPUTING See SIGBIO NEWSLETTER **1203**

ASSOCIATION FOR COMPUTING MACHINERY. SPECIAL INTEREST GROUP ON DESIGN AUTOMATION See SIGDA NEWSLETTER **1221**

Alphabetical Title Index — ASSOCIATION

ASSOCIATION FOR COMPUTING MACHINERY. SPECIAL INTEREST GROUP ON MANAGEMENT OF DATA *See* SIGMOD RECORD **1255**

ASSOCIATION FOR COMPUTING MACHINERY. SPECIAL INTEREST GROUP ON NUMERICAL MATHEMATICS *See* SIGNUM NEWSLETTER **1203**

ASSOCIATION FOR COMPUTING MACHINERY. SPECIAL INTEREST GROUP ON SYMBOLIC & ALGEBRAIC MANIPULATION *See* SIGSAM BULLETIN **1203**

ASSOCIATION FOR CONSUMER RESEARCH (U.S.) *See* ADVANCES IN CONSUMER RESEARCH **1293**

ASSOCIATION FOR EDUCATION IN JOURNALISM. COMMITTEE ON THE STATUS OF WOMEN IN JOURNALISM EDUCATION *See* STATUS NEWS **2924**

ASSOCIATION FOR EDUCATIONAL DATA SYSTEMS *See* HANDBOOK AND DIRECTORY - ASSOCIATION FOR EDUCATIONAL DATA SYSTEMS **1749**

ASSOCIATION FOR EDUCATIONAL DATA SYSTEMS *See* PROCEEDINGS OF THE AEDS CONVENTION **1868**

ASSOCIATION FOR HOLISTIC HEALTH (U.S.) *See* NATIONAL DIRECTORY OF HOLISTIC HEALTH PROFESSIONALS, THE **3618**

ASSOCIATION FOR HOSPITAL MEDICAL EDUCATION *See* ROSTER OF MEMBERS - ASSOCIATION FOR HOSPITAL MEDICAL EDUCATION **3637**

ASSOCIATION FOR INVESTMENT MANAGEMENT AND RESEARCH *See* MEMBERSHIP DIRECTORY - ASSOCIATION FOR INVESTMENT MANAGEMENT AND RESEARCH **906**

ASSOCIATION FOR INVESTMENT MANAGEMENT AND RESEARCH. CORPORATE INFORMATION COMMITTEE *See* REPORT OF ASSOCIATION FOR INVESTMENT MANAGEMENT AND RESEARCH CORPORATE INFORMATION COMMITTEE **912**

ASSOCIATION FOR JEWISH STUDIES *See* AJS REVIEW **5045**

ASSOCIATION FOR LIBRARY SERVICE TO CHILDREN *See* ALSC NEWSLETTER **3189**

ASSOCIATION FOR NATIVE DEVELOPMENT IN THE PERFORMING AND VISUAL ARTS *See* NEWSLETTER - ASSOCIATION FOR NATIVE DEVELOPMENT IN THE PERFORMING AND VISUAL ARTS **326**

ASSOCIATION FOR POPULATION/FAMILY PLANNING LIBRARIES AND INFORMATION CENTERS, INTERNATIONAL *See* A.P.L.I.C. SPECIAL PUBLICATION **3186**

ASSOCIATION FOR POPULATION/FAMILY PLANNING LIBRARIES AND INFORMATION CENTERS, INTERNATIONAL. CONFERENCE *See* PROCEEDINGS OF THE ... ANNUAL CONFERENCE / ASSOCIATION FOR POPULATION/FAMILY PLANNING LIBRARIES AND INFORMATION CENTERS INTERNATIONAL **2285**

ASSOCIATION FOR PRESERVATION TECHNOLOGY *See* COMMUNIQUE - ASSOCIATION FOR PRESERVATION TECHNOLOGY **295**

ASSOCIATION FOR PSYCHOANALYTIC MEDICINE *See* BULLETIN - ASSOCIATION FOR PSYCHOANALYTIC MEDICINE **3922**

ASSOCIATION FOR RESEARCH IN NERVOUS AND MENTAL DISEASE *See* RESEARCH PUBLICATIONS - ASSOCIATION FOR RESEARCH IN NERVOUS AND MENTAL DISEASE **3845**

ASSOCIATION FOR RESEARCH ON NONPROFIT ORGANIZATIONS AND VOLUNTARY ACTION *See* ARNOVA NEWS **5274**

ASSOCIATION FOR RETARDED CHILDREN OF BRITISH COLUMBIA. ANNUAL CONFERENCE (MINUTES) (CN/0316-9332) [02247376] **5274**

ASSOCIATION FOR RETARDED CHILDREN OF BRITISH COLUMBIA. CONFERENCE *See* ASSOCIATION FOR RETARDED CHILDREN OF BRITISH COLUMBIA. ANNUAL CONFERENCE (MINUTES) **5274**

ASSOCIATION FOR RETARDED CITIZENS OF MULTNOMAH COUNTY *See* ARC REMARKS **1875**

ASSOCIATION FOR SCOTTISH LITERARY STUDIES *See* SCOT LIT **3434**

ASSOCIATION FOR SCOTTISH LITERARY STUDIES *See* ASSOCIATION FOR SCOTTISH LITERARY STUDIES **3337**

ASSOCIATION FOR SCOTTISH LITERARY STUDIES (UK) [03377291] **3337**

ASSOCIATION FOR SOCIAL ANTHROPOLOGY IN OCEANIA *See* ASAO MONOGRAPH **231**

ASSOCIATION FOR SOCIAL WORK EDUCATION IN AFRICA *See* ASWEA: JOURNAL FOR SOCIAL WORK EDUCATION IN AFRICA **5274**

ASSOCIATION FOR SUPERVISION AND CURRICULUM DEVELOPMENT *See* ASCD UPDATE **1888**

ASSOCIATION FOR THE ADVANCEMENT OF AGRICULTURAL SCIENCES IN AFRICA *See* AAASA NEWSLETTER **42**

ASSOCIATION FOR THE ADVANCEMENT OF BALTIC STUDIES *See* NEWSLETTER - ASSOCIATION FOR THE ADVANCEMENT OF BALTIC STUDIES, INC **5211**

ASSOCIATION FOR THE ADVANCEMENT OF BALTIC STUDIES. AABS NEWSLETTER *See* BALTIC STUDIES NEWSLETTER **5192**

ASSOCIATION FOR THE ADVANCEMENT OF MEDICAL INSTRUMENTATION *See* AAMI MEMBERSHIP DIRECTORY **3543**

ASSOCIATION FOR THE ADVANCEMENT OF MEDICAL INSTRUMENTATION *See* PROCEEDINGS OF THE ANNUAL AAMI/FDA CONFERENCE ON MEDICAL DEVICE REGULATION **3696**

ASSOCIATION FOR THE ADVANCEMENT OF MEDICAL INSTRUMENTATION *See* STANDARDS MONITOR **3642**

ASSOCIATION FOR THE ADVANCEMENT OF SCANDINAVIAN STUDIES IN CANADA. MEETING *See* SCANDINAVIAN-CANADIAN STUDIES **2759**

ASSOCIATION FOR THE ANTHROPOLOGICAL STUDY OF PLAY *See* NEWSLETTER - THE ASSOCIATION FOR THE ANTHROPOLOGICAL STUDY OF PLAY **4853**

ASSOCIATION FOR THE EDUCATION OF TEACHERS IN SCIENCE *See* AETS YEARBOOK **5081**

ASSOCIATION FOR THE STUDY OF CANADIAN RADIO AND TELEVISION *See* BULLETIN - ASSOCIATION FOR THE STUDY OF CANADIAN RADIO AND TELEVISION **1128**

ASSOCIATION FOR THE STUDY OF THE WORLD REFUGEE PROBLEM *See* A.W.R. BULLETIN **5269**

ASSOCIATION FOR TROPICAL BIOLOGY *See* MEMBERSHIP DIRECTORY **464**

ASSOCIATION FOR WOMEN IN MATHEMATICS *See* NEWSLETTER - ASSOCIATION FOR WOMEN IN MATHEMATICS **5562**

ASSOCIATION FRANCAISE DE GEMMOLOGIE *See* REVUE DE GEMMOLOGIE A.F.G **2915**

ASSOCIATION FRANCAISE D'OBSERVATEURS D'ETOILES VARIABLES *See* BULLETIN DE L'ASSOCIATION FRANCAISE D'OBSERVATEURS D'ETOILES VARIABLES **394**

ASSOCIATION FRANCAISE POUR L'ETUDE ET LE DEVELOPPEMENT DES APPLICATIONS DE L'ENERGIE SOLAIRE *See* CAHIERS DE L'AFEDES **1934**

ASSOCIATION GENERALE DES HYGIENISTES ET TECHNICIENS MUNICIPAUX (FRANCE) *See* ANNUAIRE / ASSOCIATION GENERALE DES HYGIENISTES ET TECHNICIENS MUNICIPAUX **4765**

ASSOCIATION GENERALE DES HYGIENISTES ET TECHNICIENS MUNICIPAUX (FRANCE). ANNUAIRE DES MEMBRES *See* ANNUAIRE / ASSOCIATION GENERALE DES HUGIENISTES ET TECHNICIENS MUNICIPAUX **4765**

ASSOCIATION GUILLAUME BUDE *See* BULLETIN DE L'ASSOCIATION GUILLAUME BUDE **3270**

ASSOCIATION HANDBOOK *See* HANDBOOK / ASSOCIATION OF AMERICAN LAW SCHOOLS **2976**

ASSOCIATION HENRI CAPITANT DES AMIS DE LA CULTURE JURIDIQUE FRANCAISE *See* TRAVAUX DE L'ASSOCIATION HENRI CAPITANT POUR LA CULTURE JURIDIQUE FRANCAISE **1300**

ASSOCIATION INTERNATIONALE DES ETUDES BYZANTINES *See* BULLETIN D'INFORMATION ET DE COORDINATION **2681**

ASSOCIATION INTERNATIONALE D'ETUDES PATRISTIQUES *See* BULLETIN D'INFORMATION ET DE LIAISON DE L'ASSOCIATION INTERNATIONALE D'ETUDES PATRISTIQUES **4941**

ASSOCIATION LAW AND POLICY (US) **2937**

ASSOCIATION LEONARD-DE-VINCI (FR/0224-0718) [I02240718] **343**

ASSOCIATION MANAGEMENT (US) [05509074] **860**

ASSOCIATION MANAGEMENT (US/0004-5578) [01514548] **640**

ASSOCIATION MANAGEMENT WATFORD (UK/0144-9613) [I01449613] **860**

ASSOCIATION MARKETING (US/0890-9709) [14507867] **921**

ASSOCIATION MATHEMATIQUE DU QUEBEC *See* BULLETIN AMQ **3497**

ASSOCIATION MEETINGS (US/1042-3141) [19005348] **756**

ASSOCIATION MONDIALE DES MEDECINS FRANCOPHONES (1982) (CN/0820-7399) [09456993] **3553**

ASSOCIATION NATIONALE DE LA RECHERCHE TECHNIQUE *See* INFORMATION ET DOCUMENTATION - ASSOCIATION NATIONALE DE LA RECHERCHE TECHNIQUE **3215**

ASSOCIATION NATIONALE DE LA RECHERCHE TECHNIQUE *See* MEMBRES DE L'ASSOCIATION NATIONALE DE LA RECHERCHE TECHNIQUE ET LEURS TRAVAUX, LES **5128**

ASSOCIATION NEWS - INDUSTRIAL FIRST AID ATTENDANTS ASSOCIATION OF BRITISH COLUMBIA (CN/0844-0506) [19586033] **3795**

ASSOCIATION OF ACADEMIC HEALTH CENTERS (U.S.) *See* DIRECTORY - ASSOCIATION OF ACADEMIC HEALTH CENTERS (U.S.) **3779**

ASSOCIATION OF ACADEMIC HEALTH CENTERS (U.S.) *See* MEMBERSHIP DIRECTORY **3789**

ASSOCIATION OF ACADEMIC HEALTH CENTERS (U.S.). DIRECTORY *See* MEMBERSHIP DIRECTORY **3789**

ASSOCIATION OF AFRICAN UNIVERSITIES *See* INFORMATION: BULLETIN DE L'A.U.A **1830**

ASSOCIATION OF AMERICAN CHAMBERS OF COMMERCE IN LATIN AMERICA *See* AACCLA REPORT **817**

ASSOCIATION OF AMERICAN FEED CONTROL OFFICIALS *See* OFFICIAL PUBLICATION - ASSOCIATION OF AMERICAN FEED CONTROL OFFICIALS **203**

ASSOCIATION OF AMERICAN GEOGRAPHERS *See* AAG NEWSLETTER **2553**

ASSOCIATION OF AMERICAN GEOGRAPHERS *See* ANNALS OF THE ASSOCIATION OF AMERICAN GEOGRAPHERS **2554**

ASSOCIATION OF AMERICAN GEOGRAPHERS *See* ABSTRACTS, ANNUAL MEETING - ASSOCIATION OF AMERICAN GEOGRAPHERS **2553**

ASSOCIATION OF AMERICAN LAW SCHOOLS *See* PLACEMENT BULLETIN - ASSOCIATION OF AMERICAN LAW SCHOOLS **3029**

ASSOCIATION OF AMERICAN LAW SCHOOLS *See* HANDBOOK / ASSOCIATION OF AMERICAN LAW SCHOOLS **2976**

ASSOCIATION OF AMERICAN LAW SCHOOLS. SECTION ON WOMEN IN LEGAL EDUCATION *See* NEWSLETTER - ASSOCIATION OF AMERICAN LAW SCHOOLS. SECTION ON WOMEN IN LEGAL EDUCATION **3017**

ASSOCIATION OF AMERICAN MEDICAL COLLEGES *See* AAMC CURRICULUM DIRECTORY **1806**

ASSOCIATION OF AMERICAN MEDICAL COLLEGES *See* REPORT ON MEDICAL SCHOOL FACULTY SALARIES **1844**

ASSOCIATION OF AMERICAN MEDICAL COLLEGES *See* AAMC DIRECTORY OF AMERICAN MEDICAL EDUCATION **1806**

ASSOCIATION OF AMERICAN PESTICIDE CONTROL OFFICIALS, INC *See* OFFICIAL PUBLICATION - ASSOCIATION OF AMERICAN PESTICIDE CONTROL OFFICIALS, INC **4246**

ASSOCIATION OF AMERICAN PHYSICIANS *See* TRANSACTIONS OF THE ASSOCIATION OF AMERICAN PHYSICIANS **3647**

ASSOCIATION OF AMERICAN PLANT FOOD CONTROL OFFICIALS *See* OFFICIAL PUBLICATION - ASSOCIATION OF AMERICAN PLANT FOOD CONTROL OFFICIALS **116**

ASSOCIATION OF AMERICAN PUBLISHERS *See* EXHIBITS DIRECTORY - ASSOCIATION OF AMERICAN PUBLISHERS **4815**

ASSOCIATION OF AMERICAN PUBLISHERS *See* ANNUAL REPORT / ASSOCIATION OF AMERICAN PUBLISHERS **4812**

ASSOCIATION OF AMERICAN RAILROADS *See* STANDARD TRANSPORTATION COMMODITY CODE **5437**

ASSOCIATION OF AMERICAN RAILROADS. COMMUNICATION AND SIGNAL DIVISION. MEETING *See* TECHNICAL PAPERS PRESENTED AT GENERAL SESSIONS AND COMMITTEE WORKSHOPS. ANNUAL MEETING **5437**

5945

ASSOCIATION — Alphabetical Title Index

ASSOCIATION OF AMERICAN RAILROADS. COMMUNICATION AND SIGNAL DIVISION. TECHNICAL CONFERENCE See ANNUAL TECHNICAL CONFERENCE 5429

ASSOCIATION OF AMERICAN RAILROADS. ECONOMICS AND FINANCE DEPT See RAILROAD REVENUES, EXPENSES, AND INCOME: CLASS I RAILROADS IN THE UNITED STATES 5435

ASSOCIATION OF AMERICAN RAILROADS. MECHANICAL DIVISION See CIRCULAR - ASSOCIATION OF AMERICAN RAILROADS, MECHANICAL DIVISION 5430

ASSOCIATION OF AMERICAN UNIVERSITY PRESSES See DIRECTORY / ASSOCIATION OF AMERICAN UNIVERSITY PRESSES 4813

ASSOCIATION OF ARAB-AMERICAN UNIVERSITY GRADUATES See AAUG MONOGRAPH SERIES 4514

ASSOCIATION OF ASPHALT PAVING TECHNOLOGISTS See ASPHALT PAVING TECHNOLOGY 2018

ASSOCIATION OF BANK HOLDING COMPANIES See BANK HOLDING COMPANY FACTS 775

ASSOCIATION OF BIOMEDICAL COMMUNICATIONS DIRECTORS See JOINT MEMBERSHIP DIRECTORY / THE ASSOCIATION OF BIOMEDICAL COMMUNICATIONS DIRECTORS, THE ASSOCIATION OF MEDICAL ILLUSTRATORS, THE HEALTH SCIENCES COMMUNICATIONS ASSOCIATION 1114

ASSOCIATION OF BRITISH THEOLOGICAL AND PHILOSOPHICAL LIBRARIES See BULLETIN OF THE ASSOCIATION OF BRITISH THEOLOGICAL AND PHILOSOPHICAL LIBRARIES 3198

ASSOCIATION OF BRITISH WILD ANIMAL KEEPERS See PROCEEDINGS OF SYMPOSIUM ... OF THE ASSOCIATION OF BRITISH WILD ANIMAL KEEPERS 2202

ASSOCIATION OF BUILDING CONTRACTORS OF QUEBEC See AECQ STRATEGY 598

ASSOCIATION OF CALIFORNIA SCHOOL ADMINISTRATORS See EDCAL 1737

ASSOCIATION OF CANADIAN ARCHIVISTS See ACA BULLETIN 2478

ASSOCIATION OF CANADIAN PUBLISHERS See A C P NEWSLETTER 4811

ASSOCIATION OF CANADIAN PUBLISHERS See A C P NOTEBOOK 4811

ASSOCIATION OF CANADIAN UNIVERSITY PRESSES See DIRECTORY OF MEMBERS / ASSOCIATION OF CANADIAN UNIVERSITY PRESSES 4814

ASSOCIATION OF CHARTERED PHYSIOTHERAPISTS IN OBSTETRICS AND GYNAECOLOGY NEWSLETTER (UK) 3757

ASSOCIATION OF CLASSROOM TEACHERS See OFFICIAL REPORT - ASSOCIATION OF CLASSROOM TEACHERS 1868

ASSOCIATION OF CLINICAL PATHOLOGISTS (GREAT BRITAIN) See BROADSHEET - ASSOCIATION OF CLINICAL PATHOLOGISTS 3893

ASSOCIATION OF COLLEGE ADMISSIONS COUNSELORS. MEMBERSHIP DIRECTORY See MEMBERSHIP DIRECTORY - NATIONAL ASSOCIATION OF COLLEGE ADMISSIONS COUNSELORS 1835

ASSOCIATION OF COLLEGE AND RESEARCH LIBRARIES See ACRL PUBLICATIONS IN LIBRARIANSHIP 3187

ASSOCIATION OF COLLEGE AND UNIVERSITY AUDITORS See PROCEEDINGS : ANNUAL CONFERENCE - ASSOCIATION OF COLLEGE AND UNIVERSITY AUDITORS 750

ASSOCIATION OF COLLEGE AND UNIVERSITY CONCERT MANAGERS (U.S.). PROFILE SURVEY See PROFILE SURVEY - ASSOCIATION OF COLLEGE, UNIVERSITY AND COMMUNITY ART ADMINISTRATORS 328

ASSOCIATION OF COLLEGE, UNIVERSITY AND COMMUNITY ARTS ADMINISTRATORS See ASSOCIATION OF COLLEGE, UNIVERSITY AND COMMUNITY ARTS ADMINISTRATORS, INC 315

ASSOCIATION OF COLLEGE, UNIVERSITY AND COMMUNITY ARTS ADMINISTRATORS See ACUCAA BULLETIN 383

ASSOCIATION OF COLLEGE, UNIVERSITY AND COMMUNITY ARTS ADMINISTRATORS See PROFILE SURVEY - ASSOCIATION OF COLLEGE, UNIVERSITY AND COMMUNITY ART ADMINISTRATORS 328

ASSOCIATION OF COLLEGE, UNIVERSITY AND COMMUNITY ARTS ADMINISTRATORS, INC (US/0097-7276) [01798302] 1860, 315

ASSOCIATION OF COLLEGES AND UNIVERSITIES OF THE STATE OF NEW YORK See NEWS FROM, ACUSNY 1837

ASSOCIATION OF COLLEGES OF APPLIED ARTS AND TECHNOLOGY OF ONTARIO See ACAATO HANDBOOK 1806

ASSOCIATION OF COLLEGIATE SCHOOLS OF ARCHITECTURE See NEWS - ASSOCIATION OF COLLEGIATE SCHOOLS OF ARCHITECTURE 304

ASSOCIATION OF COMMONWEALTH UNIVERSITIES See CHECKLIST OF UNIVERSITY INSTITUTIONS IN THE COMMONWEALTH 1815

ASSOCIATION OF CONSULTING CHEMISTS AND CHEMICAL ENGINEERS See CONSULTING SERVICES 973

ASSOCIATION OF CONSULTING ENGINEERS (MALAYSIA) See ASSOCIATION OF CONSULTING ENGINEERS MALAYSIA YEARBOOK, THE 1965

ASSOCIATION OF CONSULTING ENGINEERS MALAYSIA YEARBOOK, THE (MY) [14517312] 1965

ASSOCIATION OF CONSULTING ENGINEERS OF QUEBEC See REPERTOIRE - ASSOCIATION DES INGENIEURS-CONSEILS DU QUEBEC 1993

ASSOCIATION OF CONSULTING ENGINEERS WHO'S WHO & YEAR BOOK (UK) [18089323] 1965

ASSOCIATION OF CONSULTING FORESTERS OF AMERICA See CONSULTANT - ASSOCIATION OF CONSULTING FORESTERS OF AMERICA, THE 2378

ASSOCIATION OF COUNCILS OF PHYSICIANS AND DENTISTS OF QUEBEC See A C P D Q BULLETIN 1314

ASSOCIATION OF COUNTY COUNCILS See BRIEF OUTLINE OF ACTIVITIES OF THE COMMITTEES OF THE ASSOCIATION 4634

ASSOCIATION OF COUNTY COUNCILS See YEAR BOOK - ASSOCIATION OF COUNTY COUNCILS 4695

ASSOCIATION OF DATA PROCESSING SERVICE ORGANIZATIONS See ANNUAL ADAPSO INDUSTRY REPORT 1235

ASSOCIATION OF DEPARTMENTS OF ENGLISH See ADE BULLETIN 3261

ASSOCIATION OF DEPARTMENTS OF FOREIGN LANGUAGES (U.S.) See ADFL BULLETIN 3261

ASSOCIATION OF EARTH SCIENCE EDITORS See AESE BLUELINE 1351

ASSOCIATION OF ENERGY ENGINEERS See AEE DIRECTORY OF ENERGY PROFESSIONALS, THE 2109

ASSOCIATION OF ENGINEERING GEOLOGISTS See AEG NEWS 2018

ASSOCIATION OF ENGINEERING GEOLOGISTS See BULLETIN - ASSOCIATION OF ENGINEERING GEOLOGISTS 1368

ASSOCIATION OF EUROPEAN AIRLINES See TRAFFIC AND OPERATING DATA OF AEA AIRLINES 37

ASSOCIATION OF EUROPEAN PAEDIATRIC CARDIOLOGISTS See PROCEEDINGS - ASSOCIATION OF EUROPEAN PAEDIATRIC CARDIOLOGISTS 3910

ASSOCIATION OF EXPLORATION GEOCHEMISTS SPECIAL PUBLICATION (NE) [08255755] 961

ASSOCIATION OF GEOSCIENTISTS FOR INTERNATIONAL DEVELOPMENT See AGID NEWS 1351

ASSOCIATION OF HALFWAY HOUSE ALCOHOLISM PROGRAMS OF NORTH AMERICA See DIRECTORY - ASSOCIATION OF HALFWAY HOUSE ALCOHOLISM PROGRAMS OF NORTH AMERICA 1342

ASSOCIATION OF HISTORIANS OF AMERICAN ART See ASSOCIATION OF HISTORIANS OF AMERICAN ART NEWSLETTER 343

ASSOCIATION OF HISTORIANS OF AMERICAN ART. A.H.A.A. NEWSLETTER See ASSOCIATION OF HISTORIANS OF AMERICAN ART NEWSLETTER 343

ASSOCIATION OF HISTORIANS OF AMERICAN ART NEWSLETTER (GW) [27764861] 343

ASSOCIATION OF INDIAN UNIVERSITIES See PROCEEDINGS - ASSOCIATION OF INDIAN UNIVERSITIES 1774

ASSOCIATION OF INTERNATIONAL BOND DEALERS See MEMBERS' REGISTER / AIBD, THE ASSOCIATION OF INTERNATIONAL BOND DEALERS 906

ASSOCIATION OF INTERNATIONAL BOND DEALERS. MEMBERS' REGISTER See MEMBERS' REGISTER 906

ASSOCIATION OF IRON AND STEEL ENGINEERS See PROCEEDINGS 2076

ASSOCIATION OF IRON AND STEEL ENGINEERS See YEAR BOOK - ASSOCIATION OF IRON AND STEEL ENGINEERS 2086

ASSOCIATION OF ISLAND MARINE LABORATORIES OF THE CARIBBEAN See MEETING - ASSOCIATION OF ISLAND MARINE LABORATORIES OF THE CARIBBEAN 1452

ASSOCIATION OF JESUIT COLLEGES AND UNIVERSITIES See DIRECTORY / ASSOCIATION OF JESUIT COLLEGES AND UNIVERSITIES JESUIT SECONDARY EDUCATION ASSOCIATION 1820

ASSOCIATION OF JEWISH LIBRARIES See AJL NEWSLETTER 3188

ASSOCIATION OF JEWISH LIBRARIES See MEMBERSHIP DIRECTORY 3230

ASSOCIATION OF JEWISH REFUGEES IN GREAT BRITAIN See AJR INFORMATION 4515

ASSOCIATION OF LAW LIBRARIES OF UPSTATE NEW YORK See NEWSLETTER - ASSOCIATION OF LAW LIBRARIES OF UPSTATE NEW YORK 3235

ASSOCIATION OF LIFE INSURANCE MEDICAL DIRECTORS OF AMERICA See TRANSACTIONS OF THE ASSOCIATION OF LIFE INSURANCE MEDICAL DIRECTORS OF AMERICA, ANNUAL MEETING 2894

ASSOCIATION OF MINE MANAGERS OF SOUTH AFRICA See PAPERS AND DISCUSSIONS - ASSOCIATION OF MINE MANAGERS OF SOUTH AFRICA 2147

ASSOCIATION OF NORTH AMERICAN MISSIONS See ROUNDTABLE 4994

ASSOCIATION OF NORTH DAKOTA GEOGRAPHERS See BULLETIN OF THE ASSOCIATION OF NORTH DAKOTA GEOGRAPHERS 2557

ASSOCIATION OF OFFICIAL ANALYTICAL CHEMISTS See JOURNAL - ASSOCIATION OF OFFICIAL ANALYTICAL CHEMISTS 98

ASSOCIATION OF OFFICIAL SEED CERTIFYING AGENCIES See ANNUAL REPORT OF THE ASSOCIATION OF OFFICIAL SEED CERTIFYING AGENCIES 163

ASSOCIATION OF ONTARIO HOUSING AUTHORITIES See SEMINAR PAPERS - ASSOCIATION OF ONTARIO HOUSING AUTHORITIES 2835

ASSOCIATION OF OPERATING ROOM NURSES See AORN JOURNAL 3851

ASSOCIATION OF OPERATING ROOM NURSES See AORN JOURNAL 3851

ASSOCIATION OF OPERATIVE MILLERS See TECHNICAL BULLETINS / ASSOCIATION OF OPERATIVE MILLERS 937

ASSOCIATION OF ORTHODOX JEWISH SCIENTISTS See PROCEEDINGS OF THE ASSOCIATIONS OF ORTHODOX JEWISH SCIENTISTS 5052

ASSOCIATION OF PACIFIC COAST GEOGRAPHERS See YEARBOOK - ASSOCIATION OF PACIFIC COAST GEOGRAPHERS 2579

ASSOCIATION OF PHYSICIAN ASSISTANT PROGRAMS See NATIONAL PHYSICIAN ASSISTANT PROGRAM PROFILE, THE 3619

ASSOCIATION OF PROFESSIONAL ENGINEERS AND GEOSCIENTISTS OF THE PROVINCE OF BRITISH COLUMBIA See DIRECTORY OF THE ASSOCIATION OF PROFESSIONAL ENGINEERS AND GEOSCIENTISTS OF THE PROVINCE OF BRITISH COLUMBIA 1971

ASSOCIATION OF PROFESSIONAL ENGINEERS OF ONTARIO See REPORT ON SALARIES 1707

ASSOCIATION OF PSYCHOLOGY INTERNSHIP CENTERS (U.S.) See DIRECTORY, INTERNSHIP PROGRAMS IN PROFESSIONAL PSYCHOLOGY (INCLUDING POST-DOCTORAL TRAINING PROGRAMS) 4585

ASSOCIATION OF PUBLIC ANALYSTS (GREAT BRITAIN) See JOURNAL OF THE ASSOCIATION OF PUBLIC ANALYSTS 4787

ASSOCIATION OF RAILWAY PRESERVATION SOCIETIES See A.R.P.S. YEAR BOOK & STEAM PRESERVATION GUIDE 5429

ASSOCIATION OF RECORDS MANAGERS AND ADMINISTRATORS. EDMONTON CHAPTER See SCOPE NOTES (EDMONTON) 2483

ASSOCIATION OF RESEARCH LIBRARIES See MINUTES OF THE MEETING - ASSOCIATION OF RESEARCH LIBRARIES 3231

ASSOCIATION OF RESEARCH LIBRARIES See ARL 3191

ASSOCIATION OF RESEARCH LIBRARIES See ARL ANNUAL SALARY SURVEY 1654

ASSOCIATION OF RESEARCH LIBRARIES See ARL STATISTICS 3257

ASSOCIATION OF RESEARCH LIBRARIES. MEETING See PROCEEDINGS OF THE ... MEETING / ASSOCIATION OF RESEARCH LIBRARIES 3242

ASSOCIATION OF RESEARCH LIBRARIES. SYSTEMS AND PROCEDURES EXCHANGE CENTER See KIT - ASSOCIATION OF RESEARCH LIBRARIES. SYSTEMS AND PROCEDURES EXCHANGE CENTER 3221

ASSOCIATION OF SOCIAL ANTHROPOLOGISTS OF THE COMMONWEALTH See ASA STUDIES 231

ASSOCIATION OF SOUTHEASTERN BIOLOGISTS See ASB BULLETIN, THE 443

ASSOCIATION OF SUPERINTENDENTS OF INSURANCE OF THE PROVINCES OF CANADA See MINUTES OF PROCEEDINGS OF THE ANNUAL CONFERENCE - ASSOCIATION OF SUPERINTENDENTS OF INSURANCE OF THE PROVINCES OF CANADA 3010

ASSOCIATION OF SURVEYORS OF PAPUA NEW GUINEA See JOURNAL OF THE ASSOCIATION OF SURVEYORS OF PAPUA NEW GUINEA, THE 2026

ASSOCIATION OF SYSTEMATICS COLLECTIONS See NEWSLETTER - ASSOCIATION OF SYSTEMATICS COLLECTIONS 4094

ASSOCIATION OF TEACHER EDUCATORS See ATE NEWS LETTER 1888

ASSOCIATION OF TEACHERS OF ENGLISH OF NOVA SCOTIA See A T E N S CONFERENCE REPORT 3357

ASSOCIATION OF THE BAR OF THE CITY OF NEW YORK See RECORD OF THE ASSOCIATION OF THE BAR OF THE CITY OF NEW YORK, THE 3036

ASSOCIATION OF THE BAR OF THE CITY OF NEW YORK. SPECIAL COMMITTEE ON CRIMINAL JUSTICE See DISCUSSION PAPER - SPECIAL COMMITTEE ON CRIMINAL JUSTICE 3163

ASSOCIATION OF TRACK AND FIELD STATISTICIANS See ANNUAL - ASSOCIATION OF TRACK AND FIELD STATISTICIANS 4856

ASSOCIATION OF TRANSLATORS AND INTERPRETERS OF ONTARIO See DIRECTORY OF MEMBERS OF THE ASSOCIATION OF TRANSLATORS AND INTERPRETERS OF ONTARIO 3277

ASSOCIATION OF TRANSLATORS AND INTERPRETERS OF ONTARIO. REPERTOIRE See DIRECTORY OF MEMBERS OF THE ASSOCIATION OF TRANSLATORS AND INTERPRETERS OF ONTARIO 3277

ASSOCIATION OF TRIAL LAWYERS OF AMERICA. CONVENTION See ANNUAL CONVENTION REFERENCE MATERIALS 2934

ASSOCIATION OF UNIVERSITY PROGRAMS IN HEALTH ADMINISTRATION See PROGRAM NOTES - ASSOCIATION OF UNIVERSITY PROGRAMS IN HEALTH ADMINISTRATION 3791

ASSOCIATION OF UNIVERSITY TEACHERS OF ECONOMICS See CONTEMPORARY ECONOMIC ANALYSIS 1590

ASSOCIATION OUVRIERE CANADIENNE See JOURNAL DE L'ASSOCIATION OUVRIERE CANADIENNE 1681

ASSOCIATION POUR LA SANTE ET LA SECURITE DU TRAVAIL, SECTEUR AFFAIRES SOCIALES See REPERTOIRE DES ACTIVITES DE FORMATION ET D'INFORMATION 2868

ASSOCIATION POUR LES ETUDES D'AMENAGEMENT ET D'URBANISME DE LA REUNION See ACTIVITES - ASSOCIATION POUR LES ETUDES D'AMENAGEMENT ET D'URBANISME DE LA REUNION 2813

ASSOCIATION POUR L'ETUDE TAXOMONIQUE DE LA FLORE D'AFRIQUE TROPICALE See BULLETIN - ASSOCIATION POUR L'ETUDE TAXONOMIQUE DE LA FLORE D'AFRIQUE TROPICALE 504

ASSOCIATION PROFESSIONELLE DES INHALOTHERAPEUTES DU QUEBEC See INFORM - A P I Q, L' 3914

ASSOCIATION PROFESSIONNELLE DES BANQUES. COMITE D'ETUDES TECHNIQUES ET DE NORMALISATION BANCAIRE See COMPTE RENDU - ASSOCIATION PROFESSIONNELLE DES BANQUES, COMITE D'ETUDES TECHNIQUES ET DE NORMALISATION BANCAIRE 784

ASSOCIATION PROVINCIALE DES CONSTRUCTEURS D'HABITATIONS DU QUEBEC See BULLETIN TRIMESTRIEL ECONOMIQUE (MONTREAL) 606

ASSOCIATION PUBLISHING (US/1055-2545) [23129205] 4812

ASSOCIATION QUEBECOISE DE TELEDETECTION See NOUVELLES DE L'A.Q.T 4413

ASSOCIATION QUEBECOISE DU TRANSPORT ET DES ROUTES See INFORMATION - L'ASSOCIATION QUEBECOISE DU TRANSPORT ET DES ROUTES 5384

ASSOCIATION QUEBECOISE POUR L'ETUDE DU QUATERNAIRE See BULLETIN - A Q Q U A 1368

ASSOCIATION SOURCE (US/1066-8691) [27076217] 640

ASSOCIATION SPORTIVE UNIVERSITAIRE DU QUEBEC See ANNUAIRE DU SPORT UNIVERSITAIRE QUEBECOIS ET CALENDRIERS DES ACTIVITES 4883

ASSOCIATION-STERLING FILMS See FREE LOAN FILMS 4071

ASSOCIATION SUISSE DES ELECTRICIENS, L' See BULLETIN DE L'ASSOCIATION SUISSE DES ELECTRICIENS 2037

ASSOCIATION TRENDS (US/0196-1942) [05780645] 640

ASSOCIATIONS CANADA (CN/1186-9798) [25066491] 5228

ASSOCIATIONS CANADA (CN/1186-9798) [25066495] 5228

ASSOCIATIONS OF DELAWARE VALLEY (US/0161-0023) [03561753] 5228

●ASSOCIATIONS QUEBEC (CN/1188-4274) [26923671] 5229

ASSOCIATIONS REPORT (US/0744-1088) [08035576] 860

ASSOCIATIONS YELLOW BOOK (US/1054-4070) [22877250] 640, 1923

ASSOCIAZIONE BANCARIA ITALIANA See ANNUARIO DELLE AZIENDE DI CREDITO E FINANZIARE 772

ASSOCIAZIONE COTONIERA ITALIANA See RAPPORTO SULLA INDUSTRIA COTONIERA ITALIANA 1623

ASSOCIAZIONE ITALIANA BIBLIOTECHE. BOLLETTINO D'INFORMAZIONI - ASSOCIAZIONE ITALIANA BIBLIOTECHE See BOLLETTINO AIB 3196

ASSOCIAZIONE ITALIANA EDITORI See ELENCO DEI QUOTIDIANI E PERIODICI ITALIANI 415

ASSOCIAZIONE ITALIANA EDITORI See CATALOGO DEI LIBRI IN COMMERCIO: AUTORI 412

ASSOCIAZIONE ITALIANA EDITORI See CATALOGO DEI LIBRI IN COMMERCIO: SOGGETTI 412

ASSOCIAZIONE ITALIANA EDITORI See CATALOGO DEI LIBRI IN COMMERCIO: TITOLI 412

ASSOCIAZIONE NAZIONALE FRE INDUSTRIE AUTOMOBILISTICHE See NOTIZIARIO STATISTICO - ANFIA 5401

ASSOCIAZIONE NAZIONALE INDUSTRIA MECCANICA VARIA ED AFFINE See REPERTORIO ASSOCIATE ANIMA 1624

ASSOCIAZIONE NAZIONALE INDUSTRIE ELETTROTECNICHE ED ELETTRONICHE. CONSIGLIO DIRETTIVO See RELAZIONE DEL CONSIGLIO DIRETTIVO ALLA ASSEMBLEA GENERALE DEI SOCI 1624

ASSOCIAZIONE TECNICA ITALIANA PER LA CELLULOSA E LA CARTA See RIUNIONE ANNUALE - ATICELCA 4238

ASSU NEWS (CN/0711-1975) [08569968] 5780

ASSUMPTION PIONEER, THE (US) [17636299] 5683

ASSUMPTIONS FOR THE ANNUAL ENERGY OUTLOOK (US) [21253009] 1933

ASSUNTOS EUROPEUS (PO) [09181710] 2937

ASSUR (US/0145-6334) [02762682] 2646

ASSURANCE COMPANIES / DEPARTMENT OF INDUSTRY, COMMERCE, AND ENERGY (IE) [08466852] 2874

ASSURANCE FRANCAISE (FR/0004-6019) [04930709] 2874

ASSURANCE I.A.R.D. AU CANADA (CN/0714-430X) [09086744] 2874

ASSURANCES (CN/0004-6027) [02230422] 2874

ASSURANCES SOCIALES (FR) 5192

ASSURE THE FREE APPROPRIATE PUBLIC EDUCATION OF ALL CHILDREN WITH DISABILITIES : ANNUAL REPORT TO CONGRESS ON THE IMPLEMENTATION OF THE INDIVIDUALS WITH DISABILITIES EDUCATION ACT / PREPARED BY THE DIVISION OF INNOVATION AND DEVELOPMENT, OFFICE OF SPECIAL EDUCATION PROGRAMS, U.S. OFFICE OF SPECIAL EDUCATION AND REHABILITATIVE SERVICES, TO (US) [24105340] 1875

ASSUREUR DES COMMERCES, L' (CN/1186-835X) [24623528] 2874

ASSUREUR VIE A L'ECOUTE (CN/0715-8564) [10845264] 2874

ASSURVIE (CN/0706-635X) [04879739] 2874

ASSYRIOLOGICAL STUDIES (US/0066-9903) [01554129] 3267

ASTA AGENCY MANAGEMENT (US/0896-4114) [16685660] 5462

ASTC NEWSLETTER (US/0895-7371) [16768661] 5086

ASTE NEWSLETTER (US/0736-6140) [09179473] 1965

ASTED See REGLEMENTS - A S T E D 3245

ASTED See GUIDE GENERAL DES COMITES - ASTED 3212

ASTED See NOUVELLES - ASTED 3237

ASTERISK (US/0097-8116) [01799088] 4101

ASTERISK (NEW YORK, N.Y.) (US/0731-1001) [24206829] 1255

ASTERISQUE (FR/0303-1179) [01640026] 3496

ASTHMA & ALLERGY ADVOCATE (US/0899-7470) [18203973] 3667

●ASTHMA MANAGEMENT (US/1050-5253) [21526809] 3948

ASTHMA UPDATE (US/8756-4734) [11564632] 3948

ASTHMA WELFARER (AT) 3948

ASTICOU (HULL) (CN/0066-992X) [03384256] 2722

ASTIN BULLETIN (UK/0515-0361) [07610866] 2874

ASTIS BIBLIOGRAPHY (CN/0226-1685) [06511349] 5086, 5173

ASTM DIRECTORY (US) [02887195] 2100

ASTM GEOTECHNICAL TESTING JOURNAL (US/0149-6115) [03528691] 1965

ASTM SPECIAL TECHNICAL PUBLICATION (US/0066-0558) [02453278] 1966

ASTM SPECIAL TECHNICAL PUBLICATION (US/0066-0558) [06959147] 2100

ASTM STANDARDS IN BUILDING CODES (US) [03759015] 599

ASTM STANDARDS INTERNATIONAL (US) 2101

ASTM YEAR BOOK (US/0090-8045) [02187242] 2101

ASTMS JOURNAL (UK) [05141414] 5086

ASTORIA SOUTH FULTON ARGUS, THE (US) [28364080] 5658

ASTR, AMERICAN SOCIETY FOR THEATRE RESEARCH NEWSLETTER (US/0044-7927) [01780032] 5361

ASTRA MILANO (IT/0392-226X) [I0392226X] 389

ASTRAD : ASEAN TRADE DIRECTORY (SI) [17978203] 823

ASTRADO, L' (FR/0004-6116) [06728194] 3364

ASTRAGALO (IT) 389

ASTRAPI PARIS. 1978 (FR/0220-1186) [I02201186] 5192

●ASTRO AGENTS (US/1065-7584) [26716389] 389

●ASTRO CASTER (US/1065-7533) [26716320] 390

ASTRO INVESTOR (US) 891

ASTRO (MONTREAL) (CN/1185-197X) [24257327] 4240

ASTRO-NEWS (BATON ROUGE, LA.) (US/0743-4227) [10574491] 390

ASTRO-TALK (US/0740-6738) [09988100] 1284

ASTRO-WEATHER (CENTRAL TIME ED.) (US/1056-9634) [23903762] 1420

●ASTRO-WEATHER (EASTERN TIME ED.) (US/1056-9642) [23903781] 1420

●ASTRO-WEATHER (MOUNTAIN TIME ED.) (US/1056-9669) [23903831] 1420

ASTROFIZICESKIE ISSLEDOVANIJA (RU/0320-9318) [04798581] 391

ASTROFIZICHESKIE ISSLEDOVANIIA (BU/0324-1459) [02369502] 391

ASTROFIZICHESKIE ISSLEDOVANIIA (US/0190-2709) [04698159] 391

ASTROFIZIKA (AI/0571-7132) [01829309] 4398, 391

ASTROGRAPH (ARLINGTON), THE (US/0094-1417) [01793833] 4367, 391

ASTROLOGICAL MAGAZINE, THE (II/0004-6140) [06723465] 390

ASTROLOGICAL   Alphabetical Title Index

ASTROLOGICAL REVIEW, THE (US/0044-9784) [03451255] **390**

ASTROLOGUE (FR) **390**

ASTROLOGY & PARAPSYCHOLOGY TODAY (US/0885-7148) [12716762] 4240, **390**

ASTROLOGY ANNUAL CALENDAR EPHEMERIS, THE (US/0363-4310) [02600621] **390**

ASTROLOGY ANNUAL REFERENCE BOOK, THE (US/0363-4140) [02600652] **390**

ASTROLOGY GUIDE (US/0004-6191) [03974861] **390**

ASTROLOGY (NEW YORK) (US/0195-0851) [04709383] **390**

ASTROLOGY QUARTERLY (UK) **390**

ASTRONAUTICAL RESEARCH (NE/0304-8705) [01783721] **12**

ASTRONAUTICS (UK) [20291454] **12**

ASTRONAUTIK (GW/0004-6221) [06203638] **12**

ASTRONAUTYKA (PL/0004-623X) [07332143] **12**

ASTRONOMI VE FIZIK DERGISI / ISTANBUL UNIVERSITESI, FEN FAKULTESI (TU/1015-5295) [22579362] 4398, **391**

ASTRONOMIA, L' (IT/0392-2308) [10454889] **391**

ASTRONOMICAL ALMANAC, THE (US/0737-6421) [06721508] **391**

ASTRONOMICAL AND ASTROPHYSICAL TRANSACTIONS (US/1055-6796) [23272677] **391**

ASTRONOMICAL CALENDAR (US/1051-6174) [02905802] **391**

ASTRONOMICAL DATA CENTER BULLETIN (US/0888-8353) [06996145] **391**

ASTRONOMICAL HANDBOOK FOR SOUTHERN AFRICA (SA) [05144035] **391**

ASTRONOMICAL HERALD (JA/0374-2466) [10465790] **391**

ASTRONOMICAL JOURNAL (NEW YORK), THE (US/0004-6256) [01518488] **392**

ASTRONOMICAL PAPERS (US/0097-7055) [01399755] **392**

ASTRONOMICAL SOCIETY OF AUSTRALIA *See* PROCEEDINGS - ASTRONOMICAL SOCIETY OF AUSTRALIA **398**

ASTRONOMICAL SOCIETY OF NEW YORK *See* NEWS LETTER OF THE ASTRONOMICAL SOCIETY OF NEW YORK **397**

ASTRONOMICAL SOCIETY OF SOUTHERN AFRICA *See* MONTHLY NOTES OF THE ASTRONOMICAL SOCIETY OF SOUTHERN AFRICA **397**

ASTRONOMICAL SOCIETY OF THE PACIFIC *See* PUBLICATIONS OF THE ASTRONOMICAL SOCIETY OF THE PACIFIC **398**

ASTRONOMICESKIJ CIRKULJAR, IZDAVAEMYJ BJURO ASTRONOMICESKIH SOOBSCENIJ AKADEMII NAUK SSSR (RU/0373-191X) [04699062] **392**

ASTRONOMICESKIJ VESTNIK (RU/0320-930X) [06731781] **392**

ASTRONOMICHESKI KALENDAR NA OBSERVATORIIATA V SOFIIA / BULGARSKA AKADEMIIA NA NAUKITE, OTDELENIE ZA MATEMATICHESKI I FIZICHESKI NAUKI, SEKTSIIA PO ASTRONOMIIA *CEASED.* (BU) [20743020] **392**

ASTRONOMICHESKII EZHEGODNIK NA ... G. / INSTITUT TEORETICHESKOI ASTRONOMII ROSSIISKOI AKADEMII NAUK (RU/0373-3343) [29809473] **392**

ASTRONOMICHESKII EZHEGODNIK SSSR (RU/0373-3343) [01850654] **392**

ASTRONOMICHESKII ZHURNAL (RU/0004-6299) [08890468] **392**

ASTRONOMIE (FR) [02254114] **392**

ASTRONOMIE MAGAZINE, L' (FR) [24624872] **392**

ASTRONOMIE-QUEBEC (CN) [24861014] **392**

ASTRONOMISCH-GEODAETISCHE ARBEITEN IN DER SCHWEIZ : ORGAN DER SCHWEIZERISCHEN NATURFORSCHENDEN GESELLSCHAFT / HERAUSGEGEBEN VON DER SCHWEIZERISCHEN GEODATISCHEN KOMMISSION (SZ) [06765765] **392**

ASTRONOMISCHE NACHRICHTEN (GW/0004-6337) [01518495] **392**

ASTRONOMISK TIDSSKRIFT (DK/0004-6345) [02257917] **392**

ASTRONOMY AND ASTROPHYSICS ABSTRACTS (GW/0067-0022) [01518498] 392, **402**

ASTRONOMY AND ASTROPHYSICS (BERLIN) (GW/0004-6361) [01518497] **392**

ASTRONOMY AND ASTROPHYSICS MONTHLY INDEX (US/0147-4669) [03176126] **392**

ASTRONOMY AND ASTROPHYSICS REVIEW, THE (GW/0935-4956) [19863876] **392**

ASTRONOMY & ASTROPHYSICS. SUPPLEMENT SERIES (FR/0365-0138) [02445085] **392**

●ASTRONOMY LETTERS (US/1063-7737) [26141853] **392**

ASTRONOMY (MILWAUKEE) (US/0091-6358) [01787772] **393**

●ASTRONOMY REPORTS (US/1063-7729) [26141940] **393**

●ASTROPARTICLE PHYSICS (NE/0927-6505) [28080665] **4398**

ASTROPHYSICAL JOURNAL. SUPPLEMENT SERIES, THE (US/0067-0049) [02413276] 4398, **393**

ASTROPHYSICAL JOURNAL, THE (US/0004-637X) [01518501] **393**

ASTROPHYSICAL LETTERS AND COMMUNICATIONS (US/0888-6512) [13684322] **393**

ASTROPHYSICS (US/0571-7256) [01518503] **4398**

ASTROPHYSICS AND SPACE SCIENCE (NE/0004-640X) [01518504] 12, **393**

ASTROPHYSICS AND SPACE SCIENCE LIBRARY (NE/0067-0057) [01644267] **393**

ASTRUIM (NE) 12, **393**

ASTURNATURA (SP) [01796433] **443**

ASTUTE INVESTOR (KINGSTON, TENN.), THE (US/0736-7643) [09202868] **891**

ASVASANA SAMITI (VIDHANAPARISHAD) AHAVALA (II) [02239624] **4631**

ASWEA: JOURNAL FOR SOCIAL WORK EDUCATION IN AFRICA (ET) [01795280] **5274**

ASWLC (US/0162-5934) [04185494] **1126**

ASYMPTOTIC ANALYSIS (NE/0921-7134) [17886937] **3496**

AT A DISTANCE (US) **1726**

AT A GLANCE (CN/0708-0263) [04784086] **3192**

AT EASE (US/0190-4280) [04711090] 4037, **4936**

AT HOME IN CANADA'S CAPITAL (CN/0225-9761) [06166666] **4834**

AT ISSUE (REGINA, SASK.) (CN/0714-8801) [09088959] **2722**

AT MI (SAINT GALLEN, SWITZERLAND) (SZ) [20323092] **5055**

AT NEWSLETTER *See* ATNF NEWSLETTER **393**

AT PRESS (UK/0951-8827) [I09518827] **4631**

●AT RANDOM (US/1062-0036) [25473736] 2917, **4812**

AT SOURCE : A QUARTERLY FOR DEVELOPMENT (NE/0920-7996) [15735521] **5086**

AT THE CENTRE (HAMILTON) *CEASED.* (CN/0226-9422) [09590538] **2859**

AT THE CROSSROADS : FEMINISM, SPIRITUALITY AND NEW PARADIGM SCIENCE EXPLORING EARTHLY AND UNEARTHLY REALITY (US) 4185, **5551**

AT THE DUNLOP (CN/0822-417X) [09822979] **4084**

AT THE LIBRARY (CN/0702-7559) [03680287] **3192**

AT THE MUSEUM (US/1065-1101) [25384494] **343**

AT-THE-PARK (CHICAGO, ILL.) (US/1048-9118) [21108257] **4857**

AT THE WHEEL POSTER (US) **640**

●AT WORK (SAN FRANCISCO, CALIF.) (US/1061-9925) [25513131] **4201**

●AT YOUR BEST (US/1065-5190) [26623025] **2596**

AT YOUR SERVICE (BIRMINGHAM, ALA.) (US/1042-6469) [19099239] **3192**

ATA *See* ATA INGEGNERIA AUTOMOTORISTICA **5404**

ATA HANDBOOK (US/0360-5205) [02244543] **2784**

ATA INGEGNERIA AUTOMOTORISTICA (IT) [07820405] **5404**

ATA JOURNAL. ASIA THEOLOGICAL ASSOCIATION. INDIA (II) **4936**

ATA NEWS (II) **4936**

ATAC, ASOCIACION DE TECNICOS AZUCAREROS DE CUBA (CU/0366-242X) [02951268] **2328**

ATACC NEWSLETTER (CN/0828-6949) [12266746] 1888, **1222**

ATAH (IS) [06587078] **2646**

ATALA (US/0160-5674) [03695746] **5605**

ATALANTA (MUNCHEN) (GW/0171-0079) [06688813] **5605**

ATALAYA CULTURAL : REVISTA DE POESIA, ARTE Y LITERATURA (SP) **3460**

ATAMA-SAIMSA (II) [02397056] **4936**

AT&T DATALINE (US/1041-2530) [18695227] **1149**

AT&T TECHNICAL JOURNAL (US/8756-2324) [11492357] **1149**

AT&T TECHNOLOGY (US/0889-8979) [14091383] **1149**

AT&T TECHNOLOGY, PRODUCTS, SYSTEMS, AND SERVICES (US) **1104**

ATARI EXPLORER (US/0882-3340) [11835345] **1264**

ATARI MAGAZINE (FR/0992-2016) [I09922016] **1264**

ATARI USER (UK/0266-545X) [I0266545X] **1264**

ATARIAN VIDEO GAME MAGAZINE (US/1043-9064) [19601286] **4857**

ATARISTE (CN/0847-5644) [21485971] **1265**

ATAS DA SOCIEDADE BOTANICA DO BRASIL, SECCAO RIO DE JANEIRO (BL) [08245823] **500**

ATASCADERO NEWS (US) [12904257] **5633**

ATB METALLURGIE (BRUSSELS, BELGIUM) (BE/0001-2696) [12149475] **3998**

●ATC MARKET REPORT (US/1070-5740) [28399181] **12**

ATCC QUALITY CONTROL METHODS FOR CELL LINES (US) [17217349] **532**

ATCC QUARTERLY NEWSLETTER (US/0894-9026) [14076948] **443**

ATCHISON COUNTY MAIL, THE (US) [13587950] **5699**

ATCHISON DAILY GLOBE (ATCHISON, KAN. : 1884) (US) [08808079] **5674**

ATCHISON MAGAZINE (US/1053-668X) [22605027] **2528**

ATCP (MX) [06353662] **4232**

●ATD, N.A.D.A. OFFICIAL HEAVY DUTY TRUCK GUIDE (US/1066-6494) [27022516] **5404**

ATE NEWS LETTER (US/0001-2718) [01460496] **1888**

ATEISMO E DIALOGO (VC) [05933214] **4936**

ATEIZM I RELIGIIA, VOPROSY I OTVETY (RU) [14162046] **4936**

ATELIER (NE) [06723500] **4222**

ATELIER ASEMI (FR/0993-538X) [I0993538X] **231**

ATELIER PARIS, L' *CEASED.* (FR/0980-9465) [I09809465] 2771, **2898**

ATEMCOP (SP/0211-8319) [I02118319] **599**

ATEMWEGS- UND LUNGENKRANKHEITEN (GW/0341-3055) [02308614] **3948**

ATENCAO (BL) [06184252] **2551**

ATENCION MEDICA (MX/0185-6235) [07540501] **3553**

ATENCION MEDICA MADRID (SP/0212-7601) [I02127601] **3553**

ATENCION PRIMARIA (SP/0212-6567) [24245957] **3736**

ATENE E ROMA (IT/0004-6493) [01518509] **1074**

ATENEA (CONCEPCION, CHILE: 1972) (CL/0004-6507) [02934458] **2611**

ATENEA (MAYAGUEZ, P.R.) (PR/0885-6079) [02937856] 5086, **343**

ATENEO VENETO : REVISTA DI SCIENZE, LETTERE ED ARTI (IT/0004-6558) [02183961] **315**

ATENEUM HELSINKI (FI/0789-9343) [I07899343] 4084, **343**

ATENEUM KAPANSKIE (PL) [05473092] **5024**

ATERET ZEKENIM (US) [07746306] **5046**

ATF BACKGROUND NOTES (AT/0812-0676) [I08120676] **1888**

ATHA (US/0883-5810) [12191168] **343**

ATHABASCA UNIVERSITY *See* FACT BOOK / ATHABASCA UNIVERSITY **1823**

ATHANOR (IT) [24769028] **3267**

ATHANOR (TALLAHASSEE, FLA.) (US/0732-1619) [08142249] **343**

ATHANOR (WESTMOUNT) (CN/0709-9592) [06033272] **3460**

ATHAREP (FR/0985-0120) [I09850120] 4384, **5274**

ATHELINGS (US/0149-0125) [03406682] **2528**

ATHENA (ATHENI) (GR/1011-1557) [06972990] 4084, **1089**

Alphabetical Title Index — ATLANTIC

ATHENA MAGAZINE (GR) [13726534] **4464**

ATHENA MEDITERRANEA (IT) [02829902] **315**

ATHENAEUM ANNOTATIONS (US) [05292333] **370**

ATHENAEUM (PAVIA, ITALY) (IT/0004-6574) [01518518] **1074**

ATHENAI (US) [10077676] **5691**

ATHENAIOS (GR) [05200364] **1089**

ATHENAUM : JAHRBUCH FUR ROMANTIK (GW) [24656687] **3364**

ATHENAUMS MONOGRAFIEN. ALFERTUMSWISSENSCHAFT (GW) [18240248] **2677**

ATHENIAN (ATHENS, GREECE) (GR) [06069837] **3267**

ATHENS DAILY NEWS, ATHENS BANNER-HERALD (US/0898-3712) [17795784] **5652**

ATHENS DAILY REVIEW (US/1040-6522) [13658134] **5746**

ATHENS LC NEWS COURIER (US/0739-1307) [09690894] **5625**

ATHENS MAGAZINE (ATHENS, GA. 1989) (US/1053-623X) [28250014] **2528**

ATHENS NEWS (ATHENS, OHIO) (US/0882-8695) [12010891] **5726**

ATHENS OBSERVER, THE (US/0744-4001) [08244929] **5652**

ATHENS STOCK EXCHANGE. INVESTMENT REPORT *See* GREEK BUSINESS MONITOR **678**

ATHENS WEEKLY REVIEW (US) [13958533] **5746**

ATHEROGENESE (WIEN) (AU/0250-4677) [04382415] **3699**

ATHEROSCLEROSIS (NE/0021-9150) [01518525] **3699**

ATHEROSCLEROSIS REVIEWS (US/0362-1650) [02196754] **3699**

ATHIOPIEN : WIRTSCHAFTLICHE ENTWICKLUNG (GW) [05699769] **1547**

ATHIOPIEN WIRTSCHAFTSLAGE (GW) [03525769] **1464**

ATHLETE, THE (US/0892-6166) [14873904] **4884**

ATHLETES IN ACTION (US/0004-6639) [04157119] **4884**

ATHLETIC ADMINISTRATION (US/0044-9873) [02256021] **4884**, **1855**

ATHLETIC BUSINESS (US/0747-315X) [10514025] **4884**, **640**

ATHLETIC DIRECTORY (US) **4884**

ATHLETIC MANAGEMENT (US) [25165820] **1888**, **4884**

ATHLETIC TRAINING *See* JOURNAL OF ATHLETIC TRAINING **1856**

●ATHLETIC TRAINING (ST. LOUIS, MO.) (US/1076-5786) [30535863] **3953**

ATHLETICS (UK) [05328377] **4884**

ATHLETICS COACH (UK/0267-0267) [08407438] **4884**

ATHLETICS EMPLOYMENT WEEKLY (US/0888-4870) [13606879] **4884**, **4201**

ATHLETICS TODAY *CEASED.* (UK/0269-1302) [02691302] **4884**

ATHLETICS (TORONTO. 1981) (CN/0229-4966) [09000592] **4884**

ATHLETICS WEEKLY (UK/0004-6671) [00046621] **4884**

ATHLON'S PRO FOOTBALL (US/0734-2888) [08705253] **4884**

ATHOL DAILY NEWS (US) [19575988] **5687**

ATI DIRECTORY (US/1047-692X) [17460235] **5348**

ATIKOKAN PROGRESS (CN) **5780**

ATILYIH (UA) [05672234] **2646**

ATIMARSA (II) [02245564] **3267**

ATIP. ASSOCIATION TECHNIQUE DE L'INDUSTRIE PAPETIERE 1989 (FR/0997-7554) [I09977554] **4232**

ATIP WORKING PAPER (BS) [25565579] **63**

ATIPCA. ASOCIACION DE TECNICOS DE LA INDUSTRIA PAPELERA Y CELULOSICA ARGENTINA (AG/0325-6901) [I03256901] **4232**

ATIQOT (IS) [26019137] **343**

ATIRA TECHNICAL DIGEST (II/0378-8148) [09290250] **5348**

ATIVIDADES DA SUDENE: CEARA (BL) [01798457] **1598**

ATIVIDADES DESENVOLVIDAS (BL) [01787526] **5086**

ATJ NEWSLETTER (US/0894-6728) [11479270] **1888**, **3267**

ATKIN'S ENCYCLOPAEDIA OF COURT FORMS IN CIVIL PROCEEDINGS (UK) [03893312] **3088**

ATLA ADVOCATE (US/0746-4177) [10030128] **2937**

ATLA : ALTERNATIVES TO LABORATORY ANIMALS (UK/0261-1929) [10628192] **480**, **578**, **3979**

ATLA BIBLIOGRAPHY SERIES (US) [03315994] **5012**

ATLA MASTERS AT WORK (US/8755-9390) [11424758] **2937**

ATLA MONOGRAPH SERIES (US) [03316011] **4936**, **3192**

ATLAL (SU) [05121739] **260**

ATLANTA (ATLANTA) (US/0004-6701) [02445094] **823**

ATLANTA BUSINESS CHRONICLE (US/0164-8071) [04138747] **640**

ATLANTA BUSINESS MAKERS & SHAKERS SERIES (US/1054-5182) [22913807] **640**

ATLANTA CONSTITUTION : A GEORGIA INDEX, THE (US/0093-1179) [01791484] **408**

ATLANTA CONSTITUTION (ATLANTA, GA. : 1897) (US) [08821030] **5652**

ATLANTA DAILY WORLD (US) [08807951] **2255**

ATLANTA FEDERAL ARCHIVES & RECORDS CENTER (GA.). ARCHIVES BRANCH *See* MICROFILM LIST **2482**

ATLANTA (GA.). BUREAU OF PLANNING *See* OFFICIAL COMPREHENSIVE DEVELOPMENT PLAN **2830**

ATLANTA HISTORY (US/0896-3975) [16507758] **2722**

ATLANTA JEWISH TIMES, THE (US/0892-3345) [15202466] **5652**

ATLANTA JOURNAL (ATLANTA, GA. : 1889) (US) [08807964] **5652**

ATLANTA JOURNAL, THE ATLANTA CONSTITUTION INDEX (ANNUAL) (US/0731-9029) [13138281] **2528**

ATLANTA KIDS MAGAZINE *SUSPENDED.* (US/1042-9271) [19252490] **1060**

ATLANTA LAKE LIFE (US) **4848**

ATLANTA LAW LIBRARIES ASSOCIATION NEWSLETTER (US) [28989763] **2937**

ATLANTA REGIONAL COMMISSION *See* MAJOR DEVELOPMENT ANNOUNCEMENTS ANNUAL REPORT / ATLANTA REGIONAL COMMISSION **2827**

ATLANTA SINGLES (US/0897-4608) [17537949] **2485**

ATLANTA SMALL BUSINESS MONTHLY, THE (US) [19730141] **640**

ATLANTA TRIBUNE (ROSWELL, GA.) (US/1064-3877) [23544593] **640**

ATLANTA VOICE, THE (US) [04423131] **5652**

ATLANTE *CEASED.* (IT/0004-6736) [02240675] **2555**

ATLANTIC *CEASED.* (UK) [07118547] **823**

ATLANTIC ADVOCATE, THE *CEASED.* (CN/0004-6744) [02277361] **2722**

ATLANTIC BAPTIST, THE (CN/0004-6752) [01776375] **5055**

ATLANTIC BEEF (CN/1184-0021) [23004423] **206**

●ATLANTIC BOOKS TODAY (CN/1192-3652) [27649288] **4823**

ATLANTIC (BOSTON, MASS. : 1981) *See* ATLANTIC MONTHLY (1993), THE **2485**

ATLANTIC (BOSTON, MASS. : 1981), THE (US/0276-9077) [07320717] **2528**

●ATLANTIC BUSINESS REPORT (CN/1192-0203) [27019125] **641**

ATLANTIC CANADA ECONOMICS ASSOCIATION *See* ANNUAL CONFERENCE OF THE ATLANTIC CANADA ECONOMICS ASSOCIATION **1462**

ATLANTIC CANADA RESEARCH LETTER (CN/0823-6933) [10061644] **2722**

ATLANTIC CHAMBER JOURNAL (CN/0835-426X) [17661939] **818**

ATLANTIC CHARISMATIC (CN/0821-6479) [09766520] **5024**

ATLANTIC CITY MAGAZINE (US/0194-9993) [05184334] **2485**

ATLANTIC CO-OPERATOR, THE (CN/0703-5357) [03184848] **1541**

ATLANTIC COAST COLLEGIATE SPORTS MAGAZINE (US/1060-362X) [24947922] **4884**

ATLANTIC COASTAL ACTION PROGRAM (CANADA) *See* ACAP NEWS **2185**

ATLANTIC COASTAL KAYAKER (US) **4884**

ATLANTIC CONSTRUCTION JOURNAL (CN/0842-9588) [19762879] **599**

ATLANTIC CONTROL STATES BEVERAGE JOURNAL (US/0044-9881) [04967988] **5070**

ATLANTIC CONTROL STATES/NORTH CAROLINA BEVERAGE JOURNAL (US/1054-657X) [22928169] **2363**

ATLANTIC CONTROL STATES/VIRGINIA BEVERAGE JOURNAL (US/1054-6561) [22928136] **2363**

ATLANTIC CONTROL STATES/WEST VIRGINIA BEVERAGE JOURNAL (US) [22928037] **2363**

ATLANTIC COUNTY (N.J.) HISTORICAL SOCIETY *See* YEARBOOK, WITH HISTORICAL AND GENEALOGICAL JOURNAL **2767**

ATLANTIC ECONOMIC JOURNAL (US/0197-4254) [02529544] **1464**

ATLANTIC ECONOMIC SOCIETY *See* BEST PAPERS PROCEEDINGS / ATLANTIC ECONOMIC SOCIETY **1464**

ATLANTIC ENERGY NEWS (CN/0821-2600) [09428177] **1933**

ATLANTIC FIREFIGHTER (CN/0838-679X) [18056527] **2288**

ATLANTIC FORESTRY JOURNAL *CEASED.* (CN/0832-5502) [17883706] **2375**

ATLANTIC GEOLOGY (CN/0843-5561) [20589820] **1366**

ATLANTIC INSIGHT *CEASED.* (CN/0708-5400) [05258175] **2485**

ATLANTIC JOURNAL OF OPPORTUNITY (CN/1183-0069) [23247659] **1598**

ATLANTIC LEGAL TELEPHONE DIRECTORY (CN/0826-2896) [13435559] **3139**

ATLANTIC LIFE BUSINESS (CN/0225-7629) [06460765] **641**

ATLANTIC LIFESTYLE BUSINESS (CN/1184-051X) [23236446] **641**

ATLANTIC LOTO (CANADA) *See* ANNUAL REVIEW - ATLANTIC LOTTERY, CANADA **4630**

ATLANTIC MATHEMATICS BULLETIN (CN/0705-9078) [04098006] **3496**

●ATLANTIC MINING JOURNAL (CN/0840-6693) [19762893] **2134**

●ATLANTIC MONTHLY (1993), THE (US/1072-7825) [29046351] **2485**

ATLANTIC NATURALIST (US/0004-6809) [01518542] **5615**, **2187**

ATLANTIC NEWS-TELEGRAPH (US/8756-6400) [11627499] **5668**

ATLANTIC NUMISMATIST, THE (CN/0708-3181) [05533961] **2779**

ATLANTIC PAPERS, THE (US) [01604651] **4516**

ATLANTIC POST CALLS (CN/0226-627X) [06473485] **2797**

ATLANTIC PROVINCES BOOK REVIEW *See* ATLANTIC BOOKS TODAY **4823**

ATLANTIC PROVINCES BOOK REVIEW, THE (CN/0316-5981) [02624626] **3337**

ATLANTIC PROVINCES LIBRARY ASSOCIATION *See* APLA BULLETIN **3191**

ATLANTIC PROVINCES LIBRARY ASSOCIATION *See* MEMBERSHIP DIRECTORY AND HANDBOOK **3230**

ATLANTIC PROVINCES REPORTS (CN/0713-8970) [02243090] **2937**

ATLANTIC REGION ... AVIATION BUSINESS DIRECTORY (CN/1183-5435) [24623645] **641**, **12**

ATLANTIC REPORT (HALIFAX, N.S.) (CN/0004-6841) [02226692] **1547**

ATLANTIC REPORTER DIGEST (US) [02352510] **2937**

ATLANTIC SALMON FEDERATION *See* ANNUAL REPORT / THE ATLANTIC SALMON FEDERATION **2295**

ATLANTIC SALMON JOURNAL, THE (CN/0044-992X) [02302539] **2296**

ATLANTIC SCHOOL OF THEOLOGY *See* ANGELOS (HALIFAX) **4934**

ATLANTIC SERIES : A COLLECTION OF STUDIES ON SUBJECTS RELATED TO THE NORTH ATLANTIC TREATY ORGANIZATION (NE/0571-7868) [01518548] **4516**

ATLANTIC SILENT NEWS (CN/1184-115X) [23598677] **4384**

ATLANTIC SPECTRUM (CN/0317-3240) [02248142] **1910**, **1810**

ATLANTIC STATES MARINE FISHERIES COMMISSION *See* ANNUAL REPORT OF THE ATLANTIC STATES MARINE FISHERIES COMMISSION **2295**

●ATLANTIC TIDE & CURRENT ALMANAC (NORTHEAST ED.) (US/1064-0142) [26190953] **4175**

ATLANTIC TRADE REPORT & GLOBAL DEFENSE INDUSTRY (US/1053-2404) [22368481] **4037**

ATLANTIC TRANSPORTATION JOURNAL (CN/0842-9596) [19762853] **5377**

ATLANTIC TRUCKING (CN/0830-1808) [15166954] **5377**

ATLANTIC — Alphabetical Title Index

ATLANTIC UNION GLEANER, THE (US) [12049293] **4936**

ATLANTICA (BL/0102-1656) [05200164] 1446, **553**

ATLANTIDA (VE) [02245005] **5192**

ATLANTIDE-REPORT: SCIENTIFIC RESULTS OF THE DANISH EXPEDITION TO THE COASTS OF TROPICAL WEST AFRICA, 1945-1946 (DK) [04887580] **553**

ATLANTIS (WOLFVILLE) (CN/0702-7818) [03409640] **5551**

ATLAS AND TEXT ASPIRATION BIOPSY CYTOLOGY (US) **532**

ATLAS/DATA ABSTRACT FOR THE UNITED STATES AND SELECTED AREAS (US) [15788265] **4037**

ATLAS DE LA REVOLUTION FRANCAISE (FR) [18238847] **5192**

ATLAS DES STRUCTURES AGRAIRES AU SUD DU SAHARA (FR/0067-0286) [03208148] **63**

ATLAS (LONDON, ENGLAND : 1985) (UK/0267-484X) [14908364] **343**

ATLAS OF ALBERTA'S CRUDE BITUMEN RESERVES (CN/0825-2483) [09371835] **4251**

ATLAS OF MOLECULAR STRUCTURES IN BIOLOGY (UK) [01075876] **443**

ATLAS OF PROTEIN SEQUENCE AND STRUCTURE. SUPPLEMENT (US) [08696039] **480**

●ATLAS OF THE ORAL AND MAXILLOFACIAL SURGERY CLINICS OF NORTH AMERICA (US/1061-3315) [25253455] **3960**

●ATLAS OF THE UROLOGIC CLINICS OF NORTH AMERICA (US/1063-5777) [26074900] **3988**

ATLAS OF TUMOR PATHOLOGY (US/0160-6344) [01777663] **3809**

ATLAS SERIES - GEOLOGICAL SURVEY OF ALABAMA (US/0160-4236) [02254402] **1366**

ATLAS SPEKTROV KHIMICHESKIKH PRODUKTOV (RU) [20347415] **961**

ATLASECO DE POCHE (FR) [15188320] **1547**

ATLETICA LEGGERA *CEASED.* (IT/0392-2251) [I03922251] 4884, **2596**

ATLETICA : RIVISTA MENSILE DELLA FIDAL (IT) **4884**

ATLETICASTUDI (IT) [12656984] **4884**

ATLETIKA : VYDAVA CESKOSLOVENSKY SVAZ TELESNE VYCHOVY (XR) [13391898] **4884**

ATLETIK'EN (DK/0905-3883) [I09053883] **4884**

ATLIN NUGGET, THE (CN/0226-6296) [06472266] **5780**

●ATM NEWSLETTER (US/1067-5221) [27254493] **4398**

ATMA VISVASA (II) [09698114] **4936**

ATMODA ATPUTAI : LTF NEDELAS LAIKRAKSTS (LV) [23230653] **2513**

ATMORE ADVANCE, THE (US/0746-1968) [09848767] **5625**

ATMOSFERA (MX/0187-6236) [17992364] **1420**

ATMOSPHERE CRISIS, THE (US/1043-5972) [19493944] **5192**

ATMOSPHERE-OCEAN (CN/0705-5900) [03947793] **1420**

●ATMOSPHERE-OCEAN SYSTEM, THE (US/1063-7184) [26123849] **1446**

●ATMOSPHERIC AND OCEANIC OPTICS (RU) [26869388] **1420**

●ATMOSPHERIC ENVIRONMENT (UK/1352-2310) [29926349] **1351**

ATMOSPHERIC ENVIRONMENT. PART A, GENERAL TOPICS (UK/0960-1686) [21110040] **2225**

ATMOSPHERIC ENVIRONMENT. PART B, URBAN ATMOSPHERE (UK/0957-1272) [20808935] **2161**

ATMOSPHERIC OZONE ... SOLAR RADIATION (PL/0138-0184) [14049886] **4433**

ATMOSPHERIC PHYSICS AND CHEMISTRY LABORATORY *See* COLLECTED REPRINTS - ATMOSPHERIC PHYSICS AND CHEMISTRY LABORATORY **4400**

ATMOSPHERIC PROGRAMS BULLETIN (US) [24398606] **5086**

ATMOSPHERIC RESEARCH (NE/0169-8095) [14208926] **1420**

ATMOSPHERIC SCIENCE PAPER (US/0067-0340) [03227371] **1420**

ATN: AUSTRALIAN TRANSPORT NEWS (AT) 5377, **823**

ATNF NEWSLETTER (AT) [22149281] **393**

ATO ALIVE (US/0899-1537) [18010106] **1089**

ATOKA COUNTY TIMES, THE (US) [23715629] **5731**

ATOLL RESEARCH BULLETIN (US/0077-5630) [01124628] **1366**

ATOM INDONESIA (IO/0126-1568) [03822478] **4446**

ATOM (LONDON, ENGLAND) (UK/0004-7015) [01518570] 1933, **4446**

ATOM TABLOID. MIDDLESEX COUNTY EDITION, THE (US/0192-5741) [05085535] **5709**

ATOMEDIA, PHILIPPINES (PH/0115-3757) [02703633] **2154**

ATOMIC ABSORPTION AND EMISSION SPECTROMETRY ABSTRACTS (UK/0309-1813) [01145608] **1013**

ATOMIC DATA AND NUCLEAR DATA TABLES (US/0092-640X) [01791173] **4446**

ATOMIC ENERGY CLEARING HOUSE (US/0519-3389) [01828924] **1933**

ATOMIC ENERGY CONTROL BOARD *See* ANNUAL REPORT **1932**

ATOMIC ENERGY IN AUSTRALIA (AT/0004-7090) [01850452] **1933**

ATOMIC ENERGY LAW JOURNAL (US/0004-7104) [01518575] 1933, **2937**

●ATOMIC ENERGY (NEW YORK, N.Y.) (US/1063-4258) [26025399] **2154**

ATOMIC ENERGY NEWSLETTER (US) [08473143] **2154**

ATOMIC INDUSTRIAL FORUM *See* PROGRAM REPORT - ATOMIC INDUSTRIAL FORUM **1953**

ATOMIC INDUSTRY, THE (US/0519-3486) [01240367] **1933**

ATOMIC SPECTROSCOPY (US/0195-5373) [05509794] **1013**

ATOMIC VETERANS' NEWSLETTER (US/0736-9255) [09269313] **4037**

ATOMIZATION AND SPRAYS (US/1044-5110) [19822075] **2008**

ATOMNAIA ENERGIIA (RU/0004-7163) [01518577] 4446, **1933**

ATOMNAIA ENERGIIA. ENGLISH. SOVIET ATOMIC ENERGY *See* ATOMIC ENERGY (NEW YORK, N.Y.) **2154**

ATOMNAIA TEKHNIKA ZA RUBEZHOM (RU/0320-9326) [09178332] **1933**

ATOMNO-VODORODNAIA ENERGETIKA I TEKHNOLOGIIA (RU) [07638221] **2154**

ATOMNYE ELEKTRICHESKIE STANTSII (RU) [20749870] **2154**

ATOMO E INDUSTRIA *CEASED.* (IT/0004-7171) [01850401] **2154**

ATOMS & WASTE (US/1056-5663) [23740008] **2225**

ATOMS IN JAPAN (JA) [02445113] 2154, **1933**

ATOMWIRTSCHAFT, ATOMTECHNIK (GW/0365-8414) [03146592] **2154**

ATORIE (JA) [13313423] **343**

ATOSSEMENT VOTRE (CN/0826-5321) [11377313] **2296**

ATOUT CHAT (FR/0769-6027) [I07696027] **5577**

ATPASES (UK/0261-4553) 480, **3553**

ATPCO CARGO TARIFF SET (US/0279-9642) [07495002] **12**

ATPCO PASSENGER TARIFF SET *CEASED.* (US/0273-6284) [06765695] **12**

ATQ. THE AMERICAN TRANSCENDENTAL QUARTERLY (US) [03580105] **3364**

ATR; AUSTRALIAN TELECOMMUNICATION RESEARCH (AT/0001-2777) [06640047] **1149**

ATRI TURF NOTES (AT/0729-9397) [I07299397] **2797**

ATRIA (CN/0824-4251) [10386350] **4084**

ATRIAL NATRIURETIC FACTORS (UK/0268-1641) [I02681641] 430, 578, **3699**

●ATRIUM GROUP ADVISORY, THE (US/1065-092X) [26498375] **3192**

ATRIUM (LONDON) (UK/0951-8088) [I09518088] **292**

ATROPOS (CN/0708-5389) [05362257] **3364**

ATS FOCUS (AT/0727-3096) [I07273096] **5086**

ATS VIDEO MAGAZINE *CEASED.* (US) **1126**

ATSIS JOURNAL (US/0277-643X) [07610557] **2874**

ATT TRAVEL DIRECTORY (HK) **5462**

ATTACKS ON JUSTICE : THE HARASSMENT AND PERSECUTION OF JUDGES AND LAWYERS (SZ) [22948602] **3139**

ATTAKAPAS GAZETTE (US/0571-8236) [05666717] **2722**

ATTENDANCE AND ENROLLMENT ACCOUNTING AND REPORTING IN CALIFORNIA PUBLIC SCHOOLS (US) [05011462] **1860**

ATTENTE (LONGUEUIL) *CEASED.* (CN/1183-0891) [23243319] **2528**

ATTENTION AND PERFORMANCE (US/1047-0387) [09295270] **4575**

ATTI (IT) [08130425] **5192**

ATTI (CI) [02239757] 231, **2677**

ATTI A.G.I (IT/0066-9830) [01951181] **542**

ATTI - COLLEGIO REGIONALE LOMBARDO DEGLI ARCHITETTI (IT/0530-9778) [03192156] **292**

ATTI DEI CIVICI MUSEI DI STORIA ED ARTE (IT) [04803857] **4084**

ATTI DEL CONVEGNO NAZIONALE - SOCIETA ITALIANA DELLE SCIENZE VETERINARIE (IT/0392-0674) [05772357] **5505**

ATTI DELLA ACCADEMIA DELLE SCIENZE DI TORINO. CLASSE DI SCIENZE FISICHE, MATEMATICHE E NATURALI (IT/0001-4419) [09177824] **5086**

ATTI DELLA ACCADEMIA LIGURE DI SCIENZE E LETTERE (IT/0392-2219) [09733974] **5086**

ATTI DELLA ACCADEMIA MEDICA LOMBARDA (IT/0001-4427) [01146169] **3553**

ATTI DELLA ACCADEMIA NAZIONALE DEI LINCEI. MEMORIE CLASSE DI SCIENZE MORALI STORICHE E FILOLOGICHE (IT/0391-8149) [I03918149] **2842**

ATTI DELLA ACCADEMIA NAZIONALE DEI LINCEI. RENDICONTI LINCEI. MATEMATICA E APPLICAZIONI (IT/1120-6330) [21899184] **3496**

ATTI DELLA ACCADEMIA NAZIONALE DEI LINCEI. RENDICONTI LINCEI. SCIENZE FISICHE E NATURALI (IT/1120-6349) [21899297] **5086**

ATTI DELLA. ACCADEMIA PELORITANA *See* ATTI DELLA ACCADEMIA PELORITANA DEI PERICOLANTI. CLASSE DI SCIENZE MEDICO-BIOLOGICHE **3553**

ATTI DELLA. ACCADEMIA PELORITANA *See* ATTI DELLA ACCADEMIA PELORITANA DEI PERICOLANTI. CLASSE I DI SCIENZE FIS., MAT. E NATURALI **4398**

ATTI DELLA ACCADEMIA PELORITANA DEI PERICOLANTI. CLASSE DI SCIENZE MEDICO-BIOLOGICHE (IT) [09554663] **3553**

ATTI DELLA ACCADEMIA PELORITANA DEI PERICOLANTI. CLASSE I DI SCIENZE FIS., MAT. E NATURALI (IT) [09703105] **4398**

ATTI DELLA ACCADEMIA PONTANIANA (IT) [03978088] **1074**

ATTI DELLA ACCADEMIA ROVERETANA DEGLI AGIATI (IT/0365-0081) [01649939] **1074**

ATTI DELLA ACCODEMIA PELORITANA DEI PERICOLANTI, CLASSE DI SCIENCE MEDICO-BIOLOGICHE (IT/0365-0294) [11824039] **443**

ATTI DELLA FONDAZIONE GIORGIO RONCHI (1976) (IT/0391-2051) [04122907] **4433**

ATTI DELLA PONTIFICIA ACCADEMIA ROMANA DI ARCHEOLOGIA. MEMORIE (IT) [06831380] **260**

ATTI DELLA PONTIFICIA ACCADEMIA ROMANA DI ARCHEOLOGIA. SERIE III, RENDICONTI (IT) [01762638] **260**

ATTI DELLA REALE ACCADEMIA PELORITANA, CLASSE DI SCIENCEIISICHE, MATHEMATICHE E BIOLOGICHE *See* ATTI DELLA ACCODEMIA PELORITANA DEI PERICOLANTI, CLASSE DI SCIENCE MEDICO-BIOLOGICHE **443**

ATTI DELLA SOCIETA DEI NATURALISTI E MATEMATICI DI MODENA (IT) [02460467] 3496, **5086**

ATTI DELLA SOCIETA ITALIANA DI SCIENZE NATURALI E DEL MUSEO CIVICO DI STORIA NATURALE DI MILANO (IT/0037-8844) [06686342] **4162**

ATTI DELLA SOCIETA LIGURE DI STORIA PATRIA (IT/01947466) **2677**

ATTI DELLA SOCIETA PELORITANA DI SCIENZE (IT) [21258920] **5086**

ATTI DELL'ACCADEMIA DI SCIENZE, LETTERE E ARTI DI UDINE (IT) [05461828] **315**

ATTI DELL'ISTITUTO ITALIANO DI NAVIGAZIONE (IT/01799612) **4175**

ATTI DELL'ISTITUTO SPERIMENTALE PER LA VALORIZZAZIONE TECNOLOGICA DEI PRODOTTI AGRICOLI, MILANO (IT) [08774287] **63**

ATTI E MEMORIE / ACCADEMIA CLEMENTINA (IT/0394-7157) [22423094] **343**

ATTI E MEMORIE (ACCADEMIA NAZIONALE DI SCIENZE, LETTERE E ARTI (MODERA, ITALY) : 1984) (IT) [19948199] **2842**

ATTI E MEMORIE / ACCADEMIA VIRGILIANA DI MANTOVA (IT/0365-4710) [22613627] **2842**

AUDIOCASSETTE

ATTI E MEMORIE DELLA ACCADEMIA DI AGRICOLTURA, SCIENZE E LETTERE DI VERONA (IT/0365-0014) [08569676] **63**

ATTI E MEMORIE DELLA ACCADEMIA PETRARCA DI LETTERE, ARTI E SCIENZE (IT/0393-2397) [I03932397] **2842**

ATTI E MEMORIE DELLA S.O.T.I.M.I. : UFFICIALE DELLA SOCIETA DI ORTOPEDIA E TRAUMATOLOGIA DELL'ITALIA MERIDIONALE ED INSULARE (IT) [18582024] **3880**

ATTI E MEMORIE DELLA SOCIETA DALMATA DI STORIA PATRIA (IT/0393-5566) [I03935566] **2677**

ATTI E MEMORIE DELLA SOCIETA ISTRIANA DI ARCHEOLOGIA E STORIA PATRIA (IT) [04818355] **260**

ATTI E MEMORIE DELLA SOCIETA MAGNA GRECIA (IT/0583-7952) [01942111] **2611**

ATTI E MEMORIE DELLA SOCIETA TIBURTINA DI STORIA E D'ARTE (IT) [07030038] **343, 2611**

ATTI E MEMORIE DELLA SOCIETA TIBURTINA DI STORIA E D'ARTE GIA ACCADEMIA DEGLI AGEVOLI E COLONIA DEGLI ARCADI SIBILLINI (IT/0394-1663) [I03941663] **2842**

ATTI E MEMORIE DELL'ACCADEMIA TOSCANA DI SCIENZE E LETTERE LA COLOMBARIA (IT/0392-0836) [08771901] **2842**

ATTI E MEMORIE - DEPUTAZIONE DI STORIA PATRIA PER LE ANTICHE PROVINCIE MODENESI (IT/0418-7296) [06587050] **2677**

ATTI E MEMORIE - DEPUTAZIONE DI STORIA PATRIA PER LE PROVINCIE DI ROMAGNA (IT/0393-7240) [I03937240] **2677**

ATTI E MEMORIE / SOCIETA SAVONESE DI STORIA PATRIA (IT/0392-033X) [02729432] **2677**

ATTI ERASSEGNA TECNICA - SOCIETA DEGLI INGEGNERI E DEGLI ARCHITETTI IN TORINO (IT/0373-3475) [I03733475] **293, 1966**

ATTI - INSTITUTO VENETO DI SCIENZE, LETTERE ED ARTI. CLASSE DI SCIENZE FISICHE, MATEMATICHE E NATURALI (IT/0392-6680) [08580408] **3496, 5086**

ATTI / ISTITUTO VENETO DI SCIENZE, LETTERE ED ARTI (IT) [01198587] **2842**

ATTI, ISTITUTO VENETO DI SCIENZE, LETTERE ED ARTI. CLASSE DI SCIENZE MORALI, LETTERE ED ARTI (IT/0392-1336) [06835268] **3364**

ATTI PARLAMENTARI. RESOCONTI STENOGRAFICI DELLE SEDUTE (IT) [05973515] **2938**

ATTI - PAVIA. UNIVERSITA. ISTITUTO BOTANICO E LABORATORIO CRITTOGAMICO (IT) [05157206] **500**

ATTI TICINENSI DI SCIENZE DALLA TERRA (IT/0394-0691) [20327711] **1366**

ATTI UFFICIALI (IT) [03875356] **2938**

ATTI UFFICIALI / ISTITUTO NAZIONALE DELLA PREVIDENZA SOCIALE (IT/0021-2520) [01963634] **2874**

ATTICA HUB (US) [16911940] **5726**

ATTITUDE (BROOKLYN (NEW YORK, N.Y.)) (US/0882-3472) [09205747] **1310**

ATTITUDE (MONTREAL) (CN/0712-1954) [08898796] **2793**

ATTITUDES & ARABESQUES (US/0889-8847) [06482007] **1310**

ATTIVITA FISICA & SPORT (IT/1120-3633) [I11203633] **4884**

ATTORNEY-CPA, THE (US/0571-8279) [05949662] **738, 2938**

ATTORNEY FEE AWARDS REPORTER (US/0732-7552) [08424920] **2938**

ATTORNEY GENERAL'S ADVISORY COMMITTEE OF UNITED STATES ATTORNEYS ANNUAL REPORT / U.S. DEPARTMENT OF JUSTICE, EXECUTIVE OFFICE FOR UNITED STATES ATTORNEYS, THE (US) [25749053] **4631**

ATTORNEY GENERAL'S DIGEST, THE (US) [07200567] **2938**

ATTORNEY GENERAL'S OPINIONS (US/0455-0315) [01784549] **3139**

ATTORNEY GENERAL'S REPORT ON FEDERAL LAW ENFORCEMENT AND CRIMINAL JUSTICE ASSISTANCE ACTIVITIES *CEASED.* (US/0161-6307) [03957991] **3158**

ATTORNEYS AND AGENTS REGISTERED TO PRACTICE BEFORE THE U.S. PATENT AND TRADEMARK OFFICE (US/0361-3844) [02246063] **2938**

ATTORNEYS COMPUTER REPORT (US/0745-421X) [09146602] **2938**

ATTORNEYS' DICTIONARY OF MEDICINE (US) [01715184] **3740**

ATTORNEYS' DIRECTORY OF SAN DIEGO COUNTY (US/0193-9300) [05259667] **3078**

ATTORNEYS GENERAL OF THE STATES AND OTHER JURISDICTIONS, THE (US) [03298331] **3139**

ATTORNEY'S GUIDE TO STATE BAR ADMISSION REQUIREMENTS (US/1057-5596) [24059131] **2938**

ATTORNEYS MARKETING REPORT (US/0745-1369) [08859610] **921, 2938**

ATTORNEYS PERSONNEL REPORT (US/8750-2763) [11202133] **938, 2938**

ATTORNEYS' TEXTBOOK OF MEDICINE (US) [01751408] **3740**

ATTRACT WILDLIFE, IMPROVE OUR ENVIRONMENT (US) [11521159] **2187**

ATTRACTION (CN/0828-6213) [12069296] **823**

ATTUALITA CINEMATOGRAFICHE (IT) [03529713] **4064**

ATTUALITA IN CHIRURGIA *CEASED.* (IT/0390-5527) [04796624] **3960**

ATTUALITA IN PSICOLOGICA (IT) **4575**

ATUACAO DO MINTER (BL) [04403112] **1547**

ATUAGAGDLIUTIT (GL) [02241191] **2555**

ATUAGATSANGA / LABRADOR CRAFT PRODUCERS ASSOCIATION (CN/0715-5093) [09499062] **370**

ATUALIDADES MEDICAS (BL/0001-1800) [03050300] **3553**

ATULU, L' (CN/0226-3688) [07294888] **3192**

ATV CANADA (CN/0829-6154) [13368963] **5377, 1966**

ATV NEWS *CEASED.* (US/0744-7809) [08551145] **4080**

ATV SPORTS *CEASED.* (US/0892-3183) [15140995] **4884**

ATW NEWS *CEASED.* (GW/0341-4213) [I03414211] **4446**

ATWATER SIGNAL (US) [26582878] **5633**

ATWOOD HERALD, THE (US) [25472196] **5658**

ATZ. AUTOMOBILTECHNISCHE ZEITSCHRIFT (GW/0001-2785) [01518918] **5404**

AU. ARQUITETURA E URBANISMO (BL/0102-8979) [I01028979] **293**

AU COEUR DE L'AFRIQUE (BD) [06668993] **4937**

AU COURANT - CANADIAN COUNCIL FOR INTERNATIONAL CO-OPERATION (CN/1181-604X) [22928666] **2907**

AU-COURANT (HYDRO-QUEBEC. BIBLIOTHEQUE) (CN/0229-8937) [08124516] **408**

AU COURANT (OTTAWA. EDITION FRANCAIS) (CN/0226-2258) [09986069] **1464**

AU COURANT (OTTAWA. ENGLISH EDITION) *CEASED.* (CN/0226-224X) [07475339] **1547**

AU COURANT (PUBLIC SERVICE COMMISSION. NATIONAL CAPITAL REGIONAL OFFICE) (CN/0228-1139) [06758398] **4631**

AU FIL DES COLLECTIONS (CN/0711-7086) [11050374] **4084**

AU FIL DES EVENEMENTS (CN/0225-1965) [I02251965] **1726**

AU FIL DU BOIS *CEASED.* (CN/0383-0047) [02811396] **2399**

AU JOUR LE SIECLE (FR) [08442844] **3337**

AU LENDEMAIN DE L'ECOLE SECONDAIRE (CN/0228-5347) [07817327] **1910**

AU NATUREL (MONTREAL) (CN/0715-4690) [09313133] **4768**

AU "PAYS" DE MATANE (CN/0836-3102) [16888269] **2438, 2722**

AU POINT (CN/0824-3069) [10339409] **1810**

AU SERVICE DE L ENSEIGNMENT INFORMATIQUE (FR) **1171**

AU SERVICE DE L'ENSEIGNEMENT. FRANCAIS (FR/0996-4703) [I09964703] **3267, 1888**

AUA UPDATE SERIES (US/0740-7386) [08295308] **3988**

AUBE (CN/0229-3587) [08036535] **3827**

AUBELLE, L' (CN/0316-3733) [02842733] **2375**

AUBURN CITIZEN (US) [18329587] **5658**

AUBURN JOURNAL (US) [28239891] **5633**

AUBURN NEWS, THE (US) [19570990] **5687**

AUBURN PLAINSMAN, THE (US/1071-1279) [28555179] **5625**

AUBURN UNIVERSITY. WATER RESOURCES RESEARCH INSTITUTE *See* WRRI BULLETIN **5549**

AUCKLAND INSTITUTE AND MUSEUM *See* ANNUAL REPORT / AUCKLAND INSTITUTE AND MUSEUM **5083**

AUCKLAND INSTITUTE AND MUSEUM *See* RECORDS OF THE AUCKLAND INSTITUTE AND MUSEUM **5145**

AUCKLAND UNIVERSITY LAW REVIEW (NZ/0067-0510) [02204334] **3105, 3089**

AUCKLAND-WAIKATO HISTORICAL JOURNAL (NZ/0111-7653) [09673447] **2611**

AUCTION CATALOGUES OF MUSIC (NE) [07383904] **4101**

AUCTION EXCHANGE, THE (US/0199-0950) [05587526] **5691**

AUCTION PRICES OF AMERICAN ARTISTS (UK/0144-3690) [07240216] **343**

AUCTION PRICES REALIZED. U.S. COINS (US/0737-6634) [08713799] **2779**

AUCTIONEER, THE (US) [07068639] **315**

AUCTIONEERS' ASSOCIATION OF ALBERTA *See* LIST OF MEMBERS / AUCTIONEERS' ASSOCIATION OF ALBERTA **929**

● AUDACITY (NEW YORK, N.Y.) (US/1064-4555) [26287888] **1547**

AUDARENA STADIUM ... INTERNATIONAL GUIDE TO FACILITIES, SUPPLIES & SERVICES (US) [22589413] **756**

AUDECIBEL (US/0004-7473) [01518595] **4384**

AUDENSHAW PAPERS (UK/0004-7481) [02285577] **4937**

AUDIBLE (TORONTO) (CN/0710-2038) [08327399] **1855, 4884**

AUDIENCIA (BL) [02773288] **1126**

AUDIO AMATEUR (US/0004-7546) [01782006] **5315**

AUDIO & ELECTRONICS DIGEST (US/0164-8985) [04297879] **5315**

AUDIO ARTS MAGAZINE SOUND RECORDING (UK) [12061103] **5315**

AUDIO CRITIC, THE (US/0146-4701) [02957339] **5315**

AUDIO-DIGEST. OBSTETRICS AND GYNECOLOGY (US/0571-8635) [01778668] **3757**

AUDIO (DURANGO, COLO.) (US/0883-8437) [11394884] **5315**

AUDIO ENGINEERING SOCIETY *See* PREPRINTS OF PAPERS PRESENTED AT THE AES CONVENTIONS **5318**

AUDIO-FILE (CN/0823-7859) [10805565] **3192**

● AUDIO JOURNAL OF ONCOLOGY (UK/1350-9667) **3553**

AUDIO LAWYER, THE (US) [10351343] **2938**

AUDIO (PHILADELPHIA, PA.) (US/0004-752X) [05369652] **5315**

AUDIO VIDEO *CEASED.* (SW/0282-6364) [13243913] **5315**

AUDIO/VIDEO INTERIORS (US/1041-5378) [18798036] **1293, 5315**

AUDIO VIDEO TOTAAL (NE/0922-2367) [I09222367] **1293**

AUDIO VISUAL (UK/0305-2249) [05073185] **1104**

AUDIO VISUAL CATALOGUE / LIBRARY, JUSTICE INSTITUTE OF BRITISH COLUMBIA (CN/1187-5453) [25352177] **408**

AUDIO VISUAL CATALOGUE - PACIFIC VOCATIONAL INSTITUTE (CN/0822-823X) [11607488] **1888**

AUDIO VISUAL DIRECTORY (UK/0956-2931) [20906015] **1126**

AUDIO VISUAL DIRECTORY (UK) [08505467] **5315**

● AUDIO-VISUAL GUIDE, RESOURCES IN GERONTOLOGY & GERIATRICS (US) [25030574] **3749**

AUDIO VISUAL MAGAZINE (UK) **1171**

AUDIO-VISUAL PRESENTATIONS / CANADIAN JEWISH CONGRESS, AUDIO-VISUAL DEPARTMENT (CN/0821-5529) [09678201] **5315**

AUDIO-VISUAL RESOURCES FOR GERONTOLOGICAL AND GERIATRIC EDUCATION *See* AUDIO-VISUAL GUIDE, RESOURCES IN GERONTOLOGY & GERIATRICS **3749**

AUDIO VISUEEL MAGAZINE (NE) **1888**

AUDIO WEEK (US/1044-7601) [19888787] **5315**

● AUDIOCASSETTE & COMPACT DISC FINDER : A SUBJECT GUIDE TO EDUCATIONAL AND LITERARY MATERIALS ON AUDIOCASSETTES AND COMPACT DISCS (US) [27166188] **1888, 3364**

AUDIOCASSETTE FINDER *See* AUDIOCASSETTE & COMPACT DISC FINDER : A SUBJECT GUIDE TO EDUCATIONAL AND LITERARY MATERIALS ON AUDIOCASSETTES AND COMPACT DISCS **3364**

AUDIOFILE — Alphabetical Title Index

●AUDIOFILE (PORTLAND, ME.) (US/1063-0244) [25844569] **1104**

AUDIOLOGIA ITALIANA : ORGANO UFFICIALE DELLA SOCIETA ITALIANA DI AUDIOLOGIA (IT) [15259299] **3886**

AUDIOLOGISCHE AKUSTIK. AUDIOLOGICAL ACOUSTICS (GW/0172-8261) [06170353] **4384**

AUDIOLOGY (SZ/0020-6091) [02257954] **3886**

AUDIO'S GUIDE TO SURROUND SOUND (US/1055-9566) [23277211] **5315**

AUDIOTEX BRIEFING (UK) **1149**

AUDIOTEX DIRECTORY & BUYER'S GUIDE (US/1042-6329) [19097430] **1149**

AUDIOTEX NEWS (US/1063-1348) [25898791] **1149**

AUDIOTEX NOW (US) **1150**

AUDIOTEX UPDATE (US/1045-5795) [20157265] **1104, 1282**

AUDIOVISION AND PROSOUND (AT/0816-9330) [I08169330] **5315**

AUDIOVISIONE (ROMA) (IT/0303-7622) [01793966] **5315**

AUDIOVISIVI *SUSPENDED*. (IT/0004-7627) **4064**

AUDIOVISUAL CATALOG - NIDA RESOURCE CENTER (US) [06622528] **1341**

AUDIOVISUAL JOURNAL OF CATARACT & IMPLANT SURGERY (US/1067-9812) [16410111] **3872**

AUDIOVISUAL LIBRARIAN, THE (UK/0302-3451) [01793312] **3192**

AUDIT ACTION LETTER INFORMATION BONUS, THE (US/0363-7387) [02482110] **3554, 738**

AUDIT ACTION LETTER, THE (US/0363-5473) [02433348] **3554**

AUDIT BRIEFING (UK/0958-367X) [I0958367X] **4712**

AUDIT BUREAU OF CIRCULATIONS *See* MEMBERSHIP ROSTER - AUDIT BUREAU OF CIRCULATIONS **762**

AUDIT GUIDE AND STANDARDS FOR COMMUNITY DEVELOPMENT BLOCK GRANT RECIPIENTS (US) [03121684] **2815, 5274**

AUDIT GUIDE FOR AUDITS OF HUD APPROVED NONSUPERVISED MORTGAGES FOR USE BY INDEPENDENT PUBLIC ACCOUNTANTS (US) [02924151] **2815, 739**

AUDIT OF ACCOUNTS AND FINANCIAL STATEMENTS ; REPORT TO THE GENERAL ASSEMBLY OF THE ORGANIZATION OF AMERICAN STATES BY THE BOARD OF EXTERNAL AUDITORS *CEASED*. (US) [05282723] **739**

AUDIT OF FEDERAL CROP INSURANCE CORPORATION *See* AUDIT OF THE FINANCIAL STATEMENTS OF FEDERAL CROP INSURANCE CORPORATION **2874**

AUDIT OF NEW YORK STATE AGENCIES (US/0095-5817) [01798248] **4712, 739**

AUDIT OF PAYMENTS FROM SPECIAL BANK ACCOUNT TO LOCKHEED AIRCRAFT CORPORATION FOR THE C-5A AIRCRAFT PROGRAM (US) [03952024] **12, 739**

AUDIT OF SAINT LAWRENCE SEAWAY DEVELOPMENT CORPORATION FINANCIAL STATEMENTS (US/0272-3522) [06781870] **4631, 739**

AUDIT OF THE FINANCIAL STATEMENTS OF FEDERAL CROP INSURANCE CORPORATION (US/0193-2918) [05149014] **2874**

AUDIT OF THE HOUSE MAJORITY PRINTING CLERK (US) [08937293] **739**

AUDIT OF THE RURAL TELEPHONE BANK, DEPARTMENT OF AGRICULTURE (WASHINGTON) (US/0091-3820) [01786562] **1150**

AUDIT OF THE SENATE BUILDING BEAUTY SHOP FOR THE FISCAL YEAR ENDED ... / BY THE COMPTROLLER GENERAL OF THE UNITED STATES (US) [05868416] **402**

AUDIT OF THE UNITED STATES CAPITOL HISTORICAL SOCIETY FOR THE YEAR ENDED ... (US/0091-5483) [01787141] **2722**

AUDIT REPORT, AUSTIN STATE SCHOOL (US) [03937315] **1875**

AUDIT REPORT: AUSTIN STATE SCHOOL FARM COLONY *See* AUDIT REPORT, AUSTIN STATE SCHOOL **1875**

AUDIT REPORT. BOARD OF MEDICAL EXAMINERS (US/0148-3439) [03295203] **3554**

AUDIT REPORT, BOARD OF PODIATRY (US/0149-1903) [03440124] **3554**

AUDIT REPORT. BOARD OF PSYCHOLOGY (US/0148-3420) [03294928] **4575**

AUDIT REPORT, CLEVELAND STATE COMMUNITY COLLEGE (TENNESSEE) (US/0148-0480) [03256394] **1810**

AUDIT REPORT, COMMISSION ON AGING (US/0147-8117) [03230677] **5178**

AUDIT REPORT, COMMISSION TO CONTROL THE SUPREME COURT BUILDING AT NASHVILLE (US/0148-3870) [03294909] **4631**

AUDIT REPORT, DEPARTMENT OF ARKANSAS NATURAL AND CULTURAL HERITAGE, ARKANSAS TERRITORIAL CAPITOL RESTORATION COMMISSION (US) [04199598] **4712**

AUDIT REPORT, DEPARTMENT OF EDUCATION, ALVIN C. YORK AGRICULTURAL INSTITUTE (US/0148-2777) [03280102] **63**

AUDIT REPORT, DEPARTMENT OF EDUCATION CENTRAL OFFICE (US/0148-0421) [03256417] **1726**

AUDIT REPORT, DEPARTMENT OF EDUCATION, DIVISION OF VOCATIONAL TECHNICAL EDUCATION (US/0148-0456) [03256430] **1910**

AUDIT REPORT, DEPARTMENT OF EDUCATION, TENNESSEE ASSOCIATION OF THE FUTURE FARMERS OF AMERICA (US/0148-043X) [03259023] **63**

AUDIT REPORT, DEPARTMENT OF EDUCATION, TENNESSEE SCHOOL FOR THE BLIND (US/0147-8125) [03230857] **1726**

AUDIT REPORT, DEPARTMENT OF EDUCATION, TENNESSEE SCHOOL FOR THE DEAF (US/0147-8133) [03230819] **1726**

AUDIT REPORT, DEPARTMENT OF GENERAL SERVICES, MOTOR VEHICLE MANAGEMENT DIVISION (US/0148-5202) [03317833] **4631**

AUDIT REPORT, DEPARTMENT OF INSURANCE, STATE BOARD OF ACCOUNTANCY (US/0148-0448) [03256526] **739**

AUDIT REPORT, DEPARTMENT OF INSURANCE, TENNESSEE BOARD OF BARBER EXAMINERS (US/0148-0464) [03258977] **2874, 4712**

AUDIT REPORT, DEPARTMENT OF INSURANCE, TENNESSEE REAL ESTATE COMMISSION (US) [03256472] **4834**

AUDIT REPORT, DEPARTMENT OF JUDICIAL, STATE PROSECUTIONS (US/0148-3854) [03294934] **3158**

AUDIT REPORT, DEPARTMENT OF MILITARY *See* AUDIT REPORT MILITARY DEPARTMENT OF TENNESSEE NASHVILLE TENNESSEE FOR THE YEAR ENDED JUNE 30 **4037**

AUDIT REPORT, DEPARTMENT OF MILITARY - TENNESSEE DIVISION OF STATE AUDIT (US/0148-3447) [03295129] **4037**

AUDIT REPORT, DEPARTMENT OF PARKS AND TOURISM, MONUMENTS AND HISTORICAL SITES DIVISION, ARKANSAS TERRITORIAL CAPITOL RESTORATION (US/0146-5503) [02969737] **4712**

AUDIT REPORT, DIVISION OF PRINTING (US/0148-3862) [03294924] **4631**

AUDIT REPORT. FLEET ADMIRAL CHESTER W. NIMITZ MEMORIAL NAVAL MUSEUM COMMISSION (US) [05633530] **4175**

AUDIT REPORT, GOVERNMENT OF GUJARAT *See* REPORT OF THE COMPTROLLER AND AUDITOR-GENERAL OF INDIA. GOVERNMENT OF GUJARAT **4745**

AUDIT REPORT, GOVERNMENT OF ORISSA (II) [02634802] **4712**

AUDIT REPORT, HARLINGEN STATE CHEST HOSPITAL (US) [04323751] **3777**

AUDIT REPORT, IDAHO DEPARTMENT OF EDUCATION FOR THE FISCAL YEARS ENDED JUNE 30 ... (US) [10478397] **1726**

AUDIT REPORT MILITARY DEPARTMENT OF TENNESSEE NASHVILLE TENNESSEE FOR THE YEAR ENDED JUNE 30 (US) [13335448] **4037**

AUDIT REPORT ON FINAL ACCOUNTS FOR FISCAL ..., THE (JA) [11590129] **4712**

AUDIT REPORT : SECRETARY OF STATE - GEORGIA. DEPT. OF AUDITS AND ACCOUNTS (US) [05359305] **4631**

AUDIT REPORT, STATE COMPTROLLER OF PUBLIC ACCOUNTS, AUSTIN, TEXAS, YEAR ENDED AUGUST 31 ... (US) [08634594] **4712**

AUDIT REPORT, STATE OF NEVADA, CLARK COUNTY TAXICAB AUTHORITY (US/0160-5356) [03685803] **4631**

AUDIT REPORT - STATE OF NEVADA. DEPARTMENT OF ADMINISTRATION. PERSONNEL DIVISION (US/0093-0202) [01791522] **4631**

AUDIT REPORT, STATE OF NEVADA DEPARTMENT OF COMMERCE, BANKING AND SAVINGS AND LOAN DIVISIONS (US/0160-5283) [03691761] **773**

AUDIT REPORT, STATE OF NEVADA DEPARTMENT OF COMMERCE, DIRECTOR'S OFFICE (US/0160-5321) [03691754] **823**

AUDIT REPORT, STATE OF NEVADA, DEPARTMENT OF COMMERCE, HOUSING DIVISION (US/0160-5380) [03685760] **1654, 4631**

AUDIT REPORT, STATE OF NEVADA, DEPARTMENT OF COMMERCE, REAL ESTATE DIVISION (US/0160-5348) [03685781] **4631**

AUDIT REPORT, STATE OF NEVADA, DEPARTMENT OF COMMERCE, REAL ESTATE EDUCATION RESEARCH AND RECOVERY FUND (US/0160-533X) [03685745] **4631**

AUDIT REPORT, STATE OF NEVADA DEPARTMENT OF COMMERCE, STATE FIRE MARSHAL DIVISION (US/0160-5291) [03691774] **2288**

AUDIT REPORT - STATE OF NEVADA. DEPARTMENT OF CONSERVATION AND NATURAL RESOURCES. DIVISION OF STATE PARKS (US/0093-6596) [01791525] **2187**

AUDIT REPORT - STATE OF NEVADA. DEPARTMENT OF CONSERVATION AND NATURAL RESOURCES. DIVISION OF STATE PARKS *See* STATE OF NEVADA, DEPARTMENT OF CONSERVATION AND NATURAL RESOURCES, DIVISION OF STATE PARKS AUDIT REPORT **2206**

AUDIT REPORT, STATE OF NEVADA DEPARTMENT OF GENERAL SERVICES, PURCHASING DIVISION, DONATED COMMODITIES REVOLVING FUND (US/0160-5755) [03691800] **4712**

AUDIT REPORT, STATE OF NEVADA DEPARTMENT OF PAROLE AND PROBATION, PAROLEE'S REVOLVING LOAN FUND; PRISONER'S WORK RELEASE REVOLVING LOAN FUND (US/0149-225X) [03440804] **3158**

AUDIT REPORT - STATE OF NEVADA. NEVADA STATE COUNCIL ON THE ARTS (US/0093-075X) [01791375] **315**

AUDIT REPORT - STATE OF NEVADA. NEVADA STATE MUSEUM (US/0093-1586) [05622165] **4084**

AUDIT REPORT, STATE OF NEVADA, OFFICE OF THE GOVERNOR (US) [04083022] **4631**

AUDIT REPORT - STATE OF NEVADA. PUBLIC SERVICE COMMISSION (US/0092-9239) [01791526] **4631**

AUDIT REPORT, TEXAS BOARD OF CHIROPRACTIC EXAMINERS (US) [04948916] **4379**

AUDIT REPORT. TEXAS BOARD OF LICENSURE FOR NURSING HOME ADMINISTRATORS (US) [05261074] **4631, 3777**

AUDIT REPORT. TEXAS COMMISSION ON ALCOHOLISM (US/0737-6383) [03949403] **1341**

AUDIT REPORT, TEXAS EMPLOYMENT COMMISSION (US) [04507826] **1654**

AUDIT REPORT, TEXAS HISTORICAL COMMISSION (US) [04633748] **2722**

AUDIT RISK ALERT (US/1067-5418) [23113423] **739**

AUDIT TUNBRIDGE WELLS (UK/0961-124X) [I0961124X] **641**

AUDITED ANNUAL FINANCIAL REPORT / PUBLIC UTILITY COMMISSION OF TEXAS (US) [12853009] **4760**

AUDITING (US/0278-0380) [07687767] **739**

AUDITING AND REPORTING (UK) [15093987] **739**

AUDITING PRACTICES BOARD AND INTERNATIONAL FEDERATION OF ACCOUNTANTS (UK) **739**

AUDITING PRACTICES BOARD PAPERS (UK) **739**

AUDITING RESEARCH MONOGRAPH (US/0146-9819) [03063205] **739**

AUDITION & PAROLE (FR/0222-3856) [07218955] **4384**

AUDITION NEWS (US) **383**

AUDITOR-GENERAL'S REPORT TO THE LEGISLATIVE ASSEMBLY ON HIS AUDIT OF THE TREASURER'S ANNUAL STATEMENT FOR THE FINANCIAL YEAR ENDED 30TH JUNE ..., THE (AT) [09294148] **4712**

AUDITOR, THE (US/0044-9997) [04043626] **4937**

●AUDITOR-TRAK (ATLANTA, GA.) (US/1063-4053) [26018469] **739**

AUDITOR'S ANNUAL REPORT OF EL PASO COUNTY, TEXAS (US) [25380658] **4712**

AUDITORS FACT BOOK (UK) **739**

AUDITOR'S REPORT AND FINANCIAL STATEMENTS FOR THE YEAR ENDED DECEMBER 31 ... (CN/0845-0722) [20614305] **4712**

Alphabetical Title Index — AUSSTEUER

AUDIVIDEO INTERNATIONAL (US/0362-1162) [02302366] **5315**

AUDUBON (US/0097-7136) [01587520] 5615, **2187**

AUDUBON ACTIVIST (US/0898-915X) [14391685] 2187, **2211**

AUDUBON CONSERVATION REPORT (US/0571-8805) [03711398] **2187**

AUDUBON NATURALIST NEWS : A PUBLICATION OF THE AUDUBON NATURALIST SOCIETY OF THE CENTRAL ATLANTIC STATES (US/0888-6555) [07968969] **4162**

AUDUBON SOCIETY OF RHODE ISLAND See REPORT - AUDUBON SOCIETY OF RHODE ISLAND **2203**

AUERBACH COMPUTER CHARACTERISTICS DIGEST See AUERBACH GUIDE TO COMPUTING EQUIPMENT SPECIFICATIONS **1256**

AUERBACH COMPUTER PROGRAMMING MANAGEMENT CEASED. (US/0746-7273) [10248493] **1278**

AUERBACH DATA BASE MANAGEMENT (US/0735-9977) [06228740] **1253**

AUERBACH DATA CENTER OPERATIONS MANAGEMENT (US/0736-3648) [06234330] **1255**

AUERBACH DATA COMMUNICATIONS EQUIPMENT DIGEST (US/0090-3590) [01783657] **2036**

AUERBACH DATA COMMUNICATIONS MANAGEMENT (US/0736-0002) [06228735] **1256**

AUERBACH DATA SECURITY MANAGEMENT (US/0746-7281) [10241024] **1225**

AUERBACH DATA WORLD (US/0190-6585) [04661279] **1256**

AUERBACH DATAGRAM. DATA SECURITY MANAGEMENT (US/0742-0978) [10262468] **860**

AUERBACH EDP AUDITING (US/0746-7265) [10248817] 1256, **739**

AUERBACH GUIDE TO COMPUTING EQUIPMENT SPECIFICATIONS (US/0361-2783) [02246065] **1256**

AUERBACH INFORMATION MANAGEMENT (US/1045-7879) [19967202] **1256**

AUERBACH PUBLISHERS See AUERBACH DATA WORLD **1256**

AUERBACH REPORTER (US/0731-9304) [03611549] **1235**

AUERBACH SYSTEMS DEVELOPMENT MANAGEMENT (US/0735-9985) [06228750] **1246**

AUFBAU (NEW YORK, N.Y.) (US/0004-7813) [02251108] **5713**

AUFBEREITUNGS-TECHNIK (GW/0004-783X) [01518617] **2134**

AUFKLARUNG (GW/0178-7128) [15292746] **2677**

AUFSATZE UND JAHRESBERICHT - KARL-MARX-UNIVERSITAT MUSIKINSTRUMENTEN-MUSEUM (GW) [04407541] **4101**

AUFSCHLUSS (GW/0004-7856) [06432965] 1438, **1366**

AUFSCHLUSS. SONDERHEFT (GW/0519-4334) [06301164] **1438**

AUFSTIEG UND NIEDERGANG DER ROEMISCHEN WELT (GW) **2677**

AUFTRAG (BASEL. 1967) (SZ/0004-7880) [01712517] **4937**

AUGENOPTIK (SZ/0004-7910) [05861027] **4215**

AUGENOPTIKER, DER (GW/0004-7929) [05900382] 4215, **3872**

AUGMENTATIVE AND ALTERNATIVE COMMUNICATION (US/0743-4618) [10587086] **1104**

AUGMENTATIVE COMMUNICATION NEWS (US/0897-9278) [17667960] 1300, **1293**

AUGSBA REVIEW / THE ATLANTA UNIVERSITY, GRADUATE SCHOOL OF BUSINESS, THE (US) [08577836] **860**

AUGUST DERLETH SOCIETY See NEWSLETTER - AUGUST DERLETH SOCIETY **3416**

AUGUST THYSSEN-HUTTE See TECHNISCHE BERICHTE - THYSSEN **4021**

AUGUST VOLLMER CRIMINALISTIC SERIES (US/0067-0561) [01518622] **3158**

AUGUSTA ADVOCATE, THE (US) [21314634] **5631**

AUGUSTA AREA TIMES (US/0749-7083) [08786751] **5765**

AUGUSTA (AUGUSTA, GA.) (US/1064-038X) [26196572] **2722**

AUGUSTA CHRONICLE (1885), THE (US/0747-1343) [09609029] **5652**

AUGUSTA DAILY GAZETTE, THE (US) [09856509] **5674**

AUGUSTA EAGLE, THE (US) [13474539] **5658**

AUGUSTA FOCUS (US/0746-4657) [10052848] **5652**

AUGUSTA HISTORICAL BULLETIN (US/0571-8899) [07992273] **2722**

AUGUSTA MAGAZINE See AUGUSTA (AUGUSTA, GA.) **2722**

AUGUSTA MELBOURNE (AT/1033-8934) [I10338934] **293**

AUGUSTAN (US) [80648766] **2438**

AUGUSTAN SOCIETY OMNIBUS, THE (US/0272-5525) [16402244] **2438**

●AUGUSTANA COLLEGE LIBRARY PUBLICATIONS (US) [26284322] **3193**

AUGUSTANA LIBRARY PUBLICATIONS See AUGUSTANA COLLEGE LIBRARY PUBLICATIONS **3193**

AUGUSTINIAN HERITAGE (US/0888-2274) [13505733] **4937**

AUGUSTINIAN JOURNEY (US/1057-9338) [24170371] **4937**

AUGUSTINIAN STUDIES (US/0094-5323) [01800145] **5024**

AUGUSTINIANA (BE/0004-8003) [01697214] 5024, **2611**

AUGUSTINIANUM (IT/0004-8011) [01772009] 4937, **4342**

AUGUSTINUS (SP/0004-802X) [03387912] **4937**

AUJOURD'HUI CREDO (CN/0383-2554) [02453063] **4937**

AUJOURD'HUI L'AFRIQUE (FR) [04927031] **4464**

AUK, THE (US/0004-8038) [01518634] **5615**

AUKTION (GW) [01796011] 4823, **377**

AUKTION (GODEBERT M REISS) (GW) [01796010] **408**

AULA (DR) [01785659] **1726**

AULA ORIENTALIS (SP/0212-5730) [10165627] **2646**

AULA : TARSADALOM ES GAZDASAG : A BUDAPESTI KOZGAZDASAGTUDOMANYI EGYETEM FOLYOIRATA (HU/0866-6865) [23125159] **1464**

AUNT EDNA'S READING LIST (US) [20702664] **5551**

AURA (PL/0137-3668) [I01373668] **2211**

AURA (BIRMINGHAM, ALA.) (US/0889-7433) [02794398] **3364**

AURA (BUFFALO) (US/0147-4855) [03175414] **4367**

AURA (FORT WORTH, TEX.) (US/1054-5441) [22918145] **2528**

AUREA PARMA (IT/0004-8062) [02186056] 3364, **2842**

AUREALIS MT. WAVERLEY (AT/1035-1205) [I10351205] **3364**

AURELIA SENTINEL (US) [16700178] **5668**

AURICLE (US) **4384**

AURIS, NASUS, LARYNX (JA/0385-8146) [03700759] **3886**

AURISA NEWS (AT/0811-3130) [I08113130] **2815**

AURORA ADVERTISER (AURORA, MO. : 1914), THE (US/1041-1275) [13343592] **5702**

AURORA-BUCHREIHE (GW/0171-6530) [03386651] 3337, **430**

AURORA COUNTY ARGUS See STICKNEY ARGUS, THE **5744**

AURORA (GRAND CENTRE) (CN/0714-7058) [09379041] **3193**

AURORA (GREENWOOD) (CN/0821-5499) [09674448] **4037**

AURORA SENTINEL (US) [14393760] **5642**

AURORA (WUERZBURG) (GW) [01518642] 343, **3364**

AURORE. TRAITE, L' (CN/0228-9148) [07817602] **4937**

AUS DEM WALDE (GW/0519-4555) [05391390] **2375**

AUS.GEO NEWS (AT/1035-9338) [24088189] **1366**

AUS HESSISCHEN MUSEEN (GW/0935-7157) [I09357157] **343**

AUSBILDUNG UND BERATUNG IN LAND- UND HAUSWIRTSCHAFT / LAND- UND HAUSWIRTSCHAFTLICHER AUSWERTUNGS- UND INFORMATIONSDIENST (GW/0045-0049) [05391502] **2788**

AUSCON CLAYTON (AT/1035-3437) [I10353437] **315**

AUSFUHR NORDRHEIN-WESTFALENS, DIE (GW) [01796611] **824**

AUSGABE DER NEUEN BUNDESLANDER (GW) **1464**

AUSGEWAHLTE ZAHLEN FUER DIE BAUWIRTSCHAFT (GW) [04272881] **599**

AUSGEWAHLTE ZAHLEN ZUR ENERGIEWIRTSCHAFT / HERAUSGEBER STATISTISCHES BUNDESAMT (GW) [11763190] **1933**

AUSGRABUNGEN IN BERLIN (GW/0341-8499) [01804310] **2677**

AUSGRABUNGEN UND FUNDE (GW/0004-8127) [I00048127] **260**

AUSGRABUNGEN UND FUNDE IN WESTFALEN-LIPPE / IM AUFTRAG DES LANDSCHAFTSVERBANDES WESTFALEN-LIPPE HERAUSGEGEBEN VON WESTFALISCHES MUSEUM FUER ARCHAOLOGIE, AMT FUER BODENDENKMALPFLEGE (GW/0175-6133) [11604183] **2677**

AUSIMM BULLETIN / THE AUSTRALASIAN INSTITUTE OF MINING AND METALLURGY, THE (AU/1034-6775) [21472866] 1438, **2134**

AUSIMM PROCEEDINGS (AT/1034-6783) [22286371] **2134**

AUSKUNFT (GW/0720-7123) [I07207123] **3193**

AUSLANDER (GW) [06306166] **5322**

AUSLANDISCHE MESSEN, AUSSTELLUNGEN, KONGRESSE (AU) [02943022] **1598**

AUSLANDISCHES WIRTSCHAFTS- UND STEUERRECHT (GW) [21416079] **2938**

AUSLANDSDEUTSCHE LITERATUR DER GEGENWART (GW) [05511186] **3364**

AUSLANDSOSTERREICHER, DER (AU) [02377319] **2677**

AUSLANDSSCHULVERZEICHNIS (GW) [05657490] **1726**

AUSLEGUNG (US/0733-4311) [05081985] **4342**

AUSONIA (IT/0004-8143) [02257967] **2513**

AUSRA (PL/0137-8570) [23005309] **2256**

AUSSENDANDEL. REIHE 2, AUSSENHANDEL NACH WAREN UND LANDERN (SPEZIALHANDEL) (GW/0170-2955) [04340810] **824**

AUSSENDIENST-INFORMATIONEN. TRAININGSKURS FUR SYSTEMATISCHES VERKAUFEN (GW/0933-8357) [I09338357] **2874**

AUSSENHANDEL, DER (GW) [02499950] 824, **726**

AUSSENHANDEL; LANDER UND WARENGLIEDERUNG (AU) [05064533] **824**

AUSSENHANDEL NORDRHEIN-WESTFALENS : AUS- UND EIN-FUHR. VORLAEUFIGE ERGEBNISSE, DER (GW) [04187919] **824**

AUSSENHANDEL NORDRHEIN-WESTFALENS, DER (GW) [03217375] 824, **726**

AUSSENHANDEL. REIHE 1: ZUSAMMENFASSENDE UBERSICHTEN FUER DEN AUSSENHANDEL (GW) [03951283] **824**

AUSSENHANDEL. REIHE 3: AUSSENHANDEL NACH LAENDERN UND WARENGRUPPEN, SPEZIALHANDEL (GW/0170-7825) [03901769] **824**

AUSSENHANDEL. REIHE 4: GENERALHANDEL. EIN- UND AUSFUHR VON MINERALOEL (GW/0072-1670) [02032484] **4251**

AUSSENHANDEL. REIHE 4.1 : EIN- UND AUSFUHR VON MINERALOL, GENERALHANDEL (GW) [04231666] **4251**

AUSSENHANDEL. REIHE 5.2, HANDEL MIT DEN STAATSHANDELSLANDERN / HERAUSGEBER STATISTISCHES BUNDESAMT (GW) [08331852] **824**

AUSSENHANDEL. REIHE 8 : AUSSENHANDEL NACH DEM INTERNATIONALEN WARENVERZEICHNIS FUR DEN AUSSENHANDEL, SITC-REV. II, UND LANDERN, SPEZIALHANDEL (GW) [06946365] **824**

AUSSENHANDEL. REIHE S. 6, SYSTEMATIKEN IN DER AUSSENHANDELSSTATISTIK / STATISTISCHES BUNDESAMT (GW) [24151570] **5322**

AUSSENPLANUNG (GW/0004-8194) [01518651] **4516**

AUSSENPOLITIK (ENGLISH EDITION) (GW/0587-3835) [00854274] **4516**

AUSSENPOLITISCHER BERICHT DES BUNDESMINISTERS FUER AUSWARTIGE ANGELEGENHEITEN (AU) [03216607] **4516**

AUSSENWIRTSCHAFT (SZ/0004-8216) [02088475] **824**

AUSSENWIRTSCHAFT: ZEITSCHRIFT FUER INTERNATIONALE WIRTSCHAFTSBEZIEHUNGEN (SZ/0004-8216) [05022814] **4516**

AUSSIE SPORTS ACTION (AT/1035-4573) [I10354573] **4884**

AUSSTEUER, BETT & COUCH See HAUSTEX **5351**

AUSTASIA — Alphabetical Title Index

AUSTASIA AQUACULTURE MAGAZINE (AT/0818-5522) [16128429] **2296**

AUSTASIA AQUACULTURE TRADE DIRECTORY (AT) [20173459] **2296**

AUSTELL NEIGHBOR, THE (US/0191-7382) [04960890] **5652**

AUSTIN AMERICAN-STATESMAN (US) [16968488] **5746**

AUSTIN AREA LEGAL RECORD *See* AUSTIN DAILY RECORD **2938**

AUSTIN BOOKWORKERS (US) [23239645] **4823**

AUSTIN BUSINESS EXECUTIVE (US/0742-3543) [09884204] **641**

AUSTIN BUSINESS JOURNAL (US/0892-869X) [07426817] **641**

AUSTIN CHRONICLE (SCOTTSBURG, IND.), THE (US/0740-4581) [09952928] **5746**

AUSTIN CHRONICLE, THE (US/1074-0740) [08620367] **4101, 5361, 2528**

●AUSTIN DAILY RECORD (US/1065-7460) [26704579] **2938**

AUSTIN GENEALOGICAL SOCIETY : [QUARTERLY] (US) [18595107] **2438**

AUSTIN HERALD (US) [01697007] **5694**

AUSTIN HOMES & GARDENS *SUSPENDED.* (US/0199-1531) [05215715] 293, **2898**

AUSTIN INSURANCE REPORT. ADMINISTRATIVE EDITION (US/0279-9006) [07344815] **2874**

AUSTIN LAWYER *See* AUSTIN LAWYER'S MAGAZINE **2938**

AUSTIN LAWYER'S MAGAZINE *CEASED.* (US/1063-1534) [25910399] **2938**

AUSTIN LIGHT, THE (US) [06203422] **5746**

AUSTIN MAGAZINE *CEASED.* (US/0890-0574) [13535653] **2528**

AUSTIN PERSPECTIVE (US/0895-6901) [16744678] **1598**

AUSTIN PRESBYTERIAN THEOLOGICAL SEMINARY *See* WINDOWS (AUSTIN, TEX.) **5009**

●AUSTIN REAL ESTATE FINANCE SOURCEBOOK (US/1071-5142) [28658879] **4834**

AUSTIN STATE SCHOOL *See* AUDIT REPORT, AUSTIN STATE SCHOOL **1875**

AUSTIN TEXAS MAGAZINE (US/1058-837X) [24402523] **818**

AUSTRALASIA OIL SERVICE (UK) **4251**

AUSTRALASIAN AIRPOWER *See* FLIGHTPATH **21**

AUSTRALASIAN ANGORA MOHAIR JOURNAL (AT) [14279095] **3183**

AUSTRALASIAN BEEKEEPER, THE (AT/0004-8313) [01518659] **63**

AUSTRALASIAN BIOTECHNOLOGY (AT/1036-7128) [24626190] **3685**

AUSTRALASIAN BUS AND COACH (AT) **5404, 5377**

AUSTRALASIAN CATHOLIC RECORD, THE (AT/0727-3215) [05136645] **5024**

AUSTRALASIAN CORROSION ENGINEERING *CEASED.* (AT/0004-833X) [02445132] 2101, **2008**

AUSTRALASIAN CYCLING AND TRIATHLON NEWS (AT/0819-3363) [l08193363] **4884**

AUSTRALASIAN DRAMA STUDIES (AT/0810-4123) [10228040] **5361**

AUSTRALASIAN FURNISHING TRADE JOURNAL (AT) **2898**

AUSTRALASIAN GAY AND LESBIAN LAW JOURNAL (AT) **2938, 5187**

AUSTRALASIAN HEALTH AND HEALING (AT/0812-3896) [l08123896] **2596**

AUSTRALASIAN INDUSTRY REPORTER (NZ/0114-6106) [l01146106] **1598**

AUSTRALASIAN INSTITUTE OF MINING AND METALLURGY *See* CONFERENCE SERIES - AUSTRALASIAN INSTITUTE OF MINING AND METALLURGY **2138**

AUSTRALASIAN INSTITUTE OF MINING AND METALLURGY *See* DIRECTORY / THE AUSTRALASIAN INSTITUTE OF MINING AND METALLURGY **4001**

AUSTRALASIAN INSTITUTE OF MINING AND METALLURGY *See* MONOGRAPH SERIES **2147**

AUSTRALASIAN INSTITUTE OF MINING AND METALLURGY *See* PUBLICATIONS INDEX / THE AUSTRALASIAN INSTITUTE OF MINING AND METALLURGY ; PRODUCED BY AUSTRALIAN MINERAL FOUNDATION **2149**

AUSTRALASIAN JOURNAL OF AMERICAN STUDIES : AJAS (AT/0705-7113) [09499265] **2722**

AUSTRALASIAN JOURNAL OF COMBINATORICS, THE (AT/1034-4942) [24802444] 1171, **3496**

AUSTRALASIAN JOURNAL OF DERMATOLOGY, THE (AT/0004-8380) [01518662] **3718**

AUSTRALASIAN JOURNAL OF PHILOSOPHY (AT/0004-8402) [02923644] **4342**

AUSTRALASIAN JOURNAL OF SPECIAL EDUCATION (AT/1030-0112) [l10300112] **1875**

AUSTRALASIAN MANUFACTURER (AT) [09837873] **3475**

AUSTRALASIAN PAINT AND PANEL (AT/0816-3596) [l08163596] **4222**

AUSTRALASIAN PHYSICAL & ENGINEERING SCIENCES IN MEDICINE (AT/0158-9938) [08581681] 494, **3685**

AUSTRALASIAN PLANT PATHOLOGY (AT/0815-3191) [06072212] **500**

AUSTRALASIAN POST (AT/0004-8437) [l00048437] **5777**

AUSTRALASIAN PUBLIC LIBRARIES AND INFORMATION SERVICES (AT/1030-5033) [20557073] **3193**

AUSTRALASIAN RADIOLOGY (AT/0004-8461) [01713507] **3939**

AUSTRALASIAN RELIGION INDEX (AT/1033-2626) [20456422] **4937**

AUSTRALASIAN SCIENCE MAG (AT/1036-0875) [l10360875] **5087**

AUSTRALASIAN SEDIMENTOLOGISTS GROUP FIELD GUIDE SERIES (AT) [16873835] **1366**

AUSTRALASIAN SHIPPING RECORD (AT) [07117203] **5447**

AUSTRALASIAN SHIPS & PORTS (AT/1032-3449) [l10323449] **5447**

AUSTRALASIAN SPORTING SHOOTER (AT/0810-5928) [l08105928] **4884**

AUSTRALASIAN STAMP CATALOGUE (AT) [06834954] **2784**

AUSTRALASIAN TAX REPORTS (AT) [01518666] **4712**

AUSTRALASIAN TEXTILES (AT/0725-086X) [10818993] **5348**

AUSTRALASIAN UNIVERSITIES LAW SCHOOLS ASSOCIATION *See* DIRECTORY OF MEMBERS **2962**

AUSTRALASIAN WEEKLY MANUFACTURER (US) [18251645] **3475**

AUSTRALASIAN WELDING JOURNAL (AT) **4026**

AUSTRALASIAN WHEELS FOR THE MIND (AT) [l10350640] **1171**

AUSTRALIA *See* COMMONWEALTH OF AUSTRALIA GAZETTE. PERIODIC **2954**

AUSTRALIA *See* COMMONWEALTH OF AUSTRALIA GAZETTE. PUBLIC SERVICE **2954**

AUSTRALIA *See* AUSTRALIAN TREATY SERIES **3124**

AUSTRALIA *See* AUSTRALIAN GOVERNMENT GAZETTE **4631**

AUSTRALIA. ADMINISTRATIVE APPEALS TRIBUNAL *See* ADMINISTRATIVE APPEALS REPORTS **4624**

AUSTRALIA AND NEW ZEALAND JOURNAL OF DEVELOPMENTAL DISABILITIES (AT/0726-3864) [08582450] **4575, 4384**

AUSTRALIA AND TOMORROWS PACIFIC / FOR AUSTRALIA (AT/1033-839X) [l1033839X] **4631**

AUSTRALIA AND WORLD AFFAIRS (AT/1033-6192) [l10336192] **4516**

AUSTRALIA. ARBITRATION INSPECTORATE *See* ANNUAL REPORT - AUSTRALIAN ARBITRATION INSPECTORATE **1648**

AUSTRALIA AT A GLANCE (AT/1031-0541) [l10310541] **1923**

AUSTRALIA. BUREAU OF METEOROLOGY *See* AUSTRALIAN RADIATION RECORDS **1420**

AUSTRALIA. BUREAU OF METEOROLOGY *See* MONTHLY WEATHER REVIEW : WESTERN AUSTRALIA **1432**

AUSTRALIA. BUREAU OF METEOROLOGY *See* MONTHLY WEATHER REVIEW : NEW SOUTH WALES **1432**

AUSTRALIA. BUREAU OF METEOROLOGY *See* MONTHLY WEATHER REVIEW : QUEENSLAND **1432**

AUSTRALIA. BUREAU OF METEOROLOGY *See* MONTHLY WEATHER REVIEW : SOUTH AUSTRALIA **1432**

AUSTRALIA. BUREAU OF METEOROLOGY *See* MONTHLY WEATHER REVIEW : TASMANIA **1432**

AUSTRALIA. BUREAU OF METEOROLOGY. WAETHER REVIEW: TASMANIA *See* MONTHLY WEATHER REVIEW : TASMANIA **1432**

AUSTRALIA. BUREAU OF METEOROLOGY. WEATHER REVIEW: QUEENSLAND *See* MONTHLY WEATHER REVIEW : QUEENSLAND **1432**

AUSTRALIA. BUREAU OF METEOROLOGY. WEATHER REVIEW: SOUTH AUSTRALIA & NORTHERN TERRITORY *See* MONTHLY WEATHER REVIEW : SOUTH AUSTRALIA **1432**

AUSTRALIA. BUREAU OF MINERAL RESOURCES, GEOLOGY AND GEOPHYSICS *See* BULLETIN - DEPARTMENT OF NATURAL RESOURCES, BUREAU OF MINERAL RESOURCES, GEOLOGY AND GEOPHYSICS **1352**

AUSTRALIA. BUREAU OF MINERAL RESOURCES, GEOLOGY AND GEOPHYSICS *See* BMR JOURNAL OF AUSTRALIAN GEOLOGY AND GEOPHYSICS **1367**

AUSTRALIA. BUREAU OF MINERAL RESOURCES, GEOLOGY AND GEOPHYSICS *See* 1:250,000 GEOLOGICAL SERIES EXPLANATORY NOTES. AUSTRALIAN NATIONAL GRID SHEET **1364**

AUSTRALIA. BUREAU OF MINERAL RESOURCES, GEOLOGY AND GEOPHYSICS. BMR JOURNAL OF AUSTRALIAN GEOLOGY AND GEOPHYSICS *See* AGSO JOURNAL OF AUSTRALIAN GEOLOGY & GEOPHYSICS **1365**

AUSTRALIA. BUREAU OF STATISTICS. WESTERN AUSTRALIAN OFFICE *See* STATISTICS OF WESTERN AUSTRALIA: RURAL INDUSTRIES **156**

AUSTRALIA. COMMONWEALTH BUREAU OF CENSUS AND STATISTICS. SOUTH AUSTRALIAN OFFICE. MONTHLY SUMMARY OF STATISTICS *See* MONTHLY SUMMARY OF STATISTICS, SOUTH AUSTRALIA **4698**

AUSTRALIA. COMMONWEALTH BUREAU OF CENSUS AND STATISTICS. TRADE UNION STATISTICS: AUSTRALIA *See* TRADE UNION STATISTICS: AUSTRALIA **1540**

AUSTRALIA. COMMONWEALTH BUREAU OF CENSUS AND STATISTICS. WESTERN AUSTRALIAN OFFICE. WESTERN AUSTRALIA ROAD TRAFFIC ACCIDENTS INVOLVING CASUALTIES *See* ROAD TRAFFIC ACCIDENTS INVOLVING CASUALTIES **5443**

AUSTRALIA. COMMONWEALTH GOVERNMENT PRINTING OFFICE. PUBLICATIONS BRANCH *See* AUSTRALIAN GOVERNMENT PUBLICATIONS. MONTHLY LIST **4631**

AUSTRALIA. COMMONWEALTH SCIENTIFIC AND INDUSTRIAL RESEARCH ORGANIZATION. DIVISION OF APPLIED GEOMECHANICS *See* GEOMECHANICS COMPUTING PROGRAMME **1380**

AUSTRALIA. COMMONWEALTH SCIENTIFIC AND INDUSTRIAL RESEARCH ORGANIZATION. DIVISION OF FOREST RESEARCH *See* DIVISIONAL REPORT - CSIRO DIVISION OF FOREST RESEARCH **2378**

AUSTRALIA. COMMONWEALTH SCIENTIFIC AND INDUSTRIAL RESEARCH ORGANIZATION. DIVISION OF SOILS *See* SOILS AND LAND USE SERIES **187**

AUSTRALIA COUNCIL *See* ANNUAL REPORT - AUSTRALIA COUNCIL **312**

AUSTRALIA DEPARTMENT OF FOREIGN AFFAIRS AND TRADE *See* ANNUAL REPORT / DEPARTMENT OF FOREIGN AFFAIRS AND TRADE **822**

AUSTRALIA DEPARTMENT OF PRIMARY INDUSTRIES AND ENERGY BASIC FISH STATISTICS (AT) **2297**

AUSTRALIA. DEPT. OF ABORIGINAL AFFAIRS *See* REPORT - DEPARTMENT OF ABORIGINAL AFFAIRS **244**

AUSTRALIA. DEPT. OF ABORIGINAL AFFAIRS. WESTERN AUSTRALIA *See* NEWSLETTER - DEPARTMENT OF ABORIGINAL AFFAIRS, WESTERN AUSTRALIA **242**

AUSTRALIA. DEPT. OF EDUCATION *See* TERTIARY AND RESIDENTIAL COLLEGE FEES **1850**

AUSTRALIA. DEPT. OF INDUSTRY, TECHNOLOGY AND COMMERCE *See* ANNUAL REPORT / DEPARTMENT OF INDUSTRY, TECHNOLOGY AND COMMERCE **4627**

AUSTRALIA. DEPT. OF NATIONAL DEVELOPMENT *See* SUMMARY OF ACTIVITIES / COMMONWEALTH OF AUSTRALIA, DEPARTMENT OF NATIONAL DEVELOPMENT **4689**

AUSTRALIA. DEPT. OF OVERSEAS TRADE *See* WINNING EXPORTS **857**

AUSTRALIA. DEPT. OF SCIENCE. ANTARCTIC DIVISION *See* REPORT - DEPARTMENT OF SCIENCE, ANTARCTIC DIVISION **5145**

AUSTRALIA. DEPT. OF TERRITORIES *See* TERRITORY OF NORFOLK ISLAND; REPORT **4690**

Alphabetical Title Index — AUSTRALIAN

AUSTRALIA. DEPT. OF THE ENVIRONMENT AND CONSERVATION *See* REPORT - DEPARTMENT OF THE ENVIRONMENT AND CONSERVATION **2181**

AUSTRALIA. DEPT. OF THE NAVY *See* ANNUAL SUMMARY OF AUSTRALIAN NOTICES TO MARINERS **4174**

AUSTRALIA. DEPT. OF TRANSPORT AND COMMUNICATIONS *See* ANNUAL REPORT / DEPARTMENT OF TRANSPORT AND COMMUNICATIONS **5376**

AUSTRALIA. DIVISION OF NATIONAL MAPPING *See* COMMONWEALTH OF AUSTRALIA NATIONAL REPORT **2581**

AUSTRALIA. DIVISION OF NATIONAL MAPPING *See* THEMATIC MAPPING BULLETIN **2583**

AUSTRALIA. FEDERAL COURT *See* FEDERAL COURT REPORTS, THE **2969**

AUSTRALIA. FISHING INDUSTRY RESEARCH COMMITTEE *See* ANNUAL REPORT - FISHING INDUSTRY RESEARCH COMMITTEE **2294**

AUSTRALIA. FOREIGN INVESTMENT REVIEW BOARD *See* REPORT / FOREIGN INVESTMENT REVIEW BOARD **912**

AUSTRALIA. HIGH COURT *See* COMMONWEALTH LAW REPORTS, THE **2953**

AUSTRALIA. HOSPITALS AND HEALTH SERVICES COMMISSION *See* ANNUAL REPORT - HOSPITALS AND HEALTH SERVICES COMMISSION **3776**

AUSTRALIA. INDUSTRY RESEARCH AND DEVELOPMENT BOARD *See* ANNUAL REPORT / INDUSTRY RESEARCH AND DEVELOPMENT BOARD **1597**

AUSTRALIA. INSPECTOR-GENERAL IN BANKRUPTCY *See* ANNUAL REPORT BY THE INSPECTOR-GENERAL IN BANKRUPTCY ON THE OPERATION OF THE BANKRUPTCY ACT 1966 **3138**

AUSTRALIA-JAPAN RESEARCH CENTRE *See* NEWSLETTER / AUSTRALIA-JAPAN RESEARCH CENTRE **5133**

AUSTRALIA MUSIC CENTRE *See* LIBRARY BULLETIN **3224**

AUSTRALIA NOW *CEASED.* (AT/0045-0197) [01518766] **2668**

AUSTRALIA. OVERSEAS TELECOMMUNICATIONS COMMISSION *See* FIGURES FOR THE YEAR ENDED MARCH 31 ... / THE OVERSEAS TELECOMMUNICATIONS COMMISSION (AUSTRALIA) **1155**

AUSTRALIA. PARLIAMENT. HOUSE OF REPRESENTATIVES *See* VOTES AND PROCEEDINGS OF THE HOUSE OF REPRESENTATIVES **4694**

AUSTRALIA. PARLIAMENT. HOUSE OF REPRESENTATIVES *See* PARLIAMENTARY DEBATES, HOUSE OF REPRESENTATIVES, WEEKLY HANSARD **4672**

AUSTRALIA. PARLIAMENT. JOINT COMMITTEE OF PUBLIC ACCOUNTS *See* REPORT : EXPENDITURE FROM THE CONSOLIDATED REVENUE FUND **4744**

AUSTRALIA. PARLIAMENT. LEGAL AID REVIEW COMMITTEE *See* REPORT OF THE LEGAL AID REVIEW COMMITTEE **3180**

AUSTRALIA. PARLIAMENT. SENATE *See* JOURNALS OF THE SENATE / THE PARLIAMENT OF THE COMMONWEALTH OF AUSTRALIA **4659**

AUSTRALIA. PARLIAMENT. SENATE *See* PARLIAMENTARY DEBATES, SENATE, WEEKLY HANSARD **4672**

AUSTRALIA. PARLIAMENT. STANDING COMMITTEE ON PUBLIC WORKS *See* GENERAL REPORT / THE PARLIAMENT OF THE COMMONWEALTH OF AUSTRALIA, PARLIAMENTARY STANDING COMMITTEE ON PUBLIC WORKS **4761**

AUSTRALIA. PATENT, TRADE MARKS, AND DESIGNS OFFICE *See* ANNUAL RECORD OF TRADE MARKS OFFICE PROCEEDINGS **1301**

AUSTRALIA. PIG MEAT PROMOTION ADVISORY COMMITTEE *See* ANNUAL REPORT OF THE PIG MEAT PROMOTION ADVISORY COMMITTEE FOR THE YEAR ENDED 30 JUNE ... / DEPARTMENT OF PRIMARY INDUSTRY **4628**

AUSTRALIA. PRICES JUSTIFICATION TRIBUNAL *See* ANNUAL REPORT - PRICES JUSTIFICATION TRIBUNAL (AUSTRALIA) **1590**

AUSTRALIA. PUBLIC SERVICE BOARD *See* ANNUAL REPORT - PUBLIC SERVICE BOARD (AUSTRALIA) **4701**

AUSTRALIA. PUBLIC SERVICE BOARD *See* ARBITRATION REPORTS **2936**

AUSTRALIA. PUBLIC SERVICE BOARD. PROJECT SERVICES BRANCH. STATISTICAL SECTION *See* SURVEY OF TEMPORARY AND EXEMPT EMPLOYMENT **1713**

AUSTRALIA. PUBLIC SERVICE BOARD. PROJECT SERVICES BRANCH. STATISTICAL SECTION *See* STATISTICS OF EMPLOYMENT UNDER THE PUBLIC SERVICE ACT **1539**

AUSTRALIA. PUBLIC SERVICE BOARD. PROJECT SERVICES BRANCH. STATISTICAL SECTION *See* STATISTICS OF PROMOTIONS AND APPEALS **1539**

AUSTRALIA. REMUNERATION TRIBUNAL *See* REVIEW / REMUNERATION TRIBUNAL **3040**

AUSTRALIA. TAXATION BOARD OF REVIEW *See* COMMONWEALTH TAXATION BOARD OF REVIEW DECISIONS. NEW SERIES **2954**

AUSTRALIA. TRADE MARKS OFFICE *See* ALPHABETICAL INDEX OF CONSTITUENT PARTICULARS OF TRADE MARKS **1301**

AUSTRALIA. TRADE PRACTICES COMMISSION *See* ANNUAL REPORT / TRADE PRACTICES COMMISSION **3095**

AUSTRALIAN ABORIGINAL STUDIES (CANBERRA, A.C.T. : 1983) (AT/0729-4352) [10372177] 2256, **2668**

AUSTRALIAN ABORIGINES IN THE NEWS. GEOGRAPHIC GUIDE TO HEADINGS AND INDEX TO THE CLIPPINGS *CEASED.* (AT/0811-2908) [I08112908] **2256**

AUSTRALIAN ACADEMIC AND RESEARCH LIBRARIES (AT/0004-8623) [01738582] **3193**

AUSTRALIAN ACADEMY OF SCIENCE *See* YEARBOOK - AUSTRALIAN ACADEMY OF SCIENCE **5171**

AUSTRALIAN ACADEMY OF SCIENCE *See* YEAR BOOK / AUSTRALIAN ACADEMY OF SCIENCE **5171**

AUSTRALIAN ACADEMY OF THE HUMANITIES *See* PROCEEDINGS - THE AUSTRALIAN ACADEMY OF THE HUMANITIES **2852**

AUSTRALIAN ACCOUNTANT, THE (AT/0004-8631) [01518768] **739**

AUSTRALIAN ACCOUNTING REVIEW (AT) **739**

AUSTRALIAN ADMINISTRATIVE LAW BULLETIN, THE (AT/0816-3030) [I08163030] **2938**

AUSTRALIAN ADMINISTRATOR *See* CHANGING EDUCATION **1861**

AUSTRALIAN ADMINISTRATOR (AT/0158-7447) [I01587447] **1860**

AUSTRALIAN ADVERSE DRUG REACTIONS BULLETIN (AT/0812-3837) [17355410] **1341**

AUSTRALIAN ALPINE NEWS (AT) **4884**

AUSTRALIAN-AMERICAN BUSINESS REVIEW, THE (US/0278-3940) [07780666] **641**

AUSTRALIAN AND NEW ZEALAND BIOTECHNOLOGY DIRECTORY (AT/1032-8068) [25571665] **3686**

● AUSTRALIAN AND NEW ZEALAND CATALOGUE OF NEW FILMS AND VIDEOS, THE (AT/1035-8005) [I10358005] **4064**

AUSTRALIAN AND NEW ZEALAND GAS INDUSTRY STATISTICS, THE (AT) [24931741] **4251**

AUSTRALIAN & NEW ZEALAND INSURANCE CASES (AT/0728-5736) [I07285736] **2874**

AUSTRALIAN & NEW ZEALAND JOURNAL OF CRIMINOLOGY, THE (AT/0004-8658) [01205158] **3158**

AUSTRALIAN AND NEW ZEALAND JOURNAL OF FAMILY THERAPY, THE (AT/0814-723X) [12918281] **2276**

AUSTRALIAN AND NEW ZEALAND JOURNAL OF MEDICINE (AT/0004-8291) [01518771] **3795**

AUSTRALIAN AND NEW ZEALAND JOURNAL OF OBSTETRICS AND GYNAECOLOGY (AT/0004-8666) [01518772] **3757**

AUSTRALIAN AND NEW ZEALAND JOURNAL OF OPHTHALMOLOGY (AT/0814-9763) [12166623] **3872**

AUSTRALIAN AND NEW ZEALAND JOURNAL OF PSYCHIATRY (AT/0004-8674) [02257989] **3921**

AUSTRALIAN & NEW ZEALAND JOURNAL OF SERIALS LIBRARIANSHIP *CEASED.* (US/0898-3283) [17786063] **3193**

AUSTRALIAN AND NEW ZEALAND JOURNAL OF SOCIOLOGY, THE (AT/0004-8690) [01157042] **5240**

AUSTRALIAN AND NEW ZEALAND JOURNAL OF SURGERY (AT/0004-8682) [01518774] **3960**

AUSTRALIAN & NEW ZEALAND JOURNAL OF VOCATIONAL EDUCATION RESEARCH (AT/1039-4001) **1911**

AUSTRALIAN AND NEW ZEALAND PC USER (AT) **1265**

AUSTRALIAN & NEW ZEALAND PHYSICIST : A PUBLICATION OF THE AUSTRALIAN INSTITUTE OF PHYSICS & THE NEW ZEALAND INSTITUTE OF PHYSICS, THE (AT/1036-3831) [25183755] **4398**

AUSTRALIAN & NEW ZEALAND STUDIES IN CANADA (CN/0843-5049) [20279177] **3364**

AUSTRALIAN AND NEW ZEALAND STUDIES IN GERMAN LANGUAGE AND LITERATURE (SZ/0171-6867) [03385322] 3267, **3364**

AUSTRALIAN & NEW ZEALAND THEATRE RECORD : ANZTR (AT) [18431730] **5361**

AUSTRALIAN AND NEW ZEALAND WINE INDUSTRY DIRECTORY (AT/1033-7954) [I10337954] **2363**

AUSTRALIAN AND NEW ZEALAND WINE INDUSTRY JOURNAL (AT) [I08192421] **2363**

AUSTRALIAN ANTARCTIC AND SUB-ANTARCTIC RESEARCH PROGRAMMES ... COMMENTS ON CURRENT ACTIVITIES AND ... PROPOSED PROGRAMMES / AUSTRALIAN ACADEMY OF SCIENCE, NATIONAL COMMITTEE FOR ANTARCTIC RESEARCH (AT/0817-1866) [01798853] **1402**

AUSTRALIAN ANTIQUE BOTTLE COLLECTOR (AT) [09523368] **250**

AUSTRALIAN ANTIQUE BOTTLES & COLLECTABLES (AT) 2771, **250**

AUSTRALIAN ANTIQUE COLLECTOR, THE (AT) [08995971] **250**

AUSTRALIAN APPAREL MANUFACTURER (AT) [12929032] 1081, **5348**

AUSTRALIAN AQUACULTURE (AT/0159-6365) [I01596365] **2297**

AUSTRALIAN ARCHAEOLOGY (AT/0312-2417) [08744833] **260**

AUSTRALIAN ART EDUCATION (AT/1032-1942) [I10321942] 1888, **343**

AUSTRALIAN ARTIST (AT/0813-8095) [I08138095] **343**

AUSTRALIAN, ASIAN AND PACIFIC ELECTRICAL WORLD (AT/1031-6914) [I10316914] **2036**

AUSTRALIAN ASSOCIATION OF GERONTOLOGY *See* PROCEEDINGS OF THE AUSTRALIAN ASSOCIATION OF GERONTOLOGY **3754**

AUSTRALIAN AUTHOR, THE (AT/0045-026X) [01805573] **3364**

AUSTRALIAN AUTISM REVIEW *CEASED.* (AT/0312-8857) [04287814] **4575**

AUSTRALIAN AVIATION (AT/0813-0876) [I08130876] **12**

AUSTRALIAN BANKER (AT/0814-2912) [10773005] **773**

AUSTRALIAN BANKING STATISTICS - RESERVE BANK OF AUSTRALIA (AT/1034-9685) [I10349685] **773**

AUSTRALIAN BAR REVIEW (AT/0814-8589) [15144213] **2938**

AUSTRALIAN BASKETBALLER (AT/0811-2541) [I08112541] **4885**

AUSTRALIAN BEAUTY COUNTER *CEASED.* (AT/0726-2566) [I07262566] **402**

AUSTRALIAN BEAUTY THERAPIST (AT/0156-9821) [I01569821] **402**

AUSTRALIAN BEE JOURNAL (AT/0045-0294) [11307162] **63**

AUSTRALIAN "BEGG ORTHODONTICS" NEWSLETTER (AT/1034-6066) [20351188] **1317**

AUSTRALIAN BIBLICAL REVIEW (AT/0045-0308) [01779549] **5014**

AUSTRALIAN BIBLIOGRAPHIC NETWORK *See* ABN NEWS / NATIONAL LIBRARY OF AUSTRALIA, AUSTRALIAN BIBLIOGRAPHIC NETWORK **3186**

AUSTRALIAN BICENTENNIAL AUTHORITY *See* ANNUAL REPORT ... ON ACTIVITIES TO 30 JUNE ... / THE AUSTRALIAN BICENTENNIAL AUTHORITY **4629**

AUSTRALIAN BIRD WATCHER (AT/0045-0316) [03217544] **5615**

AUSTRALIAN BIRDKEEPER (AT/1030-8954) [I10308954] **5615**

AUSTRALIAN BIRDS : JOURNAL OF THE N. S. W. FIELD ORNITHOLOGISTS CLUB (AT/0311-8150) [05153378] **5615**

AUSTRALIAN BLOODHORSE REVIEW (AT) **2797**

AUSTRALIAN BOOK AUCTION RECORDS / COMPILED BY MARGARET WOODHOUSE (AT) [08096291] **4823**

AUSTRALIAN BOOK COLLECTOR (AT/1034-0785) [I10340785] **4823**

AUSTRALIAN BOOK COLLECTORS PRICE GUIDE (AT) **408**

AUSTRALIAN BOOK REVIEW (AT/0155-2864) [04744283] **3337**

AUSTRALIAN BOOK SCENE (AT) [08413225] **4812**

AUSTRALIAN BOOKS ; A SELECT LIST (AT) [06644419] **4823**

AUSTRALIAN
Alphabetical Title Index

AUSTRALIAN BOOKS IN PRINT (AT) [05332586] **3193**

AUSTRALIAN BOOKSELLER & PUBLISHER (AT) [04486256] **4823**

AUSTRALIAN BROADCASTING TRIBUNAL *See* ANNUAL REPORT - AUSTRALIAN BROADCASTING TRIBUNAL **1126**

AUSTRALIAN BUILDING, CONSTRUCTION AND HOUSING (AT/1032-240X) [I1032240X] **599**

AUSTRALIAN BULLETIN OF LABOUR (AT/0311-6336) [05261326] **1654**

AUSTRALIAN BULLETIN OF LABOUR. SUPPLEMENT (AT) [04643255] **1464, 1654**

AUSTRALIAN BUREAU OF STATISTICS *See* GOVERNMENT FINANCIAL ESTIMATES: AUSTRALIA **4728**

AUSTRALIAN BUREAU OF STATISTICS *See* BEEKEEPING, AUSTRALIA **65**

AUSTRALIAN BUREAU OF STATISTICS *See* MONTHLY SUMMARY OF STATISTICS, AUSTRALIA **5333**

AUSTRALIAN BUREAU OF STATISTICS *See* AUSTRALIAN NATIONAL ACCOUNTS; INPUT-OUTPUT TABLES **4696**

AUSTRALIAN BUREAU OF STATISTICS *See* EMPLOYED WAGE AND SALARY EARNERS **1665**

AUSTRALIAN BUREAU OF STATISTICS *See* CENSUS OF MINING ESTABLISHMENTS: INDUSTRY CONCENTRATION STATISTICS, AUSTRALIA **2003**

AUSTRALIAN BUREAU OF STATISTICS *See* PERSONS NOT IN THE LABOUR FORCE **1537**

AUSTRALIAN BUREAU OF STATISTICS *See* SOCIAL INDICATORS **5308**

AUSTRALIAN BUREAU OF STATISTICS *See* MOTOR VEHICLE CENSUS, TASMANIA **5420**

AUSTRALIAN BUREAU OF STATISTICS *See* PUBLICATIONS OF THE AUSTRALIAN BUREAU OF STATISTICS **5336**

AUSTRALIAN BUREAU OF STATISTICS *See* CONSUMER PRICE INDEX **1531**

AUSTRALIAN BUREAU OF STATISTICS *See* TEACHER EDUCATION **1905**

AUSTRALIAN BUREAU OF STATISTICS *See* CATALOGUE OF PUBLICATIONS **5325**

AUSTRALIAN BUREAU OF STATISTICS *See* TAXATION REVENUE, AUSTRALIA **4701**

AUSTRALIAN BUREAU OF STATISTICS *See* OVERSEAS ARRIVALS AND DEPARTURES, AUSTRALIA **5401**

AUSTRALIAN BUREAU OF STATISTICS *See* TRADE UNION STATISTICS: AUSTRALIA **1540**

AUSTRALIAN BUREAU OF STATISTICS. MARRIAGES *See* MARRIAGES, AUSTRALIA **2287**

AUSTRALIAN BUREAU OF STATISTICS. NEW SOUTH WALES OFFICE *See* MONTHLY SUMMARY OF STATISTICS, NEW SOUTH WALES **4698**

AUSTRALIAN BUREAU OF STATISTICS PUBLICATIONS TO BE RELEASED IN .... (AT/1032-0512) [I10320512] **408**

AUSTRALIAN BUREAU OF STATISTICS. QUEENSLAND OFFICE *See* PUBLIC FINANCE: GOVERNMENT AUTHORITIES **4743**

AUSTRALIAN BUREAU OF STATISTICS. QUEENSLAND OFFICE *See* MONTHLY SUMMARY OF STATISTICS **4698**

AUSTRALIAN BUREAU OF STATISTICS. QUEENSLAND OFFICE. QUEENSLAND STATISTICS *See* MONTHLY SUMMARY OF STATISTICS **4698**

AUSTRALIAN BUREAU OF STATISTICS. SOUTH AUSTRALIAN OFFICE *See* PUBLIC FINANCE **4743**

AUSTRALIAN BUREAU OF STATISTICS. SOUTH AUSTRALIAN OFFICE *See* MONTHLY SUMMARY OF STATISTICS, SOUTH AUSTRALIA **4698**

AUSTRALIAN BUREAU OF STATISTICS. TASMANIAN OFFICE *See* BEE FARMING STATISTICS, TASMANIA **151**

AUSTRALIAN BUREAU OF STATISTICS. TASMANIAN OFFICE *See* EDUCATION **1738**

AUSTRALIAN BUREAU OF STATISTICS. TASMANIAN OFFICE *See* MINING TASMANIA **2006**

AUSTRALIAN BUREAU OF STATISTICS. TASMANIAN OFFICE *See* ROAD TRAFFIC ACCIDENTS INVOLVING CASUALTIES, TASMANIA **5443**

AUSTRALIAN BUREAU OF STATISTICS. TASMANIAN OFFICE *See* FRUIT, TASMANIA **1607**

AUSTRALIAN BUREAU OF STATISTICS. WESTERN AUSTRALIAN OFFICE *See* CENSUS OF TOURIST ACCOMMODATION ESTABLISHMENTS, WESTERN AUSTRALIA **2804**

AUSTRALIAN BUREAU OF STATISTICS. WESTERN AUSTRALIAN OFFICE *See* ROAD TRAFFIC ACCIDENTS INVOLVING CASUALTIES **5443**

AUSTRALIAN BUSINESS *See* ABM **636**

AUSTRALIAN BUSINESS BRIEF AND HANSARD SERVICE (AT) **641**

AUSTRALIAN BUSINESS INDEX (AT/0725-3109) [I07253109] **5274**

AUSTRALIAN BUSINESS LAW REVIEW (AT/0310-1053) [01796619] **3096**

AUSTRALIAN BUYING REFERENCE, THE (AT) [15169903] **1598, 949**

AUSTRALIAN CAMBODIAN QUARTERLY (AT) [21924833] **2908**

AUSTRALIAN CAMERA CRAFT AND SHOOTING VIDEO (AT/1035-641X) [I1035641X] **4367**

AUSTRALIAN CAMERA CRAFT MAGAZINE (AT/0158-2658) [I01582658] **4367**

AUSTRALIAN-CANADIAN STUDIES (AT/0810-1906) [11924482] **2722**

AUSTRALIAN CANEGROWER (AT/0157-3039) [06132317] **63**

●AUSTRALIAN CAPITAL TERRITORY IN FOCUS (AT/1039-6594) [28646094] **4696**

AUSTRALIAN CAPITAL TERRITORY LEGISLATION CATALOGUE (AT/1035-2295) [I10352295] **2938**

AUSTRALIAN CAPITAL TERRITORY STATISTICAL SUMMARY (AT/0067-1754) [01798269] **5322**

AUSTRALIAN CATTLE MAGAZINE, THE (AT) [04062826] **206**

AUSTRALIAN CERAMIC CONFERENCE *See* PROCEEDINGS OF THE AUSTRALIAN CERAMIC CONFERENCE **2593**

AUSTRALIAN CHAMBER OF SHIPPING *See* ANNUAL REPORT / AUSTRALIAN CHAMBER OF SHIPPING **5447**

AUSTRALIAN CHAROLAIS NEWS (AT) [06322330] **206**

AUSTRALIAN CHEMICAL ENGINEERING (AT/0004-8828) [02240483] **2008**

AUSTRALIAN CHILD AND FAMILY WELFARE (AT/0312-8970) [I03128970] **5274**

AUSTRALIAN CHILD & FAMILY WELFARE *See* CHILDREN AUSTRALIA **5278**

AUSTRALIAN CHRISTIAN (AT/0004-8852) [I00048852] **4937**

AUSTRALIAN CITRUS NEWS (AT/0004-8283) [02403713] **2328**

AUSTRALIAN CIVIL ENGINEERING TRANSACTIONS (AT) **2018**

AUSTRALIAN CLAY JOURNAL AND CERAMIC NEWS (AT/1035-4611) [I10354611] **2586**

AUSTRALIAN CLINICAL REVIEW (AT/0726-3139) [09161570] **3554**

AUSTRALIAN COAL GEOLOGY : JOURNAL OF THE COAL GEOLOGY GROUP OF THE GEOLOGICAL SOCIETY OF AUSTRALIA (AT/0725-4938) [14390205] **1366**

AUSTRALIAN COAL INDUSTRY RESEARCH LABORATORIES *See* ANNUAL REPORT / AUSTRALIAN COAL INDUSTRY RESEARCH LABORATORIES **2133**

AUSTRALIAN COAL INDUSTRY RESEARCH LABORATORIES *See* RESEARCH REVIEW / ACIRL COAL RESEARCH **2150**

AUSTRALIAN COAL JOURNAL *CEASED*. (AT) **2134**

AUSTRALIAN COAL REPORT (AT/0157-4566) [I01574566] **1933**

AUSTRALIAN COIN REVIEW (AT/0004-8887) [I00048887] **2779**

AUSTRALIAN COLLEGE OF EDUCATION VICTORIAN CHAPTER NEWSLETTER (AT) **1726**

AUSTRALIAN COLLEGE OF MIDWIVES INCORPORATED JOURNAL (AT/1031-170X) [19272441] **3554**

●AUSTRALIAN COMMODITIES (AT) **64**

AUSTRALIAN COMMONWEALTH SPECIALISTS' CATALOGUE, THE *CEASED*. (AT) [07442400] **2784**

AUSTRALIAN COMMUNICATION REVIEW (AT/0726-3252) [I07263252] **1104**

AUSTRALIAN COMPANY LAW CASES (AT) [11490425] **3096**

AUSTRALIAN COMPANY LAW REPORTS (AT/0313-8445) [08351541] **3096**

AUSTRALIAN COMPUTER JOURNAL, THE (AT/0004-8917) [00850766] **1256**

AUSTRALIAN CONCRETE CONSTRUCTION (AT/1031-3249) [I10313249] **599**

AUSTRALIAN CONSERVATION FOUNDATION *See* ANNUAL REPORT **2186**

AUSTRALIAN CONSULTING ENGINEER / JOURNAL FO THE ASSOCIATION OF CONSULTING ENGINEERS (AT) **1966**

AUSTRALIAN CONSUMER DIRECTORY (AT) **1300**

AUSTRALIAN CONSUMER SALES AND CREDIT LAW REPORTER (AT/0726-5956) [I07265956] **2938**

AUSTRALIAN CORPORATE TREASURE (AT) **641**

AUSTRALIAN CORPORATIONS AND SECURITIES REPORTS (AT/1033-7466) [23528360] **3096**

AUSTRALIAN CORPORATIONS DOING BUSINESS ABROAD (US) [08940520] **641**

AUSTRALIAN COTTON GROWER (AT/0159-1290) [28923926] **164**

AUSTRALIAN COUNCIL FOR EDUCATIONAL RESEARCH *See* ACER NEWSLETTER **1722**

AUSTRALIAN COUNCIL OF SOCIAL SERVICE *See* ANNUAL REPORT / AUSTRALIAN COUNCIL OF SOCIAL SERVICE **5272**

AUSTRALIAN COUNTRY LOOKS (AT) **2898**

AUSTRALIAN COUNTRY STYLE (AT/1033-6060) [I10336060] **2510**

AUSTRALIAN CRICKET *CEASED*. (AT/0004-895X) [I0004895X] **4885**

AUSTRALIAN CRIMINAL REPORTS, THE (AT) [07881694] **3105**

AUSTRALIAN CRIMINOLOGY INFORMATION BULLETIN *CEASED*. (AT/1034-6627) [22518270] **3158**

●AUSTRALIAN CRITICAL CARE : OFFICIAL JOURNAL OF THE CONFEDERATION OF AUSTRALIAN CRITICAL CARE NURSES (AT/1036-7314) [25963298] **3851**

AUSTRALIAN CROQUET GAZETTE (AT/0817-6604) [I08176604] **4885**

AUSTRALIAN CULTURAL HISTORY (AT/0728-8433) [11082506] **2668**

AUSTRALIAN CURRENT LAW. LEGISLATION (AT/1036-0425) [23676848] **2938**

AUSTRALIAN CURRENT LAW. REPORTER (AT/1036-0417) [23676917] **2938**

AUSTRALIAN CYCLIST (AT) [I10343016] **428**

AUSTRALIAN DAIRY CORPORATION *See* ANNUAL REPORT / AUSTRALIAN DAIRY CORPORATION **191**

AUSTRALIAN DAIRY FOODS (AT) [08010832] **192**

AUSTRALIAN DATABASE DEVELOPMENT ASSOCIATION NEWSLETTER (AT/0811-4927) [I08114927] **1253**

AUSTRALIAN DECORATING CRAFTS (AT) **370**

AUSTRALIAN DEER (AT) [17454492] **2187**

AUSTRALIAN DEER FARMING (AT/1034-6171) [I10346171] **226, 64**

AUSTRALIAN DEFENCE 2000 *CEASED*. (AT/1030-9667) [19117893] **4037**

AUSTRALIAN DEFENCE FORCE ACADEMY *See* ANNUAL REPORT / AUSTRALIAN DEFENCE FORCE ACADEMY **4034**

AUSTRALIAN DEFENCE FORCE JOURNAL : JOURNAL OF THE AUSTRALIAN PROFESSION OF ARMS (AT/0314-1039) [23597298] **4037**

AUSTRALIAN DENTAL ASSOCIATION *See* FACTS AND FIGURES. AUSTRALIAN DENTISTRY **1323**

AUSTRALIAN DENTAL JOURNAL (AT/0045-0421) [01518791] **1317**

AUSTRALIAN DENTAL PRACTICE (AT/1320-2340) [25627624] **1317**

AUSTRALIAN DESIGN RULES (AT) **5404**

AUSTRALIAN DESIGN SERIES (AT) **2898**

AUSTRALIAN DIGEST, THE (AT/0067-1843) [01518792] **2938**

AUSTRALIAN DIGITAL MUSIC (AT) **4101**

AUSTRALIAN DISABILITY REVIEW (AT/0813-4537) [16921063] **4384**

AUSTRALIAN DISPUTE RESOLUTION JOURNAL (AT/1034-3059) [23849096] **2938**

AUSTRALIAN DOLL DIRECTORY (AT/0816-3294) [I08163294] **2771**

Alphabetical Title Index — AUSTRALIAN

AUSTRALIAN DRIED FRUITS CORPORATION *See* REPORT FOR THE ... PERIOD OF THE AUSTRALIAN DRIED FRUITS CORPORATION FOR THE PERIOD ... **126**

AUSTRALIAN DRIED FRUITS JOURNAL *See* AUSTRALIAN DRIED FRUITS NEWS **2328**

AUSTRALIAN DRIED FRUITS NEWS (AT/0815-208X) [01077290] **2328**

AUSTRALIAN DRILLING (AT/1037-3535) [I10373535] **1966**

AUSTRALIAN EARLY CHILDHOOD NEWSLETTER (AT/1030-0236) [I10300236] **1802**

AUSTRALIAN EARTH SCIENCES INFORMATION SYSTEM *See* AESIS QUARTERLY **1361**

AUSTRALIAN ECONOMIC HISTORY REVIEW (AT/0004-8992) [04814156] **1547**

AUSTRALIAN ECONOMIC INDICATORS (AT/1035-865X) [I1035865X] 1530, **1464**

AUSTRALIAN ECONOMIC PAPERS (AT/0004-900X) [01518795] 1547, **1590**

AUSTRALIAN ECONOMIC REVIEW (AT/0004-9018) [02257995] **1464**

AUSTRALIAN ECONOMY: BUSINESS FORECASTS, THE (AT/0084-7348) [01798962] **1547**

AUSTRALIAN EDUCATION DIRECTORY / DEPT. OF EDUCATION AND YOUTH AFFAIRS (AT/0811-3165) [11230033] **1726**

AUSTRALIAN EDUCATION INDEX (AT/0004-9026) [02071510] 1726, **1793**

AUSTRALIAN EDUCATION REVIEW / AUSTRALIAN COUNCIL FOR EDUCATIONAL RESEARCH (AT) [05918798] **1726**

AUSTRALIAN EDUCATIONAL AND DEVELOPMENTAL PSYCHOLOGIST (AT/0816-5122) [I08165122] 1726, **4575**

AUSTRALIAN EDUCATIONAL COMPUTING (AT/0816-9020) [I08169020] 1888, **1222**

AUSTRALIAN EDUCATIONAL RESEARCHER (AT/0311-6999) [I03116999] **1810**

AUSTRALIAN EDUCATOR (AT) **1888**

AUSTRALIAN ELECTRONICS ENGINEERING (AT/0004-9042) [07189705] **2036**

AUSTRALIAN ENERGY MANAGEMENT NEWS (AT/0817-4113) [I08174113] **1933**

AUSTRALIAN ENERGY RESEARCH (AT/0815-0575) [I08150575] **1933**

AUSTRALIAN ENERGY STATISTICS / DEPARTMENT OF NATIONAL DEVELOPMENT AND ENERGY (AT/0727-2596) [08468288] 1933, **1961**

AUSTRALIAN ENTOMOLOGICAL MAGAZINE (AT/0311-1881) [01326832] **5605**

● AUSTRALIAN ENTOMOLOGIST, THE (AT/1320-6133) [28537951] **5605**

AUSTRALIAN EQUINE VETERINARIAN (AT/1032-6626) **2797**

AUSTRALIAN EVANGEL (AT/0812-4353) [I08124353] 5055, **4937**

AUSTRALIAN EXPATRIATE, THE (US/1064-010X) [25277338] **2668**

AUSTRALIAN FAMILY MELBOURNE (AT/0811-3661) [I08113661] **2276**

AUSTRALIAN FAMILY PHYSICIAN (AT/0300-8495) [05918923] **3737**

AUSTRALIAN FARM JOURNAL (AT/1036-6474) [24888791] **64**

AUSTRALIAN FARM MANAGER, THE (AT/1035-1914) [I10351914] **64**

AUSTRALIAN FARMERS' AND DEALERS' JOURNAL (AT/1036-4242) [I10364242] **158**

AUSTRALIAN FASHION QUARTERLY *CEASED.* (AT) **1081**

AUSTRALIAN FEDERAL TAX REPORTER (AT/0310-7817) [I03107817] **4712**

AUSTRALIAN FEMINIST STUDIES (AT/0816-4649) [16151817] **5551**

AUSTRALIAN FILM DATA (AT/1031-5462) [19842541] 4367, **4064**

AUSTRALIAN FILMS *CEASED.* (AT/0045-0448) [06039614] **4064**

AUSTRALIAN FINANCIAL REVIEW, THE (AT) [02445140] **773**

AUSTRALIAN FISHERIES (AT/0004-9115) [07622794] **2297**

AUSTRALIAN FLYING (AT/0004-9123) [I00049123] **12**

AUSTRALIAN FOLKLORE (AT/0819-0852) [18340974] **2318**

AUSTRALIAN FOREIGN AFFAIRS AND TRADE *CEASED.* (AT/1033-5722) [20378486] **824**

AUSTRALIAN FOREST GROWER (AT) [07627004] **2375**

AUSTRALIAN FOREST INDUSTRIES JOURNAL (1982) (AT/0812-2792) [09359927] **2375**

AUSTRALIAN FOREST RESEARCH *CEASED.* (AT/0004-914X) [01518801] **2375**

AUSTRALIAN FORESTRY (AT/0004-9158) [01518802] **2375**

AUSTRALIAN FRANCHISING (AT/1031-5810) [I10315810] **641**

AUSTRALIAN FRANCHISING *See* FRANCHISING **677**

AUSTRALIAN FRIEND (SYDNEY, N.S.W.) (AT) [10113224] **4937**

AUSTRALIAN GAMESTAR (AT) **4857**

AUSTRALIAN GARDEN HISTORY (AT/1033-3673) [I10333673] **2409**

AUSTRALIAN GARDEN JOURNAL, THE (AT/0812-9495) [I08129495] **2409**

AUSTRALIAN GAS INDUSTRY DIRECTORY, THE (AT/0727-3525) [05724567] **4251**

AUSTRALIAN GAS JOURNAL, THE (AT/0004-9166) [02445141] **4251**

AUSTRALIAN GAY AND LESBIAN LAW JOURNAL *See* AUSTRALASIAN GAY AND LESBIAN LAW JOURNAL **5187**

AUSTRALIAN GEM & TREASURE HUNTER (AT/0159-6322) [06272649] **4869**

AUSTRALIAN GEMMOLOGIST (AT/0004-9174) [03755071] **2913**

AUSTRALIAN GEOGRAPHER (AT/0004-9182) [01518804] **2555**

AUSTRALIAN GEOGRAPHIC : THE JOURNAL OF THE AUSTRALIAN GEOGRAPHIC SOCIETY (AT/0816-1658) [18333455] **2555**

AUSTRALIAN GEOGRAPHICAL STUDIES (AT/0004-9190) [01518805] **2555**

AUSTRALIAN GEOLOGIST, THE (AT/0312-4711) [03526754] **1366**

AUSTRALIAN GEOMAGNETISM REPORT (AT/1035-1515) [I10351515] **1351**

AUSTRALIAN GEOMECHANICS (AT/0818-9110) **2101**

AUSTRALIAN GEOMECHANICS NEWS *See* AUSTRALIAN GEOMECHANICS **2101**

AUSTRALIAN GEOSCIENCE : ANNUAL REPORT OF THE AUSTRALIAN GEOSCIENCE COUNCIL INC., THE COUNCIL OF EARTH SCIENCE SOCIETIES IN AUSTRALIA (AT) [17657353] **1351**

AUSTRALIAN GEOSCIENCE COUNCIL *See* AUSTRALIAN GEOSCIENCE : ANNUAL REPORT OF THE AUSTRALIAN GEOSCIENCE COUNCIL INC., THE COUNCIL OF EARTH SCIENCE SOCIETIES IN AUSTRALIA **1351**

AUSTRALIAN GIFTGUIDE (AT/0312-5327) [03125327] 952, **2583**

AUSTRALIAN GLIDING (AT) [09134831] **12**

AUSTRALIAN GLIDING YEAR BOOK (AT) [02811866] **4885**

AUSTRALIAN GOAT FARMER (AT/0818-8203) [I08188203] **206**

AUSTRALIAN GOAT WORLD, THE (AT) [05451811] **206**

AUSTRALIAN GOLD, GEM AND TREASURE MAGAZINE (AT/0817-654X) [I0817654X] **3998**

AUSTRALIAN GOLF DIGEST ... HANDBOOK (AT/1034-3938) [I10343938] **4885**

AUSTRALIAN GOURMET TRAVELLER 1989 (AT/1034-9006) [I10349006] 5462, **2328**

AUSTRALIAN GOVERNMENT GAZETTE (AT) [01790004] **4631**

AUSTRALIAN GOVERNMENT PUBLICATIONS (AT/0067-1878) [18758332] **4631**

AUSTRALIAN GOVERNMENT PUBLICATIONS. MONTHLY LIST (AT) [01518695] **4631**

AUSTRALIAN GRADE TEACHER (AT) **1802**

AUSTRALIAN GRAIN (AT) [26105253] **164**

AUSTRALIAN GRAPEGROWER AND WINEMAKER (AT/0727-3606) [05451846] **2363**

AUSTRALIAN GYMNAST (AT) **4885**

AUSTRALIAN HAND WEAVER AND SPINNER / HAND WEAVERS AND SPINNERS GUILD OF NEW SOUTH WALES, THE (AT) [11149930] **5183**

AUSTRALIAN HEALTH CARE SYSTEM, THE (AT/0810-7491) [11822599] **4768**

AUSTRALIAN HEALTH REVIEW (AT/0156-5788) [08857179] **3777**

AUSTRALIAN HI-FI (AT/0159-0030) [I01590030] **4367**

AUSTRALIAN HIGH COURT AND FEDERAL COURT PRACTICE (AT) **2938**

AUSTRALIAN HISTORICAL ASSOCIATION *See* AUSTRALIAN HISTORICAL ASSOCIATION BULLETIN **2668**

AUSTRALIAN HISTORICAL ASSOCIATION BULLETIN (AT) [05261091] **2668**

AUSTRALIAN HISTORICAL BIBLIOGRAPHY. BROADSHEET (AT/0810-5340) [I08105340] **2668**

AUSTRALIAN HISTORICAL GEOGRAPHY : A BULLETIN OF THE REFERENCE SECTION OF AUSTRALIA 1788-1988 : A BICENTENNIAL HISTORY (AT/0158-149X) [10745155] **2555**

AUSTRALIAN HISTORICAL STUDIES (AT/1031-461X) [18172751] **2668**

AUSTRALIAN HISTORY TEACHER (AT/0312-2530) [I03122530] **1888**

AUSTRALIAN HOME BEAUTIFUL (AT/0007-928X) [I0007928X] **2898**

AUSTRALIAN HOME BUILDER *See* AUSTRALIAN HOME BEAUTIFUL **2898**

AUSTRALIAN HORSE AND RIDER (AT/0728-1226) [I07281226] **2797**

AUSTRALIAN HORTICULTURE (AT/0726-2256) [09348452] **2409**

AUSTRALIAN HOSPITAL (AT) [25007373] **3777**

AUSTRALIAN HOSPITAL ENGINEER (AT/0727-730X) [I0727730X] **3777**

AUSTRALIAN HOUSE AND GARDEN (AT) [05451883] 2409, **2898**

AUSTRALIAN HUMANIST, THE (AT/0004-9328) [03390629] **2842**

AUSTRALIAN ILLAWARRA DAIRYMAN (AT/1034-9553) [I10349553] **192**

AUSTRALIAN INCOME TAX GUIDE (AT) [04052656] **4712**

AUSTRALIAN INCOME TAX LEGISLATION IN 2 VOLUMES. 2. REGULATIONS, RATING ACTS, INTERNATIONAL AGREEMENTS, OTHER LEGISLATION (AT/0810-5499) [I08105499] **4712**

AUSTRALIAN INDUSTRIAL LAW REVIEW (AT/0726-5883) [I07265883] **2938**

AUSTRALIAN INDUSTRIAL RELATIONS COMMISSION AWARDS : GARDENING, NURSERIES AND GREENKEEPING (UK) **2409**

AUSTRALIAN INDUSTRY TRENDS (AT/1030-7664) [20189835] **1598**

AUSTRALIAN INSOLVENCY BULLETIN (AT/1033-9345) [I10339345] **2938**

AUSTRALIAN INSTITUTE OF ABORIGINAL AND TORRES STRAIT ISLANDER STUDIES *See* ANNUAL BIBLIOGRAPHY / AUSTRALIAN INSTITUTE OF ABORIGINAL AND TORRES STRAIT ISLANDER STUDIES **2276**

AUSTRALIAN INSTITUTE OF CRIMINOLOGY *See* PROCEEDINGS OF THE RESIDENTIAL CONFERENCE OF THE AUSTRALIAN INSTITUTE OF CRIMINOLOGY **3173**

AUSTRALIAN INSTITUTE OF FAMILY STUDIES. BOARD OF MANAGEMENT *See* ANNUAL REPORT / BOARD OF MANAGEMENT, AUSTRALIAN INSTITUTE OF FAMILY STUDIES **2276**

AUSTRALIAN INTELLECTUAL PROPERTY CASES (AT/0814-9046) [I08149046] **2938**

AUSTRALIAN INTERNATIONAL LAW NEWS (AT/0811-9260) [10912006] **3124**

AUSTRALIAN INVESTMENT (AT/1031-4822) [I10314822] **891**

AUSTRALIAN INVESTOR (AT/0812-129X) [I0812129X] **641**

AUSTRALIAN JERSEY JOURNAL (AT) [02841869] **206**

AUSTRALIAN JEWISH DEMOCRAT (AT) [28735379] **5046**

AUSTRALIAN JOURNAL OF ADULT AND COMMUNITY EDUCATION (AT/1035-0462) [22147663] **1799**

AUSTRALIAN JOURNAL OF ADVANCED NURSING (AT/0813-0531) [10902438] **3852**

AUSTRALIAN JOURNAL OF AGRICULTURAL ECONOMICS, THE (AT/0004-9395) [01518808] **64**

AUSTRALIAN JOURNAL OF AGRICULTURAL RESEARCH (AT/0004-9409) [01518809] **64**

AUSTRALIAN JOURNAL OF ANTHROPOLOGY, THE (AT/1035-8811) [23262826] **231**

AUSTRALIAN JOURNAL OF ART (AT/0314-6464) [05037582] **343**

AUSTRALIAN JOURNAL OF ASTRONOMY (AT/0814-5628) [12596383] **393**

AUSTRALIAN — Alphabetical Title Index

AUSTRALIAN JOURNAL OF AUDIOLOGY, THE (AT/0157-1532) [06818504] **3886**

AUSTRALIAN JOURNAL OF BOTANY (AT/0067-1924) [01518812] **501**

AUSTRALIAN JOURNAL OF CHEMISTRY (AT/0004-9425) [01518813] **961**

AUSTRALIAN JOURNAL OF CHINESE AFFAIRS, THE (AT/0156-7365) [05895676] **2501**

AUSTRALIAN JOURNAL OF CLINICAL AND EXPERIMENTAL HYPNOSIS (AT/0156-0417) [06431400] **2857**

AUSTRALIAN JOURNAL OF CLINICAL HYPNOTHERAPY AND HYPNOSIS, THE (AT/0810-0713) [12387255] **2857**

AUSTRALIAN JOURNAL OF COAL MINING TECHNOLOGY AND RESEARCH, THE (AT/0727-419X) [09104529] **2134**

AUSTRALIAN JOURNAL OF COMMUNICATION (AT/0811-6202) [10385163] **1104**

AUSTRALIAN JOURNAL OF CORPORATE LAW (AT/1037-4124) [25312395] **3096**

AUSTRALIAN JOURNAL OF DAIRY TECHNOLOGY, THE (AT/0004-9433) [01518814] **192**

AUSTRALIAN JOURNAL OF EARLY CHILDHOOD (AT/0312-5033) [06759326] **1802**

AUSTRALIAN JOURNAL OF EARTH SCIENCES (AT/0812-0099) [11297431] **1351**

AUSTRALIAN JOURNAL OF ECOLOGY (AT/0307-692X) [02462674] **2211**

AUSTRALIAN JOURNAL OF EDUCATION, THE (AT/0004-9441) [01518817] **1726**

AUSTRALIAN JOURNAL OF EDUCATIONAL TECHNOLOGY (AT/0814-673X) [I0814673X] **1810**

AUSTRALIAN JOURNAL OF ENVIRONMENTAL EDUCATION (AT/0814-0626) [I08140626] 2211, **1726**

AUSTRALIAN JOURNAL OF EXPERIMENTAL AGRICULTURE (AT/0816-1089) [12490171] **64**

AUSTRALIAN JOURNAL OF FAMILY LAW (AT/0817-623X) [19101597] **3119**

AUSTRALIAN JOURNAL OF FORENSIC SCIENCES, THE (AT/0045-0618) [01518820] **3740**

AUSTRALIAN JOURNAL OF FRENCH STUDIES (AT/0004-9468) [01518821] **3364**

AUSTRALIAN JOURNAL OF GEODESY, PHOTOGRAMMETRY, AND SURVEYING (AT/0159-8910) [06869423] 2555, **2018**

AUSTRALIAN JOURNAL OF HISTORICAL ARCHAEOLOGY, THE (AT/0810-1868) [10154624] **260**

AUSTRALIAN JOURNAL OF HOSPITAL PHARMACY (AT/0310-6810) [01002924] **4293**

AUSTRALIAN JOURNAL OF HUMAN COMMUNICATION DISORDERS (AT/0310-6853) [00879796] **4384**

AUSTRALIAN JOURNAL OF INFOMATION SYSTEMS, THE (AT/1039-7841) **1727**

AUSTRALIAN JOURNAL OF INSTRUMENTATION AND CONTROL (AT) [16767172] **1966**

AUSTRALIAN JOURNAL OF INTERNATIONAL AFFAIRS (AT/1035-7718) [22465969] **4516**

AUSTRALIAN JOURNAL OF JEWISH STUDIES (AT/1037-0838) [26241563] **2256**

AUSTRALIAN JOURNAL OF LABOUR LAW (AT/1030-7222) [19760687] **3144**

● AUSTRALIAN JOURNAL OF LANGUAGE AND LITERACY / ARA, THE (AT/1038-1562) [26146610] **3267**

AUSTRALIAN JOURNAL OF LAW AND SOCIETY (AT/0729-3356) [09068581] **2938**

AUSTRALIAN JOURNAL OF LINGUISTICS (AT/0726-8602) [08206174] **3267**

AUSTRALIAN JOURNAL OF LITURGY (AT/1030-617X) [I1030617X] **4937**

AUSTRALIAN JOURNAL OF MANAGEMENT (AT/0312-8962) [04748496] 1464, **860**

AUSTRALIAN JOURNAL OF MARINE AND FRESHWATER RESEARCH (AT/0067-1940) [01518823] 553, **1446**

AUSTRALIAN JOURNAL OF MARRIAGE & FAMILY (AT/1034-652X) [21591221] **2276**

AUSTRALIAN JOURNAL OF MEDICAL LABORATORY SCIENCE See AUSTRALIAN JOURNAL OF MEDICAL SCIENCE **3554**

● AUSTRALIAN JOURNAL OF MEDICAL SCIENCE (AT/1038-1643) [28013863] **3554**

AUSTRALIAN JOURNAL OF MINING (AT/0817-9646) [I08179646] **2134**

AUSTRALIAN JOURNAL OF MUSIC EDUCATION (AT/0004-9484) [01793025] **4101**

AUSTRALIAN JOURNAL OF MUSIC THERAPY, THE (AT/1036-9457) [I10369457] 4101, **3554**

AUSTRALIAN JOURNAL OF NUTRITION AND DIETETICS (AT/1032-1322) [20142084] **4187**

● AUSTRALIAN JOURNAL OF OTO-LARYNGOLOGY : THE OFFICIAL JOURNAL OF THE AUSTRALIAN SOCIETY OF OTO-LARYNGOLOGY HEAD AND NECK SURGERY (AT/1037-2105) [26025110] **3887**

AUSTRALIAN JOURNAL OF PHARMACY (AT/0311-8002) [06664478] **4293**

AUSTRALIAN JOURNAL OF PHYSICS (AT/0004-9506) [01518825] **4398**

AUSTRALIAN JOURNAL OF PHYSIOTHERAPY, THE (AT/0004-9514) [05199682] **4379**

AUSTRALIAN JOURNAL OF PLANT PHYSIOLOGY (AT/0310-7841) [00963644] **501**

AUSTRALIAN JOURNAL OF POLITICAL SCIENCE (AT/1036-1146) [23018344] **4464**

AUSTRALIAN JOURNAL OF POLITICS AND HISTORY, THE (AT/0004-9522) [01518826] **4464**

AUSTRALIAN JOURNAL OF PSYCHOLOGY (AT/0004-9530) [01518827] **4575**

AUSTRALIAN JOURNAL OF PSYCHOTHERAPY (AT/0728-6155) [12085520] **4575**

AUSTRALIAN JOURNAL OF PUBLIC ADMINISTRATION (AT/0313-6647) [02395982] **4631**

AUSTRALIAN JOURNAL OF PUBLIC HEALTH (AT/1035-7319) [23435208] **4768**

AUSTRALIAN JOURNAL OF READING See AUSTRALIAN JOURNAL OF LANGUAGE AND LITERACY / ARA, THE **3267**

AUSTRALIAN JOURNAL OF REMEDIAL EDUCATION (AT/0726-5115) [I07265115] 1875, **1727**

● AUSTRALIAN JOURNAL OF RURAL HEALTH, THE (AT/1038-5282) [28774470] **3554**

AUSTRALIAN JOURNAL OF SCIENCE AND MEDICINE IN SPORT (AT) [11479123] **3953**

AUSTRALIAN JOURNAL OF SOCIAL ISSUES, THE (AT/0157-6321) [00850143] **5274**

AUSTRALIAN JOURNAL OF SOIL AND WATER CONSERVATION (AT/1032-2426) [I10322426] **5530**

AUSTRALIAN JOURNAL OF SOIL RESEARCH (AT/0004-9573) [01518830] **164**

AUSTRALIAN JOURNAL OF STATISTICS (AT/0004-9581) [01518831] **5322**

AUSTRALIAN JOURNAL OF TAFE RESEARCH AND DEVELOPMENT (AT/0816-2018) [I08162018] 1911, **1810**

AUSTRALIAN JOURNAL OF TAFE RESEARCH & DEVELOPMENT See AUSTRALIAN & NEW ZEALAND JOURNAL OF VOCATIONAL EDUCATION RESEARCH **1911**

AUSTRALIAN JOURNAL OF TEACHER EDUCATION, THE (AT/0313-5373) [04388517] **1888**

AUSTRALIAN JOURNAL OF ZOOLOGY (AT/0004-959X) [01518832] **5577**

AUSTRALIAN JOURNAL ON AGEING (AT/0726-4240) [09234990] **3749**

AUSTRALIAN JOURNALISM REVIEW : AJR (AT/0810-2686) [10250149] **2917**

AUSTRALIAN KEY BUSINESS DIRECTORY See KEY BUSINESS DIRECTORY OF AUSTRALIA : KBD **688**

AUSTRALIAN KEY BUSINESS DIRECTORY, THE (AT) [04184195] **641**

AUSTRALIAN LAW JOURNAL REPORTS, THE (AT) [05859062] **2939**

AUSTRALIAN LAW JOURNAL, THE (AT/0004-9611) [01518834] **2938**

● AUSTRALIAN LAW LIBRARIAN (AT/1039-6616) [28155531] **2939**

AUSTRALIAN LAW NEWS (AT) [20709676] **2939**

AUSTRALIAN LAW REPORTS (AT/0310-0014) [01792860] **2939**

AUSTRALIAN LAWYER (AT) [I10398775] **2939**

AUSTRALIAN LEFT REVIEW CEASED. (AT/0004-9638) [02223347] **4465**

AUSTRALIAN LEGAL DIRECTORY (AT) [06985688] **2939**

AUSTRALIAN LEGAL MONTHLY DIGEST (AT/0004-9646) [01518838] 2939, **3078**

AUSTRALIAN LIBRARIES : ALED (AT/1031-5187) [20927967] **3193**

AUSTRALIAN LIBRARY JOURNAL, THE (AT/0004-9670) [01518840] **3193**

AUSTRALIAN LIBRARY REVIEW (AT/1034-8042) [27833933] **3193**

AUSTRALIAN LIBRARY TECHNICIANS ASSOCIATION NEWS (AT/1036-1820) [I10361820] **3193**

AUSTRALIAN LIQUOR TRADER CEASED. (AT/1033-6044) [I10336044] **2364**

AUSTRALIAN LITERARY AWARDS AND FELLOWSHIPS (AT/1036-1669) [I10361669] **3337**

AUSTRALIAN LITERARY STUDIES (AT/0004-9697) [00849640] **3338**

AUSTRALIAN LITHOGRAPHER, PRINTER AND PACKAGER, THE SUSPENDED. (AT) [10756117] 4218, **4563**

AUSTRALIAN MACHINERY See AUSTRALIAN MACHINERY AND PRODUCTION ENGINEERING **2110**

AUSTRALIAN MACHINERY AND PRODUCTION ENGINEERING (AT/0004-9719) [02445150] 3475, **2110**

AUSTRALIAN MACUSER (AT) **1171**

AUSTRALIAN MAD MAGAZINE (AT) **4857**

AUSTRALIAN MAMMALOGY (AT/0310-0049) [03699542] **5577**

AUSTRALIAN MANUFACTURING COUNCIL See ANNUAL REPORT / AUSTRALIAN MANUFACTURING COUNCIL **3475**

AUSTRALIAN MAP CIRCLE See NEWSLETTER / AUSTRALIAN MAP CIRCLE **2570**

AUSTRALIAN MARINE SCIENCE BULLETIN (AT/0157-6429) [I01576429] **553**

AUSTRALIAN MARINE SCIENCES ASSOCIATION See AMSA HANDBOOK **552**

AUSTRALIAN MARKETING RESEARCHER (AT/0727-8349) [03764493] **921**

AUSTRALIAN MASTER TAX GUIDE (AT) [01795232] **4712**

AUSTRALIAN MATHEMATICAL SOCIETY See GAZETTE - AUSTRALIAN MATHEMATICAL SOCIETY **3506**

AUSTRALIAN MATHEMATICAL SOCIETY LECTURE SERIES (UK/0950-2815) [13151546] **3496**

AUSTRALIAN MATHEMATICS TEACHER, THE (AT/0045-0685) [09930103] 1888, **3496**

AUSTRALIAN MEAT INDUSTRY BULLETIN, THE (AT/0156-2681) [08069457] **206**

AUSTRALIAN MEDIA DIRECTORY (AT) **1104**

AUSTRALIAN MEDICAL RECORD JOURNAL / MEDICAL RECORD ASSOCIATION OF AUSTRALIA (AT/0817-3907) [18352762] **3777**

AUSTRALIAN MEDICINE : NEWSMAGAZINE OF THE AUSTRALIAN MEDICAL ASSOCIATION (AT) [23176441] **3554**

AUSTRALIAN METEOROLOGICAL MAGAZINE (AT/0004-9743) [01518845] **1420**

AUSTRALIAN MINER, THE (AT) [08918136] **2134**

AUSTRALIAN MINERAL DEVELOPMENT LABORATORIES See ANNUAL REPORT - AMDEL **3998**

AUSTRALIAN MINERAL INDUSTRIES RESEARCH ASSOCIATION See AMIRA ... ANNUAL REPORT / AUSTRALIAN MINERAL INDUSTRIES RESEARCH ASSOCIATION LIMITED **2133**

AUSTRALIAN MINERALOGIST CEASED. (AT/0819-6508) [17845263] 1438, **2134**

AUSTRALIAN MINES AND METALS ASSOCIATION See DIRECTORS' REPORT - AUSTRALIAN MINES AND METALS ASSOCIATION **2138**

AUSTRALIAN MINING (AT/0004-976X) [09010421] **2134**

AUSTRALIAN MINING AND PETROLEUM LAW ASSOCIATION YEARBOOK (AT/0812-857X) [11511962] 4251, 2134, **2939**

AUSTRALIAN MINING'S PRODUCT REGISTER CEASED. (AT) [17307158] **2134**

AUSTRALIAN MONEY MARKET WEEKLY (AT) [I01567713] **921**

AUSTRALIAN MOTHER AND BABY (AT/1031-4830) [I10314830] **2277**

AUSTRALIAN MUNICIPAL JOURNAL, THE (AT/0004-9808) [01804411] **4631**

AUSTRALIAN MUSEUM See RECORDS OF THE AUSTRALIAN MUSEUM **5596**

AUSTRALIAN MUSIC STUDIES (AT/0727-4025) [11734537] **4101**

AUSTRALIAN MUSIC THERAPY ASSOCIATION. NATIONAL CONFERENCE See PROCEEDINGS OF THE ... NATIONAL CONFERENCE OF THE AUSTRALIAN MUSIC THERAPY ASSOCIATION HELD IN ..., THE **4147**

Alphabetical Title Index — AUSTRALIAN

AUSTRALIAN NATIONAL ACCOUNTS. CAPITAL STOCK (AT/1033-3010) [I10333010] 4712, **4696**

AUSTRALIAN NATIONAL ACCOUNTS FINANCIAL ACCOUNTS (AT/1038-4286) [I10384286] 4712, **4696**

AUSTRALIAN NATIONAL ACCOUNTS. FLOW OF FUNDS DEVELOPMENTAL ESTIMATES *See* AUSTRALIAN NATIONAL ACCOUNTS FINANCIAL ACCOUNTS **4696**

AUSTRALIAN NATIONAL ACCOUNTS. GROSS PRODUCT, EMPLOYMENT AND HOURS WORKED *CEASED.* (AT/1030-9047) [I9964734] **1654**

AUSTRALIAN NATIONAL ACCOUNTS INPUT-OUTPUT TABLES (AT) [03042858] 4712, **4696**

AUSTRALIAN NATIONAL ACCOUNTS, INPUT-OUTPUT TABLES, COMMODITY DETAILS (AT/0727-1476) [I07271476] 1598, **1530**

AUSTRALIAN NATIONAL ACCOUNTS : NATIONAL INCOME AND EXPENDITURE (AT/0067-1983) [01799618] 4712, **4696**

AUSTRALIAN NATIONAL ACCOUNTS. STATE ACCOUNTS (AT) [16991068] 4712, **4696**

AUSTRALIAN NATIONAL BIBLIOGRAPHY *CEASED.* (AT/0004-9816) [01518850] **2496**

AUSTRALIAN NATIONAL DAIRY COMMITTEE *See* ANNUAL REPORT - AUSTRALIAN NATIONAL DAIRY COMMITTEE **191**

AUSTRALIAN NATIONAL GALLERY *See* ANNUAL REPORT / AUSTRALIAN NATIONAL GALLERY **4083**

AUSTRALIAN NATIONAL RAILWAYS COMMISSION *See* ANNUAL REPORT / AUSTRALIAN NATIONAL RAILWAYS COMMISSION **5429**

AUSTRALIAN NATIONAL UNIVERSITY, CANBERRA. FORESTRY STUDENTS' SOCIETY *See* FORESTRY LOG **2382**

AUSTRALIAN NATIONAL UNIVERSITY. RESEARCH SCHOOL OF EARTH SCIENCES *See* ANNUAL REPORT / AUSTRALIAN NATIONAL UNIVERSITY RESEARCH SCHOOL OF EARTH SCIENCES **1351**

AUSTRALIAN NATIONAL UNIVERSITY. RESEARCH SCHOOL OF PACIFIC STUDIES. DEPT. OF ECONOMICS *See* ANNUAL REPORT FOR ... / THE AUSTRALIAN NATIONAL UNIVERS TY, DEPARTMENT OF ECONOMICS, RESEARCH SCHOOL OF PACIFIC STUDIES **1462**

AUSTRALIAN NATURAL HISTORY (AT/0004-9840) [04522277] **4162**

AUSTRALIAN NEW ZEALAND LAN MAGAZINE (AU) **1240**

AUSTRALIAN NUCLEAR SCIENCE AND TECHNOLOGY ORGANISATION *See* ANNUAL REPORT / AUSTRALIAN NUCLEAR SCIENCE AND TECHNOLOGY ORGANISATION **2154**

AUSTRALIAN NUGGET JOURNAL (AT/1030-7915) [I10307915] 2780, **3998**

AUSTRALIAN NUMISMATIC JOURNAL (AT/0004-9875) [01812500] **2771**

AUSTRALIAN NUMISMATIC JOURNAL (AT/0004-9875) [08933293] **2780**

AUSTRALIAN NURSES JOURNAL *See* AUSTRALIAN NURSING JOURNAL, THE **3852**

AUSTRALIAN NURSES' JOURNAL (AT/0045-0758) [04522199] **3852**

● AUSTRALIAN NURSING JOURNAL (JULY 1993) (AT) [29369396] **3852**

AUSTRALIAN NURSING JOURNAL (JUNE 1993) *See* AUSTRALIAN NURSING JOURNAL (JULY 1993) **3852**

AUSTRALIAN NURSING JOURNAL, THE (AT) [28601392] **3852**

AUSTRALIAN NUTGROWER (AT/0819-7849) [I08197849] **164**

AUSTRALIAN OCCUPATIONAL THERAPY JOURNAL (AT/0045-0766) [05058650] **1875**

AUSTRALIAN OFFICIAL JOURNAL OF PATENTS (CANBERRA, A.C.T. : 1987) (AT) [16439772] **1301**

AUSTRALIAN OFFICIAL JOURNAL OF TRADE MARKS (AT) [16439810] **1301**

AUSTRALIAN OIL & GAS DIRECTORY (AT/0157-728X) [I0157728X] **4251**

AUSTRALIAN OIL AND GAS EXPLORERS DIRECTORY (AT) **4251**

AUSTRALIAN OLYMPIAN (AT) **4885**

AUSTRALIAN ORCHID REVIEW (AT/0045-0782) [03196743] **2409**

AUSTRALIAN ORIENTEER JAMISON (AT/0818-6510) [I08186510] **4885**

AUSTRALIAN ORTHOPTIC JOURNAL (AT/0814-0936) [10096392] **3872**

AUSTRALIAN OUTLOOK. LONDON (UK/0301-5785) [I03015785] **2510**

AUSTRALIAN PACKAGING (AT/0004-9921) [06544272] **4218**

AUSTRALIAN PAEDIATRIC NURSE (AT/1036-5060) [I10365060] **3852**

AUSTRALIAN PARAPSYCHOLOGICAL REVIEW (AT/1035-9621) [I10359621] **4240**

AUSTRALIAN PARKS AND RECREATION (AT/0311-8223) [02153842] 4848, **4706**

AUSTRALIAN PC USER *See* AUSTRALIAN AND NEW ZEALAND PC USER **1265**

AUSTRALIAN PERIODICALS IN PRINT (AT) [18003377] **408**

AUSTRALIAN PERSONAL COMPUTER (AT/0725-4415) [I07254415] **1265**

AUSTRALIAN PETROLEUM ACCUMULATIONS (AT) [19708915] **4251**

AUSTRALIAN PETROLEUM ACCUMULATIONS REPORT / DEPARTMENT OF RESOURCES AND ENERGY, BUREAU OF MINERAL RESOURCES, GEOLOGY AND GEOPHYSICS (AT/0817-9263) [15638474] **4251**

AUSTRALIAN PETROLEUM EXPLORATION ASSOCIATION *See* APEA JOURNAL, THE **4250**

AUSTRALIAN PETROLEUM SERVICES INDEX (AT/0813-3514) [I08133514] **4283**

AUSTRALIAN PHARMACIST / PHARMACEUTICAL SOCIETY OF AUSTRALIA (AT/0728-4632) [18582138] **4293**

AUSTRALIAN PHOTOGRAPHY (AT/0004-9964) [I00049964] **4367**

AUSTRALIAN PHOTOGRAPHY DIRECTORY (AT/0816-3669) [I08163669] **4367**

AUSTRALIAN PHYSIOLOGICAL AND PHARMACOLOGICAL SOCIETY *See* PROCEEDINGS OF THE AUSTRALIAN PHYSIOLOGICAL AND PHARMACOLOGICAL SOCIETY **585**

AUSTRALIAN PIPELINER (AT/0310-1258) [I03101258] **4251**

AUSTRALIAN PLANNER : JOURNAL OF THE ROYAL AUSTRALIAN PLANNING INSTITUTE (AT/0729-3682) [08595155] **2815**

AUSTRALIAN PLANNING APPEAL DECISIONS *CEASED.* (AT/0728-6309) [09558396] 2815, **2939**

AUSTRALIAN PLANT INTRODUCTION REVIEW (AT) [03570495] **2410**

AUSTRALIAN PLANTS (AT/0005-0008) [02403686] 501, **2410**

AUSTRALIAN PLAYWRIGHTS (NE/0921-2531) [18886502] 3364, **5361**

AUSTRALIAN PLUMBING INDUSTRY MAGAZINE (AT/0817-6337) [I08176337] **2603**

AUSTRALIAN PODIATRIST (AT/0311-3612) [I03113612] **3917**

AUSTRALIAN POETRY *CEASED.* (AT) [01518858] **3460**

AUSTRALIAN POLICE JOURNAL (AT/0005-0024) [01785490] **3158**

AUSTRALIAN POLITICAL DIRECTORY (AT) **4465**

AUSTRALIAN POLL DORSET JOURNAL (AT) [03292203] **206**

AUSTRALIAN POWERBOAT (AT/0313-766X) [I0313766X] **591**

AUSTRALIAN PRESBYTERIAN LIFE (AT) [04903969] **5055**

AUSTRALIAN PRESCRIBER (AT/0312-8008) [04295780] **3554**

AUSTRALIAN PRIMATOLOGY (AT/0817-9573) [I08179573] **5577**

AUSTRALIAN PRINTER MAGAZINE (AT) [20284798] **4563**

AUSTRALIAN PRISONERS (AT/0813-2364) [13284440] **3078**

AUSTRALIAN PRIVATE DOCTOR : THE JOURNAL OF PRIVATE DOCTORS OF AUSTRALIA (AT) [18467012] **3554**

AUSTRALIAN PRODUCT LIABILITY REPORTER (AT/1034-4608) [I10344608] **4768**

AUSTRALIAN PROFESSIONAL MARKETING (AT) **921**

AUSTRALIAN PROFILE (AT) **1464**

AUSTRALIAN PROJECT MANAGER (AT) **861**

AUSTRALIAN PROPERTY MARKET INVESTMENT STRATEGY REPORT (AT/1035-364X) [I1035364X] **891**

AUSTRALIAN PROSTHODONTIC JOURNAL (AT/0819-0887) [18352912] **1317**

AUSTRALIAN PSYCHOLOGIST (AT/0005-0067) [02418905] **4575**

AUSTRALIAN PURCHASING AND SUPPLY (WATERLOO) (AT/1035-0357) [I10350357] **949**

AUSTRALIAN QUARTER HORSE MAGAZINE (AT) **2797**

AUSTRALIAN QUARTERLY (AT/0005-0091) [05882348] **2668**

AUSTRALIAN RADIATION RECORDS (AT) [20316260] **1420**

AUSTRALIAN RATIONALIST (AT) **4342**

AUSTRALIAN RECORD AND MUSIC REVIEW (AT/1033-1352) [I10331352] **4101**

AUSTRALIAN REFRIGERATION, AIR CONDITIONING AND HEATING (AT) [06001872] **2603**

AUSTRALIAN RELIGION STUDIES REVIEW (AT/1031-2943) [I10312943] **4937**

AUSTRALIAN REPRESENTATIVE BASINS PROGRAM REPORT SERIES (AT/0314-2523) [04008408] **5530**

AUSTRALIAN RESOURCES GUIDE (AT) **4631**

AUSTRALIAN REVIEW OF APPLIED LINGUISTICS (AT/0155-0640) [I01550640] **3267**

AUSTRALIAN ROAD AND TRACK (AT/1036-3254) [I10363254] **5404**

AUSTRALIAN ROAD RESEARCH *See* ROAD & TRANSPORT RESEARCH : [A JOURNAL OF AUSTRALIAN AND NEW ZEALAND RESEARCH AND PRACTICE] **5443**

AUSTRALIAN ROAD RESEARCH BOARD *See* PROCEEDINGS [OF THE CONFERENCE] **5442**

AUSTRALIAN ROAD RESEARCH BOARD *See* RESEARCH REPORT - AUSTRALIAN ROAD RESEARCH BOARD **5443**

AUSTRALIAN ROAD RESEARCH BOARD *See* ARRB RESEARCH REPORT ARR **5377**

AUSTRALIAN ROWING (AT/0727-3126) [I07273126] **4885**

AUSTRALIAN RUGBY NEWS *CEASED.* (AT) **4885**

AUSTRALIAN RUNNER (AT) **4885**

AUSTRALIAN SAFETY NEWS (AT/0005-0180) [I00050180] **2859**

AUSTRALIAN SAILING (AT/0726-5646) [I07265646] **591**

AUSTRALIAN SCIENCE TEACHERS' JOURNAL, THE (AT/0045-0855) [01737884] **5087**

AUSTRALIAN SEA HERITAGE (AT/0813-0523) [I08130523] **2611**

AUSTRALIAN SECRETARY (AT/0314-4275) [I03144275] **641**

AUSTRALIAN SENIOR MATHEMATICS JOURNAL (AT) [I08194564] 1888, **3496**

AUSTRALIAN SHELL NEWS (AT/0310-1304) [11648241] **5577**

AUSTRALIAN SHOOTERS JOURNAL (AT/0005-0245) [I00050245] **4885**

AUSTRALIAN SHOPFITTING TRADE JOURNAL (AT) **4210**

AUSTRALIAN SKIING (AT) **4848**

AUSTRALIAN SKIING SURRY HILLS *See* AUSTRALIAN SKIING **4848**

AUSTRALIAN SKIING SURRY HILLS (AT/0818-9307) [I08189307] **4885**

AUSTRALIAN SLAVONIC AND EAST EUROPEAN STUDIES : JOURNAL OF THE AUSTRALIAN AND NEW ZEALAND SLAVISTS' ASSOCIATION AND OF THE AUSTRALASIAN ASSOCIATION FOR STUDY OF THE SOCIALIST COUNTRIES (AT/0818-8149) [17495632] 5192, **3267**

AUSTRALIAN SMALL BUSINESS & INVESTING (AT) **641**

AUSTRALIAN SMALL BUSINESS REVIEW *See* AUSTRALIAN SMALL BUSINESS & INVESTING **641**

AUSTRALIAN SOCCER WEEKLY (AT/0727-6850) [I07276850] **4885**

AUSTRALIAN SOCIAL WORK (AT/0312-407X) [02582797] **5274**

AUSTRALIAN SOCIETY (AT/0729-8595) [09747991] **2510**

AUSTRALIAN SOCIETY FOR BIOCHEMISTRY AND MOLECULAR BIOLOGY. CONFERENCE *See* PROCEEDINGS OF THE AUSTRALIAN SOCIETY FOR BIOCHEMISTRY AND MOLECULAR BIOLOGY : ABSTRACTS OF PAPERS PRESENTED AT THE ... ANNUAL CONFERENCE OF THE SOCIETY HELD ... **492**

AUSTRALIAN SOCIETY FOR SPORTS HISTORY BULLETIN (AT/0817-2048) [I08172048] **4885**

AUSTRALIAN SOCIETY OF ANIMAL PRODUCTION. CONFERENCE *See* PROCEEDINGS OF THE AUSTRALIAN SOCIETY OF ANIMAL PRODUCTION **219**

AUSTRALIAN SOCIETY OF INDEXERS NEWSLETTER (AT/0314-3767) [I03143767] 3257, **3193**

AUSTRALIAN SPORTS DIRECTORY (AT/0157-6542) [I01576542] **4885**

AUSTRALIAN STANDARD (AT/0158-3999) [I01583999] **64**

AUSTRALIAN — Alphabetical Title Index

AUSTRALIAN STANDARD DIAGNOSTIC TECHNIQUES FOR ANIMAL DISEASES (AT) [19485372] **5505**

AUSTRALIAN STOCK HORSE JOURNAL (AT/0817-8550) [I08178550] **2797**

AUSTRALIAN STRING TEACHER (AT/0312-9950) [I03129950] **4101**

AUSTRALIAN STUDIES (UK/0954-0954) [18770665] **2669**

AUSTRALIAN STUDIES (AUSTRALIAN STUDIES ASSOCIATION) (AT) [20441041] **2669**

AUSTRALIAN SUGAR CRAFT (AT/1033-6656) [I10336656] **2328**

AUSTRALIAN SUGAR YEAR BOOK, THE (AT/0067-2173) [03393901] **2328**

AUSTRALIAN SUPER REVIEW (AT/0819-341X) [I0819341X] **773**

AUSTRALIAN SURFING WORLD (AT) **4885**

AUSTRALIAN SURVEYOR (AT/0005-0326) [03189538] **2019**

AUSTRALIAN SYSTEMATIC BOTANY (AT/1030-1887) [18489688] **501**

AUSTRALIAN SYSTEMATIC BOTANY SOCIETY NEWSLETTER (AT/1034-1218) [16657170] **501**

AUSTRALIAN TABLE TENNIS (AT/0814-3668) [I08143668] **4885**

AUSTRALIAN TAFE TEACHER (AT/0815-3701) [I08153701] 1810, **1911**

AUSTRALIAN TAX CASES (AT/0726-5859) [03953784] **4712**

AUSTRALIAN TAX FORUM (AT/0812-695X) [10961172] **4712**

AUSTRALIAN TAX REVIEW (AT/0311-094X) [06841449] **2939**

AUSTRALIAN TEACHER *See* AUSTRALIAN EDUCATOR **1888**

AUSTRALIAN TEACHER OF THE DEAF (AT/0005-0334) [01911587] 4384, **1875**

AUSTRALIAN TEACHER, THE (AT) [06482507] **1888**

AUSTRALIAN THERAPEUTIC DEVICE BULLETIN / DEPARTMENT COMMUNITY SERVICES AND HEALTH (AT/1030-1933) [29573508] **3554**

AUSTRALIAN TOBACCO GROWERS' BULLETIN (AT/0567-1159) [05452655] **5372**

AUSTRALIAN TORTS REPORTS (AT/0814-9054) [15230022] **2939**

AUSTRALIAN TOURIST COMMISSION *See* STATISTICAL REVIEW - AUSTRALIAN TOURIST COMMISSION **5491**

AUSTRALIAN TOXIC NETWORK NEWS (AT/1035-0764) [I10350764] **2225**

AUSTRALIAN TRADE PRACTICES REPORTER 1975 (AT/0313-623X) [I0313623X] **824**

AUSTRALIAN TRADE UNION MONITOR *See* AUSTRALIA'S SUPER UNIONS **824**

AUSTRALIAN TRAINING REVIEW (AT/1037-3292) [I10373292] **1911**

AUSTRALIAN TRANSPORT (AT/0005-0385) [01809289] **5377**

AUSTRALIAN TREATY SERIES (AT) [22188229] **3124**

AUSTRALIAN UNIVERSITIES' REVIEW, THE (AT) [15051005] **1810**

AUSTRALIAN VETERINARY JOURNAL (AT/0005-0423) [05070935] **5505**

AUSTRALIAN VETERINARY PRACTITIONER (AT/0310-138X) [02217017] **5505**

AUSTRALIAN WATER RESOURCES COUNCIL *See* AUSTRALIAN WATER RESOURCES COUNCIL - TECHNICAL PAPER **5530**

AUSTRALIAN WATER RESOURCES COUNCIL OCCASIONAL PAPERS SERIES (AT) [10205896] **5530**

AUSTRALIAN WATER RESOURCES COUNCIL - TECHNICAL PAPER (AT/0155-2643) [02108271] **5530**

AUSTRALIAN WATER RESOURCES COUNCIL WATER MANAGEMENT SERIES (AT/0728-9502) [09213203] **5530**

AUSTRALIAN WATER RESOURCES COUNCIL WATER RESOURCES SERIES (AT) [09975786] **5531**

AUSTRALIAN WEEDS RESEARCH NEWSLETTER (AT) [05452887] **164**

AUSTRALIAN WELDING JOURNAL (AT/0005-0431) [06352260] **4026**

AUSTRALIAN WELDING RESEARCH (AT/0045-0960) [08945431] **4026**

AUSTRALIAN WINE AND BRANDY CORPORATION *See* ANNUAL REPORT FOR THE YEAR ENDED 30TH JUNE ... / AUSTRALIAN WINE AND BRANDY CORPORATION **2363**

AUSTRALIAN WOMEN'S BOOK REVIEW (AT/1033-9434) [24488443] 3364, **5551**

AUSTRALIAN WOMEN'S WEEKLY SALUTE TO BEAUTIFUL AUSTRALIA, THE (AT) [11681026] **2510**

AUSTRALIAN WOMEN'S WEEKLY, THE (AT/0005-0458) [I00050458] **5551**

AUSTRALIAN WOODWORKER (AT/0818-0261) [I08180261] **633**

AUSTRALIAN WOOL SALE STATISTICS; STATISTICAL ANALYSIS (AT/0311-9882) [03058319] **5360**

AUSTRALIAN WORKER : OFFICIAL JOURNAL OF THE AUSTRALIAN WORKERS' UNION, THE (AT) [08998495] **1654**

AUSTRALIAN WRITER'S JOURNAL, THE (AT/1035-8803) [I10358803] **3460**

AUSTRALIAN YEAR BOOK OF INTERNATIONAL LAW, THE (AT/0084-7658) [02126048] **3124**

AUSTRALIAN ZOOLOGICAL REVIEWS (AT) [20405733] **5577**

AUSTRALIAN ZOOLOGIST, THE (AT/0067-2238) [01782007] **5577**

AUSTRALIANA (AT) [12187422] **2510**

AUSTRALIANA SOCIETY NEWSLETTER *See* AUSTRALIANA **2510**

AUSTRALIA'S HEALTH / AUSTRALIAN INSTITUTE OF HEALTH (AT/1032-6138) [19905249] **4768**

AUSTRALIA'S IDENTIFIED PETROLEUM RESOURCES / BUREAU OF MINERAL RESOURCES, GEOLOGY & GEOPHYSICS (AT) [11117990] **4251**

AUSTRALIA'S MINING MONTHLY (AT) [12442964] **2134**

AUSTRALIA'S OVERSEAS AID PROGRAM (AT) [20081524] **2908**

AUSTRALIA'S PARENTS : THE PRACTICAL PARENTING MAGAZINE (AT) **2277**

AUSTRALIA'S POPULATION TRENDS AND PROSPECTS (AT/0814-4370) [12362011] **4549**

AUSTRALIA'S SUPER UNIONS (AT) 1654, **824**

AUSTRALIA'S SURFING LIFE (AT/1036-3491) [I10363491] **4885**

AUSTRALIA'S SURFING LIFE ANNUAL (AT/1033-6001) [I10336001] **4885**

AUSTRALIA'S TOP 500 COMPANIES (AT/0817-3192) [I08173192] **726**

AUSTRALIEN ENERGIEWIRTSCHAFT / BUNDESSTELLE FUER AUSSENHANDELSINFORMATION (GW) [07436392] **1933**

AUSTRALIEN, FORSCHUNGSPOLITIK UND FORSCHUNGSPRAXIS / BUNDESSTELLE FUER AUSSENHANDELSINFORMATION (GW) [11507509] **4465**

AUSTRALIEN, WIRTSCHAFTLICHE ENTWICKLUNG / BUNDESSTELLE FUR AUSSENHANDELSINFORMATION (GW) [09346018] **1547**

AUSTRIA *See* BUNDESGESETZBLATT FUER DIE REPUBLIK OSTERREICH **2945**

AUSTRIA (UK) [04799403] **5462**

AUSTRIA AND THE BAVARIAN ALPS *See* AUSTRIA **5462**

AUSTRIA. BUNDESAMT FUR EICH- UND VERMESSUNGSWESEN *See* AMTSBLATT FUER DAS VERMESSUNGSWESEN **2018**

AUSTRIA. BUNDESKAMMER DER GEWERBLICHEN WIRTSCHAFT, VIENNA. ABTEILUNG FUR STATISTIK UND DOKUMENTATION *See* AUSSENHANDEL; LANDER UND WARENGLIEDERUNG **824**

AUSTRIA. BUNDESKAMMER DER GEWERBLICHEN WIRTSCHAFT, VIENNA. ABTEILUNG FUR STATISTIK UND DOKUMENTATION *See* FORSCHUNG UND DOKUMENTATION IN OSTERREICH **1562**

AUSTRIA. BUNDESMINISTERIUM FUER AUSWARTIGE ANGELEGENHEITEN *See* AUSSENPOLITISCHER BERICHT DES BUNDESMINISTERS FUER AUSWARTIGE ANGELEGENHEITEN **4516**

AUSTRIA. BUNDESMINISTERIUM FUER BAUTEN UND TECHNIK. BUNDESSTRASSENVERWALTUNG *See* BERICHT UBER DIE FORDERUNG VON FORSCHUNGS- UND ENTWICKLUNGSVORHABEN UND UBER DIE ERTEILUNG VON FORSCHUNGS- UND ENTWICKLUNGSAUFTRAGEN **5439**

AUSTRIA. BUNDESMINISTERIUM FUR FINANZEN *See* BUNDESVORANSCHLAG **4715**

AUSTRIA. BUNDESMINISTERIUM FUR SOZIALE VERWALTUNG *See* BERICHT UBER DIE SOZIALE LAGE. SOZIALBERICHT, TATIGKEITSBERICHT DES BUNDESMINISTERIUMS FUER SOZIALE VERWALTUNG **5274**

AUSTRIA. BUNDESMINISTERIUM FUR UNTERRICHT UND KUNST *See* EDUCATIONAL RESEARCH IN AUSTRIA **1742**

AUSTRIA. BUNDESMINISTERIUM FUR WISSENSCHAFT UND FORSCHUNG *See* BERICHT DER BUNDESREGIERUNG AN DEN NATIONALRAT **5087**

AUSTRIA. BUNDESMINISTERIUM FUR WISSENSCHAFT UND FORSCHUNG *See* HOCHSCHULBERICHT **1829**

AUSTRIA. BUNDESMINISTERIUM FUR WISSENSCHAFT UND FORSCHUNG *See* FORSCHUNGSFORDERUNGEN UND FORSCHUNGSAUFTRAGE **5106**

AUSTRIA. GENERALDIREKTION DER OSTERREICHISCHEN BUNDESBAHNEN *See* FAHRPLANE **5382**

AUSTRIA. GENERALDIREKTION FUR DIE POST UND TELEGRAPHENVERWALTUNG *See* GESCHAFTSBERICHT **1145**

AUSTRIA. GENERALDIREKTION FUR DIE POST- UND TELEGRAPHENVERWALTUNG. FERNMELDETSCHISCHES ZENTRALAMT *See* AMTLICHES VERZICHNISUDER FERNSCHREIBTEILNEHMER (TELEX-VERZEICHNIS) **1148**

AUSTRIA. GEOLOGISCHE BUNDESANSTALT *See* JAHRBUCH DER GEOLOGISCHEN BUNDESANSTALT **1384**

AUSTRIA, LOWER. LANDESAMTSDIREKTION. PRESSEDIENST, STATISTIK *See* STEUERAUFKOMMEN DER GEMEINDEN NIEDEROSTERREICHS, DAS **4750**

AUSTRIA. NATIONALRAT *See* NATIONALRAT UND BUNDESRAT AMTLICHES VERZEICHNIS DER MITGLIEDER, AUSSCHUSSE UND KLUBS **4668**

AUSTRIA. NATIONALRAT. NATIONALRAT UND BUNDESRAT BURO, MITGLIEDER, AUSSCHUSSE, KLUBS *See* NATIONALRAT UND BUNDESRAT AMTLICHES VERZEICHNIS DER MITGLIEDER, AUSSCHUSSE UND KLUBS **4668**

AUSTRIA / PREPARED BY AMERICAN EMBASSY, VIENNA (US) [17404706] **1654**

AUSTRIA. RECHNUNGSHOF *See* BUNDESRECHNUNGSABSCHLUSS **4715**

AUSTRIA. STAATSARCHIV *See* MITTEILUNGEN DES OSTERREICHISCHEN STAATSARCHIVS **2482**

AUSTRIA TODAY (AU/0304-8713) [02240919] **2513**

AUSTRIA, UPPER. LANDESSCHULRAT *See* VERORDNUNGSBLATT DES LANDESSCHULRATES FUER OBEROESTERREICH **1789**

AUSTRIA, UPPER. LANDESSCHULRAT. VERORDNUNGSBLATT FUER DEN DIENSTBEREICH *See* VERORDNUNGSBLATT DES LANDESSCHULRATES FUER OBEROESTERREICH **1789**

AUSTRIA. ZENTRAL-ARBEITSINSPEKTORAT *See* AMTSTATIGKEIT DER ARBEITSINSPEKTORATE IM JAHRE, DIE **1643**

AUSTRIA. ZENTRALANSTALT FUER METEOROLOGIE UND GEODYNAMIK *See* JAHRBUCHER DER ZENTRALANSTALT FUER METEOROLOGIE UND GEODYNAMIK **1426**

AUSTRIACA (FR/0396-4590) [05795546] **2677**

AUSTRIAN BUSINESS (US) [08514460] **641**

AUSTRIAN HISTORY YEARBOOK (US/0067-2378) [01518889] **2677**

AUSTRIAN JOURNAL OF PUBLIC AND INTERNATIONAL LAW 1991 (AU/0942-010X) [I0942010X] **3124**

AUSTRIAN STUDIES (UK/1350-7532) [22735926] 2611, **3364**

AUSTROBAILEYA (AT/0155-4131) [03785796] **501**

AUSWAHLLISTE DER NEUERWERBUNGEN (GW) [03188389] **408**

AUSZUEGE AUS DEN EUROPAISCHEN PATENTSCHRIFTEN *See* AUSZUGE AUS DEN EUROPAISCHEN PATENTSCHRIFTEN. TEIL I, GRUND- UND ROHSTOFFINDUSTRIE, CHEMIE UND HUTTENWESEN, BAUWESEN, BERGBAU **1301**

AUSZUEGE AUS DEN EUROPAISCHEN PATENTSCHRIFTEN *See* AUSZUGE AUS DEN EUROPAISCHEN PATENTSCHRIFTEN. TEIL III, UBRIGE VERARBEITUNGSINDUSTRIE UND ARBEITSVERFAHREN, MASCHINEN- UND FAHRZEUGBAU, ERNAHRUNG, LANDWIRTSCHAFT **1301**

AUSZUEGE AUS DEN EUROPAISCHEN PATENTSCHRIFTEN *See* AUSZUGE AUS DEN EUROPAISCHEN PATENTSCHRIFTEN. TEIL II, ELEKTROTECHNIK, PHYSIK, FEINMECHANIK UND OPTIK, AKUSTIK **1301**

AUSZUG AUS DEN TATIGKEITSBERICHTEN DER GRUPPEN UND ABTEILUNGEN DES AMTES DER NO LANDESREGIERUNG, EIN (AU) [11005434] **4631**

AUSZUGE AUS DEN EUROPAISCHEN PATENTSCHRIFTEN. TEIL I, GRUND- UND ROHSTOFFINDUSTRIE, CHEMIE UND HUTTENWESEN, BAUWESEN, BERGBAU (GW/0941-0007) [I09410007] **1301**

AUSZUGE AUS DEN EUROPAISCHEN PATENTSCHRIFTEN. TEIL II, ELEKTROTECHNIK, PHYSIK, FEINMECHANIK UND OPTIK, AKUSTIK (GW/0941-0015) [I09410015] **1301**

AUSZUGE AUS DEN EUROPAISCHEN PATENTSCHRIFTEN. TEIL III, UBRIGE VERARBEITUNGSINDUSTRIE UND ARBEITSVERFAHREN, MASCHINEN- UND FAHRZEUGBAU, ERNAHRUNG, LANDWIRTSCHAFT (GW/0941-0023) [I09410023] **1301**

AUSZUGE AUS DEN GEBRAUCHSMUSTERN. AUSGABE A (GW/0005-0571) [I00050571] **1301**

AUT AUT (IT/0005-0601) [01788648] **3364, 4342**

AUTHENTIK AUTHENTIK IN ENGLISH (IE/0791-0797) [I07910797] **3267**

AUTHOR BIOGRAPHIES MASTER INDEX (US/0741-8655) [04155798] **430**

AUTHOR INDEX - CARLETON UNIVERSITY (CN/0823-129X) [10763759] **408**

AUTHOR LISTING - MIDWESTERN REGIONAL LIBRARY SYSTEM (CN/0710-6580) [08144117] **408**

AUTHOR (LONDON. 1949) (UK/0005-0628) [05146394] **3364**

AUTHOR SERIES (US/0567-1744) [02618048] **2722**

AUTHORITY (WASHINGTON, D.C.), THE (US/8750-8788) [11876574] **2815**

AUTHORIZED OA DEALER REPORT, THE **SUSPENDED.** (US/0889-9886) [14124079] **824**

AUTHORLINE - SAS INSTITUTE (US/1058-8906) [24423364] **3365**

AUTHORS & ARTISTS FOR YOUNG ADULTS (US/1040-5682) [18449873] **3365**

AUTHORS GUILD BULLETIN (US/0404-3030) [05022782] **3365**

AUTHOR'S NEWS (CN/0713-0171) [08569841] **4812**

AUTHORWARE MAGAZINE (US) **1171**

AUTISM RESEARCH REVIEW INTERNATIONAL, THE (US/0893-8474) [15670246] 3554, **4575**

AUTO (IT) [08492184] **5404**

AUTO ADVERTISING REPORT (US/0885-8292) [12746856] 5404, **756**

●AUTO AGE DEALER BUSINESS (US/1070-8294) [26847887] **5404**

AUTO AGE (VAN NUYS, CALIF.) (US/0894-1270) [14292829] **5404**

AUTO AGE (VAN NUYS, CALIF.) *See* AUTO AGE DEALER BUSINESS **5404**

AUTO AND DESIGN (IT/0393-8387) [08218782] **5404**

AUTO AND FLAT GLASS JOURNAL (US/0005-0717) [02445165] **2586**

AUTO & SPORT (IT) **5404**

AUTO & TRUCK INTERNATIONAL (US/1065-6685) [26669612] **5404**

AUTO & TRUCK INTERNATIONAL EN ESPANOL (US/1065-6693) [26669782] **5404**

AUTO BILD (GW) **5404**

AUTO/BIOGRAPHY STUDIES (US/0898-9575) [16415282] **430**

AUTO CLUB NEWS (LOS, ANGELES CALIF.) (US/0746-8504) [10340045] **5404**

AUTO CLUB NEWS PICTORIAL *See* AUTO CLUB NEWS (LOS, ANGELES CALIF.) **5404**

AUTO EN MOTORTECHNIEK (NE) **5404**

AUTO EXKLUSIV (SZ) [11329685] **5404**

AUTO EXPERTISE (FR/0150-7230) [I01507230] **5404**

AUTO GALLERY (US/0890-9121) [14450765] **2110**

AUTO HEBDO PARIS. 1976 (FR/0395-4366) [I03954366] **5439**

AUTO HEBDO SPORT (SP) **5404**

AUTO INDEX (SZ) **5404**

AUTO INDEX, THE (US/0145-6776) [02766669] **5404**

AUTO-INDUSTRIE EN ASSEMBLAGEBEDRIJVEN, AUTO-ONDERDELENINDUSTRIE, VLIEGTUIGBOUW- EN VLIEGTUIGREPARATIEBEDRIJVEN / CENTRAAL BUREAU VOOR DE STATISTIEK, HOOFDAFDELING STATISTIEKEN VAN INDUSTRIE EN BOUWNIJVERHEID (NE) [10607403] **5404**

AUTO INDUSTRY AUSTRALIA (AT) **5404**

AUTO INDUSTRY MAGAZINE (US/0746-3774) [10008117] **5404**

AUTO-JOURNAL (PARIS), L' (FR/0005-0768) [04250318] **5404**

AUTO KATALOG (GW) **5404**

AUTO LAUNDRY NEWS (US/0005-0776) [03262955] **5404**

AUTO MAGAZINE (HK) **5405**

AUTO MARKET REPORT (AT/1035-1051) [I10351051] **5405**

AUTO MERCHANDISING NEWS (US/0192-186X) [05132535] 5405, **641**

AUTO MODIFIEE, L' (CN/0822-1006) [10224844] 5405, **4885**

AUTO-MOTO MONTLHERY (FR/0769-8933) [I07698933] **5439**

AUTO, MOTOR UND SPORT (GW/0005-0806) [I00050806] 4885, **5405**

AUTO MUNDO DEPORTIVO (US) **4885**

AUTO PLUS PARIS (FR/0992-8154) [I09928154] **5405**

AUTO PREVENTION (CN/0825-4990) [11245761] **5405**

AUTO PRICES ALMANAC (US/1042-0855) [18760430] **5405**

AUTO-QUEBEC (CN/0821-7343) [09818964] **5405**

●AUTO RACEPAGES (US/1059-8367) [24779700] **4885**

AUTO RACING DIGEST (US/0090-8029) [01786053] 5405, **4885**

AUTO RACING MEMORIES & MEMORABILIA (US/0743-7129) [10649151] 5405, **4885**

AUTO RACING/USA (DALLAS, TEX.) (US/8756-9353) [11664775] 5405, **4885**

AUTO RACING USA (FRANKLIN LAKES, N.J.) (US/0164-369X) [04635490] 5405, **4885**

AUTO REVUE LUXEMBOURG (LU) **5405**

AUTO SERVICE INSIDER (US/1053-4318) [22530117] **5405**

AUTO SERVICE TODAY (US/1042-7414) [19121671] **5377**

AUTO SOUND & SECURITY (US/1065-0792) [26513478] **5405**

AUTO SPORT (JA) **5405**

AUTO SPORT (CN/0714-7104) [09157032] 5405, **4885**

AUTO SPORT (MONTREAL. 1992) (CN/1191-3401) [26714712] **4885**

●AUTO SPORTS MOTEUR, L' (CN/1193-509X) [27165180] **4885**

AUTO STEREO PARIS (FR/0245-4548) [I02454548] **5405**

AUTO-TRAIN MAGAZINE (US/0092-6515) [01789626] **5429**

AUTO TRIM & RESTYLING NEWS (US/1049-9601) [21359517] **5405**

AUTO VERTE PARIS. 1979 (FR/0222-3996) [I02223996] **5405**

AUTOBUS (IT) [07544374] **5361**

●AUTOCAD USER (CN) [30377349] 1222, **1171**

●AUTOCAD WORLD (US/1060-1317) [24877690] **1171**

AUTOCAR & MOTOR (UK/0955-5889) [18670416] **5405**

●AUTOCEPHALOUS ORTHODOX CHURCHES, THE (US/1059-1001) [24479742] **4937**

AUTOCLUB (AG) [05059779] **5405**

AUTOGESTION Y SOCIALISMO (SP) [06434303] **4540**

AUTOGLASS (MCLEAN, VA.) (US/1047-2061) [20639589] 5405, **2586**

AUTOGRAFO : QUADRIMESTRALE DEL CENTRO DI RICERCA SULLA TRADIZIONE MANOSCRITTA DI AUTORI CONTEMPORANEI, UNIVERSITA DI PAVIA (IT) [11837554] **3365**

●AUTOGRAPH COLLECTOR (US/1071-3425) [25588635] **2438**

AUTOGRAPH COLLECTOR'S MAGAZINE *See* AUTOGRAPH COLLECTOR **2438**

AUTOHARP (US/0091-8687) [05439194] **4101**

AUTOHARP QUARTERLY (US/1071-1619) [23883338] **4101**

AUTOHARPOHOLIC, THE **CEASED.** (US/0736-3796) [09106785] **4101**

AUTOHEBDO (FR) **5439**

AUTOIMMUNE DISEASES (UK/0142-8365) [I01428365] **3667**

AUTOIMMUNITY (CHUR, SWITZERLAND) (SZ/0891-6934) [14960385] **3667**

AUTOINC (US/1047-5559) [20715626] **5405**

AUTOINTELLIGENCE NEW CAR DECISION MAKER. VOL. 1, SMALL CARS, SPORTY CARS, MID-SIZE SEDANS **CEASED.** (US/1065-9137) [26790966] **5405**

AUTOINTELLIGENCE NEW CAR DECISION MAKER. VOL. 2, LARGE, LUXURY & HIGH PERFORMANCE CARS, SPORT UTILITY VEHICLES, STATION WAGONS & COMPACT VANS **CEASED.** (US/1065-9145) [26791042] **5405**

AUTOKOZLEKEDES (BUDAPEST. 1964) (HU/0587-2243) [01793323] **5405**

AUTOMATED AGENCY REPORT, THE (US/1051-3396) [21952518] **2036**

AUTOMATED BUILDER (US/0899-5540) [18131336] **2815**

AUTOMATED LAW OFFICE CONSULTANT, THE (US/0740-6819) [09007715] 861, **2939**

AUTOMATED MANUFACTURING STRATEGY (NE/0951-7162) [15479621] 3475, **1217**

AUTOMATED MEDICAL PAYMENTS DIRECTORY (US) **739**

AUTOMATED MEDICAL PAYMENTS NEWS (US) 739, **3554**

AUTOMATED OFFICE ABSTRACTS (UK/0957-3224) [I09573224] **1217**

AUTOMATED OFFICE SYSTEMS (US/0739-8743) [07981178] **4210**

AUTOMATED SOFTWARE ENGINEERING (US/0928-8910) **1284**

AUTOMATIC CONTROL AND COMPUTER SCIENCES (US/0146-4116) [02496941] **1217**

AUTOMATIC DATA PROCESSING ACTIVITIES SUMMARY IN THE UNITED STATES GOVERNMENT (US/0163-111X) [04175658] **4631**

AUTOMATIC DOCUMENTATION AND MATHEMATICAL LINGUISTICS (US/0005-1055) [00819182] 3267, **3193**

AUTOMATIC I.D. NEWS (US/0890-9768) [12628118] 952, **1171**

AUTOMATIC MACHINING (US/0005-1071) [04935135] **2110**

●AUTOMATIC MERCHANDISER (US/1061-1797) [25213455] 1599, **2328**

AUTOMATIC MERCHANDISING IN CANADA (CN/0227-1850) [06562621] **1599**

AUTOMATIC MUSICAL INSTRUMENTS PRICING GUIDE (US/0148-818X) [03375562] **4101**

AUTOMATIC SPRINKLER AND STANDPIPE SYSTEMS (US) **2288**

AUTOMATIC SPRINKLER SYSTEMS HANDBOOK (US) **2288**

AUTOMATIC TAXFINDER AND TAX PREPARER'S HANDBOOK (US/0092-6876) [01787087] **4712**

AUTOMATICA E INSTRUMENTACION (SP/0213-3113) [I02133113] 2097, **1217**

AUTOMATICA (OXFORD) (UK/0005-1098) [01518903] **1217**

AUTOMATIE (NE/0005-1128) [09327705] **1217**

AUTOMATION (JA) **1217**

AUTOMATION AND CONTROL (NZ/0110-6295) [04064800] 2097, **1217**

AUTOMATION AND REMOTE CONTROL (US/0005-1179) [01518905] **1218**

AUTOMATION (CLEVELAND, OHIO: 1987) *See* PENTON'S CONTROLS & SYSTEMS **3486**

●AUTOMATION IN CONSTRUCTION (NE/0926-5805) [26384885] 1231, **599**

AUTOMATION IN LIBRARIES (CN) [06335824] **3193**

AUTOMATION (LONDON) (UK/0005-1152) [08071269] **1218**

AUTOMATION NEWS (NEW YORK, N.Y.) **CEASED.** (US/0736-3737) [09114303] **1218**

AUTOMATION SURVEY (US/0160-6441) [03712167] **773**

AUTOMATION SYSTEMS (CN/1181-7003) [23238192] **1218**

AUTOMATION SYSTEMS (MISSISSAUGA, ONT.) *See* MANUFACTURING & PROCESS AUTOMATION **1220**

AUTOMATIQUE-PRODUCTIQUE INFORMATIQUE INDUSTRIELLE (FR/0296-1598) [12362987] **2110**

AUTOMATISIERUNGSTECHNIK - AT (GW) [11942795] **2110**

AUTOMATISIERUNGSTECHNISCHE PRAXIS : ATP (GW/0178-2320) [11966200] **2110**

AUTOMATIZACE (XR/0005-125X) [09692869] **1218**

AUTOMATIZACION DE LA PRODUCCION (SP/0213-2672) [I02132672] **1599**

AUTOMATIZACION INTEGRADA Y REVISTA DE ROBOTICA (SP) **2110**

AUTOMATIZALAS — Alphabetical Title Index

AUTOMATIZALAS (HU/0133-1620) [02727446] 2110, **1218**

AUTOMATIZALAS ES ROBOTTECHNIKA (HU/0865-7580) [I08657580] **2036**

AUTOMATIZALASI, SZAMTASTECHNIKAI ES MERESTECHNIKAI SZAKIRODALMI TAJEKOZTATO (HU/0231-0643) [I02310643] **1218**

AUTOMAZIONE E STRUMENTAZIONE (IT) [06409463] **1218**

AUTOMAZIONE INTEGRATA (IT/0393-3911) [I03933911] **5087**

AUTOMAZIONE NAVALE, L' (IT/0392-2294) [I03922294] **591**

AUTOMAZIONE OGGI (IT/0392-8829) [I03928829] **2110**

AUTOMEDICA (NEW YORK) (US/0095-0963) [01792455] **3686**

AUTOMOBIL-INDUSTRIE (GW/0005-1306) [04747896] **5405**

AUTOMOBIL (JOHANNESBURG) (SA/0304-8721) [02242815] **5405**

AUTOMOBIL-PRODUKTION (GW/0934-0394) [I09340394] **5405**

AUTOMOBILE (IT/0005-1349) [I00051349] **4885**

AUTOMOBILE ABSTRACTS (NUNEATON. 1975) (UK/0309-0817) [08012916] **5405**

AUTOMOBILE ALMANAC (US/0067-2513) [02250656] **5405**

AUTOMOBILE ASSOCIATION (GREAT BRITAIN) See AA GUIDE TO CAMPING AND CARAVANNING **5500**

AUTOMOBILE ASSOCIATION OF KENYA See MEMBERS' HANDBOOK - AUTOMOBILE ASSOCIATION OF KENYA **5418**

AUTOMOBILE ASSOCIATION OF ZAMBIA See AA HANDBOOK **5403**

AUTOMOBILE BUYERS' GUIDE (II) [05142949] **5405**

AUTOMOBILE CLUB DE MADAGASCAR. SERVICE DU GUIDE ROUTIER. GUIDE ROUTIER See GUIDE ROUTIER ET TOURISTIQUE: MADAGASCAR, REUNION, MAURICE, COMORES ET SEYCHELLES **5479**

AUTOMOBILE (COBHAM) (UK/0955-1328) [26781875] **5405**

AUTOMOBILE (DON MILLS) (CN/0005-1330) [02230510] **5405**

AUTOMOBILE INDUSTRY TRENDS (US/0198-781X) [04453568] **5405**

AUTOMOBILE INSURANCE EXPERIENCE (CN/0317-7815) [02248146] **2874**

AUTOMOBILE INSURANCE LOSSES COLLISION COVERAGES VARIATIONS BY MAKE AND SERIES (US/0093-0466) [01789043] 5405, **2875**

AUTOMOBILE INSURANCE LOSSES, INJURY COVERAGES. CLAIM FREQUENCY RESULTS FOR ... MODELS (US/0734-547X) [04484007] **2875**

AUTOMOBILE INTERNATIONAL (US/0099-2615) [05165140] **5405**

AUTOMOBILE, L' (FR) [07879371] **5405**

AUTOMOBILE LEGAL ASSOCIATION See ALA SIGHTS TO SEE BOOK **5403**

AUTOMOBILE MAGAZINE, L' (FR/0982-9156) [I09829156] **5406**

AUTOMOBILE (NEW YORK, N.Y. : 1988) (US/0897-8360) [17638416] **5406**

AUTOMOBILE QUARTERLY (US/0005-1438) [01518915] **5406**

AUTOMOBILE RED BOOK (US/0736-7953) [09221613] **5406**

AUTOMOBILE REVUE (SZ) [07442939] **5406**

AUTOMOBILE WORLD See AUTOMOBILE INTERNATIONAL **5405**

AUTOMOBILE YEAR (SZ) [07447024] **5406**

AUTOMOBILES CITROEN (FIRM) See AUTOMOBILES CITROEN. RAPPORT **5406**

AUTOMOBILES CITROEN. RAPPORT (FR) [04273005] **5406**

AUTOMOBILES CLASSIQUES (FR/0759-6065) [I07596065] **5406**

AUTOMOBILES CLASSIQUES (ENGLISH EDITION) (US/0742-7417) [10422237] **5406**

AUTOMOTIVE AIR CONDITIONING AND HEATING SERVICE MANUAL : BOOK SUPPLEMENT (US/0194-0023) [05278794] 2603, **5406**

AUTOMOTIVE AND MARINE SERVICE STATION CODE (US) 2288, **4251**

● AUTOMOTIVE & TRANSPORTATION INTERIORS (US/1071-1430) [28557404] **5406**

AUTOMOTIVE BODY REPAIR NEWS (US/0192-0995) [05069829] **5406**

AUTOMOTIVE BOOSTER OF CALIFORNIA, THE (US/0191-6459) [04968706] **5406**

AUTOMOTIVE, BURGLARY PROTECTION, MECHANICAL EQUIPMENT DIRECTORY (US) [04443269] **5406**

AUTOMOTIVE BUSINESS NEWS (UK) 5406, **641**

AUTOMOTIVE BUYER See AUTOMOTIVE WEEK **5407**

AUTOMOTIVE CHAIN STORE (NEW YORK, N.Y.) (US/0746-2077) [09865166] **5406**

AUTOMOTIVE COOLING JOURNAL : ACJ (US/0005-1497) [14174478] **5406**

AUTOMOTIVE DAILY NEWS See AUTOMOTIVE NEWS **5406**

AUTOMOTIVE ELECTRONICS JOURNAL *CEASED.* (US/1054-4828) [20786358] **5406**

AUTOMOTIVE ENGINE REBUILDERS ASSOCIATION (U.S.) See PROCEEDINGS ... OF THE ANNUAL CONVENTION / AUTOMOTIVE ENGINE REBUILDERS ASSOCIATION (U.S.) **5423**

AUTOMOTIVE ENGINEER (UK/0307-6490) [01829098] **5406**

AUTOMOTIVE ENGINEERING (US/0098-2571) [02240909] **2110**

AUTOMOTIVE EXECUTIVE (1979) (US/0195-1564) [05323107] **5406**

AUTOMOTIVE FLEET (US/0005-1519) [02554683] **5406**

AUTOMOTIVE FUEL ECONOMY PROGRAM. ANNUAL REPORT TO THE CONGRESS (US/0146-5236) [06510443] **4251**

AUTOMOTIVE INDUSTRY DATA LTD (UK/0951-158X) [I0951158X] **5406**

AUTOMOTIVE INDUSTRY DATA YEARBOOK (UK) **5406**

● AUTOMOTIVE INTELLIGENCE REPORTS' METALWORKING (US/1071-3220) [28614529] **3998**

AUTOMOTIVE INTERIORS INTERNATIONAL (UK/0967-0386) [I09670386] **5406**

AUTOMOTIVE INVESTOR (US/0898-2155) [17745004] 2771, **5406**

AUTOMOTIVE LEASE GUIDE (US) **5406**

AUTOMOTIVE LITERATURE INDEX (US/0732-9350) [07289023] **5406**

AUTOMOTIVE LITIGATION REPORTER (US/0278-4726) [07871036] **2939**

AUTOMOTIVE MARKET REPORT (US/0733-2084) [08529624] **921**

AUTOMOTIVE MARKETER *CEASED.* (CN/0702-8318) [03418035] **5406**

AUTOMOTIVE NEWS (US/0005-1551) [01518922] **5406**

AUTOMOTIVE NEWS. MARKET DATA BOOK (US) [04354955] **5407**

AUTOMOTIVE PARTS INTERNATIONAL (US/0896-3614) [14582384] **5407**

AUTOMOTIVE PRODUCTS REPORT *CEASED.* (US/8750-4103) [11380438] **5407**

AUTOMOTIVE Q & A (US/0196-0156) [05739112] **5407**

AUTOMOTIVE REBUILDER (US/0567-2317) [02251568] 641, **5407**

AUTOMOTIVE RECYCLING (US/1058-9376) [24438972] 3998, **5407**

AUTOMOTIVE RESEARCH. LONG-TERM FORECAST REPORT (US) [24203033] **5407**

AUTOMOTIVE RETAILER (VANCOUVER) (CN/0005-1578) [02228099] **5407**

AUTOMOTIVE RETAILERS ASSOCIATION (B.C.) See MEMBERSHIP ROSTER - AUTOMOTIVE RETAILERS ASSOCIATION (WINNIPEG) **955**

AUTOMOTIVE SERVICE See AUTOMOTIVE NEWS **5406**

AUTOMOTIVE SERVICE AND BODY NEWS See AUTOMOTIVE BODY REPAIR NEWS **5406**

AUTOMOTIVE SERVICE DATA BOOK (CN/0705-6281) [04097803] **5407**

AUTOMOTIVE SERVICE INDUSTRY ASSOCIATION. MARKETING RESEARCH See AUTOMOTIVE WHOLESALING : FINANCIAL OPERATION AND PERFORMANCE ANALYSIS **1599**

AUTOMOTIVE SERVICE REPORTS (US/0273-7477) [06885567] **5407**

AUTOMOTIVE SPECIAL REPORT (UK/0957-2481) [I09572481] **5407**

AUTOMOTIVE WEEK (US/0889-3918) [13922975] **5407**

AUTOMOTIVE WHOLESALING : FINANCIAL OPERATION AND PERFORMANCE ANALYSIS (US/0163-6448) [04419779] 5407, **1599**

AUTOMOVIL INTERNACIONAL See AUTO & TRUCK INTERNATIONAL EN ESPANOL **5404**

AUTOMUNDO (IT) **1966**

AUTONEWS *CEASED.* (UK) **5407**

AUTONOMIC NERVOUS SYSTEM, THE (UK/1047-5125) [20707160] **3827**

AUTONOMIE (GW) [02487833] **4540**

AUTONOMIE LOCALI E SERVIZI SOCIALI (IT/0392-2278) [I03922278] **4631**

AUTONOMOUS LIVING (CN/0822-5168) [10082784] **2788**

AUTONOMOUS ROBOTS (NE/0929-5593) **1212**

AUTOPARTS REPORT, THE (US/1045-1978) [20107412] **5407**

AUTOPINION (OTTAWA) (CN/0836-1630) [19032989] **5407**

AUTOPISTA (SP/0567-2392) [I05672392] **5407**

AUTORES (AG) [01788327] **315**

AUTOREVISTA (SP/0005-1961) **5407**

AUTOSOUND & COMMUNICATIONS *CEASED.* (US/0194-8679) [05065260] **5315**

AUTOSPORT (TEDDINGTON) (UK/0269-946X) [17811595] **5407**

AUTOSPRINT (IT/0005-1748) **5407**

AUTOSTRADE (IT) [02221735] **5439**

AUTOTECNICA LOCATE TRIULZI (IT/1121-3450) [11213450] **2110**

AUTOTRADE (UK/0308-7476) [03087476] **5407**

AUTOTRASPORTO DI MERCI, L' (IT/1120-4133) [11204133] **5377**

AUTOUR DE NOS BOISES (CN) [25352091] **2375**

AUTOWEEK (NE) **5407**

AUTOWEEK (US/0192-9674) [04799200] **5407**

AUTOWEEK AND COMPETITION PRESS See AUTOWEEK **5407**

AUTOZEITUNG (GW) **5407**

AUTRE EUROPE, L' (FR/0759-2345) [12882736] **2677**

AUTRE MONDE (PARIS. 1987), L' (FR/0984-4759) [I09844759] **4241**

AUTRE PAROLE, L' (CN/0228-4146) [08192530] 5551, **4937**

AUTREMENT DIRE (FR/0767-5259) [I07675259] **3267**

AUTREMENT. SERIE MONDE (FR) [21470622] **5192**

AUTRES TEMPS (FR) [11293168] **4937**

AUXILIAIRES DES TRANSPORTS TERRESTRES (FR) [03388350] **5377**

AUXILIARY, BIBLIOGRAPHY OF PUBLICATIONS (US) [04794410] **408**

AV. DIE ARBEITSVORBEREITUNG (GW/0003-780X) [I0003780X] **5087**

AV KOMMUNIKACIO (HU/0237-9740) [I02379740] **1104**

AV MAGAZINE, THE (US/0274-7774) [06437473] **226**

AV MARKET PLACE (US/1044-0445) [19070443] **726**

AV UPDATE (AT/0818-2507) [I08182507] **3193**

AVA NEWS (AT/0811-6997) [20379228] **5505**

AVA-YI IRAN (CN/0711-3900) [08693707] **5780**

AVADH JOURNAL OF SOCIAL SCIENCES : AJOSS, THE (II) [12437681] **5192**

AVAILABLE FOR RESTORATION (US) [12528300] **2722**

AVALOKA *CEASED.* (US/0890-5541) [14267527] **4937**

AVALON HILL GENERAL (US/0888-1081) [06372396] **4857**

AVALON TO CAMELOT *SUSPENDED.* (US/0741-1790) [10093109] **3365**

AVANCE AGROINDUSTRIAL / EEAOC (AG/0326-1131) [26102072] **64**

AVANCES DE INVESTIGACION AGRICOLA EN ZONAS DE RIEGO Y TEMPORAL / CIAN (MX) [09106885] **64**

AVANCES EN ALIMENTACION Y MEJORA ANIMAL (SP) [04017156] **206**

AVANCES EN CIENCIAS VETERINARIAS (CL/0716-260X) [16134541] **5505**

AVANCES EN CIRUGIA (SP) [13187074] **3960**

AVANCES EN INVESTIGACION AGROPECUARIA (MX/0188-7890) **64**

AVANCES EN OBSTETRICIA Y GINECOLOGIA (SP/0210-7171) [04450628] **3757**

AVANCES EN PRODUCCION ANIMAL (CL/0378-4509) [04017541] **5505**

AVANCES EN PSICOLOGIA CLINICA LATINOAMERICANA (CK/0120-3797) [13013810] **4575**

AVANCES EN TERAPEUTICA (SP/0210-3397) [11110687] **4293**

AVANCES EN TRAUMATOLOGIA, CIRUGIA, REHABILITACION, MEDICINA PREVENTIVA Y DEL DEPORTE (SP/0214-4077) [I02144077] **3554**

AVANCES; REVISTA BOLIVIANA DE ESTUDIOS HISTORICOS Y SOCIALES (BO) [04009756] **2722**

AVANT GARDE (AMSTERDAM, NETHERLANDS) *See* AVANT GARDE CRITICAL STUDIES **315**

AVANT GARDE (AMSTERDAM, NETHERLANDS) (NE/0921-2515) [17858783] **315**

●AVANT GARDE CRITICAL STUDIES (NE) [30713990] **315**

AVANT GARDENER, THE (US/0005-1926) [01518929] **2410**

AVANT-POSTE (AMQUI) (CN/1197-1193) [29206083] **5780**

AVANT-POSTE GASPESIEN, L' *See* AVANT-POSTE (AMQUI) **5780**

AVANT-SCENE. BALLET/DANSE, L' (FR/0248-7845) [10158360] **1310**

AVANT-SCENE DU CINEMA, L' (FR/0045-1150) [01518930] **4064**

AVANT-SCENE, THEATRE, L' (FR/0045-1169) [05513077] **5361**

AVANT-SIECLE, L' (FR) [12301588] **3365**

AVANTGARDE (NEDERLANDSE ED.) (NE/0926-910X) [I0926910X] **5551**

AVANTI (IT/0391-6685) [I03916685] **5804**

AVC PRESENTATION DEVELOPMENT & DELIVERY *See* AVC PRESENTATION FOR THE VISUAL COMMUNICATOR **641**

AVC PRESENTATION DEVELOPMENT & DELIVERY (US/1062-2683) [24893464] **641**

AVC PRESENTATION FOR THE VISUAL COMMUNICATOR (US/1064-7112) [26348552] **1104**, **641**

AVCA DIRECTORY : MEMBERS, OFFICERS, ACTIVITIES, AND SECRETARIAT (AT) [11772453] **1021**

AVE: LE MAGAZINE FREUDIEN, L' (FR) [08618641] **4575**

AVE MARIA (LEMONT, ILL.) (US/0746-3499) [02243420] **5024**

●$AVE OUR PLANET (US/1065-0385) [26491291] **2161**

AVEC LE CHRIST ET LE SAINT-PERE (CN/0228-2747) [07314112] **5024**

AVEC (PENNGROVE, CALIF.) (US/0899-3750) [18081499] **3460**, **3365**

AVEGA (II/0376-5296) [01790517] **3460**

AVENANT (CN/0319-5767) [02443089] **2875**

AVENC, L' (SP/0210-0150) [03442334] **2677**

AVENEMENT, L' (SZ) **2485**

AVENGERS, THE (US/0274-5240) [05175998] **4857**

AVENGERS WEST COAST (US/1044-8195) [19907218] **4857**

AVENIR & SANTE (FR/0240-6411) [I02406411] **3852**

AVENIR DU NORD (SAINT-JEROME, QUEBEC : 1981) (CN/0714-427X) [09050379] **5780**

AVENIR MONTREAL. 1991 (CN/1187-6611) [I11876611] **1464**

AVENIRS (FR/0005-1969) [02066509] **1911**

AVENUE MAGAZINE (NE) **5551**

AVENUE (NEW YORK, N.Y.) (US/0279-1226) [07565724] **2528**

AVERAGE ANNUAL WAGES (ANNUAL PAYROLL DIVIDED BY EMPLOYMENT) AND WAGE ADJUSTMENT INDEX FOR CETA PRIME SPONSORS (US) [05061654] **1654**

AVERAGE CLASSROOM TEACHERS' & PRINCIPALS' SALARIES OF THE ... UNIFIED SCHOOL DISTRICTS OF KANSAS FOR ... AND ... (US) [03791101] **1860**

AVERAGE DAILY TRAFFIC VOLUMES ON INTERSTATE AND PRIMARY ROUTES *See* AVERAGE DAILY TRAFFIC VOLUMES ON INTERSTATE, ARTERIAL AND PRIMARY ROUTES **5439**

AVERAGE DAILY TRAFFIC VOLUMES ON INTERSTATE, ARTERIAL AND PRIMARY ROUTES (US/0094-7415) [01795008] **5439**

AVERAGE MONTHLY WORKERS COVERED BY KENTUCKY UNEMPLOYMENT INSURANCE LAW BY INDUSTRIAL DIVISION AND COUNTY (US/0149-4120) [03472239] **1654**, **2875**

AVERAGE PRICES OF USA ACADEMIC BOOKS (UK) [16187467] **4824**

AVERAGE RETAIL PRICES OF SELECTED COMMODITIES AND SERVICES (US/0093-9781) [01793294] **1590**

AVERY INDEX TO ARCHITECTURAL PERIODICALS (US) **293**

AVERY INDEX TO ARCHITECTURAL PERIODICALS. SECOND EDITION. REVISED AND ENLARGED. SUPPLEMENT (US/0196-0008) [03417556] **293**, **311**

AVERY INDEX TO ARCHITECTURAL PERIODICALS. SUPPLEMENT [MICROFORM] / COLUMBIA UNIVERSITY (US/0196-0008) [08917857] **293**

AVES (BE/0005-1993) [03676804] **5615**

AVI AVOT *CEASED.* (US) 5046, **2438**

AVIACAO EM REVISTA (BL/0102-4876) [03417420] **12**

AVIACIJA I KOSMONAVTIKA *CEASED.* (RU/0373-9821) [09284521] **12**

●AVIAKOSMICHESKAIA I EKOLOGICHESKAIA MEDITSINA (RU/0233-528X) [28260465] **12**, **3554**

AVIAN BIOLOGY (US) [02258029] **5615**

AVIAN DISEASES (US/0005-2086) [01518939] **5615**, **5505**

AVIAN PATHOLOGY (UK/0307-9457) [02199397] **5615**, **5505**

AVIAN RESEARCH : OFFICIAL JOURNAL OF THE INDIAN POULTRY CLUB (II/0970-1273) [11458891] **206**

AVIASPORT (FR/0005-2094) **4885**

AVIASTRO (1984) *CEASED.* (BE/0772-876X) [11064543] **12**

AVIATEUR AUJOURDHUI *CEASED.* (CN/0846-1414) [24257290] **12**

AVIATION ADVISORY SERVICES, LTD *See* AAS MILAVNEWS **4033**

●AVIATION, AEROSPACE & DEFENCE UPDATE (CN/1191-8004) [27391250] 4037, **12**

AVIATION & AEROSPACE (CN/0847-0588) [20989839] **13**

AVIATION & AEROSPACE NEWS *See* AVIATION, AEROSPACE & DEFENCE UPDATE **12**

AVIATION & MARINE INTERNATIONAL *See* STRATEGY & DEFENCE **4058**

AVIATION BUSINESS REPORT (CN/0711-8163) [08581192] **13**

AVIATION CANADA MAGAZINE *SUSPENDED.* (CN/1183-0204) [23230478] **13**

AVIATION CASES / CCH *CEASED.* (US) [01564307] 13, **2939**

AVIATION CONSUMER, THE (US/0147-9911) [03252217] **13**

AVIATION CONVENTION NEWS *See* AVIATION INTERNATIONAL NEWS **13**

AVIATION DAILY (US/0193-4597) [05266555] **13**

AVIATION DAILY'S AIRLINE STATISTICAL ANNUAL (US/0092-2862) [01789220] **41**

AVIATION DESIGN THIAIS (FR/0997-3753) [I09973753] **13**

AVIATION DIGEST *CEASED.* (US/0884-4755) [12378726] **13**

●AVIATION EDUCATION / PUBLISHED BY THE FEDERAL AVIATION ADMINISTRATION (US) [25740490] **13**

AVIATION EMPLOYMENT MONTHLY : AVIATION & AEROSPACE EMPLOYMENT OPPORTUNITIES (US/1050-2149) [21431536] **13**

AVIATION EQUIPMENT MAINTENANCE (US/0745-0214) [08720725] **13**

AVIATION EUROPE (WASHINGTON, D.C.) (US/1058-7004) [24358672] **13**

AVIATION GROUND EQUIPMENT MARKET (US/0891-5148) [14875124] **13**

AVIATION HERITAGE (US/1054-335X) [22846015] **13**

AVIATION HERITAGE (LEESBURG, VA.) *See* AVIATION (LEESBURG, VA.) **13**

●AVIATION HISTORY (US/1076-8858) [30471031] **13**

AVIATION INTERNATIONAL NEWS (US/0887-9877) [13142100] **13**

AVIATION / LATIN AMERICA AND THE CARIBBEAN (US/1073-5518) [29463522] **13**

AVIATION LAW REPORTS (US/0273-7310) [06880641] 13, **2939**

AVIATION (LEESBURG, VA.) *See* AVIATION HISTORY **13**

AVIATION (LEESBURG, VA.) (US/1067-4799) [27247156] **13**

AVIATION LITIGATION REPORTER (US/0737-7746) [09454138] 13, **2939**

AVIATION MAGAZINE INTERNATIONAL (FR/0005-2132) [08549538] **13**

AVIATION MECHANICS BULLETIN (US/0005-2140) [13867872] **13**

AVIATION MEDICINE (BANGALORE) (II/0250-5045) [04896062] **3554**

AVIATION MONTHLY (US/0145-1014) [02669013] **13**

AVIATION NEWS (UK) **13**

AVIATION NEWS (UK) **13**

AVIATION NEWS FROM SOUTH FLORIDA (US/1058-1014) [24220309] **13**

AVIATION NEWS (RENO) (US/0190-938X) [04782796] **13**

AVIATION (OTTAWA) (CN/0843-493X) [21094819] **13**

AVIATION QUARTERLY (US/0360-8670) [02244923] **13**

AVIATION REGULATORY DIGEST SERVICE (US) **13**

AVIATION REPORT. SYDNEY (AT/1035-9079) [I10359079] **13**

AVIATION REPORTS. CIVIL AND/OR MILITARY (UK/0005-2159) **14**

AVIATION SAFETY (RIVERSIDE, CONN.) (US/0277-1764) [07515136] 4768, **14**

AVIATION SAFETY, ULTRALIGHT AND BALLOON (CN/1184-1907) [23249136] **14**

AVIATION SPACE AND ENVIRONMENTAL MEDICINE (US/0095-6562) [02245949] 14, **3554**

AVIATION SPACE DICTIONARY (US) [07242411] **14**

AVIATION TODAY (PORT CREDIT) *CEASED.* (CN/1180-9663) [23598736] **14**

AVIATION TRADESCAN (US/0899-1928) [16916357] 14, **41**

AVIATION TRAVEL AND TIMES (US/0273-7191) [06870386] **14**

AVIATION WEEK & SPACE TECHNOLOGY (US/0005-2175) [01518944] **14**

AVIATION WEEK AND SPACE TECHNOLOGY. BUYERS' GUIDE (US) [15543494] **14**

AVIATORS HOT LINE (US/0195-0347) [05226295] **14**

AVIAZIONE (IT/0391-7738) [07447028] **14**

AVIAZIONE DI LINEA, AERONAUTICA E SPAZIO *See* AVIAZIONE DI LINEA, DIFESA E SPAZIO **14**

AVIAZIONE DI LINEA, DIFESA E SPAZIO (IT) [02512618] **14**

AVICULTEUR, L' (FR/0150-939X) [04030857] **5577**

AVICULTURAL BULLETIN (US/0567-2856) [06071200] 2187, **5615**

AVICULTURAL JOURNAL, THE *CEASED.* (CN/0317-5650) [02442952] 4285, **5615**

AVICULTURAL MAGAZINE, THE (UK/0005-2256) [01518945] **5615**

AVID (CUPERTINO, CALIF.) (US/1063-8296) [26165338] **1171**

AVIDEO (US/0747-1335) [10380646] **1104**

AVIION NEWS *CEASED.* (US/1049-2542) [21186685] **1171**

AVINEWS (NZ) [04601790] **14**

AVION COACH CORPORATION *See* AVION OWNER'S MANUAL **5407**

AVION OWNER'S MANUAL (US) [03815793] **5407**

AVIONICS INTERNATIONAL *SUSPENDED.* (UK/0955-8055) [I09558055] **14**

AVIONICS NEWS (US/0567-2899) [04396444] **14**

AVIONICS (POTOMAC, MD.) (US/0273-7639) [06908947] **14**

AVIONICS REVIEW (US/1048-9207) [21075585] **14**

●AVIRON CANADIEN (CN/1184-9789) [24860873] **591**

AVIRON (ED QUEBECOISE) (CN/0821-1477) [09747522] **5780**

AVIRON (FRANCE) (FR/1154-9041) [I11549041] **4885**

AVIS AUX NAVIGATEURS (FR/0180-9938) [01792382] **4175**

AVIS AUX NAVIGATEURS (ED. HEBDOMADAIRE) (CN) [31354435] **4175**

AVIS MUNICIPAL - VILLE DE CHARNY (CN/0820-6503) [09144411] **4631**

AVISO (HALIFAX) (CN/0830-0011) [16054595] **1889**

AVISO, THE (US) [06460730] **2939**

AVISO (WASHINGTON, D.C.) (US/0739-7747) [02088619] **4084**

AVISOS A LOS NAVEGANTES (UY) [04601889] **4175**

AVISTA FORUM (US/1041-6994) [16848767] **316**

AVKO NEWSLETTER (US) 1889, **1875**

AVMA — Alphabetical Title Index

AVMA DIRECTORY (US/0898-6657) [10418021] **5505**

AVMARK AVIATION ECONOMIST (UK/0961-2513) [I09612513] 1464, **14**

AVMARK, INC See COMMERCIAL AIRCRAFT FLEETS **16**

AVN. ALLGEMEINE VERMESSUNGS-NACHRICHTEN (GW/0002-5968) [02444532] **2019**

AVODAH U-VITUAH LEUMI (IS/0005-2299) [06028383] 2875, **1654**

AVON CONSERVATION NEWS (UK/0143-1315) [I01431315] **2677**

AVON NEWS (US) [26689836] **5644**

AVON PARK SUN (US/0163-027X) [04279359] 5648, **5649**

AVOTAYNU (US/0882-6501) [12032515] 5046, **2438**

AVP BULLETIN (US) [03457565] **14**

AVPI. AGRICULTURAL AND VETERINARY PRODUCT INDEX (AT/0816-1623) [I08161623] 5505, **64**

AVPROF AMSTERDAM (NE/0923-7054) [I09237054] 4064, **5315**

AVR. ALLGEMEINER VLIESSTOFF-REPORT (GW/0170-4060) [I01704060] **4232**

AVRORA (RU/0320-6858) [01841035] **3365**

AVRUPA (TU) [03415465] **1464**

AVRUPA TOPLULUGU See AVRUPA **1464**

AVTOEXPORT ROUND-UP (RU) [05956179] **5407**

AVTOMATICESKAJA SVARKA (KIEV) (UN/0005-111X) [09233936] 2154, **2036**

AVTOMATIKA I TELEMEHANIKA (RU/0005-2310) [02445188] **2110**

AVTOMATIKA I TELEMEKHANIKA (RU) [05218562] **2110**

AVTOMATIKA I VYCISLITEL'NAYA TEHNIKA (RIGA) (LV/0132-4160) [05587126] **1218**

AVTOMATIKA (KIEV) (UN/0572-2691) [09745005] **1218**

AVTOMATIKA, TELEMEHANIKA I SVJAZ (RU/0005-2329) [05587356] 1218, **5429**

AVTOMATIZACIJA METALLURGICESKOGO PROIZVODSTVA (RU/0320-0825) [01799316] **3998**

AVTOMETRIJA (NOVOSIBIRSK) (RU/0320-7102) [09249706] **1218**

AVTOMOBILNAJA PROMYSLENNOST (RU/0005-2337) [09727962] **5407**

AVTOMOBILNYE DOROGI (RU/0005-2353) [10228383] **5439**

AVTOMOBILNYI TRANSPORT KAZAKHSTANA (KZ) [01788253] **5407**

AVUI (SP) [23101819] **5810**

AVVENIMENTI (IT) **4465**

AVVENIRE (IT/1120-6020) [I11206020] **5804**

AVVENIRE AGRICOLE, L' (IT/0005-2361) [05456019] **64**

AWA (SG) [01786041] **5551**

AWA KONTAKTE (GW) [19968759] **4101**

AWAKE (BROOKLYN) (US/0005-237X) [06713874] **4937**

AWAL (FR/0764-7573) [15668517] **2256**

AWANYU (US/0749-1816) [02776845] 2256, **160**

AWARD RATES OF PAY INDEXES, AUSTRALIA (AT) [09967057] **1464**

AWARD WINNING ARCHITECTURE/USA (US/0093-8254) [01784434] **293**

AWARD-WINNING BOOKS FOR CHILDREN AND YOUNG ADULTS (US/1055-792X) [22589051] 1060, **3365**

AWARDS ALMANAC (US/1052-2220) [22218907] 1810, **1799**

AWARDS DIGEST (II) [03246126] **1654**

AWARDS ... FIRST DIVISION, NATIONAL RAILROAD ADJUSTMENT BOARD (US) [01768585] **5429**

AWARDS FOR COMMONWEALTH UNIVERSITY ACADEMIC STAFF See AWARDS FOR UNIVERSITY TEACHERS AND RESEARCH WORKERS **1727**

AWARDS FOR FIRST DEGREE STUDY AT COMMONWEALTH UNIVERSITIES (UK) [I09679863] **1810**

● AWARDS FOR POSTGRADUATE STUDY AT COMMONWEALTH UNIVERSITIES (UK/0960-7986) [23436567] **1811**

AWARDS FOR UNIVERSITY ADMINISTRATORS AND LIBRARIANS (UK) **1727**

● AWARDS FOR UNIVERSITY TEACHERS AND RESEARCH WORKERS (UK/0964-2706) [25334826] **1727**

AWARDS, HONORS, AND PRIZES (US/0196-6316) [01326263] **5229**

AWARDS QUARTERLY (US/0747-3109) [05262503] **501**

AWARE (US) [22193906] 1420, **4768**

AWARE (US/0162-6833) [04206300] **4937**

AWARE (UK/0017-8271) **4937**

AWARE (DARBY, PA.) (US/0742-471X) [10356322] **4768**

AWARENESS / NATIONAL ASSOCIATION FOR PARENTS OF THE VISUALLY IMPAIRED (US) [14353589] **4384**

AWASIS (JOURNAL) (CN/0823-9231) [11629619] **2256**

AWAZ (TORONTO) (CN/0715-4135) [09159529] **5780**

AWC NEWS/FORUM (US/0193-0850) [10270929] 4101, **4160**

AWHONN'S CLINICAL ISSUES IN PERINATAL AND WOMEN'S HEALTH NURSING (US/1066-3614) [26926488] **3757**

● AWI QUARTERLY (US/1071-1384) [28302721] **226**

AWIS MAGAZINE (US/1057-5839) [23747329] 5551, **5087**

AWOURA (IV) [05916695] **5551**

AWP CHRONICLE (US) [21009238] **2917**

AWP NEWSLETTER (NORFOLK) (US/0194-6498) [04912814] **3365**

AWP OFFICIAL GUIDE TO WRITING PROGRAMS / ASSOCIATED WRITING PROGRAMS, THE (US) [21586460] **1811**

AWRA MONOGRAPH SERIES (US/0894-847X) [14979548] **5531**

AWRAQ : ESTUDIOS SOBRE EL MUNDO ARABE E ISLAMICO CONTEMPORANEO (SP/0213-6635) [27722408] **2677**

AWRAQ (LONDON, ENGLAND) (UK) [11253529] **2646**

AWU (SA) [10952656] **2498**

AWWA MAINSTREAM (US/0273-3218) [07046708] **5531**

AWWA SEMINAR PROCEEDINGS (US/0271-5422) [06662854] **4760**

AXES (RIMOUSKI) (CN/0828-7465) [12204325] **4101**

AXES SCHILTIGHEIM (FR/0757-1631) [I07571631] **2111**

AXIOS (LOS ANGELES, CALIF.) (US/0278-551X) [07830951] **3338**

AXIS (JA) [15566776] **2898**

AXIS: ACADEMIC COMPUTING & INFORMATION SYSTEMS (UK/1352-8971) **1246**

AXIS (WASHINGTON) SUSPENDED. (US/0192-8007) [04359182] **3193**

AXIS (WATERLOO) (CN/0381-6796) [02606834] **3193**

AXONE (DARTMOUTH) (CN/0834-7824) [16402865] 3827, **3852**

AYLK ISTATISTIK BULTENI (TU) [22174434] **5323**

AYLMER BULLETIN (CN/0710-5401) [08655386] **5780**

AYRSHIRE CATTLE SOCIETY'S JOURNAL, THE (UK/0005-2442) [03210391] **207**

AYRSHIRE COLLECTIONS See AYRSHIRE MONOGRAPHS **260**

AYRSHIRE DIGEST (US/0005-2450) [06963019] 207, **192**

AYRSHIRE MONOGRAPHS (UK) **260**

AYRSHIRE QUARTERLY See AYRSHIRE DIGEST **192**

AYU (II/0005-2469) [02245644] **3554**

AYURVEDALOKA See AYU **3554**

AZ (AU) [23266463] **5777**

AZ-BUKI (BU) [25853990] **1727**

AZABU DAIGAKU JUI GAKUBU KENKYU HOKOKU (JA/0389-1836) [09856287] **5505**

AZACA (US/0148-5393) [03321696] **2771**

AZALEA CITY NEWS & REVIEW (US/0744-5318) [08343186] **5625**

AZANIA (KE/0067-270X) [01894719] **260**

AZANIA VRIJ (NE/0166-7602) [I01667602] **4465**

AZARBAIJAN SSR ELMLAR AKADEMIIASY See IZVESTIIA AKADEMIIA NAUK AZERBAIDZHANSKOI SSR. SERIIA BIOLOGICHESKIKH NAUK **459**

AZARBAIJAN SSR ELMLAR AKADEMIIASY See DOKLADY / AKADEMIIA NAUK AZERBAIDZHANSKOI SSR **5101**

AZERBAIDZANSKIJ MEDICINSKIJ ZURNAL (AJ/0005-2523) [05698010] **3554**

AZERBAIDZHANSKII KHIMICHESKII ZHURNAL / AKADEMIIA NAUK AZERBAIDZHANSKOI SSR (AJ/0005-2531) [02580522] 4251, **962**

AZERBAJDZANSKOR NEFTJANOE HOZJAJSTVO (AJ/0365-8554) [09348872] **3338**

AZIENDA AUTONOMA DELLE FERROVIE DELLO STATO (ITALY) See TRENO, IL **5437**

AZIENDA ITALIA (IT) **641**

AZIENDA ITALIA (IT) **861**

AZIENDA PUBBLICA TEORIA E PROBLEMI DI MANAGEMENT (IT) **4632**

AZIENDO & FISCO (IT) **4712**

AZIIA I AFRIKA SEGODNIA (RU/0005-2574) [02258041] 2513, **2502**

AZIMUT (IT) **4885**

AZIMUTH (AT/0728-4586) [I07284586] **599**

AZIONE NONVIOLENTA (IT) [15185614] **1072**

AZLE NEWS ADVERTISER (US) [17636634] **5746**

AZOVO-CHERNOMORSKI I NAUCHNO-ISSLEDOVATEL'SKII INSTITUT MORSKOGO RYBNOGO KHOZIAISTVA I OKEANOGRAFII See TRUDY - AZOVO-CHERNOMORSKI I NAUCHNO-ISSLEDOVATEL-SKI I INSTITUT MORSKOGO RYBNOGO KHOZIAISTVA I OKEANOGRAFII **558**

AZTECA : BOLETIN BIBLIOGRAFICO INTERNACIONAL / FONDO DE CULTURA ECONOMICA (MX) [23830650] **4824**

AZTLAN (US/0005-2604) [01518968] **2256**

AZUR-CAMPING-MAGAZIN (GW/0935-0454) [I09350454] **4848**

AZURE (TORONTO) (CN/0829-982X) [13999630] 343, **2898**

AZZURO (IT) **1727**

B.A.S. SPEAKER, THE (US/0195-0908) [05274049] **5316**

B.A.T. BON A TIRER (FR/0180-4979) [I01804979] **4563**

B / AGRICULTURAL EXTENSION SERVICE, UNIVERSITY OF WYOMING (US) [13338148] **64**

B. ALLAN MACKIE SCHOOL OF LOG BUILDING (CN/0820-5752) [16856762] **633**

B & B. BOUW EN BEHEER (NE/0923-5108) [I09235108] **861**

B & CJ BUILDING DIRECTORY (UK) [09244431] **599**

B & D HEIR LINES (CN/1192-1137) [27165328] **2438**

B & ID (NE) **641**

B & J. BABY & JUNIOR (GW/0005-3554) [I00053554] **1081**

B & M BULLETIN (US/0362-2711) [02206351] **5429**

● B.B. DUCKWOOD'S WORD SEARCH IN RUSSIAN (US/1060-474X) [25002346] **4857**

B.C.A (IT/0394-4719) [I03944719] **316**

B.C. ADMINISTRATOR (CN/0229-1711) [07888455] **1860**

B C & T NEWS (US/0163-447X) [04328537] **1654**

B. C. ARCHER, THE (CN/0226-7691) [06515512] **4885**

B. C. AREA ANNUAL DOCKET (CN/0227-2962) [07295156] **5055**

B.C. ARTIFICIAL INSEMINATION CENTRE See NEWSLETTER / B.C.A.I. CENTRE **216**

B. C. CATHOLIC, THE CEASED. (CN/0007-0483) [02321752] **5024**

B.C. CAVER : THE NEWSLETTER OF THE BRITISH COLUMBIA SPELEOLOGICAL FEDERATION (CN) [28955189] **1402**

B. C. COUNSELLOR, THE (CN/0225-5693) [06131669] **1875**

B. C. CROWN COUNSEL NEWSLETTER (CN/0709-2598) [06858838] **3105**

B.C. DEAF ADVOCATE, THE (CN/0228-7161) [07822886] **4384**

B.C. DIGEST (VICTORIA) (CN/0825-0103) [10768324] **2722**

B.C. EXPORTER (CN/1184-986X) [24690991] **824**

B. C. FRESH WATER FISHING GUIDE (CN/0709-7778) [06166634] **2297**

B.C. GEOGRAPHICAL SERIES (CN/0068-1571) [02344261] **2555**

B.C. GOAT NEWS (CN/1182-557X) [22769007] **207**

B.C.H.S. SLICKENS / BUTTE COUNTY HISTORICAL SOCIETY (US) [13914210] **2722**

Alphabetical Title Index — BADGER

B.C. HISTORICAL NEWS (CN/0045-2963) [01743008] **2722**

B.C. HYDRO *See* INTERIM REPORT - B. C. HYDRO **4657**

B.C. HYDRO *See* PEOPLE (VANCOUVER) **1512**

B.C. HYDRO *See* DIRECTIONS - B.C. HYDRO **4643**

B.C. HYDRO *See* ISSUES (VANCOUVER. 1990) **1497**

B.C. HYDRO. DIRECTIONS *See* ACCESS MAGAZINE (VANCOUVER) **1460**

B.C. HYDRO. ISSUES *See* ACCESS MAGAZINE (VANCOUVER) **1460**

B.C. HYDRO. PEOPLE *See* ACCESS MAGAZINE (VANCOUVER) **1460**

B.C. HYDRO. POWER SMART *See* POWER SMART ANNUAL REPORT **1953**

B.C. HYDRO. POWER SMART. TIMES *See* POWER SMART ANNUAL REPORT **1953**

B. C. JOURNAL OF SPECIAL EDUCATION (CN/0704-7509) [03791175] **1875**

B.C. LABOUR MARKET INFORMATION (CN/0317-8269) [01796122] **1654**

B C LAWYERS' TELEPHONE, FAX AND SERVICES DIRECTORY (CN/0849-6013) [21353013] 1150, **2939**

B.C. MINERAL STATISTICS ANNUAL SUMMARY TABLES (CN/0838-5998) [18973607] **2134**

B. C. MUNICIPAL YEAR BOOK (CN/0068-161X) [01786803] **4712**

B.C. MUSIC EDUCATOR (CN/0705-9019) [05360034] 1889, **4101**

B.C. NATURALIST (CN/0228-8842) [07966351] **2187**

B.C. NEWS (US) [03962589] **1541**

B. C. PEACE NEWS (CN/0708-0859) [04955087] **4516**

B.C. PROFESSIONAL ENGINEER. ANNUAL DIRECTORY NUMBER, THE (CN) [02588393] **1966**

B.C. PUBLIC SCHOOL ENROLMENT STATISTICS *See* B.C. PUBLIC SCHOOL STATISTICS **1793**

B.C. PUBLIC SCHOOL STATISTICS (US) [06467485] 1727, **1793**

B.C. REGIONAL FISHING GUIDE. CARIBOO, CHILCOTIN (CN/0824-3190) [10199176] **2297**

B.C. RETAILER (CN/1186-9208) [24690428] **952**

B.C.S. BUSINESS CHANGE SERVICE : PENNSYLVANIA (US/0163-6553) [04425161] **641**

B C S T A REPORTS (CN/0709-9363) [05842481] **1860**

B.C. SCHOOL COUNSELLORS' NEWSLETTER : A PUBLICATION OF THE BRITISH COLUMBIA SCHOOL COUNSELLORS' ASSOCIATION (CN/0848-8495) [21325855] **1860**

B.C. SCIENCE TEACHERS NEWS UPDATE (CN/0711-4974) [08652014] 1889, **5087**

B. C. SPORTS ANNUAL (CN/0315-999X) [02247665] **4886**

B C T F INFORMATIONAL REPORT (CN/0317-2996) [02248222] **1727**

B C TODAY (CN/0701-1288) [03409882] **2722**

B.C. WORKER'S HEALTH NEWSLETTER (CN/0821-2937) [10156964] **2859**

B D K. BANDE DESSINEE KEBECOISE (CN/0383-9036) [03248394] **370**

B N A TOPICS (CN/0045-3129) [02311130] **2784**

B. P. F. YEARBOOK AND PHILATELIC SOCIETIES' DIRECTORY *See* YEARBOOK AND PHILATELIC SOCIETIES' DIRECTORY **2788**

●B.P.I.A. BUSINESS PRODUCTS INDUSTRY REPORT (US/1078-5809) [31129072] **4210**

B P L BEEP, THE (CN/0701-094X) [03402761] **3193**

B.R.P.T. BULLETIN (II) [02710057] **2646**

B.S.B.I. NEWS (UK/0309-930X) [02445519] **501**

B.S.I. NEWS (UK/0005-3309) [02445521] **4029**

B.T.I. NEWSLETTER (US/0145-7934) [02538342] **4937**

B.T.O. NEWS (UK/0005-3392) [02168804] **5615**

B.V.I. YACHT CLUB *See* B.V.I. YACHT CLUB ... YEARBOOK **591**

B.V.I. YACHT CLUB ... YEARBOOK (VB) [19403370] **591**

B70 (DK/0905-4650) [23373103] **3193**

BA, BESPRECHUNGEN/ANNOTATIONEN (GW) [04228198] **4824**

BA DEGREE HANDBOOK (UK) [02366364] **1811**

BA PAPYRUS (US/1060-4030) [24980023] **370**

BAA AIRPORT TIMETABLE (UK) **14**

BABAR PARIS (FR/1163-6262) [11636262] **1060**

BABEL (AT/0005-3503) [01518992] 1889, **3267**

BABEL (FRANKFURT) (GW/0521-9744) [01518993] **3267**

BABILLARD DE R.D.P (CN/0714-9107) [09344812] **5780**

BABOON IN MEDICAL RESEARCH, THE (US/0074-8919) [08651169] **3554**

BABRAHAM (UK) **5505**

BABSON'S INVESTMENT DIGEST (US/0093-190X) [01791645] **891**

BABSON'S REPORTS, INC *See* BABSON'S INVESTMENT DIGEST **891**

BABY & PEUTER (NE/0927-1368) [09271368] **5183**

●BABY & TODDLER TEACHER GUIDE (US/1059-3292) [24568019] **4937**

BABY CONNECTION, THE (US/0894-3990) [16074590] 2277, **1727**

BABY TALK (1977) (US/0749-971X) [09229315] 3757, **3900**

●BABYBUG (PERU, ILL.) (US/1077-1131) [30698646] **1060**

BABYLON (GW) [15814466] **5046**

BACA (IO/0125-9008) [01797906] **3193**

BACCALAUREAT / MINISTERE DE L'EDUCATION NATIONALE, LE (FR) [10810853] **1811**

BACCALAUREATE EDUCATION IN NURSING. KEY TO A PROFESSIONAL CAREER IN NURSING *CEASED.* (US/0145-9694) [02784870] **3852**

BACH (US/0005-3600) [02092949] **4101**

BACH-JAHRBUCH (GW/0084-7682) [01518998] **4101**

BACH KHOA (VM) [01795032] **2502**

●BACH PERSPECTIVES (US/1072-1924) [28883911] **4101**

BACHY (US/0091-1488) [01786502] **316**

BACK FORTY (ALEXANDRIA, VA.), THE (US/1049-3972) [21216802] **2188**

BACK HOME IN KENTUCKY (US/0199-6290) [05874437] **2722**

BACK OF THE YARDS JOURNAL (US) [23103131] **5658**

BACK PAIN MONITOR *CEASED.* (US/0746-9500) [10407177] **3554**

BACK STAGE (US/0005-3635) [01519001] **4064**

BACK STAGE SHOOT (US/1055-9825) [22647616] 1126, **756**

BACK STAGE. TV FILM & TAPE PRODUCTION DIRECTORY (US/0734-9777) [08831506] **1126**

BACK TO BACK (TORONTO, ONT.) (CN/0712-9122) [08734078] **3803**

BACK TO GODHEAD (US/0005-3643) [01587737] 4937, **4342**

BACKER UND KONDITOR (GW/0005-383X) [04017680] **2328**

BACKGROUND DATA ON THE COMMON MARKET (UK) [01785253] **1547**

BACKGROUND INFORMATION / COMMISSION OF THE CHURCHES ON INTERNATIONAL AFFAIRS, WORLD COUNCIL OF CHURCHES (SZ) [07298331] 4937, **4516**

BACKGROUND PAPER - CONGRESS OF THE UNITED STATES, CONGRESSIONAL BUDGET OFFICE (US/0190-7174) [02668730] **4712**

BACKGROUND PAPER - ECONOMIC PLANNING ADVISORY COUNCIL (AT/1036-1723) [I10361723] **1464**

BACKGROUND PAPER - INSTITUTE OF LAW RESEARCH AND REFORM, UNIVERSITY OF ALBERTA (CN/0382-5744) [02740570] **2939**

BACKGROUND STUDY / SCIENCE COUNCIL OF CANADA *CEASED.* (CN/0705-4769) [08503349] **5087**

BACKGROUND TO THE BUDGET; AN ECONOMIC SURVEY (TZ) [03565862] **4712**

BACKGROUNDER (CN/0382-8352) [02743458] **824**

BACKGROUNDER / AUSTRALIA, DEPARTMENT OF FOREIGN AFFAIRS AND TRADE (AT) [12272654] **4632**

BACKGROUNDER (CANBERRA, A.C.T. : 1989) *See* INSIGHT : AUSTRALIAN FOREIGN AFFAIRS AND TRADE ISSUES **4524**

BACKGROUNDER (HERITAGE FOUNDATION (WASHINGTON, D.C.)) (US) [08366215] **4465**

BACKHOME (MOUNTAIN HOME, N.C.) (US/1051-323X) [21984953] **2528**

BACKLETTER, THE (US/0894-7376) [16267552] **3554**

BACKPACKER (US/0277-867X) [01639834] **4869**

BACKSTREETS (US/0746-990X) [10447713] **2485**

BACKSTRETCH, THE (US/0005-366X) [04013548] **2797**

BACKTRACKER, THE (US/0094-6915) [01795364] **2438**

BACKWOODS (US/1042-7732) [19224194] **64**

BACKWOODS HOME MAGAZINE (US/1050-9712) [21730515] **2485**

BACKYARDS (CN/0715-5182) [09340511] **1060**

BACONIANA (UK) [04758164] 3365, **430**

BACON'S BUSINESS/FINANCIAL DIRECTORY (US/1058-9716) [24457758] 641, **756**

BACON'S BUSINESS MEDIA DIRECTORY (US) 641, **756**

BACON'S INFORMATION INTERNATIONAL LTD *See* BACON'S INTERNATIONAL PUBLICITY CHECKER **756**

BACONS INTERNATIONAL MEDIA DIRECTORY (US) **756**

BACON'S INTERNATIONAL PUBLICITY CHECKER (US/0161-4363) [03922624] **756**

●BACON'S MAGAZINE DIRECTORY (US) [26860856] **4812**

BACON'S MEDIA ALERT *See* BACON'S MEDIA CALENDAR DIRECTORY **756**

BACON'S MEDIA ALERTS (US/0736-4644) [09135057] **756**

BACON'S MEDIA CALENDAR DIRECTORY (US) **756**

●BACON'S NEWSPAPER DIRECTORY (US) [26861024] **4812**

BACON'S PUBLICITY CHECKER (US/0162-3125) [01585986] **756**

BACON'S PUBLICITY MANUAL *See* BACON'S PUBLICITY CHECKER **756**

BACON'S RADIO TV CABLE DIRECTORY (US) **1126**

BACON'S RADIO/TV DIRECTORY (US/0891-0103) [14523749] **1126**

BACTERIAL WILT NEWSLETTER (AT/1030-8512) [I10308512] **560**

BACTERIOLOGIA, VIRUSOLOGIA, PARAZITOLOGIA, EPIDEMIOLOGIA / UNIUNEA SOCIETATILOR DE STIINTE MEDICALE DIN ROMANIA (RM) [24498798] 3554, **560**

BAD ATTITUDE (US/0896-9531) [17212182] **2793**

BAD FAITH LAW REPORT, THE (US/8756-5374) [11589333] 2875, **2939**

BAD INTERN (GW/0724-5297) [11254600] **3555**

BADAN KERJA SAMA PERGURUAN TINGGI NEGERI INDONESIA BAGIAN TIMUR *See* HASIL HASIL RAPAT LENGKAP BADAN KERJA SAMA PERGURUAN TINGGI NEGERI INDONESIA BAGIAN TIMUR **1827**

BADAN KOORDINASI KELUARGA BERENCANA NASIONAL. BIRO PROYEK KHUSUS *See* LAPORAN TAHUNAN BIRO PROYEK KHUSUS BKKBN **589**

BADAN PEMBINAAN HUKUM NASIONAL *See* BERITA BADAN PEMBINAAN HUKUM NASIONAL **2941**

BADANIA FIZJOGRAFICZNE NAD POLSKA ZACHODNIA. SERIA A: GEOGRAFIA FIZYCZNA (PL) [02325422] **1352**

BADANIA OSWIATOWE (PL) [04279503] **1911**

BADEN-WUERTTEMBERG (GERMANY). MINISTERIUM FUER ARBEIT, GESUNDHEIT UND SOZIALORDNUNG *See* JAHRESBERICHT DER GEWERBEAUFSICHT **2864**

BADEN-WURTTEMBERG (GW/0404-6307) [03102602] **2677**

BADEN-WURTTEMBERG (GERMANY). KULTUSMINISTERIUM *See* BERICHT DES KULTUSMINISTERIUMS BADEN-WURTTEMBERG ZUR BERATUNG DES HAUSHALTSPLANES **1860**

BADEN-WURTTEMBERG. LANDESARBEITSAMT *See* ARBEITSMARKT IN BADEN-WURTTEMBERG; JAHRESBERICHT, DER **1529**

BADEN-WURTTEMBERGISCHE VERWALTUNGSPRAXIS (GW/0340-3505) [I03403505] **4632**

BADGER BAPTIST (US) **4937**

BADGER BIRDER, THE (US/0408-1749) [05517727] **5577**

BADGER COMMON TATER, THE (US/0271-5864) [05509652] **164**

BADGER HERALD (US/0045-1304) [03979229] **1089**

BADGER SPORTSMAN (US/0005-3775) [03979254] 4886, **4869**

BADGER TRUCKER (US/1048-9819) [21097638] **5377**

BADIL (RABAT, MOROCCO) (MR) [11902392] **2638**

BADISCHE ANILIN- UND SODA-FABRIK. UNTERNEHMENSARCHIV *See* SCHRIFTENREIHE **1029**

BADISCHE BAUERN-ZEITUNG (GW) [05509767] **64**

BADMINTON ASSOCIATION OF ENGLAND *See* ANNUAL HANDBOOK **4883**

BADMINTON CHALLENGE (CN/0710-0051) [08124122] **4886**

BADMINTON MAGAZINE, THE *CEASED.* (US/0747-9069) [10838191] **4886**

BADMINTON NEW-NOUVEAU BRUNSWICK : NEWSLETTER (CN/0229-3862) [07888624] **4886**

BADMINTON NOW (UK) **4886**

BADMINTON REVIEW (ST. ALBERT) (CN/0822-6784) [10365083] **4886**

BADMINTON SIDELINES (AT/0813-006X) [I0813006X] **4886**

BADMINTON TODAY (CN/0841-6036) [19027460] **4886**

BADMINTON U S A (US/0045-1312) [01519012] **4886**

BADMINTONIEN (CN/0228-0698) [06758100] **4886**

BAECON BI-MONTHLY REPORTER (PH) [01303594] **64**

BAESSLER-ARVHIC (GW) [01267890] **231**

BAETICA (SP) [06670983] **2677**

BAG OF TRICKS (US/0890-6416) [14353170] **1727**

BAGAINCA (NP) [08353795] **3365**

BAGCHI INDOLOGICAL SERIES (II) [07657455] **2646**

BAGDAD. JAMI'AT BAGHDAD. FACULTY OF MEDICINE *See* JOURNAL OF THE FACULTY OF MEDICINE, BAGHDAD **3598**

BAGHDAD (IQ) [05212495] **2647**

BAGHDADER MITTEILUNGEN (GW/0418-9698) [01519016] **261**

BAGHDADER MITTEILUNGEN. BEIHEFT (GW) [02326735] **261**

BAGINA (II) [03217120] **4102**

BAGLEY FARMERS INDEPENDENT (US) [01519017] **5694**

BAGNALL'S VPO INDUSTRY NEWS (US/0195-9727) [05732356] **5377**

BAGNO OGGI E DOMANI, IL (IT) **2898**

BAGONG PAMANA (PH/0115-9321) [09153276] 316, **3365**

BAHAI NEWS (WILMETTE) (US/0195-9212) [03665115] **5042**

BAHAMAS BUSINESS GUIDE : BBG (BF) [07041387] **641**

BAHAMAS DATELINE (US/0749-5714) [09772171] **4834, 891**

BAHAMAS. DEPT. OF STATISTICS *See* QUARTERLY BULLETIN OF CONSTRUCTION STATISTICS **633**

BAHAMAS DEVELOPMENT BANK *See* ANNUAL REPORT ... / BAHAMAS DEVELOPMENT BANK **770**

BAHAMAS HANDBOOK AND BUSINESSMAN'S ANNUAL (BF/0067-2912) [01519021] 641, **5462**

BAHAMAS. MONETARY AUTHORITY *See* ANNUAL REPORT AND STATEMENT OF ACCOUNTS **770**

BAHAMAS TOURISM STATISTICS (BF) [12125543] **5500**

BAHAMIAN REVIEW (BF/0005-397X) [01519022] **2528**

BAHANA (BX/0005-3988) [02243501] **3267**

BAHASA DAN SASTRA (IO) [02933564] 3365, **3267**

BAHIA, ANUARIO DA MINERACAO (BL) [05179724] **2134**

BAHIA BLANCA, ARGENTINE REPUBLIC. UNIVERSIDAD NACIONAL DEL SUR. INSTITUTO DE ECONOMIA *See* COLECCION METODOLOGICA; PUBLICACION **1590**

BAHIA, BOLETIM INFORMATIVO SETOR MINERAL (BL) [06025240] **2134**

BAHIA, BRAZIL (STATE). COORDENACAO DA PRODUCAO MINERAL *See* BAHIA, BOLETIM INFORMATIVO SETOR MINERAL **2134**

BAHIA (BRAZIL : STATE). COORDENACAO DE ENERGIA *See* CADASTRO DE ELECTRIFICACAO DO ESTADO DA BAHIA **2037**

BAHIA, BRAZIL (STATE). DEPARTAMENTO DE GEOGRAFIA E ESTATISTICA *See* PRECO MEDIO DE GENEROS ALIMENTICIOS DE SALVADOR **1621**

BAHIA (BRAZIL : STATE). DEPARTAMENTO ESTADUAL DE ESTATISTICA *See* BOLETIM DO COMERCIO EXTERIOR DA BAHIA **825**

BAHIA, BRAZIL (STATE). PROCURADORIA GERAL DO ESTADO *See* REVISTA - PROCURADORIA GERAL DO ESTADO **3042**

BAHIA, BRAZIL (STATE). PROCURADORIA GERAL DO ESTADO *See* BOLETIM INFORMATIVO - PROCURADORIA GERAL DO ESTADO **2942**

BAHIA (BRAZIL : STATE). SECRETARIA DE EDUCACAO E CULTURA *See* BOLETIM INFORMATIVO - SECRETARIA DA EDUCACAO E CULTURA **1728**

BAHIA, BRAZIL (STATE). SERVICO DE ESTATISTICA POLICIAL E CRIMINAL *See* RELATORIO ESTATISTICO - SERVICO DE ESTATISTICA POLICIAL E CRIMINAL **3082**

BAHIA, BRAZIL (STATE). TRIBUNAL DE CONTAS *See* REVISTA DO TRIBUNAL DE CONTAS DO ESTADO DA BAHIA **751**

BAHIA ... RESENHA DE EMPRESAS / SECRETARIA DA INDUSTRIA E COMERCIO (BL) [10250192] **1547**

BAI (PK) [04634994] **4824**

BAI SURVEY OF THE CHECK COLLECTION SYSTEM (US) [18356835] **773**

BAIAVAIA USKALOS *See* BAJAVAJA USKALOS' **3365**

BAIKA GAKUEN GAKUENSHI KENKYU (JA) [08267979] **1811**

BAIKA REVIEW (JA) [03027858] **3365**

BAILAMME (IT) [21429573] 4465, **4937**

BAILEYA (US/0005-4003) [02250265] **501**

BAILLIERE'S CLINICAL ANAESTHESIOLOGY (UK/0950-3501) [18485378] **3682**

BAILLIERE'S CLINICAL ENDOCRINOLOGY AND METABOLISM (UK/0950-351X) [15347546] **3726**

BAILLIERE'S CLINICAL GASTROENTEROLOGY (UK/0950-3528) [15500931] **3743**

BAILLIERE'S CLINICAL HAEMATOLOGY (UK/0950-3536) [16415348] **3770**

●BAILLIERE'S CLINICAL INFECTIOUS DISEASES (UK/1071-6564) [26906523] **3712**

●BAILLIERE'S CLINICAL NEUROLOGY (UK/0961-0421) [26851968] **3828**

BAILLIERE'S CLINICAL OBSTETRICS AND GYNAECOLOGY (UK/0950-3552) [15708613] **3757**

●BAILLIERE'S CLINICAL PAEDIATRICS (UK/0906-6714) [109636714] **3900**

●BAILLIERE'S CLINICAL PSYCHIATRY (UK/1074-8806) [29868512] **3921**

BAILLIERE'S CLINICAL RHEUMATOLOGY (UK/0950-3579) [15811853] **3803**

BAINBRIDGE ISLAND REVIEW (BAINBRIDGE ISLAND, WASH. : 1988) *See* REVIEW (WINSLOW, WASH.), THE **5762**

BAIO-INDASUTORI (JA) [12929038] **443**

BAIOMASU HENKAN KEIKAKU KENKYU HOKOKU (JA/0913-4549) [109134549] **443**

BAIQUIEN YIKE DAXUE XUEBAO (CC/0253-3707) [07102468] **3555**

BAITHAKAKO KARYAVAHIKO SANKSHIPTA-VIVARANA (NP) [02240234] **1547**

BAIU TO TAIFU NO YOSO (JA) [03551607] **1420**

BAJAVAJA USKALOS' (CN/0408-2206) [01788409] **3365**

BAJO ARAGON, PREHISTORIA (SP) [10428035] 2677, **231**

BAJTEK (PL/0860-1674) [08601674] **1171**

●BAKER & DANIELS' INDIANA ENVIRONMENTAL COMPLIANCE UPDATE (US/1067-4209) [27206592] **3110**

BAKER & TAYLOR'S SCHOOL SELECTION GUIDE (US/0732-8052) [08433598] **1727**

BAKER CITY HERALD (US) **5733**

BAKER LIBRARY *See* HARVARD BUSINESS SCHOOL CORE COLLECTION **416**

BAKER LIBRARY *See* BAKER LIBRARY MINI-LIST **641**

BAKER LIBRARY *See* RECENT ADDITIONS TO BAKER LIBRARY **3244**

BAKER LIBRARY *See* WORKING PAPERS IN BAKER LIBRARY **723**

BAKER LIBRARY MINI-LIST (US) [03794375] **641**

BAKER STREET JOURNAL, THE (US/0005-4070) [01519032] **3365**

BAKER STREET MISCELLANEA *CEASED.* (US/0199-3844) [05001128] **1923**

BAKER VALLEY NEWS (US/0746-9888) [10447486] **5633**

BAKER'S DIGEST (US/0191-6114) [01519033] **2328**

BAKERS JOURNAL (CN/0005-4097) [02232435] **2328**

BAKERS' REVIEW (WATFORD) (UK/0005-4100) [05514040] **2328**

BAKERSFIELD CALIFORNIAN, THE (US/0276-5837) [03198151] **5633**

BAKERY NEWSLETTER (US/1049-3174) [12131313] **2328**

BAKERY PRODUCTION AND MARKETING *See* RED BOOK DIRECTORY OF MAJOR BAKERIES **935**

BAKERY PRODUCTION AND MARKETING (US/0005-4127) [02247092] **2328**

BAKERY WORLD (IE/0790-2239) [I07902239] **2328**

BAKING & SNACK SYSTEMS (US/1040-9254) [18610347] **2328**

BAKING BUYER (US/1056-6007) [23744773] **2328**

BAKING IDEAS *CEASED.* (US/0278-7245) [07863874] **2788**

BAKKERSWERELD (NE/0026-5934) [I00265934] **2328**

BAKO INFORMATIONEN *See* BAKO MAGAZINE **3475**

BAKO MAGAZINE (GW) **3475**

BAKU. MUZEI ISTORII AZERBAIDZHANA *See* MATERIALY PO ISTORII AZERBAIDZHANA **2658**

BAKUNIN (DAVIS, CALIF.) (US/1052-3154) [22258109] 316, **3338**

BALAFON (IV/0378-469X) [08106466] **2638**

BALAI PENELITIAN KESEJAHTERAAN SOSIAL *See* PELITA BPKS **5300**

BALAI PENELITIAN PERKEBUNAN BOGOR *See* STATISTIK COKLAT **1539**

BALANCE FOR WOMEN PHYSICIANS (US) **3913**

BALANCE LONDON (UK/0005-4216) [I00054216] **3555**

BALANCE OF PAYMENTS (SQ/0304-8977) [01792214] **773**

BALANCE OF PAYMENTS, AUSTRALIA (AT) [07212989] 4712, **4696**

BALANCE OF PAYMENTS, AUSTRALIA. REGIONAL SERIES ON MICROFICHE (AT/0819-6001) [I08196001] 4712, **4696**

BALANCE OF PAYMENTS MONTHLY (JA/0549-317X) [05514271] **773**

BALANCE OF PAYMENTS OF JAMAICA (JM/0259-6776) [01793530] **773**

BALANCE OF PAYMENTS STATISTICS. YEARBOOK / INTERNATIONAL MONETARY FUND (US/0252-3035) [08020910] 773, **726**

BALANCE OF PAYMENTS / TAIWAN DISTRICT, THE REPUBLIC OF CHINA (CH) [07912301] **773**

BALANCE PREVENTIVO - SOCIEDAD PRIVADA MUNICIPAL TRANSPORTES DE BARCELONA (SP/0304-8993) [01796442] **5377**

BALANCE REPORT, THE (US) [15674712] **4549**

BALANCE SHEET (CINCINNATI, OHIO), THE (US/0005-4232) [01519041] 1727, **641**

BALANCE SHEET - STATE TREASURER OF THE STATE OF OKLAHOMA (US) [05275923] **4712**

BALANCE SHEETS AND THE LENDING BANKER (UK) **739**

BALANCE SHEETS OF THE U.S. ECONOMY (US) [12274781] 4632, **4712**

BALANCED DAIRYING. ECONOMICS / TEXAS AGRICULTURAL EXTENSION SERVICE (US) [20736092] **192**

BALANCED LIVING *See* GREEN REVOLUTION (YORK, PA.) **4542**

BALANCED PERSPECTIVE ON : THE HEALTH OF KANSANS (US/0161-2212) [03285808] **4768**

BALANCES OF PAYMENTS OF OECD COUNTRIES / OECD, DEPARTMENT OF ECONOMICS AND STATISTICS (FR) [11751142] **773**

BALANCES Y ESTADISTICAS DE LA BANCA PRIVADA (SP) **773**

BALANCING THE SCALES (US/0734-1822) [08651506] **3179**

BALANCO ENERGETICO NACIONAL (BL) [02676319] **1933**

BALANCO FINANCEIRO (BL) [05973271] **773**

BALANCO GERAL / GOVERNO PARANA, SECRETARIA DE ESTADO DAS FINANCAS, COORDENACAO DA ADMINISTRACAO FINANCEIRA DO ESTADO (BL) [11479442] **4712**

BALANS (DEN HAAG) (NE/0005-4259) [I00054259] **641**

BALCANOSLAVICA (XN/0350-0179) [02441235] 231, **2677**

BALDWIN LEDGER, THE (US/0745-9335) [09612620] **5674**

BALDWIN TIMES, THE (US) [11836647] **5625**

BALDWIN'S OHIO LEGISLATIVE SERVICE (US/0092-0959) [01788317] **2939**

BALDWIN'S OHIO REVISED CODE, WITH RULES OF PRACTICE, ANNOTATED (US) [01643011] **2939**

BALDWIN'S OHIO SCHOOL LAW JOURNAL (US/1055-0100) [23056494] **1727**

BALDWIN'S OHIO TAX LAW AND RULES (US) [05842404] **4712**, **2939**

BALDWIN'S OHIO TAX SERVICE (US/0739-1234) [06480527] **4713**, **2939**

BALDWINSVILLE MESSENGER (US) **5714**

BALE CATALOGUE OF ISRAEL POSTAGE STAMPS / COMPILED AND PUBLISHED BY MICHAEL H. BALE (UK) [07902789] **2784**

BALINT-GRUPPE IN KLINIK UND PRAXIS, DIE (GW) [19584690] **4575**, **3555**

BALITA (CN/0709-0358) [05258082] **5780**

BALKAN-ARCHIV (GW/0170-8007) [07500703] **3267**

BALKAN INVESTMENT REPORT (US/0193-9947) [05283298] **892**

BALKAN STUDIES (GR/0005-4313) [01519050] **2677**

BALKANISTIKA / BULGARSKA AKADEMIIA NA NAUKITE, INSTITUT PO BALKANISTIKA (BU/0205-2512) [15809795] **2677**

● BALKANMEDIA (BU/0861-5047) [26238471] **1104**

BALKANSKO EZIKOZNANIE (BU/0324-1653) [01519052] **3267**

BALL AND ROLLER BEARING ENGINEERING (GW/0522-0629) [09159830] **2111**

BALL BEARING JOURNAL (LUTON) *CEASED.* (UK/0308-1664) [02445202] **2111**

BALL BEGINNINGS (US/8756-7237) [11698826] **2438**

BALLADE : TIDSSKRIFT FOR NY MUSIKK (NO/0332-5148) [17277075] **4102**

BALLARD NEWS-TRIBUNE (SEATTLE, WASH. : 1976) (US) [17243228] **5760**

BALLENA PRESS ANTHROPOLOGICAL PAPERS (US) [01472359] **231**

BALLENA PRESS PUBLICATIONS ON NORTH AMERICAN ROCK ART *CEASED.* (US) [05935436] **1366**, **343**

BALLET (US) [04868046] **1310**

BALLET CANADA INTERNATIONAL (CN/0824-9970) [10634840] **1310**

BALLET DANCER (US) [06034544] **1310**

BALLET-HOO (CN/0045-1347) [01718700] **1310**

BALLET IN LONDON YEARBOOK (UK) [18832329] **316**

BALLET REVIEW (US/0522-0653) [01900053] **1310**

BALLETT INTERNATIONAL (GW/0722-6268) [08712351] **1310**

BALLETT INTERNATIONAL TANZ (GW) **1311**

● BALLETT INTERNATIONAL, TANZ AKTUELL (GW) [30939039] **1311**

BALLETT-JOURNAL/DAS TANZARCHIV (GW/0720-3896) [07616763] **1311**

BALLEW FAMILY JOURNAL, THE (US/1046-4247) [09120397] **2438**

BALLINGER LEDGER, THE (US) [13918452] **5746**

BALLOON (IRVINE, CALIF.) (US/8756-4661) [11567274] **4849**, **4384**

BALLOON LIFE (US/0887-6061) [13296407] **4849**, **4886**

BALLOONING (US/0194-6854) [04944418] **14**

BALLOONS TODAY (US/1049-9970) [21364380] **2528**

BALLOT ACCESS NEWS (US/1043-6898) [18598496] **4465**

BALLROOM DANCING TIMES, THE (UK) [01519061] **1311**

BALLROOM REVIEW, THE (US/1072-5156) [28995829] **1311**

BALLS AND BURLAPS (US/0404-6927) [03757767] **2410**

BALLS AND STRIKES (US/0199-2406) [05734709] **4886**

BALLSTON JOURNAL (BALLSTON SPA, N.Y. : 1952) (US) [11692453] **5714**

BALNEOLOGIA BOHEMICA (XR/0302-8070) [01788620] **4379**

BALNEOLOGIA, GYOGYFURDOUGY, GYOGYIDEGENFORGALOM (HU/0865-9222) [I08659222] **5462**, **4849**

BALOUNE (CN/0707-9672) [06025895] **4857**

BALSANWT 'IBRIYT (IS/0792-3252) [I07923252] **3267**

BALSHANUT 'IVRIT (IS) [20929417] **3268**

BALTIC AND INTERNATIONAL MARITIME CONFERENCE *See* LIST OF MEMBERS / BALTIC AND INTERNATIONAL MARITIME CONFERENCE **5451**

BALTIC AND INTERNATIONAL MARITIME CONFERENCE *See* BIMCO BULLETIN **5447**

● BALTIC ASTRONOMY (LI) [26489398] **393**

BALTIC BUSINESS REPORT (US/1058-1057) [24220423] **892**

BALTIC INDEPENDENT, THE (ER/1018-7286) [24181112] **5800**

BALTIC NEWS (AT/0312-0317) [I03120317] **4504**

● BALTIC OBSERVER : NEWS FROM ESTONIA, LATVIA, AND LITHUANIA, THE (LV) [26402655] **5806**

BALTIC PHILATELIST NUMISMATIST, THE (CN) [05653163] **2784**

BALTIC SEA ENVIRONMENT PROCEEDINGS (FI/0357-2994) [08631373] **2188**, **1446**

● BALTIC STUDIES NEWSLETTER (US) [29865113] **5192**

BALTIMORE AFRO-AMERICAN (US) [16319249] **5685**

BALTIMORE/ANNAPOLIS (US/1052-0996) [16629043] **5192**, **641**

BALTIMORE BUSINESS JOURNAL (US/0747-1823) [10621197] **641**

BALTIMORE CHRONICLE (US) [20744678] **5685**

BALTIMORE COUNTY GUIDE TO LAWS COVERING TENANT-LANDLORD RELATIONS IN THE CITY I.E. COUNTY AND THE STATE (US) [05843743] **2939**

BALTIMORE COUNTY HERITAGE PUBLICATION, A (US/0270-0344) [06338611] **2722**

BALTIMORE ENGINEER, THE (US/0005-4496) [02554718] **1966**

BALTIMORE ENTERPRISE AND INNER HARBOR NEWS, THE (US) [20733479] **5685**

BALTIMORE EPICURE (US) [08797120] **5070**

BALTIMORE JEWISH TIMES (US/0005-450X) [03981984] **5046**

BALTIMORE MAGAZINE (US/0005-4453) [03981922] **2528**

BALTIMORE (MD.) *See* CITY OF BALTIMORE ANNUAL REPORT **4638**

BALTIMORE MENU DIRECTORY *CEASED.* (US/0896-4653) [17156667] **2328**

BALTIMORE MESSENGER (1985), THE (US/1041-0872) [18372888] **5685**

BALTIMORE MUSEUM OF ART *See* ANNUAL - BALTIMORE MUSEUM OF ART **336**

BALTIMORE NEIGHBORHOODS, INC *See* BALTIMORE COUNTY GUIDE TO LAWS COVERING TENANT-LANDLORD RELATIONS IN THE CITY I.E. COUNTY AND THE STATE **2939**

BALTISCHE BRIEFE (GW) [07429576] **2513**

BALTISCHE STUDIEN (GW/0067-3099) [01519098] **2677**

BALTISTICA (LI/0045-1371) [01519101] **3268**

BALTO-SLAVIANSKIE ISSLEDOVANIIA / AKADEMIIA NAUK SSSR, INSTITUT SLAVIANOVEDENIIA I BALKANISTIKI (RU) [08563468] **3365**, **3268**

BALUNGAN (US/0885-7113) [11762934] **4102**

BAM (US/0194-5793) [04855429] **4102**

'BAMA (US/0195-0975) [05275557] **4886**

BAMAH (JERUSALEM, ISRAEL) (IS/0045-138X) [02528591] **5361**

BAMBINO COLLEZIONI (IT) **1081**

BAMBINO INCOMPIUTO (IT) [20311297] **2277**

BAMBOO JOURNAL (JA/0289-2111) [I02892111] **164**

BAMBOO RESEARCH (CC) [09665576] **164**

BAMBOO RIDGE (US/0733-0308) [08510891] **3365**

BAMLA CHOTA GALPA (II) [03348413] **3365**

BAMPTON LECTURES IN AMERICA (US/0067-3129) [01519105] **1811**

BAN THONG TIN (NANAIMO REFUGEE CO-ORDINATION SOCIETY) (CN/0824-5193) [10857669] **5274**

BAN VIET (1987) (CN/0845-4817) [19991393] **2256**

BANACH CENTER PUBLICATIONS (PL/0137-6934) [06281036] **3496**

BANAR (CN/0225-6193) [06166558] **2528**

BANARAS HINDU UNIVERSITY *See* ABSTRACTS OF THE THESES ACCEPTED FOR THE PH D. DEGREE OF BANARAS HINDU UNIVERSITY **1806**

BANARAS HINDU UNIVERSITY. CENTRE OF ADVANCED STUDY IN PHILOSOPHY *See* YEAR BOOK - BANARAS HINDU UNIVERSITY. CENTRE OF ADVANCED STUDY IN PHILOSOPHY **4365**

BANAS (BL/0005-4585) [02954117] **773**

BANAS CLASSIFICADO INDUSTRIAL BRASILEIRO (BL) [01798241] **1599**, **824**

BANASTHALI PATRIKA, THE (II/0970-4825) [01774241] **1089**

BANATICA / COMITETUL DE CULTURA SI EDUCATIE SOCIALISTA AL JUDETULUI CARAS-SEVERIN, MUZEUL JUDETEAN RESITA (RM) [12789841] **2677**

BANBER EREVANI HAMALSARANI. HASARAKAKAN GITUTYUNNER / EREVANI PETAKAN HAMALSARAN (AI) [07548968] **5192**

BANBURY REPORT (US/0198-0068) [05753811] **443**

BANCA & LAVORO (IT) **773**

BANCA, BORSA E TITOLI DI CREDITO (IT) [01519106] **773**

BANCA ESPANOLA (SP/0210-1688) [I02101688] **773**

BANCA, IMPRESA, SOCIETA (IT) [15188718] **773**

BANCA NAZIONALE DEL LAVORO *See* BANCA NAZIONALE DEL LAVORO QUARTERLY REVIEW **1590**

BANCA NAZIONALE DEL LAVORO QUARTERLY REVIEW (IT/0005-4607) [01519107] **1590**

BANCA NAZIONALE SOMALA *See* ANNUAL REPORT AND STATEMENT OF ACCOUNTS - BANCA NAZIONALE SOMALA **770**

BANCA Y COMERCIO (MX/0005-4615) [02520966] **773**

BANCA Y FINANZAS (CK/0120-7040) [02923119] **773**

BANCAMATICA (IT/0393-7062) [I03937062] **774**

BANCAR (AG) [03449176] **774**

BANCARIA (IT/0005-4623) [02521858] **774**

BANCATIQUE (FR/0766-821X) [I0766821X] **774**

BANCHE E BANCHIERI (IT/0390-1378) [I03901378] **774**

BANCNI VESTNIK (XV/0005-4631) [04871979] **774**

BANCO CENTRAL DE CHILE *See* BOLETIN MENSUAL - BANCO CENTRAL DE CHILE **779**

BANCO CENTRAL DE LA REPUBLICA DOMINICANA *See* MEMORIA / BANCO CENTRAL DE LA REPUBLICA DOMINICA **798**

BANCO CENTRAL DE LA REPUBLICA DOMINICANA. MEMORIA ANUAL *See* MEMORIA / BANCO CENTRAL DE LA REPUBLICA DOMINICA **798**

BANCO CENTRAL DE NICARAGUA *See* INFORME ANUAL / BANCO CENTRAL DE NICARAGUA **791**

BANCO CENTRAL DE VENEZUELA *See* BOLETIN MENSUAL - BANCO CENTRAL DE VENEZUELA **779**

BANCO CENTRAL DE VENEZUELA *See* INFORME ECONOMICO **1495**

BANCO CENTRAL DEL ECUADOR *See* BOLETIN ANUARIO - BANCO CENTRAL DEL ECUADOR **5323**

BANCO CENTRAL DEL ECUADOR *See* MEMORIA DEL GERENTE GENERAL DEL BANCO CENTRAL DEL ECUADOR **798**

BANCO CENTRAL. DEPARTAMENTO EXTRANJERO *See* BOLETIN INFORMATIVO - BANCO CENTRAL **779**

BANCO CENTRAL (MADRID, SPAIN) *See* BOLETIN INFORMATIVO - BANCO CENTRAL **779**

BANCO DE BIBLIOGRAFIAS / EMBRAPA, EMPRESA BRASILEIRA DE PESQUISA AGROPECUARIA, DEPARTAMENTO DE INFORMACAO E DOCUMENTACAO (BL/0101-0697) [09607629] **64**

BANCO DE CREDITO AGRICOLA *See* MEMORIA / BANCO DE CREDITO AGRICOLA (MICROFORM) **798**

BANCO DE CREDITO AGRICOLA, MADRID. MEMORIA DE ACTIVIDADES *See* MEMORIA / BANCO DE CREDITO AGRICOLA (MICROFORM) **798**

BANCO DE CREDITO LOCAL DE ESPANA (MADRID, SPAIN) *See* BOLETIN BIMESTRAL INFORMATIVO - BANCO DE CREDITO LOCAL DE ESPANA **779**

BANCO   Alphabetical Title Index

BANCO DE DESENVOLVIMENTO DE MINAS GERAIS *See* PLANO OPERATIVO ANUAL - BANCO DE DESENVOLVIMENTO DE MINAS GERAIS **803**

BANCO DE DESENVOLVIMENTO DE MINAS GERAIS *See* PLANO DE ACAO - BANCO DE DESENVOLVIMENTO DE MINAS GERAIS **803**

BANCO DE DESENVOLVIMENTO DO CEARA *See* RELATORIO DE ATIVIDADES - BANCO DE DESENVOLVIMENTO DO CEARA **807**

BANCO DE DESENVOLVIMENTO DO ESTADO ES SAO PAULO *See* RELATORIO ANUAL **807**

BANCO DE DESENVOLVIMENTO DO PARANA *See* PARANA INFORMACOES **1578**

BANCO DE ESPANA *See* INFORME ANUAL - BANCO DE ESPANA **1567**

BANCO DE ESPANA *See* MEMORIA DE ACTIVIDADES **798**

BANCO DE ESPANA, MADRID *See* BOLETIN ESTADISTICO. INDICADORES ECONOMICOS **779**

BANCO DE GUATEMALA (1945-) *See* BOLETIN ESTADISTICO - BANCO DE GUATEMALA **779**

BANCO DE LA REPUBLICA (COLOMBIA) *See* REVISTA DEL BANCO DE LA REPUBLICA **810**

BANCO DE LA REPUBLICA ORIENTAL DEL URUGUAY *See* ANNUAL REPORT FOR THE ... FISCAL YEAR / BANCO DE LA REPUBLICA ORIENTAL DEL URUGUAY **771**

BANCO DE PORTUGAL. DEPARTAMENTO DE ESTATISTICA E ESTUDOS ECONOMICOS *See* MONTHLY BULLETIN / BANCO DE PORTUGAL, RESEARCH AND STATISTICS DEPARTMENT **799**

BANCO DE VIZCAYA *See* BOLETIN INTERNACIONAL - BANCO DE VIZCAYA **779**

BANCO DEL LIBRO *See* INFORME BIENAL - BANCO DEL LIBRO **3217**

BANCO DO ESTADO DE PERNAMBUCO *See* BANDEPE RELATORIO **774**

BANCO DO ESTADO DO ACRE *See* RELATORIO DE ATIVIDADES / BANCO DO ESTADO DO ACRE, S.A **807**

BANCO DO ESTADO DO RIO DE JANEIRO *See* RELATORIO ANUAL - BANERJ **807**

BANCO DO NORDESTE DO BRASIL. DEPARTAMENTO RURAL. DIVISAO DE ESTUDOS E PROJETOS ESPECIAIS *See* MERCADOS AGRICOLAS : INFORMACOES **108**

BANCO INDUSTRIAL DE VENEZUELA *See* RESUMEN ECONOMICO FINANCIERO **1581**

BANCO INTEROCEANICO DE PANAMA *See* SERVICIOS Y ESTADOS FINANCIEROS **811**

BANCO NACIONAL DA HABITACAO *See* BNH EM RESUMO **2816**

BANCO NACIONAL DA HABITACAO. ASSESSORIA TECNICA DE DOCUMENTACA *See* BOLETIM BIBLIOGRAFICO **2840**

BANCO NACIONAL DE AHORRO Y PRESTAMO. GERENCIA DE ESTUDIOS E INVESTIGACIONES *See* BOLETIN MENSUAL - BANCO NACIONAL DE AHORRO Y PRESTAMO, GERENCIA DE ESTUDIOS E INVESTIGACIONES **779**

BANCO NACIONAL DE COMERCIO EXTERIOR (MEXICO) *See* COMERCIO EXTERIOR **828**

BANCO NACIONAL DE DESARROLLO AGRICOLA *See* MEMORIA DE LABORES **798**

BANCO NACIONAL DE MEXICO *See* REVIEW OF THE ECONOMIC SITUATION OF MEXICO **1581**

BANCO NACIONAL DE PANAMA. ASESORIA ECONOMICA Y PLANIFICACION *See* CARTA ECONOMICA - BANCO NACIONAL DE PANAMA. ASESORIA ECONOMICA Y PLANIFICACION **1550**

BANCO REGIONAL DE DESENVOLVIMENTO DO EXTREMO SUL *See* BOLETIM ESTATISTICO - BANCO REGIONAL DE DESENVOLVIMENTO DO EXTREMO SUL **779**

BANCOS : LA REVISTA DEL MUNDO FINANCIERO *See* NEGOCIOS Y BANCOS : REVISTA PARA EL EJECUTIVO **801**

BANCOSEGUROS (UY) [02619375] **774**

BANCROFT REGISTER (US) [16006616] **5668**

BANCS D'ESSAI DU TOURISME, LES (FR/0764-3578) [I07643578] **5462**

BAND & FESTIVAL GUIDE (US/0735-4711) [08920448] **4849**, **4102**

BAND INTERNATIONAL : THE JOURNAL OF THE INTERNATIONAL MILITARY MUSIC SOCIETY (UK) [09905708] **4037**, **4102**

BAND MUSIC GUIDE (US) [05505192] **4102**

BAND NEWS (AT) **4102**

BANDAOTI XUEBAO (CC/0253-4177) [09152322] **2036**

BANDAR (SI) [02323143] **2815**

● BANDELE'S ANNUAL VENDOR'S GUIDE TO AFRICAN-AMERICAN EVENTS (US/1062-0486) [25513783] **2256**

BANDEPE RELATORIO (BL) [01785762] **774**

BANDER BLECHE ROHRE (GW/0005-3848) [02445208] **3475**

BANDER SNATCH : THE LEWIS CARROLL SOCIETY NEWSLETTER (UK) [05655739] **3365**

BANDERA BULLETIN, THE (US) [14410615] **5747**

BANDES METRIQUE ET DECIMETRIQUE, LISTE DES STATIONS DE TELEVISION, ZONE EUROPEENNE DE RADIODIFFUSION / UNION EUROPEENNE DE RADIODIFFUSION, CENTRE TECHNIQUE (BE) [27395632] **1126**

BANDIERA ROSSA (IT/0404-8172) [02258130] **4540**

BANDINDUSTRIE EN OVERIGE TEXTIELINDUSTRIE / CENTRAAL BUREAU VOOR DE STATISTIEK, HOOFDAFDELING STATISTIEKEN VAN INDUSTRIE EN BOUWNIJVERHEID (NE/0168-4914) [10987325] **5348**

BANDMASTERS REPORT (US/0092-0819) [01788344] **4102**

BANDON HISTORICAL JOURNAL (IE/0790-4304) [15814071] **2611**

B&T WEEKLY (AT) **1150**, **1127**

B&T YEAR BOOK (AT) [04065291] **1150**, **1127**

BANDWAGON (COLUMBUS, OHIO : 1957) (US/0005-4968) [01519118] **4857**

BANDWIDTH REPORT (US) **1150**

BANDWORLD (US/0887-9036) [13441360] **4102**

BANG (SP) [01787921] **3365**

BANGALORE, INDIA (CITY). NATIONAL AERONAUTICAL LABORATORY *See* NAL NEWS LETTER **29**

BANGALORE THEOLOGICAL FORUM (II/0253-9365) [02228938] **4937**

● BANGKO SENTRAL REVIEW : A MONTHLY PUBLICATION OF THE BANGKO SENTRAL NG PILIPINAS (PH) [30885197] **1464**, **774**

BANGKOK POST, THE (TH) [03198203] **5811**

BANGKOK POST WEEKLY REVIEW (TH) **642**

BANGKOK WORLD *CEASED.* (TH) [03198220] **5811**

BANGLADESH ACADEMY OF SCIENCES *See* JOURNAL OF BANGLADESH ACADEMY OF SCIENCES **5118**

BANGLADESH AGRICULTURAL SCIENCES ABSTRACTS (BG) [09506457] **64**

BANGLADESH. ARTHA BIBHAGA *See* BUDGET SUMMARY STATEMENTS **4715**

BANGLADESH BANK *See* ANNUAL REPORT - BANGLADESH BANK **770**

BANGLADESH BANK *See* BULLETIN - BANGLADESH BANK **780**

BANGLADESH BANK. STATISTICS DEPT *See* ANNUAL IMPORT PAYMENTS **822**

BANGLADESH BANK. STATISTICS DEPT *See* ECONOMIC TRENDS **1558**

BANGLADESH BANK. STATISTICS DEPT *See* QUARTERLY BALANCE OF PAYMENTS - BANGLADESH BANK. STATISTICS DEPT **804**

BANGLADESH. BUREAU OF STATISTICS *See* MONTHLY STATISTICAL BULLETIN OF BANGLADESH **5333**

BANGLADESH DEVELOPMENT STUDIES, THE (BG/0304-095X) [01798858] **1547**

BANGLADESH DIRECTORY (BG) [06492059] **2647**

BANGLADESH DIRECTORY & YEAR BOOK (II) [03067926] **824**

BANGLADESH ECONOMIST, THE (BG) [02711126] **1547**

BANGLADESH EXPORT STATISTICS (BG) [06958667] **824**, **726**

BANGLADESH EXPORTERS' DIRECTORY (BG) [08816227] **824**

BANGLADESH HORTICULTURE (BG/0379-4288) [03618541] **2410**

BANGLADESH INSTITUTE OF DEVELOPMENT STUDIES *See* REPORT ON THE BACKGROUND, CURRENT PROGRAMMES AND PLANNED DEVELOPMENT OF THE BANGLADESH INSTITUTE OF DEVELOPMENT STUDIES, A **5215**

BANGLADESH INSURANCE ACADEMY *See* JOURNAL - BANGLADESH INSURANCE ACADEMY **2885**

BANGLADESH JOURNAL OF AGRICULTURAL ECONOMICS, THE (BG) [07726305] **1464**, **64**

BANGLADESH JOURNAL OF AGRICULTURAL RESEARCH (BG/0258-7122) [03971873] **64**

BANGLADESH JOURNAL OF AGRICULTURAL SCIENCES (BG/0379-4296) [03019580] **64**

BANGLADESH JOURNAL OF AGRICULTURE (BG/0253-5408) [03561031] **64**

BANGLADESH JOURNAL OF ANIMAL SCIENCE (BG/0003-3588) [03177097] **5505**

BANGLADESH JOURNAL OF BOTANY (BG/0253-5416) [02324570] **501**

BANGLADESH JOURNAL OF CHILD HEALTH (BG/0257-3490) [I02573490] **3900**

BANGLADESH JOURNAL OF CROP SCIENCE (BG/1018-0818) [10180818] **2410**

BANGLADESH JOURNAL OF JUTE & FIBRE RESEARCH (BG/0253-5424) [04362122] **5348**

BANGLADESH JOURNAL OF MICROBIOLOGY (BG/1011-9981) [19079150] **443**

BANGLADESH JOURNAL OF NEUROSCIENCE (BG) [19346164] **3828**

BANGLADESH JOURNAL OF SCIENTIFIC AND INDUSTRIAL RESEARCH (BG/0304-9809) [01216638] **1966**, **5087**

BANGLADESH JOURNAL OF SOIL SCIENCE (BG/0253-5440) [04512804] **164**

BANGLADESH JOURNAL OF TRAINING AND DEVELOPMENT (BG/1013-0306) [I10130306] **64**

BANGLADESH JOURNAL OF ZOOLOGY (BG/0304-9027) [02241550] **5577**

BANGLADESH JUTE MILLS ASSOCIATION *See* MONTHLY SUMMARY OF JUTE GOODS STATISTICS **5333**

BANGLADESH LABOUR CASES (BG) [02482027] **3144**

BANGLADESH LALIT KALA (BG) [04072163] **343**

BANGLADESH MEDICAL JOURNAL (BG/0301-035X) [09606139] **3555**

BANGLADESH MEDICAL RESEARCH COUNCIL BULLETIN (BG/0377-9238) [02340011] **3555**

BANGLADESH OBSERVER, THE (BG) [03198242] **5778**

BANGLADESH PHARMACEUTICAL JOURNAL (BG/0301-4606) [08541074] **4293**

BANGLADESH. PLANNING COMMISSION *See* ECONOMIC REVIEW **1558**

BANGLADESH. RAPTANI UNNAYANA BYURO *See* BANGLADESH EXPORT STATISTICS **726**

BANGLADESH RENAL JOURNAL (BG/1015-0889) [16986811] **3988**

BANGLADESH SHIPPING DIRECTORY (BG) [02556849] **5447**

BANGLADESH. UNIVERSITY GRANTS COMMISSION *See* REPORT FOR THE YEAR - BANGLADESH. UNIVERSITY GRANTS COMMISSION **1844**

BANGLADESH. UNIVERSITY GRANTS COMMISSION. ANNUAL REPORT FOR THE YEAR . *See* REPORT FOR THE YEAR - BANGLADESH. UNIVERSITY GRANTS COMMISSION **1844**

BANGLADESH VETERINARIAN, THE (BG/1012-5949) [I10125949] **5505**

BANGLADESH VETERINARY JOURNAL (BG/0378-8113) [04715824] **5505**

BANGLADESH : WIRTSCHAFTLICHE ENTWICKLUNG (GW) [05136299] **1547**

BANGOR DAILY NEWS (US/0892-8738) [08818350] **5687**

BANHI (II) [09438834] **5551**

BANIJYA SANSAR (NP) [05593249] **861**

BANIN, BUKU ALAMAT NIAGA & INDUSTRI SELURUH INDONESIA (IO) [02245663] **824**

BANJO NEWSLETTER (US/0190-1559) [04624924] **4102**

BANJO SOUNDSHEET (US/0748-2728) [10899245] **4102**

BANK ACCOUNTING & FINANCE (US/0894-3958) [16068783] **774**

BANK ACQUISITION REPORT (US/0739-9936) [08973596] **774**

BANK ADVERTISING NEWS (US/0274-7111) [06533952] **774**

Alphabetical Title Index — BANKERS

BANK AL-AHLI AL-MISRI *See* ECONOMIC BULLETIN - NATIONAL BANK OF EGYPT **789**

BANK AL-KUWAYT AL-MARKAZI *See* ECONOMIC REPORT - CENTRAL BANK OF KUWAIT **789**

BANK AL-KUWAYT AL-WATANI *See* ANNUAL REPORT **770**

BANK AL-MARKAZI AL-MISRI *See* ANNUAL REPORT - CENTRAL BANK OF EGYPT **770**

BANK AL-NILAYN *See* AL-TAQRIR AL-SANAWI - BANK AL-NILAYN **769**

BANK AL-SUDAN *See* ANNUAL REPORT FOR THE YEAR ENDING 31ST DECEMBER ... / BANK OF SUDAN **771**

BANK AL-SUDAN. IDARAT AL-BUHUTH AL-IQTISADIYAH *See* FOREIGN TRADE STATISTICAL DIGEST **729**

BANK AL-SUDAN. MASLAHAT AL-IHSA *See* AL-ARD AL-IQTISADI WA-AL-MALI **5320**

BANK AL-SUDAN. MASLAHAT AL-IHSA *See* ECONOMIC AND FINANCIAL STATISTICS REVIEW **1532**

●BANK AND CORPORATE GOVERNANCE LAW REPORTER (US) [25406606] **2939, 774**

BANK AND QUOTATION RECORD (US/0005-5026) [01519121] **774**

BANK & WIRASWASTA (IO) [11612795] **774**

BANK-ARCHIV (AU) [18097644] **774**

BANK ASSET/LIABILITY MANAGEMENT (US/0896-6230) [11882162] **774**

BANK AUDITING AND ACCOUNTING REPORT (US/0522-2478) [02482276] **739, 774**

BANK AUTOMATION CONTRACT WATCH *See* BANK AUTOMATION NEWS **1218**

BANK AUTOMATION GREEN BOOK : BUYER'S GUIDE & DIRECTORY, THE (US) [22380181] **774**

BANK AUTOMATION NEWS (US) **1218**

BANK AUTOMATION NEWSLETTER *CEASED.* (US/0572-5933) [03982143] **774**

BANK BAILOUT LITIGATION NEWS (US/1047-5133) [20707243] **774**

BANK BOARD WATCH *See* THRIFT REGULATOR **814**

BANK BUMI DAYA (INDONESIA) *See* ANNUAL REPORT **770**

BANK BUMI DAYA (INDONESIA) *See* LAPORAN TAHUNAN **796**

BANK CREDIT ANALYST. INVESTMENT AND BUSINESS FORECAST, THE (CN/0822-5788) [10356332] **642, 892**

BANK, DIE (GW/0342-3182) [06221597] **774**

BANK DIRECTOR (BRENTWOOD, TENN.) (US/1070-7611) [22761245] **774**

BANK DIRECTOR'S REPORT *CEASED.* (US/0522-2494) [03982282] **774**

BANK DISASTER AND CONTINGENCY PLANNER *See* BANK AUTOMATION NEWS **1218**

BANK EKSPOR IMPOR INDONESIA *See* ANNUAL REPORT - BANK EKSPOR IMPOR INDONESIA **770**

BANK EKSPOR IMPOR INDONESIA *See* WARTA EKSIM **857**

BANK- EN EFFECTENBEDRIJF (NE) [06414917] **774**

BANK EN FINANCIENWEZEN (BE) **774**

BANK EXECUTIVES REPORT (US/0522-2508) [04043942] **774**

BANK EXPANSION QUARTERLY *CEASED.* (US/0160-130X) [03617063] **774**

BANK FACTS (CN/0711-6497) [07851919] **774**

BANK FINANCIAL MANAGEMENT INTERNATIONAL (US/0956-3288) [21487870] **774**

BANK FINANCIAL QUARTERLY (US) [16716618] **774**

BANK/FINANCIAL SERVICES MARKETING (US/0893-021X) [15320063] **774**

BANK FOR INTERNATIONAL SETTLEMENTS *See* ANNUAL REPORT - BANK FOR INTERNATIONAL SETTLEMENTS **770**

BANK FRAUD (US/1065-8165) [15503680] **774**

BANK GUIDE (PK) [03806523] **775**

BANK HOLDING COMPANY FACTS (US/0519-1572) [02579856] **775**

BANK HR : BANK HUMAN RESOURCES REPORT *CEASED.* (US) [27805207] **775**

BANK I KREDYT (PL) [02325311] **775**

BANK INCOME TAX RETURN MANUAL, THE (US/0734-8037) [04694633] **775**

BANK INDONESIA *See* DATA KREDIT PERBANKAN **787**

BANK INSURANCE SURVEY (US/0278-7644) [07860152] **2875**

BANK INSURANCE SURVEY REPORT (US/1068-025X) [27399186] **775, 2875**

BANK INVESTMENT REPRESENTATIVE (US/1055-3193) [23138746] **892, 775**

BANK LAWYER LIABILITY REPORT *See* BURAFF'S LITIGATION REPORTS. BANK LAWYER LIABILITY **3085**

BANK LETTER (US) **775**

BANK LOAN REPORT (US) [19467177] **775**

BANK MAGAZIN (GW) **775**

BANK MANAGEMENT (ROLLING MEADOWS, ILL.) (US/1049-1775) [20944652] **775**

BANK MANAGEMENT SURVEY (US) [08592569] **1654**

BANK MARKETING (US/0888-3149) [04633235] **775**

BANK MARKETING INTERNATIONAL DUBLIN (IE/0791-2765) [l07912765] **775, 921**

BANK MERGERS & ACQUISITIONS (US) [14244646] **775**

BANK MIDYEAR REVIEW. TEXAS (US/1056-0777) [23282912] **775**

BANK NEGARA INDONESIA 1946 *See* MAJALAH BANK NEGARA INDONESIA 1946 **797**

BANK NEGARA INDONESIA 1946 *See* MAJALAH BANK NEGARA INDONESIA 1946 **797**

BANK NETWORK NEWS (US) [10715669] **775**

BANK NEWS (US/0005-5123) [03711863] **775**

BANK NOTE REPORTER (US/0164-0828) [04575069] **2780**

BANK OF AMERICA *See* COMMUNITY AND THE BANK **783**

BANK OF BRITISH COLUMBIA'S PIONEER NEWS (CN/0712-5321) [09145745] **775**

BANK OF CANADA *See* TRAVAUX DE RECHERCHE - BANQUE DU CANADA **814**

BANK OF CANADA *See* BANK OF CANADA REVIEW **775**

BANK OF CANADA *See* BANK OF CANADA. ANNUAL REPORT OF THE GOVERNOR TO THE MINISTER OF FINANCE AND STATEMENT OF ACCOUNTS **775**

BANK OF CANADA. ANNUAL REPORT OF THE GOVERNOR TO THE MINISTER OF FINANCE AND STATEMENT OF ACCOUNTS (CN/0067-3587) [01794360] **775**

BANK OF CANADA REVIEW (CN/0045-1460) [00830511] **775**

BANK OF ENGLAND *See* REPORT AND ACCOUNTS - BANK OF ENGLAND **807**

BANK OF ENGLAND *See* ANNUAL REPORT UNDER THE BANKING ACT FOR ... **772**

BANK OF ENGLAND. ECONOMIC INTELLIGENCE DEPT *See* BANK OF ENGLAND STATISTICAL ABSTRACT **726**

BANK OF ENGLAND QUARTERLY BULLETIN (UK/0005-5166) [07929818] **775**

BANK OF ENGLAND STATISTICAL ABSTRACT (UK) [05504945] **775, 726**

BANK OF HAWAII. DEPT. OF BUSINESS RESEARCH *See* ANNUAL ECONOMIC REVIEW (HONOLULU) **1545**

BANK OF JAMAICA. RESEARCH DEPT *See* BALANCE OF PAYMENTS OF JAMAICA **773**

BANK OF JAPAN MONETARY AND ECONOMIC STUDIES (JA/0288-8432) [10383358] **775**

●BANK OF JAPAN QUARTERLY BULLETIN (JA/0919-1380) [27982524] **775**

BANK OF LONDON & SOUTH AMERICA *See* BANK OF LONDON & SOUTH AMERICA REVIEW **775**

BANK OF LONDON & SOUTH AMERICA REVIEW (UK/0005-5298) [02255230] **775**

BANK OF MONTREAL *See* BUSINESS REVIEW (MONTREAL) **652**

BANK OF NEW SOUTH WALES *See* ANNUAL REPORT AND NOTICE OF ORDINARY GENERAL MEETING / BANK OF NEW SOUTH WALES **770**

BANK OF ZAMBIA *See* QUARTERLY FINANCIAL AND STATISTICAL REVIEW - BANK OF ZAMBIA **805**

BANK OF ZAMBIA. QUARTERLY STATISTICAL REVIEW *See* QUARTERLY FINANCIAL AND STATISTICAL REVIEW - BANK OF ZAMBIA **805**

BANK OFFICERS SALARY SURVEY (US) [04795068] **775, 1654**

BANK- OG KREDITTSTATISTIKK: AKTUELLE TALL (NO/0333-1504) [08915524] **5323**

BANK OPERATIONS BULLETIN (US) [17294332] **775**

BANK OPERATIONS REPORT *See* BANK TECHNOLOGY REPORT **5087**

BANK OUTSOURCING REPORT *See* BANK AUTOMATION NEWS **1218**

BANK PEMBANGUNAN INDONESIA *See* BULLETIN EKONOMI BAPINDO **1466**

BANK PEMBANGUNAN INDONESIA *See* OPERATIONS OF BANK PEMBANGUNAN INDONESIA **802**

BANK PERSONNEL NEWS (US/0272-3271) [05858321] **775**

BANK PROTECTION BULLETIN (US/0091-0392) [01786087] **775**

BANK QUARTERLY (AUSTIN, TEX.) (US) [14083077] **776**

BANK RAKYAT INDONESIA *See* LAPORAN STATISTIK BRI **731**

BANK RATE MONITOR (US) [17150147] **776**

BANK RATES ON SHORT-TERM BUSINESS LOANS *See* SURVEY OF TERMS OF BANK LENDING MADE DURING ... **813**

BANK RESEARCH AND DEVELOPMENT REVIEW (BG) [08420174] **776**

BANK RESOLUTION REPORTER (US/1056-7232) [23829026] **776**

BANK RESOLUTION REPORTER *See* PROBLEM ASSET REPORTER **804**

BANK, SAVINGS & LOAN CD RATINGS / STANDARD & POOR'S (US) [18181601] **776**

BANK SECURITIES NEWS *See* BANK SECURITIES REPORT **776**

BANK SECURITIES REPORT (US/1071-2038) [28570134] **776**

BANK SECURITY REPORT (US/0162-7457) [04220558] **776**

BANK SYSTEMS + TECHNOLOGY (US/1045-9472) [20292408] **776**

BANK TAX REPORT, THE *CEASED.* (US/0162-7465) [02529077] **776**

BANK TECHNOLOGY NEWS (US/1060-3506) [24943225] **776**

BANK TECHNOLOGY REPORT *CEASED.* (US/1061-5555) [25355692] **5087**

BANK TELLER'S REPORT (US/0162-7473) [02251111] **776**

BANK VAN DE NEDERLANDSE ANTILLEN. RESEARCH DEPT *See* QUARTERLY BULLETIN - BANK VAN DE NEDERLANDSE ANTILLEN (CENTRAL BANK) **805**

BANK VOOR NEDERLANDSCHE GEMEENTEN, N.V *See* VERSLAG OVER HET BOEKJAAR ... **815**

BANK WAGE-HOUR AND PERSONNEL REPORT (US/0744-8767) [08619790] **1654**

BANK YISRAEL. MAHLEKET HA-MEHKAR *See* TAKTSIV LEUMI **1586**

BANK YISRAEL. MAHLEKET HA-MEHKAR *See* ECONOMIC REVIEW (JERUSALEM) **1485**

BANKA VE TICARET HUKUKU DERGISI (TU) [05792407] **3084**

BANKAKTIEBOLAGEN (SW) [20408432] **776**

●BANKENSTATISTIK / DEUTSCHE BUNDESBANK (GW/0943-8750) [28031396] **776, 726**

BANKER & BUSINESSMAN (PK) [01784294] **776**

BANKER & TRADESMAN (US/0005-5409) [03983283] **776, 4834**

BANKER (LONDON) (UK/0005-5395) [01519136] **776**

BANKER, THE (II/0522-2931) [01519137] **776**

BANKERS' ALMANAC AND YEAR BOOK, THE (UK) [07114550] **776**

BANKERS' ALMANAC WORLD RANKING, THE (UK) [11843756] **776**

BANKERS DIGEST (DALLAS, TEX.) (US/0005-5425) [03299026] **776**

BANKERS HANDBOOK FOR ASIA (HK) [03054751] **776**

BANKERS LETTER OF THE LAW, THE (US/0005-5433) [03983294] **3084**

BANKERS MAGAZINE (BOSTON), THE (US/0005-545X) [04739421] **776**

BANKERS MIDDLE MARKET LENDING LETTER (US/1046-1620) [20340213] **776**

BANKERS MONTHLY (US/0005-5476) [04901468] **776**

BANKERS
Alphabetical Title Index

●BANKERS NEWS (US/1069-5907) [28121147] **776**

BANKERS SCHOOLS DIRECTORY (US/0145-5850) [02767037] **776**

BANKER'S WORLD DIRECTORY, THE (BE/0376-6616) [01795171] **776**

BANKFACHKLASSE, DIE (GW/0170-6659) [I01706659] **776**

BANKHISTORISCHES ARCHIV (GW) [04605476] **776**

BANKING ABSTRACTS (IT) **777**

BANKING AND COMMERCIAL LENDING LAW : RESOURCE MATERIALS (US) [10214000] **3084**

BANKING & FINANCE (US) [10001992] **777**

BANKING & FINANCE LAW REVIEW (CN/0832-8722) [14968248] **3085**

BANKING & FINANCIAL REVIEW, THE (SI) [02683494] **777**

BANKING & FINANCIAL TRAINING (UK/0265-7988) [I02657988] **777**

BANKING ATTORNEY, THE (US) [24200564] **3085**

BANKING AUTOMATION BULLETIN FOR EUROPE (UK/1351-5543) [I13515543] **777**

BANKING COMPANY REPORT (US) **777**

BANKING INDUSTRY CONFERENCE (US/0162-5063) [04088621] **777**

BANKING IRELAND (IE/0791-1386) [19686665] **777**

BANKING LAW ANTHOLOGY (US/0737-2159) [09332276] **3085**

BANKING LAW BRIEFS *CEASED.* (US/1065-1004) [16977074] **3085**

BANKING LAW JOURNAL DIGEST (US/0271-6909) [05655484] **3085**

BANKING LAW JOURNAL, THE (US/0005-5506) [01519149] **3085**

BANKING LAW: NEW YORK BANKING LAW (US/0198-9251) [06240396] **3085**

BANKING LAW REPORT (US/0742-3942) [10330893] **3085**

BANKING LAW REPORTS (UK/0961-7256) [I09617256] **2939**

BANKING LAW REVIEW *CEASED.* (US/0898-7998) [17912515] **3085**

BANKING LEGISLATION IN THE CONGRESS (US/0094-7555) [01795124] **3085**

BANKING LEGISLATION IN THE ... SESSION, ... CONGRESS (US) [01681801] **3085**

BANKING POLICY REPORT (US/1059-1257) [23474567] **3085**

BANKING REGULATOR *CEASED.* (US/0892-1377) [14039912] **3085**

BANKING REPORTER *CEASED.* (US) **777**

BANKING REVIEW (LEXINGTON, MASS.) (US/0732-1732) [08303133] **777**

BANKING SAFETY DIGEST (US) 1464, **777**

BANKING SOFTWARE REVIEW *CEASED.* (US/0892-6778) [15234410] 1171, **777**

BANKING STATISTICS OF PAKISTAN (PK/0067-3811) [01774137] **726**

BANKING TECHNOLOGY (UK/0266-0865) [12297213] **777**

... BANKING TECHNOLOGY DIRECTORY, THE (US/1054-3317) [22737294] **777**

BANKING WEEK (US/0893-8873) [15714652] **777**

BANKING WORLD (UK/0737-6413) [09438807] **777**

BANKKAUFMANN *See* BANK MAGAZIN **775**

BANKO JANAKARI : A JOURNAL OF FORESTRY INFORMATION FOR NEPAL (NP/1016-0582) [17977159] **2375**

BANKOKU BUKKYOTO REMMEI *See* KIKANSHI; BANKOKU BUKKYOTO REMMEI KEN SEITO KOKUGO UNDO **5021**

BANKOKU NIHONJIN SHOKO KAIGISHO *See* KAIIN MEIBO - BANKOKU NIHONJIN SHOKO KAIGISHO. / LIST OF MEMBERS - JAPANESE CHAMBER OF COMMERCE, BANGKOK **820**

●BANKOV PREGLED / BULGARSKA NARODNA BANKA (BU/0861-6701) [26725009] **777**

BANKRISK (STAMFORD, CONN.) (US/1056-8115) [18201523] **777**

BANKRUPTCY COUNSELLOR (US) [18192049] **3085**

BANKRUPTCY COURT DECISIONS (US/0098-7336) [02241426] **3085**

BANKRUPTCY DEVELOPMENTS JOURNAL (US/0890-7862) [11404836] **3085**

BANKRUPTCY LAW HANDBOOK (US/0882-4924) [11903031] **3085**

BANKRUPTCY LAW LETTER (US/0744-7671) [07638524] **3085**

BANKRUPTCY LITIGATION INSTITUTE *See* ANNUAL BANKRUPTCY LITIGATION INSTITUTE **3084**

BANKRUPTCY STRATEGIST, THE (US/0747-8917) [10241090] **3085**

BANKRUPTCY STUDY GROUP JOURNAL *See* CALIFORNIA BANKRUPTCY JOURNAL **782**

BANKRUPTCY YEARBOOK AND ALMANAC, THE (US/1054-9463) [23031104] **777**

BANKS & FINANCIAL INSTITUTIONS IN SINGAPORE (SI) [03424184] **777**

BANKS IN INSURANCE REPORT (US/8756-6079) [14239346] **3085**

BANKS OF ARKANSAS, THE (US/0360-232X) [02244392] **777**

BANKS OF COLORADO, THE (US/0360-425X) [02244506] **777**

BANKS OF GEORGIA, THE (US/0361-4808) [02246428] **777**

BANKS OF ILLINOIS, THE (US/0360-4268) [02243833] **777**

BANKS OF INDIANA, THE (US/0360-4276) [02244507] **777**

BANKS OF IOWA, THE (US/0360-4284) [02243834] **777**

BANKS OF KANSAS (US/0361-4816) [02246423] **777**

BANKS OF KENTUCKY, THE (US/0361-4824) [02246422] **777**

BANKS OF LOUISIANA (US/0360-4292) [02244505] **777**

BANKS OF MICHIGAN, THE (US/0360-2338) [02244391] **777**

BANKS OF MINNESOTA (US/0360-4306) [02244532] **777**

BANKS OF MISSISSIPPI, THE (US/0361-4832) [02246425] **777**

BANKS OF MISSOURI, THE (US/0360-4314) [02244531] **778**

BANKS OF NEBRASKA (US/0361-4840) [02246424] **778**

BANKS OF NEW ENGLAND (US/0361-4859) [02246560] **778**

BANKS OF OHIO, THE (US/0360-2362) [02244389] **778**

BANKS OF OKLAHOMA (US/0360-2354) [02244388] **778**

BANKS OF PENNSYLVANIA (US/0360-2346) [02244390] **778**

BANKS OF TENNESSEE (US/0361-4867) [02246426] **778**

BANKS OF TEXAS *See* BANK MIDYEAR REVIEW. TEXAS **775**

BANKS OF THE CAROLINAS, THE (US/0361-4875) [02246914] **778**

BANKS OF THE WEST (US/0361-4883) [02246427] **778**

BANKS OF WISCONSIN (US/0360-4322) [02244533] **778**

BANKSZEMLE (HU) [I01330519] **778**

BANKUBA SHINPO (CN/0710-1236) [08375678] **5780**

BANNAWAG (PH) [03561568] **2502**

BANNER / CAMBRIDGE (US) **5685**

●BANNER (CUBA, ILL.), THE (US/1075-0096) [29918569] **207**

BANNER-GAZETTE, THE (US/0194-3545) [05423029] **5662**

BANNER (GRAND RAPIDS), THE (US/0005-5557) [01776378] **4937**

BANNER INDEPENDENT, THE (US) [14510643] **5699**

BANNER-JOURNAL (US) [13221817] **5765**

BANNER-NEWS, THE (US) [18434540] **5631**

BANNER OF TRUTH, THE (US/0408-4748) [02255231] **4937**

BANNER PRESS NEWSPAPER, THE (US/0891-1118) [14578862] **5747**

BANNER-PRESS, THE (US/8750-5800) [11544024] **5747**

BANO BIGGYAN PATRIKA (BG/0254-4539) [10042213] **2375**

BANQUE AFRIQUE PARIS (FR/0184-9719) [I01849719] **778**

BANQUE & DROIT PARIS (FR/0992-3233) [I09923233] **778**

BANQUE CENTRALE DES ETATS DE L'AFRIQUE DE L'OUEST *See* NOTES D'INFORMATION ET STATISTIQUES **5335**

BANQUE COMMERCIALE POUR L'EUROPE DU NORD *See* BANQUE COMMERCIALE POUR L'EUROPE DU NORD (EUROBANK) : RAPPORT **778**

BANQUE COMMERCIALE POUR L'EUROPE DU NORD (EUROBANK) : RAPPORT (FR) [12008298] **778**

BANQUE DE FRANCE *See* COMPTE RENDU / PRESENTE A MONSIEUR LE PRESIDENT DE LA REPUBLIQUE AU NOM DU CONSEIL GENERAL DE LA BANQUE DE FRANCE **784**

BANQUE DE FRANCE *See* BULLETIN TRIMESTRIEL DE LA BANQUE DE FRANCE **781**

BANQUE DE FRANCE. BULLETIN TRIMESTRIEL *See* BULLETIN DE LA BANQUE DE FRANCE **780**

BANQUE DE KINSHASA *See* RAPPORT ANNUEL DE LA BANQUE DE KINSHASA **806**

BANQUE DE LA REPUBLIQUE DU BURUNDI *See* RAPPORT ANNUEL DE LA BANQUE DE LA REPUBLIQUE DU BURUNDI **806**

BANQUE DES ETATS DE L'AFRIQUE CENTRALE *See* ETUDES ET STATISTIQUES - BANQUE DES ETATS DE L'AFRIQUE CENTRALE **728**

BANQUE DES ETATS DE L'AFRIQUE CENTRALE *See* RAPPORT D'ACTIVITE - BANQUE CENTRALE DES ETATS DE L'AFRIQUE CENTRALE **806**

BANQUE DES MOTS (PARIS) (FR/0067-3951) [01680873] **3268**

BANQUE ET INFORMATIQUE (FR) [I02470708] 1171, **778**

BANQUE INTERNATIONALE A LUXEMBOURG *See* ANNUAL REPORT / BANQUE INTERNATIONALE A LUXEMBOURG **770**

BANQUE INTERNATIONALE POUR L'AFRIQUE OCCIDENTALE *See* RAPPORT ET RESOLUTIONS DU CONSEIL D'ADMINISTRATION, RAPPORT DES COMMISSAIRES AUX COMPTES **806**

BANQUE INTERNATIONALE POUR L'AFRIQUE OCCIDENTALE *See* ORDINARY MEETING OF SHAREHOLDERS - BANQUE INTERNATIONALE POUR L'AFRIQUE OCCIDENTALE **802**

BANQUE MAROCAINE DU COMMERCE EXTERIEUR *See* MONTHLY INFORMATION REVIEW - BANQUE MAROCAINE DU COMMERCE EXTERIEUR **846**

BANQUE NATIONALE DE BELGIQUE *See* BULLETIN DE LA BANQUE NATIONALE DE BELGIQUE **780**

BANQUE NATIONALE POUR LE COMMERCE (MADAGASCAR) *See* RAPPORT ANNUEL - BANQUE NATIONALE POUR LE COMMERCE **806**

BANQUE NATIONALE POUR LE DEVELOPPEMENT INDUSTRIEL (MADAGASCAR) *See* RAPPORTS ANNUELS - BANQUE NATIONALE POUR LE DEVELOPPEMENT INDUSTRIEL **806**

BANQUE (PARIS. 1926) (FR/0005-5581) [02529101] **778**

BANQUE ROYALE DU CANADA *See* ECOINDICATEUR DE LA BANQUE ROYALE **1556**

BANQUIER (MONTREAL) (CN/0822-6849) [10451204] **778**

BANTAM'S AUSTRALIA (US/1057-7718) [22920125] **5462**

BANTAM'S BAHAMAS : A QUICK & EASY GUIDE (US) [22701502] **5462**

BANTAM'S HAWAII (US/1056-0939) [22444934] **5462**

BANTAM'S SCOTLAND (US/1057-770X) [22922645] **5462**

BANTAM'S SOVIET UNION (US/1057-7734) [22853583] **5462**

BANTHA TRACKS (US/0279-7933) [07261183] 2528, **5229**

BANTU MINING CORPORATION *See* ANNUAL REPORT - BANTU MINING CORPORATION **2133**

BANURAMA AL-KHALIJ (BA) [11334280] **2647**

BANYASZATI ES KOHASZATI LAPOK. BANYASZAT, KOOLAJ ES FOLDGAZ, KOHASZAT, ONETOEDE *See* BANYASZATI ES KOHASZATI LOPOK. KOOLAJ ES FOLDGAZ **2135**

BANYASZATI ES KOHASZATI LAPOK. KOHASZAT (HU/0005-5670) [09711151] **1654**

BANYASZATI ES KOHASZATI LAPOK. OENTOEDE (HU/0375-9504) [09713817] **2135**

BANYASZATI ES KOHASZATI LOPOK. KOOLAJ ES FOLDGAZ (HU/0572-6034) [06190331] **2135**

BANYASZATI SZAKIRODALMI TAJEKOZTATO (HU/0231-0651) [I02310651] **2135**

BAOBAB ARID LANDS INFORMATION NETWORK (UK/0966-9035) [I09669035] **2555**

●BAOBAB INTERNATIONAL (CN/1199-1844) [30673825] **2908**

BAOGAO - GUOJI LAOGONG JU. GUOJI LAOGONG DAHUI (TH/0255-3449) [I02553449] **1654**

BAOZHA YU CHONGJI (CC/1001-1455) [19890597] **4452**

BAPTIST & REFLECTOR (US) **5055**

Alphabetical Title Index — BAROQUE

BAPTIST BIBLE TRIBUNE (US/0745-5836) [01716455] **5056**

BAPTIST BIBLICAL HERITAGE (US) **4938**

BAPTIST BULLETIN, THE (US/0005-5689) [01776381] **5056**

BAPTIST CHALLENGE, THE (US/8756-9612) [11793071] **5056**

BAPTIST CONVENTION OF ONTARIO AND QUEBEC See BCOQ DIRECTORY **5056**

BAPTIST COURIER (US/0744-6985) [01776382] **5056**

BAPTIST DIGEST (US/0408-506X) [01590398] **5056**

BAPTIST GENERAL CONFERENCE See STANDARD (EVANSTON, ILL.), THE **5068**

BAPTIST HERALD, THE (US/0005-5700) [01776383] **4938**

BAPTIST HERITAGE IN ATLANTIC CANADA (CN) [06526952] **5056**

BAPTIST HERITAGE JOURNAL, THE (US/1059-5104) [24608777] **4938**

BAPTIST HISTORY AND HERITAGE (US/0005-5719) [01776384] **5056**

BAPTIST HORIZON; TELLING THE STORY OF CANADIAN SOUTHERN BAPTISTS (CN) [01776797] **5024**

BAPTIST HOSPITAL FUND BULLETIN (US/8750-2151) [10757012] **5274**

BAPTIST LEADER (PHILADELPHIA) (US/0005-5727) [01776386] **4938**

BAPTIST MESSAGE (US/0740-2104) [07385423] **5056**

BAPTIST MESSENGER (OKLAHOMA CITY, OKLA.) (US/0744-9518) [01776388] **5056**

BAPTIST PEACEMAKER (US/0735-5815) [08733449] **5056**

BAPTIST PRESS (US) **5056**

BAPTIST PROGRAM, THE (US/0005-5743) [01776392] **5056**

BAPTIST PROGRESS (US/0005-5751) [02254115] **5056**

BAPTIST PROGRESS (BROOKLYN) (US/0164-7423) [04409193] **5056**

BAPTIST QUARTERLY (LONDON) (UK/0005-576X) [01774829] **5056**

BAPTIST RECORD (JACKSON, MISS.), THE (US/0005-5778) [03983340] **5056**

BAPTIST REVIEW OF THEOLOGY, THE (CN/1192-4241) [27203115] **4938**

BAPTIST STANDARD (US) [01776395] **5056**

BAPTIST TIMES (UK/0005-5786) [06893673] **5056**

BAPTIST TRUE UNION (US/0883-7864) [12210357] **5056**

BAPTIST TRUMPET (LITTLE ROCK, ARK.) (US/0888-9074) [04605914] **5056**

BAPTIST UNION DIRECTORY, THE (UK/0302-3184) [01793687] **5056**

BAPTIST UNION OF WESTERN CANADA. B.C. AREA. ASSEMBLY See B. C. AREA ANNUAL DOCKET **5055**

BAPTIST WORLD (WASHINGTON, D.C.) (US/0005-5808) [01776400] **5056**

BAPTISTS TODAY (US/1072-7787) [25288018] **4938**

BAR ASSOCIATION OF HAWAII. ANNUAL DIRECTORY See ANNUAL DIRECTORY / HAWAII STATE BAR ASSOCIATION **2934**

BAR ASSOCIATION OF NASSAU COUNTY, N.Y See NASSAU COUNTY BAR ASSOCIATION ANNUAL DIRECTORY **3013**

BAR ASSOCIATION OF SRI LANKA See NEWS LETTER - BAR ASSOCIATION OF SRI LANKA **3017**

BAR (AUSTIN) (US/0092-3877) [01787472] **2939**

BAR: BEVERAGE ALCOHOL REPORTER (CN/0006-0348) [02009728] **2364**

BAR BRIEF (BEVERLY HILLS, CALIF.) (US/0749-0615) [11051207] **2939**

BAR BRITISH SERIES (UK/0143-3032) [05306902] **261**

BAR BULLETIN (US) [20667211] **2940**

BAR CODE REPORTER (US) 952, **1231**

BAR COUNCIL OF MAHARASHTRA See MAHARASHTRA BAR COUNCIL JOURNAL **3005**

BAR EXAMINER, THE (US/0005-5824) [02272493] **2940**

BAR HARBOR TIMES, THE (US) [25455044] **5685**

BAR INTERNATIONAL SERIES (UK/0143-3067) [05883233] **261**

BAR LEADER (US/0099-1031) [02242771] **2940**

BAR LETTER See NEVADA LAWYER **3015**

BAR LETTER - STATE BAR OF NEVADA (US/1052-4541) [20705766] 3089, **2940**

BAR NOTES (US/0546-4714) [01760555] **2940**

BAR QUARTERLY (UK/0307-8647) [02808929] **4824**

BAR REPORT (US/0271-2024) [06558204] **2940**

BAR VON BERLIN, DER (GW/0522-0033) [10484657] **231**

BARA AFRIKA (TZ) [10353466] **2647**

BARABOO NEWS REPUBLIC (US) [15091168] **5765**

BARAT REVIEW, THE (US) [02533251] **3365**

BARATAINKNAK A MAGYAR JEZSUITAK (CN/0228-9873) [08071280] **4938**

BARATARIA (US/0149-0354) [03428340] **3338**

BARBACANE, LA (FR) [05911073] **3460**

BARBADOS See BARBADOS LAW REPORTS **2940**

BARBADOS CONSOLIDATED INDEX TO STATUTES AND SUBSIDIARY LEGISLATION TO ... (BB) [12738075] **3124**

BARBADOS LAW REPORTS (BB) [08366746] **2940**

BARBADOS. MINISTRY OF FOREIGN AFFAIRS AND INTERNATIONAL TRADE See DIPLOMATIC AND CONSULAR LIST **831**

BARBADOS MUSEUM AND HISTORICAL SOCIETY See JOURNAL OF THE BARBADOS MUSEUM AND HISTORICAL SOCIETY, THE **4090**

BARBADOS MUSEUM AND HISTORICAL SOCIETY See ANNUAL REPORT **4083**

BARBADOS NATIONAL BANK See ANNUAL REPORT & STATEMENT OF ACCOUNTS / BARBADOS NATIONAL BANK **770**

BARBADOS. PUBLIC UTILITIES BOARD See PUBLIC UTILITIES ACT 1951 **4677**

BARBADOS. REGISTRATION OFFICE See REPORT ON VITAL STATISTICS & REGISTRATIONS **5337**

BARBADOS. STATISTICAL SERVICE See ABSTRACT OF STATISTICS - BARBADOS. STATISTICAL SERVICE **5320**

BARBARA BRABEC'S NATIONAL HOME BUSINESS REPORT (US/0741-5729) [10176657] **642**

BARBEQUE PLANET (US/0364-2194) [02611658] **3365**

BARBERTON HERALD (US/0890-8591) [10331424] **5727**

BARBIE BAZAAR (US/1040-094X) [18320000] **2583**

BARBIE FASHION (US/1055-940X) [22995511] **4857**

BARBIE (NEW YORK, N.Y. 1984) (US/0743-4898) [10626251] **1060**

BARBIE (NEW YORK, N.Y. 1990) (US/1055-601X) [23040498] **4857**

BARBIZON (CN/0826-5240) [11245859] **2788**

BARBOUR COMPENDIUM. BUILDING PRODUCTS (UK/0260-9169) [l02609169] **599**

BARBOUR DEMOCRAT, THE (US) [12646844] **5772**

BARCELONA. BIBLIOTECA CENTRAL. SECCION DE MUSICA See PUBLICACIONES **4148**

BARCELONA QUIRURGICA (SP/0304-4475) [I03044475] **3960**

BARCELONA (SPAIN) See GASETA MUNICIPAL **4650**

BARCLAYS BANK See REPORT & ACCOUNTS / BARCLAYS BANK PLC **807**

BARCLAYS BANK INTERNATIONAL. REPORT AND ACCOUNTS See REPORT & ACCOUNTS / BARCLAYS BANK PLC **807**

BARCLAYS BANK PLC MAURITIUS See EAGLEVIEW : THE STAFF MAGAZINE OF BARCLAYS BANK PLC MAURITIUS **788**

BARCLAYS BANK. REPORT & ACCOUNTS See REPORT & ACCOUNTS / BARCLAYS BANK PLC **807**

BARCLAYS CALIFORNIA SUPREME COURT SERVICE (US/0893-2506) [14253076] **2940**

BARCLAYS ECONOMIC REVIEW (UK/0956-5574) [19730561] 1633, **778**

BARCLAYS INSURANCE LAW REPORT (CALIFORNIA EDITION) (US) 2875, **2940**

BARCLAYS LAW LIBRARY (US/1044-0194) [19273481] **2940**

BARCLAYS UNITED STATES EIGHTH CIRCUIT SERVICE (US) [16852539] **2940**

BARCLAYS UNITED STATES NINTH CIRCUIT SERVICE (US/0893-2492) [14253378] **2940**

BARCLAYS UNITED STATES SECOND CIRCUIT SERVICE (US/1046-1337) [19991459] **2940**

BARCLAYS UNITED STATES SEVENTH CIRCUIT SERVICE (US/1045-9006) [19038490] **2940**

BARCLAYS UNITED STATES TENTH CIRCUIT SERVICE (US/0899-3475) [17016700] **2940**

BARDY, LE (CN/0381-6982) [02341700] **5229**

BAREEL (BE/0773-5618) [l07735618] **1918**

BAREI BORU MAGAJIN (JA) **4886**

BAREME DES COEFFICIENTS. SERIES 80 (FR) **599**

BAREME DES COEFFICIENTS. SERIES 85 (FR) **600**

BARGAIN BOOK, THE (US/0737-1373) [09297817] **2788**

BARGAIN HUNTERS AND BUDGETEERS OPPORTUNITY NEWSLETTER (US/1053-2021) [22473921] **1293**

●BARGAIN HUNTERS GUIDE. ATLANTA/ATHENS AREA (US/1060-7722) [25060929] **824**

BARGAINING CALENDAR / U.S. DEPARTMENT OF LABOR, BUREAU OF LABOR STATISTICS (US) [04763148] **1655**

BARKER TEXAS HISTORY CENTER SERIES (US) [05961930] **2611**

BARKER, THE (US/1043-0849) [19295167] **5505**

●BARLEY COUNTRY (CN/1188-8911) [26776160] **65**

BARLEY GENETICS NEWSLETTER (US/1043-5174) [01640712] **200**

BARLEY NEWSLETTER **CEASED.** (US) [05515417] **200**

BARN OCH KULTUR (SW/0037-6477) [02085722] **3193**

BARNA REPORT, THE (US/1063-1437) [25507371] **4938**

BARNAMAJ AL-ISTITHMAR AL-THULATHI LIL-AM ... / JUMHURIYAT AL-SUDAN AL-DIMUQRATIYAH, WIZARAT AL-TAKHTIT AL-QAWMI (SJ) [09457303] **1548**

BARNARD BULLETIN (US/0005-6014) [03983353] **1089**

BARNARD OCCASIONAL PAPERS ON WOMEN'S ISSUES. BARNARD COLLEGE WOMEN'S CENTER, THE **CEASED.** (US) [21058075] **5551**

BARNARD'S RETAIL MARKETING REPORT (US/0882-6218) [11902958] **861**

BARNBOKEN (SW/0347-772X) [I0347772X] **3365**

BARNER FAMILY NEWSLETTER, THE (US/0735-8695) [08403071] **2438**

BARNES ASSOCIATES See BARNES ASSOCIATES NATIONAL FUND RAISER **4334**

BARNES ASSOCIATES NATIONAL FUND RAISER (US/0272-0825) [06753878] **4334**

BARNES BULLETIN See BARNES BULLETIN 2.0 **2438**

●BARNES BULLETIN 2.0 (US/1062-6859) [25696512] **2438**

BARNES FUND RAISER See BARNES ASSOCIATES NATIONAL FUND RAISER **4334**

BARNESBORO STAR, THE (US) [02258183] **5734**

BARNESVILLE RECORD-REVIEW, THE (US) [01519204] **5694**

●BARNEY MAGAZINE (US/1075-217X) [29968594] **1060**

BARNHART DICTIONARY COMPANION, THE (US/0736-1122) [08460343] **1923**

BARNOMSORGEN I SIFFROR (SW) [10024940] **5274**

BARNSTABLE PATRIOT (US/0744-7221) [08515060] **5687**

●BARNSTORMER (FORT WAYNE, IND.), THE (US/1062-7413) [25723676] **14**

BARNWELL PEOPLE-SENTINEL, THE (US) [27892697] **5741**

BAROMETER OF SMALL BUSINESS (US/0045-1568) [01681942] **642**

BAROMETER (PORTLAND) (US/0511-8255) [05518069] **2399**

BAROMETRE PORC (FR/0154-5752) [I01545752] 2328, **207**

BAROMFITENYESZTES ES FELDOLGOZAS (HU/0133-011X) [03765755] **207**

BARON REPORT See COOK POLITICAL REPORT **4470**

BARON'S MICROCOMPUTING REPORTS (US/0746-598X) [09917748] **1265**

BAROQUE (MONTAUBAN) (FR/0067-4222) [02436251] 2843, **3365**

BARQUE'S PAKISTAN TRADE DIRECTORY AND WHC'S WHO (PK/0083-9671) [02340362] **824**

BARRE GAZETTE (BARRE, MASS. : 1839) (US) [09249041] **5687**

BARRETT TRANSPORTATION NEWSLETTER (US/0883-1777) [12191765] **5377**

BARRHAVEN INDEPENDENT (CN/0846-0396) [23454598] **5780**

BARRICADA INTERNACIONAL (ENGLISH ED.) (NQ/1013-9567) [09746287] **2511**

BARRIE PUBLIC LIBRARY *See* B P L BEEP, THE **3193**

BARRINGTON TIMES (US) [25362832] **5741**

BARRIO (WASHINGTON, D.C.), EL (US/0276-7902) [07423467] **2256**

BARRISTER (CHICAGO) (US/0094-5277) [01792273] **2940**

BARRISTER LAW JOURNAL (US) **2940**

BARRISTER (PHILADELPHIA, PA.), THE (US/0739-2494) [09693664] **2940**

BARRISTER, THE (NR/0331-0086) [05360532] **2940**

BARRISTER (UNIVERSITY OF MIAMI. SCHOOL OF LAW) (US/0408-6007) [02254954] **2940**

BARRISTERS BULLETIN (PH/0116-8657) [24171770] **2940**

BARRISTERS NEWSLETTER (US/0883-8682) [12234257] **2940**

BARROCO (BL/0525-5708) [01629701] **316**

BARRON FAMILY NEWSLETTER, THE (US/0882-8202) [11990649] **2438**

BARRON'S 300 BEST BUYS IN COLLEGE EDUCATION (US) [21908531] **1811**

● BARRON'S (CHICOPEE, MASS.) (US/1077-8039) [29933161] 892, **642**

BARRON'S EDUCATIONAL SERIES, INC *See* BARRON'S REGENTS EXAMS AND ANSWERS: 11TH YEAR MATHEMATICS **3497**

BARRON'S EDUCATIONAL SERIES, INC *See* BARRON'S REGENTS EXAMS AND ANSWERS : FRENCH LEVEL 3, COMPREHENSIVE FRENCH **3268**

BARRON'S EDUCATIONAL SERIES, INC *See* BARRON'S QUESTIONS AND ANSWERS. COMPREHENSIVE ENGLISH, 3 AND 4 **3268**

BARRON'S EDUCATIONAL SERIES, INC *See* BARRON'S REGENTS EXAMS AND ANSWERS : CHEMISTRY **962**

BARRON'S EDUCATIONAL SERIES, INC *See* BARRON'S REGENTS EXAMS AND ANSWERS, 9TH YEAR MATHEMATICS, ELEMENTARY ALGEBRA **3496**

BARRON'S EDUCATIONAL SERIES, INC *See* BARRON'S REGENTS EXAMS AND ANSWERS: 10TH YEAR MATHEMATICS **3496**

BARRON'S EDUCATIONAL SERIES, INC *See* BARRON'S REGENTS EXAMS AND ANSWERS : BUSINESS MATHEMATICS **642**

BARRON'S EDUCATIONAL SERIES, INC *See* BARRON'S REGENTS EXAMS AND ANSWERS : SPANISH LEVEL 3, COMPREHENSIVE SPANISH **3268**

BARRON'S GUIDE TO GRADUATE BUSINESS SCHOOLS (US/1043-190X) [11315242] 1811, **642**

BARRON'S GUIDE TO LAW SCHOOLS (US/1062-2489) [09144347] 2940, **1811**

BARRON'S HOW TO PREPARE FOR COLLEGE ENTRANCE EXAMINATIONS, SAT / [BY] SAMUEL C. BROWNSTEIN [AND] MITCHEL WEINER (US) [05879062] **1811**

BARRON'S MARKET LABORATORY (US/0363-1273) [02401015] **892**

BARRON'S NATIONAL BUSINESS AND FINANCIAL WEEKLY (US/0005-6073) [05344526] 892, **642**

BARRON'S PROFILES OF AMERICAN COLLEGES : DESCRIPTIONS OF THE COLLEGES / COMPILED AND EDITED BY THE COLLEGE DIVISION OF BARRON'S EDUCATIONAL SERIES (US) [24097478] **1811**

BARRON'S QUESTIONS AND ANSWERS. COMPREHENSIVE ENGLISH, 3 AND 4 (US/0191-3484) [04840204] 1727, **3268**

BARRON'S REGENTS EXAMS AND ANSWERS, 9TH YEAR MATHEMATICS, ELEMENTARY ALGEBRA (US/0362-1413) [02303849] **3496**

BARRON'S REGENTS EXAMS AND ANSWERS: 10TH YEAR MATHEMATICS (US/0191-3425) [04841065] 1727, **3496**

BARRON'S REGENTS EXAMS AND ANSWERS: 11TH YEAR MATHEMATICS (US/0146-406X) [02941877] **3497**

BARRON'S REGENTS EXAMS AND ANSWERS : BUSINESS MATHEMATICS (US/0362-0670) [02441498] 1727, 3497, **642**

BARRON'S REGENTS EXAMS AND ANSWERS : CHEMISTRY (US/0147-7374) [03220971] **962**

BARRON'S REGENTS EXAMS AND ANSWERS : FRENCH LEVEL 3, COMPREHENSIVE FRENCH (US/0146-6895) [03007010] **3268**

BARRON'S REGENTS EXAMS AND ANSWERS : SPANISH LEVEL 3, COMPREHENSIVE SPANISH (US/0191-3409) [04840324] 1727, **3268**

BARR'S POST CARD NEWS (US/0744-4540) [08275701] **1144**

BARRUTIK (SP) **226**

BARRY BERNDES' ANNUAL EDITION OF SAN DIEGO GUIDE (US/0145-8345) [02826877] **5462**

BARRY COUNTY ADVERTISER (US/0194-1542) [05355647] **5702**

BARRY FAIN'S PRIVATE BLUE BOOK OF GUN VALUES (US/0273-2874) [07043569] **4037**

BARTENDER (US/0199-8404) [06206641] **2364**

BARTH KARL GESAMTAUSGABE (SZ) **5056**

BARTLESVILLE EXAMINER-ENTERPRISE (US/0883-7015) [12185655] **5731**

BARTLETTIA : NOTES FROM THE MATTHAEI BOTANICAL GARDENS OF THE UNIVERSITY OF MICHIGAN (US) [06677971] 1811, **501**

BARTON BULLETIN OF THE BARTON HISTORICAL SOCIETY, INC, THE (US/0882-0791) [11695309] **2438**

BARTON COUNTY GENEALOGICAL SOCIETY QUARTERLY (US/1042-671X) [19031060] **2438**

BARTONIA (US/0198-7356) [01519222] **501**

BARUKAN SHO AJIA KENKYU (JA) [03754074] **2677**

BARWAL DAHLIA FARM *See* PRICE LIST / BARWAL DAHLA FARM **2428**

BASA : PUBLICACION DEL COLEGIO OFICIAL DE ARQUITECTOS DE CANARIAS (SP) [17631725] **293**

BASE (BERKELEY, CALIF.) (US/0732-7706) [08426653] **5087**

BASE DE DONNEES ECONOMIQUES, FINANCIERES ET SOCIALES RESEDA (FR/0242-2921) [07942198] **65**

BASE LINE (GOLDEN, COLO.) (US/0272-8532) [06957023] **2580**

BASE METAL CONCENTRATES (UK/0953-9794) [I09539794] **3998**

BASE METALS MONTHLY (UK/0964-7686) [I09647686] **3998**

BASE OILS REPORT. FAX SERVICE (UK) **4252**

BASE REPORT: BUDGETING, ACCOUNTABILITY, AND STAFFING EVALUATION, PERSONNEL (US/0199-963X) [06281042] **938**

BASEBALL BULLETIN *CEASED.* (US/0199-0128) [05515382] **4886**

BASEBALL CARD NEWS (US/0746-7966) [10287824] **2771**

BASEBALL CARD PRICE GUIDE MONTHLY (US/0896-7563) [17282460] **2771**

BASEBALL CARD PRICE GUIDE MONTHLY *See* SPORTS CARD PRICE GUIDE MONTHLY **4922**

BASEBALL CARD UPDATE (US/1058-0433) [24185589] 4886, **2771**

BASEBALL CARDS (US/8750-5851) [08398831] 4886, **2771**

BASEBALL CASE BOOK (US/0270-4218) [05216331] **4886**

BASEBALL DIGEST (US/0005-609X) [02790154] **4886**

BASEBALL GUIDE (US) [21216809] **4886**

BASEBALL HOBBY NEWS *CEASED.* (US/0199-946X) [06324665] 4886, **2771**

BASEBALL MAGAZINE (BELLEVILLE, ILL.) (US/1057-235X) [23982094] **4886**

BASEBALL (MONTREAL) (CN/0821-4123) [09547396] **4886**

BASEBALL QUARTERLY REVIEWS (US/1066-2448) [15651816] **4886**

BASEBALL RESEARCH JOURNAL (US/0734-6891) [08813478] **4886**

BASEBALL RULE BOOK. NATIONAL FEDERATION EDITION (US/0270-1537) [06228194] **4886**

BASEBALL RULES *See* BASEBALL RULE BOOK. NATIONAL FEDERATION EDITION **4886**

BASEBALL'S FORGOTTEN HEROES (US) [11795860] 4886, **430**

BASEHOR SENTINEL (US) [12090158] **5674**

BASELINE DATA REPORT (US/0739-6279) [09420658] **4632**

BASELINE LONDON (UK/0954-9226) [I09549226] **4564**

BASELINE, THE (CN/0229-3471) [08070961] **4886**

BASENJI, THE (US/0094-9744) [01795828] **4285**

BASES PARIS (FR/0765-1325) [I07651325] 1253, **1274**

BASES (SAO PAULO, BRAZIL) (BL/0260-6739) [07902340] **2551**

BASF AGRICULTURAL NEWS (GW/0930-0430) [I09300430] **65**

BASF-STUDIE (GW/0170-5911) [04122043] **2859**

BASH MAGAZINE, THE *CEASED.* (US/0740-5197) [19368158] **3979**

BASI RAZIONALI DELLA TERAPIA *See* G & B : GIORNALE DI CLINIA MEDICA & BASI RAZIONALI DELLA TERAPIA **3578**

BASIC 2 REPORT (US) **1127**

BASIC AND APPLIED MYOLOGY : BAM (IT/1120-9992) [25366289] **3803**

BASIC AND CLINICAL ASPECTS OF NEUROSCIENCE (GW/0941-9772) [19584712] **3828**

BASIC AND CLINICAL BIOSTATISTICS (US/1045-5523) [20156270] 443, **476**

BASIC AND CLINICAL CARDIOLOGY (US/0731-1672) [08124599] **3699**

BASIC AND CLINICAL ENDOCRINOLOGY (US/0277-7886) [07257284] **3726**

BASIC & CLINICAL IMMUNOLOGY (US/0891-2076) [09543694] **3667**

BASIC AND CLINICAL IMMUNOLOGY (NEW YORK) (US/0195-4261) [05518868] **3667**

BASIC AND CLINICAL NUTRITION (US/0270-4978) [06455328] **4187**

● BASIC AND CLINICAL ONCOLOGY (US/1073-0028) [29186471] **3809**

BASIC BIBLIOGRAPHIES FOR EDUCATORS IN HEALTH (US) [05024433] **4809**

BASIC DATA ON SEALANTS IN SELECTED EUROPEAN COUNTRIES (UK) **3475**

BASIC DATA SERIES. GROUND-WATER RELEASE (US/0160-9548) [02256427] **5531**

BASIC DOCUMENTS (SZ/0512-3003) [02253950] **4768**

BASIC DRUG LIST (US/0361-8900) [02441149] **4293**

BASIC EDUCATION (WASHINGTON, D.C.) (US/0196-4984) [05522695] **1727**

BASIC EDUCATIONAL OPPORTUNITY GRANT PROGRAM HANDBOOK (US/0190-7360) [02653765] **1727**

BASIC ENERGY STATISTICS. MAGNETIC TAPE (FR) **1933**

BASIC FACTS ABOUT CORRECTIONS IN CANADA (CN/0821-0594) [09241369] **3158**

BASIC FACTS ABOUT THE UNITED NATIONS (US/0067-4419) [06623612] **3124**

BASIC GRANTS (US/0744-0960) [07909397] **1811**

BASIC HISTOLOGY (US/0891-2106) [09654272] **532**

BASIC INFORMATION FOR INDUSTRIALISTS (AT) [08299667] 1599, **892**

BASIC INSTRUMENTS AND SELECTED DOCUMENTS. SUPPLEMENT / GENERAL AGREEMENTS ON TARIFFS AND TRADE (SZ/0072-0623) [01564993] **1633**

BASIC INVESTMENT & INDUSTRY DATA SHELF (US) [09129101] **892**

BASIC LIFE SCIENCES (US/0090-5542) [01780776] **443**

BASIC MICROBIOLOGY *CEASED.* (US/0194-0163) [04066975] **560**

BASIC PAPER - PARLIAMENT OF THE COMMONWEALTH OF AUSTRALIA, LEGISLATIVE RESEARCH SERVICE, DEPARTMENT OF THE PARLIAMENTARY LIBRARY (AT/0726-3406) [16713720] **4632**

BASIC PETROLEUM DATA BOOK (WASHINGTON, D.C. : 1981) (US/0730-5621) [07199063] **4252**

● BASIC REPORTS (UK/0966-9175) [I09669175] **4037**

BASIC REPORTS ON EUROPEAN ARMS CONTROL *See* BASIC REPORTS **4037**

BASIC RESEARCH IN CARDIOLOGY (GW/0300-8428) [01787571] **3699**

BASIC ROAD STATISTICS (UK) [04846179] **5400**

BASIC SCIENCE AND TECHNOLOGY STATISTICS (FR) [24448595] **5087**

BASIC STATE PLAN AND ANNUAL PROGRAM (US/0095-361X) [01796504] **3193**

BASIC STATISTICAL DATA OF NEW JERSEY SCHOOL DISTRICTS (US) [06857047] 1727, **1793**

Alphabetical Title Index — BAY

BASIC STATISTICS OF THE COMMUNITY (BE/0081-4873) [01158662] **5323**

BASICALLY BUCKLES **CEASED.** (US/1044-775X) [19899623] **2771**

BASICS OF SWAPS (US/1060-8362) [24244486] **892**

BASILIAN ANNALS, THE (CN/0316-9030) [02247416] **5024**

BASILIAN FATHERS See BASILIAN ANNALS, THE **5024**

BASILISCO (OVIEDO, SPAIN) (SP/0210-0088) [07849172] 2843, **4342**

BASIN BIBLIOGRAPHY (OLYMPIA) (US/0092-0355) [05640710] **5549**

BASIN RESEARCH (UK/0950-091X) [15253315] **1366**

BASIR (PK) [02239399] **5042**

BASIS (IO/0005-6138) [03776329] **2647**

BASIS AND RATES OF TAXES FOR FISCAL YEAR ... (US) [08599978] **4713**

BASIS-METAALINDUSTRIE / CENTRAAL BUREAU VOOR DE STATISTIEK, HOOFDAFDELING STATISTIEKEN VAN INDUSTRIE EN BOUWNIJVERHEID (NE/0168-3020) [11877049] 1599, **3998**

BASIT. AL-BASIT (SP) [07321553] **2677**

BASKET-BALL (FR/0755-7337) [I07557337] **4886**

BASKET BITS (US) **370**

BASKETBALL BULLETIN, THE (US/0094-9175) [01795539] **4886**

BASKETBALL CASE BOOK (US/0525-4663) [01791750] **4886**

BASKETBALL DIGEST (US/0098-5988) [02242218] **4886**

BASKETBALL FORECAST (US/0160-5747) [03698903] **4887**

BASKETBALL MONTHLY See BASKETBALL NEWS **4887**

BASKETBALL NEWS (UK) **4887**

BASKETBALL OFFICIALS MANUAL (US/0270-4226) [05273410] **4887**

BASKETBALL RULES SIMPLIFIED AND ILLUSTRATED ... FOR OFFICIALS, COACHES, PLAYERS, SPECTATORS (US/0737-5212) [09387384] **4887**

BASKETBALL TIMES (US/0744-2866) [08159008] **4887**

BASKETBALL WEEKLY (US/00C5-6170) [03984889] **4887**

BASKETMAKER (WESTLAND, MICH.) (US/0897-3458) [17542090] **370**

BASLER BEITRAEGE ZUR CHIRURGIE (SZ/1013-7459) [20042626] **3960**

BASLER BEITRAEGE ZUR GEOGRAPHIE (SZ/0067-4486) [03407561] **2556**

BASLER BEITRAGE ZUR ETHNOLOGIE (SZ/0067-4478) [02356648] **231**

BASLER JAHRBUCH FUER HISTORISCHE MUSIKPRAXIS : EINE VEROFFENTLICHUNG DER SCHOLA CANTORUM BASILIENSIS AN DER MUSIK-AKADEMIE DER STADT BASEL (SZ) [04818899] **4102**

BASLER LEHRBUCHER (SZ/1019-6242) [I10196242] **3497**

BASLER STUDIEN ZUR DEUTSCHEN SPRACHE UND LITERATUR (SZ/0067-4508) [01519236] 3365, **3268**

BASLER UND BERNER STUDIEN ZUR HISTORISCHEN UND SYSTEMATISCHEN THEOLOGIE (SZ) [05003064] **4938**

BASLER VEROFFENTLICHUNGEN ZUR GESCHICHTE DER MEDIZIN UND DER BIOLOGIE (SZ/0067-4524) [02254116] **3555**

BASLER ZAHLENSPIEGEL (SZ/0303-4380) [01793952] **1548**

BASLER ZEITSCHRIFT FUER GESCHICHTE UND ALTERTUMSKUNDE (SZ/0067-4540) [02361677] **2677**

●BASS & WALLEYE BOATS (US) [30808492] **4869**

BASS MASTER MAGAZINE (US/0199-3291) [02242219] **2297**

BASS (NEW YORK, N.Y.) (US/0742-0609) [10248969] **2297**

BASS PLAYER (US/1050-785X) [21590167] **4102**

BASS PLAYER QUARTERLY (US/0734-0206) [08652505] **4102**

BASSIN' (US/0884-4739) [12382486] 591, **2297**

BASTA! (CHICAGO, ILL.) **CEASED.** (US/1053-8631) [15114010] **4938**

BASTERIA (NE/0005-6219) [02052995] **5577**

BASTROP ADVERTISER AND COUNTY NEWS, THE (US) [13943971] **5747**

BASTROP DAILY ENTERPRISE, THE (US) [17499849] **5683**

BAT RESEARCH NEWS (US/0005-6227) [07974304] **5577**

BATAS AT KATARUNGAN (PH) [09165546] **2940**

BATATINHA : RESUMOS INFORMATIVOS (BL) [06567863] **2410**

BATAVIA ACADEMICA : BULLETIN VAN DE NEDERLANDSE WERKGROEP UNIVERSITEITSGESCHIEDENIS **CEASED.** (NE/0168-7212) [13857639] **1811**

BATCHELDER REVIEW (US/0897-7429) [17609830] **2438**

BATEAUX (FR) **591**

BATEMAN DATUM (US/0741-7632) [10187717] **2438**

BATES COUNTY NEWS-HEADLINER, THE (US/0746-1569) [09817529] **5702**

BATESVILLE GUARD (US) [22228444] **5631**

BATH & KITCHEN MARKETER **CEASED.** (CN/0225-9206) [06183488] 2603, **2898**

BATH COUNTY NEWS-OUTLOOK (US) [14396113] **5679**

BATH HISTORY (UK) [20311370] **2677**

BATHROOMS (UK/0950-0197) [I09500197] **600**

BATHS SERVICE AND RECREATION MANAGEMENT See IBRM **2807**

BATI HIGH TECH MAGAZINE (FR/1148-8859) [I11488859] **600**

BATIMENT, BATIR, LE **SUSPENDED.** (FR/0395-9376) [02245194] **600**

BATIMENT CFE See CFE BATIMENT **2038**

BATON ROUGE DAILY NEWS (US/1044-3630) [19759966] **5683**

BATON ROUGE KIDS (US/1050-8708) [21664265] **1060**

BATON ROUGE, LE (US) **2438**

BATON TWIRLING RULES AND REGULATIONS (US/0361-221X) [02246465] **383**

BATS (AUSTIN, TEX.) (US/1049-0043) [21104913] **2188**

BATTALION (COLLEGE STATION, TEX. 1893), THE (US/1055-4726) [14108790] **1089**

BATTELLE MEMORIAL INSTITUTE See ANNUAL REPORT / BATTELLE MEMORIAL INSTITUTE **5084**

BATTELLE ON AUTOMATED BANKING IN EUROPE (UK) **778**

BATTELLE TODAY (US/0145-8477) [02600402] **5087**

BATTERIES INTERNATIONAL (UK/0957-9249) [22618087] **2036**

BATTERIES (NEW YORK) (US/0146-3969) [02926397] **4398**

BATTERY AND EV TECHNOLOGY NEWS (US) **5087**

BATTERY MAN (US/0005-6359) [01519256] **1933**

BATTEUR MAGAZINE (FR/0981-8936) [I09818936] **4102**

BATTLE CREEK LABOR MARKET REVIEW See BATTLE CREEK'S LABOR MARKET NEWS **1655**

●BATTLE CREEK'S LABOR MARKET NEWS (US) [25950159] **1655**

BATTLE LAKE REVIEW (US) [01519257] **5694**

BATTLE MOUNTAIN BUGLE (US) [13776362] **5713**

BATTLEFORD TELEGRAPH (CN/0226-6377) [06473580] **5780**

BAU (SZ) **600**

BAU, UM (AU/0256-2529) [I02562529] **293**

BAUANALYSIS (GW/0340-0271) [01795579] **600**

BAUBRIEFE LANDWIRTSCHAFT (GW) **65**

BAUDETTE REGION, THE (US) [01519260] **5694**

BAUEN / ALTHAUS MODERNISIERUNG (GW) **600**

BAUEN FUER DIE LANDWIRTSCHAFT (ZEITSCHRIFT) (GW/0171-7952) [04868284] 65, **600**

BAUEN IN BETON (GW/0930-0252) [18633746] **600**

BAUEN IN STAHL (SZ/0255-3104) [I02553104] **293**

BAUEN MIT HOLZ (GW/0005-6545) [02353109] 293, **600**

BAUEN + [I.E. UND] FERTIGHAUS (GW) [01794470] **600**

BAUER FINANCIAL REPORTS OF ALL BANKS & THRIFTS (US) **778**

BAUERN-ECHO (SZ) [04017841] **65**

BAUERNHAUSER DER SCHWEIZ, DIE (SZ) **293**

BAUFORUM (AU) [02353156] **600**

BAUINGENIEUR, DER (GW/0005-6650) [01519262] 600, **2019**

BAUMEISTER (GW/0005-674X) [01519264] **293**

BAUPHYSIK (GW/0171-5445) [06263236] **2019**

BAUPLANUNG-BAUTECHNIK **CEASED.** (GW/0005-6758) [09726913] 600, **293**

BAURECHT (SZ/1017-0588) [08868407] **2940**

BAUSTATISTIK. GERATEBESTAND IM HOCH- U. TIEFBAU AM ... (AU) [11652953] 600, **632**

BAUSTOFF UMSCHAU (GW/0343-5903) [08864063] **1599**

BAUSTOFFINDUSTRIE. AUSGABE A : PRIMARBAUSTOFFE (SZ/0323-4886) [02576332] **600**

BAUSTOFFINDUSTRIE. AUSGABE B: BAUELEMENTE (GW/0323-3057) [02576343] **1599**

BAUTATIGKEIT UND WOHNUNGEN. REIHE 3: BESTAND AN WOHNUNGEN, FORTGESCHRIEBENE ERGEBNISSE (GW) [03645259] **2815**

BAUTECHNIK, DIE (GW) [01519268] **2019**

BAUTECHNIK, DIE (GW) [05902574] **293**

BAUTENSCHUTZ + BAUSANIERUNG (GW/0170-9267) [11308845] **600**

BAUVERWALTUNG (GW/0005-6847) [05260076] 600, **4632**

BAUVORAUSSCHAETZUNG (GW) [01798767] **600**

BAUWELT (BERLIN, GERMANY : WEST : 1952) (GW/0005-6855) [08115903] **293**

BAUWIRTSCHAFT, DIE (GW) [01790369] **600**

BAUWIRTSCHAFT (HAUPTVERBAND DER DEUTSCHEN BAUINDUSTRIE) (GW/0341-3810) [08273582] **600**

BAUWIRTSCHAFT UND BAUTATIGKEIT IN NORDRHEIN-WESTFALEN (GW) [02474462] **5323**

BAUWIRTSCHAFTLICHE INFORMATIONEN / BETRIEBSWIRTSCHAFTLICHES INSTITUT DER WESTDEUTSCHEN BAUINDUSTRIE (GW/0721-6173) [20512378] **600**

BAUZEITUNG (GW/0005-6871) [03011395] **600**

BAV RUNDBRIEF (GW/0405-5497) [06102823] **393**

BAVARIA (GERMANY) See ALLGEMEINES MINISTERIALBLATT DER BAYERISCHEN STAATSREGIERUNG, DES BAYERISCHEN MINISTERPRASIDENTEN, DER BAYERISCHEN STAATSKANZLEI, DES BAYERISCHEN STAATSMINISTERIUMS DER INNERN **4462**

BAVARIA (GERMANY). STAATSMINISTERIUM FUR ARBEIT UND SOZIALORDNUNG See AMTSBLATT DES BAYERISCHEN STAATSMINISTERIUMS FUER ARBEIT UND SOZIALORDNUNG **3144**

BAVARIA (GERMANY). STAATSMINISTERIUM FUR UNTERRICHT UND KULTUS See PROGNOSE ZUM LEHRERBEDARF IN BAYERN **1869**

BAVARIA (GERMANY). STAATSMINISTERIUM FUR UNTERRICHT UND KULTUS. SCHULVERZEICHNIS: REALSCHULEN, GYMNASIEN, GESAMTSCHULEN, KOLLEGS See SCHULVERZEICHNIS ... REALSCHULEN, ABENDREALSCHULEN, WIRTSCHAFTSSCHULEN, FACHOBERSCHULEN, GYMNASIEN, ABENDGYMNASIEN, GESAMTSCHULEN, KOLLEGS **1782**

BAVARIA. STAATSMINISTERIUM DER FINANZEN See AMTSBLATT DES BAYERISCHEN STAATSMINISTERIUMS DER FINANZEN **4709**

BAVARIO. STAATSMINISTERIUM FUR ERNAHRUNG, LANDWIRTSCHAFT UND FORSTEN. ABTEILUNG LANDLICHE NEUORDNUNG DURCH FLURBEREINIGUNG See PRAMIERUNG VON FLURBEREINIGUNGEN **121**

BAXLEY NEWS-BANNER, THE (US) [20412884] **5652**

BAXTER (US) **1633**

BAXTER BULLETIN (US/0745-7707) [09434950] **5631**

BAXTER SPRINGS CITIZEN (US/0455-6000) [10529681] **5674**

BAXTER'S EURAILPASS TRAVEL GUIDE (US/0146-8707) [03083920] 5462, **5429**

BAY & DELTA YACHTSMAN (US/0191-4731) [04935159] **591**

BAY AREA COMPUTER CURRENTS (US/8756-0046) [11457036] **1171**

BAY — Alphabetical Title Index

BAY AREA CONSUMERS' CHECKBOOK (US/0730-9376) [08080958] **1293**

BAY AREA GUILD NEWSLETTER (US) **2940**

BAY AREA PAGAN ASSEMBLIES NEWSLETTER See PAGAN MUSE & WORLD REPORT **4186**

BAY AREA REPORTER : B.A.A (US) [26378505] 2793, **5633**

BAY AREA REVIEW COURSE, INC See EVIDENCE **2968**

BAY AREA REVIEW COURSE, INC See CIVIL PROCEDURE **3089**

BAY AREA REVIEW COURSE, INC See TRUSTS **3066**

BAY AREA REVIEW COURSE, INC See CRIMINAL PROCEDURE **3106**

BAY AREA REVIEW COURSE, INC See PROFESSIONAL RESPONSIBILITY **3032**

BAY AREA REVIEW COURSE, INC See WILLS **3119**

BAY AREA REVIEW COURSE, INC See CRIMINAL LAW (LOS ANGELES, CALIF.) **3106**

BAY AREA REVIEW COURSE, INC See CONFLICTS OF LAW **2955**

BAY AREA REVIEW COURSE, INC See TORTS **3065**

BAY AREA REVIEW COURSE, INC See REMEDIES **3037**

BAY AREA REVIEW COURSE, INC See CONTRACTS **2956**

BAY AREA REVIEW COURSE, INC See CONSTITUTIONAL LAW **3092**

BAY AREA REVIEW COURSE, INC See CORPORATIONS **3099**

BAY CITY TIMES (1935) (US) [09497122] **5691**

BAY OF BENGAL NEWS (II) [12742432] **2297**

BAY PHIL, THE (US/8756-5153) [11697848] **2784**

BAY STATE BANNER (US) [06749070] **5687**

BAY STATE BUSINESS WORLD (US/0199-7858) [06157396] **642**

BAY STATE HISTORY (US) [13648889] **2722**

BAY STATE LIBRARIAN (US/0005-6944) [01519271] **3193**

BAY VIEWER, THE (US/0895-2817) [16412272] **5765**

BAY VOICE, THE (US/8750-7188) [11693271] **5691**

BAY WINDOWS (US/0883-4334) [12195107] **2793**

BAY ZIK (IS/0302-8178) [01790780] 2256, **3365**

BAYAN (BEIRUT, LEBANON : 1970) (LE) [10282347] **2875**

BAYER SYMPOSIUM (GW/0067-4672) [20779756] **443**

BAYERISCHE AKADEMIE DER WISSENSCHAFTEN. KOMMISSION FUER GEOMORPHOLOGIE See ARBEITEN AUS DER KOMMISSION FUER GEOMORPHOLOGIE DER BAYERISCHEN AKADEMIE DER WISSENSCHAFTEN **2555**

BAYERISCHE BLATTER FUER VOLKSKUNDE (GW/0720-8006) [03759182] **231**

BAYERISCHE BOTANISCHE GESELLSCHAFT ZUR ENFORSCHUNG DER HEIMISCHEN FLORA, MUNICH See BERICHTE DER BAYERISCHEN BOTANISCHEN GESELLSCHAFT ZUR ERFORSCHUNG DER HEIMISCHEN FLORA **501**

BAYERISCHE SCHULE, DIE (GW) [05119471] **1889**

BAYERISCHE STAATSGEMALDESAMMLUNGEN See JAHRESBERICHT / BAYERISCHE STAATSGEMALDESAMMLUNGEN **238**

BAYERISCHE STAATSSAMMLUNG FUR PALAONTOLOGIE UND HISTORISCHE GEOLOGIE See MITTEILUNGEN DER BAYERISCHE **4228**

BAYERISCHE VERWALTUNGSBLATTER (GW/0522-5337) [I05225337] 4632, **2940**

BAYERISCHE VORGESCHICHTSBLATTER (GW/0341-3918) [I03413918] **2677**

BAYERISCHES JAHRBUCH FUER VOLKSKUNDE (GW/0067-4729) [01519278] **2843**

BAYERISCHES LANDWIRTSCHAFTLICHES JAHRBUCH CEASED. (GW/0375-8621) [09727107] **65**

BAYERISCHES STAATSINSTITUT FUR HOCHSCHULFORSCHUNG UND HOCHSCHULPLANUNG See TATIGKEITSBERICHT - BAYERISCHES STAATSINSTITUT FUR HOCHSCHULFORSCHUNG UND HOCHSCHULPLANUNG **1849**

BAYERISCHES STATISTISCHES LANDESAMT See GEMEINDEDATEN **5327**

BAYERISCHES STATISTISCHES LANDESAMT See ZEITSCHRIFT DES BAVERISCHEN STATISTISCHEN LANDESAMTS **5347**

BAYERN IN ZAHLEN (GW/0005-7215) [05519394] **4550**

BAYERNKURIER (GW) [04045855] **5801**

BAYERNMETALL (GW) [03568672] **3998**

BAYLOR BUSINESS REVIEW (US/0739-1072) [09690941] **642**

BAYLOR COUNTY BANNER, THE (US) [14204455] **5747**

BAYLOR GEOLOGICAL STUDIES (US/0005-7266) [01519282] **1366**

BAYLOR LAW REVIEW (US/0005-7274) [01519283] **2940**

BAYLOR NURSING EDUCATOR (US/0270-7799) [06459046] **3852**

BAYREUTH (GW) [02341539] **2513**

BAYREUTHER GEOWISSENSCHAFTLICHE ARBEITEN (GW/0933-9418) [I09339418] **2556**

BAYREUTHER MATHEMATISCHE SCHRIFTEN (GW/0172-1062) [06780360] **3497**

BAYRUT AL-MASA (LE) [09788514] **2647**

BAYRUT TAYMZ (US/0888-6016) [13660552] **5633**

BAYSHORE SUN, THE (US) [17435752] **5747**

BAYSIDE TIMES (US) [11386762] **5714**

BAYSTATE REALTOR (US/0891-5539) [14970254] **4834**

BAYTOWN SUN, THE (US) [13987914] **5747**

BAYVIEWS (OAKLAND, CALIF.) (US/1045-6724) [20186416] 1060, **3193**

BAZAK GUIDE TO ISRAEL (IS) [04902544] **5462**

BAZAK GUIDE TO SPAIN (IS/0302-6221) [01793538] **5462**

BAZAR KATOWICE (PL/0866-9902) [I06669902] **4857**

BBA LIBRARY. BIOCHIMICA ET BIOPHYSICA ACTA LIBRARY (US/0067-2734) [02258201] **3193**

BBC ACORN USER (UK/0962-9475) [22466569] **1171**

● BBC ANNUAL REVIEW (UK) [30373241] **1127**

BBC CHARTER REVIEW SERIES, THE (UK) **4064**

BBC ENGLISH (UK/0263-550X) **3268**

BBC GOOD FOOD (UK/0957-588X) [I0957588X] **2328**

BBC MICRO USER See MICRO USER **1269**

BBC MUSIC (UK) [I09667180] **4102**

BBC MUSIC GUIDES (US/0084-8018) [02942657] **4102**

BBC NACHRICHTEN (GW/0005-2825) [09710251] **2036**

BBC RESEARCH DEPARTMENT REPORTS (UK) **1127**

BBC SYMPHONY ORCHESTRA See BBC SYMPHONY ORCHESTRA. [PROGRAMME] **4102**

BBC SYMPHONY ORCHESTRA. [PROGRAMME] (UK) [02167529] **4102**

BBC VIDEO WORLD. VIDEORECORDING (UK) [20313746] **4064**

BBC WILDLIFE (UK/0265-3656) [10332942] **2188**

● BBC WORLDWIDE : THE BBC WORLD SERVICE MAGAZINE (UK) [28624554] **1127**

BBI NEWSLETTER, THE (US/1049-4316) [21217942] 3555, **642**

BBL. BIBLIOTEKSBLADET (SW/0006-1867) [01532802] **3193**

BBP MANAGEMENT LETTER (US) **642**

BBR : WASSER UND ROHRBAU (GW/0937-3756) [28035308] 4760, **5531**

BBS CALLERS DIGEST (US/1055-2812) [23132732] **1274**

BB'S HEALTH WATCH (US/1056-6228) [23748321] **2596**

BBSAG BULLETIN (SZ) [06108750] **393**

● BBSRC BUSINESS (US) **3686**

BBT PERSPECTIVAS (BL) [22785286] **1548**

BC (BL) [06411195] **5192**

BC AGRICULTURE (CN/0847-1444) [21344646] **65**

BC ATHLETICS RECORD (CN/0822-9759) [11355464] **4887**

BC BIOTECHNOLOGY ALLIANCE BIOFAX (CN) **3686**

BC BUSINESS (CN/0829-481X) [19095410] **642**

● BC HEALTH AND DISEASE SURVEILLANCE (CN/1189-4199) [26621376] **4768**

BC MOUNTAINEER, THE (CN/0045-2998) [02308157] **4869**

BC OUTDOORS (CN/0045-3013) [02321290] **4869**

BC PHARMACIST (CN/0843-168X) [19585807] **4293**

BC STUDIES (CN/0005-2949) [01788002] **2722**

BC TOURISM ROOM REVENUES (CN/0846-9962) [25607947] **5462**

BC WOMAN TO WOMAN MAGAZINE (CN/0836-4796) [17314464] **5551**

BC-X - PACIFIC FOREST RESEARCH CENTRE (CN/0705-3274) [02442329] **2375**

BCA FORETRENDS (CN) **778**

BCA INTEREST RATE FORECAST (CN/0849-1364) [22632147] **778**

BCA NEWS (NEW YORK, N.Y.) (US/0005-2841) [08860628] 316, **642**

BCATA JOURNAL FOR ART TEACHERS (1979) (CN/0710-0744) [08143911] 1889, **343**

BCATML NEWSLETTER, THE (CN/0229-0235) [07817539] **3268**

BCBA NEWS / BUCKS COUNTY BAR ASSOCIATION (US) [08941418] **2940**

BCDISCOVERY (BRITISH COLUMBIA. DISCOVERY FOUNDATION) See DISCOVERY NEWS **3478**

BCE. BOLETIN DE DERECHO DE LAS COMUNIDADES EUROPEAS CEASED. (SP/0213-6945) [I02136945] 2940, **4516**

BCEI RECHERCHES (CN/1183-4412) [25314061] **1811**

BCG NEWSLETTER BOLTON (UK/0144-588X) [I0144588X] **4084**

BCGEU NEWS & VIEWS (CN/0710-5703) [08774100] **1655**

BCIRA ABSTRACTS OF INTERNATIONAL LITERATURE ON METAL CASTINGS PRODUCTION (UK/0268-3393) [13706694] **3998**

BCLA REPORTER (CN/0005-2876) [01537216] **3193**

BCOQ DIRECTORY (CN/0849-3103) [23238155] **5056**

BCPC MONOGRAPH (UK) [25344858] **164**

BCRA QUARTERLY : A REVIEW OF PUBLISHED LITERATURE ON COAL, COKA AND ALLIED TOPICS (UK) [18077993] 2135, **2002**

BCRA REVIEW See BCRA QUARTERLY : A REVIEW OF PUBLISHED LITERATURE ON COAL, COKA AND ALLIED TOPICS **2002**

BCS EDUCATIONAL YEARBOOK See EDUCATIONAL YEARBOOK **1893**

BCS UPDATE (US/1041-4770) [18778279] **1171**

BCTLA REVIEWS See BOOKMARK (VANCOUVER) **3197**

BD FUR BAUSTOFFE UND BAUMASCHINEN (GW) [01788934] **2019**

BDA NEWS (UK/0961-9755) [I09619755] **1317**

BDGUIDE (US) [17673867] **4102**

BDS (CULVER CITY, CALIF.) (US/1072-1061) [28865485] **4887**

BE-HOLD (BINGHAMTON, N.Y.) (US/1075-0363) [29925032] **4367**

BE-MINHAL HA-HINUKH (IS) [01784349] **1727**

BE-OR HA-TORAH (JERUSALEM) (IS) [11058582] **5046**

BEACH CONSERVATION CEASED. (AT/0313-7872) [I03137872] **2188**

BEACH HAVEN TIMES (US) [11838343] **5709**

BEACHCOMBER, THE (US/0194-6307) [04895636] **5709**

BEACHES LEADER, THE (US/1059-647X) [08322562] 5648, **5649**

BEACHWEAR FORECAST INTERNATIONAL (UK/0266-5794) [I02665794] **1081**

BEACON (1989), THE (US/1044-4289) [19784141] **5709**

BEACON (ACTON, MASS.), THE (US/0744-7930) [08560666] **5687**

BEACON (BABYLON, N.Y.) (US) [11107069] **5714**

BEACON-FORUM (US) [14948952] **5668**

BEACON FREE PRESS (US) [18997673] **5714**

BEACON (GLACE BAY) (CN/0712-4988) [09137651] **5780**

Alphabetical Title Index — BEGROTING

BEACON HILL NEWS (SEATTLE, WASH.) (US) [13685085] **5760**

BEACON (LONDON. 1917) *See* NEW BEACON **4391**

BEACON (LONDON, ENGLAND) (UK/0005-7339) [11349829] **4342**

BEACON (PARRY SOUND) (CN/0229-6802) [08027908] **5780**

BEACON REVIEW (US/0730-5184) [08042991] **3365**

BEACON (SPIRIT LAKE, IOWA) (US/1061-4516) [16409622] **5668**

BEACON TIMES (CN/0703-2102) [05788429] **5780**

BEACON (TORONTO. 1970) (CN/0382-6384) [01604451] **4938**

BEACONSFIELD (QUEBEC) *See* BEACONSFIELD REPORTER **5780**

BEACONSFIELD REPORTER (CN/0712-3027) [08818893] **5780**

BEADS OF TRUTH (US) [03177780] **4938**

BEAGLE BUGLE (US/0745-6972) [09388075] **1060**

BEAGLE : OCCASIONAL PAPERS OF THE TERRITORY MUSEUM OF ARTS AND SCIENCES, THE (AT/0811-3653) [10861706] **232, 2843**

BEAKEN (NE/0005-738X) [02570232] **1089**

BEALE'S INDUSTRY LETTER, VANCOUVER (CN/0834-5414) [16220818] **2375**

BEALOIDEAS (IE/0332-270X) [02061331] **2318**

BEAM MODIFICATION OF MATERIALS (NE/0921-8637) [I09218637] **4433**

BEAM'S DIRECTORY OF INTERNATIONAL TOURIST EVENTS (US/1052-3723) [22267617] **5462**

BEAN COMMISSION JOURNAL, THE (US/0274-5054) [06364596] **164**

BEAN HOME NEWSLETTER, THE (US/0882-4428) [11837526] **1060**

BEAN IMPROVEMENT COOPERATIVE *See* ANNUAL REPORT OF THE BEAN IMPROVEMENT COOPERATIVE **163**

BEAN MARKET NEWS (US/1066-0607) [10660607] **921, 65**

BEAR & COMPANY (US/0275-6587) [07188920] **4938**

BEAR ESSENTIALS *CEASED.* (US) [18800125] **1889**

BEAR FACTS REVIEW (AT) 370, **2583**

BEAR NEWS (US/0885-615X) [12690270] **2188**

BEAR REPORT *See* CHICAGO BEAR REPORT **4890**

BEARTOOTH WEEKLY (US) [13242084] **5705**

BEAT (LOS ANGELES, CALIF. 1989) (US/1063-5319) [20690008] **4102**

BEATRICE DAILY SUN (US) [13412877] **5706**

BEATRIX POTTER STUDIES (UK) [19652844] **3365**

BEAU-COCOA (US/0067-4737) [01789696] **3365**

BEAU LIEU (SAINTE-PETRONILLE, QUEBEC) (CN/0823-7662) [10595560] **4632**

BEAUCE MEDIA (CN/0711-3420) [08605211] **5780**

BEAUCE NOUVELLE (CN/0844-2665) [19603592] **5780**

BEAUFORT GAZETTE, THE (US) [26677653] **5741**

BEAUFORT MAGAZINE (US) **2528**

BEAUFORTIA (NE/0067-4745) [01519298] **5577**

BEAUMONT ENTERPRISE (US) [13163142] **5747**

BEAUREGARD DAILY NEWS (US) [17430699] **5683**

BEAUTIFUL BRITISH COLUMBIA (CN/0005-7460) [01776970] **5462**

BEAUTIFUL GLASS FOR HOME & OFFICE *SUSPENDED.* (US/1043-5468) [19483885] 600, **2586**

BEAUTIFUL HOME PLANS (US/0278-8810) [07889435] **293**

BEAUTY AGE *CEASED.* (US/0887-414X) [13207585] **402**

BEAUTY CLASSIC *SUSPENDED.* (US/0886-8751) [13057018] **402**

BEAUTY COUNTER LONDON (UK/0960-3751) [I09603751] **402**

BEAUTY EDUCATION (US/1052-4169) [22287048] **402**

BEAUTY FASHION (US/0005-7487) [04556996] **1081**

BEAUTY (NEW YORK) *CEASED.* (US/0094-0518) [01793778] **402**

BEAUTY TRADE (US/0405-1203) [05331894] **402**

●BEAUTYFACTS (NEW YORK, N.Y.) (US/1062-3035) [25574869] **402**

BEAUX ARTS (BE) [11589676] **343**

BEAUX ARTS MAGAZINE (FR/0757-2271) [09739357] 293, **343**

BEAUX LIVRES (FR/0763-7063) [14372371] **4824**

BEAUX LIVRES DE L'ANNEE, LES (FR) [03663675] **4824**

BEAVER COUNTY LEGAL JOURNAL, THE (US) [09883155] **2940**

BEAVER COUNTY NEWS (MILFORD, UTAH : 1956) (US/0896-3312) [11781463] **5756**

BEAVER COUNTY TIMES (SOUTHERN ED.) (US) [14348988] **5734**

BEAVER PRESS, THE (US) [11771121] **5756**

BEAVER, THE (CN/0005-7517) [01519303] **2722**

BEBIDAS (US/0005-7533) [02830175] **2364**

BEBYGGELSEHISTORISK TIDSKRIFT (SW/0349-2834) [11838220] **293**

BECHUANALAND (PROTECTORATE). ESTIMATES OF REVENUE AND EXPENDITURE *See* ESTIMATES OF REVENUE AND EXPENDITURE **4722**

BECKER COUNTY RECORD, THE (US) [20650503] **5694**

BECKETT BASEBALL CARD MONTHLY (US/0886-0599) [12827195] 4887, **2771**

BECKETT BASKETBALL MAGAZINE (US/1055-8179) [23348886] 4887, **2771**

BECKETT CIRCLE, THE (US/0732-2224) [03865618] **3365**

BECKETT FOCUS ON FUTURE STARS (US/1060-2801) [24902294] **2485**

BECKETT FOOTBALL CARD MONTHLY (US/1055-2294) [23116855] **4887**

BECKETT HOCKEY MONTHLY (US/1058-5958) [24044773] **4887**

●BECKMAN FOCUS (GW) **4029**

BECKMAN REPORT *CEASED.* (GW/0005-755X) [11307459] **4029**

BECOIS-VOLANT (CN/0820-9863) [09606650] **4887**

BED & BREAKFAST AMERICAN STYLE *SUSPENDED.* (US/0893-1194) [12404645] 5070, **5462**

BED & BREAKFAST UPDATE *CEASED.* (US/0887-7505) [13386135] 5070, **5462**

BED & BREAKFAST USA / TOURIST HOUSE ASSOCIATION OF AMERICA (US) [10704110] **5462**

BED TIMES (US/0893-5556) [15579597] **2904**

BEDFORD BULLETIN (1984) (US/8750-1570) [11059153] **5758**

BEDFORD COUNTY INQUIRER (US) [12443192] **5734**

BEDFORD GAZETTE (BEDFORD, PA.) (US/0744-8457) [02258218] **5734**

BEDFORD INSTITUTE OF OCEANOGRAPHY *See* SCIENCE REVIEW (DARTMOUTH) **1456**

BEDFORD MINUTE-MAN (US) [19934108] **5687**

BEDFORD SUN BANNER (US/0746-262X) [09898393] **5727**

BEDFORD TIMES-PRESS, THE (US) [13652910] **5668**

BEDFORD TIMES-REGISTER, THE (US) [10172623] **5727**

BEDFORDSHIRE ARCHAEOLOGY (UK) [12155080] **261**

BEDFORDSHIRE FAMILY HISTORY SOCIETY JOURNAL (UK) [08433059] **2438**

BEDFORDSHIRE HISTORICAL RECORD SOCIETY *See* PUBLICATIONS OF THE BEDFORDSHIRE HISTORICAL RECORD SOCIETY **2704**

BEDFORDSHIRE MAGAZINE, THE (UK/0005-7592) [02570271] **2678**

BEDRIJFSDOCUMENTAIRE *CEASED.* (NE) **861**

BEDRIJFSGEGEVENS VOOR DE DETAILHANDEL IN KOFFERS EN LEDERWAREN (NE) [01785427] **3183**

BEDRIJFSGEGEVENS VOOR DE DETAILHANDEL IN UURWERKEN EN GGOUDEN EN ZILVEREN WWERKEN (NE) [01786455] **2913**

BEDRIJFSGEGEVENS VOOR HET SLAGERSBEDRIJF, BEDRIJSRESULTATEN IN- EN VERKOOPBELEID, VESTIGINGSPLAATS EN RESULTAAT (NE) [03305149] **1548**

BEDRIJFSKUNDE (NE) [13202078] **861**

BEDRIJFSRESULTATEN VAN DE KLEINE ZEEVISSERIJ (NE) [03450679] **2297**

BEDRIJFSUITKOMSTEN IN DE LANDBOUW (NE) [02380650] **65**

BEDROOM MAGAZINE (US/1046-1582) [20336435] **2485**

BEDRYFSBEGROTINGS VIR DIE BOEKJARE WAT EINDIG OP ... (SA) [11296613] **4632**

BEDRYFSLEIDING *See* SOUTH AFRICAN JOURNAL OF BUSINESS MANAGEMENT **886**

●BEE CULTURE (US/1071-3190) [27214642] **65**

BEE (DANVILLE, VA.) (US/0890-0809) [13685401] **5758**

BEE FARMING STATISTICS, TASMANIA (AT) [02441191] 65, **151**

BEE SCIENCE REVIEW (US) **5087**

BEE, THE (US) [13134500] **5765**

BEE WORLD (UK/0005-772X) [02361050] **5577**

BEEBE NEWS, THE (US) [24476831] **5631**

BEEBUG *CEASED.* (UK/0263-7561) [I02637561] **1171**

BEECHER CITY JOURNAL (US/1066-7970) [22830624] **5658**

BEEDAUDJIMOWIN (CN) 4504, **2256**

BEEF BUSINESS BULLETIN (US/0744-253X) [08134600] **207**

BEEF CATTLE RESEARCH IN TEXAS (US) [03248951] **207**

BEEF DIGEST *SUSPENDED.* (US/0195-0444) [02255591] **207**

BEEF SHORTHORN RECORD (UK) [05523066] **207**

BEEF (ST. PAUL, MINN.) (US/0005-7738) [01519323] **207**

BEEFALO NICKEL (US/0747-010X) [10467118] **207**

BEEFMASTER COWMAN, THE (US/0194-4282) [04647969] **207**

BEEHIVE HISTORY (US/0883-8380) [05332356] **2722**

BEEKEEPING, AUSTRALIA (AT) [03438326] **65**

BEELD EN GELUID (NE) **5316**

BEELD EN GELUID OPINIE (NE) **5316**

BEELDENAAR, DE (NE) [03535426] **2780**

BE'EMET?! (IS/0334-973X) [I0334973X] **1060**

BEER INDUSTRY UPDATE (US) [13894394] **2364**

BEER MARKETER'S INSIGHTS (US/0300-7480) [01398649] **2364**

BEER PAPER, THE (US/0738-8799) [09676473] **2364**

BEER STATISTICS NEWS (US/0164-4831) [04750527] 2364, **2362**

BEER WHOLESALER (US/0005-7770) [05057591] **2364**

BEETHOVEN-JAHRBUCH (GW/0522-5949) [01519332] **4102**

BEETHOVEN / KONVERSATIONSHEFTE (GW) **4102**

BEETHOVEN NEWSLETTER, THE (US/0898-6185) [14158543] **4102**

BEEVILLE BEE-PICAYUNE (US/0889-8618) [12854336] **5747**

BEFFROI (CN/0832-9966) [16273897] 4342, **3365**

BEFOLKNINGEN I KOMMUNERNE (DK/0108-8076) [11046822] **4550**

BEFOLKNINGENS BEVGELSER (DK/0070-3478) [04736852] **5323**

BEFORE AND AFTER (US/1049-0035) [21104982] **4824**

BEFORE I GET OLD (SI/0129-0169) [I01290169] **4102**

BEFREIUNG (GW) [03140322] **4516**

BEGEGNUNG (SZ) [02363328] **1446**

BEGINNER TEACHER (US/0190-3950) [04719220] **4938**

BEGINNER TEACHER GUIDE (US/1059-325X) [24565396] **4938**

BEGINNER'S GARDENING (PK) [12263616] **2410**

BEGINNING (IOWA CITY, IOWA) (US/0739-6694) [09801556] **4812**

BEGINNINGS : THE OFFICIAL NEWSLETTER OF THE AMERICAN HOLISTIC NURSES' ASSOCIATION (US/1071-2984) [08075153] **3852**

BEGLEITPAPIERE FUER AUSFUHRSENDUNGEN (GW) **1464**

BEGONIAN, THE (US/0096-8684) [01394185] **2410**

BEGROTING DER INKOMSTEN EN UITGAVEN VAN DE PROVINCIE NOORD-BRABANT (NE) [01798195] **4713**

BEGROTING. TOELICHTING (NE) [11557935] **4713**

BEGROTING VAN DIE ADDISIONELE BEDRYFSUITGAWE. ESTIMATES OF THE ADDITIONAL WORKING EXPENDITURE (SA) [06408525] **5429**

BEGROTING VAN DIE UITGAWES WAT UIT INKOMSTEREKENING (SOUTH AFRICA) (SA) [01788313] 4632, **4713**

BEGROTING VAN INKOMSTE (SA) [06292692] **4713**

BEHAVIOR ANALYSIS DIGEST (US/1052-0082) [22165480] **4576**

BEHAVIOR ANALYST, THE (US/0738-6729) [06281659] **4576**

BEHAVIOR AND PHILOSOPHY (US/1053-8348) [22349340] **4576**

BEHAVIOR AND SOCIAL ISSUES (US/1064-9506) [25323962] **4576**

BEHAVIOR & SOCIETY *CEASED.* (US/0145-0034) [01001847] **5240**

BEHAVIOR GENETICS (US/0001-8244) [01519335] **543**

BEHAVIOR, HEALTH AND AGING (US/1049-085X) [21127542] **3749**

BEHAVIOR IMPROVEMENT NEWS (US/0193-6271) [04110778] **4576**

BEHAVIOR MODIFICATION (US/0145-4455) [02736617] **4576**

BEHAVIOR RESEARCH METHODS, INSTRUMENTS, & COMPUTERS : A JOURNAL OF THE PSYCHONOMIC SOCIETY, INC (US/0743-3808) [10560878] **4576**

BEHAVIOR SCIENCE RESEARCH (US/0094-3673) [01794270] **5192**

BEHAVIOR THERAPIST, THE (US/0278-8403) [06973384] **4576**

BEHAVIOR THERAPY (US/0005-7894) [00811889] **4576**

BEHAVIOR THERAPY WITH CHILDREN (US/0360-6341) [02244958] **4576**

BEHAVIORAL AND BRAIN SCIENCES, THE (US/0140-525X) [04172559] 443, **4576**

BEHAVIORAL AND NEURAL BIOLOGY (US/0163-1047) [04289652] **5577**

BEHAVIORAL & SOCIAL SCIENCES LIBRARIAN (US/0163-9269) [04537738] 5192, 4576, **3193**

BEHAVIORAL ASSESSMENT (US/0191-5401) [04901478] **4576**

BEHAVIORAL DISORDERS (US/0198-7429) [04030659] **1375**

BEHAVIORAL ECOLOGY (US/1045-2249) [20043225] **2211**

BEHAVIORAL ECOLOGY AND SOCIOBIOLOGY (GW/0340-5443) [02041353] **2212**

●BEHAVIORAL HEALTH MANAGEMENT (US/1075-6701) [29851428] **1341**

●BEHAVIORAL INTERVENTIONS (UK/1072-0847) [28856522] **3921**

BEHAVIORAL MEDICINE ABSTRACTS (US/0197-7717) [06111784] 4576, 3555, **3654**

BEHAVIORAL MEDICINE (WASHINGTON, D.C.) (US/0896-4289) [17153135] **3555**

BEHAVIORAL NEUROSCIENCE (US/0735-7044) [08998034] **4576**

BEHAVIORAL PRIMATOLOGY *CEASED.* (US/0148-3781) [03282933] **5577**

BEHAVIORAL RESEARCH IN ACCOUNTING (US/1050-4753) [20298159] **739**

BEHAVIORAL RESIDENTIAL TREATMENT (US/0884-5581) [12403958] **3921**

BEHAVIORAL SCIENCE (US/0005-7940) [01425889] **4576**

BEHAVIORAL SCIENCES & THE LAW (UK/0735-9136) [08917789] 4577, **2940**

BEHAVIORAL SCIENCES NEWSLETTER *CEASED.* (US/0361-4646) [02065326] 642, **4577**

BEHAVIORMETRIKA (JA/0385-7417) [05825723] **4577**

●BEHAVIOROLOGY (MORGANTOWN, W. VA.) (US/1047-8663) [20803572] **4577**

BEHAVIOUR (NE/0005-7959) [01519347] **443**

BEHAVIOUR & INFORMATION TECHNOLOGY (UK/0144-929X) [08602118] **5087**

BEHAVIOUR CHANGE (AT/0813-4839) [16530588] **4577**

BEHAVIOUR PROBLEMS BULLETIN *SUSPENDED.* (AT/0819-9183) [08199183] **1875**

BEHAVIOUR RESEARCH AND THERAPY (UK/0005-7967) [01519349] **3921**

BEHAVIOURAL AND COGNITIVE PSYCHOTHERAPY (UK) [28918424] **4577**

BEHAVIOURAL & POLITICAL ANIMAL STUDIES (NZ) [19224126] **5505**

BEHAVIOURAL BRAIN RESEARCH (NE/0166-4328) [06183451] **3828**

BEHAVIOURAL NEUROLOGY (UK/0953-4180) [20294000] **3828**

BEHAVIOURAL PHARMACOLOGY (UK/0955-8810) [22170289] **4293**

BEHAVIOURAL PROCESSES (NE/0376-6357) [02497823] **5577**

BEHAVIOURAL PSYCHOTHERAPY (UK/0141-3473) [06855458] **4577**

●BEHAVORIAL HEALTHCARE TOMORROW (US/1063-8490) [26176775] **4768**

BEHEER EN ONDERHOUD (NE/0165-2540) [01652540] **600**

BEHIND THE WHISTLE (US/0275-3626) [07107991] **4887**

BEHINDERTENPADAGOGIK IN THEORIE UND PRAXIS (GW/0720-5007) [09454265] **1875**

BEHORDENVERZEICHNIS NORDRHEIN-WESTFALEN / LANDSAMT FUER DATENVERARBEITUNG UND STATISTIK NORDRHEIN-WESTFALEN (GW/0522-6058) [11896452] **4632**

BEHRING INSTITUTE MITTEILUNGEN (GW/0301-0457) [02359639] **3667**

BEI-JING ZHI CHUN (US/1074-469X) [28347426] **4465**

BEIFANG LUNCONG (CC/1000-3541) [06212514] **5192**

EEIHEFT ZUM BULLETIN JUGEND + LITERATUR (GW/0172-0910) [11810804] **3365**

BEIHEFT ZUR ZEITSCHRIFT GRUPPENPSYCHOTHERAPIE UND GRUPPENDYNAMIK (GW/0085-1302) [10150007] **4577**

BEIHEFTE PAEDAGOGIK *CEASED.* (FR) **1727**

BEIHEFTE ZUM GEOLOGISCHEN JAHRBUCH *See* GEOLOGISCHES JAHRBUCH, REIHE C : HYDROGEOLOGIE, INGENIEURGEOLOGIE **1413**

BEIHEFTE ZUR INTERNATIONALEN WISSENSCHAFTLICHEN KORRESPONDENZ ZUR GESCHICHTE DER DEUTSCHEN ARBEITERBEWEGUNG (GW) [09301250] **1464**

BEIHEFTE ZUR NOVA HEDWIGIA (GW/0078-2238) [03776221] **501**

BEIHEFTE ZUR SYDOWIA (AU/1016-0019) [05735329] **574**

BEIHEFTE ZUR ZEITSCHRIFT FUER DIE NEUTESTAMENTLICHE WISSENSCHAFT UND DIE KUNDE DER AELTEREN KIRCHE (GW) [01697137] **5024**

BEIHEFTE ZUR ZEITSCHRIFT FUER ROMANISCHE PHILOLOGIE (GW/0084-5396) [01586044] 3366, **3268**

BEIJING DAXUE XUEBAO ZHEXUE SHEHUI KEXUE BAN (CC/1000-5919) [I10005919] **4342**

BEIJING GONGYE DAXUE XUEBAO (CC/0254-0037) [09232006] **5087**

BEIJING HUAGONG XUEYUAN XUEBAO ZIRAN KEXUE BAN (CC/1000-5668) [I10005668] 2008, **1021**

BEIJING INFORMATION (CC/0251-3137) [I02513137] **4465**

BEIJING LIGONG DAXUE XUEBAO (CC/1001-0645) [I10010645] **5087**

BEIJING NONGYE DAXUE XUEBAO (CC/0479-8007) [07114633] **65**

BEIJING NONGYE GONGCHENG DAXUE XUEBAO (CC/1000-1514) [25259679] **65**

BEIJING REVIEW (CC/1000-9140) [04550608] **4465**

BEIJING REVIEW (NORTH AMERICAN EDITION) (CC) [17629663] **4465**

BEIJING YIKE DAXUE XUEBAO (CC/1000-1530) [20915248] **3555**

BEIJING YIXUE (CC/0253-9713) [09234973] **3555**

BEIJING ZHONGYI XUEYUAN XUEBAO (CC/0258-8811) [22449532] **3555**

BEILSTEIN CURRENT FACTS IN CHEMISTRY [COMPUTER FILE] / BEILSTEIN INSTITUT (GW/0939-7698) [25962077] **1039**

BEILSTEINS HANDBUCH DER ORGANISCHEN CHEMIE. 4. AUFL. DRITTES UND VIERTES ERGANZUNGSWERK (GW) [02433301] **962**

BEING SINGLE (US/0896-4920) [17190961] **2485**

BEING WELL (US/1064-1424) [26234407] **3555**

BEIRA ALTA (PO) [02359684] **2678**

BEIRUT REVIEW, THE (LE/1019-0732) [I10190732] 2647, **4516**

BEITRAEGE AUS DER EV. MILITARSEELSORGE (GW/0175-7652) [20641098] **4938**

BEITRAEGE FUER DIE FORSTWIRTSCHAFT (GW/0323-4673) [01639222] **2375**

BEITRAEGE ZUE OKUMENISCHEN THEOLOGIE (GW/0067-5172) [01519413] **4938**

BEITRAEGE ZUM AUSLAENDISCHEN OEFFENTLICHEN RECHT UND VOELKERRECHT (GW/0172-4770) [01519355] **2941**

BEITRAEGE ZUM INTERNATIONALEN WIRTSCHAFTSRECHT UND ATOMENERGIERECHT (GW) [01519359] 3124, **1633**

BEITRAEGE ZUR ALEXANDER-VON-HUMBOLDT-FORSCHUNG (GW) [03410820] **5087**

BEITRAEGE ZUR ALGEBRA UND GEOMETRIE (GW) [01185927] **3497**

BEITRAEGE ZUR ALLGEMEINEN UND VERGLEICHENDEN ARCHAEOLOGIE (GW/0170-9518) [09975025] **261**

BEITRAEGE ZUR ALTBAYERISCHEN KIRCHENGESCHICHTE (GW) [20814354] **2678**

BEITRAEGE ZUR BIOLOGIE DER PFLANZEN (GW/0005-8041) [01519367] **501**

BEITRAEGE ZUR DEMOGRAPHIE (GW) [11826121] **4550**

BEITRAEGE ZUR DEUTSCHEN PHILOLOGIE (GW/0522-6341) [01519371] **3268**

BEITRAEGE ZUR DEUTSCHEN VOLKS- UND ALTERTUMSKUNDE (GW/0408-8220) [01776231] **2318**

BEITRAEGE ZUR ENTOMOLOGIE (GW/0005-805X) [01519372] **5605**

BEITRAEGE ZUR EVANGELISCHEN THEOLOGIE (GW) [02356813] **4938**

BEITRAEGE ZUR FEMINISTISCHEN THEORIE UND PRAXIS (GW/0722-0189) [06321121] **5551**

BEITRAEGE ZUR FREMDSPRACHENVERMITTLUNG AUS DEM KONSTANZER SLI (GW/0171-4155) [I01714155] **3268**

BEITRAEGE ZUR GERICHTLICHEN MEDIZIN (AU/0067-5016) [02538065] **3740**

BEITRAEGE ZUR GESCHICHTE DER ARBEITERBEWEGUNG (BERLIN, DDR) (GW/0005-8068) [02103356] **2678**

BEITRAEGE ZUR GESCHICHTE DER BIBLISCHEN EXEGESE (GW/0408-8298) [04774319] **5014**

BEITRAEGE ZUR GESCHICHTE DER DEUTSCHEN SPRACHE UND LITERATUR (TUEBINGEN) (GW/0005-8076) [01519380] **3268**

BEITRAEGE ZUR GESCHICHTE DER HUMBOLDT-UNIVERSITAT ZU BERLIN (GW/0138-4104) [09974279] **1811**

BEITRAEGE ZUR GESCHICHTE DER PHARMAZIE (GW/0341-0099) [I03410099] **4293**

BEITRAEGE ZUR GESCHICHTE DER PHILOSOPHIE UND THEOLOGIE DES MITTELALTERS. SUPPLEMENTBAND (GW) [21016140] 4938, **4342**

BEITRAEGE ZUR GESCHICHTE DER PHILOSOPHIE UND THEOLOGIE DES MITTELALTERS. TEXTE UND UNTERSUCHUNGEN (GW/0067-5024) [01519382] 4938, **4342**

BEITRAEGE ZUR GESCHICHTE DER REICHSKIRCHE IN DER NEUZEIT (GW) [06109813] **5024**

BEITRAEGE ZUR GESCHICHTE DER UNIVERSITAT MAINZ (GW/0408-8379) [02585281] **1811**

BEITRAEGE ZUR GESCHICHTE DER WISSENSCHAFT UND DER TECHNIK (GW/0522-6570) [02585361] **5087**

BEITRAEGE ZUR GESCHICHTE DES PARLAMENTARISMUS UND DER POLITISCHEN PARTEIEN / HERAUSGEGEBEN VON DER KOMMISSION FUER GESCHICHTE DES PARLAMENTARISMUS UND DER POLITISCHEN PARTEIEN (GW/0522-6643) [01519386] **4465**

BEITRAEGE ZUR GESCHICHTE DORTMUNDS UND DER GRAFSCHAFT MARK (GW/0405-2021) [02256026] **2678**

BEITRAEGE ZUR GESCHICHTE KISSLEGGS (GW) [20288264] **2678**

BEITRAEGE ZUR GREGORIANIK (GW) [13505164] **4102**

BEITRAEGE ZUR HOCHSCHULFORSCHUNG *CEASED.* (GW/0171-645X) [05820969] **1811**

BEITRAEGE ZUR HYDROLOGIE (GW/0343-0987) [09147145] **1412**

BEITRAEGE ZUR HYGIENE UND EPIDEMIOLOGIE (GW/0067-5083) [02586819] **3734**

BEITRAEGE ZUR INFUSIONSTHERAPIE (SZ/1011-6974) [18785067] **3555**

BEITRAEGE ZUR INKUNABELKUNDE : IM AUFTRAGE DER DEUTSCHEN STAATSBIBLIOTHEK ZU BERLIN (GW/0067-5091) [01519390] **4564**

BEITRAEGE ZUR INTENSIV- UND NOTFALLMEDIZIN (SZ/0254-8275) [11254305] **3555**

Alphabetical Title Index

BELGIUM

BEITRAEGE ZUR KLINISCHEN NEUROLOGIE UND PSYCHIATRIE (GW/0138-5097) [09448159] 3921, **3828**

BEITRAEGE ZUR KOLONIAL- UND UBERSEEGESCHICHTE (GW/0522-6848) [01519393] **2611**

BEITRAEGE ZUR MEERESKUNDE (GW/0067-5148) [02591709] 553, **1446**

BEITRAEGE ZUR MITTELALTERARCHAEOLOGIE IN OESTERREICH / [HERAUSGEGEBER: INSTITUT FUER UR- UND FRUEHGESCHICHTE DER UNIVERSITAET WIEN] (AU) [20272665] **261**

BEITRAEGE ZUR MITTELALTERARCHAOLOGIE IN OSTERREICH. BEIHEFT (AU) [15726198] **261**

BEITRAEGE ZUR MITTELAMERIKANISCHEN VOLKERKUNDE (GW/0438-4679) [01606549] **2723**

BEITRAEGE ZUR MUSIKWISSENSCHAFT CEASED. (GW/0005-8106) [01777422] **4102**

BEITRAEGE ZUR NAMENFORSCHUNG (GW/0005-8114) [01519405] **2438**

BEITRAEGE ZUR NATURKUNDE NIEDERSACHSENS (GW/0340-4277) [04031012] **4162**

BEITRAEGE ZUR NEUEREN LITERATURGESCHICHTE (GW/0179-4027) [01519409] **3366**

BEITRAEGE ZUR OKONOMISCHEN FORSCHUNG (GW/0175-5676) [I01755676] **1464**

BEITRAEGE ZUR ONKOLOGIE (SZ/0250-3220) [06971054] **3809**

BEITRAEGE ZUR ORTHOPADIE UND TRAUMATOLOGIE CEASED. (GW/0005-8149) [01715744] **3555**

BEITRAEGE ZUR POLITISCHEN WISSENSCHAFT (GW/0582-0421) [02594537] **4465**

BEITRAEGE ZUR REGIONALEN GEOLOGIE DER ERDE (GW/0522-7038) [01519417] **1366**

BEITRAEGE ZUR ROMANISCHEN PHILOLOGIE DES MITTELALTERS (GW/0067-5202) [01519418] **3338**

BEITRAEGE ZUR SEXUALFORSCHUNG (GW/0067-5210) [01607941] **3921**

BEITRAEGE ZUR TABAKFORSCHUNG INTERNATIONAL (GW/0173-783X) [08415862] **5372**

BEITRAEGE ZUR TROPISCHEN LANDWIRTSCHAFT UND VETERINARMEDIZIN (GW/0301-567X) [02487267] **3985**

BEITRAEGE ZUR UKRAINISCHEN LITERATURGESCHICHTE (GW) [18514646] **3366**

BEITRAEGE ZUR UMWELTGESTALTUNG (GW) [03410918] **2225**

BEITRAEGE ZUR UNIVERSITAETSGESCHICHTE (GW) [19406317] 1811, **2678**

BEITRAEGE ZUR UR- UND FRUEHGESCHICHTE DER BEZIRKE ROSTOCK, SCHWERIN UND NEUBRANDENBURG (GW) [03208809] **261**

BEITRAEGE ZUR UR- UND FRUGESCHICHTLICHEN ARCHAOLOGIE DES MITTELMEER-KULTURRAUMES (GW/0067-5245) [02594629] **261**

BEITRAEGE ZUR UROLOGIE (SZ/0250-3212) [06664795] **3988**

BEITRAEGE ZUR VOGELKUNDE (GW/0005-8211) [02250270] **5615**

BEITRAEGE ZUR VOLKSKUNDE (SZ) [10577308] **2318**

BEITRAGE UND MITTEILUNGEN (VEREIN FUER KATHOLISCHE KIRCHENGESCHICHTE IN HAMBURG UND SCHLESWIG-HOLSTEIN) (GW) [19006356] 5024, **2678**

BEITRAGE ZUM AUSLANDISCHEN UND INTERNATIONALEN PRIVATRECHT (GW) [01519356] **3124**

BEITRAGE ZUR ANAESTHESIOLOGIE, INTENSIV- UND NOTFALLMEDIZIN (AU) [30037716] **3555**

BEITRAGE ZUR DERMATOLOGIE (GW/0171-0184) [04647180] **3718**

BEITRAGE ZUR DIFFERENTIALGEOMETRIE (GW) [05160334] **3497**

BEITRAGE ZUR ERFORSCHUNG DER WIRTSCHAFTLICHEN ENTWICKLUNG (US/0522-6376) [02584212] **1548**

BEITRAGE ZUR FILM- UND FERNSEHWISSENSCHAFT : SCHRIFTENREIHE DER HOCHSCHULE FUR FILM UND FERNSEHEN DER DDR (GW) [09806972] 1150, **4064**

BEITRAGE ZUR FREMDENVERKEHRSFORSCHUNG (GW/0522-6449) [02584905] **824**

BEITRAGE ZUR GANZHEITLICHEN WIRTSCHAFTS- UND GESELLSCHAFTSLEHRE (GW/0522-6457) [02584932] **2875**

BEITRAGE ZUR GEOBOTANISCHEN LANDESAUFNAHME DER SCHWEIZ (1935) (SZ) [09145071] **501**

BEITRAGE ZUR GEOLOGIE DER SCHWEIZ. GEOTECHNISCHE SERIE (SZ) [06647307] **1367**

BEITRAGE ZUR GESCHICHTE DER FDJ (GW) [05424832] **5240**

BEITRAGE ZUR GESCHICHTE DER PHILOSOPHIE UND THEOLOGIE DES MITTELALTERS (GW/0067-5024) [10199266] 4938, **3268**

BEITRAGE ZUR GESCHICHTE DER STADTE MITTELEUROPAS (AU/0522-6554) [03418868] **2611**

BEITRAGE ZUR HISTORISCHEN THEOLOGIE (GW) [04856376] **4938**

BEITRAGE ZUR JAZZFORSCHUNG. STUDIES IN JAZZ RESEARCH (GW) [04208667] **4102**

BEITRAGE ZUR KUNSTGESCHICHTE (GW) [01519400] **316**

BEITRAGE ZUR LEHRE UND FORSCHUNG IM SPORT (GW) [02896800] **1855**

BEITRAGE ZUR MITTELRHEINISCHEN MUSIKGESCHICHTE (GW) [02368642] **4102**

BEITRAGE ZUR PALAONTOLOGIE VON OSTERREICH (AU/1017-5563) [03483946] **4226**

BEITRAGE ZUR STRUKTURFORSCHUNG (GW) [02369108] **1548**

BEITRAGE ZUR VERHALTUNGSFORSCHUNG (GW/0522-7194) [03422220] **4577**

BEITRAGE ZUR WISENSSOZIOLOGIE, BEITRAGE ZUR RELIGIONS-SOZIOLOGIE (GW) [04816806] 4938, **5240**

BEITRREAGE ZUR KUNST DES CHRISTLICHEN OSTENS (GW/0067-5121) [04919936] **343**

BEJA, PORTUGAL (CITY). CAMARA MUNICIPAL See ARQUIVO DE BEJA **2480**

BEKANNTMACHUNGEN DES PATENTAMTES DER DDR (GW) [22518898] **1301**

BEKES MEGYEI MUZEUMOK KOZLEMENYEI (HU/0139-0090) [05367283] **2678**

BEKESI ELET (HU/0522-7232) [02369236] **5087**

BEL AGE, LE (CN/0835-8702) [18595958] **5178**

BELARUSKAIA MOVA (BW/1010-3996) [04403219] **3268**

BELARUSKAIA MOVA I LITARATURA U SHKOLE See RODNAE SLOVA **3317**

BELARUSKAIA MOVA I LITERATURA U SHKOLE (BW/0234-1360) [19217225] **3268**

BELARUSKAJA LITARATURA (BW/1010-4011) [04400363] **3366**

BELAS-ARTES (PO/0253-1666) [05627981] **343**

BELASTINGBESCHOUWINGEN See MBB : BELASTINGBESCHOUWINGEN **4737**

BELASTINGDRUK IN NEDERLAND (NE/0077-670X) [08672172] **4713**

BELEGGERS BELANGEN (NE/0005-8343) [I00058343] **778**

BELEID & MAATSCHAPPIJ. JAARBOEK (NE) [17312567] 4465, **5240**

BELEIDSINFORMATICA (BE) **1218**

BELEIDSNOTA VAN GEDEPUTEERDE STATEN (NE) [06534024] **4713**

BELEM (BRAZIL) See DIARIO OFICIAL DO MUNICIPIO **2960**

BELFAGOR (IT/0005-8351) [01519430] **3338**

BELFAST. EDUCATION AND LIBRARY BOARD See REPORT OF THE BELFAST EDUCATION AND LIBRARY BOARD **1903**

BELFAST TELEGRAPH (UK/0307-5664) [14338341] **5811**

BELFAST TELEGRAPH [MICROFORM] (UK/0307-5664) [10813388] **5811**

BELGIAN AMERICAN CHAMBER OF COMMERCE IN THE UNITED STATES See DIRECTORY - BELGIAN AMERICAN CHAMBER OF COMMERCE IN THE UNITED STATES, INC, THE **819**

BELGIAN BUSINESS (BE) **642**

BELGIAN JOURNAL OF BOTANY (BE/0778-4031) [23763801] **501**

BELGIAN JOURNAL OF FOOD CHEMISTRY AND BIOTECHNOLOGY See CEREVISIA AND BIOTECHNOLOGY **3690**

BELGIAN JOURNAL OF LINGUISTICS (FR/0774-5141) [20662926] **3268**

BELGIAN JOURNAL OF OPERATIONS RESEARCH, STATISTICS AND COMPUTER SCIENCE (BE/0770-0512) [13753628] **1208**

BELGIAN JOURNAL OF ZOOLOGY (BE/0777-6276) [22164404] **5577**

BELGIAN LACES (US/1046-0462) [11965508] **2438**

BELGIAN MEDICAL YEAR-BOOK (BE/0771-5676) [06703444] **3555**

BELGIEN : ENERGIEWIRTSCHAFT (GW) [04262794] **1933**

BELGIEN : WIRTSCHAFT IN ZAHLEN UND WIRTSCHAFTSDOKUMENTATION (GW) [06234168] **1548**

BELGISCH TIJDSCHRIFT VOOR SOCIALE ZEKERHEID (BE/0775-0234) [08395253] **5274**

BELGISCH TIJDSCHRIFT VOOR TANDHEELKUNDE (BE/0775-0285) [10407623] **1317**

BELGISCHE FRUITREVUE (BE/0005-8467) [I00058467] **2328**

BELGISCHE PROTESTANTSE (BE) **5056**

BELGISCHE TUINBOUW. INTERNATIONALE EDITIE, DE (BE/0005-8483) [03744436] **2410**

BELGIUM See MONITEUR BELGE. BELGISCH STAATSBLAD **3011**

BELGIUM See PASINOMIE : COLLECTION COMPLETE DES LOIS, ARRETES ET REGLEMENTS GENERAUX... **3025**

BELGIUM See RECUEIL DES LOIS, DECRETS, ET ARRETES / ROYAUME DE BELGIQUE **3134**

BELGIUM. ADMINISTRATION DE LA MARINE ET DE LA NAVIGATION INTERIEUR See LISTE OFFICIELLE DES NAVIRES DE MER BELGES ET DE LA FLOTTE DE LA FORCE NAVALE **5451**

BELGIUM. ADMINISTRATION DES MINES See STATISTIQUES: HOUILLE, COKES, AGGLOMERES, METALLURGIE, CARRIERES. STATISTIEKEN: STEENKOLEN, COKES, AGGLOMERATEN, METAALNIJVERHEID, GROVEN **2006**

BELGIUM. ADMINISTRATION DU COMMERCE See BULLETIN DE METROLOGIE (BELGIUM) **4029**

BELGIUM. AMBASSADE (RWANDA). SECTION DE COOPERATION See EXECUTION DES PROJECTS FINANCES PAR LE PROGRAMME DE COOPERATION BELGO-RWANDAIS **1561**

BELGIUM. CENTRE NATIONAL DE DOCUMENTATION SCIENTIFIQUE ET TECHNIQUE See RAPPORT D'ACTIVITE - CENTRE NATIONAL DE DOCUMENTATION SCIENTIFIQUE ET TECHNIQUE **5144**

BELGIUM. COMITE DE CONCERTATION ET DE CONTROLE DU PETROLE See RAPPORT ANNUEL - COMITE DE CONCERTATION ET DE CONTROLE DU PETROLE **4276**

BELGIUM. COMMISSION BANCAIRE ET FINANCIERE See RAPPORT ANNUEL **806**

BELGIUM. COMMISSION ROYALE DES MONUMENTS ET DES SITES See BULLETIN DE LA COMMISSION ROYALE DES MONUMENTS ET DES SITES (BELGIUM) **2680**

BELGIUM. CONSEIL SUPERIEUR DES CLASSES MOYENNES See RAPPORT ANNUEL / CONSEIL SUPERIEUR DES CLASSES MOYENNES **4678**

BELGIUM. CONSEIL SUPERIEUR DES CLASSES MOYENNES. RAPPORT ANNUEL DU SECRETAIRE GENERAL See RAPPORT ANNUEL / CONSEIL SUPERIEUR DES CLASSES MOYENNES **4678**

BELGIUM. COUR DE CASSATION See BULLETIN DES ARRETS DE LA COUR DE CASSATION **2944**

BELGIUM. COUR DE CASSATION. BULLETIN See BULLETIN DES ARRETS DE LA COUR DE CASSATION **2944**

BELGIUM, ECONOMIC AND COMMERCIAL INFORMATION (BE/0775-1443) [08702556] 824, **1464**

BELGIUM ENVIRONMENTAL RESEARCH INDEX (BE) [05524150] **2225**

BELGIUM. INSTITUT NATIONAL DE STATISTIQUE See STATISTIQUES DE LA CONSTRUCTION ET DU LOGEMENT **633**

BELGIUM. INSTITUT NATIONAL DE STATISTIQUE See STATISTIQUES FINANCIERES **734**

BELGIUM. INSTITUT NATIONAL DE STATISTIQUE See STATISTIQUES JUDICIAIRES **3083**

BELGIUM. MINISTERE DE LA PREVOYANCE SOCIALE See RAPPORT GENERAL SUR LA SECURITE SOCIALE **5304**

BELGIUM. MINISTERE DE LA SANTE PUBLIQUE ET DE LA FAMILLE See BULLETIN DU MINISTERE DE LA SANTE PUBLIQUE ET DE LA FAMILLE **4769**

BELGIUM — Alphabetical Title Index

BELGIUM. MINISTERE DE LA SANTE PUBLIQUE ET DE LA FAMILLE. CENTRE DE TRAITEMENT DE L'INFORMATION See STATISTISCHE GEGEVENS BETREFFENDE HET GENEESHERENKORPS **3917**

BELGIUM. MINISTERE DES AFFAIRES ECONOMIQUES. CELLULE BUDGET ECONOMIQUE-ETUDES See BUDGET ECONOMIQUE DE ... VERSION REVISEE / MINISTERE DES AFFAIRES ECONOMIQUES, DIRECTION GENERALE DES ETUDES ET DE LA DOCUMENTATION, CELLULE BUDGET ECONOMIQUE-ETUDES **1549**

BELGIUM. MINISTERE DES AFFAIRES ECONOMIQUES. DIRECTION GENERALE DES ETUDES ET DE LA DOCUMENTATION See PRINCIPAUX FAITS ECONOMIQUES DANS LE DOMAINE INTERNATIONAL **1579**

BELGIUM. MINISTERE DES AFFAIRES ECONOMIQUES. DIRECTION GENERALE DES ETUDES ET DE LA DOCUMENTATION. BIBLIOTH·EQUE CENTRALE ACCROISEMENTS See LISTE MENSUELLE **1535**

BELGIUM. MINISTERE DES AFFAIRES ETRANGERES ET DU COMMERCE EXTERIEUR. TEXTES ET DOCUMENTS See TEXTES ET DOCUMENTS - MINISTERE DES AFFAIRES ETRANGERES, DU COMMERCE EXTERIEUR ET DE LA COOPERATION AU DEVELOPPEMENT **4536**

BELGIUM. MINISTERE DES FINANCES See BULLETIN DE DOCUMENTATION - BELGIQUE, MINISTERE DES FINANCES **4715**

BELGIUM. MINISTERE DES FINANCES. SERVICE D'ETUDES ET DE DOCUMENTATION See BULLETIN DE DOCUMENTATION - MINISTERE DES FINANCES, SERVICE D'ETUDES ET DE DOCUMENTATION **4715**

BELGIUM. OFFICE BELGE DU COMMERCE EXTERIEUR See INFORMATIONS DU COMMERCE EXTERIEUR **840**

BELGIUM. OFFICE NATIONAL DE SECURITE SOCIALE See RAPPORT ANNUEL - ONSS **5303**

BELGIUM. PARLEMENT. CHAMBRE DES REPRESENTANTS See QUESTIONS ET REPONSES **4678**

BELGIUM. PARLEMENT. SENAT See ANNALES PARLEMENTAIRES. PARLEMENTAIRE HANDELINGEN **4463**

BELGIUM. SERVICE DE LA PROPRIETE INDUSTRIELLE ET COMMERCIALE See RECUEIL DES BREVETS D'INVENTION **1308**

BELGIUM. [LAW, ETC.]. RECUEIL DES LOIS ET ARRETES ROYAUX DE BELGIQUE See RECUEIL DES LOIS, DECRETS, ET ARRETES / ROYAUME DE BELGIQUE **3134**

BELGIUM'S 500 LARGEST COMPANIES (BE) [05280308] **642**

BELGOLAISE See REPORTS AND BALANCE SHEET PRESENTED TO THE SHAREHOLDERS AT THEIR GENERAL MEETING **808**

BELGRAD. PRIRODNJACKI MUZEJ See GLASNIK PRIRODNJACKOG MUZEJA U BEOGRADU. SUMARSTVO I LOV SERIJA C. **2384**

BELGRAD. UNIVERZITET. ELEKTROTEHNICKI FAKULTET See PUBLIKACIJE. SERIJA : ELEKTRONIKA, TELEKOMUNIKACIJE, AUTOMATIKA **2077**

BELGRAD. UNIVERZITET. POLJOPRIVREDNI FAKULTET See ZBORNIK RADOVA POLJOPRIVREDNOG FAKULTETA **1854**

BELGRAD. ZAVOD ZA ZASTITU I NAUCNO PROUCAVANJE SPOMENIKA KULTURE NR SRBIJE SAOPSTENJA ZAVODA ZA ZASTITU I NAUCNO PROUCAVANJE SPOMENIKA KULTURE NR SRBIJE See SAOPSTENJA - REPUBLICKI ZAVOD ZA ZASTITU SPOMENIKA KULTURE SR SRBIJE **308**

BELIZE BUSINESS AND TRAVEL DIRECTORY (US) [11637995] **5462**

BELIZE CONSOLIDATED INDEX OF STATUTES AND SUBSIDIARY LEGISLATION TO ... (US) [12895496] **3124**

● BELIZE DATA GUIDE (US/1063-1461) [25903909] **5266**

BELIZE. PRIME MINISTER AND MINISTER OF FINANCE AND DEFENCE See ... BUDGET / PRESENTED BY THE PRIME MINISTER ... TO THE HOUSE OF REPRESENTATIVE ON, THE **4634**

BELIZE TIMES, THE (BH) [28869651] **5778**

BELIZE TODAY (BH) [16103016] **4632**

BELIZE, WIRTSCHAFTSDATEN / BUNDESSTELLE FUER AUSSENHANDELSINFORMATION (GW) [11455299] **1548**

BELIZEAN STUDIES (BH/0250-6831) [03491847] **2723**

BELL & HOWELL CO. INDEXING CENTER See BELL & HOWELL'S NEWSPAPER INDEX TO THE LOS ANGELES TIMES **5691**

BELL & HOWELL NEWSPAPER INDEX TO THE AMERICAN BANKER / COMPILED AND PUBLISHED BY THE INDEXING CENTER, MICRO PHOTO DIVISION, BELL & HOWELL COMPANY (US) [10879303] **778**

BELL & HOWELL NEWSPAPER INDEX TO THE CHICAGO SUN-TIMES / COMPILED AND PUBLISHED BY THE INDEXING CENTER, MICRO PHOTO DIVISION, BELL & HOWELL COMPANY (US) [06360962] **5691**

BELL & HOWELL'S NEWSPAPER INDEX TO THE CHICAGO SUN-TIMES See BELL & HOWELL NEWSPAPER INDEX TO THE CHICAGO SUN-TIMES / COMPILED AND PUBLISHED BY THE INDEXING CENTER, MICRO PHOTO DIVISION, BELL & HOWELL COMPANY **5691**

BELL & HOWELL'S NEWSPAPER INDEX TO THE LOS ANGELES TIMES (US/0195-6418) [05972227] **5691**

BELL ATLANTIC QUARTERLY (US) [12093484] **1599**

BELL FAMILY NEWSLETTER, THE (JS/0749-6168) [11140561] **2439**

BELL TOWER, THE (US/0092-8666) [01791351] **4102**

BELLAIRE TEXAN, THE (US) [16520184] **5747**

BELLCORE EXCHANGE (US/1040-2020) [17555094] **1150**

BELLE BANNER, THE (US) [19044693] **5702**

BELLE FRANCE, LA (US/8750-9180) [11907427] **5462**

BELLE GLADE EREC RESEARCH REPORT (US/0892-8606) [14336811] **65**

BELLE PLAINE NEWS (US) [12659689] **5674**

BELLE PLAINE UNION (BELLE PLAINE, IOWA : 1922) (US) [12565225] **5668**

BELLE RIVER NORTH ESSEX NEWS (CN/0834-5643) [16074661] **5780**

BELLE (SYDNEY, N.S.W.) (AT/0310-1452) [12124489] 2898, **293**

BELLE W. BARUCH LIBRARY IN MARINE SCIENCE, THE (US/0361-4360) [02076805] **1446**

BELLEFONTAINE EXAMINER (US/0747-3273) [10742362] **5727**

BELLES HISTOIRES DE POMME D'API PARIS. 1972, LES (FR/0991-8787) [I09918787] **1060**

BELLES LETTRES (ARLINGTON, VA.) (US/0884-2957) [12357950] 5551, **3366**

BELLETEN CEASED. (TU/0041-4255) [01767827] **2611**

BELLEVILLE DAILY NEWS-DEMOCRAT CEASED. (US) [08784633] **5658**

BELLEVILLE NEWS-DEMOCRAT (US/8750-1058) [10125964] **5658**

BELLEVILLE POST (US) [19610744] **5709**

BELLEVILLE TELESCOPE (BELLEVILLE, KAN. : 1923) (US/0740-0985) [09880127] **5674**

BELLEVILLE TIMES NEWS, THE (US) [19610705] **5709**

BELLEVUE KIRKLAND REDMOND (KING COUNTY WASH.) POLK DIRECTORY (US) [09793011] **2556**

BELLEVUE LEADER (US/0193-0389) [05143500] **5706**

BELLEZA Y MODA (SP/0005-8629) [I00058629] **5551**

BELLINGHAM HERALD, THE (US) [14287261] **5760**

BELLINGHAM REVIEW, THE (US/0734-2934) [03689085] **3366**

BELL'ITALIA (IT) [16919318] **2513**

BELLMAN LECTURE, THE (UK/0522-8670) [01786780] **778**

BELLMAN MEMORIAL LECTURE See BELLMAN LECTURE, THE **778**

BELLMANSSALLSKAPET See BELLMANSSTUDIER **3366**

BELLMANSSTUDIER (SW/0405-3923) [02411218] **3366**

BELLMORE LIFE (US) [21814649] **5714**

BELLMORE MERRICK OBSERVER (US) **5714**

BELLONA. KWARTALNIK WOJSKOWO-HISTORYCZNY (UK/0005-8645) [05938384] **4037**

BELLOWING ARK (US/0887-4115) [13246573] **3366**

BELL'S ALASKA, YUKON & BRITISH COLUMBIA TRAVEL GUIDE (US/1054-5034) [18687210] **5462**

BELLVILLE TIMES (BELLVILLE, TEX.) (US) [14052371] **5747**

BELMONT ABBEY COLLEGE See ALUMNI DIRECTORY / BELMONT ABBEY COLLEGE **1097**

BELMONT CITIZEN HERALD (US) [26467169] **5687**

BELMONTIA (NE/0169-4375) [02243709] **501**

BELOIT DAILY CALL, THE (US/8750-1791) [11081578] **5674**

BELOIT DAILY NEWS (US) [14703936] **5765**

BELOIT FICTION JOURNAL (US/0883-9131) [12244783] **3366**

BELOIT POETRY JOURNAL, THE (US/0005-8661) [01519482] **3460**

BELORUSSKII NAUCHNO-ISSLEDOVATEL'SKII INSTITUT ZHIVOTNOVODSTVA See SBORNIK TRUDOV - BELORUSSKII NAUCHNO-ISSLEDOVATEL'SKII INSTITUT ZHIVOTNOVODSTVA **221**

BELSER KUNSTQUARTAL (GW) [04637843] **4084**

BELTON JOURNAL AND BELL COUNTY DEMOCRAT See BELTON JOURNAL (BELTON, TEX. : 1923) **5747**

BELTON JOURNAL (BELTON, TEX. : 1923) (US/1053-9131) [13695324] **5747**

BELTSVILLE SYMPOSIA IN AGRICULTURAL RESEARCH (US/0160-3612) [03622676] **65**

BELTSVILLE SYMPOSIUM IN AGRICULTURAL RESEARCH See BELTSVILLE SYMPOSIA IN AGRICULTURAL RESEARCH **65**

BELTWAY NATURALIST, THE (US/0749-436X) [11181576] **5462**

BELZONI BANNER, THE (US) [14516716] **5700**

BENALLA ART GALLERY NEWSLETTER (AT) **343**

BENBROOK NEWS, THE (US) [17894352] **5747**

BENCH AND BAR OF MINNESOTA, THE (US/0276-1505) [10169497] **2941**

BENCH MARKS FOR SCHOOL DISTRICT BUDGETS IN TEXAS; A REPORT (US) [04199982] **1860**

BENCH SHEET See WATER ENVIRONMENT LABORATORY SOLUTIONS **2247**

BENCH SHEET, THE (US/0737-4186) [09368180] **1013**

BENCHMARK (US) [04238709] **3139**

BENCHMARK (CHARLOTTETOWN) (CN/0706-5116) [05018485] **1811**

BENCHMARK OBAN (UK/0951-6859) [I09516859] **2111**

BENCHMARK PAPERS IN ANALYTICAL CHEMISTRY (US/0145-5338) [02739931] **1013**

BENCHMARK PAPERS IN BEHAVIOR (US/0277-0032) [07222707] **4577**

BENCHMARK PAPERS IN BIOLOGICAL CONCEPTS (US/0092-5616) [05580357] **443**

BENCHMARK PAPERS IN ECOLOGY (US/0095-4640) [01154200] **2212**

BENCHMARK PAPERS IN GENETICS (US/0161-7656) [03995463] **543**

BENCHMARK PAPERS IN HUMAN PHYSIOLOGY (US/0093-5557) [04856300] **578**

BENCHMARK PAPERS IN INORGANIC CHEMISTRY (US) [01716278] **1035**

BENCHMARK PAPERS IN MICROBIOLOGY CEASED. (US/0361-4069) [02050682] **560**

BENCHMARK PAPERS IN PHYSICAL CHEMISTRY AND CHEMICAL PHYSICS (US/0277-4747) [05349966] 4398, **1050**

BENCHMARK PAPERS IN SYSTEMATIC AND EVOLUTIONARY BIOLOGY (US/0362-3157) [02200876] **443**

BENCHMARK PAPERS IN TOXICOLOGY (US/0739-4012) [09722810] **3979**

BENCHMARK PAPERS ON ENERGY (US) [02185890] **1933**

BENCHMARK REPORT / ASSOCIATION OF COMPUTER USERS (US) [05433946] **1171**

BENCHMARK - THE EUROPEAN MANAGEMENT REVIEW (UK) **861**

BENCHMARK (WASHINGTON, D.C.) SUSPENDED. (US/0743-0310) [10399667] **3092**

● BENCHMARKING BRIEFING (UK/1351-5055) [I13515055] **642**

● BENCHMARKING FOR QUALITY MANAGEMENT & TECHNOLOGY: AN INTERNATIONAL JOURNAL (UK) **861**

BENCHMARKS (DENTON, TEX.) (US/1066-0380) [I10660380] **1171**

BEND BULLETIN, THE (US) [22497168] **5733**

BEND OF THE RIVER (US/1063-9241) [08971907] **4162**

BENDEL LIBRARY JOURNAL (NR/0331-555X) [08264117] **3194**

Alphabetical Title Index BERICHT

BENDEL (NIGERIA). PUBLIC SERVICE COMMISSION See REPORT OF THE BENDEL STATE PUBLIC SERVICE COMMISSION **4705**

BENDEL STATE (NIGERIA) See HANDBOOK OF BENDEL STATE OF NIGERIA **4654**

BENDER (MATTHEW) AND COMPANY, INCORPORATED See BENDER'S FORMS OF DISCOVERY **2941**

BENDER'S DICTIONARY OF 1040 DEDUCTIONS (US/0270-5206) [05878015] 4713, **2941**

BENDER'S FEDERAL PRACTICE MANUAL (US) [01768296] **3139**

BENDER'S FEDERAL TAX WEEK (US) [19653066] **4713**

BENDER'S FORMS OF DISCOVERY (US) [01519512] **2941**

BENDER'S ... PAYROLL TAX GUIDE (US/0732-6564) [08383142] **2941**

BENDER'S TAX RETURN MANUAL FOR ... (US) [04683627] **4713**

BENDER'S UNIFORM COMMERCIAL CODE SERVICE (US) [01519513] **2941**

BENEDICTINA (IT/0392-0356) [01587313] **4938**

BENEDICTINES (US/0005-8726) [01774827] **5024**

BENEFITS & COMPENSATION INTERNATIONAL (UK/0268-764X) [23249200] 938, **2875**

●BENEFITS & COMPENSATION SOLUTIONS (US/1069-1707) [27942460] **938**

●BENEFITS & COMPENSATION UPDATE (US/1074-6293) [29767006] **1655**

BENEFITS AND PENSIONS MONITOR (CN/1191-0763) [25652402] **861**

BENEFITS CANADA (CN/0703-7732) [04589908] 642, **938**

BENEFITS (CLEARWATER, FLA.) (US/1062-1148) [18405403] 939, **1655**

BENEFITS INTERNATIONAL See BENEFITS & COMPENSATION INTERNATIONAL **2875**

BENEFITS LAW JOURNAL (US/0897-7992) [17626795] **3144**

BENEFITS NEWS ANALYSIS **SUSPENDED.** (US/0199-3100) [05771123] **642**

BENEFITS QUARTERLY (US/8756-1263) [11482605] 642, 2875, **1655**

BENEFITS TODAY **CEASED.** (US/0747-9131) [10838159] **2941**

BENELUX (BE/0251-2912) [03011347] **1548**

BENELUX REPORT (US/0747-7708) [10811179] **1599**

BENEVOLE, LE (CN/0227-1567) [06688481] **1341**

BENEVOLONS! (ST-TITE) (CN/1183-1553) [24266037] **5274**

BENGAL PAST AND PRESENT (II/0005-8807) [01774246] **2647**

BENGOUGH BULLETIN (CN/0832-2937) [16581141] **5780**

BENHAM-BLAIR & AFFILIATES. ANNUAL REPORT TO THE OKLAHOMA TURNPIKE AUTHORITY; OKLAHOMA TURNPIKE SYSTEM & WILL ROGERS TURNPIKE See ANNUAL REPORT TO THE OKLAHOMA TURNPIKE AUTHORITY **4629**

BENHAM GROUP See ANNUAL REPORT TO THE OKLAHOMA TURNPIKE AUTHORITY **4629**

BENIN. MINISTERE DU DEVELOPPEMENT RURAL ET DE L'ACTION COOPERATIVE. SERVICE DES ETUDES ET DE LA STATISTIQUE See STRUCTURE DES EXPLOITATIONS AGRICOLES TRADITIONNELLES DE LA REPUBLIQUE POPULAIRE DU BENIN **138**

BENISSIMO MILANO (IT/1121-175X) [I1121175X] **1082**

BENITO STANDARD (CN/0316-0270) [02247311] **5780**

BENJAMIN N. CARDOZO SCHOOL OF LAW See ALUMNI DIRECTORY **1097**

BENJAMINS TRANSLATION LIBRARY (NE/0929-7316) **3268**

BENNETT COLLEGE (GREENSBORO, N.C.) See ALUMNAE DIRECTORY - BENNETT COLLEGE (GREENSBORO, N.C.) **1096**

BENNETT EXCHANGE NEWSLETTER See BENNETT EXCHANGE, THE **2439**

BENNETT EXCHANGE, THE (US/0884-6510) [09013092] **2439**

BENNETTS VALLEY NEWS, THE (US) [15088832] **5734**

BENN'S GUIDE (UK/0954-8548) [19544820] **600**

BENN'S MEDIA DIRECTORY. INTERNATIONAL See BENN'S MEDIA DIRECTORY. VOLUME 2, EUROPE **1104**

BENN'S MEDIA DIRECTORY. INTERNATIONAL See BENN'S MEDIA DIRECTORY. VOLUME 3, WORLD **1105**

BENN'S MEDIA DIRECTORY. VOLUME 1, UNITED KINGDOM (UK) **1105**

BENN'S MEDIA DIRECTORY. VOLUME 2, EUROPE (UK) [26025843] **1104**

BENN'S MEDIA DIRECTORY. VOLUME 3, WORLD (UK) [26025872] **1105**

BENRI CHO / BANKUBA IJUSHA NO KAI (CN/0821-4735) [10310651] **2723**

BENSHEIMER HEFTE (GW/0522-9014) [04281109] **4938**

BENSON MAGAZINE OF RESEARCH (US/0275-1720) [07078954] **2439**

BENSON TRACE, THE (US/0734-0214) [06989614] **2439**

BENT COUNTY DEMOCRAT (US) [13073286] **5642**

BENT OF TAU BETA PI, THE (US/0005-884X) [03985061] **1966**

BENTLEY HISTORICAL LIBRARY See BENTLEY LIBRARY ANNUAL, THE **3194**

BENTLEY LIBRARY ANNUAL, THE (US/0362-6881) [02330068] **3194**

BENTON COUNTY DAILY RECORD (US) [20811446] **5631**

BENTON COUNTY NEWS (US) [01519528] **5694**

BENTON COUNTY PIONEER, THE (US/0409-0829) [03815993] **2723**

BENTON COURIER, THE (US) [24125116] **5631**

BENTON HARBOR FRUIT MARKET (1982) (US/0744-9909) [08702947] **164**

BENTON HARBOR LABOR MARKET REVIEW See BENTON HARBOR'S LABOR MARKET NEWS **1655**

●BENTON HARBOR'S LABOR MARKET NEWS (US) [25950486] **1655**

BENTON NEWS, THE (US) [13343967] **5658**

BENTON REVIEW, THE (US) [11313091] **5663**

BENZENE ANNUAL See ANNUAL BENZENE & DERIVATIVES **4249**

BEP (BE/0774-6180) [16986717] **3555**

BEPPU DAIGAKU See BEPPU DAIGAKU KIYO **2843**

BEPPU DAIGAKU KIYO (JA) [03460097] **2843**

BEQUADRO (IT) **4102**

BERATER-INFORMATION - LBL (AU/0256-4270) [I02564270] **65**

BERCEO (SP/0210-8550) [03246699] **2678**

BEREA ALUMNUS, THE (US/0005-8874) [03985136] **1101**

BEREA CITIZEN, THE (US) [12249111] **5679**

BEREA COLLEGE. APPALACHIAN CENTER See NEWSLETTER - APPALACHIAN CENTER, BEREA COLLEGE **1093**

BEREAN AMBASSADOR, THE (CN/0227-5554) [08090998] **5056**

BEREAVEMENT (UK) **5274**

BEREAVEMENT & LOSS RESOURCES (US/1071-7366) [28707184] 5274, **4577**

BEREAVEMENT CARE (UK/0268-2621) [I02682621] **5274**

BEREAVEMENT (CARMEL, IND.) (US/0897-9588) [17510596] **4577**

BERENICE (IT) [07566825] **3366**

BERETNING - DANMARKS PAEDAGOGISKE INSTITUT (DK) [06495344] **1889**

BERETNING - FAELLESUDVALGET FOR STATENS MEJERI- OG HUSDYRBRUGSFORSG (DK/0106-1542) [03809827] **207**

BERETNING FOR ... / DEN CENTRALE VIDENSKABSETISKE KOMITE (DK/0107-9786) [10200188] **3555**

BERETNING FOR FINANSARET ... (DK) [10037659] **778**

BERETNING FOR PERIODEN ... (DK) [10172288] **501**

BERETNING FOR PERIODEN ... / FRA FLLESRADET VEDRRENDE MINERALSKE RASTOFFER I GRNLAND (DK/0107-3117) [11940709] **2135**

BERETNING FOR ... / ROSKILDE UNIVERSITETSCENTER (DK) [11181015] **1811**

BERETNING FOR UNDERVISNINGSARET ... / DANMARKS BIBLIOTEKSSKOLE (DK/0107-9700) [10141680] **3194**

BERETNING FRA FINANSTILSYNET (DK/0905-0965) [21170210] 778, **2875**

BERETNING FRA LABORATORIET FOR ELEKTRONIK, DANMARKS TEKNISKE HJSKOLE (DK) [02349797] **2036**

BERETNING FRA STATENS HUSDYRBRUGSFORSG (DK/0105-6883) [02256508] **65**

BERETNING - FRA STATENS PLANTEAVLSFORSOEG OG STATENS HUSDYRBRUGSFORSOEG (DK/0906-2181) [I09062181] **65**

BERETNING OG REGNSKAB FOR ARET ... (DK) [09873198] **1150**

BERETNING OG REGNSKAB - KBENHAVNS SPORVEJE (DK) [01794341] **5377**

BERETNING OG REGNSKAB - REALKREDITRADET (DK) [02241685] **778**

BERETNING OM VIRKSOMHEDEN I ... (DK) [20052625] **3998**

BERETNING - SOCIAL- OG SUNDHEDSFORVALTNINGEN I KBENHAVN (DK) [04258532] **5274**

BEREZIL : LITERATURNO-KHUDOZHNII TA HROMADSKO-POLITYCHNYI ZHURNAL SPILKY PYSMENNYKIV UKRAINY (UN) [24359303] **3366**

BERG- UND HUTTENMANNISCHE MONATSCHEFTE. SUPPLEMENTUM **CEASED.** (AU/0067-5768) [02903381] 3999, **1438**

BERGAKADEMIE FREIBERG. SEKTION GEOWISSENSCHAFTEN See VEROFFENTLICHUNG AUS DER SEKTION GEOWISSENSCHAFTEN DER BERGAKADEMIE FREIBERG **1400**

BERGAMO ECONOMICA (IT) [03246744] **1464**

BERGAMO OGGI (IT) **5804**

BERGAMO (PROVINCE). CAMERA DI COMMERCIO, INDUSTRIA E AGRICOLTURA See BERGAMO ECONOMICA **1464**

BERGAMO SPRING CONFERENCES ON HAEMATOLOGY (UK) [19485330] **3770**

BERGAMUM (IT/0005-8955) [09366553] **2678**

BERGBAU-BERUFSGENOSSENSCHA FT. BEZIRKSVERWALTUNG CLAUSTHAL-ZELLERFELD See VERWALTUNGSBERICHT DES BEZIRKS CLAUSTHAL-ZELLERFELD DER BERGBAU-BERUFSGENOSSENSCHA FT **2152**

BERGBAU-BERUFSGENOSSENSCHA FT (GERMANY). BEZIRKSVERWALTUNG BONN See VERWALTUNGSBERICHT DES BEZIRKS BONN DER BERGBAU-BERUFSGENOSSENSCHA FT / HERAUSGEGEBEN VON DER BEZIRKSVERWALTUNG BONN DER BERGBAU-BERUFSGENOSSENSCHA FT **2871**

BERGBAU (HATTINGEN) (GW/0342-5681) [06834879] **2135**

BERGBAU-ROHSTOFFE-ENERGIE (GW/0341-4132) [04023883] **1438**

BERGBAU UND VERARBEITENDES GEWERBE (GW) [07017675] **2135**

BERGEDORFER GESPRAECHSKREIS ZU FRAGEN DER FREIEN INDUSTRIELLEN GESELLSCHAFT See PROTOKOLL **849**

BERGEN, NORWAY. VESTLANDSKE KUNSTINDUSTRIMUSEUM See ARBOK - BERGEN, NORWAY. VESTLANDSKE KUNSTINDUSTRIMUSEUM **370**

BERGER & ASSOCIATES COST CONSULTANTS See BERGER BUILDING COST FILE, UNIT PRICES. WESTERN EDITION **600**

BERGER & ASSOCIATES COST CONSULTANTS See BERGER BUILDING COST FILE, UNIT PRICES. CENTRAL EDITION, THE **600**

BERGER BUILDING & DESIGN COST FILE. UNIT PRICES. CENTRAL EDITION, THE (US/0278-2146) [07388637] **600**

BERGER BUILDING & DESIGN COST FILE. UNIT PRICES. SOUTHERN EDITION, THE (US/0732-4685) [07440223] **600**

BERGER BUILDING & DESIGN COST FILE. UNIT PRICES. WESTERN EDITION, THE (US/0278-2065) [07420517] **600**

BERGER BUILDING COST FILE, UNIT PRICES. CENTRAL EDITION, THE (US/0272-5401) [05995446] **600**

BERGER BUILDING COST FILE, UNIT PRICES. WESTERN EDITION (US/0271-3128) [06586029] **600**

BERGSMANNEN (SW/0284-0448) [18788498] **2135**

BERGWELT (GW/0340-1294) [01794169] **4869**

BERICHT (AU) [01788786] **5087**

BERICHT AUS DEM HAUS DER NATUR IN SALZBURG (AU/0302-9654) [05718495] **4162**

BERICHT

Alphabetical Title Index

BERICHT DER BAYERISCHEN BODENDENKMALPFLEGE / BAYERISCHES LANDESAMT FUER DENKMALPFLEGE (GW) [17939907] **2678**

BERICHT DER BUNDESREGIERUNG AN DEN NATIONALRAT (AU) [03423425] **5087**

BERICHT DER HISTORISCHEN VEREINIGUNG WYNENTAL *See* JAHRESSCHRIFT DER HISTORISCHEN VEREINIGUNG WYNENTAL **2694**

BERICHT DER NATURFORSCHENDEN GESELLSCHAFT AUGSBURG (GW/0343-7655) [01759438] **4163**

BERICHT DER NATURHISTORISCHEN GESELLSCHAFT HANNOVER (GW/0365-9844) [01759506] **4163**

BERICHT DER ROMISCH-GERMANISCHEN KOMMISSION (GW) [19034282] **261**

BERICHT DER STAATLICHEN DENKMALPFLEGE IM SAARLAND. ABTEILUNG BODENDENKMALPFLEGE (GW/0341-9673) [03436992] **343, 261**

BERICHT DER STAATLICHEN DENKMALPFLEGE IM SAARLAND. ABTEILUNG KUNSTDENKMALPFLEGE (GW/0341-9657) [03436957] **261**

BERICHT ... DES BUNDESVERBANDES DER DEUTSCHEN INDUSTRIE E.V (GW) [19658106] **1464**

BERICHT DES KULTUSMINISTERIUMS BADEN-WURTTEMBERG ZUR BERATUNG DES HAUSHALTSPLANES (GW/0302-6353) [01793137] **1860**

BERICHT DES PRASIDENTEN UBER DIE TATIGKEIT DES INSTITUTS (GW) [06469795] **1633**

BERICHT DES PRASIDENTEN, ZAHLENSPIEGEL (GW/0723-2659) [11172009] **1811**

BERICHT - DEUTSCHE GENOSSENSCHAFTSKASSE (GW/0417- 1888) [05044578] **1464**

BERICHT - DEUTSCHER INDUSTRIE- UND HANDELSTAG (GW/0418-9469) [05005875] **1599**

BERICHT - DEUTSCHES INSTITUT FUR INTERNATIONALE PADAGOGISCHE FORSCHUNG (GW) [04662372] **1889**

BERICHT - FORSCHUNGSFORDERUNGSFONDS FUR DIE GEWERBLICHE WIFTSCHAFT (GW) [11181553] **5087**

BERICHT / HAHN-MEITNER-INSTITUT BERLIN GMBH (GW/0072-9280) [17150578] **4398, 962**

BERICHT (HISTORISCHER VEREIN FUR DIE PFLEGE DER GESCHICHTE DES EHEMALIGEN FURSTBISTUMS ZU BAMBERG : 1979) (GW) [09698914] **2611**

BERICHT - KAMMER DER GEWERBLICHEN WIRTSCHAFT FUR TIROL (GW) [01789552] **1548**

BERICHT - KAMMER FUR LAND- UND FORSTWIRTSCHAFT IN SALZBURG (AU) [02957457] **2376, 26**

BERICHT - MAX-PLANCK-INSTITUT FUER STROMUNGSFORSCHUNG (GW/0436-1199) [02684351] **2087**

BERICHT - NATURFORSCHENDE GESELLSCHAFT BAMBERG (GW/0340-3750) [10844185] **2188**

BERICHT / OSTERREICHISCHER RAIFFEISENVERBAND (AU) [20325403] **778**

BERICHT - PENSIONSVERSICHERUNGSANSTALT DER ANGESTELLTEN (AU) [01794058] **2875, 1655**

BERICHT / STIFTERVERBAND FUR DIE DEUTSCHE WISSENSCHAFT (GW) [08210175] **5087**

BERICHT - STIFTUNG VOLKSWAGENWERK *See* BERICHT (VOLKSWAGENSTIFTUNG) **2485**

BERICHT UBER DAS BASLER MUSEUM FUER VOLKERKUNDE UND SCHWEIZERISCHE MUSEUM FUER VOLKSKUNDE FUER DAS JAHR ... (SZ) [05671868] **232**

BERICHT UBER DAS ... INTERNATIONALE KOLLOQUIUM UBER DIE VERHUTUNG VON ARBEITSUNFALLEN UND BERUFSKRANKHEITEN IN DER CHEMISCHEN INDUSTRIE (GW/0171-2144) [11311373] **2859**

BERICHT UBER DEN ... OSTERREICHISCHEN HISTORIKERTAG IN ... / VERANSTALTET VOM VERBAND OSTERREICHISCHER GESCHICHTSVEREINE IN DER ZEIT VOM ... (AU) [11855965] **2678**

BERICHT UBER DIE AUSGRABUNGEN IN OLYMPIA (GW/0418-9655) [01566497] **261**

BERICHT UBER DIE FORDERUNG VON FORSCHUNGS- UND ENTWICKLUNGSVORHABEN UND UBER DIE ERTEILUNG VON FORSCHUNGS- UND ENTWICKLUNGSAUFTRAGEN (AU) [02553795] **5439**

BERICHT UBER DIE JAHRESTAGUNG ... (GW) [12031078] **2513**

BERICHT UBER DIE KALTE-KLIMA-TAGUNG ... DES DEUTSCHEN KALTE- UND KLIMATECHNISCHEN VEREINS E.V (DKV) (GW) [16912246] **2603**

BERICHT UBER DIE SOZIALE LAGE. SOZIALBERICHT, TATIGKEITSBERICHT DES BUNDESMINISTERIUMS FUER SOZIALE VERWALTUNG (AU/0587-2200) [06714976] **5274**

BERICHT UBER DIE ... TAGUNG FUER GETREIDECHEMIE (GW) [11743268] **65**

BERICHT UBER DIE VERHANDLUNGEN DER ORDENTLICHEN SYNODE DE NORDELBISCHEN EV.-LUTH. KIRCHE (GW) [05155765] **5056**

BERICHT (VOLKSWAGENSTIFTUNG) (GW/0585-3044) [22836658] **2485**

BERICHTE AUS DEM INSTITUT FUER MEERESKUNDE AN DER CHRISTIAN-ALBRECHTS-UNIVERSITAT KIEL (GW/0341-8561) [02841095] **553**

BERICHTE AUS NAMIBIA (GW) **4465**

BERICHTE AUS TECHNIK UND WISSENSCHAFT / LINDE (GW/0942-332X) [30857680] **5087**

BERICHTE AUS WASSERGUTEWIRTSCHAFT UND GESUNDHEITSINGENIEURWESEN (GW/0722-7728) [09408138] **5087**

BERICHTE DER ABWASSERTECHNISCHEN VEREINIGUNG (GW/0515-1074) [01726892] **2225**

BERICHTE DER ARBEITSGEMEINSCHAFT FUER OKOLOGISCHE ENTOMOLOGIE IN GRAZ (AU) [03572059] **5605**

BERICHTE DER BAYERISCHEN BOTANISCHEN GESELLSCHAFT ZUR ERFORSCHUNG DER HEIMISCHEN FLORA (GW/0373-7640) [01519275] **501**

BERICHTE DER BIOLOGISCHEN ANSTALT HELGOLAND (GW/0930-8148) [09308148] **443**

BERICHTE DER BOTANISCH-ZOOLOGISCHEN GESELLSCHAFT (LH) [12219490] **5578, 502**

BERICHTE DER BUNSEN-GESELLSCHAFT FUR PHYSIKALISCHE CHEMIE *See* INTERNATIONAL JOURNAL OF PHYSICAL CHEMISTRY : BERICHTE DER BUNSEN-GESELLSCHAFT, AN **1053**

BERICHTE DER BUNSENGESELLSCHAFT FUER PHYSIKALISCHE CHEMIE (GW/0005-9021) [01537817] **1050**

BERICHTE DER DEUTSCHEN MINERALOGISCHEN GESELLSCHAFT (GW/0935-123X) [20514328] **1438**

BERICHTE DER GESELLSCHAFT FUER MATHEMATIK UND DATENVERARBEITUNG (GW/0533-9480) [105339480] **3497**

BERICHTE DER KERNFORSCHUNGSANLAGE JULICH (GW/0366-0885) [23109312] **4446**

BERICHTE DER NATURFORSCHENDEN GESELLSCHAFT ZU FREIBURG I. BR (GW/0028-0917) [01759502] **5088**

BERICHTE DER DEUTSCHEN WETTERDIENST (GW/0072-4130) [01468230] **1420**

BERICHTE DES FORSCHUNGSZENTRUMS WALDOKOSYSTEM/WALDSTERBEN REIHE B (GW) [18669361] **2376**

BERICHTE DES FORSCHUNGSZENTRUMS WALDOKOSYSTEME/WALDSTERBEN REIHE A (GW/0930-7044) [18669192] **2376**

BERICHTE DES GEOBOTANISCHEN INSTITUTES DER EIDG. TECHN. HOCHSCHULE, STIFTUNG RUBEL (SZ/0373-7896) [02841588] **502**

BERICHTE DES INSTITUTES FUER METEOROLOGIE UND GEOPHYSIK DER UNIVERSITAT FRANKFUERT/MAIN (GW/0722-382X) [02741710] **1420**

BERICHTE DES NATURWISSENSCHAFTLICH-MEDIZINISCHEN VEREINS IN INNSBRUCK (AU/0379-1416) [01759510] **5088**

BERICHTE DES VEREINS NATUR UND HEIMAT UND DES NATURHISTORISCHEN MUSEUMS ZU LUBECK (GW/0505-2793) [05767104] **4163**

BERICHTE (GERMANY (WEST). UMWELTBUNDESAMT) *See* BERICHTE / UMWELTBUNDESAMT **3110**

BERICHTE GYNAKOLOGIE, GEBURTSHILFE (GW/0722-9852) [08959570] **3757**

BERICHTE - INSTITUT FUER PHONETIK DER UNIVERSITAT ZU KOLN (GW/0930-5440) [I09305440] **3268**

BERICHTE PATHOLOGIE (GW/0722-9674) [09114676] **3893**

BERICHTE PHYSIOLOGIE, PHYSIOLOGISCHE CHEMIE UND PHARMAKOLOGIE (GW/0005-9048) [01519556] **578**

BERICHTE UBER DIE AUSGRABUNGEN IN HAITHABU (GW/0525-5791) [04535919] **261**

BERICHTE UBER LANDWIRTSCHAFT (GW/0005-9080) [01519560] **65**

BERICHTE UBER LANDWIRTSCHAFT. SONDERHEFT (GW/0301-2689) [03329904] **65**

BERICHTE / UMWELTBUNDESAMT (GW) [28091407] **3110**

BERICHTE ZUR DEUTSCHEN LANDESKUNDE (GW/0005-9099) [01519561] **2678**

BERICHTE ZUR ENTWICKLUNG IN SPANIEN, PORTUGAL UND LATEINAMERIKA (GW) [03226802] **2723**

BERICHTE ZUR LUFTFAHRTGERAETEROLLE (GW) **14**

BERICHTE ZUR RAUMFORSCHUNG UND RAUMPLANUNG (AU/0005-9102) [03112561] **2816**

BERICHTE ZUR WISSENSCHAFTSGESCHICHTE (GW/0170-6233) [05149160] **5088**

BERICHTEN OVER DE BUITENLANDSE HANDEL (BE) **4102**

BERITA BADAN PEMBINAAN HUKUM NASIONAL (IO) [02245662] **2941**

BERITA BIBLIOGRAFI (JAKARTA, INDONESIA : 1984) (IO/0216-1273) [11458212] **408**

BERITA EPIDEMIOLOGI (IO) [04306018] **3712**

BERITA ILMU PENGETAHUAN DAN TEKNOLOGI (IO) [03217419] **5088**

BERITA INDUSTRI (IO/0126-1010) [01795460] **1548**

BERITA IPTEK (IO/0125-9156) [24640000] **5088**

BERITA ISOPB (MY/0127-6581) [101276581] **2410**

BERITA KOMUNIKASI MASYARAKAT SEJARAWAN INDONESIA (IO) [02245912] **2647**

BERITA KOWANI (IO) [06834270] **5551**

BERITA MIGAS (IO) [03674592] **4252**

BERITA PEKERJAAN UMUM (IO) [05794441] **4632**

BERITA PENDIDIKAN SASTRA DAN SENI (IO) [03494324] **3366**

BERITA PENYELIDIKAN INSTITUT PENYELIDIKAN DAN KEMAJUAN PERTANIAN MALAYSIA (MY) [10312000] **65**

BERITA PERPUSTAKAAN (IO) [01797922] **3194**

BERITA PRASEJARAH (IO) [01797888] **261**

BERITA PUSAT RISET DIRGANTARA, LAPAN (IO) [06702496] **14**

BERITA SELULOSA (MY/0005-9145) [03277195] **4232**

BERKALA BIOANTHROPOLOGI INDONESIA (IO/0216-7204) [08490994] **232**

BERKALA ITB (IO) [06768038] **5088**

BERKELEY, CALIFORNIA. RADIO STATION KPFA *See* KPFA PROGRAM FOLIO **1134**

BERKELEY COUNTY HISTORICAL SOCIETY NEWSLETTER (US) **5763**

BERKELEY INSIGHTS IN LINGUISTICS AND SEMIOTICS (US/0893-6935) [15626262] **3268**

● BERKELEY JOURNAL OF EMPLOYMENT AND LABOR LAW (US/1067-7666) [27345092] **3144**

BERKELEY JOURNAL OF SOCIOLOGY (US/0067-5830) [05245732] **5240**

BERKELEY JOURNAL, THE (US) [07070851] **2611**

BERKELEY-KOELNER RECHTSSTUDIEN (GW/0409-1264) [02757791] **2941**

BERKELEY LINGUISTICS SOCIETY *See* PROCEEDINGS OF THE ANNUAL MEETING OF THE BERKELEY LINGUISTICS SOCIETY **3312**

● BERKELEY MODELS OF GRAMMAR (US/1061-6055) [25378521] **3268**

BERKELEY MONTHLY, THE (US/0191-7080) [04948178] **3338**

BERKELEY NEWSLETTER (IE/0332-026X) [04221418] **4342**

BERKELEY NEWSLETTER (BERKELEY, CALIF.) (US/0748-7169) [10994021] **962**

BERKELEY PAPERS IN HISTORY OF SCIENCE (US/0145-0379) [03253872] **5088**

BERKELEY PLANNING JOURNAL (US/1047-5192) [11336832] **2816**

BERKELEY POETRY REVIEW, THE (US) [02071719] **3338**

BERKELEY WOMEN'S LAW JOURNAL (US/0882-4312) [11830558] **2941**

BERKLEY SHOWCASE, THE (US) [06206954] **3366**

BERKS COUNTY LAW JOURNAL (US/8750-3379) [01519570] **2941**

BERKS COUNTY MEDICAL RECORD, THE (US/0736-7333) [09116044] **3555**

BERKSHIRE ARCHAEOLOGICAL JOURNAL, THE (UK/0309-3093) [08862097] **261**

BERKSHIRE COURIER (GREAT BARRINGTON, MASS. : 1848) (US) [09482243] **5687**

BERKSHIRE EAGLE, THE (US/0895-8793) [12737059] **5687**

BERKSHIRE GARDEN SUPPLY *See* SPRING CATALOGUE / BERKSHIRE GARDEN SUPPLY **2432**

BERKSHIRE GENEALOGIST, THE (US/0887-0713) [09694764] **2439**

BERKSHIRE MAGAZINE (US/1042-587X) [19090117] **2723**

●BERKSHIRE REVIEW (PITTSFIELD, MASS.), THE (US/1063-7559) [26134281] **2528**

BERLIN-BRANDENBURGISCHE BAUWIRTSCHAFT (GW/0940-3825) [I09403825] **600**

BERLIN. FREIE UNIVERSITAT. INSTITUT FUR KONZENTRATIONFORSCHUNG *See* SCHRIFTENREIHE **1847**

BERLIN. FREIE UNIVERSITAT. INSTITUT FUR METEOROLOGIE *See* TAGLICHE HOHENKARTEN DER 50-MB-FLACHE SOWIE MONATLICHE MITTELKARTEN **1435**

BERLIN. FREIE UNIVERSITAT. INSTITUT FUR METEOROLOGIE *See* TAGLICHE HOHENKARTEN DER 30-MB-FLACHE SOWIE MONATLICHE MITTELKARTEN **1435**

BERLIN. FREIE UNIVERSITAT. INSTITUT FUR PUBLIZISTIK *See* ABHANDLUNGEN UND MATERIALIEN ZUR PUBLIZISTIK **2609**

BERLIN. FREIE UNIVERSITAT. OSTEUROPA-INSTITUT *See* WIRTSCHAFTSWISSENSCHAFTLICHE VEROFFENTLICHUNGEN **1526**

BERLIN (GERMANY : WEST). SENATOR FUR FINANZEN *See* FINANZPLANUNG VON BERLIN **4726**

BERLIN. HOCHSCHULE FUER OEKONOMIE *See* WISSENSCHAFTLICHE ZEITSCHRIFT DER HOCHSCHULE FUER OEKONOMIE **1527**

BERLIN IN GESCHICHTE UND GEGENWART (GW/0175-8446) [09810203] **2678**

BERLIN JOURNAL, THE (US/8755-4003) [11292002] **5765**

BERLIN MAGAZIN (GW/0300-1644) [01784804] **2513**

BERLIN. MUSEUM FUR VOLKERKUNDE (WEST BERLIN) *See* VEROFFENTLICHUNGEN. ABTEILUNG SUDSEE **2325**

BERLIN REPORTER, THE (US/1074-3499) [20881122] **5708**

BERLIN. STAATLICHE MUSEEN. AGYPTISCHE URKUNDEN: GRIECHISCHE URKUNDEN *See* AGYPTISCHE URKUNDEN AUS DEN STAATLICHEN MUSEEN BERLIN: GRIECHISCHE URKUNDEN **253**

BERLIN. STAATLICHE MUSEEN (WEST BERLIN) *See* BILDERHEFTE **4084**

BERLIN. STAATLICHE MUSEEN (WEST BERLIN) *See* AGYPTISCHE URKUNDEN AUS DEN STAATLICHEN MUSEEN BERLIN: GRIECHISCHE URKUNDEN **253**

BERLIN. TECHNISCHE UNIVERSITAT. KOMMISSION FUR FORSCHUNG UND WISSENSCHAFTLICHEN NACHWUCHS *See* FORSCHUNG AN DER TECHNISCHEN UNIVERSITAT BERLIN **5105**

BERLIN-VERKEHR, DER (GW) [03456208] **5439**

BERLIN (WEST BERLIN). DER SENATOR FUR VERKEHR UND BETRIEBE *See* BERLIN-VERKEHR, DER **5439**

BERLIN (WEST BERLIN). SENATOR FUR WIRTSCHAFT *See* BERLINER WIRTSCHAFTSDATEN **1548**

BERLINER ABHANDLUNGEN ZUM PRESSERECHT (GW/0409-1949) [01519605] **2917**

BERLINER ARZT *See* BERLINER ARZTEBLATT **3555**

BERLINER ARZTEBLATT (GW/0172-8490) [06046862] **3555**

BERLINER BEITRAEGE ZUR ARCHAOMETRIE (GW/0344-5089) [04689223] **261**

BERLINER BEITRAEGE ZUR NAMENFORSCHUNG (GE/0572-6263) [01775015] **2678, 3268**

BERLINER BYZANTINISTISCHE ARBEITEN (GW/0067-6055) [02413777] **1074, 2678**

BERLINER DEBATTE INITIAL : ZEITSCHRIFT FUER SOCIALWISSENSCHAFTLICHEN DISKURS (GW/0863-4564) [24147033] **4465, 5192**

BERLINER GASWERKE *See* JAHRESBERICHT - BERLINER GASWERKE **979**

BERLINER GEOGRAPHISCHE ABHANDLUNGEN (GW/0523-0160) [02767152] **2556**

BERLINER GEOGRAPHISCHE STUDIEN (GW/0341-8537) [06111336] **2556**

BERLINER GEOWISSENSCHAFTLICHE ABHANDLUNGEN. REIHE A. GEOLOGIE UND PALAONTOLOGIE (GW/0172-8784) [05045406] **4226, 1367**

BERLINER HANDELS- UND FRANKFURTER BANK *See* REPORT ON THE FINANCIAL LIST - BERLINER HANDELS- UND FRANKFURTER BANK **808**

BERLINER JOURNAL FUER SOZIOLOGIE (GW) [I08631808] **5240**

BERLINER JURISTISCHE ABHANDLUNGEN (GW/0523-0209) [01519616] **2941**

BERLINER SEMINAR (GW/0172-6897) [04606203] **4293**

BERLINER SIGELVERZEICHNIS / BERLINER GESAMTKATALOG ; DEUTSCHE STAATSBIBLIOTHEK, INSTITUT FUER LEIHVERKEHR UND ZENTRALKATALOGE ; DEUTSCHES BIBLIOTHEKSINSTITUT (GW/0170-1738) [28040727] **3194**

BERLINER SIGELVERZEICHNIS MIT SYSTEMATISCHEN VERZEICHNIS DER SAMMELGEBIETE WISSENSCHAFTLICHER LITERATUR IN BERLIN (WEST) (GW) [04558397] **3194**

BERLINER THEOLOGISCHE ZEITSCHRIFT : THEOLOGIA VIATORUM NEUE FOLGE : HALBJAHRESSCHRIFT FUER THEOLOGIE IN DER KIRCHE (GW/0724-6137) [10808342] **4938**

BERLINER UND MUNCHENER TIERARZTLICHE WOCHENSCHRIFT (GW/0005-9366) [06280787] **5505**

BERLINER WIRTSCHAFTSDATEN (GW) [01788376] **1548**

BERLINGSKE TIDENDE (DK) [01519621] **5799**

●BERLITZ TRAVELER'S GUIDE TO MEXICO, THE (US/1057-4786) [24041701] **5462**

●BERLITZ TRAVELLER'S GUIDE BERLIN, THE (US/1065-6294) [26659429] **5462**

●BERLITZ TRAVELLER'S GUIDE TO AUSTRALIA, THE (US/1057-4689) [24041198] **5462**

●BERLITZ TRAVELLER'S GUIDE TO CANADA, THE (US) [24041658] **5462**

●BERLITZ TRAVELLER'S GUIDE TO ENGLAND & WALES, THE (US/1057-4735) [24041476] **5462**

●BERLITZ TRAVELLER'S GUIDE TO FRANCE, THE (US/1057-476X) [24041626] **5462**

●BERLITZ TRAVELLER'S GUIDE TO GERMANY, THE (US/1057-462X) [24037884] **5463**

●BERLITZ TRAVELLER'S GUIDE TO GREECE, THE (US) [24038021] **5463**

●BERLITZ TRAVELLER'S GUIDE TO HAWAII, THE (US/1057-4700) [24041265] **5463**

●BERLITZ TRAVELLER'S GUIDE TO IRELAND, THE (US/1057-4719) [24041302] **5463**

●BERLITZ TRAVELLER'S GUIDE TO LONDON, THE (US/1057-4751) [24041576] **5463**

●BERLITZ TRAVELLER'S GUIDE TO NEW ENGLAND, THE (US/1062-3655) [25598099] **5463**

●BERLITZ TRAVELLER'S GUIDE TO NEW YORK CITY, THE (US/1057-4743) [24041517] **5463**

●BERLITZ TRAVELLER'S GUIDE TO PORTUGAL, THE (US) [24037949] **5463**

●BERLITZ TRAVELLER'S GUIDE TO ROME AND NORTHERN ITALY, THE (US) [24037971] **5463**

●BERLITZ TRAVELLER'S GUIDE TO ROME AND SOUTHERN ITALY, THE (US) [24037992] **5463**

●BERLITZ TRAVELLER'S GUIDE TO SAN FRANCISCO & NORTHERN CALIFORNIA, THE (US/1057-4727) [24041415] **5463**

●BERLITZ TRAVELLER'S GUIDE TO SPAIN, THE (US) [24037898] **5463**

●BERLITZ TRAVELLER'S GUIDE TO THE CARIBBEAN, THE (US/1057-4697) [24041235] **5463**

●BERLITZ TRAVELLER'S GUIDE TO THE SOUTHWEST, THE (US/1062-3663) [25598139] **5463**

BERMUDA BIOLOGICAL STATION FOR RESEARCH *See* CONTRIBUTIONS FROM THE BERMUDA BIOLOGICAL STATION FOR RESEARCH **2226**

BERMUDA ISLANDS *See* APPROVED ESTIMATES OF REVENUE AND EXPENDITURE **4711**

BERMUDA JOURNAL OF ARCHAEOLOGY AND MARITIME HISTORY (BM/1013-431X) [21718259] **261**

BERMUDA MONETARY AUTHORITY *See* REPORT & ACCOUNTS - BERMUDA MONETARY AUTHORITY **807**

BERMUDIAN, THE (BM) [02769700] **4887**

BERN. SCHWEIZERISCHES GUTENBERGMUSEUM *See* SCHWEIZERISCHES GUTENBERGMUSEUM **709**

BERN (SWITZERLAND : CANTON) *See* FINANZPLAN DES KANTONS BERN **4726**

BERNAN ASSOCIATES CHECKLIST OF CONGRESSIONAL HEARINGS AND COMMITTEE PRINTS *See* CONGRESS IN PRINT **4640**

BERNAN ASSOCIATES' GOVERNMENT PUBLICATIONS NEWS (US/0897-5728) [17555641] **4632**

BERNARD BOLZANO GESAMTAUSGABE (GW) **4342**

BERNARD ZICK'S REAL ESTATE FINANCING & MORTGAGE REPORT (US/0893-9519) [15803421] **4834, 778**

BERNE TRI-WKELY NEWS (US) [14389749] **5663**

BERNER BRANCHEN- UND ADRESSBUCH (SZ) [05067897] **2678**

BERNER KUNSTMITTEILUNGEN (GW/1010-559X) [08037243] **343**

BERNICE PAUAHI BISHOP MUSEUM *See* SPECIAL PUBLICATIONS **4096**

BERNISCHER JURISTENVEREIN *See* ZEITSCHRIFT DES BERNISCHEN JURISTENVEREINS **3077**

●BERNOULLI (UK/1350-7265) **5323**

BERRIEN PRESS, THE (US) [19096440] **5652**

BERRY ALUMNI ASSOCIATION *See* BERRY ALUMNI DIRECTORY **1101**

BERRY ALUMNI DIRECTORY (US/0741-9112) [10215007] **1101**

●BERRY & VEGETABLE INFORMER (CN/1189-4172) [26621378] **2328, 65**

BERRY NEWS AND VIEWS *See* BERRY & VEGETABLE INFORMER **65**

BERTIE LEDGER-ADVANCE (US) [13118314] **5722**

BERUFLICHE AUS- UND FORTBILDUNG (GW) [02981248] **1911**

BERUFLICHE REHABILITATION, ARBEITS- UND BERUFSFORDERUNG BEHINDERTER IN DEN JAHREN (GW) [10357463] **4384**

BERUFSBILDENDE SCHULE, DIE (GW/0005-951X) [I0005951X] **1599**

BERUFSBILDUNGSBERICHT (GW) [07581770] **1911**

BERUGSBILDUNG, WIETERBILDUNG, BILDUNGSPOLITIK (GW/0175-713X) [20822271] **1727**

BERUHAZASI, EPITOIPARI, LAKASEPITESI ZSEBKONYV (HU/0139-3510) [06622420] **600**

BERUHMTE FRAUEN (GW) [18129728] **5551**

BERYTUS; ARCHAEOLOGICAL STUDIES (LE/0067-6195) [01519638] **261**

BESCHAFTIGTENENTWICKLUNG IN NORDRHEIN-WESTFALEN. ERGEBNISSE EINER REGIONAL DISAGGREGIERTEN ANALYSE, DIE (GW) [16386412] **5323**

BESCHAFTIGUNGSTHERAPIE UND REHABILITATION *See* ERGOTHERAPIE & REHABILITATION **1878**

BESCHAFTIGUNGSTHERAPIE UND REHABILITATION (GW/0340-529X) [I0340529X] **1875**

BESCHRIJVENDE RASSENLIJST VOOR GROENTEGEWASSEN. VOLLEGRONDSGROENTEN (NE) [11700102] **2410**

BESKIDEN-KALENDER (GW) [06570710] **2678**

BESSATSU BIJUTSU TECHO (JA/0287-2226) [10611246] **344**

BESSATSU BUNGEI SHUNJU (JA) [06669977] **3366**

BESSATSU DAIYAMONDO (JA) [02744705] **1548**

BESSATSU SEIKEI GEKA (JA/0287-1645) [09485496] **3960**

BESSATSU TAIYO (HEIBONSHA) (JA) [09297395] **2502**

BESSERES OBST (AU) **65**

BEST — Alphabetical Title Index

BEST (FR) **4103**

BEST AMERICAN ESSAYS, THE (US/0888-3742) [13561582] **3366**

BEST AMERICAN PLAYS (US/0067-6225) [01519646] **5362**

BEST AMERICAN POETRY, THE (US/1040-5763) [18453423] **3460**

BEST AMERICAN SHORT PLAYS, THE (US/1062-7561) [24183958] **5362**

BEST AMERICAN SHORT STORIES (BOSTON, MASS. : 1978) (US/0067-6233) [09594962] **3366**

BEST AMERICAN SPORTS WRITING, THE (US/1056-8034) [23858416] **4887**

● BEST BED & BREAKFAST IN ENGLAND, SCOTLAND & WALES, THE (UK/1054-4089) [2292391-] 5463, **2804**

BEST BED & BREAKFAST IN THE WORLD *See* BEST BED & BREAKFAST IN ENGLAND, SCOTLAND & WALES, THE **2804**

BEST BOOKS FOR CHILDREN : A CATALOG OF ... TITLES (US) [01028288] **1060**

BEST BOOKS FOR YOUNG ADULTS (US/0882-0708) [04794573] **4824**

BEST BUYS & DISCOUNT PRICES (US/0882-729X) [05067889] **1293**

BEST CANADIAN STORIES (CN/0703-9476) [03569941] **3366**

BEST EDITORIAL CARTOONS OF THE YEAR (US/0737-9498) [03040845] **377**

BEST FESTIVALS OF NORTH AMERICA (US/0882-4193) [11830872] **383**

BEST GUIDE TO AMSTERDAM & BENELUX VENUES (FOR GAY MEN AND LESBIANS) (NE) 2793, **5463**

BEST GUIDE TO GREAT BRITAIN (FOR GAY MEN) (NE) 2793, **5463**

BEST HOME PLANS (US/0146-9681) [03092621] **293**

BEST IN ADVERTISING, THE (US/1046-8242) [03549516] **756**

BEST IN ANNUAL REPORTS THE (US/0360-8743) [02244979] **642**

BEST IN COVERS & POSTERS, THE (US) [03613027] **377**

BEST IN ENVIRONMENTAL GRAPHICS, THE (US/0360-8271) [02244982] **377**

BEST IN EXHIBITION DESIGN, THE (US/1048-2644) [03458350] **756**

BEST IN PACKAGING, THE (US/0360-8689) [02244981] **4218**

BEST INVESTMENT (UK) **892**

BEST MEDIA (US/0742-4027) [10334884] **1105**

BEST MEN'S STAGE MONOLOGUES, THE (US) [24358828] **5362**

BEST 'N' MOST IN DFS, THE (SW/1100-3006) [I11003006] **824**

BEST NEWSPAPER WRITING (US/0195-895X) [05701070] **2917**

BEST OF ACLD, THE (US/0731-1370) [07588497] **1875**

● BEST OF ANDALUCIA, THE (US/1045-3091) [20066324] **5463**

● BEST OF ANDORRA, THE (US/1051-1504) [21881175] **2678**

BEST OF ARIZONA, THE (US/0891-3722) [13699022] **5463**

BEST OF BUSINESS INTERNATIONAL (UK/0959-2113) [21001977] **642**

BEST OF BUSINESS QUARTERLY *CEASED.* (US/1047-3882) [14761325] **642**

● BEST OF CATALUNYA, THE (US/1045-3083) [20066296] **5463**

BEST OF CHINA WITH HONG KONG AND MACAU, THE (US/1043-6553) [19509103] 2556, **5463**

BEST OF FILM & VIDEO *See* VIDEO THE MAGAZINE **4079**

BEST OF GOAL, THE (US/0097-9767) [01799013] **4887**

● BEST OF HAIRDO IDEAS, THE (US/1064-8844) [26443801] **402**

BEST OF HONG KONG, THE (US/1043-6545) [19509005] 2556, **5463**

BEST OF INDIA, THE (US/1040-077X) [18311680] **5463**

BEST OF KERVIN FONDREN, THE (US/1058-9910) [24455641] **3460**

BEST OF LONG RANGE PLANNING, THE *CEASED.* (US/0889-3136) [13844244] 1599, **642**

BEST OF MACAU, THE (US/1043-6537) [19508963] 2556, **5463**

● BEST OF MADRID, THE (US/1045-3075) [20066255] **5463**

BEST OF MARKETING YEARBOOK, THE (AT) **921**

BEST OF METAL, THE (US/1062-6913) [25698451] **4103**

BEST OF MOROCCO, THE (US/1040-0788) [18311618] **5463**

BEST OF NATIONAL LAMPOON, THE (US/0092-5306) [01789442] **2528**

BEST OF NEWSPAPER DESIGN (MEMBER ED.), THE (US/0737-2612) [09305584] **2917**

BEST OF PERSONAL COMPUTING, THE (US/0275-455X) [07118026] 1265, **1273**

BEST OF PHOTOJOURNALISM, THE (US/0161-4762) [03916229] **4367**

● BEST OF PORTUGAL, THE (US/1045-3105) [20066350] **5463**

BEST OF SECRETS (US) **3366**

● BEST OF SPAIN, THE (US/1045-3067) [20066189] **5463**

● BEST OF THE REPUBLIC OF KOREA, THE (US/1053-9484) [22698197] **5463**

BEST OF THE SUPERSTARS, THE (US/1053-6671) [22605069] **383**

BEST OF TV GUIDE CROSSWORDS, THE (US/1054-3422) [22849601] **4857**

BEST ON QUALITY : YEARBOOK OF INTERNATIONAL ACADEMY FOR QUALITY, THE (GW) [19003174] **4218**

BEST PAPERS PROCEEDINGS / ACADEMY OF MANAGEMENT (JS/0896-7911) [14260922] **861**

BEST PAPERS PROCEEDINGS / ATLANTIC ECONOMIC SOCIETY (US/1058-4110) [24020326] **1464**

BEST PEP ADVICE (UK) **892**

BEST PLACES TO STAY IN MEXICO (US/1055-0879) [23070674] **5463**

● BEST PLACES TO STAY IN THE MID-ATLANTIC STATES (US/1061-7353) [25426012] **2804**

● BEST PLACES TO STAY IN THE MIDWEST (US/1060-7749) [25060780] **5463**

● BEST PLACES TO STAY IN THE ROCKY MOUNTAIN STATES (US/1060-7730) [25060790] **2804**

● BEST PLACES TO STAY IN THE SOUTH (US/1060-7757) [25060768] **5463**

BEST PLAYS OF ..., THE (US/1071-6971) [28703150] **5362**

BEST PRACTICE IN HEALTH CARE COMMISSIONING (UK) **4768**

BEST RECIPES (US/0897-0386) [17373706] 2788, **2328**

BEST SCIENCE FICTION (US/0091-9217) [01787763] **3366**

BEST SCIENCE FICTION OF THE YEAR, THE (US/0095-7119) [01783771] **3366**

BEST-SELLING HOME PLANS FROM HOME MAGAZINE (US/0743-2461) [10538501] **2899**

BEST SF (US) [00945803] **3366**

BEST US STOCKS FOR CANADIAN INVESTORS (CN) **892**

BEST US STOCKS FOR CANADIAN INVESTORS (CN) **892**

BEST VACATION RENTALS. CARIBBEAN (US/1054-9757) [23041461] **5463**

BEST VACATION RENTALS, EUROPE : A TRAVELER'S GUIDE TO COTTAGES, CONDOS, AND CASTLES (US/1054-9765) [23041472] **5463**

BEST WORLD SHORT STORIES (US/0737-8580) [04950436] **3366**

BESTE AUS READER'S DIGEST, DAS (GW/0005-9668) [01519657] **2485**

BESTE KEUS VOOR KANTOOR EN BEDRIJF (BE/0772-585X) [I0772585X] **1875**

BESTE UIT READER'S DIGEST, HET (NE/0005-9692) [04367711] **2513**

BESTIA (KIRKSVILLE, MO.) (US/1041-2212) [18686580] **3366**

BESTIARIO *CEASED.* (IT) [08227827] **344**

BEST'S AGENTS GUIDE. LIFE-HEALTH (US/1064-8038) [24397383] **2875**

BEST'S AGGREGATES & AVERAGES. LIFE-HEALTH (US) [14217959] **2875**

BEST'S AGGREGATES & AVERAGES. PROPERTY-CASUALTY (US/0270-5974) [03471002] **2875**

BEST'S DIRECTORY OF RECOMMENDED INSURANCE ADJUSTERS (US/0271-0927) [06406118] **2875**

BEST'S DIRECTORY OF RECOMMENDED INSURANCE ATTORNEYS (US/0277-1551) [06906660] 2875, **2941**

BEST'S ENVIRONMENTAL CONTROL AND SAFETY DIRECTORY *See* BEST'S SAFETY DIRECTORY **2859**

BEST'S EXECUTIVE DATA SERVICE: LIFE-HEALTH INDUSTRY MARKETING RESULTS (US/0145-4420) [02740437] **2875**

BEST'S EXECUTIVE DATA SERVICE. LIFE-HEALTH INDUSTRY MARKETING RESULTS. ACCIDENT & HEALTH LINES-EXPERIENCE BY STATE (US/0743-5320) [10586589] **2875**

BEST'S EXECUTIVE DATA SERVICE. LIFE-HEALTH INDUSTRY MARKETING RESULTS. EXPERIENCE OF PUERTO RICO (US/8755-9730) [11419886] **2875**

BEST'S EXECUTIVE DATA SERVICE. LIFE-HEALTH INDUSTRY MARKETING RESULTS. LIFE LINES-EXPERIENCE BY STATE (US/0743-5312) [10587707] **2875**

BEST'S EXECUTIVE DATA SERVICE. REPORT A 4 - HIGH RISK AUTO STUDY (US) [01783990] **2875**

BEST'S EXECUTIVE DATA SERVICE. REPORT A2, EXPERIENCE OF PUERTO RICO. PROPERTY AND CASUALTY INSURANCE (US/0275-4975) [07119312] **2875**

BEST'S EXECUTIVE DATA SERVICE. REPORT A6- COMPARATIVE EXPERIENCE BY STATE (STATE LEADERS) (US/0094-3150) [01794281] **2875**

BEST'S EXECUTIVE DATA SERVICE. REPORT A7-, FIVE YEAR EXPERIENCE BY STATE (US/0198-9553) [06255255] **2875**

BEST'S FLITCRAFT COMPEND *CEASED.* (US) [01426119] **2875**

BEST'S INSURANCE MANAGEMENT REPORTS (US) [05781954] **2875**

BEST'S INSURANCE REPORTS. LIFE-HEALTH (US) [04644376] **2875**

BEST'S INSURANCE REPORTS, PROPERTY-CASUALTY (US/0148-3218) [02517130] **2876**

BEST'S INSURANCE SECURITIES RESEARCH SERVICE *CEASED.* (US/0362-8701) [02329901] **2876**

BEST'S KEY RATING GUIDE : PROPERTY-CASUALTY (US/0148-3064) [02922115] **2876**

BEST'S MARKET GUIDE (US/0572-6301) [02810408] **2876**

BEST'S RATING MONITOR (US) [18132318] **2876**

BEST'S RETIREMENT INCOME GUIDE *CEASED.* (US/0197-2405) [05974509] **2876**

BEST'S REVIEW. (LIFE-HEALTH INSURANCE EDITION) (US/0005-9706) [02063415] **2876**

BEST'S REVIEW (PROPERTY/CASUALTY INSURANCE ED.) (US/0161-7745) [02390328] **2876**

BEST'S SAFETY DIRECTORY (US/0090-7480) [01786028] **2859**

BEST'S SETTLEMENT OPTIONS MANUAL *CEASED.* (US) [01774834] **2876**

BEST'S UNDERWRITING GUIDE FOR COMMERCIAL LINES (US/0191-4510) [04397780] **2876**

BEST'S WEEKLY NEWS DIGEST (US) [01519668] **2485**

BESTSELLER BODZ (PL/0867-0218) [I08670218] **4824**

BESTUURSMEMORIAAL (BE) [07825600] **4632**

BESWA REVUE (BE/0771-4181) [10407665] **2225**

BESZELO (HU) [21624641] **2678**

BET (UK) 1889, **642**

BETA (NO/0801-3322) [I08013322] **861**

BETA NEWSLETTER (CN/0823-9363) [12064592] 1889, **642**

BETA RELEASE (CN/0710-0248) [08364115] **3726**

BETA (SAN FRANCISCO, CALIF.) (US/1058-708X) [24361938] 3712, **3667**

BETE (MIAMI, FLA.), LA (US/1051-4732) [21969474] **3366**

BETE NOIRE (UK) [17690405] **3366**

BETER (NE/0168-9908) [I01689908] **4768**

BETES ET NATURE *See* VIE DES BETES, LA **4173**

BETH MIKRA : KETAV-ET SHEL HA-HEVRAH LE-HEKER HA-MIKRA BE-YISRAEL (IS/0005-979X) [02185990] **5046**

BETHANY REPUBLICAN-CLIPPER (US) [19134785] **5702**

BETHEL COLLEGE BULLETIN (US/0005-982X) [03985911] **1089**

BETHEL COLLEGE (MCKENZIE, TENN.) *See* ALUMNI DIRECTORY - BETHEL COLLEGE (MCKENZIE, TENN.) **1097**

BETHEL COLLEGE (NORTH NEWTON, KAN.) *See* BETHEL COLLEGE BULLETIN **1089**

BETHEL COURIER (BETHEL, ME 1976), THE (US/0749-9108) [08646189] 2439, **2723**

BETHEL HOME NEWS, THE (US) [24926349] **5645**

BETHEL JOURNAL *See* BETHEL JOURNAL-PRESS, THE **5727**

Alphabetical Title Index — BFG

● BETHEL JOURNAL-PRESS, THE (US/1066-7458) [27039252] **5727**

BETHEL JOURNAL, THE (US/0746-4061) [10023890] **5727**

BETHESDA MESSENGER (US/0737-4682) [02253044] **4938**

BETHLEHEM BULLETIN (US) [17465467] **5735**

BETODLAREN (SW/0345-1410) [16281880] **2410**

BETOIRE, LA (CN/0228-4413) [08205470] **1402**

BETON (GW/0005-9846) [09678048] **600**

BETON- EN CEMENTWARENINDUSTRIE / CENTRAAL BUREAU VOOR DE STATISTIEK, HOOFDAFDELING STATISTIEKEN VAN INDUSTRIE EN BOUWNIFVERHEID (NE) [10290610] **1599**

BETON I ZHELEZOBETON (RU/0005-9889) [02396442] **600**

BETON : REVUE DU BETON PREFABRIQUE (BE) **601**

BETON- UND STAHLBETONBAU (GW/0005-9900) [10527032] **601**

BETONG (SW) **601**

BETONSTEIN-ZEITUNG *See* BETONWERK + [I.E. UND] FERTIGTEIL-TECHNIK / CONCRETE PRECASTING PLANT AND TECHNOLOGY **601**

BETONWERK + [I.E. UND] FERTIGTEIL-TECHNIK / CONCRETE PRECASTING PLANT AND TECHNOLOGY (GW/0373-4331) [07043588] **601**

BETRIEB, DER (GW/0005-9935) [03247885] **2941**

BETRIEB UND PERSONAL (GW/0341-1044) [I03411044] **939**

BETRIEBS-BERATER (GW/0340-7918) [01519676] **4713**

BETRIEBS-MANAGEMENT SERVICE *See* BETRIEBSLEITER, DER **4218**

BETRIEBSERGEBNISSE : DURCHSCHNITTSERGEBNISSE (GW) [02482963] **66**

BETRIEBSERGEBNISSE VON UMSTELLUNGS- UND BESITZFESTIGUNGSBETRIEBEN (AU) [03138127] **66**

BETRIEBSKRANKENKASSEN (GW) [01788847] **2876**

BETRIEBSLEITER, DER (GW) [04512111] **4218**

BETRIEBSTECHNIK (GW/0409-2791) [02807603] **1966**

BETRIEBSWIRT GERNSBACH, DER (GW/0172-6196) [01726196] 861, **642**

BETRIEBSWIRTSCHAFT STUTTGART, DIE (GW/0342-7064) [I03427064] **643**

BETRIEBSWIRTSCHAFTLICHE BLATTER (GW/0723-9629) [I07239629] **861**

BETRIEBSWIRTSCHAFTLICHE ERGEBNISSE VON BAERLICHEN KLEIN UND MITTELBETRIEBEN IN OBEROSTERREICH (AU) [19098160] **643**

BETRIEBSWIRTSCHAFTLICHE ERGEBNISSE VON LANDWIRTSCHAFTLICHEN BETRIEBEN IN DER STEIERMARK (AU) [02243611] **66**

BETRIEBSWIRTSCHAFTLICHE FORSCHUNGEN (GW/0409-2805) [02807807] **861**

BETRIEBSWIRTSCHAFTLICHE NACHRICHTEN FUER DIE LANDWIRTSCHAFT (GW/0179-5066) [04031135] **66**

BETRIEBSWIRTSCHAFTLICHE SCHRIFTEN (GW/0523-1035) [02807921] **861**

BETTEN-MAGAZIN, DAS *See* HAUSTEX **5351**

BETTENDORF NEWS (US) [18884045] **5668**

BETTER BEAGLING MAGAZINE (US/0736-9743) [09289660] **4285**

BETTER BEEF BUSINESS *SUSPENDED.* (US/0523-1051) [06767104] 207, **643**

BETTER BOAT *CEASED.* (US/0741-4870) [10157776] **591**

BETTER BREEDING (UK) [05620248] **192**

BETTER BUILDINGS (US/0744-530X) [08333526] **601**

● BETTER BUSINESS BULLETIN (NORTH PALM BEACH, FLA.), THE (US/1064-1270) [26210449] **643**

BETTER BUSINESS BUREAU GREATER TORONTO *See* DIRECTORY & CONSUMER GUIDE - BETTER BUSINESS BUREAU GREATER TORONTO **1296**

BETTER BUSINESS BUREAU OF SOUTHEASTERN VIRGINIA *See* MEMBERSHIP DIRECTORY / THE BETTER BUSINESS BUREAU OF SOUTHEASTERN VIRGINIA **693**

BETTER CROPS WITH PLANT FOOD (US/0006-0089) [07849141] **164**

BETTER FARMING IN SALTED AFFECTED SOILS (II) [18054334] **164**

BETTER HEARING (AT) [10687393] **4384**

BETTER HOMES AND GARDENS (US/0006-0151) [05902855] **2788**

BETTER HOMES AND GARDENS CREATIVE IDEAS (US/0278-7415) [03507194] **370**

BETTER HOMES AND GARDENS DECORATING (US) [09950614] **2904**

BETTER HOMES AND GARDENS DECORATING IDEAS (US) [06860945] **2899**

BETTER HOMES AND GARDENS DECORATING IDEAS. WINDOW & WALL IDEAS (US/0277-836X) [07632792] **2899**

BETTER HOMES AND GARDENS DECORATIVE WOODCRAFTS (US/1056-716X) [23826565] **633**

BETTER HOMES AND GARDENS HOME PLAN IDEAS (US) [01794529] **293**

BETTER HOMES AND GARDENS KITCHEN & BATH IDEAS (US) [01791154] **2899**

BETTER HOMES AND GARDENS WOOD (US/0743-894X) [10701808] **2904**

● BETTER HOMOS AND GARDENS (US) [26531843] 2410, **2793**

BETTER INVESTING (US/0006-016X) [01697020] **892**

BETTER LIVING MAGAZINE (SUNNYVALE) (US/0162-3370) [04153814] **2485**

BETTER LIVING (NEW YORK. 1981) (US/0273-6160) [06751830] **2528**

BETTER LIVING TODAY (US/0745-600X) [09355742] **2485**

BETTER MANAGEMENT (UK) **861**

BETTER NUTRITION (US/0405-668X) [02315967] **4187**

BETTER NUTRITION FOR TODAY'S LIVING (US) **4188**

BETTER RADIO AND TELEVISION (US) [01519686] **1127**

BETTER REP MANAGEMENT *CEASED.* (US/0736-7171) [09200997] **861**

BETTER ROADS (US/0006-0208) [01519687] 2019, **5439**

BETTER SCHOOLS (CHICAGO) (US/0363-373X) [02455062] **1727**

BETTER SUPERVISION (US) [08318380] **939**

BETTER TEACHING (US/1061-1495) [24863925] **1727**

BETTER TIMES (POMPANO BEACH, FLA. 1985) (US/8750-7331) [11718748] **2528**

BETTER WAYS TO DO IT (US/0090-6468) [01785307] **370**

BETTER-WORK SUPERVISOR, THE (US) [05036236] **939**

BETTER WORLD *CEASED.* (US/1061-396X) [25285249] **4577**

BETTERAVIER FRANCAIS (FR/0405-6701) [09327436] **164**

BETTY AND ME (US/0006-0267) [10677495] **4857**

BETTY AND VERONICA (US/0895-4194) [16653097] 1060, **4857**

BETTY AND VERONICA COMICS DIGEST MAGAZINE (US/0886-134X) [12680360] **4857**

● BETTY (MAMARONECK, N.Y.) (US/1064-9395) [26465264] **4857**

BETWEEN OUR SELVES (US/0882-4355) [11844144] **5192**

BETWEEN THE ISSUES (CN/0715-4259) [09149657] **2212**

BETWEEN THE LAKES (US/0894-8917) [16347410] **2723**

BETWEEN THE LINES (WASHINGTON, D.C.) (US/1049-4421) [21246283] **4465**

BETWEEN THE SHEETS *See* MICHIGAN LODGING **748**

BETWEEN THE SPECIES : A JOURNAL OF ETHICS (US) [12783763] **2249**

BETWEEN US (CN/0714-4601) [09336338] 4201, **1811**

BEVARAGE ANALYST. OREGON (US/0191-5312) [04902489] **2364**

BEVARAGE ANALYST. WASHINGTON (US/0191-5347) [04902464] **2364**

● BEVERAGE AISLE (US/1060-9180) [25107784] **2364**

BEVERAGE ALCOHOL MARKET REPORT (US/0736-220X) [09078592] **2364**

BEVERAGE ANALYST. MONTANA (US/0191-5304) [04902500] **2364**

BEVERAGE AND TOBACCO PRODUCTS INDUSTRIES (CN/0835-0019) [16869840] 5372, **2364**

BEVERAGE INDUSTRY (US/0148-6187) [02445297] **2364**

BEVERAGE INDUSTRY ANNUAL MANUAL (US/8755-0717) [02885536] **2364**

BEVERAGE INDUSTRY NEWS (US) [22637067] **2364**

BEVERAGE INDUSTRY NEWS MERCHANDISER (US/0271-9894) [06720768] **2364**

BEVERAGE MARKET, THE (US/0279-7070) [07222806] **2364**

BEVERAGE MARKETING DIRECTORY (US) [22687373] **2364**

BEVERAGE MEDIA (US/0006-0372) [03985994] **2364**

BEVERAGE RETAILER WEEKLY *CEASED.* (US/0744-4958) [08364317] **2364**

BEVERAGE WORLD (US/0098-2318) [02240712] **2364**

BEVERAGE WORLD ... DATABANK (US) [12626190] **2364**

BEVERAGE WORLD INTERNATIONAL (US) [09862786] **2364**

BEVERAGES *CEASED.* (US/0409-2945) [13406685] **2364**

BEVERLY HILLS 90210, THE OFFICIAL MAGAZINE *CEASED.* (US/1058-1596) [24233648] 1060, **383**

BEVERLY HILLS BAR ASSOCIATION *See* BAR BRIEF (BEVERLY HILLS, CALIF.) **2939**

BEVERLY HILLS BAR ASSOCIATION JOURNAL (US/1051-628X) [06328634] **2941**

BEVERLY HILLS COURIER, THE (US/0892-645X) [11308738] **5633**

BEVERLY REVIEW, THE (US/0006-0410) [03986021] **5658**

BEVERLY TIMES, THE (US) [19730555] **5687**

BEVOELKERUNG & ERWERBSTATIGKEIT : POPULATION AND EMPLOYMENT. FACHSERIE 1. EINZELVEROEFFENTLICHUNGEN (GW) **4550**

BEVOLKERUNG IN NORDRHEIN-WESTFALEN, DIE (GW) [02242671] **4561**

BEVOLKERUNG UND ERWERBSTATIGKEIT. REIHE 4.2.2, ENTGELTE UND BESCHAFTIGUNGSDAUER DER ARBEITNEHMER (GW) [17949397] 2876, **2941**

BEVOLKERUNG UND ERWERBSTATIGKEIT. REIHE 4.1.1: STAND UND ENTWICKLUNG DER ERWERBSTATIGKEIT (GW) [06176851] **1655**

BEVOLKERUNG UND ERWERBSTATIGKEIT. REIHE 4.2.1., STRUKTUR DER ARBEITNEHMER (GW) [18361309] **1655**

BEVOLKERUNG UND ERWERBSTATIGKEIT. REIHE 1, GEBIET UND BEVOLKERUNG / HERAUSGEBER STATISTISCHES BUNDESAMT (GW) [11846086] 1655, **4550**

BEVOLKERUNGSSCHUTZ : MAGAZIN FUER ZIVIL- UND KATASTROPHENSCHUTZ (GW) [20928038] **1072**

BEVOLKERUNGSSTAND UND BEVOLKERUNGSBEWEGUNG (GW) [01786140] **1918**

BEVOLKING EN GEZIN (BE/0772-764X) [03421210] **4550**

BEVOLKINGSSTATISTIEKEN - NATIONAAL INSTITUUT VOOR DE STATISTIEK (BE/0304-8888) [01795196] 4550, **4561**

BEWEGEN & HULPVERLENING (NE/0168-9711) [I01689711] **4379**

BEYOND APARTHEID *CEASED.* (NE/0923-4284) [09234284] 5240, **1464**

BEYOND BEHAVIOR (US/1074-2956) [24771484] **1876**

● BEYOND BORDERS (US/1065-2426) [26537868] **1655**

BEYOND GERMANNA (US/1073-838X) [29539836] **2439**

BEYOND LAW / MAS ALLA DEL DERECHO (CK/0121-5183) [24051236] 5240, **2941**

BEYOND SIGHT (CN/0712-2446) [08790943] **4887**

BEYOND THE BOTTOM LINE (US) 861, **778**

BEZOPASNOST TRUDA V PROMYSHLENNOSTI (RU/0409-2961) [09284512] **2135**

BFCE MULTIDEVISES (FR/1166-245X) [I1166245X] **1464**

BFG : AUSSENHANDELSDIENST (GW) [04941128] **778**

BFI — Alphabetical Title Index

BFI FILM AND TELEVISION HANDBOOK (UK) [28230878] 1127, **4064**

BFLO (US/0161-7710) [03795954] **4887**

BFLO JOURNAL (US/1055-291X) [23136832] **2723**

BFUP, BETRIEBSWIRTSCHAFTLICHE FORSCHUNG UND PRAXIS (GW/0340-5370) [103405370] **861**

BG, DIE (GW/0723-7561) [107237561] **2876**

BGA SCHRIFTEN (GW/0932-2361) [12269306] **4768**

BGF BULLETIN (AT) **66**

BGRG RESEARCH MONOGRAPH (UK) [08301005] **164**

BGS REPORTS / BRITISH GEOLOGICAL SURVEY, NATURAL ENVIRONMENT RESEARCH COUNCIL (UK) [10811713] **1367**

BGS, ZEITSCHRIFT DES BUNDESGRENZSCHUTZES (GW/0302-9468) [01792963] **2513**

BHAGIRATH (II/0006-0461) [01774248] **2087**

BHARAT PUMPS & COMPRESSORS LIMITED *See* ANNUAL REPORT AND ACCOUNTS - BHARAT PUMPS & COMPRESSORS LIMITED **2109**

BHARATA VARSHA (II/0304-9116) [02245562] **5240**

BHARATI (TORONTO) (CN/0319-6887) [02442858] **2529**

BHARATIYA JYOTIR VIJYAN PARISHAD *See* BULLETIN OF THE ASTRONOMICAL SOCIETY OF INDIA **394**

BHARATIYA NEPALI VANMAYA (II) [08721651] **3268**

BHARATIYA SUGAR (II/0970-6240) [109706240] 2328, **164**

BHARATIYA TAMBAKU *CEASED.* (II) [01783603] **5372**

BHARATIYA VIDYA (II/0378-1984) [01641211] **2647**

BHARATODAYAH (II) [04471364] **2502**

BHARI UDYOGA MANTRALAYA KI ANUDANOM KI MANGEM (II) [01797848] **1599**

BHARTIYA KRISHI ANUSANDHAN PATRIKA (II/0303-3821) [01398606] **66**

BHASHA (II/0523-1418) [01774255] 3366, **3268**

BHASHA ANI JIVANA : MARATHI-ABHYASA-PARISHAD-PATRIKA (II) [11195236] 1105, **3268**

BHAVAN'S JOURNAL (II/0006-0518) [01774256] **4342**

BHAYANGKARA (IO/0216-2563) [10768361] **3158**

BHI PLUS [COMPUTER FILE] (UK/0966-8772) 2843, **2857**

BHM. BERG- UND HUTTENMANNISCHE MONATSHEFTE (AU/0005-8912) [04215909] **1966**

BHP JOURNAL *CEASED.* (AT/0313-5942) [103135942] **3999**

BHRCA OFFICIAL GUIDE TO HOTELS AND RESTAURANTS IN GREAT BRITAIN, IRELAND AND OVERSEAS (UK) [04753620] 5070, **2804**

BHUTAN JOURNAL OF ANIMAL HUSBANDRY (BT/0259-0859) [102590859] **5505**

BHUVIJNANA (II) [07118432] **1367**

BI-ANNUAL REPORT / DETROIT CITY PLANNING COMMISSION (US) [25578482] **2816**

BI-ANNUAL REVIEW OF ALLERGY *CEASED.* (US/0278-9566) [07508229] **3667**

BI-LINGUAL MAGAZINE (NR/0189-2029) [08886906] **5447**

BI-STATE REPORTER (US/0745-4813) [09219653] **5658**

BI-YEAF (IS/0302-8194) [01784340] **14**

BIA BULLETIN (UK) **443**

BIA NEWSLETTER (UK) **3686**

BIA REPORT (GW/0173-0487) [08541613] **2859**

BIANNUAL NEWSLETTER OF THE CONFERENCE GROUP ON ITALIAN POLITICS & SOCIETY, THE (US/1077-9043) [30909795] **4516**

BIAOSTOCKIE TOWARZYSTWO NAUKOWE *See* PRACE BIAOSTOCKIEGO TOWARZYSTWA NAUKOWEGO **1842**

BIAS JOURNAL (UK) [08881457] **1599**

BIB-KRANT LEUVEN (BE/0776-068X) [0776068X] **3194**

BIB REPORT / GERMAN EDUCATION INDEX (GW) **1727**

BIB TELEVISION PROGRAMMING SOURCE BOOKS (US/1056-6104) [23747325] 4064, **1127**

BIBA (FR/0221-7996) [102217996] **1082**

BIBBIA E ORIENTE (IT/0006-0585) [02982793] **5014**

BIBEL UND GEMEINDE (GW/0006-0615) [03094425] **5014**

BIBEL UND KIRCHE (GW/0006-0623) [01774835] **5014**

BIBEL UND LITURGIE (AU/0006-064X) [01774836] **5014**

BIBELOT (DAYTON, OHIO) *SUSPENDED.* (US/0887-6053) [12959613] **4938**

BIBI (CG/0376-6624) [01795696] **5551**

BIBLE ADVENTURES (ELGIN, ILL.) (US/0162-9220) [04261402] **5014**

BIBLE ADVOCATE (BROOMFIELD, COLO.) (US/0746-0104) [09693610] **5014**

BIBLE AND SPADE (US) **4938**

BIBLE BHASHYAM (ENGLISH ED.) (II/0970-2288) [08413103] **5014**

BIBLE BOOK STUDY FOR YOUTH. BIBLE STUDY CARDS (US/1057-0217) [23915133] **5014**

BIBLE BOOK STUDY FOR YOUTH TEACHERS (US/0162-4830) [04170025] **5014**

BIBLE COLLECTORS' WORLD (US/0883-9204) [11983212] **5014**

BIBLE DISCOVERERS (US/0162-4695) [04168145] **5014**

BIBLE DISCOVERERS TEACHER (US/0162-4687) [04168392] **5014**

BIBLE DISTRIBUTOR. ENGLISH (US/0256-9361) [12119487] **5014**

BIBLE EVANGELISM *See* COMMUNICATE (KAMLOOPS) **4949**

BIBLE EXPOSITOR AND ILLUMINATOR (US) [01519707] **5014**

BIBLE-IN-LIFE STORIES (US/0162-9573) [04288145] **5014**

BIBLE JOURNEYS FOR CHRISTIANS *CEASED.* (US/0747-3893) [10786787] **5014**

BIBLE JOURNEYS FOR CHRISTIANS (US) [19786787] **4938**

BIBLE LANDS (UK/0006-0763) [04849687] 4938, **5014**

BIBLE LEAGUE QUARTERLY (UK) [01776517] **5014**

BIBLE NEWSLETTER, THE (US/0279-8069) [07267460] **5014**

BIBLE OF WEATHER FORECASTING, THE (US/0749-3584) [11123745] **1420**

BIBLE PUZZLER (UK/0965-531X) **5056**

BIBLE REVIEW (WASHINGTON, D.C.) (US/8755-6316) [11362496] **5014**

BIBLE-SCIENCE NEWSLETTER (US/0164-5587) [01695224] **5014**

BIBLE SEARCHERS : TEACHER (US/0006-0798) [03986087] **5015**

BIBLE STANDARD AND HERALD OF CHRIST'S KINGDOM, THE (US/0006-081X) [01604633] **4938**

BIBLE TEACHING FOR CONFIDENT LIVING *CEASED.* (US/0890-457X) [14231189] **5015**

BIBLE TODAY, THE (US/0006-0836) [01519711] **5015**

BIBLE TRANSLATOR, THE (UK/0260-0935) [01519712] **5015**

BIBLIA (JA) [01519713] **3194**

BIBLIA PATRISTICA (FR) **5015**

BIBLIA REVUO (IT/0006-0879) [02999314] **5015**

BIBLIA Y FE (SP/0210-5209) [04733323] **5015**

BIBLICA (IT/0006-0887) [01519715] **5015**

BIBLICA ET ORIENTALIA (IT) [01913460] **5015**

BIBLICAL ARCHAEOLOGIST, THE (US/0006-0895) [01519716] 5015, **261**

BIBLICAL ARCHAEOLOGY REVIEW (UK) 261, **5015**

BIBLICAL ARCHAEOLOGY REVIEW, THE (US/0098-9444) [02242487] 5015, **261**

BIBLICAL BULLETIN (US/0749-9280) [11286846] 4938, **5015**

BIBLICAL EVANGELIST, THE (US/0740-7998) [05933837] **4938**

BIBLICAL ILLUSTRATOR (US/0195-1351) [05302566] 1889, **4938**

● BIBLICAL INTERPRETATION (NE) [27734776] **5015**

BIBLICAL MISSIONS *SUSPENDED.* (US/0006-0909) [01779573] **5057**

BIBLICAL POLEMICS (IS/0792-4739) [107924739] **4939**

BIBLICAL PREACHING JOURNAL (US/1043-5522) [18539807] **4939**

BIBLICAL RECORDER (US/0279-8182) [07325558] **5057**

BIBLICAL REFLECTIONS ON MODERN MEDICINE (US/1047-6946) [20745336] **4939**

BIBLICAL RESEARCH (US/0067-6535) [01519718] **5015**

BIBLICAL RESEARCH MONTHLY (US/0746-4525) [01715967] **5015**

BIBLICAL SCHOLARSHIP IN NORTH AMERICA (US/0277-0474) [07485027] **5015**

BIBLICAL THEOLOGY BULLETIN (US/0146-1079) [01774838] 4939, **5015**

BIBLICAL VIEWPOINT (US/0006-0925) [01714665] **5015**

BIBLICUM (SW) [01713813] **4939**

● BIBLIO 12 (BE) [28272043] **5192**

BIBLIO 17 (FR) [11909737] **3366**

BIBLIO 1992 (BE) [21205145] **5192**

BIBLIO-CLIP : BULLETIN D'INFORMATION DU SERVICE DES BIBLIOTHEQUES DE L'UQAM (CN/1183-1219) [25313720] **3194**

BIBLIO-EXPRESS (CN/0836-0464) [18603821] **3194**

BIBLIO EXPRESS (BE) **5377**

BIBLIO INDEX UITP *See* BIBLIO EXPRESS **5377**

BIBLIO-JEUNES; NIVEAUX PRESCOLAIRE ET ELEMENTAIRE: SUPPLEMENT (CN/0701-5542) [03424973] **408**

BIBLIO-PROFILE (US/0888-7721) [11798103] **3803**

BIBLIO SERVICE (CN/0710-6319) [08315730] **1727**

BIBLIOFANTASIAC, THE (CN/0821-7572) [11193096] **3366**

BIBLIOFILIA (FLORENCE, ITALY) (IT/0006-0941) [01519723] **4824**

BIBLIOGRAFI BUKU-BUKU DALAM BAHASA MALAYSIA (MY/0127-1164) [09883417] **408**

BIBLIOGRAFI DAERAH DAERAH ISTIMEWA YOGYAKARTA (IO) [05217619] **408**

BIBLIOGRAFI DAERAH ISTIMEWA ACEH : BDIA (IO) [08843603] **151**

BIBLIOGRAFI DAERAH PROPINSI DAERAH TINGKAT I I.E. PERTAMA SULAWESI SELATAN (IO) [06492266] **408**

BIBLIOGRAFI DAERAH PROPINSI JAWA BARAT (IO) [05725383] **408**

BIBLIOGRAFI DAERAH SUMATERA UTARA (IO) [05842635] **408**

BIBLIOGRAFI OVER DANMARKS OFFENTLIGE PUBLIKATIONER (DK/0067-6543) [01519726] **4696**

BIBLIOGRAFI OVER EUROPISKE KUNSTNERES EXLIBRIS (DK) [01783812] **408**

BIBLIOGRAFIA AGROMETEOROLOGII (PL/0239-958X) [10239958X] **1420**

BIBLIOGRAFIA ANALITICA EM BEM-ESTAR SOCIAL (BL) [03338344] **5274**

BIBLIOGRAFIA BRASILEIRA DE BOTANICA (BL/0067-6586) [02254065] **502**

BIBLIOGRAFIA BRASILEIRA DE CENCIAS SOCIAIS / INSTITUTO BRASILEIRO DE BIBLIOGRAFIA E DOCUMENTACAO (BL/0067-6608) [01604155] **408**

BIBLIOGRAFIA BRASILEIRA DE ENGENHARIA *CEASED.* (BL/0100-0705) [05141270] **1966**

BIBLIOGRAFIA BRASILEIRA DE FISICA (BL/0067-6640) [01519732] **4398**

BIBLIOGRAFIA BRASILEIRA DE ODONTOLOGIA (BL) [07109883] 1317, **1337**

BIBLIOGRAFIA BRASILEIRA DE POLITICA CIENTIFICA E TECNOLOGICA (BL) [11075322] **5173**

BIBLIOGRAFIA BRASILEIRA DE QUIMICA (RIO DE JANEIRO, BRAZIL : 1984) (BL/0100-0756) [16630705] **962**

BIBLIOGRAFIA BRASILEIRA DE ZOOLOGIA (BL/0067-6691) [02408934] **5578**

BIBLIOGRAFIA BRASILEIRA DO SEMI-ARIDO (BL) [10706659] **2580**

BIBLIOGRAFIA CUBANA (CU/0574-6086) [01519737] **408**

BIBLIOGRAFIA DE EDUCACAO (BL) [03158233] **1727**

BIBLIOGRAFIA DE GALICIA / DISPOSIA NO MUSEO DE PONTEVEDRA (SP) [20477448] **3366**

BIBLIOGRAFIA DE LA LITERATURA HISPANICA (SP) **408**

BIBLIOGRAFIA DO MILHO (BL) [03055337] **151**

BIBLIOGRAFIA ESPANOLA (MADRID, SPAIN : 1958) (SP/0523-1760) [01519739] **3457**

BIBLIOGRAFIA ESPANOLA. SUPLEMENTO DE CARTOGRAFIA (SP/0214-4441) [20289017] **2556**

BIBLIOGRAFIA ESPANOLA. SUPLEMENTO DE PUBLICACIONES PERIODICAS (SP/0210-8372) [08380936] **408**

BIBLIOGRAFIA FILOSOFICA ITALIANA (IT) [07830054] **4342**

BIBLIOGRAFIA FILOSOFICA MEXICANA (MX/0185-240X) [01519741] **4365**

BIBLIOGRAFIA FORRAJERA (AG) [04267114] **2410**

BIBLIOGRAFIA GEOLOGICA SI GEOFIZICA A REPUBLICII SOCIALISTE ROMANIA (RM/1013-2104) [09296112] 1402, **1367**

BIBLIOGRAFIA GOSPODARKI I INZYNIERII WODNEJ (PL/0239-622X) [04688247] 2087, **5531**

BIBLIOGRAFIA HISTORICA MEXICANA (MX/0523-1795) [01519744] **2723**

BIBLIOGRAFIA HISTORII POLSKI XIX WIEKU (PL) [07055225] **2678**

BIBLIOGRAFIA HYDROLOGII I OCEANOLOGII (PL/0239-6246) [04379645] 1446, **1412**

BIBLIOGRAFIA IDG. A, DIRITTO COMMERCIALE (IT/0392-257X) [07832135] **3096**

BIBLIOGRAFIA IDG. B, DIRITTO CANONICO ED ECCLESIASTICO (IT/0392-2588) [07832062] **4939**

BIBLIOGRAFIA IDG. C, DIRITTO E PROCEDURA PENALE (IT/0392-2596) [13907926] **3105**

BIBLIOGRAFIA ITALIANA DI ELETTROTECNICA (IT) [01777427] **1961**

BIBLIOGRAFIA ITALIANA DI IDRAULICA *CEASED*. (IT/0006-1042) [01519747] **2087**

BIBLIOGRAFIA ITALIANA DI STORIA DELLA SCIENZA (IT) [12648193] **408**

BIBLIOGRAFIA KRAKOWA I WOJEWODZTWA MIEJSKIEGO KRAKOWSKIEGO ZA ROK ... / MIEJSKA BIBLIOTEKA PUBLICZNA W KRAKOWIE (PL) [19113478] **408**

BIBLIOGRAFIA LATINOAMERICANA. 1, TRABAJOS PUBLICADOS POR LATINOAMERICANOS EN REVISTAS EXTRANJERAS (MX) [10353036] **408**

BIBLIOGRAFIA LATINOAMERICANA. 2, TRABAJOS SOBRE AMERICA LATINA PUBLICADOS EN REVISTAS EXTRANJERAS (MX) [10357322] **409**

BIBLIOGRAFIA LATINOAMERICANA. TRABAJOS SOBRE AMERICA LATINA PUBLICADOS FUERA DE LA REGION *See* BIBLIOGRAFIA LATINOAMERICANA. 2, TRABAJOS SOBRE AMERICA LATINA PUBLICADOS EN REVISTAS EXTRANJERAS **409**

BIBLIOGRAFIA LITERARNEJ VEDY A UMELECKEJ LITERATURY. KNIHY (XO) [08252821] **3457**

BIBLIOGRAFIA METEOROLOGII: POLSKA (PL/0239-6270) [04379629] **1421**

BIBLIOGRAFIA MEXICANA (BIBLIOTECA NACIONAL DE MEXICO) (MX/0006-1069) [01519748] **409**

BIBLIOGRAFIA NAZIONALE ITALIANA *See* BIBLIOGRAFIA NAZIONALE ITALIANA BNI PERIODICI **409**

BIBLIOGRAFIA NAZIONALE ITALIANA *See* BIBLIOGRAFIA NAZIONALE ITALIANA BNI MONGRAFIA **409**

BIBLIOGRAFIA NAZIONALE ITALIANA BNI MONGRAFIA (IT) **409**

BIBLIOGRAFIA NAZIONALE ITALIANA BNI PERIODICI (IT) **409**

BIBLIOGRAFIA NAZIONALE ITALIANA. PUBBLICAZIONE MENSILE (IT/0006-1077) [01519749] **409**

BIBLIOGRAFIA PAMIATKOVEJ LITERATURY V CSSR *See* BIBLIOGRAFIA PAMIATKOVEJ LITERATURY V SLOVENSKEJ SOCIALISTICKEJ REPUBLIKE ZA ROKY **293**

BIBLIOGRAFIA PAMIATKOVEJ LITERATURY V SLOVENSKEJ SOCIALISTICKEJ REPUBLIKE ZA ROKY (XO) [19931490] **293**

BIBLIOGRAFIA PEDAGOGIKI SZKOY WYZSZEJ ZA ROK ... (PL/0239-7048) [11396271] **1811**

BIBLIOGRAFIA POMORZA ZACHODNIEGO. PISMIENNICTWO ZAGRANICZNE (PL/0138-0702) [I01380702] **409**

BIBLIOGRAFIA REGIONALNA WIELKOPOLSKI ZA R. ... / UNIWERSYTET IM. ADAMA MICKIEWICZA W POZNANIU (PL/0409-347X) [07589118] **409**

BIBLIOGRAFIA SOBRE A ECONOMIA PORTUGUESA (PO/0067-6764) [01519753] **1530**

BIBLIOGRAFIA TEOLOGICA COMENTADA DEL ARIA IBEROAMERICANA (AG) [03111112] **4939**

BIBLIOGRAFIA UMBRA / REGIONE DELL'UMBRA, UFFICIO PER I BENI E SERVIZI BIBLIOTECARI, ARCHIVISTICI, PER LE ATTIVITA DELLO SPETTACOLO SPORT E TEMPO LIBERO (IT) [19406533] **4632**

BIBLIOGRAFIA URUGUAYA DE MEDICINA : PUBLICACIONES PERIODICAS (UY) [06974994] **3655**

BIBLIOGRAFIA VENEZOLANA (INSTITUTO AUTONOMO BIBLIOTECA NACIONAL Y DE SERVICIOS DE BIBLIOTECAS (VENEZUELA)) (VE) [09642503] **409**

BIBLIOGRAFIA WYDAWNICTW CIAGYCH / BIBLIOGRAPHY OF POLISH SERIALS / BIBLIOTEKA NARODOWA, INSTYTUT BIBLIOGRAFICZNY (PL/0239-4421) [15742184] **409**

BIBLIOGRAFIA ZAWARTOSCI CZASOPISM / BIBLIOTEKA NARODOWA, INSTYTUT BIBLIOGRAFICZNY (PL/0006-1093) [01519756] **3257**

BIBLIOGRAFICHESKAIA INFORMATSIIA. MUZYKA / MINISTERSTVO KULTURY SSSR, GOSUDARSTVENNAIA ORDENA LENINA BIBLIOTEKA SSSR IMENI V.I. LENINA (RU) [05952459] **4103**

BIBLIOGRAFICHESKAIA INFORMATSIIA. SREDSTVA OBUCHENIIA V VYSSHEI I SREDNEI SPETSIALNOI SHKOLE / MINISTERSTVO VYSSHEGO I SREDNEGO SPETSIALNOGO OBRAZOVANIIA SSSR, NAUCHNO-ISSLEDOVATELSKII INSTITUT PROBLEM VYSSHEI SHKOLY (RU/0208-0087) [16848288] **1793**

BIBLIOGRAFIE NEDERLANDSE SOCIOLOGIE (NE/0167-8272) [02915769] **5240**

BIBLIOGRAFIE VAN AFRIKAANSE BOEKE *CEASED*. (SA) [03437947] **409**

BIBLIOGRAFIE VAN DE NEDERLANDSE TAAL- EN LITERATUURWETENSCHAP (NE) [04281442] **409**

BIBLIOGRAFIE VAN IN NEDERLAND VERSCHENEN KAARTEN (NE/0377-8975) [04481697] **2580**

BIBLIOGRAFIE VAN IN NEDERLAND VERSCHENEN OFFICIELE UITGAVEN BIJ RIJKSOVERHEID EN PROVINCIALE BESTUREN *CEASED*. (NE/0165-2958) [06715411] **409**

BIBLIOGRAFIE VAN NEDERLANDS NATIONAAL EN INTERNATIONAAL ONDERZOEK OP SOCIAAL-WETENSCHAPPELIJK TERREIN (NE/0922-6842) [25000038] 5192, **5226**

BIBLIOGRAFIE VAN NEDERLANDSE PROEFSCHRIFTEN / DUTCH THESES (NE/0166-9966) [06258861] **409**

BIBLIOGRAFIE VAN REGIONALE ONDERZOEKINGEN OP SOCIAAL-WETENSCHAPPELIJK TERREIN / CENTRAAL BUREAU VOOR DE STATISTIEK, AFDELING BIBLIOTHEEK EN DOCUMENTATIE (NE) [10340702] 5192, **5227**

BIBLIOGRAFIIA BIBLIOGRAFII V SSSR (RU) [18587561] **409**

BIBLIOGRAFIIA IZDANII AKADEMII NAUK SSSR; EZHEGODNIK. BIBLIOGRAPHY OF PUBLICATIONS OF THE ACADEMY OF SCIENCES OF THE USSR; A YEAR-BOOK *CEASED*. (RU/0568-5222) [01842451] **409**

BIBLIOGRAFIIA NA BULGARSKATA BIBLIOGRAFIIA (BU) [02418500] **409**

BIBLIOGRAFIJA JUGOSLAVIJE. KNJIGE, BROSURE I MUZIKALIJE (YU/0523-2201) [01519761] 3457, **4103**

BIBLIOGRAFIJA JUGOSLAVIJE SERIJSKE PUBLIKACIJE (YU/0350-0349) [03346504] **409**

BIBLIOGRAFIJA RADOVA NASTAVNIKA I SARADNIKA UNIVERZITETA U BEOGRADU I UNIVERZITETA UMETNOSTI U BEOGRADU / UNIVERZITETSKA BIBLIOTEKA SVETOZAR MARKOVIC (YU) [18287383] **1811**

BIBLIOGRAFISCHE ATTENDERINGSLIJST VOOR DOCENTEN NEERLANDISTIEK IN HET BUITENLAND / BUREAU VOOR DE BIBLIOGRAFIE VAN DE NEERLANDISTIEK, KONINKLIJKE BIBLIOTHEEK, ONDER AUSPICIEN VAN DE NEDERLANDSE TAALUNIE (NE/0920-2862) [17220177] **409**

BIBLIOGRAPHIA CARTOGRAPHICA (GW/0340-0409) [01815334] **2580**

BIBLIOGRAPHIA INTERNATIONALIS SPIRITUALITATIS / A PONTIFICIO INSTITUTO SPIRITUALITATIS O.C.D. EDITA (IT/0084-7836) [06529509] **4342**

BIBLIOGRAPHIA MISSIONARIA / PONTIFICAL MISSIONARY LIBRARY OF THE CONGREGATION FOR THE EVANGELIZATION OF PEOPLES (VC/0394-9869) [19280685] 4939, **5012**

BIBLIOGRAPHIA PATRISTICA (GW/0523-2252) [01532685] **4939**

BIBLIOGRAPHIA SCIENTIAE NATURALIS HELVETICA (SZ/0067-6829) [02708066] **5173**

BIBLIOGRAPHIC GUIDE TO ANTHROPOLOGY AND ARCHAEOLOGY (US/0896-8101) [17292151] 232, **261**

BIBLIOGRAPHIC GUIDE TO ART AND ARCHITECTURE (US/0360-2699) [02481602] 316, **334**

BIBLIOGRAPHIC GUIDE TO BLACK STUDIES (US/0360-2710) [02298816] **2276**

BIBLIOGRAPHIC GUIDE TO BUSINESS AND ECONOMICS (US/0360-2702) [02377191] **726**

BIBLIOGRAPHIC GUIDE TO CONFERENCE PUBLICATIONS (US/0360-2729) [02156492] **409**

BIBLIOGRAPHIC GUIDE TO DANCE (US/0360-2737) [02484389] **1314**

BIBLIOGRAPHIC GUIDE TO EAST ASIAN STUDIES (US/1046-8765) [20550440] **2634**

BIBLIOGRAPHIC GUIDE TO EDUCATION (US/0147-6505) [05081578] **1793**

BIBLIOGRAPHIC GUIDE TO GOVERNMENT PUBLICATIONS - FOREIGN (US/0360-280X) [02368564] **4696**

BIBLIOGRAPHIC GUIDE TO LATIN AMERICAN STUDIES (US/0162-5314) [04173064] **2634**

BIBLIOGRAPHIC GUIDE TO LAW (US/0360-2745) [02282334] **2941**

BIBLIOGRAPHIC GUIDE TO MAPS AND ATLASES (US/0197-5889) [06077566] 2556, **2580**

BIBLIOGRAPHIC GUIDE TO MICROFORM PUBLICATIONS (US/0891-3749) [14713997] **409**

BIBLIOGRAPHIC GUIDE TO MIDDLE EASTERN STUDIES (US/1058-644X) [24345758] **2768**

BIBLIOGRAPHIC GUIDE TO MUSIC (US/0360-2753) [02133707] **4160**

BIBLIOGRAPHIC GUIDE TO NORTH AMERICAN HISTORY (US/0147-6491) [03642302] **2634**

BIBLIOGRAPHIC GUIDE TO PSYCHOLOGY (US/0360-277X) [02184160] **4622**

BIBLIOGRAPHIC GUIDE TO SOVIET AND EAST EUROPEAN STUDIES (US/0162-5322) [04172935] **2634**

BIBLIOGRAPHIC GUIDE TO TECHNOLOGY (US/0360-2761) [02223294] **5173**

BIBLIOGRAPHIC GUIDE TO THEATRE ARTS (US/0360-2788) [02394250] **5372**

BIBLIOGRAPHIC INDEX (US/0006-1255) [01532691] **3457**

BIBLIOGRAPHIC RETRIEVAL SERVICES, INC *See* BRS BULLETIN **1172**

BIBLIOGRAPHIC SERIES (US/0065-8847) [01480059] 4939, **5012**

BIBLIOGRAPHIC SERIES - CENTRE FOR URBAN AND COMMUNITY STUDIES. UNIVERSITY OF TORONTO (CN/0316-4691) [02247285] **2840**

BIBLIOGRAPHIC SERIES - FRANKLIN INSTITUTE, PHILADELPHIA, PA (US/0532-6036) [01413733] **409**

BIBLIOGRAPHIC SERIES / PROFESSIONAL SERVICES DEPARTMENT, INTERNATIONAL ASSOCIATION OF ASSESSING OFFICERS (US/0741-4994) [10159357] **4696**

BIBLIOGRAPHICAL BULLETIN - LATIN AMERICAN FORESTRY INSTITUTE (VE) [03685956] 2376, **2399**

BIBLIOGRAPHICAL CENTER FOR RESEARCH. ROCKY MOUNTAIN REGION, DENVER *See* ANNUAL REPORT - BIBLIOGRAPHICAL CENTER FOR RESEARCH **3190**

BIBLIOGRAPHICAL SERIES OF SUPPLEMENTS TO BRITISH BOOK NEWS ON WRITERS AND THEIR WORK (UK) [01773764] **4824**

BIBLIOGRAPHICAL SERIES / SOUTH AFRICAN INSTITUTE OF INTERNATIONAL AFFAIRS / BIBLIOGRAFIESE REEKS / SUID-AFRIKAANSE INSTITUUT VAN INTERNASIONALE AANGELEENTHEDE *CEASED*. (SA) [05866123] **4501**

BIBLIOGRAPHICAL SOCIETY OF AMERICA *See* LIST OF MEMBERS / BIBLIOGRAPHICAL SOCIETY OF AMERICA **419**

BIBLIOGRAPHICAL SOCIETY OF AMERICA *See* PAPERS OF THE BIBLIOGRAPHICAL SOCIETY OF AMERICA, THE **422**

BIBLIOGRAPHICAL SOCIETY OF CANADA *See* BULLETIN **411**

BIBLIOGRAPHICAL SOCIETY OF CANADA *See* PAPERS OF THE BIBLIOGRAPHICAL SOCIETY OF CANADA **422**

BIBLIOGRAPHICAL SOCIETY OF CANADA *See* DIRECTORY OF MEMBERS / THE BIBLIOGRAPHICAL SOCIETY OF CANADA **415**

BIBLIOGRAPHIE ANALYTIQUE DE L'AFRIQUE ANTIQUE (IT) [01188379] **2634**

BIBLIOGRAPHIE — Alphabetical Title Index

BIBLIOGRAPHIE ANNUELLE DE LA RECHERCHE FRANCAISE EN EDUCATION / INSTITUT NATIONAL DE RECHERCHE PEDAGOGIQUE, CENTRE DE DOCUMENTATION RECHERCHE (FR) [11325513] **1793**

BIBLIOGRAPHIE ANNUELLE DE L'HISTOIRE DE FRANCE DU CINQUIEME SIECLE A 1958 (FR) [03504466] **2634**

BIBLIOGRAPHIE BILDENDE KUNST (GW) [02436054] **334**

BIBLIOGRAPHIE COURANTE D'ARTICLES DE PERIODIQUES POSTERIEURS A 1944 SUR LES PROBLEMES POLITIQUES, ECONOMIQUES, ET SOCIAUX. SUPPLEMENT (US/0097-7020) [01799311] **5192**

BIBLIOGRAPHIE COURANTE SUR FICHES D'ARTICLES DE PERIODIQUES DOCUMENTATION AFRICAINE *CEASED.* (FR) **409**

BIBLIOGRAPHIE DE BELGIQUE (BE/0006-1336) [01532712] **409**

BIBLIOGRAPHIE DE BELGIQUE. PART C (BE) **409**

BIBLIOGRAPHIE DE LA COUR INTERNATIONALE DE JUSTICE / PREPAREE PAR LA BIBLIOTHEQUE DE LA COUR (NE) [12889915] 2941, **3079**

BIBLIOGRAPHIE DE LA FRANCE. SUPPLEMENT 4. ATLAS, CARTES ET PLANS (FR/0150-5998) [05585122] **2580**

BIBLIOGRAPHIE DE LA PHILOSOPHIE (FR/0006-1352) [02445314] **4365**

BIBLIOGRAPHIE DE LA REFORME, 1450-1648; OOUVRAGES PARUS DE 1940 A 1955 (NE) [08747920] **2634**

BIBLIOGRAPHIE DE L'AFRIQUE SUD-SAHARIENNE, SCIENCES HUMAINES ET SOCIALES (BE) [09014678] **5192**

BIBLIOGRAPHIE D'ECONOMIE DES TRANSPORTS (FR) [02496942] **5400**

BIBLIOGRAPHIE DER BIBLIOTHEKSADRESSBUCHER *See* DIRECTORIES AND ASSOCIATIONS OF THE BOOK TRADE AND LIBRARIANSHIP **4828**

BIBLIOGRAPHIE DER BUCH- UND BIBLIOTHEKSGESCHICHTE BBB (GW/0723-3590) [09544936] **4821**

BIBLIOGRAPHIE DER DEUTSCHEN SPRACH- UND LITERATURWISSENSCHAFT (GW) [03217936] **3457**

BIBLIOGRAPHIE DER DEUTSCHSPRACHIGEN PSYCHOLOGISCHEN LITERATUR (GW/0303-5999) [01072818] 4577, **4622**

BIBLIOGRAPHIE DER FRANZOSISCHEN LITERATURWISSENSCHAFT (GW/0523-2465) [02454092] **3457**

BIBLIOGRAPHIE DER ORTS-, REGIONAL- UND LANDESPLANUNG (SZ) [05505375] **2816**

BIBLIOGRAPHIE DER PFLANZENSCHUTZLITERATUR (GW/0006-1387) [01532722] **2434**

BIBLIOGRAPHIE DER UBERSETZUNGEN DEUTSCHSPRACHIGER WERKE *CEASED.* (GE/0006-1409) [01532727] **3457**

BIBLIOGRAPHIE DER WIRTSCHAFTSPRESSE (GW/0006-1417) [04995384] **1530**

BIBLIOGRAPHIE DES AUTEURS MODERNES DE LANGUE FRANCAISE (FR) [04408934] **3457**

BIBLIOGRAPHIE DES MUSIKSCHRIFTTUMS (GW) [01532729] 4103, **4160**

BIBLIOGRAPHIE DES TRAVAUX EN LANGUE FRANCAISE SUR L'AFRIQUE AU SUD DU SAHARA, SCIENCES HUMAINES ET SOCIALES (FR) [05627832] 5193, **5227**

BIBLIOGRAPHIE D'ETUDES BALKANIQUES (BU/0523-2376) [01532731] **2678**

BIBLIOGRAPHIE DU BENIN (DM) [05035074] **409**

BIBLIOGRAPHIE DU QUEBEC (CN/0006-1441) [02441810] **410**

BIBLIOGRAPHIE FREMDSPRACHIGER GERMANICA (GW) [01532733] **3269**

BIBLIOGRAPHIE HOCHSCHULPLANUNG (GW) [01786807] **1793**

BIBLIOGRAPHIE ILLUSTRIERTE BUCHER DER DEUTSCHEN DEMOKRATISCHEN REPUBLIK (GW) [03603974] **410**

BIBLIOGRAPHIE - INSTITUT NATIONAL DE LA RECHERCHE AGRONOMIQUE, DEPARTEMENT D'ECONOMIE ET DE LA SOCIOLOGIE RURALES (FR/0982-3417) [19370521] 66, 5240, **151**

BIBLIOGRAPHIE INTERNATIONALE DE LA DEMOGRAPHIE HISTORIQUE (BE/0255-0849) [07047746] **4561**

BIBLIOGRAPHIE INTERNATIONALE DE L'HUMANISME ET DE LA RENAISSANCE (SZ/0067-7000) [01423248] **410**

BIBLIOGRAPHIE INTERNATIONALE D'HISTOIRE MILITAIRE / COMITE INTERNATIONAL DES SCIENCES HISTORIQUES, COMMISSION INTERNATIONALE D'HISTOIRE MILITAIRE COMPAREE, COMITE DE BIBLIOGRAPHIE (SZ/0378-7869) [06472747] **4037**

BIBLIOGRAPHIE JURISTISCHER FESTSCHRIFTEN UND FESTSCHRIFTENBEITRAGE : DEUTSCHLAND, SCHWEIZ, OSTERREICH (GW) [10613617] **3079**

BIBLIOGRAPHIE LATINOAMERICAINE D'ARTICLES / INSTITUT DES HAUTES ETUDES DE L'AMERIQUE LATINE, CENTRE DE DOCUMENTATION (FR/0752-4080) [09618601] **410**

BIBLIOGRAPHIE LINGUISTISCHER LITERATUR (GW) [05577138] 3269, **3336**

BIBLIOGRAPHIE : MODERNER FREMDSPRACHENUNTERRICHT (GW) [01786065] **410**

BIBLIOGRAPHIE MUSIK (GW) [08376328] **4160**

●BIBLIOGRAPHIE NATIONALE FRANCAISE. ATLAS, CARTES ET PLANS : BIBLIOGRAPHIE ETABLIE PAR LA BIBLIOTHEQUE NATIONALE (FR) [28228110] 2556, **2580**

BIBLIOGRAPHIE NATIONALE FRANCAISE DEPUIS 1970. CD-ROM (UK) **410**

BIBLIOGRAPHIE NATIONALE FRANCAISE. LIVRES : NOTICES ETABLES PAR LA BIBLIOTHEQUE NATIONALE (FR/1142-3250) [21224800] **410**

●BIBLIOGRAPHIE NATIONALE FRANCAISE. MUSIQUE : BIBLIOGRAPHIE ETABLIE PAR LA BIBLIOTHEQUE NATIONALE (FR) [26083159] **4103**

●BIBLIOGRAPHIE NATIONALE FRANCAISE. PUBLICATIONS EN SERIE : BIBLIOGRAPHIE ETABLIE PAR LA BIBLIOTHEQUE NATIONALE (FR) [25727939] **410**

BIBLIOGRAPHIE NATIONALE FRANCAISE. SUPPLEMENT I, PUBLICATIONS EN SERIE *See* BIBLIOGRAPHIE NATIONALE FRANCAISE. PUBLICATIONS EN SERIE : BIBLIOGRAPHIE ETABLIE PAR LA BIBLIOTHEQUE NATIONALE **410**

BIBLIOGRAPHIE NATIONALE FRANCAISE. SUPPLEMENT III. MUSIQUE *See* BIBLIOGRAPHIE NATIONALE FRANCAISE. MUSIQUE : BIBLIOGRAPHIE ETABLIE PAR LA BIBLIOTHEQUE NATIONALE **4103**

BIBLIOGRAPHIE NATIONALE FRANCAISE. SUPPLEMENT IV, ATLAS, CARTES ET PLANS *See* BIBLIOGRAPHIE NATIONALE FRANCAISE. ATLAS, CARTES ET PLANS : BIBLIOGRAPHIE ETABLIE PAR LA BIBLIOTHEQUE NATIONALE **2580**

BIBLIOGRAPHIE OCCITANE (FR) [02245799] **3336**

BIBLIOGRAPHIE PADAGOGIK. REIHE A, ZEITSCHRIFTEN- AUFSATZE (GW) [12194909] **1793**

BIBLIOGRAPHIE PADAGOGIK. REIHE B, BUCHER (GW/0176-2575) [12747252] **4809**

BIBLIOGRAPHIE PADAGOGIK. REIHE C, PROJEKTE BILDUNGSFORSCHUNG (GW) [11659744] 1727, **1793**

BIBLIOGRAPHIE PALYNOLOGIE (FR/0249-762X) [04144581] **5088**

BIBLIOGRAPHIE PHILOSOPHIE *CEASED.* (GW/0034-2262) [02258308] **4365**

BIBLIOGRAPHIE SOZIALISATION UND SOZIALPAEDAGOGIK (GW/0342-3964) [03701857] **5266**

BIBLIOGRAPHIE SPECIALE ANALYTIQUE (FR) [06742968] **3257**

BIBLIOGRAPHIE : STAAT UND RECHT (SZ) [03819640] **3079**

BIBLIOGRAPHIE : STAAT UND RECHT DER DEUTSCHEN DEMOKRATISCHEN REPUBLIK *CEASED.* (GW/0006-1468) [01532739] **3079**

BIBLIOGRAPHIE ZUR ARCHAO-ZOOLOGIE UND GESCHICHTE DER HAUSTIERE (GW/0232-4865) [03603592] **286**

BIBLIOGRAPHIE ZUR GESCHICHTE DER DEUTSCHEN ARBEITERBEWEGUNG (GW/0343-4117) [03525143] **1530**

BIBLIOGRAPHIE ZUR KUNSTGESCHICHTLICHEN LITERATUR IN OST- UND SUDOSTEUROPAISCHEN ZEITSCHRIFTEN (GW) [02629829] **334**

BIBLIOGRAPHIE ZUR SCHWEIZER KUNST, BIBLIOGRAPHIE ZUR DENKMALPFLEGE / BIBLIOGRAPHIE DE L'ART SUISSE, BIBLIOGRAPHIE DE LA CONSERVATION DES BIENS CULTURELS / ETH, EIDGENOESSISCHE TECHNISCHE HOCHSCHULE ZUERICH, INSTITUT FUER DENKMALPFLEGE (SZ/0252-9556) [16954565] **344**

BIBLIOGRAPHIE ZUR SYMBOLIK, IKONOGRAPHIE UND MYTHOLOGIE (GW/0067-706X) [00932395] **4939**

BIBLIOGRAPHIE ZUR SYMBOLIK, IKONOGRAPHIE UND MYTHOLOGIE. ERGANZUNGSBAND (GW/0939-0154) [10251860] 4241, **4939**

BIBLIOGRAPHIE DES DEUTSCHEN WETTERDIENSTES (GW/0072-4149) [05424882] **1421**

BIBLIOGRAPHIE DES FORSCHUNGSZENTRUMS JULICH (GW/0938-6513) [23000729] **410**

BIBLIOGRAPHIEN ZUR DEUTSCHEN LITERATUR DES MITTELALTERS (GW/0523-2767) [01532745] 3366, **3457**

BIBLIOGRAPHIEN ZUR PHILOSOPHIE (GW/0173-1831) [13863369] **4342**

BIBLIOGRAPHIES AND INDEXES IN AMERICAN HISTORY (US/0742-6828) [10418009] 2723, **2634**

BIBLIOGRAPHIES AND INDEXES IN AMERICAN LITERATURE (US/0742-6860) [10422078] **3457**

BIBLIOGRAPHIES AND INDEXES IN ANTHROPOLOGY (US/0742-6844) [10421990] 232, **248**

BIBLIOGRAPHIES AND INDEXES IN ECONOMICS AND ECONOMIC HISTORY (US/0749-1786) [11094599] **1530**

BIBLIOGRAPHIES AND INDEXES IN EDUCATION (US/0742-6917) [10461525] 1727, **1793**

BIBLIOGRAPHIES AND INDEXES IN GERONTOLOGY (US/0743-7560) [10662571] **3750**

BIBLIOGRAPHIES AND INDEXES IN LATIN AMERICAN AND CARIBBEAN STUDIES (US/1054-9102) [23011501] **2723**

BIBLIOGRAPHIES AND INDEXES IN LAW AND POLITICAL SCIENCE (US/0742-6909) [10428362] **4501**

BIBLIOGRAPHIES AND INDEXES IN MEDICAL STUDIES (US/0896-6591) [17241348] **3555**

●BIBLIOGRAPHIES AND INDEXES IN POPULAR CULTURE (US/1066-0658) [26833272] **410**

BIBLIOGRAPHIES AND INDEXES IN PSYCHOLOGY (US/0742-681X) [10417977] **4577**

BIBLIOGRAPHIES AND INDEXES IN RELIGIOUS STUDIES (US/0742-6836) [10418044] **4939**

BIBLIOGRAPHIES AND INDEXES IN SCIENCE AND TECHNOLOGY (US/0888-7551) [13711747] **5088**

BIBLIOGRAPHIES AND INDEXES IN SOCIOLOGY (US/0742-6895) [10428320] 5240, **5266**

BIBLIOGRAPHIES AND INDEXES IN WORLD HISTORY (US/0742-6852) [10422035] **2634**

BIBLIOGRAPHIES AND INDEXES IN WORLD LITERATURE (US/0742-6801) [10417240] **3366**

●BIBLIOGRAPHIES AND INDEXES ON SPORTS HISTORY (US/1066-3746) [26926384] **4856**

BIBLIOGRAPHIES AND LITERATURE OF AGRICULTURE (US/0163-0873) [04286110] **151**

BIBLIOGRAPHIES IN AMERICAN MUSIC (US) [06039376] 4103, **4160**

BIBLIOGRAPHIES OF BATTLES AND LEADERS (US/1056-7410) [23841328] **4061**

BIBLIOGRAPHIES OF FAMOUS PHILOSOPHERS (US) [03447813] **4365**

BIBLIOGRAPHIES OF MODERN AUTHORS (SAN BERNARDINO, CALIF.) (US/0749-470X) [11129595] **3457**

●BIBLIOGRAPHIES OF THE STATES OF THE UNITED STATES (US/1060-5711) [25036897] **410**

BIBLIOGRAPHISCHE INFORMATIONEN ZUR ITALIENISCHEN GESCHICHTE IM. 19 UND 20. JAHUNDERT (IT/1121-1938) [11211938] **410**

BIBLIOGRAPHISCHES HANDBUCH ZUR SPRACHINHALTSFORSCHUNG. PART 1 : SCHRIFTTUM ZUR SPRACHINHALTSFORSCHUNG (GW) **410**

BIBLIOGRAPHISCHES HANDBUCH ZUR SPRACHINHALTSFORSCHUNG. PART 2 : SYSTEMATISCHER TEIL. REGISTER (GW) **410**

BIBLIOGRAPHY : A SELECTED BIBLIOGRAPHY OF MATERIALS IN THE CHICAGO MUNICIPAL REFERENCE LIBRARY (US) [07893940] **410**

BIBLIOGRAPHY AND INDEX OF GEOLOGY (US/0098-2784) [02240713] 1367, **1361**

BIBLIOGRAPHY AND INDEX OF MICROPALEONTOLOGY (US/0300-7227) [01741634] 4226, **4231**

BIBLIOGRAPHY & INFORMATION SOURCE LIST (US) [04536835] **726**

BIBLIOGRAPHY AND SUBJECT INDEX OF SOUTH AFRICAN GEOLOGY (SA/0584-2360) [01606456] **1361**

BIBLIOGRAPHY (AUSTRALIA. PARLIAMENT) (AT/0813-3107) [19406612] 4632, **4696**

BIBLIOGRAPHY. BOOKS FOR CHILDREN *CEASED.* (US/0147-250X) [08136564] 3366, **1072**

BIBLIOGRAPHY - BUREAU OF MINERAL RESOURCES, GEOLOGY AND GEOPHYSICS (AT/0156-5087) [I01565087] **1352**

BIBLIOGRAPHY - COSTUME SOCIETY OF AMERICA (US) [05164069] **1088**

BIBLIOGRAPHY : F I A F MEMBERS PUBLICATIONS (CN/0074-5944) [02443258] **4080**

●BIBLIOGRAPHY FOR ADVANCEMENT EXAMINATION STUDY (US) [29352417] **4175**

BIBLIOGRAPHY FOR ADVANCEMENT STUDY *See* BIBLIOGRAPHY FOR ADVANCEMENT EXAMINATION STUDY **4175**

BIBLIOGRAPHY IN CHRISTIAN EDUCATION FOR SEMINARY AND COLLEGE LIBRARIES. ADDENDA ... (US) [04826149] 1727, **4939**

BIBLIOGRAPHY - INTERNATIONAL INSTITUTE FOR LAND RECLAMATION AND IMPROVEMENT (NE/0074-6436) [01681265] 66, **151**

BIBLIOGRAPHY (NATIONAL RESEARCH COUNCIL (U.S.) TRANSPORTATION RESEARCH BOARD) (US/0148-849X) [02366164] **5400**

BIBLIOGRAPHY OF AGRICULTURE (US/0006-1530) [07896413] 66, **151**

BIBLIOGRAPHY OF AGRICULTURE : ANNUAL CUMULATION (US/0364-829X) [02652512] **66**

BIBLIOGRAPHY OF ALASKAN GEOLOGY (US) [01715133] **1361**

BIBLIOGRAPHY OF AMERICAN LITERATURE *CEASED.* (US) [02258399] **3457**

BIBLIOGRAPHY OF AMERICAN PALEOBOTANY (US/0193-5720) [02250280] **502**

BIBLIOGRAPHY OF ASIAN STUDIES (US/0067-7159) [04285212] **2634**

BIBLIOGRAPHY OF BIOETHICS (US/0363-0161) [02322232] 2249, **3555**

BIBLIOGRAPHY OF CORPORATE SOCIAL RESPONSIBILITY (US/0160-8819) [03124662] **1599**

BIBLIOGRAPHY OF DIARRHOEAL DISEASES (US/0736-7120) [09199817] **3743**

BIBLIOGRAPHY OF ECONOMIC AND STATISTICAL PUBLICATIONS ON TANZANIA, A (TZ) [04518300] **1530**

BIBLIOGRAPHY OF ECONOMIC GEOLOGY (UK/0016-7053) [09121576] 1438, 4252, **1361**

BIBLIOGRAPHY OF EDUCATION THESES IN AUSTRALIA (AT/0811-0174) [11051815] 1811, **1793**

BIBLIOGRAPHY OF FAMILY PLANNING & POPULATION (UK/0300-1598) [01793422] **591**

BIBLIOGRAPHY OF FOSSIL VERTEBRATES (US/0272-8869) [02253045] **4231**

BIBLIOGRAPHY OF INDIAN ZOOLOGY (II/0409-4093) [02245610] **5578**

BIBLIOGRAPHY OF IRRIGATION, DRAINAGE, RIVER TRAINING AND FLOOD CONTROL. BIBLIOGRAPHIE RELATIVE AUX IRRIGATIONS, AU DRAINAGE, A LA REGULARISATION DES COURS D'EAU ET LA MAITRISE DES CRUES (II) [06850887] **5549**

BIBLIOGRAPHY OF LATIN AMERICAN AND CARIBBEAN BIBLIOGRAPHIES (US/1051-5836) [13385762] **410**

BIBLIOGRAPHY OF MODERN HEBREW LITERATURE IN TRANSLATION / BY ISAAC GOLDBERG (IS/0334-309X) [06038553] 3457, **3366**

BIBLIOGRAPHY OF MUSEUM AND ART GALLERY PUBLICATIONS AND AUDIO-VISUAL AIDS IN GREAT BRITAIN AND IRELAND, THE (UK) [04088817] **4098**

●BIBLIOGRAPHY OF NATIVE NORTH AMERICANS ON DISC (US/1064-5144) [26320587] **410**

BIBLIOGRAPHY OF NOISE, A *CEASED.* (US/0092-5756) [01783663] **2161**

BIBLIOGRAPHY OF OLD NORSE-ICELANDIC STUDIES (DK/0067-7213) [01532759] 3366, **3457**

BIBLIOGRAPHY OF PALAEARCTIC LEPIDOPTERA / SOCIETAS EUROPAEA LEPIDOPTEROLOGICA (GW) [11718541] **5606**

BIBLIOGRAPHY OF PAPER AND THIN-LAYER CHROMATOGRAPHY, AND SURVEY OF APPLICATIONS (NE/0300-631X) [02088456] **996**

BIBLIOGRAPHY OF PUBLICATIONS (AT) [04845650] **66**

BIBLIOGRAPHY OF PUBLICATIONS OF THE COASTAL ENGINEERING RESEARCH CENTER AND THE BEACH EROSION BOARD (US/0732-5304) [07446453] **410**

BIBLIOGRAPHY OF PUBLICATIONS RESULTING FROM NCHSR EXTRAMURAL RESEARCH (US/0882-8989) [11765195] **4809**

BIBLIOGRAPHY OF PUBLICATIONS / WISCONSIN CENTER FOR EDUCATION RESEARCH (US) [08805113] **1793**

BIBLIOGRAPHY OF REPRODUCTION (UK/0006-1565) [01532761] 3655, **477**

BIBLIOGRAPHY OF REPRODUCTION *See* HUMAN REPRODUCTION UPDATE **581**

BIBLIOGRAPHY OF SEISMOLOGY (UK/0523-2988) [02258314] **1362**

BIBLIOGRAPHY OF SMALL WASTEWATER FLOWS (US) [06140062] **2183**

BIBLIOGRAPHY OF SOVIET LASER DEVELOPMENTS (US/0738-0305) [08970540] 2101, **2036**

BIBLIOGRAPHY OF SYSTEMATIC MYCOLOGY (UK/0006-1573) [01564462] **574**

BIBLIOGRAPHY OF THE HISTORY OF ART : BHA (FR/1150-1588) [23526711] 344, **334**

BIBLIOGRAPHY OF THE HISTORY OF MEDICINE (US/0067-7280) [01532763] 3555, **3655**

... BIBLIOGRAPHY OF THE MIDDLE EAST : A COMPLETE AND CLASSIFIED LIST OF ALL THE BOOKS PUBLISHED IN ABOUT TEN MIDDLE EASTERN COUNTRIES, THE (SY) [01532765] **2634**

BIBLIOGRAPHY OF THE SUMMER INSTITUTE OF LINGUISTICS, AUSTRALIAN ABORIGINES BRANCH UP TO ... / COMPILED BY SANDRA RAY (AT) [07264759] **3336**

BIBLIOGRAPHY OF WATER QUALITY RESEARCH REPORTS (US/0090-2055) [01784785] 2225, **5531**

BIBLIOGRAPHY ON ATOMIC TRANSITION PROBABILITIES (US/0093-9196) [01799927] **4033**

BIBLIOGRAPHY ON CABLE TELEVISION : BCTV (US/0742-4914) [04362309] **1124**

BIBLIOGRAPHY ON COLD REGIONS SCIENCE AND TECHNOLOGY (US/0149-3825) [01165833] 1966, **5088**

BIBLIOGRAPHY ON FOREIGN AND COMPARATIVE LAW, A (US/0067-7329) [01532766] **3079**

BIBLIOGRAPHY ON HIGH PRESSURE RESEARCH *CEASED.* (US/0045-1932) [02445448] **410**

BIBLIOGRAPHY ON IRRIGATION, DRAINAGE, RIVER TRAINING AND FLOOD CONTROL *See* BIBLIOGRAPHY OF IRRIGATION, DRAINAGE, RIVER TRAINING AND FLOOD CONTROL. BIBLIOGRAPHIE RELATIVE AUX IRRIGATIONS, AU DRAINAGE, A LA REGULARISATION DES COURS D'EAU ET LA MAITRISE DES CRUES **5549**

BIBLIOGRAPHY ON OVERSEAS MARKET SURVEYS OF INDIAN PRODUCTS (II) [04116729] **410**

BIBLIOGRAPHY ON THE HIGH TEMPERATURE CHEMISTRY AND PHYSICS OF MATERIALS LONDON *CEASED.* (UK/0366-0265) [03660265] **962**

BIBLIOGRAPHY : PUBLICATIONS RESULTING FROM COUNCIL SUPPORT (US/0572-807X) [03235060] **5227**

BIBLIOGRAPHY SERIES / CENTER FOR CREATIVE PHOTOGRAPHY, UNIVERSITY OF ARIZONA (US/0739-4845) [09766795] **4367**

BIBLIOGRAPHY SERIES - NORMAN PATERSON SCHOOL OF INTERNATIONAL AFFAIRS (CARLETON UNIVERSITY) (CN/0383-2848) [03222243] 4516, **4501**

BIBLIOGRAPHY SERIES - REGIONAL SCIENCE RESEARCH INSTITUTE *SUSPENDED.* (US/0080-0619) [03503094] **1530**

BIBLIOGRAPHY SERIES - UNITED STATES. DEPT. OF JUSTICE (US/0749-5706) [09680290] **3079**

BIBLIOMATICA (SP/0211-8238) [I02118238] **3194**

●BIBLION (NEW YORK, N.Y.) (US/1064-301X) [26244071] **2843**

BIBLIONEWS AND AUSTRALIAN NOTES AND QUERIES (AT/0045-1940) [02770457] **4824**

BIBLIOPHILE, LE (FR) [06972967] **4824**

BIBLIOPHILOS (UNION CITY, PA.) (US/0730-8612) [08089587] **2529**

BIBLIOSCAN Q-Z *SUSPENDED.* (US/0148-8996) [03400530] **410**

BIBLIOTECA ANTONIO MACHADO DE TEATRO (SP) [19532007] **5362**

BIBLIOTECA CLASSICA (NE) [17947682] **4103**

BIBLIOTECA DE AUTORES ESPANOLES (SP) [02499812] **430**

BIBLIOTECA DE AUTORES ESPANOLES (SP) [15080328] **3366**

BIBLIOTECA DE ESTUDIOS MADRILENOS (SP/0409-5308) [07627988] **2678**

BIBLIOTECA DE MEXICO (MX/0188-476X) [25363436] **3366**

BIBLIOTECA DE NEUROLOGIA Y CONDUCTA (AG) [08743104] **3828**

BIBLIOTECA DEGLI "HISTORIAE MUSICAE CULTORES" (IT/0073-2516) [02776536] **3194**

BIBLIOTECA DEI QUADERNI DEL NOVECENTO FRANCESE (IT) [11095801] **2611**

BIBLIOTECA DELLA LIBERTA *CEASED.* (IT) [22961557] **4465**

BIBLIOTECA DELLA RICERCA. TESTI STRANIERI (IT) [16663649] **3366**

BIBLIOTECA DELLA RIVISTA DI STORIA DELLE SCIENZE MEDICHE E NATURALI (IT) [03269658] **4163**

BIBLIOTECA DELL'ARCHIVIO STORICO ITALIANO (IT/0409-6037) [06668572] **2480**

BIBLIOTECA (DEPUTAZIONE DI STORIA PATRIA PER LE ANTICHE PROVINCIE MODENESI) (IT) [07935477] **3194**

BIBLIOTECA DI ANTICHITA CIPRIOTE (IT) [03450606] **3194**

BIBLIOTECA DI BIBLIOGRAFIA ITALIANA / DIRETTA DA CARLO FRATI (IT/0067-7418) [01532786] **410**

BIBLIOTECA DI STORIA DELLA SCIENZA (IT/0394-5065) [I03945065] **4163**

BIBLIOTECA DI STORIA TOSCANA MODERNA E CONTEMPORANEA. STUDI E DOCUMENTI (IT) [03435995] **3194**

BIBLIOTECA DI STUDI AMERICANI *SUSPENDED.* (IT/0519-6396) [01956801] **3338**

BIBLIOTECA E SOCIETA : RIVISTA DEL CONSORZIO PER LA GESTIONE DELLE BIBLIOTECHE COMUNALE DEGLI ARDENTI E PROVINCIALE "ANSELMO ANSELMI" DI VITERBO (IT/0392-2545) [27066047] **344**

BIBLIOTECA HISPANOAMERICANA Y ESPANOLA DE AMSTERDAM (NE) [10160335] 3366, **3269**

BIBLIOTECA LUIS-ANGEL ARANGO *See* BOLETIN CULTURAL Y BIBLIOGRAFICO **3368**

BIBLIOTECA NACIONAL DE VENEZUELA *See* BOLETIN DE LA BIBLIOTECA NACIONAL (CARACAS) **2724**

BIBLIOTECA NACIONAL JOSE MARTI *See* REVISTA DE LA BIBLIOTECA NACIONAL JOSE MARTI **423**

BIBLIOTECA NACIONAL (PERU) *See* BOLETIN DE LA BIBLIOTECA NACIONAL (LIMA) **3196**

BIBLIOTECA NAPOLETANA (IT) [04981064] **3194**

BIBLIOTECA PUBLICA INFORMATIVO (BL) [05977559] **3194**

BIBLIOTECA ROMANICA HISPANICA. I. TRATADOS Y MONOGRAFIAS (SP/0519-7198) [01932354] **3366**

BIBLIOTECA ROMANICA HISPANICA. II. ESTUDIOS Y ENSAYOS (SP/0519-7201) [01931911] **3367**

BIBLIOTECA ROMANICA HISPANICA. III. MANUALES (SP/0519-721x) [01931871] **3269**

BIBLIOTECA ROMANICA HISPANICA. IV. TEXTOS (SP/0519-7228) [01931955] **3367**

BIBLIOTECA ROMANICA HISPANICA. V. DICCIONARIOS (SP/0519-7236) [01931973] **3269**

BIBLIOTECA ROMANICA HISPANICA. VI. ANTOLOGIA HISPANICA (SP/0519-7244) [01931898] **3367**

BIBLIOTECA ROMANICA HISPANICA. VII. CAMPO ABIERTO (SP/0519-7252) [01931882] **3367**

BIBLIOTECA ROMANICA HISPANICA. VIII. DOCUMENTOS (SP/0519-7260) [01931996] **3367**

BIBLIOTECA STORICA TOSCANA. SEZIONE DI STORIA DEL RISORGIMENTO (IT) [06657593] **3194**

BIBLIOTECA TEATRALE (BULZONI EDITORE) (IT) [05330183] **5362**

BIBLIOTECARIO, IL (IT) [12241266] **3194**

BIBLIOTECHE OGGI (IT/0392-8586) [11995503] **3194**

●BIBLIOTECHNOE DELO I BIBLIOGRAFIIA (RU) [29686615] **3194**

BIBLIOTECHNOE DELO I BIBLIOGRAFIIA V SSSR *See* BIBLIOTECHNOE DELO I BIBLIOGRAFIIA **3194**

BIBLIOTECOLOGIA — Alphabetical Title Index

BIBLIOTECOLOGIA Y DOCUMENTACION (AG/0325-6251) [06029350] **3194**

BIBLIOTECONOMIA (SP/0006-1778) [01532793] **1464**

BIBLIOTEK FOR LAGER (DK/0006-1786) [01532794] **3555**

● BIBLIOTEKA (RU/0869-4915) [25384784] **3194**

BIBLIOTEKA ANALIZ LITERACKICH (PL/0519-7929) [02505144] **3367**

BIBLIOTEKA "KOMSOMOLSKOI PRAVDY" (RU/0132-2133) [02505291] **3194**

BIBLIOTEKA MATEMATYCZNA (PL/0519-8356) [01532796] **3497**

BIBLIOTEKA "OGONEK." *CEASED.* (RU/0132-2095) [06320683] **3367**

BIBLIOTEKAR (BEOGRAD) (YU/0006-1816) [02500298] **3194**

BIBLIOTEKAR (MOSCOW, R.S.F.S.R.) *See* BIBLIOTEKA **3194**

BIBLIOTEKARZ (PL/0208-4333) [04302771] **3194**

BIBLIOTEKOVEDENIE (RU/0869-608X) [29122466] **3194**

BIBLIOTEKOVEDENIE I BIBLIOGRAFIJA ZA RUBEZOM (RU/0320-7838) [02258323] **3194**

BIBLIOTEKOVEDENIE I BIBLIOGRAFOVEDENIE: INOSTRANNAIA LITERATURA (RU) [05987138] **3194**

BIBLIOTEKOZNANIE, BIBLIOGRAFIIA, KNIGOZNANIE / NARODNA BIBLIOTEKA "SV. SV. KIRIL I METODII" (BU) [24817808] **3194**

BIBLIOTEKSVEJVISER (DK) [01792610] **3194**

BIBLIOTEKU ZINATNES ASPEKTI. ASPEKTY BIBLIOTEKOVEDENIIA (LV) [05213672] **3194**

BIBLIOTERM (AU/0255-2795) [14711653] **3269**

BIBLIOTHECA AEGYPTIA (US/0732-6467) [08414675] **2647**, **2638**

BIBLIOTHECA AFROASIATICA (US/0742-1117) [10279293] **3367**

BIBLIOTHECA AMERICANA (CORAL GABLES, FLA.) (US/0734-1865) [08694106] **3195**

BIBLIOTHECA ANATOMICA (SZ/0067-7833) [01532805] **3679**

BIBLIOTHECA ARNAMAGNANA (IC/0067-7841) [01532806] **3367**

BIBLIOTHECA BIBLIOGRAPHICA AURELIANA (GW/0067-7884) [01532808] **3457**

BIBLIOTHECA BOTANICA (GW/0067-7892) [01532810] **502**

BIBLIOTHECA CARDIOLOGICA (SZ/0067-7906) [01624253] **3699**

BIBLIOTHECA EPHEMERIDUM THEOLOGICARUM LOVANIENSIUM (BE) [02343096] **4939**

BIBLIOTHECA FRANCISCANA SCHOLASTICA MEDII AEVI (IT) [02781893] **4939**

BIBLIOTHECA GERMANICA (GW/0067-7477) [03105495] **3269**

BIBLIOTHECA HELVETICA ROMANA (SZ/0067-7965) [03466301] **1074**

BIBLIOTHECA HISTORICA LUNDENSIS (SW/0519-9700) [01532820] **2611**

BIBLIOTHECA HISTORICO-ECCLESIASTICA LUNDENSIS (SW) [01641971] **4939**

BIBLIOTHECA HUMANISTICA ET REFORMATORIA (NE) [02255594] **1074**

BIBLIOTHECA INDONESIA (NE/0067-8023) [03442789] **3195**

BIBLIOTHECA ISLAMICA (GW) [03486215] **5042**

BIBLIOTHECA LATINA MEDII ET RECENTIORIS AEVI (PL/0067-8031) [02782190] **2678**

BIBLIOTHECA LICHENOLOGICA (GW) [01986263] **502**

BIBLIOTHECA MEDICA CANADIANA (CN/0707-3674) [05528533] **3556**, **3195**

BIBLIOTHECA MESOPOTAMICA (US/0732-6440) [03440126] **2647**, **261**

BIBLIOTHECA MUSICA - NARODNI KNIHOVNA CR (XR/0862-9021) [08629021] **4103**

BIBLIOTHECA MUSICA THERAPEUTICA (GW) **4103**

BIBLIOTHECA MUSICAE, COLLANA DI CATALOGHI E BIBLIOGRAFIE (IT) [03054575] **4103**

BIBLIOTHECA MYCOLOGIA (GW) **502**, **443**

BIBLIOTHECA NUTRITIO ET DIETA (SZ/0067-8198) [01532832] **4188**

BIBLIOTHECA ORGANOLOGICA (NE) **4103**

BIBLIOTHECA ORIENTALIS (NE/0006-1913) [01532834] **3269**, **2647**

BIBLIOTHECA PHYCOLOGICA (GW/0067-8112) [12223388] **502**

BIBLIOTHECA PRESS UPDATE (US/0277-3597) [07583076] **3195**

BIBLIOTHECA PSYCHIATRICA (SZ/0067-8147) [01532839] **3921**

BIBLIOTHECA ROMANICA (BERNE), SERIES PRIMA : MANUALIA ET COMMENTATIONES (SZ) [01532841] **3195**

BIBLIOTHECA SACRA (1864) (US/0006-1921) [05950719] **4939**

BIBLIOTHECA THEOLOGIAE PRACTICAE (SW) [04546153] **4939**

BIBLIOTHECK (UK/0006-193X) [02512904] **410**

BIBLIOTHEEK EN SAMENLEVING (NE/0165-1048) [02103142] **3195**

BIBLIOTHEK (GW/0341-4183) [04761075] **3195**

EIBLIOTHEK (GW) [01716087] **3457**

BIBLIOTHEK DER GRIECHISCHEN LITERATUR (GW) [02776555] **1074**

BIBLIOTHEK DES BUCHWESENS (GW) [04991546] **3195**

BIBLIOTHEK FUER ZEITGESCHICHTE (GERMANY) *See* JAHRESBIBLIOGRAPHIE / BIBLIOTHEK FUER ZEITGESCHICHTE, WELTKRIEGSBUCHEREI **2620**

BIBLIOTHEKAR *CEASED.* (GW/0006-1964) [05579611] **3195**

BIBLIOTHEKS-INFO (GW/0940-7944) [05407944] **3195**

BIBLIOTHEKSDIENST (GW/0006-1972) [02513158] **3195**

BIBLIOTHEKSFORUM BAYERN (GW/0340-000X) [01788703] **3195**

BIBLIOTHEKSRECHTLICHE VORSCHRIFTEN (GW/0175-6524) [01756524] **3195**

BIBLIOTHEKSWESEN IN DER DEUTSCHEN DEMOKRATISCHEN REPUBLIK, JAHRESBERICHT, DAS (GW) [07633019] **3195**

BIBLIOTHEQUE BYZANTINE *See* ETUDES **2687**

BIBLIOTHEQUE CENTRALE DE PRET DU SAGUENAY-LAC-SAINT-JEAN *See* NOUVELLES DE LA BIBLIOTHEQUE CENTRALE DE PRET. REGION DU SAGUENAY-LAC-SAINT-JEAN **3237**

BIBLIOTHEQUE DE DROIT COMMERCIAL (FR) [01532860] **3096**

BIBLIOTHEQUE DE DROIT DU TRAVAIL ET DE LA SECURITE SOCIALE (FR) [01532861] **1655**

BIBLIOTHEQUE DE LA PLEIADE (FR) [05835790] **3195**

BIBLIOTHEQUE DE LA SORBONNE *See* LISTE QUINQUENNALE DES ENTREES EN CARACTERES CYRILLIQUES **419**

BIBLIOTHEQUE DE L'ECOLE DES CHARTES (FR/0343-6237) [01532871] **3269**, **3195**

BIBLIOTHEQUE DES ARCHIVES DE PHILOSOPHIE (FR/0523-5057) [03249851] **3195**, **4342**

BIBLIOTHEQUE DES CAHIERS DE L'INSTITUT DE LINGUISTIQUE DE LOUVAIN (BE) [06119459] **3269**

BIBLIOTHEQUE DES ECOLES FRANCAISES D'ATHENES ET DE ROME (FR) [01532874] **3195**

BIBLIOTHEQUE DES LETTRES MODERNES (SZ) [02514206] **3195**

BIBLIOTHEQUE D'ETUDE (UA) [02298739] **261**

BIBLIOTHEQUE D'HUMANISME ET RENAISSANCE (SZ/0006-1999) [01532876] **2611**

BIBLIOTHEQUE JEAN GENET (FR/0988-1999) [18672573] **3195**

BIBLIOTHEQUE NATIONALE DU CANADA *See* CULTURAL EVENTS - NATIONAL LIBRARY OF CANADA **318**

BIBLIOTHEQUE NATIONALE DU QUEBEC. SERVICE DE MICROPHOTOGRAPHIE *See* MICROEDITIONS DE LA BIBLIOTHEQUE. CATALOGUE **420**

BIBLIOTHEQUE NATIONALE DU QUEBEC. SERVICE DE MICROPHOTOGRAPHIE *See* CATALOGUE DES MICROEDITIONS **3200**

BIBLIOTHEQUE NATIONALE (FRANCE) *See* REVUE DE LA BIBLIOTHEQUE NATIONALE **3246**

BIBLIOTHEQUE PHILOSOPHIQUE (BE) [01756241] **4342**

BIBLIOTHEQUE POSTALE (1989) (CN/0848-7464) [23598728] **3195**

BIBLIOTHEQUE PUBLIQUE D'OTTAWA *See* PERIODICALS / OTTAWA PUBLIC LIBRARY **3240**

BIBLIOTHEQUE RUSSE (FR) [02734049] **3367**, **3269**

BIBLIOTHEQUE RUSSE DE L'INSTITUT D'ETUDES SLAVES (FR/0078-9976) [09432498] **3269**, **3367**

BIBLIOTH-EQUE ARCTIQUE ET ANTARCTIQUE (GW/0067-8244) [02776572] **2212**

BIBLIS (SW/0430-8417) [01532895] **4812**, **4824**

BIBLISCH-THEOLOGISCHE STUDIEN (GW) [05623421] **5015**

BIBLISCHE NOTIZEN (GW/0178-2967) [05861191] **5015**

BIBLISCHE UNTERSUCHUNGEN (GW/0523-5154) [01929610] **5015**

BIBLISCHE ZEITSCHRIFT (GW/0006-2014) [01696331] **5015**

BIBLOS (PO/0870-4112) [03021783] **3195**

BIBLOS; OSTERREICHISCHE ZEITSCHRIFT FUER BUCH- UND BIBLIOTEKSWESEN, DOKUMENTATION, BIBLIOGRAPHIE, UND BIBLIOPHILIE (AU/0006-2022) [02083176] **3195**

BIBRA BULLETIN (UK/0268-2222) [10597917] **3979**

BIBURIO: RYUKYU DAGAKU FUZOKU TOSHOKAN HO. THE UNIVERSITY OF THE RYUKYUS LIBRARY BULLETIN (JA) [03303286] **3195**

BIBURUSU (JA/0006-2030) [02778409] **3195**

BIC-CODE (FR/0249-5708) [02495708] **4218**

BIC (MONTREAL, QUEBEC : 1981) (CN/0714-7546) [09375367] **5229**

BIC US. BUSINESS INDUSTRY COORDINATOR (US) **643**

BICENTENAIRE DE LA REVOLUTION FRANCAISE : BULLET DE LA COMMISSION NATIONALE DE RECHERCHE HISTORIQUE POUR LE BICENTENAIRE DE LA REVOLUTION FRANCAISE (FR) [13082121] **2678**

BICHON FRISE REPORTER, THE (US/0199-8315) [06207999] **4285**

BICIC (BANK) *See* RAPPORT ANNUEL **806**

BICICLETTA (IT) **428**

BICYCLE ACCIDENT STATISTICS (US) [04922022] **428**, **429**

BICYCLE BLUE BOOK. BICYCLE SPECIFICATION GUIDE (US/0272-8516) [06957449] **428**

BICYCLE BLUE BOOK. UNITED STATES BICYCLE TRADE INDEX (US/0272-8524) [06957436] **428**

BICYCLE BUSINESS JOURNAL (US/0745-8126) [09496339] **428**

BICYCLE DEALER SHOWCASE (US/0361-381X) [02246350] **428**

BICYCLE FORUM (US/0193-8177) [03998687] **428**

BICYCLE GUIDE (US/0889-289X) [13844516] **428**

BICYCLE MAGAZINE (UK/0950-0669) [09500669] **428**

BICYCLE PAPER, THE (US/0742-8308) [10448784] **428**

BICYCLE RIDER (US/0895-075X) [15735798] **428**

BICYCLE SPORT (US/0743-5495) [10611532] **428**

● BICYCLE TRAVELER, THE (US/1065-1802) [26520244] **4887**

BICYCLE USA (US/0747-0371) [10440239] **428**

BICYCLES TODAY (US/0746-9454) [10406914] **428**

BICYCLING (US/0006-2073) [02246420] **428**

BICYCLING AUSTRALIA (AT/1034-8085) [10348085] **428**

BID OPENING REPORT (US/0146-9037) [03094926] **5439**

BID PROTEST DECISIONS (US) [18759490] **643**

BIDRAG (DK) [03686044] **4540**

BIEDERMANN EXPORT-HANDBUCH (GW) [10916895] **824**

BIEDERMANN (FIRM). EXPORT-HANDBUCH FUR HANDEL UND INDUSTRIE *See* BIEDERMANN EXPORT-HANDBUCH **824**

BIELEFELDER KATALOG KLASSIK (GW/0721-7153) [07943712] **5320**

BIELEFELDER KATALOG SCHALLPLATTEN, COMPACT DISCS, MUSICASSETTEN KLASSIK (GW) [14193051] **5316**

BIELLESE, IL (IT/0393-1951) [03931951] **2485**

BIEN PUBLIC, LE (FR) [20922533] **5800**

BIENENVATER (AU/0006-2146) [01532908] **5606**, **66**

BIENNAL DI VENEZIA *See* BIENNALE DI VENEZIA : CATALOGO, LA **344**

BIENNALE DI VENEZIA : CATALOGO, LA (IT) [05203449] **344**

Alphabetical Title Index **BIENNIAL**

BIENNALE INTERNAZIONALE DELLA GRAFICA D'ARTE / UNIONE FIORENTINA (IT) [09787238] **344**

BIENNIAL BUDGET REQUEST - WISCONSIN DEPARTMENT OF HEALTH AND SOCIAL SERVICES (US/0147-3492) [03144520] **5274**

BIENNIAL CONFERENCE - AUSTRALIAN & NEW ZEALAND ASSOCIATION OF EDUCATORS OF THE VISUALLY HANDICAPPED (AT/0815-8398) [I08158398] 4384, **1889**

BIENNIAL EVALUATION REPORT (US) [18041051] **1911**

BIENNIAL EVALUATION REPORT - MICHIGAN. STATE ADVISORY COUNCIL FOR VOCATIONAL EDUCATION (US) [17811241] **1911**

BIENNIAL MEMBERSHIP BOOK / GENEALOGICAL FORUM OF PORTLAND, OREGON (US) [15228297] **2439**

BIENNIAL REPORT (US) [19707568] **1655**

BIENNIAL REPORT (US) [08634988] **3158**

BIENNIAL REPORT (US) [17603715] **4084**

BIENNIAL REPORT - ADJUTANT GENERAL'S DEPARTMENT, STATE OF NORTH DAKOTA (US) [04396967] **4037**

BIENNIAL REPORT / AGRICULTURAL RESEARCH AND ADVISORY STATION, CONDOBOLIN (AT/0818-8726) [20649147] **66**

BIENNIAL REPORT - AMERICAN INSTITUTE OF INDIAN STUDIES (US/0741-9228) [10218340] **2647**

BIENNIAL REPORT AND OVERVIEW, AREA REDEVELOPMENT ADMINISTRATION (US) [03997494] **2816**

BIENNIAL REPORT AND OVERVIEW OF MINNESOTA MUNICIPAL REVENUE BONDS (US) [03861884] **892**

BIENNIAL REPORT AND STATEMENT OF ACCOUNTS - RAILWAYMEN'S UNION OF MALAYA (MY) [04224291] **1655**

BIENNIAL REPORT - ARKANSAS WATERWAYS COMMISSION (US/0093-6200) [01792138] **5447**

BIENNIAL REPORT / ATTORNEY GENERAL (US) [27396043] **3139**

BIENNIAL REPORT - CALIFORNIA ENERGY COMMISSION (US/0270-8930) [06498362] **1933**

BIENNIAL REPORT / COMMONWEALTH OF VIRGINIA, DEPARTMENT OF HEALTH REGULATORY BOARDS (US) [07759826] **4768**

BIENNIAL REPORT / CSIRO AUSTRALIAN ANIMAL HEALTH LABORATORY (AT/1034-9219) [23003049] 207, **5505**

BIENNIAL REPORT / CSIRO DIVISION OF FOREST RESEARCH (AT/0313-9093) [09578931] **2376**

BIENNIAL REPORT / CSIRO DIVISION OF GEOMECHANICS (AT/0817-1947) [14702250] **1367**

BIENNIAL REPORT / CSIRO, DIVISION OF RADIOPHYSICS (AT/0812-339X) [10580063] 393, **4398**

BIENNIAL REPORT - DEPARTMENT OF REVENUE (WISCONSIN) (US) [06806747] **4713**

BIENNIAL REPORT / DIVISION OF ENTOMOLOGY, CSIRO (AT/1037-3500) [12069604] **5606**

BIENNIAL REPORT / DIVISION OF PROTEIN CHEMISTRY, INSTITUTE OF INDUSTRIAL TECHNOLOGY (AT/0314-254X) [18156596] **962**

BIENNIAL REPORT / DIVISION OF WILDLIFE AND ECOLOGY (AT/1033-2731) [20917267] **5578**

BIENNIAL REPORT - EDUCATIONAL COMMUNICATIONS BOARD (US/0361-2120) [02246359] **1889**

BIENNIAL REPORT FROM THE OFFICE OF STATE TAX COMMISSIONER ... TO THE GOVERNOR AND THE OFFICE OF MANAGEMENT AND BUDGET, STATE OF NORTH DAKOTA (US) [11696985] **4713**

BIENNIAL REPORT / GEOLOGICAL SURVEY DIVISION, MINISTRY OF MINING, ENERGY AND TOURISM (JM) [20075288] **1367**

BIENNIAL REPORT / GLEN INNES AGRICULTURAL RESEARCH AND ADVISORY STATION (AT/0814-3595) [19744317] **66**

BIENNIAL REPORT - GOVERNOR'S ADVOCACY COMMITTEE FOR CHILDREN AND YOUTH (US/0146-2423) [02914591] **5274**

BIENNIAL REPORT (HAWAII. DEPT. OF AGRICULTURE) *See* ANNUAL REPORT / DEPARTMENT OF AGRICULTURE **60**

BIENNIAL REPORT - ILLINOIS COMMISSION ON ATOMIC ENERGY (US/0732-8222) [08426988] **4632**

BIENNIAL REPORT / INSTITUTE OF OCEANOGRAPHY, MCGILL UNIVERSITY (CN/0712-9203) [08560982] **1446**

BIENNIAL REPORT - INTERNATIONAL CARGO HANDLING CO-ORDINATION ASSOCIATION (UK) [02337939] **5447**

BIENNIAL REPORT / IOWA PRESERVES BOARD (US) [07593652] 2188, **4163**

BIENNIAL REPORT / IRCD, IOWA RURAL COMMUNITY DEVELOPMENT PROGRAM (US) [07591687] **2816**

BIENNIAL REPORT / JAPAN-UNITED STATES FRIENDSHIP COMMISSION (US) [23966566] **4516**

BIENNIAL REPORT / JOINT COMMITTEE FOR REVIEW OF ADMINISTRATIVE RULES (US) [05238489] **2941**

BIENNIAL REPORT - KANSAS ADULT AUTHORITY (US/0149-340X) [03463853] **3158**

BIENNIAL REPORT - LAND RECLAMATION COMMISSION (US) [03152598] **2225**

BIENNIAL REPORT - LEAGUE OF RED CROSS SOCIETIES (SZ/0253-0406) [06370394] **5274**

BIENNIAL REPORT / LEGISLATIVE ADVISORY COMMITTEE TO THE REGIONAL TRANSPORTATION AUTHORITY (US) [10994207] **5377**

BIENNIAL REPORT / LEGISLATIVE POST AUDIT COMMITTEE AND LEGISLATIVE DIVISION OF POST AUDIT (US) [09027828] 4632, **739**

BIENNIAL REPORT - MAINE, SOIL AND WATER CONSERVATION COMMISSION (US/0085-297X) [01799012] **2188**

BIENNIAL REPORT - MINNESOTA BOARD OF DENTISTRY (US/0149-1474) [03430083] **1317**

BIENNIAL REPORT / MINNESOTA DEPARTMENT OF CORRECTIONS (US) [07055419] **3158**

BIENNIAL REPORT - MINNESOTA DEPARTMENT OF HEALTH (US) [05587318] **4768**

BIENNIAL REPORT - MINNESOTA DEPARTMENT OF NATURAL RESOURCES (US/0090-8177) [01785673] **2188**

BIENNIAL REPORT - MINNESOTA STATE BOARD OF HEALTH *See* BIENNIAL REPORT - MINNESOTA DEPARTMENT OF HEALTH **4768**

BIENNIAL REPORT - MISSOURI DIVISION OF CORRECTIONS (US) [06628763] **3158**

BIENNIAL REPORT / MONTANA SCIENCE & TECHNOLOGY ALLIANCE (US) [24149685] **5088**

BIENNIAL REPORT / NEBRASKA PUBLIC SERVICE COMMISSION (US) [11409925] **4632**

BIENNIAL REPORT - NEVADA INDIAN COMMISSION (US/0148-8198) [03375422] **2256**

BIENNIAL REPORT - NEVADA STATE FIRE MARSHAL DIVISION (US) [04406744] **2288**

BIENNIAL REPORT - NORTH CAROLINA DEPARTMENT OF TRANSPORTATION (US) [06350581] **5377**

BIENNIAL REPORT - NORTH CAROLINA MANPOWER COUNCIL (US/0146-9150) [03131665] **1655**

BIENNIAL REPORT - NORTH CAROLINA. STATE DEPARTMENT OF SOCIAL SERVICES OF THE DEPARTMENT OF HUMAN RESOURCES (US/0093-3988) [01792288] **5274**

BIENNIAL REPORT / NORTH DAKOTA COUNCIL ON THE ARTS (US) [08942180] **316**

BIENNIAL REPORT / NORTH DAKOTA, DEPT. OF HUMAN SERVICES (US) [20256551] **5274**

BIENNIAL REPORT - NORTH DAKOTA STATE HIGHWAY DEPARTMENT (US) [05305911] **5439**

BIENNIAL REPORT - NORTH DAKOTA. STATE WATER CONSERVATION COMMISSION (US) [01586131] 2087, **5531**

BIENNIAL REPORT OF EMPLOYMENT BY GEOGRAPHIC AREA (US/8756-7156) [11273854] **4701**

BIENNIAL REPORT OF EXAMINING AND LICENSING BOARDS (US) [04171613] **4379**

BIENNIAL REPORT OF EXAMINING AND LICENSING BOARDS (US) [11983190] 4379, **3803**

BIENNIAL REPORT OF EXAMINING AND LICENSING BOARDS / ADVISORY COMMITTEE OF EXAMINERS IN MORTUARY SCIENCE (MINNESOTA) (US) [04355634] **4768**

BIENNIAL REPORT OF EXAMINING AND LICENSING BOARDS / BOARD OF ASSESSORS (US) [09693469] **4713**

BIENNIAL REPORT OF EXAMINING AND LICENSING BOARDS / BOARD OF BARBER EXAMINERS (US) [04356154] **402**

BIENNIAL REPORT OF EXAMINING AND LICENSING BOARDS - MINNESOTA. BOARD OF EXAMINERS FOR NURSING HOME ADMINISTRATORS (US) [04171568] **4768**

BIENNIAL REPORT OF EXAMINING AND LICENSING BOARDS - MINNESOTA BOARD OF NURSING (US) [07126633] **3852**

BIENNIAL REPORT OF EXAMINING AND LICENSING BOARDS / MINNESOTA BOARD OF PODIATRY (US) [04354562] **3556**

BIENNIAL REPORT OF EXAMINING AND LICENSING BOARDS / MINNESOTA BOARD OF PSYCHOLOGY (US) [06998157] **4577**

BIENNIAL REPORT OF EXAMINING AND LICENSING BOARDS / MINNESOTA BOARD OF TEACHING (US) [04355576] **1889**

BIENNIAL REPORT OF EXAMINING AND LICENSING BOARDS - MINNESOTA. ENVIRONMENTAL HEALTH SPECIALIST/SANITARIAN ADVISORY COUNCIL (US) [07613250] **2225**

BIENNIAL REPORT OF EXAMINING AND LICENSING BOARDS - MINNESOTA. STATE BOARD OF ELECTRICITY (US) [07075699] **2036**

BIENNIAL REPORT OF OFFICE OF THE COMMISSIONER OF CREDIT UNIONS (US/0364-2186) [02617389] **778**

BIENNIAL REPORT OF THE ATTORNEY GENERAL OF THE STATE OF NORTH CAROLINA *See* NORTH CAROLINA ATTORNEY GENERAL REPORTS **3142**

BIENNIAL REPORT OF THE ATTORNEY GENERAL TO THE GENERAL OF THE COMMONWEALTH OF KENTUCKY FOR THE BIENNIAL PERIOD ... AS REQUIRED BY KR 15.080 *See* BIENNIAL REPORT OF THE DEPARTMENT OF LAW TO ... GOVERNOR, COMMONWEALTH OF KENTUCKY FOR THE BIENNIAL PERIOD ... AS REQUIRED BY KRS 15.080 **3139**

BIENNIAL REPORT OF THE AUDITOR OF ACCOUNTS TO THE GENERAL ASSEMBLY OF VERMONT (US) [05668128] **4713**

BIENNIAL REPORT OF THE COMMISSIONER OF FINANCIAL INSTITUTIONS AND SUPERVISOR OF HOMESTEAD AND BUILDING AND LOAN ASSOCIATIONS (US/0097-8582) [01799346] **778**

BIENNIAL REPORT OF THE COMMISSIONER OF REVENUE SUBMITTING AN EQUALIZATION AND PROPORTIONMENT UPON THE SEVERAL CITIES AND TOWNS OF THE AMOUNT OF PROPERTY AND THE PROPORTION OF EVERY ONE THOUSAND DOLLARS OF STATE AND COUNTY TAX WHICH SHOULD BE ASSESSED UPON EACH CITY AND TOWN (US) [06201475] **4713**

BIENNIAL REPORT OF THE CONNECTICUT JUDICIAL DEPARTMENT (US) [09490510] **3139**

BIENNIAL REPORT OF THE DEPARTMENT OF LAW TO ... GOVERNOR, COMMONWEALTH OF KENTUCKY FOR THE BIENNIAL PERIOD ... AS REQUIRED BY KRS 15.080 (US) [07969256] **3139**

BIENNIAL REPORT OF THE DEPARTMENT OF PUBLIC SERVICE / STATE OF VERMONT (US) [12425892] **4760**

BIENNIAL REPORT OF THE DEPARTMENT OF WATER RESOURCES (US/0466-6992) [01606428] **5531**

BIENNIAL REPORT OF THE EXECUTIVE SECRETARY (ET) [07119486] **1548**

BIENNIAL REPORT OF THE FISH AND GAME DEPARTMENT OF THE STATE OF IDAHO (US/0073-4519) [01517021] **2297**

BIENNIAL REPORT OF THE LEGISLATIVE AUDITOR (NEVADA) (US) [05270011] **4713**

BIENNIAL REPORT ... OF THE LEGISLATIVE FINANCE COMMITTEE - NEW MEXICO (US) [07292510] **4713**

BIENNIAL REPORT OF THE MASSACHUSETTS CIVIL DEFENSE AGENCY AND OFFICE OF EMERGENCY PREPAREDNESS TO THE GOVERNOR AND GENERAL COURT (US/0097-7543) [01798438] **1072**

BIENNIAL REPORT OF THE NEW YORK STATE SCIENCE SERVICE (US/0883-1548) [06473503] **5088**

BIENNIAL REPORT OF THE NORTH CAROLINA RECREATION COMMISSION (US) [01076174] **4849**

BIENNIAL REPORT OF THE OFFICE OF CRIME VICTIMS OMBUDSMAN (US) [23665865] **3158**

BIENNIAL REPORT OF THE OFFICE OF EMERGENCY ENERGY ASSISTANCE (US/0363-6410) [02531801] **1933**

BIENNIAL
Alphabetical Title Index

BIENNIAL REPORT OF THE REGIONAL DIRECTOR TO THE ... SESSION OF THE REGIONAL COMMITTEE / WORLD HEALTH ORGANIZATION, REGIONAL OFFICE FOR THE EASTERN MEDITERRANEAN (UA) [07657062] **4768**

BIENNIAL REPORT OF THE STATE ENGINEER OF NEW MEXICO (US) [02570046] **2019**

BIENNIAL REPORT OF THE STATE GAME AND FISH COMMISSION TO THE REGULAR SESSION OF THE MISSISSIPPI LEGISLATURE (US) [01512548] **2297**

BIENNIAL REPORT OF THE STATE GEOLOGIST (VERMILLION), THE (US/0361-8285) [09840308] **1367**

BIENNIAL REPORT OF THE STATE LABORATORIES AND CONSUMER AFFAIRS DEPARTMENT (US) [04137903] **4632**

BIENNIAL REPORT OF THE TEXAS LIBRARY AND HISTORICAL COMMISSION (US/0146-5635) [01604807] **3195**

BIENNIAL REPORT OF THE TEXAS STATE LIBRARY AND ARCHIVES COMMISSION (US) [07189222] 2480, **3195**

BIENNIAL REPORT OF THE TREASURER OF STATE OF THE STATE OF ARKANSAS FOR THE BIENNIAL PERIOD BEGINNING JULY 1 ... AND ENDING JUNE 30 ... (US) [09026992] **4713**

BIENNIAL REPORT OF THE VERMONT DEPARTMENT OF LIBRARIES (US/0363-3500) [02172527] **3195**

BIENNIAL REPORT OF THE VERMONT RECREATION BOARD (US/0503-9967) [01166470] **4849**

BIENNIAL REPORT OF WISCONSIN STATE ELECTIONS BOARD (US) [05594209] **4632**

BIENNIAL REPORT - OKLAHOMA EDUCATION COUNCIL (US) [05201473] **1727**

BIENNIAL REPORT - OKLAHOMA INDIAN AFFAIRS COMMISSION (US/0360-7518) [02244716] **2256**

BIENNIAL REPORT - OKLAHOMA STATE REGENTS FOR HIGHER EDUCATION (US) [03268681] **1811**

BIENNIAL REPORT ON THE SPECIAL SUPPLEMENTAL FOOD PROGRAM FOR WOMEN, INFANTS, AND CHILDREN, AND ON THE COMMODITY SUPPLEMENTAL FOOD PROGRAM (US/0884-6081) [12380855] 4188, **2328**

BIENNIAL REPORT - OREGON BOARD OF EDUCATION (US/0091-8784) [01787375] **1727**

BIENNIAL REPORT, OREGON'S SUBMERGED AND SUBMERSIBLE LANDS (US/0092-4938) [01786835] **4632**

BIENNIAL REPORT PREPARED IN ACCORDANCE WITH THE OZONE PROTECTION PROVISION, SECTION 153 (G), OF THE CLEAN AIR ACT AMENDMENTS OF 1977 (US/0270-1596) [06325936] **2225**

BIENNIAL REPORT / SANTA BARBARA MUSEUM OF ART (US) [27124264] **4084**

BIENNIAL REPORT / SPECIAL PROGRAMME OF RESEARCH, DEVELOPMENT AND RESEARCH TRAINING IN HUMAN REPRODUCTION (SZ) [27240917] 4550, **588**

BIENNIAL REPORT - STAFF SERVICES SECTION, DIVISION OF VOCATIONAL REHABILITATION (US/0363-6070) [02506346] **1911**

BIENNIAL REPORT - STATE DEPARTMENT OF HIGHWAYS AND PUBLIC TRANSPORTATION (US/0147-8362) [03233622] **5377**

BIENNIAL REPORT / STATE OF CALIFORNIA, CALIFORNIA COASTAL COMMISSION (US) [07491736] 1446, **2188**

BIENNIAL REPORT - STATE OF FLORIDA DEPARTMENT OF STATE (US/0099-1600) [02253862] **4632**

BIENNIAL REPORT / STATE OF MICHIGAN, THE DEPARTMENT OF NATURAL RESOURCES (US) [01116693] **4632**

BIENNIAL REPORT - STATE OF MINNESOTA, DEPARTMENT OF CIVIL SERVICE (US/0540-1887) [03440607] **4701**

BIENNIAL REPORT - STATE OF MINNESOTA, DEPARTMENT OF MILITARY AFFAIRS (US) [04473164] **4037**

BIENNIAL REPORT - STATE OF MINNESOTA DEPARTMENT OF PUBLIC SERVICE (US) [05229284] 5378, **4632**

BIENNIAL REPORT - STATE OF MINNESOTA, DEPARTMENT OF REVENUE (US/0095-0645) [01796161] **4713**

BIENNIAL REPORT - STATE OF MINNESOTA, DEPARTMENT OF VETERANS AFFAIRS (US) [05063644] **4038**

BIENNIAL REPORT / STATE OF NORTH CAROLINA, DEPARTMENT OF HUMAN RESOURCES, DIVISION OF YOUTH SERVICES (US) [08920407] **3158**

BIENNIAL REPORT / STATE OF WISCONSIN, CONSERVATION WORK PROJECTS BOARD (US) [05929309] **2188**

BIENNIAL REPORT / STATE OF WISCONSIN, DEPARTMENT OF DEVELOPMENT (US) [07908023] **1548**

BIENNIAL REPORT - STATE OF WISCONSIN, DEPARTMENT OF EMPLOYMENT RELATIONS (US) [05929391] **4701**

BIENNIAL REPORT - STATE OF WISCONSIN, DEPARTMENT OF INDUSTRY, LABOR AND HUMAN RELATIONS (US) [03862532] **1655**

BIENNIAL REPORT - STATE OF WISCONSIN, DEPARTMENT OF REGULATION AND LICENSING (US/0145-8647) [02793048] **4632**

BIENNIAL REPORT - STATE OF WISCONSIN, DEPARTMENT OF VETERANS AFFAIRS (US) [03714987] **4038**

BIENNIAL REPORT - STATE OF WISCONSIN ETHICS BOARD (US/0363-9193) [02569122] 4632, **2249**

BIENNIAL REPORT - STATE OF WISCONSIN, INVESTMENT BOARD (US/0364-5495) [02667412] **4713**

BIENNIAL REPORT - STATE OF WISCONSIN, PERSONNEL COMMISSION (US) [05929180] **4701**

BIENNIAL REPORT / TENNESSEE DEPARTMENT OF EMPLOYMENT SECURITY (US) [10053084] 2876, **1655**

BIENNIAL REPORT - TENNESSEE DEPARTMENT OF REVENUE (JS/0363-5317) [02461796] **4713**

BIENNIAL REPORT - TEXAS DEPARTMENT OF HEALTH (US) [06339091] **4768**

BIENNIAL REPORT - TEXAS HISTORICAL COMMISSION (US/0360-8530) [02243831] **2723**

BIENNIAL REPORT - THE ACCOKEEK FOUNDATION (US) [01433624] **4163**

BIENNIAL REPORT / THE JUDICIAL COUNCIL OF THE STATE OF MINNESOTA (US) [17151681] **2941**

BIENNIAL REPORT TO LEGISLATURE - BUREAU OF PUBLIC LANDS (US/0148-9275) [03389874] **4632**

BIENNIAL REPORT TO THE CONGRESS ON COASTAL ZONE MANAGEMENT (US) [24253032] **4632**

BIENNIAL REPORT TO THE GOVERNOR / TEXAS PLANNING COUNCIL FOR DEVELOPMENTAL DISABILITIES *See* ANNUAL REPORT TO THE GOVERNOR / TEXAS PLANNING COUNCIL FOR DEVELOPMENTAL DISABILITIES **5273**

BIENNIAL REPORT TO THE LEGISLATURE / LEGISLATIVE COMMISSION ON MINNESOTA RESOURCES (US) [11483086] **4632**

BIENNIAL REPORT TO THE LEGISLATURE - MONTANA LEGISLATIVE ASSEMBLY. ADMINISTRATIVE CODE COMMITTEE (US) [06320348] **2941**

BIENNIAL REPORT UNDER THE GREAT LAKES WATER QUALITY AGREEMENT OF 1978 (US/0736-8410) [09025749] **5531**

BIENNIAL REPORT / UNITED STATES-ISRAEL BINATIONAL SCIENCE FOUNDATION (US) [06990667] **5088**

BIENNIAL REPORT - VIRGINIA COMMISSION OF OUTDOOR RECREATION (US/0507-0503) [01165738] **4869**

BIENNIAL REPORT / VIRGINIA DEPARTMENT OF LABOR AND INDUSTRY (US) [11143415] **1655**

BIENNIAL REPORT - VIRGINIA DIVISION OF MOTOR VEHICLES (US) [01793541] **5407**

BIENNIAL REPORT / WHEAT RESEARCH UNIT (AT) [11965095] **200**

BIENNIAL REPORT - WISCONSIN ARTS BOARD (US) [03718316] **316**

BIENNIAL REPORT - WISCONSIN. DEPT. OF AGRICULTURE, TRADE AND CONSUMER PROTECTION (US/0277-0660) [03715239] **66**

BIENNIAL REPORT / WORLD ASSOCIATION OF GIRL GUIDES AND GIRL SCOUTS (UK) [20079810] **5229**

BIENNIAL REPORT - WORLD CONFEDERATION OF ORGANIZATIONS OF THE TEACHING PROFESSION (SZ) [19378907] **1889**

BIENNIAL REPORT / WORLD HEALTH ORGANIZATION, INTERNATIONAL AGENCY FOR RESEARCH ON CANCER (FR) [17801355] **3809**

BIENNIAL RESEARCH REPORT (AT/1036-0220) [23526595] **66**

BIENNIAL RESEARCH REPORT / AGRICULTURAL RESEARCH AND ADVISORY STATION, GRAFTON (AT) [24905176] **66**

BIENNIAL RESEARCH REPORT / DIVISION OF ENERGY CHEMISTRY, CSIRO (AT) [15504591] 1021, **1933**

BIENNIAL RESEARCH REPORT (INSTITUTE OF ENERGY AND EARTH RESOURCES (AUSTRALIA). DIVISION OF MINERAL CHEMISTRY) (AT/0817-4997) [17805395] **1352**

BIENNIAL ROSTER OF REGISTERED PROFESSIONAL ENGINEERS AND LAND SURVEYORS AND ALABAMA LAW REGULATING PRACTICE OF ENGINEERING AND LAND SURVEYING (US/0146-1753) [02878848] **1966**

BIENNIAL ROSTER OF REGISTRANTS FOR THE YEAR ENDING JUNE 30 ... : REPORT OF THE STATE BOARD OF REGISTRATION FOR PROFESSIONAL ENGINEERS OF WEST VIRGINIA (US) [11978076] **1966**

BIENNIAL STATEWIDE TRANSPORTATION NEEDS REPORT TO THE ARIZONA LEGISLATURE (US) [03997746] **5378**

BIENNIAL SURVEY OF EDUCATION / DEPARTMENT OF THE INTERIOR, BUREAU OF EDUCATION (US) [01779131] **1727**

BIENNIAL SURVEY OF POWER EQUIPMENT REQUIREMENTS OF THE U.S. ELECTRIC UTILITY INDUSTRY *CEASED.* (US) [09674954] **2036**

BIENNIAL SURVEY OF UNIVERSITIES OFFERING AN ORGANIZED CURRICULUM IN COMMERCE AND BUSINESS ADMINISTRATION (US/0882-5602) [01469028] 643, **1811**

BIENNIAL SYMPOSIUM ON ANIMAL REPRODUCTION; [PROCEEDINGS] (US/0570-1244) [02600005] **5505**

BIENVILLE DEMOCRAT RINGGOLD RECORD, THE (US) [17460617] **5683**

BIER & GETRANKE (GW/0937-1958) [09371958] **2364**

●BIERE MAG (CN/1188-8555) [26758171] **2329**

BIFIDOBACTERIA AND MICROFLORA (JA/0286-9306) [10267587] **560**

BIFIDUS, FLORES ET FRUCTUS (JA/0285-7006) [10167481] **477**

BIFOCAL (US/0888-1537) [08819919] 5178, **3179**

BIG APPLE JAZZ (US/0147-6645) [03215075] **4103**

BIG BANDS, THE (US/0738-7067) [05723136] **4103**

●BIG BEAR GRIZZLY (US/1073-6867) [28739053] **5633**

BIG BEAR LIFE & THE GRIZZLY *See* BIG BEAR GRIZZLY **5633**

BIG BEAUTIFUL WOMAN (US/0192-5938) [05117765] **1082**

BIG BEND REGISTER (US/0736-7074) [09179080] **2439**

BIG BEND SENTINEL *See* MARFA INDEPENDENT AND THE BIG BEND SENTINEL, THE **5752**

BIG BLUE DISK (US/0893-2212) [16003344] **1284**

BIG BLUE REVIEW (US/1056-845X) [23877534] **4887**

BIG BOND BOOK, THE (US/1057-2848) [23997016] **892**

BIG BOOK OF METALWORKING MACHINERY (US/0045-1983) [01791659] **3999**

BIG BOOK OF PATTERNS (US) [13298073] **1082**

BIG BOOK / RANDOM LENGTHS (US) [25152425] **2376**

BIG BOPPER, THE (US/1053-9212) [22690037] **383**

BIG BYTE, THE (CN/0045-1991) [01721804] 1240, **1246**

●BIG CITY MUSIC (US/1042-9263) [19252536] **4103**

BIG COUNTRY CARIBOO MAGAZINE (CN/0703-1440) [03781926] **2723**

BIG COUNTRY VOICE, THE (CN/0382-7577) [02627706] **5780**

BIG CROSSWORDS (US/0740-3321) [09935391] **4857**

BIG DEAL (US/0146-7042) [02781390] **3367**

BIG EIGHT, THE (US/0361-588X) [02246993] **4887**

BIG FARM WEEKLY (UK) **66**

BIG FARMER ENTREPRENEUR (US/0274-6050) [06469832] **66**

BIG FISH COUNTRY FISHING GUIDE (CN/0828-7899) [12204301] **2297**

●BIG GAME HUNTING (US/1059-5767) [24639061] **4869**

BIG HORN COUNTY NEW (US/0897-8735) [17646387] **5705**

BIG LAKE WILDCAT, THE (US) [13980387] **5747**

BIG MAMA RAG **SUSPENDED.** (US/0277-7533) [02778484] **5551**

BIG PAPER **CEASED.** (UK/0954-9803) [I09549803] **824**

BIG PICTURE (ALEXANDRIA, VA.), THE (US/1064-5365) [24344780] **892**

BIG PICTURE (KNOXVILLE, TENN.) (US/1047-3831) [20704626] **2485**

BIG RED DIARY (UK) [02242987] **4540**

BIG RED NEWS (US/0745-936X) [09607792] **5714**

BIG REEL, THE (US/0744-723X) [07757081] 2771, **4064**

BIG RIVER (US/1070-8340) [28475570] **2297**

BIG SANDY & HAWKINS JOURNAL AND TRI-AREA NEWS, THE (US/0745-0702) [08801935] **5747**

BIG SANDY NEWS (LOUISA, KY. : 1974) (US/0891-2327) [12183468] **5679**

BIG SKY BUSINESS JOURNAL (US/8756-6567) [11690110] **643**

BIG SKY ECONOMICS (US/0886-4489) [04456331] **66**

BIG SPRING HERALD (US/0746-6811) [10220887] **5747**

BIG TEN CONFERENCE RECORDS BOOK (US) [22950209] **4887**

BIG TEN FOOTBALL ALMANAC (US/0197-8128) [06112831] **4887**

BIG TIMBER PIONEER (1983), THE (US/0740-1981) [09891942] **5705**

BIGAKU / BIGAKKAI HEN (JA/0520-0962) [02787595] **4342**

BIGGER, FASTER, STRONGER JOURNAL (US/0889-5988) [14102969] **4887**

BIGRE (FR/1246-6875) [I12466875] **1172**

BIGRE + GLOBULE See BIGRE **1172**

BIHADASHT-I JAHAN (IR/0252-5356) [I02525356] **2596**

BIHAR BAR COUNCIL JOURNAL (II) [04735082] **2941**

BIHAR, INDIA (STATE). DISTRICT STATISTICAL OFFICE, MONGHYR See DISTRICT STATISTICAL HANDBOOK - (INDIA) **5326**

BIHAR STATE BAR COUNCIL See BIHAR BAR COUNCIL JOURNAL **2941**

BIHAREA (RM) [04845902] **232**

BIIOGRAPHY AND GENEOLOGY MASTER INDEX (US) **2439**

BIISS JOURNAL (BG) [08401494] **4516**

BIJBLIJVEN (NE/0168-9428) [19271564] **3556**

BIJDRAGEN EN MEDEDELINGEN BETREFFENDE DE GESCHIEDENIS DER NEDERLANDEN (NE/0165-0505) [01532933] **2678**

BIJDRAGEN TIJDSCHRIFT VOOR FILOSOFIE EN THEOLOGIE (NE) [03021149] 4939, **4342**

BIJDRAGEN TOT DE DIERKUNDE (NE/0067-8546) [01532934] **5578**

BIJDRAGEN TOT DE TAAL-, LAND- EN VOLKENKUNDE (NE/0006-2294) [02855914] 2647, **232**

BIJINESU REBYU. BUSINESS REVIEW (JA) [05045673] **643**

BIJOUTIER : REVUE FRANCAISE DES BIJOUTIERS HORLOGERS, LE (FR/0766-6931) [15334627] **2916**

BIJUTSU KENKYU. THE JOURNAL OF ART STUDIES (JA/0021-907X) [01532940] **316**

BIJUTSU SHI (JA/0021-907X) [02782857] **344**

BIJUTSU TECHO (JA/0287-2218) [03250233] **344**

BIJUTSUSHIGAKU SENDAI. 1978 (JA/0387-2688) [I03872688] **344**

●BIKE (MIDDLETOWN, R.I.), THE (US/1064-492X) [26319573] **4887**

BIKE TECH **CEASED.** (US/0734-5992) [08782114] **428**

BIKER (AGOURA HILLS, CALIF.) (US/1058-7926) [24387635] **4080**

BIKHAMA (II) [08623487] **3367**

BIKORET U-FARSHANUT (IS) [02783061] 3269, **3338**

BILADI (BL) [05692481] **2723**

BILAG TIL GTO RAPPORT (DK) [11139571] **2019**

BILAKABIDE : REVISTA DE POESIA (SP) **3460**

BILAN ANNUEL, BASSE-NORMANDIE (FR) [12164941] **779**

BILAN ANNUEL BRETAGNE (FR) [07816969] **5323**

BILAN AU 30 SEPTEMBRE ... / SOCIETE NATIONALE DE COMMERCE ET DE PRODUCTION (FR) [08202058] **824**

BILAN DES ACTIVITES ECONOMIQUES DANS LE BAS-RHIN (FR) [05756671] **1548**

BILAN ECONOMIQUE ET SOCIAL (FR/1169-7075) [22592669] **1548**

BILAN EN ... DES CONDITIONS DE TRAVAIL See CONDITIONS DE TRAVAIL / MINISTERE DU TRAVAIL, DE L'EMPLOI ET DE LA FORMATION PROFESSIONNELLE, CONSEIL SUPERIEUR DE LA PREVENTION DES RISQUES PROFESSIONNELS **1661**

BILAN FORMATION-EMPLOI (FR) [18317550] **1911**

BILAN / OCTRA, LE (FR) [08148124] **5429**

BILAN/PERSPECTIVES (FR) [17939593] **5447**

BILAN SAINT-LAURENT (CN/1180-1204) [23243180] **5378**

BILAN SOCIO-ECONOMIQUE, REGION DE LA COTE-NORD (CN/1184-6259) [23659512] **1464**

BILAN SOCIO-ECONOMIQUE, REGION DE LA GASPESIE--ILES-DE-LA-MADELEINE (CN/1186-818X) [24623960] **5275**

BILANCIO E CONTABILITA DI ESERCIZIO (IT) **739**

BILANS ALIMENTAIRES ET AUTRES BILANS (FR) [02975922] 66, **151**

BILANS DES BANQUES (LE) [01789650] **779**

BILANS POLITIQUES ECONOMIQUES ET SOCIAUX HEBDOMADAIRES (FR/0755-2238) [I07552238] 4465, **643**

BILANZ (SZ) [05064515] 779, **1464**

BILANZ & BUCHHALTUNG (GW/0930-0597) [I09300597] **739**

BILANZ DER WOHNBEVOELKERUNG IN DEN GEMEINDEN DER SCHWEIZ (SZ) [10494386] **4561**

BILANZ GETREIDE-FUTTERMITTEL : BR DEUTSCHLAND, EG UND WELTMARKT (GW) [03261154] **200**

BILATERAL STUDIES IN PRIVATE INTERNATIONAL LAW (US/0067-8562) [01532943] **3124**

BILATERAL TRADE OUTLOOK (US/8755-0849) [11190900] **825**

BILD AM SONNTAG (GW/0341-4906) [I03414906] **2485**

BILD DER WISSENSCHAFT (GW/0006-2375) [02445332] **5088**

BILD UND TON (BERLIN, DDR) **CEASED.** (GW/0006-2383) [07607673] 4367, **4064**

BILDENDE KUNST (DRESDEN) **CEASED.** (GW/0006-2391) [02258339] **344**

BILDERHEFTE (GW/0522-9790) [01827616] **4084**

BILDGEBENDE VERFAHREN IN DER NEURORADIOLOGIE (GW/0932-6588) [15697897] 3939, **3828**

BILDGEBUNG (BASEL) (SZ/1012-5655) [19244679] **3939**

BILDOR NEWS (US/8750-3077) [11219995] **601**

BILDTIDNINGEN (SW/1100-5203) [I11005203] **4367**

BILDUNG IM ZAHLENSPIEGEL (GW) [02242720] **1727**

BILDUNG UND ERZIEHUNG (GW/0006-2456) [02071521] **1728**

BILDUNG UND KULTURPFLEGE IN BAYERN (GW/0935-2325) [21927143] **1728**

BILDUNG UND WISSENSCHAFT (GW/0177-4212) [02220356] 1728, **5088**

BILDUNGSFORSCHUNG UND BILDUNGSPRAXIS (SZ/0252-9955) [10837794] **1728**

BILDUNGSWESEN IN NORDRHEIN-WESTFALEN See BILDUNGSWESEN IN NORDRHEIN-WESTFALEN, DAS **1728**

BILDUNGSWESEN IN NORDRHEIN-WESTFALEN, DAS (GW) [02240721] **1728**

BILDZEITUNG (GW) **5801**

BILEN, MOTOR OG SPORT (DK) [04345250] **5407**

BILEN OG BADEN See BILEN, MOTOR OG SPORT **5407**

BILINGUAL FAMILY NEWSLETTER, THE (UK/0952-4096) [11514794] 3269, **2277**

●BILINGUAL RESEARCH JOURNAL (US) [27257539] 3269, **1728**

BILINGUAL RESOURCES (US/0197-6737) [04723665] **1876**

BILINGUAL REVIEW (US/0094-5366) [01084374] 3367, **3269**

BILINGUAL TEACHER CORPS PROGRAM, THE (US/0149-7464) [06372866] **1876**

●BILINGUALISM TODAY (US/1045-4365) [20113253] **3269**

BILL & TED'S EXCELLENT COMIC BOOK (US/1061-2351) [24995906] **4857**

BILL ATKINSON'S NEWS REPORT (US/0884-7274) [12433661] **1599**

BILL BOARD : LEGISLATIVE NEWS FOR OHIO JUDGES / OHIO JUDICIAL CONFERENCE (US/1062-4600) [25627620] **2941**

BILL-DALE MARCINKO'S AFTA (US/0193-7782) [05254976] 5187, **3338**

BILL DANIELS' ILLUSTRATED TRADE REFERENCES. PROFESSIONAL AUDIO AND COMMERCIAL/INDUSTRIAL SOUND EQUIPMENT BUYERS' GUIDE (US/0882-5432) [11880102] **4452**

BILL OF FARE (US/0892-5399) [15246629] **5070**

BILL OF FARE / TENNESSEE See TENNESSEE RESTAURANTEUR **5073**

BILL OF RIGHTS IN ACTION (US/0160-7731) [02538435] 3092, **4504**

BILL OF RIGHTS JOURNAL, THE (US/0006-2499) [01532945] 4504, **2941**

BILL PALMER'S WORD WATCHING (CN/1192-1145) [27165396] **3269**

BILL SHIPP'S GEORGIA (US/0894-9697) [16377134] 643, **4633**

BILLBOARD (CINCINNATI, OHIO. 1963) (US/0006-2510) [01532948] **4103**

BILLBOARD EN ESPANOL (US/0731-9460) [08316391] **4103**

BILLBOARD INDEX (US/0360-2516) [02243030] **5362**

BILLBOARD. INTERNATIONAL BUYER'S GUIDE OF THE MUSIC-RECORD INDUSTRY (US) [01532949] **4103**

●BILLBOARD INTERNATIONAL LATIN MUSIC BUYER'S GUIDE (US) [26773593] **4103**

BILLBOARD INTERNATIONAL TALENT & TOURING DIRECTORY (US/0732-0124) [13910485] **4103**

BILLBOARD ... RECORD RETAILING DIRECTORY (US) [23980301] 952, **4103**

BILLBOARD [MICROFORM] (US/0006-2510) [21009875] 4103, **5362**

BILLBOARD'S COUNTRY MUSICS SOURCEBOOK AND DIRECTORY See BILLBOARD'S NASHVILLE 615 / COUNTRY MUSIC SOURCEBOOK **4103**

BILLBOARD'S MUSIC & VIDEO YEARBOOK (US) [18620730] 4064, **4160**

BILLBOARD'S NASHVILLE 615 / COUNTRY MUSIC SOURCEBOOK (US/1042-2544) [28460416] **4103**

BILLED BLADET (DK/0006-2537) [02251118] **2485**

BILLERICA MINUTE-MAN (US) [19730572] **5687**

BILLERICA NEWS, THE (US) [19730565] **5687**

●BILLIARD INDUSTRY SOURCE BOOK, THE (US) [26960095] **4857**

BILLIARDS DIGEST (US/0164-761X) [04360011] **4857**

BILLIKEN (AG) [02460863] **1060**

BILLINGS COMMERCE (US/0747-1831) [10623350] **825**

BILLINGS GAZETTE (BILLINGS, MONT. : DAILY : 1914) (US) [02250284] **5705**

BILLINGSLEY YESTERDAY & TODAY (US/0899-1707) [15587810] **2439**

BILLS OF BOTH HOUSES (UK) **4633**

BILTEN DOKUMENTACIJE. SERIJA F1 : SAVREMENA ORGANIZACIJA I EKONOMIKA RADNIH ORGANIZACIJA (YU) [05690689] 1655, **1530**

BILTEN SOKOJ (YU/0352-7115) [I03527115] **4103**

BILTEN UDRUZENJA ORTODONATA JUGOSLAVIJE (YU/0350-1043) [21516923] **1317**

BILTEN ZA HEMATOLOGIJU I TRANSFUZIJU (YU/0350-2023) [01929283] **3770**

BILTEN ZA HEMLJ, SIRAK I LEKOVITO BILJE (YU/0351-9430) [18926292] 3556, **502**

BILYEU BLOOD LINES (US/1066-4831) [26949678] **2439**

BIM (CHRIST CHURCH) **SUSPENDED.** (BB/0006-2766) [02781501] **3367**

BIMBI DI ELEGANTISSIMA (IT/1121-8320) [I11218320] **1082**

BIMCO BULLETIN (DK/0901-814X) [07406369] **5447**

BIMH MENTAL HANDICAP BULLETIN (UK/0260-1222) [02601222] **3921**

BIMONTHLY REVIEW OF LAW BOOKS (US/1048-8936) [21074409] **2941**

BIN. BIBLIOGRAPHY NEWSLETTER (US/0145-3084) [02712084] **410**

BINARIO (PO) [01786909] **293**

BINARY (UK/0266-304X) [I0266304X] **560**

BINARY COMPUTING IN MICROBIOLOGY *CEASED*. (US/0266-304X) [21695593] **560**

BINDEREPORT (GW/0342-3573) [03877709] **4824**

BINDERIFEN / CENTRAL BUREAU VOOR DE STATISTIEK, HOOFDAFDELING STATISTIEKEN VAN INDUSTRIE EN BOUWNIJVERHEID (NE) [10290932] **4824**

BINDTEKEN (BE/0772-2125) [I07722125] **5268**

BINDU (II) [01799957] **3367**

BING (UK) [0178918C] **4103**

BINGDU XUEBAO (CC/1000-8721) [17725116] **560**

BINGDUXUE ZAZHI (CC/1000-3223) [18604579] **560**

BINGGONG XUEBAO (CC/1000-1093) [11353167] **4038**

BINGHAM PUBLIC LIBRARY *See* ANNUAL REPORT / BINGHAM PUBLIC LIBRARY, CIRENCESTER **3190**

BINGO (FR/0523-6207) [02531635] **2498**

BINGQI ZHISHI (CC/1000-4912) [11322895] **4038**

BINNENGEWASSER (GW/0067-8643) [01532955] **1352**

BINNENLANDS BESTUUR (NE/0167-1146) [01671146] **861**

BINNENSCHIFFAHRT UND BUNDESWASSERSTRASSEN JAHRESBERICHT (GW) [20926421] **5378**

BINNENSCHIFFAHRT : ZEITSCHRIFT FEUR BINNENSCHIFFAHRT UND WASSERSTRASSEN (GW/0939-1916) [23985062] **5378**

BINOCULAR VISION & EYE MUSCLE SURGERY QUARTERLY (US) [24914428] 3960, **3872**

BINSTED'S DIRECTORY OF FOOD TRADE MARKS AND BRAND NAMES (UK) [02253671] **2329**

BINTANG DIRECTORY (IO) [02453504] **825**

BIO-BASE (US/0742-2318) [05214949] **430**

BIO-BIBLIOGRAFIA BOLIVIANA (BO) [03020266] **410**

BIO-BIBLIOGRAPHIES IN AMERICAN LITERATURE (US/0742-695X) [10461988] **3367**

BIO-BIBLIOGRAPHIES IN ART AND ARCHITECTURE (US/1055-6826) [23274098] 311, **334**

BIO-BIBLIOGRAPHIES IN MUSIC (US/0742-6968) [10465612] **4103**

●BIO-CRITICAL SOURCE BOOKS ON MUSICAL PERFORMANCE (US/1069-5230) [28084169] **4103**

BIO-DYNAMICS (JS/0006-2863) [03338675] **66**

BIO-ELECTRONICS & BIOSENSORS (UK/0952-0384) [I09520384] **443**

BIO FAX (CN/0832-5359) [17835539] **1464**

BIO INDUSTRY (JA/0910-6545) [28106359] **5088**

BIO-INPHARMA (NZ/0113-1060) [15610982] **3686**

BIO-JOULE *CEASED*. (CN/0708-1936) [05018610] **1933**

●BIO / LA LETTRE DES BIOTECHNOLOGIES (FR/0291-2430) [27919209] **444**

BIO-MEDICAL MATERIALS AND ENGINEERING (US/0959-2989) [23264275] **3686**

BIO-MEDICAL SCOREBOARD *CEASED*. (US/0095-0971) [05298394] **3556**

BIO-NOUVELLES (CN/0319-3446) [02442264] **444**

BIO-SCIENCE RESEARCH BULLETIN (II/0970-0889) [21254520] **444**

BIO-SCIENCES (FR/0292-8418) [09832467] **3686**

BIO SYSTEMS (IE/0303-2647) [01795601] **444**

BIO/TECHNOLOGY (NEW YORK, N.Y. 1983) (US/0733-222X) [08549852] 480, **5088**

BIOACOUSTICS (BERKHAMSTED) (UK/0952-4622) [19348056] **5578**

BIOACTIVE MOLECULES (NE/0921-0687) [14640896] **480**

BIOBULLETIN (UK) **444**

BIOBUSINESS (US) 643, **726**

BIOBUSINESS SEARCH GUIDE (US/0898-5227) [13978366] **643**

BIOCATALYSIS (SZ/0886-4454) [12890509] **480**

BIOCELL (AG) **572**

BIOCENTURY : THE BERNSTEIN REPORT ON BIOBUSINESS (US) 643, **3686**

BIOCHEMICAL AND BIOPHYSICAL RESEARCH COMMUNICATIONS (US/0006-291X) [01532958] 494, **481**

●BIOCHEMICAL AND MOLECULAR MEDICINE (US) 481, **3556**

BIOCHEMICAL ARCHIVES (US/0749-5331) [11135979] **481**

BIOCHEMICAL EDUCATION (UK/0307-4412) [01446802] **481**

BIOCHEMICAL GENETICS (US/0006-2928) [01532961] 481, **543**

BIOCHEMICAL JOURNAL (LONDON. 1984) (UK/0264-6021) [10379627] **481**

BIOCHEMICAL MEDICINE AND METABOLIC BIOLOGY (US/0885-4505) [12640528] 481, **3556**

BIOCHEMICAL MEDICINE METABOLIC BIOLOGY *See* BIOCHEMICAL AND MOLECULAR MEDICINE **3556**

BIOCHEMICAL PHARMACOLOGY (UK/0006-2952) [01536391] **4293**

BIOCHEMICAL REVIEWS (II/0365-9429) [01624076] **481**

BIOCHEMICAL SOCIETY (GREAT BRITAIN) *See* BIOCHEMICAL SOCIETY TRANSACTIONS **481**

BIOCHEMICAL SOCIETY (GREAT BRITAIN). SYMPOSIA *See* BIOCHEMICAL SOCIETY SYMPOSIA **481**

BIOCHEMICAL SOCIETY SYMPOSIA (UK/0067-8694) [01536393] **481**

BIOCHEMICAL SOCIETY TRANSACTIONS (UK/0300-5127) [01786787] **481**

BIOCHEMICAL SYSTEMATICS AND ECOLOGY (UK/0305-1978) [01003245] 2212, **481**

BIOCHEMIE UND PHYSIOLOGIE DER PFLANZEN (GW/0015-3796) [02053089] **502**

BIOCHEMIST LONDON (UK/0954-982X) [I0954982X] 543, **481**

●BIOCHEMISTRY & BIOPHYSICS CITATION INDEX (US/1065-7509) [26790250] 494, **481**

BIOCHEMISTRY AND CELL BIOLOGY (CN/0829-8211) [13240569] **481**

●BIOCHEMISTRY AND MOLECULAR BIOLOGY INTERNATIONAL (AT/1069-8302) [27479240] **482**

BIOCHEMISTRY (EASTON) (US/0006-2960) [01536396] **482**

BIOCHEMISTRY INTERNATIONAL (AT/0158-5231) [06748187] **482**

BIOCHEMISTRY (NEW YORK) (US/0006-2979) [01536397] **482**

BIOCHEMISTRY (NEW YORK, N.Y. 1980) (US/0194-0538) [05313653] **482**

BIOCHEMISTRY OF DISEASE, THE (US/0146-5600) [01780783] **482**

BIOCHEMISTRY OF THE ELEMENTS (US/0887-6495) [07688186] **482**

BIOCHIMICA CLINICA (IT/0393-0564) [03930564] **482**

BIOCHIMICA ET BIOPHYSICA ACTA (NE/0006-3002) [01536398] 494, **482**

BIOCHIMICA ET BIOPHYSICA ACTA. BIOENERGETICS (NE/0005-2728) [03613936] **962**

BIOCHIMICA ET BIOPHYSICA ACTA. BIOMEMBRANES (NE/0005-2736) [03614251] 494, **482**

BIOCHIMICA ET BIOPHYSICA ACTA (BR) - REVIEWS ON BIOENERGETICS (NE/0304-4173) [04969665] **444**

BIOCHIMICA ET BIOPHYSICA ACTA (G) (NE/0304-4165) [04969968] 494, **482**

BIOCHIMICA ET BIOPHYSICA ACTA. GENE STRUCTURE AND EXPRESSION (NE/0167-4781) [08661475] **543**

BIOCHIMICA ET BIOPHYSICA ACTA. LIPIDS AND LIPID METABOLISM (NE/0005-2760) [11015086] **962**

BIOCHIMICA ET BIOPHYSICA ACTA. MOLECULAR BASIS OF DISEASE (NE/0925-4439) [23273598] 543, **482**

BIOCHIMICA ET BIOPHYSICA ACTA. MOLECULAR CELL RESEARCH (NE/0167-4889) [08529579] **532**

BIOCHIMICA ET BIOPHYSICA ACTA (MR). REVIEWS ON BIOMEMBRANES (NE/0304-4157) [04970285] **962**

BIOCHIMICA ET BIOPHYSICA ACTA. PROTEIN STRUCTURE AND MOLECULAR ENZYMOLOGY (NE/0167-4838) [08653951] 494, **482**

BIOCHIMICA ET BIOPHYSICA ACTA. SPECIALIZED SECTION ON LIPIDS AND RELATED SUBJECTS *See* BIOCHIMICA ET BIOPHYSICA ACTA. LIPIDS AND LIPID METABOLISM **962**

BIOCHIMIE (FR/0300-9084) [01536399] **483**

BIOCHROMATOGRAPHY (US/0888-4404) [13575519] **483**

BIOCONJUGATE CHEMISTRY (US/1043-1802) [19336743] **483**

BIOCONTROL NEWS AND INFORMATION (UK/0143-1404) [07077787] 66, **151**

BIOCONTROL SCIENCE & TECHNOLOGY (UK/0958-3157) [25415548] 5606, **164**

BIOCYBERNETICS AND BIOMEDICAL ENGINEERING / POLISH ACADEMY OF SCIENCES, INSTITUTE OF BIOCYBERNETICS AND BIOMEDICAL ENGINEERING (PL/0208-5216) [09726398] 1250, **3686**

BIOCYCLE (US/0276-5055) [07211144] **2225**

BIODEGRADATION (DORDRECHT) (NE/0923-9820) [22937359] 1021, **2225**

BIODETERIORATION ABSTRACTS (UK/0951-0621) [17395254] 444, 2161, **2183**

BIODIGEST DEHRA DUN (II/0970-373X) [I0970373X] **444**

BIODIVERSITY AND CONSERVATION (UK/0960-3115) [25565450] **2188**

BIOELECTRIC REPAIR AND GROWTH SOCIETY (U.S.). MEETING *See* TRANSACTIONS OF THE ... ANNUAL MEETING OF THE BIOELECTRICAL REPAIR AND GROWTH SOCIETY **475**

●BIOELECTROCHEMISTRY AND BIOENERGETICS (SZ/0302-4598) [27088930] **2036**

BIOELECTROMAGNETICS (US/0197-8462) [06152871] **3556**

BIOELECTROMAGNETICS SOCIETY NEWSLETTER (US/0889-4191) [13943636] **4398**

BIOENERGETIC ANALYSIS (US/0743-4804) [10601217] 4577, **3921**

●BIOENGINEERING ABSTRACTS (1993) (US/1068-5693) [27709356] 3686, **3655**

BIOENGINEERING CURRENT AWARENESS NOTIFICATION : BECAN (UK/0142-0674) [11664431] **3686**

BIOENGINEERING (GRAFELFING, GERMANY) *CEASED*. (GW/0178-2029) [16221966] **3686**

BIOENGINEERING NEWS *CEASED*. (US/0275-4207) [07147464] 543, **444**

BIOENGINEERING NOW (UK/0951-5291) [I09515291] **3686**

BIOESSAYS (UK/0265-9247) [11195715] **532**

BIOESTHETIQUE (CN/0707-4395) [05374935] **402**

BIOETHICS (UK/0269-9702) [15622366] 2249, **3556**

●BIOETHICS BULLETIN (WASHINGTON, D.C.) (US/1063-3596) [25990435] 2249, **2941**

●BIOETHICS FORUM (US/1065-7274) [26712953] 3556, **2249**

BIOETHICS LITERATURE REVIEW (US/0886-8913) [12967153] 3556, **2249**

BIOETHICS YEARBOOK (NE/0926-261X) [24515610] **444**

BIOETICA (IT) **2249**

BIOFACTORS (OXFORD) (UK/0951-6433) [17729868] **483**

BIOFEEDBACK AND SELF-REGULATION (US/0363-3586) [02300038] 3921, **4577**

BIOFIZIKA (RU/0006-3029) [01536402] **494**

BIOFORUM (GW) [25199634] **560**

BIOFOULING (CHUR, SWITZERLAND) (SZ/0892-7014) [15239208] **444**

BIOFUTUR (FR/0294-3506) [24162832] **3686**

BIOGENIC AMINES (UK/0168-8561) [11988763] 3556, **483**

BIOGEOCHEMISTRY (NE/0168-2563) [11749004] 2212, **2188**

BIOGEOGRAFIA (BL/0100-3526) [02414720] **2556**

●BIOGEOGRAPHICA : COMPTE-RENDU DES SEANCES DE LA SOCIETE DE BIOGEOGRAPHIE (FR) [29294430] **444**

BIOGEOTSENOLOGIIA (RU) [03375772] **2212**

BIOGERON (BLOOMINGTON, IND.) (US/1055-3150) [23138660] **3556**

BIOGERON ... LIFE EXTENSION MANUAL (US/1055-5129) [23195159] **3556**

BIOGERON RESEARCH INDEX. AGING, LONGEVITY, & LIFE EXTENSION (US/0896-596X) [17211387] **3556**

BIOGRAPHIC DIRECTORY OF SOVIET REGIONAL PARTY LEADERS (GW) [17532453] **4540**

BIOGRAPHIC REGISTER / DEPARTMENT OF STATE, U.S. FOREIGN SERVICE, INTERNATIONAL COOPERATION ADMINISTRATION, U.S. INFORMATION AGENCY, FOREIGN AGRICULTURAL SERVICE, THE (US) [06687148] 4633, **430**

BIOGRAPHICAL DICTIONARY OF ARCHITECTS IN MAINE, A (US) [23072859] **293**

Alphabetical Title Index — BIOLOGUE

BIOGRAPHICAL DIRECTORY / AMERICAN POLITICAL SCIENCE ASSOCIATION (US) [10523112] 4465, **430**

BIOGRAPHICAL DIRECTORY - AMERICAN PSYCHIATRIC ASSOCIATION *CEASED.* (US/0882-2506) [09883345] 3921, **430**

BIOGRAPHICAL DIRECTORY OF THE AMERICAN ACADEMY OF PEDIATRICS (US/0275-1712) [06922087] **3655**

BIOGRAPHICAL DIRECTORY OF THE AMERICAN PODIATRY ASSOCIATION (US/0272-3603) [06797415] **3655**

BIOGRAPHICAL DIRECTORY OF THE AMERICAN PUBLIC HEALTH ASSOCIATION (US) [06126374] **4809**

BIOGRAPHICAL DIRECTORY OF THE FELLOWS & MEMBERS OF THE AMERICAN PSYCHIATRIC ASSOCIATION (US) [04119897] **3655**

BIOGRAPHICAL MEMOIRS (US/0077-2933) [01759017] 5088, **430**

BIOGRAPHICAL MEMOIRS OF FELLOWS OF THE INDIAN NATIONAL SCIENCE ACADEMY (II/0376-6632) [01797738] **430**

BIOGRAPHICAL MEMOIRS OF FELLOWS OF THE ROYAL SOCIETY (UK/0080-4606) [01713731] **430**

BIOGRAPHIE NATIONALE (BE) [02030117] **430**

BIOGRAPHIE NATIONALE. SUPPLEMENT : PUBLIEE PAR L'ACADEMIE ROYALE DES SCIENCES, DES LETTRES ET DES BEAUX-ARTS DE BELGIQUE (BE) [07991655] 5088, **430**

BIOGRAPHIES CANADIENNES-FRANCAISES (CN/0380-0830) [02443239] **430**

BIOGRAPHY AND GENEALOGY MASTER INDEX (US/0730-1316) [07052767] 2439, **430**

BIOGRAPHY AND GENEALOGY MASTER INDEX. SUPPLEMENT (US) [08937972] 2439, **430**

BIOGRAPHY & SOCIETY / NEWSLETTER OF THE ISA RESEARCH COMMITTEE (GW) **430**

BIOGRAPHY (HONOLULU) (US/0162-4962) [04092559] 3367, **430**

BIOGRAPHY INDEX (US/0006-3053) [08264686] 430, **439**

BIOGRAPHY INDEX (CD-ROM ED.) (US/1063-3286) [26294625] **439**

●BIOGRAPHY REVIEW (US/1043-9374) [19610064] **430**

●BIOGRAPHY TODAY (US/1058-2347) [24242423] 1060, **430**

BIOHIMIJA (MOSKVA) (RU/0320-9725) [01536412] **483**

●BIOIMAGING (UK/0966-9051) [28301647] 494, **4433**

BIOINFORMATION MANAGER (GW) **444**

BIOINGENIERIA Y CLINICA (SP) **3556**

BIOINVENTION (US/0886-7461) [12967674] **3686**

BIOKHIMICHESKAIA EKOLOGIIA I MEDITSINA (RU/20366603) 483, 2212, **3556**

BIOKHIMIHA ZHIVOTNYKH I CHELOVEKA (UN/0136-9377) [05130756] **578**

BIOLA COLLEGE *See* BIOLA COLLEGE ALUMNI DIRECTORY **1101**

BIOLA COLLEGE ALUMNI DIRECTORY (US) [06254914] **1101**

BIOLAW (US) [14121994] 2249, **3556**

BIOLOGIA (XO/0006-3088) [05902273] **444**

BIOLOGIA ACUATICA (AG/0326-1638) [09611438] **444**

BIOLOGIA & CLINICA HEMATOLOGICA (SP/0210-895X) [05730714] **3770**

BIOLOGIA (BUDAPEST) (HU/0133-3844) [02241610] **444**

BIOLOGIA ET IMMUNOLOGIA REPRODUCTIONIS (BU/0204-8817) [09117366] **3556**

BIOLOGIA GALLO-HELLENICA (FR/0750-7321) [02539475] **444**

BIOLOGIA (LAHORE) (PK/0006-3096) [03816599] **444**

BIOLOGIA MORA (KIEV) (UN/0320-9695) [01348175] **553**

BIOLOGIA MORA (VLADIVOSTOK) (RU/0134-3475) [02244547] **553**

BIOLOGIA PLANTARUM (XR/0006-3134) [01536418] **502**

BIOLOGIA (POZNAN, POLAND) (PL/0208-4449) [09774715] **444**

●BIOLOGIA TANITASA SZEGED, A (HU/1216-6626) [I12166626] **444**

BIOLOGIC THERAPY OF CANCER UPDATES (US/1056-3903) [23703219] **3809**

BIOLOGICA (FI) [04760345] **502**

BIOLOGICAL ABSTRACTS (US/0006-3169) [01536423] 444, **477**

BIOLOGICAL ABSTRACTS ON COMPACT DISC (US/1058-4129) [24309122] 444, **477**

BIOLOGICAL ABSTRACTS / RRM (US/0192-6985) [05109550] 444, **477**

BIOLOGICAL ABSTRACTS / RRM ON COMPACT DISC (US/1058-4137) [24309011] **444**

BIOLOGICAL ABSTRACTS. SEMIANNUAL CUMULATIVE INDEX (US) [01536424] **444**

BIOLOGICAL AGRICULTURE & HORTICULTURE (UK/0144-8765) [09449803] 2410, **66**

●BIOLOGICAL ANALYSIS AND IMAGING METHODS (US/1077-1034) [30697702] **3556**

BIOLOGICAL & AGRICULTURAL INDEX (US/0006-3177) [06857253] 151, **477**

BIOLOGICAL & AGRICULTURAL INDEX [COMPUTER FILE] (US) [22294212] 151, **477**

BIOLOGICAL AND CULTURAL TESTS FOR CONTROL OF PLANT DISEASES (US/0887-2236) [13143157] **66**

●BIOLOGICAL & PHARMACEUTICAL BULLETIN (JA/0918-6158) [27784830] 483, **4293**

BIOLOGICAL BULLETIN (LANCASTER), THE (US/0006-3185) [01536426] **444**

BIOLOGICAL BULLETIN OF INDIA (II/0254-2900) [09473105] **444**

BIOLOGICAL CHEMISTRY HOPPE-SEYLER (GW/0177-3593) [11822321] **483**

BIOLOGICAL CONSERVATION (UK/0006-3207) [00855462] **2188**

BIOLOGICAL CONTROL (US/1049-9644) [21359340] **4244**

BIOLOGICAL CYBERNETICS (GW/0340-1200) [02241165] 445, **1250**

BIOLOGICAL EFFECTS OF NONIONIZING ELECTROMAGNETIC RADIATION (US) [05720239] **494**

BIOLOGICAL EFFECTS OF NONIONIZING ELECTROMAGNETIC RADIATION DIGEST UPDATE (PHILADELPHIA, PA.) (US/1056-9138) [23894527] **3686**

BIOLOGICAL EXTINCTION (US/0740-4492) [08630859] **445**

BIOLOGICAL FIELD STATION, COOPERSTOWN, N.Y. *See* ANNUAL REPORT - BIOLOGICAL FIELD STATION, COOPERSTOWN, NEW YORK **442**

BIOLOGICAL JOURNAL OF THE LINNEAN SOCIETY (UK/0024-4066) [00859819] **445**

BIOLOGICAL MACROMOLECULES AND ASSEMBLIES (US) [13673290] **445**

BIOLOGICAL MAGNETIC RESONANCE (US/0192-6020) [04588234] **4443**

BIOLOGICAL MASS SPECTROMETRY (UK/1052-9306) [22416643] **1013**

BIOLOGICAL MEMBRANES (NEW YORK, N.Y. : 1985) (US/0748-8653) [11018524] **445**

BIOLOGICAL MEMOIRS (II/0379-8097) [03189547] **445**

BIOLOGICAL MONITORING *CEASED.* (US/0897-7550) [17616954] **445**

BIOLOGICAL NOTES (COLUMBUS) (US/0078-3986) [01604719] **445**

BIOLOGICAL PAPERS OF THE UNIVERSITY OF ALASKA (US/0568-8604) [02444507] **445**

●BIOLOGICAL PRODUCTS (UK/0968-5685) **445**

BIOLOGICAL PSYCHIATRY (1969) (US/0006-3223) [00855449] **3921**

BIOLOGICAL PSYCHIATRY (LONDON, ENGLAND) (UK/0266-2124) [11688824] **3922**

BIOLOGICAL PSYCHOLOGY (NE/0301-0511) [00932509] 445, **4577**

BIOLOGICAL REGULATION AND DEVELOPMENT (US/0271-9355) [05344442] **445**

BIOLOGICAL REPORT (WASHINGTON, D.C.) (US/0895-1926) [12150570] 2188, **445**

●BIOLOGICAL RESEARCH (CL/0716-9760) [27997036] **445**

BIOLOGICAL RESEARCH IN NORWICH (UK/0959-6321) [I09596321] **445**

BIOLOGICAL RESEARCH REPORTS FROM THE UNIVERSITY OF JYVASKYLA (FI) [04068262] **445**

BIOLOGICAL RESPONSES IN CANCER (US/0736-7414) [09139841] **3809**

BIOLOGICAL REVIEWS OF THE CAMBRIDGE PHILOSOPHICAL SOCIETY (UK/0006-3231) [06328354] **445**

●BIOLOGICAL RHYTHM RESEARCH (NE/0929-1016) [30024358] **445**

BIOLOGICAL RHYTHMS (UK/0142-8004) [I01428004] **578**

BIOLOGICAL SCIENCE TEXTS (UK/0272-054X) [06772192] **5088**

BIOLOGICAL SCIENCES REVIEW (UK/0953-5365) [I09535365] **445**

BIOLOGICAL SCIENCES SERIES (US) [07339925] **1446**

●BIOLOGICAL SIGNALS (SZ/1016-0922) [25037362] **532**

BIOLOGICAL SOCIETY OF WASHINGTON *See* PROCEEDINGS OF THE BIOLOGICAL SOCIETY OF WASHINGTON **469**

BIOLOGICAL STRUCTURE AND FUNCTION (UK) [03264908] **445**

BIOLOGICAL STRUCTURES AND MORPHOGENESIS *CEASED.* (FR/0989-8972) [18175529] **3679**

BIOLOGICAL TECHNIQUES SERIES (UK/0892-4473) [05670453] **445**

BIOLOGICAL THERAPIES IN DENTISTRY (US/0882-1852) [11778581] **1317**

BIOLOGICAL THERAPIES IN PSYCHIATRY NEWSLETTER (US/1044-422X) [19784284] **3922**

BIOLOGICAL THERAPY (US/0733-2661) [08549812] **3774**

BIOLOGICAL TRACE ELEMENT RESEARCH (US/0163-4984) [04395472] 3893, **483**

BIOLOGICALS (UK/1045-1056) [20001827] **445**

BIOLOGICESKIE NAUKI (KZ/0303-4119) [02278249] **4163**

BIOLOGICHESKAIA FLORA MOSKOVSKOI OBLASTI (RU) [03974912] **502**

BIOLOGICHESKIE MEMBRANY (RU/0233-4755) [10528511] **446**

BIOLOGICHESKIE RESURSY I PRIRODNYE USLOVIIA MONGOLSKOI NARODNOI RESPUBLIKI (RU) [03937741] 4163, **446**

BIOLOGICHESKII ZHURNAL ARMENII (AI/0002-2969) [02541186] **446**

BIOLOGICKE LISTY (XR/0366-0486) [03126472] **446**

BIOLOGICKE PRACE (V BRATISLAVA) (XO/0037-6930) [01391091] **446**

BIOLOGICO, O *SUSPENDED.* (BL/0366-0567) [02541232] **446**

BIOLOGIE HEUTE (GW/0936-6903) [I09366903] **446**

BIOLOGIE IN UNSERER ZEIT (GW/0045-205X) [02783476] **446**

BIOLOGIE VEGETALE, SCIENCES AGRICOLES. LEXIQUE (FR/0154-0262) [07087912] 3196, **66**

BIOLOGIEUNTERRICHT, DER (GW/0006-3274) [03655341] **446**

BIOLOGIIA V SHKOLE (RU) [02545682] **446**

BIOLOGIIA VNUTRENNIKH VOD (RU) [05633657] **446**

BIOLOGIJA (LI) [03250537] **446**

●BIOLOGIJA / BIOLOGY / BIOLOGIIA (LI) [29830318] **446**

BIOLOGISCHE ABHANDLUNGEN (GW/0006-3282) [01383360] **446**

BIOLOGISCHE BUNDESANSTALT FUER LAND- UND FORSTWIRTSCHAFT. ABTEILUNG FUER PFLANZENSCHUTZMITTEL UND -GERATE *See* PFLANZENSCHUTZMITTEL-VERZEICH NIS. TEIL 1: ACKERBAU, WIESEN UND WEIDEN, HOPFENBAU, SONDERKULTUREN, NICHTKULTURLAND, GEWASSER **4247**

BIOLOGISCHE BUNDESANSTALT FUR LAND- UND FORSTWIRTSCHAFT. ABTEILUNG FUR PFLANZENSCHUTZMITTEL UND -GERATE *See* PFLANZENSCHUTZMITTEL-VERZEICH NIS. TEIL 6: ANERKANNTE PFLANZENSCHUTZ- UND VORRATSSCHUTZGERATE **160**

BIOLOGISCHE BUNDESANSTALT FUR LAND- UND FORSTWIRTSCHAFT. ABTEILUNG FUR PFLANZENSCHUTZMITTEL UND -GERATE *See* PFLANZENSCHUTZMITTEL-VERZEICH NIS. TEIL 2: GEMUSEBAU, OBSTBAU, ZIERPFLANZENBAU **4247**

BIOLOGISCHES ZENTRALBLATT (GW/0006-3304) [05887140] **446**

BIOLOGISKE MILJUNDERSGELSER I NORDGRNLAND (DK) [19643064] 2212, **446**

BIOLOGIST (LONDON) (UK/0006-3347) [02240345] **446**

BIOLOGISTE ET PRATICIEN PARIS (FR/1157-1209) [I11571209] **446**

BIOLOGUE AND THE REGIONAL BIOMASS ENERGY PROGRAM REPORTS (US/1046-0411) [20402709] **1933**

BIOLOGUE (WATERLOO) (CN/0840-8548) [19996623] **446**

BIOLOGY — Alphabetical Title Index

BIOLOGY AND ENVIRONMENT : PROCEEDINGS OF THE ROYAL IRISH ACADEMY (IE/0791-7945) [28957593] **446**

BIOLOGY AND FERTILITY OF SOILS (GW/0178-2762) [12491665] **164**

BIOLOGY & PHILOSOPHY (NE/0169-3867) [13073787] 4342, **446**

BIOLOGY BULLETIN (US) [03122891] **446**

BIOLOGY BULLETIN MONTHLY *CEASED.* (US/0890-877X) [14440285] **446**

BIOLOGY BULLETIN OF THE ACADEMY OF SCIENCES OF THE USSR *See* BIOLOGY BULLETIN OF THE RUSSIAN ACADEMY OF SCIENCES **446**

●BIOLOGY BULLETIN OF THE RUSSIAN ACADEMY OF SCIENCES (US/1062-3590) [25596606] **446**

BIOLOGY DIGEST (US/0095-2958) [02243088] 447, **477**

BIOLOGY (GUILFORD, CONN.) (US) [10321526] **447**

BIOLOGY INTERNATIONAL (FR/0253-2069) [07770429] **447**

BIOLOGY INTERNATIONAL. SPECIAL ISSUES : THE NEWS MAGAZINE OF THE INTERNATIONAL UNION OF BIOLOGICAL SCIENCES (IUBS) (FR) [11198801] **447**

BIOLOGY OF CARBOHYDRATES (US/0730-7918) [07830651] **4188**

BIOLOGY OF EXTRACELLULAR MATRIX (US/0887-3224) [13181625] **447**

BIOLOGY OF METALS *See* BIOMETALS **483**

BIOLOGY OF REPRODUCTION (US/0006-3363) [01536448] **578**

BIOLOGY OF SPORT (PL/0860-021X) [15085381] **3953**

BIOLOGY OF THE CELL (FR/0248-4900) [07381466] **532**

BIOLOGY OF THE NEONATE (SZ/0006-3126) [01798033] **3900**

BIOLOGY OF THE REPTILIA (US) [01776035] **5578**

BIOLOSKI VESTNIK (XV/0520-1969) [02546419] **447**

BIOMASS & BIOENERGY (UK/0961-9534) [25030381] **1933**

BIOMASS BULLETIN (UK/0262-7183) [09824353] **1933**

●BIOMASS BULLETIN/ WESTERN REGIONAL BIOMASS ENERGY PROGRAM (US) [25897900] **1934**

●BIOMASS DIGEST / WESTERN REGIONAL BIOMASS ENERGY PROGRAM (US) [25897951] **1934**

●BIOMASS ENERGY DIRECTORY (US/1064-7651) [26208210] **1934**

BIOMASS ENERGY INCL. ALCOHOL FUELS MONTHLY UPDATE (US/0738-4114) [09592711] **1934**

BIOMATERIALS (UK/0142-9612) [06135436] **3556**

BIOMATERIALS, ARTIFICIAL CELLS, AND IMMOBILIZATION BIOTECHNOLOGY (US/1055-7172) [23274995] **3686**

●BIOMATERIALS SCIENCE AND ENGINEERING (US/1076-6286) [30567552] **3686**

BIOMATHEMATICS (BERLIN) (GW/0067-8821) [01642611] 3497, **447**

BIOME (ENGLISH ED.) (CN/0712-9319) [08741157] **4085**

BIOMEDICA (CK/0120-4157) [08454820] **3556**

BIOMEDICA BIOCHIMICA ACTA *CEASED.* (GW/0232-766X) [09681158] 3556, **447**

BIOMEDICAL ADVANCES IN CARCINOGENESIS (US) [10865343] **3809**

BIOMEDICAL AND CLINICAL ASPECTS OF COENZYME Q : PROCEEDINGS OF THE ... INTERNATIONAL SYMPOSIUM ON THE BIOMEDICAL AND CLINICAL ASPECTS OF COENZYME Q (NE) [20791950] **962**

BIOMEDICAL AND ENVIRONMENTAL SCIENCES (US/0895-3988) [16628517] 3556, **447**

BIOMEDICAL & HEALTH RESEARCH (BE/0778-4910) [07784910] 4768, **3686**

BIOMEDICAL & HEALTH RESEARCH : NEWSLETTER / EUROPEAN COMMUNITY (BE) [24591526] **3556**

BIOMEDICAL COMMUNICATIONS *CEASED.* (US/0092-8607) [01715764] **1105**

BIOMEDICAL ENGINEERING (US/0006-3398) [01536451] **3686**

BIOMEDICAL ENGINEERING AND COMPUTATION SERIES (US/0194-2778) [05363847] **3686**

BIOMEDICAL ENGINEERING AND HEALTH SYSTEMS (US/0190-0951) [04625430] **3686**

●BIOMEDICAL ENGINEERING CITATION INDEX (US/1062-5488) [25669168] **3686**

BIOMEDICAL ETHICS REVIEWS (US/0742-1796) [09252785] 2249, **3556**

BIOMEDICAL FOUNDATIONS OF OPHTHALMOLOGY (US/0732-3484) [08337460] **3872**

BIOMEDICAL INDEX TO PHS-SUPPORTED RESEARCH (US) [21141009] **3556**

BIOMEDICAL INFORMATICS TODAY (US) [25495681] **3556**

BIOMEDICAL INSTRUMENTATION & TECHNOLOGY (US/0899-8205) [18231621] **3687**

BIOMEDICAL LABORATORY TECHNICAL REPORT (US/0730-8027) [08059981] **3556**

BIOMEDICAL LETTERS (UK/0961-088X) [24139660] 447, **3556**

●BIOMEDICAL LIBRARY ACQUISITIONS BULLETIN [COMPUTER FILE] (US/1064-699X) [26462167] 3687, **3196**

BIOMEDICAL MARKET NEWSLETTER (US) [26282178] **3687**

BIOMEDICAL MATERIALS (UK/0955-7717) [20351193] **3556**

BIOMEDICAL NEWS SOURCE MIDWEST (US/1057-7424) [24111532] **3557**

BIOMEDICAL PRODUCTS (US/0192-1266) [04963878] 447, **3687**

BIOMEDICAL PROGRESS (GW/0934-0734) [10934074] **3557**

BIOMEDICAL RESEARCH (II/0970-938X) [23176421] **3687**

BIOMEDICAL RESEARCH (TOKYO) (JA/0388-6107) [07111884] **3557**

●BIOMEDICAL REVIEWS (BU) [26671668] **3687**

BIOMEDICAL SAFETY & STANDARDS (US) [11700923] **3557**

BIOMEDICAL SCIENCE AND TECHNOLOGY *CEASED.* (US/1051-2020) [21889711] **3687**

BIOMEDICAL SCIENCES INSTRUMENTATION (US/0067-8856) [03977404] **3687**

BIOMEDICAL TECHNOLOGY & HUMAN FACTORS ENGINEERING / NTIS *See* NTIS ALERT. BIOMEDICAL TECHNOLOGY & HUMAN FACTORS ENGINEERING **3695**

BIOMEDICAL TECHNOLOGY INFORMATION SERVICE (US/0147-2682) [03127718] **3687**

●BIOMEDICAL TECHNOLOGY MANAGEMENT (US/1073-1210) [29333394] **3687**

BIOMEDICINE & PHARMACOTHERAPY (FR/0753-3322) [08634158] 447, 4293, **3557**

BIOMEDIZINISCHE TECHNIK (GW/0013-5585) [01788482] **3687**

BIOMEMBRANES (NEW YORK, N.Y.) (US/0067-8864) [01536455] **532**

●BIOMETALS (US/0966-0844) [26050776] **483**

BIOMETHODS (BASEL) (SZ/1018-6255) [17649645] **447**

BIOMETRICA (SP/0210-4199) [04018079] **3893**

BIOMETRICAL JOURNAL (GW/0323-3847) [03271168] **3497**

BIOMETRICS (US/0006-341X) [05898885] **5323**

BIOMETRIE ET ECOLOGIE (FR) [06228158] **2212**

BIOMETRIE IN DER CHEMISCH-PHARMAZEUTISCHEN INDUSTRIE (GW) [10546596] 483, **4293**

BIOMETRIE-PRAXIMETRIE *CEASED.* (BE/0006-3436) [02548350] 3497, **477**

BIOMETRIE UND INFORMATIK IN MEDIZIN UND BIOLOGIE (GW/0934-9235) [21324208] 3557, **447**

BIOMETRIKA (UK/0006-3444) [01536458] **447**

●BIOMIMETICS (NEW YORK, N.Y.) (US/1059-0153) [24458744] 447, **1966**

BIOMUDULATION UND BIOTHERAPIE DES KREBSES (GW) [19262045] **3809**

BIONATURE (II) [08721409] **447**

BIONEWS ATHENS (GR/1012-2516) [I10122516] **2161**

BIONIKA (KIEV) (UN/0374-6569) [09705324] **1250**

●BIOORGANIC & MEDICINAL CHEMISTRY (UK/0968-0896) [28698705] **962**

BIOORGANIC & MEDICINAL CHEMISTRY LETTERS (UK/0960-894X) [23245011] **1039**

BIOORGANIC CHEMISTRY (US/0045-2068) [01713886] **1039**

BIOORGANIC CHEMISTRY FRONTIERS (GW) [22178095] **962**

BIOORGANIC MARINE CHEMISTRY (GW/0935-7092) [17901280] **2212**

BIOORGANICHESKAIA KHIMIIA (RU/0132-3423) [02241756] **1039**

●BIOPEOPLE (SAN MATEO, CALIF.) (US/1065-612X) [26648715] **447**

BIOPHARM (XR) [25052236] **5506**

BIOPHARM (EUGENE, OR.) (US/1040-8304) [18580193] **4293**

BIOPHARMACEUTICS & DRUG DISPOSITION (UK/0142-2782) [05527045] **4293**

BIOPHYSICAL CHEMISTRY (NE/0301-4622) [01793925] 494, **483**

BIOPHYSICAL JOURNAL (US/0006-3495) [01390110] **494**

BIOPHYSICS (BOSTON) (US/0360-019X) [01851278] **494**

BIOPHYSICS (OXFORD) (UK/0006-3509) [01536463] **494**

BIOPOLIMERY I KLETKA (UN/0233-7657) [11822299] **447**

BIOPOLITICS ATHENS (GR/1012-2532) [I10122532] **2161**

BIOPOLYMERS (US/0006-3525) [01536466] **483**

BIOPOLYMERS SYMPOSIA (US/0523-6827) [01536467] **447**

●BIOPRACTICE : INTERNATIONAL JOURNAL OF APPLIED BIOLOGY, BIOTECHNOLOGY, AND BIONICS (GW/0940-5542) [26671874] **447**

BIOPROBES (EUGENE, OR.) (US/1064-251X) [26242940] 447, **5088**

BIOPROCESS ENGINEERING (US/0883-0878) [12061280] **1966**

BIOPROCESS ENGINEERING (BERLIN, WEST) (GW/0178-515X) [14395957] **2008**

BIOPROCESS TECHNOLOGY (US/0888-7470) [13104397] **3687**

BIORECOVERY (BERKHAMSTED) (UK/0269-7572) [18997781] **3687**

BIOREMEDIATION REPORT, THE (US/1064-2455) [26245919] **1966**

BIORESEARCH TODAY. ADDICTION *CEASED.* (US/0149-1008) [03437767] **3557**

BIORESEARCH TODAY. ALZHEIMER'S DISEASE & SENILE DEMENTIAS *CEASED.* (US/1048-1826) [20861169] **3828**

BIORESEARCH TODAY. ANTIVIRAL AGENTS *CEASED.* (US/1048-1818) [20861154] **483**

BIORESEARCH TODAY. BIO-ENGINEERING & INSTRUMENTATION *CEASED.* (US/0149-0990) [00933127] **447**

BIORESEARCH TODAY. BIRTH DEFECTS *CEASED.* (US/0149-0982) [03437539] **3557**

BIORESEARCH TODAY. CANCER A. CARCINOGENESIS *CEASED.* (US/0149-1016) [03437407] **3809**

BIORESEARCH TODAY. CANCER B. ANTICANCER AGENTS *CEASED.* (US/0149-1024) [03437474] **3809**

BIORESEARCH TODAY. CANCER C. IMMUNOLOGY *CEASED.* (US/0149-1032) [03437514] 3667, **3809**

BIORESEARCH TODAY. FOOD ADDITIVES & RESIDUES *CEASED.* (US/0149-0958) [03437657] **2329**

BIORESEARCH TODAY. FOOD & DRUG LEGISLATION *CEASED.* (US/1048-1788) [20861096] **2941**

BIORESEARCH TODAY. FOOD MICROBIOLOGY *CEASED.* (US/0149-0974) [03437596] **560**

BIORESEARCH TODAY. HUMAN & ANIMAL AGING *CEASED.* (US/0149-0966) [03437629] **3750**

BIORESEARCH TODAY. HUMAN & ANIMAL PARASITOLOGY *CEASED.* (US/0149-094X) [02252737] **447**

BIORESEARCH TODAY. INDUSTRIAL HEALTH & TOXICOLOGY *CEASED.* (US/0149-0923) [03437749] 3979, **2859**

BIORESEARCH TODAY. PESTICIDES *CEASED.* (US/0149-0907) [03437799] **4244**

BIORESEARCH TODAY. POPULATION, FERTILITY & BIRTH CONTROL *CEASED.* (US/0149-0915) [03429128] 588, **4550**

BIORESOURCE TECHOLOGY (UK/0960-8524) [23349147] 66, **2225**

BIORHEOLOGY (OXFORD) (UK/0006-355X) [02086401] **447**

BIORHEOLOGY. SUPPLEMENT (US/0891-978X) [12138456] **448**

BIOS (MADISON, N.J.) (US/0005-3155) [01536471] 448, **477**

BIOS (PARIS) (FR/0366-2284) [03179891] 4218, **2364**

BIOS : ZEITSCHRIFT FUER BIOGRAPHIEFORSCHUNG UND ORAL HISTORY (GW/0933-5315) [20815311] **3269**

Alphabetical Title Index — BIRMINGHAM

BIOSCAN (US/0887-6207) [13302338] **3687**

BIOSCENE. (BIOSCENE / BIOSIS) (US/0090-3337) [02785273] 448, **3196**

BIOSCIENCE (US/0006-3568) [01536472] **448**

●BIOSCIENCE, BIOTECHNOLOGY, AND BIOCHEMISTRY (JA/0916-8451) [25516229] 484, 1039, **3687**

BIOSCIENCE REPORTS (US/0144-8463) [07561792] **532**

BIOSCIENCE RESEARCH REPORTS. RESEARCH NOTES IN ANIMAL BEHAVIOUR (US/0741-5699) [10001307] **5578**

BIOSENSORS & BIOELECTRONICS (UK/0956-5663) [20767981] **3687, 484**

BIOSEPARATION (NE/0923-179X) [21993425] **3687**

BIOSIS See SERIAL SOURCES OF THE BIOSIS PREVIEWS DATABASE **473**

BIOSIS PREVIEWS SEARCH GUIDE (US/0898-2414) [15560228] **448**

BIOSIS PREVIEWS [ONLINE DATABASE] (US) 448, **477**

BIOSOCIAL SOCIETY SERIES (UK) [19085157] 5193, **448**

BIOSOURCES DIGEST (US/0197-7571) [04755559] **448**

●BIOSPECTROSCOPY (NEW YORK, N.Y.) (US/1075-4261) [30050145] **484**

BIOSPHERE (OTTAWA) (CN/0824-1600) [12577372] **2188**

BIOSTATISTICA (DAVENPORT, IOWA) (US/1041-7648) [18842344] 448, **477**

BIOTEC (STUTTGART) (GW/0931-1408) [16723466] 543, **3687**

BIOTEC WURZBURG (GW) [I09372725] **448**

BIOTECH BUSINESS (US/0899-5702) [18144078] **3687**

BIOTECH BUYERS' GUIDE (US/1067-2818) [20985897] **3687**

BIOTECH DAILY (US/1067-1196) [26901088] **3687**

BIOTECH FORUM EUROPE CEASED. (GW/0938-7501) [21967676] **3688**

BIOTECH INVESTOR (US/0891-3161) [14709413] **892**

BIOTECH KNOWLEDGE SOURCES (UK/0953-2226) [19564273] **3688**

BIOTECH MARKET NEWS & STRATEGIES (US/0740-1221) [09880072] **448**

BIOTECH NEWS (UK) [22449937] **3688**

BIOTECH PATENT NEWS (US/0898-2813) [17778869] **3688**

BIOTECH PRODUCTS INTERNATIONAL (BE/1016-6505) [I10166505] **5088**

BIOTECH REPORTER (US/1069-4773) [28057327] **3688**

BIOTECHNIC & HISTOCHEMISTRY (US/1052-0295) [22173428] **532**

BIOTECHNIQUES (US/0736-6205) [09171046] **3557**

BIOTECHNOLOGIE (NE) 1021, **448**

●BIOTECHNOLOGY ABSTRACTS (UK) [30626983] **3688, 3655**

BIOTECHNOLOGY ABSTRACTS [COMPUTER FILE] / DERWENT PUBLICATIONS, LTD (US) [25449120] **3688**

BIOTECHNOLOGY ADVANCES (UK/0734-9750) [08838531] **3688**

BIOTECHNOLOGY AND APPLIED BIOCHEMISTRY (US/0885-4513) [12644720] 484, **3688**

BIOTECHNOLOGY AND BIOENGINEERING (US/0006-3592) [01224461] **3688**

BIOTECHNOLOGY AND BIOENGINEERING SYMPOSIUM (US/0572-6565) [01000288] **3688**

BIOTECHNOLOGY AND BIOLOGICAL SCIENCES RESEARCH COUNCIL See BBSRC BUSINESS **3686**

BIOTECHNOLOGY AND BIOTECHNOLOGICAL EQUIPMENT (BU) **3688**

BIOTECHNOLOGY AND DEVELOPMENT MONITOR (NE) [22487415] **3688**

BIOTECHNOLOGY & GENETIC ENGINEERING REVIEWS (UK/0264-8725) [10604639] **3688**

BIOTECHNOLOGY BULLETIN (UK/0261-6904) [I02616904] **3688**

BIOTECHNOLOGY BUSINESS NEWS (UK/0965-9595) [I09659595] 643, **3688**

BIOTECHNOLOGY BUSINESS NEWS / FINANCIAL TIMES (UK) [27919162] **3688**

BIOTECHNOLOGY BUSINESS REPORT (US/0892-7987) [15307314] **3688**

BIOTECHNOLOGY CITATION INDEX (US/1057-607X) [24080859] **3689**

BIOTECHNOLOGY, CURRENT PROGRESS (US/1055-2162) [23109036] **3689**

BIOTECHNOLOGY DIRECTORY (NEW YORK, N.Y.), THE (US/1059-7352) [11854428] **3689**

BIOTECHNOLOGY EDUCATION CEASED. (US/0955-6621) [17962723] **3689**

BIOTECHNOLOGY FOCUS (GW/0935-1043) [18909919] **3689**

BIOTECHNOLOGY (FRANKFURT 1991) (GW/0938-5584) [I09385584] **3689**

BIOTECHNOLOGY HANDBOOKS (US/1052-6153) [16875957] **3689**

BIOTECHNOLOGY IN AGRICULTURE AND FORESTRY (US/0934-943X) [13786323] **3689**

BIOTECHNOLOGY IN JAPAN NEWSSERVICE CEASED. (US/0891-9283) [15036406] **3689**

BIOTECHNOLOGY IN JAPAN YEARBOOK (US) [24136129] **3689**

BIOTECHNOLOGY INFORMATION NEWS CEASED. (UK/0952-147X) [18678566] **3689**

BIOTECHNOLOGY INVESTMENT OPPORTUNITIES (US/0277-9773) [07674061] 892, **3689**

BIOTECHNOLOGY LAW REPORT (US/0730-031X) [07941731] 3740, **3689**

BIOTECHNOLOGY LETTERS (UK/0141-5492) [05026728] **3689**

BIOTECHNOLOGY MONOGRAPHS (GW/0930-8938) [12744459] **3689**

BIOTECHNOLOGY MONTHLY UPDATE (US/0738-4076) [09591992] **3689**

BIOTECHNOLOGY (NEW YORK, N.Y. : 1983) (US/0275-7559) [07228275] **3689**

BIOTECHNOLOGY NEWS (US/0273-3226) [07046745] **3689**

BIOTECHNOLOGY NEWSWATCH (US) [17372322] **3689**

BIOTECHNOLOGY PROGRESS (US/8756-7938) [11666713] **3689**

BIOTECHNOLOGY RESEARCH ABSTRACTS CEASED. (US/0733-5709) [10692418] 3689, **3655**

BIOTECHNOLOGY SOFTWARE (US/0749-0372) [11052877] **3689**

BIOTECHNOLOGY TECHNIQUES (UK/0951-208X) [15712576] **3689**

BIOTECHNOLOGY THERAPEUTICS (US/0898-2848) [17777976] **3690**

●BIOTECHNOLOGY WEEK (US/1061-3471) [25258267] **3690**

BIOTECNOLOGIA (SP) **448**

BIOTECNOLOGIA APLICADA : REVISTA DE LA SOCIEDAD IBEROLATINOAMERICANA PARA INVESTIGACIONES SOBRE INTERFERON Y BIOTECNOLOGIA EN SALUD (CU/0864-4551) [25477730] 543, **3690**

BIOTEHNIKA (YU) [01795202] **66**

BIOTEHNOLOGIA (MOSKVA) (RU/0234-2758) [15260036] **3690**

BIOTEKHNOLOGIIA (US/0890-734X) [14369024] **3690**

BIOTEKHNOLOGIIA & BIOTEKHNIKA : IZDANIE NA NATSIONALNIIA SUVET PO BIOTEKHNOLOGIIA KUM DURZHAVNIIA KOMITET ZA IZSLEDVANIIA I TEKHNOLOGII (BU) [17736913] **3690**

BIOTEKHNOLOGIIA. ENGLISH. SOVIET BIOTECHNOLOGY See RUSSIAN BIOTECHNOLOGY **3696**

BIOTHERAPY (DORDRECHT) (NE/0921-299X) [19272242] **448**

BIOTICA CEASED. (MX/0185-0326) [03995712] **448**

BIOTRANSFORMATIONS : A SURVEY OF THE BIOTRANSFORMATIONS OF DRUGS AND CHEMICALS IN ANIMALS (UK) [20161645] 5506, **3557**

BIOTREATMENT NEWS (US/1058-0239) [24183262] 2225, **5088**

BIOTRONICS (JA/0289-0011) [14973686] 448, **2410**

BIOTROP SPECIAL PUBLICATION (IO/0125-975X) [11141234] **448**

BIOTROPIA (IO/0216-5023) [18669400] **2376**

BIOTROPICA (US/0006-3606) [01536475] **448**

BIOVENTURE VIEW (US/0892-1903) [15124326] **448**

BIOVIGYANAM (II/0250-507X) [03763198] **448**

BIOWORLD TODAY (US) **5633**

BIP. BULLETIN DE L'INDUSTRIE PETROLIERE (FR/0300-4554) [03688385] **4252**

BIPAC ACTION REPORT (US/0272-1694) [06793069] 643, **4465**

BIPAC POLITICS (US/0032-3276) [01240224] **4465**

BIRA JOURNAL (UK/0263-9467) [I02639467] **4633**

BIRCH BANK ALLIANCE See BIRCH BARK ALLIANCE, THE **4446**

BIRCH BARK ALLIANCE, THE (CN/0709-082X) [05375541] **4446**

BIRD BEHAVIOUR (SI/0156-1383) [04170982] **5615**

●BIRD BREEDER (US/1073-5186) [29449576] 5615, **4285**

BIRD CONSERVATION INTERNATIONAL (UK/0959-2709) [23951080] **5615**

BIRD ISLAND UNION (US) [01536479] **5694**

BIRD KEEPER (UK/0955-4238) [I09554238] **5615**

BIRD OBSERVER (BELMONT, MASS.) (US/0893-4630) [15634118] **5615**

BIRD STUDY (UK/0006-3657) [00855538] **5615**

BIRD TALK (US/0891-771X) [15033645] **4285**

BIRD TRENDS (CN/1185-5967) [25351930] **5615**

BIRD WATCHER'S DIGEST (US/0164-3037) [04604838] **5615**

BIRD WORLD (NORTH HOLLYWOOD) (US/0199-5979) [06031730] 4286, **5615**

BIRDERS JOURNAL (CN/1188-2549) [25883012] **5616**

BIRDER'S WORLD (US/0895-495X) [16658825] **5616**

BIRDING (US/0161-1836) [03853287] **5578**

BIRDING IN SOUTHERN AFRICA (SA/0006-5838) [20938774] **5616**

BIRDING NEWS SURVEY (US/0162-0738) [04091606] **5578**

BIRDS : MAGAZINE FOR MEMBERS OF THE ROYAL SOCIETY FOR THE PROTECTION OF BIRDS (UK/0006-3665) [02551528] **5616**

BIRDS OF DISTINCTION (US) [22658918] **5616**

●BIRDS OF NORTH AMERICA, THE (US/1061-5466) [25349235] 2188, **5616**

BIRKNER (GW) **4232**

BIRK'S (US/0091-4002) [01787128] **2942**

BIRMA, WIRTSCHAFTSDATEN / BUNDESSTELLE FUR AUSSENHANDELSINFORMATION (GW) [11085820] **1548**

BIRMA WIRTSCHAFTSDATEN UND WIRTSCHAFTSDOKUMENTATION / BUNDESSTELLE FUR AUSSENHANDELSINFORMATION (GW) [07368529] **1548**

BIRMINGHAM (US/0006-369X) [03986801] 643, **2529**

BIRMINGHAM AND WARWICKSHIRE ARCHAEOLOGICAL SOCIETY See TRANSACTIONS - BIRMINGHAM AND WARWICKSHIRE ARCHAEOLOGICAL SOCIETY **284**

BIRMINGHAM AREA INDUSTRIAL DIRECTORY (US/0147-2097) [03118335] **1599**

BIRMINGHAM BUSINESS JOURNAL (US/0889-2237) [13825382] **643**

BIRMINGHAM ECCENTRIC, THE (US) [09948897] **5691**

BIRMINGHAM, ENG. UNIVERSITY. INSTITUTE FOR THE STUDY OF WORSHIP AND RELIGIOUS ARCHITECTURE See RESEARCH BULLETIN - INSTITUTE FOR THE STUDY OF WORSHIP AND RELIGIOUS ARCHITECTURE **307**

BIRMINGHAM, ENG. WEIGHTS AND MEASURES DEPT See REPORT OF THE CHIEF INSPECTOR OF WEIGHTS & MEASURES, CITY OF BIRMINGHAM **4032**

BIRMINGHAM, ENGLAND. UNIVERSITY. CENTRE FOR URBAN AND REGIONAL STUDIES See URBAN AND REGIONAL STUDIES **2837**

BIRMINGHAM GENEALOGICAL SOCIETY See ROSTER / THE BIRMINGHAM GENEALOGICAL SOCIETY, INC **2471**

BIRMINGHAM HISTORICAL SOCIETY ANNUAL PUBLICATION (US) **2723**

BIRMINGHAM METROPOLITAN ARTS COUNCIL See LIMELIGHT **324**

BIRMINGHAM MUNICIPAL TRUSTEE SAVINGS BANK See REPORT AND STATEMENT OF ACCOUNTS - BIRMINGHAM MUNICIPAL TRUSTEE SAVINGS BANK **807**

BIRMINGHAM NEWS, THE (US/0899-0050) [02665772] **5625**

BIRMINGHAM POETRY REVIEW (US/1047-2258) [19467013] **3460**

BIRMINGHAM POST & MAIL YEAR BOOK AND WHO'S WHO, THE (UK) [20938450] **430**

BIRMINGHAM — Alphabetical Title Index

BIRMINGHAM POST-HERALD (US/1040-1571) [07208782] **5625**

BIRMINGHAM SLAVONIC MONOGRAPHS (UK/0141-3805) [I01413805] **3269**

BIRMINGHAM TIMES, THE (US) [11125591] **2256**

●BIRNBAUM'S BAHAMAS, TURKS & CAICOS (US/1055-5625) [23230783] **5463**

●BIRNBAUM'S BARCELONA (US/1056-4381) [23711552] **5463**

●BIRNBAUM'S BERLIN (US/1070-9746) [28522768] **5463**

●BIRNBAUM'S BERMUDA (US/1055-5684) [23230957] **5463**

●BIRNBAUM'S BOSTON (US/1056-4357) [23711402] **5464**

BIRNBAUM'S CANADA (US/0884-1039) [11403747] **5464**

●BIRNBAUM'S CANCUN, COZUMEL, AND ISLA MUJERES (US/1055-5641) [23230850] **5464**

●BIRNBAUM'S CARIBBEAN (US) [24438512] **5464**

●BIRNBAUM'S CHICAGO (US/1056-4365) [23711438] **5464**

●BIRNBAUM'S DISNEYLAND (US) [24880432] **5464**

●BIRNBAUM'S EASTERN EUROPE (US/1056-439X) [23711572] **5464**

BIRNBAUM'S EUROPE (US/0883-2498) [11455820] **5464**

BIRNBAUM'S EUROPE FOR BUSINESS TRAVELERS (US/0749-4815) [11129285] **5464**

●BIRNBAUM'S FLORENCE (US/1056-4489) [23711751] **5464**

BIRNBAUM'S FRANCE (US/0749-2553) [11105590] **5464**

●BIRNBAUM'S GERMANY (US/1068-7238) [27774378] **5464**

BIRNBAUM'S GREAT BRITAIN (US/0896-8683) [17309651] **5464**

BIRNBAUM'S HAWAII (US/0883-2471) [11332393] **5464**

●BIRNBAUM'S HONOLULU (US/1060-3875) [24956332] **5464**

BIRNBAUM'S IRELAND (US/0896-8691) [17309679] **5464**

BIRNBAUM'S ITALY (US/0890-1139) [14153747] **5464**

●BIRNBAUM'S IXTAPA & ZIHUATENEJO (US/1055-5676) [23230941] **5464**

●BIRNBAUM'S LAS VEGAS (US/1061-5423) [25355809] **5464**

●BIRNBAUM'S LONDON (US/1056-4470) [23711736] **5464**

●BIRNBAUM'S LOS ANGELES (US/1056-4462) [23711718] **5464**

BIRNBAUM'S MEXICO (US/0884-1209) [11331184] **5464**

●BIRNBAUM'S MIAMI & FT. LAUDERDALE (US/1056-4454) [23711702] **5464**

●BIRNBAUM'S MONTREAL (US/1061-5415) [25355722] **5464**

●BIRNBAUM'S NEW ORLEANS (US/1061-5431) [25355902] **5464**

●BIRNBAUM'S NEW YORK (US/1056-4446) [23711694] **5464**

●BIRNBAUM'S PARIS (US/1056-4438) [23711676] **5464**

●BIRNBAUM'S PORTUGAL (US/1055-5668) [23231006] **5464**

●BIRNBAUM'S PUERTO VALLARTA (US/1060-3883) [24956289] **5464**

●BIRNBAUM'S ROME (US/1056-442X) [23711645] **5464**

●BIRNBAUM'S SAN FRANCISCO (US/1056-4403) [23711593] **5464**

●BIRNBAUM'S SANTA FE, TAOS, ALBUQUERQUE (US/1068-722X) [27774405] **5464**

BIRNBAUM'S SOUTH AMERICA (US/0883-2463) [11375269] **5464**

●BIRNBAUM'S SPAIN (US/1055-565X) [23230987] **5464**

BIRNBAUM'S SPAIN/PORTUGAL See BIRNBAUM'S PORTUGAL **5464**

BIRNBAUM'S THE CARIBBEAN, BERMUDA, AND THE BAHAMAS See BIRNBAUM'S BAHAMAS, TURKS & CAICOS **5463**

BIRNBAUM'S THE CARIBBEAN, BERMUDA, AND THE BAHAMAS See BIRNBAUM'S BERMUDA **5463**

BIRNBAUM'S THE CARIBBEAN, BERMUDA, AND THE BAHAMAS See BIRNBAUM'S CARIBBEAN **5464**

●BIRNBAUM'S TORONTO (US/1061-5393) [25355475] **5464**

BIRNBAUM'S UNITED STATES (US/0883-2501) [11403682] **5464**

BIRNBAUM'S USA FOR BUSINESS TRAVELERS (US/0883-251X) [11690581] **5464**

●BIRNBAUM'S VANCOUVER (US/1061-5407) [25355634] **5464**

●BIRNBAUM'S VENICE (US/1056-4411) [23711619] **5464**

●BIRNBAUM'S WASHINGTON DC (US/1061-544X) [25356598] **5464**

●BIRNBAUM'S WESTERN EUROPE (US/1056-4373) [23711517] **5465**

BIRTH (BERKELEY, CALIF.) (US/0730-7659) [08066591] **3757**

BIRTH DEFECTS ORIGINAL ARTICLE SERIES (US/0547-6844) [01536497] 578, **3757**

BIRTH GAZETTE, THE (US/0890-3255) [14222670] **3757**

BIRTH-ORIGIN STUDY OF TEXAS NEWBORNS, A (US/0891-3641) [08675393] **4550**

BIRTH-ORIGIN SURVEY OF TEXAS NEWBORNS See BIRTH-ORIGIN STUDY OF TEXAS NEWBORNS, A **4550**

BIRTH PSYCHOLOGY BULLETIN (US/0734-3124) [08752607] 4577, **3758**

BIRTH ST. LEONARDS (AT/1032-9625) [I10329625] **2277**

BIRTH TRAUMA (US/0892-7227) [15347217] 3758, **2942**

BIRTHS AND DEATHS BY JURISDICTION OF RESIDENCE. MARRIAGES AND DIVORCES BY COUNTY (US/0363-1281) [02429475] **5323**

BIRTHS, AUSTRALIA (AT) [09289147] 4550, **4561**

BIRZEIT RESEARCH REVIEW (IS) [16389441] **5088**

BIS BUTLLETI D'INFORMACIO SANITARIA (SP) **4768**

BISBEE DAILY REVIEW (US) [11363144] **5629**

BISBEE MAGAZINE (US/0890-2801) [12853755] **2723**

BISBEE OBSERVER, THE (US/0895-2450) [12384423] **5629**

BISEIBUTSU NO SEITAI (JA) [01797322] **560**

BISEIBUTSU SEITAI SHIMPOJIUMU See BISEIBUTSU NO SEITAI **560**

BISERICA ORTODOXA ROMANA (RM) [03451985] **5039**

BISHOP MUSEUM BULLETIN IN ANTHROPOLOGY (US/0893-3111) [15478045] **232**

BISHOP MUSEUM BULLETIN IN ENTOMOLOGY (US/0893-3146) [15478111] **5606**

BISHOP MUSEUM BULLETIN IN ZOOLOGY (US/0893-312X) [15478059] **5578**

BISHOP MUSEUM BULLETINS IN BOTANY (US/0893-3138) [15478075] **502**

BISHOP MUSEUM OCCASIONAL PAPERS (US/0893-1348) [13713698] **5088**

BISHOP REPORT, THE (US/1065-1012) [26508189] **643**

BISMARCK TRIBUNE, THE (US) [11987205] **5725**

BISMUTH INSTITUTE See BULLETIN - BISMUTH INSTITUTE **3999**

BISNIS (IO) [07154669] **643**

●BISNIS BULLETIN (US) [26267792] **643**

BISVARUPA (II) [11335427] **3367**

BIT (IT) [02781614] 1150, **1172**

BIT (CI) [05055738] 1231, **1256**

BIT DROPPER, THE (US/0896-2774) [16978745] **1172**

BIT FIRENZE CEASED. (IT/0394-3666) [I03943666] **3196**

BIT (NORDISK TIDSKRIFT FOR INFORMATIONSBEHANDLING) (DK/0006-3835) [02495382] **1172**

BITACORA (SP/0212-632X) [I0212632X] **591**

BITAMIN (VITAMIN) (JA) [05664653] 3557, **962**

BITAON LAMOREH LEARVIT (IS) **1728**

BITE ME (US) **2485**

BITKI KORUMA BULTENI (TU/0406-3597) [01536505] **66**

BITS (US/0197-7768) [02606600] **3460**

BITS & BYTES REVIEW (US/0891-2955) [14709338] **1172**

BITS AND PIECES (DENVER) (US/0198-8670) [06226344] **2723**

BITS & PIECES (FAIRFIELD, N.J.) (US/1050-1975) [03776648] **861**

BITS AND PIECES (NEWCASTLE) CEASED. (US/0006-3894) [01696213] **861**

BITS. BSI INFORMATION TECHNOLOGY SERVICES (UK/0955-3010) [I09553010] **5465**

BITS OF BARK FROM THE FAMILY TREE (US/0270-5583) [04284318] **2439**

BITTER OLEANDER (US) [02781642] **3460**

BITTERROOT CEASED. (US/0006-3908) [02552883] **3460**

BITTKER, BORIS I See FEDERAL INCOME TAXATION OF CORPORATIONS AND SHAREHOLDERS; FORMS **4724**

BITUME ACTUALITES (FR/0406-3678) [I04063678] **1599**

BITUMEN (GW/0006-3916) [02445350] **2019**

BITUMINOUS COAL AND LIGNITE DISTRIBUTION (US) [02255947] **1599**

BITUMINOUS COAL AND LIGNITE PRODUCTION AND MINE OPERATIONS See COAL PRODUCTION **2137**

BITUMINOUS COAL DATA See COAL DATA **1935**

BITZARON CEASED. (US/0006-3932) [01536509] 3338, **5046**

BIULETEN (UKRAINSKYI TEKHNICHNO-HOSPODARSKYI INSTYTUT (MUNICH, GERMANY)) (UN) [06629860] **1548**

BIULETENI - ABASTUMNIS ASTROPIZIKURI OBSERVATORIA. MTA QANOBILI (GS/0258-7327) [04390636] **393**

BIULETYN (PL/0373-7837) [03788465] 164, **66**

BIULETYN HISTORII SZTUKI (PL/0006-3967) [05468102] **344**

BIULETYN IGS / SZKOA GOWNA HANDLOWA, INSTYTUT GOSPODARSTWA SPOECZNEGO (PL) [26281185] **5193**

BIULETYN INFORMACYJNY (PL) [05626771] 601, **2019**

BIULETYN INFORMACYJNY : GEOLOGIA, EKONOMIKA I TECHNIKA PRAC GEOLOGICZNYCH (PL) [01785856] **1367**

BIULETYN INFORMACYJNY - INSTYTUT ZOOTECHNIKI (PL/0209-2492) [03296964] **207**

BIULETYN (INSTYTUT GEOLOGICZNY (POLAND)) (PL/0208-6603) [01350488] **1367**

BIULETYN INSTYTUTU HODOWLI I AKLIMATYZACJI ROSLIN (PL/0373-7837) [I03737837] **66**

BIULETYN INSTYTUTU LEKOW 1990 (PL/0867-700X) [I0867700X] **1089**

BIULETYN INSTYTUTU ZIEMNIAKA (PL/0137-1576) [04295269] 66, **2329**

BIULETYN LUBELSKIE TOWARZYSTWA NAUKOWEGO. MATEMATYKA, FIZYKA-CHEMIA (PL/0460-2366) [01785905] 4398, **3497**

BIULETYN MORSKIEGO INSTYTUTU RYBACKIEGO (PL/0209-0708) [19100380] 553, **2297**

BIULETYN OCENY ODMIAN - CENTRALNY OSRODEK BADANIA ODMIAN ROSLIN UPRAWNYCH W SUPI WIELKIEJ POW. SRODA WLKP (PL/0137-155X) [I0137155X] **66**

BIULETYN PERYGLACJALNY (PL/0067-9038) [01536510] **1367**

BIULETYN - POLAND. URZAD PATENTOWY (PL) [01787423] **1301**

BIULETYN POLONISTYCZNY (PL/0067-902X) [02258372] **3367**

BIULETYN - POLSKI ZWIAZEK KROTKOFALOWCOW (PL) [02244300] **2036**

BIULETYN POLSKIEGO KOMITETU NORMALIZACJI I MIAR (PL/0324-8496) [01795274] **4029**

BIULETYN POLSKIEGO TOWARZYSTWA JEZYKOZNAWCZEGO (PL/0032-3802) [02926861] **3269**

BIULETYN PRZEMYSKOWEGO INSTYTUTE AUTOMATYKI I POMIAROW (PL/0300-2438) [01784775] **2111**

BIULETYN STATYSTYCZNY (PL/0006-4025) [02266299] **5323**

BIULETYN WARZYWNICZY. BULLETIN OF VEGETABLE CROPS RESEARCH WORK. BIULLETEN PO OVOSHCHEVODSTVU (PL/0509-6839) [03788755] **2410**

BIULETYN ZWIAAZKU NAUCZYCIELSTWA POLSKIEGO W KANADZIE (CN/0821-3917) [10664606] **3269**

BIULETYN ZYDOWSKIEGO INSTYTUTU HISTORYCZNEGO W POLSCE (PL/0006-4033) [02226130] **5046**

BIULETYN ZYDOWSKIEGO INSTYTUTU HISTORYCZNEGO [MICROFORM] (PL) [10029679] **5046**

BIULLETEN (RU/0366-4899) [05667571] **5506**

Alphabetical Title Index — BLACK

BIULLETEN GLAVNOGO BOTANICHESKOGO SADA (RU/0366-502X) [03788584] **502**

BIULLETEN GOSUDARSTVENNOGO NIKITSKOGO BOTANICHESKOGO SADA (RU/0513-1634) [02881512] **502**

BIULLETEN INOSTRANNOI KOMMERCHESKOI INFORMATSII (RU) [03279845] **2513**

BIULLETEN MEZHDUNARODNYKH NAUCHNYKH SEZDOV, KONFERENTSII, KONGRESSOV, VYSTAVOK / VSESOIUZNYI INSTITUT NAUCHNOI I TEKHNICHESKOI INFORMATSII, MEZHDUNARODNYI TSENTR NAUCHNOI I TEKHNICHESKOI INFORMATSII (RU/0202-5442) [04387535] **5088**

BIULLETEN' NAUCHNO-TEKHNICHESKOI INFORMATSII MS AGROINFORM (XR) [06096582] **67**

BIULLETEN NAUCHNO-TEKHNICHESKOI INFORMATSII PO AGRONOMICHESKOI FIZIKE *See* NAUCHNO-TEKHNICHESKII BIULLETEN PO AGRONOMICHESKOI FIZIKE **111**

BIULLETEN NAUCNO-TEHNICESKOJ INFORMACII VSESOUZNOGO NAUCNO-ISSLEDOVATELSKOGO INSTITUTA RISA (RU/0202-5531) [02618238] **164**

BIULLETEN. OTDEL BIOLOGICHESKII (RU) [01590296] **448**

BIULLETEN POCHVENNOGO INSTITUTA IMENI V. V. DOKUCHAEVA (RU) [06260421] **165**

BIULLETEN RADIOASTROFIZICHESKOI OBSERVATORII AKADEMII NAUK LATVIISKOI (LV) [02242016] **393**

BIULLETEN REGISTRATSII NIR. OBSHCHESTVENNYE NAUKI. SERIIA 1 / VSESOIUZNYI NAUCHNO-TEKHNICHESKII INFORMATSIONNYI TSENTR (RU) [07905029] **5193**

BIULLETEN REGISTRATSII. OBSHCHESTVENNYE NAUKI. SERIIA 1, MARKSIZM-LENINIZM, FILOSOFIIA, SOTSIOLOGIIA, PSIKHOLOGIIA *See* BIULLETEN REGISTRATSII NIR. OBSHCHESTVENNYE NAUKI. SERIIA 1 / VSESOIUZNYI NAUCHNO-TEKHNICHESKII INFORMATSIONNYI TSENTR **5193**

BIULLETEN VERKHOVNOGO SUDA SSSR (RU/0557-5257) [01764670] **2942**

BIULLETEN VSESOIUZNOGO KARDIOLOGICHESKOGO NAUCHNOGO TSENTRA AMN SSSR (RU/0201-7369) [06312767] **3699**

BIULLETEN VSESOIUZNOGO NAUCHNO-ISSLEDOVATELSKOGO INSTITUTA ZASHCHITY RASTENII (RU/0459-0864) [04692085] **502**

● BIULLETEN VYSSHEGO ATTESTATSIONNOGO KOMITETA PRI MINISTERSTVE NAUKI, VYSSHEI SHKOLY I TEKHNICHESKOI POLITIKI ROSSIISKOI FEDERATSII (RU) [26791869] **1811**

BIULLETEN VYSSHEI ATTESTATSIONNOI KOMISSII PRI SOVETE MINISTROV SSSR *See* BIULLETEN VYSSHEGO ATTESTATSIONNOGO KOMITETA PRI MINISTERSTVE NAUKI, VYSSHEI SHKOLY I TEKHNICHESKOI POLITIKI ROSSIISKOI FEDERATSII **1811**

BIULLETIN NAUCHNO-TEKHNICHESKOI INFORMATSII VSESOIUZNOGO NAUCHNO-ISSLEDOVATELSKOGO INSTITUTA ZERNOBOBOVYKH I KRUPIANYKH KULTUR (RU/0321-026X) [03024912] **200**

BIULLETIN VSESOIUZNOGO NAUCHNO-ISSLEDOVATELSKOGO INSTITUTA FIZIOLOGII, BIOKHIMII I PITANIIA SELSKOKHOZIAISTVENNYKH ZHIVOTNYKH (RU) [02714478] **5506**

BIVOUAC (CN/0228-4448) [08071623] **5229**

BIWABIK TIMES (US) [01536514] **5694**

BIWEEKLY LIST OF PAPERS ON RADIATION CHEMISTRY AND PHOTOCHEMISTRY (US/0164-5315) [04564256] **962**

BIYOKIMYA DERGISI (TU/0250-4685) [05902764] **484**

BIZ (US/0199-8730) [06234555] **4201**

BIZANTION NEA HELLAS (CL/0716-2138) [02383864] **3367**

BIZARRE CLASSIX (US/0145-8000) [02739714] **4367**

● BIZARRE SEX AND OTHER CRIMES OF PASSION (US) **5187**

BIZNES : ZHURNAL SOIUZA MENEDZHEROV SSSR (RU/0868-6009) [24013188] **643**

BJR SUPPLEMENT (UK/0961-2653) [20952345] **3939**

BJULETEN' - KOMITETU UKRAJINCIV KANADY (CN/0503-1036) [01695338] 2256, **2723**

BJULETEN SUSPILNOJI SLUZVY KANADY (CN/0700-8198) [03436263] **5275**

BJULLETEN EKSPERIMENTALNOJ BIOLOGII I MEDICINY (RU/0365-9615) [10768731] 3557, **448**

BJULLETEN INSTITUTA ASTROFIZIKI (TA/0321-4885) [08783999] **4398**

BJULLETEN MOSKOVSKOGO OBSCESTVA ISPYTATELEJ PRIRODY. OTDEL BIOLOGICESKIJ (RU/0027-1403) [06363264] **448**

BJULLETEN MOSKOVSKOGO OBSCESTVA ISPYTATELEJ PRIRODY. OTDEL GEOLOGICESKIJ (RU/0366-1318) [04699831] **1367**

BJULLETEN VULKANOLOGICESKIH STANCIJ (RU/0366-5089) [01200512] **1367**

BK SPECIAL REPORT (US/0741-4900) [10155270] **4713**

BL BLANKET ORDER (US) [10609599] **1464**

BL/BSD NAME AUTHORITY LIST (UK/0265-8887) [I02658887] **410**

BLACFAX (US/0882-6595) [11937587] **2256**

BLACK ALUMNI NETWORK NEWSLETTER (US/1040-7758) [18522239] **1101**

BLACK AMERICAN LITERATURE FORUM *See* AFRICAN AMERICAN REVIEW **3358**

BLACK AMERICANS INFORMATION DIRECTORY (US/1045-8050) [20243171] **2256**

BLACK AND GAY (US/1055-0976) [23071660] 2793, **2256**

BLACK AND MAGENTA, THE (US) [17358636] **1089**

BLACK AND RED (US) [01773778] **1089**

BLACK & WHITE & READ ALL OVER (US/1042-9069) [19247058] **410**

● BLACK & WHITE (BIRMINGHAM, ALA.) (US/1064-0134) [26199931] **2485**

BLACK ARTS ANNUAL (US/1042-7104) [19113957] 2256, **344**

● BLACK AUTHORS BOOKS IN PRINT (US/1066-940X) [27096457] **4824**

BLACK BAG (WASHINGTON), THE (JS/0196-1594) [02254520] **3557**

BLACK BEAR (US/8756-0666) [11463657] **3367**

BLACK BEAT (US/0745-8649) [09198921] 2256, **4103**

BLACK BELT (BURBANK, CALIF.) (US/0277-3066) [04949089] **4887**

BLACK BOOK. OLD CAR ... MARKET GUIDE (US/0747-4393) [10865905] **5407**

BLACK BOOK STOCK (US/1054-464X) [22901275] 756, **4367**

BLACK BOOK USED SPECIALTY VEHICLE AND TRUCK GUIDE (CN/0318-9368) [02441919] **5407**

BLACK BOOKS BULLETIN. WORDS WORK (US) [24001373] 2256, **3367**

BLACK CAMERA : THE NEWSLETTER OF THE BLACK FILM CENTER / ARCHIVES (US) [20382618] 2256, **4064**

BLACK CAUCUS *SUSPENDED.* (US/0732-7269) [08413346] **5275**

BLACK CAUCUS OF ALA NEWSLETTER / ALA BLACK CAUCUS (US) [23133363] **3196**

BLACK CHILD ADVOCATE (US) [01625980] **5275**

BLACK COAL IN AUSTRALIA (AT) [06977104] **1599**

● BLACK COLLEGES AND UNIVERSITIES LISTING (US/1058-5680) [24333224] 1811, **2256**

BLACK COLLEGIAN (NEW ORLEANS), THE (US/0192-3757) [02258387] **1811**

BLACK CONGRESSIONAL MONITOR (US/0895-1780) [16511620] **2256**

BLACK COUNTRY BUSINESS DIRECTORY (SOUTH EDITION) (UK/0957-1035) [I09571035] **643**

BLACK COUNTRY YEAR BOOK AND WHO'S WHO (UK) **430**

BLACK DIAL DIRECTORY (CN/0701-0605) [03406350] **2723**

BLACK DIAMOND, THE *SUSPENDED.* (US/0006-4149) [02445355] **2135**

BLACK ELECTED OFFICIALS (US/0882-1593) [11281418] 2256, **4465**

BLACK ELEGANCE (US/0885-9647) [12790233] 2256, **2529**

BLACK EMPLOYMENT & EDUCATION (US/1053-704X) [22612463] **643**

BLACK ENTERPRISE (US/0006-4165) [00832966] **643**

BLACK ETHNIC COLLECTIBLES (US/1043-6677) [19525860] **2256**

BLACK FAMILY (US/0279-0718) [07506604] **2256**

BLACK FILM BULLETIN (UK) **4064**

BLACK FILM REVIEW (US/0887-5723) [13323851] **4064**

BLACK GRAPHICS INTERNATIONAL (US/0045-2165) [01548429] 2256, **316**

BLACK HAIR CARE (US/1058-0999) [24208160] **402**

BLACK HEALTH (US/1042-329X) [19008488] **4768**

BLACK HERITAGE UNVEILED NEWSLETTER (US/1042-4199) [19038096] **2611**

BLACK HILLS NATIONAL FOREST PRODUCTS NEWS (US/0194-8148) [05035295] **2376**

BLACK HILLS NUGGETS (US/0523-7203) [04179204] **2439**

BLACK HILLS PIONEER (1989), THE (US/1061-6179) [21928320] **5743**

BLACK HILLS STATE UNIVERSITY *See* ALUMNI DIRECTORY / BLACK HILLS STATE UNIVERSITY **1097**

BLACK HISTORY IS NO MYSTERY (US/1055-0550) [23065551] **2256**

● BLACK HISTORY MONTHLY (LITTLE ROCK, ARK.) (US/1054-8769) [23004425] **2256**

BLACK I (CN/0316-2753) [02290306] **3367**

BLACK ISSUES IN HIGHER EDUCATION (US/0742-0277) [10244203] 2256, **1812**

BLACK LACE (US/1049-3298) [21206764] 2256, **2793**

BLACK LECHWE (ZA/0045-219X) [01786342] **2188**

BLACK LUNG BENEFITS ACT. ANNUAL REPORT ON ADMINISTRATION OF THE ACT / U.S. DEPARTMENT OF LABOR, EMPLOYMENT STANDARDS ADMINISTRATION (US) [04758100] **1655**

BLACK MALE/FEMALE RELATIONSHIPS (US/0740-2163) [06239884] **5240**

BLACK MARIA *CEASED.* (US/0045-222X) [02786249] 5551, **3367**

BLACK MASKS (US/0887-7580) [13367772] **5362**

BLACK MESSIAH (US/0737-5522) [09342614] **3367**

BLACK MUSIC RESEARCH JOURNAL (US/0276-3605) [07353674] 2256, **4103**

BLACK NATION, THE *SUSPENDED.* (US/0740-929X) [10048089] **2256**

BLACK NEWS (US) [25161210] **5741**

BLACK NEWS DIGEST *CEASED.* (US/0045-2238) [01536536] **1655**

BLACK ODYSSEY *SUSPENDED.* (US/0164-5218) [04587523] **5465**

BLACK ORPHEUS (NR/0067-9100) [01536537] **3367**

BLACK PAGES OF AMERICA (US/1063-0473) [25846137] **2256**

BLACK PAGES OF AMERICA (BALTIMORE METROPLITAN ED.) (US/1063-0449) [24333310] 643, **2256**

BLACK PAGES OF AMERICA (HAMPTON ROADS METROPOLITAN ED.) (US/1063-0457) [24032851] 643, **2257**

BLACK PAGES OF AMERICA (WASHINGTON, D.C., METROPOLITAN ED.) (US/1060-3921) [24515632] **2257**

BLACK PASSION : INTERNATIONAL HAIR MAGAZINE (US) **402**

BLACK PHOTOGRAPHERS ANNUAL, THE (US/0090-7197) [01783715] **4367**

BLACK POLITICAL STUDIES (US/0891-9631) [15048825] **4465**

BLACK POST (US) [25162703] **2257**

BLACK PRESS INFORMATION HANDBOOK (US/0147-2828) [03139452] **5647**

BLACK PRESS PERIODICAL DIRECTORY, THE (US/0093-5697) [01784462] **2917**

BLACK RADIO EXCLUSIVE (US/0745-5992) [09356442] **1127**

BLACK RESOURCE GUIDE, THE (US/0882-0643) [07678282] **2257**

BLACK REVIEW (SA) [01796033] **2257**

BLACK REVIEW, THE (US/0190-4906) [04723156] **3367**

BLACK ROSE (US) [07476994] **4540**

BLACK SACRED MUSIC (US/1043-9455) [19612352] **4103**

BLACK SCHOLAR, THE (US/0006-4246) [01536543] **2257**

BLACK SECRETS (US/1071-9830) [28865853] **2257**

BLACK SUN (COLUMBIA, S.C. : FLORENCE ED.) (US) [21182039] **2257**

BLACK SWAMP HERITAGE (US/0892-9203) [15293880] **2529**

BLACK — Alphabetical Title Index

BLACK TALENT NEWS (US/1062-3825) [25603960] 2257, **383**

BLACK TEEN *See* SPICE **1069**

BLACK VET (US) **4038**

BLACK VIDEO GUIDE, THE (US/0882-7532) [11960720] 4367, **4064**

BLACK VIEW (US) [03030620] 4465, **2257**

BLACK VOICE NEWS, THE (US) [23164049] **2257**

BLACK VOICES *CEASED.* (AT/0812-8405) [I08128405] **232**

BLACK WARRIOR REVIEW, THE (US/0193-6301) [02786585] **3338**

BLACK WAX MAGAZINE (UK) [01792016] **4103**

BLACK WILLOW (US/0733-0073) [08496862] **3460**

BLACK WRITER MAGAZINE, THE (US) [15376658] **3367**

BLACKBOOK INTERNATIONAL REFERENCE GUIDE (US) [12153743] **1599**

BLACKCOUNTRYMAN (UK/0006-4335) [01794503] **2678**

● BLACKFIRE (US/1049-3271) [21206290] **2257**

BLACKFLASH (CN/0826-3922) [12182501] **4367**

BLACKHAWK GENEALOGICAL SOCIETY *See* QUARTERLY **2468**

BLACKPOWDER REPORT, THE (US/0746-3634) [09974544] **3476**

BLACK'S GUIDE. HOUSTON OFFICE SPACE MARKET (US/0733-5059) [08598969] **4210**

BLACK'S GUIDE. ORANGE COUNTY OFFICE SPACE MARKET (US/0738-6095) [09627080] **4210**

BLACK'S GUIDE. SUBURBAN MANHATTAN OFFICE SPACE MARKET (US/0733-5067) [07532418] **4210**

BLACK'S GUIDE TO THE METRO DENVER OFFICE SPACE MARKET (US/0733-2572) [08549071] **4210**

BLACK'S MEDICAL DICTIONARY (LONDON, ENGLAND) (UK) [01536551] **3557**

BLACK'S OFFICE LEASING GUIDE *See* BLACK'S OFFICE LEASING GUIDE. WASHINGTON / BALTIMORE METRO AREA **4210**

BLACK'S OFFICE LEASING GUIDE. CONNECTICUT/NEW YORK SUBURBS (US) [17793525] **4210**

BLACK'S OFFICE LEASING GUIDE. HOUSTON OFFICE SPACE MARKET (US) [17793559] **4210**

BLACK'S OFFICE LEASING GUIDE. PHILADELPHIA & SUBURBS, SOUTHERN NEW JERSEY, DELAWARE (US) [17793497] **4210**

BLACK'S OFFICE LEASING GUIDE. WASHINGTON / BALTIMORE METRO AREA (US) [15189122] **4210**

BLACK'S REVIEW (WASHINGTON ED.) (US/0733-5032) [08599140] **4210**

BLACKSBURG SUN *See* NEWS MESSENGER, THE **5759**

BLACKSHEAR TIMES, THE (US/0746-9330) [03439080] **5652**

BLACKSTONE VALLEY TRIBUNE (US/0745-8673) [09528612] **5687**

BLACKWELL JOURNAL-TRIBUNE (US) [12101699] **5731**

BLADE-ATLAS, THE (US) [13227422] **5765**

BLADE-EMPIRE (US) [10224271] **5674**

BLADE MAGAZINE, THE (US/0744-6179) [08440281] 4887, **2771**

BLADE, THE (US) [20180689] **5652**

BLADE (TOLEDO, OHIO) (US) [12962717] **5727**

BLAETTER DER DEUTSCHEN GESELLSCHAFT FUER VERSICHERUNGSMATHEMATIK (GW) **3497**

BLAETTER FUER FRAENKISCHE FAMILIENKUNDE (GW/0006-4424) [07695492] **2439**

BLAETTER FUER TECHNIKGESCHICHTE (AU/0067-9127) [06121310] **5089**

BLAIN FAMILY NEWSLETTER, THE (CN/0712-127X) [08693714] **2439**

BLAINE LAKE JOURNAL (CN/1184-7794) [24256986] **5780**

BLAIR PRESS, THE (US) [13109027] **5765**

BLAIREAU PARIS (FR/0982-8648) [I09828648] **3338**

BLAIR'S GUIDE VICTORIA (AT/0810-9567) [I08109567] **5465**

BLAIRSTOWN PRESS (BLAIRSTOWN, N.J. : 1877) (US) [13233166] **5709**

BLAKE (US/0160-628X) [03160132] 431, 3338, **316**

BLANCO COUNTY NEWS (US/1049-2216) [13996911] **5747**

BLAND COURIER, THE (US) [13316293] **5702**

BLASMUSIK, DIE (GW/0344-8231) [05585271] **4104**

BLAST MANUKA (AT/0819-0739) [I08190739] **2510**

● BLAST : THE BULLETIN OF LAW/SCIENCE & TECHNOLOGY / AMERICAN BAR ASSOCIATION, SECTION OF SCIENCE AND TECHNOLOGY (US) [29819464] 5089, **2942**

BLATT FUER SORTENWESEN (GW/0300-4627) [01421103] **2780**

BLATTER + BILDER (GW/05878010) **3367**

BLATTER DER CARL-ZUCKMAYER-GESELLSCHAFT (GW/05206422) **3367**

BLATTER DER RILKE-GESELLSCHAFT (SZ/1010-3597) [01785039] **3367**

BLATTER DER THOMAS MANN-GESELLSCHAFT (SZ/0082-4186) [03129072] **3367**

BLATTER DES IZ3W (GW) [01798319] **1548**

BLATTER FUER DEUTSCHE LANDESGESCHICHTE (GW/0006-4408) [02568986] **2611**

BLATTER FUER DEUTSCHE UND INTERNATIONALE POLITIK (GW/0006-4416) [02569036] **2611**

BLATTER FUER HEIMATKUNDE ... (AU/0006-4459) [03251130] 344, 2318, **2611**

BLATTER FUER VORGESETZTE (GW/0172-018X) [I0172018X] **1599**

BLATTER FUER WURTTEMBERGISCHE KIRCHENGESCHICHTE (GW/0341-9479) [01536564] 2678, **4939**

BLATTER FUR EIN NEUES BODENRECHT (SZ) [07242650] **2942**

BLAU MIT WEISS ROUNDEL *See* ROUNDEL **5424**

BLAUE JUNGS (GW) [11881552] **4175**

BLA(Y)LOCK GENEALOGY NEWS, THE (US) [17969488] **2439**

BLE. BOLETIN DE LEGISLACION EXTRANJERA (SP/0212-5617) [02125617] **3124**

BLE CONTACT / LETTRE D'INFORMATION DE L'AGPB (FR) **825**

BLECH, ROHRE, PROFILE (GW/0006-4688) [06121400] **3999**

BLESSINGS OF LIBERTY, THE (US/0006-4696) [01876663] **5193**

BLETER FAR GESHIKHTE (PL/0006-470X) [01796622] **2257**

BLEU (FR) [02422875] **1548**

BLI BULLETIN (US/0090-6379) [01785385] **1655**

BLI FACSIMILE SPECIFICATIONS GUIDE (US) [21177256] 2037, **1105**

BLIBAD : BULLETIN DE LIAISON A L'INTENTION DES BIBLIOTHECAIRES, ARCHIVISTES ET DOCUMENTALISTES AFRICAINS (GO) [07628722] **3196**

BLICK DURCH DIE WIRTSCHAFT (GW/0406-4224) [I04064224] **5801**

BLICKPUNKT SCHMERZ (GW/0178-8957) [19346040] **3557**

BLIKI : TIMARIT UN FUGLA (IC) [11207945] 5616, **4163**

BLIKOPENER DEN BOSCH (NE/0927-2720) [I09272720] 2678, **5240**

BLIMP (AU) [24478416] **4064**

BLIND ALLEYS (US/0737-9269) [09468103] **3460**

BLIND (AMSTERDAM, NETHERLANDS) (NE) [20551138] 3367, **344**

● BLIND SPOT PHOTOGRAPHY (US/1068-1647) [27456969] **4367**

BLINDNESS, VISUAL IMPAIRMENT, DEAF-BLINDNESS (US/0363-7689) [02535674] **4384**

BLINDS AND SHUTTERS (UK/0305-733X) [I0305733X] **2904**

BLISSFIELD ADVANCE (US) [12220905] **5691**

BLITZ (II) [01781400] **5803**

BLITZ CHESS (US/1053-3087) [18096725] **4857**

BLITZ LONDON *CEASED.* (UK/0263-2543) [I02632543] **316**

BLITZ (LOS ANGELES, CALIF.) (US/0889-5635) [05688671] **4104**

BLK (LOS ANGELES, CALIF.) (US/1043-0075) [19287478] **2793**

BLM. BONNIERS LITTERARA MAGASIN (SW/0005-3198) [01536733] **3367**

BLM FACTS & FIGURES FOR UTAH (US) [08467990] **4633**

BLOATED TICK *See* (THE) BRAVE NEW TICK **2796**

BLOC NOTES DE L'OBSERVATOIRE ECONOMIQUE DE PARIS (MONTHLY) (FR) [18946253] **4713**

BLOCH-ALMANACH (GW/0721-3743) [10519657] **4342**

BLOCK (ALMELO) (NE/0921-2558) [05212748] **4104**

BLOCK (EAST BARNET, HERTFORDSHIRE) *CEASED.* (UK/0143-3245) [08044538] **2513**

BLOEM & BLAD (NE) [11081611] **2434**

BLOEMBOLLENCULTUUR (NE) [05668745] **2410**

BLOEMEN EN PLANTEN (NE) [19823811] **2410**

BLONDE COUNTRY / ANNUAL HEARD REFERENCE ED (CN/0711-1797) [08465898] **207**

BLOOD (US/0006-4971) [01536582] **3770**

BLOOD ALCOHOL TESTING FOR MOTOR VEHICLE DEATHS, WISCONSIN (US/0731-2393) [04266803] **3158**

BLOOD & APHORISMS (CN/1183-1499) [11831499] **3367**

BLOOD BANK WEEK (US/0747-2420) [10656546] **3770**

BLOOD CELL BIOCHEMISTRY (US) [23181320] 449, **3770**

BLOOD CELLS (1978) (GW) [05802073] **3770**

BLOOD COAGULATION & FIBRINOLYSIS : AN INTERNATIONAL JOURNAL IN HAEMOSTASIS AND THROMBOSIS (UK/0957-5235) [23181314] **3795**

BLOOD COAGULATION FACTORS (UK/0266-6294) [I02666294] **449**

BLOOD DONOR DIGEST (CN/1180-4912) [23598340] **5275**

BLOOD-HORSE, THE (US/0006-4998) [08398192] **2797**

BLOOD PLATELETS (NE/0302-1653) [10003316] **410**

● BLOOD PRESSURE (NO/0803-7051) [27348782] **3699**

BLOOD PURIFICATION (SZ/0253-5068) [10218998] **3770**

BLOOD REVIEW, THE (US/1047-174X) [20638723] **3367**

BLOOD REVIEWS (UK/0268-960X) [15800424] **3770**

BLOOD THERAPY JOURNAL INTERNATIONAL (II/0006-5005) [07371386] **3770**

BLOOD TRANSFUSION (UK/0261-4596) [I02614596] **3795**

BLOOD VESSELS *See* JOURNAL OF VASCULAR RESEARCH **3707**

● BLOOD WEEKLY (US/1065-6073) [26648454] **3770**

BLOODLINES : (US/0890-8923) [05668857] **4286**

BLOODROOT *SUSPENDED.* (US/0161-2506) [03880428] **3367**

BLOOMBERG ENERGY HANDBOOK (US) **1934**

● BLOOMBERG (PRINCETON, N.J.) (US/1063-2123) [25927279] **892**

BLOOMFIELD DEMOCRAT (BLOOMFIELD, IOWA : 1922) (US) [13908846] **5668**

BLOOMFIELD JOURNAL, THE (US/0746-9632) [10426558] **5645**

BLOOMFIELD NEWS, THE (US) [11332979] **5663**

BLOOMSBURY REVIEW, THE (US/0276-1564) [07312342] **3338**

BLOSSOM MUSIC CENTER *See* BLOSSOM MUSIC CENTER **4104**

BLOSSOM MUSIC CENTER (US/0748-6294) [10064647] **4104**

BLOUNT COUNTIAN, THE (US/1056-3288) [21214814] **5625**

BLOUNT COUNTY HISTORICAL SOCIETY (US/1064-5489) [26326199] **2723**

BLOUNT JOURNAL, THE (US/1056-6252) [13723707] 2723, **2439**

BLOWING ROCKET, THE (US/1071-0574) [23858420] **5722**

BLS FILE OF STATE, COUNTY, AND MUNICIPAL COLLECTIVE BARGAINING AGREEMENTS (US/0362-4234) [02338372] **1655**

BLU-BOOK ... DIRECTORY (US) [19416986] **4064**

BLUE & GOLD ILLUSTRATED (US/0746-2557) [09897974] **1089**

BLUE & GRAY MAGAZINE (US/0741-2207) [10125366] **2723**

BLUE BERET (US/0744-5601) [08353747] **2485**

BLUE BOOK, AMERICAN DRUGGIST (US) [18131078] **4294**

BLUE BOOK (BALTIMORE, MD.) (US/0742-1389) [08532065] **2439**

Alphabetical Title Index — BNA

BLUE BOOK BUILDING AND CONSTRUCTION (EASTERN PENNSYLVANIA, SOUTHERN NEW JERSEY, DELAWARE ED.) (US) [19244120] **601**

BLUE BOOK BUILDING AND CONSTRUCTION (FLORIDA ED.) (US/1047-5443) [19417063] **601**

BLUE BOOK BUILDING AND CONSTRUCTION. METROPOLITAN NEW YORK, NORTHERN & CENTRAL NEW JERSEY *See* BLUE BOOK BUILDING AND CONSTRUCTION. NEW YORK, THE **601**

●BLUE BOOK BUILDING AND CONSTRUCTION. NEW YORK, THE (US) [25250983] **601**

BLUE BOOK FOR THE APPLE COMPUTER, THE (US/0739-2095) [08674985] **1172**

BLUE BOOK IL *See* TRUCK BLUE BOOK **5426**

BLUE BOOK / ILLINOIS STATE BAR ASSOCIATION (US) [14920025] **2942**

BLUE BOOK ILLUSTRATED PRICE GUIDE TO COLLECTABLE CAMERAS (US/0147-0663) [03092087] **4367**

BLUE BOOK : MEMBERSHIP DIRECTORY & BUYER'S GUIDE (US) [19279856] **2329**

BLUE BOOK - NATIONAL ASSOCIATION OF PARLIAMENTARIANS (US) [06990128] **4633**

BLUE BOOK (NEW YORK, N.Y.) (US) [07636713] 2008, **5075**

BLUE BOOK OF ADJUSTERS (US) [05248299] **2876**

BLUE BOOK OF BRITISH BROADCASTING, THE (UK) [07456020] **1127**

BLUE BOOK OF C B S STOCK REPORTS (CN/0384-7802) [03248583] **892**

BLUE BOOK OF CANADIAN BUSINESS, THE (CN/0381-7245) [02862201] **643**

●BLUE BOOK OF COLLEGE ATHLETICS FOR SENIOR, JUNIOR & COMMUNITY COLLEGES, THE (US/1067-750X) [24682763] 1812, **4887**

BLUE BOOK OF FOOD STORE OPERATORS AND WHOLESALERS (CN/0316-9537) [02247470] **2329**

BLUE BOOK OF MAJOR HOMEBUILDERS, THE *SUSPENDED.* (US/0195-8461) [02215998] **601**

BLUE BOOK OF OPTOMETRISTS, THE (US) [02572697] **4215**

BLUE BOOK OF PENSION FUNDS, THE (US/0272-2445) [06772066] 2876, **1655**

BLUE BOOK OF PHOTOGRAPHY PRICES *CEASED.* (US/0738-8322) [09692974] **4367**

●BLUE BOOK OF PRINTING AND GRAPHIC ARTS BUYERS (US/1065-8521) [26777989] 344, **377**

BLUE BOOK OF SR. COLLEGE, UNIVERSITY, AND JUNIOR & COMMUNITY COLLEGE ATHLETICS *See* BLUE BOOK OF COLLEGE ATHLETICS FOR SENIOR, JUNIOR & COMMUNITY COLLEGES, THE **4887**

●BLUE BOOK OF THE ASSOCIATION FOR PUBLIC OPINION RESEARCH, WORLD ASSOCIATION FOR PUBLIC OPINION RESEARCH : AGENCIES & ORGANIZATIONS REPRESENTED IN AAPOR MEMBERSHIP, THE (US) [26493638] **5240**

BLUE BOOK OFFICIAL LAWN EQUIPMENT TRADE-IN GUIDE *CEASED.* (US/0094-4955) [01793897] **2810**

BLUE BOOK. OFFICIAL LAWN MOWER TRADE-IN GUIDE (US) [07860008] **2410**

BLUE BOOK, THE (US) [02773608] **4633**

BLUE BOOK (TULSA), THE (US/0273-0162) [03760178] **1341**

BLUE BUFFALO (CN/0820-8352) [09523812] **3367**

BLUE CHART REPORT, THE (CN/0831-6503) [14707845] **2876**

BLUE CHIP ECONOMIC INDICATORS (US/0193-4600) [05266518] 643, **1548**

BLUE CHIP ECONOMIC WORLDSCAN *See* CURRENCY FORECASTERS DIGEST **1478**

BLUE CHIP FINANCIAL FORECASTS (US/0741-8345) [10248894] **779**

●BLUE CHIP JOB GROWTH UPDATE (US/1062-9327) [25812051] **1465**

BLUE DIAMOND GROWERS *See* ANNUAL REPORT / BLUE DIAMOND **162**

BLUE GRASS ROOTS (US/0278-8071) [07418716] **2439**

BLUE GUITAR, THE *CEASED.* (IT) [03030723] **3367**

BLUE HOTEL, THE (US) [06725288] **2804**

BLUE JAY (CN/0006-5099) [01536609] **4163**

BLUE JAY NEWS (CN/0822-9988) [11240704] **4163**

BLUE LINE MAGAZINE (CN/0847-8538) [20665994] **3158**

BLUE MOON (US/0743-2917) [10546331] **3367**

BLUE MOUND LEADER (US) [22849282] **5658**

BLUE MOUNTAIN HERITAGE (US/0743-183X) [08257569] **2439**

BLUE MOUNTAINS BRUCE TRAIL CLUB *See* NEWSLETTER - BLUE MOUNTAINS BRUCE TRAIL CLUB **4875**

BLUE PRINT (UK) **14**

BLUE RIBBON BANK REPORT (US) **779**

BLUE RIBBON FILL-IT-INS (US/0194-3111) [05422028] **4858**

BLUE RIBBON HOME PLANS (US/0899-4382) [12603570] **2899**

BLUE RIBBON, THE (US) [02811737] **2797**

BLUE RIBBON WORD-FINDS (US/0194-312X) [05421801] **4858**

BLUE RIDGE COMMUNITY COLLEGE *See* ANNUAL REPORT OF THE PRESIDENT / BLUE RIDGE COMMUNITY COLLEGE **1809**

BLUE RIDGE COUNTRY (US/1041-3456) [18728547] **2529**

BLUE RYDER (US/1058-0654) [24189238] **2529**

BLUE SHEET, THE (US/0162-3605) [02848149] **4294**

BLUE SKY GUIDE (US) **892**

BLUE SKY PRACTICE FOR PUBLIC AND PRIVATE OFFERINGS (US/0887-154X) [12658350] 4713, **2942**

BLUE SWAN REVIEW : GUIDE TO WOMEN'S FASHION CATALOGS, THE (US/1041-3936) [18757714] 5551, **1082**

BLUE UNICORN (US/0197-7016) [06069780] **3460**

BLUE VALLEY GAZETTE (STANLEY, KAN.) (US) [14089956] **5674**

BLUEBOOK (CAMBRIDGE, MASS.), THE (US/1062-9971) [24208760] **2942**

BLUEFIELD DAILY TELEGRAPH (US) [08232043] **5763**

BLUEFISH *CEASED.* (US/0741-5028) [10197452] **3460**

BLUEGRASS-BUEHNE (GW/0936-2479) [17203365] **4104**

BLUEGRASS CLUB OF NEW YORK *See* NEWSLETTER - BLUEGRASS CLUB OF NEW YORK **4140**

BLUEGRASS DIRECTORY, THE (US/0148-7396) [03357579] **4104**

BLUEGRASS MUSIC NEWS (US/0006-5129) [06130430] **4104**

BLUEGRASS REFLECTIONS (US/0361-5774) [02246708] **4104**

BLUEGRASS STAR, THE (US) [01791042] **4104**

BLUEGRASS UNLIMITED (US/0006-5137) [01788602] **4104**

BLUEJACKETS' MANUAL, THE (US) [04926893] **4175**

BLUELINE : GREEK AND MEDITERRANEAN INTELLIGENCE (GR) [11794928] **4516**

BLUELINE (POTSDAM, N.Y.) (US/0198-9901) [05785630] **3367**

BLUEPRINT FOR SOCIAL JUSTICE (US/0895-5786) [06611928] **5193**

BLUEPRINT (LONDON. 1983) (UK/0268-4926) [10768478] **293**

BLUEPRINTS - NATIONAL BUILDING MUSEUM (U.S.) (US/0742-0552) [07622121] 601, **293**

BLUES (FR) [01788944] **4104**

BLUES ACCESS (US/1066-4068) [10664068] **4104**

BLUES & SOUL (UK) [11328022] **4104**

BLUES AND SWING MAGAZINE (FR) [01788290] **4104**

BLUES LIFE (AU/0250-4421) [10109011] **4104**

BLUES LIFE JOURNAL (AU/0250-4421) [25569399] **4104**

BLUES-LINK (UK/0307-7241) [01792135] **4104**

BLUES NEWS (HELSINKI, FINLAND) *See* BN **4104**

BLUES NOTES (AU) [01788476] **4104**

BLUES UNLIMITED (UK/0006-5153) [02569308] **4104**

BLUESTONE; THE LITERARY QUARTERLY (US/0006-5188) [02790020] **3367**

●BLUFFS READER, THE (US/1062-6409) [25688745] **3368**

BLUFFTON NEWS-BANNER (US) [11438141] **5663**

BLUFFTON NEWS, THE (US) [09021986] **5727**

BLUMEA (NE/0006-5196) [02053096] **502**

BLUMEN EINZELHANDEL (GW) [10834618] **2434**

BLUTALKOHL (GW/0006-5250) [02811759] **3740**

BLYTTIA (NO/0006-5269) [02572225] **502**

BM. BANK UND MARKT + TECHNIK (GW/0933-3770) [09333770] **921**

BM. BAU- + MOBELSCHREINER (GW/0341-3659) [03413659] **2904**

BM : BERITA MAHASISWA (IO) [08855733] **1089**

BMA NEWS REVIEW (UK/0306-5472) [03065472] **3557**

BMB BURO INFORMATIKA (BE/0777-9216) [07779216] **643**

BMC. BIOMEDICAL CHROMATOGRAPHY (UK/0269-3879) [13501997] 3557, **449**

BMCIS BUILDING MAINTENANCE PRICE BOOK (UK/0261-2933) [02612933] **601**

BMD (LONDON) *CEASED.* (UK/0963-3464) [09633464] **921**

●BMD MONITOR (US/1069-8175) [28166154] **4038**

BMFT FORDERUNGSKATALOG (GW) [04911097] **5089**

BMFT-JOURNAL (GW/0724-0856) [l07240856] **5089**

BMG; BANJO, MANDOLIN, GUITAR (UK/0005-321X) [01793000] **4104**

BMI ORCHESTRAL PROGRAM SURVEY (US/0521-9604) [02066056] **4104**

BMJ. BRITISH MEDICAL JOURNAL (CLINICAL RESEARCH ED.) (UK/0959-8138) [19024268] **3557**

BMJ. BRITISH MEDICAL JOURNAL (GENERAL PRACTICE ED.) (UK) **3557**

BMJ. BRITISH MEDICAL JOURNAL (INTERNATIONAL ED.) (UK/0959-8146) [19008559] **3557**

●BMJ. BRITISH MEDICAL JOURNAL (SOUTH AFRICAN ED.) (SA/1019-8350) [l10198350] **3557**

BMJ:BRITISH MEDICAL JOURNAL. ITALIAN EDITION *SUSPENDED.* (IT) **3557**

BML : BOLLETTINO DI MICROBIOLOGIA E INDAGINI DI LABORATORIO (IT/0394-9877) [15469962] **560**

BMR JOURNAL OF AUSTRALIAN GEOLOGY AND GEOPHYSICS (AT/0312-9608) [02592477] 1402, **1367**

BMR RESEARCH NEWSLETTER (AT/0813-751X) [l0813751X] **1352**

BMS. BULLETIN DE METHODOLOGIE SOCIOLOGIQUE (FR/0759-1063) [l07591063] **5240**

BMST, BULLETIN MENSUEL DES STATISTIQUES DU TRAVAIL (FR) [25206323] **1655**

BMT ABSTRACTS : BRITISH MARITIME TECHNOLOGY ABSTRACTS (UK/0268-9650) [13220028] 4175, 5447, **4185**

BMT : BAUMASCHINENTECHNIK (GW/0942-1173) [26997412] **601**

BMT NEWS / INDIANA BUSINESS MODERNIZATION AND TECHNOLOGY CORPORATION (US) [24486856] **1599**

... BMUG NEWSLETTER, THE (US/0899-1014) [17989765] **1172**

BMW NEWS *See* BMW OWNERS NEWS **4080**

BMW OWNERS NEWS (US/8750-765X) [11735266] **4080**

BMWE JOURNAL (US/1049-3921) [16749576] **1655**

BMX ACTION (US/0747-2552) [10665755] **428**

BMX PLUS (US/0195-0320) [05226201] **428**

BN (FI/0784-7726) [07052190] **4104**

BN HISTORIAN, THE (US/1055-6265) [23245505] **2723**

BNA ADMINISTRATIVE PRACTICE MANUAL. CURRENT REPORTS (US/0896-4998) [15709159] **4633**

BNA CALIFORNIA EMPLOYEE RELATIONS REPORT (US/1058-7373) [24365049] **1655**

BNA CALIFORNIA ENVIRONMENT REPORTER (US/1052-813X) [22392854] **3110**

●BNA CALIFORNIA SAFETY & HEALTH REPORT (US/1065-3104) [26570246] **4768**

BNA CRIMINAL PRACTICE MANUAL. CURRENT REPORTS (US/0889-9312) [14095493] **2942**

BNA ONLINE (US/0747-5438) [10745056] 4812, **1274**

● BNA PENSION & BENEFITS REPORTER (US/1069-5117) [28081493] **1655**

BNA PENSION REPORTER (US/0095-7100) [02153735] 2876, **1656**

BNA POLICY AND PRACTICE SERIES (US/0005-3228) [03463998] **939**

BNAC COMMUNICATOR (US/1051-208X) [11665771] 1656, **1105**

B'NAI B'RITH INTERNATIONAL JEWISH MONTHLY, THE (US/0279-3415) [07779266] **5046**

● BNA'S AMERICANS WITH DISABILITIES ACT MANUAL. NEWSLETTER (US/1063-3111) [25970591] **4384**

BNA'S BANKING REPORT (US/0891-0634) [14558359] **3085**

BNA'S BANKRUPTCY LAW REPORTER (US/1044-7474) [19830881] **3085**

BNA'S CONSTRUCTION LABOR REPORT *See* CONSTRUCTION LABOR REPORT **1661**

BNA'S EASTERN EUROPE REPORTER (US/1058-7365) [24364993] 2942, **892**

BNA'S HEALTH CARE ELECTRONIC DATA REPORT *CEASED.* (US/1068-3798) [27667304] **3557**

● BNA'S HEALTH CARE POLICY REPORT (US/1068-1213) [27448376] **3557**

● BNA'S HEALTH LAW REPORTER (US/1064-2137) [26231924] 4768, **2942**

BNA'S LAW REPRINTS. CRIMINAL LAW SERIES *See* CIS LAW REPRINTS. CRIMINAL LAW SERIES : THE SUPREME COURT OF THE UNITED STATES PETITIONS AND BRIEFS **3105**

BNA'S LAW REPRINTS. LABOR LAW SERIES *See* CIS LAW REPRINTS. LABOR LAW SERIES : THE SUPREME COURT OF THE UNITED STATES PETITIONS AND BRIEFS **3145**

BNA'S LAW REPRINTS. SECURITIES REGULATION SERIES *See* CIS LAW REPRINTS. SECURITIES REGULATION SERIES : THE SUPREME COURT OF THE UNITED STATES PETITIONS AND BRIEFS **2950**

BNA'S LAW REPRINTS. TAX SERIES *See* CIS LAW REPRINTS. TAX SERIES : THE SUPREME COURT OF THE UNITED STATES PETITIONS AND BRIEFS **4717**

BNA'S LAW REPRINTS. TRADE REGULATION SERIES *See* CIS LAW REPRINTS. TRADE REGULATION SERIES : THE SUPREME COURT OF THE UNITED STATES PETITIONS AND BRIEFS **3097**

BNA'S MEDICARE REPORT (US/1049-7986) [21310551] **5275**

BNA'S NATIONAL ENVIRONMENT WATCH *CEASED.* (US/1049-8893) [21344195] **2162**

BNA'S PATENT, TRADEMARK & COPYRIGHT JOURNAL (US/0148-7965) [01644618] **1301**

BNA'S REVIEW OF WHAT'S NEW (US/0897-5167) [17539603] **3196**

● BNA'S STATE ENVIRONMENT & SAFETY REGULATORY MONITORING REPORT (US/1065-8076) [26749093] 4768, **2162**

BNA'S WORKERS' COMPENSATION REPORT (US/1051-4775) [21973678] 2876, **1656**

BNB NBB COMPTES ANNUELS DES ENTREPRISES BELGES. CD-ROM (BE) **739**

BNB ON CD-ROM [COMPUTER FILE] (UK/0968-3097) [25836906] **3196**

BNF NUTRITION BULLETIN (UK/0141-9684) [05089347] **4188**

BNH EM RESUMO (BL) [06005680] **2816**

BO BEDRE (DK/0006-5285) [I00065285] **2816**

BOARD (US) **1728**

BOARD (CHULA VISTA, CALIF.), THE *CEASED.* (US/0887-5510) [13306242] **1728**

BOARD CONVERTING NEWS (US) **4218**

BOARD CONVERTING NEWS ESPANOL (US) **4218**

● BOARD LEADERSHIP (US/1061-4249) [25305977] **861**

BOARD MANUFACTURE AND PROCESSING (UK/0306-4123) [01794003] **2399**

● BOARD MEMBER: NATIONAL CENTER FOR NONPROFIT BOARDS (US/1058-5419) [24324320] **861**

BOARD OF CARTAGENA AGREEMENT *See* GRUPO ANDINO : LEGISLACION ECONOMICA Y SOCIAL DE LOS PAISES MIEMBROS **2975**

BOARD OF CONTRACT APPEALS DECISIONS *CEASED.* (US/0498-3637) [04383456] **3182**

BOARD OF DIRECTORS ANNUAL STUDY (US/0161-6196) [03804510] **861**

BOARD OF DIRECTORS, COMMITTEE CHAIRMEN - CANADIAN CHAMBER OF COMMERCE (CN/0709-0285) [05322773] **818**

BOARD OF ENVIRONMENTAL STUDIES RESEARCH PAPER (AT) [15479857] **2188**

BOARD OF GOVERNORS OF THE FEDERAL RESERVE SYSTEM (U.S.) *See* ACTIONS OF THE BOARD, APPLICATIONS AND REPORTS RECEIVED DURING THE WEEK ENDING ... : ANNOUNCEMENT / BY BOARD OF GOVERNORS OF THE FEDERAL RESERVE SYSTEM **768**

BOARD OF GOVERNORS OF THE FEDERAL RESERVE SYSTEM (U.S.) *See* ANNUAL REPORT TO CONGRESS ON TRUTH IN LENDING **4710**

BOARD OF GOVERNORS OF THE FEDERAL RESERVE SYSTEM (U.S.) *See* SUMMARY REPORT, ASSETS AND LIABILITIES OF MEMBER BANKS **813**

BOARD OF GOVERNORS OF THE FEDERAL RESERVE SYSTEM (U.S.) *See* ANNUAL STATISTICAL DIGEST - BOARD OF GOVERNORS OF THE FEDERAL RESERVE SYSTEM **772**

BOARD OF GOVERNORS OF THE FEDERAL RESERVE SYSTEM (U.S.) *See* RESEARCH LIBRARY, RECENT ACQUISITIONS **3245**

BOARD OF GOVERNORS OF THE FEDERAL RESERVE SYSTEM (U.S.) *See* SECURITIES CREDIT TRANSACTIONS HANDBOOK. TRANSMITTAL / BOARD OF GOVERNORS OF THE FEDERAL RESERVE SYSTEM **811**

BOARD OF MEDICAL EXAMINERS OF MARYLAND *See* ANNUAL REPORT OF BOARD OF MEDICAL EXAMINERS **3913**

BOARD OF MEDICAL EXAMINERS OF THE STATE OF OREGON *See* DIRECTORY OF REGISTERED LICENSEES, BOARD OF MEDICAL EXAMINERS OF THE STATE OF OREGON **3913**

BOARD OF PHARMACY OF THE STATE OF ARIZONA *See* ANNUAL REPORT OF THE BOARD OF PHARMACY OF THE STATE OF ARIZONA **4291**

BOARD OF PROFESSIONAL RESPONSIBILITY OF THE SUPREME COURT OF TENNESSEE. ETHICS COMMITTEE *See* FORMAL ETHICS OPINION / BOARD OF PROFESSIONAL RESPONSIBILITY OF THE SUPREME COURT OF TENNESSEE **2250**

BOARD OF TAX APPEALS DECISIONS (US/0145-6520) [02770287] **4713**

BOARD OF THE SOUTH AUSTRALIAN MUSEUM ANNUAL REPORT (AT/0814-2262) [08142262] **4085**

BOARD OF TRADE OF THAILAND'S TRADE DIRECTORY (TH) [22678686] **825**

BOARD REPORT FOR GRAPHIC ARTISTS (US/1062-7774) [09417739] **377**

BOARDING KENNEL PROPRIETOR (US/0190-0226) [04626974] **4286**

BOARDING SCHOOLS DIRECTORY (US/0897-0645) [14629183] **1728**

BOARDROOM REPORTS (US/0045-2300) [02952233] **861**

● BOARDROOM (WILLOWDALE) (CN/1192-6201) [28312001] **861**

BOARDS AND COMMISSIONS, STATE OF ALASKA (US/0149-3205) [03457782] **4633**

BOARDWALK (SURREY) (CN/1189-3109) [25589827] **316**

BOARDWATCH MAGAZINE (US/1054-2760) [20869555] **1274**

BOAT AND MOTOR DEALER (US/0006-5366) [04968593] **591**

BOAT GUIDE (CN/0826-2802) [11046665] **592**

BOAT INTERNATIONAL (UK/0264-9136) [24057248] **592**

BOAT PENNSYLVANIA (US/0888-1561) [10880058] **592**

BOAT TECHNOLOGY INTERNATIONAL (UK/0144-4034) [06645812] **592**

BOATBUILDER (RIVERSIDE, CONN.) (US/0886-0254) [12862700] **592**

BOATING INDUSTRY MARINE BUYERS' GUIDE (US) **592**

BOATING INDUSTRY STATISTICAL YEARBOOK (US/0277-8378) [07635476] **597**

BOATING INDUSTRY, THE (US/0006-5404) [01796247] **592**

BOATING INFORMATION - A BIBLIOGRAPHY AND SOURCE LIST (US) [15098461] **592**

BOATING (NEW YORK, N.Y.) (US/0006-5374) [05739792] **592**

BOATING NEWS (VANCOUVER) (CN/0700-7388) [02789449] **592**

BOATING PRODUCT NEWS *CEASED.* (US/0190-4507) [04710804] **592**

BOATING REGISTRATION STATISTICS (US/0163-7207) [04440242] **597**

BOATING SAFETY TRAINING MANUAL (US/0190-5481) [04714615] 592, **4768**

BOATING STATISTICS (US) [08568763] **597**

BOATING WORLD (US/1059-5155) [24359419] **592**

BOATMAN NEWSLETTER (US/0883-7775) [09990687] **2439**

BOATRACING *CEASED.* (US/0890-9202) [14516184] **592**

BOATS & GEAR (US/1048-5244) [20967592] **592**

BOATS & HARBORS (US/0739-2257) [09719309] **592**

BOATS & MOTORS *See* BOAT AND MOTOR DEALER **591**

BOAVISTA NEWSLETTER (BL) [25880370] **779**

BOB CARR'S INSIDE SPORTING GOODS (US) 4887, **952**

BOB DAMRON'S ADDRESS BOOK (US) [09606890] **5187**

BOB NUROCK'S ADVISORY (US/1050-9011) [21681625] 892, **643**

BOBBIN (1987) (US/0896-3991) [17022823] **1082**

BOBINA, LA (US/0194-7249) [04978932] **1082**

BOBO (NE/0165-1196) [I01651196] **1060**

BOC WEEK (US) [12830684] **1150**

BOCA BASIC HOUSING-PROPERTY MAINTENANCE CODE, THE (US) [02172565] 601, **2942**

BOCA NATIONAL BUILDING CODE, THE (US/0897-0068) [15194269] **601**

BOCA NATIONAL FIRE PREVENTION CODE, THE (US/0897-0084) [15604173] **2288**

BOCA NATIONAL MECHANICAL CODE, THE (US/0897-0092) [15561361] **2603**

BOCA NATIONAL PLUMBING CODE, THE (US/1055-6680) [15561783] **2603**

BOCA NATIONAL PROPERTY MAINTENANCE CODE (US/1055-6192) [21470352] 2942, **2816**

BOCA RATON (US/0740-2856) [08471229] **2529**

BOCCONEA (FR/1120-4060) [24649231] **502**

BOCHUMER ANGLISTISCHE STUDIEN (NE/0169-6165) [03458496] **3269**

BOCHUMER ARBEITEN ZUR SPRACH- UND LITERATURWISSENSCHAFT (GW/0523-7971) [01536627] **3368**

BOCHUMER GEOGRAPHISCHE ARBEITEN (GW/0523-798X) [03458536] **2556**

BOCOEX INDEX, THE (US/1047-496X) [20702181] **1172**

BODEM ALPHEN AAN DEN RIJN (NE/0925-1650) [I09251650] **2162**

BODENDENKMALPFLEGE IN MECKLENBURG-VORPOMMERN : JAHRBUCH (GW) [26892280] **262**

BODENKULTUR (1964) (AU/0006-5471) [05114991] **67**

BODLEIAN LIBRARY RECORD, THE (UK/0067-9488) [01536630] **3196**

BODOBOKA (NO) [15813924] **4085**

BODY BEAUTIFUL (UK) [18574910] **4367**

BODY BOARDING (US/1047-2223) [20640436] **4887**

BODY BULLETIN (US/0275-9101) [07243236] **2596**

● BODY CONTOURING SURGERY (US/1065-2523) [26557278] **3960**

BODY FASHIONS *See* BODY FASHIONS/INTIMATE APPAREL **1082**

BODY FASHIONS DIRECTORY *See* BODY FASHIONS/INTIMATE APPAREL DIRECTORY **1082**

BODY FASHIONS/INTIMATE APPAREL (US/0360-3520) [02244083] **1082**

BODY FASHIONS/INTIMATE APPAREL DIRECTORY (US/0362-2452) [02441489] **1082**

BODY LEEDS (UK/0006-5501) [I00065501] **5407**

BODY-MIND NETWORKS (US/8756-8551) [11646290] **4768**

BODY, MIND, SPIRIT (US/0895-7657) [16787390] **4185**

BODY POLITIC XTRA (CN/0826-0508) [11734377] 4849, **2793**

BODY TALK (US/0749-1018) [11078818] **5551**

BODYCHECK (NEPEAN) (CN/1191-0100) [25589894] **4887**

BODYSHOP (CN/0045-2319) [01737979] **5408**

BODYSHOP BUSINESS (US/0730-7241) [08047177] 643, **5408**

BOECKH BUILDING COST GUIDE. COMMERCIAL (CN/0225-9389) [06141441] **601**

BOECKH BUILDING COST GUIDE. INSTITUTIONAL (CN/0225-9397) [06141448] **601**

BOECKH BUILDING COST GUIDE. LIGHT INDUSTRIAL (CN/0225-9400) [06141447] **601**

BOECKH BUILDING COST GUIDE. RESIDENTIAL (CN/0225-9419) [06141445] **601**

BOECKH BUILDING COST INDEX NUMBERS (US/0090-8681) [05580372] **601**

BOEHRINGER MANNHEIM INFORMA DE ACTUALIDADES EN ANALITICA CLINICA Y BIOQUIMICA (SP) 484, **3557**

BOEI DAIGAKKO (JAPAN) See KYOKAN KENKYU YOROKU **5125**

BOEI HANDOBUKKU (JA) [02244192] **4038**

BOEI IKA DAIGAKKO ZASSHI (JA/0385-1796) [10244630] **3558**

BOEING AIRLINER See AIRLINER / BOEING CUSTOMER SERVICES DIVISION **10**

BOEKBLAD (NE/0167-4765) [07126431] **4812**

BOEKENGIDS (BE/0006-5579) [l00065579] **410**

BOEKI GYOTAI TOKEIHYO (JA) [02831038] **825**

BOER EN DE TUINDER, DE (BE) [05583146] **67**

BOER EN TUINDER (NE) [04055025] **2410**

BOERDERIJ, DE (NE) [04055047] **67**

BOEUF DE L'EST (CN/0227-0250) [08091027] **207**

BOGAZICI UNIVERSITESI See BOGAZICI UNIVERSITESI DERGISI : MUHENDISLIK **1966**

BOGAZICI UNIVERSITESI DERGISI : MUHENDISLIK (TU/0379-587X) [02241384] **1966**

BOGAZICI UNIVERSITESI DERGISI. SOSYAL BILIMLER (TU) [02583971] **5193**

BOGENS VERDEN (DK/0006-5692) [02258412] 3368, **3196**

BOGG (ARLINGTON, VA.) (US/0882-648X) [02790073] 3338, **3368**

BOGONG (AT/0159-6586) [I01596586] **2188**

BOGOSLOVNI VESTNIK (XV/0006-5722) [04926808] **4939**

BOGTRYKKERBLADET See GRAFISKE FAG, DE **4565**

BOGUS REVIEW (US/8756-8500) [11694941] **3368**

BOHEMIA (CU/0523-8579) [02256648] **2485**

BOHEMIA (MUNCHEN) (GW/0523-8587) [01536654] **2678**

BOHLAU FORUM LITTERARUM (GW) [13684443] **3368**

BOICE LYDELL'S SPORT KARATE INTERNATIONAL (US/1064-6507) [26365353] **4887**

BOILER AND PRESSURE VESSEL SAFETY ACT AND RULES AND REGULATIONS (US) [05844549] **2942**

BOILER EXPLOSIONS ACTS, 1882 AND 1890, REPORT OF PRELIMINARY INQUIRY (UK) [02155367] **3476**

BOILERMAKER REPORTER (US) [22337253] **1656**

BOILING POINT (UK/0263-3167) [25755457] **5089**

BOIRA KENKYU (JA/0387-0162) [10244469] **1599**

BOIS DE FEU & ENERGIE NOGENT-SUR-MARNE (FR/1153-3072) [l11533072] **1934**

BOIS ET FORETS DES TROPIQUES (FR/0006-579X) [01536655] **2376**

BOIS HEBDO See BOIS NATIONAL (EDITION VERTE), LE **2376**

BOIS, LES (US) [02396586] **1812**

BOIS NATIONAL (EDITION VERTE), LE (FR) [09745448] **2376**

BOISBRIAND (1983) (CN/0822-5133) [10082770] **4633**

BOISBRIAND (QUEBEC) See BOISBRIAND (1983) **4633**

BOISE (ADA COUNTY, IDAHO) CITY DIRECTORY (US) [05059967] **2556**

BOISE STATE UNIVERSITY WESTERN WRITERS SERIES (US/0886-7348) [03221423] **431**

BOISSIERA (SZ/0373-2975) [01536659] **502**

BOISSONS DE FRANCE, JEAN PRIMUS (FR/0760-1999) [I07601999] **2365**

BOITE A NOUVELLES (CN/1180-6761) [21515348] **5780**

BOITE A OUTILS (CN/0229-9909) [08311729] **1800**

BOK OG BIBLIOTEK (NO/0006-5811) [01536660] 3196, **3257**

BOK OG SAMFUNN (OSLO, NORWAY : 1981) (NO) [07200551] **4824**

BOKAORMURINN. SKJOLDUR (IC) [23155308] **3368**

BOKIN BOBAI : NIHON BOKIN BOBAI GAKKAI SHI (JA/0385-5201) [09421925] **4294**

BOKREVY (SW/0005-2833) [02591327] **3457**

BOKSER WARSZAWA (PL/0867-2806) [I08672806] **4824**

BOKVAENNEN (SW/0006-5846) [01536664] 4824, **3368**

BOLAFFI'S ROMAN STATES AND VATICAN CITY SPECIALIZED STAMP CATALOGUE (IT) [05197680] **2784**

BOLETIM ABDF (BL/0101-7268) [05720880] **3196**

BOLETIM - ADMINISTRACAO GERAL DO ACUCAR E DO ALCOOL (PO) [04200839] **1599**

BOLETIM ANUAL DE ESTATISTICA (CAPE VERDE. DIRECCAO GERAL DE ESTATISTICA) (CV) [17484979] **4465**

BOLETIM BIBLIOGRAFICO (BL/0102-9290) [02657238] **2840**

BOLETIM BIBLIOGRAFICO SEDOC (BL) [05061782] **410**

BOLETIM / CEHILA (BL) [18219780] **2723**

BOLETIM - CENTRO DE ESTUDOS, PROCURADORIA GERAL DO ESTADO (BL) [03590472] **2942**

BOLETIM - CENTRO DE LETRAS E CIENCIAS HUMANAS (BL/0102-6968) [I01026968] **2843**

BOLETIM CLINICO DES HOSPITAIS CIVIS DE LISBOA (PO/0374-6070) [01796508] **3558**

BOLETIM - COIMBRA. UNIVERSIDADE. CENTRO DE ESTUDOS GEOGRAFICOS (PO/0587-6060) [03178071] **1074**

BOLETIM - COMISSAO GOIANA DE FOLCLORE (BL) [04928270] **2318**

BOLETIM - CONSELHO FEDERAL DE CULTURA (BL) [01791443] **5229**

BOLETIM CULTURAL - ASSEMBLEIA DISTRITAL DE LISBOA (PO/0870-0761) [I08700761] 2679, **5268**

BOLETIM CULTURAL / CAMARA MUNICIPAL DO PORTO (PO/0870-0478) [12233031] 2679, **5268**

BOLETIM DA ACADEMIA NACIONAL DE MEDICINA (BL/0001-3838) [01316173] **3558**

BOLETIM DA ASSOCIACAO COMERCIAL DE LOURENCO MARQUES (MZ) [03610206] **825**

BOLETIM DA BIBLIOTECA (BL) [06642344] **2942**

BOLETIM DA DIRECCAO GERAL DOS EDIFICIOS E MONUMENTOS NACIONAIS CEASED. (PO/0870-1466) [05658327] **293**

BOLETIM DA FACULDADE DE FARMACIA DE COIMBRA (PO/0378-9608) [04031128] **4294**

BOLETIM DA FILMOTECA ULTRAMARINA PORTUGUESA (PO/0430-4497) [03800518] **2611**

BOLETIM DA PROCURADORIA GERAL (BL) [02240902] 5378, **2942**

BOLETIM DA SOCIEDADE BRASILEIRA DE CIENCIA E TECNOLOGIA DE ALIMENTOS / SOCIEDADE BRASILEIRA DE CIENCIA E TECNOLOGIA DE ALIMENTOS, SBCTA (BL) [08376448] **4188**

BOLETIM DA SOCIEDADE BRASILEIRA DE MATEMATICA (BL/0100-3569) [01788040] **3497**

BOLETIM DA SOCIEDADE BROTERIANA (PO/0081-0657) [01587108] **502**

BOLETIM DA SOCIEDADE GEOLOGICA DE PORTUGAL (PO/0366-2101) [05097232] **1367**

BOLETIM DA SOCIEDADE PORTUGUESA DE ENTOMOLOGIA (PO/0870-7227) [I08707227] **5606**

BOLETIM DE ANTROPOLOGIA (BL/0532-260X) [01379805] **232**

BOLETIM DE ARIEL (BL) [01796218] **2551**

BOLETIM DE BIBLIOGRAFIA PORTUGUESA. DOCUMENTOS NAO TEXTUAIS See BOLETIM DE BIBLIOGRAFIA PORTUGUESA. MATERIAL NAO LIVRO **3196**

BOLETIM DE BIBLIOGRAFIA PORTUGUESA. MATERIAL NAO LIVRO (PO) **3196**

BOLETIM DE CIENCIAS DO MAR / LABORATORIO DE CIENCIAS DO MAR, UNIVERSIDADE FEDERAL DO CEARA (BL) [02573033] 1446, **553**

BOLETIM DE CIENCIAS SOCIAIS (BL) [06591363] **5193**

BOLETIM DE CONJUNTURA (BL) [01789937] **1548**

BOLETIM DE FILOLOGIA (PO/0870-4600) [01536665] **3269**

BOLETIM DE FISIOLOGIA ANIMAL (BL/0101-4242) [05032561] **578**

BOLETIM DE GEOCIENCIAS DA PETROBRAS (BL/0102-9304) [16653202] **1367**

BOLETIM DE GEOGRAFIA TEORETICA (BL) [02244121] **2556**

BOLETIM DE INDUSTRIA ANIMAL (BL/0067-9615) [10503155] 5506, **207**

BOLETIM DE INFORMACAO SOCIO-ECONOMICA / GABINETE DE ESTUDOS ECONOMICOS, MINISTERIO DO PLANO E COOPERACAO INTERNACIONAL (PG) [17247344] **1465**

BOLETIM DE LEGISLACAO ECONOMICA (PO/0870-1008) [I08701008] **779**

BOLETIM DE MERCADOS AGRICOLAS, INFORMACOES / BANCO DO NORDESTE DO BRASIL, S.A (BL) [08398055] **1599**

BOLETIM DE MINAS (PO/0006-5935) [01786910] **2135**

BOLETIM DE PESQUISA (BL/0102-292X) [15183783] 2410, **165**

BOLETIM DE PESQUISA (BL/0100-8102) [07352364] **67**

BOLETIM DE PESQUISA - EMPAER (BL/0101-966X) [26974368] **67**

BOLETIM DE PESQUISA FLORESTAL (BL/0101-1057) [11652770] **2376**

BOLETIM DE PESQUISA - UEPAE DOURADOS (BL/0102-0048) [I01020048] **200**

BOLETIM DE PESQUISA - UNIDADE DE EXECUCAO DE PESQUISA DE AMBITO ESTADUAL DE PORTO VELHO (BL/0101-6431) [15720261] **67**

BOLETIM DE RECURSOS NATURAIS (BL/0585-8658) [01798755] **2188**

BOLETIM DE ZOOLOGIA (BL/0101-3580) [02662727] **5578**

BOLETIM DO ARQUIVO HISTORICO MILITAR (PO/0870-4619) [05638032] **4038**

BOLETIM DO CENTRO DE DOCUMENTACAO 25 DE ABRIL (PO/0871-3643) [23157411] 2611, **5193**

BOLETIM DO COMERCIO EXTERIOR DA BAHIA (BL) [01791084] **825**

BOLETIM DO INSTITUTO DE ANGOLA (AO/0020-3726) [06165278] **2638**

BOLETIM DO INSTITUTO DE ARQUEOLOGIA BRASILEIRA (BL) [03594041] **262**

BOLETIM DO INSTITUTO DE ARQUEOLOGIA BRASILEIRA : SERIE ESPECIAL (BL) [02244420] **2723**

BOLETIM DO INSTITUTO DE PESCA (BL/0046-9939) [01286933] **2297**

BOLETIM DO INSTITUTO DE PESQUISAS VETERINARIAS DESIDERIO FINAMOR (BL) [09349394] **5506**

BOLETIM DO INSTITUTO DOS PRODUTOS FLORESTAIS: CORTICA See CORTICA **1602**

BOLETIM DO INSTITUTO ESTADUAL DE HEMATOLOGIA ARTHUR DE SEQUERIA CAVALCANTI (BL/0046-9963) [01214976] **3770**

BOLETIM DO INSTITUTO "LUIS DE CAMOES." (MH) [04267549] **3368**

BOLETIM DO INSTITUTO NACIONAL DE INVESTIGACAO DAS PESCAS (PO) [05723364] **553**

BOLETIM DO INSTITUTO OCEANOGRAFICO (BL/0373-5524) [08630704] 1446, **553**

BOLETIM DO INSTITUTO OCEANOGRAFICO (BL/0080-6331) [01765020] 1446, **553**

BOLETIM DO MINISTERIO DA JUSTICA (PO) [01641228] **2942**

BOLETIM DO MUSEU NACIONAL. NOVA SERIE, ZOOLOGIA (BL/0080-312X) [01714634] **5578**

BOLETIM DO MUSEU PARAENSE EMILIO GOELDI. SERIE ANTROPOLOGIA (BL/0522-7291) [11864904] **232**

BOLETIM DO NUCLEO DO NORDESTE DA SOCIEDADE BRASILEIRA DE GEOLOGIA (BL) [02244067] **1367**

BOLETIM DO SERVIDOR (BL) [03616754] **4702**

BOLETIM DO TRABALHO (BL) [03161312] **1656**

BOLETIM DO TRABALHO E EMPREGO. 2A I.E. SEGUNDA SERIE (PO) [04558520] **3144**

BOLETIM DOS MUNICIPIOS (BL) [01790028] **4633**

BOLETIM ELEITORAL (US) [03674789] **2942**

BOLETIM — Alphabetical Title Index

BOLETIM ESTATISTICO (BL) [08396472] **2859**

BOLETIM ESTATISTICO - ADMINISTRACAO DO PORTO DO RECIFE (BL) [02240664] **5400**

BOLETIM ESTATISTICO ANUAL - COMPANHIA DE ELETRICIDADE DE CEARA (BL) [03150633] 4760, **4696**

BOLETIM ESTATISTICO - BANCO REGIONAL DE DESENVOLVIMENTO DO EXTREMO SUL (BL/0302-0940) [01792461] **779**

BOLETIM ESTATISTICO - CESP (BL) [05725319] **1599**

BOLETIM ESTATISTICO - COMPANHIA PAULISTA DE FORCA E LUZ (BL) [03399584] 4760, **4696**

BOLETIM ESTATIST CO, CONSUMO E CONSUMIDORES POR CLASSE E MUNICIPIO, ESTADO DE SAO PAULO *See* ANUARIO ESTATISTICO DE ENERGIA ELECTRICA / COMPANIA ENERGETICA DE SAO PAULO, DIVISAO DE ESTUDOS DO MERCADO DE ENERGIA ELETRICA **1961**

BOLETIM ESTATISTICO DE ENERGIA ELETRICA (BL) [07495316] 1934, **1961**

BOLETIM ESTATISTICO DO CACAU (BL) [01795912] **1599**

BOLETIM ESTATISTICO / ESTADO DE SANTA CATARINA, SECRETARIA DOS TRANSPORTES E OBRAS, ADMINISTRACAO DO PORTO DE SAO FRANCISCO DO SUL (BL) [09602833] **5400**

BOLETIM ESTATISTICO MENSAL DE ENERGIA ELETRICA *See* BOLETIM ESTATISTICO DE ENERGIA ELETRICA **1961**

BOLETIM FBCN (BL) [08581570] **2188**

BOLETIM GEOMAGNETICO PRELIMINAR (PO) [03637898] **4443**

BOLETIM IG-USP. SERIE CIENTIFICA / UNIVERSIDADE DE SAO PAULO, INSTITUTO DE GEOCIENCIAS (BL) [13357035] **1367**

BOLETIM INFORMATIVO (BL) [01791870] **410**

BOLETIM INFORMATIVO (BL) [09445439] **4633**

BOLETIM INFORMATIVO ADUANEIRAS (BL) [08808749] 825, **2942**

BOLETIM INFORMATIVO / BANCO DE FOMENTO NACIONAL (PO) [20305972] **892**

BOLETIM INFORMATIVO - CENTRO DE DOCUMENTACAO E INFORMACOES EDUCACIONAIS (BL) [05773822] **1728**

BOLETIM INFORMATIVO : COMERCIO EXTERIOR - EXPORTACAO DE FUMO EM FOLHAS (BL) [01786980] **5372**

BOLETIM INFORMATIVO - CONFERENCIA NACIONAL DOS BISPOS DO BRASIL, SECRETARIADO REGIONAL LESTE 2 (BL) [05268207] **5024**

BOLETIM INFORMATIVO - CONSELHO NACIONAL DE DESPORTOS (BL) [01793433] **4887**

BOLETIM INFORMATIVO DA SECAO DE DOCUMENTACAO (BL) [02981064] **4713**

BOLETIM INFORMATIVO DA SECRETARIA DE FAZENDA (BL) [02241181] **4713**

BOLETIM INFORMATIVO DO INSTITUTO NACIONAL DE ARTES CENICAS / INACEN, MINISTERIO DA EDUCACAO E CULTURA, SECRETARIA DA CULTURA (BL) [11807103] 131-, **5362**

BOLETIM INFORMATIVO DO SETOR DE DOCUMENTACAO (BL) [03339307] **410**

BOLETIM INFORMATIVO - FUNDACAO CALOUSTE GULBENKIAN, SERVICOS DE BIBLIOTECAS (PO) [03067947] **3196**

BOLETIM INFORMATIVO MENSAL (PORTO ALEGRE, BRAZIL) (BL) [10769103] **2942**

BOLETIM INFORMATIVO - PROCURADORIA GERAL DO ESTADO (BL) [03236430] **2942**

BOLETIM INFORMATIVO - SECRETARIA DA EDUCACAO E CULTURA (BL) [02239970] **1728**

BOLETIM INFORMATIVO SIP (BL) [02405485] **4064**

BOLETIM - INSTITUTO DO AZEITE E PRODUTOS OLEAGINOSOS (PO/0304-5196) [02242198] **5089**

BOLETIM / INSTITUTO HISTORICO DA ILHA TERCEIRA (PO/0870-466X) [06701626] **2611**

BOLETIM MENSAL / BANCO CENTRAL DO BRASIL (BL/0102-5171) [08512146] **779**

BOLETIM MENSAL DAS ESTATISTICAS DA AGRICULTURA E DA PESCA (PO/0377-2152) [03355947] **67**

BOLETIM MENSAL DAS ESTATISTICAS DO COMERCIO EXTERNO. CONTINENTE, ACORES E MADEIRA / INSTITUTO NACIONAL DE ESTATISTICA, SERVICOS CENTRAIS (PO) [07523977] 825, **726**

BOLETIM MENSAL DE ESTATISTICA (AO/1010-4151) [01789784] **5323**

BOLETIM MENSAL DE ESTATISTICA (MH) [04527644] **5323**

BOLETIM PAULISTA DE GEOGRAFIA (BL/0006-6079) [02804538] **2556**

BOLETIM - PRESIDENTE PRUDENTE. FACULDADE DE FILOSOFIA, CIENCIAS E LETRAS. DEPARTAMENTO DE EDUCACAO (BL) [01785658] **1728**

BOLETIM SEMESTRAL / BANCO DE PORTUGAL, DELEGACAO REGIONAL DOS ACORES (PO) [10427678] **3085**

BOLETIM / SOCIEDADE PORTUGUESA DE QUIMICA (PO/0870-1180) [14773036] **962**

BOLETIM TECHNICO INFORMATIVO (BL) [01787599] **5193**

BOLETIM TECNICO (BL) [01791266] **1656**

BOLETIM TECNICO / BRAZIL. SERVICO DE ESTATISTICA DA PREVIDENCIA E TRABALHO *See* BOLETIM TECNICO **1656**

BOLETIM TECNICO - CAPRE (BL) [06338000] **1256**

BOLETIM TECNICO CEPED (BL/0100-1949) [04728071] **5089**

BOLETIM TECNICO - COMISSAO EXECUTIVA DO PLANO DA LAVOURA CACAUEIRA, DEPARTAMENTO ESPECIAL DA AMAZONIA (BL/0102-5511) [I01025511] **67**

BOLETIM TECNICO - COORDENDORIA DE ASSISTENCIA TECNICA INTEGRAL (BL/0100-4417) [03938041] **67**

BOLETIM TECNICO COPERSUCAR (BL) [03715981] **165**

BOLETIM TECNICO DA ESCOLA SUPERIOR DE AGRICULTURA DE LAVRAS (BL) [15207237] **67**

BOLETIM TECNICO DA PETROBRAS (BL/0006-6117) [02574206] **62**

BOLETIM TECNICO DA SECRETARIA DO SANEAMENTO, HABITACAO E OBRAS (BL) [03569746] **2225**

BOLETIM TECNICO - DEPARTAMENTO NACIONAL DE OBRAS CONTRA AS SECAS (BL/0374-6658) [05711158] 67, **2087**

BOLETIM TECNICO DO SENAC (BL) [02241279] **1728**

BOLETIM TECNICO - EMPASC (BL/0100-7416) [07867787] **67**

BOLETIM TECNICO - INSTITUTO DE PESCA (BL/0103-1767) [I01031767] **2297**

BOLETIM TRIMESTRAL - BANCO DE PORTUGAL (PO/0870-0095) [09439678] 779, **1548**

BOLETIM TRIMESTRAL DAS ESTATISTICAS DA AGRICULTURA E DA PESCA : CONTINENTE E ILHAS ADJACENTES (PO) [02471604] 67, **151**

BOLETIM TRIMESTRAL DE ESTATISTICA (FUNCHAL) (PO/0303-1705) [05693169] **5323**

BOLETIM TRIMESTRAL DE ESTATISTICA - INSTITUTO NACIONAL DE ESTATISTICA. DELEGACAO SE S. TOME E PRINCIPE (SF/0303-1675) [01792548] **5323**

BOLETIM UERJ (BL) [02163258] **1812**

BOLETIM / UNIVERSIDADE ESTADUAL DE LONDRINA, CCH, CENTRO DE LETRAS E CIENCIAS HUMANAS (BL) [10812583] 2843, **5193**

BOLETIN (BO) [01789102] **1402**

BOLETIN (CL) [05297558] **262**

BOLETIN - ACADEMIA NORTEAMERICANA DE LA LENGUA ESPANOLA (US/0884-0091) [03020203] 3368, **3269**

BOLETIN / ACADEMIA VENEZOLANA DE LA LENGUA CORRESPONDIENTE DE LA ESPANOLA (VE/1012-960X) [05660556] **3368**

BOLETIN AGROPECUARIO ANDINO (PE) [05653687] **67**

BOLETIN AGROPECUARIO (INDUSTRIA LACTEA VENEZOLANA. DEPARTAMENTO DE ASISTENCIA TECNICA AGROPECUARIA) (VE) [08852605] **67**

BOLETIN AMERICANISTA (SP/0520-4100) [04748557] **2611**

BOLETIN ANGLOHISPANO (US/0731-8111) [08252499] **2942**

BOLETIN ANTARTICO CHILENO (CL/0716-0763) [07902010] **2551**

BOLETIN ANUARIO - BANCO CENTRAL DEL ECUADOR (EC) [04388874] **5323**

BOLETIN - ARCHIVO GENERAL DE LA PROVINCIA DE SANTA FE (AG/0325-6081) [03364778] **2723**

BOLETIN (ARCHIVO NACIONAL (NICARAGUA) (NQ) [19409217] **2480**

BOLETIN ARQUEOLOGICO TARRAGONA. 1943 (SP/0034-0863) [I00340863] **262**

BOLETIN - ASOC. LATINO-AMERICANA DE FILOSOFOS CAT (BL) [02242047] **4342**

BOLETIN / ASOCIACION ARGENTINA DE ASTRONOMIA (AG/0571-3285) [04625577] **393**

BOLETIN - ASOCIACION DE BIBLIOTECAS UNIVERSITARIAS Y ESPECIALIZADAS DE NICARAGUA (NQ) [01787586] **3196**

BOLETIN ASTRONOMICO DEL OBSERVATORIO DE MADRID (SP/0373-7101) [03469162] **393**

BOLETIN ASTRONOMICO. SERIE B (EC) [01796427] **393**

BOLETIN AURIENSE (SP/0210-8445) [I02108445] **262**

BOLETIN AVGMP (VE) [02920407] **1367**

BOLETIN / BANCO DE LA REPUBLICA, JUNTA DIRECTIVA (CK) [25495737] **3085**

BOLETIN BIBLIOGRAFICO - BIBLIOTECA CENTRAL DE LA ARMADA (AG) [05366769] **411**

BOLETIN BIBLIOGRAFICO DE LA ESCUELA NACIONAL DE CIENCIAS BIOLOGICOS (MX/0185-0997) [02448595] **449**

BOLETIN BIBLIOGRAFICO DE LA PREVENCION (SP/0210-2439) [I02102439] 2859, **1656**

BOLETIN BIBLIOGRAFICO - DEPARTAMENTO DE SELECCION Y REGISTRO DE MATERIAL BIBLIOGRAFICO (UY) [06187062] **411**

BOLETIN BIBLIOGRAFICO DISTRITO FEDERAL (MEXICO) (MX) [07543107] **3079**

BOLETIN BIBLIOGRAFICO ICCE (SP) [01794552] **1793**

BOLETIN BIBLIOGRAFICO MEXICANO (MX/0185-2027) [01536671] **3457**

BOLETIN BIBLIOGRAFICO (REGIONAL CENTER FOR BOOK PROMOTION IN LATIN AMERICA AND THE CARIBBEAN) (CK/0120-1204) [05770781] **4824**

BOLETIN BIMESTRAL (MX) [06414620] **1465**

BOLETIN BIMESTRAL INFORMATIVO - BANCO DE CREDITO LOCAL DE ESPANA (SP) [02243733] **779**

BOLETIN BOLSA DE TRABAJO (MX) [05664437] **1656**

BOLETIN BOTANICO LATINOAMERICANO (US) [06262641] **502**

BOLETIN / CEHILA (CK) [07367785] **4939**

BOLETIN / CENTRO DE ESTUDIOS LEGALES Y SOCIALES (AG) [12562030] **4504**

BOLETIN / CENTRO DE ESTUDIOS MONETARIOS LATINOAMERICANOS (MX) [05301100] **779**

BOLETIN CHILENO DE PARASITOLOGIA (CL/0365-9402) [05968945] **449**

BOLETIN CHILENO DE PARASITOLOGIA (CL/0006-6176) [02574319] **449**

BOLETIN CHITAKOLLA : EDICION MENSUAL DEL CENTRO DE FORMACION E INVESTIGACION DE LAS CULTURAS INDIAS (BO) [18158795] **2257**

BOLETIN CIENTIFICO - CENTRO DE INVESTIGACIONES OCEANOGRAFICAS E HIDROGRAFICAS (CK/0120-0542) [08428841] **1447**

BOLETIN CINTERFOR, OIT (UY/0254-2420) [06785532] **1911**

BOLETIN / CIRCA, CENTRO DE INFORMACION Y REFERENCIA SOBRE CENTROAMERICA Y EL CARIBE (CR) [24557076] **2511**

BOLETIN / CIRCULO DE EMPRESARIOS (SP/0211-1535) [14361783] **861**

BOLETIN / CODECAL, CORPORACION INTEGRAL PARA EL DESARROLLO CULTURAL Y SOCIAL (CK) [21920667] **1728**

BOLETIN COMERCIAL / INSTITUTO NACIONAL DE PESCA (UY) [07939123] 2297, **1599**

BOLETIN / COMISION ANDINA DE JURISTAS (PE) [14909951] 4504, **2942**

BOLETIN - COMISION COORDINADORA DE LA INDUSTRIA SIDERURGICA (MX) [04474961] **1599**

BOLETIN - COMISION DE INTEGRACION ELECTRICA REGIONAL (UY) [03476851] **4633**

BOLETIN / COMISION NACIONAL DE PROMOCION Y PROTECCION DE LOS DERECHOS HUMANOS (NQ) [20287460] **4504**

BOLETIN - COMITE CRISTIANO DE SOLIDARIDAD MONSENOR ROMERO (MX) [13791065] 5240, **4939**

BOLETIN COPAL (PE) [09298733] **2257**

BOLETIN CULTURAL Y BIBLIOGRAFICO (CK/0404-7710) [01519108] **3368**

BOLETIN DE ANDEBU / ASOCIACION NACIONAL DE BROADCASTERS URUGUAYOS (UY) [08655886] **1127**

BOLETIN DE ANTROPOLOGIA (CK/0120-2510) [03790728] **232**

BOLETIN DE ANTROPOLOGIA AMERICANA (MX/0252-841X) [07115170] **232**

BOLETIN DE ARQUEOLOGIA / FUNDACION DE INVESTIGACIONES ARQUEOLOGICAS NACIONALES (CK) [15161341] **262**

BOLETIN DE ARTE MALAGA (SP/0211-8483) [I02118483] **344**

BOLETIN DE BELLAS ARTES (SP/0210-6531) [05994454] **344**

BOLETIN DE BIOTECNOLOGIA : ORGANO DE DIFUSION DEL COMITE PERMANENTE DE BIOTECNOLOGIA DE LA ASOCIACION INTERCIENCIA (CR/0255-7924) [18542259] **3690**

BOLETIN DE CULTIVOS TROPICALES : REVISTA DEL MINISTERIO DE EDUCACION SUPERIOR DE LA REPUBLICA DE CUBA / INCA (CU) [24601456] 165, **67**

BOLETIN DE DERECHO FISCAL (AG) [02767139] **4713**

BOLETIN DE DERECHOS HUMANOS (BO) [06523667] **4504**

BOLETIN DE DIVULGACION TECNICA / SECRETARIA DE ESTADO DE AGRICULTURA Y GANADERIA DE LA NACION, INSTITUTO NACIONAL DE TECNOLOGIA AGROPECUARIA, ESTACION EXPERIMENTAL REGIONAL AGROPECUARIA ANGUIL (AG/0325-2167) [05720126] **67**

BOLETIN DE DIVULGACIONES (MX/0417-9455) [01675743] **4163**

BOLETIN DE ESTADISTICA (BOGOTA, COLOMBIA) (CK/0120-6281) [12428031] **5323**

BOLETIN DE ESTADISTICA (MADRID, SPAIN: 1980) *See* BOLETIN MENSUAL DE ESTADISTICA/ INSTITUTO NACIONAL DE ESTADISTICA **5323**

BOLETIN DE ESTADISTICA MINERA (CL/0577-7933) [03098630] 2135, **2002**

BOLETIN DE ESTADISTICA (UNIVERSIDAD DE PANAMA. DEPARTAMENTO DE ESTADISTICA) (PN) [15687420] **5323**

BOLETIN DE ESTADISTICAS LABORALES (SP/0212-7180) [11985271] 5275, **1656**

BOLETIN DE ESTUDIOS ECONOMICOS (SP/0006-6249) [02258439] **1465**

BOLETIN DE ESTUDIOS MEDICOS Y BIOLOGICOS (MX/0067-9666) [01777912] 3828, **449**

BOLETIN DE FILOLOGIA (CL/0067-9674) [02952097] **3269**

BOLETIN DE FUENTES PARA LA HISTORIA ECONOMICA DE MEXICO (MX) [23003156] **1548**

BOLETIN DE GEOLOGIA (CARACAS) (VE/0006-6281) [01475737] **1367**

BOLETIN DE HISTORIA Y ANTIGUEDADES (CK/0006-6303) [01606508] **2723**

BOLETIN DE INFORMACION - CAMARA DE COMERCIO HISPANO COLOMBIANA (CK) [04473584] **818**

BOLETIN DE INFORMACION (CENTRO DE INFORMACION DOCUMENTAL (SPAIN)) (SP) [08515413] **2480**

BOLETIN DE INFORMACION CIENTIFICA Y TECNICA CUBANA *See* REVISTA DE INFORMACION CIENTIFICA Y TECNICA CUBANA **5148**

BOLETIN DE INFORMACION DEL CENTRO INTERAMERICANO DE ARTESANIAS Y ARTES POPULARES *See* ARTESANIAS DE AMERICA **341**

BOLETIN DE INFORMACION DEL LABORATORIO DE CARRETERAS Y GEOTECNIA (SP/0210-9085) [06883264] **5439**

BOLETIN DE INFORMACION ESTADISTICA / SISTEMA ESTATAL DE INFORMACION, COPLADE-CHIHUAHUA (MX) [23936466] **5323**

BOLETIN DE INFORMACION EXTRANJERA / MINISTERIO DE AGRICULTURA, PESCA Y ALIMENTACION, INSTITUTO DE ESTUDIOS AGRARIOS, PESQUEROS Y ALIMENTARIOS *SUSPENDED.* (SP) [17458500] **1548**

BOLETIN DE INFORMACION (MADRID, SPAIN) (SP) [12212121] **3196**

●BOLETIN DE INFORMACION SOBRE ECONOMIA CUBANA / CIEM (CU) [26381132] **1465**

BOLETIN DE INFORMACIONES CIENTIFICAS NACIONALES *SUSPENDED.* (EC) [02258443] **5089**

BOLETIN DE INVESTIGACION - FACULTAD DE AGRONOMIA (MONTEVIDEO) (UY/0797-0315) [18760968] **67**

BOLETIN DE INVESTIGACIONES E INFORMACION TURISTICA (CK) [01787786] **5465**

BOLETIN DE JURISPRUDENCIA CONSTITUCIONAL : BJC (SP) [09500592] **3092**

BOLETIN DE JURISPRUDENCIA Y RESOLUCIONES ADMINISTRATIVAS SOBRE URBANISMO Y VIVIENDA (SP) [01787418] 2816, **2942**

BOLETIN DE LA A.N.A.B.A (SP/0044-9288) [07823387] 2480, **3196**

BOLETIN DE LA ACADEMIA ARGENTINA DE LETRAS (AG/0001-3757) [01888273] 3269, **3368**

BOLETIN DE LA ACADEMIA CHILENA CORRESPONDIENTE DE LA REAL ACADEMIA ESPAÑOLA (CL/0716-5463) [01387822] **3368**

BOLETIN DE LA ACADEMIA CHILENA DE LA HISTORIA (CL/0716-5439) [01460604] **2723**

BOLETIN DE LA ACADEMIA COLOMBIANA (CK/0001-3773) [01460605] **2513**

BOLETIN DE LA ACADEMIA DE HISTORIA DEL VALLE DEL CAUCA (CK/0120-9493) [06501189] **2723**

BOLETIN DE LA ACADEMIA GALEGA DE CIENCIAS (SP/0212-9051) [14772648] **5089**

BOLETIN DE LA ACADEMIA NACIONAL DE CIENCIAS (AG/0325-2051) [02444268] **5089**

BOLETIN DE LA ACADEMIA NACIONAL DE LA HISTORIA (AG/0325-0482) [08759950] **2723**

BOLETIN DE LA ACADEMIA NACIONAL DE LA HISTORIA (CARACAS) (VE/0254-7325) [01460627] **2723**

BOLETIN DE LA ACADEMIA PUERTORRIQUEÑA DE LA HISTORIA (PR/0567-6037) [01460629] **2723**

BOLETIN DE LA ACADEMIE HONDURENA DE LA LENGUA (HO/0065-0471) [03248828] **3269**

BOLETIN DE LA ANABAD (SP/0210-4164) [I02104164] **2480**

BOLETIN DE LA ASOCIACION DE DEMOGRAFIA HISTORICA (SP/0213-1145) [11896886] **4550**

BOLETIN DE LA ASOCIACION ESPAÑOLA DE COLO-PROTOLOGIA (SP/0210-0940) [I02100940] **3558**

BOLETIN DE LA ASOCIACION ESPAÑOLA DE ENDOSCOPIA DIGESTIVA (SP/0210-1262) [I02101262] **3795**

BOLETIN DE LA ASOCIACION ESPAÑOLA DE ENTOMOLOGIA (SP/0210-8984) [05873153] **5606**

BOLETIN DE LA ASOCIACION ESPAÑOLA DE ORIENTALISTAS (SP/0571-3692) [01746613] **2647**

BOLETIN DE LA ASOCIACION MEDICA DE PUERTO RICO (PR/0004-4849) [01514474] **3558**

BOLETIN DE LA BIBLIOTECA DE LOS TRIBUNALES DEL DISTRITO FEDERAL FUNDACION ROJAS ASTUDILLO (VE/0528-0761) [05268464] **3196**

BOLETIN DE LA BIBLIOTECA DE MENENDEZ PELAYO / SOCIEDAD DE MENENDEZ PELAYO (SP/0006-1646) [11721235] **411**

BOLETIN DE LA BIBLIOTECA NACIONAL (CARACAS) (VE/1012-9464) [01473539] **2724**

BOLETIN DE LA BIBLIOTECA NACIONAL (LIMA) (PE/0031-6067) [02266013] **3196**

BOLETIN DE LA CAMARA DE CUENTAS Y DEL TRIBUNAL SUPERIOR ADMINISTRATIVO (DR) [07502306] **4713**

BOLETIN DE LA CATEDRA DE PEDIATRIA DE MADRID (SP/0377-8207) [02489588] **3901**

BOLETIN DE LA CIER (UY) [17342231] **4760**

BOLETIN DE LA ESCUELA DE CIENCIAS ANTROPOLOGICAS DE LA UNIVERSIDAD DE YUCATAN (MX) [05672342] **232**

BOLETIN DE LA INSTITUCION LIBRE DE ENSEÑANZA (SP) [17309889] **1728**

BOLETIN DE LA NORMALIZACION ESPAÑOLA UNE (SP) [04453322] **1966**

BOLETIN DE LA NORMALIZACION ESPNOLA UNE *See* UNE **4033**

BOLETIN DE LA OFICINA SANITARIA PANAMERICANA (US/0030-0632) [02258447] **4769**

BOLETIN DE LA PROVINCIA DE SAN JOSE DE LA ORDEN DE AGUSTINOS RECOLETOS (SP) [02602201] **4939**

BOLETIN DE LA REAL ACADEMIA DE BUENAS LETRAS DE BARCELONA (SP/0210-7481) [01635574] **2843**

BOLETIN DE LA REAL ACADEMIA DE CORDOBA, DE CIENCIAS, BELLAS LETRAS Y NOBLES ARTES (SP/0034-060X) [11700983] **2843**

BOLETIN DE LA REAL ACADEMIA DE LA HISTORIA (MADRID) (SP/0034-0626) [01460620] **2611**

BOLETIN DE LA REAL ACADEMIA ESPAÑOLA (SP/0210-4822) [01193036] **3269**

BOLETIN DE LA REAL SOCIEDAD GEOGRAFICA (SP) [06879213] **2556**

BOLETIN DE LA SECRETARIA DE ESTADO DE COMUNICACIONES (AG) [01798896] **1144**

BOLETIN DE LA SOCIEDAD ARAGONESA DE PEDIATRIA (SP/0211-2051) [I02112051] **3901**

BOLETIN DE LA SOCIEDAD ARGENTINA DE BOTANICA (AG/0373-580X) [02458066] **502**

BOLETIN DE LA SOCIEDAD BOLIVARIANA DEL PARAGUAY (PY/0583-7316) [01952699] **2724**

BOLETIN DE LA SOCIEDAD BOTANICA DE MEXICO (MX/0366-2128) [02456030] **503**

BOLETIN DE LA SOCIEDAD CASTELLONENSE DE CULTURA (SP/0210-1475) [02157527] **2843**

BOLETIN DE LA SOCIEDAD CHILENA DE QUIMICA (CL/0366-1644) [I03661644] **962**

BOLETIN DE LA SOCIEDAD ESPAÑOLA DE ANTROPOLOGIA BIOLOGICA (SP) [08938266] 449, **232**

BOLETIN DE LA SOCIEDAD ESPAÑOLA DE CERAMICA Y VIDRIO (1983) (SP/0366-3175) [11002768] **2586**

BOLETIN DE LA SOCIEDAD ESPAÑOLA DE HIDROLOGIA MEDICA (SP/0214-2813) [I02142813] **3558**

BOLETIN DE LA SOCIEDAD ESPAÑOLA DE HISTORIA DE LA FARMACIA (SP/0583-7472) [05803959] **4294**

BOLETIN DE LA SOCIEDAD GEOGRAFICA DE COLOMBIA (CK/0037-8577) [01765731] **2556**

BOLETIN DE LA SOCIEDAD GEOGRAFICA DE LIMA (PE/0037-8585) [01585593] **2556**

BOLETIN DE LA SOCIEDAD GEOGRAFICA Y DE HISTORIA "SUCRE" (BO/0254-7449) [I02547449] **2556**

BOLETIN DE LA SOCIEDAD GEOLOGICA DEL PERU (PE/0079-1091) [01382276] **1367**

BOLETIN DE LA SOCIEDAD MATEMATICA MEXICANA (MX/0037-8615) [07079058] **3497**

BOLETIN DE LA SOCIEDAD MICOLOGICA DE MADRID (SP/0214-140X) [20821456] **574**

BOLETIN DE LA SOCIEDAD QUIMICA DEL PERU (PE/0037-8623) [I00378623] **962**

BOLETIN DE LA SOCIEDAD VALENCIANA DE PATOLOGIA DIGESTIVA (SP/0301-1143) [10215016] **3558**

BOLETIN DE LA SOCIEDAD VALENCIANA DE PEDIATRIA (SP/0489-3824) [20863003] **3901**

BOLETIN DE LA SOCIEDAD VASCO-NAVARRA DE PEDIATRIA (SP/0037-8658) [00972457] **3901**

BOLETIN DE LEGISLACION DE LAS COMUNIDADES AUTONOMAS : BCA (SP/0212-4750) [11920603] 2942, **4633**

BOLETIN DE LEGISLACION INDUSTRIAL (SP) 1599, **2942**

BOLETIN DE LIMA (PE/0253-0015) [07618299] **5193**

BOLETIN DE LITERATURA MEDIEVAL (SP) **3368**

BOLETIN DE MINAS Y ENERGIA (CK/0120-9523) [03457122] **2135**

BOLETIN DE MUSICA *See* MUSICA (CASA DE LAS AMERICAS: 1980) **4135**

BOLETIN DE MUSICA Y DANZA (PE) [05328233] 1311, **4104**

BOLETIN DE PLAGUICIDAS / CENTRO DE INVESTIGACION Y ASISTENCIA TOXICOLOGICA (AG) [09350631] **4244**

BOLETIN DE PRECIOS (CK) [05031151] **601**

BOLETIN DE PRECIOS AGRARIOS ED. SEMANAL *CEASED.* (SP/0213-3407) [I02133407] **67**

BOLETIN DE PRENSA / COMITE PERMANENTE POR LA DEFENSA DE LOS DERECHOS HUMANOS, COMISION COORDINADORA (CK) [19830037] **4504**

BOLETIN DE PROMECAFE (CR) [10294657] **2365**

BOLETIN DE PSICOLOGIA (CU/0253-5742) [07371503] **4577**

BOLETIN DE RESENAS (CENTRO DE INFORMACION Y DOCUMENTACION AGROPECUARIO) (CU) [08602804] **67**

BOLETIN DE RESENAS. TABACO (CU) [10012479] **67**

BOLETIN DE RESUMENES DE PATENTES (SP) **1301**

BOLETIN
Alphabetical Title Index

BOLETIN DE SANIDAD VEGETAL. PLAGAS (SP/0213-6910) [14948060] 67, **4244**

BOLETIN DE SISMOS PROXIMOS (SP/0211-108X) [06337856] **1402**

BOLETIN DE SUMARIOS (SP) **2611**

BOLETIN DE SUMARIOS (SP) **5193**

BOLETIN DEL ARCHIVO GENERAL DE LA NACION (CARACAS) (VE/0042-3378) [06471926] **2480**

BOLETIN DEL ARCHIVO GENERAL DE LA NACION (SANTO DOMINGO) (DR/1012-9472) [01625187] **2480**

BOLETIN DEL ARCHIVO HISTORICO DE MIRAFLORES (VE/0042-3386) [01473465] 2724, **2480**

BOLETIN DEL BANCO DE DATOS (CL) [02242165] **4550**

BOLETIN DEL CENTRO DE CALCULO DE LA UNIVERSIDAD COMPLUTENSE (SP/0210-9743) [I02109743] **1172**

BOLETIN DEL CENTRO DE ESTUDIOS GENEALOGICOS DE CORDOBA (AG) [07371162] **2439**

BOLETIN DEL CENTRO DE INVESTIGACIONES HISTORICAS Y ESTETICAS (VE/0506-600X) [02148979] **293**

BOLETIN DEL CENTRO NACIONAL DE ALIMENTACION Y NUTRICION (SP/0211-1128) [08377864] **4188**

BOLETIN DEL CENTRO NAVAL (AG) [05543547] **4175**

BOLETIN DEL CENTRO PANAMERICANO DE FIEBRE AFTOSA (BL/0009-0131) [01640862] **3558**

BOLETIN DEL CONSEJO SUPERIOR DE DEPORTES (SP) [04078143] **1855**

BOLETIN DEL DEPARTAMENTO DE GEOLOGIA, UNI-SON (MX/0185-0873) [05321248] **1367**

BOLETIN DEL DEPARTAMENTO DE INVESTIGACION DE LAS TRADICIONES POPULARES (MX) [04455405] **2318**

BOLETIN DEL DERECHO DE AUTOR (MX) [04125942] **1301**

BOLETIN DEL FMI (US/0250-7420) [07578615] **779**

BOLETIN DEL INSTITUTO AMERICANO DE ESTUDIOS VASCOS (AG/0020-3637) [02697473] **3269**

BOLETIN DEL INSTITUTO DE ESTUDIOS ASTURIANOS (SP/0020-384X) [02098172] **2679**

BOLETIN DEL INSTITUTO DE ESTUDIOS AYMARAS (PE/0258-8536) [18502817] **2724**

BOLETIN DEL INSTITUTO DE HISTORIA ARGENTINA Y AMERICANA DOCTOR EMILIO RAVIGNANI (AG/0524-9767) [01285469] **2612**

BOLETIN DEL INSTITUTO DE INVESTIGACIONES BIBLIOGRAFICAS (MX) [20557995] **411**

BOLETIN DEL INSTITUTO DE INVESTIGACIONES ELECTRICAS (MX/0185-0059) [04320341] **2037**

BOLETIN DEL INSTITUTO DE SALUD PUBLICA DE CHILE (CL) [08349328] **4769**

BOLETIN DEL INSTITUTO DE TONANTZINTLA (MX/0303-7584) [01793973] **393**

BOLETIN DEL INSTITUTO ESPANOL DE OCEANOGRAFIA (1983) (SP/0074-0195) [11010248] **1447**

BOLETIN DEL INSTITUTO GEMOLOGICO ESPANOL (SP/0210-7228) [I02107228] **2913**

BOLETIN DEL INSTITUTO OCEANOGRAFICO DE LA UNIVERSIDAD DE ORIENTE (VE/0020-417X) [02097136] **1447**

BOLETIN DEL INSTITUTO RIVA-AGUERO (PE/0459-410X) [02263580] **1074**

BOLETIN DEL MINISTERIO DE JUSTICIA (AG) [07808505] **3139**

BOLETIN DEL MINISTERIO DE TRABAJO Y SEGURIDAD SOCIAL (SP/0214-2406) [18700346] **3144**

BOLETIN DEL MUSEO ARQUEOLOGICO NACIONAL (SP/0212-5544) [12866181] **262**

BOLETIN DEL MUSEO CHILENO DE ARTE PRECOLOMBINO (CL/0716-1530) [16813243] **232**

BOLETIN DEL MUSEO DE CIENCIAS NATURALES Y ANTROPOLOGICAS JUAN CORNELIO MOYANO (AG/0326-1484) [07956482] **262**

BOLETIN DEL MUSEO DEL HOMBRE DOMINICANO (DR) [02517690] **2724**

BOLETIN DEL MUSEO DEL PRADO (SP/0210-8143) [07937326] **4085**

BOLETIN DEL MUSEO E INSTITUTO CAMON AZNAR (SP/0211-3171) [07470606] **344**

BOLETIN DEL PROGRAMA ARQUEOLOGIA DE RESCATE / CORPOZULIA -UNIVERSIDAD DEL ZULIA, CENTRO DE ESTUDIOS HISTORICOS (VE) [09227555] 2257, **262**

BOLETIN DEL PROLAP (AG) [25505953] **4550**

BOLETIN DEL SECRETARIADO TECNICO (DR/1012-9480) [10164333] **861**

BOLETIN DEL SEMINARIO DE ESTUDIOS DE ARTE Y ARQUEOLOGIA **CEASED.** (SP) [02437211] **262**

BOLETIN DEL SEMINARIO DE ESTUDIOS DE ARTE Y ARQUEOLOGIA / UNIVERSIDAD DE VALLADOLID, FACULTAD DE FILOSOFIA Y LETRAS (SP) [07243478] 344, **262**

BOLETIN DEL SISTEMA ESTATAL DE DOCUMENTACION DEL ESTADO DE MEXICO (MX/0188-4492) [I01884492] 3196, **4633**

BOLETIN DEMOGRAFICO - CENTRO LATINOAMERICANO DE DEMOGRAFIA (CL/0378-5386) [02636534] **4550**

BOLETIN DERMATOLOGIA SANITARIO (VE/0798-4618) [I07984618] **3718**

BOLETIN DOCUMENTAL SOBRE LAS MUJERES (MX) [02661966] **5551**

BOLETIN ECONOMICO DE LA CONSTRUCCION 1956 (SP/0210-1947) [I02101947] **601**

BOLETIN ECONOMICO Y SOCIAL (BE) [02652140] **1656**

BOLETIN EPIDEMIOLOGICO DE CASTILLA Y LEON (SP/0214-3852) [I02143852] **4769**

BOLETIN EPIDEMIOLOGICO SEMANAL / MINISTERIO DE SANIDAD Y ASISTENCIA SOCIAL, DIRECCION DE SALUD PUBLICA, DEPARTAMENTO DE DEMOGRAFIA Y EPIDEMIOLOGIA, DIVISION DE EPIDEMIOLOGIA (VE) [07569344] 3712, **3734**

BOLETIN EPIDEMIOLOGICO SEMANAL - MINISTERIO DE SANIDAD Y CONSUMO. PUBLICACIONES. DOCUMENTACION Y BIBLIOTECA (SP/0210-1653) [I02101653] **3558**

BOLETIN ESTADISTICO (PY/0408-330X) [02521287] **779**

BOLETIN ESTADISTICO (AG) [01785958] **3999**

BOLETIN ESTADISTICO (PE) [01791779] **779**

BOLETIN ESTADISTICO - ASIGNACIONES FAMILIARES (UY) [06895103] **5275**

BOLETIN ESTADISTICO / BANCO CENTRAL DE LA REPUBLICA ARGENTINA, GERENCIA DE INVESTIGACIONES Y ESTADISTICAS ECONOMICAS (AG) [18373214] 779, **726**

BOLETIN ESTADISTICO - BANCO DE GUATEMALA (GT/0005-481X) [07545583] **779**

BOLETIN ESTADISTICO / BANCO NACIONAL DE AHORRO Y PRESTAMO (VE) [07505447] 779, **726**

BOLETIN ESTADISTICO / BANCOS CENTRALES DE LOS PAISES MIEMBROS DEL FLAR (CK) [24314313] **779**

BOLETIN ESTADISTICO DE BANCA MULTIPLE (MX/0185-6456) [26489437] **779**

BOLETIN ESTADISTICO DE LA OEA (US/0250-6092) [05369547] **1548**

BOLETIN ESTADISTICO - DIRECCION GENERAL DE ESTADISTICA Y CENSOS (ES) [02267425] **5323**

BOLETIN ESTADISTICO (DOMINICAN REPUBLIC. SECRETARIA DE ESTADO DE FINANZAS, DEPARTAMENTO DE ESTUDIOS ECONOMICOS) (DR) [10201714] 4713, **4696**

BOLETIN ESTADISTICO. INDICADORES ECONOMICOS (SP) [03038955] **779**

BOLETIN ESTADISTICO TRIMESTRAL (INSTITUTO NACIONAL DE ESTADISTICA). (BOLIVIA) (BL/1012-9529) [09910588] 1548, **1530**

BOLETIN ESTADISTICO TRIMESTRAL - INSTITUTO NACIONAL DE ESTADISTICA Y CENSOS **SUSPENDED.** (AG/0325-1969) [03862854] **5323**

BOLETIN GENETICO (AG/0067-9720) [I00679720] **543**

BOLETIN GENETICO. ENGLISH EDITION (AG/0325-8319) [01536682] 503, **543**

BOLETIN GEOLOGICO - INSTITUTO GEOGRAFICO NACIONAL (GT/0367-7923) [03007163] **1367**

BOLETIN GEOLOGICO Y MINERO (SP/0366-0176) [04219475] **1367**

BOLETIN - GUATEMALA (CITY) BIBLIOTECA NACIONAL (GT) [01475615] **3196**

BOLETIN HISTORIAL (CK) [03464798] **2724**

BOLETIN HISTORICO (CARACAS) (VE/0016-2701) [01299247] **2724**

BOLETIN HOSPITAL DE VINA DEL MAR (CL) [06541858] **3558**

BOLETIN ICE ECONOMICO (SP/0214-8307) [I02148307] 1465, **1966**

BOLETIN INDIGENISTA (BO) [06396748] 2724, **232**

BOLETIN INDIGENISTA VENEZOLANO (VE/0523-9133) [02258462] 2724, **232**

BOLETIN INDUSTRIAL (EC/0523-9141) [02155694] **1599**

BOLETIN INFORMATION - CEBIDE (AG/0325-8645) [09624533] **3558**

BOLETIN INFORMATIVO (SP) [07473591] **3269**

BOLETIN INFORMATIVO ANAFEM (MX) [05666573] **825**

BOLETIN INFORMATIVO (ARGENTINA.) DEPARTAMENTO GENERAL DE IRRIGACION (AG/0325-8106) [08316710] **2087**

BOLETIN INFORMATIVO (ASOCIACION DE HISTORIADORES LATINOAMERICANISTAS EUROPEOS) (GW) [09904031] **2724**

BOLETIN INFORMATIVO - BANCO CENTRAL (SP) [02244126] 1549, **779**

BOLETIN INFORMATIVO (BANCO CENTRAL HISPANOAMERICANO) *See* BOLETIN INFORMATIVO / CENTRAL HISPANO **779**

BOLETIN INFORMATIVO - CEDOCLA (MX) [02439113] **344**

● BOLETIN INFORMATIVO / CENTRAL HISPANO (SP) [26093857] **779**

BOLETIN INFORMATIVO - CENTRO DE INVESTIGACION PARA LA INTEGRACION SOCIAL (MX) [05423075] **5240**

BOLETIN INFORMATIVO / COMISION DE DERECHOS HUMANOS DE GUATEMALA (MX) [16103747] **4504**

BOLETIN INFORMATIVO / CONIECE, CORPORACION NICARAGUENSE DE EMPRESAS DE COMERCIO EXTERIOR (NQ) [22877284] **825**

BOLETIN INFORMATIVO DE LA ASOCIACION DE BIBLIOTECARIOS GRADUADOS DE LA REPUBLICA ARGENTINA (AG) [03460380] **3196**

BOLETIN INFORMATIVO DE PRECIOS Y MERCADOS (DR) [05654440] **67**

BOLETIN INFORMATIVO DEL ARCHIVO NACIONAL DE PANAMA (PN) [03603961] **2724**

BOLETIN INFORMATIVO DEL DEPARTAMENTO DE DERECHO POLITICO (SP) [07397536] **2942**

BOLETIN INFORMATIVO HONDURAS / CENTRO DE DOCUMENTACION DE HONDURAS, CEDOH (HO) [11646157] **1549**

BOLETIN INFORMATIVO / INSTITUTO DE ANTROPOLOGIA (MX) [15676729] **232**

BOLETIN INFORMATIVO - INSTITUTO DE FILOSOFIA DEL DERECHO (VE) [06100541] **2942**

BOLETIN INFORMATIVO (INTER-AMERICANA CONFERENCE ON SOCIAL SECURITY) (MX) [09700960] 2876, **5275**

BOLETIN INFORMATIVO / SIECA (GT) [28487167] **1465**

BOLETIN INFORMATIVO TECHINT (AG/0497-0292) [18115414] **1599**

BOLETIN INICA (CU) [14950991] **67**

BOLETIN / INSTITUTO DE ESTUDIOS IBEROAMERICANOS (GW) [23742441] **2679**

BOLETIN / INSTITUTO DEL MAR DEL PERU (PE/0378-7699) [01395108] **4163**

BOLETIN - INSTITUTO MEXICANO DE PLANEACION Y OPERACION DE SISTEMAS (MX) [04323731] **1599**

BOLETIN / INSTITUTO NACIONAL DE CIENCIAS AGRICOLAS (CU) [24673654] 165, **67**

BOLETIN INTERAMERICANO DE CONTABILIDAD (MX) [05049751] **739**

BOLETIN INTERNACIONAL - BANCO DE VIZCAYA (SP) [03725355] **779**

BOLETIN INTERNACIONAL / URNG, UNIDAD REVOLUCIONARIA NACIONAL GUATEMALTECA (GT) [19273568] **4465**

BOLETIN INTEXTAR DEL INSTITUTO DE INVESTIGACION TEXTIL Y DE COOPERACION INDUSTRIAL (SP) [16144388] **5348**

BOLETIN / ISIS INTERNACIONAL, RED DE SALUD DE LAS MUJERES LATINOAMERICANAS Y DEL CARIBE (CL) [27158752] **5552**

BOLETIN LURATHA / INSTITUTO NACIONAL DE ANTROPOLOGIA (BO) [09233304] **232**

BOLETIN MEDICO DEL HOSPITAL INFANTIL DE MEXICO (SPANISH EDITION) (MX/0539-6115) [10062797] **3901**

BOLETIN MENSUAL - BANCO CENTRAL DE CHILE (CL/0716-2367) [02080926] **779**

Alphabetical Title Index — BOLLETTINO

BOLETIN MENSUAL - BANCO CENTRAL DE VENEZUELA (VE/0252-8991) [02968958] **779**

BOLETIN MENSUAL - BANCO NACIONAL DE AHORRO Y PRESTAMO, GERENCIA DE ESTUDIOS E INVESTIGACIONES (VE) [03739459] **779**

BOLETIN MENSUAL DE ESTADISTICA (SP) [01963742] **5323**

● BOLETIN MENSUAL DE ESTADISTICA / INSTITUTO NACIONAL DE ESTADISTICA (SP) [25599454] **5323**

BOLETIN MENSUAL DE INFORMACION BASICA DEL SECTOR AGROPECUARIO Y FORESTAL / SECRETARIA DE AGRICULTURA Y RECURSOS HIDRAULICOS, SUBSECRETARIA DE PLANEACION, DIRECCION GENERAL DE ESTADISTICA (MX/0188-4360) [24557044] 2376, **67**

BOLETIN METEOROLOGICO (SP) **1421**

BOLETIN MEXICANO DE DERECHO COMPARADO (MX/0041-8633) [01536688] **3124**

BOLETIN / MEXICO (CITY). UNIVERSIDAD NACIONAL. INSTITUTO DE QUIMICA (MX) [01640262] **963**

BOLETIN MICOLOGICO (CL/0716-114X) [10773781] **5506**

BOLETIN MICROBIOLOGICO SEMANAL (SP) [25047263] **3712**

BOLETIN / MUSEO DE ZARAGOZA (SP/0212-548X) [11340478] **4085**

BOLETIN / MUSEO DEL ORO, BANCO DE LA REPUBLICA (CK) [05031193] **2724**

BOLETIN - OBSERVATORIO ASTRONOMICO MUNICIPAL DE ROSARIO (AG/0302-2277) [01793082] **393**

BOLETIN OFICIAL DE LA JURISDICCION ECLESIASTICA CASTRENSE (SP) [04219585] **5024**

BOLETIN OFICAL DEL ESTADO : GACETA DE MADRID (SP) [05332391] 4633, **2942**

BOLETIN OFICIAL DEL MINISTERIO DE DEFENSA (SP) [12333632] **4038**

BOLETIN OFICIAL DEL MINISTERIO DE ECONOMIA Y HACIENDA (SP) [19968918] **4633**

BOLETIN OFICIAL DEL MINISTERIO DE SANIDAD Y CONSUMO (SP/0212-9183) [28384664] 4769, **1293**

BOLETIN OFICIAL DEL TERRITORIO HISTORICO DE ALAVA (SP) **2724**

BOLETIN OFICIAL (DOMINICAN REPUBLIC. CAMARA DE CUENTAS) *See* BOLETIN DE LA CAMARA DE CUENTAS Y DEL TRIBUNAL SUPERIOR ADMINISTRATIVO **4713**

BOLETIN OFICIAL, MINISTERIO DE EDUCACION Y CIENCIA. ACTOS ADMINISTRATIVOS (SP) [09817771] 1728, **2942**

BOLETIN ORCYT / OFICINA REGIONAL DE CIENCIA Y TECNOLOGIA DE LA UNESCO PARA AMERICA LATINA Y EL CARIBE (UY) [27350169] **5089**

BOLETIN ROSTLAC / OFICINA REGIONAL DE CIENCIA Y TECNOLOGIA DE LA UNESCO PARA AMERICA LATINA Y EL CARIBE (UY) [07689413] **5089**

BOLETIN SEMESTRAL - COLEGIO DE MEXICO (MX/0543-7369) [02268297] **1089**

BOLETIN / SERVICIO NACIONAL DE GEOLOGIA Y MINERIA, CHILE (CL/0020-3939) [10263712] **1368**

BOLETIN / SIARB, SOCIEDAD DE INVESTIGACION DEL ARTE RUPESTRE DE BOLIVIA (BO) [17857574] **262**

BOLETIN SISMOLOGICO DE VENEZUELA / FUNDACION VENEZOLANA DE INVESTIGACIONES SISMOLOGICAS, DEPARTMENT DE SISMOLOGIA (VE) [18755701] **1403**

BOLETIN - SOCIEDAD NACIONAL DE MINERIA Y PETROLEO *See* MINERIA Y PETROLEO **4264**

BOLETIN TECNICO (MX/0185-2310) [11592043] **2376**

BOLETIN TECNICO - ARPEL (UY/0253-6005) [02869041] **4252**

BOLETIN TECNICO - CHILE. DIRECCION DE AGRICULTURA Y PESCA (CL/0577-7925) [03098499] **67**

BOLETIN TECNICO - ESTACION EXPERIMENTAL REGIONAL AGROPECUARIA BALCARCE (AG) [06264722] **68**

BOLETIN TECNICO - IAPAR (BL/0100-3054) [03959698] **68**

BOLETIN TECNICO / INTER-AMERICAN INSTITUTE OF AGRICULTURAL SCIENCES (CR/0574-203X) [01640777] 5089, **68**

BOLETIN TECNICO - UNIVERSIDAD DE CHILE, FACULTAD DE AGRONOMIA (CL/0304-5552) [01639465] **68**

BOLETIN TECNICO / UNIVERSIDAD DE CHILE, FACULTAD DE CIENCIAS AGRARIAS, VETERINARIAS Y FORESTALES, ESCUELA DE CIENCIAS FORESTALES (CL/0304-5560) [14106087] **2376**

BOLETIN TRIMESTRAL DE PRECIOS INTERNACIONALES DE PRODUCTOS BASICOS (US) [15182955] **825**

BOLETIN - UNIVERSIDAD DE PANAMA, DIRECCION DE PLANIFICACION UNIVERSITARIA (PN) [02477087] **1812**

BOLETIN - UNIVERSIDAD LIBRE, SECCIONAL DE PEREIRA, CENTRO DE INVESTIGACIONES (CK) [04479388] **5089**

BOLETIN - VENEZUELA. INSTITUTO AGRARIO NACIONAL (VE/0506-533X) [01477505] **68**

BOLETINES Y TRABAJOS - ACADEMIA ARGENTINA DE CIRUGIA (AG) [01342769] **3960**

BOLI YU TANGCI (CC/1000-2871) [21722478] **2586**

BOLIGTLLINGEN (DK/0107-8909) [09879268] **4550**

BOLINA ROMA (IT/1121-3108) [I11213108] **592**

BOLIVAR COMMERCIAL, THE (US) [14999861] **5700**

BOLIVAR HERALD-FREE PRESS (US) [19331492] **5702**

BOLIVIA BULLETIN (BO) [12795514] **2551**

BOLIVIA. CORTE SUPERIOR (DISTRITO JUDICIAL DE CHUQUISACA) *See* INFORME DE LABORES ... Y APERTURA DEL ANO JUDICIAL / CORTE SUPERIOR DEL DISTRITO JUDICIAL DE CHUQUISACA **2982**

BOLIVIA. DIRECCION GENERAL DE HIDROCARBUROS *See* INFORME PETROLERAS **4260**

BOLIVIA EN MARCHA / SECRETARIA NACIONAL DE TRABAJADORES (BO) [25427366] **1656**

BOLIVIA : GUIA ECLESIASTICA (BO) [04286735] **5024**

BOLIVIA. MINISTERIO DE PLANEAMIENTO Y COORDINACION *See* ENCUESTAS DE COYUNTURA (BOLIVIA) **1488**

BOLIVIA (MONTREAL) (CN/0824-3816) [10451289] **2724**

BOLIVIEN : ENERGIEWIRTSCHAFT (GW) [05725461] **1934**

BOLIVIEN, WIRTSCHAFTLICHE ENTWICKLUNG (GW) [01798760] **1549**

BOLIVIEN, WIRTSCHAFTSDATEN UND WIRTSCHAFTSDOKUMENTATION / BUNDESSTELLE FUER AUSSENHANDELSINFORMATION (GW) [10257202] **1549**

BOLLETI DE LA SOCIETAT ARQUEOLOGICA LULIANA 1978 (SP/0212-7458) [I02127458] **262**

BOLLETIN DE ARCHIVOS (SP/0210-4946) [06767838] **2480**

BOLLETINO - CENTRO DI STUDI FILOLOGICI E LINGUISTICI SICILIANI (IT/0577-277X) [03026217] **3269**

BOLLETINO - CONSOB (IT/1120-2998) [I11202998] **779**

BOLLETINO DEL CENTRO ROSSINIANO DI STUDI (IT/0411-5384) [02058658] **4104**

BOLLETINO DELL'ATLANTE LINGUISTICO ITALIANO (IT) [11026713] **3270**

BOLLETINO DELL'ISTITUTO CENTRALE PER LA PATOLOGIA DEL LIBRO. QUADERNI (IT/0392-8438) [11473177] **3196**

BOLLETINO - LEGA ITALIANA CONTRO L'EPILESSIA (IT/0394-560X) [I0394560X] **3828**

BOLLETINO : OFFICIAL PUBLICATION OF THE ITALIAN CATHOLIC FEDERATION (US/0745-256X) [08983972] **5024**

BOLLETINO TARIFFE TRASFERTE ITALIA (IT) **1656**

BOLLETINO UFFICIALE DELLA REGIONE : LOMBARDIA. TIPO B. C (IT) **4633**

BOLLETINO UFFICIALE DELLA REGIONE : MOLISE (IT) **4633**

● BOLLETTINO AIB (IT/1121-1490) [26395354] **3196**

BOLLETTINO AIPPO *See* NASCERE **2922**

BOLLETTINO ANDAMENTO COSTI INVESTIMENTO INDUSTRIA (IT) **1599**

BOLLETTINO ARCHITETTI (IT) **293**

BOLLETTINO - ASSOCIAZIONE ITALIANA VETERINARI PER PICCOLI ANIMALI (IT/0004-5977) [I00045977] **5506**

BOLLETTINO ASSOCIAZIONE REGIONALE INGEGNERI E ARCHITETTI DI PUGLIA (IT) **2019**

BOLLETTINO CERIS *See* QUADERNI CERIS **5143**

BOLLETTINO CHIMICO FARMACEUTICA (IT/0006-6648) [04055131] **4294**

BOLLETTINO (CIVICI MUSEI VENEZIANI D'ARTE E DI STORIA) (IT/0394-1027) [10736267] **4085**

BOLLETTINO COMMERCIALE FF SS (IT) **5429**

BOLLETTINO D'ARTE (IT/0391-9854) [01536690] **344**

BOLLETTINO D'ARTE. SUPPLEMENTO / MINISTERO PER I BENI CULTURALI E AMBIENTALI, UFFICIO CENTRALE PER I BENI AMBIENTALI, ARCHITETTONICI, ARCHEOLOGICI, ARTISTICI E STORICI (IT) [09833035] **344**

BOLLETTINO DEGLI INGEGNERI (IT) **601**

BOLLETTINO DEI BREVETTI PER INVENZIONI, MODELLI E MARCHI *CEASED.* (IT) [03260688] **1301**

BOLLETTINO DEI CHIMICI IGIENISTI. PARTE LEGISLATIVA. COMUNITA ECONOMICHE EUROPEE (IT) [11879788] **2942**

BOLLETTINO DEI CHIMICI IGIENISTI. PARTE LEGISLATIVA. REPUBBLICA ITALIANA (IT) [11203799] **3110**

BOLLETTINO DEI CHIMICI IGIENISTI. PARTE SCIENTIFICA (IT) [11879890] **963**

BOLLETTINO DEI CLASSICI (IT/0391-8270) [08287629] **1074**

BOLLETTINO DEI CONTRATTI (IT) **949**

BOLLETTINO DEI MUSEI COMUNALI DI ROMA (IT/0523-9346) [02785323] **4085**

BOLLETTINO DEI PREZZI : SETTIMANALE DELLA BORSA MERCI DI BARI (IT) [05724954] **825**

BOLLETTINO DEL C.I.R.V.I (IT) [09627999] **1812**

BOLLETTINO DEL CENTRO CAMUNO DI STUDI PREISTORICI (IT/0577-2168) [03032336] 262, **344**

BOLLETTINO DEL CENTRO DI STUDI PER LA STORIA DELL'ARCHITETTURA (IT) [09948868] **293**

BOLLETTINO DEL CENTRO DI STUDI VICHIANI (IT/0392-7334) [03038348] **4342**

BOLLETTINO DEL CENTRO MILANESE DI TERAPIA DELLA FAMIGLIA (IT) **2277**

BOLLETTINO DEL LABORATORIO DI ENTOMOLOGIA AGRARIA FILIPPO SILVESTRI PORTICI (IT) [05419364] **5578**

BOLLETTINO DEL LAVORO E DEI TRIBUTI (IT/0394-6592) [I03946592] **3144**

BOLLETTINO DEL MUSEO CIVICO DI PADOVA ... (IT/0393-0750) [10651136] **4085**

BOLLETTINO DEL MUSEO CIVICO DI STORIA NATURALE DI VENEZIA (IT/0505-205X) [01386704] **4163**

BOLLETTINO DEL MUSEO CIVICO DI STORIA NATURALE DI VERONA (IT/0392-0062) [02365712] 4163, **4085**

BOLLETTINO DEL SERVIZIO GEOLOGICO D'ITALIA (IT/0366-2241) [03130962] **1368**

BOLLETTINO DELL'ISTITUTO STORICO E DI CULTURA DELL'ARMA DEL GENIO (IT/0391-7088) [06680113] 1966, **4038**

BOLLETTINO DELL ISTITUTO DI FILOGIA DELL UNIVERSITA DI PADOVA (IT) **3368**

BOLLETTINO DELL'ISTITUTO DI LINGUE ESTERE / UNIVERSITA DEGLI STUDI DI GENOVA, FACOLTA DI ECONOMIA E COMMERCIO (IT/0433-3837) [20404169] **3270**

BOLLETTINO DELLA BADIA GRECA DI GROTTAFERRATA (IT) [01770821] **5024**

BOLLETTINO DELLA DEPUTAZIONE DI STORIA PATRIA PER L'UMBRIA (IT/0300-4422) [01421099] 4702, **4633**

BOLLETTINO DELLA DOMUS MAZZINIANA (IT/0012-5385) [05503864] **2679**

BOLLETTINO DELLA DOXA (IT) [06060509] **5240**

BOLLETTINO DELLA PREVENZIONE (IT) **1656**

BOLLETTINO DELLA SOCIETA DI STUDI VALDESI (IT/0037-8739) [05576548] **4939**

BOLLETTINO DELLA SOCIETA ENTOMOLOGICA ITALIANA (IT/0373-3491) [01765746] **5606**

BOLLETTINO DELLA SOCIETA GEOGRAFICA ITALIANA (IT/0037-8763) [01772449] **2556**

BOLLETTINO DELLA SOCIETA GEOGRAFICA ITALIANA (IT/0037-8755) [I00378755] **2556**

BOLLETTINO DELLA SOCIETA GEOLOGICA ITALIANA (IT/0037-8763) [01947477] **1368**

BOLLETTINO — Alphabetical Title Index

BOLLETTINO DELLA SOCIETA ITALIANA DI BIOLOGIA SPERIMENTALE (IT/0037-8771) [07163151] **449**

BOLLETTINO DELLA SOCIETA ITALIANA DI FARMACIA OSPEDALIERA (IT/0037-8798) [13037357] **4294**

BOLLETTINO DELLA SOCIETA ITALIANA DI TOPOGRAFIA E FOTOGRAMMETRIA (IT/0392-4424) [09193126] **2556**

BOLLETTINO DELLA SOCIETA MEDICO CHIRURGICA DELLA PROVINCIA DI CRIMONA (IT) [18466624] **3960**

BOLLETTINO DELLA SOCIETA PALEONTOLOGICA ITALIANA (IT/0375-7633) [01935741] **4226**

BOLLETTINO DELLA SOCIETA PAVESE DI STORIA PATRIA (IT) [05740629] **2679**

BOLLETTINO DELLA SOCIETA PER GLI STUDI STORICI, ARCHEOLOGICI ED ARTISTICI NELLA PROVINCIA DI CUNEO (IT) [21546359] 262, 344, **2679**

BOLLETTINO DELLA SOCIETA STORICA MAREMMANA (IT/0583-8002) [01942128] **2679**

BOLLETTINO DELLA SOCIETA STORICA VALTELLINESE (IT) [01952658] **2679**

BOLLETTINO DELLA UNIONE MATEMATICA ITAL ANA. A (IT/0392-4033) [02973154] **3497**

BOLLETTINO DELLA UNIONE STORIA ED ARTE (IT/0394-4727) [I03944727] **344**

BOLLETTINO DELL'ACCADEMIA GIOENIA DI SCIENZE NATURALI (IT) [16783892] **5089**

BOLLETTINO DELL'ANNO ... / SOCIETA TARQUINIENSE DI ARTE E STORIA (IT) [08158616] **2843**

BOLLETTINO DELL'ARCHIVIO PER LA STORIA DEL MOV MENTO SOCIALE CATTOLICO IN ITALIA (IT) [01731903] **4939**

BOLLETTINO DELL'ATLANTE LINGUISTICO MEDITERRANEO **CEASED.** (IT/0067-9879) [02789118] **3270**

BOLLETTINO DELLE ESTRAZIONI (IT) **818**

BOLLETTINO DELL'INSTITUTO DI ENTOMOLOGIA DELL'UNIVERSITA DEGLI STUDI DI BOLOGNA (IT/0373-5176) [04716483] **5578**

BOLLETTINO DELL'INSTITUTO SIEROTERAPICC MILANESE **CEASED.** (IT/0021-2547) [01607484] 560, 3734, **3667**

BOLLETTINO DELL'ISTITUTO DI FILOLOGIA GRECA (IT/0392-7628) [03460932] **3270**

BOLLETTINO DELL'ISTITUTO DI FILOLOGIA GRECA. SUPPLEMENTO (IT) [05579557] **3270**

BOLLETTINO DELL'ISTITUTO DI STORIA E DI ARTE DEL LAZIO MERIDIONALE (IT/0578-9850) [I05789850] 344, **2612**

BOLLETTINO DELL'ISTITUTO STORICO ARTISTICO ORVIETANO (IT/0391-8211) [05985301] **2612**

BOLLETTINO DI FARMACOSORVEGLIANZA (IT/1120-8678) [I11208678] **3558**

BOLLETTINO DI GEODESIA E SCIENZE AFFINI (IT/0006-6710) [08691758] **1352**

BOLLETTINO DI GEOFISICA TEORICA ED APPLICATA (IT/0006-6729) [02258481] **1403**

BOLLETTINO DI INFORMAZIONI COSTITUZIONALI E PARLAMENTARI. NUOVA SERIE (IT/0444-9266) [02176494] **3092**

BOLLETTINO DI ITALIANISTICA (NE/0168-7298) [11073013] **2513**

BOLLETTINO DI LEGISLAZIONE TECNICA (IT/0392-3789) [I03923789] **5089**

BOLLETTINO DI OCEANOLOGIA TEORICA ED APPLICATA (IT/0393-196X) [09549907] **1447**

BOLLETTINO DI OCULISTICA (IT/0006-677X) [11688696] **3872**

BOLLETTINO DI PESCA, PISCICOLTURA E IDROBIOLOGIA (IT/0006-6575) [02404996] **2297**

BOLLETTINO DI PSICHIATRIA BIOLOGICA (IT/0393-4853) [I03934853] **3922**

BOLLETTINO DI PSICOLOGIA APPLICATA (IT/0006-6761) [09199353] **4577**

BOLLETTINO DI STORIA DELLE SCIENZE MATEMATICHE (IT/0392-4432) [08679176] **3497**

BOLLETTINO DI STUDI E RICERCHE (IT/1121-6433) [23370536] **1812**

BOLLETTINO DI STUDI LATINI (IT/0006-6583) [02606414] 3368, **3270**

BOLLETTINO DI ZOOLOGIA (IT/0373-4137) [01536697] 449, **5578**

BOLLETTINO DI ZOOLOGIA AGRARIA E DI BACHICOLTURA (IT/0366-2403) [02606485] 5578, **68**

BOLLETTINO D'INFORMAZIONE DEGLI SLOVENI IN ITALIA *See* SLOVENI IN ITALIA **2273**

BOLLETTINO D'INFORMAZIONI / CENTRO DI RICERCHE INFORMATICHE PER I BENI CULTURALI (IT) [26002521] 2843, **316**

BOLLETTINO E MEMORIE DELLA SOCIETA PIEMONTESE DE CHIRURGIA (IT/0366-1970) [I03661970] **3961**

BOLLETTINO ECONOMICO (IT) [03688848] **1465**

BOLLETTINO ECONOMICO (ROME, ITALY) (IT/0393-2400) [10452690] **779**

BOLLETTINO ECONOMICO (VALLE D'AOSTA (ITALY). ASSESSORATO INDUSTRIA, COMMERCIO, ARTIGIANATO E TRASPORTI DELLA REGIONE) (IT) [09433515] **1549**

BOLLETTINO GEODETICO *See* BOLLETTINO DI GEODESIA E SCIENZE AFFINI **1352**

BOLLETTINO LEGGI E DECRETI (IT/0390-9131) [I03909131] **1656**

BOLLETTINO LIGUSTICO PER LA STORIA E LA CULTURA REGIONALE (IT) [02053939] **2612**

BOLLETTINO MALACOLOGICO (IT/0394-7149) [11202467] **5578**

BOLLETTINO MENSILE DI STATISTICA - ISTITUTO CENTRALE DI STATISTICA (IT/0021-3136) [02262820] **5323**

BOLLETTINO - MONUMENTI, MUSEI E GALLERIE PONTIFICIE (VC/1018-4317) [05371538] 4085, **344**

BOLLETTINO NAZIONALE PREVENZIONE INFORTUNI (IT/0392-3797) [I03923797] **1656**

BOLLETTINO PER LE FARMACODIPENDENZE E L'ALCOOLISMO (IT/0392-3126) [I03923126] **1341**

BOLLETTINO PREFILATELICO E STORICO-POSTALE (IT) [06792210] **2784**

BOLLETTINO PREZZI INGROSSO MERCATO AGRICOLO ALIMENTARE DI CREMONA (IT) **825**

BOLLETTINO PROTESTI CAMBIARI (IT) **818**

BOLLETTINO QUINDICINALE - AUTORITA GARANTE DELLA CONCORRENZA E DEL MERCATO (IT/1121-2861) [I11212861] **825**

BOLLETTINO S.I.A.M.E (IT/0393-3423) [07748421] **4379**

BOLLETTINO SCIENTIFICO DELLA FACOLTA DI ZOOTECNIA & VETERINARIA / UNIVERSITE NAZIONALE SOMALA, FACOLTA ZOOTECNIA E VETERINARIA (IT) [11563712] **5506**

BOLLETTINO STATISTICO QUADRIMESTRALE (ISTITUTO NAZIONALE DELLA PREVIDENZA SOCIALE (ITALY)) (IT) [09307546] 1656, **5275**

BOLLETTINO STATISTICO QUADRIMESTRALE (ISTITUTO NAZIONALE DELLA PREVIDENZA SOCIALE (ITALY). SERVIZIO STATISTICO ATTUARIALE) *See* BOLLETTINO STATISTICO QUADRIMESTRALE (ISTITUTO NAZIONALE DELLA PREVIDENZA SOCIALE (ITALY)) **5275**

BOLLETTINO STATISTICO (ROME, ITALY) (IT/0393-604X) [11615359] **779**

BOLLETTINO STORICO-BIBLIOGRAFICO SUBALPINO (IT/0391-6715) [01536701] **2679**

BOLLETTINO STORICO CREMONESE (IT) [03046318] **2679**

BOLLETTINO STORICO DELLA BASILICATA / A CURA DELLA DEPUTAZIONE DI STORIA PATRIA DELLA LUCANIA (IT/0394-1841) [17309629] **2679**

BOLLETTINO STORICO DELLA CITTA DI FOLIGNO / ACCADEMIA FULGINIA DI LETTERE, SCIENZE E ARTI (IT/1121-6425) [20139868] 2843, **2679**

BOLLETTINO STORICO DI TERRA D'OTRANTO / SOCIETA DI STORIA PATRIA PER LA PUGLIA, SEZIONE DI GALATINA (IT) [25357252] **2679**

BOLLETTINO STORICO PER LA PROVINCIA DI NOVARA 1947 (IT/0392-1107) [I03921107] **2679**

BOLLETTINO STORICO PIACENTINO (IT/0006-6591) [02056187] **2679**

BOLLETTINO STORICO PISANO / SOCIETA STORICA PISANA (IT/0391-1780) [02606846] **2612**

BOLLETTINO STORICO REGGIANO (IT/0392-1255) [I03921255] **2679**

BOLLETTINO STORICO VERCELLESE (IT) [09485916] **2679**

BOLLETTINO TRIBUTARIO D'INFORMAZIONI (IT/0006-6893) [I00066893] 4713, **2942**

BOLLETTINO UFFICIALE (IT) [01784013] **4465**

BOLLETTINO UFFICIALE DEGLI IDROCARBURI *See* BOLLETTINO UFFICIALE DEGLI IDROCARBURI E DELLA GEOTERMIA / MINISTERO DELL'INDUSTRIA, DEL COMMERCIO E DELL'ARTIGIANATO, DIREZIONE GENERALE DELLE MINIERE, UFFICIO NAZIONALE MINERARIO PER GLI IDROCARBURI E LA GEOTERMIA **4252**

BOLLETTINO UFFICIALE DEGLI IDROCARBURI E DELLA GEOTERMIA / MINISTERO DELL'INDUSTRIA, DEL COMMERCIO E DELL'ARTIGIANATO, DIREZIONE GENERALE DELLE MINIERE, UFFICIO NAZIONALE MINERARIO PER GLI IDROCARBURI E LA GEOTERMIA (IT/1120-544X) [26939846] 2942, **4252**

BOLLETTINO UFFICIALE DEI PROTESTI CAMBIARI (IT) **818**

BOLLETTINO UFFICIALE DEL TOTOCALCIO (IT/1121-5305) [I11215305] **2485**

BOLLETTINO UFFICIALE DELLA REGIONALE : LOMBARDIA. TIPO C (IT) **4633**

BOLLETTINO UFFICIALE DELLA REGIONE : AUTONOMA DELLA SARDEGNA (IT) **4633**

BOLLETTINO UFFICIALE DELLA REGIONE : AUTONOMA FRIULI BENEZIA GIULIA (IT) **4633**

BOLLETTINO UFFICIALE DELLA REGIONE : AUTONOMA TRENTINO ALTO ADIGE. PART III (IT) **4633**

BOLLETTINO UFFICIALE DELLA REGIONE CALABRIA (IT) **4633**

BOLLETTINO UFFICIALE DELLA REGIONE : LAZIO (IT) **4633**

BOLLETTINO UFFICIALE DELLA REGIONE : LIGURIA (IT) **4633**

BOLLETTINO UFFICIALE DELLA REGIONE : LOMBARDIA. TIPO A (IT) **4633**

BOLLETTINO UFFICIALE DELLA REGIONE : MARCHE (IT) **4633**

BOLLETTINO UFFICIALE DELLA REGIONE : PIEMONTE (IT) **4633**

BOLLETTINO UFFICIALE - MINISTERO DELLA PUBBLICA ISTRUZIONE. PARTE I. LEGI, DECRETI, REGOLAMENTI E ALTRE DISPOSIZIONI GENERALI (IT/0390-8518) [I03908518] **1860**

BOLLETTINO UFFICIALE - MINISTERO DELLA PUBBLICA ISTRUZIONE. PARTE IIE. ATTI DI AMMINISTRAZIONE (IT/0391-1985) [I03911985] **1861**

BOLLETTINO UFFICIALE - MINISTERO DELL'INDUSTRIA DEL COMMERCIO E DELL'ARTIGIANATO (IT) [04681801] **825**

BOLLETTINO UFFICIALE MINISTERO LAVORI PUBLICI (IT) **2943**

BOLLETTINO UFFICIALE PT- PART 2 (IT) **1144**

BOLLETTINO UFFICIALE REGIONE : CAMPANIA (IT) **4633**

BOLLETTINO UFFICIALE REGIONE. EMILIA ROMAGNA. PART I (IT) **4633**

BOLLETTINO UFFICIALE REGIONE : EMILIA ROMAGNA - PART II (IT) **4633**

BOLLETTINO UFFICIALE REGIONE : EMILIA ROMAGNA - PART III (IT) **4633**

BOLLETTINO UFFICIALE REGIONE : EMILIA ROMAGNA - PART IV (IT) **4633**

BOLLETTINO UFFICIALE REGIONE : PUGLIA (IT) **4633**

BOLLETTINO UFFICIALE REGIONE : TOSCANA (IT) **4633**

BOLLETTINO UFFICIALE REGIONE : UMBRIA. PART 1 & 2 (IT) **4633**

BOLLETTINO UFFICIALE REGIONE : UMBRIA. PART 3 (IT) **4633**

BOLLETTINO UFFICIALE REGIONE : UMBRIA. PART 4 (IT) **4633**

BOLLETTINO UFFICIALE REGIONE : VALLE D AOSTA (IT) **4634**

BOLLETTINO UFFICIALE REGIONE : VENETO. TYPE B (IT) **4634**

BOLLETTINO UFFICIALE SPA SRL. BARI (IT) **1599**

BOLLETTINO UFFICIALE TASSE E IMPOSTE INDIRETTE SUGLI AFFARI (IT) **818**

BOLLETTINO VARIAZIONI ANAGRAFICHE DITTE (IT) **1465**

BOLOGNA INCONTRI **CEASED.** (IT) [14269115] **344**

BOLSA DE COMERCIO DE BUENOS AIRES. BOLETIN OFICIAL *See* BOLSA, LA **825**

BOLSA DE VALORES DE SAO PAULO *See* REVISTA - BOLSA DE VALORES DE SAO PAULO **913**

BOLSA EN GRAFICOS, ACTUALIZACION, LA (SP) [02611988] **892**

BOLSA, LA (AG) [04358595] **825**

BOLSA OFICIAL DE VALORES. REVISTA *See* REVISTA - BOLSA DE VALORES DE SAO PAULO **913**

BOLTON EVENING NEWS (UK/0962-1539) [I09621539] **5811**

Alphabetical Title Index — BOOK

BOLVIEN : WIRTSCHAFTSDATEN (GW) [06229685] **1549**

BOLYAI JANOS MATEMATIKAI TARSULAT See COLLOQUIA MATHEMATICA **3500**

BOMA EXPERIENCE EXCHANGE REPORT (US/0738-2170) [09024319] **4834**

BOMB (NEW YORK, N.Y.) (US/0743-3204) [10226319] **316**

BOMB SUMMARY (US/0360-3245) [02239731] **3158**

BOMBAY (II) [06643796] **2647**

BOMBAY ART SOCIETY'S ART JOURNAL (II) [10193729] **344**

BOMBAY GIN (US/0160-4694) [03686180] **3368**

BOMBAY. J J GROUP OF HOSPITALS See JOURNAL OF J J GROUP OF HOSPITALS AND GRANT MEDICAL COLLEGE **3787**

BOMBAY MARKET (II) [02618204] **2502**

BOMBAY NATURAL HISTORY SOCIETY See JOURNAL OF THE BOMBAY NATURAL HISTORY SOCIETY **4166**

BOMBAY. PRINCE OF WALES MUSEUM OF WESTERN INDIA See BULLETIN OF THE PRINCE OF WALES MUSEUM OF WESTERN INDIA **4086**

BON APPETIT (US/0006-6990) [02483515] **2788**

BONANZA (JA) [02608308] **1549**

BONANZA BUGLE, THE (US/0896-1557) [10066609] **2724**

BOND BUYER (NEW YORK, N.Y. 1982), THE (US/0732-0469) [08256194] 779, **892**

BOND BUYER'S MUNICIPAL MARKETPLACE, THE (US/1053-8658) [22107035] **892**

BOND COUNSEL (US/1064-9476) [26863027] **892**

BOND FUND ADVISOR (US) **892**

BOND FUND SURVEY (US/0738-5579) [09631150] **779**

BOND GUIDE (US/0277-3988) [02244007] **892**

BOND LAW REVIEW (AT/1033-4505) [20446793] **2943**

BOND MANAGEMENT REVIEW (AT/1036-1456) [I10361456] **861**

BOND MARKET ROUNDUP / SALOMON BROTHERS INC (US) [04205483] **892**

BOND (MINNEAPOLIS, MINN.) (US/0279-9111) [07349401] **5057**

BONDHOLDER / IFR, THE (UK/0961-8171) [23169532] **779**

BONDWEEK (US/0278-8896) [07410088] **892**

●BONE & JOINT DISEASES (US/1063-0295) [25843390] **3803**

BONE AND MINERAL (NE/0169-6009) [13502360] **3726**

BONE AND MINERAL RESEARCH (NE/0168-051X) [09229206] **3803**

BONE MARROW TRANSPLANTATION (BASINGSTOKE) (UK/0268-3369) [14220154] **3558**

BONE (NEW YORK, N.Y.) (US/8756-3282) [11527159] **3803**

BONES (NE/0922-1433) [19693133] 232, **262**

BONHAM DAILY FAVORITE, THE (US) [18296651] **5747**

BONITA BANNER (US/0191-5479) [05011014] 5648, **5649**

BONJOUR AVERBODE (BE/0773-0306) [I07730306] **1060**

BONJOUR CHEZ-NOUS (CN/0383-7866) [03233093] **5780**

BONJOUR (NEW YORK) (US/0006-7121) [04398490] 1889, **3270**

BONJOUR QUEBEC (CN/0229-0898) [08079315] **5465**

BONJOUR (TROIS-RIVIERES-OUEST) (CN/0226-7152) [06511858] **5024**

BONN. BEETHOVENHAUS See VEROFFENTLICHUNGEN. NEUE FOLGE, REIHE 4. SCHRIFTEN ZUR BEETHOVENFORSCHUNG **4158**

BONN. UNIVERSITAT. FORSCHUNGSSTELLE FUR BUCHWISSENSCHAFT See KLEINE SCHRIFTEN **3221**

BONNE CUISINE (FR/0006-713X) **2329**

BONNE NOUVELLE (BE/0774-5230) [I07745230] **4939**

BONNE NOUVELLE DE L'ALLIANCE (CN/0701-0648) [03406520] **5057**

BONNE SOIREE (BE/0771-8020) [I07718020] **4849**

BONNE TABLE ET TOURISME : ORGANE OFFICIEL DE LA CHAINE DES ROTISSEURS, DE L'ACADEMIE DE GASTRONOMIE BRILLAT-SAVARIN, DE L'ORDRE MONDIAL DES GOURMETS DEGUSTATEURS (FR) [09414842] **2329**

BONNER ARBEITEN ZUR DEUTSCHEN LITERATUR (GW/0068-001X) [01536722] **3368**

BONNER BEITRAEGE ZUR SOZIOLOGIE / INSTITUT FUER SOZIOLOGIE DER UNIVERSITAT BONN (GW/0068-0044) [01536724] **5240**

BONNER COUNTY DAILY BEE (US/1047-6822) [18769408] **5656**

BONNER GEOGRAPHISCHE ABHANDLUNGEN (GW/0373-0468) [01536727] **2556**

BONNER GESCHICHTSBLATTER (GW/0068-0052) [03067745] **2679**

BONNER HEFTE ZUR VORGESCHICHTE (GW) [03455953] **2679**

BONNER HISTORISCHE FORSCHUNGEN (GW) [01536728] **2612**

BONNER JAHRBUCHER (GW) [02586754] **344**

BONNER JAHRBUCHER DES RHEINISCHEN LANDESMUSEUMS IN BONN (IM LANDSCHAFTSVERBAND RHEINLAND) UND DES VEREINS VON ALTERTUMSFREUNDEN IM RHEINLANDE (GW/0067-9976) [12190722] **262**

BONNER JAHRBUCHER DES RHEINISCHEN LANDESMUSEUMS IN BONN UND DES RHEINISCHEN AMTES FUER BODENDENKMALPFLEGE IM LANDSCHAFTSVERBAND RHEINLAND UND DES VEREINS VON ALTERTUMSFREUNDEN IM RHEINLANDE (GW/0938-9334) [I09389334] **2679**

BONNER MATHEMATISCHE SCHRIFTEN (GW/0524-045X) [01536730] **3497**

BONNER METEOROLOGISCHE ABHANDLUNGEN (GW/0006-7156) [02785078] **1421**

BONNER RUNDSCHAU (GW) [20873597] **5801**

BONNER ZOOLOGISCHE BEITRAEGE (GW/0006-7172) [02445391] **5578**

BONNERS FERRY HERALD (US/1064-9298) [13089671] **5656**

BONNET DE NUIT, LE (CN/1183-0832) [24256762] **3368**

BONNET-T-E'S & KIN, THE (US/0743-0957) [06317259] **2439**

BONNEVILLE POWER ADMINISTRATION See ADVANCE PROGRAM **2034**

BONNIERS SMA KONSTBOCKER (SW/0520-5700) [03030853] **344**

BONNYVILLE NOUVELLE (CN/0710-3905) [I07103905] **4887**

BONSAI BULLETIN (US) [07243405] **2410**

BONSAI CLUB INTERNATIONAL See BONSAI MAGAZINE **2410**

BONSAI CLUBS INTERNATIONAL (US/0744-3277) [07353167] **2410**

BONSAI JOURNAL OF AUSTRALIA (AT) [03210455] **2410**

BONSAI : JOURNAL OF THE AMERICAN BONSAI SOCIETY (US) [22472084] **2410**

BONSAI MAGAZINE (US/1068-6193) [27723752] **2410**

BONSAI (PHOENIX) (US/0362-4447) [02230327] **2410**

BONSAI TODAY (US/1044-2529) [19719418] **2410**

BONTEBOK (SA/0256-9175) [10326841] **2188**

BOOGIE MADRID (SP/0214-297X) [I0214297X] **4104**

BOOK - AMERICAN ANTIQUARIAN SOCIETY, THE (US/0740-8439) [10032200] **4824**

BOOK AND MAGAZINE COLLECTOR (UK) [15192943] 4824, **2771**

BOOK & PAPER GROUP ANNUAL, THE (US/0887-8978) [11535704] 4824, **344**

BOOK AS ART (MOSCOW, R.S.F.S.R.) (RU) [19212039] **4824**

BOOK AUCTION (NE) [17934371] **4824**

BOOK AUCTION RECORDS (UK/0068-0095) [07270273] **4824**

BOOK AUTHOR'S NEWSLETTER (US/1045-2966) [20074394] **3368**

BOOK BUYER'S ADVISOR See BOOKLIST'S GUIDE TO THE YEAR'S BEST BOOKS : DEFINITIVE REVIEWS OF OVER 1,000 FICTION AND NONFICTION TITLES IN ALL FIELDS **4821**

BOOK CLUB OF CALIFORNIA See QUARTERLY NEWS-LETTER - BOOK CLUB OF CALIFORNIA **4831**

BOOK CLUB OF CALIFORNIA See KEEPSAKE SERIES **3401**

BOOK COLLECTOR, THE (UK/0006-7237) [01536744] **4824**

BOOK FORUM (US/0094-9426) [01795991] **3338**

BOOK INDUSTRY TRENDS (US/0160-970X) [03791850] **4824**

BOOK LINKS (US/1055-4742) [23189539] **4824**

BOOK LIST / SOCIETY FOR OLD TESTAMENT STUDY (UK/0081-1440) [01955584] **5012**

BOOK/LOS ANGELES, THE (US/1040-6344) [18475767] **4824**

BOOK MARKETING UPDATE (US/0891-8813) [15049511] 921, **4824**

BOOK MARKETS IN THE AMERICAS, ASIA, AFRICA & AUSTRALASIA (UK) [07438468] **4824**

BOOK MARKETS IN WESTERN EUROPE (UK) [06687601] 921, **4824**

BOOK MARKS (US/0197-0437) [04248124] **3196**

BOOK-MART (DECATUR), THE (US/0161-5556) [06793351] **4825**

BOOK MODA-ALTA MODA (IT) **1082**

BOOK NEWS FOR BOOKSELLERS AND LIBRARIANS (CN/0381-7261) [03202042] **4812**

BOOK NEWSLETTER (MINNEAPOLIS, MINN.) (US/1043-352X) [19415356] 4939, **3338**

BOOK NEWSLETTER OF AUGSBURG PUBLISHING HOUSE See BOOK NEWSLETTER (MINNEAPOLIS, MINN.) **3338**

BOOK OF AMERICAN TRADE MARKS, THE (US) [05912994] **1301**

BOOK OF APPLE SOFTWARE, THE **CEASED.** (US/0736-2692) [09094729] 1265, **1284**

BOOK OF ATARI SOFTWARE, THE (US/0736-2706) [09094700] 1265, **1284**

●BOOK OF LISTS: A REFERENCE GUIDE TO ALASKA'S LEADING INDUSTRIES, THE (US) [25097068] **643**

BOOK OF LISTS (LOS ANGELES, CALIF.) (US) [15234895] **643**

BOOK OF NAMES, THE (US/0094-1255) [01793700] **756**

BOOK OF PAPERS - AMERICAN ASSOCIATION OF TEXTILE CHEMISTS AND COLORISTS. INTERNATIONAL CONFERENCE & EXHIBITION (US/0892-2713) [12301697] **5348**

BOOK OF PROFILES (US) [23914278] **1656**

BOOK OF RECORDS, NATIONALS - SOFTBALL CANADA (CN/0821-0098) [09743137] **4887**

BOOK OF SEMI STANDARDS (US/0734-1903) [05267538] **2037**

BOOK OF SPECIAL DAYS (CN/1184-2989) [24265510] **1923**

BOOK OF SUCCESSFUL FIREPLACES (US) [04986071] **2603**

BOOK OF THE OLD EDINBURGH CLUB, THE **CEASED.** (UK) [01773265] **5229**

BOOK OF THE STATES, THE (US/0068-0125) [01238839] **4634**

BOOK ON STARTING PITCHERS (US/0739-4667) [09740399] **4887**

BOOK PEDDLER, THE (US/0896-9523) [12042719] **3368**

BOOK PRODUCTION (BENN PUBLICATIONS LTD.) (UK) [07752445] 4564, **4825**

BOOK PUBLISHING CAREER DIRECTORY (US/0882-8261) [12004270] **4825**

BOOK PUBLISHING (OTTAWA) (CN/1181-6635) [23659024] **4812**

BOOK REPORT (UK) 4825, **921**

BOOK REPORT (US) **4825**

BOOK REPORT (COLUMBUS, OHIO) (US/0731-4388) [08187197] **3196**

BOOK REVIEW DIGEST (US/0006-7326) [06038062] 3338, **3356**

BOOK REVIEW DIGEST. CD-ROM (US/0006-7326) **4821**

BOOK REVIEW INDEX (US/0524-0581) [01536773] 4825, **4821**

BOOK REVIEW, THE (II) [02594657] **4825**

BOOK RIGHTS REPORT (US/1056-635X) [23751199] **4825**

BOOK SERIES (ISIS INTERNATIONAL) (IT) [18215452] **5552**

BOOK TALK (ALBUQUERQUE) (US/0145-627X) [02258493] 3338, **4825**

BOOK TRADE IN CANADA, WITH WHO'S WHERE, THE (CN/0836-8619) [12651184] 4825, **4812**

BOOK WORLD (II) [04594854] **4825**

BOOK WORLD (WASHINGTON) (US/0006-7369) [01536777] **4825**

BOOKBINDER — Alphabetical Title Index

BOOKBINDER : JOURNAL OF THE SOCIETY OF BOOKBINDERS AND BOOK RESTORERS (UK) [17569014] **4825**

BOOKBIRD (DK/0006-7377) [12712013] **3368**

BOOKER NEWS, THE (US) [14205464] **5747**

BOOKKEEPER'S JOURNAL FOR DENTAL PRACTICES, THE (US/1054-1713) [22774655] **1317**

BOOKLEGGER MAGAZINE *SUSPENDED.* (US/0092-7686) [01791024] **3196**

BOOKLET (GREAT BRITAIN. MINISTRY OF AGRICULTURE, FISHERIES AND FOOD) (UK) [08905808] 2297, **68**

BOOKLET I : GRANT APPLICATION MATERIALS *See* GRANTS-IN-AID APPLICATION AND REFERENCE MATERIALS **4653**

BOOKLET II : GRANTS-IN-AID REFERENCE MATERIALS *See* GRANTS-IN-AID APPLICATION AND REFERENCE MATERIALS **4653**

BOOKLIST (CHICAGO, ILL. 1969) (US/0006-7385) [01536781] **3196**

BOOKLIST'S GUIDE TO THE YEAR'S BEST BOOKS : DEFINITIVE REVIEWS OF OVER 1,000 FICTION AND NONFICTION TITLES IN ALL FIELDS *CEASED.* (US) [26086951] **4821**

BOOKLURE (PASADENA, CALIF.) *CEASED.* (US/1041-7834) [18897969] **3368**

BOOKMAN. PART 3, THE (BG) [07996015] **411**

BOOKMAN'S PRICE INDEX (US/0068-0141) [01536787] **253**

BOOKMARK (EDINBURGH, LOTHIAN) (UK/0260-0315) [09403926] **4825**

BOOKMARK (MOSCOW, IDAHO), THE (US/0735-0295) [01536788] **3197**

BOOKMARK, THE (US/0006-7407) [01536789] **3197**

BOOKMARK (VANCOUVER) (CN/0381-6028) [02301631] 1728, **3197**

BOOKNOTES (PORTLAND, ORE.) (US/0747-847X) [10810529] **3825**

BOOKPLATE JOURNAL, THE (UK/0264-3693) [09600101] **4825**

BOOKPLATES IN THE NEWS (US/0045-2521) [02648802] **2771**

BOOKPRESS, THE (US) [24655341] 3368, **4825**

BOOKS ABOUT BIRDS (US) [03254416] **5616**

BOOKS AND ART IN THE USSR (RU/0201-8500) [06843902] 344, **4825**

BOOKS AND ARTICLES ON ORIENTAL SUBJECTS PUBLISHED IN JAPAN. / TOHOGAKU KANKEI CHOSHO RONBUN MOKUROKU (JA/0524-0654) [02098224] **2634**

BOOKS AND PERIODICALS ONLINE (US/0951-838X) [17201641] **3257**

BOOKS & RELIGION *CEASED.* (US/0890-0841) [11908460] 4825, **4939**

BOOKS AT BOSTON SPA. MICROFORM (UK/0268-6538) [17569411] **4825**

BOOKS AT BROWN (US/0147-0787) [01570232] **4821**

BOOKS AT IOWA (US/0006-7474) [01536802] **3197**

BOOKS BY BLACK WOMEN (US/1040-0362) [18296703] **4825**

BOOKS FOR CHILDREN WASHINGTON, D.C.) *CEASED.* (US/0882-5343) [11884747] **4825**

BOOKS FOR KEEPS (UK) [19113058] **3368**

BOOKS FOR THE TEEN AGE (US/0068-0192) [01772360] **1060**

BOOKS FOR YOUR CHILDREN (UK/0006-7482) [02258498] 1060, **3338**

BOOKS FROM BRITISH COLUMBIA (CN/0823-8707) [11422279] **411**

BOOKS FROM FINLAND (FI/0006-7490) [01536806] 3368, **4821**

BOOKS FROM INDIA (II) [08104776] **4825**

BOOKS FROM ISRAEL *CEASED.* (IS/0578-932X) [04735273] **4825**

BOOKS IN ARABIC (1980) (CN/0713-4460) [10088104] **4825**

BOOKS IN ARMENIAN (CN/0705-8209) [04875380] **4825**

BOOKS IN BENGALI (1980) (CN/0713-5335) [10643513] **4825**

BOOKS IN BOSNIA AND HERZEGOVINA (BN/0352-1044) [11511616] 3460, **3368**

BOOKS IN CANADA (CN/0045-2564) [01789992] **4825**

BOOKS IN CHINESE (1980) (CN/0713-4495) [10655942] **4825**

BOOKS IN CROATIAN (CN/0713-4568) [09809021] **4825**

BOOKS IN DANISH (CN/0705-2332) [04677931] **4825**

BOOKS IN DUTCH (1980) (CN/0713-4533) [10088083] **4825**

BOOKS IN ENGLISH (UK/0045-2572) [16126399] **411**

BOOKS IN ESTONIAN (1980) (CN/0714-2129) [09751840] **4825**

BOOKS IN FINNISH (1980) (CN/0714-2382) [10088220] **4825**

BOOKS IN FRISIAN (1980) (CN/0714-2420) [10088318] **4826**

BOOKS IN GERMAN (1980) (CN/0714-2455) [09743322] **4826**

BOOKS IN GREEK (1980) (CN/0714-2471) [09743307] **4826**

BOOKS IN GUJARATI (CN/0714-2501) [09743270] **4826**

BOOKS IN HINDI (1980) (CN/0714-2528) [09743293] **4826**

BOOKS IN HUNGARIAN (1980) (CN/0714-2544) [10088235] **4826**

BOOKS IN ITALIAN (CN/0714-2609) [10088262] **4826**

BOOKS IN JAPANESE (CN/0705-6486) [04754501] **4826**

BOOKS IN LIBRARY AND INFORMATION SCIENCE (US) [01781402] **3197**

BOOKS IN LITHUANIAN (CN/0705-8225) [04589157] **4826**

BOOKS IN MARATHI (CN/0317-2406) [04875359] **4826**

BOOKS IN PANJABI (1980) (CN/0714-282X) [10339586] **4826**

BOOKS IN PERSIAN (1980) (CN/0227-2741) [09678190] **4826**

BOOKS IN POLISH (1980) (CN/0714-2773) [10082709] **4826**

BOOKS IN POLISH OR RELATING TO POLAND (UK) [02600665] **2514**

BOOKS IN PORTUGUESE (1980) (CN/0714-279X) [09639295] **4826**

BOOKS IN PRINT (NEW YORK) (US/0068-0214) [01641212] **411**

BOOKS IN PRINT PLUS (US/1062-5100) [20621102] **411**

BOOKS IN PRINT SUPPLEMENT (US/0000-0310) [02429038] **411**

BOOKS IN PRINT WITH BOOK REVIEWS PLUS [COMPUTER FILE] (US) [25074838] **3197**

BOOKS IN SCOTLAND (UK/0143-1285) [05640277] **4826**

BOOKS IN SERIES (US/0000-0906) [07098889] **4826**

BOOKS IN SOILS, PLANTS, AND THE ENVIRONMENT (US) **165**

BOOKS IN SPANISH (1980) (CN/0713-5998) [09751822] **4826**

BOOKS IN TAGALOG (1980) (CN/0824-5592) [11193195] **4826**

BOOKS IN THE EARTH SCIENCES AND RELATED TOPICS (UK/0140-7805) [05183131] **1352**

BOOKS IN UKRAINIAN (1980) (CN/0714-2927) [10643509] **4826**

BOOKS IN URDU (1980) (CN/0714-296X) [10643504] **4826**

BOOKS IN VIETNAMESE (1980) (CN/0227-2776) [09631177] **4826**

BOOKS IN YIDDISH (CN/0705-8268) [10643481] **4826**

BOOKS IRELAND (IE/0376-6039) [04255461] **4812**

BOOKS (LONDON, ENGLAND : 1944) (UK) [08433657] **4826**

BOOKS (LONDON, ENGLAND : 1987) *See* BOOKS MAGAZINE **4826**

BOOKS (LONDON,1987) (UK/0952-987X) [15535946] **4826**

● BOOKS MAGAZINE (UK/0952-987X) [27316019] **4826**

BOOKS--NOTED FOR YOU (CN/0829-4976) [13318667] **4821**

BOOKS NOW (CN/0707-6924) [04747145] 4826, **3368**

BOOKS OF THE SOUTHWEST (US/0006-7520) [02791645] **3457**

BOOKS ON DEMAND: AUTHOR GUIDE. INTERNATIONAL ED (US/0736-9034) [09253046] **4826**

BOOKS ON TRIAL (NEW YORK, N.Y.) (US/0749-5323) [11135945] **2943**

BOOKS OUT-OF-PRINT (US/0000-0736) [10220773] **4826**

BOOKS PURCHASED FOR DISPLAY PURPOSES (CN/0381-5072) [02603542] **411**

BOOKSELLER (LONDON) (UK/0006-7539) [03995789] **4821**

BOOKSELLERS ASSOCIATION OF GREAT BRITAIN AND IRELAND *See* ECONOMIC SURVEY **4828**

BOOKSELLING THIS WEEK (US) **4826**

BOOKSTORE JOURNAL (US/0006-7563) [01789289] **4939**

BOOKSTORE JOURNAL REVIEWS (US/0092-6264) [01789682] **4826**

BOOKTALK *CEASED.* (UK/0307-854X) [10307854X] **4826**

BOOKTALKER *See* NEW BOOKTALKER, THE **4830**

BOOKTALKER, THE (US) [20980820] **4827**

BOOKWATCH (SAN FRANCISCO, CALIF.), THE (US/0896-4521) [17192991] **4827**

BOOKWAYS (AUSTIN, TEX.) *CEASED.* (US/1057-6355) [24083736] **4827**

BOOKWOMAN, THE (US/0163-1128) [04294196] **4827**

BOOMBAH HERALD (US/8755-5832) [08637183] 431, **4104**

BOOMER REPORT, THE (US) [27863869] **2529**

BOOMERANG! (SAN FRANCISCO, CALIF.) (US/1052-1682) [22202561] **1060**

BOOMERANG, THE (CN/0228-2321) [07314086] **3158**

BOOMWEKERIJ (NE) **2410**

BOONE COUNTY GENEALOGICAL SOCIETY *See* KITH AND KIN OF BOONE COUNTY, WEST VIRGINIA **2457**

BOONE COUNTY HISTORIAN (US) [04556457] **2439**

BOONE COUNTY RECORDER, THE (US) [11061510] **5679**

BOONE SCOUT OF THE BOONE FAMILY ASSOCIATION OF WASHINGTON, THE (US/0145-5060) [01536817] **2439**

BOONEVILLE SENTINEL (US) [12318432] **5679**

BOONVILLE HERALD AND ADIRONDACK TOURIST (US) [13507228] **5714**

BOONVILLE STANDARD (BOONVILLE, IND. : 1906) (US) [14284591] **5663**

BOOSEY AND HAWKES, INC., NEW YORK *See* NEWSLETTER - BOOSEY AND HAWKES INC **4140**

BOOSTER, THE (US) [18386987] **5727**

BOOTBLACK (BOYNTON BEACH, FLA.) (US/1040-7405) [18507857] **3368**

BOOTHBAY REGISTER (US) [10341068] **5685**

BOOTH'S NIC BRIEF (UK/0965-450X) [0965450X] 5275, **2876**

BOOWATT (CN/0383-1353) [03202057] **2529**

BOP (US/8750-7242) [11697665] **2529**

BOPHUTHATSWANA (SOUTH AFRICA) DEPT. OF EDUCATION *See* ANNUAL REPORT / DEPARTMENT OF EDUCATION **1725**

BOPHUTHATSWANA (SOUTH AFRICA). DEPT. OF HEALTH AND SOCIAL SERVICES *See* ANNUAL REPORT / BOPHUTHATSWANA, DEPARTMENT OF HEALTH AND SOCIAL SERVICES **4765**

BOPHUTHATSWANA (SOUTH AFRICA) NURSING DIVISION *See* ANNUAL RREPORT / REPUBLIC OF BOPHUTHATSWANA, DEPARTMENT OF HEALTH AND SOCIAL WELFARE, NURSING DIVISION **3851**

BOPUXUE ZAZHI (CC/1000-4556) [21663513] **4434**

BORDEAUX. UNIVERSITE. INSTITUT DE GEOLOGIE DU BASSIN D'AQUITAINE *See* MEMOIRES DE L'INSTITUT DE GEOLOGIE DU BASSIN D'AQUITAINE **1387**

BORDER CROSSINGS (WINNIPEG, MAN.) (CN/0831-2559) [14954880] **316**

BORDER/LINES (CN/0826-967X) [12816341] **4185**

BORDERLAND REPORTER (CN/0821-6177) [09688391] **5781**

● BORDERLANDS (AUSTIN, TEX.) (US/1065-0342) [26489810] **3460**

BORDERLANDS JOURNAL, THE *CEASED.* (US/0276-9220) [06873855] **1812**

BORDERLINES (CN) **316**

BORDURES (CN/0715-741X) [09766510] **3922**

BOREAL INSTITUTE FOR NORTHERN STUDIES *See* OCCASIONAL PUBLICATION - BOREAL INSTITUTE FOR NORTHERN STUDIES **2751**

BOREAL INSTITUTE FOR NORTHERN STUDIES. LIBRARY *See* LIBRARY BULLETIN - BOREAL INSTITUTE FOR NORTHERN STUDIES **3224**

BOREAL INSTITUTE VERTICAL FILES ON NORTHERN AFFAIRS, KWIC INDEX TO CLIPPING SERVICE ON MICROFICHE (CN/0228-2046) [06966048] **2724**

BOREAL INTERNATIONAL (CN/0823-2679) [10052168] **3460**

BOREALIS (TORONTO) (CN/0840-6189) [20267865] **4706**

BOREAS (NO/0300-9483) [01773784] **1368**

BOREAS (MUNSTER) (GW/0344-810X) [04329209] **262**

BORGAZDASAG (HU/0006-7741) [02794883] **68**

BORGER NEWS-HERALD (US) [14052337] **5747**

BORGHESE, IL *CEASED.* (IT/0006-775X) [02794902] **2514**

BORGO (CN/0712-645X) [09336334] **4104**

BORGO BIOVIEWS (US/0743-9628) [07941383] **431**

BORGO CATALOGING GUIDES (US/0891-9615) [15048763] **3197**

BORGO FAMILY HISTORIES (US/0733-6764) [08641762] **2612**

BORGO LITERARY GUIDES (US/0891-9623) [15048872] **3368**

BORGO POLITICAL SCENARIOS (US/0278-9752) [07941338] **4465**

BORGO REFERENCE GUIDES (US/0891-9607) [15048416] **1923**

BORGO REFERENCE LIBRARY, THE (US/0270-3653) [06395754] **3197**

BORGYOGYASZATI ES VENEROLOGIAI SZEMLE (HU/0006-7768) [06337547] **3718**

●BORLAND C++ DEVELOPER'S JOURNAL (US/1073-4805) [29417456] **1284**

BORN-AGAIN CHRISTIAN DIRECTORY-CATALOG, THE (CN/0824-555X) [10668919] **4939**

BORN & BOGER (DK/0006-7792) [10447004] **3197**

BORN TO SHOP. ENGLAND, SCOTLAND, AND IRELAND *See* BORN TO SHOP. GREAT BRITAIN **1293**

BORN TO SHOP. FRANCE *See* BORN TO SHOP. PARIS **1293**

●BORN TO SHOP. GREAT BRITAIN (US/1071-9717) [28819085] **1293**

●BORN TO SHOP. NEW ENGLAND (US/1066-2782) [26912206] **1293**

●BORN TO SHOP. PARIS (US/1066-2790) [26912242] **1293**

BORNEO BULLETIN (BX) [03198360] **5779**

BORNEO RESEARCH BULLETIN (US/0006-7806) [00968186] **232, 2647**

BORNEO RESEARCH COUNCIL MONOGRAPH SERIES (US/1055-7792) [23302564] **232**

BORROWING IN INTERNATIONAL CAPITAL MARKETS (US) [04154790] **779**

BORSA DEI NOLI (IT) **2876**

BORSA VALORI (SERIES) (IT) [10281596] **779**

●BORSCHT (MINNEAPOLIS, MINN.) (US/1065-5212) [26626223] **316**

BORSE (WIEN) (AU/0302-0770) [01793220] **892**

BORSEN-ZEITUNG 1972 (GW/0343-7728) [103437728] **5801**

BORSENBLATT FUR DEN DEUTSCHEN BUCHHANDEL *CEASED.* (SZ) [02602119] **4812**

BORSENBLATT FUR DEN DEUTSCHEN BUCHHANDEL. FRANKFURTER AUSGABE. SONDERNUMMER (GW) [03251239] **4827**

BORSMEDDELANDEN (SW/0283-4529) [19926732] **4634**

BORTHWICK PAPERS / UNIVERSITY OF YORK, BORTHWICK INSTITUTE OF HISTORICAL RESEARCH (UK/0524-0913) [01536835] **2679**

BORTHWICK TEXTS AND CALENDARS : RECORDS OF THE NORTHERN PROVINCE (UK) [03455836] **2480**

BORZOI QUARTERLY (WHEAT RIDGE, COLO.), THE (US/0746-2875) [09926293] **4286**

BOS, BERICHTEN OVER STADSVERNIEUWING (NE/0166-9370) [04773056] **2816**

BOS NIEUWSLETTER (NE/0923-7488) [l09237488] **2376**

BOSAI KAGAKU GIJUTSU (JA) [02407187] **2556**

BOSAI ROPPO (JA) [02805900] **5275**

BOSBOUNUUS (SA) [12201725] **2376**

BOSCH BUSINESS, DEN (SW) **644**

BOSEI KANRI (JA/0520-6340) [09349381] **963**

BOSLEY NURSERIES *See* BOSLEY PLANT NEWS **2410**

BOSLEY PLANT NEWS (US) [12068034] **2410**

BOSQUE (CL/0304-8799) [02739972] **2376**

BOSSIER PRESS-TRIBUNE (US/0747-4733) [10904783] **5683**

BOSTON *See* BOSTON MAGAZINE **5465**

BOSTON AREA FRIENDS OF BLUEGRASS & OLD-TIME COUNTRY MUSIC *See* NEWSLETTER **4140**

BOSTON AUDIO SOCIETY *See* B.A.S. SPEAKER, THE **5316**

BOSTON BAR JOURNAL (US/0524-1111) [01536844] **2943**

BOSTON BRUINS OFFICIAL YEARBOOK (US/0361-6398) [02247088] **4887**

BOSTON BULLETIN ON CHEMICALS AND DISEASE (US/0894-4024) [15578911] **3979, 4294**

BOSTON BUSINESS JOURNAL, THE (US/0746-4975) [08417537] **644**

BOSTON CELTICS (US/0361-6894) [02441395] **4887**

BOSTON COLLEGE ENVIRONMENTAL AFFAIRS LAW REVIEW (US/0190-7034) [04708380] **3110**

BOSTON COLLEGE INTERNATIONAL AND COMPARATIVE LAW REVIEW (US/0277-5778) [05228055] **3125**

BOSTON COLLEGE LAW REVIEW (US/0161-6587) [03898891] **2943**

BOSTON COLLEGE. LAW SCHOOL *See* BOSTON COLLEGE LAW REVIEW **2943**

BOSTON COLLEGE. LAW SCHOOL *See* BOSTON COLLEGE ENVIRONMENTAL AFFAIRS LAW REVIEW **3110**

BOSTON COLLEGE STUDIES IN PHILOSOPHY *CEASED.* (US/0524-112X) [02251052] **4342**

BOSTON COLLEGE THIRD WORLD LAW JOURNAL (US/0276-3583) [06558685] **3125**

BOSTON COMPUTER CURRENTS (US/0897-9324) [17399574] **1235**

BOSTON, FRESH FRUIT AND VEGETABLE WHOLESALE MARKET PRICES (US) [03495097] **2329**

BOSTON GLOBE INDEX (1987), THE (US/0893-2727) [15475073] **5814**

BOSTON GLOBE, THE (US/0743-1791) [01536853] **5687**

BOSTON HERALD (1982), THE (US/0738-5854) [09310673] **5688**

BOSTON JEWISH TIMES, THE (US/8750-1961) [10941551] **5688**

BOSTON JOB BANK, THE (US) [15244426] **4201**

BOSTON MAGAZINE (US) [07711708] **5465**

BOSTON (MASS.) *See* CITY RECORD **4638**

BOSTON MONTHLY, THE (US/0194-732X) [04979163] **2529**

BOSTON MYCOLOGICAL CLUB *See* BOSTON MYCOLOGICAL CLUB BULLETIN **574**

BOSTON MYCOLOGICAL CLUB BULLETIN (US/0270-4633) [06395802] **574**

BOSTON ORGAN CLUB NEWSLETTER, THE (US/0524-1170) [09293008] **4104**

BOSTON PARENTS' PAPER, THE (US/1059-1710) [13622865] **2277**

BOSTON PHOENIX, THE (US/0163-3015) [04350940] **5688**

... BOSTON RESTAURANT GUIDE, THE (US/0731-1923) [08141036] **5070**

BOSTON REVIEW (CAMBRIDGE, MASS. : 1982) (US/0734-2306) [08614974] **4465, 3368**

BOSTON ROCK (US/0889-230X) [13826531] **4104**

BOSTON SHIPPING ASSOCIATION *See* PORT OF BOSTON HANDBOOK **5454**

BOSTON SPA SERIALS ON CD-ROM (UK) **411**

BOSTON STUDIES IN THE PHILOSOPHY OF SCIENCE (NE/0068-0346) [01536849] **5089**

BOSTON SYMPHONY ORCHESTRA *See* BOSTON SYMPHONY ORCHESTRA **4104**

BOSTON SYMPHONY ORCHESTRA (US/0006-8020) [01536882] **4104**

BOSTON SYMPHONY ORCHESTRA. CONCERT BULLETIN *See* BOSTON SYMPHONY ORCHESTRA **4104**

BOSTON TAB, THE (US/0745-2055) [08924236] **5688**

BOSTON THEOLOGICAL INSTITUTE *See* B.T.I. NEWSLETTER **4937**

BOSTON UNIVERSITY. CENTER FOR LAW AND HEALTH SCIENCES *See* ANNUAL REPORT - CENTER FOR LAW AND HEALTH SCIENCES **3739**

BOSTON UNIVERSITY. COLLEGE OF BASIC STUDIES *See* ALUMNI DIRECTORY / BOSTON UNIVERSITY, COLLEGE OF BASIC STUDIES **1097**

BOSTON UNIVERSITY. COLLEGE OF ENGINEERING *See* ALUMNAE/I DIRECTORY / BOSTON UNIVERSITY, COLLEGE OF ENGINEERING **1096**

BOSTON UNIVERSITY. DIVISION OF GENERAL EDUCATION *See* ALUMNI DIRECTORY / BOSTON UNIVERSITY, GENERAL EDUCATION **1097**

BOSTON UNIVERSITY. HUMAN RELATIONS CENTER *See* RESEARCH REPORTS AND TECHNICAL NOTES - BOSTON UNIVERSITY. HUMAN RELATIONS CENTER **1845**

BOSTON UNIVERSITY INTERNATIONAL LAW JOURNAL (US/0737-8947) [08842381] **3125**

BOSTON UNIVERSITY JOURNAL OF TAX LAW *CEASED.* (US/0741-8477) [09452643] **4713, 2943**

BOSTON UNIVERSITY LAW REVIEW (US/0006-8047) [01536885] **2943**

BOSTON UNIVERSITY. SCHOOL OF LAW *See* BOSTON UNIVERSITY LAW REVIEW **2943**

BOSTON UNIVERSITY. SCHOOL OF MEDICINE. ALUMNI ASSOCIATION *See* ALUMNI DIRECTORY - BOSTON UNIVERSITY. SCHOOL OF MEDICINE. ALUMNI ASSOCIATION **3548**

BOSTON UNIVERSITY. SCHOOL OF PUBLIC RELATIONS AND COMMUNICATIONS. COMMUNICATIONS ARTS DIVISION *See* FILM STUDIES **4070**

BOSTON UNIVERSITY STUDIES IN PHILOSOPHY AND RELIGION (US) [07759180] **4940, 4342**

BOSTON UNIVERSITY TODAY (1984) (US/8750-989X) [11248431] **1089**

BOSTON WOMAN (US/0893-5572) [15585709] **5552**

BOSTONIA (BOSTON, MASS. 1986) (US/1067-2834) [24760867] **3368**

BOSWELL ENTERPRISE, THE (US) [15123205] **5663**

BOTANIC GARDENS CONSERVATION NEWS : MAGAZINE OF THE IUCN BOTANIC GARDENS CONSERVATION SECRETARIAT (UK) [17346989] **2188**

BOTANIC GARDENS MICROPROPAGATION NEWS (UK/0962-7448) [l09627448] **503**

BOTANICA ACTA (GW/0932-8629) [17167709] **503**

BOTANICA HELVETICA (SZ/0253-1453) [08446474] **503**

BOTANICA MARINA (GW/0006-8055) [01800256] **503**

BOTANICA (NEW DELHI, INDIA) (II/0045-2629) [01536890] **503**

BOTANICAL BULLETIN OF ACADEMIA SINICA (CH/0006-8063) [01554645] **503**

BOTANICAL GAZETTE (CHICAGO, ILL.) *See* INTERNATIONAL JOURNAL OF PLANT SCIENCES **514**

BOTANICAL GAZETTE (CHICAGO, ILL.) *See* INTERNATIONAL JOURNAL OF PLANT SCIENCES. MICROFORM **514**

BOTANICAL JOURNAL OF SCOTLAND (UK) [25269273] **503**

BOTANICAL MAGAZINE, TOKYO *See* JOURNAL OF PLANT RESEARCH **516**

BOTANICAL MAGAZINE, TOKYO, THE (JA) [26287357] **503**

BOTANICAL MUSEUM LEAFLETS / HARVARD UNIVERSITY (US) [09336198] **503**

BOTANICAL REVIEW, THE (US/0006-8101) [01536897] **503**

BOTANICAL SOCIETY OF AMERICA *See* MEMBERSHIP DIRECTORY AND HANDBOOK / BOTANICAL SOCIETY OF AMERICA **517**

BOTANICAL SOCIETY OF THE BRITISH ISLES *See* LIST OF MEMBERS AND SUBSCRIBERS / BOTANICAL SOCIETY OF THE BRITISH ISLES **517**

BOTANICAL SOCIETY OF THE BRITISH ISLES *See* B.S.B.I. NEWS **501**

BOTANICAL SOCIETY OF THE BRITISH ISLES *See* CONFERENCE REPORTS **507**

BOTANICAL SURVEY OF INDIA *See* BULLETIN OF THE BOTANICAL SURVEY OF INDIA **505**

BOTANICESKIJ ZURNAL (RU/0006-8136) [05463986] **503**

BOTANIKAI KOZLEMENYEK (HU/0006-8144) [07600022] **503**

BOTANISCH ZOOLOGISCHE GESELLSCHAFT (LH) **503**

BOTANISCHE JAHRBUCHER FUER SYSTEMATIK, PFLANZENGESCHICHTE UND PFLANZENGEOGRAPHIE (GW/0006-8152) [01536907] **503**

BOTANISCHE TUINEN UTRECHT *See* INDEX SEMINUM / UNIVERSITY BOTANIC GARDENS **174**

BOTANISCHER GARTEN DER UNIVERSITAT TUBINGEN *See* HORTUS TUBIGENSIS INDEX SEMINUM **2420**

BOTE, DER (GW) [05531035] **3338**

BOTH SIDES NOW (US) **4940**

BOTHALIA (SA/0006-8241) [01536923] **504**

BOTHNIAN BAY REPORTS (FI/0355-8142) [I03558142] **1447**

BOTHWELL TIMES (CN/0834-5686) [16079004] **5781**

BOTICARIO, EL (US/0006-825X) [02915969] **4294**

BOTSCHAFT, DIE (US) [15714037] **5735**

BOTSWANA *See* ESTABLISHMENT REGISTER, INDUSTRIAL CLASS **4646**

BOTSWANA (US/0301-9020) [01793283] 1465, **644**

BOTSWANA *See* ESTIMATES OF RECURRENT REVENUE AND EXPENDITURE **4722**

BOTSWANA *See* ESTIMATES OF REVENUE AND EXPENDITURE **4722**

BOTSWANA *See* TOWN COUNCILS ESTIMATES OF REVENUE AND EXPENDITURE, RECURRENT BUDGET **4756**

BOTSWANA AGRICULTURAL MARKETING BOARD *See* ANNUAL REPORT / BOTSWANA AGRICULTURAL MARKETING BOARD **60**

BOTSWANA. DEPT. OF SURVEYS AND LANDS *See* REPORT FOR THE PERIOD ... / REPUBLIC OF BOTSWANA, MINISTRY OF LOCAL GOVERNMENT AND LANDS, DEPARTMENT OF SURVEYS AND LANDS **4680**

BOTSWANA DIRECTORY (SA) [06950207] **2556**

BOTSWANA. HIGH COURT *See* CIVIL CAUSE **2950**

BOTSWANA. HIGH COURT *See* CRIM. COMMITTAL **3105**

BOTSWANA JOURNAL OF EARTH SCIENCES (BS/1013-1493) [I10131493] **1352**

BOTSWANA. MINISTRY OF WORKS AND COMMUNICATIONS. STATISTICS UNIT *See* TRANSPORT STATISTICS **5402**

BOTSWANA NATIONAL LIBRARY SERVICE *See* REPORT ON THE NATIONAL LIBRARY SERVICE **3245**

BOTSWANA NOTES AND RECORDS (BS/0525-5090) [02612984] **2498**

BOTTIN ADMINISTRATIF (FR/1147-1999) [22839374] **4634**

BOTTIN COMMUNES (FR) [05143548] **4634**

●BOTTIN DE L'INDUSTRIE DE LA MUSIQUE AU QUEBEC (CN/1187-9580) [26497672] **4104**

BOTTIN DU MOUVEMENT ETUDIANT / PRESSE ETUDIANTE DU QUEBEC (CN/0822-8965) [10634803] **1812**

BOTTIN DU TRANSPORT (FR) [02244407] **5378**

BOTTIN ENTREPRISES. IDENTITES (FR) [21550522] **644**

BOTTIN INFORMATIQUE (FR) [16412785] **1172**

BOTTIN MONDAIN; TOUT PARIS, TOUTE LA FRANCE (FR) [03108376] **5465**

BOTTIN QUEBECOIS DES CHERCHEURS EN GENEALOGIE (CN/0826-8428) [13843813] **2439**

BOTTIN / UNION CANADIENNE DES RELIGIEUSES CONTEMPLATIVES *CEASED.* (CN/0822-8949) [11046421] **4940**

BOTTLED WATER REPORTER (US/1046-543X) [07243642] **2365**

BOTTOM LINE (CHARLESTON, S.C.), THE (US/0279-1889) [07607686] **739**

BOTTOM LINE FOR KENTUCKY CPA'S, THE (US) [06353324] **739**

BOTTOM LINE (MARKHAM) (CN/0831-5477) [13999705] **739**

BOTTOM LINE (NEW YORK, N.Y.), THE (US/0888-045X) [13470700] 861, **3197**

BOTTOM LINE ON ALCOHOL IN SOCIETY, THE (US/0891-6950) [14248000] **1341**

BOTTOM LINE, PERSONAL (US/0274-4805) [06584492] 892, **644**

BOTTOM LINE, THE (US) [06407315] **2943**

BOTTOM LINE, THE (US/1056-7798) [23886892] **644**

BOTTOM LINE'S CANADIAN INTERNAL AUDITING LETTER, THE *See* NATIONAL INTERNAL AUDITING LETTER, THE **748**

●BOTTOM TIME (US/1065-7134) [26700406] **4887**

BOTTOMLINE (US/0361-4662) [02246847] 1278, **1256**

BOTTOMLINE (WASHINGTON, D.C.) *See* SAVINGS & COMMUNITY BANKER **810**

BOTTOMLINE (WASHINGTON, D.C. : 1983) *CEASED.* (US/0740-5464) [09965449] **779**

BOUCHERIE FRANCAISE, LA (FR) [04055354] **2329**

BOUCHERVILLE (QUEBEC) *See* PROGRAMME DE LOISIR **387**

BOUEILLE, LA (CN/0226-8663) [07313859] **5781**

BOUGE (CN) **5552**

BOUKWOSTEN (NE) **601**

BOULANGER PATISSIER 1979, LE (FR/0224-5027) [I02245027] **2329**

BOULDER CITY NEWS (1948) (US) [13501005] **5707**

BOULDER COUNTY BUSINESS REPORT (US) **644**

●BOULEVARD MAGAZINE (VICTORIA) (CN/1189-6051) [27202861] **316**

BOULEVARD (NEW YORK, N.Y.) (US/0885-9337) [12769325] **3368**

BOUND BROOK CHRONICLE (1971) (US/1047-3351) [11983609] **5709**

BOUNDARY 2 (US/0190-3659) [01408678] **3368**

BOUNDARY AND ANNEXATION SURVEY (US/0272-4472) [02653818] **4634**

BOUNDARY AND SECURITY BULLETIN (UK/0967-411X) **861**

BOUNDARY AND TERRITORY BRIEFINGS (UK/0967-4128) **861**

BOUNDARY CREEK TIMES, THE (CN/0822-8671) [10620328] **5781**

BOUNDARY ELEMENTS (GW) **5089**

BOUNDARY ELEMENTS ABSTRACTS AND NEWSLETTER (UK/0957-2902) [I09572902] **1966**

●BOUNDARY ELEMENTS COMMUNICATIONS (UK) **1966**

BOUNDARY-LAYER METEOROLOGY (NE/0006-8314) [01536930] **1421**

BOUNDARY WATERS JOURNAL, THE (US/0899-2681) [17868392] **2188**

BOUNTY INFANT CARE GUIDE, THE (UK/1183-0654) [24623493] **2277**

BOUNTY NEWS (US) [01536932] **1812**

BOURBON COUNTY CITIZEN, THE (US/0747-0282) [10498670] **5679**

BOURBON NEWS-MIRROR (1971) (US/1042-5225) [15742275] **5663**

BOURBON TIMES (PARIS, KY.) (US/1040-9017) [18354576] **5679**

BOURNE COURIER (US/0895-2590) [13648878] **5688**

BOURNE SOCIETY *See* LOCAL HISTORY RECORDS - BOURNE SOCIETY **2482**

BOURSE CANADIENNE DES ECHETS (CN) **893**

BOURSE D'EMPLOIS EN REVUE, LA (CN/0228-2542) [06860207] **1656**

BOURSES DES GOUVERNEMENTS ETRANGERS *See* PROGRAMME DE BOURSES DES GOUVERNEMENTS ETRANGERS / ADMINISTRE PAR LE CONSEIL INTERNATIONAL D'ETUDES CANADIENNES **4675**

BOURSES D'ETUDES ET DE PERFECTIONNEMENT DE L'ENSEIGNEMENT SUPERIEUR (CN/0713-472X) [08878548] **1812**

●BOURSES D'EXCELLENCE POUR DES ETUDES DE CYCLES SUPERIEURS, DE PERFECTIONNEMENT ET DE REINTEGRATION A LA RECHERCHE ..., GUIDE DU BOURSIER, LES (CN/1188-6773) [26498137] **1812**

BOUSSOLE (CN/0825-9178) [12782152] **3922**

BOUT DE PAPIER (CN/0833-9864) [15466717] **2485**

BOUT DE PAPIER (CN/0833-9864) [15467009] **4517**

BOUTIQUES DE FRANCE (FR/0291-0764) [I02910764] **952**

BOUW (NE/0366-2330) [02613242] **601**

BOUWBELANGEN (NE/0006-8330) [I00068330] **601**

BOUWEN MET STAAL (NE/0166-6363) [I01666363] **5089**

BOUWKRONIEK : WEEKBLAD VOOR DE BOUW EN INDUSTRIE (BE) **601**

BOUWMARKT ROTTERDAM (NE/0166-641X) [I0166641X] 601, **1599**

BOUWRECHT (NE/0165-1528) [I01651528] 601, **2943**

BOUWTIPS. ED. GRON, FRIESLAND, DRENTHE (NE/0165-6457) [I01656457] **601**

BOUWTIPS. ED. NOORD-HOLLAND EN ZUID-HOLLAND (NE/0165-6554) [I01656554] **602**

BOUWWERELD (NE/0026-5942) [I00265942] **602**

BOVE & RHODES INSIDE REPORT ON DESKTOP PUBLISHING AND MULTIMEDIA (US/1043-6065) [19495882] **1263**

BOVE AND RHODES REPORT ON DESKTOP PUBLISHING & MULTIMEDIA *See* INSIDE REPORT ON NEW MEDIA **1189**

BOVINE PRACTITIONER, THE *SUSPENDED.* (US/0524-1685) [01213902] **5506**

BOW & ARROW HUNTING (US/0894-7856) [12642544] **4869**

BOW VALLEY VIEWS (CN/0316-697X) [02247792] **5781**

BOW WAVE *See* BOW WAVE'S BOATING **592**

BOW WAVE'S BOATING (US/0743-8125) [10674530] **592**

BOWBENDER MAGAZINE (CN/0827-2638) [11873817] **4888**

BOWDEN EYE OPENER (CN/0704-0490) [08690820] **5781**

BOWDLE PIONEER, THE (US) [12812649] **5743**

BOWDOIN COLLEGE. MUSEUM OF ART *See* OCCASIONAL PAPERS - BOWDOIN COLLEGE. MUSEUM OF ART **4094**

BOWERS BUSINESS BAROMETER (US/1058-4234) [24301680] **644**

BOWER'S DIRECTORY FOR GREATER METROPOLITAN TORONTO (CN/1182-8994) [23599039] **2556**

BOWHUNTER (FORT WAYNE) (US/0273-7434) [05088155] **4869**

BOWHUNTING WORLD (US/1043-5492) [19483291] **4869**

BOWIE BLADE-NEWS, THE (US) [19841820] **5685**

BOWIE NEWS, THE (US) [17460899] **5747**

BOWKER ANNUAL LIBRARY AND BOOK TRADE ALMANAC, THE (US) [21968036] **3197**

BOWKER ANNUAL OF LIBRARY AND BOOK TRADE INFORMATION, THE (US/0068-0540) [04170021] **3197**

BOWKER'S COMPLETE SOURCEBOOK OF PERSONAL COMPUTING *CEASED.* (US/0000-0876) [11690730] 1235, **1265**

BOWKER'S COMPLETE VIDEO DIRECTORY (US/1051-290X) [21254019] **4378**

BOWKER'S LAW BOOKS AND SERIALS IN PRINT (US/0000-0752) [11460290] **3079**

BOWLERS JOURNAL (US/0164-9183) [04235685] **4888**

BOWLEY, R. L. ISLES OF SCILLY *See* STANDARD GUIDEBOOK TO THE ISLES OF SCILLY, THE **5491**

BOWLINE (CN/0316-2532) [02247541] **592**

BOWLING DIGEST (US/8750-3603) [09798878] **4888**

BOWLING GREEN STATE UNIVERSITY BOWLING GREEN *See* ABSTRACTS OF THESES AND DISSERTATIONS (BOWLING GREEN, OHIO) **1806**

BOWLING GREEN TIMES, THE (US/0162-6701) [04200610] **5702**

BOWLING MAGAZINE (1988) (US/1050-5121) [21487601] **4888**

BOWLING PROPRIETOR (US/0006-8446) [03987006] 644, **4858**

BOWMAN FINDER (US) [01536950] **5725**

BOWMAN'S ACCOUNTING REPORT (US/0897-3482) [17462130] **739**

BOWNE DIGEST FOR CORPORATE & SECURITIES LAWYERS (US/0896-906X) [17192501] 3096, **3079**

BOWSER DIRECTORY OF SMALL STOCKS, THE (US/1053-0908) [22448548] **893**

BOWSER REPORT, THE (US/0738-7288) [09655518] **893**

BOX 749 (US/0364-3344) [02625571] **3369**

BOX 1980 (US/0362-2584) [02298220] **1341**

BOX ELDER NEWS JOURNAL (1986) (US/0892-225X) [14193458] **5756**

●BOX N' CHEST (US/1064-0096) [26190750] **3369**

BOX Y LUCHA (US) [04989397] **4888**

BOXBOARD CONTAINERS (US/0006-8497) [02244636] **4218**

BOXES AND ARROWS (US/0742-4574) [10356557] **1253**

BOXING ILLUSTRATED (US/0006-8500) [01448248] **4888**

BOXING MONTHLY (UK/0956-098X) [I0956098X] **4888**

BOXING NEWS (UK/0006-8519) [I00068519] **4888**

BOXING REGISTRY'S RATINGS GUIDE (US/1056-5353) [23734783] **4888**

BOXING TODAY (US/0274-7979) [05243890] **4888**

BOXING TODAY (NEW YORK, N.Y. 1991) (US/1054-8106) [22978783] **4888**

BOXING WEEKLY (UK/0959-8944) [I09598944] **4888**

BOXOFFICE (US/0006-8527) [05261926] **4064**

BOXWOOD BULLETIN, THE (US/0006-8535) [02445419] **5229**

BOYCOTT LAW BULLETIN (US/0162-1726) [04106438] **2943**

BOYCOTT REPORT (US/0738-5161) [03807743] **2257**

BOYERTOWN AREA TIMES, THE (US) [18617316] **5735**

BOYS' CLUBS OF AMERICA *See* JUNIOR BOOK AWARDS **3458**

BOYS' LIFE (US/0006-8608) [01536963] **1060**

BOYS' QUEST (US) **1060**

BOZEMAN DAILY CHRONICLE (US) [13415547] **5705**

BOZJA BESEDA (CN) [12285038] **4940**

BOZZE *CEASED.* (IT/0391-6723) [08829618] **4517**

BP REPORT ON THE BUSINESS OF BOOK PUBLISHING (US/0145-9457) [02517071] **4827**

BP REVIEW OF WORLD GAS (UK) [18767452] **4252**

BP SHIELD (UK) **4252**

BP STATISTICAL REVIEW OF WORLD ENERGY (UK/0263-9815) [08530077] **1934, 1961**

BP&R BRITISH PLASTICS AND RUBBER (UK/0307-6164) [02316299] **5075, 4454**

BPC, BUILDING PRODUCTS CATALOG *CEASED.* (US/0161-6293) [03973493] **602**

BPRC TECHNICAL REPORT (US/1056-8050) [23861667] **2556**

BPT-BERICHT (GW/0721-9245) [08159255] **3558**

BQSF REVIEW *CEASED.* (UK) [06492091] **2135**

BR. BAUSTOFF-RECYCLING + DEPONIETECHNIK (GW/0934-683X) [I0934683X] **5089**

BRABANTS HEEM (NE) [I0166431X] **2679**

BRABANTSE LEEUW, DE (NE) [08365925] **2439**

BRABY'S CAPE PROVINCE DIRECTORY (SA) [04020452] **2498, 5500**

BRABY'S NATAL DIRECTORY (SA) [04008443] **2485**

BRABY'S TRANSKEI BUSINESS DIRECTORY (SA) [04728507] **825**

BRACARA AUGUSTA (PO) [03256994] **2679**

BRACEBRIDGE EXAMINER (CN/0704-0210) [04879776] **5781**

BRACKEN COUNTY NEWS, THE (US) [13194658] **5679**

BRACKISHWATER AQUACULTURE ABSTRACTS (PH/0116-1377) [15499481] **2297**

BRACTON LAW JOURNAL, THE (UK/0308-4574) [04145842] **2943**

BRAD ADVERTISER & AGENCY LIST (UK/0144-6126) [I01446126] **756**

BRADEA (BL/0084-800X) [02607651] **504**

BRADENTON HERALD, THE (US) [29021149] 5648, **5649**

BRADFORD BOOK OF COLLECTOR'S PLATES, THE *CEASED.* (US/0161-2794) [03702075] **2586**

BRADFORD ERA, THE (US) [14866399] **5735**

BRADFORD JOURNAL (BRADFORD, PA. : 1973) (US) [16872564] **5735**

BRADFORD PRICE BOOK (US) **2603**

●BRADFORD STUDIES ON SOUTH EASTERN EUROPE (UK/1354-7739) **2679**

BRADFORD STUDIES ON YUGOSLAVIA (UK/0143-5043) [09875468] **2679**

BRADFORD'S DIRECTORY OF MARKETING RESEARCH AGENCIES AND MANAGEMENT CONSULTANTS IN THE UNITED STATES AND THE WORLD (US/0068-063X) [04630229] **921**

BRADLEYA *CEASED.* (UK/0265-086X) [10835159] **504**

BRADY HERALD, THE (US) [13980874] **5747**

BRADYLINE (US/1049-5312) [21247947] **5089**

BRAGANTIA : BOLETIM TECNICO DO INSTITUTO AGRONOMICO DO ESTADO DE SAO PAULO (BL/0006-8705) [01536978] **165**

BRAHMAN JOURNAL, THE (US/0192-6764) [02384268] **207**

BRAHMANA-GAURAVA (II/0304-9272) [01784146] **5040**

BRAIDWOOD INDEX, THE (US) [23443475] **5658**

BRAILLE BOOK REVIEW (US/0006-873X) [01536983] 4827, **4384**

BRAILLE BOOKS (US/0277-5247) [07586764] 4384, **4827**

BRAILLE MONITOR, THE (US/0006-8829) [01015129] **4384**

BRAILLE SCIENCE JOURNAL (UK) 5089, **4384**

BRAILLE SCORES CATALOG. INSTRUMENTAL (US/0145-3165) [07372621] 4384, **4104**

BRAILLE SCORES CATALOG. ORGAN (US/0145-3149) [04823026] 4384, **4104**

BRAILLE SCORES CATALOG. VOCAL (US/1051-1016) [09737313] 4384, **4105**

BRAILLE STAR THEOSOPHIST, THE (US/0006-8918) [03987962] 4940, **4384**

BRAIN (UK/0006-8950) [01536984] **3828**

BRAIN AND COGNITION (US/0278-2626) [07753769] 3828, **4577**

BRAIN & DEVELOPMENT (TOKYO. 1979) (JA/0387-7604) [05730754] **3828**

BRAIN AND LANGUAGE (US/0093-934X) [01793424] 3270, **3828**

BRAIN, BEHAVIOR AND EVOLUTION (SZ/0006-8977) [01536985] **3828**

BRAIN, BEHAVIOR, AND IMMUNITY (US/0889-1591) [13800590] **3828**

BRAIN DYSFUNCTION (SZ/0259-1278) [18281320] **3828**

BRAIN INJURY (UK/0269-9052) [12055327] **3828**

●BRAIN, MIND & COMMON SENSE (US/1064-671X) [26268081] **4578**

BRAIN PATHOLOGY (SZ/1015-6305) [24603872] 3893, **3829**

BRAIN RESEARCH (NE/0006-8993) [01536986] **3829**

BRAIN RESEARCH BULLETIN (US/0361-9230) [02134161] **3829**

BRAIN RESEARCH REVIEWS (NE) [19645042] **3829**

BRAIN TOPOGRAPHY (US/0896-0267) [16E85199] **3829**

BRAINERD DISPATCH (US) [01775688] **5694**

BRAINSTORMER (BELLINGHAM, MASS.) (US/1061-6675) [25394801] **861**

BRAINTREE FORUM AND OBSERVER (US) [19932092] **5688**

BRAKE & FRONT END (US/0193-726X) [05250388] 644, **5408**

BRAKE AND FRONT END SERVICE *See* BRAKE & FRONT END **5408**

BRAKES (US/0095-1854) [01796230] 5408, **4769**

BRANCH AUTOMATION NEWS *See* BANK AUTOMATION NEWS **1218**

BRANCH BANKER'S REPORT *CEASED.* (US/0162-7481) [04220598] **780**

BRANCH DEPOSIT REPORT OF FLORIDA BANK AND THRIFT INSTITUTIONS (US) [22968376] **780**

BRANCH DIRECTORY AND SUMMARY OF DEPOSITS FOR THE STATE OF NEW YORK (US/0147-3131) [03137417] **780**

BRANCH DIRECTORY AND SUMMARY OF DEPOSITS FOR THE STATE OF OHIO (US/0147-1546) [03114696] **780**

BRANCH DIRECTORY AND SUMMARY OF DEPOSITS FOR THE STATE OF PENNSYLVANIA (US/0148-3021) [03285824] **780**

BRANCH DIRECTORY AND SUMMARY OF DEPOSITS FOR THE STATES OF CALIFORNIA, NEW MEXICO, ARIZONA (US/0147-3115) [03137036] **780**

BRANCH DIRECTORY AND SUMMARY OF DEPOSITS FOR THE STATES OF CONNECTICUT, MAINE, MASSACHUSETTS, NEW HAMPSHIRE, RHODE ISLAND, VERMONT (US/0147-5002) [03181753] **780**

BRANCH DIRECTORY AND SUMMARY OF DEPOSITS FOR THE STATES OF IDAHO, NEVADA, WASHINGTON, OREGON, UTAH (US/0147-314X) [03137379] **780**

BRANCH DIRECTORY AND SUMMARY OF DEPOSITS FOR THE STATES OF INDIANA, MICHIGAN (US/0147-1538) [03114535] **780**

BRANCH DIRECTORY AND SUMMARY OF DEPOSITS FOR THE STATES OF MARYLAND, DISTRICT OF COLUMBIA, VIRGINIA (US/0147-3123) [03137446] **780**

BRANCH DIRECTORY AND SUMMARY OF DEPOSITS FOR THE STATES OF NEW JERSEY, DELAWARE (US/0147-3778) [03155086] **780**

BRANCH DIRECTORY AND SUMMARY OF DEPOSITS FOR THE STATES OF SOUTH CAROLINA, NORTH CAROLINA (US/0147-2836) [03137346] **780**

BRANCH FOUR (US/1041-3324) [18705991] **4517**

BRANCH NOTES / WATERLOO-WELLINGTON BRANCH, ONTARIO GENEALOGICAL SOCIETY (CN/0383-7505) [03248102] **2439**

BRANCHES AND ACORNS (US) [13717484] **2440**

BRANCHES & TWIGS : NEWSLETTER OF GENEALOGICAL SOCIETY OF VERMONT (US/0742-9851) [07332315] **2440**

BRANCHES (BERKELEY, CALIF.) (US/0892-6220) [15244541] **2257**

BRANCHES EXPLOITATION FORESTIERE, CARBONISATION EN FORET ET SCIERIE : RESULTATS STATISTIQUES (FR) [01794278] **2376**

BRANCHING OUT FROM ST. CLAIR COUNTY, ILLINOIS (US/8755-9749) [04031996] **2440**

BRANCHLINE (OTTAWA) (CN/0824-233X) [10634741] **5429**

BRAND & BRANDWEER (NE/0165-4675) [I01654675] **756**

BRAND BOOK, THE (UK) [01787572] **2724**

BRAND RECOGNITION STUDY : OFFICE EQUIPMENT & METHODS (CN/0380-9463) [03031913] 4210, **922**

●BRANDADVANTAGE (WILMETTE, ILL.) (US/1064-5756) [26207920] **1293**

BRANDEIS QUARTERLY, THE (US/0273-7175) [06870514] **1812**

BRANDHILFE (GW/0006-906X) [I0006906X] **2288**

BRANDING IRON OF THE BILL RICE RANCH, THE (US/0738-498X) [09612304] **4384**

BRANDING IRON, THE (US/0006-9078) [02788777] **2724**

BRANDON DIRECTORY, THE (CN/0710-7676) [08336382] **2529**

BRANDON NEWS (US) 5648, **5649**

BRANDON UNIVERSITY *See* CALENDAR - BRANDON UNIVERSITY **1813**

BRANDON UNIVERSITY. RETIREMENT PLAN *See* AUDITOR'S REPORT AND FINANCIAL STATEMENTS FOR THE YEAR ENDED DECEMBER 31 ... **4712**

BRANDON UNIVERSITY. RURAL COMMUNITY RESOURCE CENTRE *See* CENTREFOLD (BRANDON) **2817**

BRANDON VALLEY CHALLENGER (US/0746-8261) [10306719] **5743**

BRANDS AND THEIR COMPANIES (US/1047-6407) [20740000] **1302**

BRANDSCHUTZ (AUSGABE RHEINLAND-PFALZ) (GW/0340-8019) [09366010] **4769**

BRANDSTOFFEN BRUSSEL (BE/0778-5097) [I07785097] **1021**

BRANDVAERN (DK/0106-6072) [02241989] **2288**

BRANDWACHT (GW/0006-9116) [02243263] 602, **2288**

●BRANDWEEK (NEW YORK, N.Y.) (US/1064-4318) [26229873] **756**

BRANDYWINE MAGAZINE (US/0741-9880) [10262766] **2485**

BRANFORD REVIEW, THE (US/0888-1901) [08006306] **5645**

BRANGUS JOURNAL (US/0006-9132) [01536998] **207**

BRANHAM AUTOMOBILE REFERENCE BOOK, SHOWING IN ILLUSTRATED FORM THE LOCATION OF MOTOR AND SERIAL NUMBERS ON ALL PASSENGER CARS AND TRUCKS (US) [04769725] **5408**

BRANHAM'S MOTORCYCLE AND SNOWMOBILE REFERENCE (US) [04769751] **4080**

BRANNTWEINWIRTSCHAFT, DIE (GW) [05761842] **2365**

BRANSON BEACON AND WHITE RIVER LEADER *See* BRANSON TRI-LAKES DAILY NEWS **5702**

●BRANSON TRI-LAKES DAILY NEWS (US/1063-6994) [25810301] **5702**

BRANSON'S COUNTRY REVIEW (US/1066-4033) [26943380] **4105**

BRANT NEWS (CN/0707-7998) [04955106] **5781**

BRANTCHES - ONTARIO GENEALOGICAL SOCIETY. BRANT COUNTY BRANCH (CN/0848-841X) [20535876] **2440**

BRASIL (BL) [02241726] **1549**

BRASIL ATRAVES DOS TEXTOS (BL) [05339372] **2551**

BRASIL FINANCIERO *See* GRANDES COMPANHIAS, AS **678**

BRASIL
Alphabetical Title Index

BRASIL FLORESTAL **SUSPENDED.** (BL/0045-270X) [02788835] **2376**

BRASIL HOJE (1981) (BL) [09749062] **2551**

BRASIL MADEIRA (BL) [05806691] **2376**

BRASIL, MEETING FACILITIES (BL) [07154299] **2804**

BRASIL, PERSPECTIVAS INTERNACIONAIS **CEASED.** (BL) [12654907] **4517**

BRASIL PORTO ALEGRE (BL/0103-751X) [I0103751X] **3369**

BRASIL, S.A (BL) [01792035] **1599**

BRASILIA (PO) [06116881] **4085**

BRASILIANS, THE (US) [02868934] **2724**

BRASILIANS, THE (US/0741-0298) [10067886] **2724**

BRASILIEN, FORSCHUNGSPOLITIK UNE FORSCHUNGSPRAXIS / BUNDESSTELLE FUER AUSSENHANDELSINFORMATION (GW) [10257189] **5089**

BRASILIEN: WIRTSCHAFTLICHE ENTWICKLUNG (GW) [05691301] **1549**

BRASILIEN : WIRTSCHAFTLICHE ENTWICKLUNG DES BUNDESSTATES RIO GRANDE DO SUL (GW) [05136249] **1549**

BRASILIEN WIRTSCHAFTSDATEN / BUNDESSTELLE FUR AUSSENHANDELSINFORMATION (GW) [08678520] **1465**

BRASILIEN WIRTSCHAFTSDATEN UND WIRTSCHAFTSDOKUMENTATION / BUNDESSTELLE FUR AUSSENHANDELSINFORMATION (GW) [07436280] **1549**

BRASILIEN : WIRTSCHAFTSDOKUMENTATION (GW) [03382050] **1465**

BRASILINFORM. NEWS BRIEFS (BL) [13035519] **4465, 1465**

BRASS BULLETIN (SZ/0303-3848) [01793930] **4105**

BRASS MILL PRODUCTS See COPPER AND COPPER ALLOY MILL PRODUCTS **4000**

BRASS MODELER & COLLECTOR (US/1056-2346) [23592347] **2771**

BRASS RESEARCH SERIES (US/0363-454X) [02422371] **4105**

●BRASSEY'S DEFENCE YEARBOOK / EDITED BY THE CENTRE FOR DEFENCE STUDIES (UK) [28836009] **4038**

BRATISLAVA. UNIVERZITA. FAKULTA TELESNEJ VYCHOVY A SPORTU See ACTA - BRATISLAVA. UNIVERZITA. FAKULTA TELESNEJ VYCHOVY A SPORTU **4881**

BRATISLAVA. UNIVERZITA. LEKARSKA FAKULTA See FOLIA FACULTATIS MEDICAE UNIVERSITATIS COMENIANAE BRATISLAVIENSIS **3577**

BRATISLAVSKE LEKARSKE LISTY (XO/0006-9248) [01537007] **3558**

BRATSKII VESTNIK (RU/0203-5839) [02638940] **5057**

BRATSTVO (TORONTO) (CN/0006-9264) [02285019] **5229**

BRAUCH REPORT ON ELECTRONIC PUBLISHING, THE (CN/0826-9335) [13143758] **4812**

BRAUER-UND MAELZER-LEHRLING (GW/0520-7568) [02812058] **2329**

BRAUEREI FORUM (GW/0179-2466) [I01792466] **2365**

BRAUEREI-JOURNAL (GW/0172-0589) [I01720589] **2365**

BRAUEREI- UND GETRANKE-RUNDSCHAU (SZ) [27352892] **2365**

BRAUEREIEN UND MALZEREIEN IN EUROPA (GW) [05251686] **2365**

BRAUINDUSTRIE (GW/0341-7115) [03092915] **2365**

BRAUNKOHLE (DUSSELDORF. 1972) (GW/0341-1060) [01788932] **1934**

BRAUNSCHWEIGER ANGLISTISCHE ARBEITEN (GW) [03462271] **3270**

BRAUNSCHWEIGER GEOGRAPHISCHE STUDIEN (GW/0524-2444) [03469029] **2556**

BRAUNSCHWEIGER NATURKUNDLICHE SCHRIFTEN (GW/0174-3384) [07321778] **4163**

BRAUNSCHWEIGER ZEITUNG (GW) [12417389] **5801**

BRAUNSCHWEIGISCHE WISSENSCHAFTLICHE GESELLSCHAFT See ABHANDLUNGEN DER BRAUNSCHWEIGISCHEN WISSENSCHAFTLICHEN GESELLSCHAFT **5079**

BRAUNSCHWEIGISCHES JAHRBUCH (GW/0068-0745) [03109122] **2679**

BRAUWELT (1978) (GW/0724-696X) [10598855] **2329**

BRAUWELT INTERNATIONAL (GW/0934-9340) [11752562] **2365**

BRAVEAR (US/0737-0768) [09273822] **2529**

BRAVO MUNCHEN (GW/0406-9595) [I04069595] 4105, **4064**

BRAVO (TORONTO) (CN/0714-6981) [09543151] **383**

BRAXTON CITIZEN'S NEWS (US) [12688668] **5763**

BRAXTON DEMOCRAT-CENTRAL, THE (US) [12688648] **5763**

BRAYER, THE (US) [10313103] **207**

BRAY'S THE DEVON REFERENCE INFORMATION & GAZETTEER (UK) [12402381] **2556**

BRAZIL See LEGIS BANCOS INFORMATIVO. IMPOSTO DE RENDA : IR **3001**

BRAZIL (US) **3338**

BRAZIL See LEGISLACAO FEDERAL E MARGINALIA **3001**

BRAZIL See LEGISLACAO DE ENSINO DE 1O. E 2O. GRAUS. FEDERAL **3001**

BRAZIL See IMPOSTO DE RENDA NA FONTE : TABELAS PRATICAS **2980**

BRAZIL. COMISSAO DE COORDENACAO DAS ATIVIDADES DE PROCESSAMENTO ELECTRONICO See BOLETIM TECNICO - CAPRE **1256**

BRAZIL. COMISSAO DE FINANCIAMENTO DA PRODUCAO See AGRICULTURA : PERSPECTIVAS - BRAZIL. COMISSAO DE FINANCIAMENTO DA PRODUCAO **49**

BRAZIL. COMISSAO DE FINANCIAMENTO DA PRODUCAO. DEPARTAMENTO DE PESQUISAS ECONOMICAS See ANUARIO ESTATISTICO - COMISSAO DE FINANCIAMENTO DA PRODUCAO, DEPARTAMENTO DE PESQUISAS ECONOMICAS **151**

BRAZIL. COMISSAO EXECUTIVA DO PLANO DE RECUPERACAO ECONOMICO-RURAL DA LAVOURA CACAUEIRA See BOLETIM ESTATISTICO DO CACAU **1599**

BRAZIL. COMISSAO EXECUTIVA DO SAL See PERSPECTIVA DO SAL, A **1621**

BRAZIL. COMISSAO NACIONAL DE ENERGIA NUCLEAR See RELATORIO ANUAL - COMISSAO NACIONAL DE ENERGIA NUCLEAR **2158**

BRAZIL. CONGRESSO NACIONAL. CAMARA DOS DEPUTADOS. DIRETORIA LEGISLATIVA See ENDERECOS DOS SENHORES DEPUTADOS E GUIA TELEFONICO DA CAMARA DOS DEPUTADOS **4646**

BRAZIL. CONGRESSO. SENADO. SECAO DE TELEX E TELEFONIA See ENDERCOS DOS SENHORES SENADORES (BRAZIL) **4473**

BRAZIL. CONSELHO NACIONAL DE DESPORTOS See RELATORIO - CONSELHO NACIONAL DE DESPORTOS **4914**

BRAZIL. CONSELHO NACIONAL DE DESPORTOS See BOLETIM INFORMATIVO - CONSELHO NACIONAL DE DESPORTOS **4887**

BRAZIL. COORDENACAO DE ASSISTENCIA MEDICA E HOSPITALAR See CADASTRO HOSPITALAR BRASILEIRO **3777**

BRAZIL. COORDENACAO DE LEGISLACAO E NORMAS DE ENSINO See SELECAO DE PARECERES E ESTUDOS DA COORDENACAO DE LEGISLACAO E NORMAS DE ENSINO **3047**

BRAZIL. DEPARTAMENTO DE ASSUNTOS UNIVERSITARIOS See INFORME TECNICO - DEPARTAMENTO DE ASSUNTOS UNIVERSITARIOS **1830**

BRAZIL. DEPARTAMENTO DE ENSINO SUPLETIVO See PLANO DE OBJETIVOS: PIPMO - RJ **1774**

BRAZIL. DEPARTAMENTO DE POLICIA FEDERAL. DIVISAO DE COMMUNICACAO SOCIAL See INFORMATIVO **3166**

BRAZIL. DEPARTAMENTO NACIONAL DE PORTOS E VIAS NAVEGAVEIS See INFORMATIVO **5203**

BRAZIL DEVELOPMENT SERIES (BL) [01787485] **2816**

BRAZIL. DIRECTORIA DE NAVEGACAO. DIVISAO DE HIDROGRAFIA. ANAIS HIDROGRAFICOS See ANAIS HIDROGRAFICOS **5529**

BRAZIL. DIRETORIA DE ARMAMENTO E COMUNICACOES DA MARINHA See PREVISOES IONOSFERICAS MUF **1433**

BRAZIL. DIRETORIA DE HIDROGRAFIA E NAVEGACAO See LIST OF NAUTICAL CHARTS AND ITS CORRECTIONS BY NOTICES TO MARINERS: PERMANENT, PRELIMINARY AND TEMPORARY **4185**

BRAZIL. DIRETORIA DE HIDROGRAFIA E NAVEGACAO See ANAIS HIDROGRAFICOS **5529**

BRAZIL. DIVISAO DE INFORMACAO DE MERCADO AGRICOLA See INFORMATIVO ESTATISTICO DE MERCADO AGRICOLA DE GOIAS **96**

BRAZIL GOSPEL NEWS (US) [01776803] **4940**

BRAZIL HERALD (BL) [04939450] **2551**

BRAZIL INFORMATION (BL) [10423442] **2551**

BRAZIL (LONDON, ENGLAND) (UK/0267-9965) [12985059] **2485**

BRAZIL. MINISTERIO DA AGRICULTURA. SUBSECRETARIA DE PLANEJAMENTO E ORCAMENTO See PROGRAMACAO DA REGIAO NORDESTE **122**

BRAZIL. MINISTERIO DA FAZENDA. DELEGACIA ESTADUAL NA GUANABARA. SETOR DE DOCUMENTACAO See BOLETIM INFORMATIVO DO SETOR DE DOCUMENTACAO **410**

BRAZIL. MINISTERIO DA FAZENDA. INSPETORIA-GERAL DE FINANCAS See RELATORIO DAS ATIVIDADES ADMINISTRATIVAS DA INSPETORIA-GERAL DE FINANCAS DO MINISTERIO DA FAZENDA **4744**

BRAZIL. MINISTERIO DA FAZENDA. INSPETORIA-GERAL DE FINANCAS. RELATORIO DAS ATIVIDADES See RELATORIO DAS ATIVIDADES ADMINISTRATIVAS DA INSPETORIA-GERAL DE FINANCAS DO MINISTERIO DA FAZENDA **4744**

BRAZIL. MINISTERIO DA FAZENDA. NUCLEO REGIONAL DE ADMINISTRACAO NA GUANABARA. SETOR DE DOCUMENTACAO See BOLETIM INFORMATIVO **410**

BRAZIL. MINISTERIO DA JUSTICA See ARQUIVOS DO MINISTERIO DA JUSTICA **2937**

BRAZIL. MINISTERIO DAS MINAS E ENERGIA See BALANCO ENERGETICO NACIONAL **1933**

BRAZIL. MINISTERIO DAS MINAS E ENERGIA See DESTAQUES **1603**

BRAZIL. MINISTERIO DA FAZENDA. DELEGACIA NO RIO DE JANEIRO. SECAO DE COCUMENTACAO See BOLETIM INFORMATIVO DA SECAO DE DOCUMENTACAO **4713**

BRAZIL. MINISTERIO DO INTERIOR. COORDENADORIA DE COMUNICACAO SOCIAL See INTERIOR **1567**

BRAZIL. MINISTERIO DO INTERIOR. SECRETARIA GERAL See ATUACAO DO MINTER **1547**

BRAZIL. MINISTERIO DO TRABALHO See BOLETIM DO TRABALHO **1656**

BRAZIL. MINISTERIO DO TRABALHO E PREVIDENCIA SOCIAL. CENTRO DE DOCUMENTACAO E INFORMATICA See BOLETIM TECNICO **1656**

BRAZIL. MUSEU NACIONAL See BOLETIM DO MUSEU NACIONAL. NOVA SERIE, ZOOLOGIA **5578**

BRAZIL REPORT (BL/0143-5272) [01786495] **1549**

BRAZIL. SECRETARIA DA RECEITA FEDERAL. COORDENACAO DO SISTEMA DE INFORMACOES ECONOMICO-FISCAIS See IMPOSTO DE RENDA PESSOA JURIDICA **4731**

BRAZIL. SECRETARIA DE ORCAMENTO E FINANCAS See ORCAMENTO DA UNIAO. PROJETO DE LEI / SECRETARIA DE PLANEJAMENTO DA PRESIDENCIA DA REPUBLICA, SECRETARIA DE ORCAMENTO E FINANCAS **4739**

BRAZIL. SECRETARIA DE ORCAMENTO E FINANCAS. PROJETO DE LEI ORCAMENTARIA ANUAL See ORCAMENTO DA UNIAO. PROJETO DE LEI / SECRETARIA DE PLANEJAMENTO DA PRESIDENCIA DA REPUBLICA, SECRETARIA DE ORCAMENTO E FINANCAS **4739**

BRAZIL. SECRETARIA DE TECNOLOGIA INDUSTRIAL See RELATORIO DE ATIVIDADES - SECRETARIA DE TECNOLOGIA INDUSTRIAL **5145**

BRAZIL SELLING : CATTLE BREEDING & AGRO INDUSTRIES (BL) [03397533] **207**

BRAZIL SERVICE (US/0889-1761) [13812580] **1465**

BRAZIL. SERVICO DE ESTATISTICA DA EDUCACAO E CULTURA See ESTATISTICAS DA EDUCACAO NACIONAL **1795**

BRAZIL. SERVICO DE ESTATISTICA DOS TRANSPORTES. ANUARIO ESTATISTICO DOS TRANSPORTS See ANUARIO ESTATISTICO DOS TRANSPORTES **5400**

BRAZIL. SERVICO DE PISCICULTURA See PUBLICACAO. SERIE 2-M. RELATORIO DOS SERVICOS EXECUTADOS **2095**

BRAZIL. SERVICO NACIONAL DE APRENDIZAGEM COMERCIAL See BOLETIM TECNICO DO SENAC **1728**

Alphabetical Title Index — BREWING

BRAZIL. SERVICO NACIONAL DE APRENDIZAGEM COMERCIAL. ADMINISTRACAO REGIONAL EM SERGIPE See RELATORIO GERAL / SENAC, ADMINISTRACAO REGIONAL EM SERGIPE **706**

BRAZIL. SERVICO NACIONAL DE APRENDIZAGEM COMERCIAL. ADMINISTRACAO REGIONAL NO ESTADO DO PIAUI See RELATORIO DAS ATIVIDADES DO EXERCICIO DE ... **849**

BRAZIL. SERVICO NACIONAL DE APRENDIZAGEM INDUSTRIAL. DEPARTAMENTO REGIONAL DO AMAZONAS See RELATORIO - SERVICO NACIONAL DE APRENDIZAGEM INDUSTRIAL, DEPARTAMENTO REGIONAL DO AMAZONAS **1706**

BRAZIL. SERVICO NACIONAL DE APRENDIZAGEM INDUSTRIAL. DEPARTAMENTO REGIONAL DO MARANHAO See RELATORIO - DEPARTAMENTO REGIONAL DO MARANHAO, SENAI **375**

BRAZIL. SERVICO NACIONAL DE APRENDIZAGEM INDUSTRIAL. DEPARTAMENTO REGIONAL DO PARANA See RELATORIO - SERVICO NACIONAL DE APRENDIZAGEM INDUSTRIAL, DEPARTAMENTO REGIONAL DO PARANA **1706**

BRAZIL. SERVICO NACIONAL DE APRENDIZAGEM INDUSTRIAL. DEPARTAMENTO REGIONAL DO RIO GRANDE DO SUL See RELATORIO / SENAI RS **1706**

BRAZIL. SERVICO NACIONAL DE APRENDIZAGEM INDUSTRIAL. DEPARTAMENTO REGIONAL DO RIO GRANDE DO SUL. RELATORIO DAS ATIVIDADES See RELATORIO / SENAI RS **1706**

BRAZIL. SUPERINTENDENCIA DO DESENVOLVIMENTO DO NORDESTE See RELATORIO SINTETICO SOBRE O PROGRAMA DE IRRIGACAO DO NORDESTE **2095**

BRAZIL. SUPERINTENDENCIA DO DESENVOLVIMENTO DO NORDESTE See SUDENE INFORMA **1585**

BRAZIL. SUPERINTENDENCIA DO DESENVOLVIMENTO DO NORDESTE. DIVISAO DE COMERCIO See NORDESTE EM NUMEROS **5334**

BRAZIL. SUPERINTENDENCIA DO DESENVOLVIMENTO DO NORDESTE. ESCRITORIO DO CEARA See ATIVIDADES DA SUDENE: CEARA **1598**

BRAZIL. SUPREMO TRIBUNAL FEDERAL See LEX, JURISPRUDENCIA DO SUPREMO TRIBUNAL FEDERAL **3002**

BRAZIL TIMES, THE (US) [13364505] **5663**

BRAZIL. TRIBUNAL REGIONAL ELECTORAL DE SAO PAULO See BOLETIM ELEITORAL **2942**

BRAZIL WATCH (WASHINGTON, D.C. 1985) (US/0897-3067) [13770931] **1549**

BRAZILIAN-AMERICAN CHAMBER OF COMMERCE See NEWS BULLETIN - BRAZILIAN-AMERICAN CHAMBER OF COMMERCE **1638**

BRAZILIAN BIBLE QUARTERLY (BL) **4940**

●BRAZILIAN COMMUNICATION RESEARCH YEARBOOK (BL/0103-9318) [27122313] **1105**

BRAZILIAN ECONOMIC INDICATORS (US/8755-089X) [10501065] **1549**

BRAZILIAN ECONOMIC OUTLOOK (US) [11246465] **1549**

BRAZILIAN ECONOMIC STUDIES (BL/0100-2910) [02515839] **1465**

BRAZILIAN GAZETTE, THE (UK/0307-160X) [01625735] **2485**

BRAZILIAN INDEX (BL) [06293544] **780**

BRAZILIAN JOURNAL OF MEDICAL AND BIOLOGICAL RESEARCH (BL/0100-879X) [08259300] 449, **3558**

●BRAZILIAN JOURNAL OF PHYSICS (BL/0103-9733) [26186812] **4398**

BRAZILIAN JOURNAL OF VETERINARY RESEARCH AND ANIMAL SCIENCE : REVISTA DA FACULDADE DE MEDICINA VETERINARIA E ZOOTECNIA DA UNIVERSIDADE DE SAO PAULO (BL/0303-7525) [24079493] **5506**

BRAZILIAN OVERSEAS NEWSLETTER (BL) **2551**

BRAZILINFORM NEWS LETTER (BL) **2551**

BRAZILYANER IDISHE TSAYTUNG (BL) [03196026] **2647**

BRAZORIA COUNTY NEWS, THE (US) [16903067] **5747**

BRAZORIAN NEWS, THE (US) [16902585] **5747**

BRAZOSPORT FACTS, THE (US/1065-7886) [14564360] **5747**

BRE DIGEST (UK) [18488728] **2019**

BRE (HOLLYWOOD, CALIF.) (US/1063-1011) [25861776] **1127**

BRE INFORMATION PAPER (UK) [19502163] **602**

BRE NEWS OF CONSTRUCTION RESEARCH (UK/0265-9611) [11008816] **602**

BRE NEWS OF FIRE RESEARCH (UK/0265-962X) [11823200] **2288**

BREAD AND JUSTICE (US) [19419221] **5275**

BREAD BOX See VIDEO TOASTER USER **1235**

BREAD FOR THE WORLD NEWSLETTER (US/1045-1005) [20020604] **5275**

●BREAD MACHINE NEWSLETTER, THE (US/1061-2718) [25224387] **2329**

BREAD OF LIFE (ANCASTER) (CN/0821-168X) [09747533] **4940**

BREAD PUDDING UPDATE (US/1042-7139) [19114111] **2789**

BREAK POINT WITH CHARLES COLSON (US/1062-2837) [25566626] **4940**

BREAK THROUGH CAMPSIE (AT/0812-9126) [08129126] **3197**

BREAK-THROUGH (HARTNEY) (CN/0824-6653) [10852455] **4105**

BREAKAWAY (POMONA, CALIF.) (US/1048-2881) [20909620] 4940, **2277**

BREAKING NEW GROUND (US) [11957572] **4385**

BREAKING THE SIEGE : THE NEWSLETTER OF THE MIDDLE EAST JUSTICE NETWORK (US) [22248895] **4517**

BREAKING THE SILENCE (OTTAWA, ONT.) CEASED. (CN/0713-4266) [09088971] 5275, **5552**

BREAKOUT CEASED. (US/0744-8295) [08584895] **4888**

BREAKTHROUGH (ATLANTA, GA.) (US/0885-8578) [12764496] **2771**

BREAKTHROUGH (EAST ORANGE, N.J.) (US/0889-3942) [09741428] **1728**

BREAKTHROUGH FOR WOMEN (CN/0228-7293) [07805629] **5552**

BREAKTHROUGH (HAMMOND, LA.) (US/1056-0130) [23444185] **2771**

BREAKTHROUGH NEWS (US) **1728**

BREAKTHROUGH (SAN FRANCISCO, CALIF.) (US) [06839853] **4465**

BREAKTHROUGH STRATEGIES CEASED. (US/1066-260X) [I1066260X] **2485**

BREAKTHROUGHS (US) [22714690] **4038**

BREARLEY SCHOOL See ALUMNAE DIRECTORY / THE BREARLEY SCHOOL **1096**

BREAST CANCER (US/0161-0112) [03643273] **3809**

BREAST CANCER RESEARCH AND TREATMENT (NE/0167-6806) [07902538] **3809**

BREAST DISEASE (US/0888-6008) [13662709] **3558**

BREAST DISEASES (US/1043-321X) [19411752] **3758**

●BREAST DISEASES UPDATES (US/1061-4575) [25312426] **3558**

●BREAST IMPLANT LITIGATION REPORTER (US/1062-1814) [25530799] **2943**

●BREAST JOURNAL (US/1075-122X) [29944352] **3558**

●BREAST : OFFICIAL JOURNAL OF THE EUROPEAN SOCIETY OF MASTOLOGY, THE (UK/0960-9776) [26672025] **3758**

BREASTFEEDING ABSTRACTS (US/0896-4572) [08530554] 3758, **3655**

●BREATHE! (LA QUINTA, CALIF.) (US/1065-710X) [26699804] 5372, **4769**

BRECHA (MEXICO CITY, MEXICO) (MX) [17988988] **4466**

BRECHA (MONTEVIDEO, URUGUAY) (UY) [14083629] **2917**

BRECHA : PUBLICACION MENSUAL DE LA COMISION PARA LA DEFENSA DE LOS DERECHOS HUMANOS EN CENTROAMERICA, CODEHUCA (CR) [20785146] **4504**

BRECHT YEARBOOK, THE (US/0734-8665) [08815442] **3369**

BRECKENRIDGE AMERICAN (US) [14053219] **5747**

BREEDER AND FEEDER (CN/0712-5291) [09145760] **207**

BREEDER FORUM (US/1059-0625) [24492987] **4286**

●BREEDING SCIENCE (JA) **68**

BREESE JOURNAL, THE (US) [08786336] **5658**

BREEZE (CN/0700-3641) [03304208] **3197**

BREEZE (CAPE CORAL, FLA.), THE (US/1053-4504) [22532656] 5648, **5649**

BREEZE (ROCKLEDGE, PA.) (US) [12170215] **5735**

BREF (ASSOCIATION DES TISSERANDS D'ICI), EN (CN/0228-8710) [08003205] **5348**

BREF BULLETIN DE RECHERCHES SUR L'EMPLOI ET LA FORMATION (FR/0758-1858) [07581858] **1656**

BREF DE L'ACAQ, EN (CN/0835-8710) [24266590] **5178**

BREF (OTTAWA), EN (CN/0714-5578) [09084917] **1889**

BREF (PARIS) (FR/0759-6898) [07596898] **384**

BREF RHONE ALPES (FR/0006-9566) [I00069566] 644, **1549**

BREISGAU-GESCHICHTSVEREIN SCHAUINSLAND See ZEITSCHRIFT DES BREISGAU-GESCHICHTSVEREINS SCHAUINSLAND **2716**

BREIZH (FR) [04171999] **2679**

BREMER COUNTY BROWSINGS (US/0896-7415) [17282829] **2440**

BREMER COUNTY INDEPENDENT (1959) (US/0899-8698) [16077361] **5668**

BREMISCHES JAHRBUCH (GW/0341-9622) [02667571] **2679**

BREMOND PRESS, THE (US) [14288318] **5747**

BRENESIA (CR/0304-3711) [01947753] **4163**

BRENGLE BRANCHES (US/8756-0445) [11463920] **2440**

BRENNER-STUDIEN (AU) [07781648] **3369**

BRENNPUNKTE DER SPORTWISSENSCHAFT / HERAUSGEGEBEN VON DER DEUTSCHEN SPORTHOCHSCHULE KOLN (GW/0932-8823) [19818057] **4888**

BRENNSTOFF-WAERME-KRAFT (GW/0006-9612) [06012423] **1934**

BRENNSTOFFSPIEGEL (GW/0342-6580) [05851152] 4252, **1600**

BREPOLS (FIRM) See BREPOLS PUBLISHERS NEWSLETTER **4812**

BREPOLS PUBLISHERS NEWSLETTER (BE) [08638451] **4812**

BRES (NE) [05188411] **316**

BRESCIAOGGI NUOVO (IT) **5804**

BRESLAU. POLITEKNIKA See ACTA - BRESLAU. POLITEKNIKA **407**

BRESLAU. POLITEKNIKA See ACTA POLYTECHNICAE WRATISLAVIENSIS **5080**

BRETAGNE (HACHETTE (FIRM)) (FR) [18492999] **5465**

BRETAGNE LINGUISTIQUE : CAHIERS DU GROUPE DE RECHERCHE SUR L'ECONOMIE LINGUISTIQUE DE LA BRETAGNE, LA (FR) [26539728] **3270**

BRETAGNE, REVUE POLITIQUE, MARITIME ET LITTERAIRE, LA (FR) [20439677] **5800**

BRETHREN IN CHRIST CHURCH / GENERAL CONFERENCE MINUTES (US) **4940**

BRETHREN IN CHRIST HISTORY AND LIFE (US/1071-4200) [08536029] **5057**

BRETHREN LIFE AND THOUGHT (US/0006-9663) [01776524] **4940**

BRETHREN MISSIONARY HERALD (US/0161-5238) [01587083] **4940**

BREVARD BUSINESS NEWS (US/0889-5104) [13920007] **644**

BREVES DE LA DELEGATION GENERALE A LA LANGUE FRANCAISE (FR) **3270**

BREVES DU COMMISSARIAT GENERAL DE LA LANGUE FRANCAISE See BREVES DE LA DELEGATION GENERALE A LA LANGUE FRANCAISE **3270**

BREVIORA (US/0006-9698) [01415078] **5578**

BREW INFO MONTHLY INDUSTRY REVIEW (NE) **2365**

BREWER & WINE MERCHANT & BREWERS' GUARDIAN See BREWERS' GUARDIAN **2365**

BREWER (LONDON) (UK/0006-9736) [03055067] **2365**

BREWERS' ALMANAC (US) [01537062] **2365**

BREWERS BULLETIN, THE (US/0006-9701) [03988804] **2365**

BREWER'S DIGEST. BUYERS' GUIDE & DIRECTORY, THE (US) [05965027] **2365**

BREWER'S DIGEST, THE (US/0006-971X) [06067001] **2365**

BREWERS' GUARDIAN (UK/0006-9728) [02240347] **2365**

BREWING AND BEVERAGE INDUSTRY INTERNATIONAL (GW) [21878674] **2365**

BREWING & DISTILLING INTERNATIONAL (UK/0308-1265) [02987259] **2365**

BREWING — Alphabetical Title Index

BREWING INDUSTRY NEWS, THE **CEASED.** (US/0273-5768) [07082808] **2365**

BREWSTER TRIBUNE (US) [01537065] **5694**

BREWTON STANDARD, THE (US) [11793843] **5625**

BRIAN COSTELLO ON MONEY MANAGEMENT (CN/0827-2794) [11734443] **4713**

BRIAR PATCH (CN/0703-8968) [03781563] **5193**

BRICK (CN/0382-8565) [03781956] **3338**

BRICK BULLETIN (UK/0307-9325) [02445445] **602**

BRICK IN ARCHITECTURE (US/0743-0043) [0431 3335] **293**

BRICKER BRANCHES (US/0897-7879) [16069056] **2440**

BRICKER'S INTERNATIONAL DIRECTORY *See* BRICKER'S INTERNATIONAL DIRECTORY. VOL. 1, LONG-TERM UNIVERSITY-BASED EXECUTIVE PROGRAMS **862**

BRICKER'S INTERNATIONAL DIRECTORY. VOL. 1, LONG-TERM UNIVERSITY-BASED EXECUTIVE PROGRAMS (US/1054-7835) [22971330] 1812, **862**

BRICKER'S INTERNATIONAL DIRECTORY. VOL. 2, SHORT-TERM UNIVERSITY-BASED EXECUTIVE PROGRAMS (US/1054-7843) [22971460] 1812, **862**

BRICKMAN LETTER, THE (US/0748-1853) [10908467] **893**

BRIDAL APPAREL NEWS (US) **1082**

BRIDAL GUIDE (US/0882-7451) [11957488] **2277**

BRIDE GUIDE (LOS ANGELES, CALIF.), THE (US/0730-1006) [07950651] **2277**

BRIDE GUIDE (SAN DIEGO, CALIF.), THE (US/0730-0972) [07949992] **2277**

BRIDE OF CHRIST, THE (US/0197-3045) [04935697] **5057**

BRIDE'S *See* BRIDE'S & YOUR NEW HOME **2277**

BRIDES AND SETTING UP HOME (UK/0006-9787) [I00069787] 5552, **2277**

●BRIDE'S & YOUR NEW HOME (US/1059-7476) [24706604] **2277**

BRIDES OF BERKSHIRE (UK/0957-3933) [I09573933] 1082, **5552**

BRIDES OF BRISTOL BATH & AVON (UK/0957-7432) [I09577432] 1082, **5552**

BRIDES OF DEVON & CORNWALL (UK/0957-3941) [I09573941] 1082, **5552**

BRIDES OF EAST ANGLIA (UK/0957-7270) [I09577270] 1082, **5552**

BRIDES OF HERTS, BUCKS & BEDS (UK/0957-395X) [I09573955X] 1082, **5552**

BRIDES OF NORTH EAST ENGLAND (UK/0957-7440) [I09577440] 1082, **5552**

BRIDES OF SCOTLAND (UK/0957-7289) [I09577289] 1082, **5552**

BRIDES OF SOMERSET (UK/0957-3968) [I09573968] 1082, **5552**

BRIDES OF SURREY (UK/0957-3976) [I09573976] 1082, **5552**

BRIDES OF THE NORTH WEST (UK/0958-7039) [I09587039] 1082, **5552**

BRIDES OF YORKSHIRE & HUMBERSIDE (UK/0957-3984) [I09573984] 1082, **5552**

BRIDGE (NE) **4858**

BRIDGE AND FERRY DIRECTORY : INCLUDING TOLL BRIDGES, FERRIES, DOMESTIC STEAMSHIP LINES AND AUTO/PASSENGER LAND CARRIERS (US) [13616293] **5378**

BRIDGE & STRUCTURAL ENGINEER (II) **2019**

BRIDGE BUILDER (SCHENECTADY, N.Y.), THE (US/0743-8958) [08610399] **2440**

BRIDGE (GLASSBORO, N.J.), THE (US/1052-5440) [22301284] **1861**

BRIDGE (HONG KONG) (HK/1018-8983) [10116582] **4940**

BRIDGE (LAFAYETTE, IND.) (US/8750-5266) [11478084] **1089**

BRIDGE (OAK PARK, MICH.), THE (US/1052-1569) [22196528] 3460, **3369**

BRIDGE OF ETA KAPPA NU *See* BRIDGE (LAFAYETTE, IND.) **1089**

BRIDGE RIVER LILLOOET NEWS (CN) **5781**

BRIDGE (SALEM, OR.), THE (US/0741-1200) [05244420] **2724**

BRIDGE, THE (UK) [05887461] **4858**

BRIDGE TODAY! (US/1043-6383) [19502499] **4858**

BRIDGE (WASHINGTON, D.C. : 1969), THE (US/0737-6278) [02258585] **1966**

BRIDGE WORLD, THE (US/0006-9876) [01537071] **4858**

BRIDGEPORT INDEX, THE (US) [14396021] **5747**

BRIDGEPORT LAW REVIEW (US/1066-8411) [25932055] **2943**

BRIDGEPORT LEADER (US) [23830291] **5658**

BRIDGEPORT NEWS (US) [22106966] **5658**

BRIDGEPORT POST *See* CONNECTICUT POST (BRIDGEPORT, CONN.) **5645**

BRIDGEPORT POST, THE (US/1049-9164) [09264305] **5645**

BRIDGES (NEW YORK, N.Y. : 1986) **CEASED.** (US/0893-391X) [15543836] **2529**

BRIDGES (SEATTLE, WASH.) (US/1046-8358) [20542141] 5046, **5552**

BRIDGES (TORONTO) **SUSPENDED.** (CN/0824-4960) [10680879] **1728**

BRIDGETON EVENING NEWS (US) [13200431] **5709**

BRIDGEVILLE AREA NEWS (US/1047-0670) [17717057] **5735**

●BRIDGEWATER-DAVIS PACIFIC INTELLIGENCE UPDATE (US/1060-3093) [24924248] **4517**

●BRIDGEWATER TOWNSMAN, THE (US) [29947737] **5688**

BRIDGING THE GAP (CALGARY) (CN/1184-6542) [23686601] **4940**

BRIDGING THE GAP (LANCASTER) **CEASED.** (CN/0840-7738) [19465819] **2440**

BRIDGTON NEWS, THE (US) [10341031] **5685**

BRIEF (BOSTON), THE (US/0520-9617) [01537074] **2943**

BRIEF (CHICAGO. 1980), THE (US/0273-0995) [06661398] 2876, **2943**

●BRIEF (FORT LAUDERDALE, FLA.) (US/1062-5690) [25669133] **862**

BRIEF (HOUSTON, TEX.) (US/0899-3009) [18060199] **862**

BRIEF OUTLINE OF ACTIVITIES OF THE COMMITTEES OF THE ASSOCIATION (UK) [04148228] **4634**

BRIEF OUTLINE OF THE OKLAHOMA REVENUE SYSTEM, A (US/0149-2020) [03434890] **4713**

BRIEF TIMES REPORTER, THE (US/0164-789X #y 0164-789) [04348419] **2943**

BRIEF TO THE ONTARIO COUNCIL ON UNIVERSITY AFFAIRS / RYERSON POLYTECHNICAL INSTITUTE (CN/0821-4050) [10314571] **1812**

BRIEF TO THE ONTARIO COUNCIL ON UNIVERSITY AFFAIRS (YORK UNIVERSITY) (CN/0706-6775) [04801034] **1812**

BRIEFING (TU) [06643984] 1465, **4466**

BRIEFING (US) [11315033] **1812**

BRIEFING BOOK ON MAJOR POLICY ISSUES (US/0276-9743) [07444981] **1656**

BRIEFING / NORTH-SOUTH INSTITUTE (CN) [08319374] **2556**

BRIEFING PAPER (UK) [08536127] **4504**

BRIEFING PAPER ON SOUTHERN AFRICA / INTERNATIONAL DEFENCE & AID FUND (UK/0262-3781) [09129724] **4038**

BRIEFING PAPERS (WASHINGTON, D.C.) (US/0007-0025) [01607356] **1549**

BRIEFING (SAO PAULO, BRAZIL) (BL) [10054327] **644**

BRIEFING (SHAWNEE MISSION, KAN.) **CEASED.** (US/1060-2941) [24915977] **5193**

BRIEFING--TERRORISM AND LOW INTENSITY CONFLICT *See* BRIEFING (SHAWNEE MISSION, KAN.) **5193**

BRIEFING, THE COMPREHENSIVE SOURCE FOR INTERNATIONAL SECURITY INTELLIGENCE **CEASED.** (US/1060-2941) **4517**

BRIEFINGS ON HOSPITAL SAFETY (US) **3777**

BRIEFINGS ON JCAHO (US/1054-6995) [22942577] **4769**

●BRIEFINGS ON LONG-TERM CARE REGULATIONS (US/1076-6014) [30571614] **4769**

BRIEFLET (US) [01510447] **68**

BRIEFLY SPEAKING (CN/0715-3759) [09137751] **2943**

BRIEFS / AMERICAN ASSOCIATION OF COLLEGES FOR TEACHER EDUCATION (US) [16840942] 1728, **2943**

BRIEFS / AMERICAN INSTITUTE OF FISHERY RESEARCH BIOLOGISTS (US/8755-0075) [11284245] 1447, **2297**

BRIEFS/ BREAD RESEARCH INSTITUTE OF AUSTRALIA (AT/0818-8653) [I08188653] **2329**

BRIEFS OF ACCIDENTS INVOLVING AMATEUR-HOME BUILT AIRCRAFT, U.S. GENERAL AVIATION (US/0362-8884) [02379283] 4769, **14**

BRIEFS OF ACCIDENTS INVOLVING COMMUTER AIR CARRIERS AND ON-DEMAND AIR TAXI OPERATIONS, U.S. GENERAL AVIATION (US) [04200118] **14**

BRIEFS OF ACCIDENTS INVOLVING MIDAIR COLLISIONS, U.S. GENERAL AVIATION (US/0360-392X) [02243896] **14**

BRIEFS OF ACCIDENTS INVOLVING MISSING AIRCRAFT, U.S. GENERAL AVIATION *See* BRIEFS OF ACCIDENTS INVOLVING MISSING AND MISSING LATER RECOVERED AIRCRAFT, U.S. GENERAL AVIATION **15**

BRIEFS OF ACCIDENTS INVOLVING MISSING AND MISSING LATER RECOVERED AIRCRAFT, U.S. GENERAL AVIATION (US/0360-6813) [02244807] **15**

BRIEFS OF ACCIDENTS INVOLVING ROTORCRAFT, U.S. GENERAL AVIATION / NATIONAL TRANSPORTATION SAFETY BOARD (US) [02239253] **15**

BRIEFS OF ACCIDENTS INVOLVING WEATHER AS A CAUSE/FACTOR, U.S. GENERAL AVIATION *See* BRIEFS OF FATAL ACCIDENTS INVOLVING WEATHER AS A CAUSE/FACTOR, U.S. GENERAL AVIATION **15**

BRIEFS OF AIRCRAFT ACCIDENTS INVOLVING TURBINE POWERED AIRCRAFT, U.S. GENERAL AVIATION (US/0091-1399) [01785497] 4769, **15**

BRIEFS OF FATAL ACCIDENTS INVOLVING WEATHER AS A CAUSE-FACTOR, U.S. GENERAL AVIATION (US/0360-7127) [02244811] 4769, **15**

BRIERCREST ECHO (CN/0821-5839) [09670422] **4940**

BRIGADA (MANAGUA, NICARAGUA) (NQ) [06669669] 4466, **1465**

BRIGANTIA (PO/0870-8339) [09010712] **2679**

BRIGHAM YOUNG UNIVERSITY *See* GEOLOGY STUDIES. SPECIAL PUBLICATIONS **1380**

BRIGHAM YOUNG UNIVERSITY. COLLEGE OF ENGINEERING AND TECHNOLOGY *See* ALUMNI DIRECTORY / BRIGHAM YOUNG UNIVERSITY, COLLEGE OF ENGINEERING AND TECHNOLOGY **1097**

●BRIGHAM YOUNG UNIVERSITY EDUCATION AND LAW JOURNAL (US) [28133032] **2943**

BRIGHAM YOUNG UNIVERSITY ... FIRESIDE AND DEVOTIONAL SPEECHES (US/0740-4107) [09939183] **4940**

BRIGHAM YOUNG UNIVERSITY JOURNAL OF LAW AND EDUCATION *See* BRIGHAM YOUNG UNIVERSITY EDUCATION AND LAW JOURNAL **2943**

BRIGHAM YOUNG UNIVERSITY LAW REVIEW (US/0360-151X) [02243706] **2943**

BRIGHAM YOUNG UNIVERSITY STUDIES (1984) (US/0007-0106) [12595965] **4940**

BRIGHT **CEASED.** (US/0892-8673) [15295848] **2529**

BRIGHT (MIDDLETOWN, CALIF.), THE (US/1056-778X) [23851994] **4940**

BRIGHTON ARGUS (US) [13277107] **5691**

BRIGHTON CROP PROTECTION CONFERENCE--WEEDS (UK/0955-1514) [21233857] **165**

BRIGHTON INDEPENDENT, THE (CN/0834-5899) [16164493] **5781**

BRIGHTON PARK AND MCKINLEY PARK LIFE (US) [28194049] **5658**

BRIGHTON PITTSFORD POST (US) **5714**

BRIGITTE (GW) [03305295] **1082**

BRILLIANT CORNERS (US/0161-1577) [02796067] **316**

BRILLION NEWS, THE (US/0749-7210) [11167100] **5765**

BRILL'S INDOLOGICAL LIBRARY (NE/0925-2916) [I09252916] **2647**

BRILL'S JAPANESE STUDIES LIBRARY (NE/0925-6512) [I09256512] **2647**

BRILL'S SERIES IN JEWISH STUDIES (NE/0926-2261) [I09262261] **5046**

BRILL'S STUDIES IN EPISTEMOLOGY, PSYCHOLOGY AND PSYCHIATRY (NE/0924-0314) [I09240314] 3922, **4578**

BRILL'S STUDIES IN INTELLECTUAL HISTORY (NE/0920-8607) [I09208607] **2612**

BRIMLEYANA (US/0193-4406) [04904283] **5578**

BRINGING RELIGION HOME (US) **4940**

BRINKLEY ARGUS, THE (US) [23188087] **5631**

Alphabetical Title Index — BRITISH

BRINKMAN'S CUMULATIEVE CATALOGUS VAN BOEKEN (NE/0007-0165) [07081010] **411**

BRIO (POMONA, CALIF.) (US/1048-2873) [20909575] 4940, **2277**

BRIO (UNITED KINGDOM BRANCH, INTERNATIONAL ASSOCIATION OF MUSIC LIBRARIES) (UK/0007-0173) [01537097] 3197, **4105**

BRISBANE CITY COUNCIL *See* ANNUAL REPORT OF THE AUDITOR-GENERAL UPON THE BOOKS AND ACCOUNTS OF THE BRISBANE CITY COUNCIL **4710**

BRISBANE CITY COUNCIL. ANNUAL REPORT *See* ANNUAL REPORT OF THE AUDITOR-GENERAL UPON THE BOOKS AND ACCOUNTS OF THE BRISBANE CITY COUNCIL **4710**

BRISE DE L'EST, LA (CN/0384-9058) [03248413] **5275**

BRISE-GLACE, LE (FR) [19907647] **4466**

BRISEBOIS ET COMPAGNIE (CN/0383-8498) [03412325] **4858**

BRISES. BULLETIN DE RECHERCHES SUR L'INFORMATION EN SCIENCES ECONOMIQUES HUMAINES ET SOCIALES (FR/0293-7166) [l02937166] **2485**

BRISTOL ADVANCES IN THERAPEUTICS (UK/0262-8732) [07332109] **3558**

BRISTOL AND GLOUCESTERSHIRE ARCHAEOLOGICAL SOCIETY *See* TRANSACTIONS - BRISTOL AND GLOUCESTERSHIRE ARCHAEOLOGICAL SOCIETY **284**

BRISTOL BAYTIMES (US) **5628**

BRISTOL, ENG. UNIVERSITY. SPELAEOLOGICAL SOCIETY *See* PROCEEDINGS - UNIVERSITY OF BRISTOL SPELAEOLOGICAL SOCIETY **1409**

BRISTOL FOLK NEWS (UK) [01787559] **4105**

BRISTOL HERALD COURIER, BRISTOL VIRGINIA-TENNESSEE (US/8750-6505) [11619976] **5758**

BRISTOL PILOT (US) [20584659] **5735**

BRISTOL PRESS, THE (US) [10384434] **5645**

BRISTOL RECORD SOCIETY *See* PUBLICATIONS ... **5235**

BRITAIN (UK/0068-1075) [01751424] **2514**

BRITAIN AND EUROPE (UK) [04286267] **2679**

BRITAIN BY BRITRAIL. WRITTEN BY GEORGE WRIGHT FERGUSON (US) [06897134] 5430, **5465**

BRITAIN VOTES : A HANDBOOK OF PARLIAMENTARY ELECTION RESULTS / COMPILED AND EDITED BY F.W.S. CRAIG (UK) [19735094] **4634**

BRITAIN'S COMPUTER INDUSTRY (UK) **1236**

BRITAINS TOP 500 ELECTRONIC & ELECTRICAL COMPANIES (UK) [11903128] **2037**

BRITAIN'S TOP 1,000 FOREIGN OWNED COMPANIES (UK) [06445940] 893, **922**

BRITAIN'S TOP PRIVATELY OWNED COMPANIES (UK) [22700377] **644**

BRITANNIA MONOGRAPH SERIES (UK/0953-542X) [12232651] **411**

BRITANNIA (SOCIETY FOR THE PROMOTION OF ROMAN STUDIES) (UK/0068-113X) [01915410] **1075**

BRITANNIA (TORONTO) (CN/0823-7743) [10768299] **2514**

BRITANNICA BOOK OF THE YEAR (US/0068-1156) [00911926] **1923**

BRITEQ PRESSE (CN/0706-1056) [05533521] 2376, **1934**

BRITISH ACADEMY *See* BRITISH ACADEMY DIRECTORY, THE **5229**

BRITISH ACADEMY DIRECTORY, THE (UK) [19006259] **5229**

BRITISH ACCOUNTING REVIEW RESEARCH REGISTER, THE (UK) [20002664] **740**

BRITISH ACCOUNTING REVIEW, THE (UK/0890-8389) [12406858] **740**

BRITISH ADHESIVES AND SEALANTS ASSOCIATION *See* ADHESIVES & SEALANTS YEARBOOK AND DIRECTORY /BASA, BRITISH ADHESIVES AND SEALANTS ASSOCIATION **3997**

BRITISH AGENCIES FOR ADOPTION AND FOSTERING *See* ANNUAL REVIEW / BRITISH AGENCIES FOR ADOPTION AND FOSTERING **5273**

BRITISH AGENCIES FOR ADOPTION AND FOSTERING *See* REPORT & ACCOUNTS / BRITISH AGENCIES FOR ADOPTION AND FOSTERING **5305**

BRITISH AID STATISTICS (UK/0068-1210) [02244174] **5323**

BRITISH ALTERNATIVE THEATRE DIRECTORY (UK/0142-5218) [05744942] **5362**

BRITISH-AMERICAN DEAL REVIEW, THE (US/1044-2944) [19752162] **1633**

BRITISH AND COLONIAL PHARMACIST. YEARBOOK (UK) [20659672] **4294**

BRITISH AND IRISH AUTHORS (UK) **3369**

BRITISH AND IRISH STUDIES IN GERMAN LANGUAGE AND LITERATURE (SZ/0171-6662) [03462174] **3270**

BRITISH ARCHAEOLOGICAL ABSTRACTS *See* BRITISH ARCHAEOLOGICAL BIBLIOGRAPHY **286**

BRITISH ARCHAEOLOGICAL ASSOCIATION *See* CONFERENCE TRANSACTIONS - BRITISH ARCHAEOLOGICAL ASSOCIATION **266**

BRITISH ARCHAEOLOGICAL ASSOCIATION *See* JOURNAL OF THE BRITISH ARCHAEOLOGICAL ASSOCIATION **272**

●BRITISH ARCHAEOLOGICAL BIBLIOGRAPHY (UK/0964-7104) [25959781] 262, **286**

BRITISH ARCHER, THE (UK/0007-0289) [05714203] **4888**

BRITISH ART DIRECTORS ANNUAL (UK) **344**

BRITISH ASSOCIATION FOR PSYCHOPHARMACOLOGY MONOGRAPH (UK/0264-2689) [07791463] 4294, **3922**

BRITISH ASTRONOMICAL ASSOCIATION *See* BRITISH ASTRONOMICAL ASSOCIATION CIRCULAR **393**

BRITISH ASTRONOMICAL ASSOCIATION CIRCULAR (UK/0264-4185) [02672186] **393**

BRITISH ASTRONOMICAL ASSOCIATION, LONDON *See* HANDBOOK OF THE BRITISH ASTRONOMICAL ASSOCIATION, THE **395**

BRITISH BAKER (UK/0007-0300) [02044363] **2329**

BRITISH BANDSMAN (UK) [01639948] **4105**

BRITISH BEE JOURNAL (UK/0007-0327) [04236609] **5578**

BRITISH BIRDS (UK/0007-0335) [0^537138] **5616**

BRITISH BOOK NEWS *CEASED*. (UK/0007-0343) [01537139] **4827**

BRITISH BOOK TRADE DIRECTORY, THE (UK) [05962046] **4812**

BRITISH-BORNEO PETROLEUM SYNDICATE *See* ANNUAL REPORT, YEAR TO 31ST MARCH ... / BRITISH-BORNEO PETROLEUM SYNDICATE, P.L.C **4250**

BRITISH-BORNEO PETROLEUM SYNDICATE. ANNUAL REPORT *See* ANNUAL REPORT, YEAR TO 31ST MARCH ... / BRITISH-BORNEO PETROLEUM SYNDICATE, P.L.C **4250**

BRITISH BROADCASTING CORPORATION *See* BBC ANNUAL REVIEW **1127**

BRITISH BROADCASTING CORPORATION. ANNUAL REPORT & ACCOUNTS *See* BBC ANNUAL REVIEW **1127**

BRITISH BROADCASTING CORPORATION. MONITORING SERVICE *See* MONITORING REPORT, THE **1135**

BRITISH BULLETIN OF PUBLICATIONS ON LATIN AMERICA, THE CARIBBEAN, PORTUGAL AND SPAIN / CANNING HOUSE, HISPANIC AAN LUSO-BRAZILIAN COUNCIL (UK/0268-2400) [05828316] **4827**

BRITISH CACTUS & SUCCULENT JOURNAL (UK/0264-3405) [09491732] **504**

BRITISH CAR (US/1052-0929) [22189809] **5408**

BRITISH CATALOGUE OF MUSIC, THE (UK/0068-1407) [01537143] **4105**

BRITISH CATTLE BREEDERS' CLUB *See* DIGEST - BRITISH CATTLE BREEDERS' CLUB **210**

BRITISH CATTLE VETERINARY ASSOCIATION *See* BRITISH CATTLE VETERINARY ASSOCIATION PROCEEDINGS FOR ... **5506**

BRITISH CATTLE VETERINARY ASSOCIATION PROCEEDINGS FOR ... (UK) [10676933] **5506**

BRITISH CERAMIC PROCEEDINGS (UK/0268-4373) [11752421] **2586**

BRITISH CERAMIC RESEARCH ASSOCIATION *See* SPECIAL PUBLICATION - BRITISH CERAMIC RESEARCH ASSOCIATION **2594**

BRITISH CERAMIC REVIEW (UK/0306-7076) [06538368] **2586**

●BRITISH CERAMIC TRANSACTIONS (UK/0967-9782) [27781150] **2586**

BRITISH CERAMIC TRANSACTIONS AND JOURNAL (UK/0266-7606) [11244783] **2586**

BRITISH CHAROLAIS CATTLE SOCIETY *See* BRITISH CHAROLAIS HERD BOOK, CONTAINING THE AGES AND PEDIGREES OF BRITISH CHAROLAIS CATTLE WITH SUPPLEMENTARY REGISTER, THE **207**

BRITISH CHAROLAIS HERD BOOK, CONTAINING THE AGES AND PEDIGREES OF BRITISH CHAROLAIS CATTLE WITH SUPPLEMENTARY REGISTER, THE (UK) [05765524] **207**

BRITISH CHESS MAGAZINE, THE (UK/0007-0440) [05233247] **4858**

BRITISH CIVIL AIRWORTHINESS REQUIREMENTS (UK) **15**

BRITISH CIVIL AIRWORTHINESS REQUIREMENTS AMENDMENT SERVICE (UK) **15**

BRITISH CLOTHING INDUSTRY YEAR BOOK / SPONSORED BY THE CLOTHING EXPORT COUNCIL OF GREAT BRITAIN, THE (UK) [07635910] **1082**

BRITISH COLUMBIA *See* BRITISH COLUMBIA GAZETTE. PART II, REGULATIONS, THE **2943**

BRITISH COLUMBIA *See* PROVINCE OF BRITISH COLUMBIA BUDGET **4742**

BRITISH COLUMBIA (CN/0704-6278) [13529389] **3476**

BRITISH COLUMBIA *See* ESTIMATES - PROVINCE OF BRITISH COLUMBIA **4722**

BRITISH COLUMBIA ACID MINE DRAINAGE TASK FORCE *See* ANNUAL REPORT / BRITISH COLUMBIA ACID MINE DRAINAGE TASK FORCE **2133**

BRITISH COLUMBIA, ALBERTA, SASKATCHEWAN AND MANITOBA GROCER *See* GROCER TODAY **838**

BRITISH COLUMBIA. ALCOHOL AND DRUG COMMISSION *See* ANNUAL REPORT TO THE LEGISLATURE OF THE ALCOHOL AND DRUG COMMISSION (VICTORIA) **1341**

●BRITISH COLUMBIA & ALBERTA HOME BUSINESS REPORT (CN/1191-8640) [27649116] **644**

BRITISH COLUMBIA. AQUATIC PLANT MANAGEMENT PROGRAM *See* AQUATIC PLANT MANAGEMENT PROGRAM PROPOSALS FOR ... **2409**

BRITISH COLUMBIA ASSOCIATION FOR COMMUNITY LIVING NEWS (CN/0849-9888) [22135169] 5275, **3922**

BRITISH COLUMBIA ASSOCIATION OF HOSPITALS AND HEALTH ORGANIZATIONS *See* MINUTES OF ANNUAL MEETING - BRITISH COLUMBIA ASSOCIATION OF HOSPITALS AND HEALTH ORGANIZATIONS **3789**

BRITISH COLUMBIA ASSOCIATION OF HOSPITALS AND HEALTH ORGANIZATIONS *See* REPORTS - BRITISH COLUMBIA ASSOCIATION OF HOSPITALS AND HEALTH ORGANIZATIONS **3792**

BRITISH COLUMBIA BIRDS (CN/1183-3521) [29593032] **5616**

BRITISH COLUMBIA BOARD OF PAROLE *See* ANNUAL REPORT - BRITISH COLUMBIA BOARD OF PAROLE **3157**

BRITISH COLUMBIA BUSINESS INDICATORS (CN/1184-9207) [24296413] **644**

... BRITISH COLUMBIA COLLECTIVE BARGAINING REVIEW AND OUTLOOK, THE (CN/0829-8319) [16517226] **1656**

BRITISH COLUMBIA COUNCIL FOR THE FAMILY *See* NEWSLETTER - BRITISH COLUMBIA COUNCIL FOR THE FAMILY **2284**

BRITISH COLUMBIA DECISIONS, STATUTE CITATOR (CN/0715-4798) [09204483] **2943**

BRITISH COLUMBIA. DEPT. OF ECONOMIC DEVELOPMENT *See* MANUFACTURING OPPORTUNITIES **3484**

BRITISH COLUMBIA. DEPT. OF HUMAN RESOURCES *See* LEAFLETS, FOLDERS, ETC. - DEPT. OF HUMAN RESOURCES **4661**

BRITISH COLUMBIA. DEPT. OF LABOUR. RESEARCH AND PLANNING BRANCH *See* B.C. LABOUR MARKET INFORMATION **1654**

BRITISH COLUMBIA. DEPT. OF LABOUR. RESEARCH BRANCH *See* WORKING CONDITIONS IN BRITISH COLUMBIA INDUSTRY **1719**

BRITISH COLUMBIA ECONOMIC AND STATISTICAL REVIEW (CN/0847-1525) [20784546] **1465**

BRITISH COLUMBIA. EDUCATIONAL DATA SERVICES *See* B.C. PUBLIC SCHOOL STATISTICS **1793**

BRITISH COLUMBIA ENERGY SUPPLY AND DEMAND FORECAST *See* BRITISH COLUMBIA ENERGY SUPPLY AND REQUIREMENTS FORECAST. TECHNICAL REPORT **1934**

BRITISH — Alphabetical Title Index

BRITISH COLUMBIA ENERGY SUPPLY AND REQUIREMENTS FORECAST. SUMMARY REPORT (CN/0827-0333) [13171979] **1934**

BRITISH COLUMBIA ENERGY SUPPLY AND REQUIREMENTS FORECAST. TECHNICAL REPORT (CN/0827-0325) [13171469] **1934**

BRITISH COLUMBIA. ENVIRONMENTAL APPEAL BOARD *See* ANNUAL REPORT / ENVIRONMENTAL APPEAL BOARD **3109**

BRITISH COLUMBIA FEDERATION OF LABOUR (C.L.C.). CONVENTION *See* SUMMARY OF PROCEEDINGS. ANNUAL CONVENTION - B.C. FEDERATION OF LABOUR (CLC) **1712**

BRITISH COLUMBIA FERRY CORPORATION *See* DOLPHIN UPDATE **5449**

BRITISH COLUMBIA. FIELD CROPS BRANCH *See* GUIDE TO THE USE OF FERTILIZERS FOR VANCOUVER ISLAND, ZONE 1 **91**

BRITISH COLUMBIA. FINANCIAL INSTITUTIONS COMMISSION *See* ANNUAL REPORT / FINANCIAL INSTITUTIONS COMMISSION **771**

BRITISH COLUMBIA. FIRST PROGRAM *See* TIRE TALK **5312**

BRITISH COLUMBIA GAZETTE MICROFORM, THE (CN/0007-0505) [11463204] **4634**

BRITISH COLUMBIA GAZETTE. PART II, REGULATIONS, THE (CN/0824-7986) [05297025] **2943**

BRITISH COLUMBIA GENEALOGIST, THE (CN/0315-3835) [01720692] **2440**

BRITISH COLUMBIA GOVERNMENT EMPLOYEES' UNION *See* BCGEU NEWS & VIEWS **1655**

BRITISH COLUMBIA GOVERNMENT PUBLICATIONS MONTHLY CHECKLIST **SUSPENDED.** (CN/0316-0823) [02240565] **411**

BRITISH COLUMBIA GROWER (CN/0709-0102) [05258161] **68**

BRITISH COLUMBIA HISTORICAL NEWS : JOURNAL OF THE B.C. HISTORICAL FEDERATION (CN) [25024616] **2724**

BRITISH COLUMBIA HOLSTEIN NEWS (CN/0824-4774) [10634783] **192**

BRITISH COLUMBIA. HOSPITAL PROGRAMS. RESEARCH DIVISION *See* STATISTICS OF HOSPITAL CASES DISCHARGED. BRITISH COLUMBIA **3662**

BRITISH COLUMBIA. HOSPITAL PROGRAMS. RESEARCH DIVISION *See* STATISTICS OF HOSPITALIZED ACCIDENTS : BRITISH COLUMBIA **3662**

BRITISH COLUMBIA. INDUSTRIAL RELATIONS COUNCIL *See* ANNUAL REPORT / BRITISH COLUMBIA, INDUSTRIAL RELATIONS COUNCIL **1597**

BRITISH COLUMBIA. JUSTICE DEVELOPMENT COMMISSION *See* ANNUAL REPORT - JUSTICE DEVELOPMENT COMMISSION (BRITISH COLUMBIA) **2934**

BRITISH COLUMBIA LABOUR RELATIONS BOARD DECISIONS (CN/0715-5808) [09379008] **3144**

BRITISH COLUMBIA LAW REPORTS (CALGARY) (CN/0703-3060) [04589481] **2943**

BRITISH COLUMBIA LEGAL TELEPHONE DIRECTORY, THE (CN/0521-0585) [02247992] **3139**

BRITISH COLUMBIA. LEGISLATIVE ASSEMBLY *See* OFFICIAL REPORT OF DEBATES OF THE LEGISLATIVE ASSEMBLY **3021**

BRITISH COLUMBIA. LEGISLATIVE ASSEMBLY. SELECT STANDING COMMITTEE ON FINANCE, CROWN CORPORATIONS AND GOVERNMENT SERVICES *See* REPORT - BRITISH COLUMBIA. LEGISLATIVE ASSEMBLY. SELECT STANDING COMMITTEE ON FINANCE, CROWN CORPORATIONS AND GOVERNMENT SERVICES **807**

BRITISH COLUMBIA LIBRARY ASSOCIATION *See* BCLA REPORTER **3193**

BRITISH COLUMBIA. LIQUOR DISTRIBUTION BRANCH *See* FINANCIAL STATEMENTS / BRITISH COLUMBIA LIQUOR DISTRIBUTION BRANCH **2367**

BRITISH COLUMBIA LUMBERMAN (CN) [02686209] **2399**

BRITISH COLUMBIA MEDIA GUIDE (CN/1183-0212) [24367934] **1105**

BRITISH COLUMBIA MEDICAL JOURNAL (CN/0007-0556) [01586013] **3558**

BRITISH COLUMBIA MEDICAL LIBRARY SERVICE *See* RECENT AND RECOMMENDED MEDICAL BOOKS **3633**

BRITISH COLUMBIA MIGRATION HIGHLIGHTS (CN/1186-7965) [24623964] **4550**

BRITISH COLUMBIA MINERAL EXPLORATION REVIEW (CN/0846-0051) [15746087] **2135**

BRITISH COLUMBIA. MINERAL RESOURCES DIVISION *See* SUMMARY OF OPERATIONS / MINERAL RESOURCES DIVISION **2151**

BRITISH COLUMBIA. MINISTRY OF AGRICULTURE AND FOOD *See* AGRICULTURAL AID TO DEVELOPING COUNTRIES **2907**

BRITISH COLUMBIA. MINISTRY OF EDUCATION *See* THE POINT (VICTORIA), TO **1787**

BRITISH COLUMBIA. MINISTRY OF ENERGY, MINES AND PETROLEUM RESOURCES *See* DANGEROUS AND/OR UNUSUAL OCCURRENCES **2861**

BRITISH COLUMBIA. MINISTRY OF ENERGY, MINES AND PETROLEUM RESOURCES *See* FATAL ACCIDENT SUMMARY (VICTORIA) **2862**

BRITISH COLUMBIA. MINISTRY OF ENERGY, MINES AND PETROLEUM RESOURCES. RESOURCE MANAGEMENT BRANCH *See* PLAN - BRITISH COLUMBIA. RESOURCE MANAGEMENT BRANCH **1359**

BRITISH COLUMBIA. MINISTRY OF ENVIRONMENT *See* ANNUAL REPORT - BRITISH COLUMBIA. MINISTRY OF ENVIRONMENT (1989) **2160**

BRITISH COLUMBIA. MINISTRY OF FINANCE AND CORPORATE RELATIONS *See* RESPONSE TO THE ... REPORT OF THE AUDITOR GENERAL - PROVINCE OF BRITISH COLUMBIA. FINANCE AND CORPORATE RELATIONS **809**

BRITISH COLUMBIA. MINISTRY OF FORESTS *See* FIVE YEAR FOREST AND RANGE RESOURCE PROGRAM **2379**

BRITISH COLUMBIA. MINISTRY OF FORESTS AND LANDS *See* COMPREHENSIVE PUBLICATION LIST - MINISTRY OF FORESTS AND LANDS (VICTORIA) **2378**

BRITISH COLUMBIA. MINISTRY OF HEALTH *See* ANNUAL REPORT - MINISTRY OF HEALTH (VICTORIA) **4766**

BRITISH COLUMBIA. MINISTRY OF HEALTH *See* NEWSLETTER - MINISTRY OF HEALTH (VICTORIA) **4793**

BRITISH COLUMBIA. MINISTRY OF LABOUR AND CONSUMER SERVICES *See* ANNUAL REPORT - MINISTRY OF LABOUR AND CONSUMER SERVICES (VICTORIA) **1649**

BRITISH COLUMBIA. MINISTRY OF PARKS *See* ANNUAL REPORT - MINISTRY OF PARKS (VICTORIA) **4705**

BRITISH COLUMBIA. MINISTRY OF SOCIAL SERVICES AND HOUSING *See* BUSINESS PLAN (VICTORIA) **4715**

BRITISH COLUMBIA MONTHLY (VANCOUVER. 1972) (CN/0382-5272) [02310459] **2529**

BRITISH COLUMBIA MOTOR TRANSPORT ASSOCIATION *See* DIRECTORY - BRITISH COLUMBIA MOTOR TRANSPORT ASSOCIATION **5381**

BRITISH COLUMBIA. OFFICE OF THE AUDITOR GENERAL *See* ANNUAL REPORT OF THE AUDITOR GENERAL OF BRITISH COLUMBIA TO THE LEGISLATIVE ASSEMBLY **4710**

BRITISH COLUMBIA. OFFICE OF THE AUDITOR GENERAL *See* REPORT TO THE LEGISLATIVE ASSEMBLY OF BRITISH COLUMBIA ON THE PUBLIC ACCOUNTS **4746**

BRITISH COLUMBIA. OFFICE OF THE AUDITOR GENERAL. REPORT OF THE AUDITOR GENERAL FOR THE YEAR ENDED 31 MARCH . *See* ANNUAL REPORT OF THE AUDITOR GENERAL OF BRITISH COLUMBIA TO THE LEGISLATIVE ASSEMBLY **4710**

BRITISH COLUMBIA. OFFICE OF THE OMBUDSMAN *See* ANNUAL REPORT TO THE LEGISLATIVE ASSEMBLY - PROVINCE OF BRITISH COLUMBIA. OMBUDSMAN **4629**

BRITISH COLUMBIA ORCHARD INDUSTRY MUSEUM *See* ORCHARD (KELOWNA) **117**

BRITISH COLUMBIA PLACE LTD *See* ANNUAL REPORT / BRITISH COLUMBIA PLACE LTD **4834**

BRITISH COLUMBIA POLICE JOURNAL (CN/0706-2893) [04631548] **3158**

BRITISH COLUMBIA POLITICS & POLICY (CN/0835-2925) [16515477] **4466**

BRITISH COLUMBIA. PREMIER'S ADVISORY COUNCIL FOR PERSONS WITH DISABILITIES *See* DIRECTIONS - BRITISH COLUMBIA PREMIER'S ADVISORY COUNCIL FOR PERSONS WITH DISABILITIES **4386**

BRITISH COLUMBIA. PROVINCIAL AGRICULTURAL LAND COMMISSION *See* ANNUAL REPORT - PROVINCIAL AGRICULTURAL LAND COMMISSION (BRITISH COLUMBIA) **61**

BRITISH COLUMBIA PROVINCIAL MUSEUM *See* OCCASIONAL PAPERS OF THE BRITISH COLUMBIA PROVINCIAL MUSEUM **4169**

BRITISH COLUMBIA. PURCHASING COMMISSION *See* CUSTOMER INFORMATION - BRITISH COLUMBIA. PURCHASING COMMISSION **949**

BRITISH COLUMBIA. REGISTRAR OF REGULATIONS *See* INDEX OF CURRENT B.C. REGULATIONS **2981**

BRITISH COLUMBIA REPORT (CN) **2724**

BRITISH COLUMBIA REPORT (VANCOUVER) (CN/0847-2998) [22281340] **2724**

● BRITISH COLUMBIA SCHOOL BUS (CN/1189-4717) [26497882] **1728, 5378**

BRITISH COLUMBIA SCHOOL TRUSTEES ASSOCIATION *See* B C S T A REPORTS **1860**

BRITISH COLUMBIA SCHOOL TRUSTEES ASSOCIATION. GENERAL MEETING *See* REPORT OF PROCEEDINGS. ANNUAL GENERAL MEETING - BRITISH COLUMBIA SCHOOL TRUSTEES ASSOCIATION **1778**

BRITISH COLUMBIA SOIL SURVEY, REPORT (CN/0375-5886) [02248865] **165**

BRITISH COLUMBIA SPORT FISHING (CN/0827-2042) [11847684] **2297**

BRITISH COLUMBIA SPORT SALMON FISHING NEWS (CN/0711-3862) [08489271] **4888, 2297**

BRITISH COLUMBIA SPORTS HALL OF FAME AND MUSEUM (CN/0228-3263) [07313296] **4888**

BRITISH COLUMBIA SYSTEMS CORPORATION *See* ANNUAL REPORT / BCSC, BRITISH COLUMBIA SYSTEMS CORPORATION **1597**

BRITISH COLUMBIA TEACHERS' FEDERATION *See* COLLECTIVE BARGAINING HANDBOOK **939**

BRITISH COLUMBIA TEACHERS' FEDERATION *See* BRITISH COLUMBIA TEACHERS' FEDERATION : SALARY AGREEMENT **1861**

BRITISH COLUMBIA TEACHERS' FEDERATION *See* MEMBERS' GUIDE TO THE BCTF **1900**

BRITISH COLUMBIA TEACHERS' FEDERATION. LEARNING CONDITIONS COMMITTEE *See* B C T F INFORMATIONAL REPORT **1727**

BRITISH COLUMBIA TEACHERS' FEDERATION : SALARY AGREEMENT (CN/0712-3760) [08898747] **1861**

BRITISH COLUMBIA TRADE DEVELOPMENT CORPORATION *See* ANNUAL REPORT - BRITISH COLUMBIA TRADE DEVELOPMENT CORPORATION **822**

BRITISH COLUMBIA TRADE DEVELOPMENT CORPORATION *See* B.C. EXPORTER **824**

BRITISH COLUMBIA TRANSFER GUIDE (CN/1180-3630) [22773382] **1812**

BRITISH COLUMBIA WEEKLY LAW DIGEST (CN/0713-8865) [09096484] **2943**

BRITISH COLUMBIA'S WEDDING BELLS (CN/0840-464X) [20243346] **5268, 2277**

BRITISH COMBUSTION (UK/0307-1219) [02243792] **2111**

BRITISH COMPANIES SECRETARY'S PRACTICE MANUAL (UK) **644**

BRITISH COMPANY CASES (UK/0269-0535) [23475639] **3096**

BRITISH COMPANY LAW & PRACTICE (UK) [12038216] **3096**

BRITISH CONSTRUCTION EQUIPMENT AND CRANES (UK) [08997555] **602**

BRITISH CONTACT LENS ASSOCIATION *See* JOURNAL OF THE BRITISH CONTACT LENS ASSOCIATION **3876**

BRITISH CORROSION JOURNAL (UK/0007-0599) [01537226] **2101, 2008**

BRITISH COUNTRY MUSIC ASSOCIATION *See* BRITISH COUNTRY MUSIC ASSOCIATION YEARBOOK **4105**

BRITISH COUNTRY MUSIC ASSOCIATION YEARBOOK (UK/0308-4698) [02244714] **4105**

BRITISH DEAF NEWS (UK/0007-0602) [02980849] **4385**

BRITISH DEFENCE DIRECTORY (UK/0272-4782) [06848518] **4038**

BRITISH DEFENCE EQUIPMENT CATALOGUE (UK) [08084833] **4038**

BRITISH DENTAL JOURNAL (UK/0007-0610) [01537229] **1317**

BRITISH DENTAL SURGERY ASSISTANT (UK/0007-0629) [06464156] **1317**

BRITISH DESIGN AND ART DIRECTION *See* BRITISH DESIGN & ART DIRECTION : D & AD **377**

BRITISH DESIGN & ART DIRECTION : D & AD (UK) [10304281] **377**

BRITISH DIGEST ILLUSTRATED (US/0196-7517) [05884663] **2514**

BRITISH ECONOMY SURVEY (UK/0263-3523) [03122828] **1465**

BRITISH EDUCATION INDEX (UK/0007-0637) [01537230] 1728, **1793**

BRITISH EDUCATIONAL RESEARCH JOURNAL (UK/0141-1926) [05343940] **1728**

●BRITISH ELECTIONS AND PARTIES YEARBOOK (UK/0968-2481) [25375368] **4634**

BRITISH EQUAL OPPORTUNITIES CASES (UK/0953-5705) [20019937] **2943**

BRITISH EXPORTS TO NORTH AMERICA (UK) [22742766] **825**

BRITISH FARMER 1985 (UK/0267-6338) [I02676338] **68**

BRITISH FARMER AND STOCK BREEDER. YEARBOOK AND FARM DIARY (UK) [02253183] **68**

BRITISH FEDERATION OF MUSIC FESTIVALS *See* YEAR BOOK - BRITISH FEDERATION OF MUSIC FESTIVALS **389**

BRITISH FOOD JOURNAL (1966) (UK/0007-070X) [09261797] **2329**

BRITISH FOOD MANUFACTURING INDUSTRIES RESEARCH ASSOCIATION *See* SCIENTIFIC AND TECHNICAL SURVEYS - BRITISH FOOD MANUFACTURING INDUSTRIES RESEARCH ASSOCIATION **2357**

BRITISH GAS (FIRM) *See* ANNUAL REPORT AND ACCOUNTS / BRITISH GAS **1597**

BRITISH GAS (FIRM) *See* DIRECTORS' REPORT AND ACCOUNTS / BRITISH GAS **4254**

BRITISH GAS (FIRM). ANNUAL REPORT AND ACCOUNTS *See* DIRECTORS' REPORT AND ACCOUNTS / BRITISH GAS **4254**

BRITISH GEOLOGICAL LITERATURE (UK/0140-7813) [03234609] **1368**

BRITISH GEOLOGIST (UK) [02998128] **1368**

BRITISH GEOMORPHOLOGICAL RESEARCH GROUP *See* TECHNICAL BULLETIN - BRITISH GEOMORPHOLOGICAL RESEARCH GROUP **1361**

BRITISH GLASS INDUSTRY RESEARCH ASSOCIATION *See* DIGEST OF INFORMATION AND PATENT REVIEW **2588**

BRITISH GOAT SOCIETY *See* BRITISH GOAT SOCIETY'S YEAR BOOK FOR..., THE **192**

BRITISH GOAT SOCIETY *See* HERD BOOK - BRITISH GOAT SOCIETY **195**

BRITISH GOAT SOCIETY'S YEAR BOOK FOR..., THE (UK) [05765729] 207, **192**

BRITISH GRASSLAND SOCIETY *See* OCCASIONAL SYMPOSIUM **5517**

BRITISH HEART JOURNAL (UK/0007-0769) [01537247] **3699**

BRITISH HERITAGE (US/0195-2633) [05432407] **2485**

BRITISH HERITAGE SERIES (UK) [18004090] **4105**

BRITISH HERPETOLOGICAL SOCIETY BULLETIN, THE (UK) [07251336] **5578**

BRITISH HOMEOPATHIC JOURNAL, THE (UK/0007-0785) [02981050] **3558**

BRITISH HOMING WORLD (UK) [03860071] **5616**

BRITISH HONDURAS. PUBLIC WORKS DEPARTMENT *See* ANNUAL REPORT OF THE PUBLIC WORKS DEPARTMENT (BELIZE) **4629**

BRITISH HOTELIER AND RESTAURANTEUR *See* VOICE OF THE HOSPITALITY ASSOCIATION **2810**

BRITISH HOTELIER & RESTAURATEUR : OFFICIAL MAGAZINE OF THE BRITISH HOTELS, RESTAURANTS & CATERERS ASSOCIATION (UK) [09582173] 5070, **2804**

BRITISH HUMANITIES INDEX (UK/0007-0815) [01537252] 2843, **2857**

BRITISH INSTITUTE OF INTERNATIONAL AND COMPARATIVE LAW *See* COMPARATIVE LAW SERIES **3126**

BRITISH INSTITUTE OF INTERNATIONAL AND COMPARATIVE LAW *See* NEWSLETTER - BRITISH INSTITUTE OF INTERNATIONAL AND COMPARATIVE LAW **3133**

BRITISH INSTITUTE STUDIES IN INTERNATIONAL & COMPARATIVE LAW (UK/0524-627X) [01537258] **3125**

BRITISH INSURANCE INDUSTRY, THE (UK) [11730395] **2876**

BRITISH INTERNATIONAL TAX AGREEMENTS (UK) **4713**

BRITISH ISLES AND IRELAND TRAVEL GUIDE (US/0095-1579) [01795705] **5465**

BRITISH JEWELLER 1983 (UK/0266-2558) [I02662558] **2913**

BRITISH JOURNAL FOR EIGHTEENTH-CENTURY STUDIES, THE (UK/0141-867X) [04144241] 2679, **3369**

●BRITISH JOURNAL FOR THE HISTORY OF PHILOSOPHY (UK/0960-8788) **4342**

BRITISH JOURNAL FOR THE HISTORY OF SCIENCE, THE (UK/0007-0874) [01537266] **5089**

BRITISH JOURNAL FOR THE PHILOSOPHY OF SCIENCE, THE (UK/0007-0882) [01537267] 4343, **5089**

BRITISH JOURNAL OF ACADEMIC LIBRARIANSHIP (UK/0269-0497) [13896729] **3197**

BRITISH JOURNAL OF ACUPUNCTURE *See* EUROPEAN JOURNAL OF ORIENTAL MEDICINE **3575**

BRITISH JOURNAL OF ACUPUNCTURE (UK/0143-4977) [11603016] **3558**

BRITISH JOURNAL OF ADDICTION (UK/0952-0481) [06652609] **1341**

BRITISH JOURNAL OF AESTHETICS (UK/0007-0904) [01537270] **344**

BRITISH JOURNAL OF ANAESTHESIA (UK/0007-0912) [01537271] **3682**

BRITISH JOURNAL OF AUDIOLOGY (UK/0300-5364) [01786029] **3887**

●BRITISH JOURNAL OF BIOMEDICAL SCIENCE (UK/0967-4845) [27845663] **3690**

BRITISH JOURNAL OF CANADIAN STUDIES (UK/0269-9222) [15188258] **2724**

BRITISH JOURNAL OF CANCER (UK/0007-0920) [01537274] **3809**

BRITISH JOURNAL OF CANCER. SUPPLEMENT, THE (UK/0306-9443) [01395847] **3809**

BRITISH JOURNAL OF CLINICAL AND SOCIAL PSYCHIATRY (UK/0951-0192) [I0951O192] **3922**

BRITISH JOURNAL OF CLINICAL PHARMACOLOGY (UK/0306-5251) [01266516] **4294**

BRITISH JOURNAL OF CLINICAL PRACTICE. SYMPOSIUM SUPPLEMENT (UK/0262-8767) [06756832] 4294, **3559**

BRITISH JOURNAL OF CLINICAL PRACTICE, THE (UK/0007-0947) [01537276] 4294, **3558**

BRITISH JOURNAL OF CLINICAL PSYCHOLOGY, THE (UK/0144-6657) [07198489] **4578**

BRITISH JOURNAL OF CRIMINOLOGY, DELINQUENCY AND DEVIANT SOCIAL BEHAVIOR, THE (UK/0007-0955) [01537277] **3158**

BRITISH JOURNAL OF CURRICULUM AND ASSESSMENT (UK/0960-796X) [I0960796X] **1889**

BRITISH JOURNAL OF DERMATOLOGY (1951) (UK/0007-0963) [05928691] **3718**

BRITISH JOURNAL OF DERMATOLOGY. SUPPLEMENT (UK/0366-077X) [01645907] **3718**

●BRITISH JOURNAL OF DEVELOPMENTAL DISABILITIES, THE (UK) [27525286] **1876**

BRITISH JOURNAL OF DEVELOPMENTAL PSYCHOLOGY, THE (UK/0261-510X) [09424051] **4578**

BRITISH JOURNAL OF DISORDERS OF COMMUNICATION. MONOGRAPH (UK) [06431917] 1105, **4385**

BRITISH JOURNAL OF EDUCATION AND WORK (UK) [17866039] 4201, **1728**

BRITISH JOURNAL OF EDUCATIONAL PSYCHOLOGY, THE (UK/0007-0998) [01537283] 1889, **4578**

BRITISH JOURNAL OF EDUCATIONAL STUDIES (UK/0007-1005) [01537284] **1728**

BRITISH JOURNAL OF EDUCATIONAL TECHNOLOGY (UK/0007-1013) [01126749] **1889**

BRITISH JOURNAL OF ENTOMOLOGY AND NATURAL HISTORY (UK/0952-7583) [18316915] 5578, **4163**

BRITISH JOURNAL OF FAMILY PLANNING, THE (UK/0144-8625) [06084262] **588**

BRITISH JOURNAL OF GENERAL PRACTICE, THE (UK/0960-1643) [20966338] **3737**

BRITISH JOURNAL OF GUIDANCE & COUNSELLING (UK/0306-9885) [02243755] **1911**

BRITISH JOURNAL OF HAEMATOLOGY (UK/0007-1048) [01537286] **3771**

BRITISH JOURNAL OF HEALTHCARE COMPUTING, THE (UK/0265-5217) [12812821] **1172**

●BRITISH JOURNAL OF HOLOCAUST EDUCATION (UK/0966-095X) [I0966095X] **2679**

BRITISH JOURNAL OF HOSPITAL MEDICINE (UK/0007-1064) [02811678] **3559**

BRITISH JOURNAL OF IN-SERVICE EDUCATION (UK) [05122050] **1889**

BRITISH JOURNAL OF INDUSTRIAL MEDICINE (UK/0007-1072) [01537287] **2859**

BRITISH JOURNAL OF INDUSTRIAL RELATIONS (UK/0007-1080) [01782012] 862, **1656**

BRITISH JOURNAL OF MANAGEMENT (UK/1045-3172) [20070828] **862**

BRITISH JOURNAL OF MATHEMATICAL & STATISTICAL PSYCHOLOGY, THE (UK/0007-1102) [06010380] 4578, **4622**

BRITISH JOURNAL OF MEDICAL ECONOMICS, THE (UK/0962-1423) [27977735] 3559, **1465**

BRITISH JOURNAL OF MEDICAL PSYCHOLOGY (UK/0007-1129) [01537291] **4578**

BRITISH JOURNAL OF MENTAL SUBNORMALITY (UK/0374-633X) [01319219] **1876**

BRITISH JOURNAL OF MIDDLE EASTERN STUDIES (UK) [25037241] **2768**

BRITISH JOURNAL OF MIDWIFERY (UK) **3758**

BRITISH JOURNAL OF MUSIC EDUCATION : BJME (UK/0265-0517) [11269602] **4105**

BRITISH JOURNAL OF NEUROSURGERY (UK/0268-8697) [16716669] 3961, **3829**

BRITISH JOURNAL OF NON-DESTRUCTIVE TESTING (UK/0007-1137) [02445478] 2111, **2101**

●BRITISH JOURNAL OF NURSING : BJN (UK/0966-0461) [25976498] **3852**

BRITISH JOURNAL OF NUTRITION, THE (UK/0007-1145) [01537294] **4188**

BRITISH JOURNAL OF OBSTETRICS AND GYNAECOLOGY (UK/0306-5456) [01260948] **3758**

BRITISH JOURNAL OF OBSTETRICS AND GYNAECOLOGY. SUPPLEMENT (UK/0140-7686) [01407686] **3758**

BRITISH JOURNAL OF OCCUPATIONAL THERAPY, THE (UK/0308-0226) [02253539] **1876**

BRITISH JOURNAL OF OPHTHALMOLOGY (UK/0007-1161) [01537295] **3872**

BRITISH JOURNAL OF OPTOMETRY AND DISPENSING (UK) **4215**

BRITISH JOURNAL OF ORAL & MAXILLOFACIAL SURGERY, THE (UK/0266-4356) [10519906] 1317, **3961**

BRITISH JOURNAL OF ORTHODONTICS (UK/0301-228X) [01590285] **1317**

BRITISH JOURNAL OF PHARMACOLOGY (UK/0007-1188) [01240522] **4294**

BRITISH JOURNAL OF PHOTOGRAPHY (UK/0007-1196) [05928805] **4367**

BRITISH JOURNAL OF PHYSICAL EDUCATION (UK/0144-3569) [10166683] **1855**

BRITISH JOURNAL OF PHYSICAL EDUCATION. PRIMARY SUPPLEMENT (UK) **1855**

BRITISH JOURNAL OF PHYTOTHERAPY, THE (UK/0959-6879) [I09596879] **504**

BRITISH JOURNAL OF PLASTIC SURGERY (UK/0007-1226) [01537302] **3961**

BRITISH JOURNAL OF PODIATRIC MEDICINE & SURGERY (UK/0955-8160) [20857438] **3917**

BRITISH JOURNAL OF POLITICAL SCIENCE (UK/0007-1234) [01180372] **4466**

BRITISH JOURNAL OF PROJECTIVE PSYCHOLOGY (UK) [18838461] **4578**

BRITISH JOURNAL OF PSYCHIATRY. SUPPLEMENT, THE (UK/0960-5371) [18854892] **3922**

BRITISH JOURNAL OF PSYCHIATRY, THE (UK/0007-1250) [01537306] **3922**

BRITISH JOURNAL OF PSYCHOLOGY (1955) (UK/0007-1269) [06370793] **4578**

BRITISH JOURNAL OF PSYCHOTHERAPY (UK/0265-9883) [12005655] **3922**

BRITISH JOURNAL OF RADIOLOGY, THE (UK/0007-1285) [01537310] **3939**

BRITISH JOURNAL OF RELIGIOUS EDUCATION (UK/0141-6200) [04256962] **4940**

BRITISH JOURNAL OF RHEUMATOLOGY (UK/0263-7103) [09272712] **3803**

BRITISH — Alphabetical Title Index

BRITISH JOURNAL OF SERIALS LIBRARIANSHIP See EUROPEAN JOURNAL OF SERIALS LIBRARIANSHIP 3209

BRITISH JOURNAL OF SEXUAL MEDICINE *CEASED.* (UK/0301-5572) [06464121] 5187, **3559**

BRITISH JOURNAL OF SOCIAL PSYCHOLOGY, THE (UK/0144-6665) [07198463] **4578**

BRITISH JOURNAL OF SOCIAL WORK, THE (UK/0045-3102) [01537313] **5275**

BRITISH JOURNAL OF SOCIOLOGY OF EDUCATION (UK/0142-5692) [06546273] 1728, **5241**

BRITISH JOURNAL OF SOCIOLOGY, THE (UK/0007-1315) [01537314] **5240**

BRITISH JOURNAL OF SPECIAL EDUCATION (UK/0952-3383) [11990888] **1876**

BRITISH JOURNAL OF SPORTS MEDICINE (UK/0306-3674) [01021858] **3953**

BRITISH JOURNAL OF SURGERY (UK/0007-1323) [01537315] **3961**

BRITISH JOURNAL OF SURGERY (SPANISH EDITION), THE (SP) **3961**

BRITISH JOURNAL OF THEATRE NURSING : NATNEWS : THE OFFICIAL JOURNAL OF THE NATIONAL ASSOCIATION OF THEATRE NURSES, THE (UK) [25545581] 3961, **3852**

BRITISH JOURNAL OF THEOLOGICAL EDUCATION (UK) **4940**

BRITISH JOURNAL OF THERAPY & REHABILITATION (UK) **4379**

BRITISH JOURNAL OF UROLOGY (UK/0007-1331) [01537316] **3988**

BRITISH JOURNAL OF VISUAL IMPAIRMENT, THE (UK/0264-6196) [09850026] **4385**

BRITISH LEGION JOURNAL See JOURNAL - ROYAL BRITISH LEGION **5232**

BRITISH LEPROSY RELIEF ASSOCIATION See LEPRA REPORT **3604**

BRITISH LIBRARIANSHIP AND INFORMATION WORK (UK) [09311677] **3197**

BRITISH LIBRARY See CATALOGUE OF PRINTED MUSIC IN THE BRITISH LIBRARY : ACCESSIONS **4108**

BRITISH LIBRARY See BRITISH LIBRARY JOURNAL, THE **3197**

BRITISH LIBRARY See BRITISH LIBRARY NEWS **3197**

BRITISH LIBRARY. BIBLIOGRAPHIC SERVICES See BRITISH LIBRARY BIBLIOGRAPHIC SERVICES NEWSLETTER **411**

BRITISH LIBRARY BIBLIOGRAPHIC SERVICES NEWSLETTER (UK/0268-9707) [13507402] **411**

BRITISH LIBRARY. BOARD See ANNUAL REPORT - BRITISH LIBRARY **3190**

BRITISH LIBRARY. DOCUMENT SUPPLY CENTRE See INDEX OF CONFERENCE PROCEEDINGS / THE BRITISH LIBRARY, DOCUMENT SUPPLY CENTRE **3214**

BRITISH LIBRARY. DOCUMENT SUPPLY CENTRE See CURRENT SERIALS RECEIVED **3205**

BRITISH LIBRARY. DOCUMENT SUPPLY CENTRE See BRITISH REPORTS, TRANSLATIONS AND THESES RECEIVED BY THE BRITISH LIBRARY DOCUMENT SUPPLY CENTRE **3197**

BRITISH LIBRARY. DOCUMENT SUPPLY CENTRE See BOOKS AT BOSTON SPA. MICROFORM **4825**

BRITISH LIBRARY. DOCUMENT SUPPLY CENTRE See INDEX OF CONFERENCE PROCEEDINGS. ANNUAL CUMULATION **3214**

BRITISH LIBRARY JOURNAL, THE (UK/0305-5167) [02243754] **3197**

BRITISH LIBRARY. LENDING DIVISION See KEYWORD INDEX TO SERIAL TITLES **2489**

BRITISH LIBRARY. LENDING DIVISION See INDEX OF CONFERENCE PROCEEDINGS RECEIVED **3214**

BRITISH LIBRARY MUSIC FACSIMILES (UK) [07083282] **4105**

BRITISH LIBRARY. NATIONAL BIBLIOGRAPHIC SERVICE See SELECT : NATIONAL BIBLIOGRAPHIC SERVICE NEWSLETTER **3248**

BRITISH LIBRARY NEWS (UK/0307-9481) [05038990] **3197**

BRITISH LIBRARY REFERENCE DIVISION NEWSPAPER LIBRARY NEWSLETTER (UK/0144-9958) [07994198] **3197**

BRITISH LIBRARY. RESEARCH AND DEVELOPMENT DEPT See REPORT / BRITISH LIBRARY, RESEARCH AND DEVELOPMENT DEPARTMENT **3245**

BRITISH MARQUE CAR CLUB NEWS (US/1056-8468) [23877612] 2772, **5408**

BRITISH MEDICAL BULLETIN (UK/0007-1420) [00855519] **3559**

BRITISH MEDICAL JOURNAL ED. ESPANOLA (SP/0213-3954) [02133954] **3795**

BRITISH MEDICAL JOURNAL. ITALIAN EDITION See BMJ:BRITISH MEDICAL JOURNAL. ITALIAN EDITION **3557**

BRITISH MEDICAL JOURNAL (PRACTICE OBSERVED ED.) (UK/0267-0631) [09632070] **3559**

BRITISH MEDICINE (LONDON : 1972) *CEASED.* (UK/0140-2722) [01777909] **3559**

BRITISH MINIATURE ELECTRONIC COMPONENTS DATA ANNUAL (UK/0068-2276) [03138809] **2037**

BRITISH MUSEUM. DEPT. OF PRINTED BOOKS See GENERAL CATALOGUE OF PRINTED BOOKS / BRITISH MUSEUM **4088**

BRITISH MUSEUM MAGAZINE (UK/0965-8297) [I09658297] **4085**

BRITISH MUSEUM MAGAZINE : JOURNAL OF THE BRITISH MUSEUM SOCIETY (UK) [25588337] **4085**

BRITISH MUSEUM (NATURAL HISTORY) See ANNUAL BIBLIOGRAPHY OF THE HISTORY OF NATURAL HISTORY **429**

BRITISH MUSEUM (NATURAL HISTORY) See REPORT ON THE BRITISH MUSEUM (NATURAL HISTORY) **4171**

BRITISH MUSEUM (NATURAL HISTORY). DEPT. OF LIBRARY SERVICES See SERIAL PUBLICATIONS IN THE BRITISH MUSEUM, NATURAL HISTORY LIBRARY ON MICROFICHE **4172**

BRITISH MUSIC (UK/0958-5664) [23274177] **4105**

BRITISH MUSIC EDUCATION YEARBOOK (UK/0266-2329) [12651863] **4105**

BRITISH MUSIC YEARBOOK (UK/0306-5928) [02245045] **4105**

BRITISH MYCOLOGICAL SOCIETY See BRITISH MYCOLOGICAL SOCIETY SYMPOSIUM SERIES **574**

BRITISH MYCOLOGICAL SOCIETY SYMPOSIUM SERIES (UK/0275-0287) [06186833] **574**

BRITISH NATIONAL BIBLIOGRAPHY (UK/0007-1544) [01537342] 3197, **3257**

BRITISH NATIONAL COMMITTEE FOR GEODESY AND GEOPHYSICS. GEODESY SUBCOMMITTEE See UNITED KINGDOM GEODESY REPORT **2578**

BRITISH NATIONAL COMMITTEE FOR GEOGRAPHY. CARTOGRAPHY SUBCOMMITTEE See CARTOGRAPHIC ACTIVITIES IN THE UNITED KINGDOM, REPORT **2581**

BRITISH NATIONAL FORMULARY (LONDON, ENGLAND : 1966) (UK) [13987875] **4294**

BRITISH NEWSPAPERS : HISTORY AND GUIDE FOR COLLECTORS (UK) [13064169] **5811**

BRITISH NON-FERROUS METALS DIRECTORY, THE (UK) [20298930] **3999**

BRITISH NUMISMATIC JOURNAL (UK/0143-8956) [03140892] **2780**

BRITISH NUTRITION FOUNDATION See BNF NUTRITION BULLETIN **4188**

BRITISH ORNITHOLOGISTS' CLUB See BULLETIN OF THE BRITISH ORNITHOLOGIST'S CLUB **5616**

BRITISH ORTHOPTIC JOURNAL (UK/0068-2314) [01586859] **3873**

BRITISH OVERSEAS TRADE BOARD See REPORT - BRITISH OVERSEAS TRADE BOARD **850**

BRITISH PERFORMING ARTS NEWS LETTER / ARC (UK) [08161214] **384**

BRITISH PERFORMING ARTS YEARBOOK (UK/0951-5208) [18651754] **384**

BRITISH PERSONNEL MANAGEMENT (UK) **939**

BRITISH PHARMACEUTICAL INDUSTRY (UK) **4294**

BRITISH PHARMACOPIA, THE (UK) [01537352] **4294**

BRITISH PHARMACOPOEIA (VETERINARY) (UK) [03399462] **5506**

BRITISH PHYCOLOGICAL JOURNAL (UK/0007-1617) [02698246] **504**

BRITISH POULTRY SCIENCE (UK/0007-1668) [01537355] **207**

BRITISH PRESS, THE (UK) [19099158] **5811**

BRITISH PRINTER, THE (UK/0007-1684) [01537357] **4564**

BRITISH PTERIDOLOGICAL SOCIETY See BRITISH PTERIDOLOGICAL SOCIETY BULLETIN **504**

BRITISH PTERIDOLOGICAL SOCIETY BULLETIN (UK/0301-9195) [01793284] **504**

BRITISH PUBLIC OPINION (UK/0144-1329) [07102914] 4466, **5241**

BRITISH QUALIFICATIONS (UK/0141-5972) [04013638] 1812, **4210**

BRITISH QUARRYING & SLAG FEDERATION See BQSF REVIEW **2135**

BRITISH RAILWAYS BOARD See PASSENGER TIMETABLE : GREAT BRITAIN INTER-CITY, LOCAL AND SUBURBAN SERVICES, IRISH, CHANNEL ISLAND, COASTAL SERVICES **5433**

BRITISH RAILWAYS BOARD See PASSENGER TIMETABLE : INTERNATIONAL, INTER-CITY, SEALINK, SEASPEED SERVICES, GREAT BRITAIN-CONTINENT OF EUROPE **5433**

BRITISH RATE & DATA DIRECTORIES AND ANNUALS (UK) [01788151] **411**

BRITISH RECORDS ASSOCIATION See REPORT OF COUNCIL, ACCOUNTS, AND MINUTES OF ANNUAL GENERAL MEETING **2483**

BRITISH RECORDS ASSOCIATION See LIST OF MEMBERS - BRITISH RECORDS ASSOCIATION **2482**

BRITISH RED CROSS SOCIETY See REVIEW OF ... / BRITISH RED CROSS **5306**

BRITISH REPORTS, TRANSLATIONS AND THESES RECEIVED BY THE BRITISH LIBRARY DOCUMENT SUPPLY CENTRE (UK/0959-4922) [13818982] **3197**

BRITISH REVIEW OF BULIMIA + ANOREXIA NERVOSA (UK/0950-3005) [16921049] **3559**

BRITISH REVIEW OF ECONOMIC ISSUES (UK/0141-4739) [05454857] **1465**

BRITISH REVIEW OF NEW ZEALAND STUDIES : BRONZS (UK/0951-6204) [19652630] **5193**

BRITISH ROBOT ASSOCIATION. CONFERENCE See PROCEEDINGS OF THE ... ANNUAL BRITISH ROBOT ASSOCIATION CONFERENCE **1216**

BRITISH ROWING ALMANACK AND ARA YEAR BOOK (UK) [11050694] **4849**

BRITISH SCHOOL AT ROME See PAPERS OF THE BRITISH SCHOOL AT ROME **278**

BRITISH SCHOOL OF ARCHAEOLOGY IN JERUSALEM See REPORT AND ACCOUNTS **280**

BRITISH SCHOOLS EXPLORING SOCIETY See REPORT - BRITISH SCHOOLS EXPLORING SOCIETY **5145**

BRITISH SCIENCE FICTION BOOK INDEX (UK) [11683065] **3369**

BRITISH SOCIETY FOR CELL BIOLOGY See BRITISH SOCIETY FOR CELL BIOLOGY SYMPOSIUM **449**

BRITISH SOCIETY FOR CELL BIOLOGY SYMPOSIUM (UK/0309-1805) [02828222] **449**

BRITISH SOCIETY FOR PHENOMENOLOGY See JBSP. JOURNAL OF THE BRITISH SOCIETY FOR PHENOMENOLOGY **4350**

BRITISH SOCIETY FOR THE HISTORY OF SCIENCE See BSHS MONOGRAPHS **5090**

BRITISH SOLOMON ISLANDS See DEVELOPMENT PLAN - BRITISH SOLOMON ISLANDS PROTECTORATE **1555**

BRITISH STANDARD (UK) [02100785] **4029**

BRITISH STANDARDS INSTITUTION See BRITISH STANDARD **4029**

BRITISH STANDARDS INSTITUTION See B.S.I. NEWS **4029**

BRITISH STANDARDS INSTITUTION See BSI NEWS **4029**

BRITISH STEEL (UK/0007-182X) [01537378] 3999, **1600**

BRITISH STEEL CORPORATION See IRON AND STEEL INDUSTRY. ANNUAL STATISTICS FOR THE UNITED KINGDOM **1612**

BRITISH STEEL CORPORATION STATISTICAL SERVICES See INTERNATIONAL STEEL STATISTICS, UNITED KINGDOM **4025**

BRITISH SUGAR BEET REVIEW (UK/0007-1854) [09275963] **165**

BRITISH SUGAR NEWS (UK/0141-1969) [I01411969] **165**

BRITISH SULPHUR AMONIA QUARTERLY MARKET REPORT (UK) **963**

BRITISH TAX ENCYCLOPEDIA (UK) 1923, **4714**

BRITISH TAX GUIDE (US) [04401712] **4714**

BRITISH TAX REPORT (UK/0141-2876) [05789862] **4714**

BRITISH TAX REVIEW (UK/0007-1870) [01537382] **4714**

BRITISH TELECOM *See* BRITISH TELECOM GUIDE **1150**

BRITISH TELECOM GUIDE (UK) [07633191] **1150**

BRITISH TELECOMMUNICATIONS ENGINEERING (UK/0262-401X) [08735559] **1150**

BRITISH THEATRE REVIEW (UK) [02509817] **5362**

BRITISH TOURIST AUTHORITY *See* DIGEST OF TOURIST STATISTICS **5468**

BRITISH TOURIST AUTHORITY *See* ANNUAL REPORT OF THE BRITISH TOURIST AUTHORITY **5461**

BRITISH TOYS & HOBBIES (UK/0308-6712) [03086712] **2772**

BRITISH TRANSPORT DOCKS BOARD *See* REPORT AND ACCOUNTS - BRITISH TRANSPORT DOCKS BOARD **5455**

BRITISH TRAVEL LETTER (US/1041-4010) [18758795] **5465**

BRITISH TRUST FOR ORNITHOLOGY *See* B.T.O. NEWS **5615**

BRITISH TRUST FOR ORNITHOLOGY *See* ANNUAL REPORT AND ACCOUNTS - BRITISH TRUST FOR ORNITHOLOGY **5614**

BRITISH UNIVERSITIES' GUIDE TO GRADUATE STUDY (UK) [12142428] **1812**

BRITISH VALUE ADDED TAX REPORTER (UK) **4714**

BRITISH VETERINARY JOURNAL, THE (UK/0007-1935) [01537387] **5506**

BRITISH VIRGIN ISLANDS CONSOLIDATED INDEX OF STATUTES AND SUBSIDIARY LEGISLATION TO ... (BB) [12435766] **3125**

BRITISH WATER SUPPLY YEAR BOOK, THE (UK) [01789235] **5531**

BRITISH WATERWORKS YEAR BOOK AND DIRECTORY WITH STATISTICAL TABLES *See* BRITISH WATER SUPPLY YEAR BOOK, THE **5531**

BRITISH WILDLIFE (UK) [I09580956] 2189, **4869**

BRITISH YEAR BOOK OF INTERNATIONAL LAW, THE (UK/0068-2691) [01537393] **3125**

BRITT NEWS-TRIBUNE, THE (US) [16145786] **5668**

BRITTANY (FRANCE) *See* ANNUAIRE / ETABLISSEMENT PUBLIC REGIONAL DE BRETAGNE **4626**

BRITTONIA (US/0007-196X) [01537395] **504**

BRIXIA SACRA 1966 (IT/0392-1158) [I03921158] **2679**

BRMNA JOURNAL (CN/0229-0553) [08072167] **5430**

BRNE. VYSOKA SKOLA ZEMEDELSKA. FAKULTA PROVOZNE EKONOMICKA *See* ACTA UNIVERSITATIS AGRICULTURAE FACULTAS AGROECONOMICA **43**

BRNEKLINIKENS VEJLEDNINGER (DK/0106-3308) [03716323] **4385**

BRNO STUDIES IN ENGLISH (XR/0524-6881) [03198277] **3270**

BROAD TOP BULLETIN (US) [14988553] **5735**

BROADBAND NETWORKING NEWS (US/1059-0544) [24466909] **1127**

BROADCAST ACTIONS (US) [03457170] **1127**

BROADCAST BANKER/BROKER (US/0889-2644) [13829133] **780**

BROADCAST (BORDON) (UK/0040-2788) [14589806] **1127**

BROADCAST CABLE FINANCIAL JOURNAL (US) [22459630] **1127**

●BROADCAST CABLE FINANCIAL JOURNAL & CREDITOPICS (US) [27637139] **1127**

BROADCAST DATABOOK *See* ... BROADCAST FINANCIAL RECORD, THE **1127**

BROADCAST ENGINEERING NEWS (AT/0155-3720) [I01553720] **1127**

BROADCAST ENGINEERING (OVERLAND PARK) (US/0007-1994) [01537398] **1127**

BROADCAST EQUIPMENT BUYERS GUIDE (SHAWNEE MISSION, KAN.) (US/0882-5688) [11879660] **1127**

BROADCAST FINANCIAL & LEGAL SERVICES GUIDE (US) [19213343] **1127**

BROADCAST FINANCIAL JOURNAL (US/0161-9063) [04048747] **1127**

... BROADCAST FINANCIAL RECORD, THE (US) [18664600] **1127**

BROADCAST HARDWARE INTERNATIONAL (UK/0269-493X) [22106982] **1127**

BROADCAST (INTERNATIONAL) (UK) **1127**

BROADCAST. INTERNATIONAL EDITION (UK) **1127**

BROADCAST INVESTOR (US/0146-0110) [02827898] 780, **1127**

BROADCAST INVESTOR CHARTS (US/0736-9069) [09243216] 1127, **893**

BROADCAST MAGAZINE (NE) **1127**

BROADCAST MUSIC, INC *See* BMI ORCHESTRAL PROGRAM SURVEY **4104**

BROADCAST RULES (US) **1127**

... BROADCAST SERVICES GUIDE, THE (US) [23918852] **1127**

BROADCAST STATS (US/0749-2936) [11101064] 1127, **1124**

BROADCAST SYSTEMS ENGINEERING (UK/0267-565X) [12325620] **1128**

BROADCAST SYSTEMS INTERNATIONAL (UK/0959-5813) [I09595813] **1128**

BROADCAST TECHNICAL DATA AND APPLICATION INFORMATION MANUAL (US/0899-6725) [18180816] **4398**

BROADCAST + TECHNOLOGY (CN/0709-9797) [17311668] **1128**

BROADCASTER DIRECTORY (CN) **1128**

BROADCASTER (TORONTO) (CN/0008-3038) [01743566] **1128**

BROADCASTING ABOARD *See* BROADCASTING & CABLE INTERNATIONAL **1128**

BROADCASTING ABROAD (US/1064-6124) [26341191] **1128**

●BROADCASTING & CABLE (US/1068-6827) [27653186] **1128**

BROADCASTING & CABLE INTERNATIONAL (US) **1128**

BROADCASTING & CABLE MARKET PLACE (US/0000-1384) [25265849] **1128**

●BROADCASTING & CABLE YEARBOOK (US/0000-1511) [27375818] **1124**

BROADCASTING AND GOVERNMENT (US/0737-3120) [09346508] **1128**

BROADCASTING AND THE LAW (US/0161-5823) [11641286] 1128, **2943**

BROADCASTING CORPORATION OF NEW ZEALAND *See* REPORT OF THE BROADCASTING CORPORATION OF NEW ZEALAND **1138**

BROADCASTING SYSTEMS & OPERATIONS *See* INTERNATIONAL BROADCASTING **1133**

BROADCASTING TRIBUNAL (NEW ZEALAND) *See* REPORT OF THE BROADCASTING TRIBUNAL FOR THE YEAR ENDED 31 MARCH ... **1138**

BROADCASTING (WASHINGTON, D.C. : 1957) *See* BROADCASTING & CABLE **1128**

BROADCASTING (WASHINGTON, D.C. 1957) (US/0007-2028) [06318655] **1128**

BROADCASTING YEARBOOK (WASHINGTON, D.C. : 1990) *See* BROADCASTING & CABLE MARKET PLACE **1128**

BROADLY GRADED TEACHER'S RESOURCE GUIDE (US/0744-7345) [08516406] **1889**

BROADSHEET - ASSOCIATION OF CLINICAL PATHOLOGISTS (UK/0308-2555) [11131388] **3893**

BROADSHEET / GOSSE BIRD CLUB (JM) [06912714] **5616**

BROADSIDE CRITICS SERIES (US) [02999879] **3338**

BROADSIDE (NEW YORK, N.Y. : 1940) (US/0068-2748) [01537404] **5362**

BROADSIDE (NEW YORK, N.Y. 1962) *CEASED.* (US/0740-7955) [01696692] **4105**

BROADWATER MARKET LETTER (CN/0711-7590) [08559528] **68**

BROADWOVEN GRAY FABRIC PRODUCTION. SEASONAL ADJUSTMENT SUPPLEMENT (US/0730-0905) [07934672] **5348**

BROCHURE FOR ... / INSTITUTE OF STATISTICS AND APPLIED ECONOMICS (UG) [23752505] **1530**

BROCKPORT POST, THE (US) [08615957] **5714**

BROCKWAY RECORD *See* COUNTY NEIGHBORS (PUNXSUTAWNEY, PA.) **5735**

BROCKWAY RECORD, THE (US/1054-755X) [15088845] **5735**

BROILER INDUSTRY (US/0007-2176) [02445502] **207**

BROILER MARKETING FACTS (US/0360-3911) [02244278] **922**

BROILER MARKETING GUIDE *See* BROILER MARKETING FACTS **922**

BROJ STOKE I STOCNA PROIZVODNJA / SOCIJALISTICKA REPUBLIKA HRVATSKA, REPUBLICKI ZAVOD ZA STATISTIKU (CI) [09873910] **207**

BROJ STOKE I STOCNA PROIZVODNJA U SR HRVATSKOJ *See* BROJ STOKE I STOCNA PROIZVODNJA / SOCIJALISTICKA REPUBLIKA HRVATSKA, REPUBLICKI ZAVOD ZA STATISTIKU **207**

BROKEN BENCH REVIEW *SUSPENDED.* (US/0739-652X) [08469041] **3085**

BROKEN CUE NEWS, THE (CN/0317-0187) [02247573] **4858**

BROKEN SPOKE, THE (CN/0045-3226) [03418051] **5408**

BROKER (LONDON) (UK/0961-2114) [I09612114] **2876**

BROKER REPORT INDEX (AT/1033-0682) [I10330682] **893**

BROKER WORLD (US/0273-6551) [06798832] **2876**

BROMATOLOGIA I CHEMIA TOKSYKOLOGICZNA (PL/0365-9445) [01410558] **3979**

BROMELIAD SOCIETY *See* JOURNAL OF THE BROMELIAD SOCIETY **516**

BROMELIADS (UK) [03886847] **504**

BROMINE (US) [24177633] **2135**

BROMINE IN ... (US) [03025868] 1438, 2135, **1362**

BRONSON JOURNAL (US) **5691**

BRONTE NEWSLETTER (US/0737-6340) [08897122] **3369**

BRONTE SOCIETY *See* BRONTE SOCIETY PUBLICATIONS. TRANSACTIONS **3369**

BRONTE SOCIETY GAZETTE (UK) [22446959] **3369**

BRONTE SOCIETY PUBLICATIONS. TRANSACTIONS (UK/0309-7765) [08336755] **3369**

BRONX COUNTY HISTORICAL SOCIETY *See* BRONX COUNTY HISTORICAL SOCIETY JOURNAL, THE **2724**

BRONX COUNTY HISTORICAL SOCIETY JOURNAL, THE (US/0007-2249) [06989881] **2724**

BRONX PRESS-REVIEW (US) [09689812] **5714**

BRONX TIMES REPORTER (US/8750-4499) [11416187] **5714**

BROOKE COUNTY REVIEW (US) **5763**

BROOKE NEWS (US) [12698602] **5763**

BROOKFIELD JOURNAL, THE (US) [25635671] **5645**

BROOKFIELD NEWS, THE (US) [13030644] **5765**

BROOKFIELD ZOO BISON (US/8756-3479) [11540694] **5578**

BROOKGREEN GARDENS NEWSLETTER (US/0897-0785) [15810419] **2410**

BROOKGREEN JOURNAL (US/0884-8815) [12494143] 2410, 2724, **345**

BROOKHAVEN BULLETIN / BROOKHAVEN NATIONAL LABORATORY (US) [08920272] **5090**

BROOKHAVEN HIGHLIGHTS (US/0092-1548) [03028138] **4446**

BROOKHAVEN NATIONAL LABORATORY *See* DIRECTORY / BROOKHAVEN NATIONAL LABORATORY **5100**

BROOKHAVEN NATIONAL LABORATORY. DEPT. OF ENERGY AND ENVIRONMENT *See* ANNUAL SUMMARY OF PROGRAMS IN ENERGY SCIENCES **1932**

BROOKHAVEN NATIONAL LABORATORY. DEPT. OF ENERGY AND ENVIRONMENT *See* ANNUAL HIGHLIGHTS OF THE ENERGY TECHNOLOGY PROGRAMS **1932**

BROOKINGS DISCUSSION PAPERS IN INTERNATIONAL ECONOMICS (US) [11227672] **1633**

BROOKINGS INSTITUTION *See* GENERAL SERIES REPRINT **5200**

BROOKINGS PAPERS ON ECONOMIC ACTIVITY (US/0007-2303) [01167459] **1465**

BROOKINGS PAPERS ON ECONOMIC ACTIVITY. MICROECONOMICS (US/1057-8641) [19985852] **1465**

BROOKINGS REGISTER, THE (US) [12862643] **5743**

BROOKINGS REVIEW, THE (US/0745-1253) [08853284] **5193**

BROOKLINE CITIZEN (US) [19730583] **5688**

BROOKLINE TAB, THE (US/0745-2071) [08924170] **5688**

BROOKLYN BARRISTER (US/0007-232X) [01537438] **2944**

BROOKLYN. BOTANIC GARDEN *See* CONTRIBUTIONS - BROOKLYN BOTANIC GARDEN **507**

BROOKLYN BOTANIC GARDEN *See* ANNUAL REPORT / BROOKLYN BOTANIC GARDEN **499**

BROOKLYN — Alphabetical Title Index

BROOKLYN BOTANIC GARDEN 21ST CENTURY GARDENING SERIES (US) **2410**

BROOKLYN BOTANIC GARDEN RECORD *See* ANNUAL REPORT / BROOKLYN BOTANIC GARDEN **499**

BROOKLYN CENTER POSTNEWS (US) [21792964] **5694**

BROOKLYN COLLEGE. INSTITUTE FOR STUDIES IN AMERICAN MUSIC *See* I.S.A.M. MONOGRAPHS **4122**

BROOKLYN COLLEGE. INSTITUTE FOR STUDIES IN AMERICAN MUSIC *See* NEWSLETTER - INSTITUTE FOR STUDIES IN AMERICAN MUSIC **4141**

BROOKLYN COURIER (US/0744-7728) [08547442] **5714**

BROOKLYN ENGINEER, THE (US/0271-6437) [05985385] **1966**

BROOKLYN EXPONENT (US) [13440177] **5691**

BROOKLYN GRAPHIC, THE (US/0740-2260) [09922027] **5714**

BROOKLYN HEIGHTS PRESS & COBBLE HILL NEWS (US/0007-2346) [03989026] **5714**

BROOKLYN JOURNAL OF INTERNATIONAL LAW (US/0740-4824) [02246433] **3125**

BROOKLYN LAW REVIEW (US/0007-2362) [01537455] **2944**

BROOKLYN LITERARY REVIEW (US/0883-2846) [12047686] 3338, **1101**

BROOKLYN MUSEUM *See* REPORT **4095**

BROOKLYN PAPER, THE (US/0885-839X) [12737272] **5714**

BROOKLYN RECORD *CEASED.* (US/0740-2643) [09929751] **5714**

BROOKLYN TRIBUNE, THE (US) [08402436] **2724**

BROOKS FAMILY QUERY EXCHANGE, THE (US/0736-7066) [09179578] **2440**

BROOKS' STANDARD RATE BOOK, THE (US/0193-2314) [03768676] 4064, **1656**

BROOKSHIRE BANNER (US/0746-0678) [09723232] **5747**

BROOKSHIRE ROYAL BANNER *See* BROOKSHIRE BANNER **5747**

BROOKVILLE AMERICAN (BROOKVILLE, IND. : 1873) (US) [08786904] **5663**

BROOKVILLE AMERICAN (BROOKVILLE, PA.) (US) [15088850] **5735**

BROOKVILLE DEMOCRAT, THE (US) [12791327] **5663**

BROOM, BRUSH & MOP (US/0890-2933) [09169781] **1600**

BROOMFIELD ENTERPRISE (US) [20227733] **5642**

BROOMSTICK *CEASED.* (US/0883-9611) [08147254] **5552**

BROSCHURE ... DES FORSCHUNGSINSTITUTS FUR DIE ZAHNARZTLICHE VERSORGUNG (GW) [10502394] **1317**

BROSSARD ECLAIR (CN/0713-620X) [08967784] **5781**

BROT & BACKWAREN (GW/0172-8180) [01728180] **2329**

BROT UND ROSEN (ASSOCIATION) *See* FRAUENHANDBUCH / BROT UND ROSEN **589**

BROTERIA 1925 (PO/0870-7618) [08707618] **2843**

BROTHERHOOD ACTION (AT/0300-4678) [01429520] **5229**

BROWARD ECONOMIC HANDBOOK (US) **1465**

BROWARD LEGACY (US/0148-0340) [03258829] **2724**

BROWARD REVIEW (US/0887-4751) [13259613] **3096**

BROWARD STREET ATLAS (US) **1923**

BROWARD TIMES, THE (US/1065-1462) [26515574] **2257**

BROWBEAT (US/1075-0371) **4105**

BROWER FAMILY CIRCLE, THE (US) [06063570] **2440**

BROWN AND WHITE, THE (US) [09258406] **1089**

BROWN BOOK (OAKLAND, CALIF.), THE (US/0882-0651) [11741122] **1265**

"BROWN CHART" FOR ALL LINES OF GENERAL INSURANCE, PROVINCIAL RESULTS : ... REPORT, THE (CN/0227-437X) [06106256] **2876**

BROWN COMPANY *See* BROWN COMPANY ANNUAL REPORT **644**

BROWN COMPANY ANNUAL REPORT (US/0277-7541) [05297076] **644**

BROWN COUNTY DEMOCRAT (NASHVILLE, IND.) (US) [12096395] **5663**

BROWN DEER HERALD (US) **5765**

BROWN FAMILY NEWS AND GENEALOGICAL SOCIETY, THE *CEASED.* (US/1068-9931) [24437067] **2440**

BROWN GOLD (US/0007-2494) [03989173] **4940**

BROWN JUDAIC STUDIES (US/0147-927X) [03250610] **5046**

BROWN SWISS BULLETIN, THE (US/0007-2516) [01537479] **207**

BROWN SWISS CATTLE BREEDERS' ASSOCIATION *See* BROWN SWISS BULLETIN, THE **207**

BROWN UNIVERSITY CHILD AND ADOLESCENT BEHAVIOR LETTER, THE (US/1058-1073) [24221094] **4578**

BROWN UNIVERSITY. DEPARTMENT OF OCEANOGRAPHY *See* TECHNICAL REPORT - DEPARTMENT OF OCEANOGRAPHY **1457**

BROWN UNIVERSITY DIGEST OF ADDICTION THEORY AND APPLICATION (US/1040-6328) [16626488] **1341**

BROWN UNIVERSITY FAMILY THERAPY LETTER *See* PSYCHOTHERAPY LETTER, THE **4614**

BROWN UNIVERSITY FAMILY THERAPY LETTER, THE (US/1045-5051) [20149391] **2277**

● BROWN UNIVERSITY GERIATRIC RESEARCH APPLICATION DIGEST, THE (US/1067-7372) [27335395] **3750**

BROWN UNIVERSITY LONG TERM CARE LETTER *See* BROWN UNIVERSITY LONG TERM CARE QUALITY LETTER **4769**

BROWN UNIVERSITY LONG-TERM CARE LETTER, THE (US/1042-1386) [18946266] **4769**

BROWN UNIVERSITY LONG TERM CARE QUALITY LETTER (US) **4769**

BROWN UNIVERSITY STD UPDATE, THE (US/0898-8323) [17927717] 3712, **4769**

BROWNE RECORDS (UK) [04613760] **2440**

BROWNFIELD NEWS AND TERRY COUNTY HERALD, THE (US) [13983104] **5747**

BROWNING NEWSLETTER (BURLINGTON, VT.), THE (US/0896-3045) [15534015] **5090**

BROWNING SOCIETY (LONDON, ENGLAND) *See* BROWNING SOCIETY NOTES **3369**

BROWNING SOCIETY NOTES *CEASED.* (UK/0950-6349) [18066252] **3369**

BROWN'S BUSINESS REPORTER (US/1066-2421) [I10662421] **644**

BROWN'S DIRECTORY OF INSTRUCTIONAL PROGRAMS (7-12). FOREIGN LANGUAGE (US/1053-7406) [22621173] **1889**

BROWN'S DIRECTORY OF INSTRUCTIONAL PROGRAMS (7-12). LANGUAGE ARTS / PREPARED AND COMPILED BY BROWN PUBLISHING NETWORK (US/1053-7392) [22621143] **1889**

BROWN'S DIRECTORY OF INSTRUCTIONAL PROGRAMS (7-12). MATHEMATICS (US/1053-7422) [22621223] 3497, **1889**

BROWN'S DIRECTORY OF INSTRUCTIONAL PROGRAMS (7-12). SCIENCE/HEALTH (US/1053-7430) [22621260] 1889, **5090**

BROWN'S DIRECTORY OF INSTRUCTIONAL PROGRAMS (7-12). SOCIAL STUDIES / PREPARED AND COMPILED BY BROWN PUBLISHING NETWORK (US/1053-7414) [22621194] **1889**

● BROWN'S DIRECTORY OF INSTRUCTIONAL PROGRAMS (7-12). TECHNICAL/VOCATIONAL EDUCATION, HOME ECONOMICS (US/1075-2307) [29645030] **1911**

BROWN'S DIRECTORY OF INSTRUCTIONAL PROGRAMS (7-12). VOCATIONAL EDUCATION *See* BROWN'S DIRECTORY OF INSTRUCTIONAL PROGRAMS (7-12). TECHNICAL/VOCATIONAL EDUCATION, HOME ECONOMICS **1911**

BROWN'S DIRECTORY OF INSTRUCTIONAL PROGRAMS (7-12). VOCATIONAL EDUCATION (US/1053-7449) [22621287] **1911**

BROWN'S DIRECTORY OF INSTRUCTIONAL PROGRAMS (K-8). LANGUAGE ARTS/SPELLING/HANDWRITING (US/1053-735X) [22620555] **1889**

BROWN'S DIRECTORY OF INSTRUCTIONAL PROGRAMS (K-8). MATHEMATICS / PREPARED AND COMPILED BY BROWN PUBLISHING NETWORK (US/1053-7376) [22620701] 3497, **1802**

BROWN'S DIRECTORY OF INSTRUCTIONAL PROGRAMS (K-8). READING (US/1053-7333) [22620469] **1802**

BROWN'S DIRECTORY OF INSTRUCTIONAL PROGRAMS (K-8). SCIENCE/HEALTH / PREPARED AND COMPILED BY BROWN PUBLISHING NETWORK (US/1053-7384) [22621087] 5090, **1889**

BROWN'S DIRECTORY OF INSTRUCTIONAL PROGRAMS (K-8). SOCIAL STUDIES (US/1053-7368) [22620659] **1889**

BROWN'S DIRECTORY OF INSTRUCTIONAL PROGRAMS (K-8). WHOLE LANGUAGE/LITERATURE (US/1053-7341) [22620498] **1890**

BROWN'S DIRECTORY OF NORTH AMERICAN AND INTERNATIONAL GAS COMPANIES (US/0197-8098) [04473010] **4252**

BROWN'S NAUTICAL ALMANAC (UK/0068-290X) [I0068290X] **4175**

BROWN'S NAUTICAL ALMANAC; DAILY TIDE TABLES (UK/0068-290X) [06226477] **4175**

BROWNS NEWS/ILLUSTRATED (US/0278-9973) [07954750] **4888**

BROWNSTONE MYSTERY GUIDES (US/1055-6869) [23269702] **3369**

BROWNSTONER, THE (US/0883-962X) [03252649] 602, **293**

BROWNSVILLE HERALD (BROWNSVILLE, TEX. : 1910) (US/0894-2064) [12903289] **5747**

BROWNSVILLE STATES-GRAPHIC (US/0893-3839) [15509067] **5744**

BROWNSVILLE TIMES, THE (US/0746-6412) [10195830] **5747**

BROWNWOOD BULLETIN (US) [14247616] **5747**

BROWSE (WEST HILL. 1991) (CN/1184-2709) [24265611] **5579**

BRS BULLETIN (US/0196-7223) [04656091] 3197, **1172**

BRUCE & GREY BRANCH OF O.G.S (CN/0849-0848) [22470916] **2440**

BRUCE BULLETIN (CN/1184-7387) [24256529] **2440**

BRUCE DAVID COHEN'S THE GOOD LIFE (US/0742-8189) [10463472] **2529**

BRUCE REPORT, THE (US/1055-3525) [23157812] **862**

BRUCE TRAIL NEWS (CN/0383-9249) [03219813] **4869**

BRUCELLOSIS SURVEILLANCE (ANNUAL SUMMARY) *CEASED.* (US/0090-1156) [01794857] **4769**

BRUCKE-ARCHIV (GW/0300-2039) [01784747] **345**

BRUCKE-ARCHIVE (GW) [06723362] **4085**

BRUCKE, DIE (AU) [02716505] **2679**

BRUCKE-MUSEUM *See* BRUCKE-ARCHIV **345**

BRUCKMANNS PANTHEON (GW/0720-0056) [07090303] **345**

BRUEL & KJAER TECHNICAL REVIEW *CEASED.* (DK/0007-2621) [07314347] **1967**

BRUG, DE (NE) [06057531] **5806**

BRUKDOWN (BH) [03908633] **2724**

BRUNDTLAND BULLETIN / THE CENTRE FOR OUR COMMON FUTURE (SZ) [24270760] **2162**

BRUNEI MUSEUM JOURNAL (BX) [01792199] **4085**

BRUNN. UNIVERSITA. FILOSOFICKA FAKULTA *See* SBORNIK PRACI FILOSOFICKE FACULTY BRNENSKE UNIVERSITY **1904**

BRUNN. VYSOKA SKOLA ZEMEDELSKA. FAKULTA LESNICKA *See* ACTA UNIVERSITATIS AGRICULTURAE FACULTAS SILVICULTURAE **2373**

BRUNSWICK BUSINESS JOURNAL, THE (CN/0829-5239) [13318974] **644**

BRUNSWICK NEWS, THE (US) [21707708] **5652**

BRUNSWICK TAX REPORT, THE (CN/0828-5365) [12177978] **4714**

BRUNSWICKER (BRUNSWICK, MO. : 1916) (US) [13433411] **5702**

BRUNTON'S MISCELLANY (UK) [04202668] **3369**

BRUSH DECORATION (US/0009-0328) **2586**

BRUSH-MORGAN COUNTY NEWS-TRIBUNE (US) [21479842] **5642**

BRUSHES INTERNATIONAL DIRECTORY (UK/0966-4890) [I09664890] **2810**

BRUSHWARE (WASHINGTON, D.C.) (US/0007-2710) [04047185] **2810**

BRUSSELS BRIEFING (UK) 602, **2019**

BRUSSELS. CENTRE DE RECHERCHES SCIENTIFIQUES ET TECHNIQUES DE L'INDUSTRIE DES FABRICATIONS METALLIQUES *See* SECTION : CONSTRUCTION ELECTRIQUE **2080**

Alphabetical Title Index — BUDGET

BRUSSELS. INSTITUT ROYAL DES SCIENCES NATURELLES DE BELGIQUE *See* MEMOIRES. DEUXIEME SERIE (BRUXELLES) **4167**

BRUSSELS. INSTITUT ROYAL METEOROLOGIQUE DE BELGIQUE *See* BULLETIN MENSUEL: POLLUTION ATMOSPHERIC, FUMEE ET SO2. MAANDBERICHT: LUCHTVERONTREINIGING, ROOK EN SO2 **2225**

BRUSSELS. INSTITUT ROYAL METEOROLOGIQUE DE BELGIQUE *See* OBSERVATIONS CLIMATOLOGIQUES **1433**

BRUSSELS. MUSEES ROYAUX DES BEAUX-ARTS DE BELGIQUE *See* ANNUAIRE DES MUSEES ROYAUX DES BEAUX-ARTS DE BELGIQUE **4083**

BRUSSELS MUSEUM OF MUSICAL INSTRUMENTS BULLETIN, THE *SUSPENDED.* (BE) [02152131] **4105**

BRUSSELS. OBSERVATOIRE ROYAL DE BELGIQUE *See* BULLETIN D'OBSERVATIONS: MAREES TERRESTRES. WAARNEMINGSBERICHTEN: AARDGETIJDEN **1352**

BRUSSELS. UNIVERSITE LIBRE. INSTITUT DE PHONETIQUE *See* RAPPORT D'ACTIVITES DE L'INSTITUT DE PHONETIQUE **3314**

BRUSSELS. UNIVERSITE LIBRE. INSTITUT DE SOCIOLOGIE SOVAY *See* REVUE DE L'INSTITUT DE SOCIOLOGIE **5217**

BRUTIUM (IT/0392-3894) [I03923894] **2680**

BRUTUS MAGAZINE (JA) **3994**

BRW : THE MAGAZINE OF AUSTRALIAN & NEW ZEALAND BUSINESS *CEASED.* (AT) [24677031] **644**

BRYAN-COLLEGE STATION EAGLE (US/0739-8727) [09824088] **5747**

BRYANT BACKTRAILS (US/0146-1990) [02884251] **2440**

BRYANT COLLEGE *See* ALUMNI DIRECTORY / BRYANT COLLEGE **1097**

BRYGMESTEREN (DK/0007-2737) [03438138] **2365**

BRYN MAWR CLASSICAL REVIEW (US/1055-7660) [23226497] **1075**

BRYNWT WSTYH HBRTYT (IS/0334-4525) [I03344525] **5275**

BRYOLOGISCHE BEITRAEGE (GW/0723-2470) [09015429] **504**

BRYOLOGIST, THE (US/0007-2745) [01537534] **504**

BRYOPHYTORUM BIBLIOTHECA (GW/0258-3348) [03149451] **504**

BSA ANNUAL REPORT (UK/0953-9905) [I09539905] **602**

BSAP OCCASIONAL PUBLICATION (UK/0263-967X) [07811003] **5506**

BSBI ABSTRACTS (UK/0307-2657) [01773785] **449**

BSCS JOURNAL, THE (US/0737-7460) [05962214] **449**

BSES BULLETIN (AT/0810-3240) [09451431] **165**

BSHS MONOGRAPHS (UK) [06850303] **5090**

BSHS NEWSLETTER (UK/0144-6347) [I01446347] **5090**

BSI BUYERS GUIDE (UK) [06201193] **4029**

BSI HISTORY PROJECT, THE (US/1045-4489) [20127419] **3197**

BSI NEWS (UK/0005-3309) [01537376] **4029**

BSI STANDARDS CATALOGUE (UK) [17623924] **4029**

BSP BAREME SOCIAL PERIODIQUE (FR/0767-9866) [I07679866] **5193**

BT 2 CANNES (FR/0005-3414) [I00053414] **1728**

BT (CANNES, FRANCE) (FR) [18516891] **1060**

BT CATALYST (US/1040-9416) [18031850] **3690**

BT TECHNOLOGY JOURNAL / BT LABORATORIES (UK) [24486562] **1150**

BTA JOURNAL *CEASED.* (US/0895-0067) [07096302] 1890, **644**

BTH. BODENBELAGE, TAPETEN, HEIMTEXTILIEN. FUSSBODEN-ZEITUNG (GW/0933-2855) [I09332855] **633**

BTI : BULLETIN TECHNIQUE D'INFORMATION (FR) [24383190] **68**

BTI UNION LIST OF SERIALS. MICROFORM (US) [08918604] **4940**

BTJ. BIBLIOTHEQUE DE TRAVAIL JUNIOR (FR/0005-3120) [I00053120] **1728**

BTL (GW) [09776673] **4210**

BTN (BIRMINGHAM, ALA.) (US/1055-4548) [23187412] **1150**

BTS : BUERO, TECHNIK, SYSTEME (GW/0935-0276) [26206630] **4210**

BTS BUEROTECHNISCHE SAMMLUNG, DAS RATIONELLE BUERO (GW/0341-1370) [18610352] **4210**

BUBBA MAGAZINE (US/1068-3208) [27409651] **2529**

BUC ... NEW BOAT PRICE GUIDE *CEASED.* (US/0195-346X) [07663929] **592**

BUC USED BOAT PRICE GUIDE (US/0735-973X) [07723586] **592**

BUCERUS MARTIN OPERA OMNIA (GW) **4105**

BUCH (AU/0003-6277) [23275320] **4827**

BUCH DER ZEIT (GW/0007-2761) [06306237] **4812**

BUCH UND BIBLIOTHEK (GW/0340-0301) [02693858] **3197**

BUCHALTER SZCZECIN (PL/0867-7204) [I08677204] **740**

BUCHAREST. INSTITUTUL DE STUDII SI CERCETARI HIDROTEHNICE. STUDII DE ALIMENTARI CU APA *See* STUDI ALIMENTARI CU APA **5540**

BUCHEREI DES AUGENARZTES (GW/0068-3361) [01537576] **3873**

BUCHEREI DES FRAUENARZTES (GW/0068-337X) [01537577] **3758**

BUCHEREI DES ORTHOPADEN (GW/0068-3388) [01589526] **3880**

BUCHEREI DES PADIATERS (GW/0373-3165) [01645393] **3901**

BUCHEREI DES PNEUMOLOGEN (GW/0342-4456) [03551189] **3948**

BUCHERPICK (SZ) [09158733] **4827**

BUCHHALTUNGSERGEBNISSE SCHWEIZERISCHER UNTERNEHMUNGEN (SZ) [13724065] **644**

BUCHREIHE DER ANGLIA (GW/0340-5435) [05901946] 3270, **3369**

BUCHREIHE DER CUSANUS-GESELLSCHAFT (GW/0070-2234) [03038518] **5024**

BUCHREIHE DER SUDOSTDEUTSCHEN HISTORISCHEN KOMMISSION (GW/0562-5270) [03111119] **2680**

BUCHREIHE DER ZEITSCHRIFT FUER CELTISCHE PHILOLOGIE (GW) [12756134] **3270**

● BUCK NAKED CRIME FIGHTER (US/1068-6800) [27759176] **4858**

BUCKER JUNGMANN NEWSLETTER *See* BUCKER NEWS LETTER, THE **15**

BUCKER NEWS LETTER, THE (US/0889-4388) [14047398] **15**

BUCKEYE BEVERAGE JOURNAL *See* OHIO BEVERAGE JOURNAL **2370**

BUCKEYE FARM NEWS (US/0007-2834) [04131132] **68**

● BUCKEYE INDEPENDENT, THE (US/1065-3880) [26610811] **5629**

BUCKEYE OSTEOPATH *See* BUCKEYE OSTEOPATHIC PHYSICIAN **4294**

BUCKEYE OSTEOPATHIC PHYSICIAN (US/0898-3070) [06647337] 3559, **4294**

BUCKEYE REVIEW (US/0045-3285) [03989242] **2257**

BUCKEYE SPORTS BULLETIN (US/0883-6833) [12201568] **4888**

BUCKEYE VALLEY NEWS (US) **5629**

BUCKINGHAMSHIRE RECORD SOCIETY *See* PUBLICATIONS **2703**

BUCKLEY-LITTLE CATALOGUE OF BOOKS AVAILABLE FROM AUTHORS, THE (US/0749-615X) [10897621] **411**

BUCKLEY ON THE COMPANIES ACTS (UK) **3096**

BUCKMASTERS WHITETAIL MAGAZINE (US/0895-481X) [16657177] **4869**

BUCKNELL REVIEW (US/0007-2869) [04412203] **3338**

BUCKNELL UNIVERSITY *See* ANNUAL REPORT - BUCKNELL UNIVERSITY **1809**

BUCKNELL UNIVERSITY. REPORT TO THE PRESIDENT *See* ANNUAL REPORT - BUCKNELL UNIVERSITY **1809**

BUCKS AND BERKS COUNTRYSIDE (UK) [10759938] **2680**

BUCKSKIN BULLETIN (US/0045-3307) [02505557] **2724**

BUCYRUS-ERIE COMPANY *See* REPORT - BUCYRUS-ERIE COMPANY **707**

BUDAPEST. MAGYAR TESTNEVELESI FOISKOLA *See* TUDOMANYOS KOZLEMENYEK **1859**

BUDAPEST. MEZOGAZDASAGI GEPKISERLETI INTEZET *See* MEZOGAZDASAGI GEPESITESI TANULMANYOK **160**

BUDAPEST REGISEGEI (HU/0133-1892) [01537562] **2680**

BUDAPEST REVIEW OF BOOKS (HU/1215-735X) [25729154] **4827**

BUDAPEST STATISZTIKAI ZSEBKONYVE (HU/0438-2242) [01240390] **5323**

BUDAPEST. TUDOMANY-EGYETEM. ALLAM- ES JOGTUDOMANYI KAR *See* BUDAPESTI EOETVOES LORAND TUDOMANYEGYETEM ALLAM ES JOGTUDOMANYI KARANAK ACTAI **2944**

BUDAPESTI EOETVOES LORAND TUDOMANYEGYETEM ALLAM ES JOGTUDOMANYI KARANAK ACTAI (HU/0524-904X) [03269933] **2944**

BUDAPESTI KOZLEKEDESI VALLALAT *See* VAROSI KOZLEKEDES **5399**

BUDAPESTI STATISZTIKAI TAJEKOZTATO (HU) [02325193] **5323**

BUDAVOX TELECOMMUNICATION REVIEW *CEASED.* (HU/0007-2907) [09586631] **1150**

BUDAYA (SHOREVIEW, MINN.) (US/1051-9483) [22152984] **2647**

BUDDHIPRAKASA (II) [06335883] **3369**

BUDDHISM AT THE CROSSROADS *SUSPENDED.* (CN/1181-8360) [22730601] **5020**

BUDDHIST-CHRISTIAN STUDIES (US/0882-0945) [08420636] **5020**

BUDDHIST STUDIES (II) [02383953] **5020**

BUDDHIST TEXT INFORMATION (US/0360-6112) [01906629] **5012**

BUDDHISTS FOR PEACE (MP) [09524324] **5020**

BUDDY (DALLAS, TEX.) (US/0192-9097) [05134794] **4105**

BUDESHTE (FR) [04319363] **2514**

BUDGET (II/0448-2352) [01779418] **4714**

● BUDGET (SA) [24779012] **4714**

BUDGET. ADDITIONAL INFORMATION : ESTIMATES (CN/0706-0335) [04520885] **4714**

BUDGET ADDRESS (AQ) [20818255] **4714**

BUDGET ADDRESS OF THE CHAIRMAN OF THE MANAGEMENT COMMITTEE (JOHANNESBURG, SOUTH AFRICA) *See* BUDGET **4714**

BUDGET - ALBERTA WHEAT POOL (CN/0843-2309) [19551807] **165**

BUDGET AMENDMENT REPORT (US) [05186188] **4714**

BUDGET ANALYSES OF STATE AGENCIES : REPORT OF THE LEGISLATIVE FINANCE COMMITTEE TO THE ... LEGISLATURE (US) [10866976] **4714**

● BUDGET ANALYSIS FOR SFY ... / STATE OF NEW YORK, LEGISLATIVE COMMISSION ON STATE-LOCAL RELATIONS (US) [26513819] **4714**

BUDGET AS ADOPTED BY THE BOARD OF COMMISSIONERS (US/0145-7837) [02782158] **4634**

BUDGET - BOARD FOR INTERNATIONAL BROADCASTING (US) [03948326] **1128**

BUDGET. BUDGET SPEECH AND ADDITIONAL INFORMATION (CN/0839-8429) [17204233] **4714**

BUDGET. COMMUNIQUES (QUEBEC) (CN/0226-4390) [06861062] **4634**

BUDGET DE L'ETAT - MINISTERE DES FINANCES (LU) [06514925] **4714**

BUDGET DE PROGRAMMES / SECRETARIAT GENERAL POUR L'ADMINISTRATION, ACTION SOCIALE DES ARMEES (FR) [07337018] **4038**

BUDGET D'EQUIPEMENT ET DE RECHERCHE (CM) [05259584] **3270**

BUDGET DER BUNDESHAUPTSTADT WIEN (AU) [03472687] **780**

BUDGET DES DEPENSES PRINCIPAL DE LA PROVINCE DU MANITOBA (CN/0848-6220) [23257748] **4714**

BUDGET D'INVESTISSEMENT ET D'EQUIPEMENT (TG) [06451276] **4714**

BUDGET. DISCOURS SUR LE BUDGET ET RENSEIGNEMENTS SUPPLEMENTAIRES (CN/0839-8445) [18457363] **4714**

BUDGET : ECONOMIC BACKGROUND (HK) [05000692] **1549**

BUDGET ECONOMIQUE DE ... VERSION REVISEE / MINISTERE DES AFFAIRES ECONOMIQUES, DIRECTION GENERALE DES ETUDES ET DE LA DOCUMENTATION, CELLULE BUDGET ECONOMIQUE-ETUDES (BE) [10991881] **1549**

BUDGET ESTIMATES / PARLIAMENT OF NEW SOUTH WALES (AT) [14643679] **4634**

BUDGET: ESTIMATES (QUEBEC) (CN/0705-3401) [04567209] **4714**

BUDGET ESTIMATES - U.S. NUCLEAR REGULATORY COMMISSION (US) [08081085] **4634**

BUDGET

Alphabetical Title Index

BUDGET FOR THE FINANCIAL YEAR / REPUBLIC OF SINGAPORE, THE (SI/0129-4679) [04197042] **780**

BUDGET / GOVERNMENT OF INDIA, MINISTRY OF FINANCE (II/0536-9290) [01589703] **5430, 4714**

BUDGET - GREATER LONDON COUNCIL (UK) [02246527] **4714**

BUDGET GUIDELINES : CONDOMINIUMS, PLANNED DEVELOPMENTS, STOCK COOPERATIVES, COMMUNITY ASSOCIATIONS (US/0273-1169) [06985632] **2816**

BUDGET HIGHLIGHTS - UNITED STATES. DEPT. OF ENERGY. OFFICE OF THE CONTROLLER (US/0743-5487) [09768163] **4634**

BUDGET IN BRIEF (US) [06284608] **4714**

BUDGET IN BRIEF / GEORGIA. BUDGET BUREAU *See* BUDGET IN BRIEF / STATE OF GEORGIA **4714**

BUDGET IN BRIEF - MANIPUR (INDIA). DEPT. OF STATISTICS (II) [01797706] **4714**

BUDGET IN BRIEF / STATE OF GEORGIA (US) [05827344] **4714**

BUDGET IN BRIEF / U.S. DEPARTMENT OF ENERGY (US/0272-8435) [06021074] **4714**

BUDGET IRELAND (IE) [09477562] **4714**

BUDGET - LOS ANGELES (US/0090-242X) [01784869] **4714**

BUDGET MESSAGE (US) [07851777] **4714**

BUDGET / MINISTERE DE L'ECONOMIE ET DU PLAN, SOCIETE DE DEVELOPPEMENT DU NKAM (CM) [07118631] **780**

BUDGET MONITOR (AT) **4714**

BUDGET - NATIONAL TRANSPORTATION SAFETY BOARD (US/0147-7382) [03138048] **5378**

BUDGET OF THE UNITED STATES GOVERNMENT (US/0163-2000) [00932137] **4714**

BUDGET PREPARATION MANUAL (US) [03853478] **4715**

● BUDGET PRESENTATION TO THE GENERAL ASSEMBLY OF THE COMMONWEALTH OF PENNSYLVANIA - UNIVERSITY OF PITTSBURGH (US) [23728146] **4715**

... BUDGET / PRESENTED BY THE PRIME MINISTER ... TO THE HOUSE OF REPRESENTATIVE ON, THE (BH) [19285111] **4634**

BUDGET PROPOSED FOR THE DEPARTMENT OF LABOR AND RELATED AGENCIES, THE (US/0161-4770) [03122663] **4715, 1656**

BUDGET RECOMMENDATIONS. EXECUTIVE SUMMARY / MASSACHUSETTS EXECUTIVE OFFICE OF HUMAN SERVICES (US) [07522881] **5275**

BUDGET RECOMMENDATIONS FOR THE CONNECTICUT SYSTEM OF HIGHER EDUCATION (US) [02241699] **1812**

BUDGET. RENSEIGNEMENTS SUPPLEMENTAIRES : IMPOTS (CN/0711-8651) [06281924] **4715**

BUDGET. RENSEIGNEMENTS SUPPLEMENTAIRES : REFORME DE LA FISCALITE MUNICIPALE (CN/0707-9230) [06240199] **4715**

BUDGET REQUEST - STATE DEPARTMENT OF PUBLIC INSTRUCTION (US/0145-9902) [02826583] **1812**

BUDGET REQUEST - U.S. CONSUMER PRODUCT SAFETY COMMISSION (US/0193-0362) [04660858] **1294, 4634**

BUDGET REQUESTS - STATE BOARD OF REGENTS (US/0361-5901) [02308378] **1728**

BUDGET REVISIONS - EXECUTIVE OFFICE OF THE PRESIDENT, OFFICE OF MANAGEMENT AND BUDGET (US/0146-907X) [03058422] **4715**

BUDGET SPEECH AND TAX PROPOSALS (MY) [08482806] **4715**

BUDGET SPEECH DELIVERED BY THE MINISTER FOR FINANCE ... IN THE HOUSE OF REPRESENTATIVES ON (GD) [19292203] **4715**

BUDGET SPEECH - MEGHALAYA (INDIA) (II) [01784176] **4715**

BUDGET SPEECH - MILITARY ADMINISTRATOR, IMO STATE OF NIGERIA (NR) [06280950] **4715**

BUDGET SPEECH - MINISTER OF FINANCE (MF) [04614630] **4715**

BUDGET SPEECH OF HIS EXCELLENCY THE MILITARY GOVERNOR (NR) [01785288] **4715**

BUDGET SPEECH / PRESENTED BY THE TREASURER OF VICTORIA ON THE OCCASION OF THE BUDGET (AT) [19085849] **4715**

BUDGET - STATE OF NORTH CAROLINA, THE (US/0147-2984) [03251248] **4715**

BUDGET : STATISTICAL SURVEY (SA) [01784911] **4715, 4696**

BUDGET (SUGARCREEK, OHIO : 1928) (US) [19491996] **5727**

BUDGET SUMMARY AND PROGRAM BUDGET EXPENDITURES / PRESENTED BY THE TREASURER OF VICTORIA FOR THE INFORMATION OF HONOURABLE MEMBERS ON THE OCCASION OF THE BUDGET (AT) [19116614] **4715**

BUDGET SUMMARY STATEMENTS (BG) [20379542] **4715**

BUDGET SUMMARY STATEMENTS / BANGLADESH. ARTHA MANTRANALAYA *See* BUDGET SUMMARY STATEMENTS **4715**

BUDGET. SUPPLEMENT (VIRGINIA. GOVERNOR) (US) [06322353] **4715**

... BUDGET, THE (HK) [15343967] **4714**

BUDGET TRAVEL IN CANADA (UNITED STATES EDITION) (US) [10730089] **5465**

BUDGET TUNISIEN, LE (TI) [07181344] **4715**

BUDGET / VILLE DE MONTREAL (CN/0227-9142) [09100449] **4715**

BUDGET / VIRGIN ISLANDS OF THE UNITED STATES. GOVERNOR *See* VIRGIN ISLANDS OF THE UNITED STATES. GOVERNOR. BUDGET **4758**

BUDGET-WISE HOUSE PLANS (US/0748-5549) [09822162] **293**

BUDGETING FOR BASIC NEEDS AND BUDGETING FOR MINIMUM ADEQUATE STANDARD OF LIVING (CN/0822-7918) [10638925] **2789**

BUDKAVLEN (FI) [05665643] **2680**

BUDO (JA) [03278155] **4888**

BUDOWNICTWO OKRETOWE I GOSPODARKA MORSKA : ORGAN SEKCJI OKRETOWCOW PRZY ZARZADZIE GOWNYM STOWARZYSZENIA INZYNIEROW I TECHNIKOW MECHANIKOW POLSKICH (PL) [30604228] **5447**

BUDOWNICTWO ROLNICZE (PL/0324-8674) [03036293] **602**

BUDZETY GOSPODARSTW DOMOWYCH (PL) [03011378] **1465**

BUECHERSCHIFF; DIE DEUTSCHE BUECHERZEITUNG (GW/0007-3059) [02987199] **4827**

BUEHNE (AU/0007-3075) [02258689] **4105**

BUEHNENTECHNISCHE RUNDSCHAU (GW/0007-3091) [02445546] **5362**

BUELNA (MX) [06515482] **1812**

BUENA SALUD (US/0896-2642) [16997412] **4769**

BUENA VISTA COLLEGE *See* ALUMNI DIRECTORY / BUENA VISTA COLLEGE **1097**

BUENASALUD (ED. NACIONAL) (PR/1053-5543) [22575098] **2596**

BUENDERWALD (SZ) **5229**

BUENHOGAR (HEARST CORPORATION) (US) [08901228] **5552, 2789**

BUENOS AIRES. CAMARA DE COMERCIO *See* INFORMATIVO MENSUAL **840**

BUENOS AIRES HERALD (AG) [12426256] **5777**

BUENOS AIRES. UNIVERSIDAD NACIONAL. INSTITUTO DE ENFERMEDADES INFECCIOSAS *See* PUBLICACION **3631**

BUFANDA DEL SOL, LA (EC/0304-1417) [01795310] **3369**

BUFFALO AND ERIE COUNTY HISTORICAL SOCIETY *See* NEWSLETTER - BUFFALO AND ERIE COUNTY HISTORICAL SOCIETY **2749**

BUFFALO BULLETIN (TH/0125-6726) [I01256726] **5579**

BUFFALO BULLETIN, THE (US) [26075221] **5765**

BUFFALO BUSINESS JOURNAL (US/0882-2859) [11690497] **644**

BUFFALO CENTER TRIBUNE (US) [16769304] **5669**

BUFFALO CHIPS *CEASED.* (US/0736-2463) [09075221] **2440**

BUFFALO (CUSTER) (US/0196-9137) [04292550] **208**

BUFFALO EVENING NEWS OFFICE ALMANAC (US) [06232888] **2529**

BUFFALO FRUIT AND VEGETABLE REPORT (US/0744-3447) [08205374] **68**

BUFFALO GROVE COUNTRYSIDE *See* COUNTRYSIDE (BARRINGTON, ILL.) **5659**

BUFFALO JEWISH REVIEW (US) [12618614] **5714**

BUFFALO JOURNAL (TH/0857-1554) [I08571554] **5090**

BUFFALO LAW JOURNAL (US/0197-4955) [06026137] **2944**

BUFFALO LAW REVIEW (US/0023-9356) [01537639] **2944**

BUFFALO MUNICIPAL HOUSING AUTHORITY *See* HANDBOOK AND REPORT TO THE COMMISSIONERS - BUFFALO MUNICIPAL HOUSING AUTHORITY **2823**

BUFFALO NEWS, THE (US/0745-2691) [08882862] **5714**

BUFFALO PSYCHIATRIC CENTER. BOARD OF VISITORS *See* ANNUAL REPORT OF THE BOARD OF VISITORS OF THE BUFFALO PSYCHIATRIC CENTER TO THE DEPARTMENT OF MENTAL HYGIENE **3920**

BUFFALO SOCIETY OF NATURAL SCIENCES *See* BULLETIN OF THE BUFFALO SOCIETY OF NATURAL SCIENCES **4164**

● BUFFALO SPORTS NEWS, THE (US/1065-2140) [26524109] **4888**

BUFFALO SPREE (US/0300-7499) [01426997] **2529**

BUGEY, LE (FR/1148-7771) [I11487771] **2612**

BUGLE (US/0889-6445) [13979984] **2189**

BUGLE CALL (COTTONWOOD, ARIZ.) *See* BUGLE (COTTONWOOD, ARIZ.), THE **5629**

BUGLE (COTTONWOOD, ARIZ.), THE (US/1054-2876) [22833844] **5629**

BUHL HERALD, THE (US) [18831932] **5656**

BUHNE (VIENNA, AUSTRIA : 1958) (AU/0007-3075) [01779595] **5362**

BUHUTH, EL (SJ) [03308041] **5090**

BUICK ... ELECTRICAL SYSTEMS MANUAL. PARK AVENUE, PARK AVENUE ULTRA (US) [21997359] **5408**

BUILD; JOURNAL OF THE INDUSTRY (IE/0007-3229) [02993827] **602**

BUILD (WELLINGTON) (NZ/0110-4381) [I01104381] **602**

BUILD YOUR DREAM HOME DESIGNS *CEASED.* (US) [21051590] **294**

BUILDCORE INDEX (CN/0227-0595) [07965915] **602**

BUILDER & CONTRACTOR (US/0273-7965) [06922900] **602**

BUILDER/DEALER (US/0892-824X) [15295681] **602**

BUILDER DEVELOPER WEST (US/0273-6225) [06753307] **602**

BUILDER DIRECTORY, HONG KONG (HK) [07155007] **602**

BUILDER (WASHINGTON, D.C. : 1981) (US/0744-1193) [08040199] **602**

BUILDER'S BEST HOME DESIGNS (US/1055-3460) [23157763] **602**

BUILDERS MERCHANTS JOURNAL (TONBRIDGE AND MALLING, KENT : 1985) (UK/0268-1323) [13378043] **602**

BUILDERS (WASHINGTON, D.C. 1979), THE (US/0190-5996) [04730484] **602**

BUILDING A MARRIAGE (US/0742-9363) [10480211] **2277**

● BUILDING ACOUSTICS (UK/1351-010X) [I1351010X] **602**

BUILDING ACTIVITY BULLETIN (NZ) [10365341] **602**

BUILDING ACTIVITY, WESTERN AUSTRALIA (AT) [17251220] **632, 2840**

BUILDING AND CIVIL ENGINEERING RESEARCH FOCUS (UK/0960-5185) [I09605185] **2019**

BUILDING AND CONSTRUCTION AND CAZALYS CONTRACT REPORTER (AT) **602**

BUILDING AND CONSTRUCTION LAW (AT/0815-6050) [I08156050] **2944, 602**

BUILDING AND CONSTRUCTION MARKET FORECAST (US) **602**

BUILDING & CONSTRUCTION NEWS (SI/0217-5541) [I02175541] **602**

BUILDING AND CONSTRUCTION TRADES TODAY (CN/1186-1398) [24368019] **602**

BUILDING AND ENVIRONMENT (UK/0360-1323) [02177041] **602**

BUILDING AND RELATED STATISTICS, TASMANIA (AT/0811-0913) [16965192] **603, 632**

BUILDING AND REMODELING (US/0194-1569) [04928978] **603**

BUILDING AND WOOD (SZ) [02441374] **1656**

BUILDING AUTOMATION (IT) **603**

BUILDING BLOCKS (US/0195-1580) [05323439] **1060, 3369**

BUILDING CONSERVATION (UK/0143-2249) [05772854] **603**

BUILDING CONSTRUCTION COST DATA *See* MEANS BUILDING CONSTRUCTION COST DATA **620**

BUILDING CONSTRUCTION EMPLOYERS' ASSOCIATION OF CHICAGO See DIRECTORY AND GUIDE - BUILDING CONSTRUCTION EMPLOYERS' ASSOCIATION OF CHICAGO, INC **2961**

BUILDING CONSTRUCTION IN THE BUFFALO AREA / PREPARED BY RESEARCH AND STATISTICS DEPT., BUFFALO CHAMBER OF COMMERCE (US) [07506202] 603, **632**

BUILDING CONSTRUCTION MATERIALS AND EQUIPMENT (AT/1031-3745) [I10313745] **603**

BUILDING CONSTRUCTION NEWS (US/0192-7590) [05138654] **603**

BUILDING CONTROL (UK/0265-6493) [I02656493] **603**

BUILDING COST FILE. WESTERN EDITION (US/0194-0295) [03249277] **603**

BUILDING COST GUIDE. AGRICULTURAL (CN/0821-7327) [09819063] **603**

BUILDING COST GUIDE. MOBILE HOME (CN/0821-7300) [09819066] **603**

BUILDING COST GUIDE. YARD IMPROVEMENTS (CN/0821-7319) [09819061] **603**

BUILDING COST MANUAL (US/0732-5789) [06018886] **603**

BUILDING DESIGN (UK/0007-3423) [04677701] **294**

BUILDING DESIGN & CONSTRUCTION (US/0007-3407) [02246731] 603, **294**

BUILDING ECONOMIC ALTERNATIVES (US/0885-9930) [12812687] **1465**

BUILDING ECONOMICS *CEASED.* (US/0885-9299) [12770560] **603**

BUILDING ECONOMIST, THE (AT/0007-3431) [03301543] **603**

BUILDING ENGINEER (UK) [29354920] **603**

BUILDING ESTIMATOR'S REFERENCE BOOK, THE (US) [03463530] **603**

BUILDING IDEAS (DES MOINES) (US/0093-0938) [05971701] **294**

BUILDING IN CHINA (CC/1000-9507) [15617422] 294, **603**

BUILDING INDUSTRY REVIEW (AT) **603**

BUILDING INDUSTRY TECHNOLOGY / NTIS See NTIS ALERT. BUILDING INDUSTRY TECHNOLOGY **623**

BUILDING LAW MONTHLY (UK/0266-0628) [I02660628] 603, **2944**

BUILDING (LONDON. ENGLAND) (UK/0007-3318) [01537651] **603**

● BUILDING MANAGEMENT & DESIGN (CN/1191-9841) [27809708] **862**

BUILDING MANUAL See HOUSE BEAUTIFUL'S HOME BUILDING **616**

BUILDING MARKET REPORT (UK/0267-2561) [I02672561] **603**

BUILDING MATERIAL RETAILER (US) [11503012] **603**

BUILDING MATERIALS & EQUIPMENT SOUTHEAST ASIA (PH) [03375387] **603**

BUILDING MATERIALS DIRECTORY / UNDERWRITERS' LABORATORIES, INC (US) [03999126] **603**

BUILDING OFFICIAL AND CODE ADMINISTRATOR, THE (US/0007-3547) [01780789] **603**

BUILDING OFFICIALS AND CODE ADMINISTRATORS INTERNATIONAL See BOCA NATIONAL PROPERTY MAINTENANCE CODE **2816**

BUILDING OFFICIALS AND CODE ADMINISTRATORS INTERNATIONAL See BOCA NATIONAL BUILDING CODE, THE **601**

BUILDING OFFICIALS AND CODE ADMINISTRATORS INTERNATIONAL See BOCA NATIONAL FIRE PREVENTION CODE, THE **2288**

BUILDING OFFICIALS AND CODE ADMINISTRATORS INTERNATIONAL See BOCA NATIONAL PLUMBING CODE, THE **2603**

BUILDING OFFICIALS AND CODE ADMINISTRATORS INTERNATIONAL See BOCA BASIC HOUSING-PROPERTY MAINTENANCE CODE, THE **2942**

BUILDING OFFICIALS AND CODE ADMINISTRATORS INTERNATIONAL See BOCA NATIONAL MECHANICAL CODE, THE **2603**

BUILDING OKLAHOMA (OKLAHOMA CITY, OKLA. 1989) (US/1071-2879) [28618968] **603**

BUILDING OPERATING MANAGEMENT (US/0007-3490) [02062366] 862, **603**

BUILDING OPERATING MANAGER (CN/0227-6631) [07869968] **603**

BUILDING OWNER & PROPERTY MANAGER See BUILDING MANAGEMENT & DESIGN **862**

BUILDING OWNERS AND MANAGERS ASSOCIATION INTERNATIONAL See MEMBERSHIP/COMMITTEE DIRECTORY - BUILDING OWNERS AND MANAGERS ASSOCIATION INTERNATIONAL **4840**

BUILDING-PERMIT ACTIVITY IN FLORIDA (ANNUAL) (US/0270-9317) [06534788] **603**

BUILDING-PERMIT ACTIVITY IN FLORIDA (MONTHLY) (US/0007-3555) [05896008] **603**

BUILDING PERMITS (CN/0318-8809) [01786539] 2944, **604**

BUILDING PERMITS (US/0419-8174) [04898915] **604**

BUILDING PERMITS, ANNUAL SUMMARY (CN/0575-7975) [01786538] 604, **632**

BUILDING PRACTICE NOTE (CN/0701-5216) [02731956] **604**

BUILDING PRODUCT NEWS (AT) **604**

BUILDING PRODUCTS (CLEVELAND, OHIO) (US/1041-9152) [18884857] **604**

BUILDING PRODUCTS DIGEST (US/0742-5694) [10365523] 644, **2399**

BUILDING PROJECTS STATUS REPORT : A REPORT TO THE WISCONSIN LEGISLATURE (US) [09395839] **604**

BUILDING REFURBISHMENT (UK/0957-5790) [I09575790] **604**

BUILDING REGULATION (US) [07969295] 604, **2944**

● BUILDING RENOVATION (CLEVELAND, OHIO) (US/1070-5988) [28406725] **604**

BUILDING RESEARCH (AT/0312-617X) [02400127] **604**

BUILDING RESEARCH AND DEVELOPMENT IN AUSTRALIA / PREPARED BY BUILDING RESEARCH AND DEVELOPMENT ADVISORY COMMITTEE (BRDAC) (AT) [17975400] **604**

BUILDING RESEARCH AND INFORMATION : THE INTERNATIONAL JOURNAL OF RESEARCH, DEVELOPMENT AND DEMONSTRATION (UK/0961-3218) [23808095] **604**

BUILDING RESEARCH ESTABLISHMENT UPDATE (UK) **604**

● BUILDING RESEARCH JOURNAL (US/1065-4968) [26617525] **604**

BUILDING RESEARCH STATION (GREAT BRITAIN) See ENGINEERING PAPERS **2023**

BUILDING REVIEW (AT) [05000588] **604**

BUILDING SCIENCE ABSTRACTS (UK/0007-3636) [01792402] **604**

BUILDING SCIENCES (US) [05656841] **604**

BUILDING SERVICES & ENVIRONMENTAL ENGINEER (UK/0142-310X) [05249236] **2019**

BUILDING SERVICES CONTRACTOR (US/0007-3644) [05094136] **604**

BUILDING SERVICES ENGINEERING RESEARCH & TECHNOLOGY (UK/0143-6244) [07859922] **604**

BUILDING SERVICES : THE CIBSE JOURNAL (UK) [12276427] 2604, **604**

BUILDING STANDARDS (US/0270-1197) [02445552] **604**

BUILDING STATISTICS IN KARNATAKA STATE See BUILDINGS STATISTICS IN KARNATAKA STATE **632**

BUILDING STATISTICS (PAPUA NEW GUINEA. NATIONAL STATISTICAL OFFICE) (PP) [09778355] **604**

BUILDING STONE MAGAZINE (US/0749-6133) [06459203] **604**

BUILDING SUPPLY & HOME CENTERS (US/0890-9008) [12221377] 2810, **604**

● BUILDING SUPPLY HOME CENTERS (MIDWEST ED.) (US/1075-8038) [30305075] **605**

● BUILDING SUPPLY HOME CENTERS (NORTHEAST ED.) (US/1075-802X) [30304951] **605**

● BUILDING SUPPLY HOME CENTERS (SOUTH ED.) (US/1075-8054) [30305340] **605**

● BUILDING SUPPLY HOME CENTERS (WEST ED.) (US/1075-8046) [30305407] **605**

BUILDING SURVEYOR MELBOURNE (AT/0728-9820) [I07289820] 2019, **605**

BUILDING SYSTEMS BUILDER (US/1064-5896) [23641165] **605**

● BUILDING SYSTEMS BUILDER (US/1064-5896) [26341165] **605**

BUILDING TECHNICAL FILE *CEASED.* (UK) [I02646978] **605**

BUILDING TECHNOLOGY PROJECT SUMMARIES (US/0149-1679) [03435713] **605**

BUILDING : THE NEWSMAGAZINE FOR CANADA'S DEVELOPMENT INDUSTRY (CN) [24252301] **605**

BUILDING THERMAL ENVELOPE SYSTEMS AND MATERIALS (BTESM) AND RESEARCH UTILIZATION/TECHNOLOGY TRANSFER PROGRESS REPORT FOR DOE OFFICE OF BUILDING AND COMMUNITY SYSTEMS : MONTHLY PROGRESS REPORT (US) [24159913] **605**

BUILDING TIMES MAGAZINE (US/0897-8115) [17636537] **4940**

BUILDING TODAY (UK) [17223475] **605**

BUILDING TRADES INDEX, STATE OF WYOMING (US) [09270519] **1656**

BUILDING TRADESMAN, THE (US/0007-3717) [02258693] **605**

BUILDING WITH STEEL (LONDON. 1969) (UK/0140-8488) [I01408488] **605**

● BUILDINGS & FACILITIES MANAGEMENT FOR THE PUBLIC SECTOR (UK/0965-7231) [I09657231] **605**

BUILDINGS (CEDAR RAPIDS. 1947) (US/0007-3725) [01537672] 862, **605**

BUILDINGS ENERGY TECHNOLOGY (US/0891-3730) [14713964] 605, **1934**

BUILDINGS STATISTICS IN KARNATAKA STATE (II) [03469256] 605, **632**

BUILT ENVIRONMENT (LONDON, 1978) (UK/0263-7960) [04683863] **2816**

BU$INESS OF HERBS, THE (US/0736-9050) [09251140] 644, **2411**

BUITENLANDSE PROJECTEN / EXPORTBEVORDERINGS- EN VOORLICHTINGSDIENST, EVD (NE/0166-946X) [11295013] **1549**

BUITENSCHOOLS MONDELING ONDERWIJS / CENTRAAL BUREAU VOOR DE STATISTIEK, HOOFDAFDELING STATISTIEKEN VAN ONDERWIJS EN WETENSCHAPPEN (NE/0168-8529) [11884736] **1729**

BUKHGALTERSKII UCHET (RU/0007-3776) [03010552] **740**

BUKKA REPOTO (JA) [02556784] **1590**

BUKKA SHISU GEPPO. PRICE INDEXES MONTHLY (JA) [05691116] **1590**

BUKKU ENDO TSUSHIN (JA) [05671010] **3369**

BUKKYO BUNGAKU KENKYU (JA) [02550512] **3369**

BUKKYO GEIJUTSU (JA/0004-2889) [03010507] **345**

BUKKYO SHIGAKU KENKYU (JA) [02244675] **5021**

BUKKYO SHISO SHI (JA) [06909286] **5021**

BUKKYOSHI KENKYU (RYUKOKU DAIGAKU. BUKKYOSHI KENKYUKAI) (JA) [08671778] **5021**

BUKU DAFTAR ANGGOTA KAMAR DAGANG DAN INDUSTRI DI JAWA BARAT (IO) [06494779] **818**

BUKU MAKLUMAT PERANGKAAN GETAH BAGI MALAYSIA. RUBBER STATISTICS HANDBOOK OF MALAYSIA (MY) [04145949] 5075, **5078**

BUKU PANDUAN - UNIVERSITI PERTANIAN MALAYSIA (MY) [02776410] **68**

BUKU PENUNTUN PERUSAHAAN NEGARA (IO) [04485343] **644**

BUKU PETUNJUK BANK BANK SWASTA NASIONAL (IO) [02652920] **780**

BUKU PETUNJUK GEREJA KATOLIK INDONESIA (IO) [03176919] **5024**

BUKU SAKU STATISTIK INDONESIA (IO) [04212405] **5324**

BUKU TAHUNAN ... PROPINSI SUMATERA UTARA (IO) [11271955] **2647**

BULETIN DE INFORMARE STIINTIFICA. GEOLOGIE, GEOGRAFIE / ACADEMIA REPUBLICII POPULARE ROMINE, CENTRUL DE DOCUMENTARE STIINTIFICA (RM) [05820607] 2556, **1368**

BULETIN DEPARTEMEN STUDIUM GENERALE IKIP YOGYAKARTA (IO) [02240291] **1890**

BULETIN I SHKENCAVE NATYRORE / UNIVERSITETI I TIRANES "ENVER HOXHA," FAKULTETI I SHKENCAVE NATYRORE (AA) [21207294] **1352**

BULETIN I UNIVERSITETIT SHTETEROR TE TIRANES. SERIA SHKENCAT SHOGERORE See STUDIME HISTORIKE **2712**

BULETIN IKIP PADANG (IO) [02732719] **1729**

BULETIN NG KAPISANANG PANGKASAYSAYAN NG PILIPINAS See HISTORICAL BULLETIN / PHILIPPINE HISTORICAL ASSOCIATION **2652**

BULETIN PENDIDIKAN (MX) [03625782] **1729**

BULETIN PENELITIAN HUTAN (IO/0215-028X) [12893778] **2376**

BULETIN PENELITIAN INSTITUT PERTANIAN BOGOR (IO/0216-3500) [11489889] **68**

BULETIN   Alphabetical Title Index

BULETIN PENELITIAN KEHUTANAN (IO/0215-0190) [I02150190] **2376**

BULETIN PERKEBUNAN (IO) [17647232] **68**

BULETIN PERSATUAN GEOLOGI MALAYSIA (MY/0126-6187) [08246074] **1368**

BULETIN SEKOLAH PEMBANGUNAN (IO) [02239651] **1729**

BULETIN STIINTIFIC. CHEMISTRY AND MATERIALS SCIENCE / IPB (RM) [26685608] **2101**, **963**

BULETIN SUKU TAHUNAN (MY/0127-8428) [15581614] **1549**

BULETIN VURH VODNANY (CZ/0007-389X) [14765827] **2297**

BULETINI I SHKENCAVE BUJQESORE (AA/0563-573X) [01767528] **68**

BULETINI I SHKENCAVE GJEOLOGJIKE (AA/0254-5276) [21462519] **1368**

BULETINI I SHKENCAVE ZOOTEKNIKE E VETERINARE (AA/0259-2843) [I02592843] **5579**

BULETINUL ACADEMIEI DE STIINTE A REPUBLICII MOLDOVA. ECONOMIE SI SOCIOLOGIE (MV) [27661495] 5241, **1465**

BULETINUL (BIBLIOTECA ROMANA. INSTITUTUL ROMAN DE CERCETARI) See BULETINUL BIBLIOTECII ROMANE **2680**

BULETINUL BIBLIOTECII ROMANE (GW) [08134650] **2680**

BULETINUL INFORMATIV AL ACADEMIEI DE STIINTE AGRICOLE SI SILVICE (RM/1010-3589) [15191795] **2376**

BULETINUL INSTITUTUL AGRONOMIC CLUJ-NAPOCA. SERIA ZOOTEHNIE SI MEDICINA VETERINARA (RM/0557-4668) [06319031] **208**

BULETINUL INSTITUTULUI AGRONOMIC CLUJ-NAPOCA. SERIA AGRICULTURA (RM/0557-465X) [06319037] **68**

BULETINUL INSTITUTULUI DE PETROL SI GAZE (RM/0376-4516) [02949023] **4252**

BULETINUL INSTITUTULUI POLITEHNIC BUCURESTI. SERIA ENERGETICA (RM/1012-3202) [14182252] **2111**

BULETINUL OFICIAL AL REPUBLICII SOCIALISTE ROMANIA. PARTEA A III-A. SUPLIMENT (RM) [02246529] **2944**

BULETINUL SIINTIFIC SI TEHNIC AL INSTITUTULUI POLITEHNIC "TRAIAN VUIA" TIMISOARA. SERIA ELECROTEHNICA (RM) [12036172] **5090**

BULETINUL STIINTIFIC AL INSTITUTULUI POLITECHNIC CLUJ: SERIA CONSTRUCTII (RM/0378-1267) [02142645] **2019**

BULETINUL STIINTIFIC / INSTITUTUL DE CONSTRUCTII BUCURESTI (RM/0524-8159) [02703580] **2019**

BULETINUL STIINTIFIC SI TEHNIC AL INSTITUTULUI POLITEHNIC TRAIAN VUIA TIMISOARA. SERIA CHIMIE (RM) [12036230] **1021**

BULETINUL STIINTIFIC SI TEHNIC AL INSTITUTULUI POLITEHNIC "TRAIAN VUIA" TIMISOARA. SERIA CHIMIE (RM/0378-9675) [07425301] **2008**

BULETINUL STIINTIFIC SI TEHNIC AL INSTITUTULUI POLITEHNIC "TRAIAN VUIA" TIMISOARA. SERIA CONSTRUCTII (RM) [12036269] **605**

BULETINUL STIINTIFIC SI TEHNIC AL INSTITUTULUI POLITEHNIC "TRAIAN VUIA" TIMISOARA. SERIA MECANICA (RM) [12036054] **2111**

BULETINUL UNIVERSITATII DIN BRASOV. SERIA B : ECONOMIE FORESTIERA (RM) [06437999] **2376**

BULETINUL UNIVERSITATII DIN GALATI. FASCICULA I, STIINTE SOCIALE SI UMANISTE (RM) [09096853] **3270**

BULETINUL UNIVERSITATII DIN GALATI. FASCICULA II, MATEMATICA, FIZICA, MECANICA TEORETICA (RM/0254-4385) [09096008] **3497**

BULETINUL UNIVERSITATII DIN GALATI. FASCICULA III, ELECTROTEHNICA, ELECTRONICA, AUTOMTICA [SIC], INFORMATICA (RM) [09095633] **2037**

BULETINUL UNIVERSITATII DIN GALATI. FASCICULA V, TEHNOLOGII IN CONSTRUCTII SIC DE MASINI, METALURGIE (RM/0254-5543) [09095586] **3999**

BULGARIA. GLAVNA DIREKTSIIA NA STATISTIKATA See STATISTICA **5342**

BULGARIAN ACADEMIC BOOKS (BU/0324-0509) [02241724] **4827**

BULGARIAN CHEMICAL COMMUNICATIONS (BU/0324-1130) [30454458] **963**

BULGARIAN CO-OPERATIVE REVIEW (BU) [04403235] **1541**

BULGARIAN FILMS CEASED. (BU/0204-8884) [03009476] **4064**

BULGARIAN FOREIGN TRADE SUSPENDED. (BU/0007-392X) [02258700] 1633, **825**

BULGARIAN HISTORICAL REVIEW (BU/0324-0207) [01794570] **2680**

BULGARIAN JOURNAL OF METEOROLOGY & HYDROLOGY (BU/0861-0762) [23290316] 1412, **1421**

BULGARIAN JOURNAL OF PHYSICS (BU/0323-9217) [02242931] **4398**

BULGARIAN QUARTERLY CEASED. (LH/0861-556X) [25315892] **316**

BULGARIAN STUDIES ASSOCIATION See NEWSLETTER - BULGARIAN STUDIES ASSOCIATION **2624**

BULGARIAN STUDIES GROUP. NEWSLETTER See NEWSLETTER - BULGARIAN STUDIES ASSOCIATION **2624**

BULGARIEN VOLKSWIRTSCHAFTSPLAN FUR ... / BUNDESSTELLE FUR AUSSENHANDELSINFORMATION (GW) [07436803] **1549**

BULGARISTIKA (BU/0205-3209) [17572753] **2680**

BULGARSKA AKADEMIIA NA NAUKITE See SBORNIK ZA NARODNI UMOTVORENIJA I NARODOPIS **3319**

BULGARSKA AKADEMIIA NA NAUKITE See SPISANIE NA BULGARSKATA AKADEMIIA NA NAUKITE **5159**

BULGARSKA AKADEMIIA NA NAUKITE, SOFIA. INSTITUT PO TEKHNICHESKA MEKHANIKA See IZVESTIJA NA INSTITUT PO TEHNICESKA MEHANIKA **2117**

BULGARSKA AKADEMIIA NA NAUKITE, SOFIA. INSTITUT PO VODNI PROBLEMI See IZVESTIIA **5535**

BULGARSKA AKADEMIIA NA NAUKITE, SOFIA. ARKHIVEN INSTITUT See IZVESTIIA NA ARKHIVNIIA INSTITUT **2481**

BULGARSKA AKADEMIIA NA NAUKITE, SOFIA. INSTITUT ZA BULGARSKI EZIK See IZVESTIIA NA INSTITUTA ZA BULGARSKI EZIK **3288**

BULGARSKA AKADEMIIA NA NAUKITE, SOFIA. INSTITUT ZA PRAVNI NAUKI See IZVESTIIA NA INSTITUTA ZA PRAVNI NAUKI **2985**

BULGARSKA AKADEMIIA NA NAUKITE, SOFIA. TSENTRALNA KHELMINTOLOGICHNA LABORATORIIA See IZVESTIIA **5117**

BULGARSKI GLAS (SP) [06872770] 3369, **4466**

BULGARSKI JAZIK (BU/0005-4283) [01537686] **3270**

BULGARSKI KNIGOPIS (BU) [02726797] 4812, **4821**

BULGARSKO GEOFIZICHNO SPISANIE (BU/0323-9918) [02672959] **1403**

BULGARSKO GEOLOGICHESKO DRUZHESTVO See SPISANIE NA BALGARSKOTO GEOLOGICESKO DRUZESTVO **1398**

BULGARSKO MUZIKOZNANIE (SOFIA, BULGARIA : 1979) (BU/0204-823X) [06318783] **4105**

BULGARSKOTO MUZIKALNO IZPULNITELSTVO PO SVETA (BU) [05593670] **4105**

BULK HANDLING (UK) [13343401] **4218**

BULK MATERIALS INTERNATIONAL (UK) [20782843] **3476**

BULK SOLIDS HANDLING (GW/0173-9980) [08408311] **1967**

BULK WHEAT (AT/0156-2452) [08458457] **68**

BULK'S NURSERIES See WHOLESALE PRICE LIST / BULK'S NURSERIES **2433**

BULK'S NURSERIES (FREEHOLD, N.J.). WHOLESALE PRICE LIST See WHOLESALE PRICE LIST / BULK'S NURSERIES **2433**

BULL & BEAR (US/0319-1362) [01727867] **893**

BULL AND BRANCH : NEWSLETTER OF THE FRIENDS OF THE DARD HUNTER PAPER MUSEUM (US) [25618944] **4232**

BULL GATOR (US/0745-1083) [08820184] **1089**

BULLDOG (LOS ANGELES, CALIF.) (US/0744-1797) [08085285] **4201**

BULLDOG REPORTER (US) **1294**

BULLDOG REPORTER'S WESTERN MEDIA CONTACTS (US) **1294**

BULLDOZER (CN/0821-0357) [09666946] **3158**

BULLETEN - CANADA-USSR BUSINESS COUNCIL (CN/1183-0190) [23238229] **644**

BULLETEN' MOSKOVSKOGO OBSESTVA ISPYTATELEJ PRIRODY. NOVAA SERIA. OTDEL BIOLOGICESKIJ (UK/0007-7682) [I00077682] **449**

BULLETIN 78 (CN/0382-4713) [03959979] **4888**

BULLETIN A B Q (CN/0380-7150) [02125747] **3197**

BULLETIN A L'USAGE DES TRAPPEURS (CN/0709-2172) [05377951] 4869, **4888**

BULLETIN - A Q Q U A (CN/0381-9841) [02606825] **1368**

BULLETIN : A VDOT MONTHLY NEWSPAPER (US) [16074270] **5378**

BULLETIN - ACADEMIE SERBE DES SCIENCES ET DES ARTS, CLASSE DES SCIENCES NATURELLES ET MATHEMATIQUES. SCIENCES NATURELLES (YU/0352-5740) [05929329] **5090**

BULLETIN - ACADEMIE SERBE DES SCIENCES ET DES ARTS. CLASSE DES SCIENCES SOCIALES (YU/0561-7359) [01081454] **5193**

BULLETIN ADMINISTRATIF DES ASSURANCES (FR) [07198695] 2876, **2944**

BULLETIN ADMINISTRATIF DES ASSURANCES - FRANCE. MINISTERE DE L'ECONOMIE ET DES FINANCES See BULLETIN ADMINISTRATIF DES ASSURANCES **2944**

BULLETIN AEF (CN/0827-0139) [16220429] **5552**

BULLETIN AFRICAIN DE GEOSCIENCE (NR/0189-9392) [I01899392] **1352**

BULLETIN - AGENCE DE PRESSE LIBRE DU QUEBEC (CN/0701-1229) [03406073] **2917**

BULLETIN AGRICOLE, DISTRICT DE TIMISKAMING (CN/0708-5702) [05325786] **68**

BULLETIN AGRICOLE DU RWANDA (RW) [03942682] **68**

BULLETIN - AGRICULTURAL EXPERIMENT STATION, RIO PIEDRAS (PR/0097-5486) [01459553] **68**

BULLETIN AGRONOMIQUE PETIT-BOURG (GP/0765-0787) [I07650787] **68**

BULLETIN - AIDE AUX CROYANTS DE L'URSS (FR/1142-2300) [I11422300] **4940**

BULLETIN (ALABAMA AGRICULTURAL EXPERIMENT STATION) (US) [15719752] **68**

BULLETIN (ALABAMA MUSEUM OF NATURAL HISTORY) (US/0196-1039) [02027012] **4163**

BULLETIN - ALBERT HOFMANN FOUNDATION (US/1068-4409) [27674418] **4578**

BULLETIN / ALBERTA RESEARCH COUNCIL SUSPENDED. (CN/0383-5359) [03300857] **5090**

BULLETIN (ALBERTA TEACHERS' ASSOCIATION. SCIENCE COUNCIL) (CN/0820-7941) [09523747] **5090**

BULLETIN ALGEMENE SOCIALE GEOGRAFIE. SERIE 1 (NE) [05351897] **1549**

BULLETIN / ALLEN MEMORIAL ART MUSEUM (US) [16785886] **345**

BULLETIN (AMARILLO GENEALOGICAL SOCIETY) See REFLECTOR (AMARILLO, TEX.), THE **2469**

BULLETIN - AMERICAN ACADEMY OF ARTS AND SCIENCES (US/0002-712X) [04038464] **316**

BULLETIN / AMERICAN ACADEMY OF ORTHOPAEDIC SURGEONS (US/1049-9741) [02254820] **3880**

BULLETIN - AMERICAN ACADEMY OF OTOLARYNGOLOGY-HEAD AND NECK SURGERY, THE (US/0731-8359) [08246980] **3887**

BULLETIN / AMERICAN ANIMAL HOSPITAL ASSOCIATION (US) [06663807] **5506**

BULLETIN / AMERICAN ASSOCIATION FOR THE HISTORY OF NURSING (US/0898-6622) [13050712] **3852**

BULLETIN / AMERICAN ASSOCIATION OF UNIVERSITY WOMEN (US/1058-9988) [24457210] 5552, **1812**

BULLETIN - AMERICAN ASTRONOMICAL SOCIETY (US/0002-7537) [01479434] 394, **402**

●BULLETIN / AMERICAN COLLEGE OF RADIOLOGY (US) [30472536] **3939**

BULLETIN / AMERICAN CONIFER SOCIETY (US/8755-0490) [10797068] **504**

BULLETIN - AMERICAN CONTRACT BRIDGE LEAGUE (1993), THE (US/1071-3131) [28605247] **4858**

BULLETIN (AMERICAN FEDERATION OF ASTROLOGERS) See TODAY'S ASTROLOGER **390**

BULLETIN - AMERICAN FEDERATION OF ASTROLOGERS (US/0735-4797) [08920393] **390**

BULLETIN - AMERICAN LUNG ASSOCIATION (US/0092-5659) [01787626] **3948**

BULLETIN - AMERICAN ORCHID SOCIETY (US) [07603384] **2411**

Alphabetical Title Index — BULLETIN

BULLETIN (AMERICAN PSYCHOLOGICAL ASSOCIATION. DIVISION OF CONSULTING PSYCHOLOGY) *See* JOURNAL - AMERICAN PSYCHOLOGICAL ASSOCIATION. DIVISION OF CONSULTING PSYCHOLOGY **4592**

BULLETIN - AMERICAN RAILWAY ENGINEERING ASSOCIATION (US/0003-0694) [05633346] **5430**

BULLETIN / AMERICAN SOCIETY OF CARTOGRAPHERS (US/0044-7943) [07640312] **2580**

BULLETIN - AMERICAN SOCIETY OF PLANT PHYSIOLOGISTS (US) [03797246] **504**

BULLETIN / AMERICAN SUNBATHING ASSOCIATION, THE (US/0279-8158) [07269172] **4849**

BULLETIN AMI (CN/1187-2233) [25314099] **3559**

BULLETIN - AMIS DE GUSTAVE COURBET (FR/0983-3943) [I09833943] **345**

BULLETIN (AMNESTY INTERNATIONAL. CANADIAN SECTION-ENGLISH-SPEAKING) (CN/0831-9227) [15241268] **4504**

BULLETIN AMQ (CN/0316-8832) [02275598] **3497**

BULLETIN ANALYTIQUE BULLETIN BIBLIOGRAPHIQUE DE LA VIGNE & DU VIN (FR) **1600**

BULLETIN ANALYTIQUE - CIE (FR/0243-5314) [I02435314] **2329**

BULLETIN ANALYTIQUE - CTCPA *See* CT INFOS PARIS **2332**

BULLETIN ANALYTIQUE DE DOCUMENTATION POLITIQUE, ECONOMIQUE ET SOCIALE CONTEMPORAINE / FONDATION NATIONAL DES SCIENCES POLITIQUES (FR/0007-4071) [01337034] **5193**

BULLETIN ANALYTIQUE D'HISTOIRE ROMAINE / UNIVERSITE DE STRASBOURG, GROUPE DE RECHERCHE D'HISTOIRE ROMAINE (FR/0525-1044) [02728544] **2612**

BULLETIN ANALYTIQUE PETROLIER (FR/0007-4101) [I00074101] **4252**

BULLETIN ANALYTIQUE PETROLIER ET SES *See* NOTES D'INFORMATION ECONOMIQUE **1508**

BULLETIN & I.E. ET ANNALES DE LA SOCIETE ROYALE BELGE D'ENTOMOLOGIE (BE/0374-6038) [01714913] **5579**

BULLETIN ANNUEL - ADMINISTRATION GENERALE DES CONTRIBUTIONS (HAITI (REPUBLIC)) (HT) [05160443] **4715**

BULLETIN ANNUEL DE LA SOCIETE D'ARCHEOLOGIE ET D'HISTOIRE DU TONNEROIS (FR/1148-795X) [I1148795X] **262**

BULLETIN ANNUEL DES STATISTIQUES - REPUBLIQUE TUNISIENNE, OFFICE DES PORTS NATIONAUX (TI) [02240341] **5448**

BULLETIN ANNUEL / MUSEE D'ETHNOGRAPHIE DE LA VILLE DE GENEVE (SZ) [16113661] **232**

BULLETIN ANNUEL (SOCIETE DES PROFESSEURS FRANCAIS EN AMERIQUE) *See* BULLETIN / SOCIETE DES PROFESSEURS FRANCAIS EN AMERIQUE **1861**

BULLETIN ANTIEKE BESCHAVING : BABESCH (NE/0165-9367) [03901403] **2612**

BULLETIN APICOLE DE DOCUMENTATION SCIENTIFIQUE ET TECHNIQUE D'INFORMATION (FR/0521-6761) [03006519] **5579**

BULLETIN - AQUACULTURE ASSOCIATION OF CANADA (CN/0840-5417) [19298862] **449**

BULLETIN - AQUACULTURE ASSOCIATION OF CANADA (CN/0840-5417) [19298841] **449**

BULLETIN ARBIDO (SZ/0258-0764) [13980218] **3198**

BULLETIN ARCHEOLOGIQUE DE PROVENCE (FR/0221-8321) [11106532] **262**

BULLETIN ARCHEOLOGIQUE DU COMITE DES TRAVAUX HISTORIQUES ET SCIENTIFIQUES (FR/0071-8394) [02030523] 250, **262**

BULLETIN ARCHEOLOGIQUE DU COMITE DES TRAVAUX HISTORIQUES ET SCIENTIFIQUES. FASCICULE A, ANITQUITES NATIONALES / MINISTERE DE L'EDUCATION NATIONALE (FR/0997-5322) [09500756] 250, **262**

BULLETIN ARCHEOLOGIQUE DU COMITE DES TRAVAUX HISTORIQUES ET SCIENTIFIQUES. FASCICULE B, AFRIQUE DU NORD (FR/0997-5306) [09500814] **262**

BULLETIN ARCHEOLOGIQUE DU COMITES DES TRAVAUX HISTORIQUES ET SCIENTIFIQUES *See* BULLETIN ARCHEOLOGIQUE DU COMITE DES TRAVAUX HISTORIQUES ET SCIENTIFIQUES. FASCICULE B, AFRIQUE DU NORD **262**

BULLETIN ARCHEOLOGIQUE DU VEXIN FRANCAIS / CENTRE DE RECHERCHES ARCHEOLOGIQUES DU VEXIN FRANCAIS (FR/1140-7409) [22613577] **262**

BULLETIN ARPEA (SZ) **5229**

BULLETIN (ARTICLE 19 ORGANIZATION) (UK/1011-3983) [20478142] **4504**

BULLETIN - ASMP--THE SOCIETY OF PHOTOGRAPHERS IN COMMUNICATIONS (US/0361-9168) [02386372] **4367**

BULLETIN ASPEA (SZ) **1934**

BULLETIN / ASSOCIATION CANADIENNE DE LINGUISTIQUE (CN/0825-2823) [11355352] **3270**

BULLETIN - ASSOCIATION CANADIENNE POUR L'AVANCEMENT DES ETUDES NEERLANDAISES (CN/0823-9487) [11802896] **2680**

BULLETIN - ASSOCIATION D'EDUCATION DU QUEBEC (CN/0712-9793) [08890760] **1729**

BULLETIN - ASSOCIATION DES AMIS DE RABELAIS ET DE LA DEVINIERE (FR/0571-5350) [01779528] **3369**

BULLETIN - ASSOCIATION DES CONSEILLERS EN ORGANISATION ET METHODES DE QUEBEC, LE (CN/0226-8434) [06562630] **862**

BULLETIN - ASSOCIATION DES MEDECINS DE LANGUE FRANCAISE DU CANADA (1977) (CN/0702-7656) [03453032] **3559**

BULLETIN - ASSOCIATION DES PATHOLOGISTES DU QUEBEC (CN/1187-7758) [25796407] **3893**

BULLETIN - ASSOCIATION DES PROFESSEURS D'HISTOIRE LOCALE DU QUEBEC (CN/0318-5486) [02442092] **2724**

BULLETIN - ASSOCIATION FOR PSYCHOANALYTIC MEDICINE (US/0004-542X) [04138049] **3922**

BULLETIN - ASSOCIATION FOR THE ADVANCEMENT OF AUTOMOTIVE MEDICINE (US/1042-7708) [18237394] 4769, **5439**

BULLETIN (ASSOCIATION FOR THE BIBLIOGRAPHY OF HISTORY (U.S.)) (US/0892-4600) [15203946] **2635**

BULLETIN - ASSOCIATION FOR THE STUDY OF CANADIAN RADIO AND TELEVISION (CN/0709-0676) [05585013] **1128**

BULLETIN - ASSOCIATION FRANCAISE DES PONTS ET CHARPENTES (FR/0150-6021) [I01506021] **605**

BULLETIN - ASSOCIATION INTERNATIONALE D'ETUDES DU SUD-EST EUROPEEN (RM/0004-5551) [08177254] **2680**

BULLETIN / ASSOCIATION OF CANADIAN MAP LIBRARIES AND ARCHIVES (CN/0840-9331) [18900242] **2581**

BULLETIN / ASSOCIATION OF CHRISTIAN ECONOMISTS (US/0896-307X) [16997388] **1465**

BULLETIN (ASSOCIATION OF CONTEMPORARY HISTORIANS (GREAT BRITAIN)) (UK) [07163004] **2680**

BULLETIN - ASSOCIATION OF ENGINEERING GEOLOGISTS (US/0004-5691) [01794026] **1368**

BULLETIN - ASSOCIATION POUR L'ETUDE TAXONOMIQUE DE LA FLORE D'AFRIQUE TROPICALE (NE) [02914422] **504**

BULLETIN - ASSOCIATION QUEBECOISE POUR L'ETUDE DE L'IMPRIME (CN/0838-5459) [18958405] **431**

BULLETIN (AUSTIN, TEX.), THE (US/0895-0326) [16412291] **1172**

BULLETIN - AUSTRALIA, BUREAU OF MINERAL RESOURCES, GEOLOGY AND GEOPHYSICS (AT/0084-7089) [07723360] 1403, 1438, **1368**

BULLETIN / AUSTRALIAN MUSIC THERAPY ASSOCIATION (AT/0156-5184) [26927719] 3559, **4105**

BULLETIN B - OKLAHOMA STATE UNIVERSITY. AGRICULTURAL EXPERIMENT STATION (US/0886-473X) [05921785] **68**

BULLETIN BAKHTINE, LE (CN/0821-6886) [10436273] **3338**

BULLETIN - BANGLADESH BANK (BG/0304-9345) [01799020] **780**

BULLETIN BAUDELAIRIEN (US/0007-4128) [01537690] **3460**

BULLETIN / BIBLIOGRAPHICAL SOCIETY OF AUSTRALIA AND NEW ZEALAND (AT/0084-7852) [06878681] **3198**

BULLETIN BIBLIOGRAPHIQUE (FR/0335-7414) [00947193] **4809**

BULLETIN BIBLIOGRAPHIQUE (FR/0335-0266) [03890331] **411**

BULLETIN BIBLIOGRAPHIQUE AMERIQUE LATINE / RESEAU DOCUMENTAIRE AMERIQUE LATINE, GRECO 26, CNRS (FR/0292-8515) [08527555] **411**

BULLETIN BIBLIOGRAPHIQUE ANNUEL (CM) [07111418] **411**

BULLETIN BIBLIOGRAPHIQUE - CENTRE DE RECHERCHE ET D'ETUDE POUR LA DIFFUSION DU FRANCAIS (FR/0765-1937) [07651937] **411**

BULLETIN BIBLIOGRAPHIQUE DE DOCUMENTATION TECHNIQUE / GROUPEMENT DE DOCUMENTATION DES INDUSTRIES EXTRACTIVES *CEASED.* (FR/0395-7322) [11416395] **411**

BULLETIN BIBLIOGRAPHIQUE DE LA SOCIETE INTERNATIONALE ARTHURIENNE (FR/0074-1388) [01771689] **3457**

BULLETIN BIBLIOGRAPHIQUE DE LA SOCIETE RENCESVALS (FR/0583-8797) [01788994] **3369**

BULLETIN BIBLIOGRAPHIQUE DU FONDS DOCUMENTAIRE DU CENTRE DE DOCUMENTATION DE L'IPD-AOS / INSTITUT PANAFRICAIN POUR LE DEVELOPPEMENT, DIRECTION REGIONALE DE L'OUEST SAHEL (IPD-AOS) (UV) [07299133] **1530**

BULLETIN BIBLIOGRAPHIQUE FONDERIE (FR/0249-4418) [I02494418] **4025**

BULLETIN BIBLIOGRAPHIQUE - INSTITUT NATIONALE DE LA STATISTIQUE ET DES ETUDES ECONOMIQUES (FR/0020-2398) [09719849] **1530**

BULLETIN BIBLIOGRAPHIQUE INTERNATIONAL DU MACHINISME AGRICOLE (FR/0007-4160) [03006564] **152**

BULLETIN BIBLIOGRAPHIQUE O.R.S.T.O.M. SANTE (FR/0998-678X) **3655**

BULLETIN BIBLIOGRAPHIQUE SPELEOLOGIQUE (SZ/0253-8296) [01798903] **5173**

BULLETIN BIMENSUEL DES TIRAGES (FR) **4564**

BULLETIN - BISMUTH INSTITUTE (BE/0379-0401) [03348234] 2037, **3999**

BULLETIN / BODENKUNDLICHE GESELLSCHAFT DER SCHWEIZ (SZ) [17660013] **165**

BULLETIN - BRANZ (NZ/1170-8395) [I11708395] **605**

BULLETIN / BRITISH ARACHNOLOGICAL SOCIETY (UK/0524-4994) [01537128] **5579**

BULLETIN / BRITISH ECOLOGICAL SOCIETY (UK/0306-8307) [07268692] **2162**

BULLETIN / BRITISH SOCIETY FOR MUSIC THERAPY (UK/0953-7511) [18193605] 3559, **4105**

BULLETIN / BUREAU OF BUSINESS RESEARCH, COLLEGE OF BUSINESS ADMINISTRATION, UNIVERSITY OF TOLEDO (US) [24433095] **644**

BULLETIN - C P A A C M P A (CN/0701-0575) [03406370] **1144**

BULLETIN - C.R.I.D.E.V (FR/0397-9717) [I03979717] **4505**

BULLETIN - CALCUTTA STATISTICAL ASSOCIATION (II/0008-0683) [01552348] **5324**

BULLETIN (CALIFORNIA CENTRAL COAST GENEALOGICAL SOCIETY : 1993) (US/1077-095X) [30697073] **2440**

BULLETIN - CALIFORNIA. DEPT. OF WATER RESOURCES (US/0084-8263) [01213170] **5531**

BULLETIN / CALIFORNIA DIVISION OF MINES AND GEOLOGY (US/0008-1000) [08339636] **2135**

BULLETIN - CALIFORNIA WATER POLLUTION CONTROL ASSOCIATION (US/0008-1620) [02520317] **2225**

BULLETIN CAN/OLE (CN/0708-1502) [04880090] **5090**

BULLETIN - CANADA POST (CN/0708-0646) [03980396] **1144**

BULLETIN (CANADIAN ACADEMY OF CHILD PSYCHIATRY) *See* CANADIAN CHILD PSYCHIATRIC BULLETIN, THE **3922**

BULLETIN - CANADIAN ASSOCIATION FOR COMPOSITE STRUCTURES AND MATERIALS (CN/1187-6859) [26066550] **2101**

BULLETIN - CANADIAN ASSOCIATION FOR UNIVERSITY CONTINUING EDUCATION (CN/0823-1168) [09929509] **1812**

BULLETIN - CANADIAN ASSOCIATION OF COLLEGE AND UNIVERSITY STUDENT SERVICES (CN/0711-2416) [08482300] **1812**

BULLETIN - CANADIAN ASSOCIATION OF JOURNALISTS *CEASED.* (CN/1184-0641) [23659155] **2917**

BULLETIN - CANADIAN AURAL/ORAL HISTORY ASSOCIATION (CN/0318-9600) [02442145] **2724**

BULLETIN - CANADIAN BOTANICAL ASSOCIATION (CN/0008-3046) [01820035] **504**

BULLETIN
Alphabetical Title Index

BULLETIN - CANADIAN COMMISSION FOR UNESCO (CN/0008-4557) [03300561] 1729, **5193**

BULLETIN / CANADIAN ENVIRONMENTAL NETWORK (CN/1183-4528) [24257300] **2162**

BULLETIN / CANADIAN ENVIRONMENTAL NETWORK (CN/1183-4528) [24257295] **2162**

BULLETIN / CANADIAN EQUESTRIAN FEDERATION (CN/0838-1690) [19898227] **2797**

BULLETIN - CANADIAN ETHNIC STUDIES ASSOCIATION (CN/0315-8705) [01852263] **2257**

BULLETIN - CANADIAN FARM AND INDUSTRIAL EQUIPMENT INSTITUTE (CN/0821-7513) [09819013] **158**

BULLETIN - CANADIAN FEDERATION FOR THE HUMANITIES (CN/0707-8048) [04955145] **2843**

BULLETIN / CANADIAN INSTITUTE OF ACTUARIES (CN/1180-3681) [23238098] **2876**

BULLETIN - CANADIAN INTRAMURAL RECREATION ASSOCIATION (CN/1187-0818) [25066847] **4849**

BULLETIN - CANADIAN MEDICAL ASSOCIATION *CEASED*. (CN/1186-0006) [24257281] **3559**

BULLETIN - CANADIAN NUCLEAR SOCIETY (CN/0714-7074) [19294611] **4446**

BULLETIN - CANADIAN POLITICAL SCIENCE ASSOCIATION (1979) (CN/0832-008X) [15167563] **4466**

BULLETIN - CANADIAN RELIGIOUS CONFERENCE (CN/0316-8743) [02247490] **4940**

BULLETIN - CANADIAN SOCIETY FOR ARCHAEOLOGY ABROAD, THE (CN/0384-6547) [03304112] **262**

BULLETIN / CANADIAN SOCIETY FOR MESOPOTAMIAN STUDIES (CN/0844-3416) [19117748] 2647, **262**

BULLETIN - CANADIAN SOCIETY OF BIBLICAL STUDIES (CN/0068-970X) [03196207] 5015, **5012**

BULLETIN - CANADIAN SOCIETY OF LABORATORY TECHNOLOGISTS (CN/0381-5838) [02729361] **5090**

BULLETIN - CANADIAN SOCIETY OF ZOOLOGISTS (CN/0319-6674) [01913403] **5579**

BULLETIN - CANADIAN TALENT LIBRARY (CN/0319-664X) [01928080] 384, **3198**

BULLETIN / CANADIAN WATER AND WASTEWATER ASSOCIATION (CN/0836-0278) [19272323] **5531**

BULLETIN CANADIEN D'HISTOIRE DE LA MEDECINE (CN/0823-2105) [23242495] **3559**

BULLETIN / CAPE COD GENEALOGICAL SOCIETY (US/1075-3605) [30047088] **2440**

BULLETIN - CAPE TOWN. UNIVERSITY OF CAPE TOWN. DEPARTMENT OF GEOLOGY (SA/0576-6850) [03111570] **1368**

BULLETIN (CARDINAL OTUNGA HIGH SCHOOL HISTORICAL SOCIETY) (KE) [09613825] **2612**

BULLETIN / CASCA, CANADIAN ANTHROPOLOGY SOCIETY (CN/1187-0826) [23882884] **232**

BULLETIN (CATHOLIC CHURCH. PONTIFICIUM CONSILIUM PRO DIALOGO INTER RELIGIONES) (IT) [19696223] **5024**

BULLETIN - CAVE EXPLORATION GROUP OF EAST AFRICA (KE/1013-784X) [02400976] **1403**

BULLETIN / CEA (CN) **1729**

BULLETIN - CEDRI (FR/0988-7199) [I09887199] **1918**

BULLETIN - CENTER FOR THE STUDY OF WORLD RELIGIONS, HARVARD UNIVERSITY (US/0163-6561) [04447495] **4940**

BULLETIN - CENTRAL GLASS AND CERAMIC RESEARCH INSTITUTE (II) [02732511] **2586**

BULLETIN - CENTRAL INLAND FISHERIES RESEARCH INSTITUTE BARRACKPORE (II/0008-9427) [01982165] **2297**

BULLETIN - CENTRAL STATES ANTHROPOLOGICAL SOCIETY (U.S.) (US/0577-0963) [03020866] **232**

BULLETIN (CENTRE DE RECHERCHES DE REFLEXION ET D'INFORMATION FEMINISTES (PARIS, FRANCE)) (FR) [10285483] **5552**

BULLETIN - CENTRE D'ETUDES DE MUSIQUE ORIENTALE (FR) [03530361] **4105**

BULLETIN (CENTRE FOR ECONOMIC POLICY RESEARCH (GREAT BRITAIN)) (UK/0265-7996) [12993195] **1466**

BULLETIN - CENTRE INTERNATIONAL DE RECHERCHES SUR L'ANARCHISME (SZ) [07219660] **4540**

BULLETIN - CENTRE INTERUNIVERSITAIRE D'ETUDES EUROPEENNES (CN/0319-1095) [02442094] **2680**

● BULLETIN / CENTRE PIERRE LEON D'HISTOIRE ECONOMIQUE ET SOCIALE (FR/1241-9257) [28698254] **1549**

BULLETIN - CHAMBER OF MINES PRECAMBRIAN RESEARCH UNIT (SA) [05734948] **1368**

BULLETIN - CHAMBRE DE COMMERCE ET D'INDUSTRIE D'ANVERS (BE) [01787208] **1549**

BULLETIN - CHINESE HISTORICAL SOCIETY OF AMERICA (US/0577-9065) [03126841] 2257, **2724**

BULLETIN - CHUO DAIGAKU, TOKYO. FACULTY OF SCIENCE AND ENGINEERING (JA/0578-2228) [01541842] 5090, **1967**

BULLETIN CILA *See* BULLETIN SUISSE DE LINGUISTIQUE APPLIQUEE **3271**

BULLETIN - CITE DE COTE SAINT-LUC (CN/0712-9661) [08890875] **4634**

BULLETIN / CIVIL LIBERTIES ACTION SECURITY PROJECT (CN/0824-4448) [10513365] **4505**

BULLETIN / CLASSICAL ASSOCIATION OF NEW ENGLAND (US) [09149420] **1075**

BULLETIN CLIMATIQUE MENSUEL (FR) **1421**

BULLETIN - COASTAL SOCIETY (US/0277-8815) [06634549] **1352**

BULLETIN / COLLEGE D'ENSEIGNEMENT GENERAL ET PROFESSIONNEL VIEUX MONTREAL *See* JOINT **1832**

BULLETIN / COLLEGE OF DENTAL SURGEONS OF BRITISH COLUMBIA, THE (CN/0843-3690) [22366539] **1317**

BULLETIN / COLLEGE OF FORESTRY, WILDLIFE AND RANGE SCIENCES (US) [03406919] **2189**

BULLETIN - COLOMBO, CEYLON. FISHERIES RESEARCH STATION (CE/0588-4225) [01564116] **2297**

BULLETIN / COLONIAL WATERBIRD SOCIETY (US) [25310472] **5616**

BULLETIN (COLORADO GEOLOGICAL SURVEY) (US/0375-6157) [02533861] **1368**

BULLETIN COMITE ECONOMIQUE ET SOCIAL DES COMMUNAUTES (SP) **1466**

BULLETIN (COMMISSAIRE A L'INFORMATION ET A LA PROTECTION DE LA VIE PRIVEE/ONTARIO) *See* PERSPECTIVES / COMMISSAIRE A L'INFORMATION ET A LA PROTECTION DE LA VIE PRIVEE/ONTARIO **4673**

BULLETIN - COMMISSION DE LA CARTE GEOLOGIQUE DU MONDE (FR/0414-0575) [01794625] **1368**

BULLETIN (COMMISSION DES VALEURS MOBILIERES DU QUEBEC) (CN/0835-1384) [23264554] **893**

BULLETIN COMMISSION HISTORIQUE DU NORD (FR) **2680**

BULLETIN. COMMISSION ON INSURANCE TERMINOLOGY (US/0588-7127) [03313345] **2876**

BULLETIN COMPTABLE & FINANCIER (FR/0220-2352) [I02202352] **740**

BULLETIN - CONFERENCE RELIGIEUSE CANADIENNE (CN/0316-8751) [02247489] **4940**

BULLETIN / CONNECTICUT AGRICULTURE EXPERIMENT STATION (US/0097-0905) [01399719] **68**

BULLETIN / CONNECTICUT LABOR DEPARTMENT (US) [06682083] **1656**

BULLETIN - CONNECTICUT RIVER VALLEY COVERED BRIDGE SOCIETY (US/0090-8547) [01785863] **2019**

BULLETIN - CONSEIL DES AFFAIRES FRANCO-ONTARIENNES (CN/0706-5361) [04589801] **4634**

BULLETIN, CONVERSION AU SYSTEME METRIQUE (CN/0228-2690) [06859903] **4029**

BULLETIN - COOPERATIVE EXTENSION SERVICE (ATHENS) (US/0092-9077) [05519058] **1541**

BULLETIN - COPYRIGHT BOARD CANADA (CN/1185-7250) [25127783] **1302**

BULLETIN - CORPORATION PROFESSIONNELLE DES DIETETISTES DU QUEBEC (CN/0319-7808) [01985686] **4188**

BULLETIN - CORPORATION PROFESSIONNELLE DES MEDECINS DU QUEBEC (CN/0315-2979) [02546026] **3559**

BULLETIN - CORPUS CHRISTI GEOLOGICAL SOCIETY (US/0739-5620) [04636306] **1368**

BULLETIN - COSMOS CLUB (WASHINGTON, D.C.) (US/0742-8995) [05461954] **5229**

BULLETIN - COUNCIL FOR RESEARCH IN MUSIC EDUCATION (US/0010-9894) [01565242] 1729, **4105**

BULLETIN / COUNCIL OF SOCIETIES FOR THE STUDY OF RELIGION (US/1060-1635) [17577253] **4940**

BULLETIN - COUNTY OF CARLETON LAW ASSOCIATION (CN/1183-9791) [25796577] **2944**

BULLETIN (CRANBROOK INSTITUTE OF SCIENCE) *SUSPENDED*. (US/0070-1416) [01307840] **5090**

BULLETIN - CREDIT SUISSE (ENGLISH ED.) (SZ/1016-1570) [01565401] **780**

BULLETIN CRITIQUE DES ANNALES ISLAMOLOGIQUES (UA/0259-7373) [15705353] 1075, **5042**

BULLETIN CRITIQUE DU LIVRE FRANCAIS (FR/0007-4209) [01537694] **3338**

BULLETIN / CROIX-ROUGE LIBANAISE (LE/0253-9349) [06908297] **4769**

BULLETIN (CROZET, VA.) (US) [10656666] **2876**

BULLETIN CRR (BE/0777-2572) [I07772572] **5439**

BULLETIN / CSD (SA) [28407011] **5193**

BULLETIN / DALLAS MUSEUM OF ART (US) [11358077] **345**

BULLETIN D'ARCHEOLOGIE ALGERIENNE (FR/0525-1133) [02712986] **262**

BULLETIN D'ARCHEOLOGIE MAROCAINE / ROYAUME DU MAROC, MINISTERE D'ETAT CHARGE DES AFFAIRES CULTURELLES, DIVISION DE L'ARCHEOLOGIE , DES MONUMENTS HISTORIQUES, DES SITES ET DES MUSEES, SERVICE DE L'ARCHEOLOGIE (MR/0068-4015) [02713064] **262**

BULLETIN D'ARCHEOLOGIE SUD-EST EUROPEENNE (RM) [01786270] **263**

BULLETIN D'AUDIOPHONOLOGIE, ANNALES SCIENTIFIQUES DE L'UNIVERSITE DE FRANCHE-COMTE. MEDECINE & PHARMACIE (FR/0764-8103) [I07648103] **3559**

BULLETIN D'AUDIOPHONOLOGIE BESANCON (FR/0338-9405) [I03389405] **5316**

BULLETIN - DAVID AND ALFRED SMART MUSEUM OF ART (US/1067-8808) [27355078] **345**

BULLETIN - DAYTON ART INSTITUTE (US) [03798986] **345**

BULLETIN DBSF (CN/1183-269X) [24267063] **5275**

BULLETIN DE BIBLIOGRAPHIE BIBLIQUE (SZ) **411**

BULLETIN DE CHATEAUGUAY, LE (CN/0712-6808) [09379141] **4634**

BULLETIN DE CORRESPONDANCE HELLENIQUE (GR/0007-4217) [01537699] **4343**

BULLETIN DE CORRESPONDANCE HELLENIQUE. SUPPLEMENT (FR) [03485520] **2843**

BULLETIN DE DOCUMENTATION (FR) [07483697] **2860**

BULLETIN DE DOCUMENTATION - ASSOCIATION TECHNIQUE DE L'INDUSTRIE DES LIANTS HYDRAULIQUES (FR) [17748461] **2087**

BULLETIN DE DOCUMENTATION - BELGIQUE, MINISTERE DES FINANCES (BE) [05199242] **4715**

BULLETIN DE DOCUMENTATION ET D'INFORMATION - DIRECTION DES ETUDES GENERALES (FR) [04397703] **5430**

BULLETIN DE DOCUMENTATION (FRANCE. SECRETARIAT D'ETAT AUPRES DU PREMIER MINISTRE CHARGE DE L'ENVIORNNEMENT ET DE LA QUALITE DE LA VIE) *See* BULLETIN DE DOCUMENTATION / MINISTERE DE L'ENVIRONNEMENT **2162**

BULLETIN DE DOCUMENTATION INRS (FR/0376-6187) [01228963] **2860**

BULLETIN DE DOCUMENTATION - MINISTERE DE LA QUALITE DE LA VIE (FR) [04459149] **2225**

BULLETIN DE DOCUMENTATION / MINISTERE DE L'ENVIRONNEMENT (FR/0980-949X) [19418460] **2162**

BULLETIN DE DOCUMENTATION - MINISTERE DES FINANCES, SERVICE D'ETUDES ET DE DOCUMENTATION (BE/0777-2238) [07989612] **4715**

BULLETIN DE DROIT COMPARE DU TRAVAIL ET DE LA SECURITE SOCIALE (FR/0753-2601) [11511021] **3144**

BULLETIN DE DROIT IMMOBILIER (CN/0829-1802) [13318589] **2944**

BULLETIN DE FRANCAIS 30 (CN/0848-7316) [23455485] **3270**

BULLETIN DE GEOGRAPHIE D'AIX-MARSEILLE *See* BULLETIN DE LA SOCIETE DE GEOGRAPHIE DE MARSEILLE **2556**

BULLETIN DE GESTION FISCALE DES ENTREPRISES (FR/0982-8044) [I09828044] **825**

●BULLETIN DE LA BANQUE DE FRANCE (FR) [29918724] **780**

BULLETIN DE LA BANQUE NATIONALE DE BELGIQUE (BE/0005-5611) [06383672] **780**

BULLETIN DE LA BANQUE ROYALE (CN/0227-5961) [07821319] **780**

BULLETIN DE LA BIBLIOTHEQUE FORNEY ET DE SES AMIS (FR/1167-3648) [26998453] **5229**

BULLETIN DE LA CATHEDRALE DE STRASBOURG (FR/0153-3851) [05837016] **4940**, **294**

BULLETIN DE LA CHAMBRE DE COMMERCE, D'AGRICULTURE, D'INDUSTRIE ET D'ARTISANAT DU NIGER (NG) [04183154] **1549**

BULLETIN DE LA CHAMBRE DE COMMERCE D'INDUSTRIE ET AGRICULTURE DE MAURITANIE (MU/0302-1343) [01793104] **818**

BULLETIN DE LA CHAMBRE SYNDICALE DE LA SIDERURGIE FRANCAISE. SERIE ROUGE (FR) [08021918] 3999, **1600**

BULLETIN DE LA CHAMBRE SYNDICALE DE LA SIDERURGIE FRANCAISE. SERIE VERTE, STATISTIQUES MENSUELLES (FR) [08021357] 3999, **1600**

BULLETIN DE LA CHAMBRE SYNDICALE DE LA SIDERURGIE FRANCAISE. [SERIE BLEUE] (FR) [08026968] 3999, **1600**

BULLETIN DE LA CHAMBRE SYNDICALE DE LA SIDERURGIE. SERIE BLEUE, STATISTIQUES ANNUELLES, COMMERCE EXTERIEUR *See* BULLETIN DE LA CHAMBRE SYNDICALE DE LA SIDERURGIE FRANCAISE. [SERIE BLEUE] **1600**

BULLETIN DE LA CHAMBRE SYNDICALE DE LA SIDERURGIE. SERIE ROSE, STATISTIQUES ANNUELLES, PRODUCTION *See* BULLETIN DE LA CHAMBRE SYNDICALE DE LA SIDERURGIE FRANCAISE. SERIE ROUGE **1600**

BULLETIN DE LA CLASSE DE BEAUX-ARTS ACADEMIE ROYALE DE BELGIQUE (BE/0378-0716) [05399180] **316**

BULLETIN DE LA CLASSE DES LETTRES ET DES SCIENCES MORALES ET POLITIQUES (BE) [05399168] **3339**

BULLETIN DE LA CLASSE DES SCIENCES. ACADEMIE ROYALE DE BELGIQUE (BE/0001-4141) [01460691] **5090**

BULLETIN DE LA COMMISSION BANCAIRE (FR/1142-2858) [I11422858] 780, **644**

BULLETIN DE LA COMMISSION DEPARTEMENTALE DES ANTIQUITES DE LA SEINE-MARITIME (FR/0246-5825) [I02465825] **2680**

BULLETIN DE LA COMMISSION DEPARTEMENTALE D'HISTOIRE ET D'ARCHEOLOGIE DU PAS-DE-CALAIS (FR/0750-1331) [09882456] 2680, **294**

BULLETIN DE LA COMMISSION HISTORIQUE DU DEPARTEMENT DU NORD (FR/1140-7387) [I11407387] **2680**

BULLETIN DE LA COMMISSION ROYALE DES MONUMENTS ET DES SITES (BELGIUM) (BE/0522-7496) [01772051] **2680**

●BULLETIN DE LA COMMUNICATION PARLEE (FR) [24951042] **3270**

BULLETIN DE LA CONCURRENCE ET DE LA CONSOMMATION (FR) **1600**

BULLETIN DE LA DIANA MONTBRISON (FR/1148-7860) [I11487860] **2680**

BULLETIN DE LA DIRECTION DES ETUDES ET RECHERCHES, ELECTRICITE DE FRANCE - SERIE C. MATHEMATIQUES, INFORMATIQUE (FR/0013-4511) [08511184] **3497**

BULLETIN DE LA DIRECTION DES ETUDES ET RECHERCHES. SERIE A. NUCLEAIRE, HYDRAULIQUE, THERMIQUE (FR/0013-449X) [02321968] **2087**

BULLETIN DE LA DIRECTION DES ETUDES ET RECHERCHES. SERIE B. RESEAUX ELECTRIQUES, MATERIELS ELECTRIQUES (FR/0013-4503) [07744315] **2037**

BULLETIN DE LA F.A.A.F., N.-B, LE (CN/1187-4392) [25590027] **69**

BULLETIN DE LA FEDERATION DE MONTREAL DES CAISSES DESJARDINS (CN/0701-1601) [03520216] **825**

BULLETIN DE LA FEDERATION INTERNATIONALE POUR L'ECONOMIE FAMILIALE *See* ECONOMIE FAMILIALE, L' **2789**

BULLETIN DE LA FONDATION DE L'UQAM (ENGLISH ED.) (CN/1180-5242) [22935078] **1812**

BULLETIN DE LA FONDATION JULIEN ET LAURE VANHOVE-VONNECHE (BE) [20975634] **294**

BULLETIN DE LA GENERALE DE BANQUE (BE) [18994066] **780**

BULLETIN DE L'A.I.M (FR/0007-4314) [04774328] **4940**

BULLETIN DE LA MAISON FRANCO-JAPONAISE (JA/0495-7725) [01589495] **2843**

BULLETIN DE LA REVUE DE LA SOCIETE D'ARCHEOLOGIE ET D'HISTOIRE DU PAYS DE LORIENT (FR/0249-9320) **263**

BULLETIN DE LA SANTE PUBLIQUE *See* BULLETIN DU MINISTERE DE LA SANTE PUBLIQUE ET DE LA FAMILLE **4769**

BULLETIN DE LA SDIE (CN/1184-8774) [24368395] **3125**

BULLETIN DE LA SECTION DE LINGUISTIQUE DE LA FACULTE DES LETTRES DE LAUSANNE (SZ) [17193147] **3270**

BULLETIN DE LA SOCIETE AMERICAINE DE PHILOSOPHIE DE LANGUE FRANCAISE (US/1042-6833) [19106773] **4343**

BULLETIN DE LA SOCIETE ARCHEOLOGIQUE CHAMPENOISE 1954 (FR/1145-7295) [I11457295] **263**

BULLETIN DE LA SOCIETE ARCHEOLOGIQUE DE TARN-ET-GARONNE (FR/1153-2661) [I11532661] **316**

BULLETIN DE LA SOCIETE ARCHEOLOGIQUE DE TOURAINE (FR/1153-2521) [I11532521] **263**

BULLETIN DE LA SOCIETE ARCHEOLOGIQUE D'EURE-ET-LOIR (FR/1149-6770) [I11496770] **263**

BULLETIN DE LA SOCIETE ARCHEOLOGIQUE DU FINISTERE (FR/0249-6763) [02996690] **263**

BULLETIN DE LA SOCIETE ARCHEOLOGIQUE ET HISTORIQUE DE L'ORLEANAIS 1959 (FR/0337-579X) [I0337579X] 2680, **263**

BULLETIN DE LA SOCIETE ARCHEOLOGIQUE ET HISTORIQUE DES HAUTS CANTONS DE L'HERAULT (FR/0182-3876) [I01823876] 2680, **263**

BULLETIN DE LA SOCIETE ARCHEOLOGIQUE ET HISTORIQUE DU LIMOUSIN (FR/0184-7651) [I01847651] **263**

BULLETIN DE LA SOCIETE ARCHEOLOGIQUE ET HISTORIQUE DU LIMOUSIN (FR/0184-7651) [03018650] **263**

BULLETIN DE LA SOCIETE ARCHEOLOGIQUE, HISTORIQUE ET ARTISTIQUE, LE VIEUX PAPIER, POUR L'ETUDE DE LA VIE ET DES MRS D'AUTREFOIS (FR/1145-7325) [01642824] 345, 2680, **263**

BULLETIN DE LA SOCIETE ARCHEOLOGIQUE HISTORIQUE LITTERAIRE & SCIENTIFIQUE DU GERS (FR/0037-8895) [I00378895] 2680, **263**

BULLETIN DE LA SOCIETE ARCHEOLOGIQUE, HISTORIQUE, LITTERAIRE & SCIENTIFIQUE DU GERS (FR/0037-8895) [03065277] **5193**

BULLETIN DE LA SOCIETE ARIEGEOISE DES SCIENCES LETTRES ET ARTS (FR/0988-1557) [I09881557] **316**

BULLETIN DE LA SOCIETE ASTRONOMIQUE DE FRANCE ET REVUE MENSUELLE D'ASTRONOMIE DE METEOROLOGIE ET DE PHYSIQUE DU GLOBE *See* ASTRONOMIE **392**

BULLETIN DE LA SOCIETE BELFORTAINE D'EMULATION (FR) [07087651] **2680**

BULLETIN DE LA SOCIETE BELGE DE GEOLOGIE (BE/0379-1807) [02441229] **1368**

BULLETIN DE LA SOCIETE BELGE D'ETUDES GEOGRAPHIQUES (BE/0037-8925) [01765761] **2556**

BULLETIN DE LA SOCIETE BELGE D'OPHTALMOLOGIE (BE/0081-0746) [01765762] **3873**

BULLETIN DE LA SOCIETE BOTANIQUE DE FRANCE. ACTUALITES BOTANIQUES (FR/0181-1789) [04704577] **504**

BULLETIN DE LA SOCIETE CHIMIQUE DE FRANCE (PARIS, FRANCE : 1985) (FR/0037-8968) [12067665] **963**

BULLETIN DE LA SOCIETE D'AGRICULTURE, SCIENCES ET ARTS DE LA SARTHE (FR/0373-952x) [02586232] **316**

BULLETIN DE LA SOCIETE D'ARCHEOLOGIE COPTE (UA) [07940417] **2638**

BULLETIN DE LA SOCIETE D'ART ET D'HISTOIRE DU DIOCESE DE LIEGE (BE/0776-1295) [01772462] 5024, **2843**

BULLETIN DE LA SOCIETE DE BORDA (FR/0337-0267) [I03370267] **2680**

BULLETIN DE LA SOCIETE DE GEOGRAPHIE DE MARSEILLE (FR) [04879350] **2556**

BULLETIN DE LA SOCIETE DE L'HISTOIRE DE L'ART FRANCAIS (FR/0301-4126) [01681075] **345**

BULLETIN DE LA SOCIETE DE L'HISTOIRE DE PARIS ET DE L'ILE-DE-FRANCE (FR/1148-7968) [01772474] **2680**

BULLETIN DE LA SOCIETE DE L'HISTOIRE DU PROTESTANTISME FRANCAIS (1981) (FR/0037-9050) [08424388] **5057**

BULLETIN DE LA SOCIETE DE LINGUISTIQUE DE PARIS (FR/0037-9069) [01586895] **3270**

BULLETIN DE LA SOCIETE DE MYTHOLOGIE FRANCAISE (FR/1151-2709) [21429592] **2318**

BULLETIN DE LA SOCIETE DE PATHOLOGIE EXOTIQUE (FR) [26671780] 3985, **3893**

BULLETIN DE LA SOCIETE DE PATHOLOGIE EXOTIQUE (FR/0475-042X) [14244925] **3559**

BULLETIN DE LA SOCIETE DE PHARMACIE DE BORDEAUX (FR/0037-9093) [10698400] **4294**

BULLETIN DE LA SOCIETE DE PHARMACIE DE LILLE (FR/0366-3507) [09733989] **4294**

BULLETIN DE LA SOCIETE DE PHARMACIE DE L'OUEST (FR/0291-8374) [I02918374] **4294**

BULLETIN DE LA SOCIETE DE PHILOSOPHIE DU QUEBEC *CEASED.* (CN/0701-1385) [03406545] **4343**

BULLETIN DE LA SOCIETE DES AMIS DE LA BIBLIOTHEQUE DE L'ECOLE POLYTECHNIQUE (FR/0989-3059) [I09893059] **5090**

BULLETIN DE LA SOCIETE DES AMIS DE LA BIBLIOTHEQUE FORNEY *See* BULLETIN DE LA BIBLIOTHEQUE FORNEY ET DE SES AMIS **5229**

BULLETIN DE LA SOCIETE DES AMIS DE MONTAIGNE (FR) [10405453] **5229**

BULLETIN DE LA SOCIETE DES AMIS DES SCIENCES ET DES LETTRES DE POZNAN. SERIE D. SCIENCES BIOLOGIQUES (PL/0079-4570) [01652498] **449**

BULLETIN DE LA SOCIETE DES AMIS DU CHATEAU DE PAU (FR/0339-0195) [I03390195] 4085, **2680**

BULLETIN DE LA SOCIETE DES AMIS DU VIEUX CHINON (FR/0988-1875) [I09881875] 4085, **2680**

BULLETIN DE LA SOCIETE DES ANTIQUAIRES DE L'OUEST ET DES MUSEES DE POITIERS (FR/0037-9190) [05810150] **4085**

BULLETIN DE LA SOCIETE DES ETUDES LITTERAIRES, SCIENTIFIQUES ET ARTISTIQUES DU LOT (FR/0755-2483) [I07552483] **2843**

BULLETIN DE LA SOCIETE DES ETUDES OCEANIENNES (FP) [09510786] **2669**

BULLETIN DE LA SOCIETE DES ETUDES OCEANIENNES (POLYNESIE ORIENTALE) (FP) [07712617] 232, **2669**

BULLETIN DE LA SOCIETE DES FOUILLES ARCHEOLOGIQUES ET DES MONUMENTS HISTORIQUES DE L'YONNE (FR/0762-8129) [I07628129] **263**

BULLETIN DE LA SOCIETE DES LETTRES, SCIENCES ET ARTS DE LA CORREZE (FR/1148-8557) [01765792] **2843**

BULLETIN DE LA SOCIETE DES SCIENCES HISTORIQUES ET NATURELLES DE L'YONNE (FR/0164-3940) [01643940] 4163, **2680**

BULLETIN DE LA SOCIETE DES SCIENCES MEDICALES DU GRAND-DUCHE DE LUXEMBOURG (LU/0037-9247) [01424749] **3559**

BULLETIN DE LA SOCIETE D'ETUDES DES HAUTES-ALPES (FR/0243-7686) [08630818] **2680**

BULLETIN DE LA SOCIETE D'ETUDES ET DE RECHERCHES HISTORIQUES DU PAYS DE RETZ (FR/0294-3484) [I02943484] 1812, **2680**

BULLETIN DE LA SOCIETE D'ETUDES HISTORIQUES DE LA NOUVELLE-CALEDONIE *See* BULLETIN (SOCIETE D'ETUDES HISTORIQUES DE LA NOUVELLE CALEDONIE) **2669**

BULLETIN DE LA SOCIETE D'ETUDES POUR LA CONNAISSANCE D'EDOUARD MANET (FR/0081-0932) [01765802] **1729**

BULLETIN DE LA SOCIETE D'ETUDES SCIENTIFIQUES DE L'AUDE (FR/0153-9175) [I01539175] **5090**

BULLETIN DE LA SOCIETE D'ETUDES SCIENTIFIQUES ET ARCHEOLOGIQUES DE DRAGUIGNAN ET DU VAR (FR/0153-937X) [I0153937X] **263**

BULLETIN DE LA SOCIETE D'HISTOIRE ET D'ARCHEOLOGIE DE GENEVE (SZ/1017-849X) [I1017849X] 263, **2680**

BULLETIN — Alphabetical Title Index

BULLETIN DE LA SOCIETE D'HISTOIRE ET D'ARCHEOLOGIE DE L'ARRONDISSEMENT DE PROVINS *See* PROVINS ET SA REGION : BULLETIN DE LA SOCIETE D'HISTOIRE ET D'ARCHEOLOGIE DE PROVINS **279**

BULLETIN DE LA SOCIETE D'HISTOIRE ET D'ARCHEOLOGIE DE VICHY ET DE SES ENVIRONS (FR/1153-3277) [I11533277] 263, **2680**

BULLETIN DE LA SOCIETE D'HISTOIRE MODERNE (FR/0991-1367) [02168685] **2612**

BULLETIN DE LA SOCIETE D'HISTOIRE NATURELLE DE L'AFRIQUE DU NORD (AE/0374-0994) [01765807] **4163**

BULLETIN DE LA SOCIETE D'HISTOIRE NATURELLE DE TOULOUSE (FR/0366-3477) [07392582] **4163**

BULLETIN DE LA SOCIETE ENTOMOLOGIQUE DE FRANCE (FR/0037-928X) [01765811] **5606**

BULLETIN DE LA SOCIETE ENTOMOLOGIQUE D'EGYPTE (UA) [11674231] **5606**

BULLETIN DE LA SOCIETE FRANCAISE DE CANCEROLOGIE PRIVEE (FR/0753-7417) [107537417] **3810**

BULLETIN DE LA SOCIETE FRANCAISE DE NUMISMATIQUE (FR/0037-9344) [05905405] **2780**

BULLETIN DE LA SOCIETE FRANCAISE DE PARASITOLOGIE (FR/0761-8328) [11256804] **449**

BULLETIN DE LA SOCIETE FRANCAISE DE PHILOSOPHIE (FR/0037-9352) [05753088] **4343**

BULLETIN DE LA SOCIETE FRANCAISE DE PHYSIQUE (FR/0037-9360) [11332493] **4398**

BULLETIN DE LA SOCIETE FRANCAISE D'EGYPTOLOGIE (FR) [01955452] **2638**

BULLETIN DE LA SOCIETE FRANCAISE D'ETUDE DU DIX-HUITIEME SIECLE (FR) [04048307] **2680**

BULLETIN DE LA SOCIETE FRANCAISE DU RORSCHACH ET DES METHODES PROJECTIVES (FR/0373-6261) [I03736261] **4578**

BULLETIN DE LA SOCIETE GEOLOGIQUE DE FRANCE (FR/0037-9409) [01765827] **1368**

BULLETIN DE LA SOCIETE HISTORIQUE DE SAINT-BONIFACE (CN/0384-0158) [02498891] **2681**

BULLETIN DE LA SOCIETE HISTORIQUE ET ARCHELOGIQUE DE CORBEIL, DE L'ESSONNE ET DU HUREPOIX (FR/1154-368X) [20615844] 263, **2681**

BULLETIN DE LA SOCIETE HISTORIQUE ET ARCHEOLOGIQUE DE LANGRES (FR/1148-859X) [03005933] 263, **2681**

BULLETIN DE LA SOCIETE HISTORIQUE ET ARCHEOLOGIQUE DU PERIGORD (FR/1141-135X) [I1141135X] 263, **2681**

BULLETIN DE LA SOCIETE HISTORIQUE ET FOLKLORIQUE FRANCAISE (US) [03031842] **2318**

BULLETIN DE LA SOCIETE HISTORIQUE ET SCIENTIFIQUE DES DEUX-SEVRES (FR/0751-5294) [02996527] **2681**

BULLETIN DE LA SOCIETE INDUSTRIELLE DE MULHOUSE (FR/0037-9441) [01765834] **5090**

BULLETIN DE LA SOCIETE INTERNATIONALE DE DEFENSE SOCIALE *See* CAHIERS DE DEFENSE SOCIALE **3159**

BULLETIN DE LA SOCIETE MATHEMATIQUE DE BELGIQUE. SER. B *See* BULLETIN OF THE BELGIAN MATHEMATICAL SOCIETY, SIMON STEVIN **3498**

BULLETIN DE LA SOCIETE MATHEMATIQUE DE BELGIQUE. SERIE A (BE/0771-1204) [07187706] **3497**

BULLETIN DE LA SOCIETE MATHEMATIQUE DE BELGIQUE. SERIE B (BE/0771-1158) [04683455] **3497**

BULLETIN DE LA SOCIETE MATHEMATIQUE DE FRANCE (FR/0037-9484) [01765846] **3497**

BULLETIN DE LA SOCIETE MEDICALE D'AFRIQUE NOIRE DE LANGUE FRANCAISE (SG/0049-1101) [05433948] **3559**

BULLETIN DE LA SOCIETE MERIDIONALE DE SPELEOLOGIE ET DE PREHISTOIRE 1976 (FR/0750-6570) [I07506570] **263**

BULLETIN DE LA SOCIETE NATIONALE DES ANTIQUAIRES DE FRANCE (FR) [19697758] **2681**

BULLETIN DE LA SOCIETE NEUCHATELOISE DE GEOGRAPHIE (SZ/0373-3076) [01680728] **2556**

BULLETIN DE LA SOCIETE PAUL CLAUDEL (FR/0037-9506) [05085255] 431, **3369**

BULLETIN DE LA SOCIETE PREHISTORIQUE FRANCAISE (FR) [05309466] **263**

BULLETIN DE LA SOCIETE RAMOND (FR) [19752301] **2681**

BULLETIN DE LA SOCIETE ROYALE BELGE D'ETUDES GEOLOGIQUES ET ARCHEOLOGIQUES LES CHERCHEURS DE WALLONIE (BE/0776-0086) [07760086] 263, **1368**

BULLETIN DE LA SOCIETE ROYALE DES SCIENCES DE LIEGE (BE/0037-9565) [01424917] **5090**

BULLETIN DE LA SOCIETE ROYALE LE VIEUX-LIEGE (BE/0776-1309) [10692513] **2681**

BULLETIN DE LA SOCIETE SCHONGAUER DE COLMAR (FR/1148-8298) [I11488298] **2681**

BULLETIN DE LA SOCIETE SCIENTIFIQUE DE BRETAGNE (FR/0037-9581) [01765867] **5090**

BULLETIN DE LA SOCIETE SCIENTIFIQUE HISTORIQUE ET ARCHEOLOGIQUE DE LA CORREZE (FR) [01765866] **263**

BULLETIN DE LA SOCIETE THEOPHILE GAUTIER (FR/0221-7945) [07261538] **3369**

BULLETIN DE LA SOCIETE VAUDOISE DES SCIENCES NATURELLES (SZ/0037-9603) [01765872] **4163**

BULLETIN DE LA SOCIETE VERSAILLAISE DE SCIENCES NATURELLES *See* BULLETIN DES NATURALISTES DES YVELINES / PUBLICATION DE L'ASSOCIATION DES NATURALISTES DES YVELINES **4163**

BULLETIN DE LA SOCIETE ZOOLOGIQUE DE FRANCE (FR/0037-962X) [01715809] **5579**

BULLETIN DE L'ACADEMIE DENTAIRE (FR) [05121253] **1318**

BULLETIN DE L'ACADEMIE DES SCIENCES AGRICOLES ET FORESTIERES (RM/0378-8997) [02686824] **69**

BULLETIN DE L'ACADEMIE DES SCIENCES ET LETTRES DE MONTPELLIER (FR) [03262981] **2843**

BULLETIN DE L'ACADEMIE DU VAR (FR/1148-7852) [I11487852] **1075**

BULLETIN DE L'ACADEMIE NATIONALE DE CHIRURGIE DENTAIRE (FR/0339-9710) [20223834] 1318, **3961**

BULLETIN DE L'ACADEMIE NATIONALE DE MEDECINE (FR/0001-4079) [01080919] **3559**

BULLETIN DE L'ACADEMIE ROYALE DE BELGIQUE CLASSE DES LETTRES (BE) **1812**

BULLETIN DE L'ACADEMIE ROYALE DE BELGIQUE CLASSE DES SCIENCES (BE) **5090**

BULLETIN DE L'ACADEMIE ROYALE DE LANGUE ET DE LITTERATURE FRANCAISES (BE/0378-0708) [01460680] 3369, **3270**

BULLETIN DE L'ACADEMIE VETERINAIRE DE FRANCE (FR/0001-4192) [01412010] **5506**

BULLETIN DE L'ACHETEUR, LE (FR/0757-2859) [01572859] **294**

BULLETIN DE L'ADMINISTRATION DES PRISONS *See* BULLETIN DE L'ADMINISTRATION PENITENTIAIRE (BELGIUM. MINISTERE DE LA JUSTICE) **3159**

BULLETIN DE L'ADMINISTRATION PENITENTIAIRE (BELGIUM. MINISTERE DE LA JUSTICE) (BE) [10352760] **3159**

BULLETIN DE L'AFRIQUE NOIRE (FR/0045-3501) [02445562] **1466**

BULLETIN DE L'AGE D'OR, LE (CN/0229-866X) [08655373] **5178**

BULLETIN DE L'AGMF (FR) **3560**

BULLETIN DE L'AIDE JURIDIQUE (CN/0701-1598) [03425156] **3179**

BULLETIN DE L'ALCAM (CM/0258-1302) [02960246] **3270**

BULLETIN DE L'AMIE (CN/1187-5038) [25652335] **5275**

BULLETIN DE L'AMIE (LA POCATIERE, QUEBEC) *See* REVUE DE L'AMIE **5306**

BULLETIN DE L'ANIMATEUR, LE (CN/0228-1503) [06858779] **5229**

BULLETIN DE L'AQDR, LE (CN/0226-9880) [08099320] **5275**

BULLETIN DE L'ASSOCIATION DE GEOGRAPHES FRANCAIS (FR/0004-5322) [01514506] **2556**

BULLETIN DE L'ASSOCIATION DE PARENTS DU COLLEGE VIEUX MONTREAL (CN/0380-4941) [02578349] **1812**

BULLETIN DE L'ASSOCIATION DES BIBLIOTHECAIRES FRANCAIS (FR) [08506588] **3198**

BULLETIN DE L'ASSOCIATION DES NATURALISTES DU MALI (ML) [02682037] **4163**

BULLETIN DE L'ASSOCIATION DES PROFESSEURS DE MATHEMATIQUES ET L'ENSEIGNEMENT PUBLIC (FR) [05705860] 1890, **3498**

BULLETIN DE L'ASSOCIATION FRANCAISE D'OBSERVATEURS D'ETOILES VARIABLES (FR) [01514538] **394**

BULLETIN DE L'ASSOCIATION GUILLAUME BUDE (FR/0184-6957) [01514542] **3270**

BULLETIN DE L'ASSOCIATION INTERNATIONALE POUR L'HISTOIRE DU VERRE (BE) [09026336] **2586**

BULLETIN DE L'ASSOCIATION PROFESSIONNELLE DES GEOLOGUES ET DES GEOPHYSICIENS DU QUEBEC (CN/0849-0643) [22135406] 1403, **1368**

BULLETIN DE L'ASSOCIATION QUEBECOISE DE TELEDETECTION (CN/0715-7746) [10314436] **2037**

BULLETIN DE L'ASSOCIATION SCIENTIFIQUE LIEGEOISE POUR LA RECHERCHE ARCHEOLOGIQUE (BE) [09704702] **263**

BULLETIN DE L'ASSOCIATION SUISSE DES ELECTRICIENS (SZ/0004-587X) [06362811] **2037**

BULLETIN DE L'ASSOCIATION TECHNIQUE MARITIME ET AERONAUTIQUE (FR/0066-9814) [08889049] **4175**

BULLETIN DE LAUDEM (CN/1181-9189) [23237408] **4106**

BULLETIN DE L'ECOLE ANTIQUE DE NIMES (FR) [24692099] **2681**

BULLETIN DE L'ECOLE FRANCAISE D'EXTREME-ORIENT (FR/0336-1519) [01567351] **2647**

BULLETIN DE L'ELEVAGE FRANCAIS (FR/0398-091X) [0398091X] **208**

BULLETIN DE L'ENTRAIDE MISSIONNAIRE (CN/0382-9472) [02399025] **4941**

BULLETIN DE L'I.N.A.O (FR/0399-6174) [I03996174] **825**

BULLETIN DE LIAISON (CN) **4941**

BULLETIN DE LIAISON ACCESSSIBLE (CN/1189-3524) [25796562] **5275**

BULLETIN DE LIAISON - ASEQUA (SG/0304-5854) [02900678] **1369**

BULLETIN DE LIAISON / ASSOCIATION DES RELATIONNISTES DU QUEBEC (CN/0714-2080) [08967910] **756**

BULLETIN DE LIAISON - CENTRE DE LINGUISTIQUE THEORIQUE ET APPLIQUEE, UNIVERSITE NATIONALE DU ZAIRE (CG) [04218017] **3270**

BULLETIN DE LIAISON / CENTRE REGIONAL D'ETUDES DE POPULATION (CX) [07591823] **4550**

BULLETIN DE LIAISON DE DEMOGRAPHIE AFRICAINE (CM/1013-1396) [06835380] **4550**

BULLETIN DE LIAISON DE LA RECHERCHE EN INFORMATIQUE ET AUTOMATIQUE (FR/0303-1276) [03830465] **1218**

BULLETIN DE LIAISON / DEPARTEMENT DES ETUDES DE POPULATION (CX) [23196464] **4550**

BULLETIN DE LIAISON DES LABORATOIRES DES PONTS ET CHAUSSEES (FR/0458-5860) [03850105] 605, **1967**

BULLETIN DE LIAISON DU CNDT (FR/0995-3671) [I09953671] **1342**

BULLETIN DE LIAISON DU COMITE INTERAFRICAIN D'ETUDES HYDRAULIQUES (UV/0379-3478) [07519217] **2088**

BULLETIN DE LIAISON DU CONSEIL DE LA JEUNESSE SCIENTIFIQUE (CN/0317-9273) [02248271] **5090**

BULLETIN DE LIAISON ET D'INFORMATION DE L'AFEC (FR) **1729**

BULLETIN DE LIAISON / FEDERATION DES ASSOCIATIONS DE FAMILLES MONOPARENTALES DU QUEBEC (CN/0822-6768) [10595504] **2277**

BULLETIN DE LIAISON - GROUPE POLYPHENOLS (FR/0242-8466) [I02428466] **963**

BULLETIN DE LIAISON: INVENTAIRE DESCRIPTIF DES UNITES DE RECHERCHE ET DE FORMATION EN SCIENCES SOCIALES, AMERIQUE LATINE. LIAISON BULLETIN: DIRECTORY OF SOCIAL SCIENCE RESEARCH AND TRAINING UNITS, LATIN AMERICA (US) [03298729] **5193**

BULLETIN DE LIAISON / PRESSE ETUDIANTE DU QUEBEC (CN/0824-9180) [10517660] **1812**

BULLETIN DE LIAISON - SECTEUR PUBLIC (CN/0705-6257) [04783805] **1656**

BULLETIN DE LIAISON - SOCIETE CANADIENNE D'HISTOIRE DE L'EGLISE CATHOLIQUE (CN/1183-6490) [25652185] **5024**

BULLETIN DE L'INSTITUT ALGERIEN DE NORMALISATION ET DE PROPRIETE INDUSTRIELLE (AE) [07038464] **1302**

BULLETIN DE L'INSTITUT ARCHEOLOGIQUE LIEGEOIS (BE/0776-1260) [I07761260] **263**

BULLETIN DE L'INSTITUT DE GEOLOGIE DU BASSIN D'AQUITAINE (FR/0524-0832) [02436493] 1447, **1369**

BULLETIN DE L'INSTITUT DE READAPTATION DE MONTREAL, LE (CN/0316-4454) [11100349] **5275**

BULLETIN DE L'INSTITUT DES ACTUAIRES FRANCAIS (FR/1153-2254) [I11532254] **644**

BULLETIN DE L'INSTITUT D'HISTOIRE DE L'AMERIQUE FRANCAISE (CN/0712-2187) [08867639] **2724**

BULLETIN DE L'INSTITUT D'HISTOIRE DU TEMPS PRESENT (PARIS, FRANCE : 1981) (FR/0247-0101) [09586294] **2612**

BULLETIN DE L'INSTITUT FONDAMENTAL D'AFRIQUE NOIRE. SERIE A: SCIENCES NATURELLES (SG/0018-9634) [01415270] **449**

BULLETIN DE L'INSTITUT FRANCAIS D'ARCHEOLOGIE ORIENTALE (UA) [01538089] **263**

BULLETIN DE L'INSTITUT FRANCAIS D'ETUDES ANDINES (PE/0303-7495) [01793981] **2724**

BULLETIN DE L'INSTITUT HISTORIQUE BELGE DE ROME (BE/0073-8530) [01590468] **2481**

BULLETIN DE L'INSTITUT INTERNATIONAL DE DROIT D'EXPRESSION FRANCAISE (FR/1019-0600) [I10190600] **2944**

BULLETIN DE L'INSTITUT INTERNATIONAL DE STENOGRAPHIE DUPLOYE *See* VERITE STENOGRAPHIQUE, LA **718**

BULLETIN DE L'INSTITUT INTERNATIONAL DU FROID (FR/0020-6970) [12150954] **2604**

BULLETIN DE L'INSTITUT NATIONAL SCIENTIFIQUE ET TECHNIQUE D'OCEANOGRAPHIE ET DE PECHE (TI/0579-7926) [04139599] **553**

BULLETIN DE L'INSTITUT OCEANOGRAPHIQUE (MONACO) (MC/0304-5722) [01614778] **1447**

BULLETIN DE L'INSTITUT PASTEUR (FR/0020-2452) [02258720] **3667**

BULLETIN DE L'INSTITUT ROYAL DU PATRIMOINE ARTISTIQUE. MICROFORM (US) [04706354] **316**

BULLETIN DE L'INSTITUT SCIENTIFIQUE (RABAT) (MR/0253-3243) [06848438] **5090**

BULLETIN DE L'IRDAP : UN SERVICE D'INFORMATION DE L'INSTITUT DE RECHERCHES EN DONS ET EN AFFAIRES PUBLIQUES (CN/1186-8759) [24690722] **5275**

BULLETIN DE L'IREPP *See* CAHIERS DE L'IREPP, LES **1144**

BULLETIN DE L'IREPP (FR/0994-3749) [I09943749] **1144**

BULLETIN DE L'IRES (BE/0770-4585) [I07704585] **1466**

BULLETIN DE LITTERATURE ECCLESIASTIQUE (FR/0007-4322) [05700161] **5025**

BULLETIN DE L'OEUVE DE LA CATHEDRALE DE METZ (FR/0241-2977) [I02412977] **294**

BULLETIN DE L'OIV (FR/0029-7127) [04060759] **69**

BULLETIN DE L'ORDRE DES MEDECINS (FR/0030-4565) [I00304565] **3560**

BULLETIN DE L'ORGANISATION INTERNATIONALE DE METROLOGIE LEGALE (FR/0473-2812) [I04732812] **4029**

BULLETIN DE L'UNION DES ARTISTES, LE (CN/0383-9397) [02916092] **1656**

BULLETIN DE L'UNION DES PHYSICIENS (FR/0366-3876) [11333021] **4399**

BULLETIN DE L'UNION INTERNATIONALE CONTRE LA TUBERCULOSE ET LES MALADIES RESPIRATOIRES *CEASED.* (FR/1011-7903) [I10117903] 4769, **3949**

BULLETIN DE MATHEMATIQUES ET SCIENCES (CN/0848-7510) [23263597] 5091, **3498**

BULLETIN DE METROLOGIE (BELGIUM) (BE) [01799189] **4029**

BULLETIN DE NOUVELLES - CORPORATION PROFESSIONNELLE DES TRAVAILLEURS SOCIAUX DU QUEBEC (CN/0713-4290) [09096430] **5275**

BULLETIN DE NOUVELLES / FEDERATION QUEBECOISE DES SPORTS AERIENS, SECTEUR PARACHUTISME (CN/0826-1326) [11100306] **4888**

BULLETIN DE NOUVELLES / FEDERATION QUEBECOISE DES SPORTS AERIENS, SECTEUR VOL LIBRE (CN/0822-854X) [10935173] **4888**

BULLETIN DE NOUVELLES - PRESSE ETUDIANTE DU QUEBEC (CN/0228-1252) [09050502] **1089**

BULLETIN DE NOUVELLES - SOCIETE CANADIENNE DE DROIT CANONIQUE (CN/0703-1963) [05789483] **5025**

BULLETIN DE PHILOSOPHIE MEDIEVALE (BE/0068-4023) [03755357] **4343**

BULLETIN DE PSYCHOLOGIE (FR/0007-4403) [08660496] **4578**

BULLETIN DE PSYCHOLOGIE SCOLAIRE ET D'ORIENTATION (BE/0007-4411) [03065300] **4578**

BULLETIN DE RCI (CN/1182-4573) [23248122] **1128**

BULLETIN DE RECHERCHE - UNIVERSITE DE SHERBROOKE. DEPARTEMENT DE GEOGRAPHIE (CN/0710-0868) [08401477] **2557**

BULLETIN DE RECHERCHES DE LA DIVISION DES RECHERCHES SUR LE BATIMENT (CN) [03992159] **605**

BULLETIN DE RENSEIGNEMENTS, LA TAXE DE VENTE AU DETAIL / DIRECTION DE LA TAXE DE VENTE AU DETAIL (CN/1183-6474) [24402109] **4715**

BULLETIN DE SAINT-SULPICE (US) **4941**

BULLETIN DE STATISTIQUE (CHAD) (CD) [01795183] **5324**

BULLETIN DE STATISTIQUE / CHAD. DIRECTION DE LA STATISTIQUE ET DES ETUDES ECONOMIQUES *See* BULLETIN DE STATISTIQUE (CHAD) **5324**

BULLETIN DE STATISTIQUE - DIRECTION DE LA STATISTIQUE ET DE LA DOCUMENTATION (RWANDA) (RW/0304-9426) [01794611] **5324**

BULLETIN DE STATISTIQUE - DIRECTION DE LA STATISTIQUE ET DE LA DOCUMENTATION. SUPPLEMENT ANNUEL (RWANDA) (RW) [01799407] **5324**

BULLETIN DE STATISTIQUE - INSTITUT NATIONAL DE STATISTIQUE (BE/0045-1703) [21947160] **5324**

BULLETIN DE STATISTIQUE - REPUBLIQUE DU NIGER, MINISTERE DU DEVELOPPEMENT ET DE LA COOPERATION, DIRECTION DE LA STATISTIQUE (NG) [02246163] **5324**

BULLETIN DE STATISTIQUES - COMMISSION DES VALEURS MOBILIERES DU QUEBEC (CN/0706-1498) [06300084] **893**

BULLETIN DE STIMAREC (FR) **3700**

BULLETIN DE TELECOMMUNICATION (SZ) **1150**

BULLETIN DE THEOLOGIE AFRICAINE (CG/0253-9969) [09120321] **4941**

BULLETIN DE THEOLOGIE ANCIENNE ET MEDIEVALE (BE/0007-442X) [01774852] **4941**

BULLETIN D'ECOLOGIE (FR/0395-7217) [11087449] **2212**

BULLETIN DEI VERBUM (GW) **5025**

BULLETIN / DEMOCRACY INTERNATIONAL COMMITTEE TO AID DEMOCRATIC DISSIDENTS IN YUGOSLAVIA (US) [17206868] **4466**

BULLETIN DEPARTEMEN PENDIDIKAN EKONOMI (IO) [01790751] **1590**

BULLETIN - DEPARTMENT OF AGRICULTURAL ECONOMICS (UK) [02732990] 1466, **69**

BULLETIN - DEPARTMENT OF GEOLOGY, AHMADU BELLO UNIVERSITY (NR) [06730224] **1369**

BULLETIN - DEPARTMENT OF NATURAL RESOURCES, BUREAU OF MINERAL RESOURCES, GEOLOGY AND GEOPHYSICS (AT) [06367681] **1352**

BULLETIN - DEPARTMENT OF NORTHERN AFFAIRS AND NATIONAL RESOURCES, WATER RESOURCES BRANCH (US) [01147710] **5531**

BULLETIN / DEPARTMENT OF THE INTERIOR, BUREAU OF MINES (US/0082-9129) [01282174] **2135**

BULLETIN - DEPT. OF AGRICULTURE (AT) [03309699] **69**

BULLETIN DER BOLSCHEWIKI-LENINISTEN (AU) [03497506] **4540**

BULLETIN DER VEREINIGUNG SCHWEIZ. PETROLEUM-GEOLOGEN UND- INGENIEURE (SZ/0366-4848) [07567863] **4252**

BULLETIN DES AGRICULTEURS (CN/0007-4446) [02353601] **69**

BULLETIN DES AMIS D'ANDRE GIDE (FR/0044-8133) [06584885] **3369**

BULLETIN DES AMIS DE MONTAIGNE *See* BULLETIN DE LA SOCIETE DES AMIS DE MONTAIGNE **5229**

BULLETIN DES AMIS DE MONTLUCON (FR/1140-7425) [11407425] **2681**

BULLETIN DES AMIS DES MONUMENTS ROUENNAIS (FR/0337-7113) [I03377113] **2681**

BULLETIN DES ANGLICISTES MEDIEVISTES (FR/0240-8805) [I02408805] **3270**

BULLETIN DES ANNONCES LEGALES OBLIGATOIRES (FR) [05471434] **780**

BULLETIN DES ANTIQUITES LUXEMBOURGEOISES (LU/1016-961X) [I1016961X] **2681**

BULLETIN DES ARBEITSKREISES "ZWEITER WELTKRIEG" *See* BULLETIN, FASCHISMUS/ZWEITER WELTKRIEG **2681**

BULLETIN DES ARRETS DE LA COUR DE CASSATION (FR) [02244550] **2944**

BULLETIN DES AUTOROUTES FRANCAISES (FR/0295-608X) [I0295608X] **5439**

BULLETIN DES BIBLIOTHEQUES DE FRANCE (FR/0006-2006) [01537710] **3198**

BULLETIN DES C.G.A (CN/0229-9461) [08143895] **740**

BULLETIN DES CENTRES DE RECHERCHES EXPLORATION-PRODUCTION ELF-AQUITAINE (FR/0396-2687) [03512550] **1369**

BULLETIN DES COMMUNAUTES EUROPEENNES (BE/0588-6902) [04156978] **1466**

BULLETIN DES COURS ET DES LABORATOIRES D'ESSAIS DES CONSTRUCTIONS DU GENIE CIVIL ET D'HYDRAULIQUE FLUVIALE (BE) [20316247] **2019**

BULLETIN DES DESSINS ET MODELES INTERNATIONAUX : PUBLICATION MENSUELLE DU BUREAU INTERNATIONAL DE L'ORGANISATION MONDIALE DE LA PROPRIETE INTELLECTUELLE (SZ/0250-7730) [09561311] **3476**

BULLETIN DES ETUDES AFRICAINES (FR/0249-728X) [09353855] **2498**

BULLETIN DES ETUDES PORTUGAISES ET BRESILIENNES *CEASED.* (PO/0379-4954) [03657263] **3270**

BULLETIN DES ETUDES VALERYENNES (FR/0335-508X) [03493358] **3369**

BULLETIN DES G.T.V (FR/0399-2519) [04152160] **5506**

BULLETIN DES MARCHES DELEGATION GENERALE POUR L'ARMEMENT (FR) **4038**

BULLETIN DES MEMBRES - SYNDICAT DES FONCTIONNAIRES PROVINCIAUX DU QUEBEC (CN/0380-1705) [02443335] **1656**

BULLETIN DES MUSEES ET MONUMENTS LYONNAIS (FR/0521-7032) [03301572] **4085**

BULLETIN DES MUSEES ROYAUX D'ART ET D'HISTOIRE (BE) [01716719] **4085**

●BULLETIN DES NATURALISTES DES YVELINES / PUBLICATION DE L'ASSOCIATION DES NATURALISTES DES YVELINES (FR/1167-9786) [26787092] **4163**

BULLETIN DES RECHERCHES AGRONOMIQUES DE GEMBLOUX (BE/0435-2033) [02715408] **69**

BULLETIN DES SCHWEIZERISCHEN ELEKTROTECHNISCHEN VEREINS (ZURICH) (SZ/0036-1321) [01918872] **2037**

BULLETIN DES SCIENCES MATHEMATIQUES (FR/0007-4497) [04246988] **3498**

BULLETIN DES SEANCES - ACADEMIE ROYALE DES SCIENCES D'OUTRE-MER (BE/0001-4176) [05198503] **5091**

BULLETIN DES SOCIETES CHIMIQUES BELGES (BE/0037-9646) [06112872] **963**

BULLETIN DES SOCIETES D'HISTOIRE ET D'ARCHEOLOGIE DE LA MEUSE (FR/0525-1249) [02720177] 263, **2681**

BULLETIN DES SOCIETES D'OPHTALMOLOGIE DE FRANCE (FR/0081-1270) [02715801] **3873**

BULLETIN DES STATISTIQUE - DIRECTION DE L'OFFICE GENERAL DES STATISTIQUES. RWANDA *See* BULLETIN DE STATISTIQUE - DIRECTION DE LA STATISTIQUE ET DE LA DOCUMENTATION (RWANDA) **5324**

BULLETIN DES TRANSPORTS ET DE LA LOGISTIQUE PARIS (FR/1157-1055) [11571055] **5378**

BULLETIN DES TRANSPORTS INTERNATIONAUX FERROVIAIRES / ZEITSCHRIFT FUER DEN INTERNATIONALEN EISENBAHNVERKEHR (SZ/1011-3797) [15504743] **5430**

BULLETIN DES TRAVAUX DE LA SOCIETE DE PHARMACIE DE LYON (FR/0037-9107) [01424948] **4294**

BULLETIN D'ESTHETIQUE DERMATOLOGIQUE ET COSMETOLOGIE (FR/0765-9261) [I07659261] **402**

BULLETIN D'ETUDES KARAITES (FR) [12412045] **5046**

BULLETIN D'ETUDES ORIENTALES (UA/0253-1623) [01775695] **2647**

BULLETIN D'ETUDES PARNASSIENNES ET SYMBOLISTES (FR/0997-3907) [19504810] **3461**

BULLETIN

Alphabetical Title Index

BULLETIN D'HISTOIRE CISTERCIENNE / BULLETIN OF CISTERICAN HISTORY (BE) [20448495] 2681, 5025, **5012**

BULLETIN D'HISTOIRE DE LA REVOLUTION FRANCAISE (FR/0766-4516) [I07664516] **2681**

BULLETIN D'HISTOIRE DE L'ELECTRICITE (FR) [14970724] **2037**

BULLETIN DIGEST (US/0744-768X) [08550137] **4941**

BULLETIN D'INFORMATION - ASSOCIATION INTERNATIONALE DE STANDARDISATION BIOLOGIQUE. NEWSLETTER - INTERNATIONAL ASSOCIATION OF BIOLOGICAL STANDARDIZATION (SZ) [03492632] **4295**

BULLETIN D'INFORMATION - B.N.I.S.T *See* BULLETIN D'INFORMATION - M.I.D.I.S.T **5091**

BULLETIN D'INFORMATION - BUREAU GRAVIMETRIQUE INTERNATIONAL (FR/0373-9023) [01786271] **4399**

BULLETIN D'INFORMATION - CENTRE DE DONNEES STELLAIRES (FR) [06009663] **394**

BULLETIN D'INFORMATION (CENTRE NATIONAL DU MACHINISME AGRICOLE, DU GENIE RURAL, DES EAUX ET DES FORETS (FRANCE) (FR/0249-4779) [13399650] **158**

BULLETIN D'INFORMATION - CENTRE NATIONAL POUR L'EXPLOITATION DES OCEANS (FR/0395-8671) [01421349] **1447**

BULLETIN D'INFORMATION - COMITE EURO-INTERNATIONAL DU BETON (FR/0378-9489) [06740259] **605**

BULLETIN D'INFORMATION - COMITE INTERNATIONAL DES SCIENCES HISTORIQUES (FR/0074-2783) [14399090] **5091**

BULLETIN D'INFORMATION - CONSEIL DES UNIVERSITES (SAINTE-FOY) (CN/0714-3370) [09594517] **1812**

BULLETIN D'INFORMATION - CONSEIL REGIONAL DE DEVELOPPEMENT DE L'OUTAOUAIS (07) (CN/0226-5540) [06315847] **1466**

BULLETIN D'INFORMATION DE L'APCRIQ *See* CAMIONNEURS/TRUCKERS MAGAZINE **5408**

BULLETIN D'INFORMATION DE L'APCRIQ (CN/1181-7941) [24368351] **5378**

BULLETIN D'INFORMATION DES GEOLOGUES DU BASSIN DE PARIS (FR/0374-1346) [04617830] **1369**

BULLETIN D'INFORMATION DES LABORATOIRES DES SERVICES VETERINAIRES *SUSPENDED.* (FR/0243-7880) [11081622] **5506**

BULLETIN D'INFORMATION DU BITS (BE) **5465**

BULLETIN D'INFORMATION DU CENTRE DE DOCUMENTATION SUR LE LAOS (FR) [20412416] **1466**

BULLETIN D'INFORMATION DU CENTRE DE DONNEES STELLAIRES (FR/0242-6536) [07333967] **394**

BULLETIN D'INFORMATION DU MINISTERE DE L'AGRICULTURE (FRANCE) (FR) [02244829] **69**

BULLETIN D'INFORMATION ET DE COORDINATION (GR) [02240946] **2681**

BULLETIN D'INFORMATION ET DE DOCUMENTATION (FR) [03376007] **4517**

BULLETIN D'INFORMATION ET DE DOCUMENTATION - CENTRE NATIONAL DE FORMATION, DOCUMENTATION ET COOPERATION INTERNATIONALE DE LA DIRECTION GENERALE DE LA CONCURRENCE, DE LA CONSOMMATION ET DE LA REPRESSION DES FRAUDES (FR/0989-5086) [I09895086] **1466**

BULLETIN D'INFORMATION ET DE DOCUMENTATION GENERALE *See* BULLETIN DE DOCUMENTATION ET D'INFORMATION - DIRECTION DES ETUDES GENERALES **5430**

BULLETIN D'INFORMATION ET DE LIAISON - ASSOCIATION DES SERVICES GEOLOGIQUES AFRICAINS (FR/0396-8863) [03350787] **1369**

BULLETIN D'INFORMATION ET DE LIAISON DE L'ASSOCIATION INTERNATIONALE D'ETUDES PATRISTIQUES (FR) [01514545] **4941**

BULLETIN D'INFORMATION - FOIRE INTERNATIONALE DU LIVRE DE MONTREAL (CN/0700-5083) [03400109] **4827**

BULLETIN D'INFORMATION / FRANCE. BUREAU NATIONAL DE METROLOGIE *See* BULLETIN DU BUREAU NATIONAL DE METROLOGIE **4029**

BULLETIN D'INFORMATION. INFORMATION BULLETIN (FR/0525-6240) [03923339] **5372**

BULLETIN D'INFORMATION (INSTITUT GEOGRAPHIQUE NATIONAL (FRANCE) : 1981) (FR) [12041636] **2557**

BULLETIN D'INFORMATION IRAZ / INSTITUT DE RECHERCHE AGRONOMIQUE ET ZOOTECHNIQUE (BD) [25986529] 5579, **69**

BULLETIN D'INFORMATION - M.I.D.I.S.T (FR/0243-3664) [10564144] **5091**

BULLETIN D'INFORMATION. RETAIL SALES TAX ACT. LOI SUR LA TAXE DE VENTE AU DETAIL (CN/0226-3033) [06467954] **2944**

BULLETIN D'INFORMATION SPORTIVE BRUXELLES (BE/1012-0491) [I10120491] **4888**

BULLETIN D'INFORMATION / STATION EXPERIMENTALE D'AVICULTURE DE PLOUFRAGAN (FR) [05925717] **208**

BULLETIN D'INFORMATION SUR L'ALCOOLISME (FR/0241-2284) [10606863] **1342**

BULLETIN D'INFORMATION SUR LES ACTIVITES JURIDIQUES AU SEIN DU CONSEIL DE L'EUROPE ET DANS LES ETATS MEMBRES : BULLETIN D'INFORMATION DE LA DIRECTION DES AFFAIRES JURIDIQUES DU CONSEIL DE L'EUROPE (FR) [09930047] **3125**

BULLETIN D'INFORMATION SUR LES ETOILES BE (FR/0296-3140) [13684567] **1729**

BULLETIN D'INFORMATION SUR L'EXECUTION DU PLAN (SG) [16649530] **1549**

BULLETIN D'INFORMATION TOXICOLOGIQUE (CN/0829-5557) [14516863] **3979**

BULLETIN D'INFORMATION UFOLOGIQUE (CN/0828-4938) [11888291] **15**

BULLETIN D'INFORMATION - UNION DES MUNICIPALITES DE LA PROVINCE DE QUEBEC (CN/0316-5140) [02247455] **4634**

BULLETIN D'INFORMATION - URSI (BE/0041-543X) [I0041543X] **1128**

BULLETIN D'INFORMATIONS ARCHITECTURALES (FR/0223-5331) [07408030] **294**

BULLETIN D'INFORMATIONS CEA / SECRETARIAT GENERAL (SZ) [08828791] **69**

BULLETIN D'INFORMATIONS DE L'ASSOCIATION DES BIBLIOTHECAIRES FRANCAIS (FR/0004-5365) [08890659] **3198**

BULLETIN D'INFORMATIONS ET DE RECHERCHES (FR/0180-8567) [04151772] **3369**

BULLETIN D'INFORMATIONS PROUSTIENNES (FR/0338-0548) [03087070] **3339**

BULLETIN D'INFORMATIONS SCIENTIFIQUES - INSTITUT PASTEUR (FR/1144-3464) [I11443464] **5091**

BULLETIN D'INFORMATIONS SOCIALES *CEASED.* (SZ/0378-5394) [I03785394] **1656**

BULLETIN D'INVENTAIRE DES INSECTES DU QUEBEC *SUSPENDED.* (CN/0704-4666) [06082767] **5606**

BULLETIN / DIPLOMATIC SERVICE ORNITHOLOGICAL SOCIETY (UK) [17002861] **5616**

BULLETIN - DIVISION OF GEOLOGY (US/0096-7866) [05019199] **1369**

BULLETIN - DIVISION OF GEOLOGY AND EARTH RESOURCES (OLYMPIA) (US) [01286515] **1369**

BULLETIN D'OBSERVATIONS: MAREES TERRESTRES. WAARNEMINGSBERICHTEN: AARDGETIJDEN (BE/0524-787X) [02980929] **1352**

BULLETIN DOCUMENTAIRE MENSUEL - AGENCE MAURITANIENNE DE PRESSE (MU) [03265170] **2638**

BULLETIN - DOLMETSCH FOUNDATION (UK/0419-618X) [01566874] **4106**

BULLETIN DU BIBLIOPHILE (FR) [01537722] **411**

BULLETIN DU BRGM (FR) **1369**

BULLETIN DU BUREAU INTERNATIONAL D'EDUCATION *CEASED.* (FR/0303-3899) [20983722] **1729**

BULLETIN DU BUREAU NATIONAL DE METROLOGIE (FR/0982-2232) [20067681] **4029**

BULLETIN DU C. R. I. U (CN/0380-1977) [02604196] **2816**

BULLETIN DU CANCER (FR/0007-4551) [01537725] **3810**

BULLETIN DU CANGE / UNION ACADEMIQUE INTERNATIONALE (BE) [01537726] 2681, **3271**

BULLETIN DU CENTRE DE QUEBEC DE LA S R A C (CN/0382-9804) [03209849] **394**

BULLETIN DU CENTRE DE RECHERCHES D'HISTOIRE DES MOUVEMENTS SOCIAUX ET DU SYNDICALISME (FR/0220-2018) [05291103] **5194**

BULLETIN DU CENTRE GENEVOIS D'ANTHROPOLOGIE / MUSEE D'ETHNOGRAPHIE, DEPARTEMENT D'ANTHROPOLOGIE (BE/0777-5466) [20502433] **232**

BULLETIN DU CENTRE PROTESTANT D'ETUDES (SZ) [03008386] **5057**

BULLETIN DU CERCLE D'ETUDES DES METAUX (FR/0366-4104) [09803450] **3999**

BULLETIN DU CIETA (FR) [22337995] **5348**

BULLETIN DU COMITE DES ARCHIVES D'ENTERPRISES / CONSEIL INTERNATIONAL DES ARCHIVES *CEASED.* (BE) [11195682] **644**

BULLETIN DU COMITE FRANCAIS DE CARTOGRAPHIE (FR/0588-618X) [05875124] **2581**

BULLETIN DU CONSEIL DE LA LANGUE FRANCAISE (CN/0825-6926) [11873789] **3271**

BULLETIN DU CREDIT COMMUNAL (BE) [27942637] **780**

BULLETIN DU DROIT D'AUTEUR (INT/0304-2928) [I03042928] **1302**

BULLETIN DU FMI (US/0250-7412) [07578687] **780**

BULLETIN DU GROUPE D'HISTOIRE ET D'ARCHEOLOGIE DE BUZANCAIS (FR/0988-9477) [I09889477] 263, **2681**

BULLETIN DU GROUPEMENT D'INFORMATIONS MUTUELLES AMPERE (SZ/0434-6971) [06534366] **4399**

BULLETIN DU GROUPEMENT INTERNATIONAL POUR LA RECHERCHE SCIENTIFIQUE EN STOMATOLOGIE & ODONTOLOGIE (BE/0250-4693) [04705597] **1318**

BULLETIN DU HOT-CLUB DE FRANCE (FR/0755-7272) [20080550] **4106**

BULLETIN DU JAPON (EDITION CANADIENNE) (CN/0521-7059) [09313031] **825**

BULLETIN DU JARDIN BOTANIQUE NATIONAL DE BELGIQUE (BE/0303-9153) [I03039153] **504**

BULLETIN DU JARDIN BOTANIQUE NATIONAL DE BELGIQUE (BE/0524-7837) [02400220] **504**

BULLETIN DU MINISTERE DE LA SANTE PUBLIQUE ET DE LA FAMILLE (BE/0304-9450) [01794159] **4769**

BULLETIN DU MOUVEMENT TRI-ACTION, LE (CN/0823-289X) [10224811] **825**

BULLETIN DU MUSEE BASQUE (FR) [11488395] 263, **2681**

BULLETIN DU MUSEE BASQUE (FR/1148-8395) [I11488395] **4085**

BULLETIN DU MUSEE D'ANTHROPOLOGIE PREHISTORIQUE DE MONACO (MC/0544-7631) [02264315] **232**

BULLETIN DU MUSEE DE BEYROUTH (FR/0399-0060) [01901011] **4085**

BULLETIN DU MUSEE HONGROIS DES BEAUX-ARTS (HU) [01537558] 263, 345, **4085**

BULLETIN DU MUSEE INGRES (FR/0540-7575) [07317243] 345, **4085**

BULLETIN DU MUSEE NATIONAL DE VARSOVIE (PL/0027-3791) [01769398] **4085**

BULLETIN DU MUSEUM NATIONAL D'HISTOIRE NATURELLE. SECTION A : ZOOLOGIE, BIOLOGIE ET ECOLOGIE ANIMALES (FR/0181-0626) [05297804] **5579**

BULLETIN DU MUSEUM NATIONAL D'HISTOIRE NATURELLE. SECTION B : ADANSONIA, BOTANIQUE, PHYTOCHIMIE (FR/0240-8937) [08093302] **504**

BULLETIN DU MUSEUM NATIONAL D'HISTOIRE NATURELLE. SECTION C : SCIENCES DE LA TERRE : PALEONTOLOGIE, GEOLOGIE, MINERALOGIE (FR/0181-0642) [05297899] **4163**

BULLETIN DU POSTE D'EXPANSION ECONOMIQUE (FR) **1633**

BULLETIN DU PROGRAMME D'EDUCATION SCOLAIRE SUR LES PECHES (CN/1186-2785) [24401869] **4870**

BULLETIN DU PROGRAMME DES EXAMENS EN VUE DU DIPLOME. FRANCAIS 30 (CN/1191-677X) [27194022] **1729**

BULLETIN DU SERVICE DE LA PROTECTION DES VEGETAUX (TG/1015-8219) [I10158219] **69**

BULLETIN DU SERVICE DE L'ATTACHE D'ARMEMENT A LONDRES (FR) **4634**

BULLETIN DU SERVICE SOCIAL DES CAISSES D'ASSURANCE MALADIE (FR) [03863381] 5275, **2876**

BULLETIN DU STATEC / SERVICE CENTRAL DE LA STATISTIQUE ET DES ETUDES ECONOMIQUES (LU/0076-1583) [04344729] 1466, **1530**

BULLETIN DU TRIMESTRE / ASSOCIATION INTERNATIONALE DES SECRETAIRES PROFESSIONNELLES, SECTION DE L'OUTAOUAIS (CN/0711-5830) [09631064] **862**

Alphabetical Title Index — BULLETIN

BULLETIN DU XVII SIECLE (FR) 2612, **3369**

BULLETIN - EARLY SITES RESEARCH SOCIETY (US/0192-6993) [04344518] **5229**

BULLETIN / EASTERN FISHERMEN'S FEDERATION (CN/0821-6576) [09766506] **2297**

BULLETIN - EASTERN STATES ARCHEOLOGICAL FEDERATION (U.S.). MEETING (US/0749-0100) [10243396] **263**

BULLETIN / ECONOMIC AND SOCIAL COMMITTEE OF THE EUROPEAN COMMUNITIES (BE/0256-5846) [06995696] **1549**

BULLETIN - EDUCATIONAL RECORDS BUREAU (US) [01644314] **1729**

BULLETIN EKONOMI BAPINDO (IO) [05896017] **1466**

BULLETIN EKONOMI DAN MANAGEMENT (IO) [01784330] 862, **1466**

BULLETIN - ENTOMOLOGICAL SOCIETY OF CANADA (CN/0071-0741) [01568018] **5579**

BULLETIN - ENTOMOLOGICAL SOCIETY OF NEW ZEALAND (NZ/0110-4527) [02253063] **5579**

BULLETIN - ENVIRONMENT COUNCIL OF ALBERTA (CN/0227-3462) [06635627] **2162**

BULLETIN - ENVIRONMENTAL PROTECTION AUTHORITY, WESTERN AUSTRALIA (AT/1030-0120) [I10300120] **2162**

BULLETIN EPIDEMIOLOGIQUE HEBDOMADAIRE : BEH / REPUBLIQUE FRANCAISE, MINISTERE DE LA SOLIDARITE, DE LA SANTE ET DE LA PROTECTION SOCIALE, DIRECTION GENERALE DE LA SANTE (FR/0245-7466) [26501350] 3712, **3734**

BULLETIN ET MEMOIRES DE LA SOCIETE ARCHEOLOGIQUE DU DEPARTEMENT D'ILLE-ET-VILAINE (FR/0750-1412) [I07501412] **263**

BULLETIN ET MEMOIRES DE L'ACADEMIE ROYALE DE MEDECINE DE BELGIQUE (BE/0377-8231) [02381276] **3560**

BULLETIN ET MEMOIRES - SOCIETE D'EMULATION DE MONTBELIARD (FR/1162-8774) [I11628774] **2681**

BULLETIN - EUROPEAN PARLIAMENT (LU/0423-7846) [01786234] 4634, **3125**

BULLETIN - EXPERIMENT STATION, RIO PIEDRAS *See* BULLETIN - AGRICULTURAL EXPERIMENT STATION, RIO PIEDRAS **68**

BULLETIN, FASCHISMUS/ZWEITER WELTKRIEG (GW) [28143153] **2681**

BULLETIN - FEDERATION DES ETUDIANTS DE L'U. DE O (CN/0822-9376) [10862189] **1089**

BULLETIN / FEDERATION INTERNATIONALE DE GYMNASTIQUE (SZ/0428-1659) [08660451] **4888**

BULLETIN FINANCIER - BANQUE BRUXELLES LAMBERT (BE/0771-6273) [I07716273] **780**

BULLETIN FISCAL & FEUILLET RAPIDE: BFFR (FR) **1466**

BULLETIN FISCAL FRANCIS LEFEBVRE (FR/0242-5912) [12211341] **4715**

BULLETIN - FISHERIES COUNCIL OF CANADA *CEASED.* (CN/0046-3973) [02399011] **2297**

BULLETIN - FLORIDA. UNIVERSITY, GAINESVILLE. BUREAU OF EDUCATIONAL RESEARCH (US) [01348908] **1729**

BULLETIN - FONDATION DE L'UQAM (CN/0849-0724) [22154480] **1813**

BULLETIN / FONDS DE RECHERCHES ET DE DEVELOPPEMENT FORESTIER (CN/0822-773X) [10638918] **2376**

BULLETIN FOR BIBLICAL RESEARCH (US/1065-223X) [25782760] 5046, **5015**

BULLETIN FOR COLLEGES OF TEACHER EDUCATION IN COOPERATION, THE (SW/0283-7536) [I02837536] **1813**

BULLETIN FOR INTERNATIONAL FISCAL DOCUMENTATION (NE/0007-4624) [01753423] **4715**

BULLETIN - FOREST PRODUCTS RESEARCH. DEPARTMENT OF THE ENVIRONMENT (UK) [04093145] **2376**

BULLETIN - FOREST, WILDLIFE AND RANGE EXPERIMENT STATION (US/0073-4586) [03406876] **2189**

BULLETIN - FORESTS COMMISSION, VICTORIA (AT/0085-7742) [01769084] **2376**

BULLETIN - FORESTS DEPARTMENT (AT/0085-8129) [01644402] **2376**

BULLETIN FRANCAIS DE LA PECHE ET DE LA PISCICULTURE (FR/0767-2861) [12483886] **2298**

BULLETIN - FRANCE. PARLEMENT (1946-). ASSEMBLEE NATIONALE (FR/0755-2793) [02239479] **4634**

BULLETIN FRANCOPHONE DE LIAISON ET DE DOCUMENTATION SUR LES DROITS DE L'HOMME (SW) [18152107] **4505**

BULLETIN FROM SADRAC (SW/0281-0999) [I02810999] **4295**

BULLETIN FROM THE HILL (US/8755-450X) [08127282] **4941**

BULLETIN FROM WISCONSIN LIVE STOCK BREEDERS' ASSOCIATION, THE (US/0194-3707) [05469294] **208**

BULLETIN / GDR COMMITTEE FOR HUMAN RIGHTS (GW) [02713051] **4505**

BULLETIN / GENEALOGICAL FORUM OF OREGON, INC (US) [15131561] **2440**

BULLETIN - GENEALOGICAL SOCIETY OF OLD TYRON COUNTY (US/0092-7953) [01791470] **2440**

BULLETIN - GENERAL ELECTRIC COMPANY. RESEARCH LABORATORY (US/0433-342X) [01442963] **2037**

BULLETIN - GENETICS SOCIETY OF CANADA (CN/0316-4357) [02442281] **543**

BULLETIN GEODESIQUE (FR/0007-4632) [02445568] **1403**

BULLETIN - GEOLOGICAL SURVEY OF ALABAMA (US/0097-3262) [01374708] **1369**

BULLETIN / GEOLOGICAL SURVEY OF CANADA (CN/0068-7626) [01552909] **1369**

BULLETIN / GEOLOGICAL SURVEY OF FINLAND (FI) [12303280] **1369**

BULLETIN / GEOLOGICAL SURVEY OF GUYANA (GY/0072-9116) [01604788] **1369**

BULLETIN / GEOLOGICAL SURVEY OF IRELAND (IE/0085-0985) [03901345] **1369**

BULLETIN - GEOLOGICAL SURVEY OF NEW SOUTH WALES (AT/0155-5561) [03978608] **1369**

BULLETIN / GEOLOGICAL SURVEY OF NEW SOUTH WALES (AT) [02351128] **1369**

BULLETIN / GEOLOGICAL SURVEY OF SOUTH AUSTRALIA (AT/0016-7671) [01343674] **1352**

BULLETIN / GEOLOGICAL SURVEY OF WESTERN AUSTRALIA (AT/0085-8137) [01769695] **1369**

BULLETIN (GEOLOGICAL SURVEY OF WYOMING) (US/0096-6053) [01328009] **1369**

BULLETIN - GEOLOGICAL SURVEY (PRETORIA) (SA/1015-8049) [01383169] **1369**

BULLETIN GEOLOGIQUE (SAINTE-FOY) (CN/0227-1575) [06562933] **1369**

BULLETIN - GEORGIA. DEPT. OF EDUCATION (US) [01447227] **1890**

BULLETIN - GEORGIA MUSEUM OF ART, THE UNIVERSITY OF GEORGIA *CEASED.* (US/0147-1902) [01578078] 345, **4085**

BULLETIN - GEORGIA. UNIVERSITY. COLLEGE OF AGRICULTURE. EXTENSION SERVICE (US) [01440639] **69**

BULLETIN - GEORGIAN BAY REGIONAL LIBRARY SYSTEM (CN/0380-8076) [02583576] **3198**

BULLETIN / GEOTHERMAL RESOURCES COUNCIL (US/0160-7782) [03765238] **1934**

BULLETIN / GERMAN GENEALOGICAL SOCIETY OF AMERICA *SUSPENDED.* (US/1047-6121) [16744411] **2440**

BULLETIN (GERMANY (WEST). PRESSE- UND INFORMATIONSAMT : 1979). ENGLISH (GW) [05627898] **4634**

BULLETIN - GREAT BRITAIN DEPARTMENT OF SCIENTIFIC AND INDUSTRIAL RESEARCH. ROAD RESEARCH BOARD (UK) [20316525] **5439**

BULLETIN - GREATER ST. LOUIS DENTAL SOCIETY (US/0360-2575) [01838792] **1318**

BULLETIN - HARVARD UNIVERSITY. BLACK ROCK FOREST. CORNWALL, NEW YORK (US) [01828285] **1813**

BULLETIN - HCEIA (FR/0992-6151) [16863798] **1342**

BULLETIN - HEALTH SCIENCES ASSOCIATION OF ALBERTA (CN/0712-4775) [09674428] 4769, **1657**

BULLETIN HISPANIQUE (FR/0007-4640) [01196199] **3370**

BULLETIN HISTORIQUE ET ARTISTIQUE DU CALAISIS (FR/0521-713X) [I0521713X] 345, **2681**

BULLETIN HISTORIQUE ET SCIENTIFIQUE DE L'AUVERGNE 1933 (FR/1153-2599) [I11532599] **2843**

BULLETIN / HOLMES SAFETY ASSOCIATION (US/0271-3888) [05140851] **2860**

● BULLETIN / HOSPITAL FOR JOINT DISEASES (US/0018-5647) [26884740] **3804**

BULLETIN - HOT CLUB DE FRANCE (FR/0755-7272) [01788964] **4106**

BULLETIN - HUDSON FAMILY ASSOCIATION, SOUTH (US/0363-8847) [02546490] **2440**

BULLETIN HUKUM (IO) [09126834] **3182**

● BULLETIN / HUMAN FACTORS AND ERGONOMICS SOCIETY (US/0438-1629) [27988896] **1250**

BULLETIN - HUMAN FACTORS SOCIETY (US/0438-1629) [04293009] **1250**

BULLETIN - HYMN SOCIETY OF GREAT BRITAIN AND IRELAND (UK/0018-828X) [01752446] 4941, **4106**

BULLETIN - I C S S (CN/0700-8090) [03399958] **4888**

BULLETIN - ILLINOIS GEOGRAPHICAL SOCIETY (US/0019-2031) [01775250] **2557**

BULLETIN (ILLINOIS. NATURAL HISTORY SURVEY DIVISION) (US/0073-4918) [01752599] **4163**

BULLETIN - ILLINOIS STATE WATER SURVEY (US/0360-9804) [01152420] **5531**

BULLETIN INDEX-DIGEST SYSTEM. SERVICE FOUR. EXCISE TAX (US/0363-8499) [02459497] **2944**

BULLETIN INDEX-DIGEST SYSTEM. SERVICE ONE. INCOME TAX (US/0363-3594) [02403463] **2944**

BULLETIN INDEX-DIGEST SYSTEM. SERVICE THREE. EMPLOYMENT TAXES (US/0363-8502) [02459520] **3144**

BULLETIN INDEX-DIGEST SYSTEM. SERVICE TWO. ESTATE AND GIFT TAX (US/0363-8456) [02459509] **3117**

BULLETIN - INDIAN GEOLOGISTS' ASSOCIATION (II/0379-5098) [03582811] **1369**

BULLETIN - INDIAN MUSEUM (II/0019-5987) [01774657] **4085**

BULLETIN - INDIAN SOCIETY OF SOIL SCIENCE (II/0366-0672) [01752982] **165**

BULLETIN - INSTITUT DES AGRONOMES DU N.-B. INSTITUT AGRICOLE DU CANADA *CEASED.* (CN/0712-8835) [08828205] **69**

BULLETIN - INSTITUT NATIONAL DE RECHERCHE SUR LES EAUX (CN/0836-0987) [I08360987] **5531**

BULLETIN - INSTITUT ROYAL DES SCIENCES NATURELLES DE BELGIQUE. BIOLOGIE (BE/0303-9137) [01685540] **449**

BULLETIN - INSTITUT ROYAL DES SCIENCES NATURELLES DE BELGIQUE. ENTOMOLOGIE (BE/0303-9129) [01674573] **5579**

BULLETIN - INSTITUT ROYAL DES SCIENCES NATURELLES DE BELGIQUE. SCIENCES DE LA TERRE (BE/0303-9110) [01685628] **1352**

BULLETIN (INSTITUT ROYAL DU PATRIMOINE ARTISTIQUE (BRUXELLES)) (BE/0085-1892) [01537515] **345**

BULLETIN - INSTITUT SIMONE DE BEAUVOIR (CN/0840-4011) [19216390] **5552**

BULLETIN / INSTITUTE FOR ANTIQUITY AND CHRISTIANITY (US/0739-0459) [06572350] **4941**

BULLETIN / INSTITUTE FOR THEOLOGICAL ENCOUNTER WITH SCIENCE AND TECHNOLOGY (US/1073-5976) [29484414] 5091, **4941**

BULLETIN / INSTITUTE OF ADVANCED LEGAL STUDIES (UNIVERSITY OF LONDON) (UK/0963-9675) [29869245] **2944**

BULLETIN - INSTITUTE OF CLASSICAL STUDIES (UK/0076-0730) [01695663] **1075**

BULLETIN - INSTITUTE OF MATHEMATICAL STATISTICS (US/0146-3942) [01211149] **5324**

BULLETIN - INSTITUTE OF MATHEMATICS AND ITS APPLICATIONS (UK/0950-5628) [04093455] **3498**

BULLETIN - INTER-AMERICAN TROPICAL TUNA COMMISSION (US/0074-0993) [01643146] 1447, **449**

BULLETIN (INTER PARES (ORGANIZATION)) (CN/0715-4267) [09159593] **2908**

BULLETIN INTERIEUR - ASSOCIATION POUR LA PROTECTION CONTRE LES RAYONNEMENTS IONISANTS (FR/0376-5954) [01415205] **4434**

BULLETIN - INTERNATIONAL ASSOCIATION FOR MOBILIZATION OF CREATIVITY (CN/0705-3029) [03900353] **3560**

BULLETIN (INTERNATIONAL ASSOCIATION OF LIGHTHOUSE AUTHORITIES) (FR/0379-2811) [08257877] **4175**

BULLETIN - INTERNATIONAL ASSOCIATION OF ORIENTALIST LIBRARIANS (US/0161-7397) [04024179] **3198**

BULLETIN — Alphabetical Title Index

BULLETIN / INTERNATIONAL COMMITTEE OF THE RED CROSS (SZ) [07261780] **5275**

BULLETIN - INTERNATIONAL COUNCIL ON ARCHIVES (FR/0252-9785) [I02529785] **2481**

BULLETIN - INTERNATIONAL DAIRY FEDERATION (BE/0259-8434) [I02598434] **192**

BULLETIN (INTERNATIONAL DAIRY FEDERATION) (BE/0250-5118) [05896740] **192**

BULLETIN INTERNATIONAL DES SCIENCES DE LA MER (INT/0251-4451) [I02514451] **1447**

BULLETIN INTERNATIONAL D'INFORMATIONS (FR/0153-288X) [11033076] **4295**

BULLETIN - INTERNATIONAL INSTITUTE FOR CONSERVATION OF HISTORIC AND ARTISTIC WORKS (UK) [02078773] **316**

BULLETIN - INTERNATIONAL INSTITUTE FOR LAND RECLAMATION AND IMPROVEMENT (NE/0074-6444) [01607805] **2189**

BULLETIN - INTERNATIONAL NORTH PACIFIC FISHERIES COMMISSION (CN/0074-7157) [02248191] **2298**

BULLETIN / INTERNATIONAL OLD LACERS (US) [07316595] **5348**

BULLETIN - INTERNATIONAL TYPOGRAPHICAL UNION, THE (US/0020-904X) [04576498] **4564**

BULLETIN - IRISH BIOGEOGRAPHICAL SOCIETY (IE/0332-1185) [I03321185] **2557**

BULLETIN / IRISH COUNCIL FOR CIVIL LIBERTIES (IE/0332-1584) [13381564] **4505**

BULLETIN / IRISH MATHEMATICAL SOCIETY (IE/0790-1690) [14232141] **3498**

BULLETIN - JOINT ASSOCIATION OF CLASSICAL TEACHERS (UK/0267-8349) [I02678349] **1729**

BULLETIN JOLY PARIS (FR/0997-5047) [I09975047] **825**

BULLETIN - JOURNAL OF THE TOKYO WOMEN'S MEDICAL COLLEGE (JA/0495-7792) [01587261] **3560**

BULLETIN - JUGOSLAVENSKA ADAKEMIJA ZNANOSTI I UMJETNOSTI, RAZRED ZA LIKOVNE UMJETNOSTI (CI) [06829719] **345**

BULLETIN JURIDIQUE (CN/0701-0303) [03406248] 605, **2944**

BULLETIN - KANSAS AGRICULTURAL EXPERIMENT STATION (US/0097-0484) [01371916] **69**

BULLETIN (KANSAS GEOLOGICAL SURVEY) (US/0097-4471) [01375907] **1369**

BULLETIN - KANSAS ORNITHOLOGICAL SOCIETY (US/0022-8729) [04120497] **5616**

BULLETIN (KANSAS. STATE DEPT. OF EDUCATION) (US) [02239933] **1729**

BULLETIN: KAWARTHA BRANCH, ONTARIO GENEALOGICAL SOCIETY, THE (CN/0842-5159) [19580026] **2440**

BULLETIN KFT : MEDIA KARYAWAN FILM DAN TELEVISI INDONESIA (IO/0216-3411) [11013843] 4064, **1128**

BULLETIN - KING COUNTY MEDICAL SOCIETY, THE (US/0023-1592) [06336977] **3913**

BULLETIN - KNOB (NE/0166-0470) [I01660470] **5806**

BULLETIN - KODALY MUSICAL TRAINING INSTITUTE INC (US/0094-3258) [01792549] **4106**

BULLETIN LA PARENTELE : BULLETIN DE L'ASSOCIATION DES FAMILLES MARCHAND (CN/1183-4455) [24257022] **2440**

BULLETIN / LABOUR HERITAGE WOMEN'S RESEARCH COMMITTEE (UK) [19006368] 1657, **5552**

BULLETIN L'AFRI (FR) [1218]

BULLETIN / LARF, LATIN AMERICAN RESERVE FUND (CK) [24064284] **780**

BULLETIN / LAWYERS COMMITTEE FOR HUMAN RIGHTS (US/0897-1358) [12414557] **4505**

BULLETIN - LE MONDE BICYCLETTE (CN/0705-0623) [04746601] **428**

BULLETIN LEGISLATIF BELGE (BE) [03006378] **2944**

BULLETIN (LEMBAGA PENELITIAN PETERNAKAN (INDONESIA)) (IO/0125-9660) [09634536] **208**

BULLETIN LINGUISTIQUE, ETHNOLOGIQUE ET TOPONYMIQUE (LU) [03739167] **3271**

BULLETIN - LIQUE HAITIENNE DES DROITS HUMAINS (HT) [06522317] **4505**

● BULLETIN LS (CN/1193-2325) [26714934] **3198**

BULLETIN - LUTHERAN THEOLOGICAL SEMINARY, GETTYSBURG (US/0362-0581) [02045836] **5057**

BULLETIN - LUZERNE COUNTY MEDICAL SOCIETY, THE (US/0098-5880) [01452297] **3560**

BULLETIN (MADJELIS ILMU PENGETAHUAN) *See* BULLETIN **5090**

BULLETIN - MADRAS INSTITUTE OF DEVELOPMENT STUDIES (II) [01783605] **1549**

BULLETIN - MAINE ARCHAEOLOGICAL SOCIETY (US/0542-1292) [04097006] **263**

BULLETIN / MALAWI NATIONAL LIBRARY SERVICE BOARD (MW) [09538757] **3198**

BULLETIN - MANITOBA DENTAL ASSOCIATION (CN/0701-1725) [03409783] **1318**

BULLETIN / MANITOBA NATURALISTS SOCIETY (CN/0823-2911) [10513406] **4164**

BULLETIN MARCEL PROUST (FR) [27110820] **3370**

BULLETIN MARIE DE L'INCARNATION (CN/1186-8937) [24690482] **4941**

BULLETIN - MARION COUNTY MEDICAL SOCIETY (US/0098-5872) [01450634] **3560**

BULLETIN (MARKAZ AL-BUHUTH AL-ANTHRUBULUJIYAH WA-MA QABLA AL-TARIKH (ALGERIA)) (AE) [08422045] **232**

BULLETIN - MARO PROGRESSIVE LEARNING SYSTEMS (CN/0702-8296) [03436694] **1803**

BULLETIN MATCH (CN/0229-5814) [07888649] **5552**

BULLETIN MATHEMATIQUE DE LA SOCIETE DES SCIENCES MATHEMATIQUES DE LA REPUBLIQUE SOCIALISTE DE ROUMAINE (RM/0373-2908) [08778480] **3498**

BULLETIN - MEDELHAVSMUSEET (SW/0585-3214) [01983376] **263**

BULLETIN MENSUAL D'INFORMATION DE LA CHAMBRE NATIONALE DE COMMERCE (CX) [08515934] **818**

BULLETIN MENSUEL / BANQUE DE FRANCE (FR) [21989739] **780**

BULLETIN MENSUEL - BANQUE DE LA REPUBLIQUE DU BURUNDI (BD/1013-5332) [07685556] **780**

BULLETIN MENSUEL - CHAMBRE DE COMMERCE, D'AGRICULTURE ET D'INDUSTRIE DE LA REPUBLIQUE TOGOLAISE (TG/0303-7460) [05705686] **1549**

BULLETIN MENSUEL DE DOCUMENTATION *See* DOCUMENTATION - SNCB, DIRECTION DU PERSONNEL ET DES SERVICES SOCIAUX **5431**

BULLETIN MENSUEL DE LA BANQUE DE LA REPUBLIQUE DU BURUNDI *See* BULLETIN MENSUEL - BANQUE DE LA REPUBLIQUE DU BURUNDI **780**

BULLETIN MENSUEL DE LA SOCIETE LINNEENNE DE LYON (FR/0366-1326) [01765840] **4164**

BULLETIN MENSUEL DE LA SOCIETE VETERINAIRE PRATIQUE DE FRANCE (FR/0395-7500) [03246179] **5506**

BULLETIN MENSUEL DE L'ENERGIE ELECTRIQUE (BE) [02337664] **4760**

BULLETIN MENSUEL DE L'OFFICE NATIONAL DE L'EMPLOI (BE/0771-1182) [12763192] **1657**

BULLETIN MENSUEL DE STATISTIQUE (FR/0007-4713) [09491678] **5324**

BULLETIN MENSUEL DE STATISTIQUE AGRICOLE (PARIS) (FR/0997-1122) [19903096] 69, **152**

BULLETIN MENSUEL DE STATISTIQUE - DIRECTION DE LA STATISTIQUE ET DES ETUDES ECONOMIQUES (GABON) (GO/0304-9485) [01796707] **1530**

BULLETIN MENSUEL DE STATISTIQUE IINDUSTRIELLE (FR/0151-0770) [05236245] 1600, **1530**

BULLETIN MENSUEL DE STATISTIQUE - INSTITUT NATIONAL DE LA STATISTIQUE (AL-MAHAD) (TI) [02246911] **5324**

BULLETIN MENSUEL DE STATISTIQUE (LOME, TOGO) (TG) [01787886] **5324**

BULLETIN MENSUEL DE STATISTIQUE / REPUBLIQUE DU MALI, MINISTERE D'ETAT CHARGE DU PLAN ET DE LA COORDINATION DES AFFAIRES ECONOMIQUES ET FINANCIERES, SERVICE DE LA STATISTIQUE GENERALE ET DE LA COMPTABILITE ECONOMIQUE NATIONALE (ML) [02239804] **5324**

BULLETIN MENSUEL DE STATISTIQUES (GABON. DIRECTION COMMERCIALE ET DE L'EXPLOITATION) (GO) [19094565] **5324**

BULLETIN MENSUEL DES AVIS TECHNIQUES (FR) [19098793] **5091**

BULLETIN MENSUEL DES STATISTIQUES - DIRECTION DE LA STATISTIQUE ET DE LA COMPTABILITE ECONOMIQUE (CONGO (BRAZZAVILLE)) (CG) [02891202] **5324**

BULLETIN MENSUEL DES STATISTIQUES DU TRAVAIL. SUPPLEMENT (PARIS, FRANCE : 1982) (FR) [12219750] 1657, **1530**

BULLETIN MENSUEL D'INFORMATION DU CENTRE DE CREATION INDUSTRIELLE (FR/0397-7102) [12835720] **345**

BULLETIN MENSUEL D'INFORMATION ET DE LIAISON DES CHAMBRES D'AGRICULTURE (FR) **69**

BULLETIN MENSUEL D'INFORMATION (FRANCE. SERVICE DE CONSERVATION DES GISEMENTS) (FR/0290-0556) [08483327] **4252**

BULLETIN MENSUEL. OBSERVATIONS CLIMATOLOGIQUES / INSTITUT ROYAL METEOROLOGIQUE DE BELGIQUE / MAANDBERICHT. KLIMATOLOGISCHE WAARNEMINGEN / KONINKLIJK METEOROLOGISCH INSTITUUT VAN BELGIEE (BE/0029-7682) [10489265] **4029**

BULLETIN MENSUEL: OBSERVATIONS IONOSPHERIQUES *See* BULLETIN MENSUEL : OBSERVATIONS IONOSPHERIQUES ET DU RAYONNEMENT COSMIQUE **1421**

BULLETIN MENSUEL : OBSERVATIONS IONOSPHERIQUES ET DU RAYONNEMENT COSMIQUE (BE) [05519404] **1421**

BULLETIN MENSUEL: POLLUTION ATMOSPHERIC, FUMEE ET SO2. MAANDBERICHT: LUCHTVERONTREINIGING, ROOK EN SO2 (BE/0524-7802) [03000405] **2225**

BULLETIN - METROPOLITAN MUSEUM OF ART (US/0026-1521) [01624350] 345, **4085**

BULLETIN - MICHIGAN. GEOLOGICAL SURVEY DIVISION (US/0539-7545) [01757290] **1369**

BULLETIN (MICHIGAN HISTORICAL COLLECTIONS) (US/0196-6170) [01757331] **2724**

BULLETIN - MICROSCOPICAL SOCIETY OF CANADA (CN/0383-1825) [03202314] **572**

BULLETIN / MIDWEST KODALY MUSIC EDUCATORS OF AMERICA (US) [09089132] **4106**

BULLETIN - MILITARY HISTORICAL SOCIETY (UK/0026-4008) [06328286] **4038**

BULLETIN - MINERAL RESOURCES DIVISION (SUVA) (FJ/0379-1580) [03693611] **1370**

BULLETIN - MINNESOTA GEOLOGICAL SURVEY (US/0076-9169) [01589732] **1370**

BULLETIN (MISSISSIPPI AGRICULTURAL AND FORESTRY EXPERIMENT STATION) (US/0898-0497) [05896186] 2376, **69**

BULLETIN - MISSISSIPPI BOARD OF WATER COMMISSIONERS (US/0462-8128) [07039846] **5531**

BULLETIN - MISSISSIPPI DEPARTMENT OF ENVIRONMENTAL QUALITY, BUREAU OF GEOLOGY (US/0271-8537) [06701518] **1370**

BULLETIN MMPI *See* MMPI **4074**

BULLETIN (MONTREAL CITIZENSHIP COUNCIL) (CN/0229-4001) [08036476] **5194**

BULLETIN MONUMENTAL (FR/0007-473X) [01537742] **345**

BULLETIN - MORAVIAN THEOLOGICAL SEMINARY, THE (US/0540-8644) [01642265] **4941**

BULLETIN MORAVSKE GALERIE V BRNE / MG (XR) [14998628] **345**

BULLETIN - MOUNT DESERT ISLAND BIOLOGICAL LABORATORY (1934) (US/0097-0883) [04699893] **450**

BULLETIN MUNICIPAL - CONSEIL MUNICIPAL DE SAINT-LOUIS-DE-TERREBONNE (CN/0711-7744) [08716784] **4634**

BULLETIN MUNICIPAL / OUTREMONT (CN/0820-9278) [09606613] **4634**

BULLETIN MUNICIPAL / VILLE DE MONTREAL-NORD (CN/0822-0395) [10420473] **4634**

BULLETIN - MUSEES ROYAUX DES BEAUX-ARTS DE BELGIQUE (BE/0027-3856) [01537518] **345**

BULLETIN - MUSEUM OF FAR EASTERN ANTIQUITIES (SW/0081-5691) [03057592] 4085, **264**

BULLETIN - MUSEUM OF INDIAN ARCHAEOLOGY. UNIVERSITY OF WESTERN ONTARIO (CN/0709-2628) [06702754] 264, **4085**

BULLETIN / MUSIKRAT DER DEUTSCHEN DEMOKRATISCHEN REPUBLIK, SEKTION DDR DES INTERNATIONALEN MUSIKRATES (GW/0433-678X) [04969557] **4106**

BULLETIN - NANZAN INSTITUTE FOR RELIGION AND CULTURE (JA/0386-720X) [04877206] **4941**

Alphabetical Title Index — BULLETIN

BULLETIN (NATIONAL ASSOCIATION OF RAILROAD AND UTILITIES COMMISSIONERS) *See* BULLETIN NATIONAL ASSOCIATION OF REGULATORY UTILITY COMMISSIONERS **4634**

BULLETIN NATIONAL ASSOCIATION OF REGULATORY UTILITY COMMISSIONERS (US/0027-8645) [03491582] **4634**

BULLETIN / NATIONAL COUNCIL FOR THE SOCIAL STUDIES (US/0077-4049) [01759152] 1890, **5194**

BULLETIN NATIONAL DU CCA (CN/0822-9309) [11073610] **5275**

BULLETIN, NATIONAL EMPLOYMENT LISTING SERVICE FOR THE CRIMINAL JUSTICE SYSTEM *CEASED.* (US/0194-0767) [04333113] 3159, **4201**

BULLETIN - NATIONAL FOUNDATION FOR UNEMPLOYMENT COMPENSATION & WORKERS' COMPENSATION (U.S.) (US/0882-3669) [11857255] **1657**

BULLETIN - NATIONAL INSTITUTES OF HEALTH (U.S.) (US) [05140135] **4769**

BULLETIN - NATIONAL MUSEUM, NEW DELHI (II/0418-5730) [01681258] **4086**

BULLETIN - NATIONAL PSYCHOLOGICAL ASSOCIATION FOR PSYCHOANALYSIS (US/0077-5339) [05013548] **4579**

BULLETIN (NATIONAL SCIENCE FOUNDATION (U.S.)) (US/0145-0670) [02538502] **5091**

BULLETIN - NATIONAL SHEVCHENKO MUSICAL ENSEMBLE GUILD OF CANADA (CN/0703-9999) [05376496] **4106**

BULLETIN - NATIONAL TROPICAL BOTANICAL GARDEN (US/1057-3968) [20766782] **505**

BULLETIN - NATIONALMUSEUM (SW/0347-7835) [03831523] **317**

BULLETIN - NEPAL BANK LIMITED (NP/0550-9246) [06678202] **781**

BULLETIN - NEVADA BUREAU OF MINES *See* BULLETIN - NEVADA BUREAU OF MINES AND GEOLOGY **1370**

BULLETIN - NEVADA BUREAU OF MINES AND GEOLOGY (US/0097-191X) [01695548] 2135, **1370**

BULLETIN - NEW JERSEY ACADEMY OF SCIENCE, THE (US/0028-5455) [00834332] **5091**

BULLETIN - NEW JERSEY AGRICULTURAL EXPERIMENT STATION, RUTGERS UNIVERSITY (US/0096-6398) [01423104] **69**

BULLETIN (NEW JERSEY GEOLOGICAL SURVEY) (US) [10647611] 1438, **1370**

BULLETIN - NEW JERSEY MOTOR TRUCK ASSOCIATION (US/0028-5838) [04130945] **5378**

BULLETIN - NEW MEXICO BUREAU OF MINES & MINERAL RESOURCES (US/0096-4581) [06563064] **2135**

BULLETIN / NEW MEXICO STATE UNIVERSITY, AGRICULTURAL EXPERIMENT STATION (US/0149-9866) [03596640] **69**

BULLETIN (NEW SERIES) OF THE AMERICAN MATHEMATICAL SOCIETY (US/0273-0979) [04672985] **3498**

BULLETIN (NEW YORK STATE ARCHEOLOGICAL ASSOCIATION : 1987) (US/1046-2368) [17823564] **264**

BULLETIN - NEW YORK STATE MUSEUM (1976) (US/0278-3355) [05152333] **4086**

BULLETIN. (NEW YORK (STATE). OFFICE OF JUSTICE SYSTEMS ANALYSIS. BUREAU OF STATISTICAL SERVICES) (US) [18890976] **3159**

BULLETIN (NEW YORK STATE SCHOOL OF INDUSTRIAL AND LABOR RELATIONS) (US/0070-0134) [01565138] 1466, **1657**

BULLETIN - NEW ZEALAND, GEOLOGICAL SURVEY BRANCH *See* NEW ZEALAND GEOLOGICAL SURVEY BULLETIN **1389**

BULLETIN - NEW ZEALAND. SOIL BUREAU (NZ) [08967505] **165**

BULLETIN - NEW ZEALAND. SOIL BUREAU (NZ/0077-9644) [01760246] **69**

BULLETIN / NEWCASTLE AND HUNTER DISTRICT HISTORICAL SOCIETY *CEASED.* (AT) [16941714] **2669**

BULLETIN / NORGES GEOLOGISKE UNDERSKELSE (NO/0332-5768) [12019005] **1352**

BULLETIN - NORTH AMERICAN GLADIOLUS COUNCIL (US/0029-2370) [04090217] **505**

BULLETIN - NORTH CAROLINA, DEPARTMENT OF NATURAL RESOURCES AND COMMUNITY DEVELOPMENT, DIVISION OF LAND RESOURCES, GEOLOGICAL SURVEY SECTION (US/0270-5001) [06060835] **1370**

BULLETIN - NORTH CAROLINA MUSEUM OF ART *SUSPENDED.* (US/0029-2567) [02772671] 345, **4086**

BULLETIN - NORTH DAKOTA LEAGUE OF CITIES (US/0279-800X) [01695335] **4634**

BULLETIN - NORTHERN ARIZONA GENEALOGICAL SOCIETY (US/1070-8677) [22752889] **2440**

BULLETIN OAQ (CN/0822-6644) [10440958] **294**

BULLETIN OEPP (FR/0250-8052) [02920704] **165**

BULLETIN OF AGRICULTURAL PRICES (INDIA) (II/0445-5983) [01587966] 1466, **69**

BULLETIN OF AMERICAN GARDEN HISTORY, A (US/0897-0599) [14048752] **2411**

●BULLETIN OF AMERICAN ODONATOLOGY (US/1061-3781) [25278340] **5579**

BULLETIN OF ANIMAL HEALTH AND PRODUCTION IN AFRICA (KE/0378-9721) [02800979] 5506, **208**

BULLETIN OF ASIAN GEOGRAPHY (US/0732-2186) [03500090] **2557**

●BULLETIN OF ASIAN-PACIFIC ECONOMIC AND POLITICAL ISSUES (US) 4466, **1549**

BULLETIN OF BIBLIOGRAPHY (1979) (US/0190-745X) [04752631] **412**

BULLETIN OF CANADIAN PETROLEUM GEOLOGY (CN/0007-4802) [01537746] 1370, **4252**

BULLETIN OF CANADIAN WELFARE LAW (CN/0317-8021) [03210314] **5275**

BULLETIN OF CARNEGIE MUSEUM OF NATURAL HISTORY (US/0145-9058) [02805151] 264, **4164**

BULLETIN OF CENTRE FOR INFORMATICS (JA/0911-3622) [15099809] **3198**

BULLETIN OF COMPARATIVE LABOUR RELATIONS (NE/0770-3724) [05542209] **3145**

BULLETIN OF CONCERNED ASIAN SCHOLARS (US/0007-4810) [06740690] 4466, **2647**

BULLETIN OF CROP AND LIVESTOCK STATISTICS (TZ) [04348264] 165, 208, **152**

BULLETIN OF CZECHOSLOVAK LAW *CEASED.* (XR) [01537748] **2944**

BULLETIN OF DENTAL EDUCATION (US/0007-4837) [02258741] **1318**

BULLETIN OF DR. WILLIAMS'S LIBRARY (UK) [06668260] **4941**

BULLETIN OF EARTH SCIENCES (II) [01791133] **1352**

BULLETIN OF EASTERN CARIBBEAN AFFAIRS (BB) [03099419] **2511**

BULLETIN OF ECONOMIC RESEARCH (UK/0307-3378) [02445572] 1466, **1590**

BULLETIN OF ELECTROCHEMISTRY (II/0256-1654) [14340443] **1034**

BULLETIN OF ENDEMIC DISEASES (IQ/0007-4845) [03010718] 3712, **4769**

BULLETIN OF ENTOMOLOGICAL RESEARCH (UK/0007-4853) [01537749] **5606**

BULLETIN OF ENTOMOLOGY (II/0013-8762) [01537750] **5606**

BULLETIN OF ENVIRONMENTAL CONTAMINATION AND TOXICOLOGY (US/0007-4861) [01537751] 2225, **3979**

BULLETIN OF ETHIOPIAN MANUSCRIPTS (ET) [02537638] **412**

●BULLETIN OF EUROPEAN POLITICAL AND ECONOMIC ISSUES (US) 1549, **4466**

BULLETIN OF EXPERIMENTAL BIOLOGY AND MEDICINE (US/0007-4888) [02711392] 450, **3560**

BULLETIN OF FISHERY STATISTICS (IT) [16307405] **2298**

BULLETIN OF GRAIN TECHNOLOGY (II/0007-4896) [01537755] **200**

BULLETIN OF HAFFKINE INSTITUTE (II/0304-9515) [01216308] **3712**

BULLETIN OF HERPETOLOGY *See* HERPETOFAUNA **5585**

BULLETIN OF HIGHER EDUCATION (II) [03367419] **1813**

BULLETIN OF HISPANIC STUDIES (UK/0007-490X) [04900237] **3271**

BULLETIN OF HISTORICAL RESEARCH IN MUSIC EDUCATION, THE (US/0739-5639) [08292873] **4106**

BULLETIN OF HUMAN RIGHTS (SZ) [05666829] **4505**

BULLETIN OF INDONESIAN ECONOMIC STUDIES (AT/0007-4918) [02291792] **1466**

BULLETIN OF INFORMATICS AND CYBERNETICS (JA/0286-522X) [08986159] **1250**

BULLETIN OF INFORMATION ON CURRENT RESEARCH ON HUMAN SCIENCES CONCERNING AFRICA. BULLETIN D'INFORMATION SUR LES RECHERCHES DANS LES SCIENCES HUMAINES CONCERNANT L'AFRIQUE (BE) [05267820] **5194**

BULLETIN OF INFORMATION - REGIONAL CENTRE FOR BOOK PROMOTION IN AFRICA (CM) [05521775] **4827**

●BULLETIN OF INTERNATIONAL TRADE ISSUES (US) **825**

BULLETIN OF IRANIAN MATHEMATICAL SOCIETY (IR/1018-6301) [I10186301] **3498**

BULLETIN OF JAPANESE SOCIETY OF PHYCOLOGY, THE (JA) [03820399] **4295**

BULLETIN OF JUDAEO-GREEK STUDIES (UK/0954-1179) [17345920] 2612, **5046**

BULLETIN OF LABOUR STATISTICS (SZ/0007-4950) [01537758] 1657, **1530**

BULLETIN OF LATIN AMERICAN RESEARCH (UK/0261-3050) [08228597] **2725**

BULLETIN OF LAW, SCIENCE & TECHNOLOGY (US/0362-3769) [02135067] 5091, **2944**

BULLETIN OF LEGAL DEVELOPMENTS (UK/0007-4969) [01537759] **3125**

BULLETIN OF MAGNETIC RESONANCE (US/0163-559X) [04415485] **4443**

BULLETIN OF MARINE SCIENCE (US/0007-4977) [05516608] **1447**

BULLETIN OF MATERIALS SCIENCE (II/0250-4707) [07821397] **5091**

BULLETIN OF MATHEMATICAL BIOLOGY (US/0092-8240) [02241208] **450**

BULLETIN OF MECHANICAL ENGINEERING LABORATORY (JA/0374-2725) [01792027] **2111**

BULLETIN OF MEDICAL ETHICS (UK) [23273791] 3560, **2249**

BULLETIN OF MEDIEVAL CANON LAW (US/0146-2989) [01537764] **2944**

BULLETIN OF MOLECULAR BIOLOGY AND MEDICINE (IT/0391-481X) [03582637] **560**

BULLETIN OF MONUMENTAL BRASS SOCIETY (UK/0306-1612) [I03061612] **264**

BULLETIN OF NEW ZEALAND ART HISTORY (NZ/0110-4888) [25110194] **345**

BULLETIN OF NICCA / NICARAGUAN CENTER FOR COMMUNITY ACTION (US) [21261994] **2816**

BULLETIN OF NRLM (JA/0368-6051) [08959079] **4029**

BULLETIN OF NUMBER THEORY AND RELATED TOPICS. BOLETIN DE TEORIA DE NUMEROS Y TEMAS CONEXOS (AG) [04911859] **3498**

BULLETIN OF OCCUPATIONAL EDUCATION (US) [03013172] **1911**

BULLETIN OF OUTSTANDING ACQUISITIONS OF THE METROPOLITAN TORONTO CENTRAL LIBRARY (CN/0383-2791) [03258780] **3198**

BULLETIN OF PALEOMALACOLOGY *CEASED.* (US/0897-2451) [17435563] **4226**

BULLETIN OF PEACE PROPOSALS (NO/0007-5035) [01537766] **4466**

BULLETIN OF PHARMACEUTICAL SCIENCES (UA) **4295**

BULLETIN OF PHARMACY (TU/0367-0236) [09348537] **4295**

BULLETIN OF PHYSICAL EDUCATION (UK/0521-0011) [01537133] **1855**

BULLETIN OF POSTGRADUATE INSTITUTE OF MEDICAL EDUCATION AND RESEARCH, CHANDIGARH (II/0302-2404) [02683131] **3560**

BULLETIN OF PRECISION AND INTELLIGENCE LABORATORY (JA/0916-8311) [26666175] **3476**

BULLETIN OF PROCEEDINGS - CANADA. SUPREME COURT (CN/1193-8536) [I11938536] **2944**

BULLETIN OF PROCEEDINGS IN ... - NSW INSTITUTE FOR EDUCATIONAL RESEARCH (AT/0728-7186) [I07287186] **1729**

BULLETIN OF PROCEEDINGS TAKEN IN THE SUPREME COURT OF CANADA *See* BULLETIN OF PROCEEDINGS - CANADA. SUPREME COURT **2944**

BULLETIN OF PROCEEDINGS TAKEN IN THE SUPREME COURT OF CANADA (CN/0384-2487) [03216449] **2944**

BULLETIN OF PURE & APLIED SIENCES. SEC. F, GEOLOGY (II/0970-4639) [21271812] **1370**

BULLETIN OF PURE & APPLIED SCIENCES. SEC. D, PHYSICS (II) [21271805] **4399**

BULLETIN OF PURE & APPLIED SCIENCES. SEC. E, MATHEMATICS (II/0970-6577) [21271746] **3498**

BULLETIN Alphabetical Title Index

BULLETIN OF PURE & APPLIED SCIENCES. SECTION A, ANIMAL SCIENCE (II/0970-0765) [12020241] **5579**

BULLETIN OF PURE & APPLIED SCIENCES. SECTION B, PLANT SCIENCES (II) [12020225] **505**

BULLETIN OF PURE & APPLIED SCIENCES. SECTION C, CHEMISTRY (II) [27923252] **963**

BULLETIN OF QUANTITATIVE AND COMPUTER METHODS IN SOUTH ASIAN STUDIES (UK/0301-9330) [02713929] **2647**

BULLETIN OF RADIATION PROTECTION (II/0253-6897) [09176554] **4399**

BULLETIN OF REHABILITATION COUNSELING *See* REHABILITATION COUNSELING BULLETIN **1884**

BULLETIN OF RESEARCH IN MUSIC EDUCATION *See* PMEA NEWS **4146**

BULLETIN OF RESEARCH IN THE HUMANITIES *See* BIBLION (NEW YORK, N.Y.) **2843**

BULLETIN OF RESEARCH THESES AND DISSERTATIONS (II) [13650036] **1729**

BULLETIN OF SCIENCE, TECHNOLOGY & SOCIETY (US/0270-4676) [06427579] **5091**

BULLETIN ... OF SEISMICITY OF THE SOUTHEASTERN UNITED STATES (US/0270-8329) [04575498] **1403**

BULLETIN OF SELENIUM-TELLURIUM, THE (US/0582-5063) [08841246] **2135**

BULLETIN OF STATISTICS ON WORLD TRADE IN ENGINEERING PRODUCTS (US/0084-8174) [01486967] **2002**

BULLETIN OF STATISTICS RELATING TO THE MINING INDUSTRY OF MALAYSIA (MY) [01792673] 2135, **2002**

●BULLETIN OF TALL TIMBERS RESEARCH, INC (US) [26187068] 2212, **2376**

BULLETIN OF TANZANIAN AFFAIRS (UK/0952-2948) [04842268] **2638**

BULLETIN OF TAU BETA PI, THE (US/8755-5670) [11347591] **5229**

BULLETIN OF TEACHING & LEARNING *See* TEACHING & LEARNING BULLETIN **1906**

BULLETIN OF THE 8TH DISTRICT DENTAL SOCIETY (US/0190-0277) [04588719] **1318**

BULLETIN OF THE ABERDEEN UNIVERSITY AFRICAN STUDIES GROUP (UK/0001-3196) [04680951] **2638**

BULLETIN OF THE ACADEMY OF MEDICINE, TORONTO (CN/0001-4311) [01375747] **3560**

BULLETIN OF THE ACADEMY OF SCIENCES OF THE USSR, DIVISION OF CHEMICAL SCIENCE *See* BULLETIN OF THE RUSSIAN ACADEMY OF SCIENCES, DIVISION OF CHEMICAL SCIENCE **963**

BULLETIN OF THE ACADEMY OF SCIENCES OF THE USSR. PHYSICAL SERIES *See* BULLETIN OF THE RUSSIAN ACADEMY OF SCIENCES. PHYSICS **4399**

BULLETIN OF THE AGRICULTURAL EXPERIMENT STATION OF THE LOUISIANA STATE UNIVERSITY AND A & M COLLEGE (US/0096-7874) [03636030] **69**

BULLETIN OF THE ALLAHABAD MATHEMATICAL SOCIETY (II) [25544672] **3498**

BULLETIN OF THE ALLYN MUSEUM (US/0097-3211) [01451276] 5579, **4086**

BULLETIN OF THE AMATEUR ENTOMOLOGISTS' SOCIETY, THE (UK/0266-836X) [03550343] **5606**

BULLETIN OF THE AMERICAN ACADEMY OF PSYCHIATRY AND THE LAW (US/0091-634X) [01787774] 2944, **3922**

BULLETIN OF THE AMERICAN COLLEGE OF SURGEONS (US/0002-8045) [01479682] **3961**

BULLETIN OF THE AMERICAN DAHLIA SOCIETY, INC (US/0002-8150) [01479748] **2411**

BULLETIN OF THE AMERICAN HISTORICAL COLLECTION (PH) [03138864] 431, **2725**

BULLETIN OF THE AMERICAN HISTORICAL COLLECTION (PH/0115-3226) [02743124] **2647**

BULLETIN OF THE AMERICAN IRIS SOCIETY (US/0747-4172) [01480087] **2411**

BULLETIN OF THE AMERICAN METEOROLOGICAL SOCIETY (US/0003-0007) [01480420] **1421**

BULLETIN OF THE AMERICAN MUSEUM OF NATURAL HISTORY (US/0003-0090) [01287364] **4164**

BULLETIN OF THE AMERICAN PENSTEMON SOCIETY (US/0065-9584) [05259757] **2411**

BULLETIN OF THE AMERICAN PHYSICAL SOCIETY (US/0003-0503) [01376201] **4399**

BULLETIN OF THE AMERICAN ROCK GARDEN SOCIETY (US/0003-0864) [02444751] **2411**

BULLETIN OF THE AMERICAN SCHOOLS OF ORIENTAL RESEARCH (US/0003-097X) [05748058] **264**

BULLETIN OF THE AMERICAN SOCIETY FOR INFORMATION SCIENCE (US/0095-4403) [01796756] **3198**

BULLETIN OF THE AMERICAN SOCIETY OF NEWSPAPER EDITORS, THE (US/0003-1178) [04042765] **2917**

BULLETIN OF THE AMERICAN SOCIETY OF PAPYROLOGISTS, THE (US/0003-1186) [01994479] **264**

BULLETIN OF THE ANCIENT ORIENT MUSEUM (JA) [08338946] 264, **4086**

BULLETIN OF THE ANGLO-ISRAEL ARCHAEOLOGICAL SOCIETY (UK/0266-2442) [11892009] **264**

BULLETIN OF THE ANNA FREUD CENTRE (UK/0267-3061) [13139244] **3922**

BULLETIN OF THE ANTIQUE AUTOMOBILE CLUB OF AMERICA *See* ANTIQUE AUTOMOBILE, THE **5404**

BULLETIN OF THE ARCHAEOLOGICAL INSTITUTE OF AMERICA (US) [05503973] **264**

BULLETIN OF THE ARCHAEOLOGICAL SOCIETY OF CONNECTICUT (US/0739-5612) [01481820] 2612, **264**

BULLETIN OF THE ARCHAEOLOGICAL SOCIETY OF DELAWARE (US/0003-8067) [01481821] **264**

BULLETIN OF THE ARCHAEOLOGICAL SOCIETY OF NEW JERSEY (US/0196-8319) [01888318] 2257, **264**

BULLETIN OF THE ASIA INSTITUTE (US/0890-4464) [14252536] **2647**

BULLETIN OF THE ASSOCIATION FOR BUSINESS COMMUNICATION, THE (US/8756-1972) [11492251] 1890, **862**

BULLETIN OF THE ASSOCIATION OF BRITISH THEOLOGICAL AND PHILOSOPHICAL LIBRARIES (UK/0305-781X) [01589531] **3198**

BULLETIN OF THE ASSOCIATION OF COLLEGE UNIONS-INTERNATIONAL, THE (US/0004-5659) [05517020] **1861**

BULLETIN OF THE ASSOCIATION OF NORTH DAKOTA GEOGRAPHERS (US/0192-4281) [01518438] **2557**

BULLETIN OF THE ASTRONOMICAL SOCIETY OF INDIA (II/0304-9523) [02245932] 4399, **394**

BULLETIN OF THE ATOMIC SCIENTISTS (US/0096-3402) [01242732] 4517, **5091**

BULLETIN OF THE AUSTRALIAN LITTORAL SOCIETY (AT/0157-308X) [I0157308X] 5531, **2189**

BULLETIN OF THE AUSTRALIAN MATHEMATICAL SOCIETY (AT/0004-9727) [01518843] **3498**

BULLETIN OF THE AUSTRALIAN METEOROLOGICAL AND OCEANOGRAPHIC SOCIETY (AT/1035-6576) [I10356576] 1447, **1421**

BULLETIN OF THE AUSTRALIAN PSYCHOLOGICAL SOCIETY (AT) [07610961] **4579**

BULLETIN OF THE AUSTRALIAN SOCIETY OF LEGAL PHILOSOPHY (AT/0726-5239) [I07265239] **2945**

●BULLETIN OF THE BELGIAN MATHEMATICAL SOCIETY, SIMON STEVIN (BE) [30050995] **3498**

BULLETIN OF THE BIOLOGICAL SOCIETY OF WASHINGTON (US/0097-0298) [07890077] **4164**

BULLETIN OF THE BOTANICAL SURVEY OF INDIA (II/0006-8128) [01752752] **505**

BULLETIN OF THE BRACKISHWATER AQUACULTURE DEVELOPMENT CENTRE (IO/0126-1924) [06384768] **2298**

BULLETIN OF THE BRITISH MUSEUM (NATURAL HISTORY) BOTANY (UK/0068-2292) [06608510] **505**

BULLETIN OF THE BRITISH MUSEUM (NATURAL HISTORY). ENTOMOLOGY SERIES (UK/0524-6431) [08274129] **5606**

BULLETIN OF THE BRITISH MUSEUM (NATURAL HISTORY). GEOLOGY SERIES (UK) [10503220] 1370, **4164**

BULLETIN OF THE BRITISH MUSEUM (NATURAL HISTORY). HISTORICAL SERIES *CEASED*. (UK/0068-2306) [01330664] **4164**

BULLETIN OF THE BRITISH MUSEUM (NATURAL HISTORY). ZOOLOGY SERIES (UK/0007-1498) [08274157] **5579**

BULLETIN OF THE BRITISH ORNITHOLOGIST'S CLUB (UK/0007-1595) [08601562] **5616**

BULLETIN OF THE BUFFALO SOCIETY OF NATURAL SCIENCES (US/0096-4131) [01277606] **4164**

BULLETIN OF THE BUREAU OF EDUCATIONAL AND PSYCHOLOGICAL RESEARCH, CALCUTTA (II/0376-6675) [01784223] 1729, **4579**

BULLETIN OF THE CALCUTTA MATHEMATICAL SOCIETY (II/0008-0659) [01552345] **3498**

BULLETIN OF THE CALCUTTA SCHOOL OF TROPICAL MEDICINE (II/0068-5372) [01380677] **3985**

BULLETIN OF THE CALIFORNIA INSECT SURVEY (US/0068-5631) [01330693] **5606**

BULLETIN OF THE CALIFORNIA NATIVE PLANT SOCIETY (US/1046-1442) [05168059] **505**

BULLETIN OF THE CANADIAN BIOCHEMICAL SOCIETY (CN/0008-302X) [01844476] **484**

●BULLETIN OF THE CANADIAN SOCIETY OF BIOCHEMISTRY AND MOLECULAR BIOLOGY (CN/1197-6578) [27995265] **484**

BULLETIN OF THE CAPE CODE GENEALOGICAL SOCIETY *See* BULLETIN / CAPE COD GENEALOGICAL SOCIETY **2440**

BULLETIN OF THE CENTER FOR CHILDREN'S BOOKS (US/0008-9036) [04123300] 1060, **3370**

BULLETIN OF THE CENTRE FOR TASMANIAN HISTORICAL STUDIES (AT/0816-6617) [17889489] **2612**

BULLETIN OF THE CHEMICAL SOCIETY OF ETHIOPIA (ET/1011-3924) [I10113924] **1021**

BULLETIN OF THE CHEMICAL SOCIETY OF JAPAN (JA/0009-2673) [01760395] **963**

BULLETIN OF THE CHICAGO ACADEMY OF SCIENCES (US/0009-3491) [01238712] **5091**

BULLETIN OF THE CHRISTIAN INSTITUTE OF SIKH STUDIES (II/0254-9182) [03822582] **4941**

BULLETIN OF THE CLEVELAND MUSEUM OF ART, THE *CEASED*. (US/0009-8841) [01554906] 4086, **345**

BULLETIN OF THE COMEDIANTES (US/0007-5108) [02574675] **3370**

BULLETIN OF THE CONGREGATIONAL LIBRARY (US/0010-5821) [01537775] 4941, **3198**

BULLETIN OF THE CORTLAND COUNTY HISTORICAL SOCIETY (US) [09091722] **2725**

BULLETIN OF THE CRIMINOLOGICAL RESEARCH DEPARTMENT (JA) [01783739] **3159**

BULLETIN OF THE DEPARTMENT OF ANTHROPOLOGY, DIBRUGARH UNIVERSITY, THE (II) [04536399] **233**

BULLETIN OF THE DEPARTMENT OF GEOGRAPHY, UNIVERSITY OF TOKYO (JA/0082-478X) [03624538] **2557**

BULLETIN OF THE DEPARTMENT OF INTERNATIONAL AFFAIRS, AFL-CIO, THE (US/0890-6165) [14349602] 1657, **4517**

BULLETIN OF THE DEPARTMENT OF MARINE SCIENCES (II/0970-9878) [02246650] **553**

BULLETIN OF THE DETROIT INSTITUTE OF ARTS (US/0011-9636) [01566317] **345**

BULLETIN OF THE DISASTER PREVENTION RESEARCH INSTITUTE (JA/0454-7675) [01782989] **2019**

BULLETIN OF THE EARTHQUAKE RESEARCH INSTITUTE, UNIVERSITY OF TOKYO (JA) [02268603] **1403**

BULLETIN OF THE EARTHQUAKE RESISTANT STRUCTURE RESEARCH CENTER (JA) **1967**

BULLETIN OF THE ECOLOGICAL SOCIETY OF AMERICA (US/0012-9623) [01380772] **2212**

BULLETIN OF THE EGYPTOLOGICAL SEMINAR (US/0270-210X) [06166120] 2638, **264**

BULLETIN OF THE ENTOMOLOGICAL SOCIETY OF EGYPT. ECONOMIC SERIES (UA/0081-0991) [03130590] **5579**

BULLETIN OF THE ESSEX COUNTY MEDICAL SOCIETY, THE (US/0014-0937) [01380827] **3560**

BULLETIN OF THE EUROPEAN ASSOCIATION FOR JAPANESE STUDIES (UK) [03993377] **2502**

BULLETIN OF THE EUROPEAN ASSOCIATION FOR THEORETICAL COMPUTER SCIENCE (NE/0252-9742) [15234980] **1172**

BULLETIN OF THE EUROPEAN ASSOCIATION OF FISH PATHOLOGISTS (NE/0108-0288) [11036305] **2298**

BULLETIN OF THE EUROPEAN COMMUNITIES (BE/0378-3693) [01537777] **4634**

BULLETIN OF THE EUROPEAN COMMUNITIES. SUPPLEMENT (LU) [06260951] **4635**

●BULLETIN OF THE EUROPEAN UNION. SUPPLEMENT (LU) [30684514] **4635**

BULLETIN OF THE EVANGELICAL PHILOSOPHICAL SOCIETY (US) [08104860] 4941, **4343**

BULLETIN OF THE FACULTY OF EARTH SCIENCES (SA/1012-8832) [09287034] **1352**

BULLETIN OF THE FACULTY OF ENGINEERING, YOKOHAMA NATIONAL UNIVERSITY (JA/0513-2592) [04269178] **1967**

BULLETIN OF THE FACULTY OF PHARMACY (UA/0575-1373) [01380880] **4295**

BULLETIN OF THE FACULTY OF SCIENCE, ASSIUT UNIVERSITY (UA/0366-4740) [02130491] **5091**

BULLETIN OF THE FACULTY OF SCIENCE, IBARAKI UNIVERSITY. SERIES A : MATHEMATICS (JA) [02698874] **3498**

BULLETIN OF THE FIJI MUSEUM (FJ) [09138335] **4086**

BULLETIN OF THE FLORIDA MUSEUM OF NATURAL HISTORY. BIOLOGICAL SCIENCES (US/1052-3669) [21934045] 4086, **4164**

BULLETIN OF THE FOLKLORE STUDIES ASSOCIATION OF CANADA (CN/0705-1115) [03963463] **2318**

BULLETIN OF THE FRIENDS OF JADE, THE (US/0261-7080) [07943385] **370**

BULLETIN OF THE FRIENDS OF THE OWEN D. YOUNG LIBRARY (US/0734-2012) [08673186] **3198**

BULLETIN OF THE FRUIT TREE RESEARCH STATION. SERIES B. (OKITSU) (JA) [02254573] 165, **69**

BULLETIN OF THE GENERAL THEOLOGICAL CENTER OF MAINE (US/1052-8202) [19506521] **4941**

BULLETIN OF THE GEOGRAPHICAL SURVEY INSTITUTE (JA) [04747844] **2557**

BULLETIN OF THE GEOLOGICAL INSTITUTIONS OF THE UNIVERSITY OF UPPSALA (SW/0302-2749) [10321597] **1370**

BULLETIN OF THE GEOLOGICAL, MINING AND METALLURGICAL SOCIETY OF INDIA (II/0016-7576) [01570680] **1370**

BULLETIN OF THE GEOLOGICAL SOCIETY OF DENMARK (DK/0011-6297) [01570701] **1370**

BULLETIN OF THE GEOLOGICAL SOCIETY OF FINLAND (FI/0367-5211) [03107329] **1370**

BULLETIN OF THE GEORGIA HERPETOLOGICAL SOCIETY (US/0363-2172) [02384435] **5579**

BULLETIN OF THE GHANA GEOGRAPHICAL ASSOCIATION (GH/0016-9536) [01455461] **2557**

BULLETIN OF THE GLOBAL VOLCANISM NETWORK (US/1050-4818) [21208475] **1352**

BULLETIN OF THE GLOUCESTER COUNTY HISTORICAL SOCIETY (US/0887-5413) [05973894] 2440, **2725**

BULLETIN OF THE GUILD OF CARILLONNEURS IN NORTH AMERICA (US/0827-5955) [04760537] **4106**

BULLETIN OF THE HEGEL SOCIETY OF GREAT BRITAIN, THE (UK/0263-5232) [08231086] **4343**

BULLETIN OF THE HENRY MARTYN INSTITUTE OF ISLAMIC STUDIES (HYDERABAD, INDIA) (II) [16503293] **5042**

BULLETIN OF THE HIGH INSTITUTE OF PUBLIC HEALTH, THE (UA/0379-7988) [04256539] **4769**

BULLETIN OF THE HIROSHIMA AGRICULTURAL COLLEGE (JA/0440-8772) [03325176] **69**

BULLETIN OF THE HISTORICAL SOCIETY OF MONTGOMERY COUNTY, PENNSYLVANIA (US/0362-8590) [01681070] **2725**

BULLETIN OF THE HISTORY OF DENTISTRY (US/0007-5132) [01537778] **1318**

BULLETIN OF THE HISTORY OF MEDICINE (US/0007-5140) [01537779] **3560**

BULLETIN OF THE HOSPITAL FOR JOINT DISEASES ORTHOPAEDIC INSTITUTE See BULLETIN / HOSPITAL FOR JOINT DISEASES **3804**

BULLETIN OF THE HOUSTON GEOLOGICAL SOCIETY, THE (US/0018-6686) [02922938] **1370**

BULLETIN OF THE HUNT INSTITUTE FOR BOTANICAL DOCUMENTATION (US/0192-3641) [05014784] **505**

BULLETIN OF THE ILLINOIS STATE FLORISTS' ASSOCIATION (US) [05880501] **2434**

BULLETIN OF THE IMPERIAL EARTHQUAKE INVESTIGATION COMMITTEE See BULLETIN OF THE EARTHQUAKE RESEARCH INSTITUTE, UNIVERSITY OF TOKYO **1403**

BULLETIN OF THE INDIAN INSTITUTE OF HISTORY OF MEDICINE (II/0304-9558) [01612737] **3560**

BULLETIN OF THE INDIAN SOCIETY OF EARTHQUAKE TECHNOLOGY (II) [07706445] **1403**

BULLETIN OF THE INDIAN VACUUM SOCIETY (II/0970-2334) [25194990] **4399**

BULLETIN OF THE INSTITUTE FOR CHEMICAL RESEARCH, KYOTO UNIVERSITY (JA/0023-6071) [01755349] **963**

BULLETIN OF THE INSTITUTE FOR CONTINUING DENTAL EDUCATION OF THE QUEENS COUNTY DENTAL SOCIETY (US/0739-1773) [09716374] **1318**

BULLETIN OF THE INSTITUTE OF ARCHAEOLOGY / UNIVERSITY OF LONDON, INSTITUTE OF ARCHAEOLOGY (UK/0076-0722) [02212200] **264**

BULLETIN OF THE INSTITUTE OF CHEMISTRY. ACADEMIA SINICA (CH/0366-0370) [03145892] **963**

BULLETIN OF THE INSTITUTE OF COMBINATORICS AND ITS APPLICATIONS (CN/1183-1278) [25586422] **3498**

BULLETIN OF THE INSTITUTE OF EARTH SCIENCES, ACADEMIA SINICA (CH/0258-0314) [09848951] **1352**

BULLETIN OF THE INSTITUTE OF MARITIME AND TROPICAL MEDICINE IN GDYNIA (PL/0324-8542) [01950675] **3985**

BULLETIN OF THE INSTITUTE OF MATHEMATICS, ACADEMIA SINICA (CH/0304-9825) [02441394] **3498**

BULLETIN OF THE INSTITUTE OF POST GRADUATE MEDICAL EDUCATION AND RESEARCH (II/0575-1772) [01552343] **3560**

BULLETIN OF THE INSTITUTE OF TRADITIONAL CULTURES (II/0541-7562) [01714048] **5194**

BULLETIN OF THE INSTITUTE OF TROPICAL AGRICULTURE, KYUSHU UNIVERSITY (JA/0915-499X) [I0915499X] **69**

BULLETIN OF THE INSTITUTE OF ZOOLOGY, ACADEMIA SINICA See ZOOLOGICAL STUDIES **5602**

BULLETIN OF THE INSTITUTE OF ZOOLOGY, ACADEMIA SINICA See ZOOLOGICAL RECORD **5601**

BULLETIN OF THE INSTITUTION OF ENGINEERS (INDIA) (II/0020-3343) [01753269] **2037**

BULLETIN OF THE INTERNATIONAL ASSOCIATION FOR SHELL AND SPATIAL STRUCTURES (SP/0304-3622) [02262488] **605**

BULLETIN OF THE INTERNATIONAL ASSOCIATION OF ENGINEERING GEOLOGY (GW/0074-1612) [01779784] **2019**

BULLETIN OF THE INTERNATIONAL CENTRE FOR HEAT AND MASS TRANSFER *CEASED.* (US/0888-6911) [13691995] 2008, **2111**

BULLETIN OF THE INTERNATIONAL COMMITTEE ON URGENT ANTHROPOLOGICAL AND ETHNOLOGICAL RESEARCH (AU/0538-5865) [02447750] **233**

BULLETIN OF THE INTERNATIONAL COUNCIL FOR BIRD PRESERVATION (UK) [01424354] 5616, **2189**

BULLETIN OF THE INTERNATIONAL COUNCIL FOR TRADITIONAL MUSIC (US/0739-1390) [08046680] **4106**

BULLETIN OF THE INTERNATIONAL GROUP FOR THE STUDY OF MIMOSOIDEAE (FR) [16152510] **2411**

BULLETIN OF THE INTERNATIONAL INSTITUTE OF SEISMOLOGY AND EARTHQUAKE ENGINEERING (JA/0074-655X) [06201178] **1403**

BULLETIN OF THE INTERNATIONAL ORGANIZATION FOR SEPTUAGINT AND COGNITE STUDIES (US/0145-3890) [01714866] **5046**

BULLETIN OF THE INTERNATIONAL PEAT SOCIETY (FI/0355-1008) [09965516] **1934**

BULLETIN OF THE INTERNATIONAL PEDIATRIC ASSOCIATION *SUSPENDED.* (FR/0245-9337) [02949775] **3901**

BULLETIN OF THE INTERNATIONAL SEISMOLOGICAL CENTRE (UK/0020-8671) [04029396] **1403**

BULLETIN OF THE INTERNATIONAL SOCIETY OF SOIL SCIENCE. BULLETIN DE L'ASSOCIATION INTERNATIONALE DE LA SCIENCE DU SOL. MITTEILUNGEN DER INTERNATIONALEN BODENKUNDLICHEN GESELLSCHAFT (IT/0020-8760) [01695795] **165**

BULLETIN OF THE INTERNATIONAL STATISTICAL INSTITUTE (GW/0074-8609) [01604594] **5324**

BULLETIN OF THE INTERNATIONAL TEST COMMISSION AND OF THE DIVISION OF PSYCHOLOGICAL ASSESSMENT OF THE IAAP (FR/1013-9974) [11609412] **4579**

BULLETIN OF THE INTERNATIONAL UNION AGAINST TUBERCULOSIS AND LUNG DISEASE See TUBERCLE AND LUNG DISEASE : THE OFFICIAL JOURNAL OF THE INTERNATIONAL UNION AGAINST TUBERCULOSIS AND LUNG DISEASE **3952**

BULLETIN OF THE IRISH GEORGIAN SOCIETY (IE) [11947474] **2514**

BULLETIN OF THE JAPANESE SOCIETY OF SCIENTIFIC FISHERIES (JA) 553, **2298**

BULLETIN OF THE JEWISH HISTORICAL SOCIETY OF ENGLAND (UK) [10794693] **5046**

BULLETIN OF THE JOHN RYLANDS UNIVERSITY LIBRARY OF MANCHESTER (UK/0301-102X) [01780973] **2843**

BULLETIN OF THE KANAGAWA DENTAL COLLEGE (JA/0385-1443) [07910533] **1318**

BULLETIN OF THE KOHNO CLINICAL MEDICINE RESEARCH INSTITUTE (JA) [18976168] **3560**

BULLETIN OF THE KOREAN CHEMICAL SOCIETY (KO/0253-2964) [08704850] 5091, **963**

BULLETIN OF THE KOREAN MATHEMATICAL SOCIETY (KO/1015-8634) [I10158634] **3498**

BULLETIN OF THE KOREAN RESEARCH CENTER See JOURNAL OF SOCIAL SCIENCES AND HUMANITIES (SEOUL) **2849**

BULLETIN OF THE KYUSHU UNIVERSITY FORESTS (JA) [01755363] **2376**

●BULLETIN OF THE LEBEDEV PHYSICS INSTITUTE (US/1068-3356) [27352022] **4399**

BULLETIN OF THE LONDON MATHEMATICAL SOCIETY, THE (UK/0024-6093) [01638894] **3498**

BULLETIN OF THE LOUDOUN COUNTY HISTORICAL SOCIETY, INC (US/0458-3108) [02243595] **2725**

BULLETIN OF THE MALAYSIAN MATHEMATICAL SOCIETY (MY/0126-6705) [02246020] **3498**

BULLETIN OF THE MARINE ENGINEERING SOCIETY IN JAPAN (JA/0388-0079) [08940683] **1967**

BULLETIN OF THE MARINE PARK RESEARCH STATIONS (JA) [02510063] **553**

BULLETIN OF THE MARX MEMORIAL LIBRARY - LONDON (UK) [10080378] **4540**

BULLETIN OF THE MARYLAND HERPETOLOGICAL SOCIETY (US/0025-4231) [01455250] **5579**

BULLETIN OF THE MASSACHUSETTS ARCHAEOLOGICAL SOCIETY (US/0148-1886) [01756815] **264**

BULLETIN OF THE MATHEMATICAL ASSOCIATION OF INDIA (II/0025-5556) [10085046] **3499**

BULLETIN OF THE MEDICAL LIBRARY ASSOCIATION (US/0025-7338) [01756998] **3198**

BULLETIN OF THE MEDICAL STAFF OF THE METHODIST HOSPITALS OF DALLAS (US/0045-9550) [02721307] **3777**

BULLETIN OF THE MENNINGER CLINIC (US/0025-9284) [01624125] **3922**

BULLETIN OF THE MICHIGAN DENTAL HYGIENISTS' ASSOCIATION, THE (US/0746-5564) [06819278] **1318**

BULLETIN OF THE MINERAL RESEARCH AND EXPLORATION (TU) [18619681] 1438, **2135**

BULLETIN OF THE MODERN GREEK STUDIES ASSOCIATION (US/0047-7702) [06571367] **2681**

BULLETIN OF THE MUSEUM OF COMPARATIVE ZOOLOGY (US/0027-4100) [01641426] **5579**

BULLETIN OF THE NATIONAL BRAILLE ASSOCIATION, INC (US/0550-5666) [01799005] 4385, **1876**

BULLETIN OF THE NATIONAL GALLERY IN PRAGUE (XR/0862-8912) [27049834] **345**

BULLETIN OF THE NATIONAL GEOPHYSICAL RESEARCH INSTITUTE See ORGANISATION DE L'ENSEIGNEMENT EN FRANCE, L' **1868**

BULLETIN OF THE NATIONAL GUILD OF CATHOLIC PSYCHIATRISTS, INC, THE *SUSPENDED.* (US/0547-7115) [01796798] 5025, **3922**

BULLETIN OF THE NATIONAL SCIENCE MUSEUM. SERIES A, ZOOLOGY (JA/0385-2423) [09425012] **5579**

BULLETIN OF THE NATIONAL SCIENCE MUSEUM. SERIES B, BOTANY (JA/0385-2431) [02376342] **505**

BULLETIN — Alphabetical Title Index

BULLETIN OF THE NATIONAL SCIENCE MUSEUM. SERIES D, ANTHROPOLOGY (JA/0385-3039) [02739060] **233**

BULLETIN OF THE NATIONAL SCIENCE MUSEUM. SERIES E, (PHYSICAL SCIENCES & ENGINEERING) (JA/0387-8511) [08136101] **5091**

BULLETIN OF THE NATIONAL UNIVERSITIES COMMISSION (NR) [04015868] **1813**

● BULLETIN OF THE NATURAL HISTORY MUSEUM. BOTANY SERIES (UK/0968-0446) [28434157] **505**

● BULLETIN OF THE NATURAL HISTORY MUSEUM. ENTOMOLOGY SERIES (UK/0968-0454) [28624498] **5606**

● BULLETIN OF THE NATURAL HISTORY MUSEUM. GEOLOGY SERIES (UK/0968-0462) [28434155] **1370**

● BULLETIN OF THE NATURAL HISTORY MUSEUM. ZOOLOGY SERIES (UK/0968-0470) [28624665] **5579**

BULLETIN OF THE NEEDLE AND BOBBIN CLUB, THE **SUSPENDED.** (US/0273-0197) [01642417] **5183**

BULLETIN OF THE NEW YORK ACADEMY OF MEDICINE (1925) (US/0028-7091) [03776029] **3560**

BULLETIN OF THE NEW ZEALAND NATIONAL SOCIETY FOR EARTHQUAKE ENGINEERING (NZ/0110-0718) [02240743] **2019**

BULLETIN OF THE NFGS (UK) [17396388] **5316**

BULLETIN OF THE NIIGATA AIRGLOW OBSERVATORY (JA/0388-0125) [01795814] **1421**

BULLETIN OF THE NINTH DISTRICT DENTAL SOCIETY (US/0070-3710) [11498829] **1318**

BULLETIN OF THE NUTRITION FOUNDATION OF THE PHILIPPINES (PH) [08366547] **4188**

BULLETIN OF THE NUTRITION INSTITUTE OF THE UNITED ARAB REPUBLIC (UA/0366-1393) [I03661393] **4188**

BULLETIN OF THE OCEAN RESEARCH INSTITUTE, UNIVERSITY OF TOKYO (JA/0564-6898) [01167316] **1447**

BULLETIN OF THE OCMA, THE (US/0199-7378) [06118242] **3560**

BULLETIN OF THE OHIO BIOLOGICAL SURVEY (US/0078-3994) [09693280] **450**

BULLETIN OF THE OIL AND NATURAL GAS COMMISSION (II/0537-0094) [06157922] **4252**

BULLETIN OF THE OKLAHOMA ANTHROPOLOGICAL SOCIETY (US/0078-432X) [04303466] 2257, **233**

BULLETIN OF THE ORANGE COUNTY MEDICAL ASSOCIATION **See** BULLETIN OF THE OCMA, THE **3560**

BULLETIN OF THE ORIENTAL CERAMIC SOCIETY OF HONG KONG, THE (HK) [02735450] **2586**

BULLETIN OF THE OSAKA MEDICAL COLLEGE (JA) [20626668] **3560**

BULLETIN OF THE PAN AMERICAN HEALTH ORGANIZATION (US/0301-5750) [01778334] **4769**

BULLETIN OF THE PEAK DISTRICT MINES HISTORICAL SOCIETY (UK/0031-3637) [06687259] **2135**

BULLETIN OF THE PERMANENT INTERNATIONAL ASSOCIATION OF NAVIGATION CONGRESSES (BE/0374-1001) [01643427] 4175, **2088**

BULLETIN OF THE PHILADELPHIA HERPETOLOGICAL SOCIETY **SUSPENDED.** (US/0553-9587) [10992630] **5579**

BULLETIN OF THE POLISH ACADEMY OF SCIENCES. BIOLOGY (PL/0239-751X) [13115575] **450**

BULLETIN OF THE POLISH ACADEMY OF SCIENCES. CHEMISTRY (PL/0239-7285) [10321472] **963**

BULLETIN OF THE POLISH ACADEMY OF SCIENCES. EARTH SCIENCES (PL/0239-7277) [10987488] **1352**

BULLETIN OF THE POLISH ACADEMY OF SCIENCES. MATHEMATICS (PL/0239-7269) [10010587] **3499**

BULLETIN OF THE POLISH ACADEMY OF SCIENCES. TECHNICAL SCIENCES (PL/0239-7528) [11454539] **5091**

BULLETIN OF THE POLONUS PHILATELIC SOCIETY (US/0477-4612) [10465110] **2784**

BULLETIN OF THE PRINCE OF WALES MUSEUM OF WESTERN INDIA (II/0523-9702) [01779586] **4086**

BULLETIN OF THE PSYCHONOMIC SOCIETY (US/0090-5054) [01788365] **4579**

BULLETIN OF THE RAMAKRISHNA MISSION INSTITUTE OF CULTURE (II/0033-9156) [01639690] **2843**

BULLETIN OF THE REED ORGAN SOCIETY, INC (US/0736-9549) [09266712] **4106**

BULLETIN OF THE RESEARCH LABORATORY FOR NUCLEAR REACTORS (JA/0387-6144) [I03876144] **2154**

BULLETIN OF THE ROYAL COLLEGE OF PATHOLOGISTS (UK/0959-972X) [I0959972X] **3893**

BULLETIN OF THE RUSSIAN ACADEMY OF SCIENCES, DIVISION OF CHEMICAL SCIENCE (US/1063-5211) [26049442] **963**

● BULLETIN OF THE RUSSIAN ACADEMY OF SCIENCES. PHYSICS (US/1062-8738) [25776353] **4399**

BULLETIN OF THE SCHOOL OF ORIENTAL AND AFRICAN STUDIES (UK/0041-977X) [07408456] **3271**

BULLETIN OF THE SCIENCE FICTION WRITERS OF AMERICA (US/0192-2424) [04973550] **3370**

BULLETIN OF THE SCOTTISH GEORGIAN SOCIETY (UK/0950-5644) [02069937] **294**

BULLETIN OF THE SCOTTISH INSTITUTE OF MISSIONARY STUDIES, THE (UK/0048-9778) [04788009] **4941**

BULLETIN OF THE SECTION OF LOGIC (PL) [12747050] **3499**

BULLETIN OF THE SEISMOGRAPHIC STATIONS (US/0041-9435) [12601043] **1403**

BULLETIN OF THE SEISMOLOGICAL SOCIETY OF AMERICA (US/0037-1106) [01604335] **1403**

BULLETIN OF THE SOCIETY FOR AFRICAN CHURCH HISTORY, THE **SUSPENDED.** (UK/0081-1297) [02639711] **4941**

BULLETIN OF THE SOCIETY FOR AMERICAN ARCHAEOLOGY (US/0741-5672) [09778309] **264**

BULLETIN OF THE SOCIETY FOR ITALIAN STUDIES **CEASED.** (UK/0264-2190) [07829080] **3271**

BULLETIN OF THE SOCIETY OF CARTOGRAPHERS, THE (UK) [23272081] **2581**

BULLETIN OF THE SOCIETY OF VECTOR ECOLOGISTS (US/0146-6429) [19284905] **2212**

BULLETIN OF THE SOUTHERN ASSOCIATION OF AFRICANISTS, THE (US/0164-0666) [04556684] **2638**

BULLETIN OF THE SOUTHERN CALIFORNIA PALEONTOLOGICAL SOCIETY (US/0160-4937) [03694844] **4226**

BULLETIN OF THE SUTTON HOO RESEARCH COMMITTEE **CEASED.** (UK/0953-6191) [12016665] **264**

BULLETIN OF THE TECHNICAL UNIVERSITY OF ISTANBUL (TU/0254-4121) [09776081] **5091**

BULLETIN OF THE TEXAS ARCHEOLOGICAL SOCIETY (US/0082-2930) [03126356] **264**

BULLETIN OF THE TEXAS ORNITHOLOGICAL SOCIETY (US/0040-4543) [04266153] **5616**

BULLETIN OF THE TOKYO INSTITUTE OF TECHNOLOGY (JA/0495-8020) [03319469] **5091**

BULLETIN OF THE TOKYO METROPOLITAN REHABILITATION CENTER FOR THE PHYSICALLY AND MENTALLY HANDICAPPED (JA/0388-0168) [I03880168] **1876**

BULLETIN OF THE TOKYO UNIVERSITY FORESTS (JA) [01767583] **2377**

BULLETIN OF THE TORREY BOTANICAL CLUB, THE (US/0040-9618) [01639180] 2212, **505**

BULLETIN OF THE TRIBAL RESEARCH AND DEVELOPMENT INSTITUTE BHOPAL (II) [01606780] **1549**

BULLETIN OF THE UNESCO PRINCIPAL REGIONAL OFFICE FOR ASIA AND THE PACIFIC **SUSPENDED.** (TH) [19603807] **1729**

BULLETIN OF THE UNESCO REGIONAL OFFICE OF SCIENCE AND TECHNOLOGY FOR AFRICA (KE/0304-9590) [01796017] **5091**

BULLETIN OF THE UNIVERSITY OF AGRICULTURAL SCIENCES, GODOLLO (HU/0237-8930) [17458907] **70**

BULLETIN OF THE UNIVERSITY OF NEBRASKA STATE MUSEUM (US/0093-6812) [01759563] 4086, **4164**

BULLETIN OF THE UNIVERSITY OF OSAKA PREFECTURE. SERIES B: AGRICULTURE AND BIOLOGY (JA/0366-3353) [01761541] **70**

BULLETIN OF THE VETERINARY INSTITUTE IN PUAWY (PL/0042-4870) [05914744] **5506**

BULLETIN OF THE WATAUGA ASSOCIATION OF GENEALOGISTS (US/0091-8857) [I00918857] **2440**

BULLETIN OF THE WEST-CENTRAL KENTUCKY FAMILY RESEARCH ASSOCIATION (US) **2440**

BULLETIN OF THE WEST VIRGINIA ASSOCIATION OF COLLEGE ENGLISH TEACHERS, THE (US/0887-4409) [03476082] **3370**

BULLETIN OF THE WHATCOM GENEALOGICAL SOCIETY (US/0748-2507) [04032173] **2440**

BULLETIN OF THE WORLD HEALTH ORGANIZATION (SZ/0042-9686) [01588496] 4769, **3560**

BULLETIN OF THE YAMAGUCHI MEDICAL SCHOOL (JA/0513-1812) [01590539] **3560**

BULLETIN OF THE ZOOLOGICAL SURVEY OF INDIA (II/0255-9587) [04356521] **5580**

BULLETIN OF TIBETOLOGY (II/0525-1516) [02163533] **2647**

BULLETIN OF TOKYO DENTAL COLLEGE, THE (JA/0040-8891) [01606749] **1318**

BULLETIN OF TOKYO MEDICAL AND DENTAL UNIVERSITY, THE (JA/0040-8921) [01589025] 1318, **3561**

BULLETIN OF UNIVERSITY OF OSAKA PREFECTURE. SERIES A : ENGINEERING AND NATURAL SCIENCES (JA/0474-7844) [04971051] **1967**

BULLETIN OF VOLCANOLOGY (GW/0258-8900) [13622617] **1403**

BULLETIN OF ZOOLOGICAL NOMENCLATURE, THE (UK/0007-5167) [01753468] **5580**

BULLETIN - OFFICE DE LA CONSTRUCTION DU QUEBEC (CN/0708-3912) [04526931] 606, **4635**

BULLETIN - OFFICE DES RECHERCHES SUR LES PECHERIES DU CANADA (CN) [02868815] 2298, **5580**

BULLETIN - OFFICE INTERNATIONAL DES EPIZOOTIES (PARIS) (FR/0300-9823) [01424965] **5506**

BULLETIN OFFICIEL (FR) [01791183] **4635**

BULLETIN OFFICIEL D'ANNONCES DES DOMAINES (FRANCE. MINISTERE DE L'ECONOMIC ET DES FINANCES : 20 JUIN 1981) (FR) [08937027] **4635**

BULLETIN OFFICIEL D'ANNONCES DES DOMAINES (FRANCE. MINISTERE DU BUDGET) **See** BULLETIN OFFICIEL D'ANNONCES DES DOMAINES (FRANCE. MINISTERE DE L'ECONOMIC ET DES FINANCES : 20 JUIN 1981) **4635**

BULLETIN OFFICIEL DE LA PROPRIETE INDUSTRIELLE BREVETS D'INVENTION ABREGES ET LISTES (FR/0750-7674) [09024674] 1302, **1310**

BULLETIN OFFICIEL DE LA PROPRIETE INDUSTRIELLE (PARIS, FRANCE) (FR) [04383612] **1302**

BULLETIN OFFICIEL DE LA PROPRIETE INDUSTRIELLE. TABLE PAR DENOMINATIONS DE MARQUES DE FABRIQUE, DE COMMERCE OU DE SERVICE **See** TABLE PAR DENOMINATIONS DE MARQUES DE FABRIQUE, DE COMMERCE OU DE SERVICE **5161**

BULLETIN OFFICIEL DE LA SOCIETE FRANCAISE DE PSYCHO-PROPHYLAXIE OBSTETRIQUE (FR) [01427424] **3758**

BULLETIN OFFICIEL DE LA SOCIETE INTERNATIONALE DE PSYCHO-PROPHYLAXIE OBSTETRICALE (FR/0037-9468) [01427445] **3758**

BULLETIN OFFICIEL DES AFFAIRES SOCIALES (FR) **5194**

BULLETIN OFFICIEL DES ANNONCES CIVILES ET COMMERCIALES (FR) [04512451] 825, **2945**

BULLETIN OFFICIEL DES ANNONCES COMMERCIALES **See** BULLETIN OFFICIEL DES ANNONCES CIVILES ET COMMERCIALES **2945**

BULLETIN OFFICIEL DES ANNONCES DES MARCHES PUBLICS (FR/0429-2944) [I04292944] **4635**

BULLETIN OFFICIEL DES ARMEES (FR) **4038**

BULLETIN OFFICIEL DES ASSURANCES / REPUBLIQUE FRANCAISE, MINISTERE DE L'ECONOMIE (FR) [07920689] 2876, **2945**

BULLETIN OFFICIEL DES DECORATIONS, MEDAILLES ET RECOMPENSES / REPUBLIQUE FRANCAISE (FR) [11691567] **4038**

BULLETIN OFFICIEL DES DOUANES (FR/0427-2129) [I04272129] **5378**

BULLETIN OFFICIEL DES IMPOTS (FR/0982-801X) [I0982801X] **825**

BULLETIN OFFICIEL DES IMPOTS / ACCORDS INTERNATIONAUX 132 (FR) **1633**

BULLETIN OFFICIEL DES IMPOTS / CONTROLE DE L'IMPOT 133 (FR) **1466**

BULLETIN OFFICIEL DES IMPOTS / FISCALITE DIRECTE DES ENTERPRISES 127 (FR) **1466**

BULLETIN OFFICIEL DES IMPOTS / FISCALITE DIRECTE DES PERSONNES 126 (FR) **1466**

BULLETIN

BULLETIN OFFICIEL DES IMPOTS / TAXE SUR LE CHIFFRE D'AFFAIRES 128 (FR) **1466**

BULLETIN OFFICIEL DES IMPOTS / TEXTES LEGAUX ET REGLEMENTAIRES 139 (FR) **1466**

BULLETIN OFFICIEL DES MINISTERES CHARGES DE L'EMPLOI ET DU TRAVAIL (FR) [09244402] **1657**

BULLETIN OFFICIEL DES SERVICES DU PREMIER MINISTRE (FR/0249-6046) [09711188] **4702**

BULLETIN OFFICIEL DU BIT. SERIES A (SZ) **1657**

BULLETIN OFFICIEL DU BIT. SERIES B (SZ) **1657**

BULLETIN OFFICIEL DU MINISTERE DE LA JUSTICE (FRANCE) (FR/0750-0416) [10595891] **2945**

BULLETIN OFFICIEL DU MINISTERE DE L'EDUCATION NATIONALE. NO SPECIAL : BO (FR/0291-6207) [10810009] **1729**

BULLETIN OFFICIEL DU MINISTERE DE L'EDUCATION NATIONALE (PARIS, FRANCE : 1981) (FR/0291-5871) [08199860] **1729**

BULLETIN OFFICIEL DU MINISTERE DE L'ENVIRONNEMENT ET DU CADRE DE VIE ET DU MINISTERE DES TRANSPORTS (FR) [07684250] **3110**

BULLETIN OFFICIEL DU MINISTERE DE L'EQUIPEMENT *See* BULLETIN OFFICIEL DU MINISTERE DE L'EQUIPEMENT ET DE L'AMENAGEMENT DU TERRITOIRE **2816**

BULLETIN OFFICIEL DU MINISTERE DE L'EQUIPEMENT ET DE L'AMENAGEMENT DU TERRITOIRE (FR) [04838243] **2816**

BULLETIN OFFICIEL DU MINISTERE DE L'INTERIEUR *See* REPERTOIRE MENSUEL DU MINISTERE DE L'INTERIEUR **4680**

BULLETIN OFFICIEL DU MINISTERE DELEGUE CHARGE DE LA MER (FR/0767-1288) [21021228] **3180**

BULLETIN OFFICIEL DU MINISTERE DES TRANSPORTS MARINE MARCHANDE (FRANCE) (FR) [08031185] **3180**

BULLETIN OFFICIEL DU SECRETARIAT D'ETAT AUX DEPARTEMENTS ET TERRITOIRES D'OUTRE-MER (FRANCE) (FR) [02723966] 4635, **2945**

BULLETIN OFFICIEL (FRANCE. MINISTERE DES RELATIONS EXTERIEURES) (FR/0751-0772) [11713761] **4517**

BULLETIN OFFICIEL. SECTION II : AVIATION CIVILE ET METEOROLOGIE (FR) [03097546] **15**

BULLETIN - OHIO. DIVISION OF GEOLOGICAL SURVEY (US/0097-5478) [01924773] **1370**

BULLETIN - OHIO. DIVISION OF GEOLOGICAL SURVEY (US) [06395130] **1370**

BULLETIN (OHIO. DIVISION OF WATER) (US/0097-2576) [01152437] **5531**

BULLETIN - OHIO FLORISTS' ASSOCIATION (US/0030-090X) [04845453] **2434**

BULLETIN - OKLAHOMA GEOLOGICAL SURVEY (US/0078-4389) [01688234] **1370**

BULLETIN ON CURRENT RESEARCH IN SOVIET AND EAST EUROPEAN LAW (US) [01624143] **3125**

BULLETIN ON FOOD STATISTICS (II/0536-8502) [01696619] **2329**

BULLETIN ON MOTOR VEHICLE STATISTICS (CE) [08470803] **5400**

BULLETIN ON NARCOTICS *CEASED*. (SZ/0007-523X) [01537787] **1342**

BULLETIN ON THE RHEUMATIC DISEASES (US/0007-5248) [05984797] **3804**

BULLETIN ON TRAINING (US/0272-8486) [05383417] **939**

BULLETIN - ONTARIO DIVISION. CANADIAN RED CROSS SOCIETY (CN/0715-366X) [09313095] **4769**

BULLETIN - ONTARIO HANDWEAVERS AND SPINNERS (CN/1182-5561) [22769099] 2772, **370**

BULLETIN - ONTARIO. SOCIAL ASSISTANCE REVIEW BOARD (CN/1187-4996) [25352051] **5275**

BULLETIN - ONTARIO. SOCIAL ASSISTANCE REVIEW BOARD (CN/1187-4996) [25352048] **4635**

BULLETIN - ORIENTAL BIRD CLUB (UK) [17277261] **5229**

BULLETIN - ORNITHOLOGICAL SOCIETY OF THE MIDDLE EAST (UK) [05901315] **5616**

BULLETIN ORNITHOLOGIQUE (ORSAINVILLE) (CN/0007-5256) [02294156] **5616**

BULLETIN / OVERHOLSER FAMILY ASSOCIATION (US/0742-8472) [10441492] **2441**

BULLETIN - OVERSEAS DEVELOPMENT NATURAL RESOURCES INSTITUTE (UK/0952-8245) [l09528245] 450, **70**

BULLETIN - OXFORD UNIVERSITY EXPLORATION CLUB (UK) [06456750] **2557**

BULLETIN OZANAM / SOCIETE DE SAINT-VINCENT DE PAUL, HULL ET GATINEAU (CN/0823-7883) [10768455] **4941**

BULLETIN P 3 - INSTITUT KEGURUAN DAN ILMU PENDIDIKAN, YOGYAKARTA, INDONESIA. PUSAT PENELITIAN PENDIDIKAN (IO/0304-9612) [02326019] **1729**

BULLETIN / PACIFIC MARINE FISHERIES COMMISSION (US/0078-7582) [01761684] **2298**

BULLETIN / PACIFIC SEABIRD GROUP (US/0740-3771) [06050248] 2189, **5616**

BULLETIN - PATENT AND TRADE INSTITUTE OF CANADA (1990) (CN/0849-3154) [23238132] **1302**

BULLETIN - PEABODY MUSEUM OF NATURAL HISTORY *SUSPENDED*. (US/0079-032X) [01674406] **4164**

BULLETIN PEDAGOGIQUE IUT: SERIE C, ABONNEMENT (FR) **1876**

BULLETIN PEDAGOGIQUE IUT: SERIE E, EXPRESSIONS (FR) **1876**

BULLETIN PENELITIAN HORTIKULTURA (IO/0126-1436) [03104941] **2411**

BULLETIN PENELITIAN KESEHATAN (IO/0303-3236) [03737743] **4769**

BULLETIN - PENNSYLVANIA FLOWER GROWERS (US/0031-448X) [05224319] 4244, **2435**

BULLETIN - PENNSYLVANIA STATE UNIVERSITY, COLLEGE OF AGRICULTURE, AGRICULTURAL EXPERIMENT STATION (US/0362-4013) [01762039] **70**

BULLETIN PERIODIQUE DE LA PRESSE TCHCOSLOVAQUE ... (BE) [01332196] **2681**

BULLETIN PERKARETAN (IO/0216-7867) [21474542] 165, **70**

BULLETIN PERPUSTAKAAN DAN DOKUMENTASI (IO/0304-5773) [02239814] **3198**

BULLETIN PERTAMINA (IO) [02866135] **4252**

BULLETIN (PEWTER COLLECTORS' CLUB OF AMERICA) (US) [09086135] **2772**

BULLETIN - PHILADELPHIA MUSEUM OF ART (US/0031-7314) [02432439] 4086, **345**

BULLETIN / PLANNED PARENTHOOD FEDERATION OF CANADA (CN/0842-9375) [23686572] **588**

BULLETIN / POLISH GENEALOGICAL SOCIETY, CALIFORNIA (US/1056-568X) [23666666] **2441**

BULLETIN - PORTLAND ART ASSOCIATION (OR.) (US/0887-4395) [06657853] **345**

BULLETIN - PRINTING HISTORICAL SOCIETY (UK/0144-7505) [07414858] **4564**

BULLETIN - PROFESSIONAL CORPORATION OF PHYSICIANS OF QUEBEC (CN/0315-2979) [02546004] **3561**

BULLETIN PROVINCIAL (CANADIAN CHILD AND YOUTH DRAMA ASSOCIATION. NEW BRUNSWICK) (CN/0228-8079) [08046005] **5362**

BULLETIN PSILOG, LE (CN/0706-120X) [08693679] **4241**

BULLETIN - PUBLIC SERVICE ALLIANCE OF CANADA (1978) (CN/0713-6668) [08955913] **1657**

BULLETIN - PUBLIC SERVICE COMMISSION OF CANADA (CN/0706-0564) [02249257] **4635**

BULLETIN - QUEENSLAND. UNIVERSITY, BRISBANE. DEPT. OF CIVIL ENGINEERING *CEASED*. (AT/0041-9966) [01434881] **2019**

BULLETIN QUOTIDIEN D'AFRIQUE (FR/0007-5264) [14576513] **2498**

BULLETIN QUOTIDIEN (TEXTES DU JOUR ET PRESSE ETRANGERE) (FR) [01357625] **2612**

BULLETIN - RAILROAD STATION HISTORICAL SOCIETY, THE (US/0147-0027) [03061703] **5430**

BULLETIN / RAJENDRA MEMORIAL RESEARCH INSTITUTE OF MEDICAL SCIENCES (II/0255-7207) [09928493] **3561**

BULLETIN - RAPAL (UK/0269-8854) [I02698854] **1800**

BULLETIN - REGIONAL INSTITUTE OF HIGHER EDUCATION AND DEVELOPMENT (SI/0129-7023) [02719998] **1813**

BULLETIN REGIONAL SUR LE MARCHE DU TRAVAIL (REGION DES CANTONS DE L'EST) (CN/0710-9857) [08674165] **1657**

BULLETIN REGIONAL SUR LE MARCHE DU TRAVAIL (REGION LAURENTIDES-LANAUDIERE) (CN/0710-9865) [08674162] **1657**

BULLETIN / REGROUPEMENT DES PROFESSIONNELS DE LA DANSE DU QUEBEC (CN/0840-9633) [19762173] **1311**

BULLETIN / RESERVE BANK OF AUSTRALIA (AT/0725-0320) [08324725] **781**

BULLETIN / RESERVE BANK OF NEW ZEALAND (NZ/0034-5539) [01865303] **781**

BULLETIN ROUTIER; QUEBEC (CN/0226-1014) [06273463] **4635**

BULLETIN / ROYAL ASTRONOMICAL SOCIETY OF CANADA (CN/1187-1571) [25066205] **394**

BULLETIN (ROYAL PHOTOGRAPHIC SOCIETY OF GREAT BRITAIN. COLOUR GROUP) (UK) [10495306] **4367**

BULLETIN - ROYAL SOCIETY OF NEW ZEALAND (NZ/0370-6559) [06271804] **5091**

BULLETIN - ROYAL TROPICAL INSTITUTE (NE/0922-7911) [l09227911] **450**

BULLETIN - SACRAMENTO COUNTY MEDICAL SOCIETY *See* SACRAMENTO MEDICINE **3638**

BULLETIN / SASKATCHEWAN CHORAL FEDERATION (CN/0838-6730) [18112323] **4106**

BULLETIN - SASKATCHEWAN GENEALOGICAL SOCIETY (CN/0048-9182) [02134975] **2441**

BULLETIN (SCHWEIZERISCHE VEREINIGUNG FOR ATOMENERGIE) *See* SVA BULLETIN : OFFIZIELLES ORGAN DER SVA UND DESOAF **4451**

●BULLETIN / SCIENCE FICTION AND FANTASY WRITERS OF AMERICA (US) [27457545] 3339, **3370**

BULLETIN SCIENTIFIQUE AIM (BE) **1967**

BULLETIN SCIENTIFIQUE DE L'ASSOCIATION DES INGENIEURS ELECTRICIENS SORTIS DE L'INSTITUT ELECTROTECHNIQUE MONTEFIORE (FR/0302-2676) [02653211] **2037**

BULLETIN SCIENTIFIQUE. SECTION B, SCIENCES HUMAINES (CI/0350-1604) [01765068] **2843**

●BULLETIN - SEARCH FOR COMMON GROUND (ORGANIZATION). INITIATIVE FOR PEACE AND COOPERATION IN THE MIDDLE EAST (US/1065-0237) [25527534] **4517**

BULLETIN - SEATTLE GENEALOGICAL SOCIETY (US/0559-2526) [01765329] **2441**

BULLETIN SEMENCES (FR) **450**

BULLETIN SEMESTRIEL DE STATISTIQUE (FT) [14125613] 5465, **825**

BULLETIN SEMESTRIEL D'INFORMATION SUR L'EXECUTION DU PLAN *See* BULLETIN D'INFORMATION SUR L'EXECUTION DU PLAN **1549**

BULLETIN SERIES. MUSEUM OF NORTH ARIZONA (US) [23818983] **4086**

BULLETIN - SHAWNEE COUNTY HISTORICAL SOCIETY (US/0362-1731) [01605962] **2725**

BULLETIN SIGNALETIQUE. 22, SCIENCES DE LA TERRE (FR) [09313699] 1438, **1362**

BULLETIN SIGNALETIQUE. 110 (FR) [04308879] 3499, **3542**

BULLETIN SIGNALETIQUE. 120, GEOPHYSIQUE EXTERNE, ASTRONOMIE ET ASTROPHYSIQUE / CENTRE NATIONAL DE LA RECHERCHE SCIENTIFIQUE (FR/0240-849X) [08248332] 1403, **402**

BULLETIN SIGNALETIQUE. 140: ELECTROTECHNIQUE (FR) [02164079] 2037, **2002**

BULLETIN SIGNALETIQUE. 160: PHYSIQUE DE L'ETAT CONDENSE (FR) [05356039] **4427**

BULLETIN SIGNALETIQUE. 160: STRUCTURE DE LA MATIERE I-PHYSIQUE DE L'ETAT CONDENSE, PHYSIQUE ATOMIQUE ET MOLECULAIRE, SPECTROSCOPIE *See* BULLETIN SIGNALETIQUE. 160: PHYSIQUE DE L'ETAT CONDENSE **4427**

BULLETIN SIGNALETIQUE. 161, STRUCTURE DE L'ETAT CONDENSE, CRISTALLOGRAPHIE / CENTRE NATIONAL DE LA RECHERCHE SCIENTIFIQUE (FR/0304-1298) [04215954] **1031**

BULLETIN SIGNALETIQUE. 165: ATOMES ET MOLECULES, FLUIDES ET PLASMAS (FR) [02357061] **4399**

BULLETIN SIGNALETIQUE. 170, CHIMIE / CENTRE NATIONAL DE LA RECHERCHE SCIENTIFIQUE (FR) [09188683] **963**

BULLETIN — Alphabetical Title Index

BULLETIN SIGNALETIQUE. 171, CHIMIE GENERALE ET CHIMIE PHYSIQUE / CENTRE NATIONAL DE LA RECHERCHE SCIENTIFIQUE (FR/0240-8465) [07414988] **1050**

BULLETIN SIGNALETIQUE. 172, CHIMIE ANALYTIQUE / CENTRE NATIONAL DE LA RECHERCHE SCIENTIFIQUE (FR/0240-8473) [07410121] **1014**

BULLETIN SIGNALETIQUE 221: GISEMENTS METALLIQUES ET NON METALLIQUES, ECONOMIE MINIERE (FR) [03647376] **3999**

BULLETIN SIGNALETIQUE 320: BIOCHEMIE. BIOPHYSIQUE. CHEMIE ANALYTIQUE BIOLOGIQUE. BIOPHYSIQUE. GENIE BIOLOGIQUE ET MEDICAL (FR/0007-5434) [01569983] **450**

BULLETIN SIGNALETIQUE. 364, PROTOZOAIRES ET INVERTEBRES, ZOOLOGIE GENERALE ET APPLIQUEE (FR/0181-0006) [05157007] **5580**

BULLETIN SIGNALETIQUE. 740, METAUX, METALLURGIE (FR/0007-5655) [01326009] **3999**

BULLETIN SIGNALETIQUE. 780: POLYMERES, PEINTURES, BOIS, CUIRS (FR/0397-7730) [04454447] **1039**

BULLETIN SIGNALETIQUE. 800 : GENIE CHEMIQUE, INDUSTRIES CHEMIQUE ET PARACHIMIQUE (FR/0007-568X) [01329702] **1021**

BULLETIN SIGNALETIQUE. 885: NUISANCES (FR/0301-3499) [02341781] **2225**

BULLETIN SIGNALETIQUE. 890 (FR) [04219213] **2111**

BULLETIN SIGNALETIQUE. 891: INDUSTRIES MECANIQUES (FR/0223-4246) [06931909] **2111**

BULLETIN SIGNALETIQUE. 900 (FR) [04219479] **5091**

BULLETIN SIGNALETIQUE (CENTRE D'INFORMATION ET DE DOCUMENTATION SUR LE VIETNAM CONTEMPORAIN) (FR) [17553355] **5091**

BULLETIN SIGNALETIQUE CHEMIE GENERALE ANALYTIQUE MINERALE ORGANIQUE SECT 917 *CEASED.* (FR) 963, **1438**

BULLETIN SIGNALETIQUE DES TELECOMMUNICATIONS (FR/0007-5302) [02258773] **1150**

BULLETIN SIGNALETIQUE - DOC MNE (FR/0989-1994) [I09891994] **208**

BULLETIN SIGNALETIQUE - INSTITUT NATIONAL AGRONOMIQUE EL HARRACH (AE/1011-999X) [I1011999X] **70**

BULLETIN SIGNALETIQUE SCIENCES AGRONOMIQUES ZOOLOGIE DES INVERTEBRES SECTION 980 (FR) **5580**

BULLETIN SIGNALETIQUE SCIENCES BIOLOGIQUES ET BIOMEDICALES SECTION 931 (FR) **450**

BULLETIN SIGNALETIQUE: SECTION 527. HISTOIRE ET SCIENCES DES RELIGIONS *See* FRANCIS : HISTOIRE DES SCIENCES ET DES RELIGIONS. 527 **2616**

BULLETIN SIGNALETIQUE UCD DE JOUY-EN-JOSAS (FR/1164-5431) [I11645431] **5580**

BULLETIN SIGNALETIQUE. [SECTION] 140. ELECTROTECHNIQUE (FR/0301-3308) [02339897] **2037**

BULLETIN SIGNALETIQUE. [SECTION] 761. MICROSCOPIE ELECTRONIQUE, DIFFRACTION ELECTRONIQUE (FR/0007-5663) [02339169] **572**

BULLETIN - SIOUX FALLS COLLEGE (SIOUX FALLS, S.D.) (US/0745-2829) [04441464] **1813**

BULLETIN SKI NAUTIQUE (CN/0824-0906) [11825349] **4888**

BULLETIN SOCIALE GEOGRAFIE ONTWIKKELINGSLANDEN; SERIE 2 (UTRECHT) (NE) [05346584] **5241**

BULLETIN - SOCIETE ACADEMIQUE DU BAS-RHIN POUR LE PROGRES DES SCIENCES, DES LETTRES, DES ARTS ET DE LA VIE ECONOMIQUE (FR/1160-5634) [I11605634] 2843, **317**

BULLETIN - SOCIETE ARCHEOLOGIQUE DE SENS (FR/1149-932X) [I1149932X] **264**

BULLETIN - SOCIETE BOTANIQUE DU QUEBEC (CN/0228-975X) [10926592] **505**

BULLETIN - SOCIETE CHATEAUBRIAND (FR/0081-0754) [01941200] **3370**

BULLETIN / SOCIETE D'EGYPTOLOGIE, GENEVE (SZ) [10527817] **265**

BULLETIN - SOCIETE DES AMIS DU JARDIN VAN DEN HENDE INC (CN/0711-6446) [09166854] **2411**

BULLETIN - SOCIETE DES DIPLOMES DE L'ECOLE DE BIBLIOTHECONOMIE DE L'UNIVERSITE DE MONTREAL (CN/0700-5431) [03400125] **3198**

BULLETIN - SOCIETE DES JEUX DU QUEBEC (CN/0381-0003) [03304078] **4858**

BULLETIN / SOCIETE DES PROFESSEURS FRANCAIS EN AMERIQUE (US/0887-607X) [11507246] **1861**

BULLETIN (SOCIETE D'ETUDES HISTORIQUES DE LA NOUVELLE CALEDONIE) (NL) [08804847] **2669**

BULLETIN - SOCIETE D'HISTOIRE DE HUNINGUE ET DE SA REGION (FR/0997-1734) [I09971734] **2681**

BULLETIN - SOCIETE D'HISTOIRE DU CANTON DE LAPOUTROIE VAL D'ORBEY (FR/0753-8413) [16403144] **2681**

BULLETIN - SOCIETE D'HISTOIRE DU PROTESTANTISME BELGE (BE) [01947328] **5057**

BULLETIN / SOCIETE FRANCAISE DE PHOTOGRAMMETRIE *See* BULLETIN - SOCIETE FRANCAISE DE PHOTOGRAMMETRIE ET DE TELEDETECTION **4367**

BULLETIN - SOCIETE FRANCAISE DE PHOTOGRAMMETRIE ET DE TELEDETECTION (FR/0244-6014) [06599169] **4367**

BULLETIN / SOCIETE GEOGRAPHIQUE DE LIEGE (BE) [07125723] **2557**

BULLETIN / SOCIETE INTERNATIONALE D'ETUDES YOURCENARIENNES (FR/0987-7940) [20147969] **3370**

BULLETIN - SOCIETE LANGUEDOCIENNE DE GEOGRAPHIE (FR/0373-3297) [12190436] **2557**

BULLETIN / SOCIETE SUISSE DES AMERICANISTES (SZ/0582-1592) [01929438] **233**

BULLETIN - SOCIETY FOR SPANISH AND PORTUGUESE HISTORICAL STUDIES (U.S.) (US/0739-1824) [04071192] **2681**

BULLETIN / SOCIETY FOR THE STUDY OF ARCHITECTURE IN CANADA (CN/0228-0744) [08811595] **294**

BULLETIN - SOCIETY OF WETLAND SCIENTISTS (U.S.) (US/0732-9393) [08501431] 1352, **450**

BULLETIN SOLIDARNOSC (US/0738-2154) [08500920] **1657**

BULLETIN - SOMERSET INDUSTRIAL ARCHAEOLOGICAL SOCIETY (UK/0954-7029) [I09547029] **265**

BULLETIN - SOTRAC (CN/0823-5392) [10381574] **2189**

BULLETIN / SOUTH DAKOTA GEOLOGICAL SURVEY (US/0085-6479) [01714986] **1370**

BULLETIN / SOUTHERN CALIFORNIA ACADEMY OF SCIENCES (US/0038-3872) [01766177] **5092**

BULLETIN - SOUTHERN CALIFORNIA DENTAL LABORATORY ASSOCIATION (US/0038-3945) [05317219] **1318**

BULLETIN SPECIAL - INSTITUT TECCART (CN/0822-5508) [10082641] **2037**

BULLETIN - SPECIAL LIBRARIES ASSOCIATION, EASTERN CANADA CHAPTER (CN/0824-7749) [04975746] **3198**

BULLETIN - SPECIAL LIBRARIES ASSOCIATION. EDUCATION DIVISION (US/1052-9454) [12227997] **3198**

BULLETIN (SPECIAL LIBRARIES ASSOCIATION. FLORIDA CHAPTER) (US/0740-9753) [10075742] **3198**

BULLETIN - SPECIAL LIBRARIES ASSOCIATION. GEOGRAPHY AND MAP DIVISION (US/0036-1607) [01766321] 2581, **2557**

BULLETIN - SPECIAL LIBRARIES ASSOCIATION, NORTH CAROLINA CHAPTER (US/0195-9077) [05713440] **3198**

BULLETIN - SPECIAL LIBRARIES ASSOCIATION. SAN FRANCISCO BAY REGION CHAPTER (US/0277-2124) [02464731] **3199**

BULLETIN SROP (NE) [02954556] **450**

BULLETIN SSQ RESPECTING SOCIAL LAWS (CN/0822-5699) [10216611] 5275, **2945**

BULLETIN SSQ SUR LES LOIS SOCIALES. FRANCAIS (CN/0713-8431) [09054451] **5276**

BULLETIN - STATE BANK OF PAKISTAN (PK/0039-0011) [01774136] **781**

BULLETIN / STATE BOARD OF ACCOUNTANCY (US) [05777916] **740**

BULLETIN / STATE COMMUNITIES AID ASSOCIATION (US) [13289823] **5276**

BULLETIN - STATE GEOLOGICAL AND NATURAL HISTORY SURVEY OF CONNECTICUT (US/0095-8638) [01320727] **4164**

BULLETIN - STATE OF ALASKA, ALASKA OIL AND GAS CONSERVATION COMMISSION (US) [05326758] 4252, **2189**

BULLETIN / STATE OF MONTANA, BUREAU OF MINES AND GEOLOGY (US/0077-1090) [01715196] **1370**

BULLETIN - STATE OF WASHINGTON DIVISION OF POWER RESOURCES (US/0509-7754) [01247660] 825, **1934**

BULLETIN STATISTIK DEPARTEMEN SOSIAL (INDONESIA) (IO) [02724437] **5276**

BULLETIN STATISTIQUE (BD) [22197224] **5324**

BULLETIN STATISTIQUE DE LA DGAC / MINISTERE DES TRANSPORTS, AVIATION CIVILE (FR/0181-1517) [11050774] **41**

BULLETIN STATISTIQUE - DIRECTION GENERALE DE L'ENSEIGNEMENT COLLEGIAL (CN/0229-0766) [08289407] 1813, **1793**

BULLETIN STATISTIQUE DU SECRETARIAT GENERAL A L'AVIATION CIVILE (FR/0302-8607) [02239832] **41**

BULLETIN STATISTIQUE INTERNATIONAL : CHOCOLAT SUCRE BISCUITERIE (BE) **2329**

BULLETIN - STUDENT COUNSELLING AND RESEARCH UNIT, UNIVERSITY OF NEW SOUTH WALES (AT/0158-2631) [I01582631] **4201**

BULLETIN SUISSE DE LINGUISTIQUE APPLIQUEE (SZ) **3271**

BULLETIN (SUOMEN PANKKI) (FI/0784-6509) [17651857] **781**

BULLETIN SUR LA PME (CN/0824-3735) [10415685] **1600**

BULLETIN SUR L'ENERGIE (OTTAWA, ONT.) (CN/0823-1486) [09938385] **1934**

BULLETIN SUR LES COMPOSITES (CN/1187-127X) [25066886] **4454**

BULLETIN SUR LES RELATIONS DU TRAVAIL (EDITION ANGLAISE) (CN/0704-0873) [04589949] **1657**

BULLETIN - SVENSKT MUSIKHISTORISKT ARKIV (SW/0586-0709) [02067757] **4106**

BULLETIN - SVETOVY KONGRES SLOVAKOV (CN/0317-4018) [01793840] **2681**

BULLETIN - SWAZILAND, GEOLOGICAL SURVEY AND MINES DEPARTMENT (SQ/0082-0008) [02009431] **1370**

BULLETIN (SYDNEY) (AT/0007-4039) [02258709] **2510**

BULLETIN (TALL TIMBER RESEARCH STATION) *See* BULLETIN OF TALL TIMBERS RESEARCH, INC **2376**

BULLETIN TECHNIQUE APICOLE (FR/0335-3710) [02918709] **5580**

BULLETIN TECHNIQUE DE L INSEMINATION ARTIFICIELLE (FR/0153-6281) [I01536281] 208, **5506**

BULLETIN TECHNIQUE D'INFORMATION DES INGENIEURS DES SERVICES AGRICOLE, DIRECTIONS DEPARTEMENTALES ET ETABLISSEMENTS D'ENSEIGNEMENT *See* BULLETIN TECHNIQUE D'INFORMATION (FRANCE. MINISTERE DE L'AGRICULTURE ET DU DEVELOPPEMENT RURAL) **70**

BULLETIN TECHNIQUE D'INFORMATION (FRANCE. MINISTERE DE L'AGRICULTURE ET DU DEVELOPPEMENT RURAL) (FR/0303-1721) [01792626] **70**

BULLETIN TECHNIQUE DU BUREAU VERITAS (FR/0007-5752) [04139998] **4175**

BULLETIN TECHNIQUE DU MACHINISME ET DE L'EQUIPMENT AGRICOLES (FR) [13802612] **158**

BULLETIN TECHNIQUE - GATTEFOSSE REPORT (FR/1149-0306) [I11490306] **5092**

BULLETIN TECHNIQUE / INSTIUT CANADIEN DE TOLE D'ACIER EN BATIMENT (CN/0826-452X) [11240730] **2019**

BULLETIN TECHNIQUE - OFFICE NATIONAL DES FORETS (FR/0395-7497) [I03957497] **2377**

BULLETIN - TEXAS AGRICULTURAL EXPERIMENT STATION (US/0096-6061) [01431525] **70**

BULLETIN, THE (US) [22866923] **1317**

BULLETIN - THE AMERICAN ASSOCIATION OF VARIABLE STAR OBSERVERS (US/0516-9518) [01909495] **394**

BULLETIN / THE DAYTON ART INSTITUTE (US/0883-9239) [12248358] **346**

BULLETIN - THE INSTITUTE OF MEAT (UK) [01162006] **2329**

BULLETIN / THE J. PAUL GETTY TRUST (US/1041-9063) [14576565] **346**

BULLETIN / THE JAPANESE AMERICAN LIBRARY (US/0893-8601) [15620696] **2257**

BULLETIN / THE MAJOR PROJECT OF EDUCATION IN LATIN AMERICA AND THE CARIBBEAN (CL) [25119387] **1729**

BULLETIN - THE MARIE SELBY BOTANICAL GARDENS (US/0197-6265) [03623404] **505**

BULLETIN / THE NATIONAL EATING DISORDER INFORMATION CENTRE (CN/0836-6845) [17500133] 4188, **3829**

Alphabetical Title Index **BULLETINS**

BULLETIN - THE ST. LOUIS ART MUSEUM (US/0009-7691) [02571136] 346, **4086**

BULLETIN - THE UNIVERSITY OF NEW MEXICO ART MUSEUM (US/0077-8583) [01776109] 346, **4086**

BULLETIN TO MANAGEMENT (US/0525-2156) [02445580] **939**

BULLETIN TO MEMBERS / ARUSHA CHAMBER OF COMMERCE, AGRICULTURE & INDUSTRY (TZ) [08059450] **818**

BULLETIN - TOURING OFFICE OF THE CANADA COUNCIL (CN/0703-6078) [02249118] **384**

BULLETIN (TOY TRAIN OPERATING SOCIETY : 1973) (US) [10137853] 5430, **2772**

BULLETIN TRIMESTRIEL (BE) [06597020] **4715**

BULLETIN TRIMESTRIEL - CERCLE D'ETUDES NUMISMATIQUES (BE/0009-0344) [I00090344] **2780**

BULLETIN TRIMESTRIEL DE LA BANQUE DE FRANCE (FR/0150-7583) [04445856] **781**

BULLETIN TRIMESTRIEL DE LA FONDATION AUSCHWITZ (BE/0772-6961) [16949029] **2681**

BULLETIN TRIMESTRIEL DE LA SOCIETE BELGE DE PHOTOGRAMMETRIE-TELEDETECTION ET CARTOGRAPHIE (BE) [27327062] **4367**

BULLETIN TRIMESTRIEL DE LA SOCIETE BELGE DE PHOTOGRAMM,ETRIE ET DE T,EL,EDETECTION See BULLETIN TRIMESTRIEL DE LA SOCIETE BELGE DE PHOTOGRAMMETRIE-TELEDETECTION ET CARTOGRAPHIE **4367**

BULLETIN TRIMESTRIEL DE LA SOCIETE DES ANTIQUAIRES DE PICARDIE (FR/0037-9204) [I00379204] **2681**

BULLETIN TRIMESTRIEL DE LA SOCIETE MYCOLOGIQUE DE FRANCE (FR/0395-7527) [01765848] **574**

BULLETIN TRIMESTRIEL DE STATISTIQUE (BANGUI, CENTRAL AFRICAN REPUBLIC) (CX) [12546586] **5324**

BULLETIN TRIMESTRIEL DE STATISTIQUES - DIRECTION DES STATISTIQUES ET DE LA COMPTABILITE NATIONALE (AE) [02887642] **5324**

BULLETIN TRIMESTRIEL DI L'INSTITUT ARCHEOLOGIQUE DU LUXEMBOURG (BE/0020-2177) [02697567] 2681, **265**

BULLETIN TRIMESTRIEL ECONOMIQUE (MONTREAL) (CN/0227-1044) [06703482] **606**

BULLETIN TRIMESTRIEL / INSTITUT MONETAIRE LUXEMBOURGEOIS (LU) [12072336] **781**

BULLETIN TRIMESTRIEL / SOCIETE FORESTIERE DE FRANCHE-COMTE ET DES PROVINCES DE L'EST (FR) [30497984] **2377**

BULLETIN (TRINIDAD AND TOBAGO. CENTRAL STATISTICAL OFFICE) (TR) [09856324] **5324**

BULLETIN - U.S. COAST GUARD ACADEMY ALUMNI ASSOCIATION (US/0191-9814) [04939151] 4175, **1101**

BULLETIN - U.S. DEPT. OF LABOR, EMPLOYMENT STANDARDS ADMINISTRATION, WOMEN'S BUREAU (US/0083-3606) [01768698] 5552, **1657**

BULLETIN - UK CENTRE FOR ECONOMIC AND ENVIRONMENTAL DEVELOPMENT (UK/0268-7402) [I02687402] 2162, **1466**

BULLETIN / UKRAINIAN CANADIAN COMMITTEE, SASKATCHEWAN PROVINCIAL COUNCIL, THE (CN/0845-4493) [20135188] **2725**

BULLETIN - UNDERHILL SOCIETY OF AMERICA (US/0501-0918) [03493313] **2725**

BULLETIN UNION INTERNATIONALE DE PENTATHLON MODERNE ET BIATHLON (AU) 2596, **4888**

BULLETIN - UNITED ARAB EMIRATES CURRENCY BOARD (TS) [02506450] **1549**

BULLETIN - UNITED BIBLE SOCIETIES (UK/0041-719X) [02212212] **5015**

BULLETIN - UNITED NATIONS ASSOCIATION IN CANADA (CN/0317-6460) [03258704] **3125**

BULLETIN / UNITED NATIONS CENTRE FOR REGIONAL DEVELOPMENT (JA) [08038708] **2816**

BULLETIN - UNITED PLANTERS' ASSOCIATION OF SOUTHERN INDIA, SCIENTIFIC DEPARTMENT (II/0498-1308) [03592485] **165**

BULLETIN (UNITED STATES. BUREAU OF JUSTICE STATISTICS) (US/0742-7271) [07452466] 3159, **3079**

BULLETIN - UNITED STATES. BUREAU OF LABOR STATISTICS (US/0082-9021) [01714756] **1530**

BULLETIN (UNITED STATES. OFFICE OF MANAGEMENT AND BUDGET) (US) [06630375] **4635**

BULLETIN - UNITED STEELWORKERS OF AMERICA. LOCAL 7896 (FITCHBURG, MASS.), THE (US/0730-8469) [08081279] **1657**

BULLETIN UNIVERSITAS UDAYANA (IO) [02240469] **1813**

BULLETIN - UNIVERSITE DE GENEVE, DEPARTEMENT D'HISTOIRE ECONOMIQUE (SZ) [04967433] **1550**

BULLETIN, UNIVERSITY-INDUSTRY PROGRAMS (CN/0838-1380) [25590170] **3561**

BULLETIN - UNIVERSITY OF ARKANSAS, FAYETTEVILLE. AGRICULTURAL EXPERIMENT STATION (US/0097-3491) [08624158] **70**

BULLETIN - UNIVERSITY OF ARKANSAS, FAYETTEVILLE CAMPUS). ENGINEERING EXPERIMENT STATION (US/0097-5273) [01514136] **1967**

BULLETIN - UNIVERSITY OF CALIFORNIA (SYSTEM). DIVISION OF AGRICULTURE AND NATURAL RESOURCES (US/1044-4823) [19804373] 2189, **70**

BULLETIN - UNIVERSITY OF DELAWARE, AGRICULTURAL EXPERIMENT STATION (US/0097-1367) [01431470] **70**

BULLETIN - UNIVERSITY OF FLORIDA, AGRICULTURAL EXPERIMENT STATIONS (US/0096-607X) [01287440] **70**

BULLETIN / UNIVERSITY OF HEALTH SCIENCES, ANTIGUA, SCHOOL OF MEDICINE (AQ) [19467427] **3561**

BULLETIN - UNIVERSITY OF KANSAS MEDICAL CENTER, THE (US/0199-1256) [03734070] **3777**

BULLETIN - UNIVERSITY OF MELBOURNE GALLERY SOCIETY AND THE DEPARTMENT OF FINE ARTS (AT/0818-9382) [I08189382] **346**

BULLETIN - UNIVERSITY OF MICHIGAN. MUSEUM OF ART (US/0076-8391) [04422532] 346, **4086**

BULLETIN / UNIVERSITY OF READING, AGRICULTURAL EXTENSION AND RURAL DEVELOPMENT CENTRE (UK) [19891835] **70**

BULLETIN / UNIVERSITY OF TENNESSEE, AGRICULTURAL EXPERIMENT STATION (US/0040-3148) [02298622] **70**

BULLETIN / (UNIVERSITY OF WESTERN ONTARIO, DEPT. OF PSYCHIATRY) (CN/0711-6012) [09816390] **3922**

BULLETIN - UNIVERSITY RELATIONS AND INFORMATION OFFICE, UNIVERSITY OF MANITOBA (CN/0706-8549) [04433037] **1813**

BULLETIN USTREDNEHO VYBORU NARODNEHO FRONTU SLOVENSKEJ SOCIALISTICKEJ REPUBLIKY (XO) [02441270] **4635**

BULLETIN USUEL DES LOIS ET ARRETES (BRUXELLES) (BE/0773-7467) [I07737467] **4635**

BULLETIN - UTAH GEOLOGICAL AND MINERAL SURVEY (US/0098-4825) [02240340] **1370**

BULLETIN VAN HET RYKSMUSEUM (NE/0165-9510) [04272788] 346, **4086**

BULLETIN VAN STATISTIEK / REPUBLIEK VAN SUID-AFRIKA, SENTRALE STATISTIEKDIENS (SA/0034-5024) [09414265] **4696**

BULLETIN VAN STATISTIEK (SOUTH AFRICA. DEPT. OF STATISTICS) See BULLETIN VAN STATISTIEK / REPUBLIEK VAN SUID-AFRIKA, SENTRALE STATISTIEKDIENS **4696**

BULLETIN - VERMONT FISH AND GAME DEPARTMENT (US/0506-7510) [01533558] **2189**

BULLETIN / VERMONT GEOLOGICAL SURVEY (US/0083-5757) [01306713] **1370**

BULLETIN / VILLE DE MONT-LAURIER (CN/0710-3689) [08693624] **4635**

BULLETIN / VIRGINIA AGRICULTURAL EXPERIMENT STATION (US/0096-6088) [08769619] **70**

BULLETIN - VIRGINIA MUSEUM OF FINE ARTS (US/0363-3519) [02410390] **4086**

BULLETIN - VIRGINIA. TRUCK EXPERIMENT STATION, NORFOLK (US) [01559141] **2411**

BULLETIN VOYAGES (CN/0706-215X) [06316115] **5465**

BULLETIN (VYZKUMNY USTAV GEODETICKY, TOPOGRAFICKY A KARTOGRAFICKY (PRAGUE, CZECHOSLOVAKIA)) (XR) [07902079] **1370**

●BULLETIN / WAMP, WEST AFRICAN MUSEUMS PROGRAMME (UK) [28479380] **4086**

BULLETIN - WASHINGTON DEPARTMENT OF NATURAL RESOURCES, DIVISION OF GEOLOGY AND EARTH RESOURCES (US/0271-8545) [06701548] 2189, **1371**

BULLETIN - WATAUGA ASSOCIATION OF GENEALOGISTS (US) [01786572] **2441**

BULLETIN - WATER RESEARCH INSTITUTE (MORGANTOWN) (US/0512-4727) [01185724] **5531**

BULLETIN - WATER RESOURCES RESEARCH CENTER (DURHAM) (US/0548-4901) [01541643] **5531**

BULLETIN - WELDING RESEARCH COUNCIL (U.S.) (US/0043-2326) [03455081] **4026**

BULLETIN / WEST AFRICAN MUSEUMS PROJECT, DAKAR (UK) [21541900] **4086**

BULLETIN / WEST TEXAS GEOLOGICAL SOCIETY (US/0739-5957) [09768819] **1371**

BULLETIN - WEST VIRGINIA DEPARTMENT OF NATURAL RESOURCES, WILDLIFE RESOURCES DIVISION (US) [05538463] **2189**

BULLETIN - WEST VIRGINIA GEOLOGICAL AND ECONOMIC SURVEY (US/0083-8500) [01283135] 1466, **1371**

BULLETIN - WEST VIRGINIA SPELEOLOGICAL SURVEY (US/0161-0392) [03819083] **1403**

BULLETIN / WEST VIRGINIA UNIVERSITY AGRICULTURAL AND FORESTRY EXPERIMENT STATION (US/0748-1268) [04300679] 2377, **70**

BULLETIN / WESTERN SYDNEY CLEARINGHOUSE (AT) [19223985] **5227**

BULLETIN (WISCONSIN. BUREAU OF LOCAL FINANCIAL ASSISTANCE) (US) [03778560] **4715**

BULLETIN - WISCONSIN GEOLOGICAL AND NATURAL HISTORY SURVEY (US/0375-8265) [01697283] **1371**

BULLETIN - WISCONSIN VETERINARY MEDICAL ASSOCIATION (US/0512-1345) [01695352] **5506**

BULLETIN - WORKERS LEAGUE (U.S.). CENTRAL COMMITTEE (US/0279-0165) [07441765] **4540**

BULLETIN (WORLD FEDERATION OF BUILDING AND WOODWORKERS UNIONS) (NE) [07763868] **1657**

BULLETIN / WORLD METEOROLOGICAL ORGANIZATION (SZ) [23291277] **1421**

BULLETIN / WORLD VETERINARY ASSOCIATION (SP) [18669495] **5507**

BULLETIN / YAKIMA VALLEY GENEALOGICAL SOCIETY (US/0513-6776) [05454306] **2441**

BULLETIN / YALE UNIVERSITY ART GALLERY (US/0084-3539) [02243316] **346**

BULLETIN / YALE UNIVERSITY, SCHOOL OF FORESTRY AND ENVIRONMENTAL STUDIES (US/0361-4425) [01545677] **2377**

BULLETIN - YELL COUNTY HISTORICAL & GENEALOGICAL ASSOCIATION (ARK.) (US/0892-5895) [07761062] **2441**

BULLETIN - YORK UNIVERSITY, TORONTO. INSTITUTE FOR BEHAVIOURAL RESEARCH (CN) [05724306] **4579**

BULLETIN / YORKSHIRE NATURALISTS' UNION (UK/0265-6833) [19587370] **4164**

BULLETIN - ZAMBIAN ORNITHOLOGICAL SOCIETY (ZA/0378-4525) [01787486] **5616**

BULLETIN ZOOLOGISCH MUSEUM, UNIVERSITEIT VAN AMSTERDAM (NE/0165-9464) [03584149] **5580**

BULLETIN - [ECONOMICS DEPARTMENT, FEDERAL HOME LOAN BANK OF INDIANAPOLIS] (US) [01795074] **781**

BULLETIN / [PREPARED BY ECONOMIC RESEARCH DEPARTMENT, THE CENTRAL BANK OF THE ISLAMIC REPUBLIC OF IRAN] (IR) [18576530] **781**

BULLETINS (US/1076-8939) **644**

BULLETINS DE LA SOCIETE D ETUDES HISTORIQUES DE LA NOUVELLE CALEDONIE (NL) **2612**

BULLETINS ET MEMOIRES (FR/0081-1092) [01765820] **3873**

BULLETINS ET MEMOIRES DE LA SOCIETE D'ANTHROPOLOGIE DE PARIS (FR/0037-8984) [01427596] **233**

BULLETINS ET MEMOIRES (SOCIETE ARCHEOLOGIQUE ET HISTORIQUE DE LA CHARENTE : 1983) (FR/0397-579X) [10678652] **2681**

BULLETINS OF AMERICAN PALEONTOLOGY (US/0007-5779) [01537796] **4226**

BULLETINS OF THE GEOLOGICAL SURVEY OF INDIA (II/0445-622X) [01321386] **1412**

BULLETINS — Alphabetical Title Index

BULLETINS OF THE GEOLOGICAL SURVEY OF INDIA. SERIES A : ECONOMIC GEOLOGY (II/0536-8782) [02659135] **1371**

BULLETTINO DELLA COMMISSIONE ARCHEOLOGICA COMUNALE DI ROMA (IT) [01716088] **265**

BULLETTINO DELLA DEPUTAZIONE ABRUZZESE DI STORIA PATRIA (IT/0394-5006) [I03945006] **2681**

BULLETTINO DELL'ISTITUTO DI DIRITTO ROMANO (IT) [01754027] **2945**

BULLETTINO DELL'ISTITUTO STORICO ITALIANO PER IL MEDIO EVO E ARCHIVIO MURATORIANO (IT) [01714181] **2681**

BULLETTINO SENESE DI STORIA PATRIA (IT) [01537800] **2612**

BULLETTINO STORICO EMPOLESE (IT/0007-5795) [03282810] 5465, **2682**

BULLETTINO STORICO PISTOIESE (IT/0007-5809) [02168217] **2682**

BULLION, THE (NR) [06726710] **781**

BULLISH CONSENSUS, THE (US/0889-7840) [14114325] **1466**

BULLISIANA (CN/0705-9108) [08923992] **394**

BULL'S EYE (LYNBROOK, N.Y.) (US/1041-3669) [18733409] **2917**

BULL'S-EYE NEWS (US/0885-0771) [12559990] **4888**

BULLS (OTHER THAN FRIESIAN) WITH IMPROVED CONTEMPORARY COMPARISONS (UK) [05167539] **208**

BULLSEYE DIRECTORY OF BUY-SIDE TRADERS (US) **825**

BULLSEYE (NORTH LAS VEGAS) (US/0193-5178) [06802889] **2529**

BULWARK (CHICAGO, ILL.), THE (US/0741-5788) [10206074] **4505**

BULWARK, OR, REFORMATION JOURNAL IN DEFENCE OF THE TRUE INTERESTS OF MAN AND OF SOCIETY, ESPECIALLY IN REFERENCE TO THE RELIGIOUS, SOCIAL AND POLITICAL BEARINGS OF POPERY See BULWARK, THE **5057**

BULWARK, THE (UK/0045-3536) [09879900] **5057**

BUMAZHNAIA PROMYSHLENNOST See TSELLIULOZA, BUMAGA, KARTON **4239**

BUMMEI (JA) [04015516] **2612**

BUMMEI JIHYO (JA) [04426752] **5229**

BUMPER (NE/0167-6520) [I01676520] 3461, **3370**

BUMPER STICKERS FOR SALE (US/0740-3216) [09921320] **922**

BUND DER EVANGELISCHEN KIRCHEN IN DER DDR See MITTEILUNGSBLATT DES BUNDES DER EVANGELISCHEN KIRCHEN IN DER DEUTSCHEN DEMOKRATISCHEN REPUBLIK **5064**

BUNDERVERBAND DER DEUTSCHEN GAS- UND WASSERWIRTSCHAFT See JAHRESBERICHT - BUNDESVERBAND DER DEUTSCHEN GAS- UND WASSERWIRTSCHAFT **2196**

BUNDES-TELEFONBUCH FUER DIE GEWERBLICHE WIRTSCHAFT DER BUNDESREPUBLIK DEUTSCHLAND MIT BERLIN (WEST) (GW) [11330012] **1600**

BUNDESANSTALT FUER ARBEIT See INFORMATIONEN FUER DIE BERATUNGS- UND VERMITTLUNGSDIENSTE **1679**

BUNDESANSTALT FUERFUER ARBEIT (GERMANY). JAHRESZAHLEN, ARBEITSSTATISTIK See AMTLICHE NACHRICHTEN DER BUNDESANSTALT FUER ARBEIT. ARBEITSSTATISTIK ... JAHRESZAHLEN **5320**

BUNDESANSTALT FUER GEOWISSENSCHAFTEN UND ROHSTOFFE See TATIGKEITSBERICHT - BUNDESANSTALT FUER GEOWISSENSCHAFTEN UND ROHSTOFFE **1399**

BUNDESANSTALT FUER GEWASSERKUNDE (GERMANY) See JAHRESBERICHT DER BUNDESANSTALT FUER GEWASSERKUNDE / BFG **1415**

BUNDESANSTALT FUER MATERIALFORSCHUNG UND -PRUFUNG (GERMANY) See AMTS- UND MITTEILUNGSBLATT / BAM, BUNDESANSTALT FUER MATERIALFORSCHUNG UND -PRUFUNG **1964**

BUNDESANSTALT FUER STRASSENWESEN (GERMANY). BEREICH UNFALLFORSCHUNG See FORSCHUNGSPROGRAMM - BUNDESANSTALT FUER STRASSENWESEN, BEREICH UNFALLFORSCHUNG **5440**

BUNDESANZEIGER (GW/0344-7634) [01751143] **4635**

BUNDESARBEITSBLATT (GW/0007-5868) [01537803] **1657**

BUNDESBAHN, DIE (GW/0007-5876) [08558282] **5430**

BUNDESBAHN-VERSICHERUNGSANSTALT See GESCHAFTSBERICHT DER BUNDESBAHN-VERSICHERUNGSANSTALT **1676**

BUNDESBAUBLATT (GW/0007-5884) [02778911] **2816**

BUNDESFIRMENREGISTER. BAND 1, NORD- UND WESTDEUTSCHLAND 1986 (GW/0931-5918) [I09315918] **644**

BUNDESFORSCHUNGSANSTALT FUER FORST- UND HOLZWIRTSCHAFT (GERMANY) See MITTEILUNGEN DER BUNDESFORSCHUNGSANSTALT FUER FORST- UND HOLZWIRTSCHAFT REINBEK BEI HAMBURG **2388**

BUNDESGESETZBLATT (GW) [08939065] **2945**

BUNDESGESETZBLATT FUER DIE REPUBLIK OSTERREICH (AU) [06027169] **2945**

BUNDESGESUNDHEITSBLATT (GW/0007-5914) [06364700] **4770**

BUNDESKAMMER DER GEWERBLICHEN WIRTSCHAFT (AUSTRIA). SEKTION INDUSTRIE See MONATSBEZUEGE DER ANGESTELLTEN IN DER INDUSTRIE OSTERREICHS **1691**

BUNDESMARINE (GW) [02981161] **4175**

BUNDESRECHNUNGSABSCHLUSS (AU) [04098628] **4715**

BUNDESREPUBLIK DEUTSCHLAND STAATSHANDBUCH. LANDESAUSGABE LAND NORDRHEIN-WESTFALEN, DIE (GW) [10030178] **4635**

BUNDESSTELLE FUER AUSSENHANDELSINFORMATION (GERMANY) See NIEDERLANDE: WIRTSCHAFT IN ZAHLEN UND WIRTSCHAFTSDOKUMENTATION **1575**

BUNDESSTELLE FUER AUSSENHANDELSINFORMATION (GERMANY) See GHANA: ENERGIEWIRTSCHAFT **1945**

BUNDESSTELLE FUER AUSSENHANDELSINFORMATION (GERMANY) See PORTUGAL, AZOREN UND MADEIRA : WIRTSCHAFT IN ZAHLEN UND WIRTSCHAFTSDOKUMENTATION **1578**

BUNDESSTELLE FUER AUSSENHANDELSINFORMATION (GERMANY) See IRLAND : WIRTSCHAFTLICHE ENTWICKLUNGEN **1568**

BUNDESSTELLE FUER AUSSENHANDELSINFORMATION (GERMANY) See MACAN : WIRTSCHAFTLICHE ENTWICKLUNG **1573**

BUNDESSTELLE FUER AUSSENHANDELSINFORMATION (GERMANY) See EL SALVADOR: WIRTSCHAFTLICHE ENTWICKLUNG **1559**

BUNDESSTELLE FUER AUSSENHANDELSINFORMATION (GERMANY) See EL SALVADOR: ENERGIEWIRTSCHAFT **1937**

BUNDESSTELLE FUER AUSSENHANDELSINFORMATION (GERMANY) See OMAN: ENERGIEWIRTSCHAFT **1952**

BUNDESSTELLE FUER AUSSENHANDELSINFORMATION (GERMANY) See ZENTRALAFRIKANISHCHES KAISERREICH: WIRTSCHAFTLICHE ENTWICKLUNG **1589**

BUNDESSTELLE FUER AUSSENHANDELSINFORMATION (GERMANY) See DEMOKRATISCHE VOLKSREPUBLIK JEMEN: ENERGIEWIRTSCHAFT **1936**

BUNDESSTELLE FUER AUSSENHANDELSINFORMATION (GERMANY) See FINNLAND: WIRTSCHAFTLICHE ENTWICKLUNG **1561**

BUNDESSTELLE FUER AUSSENHANDELSINFORMATION (GERMANY) See WIRTSCHAFTLICHE ENTWICKLUNG: NICARAGUA **1589**

BUNDESSTELLE FUER AUSSENHANDELSINFORMATION (GERMANY) See ISLAND: ENERGIEWIRTSCHAFT **1948**

BUNDESSTELLE FUER AUSSENHANDELSINFORMATION (GERMANY) See WIRTSCHAFTLICHE ENTWICKLUNG: MADAGASKAR **1588**

BUNDESSTELLE FUER AUSSENHANDELSINFORMATION (GERMANY) See KENIA: WIRTSCHAFTSDATEN UND WIRTSCHAFTSDOKUMENTATION **1570**

BUNDESSTELLE FUER AUSSENHANDELSINFORMATION (GERMANY) See BELGIEN : WIRTSCHAFT IN ZAHLEN UND WIRTSCHAFTSDOKUMENTATION **1548**

BUNDESSTELLE FUER AUSSENHANDELSINFORMATION (GERMANY) See NIEDERLANDE : ENERGIEWIRTSCHAFT **1951**

BUNDESSTELLE FUER AUSSENHANDELSINFORMATION (GERMANY) See JAPAN: ENERGIEWIRTSCHAFT **1948**

BUNDESSTELLE FUER AUSSENHANDELSINFORMATION (GERMANY) See KUBA : WIRTSCHAFTLICHE ENTWICKLUNG **1571**

BUNDESSTELLE FUER AUSSENHANDELSINFORMATION (GERMANY) See SOMALIA : WIRTSCHAFTLICHE ENTWICKLUNG **1521**

BUNDESSTELLE FUER AUSSENHANDELSINFORMATION (GERMANY) See BANGLADESH : WIRTSCHAFTLICHE ENTWICKLUNG **1547**

BUNDESSTELLE FUER AUSSENHANDELSINFORMATION (GERMANY) See SAUDI-ARABIEN: WIRTSCHAFTLICHE ENTWICKLUNG **1519**

BUNDESSTELLE FUER AUSSENHANDELSINFORMATION (GERMANY) See REPUBLIK KOREA : WIRTSCHAFTSDATEN UND WRITSCHAFTSDOKUMENTATION **1581**

BUNDESSTELLE FUER AUSSENHANDELSINFORMATION (GERMANY) See VOLKSREPUBLIK KONGO : WIRTSCHAFTLICHE ENTWICKLUNG **1588**

BUNDESSTELLE FUER AUSSENHANDELSINFORMATION (GERMANY) See TOGO : WIRTSCHAFTLICHE ENTWICKLUNG **1587**

BUNDESSTELLE FUER AUSSENHANDELSINFORMATION (GERMANY) See AFGHANISTAN, PAKISTAN : ENERGIEWIRTSCHAFT **1931**

BUNDESSTELLE FUER AUSSENHANDELSINFORMATION (GERMANY) See GUYANA : WIRTSCHAFTLICHE ENTWICKLUNG **1565**

BUNDESSTELLE FUER AUSSENHANDELSINFORMATION (GERMANY) See ECUADOR : ENERGIEWIRTSCHAFT **1937**

BUNDESSTELLE FUER AUSSENHANDELSINFORMATION (GERMANY) See BRASILIEN: WIRTSCHAFTLICHE ENTWICKLUNG **1549**

BUNDESSTELLE FUER AUSSENHANDELSINFORMATION (GERMANY) See QATAR: WIRTSCHAFTLICHE ENTWICKLUNG **1579**

BUNDESSTELLE FUER AUSSENHANDELSINFORMATION (GERMANY) See SINGAPUR : ENERGIEWIRTSCHAFT **1957**

BUNDESSTELLE FUER AUSSENHANDELSINFORMATION (GERMANY) See PANAMA : WIRTSCHAFTLICHE ENTWICKLUNG **1577**

BUNDESSTELLE FUER AUSSENHANDELSINFORMATION (GERMANY) See SAMBIA : ENERGIEWIRTSCHAFT **1625**

BUNDESSTELLE FUER AUSSENHANDELSINFORMATION (GERMANY) See BELGIEN : ENERGIEWIRTSCHAFT **1933**

BUNDESSTELLE FUER AUSSENHANDELSINFORMATION (GERMANY) See WIRTSCHAFTLICHE ENTWICKLUNG : MOCAMBIQUE **1589**

BUNDESSTELLE FUER AUSSENHANDELSINFORMATION (GERMANY) See LIBANON : WIRTSCHAFTSDATEN UND WIRTSCHAFTSDOKUMENTATION **1572**

BUNDESSTELLE FUER AUSSENHANDELSINFORMATION (GERMANY) See POLEN : VOLKSWIRTSCHAFTSPLAN UND BUDGETDATEN **1578**

BUNDESSTELLE FUER AUSSENHANDELSINFORMATION (GERMANY) See OBERVOLTA : WIRTSCHAFTSDATEN UND WIRTSCHAFTSDOKUMENTATION **1576**

BUNDESSTELLE FUER AUSSENHANDELSINFORMATION (GERMANY) See JAMAIKA : WIRTSCHAFTLICHE ENTWICKLUNG **1568**

BUNDESSTELLE FUER AUSSENHANDELSINFORMATION (GERMANY) See GABUN : ENERGIEWIRTSCHAFT **1607**

BUNDESSTELLE FUER AUSSENHANDELSINFORMATION (GERMANY) See GHANA : WIRTSCHAFTSDATEN UND WIRTSCHAFTSDOKUMENTATION **1564**

BUNDESSTELLE FUER AUSSENHANDELSINFORMATION (GERMANY) See IRLAND : WIRTSCHAFT IN ZAHLEN UND WIRTSCHAFTSDOKUMENTATION 1568

BUNDESTEFUERLLE FUER AUSSENHANDELSINFORMATION (GERMANY) See WIRTSCHAFTLICHE ENTWICKLUNG: AFGHANISTAN 1588

BUNDESSTELLE FUER AUSSENHANDELSINFORMATION (GERMANY) See FRANKREICH : ENERGIEWIRTSCHAFT 1944

BUNDESSTELLE FUER AUSSENHANDELSINFORMATION (GERMANY) See ARABISCHE REPUBLIK JEMEN : WIRTSCHAFTLICHE ENTWICKLUNG 1546

BUNDESSTELLE FUER AUSSENHANDELSINFORMATION (GERMANY) See ZOLLDIENST 3078

BUNDESSTELLE FUER AUSSENHANDELSINFORMATION (GERMANY) See KOLUMBIEN : WIRTSCHAFTLICHE ENTWICKLUNG 1571

BUNDESSTELLE FUER AUSSENHANDELSINFORMATION (GERMANY) See GHANA : WIRTSCHAFTLICHE ENTWICKLUNG 1564

BUNDESSTELLE FUER AUSSENHANDELSINFORMATION (GERMANY) See MALAYSIA : WIRTSCHAFTSDATEN UND WIRTSCHAFTSDOKUMENTATION 1573

BUNDESSTELLE FUER AUSSENHANDELSINFORMATION (GERMANY) See WIRTSCHAFTLICHE ENTWICKLUNG : GUATEMALA 1588

BUNDESSTELLE FUER AUSSENHANDELSINFORMATION. (GERMANY) See WIRTSCHAFTLICHE ENTWICKLUNG : VENEZUELA 1589

BUNDESSTELLE FUER AUSSENHANDELSINFORMATION (GERMANY) See TRINIDAD UND TOBAGO : WIRTSCHAFTLICHE ENTWICKLUNG 1525

BUNDESSTELLE FUER AUSSENHANDELSINFORMATION (GERMANY) See DANEMARK : WIRTSCHAFTLICHE ENTWICKLUNG 1555

BUNDESSTELLE FUER AUSSENHANDELSINFORMATION (GERMANY) See MALAYSIA : WIRTSCHAFTLICHE ENTWICKLUNG 1504

BUNDESSTELLE FUER AUSSENHANDELSINFORMATION (GERMANY) See LIBANON : WIRTSCHAFTLICHE ENTWICKLUNG 1572

BUNDESSTELLE FUER AUSSENHANDELSINFORMATION (GERMANY) See PORTUGAL : ENERGIEWIRTSCHAFT 1953

BUNDESSTELLE FUER AUSSENHANDELSINFORMATION (GERMANY) See ITALIEN : WIRTSCHAFTLICHE ENTWICKLUNG 1568

BUNDESSTELLE FUER AUSSENHANDELSINFORMATION (GERMANY) See ZAIRE : LUFTVERKEHR 40

BUNDESSTELLE FUER AUSSENHANDELSINFORMATION (GERMANY) See GRIECHENLAND : WIRTSCHAFTSDATEN UND WIRTSCHAFTSDOKUMENTATION 1564

BUNDESSTELLE FUER AUSSENHANDELSINFORMATION (GERMANY) See REPUBLIK KOREA : ENERGIEWIRTSCHAFT 1955

BUNDESSTELLE FUER AUSSENHANDELSINFORMATION (GERMANY) See SCHWEDEN : WIRTSCHAFTLICHE ENTWICKLUNG 1583

BUNDESSTELLE FUER AUSSENHANDELSINFORMATION (GERMANY) See INDONESIEN : WIRTSCHAFTLICHE ENTWICKLUNG 1567

BUNDESSTELLE FUER AUSSENHANDELSINFORMATION (GERMANY) See RUMANIEN: VOLKSWIRTSCHAFTSPLAN UND BUDGETDATEN 1582

BUNDESSTELLE FUER AUSSENHANDELSINFORMATION (GERMANY) See REPUBLIK SUDAFRIKA : ENERGIEWIRTSCHAFT 1955

BUNDESSTELLE FUER AUSSENHANDELSINFORMATION (GERMANY) See FRANKREICH : WIRTSCHAFT IN ZAHLEN UND WIRTSCHAFTSDOKUMENTATION 1562

BUNDESSTELLE FUER AUSSENHANDELSINFORMATION (GERMANY) See ISLAND : WIRTSCHAFT IN ZAHLEN 1568

BUNDESSTELLE FUER AUSSENHANDELSINFORMATION (GERMANY) See INDONESIEN : WIRTSCHAFTSDATEN UND WIRTSCHAFTSDOKUMENTATION 1567

BUNDESSTELLE FUER AUSSENHANDELSINFORMATION (GERMANY) See NEPAL : WIRTSCHAFTLICHE ENTWICKLUNG 1575

BUNDESSTELLE FUER AUSSENHANDELSINFORMATION (GERMANY) See QATAR : ENERGIEWIRTSCHAFT 1954

BUNDESSTELLE FUER AUSSENHANDELSINFORMATION (GERMANY) See MALAWI : WIRTSCHAFTLICHE ENTWICKLUNG 1573

BUNDESSTELLE FUER AUSSENHANDELSINFORMATION (GERMANY) See ITALIEN : WIRTSCHAFT IN ZAHLEN UND WIRTSCHAFTSDOKUMENTATION 1568

BUNDESSTELLE FUER AUSSENHANDELSINFORMATION (GERMANY) See FINNLAND : WIRTSCHAFT IN ZAHLEN UND WIRTSCHAFTSDOKUMENTATION 1561

BUNDESSTELLE FUER AUSSENHANDELSINFORMATION (GERMANY) See KAMERUN : EINFUHRPROGRAMM 843

BUNDESSTELLE FUER AUSSENHANDELSINFORMATION (GERMANY) See JORDANIEN : WIRTSCHAFTSDATEN UND WIRTSCHAFTSDOKUMENTATION 1569

BUNDESSTELLE FUER AUSSENHANDELSINFORMATION (GERMANY) See BOLIVIEN : ENERGIEWIRTSCHAFT 1934

BUNDESSTELLE FUER AUSSENHANDELSINFORMATION (GERMANY) See SWASILAND : WIRTSCHAFTLICHE ENTWICKLUNG 1586

BUNDESSTELLE FUER AUSSENHANDELSINFORMATION (GERMANY) See TOGO : WIRTSCHAFTSDATEN UND WIRTSCHAFTSDOKUMENTATION 1587

BUNDESSTELLE FUER AUSSENHANDELSINFORMATION (GERMANY) See GABUN : WIRTSCHAFTLICHE ENTWICKLUNG 5327

BUNDESSTELLE FUER AUSSENHANDELSINFORMATION (GERMANY) See USA: WIRTSCHAFT IN ZAHLEN 1588

BUNDESSTELLE FUER AUSSENHANDELSINFORMATION (GERMANY) See ZAIRE : ENERGIEWIRTSCHAFT 1961

BUNDESSTELLE FUER AUSSENHANDELSINFORMATION (GERMANY) See SYRIEN : WIRTSCHAFTLICHE ENTWICKLUNG 1586

BUNDESSTELLE FUER AUSSENHANDELSINFORMATION (GERMANY) See LIBERIA : WIRTSCHAFTLICHE ENTWICKLUNG 1572

BUNDESSTELLE FUER AUSSENHANDELSINFORMATION (GERMANY) See SCHWEIZ : ENERGIEWIRTSCHAFT 1956

BUNDESSTELLE FUER AUSSENHANDELSINFORMATION (GERMANY) See WESTEUROPA : QUELLEN ZUM MARKT FUER ELEKTROHAUSGERATE 2812

BUNDESSTELLE FUER AUSSENHANDELSINFORMATION (GERMANY) See ELFENBEINKUSTE : WIRTSCHAFTLICHE ENTWICKLUNG 1559

BUNDESSTELLE FUER AUSSENHANDELSINFORMATION (GERMANY) See BRASILIEN : WIRTSCHAFTLICHE ENTWICKLUNG DES BUNDESSTATES RIO GRANDE DO SUL 1549

BUNDESSTELLE FUER AUSSENHANDELSINFORMATION (GERMANY) See LUXEMBURG : WIRTSCHAFT IN ZAHLEN UND WIRTSCHAFTSDOKUMENTATION 1573

BUNDESSTELLE FUER AUSSENHANDELSINFORMATION (GERMANY) See NEUSEELAND: ENERGIEWIRTSCHAFT 2123

BUNDESSTELLE FUER AUSSENHANDELSINFORMATION (GERMANY) See SINGAPUR : WIRTSCHAFTLICHE ENTWICKLUNG 1584

BUNDESSTELLE FUER AUSSENHANDELSINFORMATION (GERMANY) See ATHIOPIEN WIRTSCHAFTSLAGE 1464

BUNDESSTELLE FUER AUSSENHANDELSINFORMATION (GERMANY) See ATHIOPIEN : WIRTSCHAFTLICHE ENTWICKLUNG 1547

BUNDESSTELLE FUER AUSSENHANDELSINFORMATION (GERMANY) See ZYPERN, TURKISCH VERWALTETER TEIL : WIRTSCHAFTLICHE ENTWICKLUNG 1589

BUNDESSTELLE FUER AUSSENHANDELSINFORMATION (GERMANY) See SRI LANKA : ENERGIEWIRTSCHAFT 1958

BUNDESSTELLE FUER AUSSENHANDELSINFORMATION (GERMANY) See SCHWEDEN : WIRTSCHAFT IN ZAHLEN UND WIRTSCHAFTSDOKUMENTATION 1583

BUNDESSTELLE FUER AUSSENHANDELSINFORMATION (GERMANY) See USA : ENERGIEWIRTSCHAFT 1960

BUNDESSTELLE FUER AUSSENHANDELSINFORMATION (GERMANY) See WIRTSCHAFTLICHE ENTWICKLUNG : AGYPTEN 1588

BUNDESSTELLE FUER AUSSENHANDELSINFORMATION (GERMANY) See BRASILIEN : WIRTSCHAFTSDOKUMENTATION 1465

BUNDESSTELLE FUER AUSSENHANDELSINFORMATION (GERMANY) See VEREINIGTE ARABISCHE EMIRATE : WIRTSCHAFTLICHE ENTWICKLUNG 1525

BUNDESSTELLE FUER AUSSENHANDELSINFORMATION (GERMANY) See TRINIDAD UND TOBAGO : ENERGIEWIRTSCHAFT 1959

BUNDESSTELLE FUER AUSSENHANDELSINFORMATION (GERMANY) See QATAR : WIRTSCHAFTSDATEN UND WIRTSCHAFTSDOKUMENTATION 1579

BUNDESSTELLE FUER AUSSENHANDELSINFORMATION (GERMANY) See WIRTSCHAFTLICHE ENTWICKLUNG : KUWAIT 1588

BUNDESSTELLE FUER AUSSENHANDELSINFORMATION (GERMANY) See SENEGAL : WIRTSCHAFTLICHE ENTWICKLUNG 1583

BUNDESSTELLE FUER AUSSENHANDELSINFORMATION (GERMANY) See NIEDERLANDE : WIRTSCHAFTLICHE ENTWICKLUNG UND PROGNOSE 1575

BUNDESSTELLE FUER AUSSENHANDELSINFORMATION (GERMANY) See THAILAND : WIRTSCHAFTLICHE ENTWICKLUNG 1587

BUNDESSTELLE FUER AUSSENHANDELSINFORMATION (GERMANY) See ALGERIEN : WIRTSCHAFTSDATEN UND WIRTSCHAFTSDOKUMENTATION 1545

BUNDESSTELLE FUER AUSSENHANDELSINFORMATION (GERMANY) See TOGO : ENERGIEWIRTSCHAFT 1959

BUNDESSTELLE FUER AUSSENHANDELSINFORMATION (GERMANY) See KAMERUN : WIRTSCHAFTLICHE ENTWICKLUNG 1570

BUNDESSTELLE FUER AUSSENHANDELSINFORMATION (GERMANY) See CHILE : ENERGIEWIRTSCHAFT 1935

BUNDESSTELLE FUER AUSSENHANDELSINFORMATION (GERMANY) See MAURITIUS : WIRTSCHAFTSDATEN UND WIRTSCHAFTSDOKUMENTATION 1574

BUNDESSTELLE FUER AUSSENHANDELSINFORMATION (GERMANY) See ZYPERN : ENERGIEWIRTSCHAFT 1961

BUNDESSTELLE FUER AUSSENHANDELSINFORMATION (GERMANY) See PERU: WIRTSCHAFTSDATEN UND WIRTSCHAFTSDOKUMENTATION 1578

BUNDESSTELLE FUER AUSSENHANDELSINFORMATION (GERMANY) See WESTEUROPA QUELLEN ZUM KRAFTFAHRZEUGMARKT 5428

BUNDESSTELLE FUER AUSSENHANDELSINFORMATION (GERMANY) See WIRTSCHAFTLICHE ENTWICKLUNG : ZYPERN 1589

BUNDESSTELLE FUER AUSSENHANDELSINFORMATION (GERMANY) See BOLVIEN : WIRTSCHAFTSDATEN 1549

BUNDESSTELLE FUER AUSSENHANDELSINFORMATION (GERMANY) See AGUPTEM : ENERGIEWIRTSCHAFT 1931

BUNDESSTELLE FUER AUSSENHANDELSINFORMATION (GERMANY) See KUWAIT : WIRTSCHAFTSDATEN UND WIRTSCHAFTSDOKUMENTATION 1571

BUNDESSTELLE FUER AUSSENHANDELSINFORMATION (GERMANY) See PAKISTAN : ENERGIEWIRTSCHAFT **1952**

BUNDESSTELLE FUER AUSSENHANDELSINFORMATION (GERMANY) See ZAIRE : WIRTSCHAFTLICHE ENTWICKLUNG **1589**

BUNDESSTELLE FUER AUSSENHANDELSINFORMATION (GERMANY) See NIGERIA : ENERGIEWIRTSCHAFT **1951**

BUNDESSTEUERBLATT (GW) [01782617] **4715**

BUNDESVERBAND DER BETRIEBSKRANKENKASSEN (GERMANY) See BETRIEBSKRANKENKASSEN **2876**

BUNDESVERBAND DER OBST- UND GEMUESEVERWERTUNGSINDUSTRIE See INDUSTRIELLE OBST- UND GEMUESEVERWERTUNG, DIE **2344**

BUNDESVERBAND DER ORTSKRANKENKASSEN See STATISTIK DER ORTSKRANKENKASSEN IN DER BUNDESREPUBLIK DEUTSCHLAND : ALTERSGLIEDERUNG DER MITGLIEDER **2898**

BUNDESVEREINIGUNG DER DEUTSCHEN ARBEITGEBERVERBANDE See SAE, SAMMLUNG ARBEITSRECHTLICHER ENTSCHEIDUNGEN **3154**

BUNDESVERSONGUNGSBLATT IM BUNDESARBEITSBLATT See BUNDESVERSORGUNGSBLATT **4038**

BUNDESVERSORGUNGSBLATT (GW) [02556239] **4038**

BUNDESVORANSCHLAG (AU) [12734980] **4715**

BUNESKAMMER DER GEWERBLICHEN WIRTSCHAFT (AUSTRIA). SEKTION INDUSTRI See ARBEITER IM ANGESTELLTENVERHALTNIS IN DER INDUSTRIE OSTERREICHS **1651**

BUNGA RAMPAI ILMU SASTRA (IO) [06825174] **3370**

BUNGAKU (JA) [23191470] **3370**

BUNGAKU KUKAN (JA) [05619919] **3370**

BUNGAKUKAI (JA) [01537809] **2502**

BUNGAKUKAI (JA) [13369569] **3370**

BUNGEI GENGO KENKYU: BUNGEIHEN (JA) [04403343] **3370**

BUNGEI KENKYU (JA) [07044701] **3370**

BUNGEI SHUNJU (JA) [01537812] **2502**

BUNGEI (TOKYO, JAPAN : 1962) (JA/0525-1885) [01537810] **2502**

BUNGEI YOKOHAMA (JA) [05656288] **3370**

BUNKA (JA) [02245281] **5229**

BUNKAGAKU NENPO (JA) [04375635] **5241**

BUNKAGAKU NENPO (KOBE DAIGAKU. BUNKAGAKU KENKYUKA) (JA) [08759628] **5194**, **2843**

BUNKAZAI NO HOZON (JA) [08157349] **4086**, **2647**

BUNKER BANNER / BUNKER FAMILY ASSOCIATION OF AMERICA (US) [08758991] **2441**

BUNKER HILL GAZETTE-NEWS, THE (US) [23283890] **5658**

BUNKERFUELS REPORT (US/0739-294X) [09719251] **4252**

BUNKO KENKYU (JA/0038-7002) [03093491] **4434**

BUNRIN (JA) [10173020] **3370**

BUNSEKI (JA/0386-2178) [02200852] **1014**

BUNSEKI (JA) [04856507] **1014**

BUNSEKI KAGAKU (JA/0525-1931) [03061122] **1014**

BUNTE HUND, DER (GW/0721-183X) [l0721183X] **1060**

BUNTE ILLUSTRIERTE (GW) [01537818] **2514**

BUNTINGS' ... BERRIES (US) [12223453] **2411**

BUNTINGS' NURSERIES See BUNTINGS' ... BERRIES **2411**

BUNYAN STUDIES (UK/0954-0970) [19074833] **3370**

BUOYANT FLIGHT (US/0361-5065) [02246093] **15**

BUR (CHICAGO, ILL.), THE (US/0007-6007) [11217527] **1318**

●BURAFF'S LITIGATION REPORTS. BANK LAWYER LIABILITY (US/1067-618X) [27230769] **3085**

BURBANK BANNER (US/1071-7013) [24281095] **2441**

BURBANK FAMILY NEWS (US/0736-4040) [09104876] **2441**

BURDA INTERNATIONAL (IT) **1082**

BURDA-MODEN (1964) (GW/0007-6031) [06281876] **1082**

BURDA MODEN SONDERHEFT FUER MAEDCHEN UND JUNGEN (GW) **1082**

BUREAU CANADIEN DE LA RADIO See RADIO (MONTREAL) **1137**

BUREAU COUNTY REPUBLICAN, THE (US/0894-1181) [09140664] **5658**

BUREAU DE LA PROTECTION CIVILE DU QUEBEC See RAPPORT ANNUEL / BUREAU DE LA PROTECTION CIVILE DU QUEBEC **4054**

BUREAU DE LA STATISTIQUE DU QUEBEC See PUBLICATIONS DU BUREAU DE LA STATISTIQUE DU QUEBEC, LES **423**

BUREAU DE LA STATISTIQUE DU QUEBEC See RAPPORT D'ACTIVITES / LE BUREAU DE LA STATISTIQUE DU QUEBEC **5337**

BUREAU DE LA STATISTIQUE DU QUEBEC. SERVICE DES FINANCES, DES GOUVERNEMENTS ET DES INSTITUTIONS A BUT NON LUCRATIF See STATISTIQUES FINANCIERES DU GOUVERNEMENT DU QUEBEC **4700**

BUREAU DE L'ENSEIGNEMENT NATIONAL CATHOLIQUE See STATISTIQUES DE L'ENSEIGNEMENT PRIMAIRE ET SECONDAIRE **5036**

BUREAU DE L'ENSEIGNEMENT NATIONAL CATHOLIQUE. SERVICE STATISTIQUE See ECOLES SECONDAIRES, LES **1737**

BUREAU DE LIAISON DES AGENTS DE COOPERATION TECHNIQUE See NOTICE D'INFORMATION A L'USAGE DES AGENTS DE LA COOPERATION : REPUBLIQUE DU SENEGAL **2642**

BUREAU DE RECHERCHE SUR L'INDUSTRIE DE LA TOURBE DANS L'EST DU QUEBEC See BRITEQ PRESSE **1934**

BUREAU DE RECHERCHES ET DE PARTICIPATIONS MINIERES See ACTIVITIES / BUREAU DE RECHERCHES ET DE PARTICIPATIONS MINIERES **2132**

BUREAU DE RECHERCHES ET DE PARTICIPATIONS MINIERES : RAPPORT (MR) [19462612] **2135**, **1421**

BUREAU D'ETUDES AUTOMATISMES (FR/0296-8517) [12993060] **1250**, **1218**

BUREAU INTERNATIONAL DE L'HEURE, PARIS See RAPPORT ANNUEL - BUREAU INTERNATIONAL DE L'HEURE **399**

BUREAU INTERNATIONAL DU TRAVAIL ABONNEMENT GROUPE (SZ) **1657**

BUREAU MEMORANDUM (US/0162-0150) [04082275] **4385**

BUREAU NEWS / BUREAU OF WHOLESALE SALES REPRESENTATIVES (US/0747-4598) [10889294] **644**

BUREAU OF BUSINESS PRACTICE MANAGEMENT LETTER, THE (US) [19122558] **862**

BUREAU OF CORRECTION ANNUAL REPORT (US) [08091351] **3159**

BUREAU OF EDUCATIONAL AND PSYCHOLOGICAL RESEARCH, CALCUTTA See BULLETIN OF THE BUREAU OF EDUCATIONAL AND PSYCHOLOGICAL RESEARCH, CALCUTTA **4759**

BUREAU OF FISHERIES LABORATORY See MISCELLANEOUS REPORT - BUREAU OF FISHERIES LABORATORY **2308**

BUREAU OF JUSTICE STATISTICS ANNUAL REPORT / U.S. DEPARTMENT OF JUSTICE, BUREAU OF JUSTICE STATISTICS (US) [14204555] **3159**, **3079**

BUREAU OF MINES INFORMATION CIRCULAR (US/1066-5544) [01728697] **2135**

BUREAU OF MINES RESEARCH (US/0737-626X) [01730827] **3999**, **2135**

BUREAU OF MINES TECHNICAL PROGRESS REPORT (US/0362-725X) [01729880] **2135**

BUREAU OF NATIONAL AFFAIRS (WASHINGTON, D.C.) See CHEMICAL REGULATION REPORTER **2949**

BUREAU OF NATIONAL AFFAIRS (WASHINGTON, D.C.) See BNA PENSION REPORTER **1656**

BUREAU OF NATIONAL AFFAIRS (WASHINGTON, D.C.) See ANTITRUST & TRADE REGULATION REPORT **3095**

BUREAU OF NATIONAL AFFAIRS (WASHINGTON, D.C.) See MEDIA LAW REPORTER **3008**

BUREAU OF NATIONAL AFFAIRS (WASHINGTON, D.C.) See BNA POLICY AND PRACTICE SERIES **939**

BUREAU OF NATIONAL AFFAIRS (WASHINGTON, D.C.) See FEDERAL CONTRACTS REPORT **2969**

BUREAU OF NAVAL PERSONNEL MANUAL (US) [02786217] **939**

BUREAU OF RADIOLOGICAL HEALTH PUBLICATIONS SUBJECT INDEX (US/0194-1399) [08743275] **3939**

BUREAU OF RECLAMATION PROGRESS (US/0565-0674) [02291029] **70**

BUREAU OF RESEARCH & PUBLICATIONS ON TRIPURA See B.R.P.T. BULLETIN **2646**

BUREAU OF WHOLESALE SALES REPRESENTATIVES (U.S.) See BUREAU NEWS / BUREAU OF WHOLESALE SALES REPRESENTATIVES **644**

BUREAU SPECIALIST See UNITED STATES SPECIALIST, THE **1147**

BUREAU SUISSE (SZ) **4210**, **645**

BUREAU VERITAS See BULLETIN TECHNIQUE DU BUREAU VERITAS **4175**

BUREAUCRAT See PUBLIC MANAGER (POTOMAC, MD.), THE **4676**

BUREAUCRAT, THE (NR) [06629560] **4702**

BUREAUX D'ETUDES 1990 (FR/1148-7305) [l11487305] **1172**

BUREAUX ET SYSTEMES See BUREAU SUISSE **645**

BUREAUX ET SYSTEMES (SZ/0257-8328) [l02578328] **4210**, **862**

BURENIE (MOSKVA) (RU/0521-8136) [10120469] **756**

BURGEN UND SCHLOSSER (GW/0007-6201) [03374296] **2682**

BURGENLANDISCHE HEIMATBLATTER (AU/1018-6107) [l10186107] **5580**

BURGENLANDISCHER AGRAR KURIER (AU) [05951239] **70**

BURGENSE (SP/0521-8195) [02732674] **4941**

BURIED HISTORY (AT/0007-6260) [01714589] **265**

BURIED TREASURE (WESTLAKE, OHIO) SUSPENDED. (US/1043-0806) [19299995] **1060**

BURIED TREASURES (US/0882-5653) [11810144] **2441**

BURIED VALLEY INVESTIGATION (US/0473-9434) [01152426] **1412**

BURKBURNETT INFORMER STAR (US) [13994394] **5747**

BURKE & NOVI NOTIZIE FLASH DELLA SETTIMANA (IT) **2486**

BURKE COUNTY TRIBUNE (US) [01537836] **5725**

BURKE'S IRISH FAMILY RECORDS (UK) [03495001] **2441**

BURKE'S PRESIDENTIAL FAMILIES OF THE UNITED STATES OF AMERICA (UK) [07359463] **4466**

BURKINA FASO See JOURNAL OFFICIEL DU BURKINA FASO **4659**

BURLESON COUNTY CITIZEN-TRIBUNE AND THE CALDWELL NEWS (US) [16988489] **5747**

BURLESON FAMILY BULLETIN (US/0730-1405) [07941885] **2441**

BURLINGTON CORPORATION. ANNUAL REPORT See ANNUAL REPORT / BURLINGTON INDUSTRIES INC **1597**

BURLINGTON COUNTY TIMES (WILLINGBORO, N.J.) (US) [15288442] **5709**

BURLINGTON FREE PRESS (1923), THE (US/0894-8844) [09390458] **5760**

BURLINGTON INDUSTRIES See ANNUAL REPORT / BURLINGTON INDUSTRIES INC **1597**

BURLINGTON MAGAZINE (UK/0007-6287) [05461534] **346**

BURLINGTON NEWS, THE (US) [29435309] **5688**

BURLINGTON STANDARD-PRESS (US/0749-7261) [11166890] **5765**

BURMA RESEARCH SOCIETY See JOURNAL OF THE BURMA RESEARCH SOCIETY **2656**

BURMA RESEARCH SOCIETY. JOURNAL OF THE BURMA RESEARCH SOCIETY See MYANMA NAING NGAN THUTEITHANA ATHIN GYANE. THE JOURNAL OF THE BURMA RESEARCH SOCIETY **2659**

BURMA (UNION). MINISTRY OF FOREIGN AFFAIRS See CONSULAR LIST AND LIST OF INTERNATIONAL ORGANIZATIONS **4519**

BURMASS' TEX-OK-KAN OIL DIRECTORY (US/8755-1489) [11194085] **4252**

BURNET BULLETIN (US) [10151550] **5747**

BURNETT COUNTY SENTINEL (GRANTSBURG, WIS. : 1962) (US) [15151393] **5766**

BURNETT FAMILY NEWSLETTER (US/0730-4978) [08011724] **2441**

BURNING BUSH (US/0007-6309) **5057**

BURNS CHRONICLE (UK) [25404193] **3370**, **431**

BUSINESS

BURNS : JOURNAL OF THE INTERNATIONAL SOCIETY FOR BURN INJURIES (UK/0305-4179) [20002337] **3561**

BURNSVILLE CURRENT, THE (US/0193-3000) [05165130] **5694**

BUROTECHNIK *See* OFFICE-MANAGEMENT (BADEN-BADEN) **880**

BURPEE GARDENS (US/0749-4653) [10337544] **2411**

BURPEE SPRING FLOWERING BULBS : ... PRE-SEASON SALE CATALOG (US) [12011491] **2411**

BURPEE'S IMPORTED DUTCH BULBS : ... WHOLESALE PRICES FOR THE TRADE (US) [12011336] **2411**

BURRELLE'S BLACK HISPANIC MEDIA DIRECTORY **SUSPENDED.** (US) **1105**

BURRELLE'S BLACK MEDIA DIRECTORY (US/0748-4259) [10036991] 2257, **1105**

BURRELLE'S NEW ENGLAND MEDIA DIRECTORY **SUSPENDED.** (US/0883-9999) [18568885] **1105**

BURRELLE'S NEW JERSEY MEDIA DIRECTORY **SUSPENDED.** (US/0883-9978) [07119047] **1105**

BURRELLE'S ... PENNSYLVANIA MEDIA DIRECTORY (US/0276-7872) [07268421] **1105**

BURRELLE'S WOMEN'S MEDIA DIRECTORY (US/0748-4240) [10086502] 5552, **1105**

BURRTON GRAPHIC (BURRTON, KAN. : 1893) *See* HARVEY COUNTY INDEPENDENT, THE **5676**

BURT FRANKLIN RESEARCH AND SOURCE WORKS SERIES (US/0068-4341) [04909560] **2612**

BURTON GROUP NEWS ANALYSIS (US) **1240**

BURTON GROUP REPORT (US) **645**

BURUNDI EN IMAGES / REPUBLIQUE DU BURUNDI, MINISTERE DE L'INFORMATION, DIRECTION GENERALE DES PUBLICATIONS DE PRESSE, DEPARTEMENT DE LA PRESSE PERIODIQUE, LE (BD) [07867496] **2638**

BURUNDI, WIRTSCHAFTDATEN UND WIRTSCHAFTSDOKUMENTATION / BUNDESSTELLE FUER AUSSENHANDELSINFORMATION (GW) [07845483] **1550**

BURWELL DIRECTORY OF INFORMATION BROKERS (US) [23686495] **3199**

BUS AND COACH STATISTICS, GREAT BRITAIN (UK) [20876655] **5378**

BUS DATABASE (US) **1172**

BUS ET CAR (FR/0399-2535) [03992535] **5378**

BUS RIDE (US/0192-8902) [03064294] **5378**

BUS RIDE: BUS INDUSTRY DIRECTORY (US/0363-3764) [02454353] **5378**

BUS (ST-LAURENT) (CN/0835-0280) [16798804] **1729**

BUS TOURS MAGAZINE (US/0199-6096) [06046553] **5465**

BUS VERKEHR (GW) [11789326] **5378**

BUS WORLD (US/0162-9689) [04258461] **5378**

BUSARL : BOLOGNA (IT) **818**

BUSARL : CAMPOBASSO (IT) **818**

BUSARL : FIRENZE (IT) **818**

BUSARL : LIGURIA (IT) **781**

BUSARL : MILAN (IT) **818**

BUSARL : NAPOLI (IT) **818**

BUSARL : PERUGIA (IT) **4635**

BUSARL : TRIESTE (IT) **4635**

BUSEFAL. BULLETIN POUR LES SOUS ENSEMBLES FLOUS ET LEURS APPLICATIONS (FR/0296-3698) [02963698] **1089**

BUSES SHEPPERTON (UK/0007-6392) [00076392] **5378**

BUSES YEARBOOK (UK) [19336476] **5378**

BUSH FIRE BULLETIN (AT) [07563627] **2288**

BUSH-MEETING DUTCH, THE (US/1071-0523) [12934289] 2441, **4941**

BUSHDRIVER (AT/0155-0535) [01550535] **5408**

BUSHU KYODO SHIRYO (JA) [01797398] **2647**

BUSHWHACKER *See* BUSHWHACKER MUSINGS : VERNON COUNTY HISTORICAL SOCIETY NEWSLETTER **2725**

BUSHWHACKER MUSINGS : VERNON COUNTY HISTORICAL SOCIETY NEWSLETTER (US/1070-8243) [28473795] 2441, **2725**

BUSINESS ACCOUNTING FOR LAWYERS NEWSLETTER / PRACTISING LAW INSTITUTE (US/0885-1034) [10900797] **3096**

BUSINESS ACRONYMS (US/0899-3726) [18109884] 825, **645**

BUSINESS ADVISORY REVIEW (CN/0823-9665) [11559805] **645**

BUSINESS ADVOCATE, THE (US/0193-4414) [05215683] **3096**

BUSINESS ADVOCATE (WASHINGTON, D.C. : 1983), THE (US/0746-3669) [09977384] **3096**

●BUSINESS AFFIRMATIVE ACTION DIRECTORY (US) [25006349] 2257, **1600**

BUSINESS AFRICA / ECONOMIST INTELLIGENCE UNIT (UK) [27571189] **645**

BUSINESS ALABAMA MONTHLY (US/1050-091X) [20876991] **645**

BUSINESS AMERICA (US/0190-6275) [04320918] **825**

BUSINESS & ACQUISITION NEWSLETTER (US/0738-7253) [09655148] **645**

BUSINESS AND COMMERCIAL AVIATION (US/0191-4642) [07320376] **15**

BUSINESS & COMPUTING COMMUNICATIONS *See* WHAT'S NEW IN COMPUTING **1207**

BUSINESS AND DEVELOPMENT NEWS (MW/0304-9647) [01798175] **1600**

BUSINESS AND ECONOMIC HISTORY (US/0894-6825) [03757511] **645**

BUSINESS & ECONOMIC REPORT (US/1043-6227) [10989908] **1550**

BUSINESS AND ECONOMIC REVIEW (COLUMBIA) (US/0007-6465) [01537867] **862**

BUSINESS & ECONOMICS REVIEW (UK/0951-919X) [18437998] 1466, **645**

BUSINESS & ECONOMICS (SPRINGFIELD, VA.) *See* NTIS ALERT. BUSINESS & ECONOMICS **700**

BUSINESS AND FINANCE (E/0007-6473) [02252939] **781**

BUSINESS & FINANCE CAREER DIRECTORY (US/1064-8127) [20698132] **781**

BUSINESS AND FINANCE IN SCOTLAND (UK) **781**

BUSINESS AND GOVERNMENT (UK) 4635, **645**

BUSINESS AND GOVERNMENT SALARY AND WAGE SURVEYS (NEW JERSEY) (US) [05066213] **1657**

BUSINESS AND HEALTH (US/0739-9413) [09839332] 4770, **645**

BUSINESS AND INCENTIVE STRATEGIES (US/1064-430X) [26281765] **756**

BUSINESS & INDUSTRY (US/0021-0463) [01537868] **645**

●BUSINESS AND LEGAL START-UP DIRECTORY FOR ENTREPRENEURS, THE (US/1061-8635) [25482203] **645**

BUSINESS AND MANAGEMENT EDITIONS: BMB (BE) **862**

BUSINESS & MANAGEMENT EDUCATION FUNDING ALERT (US/1042-5217) [19075806] **1813**

BUSINESS & PROFESSIONAL ETHICS JOURNAL (US/0277-2027) [07520096] 2249, **645**

BUSINESS & PROFESSIONAL WOMAN (OTTAWA) (CN/0045-3587) [01736769] 645, **5552**

BUSINESS AND SOCIETY (US/0007-6503) [01537869] **645**

BUSINESS AND SOCIETY BRIEFING (US/1065-5875) [26641016] **645**

BUSINESS AND SOCIETY REVIEW (1974) (US/0045-3609) [02240366] **645**

BUSINESS & STREET DIRECTORY FOR ... ADELAIDE CITY & SUBURBS, INCLUDING ELIZABETH & SALISBURY (AT) [10201074] **645**

BUSINESS & STREET DIRECTORY FOR PERTH CITY & SUBURBS (AT) [08324030] 1923, **645**

BUSINESS & TAX PLANNING QUARTERLY *CEASED.* (US/0898-1841) [17742544] **645**

BUSINESS & TELECOM (NEDERLANDSE ED.) (BE/0778-7588) [07787588] 1150, **645**

BUSINESS & THE CONTEMPORARY WORLD (WALTHAM, MASS. 1991) (GW/1062-6158) [25000937] **645**

BUSINESS AND THE ENVIRONMENT (US/1052-7206) [22361839] **2162**

BUSINESS & THE LAW (CN/0825-4982) [11607479] **3096**

BUSINESS AND THE MEDIA (US/0270-3572) [06395730] **1105**

BUSINESS ARCHIVES (UK/0007-6538) [15178342] **3199**

BUSINESS ASAP [COMPUTER FILE] (US) 646, **726**

BUSINESS ASIA (HK/0572-7545) [02066333] **646**

BUSINESS ASSISTANCE MONOGRAPH SERIES, THE (US/0146-4744) [02942051] 781, **646**

BUSINESS ASSOCIATION REVIEW (US) [03064379] **646**

BUSINESS ASSOCIATIONS IN WASHINGTON STATE (US) [06850959] **825**

BUSINESS ATLANTA (US/0192-0855) [04905261] **646**

BUSINESS AVIATION (US) **15**

BUSINESS AVIATION SAFETY (US/0890-8664) [14510646] **15**

BUSINESS BANKER INTERNATIONAL *CEASED.* (IE/0956-1498) [21363941] **781**

BUSINESS BASICS (US) [06994000] **646**

BUSINESS BASICS - GUIDE TO BUSINESS FORMS (UK) **646**

BUSINESS BASICS - GUIDE TO NATIONAL INSURANCE (UK) **646**

BUSINESS BASICS - PROPERTY (UK) **646**

●BUSINESS BASICS STAFF BULLETIN (UK/1352-5581) [113525581] **646**

BUSINESS BASICS - TAX (UK) **646**

BUSINESS BLUE-BOOK OF SOUTH AFRICA (SA) [05819629] **646**

BUSINESS BOOK REVIEW (US/0741-8132) [10205287] **646**

BUSINESS BRIEFING (UK) **646**

BUSINESS BRIEFING LOOSELEAF (UK) **740**

BUSINESS BRIEFS (DETROIT, MICH.) (US/0890-2178) [04300409] **646**

BUSINESS BULLETIN (US) [20578174] **893**

BUSINESS BULLETIN (FRANKFORT, KY.) (US/0899-6830) [18183883] **646**

BUSINESS CHINA (HK) [04384429] **922**

BUSINESS CHRONICLE (II) [01784201] 1466, **646**

●BUSINESS CLAIMS CASUALTY BULLETIN (US/1075-9018) [30327007] **2877**

BUSINESS COMMERCIAL AVIATION (US/0007-6570) [03064340] **15**

BUSINESS COMMUNICATIONS (JA) **646**

BUSINESS COMMUNICATIONS (UK) 1150, **646**

BUSINESS COMMUNICATIONS REVIEW (US/0162-3885) [04163601] **646**

BUSINESS COMPUTER INDEX, THE (US/0741-2363) [10108293] 646, **1172**

BUSINESS COMPUTER NEWS (CN/0838-438X) [19762939] 1265, **646**

BUSINESS COMPUTING (GW) **1172**

BUSINESS COMPUTING & COMMUNICATIONS *See* WHAT'S NEW IN COMPUTING **1245**

BUSINESS COMPUTING & COMMUNICATIONS (UK/0265-1564) [02651564] **1172**

●BUSINESS CONCEPTS (US/1055-8217) [23352003] **646**

BUSINESS CONDITIONS (NEW YORK) (US/0146-7425) [03027048] **646**

BUSINESS CONNEXIONS (CN) [25730478] **646**

BUSINESS CONTACT (RU/0235-764X) [22166685] **826**

BUSINESS CONTACT EXPRESS (RU) [24401598] **646**

BUSINESS CONTACT : JOURNAL OF THE BELGIAN CHAMBER OF COMMERCE IN GREAT BRITAIN (UK) [09668400] **818**

BUSINESS CONTACTS IN FINLAND (FI/0355-0346) [01799335] **646**

BUSINESS COUNCIL BULLETIN (AT/0814-4273) [26190619] **646**

BUSINESS CREDIT (US/0897-0181) [17358534] **781**

BUSINESS CRIMES BULLETIN (US) 3159, **646**

BUSINESS CURRENTS. TECHNICAL REPORT (US/0736-4415) [09125295] **939**

BUSINESS DATA PROCESSING: A WILEY SERIES (US/0193-9734) [05279782] 1256, **646**

BUSINESS DATE (AT) 1729, **646**

BUSINESS DATELINE (US) 646, **727**

BUSINESS DAY (SA) [17376037] **5810**

BUSINESS DAY'S 1000 TOP CORPORATIONS IN THE PHILIPPINES (PH) [11011798] **647**

BUSINESS DAY'S PHILIPPINES' LARGEST EXPORTERS (PH) [08593049] **826**

BUSINESS — Alphabetical Title Index

BUSINESS DIARY (UK) **647**

BUSINESS DIGEST (US/1046-168X) [20341557] **647**

BUSINESS DIGEST (DANBURY, CONN.) (US/8750-9520) [11951059] **647**

BUSINESS DIGEST (HYANNIS, MASS.) (US/0895-3791) [16581206] **647**

BUSINESS DIGEST PARIS (FR/1167-2064) [11672064] **647**

BUSINESS DIGEST (PORTSMOUTH, N.H.) **CEASED.** (US/0747-1629) [10617537] **647**

BUSINESS DIRECTIONS (AT/1031-2315) [I10312315] **647**

BUSINESS DIRECTORY (TH) [02245019] **647**

BUSINESS DIRECTORY : A COMPREHENSIVE GUIDE FOR BUYING BUSINESS-TO-BUSINESS GOODS AND SERVICES IN THE HAMILTON/BURLINGTON AREA (CN/1184-9819) [24690761] **647**

BUSINESS DIRECTORY (AGANA) (GU/0072-7865) [01353024] **647**

BUSINESS DIRECTORY & COMMUNITY GUIDE (US) [20026826] **818**

BUSINESS DIRECTORY & RESOURCE GUIDE (US) [19469886] **647**

BUSINESS DIRECTORY / NATIONAL FOOTBALL LEAGUE RETIRED PLAYERS ASSOCIATION (US) [12032988] **4888**

BUSINESS DIRECTORY OF HONG KONG (HK) [04139304] **647**

BUSINESS DIRECTORY ... OF THE HUNGARIAN CHAMBER OF COMMERCE (HU) [22923329] **818**

BUSINESS DOCUMENTS (US) **647**

BUSINESS DYNAMICS (100 MILE HOUSE) **CEASED.** (CN/0831-7291) [15587078] 862, **647**

BUSINESS EASTERN EUROPE (UK) [02395961] **647**

BUSINESS ECONOMICS (CLEVELAND, OHIO) (US/0007-666X) [01537881] 647, **1466**

BUSINESS ECONOMICS. MEMBERSHIP DIRECTORY (US) [13573530] **1466**

BUSINESS ECONOMIST (UK/0306-5049) [01077976] 1466, **647**

BUSINESS EDUCATION (UK/0144-2813) [11795178] **647**

BUSINESS EDUCATION FORUM (US/0007-6678) [05933640] 1911, **647**

BUSINESS EDUCATION INDEX (US/0068-4414) [01537885] 647, 1729, **727**

BUSINESS EDUCATION NEWS (FREDERICTON) (CN/0710-7714) [08336326] 1729, **647**

BUSINESS-EDUCATION REPORT (US/1068-2198) [27472400] 647, **1729**

BUSINESS EDUCATION TODAY (UK) [17486724] 647, **1729**

BUSINESS EDUCATION TODAY (UK/0951-1512) [I09511512] 1890, **647**

BUSINESS ELECTRONICS NETWORKS (US/0731-0102) [08107389] **647**

BUSINESS ENGLISH (JA) **647**

BUSINESS ENVIRONMENT RISK INFORMATION (US/0738-5595) [09611599] **893**

BUSINESS ENVIRONMENTAL FORUM (AT) **647**

BUSINESS EQUIPMENT DIGEST (UK/0007-6708) [I00076708] **4210**

●BUSINESS ETHICS: A EUROPEAN REVIEW (UK/0962-8770) [25652399] 647, **2249**

BUSINESS ETHICS (MADISON, WIS.) (US/0894-6582) [16163587] 647, **2249**

BUSINESS ETHICS QUARTERLY (US/1052-150X) [22196487] 2249, **647**

BUSINESS ETHICS RESOURCE (US/1064-0223) [20975465] 2249, **648**

●BUSINESS ETHICS REVIEW (US/1061-0081) [25155364] **2249**

●BUSINESS EUROPA (UK/0966-3541) [27126331] **648**

BUSINESS EUROPE (UK/0007-6724) [02258796] 4517, **648**

BUSINESS EXPECTATIONS (US) [06799107] **648**

BUSINESS FACILITIES (US/0746-0023) [09335820] **648**

BUSINESS FAILURE RECORD (US) [12848830] **648**

BUSINESS FAX (US/0897-2052) [17455759] **1150**

BUSINESS FINLAND (FI/0785-5540) [20603384] **648**

BUSINESS FIRMS DIRECTORY OF THE DELAWARE VALLEY (US/0091-2581) [01786902] **648**

BUSINESS FIRST (US) **648**

BUSINESS FIRST (BUFFALO, N.Y.) (US/0749-9418) [11241106] **648**

BUSINESS FIRST (COLUMBUS, OHIO) (US/0748-6146) [10979783] **648**

BUSINESS FIRST (LOUISVILLE, KY.) (US/0748-6138) [10979806] **648**

BUSINESS FLYER, THE (US/0893-3073) [15501910] **648**

BUSINESS FOR CENTRAL NEW JERSEY (US/1042-8704) [18180957] **862**

BUSINESS FORECASTING CONFERENCE. UCLA BUSINESS FORECAST FOR THE NATION AND CALIFORNIA IN . *See* UCLA BUSINESS FORECAST FOR CALIFORNIA, THE **1525**

BUSINESS FORMATIONS AND FAILURES (CN/1184-9223) [24296407] **648**

BUSINESS FORMS, LABELS & SYSTEMS (US/1044-758X) [19898127] **4211**

BUSINESS FORUM (LOS ANGELES, CALIF.) (US/0733-2408) [08425442] **648**

BUSINESS GUIDE BOOK TO DJAKARTA *See* BUSINESS GUIDE : JAKARTA **648**

BUSINESS GUIDE HUNGARY (HU/0238-180X) [20974666] 5465, **648**

BUSINESS GUIDE : JAKARTA (IO) [02479328] **648**

BUSINESS GUIDE, THE (CN/0847-3900) [21417028] **648**

BUSINESS GUIDE TO ATLANTA (US/1045-3822) [20083056] **648**

BUSINESS, HEALTH AND EDUCATIONAL DISCIPLINES (US/0360-7208) [01920026] 4770, **648**

BUSINESS HISTORY (UK/0007-6791) [01537892] **648**

BUSINESS HISTORY CONFERENCE *See* BUSINESS AND ECONOMIC HISTORY **645**

BUSINESS HISTORY REVIEW (US/0007-6805) [05984700] **648**

BUSINESS HISTORY REVIEW (US/0007-6805) [06285449] **648**

BUSINESS IDEAS NEWSLETTER (US/0738-7024) [08166473] **649**

BUSINESS IN BROWARD (US) **649**

BUSINESS IN BROWARD (US) [21899631] **1466**

BUSINESS IN NEBRASKA (US/0007-683X) [05347963] **649**

BUSINESS IN PALM BEACH COUNTY (US) **649**

BUSINESS IN THAILAND (TH/0125-0140) [01789647] **649**

BUSINESS IN THE EX-USSR *See* DELOVIE LYUDI **787**

BUSINESS IN VANCOUVER (CN/0849-5017) [21201067] **649**

BUSINESS INDEX (US/0273-3684) [06888173] 649, **727**

BUSINESS INDIA (II/0254-5268) [04525594] 1467, **649**

BUSINESS INDICATORS (AT) [21115183] **649**

BUSINESS INDICATORS. CD-ROM (US) **1550**

BUSINESS-INDUSTRY POLITICAL ACTION COMMITTEE. POLITICAL ACTION DIVISION *See* BIPAC ACTION REPORT **4465**

BUSINESS, INDUSTRY, TECHNOLOGY SERVICES (US) [01775698] **5092**

BUSINESS INFORMATION ALERT (US/1042-0746) [18729155] 649, **3199**

●BUSINESS INFORMATION BASICS (UK/0953-9263) **649**

●BUSINESS INFORMATION FROM GOVERNMENT (UK/0966-2138) [I09662138] **649**

BUSINESS INFORMATION FROM YOUR PUBLIC LIBRARY (US/0892-6034) [15242822] 3199, **649**

BUSINESS INFORMATION REVIEW (UK/0266-3821) [12266742] **3199**

BUSINESS INQUIRY (US/0007-6856) [03064628] **649**

BUSINESS INSIGHT (US/1056-6244) [23603609] **649**

BUSINESS INSIGHTS : SCHOOL OF BUSINESS ADMINISTRATION QUARTERLY MAGAZINE, CALIFORNIA STATE UNIVERSITY, LONG BEACH (US/0270-2266) [11381543] **649**

BUSINESS INSURANCE (US/0007-6864) [01785372] **2877**

BUSINESS INSURANCE. DIRECTORY OF CORPORATE BUYERS OF INSURANCE, BENEFIT PLANS AND RISK MANAGEMENT SERVICES (US/0747-7937) [10464954] **649**

BUSINESS INSURANCE. EDITORIAL INDEX **CEASED.** (US/0275-0317) [07074102] **2877**

BUSINESS INTERCOMMUNICATIONS INC *See* WHITE PAPER ON JAPANESE TRADE **857**

BUSINESS INTERNATIONAL (US/0007-6872) [01537899] **649**

BUSINESS INTERNATIONAL CORPORATION *See* BUSINESS INTERNATIONAL MONEY REPORT **781**

BUSINESS INTERNATIONAL CORPORATION *See* INVESTING, LICENSING AND TRADING CONDITIONS ABROAD **684**

BUSINESS INTERNATIONAL CORPORATION. BUSINESS INTERNATIONAL MONEY REPORT *See* FINANCE & TREASURY **898**

BUSINESS INTERNATIONAL MONEY REPORT (US/0161-0384) [01388221] **781**

BUSINESS JAPAN *See* JAPAN 21ST **685**

BUSINESS JOURNAL (GW) [06294564] **649**

BUSINESS JOURNAL (1988), THE (US/1048-8812) [21058456] **649**

BUSINESS JOURNAL (CHARLOTTE, N.C.) (US/0887-5588) [13306307] **649**

BUSINESS JOURNAL (MILWAUKEE, WIS.), THE (US/0740-2899) [09912188] **649**

BUSINESS JOURNAL (NEW YORK) (US) **649**

BUSINESS JOURNAL OF NEW JERSEY (JAMESBURG, N.J : 1985) (US/0889-3403) [13868705] **649**

BUSINESS JOURNAL OF THE PERMIAN BASIN (US) [15687804] **650**

BUSINESS JOURNAL OF UPPER EAST TENNESSEE AND SOUTHWEST VIRGINIA (US/1040-6360) [18494065] **650**

BUSINESS JOURNAL (PHOENIX, ARIZ.), THE (US/0895-1632) [16510904] **650**

BUSINESS JOURNAL (PORTLAND, OR.), THE (US/0742-6550) [10399453] **650**

BUSINESS JOURNAL (SACRAMENTO, CALIF.) (US/8756-5897) [11605271] **650**

BUSINESS JOURNAL / SONOMA & MARIN (US) **650**

BUSINESS JOURNAL (WICHITA) (US/0091-3537) [05881418] **650**

BUSINESS KOREA (KO) [10516467] **650**

BUSINESS KOREA YEARBOOK ON KOREAN ECONOMY AND BUSINESS (KO) [14235576] **650**

BUSINESS LATIN AMERICA (UK/0007-6880) [02066545] **650**

BUSINESS LAW BRIEF (UK) [10480212] **3096**

BUSINESS LAW EUROPE (UK) **2945**

BUSINESS LAW EUROPE (GW) [23737971] **3096**

BUSINESS LAW HANDBOOK (UK) **3096**

BUSINESS LAW JOURNAL (CORAL GABLES, FLA.), THE (US/1047-2819) [20650544] **3096**

BUSINESS LAW MONOGRAPHS (US) [11423996] **3096**

BUSINESS LAW REPORTER (US/0277-1713) [07520138] **3096**

BUSINESS LAW REPORTS (CN/0703-5551) [03257383] **3096**

BUSINESS LAW REVIEW (UK) [06977142] **3096**

BUSINESS LAW REVIEW LONDON (UK/0143-6295) [I01436295] **3096**

BUSINESS LAW SECTION NEWSLETTER (US/1054-0326) [22716971] **3096**

●BUSINESS LAW TODAY / THE MAGAZINE OF THE ABA SECTION OF BUSINESS LAW (US/1059-9436) [24832460] **3097**

BUSINESS LAWYER, THE (US/0007-6899) [01537903] 3085, **3097**

BUSINESS LAWYER UPDATE *See* BUSINESS LAW TODAY / THE MAGAZINE OF THE ABA SECTION OF BUSINESS LAW **3097**

BUSINESS LAWYER UPDATE, THE (US/0884-1977) [12322237] **3097**

BUSINESS LEADER (RALEIGH, N.C.) (US/1060-8230) [25065440] **650**

BUSINESS LEADS AND SALES TARGETS (US/0190-6208) [04735302] **650**

BUSINESS LEADS INTERNATIONAL (US/1050-5474) [21534157] **650**

BUSINESS LEGAL MATERIALS, RUSSIA (US/1066-2596) [I10662596] 650, **2945**

BUSINESS LIBRARY NEWSLETTER (US/0191-4006) [04863659] 650, **3199**

BUSINESS LIBRARY REVIEW (US/1045-7798) [20228861] 1467, **650**

BUSINESS LIFE (1980) (CN/0714-8585) [09145837] **650**

BUSINESS

BUSINESS LINE (SYLMAR, CALIF.) ***SUSPENDED.*** (US/0898-3526) [17791716] **650**

BUSINESS (LUXEMBOURG) (LU) **650**

BUSINESS MACHINE DEALER (US/1055-7822) [23305391] **4211**

BUSINESS (MADISON) (US/0192-7450) [05105598] **650**

BUSINESS MAILERS REVIEW (US/0739-3873) [09725221] 922, **650**

BUSINESS/MANAGEMENT (GUILFORD, CONN.) (US/0276-3923) [07145158] **862**

BUSINESS MARKETING (US/0745-5933) [09306784] **922**

BUSINESS MEDIA WEEK (US/8756-9639) [11773448] 1105, 1236, **650**

BUSINESS MEMO FROM BELGIUM (US/0007-6945) [01537908] **893**

BUSINESS MEXICO (MX/0187-1455) [23709222] **650**

BUSINESS MIDDLE EAST (UK) **650**

●BUSINESS MN (RU) [25243879] **5809**

BUSINESS MONITOR PRODUCTION SERIES. MISCELLANEOUS MONITORS (UK) **893**

BUSINESS MONITOR PRODUCTION SERIES. PRODUCTION MONITORS (UK) **650**

BUSINESS NEW HAMPSHIRE MAGAZINE (US/1046-9575) [20571439] **650**

BUSINESS/NEW YORK ***CEASED.*** (US/8750-927X) [11921327] **651**

BUSINESS NEWS CONFIDENTIAL (US) **651**

BUSINESS NEWS (EUGENE, OR.), THE (US/1064-1661) [26221772] **651**

BUSINESS NEWS FROM POLAND (PL) **651**

BUSINESS NEWS INDEX ***See*** AUTOMOTIVE BUSINESS NEWS **641**

BUSINESS NEWS (MACOMB) (US/0192-9461) [05131473] **651**

BUSINESS NEWS, SAN DIEGO (US/0738-6869) [09667184] **651**

BUSINESS NEWS (ST. JOHN'S, NFLD.) (CN/0834-020X) [16308619] **651**

BUSINESS NEWSLETTERS DIRECTORY (UK/0967-6376) **651**

BUSINESS, NORTH CAROLINA (US/0279-4276) [07867540] **651**

BUSINESS NORTHWEST (CN/0846-1058) [24266791] **651**

BUSINESS OF FILM, THE (UK) [21125560] **4064**

BUSINESS OF FUR, THE (US/0740-6258) [10027552] **3183**

●BUSINESS OF MANAGED CARE (US/1072-1932) [28883876] **3777**

BUSINESS ONE IRWIN BUSINESS AND INVESTMENT ALMANAC ***See*** IRWIN BUSINESS AND INVESTMENT ALMANAC, THE **684**

... BUSINESS ONE IRWIN BUSINESS AND INVESTMENT ALMANAC, THE (US/1057-5014) [22919468] **651**

BUSINESS ONE IRWIN INVESTOR'S HANDBOOK, THE (US/1062-0028) [23368467] **893**

BUSINESS OPINION (NZ) [03505073] 1467, **651**

BUSINESS OPPORTUNITIES HANDBOOK (US/1042-6175) [17193559] 1294, **651**

BUSINESS OPPORTUNITIES IN EASTERN EUROPE (US/1051-0273) [21790936] **651**

BUSINESS OPPORTUNITIES JOURNAL (US/0193-3221) [04856402] 4835, **893**

BUSINESS ORGANIZATIONS, AGENCIES, AND PUBLICATIONS DIRECTORY (US/0888-1413) [13490653] **651**

BUSINESS OUTLOOK FOR WEST MICHIGAN (US) [13231178] **651**

BUSINESS OUTLOOK IN CANADA : A DISCUSSION BY THE CONFERENCE BOARD'S CANADIAN ECONOMIC FORUM (CN) [04141671] **1550**

BUSINESS OUTLOOK IN THE PHILIPPINES AND ASIA (PH/0115-0235) [03329473] **651**

BUSINESS OUTLOOK (WELLINGTON) ***See*** NATIONAL BUSINESS OUTLOOK **800**

BUSINESS OWNER (HICKSVILLE, N.Y.), THE (US/0190-4914) [03622870] **651**

●BUSINESS OWNER (NEWPORT BEACH, CALIF.) (US/1064-4598) [26288791] **651**

BUSINESS PARTNER HUNGARY ***CEASED.*** (HU/0237-3831) [I02373831] **826**

BUSINESS PEOPLE MAGAZINE (WINNIPEG. 1990) (CN/0849-3901) [23238141] **651**

BUSINESS PERIODICALS INDEX (US/0007-6961) [05574615] **727**

BUSINESS PERIODICALS INDEX. CD-ROM (US/0007-6961) **727**

BUSINESS PERSPECTIVES (MEMPHIS, TENN.) (US/0896-3703) [16978704] **651**

BUSINESS PHILADELPHIA (US/1051-7510) [22102009] **651**

BUSINESS PICTURE, THE (US/1064-2471) [26245261] **651**

BUSINESS PLAN (VICTORIA) (CN/0846-0620) [23659448] **4715**

●BUSINESS PLANS HANDBOOK (US) **651**

BUSINESS PRESS (CN/0707-493X) [04754918] **651**

BUSINESS PRESS (FORT WORTH, TEX.), THE (US/1045-8697) [19888865] **651**

●BUSINESS PROCESS RE-ENGINEERING & MANAGEMENT JOURNAL (UK/1355-2546) **862**

BUSINESS PROFILE SERIES. THE PEOPLE'S REPUBLIC OF CHINA / THE HONGKONG AND SHANGHAI BANKING CORPORATION (HK) [08377984] **651**

BUSINESS PROFITABILITY DATA (US/1045-232X) [08424959] **651**

●BUSINESS PUBLICATION ADVERTISING SOURCE (US) [28643451] **756**

BUSINESS PUBLICATION RATES AND DATA (US/0038-948X) [06188313] **651**

BUSINESS PUBLICATIONS INDEX AND ABSTRACTS (US/0739-618X) [09772878] 652, **727**

BUSINESS PUBLICATIONS INDEX AND ABSTRACTS. SUBJECT/AUTHOR CITATIONS ***CEASED.*** (US) [10316291] **652**

BUSINESS PUBLISHER (US) **4812**

BUSINESS PUBLISHING (CAROL STREAM, ILL.) (US/1060-2208) [24890349] 1263, **4812**

BUSINESS PUERTO RICO (PR) [11299463] **652**

BUSINESS QUARTERLY, THE (CN/0007-6996) [01801613] **652**

BUSINESS QUEENSLAND (AT/1038-1430) [I10381430] **652**

BUSINESS RADIO (US/0746-8911) [10378132] **1150**

BUSINESS RANKINGS ANNUAL (US/1043-7908) [19564062] **652**

BUSINESS RECORD (DES MOINES, IOWA) (US/0746-410X) [10014322] **652**

BUSINESS RECORD (DES MOINES, IOWA) ***See*** DES MOINES BUSINESS RECORD **665**

●BUSINESS RECORD, THE (US/1068-2899) [27293488] **652**

BUSINESS REFERRAL DIRECTORY / GREATER SAN DIEGO CHAMBER OF COMMERCE (US/1068-3038) [08732098] **652**

BUSINESS REGULATION LAW REPORT: WAGE AND PRICE CONTROL (US/0094-2502) [01793348] **3097**

BUSINESS REORGANIZATIONS UNDER THE BANKRUPTCY CODE (US/0733-4613) [08556436] **3086**

BUSINESS REPORT (CN/0833-062X) [17314576] 1876, **652**

BUSINESS REPORT (JA) [26912268] **5430**

BUSINESS RESEARCH BULLETIN (US/0362-823X) [02351468] **652**

BUSINESS RESEARCH GUIDE HEADLAND (UK/0957-9869) [I09579869] **652**

BUSINESS REVIEW (TH/0125-0477) [01791936] **652**

●BUSINESS REVIEW (UK/1354-1110) **652**

BUSINESS REVIEW AND ECONOMIC NEWS FROM ISRAEL (US/0149-0826) [03427307] **1467**

BUSINESS REVIEW (MONTREAL) ***CEASED.*** (CN/0005-531X) [01519133] **652**

BUSINESS REVIEW (PHILADELPHIA) (US/0007-7011) [01591471] 652, **1467**

BUSINESS REVIEW (WASHINGTON ED.), THE (US/0745-9351) [09611936] **652**

BUSINESS REVIEW WEEKLY : BRW (AT/0727-758X) [10249354] **652**

BUSINESS REVIEWS (US) [04311408] **652**

BUSINESS RISK SERVICE (GW) **652**

BUSINESS ROUNDS (CN/1180-260X) [24256447] **3913**

BUSINESS (SAINT LOUIS, MO.) (US) [10042421] 1467, **652**

BUSINESS SCOTLAND ***CEASED.*** (UK/0144-6096) [02998697] **652**

●BUSINESS SERIALS (US/1056-3512) [23668972] **652**

BUSINESS SERVICES (CN/0838-2182) [19544051] **1600**

BUSINESS SOFTWARE DIRECTORY (US/0887-9478) [13439321] **1284**

BUSINESS SOFTWARE REVIEW (US/0885-8055) [12732916] **1172**

BUSINESS SOURCE, THE (US/1181-8131) [23658899] **652**

●BUSINESS SOURCE. [COMPUTER FILE] (US) [29353716] 652, **727**

BUSINESS SPAIN (UK) **652**

BUSINESS SPEAKER'S DIGEST (US/1055-3568) [23157996] **652**

BUSINESS STATISTICS (BIENNIAL) (US/0083-2545) [01227582] 652, **727**

BUSINESS STATISTICS LONDON (UK/0967-6392) [I09676392] **5324**

BUSINESS STATISTICS, NEW YORK STATE (US) [04577284] 652, **727**

BUSINESS STRATEGIES / CCH (US) [10177361] **653**

BUSINESS STRATEGY REVIEW (UK/0955-6419) [22516151] **653**

BUSINESS STUDIES (UK/0953-685X) [21491699] 1729, **653**

BUSINESS STUDIES, THE (PK) [05525389] **653**

BUSINESS SYSTEMS AND EQUIPMENT (LONDON, 1972) ***CEASED.*** (UK/0007-7097) [08959902] **4211**

BUSINESS TAX INTERPRETATIONS (US/0146-0587) [02123086] 653, **4715**

BUSINESS TAX REPORT (US/0897-9979) [17691810] **3097**

BUSINESS TELECOMMUNICATIONS DIRECTORY ***CEASED.*** (US/1041-6137) [18831593] **1150**

●BUSINESS THEATER (US/1064-475X) [26294183] **5362**

BUSINESS TIMES (EAST HARTFORD, CONN.), THE (US/0744-172X) [08086655] **653**

BUSINESS TIMES SINGAPORE (SI) 653, **5810**

BUSINESS TIMES [MICROFORM] (MY) [19834552] **5806**

BUSINESS-TO-BUSINESS DIRECT MARKETER, THE (US/0897-7127) [17629265] **922**

BUSINESS TO BUSINESS (PITTSFORD, N.Y.) (US/0897-9065) [15547447] **653**

BUSINESS TO BUSINESS QUINTE ***CEASED.*** (CN/1186-0340) [24266735] **653**

BUSINESS TO BUSINESS SOUTH AUSTRALIA (AT/1033-9612) [I10339612] **653**

BUSINESS TODAY (US/0007-7100) [01537918] **653**

●BUSINESS TODAY (II) [26482979] **653**

BUSINESS TODAY, CONSTRUCTION NEWS (CN/1187-4635) [25652233] **606**

BUSINESS TOKYO ***CEASED.*** (JA/0914-0026) [15641679] **653**

BUSINESS (TORONTO) (CN/0708-5842) [05528624] 653, **5552**

BUSINESS TRAVEL MANAGEMENT (US/1046-5057) [20433523] 5465, **653**

BUSINESS TRAVEL NEWS (US/8750-3670) [11349490] 5465, **653**

BUSINESS TRAVEL REVIEW ***CEASED.*** (US/0746-9497) [10407142] 653, **5465**

BUSINESS TRAVELER INTERNATIONAL (UK/0955-7288) [18894485] **5465**

BUSINESS TRAVELER'S REPORT ***CEASED.*** (US/0270-7969) [06497751] 653, **5465**

BUSINESS TRAVELLER AND LEISURE TIME PLANNER (CN/0834-0552) [15731079] 653, **5465**

BUSINESS TRAVELLER ASIA-PACIFIC ED (HK/0255-7312) [I02557312] **5465**

BUSINESS TRENDS (PETALUMA, CALIF.) ***CEASED.*** (US/0194-9225) [05114254] **653**

BUSINESS UNIV. JOURNAL, THE ***CEASED.*** (US/0882-8547) [11648365] **1172**

BUSINESS UPDATE (SANTA ANA, CALIF.) ***CEASED.*** (US/8750-7803) [11759968] **818**

BUSINESS VALUATOR (CN/0703-1939) [03660593] **740**

BUSINESS VENEZUELA (VE/1013-2120) [02690609] **653**

BUSINESS VENTURES ***See*** BUSINESS OPPORTUNITIES JOURNAL **893**

BUSINESS VISUALIZATION ***CEASED.*** (US/1056-7852) [23853054] 653, **1172**

BUSINESS — Alphabetical Title Index

BUSINESS WEEK (US/0007-7135) [01537921] **653**

BUSINESS WEEK (INDUSTRIAL ED.) (US/0739-8395) [09431646] **653**

BUSINESS WHO'S WHO OF AUSTRALIA, THE (AT/0068-4503) [01537922] **727**

BUSINESS WHO'S WHO PRODUCTS AND TRADENAMES GUIDE (AT/1031-1343) [I10311343] 653, **727**

BUSINESS WHO'S WHO, THE (UK/0308-0390) [02239427] **431**

BUSINESS WIRE NEWSLETTER (US) **653**

●BUSINESS WOMEN'S NETWORK DIRECTORY, THE (US/1076-7363) [30596892] 5552, **653**

BUSINESS WORCESTER (US/0738-8977) [09679172] **654**

BUSINESS WORLD (II) [07992270] 654, **1550**

BUSINESS YELLOW PAGES OF AMERICA ON CD-ROM *CEASED.* (CN) **654**

BUSINESSBEAT (CN/0227-0331) [07888548] **654**

BUSINESSCOPE (MY/0126-7930) [01797933] **654**

BUSINESSES AND ASSETS (UK) [15179035] **893**

BUSINESSGRAM (TAMPA, FLA.) (US/1064-2412) [26246552] **654**

BUSINESSLETTER (LIVESTOCK MARKETING ASSOCIATION) *See* LMA BUSINESSLETTER, THE **215**

BUSINESSLINK *CEASED.* (US) [16322478] 2277, **654**

BUSINESSMAN'S DIRECTORY, THE REPUBLIC OF CHINA / CHUNG-HUA MIN KUO KUNG SHANG CHI YEH CHIH NAN (CH) [01797597] **654**

BUSINESSMAN'S GUIDE TO THE ARAB WORLD (US/0275-1690) [06654269] **654**

BUSINESSMEN'S EXPECTATIONS *See* BUSINESS EXPECTATIONS **648**

BUSINESSWEST (SPRINGFIELD, MASS.) (US/1049-9822) [19658044] **654**

●BUSINEST (CN/1189-458X) [26715157] **1600**

BUSINFO *CEASED.* (US/0882-4436) [11835979] **654**

BUSKAP OG AVDRATT (NO/0007-7194) [03970418] **208**

BUSQUEDA (UY) [02903576] **1550**

BUSS *CEASED.* (US/0193-6832) [05251321] **1265**

BUSSEIKEN DAYORI (TOKYO) (JA/0385-9843) [04030117] **4427**

BUTADIENE ANNUAL (US/0740-1760) [09879310] **1600**

BUTCE GELIRLERI YLLG (TU) [02452819] **4716**

BUTCHER & PROCESSOR (UK/0268-1781) [I02681781] **2329**

BUTLER BULLETIN, THE (US) [15698154] **5663**

BUTLER COUNTY BANNER (US/0745-7006) [09387214] **5679**

●BUTLER COUNTY BANNER AND THE GREEN RIVER REPUBLICAN, THE (US/1064-895X) [26450171] **5679**

BUTLER COUNTY NEWS (GEORGIANA, ALA.) (US/0741-3319) [10149926] **5625**

BUTLER EAGLE (BUTLER, PA. : DAILY) (US/0744-401X) [02258809] **5735**

BUTLLETI DE LA CAMBRA OFICIAL DE COMERC, INDUSTRIA I NAVEGACIO DE BARCELONA (SP) [08985689] **826**

BUTLLETI DE LA SOCIETAT CATALANA DE PEDIATRIA (SP/0210-721X) [04746378] **3901**

BUTLLETI DE LES SOCIETATS CATALANES DE FISICA, QUIMICA, MATEMATIQUES I TECNOLOGIA (SP/1130-4758) [I11304758] 963, 3499, **4399**

BUTLLETI EPIDEMIEOLOGIC GENERALITAT VALENCIANA (SP/0212-6176) [I02126176] **3561**

BUTLLETI EPIDEMIOLOGIC DE CATALUNYA (SP/0211-6340) [I02116340] **3561**

BUTLLETI OFICIAL DEL PARLAMENT DE CATALUNYA (SP) [07901834] **4635**

BUTLLETI OFICIAL DEL PRINCIPAT D'ANDORRA (AN/1013-7777) [23228173] **2945**

BUTSURI TANKO CHOSA KENKYU ICHIRAN (JA) [03763958] **2136**

BUTSURI TANKO / GEOPHYSICAL EXPLORATION (JA/0521-9191) [03093452] **1403**

BUTT (US/0146-7182) [02803785] **4827**

BUTTE COUNTY HISTORICAL SOCIETY (CALIF.) *See* B.C.H.S. SLICKENS / BUTTE COUNTY HISTORICAL SOCIETY **2722**

BUTTERFLIES OF EUROPE (GW) [10735424] **5580**

BUTTERFLIES OF THE NEOTROPICAL REGION SERIES (UK) **450**

BUTTERICK HOME CATALOG (1985) (US/0895-6871) [12316475] **5183**

BUTTERWORTH LECTURES (UK/0959-3438) [I09593438] **2945**

BUTTERWORTH'S BUDGET TAX TABLES (UK) **4716**

BUTTERWORTHS COMPANY LAW CASES (UK) [11241952] **3097**

BUTTERWORTH'S CONSTRUCTION LAW MANUAL (UK) 606, **2945**

BUTTERWORTHS CURRENT LAW (NZ/0110-070X) [02441136] **3125**

BUTTERWORTHS EC CASE CITATOR AND SERVICE (UK/0968-1418) [I09681418] **2945**

●BUTTERWORTH'S EC LEGISLATION IMPLEMENTATOR (UK/0969-3912) [I09693912] **2945**

BUTTERWORTHS INDEX AND NOTER-UP TO THE SOUTH AFRICAN LAW REPORTS (SA) [07120784] **2945**

BUTTERWORTHS INTERNATIONAL MEDICAL REVIEWS. CARDIOLOGY (UK/0260-0064) [09047657] **3700**

BUTTERWORTHS INTERNATIONAL MEDICAL REVIEWS. CLINICAL PHARMACOLOGY AND THERAPEUTICS (UK/0260-0099) [08697329] **4295**

BUTTERWORTHS INTERNATIONAL MEDICAL REVIEWS. UROLOGY (UK/0260-0196) [10331352] **3988**

BUTTERWORTHS JOURNAL OF INTERNATIONAL BANKING AND FINANCIAL LAW (UK/0269-2694) [14929749] 1633, **3086**

BUTTERWORTHS LAW DIGEST MALAYSIA, SINGAPORE AND BRUNEI (SI/0951-5720) [19088257] **2945**

BUTTERWORTHS LEGAL SERVICES DIRECTORY (UK) **3159**

BUTTERWORTHS ORANGE TAX HANDBOOK (UK) [04770869] 4716, **2945**

BUTTERWORTH'S UK TAX GUIDE (UK) [09361578] 4716, **2945**

BUTTERWORTHS YELLOW TAX HANDBOOK (UK) [04428887] 4716, **2945**

BUTTON BULLETIN *See* NATIONAL BUTTON BULLETIN, THE **2775**

BUTYLENES ANNUAL (US/0277-1853) [07494145] **1600**

BUVAR (HU/0007-7356) [05952451] **450**

BUVISINDI (REYKJAVIK) (IC/1012-6910) [21460656] **70**

BUXTEHUDE DIETRICH COLLECTED WORKS SERIES : WERKE GESAMTAUSGABE (GW) **4106**

BUY BLACK (US/0742-5589) [10361908] **952**

BUY BOOKS WHERE, SELL BOOKS WHERE (US/0732-6599) [05973059] **4812**

BUYER (MONITOR PRESS) (UK) [07298297] **949**

BUYERISM NEWSLETTER (US) **654**

BUYERS BOOK OF AMERICAN CRAFTS, THE (US/0272-6246) [06545648] **370**

BUYER'S DIRECTORY OF SUPPLIERS FOR GENERAL MERCHANDISE BUYERS (US/0361-4247) [02246532] **949**

BUYERS' GUIDE (UK/0306-204X) [01799301] **2587**

BUYER'S GUIDE - AMERICAN ASSOCIATION OF TEXTILE CHEMISTS AND COLORISTS (US/0065-7352) [05018254] **5348**

BUYERS' GUIDE & DEALER DIRECTORY: NORTHEASTERN AREA (US/0145-5915) [02764778] 2399, **826**

BUYERS GUIDE (COMPUTER SECURITY INSTITUTE (SAN FRANCISCO, CALIF.)) *See* COMPUTER SECURITY PRODUCTS BUYERS GUIDE **1226**

BUYERS GUIDE (ENGINEER (LONDON, ENGLAND)) (UK/0071-0288) [01567891] 949, **1967**

BUYERS' GUIDE FOR COSMETICS & TOILETRIES MANUFACTURERS SUPPLIERS (UK/0955-7105) [I09557105] **402**

BUYERS' GUIDE FOR THE MASS ENTERTAINMENT INDUSTRY (US/0362-6180) [02328646] **4849**

BUYER'S GUIDE (HINSDALE, ILL.) (US/0078-2610) [04089856] 1934, **2154**

BUYER'S GUIDE (NATIONAL GLASS ASSOCIATION (U.S.)) (US/1055-9302) [23085333] **2587**

BUYERS GUIDE - NATIONAL SOFT DRINK ASSOCIATION (US/1056-280X) [23588046] **2365**

BUYERS GUIDE - NATIONAL TOOLING & MACHINING ASSOCIATION (US/0736-7112) [07879152] 2111, **949**

BUYER'S GUIDE OF PRODUCTS AND SERVICES IN THE ST. LOUIS REGION (US/0741-8205) [10186732] **826**

BUYER'S GUIDE REPORTS. NEW CAR PRICES (MILWAUKEE, WIS. : 1989) *See* PACE BUYER'S GUIDES. NEW CAR PRICES **5422**

BUYER'S GUIDE REPORTS : SHOPPER'S GUIDE (US/0149-0338) [03415650] **1294**

BUYER'S GUIDE REPORTS. TRUCK & VAN PRICES (US) [18820758] 1294, **5378**

BUYER'S GUIDE REPORTS. USED CAR PRICES (MILWAUKEE, WIS. : 1988) *See* PACE BUYER'S GUIDES. USED CAR PRICES **5422**

BUYERS' GUIDE, THE REPUBLIC OF CHINA (CH) [02652902] **826**

BUYER'S GUIDE / THOROUGHBRED TIMES, BLOODSTOCK RESEARCH, THE (US/1057-9907) [24167986] **2797**

BUYER'S GUIDE TO ENVIRONMENTAL MEDIA (US) [02252741] **2162**

BUYERS GUIDE TO INDIAN ART (US/0095-3083) [01796472] 2257, **346**

BUYERS GUIDE TO JAPAN'S INORGANIC CHEMICALS (JA) [02245988] **1021**

BUYER'S GUIDE TO MEDICAL TOYS & BOOKS FOR TODDLERS THROUGH TEENS *CEASED.* (US/1040-7065) [18515608] 1060, **2583**

BUYER'S GUIDE TO MICROGRAPHIC EQUIPMENT, PRODUCTS AND SERVICES (US/0362-0131) [02441237] **4367**

BUYERS GUIDE TO OUTDOOR ADVERTISING, THE (US/0095-5531) [01798040] **756**

BUYER'S GUIDE TO REACTIVE CURE SYSTEMS, UV-IR-EB (US) [14222547] **1021**

BUYER'S GUIDE TO THE WORLD OF TAPE (US/0090-9033) [01785764] **5316**

BUYING AND SELLING LAW (UK) **2945**

BUYING FOR BABY (AT) **2277**

BUYING FOR LIBRARIES *CEASED.* (UK) [11558326] **3199**

BUYING GUIDE (US) [15151343] **4434**

BUYING GUIDE TO CAR STEREO SYSTEMS (US/0272-2291) [06769723] **5316**

BUYING OFFICES & ACCOUNTS (US) [17858666] **1082**

BUYING STRATEGY FORECAST FOR PURCHASING MANAGERS (US/0733-0103) [08508952] **949**

BUYOUTS DIRECTORY OF LBO FINANCING SOURCES *See* DIRECTORY OF BUYOUT FINANCING SOURCES **788**

BUYOUTS (WELLESLEY HILLS, MASS.) (US/1040-0990) [18319939] **654**

BUZANTINA (THESSALONIKE) (GR/1105-0772) [05724757] **2682**

BUZZ (LOS ANGELES, CALIF.) (US/1053-3605) [22517029] **2529**

BUZZ (THUNDER BAY) (CN/0701-2837) [03403044] **4941**

BUZZWORM (BOULDER, COLO.) (US/0898-2996) [17781516] **2189**

BUZZWORM'S EARTH JOURNAL *CEASED.* (US/1073-5852) [29297114] **2162**

BVDA JOURNAL : BRITISH VETERINARY DENTAL ASSOCIATION (UK) **5507**

BVR, BERNISCHE VERWALTUNGSRECHTSPRECHUNG (GW) [04319997] **3092**

●BWC NEWS (US) [25563315] 2860, **1657**

BWLETIN Y BWRDD GWYBODAU CELTAIDD (UK/0142-3363) [01775132] **3271**

BWR TWRH (IS/0333-6298) [I03336298] **5046**

BY APPOINTMENT ONLY (CN/0824-5355) [10668948] **5552**

BY-LAWS, RULES AND REGULATIONS. INTERNATIONAL MONETARY FUND (US/0250-7307) [01714091] **4635**

BY OG BYGD (NO/0084-8212) [01697077] **4086**

●BY THE YEAR 2000: REPORT OF THE FCCSET COMMITTEE ON EDUCATION AND HUMAN RESOURCES (US) [25424849] 5092, **1729**

BYDGOSKIE TOWARZYSTWO NAUKOWE. WYDZIAL NAUK HUMANISTYCZNYCH *See* PRACE. SERIA A **2852**

BYDGOSKIE TOWARZYSTWO NAUKOWE. WYDZIAL NAUK TECHNICZNYCH *See* PRACE. SERIA B **1991**

BYE CADMOS (US/0363-5236) [01949510] **3370**

Alphabetical Title Index C2C

BYELORUSSIAN YOUTH (US/0736-2625) [01078028] **2682**

BYGG & TEKNIK (SW/0281-658X) [10931552] **606**

BYGG OCH TRAVARUHANDELN (SW) [02484618] **2399**

BYGGE - OG BOLIGPOLITISKE UDVIKLING (DENMARK), DEN (DK) [01783830] **606**

BYGGEKUNST (NO/0007-7518) [01537946] **294**

BYGGMASTAREN (SW/0007-7550) [03387563] **294**

BYGGNADSKULTUR (SW/0348-6885) [I03486885] **606**

BYGGREFERAT (SW/0345-1941) [I03451941] **294**

BYGNINGSARKOLOGISKE STUDIER (DK/0109-6249) [13740344] **294**

BYGNINGSSTATISKE MEDDELELSER (DK/0106-3715) [03764459] **2020**

BYLAWS & DIRECTORY / ONTARIO SCHOOL COUNSELLORS' ASSOCIATION (CN/1182-5529) [22769105] **1861**

BYLAWS, RULES, AND SPECIFICATIONS - WOMEN'S INTERNATIONAL BOWLING CONGRESS (US/0191-1902) [04785921] **4888**

BYLINE (EVANSTON, ILL.) (US/0731-5449) [08227389] 1128, **2917**

BYLINE (OKLAHOMA CITY, OKLA.) (US/0744-4249) [08256916] **2918**

BYOIN KANRI KENKYUJO *See* BYOIN KANRI KENKYUJO. ANNUAL REPORT OF THE NATIONAL INSTITUTE OF HOSPITAL ADMINISTRATION **3777**

BYOIN KANRI KENKYUJO. ANNUAL REPORT OF THE NATIONAL INSTITUTE OF HOSPITAL ADMINISTRATION (JA) [04264826] **3777**

BYOIN NEMPO (JA) [02971472] **4770**

BYOIN YAKUGAKU (JA/0389-9098) [10296866] **4295**

BYOIN YORAN (JA) [02300429] **3777**

BYOJAKUJI NO JIREI KENKYU (JA) [10672750] **3901**

BYOTAI SEIRI (OSAKA. 1982) (JA/0286-2190) [10388480] 3561, **4343**

BYPLAN (DK/0007-7658) [01537952] **2816**

BYRON JOURNAL (UK/0301-7257) [01792544] **3339**

BYRON REVIEW (US) [01537954] **5695**

BYRON SOCIETY. AMERICAN COMMITTEE *See* NEWSLETTER - BYRON SOCIETY **5234**

BYTE (US/0360-5280) [02244730] **1273**

BYTE BUYER, THE (US/0889-8200) [14092915] **1172**

BYTOWN FIRE BRIGADE NEWSLETTER, THE (CN/0846-3255) [25066287] **2288**

BYTOWN TIMES (CN/0712-2799) [08818913] **2916**

BYU JOURNAL OF PUBLIC LAW, THE (US/0896-2383) [16759621] **2945**

BYURAKANI ASTGHADITARAN *See* SOOBSCENIJA BJURAKANSKOJ OBSERVATORII **400**

BYWORD NEW DELHI (II/0971-2852) [I09712852] **2486**

BYWORDS (OTTAWA) (CN/1181-8697) [24368178] **3461**

BYZANTINA KAI METABYZANTINA (US/0742-1141) [10002908] 2682, **2647**

BYZANTINA NEERLANDICA (NE/0525-4507) [03509543] **2682**

BYZANTINA VINDOBONENSIA (AU/0525-3292) [02723694] **2682**

BYZANTINE AND MODERN GREEK STUDIES (UK/0307-0131) [02638552] **2682**

BYZANTINE CATHOLIC WORLD, THE (US/0744-2289) [02258814] **5735**

BYZANTINE STUDIES (US/0095-4608) [01620336] **2682**

BYZANTINISCH-NEUGRIECHISCHE JAHRBUCHER; INTERNATIONALES WISSENSCHAFTLICHES ORGAN (GW) [02445610] **3370**

BYZANTINISCHE FORSCHUNGEN (NE) [01537959] **2682**

BYZANTINISCHE ZEITSCHRIFT (GW/0007-7704) [01537961] 3370, **2682**

BYZANTINO BULGARICA (BU/0204-9864) [02124677] 2843, **2682**

BYZANTINOSLAVICA (XR/0007-7712) [01537962] 1075, **3457**

BYZANTION (BRUXELLES) (BE/0378-2506) [01188035] 2682, **3370**

BZZLLETIN (NE/0165-0858) [I01650858] **3461**

CP3SI NEWS (US/0749-4408) [11177127] **4038**

C.A.B. INTERNATIONAL *See* REPORT FOR ... / C.A.B. INTERNATIONAL **125**

C A C A RODEO NEWS *See* C C A RODEO NEWS **4889**

C.A.C.U.L WORKSHOP ON LIBRARY AUTOMATION *See* AUTOMATION IN LIBRARIES **3193**

C A F C DIALOGUE (CN/0706-1382) [06511741] **2288**

C A L ANTHOLOGY (US) **3370**

C A MONOGRAPHS, A (US/0514-8863) [01460598] **1031**

C.A.P. JOURNAL / THE CANADIAN ASSOCIAION OF PRINCIPALS (CN/1183-1995) [24690458] **1861**

C.A.P. MONITOR (UK) [08981929] **70**

C.A.R.A. CENTRE AIXOIS DE RECHERCHES ANGLAISES (FR/0240-8864) [I02408864] 3370, **3271**

C.A.R.E. PACKAGE, THE (US/1064-2609) [26239139] 1060, **3370**

C.A.R.P. NEWS (CANADIAN ASSOCIATION OF RETIRED PERSONS) *See* CARP. CANADIAN ASSOCIATION OF RETIRED PERSONS **5178**

C.A.R. SCOPE (CN/0068-8258) [01814013] **3561**

C A S A S NEWS (CN/0706-9782) [04747010] **70**

C. A. S. C. RACE REGULATIONS (CN/0381-9906) [02624848] 5408, **4889**

C/A/S/E OUTLOOK (US/0895-2108) [16557427] **1172**

C. A. U. T. G. NEWSLETTER (CN/0384-5311) [03258518] **3271**

● C & D DEBRIS RECYCLING (US) **2225**

C & L APPLICATIONS (UK/0957-4085) [20768937] 1172, **3199**

C B C ENGINEERING REVIEW (CN/0068-8401) [04080260] **1128**

C.B.M.S. NEWSLETTER (US/0092-5063) [01789060] **4106**

C. B. REVIEW (PH/0115-1401) [01796126] **1467**

C.C.A.I. MONTHLY NEWSLETTER (II/0376-7787) [01797761] **1294**

C C A RODEO NEWS (CN/0382-4055) [02943147] **4889**

C C C N (CALIFORNIA COMMUNITY CARE NEWS) (US) **2529**

C.C.G.S. NEWSLETTER (US) [08369838] **2441**

C C N G REPORT (CN/0384-5702) [03348806] **1240**

C-C O R E NEWS (CN/0381-6486) [03230259] 1352, **1967**

C C U M C LEADER (US) 1105, **1813**

● C/C++ USERS JOURNAL (US) **1172**

C-CORE PUBLICATION (CN/0229-5628) [07888612] **1967**

C E A HANDBOOK (CN/0068-8657) [02441651] **1861**

C. E. D. PRESS REACTION (US) [03306582] **1467**

C.E.D.R.E.S.--ETUDES, REVUE ECONOMIQUE ET SOCIALE VOLTAIQUE (UV) [10425610] **1550**

C. E. G. BULLETIN (II/0303-8556) [02240202] **2136**

C.E.S.A.O. AUJOURD'HUI, LE (UV) [04177159] **5194**

C.F.A. DIGEST, THE (US/0046-9777) [02518339] 893, **781**

C.F.O. JOURNAL (US/0362-9902) [02397632] **5616**

C.F.P. CHAUD FROID PLOMBERIE (FR/0750-1552) [I07501552] **2604**

C.F. RAMUZ (FR/0294-0078) [10298011] **3370**

C-FAR NEWSLETTER (CN/0849-1259) [21113601] **2908**

C. H. A. C. REVIEW (CN/0226-5923) [06859255] 5025, **3777**

C H L A/A B S C NEWSLETTER (CN/0700-5474) [03959989] **3199**

C H P C PROGRESS (US/0526-6459) [03129703] **2816**

C H R A RECORDER (CN/0227-3748) [06703082] **4770**

C.H.W. LETTER (CN/0834-1508) [16219983] **893**

C I E N, CANADIAN INDUSTRIAL EQUIPMENT NEWS (CN/0319-5902) [01894355] **3476**

C I E S NEWSLETTER (US/0010-4043) [01564545] **1729**

C I M REPORTER (CN/0701-0710) [03406171] **2136**

C.I.R.I.E.C. ESPANA (SP/0213-8093) [02138093] **1467**

C I S; CHROMOSOMES INFORMATION SERVICE (JA/0574-9549) [03144068] **543**

C. J. ARQUITETURA (BL) [02163796] **294**

C.J. THE AMERICAS (US/0896-9922) [17363629] **3159**

● C-JEUNES (CN/1195-9231) [31000988] **5276**

C-L-A-S-S FORUM (US/1052-4754) [18735823] **3199**

C.L.C. CONTEMPORARY LITERARY CRITICISM (US/0091-3421) [01799898] **3339**

C-L/CLL. COUNSELING-LEARNING COMMUNITY LANGUAGE LEARNING NEWSLETTER (US/0197-6893) [06081685] **3271**

C L I C 'S LEGAL MATERIALS LETTER *CEASED.* (CN/0704-0393) [03960146] **2945**

C-LECT (US) **1813**

C LIBRARY. CD-ROM (US) **1276**

C.M.L.R. ANTITRUST REPORTS (UK) [23735600] 826, **3097**

C-MAGAZIN (GW/0935-0373) [I09350373] **4941**

● C MAGAZINE (1992) (CN/1193-8625) [27809663] **317**

C.O.A. BULLETIN (US/0526-6742) [05295675] **4770**

C. O. E. Q. JOURNAL, THE (CN/0706-4667) [06131620] 4870, **1729**

C/O : JOURNAL OF ALTERNATIVE HUMAN SERVICES (US/0192-0618) [04676886] **5276**

C O R S BULLETIN (CN/0315-1417) [01887557] **1236**

C.O.S.-M.O.S. DIGITAL INTEGRATED CIRCUITS (US/0093-8270) [01791534] **2037**

C.P.A *See* CPA LETTER, THE **742**

C P A C REVIEW (CN/0315-4920) [02443086] **2816**

C.P.C. : [PUBLICATIONS] / CONSERVATIVE POLITICAL CENTRE (UK) [06895297] **4466**

C P H A HEALTH DIGEST (CN/0703-5624) [03960019] **4770**

C P S NEWS LETTER (TORONTO) (CN/0384-7632) [03230489] **2784**

C R E S S SPECTROSCOPIC REPORT (CN/0318-1634) [02441791] **4399**

C R S PERSPECTIVES (CN/0228-1821) [06860062] **2136**

C R U S NEWS *See* INFORMATION RESEARCH NEWS **3216**

C++ REPORT, THE (US/1040-6042) [18474354] **1278**

C.S.A. NEWSLETTER - CANADIAN SOCIETY OF AGRONOMY (1983) (CN/0826-2942) [11180164] **165**

C S E MONOGRAPH SERIES IN EVALUATION (US) [02255247] **1729**

C.S.N.D.T. JOURNAL (CN/0826-9343) [13292561] **4427**

C.S.P.G. SEMINAR (CN/0733-5423) [03398591] **1371**

C S S E NEWS (CN/0382-8018) [02851871] **1730**

C.S.S. NEED ANALYSIS (US/0092-9883) [01783703] **1813**

C-SPAN UPDATE (US/0746-3812) [10007954] **5647**

C-STORE WEEK *See* U.S. OIL WEEK **4281**

C (TORONTO. 1987) (CN/0838-0392) [22159246] **346**

C (TORONTO, ONT. : 1987) *See* C MAGAZINE (1992) **317**

C.U.S.I.P. DIRECTORY (US/0091-2212) [01786921] **893**

C.U.S.I.P. DIRECTORY. CORPORATE DIRECTORY (US/0091-3804) [01786887] **893**

C USERS GROUP LIBRARY DIRECTORY (US) 3199, **1284**

C USER'S GROUP LIBRARY DIRECTORY, THE (US) **1278**

C USERS JOURNAL, THE (US/0898-9788) [17192242] **1278**

C W C DATAFILE (CN/0318-2215) [02441793] **633**

C. W. E. A. NEWS (CN/0226-8442) [07298380] **4399**

C1 MOLECULE CHEMISTRY *CEASED.* (SZ/0275-7567) [07228194] **1035**

C2C ABSTRACTS JAPAN. ANALYTICAL CHEMISTRY *CEASED.* (US/1049-1260) [21139555] 1014, **996**

C2C ABSTRACTS JAPAN. CERAMICS (US/1049-1252) [21139900] 2587, **2595**

C2C ABSTRACTS JAPAN. CHEMICAL ENGINEERING (US/1049-1279) [21139730] 2008, **996**

C2C ABSTRACTS JAPAN. CRYSTALLOGRAPHY (US/1049-1287) [21139800] 1031, **996**

C2C ABSTRACTS JAPAN. HYDROCARBONS (US/1049-1295) [21139833] 963, **996**

Alphabetical Title Index

C2C ABSTRACTS JAPAN. INORGANIC CHEMISTRY (US/1049-1309) [21139574] 1035, **996**

C2C ABSTRACTS JAPAN. MATERIALS SCIENCES (US/1049-1317) [21139766] 5092, **5174**

C2C ABSTRACTS JAPAN. METALS (US/1049-1384) [21139915] 3999, **4025**

C2C ABSTRACTS JAPAN. ORGANIC CHEMISTRY (US/1049-1325) [21139709] **1040**

C2C ABSTRACTS JAPAN. PHYSICAL CHEMISTRY (US/1049-1333) [21139591] 1050, **996**

C2C ABSTRACTS JAPAN. PLASTICS (US/1049-1341) [21139867] 4454, **4461**

C2C ABSTRACTS JAPAN. POLYMER CHEMISTRY (US/1049-135X) [21139641] 963, **996**

C2C ABSTRACTS JAPAN. SURFACE CHEMISTRY (US/1049-1368) [21139684] 964, **997**

C2C ABSTRACTS JAPAN. TEXTILES (US/1049-1376) [21139847] 5348, **5360**

C2C CURRENTS JAPAN. CHEMISTRY *CEASED.* (US/1049-1228) [21139463] **964**

C2C CURRENTS JAPAN. COMPUTERS (US/1049-1244) [21139523] **1172**

C2C CURRENTS JAPAN. ELECTRONICS (US/1049-1236) [21139505] **2037**

C2C CURRENTS JAPAN. MANUFACTURING (US/1051-7545) [22102572] **3476**

C2C CURRENTS JAPAN. MATERIALS *CEASED.* (US/1049-121X) [21139431] **654**

C3I FORECAST (US) **4038**

C3I REPORT (US/0889-4728) [13899212] **4038**

●C4I NEWS (US/1071-1317) [28555717] 1105, **1212**

CA (US/0007-9235) [01044790] **3810**

CA CRAFT CONNECTION, THE (US/1042-6280) [19095348] **370**

CA MAGAZINE (CN/0317-6878) [01787882] **740**

CA MAGAZINE (UK) [26250359] **740**

CA MAGAZINE (CN/0832-9117) [18241890] **740**

CA M'INTERESSE (FR/0243-1335) [02431335] **2514**

CA NEWSERVICE (US) [11484465] **4941**

CA QUARTERLY (AU/0258-3577) [08677960] **1467**

CA QUICK SEARCH [COMPUTER FILE] (US) 606, 2020, **2002**

CA : REVISTA OFICIAL DEL COLEGIO DE ARQUITECTOS DE CHILE (CL) [14258302] **294**

CA SELECTS: ACID RAIN & ACID AIR (US/0885-0097) [12533845] 964, **997**

CA SELECTS: ADHESIVES (US/0162-7686) [04223631] 964, **997**

CA SELECTS: AIDS & RELATED IMMUNODEFICIENCIES (US/1040-7111) [18508863] 3667, **997**

CA SELECTS: AIR POLLUTION (BOOKS & REVIEWS) (US/0895-5980) [16693768] 2225, **997**

CA SELECTS: ALKYLATION & CATALYSTS (US/0895-5964) [16700354] 1040, **997**

●CA SELECTS: ALUMINUM-LITHIUM & ALUMINUM-CERIUM ALLOYS (US/1066-1166) [26861187] 964, **997**

CA SELECTS: ALZHEIMER'S DISEASE & RELATED MEMORY DYSFUNCTIONS (US/1047-8183) [20788312] **997**

CA SELECTS: AMINO ACIDS, PEPTIDES & PROTEINS (US/0275-701X) [07228507] 1040, **997**

CA SELECTS: ANALYTICAL ELECTROCHEMISTRY (US/0160-8959) [04044774] 1034, **997**

CA SELECTS: ANIMAL LONGEVITY & AGING (US/0162-7694) [04223666] 484, **997**

CA SELECTS: ANTI-INFLAMMATORY AGENTS & ARTHRITIS (US/0148-2394) [03691408] 4295, 3561, **997**

CA SELECTS: ANTIBACTERIAL AGENTS (US/1045-8522) [20282483] 964, **997**

CA SELECTS: ANTIOXIDANTS (US/0275-7028) [07228468] 964, **997**

CA SELECTS: ANTITUMOR AGENTS (US/0148-2386) [03691409] 4295, **997**

CA SELECTS: ARTIFICIAL SWEETENERS (US/0890-1813) [14169748] 1021, 2329, **997**

CA SELECTS: ASYMMETRIC SYNTHESIS & INDUCTION (US/0890-183X) [14169844] 964, **998**

CA SELECTS: ATHEROSCLEROSIS & HEART DISEASE (US/0148-2378) [03691410] 4295, 3700, **998**

CA SELECTS: ATOMIC SPECTROSCOPY (US/0195-4911) [05510910] 964, **998**

CA SELECTS: AUTOMATED CHEMICAL ANALYSIS (US/0740-0683) [09887103] 964, **998**

CA SELECTS: B-LACTAM ANTIBIOTICS (US/0148-2459) [03688771] 4295, **998**

CA SELECTS: BATTERIES & FUEL CELLS (US/0162-7708) [04223722] 964, **998**

CA SELECTS: BIOGENIC AMINES & THE NERVOUS SYSTEM (US/0162-7716) [04223763] 964, **998**

CA SELECTS: BIOLOGICAL INFORMATION TRANSFER *CEASED.* (US/0162-7724) [04223789] 964, **998**

●CA SELECTS: BISMUTH CHEMISTRY (US/1061-5342) [25344851] 964, **998**

CA SELECTS: BLOCK & GRAFT POLYMERS (US/0734-8851) [08817095] 964, **998**

CA SELECTS: BLOOD COAGULATION (US/0162-7732) [04223852] 484, **998**

CA SELECTS: CARBOHYDRATES (CHEMICAL ASPECTS) (US/0740-0756) [09885801] 964, **998**

CA SELECTS: CARBON & GRAPHITE FIBERS (US/0890-1856) [14169910] 964, **998**

CA SELECTS: CARBON & HETEROATOM NMR (US/0190-9401) [04771432] 964, **998**

CA SELECTS: CARBON FIBER COMPOSITES (US/0895-5956) [16700184] 964, **998**

CA SELECTS: CARCINOGENS, MUTAGENS & TERATOGENS (US/0148-2408) [03691411] 484, **998**

CA SELECTS: CATALYSIS (APPLIED AND PHYSICAL ASPECTS) (US/0146-440X) [03175885] 964, **999**

CA SELECTS: CATALYSIS (ORGANIC REACTIONS) (US/0146-4396) [03176424] 1040, **999**

CA SELECTS: CATALYST REGENERATION (US/0734-8800) [08819662] 964, **999**

CA SELECTS: CATALYTIC & KINETIC ANALYSIS (US/0890-1864) [14169934] 964, **999**

CA SELECTS: CERAMIC MATERIALS (JOURNALS) (US/0895-5948) [16700160] 2587, **999**

CA SELECTS: CERAMIC MATERIALS (PATENTS) (US/0885-0100) [12534195] 964, **999**

CA SELECTS: CHELATING AGENTS (US/0734-8797) [08822542] 964, **999**

CA SELECTS: CHEMICAL ENGINEERING OPERATIONS (US/1040-712X) [18508950] 2008, **999**

CA SELECTS: CHEMICAL HAZARDS, HEALTH, & SAFETY (US/0190-9398) [04771356] 964, **999**

CA SELECTS: CHEMICAL INSTRUMENTATION (US/0195-4938) [05510939] 964, **999**

CA SELECTS: CHEMICAL PROCESSING APPARATUS (US/0195-4946) [05510990] 964, 2008, **999**

CA SELECTS: CHEMICAL VAPOR DEPOSITION (US/0885-0119) [12534217] 964, **999**

CA SELECTS: CHEMILUMINESCENCE (US/1040-7138) [18509034] 1050, **999**

CA SELECTS: CHEMISTRY OF IR, OS, RH, & RU (US/1040-7146) [18509086] 964, **999**

CA SELECTS: COAL SCIENCE & PROCESS CHEMISTRY (US/0146-4426) [03176267] 964, 2008, **999**

CA SELECTS: COATINGS, INKS, & RELATED PRODUCTS (US/0275-7036) [07231970] 1050, **999**

CA SELECTS: COLLOIDS (APPLIED ASPECTS) (US/0160-8967) [04043864] 964, **1000**

CA SELECTS: COLLOIDS (MACROMOLECULAR ASPECTS) (US/0190-9444) [04770708] 964, **1000**

CA SELECTS: COLLOIDS (PHYSICOCHEMICAL ASPECTS) (US/0160-8975) [04043831] 964, **1000**

CA SELECTS: COLOR SCIENCE (US/0885-0127) [12534180] 964, **1000**

CA SELECTS: COLORANTS & DYES (US/0734-8789) [08819616] 964, **1000**

●CA SELECTS: COMPOSITE MATERIALS (CERAMIC) (US/1066-1158) [26861104] 2587, **1000**

●CA SELECTS: COMPOSITE MATERIALS (METALLIC) (US/1066-114X) [26861064] 964, **1000**

CA SELECTS: COMPOSITE MATERIALS (POLYMERIC) (US/1040-7154) [18509191] 964, **1000**

CA SELECTS: COMPUTERS IN CHEMISTRY (US/0160-9025) [04044733] 964, 1173, **1000**

CA SELECTS: CONDUCTIVE POLYMERS (US/0885-0135) [12534161] 964, **1000**

CA SELECTS: CONTROLLED RELEASE TECHNOLOGY (US/0740-0748) [09879970] 964, **1000**

CA SELECTS: CORROSION (US/0146-4434) [03176598] 2008, 2101, **1000**

CA SELECTS: CORROSION-INHIBITING COATINGS (US/0749-7296) [11181057] 2008, **1000**

CA SELECTS: COSMETIC CHEMICALS (US/0275-7044) [07232029] 964, **1000**

CA SELECTS: CROSSLINKING REACTIONS (US/0740-0721) [09879924] 964, **1000**

CA SELECTS: CRYSTAL GROWTH (US/0162-7740) [04223880] 964, 1031, **1000**

CA SELECTS: DETERGENTS, SOAPS, & SURFACTANTS (US/0162-7767) [04223901] 964, **1001**

CA SELECTS: DISTILLATION TECHNOLOGY (US/0275-7052) [07231938] 964, **1001**

CA SELECTS: DRILLING MUDS (US/0749-730X) [11181007] 964, 2008, **1001**

CA SELECTS: DRUG & COSMETIC TOXICITY (US/0162-7775) [04223929] 964, 4295, **1001**

CA SELECTS: DRUG DELIVERY SYSTEMS & DOSAGE FORMS (US/1040-7162) [18509273] 4295, **1001**

CA SELECTS: ELECTRICALLY CONDUCTIVE ORGANICS (US/0885-0143) [12534141] 964, **1001**

CA SELECTS: ELECTROCHEMICAL ORGANIC SYNTHESIS (US/0734-8770) [08819549] 964, **1001**

CA SELECTS: ELECTROCHEMICAL REACTIONS (US/0146-4442) [03176556] 964, **1001**

CA SELECTS: ELECTRODEPOSITION (US/0162-7783) [04223952] 964, **1001**

CA SELECTS: ELECTRON & AUGER SPECTROSCOPY (US/0146-4450) [03176516] 964, **1001**

CA SELECTS: ELECTRON SPIN RESONANCE (CHEMICAL ASPECTS) (US/0146-4469) [03176480] 964, **1001**

CA SELECTS: ELECTRONIC CHEMICALS & MATERIALS (US/0885-0151) [12533738] 964, **1001**

CA SELECTS: ELECTROPHORESIS (US/0195-4962) [05511172] 964, **1001**

CA SELECTS: EMULSIFIERS & DEMULSIFIERS (US/0734-8754) [08817206] 964, **1001**

CA SELECTS: EMULSION POLYMERIZATION (US/0195-4970) [05511208] 964, **1001**

CA SELECTS: ENERGY REVIEWS & BOOKS (US/0162-7791) [04224018] 964, **1002**

CA SELECTS: ENHANCED PETROLEUM RECOVERY (US/0734-8746) [08819038] 964, **1002**

CA SELECTS: ENVIRONMENTAL POLLUTION (US/0160-9041) [04044031] 964, 2226, **1002**

CA SELECTS: ENZYME APPLICATIONS (US/0895-593X) [16700141] 1040, **1002**

CA SELECTS: ENZYME ASSAYS (US/0895-5808) [16693818] 450, **1002**

CA SELECTS: EPOXY RESINS (US/0275-7060) [07231058] 964, **1002**

CA SELECTS: FATS & OILS (US/0275-7079) [07228890] 964, **1002**

CA SELECTS: FERMENTATION CHEMICALS (US/0740-0713) [09878979] 964, **1002**

CA SELECTS: FIBER OPTICS & OPTICAL COMMUNICATION (US/0890-1872) [14169974] 965, **1002**

CA SELECTS: FIBER-REINFORCED PLASTICS (US/0734-869X) [08819164] 965, **1002**

CA SELECTS: FLAMMABILITY (US/0162-7805) [04224094] 965, **1002**

CA SELECTS: FLAVORS & FRAGRANCES (US/0148-2327) [03691433] 965, **1002**

CA SELECTS: FLUIDIZED SOLIDS TECHNOLOGY (US/0195-4989) [05511263] 965, **1002**

CA SELECTS: FLUOROPOLYMERS (US/0895-5921) [16700099] 1040, **1002**

CA SELECTS: FOOD & FEED ANALYSIS (US/0895-5913) [16700002] 5324, 2329, **1002**

CA SELECTS: FOOD, DRUGS, & COSMETICS (US/1051-3914) [21947274] 4295, 2329, **1002**

CA SELECTS: FOOD TOXICITY (US/0162-7813) [04224122] 4295, 2329, **1003**

CA SELECTS: FORENSIC CHEMISTRY (US/0362-9880) [03285868] 965, **1003**

CA SELECTS: FORMULATION CHEMISTRY (US/0890-1880) [14169997] 965, 4295, **1003**

Alphabetical Title Index — CA

CA SELECTS: FREE RADICALS (BIOCHEMICAL ASPECTS) (US/0895-5905) [16699892] 450, **1003**

CA SELECTS: FREE RADICALS (ORGANIC ASPECTS) (US/0895-5972) [16693652] 1050, **1003**

CA SELECTS: FUEL & LUBRICANT ADDITIVES (US/0195-4997) [05619949] 965, **1003**

CA SELECTS: FUNGICIDES (US/0160-9068) [04044669] 70, 965, **1003**

CA SELECTS: GAS CHROMATOGRAPHY (US/0146-4477) [03176448] 965, **1003**

CA SELECTS: GASEOUS WASTE TREATMENT (US/0160-9076) [04045341] 965, 2008, **1003**

CA SELECTS: GEL PERMEATION CHROMATOGRAPHY (US/0146-4485) [03175931] 965, **1003**

●CA SELECTS: GEOCHEMISTRY (US/1066-5730) [26995528] 965, **1003**

CA SELECTS: HEAT-RESISTANT & ABLATIVE POLYMERS (US/0162-7821) [04224187] 965, **1003**

CA SELECTS: HERBICIDES (US/0160-9084) [04044602] 70, 965, **1003**

CA SELECTS: HIGH PERFORMANCE LIQUID CHROMATOGRAPHY (US/0195-5217) [05620006] 965, **1003**

CA SELECTS: HOT-MELT ADHESIVES (US/0895-5891) [16699811] 965, **1003**

CA SELECTS: HYPERTENSION & ANTIHYPERTENSIVES (US/1051-3922) [21947321] 3700, **1003**

CA SELECTS: INFRARED SPECTROSCOPY (ORGANIC ASPECTS) (US/0190-9428) [04770771] 965, **1004**

CA SELECTS: INFRARED SPECTROSCOPY (PHYSICOCHEMICAL ASPECTS) (US/0190-9436) [04770586] 965, **1004**

CA SELECTS: INITIATION OF POLYMERIZATION (US/0734-8843) [08820010] 965, **1004**

CA SELECTS: INORGANIC ANALYTICAL CHEMISTRY (US/0275-7087) [07228849] 965, **1004**

CA SELECTS: INORGANIC & ORGANOMETALLIC REACTION MECHANISMS (US/0195-5012) [05620075] 965, **1004**

CA SELECTS: INORGANIC CHEMICALS & REACTIONS (US/0275-7095) [07228806] 1035, **1004**

CA SELECTS: INSECTICIDES (US/0160-9092) [04043908] 70, 965, **1004**

CA SELECTS: ION CHROMATOGRAPHY (US/0890-1899) [14170022] 1014, **1004**

CA SELECTS: ION-CONTAINING POLYMERS (US/0195-5020) [05620254] 965, **1004**

CA SELECTS: ION EXCHANGE (US/0146-4493) [03176020] 965, **1004**

CA SELECTS: ISOMERIZATION & CATALYSTS (US/0895-5883) [16699734] 1040, **1004**

CA SELECTS: LASER APPLICATIONS (US/0195-5039) [05620311] 965, 2008, **1004**

CA SELECTS: LASER-INDUCED CHEMICAL REACTIONS (US/0885-0178) [12533894] 965, 2008, **1004**

CA SELECTS: LIQUID CRYSTALS (US/0148-2351) [03691558] 1031, **1004**

CA SELECTS: LIQUID WASTE TREATMENT (US/0160-9106) [04044001] 965, **1004**

CA SELECTS: LUBRICANTS, GREASES & LUBRICATION (US/0734-8738) [08817263] 965, **1004**

CA SELECTS: MASS SPECTROMETRY (US/0362-9872) [03285681] 965, **1005**

CA SELECTS: MEMBRANE SEPARATION (US/1040-7197) [18509774] 1021, **1005**

CA SELECTS: MEMORY & RECORDING DEVICES & MATERIALS (US/0890-1821) [14169797] 1173, **1005**

●CA SELECTS: METALLIC GLASSES (US/1062-8681) [25774359] 965, **1005**

CA SELECTS: METALLO ENZYMES & METALLO COENZYMES (US/0160-9114) [04044529] 965, **1005**

●CA SELECTS: MOLECULAR MODELING (BIOCHEMICAL ASPECTS) (US/1059-2784) [24529769] 484, **1005**

CA SELECTS: NATURAL PRODUCT SYNTHESIS (US/0740-0691) [09878743] 965, **1005**

CA SELECTS: NEW ANTIBIOTICS (US/0895-5875) [16699694] 4295, **1005**

CA SELECTS: NEW BOOKS IN CHEMISTRY (US/0148-2416) [03691584] 965, **1005**

CA SELECTS: NEW PLASTICS (US/0734-8673) [08819201] 965, **1005**

CA SELECTS: NITROGEN FIXATION (US/1047-8108) [20787784] 70, 484, **1005**

CA SELECTS: NONLINEAR OPTICAL MATERIALS (US/0895-5867) [16700464] 1021, **1005**

CA SELECTS: NOVEL NATURAL PRODUCTS (US/0734-872X) [08819115] 965, **1005**

CA SELECTS: NOVEL PESTICIDES & HERBICIDES (US/0734-7318) [11180952] 70, **1005**

CA SELECTS: NOVEL POLYMERS FROM PATENTS (US/0734-8819) [08819705] 965, **1005**

CA SELECTS: NOVEL SULFUR HETEROCYCLES (US/0275-7109) [07228760] 965, **1005**

CA SELECTS: OMEGA THREE FATTY ACIDS & FISH OIL (US/1052-1984) [22218049] 965, 2298, **1006**

CA SELECTS: OPTICAL & PHOTOSENSITIVE MATERIALS (US/0195-5063) [05620738] 965, **1006**

CA SELECTS: OPTIMIZATION OF ORGANIC REACTIONS (US/0195-5071) [05620777] 965, 2008, **1006**

CA SELECTS: ORGANIC ANALYTICAL CHEMISTRY (US/0275-7117) [07228723] 965, **1006**

CA SELECTS: ORGANIC OPTICAL MATERIALS (US/0885-0186) [12534111] 1040, **1006**

CA SELECTS: ORGANIC REACTION MECHANISMS (US/0162-7848) [04224245] 965, **1006**

CA SELECTS: ORGANIC STEREOCHEMISTRY (US/0195-508X) [05620799] 965, **1006**

CA SELECTS: ORGANO-TRANSITION METAL COMPLEXES (US/0160-9130) [04043941] 965, **1006**

CA SELECTS: ORGANOFLUORINE CHEMISTRY (US/0160-905X) [04044500] 965, **1006**

CA SELECTS: ORGANOMETALLICS IN ORGANIC SYNTHESIS (US/0895-5859) [16699669] 1040, **1006**

CA SELECTS: ORGANOPHOSPHORUS CHEMISTRY (US/0162-783X) [04224217] 965, **1006**

CA SELECTS: ORGANOSILICON CHEMISTRY (US/0362-9899) [03285891] 965, **1006**

CA SELECTS: ORGANOSULFUR CHEMISTRY (JOURNALS) (US/1040-7189) [18509492] 965, **1006**

CA SELECTS: ORGANOTIN CHEMISTRY (US/0195-5101) [05621653] 965, **1006**

CA SELECTS: OXIDATION CATALYSTS (US/1040-7170) [18509446] 965, **1006**

CA SELECTS: OXIDE SUPERCONDUCTORS (US/1040-7219) [18509825] 1040, **1006**

CA SELECTS: PAINT ADDITIVES (US/0734-8762) [08819501] 1050, **1007**

CA SELECTS: PAPER ADDITIVES (US/0734-8711) [08819479] 965, **1007**

CA SELECTS: PAPER & THIN-LAYER CHROMATOGRAPHY (US/0146-4515) [03176102] 965, **1007**

CA SELECTS: PAPER CHEMISTRY (US/1040-7200) [18509798] 4232, **1007**

CA SELECTS: PHARMACEUTICAL ANALYSIS (US/0890-1902) [14170040] 4295, **1007**

CA SELECTS: PHARMACEUTICAL CHEMISTRY (JOURNALS) (US/0890-1910) [14170082] 4295, **1007**

CA SELECTS: PHARMACEUTICAL CHEMISTRY (PATENTS) (US/0890-1929) [14170111] 4295, **1007**

CA SELECTS: PHASE TRANSFER CATALYSIS (US/0885-0194) [12534082] 965, 2008, **1007**

CA SELECTS: PHOTOBIOCHEMISTRY (US/0148-2335) [03691609] 484, **1007**

CA SELECTS: PHOTOCHEMICAL ORGANIC SYNTHESIS (US/0885-0208) [12534055] 1040, **1007**

CA SELECTS: PHOTOCHEMISTRY (US/0362-9856) [03285653] 965, **1007**

CA SELECTS: PHOTORESISTS (US/0885-0216) [12533922] 965, **1007**

CA SELECTS: PHOTOSENSITIVE POLYMERS (US/0749-7326) [11180879] 965, **1007**

CA SELECTS: PLASMA & REACTIVE ION ETCHING (US/0749-7334) [11180830] 965, 2037, **1007**

CA SELECTS: PLASTIC FILMS (US/0195-511X) [05621686] 965, **1007**

CA SELECTS: PLASTICS ADDITIVES (US/0734-8681) [08819420] 965, **1007**

CA SELECTS: PLASTICS FABRICATION & USES (US/0275-7125) [07228646] 965, **1007**

CA SELECTS: PLASTICS MANUFACTURING & PROCESSING (US/0275-7133) [07228620] 965, **1008**

CA SELECTS: PLATINUM & PALLADIUM CHEMISTRY (US/0890-1937) [14170150] 965, **1008**

CA SELECTS: POLLUTION MONITORING (US/0160-9149) [04044801] 965, **1008**

CA SELECTS: POLYACRYLATES (JOURNALS) (US/0890-1945) [14170169] 965, 2008, **1008**

CA SELECTS: POLYESTERS (US/0734-8703) [08819444] 966, **1008**

CA SELECTS: POLYIMIDES (US/0895-5840) [16699600] 2008, **1008**

CA SELECTS: POLYMER BLENDS (US/0734-8827) [08819858] 966, **1008**

CA SELECTS: POLYMER DEGRADATION (US/0734-8835) [08819918] 966, **1008**

CA SELECTS: POLYMER MORPHOLOGY (US/0195-5128) [05623337] 966, **1008**

CA SELECTS: POLYMERIZATION KINETICS & PROCESS CONTROL (US/0885-0224) [12533705] 966, 2008, **1008**

CA SELECTS: POLYURETHANES (US/0740-0705) [09878945] 966, **1008**

CA SELECTS: PORPHYRINS (US/0195-5136) [05623338] 966, **1008**

CA SELECTS: PROSTAGLANDINS (US/0148-2343) [03691663] 966, **1008**

CA SELECTS: PROTON MAGNETIC RESONANCE (US/0190-941X) [04771297] 966, **1008**

CA SELECTS: PSYCHOBIOCHEMISTRY (US/0362-9848) [03285927] 484, **1008**

CA SELECTS: QUATERNARY AMMONIUM COMPOUNDS (US/0890-1953) [14170186] 966, **1009**

CA SELECTS: RADIATION CHEMISTRY (US/0146-4523) [03176129] 966, **1009**

CA SELECTS: RADIATION CURING (US/0749-7342) [11180777] 966, **1009**

CA SELECTS: RAMAN SPECTROSCOPY (US/0148-2432) [03691694] 966, **1009**

CA SELECTS: RECOVERY & RECYCLING OF WASTES (US/0160-9157) [04045271] 966, **1009**

CA SELECTS: SELENIUM & TELLURIUM CHEMISTRY (US/0749-7350) [11180729] 966, **1009**

●CA SELECTS: SHAPE MEMORY ALLOYS (US/1062-869X) [25774440] 966, **1009**

CA SELECTS: SILICAS & SILICATES (US/0890-1961) [14170219] 966, **1009**

CA SELECTS: SILOXANES & SILICONES (US/0895-5832) [16699529] 1040, **1009**

CA SELECTS: SILVER CHEMISTRY (US/0148-2440) [03691887] 966, **1009**

CA SELECTS: SOLAR ENERGY (US/0148-236X) [03691922] 966, 1934, **1009**

CA SELECTS: SOLID & RADIOACTIVE WASTE TREATMENT (US/0160-9165) [04043978] 966, 2008, **1009**

CA SELECTS: SOLID STATE NMR (US/0895-5824) [16694432] 4443, **1009**

CA SELECTS: SOLVENT EXTRACTION (US/0146-4531) [03176165] 966, **1009**

CA SELECTS: SPECTROCHEMICAL ANALYSIS (US/0885-0232) [12533673] 966, **1009**

CA SELECTS: STEROIDS (BIOCHEMICAL ASPECTS) (US/0160-9173) [04045430] 484, **1009**

CA SELECTS: STEROIDS (CHEMICAL ASPECTS) (US/0160-9181) [04045519] 966, **1009**

●CA SELECTS: STRESS CORROSION - METALS (US/1066-1174) [26861235] 3999, **1010**

CA SELECTS: STRUCTURE-ACTIVITY RELATIONSHIPS (US/0895-5816) [16693923] 1035, **1010**

CA SELECTS: SURFACE ANALYSIS (US/0195-5152) [05623341] 966, 2008, **1010**

CA SELECTS: SURFACE CHEMISTRY (PHYSICOCHEMICAL ASPECTS) (US/0146-454X) [03176206] 966, **1010**

CA SELECTS: SYNFUELS (US/0195-5160) [05623344] 966, **1010**

CA SELECTS: SYNTHETIC HIGH POLYMERS (US/0275-7168) [07232001] 966, **1010**

CA SELECTS: SYNTHETIC MACROCYCLIC COMPOUNDS (US/0195-5179) [05623346] 966, **1010**

●CA SELECTS: TECHNICAL CERAMICS (US/1062-8703) [25774499] 966, **1010**

CA SELECTS: THERMAL ANALYSIS (US/0195-5187) [05623349] 966, **1010**

CA SELECTS: THERMOCHEMISTRY (US/0162-7864) [04224310] 966, **1010**

CA SELECTS: TRACE ELEMENT ANALYSIS (US/0160-919X) [04044755] 966, **1010**

CA Alphabetical Title Index

CA SELECTS: ULTRAFILTRATION (US/0195-5195) [05623362] 966, 2008, **1010**

CA SELECTS: ULTRAVIOLET & VISIBLE SPECTROSCOPY (US/0195-5209) [05623372] 966, **1010**

CA SELECTS: WATER-BASED COATINGS (US/0749-7369) [11180640] 966, **1010**

CA SELECTS: WATER TREATMENT (US/0740-073X) [09886921] 966, 2008, **1010**

CA SELECTS: X-RAY ANALYSIS & SPECTROSCOPY (US/0162-7872) [04224344] 966, **1010**

CA SELECTS: ZEOLITES (US/0190-4949) [04719643] 966, **1011**

CA TECHNIEK (NE/0925-7977) [I09257977] **1173**

CA VA (US/0007-9243) [03981376] 3271, **1890**

CAA MAGAZINE (US/0279-6945) [07207205] **4889**

CAAS NEWS (US/8755-3732) [11183770] 781, 1173, **4835**

CAAT TRACKS (CN/0829-254X) [15367805] **3199**

CAAT TRACKS : INTERLIBRARY LOANS MANUAL (CN/1191-1468) [25882953] **3199**

CAAXAAN FAAXEE / JS (SG) [11790718] 4466, **2638**

CAB ABSTRACTS ON CD-ROM [COMPUTER FILE] (US) [21397582] **70**

CAB ABSTRACTS ONLINE MANUAL (UK) [20793400] **1274**

CAB ANNUAL REPORT (UK) [09461286] **70**

CAB, CURRENT AWARENESS BULLETIN (US) [02760935] **3999**

CAB FARE (US/0732-1236) [08326121] **5378**

CAB INTERNATIONAL DATABASE NEWS (UK/0951-6050) [I09516050] **1253**

CAB INTERNATIONAL NEWS (UK/0308-8480) [15683562] **71**

CABARET VERT (CN/1183-3440) [25423809] **3370**

CABBAGES AND KINGS (AT/0310-1584) [06553083] **2669**

CABELL RECORD (US/1041-2255) [12768309] **5763**

CABELL'S DIRECTORY OF PUBLISHING OPPORTUNITIES IN BUSINESS, ADMINISTRATION AND ECONOMICS *See* CABELL'S DIRECTORY OF PUBLISHING OPPORTUNITIES IN BUSINESS AND ECONOMICS **4812**

CABELL'S DIRECTORY OF PUBLISHING OPPORTUNITIES IN BUSINESS AND ECONOMICS (US) [13197625] 654, **4812**

CABELL'S DIRECTORY OF PUBLISHING OPPORTUNITIES IN EDUCATION (US) [11945201] 1730, **4812**

CABINET MAKER LONDON. 1990 (UK/0964-4199) [I09644199] **633**

CABINET MANUFACTURING & FABRICATIONS (US/1041-2166) [18680356] **3476**

CABINETMAKER (CHICAGO, ILL.) (US/1048-0196) [20840854] **633**

CABINETS MINISTERIELS (FR) **4635**

CABINETS MINISTERIELS (FR/0759-2736) [I07592736] **4466**

CABIRION AND GAY BOOKS BULLETIN, THE (US/1043-383X) [11326393] 3370, **2793**

CABLE AND PAY TV NEWSLETTER (AT/1322-3534) **1128**

CABLE & SATELLITE EUROPE (UK) [17464081] **1150**

CABLE & SATELLITE EXPRESS (UK/0268-215X) [I0268215X] **1128**

CABLE & SATELLITE YEARBOOK (UK) [15604014] **1150**

CABLE AVAILS (US/1057-7378) [24111278] **756**

CABLE COMMUNICATIONS. ANNUAL DIRECTORY AND BUYERS' GUIDE (CN) [02443349] **1150**

CABLE COMMUNICATIONS IN MINNESOTA (US/0733-8600) [04671198] **1128**

CABLE COMMUNICATIONS MAGAZINE (CN/0318-0069) [10615498] **1128**

CABLE COMMUNIQUE (BI-HEBDOMADAIRE. EDITION FRANCAISE) (CN/0710-2259) [08659342] **1128**

CABLE COMMUNIQUE (BI-HEBDOMADAIRE). FRANCAIS *See* COMMUNIQUE - ASSOCIATION CANADIENNE DE TELEVISION PAR CABLE (1992) **1130**

CABLE COMMUNIQUE (BIWEEKLY. ENGLISH ED.) *See* COMMUNIQUE - CANADIAN CABLE TELEVISION ASSOCIATION 1992 **1130**

CABLE COMMUNIQUE (BIWEEKLY. ENGLISH EDITION) (CN/0710-2240) [08659341] **1128**

CABLE CONTACTS *CEASED*. (US/1053-9026) [22646181] **1129**

CABLE CONTACTS YEARBOOK (US/1048-3764) [09130594] **1150**

CABLE GUIDE (US/0191-4871) [04935036] **1129**

CABLE GUIDE (WYOMING, MI) (US) **1129**

CABLE HANDBOOK (US/0364-8761) [02671726] **1129**

CABLE IN THE CLASSROOM (US/1054-5409) [22916047] 1730, **1129**

CABLE INDUSTRY DIRECTORY (US) **1150**

CABLE MADRID (SP/0214-1868) [I02141868] **1129**

●CABLE NETWORK INVESTOR (US/1062-3515) [25590314] 893, **781**

CABLE PRODUCT NEWS (US/0733-5504) [08608994] **1129**

CABLE REPORT (US) [03067476] **2037**

CABLE SERVICES REPORT (US) [05162834] **1129**

CABLE SYSTEM MANAGER (US/1059-681X) [24679548] **1105**

CABLE T.V. AND NEW MEDIA LAW & FINANCE (US/1068-3631) [12705344] 2945, **1129**

CABLE-TELCO REPORT, THE (US/1050-0553) [21389530] **1150**

CABLE TELEVISION (CN/0703-7244) [01792118] **1129**

CABLE TELEVISION LAW : MUNICIPAL LAW OFFICERS EDITION (US/0161-6811) [03983848] 1129, **2945**

CABLE TELEVISION SERVICE APPLICATIONS *See* CABLE TELEVISION SERVICE REGISTRATIONS **1129**

CABLE TELEVISION SERVICE REGISTRATIONS (US) [06730647] **1129**

CABLE TV ADVERTISING (US/0270-885X) [06507764] **756**

CABLE TV BANKER/BROKER (US/0893-2131) [15467287] **1600**

●CABLE TV FINANCE (1992) (US/1061-5652) [25364249] **1129**

CABLE TV FRANCHISING *See* CABLE TV REGULATION (1993) **1129**

CABLE TV FRANCHISING (US/0731-0269) [08117803] **1129**

CABLE TV INVESTOR (US/0731-0250) [08117886] 893, **1129**

CABLE TV INVESTOR CHARTS (US/0732-7757) [08433468] **1129**

CABLE TV LAW REPORTER (US/0749-7652) [11189974] 1129, **2945**

CABLE TV MAGAZINE (US/0277-1462) [07498720] **1129**

CABLE TV PROGRAMMING (US/0278-503X) [07817522] **1129**

●CABLE TV REGULATION (1993) (US/1068-9826) [27872713] **1129**

CABLE TV RULES (US) **1129**

CABLE TV TAX LETTER (US/0730-6202) [08048344] 4716, **1129**

CABLE TV TECHNOLOGY (US/0276-5713) [07382679] **1129**

CABLE-VIDEO INDEX, THE (US) [10489913] **1129**

CABLE VIEWER MAGAZINE (US/0745-6891) [09396049] **1129**

CABLE VISION (US/0361-8374) [02441475] **1129**

CABLE WEEK. ORANGE-SEMINOLE-OSEOLA ED (US/0744-2327) [08120284] **1129**

CABLE WORLD (US/1042-7228) [19119497] **1150**

CABLECASTER DIRECTORY (CN) **1129**

CABLECASTER (TORONTO) (CN/0840-9153) [19762839] **1129**

CABLEFAX (DENVER, COLO.) (US/1069-6644) [28130387] **1105**

CABLEOPTICS NEWSLETTER (US/1051-1938) [21887451] **1150**

CABLEPLUS MAGAZINE (US/0884-8025) [12489399] **1129**

CABLESPORTS *See* PHILLIPS BUSINESS INFORMATION'S INTERACTIVE VIDEO NEWS **4372**

CABLESPORTS NEWSLETTER (US) 4889, **1129**

CABLETIME (US/0745-2969) [09038901] **1150**

CABLING INSTALLATION & MAINTENANCE (US/1073-3108) [29331493] **1105**

CABO (SA/0379-4830) [01788185] **2638**

CABO-VERSLAG / CENTRUM VOOR AGROBIOLOGISCH ONDERZOEK (NE) [14105923] **71**

CABOT MARKET LETTER, THE (US/0733-8554) [08484386] **893**

CABOT'S MUTUAL FUND NAVIGATOR (US/1041-9454) [18887960] **4716**

CABRA & BODES (BL/0102-7344) [I01027344] 2330, **165**

CAC NEWS - CHICAGO ARTISTS' COALITION (US/0890-5908) [13585370] **346**

CACD JOURNAL (US/1052-3103) [21710100] **5276**

CACHE REGISTER, THE (US/0731-079X) [08120303] **1236**

CACTACEAS Y SUCULENTAS MEXICANAS (MX/0526-717X) [02729619] **505**

CACTUS AND SUCCULENT JOURNAL (AT) [03266424] 505, **2411**

CACTUS AND SUCCULENT JOURNAL (SANTA BARBARA) (US/0007-9367) [01538018] **2411**

CACTUS AND SUCCULENT JOURNAL WOOLLAHRA (AT/0526-7196) [I05267196] 505, **2411**

CAD CAM (GW) **1227**

CAD CAM (UK) **1231**

CAD/CAM ABSTRACTS (US/0882-1437) [11601894] 1227, **1231**

CAD/CAM, CAE, SURVEY, REVIEW, AND BUYERS' GUIDE (US/1043-6448) [11881887] **1173**

CAD/CAM DIGEST (UK/0263-6190) [06856012] 1227, **1231**

CAD/CAM MANAGEMENT STRATEGIES *CEASED*. (US/0741-0042) [10062170] **1218**

CAD CAM REPORT (GW) **1227**

CAD/CAM WATCH (US/1052-0856) [22185944] **1173**

CAD/CIM ALERT (US/8756-842X) [11668702] 1227, **1231**

CAD EDUCATOR, THE (US/8755-8637) [11455208] **1231**

CAD EVOLUTION (US/0896-3266) [17012823] **1967**

CAD INDUSTRY DIRECTORY (HARDWARE ED.) (US/1055-8926) [23364617] **1231**

CAD MAGAZINE (NE) **1231**

CAD SYSTEMS (CN/1183-9414) [26066772] **1231**

CAD USER (UK/0959-6259) [I09596259] **1222**

CAD USER AUSTRALIA NEW ZEALAND (AT/1037-8529) [I10378529] **1173**

CAD WORLD *CEASED*. (US/0892-4821) [15307571] **1173**

CADALYST (US/0820-5450) [16687894] **1231**

CADASTRO DAS INSTITUICOES DE PESQUISA, PESQUISADORES E SUAS ATIVIDADES NO RIO GRANDE DO SUL : I. MEDICINA VETERINARIA (BL) [03043246] **5507**

CADASTRO DAS INSTITUICOES DE PESQUISA, PESQUISADORES E SUAS ATIVIDADES NO RIO GRANDE DO SUL : II. AGRONOMIA E ZOOTECNIA (BL) [03027735] **71**

CADASTRO DAS INSTITUICOES DE PESQUISA, PESQUISADORES E SUAS ATIVIDADES NO RIO GRANDE DO SUL: III. GEOLOGIA (BL) [04918113] **1371**

CADASTRO DE ELECTRIFICACAO DO ESTADO DA BAHIA (BL) [04074331] **2037**

CADASTRO HOSPITALAR BRASILEIRO (BL) [02664566] **3777**

CADASTRO INDUSTRIAL (BL) [02241594] **1550**

CADASTRO INDUSTRIAL DO DISTRITO FEDERAL (BL) [02242042] **1550**

CADASTRO INDUSTRIAL DO ESPIRITO SANTO (BL) [21253390] **1550**

CADASTRO INDUSTRIAL DO PARA (BL) [01791815] **1550**

CADASTRO INDUSTRIAL: ESTADO DO RIO GRANDE DO NORTE (BL) [01793030] **1550**

CADASTROS: ESTABELECIMENTOS HOSPITALARES, ESTABELECIMENTOS PARA-HOSPITALARES, ESTABELECIMENTOS DE SERVICOS OFICIAIS DE SAUDE PUBLICA (BL) [02242317] **3777**

CADCAM LONDON (UK/0963-5750) [I09635750] **1231**

CADDET NEWSLETTER (NE) [19617307] 2189, **1934**

CADDO CITIZEN (US) [18311480] **5683**

CADENCE (US/0162-6973) [03589146] **4106**

CADENCE (US) **5691**

CADENCE (AUSTIN, TEX.) (US/0887-9141) [13415019] **1173**

CADENCE INVESTMENT ADVISORS PERFORMANCE SURVEY (US) **893**

Alphabetical Title Index — CAHIERS

CADENCE UNIVERSE PERFORMANCE REPORT (US) [12389522] **893**

CADENZA (LOLO, MONT.) (US/0007-9405) [02511117] **4106**

CADENZA (SASKATOON) (CN/0703-8380) [03956649] **4106**

CADERNO DE DIREITO ECONOMICO (BL) [10534856] **2945**

CADERNO DE MUSICA (BL) [09504734] **4106**

CADERNO DE PESQUISAS TRIBUTARIAS (BL) [03617108] 4716, **2946**

CADERNOS ABESC (BL) [03031222] 1730, **4941**

CADERNOS BRASILEIROS DE ARQUITETURA (BL) [05968847] **294**

CADERNOS DCP (BL) [01796562] **4466**

CADERNOS DE ADMINISTRACAO MUNICIPAL / IMAM (BL) [06492501] **4635**

CADERNOS DE ARQUEOLOGIA (BRAGA, PORTUGAL) (PO/0870-6425) [18904917] **265**

CADERNOS DE CAMPO : REVISTA DOS ALUNOS DE POS-GRADUACAO EM ANTROPOLOGIA (BL) [26334235] **233**

CADERNOS DE CIENCIAS SOCIAIS (BL) [25824011] **5194**

CADERNOS DE CIRURGIA (SAO BERNARDO DO CAMPO) (BL/0100-0462) [01731066] **3961**

CADERNOS DE CONSULTA PSICOLOGICA (PO/0871-7516) [26001925] **4579**

CADERNOS DE DIREITO PRIVADO (BL) [06840180] **3089**

CADERNOS DE ECONOMIA. REVISTA DE ANALISE (PO) **1467**

CADERNOS DE ESTUDOS BRASILEIROS *CEASED.* (BL) [04364319] **1550**

CADERNOS DE ESTUDOS LINGUISTICOS / UNIVERSIDADE ESTADUAL DE CAMPINAS, INSTITUTO DE ESTUDOS DA LINGUAGEM, DEPARTAMENTO DE LINGUISTICA (BL/0102-5767) [11620607] **3271**

CADERNOS DE FOLCLORE (BL) [01538020] **2318**

CADERNOS DE HISTORIA E FILOSOFIA DA CIENCIA (BL) [10509166] **5092**

CADERNOS DE HISTORIA E FILOSOFIA DA CIENCIA. SUPLEMENTO (BL) [12240703] **5092**

CADERNOS DE LINGUISTICA E TEORIA DA LITERATURA *CEASED.* (BL/0101-3548) [20122961] **3271**

CADERNOS DE OPINAO (BL) [02244949] **2514**

CADERNOS DE PESQUISA / FUNDACAO CARLOS CHAGAS (BL) [02240038] **1876**

CADERNOS DE PSICOLOGIA APLICADA (BL) [02414546] **4579**

CADERNOS DE SAUDE PUBLICA / MINISTERIO DA SAUDE, FUNDACAO OSWALDO CRUZ, ESCOLA NACIONAL DE SAUDE PUBLICA (BL/0102-311X) [15717205] **4770**

CADERNOS DE TECNOLOGIA E CIENCIA (BL/0101-2991) [04846467] **5092**

CADERNOS DO CEAS (BL/0102-9711) [01490971] **5241**

CADERNOS DO CEDI (BL/0103-5673) [I01035673] **5241**

CADERNOS DO RIO GRANDE DE NORTE (BL) [02240606] **2725**

CADERNOS FUNDAP (BL/0101-3211) [08244067] **4466**

CADERNOS MUNICIPAIS (PO) [10050105] **4635**

CADERNOS PEDAGOGICOS (BL) [01792389] **1890**

CADET JOURNAL & GAZETTE (UK) **4038**

CADILAC EVENING NEWS (US/0745-3655) [09097221] **5691**

CADIZ RECORD, THE (US) [14146497] **5679**

CADMIUM ABSTRACTS (UK/0309-1139) [02820766] **3999**

CADMOS (SW) [04382961] **2682**

CADOTT SENTINEL, THE (US/0885-0798) [12565444] **5766**

CADRES (FR/0526-7463) [03591696] **781**

CADRES CFDT (FR/0398-3145) [04687293] **1657**

CADRES ET MAITRISES (FR) **1730**

CADRES ET PROFESSION *See* CADRES CFDT **1657**

CADRIOLOGIA & HIPERTENSION (SP/1130-4014) [I11304014] **3700**

CADSCAN (UK) [14633327] **3999**

CADUCEE, LE (CN/0226-3467) [06562748] **862**

CADUCEUS (SPRINGFIELD, ILL.) (US/0882-6447) [11800401] **3561**

CAEL FORUM & NEWS (US) **1876**

CAEL NEWS *See* CAEL FORUM & NEWS **1876**

CAEL NEWS / COUNCIL FOR THE ADVANCEMENT OF EXPERIENTIAL LEARNING (US) [07262396] **1876**

CAERNARVONSHIRE HISTORICAL SOCIETY *See* TRANSACTIONS. TRAFODION **2484**

CAESARAUGUSTA (SP/0007-9502) [07906846] 2780, **265**

CAESARODUNUM : BULLETIN DE L'INSTITUT D'ETUDES LATINES DE LA FACULTE DES LETTRES ET SCIENCES HUMAINES D'ORLEANS-TOURS (FR/0245-5196) [03277219] **1075**

CAFE, CACAO, THE (FR/0007-9510) [02729853] **165**

CAFE D'AFRIQUE / ORGANISATION INTERAFRICAINE DU CAFE (IV) [10613292] **2365**

CAFE PERU - CENTRAL DE COOPERATIVAS AGRARIAS CAFE PERU (PE/1010-3503) [05659900] **165**

CAFE: RESULTADOS OBTIDOS (BL) [02242526] **2365**

CAFE SOLO (US/0007-9537) [01538024] **3461**

CAFES ET RESTAURANTS CHOUETTES (CN/0711-6322) [08651747] **5070**

● CAFETAL: REVISTA BIMESTRAL DE ANACAFE (GT) [25880552] **2365**

CAFFE; SATIRICO DI LETTERATURA E ATTUALITA, IL (IT/0007-9553) [03598598] **3370**

● CAGED BIRD HOBBYIST (US/1062-7383) [25723360] 2772, **5616**

CAGRINDEX : ABSTRACTS OF THE AGRICULTURAL LITERATURE OF THE CARIBBEAN (TR) 3370, **71**

CAGRINDEX / CAGRIS, CARIBBEAN INFORMATION SYSTEM FOR THE AGRICULTURAL SCIENCES (TR/0255-8319) [21800382] 3370, **71**

CAHHS INSIGHT (US/0896-7997) [15473288] **3777**

CAHIER - CENTRE DE RECHERCHES SUR L'ANTIQUITE TARDIVE ET LE HAUT MOYEN-AGE (FR/0292-1979) [I02921979] **2682**

CAHIER DE CONJONCTURE DE L'ANDESE, LE *See* CAHIERS VERTS DE L'ECONOMIE PARIS, LES **1467**

CAHIER DE CONJONCTURE DE L'ANDESE, LE (FR/0986-7236) [I09867236] **1633**

● CAHIER DE L'ENVOLEE LUMIERE (CN/1188-6749) [26715168] **4941**

CAHIER DE RECHERCHE - FACULTE DE L'AMENAGEMENT, UNIVERSITE DE MONTREAL (CN/0711-2475) [09340450] **2816**

CAHIER DE RECHERCHE - FACULTE DES SCIENCES SOCIALES. DEPARTMENT DE SCIENCE ECONOMIQUE. UNIVERSITE D'OTTAWA (CN/0225-3860) [06033097] **1467**

CAHIER - DEPARTEMENT D'ECONONOMIQUE, FACULTE DES SCIENCES SOCIALES, UNIVERSITE LAVAL (CN/0714-5659) [09340954] **1467**

CAHIER DES ARTS ET DES ARTISTES (FR/0765-9326) [I07659326] **346**

CAHIER DES JOURNEES HORTICOLES ORNEMENTALES (CN/0828-7449) [08287449] **2411**

CAHIER D'ETHOLOGIE APPLIQUEE (BE/0770-3767) [I07703767] **5580**

● CAHIER D'INFORMATION ..., INDUSTRIE, MICT, QUEBEC (CN/1189-4067) [26290455] **1600**

CAHIER D'INFORMATION - MINISTERE DE L'AGRICULTURE DES PECHES ET DE L'ALIMENTATION. DIRECTION GENERALE DES PECHES MARITIMES. DIRECTION DE LA RECHERCHE SCIENTIFIQUE ET TECHNIQUE (CN/0712-0613) [11264835] **2298**

CAHIER GENERAL DES CHARGES POUR TRAVAUX DE CONSTRUCTION PRIVEE *CEASED.* (BE) **606**

CAHIER HISTORIQUE (CN/0705-2944) [04129801] **2725**

CAHIER - INSTITUT NATIONAL DE PREPARATION PROFESSIONELLE (CG) [01788643] **1657**

CAHIER - LA SAUVRGARDE DE L'ART FRANCAIS (FR) [07035204] **346**

CAHIER MALEVITCH (SZ) [10054708] **346**

CAHIER - SOCIETE D'HISTOIRE DES PAYS-D'EN-HAUT (1989) (CN/0846-5312) [20781874] **2612**

CAHIER - SOCIETE HISTORIQUE DU MARIGOT, LONGUEUIL (1980) (CN/0711-0529) [08465948] **2725**

CAHIER SPECIAL D'INFORMATION - DIRECTION GENERAL DES PECHES MARITIMES. DIRECTION DE LA RECHERCHE SCIENTIFIQUE ET TECHNIQUE (CN/0832-7858) [08964189] **2298**

CAHIER TECHNIQUE - DIRECTION GENERALE DE LA PLANIFICATION. OFFICE DE PLANIFICATION ET DE DEVELOPPEMENT DU QUEBEC (CN/0712-0370) [08850967] **2816**

CAHIER TECHNIQUE DU BIOLOGISTE, LE (FR) **450**

CAHIER (UNIVERSITE DE MONTREAL. DEPARTEMENT DE SCIENCES ECONOMIQUES) (CN/0709-9231) [03520222] **1467**

CAHIERS (BE/0771-6435) [13432746] 4517, **2612**

CAHIERS (FR) [06597049] **3370**

● CAHIERS AFIDES (CN/1188-5033) [26497897] **1730**

CAHIERS AFRICAINS D'ADMINISTRATION PUBLIQUE *CEASED.* (MR/0007-9588) [02323722] **4635**

CAHIERS ALSACIENS D'ARCHEOLOGIE, D'ART ET D'HISTOIRE (FR/0575-0385) [03493561] 346, 2682, **265**

CAHIERS ARCHEOLOGIQUES (FR/0068-4945) [01538026] **265**

CAHIERS - ASSOCIATION INTERNATIONALE DES ENTRETIENS ECOLOGIQUES (FR/0759-2310) [I07592310] **2212**

CAHIERS BEI / BANQUE EUROPEENNE D'INVESTISSEMENT (LU/0257-7755) [14096130] 781, **893**

CAHIERS BERNARD LAZARE (FR) [03500665] **5046**

CAHIERS BIBLIOGRAPHIQUES DE CHIMIE ORGANOMETALLIQUE (FR) [12229774] **966**

CAHIERS BINET SIMON (FR) [24993826] 1730, **4579**

CAHIERS BLEUS (FR/0338-7208) [15028920] **3370**

CAHIERS BLEUS VETERINAIRES, LES (GW/0526-765X) [06003671] **5507**

CAHIERS BRUXELLOIS (BE/0007-9626) [03277330] **2682**

CAHIERS - CEGEP DE LIMOILOU. DEPARTEMENT DE FRANCAIS (CN/1183-4110) [25589774] **3370**

CAHIERS - CEGEP DE LIMOILOU. DEPARTEMENT DE FRANCAIS (CN/1183-4110) [24623497] **3370**

CAHIERS CELINE (FR/0398-6659) [I03986659] **3370**

CAHIERS - CENTRE D'ETUDES DE RECHERCHE OPERATIONNELLE (BE/0008-9737) [02445776] **1173**

CAHIERS CHARLES V (FR) [11106520] 3371, **2682**

CAHIERS COLETTE (FR/0291-2120) [04212712] **3371**

CAHIERS / COMEDIE-FRANCAISE, LES (FR/0759-125X) [24832281] **5362**

CAHIERS CONFRONTATION *CEASED.* (FR) [06950307] **4579**

CAHIERS CRITIQUES DE LA LITTERATURE (FR) [03594261] **3339**

CAHIERS D'ANESTHESIOLOGIE (FR/0007-9685) [03067753] **3682**

CAHIERS D'ANIMATION MISSIONNAIRE (CN/0381-7652) [02433671] **4941**

CAHIERS D'ANTHROPOLOGIE ET BIOMETRIE HUMAINE (FR/0758-2714) [09844753] **233**

CAHIERS D'ARCHEOLOGIE ET D'HISTORIE DU BERRY (FR/0007-9693) [03298154] **265**

CAHIERS D'ARCHEOLOGIE SUBAQUATIQUE (FR) [03093531] **265**

CAHIERS DE BIBLIOLOGIE (CN/0228-6556) [07805549] **4827**

CAHIERS DE BIOLOGIE MARINE (FR/0007-9723) [01538032] **553**

CAHIERS DE BIOLOGIE (OTTAWA. 1973) (CN/0703-0967) [06273220] **450**

CAHIERS DE CANCEROLOGIE. BIOLOGIE CLINIQUE THERAPEUTIQUE (FR) 450, **3810**

CAHIERS DE CAP-ROUGE (CN/0227-2822) [I02272822] **1090**

CAHIERS DE CHROMOTOGRAPHIE (FR) 966, **4367**

CAHIERS DE CIVILISATION MEDIEVALE (FR/0007-9731) [01538035] **2682**

CAHIERS DE CIVILISATION MEDIEVALE. BIBLIOGRAPHIE (FR/0240-8678) [I02408678] **2635**

CAHIERS DE CIVILISATION MEDIEVALE. SUPPLEMENT (FR/0068-5011) [03068068] **2612**

CAHIERS DE CLIO (BE/0575-0598) [03068090] **5241**

CAHIERS
Alphabetical Title Index

CAHIERS DE COURS DE L'HOLANTHROPE, LES (CN/0318-7349) [02443070] **4241**

CAHIERS DE DEFENSE SOCIALE (FR) [03484471] **3159**

CAHIERS DE DROIT EUROPEEN (BE/0007-9758) [01538038] **2946**

CAHIERS DE DROIT FISCAL INTERNATIONAL (NE) [03598397] **4716**

CAHIERS DE DROIT (QUEBEC) (CN/0007-974X) [02301743] **2946**

CAHIERS DE FONTENAY, LES (FR/0395-8418) [10248373] **2844**

CAHIERS DE GEOGRAPHIE DU QUEBEC (CN/0007-9766) [09951461] **2557**

CAHIERS DE GEOGRAPHIE (PARIS, FRANCE) (FR) [15524950] **2557**

CAHIERS DE KINESITHERAPIE (FR/0007-9782) [00079782] **3774, 3953**

CAHIERS DE LA CINEMATHEQUE, LES (FR/0764-8499) [03825624] **4064**

CAHIERS DE LA DAFI (FR/0765-104X) [02198221] **265**

CAHIERS DE LA DOCUMENTATION (BE/0007-9804) [01538041] **3199**

CAHIERS DE LA FONCTION PUBLIQUE ET DE L'ADMINISTRATION (FR/0753-4418) [07534418] **4635**

CAHIERS DE LA FONDATION, LES (FR/0983-1851) [09831851] **654**

CAHIERS DE LA GUITARE, LES (FR/0294-6939) [12270424] **4106**

CAHIERS DE LA HAUTE-LOIRE LE PUY (FR/0575-0717) [05750717] **2682**

CAHIERS DE LA MUTUALITE DANS L'ENTREPRISE, LES (FR/0294-4049) [02944049] **1467**

●CAHIERS DE LA NCT (CN/1188-1461) [26497673] **5362**

CAHIERS DE LA NOUVELLE, LES (FR/0294-0442) [10472085] **3371**

CAHIERS DE LA PEINTURE, LES (FR/0769-1912) [07691912] **346**

CAHIERS DE LA PHOTOGRAPHIE, LES (FR) [07727063] **4367**

CAHIERS DE LA PUERICULTRICE (FR/0007-9820) [00079820] **3852**

CAHIERS DE LA RECHERCHE AGRONOMIQUE, LES (MR/0525-7951) [01538043] **71**

CAHIERS DE LA RECHERCHE ARCHITECTURALE, LES (FR/0150-9535) [05217422] **294**

CAHIERS DE LA RECHERCHE DEVELOPPEMENT, LES (FR/0760-579X) [12932642] **71**

CAHIERS DE LA REVUE DE THEOLOGIE ET DE PHILOSOPHIE (SZ/0250-6971) [04758604] **4343, 4941**

CAHIERS DE LA ROTONDE (FR/0183-536X) [07633870] **1075**

CAHIERS DE LA SECURITE INTERIEURE / INSTITUT DES HAUTES ETUDES DE LA SECURITE INTERIEURE, LES (FR) [23195637] **3159**

CAHIERS DE LA SEIGNEURIE DE CHAMBLY (CN/0228-0930) [08063571] **2725**

CAHIERS DE LA TERRE CUITE, LES (FR/0335-1688) [04153101] **2587**

CAHIERS DE LA WALLONIE ET DE BRUXELLES / GROUPE DE SOCIOLOGIE WALLONNE, LES *CEASED.* (BE/0771-6680) [11889836] **5241**

CAHIERS DE L'ACADEMIE ANQUETIN NEUILLY-SUR-SEINE, LES (FR/0999-2413) [09992413] **1090**

CAHIERS DE L'ACADEMIE (MONTREAL) (CN/0824-6602) [10926523] **2784**

CAHIERS DE L'AFEDES (FR) [20062318] **1934**

CAHIERS DE L'AMENAGEMENT : PUBLICATION DE L'UNITE DE RECHERCHE EN AMENAGEMENT TERRITORIAL / MINISTERE DE L'AMENAGEMENT DU TERRITOIRE, DE L'URBANISME ET DE LA CONSTRUCTION, AGENCE NATIONALE POUR L'AMENAGEMENT DU TERRITOIRE (AE) [19256876] **2816**

CAHIERS DE L'ANALYSE DES DONNEES, LES (FR/0339-3097) [03804453] **5324**

●CAHIERS DE L'ANIMATION, LES (FR/1243-6852) [12436852] **1730**

CAHIERS DE L'APF (FR) [02917097] **4941**

CAHIERS DE L'ARMUQ, LES (CN/0821-1817) [10441488] **4106**

CAHIERS DE L'ASSOCIATION INTERNATIONALE DES ETUDES FRANCAISES (FR/0571-5865) [01238315] **3271**

CAHIERS DE L'ATLAS DE FRANCHE-COMTE (FR) [03813447] **2557**

CAHIERS DE L'ECOLE SAINT-JEAN *CEASED.* (FR/0761-7232) [07617232] **2612**

CAHIERS DE L'EUPHRATE / CENTRE NATIONAL DE LA RECHERCHE SCIENTIFIQUE, CENTRE DE RECHERCHES ARCHEOLOGIQUES, CENTRE REGIONAL DE PUBLICATIONS : SOPHIA-ANTIPOLIS (FR) [07861787] **2647, 265**

CAHIERS DE L'EUROPE PARIS (FR/1148-4683) [11484683] **2946, 5276**

CAHIERS DE LEXICOLOGIE (FR/0007-9871) [01715490] **3271**

CAHIERS DE L'EXPANSION REGIONALE *See* INTER REGIONS **2825**

CAHIERS DE L'EXPANSION REGIONALE, LES (FR/0014-4711) [05713335] **2816**

CAHIERS DE L'EXPRESS (PARIS), LES (FR/1145-0320) [11450320] **2514**

CAHIERS DE L'I.H.T.P, LES (FR/0769-4504) [07694504] **2612**

CAHIERS DE L'ICP RAPPORT DE RECHERCHE, LES (FR/1163-765X) [I1163765X] **3271**

CAHIERS DE L'IMAGINAIRE, LES (FR/0243-2226) [15926060] **3371**

CAHIERS DE L'INGENIERIE (FR) **1967**

CAHIERS DE LINGUISTIQUE. ASIE ORIENTALE (FR/0153-3320) [03864330] **3271**

CAHIERS DE LINGUISTIQUE FRANCAISE (SZ/0259-6199) [02596199] **3271**

CAHIERS DE LINGUISTIQUE HISPANIQUE MEDIEVALE (FR) [03342408] **3271**

CAHIERS DE LINGUISTIQUE THEORIQUE ET APPLIQUEE (RM/0007-988X) [02258837] **3271**

CAHIERS DE L'INSTITUT D'AMENAGEMENT ET D'URBANISME DE LA REGION D'ILE-DE-FRANCE (FR/0153-6184) [04580125] **2816**

CAHIERS DE L'INSTITUT DE LINGUISTIQUE DE LOUVAIN (BE/0771-6524) [07716524] **3271**

CAHIERS DE L'INSTITUT DU MOYENAGE GREC ET LATIN / UNIVERSITE DE COPENHAGUE (DK/0591-0358) [01001593] **3271**

CAHIERS DE L'IPAG NANCY (FR/1145-5268) [11455268] **4466**

CAHIERS DE L'IPC (FR) **1090**

●CAHIERS DE L'IREPP, LES (FR/1240-2095) [12402095] **1144**

CAHIERS DE LITTERATURE ORALE (FR/0396-891X) [04600699] **2318**

CAHIERS DE L'OBSERVATION DU CHANGEMENT SOCIAL / ATP OBSERVATION CONTINUE DU CHANGEMENT SOCIAL ET CULTURAL (FR) [08981428] **5241**

CAHIERS DE L'ORIENT, LES (FR/0767-6468) [15035685] **2612**

CAHIERS DE MARIEMONT, LES (BE/0776-1317) [I0776I317] **4086**

CAHIERS DE MARS, LES (FR/1169-0402) [11690402] **4038**

CAHIERS DE MEDECINE DU TRAVAIL (BE/0376-7639) [01383540] **2860, 3561**

CAHIERS DE MEDECINE INTERPROFESSIONNELLE (FR/0007-9936) [00079936] **3561**

CAHIERS DE MICROPALEONTOLOGIE (FR/0068-5054) [01989623] **4226**

CAHIERS DE MUSIQUES TRADITIONNELLES (SZ) [20222995] **4106**

CAHIERS DE NOTES DOCUMENTAIRES (FR/0007-9952) [13206020] **4770**

CAHIERS DE NUTRITION ET DE DIETETIQUE (FR/0007-9960) [03599127] **4188**

CAHIERS DE PHILOSOPHIE POLITIQUE ET JURIDIQUE (FR/1144-4924) [I1444924] **1060**

CAHIERS DE PROPRIETE INTELLECTUELLE (CN/0840-7266) [19730574] **1302**

CAHIERS DE PROTHESE, LES (FR/0397-1643) [02718517] **1318**

CAHIERS DE PSYCHOLOGIE COGNITIVE (FR/0249-9185) [10625256] **4579**

CAHIERS DE RECHERCHE SOCIOLOGIQUE (CN/0831-1048) [13784477] **5241**

CAHIERS DE RHEOLOGIE, LES (FR/1149-0039) [27860762] **450**

CAHIERS DE SAINT-MICHEL DE CUXA, LES (FR/1140-7530) [02258840] **346**

CAHIERS DE SEXOLOGIE CLINIQUE (FR/0336-5913) [03365913] **5187**

CAHIERS DE SOCIOLOGIE ECONOMIQUE ET CULTURELLE, ETHNOPSYCHOLOGIE (FR/0761-9871) [11501239] **233, 4579, 5241**

CAHIERS DE SOCIOLOGIE ET DE DEMOGRAPHIE MEDICALES (FR/0007-9995) [00079995] **4770**

CAHIERS DE SPIRITUALITE IGNATIENNE (CN/0705-8942) [04518911] **4941**

CAHIERS DE STATISTIQUES AGRICOLES (FR) [02243801] **71**

CAHIERS DE TOPOLOGIE ET GEOMETRIE DIFFERENTIELLE CATEGORIQUES (FR) [12368868] **3499**

CAHIERS DE TUNISIE (TI/0008-0012) [01538054] **2638**

CAHIERS DEBUSSY (FR/0395-1200) [03349438] **4106**

CAHIERS D'ECONOMIE ET SOCIOLOGIE RURALES (FR/0755-9208) [22357001] **71, 1467, 5194**

CAHIERS D'ECONOMIE POLITIQUE (FR/0339-3437) [05917921] **4466**

CAHIERS D'ENSEIGNEMENT DE LA SOFCOT (FR/0338-3849) [02079028] **3561**

CAHIERS DES AMERIQUES LATINES (PARIS, FRANCE : 1985) (FR) [12685246] **2725**

CAHIERS DES AMIS DE ROBERT BRASILLACH (SZ/0409-8536) [03075518] **3371**

CAHIERS DES ARTS ET TECHNIQUES D'AFRIQUE DU NORD (FR) [03491077] **370**

CAHIERS DES COMITES DE PREVENTION DU BATIMENT ET DES TRAVAUX PUBLICS (FR/0010-244X) [08664945] **606, 2860**

CAHIERS DES DIX (CN/0575-089X) [02247928] **2725**

CAHIERS DES ETUDES ANCIENNES (CN/0317-5065) [01789189] **2612**

CAHIERS DES ETUDES RURALES (FR) [02746813] **5241**

CAHIERS DES INGENIEURS AGRONOMES (FR/0575-0865) [02749667] **1967**

CAHIERS DES NATURALISTES (FR/0008-0039) [06003789] **5194**

CAHIERS DES RELIGIONS AFRICAINES (CG/0008-0047) [02258833] **4942**

CAHIERS DES SCIENCES HUMAINES (FR/0768-9829) [14403816] **5194**

CAHIERS D'ETUDE DE SOCIOLOGIE CULTURELLE (FR) [03075576] **5241**

CAHIERS D'ETUDES AFRICAINES (FR/0008-0055) [01538061] **2638**

CAHIERS D'ETUDES CATHARES (FR/0008-0063) [03261825] **4942**

CAHIERS D'ETUDES COMTOISES (FR/0575-0512) [03075611] **2682**

CAHIERS D'ETUDES ET DE RECHERCHES FRANCOPHONES SANTE ET DEVELOPPEMENT (FR) **4466**

CAHIERS D'ETUDES GERMANIQUES (FR/0751-4239) [07683007] **3371**

CAHIERS D'ETUDES MEDIEVALES (FR) [06270561] **2682**

CAHIERS D'ETUDES ROMANES : C.E.R (FR/0244-6103) [07308868] **1075**

CAHIERS D'HERALDIQUE (FR/0339-9354) [I03399354] **2441**

CAHIERS D'HISTOIRE (FR/0008-008X) [02068221] **2612**

CAHIERS D'HISTOIRE DE DEUX-MONTAGNES (CN/0226-7063) [06511773] **2725**

CAHIERS D'HISTOIRE DE LA RIVIERE DU NORD, LES (CN/0824-796X) [11734440] **2725**

CAHIERS D'HISTOIRE DE LA SOCIETE D'HISTOIRE DE BELOEIL-MONT-SAINT-HILAIRE, LES (CN/0225-5359) [08063899] **2612**

CAHIERS D'HISTOIRE DE L'ART CONTEMPORAIN. DOCUMENTS (FR) [01791917] **346**

CAHIERS D'HISTOIRE DE L'INSTITUT DE RECHERCHES MARXISTES (FR/0221-5047) [07238902] **4540, 2682**

CAHIERS D'HISTOIRE DE L'UNIVERSITE LAVAL, LES (CN/0701-4031) [12030705] **2725**

CAHIERS D'HISTOIRE EGYPTIENNE (UA) [02749844] **2638**

CAHIERS D'HISTOIRE ET DE PHILOSOPHIE DES SCIENCES (FR/0221-3664) [06407662] **5092**

CAHIERS D'HISTOIRE (MONTREAL) (CN/0712-2330) [08898800] **2613**

CAHIERS D'HISTOIRE (QUEBEC) *CEASED.* (CN/0704-6952) [03491198] **2725**

CAHIERS D'INFORMATION DU DIRECTEUR DE PERSONNEL, LES (FR/0397-2143) [I03972143] **939**

●CAHIERS D'ONCOLOGIE (FR/0941-3804) [28710206] **3810**

CAHIERS D'OTO. RHINO. LARYNGOLOGIE, DE CHIRURGIE CERVICO. FACIALE ET D'AUDIOPHONOLOGIE, LES (FR/0395-3971) [10601254] **3887**

CAHIERS D'OUTRE-MER
(FR/0373-5834) [01538065] **2557**

CAHIERS DU BARREAU DE PARIS,
LES (FR/0982-3573) [17730389] **2946**

CAHIERS DU C.E.R.M.T.R.I, LES
(FR/0292-4943) [09631273] **412**

CAHIERS DU C.R.E.S.M, LES
(FR/0336-5042) [06683432] **2682**

CAHIERS DU CEDAF, LES
(BE/0250-1619) [03012026] 2638, **5194**

CAHIERS DU CENTRE D'ETUDES DE
L'ASIE DE L'EST (CN/0839-4555)
[17597354] **2844**

CAHIERS DU CENTRE
INTERDISCIPLINAIRE DES SCIENCES
DU LANGAGE (FR/0759-1586)
[19224145] **3271**

CAHIERS DU CENTRE SCIENTIFIQUE
ET TECHNIQUE DU BATIMENT
(FR/0008-9850) [03029670] **5092**

CAHIERS DU CENTRE UNIVERSITAIRE
DE LA REUNION (RE/0337-6176)
[02239983] **3272**

CAHIERS DU CETAI / CENTRE
D'ETUDES EN ADMINISTRATION
INTERNATIONALE, LES
(CN/0825-5822) [11245767] **1633**

CAHIERS DU CINEMA (FR/0008-011X)
[01538067] **4064**

CAHIERS DU COMMUNISME
(FR/0008-0136) [03718983] **4540**

CAHIERS DU CRABB
MONT-SAINT-AIGNAN, LES
(FR/1152-8427) [11528427] **781**

CAHIERS DU CREDIT MUTUEL
(FR/0395-8175) [03958175] **781**

CAHIERS DU CRELEF (FR) **1890**

CAHIERS DU CRIC (FR/0762-6193)
[15650630] **3371**

CAHIERS DU CURDES (BD) [12998130]
5194, **1467**

CAHIERS DU DEPARTEMENT DES
LANGUES ET DES SCIENCES DU
LANGAGE (SW/0256-1565) [13621736]
3272

CAHIERS DU DESSIN FRANCAIS (FR)
[12993698] **377**

CAHIERS DU DIX-SEPTIEME
(US/1040-3647) [16159695] **3371**

CAHIERS DU DOUBLE, LES (FR)
[05065318] **4466**

CAHIERS DU G.E.R.M, LES
(BE/0771-0313) [07710313] **3561**

CAHIERS DU GERAD (CN/0711-2440)
[10763985] **1467**

CAHIERS DU GRIDEQ (CN/0824-9547)
[05967477] 1657, **1541**

CAHIERS DU GROUPE DE
RECHERCHES SUR L'ARMEE
ROMAINE ET LES PROVINCES (FR)
[04181673] **2682**

CAHIERS DU JAZZ (FR) **4106**

CAHIERS DU LABRAPS (CN/0824-0736)
[11825359] **1813**

CAHIERS DU LACITO PARIS
(FR/0994-7736) [09947736] **3272**

CAHIERS DU MONDE HISPANIQUE ET
LUSO-BRESILIEN (FR/0008-0152)
[03498291] **3371**

CAHIERS DU MONDE HISPANIQUE ET
LUSO-BRESILIEN (FR/0008-0152)
[02258841] **2725**

●CAHIERS DU MONDE RUSSE (FR)
[30835668] **2682**

CAHIERS DU MONDE RUSSE ET
SOVIETIQUE (FR/0008-0160)
[01538068] **2682**

CAHIERS DU MUSEE NATIONAL D'ART
MODERNE (FR/0181-1525) [06078768]
346

CAHIERS DU PATRIMOINE
(FORT-DE-FRANCE, MARTINIQUE)
(MQ) [19746731] **2725**

CAHIERS DU PISTOLIER ET DU
CARABINIER (FR) **4889**

CAHIERS DU QUATERNAIRE
(FR/0246-5582) [10681119] **1371**

CAHIERS DU SCENARIO BRUXELLES,
LES (BE/0775-9479) [07759479] **4064**

CAHIERS DU SEMINAIRE D'HISTOIRE
DES MATHEMATIQUES (FR)
[07264192] **3499**

CAHIERS DU TEMOIGNAGE
CHRETIEN (FR) [08500953] **4942**

CAHIERS DU TOURISME. SERIE A,
LES (FR/0068-5151) [I00685151] **5465**

CAHIERS DU YACHTING See
NEPTUNE YACHTING **594**

CAHIERS ECONOMIQUES (BE)
[05355662] 1467, **1530**

CAHIERS ECONOMIQUES DE
BRUXELLES (BE/0008-0195)
[02755957] **1467**

CAHIERS ECONOMIQUES ET
MONETAIRES (FR/0396-4701)
[03613241] 1467, **781**

CAHIERS ECONOMIQUES ET
SOCIAUX (KINSHASA) (CG/0008-0209)
[02258843] **1550**

CAHIERS ELISABETHAINES
(FR/0184-7678) [01086703] **3339**

CAHIERS ETHNOLOGIQUES
(FR/0249-5635) [08704499] **233**

CAHIERS EVANGILE (FR/0222-9714)
[03701971] **4942**

CAHIERS FERDINAND DE SAUSSURE
(SZ/0068-516X) [01538069] **3272**

CAHIERS FRANCAIS, LES
(FR/0008-0217) [02251128] **2682**

CAHIERS FRANCO-CANADIENS DE
LOUEST (CN/0843-9559) [22159248]
2318, 3371, **3272**

CAHIERS FRANCO POLONAIS (FR)
3371

CAHIERS GEN-HISTO (CN/0225-9303)
[06183456] **2441**

CAHIERS GEOGRAPHIQUES DE
ROUEN (FR/0181-0839) [01810839]
2557

CAHIERS GEOLOGIQUES
(FR/0008-0241) [02756211] **1371**

CAHIERS GERARD DE NERVAL
(FR/0222-1578) [07547503] **3371**

CAHIERS HAUT-MARNAIS, LES
(FR/0008-025X) [02098363] 3371, **2613**

CAHIERS HENRI BOSCO (FR)
[10967897] 3339, **431**

CAHIERS HOSPITALIERS:
PERSONNEL AND FORMATION
(FR/0295-4591) [I02954591] **3777**

CAHIERS INTEGRES DE MEDECINE
(FR) [03075633] **3561**

CAHIERS INTERNATIONAUX DE
PSYCHOLOGIE SOCIALE, LES
(BE/0777-0707) [07770707] **4579**

CAHIERS INTERNATIONAUX DE
SOCIOLOGIE (FR/0008-0276)
[01538071] **5241**

CAHIERS INTERNATIONAUX DE
SYMBOLISME (BE/0008-0284)
[01538072] **4579**

CAHIERS INTERNATIONAUX
D'HISTOIRE ECONOMIQUE ET
SOCIALE (SZ/1010-3643) [02241143]
1550

CAHIERS IVAN TOURGUENIEV,
PAULINE VIARDOT, MARIA MALIBRAN
(FR/0399-1326) [06413747] **2613**

CAHIERS IVOIRIENS DE RECHERCHE
LINGUISTIQUE / INSTITUT DE
LINGUISTIQUE
APPLIQUU.N.A.C.I-ABIDJAN
(IV/0252-9386) [03822712] **3272**

CAHIERS JEAN-COCTEAU (PARIS)
(FR/0068-5178) [00972365] **3371**

CAHIERS JEAN GIRAUDOUX
(FR/0150-6943) [01794802] **3371**

CAHIERS JURIDIQUES ET FISCAUX
DE L'EXPORTATION (FR/0242-0627)
[I02420627] **826**

CAHIERS LEON TROTSKY
(FR/0181-0790) [08228927] **4540**

CAHIERS LEOPOLD DELISLE
(FR/0399-1415) [02069666] 265, **2682**

CAHIERS LIGURES DE PREHISTOIRE
ET DE PROTOHISTOIRE (IT/1012-0238)
[13872457] 265, **2613**

CAHIERS LINGUISTIQUES D'OTTAWA
(CN/0315-3967) [02247829] **3272**

CAHIERS LORRAINS, LES
(FR/0758-6760) [03498344] 265, **2682**

CAHIERS MANAGEMENT
INFORMATIQUE (FR) **1256**

CAHIERS MARCEL PROUST
(FR/0068-5186) [03075783] **3371**

CAHIERS MARXISTES (BE) [09636254]
4540

CAHIERS MAYNARD (FR) [04151950]
3461

CAHIERS MEDICAUX (FR/0338-1439)
[01891312] **3561**

CAHIERS NATURALISTES, LES
(FR/0008-0365) [01538075] **3371**

CAHIERS NEPALAIS (FR) [03075646]
1352, **2557**

CAHIERS O.R.S.T.O.M. SERIE
ENTOMOLOGIE MEDICALE ET
PARASITOLOGIE *CEASED.*
(FR/0029-7224) [10002097] **5606**

CAHIERS O.R.S.T.O.M: SERIE
HYDROBIOLOGIE (FR/0008-0381)
[03075713] **450**

CAHIERS O.R.S.T.O.M. SERIE
PEDOLOGIE (FR/0029-7259)
[10130833] **1352**

CAHIERS OBSIDIANE, LES
(FR/0182-2373) [08710894] **2514**

CAHIERS PAUL CLAUDEL
(FR/0575-1144) [01263815] **3371**

CAHIERS PAUL LEAUTAUD
(CN/0713-4258) [09808963] **3371**

CAHIERS PAUL-LOUIS COURIER
(FR/0084-8239) [03510534] 431, **3371**

CAHIERS PEDAGOGIQUES (COMITE
UNIVERSITAIRE D'INFORMATION
PEDAGOGIQUE) See CAHIERS
PEDAGOGIQUES (FEDERATION DES
CERCLES DE RECHERCHE ET
D'ACTION PEDAGOGIQUES
(FRANCE)) **1730**

CAHIERS PEDAGOGIQUES DE LA
MONTEREGIE, LES (CN/1185-6629)
[25352098] **1730**

CAHIERS PEDAGOGIQUES
(FEDERATION DES CERCLES DE
RECHERCHE ET D'ACTION
PEDAGOGIQUES (FRANCE)) (FR)
[07618288] **1730**

CAHIERS PERCHERONS
(FR/0526-8443) [I05268443] 2557, **2514**

CAHIERS PHILOSOPHIQUES
(FR/0241-2799) [I02412799] **4343**

CAHIERS PHILOSOPHIQUES
AFRICAINS (CG) [01787865] **4343**

CAHIERS POUR CROIRE
AUJOURD'HUI (FR/0987-2213)
[I09872213] **4942**

CAHIERS POUR L'ANALYSE
CONCRETE (FR) [04065397] **1657**

CAHIERS PROFESSIONNELS, LES
(CN/1188-4045) [25796550] **5276**

CAHIERS QUEBECOIS DE
DEMOGRAPHIE (CN/0380-1721)
[02578464] **4550**

CAHIERS RATIONALISTES, LES (FR)
[03075767] 2844, **5092**

CAHIERS ROGER NIMIER
(FR/0246-2648) [07868977] **3371**

CAHIERS ROUMAINS D'ETUDES
LITTERAIRES (RM/0257-7526)
[02069846] **3339**

CAHIERS - S.E.M.A (FR/0153-5552)
[08740398] **2860**

CAHIERS SAINT DOMINIQUE (FR)
5025

CAHIERS SAINT-EXUPERY (FR)
[06755320] **3371**

CAHIERS SAINT-JOHN PERSE
(FR/0181-7779) [04799631] **3371**

CAHIERS SAINT-SIMON
(FR/0409-8846) [05237445] 3371, **2613**

CAHIERS SAVOYARDS DE
GENEALOGIE (FR/0756-9750)
[12936485] **2441**

CAHIERS SCIENTIFIQUES (FR)
[05998240] **2377**

CAHIERS SCIENTIFIQUES DU
TRANSPORT CAEN, LES
(FR/1150-8809) [I11508809] 5378, **1467**

CAHIERS SIMONE WEIL
(FR/0181-1126) [09753624] **4343**

CAHIERS SLAVES (FR) [17374420]
4505

CAHIERS--SOCIETE HISTORIQUE
ACADIENNE, LES (CN/0049-1098)
[02172336] 2441, **2725**

CAHIERS SPINOZA (FR/0152-593X)
[03792932] **4343**

CAHIERS STAELIENS (FR/0575-1276)
[03112470] **3339**

CAHIERS - SYSTEMA (FR/0243-6299)
[I02436299] **5092**

CAHIERS TECHNIQUES DU BATIMENT
(FR/0241-6794) [I02416794] **606**

CAHIERS THEATRE LOUVAIN
CEASED. (BE/0771-4653) [20277447]
5362

CAHIERS VAN DE STICHTING
BIO-WETENSCHAPPEN EN
MAATSCHAPPIJ (NE/0921-3457)
[13039241] **3561**

CAHIERS VASILE STANCIU (FR)
[18095507] **3159**

●CAHIERS VERTS DE L'ECONOMIE
PARIS, LES (FR/1167-5217) [11675217]
1467

CAHIERS VILFREDO PARETO
(SZ/0008-0497) [01538084] **5194**

CAHIERS ZAIROIS DE LA RECHERCHE
ET DU DEVELOPPEMENT (CG)
[01786059] 4635, **4466**

CAHIERS ZAIROIS D'ETUDES
POLITIQUES ET SOCIALES
(CG/0304-2707) [01791016] **1550**

CAHNERS ECONOMIC OUTLOOK (US)
1467

CAHPER JOURNAL TIMES See
CAHPERD JOURNAL TIMES **4770**

CAHPERD JOURNAL TIMES
(US/0273-6896) [06866819] 4849, **4770**

CAHR NEWSLETTER (CH) [18515218]
4505

CAHS JOURNAL, THE (CN/0007-7771)
[02908389] **15**

CAI NEWS / WASHINGTON
METROPOLITAN CHAPTER
(US/0277-2949) [07529782] **654**

CAIET DE INFORMARE: GEOGRAFIE
(RM) [01790981] **2557**

CAILIAO BAOHU (CC/1001-1560)
[I10011560] **966**

CAIMAN BARBUDO (MICROFICHE)
(CU) [04366086] **3339**

CAIN AND SCOTT APARTMENT
INVESTMENT STUDY, THE
(US/1042-8631) [19231490] **4835**

CAIN
Alphabetical Title Index

CAIN AND SCOTT COMMERCIAL INVESTMENT STUDY, THE (US/0896-6435) [17238706] **4835**

CAIN AND SCOTT MARKET SUMMARY See APARTMENT LETTER, THE **772**

CAIN AND SCOTT MARKET SUMMARY, THE (US/1043-3678) [19412460] **4835**

CAIRN, THE (CN/0701-0281) [03406145] **4086**

CAIRO (II/0376-7647) [02241804] **2638**

CAIRO. INSTITUT FRANCAIS D'ARCHEOLOGIE ORIENTALE See TEXTES ARABES ET ETUDES ISLAMIQUES **284**

CAIRO MESSENGER, THE (US) [19617244] **5652**

CAIRO PAPERS IN SOCIAL SCIENCE (UA) [04064882] **5194**

CAIRO PRESS REVIEW See CPR, CAIRO PRESS REVIEW **2486**

CAISSE CENTRALE DE COOPERATION ECONOMIQUE (FRANCE) See ANNUAL REPORT - CAISSE CENTRALE DE COOPERATION ECONOMIQUE **2907**

CAISSE CENTRALE DE COOPERATION ECONOMIQUE (FRANCE) See RAPPORT ANNUEL - CAISSE CENTRALE DE COOPERATION ECONOMIQUE **2911**

CAISSE DE DEPOT ET PLACEMENT DU QUEBEC See FINANCIAL STATEMENTS & FINANCIAL STATISTICS / CAISSE DE DEPOT ET PLACEMENT DU QUEBEC **4649**

CAISSE DE DEPOT ET PLACEMENT DU QUEBEC. DIRECTION DES ETUDES ECONOMIQUES See CYCLES ET TENDANCES **1590**

CAISSE DES DEPOTS ET CONSIGNATIONS (FRANCE) See PLAN DE LA CAISSE DES DEPOTS, LE **4741**

CAISSE-EXPRESS (CN/0226-8655) [06859320] **1541**

CAISSE NATIONALE DE L'ASSURANCE MALADIE DES TRAVAILLEURS SALARIES See RAPPORT D'ACTIVITIE - CAISSE NATIONALE DE L'ASSURANCE MALADIE DES TRAVAILLEURS SALARIES **1705**

CAISSE NATIONALE DES ALLOCATIONS FAMILIALES See STATISTIQUES ET RESULTATS COMPLEMENTAIRES **2287**

CAISSE NATIONALE DES ALLOCATIONS FAMILIALES See ACTION SOCIALE DES CAISSES D'ALLOCATIONS FAMILIALES, L' **5269**

CAISSE NATIONALE DES AUTOROUTES See RAPPORT ANNUEL DE LA CAISSE NATIONALE DES AUTOROUTES **5442**

CAISSE NATIONALE DES AUTOROUTES. CONSEIL D'ADMINISTRATION See RAPPORT ANNUEL DU CONSEIL D'ADMINISTRATION SUR L'ACTIVITE DE LA CAISSE NATIONALE DES AUTOROUTES EN ... **5443**

CAJA COSTARRICENSE DE SEGURO SOCIAL See ANUARIO ESTADISTICO - DEPTO ACTUARIAL Y ESTADISTICO **5273**

CAJA DE SEGURO SOCIAL (PANAMA) See MEMORIA QUE PRESENTA EL DIRECTOR GENERAL ... A LA HONORABLE ASAMBLEA DE REPRESENTANTES DE CORREGIMIENTOS **5296**

CAJAL CLUB See PROCEEDINGS OF THE CAJAL CLUB **3680**

CAJANUS (JM/0376-7655) [01362112] 2330, **4188**

CAKALELE (HONOLULU, HAWAII) (US/1053-2285) [22484068] **2647**

CAKAVSKA RIC (CI/0350-7831) [03081890] **3272**

CAKE DECORATING (US/0749-1824) [03779516] **2330**

CAL NEWS (CN/0711-7256) [08854776] **1294**

CAL-OSHA REPORTER (US/1054-1209) [06398041] **2860**

CAL POLY SCHOLAR, THE (US/0899-5281) [18124007] **1813**

● CAL SCIENCES (US/1061-3552) [25262428] **5092**

CAL-TAX LETTER (US) **4716**

CAL-TAX NEWS (US/0008-0543) [01552335] **4716**

CALABRIA MIA (DOWNSVIEW, ONT.) (CN/0827-2255) [11564280] **2682**

CALAMO (SP) [14090808] **2638**

CALAO (FR/0335-6469) [I03356469] **1060**

CALAVO NEWSLETTER (US/0008-0578) [03106165] **165**

CALC REPORT (US/0739-9189) [08946038] 5241, **4942**

CALCIFIED TISSUE ABSTRACTS (UK/0008-0586) [01983812] 532, **3655**

CALCIFIED TISSUE INTERNATIONAL (US/0171-967X) [04923138] **578**

● CALCIUM AND CALCIFIED TISSUE ABSTRACTS (US/1069-5540) [28102470] 532, **3655**

CALCIUM ANTAGONISMUS AKTUELL (GW/0724-7141) [12155451] **3561**

CALCOLO (IT/0008-0624) [02735374] 1256, **3499**

CALCULATOR (US) [02241539] **1730**

CALCULATOR LIB (US/0363-0102) [02400972] **1173**

CALCULUS OF VARIATIONS AND PARTIAL DIFFERENTIAL EQUATIONS (GW) **3499**

CALCUTTA. CENTRAL GLASS AND CERAMIC RESEARCH INSTITUTE See BULLETIN - CENTRAL GLASS AND CERAMIC RESEARCH INSTITUTE **2586**

CALCUTTA ELECTRIC SUPPLY CORPORATION See REPORT AND ACCOUNTS - CALCUTTA ELECTRIC SUPPLY CORPORATION **1624**

CALCUTTA HISTORICAL JOURNAL, THE (II) [06744867] **2648**

CALCUTTA. INSTITUTE OF POST GRADUATE MEDICAL EDUCATION AND RESEARCH See BULLETIN OF THE INSTITUTE OF POST GRADUATE MEDICAL EDUCATION AND RESEARCH **3560**

CALCUTTA JOURNAL OF POLITICAL STUDIES, THE (II) [08036300] **4466**

CALCUTTA LAW JOURNAL (II) [01755594] **2946**

CALCUTTA MATHEMATICAL SOCIETY See BULLETIN OF THE CALCUTTA MATHEMATICAL SOCIETY **3498**

CALCUTTA MEDICAL JOURNAL (II/0008-0667) [01552346] **3561**

CALCUTTA REVIEW SUSPENDED. (II/0045-3846) [02445636] **1090**

CALCUTTA STATISTICAL ASSOCIATION See BULLETIN - CALCUTTA STATISTICAL ASSOCIATION **5324**

CALCUTTA. UNIVERSITY. DEPT. OF PHILOSOPHY See JOURNAL OF THE DEPARTMENT OF PHILOSOPHY **4351**

CALDASIA (CK/0366-5232) [01552350] **4164**

CALDERONIANA (GW) [03489871] **5362**

CALDWELL COUNTY GENEALOGICAL SOCIETY, INC (US/0747-4849) [10705836] **2441**

CALDWELL COUNTY TIMES (US) [14125217] **5680**

CALDWELL INFORMER (US/0883-1645) [12065664] **5722**

CALDWELL MESSENGER (CALDWELL, KAN. 1942), THE (US/0897-4551) [08782163] **5674**

CALDWELL PROGRESS (1942) (US) [16893487] **5709**

CALEDON CITIZEN (CN/0823-9681) [11559823] **5781**

CALEDON COMMENT (CN/0821-235X) [10381825] **4870**

CALEDONIA ADVERTISER (US) [10549564] **5714**

CALEDONIA TIMES (CN/0701-0729) [03436216] **4942**

CALEDONIAN (PRINCE GEORGE) (CN/0381-856X) [08489197] **3371**

CALEDONIAN-RECORD (SAINT JOHNSBURY, VT.) (US/1054-3716) [12180513] **5757**

CALENDAR (US) [23610052] **346**

CALENDAR - BRANDON UNIVERSITY (CN/0316-8638) [02247249] **1813**

CALENDAR FOR NEW MUSIC, THE (US/0886-4594) [12892146] **4106**

CALENDAR / KENYATTA UNIVERSITY (KE) [17252740] **1813**

CALENDAR / MCGILL UNIVERSITY (CN/0383-7793) [01756912] **1813**

CALENDAR OF COLLECTIVE BARGAINING, NEW YORK STATE (US) [05180909] 1467, **1657**

CALENDAR OF EVENTS. TRADE FAIRS AND EXHIBITIONS (GW) [07766815] **5092**

CALENDAR OF EVENTS (VICTORIA. 1979) (CN/0709-2121) [05377978] **2486**

CALENDAR OF EXPIRING COLLECTIVE AGREEMENTS (CN/0381-4130) [03424733] **1657**

CALENDAR OF FESTIVALS (US/0271-9096) [06689203] **5268**

CALENDAR OF LITERARY FACTS, A (US) [20362147] **3371**

CALENDAR OF REGULAR MEETINGS OF THE ART ORGANIZATIONS IN NEW YORK CITY ... (US) [04563145] **346**

CALENDAR OF THE UNIVERSITY OF QUEENSLAND (AT) [06661521] **1813**

CALENDAR OF THE UNIVERSITY OF VICTORIA COLLEGE, COBOURG, FOR THE ACADEMIC YEAR ... (CN/1182-6002) [I11826002] **1730**

CALENDAR / ROYAL PHARMACEUTICAL SOCIETY OF GREAT BRITAIN (UK) [20818288] **4295**

CALENDAR / UNIVERSITY ART MUSEUM BERKELEY (US/0890-8850) [09909465] **4086**

CALENDAR (WINFIELD) (CN/0715-5778) [09403329] **5781**

CALENDAR YEAR REPORT / NATIONAL MANPOWER AND YOUTH COUNCIL (PH) [08225993] **1657**

CALENDARIO DEL POPOLO, IL (IT/0393-3741) [I03933741] **2613**

CALENDARIO TURISTICO (PE) [03175638] **5465**

CALENDARS OF THE UNITED STATES HOUSE OF REPRESENTATIVES AND HISTORY OF LEGISLATION (US/0364-0558) [01768279] **4635**

CALENDRIER MURAL (FR) **4849**

CALEPINS DE BIBLIOGRAPHIE (FR/0068-5429) [03075911] **412**

CALF NEWS (US/0007-7798) [03075938] **208**

CALGARY, ALBERTA, CITY DIRECTORY (CN/0226-000X) [06245238] **2557**

CALGARY (ALTA.) See MUNICIPAL HANDBOOK : THE CITY OF CALGARY **4667**

CALGARY & AREA AIRPORT BUSINESS DIRECTORY See CALGARY & AREA AVIATION BUSINESS DIRECTORY **5378**

● CALGARY & AREA AVIATION BUSINESS DIRECTORY (CN/1183-7853) [25423610] **5378**

CALGARY CITY SCENE (CN/0711-3684) [08454742] **5781**

CALGARY COMMERCE (CN/0707-8064) [04875850] **826**

CALGARY COMMUNITY SERVICES DIRECTORY (CN/0824-5444) [11777596] **5276**

CALGARY CORD, THE (CN/0380-9129) [02743472] **4385**

CALGARY ECONOMIC DEVELOPMENT NEWS (CN/0844-4552) [20174029] **1467**

CALGARY EVANGELICAL DIRECTORY (CN/0228-9229) [08071250] **4942**

CALGARY FOLK CLUB (CN/0821-2791) [09403285] **4106**

CALGARY HERALD (CN/0828-1815) [12027207] **5781**

CALGARY INDUSTRIAL LAND SURVEY (CN/0823-7980) [11193187] **2816**

CALGARY INSTITUTE FOR THE HUMANITIES See NEWSLETTER / THE CALGARY INSTITUTE FOR THE HUMANITIES **2851**

CALGARY INSTITUTE FOR THE HUMANITIES SERIES (CN) **2844**

CALGARY PUBLIC LIBRARY See MAGAZINES AND NEWSPAPERS - CALGARY PUBLIC LIBRARY **5789**

CALGARY PUBLIC LIBRARY See HAPPENINGS **3213**

CALGARY SUN (CN) **5781**

CALGARY WOMEN'S NEWSPAPER (CN/0702-9241) [03436755] **5552**

CALGARY WORKING PAPERS IN LINGUISTICS (CN/0823-0579) [12045326] **3272**

CALGARY Y F C FOCUS (CN/0319-3829) [02442829] **4942**

CALGARY YOUTH FOR CHRIST See CALGARY Y F C FOCUS **4942**

CALHOUN CHRONICLE AND THE GRANTSVILLE NEWS, THE (US/1040-399X) [12766699] **5763**

CALHOUN COUNTY ADVOCATE (US/0746-8512) [10339969] **5669**

CALHOUN COUNTY JOURNAL (BRUCE, MISS.) (US) [14817946] **5700**

CALHOUN NEWS, THE (US) [28395918] **5658**

CALHOUN TIMES AND GORDON COUNTY NEWS (US) [21977931] **5652**

CALI, COLOMBIA. UNIVERSIDAD DEL VALLE. DIVISION DE INGENIERIA See REVISTA - CALI, COLOMBIA. UNIVERSIDAD DEL VALLE. DIVISION DE INGENIERIA **1994**

CALIBAN (ANN ARBOR, MICH.) (US/0890-7269) [14366999] **3461**

CALIBAN (TOULOUSE, FRANCE) (FR/0575-2124) [02246007] **3371**

CALICO JOURNAL (US/0742-7778) [10321961] 3272, **1222**

CALIDAD DEL AGUA - GUATEMALA. INSTITUTO GEOGRAFICO NACIONAL (GT) [03217166] **2226**

CALIDRIS (SW/0346-9395) [I03469395] **5580**

CALIFORNIA See VEHICLE CODE **5427**

CALIFORNIA See LAWS RELATING TO FIRES AND FIREMEN, STATE OF CALIFORNIA **2997**

CALIFORNIA

CALIFORNIA See WORKERS' COMPENSATION LAWS OF CALIFORNIA, THE 3155

CALIFORNIA See COLLECTION AGENCY ACT WITH RULES AND REGULATIONS - (CALIFORNIA) 2952

CALIFORNIA See PLANNING, ZONING, AND DEVELOPMENT LAWS 3029

CALIFORNIA See CALIFORNIA LAWS FOR PSYCHOTHERAPISTS 3119

CALIFORNIA See FISH AND GAME CODE 4872

CALIFORNIA See FINAL BUDGET SUMMARY / STATE OF CALIFORNIA 4724

CALIFORNIA See WEST'S ANNOTATED CALIFORNIA CODES 3074

CALIFORNIA See LAWS RELATING TO THE PRACTICE OF OPTOMETRY, WITH RULES AND REGULATIONS 2997

CALIFORNIA See CALIFORNIA PHARMACY LAWS, WITH RULES AND REGULATIONS 2946

CALIFORNIA See CALIFORNIA RULES OF COURT. FEDERAL 3139

CALIFORNIA See COMPILATION OF LAWS RELATING TO THE PRACTICE OF VETERINARY MEDICINE, SURGERY AND ANIMAL HEALTH TECHNOLOGY WITH RULES AND REGULATIONS, GENERAL PROVISIONS OF THE BUSINESS AND PROFESSIONS CODE, INCLUDING THE CONSUMER AFFAIRS 5508

CALIFORNIA See EDUCATION CODE / STATE OF CALIFORNIA 1738

CALIFORNIA See STATE LAWS GOVERNING BOXING AND WRESTLING IN CALIFORNIA, WITH RULES AND REGULATIONS 3058

CALIFORNIA ACADEMIC LIBRARIES LIST OF SERIALS MICROFORM (US/0198-8433) [06771529] 3199

CALIFORNIA ACADEMY OF SCIENCES See SELECTED NEW ACQUISITIONS / CALIFORNIA ACADEMY OF SCIENCES, LIBRARY 3248

CALIFORNIA ACADEMY OF SCIENCES. LIBRARY See SELECTED NEW ACQUISITIONS / CALIFORNIA ACADEMY OF SCIENCES, LIBRARY 3248

CALIFORNIA ACADEMY OF SCIENCES, SAN FRANCISCO See PROCEEDINGS OF THE CALIFORNIA ACADEMY OF SCIENCES, 4TH SERIES 5140

CALIFORNIA ACCOUNTANCY ACT WITH RULES AND REGULATIONS (US/0095-6147) [01796641] 740

CALIFORNIA ACCOUNTANT See SUCCESSFUL CALIFORNIA ACCOUNTANT, THE 752

CALIFORNIA ACCOUNTANT, THE (US/0744-9895) [06402947] 740

CALIFORNIA ACTION SERVICE (US) 4635

CALIFORNIA ADMINISTRATIVE CODE (US) [06327802] 4635

CALIFORNIA. ADMINISTRATIVE OFFICE OF THE COURTS See NEWS RELEASE - CALIFORNAIA. ADMINISTRATIVE OFFICE OF THE COURTS 3142

CALIFORNIA ADVOCATE, THE (US) [10554372] 5633

CALIFORNIA AFL-CIO NEWS (US/0008-0802) [06165988] 1657

CALIFORNIA AGENCY FOR RESEARCH IN EDUCATION See CALIFORNIA SCHOOL DISTRICT FINANCIAL ANALYSES 1730

CALIFORNIA AGRICULTURAL DIRECTORY (BERKELEY, CALIF.) (US/0575-5298) [02734125] 71

CALIFORNIA AGRICULTURAL EXPERIMENT STATION See ECONOMIC RESEARCH OF INTEREST TO AGRICULTURE / UNIVERSITY OF CALIFORNIA, DIVISION OF AGRICULTURAL SCIENCES, AGRICULTURAL EXPERIMENT STATION 153

CALIFORNIA AGRICULTURAL EXPORTER (US) [19825341] 71

CALIFORNIA AGRICULTURAL EXPORTS (US) [15123766] 826, 71

CALIFORNIA AGRICULTURAL EXPORTS ANNUAL BULLETIN AND STATISTICAL APPENDIX (US/1064-9670) [26478642] 826, 71

CALIFORNIA AGRICULTURAL EXPORTS APPENDIX (US) [16508254] 826, 71

CALIFORNIA AGRICULTURE (BERKELEY, CALIF.) (US/0008-0845) [01552530] 71

CALIFORNIA AGRICULTURE STATISTICAL REVIEW (US) [15123459] 71, 152

CALIFORNIA AIR QUALITY DATA (US/0008-087X) [04264794] 2226

CALIFORNIA. AIR RESOURCES BOARD. TECHNICAL SERVICES DIVISION See CALIFORNIA AIR QUALITY DATA 2226

CALIFORNIA - ALASKA OIL AND GAS REVIEW (US) [02762673] 4252

CALIFORNIA ALLIANCE FOR THE MENTALLY ILL (US) [26038546] 3922

CALIFORNIA ALMANAC (US/0748-4402) [10493120] 5324

CALIFORNIA ALMOND GROWERS EXCHANGE, SACRAMENTO, CALIF See ALMOND FACTS 2408

CALIFORNIA AND HAWAII PUBLISHING MARKET PLACE (US/1058-2096) [22756626] 4813

CALIFORNIA AND WESTERN STATES GRAPE GROWER (US/0092-2145) [05140959] 166

CALIFORNIA ANGLER CEASED. (US/8750-8907) [11964904] 2298

CALIFORNIA ANTHROPOLOGIST (US/0272-5452) [02765135] 265, 233

CALIFORNIA APARTMENT INVESTMENT SURVEY (SACRAMENTO COUNTY ED.), THE (US/1056-2486) [23599905] 2816

CALIFORNIA APPAREL NEWS (US/0008-0896) [03981423] 1082

CALIFORNIA ARBITRATIONS (US/1044-9345) [19095216] 2946

CALIFORNIA ARCHITECTURE AND ARCHITECTS (US/1040-4317) [11046680] 294

CALIFORNIA-ARIZONA COTTON (US/0008-090X) [02756456] 166

CALIFORNIA-ARIZONA FARM PRESS (US/0164-5331) [04563043] 71

CALIFORNIA ARTS ADVOCATE (US) 317

CALIFORNIA ARTS COUNCIL See STATE OF THE ARTS : A PUBLICATION OF THE CALIFORNIA ARTS COUNCIL 365

CALIFORNIA ASSESSMENT PROGRAM RESULTS FOR EDUCATIONALLY HANDICAPPED PUPILS IN THE PRIMARY GRADES (US/0364-4561) [02638382] 1876

CALIFORNIA ASSOCIATION FOR HEALTH, PHYSICAL EDUCATION, RECREATION, AND DANCE See CAHPERD JOURNAL TIMES 4770

CALIFORNIA ASSOCIATION OF MACHINE EMBROIDERY (US/0882-2697) [11794227] 5183

CALIFORNIA ASSOCIATION OF RESIDENTIAL CARE HOMES See CARCH NEWS 3778

CALIFORNIA. ATTORNEY GENERAL'S OFFICE See OPINIONS OF THE ATTORNEY GENERAL OF CALIFORNIA 3142

CALIFORNIA AUCTIONEER COMMISSION See INFORMATION BULLETIN / CALIFORNIA AUCTIONEER COMMISSION 682

CALIFORNIA AVOCADO SOCIETY See YEARBOOK OF THE CALIFORNIA AVOCADO SOCIETY 2434

CALIFORNIA BANKRUPTCY JOURNAL (US/1047-0743) [20591869] 782

CALIFORNIA BLUE BOOK CEASED. (US) [02743957] 1082

CALIFORNIA. BOARD OF REGISTRATION FOR PROFESSIONAL ENGINEERS See ROSTER OF PROFESSIONAL ENGINEERS AND LAND SURVEYORS 1994

CALIFORNIA BOWLING NEWS (US/0008-0918) [03981480] 4889

CALIFORNIA BRIDE. LOS ANGELES EDITION CEASED. (US/0742-4493) [10371702] 2277

CALIFORNIA BUILDER (US/0527-2009) [02761519] 606

CALIFORNIA BUILDER & ENGINEER (US/0045-3900) [02246754] 2020

CALIFORNIA. BUREAU OF CRIMINAL STATISTICS See REFERENCE TABLES. DRUG ARRESTS AND DISPOSITIONS (SACRAMENTO) 3174

CALIFORNIA. BUREAU OF CRIMINAL STATISTICS AND SPECIAL SERVICES See HOMICIDE IN CALIFORNIA 3165

CALIFORNIA. BUREAU OF MARKET NEWS See FOOD PRICE SPREADS IN CALIFORNIA 2339

CALIFORNIA. BUREAU OF SCHOOL APPORTIONMENTS AND REPORTS See CALIFORNIA TEACHERS SALARIES AND SALARY SCHEDULES 1861

CALIFORNIA. BUREAU OF SCHOOL APPORTIONMENTS AND REPORTS See SCHOOL DISTRICTS THAT WERE GRANTED WAIVERS OF ADMINISTRATOR-TEACHER RATIO LIMITS 1871

CALIFORNIA. BUREAU OF SCHOOL APPORTIONMENTS AND REPORTS. DIVISION OF FINANCIAL RESOURCES AND DISTRIBUTION OF AID See SALARIES OF CERTIFICATED EMPLOYEES IN CALIFORNIA PUBLIC SCHOOLS 1709

CALIFORNIA BUSINESS (US/0008-0926) [02763580] 654

CALIFORNIA BUSINESS LAW PRACTITIONER (US/0892-2349) [14047856] 3097

CALIFORNIA BUSINESS LAW REPORTER (US/0199-669X) [06075602] 3097

CALIFORNIA CABLETTER (US/0740-0527) [09856901] 1150

CALIFORNIA CAL-LIOPE (US/0279-6449) [07134133] 1658

CALIFORNIA CAREER CRIMINAL APPREHENSION PROGRAM. ANNUAL REPORT TO THE LEGISLATURE / STATE OF CALIFORNIA, OFFICE OF CRIMINAL JUSTICE PLANNING (US) [08713687] 3159

CALIFORNIA CATTLEMAN (US/0008-0942) [02772992] 208

CALIFORNIA. CENTER FOR HEALTH STATISTICS See ANNUAL REPORT: STATE HOSPITALS FOR THE MENTALLY DISORDERED 3776

CALIFORNIA CERTIFIED ORGANIC FARMERS CERTIFICATION HANDBOOK (US) [25680016] 71

CALIFORNIA CHILDREN SERVICES INFORMATION AND STATISTICS FOR FISCAL YEARS ... (US) [08055308] 4809

CALIFORNIA CHRONICLE : NEWS FROM THE CALIFORNIA HISTORICAL SOCIETY (US) [17255936] 2725

CALIFORNIA, CITIES, TOWNS & COUNTIES (US/0891-2718) [14687308] 4636

CALIFORNIA CITY SPORTS MAGAZINE (US) 4889

CALIFORNIA. COASTAL AREA LABOR MARKET INFORMATION GROUP See LABOR MARKET REVIEW: VALLEJO-FAIRFIELD-NAPA STANDARD METROPOLITAN STATISTICAL AREA 1684

CALIFORNIA. COASTAL AREA LABOR MARKET INFORMATION GROUP See LABOR MARKET REVIEW : SANTA CRUZ STANDARD METROPOLITAN STATISTICAL AREA 1684

CALIFORNIA. COASTAL AREA LABOR MARKET INFORMATION GROUP See LABOR MARKET REVIEW : SAN FRANCISCO-OAKLAND STANDARD METROPOLITAN STATISTICAL AREA 1684

CALIFORNIA. COASTAL AREA LABOR MARKET INFORMATION GROUP See LABOR MARKET REVIEW: SALINAS-SEASIDE-MONTEREY STANDARD METROPOLITAN STATISTICAL AREA 1684

CALIFORNIA. COASTAL AREA LABOR MARKET INFORMATION GROUP See ANNUAL PLANNING REPORT : SAN FRANCISCO-OAKLAND STANDARD METROPOLITAN STATISTICAL AREA, BALANCE OF ALAMEDA COUNTY, ALAMEDA COUNTY EXCEPT CITIES OF OAKLAND AND BERKELEY 1648

CALIFORNIA. COASTAL AREA LABOR MARKET INFORMATION GROUP See ANNUAL PLANNING REPORT : VALLEJO-FAIRFIELD-NAPA STANDARD METROPOLITAN STATISTICAL AREA, NAPA COUNTY 1648

CALIFORNIA. COASTAL AREA LABOR MARKET INFORMATION GROUP See LABOR MARKET REVIEW : SANTA ROSA STANDARD METROPOLITAN STATISTICAL AREA 1684

CALIFORNIA. COASTAL AREA LABOR MARKET INFORMATION GROUP See ANNUAL PLANNING INFORMATION. HUMBOLDT COUNTY 1646

CALIFORNIA. COASTAL AREA LABOR MARKET INFORMATION GROUP See ANNUAL PLANNING INFORMATION : SAN FRANCISCO-OAKLAND STANDARD METROPOLITAN STATISTICAL AREA, CONTRA COSTA COUNTY, EXCLUDING THE CITY OF RICHMOND 1647

CALIFORNIA. COASTAL AREA LABOR MARKET INFORMATION GROUP See LABOR MARKET REVIEW : SAN JOSE STANDARD METROPOLITAN STATISTICAL AREA 1684

CALIFORNIA. COASTAL AREA LABOR MARKET INFORMATION GROUP See ANNUAL PLANNING INFORMATION : VALLEJO-FAIRFIELD-NAPA STANDARD METROPOLITAN STATISTICAL AREA, NAPA COUNTY 1648

CALIFORNIA. COASTAL AREA LABOR MARKET INFORMATION GROUP See ANNUAL PLANNING INFORMATION: SAN FRANCISCO-OAKLAND STANDARD METROPOLITAN STATISTICAL AREA, CITY OF BERKELEY 1647

CALIFORNIA. COASTAL AREA LABOR MARKET INFORMATION GROUP See ANNUAL PLANNING INFORMATION : SAN FRANCISCO-OAKLAND STANDARD METROPOLITAN STATISTICAL AREA, CITY OF RICHMOND 1647

CALIFORNIA COASTAL COMMISSION See BIENNIAL REPORT / STATE OF CALIFORNIA, CALIFORNIA COASTAL COMMISSION 2188

CALIFORNIA — Alphabetical Title Index

CALIFORNIA COLLEGE OF ARTS AND CRAFTS (OAKLAND, CALIF.) *See* ALUMNI DIRECTORY - CALIFORNIA COLLEGE OF ARTS AND CRAFTS (OAKLAND, CALIF.) **1097**

CALIFORNIA COLLEGES AND UNIVERSITIES / CALIFORNIA POSTSECONDARY EDUCATION COMMISSION (US) [14627869] 1730, **1813**

CALIFORNIA. COMMISSION FOR ECONOMIC DEVELOPMENT *See* ANNUAL REPORT - CALIFORNIA. COMMISSION FOR ECONOMIC DEVELOPMENT **1462**

CALIFORNIA. COMMISSION ON PEACE OFFICER STANDARDS AND TRAINING *See* POST ALLOCATION OF FUNDS AND TRAINING ACTIVITY SUMMARY **3173**

CALIFORNIA COMMISSIONER OF CORPORATIONS CURRENT OFFICIAL OPINIONS ISSUED PURSUANT TO THE CORPORATE SECURITIES LAW OF 1968 (US/0360-0955) [02243691] **3097**

CALIFORNIA COMMISSIONER OF CORPORATIONS CURRENT OFFICIAL OPINIONS ISSUED PURSUANT TO THE FRANCHISE INVESTMENT LAW (US/0362-1804) [02441137] **654**

CALIFORNIA COMMUNITIES (US/0194-2913) [05370705] **2816**

CALIFORNIA COMMUNITY COLLEGES. OFFICE OF THE CHANCELLOR *See* FACULTY AND ADMINISTRATIVE SALARIES **1864**

CALIFORNIA COMMUNITY FOUNDATION *See* YEAR BOOK / CALIFORNIA COMMUNITY FOUNDATION **4695**

CALIFORNIA COMMUNITY HEALTH INSTITUTE. SEMINAR *See* PROCEEDINGS OF THE ANNUAL SEMINAR OF THE CALIFORNIA COMMUNITY HEALTH INSTITUTE **4796**

CALIFORNIA. CONCILIATION SERVICE. REPORT *See* REPORT / STATE OF CALIFORNIA, MEDIATION/CONCILIATION SERVICE **1707**

CALIFORNIA CONGRESS OF PARENTS, TEACHERS, AND STUDENTS. LOS ANGELES TENTH DISTRICT *See* PTA BULLETIN **1869**

CALIFORNIA CONNECTIONS / DEPARTMENT OF DEVELOPMENTAL SERVICES (US) [25006939] **4385**

CALIFORNIA CONNECTIONS PUBLICATIONS *CEASED*. (US/0893-0694) [15342486] **1658**

CALIFORNIA CONSTRUCTION REVIEW (US) [18030585] **606**

CALIFORNIA COOPERATIVE OCEANIC FISHERIES INVESTIGATIONS *See* REPORTS - CALIFORNIA COOPERATIVE OCEANIC FISHERIES INVESTIGATIONS **2311**

CALIFORNIA CORRECTIONAL NEWS (US/0194-1682) [02380848] **3159**

CALIFORNIA COUNTRY (US/0194-5165) [04786525] **2529**

CALIFORNIA COUNTY (US/0743-0868) [10515974] **2529**

CALIFORNIA COUNTY FACT BOOK *CEASED*. (US/0590-0158) [02768560] **2557**

CALIFORNIA COURTS COMMENTARY (US/0527-2173) [05188895] **3139**

CALIFORNIA CRIPPLED CHILDREN SERVICES STATISTICAL REPORT (US/0190-1591) [04609146] 5276, **5266**

CALIFORNIA. CROP AND LIVESTOCK REPORTING SERVICE *See* CALIFORNIA FIELD CROP REVIEW **166**

CALIFORNIA CROP AND LIVESTOCK REPORTING SERVICE *See* CALIFORNIA DAIRY INDUSTRY STATISTICS: MANUFACTURED DAIRY PRODUCTS, MILK PRODUCTION, UTILIZATION AND PRICES **192**

CALIFORNIA. CROP AND LIVESTOCK REPORTING SERVICE *See* PRODUCTION AND MARKETING EGGS, CHICKENS AND TURKEYS, CALIFORNIA **219**

CALIFORNIA CROP AND LIVESTOCK REPORTING SERVICE *See* CALIFORNIA FRUIT & NUT ACREAGE **166**

CALIFORNIA CULINARY ACADEMY *See* ALUMNI DIRECTORY / THE CALIFORNIA CULINARY ACADEMY **1099**

CALIFORNIA DAIRY INDUSTRY STATISTICS: MANUFACTURED DAIRY PRODUCTS, MILK PRODUCTION, UTILIZATION AND PRICES (US) [02775929] **192**

CALIFORNIA DAIRY INFORMATION BULLETIN (US/0892-4406) [15236953] **192**

CALIFORNIA DEMOCRAT (US) [12298843] **5702**

CALIFORNIA DENTAL HYGIENISTS' ASSOCIATION JOURNAL (US) **1318**

CALIFORNIA. DEPT. OF CONSERVATION *See* CONSERVATION (SACRAMENTO) **2190**

CALIFORNIA. DEPT. OF CONSUMER AFFAIRS *See* REPORT TO THE GOVERNOR AND THE LEGISLATURE - STATE OF CALIFORNIA, DEPARTMENT OF CONSUMER AFFAIRS **1299**

CALIFORNIA. DEPT. OF CORPORATIONS *See* CALIFORNIA COMMISSIONER OF CORPORATIONS CURRENT OFFICIAL OPINIONS ISSUED PURSUANT TO THE FRANCHISE INVESTMENT LAW **654**

CALIFORNIA. DEPT. OF CORPORATIONS *See* CALIFORNIA COMMISSIONER OF CORPORATIONS CURRENT OFFICIAL OPINIONS ISSUED PURSUANT TO THE CORPORATE SECURITIES LAW OF 1968 **3097**

CALIFORNIA. DEPT. OF CORRECTIONS *See* ANNUAL RESEARCH REVIEW - CALIFORNIA DEPARTMENT OF CORRECTIONS **3158**

CALIFORNIA. DEPT. OF DEVELOPMENTAL SERVICES *See* ANNUAL CHAPTER 1 EDUCATION REPORT PROGRAM INFORMATION / CALIFORNIA HEALTH AND WELFARE AGENCY, STATE DEPARTMENT OF DEVELOPMENTAL SERVICES **1724**

CALIFORNIA DEPT. OF EDUCATION. DIVISION OF FINANCIAL SERVICES. LOCAL ASSISTANCE BUREAU *See* ENROLLMENT IN CALIFORNIA'S PRIVATE ELEMENTARY SCHOOLS AND HIGH SCHOOLS **1744**

CALIFORNIA. DEPT. OF FAIR EMPLOYMENT AND HOUSING *See* ANNUAL REPORT / CALIFORNIA DEPARTMENT OF FAIR EMPLOYMENT AND HOUSING **1648**

CALIFORNIA. DEPT. OF FAIR EMPLOYMENT AND HOUSING. OFFICE OF PUBLIC INFORMATION AND EDUCATION *See* ANNUAL REPORT - CALIFORNIA. DEPT. OF FAIR EMPLOYMENT AND HOUSING. OFFICE OF PUBLIC INFORMATION AND EDUCATION **4627**

CALIFORNIA. DEPT. OF FINANCE *See* CALIFORNIA ECONOMIC INDICATORS **1550**

CALIFORNIA. DEPT. OF FOOD AND AGRICULTURE *See* FINAL GRAPE CRUSH REPORT **87**

CALIFORNIA. DEPT. OF FORESTRY *See* ANNUAL REPORT - CALIFORNIA. DEPT. OF FORESTRY **2374**

CALIFORNIA. DEPT. OF FORESTRY *See* VOLUNTEERS IN FIRE PREVENTION **2293**

CALIFORNIA. DEPT. OF GENERAL SERVICES *See* STATE OF CALIFORNIA TELEPHONE DIRECTORY **1164**

CALIFORNIA. DEPT. OF HEALTH *See* ANNUAL REPORT TO THE GOVERNOR AND LEGISLATURE ON PREPAID HEALTH PLANS, PHPS **2874**

CALIFORNIA. DEPT. OF HEALTH. SOCIAL SERVICES DIVISION *See* PROPOSED, STATE OF CALIFORNIA, ANNUAL STATEWIDE SOCIAL SERVICES PLAN **5302**

CALIFORNIA DEPT. OF HOUSING AND COMMUNITY DEVELOPMENT *See* ANNUAL REPORT - DEPARTMENT OF HOUSING & COMMUNITY DEVELOPMENT **2814**

CALIFORNIA. DEPT. OF HOUSING AND COMMUNITY DEVELOPMENT *See* CALIFORNIA HOUSING PLAN, THE **2817**

CALIFORNIA. DEPT. OF INDUSTRIAL RELATIONS. DIVISION OF APPRENTICESHIP STANDARDS *See* CHARACTERISTICS OF REGISTERED APPRENTICES IN CALIFORNIA **1659**

CALIFORNIA. DEPT. OF INDUSTRIAL RELATIONS. DIVISION OF LABOR STATISTICS AND RESEARCH *See* MAJOR MEDICAL PLANS : SELECTED COLLECTIVE BARGAINING AGREEMENTS, CALIFORNIA **2887**

CALIFORNIA. DEPT. OF JUSTICE *See* INFORMATION PAMPHLET - CALIFORNIA. DEPT. OF JUSTICE **3107**

CALIFORNIA. DEPT. OF MENTAL HEALTH. GRANTS SECTION *See* CALIFORNIA STATE PLAN FOR COMMUNITY MENTAL HEALTH CENTERS **4770**

CALIFORNIA. DEPT. OF MOTOR VEHICLES *See* ORGANIZATION CHART MANUAL / STATE OF CALIFORNIA, DEPARTMENT OF MOTOR VEHICLES **5422**

CALIFORNIA. DEPT. OF PARKS AND RECREATION *See* STEWARDSHIP REPORT, A **4708**

CALIFORNIA. DEPT. OF PARKS AND RECREATION *See* CALIFORNIA RECREATION ACTION PROGRAM REPORT **4849**

CALIFORNIA. DEPT. OF REHABILITATION. COMMUNITY RESOURCES DEVELOPMENT SECTION *See* CALIFORNIA STATE PLAN FOR REHABILITATION FACILITIES **5276**

CALIFORNIA. DEPT. OF TRANSPORTATION *See* ANNUAL FINANCIAL REPORT, STATE OWNED TOLL BRIDGES **5376**

CALIFORNIA. DEPT. OF TRANSPORTATION *See* PROGRESS REPORT ON TRIP ENDS GENERATION RESEARCH COUNTS (SAN FRANCISCO) **5390**

CALIFORNIA. DEPT. OF WATER RESOURCES *See* KAWEAH RIVER FLOWS, DIVERSIONS AND STORAGE **1416**

CALIFORNIA. DEPT. OF WATER RESOURCES *See* CALIFORNIA WATER PLAN OUTLOOK, SUMMARY REPORT, THE **5531**

CALIFORNIA. DEPT. OF WATER RESOURCES *See* INVENTORY OF WASTE WATER PRODUCTION AND WASTE WATER RECLAMATION PRACTICES IN CALIFORNIA **2233**

CALIFORNIA. DEPT. OF WATER RESOURCES *See* DAMS WITHIN JURISDICTION OF THE STATE OF CALIFORNIA **2088**

CALIFORNIA. DEPT. OF WATER RESOURCES *See* DEPARTMENT PUBLICATIONS - STATE OF CALIFORNIA, RESOURCES AGENCY, DEPARTMENT OF WATER RESOURCES **5532**

CALIFORNIA. DEPT. OF WATER RESOURCES *See* CALIFORNIA WATER PLAN OUTLOOK, THE **5531**

CALIFORNIA. DEPT. OF WATER RESOURCES. DIVISION OF OPERATIONS AND MAINTENANCE *See* STATE WATER PROJECT ANNUAL REPORT OF OPERATIONS **5539**

CALIFORNIA. DEPT. OF WATER RESOURCES. SOUTHERN DISTRICT *See* WATERMASTER SERVICE IN THE WEST COAST BASIN, LOS ANGELES COUNTY **5548**

CALIFORNIA. DEVELOPMENTAL DISABILITIES PLANNING AND ADVISORY COUNCIL *See* STATE PLAN ANNUAL REVISION, DEVELOPMENTAL DISABILITIES SERVICES AND FACILITIES CONSTRUCTION ACT OF 1970 **5311**

CALIFORNIA DIRECTORY OF JUSTICE AGENCIES FOR JUVENILE AND ADULT (US) [20838694] **3159**

CALIFORNIA DIVING NEWS (US) **4889**

CALIFORNIA. DIVISION OF FORESTRY *See* DIVISION OF FORESTRY IN THE CALIFORNIA CONSERVATION CAMP PROGRAM, THE **2378**

CALIFORNIA. DIVISION OF HIGHWAYS. DISTRICT 7 *See* FREEWAY EVOLUTION, THE **5440**

CALIFORNIA. DIVISION OF MINES AND GEOLOGY *See* COUNTY REPORT - CALIFORNIA. DIVISION OF MINES AND GEOLOGY **1372**

CALIFORNIA. DIVISION OF OIL AND GAS *See* ANNUAL REPORT OF THE STATE OIL AND GAS SUPERVISOR **4283**

CALIFORNIA DUI REPORT (US/0892-9033) [15290025] 1342, **3105**

CALIFORNIA DURABLE POWER OF ATTORNEY HANDBOOK (US) [18397902] **2946**

CALIFORNIA ECONOMIC INDICATORS (US/0364-2895) [02782955] **1550**

CALIFORNIA EMPLOYER (US/0098-1435) [02240510] **1658**

CALIFORNIA EMPLOYER ADVISOR (US/1058-4293) [24296472] **1658**

CALIFORNIA EMPLOYER CONTRIBUTIONS TO THE UNEMPLOYMENT FUND (US/0091-3545) [01786667] 2877, **1658**

CALIFORNIA. EMPLOYMENT DATA AND RESEARCH DIVISION *See* ANNUAL PLANNING INFORMATION, CALIFORNIA **1645**

CALIFORNIA. EMPLOYMENT DEVELOPMENT DEPT *See* CALIFORNIA MANPOWER **1658**

CALIFORNIA. EMPLOYMENT DEVELOPMENT DEPT. NORTHERN CALIFORNIA EMPLOYMENT DATA AND RESEARCH SECTION *See* AREA MANPOWER REVIEW: CITY OF OAKLAND **1652**

CALIFORNIA. EMPLOYMENT DEVELOPMENT DEPT. NORTHERN CALIFORNIA EMPLOYMENT DATA AND RESEARCH SECTION *See* AREA MANPOWER REVIEW : SOLANO COUNTY **1652**

CALIFORNIA. EMPLOYMENT DEVELOPMENT DEPT. NORTHERN CALIFORNIA EMPLOYMENT DATA AND RESEARCH SECTION *See* AREA MANPOWER REVIEW : SAN FRANCISCO CITY AND COUNTY **1652**

CALIFORNIA. EMPLOYMENT DEVELOPMENT DEPT. NORTHERN CALIFORNIA EMPLOYMENT DATA AND RESEARCH SECTION *See* AREA MANPOWER REVIEW : SACRAMENTO STANDARD METROPOLITAN STATISTICAL AREA. PLACER COUNTY SUPPLEMENT **1652**

Alphabetical Title Index CALIFORNIA

CALIFORNIA. EMPLOYMENT DEVELOPMENT DEPT. NORTHERN CALIFORNIA EMPLOYMENT DATA AND RESEARCH SECTION *See* AREA MANPOWER REVIEW : MARIN COUNTY **1652**

CALIFORNIA. EMPLOYMENT DEVELOPMENT DEPT. NORTHERN CALIFORNIA EMPLOYMENT DATA AND RESEARCH SECTION *See* AREA MANPOWER REVIEW : CITY OF RICHMOND **1652**

CALIFORNIA. EMPLOYMENT DEVELOPMENT DEPT. NORTHERN CALIFORNIA EMPLOYMENT DATA AND RESEARCH SECTION *See* AREA MANPOWER REVIEW : SACRAMENTO-YOLO PLANNING AREA **1652**

CALIFORNIA. EMPLOYMENT DEVELOPMENT DEPT. NORTHERN CALIFORNIA EMPLOYMENT DATA AND RESEARCH SECTION *See* AREA MANPOWER REVIEW : CITY OF BERKELEY **1652**

CALIFORNIA. EMPLOYMENT DEVELOPMENT DEPT. NORTHERN CALIFORNIA EMPLOYMENT DATA AND RESEARCH SECTION *See* AREA MANPOWER REVIEW : SAN MATEO COUNTY **1652**

CALIFORNIA. EMPLOYMENT DEVELOPMENT DEPT. NORTHERN CALIFORNIA EMPLOYMENT DATA RESEARCH SECTION *See* AREA MANPOWER REVIEW : VALLEJO-FAIRFIELD-NAPA SMSA. NAPA COUNTY SUPPLEMENT **1529**

CALIFORNIA EMPLOYMENT LAW LETTER (US/1049-9334) [21356880] **3145**

CALIFORNIA ENERGY COMMISSION *See* SECURING CALIFORNIA'S ENERGY FUTURE : ... BIENNIAL REPORT TO THE GOVERNOR AND THE LEGISLATURE / CALIFORNIA ENERGY COMMISSION **1956**

CALIFORNIA ENERGY COMMISSION *See* BIENNIAL REPORT - CALIFORNIA ENERGY COMMISSION **1933**

CALIFORNIA ENERGY PRICES (US/0748-8246) [10992843] **1934**

CALIFORNIA ENGINEER (US/0008-1027) [03981561] **1967**

CALIFORNIA ENGLISH (US/0279-1161) [02612577] **3371**

CALIFORNIA ENVIRONMENTAL DIRECTORY (US/0148-0324) [03262362] **2162**

CALIFORNIA ENVIRONMENTAL INSIDER (US/0895-2299) [16643490] **2162**

CALIFORNIA ENVIRONMENTAL LAW REPORTER (US/1061-365X) [24337565] **3110**

CALIFORNIA. EXECUTIVE DEPARTMENT *See* EXECUTIVE ORDER / EXECUTIVE DEPARTMENT, STATE OF CALIFORNIA **2968**

CALIFORNIA EXECUTIVE. SOUTHERN CALIFORNIA, THE (US) [16892315] **654**

CALIFORNIA EXPLORER (US/0164-8748) [04312931] **4870**, **5465**

CALIFORNIA EYE, THE (US/0279-0246) [07445042] **4466**

CALIFORNIA FAMILY LAW MONTHLY (US/0882-7842) [11467245] **3119**

CALIFORNIA FAMILY LAW REPORT (US/0164-7040) [04390366] **3119**

CALIFORNIA FARMER (US/0008-1051) [02211625] **71**

CALIFORNIA-FEDERAL PERSONNEL LAW UPDATE (US) [15355808] **3145**

CALIFORNIA FIELD CROP REVIEW (US/0279-2648) [06165623] **166**

CALIFORNIA FIELD CROPS STATISTICS (1987) *CEASED.* (US) [17940535] **166**, **152**

CALIFORNIA FIRE CONTROL NOTES (CALIFORNIA. DEPT. OF FORESTRY) (US) [09839883] **2288**

CALIFORNIA FIRE SERVICE, THE (US/1048-5074) [20960998] **2288**

CALIFORNIA FISH AND GAME (US/0008-1078) [01552544] **2189**

CALIFORNIA, FOLKS & LORE (US/0889-1648) [13843515] **2318**

CALIFORNIA FOOD (US/1047-9481) [20820874] **2330**

CALIFORNIA FORESTRY NOTE (US/0889-0102) [06692584] **2377**

CALIFORNIA FRESH FRUIT AND VEGETABLE SHIPMENTS BY RAIL, TRUCK, AND AIR (US/0270-384X) [06383350] **2330**

CALIFORNIA FRUIT & NUT ACREAGE (US/0527-2181) [04171056] **166**

CALIFORNIA FRUIT & NUT REVIEW (US/0279-263X) [07707936] **71**

CALIFORNIA FRUIT & NUT STATISTICS (US) [14197056] **166**, **152**

CALIFORNIA FRUIT GROWER ANNUAL (US/1061-9658) [24079514] **2330**

CALIFORNIA FRUIT NEWS *See* PACIFIC FRUIT NEWS **2352**

CALIFORNIA FUTURE FARMER (US/0008-1108) [03981737] **71**

CALIFORNIA GAME & FISH (US/1056-0122) [23444227] **4870**

CALIFORNIA GARDEN (US/0008-1116) [03110378] **2411**

CALIFORNIA GEOGRAPHER, THE (US/0575-5700) [01552545] **2557**

CALIFORNIA GEOLOGY (US/0026-4555) [01552401] **1371**

CALIFORNIA GOLD BOOK (US/0194-0406) [02406521] **2365**

CALIFORNIA GOVERNMENT AND POLITICS ANNUAL (US/0084-8271) [01789727] **4466**

CALIFORNIA GOVERNMENT CONTRACTS (US/0271-2741) [06575066] **2946**

CALIFORNIA GOVERNMENT TORT LIABILITY PRACTICE / ARVO VAN ALSTYNE (US) [09819330] **2946**

CALIFORNIA. GOVERNOR *See* GOVERNOR'S BUDGET - CALIFORNIA **4729**

CALIFORNIA GOVERNOR'S COMMITTEE FOR EMPLOYMENT OF DISABLED PERSONS *See* COMMUNIQUE / CALIFORNIA GOVERNOR'S COMMITTEE FOR EMPLOYMENT OF DISABLED PERSONS **4385**

CALIFORNIA. GOVERNOR'S EARTHQUAKE COUNCIL *See* REPORT OF THE GOVERNOR'S EARTHQUAKE COUNCIL **5305**

CALIFORNIA GRANGE NEWS (US/0008-1124) [03981654] **5633**

CALIFORNIA GRAPEVINE (US/0273-8961) [07014310] **2365**

CALIFORNIA GROCER (US) **2330**

CALIFORNIA GROWER (VISTA, CALIF.) (US/0888-1715) [12678035] **166**, **71**

CALIFORNIA HANDBOOK, THE *CEASED.* (US/0068-5615) [01777450] **2529**

CALIFORNIA HAZARDOUS MATERIALS PROGRAM COMMENTARY (CN) **2226**

CALIFORNIA HAZARDOUS MATERIALS PROGRAM MATRIX (CN) **2226**

CALIFORNIA. HEALTH AND WELFARE AGENCY *See* TITLE XX COMPREHENSIVE ANNUAL SERVICES PROGRAM PLAN **5312**

●CALIFORNIA HEALTH CARE IN PERSPECTIVE (US/1065-4070) [26604702] **4770**

CALIFORNIA HEALTH LAW REPORT *CEASED.* (US) **2946**

CALIFORNIA. HEALTH MANPOWER POLICY COMMISSION *See* ANNUAL REPORT TO THE CALIFORNIA LEGISLATURE - CALIFORNIA. HEALTH MANPOWER POLICY COMMISSION **3913**

CALIFORNIA HIGH WATER (1979-80) (US) [08329229] **1421**, **1413**

CALIFORNIA HIGHWAY PATROLMAN, THE (US/0008-1140) [03981896] **3159**

CALIFORNIA HISTORIAN (US/0575-5751) [02960265] **2725**

CALIFORNIA HISTORICAL LANDMARKS (US) [08006908] **2725**

CALIFORNIA HISTORICAL SOCIETY *See* CALIFORNIA CHRONICLE : NEWS FROM THE CALIFORNIA HISTORICAL SOCIETY **2725**

CALIFORNIA HISTORY ACTION (US/0882-357X) [11822780] **2725**

CALIFORNIA HISTORY (SAN FRANCISCO) (US/0162-2897) [03937507] **2726**

CALIFORNIA HIV TESTING AND COUNSELING MONTHLY REPORT (US) [22771474] **3712**, **3667**

CALIFORNIA HOMES AND LIFESTYLES (US/1060-3190) [24931642] **2899**

CALIFORNIA HONEY REPORT (US/0279-4551) [07887003] **71**

CALIFORNIA HORSE RACING BOARD *See* ANNUAL REPORT OF THE CALIFORNIA HORSE RACING BOARD FOR THE PERIOD JULY 1 ... TO JUNE 30 ... **2797**

CALIFORNIA HORSE REVIEW (US/0091-441X) [05298491] **2797**

CALIFORNIA HORSEMAN'S NEWS (US/0273-8287) [06955140] **2797**

CALIFORNIA HOSPITALS (US/0896-2766) [14817298] **3777**

CALIFORNIA HOUSING PLAN, THE (US/0741-6083) [09470658] **2817**

CALIFORNIA IN PERSPECTIVE (US/1065-5344) [26499424] **5324**

CALIFORNIA IN PRINT (US/0738-694X) [07778684] **4636**

CALIFORNIA INDIAN EDUCATION CENTERS (US/0145-0735) [02707186] **2257**, **1730**

CALIFORNIA INNTOUCH (US/0274-6093) [06469854] **2804**

CALIFORNIA INSTITUTE OF TECHNOLOGY *See* CALTECH **5092**

CALIFORNIA INSTITUTE OF TECHNOLOGY, PASADENA. ENVIRONMENTAL QUALITY LABORATORY *See* EQL REPORT **2230**

CALIFORNIA INSURANCE LAW & REGULATION REPORTER (US/1047-6466) [20771090] **2946**

CALIFORNIA INSURANCE LAW REPORT (US/0890-4871) [14237451] **2877**, **2946**

CALIFORNIA INSURANCE NEWS / CALIFORNIA, DEPARTMENT OF INSURANCE (US) [24308444] **2877**

CALIFORNIA INTERMOUNTAIN NEWS (US/0739-4438) [09734764] **5633**

CALIFORNIA INTERNATIONAL PRACTITIONER, THE (US) [21277937] **3125**

CALIFORNIA INTERNATIONAL TRADE REGISTER (US/0270-4862) [06461551] **1633**, **1467**

CALIFORNIA JAZZ NOW (US/1067-5213) [27255069] **4106**

CALIFORNIA JOB DEVELOPMENT CORPORATION LAW EXECUTIVE BOARD *See* ANNUAL REPORT - CALIFORNIA JOB DEVELOPMENT CORPORATION LAW EXECUTIVE BOARD **639**

CALIFORNIA JOB JOURNAL (US/0892-6395) [10001001] **1658**

CALIFORNIA JOURNAL (US/0008-1205) [01552556] **4466**

CALIFORNIA JOURNAL ALMANAC OF STATE GOVERNMENT AND POLITICS (US/0190-969X) [03639720] **4636**

CALIFORNIA JOURNAL NEWSFILE (US) [10593018] **2529**

●CALIFORNIA JOURNAL'S ELECTION WEEKLY (US) [25452991] **4636**, **4466**

CALIFORNIA LABOR LETTER (US) **1658**

CALIFORNIA LAND USE AND PLANNING LAW (US/1052-8946) [13279318] **2817**

CALIFORNIA LAND USE LAW & POLICY REPORTER (US/1058-8205) [24386720] **4835**, **2946**

CALIFORNIA LANDSCAPE MAGAZINE (US/0888-1502) [13449920] **2411**

●CALIFORNIA LANDSCAPING (US) [26066464] **2411**

CALIFORNIA LAW REVIEW (US/0008-1221) [01552564] **2946**

CALIFORNIA LAWS FOR PSYCHOTHERAPISTS (US) [06175636] **3922**, **3119**

CALIFORNIA. LAWS, STATUTES, ETC. PHARMACY LAWS OF CALIFORNIA AND ADMINISTRATIVE RULES OF BOARD OF PHARMACY *See* CALIFORNIA PHARMACY LAWS, WITH RULES AND REGULATIONS **2946**

CALIFORNIA LAWYER (US/0279-4063) [07810967] **2946**

CALIFORNIA LAWYERS (US/1052-2379) [20928657] **2946**

CALIFORNIA LEGAL DIRECTORY, THE (US) [04009835] **2946**

CALIFORNIA. LEGISLATURE. ASSEMBLY. COMMITTEE ON CRIMINAL JUSTICE *See* NEW STATUTES AFFECTING THE CRIMINAL LAW **3108**

CALIFORNIA. LEGISLATURE. ASSEMBLY. OFFICE OF RESEARCH *See* HEARINGS AND REPORTS OF COMMITTEES OF THE CALIFORNIA LEGISLATURE : A LISTING **2978**

CALIFORNIA. LEGISLATURE. ASSEMBLY. OFFICE OF RESEARCH *See* AOR REPORTER **4630**

CALIFORNIA LIBRARIES (US/1056-1528) [23133725] **3199**

CALIFORNIA LIBRARY DIRECTORY (US/0740-7688) [09696151] **3199**

CALIFORNIA LIBRARY LAWS (US/0097-9902) [03146990] **3199**, **2946**

CALIFORNIA LIBRARY STATISTICS (US/0741-031X) [09579479] **3199**, **3257**

CALIFORNIA LIBRARY TRUSTEES DIRECTORY (US/8755-7711) [11230047] **3199**

CALIFORNIA LICENSED CONTRACTOR, THE (US/0362-7136) [02323847] **606**

CALIFORNIA LIVESTOCK REVIEW *CEASED.* (US/0279-2621) [07709945] **208**

CALIFORNIA LOCAL PROBATE RULES (US/0883-6116) [07982826] **2946**

CALIFORNIA MACADAMIA SOCIETY *See* YEARBOOK - CALIFORNIA MACADAMIA SOCIETY **2434**

CALIFORNIA MANAGEMENT REVIEW (US/0008-1256) [05755713] **862**

CALIFORNIA MANPOWER (US/0096-980X) [01798725] **1658**

CALIFORNIA
Alphabetical Title Index

CALIFORNIA MANUFACTURERS REGISTER (US/0068-5739) [03178275] 949, **3476**

CALIFORNIA MASTER PLAN FOR SPECIAL EDUCATION, ANNUAL EVALUATION REPORT (US/0145-4463) [02739581] **1876**

CALIFORNIA MEDICAL ASSISTANT, THE (US) **3561**

CALIFORNIA MEDICAL ASSOCIATION. BUREAU OF RESEARCH AND PLANNING *See* SOCIOECONOMIC REPORT **3642**

CALIFORNIA MILITARY MONITOR (US) [19320798] **4038**

CALIFORNIA MINING JOURNAL (US/0008-1299) [03981960] **2136**

CALIFORNIA MONTHLY (US/0008-1302) [03982138] **1090**

CALIFORNIA MOSQUITO AND VECTOR CONTROL ASSOCIATION *See* PROCEEDINGS AND PAPERS OF THE ANNUAL CONFERENCE OF THE CALIFORNIA MOSQUITO AND VECTOR CONTROL ASSOCIATION **2239**

CALIFORNIA MUNICIPAL BOND ADVISOR (US/0749-2375) [11093980] **893**

... CALIFORNIA MUSIC DIRECTORY, THE *SUSPENDED.* (US) [12092631] **4107**

CALIFORNIA MUSIC EDUCATORS ASSOCIATION *See* CMEA NEWS **4110**

CALIFORNIA NEIGHBORHOODS (US) **2817**

●CALIFORNIA/NEVADA HORSEMAN'S DIRECTORY (US/1061-1754) [25214286] **2797**

CALIFORNIA NEVADA UNITED METHODIST REPORTER *See* CALIFORNIA NEVADA UNITED METHODIST REVIEW **5057**

CALIFORNIA-NEVADA UNITED METHODIST REPORTER, THE (US/0892-6646) [15266777] **5057**

CALIFORNIA NEVADA UNITED METHODIST REVIEW (US) **5057**

CALIFORNIA. NORTHERN AREA LABOR MARKET INFORMATION GROUP *See* ANNUAL PLANNING INFORMATION. BUTTE COUNTY **1645**

CALIFORNIA NOTARY BULLETIN (US/1059-9487) [24817809] **4636**

CALIFORNIA NURSE (US/0008-1310) [01552571] **3852**

CALIFORNIA. OFFICE OF ADMINISTRATIVE LAWS *See* ANNIVERSARY REPORT **3092**

CALIFORNIA. OFFICE OF CRIMINAL JUSTICE PLANNING *See* COMPREHENSIVE PLAN FOR CRIMINAL JUSTICE **3160**

CALIFORNIA. OFFICE OF CRIMINAL JUSTICE PLANNING *See* CALIFORNIA CAREER CRIMINAL APPREHENSION PROGRAM. ANNUAL REPORT TO THE LEGISLATURE / STATE OF CALIFORNIA, OFFICE OF CRIMINAL JUSTICE PLANNING **3159**

CALIFORNIA. OFFICE OF EMERGENCY SERVICES *See* ANNUAL REPORT / CALIFORNIA OFFICE OF EMERGENCY SERVICES **5272**

CALIFORNIA. OFFICE OF STATE CONTROLLER *See* ANNUAL REPORT OF THE STATE OF CALIFORNIA FOR THE FISCAL YEAR ENDED JUNE 30 ... **4710**

CALIFORNIA. OFFICE OF STATEWIDE HEALTH PLANNING AND DEVELOPMENT *See* HEALTH MANPOWER PILOT PROJECTS PROGRAM. ANNUAL REPORT TO THE LEGISLATURE AND THE HEALING ARTS LICENSING BOARDS **3914**

CALIFORNIA. OFFICE OF THE STATE FIRE MARSHAL *See* SUMMARY & ANALYSIS : CALIFORNIA FIRE INCIDENT REPORTING SYSTEM **2293**

CALIFORNIA OPINION INDEX (US/0271-1095) [05762937] **5241**

CALIFORNIA OPTOMETRY (US/0273-804X) [06022776] **4215**

CALIFORNIA ORNAMENTAL CROPS REPORT (US/0744-2653) [08167415] **2435**

CALIFORNIA PARALEGAL MAGAZINE *CEASED.* (US/1040-2640) [18362771] **2946**

CALIFORNIA PARKS & RECREATION (US/0733-5326) [05983364] **4706**

CALIFORNIA PEACE OFFICER, THE (US/0199-7025) [06083562] **3159**

CALIFORNIA PEDIATRICIAN (US/0882-3421) [11808205] **3901**

CALIFORNIA PERIODICALS INDEX *CEASED.* (US/0730-1367) [03879360] **412**

CALIFORNIA PERIODICALS ON MICROFILM *CEASED.* (US) **412**

CALIFORNIA PERSONAL LINES (US) **654**

CALIFORNIA PHARMACIST (US/0739-0483) [01552572] **4295**

CALIFORNIA PHARMACY LAWS, WITH RULES AND REGULATIONS (US) [03877362] 4295, **2946**

●CALIFORNIA PHILANTHROPY REPORT (US/1065-7282) [26713905] **4334**

CALIFORNIA PHYSICIAN (US/8750-1813) [11082529] **3561**

CALIFORNIA PLANNING & DEVELOPMENT REPORT (US/0891-382X) [14714291] **2817**

CALIFORNIA PLANT PATHOLOGY *SUSPENDED.* (US/0094-3800) [04186500] **505**

CALIFORNIA POLICY CHOICES (US/0742-0927) [10262513] **4636**

CALIFORNIA POLITICAL ALMANAC (US) [21420576] **4466**

CALIFORNIA POLITICAL WEEK (US/0195-6175) [05527170] **4636**

CALIFORNIA POLL *See* FIELD POLL, THE **5245**

CALIFORNIA POLL, THE (US/0195-4520) [05455633] **4561**

CALIFORNIA POSTSECONDARY EDUCATION COMMISSION *See* ANALYSIS OF THE ... GOVERNOR'S BUDGET : A STAFF REPORT TO THE CALIFORNIA POSTSECONDARY EDUCATION COMMISSION **1808**

CALIFORNIA POTATO & ONION REPORT (US/0744-4834) [08308575] **2330**

CALIFORNIA POULTRY LETTER (US/0886-5124) [07566327] **208**

CALIFORNIA POULTRY REPORT (US/0744-6160) [08440782] **208**

CALIFORNIA PRISONER, THE (US/0884-0075) [09090030] **3159**

CALIFORNIA PRIVATE POSTSECONDARY EDUCATION DIRECTORY / PREPARED BY THE OFFICE OF PRIVATE POSTSECONDARY EDUCATION, CALIFORNIA STATE DEPARTMENT OF EDUCATION (US) [09411017] **1813**

CALIFORNIA PRIVATE SCHOOL DIRECTORY (US/0098-5147) [02241417] **1730**

CALIFORNIA PROFESSOR (US/0008-1418) [03982255] **1813**

CALIFORNIA PROPERTY TAX CONFERENCE *See* CALIFORNIA PROPERTY TAX CONFERENCE **4716**

CALIFORNIA PROPERTY TAX CONFERENCE (US/0146-1826) [02879801] **4716**

CALIFORNIA PSYCHOLOGIST, THE (US/0890-0302) [14147751] **4579**

CALIFORNIA PUBLIC EMPLOYEE RELATIONS : CPER SERIES (US/0194-3073) [05391213] **1658**

CALIFORNIA PUBLIC EMPLOYEE RELATIONS PROGRAM *See* CPER BULLETIN **1661**

CALIFORNIA. PUBLIC EMPLOYEES' RETIREMENT SYSTEM *See* ANNUAL FINANCIAL REPORT AND REPORT OF OPERATIONS / PUBLIC EMPLOYEES' RETIREMENT SYSTEM, STATE OF CALIFORNIA **4626**

CALIFORNIA. PUBLIC EMPLOYEES' RETIREMENT SYSTEM. BOARD OF ADMINISTRATION *See* JUDGES' RETIREMENT SYSTEM : ANNUAL FINANCIAL REPORT AND REPORT OF OPERATIONS FOR THE FISCAL YEAR ENDED JUNE 30 ... / ADMINISTERED BY THE BOARD OF ADMINISTRATION, PUBLIC EMPLOYEES' RETIREMENT SYSTEM **3141**

CALIFORNIA PUBLIC FINANCE (US) **4716**

CALIFORNIA PUBLIC SCHOOL DIRECTORY (US/0068-5771) [01783470] 1730, **1923**

CALIFORNIA PUBLIC UTILITIES COMMISSION *See* DECISIONS OF THE PUBLIC UTILITIES COMMISSION OF THE STATE OF CALIFORNIA **4760**

CALIFORNIA PUBLISHER (US/0008-1434) [02064518] **4813**

CALIFORNIA PUBLISHING MARKETPLACE (US) [20043322] **4813**

CALIFORNIA QUARTERLY *SUSPENDED.* (US/0045-3978) [01795162] **3371**

CALIFORNIA READER, THE (US/0892-6964) [06414705] **3272**

CALIFORNIA REAL ESTATE (1975) (US/0008-1450) [04092315] **4835**

CALIFORNIA REAL ESTATE TRENDS. FORECAST FOR HOUSING AND THE ECONOMY (US/1053-4164) [22348216] **4835**

CALIFORNIA REAL PROPERTY JOURNAL (US/1052-2921) [10078330] 4835, **2946**

CALIFORNIA RECREATION ACTION PROGRAM REPORT (US) [08942675] **4849**

CALIFORNIA. RECREATION COMMISSION *See* PUBLICATION - STATE OF CALIFORNIA RECREATION COMMISSION **4853**

CALIFORNIA REDWOOD ASSOCIATION *See* REDWOOD NEWS **2404**

●CALIFORNIA REGULATORY LAW BULLETIN (US/1072-7833) [28588449] **2946**

CALIFORNIA REGULATORY LAW REPORTER, THE (US/0739-7860) [07533749] **2946**

CALIFORNIA REGULATORY NOTICE REGISTER (US/1041-2654) [17495761] **2946**

CALIFORNIA REPORT ON AUTOMOTIVE MARKETING, THE (US/1042-9603) [19274211] 922, **5408**

CALIFORNIA REPUBLIC *CEASED.* (US/1061-3900) [23195010] **2529**

CALIFORNIA RISK MANAGEMENT REPORT FOR THE FEMALE EXECUTIVE *See* RISK MANAGEMENT FOR EXECUTIVE WOMEN **2892**

CALIFORNIA ROAD ATLAS AND TRAVEL GUIDE. ZIP CODE EDITION (US/0737-884X) [09548592] 5465, **2557**

CALIFORNIA ROSTER OF FEDERAL STATE COUNTY & CITY OFFICIALS (US) **4702**

CALIFORNIA RULES OF COURT. FEDERAL (US/1044-1115) [17826526] **3139**

CALIFORNIA SALES GUIDE TO HIGH-TECH COMPANIES (US/1041-0260) [18611234] **5092**

CALIFORNIA SCHOOL BOARDS JOURNAL (US/0895-6073) [16694695] **1861**

CALIFORNIA. SCHOOL CODE OF THE STATE OF CALIFORNIA *See* EDUCATION CODE / STATE OF CALIFORNIA **1738**

CALIFORNIA SCHOOL DISTRICT FINANCIAL ANALYSES (US/0098-6526) [02239692] **1730**

CALIFORNIA SCHOOL EMPLOYEE, THE (US/0008-1515) [03982463] **1861**

CALIFORNIA SCHOOL LAW DIGEST (US/0094-2057) [01794131] 1730, **2946**

CALIFORNIA SENIOR CITIZEN (US/0748-5727) [10965611] **5633**

CALIFORNIA SERVICES REGISTER (US/0271-6615) [06674195] 939, **654**

CALIFORNIA SLAVIC STUDIES *CEASED.* (US/0068-5798) [01552577] **2683**

CALIFORNIA SOCIETY OF CERTIFIED PUBLIC ACCOUNTANTS *See* DIRECTORY OF MEMBERS - CALIFORNIA SOCIETY, CERTIFIED PUBLIC ACCOUNTANTS **743**

CALIFORNIA SOCIETY OF CERTIFIED PUBLIC ACCOUNTANTS. DIRECTORY OF THE CALIFORNIA SOCIETY OF CERTIFIED PUBLIC ACCOUNTANTS *See* DIRECTORY OF MEMBERS - CALIFORNIA SOCIETY, CERTIFIED PUBLIC ACCOUNTANTS **743**

CALIFORNIA SOCIOLOGIST (US/0162-8712) [04025459] **5241**

CALIFORNIA SOUTHERN BAPTIST, THE (US/0008-1558) [03984343] **5057**

CALIFORNIA SPORTSCAR CLUB NEWS (US/0747-0223) [10470841] **5408**

CALIFORNIA STAATS-ZEITUNG (US/0890-1473) [12093964] **5633**

CALIFORNIA STALLION REGISTER (US) [02800883] **2797**

CALIFORNIA STATE AGENCIES' WATER QUALITY RELATED ACTIVITIES (US) [05908936] **5531**

CALIFORNIA. STATE BANKING DEPT *See* WEEKLY BULLETIN - CALIFORNIA. STATE BANKING DEPT **816**

CALIFORNIA. STATE BOARD OF ACCOUNTANCY. REGISTER *See* CALIFORNIA ACCOUNTANCY ACT WITH RULES AND REGULATIONS **740**

CALIFORNIA. STATE BOARD OF EQUALIZATION *See* TAXABLE SALES IN CALIFORNIA. SALES AND USE TAX (ANNUAL) **4754**

CALIFORNIA. STATE DEPT. OF EDUCATION *See* REGIONAL OCCUPATIONAL CENTERS AND PROGRAMS **1915**

CALIFORNIA. STATE DEPT. OF EDUCATION *See* CALIFORNIA STATE PLAN FOR VOCATIONAL EDUCATION **1911**

CALIFORNIA. STATE DEPT. OF EDUCATION *See* ENROLLMENT REPORT OF APPRENTICES IN CALIFORNIA PUBLIC SECONDARY AND ADULT SCHOOLS AND COMMUNITY COLLEGES **1913**

CALIFORNIA. STATE DEPT. OF EDUCATION *See* CALIFORNIA VOCATIONAL EDUCATION ACCOUNTABILITY REPORT **1911**

CALIFORNIA. STATE DEPT. OF EDUCATION *See* EXPERIMENTAL EDUCATION PROGRAMS FOR HANDICAPPED CHILDREN **1879**

CALIFORNIA. STATE DEPT. OF EDUCATION *See* SUMMARY REPORT FOR THE PROFESSIONAL DEVELOPMENT AND PROGRAM IMPROVEMENT CENTERS PROGRAM **1873**

CALIFORNIA. STATE DEPT. OF EDUCATION *See* CALIFORNIA MASTER PLAN FOR SPECIAL EDUCATION, ANNUAL EVALUATION REPORT **1876**

CALIFORNIA. STATE DEPT. OF EDUCATION. BUREAU OF MANAGEMENT SERVICE *See* ATTENDANCE AND ENROLLMENT ACCOUNTING AND REPORTING IN CALIFORNIA PUBLIC SCHOOLS **1860**

CALIFORNIA. STATE DEPT. OF EDUCATION. DIVISION OF FINANCIAL SERVICES. LOCAL ASSISTANCE BUREAU *See* RATIOS OF CALIFORNIA PUBLIC SCHOOL NONTEACHING EMPLOYEES TO CLASSROOM TEACHERS **1869**

CALIFORNIA. STATE DEPT. OF EDUCATION. OFFICE OF CHILD DEVELOPMENT *See* ALTERNATIVE CHILD CARE PROGRAMS **5271**

CALIFORNIA. STATE DEPT. OF EDUCATION. OFFICE OF PROGRAM EVALUATION *See* SCHOOL ACHIEVEMENT IN EARLY CHILDHOOD EDUCATION **1805**

CALIFORNIA. STATE DEPT. OF EDUCATION. OFFICE OF PROGRAM EVALUATION *See* RESEARCH, PROGRAM DEVELOPMENT, AND EVALUATION IN CALIFORNIA SPECIAL EDUCATION **1884**

CALIFORNIA. STATE DEPT. OF EDUCATION. OFFICE OF PROGRAM EVALUATION *See* CHILD DEVELOPMENT PROGRAM EVALUATION REPORT (CALIFORNIA) **1731**

CALIFORNIA. STATE DEPT. OF EDUCATION. OFFICE OF PROGRAM EVALUATION *See* CALIFORNIA ASSESSMENT PROGRAM RESULTS FOR EDUCATIONALLY HANDICAPPED PUPILS IN THE PRIMARY GRADES **1876**

CALIFORNIA. STATE DEPT. OF EDUCATION. OFFICE OF PROGRAM EVALUATION *See* CALIFORNIA INDIAN EDUCATION CENTERS **1730**

CALIFORNIA. STATE DEPT. OF EDUCATION. OFFICE OF PROGRAM EVALUATION *See* AMERICAN INDIAN EARLY CHILDHOOD EDUCATION **1802**

CALIFORNIA. STATE DEPT. OF EDUCATION. OFFICE OF PROGRAM EVALUATION AND RESEARCH *See* BILINGUAL TEACHER CORPS PROGRAM, THE **1876**

CALIFORNIA. STATE DEPT. OF EDUCATION. OFFICE OF PROGRAM EVALUATION AND RESEARCH *See* INNOVATIVE PROGRAMS FOR CHILD CARE : EVALUATION REPORT **1804**

CALIFORNIA. STATE DEPT. OF EDUCATION. SPECIAL EDUCATION PROGRAMS SECTION *See* EXPERIMENTAL EDUCATION PROGRAMS IN SPECIAL EDUCATION **1879**

CALIFORNIA. STATE DEPT. OF EDUCATION. SPECIAL EDUCATION PROGRAMS SECTION *See* ENROLLMENT OF CHILDREN IN EDUCATIONALLY HANDICAPPED PROGRAMS IN EXCESS OF LEGAL LIMITATION **1878**

CALIFORNIA STATE EMPLOYEE, THE (US/0008-1566) [03990252] **1658**

CALIFORNIA STATE GOVERNMENT DIRECTORY, THE (US) [20129073] **4636**

CALIFORNIA STATE LIBRARY *See* CALIFORNIA STATE LIBRARY NEWSLETTER **3199**

CALIFORNIA STATE LIBRARY *See* CALIFORNIA LIBRARY LAWS **2946**

CALIFORNIA STATE LIBRARY NEWSLETTER (US/0276-6973) [07262404] **3199**

CALIFORNIA. STATE MEDIATION/CONCILIATION SERVICE *See* REPORT / STATE OF CALIFORNIA, MEDIATION/CONCILIATION SERVICE **1707**

CALIFORNIA STATE PLAN FOR COMMUNITY MENTAL HEALTH CENTERS (US/0191-9806) [04915321] **4770**

CALIFORNIA STATE PLAN FOR REHABILITATION FACILITIES (US) [06618219] **5276**

CALIFORNIA STATE PLAN FOR VOCATIONAL EDUCATION (US) [04101445] **1911**

CALIFORNIA STATE PSYCHOLOGICAL ASSOCIATION *See* DIRECTORY, HANDBOOK - CALIFORNIA STATE PSYCHOLOGICAL ASSOCIATION **4585**

CALIFORNIA STATE PSYCHOLOGIST *See* CALIFORNIA PSYCHOLOGIST, THE **4579**

CALIFORNIA STATE UNIVERSITY, NORTHRIDGE *See* ALUMNI DIRECTORY / CALIFORNIA STATE UNIVERSITY, NORTHRIDGE **1097**

CALIFORNIA. STATE WATER RESOURCES CONTROL BOARD *See* CALIFORNIA STATE AGENCIES' WATER QUALITY RELATED ACTIVITIES **5531**

CALIFORNIA. STATE WATER RESOURCES CONTROL BOARD *See* PUBLICATION - CALIFORNIA STATE WATER RESOURCES CONTROL BOARD **5537**

CALIFORNIA STATEWIDE HOUSING PLAN ... UPDATE *See* CALIFORNIA HOUSING PLAN, THE **2817**

CALIFORNIA STATISTICAL ABSTRACT (US/0575-6200) [02253682] **5325**

CALIFORNIA STRAWBERRY REPORT (US/0194-8504) [05058403] **2330**

CALIFORNIA STUDIES IN THE HISTORY OF ART (US/0068-5909) [01552581] **346**

CALIFORNIA SUPREME COURT SERVICE (US/0164-3339) [04318871] **3139**

CALIFORNIA TAX LAWYER (US) **4716**

CALIFORNIA TEACHER (US/0410-3556) [03990289] **1890**

CALIFORNIA TEACHERS SALARIES AND SALARY SCHEDULES (US/0147-1406) [03131137] **1861**

CALIFORNIA TECH, THE (US/0008-1582) [03984028] **1090**

●CALIFORNIA TECHNOLOGY REGISTER (US/1059-7085) [24681225] **5092**

CALIFORNIA TECHNOLOGY STOCK LETTER (US/8756-2154) [12396304] **893**

CALIFORNIA THEATRE ANNUAL (US/0733-5806) [08201846] **5362**

CALIFORNIA TODAY (US/0739-8042) [09805385] **2162**

CALIFORNIA TOMATO GROWER, THE (US/0527-3277) [05527095] **166**

CALIFORNIA TORT REPORTER (US/0744-6756) [06587855] **2947**

CALIFORNIA TRADESHOW & EXHIBIT CALENDAR (US/1054-8955) [23019285] **757**

CALIFORNIA TRANSPORTATION COMMISSION *See* ANNUAL REPORT TO CALIFORNIA LEGISLATURE / CALIFORNIA TRANSPORTATION COMMISSION **5377**

CALIFORNIA TRIAL LAWYERS JOURNAL *See* JOURNAL / CALIFORNIA TRIAL LAWYERS ASSOCIATION **2986**

CALIFORNIA TRUCKER (US/1049-1023) [21145356] **5378**

CALIFORNIA TURFGRASS CULTURE (US/0527-1622) [05424574] **2411**

CALIFORNIA. UNEMPLOYMENT INSURANCE APPEALS BOARD *See* INDEX-DIGEST OF PRECEDENT DECISIONS **2882**

CALIFORNIA UNION LIST OF PERIODICALS (US/0095-8034) [01798723] **412**

CALIFORNIA. UNIVERSITY, BERKELEY. AGRICULTURAL EXTENSION SERVICE *See* LIVESTOCK FACT SHEET **214**

CALIFORNIA. UNIVERSITY, BERKELEY. COOPERATIVE EXTENSION SERVICE *See* GROWING POINTS, CENTRAL COAST COUNTRIES **2418**

CALIFORNIA. UNIVERSITY, BERKELEY. EARTHQUAKE ENGINEERING RESEARCH CENTER *See* REPORT **2030**

CALIFORNIA. UNIVERSITY. INSTITUTE OF TRANSPORTATION AND TRAFFIC ENGINEERING *See* SHORT COURSE IN AIRPORT MANAGEMENT **35**

CALIFORNIA. UNIVERSITY, LOS ANGELES *See* U C L A GENERAL CATALOG **1851**

CALIFORNIA UPDATE : LEGISLATION, REGULATIONS AND NEWS AFFECTING INDIVIDUALS WITH SPECIAL NEEDS / EDITED BY DOUGLAS BRITTON (US) [09995733] **5276**

CALIFORNIA VEGETABLE REVIEW (US/0279-2613) [07709926] **71**

CALIFORNIA VETERINARIAN, THE (US/0008-1612) [01552587] **5507**

CALIFORNIA VOCATIONAL EDUCATION ACCOUNTABILITY REPORT (US) [06363582] **1911**

CALIFORNIA VOTER (US) [05187382] **4466**

CALIFORNIA WASTE MANAGEMENT BOARD *See* PROGRESS AND CHALLENGE, WASTE-TO-ENERGY PROJECTS **2240**

CALIFORNIA WATER (US/0195-8658) [04951356] **5531**

CALIFORNIA WATER LAW & POLICY REPORTER (US/1053-4938) [22545294] **3110**

CALIFORNIA WATER PLAN OUTLOOK, SUMMARY REPORT, THE (US/0147-9806) [03263489] **5531**

CALIFORNIA WATER PLAN OUTLOOK, THE (US/0147-9164) [03251075] **5531**

CALIFORNIA WATER POLLUTION CONTROL ASSOCIATION *See* BULLETIN - CALIFORNIA WATER POLLUTION CONTROL ASSOCIATION **2225**

CALIFORNIA WATER RESOURCES CENTER. ARCHIVES *See* ARCHIVES REPORT / CALIFORNIA WATER RESOURCES CENTER, UNIVERSITY OF CALIFORNIA **5530**

CALIFORNIA WEED SCIENCE SOCIETY PROCEEDINGS (US) **2411**

CALIFORNIA WESTERN INTERNATIONAL LAW JOURNAL (US/0886-3210) [01768750] **3125**

CALIFORNIA WESTERN LAW REVIEW (US/0008-1639) [01552589] **2947**

CALIFORNIA WINE PURCHASING GUIDE (US) [08648257] **2365**

CALIFORNIA WINE REPORT / UNITED STATES DEPARTMENT OF AGRICULTURE, AGRICULTURAL MARKETING SERVICE, FRUIT AND VEGETABLE MARKET NEWS SERVICE *CEASED.* (US) **2366**

CALIFORNIA WINE WINNERS (US/0883-4423) [12001171] **2366**

CALIFORNIA WOMAN, THE (US/0008-1663) [03990303] **5552**

CALIFORNIA WORKERS' COMP ADVISOR *See* WORKERS' COMP ADVISOR (CALIFORNIA ED.) **2896**

CALIFORNIA WORKERS' COMPENSATION ENQUIRER (US/0883-9867) [12277885] **1658**, **2877**

CALIFORNIA WORKERS' COMPENSATION REPORTER (US/0363-129X) [02422970] **3145**

CALIFORNIA ZIP+4 STATE DIRECTORY / PREPARED BY THE ADDRESS INFORMATION SYSTEMS DIVISION, DELIVERY SYSTEMS DEPARTMENT (US) [11571428] **1144**

CALIFORNIAI MAGYARSAG (US/0744-8600) [08601878] **2257**

CALIFORNIAN (CUPERTINO, CALIF.), THE (US/0742-5465) [09263910] **2726**

CALIFORNIAN (EL CAJON, CALIF.), THE (US/0898-1817) [16729111] **5633**

CALIFORNIAN (TEMECULA, CALIF.), THE (US/1045-5868) [20148951] **5633**

CALIFORNIANS (SAN FRANCISCO, CALIF.), THE (US/0745-5895) [09306190] **2726**

CALIFORNIA'S THE GREEN BOOK (US/0741-2371) [19293615] **4636**

CALIOPE (BL) [17534958] **1075**

CALIOPE Y POLIMNIA : REVISTA DE POESIA Y CUENTOS (SP) **3461**

CALIPER (TORONTO) (CN/0045-4001) [02251133] **4385**

CALL-A.P.P.L.E *CEASED.* (US/8755-4909) [08898855] **1265**

CALL AND POST (US) [09964681] **5727**

CALL AND POST (CINCINNATI ED.) (US) [17937562] **5727**

CALL BOARD (SAN FRANCISCO, CALIF.) (US/1064-0703) [26204898] **5362**

●CALL CENTER MAGAZINE (US/1064-5543) [26327162] **1151**

CALL (KANSAS CITY, MO. : 1933 : CITY ED.) (US) [16736831] **5702**

CALL NEWS AND REVIEWS (US/8755-7134) [11390265] **3272**

CALL-NEWS DISPATCH *See* WASHINGTON COUNTY NEWS **5628**

CALL-NEWS DISPATCH, THE (US) [16505774] **5625**

CALL OF THE PLATEAU (US/0575-6383) [02909510] **2726**

CALL SHEET / SCREEN ACTORS GUILD (US) [30130552] **4064**

CALL, THE (US) [18664615] **5735**

CALLAGHAN'S LAW REVIEW DIGEST (US/1048-5392) [12047205] **2947**

CALLAHAN COUNTY STAR (US) [13978814] **5747**

CALLALOO (US/0161-2492) [03880433] **317**, **2257**, **3371**

CALLBOARD (CN) [05178992] **5362**

CALLIGRAFREE *See* CALLIGRAFREE SCRIBE **377**

CALLIGRAFREE SCRIBE (US/0145-1731) [02705378] **377**

CALLIGRAPH (US/0749-954X) [09265398] **377**

CALLIGRAPHY REVIEW (NORMAN, OKLA.) (US/0895-7819) [16796362] **377**

CALLING THE WORLD (US/0360-3539) [02241553] **1151**

CALLIOPE (BRISTOL, R.I.) (US/0889-7158) [14064187] **3371**

CALLIOPE (PETERBOROUGH, N.H.) (US/1050-7086) [21577362] **1061**, **2613**

CALORIE CONTROL COMMENTARY (US/1049-1791) [09005629] **4188**

CALOTTE, LA (CN/0823-3594) [11607539] **3922**

CALPHAD (US/0364-5916) [03738764] **1050**

CALS CE REPORT (US) **3476**

● CALS JOURNAL (US/1061-2572) [25222697] **1173**

CALS REPORT (US/0897-991X) [17687831] **3476**

CALSMA ISTATISTIKLERI VE ISGUCU MALIYETI (TU) [22856673] **1658**

CALTECH (US/0160-502X) [03695728] **5092**

CALUMET JOURNAL (CN/0712-1016) [08559520] **2257**

CALUMET PRESS, THE (US) [15504440] **5663**

CALUNDERWRITER (US/0199-2414) [05734664] **2877**

CALVACADE OF ACTS & ATTRACTIONS (US) [02244439] **384**

CALVARY BAPTIST THEOLOGICAL JOURNAL (US/8756-0429) [11454620] **5057**

CALVERT CO. MARYLAND GENEALOGY NEWSLETTER (US/0895-8939) [20960613] **2441**

CALVERT INDEPENDENT (US) [18712368] **5685**

CALVIN SYNOD HERALD (US/0161-6900) [03636025] **5727**

CALVIN THEOLOGICAL JOURNAL (US/0008-1795) [01774859] **4942**

CALVINISM TODAY (UK/0961-7272) [l09617272] **4942**

CALVINIST CONTACT (CN/0410-3882) [02321362] **5057**

CALYPSO (TR) [01785086] **4107**

CALYPSO LOG (LOS ANGELES, CALIF.) (US/8756-6354) [05004211] 553, **1447**

CALYX (CORVALLIS) (US/0147-1627) [03114927] 5552, **3371**

CALYX (TORONTO) (CN/1183-3181) [24368638] **3901**

CALZADO Y TENERIA (MX) [06664249] **1082**

CAM MAGAZINE (US/0883-7880) [12210949] **606**

CAM NEWSLETTER (US) **4086**

CAM REPORT (US/0745-4341) [05685930] **4201**

CAMAC BULLETIN (IT) [01785249] 1256, **2037**

CAMAGUEYANO, EL (US) [04401144] **2726**

CAMARA DE COMERCIO DE GUATEMALA (GT) [04842440] **826**

CAMARA DE COMERCIO HISPANO-COLOMBIANA See BOLETIN DE INFORMACION - CAMARA DE COMERCIO HISPANO COLOMBIANA **818**

CAMARA NACIONAL DE MINERIA, LA PAZ, BOLIVIA See CARTA SEMANAL **1438**

CAMARA VENEZOLANO BRITANICA DE COMERCIO E INDUSTRIA See ANUARIO - CAMARA VENEZOLANO BRITANICA DE COMERCIO E INDUSTRIA **823**

● CAMAROS (LOS ANGELES, CALIF.) (US/1059-5740) [24639009] **5408**

CAMAS-WASHOUGAL POST RECORD & BUYER'S BONUS, THE (US) [17023401] **5760**

CAMBIO (NQ) [28387515] **2511**

CAMBIO 16 (SP) [02093605] **1550**

CAMBIOS : MUNICIPIO Y POLITICAS PUBLICAS (AG) [25735917] **4636**

CAMBODIA TODAY (US) [05255495] **2648**

CAMBORNE SCHOOL OF MINES See JOURNAL - CAMBORNE SCHOOL OF MINES **2141**

CAMBRIA (UK/0306-9796) [04297603] **2557**

CAMBRIA COUNTY LEGAL JOURNAL (US) **2947**

CAMBRIAN LAW REVIEW, THE (UK/0084-8328) [01788540] **2947**

● CAMBRIAN MEDIEVAL CELTIC STUDIES (UK) [29451318] **3272**

CAMBRIDGE & DISTRICT CHAMBER OF COMMERCE & INDUSTRY (CAMBRIDGESHIRE) See DIRECTORY / CAMBRIDGE & DISTRICT CHAMBER OF COMMERCE & INDUSTRY **819**

CAMBRIDGE ANTHROPOLOGY (UK) [03887502] **233**

CAMBRIDGE ARCHAEOLOGICAL JOURNAL (UK/0959-7743) [24202366] **265**

CAMBRIDGE BIBLE COMMENTARY ON THE NEW ENGLISH BIBLE. OLD TESTAMENT (UK) **5015**

CAMBRIDGE BIBLIOGRAPHICAL SOCIETY See TRANSACTIONS OF THE CAMBRIDGE BIBLIOGRAPHICAL SOCIETY **426**

CAMBRIDGE CHRONICLE (US) [19907105] **5688**

CAMBRIDGE CHRONICLE, THE (US) [27213329] **5658**

CAMBRIDGE CLASSICAL TEXTS AND COMMENTARIES (UK/0068-6638) [02834933] **1075**

CAMBRIDGE COMPUTER SCIENCE TEXTS (UK) [06493332] **1173**

CAMBRIDGE EDITION OF THE WORKS OF D.H. LAWRENCE (UK) **3372**

CAMBRIDGE EVENING NEWS (UK/0963-4029) [l09634029] **5811**

CAMBRIDGE FUTURES CHARTS (UK/0961-0480) **1467**

CAMBRIDGE GEOGRAPHICAL STUDIES (UK/0068-6654) [06524147] **2558**

CAMBRIDGE GREEK & LATIN CLASSICS (UK) **1075**

CAMBRIDGE GUIDE TO THE ARTS IN BRITAIN (UK) [15628127] **317**

CAMBRIDGE HISTORY OF CHINA (UK) **2648**

CAMBRIDGE HISTORY OF IRAN CEASED. (UK) **2648**

CAMBRIDGE HISTORY OF LATIN AMERICA (UK) **2726**

CAMBRIDGE HISTORY OF MODERN FRANCE, THE (UK) [10587798] **2683**

CAMBRIDGE JOURNAL OF ECONOMICS (UK/0309-166X) [03020038] **1467**

CAMBRIDGE JOURNAL OF EDUCATION (UK/0305-764X) [02845361] **1890**

CAMBRIDGE LATIN AMERICAN STUDIES (UK/0068-6689) [01552633] **2726**

CAMBRIDGE LAW JOURNAL, THE (UK/0008-1973) [02277447] **2947**

CAMBRIDGE MEDIEVAL CELTIC STUDIES (UK/0260-5600) [07818503] **3272**

CAMBRIDGE NEWS (CAMBRIDGE, WIS.) (US/0749-7202) [11167133] **5766**

CAMBRIDGE NONLINEAR SCIENCE SERIES (UK/0963-7141) [l09637141] **5092**

CAMBRIDGE, ONTARIO, CANADA ... TOURIST GUIDEBOOK (CN/1186-947X) [24690411] **5465**

CAMBRIDGE OPERA JOURNAL (UK/0954-5867) [19282923] **4107**

CAMBRIDGE PAPERS IN SOCIAL ANTHROPOLOGY CEASED. (UK/0068-6719) [02845773] **233**

CAMBRIDGE PHILOLOGICAL SOCIETY See PROCEEDINGS OF THE CAMBRIDGE PHILOLOGICAL SOCIETY. SUPPLEMENT **3312**

CAMBRIDGE PHILOLOGICAL SOCIETY See PROCEEDINGS OF THE CAMBRIDGE PHILOLOGICAL SOCIETY **3312**

CAMBRIDGE PHILOSOPHICAL SOCIETY See MATHEMATICAL PROCEEDINGS OF THE CAMBRIDGE PHILOSOPHICAL SOCIETY **3519**

CAMBRIDGE QUARTERLY (UK/0008-199X) [01552643] 317, **3339**

● CAMBRIDGE QUARTERLY OF HEALTHCARE ETHICS : CQ : THE INTERNATIONAL JOURNAL FOR HEALTHCARE ETHICS COMMITTEES (US/0963-1801) [25292033] 2249, **3561**

CAMBRIDGE READINGS IN THE LITERATURE OF MUSIC (US) **4107**

CAMBRIDGE REPORT ON CORPORATE MERGERS AND CORPORATE POLICY, THE (US/0273-6357) [06769873] **782**

CAMBRIDGE REVIEW OF INTERNATIONAL AFFAIRS (UK/0955-7571) [20612707] 2613, **4467**

CAMBRIDGE REVIEW, THE (UK/0008-2007) [01771144] **1090**

CAMBRIDGE SCIENTIFIC BIOCHEMISTRY ABSTRACTS: PART 1 BIOLOGICAL MEMBRANES CEASED. (US/8756-7504) [11666545] **484**

CAMBRIDGE SCIENTIFIC BIOCHEMISTRY ABSTRACTS: PART 2 NUCLEIC ACIDS (US/8756-7512) [11666609] 484, **477**

CAMBRIDGE SCIENTIFIC BIOCHEMISTRY ABSTRACTS: PART 3 AMINO-ACIDS, PEPTIDES & PROTEINS CEASED. (US/8756-7520) [11666454] **484**

CAMBRIDGE SOUTH ASIAN STUDIES (UK/0575-6863) [01552644] **2648**

CAMBRIDGE STAR, THE (US) [01552645] **5695**

CAMBRIDGE STUDIES IN ADVANCED MATHEMATICS (UK/0950-6330) [09312543] **3499**

CAMBRIDGE STUDIES IN ANGLO-SAXON ENGLAND (UK) [22874748] **2683**

CAMBRIDGE STUDIES IN BIOLOGICAL ANTHROPOLOGY (UK/0957-0306) [13335322] **233**

CAMBRIDGE STUDIES IN CRIMINOLOGY (UK) [02845878] **3159**

CAMBRIDGE STUDIES IN EARLY MODERN HISTORY (UK) **2613**

CAMBRIDGE STUDIES IN ENGLISH LEGAL HISTORY (UK) [01552647] **2947**

CAMBRIDGE STUDIES IN FRENCH (UK/0950-6322) [08683547] 3339, **4343**

CAMBRIDGE STUDIES IN INTERNATIONAL AND COMPARATIVE LAW (UK) [01552648] **3125**

CAMBRIDGE STUDIES IN LINGUISTICS (UK/0068-676X) [01552649] **3272**

CAMBRIDGE STUDIES IN MATHEMATICAL BIOLOGY (UK/0263-9424) [07101821] **450**

CAMBRIDGE STUDIES IN MODERN BIOLOGY (UK) [07382655] **450**

CAMBRIDGE STUDIES IN MODERN OPTICS (UK) [13561220] **4434**

CAMBRIDGE STUDIES IN ORAL AND LITERATE CULTURE (UK) [08234638] **5241**

CAMBRIDGE STUDIES IN POPULATION, ECONOMY AND SOCIETY IN PAST TIME (UK/0954-0547) [l09540547] **4550**

CAMBRIDGE STUDIES IN RUSSIAN LITERATURE (UK/0950-6292) [08696709] **3372**

CAMBRIDGE STUDIES IN SOCIAL AND CULTURAL ANTHROPOLOGY (UK) [23114697] **233**

CAMBRIDGE STUDIES IN SOCIOLOGY (UK) [01552652] **5241**

CAMBRIDGE TAB, THE (US/0745-2063) [08924207] **5688**

CAMBRIDGE TRACTS IN MATHEMATICS (UK/0950-6284) [01775023] **3499**

CAMBRIDGE TRACTS IN THEORETICAL COMPUTER SCIENCE (UK) [18102884] **1173**

CAMBRIDGE. UNIVERSITY. DEPT. OF ENGINEERING See UNIVERSITY OF CAMBRIDGE. DEPARTMENT OF ENGINEERING. CUED/C-MAT **2000**

CAMBRIDGE. UNIVERSITY. DEPT. OF ENGINEERING See UNIVERSITY OF CAMBRIDGE. DEPARTMENT OF ENGINEERING. CUED/A-TURBO **2000**

CAMBRIDGE UNIVERSITY GUIDE TO COURSES (UK) [22547448] **1090**

CAMBRIDGE UNIVERSITY LIBRARY See LIST OF SERIALS AVAILABLE IN CAMBRIDGE UNIVERSITY LIBRARY AND IN OTHER LIBRARIES CONNECTED WITH THE UNIVERSITY [MICROFORM] **3228**

CAMBRIDGE UNIVERSITY REPORTER (UK/0008-2015) [03536185] **1090**

CAMCORDER CEASED. (JA) [21432474] **4367**

CAMCORDER USER (UK) [l09542108] **4367**

CAMCORDER (VENTURA, CALIF.) (US/1048-8804) [21063669] **4367**

CAMCORE BULLETIN ON TROPICAL FORESTRY (US/1057-1736) [11064733] **2377**

CAMDEN COUNTY TRIBUNE (US/1055-6559) [19704287] **5652**

CAMDEN HERALD, THE (US) [10411018] **5685**

CAMDEN HISTORY REVIEW (UK/0305-4756) [03566621] **2683**

CAMDEN NEWS, THE (US) [16997701] **5631**

CAMEL FORUM (SO/0281-7985) [21401385] **5507**

CAMEL NEWSLETTER (SY) [15062951] **5507**

CAMELLIA JOURNAL, THE (US/0008-204X) [02400381] **2411**

CAMELLIA NOMENCLATURE (US) [07420985] **2411**

CAMELLIA REVIEW, THE (US) [02400406] **5229**

CAMEL'S CALF, THE (US/0164-8594) [04309102] **4185**

CAMEO (NEW YORK) (US/0197-3363) [05984658] **5074**

CAMERA & DARKROOM (US/1056-8484) [25489938] **4367**

CAMERA AUSTRIA (AU/1015-1915) [09878990] **4367**

CAMERA AUSTRIA INTERNATIONAL (AU) [25807113] **4368**

CAMERA CANADA (CN/0008-2090) [01805849] **4368**

Alphabetical Title Index — CANA

CAMERA DE COMERCIANTES EN ARTEFACTOS PARA EL HOGAR See REVISTA - CAMERA DE COMERCIANTES EN ARTEFACTOS PARA EL HOGAR **2907**

CAMERA DI COMMERCIO, INDUSTRIA, ARTIGIANATO E AGRICOLTURA DI MILANO See NOTIZIARIO COMMERCIALE **848**

CAMERA DI COMMERCIO, INDUSTRIA, ARTIGIANATO E AGRICOLTURA DI MILANO See SCAMBI COMMERCIALI CON L'ESTERO, GLI **850**

CAMERA DI COMMERCIO, INDUSTRIA, ARTIGIANATO E AGRICOLTURA, MILAN See SITUAZIONE ECONOMICA PROVINCIALE **135**

CAMERA DI COMMERCIO, INDUSTRIA E AGRICOLTURA DI MILANO. NOTIZIARIO COMMERCIALE See NOTIZIARIO COMMERCIALE **848**

CAMERA DI COMMERCIO, INDUSTRIA E AGRICOLTURA DI TERNI See RASSEGNA ECONOMICA: TERNI **1515**

CAMERA (DURANGO, COLO.) (US/0883-489X) [12099905] **4368**

CAMERA INTERNATIONAL (FR/0765-9849) [12748430] **4368**

CAMERA (LUCERNE, SWITZERLAND) See FOTOMAGAZIN **4369**

CAMERA OBSCURA (BERKELEY) (US/0270-5346) [04818143] **4065**

CAMERA STYLO (FR/0248-8868) [02488868] **4065**

CAMERART (JA/0008-2082) [02251577] **4368**

CAMERART PHOTO TRADE DIRECTORY (JA) [02951792] **4368**

●CAMERAWORK (US) [26435583] **4368**

CAMERON CHRONICLE (US/8750-202X) [11110684] **5747**

CAMERON CITIZEN OBSERVER, THE (US) [19758357] **5702**

CAMERON COUNTY ECHO (US) [15027018] **5735**

CAMERON HERALD (CAMERON, TEX.) (US) [14072349] **5747**

●CAMERON'S FOODSERVICE MARKETING REPORTER (US) [27905223] **2330**

CAMERON'S FOODSERVICE PROMOTIONS REPORTER (US/0735-5548) [08950181] 5070, **757**

CAMERON'S READYART BULLETIN (US/0894-8186) [16260247] **346**

CAMEROON. DEPT. OF STATISTICS AND NATIONAL ACCOUNTS See NOTE ANNUELLE DE STATISTIQUE - DIRECTION DE LA STATISTIQUE ET DE LA COMPTABILITE NATIONALE **5335**

CAMEROON. EMBASSY (U.S.) PRESS AND INFORMATION SERVICE See NOUVELLES DU CAMEROUN **2642**

CAMEROON INTER-PORTS : ORGANE DE LIAISON ET D'INFORMATION DE L'OFFICE NATIONAL DES PORTS DU CAMEROUN (CM) [07373271] **5448**

CAMEROON MONITOR : BULLETIN OF THE COMMITTEE FOR HUMAN RIGHTS IN CAMEROON (UK) [14765584] **4505**

CAMEROON NATIONAL PORTS AUTHORITY See RAPPORT ANNUEL - OFFICE NATIONAL DES PORTS DU CAMEROUN **5455**

CAMEROON. SERVICE PROVINCIAL DE STATISTIQUE DU CENTRE-SUD See RAPPORT D'ACTIVITE - SERVICE PROVINCIAL DE STATISTIQUE DU CENTRE-SUD **5337**

CAMEROON. SERVICE PROVINCIAL STATISTIQUE DU NORD CAMEROUN See RAPPORT D'ACTIVITES - REPUBLIQUE UNIE DU CAMEROUN, SERVICE PROVINCIAL STATISTIQUE DU NORD CAMEROUN **5337**

CAMEROON TRIBUNE (CM) [29609464] **5779**

CAMEROON YEAR BOOK (CM) [01792500] **2498**

CAMEROUN 3E REPUBLIQUE (CM/0376-7612) [01793939] **1550**

CAMEROUN AGRICOLE, PASTORAL ET FORESTIER, LE (CM/0527-4257) [04107355] **71**

CAMEROUN, GUIDE ECONOMIQUE BELIBI (CM) [07506993] **1550**

CAMEROUN SELECTION (FR/0241-0257) [02410257] **826**

●CAMFORD CHEMICAL REPORT (CN/1187-8746) [26497505] **966**

CAMILLA ENTERPRISE, THE (US) [21767118] **5652**

CAMINANDO! (CN) **4505**

CAMINHOS DO TURISMO (BL) [02242052] **5465**

CAMINO (IT) **2904**

CAMINOS (UY) [26920188] **4540**

CAMINOS (SAN BERNARDINO) (US/0196-6847) [05873884] **2529**

CAMINUS QUARTERLY POOL PRICE REVIEW (UK) **2037**

●CAMIONNEURS/TRUCKERS MAGAZINE (CN/1192-3857) [27649193] **5408**

CAMLS NEWS (US/0730-093X) [06134818] **3199**

CAMMAC MONTREAL See NOUVELLES DE CAMMAC MONTREAL **4142**

CAMMINANDO INSIEME (IT/1121-2993) [11212993] **3339**

CAMOES CENTER QUARTERLY (US/1042-864X) [19231404] **2613**

CAMP DITES-VOUS? (CN/1181-8689) [23242545] **4849**

CAMP FIRE GIRL See CAMP FIRE LEADERSHIP **5229**

CAMP FIRE, INC See ANNUAL REPORT - CAMP FIRE, INC **5228**

CAMP FIRE LEADERSHIP CEASED. (US/0092-1289) [01788943] **5229**

CAMP RESORT LAW REPORT (US/0748-2396) [10918434] 4835, **2947**

CAMP ROLLAND-GERMAIN See TRAVAUX DES CAMPEUSES D'ETE AU CAMP ROLLAND-GERMAIN (1976) **4173**

CAMPAGNE (IT) **2486**

CAMPAGNES OCEANOGRAPHIQUES FRANCAISES (FR/0761-3989) [07613989] **1447**

CAMPAIGN AUSTRALIA (AT) [19409106] **2793**

CAMPAIGN FINANCE LAW (US/0884-8351) [08559601] 4467, **2947**

CAMPAIGN FOR YALE See LOOK HERE **1834**

CAMPAIGN LAW REPORTER (US/0094-1921) [01794047] 2947, **4467**

CAMPAIGN (LONDON. 1968) (UK/0008-2309) [01552661] **757**

CAMPAIGN PEOPLE (US/0733-9771) [08658114] **4467**

CAMPAIGN PRACTICES REPORTS CEASED. (US/0361-056X) [01588488] 4467, **2947**

CAMPAIGN PRESS ADVERTISING AWARDS (UK) [06048108] **757**

CAMPAIGN (WASHINGTON, D.C. 1991) (US/1061-964X) [24458464] **4467**

CAMPAIGNER (UK) [23062458] **226**

CAMPAIGNER (NEW YORK) (US/0045-4109) [01789719] **4540**

CAMPAIGNER SPECIAL REPORT, THE (US/0161-9039) [04048484] **4636**

CAMPAIGNETWORKS (LIBERTY, MO.) (US/0899-7438) [18202895] **4467**

CAMPANA (SP) **2257**

CAMPANA CONTRA EL HAMBRE EN EL MUNDO (SP) **5276**

CAMPANIA SACRA / PONTIFICIA FACOLTA TEOLOGICA DELL'ITALIA MERIDIONALE, SEZIONE DI CAPODIMONTE (IT) [05078380] **2683**

CAMPANILE, THE (US) [03690732] **1813**

CAMPANILOIS (SAINTE-FOY) (CN/1183-5672) [24267105] **2726**

CAMPBELL COUNTY RECORDER, THE (US) [12967577] **5680**

CAMPBELL LAW REVIEW (US/0198-8174) [05528584] **2947**

CAMPBELL RIVER DIRECTORY (BUSINESS EDITION) (CN/0319-5058) [02443152] **2558**

CAMPBELL RIVER UPPER ISLANDER, THE (CN/0318-9538) [02441904] **5781**

CAMPBELL'S LIST (US/0742-8987) [01552663] **2947**

CAMPBOOK. EASTERN CANADA (US) [06469247] **4870**

CAMPBOOK. MIDEASTERN (US/0734-2705) [06469314] **4870**

CAMPBOOK. NORTH CENTRAL (US/0732-2585) [08317181] **4870**

CAMPBOOK. NORTHEASTERN (US/0732-7315) [08394488] **4870**

CAMPBOOK. NORTHWESTERN (US/0732-2577) [08316037] **4870**

CAMPBOOK. SOUTH CENTRAL (US/0731-535X) [06469357] **4870**

CAMPBOOK. SOUTHEASTERN (US/0731-5112) [06469370] **4870**

CAMPBOOK. SOUTHWESTERN (US/0731-8103) [06469379] **4870**

CAMPBOOK. WESTERN CANADA AND ALASKA (US/0732-5347) [06469263] **4870**

CAMPER'S GUIDE TO AREA CAMPGROUNDS (US/0094-0054) [01792913] **4870**

CAMPESINO, EL (CL) [05147048] **71**

CAMPGROUND DIRECTORY, MID ATLANTIC See ANDERSON'S CAMPGROUND DIRECTORY **4869**

CAMPING AND RV MAGAZINE (US/0896-5706) [17205788] 4870, **4849**

CAMPING AND TRAILERING GUIDE (US/0361-5812) [02246962] **4870**

CAMPING CANADA (CN/0384-9856) [03406549] **4870**

CAMPING, CARAVANING FRANCE (FR) [05429222] **4870**

CAMPING, CARAVANING (MONTREAL) (CN/1187-1334) [25127360] **4870**

CAMPING CLUES (CN/0822-6474) [10224848] **4870**

CAMPING-FUHRER. BAND 1: SUDEUROPA (GW) [03456144] **4870**

CAMPING FUHRER BAND II : DEUTSCHLAND, MITTEL- UND NORD-EUROPA (GW) [03734224] **4870**

CAMPING HOTLINE (US/8755-9773) [11424725] **4870**

CAMPING MAGAZINE, THE (US/0740-4131) [01552665] **4870**

CAMPING QUATRO RODAS (BL) [08913522] **4870**

CAMPING TRAILER & TRAVEL TRAILER TRADE-IN-GUIDE (US/0736-1939) [09063237] 5465, **5378**

CAMPNEWS (PHILADELPHIA, PA.) (US/0746-1259) [09788443] **4870**

CAMPO, EL (SP/0212-2146) [02012799] **72**

CAMPO; REVISTA MENSUAL AGRICOLA Y GANADERA (MX/0008-2473) [02510807] **72**

●CAMPO Y TECNOLOGIA (AG) [26632133] **5092**

CAMPUS (IT) **2486**

CAMPUS ACTIVITIES PROGRAMMING (US/0746-2328) [09869089] 384, **1813**

CAMPUS: AMERICA'S STUDENT NEWSPAPER (US) [25061711] **1813**

CAMPUS BOOK STORES (CN/0380-6286) [02443770] 4827, **4821**

CAMPUS CANADA (TORONTO, ONT.) (CN/0829-3309) [13104220] **1090**

CAMPUS CRIME (US/1054-3821) [22874411] **3159**

CAMPUS DIGEST (CN/0823-4531) [11193177] **1090**

CAMPUS ECOLOGIST, THE (US/0889-7344) [14066259] 1813, **2212**

CAMPUS-FREE COLLEGE DEGREES (US/1043-2086) [19340260] **1813**

CAMPUS LAW ENFORCEMENT JOURNAL (US/0739-0394) [03101546] **3159**

CAMPUS LIFE (WHEATON, ILL.) (US/0008-2538) [01552667] **1061**

CAMPUS (LONDON, ENGLAND) See CURRENT (LONDON, ENGLAND) **2514**

CAMPUS MINISTRY WOMEN (ORGANIZATION) See NEWSLETTER - CAMPUS MINISTRY WOMEN (ORGANIZATION) **5562**

CAMPUS OPPORTUNITIES FOR STUDENTS WITH LEARNING DIFFERENCES / BY JUDITH M. CROOKER (US) [20680759] **1876**

CAMPUS OUTREACH (US/1046-6975) [20495344] **1813**

CAMPUS REPORT (STANFORD) (US/0049-2108) [04040582] **1090**

●CAMPUS SAFETY JOURNAL (US/1066-0739) [26834438] **3159**

CAMPUS SAFETY NEWSLETTER / NATIONAL SAFETY COUNCIL (US) [05276836] 1813, **4770**

CAMPUS SAFETY REPORT NEWSLETTER (US/0885-3398) [12617038] **4770**

CAMPUS SECURITY REPORT (US/1055-4319) [23173087] **4770**

CAMPUS TECH See EDUCATORS' TECH EXCHANGE : AN EDUTECH PUBLICATION FOR THE ACADEMIC COMPUTING COMMUNITY **1223**

CAMPUS TECH (US/1065-9447) [26813170] **1730**

CAMPUS TIMES, THE (US) [23806023] **1090**

CAMPUS TRENDS / AMERICAN COUNCIL ON EDUCATION, HIGHER EDUCATION PANEL (US) [14226294] **1813**

CAMPUS VOICE (KNOXVILLE, TENN.) (US/1047-3874) [20715637] **1813**

CAMPUS WATCH (US/1050-5644) [21542605] **1814**

●CAMPUS-WIDE INFORMATION SYSTEMS (US/1065-0741) [26498645] 1240, **1218**

CAMPUSKRANT (BE) **1090**

CAMROSE REVIEW, THE (CN/0823-6712) [10003743] **3372**

CAN SHIPMENTS REPORT (US) [13565480] 3999, **3476**

CAN TECHNOLOGY INTERNATIONAL (US) **4218**

CANA, INC (US/1060-8532) [25072276] 3682, **3852**

CANADA

Alphabetical Title Index

CANADA See MARTIN'S RELATED CRIMINAL STATUTES 3108

CANADA See ESTIMATES. PART III, IMMIGRATION APPEAL BOARD 1918

CANADA See ESTIMATES. PART III, ECONOMIC COUNCIL OF CANADA 4646

CANADA See ESTIMATES. PART III, AUDITOR GENERAL OF CANADA 4646

CANADA See ESTIMATES. PART III, FEDERAL COURT OF CANADA 2967

CANADA See ESTIMATES. PART III, MINISTRY OF STATE, ECONOMIC AND REGIONAL DEVELOPMENT 1560

CANADA See ESTIMATES. PART III, PRIVY COUNCIL OFFICE 4646

CANADA See ESTIMATES. PART III, TARIFF BOARD 2967

CANADA See ESTIMATES. PART III, CANADIAN INTERNATIONAL DEVELOPMENT AGENCY 1560

CANADA See ESTIMATES. PART III, SUPPLY AND SERVICES CANADA 4646

CANADA See ANNOTATED TREMEEAR'S CRIMINAL CODE 3105

CANADA See ESTIMATES. PART III, DEPARTMENT OF FINANCE CANADA 4722

CANADA See QUARTERLY STATEMENTS OF FINANCIAL OPERATIONS ENDING ... 4743

CANADA See ESTIMATES. PART III, HEALTH AND WELFARE CANADA, HEALTH AND SOCIAL SERVICES PROGRAM, INCOME SECURITY PROGRAM, FITNESS AND AMATEUR SPORT PROGRAM 5285

CANADA See FINANCIAL RESULTS - GOVERNMENT OF CANADA 4725

CANADA See ESTIMATES. PART III, ENVIRONMENT CANADA, PARKS CANADA PROGRAM 2193

CANADA See ESTIMATES. PART III, FISHERIES AND OCEANS 2300

CANADA See ESTIMATES. PART III, NATIONAL FILM BOARD 4068

CANADA See TRANSPORTATION OF DANGEROUS GOODS REGULATIONS 2245

CANADA See ESTIMATES. PART III, NATIONAL RESEARCH COUNCIL CANADA 4646

CANADA See ESTIMATES. PART III, NORTHERN PIPELINE AGENCY 1560

CANADA See ESTIMATES. PART III, HEALTH AND WELFARE CANADA 4775

CANADA See ESTIMATES. PART III, CANADIAN INTERGOVERNMENTAL CONFERENCE SECRETARIAT 4646

CANADA See ESTIMATES. PART III, NATIONAL LIBRARY OF CANADA 3209

CANADA See ESTIMATES. PART III, REVENUE CANADA, CUSTOMS AND EXCISE 4722

CANADA See ESTIMATES. PART III, TAX REVIEW BOARD 2967

CANADA See ESTIMATES. PART III, RESTRICTIVE TRADE PRACTICES COMMISSION OF CANADA 2967

CANADA See ESTIMATES. PART III, AGRICULTURE CANADA 82

CANADA See ESTIMATES. PART III, CANADIAN HUMAN RIGHTS COMMISSION 4507

CANADA See ESTIMATES. PART III, SECRETARY OF STATE, OFFICIAL LANGUAGES PROGRAM 3280

CANADA See ESTIMATES. PART III, SUPREME COURT OF CANADA 2967

CANADA See CANADA GAZETTE. PART 1 2947

CANADA See ESTIMATES. PART III, LAW REFORM COMMISSION OF CANADA 2967

CANADA See ESTIMATES. PART III, CONSUMER AND CORPORATE AFFAIRS EXPENDITURE PLAN 4646

CANADA See INFO SOURCE. GUIDE TO SOURCES OF FEDERAL GOVERNMENT INFORMATION 4656

CANADA See ESTIMATES. PART III, ENERGY, MINES AND RESOURCES CANADA, MINERALS AND EARTH SCIENCES PROGRAM 2114

CANADA See ESTIMATES. PART III, OFFICE OF THE COMMISSIONER OF OFFICIAL LANGUAGES 3280

CANADA See ESTIMATES. PART III, ROYAL CANADIAN MOUNTED POLICE 3164

CANADA See CODE CRIMINEL, L.R.C. (1985), CH. C-46, ET LOIS CONNEXES 2951

CANADA See ESTIMATES. PART III, CANADIAN ADVISORY COUNCIL ON THE STATUS OF WOMEN 5555

CANADA See ESTIMATES. PART III, NATIONAL ARCHIVES OF CANADA 2481

CANADA See ESTIMATES. PART III, DEPARTMENT OF JUSTICE CANADA, CANADIAN UNITY INFORMATION OFFICE PROGRAM 2967

CANADA See ESTIMATES. PART III, PUBLIC SERVICE STAFF RELATIONS BOARD 1668

CANADA See CANADA GAZETTE. PART 2 2947

CANADA See ESTIMATES. PART III, INVESTMENT CANADA 897

CANADA See ESTIMATES. PART III, NATIONAL ENERGY BOARD 1943

CANADA See INCOME TAX ACT ... ANNOTATED 2981

CANADA See ESTIMATES. PART III, VETERANS AFFAIRS CANADA 4043

CANADA See ESTIMATES. PART III, NATIONAL MUSEUMS OF CANADA 4087

CANADA See INCOME TAX ACT 4731

CANADA See ESTIMATES. PART I, THE GOVERNMENT EXPENDITURE PLAN 4722

CANADA See ESTIMATES. PART III, REVENUE CANADA, TAXATION 4722

CANADA See ESTIMATES. PART III, TREASURY BOARD OF CANADA, COMPTROLLER GENERAL 743

CANADA See ESTIMATES. PART III, PUBLIC SERVICE COMMISSION OF CANADA 4646

CANADA See ESTIMATES. PART III, STATUS OF WOMEN CANADA 5555

CANADA See CANADA GAZETTE. PART 3 2529

CANADA See ESTIMATES. PART III, TRANSPORT CANADA 5381

CANADA See ESTIMATES. PART III, NATIONAL TRANSPORTATION AGENCY OF CANADA 5381

CANADA See ESTIMATES. PART III, CANADIAN RADIO-TELEVISION AND TELECOMMUNICATIONS COMMISSION 1154

CANADA See ESTIMATES. PART III, EMPLOYMENT AND IMMIGRATION CANADA 1668

CANADA See ESTIMATES. PART III, ENVIRONMENT CANADA 1560

CANADA See ESTIMATES. PART III, WESTERN ECONOMIC DIVERSIFICATION CANADA 1489

CANADA See ESTIMATES. PART III, ENERGY, MINES AND RESOURCES CANADA 2138

CANADA See ESTIMATES. PART III, CANADA LABOUR RELATIONS BOARD 3148

CANADA See ESTIMATES. PART III, NATURAL SCIENCES AND ENGINEERING RESEARCH COUNCIL OF CANADA 5103

CANADA See MARTIN'S ANNUAL CRIMINAL CODE 3108

CANADA See ESTIMATES. PART III, MEDICAL RESEARCH COUNCIL 3575

CANADA See ESTIMATES. PART III, SCIENCE COUNCIL OF CANADA 5103

CANADA See ESTIMATES. PART III, NATIONAL DEFENCE 4043

CANADA See ESTIMATES. PART III, ATOMIC ENERGY CONTROL BOARD 1560

CANADA See ESTIMATES. PART III, CORRECTIONAL SERVICE CANADA 3164

CANADA See ESTIMATES. PART III, SOCIAL SCIENCES AND HUMANITIES RESEARCH COUNCIL 5199

CANADA See MIGRATORY BIRDS CONVENTION ACT AND MIGRATORY BIRD REGULATIONS 2198

CANADA See ESTIMATES. PART III, DEPARTMENT OF COMMUNICATIONS 1154

CANADA See ESTIMATES. PART III, INDIAN AND NORTHERN AFFAIRS CANADA 2732

CANADA (CN) [23127777] 826

CANADA See ESTIMATES. PART III, DEPARTMENT OF FOREIGN AFFAIRS AND INTERNATIONAL TRADE 4722

CANADA See ESTIMATES. PART III, EXTERNAL AFFAIRS AND INTERNATIONAL TRADE CANADA. EXPENDITURE PLAN 4722

CANADA See ESTIMATES. PART III, INDIAN AND NORTHERN AFFAIRS CANADA AND CANADIAN POLAR COMMISSION 2260

CANADA See ESTIMATES. PART III, INDUSTRY, SCIENCE AND TECHNOLOGY CANADA. EXPENDITURE PLAN 1606

CANADA See ESTIMATES. PART III, NATURAL RESOURCES CANADA 2193

CANADA See ESTIMATES. PART III, SOLICITOR GENERAL CANADA 2967

CANADA See ESTIMATES. PART III, TRANSPORTATION SAFETY BOARD OF CANADA. EXPENDITURE PLAN 4646

CANADA See INFO SOURCE (ED. FRANCAISE) 4656

CANADA See INFO SOURCE (ENGLISH ED.) 4656

CANADA, A PORTRAIT (CN/0840-6014) [19862489] 1550

CANADA A-Z (CN/0824-4766) [10513419] 4252

CANADA. ADVISORY COMMITTEE ON NORTHERN DEVELOPMENT See PROGRAMME ANNUEL DES DEPENSES DANS LE NORD 4742

CANADA. AGENCE DES TELECOMMUNICATIONS GOUVERNEMENTALES See ANNUAL REPORT - CANADA. GOVERNMENT TELECOMMUNICATIONS AGENCY 1149

CANADA. AGRICULTURAL STABILIZATION BOARD See ANNUAL REPORT TO THE MINISTER OF AGRICULTURE (AGRICULTURAL STABILIZATION BOARD) 61

CANADA. AGRICULTURE CANADA See AGRICULTURE CANADA ANNUAL REPORT 53

CANADA. AGRICULTURE CANADA See ANNUAL REPORT OF OPERATIONS UNDER THE MEAT IMPORT ACT 206

CANADA. AGRICULTURE CANADA See ANNUAL REPORT OF THE MINISTER UNDER THE CROP INSURANCE ACT 61

CANADA. AGRICULTURE CANADA. RESEARCH BRANCH See DIRECTORY OF RESEARCH / RESEARCH BRANCH / ANNUAIRE DE LA RECHERCHE / DIRECTION GENERALE DE LA RECHERCHE 79

CANADA. AGRICULTURE CANADA. RESEARCH STATION (SUMMERLAND, B.C.) See RESEARCH BRANCH REPORT - RESEARCH STATION, SUMMERLAND, BRITISH COLUMBIA 184

CANADA AIR PILOT (CN) 15

CANADA AIR PILOT. WATER AERODROME SUPPLEMENT / COMPILED AND ISSUED BY SURVEYS AND MAPPING BRANCH, DEPARTMENT OF MINES & TECHNICAL SURVEYS, THE (CN) [24924842] 15

CANADA--ALBERTA SOIL CONSERVATION INITIATIVE See ANNUAL REPORT - CANADA-ALBERTA SOIL CONSERVATION INITIATIVE 162

CANADA AMONG NATIONS (CN/0832-0683) [14627669] 4517

CANADA & THE WORLD CEASED. (CN/0043-8170) [01803871] 5194

CANADA & THE WORLD BACKGROUNDER (CN) 5194

CANADA. ATMOSPHERIC ENVIRONMENT SERVICE See ICE SUMMARY AND ANALYSIS: EASTERN CANADIAN SEABOARD 1415

CANADA. ATMOSPHERIC ENVIRONMENT SERVICE See ANNUAL METEOROLOGICAL SUMMARY, TORONTO, ONTARIO, WITH COMPARATIVE DATA 1420

CANADA. ATMOSPHERIC ENVIRONMENT SERVICE See ANNUAL RECORD OF OPERATIONS - ATMOSPHERIC ENVIRONMENT SERVICE 1420

CANADA. ATMOSPHERIC ENVIRONMENT SERVICE See MONTHLY RADIATION SUMMARY 1431

CANADA. ATMOSPHERIC ENVIRONMENT SERVICE See MONTHLY RECORD: METEOROLOGICAL OBSERVATIONS IN CANADA 1431

CANADA. ATMOSPHERIC ENVIRONMENT SERVICE See CLIMATIC DATA SHEETS 1422

CANADA. ATMOSPHERIC ENVIRONMENT SERVICE See OZONE DATA FOR THE WORLD 1433

CANADA. ATOMIC ENERGY CONTROL BOARD See PUBLICATIONS CATALOGUE - ATOMIC ENERGY CONTROL BOARD 1954

CANADA. BANKRUPTCY BRANCH See ANNUAL REPORT. SUPERINTENDENT OF BANKRUPTCY (OTTAWA) 3084

CANADA, BELGIUM, LUXEMBOURG (CN/0380-3570) [01965970] 818

CANADA BOOK AUCTIONS RECORDS (CN/0711-7299) [07917595] 4827

CANADA. BUREAU DU VERIFICATEUR GENERAL See RAPPORT DU VERIFICATEUR GENERAL DU CANADA A LA CHAMBRE DES COMMUNES (1979) 4678

CANADA. BUREAU OF STATISTICS See ANNUAL REVIEW OF THE EMPLOYMENT SITUATION (CANADA) 1650

CANADA BUSINESS CORPORATIONS ACT WITH REGULATIONS (CN/0317-6649) [02441890] 3097

CANADA. CANADA POST See BULLETIN - CANADA POST 1144

Alphabetical Title Index — CANADA

CANADA. CANADIAN STUDIES AND SPECIAL PROJECTS DIRECTORATE *See* INFORMATION AND APPLICATION GUIDE / CANADIAN STUDIES AND SPECIAL PROJECTS DIRECTORATE **2739**

CANADA. CENTRE DE RECHERCHES FORESTIERES DES LAURENTIDES *See* INVENTAIRE DES INSECTES ET DES MALADIES DES ARBRES, AU QUEBEC **2385**

CANADA CENTRE FOR MINERAL AND ENERGY TECHNOLOGY *See* ANNUAL REPORT / CANMET **1437**

CANADA CENTRE FOR MINERAL AND ENERGY TECHNOLOGY *See* CANMET BUSINESS PLAN **4636**

CANADA CENTRE FOR MINERAL AND ENERGY TECHNOLOGY *See* MINTEC : MINING TECHNOLOGY ABSTRACTS **2006**

CANADA CHINCHILLA (CN/0823-2504) [10032095] **5507**

CANADA. COAST GUARD *See* LISTS OF LIGHTS, BUOYS AND FOG SIGNALS. INLAND WATERS **4178**

CANADA. COAST GUARD *See* LIST OF LIGHTS, BUOYS AND FOG SIGNALS. PACIFIC COAST **4178**

CANADA. COAST GUARD *See* LIST OF LIGHTS, BUOYS AND FOG SIGNALS. ATLANTIC COAST **4178**

CANADA. COAST GUARD. AIDS AND WATERWAYS BRANCH *See* ANNUAL EDITION: NOTICES TO MARINERS **4174**

CANADA. COAST GUARD. AIDS AND WATERWAYS BRANCH *See* LIVRE DES FEUX, DES BOUEES ET DES SIGNAUX DE BRUME. COTE DU PACIFIQUE **4178**

CANADA. COAST GUARD. AIDS AND WATERWAYS BRANCH *See* EDITION ANNUELLE : AVIS AUX NAVIGATEURS **4176**

CANADA. COMMISSION CANADIENNE DES DROITS DE LA PERSONNE *See* ANNUAL REPORT - CANADIAN HUMAN RIGHTS COMMISSION **4504**

● CANADA COMMUNICABLE DISEASE REPORT (CN/1188-4169) [26498061] **3712, 4770**

● CANADA COMMUNICABLE DISEASE REPORT (CN/1188-4169) [26498063] **3712, 4770**

CANADA. CONSEIL DU TESOR *See* ORIENTATION A LA GESTION FINANCIERE **802**

CANADA. CONSUMER AND CORPORATE AFFAIRS *See* LOBBYISTS REGISTRATION ACT ANNUAL REPORT **4481**

CANADA CORPORATIONS BULLETIN (CN/0848-4686) [15506470] **3097**

CANADA. CORRECTIONAL INVESTIGATOR *See* ANNUAL REPORT OF THE CORRECTIONAL INVESTIGATOR **3157**

CANADA COUNCIL. TOURING OFFICE *See* BULLETIN - TOURING OFFICE OF THE CANADA COUNCIL **384**

CANADA. CUSTOMS AND EXCISE *See* LIST OF LICENCES UNDER THE EXCISE TAX ACT **690**

CANADA. DEPARTMENT OF EXTERNAL AFFAIRS *See* DOCUMENTS ON CANADIAN EXTERNAL RELATIONS **4520**

CANADA. DEPARTMENT OF FISHERIES. ECONOMICS SERVICE *See* STATISTICAL BASEBOOK SERIES - ECONOMICS SERVICE, DEPARTMENT OF FISHERIES OF CANADA **2317**

CANADA. DEPARTMENT OF MANPOWER AND IMMIGRATION *See* QUARTERLY IMMIGRATION BULLETIN **1921**

CANADA. DEPARTMENT OF MINES AND TECHNICAL SURVEYS *See* REPORT ON THE ADMINISTRATION OF THE EMERGENCY GOLD MINING ASSISTANCE ACT **2150**

CANADA. DEPARTMENT OF NORTHERN AFFAIRS AND NATIONAL RESOURCES. WATER RESOURCES BRANCH *See* BULLETIN - DEPARTMENT OF NORTHERN AFFAIRS AND NATIONAL RESOURCES, WATER RESOURCES BRANCH **5531**

CANADA. DEPT. OF AGRICULTURE. ECONOMICS BRANCH *See* ECONOMICS BRANCH PUBLICATION **81**

CANADA. DEPT. OF AGRICULTURE. RESEARCH BRANCH *See* NEW BRUNSWICK SOIL SURVEY, REPORT **111**

CANADA. DEPT. OF AGRICULTURE. RESEARCH PROGRAM SERVICES SECTION *See* INSECT LIBERATIONS IN CANADA **5609**

CANADA. DEPT. OF ENERGY, MINES AND RESOURCES. SCIENCE AND TECHNOLOGY SECTOR *See* EMR; ACTIVITIES OF THE SCIENCE AND TECHNOLOGY SECTOR **1937**

CANADA. DEPT. OF EXTERNAL AFFAIRS *See* CANADIAN REPRESENTIVES ABROAD AND REPRESENTATIVES OF OTHER COUNTRIES IN CANADA **4517**

CANADA. DEPT. OF EXTERNAL AFFAIRS *See* STATEMENTS AND SPEECHES / EXTERNAL AFFAIRS, CANADA **4535**

CANADA. DEPT. OF FINANCE *See* COMPTE RENDU DE LA SITUATION ECONOMIQUE **1552**

CANADA. DEPT. OF FISHERIES AND OCEANS *See* FISHERIES DEVELOPMENT ACT, ANNUAL REPORT **2302**

CANADA. DEPT. OF FISHERIES AND OCEANS *See* ANNUAL REPORT / DEPARTMENT OF FISHERIES AND OCEANS **2294**

CANADA. DEPT. OF FISHERIES AND OCEANS. NEWFOUNDLAND REGION *See* ANNUAL REVIEW / NEWFOUNDLAND REGION **2295**

CANADA. DEPT. OF FISHERIES AND OCEANS. NEWFOUNDLAND REGION. ANNUAL REPORT *See* ANNUAL REVIEW / NEWFOUNDLAND REGION **2295**

CANADA. DEPT. OF INDUSTRY, TRADE, AND COMMERCE *See* REVUE ANNUELLE - INDUSTRIE ET COMMERCE **850**

CANADA. DEPT. OF LABOUR. LEGISLATIVE RESEARCH BRANCH *See* LABOUR STANDARDS IN CANADA **1686**

CANADA. DEPT. OF NATIONAL DEFENCE *See* DEFENCE (OTTAWA. 1971) **4040**

CANADA. DEPT. OF THE SECRETARY OF STATE OF CANADA. DEPARTMENTAL LIBRARY *See* LISTE DES RAPPORTS ANNUELS, BIBLIOTHEQUE PRINCIPALE JE, LIST OF ANNUAL REPORTS, MAIN LIBRARY (JE) **4662**

CANADA. DEPT. OF TRANSPORT. AIR REGULATIONS *See* AIR REGULATIONS AND AERONAUTICS ACT **8**

CANADA. DIRECTION DE LA RECHERCHE SUR LA CONSOMMATION *See* RAPPORT DE LA DIRECTION DES RECHERCHES SUR LA CONSOMMATION **1515**

CANADA. DIRECTION DES EXPLOSIFS *See* SECURITE ET CONTROLE DES EXPLOSIFS AU CANADA **2150**

CANADA DISEASES WEEKLY REPORT *See* CANADA COMMUNICABLE DISEASE REPORT **4770**

CANADA. DOUANES ET ACCISE *See* MODIFICATION AU TARIF **846**

CANADA. DOUANES ET ACCISE *See* MODIFICATION AU TARIF **846**

CANADA EMPLOYMENT AND IMMIGRATION UNION. NATIONAL CONVENTION *See* CONVENTION REPORT / CANADA EMPLOYMENT AND IMMIGRATION UNION **1661**

CANADA. ENVIRONMENT CANADA *See* CANADA WATER ACT : ANNUAL REPORT, THE **5531**

CANADA. ENVIRONMENT CANADA *See* ENVIROSOURCE (HULL. ENGLISH ED.) **4646**

CANADA. ENVIRONMENT CANADA *See* ANNUAL REPORT - ENVIRONMENT CANADA (1980) **2160**

CANADA. ENVIRONMENTAL PROTECTION SERVICE *See* NATIONAL AIR POLLUTION SURVEILLANCE **2237**

CANADA. ENVIRONNEMENT CANADA *See* ENVIROSOURCE (HULL. ED. FRANCAISE) **2171**

CANADA. ESTIMATES. PART III, ENERGY, MINES AND RESOURCES CANADA *See* ESTIMATES. PART III, NATURAL RESOURCES CANADA **2193**

CANADA. ESTIMATES. PART III, EXTERNAL AFFAIRS AND INTERNATIONAL TRADE CANADA. EXPENDITURE PLAN *See* ESTIMATES. PART III, DEPARTMENT OF FOREIGN AFFAIRS AND INTERNATIONAL TRADE **4722**

CANADA. ESTIMATES. PART III, INDIAN AND NORTHERN AFFAIRS CANADA *See* ESTIMATES. PART III, INDIAN AND NORTHERN AFFAIRS CANADA AND CANADIAN POLAR COMMISSION **2260**

CANADA. ESTIMATES. PART III, MINISTRY OF STATE, SCIENCE AND TECHNOLOGY CANADA *See* ESTIMATES. PART III, INDUSTRY, SCIENCE AND TECHNOLOGY CANADA. EXPENDITURE PLAN **1606**

CANADA. ESTIMATES. PART III, REGIONAL INDUSTRIAL EXPANSION *See* ESTIMATES. PART III, INDUSTRY, SCIENCE AND TECHNOLOGY CANADA. EXPENDITURE PLAN **1606**

CANADA. ESTIMATES. PART III, SOLICITOR GENERAL SECRETARIAT *See* ESTIMATES. PART III, SOLICITOR GENERAL CANADA **2967**

CANADA. EXPLOSIVES BRANCH *See* EXPLOSIVE SAFETY AND CONTROL IN CANADA **2012**

CANADA. EXTERNAL AFFAIRS AND INTERNATIONAL TRADE CANADA *See* ANNUAL REPORT / EXTERNAL AFFAIRS AND INTERNATIONAL TRADE CANADA **4515**

CANADA. EXTERNAL AFFAIRS AND INTERNATIONAL TRADE CANADA. LIBRARY *See* ACCESSIONS LIST - EXTERNAL AFFAIRS AND INTERNATIONAL TRADE CANADA. LIBRARY **3186**

CANADA. FARM DEBT REVIEW BOARD *See* OPERATIONAL REVIEW ... FARM DEBT REVIEW BOARDS **117**

CANADA. FARM DEBT REVIEW BOARD. ANNUAL REPORT ... FARM DEBT REVIEW BOARDS *See* OPERATIONAL REVIEW ... FARM DEBT REVIEW BOARDS **117**

CANADA. FEDERAL COURT *See* CANADA FEDERAL COURT REPORTS **2947**

CANADA FEDERAL COURT REPORTS (CN/0384-2568) [02885615] **2947**

CANADA. FISHERIES AND MARINE SERVICE. NEWFOUNDLAND REGION *See* NEWFOUNDLAND FISHERIES **2309**

CANADA. FISHERIES RESEARCH BOARD *See* ANNUAL REPORT - FISHERIES RESEARCH BOARD OF CANADA **2294**

CANADA FLIGHT SUPPLEMENT (CN) **15**

CANADA. FORESTRY BRANCH. FORESTRY BRANCH PUBLICATION *See* PUBLICATION - CANADIAN FORESTRY SERVICE **2391**

CANADA. FORESTRY CANADA. SCIENCE AND SUSTAINABLE DEVELOPMENT DIRECTORATE *See* ARNEWS ANNUAL REPORT **2375**

CANADA. FORETS CANADA *See* ETAT DES FORETS AU CANADA, RAPPORT AU PARLEMENT, L' **2379**

CANADA. GARDE COTIERE *See* LIVRE DES FEUX, DES BOUEES ET DES SIGNAUX DE BRUME. EAUX INTERIEURES **4178**

CANADA. GARDE COTIERE. DIRECTION DES AIDES ET DES VOIES NAVIGABLES *See* AVIS AUX NAVIGATEURS (ED. HEBDOMADAIRE) **4175**

CANADA GAZETTE. PART 1 (CN/0045-4192) [02248646] **2947**

CANADA GAZETTE. PART 2 (CN/0045-4206) [10446023] **2947**

CANADA GAZETTE. PART 3 (CN/0705-9485) [02248489] **2529**

CANADA. GOVERNMENT TELECOMMUNICATIONS AGENCY *See* ANNUAL REPORT - CANADA. GOVERNMENT TELECOMMUNICATIONS AGENCY **1149**

CANADA. GRAIN COMMISSION. ECONOMICS AND STATISTICS DIVISION *See* CANADIAN GRAIN POSITION **1600**

CANADA GRAINS COUNCIL *See* CANADIAN GRAINS INDUSTRY; STATISTICAL HANDBOOK **152**

CANADA GREEN (CN/0703-5667) [03951160] **2412**

CANADA GUNSPORT (CN/0383-1191) [03219736] **4889**

CANADA HEALTH ACT ANNUAL REPORT (CN/0842-3202) [13515059] **5276**

CANADA. HEALTH AND WELFARE CANADA *See* CANADA HEALTH ACT ANNUAL REPORT **5276**

CANADA. HEALTH AND WELFARE CANADA *See* FILM LIBRARY CATALOGUE / NATIONAL HEALTH AND WELFARE **3210**

CANADA. HEALTH AND WELFARE CANADA. EQUAL OPPORTUNITY FOR WOMEN *See* ANNUAL REPORT INCLUDING ... OBJECTIVES AND ACTION PLANS - EQUAL OPPORTUNITIES FOR WOMEN **5551**

CANADA. IMMIGRATION APPEAL BOARD *See* ANNUAL REPORT OF THE YEAR ENDING DECEMBER 31 ... / CANADA. IMMIGRATION APPEAL BOARD **1918**

CANADA IN TRANSIT (CN/1191-0577) [25796294] **5378**

CANADA. INDIAN AND NORTHERN AFFAIRS CANADA *See* ANNUAL NORTHERN EXPENDITURE PLAN **4709**

CANADA. INDUSTRY, TRADE AND COMMERCE *See* SERVICE COMMERCIAL DU CANADA A L'ETRANGER **851**

CANADA. INDUSTRY, TRADE AND COMMERCE *See* FEDERAL INCENTIVES TO INDUSTRY **1606**

CANADA. INFORMATION CANADA. PHOTOTHEQUE. COMMERCIAL PRICE LIST *See* COMMERCIAL PRICE LIST - N.F.B. PHOTOTHEQUE **4067**

CANADA

Alphabetical Title Index

CANADA. INFORMATION COMMISSIONER OF CANADA *See* ANNUAL REPORT, INFORMATION COMMISSIONER **4627**

CANADA. INLAND WATERS DIRECTORATE *See* HISTORICAL STREAMFLOW SUMMARY, ALBERTA **1414**

CANADA. INLAND WATERS DIRECTORATE *See* HISTORICAL STREAMFLOW SUMMARY: BRITISH COLUMBIA **1414**

CANADA. INLAND WATERS DIRECTORATE *See* HISTORICAL STREAMFLOW SUMMARY : YUKON TERRITORY AND NORTHWEST TERRITORIES **1414**

CANADA. INLAND WATERS DIRECTORATE *See* HISTORICAL STREAMFLOW SUMMARY : ATLANTIC PROVINCES **1414**

CANADA. INLAND WATERS DIRECTORATE *See* TECHNICAL BULLETIN **2244**

CANADA. INLAND WATERS DIRECTORATE *See* HISTORICAL STREAMFLOW SUMMARY: MANITOBA **1414**

CANADA INSTITUTE FOR SCIENTIFIC AND TECHNICAL INFORMATION *See* BULLETIN CAN/OLE **5090**

CANADA. INTERNATIONAL DEVELOPMENT AGENCY *See* THOUGHTS ON INTERNATIONAL DEVELOPMENT **1640**

CANADA-JAPAN SOCIETY OF VANCOUVER *See* NEWS FROM CANADA-JAPAN SOCIETY OF VANCOUVER **5234**

CANADA-JAPAN TRADE COUNCIL *See* NEWSLETTER - CANADA JAPAN TRADE COUNCIL **1638**

CANADA JEWISH TRAVEL GUIDE (US) **5046, 5465**

CANADA JOURNAL (DEUTSCHE AUSG.) (CN/0829-0814) [14960857] **5465, 654**

CANADA. LABOUR CANADA *See* ANNUAL REVIEW - LABOUR CANADA **1650**

CANADA LAND INVENTORY *See* REPORT - CANADA LAND INVENTORY **4680**

CANADA LAND INVENTORY *See* CLI REPORT **2190**

CANADA LAND INVENTORY. REPORT *See* CLI REPORT **2190**

CANADA LEGAL DIRECTORY (CN/0315-8322) [02247863] **3139**

CANADA. LIBRARY OF PARLIAMENT *See* ANNUAL REPORT OF THE PARLIAMENTARY LIBRARIAN **3191**

CANADA. LIBRARY OF PARLIAMENT *See* NEWSPAPERS AND PERIODICALS CURRENTLY RECEIVED BY THE LIBRARY OF PARLIAMENT INCLUDING THE READING ROOM OF THE HOUSE OF COMMONS **4699**

CANADA. LIBRARY OF PARLIAMENT *See* PERIODICALS AND NEWSPAPERS IN THE COLLECTIONS OF THE LIBRARY OF PARLIAMENT **3259**

CANADA. LIBRARY OF PARLIAMENT. INFORMATION AND TECHNICAL SERVICES BRANCH *See* SELECTIVE ACQUISITIONS **3248**

CANADA LUTHERAN (NATIONAL ED.) (CN/0832-0179) [13515394] **5057**

CANADA. MAP OFFICE *See* CONTOURS (OTTAWA) **2559**

CANADA. MARKETING AND TRADE DIVISION *See* ANIMAL AND ANIMAL PRODUCTS; OUTLOOK **205**

CANADA. MINES BRANCH *See* MINES BRANCH MONOGRAPH (OTTAWA) **2145**

CANADA. MINISTRY OF STATE, SCIENCE AND TECHNOLOGY *See* FEDERAL SCIENCE EXPENDITURES AND PERSONNEL **4648**

CANADA. MINISTRY OF STATE, SCIENCE AND TECHNOLOGY *See* SCIENTIFIC ACTIVITIES : FEDERAL GOVERNMENT COSTS AND EXPENDITURES **5154**

CANADA. MINISTRY OF STATE, SCIENCE AND TECHNOLOGY *See* MEDIA IMPACT **1116**

CANADA. MINISTRY OF TRANSPORT *See* AIR REGULATIONS AND AERONAUTICS ACT **8**

CANADA. MINISTRY OF TRANSPORT. ROLE OF THE AUTOMOBILE STUDY *See* WORKING PAPER - ROLE OF THE AUTOMOBILE STUDY, TRANSPORT CANADA **5428**

CANADA. NATIONAL ADVISORY COUNCIL ON AGING *See* EXPRESSION (OTTAWA) **5285**

CANADA. NATIONAL CAPITAL COMMISSION *See* CANADA'S CAPITAL, OURS IN COMMON. ANNUAL REPORT **2817**

CANADA. NATIONAL FARM PRODUCTS MARKETING COUNCIL *See* ANNUAL REPORT - NATIONAL FARM PRODUCTS MARKETING COUNCIL **61**

CANADA (NEW YORK, N.Y. 1983) (US/0883-2641) [09844393] **5465**

CANADA NEWS (AUBURNDALE, FLA.) (US/0889-0412) [13912533] **5648, 5649**

CANADA NORMANDIE (CN/0318-6814) [01812343] **2529**

CANADA. NORTHERN ECONOMIC DEVELOPMENT BRANCH. MINING SECTION *See* MINING STATISTICS : NORTH OF 60 **2006**

CANADA NOW (CN/0704-7991) [03991695] **2726**

CANADA. OFFICE DES RECHERCHES SUR LES PECHERIES *See* BULLETIN - OFFICE DES RECHERCHES SUR LES PECHERIES DU CANADA **5580**

CANADA. OFFICE OF PRIVATIZATION AND REGULATORY AFFAIRS *See* FEDERAL REGULATORY PLAN **4648**

CANADA. OFFICE OF SPECIAL IMPORT POLICY *See* NOTICE TO IMPORTERS **848**

CANADA. OFFICE OF THE AUDITOR GENERAL. COMMUNICATIONS ADVISORY GROUP *See* OPINIONS **4671**

CANADA. OFFICE OF THE COMMISSIONER OF OFFICIAL LANGUAGES *See* ANNUAL REPORT - COMMISSIONER OF OFFICIAL LANGUAGES **3265**

CANADA. OFFICE OF THE UMPIRE *See* DECISION OF THE UMPIRE **3146**

CANADA OFFSHORE BUYERS GUIDE (CN/0822-8698) [10643472] **4252**

CANADA ON STAGE (CN/0380-9455) [03291591] **5362**

CANADA. PARLEMENT. CHAMBRE DES COMMUNES. COMITE PERMANENT DE LA GESTION ET DES SERVICES AUX DEPUTES *See* MINUTES OF PROCEEDINGS AND EVIDENCE OF THE STANDING COMMITTEE ON MANAGEMENT AND MEMBERS' SERVICES **3010**

CANADA. PARLEMENT. CHAMBRE DES COMMUNES. COMITE PERMANENT DES LANGUES OFFICIELLES *See* MINUTES OF PROCEEDINGS AND EVIDENCE OF THE STANDING COMMITTEE ON OFFICIAL LANGUAGES **3302**

CANADA. PARLEMENT. CHAMBRE DES COMMUNES. COMITE SPECIAL CHARGE DE L'EXAMEN DE LA LOI CONCERNANT LES DOUANES *See* MINUTES OF PROCEEDINGS AND EVIDENCE OF THE SPECIAL COMMITTEE ON THE ACT RESPECTING CUSTOMS **4665**

CANADA. PARLEMENT. CHAMBRE DES COMMUNES. COMITE SPECIAL SUR LA REFORME DE LA REGLEMENTATION *See* MINUTES OF PROCEEDINGS AND EVIDENCE OF THE SPECIAL COMMITTEE ON REGULATORY REFORM **3010**

CANADA. PARLEMENT. CHAMBRE DES COMMUNES. COMITE SPECIAL SUR LES ACCORDS FISCAUX ENTRE LE GOUVERNEMENT FEDERAL ET LES PROVINCES *See* MINUTES OF PROCEEDINGS AND EVIDENCE OF THE SPECIAL COMMITTEE ON THE FEDERAL- PROVINCIAL FISCAL ARRANGEMENTS **4665**

CANADA. PARLEMENT. CHAMBRE DES COMMUNES. COMITE SPECIAL SUR L'OBJET DU PROJET DE LOI C-80 (ARMES A FEU) *See* MINUTES OF PROCEEDINGS AND EVIDENCE OF THE SPECIAL COMMITTEE ON SUBJECT MATTER OF BILL C-80 (FIREARMS) **4665**

CANADA. PARLEMENT. CHAMBRE DES COMMUNES. COMIT,E SP,ECIAL CHARG,E DE LA R,EFORME ,ELECTORALE *See* MINUTES OF PROCEEDINGS AND EVIDENCE OF THE SPECIAL COMMITTEE ON ELECTORAL REFORM (FRENCH EDITION) **4482**

CANADA. PARLEMENT. CHAMBRE DES COMMUNES. PROCES-VERBAUX DE LA CHAMBRE DES COMMUNES DU CANADA *See* VOTES AND PROCEEDINGS (OTTAWA) **4694**

CANADA. PARLEMENT. CHAMBRE DES COMMUNES. SOUS-COMITE DE LA BANQUE DU CANADA *See* MINUTES OF PROCEEDINGS AND EVIDENCE OF THE SUB-COMMITTEE ON THE BANK OF CANADA OF THE STANDING COMMITTEE ON FINANCE **799**

CANADA. PARLEMENT. CHAMBRE DES COMMUNES. SOUS-COMITE DES AFFAIRES EMANANT DES DEPUTES *See* MINUTES OF PROCEEDINGS AND EVIDENCE OF THE SUB-COMMITTEE ON PRIVATE MEMBERS BUSINESS OF THE STANDING COMMITTEE ON HOUSE MANAGEMENT **4666**

CANADA. PARLEMENT. CHAMBRE DES COMMUNES. SOUS-COMITE DES PROGRAMMES DU MEER (QUEBEC) *See* MINUTES OF PROCEEDINGS AND EVIDENCE OF THE SUB-COMMITTEE ON DREE PROGRAMMES (QUEBEC) OF THE STANDING COMMITTEE ON REGIONAL DEVELOPMENT **4665**

CANADA. PARLEMENT. CHAMBRE DES COMMUNES. SOUS-COMITE DES QUESTIONS DE SANTE *See* MINUTES OF PROCEEDINGS AND EVIDENCE OF THE SUB-COMMITTEE ON HEALTH ISSUES OF THE STANDING COMMITTEE ON HEALTH AND WELFARE, SOCIAL AFFAIRS, SENIORS AND THE STATUS OF WOMEN **4791**

CANADA. PARLEMENT. CHAMBRE DES COMMUNES. SOUS-COMITE DU DEVELOPPEMENT ET DROITS DE LA PERSONNE *See* MINUTES OF PROCEEDINGS AND EVIDENCE OF THE SUB-COMMITTEE ON DEVELOPMENT AND HUMAN RIGHTS OF THE STANDING COMMITTEE ON EXTERNAL AFFAIRS AND INTERNATIONAL TRADE **4510**

CANADA. PARLEMENT. CHAMBRE DES COMMUNES. SOUS-COMITE SUR LA CONDITION FEMININE *See* MINUTES OF PROCEEDINGS AND EVIDENCE OF THE SUB-COMMITTEE ON THE STATUS OF WOMEN OF THE STANDING COMMITTEE ON HEALTH AND WELFARE, SOCIAL AFFAIRS, SENIORS AND ON THE STATUS OF WOMEN **5561**

CANADA. PARLEMENT. CHAMBRE DES COMMUNES. SOUS-COMITE SUR LA LEGISLATION SUR LES INSTITUTIONS FINANCIERES *See* MINUTES OF PROCEEDINGS AND EVIDENCE OF THE SUB-COMMITTEE ON FINANCIAL INSTITUTIONS LEGISLATION OF THE STANDING COMMITTEE ON FINANCE **798**

CANADA. PARLEMENT. CHAMBRE DES COMMUNES. SOUS-COMITE SUR LA SECURITE NATIONALE *See* MINUTES OF PROCEEDINGS AND EVIDENCE OF THE SUB-COMMITTEE ON NATIONAL SECURITY OF THE STANDING COMMITTEE ON JUSTICE AND THE SOLICITOR GENERAL **4666**

CANADA. PARLEMENT. CHAMBRE DES COMMUNES. SOUS-COMITE SUR LA VOIE MARITIME DU SAINT-LAURENT *See* MINUTES OF PROCEEDINGS AND EVIDENCE OF THE SUB-COMMITTEE ON THE ST. LAWRENCE SEAWAY OF THE STANDING COMMITTEE ON TRANSPORT (FRENCH EDITON) **5387**

CANADA. PARLEMENT. CHAMBRE DES COMMUNES. SOUS-COMITE SUR LE NORAD *See* MINUTES OF PROCEEDINGS AND EVIDENCE OF THE SUB-COMMITTEE ON NORAD OF THE STANDING COMMITTEE ON EXTERNAL AFFAIRS AND INTERNATIONAL TRADE **846**

CANADA. PARLEMENT. CHAMBRE DES COMMUNES. SOUS-COMITE SUR LES INSTITUTIONS FINANCIERES INTERNATIONALES *See* MINUTES OF PROCEEDINGS AND EVIDENCE OF THE SUB-COMMITTEE ON INTERNATIONAL FINANCIAL INSTITUTIONS OF THE STANDING COMMITTEE ON FINANCE (ENGLISH EDITION) **799**

CANADA. PARLEMENT. COMITE DE LIAISON AVEC LES AUTOCHTONES *See* MINUTES OF PROCEEDINGS AND EVIDENCE OF THE ABORIGINAL LIAISON COMMITTEE OF THE SPECIAL JOINT COMMITTEE ON A RENEWED CANADA (FRENCH EDITION) **2747**

CANADA. PARLEMENT. SENAT. SOUS-COMITE SUR LA SECURITE ET DEFENSE NATIONALE *See* PROCEEDINGS OF THE SUBCOMMITTEE ON SECURITY AND NATIONAL DEFENCE (FRENCH EDITION) **4054**

CANADA. PARLIAMENT *See* STATUS OF BILLS REPORT **3059**

CANADA. PARLIAMENT. ABORIGINAL LIAISON COMMITTEE *See* MINUTES OF PROCEEDINGS AND EVIDENCE OF THE ABORIGINAL LIAISON COMMITTEE OF THE SPECIAL JOINT COMMITTEE ON A RENEWED CANADA (ENGLISH EDITION) **2746**

CANADA. PARLIAMENT. HOUSE OF COMMONS *See* LIST OF MEMBERS OF THE HOUSE OF COMMONS OF CANADA **4662**

CANADA. PARLIAMENT. HOUSE OF COMMONS *See* ORDER PAPER AND NOTICE PAPER **4671**

CANADA. PARLIAMENT. HOUSE OF COMMONS *See* HOUSE OF COMMONS DEBATES (OTTAWA. DAILY ED.) **4654**

CANADA. PARLIAMENT. HOUSE OF COMMONS *See* HOUSE OF COMMONS DEBATES (OTTAWA. RETROSPECTIVE COMPILATION) **4654**

CANADA. PARLIAMENT. HOUSE OF COMMONS *See* VOTES AND PROCEEDINGS (OTTAWA) **4694**

CANADA. PARLIAMENT. HOUSE OF COMMONS. SPECIAL COMMITTEE ON A NORTHERN GAS PIPELINE *See* MINUTES OF PROCEEDINGS AND EVIDENCE OF THE SPECIAL COMMITTEE ON A NORTHERN GAS PIPELINE **4264**

Alphabetical Title Index — CANADA

CANADA. PARLIAMENT. HOUSE OF COMMONS. SPECIAL COMMITTEE ON CANADA-UNITED STATES AIR TRANSPORT SERVICES *See* MINUTES OF PROCEEDINGS AND EVIDENCE OF THE SPECIAL COMMITTEE ON CANADA-UNITED STATES AIR TRANSPORT SERVICES **28**

CANADA. PARLIAMENT. HOUSE OF COMMONS. SPECIAL COMMITTEE ON ELECTORAL REFORM *See* MINUTES OF PROCEEDINGS AND EVIDENCE OF THE SPECIAL COMMITTEE ON ELECTORAL REFORM **4482**

CANADA. PARLIAMENT. HOUSE OF COMMONS. SPECIAL COMMITTEE ON EMPLOYMENT OPPORTUNITIES FOR THE '80S. SUB-COMMITTEE B *See* MINUTES OF PROCEEDINGS AND EVIDENCE OF SUB-COMMITTEE B OF THE SPECIAL COMMITTEE ON EMPLOYMENT OPPORTUNITIES FOR THE '80S **1691**

CANADA. PARLIAMENT. HOUSE OF COMMONS. SPECIAL COMMITTEE ON PENSION REFORM *See* MINUTES OF PROCEEDINGS AND EVIDENCE OF THE SPECIAL COMMITTEE ON PENSION REFORM **1691**

CANADA. PARLIAMENT. HOUSE OF COMMONS. SPECIAL COMMITTEE ON THE ACT RESPECTING CUSTOMS *See* MINUTES OF PROCEEDINGS AND EVIDENCE OF THE SPECIAL COMMITTEE ON THE ACT RESPECTING CUSTOMS **4737**

CANADA. PARLIAMENT. HOUSE OF COMMONS. SPECIAL COMMITTEE ON TRENDS IN FOOD PRICES *See* MINUTES OF PROCEEDINGS AND EVIDENCE OF THE SPECIAL COMMITTEE ON TRENDS IN FOOD PRICES **2350**

CANADA. PARLIAMENT. HOUSE OF COMMONS. STANDING COMMITTEE ON HOUSE MANAGEMENT *See* MINUTES OF PROCEEDINGS AND EVIDENCE OF THE STANDING COMMITTEE ON HOUSE MANAGEMENT **4665**

CANADA. PARLIAMENT. HOUSE OF COMMONS. STANDING COMMITTEE ON MULTICULTURALISM AND CITIZENSHIP *See* MINUTES OF PROCEEDINGS AND EVIDENCE OF THE STANDING COMMITTEE ON MULTICULTURALISM AND CITIZENSHIP **2539**

CANADA. PARLIAMENT. HOUSE OF COMMONS. STANDING COMMITTEE ON NORTHERN PIPELINES *See* MINUTES OF PROCEEDINGS AND EVIDENCE OF THE STANDING COMMITTEE ON NORTHERN PIPELINES **4264**

CANADA. PARLIAMENT. HOUSE OF COMMONS. SUB-COMMITTEE OF THE STANDING COMMITTEE ON AGRICULTURE ON FARM CREDIT ARRANGEMENTS *See* MINUTES OF PROCEEDINGS AND EVIDENCE OF THE SUB-COMMITTEE OF THE STANDING COMMITTEE ON AGRICULTURE ON FARM CREDIT ARRANGEMENTS **108**

CANADA. PARLIAMENT. HOUSE OF COMMONS. SUB-COMMITTEE OF THE STANDING COMMITTEE ON EXTERNAL AFFAIRS AND NATIONAL DEFENSE ON ARMED FORCES RESERVES *See* SUB-COMMITTEE OF THE STANDING COMMITTEE ON EXTERNAL AFFAIRS AND NATIONAL DEFENCE ON ARMED FORCES RESERVES **4058**

CANADA. PARLIAMENT. HOUSE OF COMMONS. SUB-COMMITTEE ON DEVELOPMENT AND HUMAN RIGHTS *See* MINUTES OF PROCEEDINGS AND EVIDENCE OF THE SUB-COMMITTEE ON DEVELOPMENT AND HUMAN RIGHTS OF THE STANDING COMMITTEE ON EXTERNAL AFFAIRS AND INTERNATIONAL TRADE **4510**

CANADA. PARLIAMENT. HOUSE OF COMMONS. SUB-COMMITTEE ON FINANCIAL INSTITUTIONS LEGISLATION *See* MINUTES OF PROCEEDINGS AND EVIDENCE OF THE SUB-COMMITTEE ON FINANCIAL INSTITUTIONS LEGISLATION OF THE STANDING COMMITTEE ON FINANCE **3087**

CANADA. PARLIAMENT. HOUSE OF COMMONS. SUB-COMMITTEE ON HEALTH ISSUES *See* MINUTES OF PROCEEDINGS AND EVIDENCE OF THE SUB-COMMITTEE ON HEALTH ISSUES OF THE STANDING COMMITTEE ON HEALTH AND WELFARE, SOCIAL AFFAIRS, SENIORS AND THE STATUS OF WOMEN **4791**

CANADA. PARLIAMENT. HOUSE OF COMMONS. SUB-COMMITTEE ON INDIAN WOMEN AND THE INDIAN ACT *See* MINUTES OF PROCEEDINGS AND EVIDENCE OF THE SUB-COMMITTEE ON INDIAN WOMEN AND THE INDIAN ACT OF THE STANDING COMMITTEE ON INDIAN AFFAIRS AND NORTHERN DEVELOPMENT **2267**

CANADA. PARLIAMENT. HOUSE OF COMMONS. SUB-COMMITTEE ON INTERNATIONAL DEVELOPMENT *See* MINUTES OF PROCEEDINGS AND EVIDENCE OF THE SUB-COMMITTEE ON INTERNATIONAL DEVELOPMENT OF THE STANDING COMMITTEE ON EXTERNAL AFFAIRS AND NATIONAL DEFENSE **2911**

CANADA. PARLIAMENT. HOUSE OF COMMONS. SUB-COMMITTEE ON INTERNATIONAL FINANCIAL INSTITUTIONS *See* MINUTES OF PROCEEDINGS AND EVIDENCE OF THE SUB-COMMITTEE ON INTERNATIONAL FINANCIAL INSTITUTIONS OF THE STANDING COMMITTEE ON FINANCE **799**

CANADA. PARLIAMENT. HOUSE OF COMMONS. SUB-COMMITTEE ON INTERNATIONAL TRADE *See* MINUTES OF PROCEEDINGS AND EVIDENCE OF THE SUB-COMMITTEE ON INTERNATIONAL TRADE OF THE STANDING COMMITTEE ON EXTERNAL AFFAIRS AND INTERNATIONAL TRADE **846**

CANADA. PARLIAMENT. HOUSE OF COMMONS. SUB-COMMITTEE ON PRIVATE MEMBERS BUSINESS *See* MINUTES OF PROCEEDINGS AND EVIDENCE OF THE SUB-COMMITTEE ON PRIVATE MEMBERS BUSINESS OF THE STANDING COMMITTEE ON HOUSE MANAGEMENT **4666**

CANADA. PARLIAMENT. HOUSE OF COMMONS. SUB-COMMITTEE ON THE BANK OF CANADA *See* MINUTES OF PROCEEDINGS AND EVIDENCE OF THE SUB-COMMITTEE ON THE BANK OF CANADA OF THE STANDING COMMITTEE ON FINANCE **799**

CANADA. PARLIAMENT. HOUSE OF COMMONS. SUB-COMMITTEE ON THE PENITENTIARY SYSTEM IN CANADA *See* MINUTES OF PROCEEDINGS AND EVIDENCE OF THE SUB-COMMITTEE ON THE PENITENTIARY SYSTEM IN CANADA **3169**

CANADA. PARLIAMENT. HOUSE OF COMMONS. SUB-COMMITTEE ON THE ST. LAWRENCE SEAWAY *See* MINUTES OF PROCEEDINGS AND EVIDENCE OF THE SUB-COMMITTEE ON THE ST. LAWRENCE SEAWAY OF THE STANDING COMMITTEE ON TRANSPORT **5387**

CANADA. PARLIAMENT. SENATE *See* DEBATES OF THE SENATE **4471**

CANADA. PARLIAMENT. SENATE. COMMITTEE ON PRIVILEGES, STANDING RULES AND ORDERS *See* PROCEEDINGS OF THE STANDING SENATE COMMITTEE ON PRIVILEGES, STANDING RULES AND ORDERS **4675**

CANADA. PARLIAMENT. SENATE. COMMITTEE ON STANDING RULES AND ORDERS. PROCEEDINGS OF THE COMMITTEE ON STANDING RULES AND ORDERS *See* PROCEEDINGS OF THE STANDING SENATE COMMITTEE ON PRIVILEGES, STANDING RULES AND ORDERS **4675**

CANADA. PARLIAMENT. SENATE. SPECIAL COMMITTEE ON A NORTHERN GAS PIPELINE *See* PROCEEDINGS OF THE SPECIAL COMMITTEE OF THE SENATE ON A NORTHERN GAS PIPELINE **4275**

CANADA. PARLIAMENT. SENATE. SPECIAL COMMITTEE ON NATIONAL DEFENCE *See* PROCEEDINGS OF THE SPECIAL COMMITTEE OF THE SENATE ON NATIONAL DEFENCE **4054**

CANADA. PARLIAMENT. SENATE. SPECIAL COMMITTEE ON SCIENCE POLICY *See* PROCEEDINGS OF THE SPECIAL COMMITTEE OF THE SENATE ON SCIENCE POLICY **5142**

CANADA. PARLIAMENT. SENATE. SPECIAL COMMITTEE ON THE NORTHERN PIPELINE *See* PROCEEDINGS OF THE SPECIAL COMMITTEE OF THE SENATE ON THE NORTHERN PIPELINE **4275**

CANADA. PARLIAMENT. SENATE. SPECIAL SENATE COMMITTEE ON RETIREMENT AGE POLICIES *See* PROCEEDINGS OF THE SPECIAL SENATE COMMITTEE ON RETIREMENT AGE POLICIES **1703**

CANADA. PARLIAMENT. SENATE. STANDING COMMITTEE ON AGRICULTURE AND FORESTRY *See* PROCEEDINGS OF THE STANDING SENATE COMMITTEE ON AGRICULTURE AND FORESTRY **122**

CANADA. PARLIAMENT. SENATE. STANDING COMMITTEE ON BANKING, TRADE AND COMMERCE *See* PROCEEDINGS OF THE STANDING SENATE COMMITTEE ON BANKING, TRADE AND COMMERCE **849**

CANADA. PARLIAMENT. SENATE. STANDING COMMITTEE ON FISHERIES *See* PROCEEDINGS OF THE STANDING SENATE COMMITTEE ON FISHERIES **2311**

CANADA. PARLIAMENT. SENATE. STANDING COMMITTEE ON FOREIGN AFFAIRS *See* PROCEEDINGS OF THE STANDING SENATE COMMITTEE ON FOREIGN AFFAIRS **4532**

CANADA. PARLIAMENT. SENATE. STANDING COMMITTEE ON LEGAL AND CONSTITUTIONAL AFFAIRS *See* PROCEEDINGS OF THE STANDING SENATE COMMITTEE ON LEGAL AND CONSTITUTIONAL AFFAIRS **3093**

CANADA. PARLIAMENT. SENATE. STANDING COMMITTEE ON NATIONAL FINANCE *See* PROCEEDINGS OF THE STANDING SENATE COMMITTEE ON NATIONAL FINANCE **4675**

CANADA. PARLIAMENT. SENATE. STANDING COMMITTEE ON TRANSPORT AND COMMUNICATIONS *See* PROCEEDINGS OF THE STANDING SENATE COMMITTEE ON TRANSPORT AND COMMUNICATIONS **1119**

CANADA. PARLIAMENT. SENATE. SUB-COMMITTEE ON CHILDHOOD EXPERIENCES AS CAUSES OF CRIMINAL BEHAVIOUR *See* PROCEEDINGS OF THE SUBCOMMITTEE ON CHILDHOOD EXPERIENCES AS CAUSES OF CRIMINAL BEHAVIOUR **3173**

CANADA. PARLIAMENT. SENATE. SUBCOMMITTEE ON NATIONAL DEFENCE *See* PROCEEDINGS OF THE SUBCOMMITTEE ON NATIONAL DEFENCE **4054**

CANADA. PARLIAMENT. SENATE. SUBCOMMITTEE ON OFF-TRACK BETTING *See* PROCEEDINGS OF THE SUBCOMMITTEE ON OFF-TRACK BETTING **2801**

CANADA. PARLIAMENT. SENATE. SUBCOMMITTEE ON SECURITY AND NATIONAL DEFENCE *See* PROCEEDINGS OF THE SUBCOMMITTEE ON SECURITY AND NATIONAL DEFENCE **4054**

CANADA. PARLIAMENT. SPECIAL JOINT COMMITTEE ON IMMIGRATION POLICY *See* MINUTES OF PROCEEDINGS AND EVIDENCE OF THE SPECIAL JOINT COMMITTEE OF THE SENATE AND OF THE HOUSE OF COMMONS ON IMMIGRATION POLICY **1920**

CANADA. PARLIAMENT. SPECIAL JOINT COMMITTEE ON SENATE REFORM *See* MINUTES OF PROCEEDINGS AND EVIDENCE OF THE SPECIAL JOINT COMMITTEE OF THE SENATE AND OF THE HOUSE OF COMMONS ON SENATE REFORM **4665**

CANADA. PARLIAMENT. SPECIAL JOINT COMMITTEE ON THE PROCESS FOR AMENDING THE CONSTITUTION OF CANADA *See* MINUTES OF PROCEEDINGS AND EVIDENCE OF THE SPECIAL JOINT COMMITTEE OF THE SENATE AND THE HOUSE OF COMMONS ON PROCESS FOR AMENDING THE CONSTITUTION OF CANADA **4482**

CANADA. PARLIAMENT. STANDING JOINT COMMITTEE ON REGULATIONS AND OTHER STATUTORY INSTRUMENTS *See* INDEX OF PROCEEDINGS / CANADA. PARLIAMENT. STANDING JOINT COMMITTEE ON REGULATIONS AND OTHER STATUTORY INSTRUMENTS **2981**

CANADA. PARLIAMENT. STANDING JOINT COMMITTEE ON REGULATIONS AND OTHER STATUTORY INSTRUMENTS *See* REPORT OF THE STANDING JOINT COMMITTEE OF THE SENATE AND OF THE HOUSE OF COMMONS ON REGULATIONS AND OTHER STATUTORY INSTRUMENTS **3038**

CANADA. PATENT OFFICE *See* PATENT OFFICE RECORD, THE **1307**

CANADA PENSION PLAN CONTRIBUTION AND UNEMPLOYMENT INSURANCE PREMIUM TABLES (CN/0713-1755) [08977592] 2877, **1658**

CANADA POST CORPORATION *See* PERFORMANCE (OTTAWA) **1146**

CANADA. POST OFFICE DEPARTMENT *See* CANADA POSTAL GUIDE **1144**

CANADA POSTAL GUIDE (CN) [01552983] **1144**

CANADA POULTRYMAN (CN/0008-2732) [01808271] **208**

CANADA. PRAIRIE FARM REHABILITATION ADMINISTRATION *See* ANNUAL REPORT - PRAIRIE FARM REHABILITATION ADMINISTRATION **61**

CANADA. PRIVACY COMMISSIONER OF CANADA *See* ANNUAL REPORT OF THE PRIVACY COMMISSIONER **2935**

CANADA. PUBLIC SERVICE STAFF RELATIONS BOARD *See* PUBLIC SERVICE STAFF RELATIONS BOARD DECISIONS **3033**

CANADA-QUEBEC ST. LAWRENCE RIVER WORKING GROUP *See* STUDY OF THE ST. LAWRENCE RIVER; REPORT FOR THE FISCAL YEAR **1418**

CANADA QUILTS (CN/0381-7369) [03209966] **5183**

CANADA REGISTER (US/1052-1208) [22191864] **4835**

CANADA REPORT *CEASED*. (CN/0384-9252) [03285021] **826**

CANADA

Alphabetical Title Index

CANADA. RESTRICTIVE TRADE PRACTICES COMMISSION See ANNUAL REPORT FOR THE YEAR ENDED MARCH 31 ... / RESTRICTIVE TRADE PRACTICES COMMISSION (CANADA) **3095**

CANADA RIDES (CN/0300-4511) [01804042] **2529**

CANADA. ROAD SAFETY See ROAD SAFETY ANNUAL REPORT **5443**

CANADA. ROYAL COMMISSION ON ENERGY See REPORT - ROYAL COMMISSION ON ENERGY (OTTAWA) **1955**

CANADA SAFETY COUNCIL CONFERENCE See CONGRES ANNUEL - CONSEIL CANADIEN DA LA SECURITE **4772**

CANADA. SECRETARIAT D'ETAT DU CANADA. BIBLIOTHEQUE MINISTERIELLE See LISTE DES RAPPORTS ANNUELS, BIBLIOTHEQUE PRINCIPALE JE **4662**

CANADA. SERVICES EPIDEMIOLOGIQUES See CANADA COMMUNICABLE DISEASE REPORT **4770**

CANADA SKI (CN/0045-4222) [01808748] **4889**

CANADA. SOLICITOR GENERAL CANADA See ANNUAL REPORT / SOLICITOR GENERAL CANADA **3157**

CANADA SPECIALIZED POSTAGE STAMP CATALOGUE (CN/0702-9268) [03453099] **2784**

CANADA. STATISTICS CANADA See LABOUR FORCE INFORMATION **1535**

CANADA. STATISTICS CANADA. AVIATION STATISTICS CENTRE See AIR CARRIER OPERATIONS IN CANADA **7**

CANADA. STATISTICS CANADA AVIATION STATISTICS CENTRE See AIR PASSENGER ORIGIN AND DESTINATION. CANADA-UNITED STATES **7**

CANADA. STATISTICS CANADA. AVIATION STATISTICS CENTRE See AIR PASSENGER ORIGIN AND DESTINATION. DOMESTIC REPORT **8**

CANADA. STATISTICS CANADA. BUSINESS FINANCE DIVISION See INTER-CORPORATE OWNERSHIP **1612**

CANADA. STATISTICS CANADA. BUSINESS FINANCE DIVISION See CORPORATION TAXATION STATISTICS (OTTAWA) **4697**

CANADA. STATISTICS CANADA. COMMUNICATIONS SECTION See TELEPHONE STATISTICS **1125**

CANADA. STATISTICS CANADA. EDUCATION, SCIENCE AND CULTURE DIVISION. PROJECTIONS SECTION See EDUCATION IN CANADA **1794**

CANADA. STATISTICS CANADA. EXTERNAL TRADE DIVISION See COMMERCE DU CANADA: EXPORTATIONS PAR MERCHANDISES **828**

CANADA. STATISTICS CANADA. FORESTRY SECTION See CANADIAN FORESTRY STATISTICS **2399**

CANADA. STATISTICS CANADA GROSS NATIONAL PRODUCT DIVISION See NATIONAL INCOME AND EXPENDITURE ACCOUNTS : THE ANNUAL ESTIMATES **1575**

CANADA. STATISTICS CANADA. HORTICULTURAL CROPS UNIT See GREENHOUSE INDUSTRY **2417**

CANADA. STATISTICS CANADA. HORTICULTURAL CROPS UNIT See SURVEY OF CANADIAN NURSERY TRADES INDUSTRY **2432**

CANADA. STATISTICS CANADA. HOSPITALS SECTION See HOSPITAL STATISTICS. VOLUME 1. BEDS, SERVICES, PERSONNEL **3660**

CANADA. STATISTICS CANADA. INDUSTRY PRODUCT DIVISION See SURVEY OF PRODUCTION **1628**

CANADA. STATISTICS CANADA. LIVESTOCK AND ANIMAL PRODUCTS SECTION See STOCKS OF DAIRY AND FROZEN POULTRY PRODUCTS **222**

CANADA. STATISTICS CANADA. PUBLIC FINANCE DIVISION See LOCAL GOVERNMENT EMPLOYMENT **1688**

CANADA. STATISTICS CANADA. SCIENCE STATISTICS SECTION See SELECTED STATISTICS ON TECHNOLOGICAL INNOVATION IN INDUSTRY **1538**

CANADA. STATISTICS CANADA. SURFACE TRANSPORT SECTION See RAILWAY TRANSPORT **5436**

CANADA. STATISTICS CANADA. VITAL STATISTICS SECTION See CANADIAN SUICIDE RATIOS BY LOCAL AREAS AND BY URBAN CENTRES **5276**

CANADA. STATISTIQUE CANADA. DIVISION DES INDUSTRIES MANUFACTURIERES ET PRIMAIRES See PRIMARY IRON AND STEEL **4016**

CANADA. STATISTIQUE CANADA. DIVISION DES INDUSTRIES MANUFACTURIERES ET PRIMAIRES See GYPSUM PRODUCTS **632**

CANADA. STATISTIQUE CANADA. DIVISION DES INDUSTRIES MANUFACTURIERES ET PRIMAIRES See GAS UTILITIES **4258**

CANADA. STATISTIQUE CANADA. DIVISION DES INDUSTRIES MANUFACTURIERES ET PRIMAIRES See OIL PIPE LINE TRANSPORT (MONTHLY ED.) **4270**

CANADA. STATISTIQUE CANADA. DIVISION DES INDUSTRIES MANUFACTURIERES ET PRIMAIRES See PRINTING, PUBLISHING AND ALLIED INDUSTRIES **4568**

CANADA. STATISTIQUE CANADA. DIVISION DES INDUTRIES MANUFACTURIERES ET PRIMAIRES See FACTORY SALES OF ELECTRIC STORAGE BATTERIES **2054**

CANADA. STATISTIQUE CANADA. SECTION DES STATISTIQUES DE L'EMPLOI ET DE LA REMUNERATION See EMPLOYMENT, EARNINGS AND HOURS **1532**

CANADA. STATISTIQUE CANADA. SECTION DES TRANSPORTS DE SURFACE See RAILWAY CARLOADINGS (MONTHLY ED.) **5435**

CANADA. SUPPLY AND SERVICES CANADA See REPORTER (SUPPLY AND SERVICES CANADA) **4682**

CANADA. SUPREME COURT See CANADA SUPREME COURT REPORTS **2947**

CANADA. SUPREME COURT See SUPREME COURT OF CANADA DECISIONS. CIVIL AND CRIMINAL CASES **3061**

CANADA. SUPREME COURT See BULLETIN OF PROCEEDINGS TAKEN IN THE SUPREME COURT OF CANADA **2944**

CANADA SUPREME COURT REPORTS (CN/0045-4230) [01552999] **2947**

CANADA. TAX APPEAL BOARD See CANADA. TAX APPEAL BOARD CASES. INDEX. SUPPLEMENT **2947**

CANADA. TAX APPEAL BOARD CASES. INDEX. SUPPLEMENT (CN/0317-2821) [02248057] 4716, **2947**

CANADA. TAXATION See INCOME TAX RULING **4731**

CANADA. TAXATION See TAXATION STATISTICS (OTTAWA) **4701**

CANADA: THE STATE OF THE FEDERATION (CN/0827-0708) [14707113] **4636**

CANADA TODAY (LONDON) (UK/0306-8145) [03917862] **2529**

CANADA TODAY (WASHINGTON) CEASED. (US/0045-4257) [01553023] **2529**

CANADA TOMORROW (TORONTO, ONT.) See FUTURE CONSUMER NEWSLETTER **1592**

CANADA TOMORROW (TORONTO, ONT.) (CN/0828-4474) [12177970] **654**

CANADA. TRANSPORT CANADA. STRATEGIC PLANNING See TRANSPORT CANADA CORPORATE PRIORITIES **854**

CANADA. TREASURY BOARD. REGULATORY AFFAIRS See FEDERAL REGULATORY PLAN **4648**

CANADA-U.S. BUSINESS LAW REVIEW CEASED. (CN/1180-4823) [22364058] **3097**

CANADA-U.S. OUTLOOK (US/1044-3223) [19751671] **4716**

CANADA-U.S. TRADE DISPUTES (CN/1185-9679) [25467976] **826**

CANADA. UNEMPLOYMENT INSURANCE COMMISSION See DIGEST OF BENEFIT ENTITLEMENT PRINCIPLES **1663**

CANADA-UNITED STATES LAW JOURNAL (US/0163-6391) [04419409] **3125**

CANADA. URBAN AFFAIRS CANADA See ANNUAL REPORT - URBAN AFFAIRS (OTTAWA) **4630**

CANADA (WASHINGTON, D.C. 1985) (US/0883-8135) [12228031] **2726**

●CANADA WATCH (CN/1191-7733) [27203198] **4636**

CANADA WATER ACT : ANNUAL REPORT, THE (CN/0227-4787) [06766782] **5531**

CANADA. WATER RESOURCES DOCUMENT REFERENCE CENTRE See WATDOC NEWSLETTER **5541**

CANADA WATER YEAR BOOK (CN/0708-4285) [02246241] 1413, **5531**

CANADA WEST TRAVEL NEWS (CN/1183-1987) [23598521] **5465**

CANADA WILDLIFE SERVICE See PROGRESS NOTES - CANADIAN WILDLIFE SERVICE **470**

CANADA YEARBOOK (CN/0068-8142) [01784899] **1923**

CANADAN UUTISET (CN/0008-2775) [16386080] **5781**

CANADA'S BUSINESS CLIMATE (CN/0045-4303) [01810649] 1467, **654**

CANADA'S CAPITAL, OURS IN COMMON. ANNUAL REPORT (CN/1185-653X) [25796679] **2817**

CANADA'S DATA PROCESSING MARKET (CN/0704-7932) [04955037] **1256**

CANADA'S FOREST INVENTORY / BY G.M. BONNOR (CN) [10058096] **2377**

CANADA'S FURNITURE MARKET (CN/0319-0803) [03258705] **2904**

CANADA'S HOUSING CRISIS (CN/0824-3727) [10398366] **2817**

CANADA'S IMMIGRATION & CITIZENSHIP BULLETIN (CN/0843-7564) [20977312] **1918**

CANADA'S MEN (CN/0835-8478) [19227634] 1658, **1530**

CANADA'S MENTAL HEALTH SUSPENDED. (CN/0008-2791) [02442426] **4770**

CANADA'S MINERAL PRODUCTION, PRELIMINARY ESTIMATES (CN/0380-7797) [02585825] **2136**

CANADA'S OLDER WORKERS (CN/0835-8494) [19948552] 1658, **1530**

CANADA'S UNIONIZED WORKERS (CN/0835-8559) [22596263] 1658, **1531**

CANADA'S WHO'S WHO OF THE POULTRY INDUSTRY (CN/0068-8134) [02247757] **431**

CANADA'S WOMEN (CN/0835-846X) [18933718] 1658, **1531**

CANADA'S YOUTH (CN/0835-8486) [20053503] 1658, **1531**

CANADAWORKS! : THE SERVICE EMPLOYEES INTERNATIONAL UNION MAGAZINE (CN/0841-6060) [19119904] **1658**

CANADEAN WORLD NEW PRODUCTS (UK/0260-7352) [07088896] 2366, **2330**

CANADEXPORT (ENGLISH ED.) (CN/0823-3330) [11744792] **826**

CANADIAN ACADEMIC ACCOUNTING ASSOCIATION. CONFERENCE See PROCEEDINGS. ANNUAL CONFERENCE - CANADIAN ACADEMIC ACCOUNTING ASSOCIATION **750**

CANADIAN ACOUSTICS (CN/0711-6659) [08882586] **2162**

CANADIAN ACOUSTICS (CN/0711-6659) [08882587] **4107**

CANADIAN ADMINISTRATOR, THE (CN/0008-2813) [01810571] **1861**

CANADIAN ADVENTIST MESSENGER (CN/0702-5084) [03782108] **5057**

CANADIAN ADVERTISING ADVISORY BOARD. ADVERTISING STANDARDS COUNCIL See REPORT ON COUNCIL ACTIVITY - CANADIAN ADVERTISING ADVISORY BOARD. ADVERTISING STANDARDS COUNCIL **765**

CANADIAN ADVERTISING AND SALES ASSOCIATION See THIS IS THE VOICE OF CASA **767**

CANADIAN ADVERTISING RATES & DATA (CN/0038-9498) [04695904] **757**

CANADIAN AERONAUTICS AND SPACE JOURNAL (CN/0008-2821) [01553029] **15**

CANADIAN AFTERMARKET, THE (CN/0821-2651) [09432728] **5408**

CANADIAN AGGREGATES (CN/0836-799X) [17743078] **606**

CANADIAN AGRICULTURAL ECONOMICS AND FARM MANAGEMENT SOCIETY. MEETING See ANNUAL MEETING PROCEEDINGS **60**

CANADIAN AGRICULTURAL ECONOMICS SOCIETY. WORKSHOP See PROCEEDINGS OF THE WORKSHOP OF THE CANADIAN AGRICULTURAL ECONOMICS SOCIETY **122**

CANADIAN AGRICULTURAL ENGINEERING (CN/0045-432X) [01553031] 1967, **158**

CANADIAN AGRICULTURAL INSECT PEST REVIEW, THE (CN/0068-8185) [02754764] **72**

CANADIAN AIRCRAFT OPERATOR, THE (CN/0008-2848) [01811406] **15**

CANADIAN ALMANAC & DIRECTORY (CN/0068-8193) [02248021] **1924**

CANADIAN ALPINE JOURNAL, THE (CN/0068-8207) [02247165] **4870**

CANADIAN AMATEUR (1987) (CN/0834-3977) [16847861] 1129, **2037**

CANADIAN AMATEUR FOOTBALL ASSOCIATION See CANADIAN RULE BOOK FOR TACKLE FOOTBALL **4889**

CANADIAN AMATEUR HOCKEY ASSOCIATION See CONSTITUTION, BY-LAWS, REGULATIONS, HISTORY / CANADIAN AMATEUR HOCKEY ASSOCIATION **4891**

CANADIAN AMATEUR HOCKEY ASSOCIATION See HOCKEY AMATEUR **4898**

CANADIAN AMATEUR SOFTBALL ASSOCIATION See BOOK OF RECORDS, NATIONALS - SOFTBALL CANADA **4887**

Alphabetical Title Index — CANADIAN

CANADIAN AMATEUR SYNCHRONIZED SWIMMING ASSOCIATION *See* ANNUAL GUIDE TO SYNCHRONIZED SWIMMING **4883**

CANADIAN AMATEUR SYNCHRONIZED SWIMMING ASSOCIATION *See* COMMUNIQUE - SYNCHRO SWIM CANADA **4891**

CANADIAN-AMERICAN PUBLIC POLICY (US/1047-1073) [20607947] **826**

CANADIAN-AMERICAN SLAVIC STUDIES (US/0090-8290) [00844052] **2683**

CANADIAN AMPUTEE SPORTS ASSOCIATION (CN/0823-6674) [10036693] **4385, 4889**

CANADIAN ANALYST, THE *CEASED.* (CN/0527-8759) [01844348] **2529**

CANADIAN ANCESTRAL TIES (US/1041-1240) [18648014] **2441**

CANADIAN AND INTERNATIONAL EDUCATION (CN/0315-1409) [01774885] **1730**

CANADIAN AND PROVINCIAL GOLF RECORDS (CN/0316-8131) [02247184] **4889**

CANADIAN ANGLER (CN) [29206038] **4870, 2298**

CANADIAN ANNUAL REVIEW OF POLITICS AND PUBLIC AFFAIRS (CN/0315-1433) [01783711] **4467**

CANADIAN APPAREL MANUFACTURER *See* APPAREL (SAINTE-ANNE-DE-BELLEVUE) **1081**

CANADIAN APPLIED MATHEMATICS QUARTERLY (US) [28138965] **3499**

CANADIAN APPRAISER, THE (CN/0827-2697) [11131266] **4835**

CANADIAN AQUATICS (CN/0712-5135) [09106527] **4889**

CANADIAN ARAB FEDERATION *See* NEWSLETTER OF THE C A F **5252**

CANADIAN ARABIAN HORSE STUD BOOK (CN) [06010435] **2797**

CANADIAN ARABIAN RACING REFERENCE (CN/0824-1414) [11807802] **2797**

CANADIAN ARCHITECT, THE (CN/0008-2872) [01553038] **294**

CANADIAN ART. CATALOGUE OF THE NATIONAL GALLERY OF CANADA (CN/0826-9726) **346**

CANADIAN ART INVESTOR'S GUIDE, THE (US/0384-1588) [03258654] **893, 346**

CANADIAN ART SALES INDEX ..., THE (CN/0229-8961) [08079098] **346**

CANADIAN ART (TORONTO, 1984) (CN/0825-3854) [12045245] **346**

CANADIAN ARTHRITIS AND RHEUMATISM SOCIETY *See* C.A.R. SCOPE **3561**

CANADIAN ARTIFICIAL INTELLIGENCE NEWSLETTER (CN/0823-9339) [12168397] **1212**

CANADIAN ARTISTS IN EXHIBITION (CN/0316-6015) [01784487] **346**

CANADIAN ASSOCIATION FOR GRADUATE STUDIES *See* STATISTICAL REPORT - CANADIAN ASSOCIATION FOR GRADUATE STUDIES **1848**

CANADIAN ASSOCIATION FOR INFORMATION SCIENCE *See* MEMBERSHIP DIRECTORY - CANADIAN ASSOCIATION FOR INFORMATION SCIENCE **3230**

CANADIAN ASSOCIATION FOR LABORATORY ANIMAL SCIENCE. CONVENTION *See* PROCEEDINGS OF THE CANADIAN ASSOCIATION FOR LABORATORY ANIMAL SCIENCE **5519**

CANADIAN ASSOCIATION FOR UNIVERSITY CONTINUING EDUCATION *See* HANDBOOK / CANADIAN ASSOCIATION FOR UNIVERSITY CONTINUING EDUCATION **1827**

CANADIAN ASSOCIATION OF ADMINISTRATIVE SCIENCES *See* PROCEEDINGS. ANNUAL CONFERENCE - CANADIAN ASSOCIATION OF ADMINISTRATIVE SCIENCES **882**

CANADIAN ASSOCIATION OF APPLIED LINGUISTICS. MEETING *See* ACTES. / ASSOCIATION CANADIENNE DE LINGUISTIQUE APPLIQUEE **3261**

CANADIAN ASSOCIATION OF COLLEGE AND UNIVERSITY STUDENT SERVICES *See* MEMBERSHIP DIRECTORY - CANADIAN ASSOCIATION OF COLLEGE AND UNIVERSITY STUDENT SERVICES **1835**

CANADIAN ASSOCIATION OF FIRE CHIEFS *See* C A F C DIALOGUE **2288**

CANADIAN ASSOCIATION OF GEOGRAPHERS *See* DIRECTORY - CANADIAN ASSOCIATION OF GEOGRAPHERS **2559**

CANADIAN ASSOCIATION OF GRADUATE SCHOOLS. STATISTICAL REPORT - CANADIAN ASSOCIATION OF GRADUATE SCHOOLS *See* STATISTICAL REPORT - CANADIAN ASSOCIATION FOR GRADUATE STUDIES **1848**

CANADIAN ASSOCIATION OF IMMERSION TEACHERS. NATIONAL CONVENTION *See* ACTES DU CONGRES / ASSOCIATION CANADIENNE DES PROFESSEURS D'IMMERSION **1722**

CANADIAN ASSOCIATION OF LAW LIBRARIES *See* DIRECTORY / CANADIAN ASSOCIATION OF LAW LIBRARIES **3206**

CANADIAN ASSOCIATION OF MUSIC LIBRARIES *See* MEMBERSHIP LIST - CANADIAN ASSOCIATION OF MUSIC LIBRARIES (1984) **3231**

CANADIAN ASSOCIATION OF PATHOLOGISTS *See* DIRECTORY - CANADIAN ASSOCIATION OF PATHOLOGISTS **3894**

CANADIAN ASSOCIATION OF PHYSICAL ANTHROPOLOGY NEWSLETTER (CN) [23922794] **233**

CANADIAN ASSOCIATION OF RADIOLOGISTS JOURNAL (CN/0846-5371) [13675053] **3939**

CANADIAN ASSOCIATION OF RHODES SCHOLARS *See* NEWSLETTER / CANADIAN ASSOCIATION OF RHODES SCHOLARS **1837**

CANADIAN ASSOCIATION OF SLAVISTS *See* NEWSLETTER - CANADIAN ASSOCIATION OF SLAVISTS **2520**

CANADIAN ASSOCIATION OF SOCIAL WORKERS *See* INFORMATION - CANADIAN ASSOCIATION OF SOCIAL WORKERS **5289**

CANADIAN ASSOCIATION OF SPECIAL LIBRARIES AND INFORMATION SERVICES. CALGARY CHAPTER *See* UNION LIST OF PERIODICALS / CASLIS, CALGARY CHAPTER **3254**

CANADIAN ASSOCIATION OF SPECIAL LIBRARIES AND INFORMATION SERVICES. EDMONTON CHAPTE *See* SPECIAL LIBRARIES IN THE EDMONTON AREA (1981) **3250**

CANADIAN ASSOCIATION OF THE DEAF *See* DEAF CANADA **4386**

CANADIAN ASSOCIATION OF THE DEAF *See* SOURDS DU CANADA **4393**

CANADIAN ASSOCIATION OF UNIVERSITY SCHOOLS OF MUSIC *See* DIRECTORY OF THE CANADIAN ASSOCIATION OF UNIVERSITY SCHOOLS OF MUSIC **4115**

CANADIAN ASSOCIATION OF UNIVERSITY TEACHERS OF GERMAN *See* C. A. U. T. G. NEWSLETTER **3271**

CANADIAN ASSOCIATION OF UNIVERSITY TEACHERS OF GERMAN *See* CAUTG BULLETIN **1890**

CANADIAN ASSOCIATION OF UNIVERSITY TEACHERS OF GERMAN. C.A.U.T.G. NEWSLETTER *See* CAUTG BULLETIN **1890**

CANADIAN ASSOCIATION OF YOUTH ORCHESTRAS *See* CAYO PUBLICATION **4108**

CANADIAN ASSOCIATION ON GERONTOLOGY *See* NEWSLETTER - CANADIAN ASSOCIATION ON GERONTOLOGY **5180**

CANADIAN ATV DEALERS BLUE BOOK (CN/0832-9990) [16580474] **826**

CANADIAN AUCTIONEER, THE (CN/0823-6429) [09951401] **862**

CANADIAN AURAL/ORAL HISTORY ASSOCIATION *See* BULLETIN - CANADIAN AURAL/ORAL HISTORY ASSOCIATION **2724**

●CANADIAN AUTHOR (1992) (CN/1193-9974) [28482380] **3372**

CANADIAN AUTHOR & BOOKMAN (CN/0008-2937) [04426690] **3372**

CANADIAN AUTOMOBILE ASSOCIATION *See* COMMUNIQUE - CANADIAN AUTOMOBILE ASSOCIATION **5412**

CANADIAN AUTOMOBILE SPORT CLUBS *See* C. A. S. C. RACE REGULATIONS **4889**

CANADIAN AUTOMOBILE SPORT CLUBS *See* RALLY REGULATIONS (WILLOWDALE) **4914**

CANADIAN AUTOMOTIVE FLEET (CN/0828-2161) [14375037] **5378**

CANADIAN AUTOMOTIVE FLEET. FACT BOOK (US/1187-5356) [26066723] **5378**

CANADIAN AUTOMOTIVE TECHNICIAN (CN/1180-2065) [22286037] **5408**

●CANADIAN AUTOWORLD (CN/1192-2745) [28166198] **5408**

CANADIAN AVIATION HISTORICAL SOCIETY *See* CAHS JOURNAL, THE **15**

CANADIAN AVIATION NEWS (1984) (CN/0829-2132) [13191806] **15**

CANADIAN AWARDS AND PRIZES (CN) **2530**

CANADIAN AYRSHIRE REVIEW (CN/0008-2961) [01827225] **72**

CANADIAN BADMINTON ASSOCIATION *See* HANDBOOK - CANADIAN BADMINTON ASSOCIATION **4898**

CANADIAN BALANCE OF INTERNATIONAL PAYMENTS, THE (CN/0318-8817) [01788315] **4716**

CANADIAN BAND JOURNAL (CN/0831-0203) [I08310203] **4107**

CANADIAN BANKER (1983) (CN/0822-6830) [09937114] **782**

CANADIAN BANKING REVIEW / CANADIAN BOND RATING SERVICE *CEASED.* (CN/0836-3021) [14176249] **782, 727**

CANADIAN BANKRUPTCY REPORTS (CN/0068-8347) [01553051] **3086**

CANADIAN BAPTIST, THE (CN/0008-2988) [01642058] **4942**

CANADIAN BAR ASSOCIATION *See* ... YEAR BOOK OF THE CANADIAN BAR ASSOCIATION AND THE MINUTES OF PROCEEDINGS OF THE ... ANNUAL MEETING, THE **3077**

CANADIAN BAR ASSOCIATION. ALBERTA BRANCH *See* ANNUAL REPORT - CANADIAN BAR ASSOCIATION. ALBERTA BRANCH **2934**

CANADIAN BAR ASSOCIATION. ALBERTA BRANCH. MID-WINTER MEETING *See* PAPERS PRESENTED AT THE MID-WINTER MEETING OF THE ALBERTA BRANCH OF THE CANADIAN BAR ASSOCIATION **3024**

CANADIAN BAR REVIEW. REVUE DU BARREAU CANADIEN, THE (CN/0008-3003) [01553057] **2947**

CANADIAN BAR REVIEW, THE (CN/0008-3003) [02168670] **3125**

CANADIAN BASE METAL EQUITIES (CN/1186-1983) [24267038] **893**

CANADIAN BEEKEEPING (CN/0576-4688) [01846898] **72**

CANADIAN BIKER MAGAZINE, THE (CN/0820-8344) [09528083] **4080**

CANADIAN BIOCHEMICAL SOCIETY *See* BULLETIN OF THE CANADIAN BIOCHEMICAL SOCIETY **484**

CANADIAN BIOCHEMICAL SOCIETY. BULLETIN OF THE CANADIAN BIOCHEMICAL SOCIETY *See* BULLETIN OF THE CANADIAN SOCIETY OF BIOCHEMISTRY AND MOLECULAR BIOLOGY **484**

CANADIAN BIODIVERSITY *See* GLOBAL BIODIVERSITY **456**

CANADIAN BIODIVERSITY (CN/1183-3254) [23509185] **450**

●CANADIAN BIOTECH NEWS (CN/1188-455X) [26883966] **3690**

CANADIAN BLACK BOOK (CN/0705-6966) [04097810] **5408**

CANADIAN BLACK BOOK. ONTARIO (CN/0384-8434) [03264513] **5408**

CANADIAN BLACK BOOK, USED TRUCK AND VAN GUIDE (CN/1187-4376) [25590026] **5408**

CANADIAN BOATING (CN/0045-4494) [I00454494] **592**

CANADIAN BOND PRICES (CN/0828-170X) [11839426] **654**

CANADIAN BOOK OF CHARITIES (CN/0226-0409) [06264740] **5276**

CANADIAN BOOK OF CORPORATE MANAGEMENT (CN/0707-2902) [04653856] **863**

CANADIAN BOOK REVIEW ANNUAL (CN/0383-770X) [02844655] **3339**

CANADIAN BOOKS FOR YOUNG PEOPLE (CN) [07770663] **3372**

CANADIAN BOOKS IN PRINT. AUTHOR AND TITLE INDEX (CN/0068-8398) [02280727] **4827**

CANADIAN BOOKS IN PRINT. SUBJECT INDEX (CN/0315-1999) [02979006] **4827, 4821**

CANADIAN BOOKSELLER (TORONTO) (CN/0225-2392) [06136608] **4827**

CANADIAN BOTANICAL ASSOCIATION *See* DIRECTORY OF THE CANADIAN BOTANICAL ASSOCIATION & CANADIAN SOCIETY OF PLANT PHYSIOLOGISTS **508**

CANADIAN BOTANICAL ASSOCIATION *See* BULLETIN - CANADIAN BOTANICAL ASSOCIATION **504**

CANADIAN BOWHUNTING (CN/0846-3182) [25066644] **4870**

CANADIAN BRIDGE DIGEST (1977) (CN/0707-9524) [04955160] **4858**

CANADIAN BROADCASTING CORPORATION *See* C B C ENGINEERING REVIEW **1128**

CANADIAN BROADCASTING CORPORATION *See* ANNUAL REPORT - CANADIAN BROADCASTING CORPORATION **1126**

CANADIAN
Alphabetical Title Index

CANADIAN BROADCASTING CORPORATION. MERCHANDISING See CBC JAZZ AND POPULAR RECORD CATALOGUE **4108**

CANADIAN BROADCASTING CORPORATION. MERCHANDISING See CBC CLASSICAL CATALOGUE **4108**

CANADIAN BUILDING DIGEST **CEASED.** (CN/0008-3097) [02248850] **606**

CANADIAN BULLETIN OF FISHERIES AND AQUATIC SCIENCES (CN/0706-6503) [06110887] **2298**

CANADIAN BUSINESS. 500 (CN) [16349476] **654**

CANADIAN BUSINESS (1977) (CN/0008-3100) [10310521] **654**

CANADIAN BUSINESS CHARTBOOK (CN) [01780805] **655**

CANADIAN BUSINESS CONDITIONS (CN/0383-5893) [02885347] **655**

CANADIAN BUSINESS ECONOMICS (CN/0705-6330) [04783851] **655, 1467**

CANADIAN BUSINESS EDUCATION INDEX (CN/0709-2946) [08659487] **655**

CANADIAN BUSINESS INDEX (CN/0227-8669) [06972315] **655, 727**

CANADIAN BUSINESS LAW JOURNAL, THE (CN/0319-3322) [02443090] **3097**

CANADIAN BUSINESS REVIEW, THE (CN/0317-4026) [01794541] **655, 1467**

CANADIAN BUSINESS SERVICE See BLUE BOOK OF C B S STOCK REPORTS **892**

CANADIAN BUSINESS SERVICE. SUMMARY REVIEW SERVICE See BLUE BOOK OF C B S STOCK REPORTS **892**

CANADIAN C.S. LEWIS JOURNAL, THE (CN/0711-2173) [08690308] **431, 3372**

CANADIAN CAMPER, THE (CN/0316-280X) [01837845] **4870**

CANADIAN (CANADIAN AIRLINES INTERNATIONAL) (CN) **2530**

CANADIAN CANCER SOCIETY. MANITOBA DIVISION See COMMUNIQUE - MANITOBA DIVISION, CANADIAN CANCER SOCIETY **3815**

CANADIAN CANON LAW SOCIETY See BULLETIN DE NOUVELLES - SOCIETE CANADIENNE DE DROIT CANONIQUE **5025**

CANADIAN CAPITAL PROJECTS (CN/0828-0622) [16082858] **893**

●CANADIAN CASE AND STATUTE CITATIONS (CN/1188-3081) [25417700] **2947**

CANADIAN CASE AND STATUTE CITATIONS / REFERENCES JURISPRUDENTIELLES ET LEGISLATIVES CANADIENNES **CEASED.** (CN/1188-3081) [25404240] **2947**

CANADIAN CASES ON EMPLOYMENT LAW (CN/0824-2607) [10638879] **3145**

CANADIAN CASES ON THE LAW OF INSURANCE (CN/0824-2585) [10513397] **2877, 2947**

CANADIAN CASES ON THE LAW OF TORTS (CN/0701-1733) [04097950] **3089**

CANADIAN CAVER, THE (CN/0833-0948) [16079933] **2558, 4870**

CANADIAN CD-ROM NEWS **CEASED.** (CN/0848-8649) [20667973] **1173**

CANADIAN CENTENARY SERIES, THE (CN) [01771157] **2726**

CANADIAN CENTRE FOR MANAGEMENT DEVELOPMENT See ANNUAL REPORT / CANADIAN CENTRE FOR MANAGEMENT DEVELOPMENT **4627**

CANADIAN CENTRE FOR OCCUPATIONAL HEALTH AND SAFETY See AT THE CENTRE (HAMILTON) **2859**

CANADIAN CERAMICS (CN/0316-1137) [02247736] **2587**

CANADIAN CERAMICS QUARTERLY (CN/0831-2974) [12642673] **2587**

CANADIAN CHALLENGE (CN/0828-6930) [12199481] **4942**

CANADIAN CHAMBER OF COMMERCE See BOARD OF DIRECTORS, COMMITTEE CHAIRMEN - CANADIAN CHAMBER OF COMMERCE **818**

CANADIAN CHAMPION (CN/0834-6925) [16349606] **5781**

CANADIAN CHEMICAL NEWS (CN/0823-5228) [10399941] **1021**

CANADIAN CHESS CHAT (CN) [04178294] **4858**

●CANADIAN CHILD PSYCHIATRIC BULLETIN, THE (CN/1188-7605) [26715083] **3922**

CANADIAN CHILDREN (CN/0833-7519) [16284809] **1803**

CANADIAN CHILDREN'S LITERATURE (CN/0319-0080) [02442026] **3372**

CANADIAN CHURCH HISTORICAL SOCIETY See JOURNAL OF THE CANADIAN CHURCH HISTORICAL SOCIETY **4970**

CANADIAN CITATIONS See CANADIAN CASE AND STATUTE CITATIONS / REFERENCES JURISPRUDENTIELLES ET LEGISLATIVES CANADIENNES **2947**

CANADIAN CIVIL AIRCRAFT REGISTER (CN/0527-6497) [16081404] **15**

CANADIAN CIVIL AVIATION (CN/0826-6026) [11774531] **15**

CANADIAN CIVIL ENGINEER (CN/0825-7515) [11852343] **2020**

CANADIAN CLEANER & LAUNDERER (CN/0008-3224) [09048108] **1600**

CANADIAN CLOTHING JOURNAL **SUSPENDED.** (CN/0008-3232) [01819922] **1082**

CANADIAN CO-OPERATIVE WOOLGROWERS MAGAZINE, THE (CN/0829-075X) [10168247] **1600, 1541**

CANADIAN COAST GUARD See LIVRE DES FEUX, DES BOUEES ET DES SIGNAUX DE BRUME: EAUX INTERIEURES (A L'OUEST DE MONTREAL ET A L'EST DE LA COLOMBIE-BRITANNIQUE) **4178**

CANADIAN COAST GUARD AIDS AND WATERWAYS DIRECTORATE NOTICE TO MARINERS See NOTICE TO MARINERS (ANNUAL EDITION 1976) **4181**

CANADIAN COIN BOX MAGAZINE (CN/0045-4575) [l00454575] **655**

CANADIAN COIN NEWS (CN/0702-3162) [03412307] **2780**

CANADIAN COMMENT (CN/1186-1568) [24280011] **2037**

CANADIAN COMMISSION FOR UNESCO See BULLETIN - CANADIAN COMMISSION FOR UNESCO **5193**

CANADIAN COMMUNICATION ASSOCIATION See COMMUNIQUE / CANADIAN COMMUNICATION ASSOCIATION **1108**

CANADIAN COMMUNICATIONS LAW REVIEW (CN/0317-0055) [02247551] **1105, 2947**

CANADIAN COMMUNICATIONS NETWORK LETTER (CN/0825-3021) [11868888] **1151**

CANADIAN COMMUNICATIONS REGULATION & POLICY (CN/0711-1967) [08858259] **1151**

CANADIAN COMMUNICATIONS REPORTS (CN/0316-3083) [02247188] **1129**

CANADIAN COMMUNITY COLLEGE PROGRAMMES. INTERNATIONAL EDITION (CN/0226-0530) [06264993] **1814**

CANADIAN COMMUNITY COLLEGE PROGRAMMES (NATIONAL EDITION) (CN/0226-0522) [06460665] **1814**

CANADIAN COMPETITION POLICY RECORD (CN/0228-1961) [06858661] **1600**

CANADIAN COMPOSER (CN/1180-3762) [21683269] **4107**

CANADIAN COMPOSER (CN/0008-3259) [16221220] **4107**

CANADIAN COMPOSER, THE **CEASED.** (CN/0008-3259) [02443360] **4107**

CANADIAN COMPUTER DEALER NEWS SOURCE GUIDE See COMPUTER DEALER NEWS SOURCE GUIDE **1236**

CANADIAN COMPUTER LAW REPORTER **CEASED.** (CN/0822-6709) [11193101] **1173, 2947**

CANADIAN COMPUTER RESELLER (CN/0840-7312) [19027320] **1173**

CANADIAN CONFERENCE OF THE ARTS See ARTS BULLETIN OF THE CANADIAN CONFERENCE OF THE ARTS **314**

CANADIAN CONSERVATION INSTITUTE See ICC **352**

CANADIAN CONSERVATION INSTITUTE. MUSEOLOGICAL RESOURCE CENTRE See INDEX TO MUSEOLOGICAL LITERATURE **4089**

CANADIAN CONSTRUCTION ASSOCIATION See PREVIEW - CANADIAN CONSTRUCTION ASSOCIATION **624**

CANADIAN CONSTRUCTION CATALOGUE FILE (CN/0082-0431) [02441930] **606**

CANADIAN CONSULTING ENGINEER (CN/0008-3267) [02606789] **1967**

CANADIAN CONSUMER (1963) **CEASED.** (CN/0008-3275) [01851172] **1294**

CANADIAN CONTRACTOR REPORT OF HYDROGRAPHY AND OCEAN SCIENCES (CN/0711-6748) [11200984] **1447**

CANADIAN CONTROLS AND INSTRUMENTATION. BUYERS' GUIDE (CN) [02443047] **3476**

CANADIAN COPPER (CN/0008-3291) [01861119] **3999**

CANADIAN COPYRIGHT INSTITUTE (CN/0824-5452) [10680888] **1302**

CANADIAN CORPORATE COUNSEL (CN/1188-2026) [l11882026] **655**

CANADIAN CORPORATE LAW REPORTER **CEASED.** (CN/0835-9245) [19573878] **3097**

CANADIAN COUNCIL OF CHURCHES. ASSEMBLY See PROCEEDINGS OF THE ... TRIENNIAL ASSEMBLY (... MEETING) OF THE CANADIAN COUNCIL OF CHURCHES, THE **4988**

CANADIAN COUNCIL OF MINISTERS OF THE ENVIRONMENT See ANNUAL REPORT - CANADIAN COUNCIL OF MINISTERS OF THE ENVIRONMENT **2160**

CANADIAN COUNCIL OF PROFESSIONAL ENGINEERS See CCPE NEWS **1967**

CANADIAN COUNCIL ON INTERNATIONAL LAW See PROCEEDINGS OF THE ANNUAL CONFERENCE - CANADIAN COUNCIL ON INTERNATIONAL LAW **3134**

CANADIAN COUNCIL ON SOCIAL DEVELOPMENT See ANNUAL REPORT - CANADIAN COUNCIL ON SOCIAL DEVELOPMENT **5239**

CANADIAN COUNTY CONNECTIONS **CEASED.** (US/0732-0590) [07864781] **2441**

CANADIAN COWBOYS ASSOCIATION See C C A RODEO NEWS **4889**

CANADIAN CREDIT REVIEW **CEASED.** (CN/0827-4312) [11588944] **782**

CANADIAN CRICKETER, THE (CN/0228-9504) [08071544] **4889**

CANADIAN CRIME STATISTICS (CN/0824-0337) [12332565] **3159, 3079**

CANADIAN CRIMINAL CASES (BOUND CUMULATION) (CN/0008-3348) [11382323] **3105**

CANADIAN CRITICAL CARE NURSING JOURNAL **CEASED.** (CN/0826-6778) [11825466] **3852**

CANADIAN CURLING NEWS (CN/0045-4648) [16679507] **4889**

CANADIAN CURRENT TAX (CN/0317-6495) [09519560] **740, 2947**

CANADIAN CUSTOMS AND EXCISE REPORTS (CN/0228-3409) [06860421] **2948**

CANADIAN DAIRY COMMISSION See ANNUAL REPORT / THE CANADIAN DAIRY COMMISSION / RAPPORT ANNUEL / LA COMMISSION CANADIENNE DU LAIT **192**

CANADIAN DANCE NEWS (CN/0228-1767) [06859643] **1311**

CANADIAN DANCERS NEWS (1988) (CN/0843-218X) [20136048] **1311**

CANADIAN DATA REPORT OF FISHERIES AND AQUATIC SCIENCES (CN/0706-6465) [09377256] **1447, 2298**

CANADIAN DATA REPORT OF HYDROGRAPHY AND OCEAN SCIENCES (CN/0711-6721) [12054342] **2298**

CANADIAN DATASYSTEMS (CN/0008-3364) [01843946] **1256**

CANADIAN DATASYSTEMS. REFERENCE MANUAL (CN) [02943380] **1236**

CANADIAN DEFENCE QUARTERLY (TORONTO) (CN/0315-3495) [01821404] **4038**

CANADIAN DEFENCE UPDATE See AVIATION, AEROSPACE & DEFENCE UPDATE **12**

CANADIAN DENTAL ASSISTANTS' ASSOCIATION : JOURNAL (CN/0833-8264) [15166800] **1318**

CANADIAN DENTAL ASSOCIATION See JOURNAL - CANADIAN DENTAL ASSOCIATION **1325**

CANADIAN DENTAL ASSOCIATION See JOURNAL - CANADIAN DENTAL ASSOCIATION (FRENCH EDITION) **1325**

CANADIAN DENTAL ASSOCIATION See DIRECTORY OF CANADIAN DENTAL ASSOCIATION **1322**

CANADIAN DENTAL FACULTY AND STAFF REGISTER (CN/0708-2002) [05018239] **1318**

CANADIAN DEPRECIATION GUIDE (CN/0068-8649) [02247183] **2948**

CANADIAN DIMENSION (CN/0008-3402) [01774886] **4467**

●CANADIAN DIRECTORY OF EFFICIENCY AND ALTERNATIVE ENERGY TECHNOLOGIES (CN) [26133312] **2136**

CANADIAN DIRECTORY OF INDUSTRIAL DISTRIBUTORS (CN/0708-7241) [05533992] **826**

CANADIAN DIRECTORY OF SCHOOLS (CN) **1730**

CANADIAN DIRECTORY OF SHOPPING CENTRES (CN/0822-7799) [10440744] **952**

CANADIAN DISCIPLE (CN/0008-3410) [01872003] **4942**

CANADIAN DRUG IDENTIFICATION CODE (CN/0824-2666) [03511304] **4295**

CANADIAN ECONOMIC COMMENT (CN/0318-1391) [02441696] **1468**

CANADIAN ECONOMIC OBSERVER (CN/0835-9148) [17470086] **1468**

CANADIAN ECUMENICAL NEWS (CN/0227-8782) [06959334] **4942**

CANADIAN EDUCATION ASSOCIATION *See* NEWSLETTER - CANADIAN EDUCATION ASSOCIATION **1867**

CANADIAN EDUCATION ASSOCIATION *See* C E A HANDBOOK **1861**

CANADIAN EDUCATION INDEX (CN/0008-3453) [02248101] 1730, **1793**

CANADIAN ELECTRICAL ASSOCIATION. ENGINEERING AND OPERATING DIVISION *See* TRANSACTIONS - ENGINEERING AND OPERATING DIVISION. CANADIAN ELECTRICAL ASSOCIATION **2084**

CANADIAN ELECTRONICS ENGINEERING ANNUAL BUYER'S GUIDE (CN) [12587694] **2037**

CANADIAN ELECTRONICS ENGINEERING ANNUAL BUYERS' GUIDE AND CATALOG DIRECTORY (CN/0317-0292) [02247626] **2037**

CANADIAN ELECTRONICS MARKET, THE (CN/0381-9396) [03258659] **2038**

CANADIAN ELECTRONICS (WILLOWDALE) (CN/1187-6026) [25882796] **2038**

CANADIAN EMERGENCY NEWS (CN/0847-947X) [20787182] 5276, **4770**

CANADIAN EMPLOYEE BENEFIT PLANS (US) [12880086] **1658**

●CANADIAN EMPLOYMENT LAW FOR U.S. COMPANIES (US/1073-5720) [29482911] **3145**

CANADIAN EMPLOYMENT LAW TODAY (CN/0843-090X) [19915439] **3145**

CANADIAN ENERGY NEWS (CN/0319-3403) [01868706] **1934**

CANADIAN ENERGY TRENDS MONTHLY (1991) (CN/1196-0833) **1934**

CANADIAN ENTOMOLOGIST, THE (CN/0008-347X) [01553087] **5606**

CANADIAN ENTREPRENEUR MAGAZINE (CN/0229-6551) [08070786] **826**

CANADIAN ENVIRONMENT *See* AQUAREF **5549**

CANADIAN ENVIRONMENTAL DIRECTORY (CN/1187-1202) [24571263] **2162**

CANADIAN ENVIRONMENTAL LAW REPORTS (CN/0707-7874) [17480453] **3110**

CANADIAN ENVIRONMENTAL PROTECTION (CN) **2162**

CANADIAN ENVIRONMENTAL REGULATION & COMPLIANCE NEWS (CN/1181-795X) [25066676] **2162**

CANADIAN EQUINE SPORTS (CN/0319-2997) [02442298] **4889**

CANADIAN ETHNIC STUDIES (CN/0008-3496) [01553089] **2257**

CANADIAN ETHNIC STUDIES ASSOCIATION *See* BULLETIN - CANADIAN ETHNIC STUDIES ASSOCIATION **2257**

CANADIAN ETHNOLOGY SOCIETY *See* PAPERS FROM THE ... ANNUAL CONGRESS / CANADIAN ETHNOLOGY SOCIETY **243**

CANADIAN EXPORTER (SCARBORO) (CN/0226-0263) [06212987] **826**

CANADIAN FACILITY MANAGEMENT *See* CANADIAN FACILITY MANAGEMENT & DESIGN **863**

●CANADIAN FACILITY MANAGEMENT & DESIGN (CN/1193-7505) [27272177] **863**

CANADIAN FAMILY LAW QUARTERLY (CN/0832-6983) [15624866] **3119**

CANADIAN FAMILY PHYSICIAN (CN/0008-350X) [01855088] **3737**

CANADIAN FAR EASTERN NEWSLETTER, THE *CEASED.* (CN/0045-4737) [01867729] **4517**

CANADIAN FARM & HOME ALMANAC (1978) (US/0704-9412) [04129735] **2530**

CANADIAN FARM AND INDUSTRIAL EQUIPMENT INSTITUTE *See* INDUSTRY OUTLOOK UPDATE ... **159**

CANADIAN FARM BUILDING CODE (CN/0700-1320) [03789924] 72, **606**

CANADIAN FARMTAX (CN/0823-6089) [09818922] **4716**

●CANADIAN FEDERAL GOVERNMENT HANDBOOK (CN/1189-4709) [26888991] **4636**

CANADIAN FEDERATION FOR THE HUMANITIES *See* BULLETIN - CANADIAN FEDERATION FOR THE HUMANITIES **2843**

CANADIAN FEDERATION OF BIOLOGICAL SOCIETIES. MEETING *See* PROGRAMME, PROCEEDINGS / CANADIAN FEDERATION OF BIOLOGICAL SOCIETIES **585**

CANADIAN FEDERATION OF UNIVERSITY WOMEN *See* JOURNAL - CANADIAN FEDERATION OF UNIVERSITY WOMEN **5559**

CANADIAN FICTION MAGAZINE (CN/0045-477X) [01862152] **3372**

CANADIAN FIELD HOCKEY ASSOCIATION *See* HANDBOOK AND DIRECTORY - CANADIAN FIELD HOCKEY ASSOCIATION **4898**

CANADIAN FILM-MAKERS DISTRIBUTION CENTRE *See* CANADIAN FILM-MAKERS DISTRIBUTION CENTRE CATALOGUE **4065**

CANADIAN FILM-MAKERS DISTRIBUTION CENTRE CATALOGUE (CN/0315-2715) [06017494] **4065**

CANADIAN FINANCE LETTER (CN/0848-0435) [20985120] **893**

CANADIAN FIREFIGHTER, THE (CN/0704-6391) [03790895] **2288**

CANADIAN FISH FANCIERS (CN/0702-7966) [03412170] **2298**

CANADIAN FISHERIES AND OCEAN INDUSTRIES DIRECTORY, THE (CN/0710-7641) [08340644] **2298**

CANADIAN FISHERIES ANNUAL STATISTICAL REVIEW (CN/0713-2158) [09234525] 2298, **2317**

CANADIAN FISHERIES. ANNUAL STATISTICAL REVIEW / ECONOMIC POLICY BRANCH, ECONOMIC DEVELOPMENT DIRECTORATE, FISHERIES AND OCEANS (CN) [09087038] 2298, **2317**

CANADIAN FISHERIES, LANDINGS (CN/0713-1348) [08741199] **2298**

CANADIAN FLIGHT (CN/0008-3577) [01861644] **16**

CANADIAN FLORIST, GREENHOUSE AND NURSERY (CN/0008-3585) [01950364] **2435**

CANADIAN FOLK MUSIC BULLETIN (CN/0829-5344) [10121662] **4107**

CANADIAN FOLK MUSIC JOURNAL (CN/0318-2568) [02585405] **4107**

CANADIAN FOLKLORE (FOLKLORE STUDIES ASSOCIATION OF CANADA) (CN/0225-2899) [07865676] **2318**

CANADIAN FOOTBALL LEAGUE *See* OFFICIAL PLAYING RULES FOR THE CANADIAN FOOTBALL LEAGUE, THE **4910**

CANADIAN FOOTWEAR JOURNAL (CN/0705-1433) [03963447] **1082**

CANADIAN FOREST INDUSTRIES (CN/0318-4277) [01553095] **2399**

CANADIAN FORESTRY STATISTICS (CN/0575-805X) [02443463] 2377, **2399**

CANADIAN FORUM (CN/0008-3631) [01553097] **3339**

CANADIAN FREE TRADER (CN/0831-4527) [14516839] **826**

CANADIAN FRIEND, THE (CN/0382-7658) [02337078] **4942**

CANADIAN FRUITGROWER (CN/0045-4885) [01880104] **2412**

CANADIAN FUNERAL DIRECTOR (CN/0319-3225) [01856260] **2406**

CANADIAN FUNERAL NEWS (CN/0382-5876) [02802295] **2406**

CANADIAN FURNITURE AND FURNISHINGS DIRECTORY (CN/0826-6204) [12064642] **2904**

CANADIAN FUTURES (CN/0705-5463) [04784025] **1468**

CANADIAN GARDEN NEWS (CN/0828-7619) [12199524] **2412**

CANADIAN GARDENING (CN/0847-3463) [22928808] **2412**

CANADIAN GAS ASSOCIATION *See* DIRECTORY / CANADIAN GAS ASSOCIATION **4760**

CANADIAN GAS FACTS (CN/0316-3547) [02239504] 4253, **4760**

CANADIAN GAS PRICE REPORTER (CN) **4253**

CANADIAN GAS RATES (CN/1194-2967) [11942967] 4253, **4760**

CANADIAN GEMMOLOGIST (CN/0226-7446) [08071563] **2913**

CANADIAN GENERAL AVIATION NEWS (CN/0226-5648) [06316132] **16**

CANADIAN GENERAL STANDARDS BOARD *See* QUARTERLY JOURNAL - CANADIAN GENERAL STANDARDS BOARD **4677**

CANADIAN GEOGRAPHER (CN/0008-3658) [01553098] **2558**

CANADIAN GEOGRAPHIC (CN/0706-2168) [04174172] **2558**

CANADIAN GEOPHYSICAL BULLETIN *CEASED.* (CN/0068-8819) [02248985] **1403**

CANADIAN GEOSCIENCE COUNCIL *See* GEOSCIENCES IN CANADA (1976) **1356**

CANADIAN GEOTECHNICAL JOURNAL (CN/0008-3674) [02248677] **1352**

CANADIAN GEOTHERMAL RESOURCES ASSOCIATION *See* NEWSLETTER - CANADIAN GEOTHERMAL RESOURCES ASSOCIATION **1389**

CANADIAN-GERMAN FOLKLORE (CN/0576-5277) [02934651] **2318**

CANADIAN GIDEON (CN/0316-2907) [02362489] **4942**

CANADIAN GLADIOLUS SOCIETY *See* ANNUAL - CANADIAN GLADIOLUS SOCIETY **2409**

●CANADIAN GLOBAL ALMANAC, THE (CN/1187-4570) [25796384] **1924**

CANADIAN GOAT SOCIETY *See* QUARTERLY - CANADIAN GOAT SOCIETY **220**

CANADIAN GOVERNMENT BOND REGISTER (CN/1180-3584) [23302876] **893**

CANADIAN GOVERNMENT PUBLICATIONS: CATALOGUE (CN/0318-675X) [03217896] **4697**

CANADIAN GRAIN COMMISSION *See* ANNUAL REPORT - CANADIAN GRAIN COMMISSION **60**

CANADIAN GRAIN COMMISSION. ECONOMICS AND STATISTICS DIVISION *See* VISIBLE GRAIN SUPPLIES AND DISPOSITION **204**

CANADIAN GRAIN COMMISSION. ECONOMICS AND STATISTICS DIVISION *See* GRAIN STATISTICS WEEKLY **153**

CANADIAN GRAIN POSITION (CN) [01783972] **1600**

CANADIAN GRAINS INDUSTRY; STATISTICAL HANDBOOK (CN) [03227491] 200, **152**

CANADIAN GRAPHIC COLLECTOR (CN/0705-2197) [03991879] **377**

CANADIAN GROCER (CN/0008-3704) [01869060] **2330**

CANADIAN GUERNSEY JOURNAL (CN/0831-3008) [15992585] **192**

CANADIAN GUIDE *CEASED.* (CN/0008-3712) [01868133] **2530**

CANADIAN GUIDER (CN/0300-435X) [01865939] **1730**

CANADIAN GUNNER (SHILO. 1965) (CN/0068-8843) [02603597] **4038**

CANADIAN HAIRDRESSER (CN/0008-3720) [01866220] **402**

CANADIAN HANDGUN (CN/0045-4915) [01880814] **2810**

CANADIAN HEALTH CARE GUILD *See* CHCG PULSE **3853**

CANADIAN HEALTH CARE MANAGEMENT (CN) **3777**

CANADIAN HEALTH RECORD ASSOCIATION *See* C H R A RECORDER **4770**

CANADIAN HEALTHCARE MANAGER (CN) **3777**

CANADIAN HEAVY EQUIPMENT GUIDE (CN/0832-6533) [15466681] **606**

CANADIAN HEREFORD DIGEST (CN/0008-3739) [01877223] **208**

CANADIAN HIGHWAY CARRIERS GUIDE *CEASED.* (CN/0702-8733) [03680494] 863, **5378**

CANADIAN HISTORICAL ASSOCIATION *See* DIRECTORY OF MEMBERS / THE CANADIAN HISTORICAL ASSOCIATION **2731**

CANADIAN HISTORICAL REVIEW (CN/0008-3755) [01553108] **2726**

CANADIAN HOCKEY LEAGUE *See* RECORD BOOK / CANADIAN HOCKEY LEAGUE **4914**

CANADIAN HOME ECONOMICS JOURNAL (CN/0008-3763) [01553109] **2789**

CANADIAN HORSEMAN (GUELPH) (CN/0840-6200) [20160280] **2797**

CANADIAN HORSESHOE PITCHERS YEAR BOOK (CN/0703-7074) [03453096] **4889**

CANADIAN HORTICULTURAL HISTORY *SUSPENDED.* (CN/0828-8259) [14709583] **2412**

CANADIAN HORTICULTURAL THERAPY ASSOCIATION NEWSLETTER (US) **2412**

CANADIAN HOSPITAL ASSOCIATION COMMITTEE RESEARCH REPORT (CN/0228-8907) [05977027] **3777**

CANADIAN HOSPITAL DIRECTORY (CN/0068-8932) [02247192] **3777**

CANADIAN HOSPITAL DIRECTORY & DIRECTORY OF LONG TERM CARE CENTERS IN CANADA *See* GUIDE TO CANADIAN HEALTH CARE FACILITIES **3780**

CANADIAN — Alphabetical Title Index

CANADIAN HOSPITAL ENGINEERING JOURNAL (CN/0821-2236) [09403358] **3778**

CANADIAN HOSPITAL FORUM (CN/1187-3779) [25314171] **3778**

CANADIAN HOSPITALITY (CN/0229-4427) [07888591] **2804**

CANADIAN HOTEL AND RESTAURANT (1990) (CN/1182-9923) [24257176] 5070, **2804**

CANADIAN HOTEL & RESTAURANT. SOURCES DIRECTORY (CN) [02578396] 5070, **2804**

CANADIAN HOUSE AND HOME (CN/0826-7642) [11868873] **2904**

CANADIAN HOUSING (CN/0826-7278) [12782146] **2817**

CANADIAN HOUSING INFORMATION CENTRE *See* ACQUISITIONS - CANADIAN HOUSING INFORMATION CENTRE **2813**

CANADIAN HOUSING INFORMATION CENTRE *See* ACQUISITIONS LIST - CANADIAN HOUSING INFORMATION CENTRE **2813**

CANADIAN HOUSING INFORMATION CENTRE. ACQUISITIONS *See* ACQUISITIONS LIST - CANADIAN HOUSING INFORMATION CENTRE **2813**

CANADIAN HOUSING. MONTHLY ANALYSIS (CN/0823-020X) [09822910] **2817**

CANADIAN HR REPORTER (CN/0838-228X) [18047808] **939**

CANADIAN HUMAN RIGHT REPORTER (CN/0226-2177) [07208097] **4505**

CANADIAN HUMAN RIGHTS YEARBOOK (CN/0824-5266) [10141922] **4505**

CANADIAN HUNTING & SHOOTING MAGAZINE, THE (CN/0846-3042) [25066667] **4870**

CANADIAN HYDROMETALLURGISTS *See* PROCEEDINGS OF THE ANNUAL MEETING OF THE CANADIAN HYDROMETALLURGISTS **4016**

CANADIAN IMPERIAL BANK OF COMMERCE. INFORMATION CENTRE *See* SELECTION OF RECENT ACQUISITIONS - CANADIAN IMPERIAL BANK OF COMMERCE, INFORMATION CENTRE, A **1520**

CANADIAN IMPORTS BY DOMESTIC AND FOREIGN CONTROLLED ENTERPRISES (CN/0830-0097) [08445508] **826**

CANADIAN INDEPENDENT ADJUSTER, THE (CN/0008-3828) [01861697] **2877**

CANADIAN INDEPENDENT SCHOOL JOURNAL (CN/0229-3129) [07858017] **1730**

CANADIAN INDEX TO GEOSCIENCE DATA. BRITISH COLUMBIA (CN) [02997262] **1353**

CANADIAN INDEX TO GEOSCIENCE DATA. MANITOBA (CN) [02997284] **1353**

CANADIAN INDEX TO GEOSCIENCE DATA. ONTARIO (CN) [02997311] **1353**

CANADIAN INDEX TO GEOSCIENCE DATA. QUEBEC (CN) [02997325] **1353**

●CANADIAN INDEX (TORONTO) (CN/1192-4160) [27757791] 5814, **5781**

CANADIAN INDIA STAR, THE (CN/0319-8715) [02578134] **2648**

CANADIAN INDUSTRIAL RELATIONS ASSOCIATION *See* CIRA NEWSLETTER **1659**

CANADIAN INDUSTRIAL RELATIONS RESEARCH INSTITUTE. MEETING *See* RAPPORT DU ... CONGRES DE L'INSTITUT CANADIEN DE RECHERCHE EN RELATIONS INDUSTRIELLES **1705**

CANADIAN INDUSTRIAL TRANSPORTATION LEAGUE *See* CITL MEMBERSHIP DIRECTORY **5379**

CANADIAN INDUSTRIES LIMITED *See* CONTACT C I L **1602**

CANADIAN INDUSTRY REPORT OF FISHERIES AND AQUATIC SCIENCES (CN/0704-3694) [06296367] **2298**

CANADIAN INFORMATION INDUSTRY ASSOCIATION (CN/0227-8804) [08099424] **3199**

CANADIAN INFORMATION PROCESSING *CEASED.* (CN/1182-3097) [21475287] **1173**

CANADIAN INSTITUTE OF ACTUARIES *See* YEARBOOK - CANADIAN INSTITUTE OF ACTUARIES **2897**

CANADIAN INSTITUTE OF ACTUARIES. GENERAL MEETING *See* PROCEEDINGS / CANADIAN INSTITUTE OF ACTUARIES **2890**

CANADIAN INSTITUTE OF FOOD SCIENCE AND TECHNOLOGY *See* NATIONAL DIRECTORY / CANADIAN INSTITUTE OF FOOD SCIENCE AND TECHNOLOGY **2350**

CANADIAN INSTITUTE OF FOOD SCIENCE AND TECHNOLOGY. CANADIAN INSTITUTE OF FOOD SCIENCE AND TECHNOLOGY JOURNAL *See* FOOD RESEARCH INTERNATIONAL **2339**

CANADIAN INSTITUTE OF INTERNATIONAL AFFAIRS. ADVISORY COMMITTEE ON CANADA-UNITED STATES STUDIES *See* CUSSNEWS **5244**

CANADIAN INSTITUTE OF MINING AND METALLURGY *See* C I M REPORTER **2136**

CANADIAN INSTITUTE OF MINING AND METALLURGY *See* TRANSACTIONS - CANADIAN INSTITUTE OF MINING AND METALLURGY **2152**

CANADIAN INSTITUTE OF MINING, METALLURGY AND PETROLEUM *See* CIM DIRECTORY **2136**

CANADIAN INSURANCE (CN/0008-3879) [01855752] **2877**

CANADIAN INSURANCE CLAIMS DIRECTORY (CN/0318-0352) [02248313] **2877**

CANADIAN INSURANCE LAW REPORTER (CN/0588-6562) [03219762] 2877, **2948**

CANADIAN INSURANCE LAW REVIEW (CN/0836-0456) [19418058] 2877, **2948**

CANADIAN INTELLECTUAL PROPERTY REPORTS (CN/0824-2623) [11355363] **1302**

CANADIAN INTELLECTUAL PROPERTY REVIEW (CN/0825-7256) [18450528] **1302**

CANADIAN INTELLIGENCE SERVICE (CN/0576-5501) [02359057] **4636**

CANADIAN INTERCONNECT DIRECTORY, THE (CN/0828-0150) [12204328] **1151**

CANADIAN INTERIORS (CN/0008-3887) [01855305] **2899**

CANADIAN INTERNATIONAL DEVELOPMENT AGENCY. DEVELOPMENT INFORMATION CENTRE *See* LISTE DES PERIODIQUES / CENTRE D'INFORMATION SUR LE DEVELOPPEMENT **2911**

CANADIAN INTERNATIONAL TRADE TRIBUNAL *See* NOTICE OF DECISION ON PUBLIC INTEREST REPRESENTATIONS **848**

CANADIAN INTERUNIVERSITY ATHLETIC UNION *See* DIRECTORY - CANADIAN INTERUNIVERSITY ATHLETIC UNION **4892**

CANADIAN INVESTMENT REVIEW (CN/0840-6863) [19486531] **894**

CANADIAN INVESTOR (TORONTO. 1984) (CN/0840-4917) [19903886] **894**

CANADIAN IRIS SOCIETY NEWSLETTER (CN/0715-3775) [09145754] **5229**

CANADIAN ISBN PUBLISHER'S DIRECTORY (CN/0228-8753) [08192862] **4827**

CANADIAN ISSUES (ASSOCIATION FOR CANADIAN STUDIES) (CN/0318-8442) [02443257] **2726**

CANADIAN JERSEY BREEDER (CN/0008-3909) [01883093] 192, **208**

CANADIAN JEWELLER (CN/0008-3917) [01868292] **2913**

CANADIAN JEWISH CONGRESS *See* CONGRES JUIF CANADIEN RAPPORT INTERIMAIRE **2258**

CANADIAN JEWISH CONGRESS. AUDIO-VISUAL DEPT *See* AUDIO-VISUAL PRESENTATIONS / CANADIAN JEWISH CONGRESS, AUDIO-VISUAL DEPARTMENT **5315**

CANADIAN JEWISH CONGRESS. NATIONAL ARCHIVES *See* NATIONAL ARCHIVES NEWSLETTER **2482**

CANADIAN JEWISH NEWS MONTREAL ED (CN) [I0837287X] **5046**

CANADIAN JEWISH NEWS (TORONTO) (CN/0008-3941) [05253026] **2257**

CANADIAN JOURNAL FOR THE STUDY OF ADULT EDUCATION (CN/0835-4944) [16876663] **1800**

CANADIAN JOURNAL OF ADMINISTRATIVE LAW & PRACTICE (CN/0835-6742) [17236310] **3092**

CANADIAN JOURNAL OF ADMINISTRATIVE SCIENCES (CN/0825-0383) [22569170] **863**

CANADIAN JOURNAL OF AFRICAN STUDIES (CN/0008-3968) [01553126] **2638**

CANADIAN JOURNAL OF AGRICULTURAL ECONOMICS (CN/0008-3976) [02247938] 1468, **72**

CANADIAN JOURNAL OF ANAESTHESIA (CN/0832-610X) [15097573] **3682**

CANADIAN JOURNAL OF ANIMAL SCIENCE (CN/0008-3984) [01553129] **208**

●CANADIAN JOURNAL OF APPLIED PHYSIOLOGY (US/1066-7814) [27047096] 2596, **579**

CANADIAN JOURNAL OF APPLIED SPECTROSCOPY (CN/1183-7306) [22589033] **4434**

CANADIAN JOURNAL OF ARCHAEOLOGY (CN/0705-2006) [03991846] **265**

CANADIAN JOURNAL OF BEHAVIOURAL SCIENCE (CN/0008-400X) [01553131] 5194, **4579**

CANADIAN JOURNAL OF BOTANY (CN/0008-4026) [02248671] **505**

CANADIAN JOURNAL OF CARDIOLOGY (CN/0828-282X) [11882527] **3700**

CANADIAN JOURNAL OF CARDIOVASCULAR NURSING (CN/0843-6096) [20223401] **3700**

CANADIAN JOURNAL OF CHEMICAL ENGINEERING, THE (CN/0008-4034) [01553135] **2008**

CANADIAN JOURNAL OF CHEMISTRY (CN/0008-4042) [02248672] **966**

CANADIAN JOURNAL OF CIVIL ENGINEERING (CN/0315-1468) [02240907] **2020**

CANADIAN JOURNAL OF CME (CN/0843-994X) [20665472] **3561**

CANADIAN JOURNAL OF COMMUNICATION (CN/0705-3657) [03900226] **1105**

CANADIAN JOURNAL OF COMMUNITY MENTAL HEALTH (CN/0713-3936) [09379069] **5276**

CANADIAN JOURNAL OF COUNSELLING (CN/0828-3893) [13171814] 1911, **1876**

CANADIAN JOURNAL OF CRIMINOLOGY (CN/0704-9722) [03563755] **3159**

CANADIAN JOURNAL OF DERMATOLOGY, THE (CN/0843-4247) [20665329] **3718**

CANADIAN JOURNAL OF DIAGNOSIS (CN/0839-1866) [19078320] **3561**

CANADIAN JOURNAL OF DRAMA AND THEATRE, THE *CEASED.* (CN/1183-1243) [25066707] **5362**

CANADIAN JOURNAL OF EARLY CHILDHOOD EDUCATION *CEASED.* (CN/0226-7071) [07857963] **1803**

CANADIAN JOURNAL OF EARTH SCIENCES (CN/0008-4077) [02248673] **1353**

CANADIAN JOURNAL OF ECONOMICS, THE (CN/0008-4085) [01553140] **1468**

CANADIAN JOURNAL OF EDUCATION (CN/0380-2361) [02603472] **1730**

CANADIAN JOURNAL OF EDUCATIONAL COMMUNICATION (CN/0710-4340) [08811547] 1730, **1105**

CANADIAN JOURNAL OF ELECTRICAL AND COMPUTER ENGINEERING (CN/0840-8688) [18830717] 2038, **1227**

●CANADIAN JOURNAL OF EXPERIMENTAL PSYCHOLOGY (CN/1196-1961) [27872989] **4579**

CANADIAN JOURNAL OF FAMILY LAW (CN/0704-1225) [03858060] **3120**

CANADIAN JOURNAL OF FISHERIES AND AQUATIC SCIENCES (CN/0706-652X) [05974034] **2298**

CANADIAN JOURNAL OF FOREST RESEARCH (CN/0045-5067) [02248722] **2377**

CANADIAN JOURNAL OF GASTROENTEROLOGY, THE (CN/0835-7900) [18349849] **3743**

CANADIAN JOURNAL OF GERIATRICS, THE (CN/0845-2970) [18318015] **3750**

CANADIAN JOURNAL OF HERBALISM (CN/0848-9629) [21530544] **2412**

CANADIAN JOURNAL OF HIGHER EDUCATION (1975) (CN/0316-1218) [02442199] **1814**

CANADIAN JOURNAL OF HISTORY (CN/0008-4107) [01553144] **2613**

CANADIAN JOURNAL OF HISTORY OF SPORT (CN/0712-9815) [07616520] 1855, **4889**

CANADIAN JOURNAL OF HOSPITAL PHARMACY (CN/0008-4123) [17311890] **4295**

●CANADIAN JOURNAL OF HUMAN SEXUALITY, THE (CN/1188-4517) [27193661] **5187**

CANADIAN JOURNAL OF INFECTION CONTROL : THE OFFICIAL JOURNAL OF THE COMMUNITY & HOSPITAL INFECTION CONTROL ASSOCIATION-CANADA, THE (CN/1183-5702) [24845132] **4770**

CANADIAN JOURNAL OF INFECTIOUS DISEASES, THE (CN/1180-2332) [22426092] **3712**

●CANADIAN JOURNAL OF INFORMATION AND LIBRARY SCIENCE, THE (CN/1195-096X) [28082254] **3199**

CANADIAN JOURNAL OF INFORMATION SCIENCE (CN/0380-9218) [03219811] **3199**

CANADIAN JOURNAL OF INFORMATION SCIENCE *See* CANADIAN JOURNAL OF INFORMATION AND LIBRARY SCIENCE, THE **3199**

CANADIAN JOURNAL OF INSURANCE LAW (CN/0822-109X) [10759700] 2877, 2948

CANADIAN JOURNAL OF IRISH STUDIES, THE (CN/0703-1459) [03781898] 3372

CANADIAN JOURNAL OF ITALIAN STUDIES (CN/0705-3002) [03722912] 3372

CANADIAN JOURNAL OF LATIN AMERICAN AND CARIBBEAN STUDIES (CN/0826-3663) [11930339] 2726

CANADIAN JOURNAL OF LAW AND JURISPRUDENCE, THE (CN/0841-8209) [17969162] 2948

CANADIAN JOURNAL OF LAW AND SOCIETY (CN/0829-3201) [14162899] 2948

CANADIAN JOURNAL OF LIFE INSURANCE (CN/0706-5582) [04631853] 2877

CANADIAN JOURNAL OF LINGUISTICS (CN/0008-4131) [01553146] 3272

CANADIAN JOURNAL OF MARKETING RESEARCH (CN/0829-4836) [15372816] 922

CANADIAN JOURNAL OF MATHEMATICS (CN/0008-414X) [01553147] 3499

CANADIAN JOURNAL OF MEDICAL RADIATION TECHNOLOGY (CN/0820-5930) [15623105] 3939

CANADIAN JOURNAL OF MEDICAL TECHNOLOGY (CN/0008-4158) [01779391] 3562

CANADIAN JOURNAL OF MEDICAL TECHNOLOGY (ED. FRANCAISE) (CN/0828-7643) [16860997] 3562

CANADIAN JOURNAL OF MICROBIOLOGY (CN/0008-4166) [01553149] 560

CANADIAN JOURNAL OF NATIVE EDUCATION (CN/0710-1481) [08185769] 2258, 1730

CANADIAN JOURNAL OF NATIVE STUDIES, THE (CN/0715-3244) [08137717] 2726

CANADIAN JOURNAL OF NETHERLANDIC STUDIES (CN/0225-0500) [06960378] 2683

CANADIAN JOURNAL OF NEUROLOGICAL SCIENCES (CN/0317-1671) [01793789] 3829

CANADIAN JOURNAL OF NURSING ADMINISTRATION (CN/0838-2948) [18921360] 3852

CANADIAN JOURNAL OF NURSING RESEARCH, THE (CN/0844-5621) [19034331] 3852

CANADIAN JOURNAL OF OB/GYN & WOMEN'S HEALTH CARE, THE (CN/1183-2517) [26497800] 3758

CANADIAN JOURNAL OF OCCUPATIONAL THERAPY (1939) (CN/0008-4174) [01861310] 3750, 3922

CANADIAN JOURNAL OF ONCOLOGY, THE (CN/1183-2509) [25314015] 3810

CANADIAN JOURNAL OF OPHTHALMOLOGY (CN/0008-4182) [01553150] 3873

CANADIAN JOURNAL OF OPTOMETRY (CN/0045-5075) [01821244] 4215

CANADIAN JOURNAL OF PEDIATRICS, THE (CN/0843-4263) [20293910] 3901

CANADIAN JOURNAL OF PHILOSOPHY (CN/0045-5091) [01553152] 4343

CANADIAN JOURNAL OF PHYSICS (CN/0008-4204) [01553153] 4399

CANADIAN JOURNAL OF PHYSIOLOGY AND PHARMACOLOGY (CN/0008-4212) [01553154] 4295, 579

CANADIAN JOURNAL OF PLANT PATHOLOGY (CN/0706-0661) [05339407] 505

CANADIAN JOURNAL OF PLANT SCIENCE (CN/0008-4220) [01553155] 2412, 505

CANADIAN JOURNAL OF POLITICAL SCIENCE (CN/0008-4239) [01553156] 4467

CANADIAN JOURNAL OF PROGRAM EVALUATION, THE (CN/0834-1516) [14929567] 4636

CANADIAN JOURNAL OF PSYCHIATRY (CN/0706-7437) [04678455] 3923

CANADIAN JOURNAL OF PSYCHOLOGY See CANADIAN JOURNAL OF EXPERIMENTAL PSYCHOLOGY 4579

CANADIAN JOURNAL OF PSYCHOLOGY (CN/0008-4255) [01553157] 4579

CANADIAN JOURNAL OF PUBLIC HEALTH (US/0008-4263) [06733573] 4770

CANADIAN JOURNAL OF PUBLIC HEALTH (CN/0008-4263) [01553158] 4770

CANADIAN JOURNAL OF QUALITY IN HEALTH CARE, THE (CN/1185-9814) [25796500] 4770

CANADIAN JOURNAL OF REGIONAL SCIENCE, THE (CN/0705-4580) [04589210] 2817

CANADIAN JOURNAL OF REHABILITATION (CN/0828-0827) [17511968] 4379

CANADIAN JOURNAL OF REMOTE SENSING (CN/0703-8992) [02167038] 16

CANADIAN JOURNAL OF RESEARCH IN EARLY CHILDHOOD EDUCATION, THE (CN/0827-0899) [13324253] 1803

CANADIAN JOURNAL OF SCHOOL PSYCHOLOGY (CN/0829-5735) [13453647] 4579, 1730

CANADIAN JOURNAL OF SOCIOLOGY (CN/0318-6431) [02248412] 5241

CANADIAN JOURNAL OF SOIL SCIENCE (US/0008-4271) [17240842] 2212, 1371

CANADIAN JOURNAL OF SOIL SCIENCE (CN/0008-4271) [01553166] 166

CANADIAN JOURNAL OF SPECIAL EDUCATION (CN/0827-3391) [13448571] 1876

CANADIAN JOURNAL OF SPORT SCIENCES (US/0833-1235) [15743331] 3953

CANADIAN JOURNAL OF STATISTICS, THE (CN/0319-5724) [01880906] 5325

CANADIAN JOURNAL OF SURGERY (CN/0008-428X) [01553168] 3961

CANADIAN JOURNAL OF UNIVERSITY CONTINUING EDUCATION (CN/0318-9090) [06017055] 1800

●CANADIAN JOURNAL OF URBAN RESEARCH (CN/1188-3774) [26844235] 2817

CANADIAN JOURNAL OF VETERINARY RESEARCH (CN/0830-9000) [13561247] 5507

CANADIAN JOURNAL OF WOMEN AND THE LAW (CN/0832-8781) [13902155] 5552, 2948

CANADIAN JOURNAL OF ZOOLOGY (CN/0008-4301) [02248676] 5580

CANADIAN JOURNAL ON AGING (CN/0714-9808) [09586298] 3750

CANADIAN KEY BUSINESS DIRECTORY (CN/0315-0879) [01798454] 655

CANADIAN L P & TAPE CATALOGUE, THE (CN/0381-9507) [02641714] 5316

CANADIAN LABOUR ARBITRATION SUMMARIES (CN/0831-7348) [15609116] 3145

CANADIAN LABOUR CONGRESS See MEMORANDUM TO THE GOVERNMENT OF CANADA BY THE CANADIAN LABOUR CONGRESS 1690

CANADIAN LABOUR CONGRESS. CONSTITUTIONAL CONVENTION See PROCEEDINGS - CANADIAN LABOUR CONGRESS, CONSTITUTIONAL CONVENTION 1703

CANADIAN LABOUR FORCE DEVELOPMENT BOARD See REPORT ON THE BUDGET FOR THE DEVELOPMENT USES OF UNEMPLOYMENT INSURANCE 5305

CANADIAN LABOUR FORCE DEVELOPMENT BOARD See REPORT ON THE ... BUDGET FOR THE DEVELOPMENTAL USES OF UNEMPLOYMENT INSURANCE 1707

CANADIAN LABOUR RELATIONS BOARDS REPORTS (CN/0317-0535) [02247649] 3145

CANADIAN LACEMAKER GAZETTE (CN/0824-1856) [11816202] 5183

CANADIAN LAW INFORMATION COUNCIL See C L I C 'S LEGAL MATERIALS LETTER 2945

CANADIAN LAW LIBRARIES (CN/1180-176X) [22122265] 3200, 2948

CANADIAN LAW LIST (1951) (CN/0084-8573) [02247906] 3139

CANADIAN LAW SYMPOSIA INDEX (CN) 3079

CANADIAN LAWYER (CN/0703-2129) [03715322] 2948

CANADIAN LEGAL & LEGISLATIVE BENEFITS REPORTER (US/0740-1043) [09878825] 3145

CANADIAN LEGAL FAX DIRECTORY (CN/0843-7084) [20493820] 3140

CANADIAN LEGAL LITERATURE (CN/0832-9257) [23249681] 2948, 3079

CANADIAN LEGAL SERVICES DIRECTORY (CN/1184-7190) [24266843] 2948

CANADIAN LEGISLATURES (CN/0715-7118) [09475999] 4636

CANADIAN LIBRARY ASSOCIATION See PROGRAM - CANADIAN LIBRARY ASSOCIATION, CONFERENCE 3242

CANADIAN LIBRARY ASSOCIATION See DIRECTORY OF MEMBERS / CANADIAN LIBRARY ASSOCIATION 3207

CANADIAN LIBRARY JOURNAL (CN/0008-4352) [01553177] 3200

CANADIAN LIFE AND HEALTH INSURANCE ASSOCIATION See DIRECTORY - CANADIAN LIFE AND HEALTH INSURANCE ASSOCIATION 2878

CANADIAN LIFE AND HEALTH INSURANCE FACTS (CN/0836-4001) [15002286] 2877

CANADIAN LINGUISTIC ASSOCIATION See BULLETIN / ASSOCIATION CANADIENNE DE LINGUISTIQUE 3270

CANADIAN LINK CEASED. (CN/1182-722X) [23238124] 2258

CANADIAN LITERARY PERIODICALS INDEX (CN) 3372, 4821

CANADIAN LITERATURE (CN/0008-4360) [01553179] 3372

CANADIAN LIVING (CN/0382-4624) [02788432] 5552

CANADIAN LOCAL HISTORIES TO 1950: A BIBLIOGRAPHY (CN/0068-9165) [02922265] 2635

CANADIAN LOCATIONS OF JOURNALS INDEXED FOR MEDLINE (CN/0707-7629) [05072026] 3200

CANADIAN LODGING OUTLOOK (CN/1185-5738) [24860990] 2804

CANADIAN LOSS PREVENTION (CN/0228-8958) [07817255] 863

CANADIAN LOYALISTS' ASSOCIATION See OTTAWA NEWSLETTER 5300

CANADIAN MACHINERY AND METALWORKING (CN/0008-4379) [01792622] 2111

CANADIAN MAGAZINE INDEX (CN/0829-8777) [14879889] 2530, 2496

CANADIAN MAGAZINE INDEX (TORONTO, ONT.) See CANADIAN INDEX (TORONTO) 5781

CANADIAN MANAGEMENT CENTRE PRESENTS MANAGEMENT DEVELOPMENT PROGRAMMES (CN/0709-5384) [05528825] 863

CANADIAN MANAGEMENT CENTRE (TORONTO, ONT.) See CANADIAN MANAGEMENT CENTRE PRESENTS MANAGEMENT DEVELOPMENT PROGRAMMES 863

CANADIAN MANAGER (CN/0045-5156) [01887924] 863

CANADIAN MANUFACTURER (1908) CEASED. (CN/0382-8069) [02353453] 3476

CANADIAN MANUSCRIPT REPORT OF FISHERIES AND AQUATIC SCIENCES (CN/0706-6473) [09399082] 2298

CANADIAN MAPLE LEAF BUSINESS REPORT, THE See CANADIAN MAPLE LEAF REPORT, THE 1468

●CANADIAN MAPLE LEAF REPORT, THE (CN/1187-919X) [26497768] 1468

CANADIAN MARATHON ANNUAL (CN/0709-0269) [05258067] 2596, 4889

CANADIAN MARITIME INDUSTRIES ASSOCIATION. TECHNICAL CONFERENCE See PAPERS PRESENTED TO THE ... ANNUAL TECHNICAL CONFERENCE / CANADIAN MARITIME INDUSTRIES ASSOCIATION 5454

●CANADIAN MARKET PULP (CN/1193-2988) [26715164] 4232

CANADIAN MARKET PULP STATISTICS (CN/0836-6756) [15567046] 4232

CANADIAN MARKETS (1986) (CN/0832-2503) [14523822] 922, 727

CANADIAN MASTER TAX GUIDE (CN/0316-1331) [02247869] 4716

CANADIAN MATHEMATICAL BULLETIN (CN/0008-4395) [01553183] 3499

CANADIAN MATHEMATICAL SOCIETY See CONFERENCE PROCEEDINGS / CANADIAN MATHEMATICAL SOCIETY 3502

CANADIAN MATHEMATICAL SOCIETY. NOTES See CMS NOTES 3500

CANADIAN MEDIA DIRECTORS COUNCIL MEDIA DIGEST (CN/0829-1888) [02272457] 5194

CANADIAN MEDIA LIST, THE (CN/0849-2883) [22934566] 1105

CANADIAN MEDICAL AND BIOLOGICAL ENGINEERING SOCIETY See NEWSLETTER - CANADIAN MEDICAL AND BIOLOGICAL ENGINEERING SOCIETY 3695

CANADIAN MEDICAL ASSOCIATION See BULLETIN - CANADIAN MEDICAL ASSOCIATION 3559

... CANADIAN MEDICAL DEVICE DIRECTORY, THE (CN/0838-9845) [17160779] 3562

CANADIAN MEDICAL DIRECTORY (CN/0068-9203) [02441979] 3913

CANADIAN MEDICAL EDUCATION STATISTICS (CN/0225-9451) [06141451] 1730, 3562, 3655

CANADIAN MEDICAL LIVES (CN) [21591696] 3562

CANADIAN MEETING PLANNER (CN/0822-8027) [10436245] 655

CANADIAN MERCHANDISE MART (CN/0068-9238) [03436705] 1082

CANADIAN — Alphabetical Title Index

CANADIAN METALLURGICAL QUARTERLY (US/0008-4433) [17314390] **3999**

CANADIAN METALLURGICAL QUARTERLY (CN/0008-4433) [02583332] **3999**

CANADIAN METEOROLOGICAL AND OCEANOGRAPHIC SOCIETY. CONGRESS *See* PROGRAMME WITH ABSTRACTS - CANADIAN METEOROLOGICAL AND OCEANOGRAPHIC SOCIETY **1455**

●CANADIAN MILITARY HISTORY (CN/1195-8472) [29494799] **4038**

CANADIAN MILITARY JOURNAL *CEASED.* (CN/0008-4468) [02328232] **4038**

CANADIAN MILL PRODUCT NEWS (CN/1186-2033) [24368311] **4233**

CANADIAN MINERAL INDUSTRY MONTHLY REPORT *See* MINERAL INDUSTRY QUARTERLY REPORT **1441**

CANADIAN MINERAL PROCESSORS *See* PROCEEDINGS OF THE ANNUAL MEETING OF THE CANADIAN MINERAL PROCESSORS **4016**

CANADIAN MINERALOGIST, THE (CN/0008-4476) [01553191] **1438**

CANADIAN MINERALS YEARBOOK (CN/0068-9270) [03085132] 2136, **1438**

CANADIAN MINES HANDBOOK (CN/0068-9289) [01553193] **2136**

CANADIAN MINES, PERSPECTIVE (CN/0823-5716) [10526726] **2136**

CANADIAN MINING JOURNAL (CN/0008-4492) [01553195] **2136**

CANADIAN MINING LIFE & EXPLORATION NEWS (CN/1184-9738) [24690830] **2136**

CANADIAN MINING SOURCEBOOK (CN) **2136**

CANADIAN MODERN LANGUAGE REVIEW, THE (CN/0008-4506) [01080724] **3272**

CANADIAN MONEYSAVER (CN/0713-3286) [09067801] **894**

CANADIAN MOONLIGHTER'S DIGEST (CN/0826-4899) [11734455] **1658**

CANADIAN MOTORCYCLE RIDER (CN/0710-0590) [08340642] **4081**

CANADIAN MOTORSPORT ANNUAL..., THE (CN/0711-3064) [08465875] **5408**

●CANADIAN MULTI MEDIA MAGAZINE, THE (CN/1188-5556) [26714637] **1105**

CANADIAN MULTICULTURAL SCENE (CN/0707-7300) [04747035] **2258**

CANADIAN MULTICULTURALISM COUNCIL *See* REPORT OF THE CANADIAN MULTICULTURALISM COUNCIL **2757**

CANADIAN MUSEUM OF NATURE. LIBRARY SERVICES *See* ACQUISITIONS LIST - CANADIAN MUSEUM OF NATURE. LIBRARY SERVICES **3187**

CANADIAN MUSIC EDUCATOR, THE (CN/0008-4549) [01884702] 1730, **4107**

CANADIAN MUSIC THERAPY JOURNAL (CN/0319-6283) [02442831] 3562, **4107**

CANADIAN MUSICAL HERITAGE, THE (CN) [10502164] **4107**

CANADIAN MUSICIAN (CN/0708-9635) [05133704] **4107**

CANADIAN MUSLIM, THE (CN/0707-2945) [04653864] **5042**

CANADIAN NATIONAL *See* ANNUAL REPORT / CANADIAN NATIONAL **5376**

CANADIAN NATIONAL *See* RAPPORT ANNUEL / CANADIAN NATIONAL **5390**

CANADIAN NATIONAL LIVE STOCK RECORDS *See* CANADIAN ARABIAN HORSE STUD BOOK **2797**

CANADIAN NATIONAL RAILWAYS *See* RAPPORT ANNUEL / CANADIAN NATIONAL **5390**

CANADIAN NATIVE LAW REPORTER (CN/0225-2279) [05367123] **2948**

CANADIAN NATURAL GAS FOCUS (CN/0847-0316) [21205834] **4253**

●CANADIAN NATURAL GAS MARKET REPORT (CN/1196-0906) [28558057] **4253**

CANADIAN NETWORK PAPERS (CN/0226-8760) [07954313] **3200**

CANADIAN NEWS FACTS (CN/0008-4565) [01553201] **2530**

CANADIAN NEWS INDEX TORONTO (CN/0225-7459) [06210577] **5781**

CANADIAN NEWS INDEX (TORONTO) (CN/0225-7459) [08079032] 5814, **5781**

CANADIAN NEWSLETTER FOR OPEN GOVERNMENT, THE (CN/0703-1378) [03660538] **4636**

CANADIAN NEWSPAPER CIRCULATION FACTBOOK (CN/1043-7495) [19545801] **5781**

CANADIAN NUCLEAR ASSOCIATION. INTERNATIONAL CONFERENCE *See* ANNUAL INTERNATIONAL CONFERENCE / CANADIAN NUCLEAR ASSOCIATION **2154**

CANADIAN NUCLEAR SOCIETY. CONFERENCE *See* ANNUAL CONFERENCE. PROCEEDINGS - CANADIAN NUCLEAR SOCIETY **2154**

CANADIAN NUCLEAR SOCIETY. CONFERENCE *See* ANNUAL CONFERENCE. CONFERENCE SUMMARIES - CANADIAN NUCLEAR SOCIETY **2153**

CANADIAN NUMISMATIC ASSOCIATION *See* ANNUAL CONVENTION - CANADIAN NUMISMATIC ASSOCIATION **2779**

CANADIAN NUMISMATIC JOURNAL, THE (CN/0008-4573) [01873742] **2780**

CANADIAN NURSE (1924) (CN/0008-4581) [01553202] **3852**

CANADIAN NURSING HOME (CN/0847-5520) [24690788] **3778**

CANADIAN NURSING MANAGEMENT (CN) **3852**

CANADIAN OBITUARY RECORD (CN/0846-0019) [20185845] **2406**

CANADIAN OCCUPATIONAL HEALTH & SAFETY NEWS (CN/0709-5252) [05528890] **2860**

CANADIAN OCCUPATIONAL SAFETY (CN/0008-4611) [01873920] **2860**

CANADIAN OCCUPATIONAL SAFETY AND HEALTH LAW MONTHLY REPORT (CN/0825-608X) [11734668] 2860, **2948**

CANADIAN OFFICIAL, THE (CN/1183-4269) [25423800] **4889**

CANADIAN OIL AND GAS (CN/0384-8965) [01771107] **4253**

CANADIAN OIL & GAS HANDBOOK *CEASED.* (CN/0710-622X) [07078135] **4253**

CANADIAN OIL INDUSTRY MERGER AND ACQUISITION REPORT (CN/1181-8077) [24368364] **4253**

CANADIAN OIL REGISTER (CN/0068-9394) [02247974] **4253**

CANADIAN ONCOLOGY NURSING JOURNAL (CN/1181-912X) [24267070] 3810, **3853**

CANADIAN ONCOLOGY NURSING JOURNAL (CN/1181-912X) [24267067] 3810, **3853**

CANADIAN OPERA COMPANY (CN/0710-2666) [08260399] **4107**

CANADIAN OPERA COMPANY NEWS (1986) (CN/0820-4896) [16850398] **4107**

CANADIAN OPERATING ROOM NURSING JOURNAL (CN/0712-6778) [09863921] **3853**

CANADIAN OPERATIONAL RESEARCH SOCIETY *See* C O R S BULLETIN **1236**

CANADIAN ORAL HISTORY ASSOCIATION *See* JOURNAL - CANADIAN ORAL HISTORY ASSOCIATION **2740**

CANADIAN ORCHESTRAS AND YOUTH ORCHESTRAS DIRECTORY (CN/1189-9956) [30673783] **4107**

CANADIAN ORCHID JOURNAL, THE (CN/0824-1554) [11183747] **2412**

CANADIAN ORNAMENTAL PHEASANT AND GAME BIRD ASSOCIATION *See* MAGAZINE - CANADIAN ORNAMENTAL PHEASANT AND GAME BIRD ASSOCIATION **2774**

CANADIAN ORTHO-PROS, THE (CN/0714-878X) [09099760] **3881**

CANADIAN ORTHODOX MISSIONARY, THE (US/0893-7796) [15649115] **5039**

CANADIAN ORTHOPAEDIC NURSES' ASSOCIATION *See* CONA JOURNAL **3854**

CANADIAN OUTBOARD MOTOR DEALERS BLUE BOOK (CN/1183-5990) [24623650] **592**

CANADIAN OUTLOOK, EXECUTIVE SUMMARY (CN/0832-0500) [15134104] **1590**

CANADIAN PACKAGING (CN/0008-4654) [01882984] **4218**

CANADIAN PACKAGING. BUYERS GUIDE (CN) [02443248] **4218**

CANADIAN PALLIATIVE CARE DIRECTORY, THE (CN/0715-9471) [10334981] **3778**

CANADIAN PAPER ANALYST (CN/0705-6710) [04079996] **4233**

●CANADIAN PAPERMAKER (CN/1191-887X) [26926275] **4233**

CANADIAN PAPERS IN RURAL HISTORY (CN) [04865795] **72**

CANADIAN PARKS SERVICE *See* NORTHERN YUKON NATIONAL PARK **4707**

CANADIAN PARLIAMENTARY GUIDE (CN/0315-6168) [02248417] **4636**

CANADIAN PARLIAMENTARY HANDBOOK (CN/0714-8143) [09086712] **4467**

CANADIAN PARLIAMENTARY REVIEW (CN/0229-2548) [07869888] **4636**

CANADIAN PATENT (CN/1181-3969) [111813369] **1302**

CANADIAN PATENT REPORTER (CN/0008-4689) [01553206] **1302**

CANADIAN PAYMENTS ASSOCIATION *See* DIRECTORY - CANADIAN PAYMENTS ASSOCIATION **787**

CANADIAN PC MARKET, THE *See* TRENDS IN THE CANADIAN PC MARKET **1273**

CANADIAN PEACE OFFICER (CN/0318-806X) [02443067] **3159**

CANADIAN PEACE REPORT (CN/0838-5041) [20377879] **4517**

CANADIAN PERIODICAL INDEX (1964) (CN/0008-4719) [02336854] **412**

CANADIAN PEST MANAGEMENT SOCIETY. MEETING *See* PROCEEDINGS OF THE ANNUAL MEETING - CANADIAN PEST MANAGEMENT SOCIETY **4247**

CANADIAN PETROLEUM TAX JOURNAL (CN/0838-0961) [18603646] **4716**

CANADIAN PETROLEUM TAX SOCIETY *See* MEMBERSHIP ROSTER / CANADIAN PETROLEUM TAX SOCIETY **4737**

CANADIAN PHILATELIC SOCIETY *See* C P S NEWS LETTER (TORONTO) **2784**

CANADIAN PHILATELIST (CN/0045-5253) [01891482] **2784**

CANADIAN PHILOSOPHICAL REVIEWS (CN/0228-491X) [07872835] **4343**

CANADIAN PHOTOGRAPHY. BUYING GUIDE (CN) [02443016] **4368**

CANADIAN PLAINS BULLETIN (CN/0316-0343) [02441551] 2162, **2726**

CANADIAN PLAINS PROCEEDINGS (CN/0317-6401) [03886290] 72, **2726**

CANADIAN PLAINS STUDIES (CN) [03936516] 5194, **2726**

CANADIAN PLANT DISEASE SURVEY (CN/0008-476X) [02587741] 506, **72**

CANADIAN PLASTICS (CN/0008-4778) [01897900] **4454**

CANADIAN PLASTICS AUTOMOTIVE DIRECTORY (CN/0843-2392) [20286568] 4454, **5408**

CANADIAN PLASTICS DIRECTORY & BUYER'S GUIDE (CN/0068-9459) [02247287] **4454**

CANADIAN PLASTICS STATISTICAL YEAR BOOK (CN/0828-5810) [10222371] 4454, **4461**

CANADIAN PLUMBING CODE (CN/0700-1223) [07142331] **2604**

CANADIAN POCKETAX (ENGLISH EDITION) (CN/0382-7585) [02627656] **4716**

CANADIAN PODIATRY ASSOCIATION NEWSLETTER *CEASED.* (CN/0820-8212) [09457260] **3917**

CANADIAN PODIUM, THE (CN/0226-1979) [06299516] **1550**

CANADIAN POETRY ANNUAL, THE (CN/0383-1574) [02729648] **3461**

CANADIAN POETRY (LONDON, ONT.) (CN/0704-5646) [05788366] **3461**

CANADIAN POLICE CHIEF NEWSLETTER (CN/0713-4517) [08349979] **3159**

CANADIAN POLICE COLLEGE *See* CANADIAN POLICE COLLEGE JOURNAL **3159**

CANADIAN POLICE COLLEGE JOURNAL *CEASED.* (CN/0705-8810) [04433336] **3159**

CANADIAN POLISH CONGRESS. MEETING *See* KONGRES POLONII KANADYJSKIEJ **2743**

CANADIAN POOL & PATIO CONSUMERS HANDBOOK (CN/0711-6470) [08562643] **4849**

CANADIAN PORTS AND SEAWAY DIRECTORY *CEASED.* (CN/0068-9467) [02585303] **5448**

CANADIAN POSTMASTERS AND ASSISTANTS ASSOCIATION *See* BULLETIN - C P A A C M P A **1144**

CANADIAN POWER ILLUSTRATED (CN/0847-1061) [21485740] **592**

CANADIAN PRINT & PORTFOLIO *SUSPENDED.* (CN/0824-6904) [11073598] **377**

CANADIAN PRINTER (CN/0849-0767) [22185792] **4564**

CANADIAN PROCESS EQUIPMENT & CONTROL NEWS (CN/0318-0859) [01903149] 655, **2101**

CANADIAN PROFESSIONAL REAL ESTATE DIRECTORY FOR THE PROVINCE OF BRITISH COLUMBIA (CN/0709-0757) [05362567] **4835**

CANADIAN PROPERTY AND CASUALTY INSURANCE SERVICE : QUARTERLY REPORT (CN) [06687974] **2877**

Alphabetical Title Index — CANADIAN

CANADIAN PSYCHIATRIC ASSOCIATION See MEMBERSHIP DIRECTORY - CANADIAN PSYCHIATRIC ASSOCIATION. REPERTOIRE DES MEMBRES - ASSOCIATION DES PSYCHIATRES DU CANADA **3930**

CANADIAN PSYCHOLOGICAL ASSOCIATION See DIRECTORY OF THE CANADIAN PSYCHOLOGICAL ASSOCIATION **4585**

CANADIAN PSYCHOLOGY (CN/0708-5591) [06518844] **4579**

CANADIAN PUBLIC ADMINISTRATION (CN/0008-4840) [01553218] **4636**

CANADIAN PUBLIC HEALTH ASSOCIATION See PROCEEDINGS OF THE ANNUAL MEETING OF THE CANADIAN PUBLIC HEALTH ASSOCIATION **4796**

CANADIAN PUBLIC HEALTH ASSOCIATION See C P H A HEALTH DIGEST **4770**

CANADIAN PUBLIC PERSONNEL MANAGEMENT ASSOCIATION. OTTAWA-HULL CHAPTER See PERSONNEL (OTTAWA) **4673**

CANADIAN PUBLIC POLICY (CN/0317-0861) [02247694] **4636**, **1468**

CANADIAN PUBLIC RELATIONS SOCIETY See CPRS CROSS-REFERENCE LIST **758**

CANADIAN PUBLIC SERVICE WORKER'S BULLETIN (CN/0382-8700) [03230391] **1658**

CANADIAN PUBLISHERS' DIRECTORY (CN/0008-4859) [02510184] **4813**

CANADIAN PULP AND PAPER ASSOCIATION See STATISTICAL BULLETIN - CANADIAN PULP AND PAPER ASSOCIATION **4239**

CANADIAN PULP AND PAPER ASSOCIATION See ANNUAL NEWSPRINT SUPPLEMENT - CANADIAN PULP AND PAPER ASSOCIATION **4232**

CANADIAN PULP AND PAPER ASSOCIATION See CANADIAN PULP AND PAPER ASSOCIATION. NEWSPRINT DATA **4233**

CANADIAN PULP AND PAPER ASSOCIATION See REFERENCE TABLES - CANADIAN PULP AND PAPER ASSOCIATION **4238**

CANADIAN PULP AND PAPER ASSOCIATION. NEWSPRINT DATA (CN/0068-9491) [01792093] **4564**, **4233**

CANADIAN PULP AND PAPER ASSOCIATION. TECHNICAL SECTION See TECHNICAL SECTION PROCEEDINGS (MONTREAL) **4239**

CANADIAN PULP AND PAPER ASSOCIATION. TECHNICAL SECTION. MEETING See PREPRINTS A / TECHNICAL SECTION, CANADIAN PULP AND PAPER ASSOCIATION **4237**

CANADIAN PULP AND PAPER ASSOCIATION. TECHNICAL SECTION. MEETING See PREPRINTS B / TECHNICAL SECTION, CANADIAN PULP AND PAPER ASSOCIATION **4237**

CANADIAN PULP AND PAPER ASSOCIATION. WOODLANDS SECTION See WOODLANDS SECTION NEWS BULLETIN **4240**

CANADIAN PULP AND PAPER CAPACITY (CN/0823-2873) [10057223] **4233**

CANADIAN QUAKER HISTORY JOURNAL CEASED. (CN/1180-968X) [23295913] 2613, **2258**

CANADIAN QUARTERLY ECONOMIC REVIEW (CN/0715-4542) [09204487] **1550**

CANADIAN QUILL (CN/0714-5721) [09071186] **3272**

CANADIAN RACING PIGEON UNION See YEAR BOOK - CANADIAN RACING PIGEON UNION **4931**

CANADIAN RADIO-TELEVISION AND TELECOMMUNICATIONS COMMISSION See TETE-A-TETE (OTTAWA. 1991) **1141**

CANADIAN RAIL (CN/0008-4875) [01913063] **5430**

CANADIAN RAILWAY CLUB See CANADIAN RAILWAY CLUB NEWS **5430**

CANADIAN RAILWAY CLUB NEWS (CN/0226-157X) [06468530] **5430**

CANADIAN RAILWAY MODELLER (CN/0849-2964) [22928750] **5430**

CANADIAN RATIOS FOR PROFIT PLANNING (CN/0317-2074) [02247879] **1600**

CANADIAN REAL ESTATE (1983) See CANADIAN REALTOR NEWS **4835**

CANADIAN REAL ESTATE (DON MILLS. 1983) (CN/0823-8197) [11847706] **4835**

●CANADIAN REALTOR NEWS (CN/1193-8021) [27649058] **4835**

CANADIAN REALTY NEWS (EDITION FRANCAISE) (CN/0381-7687) [03213231] **4835**

CANADIAN RECORD CATALOGUE CEASED. (CN/0714-8070) [09074981] **4107**

CANADIAN RECORD, THE (US) [14062638] **5747**

CANADIAN RECREATIONAL VEHICLE GUIDE (CN/0710-4405) [08469664] **5379**

CANADIAN RED BOOK (CN/0045-527X) [01906030] **5408**

CANADIAN RED CROSS SOCIETY. NEW BRUNSWICK DIVISION See REPORT - CANADIAN RED CROSS SOCIETY. NEW BRUNSWICK DIVISION **5305**

CANADIAN REFERENCE DIRECTORY ON BUSINESS PLANNING AND FUNDING (CN) **655**

CANADIAN REHABILITATION COUNCIL FOR THE DISABLED See EMPLOYMENT BULLETIN (TORONTO. 1971) **1666**

CANADIAN REINER, THE (CN/0820-6813) [10156846] **2798**

CANADIAN RELIGIOUS CONFERENCE See BULLETIN - CANADIAN RELIGIOUS CONFERENCE **4940**

CANADIAN RELIGIOUS CONFERENCE See DIRECTORY - CANADIAN RELIGIOUS CONFERENCE **4953**

CANADIAN RENTAL SERVICE (CN/0383-7920) [03230485] **1600**

CANADIAN REPRESENTIVES ABROAD AND REPRESENTATIVES OF OTHER COUNTRIES IN CANADA (CN) [02888782] **4517**

CANADIAN RESIDENTIAL HEATING SURVEY (1990) (CN/1184-177X) [23599045] **2604**

CANADIAN RESOUCRES REVIEW (CN/1196-1376) [31235258] **2377**

CANADIAN RESOURCES & PENNYMINES ANALYST (CN/1182-1590) [22378699] **894**

CANADIAN RETAILER (CN/0226-9864) [08071827] **952**

CANADIAN REVIEW OF AMERICAN STUDIES (CN/0007-7720) [01553229] **2530**

CANADIAN REVIEW OF ART EDUCATION, RESEARCH AND ISSUES (CN/0706-8107) [04433000] **346**

CANADIAN REVIEW OF COMPARATIVE LITERATURE (CN/0319-051X) [01727228] **3372**

CANADIAN REVIEW OF PHYSICAL ANTHROPOLOGY See CANADIAN ASSOCIATION OF PHYSICAL ANTHROPOLOGY NEWSLETTER **233**

CANADIAN REVIEW OF SOCIAL POLICY (1987) (CN/0836-303X) [16888292] **5276**

CANADIAN REVIEW OF SOCIOLOGY AND ANTHROPOLOGY, THE (CN/0008-4948) [01553230] **5241**, **233**

CANADIAN REVIEW OF STUDIES IN NATIONALISM (CN/0317-7904) [01798071] **5194**, 2613, **2635**

CANADIAN RIGHTS REPORTER. SECOND SERIES (CN/0715-4860) [24158311] 3092, **4505**

CANADIAN ROOFING CONTRACTORS' ASSOCIATION See DIRECTORY - CANADIAN ROOFING CONTRACTORS' ASSOCIATION **613**

CANADIAN ROSE ANNUAL (1983) (CN/0826-743X) [11830175] **2412**

CANADIAN ROSE ROOTS (CN/0824-6637) [10857610] **2441**

CANADIAN RULE BOOK FOR TACKLE FOOTBALL (CN/1185-9792) [25423684] **4889**

CANADIAN SAILINGS (CN/0821-5944) [09670534] **5448**

CANADIAN SAILOR (CN/0008-4972) [02356101] **5448**

CANADIAN SALES TAX REPORTS (AT) **4716**

CANADIAN SCENE (TORONTO. 1951) CEASED. (CN/0319-6577) [01913098] **2530**

CANADIAN SCHOOL EXECUTIVE (1982) (CN/0228-0914) [09692630] **1861**

CANADIAN SCIENCE (DOWNSVIEW, ONT.) CEASED. (CN/0712-4848) [09816281] **5092**

CANADIAN SCIENCE WRITER'S ASSOCIATION See NEWSLETTER - CANADIAN SCIENCE WRITER'S ASSOCIATION **2922**

CANADIAN SECURITIES COURSE, THE (CN/0317-9451) [02441944] **894**

CANADIAN SECURITIES INSTITUTE See CANADIAN SECURITIES COURSE, THE **894**

CANADIAN SECURITY (CN/0709-3403) [06270085] **5176**

CANADIAN SEED GROWERS' ASSOCIATION See ANNUAL REPORT AND MINUTES OF THE ANNUAL MEETING - CANADIAN SEED GROWERS' ASSOCIATION **162**

CANADIAN SEISMIC AGREEMENT (US) [08512647] **1403**

CANADIAN SELECT HOMES (CN) **2899**

CANADIAN SENIORITY (CN) **5178**

CANADIAN SERIALS DIRECTORY (CN/0000-0345) [01779647] **3200**

CANADIAN SHAREOWNER (CN/0836-0960) [17748446] **894**

CANADIAN SHIPBUILDING, OFFSHORE AND MARINE INDUSTRIES (CN/0836-5164) [17314027] **5448**

CANADIAN SHORT STORY INDEX (CN) 3372, **3458**

CANADIAN SLAVONIC PAPERS (CN/0008-5006) [01553234] **3272**

CANADIAN SOCCER ASSOCIATION See TECHNICAL MANUAL - CANADIAN SOCCER ASSOCIATION **4925**

CANADIAN SOCIAL SCIENCE DATA CATALOG (CN) [04551308] **5194**

CANADIAN SOCIAL STUDIES : THE HISTORY AND SOCIAL SCIENCE TEACHER (CN/1191-162X) [24987753] **1890**

CANADIAN SOCIAL TRENDS (CN/0831-5698) [15214636] **5241**

CANADIAN SOCIAL WORK REVIEW (CN/0820-909X) [10702357] **5276**

CANADIAN SOCIETY FOR ARCHAEOLOGY ABROAD See BULLETIN - CANADIAN SOCIETY FOR ARCHAEOLOGY ABROAD, THE **262**

CANADIAN SOCIETY FOR CHEMICAL ENGINEERING See MEMBERSHIP DIRECTORY / CANADIAN SOCIETY FOR CHEMICAL ENGINEERING **2015**

CANADIAN SOCIETY FOR CIVIL ENGINEERING. CONFERENCE See PROCEEDINGS - CANADIAN SOCIETY FOR CIVIL ENGINEERING **2029**

CANADIAN SOCIETY FOR COMPUTATIONAL STUDIES OF INTELLIGENCE. CONFERENCE See PROCEEDINGS OF THE ... BIENNIAL CONFERENCE OF THE CANADIAN SOCIETY FOR COMPUTATIONAL STUDIES OF INTELLIGENCE **1216**

CANADIAN SOCIETY FOR EIGHTEENTH-CENTURY STUDIES See MAN AND NATURE **2622**

CANADIAN SOCIETY FOR HORTICULTURAL SCIENCE. MEETING See PROCEEDINGS OF THE CANADIAN SOCIETY FOR HORTICULTURAL SCIENCE **2429**

CANADIAN SOCIETY FOR INDUSTRIAL SECURITY See MEMBERSHIP DIRECTORY / CANADIAN SOCIETY FOR INDUSTRIAL SECURITY **2865**

CANADIAN SOCIETY FOR MUSICAL TRADITIONS See FOLK MUSIC CATALOGUE **4118**

CANADIAN SOCIETY FOR RENAISSANCE STUDIES See DIRECTORY / CANADIAN SOCIETY FOR RENAISSANCE STUDIES **2685**

CANADIAN SOCIETY FOR THE STUDY OF EDUCATION See C S S E NEWS **1730**

CANADIAN SOCIETY OF AGRONOMY See C.S.A. NEWSLETTER - CANADIAN SOCIETY OF AGRONOMY (1983) **165**

CANADIAN SOCIETY OF ANIMAL SCIENCE See MEMBERSHIP DIRECTORY / THE CANADIAN SOCIETY OF ANIMAL SCIENCE **5516**

CANADIAN SOCIETY OF ANIMAL SCIENCE See CANADIAN SOCIETY OF ANIMAL SCIENCE. PROCEEDINGS OF THE ANNUAL MEETING OF THE GENERAL SOCIETY AND THE WESTERN BRANCH **5507**

CANADIAN SOCIETY OF ANIMAL SCIENCE. PROCEEDINGS OF THE ANNUAL MEETING OF THE GENERAL SOCIETY AND THE WESTERN BRANCH (CN/0318-1839) [01771164] **5507**

CANADIAN SOCIETY OF BIBLICAL STUDIES See BULLETIN - CANADIAN SOCIETY OF BIBLICAL STUDIES **5012**

CANADIAN SOCIETY OF BIOCHEMISTRY AND MOLECULAR BIOLOGY See BULLETIN OF THE CANADIAN SOCIETY OF BIOCHEMISTRY AND MOLECULAR BIOLOGY **484**

CANADIAN SOCIETY OF CHILDREN'S AUTHORS, ILLUSTRATORS AND PERFORMERS See CANSCAIP NEWS **1061**

CANADIAN SOCIETY OF CHURCH HISTORY See PAPERS OF THE CANADIAN SOCIETY OF CHURCH HISTORY **4985**

CANADIAN SOCIETY OF CLINICAL CHEMISTS See CSCC NEWS **973**

CANADIAN SOCIETY OF ENVIRONMENTAL BIOLOGISTS See NEWSLETTER - CANADIAN SOCIETY OF ENVIRONMENTAL BIOLOGISTS **2200**

CANADIAN SOCIETY OF FORENSIC SCIENCE See CANADIAN SOCIETY OF FORENSIC SCIENCE JOURNAL **3740**

CANADIAN SOCIETY OF FORENSIC SCIENCE JOURNAL (CN/0008-5030) [01915058] **3740**

CANADIAN
Alphabetical Title Index

CANADIAN SOCIETY OF LABORATORY TECHNOLOGISTS *See* ROSTER DE L'ACTL **3637**

CANADIAN SOCIETY OF LABORATORY TECHNOLOGISTS *See* BULLETIN - CANADIAN SOCIETY OF LABORATORY TECHNOLOGISTS **5090**

CANADIAN SOCIETY OF MICROBIOLOGISTS *See* NEWSLETTER - CANADIAN SOCIETY OF MICROBIOLOGISTS / BULLETIN DE NOUVELLES - SOCIETET CANADIENNE DES MICROBIOLOGISTES **568**

CANADIAN SOCIETY OF PAINTERS IN WATER COLOUR *See* ANNUAL EXHIBITION OF THE CANADIAN SOCIETY OF PAINTERS IN WATER COLOUR **336**

CANADIAN SOCIETY OF PETROLEUM GEOLOGISTS *See* REPRINT SERIES - CANADIAN SOCIETY OF PETROLEUM GEOLOGISTS **1395**

CANADIAN SOCIETY OF ZOOLOGISTS *See* BULLETIN - CANADIAN SOCIETY OF ZOOLOGISTS **5579**

CANADIAN SOCIETY OF ZOOLOGISTS *See* DIRECTORY / CANADIAN SOCIETY OF ZOOLOGISTS **5581**

CANADIAN SOLAR DIRECTORY (1983) (CN/0823-0226) [09816155] **1934**

CANADIAN SOURCES OF ENVIRONMENTAL INFORMATION (CN/0832-9176) [16530822] **2226**

CANADIAN SPECIAL PUBLICATION OF FISHERIES AND AQUATIC SCIENCES (CN/0706-6481) [08828310] **2299**

CANADIAN SPECTROSCOPIC NEWS (1972) (CN/0381-5447) [02171549] **4434**

CANADIAN SPEECH COMMUNICATION JOURNAL *CEASED.* (CN/0715-5999) [03107737] **1105**

CANADIAN SPEECHES, ISSUES OF THE DAY (CN/1191-0860) [26122728] **1105**

CANADIAN SPORTS AWARDS, ATHLETE OF THE MONTH (CN/0823-874X) [11431477] **4889**

CANADIAN SPORTSCARD COLLECTOR (CN/1185-1856) [24368609] **2772**

CANADIAN SPORTSMAN, THE (CN/0008-5073) [01936005] **2798**

CANADIAN STAGE PRESS *CEASED.* (CN/1184-2695) [24265649] **5362**

CANADIAN STAMP DEALERS' ASSOCIATION *See* DIRECTORY - CANADIAN STAMP DEALERS' ASSOCIATION **2785**

CANADIAN STAMP NEWS (CN/0702-3154) [03412309] **2784**

CANADIAN STANDARDS ASSOCIATION *See* LIST OF CERTIFIED HEALTH CARE PRODUCTS AND SERVICES **3605**

CANADIAN STANDARDS ASSOCIATION *See* LIST OF CERTIFIED PLUMBING PRODUCTS (1983) **2606**

CANADIAN STANDARDS ASSOCIATION *See* INFORMATION UPDATE - CANADIAN STANDARDS ASSOCIATION **1978**

CANADIAN STANDARDS ASSOCIATION *See* LIST OF CERTIFIED ELECTRICAL EQUIPMENT (1988) **2071**

CANADIAN STANDARDS ASSOCIATION *See* LIST OF CSA CERTIFIED ELEVATOR EQUIPMENT **2120**

CANADIAN STANDARDS ASSOCIATION *See* LIST OF CSA CERTIFIED COMFORT CONDITIONING EQUIPMENT **2606**

CANADIAN STANDARDS ASSOCIATION *See* LIST OF CSA CERTIFIED HEALTH CARE PRODUCTS AND SERVICES **3605**

CANADIAN STANDARDS ASSOCIATION. LIST OF CERTIFIED COMFORT CONDITIONING EQUIPMENT *See* LIST OF CSA CERTIFIED COMFORT CONDITIONING EQUIPMENT **2606**

CANADIAN STANDARDS ASSOCIATION. LIST OF CERTIFIED HEALTH CARE PRODUCTS AND SERVICES *See* LIST OF CSA CERTIFIED HEALTH CARE PRODUCTS AND SERVICES **3605**

CANADIAN STATISTICS INDEX *See* DIRECTORY OF STATISTICS IN CANADA **5326**

CANADIAN STEEL STOCKS (CN/1186-1029) [24266103] **894**

CANADIAN STRATEGIC FORECAST, THE (CN/0843-6940) [20957005] **4467**

CANADIAN STRATEGIC REPORT (US/0196-7886) [05901588] **4039**

CANADIAN STUDIES DIRECTORATE *See* INFORMATION AND APPLICATION GUIDE / CANADIAN STUDIES AND SPECIAL PROJECTS DIRECTORATE **2739**

CANADIAN STUDIES IN GERMAN LANGUAGE AND LITERATURE (SZ/0171-6859) [02215123] **3272, 3372**

CANADIAN STUDIES IN POPULATION (CN/0380-1489) [02443320] **4550**

CANADIAN SUICIDE RATIOS BY LOCAL AREAS AND BY URBAN CENTRES (CN) [01799154] **5276**

CANADIAN TALENT LIBRARY *See* BULLETIN - CANADIAN TALENT LIBRARY **3198**

CANADIAN TAX AND TRADE BRIEFS (US/0160-4708) [01481106] **4716**

CANADIAN TAX DIGEST (ANNUAL EDITION) (CN/0229-8031) [08070739] **4716**

CANADIAN TAX FOUNDATION *See* PROVINCIAL AND MUNICIPAL FINANCES **4742**

CANADIAN TAX FOUNDATION *See* REPORT OF PROCEEDINGS OF THE TAX CONFERENCE CONVENED BY THE CANADIAN TAX FOUNDATION **4745**

CANADIAN TAX JOURNAL (CN/0008-5111) [01553248] **740, 4716**

CANADIAN TAX NEWS (CN/0319-2431) [01904600] **4716, 2948**

CANADIAN TAX PAPERS (CN/0008-512X) [03258718] **4716**

CANADIAN TAX PLANNERS *See* CANADIAN TAX PLANNER'S NEWSLETTER **740**

CANADIAN TAX PLANNER'S NEWSLETTER (CN/0227-8375) [06702807] **740**

CANADIAN TAXPAYER (CN/0225-0608) [06136335] **4716**

CANADIAN TEACHERS' FEDERATION *See* INTERNATIONAL PROGRAMS, GENERAL REPORT / CANADIAN TEACHERS' FEDERATION AND ITS MEMBERS **1897**

CANADIAN TEACHERS' FEDERATION *See* CANADIAN TEACHERS' FEDERATION, ITS OBJECTIVES, ITS POLICY **1890**

CANADIAN TEACHERS' FEDERATION, ITS OBJECTIVES, ITS POLICY (CN/0229-4273) [07966333] **1890**

CANADIAN TECHNICAL ASPHALT ASSOCIATION. CONFERENCE *See* PROCEEDINGS OF THE ANNUAL CONFERENCE OF CANADIAN TECHNICAL ASPHALT ASSOCIATION **2029**

CANADIAN TECHNICAL REPORT OF FISHERIES AND AQUATIC SCIENCES (CN/0706-6457) [06524091] **553, 2299**

CANADIAN TECHNICAL REPORT OF HYDROGRAPHY AND OCEAN SCIENCES (CN/0711-6764) [09304701] **1447**

CANADIAN TECHNOLOGY MONTHLY (CN/1186-1037) [24266210] **894**

CANADIAN TESTING ASSOCIATION *See* DIRECTORY - CANADIAN TESTING ASSOCIATION **865**

CANADIAN TEXTILE JOURNAL (CN/0008-5170) [01553250] **5348**

CANADIAN TEXTILES INSTITUTE *See* ESTIMATED POUNDAGE EQUIVALENTS **5350**

CANADIAN THEATRE REVIEW (CN/0315-0836) [01081487] **5362**

CANADIAN THEOSOPHIST, THE (CN/0045-544X) [01917257] **4343, 4942**

CANADIAN THESES (CN/0068-9874) [16292087] **412**

CANADIAN THOROUGHBRED (CN/0830-0593) [15271266] **2798**

CANADIAN TIDE AND CURRENT TABLES. PACIFIC COAST (CN/0576-2243) [08190455] **1447**

CANADIAN TOBACCO GROWER, THE (CN/0008-5189) [01936075] **5372**

CANADIAN TOKEN, THE (CN/0703-895X) [03589225] **2772**

CANADIAN TOURIST TRAVEL GUIDE (CN/0845-8987) [20777067] **5465**

CANADIAN TOY & DECORATION FAIR *See* CANADIAN TOY & DECORATION FAIR : DIRECTORY **2583**

CANADIAN TOY & DECORATION FAIR : DIRECTORY (CN/0834-2202) [16309251] **2583**

CANADIAN TOY TESTING COUNCIL *See* TOY REPORT **2585**

CANADIAN TRACK AND FIELD ASSOCIATION *See* RULES AND BY-LAWS / CANADIAN TRACK AND FIELD ASSOCIATION **4915**

CANADIAN TRACKSIDE GUIDE (CN/0829-3023) [12426013] **5430**

CANADIAN TRADE & COMMODITY TAX CASES COMBINATIONS (CN) **826**

CANADIAN TRANSPORT (CN/0045-5466) [01935369] **5430**

CANADIAN TRANSPORTATION LOGISTICS (CN/1187-4295) [24765191] **5448**

CANADIAN TRANSPORTATION LOGISTICS GUIDE (CN) **5379**

CANADIAN TRANSPORTATION RESEARCH FORUM. MEETING *See* PROCEEDINGS ... ANNUAL MEETING OF THE CANADIAN TRANSPORTATION RESEARCH FORUM **5390**

CANADIAN TRAVEL COURIER (CN/0008-5219) [01553251] **5465**

CANADIAN TRAVEL PRESS WEEKLY (CN/0831-9138) [15264606] **5465**

CANADIAN TRAVEL SURVEY. DOMESTIC TRAVEL (CN/0229-821X) [08124354] **5466**

CANADIAN TRAVELLER (TORONTO, ONT.) (CN/0848-158X) [21201051] **1061**

CANADIAN TREASURER (CN/0845-7328) [20183889] **782, 655**

CANADIAN TREASURY MANAGEMENT REVIEW (CN/0829-4003) [19032562] **863, 782**

CANADIAN TREASURY SERVICES (US/0883-0622) [11906567] **4716**

CANADIAN TRIBUNE (TORONTO, ONT.) *See* TRIBUNE, THE **5796**

CANADIAN ULTRALIGHT NEWS (CN/0821-6673) [09774775] **16**

CANADIAN UNDERWRITER (CN/0008-5251) [01917550] **2877**

CANADIAN UNDERWRITER. ANNUAL STATISTICAL REVIEW (CN/0317-1264) [02585401] **2877, 2897**

CANADIAN UNION CATALOGUE OF LIBRARY MATERIALS FOR THE HANDICAPPED [MICROFORM] / CATALOGUE COLLECTIF CANADIEN DES DOCUMENTS DE BIBLIOTHEQUE POUR LES PERSONNES HANDICAPEES (CN/0822-2576) [18121996] **3200**

CANADIAN UNION OF PUBLIC EMPLOYEES. CONVENTION *See* PROCEEDINGS - CONVENTION, CANADIAN UNION OF PUBLIC EMPLOYEES **1703**

CANADIAN UNION OF PUBLIC EMPLOYEES. CONVENTION *See* CONVENTION REPORT - C U P E **1661**

CANADIAN UNITARIAN, THE (CN/0527-9860) [01917144] **4942**

CANADIAN UNIVERSITY DISTANCE EDUCATION DIRECTORY / REPERTOIRE DE L'ENSEIGNEMENT A DISTANCE DANS LES UNIVERSITES CANADIENNES (CN/0827-1224) [13434932] **1814**

CANADIAN UNIVERSITY MUSIC REVIEW (CN/0710-0353) [07936807] **4107**

CANADIAN UNIVERSITY PRESS *See* SUMMER NEWS SERVICE - CANADIAN UNIVERSITY PRESS **1849**

CANADIAN UNIVERSITY PRESS *See* FEATURE - CANADIAN UNIVERSITY PRESS **1823**

CANADIAN UNIVERSITY PRESS *See* SUMMER REVIEW SERVICE - CANADIAN UNIVERSITY PRESS **1849**

CANADIAN URBAN TRANSIT ASSOCIATION. MEETING *See* ANNUAL MEETING. PROCEEDINGS. CANADIAN URBAN TRANSIT ASSOCIATION **5376**

CANADIAN VENDING MAGAZINE (L989) (CN/0848-8975) [21400892] **1600**

CANADIAN (VERNON, B.C.) (CN/0836-3196) [16876216] **655**

CANADIAN VET SUPPLIES *CEASED.* (CN/0825-754X) [11807706] **5507**

CANADIAN VETERINARY JOURNAL (CN/0008-5286) [19903137] **5507**

CANADIAN VETERINARY PHARMACEUTICALS & BIOLOGICALS (US/0740-0586) [09869256] **5507**

CANADIAN VIEWPOINT (WILLOW GROVE, PA.) (US/0277-9285) [07659047] **3200**

CANADIAN VOCATIONAL JOURNAL (CN/0045-5520) [01926667] **1911**

CANADIAN VOLLEYBALL ASSOCIATION *See* RULE BOOK / CANADIAN VOLLEYBALL ASSOCIATION **4915**

CANADIAN WAR MUSEUM *See* HISTORICAL PUBLICATIONS - CANADIAN WAR MUSEUM **2737**

CANADIAN WASTE MATERIALS EXCHANGE BULLETIN (CN) **2226**

CANADIAN WATER RESOURCES JOURNAL (CN/0701-1784) [03409867] **5531**

CANADIAN WATER WELL (CN/1180-050X) [24267088] **5532**

CANADIAN WELDER AND FABRICATOR. DIRECTORY AND BUYERS' GUIDE (CN) [02585103] **4026**

CANADIAN WEST (1985) (CN/0829-5026) [13907797] **2726**

CANADIAN WHEAT BOARD *See* ANNUAL REPORT / THE CANADIAN WHEAT BOARD **200**

CANADIAN WHO'S WHO, THE (CN/0068-9963) [02604443] **431**

CANADIAN WILDLIFE ADMINISTRATION (CN/0822-2320) [10109976] **2189**

CANADIAN WIND ENGINEERING ASSOCIATION See C. W. E. A. NEWS **4399**

CANADIAN WOMEN'S FIELD HOCKEY ASSOCIATION See HANDBOOK AND DIRECTORY - CANADIAN WOMEN'S FIELD HOCKEY ASSOCIATION **4898**

CANADIAN WOMEN'S PERIODICALS INDEX (CN/0847-2882) [21111218] **5552**

CANADIAN WOMEN'S STUDIES (CN/0713-3235) [09951504] **5553**

CANADIAN WOOD COUNCIL See C W C DATAFILE **633**

●CANADIAN WOOD PRODUCTS (1992) (CN/1183-9139) [25796398] **1600**

CANADIAN WORKERS' ASSOCIATION See NEWSPAPER OF THE CANADIAN WORKERS' ASSOCIATION **1695**

CANADIAN WORKSHOP (CN/0704-0717) [03797387] **633**

CANADIAN WORLD ALMANAC AND BOOK OF FACTS, THE See CANADIAN GLOBAL ALMANAC, THE **1924**

CANADIAN WORLD FEDERALIST (1975) (CN/0382-8662) [03202040] 4517, **3125**

CANADIAN WRESTLER (1985) (CN/0831-229X) [14516799] **4889**

CANADIAN WRITER'S JOURNAL (CN/0827-293X) [11825370] **3372**

CANADIAN YACHTING (CN/0384-0999) [03248479] **592**

CANADIAN YEARBOOK OF INTERNATIONAL LAW (CN/0069-0058) [02442067] **3125**

CANADIAN YOUNG ASTRONAUT, THE *CEASED.* (CN/0831-2060) [16687803] **16**

CANADIANA (CN/0008-5391) [02248879] **412**

CANADIANA AUTHORITIES (CN/0225-1574) [08428116] **3200**

CANADIANA GERMANICA (CN/0703-1599) [03963397] **2683**

CANADIANA ROMANICA (GW/0933-2421) [I09332421] **3372**

CANADIANS FOR A DEMOCRATIC WORKPLACE See NEWSLETTER - CANADIANS FOR A DEMOCRATIC WORKPLACE **1694**

CANADO-AMERICAIN, LE (US/0576-6478) [03814917] **2530**

CANAL & RIVERBOAT (UK/0141-2302) **4870**

●CANAL DE PANAMA HOY / CENTRO DE ESTUDIOS LATINOAMERICANOS "JUSTO AROSEMENA." (PN) [26573124] **2726**

CANAL HISTORY AND TECHNOLOGY PROCEEDINGS (US/0892-3515) [14268552] **2088**

CANAL-ISEP (CN/0711-7027) [08878492] **4636**

CANAL PARIS *CEASED.* (FR/0151-4989) [I01514989] **317**

CANAL TIMES : NEW YORK STATE CANAL SYSTEM NEWS (US) [22284357] **5448**

CANAL ZONE STUDY GROUP (US/0746-004X) [09670810] **2784**

CANALES (NEW YORK, N.Y.) (US/1042-3281) [11507367] **2486**

CANALS CANADA (CN/0826-1954) [11360542] **5379**

CANARD ENCHAINE, LE (FR/0008-5405) [02258971] **4467**

CANARSIE COURIER (US) **5714**

CANBERRA ANTHROPOLOGY (AT/0314-9099) [05593512] **233**

CANBERRA BIRD NOTES (AT/0314-8211) [I03148211] **5616**

CANBERRA BULLETIN OF PUBLIC ADMINISTRATION (AT/0811-6318) [I08116318] **4636**

CANBERRA HISTORICAL JOURNAL (AT/0313-5977) [05702459] **2669**

CANBERRA LINGUIST (AT/0311-4627) [I03114627] 1890, **3272**

CANBY HERALD (US) **5733**

CANBY NEWS (US/0745-7251) [09400539] **5695**

CANCELLED LEAVES (CN/0706-6899) [04879562] **3372**

CANCER (US/0008-543X) [01553275] **3810**

CANCER AND METASTASIS REVIEWS (NE/0167-7659) [12009081] **3810**

CANCER BIOCHEMISTRY BIOPHYSICS (US/0305-7232) [01181846] 484, 495, **3810**

CANCER BIOLOGY (US/0363-017X) [02322368] **3810**

●CANCER BIOTHERAPY (US/1062-8401) [25797283] **3810**

CANCER BULLETIN - M.D. ANDERSON CANCER CENTER, THE (US) [24172687] **3810**

CANCER BULLETIN OF THE UNIVERSITY OF TEXAS M.D. ANDERSON HOSPITAL AND TUMOR INSTITUTE AT HOUSTON See CANCER BULLETIN - M.D. ANDERSON CANCER CENTER, THE **3810**

CANCER CAUSES & CONTROL : CCC (UK/0957-5243) [22459434] **3810**

CANCER (CD-ROM ED.) (US/1045-7410) [20223671] **3810**

CANCER CHEMOTHERAPY AND BIOLOGICAL RESPONSE MODIFIERS (NE/0921-4410) [17464864] **3810**

CANCER CHEMOTHERAPY AND PHARMACOLOGY (GW/0344-5704) [04084336] **3810**

CANCER CHEMOTHERAPY REPORT (UK) [19805157] **3811**

CANCER CHRONICLES, THE (US/1044-6508) [19860981] **3811**

CANCER COMMUNICATIONS See ONCOLOGY RESEARCH **3822**

CANCER CONTROL JOURNAL (US/0191-3794) [04823490] **3811**

CANCER DATA (NZ/0548-9415) [08265798] **3811**

CANCER DETECTION AND PREVENTION (US/0361-090X) [02701243] **3811**

CANCER DETECTION AND PREVENTION. SUPPLEMENT (US/1043-6995) [17001387] **3811**

CANCER ECONOMICS (US/1053-9611) [16627304] **3811**

CANCER EN PUERTO RICO / ESTADO LIBRE ASOCIADO DE PUERTO RICO, DEPARTAMENTO DE SALUD, PROGRAMA CONTROL DEL CANCER, REGISTRO CENTRAL DEL CANCER (PR/0896-9566) [08498401] **3811**

CANCER EPIDEMIOLOGY, BIOMARKERS & PREVENTION (US/1055-9965) [23441645] 3734, **3811**

CANCER FACTS AND FIGURES (US/0069-0147) [02254523] **3811**

CANCER FORUM (AT/0311-306X) [01351021] **3811**

CANCER FOUNDATION OF WESTERN AUSTRALIA See ANNUAL REPORT FOR THE PERIOD ... / CANCER FOUNDATION OF WESTERN AUSTRALIA INC **3808**

●CANCER GENE THERAPY (US/0929-1903) [30637792] **3811**

CANCER GENETICS AND CYTOGENETICS (US/0165-4608) [04853076] **3811**

CANCER IMMUNOLOGY AND IMMUNOTHERAPY (GW/0340-7004) [09799069] **3811**

CANCER IN CANADA (1989) (CN/1195-406X) [30804482] **3811**

CANCER IN ILLINOIS (US/0277-7215) [07616286] **3811**

CANCER IN NEW SOUTH WALES : INCIDENCE AND MORTALITY (AT/0157-2547) [06825548] **3811**

CANCER INVESTIGATION (US/0735-7907) [08996676] **3811**

CANCER JOURNAL (VILLEJUIF), THE (FR/0765-7846) [13673692] **3811**

CANCER LETTER, THE (US/0096-3917) [01161592] **3811**

CANCER LETTERS (NE/0304-3835) [01874893] **3811**

CANCER MANAGEMENT (US/0193-1415) [05077491] **3812**

CANCER MORTALITY TRENDS IN AUSTRALIA / EPIDEMIOLOGY BRANCH, HEALTH DEPARTMENT OF WESTERN AUSTRALIA (AT) [19085049] **3812**

CANCER NEWS (NEW YORK, N.Y.) (US/0008-5464) [01553284] **3812**

CANCER NEWSLINE (US/0276-3974) [05236404] **3812**

CANCER NURSING (US/0162-220X) [03804001] 3812, **3853**

CANCER NURSING NEWS (US/0734-1873) [08690565] 3812, **3853**

CANCER PAIN RELEASE (US/1013-3097) [18765383] **3812**

CANCER PHARMACOLOGY ANNUAL, THE (NE/0920-7848) [09751932] **3812**

●CANCER PRACTICE (US/1065-4704) [26612360] **3812**

CANCER PREVENTION (BALTIMORE, MD.) *CEASED.* (US/1043-8491) [19579899] **3812**

CANCER REPORT (NEW YORK) (US/0190-5112) [04684257] **3812**

CANCER RESEARCH (BALTIMORE) (US/0008-5472) [01553285] **3812**

●CANCER RESEARCH, THERAPY & CONTROL (SZ/1064-0525) [26208053] **3812**

●CANCER RESEARCHER WEEKLY (US/1071-7226) [28704414] **3812**

CANCER SEMINAR (US/0069-0171) [01696649] **3812**

CANCER SURVEY (COLD SPRINGS HARBOR, N.Y.) (US/1050-849X) [21654052] **3812**

CANCER SURVEYS (US/0261-2429) [08790612] **3812**

CANCER THERAPY AND CONTROL (SZ/0896-5080) [17197674] **3812**

CANCER THERAPY REPORTS *CEASED.* (US/1050-9992) [21742749] **3812**

CANCER THERAPY UPDATE *CEASED.* (US/0924-6533) [23364608] **3812**

CANCER TOPICS. VERSION ESPANOLA (SP/0212-2618) [I02122618] **3812**

CANCER TREATMENT AND RESEARCH (NE/0927-3042) [07931224] **3812**

CANCER TREATMENT REVIEWS (UK/0305-7372) [01181754] **3812**

CANCER VICTORS JOURNAL (US/0891-0766) [14275764] **3813**

●CANCER WATCH (US/1059-3802) [24603302] **3813**

CANCERGRAM. SERIES CB19, ANTITUMOR AND ANTIVIRAL AGENTS MECHANISM OF ACTION *CEASED.* (US/1057-588X) [19070453] **3813**

CANCERGRAM. SERIES CB20 ANTITUMOR AND ANTIVIRAL AGENTS EXPERIMENTAL THERAPEUTICS TOXICOLOGY PHARMACOLOGY *CEASED.* (US/1057-5898) [18891616] **3813**

CANCERGRAM. SERIES CT01 CANCER DETECTION AND MANAGEMENT BIOLOGICAL MARKERS *CEASED.* (US/1057-5901) [19090658] **3813**

CANCERGRAM. SERIES CT02 CANCER DETECTION AND MANAGEMENT NUCLEAR MEDICINE *CEASED.* (US/1057-591X) [19277146] 3847, **3813**

CANCERGRAM. SERIES CT05 LYMPHOMAS DIAGNOSIS TREATMENT *CEASED.* (US/1057-5936) [19060456] **3813**

CANCERGRAM. SERIES CT06, CLINICAL CANCER IMMUNOLOGY AND BIOLOGICAL THERAPY *CEASED.* (US/1057-5944) [19279188] **3813**

CANCERGRAM. SERIES CT08 LUNG CANCER. DIAGNOSIS TREATMENT *CEASED.* (US/1057-5960) [19054487] **3813**

CANCERGRAM. SERIES CT09 BREAST CANCER DIAGNOSIS TREATMENT PRE-CLINICAL BIOLOGY *CEASED.* (US/1057-5979) [18885484] **3813**

CANCERGRAM. SERIES CT10 PEDIATRIC ONCOLOGY *CEASED.* (US/1057-9087) [19280534] 3901, **3813**

CANCERGRAM. SERIES CT11 NEOPLASIA OF THE HEAD AND NECK DIAGNOSIS TREATMENT *CEASED.* (US/1057-9079) [19060444] **3813**

CANCERGRAM. SERIES CT12 SARCOMAS AND RELATED TUMORS. DIAGNOSIS TREATMENT *CEASED.* (US/1057-9060) [19060470] **3813**

CANCERGRAM. SERIES CT14 CANCER DETECTION AND MANAGEMENT DIAGNOSTIC RADIOLOGY *CEASED.* (US/1057-5928) [19068660] **3813**

CANCERGRAM. SERIES CT15, CLINICAL TREATMENT OF CANCER. RADIATION THERAPY *CEASED.* (US/1057-9052) [19367148] 3939, **3813**

CANCERGRAM. SERIES CT16, GENITO-URINARY CANCERS. DIAGNOSIS, TREATMENT *CEASED.* (US/1057-9109) [18869307] **3813**

CANCERGRAM. SERIES CT17 GYNECOLOGIC TUMORS. DIAGNOSIS TREATMENT *CEASED.* (US/1057-9117) [18891883] **3813**

CANCERGRAM. SERIES CT18, NERVOUS SYSTEM MALIGNANCIES. DIAGNOSIS, TREATMENT *CEASED.* (US/1057-9125) [19807145] 3829, **3814**

CANCERGRAM. SERIES CT19, UPPER GASTRINTESTINAL TUMORS DIAGNOSIS, TREATMENT *CEASED.* (US) [19068538] **3814**

CANCERGRAM. SERIES CT20 REHABILITATION AND SUPPORTIVE CARE *CEASED.* (US) [19668292] **3814**

CANCERGRAM. SERIES CT21 ENDOCRINE TUMORS. DIAGNOSIS TREATMENT PATHOPHYSIOLOGY *CEASED.* (US/1057-9133) [19068565] **3814**

CANCERGRAM. SERIES CT22 MELANOMA AND OTHER SKIN CANCER DIAGNOSIS TREATMENT *CEASED.* (US/1057-9141) [19090578] **3814**

CANCERGRAM. SERIES CT23, LEUKEMIAS AND MULTIPLE MYELOMA. DIAGNOSIS, TREATMENT *CEASED.* (US/1057-915X) [21480788] **3814**

CANCERMONTHLY (AIDS RELATED CANCER ED.) (US/1059-8960) [24801845] **3814**

●CANCERMONTHLY (BREAST CANCER ED.) (US/1059-8928) [24801548] **3814**

CANCERMONTHLY — Alphabetical Title Index

CANCERMONTHLY (BUSINESS AND FINANCE ED.) (US/1059-9029) [24802276] **3814**

CANCERMONTHLY (CANCER TREATMENT/GENE THERAPY ED.) (US/1059-8979) [24801885] **3814**

●CANCERMONTHLY (CARCINOGENESIS AND EPIDEMIOLOGY ED.) (US/1059-8944) [24801751] **3814**

CANCERMONTHLY (EDUCATION AND HEALTHCARE ED.) (US/1059-9010) [24801996] 3814, **4770**

CANCERMONTHLY (INTERNATIONAL ACTIVITIES ED.) (US/1059-9037) [24802505] **3814**

●CANCERMONTHLY (JOURNAL ED.) (US/1059-8987) [24801916] **3814**

●CANCERMONTHLY (RESEARCH ED.) (US/1059-8995) [24801935] **3814**

●CANCERMONTHLY (SMOKING AND LUNG CANCER ED.) (US/1059-8936) [24801597] **3814**

CANCERMONTHLY (SOLID TUMOR ED.) (US/1059-8952) [24801787] **3814**

CANCEROLOGIE (FR/0220-7346) [05080385] **3814**

CANCERWEEKLY See CANCER RESEARCHER WEEKLY **3812**

CANCERWEEKLY (ATLANTA, GA.) (US/1071-7218) [23835828] **3814**

CANCHIM : RESUMOS INFORMATIVOS (BL) [05724877] 4942, **5025**

CANCORP DOCUMENTS SERVICE (CN/1181-3385) [22768932] **655**

CANDID FACTS (CN/0226-2347) [06702975] **3795**

CANDLE COMPUTER REPORT (US/1071-2976) [28641037] **1173**

CANDOLLEA (SZ/0373-2967) [01553291] **506**

CANDY APPLE See FROMMER'S FAMILY TRAVEL GUIDE. NEW YORK CITY WITH KIDS **5477**

CANDY BUYERS' DIRECTORY; A CLASSIFIED DIRECTORY OF CANDY MANUFACTURERS SELLING NATIONALLY OR SECTIONALLY, THE (US) [06212375] **2330**

CANDY INDUSTRY (1982) (US/0745-1032) [08820994] **2330**

CANDY INDUSTRY BUYING GUIDE (US/0739-8921) [09104005] **2330**

CANDY INDUSTRY CATALOG & FORMULA BOOK (US) [06464174] **2330**

CANDY MARKETER (1985) *CEASED.* (US/0886-3741) [11849577] **2330**

CANDY WHOLESALER (US/0162-5136) [04163683] **2330**

CANEFARM NEWS (PH) [08276550] **166**

CANELOBRE (SP) [12739768] **317**

CANENTE (SP/0213-7895) [19690610] **3372**

CANEY CHRONICLE (CANEY, KAN. : 1958) (US) [12190846] **5674**

CANFAX (CN) 208, **5507**

CANINE CHRONICLE (US/0746-1410) [09797476] **4286**

CANINE PRACTICE (1990) (US/1057-6622) [22177738] **5507**

CANISIUS COLLEGE See ALUMNI DIRECTORY / CANISIUS COLLEGE **1097**

CANMAKER AND CANNER, THE (UK/0953-8690) [I09535690] **4218**

CANMAKING & CANNING INTERNATIONAL (UK) [18369673] 3476, **4218**

CANMET BUSINESS PLAN (CN/0844-9228) [20308264] **4636**

CANMET REPORT (CN/0705-5196) [02918495] **1438**

CANMORE LEADER (CN/0824-3646) [10386386] **5781**

CANNATA REPORT (US) **4211**

CANNED AND FROZEN FRUITS AND VEGETABLES (CN/0702-6528) [03439914] **2330**

CANNED FISHERY PRODUCTS, ANNUAL SUMMARY See PROCESSED FISHERY PRODUCTS, ANNUAL SUMMARY **2311**

CANNING HANDBOOK, THE (UK) [10702242] **3999**

CANNON FALLS BEACON (US) [01553294] **5695**

CANNONS OF CONSTRUCTION, THE (CN/0319-7085) [01940750] **2948**

●CANOE & KAYAK (US) [29681851] **592**

CANOE AND KAYAK RACING NEWS *CEASED.* (US) 4889, **592**

CANOE (CAMDEN, ME.) (US/0360-7496) [02244561] **592**

CANOLA DIGEST (CN/0715-3651) [09159469] **72**

CANON LAW ABSTRACTS (UK/0008-5650) [01774890] 4942, **5012**

CANOPY INTERNATIONAL (PH/0115-0960) [08774870] **2377**

CANOTTAGGIO (IT) **4889**

CANPARA (1976) (CN/0227-5880) [08023777] **4889**

CANPLAY (CN/0829-3627) [13232071] **5362**

CANQUA NEWSLETTER (CN/1183-8566) [25652356] **1353**

CANSCAIP NEWS (CN/0708-594X) [05376460] 3372, **1061**

CANSPA COMMUNICATOR (CN/0823-0145) [09809057] **4849**

CANTABRIA MEDICA (SP) **3562**

CANTANTIBUS ORGANIS; SAMMLUNG VON ORGELSTUCKEN ALTER MEISTER (GW) [05809962] **4107**

CANTERAS Y EXPLOTACIONES (SP/0008-5677) [I00085677] **2111**

CANTERBURY AND YORK SOCIETY (SERIES) (UK/0262-995X) [09029937] **5229**

CANTERBURY LAW REVIEW, THE (NZ/0112-0581) [07338675] **2948**

CANTIGUEIROS (LEXINGTON, KY.) (US/0898-8463) [17932108] 4107, **3372**

CANTIO SACRA (GW) [04959748] **4107**

CANTON EAGLE, THE (US/0192-6446) [05061746] **5691**

CANTON HERALD (CANTON, TEX.) (US/0894-2560) [14072400] **5748**

CANTON INDEPENDENT-SENTINEL, THE (US) [13569357] **5735**

CANTON PILOT, THE (US) [11892046] **5674**

CANTONS (CN/0713-0139) [08701010] **5781**

CANTRILL'S FILMNOTES (AT/0158-4154) [03011071] **4065**

CANTWELL TAPESTRY, A (US/0094-6907) [01794657] **2441**

CANYE KEXUE (CC/0257-4799) [24469852] **5606**

CANYON COURIER WEEKENDER, THE (US/0192-0197) [05094183] **5642**

CANYON CRIER NEWS (US/0746-9926) [10447328] **5633**

CANYON ECHO (US/0164-7024) [04390477] **2530**

CANYON LEGACY (US/0897-3423) [17465303] 4164, **2613**

CANYON NEWS (CANYON, TEX. : 1926) (US) [14064895] **5748**

CAO/CAM/CAE PRODUCTS DATABASE (US) 1264, 1284, **1244**

CAO TIMES (US/0146-3365) [02917631] **390**

CAO'S IN NEDERLAND (NE) [06233597] **939**

CAOUTCHOUCS & PLASTIQUES PARIS (FR/1154-1105) [I11541105] **5075**

CAP-AUX-DIAMANTS (CN/0829-7983) [13435646] **2726**

CAP BLACK BOOK (UK) **5408**

CAP BLACK BOOK. CARS, TRADE & RETAIL VALUES (UK) **5408**

CAP LEGISLATION (UK/0953-5586) [I09535586] 2948, **72**

CAP MONITOR (UK/0142-5633) [I01425633] **72**

CAP MONITOR UPDATES (UK) **72**

CAP TODAY (US/0891-1525) [14641603] **3893**

CAP WEEKLY (UK/0953-5594) [I09535594] **72**

CAPABILITIES (CHICAGO, ILL.) (US/1055-7156) [23274903] **1967**

CAPACITOR AND RESISTOR TECHNOLOGY SYMPOSIUM (US/0887-7491) [13385782] **1967**

CAPACITOR INDUSTRY NEWSLETTER : BIMONTHLY NEWS FOR THE FILM CAPACITOR TRADE AND ALLIED DIELECTRIC MARKETS (US/1056-6813) [23825348] **1600**

CAPACITY CHANGES IN LEAD AND ZINC IN THE 1980'S (UK) **3999**

CAPACITY MANAGEMENT REVIEW (US/1049-2194) [21124778] **1173**

CAPACITY UTILIZATION, MANUFACTURING AND MATERIALS (US) [03458628] **3476**

CAPAHA ARROW, THE (US/0008-5774) [03990475] **1090**

CAPE (UK) [24317017] 3372, **317**

CAPE BRETON DEVELOPMENT CORPORATION (CANADA) See ANNUAL REPORT / CAPE BRETON DEVELOPMENT CORPORATION **4627**

CAPE BRETON'S MAGAZINE (CN/0319-4639) [01941799] **2726**

CAPE COD HOME & GARDEN (US/1049-460X) [21244886] **2412**

CAPE COD LIFE (US/0199-7238) [06103495] **2530**

CAPE COD NEWS (SANDWICH, MASS.) (US/0192-8465) [05119801] **5688**

CAPE COD TIMES (US/0747-1467) [10577867] **5688**

CAPE CODDER, THE (US) [13719833] **5688**

CAPE DIVISION, CAPE OF GOOD HOPE. DIVISIONAL COUNCIL See VERSLAG DEUR DIE VOORSITTER OOR DIE RAAD SE BEDRYWIGHEDE **4693**

CAPE DORSET PRINTS (CN/0319-0463) [02443033] **377**

CAPE ISLAND SOUND (US/0094-9167) [01794306] **3461**

CAPE LIBRARIAN, THE (SA/0008-5790) [02258983] **3200**

CAPE MAY COUNTY HERALD (US) [13885932] **5709**

CAPE MAY STAR AND WAVE (US) [15736303] **5709**

CAPE NATURALIST, THE (US) [07243266] **4164**

CAPE OF GOOD HOPE. CAPE SCHOOL BOARD See ANNUAL REPORT - CAPE OF GOOD HOPE. CAPE SCHOOL BOARD **1860**

CAPE OF GOOD HOPE (SOUTH AFRICA) See ESTIMATES OF PROVINCIAL REVENUE TO BE COLLECTED AND EXPENDITURE TO BE DEFRAYED FROM THE PROVINCIAL REVENUE FUND DURING THE YEAR ... / REPUBLIC OF SOUTH AFRICA, PROVINCE OF THE CAPE OF GOOD HOPE **4722**

CAPE OF GOOD HOPE (SOUTH AFRICA). DEP. OF NATURE CONSERVATION. INVESTIGATIONAL REPORT See BONTEBOK **2188**

CAPE OF GOOD HOPE (SOUTH AFRICA). DEPT. OF NATURE CONSERVATION See INVESTIGATIONAL REPORT - DEPARTMENT OF NATURE CONSERVATION **4166**

CAPE OUTLOOK / COUNCIL FOR AMERICAN PRIVATE EDUCATION (US) [15340824] **1730**

CAPE ROCK, THE (US/0146-2199) [02045813] 4368, **3461**

CAPE TIMES (MICROFICHE) (SA) [03505845] **5810**

CAPE TOWN. CITY TREASURER'S DEPT See ESTIMATES OF INCOME & EXPENDITURE **4722**

CAPE TOWN. UNIVERSITY OF CAPE TOWN. DEPARTMENT OF GEOLOGY See BULLETIN - CAPE TOWN. UNIVERSITY OF CAPE TOWN. DEPARTMENT OF GEOLOGY **1368**

CAPE VERDEAN (US) [13571677] **2530**

CAPEARTS (US/0743-0922) [10493532] **370**

CAPELL'S CIRCULATION REPORT (US/0736-9077) [09243313] **4813**

CAPILANO REVIEW, THE (CN/0315-3754) [01947161] **3372**

CAPITAL (II) [01774271] **1550**

CAPITAL (FR) [29209490] **1468**

CAPITAL (GW) 1468, **655**

CAPITAL (ALBANY, N.Y.) (US/1044-4769) [19796213] **2486**

CAPITAL & CLASS (UK/0309-8168) [03388313] 1633, **1590**

CAPITAL AND REVENUE ESTIMATES - INNER LONDON EDUCATION AUTHORITY (UK) [05753318] **1861**

CAPITAL AREA PLANNING COUNCIL See ANNUAL REPORT - CAPITAL AREA PLANNING COUNCIL **2814**

CAPITAL AREA PLANNING COUNCIL See REGIONAL DIRECTORY - CAPITAL AREA PLANNING COUNCIL **4679**

CAPITAL BAPTIST (US/0528-0559) [01716567] **5057**

●CAPITAL BUDGET (US) [23183735] **4716**

CAPITAL BUDGET AND SIX YEAR IMPROVEMENT PROGRAM (US/0363-0870) [02409739] **4716**

CAPITAL BUDGET (GEORGIA) (US) [06179251] **4716**

CAPITAL CHEMIST, THE (US/0411-0080) [06149287] **966**

CAPITAL COGS (US) [06229559] **5229**

CAPITAL COMPUTER DIGEST (US/0893-3049) [15513552] **1173**

CAPITAL CONSORTIUM'S NORTH CAROLINA GIVING (US/1042-2285) [18976835] **5276**

CAPITAL DISTRICT BUSINESS REVIEW (US/0747-3699) [10773783] **655**

CAPITAL ENERGY LETTER *CEASED.* (US/0195-5292) [05619688] **1935**

Alphabetical Title Index — CARD

CAPITAL EXPENDITURE AND DEBT FINANCING STATISTICS / CIPFA, STATISTICAL INFORMATION SERVICE (UK/0263-2985) [10760584] 4716, **4697**

CAPITAL EXPENDITURE BY PRIVATE BUSINESSES (PAPUA NEW GUINEA) (PP) [01793206] **894**

CAPITAL FEASTS (US/0148-4516) [03315191] **5070**

CAPITAL FOR SHIPPING / COMPILED BY MARITIME CONSULTANTS LIMITED (UK) [19947037] **5448**

CAPITAL GAIN$ (US/8756-4114) [11693092] **782**

CAPITAL (HAMBURG) (GW/0008-5847) [03263114] **1550**

CAPITAL HUMANO (SP) [15540518] **1468**

●CAPITAL IDEAS / FROM THE NATIONAL TAXPAYERS UNION FOUNDATION (US/1065-8114) [26750348] **4716**

●CAPITAL IMPROVEMENT PROGRAM (US) [18118756] **5379**

CAPITAL IMPROVEMENT PROGRAM (FAIRFAX) (US/0147-7749) [03225047] 1600, **4636**

●CAPITAL IMPROVEMENT PROGRAM, FISCAL YEARS ... / STATE OF MARYLAND, DEPARTMENT OF STATE PLANNING (US) [17595316] **4716**

CAPITAL IMPROVEMENTS PROGRAM FOR CHICAGO (US/0149-1059) [03429274] **4716**

CAPITAL IMPROVEMENTS PROGRAM STATUS REPORT, FINANCIAL SUMMARY (US/0160-0109) [03587157] **894**

CAPITAL INTERNATIONAL (IT) [15001885] **2514**

CAPITAL INVESTMENT FORECASTS AND TRENDS IN INDUSTRY (US) 894, **1600**

CAPITAL JOURNAL (ALBANY, N.Y.) (US/0891-9836) [15050008] **1468**

CAPITAL JOURNAL (PIERRE, S.D.) (US/0893-5564) [15525387] **5743**

CAPITAL MARKETS GUIDE (US) **894**

CAPITAL MARKETS STRATEGIES (UK) **782**

CAPITAL (MILAN, ITALY) (IT) [10296933] **1468**

CAPITAL NEWS (AT/0812-1494) [I08121494] **4107**

CAPITAL NURSING (US) [11435327] **3853**

CAPITAL OUTLAY BUDGET (LOUISIANA) (US) [04603265] **4716**

CAPITAL PC MONITOR *See* MONITOR (ROCKVILLE, MD.) **1270**

CAPITAL PRESS (US/0740-3704) [09953335] **5733**

CAPITAL PROJECT RECOMMENDATIONS FOR THE STATE OF NEW MEXICO *See* CAPITAL BUDGET **4716**

CAPITAL PROJECTS (US/0146-8952) [03050055] **4716**

CAPITAL PUNISHMENT (PLANO, TEX.) (US) [14996388] **3160**

CAPITAL REGION CREATIVE SERVICES DIRECTORY, THE (CN/0822-918X) [10668980] **317**

CAPITAL REGION DEVELOPMENTS (CN/1180-9132) [22159235] **1600**

CAPITAL (RHINEBECK, N.Y.), THE (US/0885-4718) [12680098] **2441**

CAPITAL SOURCE, THE (US/0898-6916) [12224201] 4201, **4636**

CAPITAL SPORTS FOCUS (US/1041-5742) [18802613] **4889**

CAPITAL SPOTLIGHT, THE (US/0411-0137) [20448216] **5647**

CAPITAL TAX PLANNING (UK) **4716**

CAPITAL TAXES : A QUARTERLY COMMENTARY (UK) [13409406] **4716**

CAPITAL TAXES NEWS AND REPORTS (UK/0964-9204) [I09649204] **4717**

CAPITAL, THE (US) [09236150] **5685**

CAPITAL TIMES, THE (US/0749-4068) [07351334] **5766**

CAPITAL UNIVERSITY. LAW AND GRADUATE CENTER *See* ALUMNI DIRECTORY / CAPITAL UNIVERSITY LAW AND GRADUATE CENTER **1097**

CAPITAL UNIVERSITY LAW REVIEW (US/0198-9693) [01553315] **3160**

CAPITAL UPDATE (US) [19098802] **3853**

CAPITAL VOICE (US/0008-5898) [03990504] **4942**

CAPITALE SUD *SUSPENDED*. (IT) [22144316] **1468**

CAPITALISM (LONDON, ONT.) (CN/0821-2643) [09414460] **4467**

CAPITALISM, NATURE, SOCIALISM (US/1045-5752) [19480060] **2212**

CAPITALIST, THE (II) [05863570] **2648**

●CAPITATION & MEDICAL PRACTICE (US/1076-1047) [30411190] **3562**

CAPITOL ADVANTAGE (US) **4636**

CAPITOL CURRENTS (US/1064-6957) [21055635] **4637**

CAPITOL HILL TIMES (US) [11458216] **5760**

CAPITOL NEWSLETTER (US) **4637**

CAPITOL REPORTER (US) 2877, **782**

CAPITOL REPORTS, INC *See* WASHINGTON CREDIT LETTER PRIVACY REPORT **3072**

CAPITOL REPORTS, INC *See* WASHINGTON CREDIT LETTER DIGEST **3072**

CAPITOL REVIEW, THE (US/0746-3294) [09925500] **5748**

CAPITOL UPDATE (US/0889-4841) [14083442] **4637**

CAPITOL WEEKLY (US/1049-1767) [19695186] **2918**

CAPPER'S (US/0892-1148) [15080775] **5674**

CAPSICUM NEWSLETTER (IT) [13681340] **2412**

CAPSTONE LETTER (US) **1173**

CAPSULE (US) 3750, **5178**

●CAPSULES AND COMMENTS IN CRITICAL CARE NURSING (US/1066-4815) [26949667] **3853**

CAPSULES AND COMMENTS IN MATERNITY AND GYNECOLOGIC NURSING (US) 3758, **3853**

●CAPSULES & COMMENTS IN NURSING LEADERSHIP & MANAGEMENT (US/1068-6088) [27720021] **3853**

●CAPSULES AND COMMENTS IN ONCOLOGY NURSING (US/1066-4114) [26949726] 3814, **3853**

●CAPSULES & COMMENTS IN PEDIATRIC NURSING (US) [29333708] **3853**

CAPSULES AND COMMENTS IN PERIOPERATIVE NURSING (US) **3853**

●CAPSULES AND COMMENTS IN PSYCHIATRIC NURSING (US) [29457699] 3923, **3853**

CAPT. LILLIE'S BRITISH COLUMBIA COAST GUIDE AND RADIOTELEPHONE DIRECTORY (CN/0822-9481) [11046539] **4175**

CAPTAIN AMERICA (US/0274-5267) [04481475] **1061**

CAPTAIN CANUCK (CN/0383-0462) [03199492] **4858**

CAPTAIN GEORGE'S YELLOW JOURNAL (CN/0317-6134) [02441676] **4858**

CAPTAIN N, THE GAME MASTER (US/1049-1473) [21141739] **4858**

CAPTAIN PLANET AND THE PLANETEERS (US/1060-8745) [24496442] **4858**

CAPTAIN'S MATE (US/0094-5889) [01794397] **4889**

CAPTIVE INSURANCE COMPANY DIRECTORY (US/1056-814X) [09277119] **2877**

CAPTIVE INSURANCE COMPANY REPORTS (US/1056-8158) [09184148] **2877**

CAPTIVE INSURANCE COMPANY REVIEW (UK/0262-7701) [I02627701] **2877**

●CAPTN. JACK'S TIDE AND ... CURRENT ALMANAC (US/1045-4543) [24466868] 1924, **4175**

CAR (UK/0008-5987) [03881496] **5408**

CAR AND ACCESSORY TRADER (UK) **5408**

CAR AND DRIVER (US/0008-6002) [04814147] **5408**

CAR AND DRIVER BUYERS GUIDE TO ... NEW CARS (US) [23068259] **5408**

CAR AND DRIVER JAPAN (JA) **5408**

CAR AND DRIVER ROAD TEST ANNUAL (US/8755-626X) [10777021] **5409**

CAR AND DRIVER YEARBOOK (DANBURY, CONN.) (US/1050-9682) [21727926] **5409**

CAR AND LOCOMOTIVE CYCLOPEDIA OF AMERICAN PRACTICE (US) [05245643] **5430**

CAR AUDIO AND ELECTRONICS (US/0898-3720) [17795211] **5316**

CAR BOOK, THE (US/0893-1208) [11900117] **5409**

CAR CARE (US/0275-391X) [07107785] **5409**

CAR CARE GUIDE (US/0162-3443) [03603846] **5409**

CAR CARE MALL NEWS (US) **5409**

CAR COLLECTING & INVESTING *CEASED*. (US/1042-7406) [19121702] **5409**

●CAR COLLECTOR & CAR CLASSICS (US) [28452246] **5409**

CAR COLLECTOR & CAR CLASSICS MAGAZINE (US/1057-4441) [24038154] 250, **5409**

CAR CORRAL (US/1045-7216) [20215310] 250, **5409**

CAR CRAFT (US/0008-6010) [05937573] **5409**

CAR CRAFT ANNUAL (US/0743-3182) [10527917] **5409**

CAR DEALER INSIDER (1990) (US/1052-407X) [22283492] **5409**

CAR-DEL SCRIBE *CEASED*. (US/0008-6029) [04145231] **2441**

CAR MECHANICS (UK/0008-6037) [04689244] **5409**

CAR MODELER (US/1048-6194) [20990026] **2772**

CAR (MONTREAL, QUEBEC) (CN/0712-8614) [08734120] **5409**

CAR PRICES *CEASED*. (US/0739-1722) [04591142] **5409**

CAR RENTAL & LEASING INSIDER (US/1052-4118) [22284404] **5409**

CAR SERVICE MANUAL (US/0743-6084) [10602064] **5409**

CAR STEREO (DURANGO, COLO.) (US/1046-3852) [18110748] **5409**

CAR STEREO (NEW YORK) (US/0272-7943) [06905051] 5409, **2038**

CAR STEREO REVIEW (LOS ANGELES, CALIF.) (US/0894-3443) [16001395] **5316**

CAR STYLING (JA) [17494301] **5409**

CARABELA (SP/0213-9715) [I02139715] **3272**

CARABINIERE, IL (IT) [19572313] **2486**

CARABO, EL (SP) [04405024] **5194**

CARACAS. BIBLIOTECA DE LOS TRIBUNALES DEL DISTRITO FEDERAL FUNDACION ROJAS ASTUDILLO *See* BOLETIN DE LA BIBLIOTECA DE LOS TRIBUNALES DEL DISTRITO FEDERAL FUNDACION ROJAS ASTUDILLO **3196**

CARACAS. UNIVERSIDAD SANTA MARIA. FACULTAD DE DERECHO *See* REVISTA DE LA FACULTAD DE DERECHO **3041**

CARACTERE (FR/0008-6126) [02062570] **4564**

CARACTERE 1980 (FR/0247-039X) [I0247039X] **4564**

CARAM DIGEST *See* CARIBBEAN DIGEST **2258**

CARAPHIN NEWS (CR/1018-1210) [I10181210] 5507, **506**

CARAVAN BUSINESS (UK/0268-5558) **5466**

CARAVEL MAGAZINE (US/0008-6207) [01553335] **2530**

CARBENES. EDITED BY MAITLAND JONES, JR. [AND] ROBERT A. MOSS (US) [04179642] **1040**

CARBOHYDRATE CHEMISTRY (UK/0576-7172) [01553337] **1040**

CARBOHYDRATE CHEMISTRY & METABOLISM ABSTRACTS (UK/0301-8679) [01793222] **966**

CARBOHYDRATE POLYMERS (UK/0144-8617) [08036109] **1040**

CARBOHYDRATE RESEARCH (NE/0008-6215) [01553338] 484, **1040**

CARBON COUNTY LAW JOURNAL, THE (US/0090-8789) [01785857] **2948**

CARBON COUNTY NEWS (RED LODGE, MONT. : 1936) (US) [11683242] **5705**

CARBON DIOXIDE EFFECTS RESEARCH AND ASSESSMENT PROGRAM. CARBON DIOXIDE RESEARCH PROGRESS REPORT (US) [06285709] **2226**

CARBON (NEW YORK) (US/0008-6223) [01926664] **1035**

CARBONATES AND EVAPORITES (US/0891-2556) [14268278] **1371**

CARBONDALE NEWS (CARBONDALE, PA. : 1961) (US/0746-3510) [09957612] **5735**

CARCH NEWS (US/0163-2213) [04318915] **3778**

CARCINOGENESIS. A COMPREHENSIVE SURVEY (US/0147-4006) [03146775] **3814**

CARCINOGENESIS (NEW YORK) (US/0143-3334) [06123551] **3814**

CARD COLLECTOR'S PRICE GUIDE (US/1059-9142) [24808082] **2772**

●CARD DECK ADVERTISING SOURCE (US/1071-4626) [28642734] **757**

CARD DECK RATES AND DATA *See* CARD DECK ADVERTISING SOURCE **757**

CARD INDUSTRY DIRECTORY (US/1051-6778) [20859302] **740**

CARD — Alphabetical Title Index

CARD NEWS (US/0894-0797) [15747547] **782**

CARD REPORT (AMES, IOWA. 1986) (US/0886-3970) [12897920] **72**

CARD WORKING PAPER SERIES (US) [20175003] **72**

CARDAMOM STATISTICS (INDIA) (II) [02357670] 2330, **2362**

CARDEALS (WASHINGTON, D.C.) (US/1056-912X) [23893018] **4889**

CARDFAX (US) **1601**

CARDIAC ALERT (US/0194-2557) [05365701] **3700**

CARDIAC IMAGING VIDEO JOURNAL *CEASED.* (NE) **3700**

CARDIAC IMPULSE *CEASED.* (US/0892-4082) [12397932] **3700**

CARDIAC SURGERY *CEASED.* (US/0887-9850) [13505779] 3700, **3961**

CARDIAC/THORACIC SURGERY (US/0163-7029) [04442503] **3961**

CARDINAL NEWS, THE (US) [09349329] 2189, **5580**

CARDINAL YEARBOOK, THE (US/0098-2598) [02240991] **1814**

CARDIO *CEASED.* (US/0742-9622) [10476441] **3700**

CARDIO INTERNATIONAL *CEASED.* (US) **3700**

CARDIO INTERVENTION *CEASED.* (US) [29373824] **3700**

CARDIO-VASCULAR NURSING (US/0008-6355) [01605574] 3700, **3853**

CARDIOLOGIA ... BARCELONA (SP/0213-8115) [I02138115] **3700**

CARDIOLOGIA PER IMMAGINI (IT/1120-3730) [I11203730] **3700**

CARDIOLOGIA (ROMA) (IT/0393-1978) [09292060] **3700**

CARDIOLOGIC CONSULTATION (US/0741-7454) [08448208] **3700**

CARDIOLOGIE PRATIQUE PARIS (FR/0766-3633) [I07663633] **3700**

CARDIOLOGIE TROPICALE (IV/0253-5580) [08418102] **3985**

CARDIOLOGISCH-ANGIOLOGISCHES BULLETIN (GW/0179-7166) [15899364] **3700**

CARDIOLOGIST'S COMPENDIUM OF DRUG THERAPY, THE (US/0276-4296) [07370503] **3700**

CARDIOLOGISTS' LEGAL LETTER (US/0741-515X) [10133872] 3700, **2948**

CARDIOLOGY (SZ/0008-6312) [02064881] **3700**

CARDIOLOGY BOARD REVIEW (US/0888-8418) [13735506] **3700**

CARDIOLOGY CLINICS (US/0733-8651) [08649074] **3700**

CARDIOLOGY CONSULTANT (CN/1181-9030) [24256404] **3700**

CARDIOLOGY DIGEST (1979) (US/0008-6347) [05922151] **3701**

CARDIOLOGY IN PRACTICE *SUSPENDED.* (UK/0262-5547) [08743694] **3701**

●CARDIOLOGY IN REVIEW (US/1061-5377) [25354725] **3701**

●CARDIOLOGY IN THE ELDERLY (US/1058-3661) [24279340] 3750, **3701**

CARDIOLOGY IN THE YOUNG (US/1047-9511) [20821740] **3701**

●CARDIOLOGY JOURNAL CLUB JOURNAL (US) **3701**

CARDIOLOGY MANAGEMENT *CEASED.* (US/0892-9327) [15337449] **3701**

CARDIOLOGY (NEW YORK, N.Y.) (US/0275-0066) [07068923] **3701**

CARDIOLOGY TIMES (US/0278-4157) [07821312] **3701**

CARDIOLOGY UPDATE (US/0163-1675) [04307293] **3701**

CARDIOLOGY WORLD NEWS (US/0883-4946) [12153514] **3701**

CARDIOMYOLOGY *CEASED.* (IT/0394-073X) [10271613] **450**

CARDIOPULMONARY PHYSICAL THERAPY JOURNAL (US) 3701, **4379**

CARDIOSCIENCE (IT/1015-5007) [22106908] **3701**

CARDIOSTIMOLAZIONE (IT) [18581995] **3701**

CARDIOTHORACIC AND VASCULAR ANESTHESIA UPDATE (US/1046-1795) [20346768] 3701, **3682**

CARDIOTHORACIC SURGERY (US/0893-8725) [14066926] 3961, **3701**

CARDIOVASCULAR AND INTERVENTIONAL RADIOLOGY (US/0174-1551) [06118549] 3701, **3939**

CARDIOVASCULAR CLINICS *CEASED.* (US/0069-0384) [01553349] **3701**

CARDIOVASCULAR DRUG REVIEWS (US/0897-5957) [17560326] **3701**

CARDIOVASCULAR DRUGS (US/0161-5734) [03971405] **3701**

CARDIOVASCULAR DRUGS AND THERAPY (US/0920-3206) [15991683] **3701**

CARDIOVASCULAR MEDICINE (NEW YORK, N.Y. : 1984) *See* PRIMARY CARDIOLOGY **3709**

●CARDIOVASCULAR NETWORK NEWS (US/1076-4763) [30492288] **3701**

CARDIOVASCULAR NEWS (US/0747-461X) [08479716] **3701**

●CARDIOVASCULAR PATHOLOGY (US/1054-8807) [23004510] 3893, **3701**

CARDIOVASCULAR PHARMACOLOGY (UK/0263-7243) [I02637243] **3701**

CARDIOVASCULAR PHYSIOLOGY (UK/0142-8012) [I01428012] **579**

CARDIOVASCULAR PHYSIOLOGY (LONDON, ENGLAND) (US/0363-387X) [02385982] 579, **3701**

CARDIOVASCULAR RESEARCH (UK/0008-6363) [01553351] **3702**

CARDIOVASCULAR REVIEW (BALTIMORE) (US/0271-4779) [06617824] **3702**

CARDIOVASCULAR REVIEWS & REPORTS (US/0197-3118) [06005714] **3702**

CARDIOVASCULAR REVIEWS & REPORTS EDICION ESPANOLA (SP/0211-6553) [I02116553] 3893, **3702**

CARDIOVASCULAR RISK FACTORS (CN/0842-537X) [19763736] **3702**

CARDIOVASCULAR SURGERY (US) [01586259] 3702, **3961**

●CARDIOVASCULAR SURGERY : OFFICIAL JOURNAL OF THE INTERNATIONAL SOCIETY FOR CARDIOVASCULAR SURGERY (UK/0967-2109) [27721553] **3702**

CARDOZO ARTS & ENTERTAINMENT LAW JOURNAL (US/0736-7694) [08791727] 384, **2948**

CARDOZO LAW REVIEW (US/0270-5192) [06428933] **2948**

CARDOZO STUDIES IN LAW AND LITERATURE (US/1043-1500) [19329285] 3372, **2948**

CARDS INTERNATIONAL (US/0956-5558) [21487829] **655**

CARDSTON CHRONICLE, THE (CN/0227-1192) [06635055] **5781**

CARE BEARS *CEASED.* (US/0894-3389) [12713751] **1061**

CARE CASSETTES (US/0739-3113) [12001133] **4942**

CARE CONNECTION, THE (CN/0843-9966) [20985453] **3853**

CARE HOME MANAGEMENT (UK) **2789**

CARE HOME MANAGEMENT RECORDS AND PROCEDURES (UK) **2789**

CARE IN PLACE: THE INTERNATIONAL JOURNAL OF NETWORKS AND COMMUNITY (UK) **5276**

CARE IN THE HOME (UK/0300-5909) [10171794] **4771**

CARE OF THE CRITICALLY ILL (UK/0266-0970) [24914374] **3562**

CARE OF THE ELDERLY (UK/0955-4262) [22238815] **3750**

CARE OF THE SURGICAL PATIENT (US) **3961**

CARE ON THE ROAD BIRMINGHAM (UK/0045-5768) [I00455768] **5439**

CAREE COMMUNICATOR (US/0732-9245) [08485299] 5039, **5057**

CAREE NEWSLETTER *See* CAREE COMMUNICATOR **5057**

CAREER CANDIDATES (CN/0703-5314) [03439602] **4201**

CAREER CENTER BULLETIN, THE (US) [10343549] **4201**

CAREER CHOICES NEWSLETTER, THE (US/0888-2770) [13533794] **4201**

CAREER DEVELOPMENT, DROPOUT PREVENTION PROGRAM, EXPERIMENTAL PROGRAMS, TEACHER LEADERSHIP PROGRAM, REGIONAL SERVICE UNITS (US/0094-5374) [01794183] **1911**

CAREER DEVELOPMENT FOR EXCEPTIONAL INDIVIDUALS (US/0885-7288) [05543328] **1911**

CAREER DEVELOPMENT QUARTERLY, THE (US/0889-4019) [13871624] **4201**

CAREER DIRECTIONS (US) [06583726] **4201**

●CAREER DIRECTORY (TORONTO. 1992) (CN/0846-3514) [25066592] **4201**

CAREER EDUCATION AND GUIDANCE (UK/0954-3732) **1730**

CAREER EDUCATION DIGEST (US) [04155886] **4201**

CAREER EDUCATION NEWS : CENTRAL NEWS SERVICE FOR THE WORLDS OF WORK AND LEARNING *CEASED.* (US) [01779651] **4202**

CAREER EDUCATION PROGRAM : PROGRAM PLAN (US/0361-1507) [02241359] **1911**

CAREER EDUCATION (WASHINGTON) (US/0270-7705) [06461282] 4202, **1911**

CAREER FOCUS FOR TODAY'S RISING BLACK PROFESSIONAL (US/1049-9954) [21364313] 2258, **4202**

CAREER FOCUS FOR TODAY'S RISING HISPANIC PROFESSIONAL (US/1049-9946) [21364292] 2258, **4202**

CAREER FOCUS FOR TODAY'S RISING PROFESSIONAL (US) 2258, **4202**

CAREER FUTURES *CEASED.* (US/1045-4314) [20123125] **4202**

CAREER GUIDE (PARSIPPANY, N.J.), THE (US/0891-0596) [11440088] **4211**

CAREER GUIDE TO PROFESSIONAL ASSOCIATIONS (US) **4202**

CAREER INFO CUS (CN/1182-9192) [23686543] **1911**

CAREER INFORMATION RESOURCE ADVISORY GROUP *See* PROFESSIONAL SCHOOLS FACTSHEETS **1842**

CAREER NEWS (WATERLOO) *CEASED.* (CN/0709-0366) [05322739] **4202**

CAREER OPPORTUNITIES. CD-ROM (US) [28160808] **4202**

CAREER OPPORTUNITIES NEWS (US/0739-5043) [09745783] **4202**

CAREER OPPORTUNITY BULLETIN (US) **4202**

CAREER OPPORTUNITY UPDATE *See* EXPERIENCED PROFESSIONAL **4204**

CAREER OPTIONS (CN) [18896959] **4202**

CAREER OUTLOOK, UNIVERSITY AND COMMUNITY COLLEGE : ADMINISTRATION/SOCIAL SCIENCES AND SERVICES (CN) [02441447] **4202**

CAREER PATHFINDER, THE (US/0885-7547) [12714590] **4202**

CAREER PILOT (US/1048-8898) [21060962] **16**

CAREER PILOT JOB REPORT (US/0891-0855) [14637207] **16**

CAREER PLANNING (US) [04068522] **4202**

CAREER PLANNING AND ADULT DEVELOPMENT JOURNAL (US/0736-1920) [09091504] **4202**

CAREER PLANNING AND ADULT DEVELOPMENT NETWORK NEWSLETTER (US/0898-1353) [17724413] **4202**

CAREER PLANNING GUIDE FOR PHYSICAL AND OCCUPATIONAL THERAPISTS (US/1059-3896) [24579725] **4379**

CAREER RESOURCE GUIDE (US/0890-5878) [14289789] **1658**

CAREER SCHOOL DIRECTORY (US/0278-1034) [05274104] 1730, **4202**

CAREER WAVES (US/1047-4293) [20690227] **4202**

CAREER WOMAN (US/1051-1075) [20583772] 4202, **5553**

CAREER WORLD (HIGHLAND PARK, ILL. 1981) (US/0744-1002) [08029104] **4202**

CAREERISM NEWSLETTER (US/1071-0418) [10074138] **4385**

CAREERISM NEWSLETTER : ZEROING IN ON CAREER AND JOB OPPORTUNITIES (US) [04734588] **4202**

CAREERS & COLLEGES (US/1065-9935) [26823770] 1814, **4202**

CAREERS & MAJORS (US/1059-5856) [24641287] **1730**

CAREERS & THE DISABLED (US/1056-277X) [23226809] 4385, **4202**

CAREERS AND THE ENGINEER (US) [20713559] **1967**

CAREERS AND THE MBA (US) [04648230] **655**

CAREERS BULLETIN (ZAMBIA) (ZA) **4202**

CAREERS (EDMONTON) (CN/0229-379X) [08469771] **4202**

CAREERS FOR GRADUATES (CN/0318-6229) [02879963] **4202**

●CAREERS GUIDANCE TODAY (UK/0969-6431) [I09696431] **4202**

CAREERS GUIDE (RH) [07035213] **4202**

CAREERS IN BUSINESS (US/0576-7334) [01553355] 655, **4202**

CAREERS IN NURSING AND OTHER HEALTH SERVICE PROFESSIONS (UK/0309-2399) [01950792] **3853**

CAREERS IN THE UNITED STATES DEPARTMENT OF THE INTERIOR (US/0502-0166) [01283091] 4637, **4202**

●CAREERS INTERNATIONAL (US/1059-3861) [24579898] **4202**

Alphabetical Title Index — CARLISLE

CAREERS OFFICER *See* CAREERS GUIDANCE TODAY **4202**

CAREERS (PORTLAND) (US/0094-6087) [01784489] **1912**

CAREERS RESEARCH AND ADVISORY CENTRE *See* DEGREE COURSE GUIDES **1819**

CAREERS (SARATOGA) (US/0193-1873) [05363757] **4203**

CAREFREE ENTERPRISE (US/0738-9604) [09697890] 2726, **2530**

CARERS WORLD (UK/0968-8838) 5178, **4385**

CARETAKER GAZETTE, THE (US/1074-3642) **4203**

CARETAS : ILUSTRACION PERUANA (PE/0576-7423) [02918591] **346**

CARF. CAMPAIGN AGAINST RACISM & FASCISM 1991 (UK/0966-1050) [I09661050] **4467**

CARF WORK HARDENING STANDARDS (US) **4379**

CARFAX (HULL, QUEBEC) (CN/0825-5326) [11180192] **3372**

CARGILL BULLETIN (US) [08681305] **72**

CARGO CLAIMS ANALYSIS *CEASED.* (UK/0265-427X) [15188646] **3180**

CARGO EXPRESS *CEASED.* (CN/0834-9797) [16856585] **16**

CARGO FACTS (US/0278-0801) [07701944] 16, **5379**

CARGO HANDLING ABSTRACTS / INTERNATIONAL CARGO HANDLING CO-ORDINATION ASSOCIATION (UK/0141-0687) [08107341] 5448, **5400**

CARGO / NORTH CAROLINA STATE PORTS AUTHORITY (US) [23377345] **5448**

CARGO SYSTEMS INTERNATIONAL (UK/0306-0985) [02441332] **5379**

CARGONEWS ASIA (HK/0252-9610) [I02529610] **5379**

CARGOWARE INTERNATIONAL (UK) [19598567] **4218**

CARGOWORLD (GW/0172-9314) [06905675] **5448**

CARGUIDE (CN/0384-9309) [03285010] **5409**

CARIB (JM) [07289410] 3272, **3372**

CARIB BASIN TRADE UPDATE (US/0888-1065) [13518968] **1601**

CARIBBEAN ABSTRACTS / EDITED AND PUBLISHED BY THE DEPARTMENT OF CARIBBEAN STUDIES OF THE ROYAL INSTITUTE OF LINGUISTICS AND ANTHROPOLOGY (NE/0925-0885) [24057322] **5227**

CARIBBEAN AFFAIRS (TR/1011-5765) [17975106] **2511**

CARIBBEAN/AMERICAN DIRECTORY (US/0275-2883) [09823140] **655**

●CARIBBEAN AND CENTRAL AMERICA REPORT (UK/0968-2732) [27318727] 782, **1468**

CARIBBEAN ARCHIVES (GP/0376-7698) [01792068] **2481**

CARIBBEAN ASSOCIATION OF NOVA SCOTIA *See* NEWSLETTER - CARIBBEAN ASSOCIATION OF NOVA SCOTIA **2749**

CARIBBEAN BARGAIN BOOK, THE (US/0270-4803) [06415595] **5466**

CARIBBEAN BUSINESS (US/0194-8326) [02977020] **655**

CARIBBEAN BUSINESS DIRECTORY (CJ) [16835634] **655**

CARIBBEAN BUSINESS TO BUSINESS GUIDE (PR) [20080612] **655**

CARIBBEAN CHALLENGE (JM/0008-6436) [03005560] **5015**

CARIBBEAN COMMUNITY *See* REPORT OF THE SECRETARY-GENERAL OF THE CARIBBEAN COMMUNITY **1639**

CARIBBEAN COMMUNITY. SECRETARIAT *See* CARICOM BULLETIN **1550**

CARIBBEAN CONNECTIONS (US/0745-2608) [09009702] **2486**

CARIBBEAN CONTACT *CEASED.* (TR) [02973748] **4942**

CARIBBEAN DATELINE (US) [08056336] **894**

CARIBBEAN DIALOGUE (CN/0384-1464) [03230440] **4467**

CARIBBEAN DIGEST (BB) [05430944] 5466, **1550**

●CARIBBEAN DIGEST (US/1063-0775) [25852058] **2258**

CARIBBEAN ECONOMIC ALMANAC *CEASED.* (TR/0069-0481) [02071483] **1468**

●CARIBBEAN ETHNOLOGY (VI/1057-2872) [23997217] **2258**

CARIBBEAN EVENTS MAGAZINE (US/1048-5171) [20961692] 5466, **2530**

CARIBBEAN FINANCE AND MANAGEMENT (JM/0256-9647) [13257506] **863**

CARIBBEAN FLITE GUIDE (US) [02241325] 5466, **16**

CARIBBEAN FOCUS (CN/0821-2295) [09403314] **2726**

CARIBBEAN FOREIGN BUSINESS INFORMATION, THE (AQ) **655**

CARIBBEAN GEOGRAPHY (JM/0252-9939) [09910219] **2558**

CARIBBEAN HANDBOOK, THE (AQ) [12077154] **5466**

CARIBBEAN INDUSTRIAL RESEARCH INSTITUTE *See* CARIRI **5092**

CARIBBEAN INSIGHT (UK/0142-4742) [08203382] **2726**

●CARIBBEAN INTERNATIONAL (ALBANY, N.Y.) (US/1058-4315) [24329570] 2530, **2511**

CARIBBEAN ISLANDS HANDBOOK (UK) [20645860] **5466**

CARIBBEAN JOURNAL OF AFRICAN STUDIES (JM/1015-6879) [05097006] **2638**

CARIBBEAN JOURNAL OF EDUCATION (JM/0376-7701) [02927958] **1730**

CARIBBEAN JOURNAL OF LEGAL INFORMATION : BULLETIN OF THE CARIBBEAN ASSOCIATION OF LAW LIBRARIANS, THE (JM/0255-7118) [18434649] 3200, **2948**

CARIBBEAN JOURNAL OF MATHEMATICAL AND COMPUTING SCIENCES (BB/1017-6764) [30311329] 1173, **3499**

CARIBBEAN JOURNAL OF MATHEMATICS (BB) [09475120] **3499**

CARIBBEAN JOURNAL OF RELIGIOUS STUDIES (JM/0253-066X) [02049913] **4942**

CARIBBEAN JOURNAL OF SCIENCE (PR/0008-6452) [01553365] **5092**

CARIBBEAN JOURNAL OF SCIENCE AND MATHEMATICS, THE *SUSPENDED.* (US/0008-6460) [02472131] **5092**

CARIBBEAN LAW AND BUSINESS (BB/1013-9230) [19987060] **3097**

CARIBBEAN LIFE & TIMES (CJ) [06432678] **2530**

CARIBBEAN MEDICAL JOURNAL (TR/0374-7042) [01778697] **3562**

CARIBBEAN MONOGRAPH SERIES (PR/0069-0511) [01781502] **2727**

CARIBBEAN NEWS *SUSPENDED.* (US) [02918777] **2530**

CARIBBEAN NEWSLETTER (NEW YORK, N.Y.) (US/0894-0223) [15796296] **2727**

CARIBBEAN PERSPECTIVES (US/1053-9700) [22712651] **2727**

CARIBBEAN PORTS HANDBOOK *SUSPENDED.* (JM) [08039442] **5448**

CARIBBEAN QUARTERLY (JM/0254-8038) [00843029] **2486**

CARIBBEAN RESEARCH INSTITUTE *See* ANNUAL REPORT **5191**

CARIBBEAN REVIEW (US/0008-6525) [01553369] **4467**

CARIBBEAN REVIEW OF BOOKS (JM/1018-2926) [25144524] **3373**

CARIBBEAN SERIES *CEASED.* (US/0069-0538) [01553370] **2727**

CARIBBEAN SHIPPING : THE JOURNAL OF THE CARIBBEAN SHIPPING ASSOCIATION (JM) [06598217] **5448**

CARIBBEAN SPORTS TRAVEL QUARTERLY (US) **592**

CARIBBEAN STUDIES (LEIDEN, NETHERLANDS) (NE) [20500487] **412**

CARIBBEAN STUDIES (NEW YORK N.Y.) (US/0275-5793) [07189284] **2727**

CARIBBEAN STUDIES NEWSLETTER (PR/0271-6577) [06075761] **2727**

CARIBBEAN STUDIES (RIO PIEDRAS, SAN JUAN, P.R.) (PR/0008-6533) [00844091] **2727**

CARIBBEAN TOURISM STATISTICAL REPORT (BB) [08941442] **5466**

CARIBBEAN TRAVEL AND LIFE (US/1052-1011) [17999626] **5466**

CARIBBEAN TRAVEL NEWS EUROPE (UK) **5466**

CARIBBEAN UPDATE (US/8756-324X) [11542442] 4517, **655**

CARIBBEAN WEEK (BB/1019-5076) [24956164] **5778**

CARIBBEAN WRITER, THE (VI/0893-1550) [15372109] **3373**

CARIBBEAN YEAR BOOK, THE (CN/0705-2731) [03567046] **2727**

CARIBBEAN YEARBOOK OF INTERNATIONAL RELATIONS, THE (NE) [03230873] **4517**

CARIBBEAN YELLOW PAGES (AQ) [20779000] **655**

CARIBE (US/0148-9968) [03410186] **3373**

CARIBE CONTEMPORANEO, EL *SUSPENDED.* (MX/0185-2426) [06912958] **1550**

CARIBOO CALLING (CN/0319-7360) [02442955] **2558**

CARIBOO MINER (CN/1185-0183) [23598297] **2136**

CARIBOO COUNTY SUN (US) [12292905] **5656**

CARIBOU, LE (CN/0704-0792) [03797382] **5781**

CARIBOU NEWS (CN/0712-2055) [08781343] **2189**

CARIBUS (US/0889-4027) [13871788] **2727**

CARICOM BULLETIN (GY) [06644859] **1550**

CARICOM PERSPECTIVE (GY) [07073809] **2551**

CARIES RESEARCH (SZ/0008-6568) [01553372] **1318**

CARILLON (CANADA. DEPT. OF VETERANS AFFAIRS) (CN/0825-7345) [11481322] **4637**

CARILLON NEWS (US/0730-5001) [07994308] **4107**

CARINDEX, SCIENCE & TECHNOLOGY (TR/1011-4866) [I10114866] **5174**

CARINDEX, SOCIAL SCIENCES AND HUMANITIES (TR) [11707391] 2844, **5194**

CARING COMMUNITY, THE (US) **5025**

CARING CONNECTION (US) **4385**

CARING FOR ANIMALS (OTTAWA, ONT.) (CN/0825-1711) [11564265] **226**

CARING : FOR THE DISABLED CARERS AND THE ELDERLY (UK) 5178, **4385**

CARING PEOPLE (WASHINGTON, D.C.) (US/1041-4959) [18782742] **2844**

CARING : THE BENEVOLENCES STORY (US) [04320209] **4942**

CARINTHIA I (AU/0008-6606) [01553374] **2683**

CARIRI (TR) [01795254] **5092**

CARISPLAN ABSTRACTS / CARIBBEAN DEVELOPMENT AND COOPERATION COMMITTEE (TR) [09925691] **1550**

CARITAS (FREIBURG IM BREISGAU) (GW/0008-6614) [01553377] **4334**

CARITAS-KORRESPONDENZ (GW/0008-6622) [I00086622] **5276**

CARLE SELECTED PAPERS (US/0098-0153) [01354923] **3562**

CARLETON GERMANIC PAPERS (CN/0317-7254) [01791548] **3373**

CARLETON INTERNATIONAL (CN/0704-5174) [11559790] **1731**

CARLETON INTERNATIONAL STUDIES (CN/0702-8334) [07091656] **4517**

CARLETON MATHEMATICAL LECTURE NOTES (CN/0318-6288) [02441957] **3499**

CARLETON MATHEMATICAL SERIES (CN/0069-0600) [02248130] **3499**

CARLETON-OTTAWA MATHEMATICAL LECTURE NOTE SERIES (CN/0827-3669) [I08273669] **3499**

CARLETON PAPERS IN APPLIED LANGUAGE STUDIES (CN/0824-7714) [11895330] **3272**

CARLETON UNIVERSITY *See* RESEARCH AND STUDIES - CARLETON UNIVERSITY **1845**

CARLETON UNIVERSITY *See* SUBMISSION TO THE ONTARIO COUNCIL ON UNIVERSITY AFFAIRS (CARLETON UNIVERSITY) **1849**

CARLETON UNIVERSITY. DEVELOPMENT OFFICE *See* NEWS BULLETIN - DEVELOPMENT OFFICE, CARLETON UNIVERSITY **1837**

CARLETON UNIVERSITY. LIBRARY *See* NEWSPAPER GEOG. LIST - CARLETON UNIVERSITY **5790**

CARLETON UNIVERSITY. LIBRARY *See* MUSIC SCORE CATALOGUE - CARLETON UNIVERSITY **4160**

CARLETON UNIVERSITY. LIBRARY *See* AUTHOR INDEX - CARLETON UNIVERSITY **408**

CARLETON UNIVERSITY. SCHOOL OF PUBLIC ADMINISTRATION *See* CAREER CANDIDATES **4201**

CARLETON UNIVERSITY STUDENT JOURNAL OF PHILOSOPHY, THE (CN/0317-073X) [02247688] **4343**

CARLINVILLE DEMOCRAT, THE (US) [11962170] **5658**

CARLISLE CITIZEN, THE (US) [14924716] **5669**

CARLISLE COUNTY NEWS, THE (US) [12401052] **5680**

CARLISLE Alphabetical Title Index

CARLISLE MERCURY, THE (US) [11061807] **5680**

CARLOAD WAYBILL STATISTICS (US/0360-4586) [05692420] **5379**

CARLSBAD CURRENT-ARGUS (US) [10260942] **5712**

CARLSBERGFONDET (COPENHAGEN, DENMARK) *See* ARSSKRIFT - CARLSBERGFONDET, FREDERIKSBORGMUSEET, NY CARLSBERGFONDET **1074**

CARLSONREPORT (US/0889-2288) [13827357] 863, **952**

CARLYLE ANNUAL (US/1050-3099) [20911357] **3373**

●CARLYLE STUDIES ANNUAL (US/1074-2670) [29665800] **3373**

CARMARTHENSHIRE ANTIQUARY, THE (UK/0142-1867) [05544020] **2683**

CARMEL (FR) **2558**

CARMEL DAILY LEDGER, THE (US) [21981941] **5663**

CARMEL PINE CONE AND CARMEL VALLEY OUTLOOK, THE (US) [28146032] **5633**

CARMELITE DIGEST (US) [13104644] **4942**

CARMELUS (IT/0008-6673) [01715907] **5025**

CARMICHAEL'S ANNUAL FRANCHISE DIRECTORY (US/0164-0208) [04556907] **655**

CARN (IE) [03526882] **4517**

CARN (CHICAGO, ILL.) (US/0890-7609) [14396413] **655**

CARNATION (US) **5229**

CARNATION NUTRITION EDUCATION SERIES (US/1049-4901) [20806229] **4188**

CARNE (IT) **2330**

CARNEGIE CORPORATION OF NEW YORK *See* ANNUAL REPORT - CARNEGIE CORPORATION OF NEW YORK **4334**

CARNEGIE ENDOWMENT FOR INTERNATIONAL PEACE *See* FINANCIAL REPORT - CARNEGIE ENDOWMENT FOR INTERNATIONAL PEACE **4521**

CARNEGIE INSTITUTION OF WASHINGTON *See* YEAR BOOK - CARNEGIE INSTITUTION OF WASHINGTON **5171**

CARNEGIE MAGAZINE (US/0008-6681) [05453926] **2844**

CARNEGIE MUSEUM OF NATURAL HISTORY *See* BULLETIN OF CARNEGIE MUSEUM OF NATURAL HISTORY **4164**

CARNEGIE QUARTERLY (US/0576-7954) [05848354] **1814**

CARNEGIE-ROCHESTER CONFERENCE SERIES ON PUBLIC POLICY (NE/0167-2231) [02673676] **1468**

CARNET MUSICAL (CN/0315-3916) [03116905] **4108**

CARNETS STATISTIQUES - CAISSE NATIONALE DE L'ASSURANCE MALADIE DES TRAVAILLEURS SALARIES (FR/0762-2929) [I07622929] **5325**

CARNICA 2000 (SP/0210-5543) [02105543] **2366**

CARNIVAL & CIRCUS BOOKING GUIDE *CEASED.* (US/0090-2985) [01784918] **4849**

CARNIVOROUS PLANT NEWSLETTER (US/0190-9215) [04011202] **506**

CARNIVOROUS PLANTS DIGEST (US/0197-7679) [04564382] **2412**

CARO BULLETIN *CEASED.* (CN/0827-357X) [12045237] **347**

CAROLINA AGENT, THE (US/1065-1292) [26513433] **2877**

CAROLINA BIOLOGY READERS (US/0148-9739) [03406897] **450**

CAROLINA BLUE (US/0274-7723) [06582840] **2486**

CAROLINA BUSINESS & FINANCE (US) **655**

CAROLINA CHEMTIPS (US/0748-0466) [10872949] **966**

CAROLINA CHRISTIAN (US/0008-672X) [03990538] **4942**

CAROLINA COMMENTS (US/0576-808X) [02047645] 2727, **2481**

CAROLINA COUNTRY (US/0008-6746) [06154179] **1541**

CAROLINA FARMER (NORTH CAROLINA ED.) (US/0744-2033) [08101283] **72**

CAROLINA FOOD DEALER, THE (US/0744-2483) [08134416] **2330**

CAROLINA GARDENER (US/1063-7451) [24485342] **2412**

CAROLINA INDIAN VOICE, THE (US/0739-1730) [06168850] **2258**

CAROLINA JOURNAL OF PHARMACY, THE (US/0528-1725) [01609721] **4295**

CAROLINA LIFE, INC *See* MOUNTAIN VACATION & TRAVEL GUIDE COVERING WESTERN NORTH CAROLINA **5485**

CAROLINA MESSENGER OF TRUTH *See* CAROLINA CHRISTIAN **4942**

CAROLINA PEACEMAKER (US) [27183769] **2258**

CAROLINA PIEDMONT *CEASED.* (US/0894-5446) [16157703] **5466**

CAROLINA PLANNING (US/0164-0070) [03338038] **2817**

CAROLINA POPULATION CENTER PAPERS (US) [09986371] **4550**

CAROLINA QUARTERLY (US/0008-6797) [01553423] **3373**

CAROLINA REAL ESTATE JOURNAL *CEASED.* (US/0742-5678) [10365824] **4835**

CAROLINA TIMES, THE (US) [02259007] **5722**

CAROLINA TIPS (US/0045-5865) [03520461] **5092**

CAROLINA WRITER (US) **3373**

CAROLINAS COMPANIES (US/0162-6353) [04178954] **655**

CAROLINAS GENEALOGICAL SOCIETY *See* CAROLINAS GENEALOGICAL SOCIETY YEARBOOK **2442**

CAROLINAS GENEALOGICAL SOCIETY BULLETIN, THE (US/0363-440X) [02473938] **2441**

CAROLINAS GENEALOGICAL SOCIETY YEARBOOK (US/0363-1826) [02430359] **2442**

CAROLINE COUNTY TIMES-RECORD, THE (US/0746-1658) [09819810] **5685**

CAROLINEA (GW/0176-3997) [10049520] **4164**

CAROLINIAN (RALEIGH), THE (US/0045-5873) [02259008] **5722**

CAROLOMAS GENEALOGICAL SOCIETY *See* CAROLINAS GENEALOGICAL SOCIETY BULLETIN, THE **2441**

CARONTAWAN (US) [04799687] **1090**

CAROUSEL NEWS & TRADER, THE (US/0892-9769) [15307337] **250**

●CARP. CANADIAN ASSOCIATION OF RETIRED PERSONS (CN/1193-8544) [27725187] **5178**

CARP NEWS (CN/0821-0128) [09674432] **5276**

CARPA BULLETIN (AT) [04926802] **4505**

CARPATHO-RUSYN AMERICAN (US/0749-9213) [05388929] **2258**

CARPENTER (US/0008-6843) [02393206] 1658, **633**

CARPENTER AND RELATED FAMILY HISTORICAL JOURNAL, THE (US/0740-6673) [09968174] **2442**

CARPENTER FAMILY COURIER (US/8755-7207) [11400774] **2442**

CARPENTER (NEW YORK, N.Y.), THE (US/0882-9055) [12015207] **633**

CARPET & FLOORCOVERINGS REVIEW (UK/0263-4236) [09662854] **5348**

CARPET & RUG INDUSTRY (US/0192-4486) [05043891] **2899**

CARPET AND RUG INSTITUTE *See* DIRECTORY AND REPORT / CARPET AND RUG INSTITUTE **5350**

CARPET AND RUG INSTITUTE *See* CARPET SPECIFIER'S HANDBOOK, THE **5348**

CARPET ANNUAL (UK/0069-0767) [I00690767] 5348, **1601**

CARPET MANAGEMENT : A QUARTERLY REVIEW OF THE INTERNATIONAL CARPET AND RUG INDUSTRY (US) 1601, **5348**

CARPET SPECIFIER'S HANDBOOK, THE (US/0095-6457) [01798517] **5348**

CARPICA (RM) [01941988] **2683**

CARRE BLEU, LE (FR/0008-6878) [02259009] **294**

CARREFOUR (CN/0706-1250) [27039950] **4343**

CARREFOUR BIO-ALIMENTAIRE (CN/1186-6217) [24401878] **2330**

CARREFOUR SALESIEN (CN/0823-9428) [11581554] **1814**

CARRELL, THE (US/0008-6894) [01553428] **3373**

CARRIAGE DRIVING (UK/0958-1820) [I09581820] **2798**

CARRIAGE JOURNAL, THE (US/0008-6916) [02977935] **2772**

CARRIAGE TRADE (SARNIA, ONT.) (CN/0831-2907) [15060229] 5183, **5348**

CARRIER PIDGIN, THE (US/0739-3474) [03863720] **3273**

CARRIER REPORT (US) **5379**

CARRIEROLOGIE (CN/0820-5000) [16747618] **1658**

CARROBBIO, IL (IT) [03689712] **2683**

CARROLL CABLES (US/0892-2152) [15122246] **2442**

CARROLL COLLEGE (HELENA, MONT.) *See* ALUMNI DIRECTORY / CARROLL COLLEGE **1097**

CARROLL COUNTY COMET (US) [14773168] **5663**

CARROLL COUNTY GENEALOGICAL QUARTERLY (US/0734-5682) [08730802] **2442**

CARROLL COUNTY HISTORICAL QUARTERLY (1992) (US/1062-841X) [25769404] **2727**

CARROLL COUNTY HISTORICAL SOCIETY (ARK.) CARROLL COUNTY HISTORICAL SOCIETY QUARTERLY *See* CARROLL COUNTY HISTORICAL QUARTERLY (1992) **2727**

CARROLL COUNTY HISTORICAL SOCIETY (ARKANSAS) *See* CARROLL COUNTY HISTORICAL SOCIETY QUARTERLY, THE **2727**

CARROLL COUNTY HISTORICAL SOCIETY QUARTERLY, THE (US/0191-6637) [03815853] **2727**

CARROLL COUNTY HISTORY JOURNAL (US) **2727**

CARROLL COUNTY INDEPENDENT CARROLL COUNTY PIONEER (US) [21349798] **5708**

CARROLL COUNTY REVIEW (US) [28272266] **5658**

CARROLL COUNTY TIMES (US/0746-7494) [10255086] **5685**

CARROLL COUSINS (US/0747-4873) [10709019] **2442**

CARROLL GARDENS COBBLE HILL NEWSPAPER, THE (US) [08254075] **5714**

CARROLL TODAY NEWS (US) [20576816] **5669**

CARROLLTON CHRONICLE (US) [14072447] **5748**

CARROLLTONIAN (US/0882-1631) [11719091] **2442**

CARROSSERIE (FR/0750-8131) [I07508131] 5409, **5379**

CARROSSIER (SZ) **1967**

CARROUSEL ART (US/0740-0780) [04793013] 347, **250**

CARROZZERIA *See* CLASSIC CAR DIGEST **5411**

CARRYING STREAM, THE (UK/0961-4532) [I09614532] **2683**

CARS (US) [13282977] **5409**

CARS (US) [02246394] **5409**

CARS & PARTS (US/0008-6975) [01553433] **5409**

CARS & PARTS ANNUAL (US) [10033179] **5409**

CARS IN PROFILE (UK) [01793412] **5409**

CARSON PRESS, THE (US/0899-7624) [01553436] **5725**

CARSON VALLEY CHRONICLE (US) [03198329] **5707**

CARSTAIRS COURIER, THE (CN/0823-7557) [10398408] **5781**

CARSWELL'S PRACTICE CASES (CN/0706-5388) [04746820] **3089**

CART NEWS MEDIA GUIDE (US/8755-7703) [11382661] **4889**

CARTA, A (BL) [03402679] **4637**

CARTA ADMINISTRATIVA (CK/0120-193X) [06419709] **4702**

CARTA AL EJECUTIVO ANDINO (PE) [04709231] **1633**

CARTA CEPRO (BL) [02162840] **1550**

CARTA DE CLACSO (AG) [05398443] **5194**

CARTA DE ESPANA (SP/0576-8233) [02068784] **2514**

CARTA DE OLIVER, LA (AG) [23986279] **3461**

CARTA ECONOMICA - BANCO NACIONAL DE PANAMA. ASESORIA ECONOMICA Y PLANIFICACION (PN) [01792309] **1550**

CARTA ECONOMICA REGIONAL : CER (MX/0187-7674) [19992418] **1468**

CARTA FINANCIERA - ANIF (CK) [03582766] **4717**

CARTA GANADERA (CK) [07525565] **208**

CARTA GEOLOGICA DE CHILE (CL/0577-8042) [01554262] **1371**

CARTA INFORMATIVA DE LA SECRETARIA PERMANENTE DE INTEGRACION ECONOMICA CENTROAMERICANA *See* BOLETIN INFORMATIVO / SIECA **1465**

CARTA INFORMATIVA PARA LOS SOCIOS (ES) [07563339] **818**

CARTA INFORMATIVA SIECA (GT) [11652627] **1468**

Alphabetical Title Index — CASHEW

CARTA-LEON DESDE WASHINGTON SOBRE ADMINISTRACION DE RECURSOS HUMANOS (US/0888-3548) [10565032] **939**

CARTA MAGNETICA DE CHILE (CL/0716-0095) **1353**

CARTA POLITICA (AG) [02973701] **1550**

CARTA POLITICA (BL) [24239733] **2727**

CARTA SEMANAL (BO) [06409887] **1438**

CARTA SERPAJ URUGUAY (UY) [21357206] **4505**

CARTACTUAL *CEASED.* (HU/0008-7009) [01553439] **2558**

CARTE ITALIANE (US/0737-9412) [09292862] 3273, **3373**

CARTE SEMIOTICHE : RIVISTA DELL'ASSOCIAZIONE ITALIANA DI STUDI SEMIOTICI *CEASED.* (IT) [14118368] **3273**

CARTEIRA DE TITULOS, PERFIL DE EMPRESAS / FUNDO DE INVESTIMENTOS DA AMAZONIA, FINAM (BL) [08074152] **4637**

CARTELLINA, LA (IT/1120-4621) [03146375] **4108**

CARTELLO METEOROLOGICO (IT) **1421**

CARTES SYNOPTIQUES DE LA CHROMOSPHERE SOLAIRE ET CATALOGUES DES FILAMENTS ET DES CENTRES D'ACTIVITE (FR) [06124006] **394**

CARTHAGE COURIER (US) [19008416] **5744**

CARTHAGE PRESS (US) [28446911] **5702**

CARTHAGE REPUBLICAN TRIBUNE (US/0889-8715) [11616284] **5714**

CARTHAGINIAN (CARTHAGE, MISS. : 1872) (US) [11652299] **5700**

CARTMEL, CARTMELL, CARTMILL FAMILY QUARTERLY, THE (US/0749-4890) [11109120] **2442**

CARTOGRAPHIC ACTIVITIES IN THE UNITED KINGDOM, REPORT (UK) [03080970] **2581**

CARTOGRAPHIC ACTIVITY IN GREAT BRITAIN REPORT *See* CARTOGRAPHIC ACTIVITIES IN THE UNITED KINGDOM, REPORT **2581**

CARTOGRAPHIC JOURNAL, THE (UK/0008-7041) [01553443] 1218, **2581**

CARTOGRAPHIC PERSPECTIVES (US/1048-9053) [19657307] **2581**

CARTOGRAPHICA (1980) (CN/0317-7173) [06809484] **2581**

CARTOGRAPHICA HELVETICA (SZ/1015-8480) [21189887] **2581**

CARTOGRAPHY (AT/0069-0805) [01553446] **2581**

CARTOGRAPHY AND GEOGRAPHIC INFORMATION SYSTEMS (US/1050-9844) [21328402] **2581**

CARTOMANIA (US/0894-2595) [15972142] **2558**

CARTONNAGES *See* CARTONNAGES EMBALLAGES MODERNES **4218**

CARTONNAGES EMBALLAGES MODERNES (FR) [15614790] **4218**

CARTOONIST PROFILES (US/0008-7068) [01775711] **377**

CARTOUCHE (US) [20474727] **294**

CARTOUCHE ENGLISH EDITION (CALGARY) (CN/1183-2045) [24368359] **2581**

CARTOUCHE FRENCH EDITION (CALGARY) (CN/1183-2045) [24368360] **2581**

CARUS MATHEMATICAL MONOGRAPHS, THE (US/0069-0813) [01553448] **3499**

CARVER (UK) **2949**

CARVER COUNTY NEWS (US) [01553450] **5695**

CARVER REPORTER (US) [24484012] **5688**

CARYOLOGIA (IT/0008-7114) [01553454] **450**

CAS BIOTECH UPDATES. AGRICULTURE (US/0890-7528) [14372980] 543, **72**

CAS BIOTECH UPDATES. ANTIBODY CONJUGATES (US/0895-6499) [16727951] **484**

CAS BIOTECH UPDATES. BIOCHEMICAL IMMOBILIZATION & BIOCATALYTIC REACTORS (US/0895-6626) [16728168] **484**

CAS BIOTECH UPDATES. BIOSENSORS (US/0884-7479) [12489453] **3690**

CAS BIOTECH UPDATES. CELL & TISSUE CULTURE (US/1040-709X) [18508709] **3690**

CAS BIOTECH UPDATES. COMMERCIAL FERMENTATION (US/1045-8565) [20282513] **1021**

CAS BIOTECH UPDATES. DNA & RNA PROBES (US/1045-8581) [20282499] **450**

CAS BIOTECH UPDATES. DNA FORMATION & REPAIR (US/0895-6618) [16728053] **543**

CAS BIOTECH UPDATES. ENVIRONMENTAL BIOTECHNOLOGY (US/0884-7452) [12439245] 2162, **3690**

CAS BIOTECH UPDATES. ENZYMES IN BIOTECHNOLOGY (US/1040-7081) [18508657] **3690**

CAS BIOTECH UPDATES. GENETIC ENGINEERING (US/0884-7460) [12439373] 543, **966**

CAS BIOTECH UPDATES. NUCLEIC ACID & PROTEIN SEQUENCES (US/1045-859X) [20282363] **450**

CAS BIOTECH UPDATES. PHARMACEUTICAL APPLICATIONS (US/0884-7487) [12489502] **4295**

CAS BIOTECH UPDATES. PRODUCT PURIFICATION & SEPARATION (US/1040-7103) [18508768] **1021**

CAS BIOTECH UPDATES. SLOW-RELEASE PHARMACEUTICALS (US/1051-3957) [21961446] **4295**

CAS. CURRENT AWARENESS SERVICE - BRITISH INSTITUTE OF MENTAL HANDICAP (UK/0143-0289) [101430289] **1793**

CAS FORUM (US/0147-2127) [03123039] 2844, **1814**

CAS JOURNAL (US/1053-7694) [21586508] **4108**

CAS NEWSLETTER / NATIONAL SPELEOLOGICAL SOCIETY, COMPUTER APPLICATIONS SECTION (US) [07406758] 1403, **1173**

CAS PAPER (UK) [09141811] **72**

CAS REPORT (UK) [18850380] **72**

CAS REPORT (COLUMBUS) (US/0162-7112) [02257269] **966**

CASA & I.E. E DECORACAO (BL) [04486263] **2899**

CASA DE CHILE EN MEXICO. CENTRO DE DOCUMENTACION Y BIBLIOTECA *See* CATALOGO - CENTRO DE DOCUMENTACION Y BIBLIOTECA, CASA DE CHILE EN MEXICO **3200**

CASA DE LAS AMERICAS *See* CASA DE LAS AMERICAS **3373**

CASA DE LAS AMERICAS (CU/0008-7157) [00844999] **3373**

CASA DEL TIEMPO (MX/0185-4275) [08610701] **2511**

CASA E GIARDINO (IT) **2412**

CASA GRANDE DISPATCH (US) [16877473] **5629**

CASA NOSTRA DE GINEBRA *See* INFORMACIO - CASA NOSTRA DE GINEBRA **2692**

CASA OGGI (IT) **2904**

CASA STILE (IT/0390-1513) [08971289] **2583**

CASA SUI CAMPI, LA (IT/1120-6381) [11206381] **2904**

CASA TESSIL REPORTER (IT/0394-882X) [I0394882X] 2904, **5348**

CASA VOGUE (IT/0008-7173) [01553456] 294, **2899**

CASA VOGUE ESPANA (SP) [22151501] **1082**

CASABELLA (MILAN, ITALY, 1965) (IT/0008-7181) [01553457] **294**

CASAULT FOL (CN/0820-7402) [09515302] **5781**

CASAVIVA (IT) [19319264] **2904**

CASCADE CAVER, THE (US/0008-7211) [07238603] **1403**

CASCADE COURIER, THE (US) [12102298] **5705**

CASCADES EAST (US/0194-8954) [05086715] **4870**

CASE 1 (US/0743-1732) [10529455] **2020**

CASE ANALYSIS IN SOCIAL SCIENCE IN SOCIAL THERAPY *CEASED.* (US/0149-6948) [03525368] 4580, **5241**

CASE COMMENTARIES AND BRIEFS (US/0736-8240) [07674012] **3105**

CASE DIGEST (LANSING) (US/0273-0642) [04645401] **4505**

CASE DIGEST (SACRAMENTO, CALIF.) (US/0890-8400) [06757821] **3105**

CASE ENFORCEMENT REPORT / DISTRICT OF COLUMBIA, OFFICE OF HUMAN RIGHTS (US) [09059936] **4505**

CASE HISTORIES OF OIL AND GAS FIELDS IN ASIA AND THE FAR EAST (US) [01783066] **4253**

CASE HISTORY - MINERAL EXPLORATION RESEARCH INSTITUTE (CN/0227-3535) [06688740] **1438**

CASE HISTORY OF AN ACCIDENT OR INCIDENT (CN/0710-0973) [08296953] **2860**

CASE IH FARM FORUM (US) [18132892] **72**

CASE IN POINT : DISTRICT ONE NEWSLETTER / COUNCIL FOR ADVANCEMENT AND SUPPORT OF EDUCATION (US) [08463057] **1876**

CASE INDUSTRY DIRECTORY (US/0898-5022) [17829541] 1967, **1173**

●CASE LAW DIGESTS (CN/1188-2948) [25313004] **2949**

CASE MANAGEMENT ADVISOR (US/1053-5500) [22571310] **3778**

CASE MANAGEMENT RESOURCE GUIDE: A DIRECTORY OF HOMECARE, REHABILITATION, MENTAL HEALTH AND LONG TERM CARE SERVICES (US/1046-0748) [20323642] **4771**

CASE MANAGER (US/1061-9259) [24044398] 3562, **2877**

CASE PRODUCT GUIDE *See* APPLICATION DEVELOPMENT TOOLS **1284**

CASE REGISTER (US/0272-2119) [06802686] **949**

CASE RESEARCH JOURNAL (US/0894-6043) [06955103] **863**

CASE SEARCH MONTHLY (UK/0959-9078) [19747238] **2949**

CASE STRATEGIES *See* APPLICATION DEVELOPMENT STRATEGIES **1171**

CASE STUDIES FOR PRACTICE (UK/0955-7989) [19743807] **5276**

●CASE STUDIES IN GREAT LAKES ARCHAEOLOGY (US/1061-4257) [25305965] **265**

CASE STUDIES IN HEALTH ADMINISTRATION (US/0193-9394) [05253227] **3778**

CASE STUDIES OF ARRANGEMENTS FOR EVALUATION AND UTILIZATION OF POPULATION CENSUS RESULTS; REPORT (US) [01484024] **4550**

CASE STUDY - AMERICAN PRODUCTIVITY CENTER (US/0741-6423) [10200015] **1601**

CASE TRENDS (US/1046-5944) [20461553] 1284, **1227**

CASE UPDATE (US/0749-7709) [10175532] **2949**

CASE WESTERN RESERVE JOURNAL OF INTERNATIONAL LAW (US/0008-7254) [01553466] **3125**

CASE WESTERN RESERVE LAW REVIEW (US/0008-7262) [01553468] **2949**

CASE WESTERN RESERVE UNIVERSITY *See* JOURNAL OF SOCIOLOGY (CLEVELAND) **5250**

CASEHANDLING MANUAL - NATIONAL LABOR RELATIONS BOARD (US) [02790391] **3145**

CASELOAD STATISTICAL REPORT ... FOR SUPREME COURT OF ALABAMA, COURT OF CRIMINAL APPEALS, COURT OF CIVIL APPEALS, CIRCUIT COURTS, DISTRICT COURTS (US) [08747449] **3079**

CASELOAD STATISTICS : STATE VOCATIONAL REHABILITATION AGENCIES (US/0566-0009) [05032492] 5276, **5266**

CASES DECIDED IN THE SUPREME COURT OF VIRGINIA (US) [03473446] **2949**

CASES IN POINT (US) [24035855] **1861**

CASES IN PUBLIC POLICY AND MANAGEMENT (US) [05158645] 863, **4637**

CASES OF COMMON REPORTABLE DISEASES *See* SELECTED REPORTABLE DISEASES BY HEALTH JURISDICTION **3716**

CASEY COUNTY NEWS, THE (US) [14200875] **5680**

CASH BOX, THE (US/0008-7289) [01553471] 4108, **5316**

CASH DISPENSERS AND AUTOMATED TELLERS (US/0148-5423) [03325689] 782, **727**

CASH FLOW. CASH- EN CREDITMANAGEMENT (NE) [I01678981] 863, **782**

CASH FLOW ENHANCEMENT REPORT (US/1053-0347) [22438803] **863**

CASH MANAGEMENT ANALYST, THE (US/0731-4507) [08197047] **1468**

CASH MANAGEMENT FORUM (US/0197-2987) [04902654] **782**

CASH MANAGEMENT PERFORMANCE REPORT *CEASED.* (US/1052-1747) [22202707] **782**

CASH MANAGEMENT TRUSTS, AUSTRALIA (AT/0813-1139) [I08131139] 782, **727**

CASH RECEIPTS FROM FARMING / IOWA CROP AND LIVESTOCK REPORTING SERVICE (US) [05979391] **72**

CASH RICH COS (US/1054-9994) [23043894] **782**

CASHEW COCHIN (II/0970-2423) [109702423] **72**

CASHTON RECORD (US) [13137564] **5766**

CASI E QUESTIONI DEL LAVORA (IT) **1658**

CASINO CHRONICLE (US/0889-9797) [09878269] 4858, **2804**

CASINO DIGEST (US/8755-6103) [11456465] **4858**

CASINO EXPLORER (US) [28922111] **4858**

CASINO PLAYER (US) [23727626] **4849**

CASINOS : THE INTERNATIONAL CASINO GUIDE (US/1040-9920) [18597839] **4858**

CASKET & SUNNYSIDE (US/0008-7327) [04912421] **2406**

CASON QUARTERLY, THE (US/0092-7694) [01789612] **2442**

: CASOPIS INFORMACNICH PRACOVNIKU, KNIHOVNIKU A UZIVATELU INFORMACI, I (XR/0862-9382) [25997709] **3200**

CASOPIS LEKARU CESKYCH (XR/0008-7335) [01553478] **3562**

CASOPIS MATICE MORAVSKE (1968) (XR/0323-052X) [04339523] **2683**

CASOPIS MORAVSKEHO MUZEA. VEDY PRIRODNI (XR/0521-2359) [03037135] 5092, **4086**

CASOPIS MORAVSKEHO MUZEA. VEDY SPOLECENSKE (XR/0323-0570) [03037172] **5194**

CASOPIS NARODNIHO MUZEA V PRAZE. RADA HISTORICKA (XR) [07339936] **5194**

CASOPIS PRO MINERALOGII A GEOLOGII (XR/0008-7378) [02961181] **1371**

CASOPIS PRO MODERNI FILOLOGII / CESKOSLOVENSKA AKADEMIE VED (NE/0862-8459) [25670147] 3373, **3273**

CASOPIS SLEZSKEHO MUZEA. SERIE A, VEDY PRIRODNI (XR/0323-0627) [07445790] **451**

CASOPIS SLEZSKEHO MUZEA. SERIE B, VEDY HISTORIKE (XR/0323-0678) [06323316] **4086**

CASOPIS SLEZSKEHO MUZEA. SERIE C. DENDROLOGIE (XR) [05544186] **506**

CASOPIS ZA KRITIKO ZNANOSTI (YU/0351-4285) [19951855] **4540**

CASOPIS ZA ZGODOVINO IN NARODOPISJE (XV/0590-5966) [01553482] **2613**

CASPER STAR-TRIBUNE (US) [09611324] **5772**

● CASS COUNTY CONNECTIONS (US/1074-5742) [27877140] **2442**

CASS COUNTY GENEALOGICAL SOCIETY QUARTERLY (US) [12868471] **2442**

CASS COUNTY REPORTER (US) [20818468] **5725**

CASS COUNTY SUN (1897) (US) [14634482] **5748**

● CASSAVA BIBLIOGRAPHIC BULLETIN (CK) **72**

CASSAVA NEWSLETTER (CK/0120-1824) [04040857] **166**

CASSAZIONE PENALE : RIVISTA MENSILE DI GIURISPRUDENZA (IT/0008-7424) **3092**

CASSELL & THE PUBLISHERS ASSOCIATION DIRECTORY OF PUBLISHING See DIRECTORY OF PUBLISHING. UNITED KINGDOM, COMMONWEALTH AND OVERSEAS **4814**

CASSELMAN CHRONICLE, THE (US/0528-2276) [05981825] **2727**

CASSETTE BOOKS (US/0363-9029) [05173930] 4385, **4827**

CASSETTE INFORMATION SERVICES (FIRM) See NEWSLETTER - CASSETTE INFORMATION SERVICES **1901**

CASSETTE NEWS. AUDIO CASSETTE (FR) **3273**

CASSIOPEIA (BRAMPTON) (CN/0227-6127) [08674302] **3373**

CASSIOPEIA (VICTORIA) (CN/0715-4747) [09340518] **394**

CASSUS BELLI (FR/0243-1327) [l02431327] 4858, **4889**

CASSVILLE DEMOCRAT (CASSVILLE, MO. : 1871) (US) [12303472] **5703**

CAST METALS (UK/0953-4962) [l09534962] **3999**

CAST ON (US) **5183**

CASTANEA (US/0008-7475) [01553496] 2212, **506**

CASTEEL *CEASED.* (US) [02445743] **3999**

CASTELLO DI ELSINORE, IL (IT) [20478076] **5362**

CASTELLUM (IT) [13770623] 4039, **294**

CASTILLA (VALLADOLID) (SP/0378-200X) [07890166] **3373**

CASTILLOS DE ESPANA (SP/0008-7505) [22144294] **294**

CASTINE PATRIOT (US) **5685**

CASTING & JEWELRY CRAFT (US/0363-5767) [02498409] **2913**

CASTING DESIGN & APPLICATION (US/1051-1237) [21878609] **3999**

CASTING WORLD *SUSPENDED.* (US/0887-9060) [13500450] **3999**

CASTINGS (AT/0008-7521) [02445745] **3999**

CASTLEGAR SUN, THE (CN/1185-1899) [24257161] **5781**

CASTLETON BANNER, THE (US) [16144149] **5663**

CASTME JOURNAL (UK/0264-3138) [l02643138] 3499, 5092, **1890**

CASTOR REVIEW (CN/0707-4956) [04746964] **5781**

CASTORO CINEMA, IL *CEASED.* (IT) [04090925] **4065**

CASTRO, EL (SP) **3461**

CASTRUM PEREGRINI (NE/0008-7556) [01553498] **3373**

CASUAL BULLETIN / ARCHIVE OF AUSTRALIAN JUDAICA (AT) [15307038] **5046**

CASUAL LIVING (US/0740-8285) [08819143] **2904**

CASUAL LIVING & SUMMER AND CASUAL FURNITURE See CASUAL LIVING **2904**

CASUALTY ACTUARIAL SOCIETY See PROCEEDINGS OF THE CASUALTY ACTUARIAL SOCIETY **2890**

CASUALTY ACTUARIAL SOCIETY See YEARBOOK - CASUALTY ACTUARIAL SOCIETY **2897**

CASUALTY ACTUARIAL SOCIETY FORUM (US/1046-6487) [20480828] **2877**

CASUALTY RETURN / LLOYD'S REGISTER OF SHIPPING (UK/0268-0815) [12754398] **2877**

CASWELL MESSENGER, THE (US/1074-5092) [13118254] **5722**

CAT FANCIERS' NEWS (US/0069-1003) [01553500] **4286**

CAT FANCY (SAN JUAN CAPISTRANO, CALIF.) (US/0892-6514) [14249006] **4286**

● CAT INDUSTRY NEWSLETTER (US/1074-7788) [28159282] **4286**

CAT LOVERS : THE OFFICIAL CLA CLUB MAGAZINE (US/1055-8438) [23359353] **4286**

CAT MEWS FOR A HEALTHIER CAT (US/0889-3152) [13844187] **5507**

CAT NEWS (SZ) 4164, **2189**

CAT WORLD (US/0163-1926) [04314239] **4286**

CAT WORLD BRIGHTON (UK/0952-2875) [l09522875] **5507**

CATALAN REVIEW (SP/0213-5949) [16078075] **2258**

CATALAN WRITING (SP/0214-3089) [18973807] **3373**

CATALIST BUSINESS AND HOUSEHOLD DIGEST OF ITHACA (US) [24767328] **655**

CATALIST BUSINESS AND HOUSEHOLD DIGEST OF SEATTLE AND VICINITY (US) [24333812] **922**

CATALOG (US) [08129829] **4039**

CATALOG AGE (US/0740-3119) [09911236] 4813, **757**

CATALOG (ARTHRITIS INFORMATION CLEARINGHOUSE (U.S.) (US/0277-9552) [07654441] **3804**

CATALOG FOR COLLEGE STORES, THE (US/0069-1011) [01787949] **656**

CATALOG - FORESTRY SUPPLIERS, INC (US/0742-7921) [05121886] **2377**

CATALOG HANDBOOK (US/1042-6167) [19092945] **656**

CATALOG MARKETER, THE (US/0730-9937) [08118063] **4813**

CATALOG MICROFORM / CENTER FOR RESEARCH LIBRARIES (US) [09040349] **3200**

CATALOG OF AMERICAN NATIONAL STANDARDS See AMERICAN NATIONAL STANDARDS CATALOG **4029**

CATALOG OF AMERICAN NATIONAL STANDARDS (US/1043-7002) [06192970] **4030**

CATALOG OF BRITANNICA FILMS (US) [03756398] **4065**

CATALOG OF CALIFORNIA STATE FUNDING SOURCES / CALIFORNIA STATE LIBRARY (US) [24098372] **4717**

CATALOG OF CAPTIONED FILMS/VIDEOS FOR THE DEAF (US) [21216895] 4065, **4385**

CATALOG OF CELL LINES (US/0737-7983) [09161224] **3893**

CATALOG OF CELL LINES / NATIONAL INSTITUTE ON AGING (US) [25539886] **3893**

CATALOG OF COPYRIGHT EENTRIES, FOURTH SERIES. PART 1, NONDRAMATIC LITERARY WORKS [MICROFORM] (US/0163-7290) [11733091] **1302**

CATALOG OF COPYRIGHT ENTRIES. FOURTH SERIES. 4, MOTION PICTURES & FILMSTRIPS. MICROFORM (US) [10297100] **1302**

CATALOG OF COPYRIGHT ENTRIES. FOURTH SERIES. PART 2. SERIALS & PERIODICALS (US/0163-7304) [10631097] **1302**

CATALOG OF COPYRIGHT ENTRIES. FOURTH SERIES. PART 3. PERFORMING ARTS (US/0163-7312) [10666961] 384, **1302**

CATALOG OF COPYRIGHT ENTRIES. FOURTH SERIES. PART 4, MOTION PICTURES & FILMSTRIPS MICROFORM (US/0163-7320) [11059663] **4065**

CATALOG OF COPYRIGHT ENTRIES. FOURTH SERIES. PART 5. VISUAL ARTS (US/0163-7339) [12541456] **1302**

CATALOG OF COPYRIGHT ENTRIES. FOURTH SERIES. PART 6. MAPS (US/0163-7347) [12533930] 2581, **1302**

CATALOG OF COPYRIGHT ENTRIES. FOURTH SERIES. PART 7. SOUND RECORDINGS (US/0163-7355) [12310008] **1302**

CATALOG OF COPYRIGHT ENTRIES. FOURTH SERIES. PART 8. RENEWALS (US/0163-7363) [11821352] **1302**

CATALOG OF CURRENT LAW TITLES (US/1044-2987) [19729879] **2949**

● CATALOG OF CURRENT LAW TITLES, ANNUAL (US/1049-796X) [21310592] **2949**

CATALOG OF FEDERAL DOMESTIC ASSISTANCE (US/0097-7799) [02239457] **1468**

CATALOG OF FEDERAL PAPERWORK REQUIREMENTS, BY INDUSTRY GROUP (US) [05962699] **656**

CATALOG OF FINE ANTIQUE CAMERAS & PHOTOGRAPHIC IMAGES (US) [04560433] 4368, **250**

CATALOG OF GOVERNMENT PATENTS (US/0748-8858) [07885671] **1302**

CATALOG OF HEALTHCARE INFORMATION AND MANAGEMENT SYSTEMS PUBLICATIONS / AHA (US) [18004214] **3778**

CATALOG OF INFORMATION ON WATER DATA. INDEX TO WATER-DATA ACQUISITION (US) [21165609] **5532**

CATALOG OF KOREA ELECTRONICS (KO) [06498892] **2038**

CATALOG OF MARKET RESEARCH REPORTS / UNITED STATES DEPARTMENT OF COMMERCE, INTERNATIONAL TRADE ADMINISTRATION (US) [11250098] **826**

CATALOG OF MEMBERSHIP PROGRAMS AND SERVICES (US/0147-2976) [03142704] **818**

CATALOG OF NATIONAL ARCHIVES MICROFILM PUBLICATIONS (US/0094-629X) [01294422] **2481**

CATALOG OF NEW FOREIGN AND INTERNATIONAL LAW TITLES (US/1043-4852) [19473314] **3126**

CATALOG OF NEW YORK STATE VISUAL ARTISTS SELECTED FOR THE CREATIVE ARTISTS PUBLIC SERVICE PROGRAM, A (US/0732-3530) [04368345] **347**

CATALOG OF PRODUCTS & SERVICES (US) [24222079] **5092**

CATALOG OF PROFESSIONAL DEVELOPMENT SEMINARS / INSTITUTE FOR ADVANCED TECHNOLOGY, CONTROL DATA CORPORATION (US) [08257680] **5092**

CATALOG OF PUBLICATIONS - OAS. CATALOGO DE PUBLICACIONES - OEA (US) [03301080] **412**

CATALOG OF PUBLICATIONS OF THE NATIONAL CENTER FOR HEALTH STATISTICS (US/0278-4912) [07062972] **4809**

CATALOG OF PUBLICATIONS - THE JAPAN FEDERATION OF COMPOSERS (JA) [01794555] **4108**

CATALOG OF ... - SOTHEBY'S IN IRELAND (IE) [20910342] 250, **347**

CATALOG OF STATE ASSISTANCE PROGRAMS (US) [21542643] **2908**

CATALOG OF STATE ASSISTANCE PROGRAMS (US/0097-9309) [01799329] 4717, **4637**

CATALOG OF TAPE RECORDED BOOKS / RECORDINGS FOR THE BLIND (US) [03006556] **4385**

CATALOG OF TELEVISION AND AUDIOVISUAL MATERIALS (US/0193-5801) [04630010] 5316, **1130**

CATALOG OF THE FLORIDA STATE ARCHIVES (US) [03922058] **2481**

Alphabetical Title Index — CATALONIA

CATALOG OF THE THEATRE AND DRAMA COLLECTIONS (US) [05162901] **5362**

CATALOG OF TISSUE TYPING ANTISERA *See* NIAID CATALOG OF TISSUE TYPING ANTISERA **568**

CATALOG OF TRAINING ACTIVITIES / U.S. DEPARTMENT OF COMMERCE, BUREAU OF THE CENSUS (US) [05022174] **5194**

●CATALOG OF TRAINING / FISH AND WILDLIFE SERVICE, U.S. DEPARTMENT OF THE INTERIOR (US) [24117603] **2212**

CATALOG OF UNIVERSITY PRESENTATIONS (US/0748-5093) [10935743] **3734, 4771**

CATALOG PRODUCT NEWS (US/1048-0633) [20845148] **949**

CATALOG SHOPPER (US/0742-4035) [10331558] **952**

CATALOG SOURCES FOR CREATIVE PEOPLE, NEWS & UPDATES (US/0732-6696) [08428413] **1924**

CATALOG. WORLD BANK PUBLICATIONS *See* WORLD BANK CATALOG OF PUBLICATIONS, THE **1540**

CATALOGER'S DESKTOP (US) [29419319] **412**

CATALOGHI D'ARTE: INDICI ANALITICI (IT) [01787123] **347**

CATALOGHI DI MOSTRE (IT/0531-9811) [01378089] **347**

CATALOGING & CLASSIFICATION QUARTERLY (US/0163-9374) [04538259] **3200**

CATALOGING SERVICE BULLETIN (US/0160-8029) [04097432] **3200**

CATALOGING SERVICE BULLETIN INDEX (US/0739-3393) [08829405] **3200**

CATALOGO BOLAFFI DELL'ARCHITETTURA ITALIANA (IT/0576-8896) [02981778] **294**

CATALOGO - CENTRO DE DOCUMENTACION Y BIBLIOTECA, CASA DE CHILE EN MEXICO (MX) [05378286] **3200**

CATALOGO COLECTIVO DE PERIODICOS DA AREA DE EDUCACAO (BL) [05818281] **1793**

CATALOGO COLETIVO DE PUBLICACOES PERIODICAS EM CIENCIAS BIOMEDICAS (BL) [04403283] **3655**

CATALOGO DAS INSTITUICOES CATOLICAS DE ENSIO SUPERIOR NO BRASIL (BL) [06894374] **5025, 1731**

CATALOGO DE ESPECIALIDADES FORMACEUTICOS (SP/0302-4296) [10260081] **4295**

CATALOGO DEGLI EDITORI ITALIANI / ASSOCIAZIONE ITALIANA EDITORI (IT) [18215375] **4813**

CATALOGO DEI LIBRI IN COMMERCIO: AUTORI (IT) [03419593] **412**

CATALOGO DEI LIBRI IN COMMERCIO: SOGGETTI (IT) [03415884] **412**

CATALOGO DEI LIBRI IN COMMERCIO: TITOLI (IT) [03415845] **412**

CATALOGO DEI PERIODICI ITALIANI (IT) [07525615] **3458**

CATALOGO DEL ARCHIVO GENERAL DE LA NACION (PE) [02240669] **2481**

CATALOGO DELLA SCULTURA ITALIANA (IT) [09364015] **347**

CATALOGO DIPINTI DELL 800 : SEMENZATO (IT) **4223**

CATALOGO DIPINTI MODERNI E ARTE CONTEMPORANIA : SEMENZATO (IT) **4223**

CATALOGO EDILE (IT) **2020**

CATALOGO GENERAL - FONDO DE CULTURA ECONOMICA, MEXICO (MX) [01293731] **1531**

CATALOGO GENERAL ... PUBLICACIONES OFICIALES (SP) [19645889] **412**

CATALOGO GENERALE DELLE ASTE : NUOVA BRERARTE *CEASED.* (IT) **347**

CATALOGO GENERALE DELLE ASTE: SOTHEBY'S (IT) **656**

CATALOGO GERAL DAS INSTITUICOES DE ENSINO SUPERIOR (BL) [02239942] **1814**

CATALOGO INDUSTRIAL VASCO-NAVARRO (SP) [01785291] **1551**

CATALOGO INTERNAZIONALE BOLAFFI D'ARTE ANTICA E DI ANTIQUARIATO (IT) [01799309] **250, 347**

CATALOGO SOFTWARE (IT) **1284**

CATALOGO STUDIO CENTRO (IT) [01795823] **347**

CATALOGUE AFNOR (FR/0750-7046) [10319270] **4030**

CATALOGUE AMENDMENT SERVICE (UK/0951-8835) [I09518835] **4637**

CATALOGUE & INDEX (UK/0008-7629) [01553503] **3200**

CATALOGUE ANNUEL DES LIVRES ET PERIODIQUES (FR) [23176353] **4637**

CATALOGUE : BRITISH SUPPLIERS TO THE OIL, GAS, PETROCHEMICAL, AND PROCESS INDUSTRIES / ENERGY INDUSTRIES COUNCIL (UK) [08519813] **4253**

CATALOGUE, CARTES POSTALES ANCIENNES DE COLLECTION (FR) [03803990] **370**

CATALOGUE COLLECTIF DES LIVRES FRANCAIS DE SCIENCES ET TECHNIQUES (FR) [08658571] **5092**

CATALOGUE DE LA PRODUCTION CINEMATOGRAPHIQUE FRANCAISE (FR/0224-7518) [11723611] **4065**

CATALOGUE DE L'EDITEUR OFFICIEL DU QUEBEC (CN/0316-1560) [12100095] **4813**

CATALOGUE DE L'INGENIERIE (FR/0245-0283) [07096853] **1967**

CATALOGUE DE LIVRES AU FORMAT DE POCHE (FR/0769-1696) [03455096] **412**

CATALOGUE DE PUBLICATIONS EUROPEENNES (CN/0847-4583) [23248001] **606**

CATALOGUE DE REPRODUCTIONS DE PEINTURES *CEASED.* (FR) [03647512] **347**

CATALOGUE DE VENTE - PARIS. MUSEE GALLIERA (FR) [05351856] **347**

CATALOGUE DES DOCUMENTS AUDIOVISUELS (CN) [06104341] **4065**

CATALOGUE DES FOURNITURES ET DU MOBILIER (CN/1187-1776) [25352119] **4211**

●CATALOGUE DES LIVRES ET PERIODIQUES PARUS EN (FR) [29528344] **4637**

CATALOGUE DES MICROEDITIONS (CN/0384-9724) [03589378] **3200**

CATALOGUE DES PRODUITS EN FRANCAIS (CN/1186-1215) [24296466] **412**

CATALOGUE DES PUBLICATIONS - MINISTERE DE L'INDUSTRIE ET DU COMMERCE, DIRECTION DES COMMUNICATIONS (CN) [02241521] **826**

CATALOGUE DES PUBLICATIONS - SERVICE GEOLOGIQUE DE MADAGASCAR *CEASED.* (MG) [02246984] **1371**

CATALOGUE DES PUBLICATIONS UNESCO (FR) [05344079] **412**

CATALOGUE DISQUES (FR) [01788915] **5316, 4108**

CATALOGUE DU SERVICE DU FILM DE RECHERCHE SCIENTIFIQUE (FR) [07889680] **5092**

CATALOGUE : FOR THE INDEPENDENT MUSIC TRADE (UK) **4108**

●CATALOGUE FRANCOPHONE CANADIEN DE DOCUMENTS EN ALPHABETISATION / GROUPE DE RESSOURCES DOCUMENTAIRES EN FRANCAIS (CN/1191-5056) [26715100] **412**

CATALOGUE - FUNNEL (CN/0826-2861) [11559816] **4065**

CATALOGUE GENERAL DES EDITIONS *See* EDITIONS / ORSTOM **415**

CATALOGUE GENERAL DES MANUSCRITS LATINS (FR) **412**

CATALOGUE / JOHN F. KENNEDY SCHOOL OF GOVERNMENT, HARVARD UNIVERSITY (US) [09287798] **1814**

CATALOGUE - LAURENCE WITTEN RARE BOOKS (US/8756-7083) [05716524] **4827**

CATALOGUE / MAPS ALBERTA (CN/0833-2045) [15190817] **2581**

CATALOGUE - NATIONAL INDIAN LAW LIBRARY (US/0092-3419) [01784478] **3079**

CATALOGUE OF 16 MM. FILMS (AT) [03876730] **4065**

CATALOGUE OF ACCESSIONED PUBLICATIONS. SUPPLEMENT (US/0162-0827) [01483881] **1447**

CATALOGUE OF AMERICAN AMPHIBIANS AND REPTILES (US) [01731778] **5580**

CATALOGUE OF BOOKS ADDED TO THE NEW SOUTH WALES PARLIAMENTARY LIBRARY FROM THE ... WITH SUBJECT-INDEX (AT) [16503909] **3200**

CATALOGUE OF BRITISH OFFICIAL PUBLICATIONS NOT PUBLISHED BY HMSO (UK/0260-5619) [07678038] **412**

CATALOGUE OF CALCAREOUS NANNOFOSSILS (IT) [02253475] **1371**

CATALOGUE OF CELL LINES AND HYBRIDOMAS / AMERICAN TYPE CULTURE COLLECTION (US) [13714606] **561**

CATALOGUE OF CONODONTS (GW) [02254716] **4226**

CATALOGUE OF DEPARTMENTALLY-OWNED FILMS HOUSED WITH FILM LIBRARY / THE GENERAL LIBRARIES (US) [06566604] **3200**

CATALOGUE OF DOCUMENTS AND PUBLICATIONS / EDUCATION SECTOR, DOCUMENTATION AND COMPUTER-ASSISTED MANAGEMENT SERVICE (FR) [18617450] **863, 1173**

CATALOGUE OF EMERGENCY MEDICINE RESIDENCY PROGRAMS (US) [23076039] **3723**

CATALOGUE OF FILAMENTOUS FUNGI / AMERICAN TYPE CULTURE COLLECTION (US) [24774870] **451**

CATALOGUE OF FORAMINIFERA. SUPPL (US/0885-7083) [01567801] **4164**

CATALOGUE OF GOVERNMENT PUBLICATIONS (KE) [01783583] **412**

CATALOGUE OF GOVERNMENT PUBLICATIONS. GOVERNMENT OF TAMIL NADU (II/0376-7744) [01797698] **412**

CATALOGUE OF ICAO PUBLICATIONS AND AUDIO VISUAL TRAINING AIDS (CN) [30958664] **41**

CATALOGUE OF IEC PUBLICATIONS COMPLETE TO ... / INTERNATIONAL ELECTROTECHNICAL COMMISSION (SZ) [19543055] **2038**

CATALOGUE OF ILO PUBLICATIONS *See* ILO CATALOGUE OF PUBLICATIONS IN PRINT **1533**

●CATALOGUE OF OTA PUBLICATIONS (US) [27807171] **5174**

CATALOGUE OF PRINTED MUSIC IN THE BRITISH LIBRARY : ACCESSIONS (UK) [02717527] **4108**

CATALOGUE OF PUBLICATIONS (AT/1032-805X) [20243249] **5325**

CATALOGUE OF PUBLICATIONS STOCKED IN GOVERNMENT PRESSES, TRIVANDRUM, ERNAKULAM AND SHORANUR (II) [01784160] **413**

CATALOGUE OF PUBLICATIONS - WORLD METEOROLOGICAL ORGANIZATION (US) [06526160] **1421**

CATALOGUE OF RARE BOOKS (JA) [03217916] **4827**

CATALOGUE OF SCRIPTS HELD AT THE SALAMANCA SCRIPT RESOURCE CENTRE (AT/0728-5256) [I07285256] **317**

CATALOGUE OF SOCIAL AND ECONOMIC DEVELOPMENT INSTITUTES AND PROGRAMMES, TRAINING / DEVELOPMENT CENTRE OF ORGANISATION FOR ECONOMIC CO-OPERATION AND DEVELOPMENT (FR) [06689373] **1468**

CATALOGUE OF STATE PROGRAMS (CARSON CITY) (US/0091-0694) [01786329] **1551**

CATALOGUE OF STATISTICAL INFORMATION ON PAPUA NEW GUINEA (PP) [01795331] **5325**

CATALOGUE OF THE ACTIVE VOLCANOES OF THE WORLD, INCLUDING SOLFATARA FIELDS (IT) [06079112] **1404**

CATALOGUE OF THE EXHIBITION - ROYAL CANADIAN ACADEMY OF ARTS (CN/0080-4290) [05424224] **347**

CATALOGUE OF UNESCO PUBLICATIONS (FR/0566-7704) [01596870] **413**

CATALOGUE OF UNITED KINGDOM OFFICIAL PUBLICATIONS [COMPUTER FILE] : UKOP (UK) [25835984] **4637**

CATALOGUE OF USED PLATE NUMBER SINGLES *See* HEBERT'S CATALOGUE OF USED PLATE NUMBER SINGLES **2785**

CATALOGUE OF YEASTS (US/1062-5151) [23890384] **506**

CATALOGUE OF YUGOSLAV PERIODICALS AND NEWSPAPERS (YU/0352-7220) [19761207] **5814, 5813**

CATALOGUE P.N.P2S, PERUM. P2S, P.T.P2S INDUSTRI KIMIA (IO) [02167504] **1601**

CATALOGUE-REPERTOIRE DES CREATEURS-CONCEPTEURS (CN/1185-9318) [25423397] **317**

CATALOGUES ET PUBLICATIONS EN VENTE (FR) [08331642] **413**

CATALOGUING AUSTRALIA (AT/0312-4371) [18272630] **3200**

CATALOGUS MUSICUS (GW/0069-116X) [01553508] **4108**

CATALOGUS VAN NEDERLANDSE ZEEKAARTEN EN ANDERE HYDROGRAFISCHE PUBLIKATICS (NE) [02458256] **2558**

CATALOGUS VAN NEDERLANDSE ZEEKAARTEN EN BOEKWERKEN *See* CATALOGUS VAN NEDERLANDSE ZEEKAARTEN EN ANDERE HYDROGRAFISCHE PUBLIKATICS **2558**

CATALONIA CULTURE (SP) [16800164] **2514**

CATALONIA

CATALONIA (SPAIN) See DIARI OFICIAL DE LA GENERALITAT DE CATALUNYA **2960**

CATALONIA (SPAIN) See DIARI OFICIAL DE LA GENERALITAT DE CATALUNYA **5810**

CATALONIA (SPAIN). PARLAMENT See DIARI DE SESSIONS DEL PARLAMENT DE CATALUNYA **4471**

CATALONIA (SPAIN). PARLEMENT See BUTLLETI OFICIAL DEL PARLAMENT DE CATALUNYA **4635**

CATALYSIS (UK/0140-0568) [03782073] **1050**

CATALYSIS IN ORGANIC SYNTHESES (US/0197-534X) [06049000] **1040**

CATALYSIS LETTERS (NE/1011-372X) [18121158] **1050**

CATALYSIS REVIEWS : SCIENCE AND ENGINEERING (US/0161-4940) [01299901] **2009**

CATALYSIS TODAY (NE/0920-5861) [16108226] **966**

CATALYST (US) [05081836] **1861**

CATALYST (ATLANTA, GA.) (US/0896-7423) [17285074] **3373**

CATALYST (BRANTFORD) (CN/0381-5005) [02578951] **3373**

CATALYST / CITIZENS FOR PUBLIC JUSTICE (CN/0824-2062) [09844936] **4942, 4467**

CATALYST (DES MOINES, IOWA : 1971), THE (US/0730-711X) [08044324] **3201**

CATALYST. (EVANSTON) (US/0528-2616) [02820963] **1731**

CATALYST FOR CHANGE (US/0739-2532) [02510997] **1861**

CATALYST FOR ENVIRONMENTAL CONTROL STATIONARY SOURCES (BE) **2162**

CATALYST (GOROKA, PAPUA NEW GUINEA) (PP/0253-2921) [03263409] **2669**

CATALYST (MENLO PARK, CALIF.), THE (US/0897-3318) [11516829] **1265, 1876**

CATALYST (MONTPELIER, VT.) CEASED. (US/0742-6534) [10408042] **1468**

CATALYST OXFORD (UK/0958-3629) [109583629] **5092**

CATALYST (PETERBOROUGH) CEASED. (CN/0008-7661) [01553511] **5241**

CATALYST (PHILADELPHIA), THE (US/0008-767X) [02251146] **967**

CATALYST REVIEW NEWSLETTER, THE (US/0898-3089) [17784723] **1050**

CATALYST (TORONTO. 1982) (CN/0824-2062) [09981985] **2727**

CATALYST (VANCOUVER. 1986) (CN/0834-2466) [16274240] **5092**

CATALYSTS & CATALYSIS See LITERATURE ABSTRACTS. CATALYSTS & CATALYSIS **4284**

CATALYSTS IN CHEMISTRY (UK/0309-5770) [03092979] **967**

CATARACT (NEW YORK, N.Y.) CEASED. (US/0740-6967) [09992528] **3873**

CATASAUQUA DISPATCH, THE (US) [10209132] **5735**

CATASTROPHISM AND ANCIENT HISTORY (US/0733-8058) [06471737] **2613**

CATAWBA COLLEGE See ALUMNI DIRECTORY / CATAWBA COLLEGE **1097**

CATCHWORD AND TRADE NAME INDEX : CATNI (UK) [07838693] 5093, **5174**

CATECHESE (FR) [01643604] **5025**

CATECHIST (US/0008-7726) [01553516] 1731, **5025**

CATECHIST'S CONNECTION, THE (US) **5025**

CATECHUMENATE (CHICAGO, ILL.) (US/1040-659X) [15151005] **4942**

CATEDRA : ORGANO DE LA FACULTAD DE CIENCIAS DE LA EDUCACION DE LA UNIVERSIDAD NACIONAL AUTONOMA DE NICARAGUA (UNAN-MANAGUA) (NQ) [26945108] **1814**

CATEGORY B CEASED. (AT/0810-2627) [I08102627] **1731**

CATEGORY REPORT (US) **2330**

CATENA (GIESSEN) (GW/0341-8162) [02417050] **166**

CATENA SUPPLEMENT (GW/0722-0723) [08624734] **1353**

CATEQUESIS LATINOAMERICANO (PY) [02918817] **5025**

CATEQUETICA (SP) [06033984] **5025**

CATERER & HOTELKEEPER (UK/0008-7777) [I00087777] 2804, **2330**

CATERING (UK) 2804, **2330**

CATERING (UK) **2330**

CATERING & HEALTH (UK/0267-3851) [18421261] **2330**

CATERING BUYERS GUIDE (UK) 2330, **949**

CATERING IMPACT (US/1057-042X) [23919097] **2330**

CATERING INDUSTRY EMPLOYEE (US/0008-7815) [06000681] 2330, **1658**

CATERING MAGAZINE (NE) [I09212191] **2330**

CATERING MANAGEMENT (AUCKLAND, N.Z.) (NZ/0113-2326) [23131414] **2330**

CATERING RECORDS AND PROCEDURES (UK) **2330**

CATERING : REVISTA DE ALIMENTACION RESTAURACION Y EQUIPAMIENTO PARA GRANDES COLECTIVIDADES CEASED. (SP) **2330**

CATERING SERVICE IDEA NEWSLETTER (US) **2330**

CATERING UPDATE (UK/0269-7696) [I02697696] **2331**

CATERPILLAR See FREEWAY/L.A **5440**

CATFISH AND AQUACULTURE NEWS (US) [22646479] **2299**

CATFISH PROCESSING / NATIONAL AGRICULTURAL STATISTICS SERVICE, UNITED STATES DEPT. OF AGRICULTURE (US) [28014099] 5325, **2299**

CATFISH (WASHINGTON, D.C.) See CATFISH PROCESSING / NATIONAL AGRICULTURAL STATISTICS SERVICE, UNITED STATES DEPT. OF AGRICULTURE **2299**

CATFISH (WASHINGTON, D.C.) (US/0735-2077) [06310860] **2299**

CATHAIR NO MART (IE/0332-4117) [15814107] **2683**

●CATHAY (US/1065-9250) [26789902] **3461**

CATHEDRA (MX) [03403387] **3373**

CATHEDRAL AGE (US/0008-7874) [01553520] 4942, **294**

CATHEDRAL CITY POST (US/0884-6189) [12401682] **5633**

CATHER STUDIES (US/1045-9871) [20306212] **3373**

CATHETERIZATION AND CARDIOVASCULAR DIAGNOSIS (US/0098-6569) [01506956] **3702**

Alphabetical Title Index

CATHOLIC See PRAY TOGETHER INSTRUCTIONS FOR LECTORS AND COMMENTATORS **4987**

CATHOLIC ACCENT, THE (US/0745-399X) [02259034] **5025**

CATHOLIC ADVANCE, THE (US/0008-7904) [04021158] **5025**

CATHOLIC ALMANAC (US/0069-1208) [01553524] **5025**

CATHOLIC ANCESTOR (UK) 5025, **2442**

CATHOLIC ANSWER, THE (US/1044-1581) [17790397] **5025**

CATHOLIC ARCHIVES : THE JOURNAL OF THE CATHOLIC ARCHIVES SOCIETY (UK/0261-4316) [09343400] **5025**

CATHOLIC BIBLICAL QUARTERLY. MONOGRAPH SERIES (US) [03520475] **5016**

CATHOLIC BULLETIN, THE (US) [01553534] **5025**

CATHOLIC CHALLENGE, THE (US/8756-7482) [11689314] **5025**

CATHOLIC CHRONICLE, THE (US/0008-7971) [04021206] **5025**

CATHOLIC CHURCH. ARCHDIOCESE OF KINSHASA (ZAIRE) See PERSONNEL ECCLESIASTIQUE / ARCHDIOCESE DE KINSHASA **5034**

CATHOLIC CHURCH. ARCHDIOCESE OF OTTAWA. ARCHBISHOP (1967- : PLOURDE) See MANUSCRIPT LETTERS OR COMMUNIQUES PUBLISHED IN THE ARCHDIOCESE OF OTTAWA **5032**

CATHOLIC CHURCH. ARCHDIOCESE OF SANTIAGO (CHILE). VICARIA DE LA SOLIDARIDAD See VICARIA DE LA SOLIDARIDAD **5038**

CATHOLIC CHURCH. CANADIAN CONFERENCE OF CATHOLIC BISHOPS See ANNUAIRE - CONFERENCE DES EVEQUES CATHOLIQUES DU CANADA **5023**

CATHOLIC CHURCH. CANADIAN CONFERENCE OF CATHOLIC BISHOPS. NATIONAL LITURGICAL OFFICE See GUIDELINES FOR PASTORAL LITURGY **5030**

CATHOLIC CHURCH. CANADIAN CONFERENCE OF CATHOLIC BISHOPS. NATIONAL LITURGICAL OFFICE See ORDO (1977) **5033**

CATHOLIC CHURCH. CONFERENCIA NACIONAL DOS BISPOS DO BRASIL See COMUNICADO MENSAL DA CONFERENCIA NACIONAL DOS BISPOS DO BRASIL **5028**

CATHOLIC CHURCH. CONFERENCIA NACIONAL DOS BISPOS DO BRASIL See DIRETORIO LITURGICO **5028**

CATHOLIC CHURCH. POPE See ACTA APOSTOLICAE SEDIS, COMMENTARIUM OFFICIALE **5022**

CATHOLIC CHURCH. ROTA ROMANA. TRIBUNAL APOSTOLICUM See DECISIONES SEU SENTENTIAE **5028**

CATHOLIC CHURCH SECRETARIATUS AD CHRISTIANORUM UNITATEM FOVENDAM See INFORMATION SERVICE **4965**

CATHOLIC CHURCH. VICARIATO GENERAL CASTRENSE See BOLETIN OFICIAL DE LA JURISDICCION ECLESIASTICA CASTRENSE **5024**

CATHOLIC COMMENTATOR, THE (US/0746-0511) [09701176] **5025**

CATHOLIC COURIER (1989) (US/1054-2728) [19290046] **5025**

CATHOLIC DIGEST (SAINT PAUL, MINN.) (US/0008-7998) [06161602] **5025**

CATHOLIC DIRECTORY See CATHOLIC DIRECTORY OF ENGLAND AND WALES, THE **5025**

CATHOLIC DIRECTORY FOR SCOTLAND, THE (UK/0306-5677) [01793890] **5025**

CATHOLIC DIRECTORY OF ENGLAND AND WALES, THE (UK) [06058667] **5025**

CATHOLIC EXPONENT, THE (US/0162-7031) [04215311] **5025**

CATHOLIC FREE PRESS, THE (US/0008-8056) [04021300] **5026**

CATHOLIC GAZETTE (UK/0008-8064) [09224540] **5026**

CATHOLIC HEALTH ASSOCIATION OF CANADA See C. H. A. C. REVIEW **3777**

CATHOLIC HEALTH WORLD (US/8756-4068) [11558213] **3778**

CATHOLIC HERALD (UK/0008-8072) [05996158] **5026**

CATHOLIC HERALD (SACRAMENTO, CALIF.) (US/0746-4185) [10029657] **5026**

CATHOLIC HISTORICAL REVIEW, THE (US/0008-8080) [01553555] **5026**

CATHOLIC INSIGHT CEASED. (US) **5026**

CATHOLIC INSTITUTE FOR INTERNATIONAL RELATIONS See CIIR ANNUAL REVIEW **4948**

CATHOLIC INTERNATIONAL (FR) [22834910] **5026**

CATHOLIC INTERNATIONAL EDUCATION OFFICE. BULLETIN. NOUVELLE SERIE See OIEC BIMESTRIEL BULLETIN **1883**

CATHOLIC JOURNALIST (US/0008-8129) [01553558] 4813, 5026, **2918**

CATHOLIC LAWYER, THE (US/0008-8137) [01553559] 5026, **2949**

CATHOLIC LEAGUE FOR RELIGIOUS & CIVIL RIGHTS NEWSLETTER (US) **4505**

CATHOLIC LIBRARY ASSOCIATION See CLA HANDBOOK AND MEMBERSHIP DIRECTORY / CATHOLIC LIBRARY ASSOCIATION **3202**

CATHOLIC LIBRARY WORLD, THE (US/0008-820X) [01553562] 5026, **3201**

CATHOLIC LIGHT, THE (US/0164-9418) [04246573] **5735**

CATHOLIC MEDICAL QUARTERLY : JOURNAL OF THE GUILD OF CATHOLIC DOCTORS (UK/0008-8226) [01776532] 5026, **3562**

CATHOLIC MESSENGER (US/0008-8234) [01553564] **5026**

●CATHOLIC MUSIC EDUCATOR (US/1059-9088) [24807645] **4108**

CATHOLIC NEAR EAST MAGAZINE (US/0164-0674) [04556515] **5026**

CATHOLIC NEW TIMES (CN/0701-0788) [03406416] **5026**

CATHOLIC NEW YORK (US/0278-1174) [07715329] **5026**

CATHOLIC NEWS & HERALD, THE (US/1060-0159) [24844446] **5026**

CATHOLIC NORTHWEST PROGRESS See PROGRESS (SEATTLE, WASH.), THE **5034**

●CATHOLIC PARENT (HUNTINGTON, IND.) (US/1069-4862) [28129732] 2277, **5026**

CATHOLIC PERIODICAL AND LITERATURE INDEX, THE (US/0008-8285) [02065864] 5026, **5012**

CATHOLIC PRESS DIRECTORY (US/0008-8307) [01553571] **5012**

CATHOLIC RECORD SOCIETY, LONDON See PUBLICATIONS. (MONOGRAPH SERIES) **5035**

CATHOLIC REGISTER, THE (CN/0383-1620) [02370610] **5026**

CATHOLIC RESOURCE NEWSLETTER (US/8756-9698) [11732303] **5026**

CATHOLIC REVIEW (BALTIMORE, MD.), THE (US/0008-8315) [04021407] **5026**

CATHOLIC SCHOOL STUDIES: A JOURNAL OF EDUCATION FOR AUSTRALIAN & NEW ZEALAND CATHOLIC SCHOOLS (AT) 5026, **1890**

CATHOLIC SENTINEL - CATHOLIC CHURCH. DIOCESE OF BAKER (OR.) (US/0162-0363) [04086271] **5026**

CATHOLIC SINGLES *CEASED.* (US/0886-8190) [13021913] 5026, **5242**

CATHOLIC SPIRIT (AUSTIN, TEX.) (US/0896-2715) [16993927] **5026**

CATHOLIC STANDARD (GY) [11760218] **4942**

CATHOLIC STANDARD AND TIMES, THE (US) [12891386] **5735**

CATHOLIC STANDARD (WASHINGTON, D.C.) (US/0411-2741) [09458506] **5026**

CATHOLIC SUN (SYRACUSE, N.Y.), THE (US/0744-267X) [08165247] **5026**

CATHOLIC TELEGRAPH (US) [21378781] **5727**

CATHOLIC TELEPHONE GUIDE (US/0147-5959) [03200866] **5026**

CATHOLIC TELEPHONE GUIDE AND DIRECTORY FOR THE ARCHDIOCESE OF NEW YORK AND THE DIOCESE OF BROOKLYN *See* CATHOLIC TELEPHONE GUIDE **5026**

CATHOLIC THEOLOGICAL SOCIETY OF AMERICA *See* PROCEEDINGS OF THE ANNUAL CONVENTION **4988**

CATHOLIC TIMES (COLUMBUS, OHIO), THE (US/0745-6050) [09359077] **5026**

CATHOLIC TIMES (MONTREAL) (CN/0703-1521) [03781908] **5026**

CATHOLIC TRANSCRIPT, THE (US) [17864375] **5645**

CATHOLIC TRENDS (US) [01553582] **5026**

CATHOLIC TWIN CIRCLE (US/0273-6136) [06769186] **5026**

CATHOLIC UNIVERSE-BULLETIN, THE (US/0162-7023) [04215378] **5027**

CATHOLIC UNIVERSITY LAW REVIEW (1975) (US/0008-8390) [01553585] **2949**

CATHOLIC UNIVERSITY OF AMERICA. GRADUATE DEPT. OF LIBRARY AND INFORMATION SCIENCE *See* ANNUAL REPORT - GRADUATE DEPT. OF LIBRARY AND INFORMATION SCIENCE, THE CATHOLIC UNIVERSITY OF AMERICA **3190**

CATHOLIC UNIVERSITY OF AMERICA. YEARBOOK *See* CARDINAL YEARBOOK, THE **1814**

CATHOLIC UPDATE (US) **5027**

CATHOLIC VIRGINIAN (US/0008-8404) [04021525] **5027**

CATHOLIC VOICE (OAKLAND, CALIF.), THE (US/0279-0645) [07491000] **5027**

CATHOLIC WEEK, THE (US/1045-7496) [12284105] **5625**

CATHOLIC WORKER, THE (US/0008-8463) [01553601] **5027**

CATHOLIC WORLD (1989), THE (US/1042-3494) [18946116] **5027**

CATHOLIC WORLD REPORT, THE (US/1058-8159) [24384074] **5027**

CATHOLIC YOUTH MINISTRY (US/0277-8165) [07646335] **5027**

CATHOLICA (MUNSTER) (GW/0008-8501) [01695820] **5027**

CATHOLICISM TODAY (US) **5027**

CATIONS OF BIOLOGICAL SIGNIFICANCE (US) [08178248] **484**

CATO JOURNAL, THE (US/0273-3072) [07036762] **5195**

CATO POLICY REPORT (US/0743-605X) [10624977] **1468**

CATONSVILLE TIMES (US/0748-5263) [10961825] **5686**

●CAT'S EAR (US/1062-6379) [25686947] **3461**

CATS MAGAZINE (US/0008-8544) [01553604] **4286**

CATSKILL MOUNTAIN NEWS (US) [08433945] **5714**

CATSKILLS GUIDE (US) **5466**

CATSKILLS, THE (US/0090-452X) [01785083] **2530**

CATTLE (AT/0310-8279) [02393515] **208**

CATTLE BUSINESS IN MISSISSIPPI (US/0897-2737) [17445599] 208, **72**

CATTLE FEEDER, THE (CN/1182-8765) [23237480] **208**

CATTLE GUARD (US/0411-289X) [06212425] **208**

CATTLE ON FEED (US/0364-202X) [01644520] **208**

CATTLE (WASHINGTON) (US/0094-3819) [04046003] **209**

CATTLEMAN (US/0008-8552) [01553607] **209**

CATTLEMEN (CN/0008-3143) [01843127] **209**

CATTW BULLETIN (CN/1184-6569) [24367972] 2918, **1890**

CATV SYSTEMS DIRECTORY, MAP SERVICE & HANDBOOK (US/0091-1984) [01786256] **1130**

CAUCE (SANTIAGO, CHILE) (CL) [10570157] **2727**

CAUCES (AG) [21507657] **4467**

CAUCHO (AG/0528-3280) [02776387] **5075**

CAUDA PAVONIS (US/1059-8308) [10571971] **2844**

CAUMASA (II) [11197285] **2648**

CAUSA INTERNATIONAL SEMINAR SERIES (NEW YORK, N.Y. : 1986) *CEASED.* (US/0891-1975) [14641177] **4517**

CAUSE & FUNCTION (US/0731-7433) [07897712] **5276**

CAUSE DI MORTE (1989) (IT/1121-0958) [23002028] **5325**

CAUSE/EFFECT (US/0164-534X) [04564048] 1890, **1814**

CAUSES OF DEATH, AUSTRALIA (AT) [09222093] 4550, **4561**

CAUSEWAYS & THEATRE PROJECTS; ANNUAL REPORT (US/0277-6286) [04995899] **5439**

CAUT BULLETIN (CN/0834-9614) [16856541] **1814**

●CAUTG BULLETIN (CN/1193-817X) [27809639] **1890**

CAUTION MAGAZINE *See* HEALTH & SAFETY SPECIFIER **4778**

CAVALCADE AND DIRECTORY OF ACTS & ATTRACTIONS *See* CALVACADE OF ACTS & ATTRACTIONS **384**

CAVALIER CHRONICLE (US) [01553611] **5725**

CAVALIER COUNTY REPUBLICAN (US) [01553612] **5725**

CAVALIER (SAINT-GERMAIN-DE-GRANTHAM) (CN/0384-6156) [03248211] **2798**

●CAVALRY JOURNAL, THE (US/1074-0252) [28318459] **2613**

CAVE EXPLORATION GROUP OF EAST AFRICA *See* BULLETIN - CAVE EXPLORATION GROUP OF EAST AFRICA **1403**

CAVE SCIENCE (1982) (UK/0263-760X) [08834386] **1404**

CAVEAT (US/0411-3012) [02999735] **2949**

CAVEAT VENDOR (US/0197-193X) [05966195] **2949**

CAVELTI'S MARKET REPORT (CN/0849-181X) [23237028] **894**

CAVES & CAVING (UK/0142-1832) [04521916] 1404, **1371**

CAVES AND KARST (US/0008-8625) [02250793] **1404**

CAVING IN THE ROCKIES (US/0736-6655) [09189572] **1404**

CAVING INTERNATIONAL (CN/0706-8166) [06769337] **4871**

CAVITATION AND MULTIPHASE FLOW FORUM (US/0884-0636) [10516600] **1967**

CAVOUR EPISTOLARIO (IT) **2613**

CAWP NEWS & NOTES (US/1060-3670) [21068410] 4467, **5553**

CAYENNE (CN/0827-0732) [13434678] **5553**

CAYMAN GAZETTE (CJ/0376-7779) [02243242] **2949**

CAYMAN ISLANDS CONSOLIDATED INDEX OF STATUTES AND SUBSIDIARY LEGISLATION TO ... (BB) [12597911] **3126**

CAYMAN ISLANDS HANDBOOK AND BUSINESSMAN'S GUIDE (BF) [01791660] **656**

CAYMAN ISLANDS HOLIDAY GUIDE *See* CAYMAN ISLANDS MAP & VISITORS GUIDE : OFFICIAL GUIDE OF THE CAYMAN ISLANDS, DEPARTMENT OF TOURISM **5466**

CAYMAN ISLANDS LAW REPORTS, THE (UK/0269-977X) [14171322] **2949**

CAYMAN ISLANDS. LEGISLATIVE ASSEMBLY *See* HANSARD OFFICIAL REPORT **4654**

CAYMAN ISLANDS. LEGISLATIVE ASSEMBLY *See* MINUTES : LEGISLATIVE ASSEMBLY OFFICIAL REPORT **4665**

CAYMAN ISLANDS MAP & VISITORS GUIDE : OFFICIAL GUIDE OF THE CAYMAN ISLANDS, DEPARTMENT OF TOURISM (CJ) [19542624] **5466**

CAYMAN ISLANDS YEARBOOK AND BUSINESS DIRECTORY, THE (CJ) [16070542] **656**

CAYO PUBLICATION (CN/0712-3272) [09000549] **4108**

CAZA FOTOGRAFICA (SP) [02441405] **4164**

CAZENOVIA REPUBLICAN (US) [09890252] **5714**

CB. CITIZENS BAND (UK/0261-0361) [02610361] **1151**

CB MAGAZINE : TRAINING TECHNOLOGISTS FOR TOMORROW (SI) **5093**

CB (MEXICO CITY, MEXICO : 1980) *CEASED.* (MX) [07756499] **3201**

CB RADIO JOURNAL (US/0145-8167) [02792582] **1105**

CB REPORT (US) [17660356] **1814**

CB VOICE *CEASED.* (US/0145-6806) [02767736] **1151**

CBA RECORD (US/0892-1822) [14949323] **2949**

CBA REPORT *See* REPORT - CINCINNATI BAR ASSOCIATION **3037**

CBAC NEWS (CN/0715-5956) [10330405] 656, **347**

CBASSE NEWSLETTER (US/0734-5119) [08767779] 1731, **5195**

CBC CLASSICAL CATALOGUE (CN/0713-1283) [08663188] **4108**

CBC FEATURES (US) [12139803] **3373**

CBC JAZZ AND POPULAR RECORD CATALOGUE (CN/0713-1291) [08663184] **4108**

CBE REPORT : A PUBLICATION OF THE ASSOCIATION FOR COMMUNITY BASED EDUCATION (US) [16639894] **1731**

CBE VIEWS (US/0164-5609) [04541852] 4813, **451**

CBI EDUCATION & TRAINING BULLETIN *CEASED.* (UK) [06634779] **1912**

CBI FORSKNING (SW/0346-6906) [07902778] **2020**

CBI NEWS (UK/0261-6661) [I02616661] **5093**

CBI RAPPORTER (SW/0346-8240) [02958551] **2020**

CBIA NEWS (US/0199-686X) [03835899] **656**

CBIE RESEARCH (CN/1183-4404) [25314060] **1731**

CBMR DIGEST (US/1043-1241) [18669845] 2258, **4108**

CBMR MONOGRAPHS (US/1042-8836) [19232906] **4108**

CBMS-NSF REGIONAL CONFERENCE SERIES IN APPLIED MATHEMATICS (US/0163-9439) [04537602] **3499**

●CBN NEWSLETTER (CK/1022-1492) [I10221492] **166**

CBP'S GUIDE TO BLACK CHARLOTTE (US/1061-8783) [25482194] **2258**

CBS BUDGETONDERZOEK / CENTRAAL BUREAU VOOR DE STATISTIEK, HOOFDAFDELING STATISTIEKEN VAN INKOMEN EN CONSUMPTIE (NE) [10129059] **1468**

CBS CARROSSERIE-, AANHANGWAGEN- EN OPLEGGERINDUSTRIE / CENTRAAL BUREAU VOOR DE STATISTIEK, HOOFDAFDELING STATISTIEKEN VAN INDUSTRIE EN BOUWNIJVERHEID (NE) [10058408] **5409**

CBS ELEKTROTECHNISCHE INDUSTRIE / CENTRAAL BUREAU VOOR DE STATISTIEK, HOOFDAFDELING STATISTIEKEN VAN INDUSTRIE EN BOUWNIJVERHEID (NE) [10058056] **2038**

CBS MAIN ALPHABETICAL & NUMERICAL CATALOGUE (UK) [02158550] **4108**

CBS NEWS *See* CBS NEWS SPECIAL REPORT **1130**

CBS NEWS *See* CBS REPORTS **1130**

CBS NEWS SPECIAL REPORT (US/0361-3135) [02051960] **1130**

CBS REPORTS (US/0361-3097) [02051476] **1130**

CBS RIJWIEL- EN MOTORRIJWIELINDUSTRIE / CENTRAAL BUREAU VOOR DE STATISTIEK, HOOFDAFDELING STATISTIEKEN VAN INDUSTRIE EN BOUWNIJVERHEID (NE) [10057844] **428**

CBS WEGVERVOERVERWANTE BEDRIJVEN / CENTRAAL BUREAU VOOR DE STATISTIEK, HOOFDAFDELING STATISTIEKEN VAN VERKEER EN VERVOER (NE) [10128979] **5379**

CBT DIRECTIONS *CEASED.* (US/0898-8498) [17933171] **1173**

CC AI (BE/0773-4182) [17063702] **1212**

●CC PERFORMANCE CAR (US/1066-4734) [26947664] **5409**

CCA NEWS / CHRISTIAN CONFERENCE OF ASIA (SI/0129-9891) [08242583] **4943**

CCAN *CEASED.* (US/0277-0407) [07485221] 1173, **606**

CCAR JOURNAL (1991) (US/1058-8760) [24079831] **5046**

CCB NATIONAL NEWSLETTER (CN/0824-3042) [10845214] **4385**

CCB : REVIEW FOR CHOCOLATE, CONFECTIONERY AND BAKERY (GW/0341-2601) [03111029] **2331**

CCBC : COOPERATIVE CHILDREN'S BOOK CENTER CIRCULAR (US) [04717660] **4827**

CCC NEWS (US/8750-2259) [11143845] **2277**

CCCO NEWS NOTES (US/0008-5952) [01553674] **4039**

●CCD ASTRONOMY (US/1074-875X) [29867457] **394**

CCEA NEWSLETTER (AT/0310-1878) [I03101878] **1861**

CCH CANADIAN LIMITED *See* CANADIAN DEPRECIATION GUIDE **2948**

CCH JOURNAL OF ASIAN PACIFIC TAXATION, THE (AT/1031-8364) [I10318364] **4717**

CCH JOURNAL OF AUSTRALIAN TAXATION, THE (AT/1032-1810) [I10321810] **4717**

CCHA MEDIA GUIDE (US) **4889**

CCHA NEWS RELEASE (US) **4889**

CCI. CLIMA COMMERCE INTERNATIONAL (GW/0009-8914) [I00098914] **2604**

CCI NEWSLETTER OTTAWA (CN/1180-3223) [I11803223] **2189**

CCI NOTES (CN/0714-6221) [25883172] **2189**

CCI NOUVELLES (CN/0822-5192) [10087984] **1967**

CCIC INFORMATION (FR) **2908**

CCIR (SZ) **1151**

CCIR (RE) [03097599] **818**

CCIS NEWSLETTER (US/0160-8711) [03783209] **1173**

CCLA NEWS NOTES (CN) **4505**

CCLM NEWSLETTER *CEASED.* (US/0273-3315) [07042307] **3373**

●CCMC NEWS (CN/1188-0783) [26758305] **606**

CCMS BUSINESS PAGES (CN/0229-7779) [08091309] **863**

CCPD ACTIVITY REPORT (SZ) [06676250] **4943**

CCPE NEWS (CN/0712-5844) [09332433] **1967**

CCPS/AICHE DIRECTORY OF CHEMICAL PROCESS SAFETY SERVICES (US/1057-1981) [23719977] 2860, **967**

CCR FUTURES TRADING GUIDE (CN/0710-3468) [08185722] **894**

CCRA NEWSLETTER : THE OFFICIAL MONTHLY NEWSLETTER OF THE CAMPUS COMPUTER RESELLERS ALLIANCE, THE (US/1058-8329) [24397271] **1244**

CCRM MARINE REPORTS (BE) **1105**

CCSSA NEWSLETTER (US) [04393494] **5195**

CCTA NEWSLETTER *See* CCTANS NEWSLETTER **1814**

CCTA NEWSLETTER (CN/1183-4056) [25652312] **1814**

●CCTANS NEWSLETTER (CN/1197-5865) [29970406] **1814**

CCTD NEWSLETTER (TH) [09071684] **2502**

CCUA NEWS *See* CHRISTIAN COMPUTER NEWS **1174**

CD BOOK (GW) 922, **949**

CD COMPUTING NEWS (US/0893-4843) [15566284] 1236, **1276**

CD COREWORKS. CD-ROM (US) **3373**

CD DATA REPORT *SUSPENDED.* (US/8755-5727) [11347361] 3201, **1276**

●CD-DIS (ARLINGTON, VA.) (US/1061-6691) [25396862] **2908**

CD-HOUSING REGISTER, THE (US/1050-3811) [21472958] **2817**

CD-I NEWS *CEASED.* (US) [17778389] **1173**

CD INTERNATIONAL. AMERICAN CD REFERENCE GUIDE (US) [25569480] **4108**

CD MARKETING (GW) **922**

CD PLUS COMPACT DISC CATALOGUE (CN/0843-9532) [22254420] **4108**

CD PLUS (FIRM) *See* CD PLUS COMPACT DISC CATALOGUE **4108**

CD PUBLISHER NEWS (US) **5316**

CD RATELINE *CEASED.* (US/0746-8431) [10319477] **782**

CD REVIEW DIGEST ANNUAL. CLASSICAL (US) [21389847] **4108**

CD REVIEW DIGEST. CLASSICAL (US/1045-0114) [19968675] **4108**

CD REVIEW DIGEST. JAZZ, POPULAR, ETC (US/1045-0122) [19968606] **4108**

CD REVIEW (HANCOCK, N.H.) (US/1044-1700) [19695398] **4108**

CD-ROM (FR) **1276**

CD-ROM APPLICATIONS FORUM (US/0892-0176) [15060352] **1173**

CD-ROM DATABASES (US) **1276**

CD-ROM DEVELOPERS LAB. CD-ROM (US) **1276**

CD-ROM DIRECTORY ON DISC, THE (US/1062-6891) [25697227] **1276**

CD-ROM DIRECTORY, THE (UK) [18796290] **1174**

CD-ROM ENDUSER (US/1042-8623) [19231671] **1174**

●CD-ROM FINDER : THE WORLD OF CD-ROM PRODUCTS FOR INFORMATION SEEKERS (US) [27986707] 1276, **3257**

CD-ROM HANDBOOK (US/1059-5260) [24617797] **3201**

CD-ROM INFORMATION PRODUCTS *CEASED.* (UK/0967-8123) 1276, **1264**

CD ROM INTERNATIONAL (FR) **1276**

CD-ROM LIBRARIAN (US/0893-9934) [15719667] 3201, **1174**

CD-ROM MARKET PLACE (US/1047-966X) [20832255] **1174**

●CD-ROM NEWS EXTRA (US/1075-1106) [27543259] **1276**

CD-ROM NEWSLETTER ALTON (UK/0954-3600) [09543600] **1276**

●CD-ROM POCKET GUIDE (US/1076-0415) [30380250] **1276**

CD-ROM ... PRODUCT GUIDE (US) [24326184] **1276**

CD-ROM PROFESSIONAL (US/1049-0833) [21127593] **1276**

CD-ROM SHOPPERS GUIDE *SUSPENDED.* (US/1048-406X) [20943685] **1174**

CD-ROM SOURCEDISC (US) **413**

CD-ROM SOURCEDISC [COMPUTER FILE], THE (US) [25321200] **1276**

●CD-ROM TODAY (US/1069-4099) [28034164] **1276**

●CD-ROM WORLD (US/1066-274X) [26912047] 3201, **1276**

CD-ROMS IN PRINT (US/0891-8198) [14996071] **1276**

CD-ROMS IN PRINT (CD-ROM VERSION) (US/1052-2638) [22231996] 3201, **1276**

CD SUMMARY (US/1058-7888) [22945192] **3712**

CD WORLDLIBRARY : THE INTERACTIVE BIBLICAL LIBRARY. CD-ROM (US) **4943**

●CDA/INVESTNET INSIDERS' CHRONICLE (US) [27322507] **894**

●CDA/SPECTRUM. 13(F) INSTITUTIONAL STOCK HOLDINGS (US) [28320146] 782, **894**

●CDA/SPECTRUM FIVE PERCENT STOCK HOLDINGS (US) [27723639] **894**

●CDA/SPECTRUM INSIDER HOLDINGS (US) [27923587] **894**

●CDA/WIESENBERGER MUTUAL FUNDS PANORAMA (US) [26018188] **894**

●CDA/WIESENBERGER MUTUAL FUNDS UPDATE (US/1066-9264) [25566912] **894**

CDB NEWS / CARIBBEAN DEVELOPMENT BANK (BB) [09959453] **782**

CDC BULLETIN : A PUBLICATION OF THE CURRICULUM DEVELOPMENT COUNCIL FOR SOUTHERN NEW JERSEY (US/1056-246X) [23600596] **1890**

CDC HIV : AIDS PREVENTION NEWSLETTER (US) [22781204] 4771, 3667, **3712**

CDC LIBRARY SERIAL HOLDINGS (US/0748-853X) [08574738] **413**

CDC LIBRARY (U.S.) *See* CDC LIBRARY SERIAL HOLDINGS **413**

CDE STOCK OWNERSHIP DIRECTORY : AGRIBUSINESS (US/0277-5646) [04961328] 72, **656**

CDE STOCK OWNERSHIP DIRECTORY : BANKING & FINANCE (US/0197-0313) [05951364] **782**

CDE STOCK OWNERSHIP DIRECTORY : ENERGY (US/0197-0321) [05951251] **782**

CDE STOCK OWNERSHIP DIRECTORY : FORTUNE 500 (US/0276-7775) [07421865] **782**

CDE STOCK OWNERSHIP DIRECTORY: TRANSPORTATION INDUSTRY (US/0162-8275) [03711906] **5379**

CDF REPORTS (US/0276-6531) [07389354] **5276**

CDF'S CHILD, YOUTH, AND FAMILY FUTURES CLEARINGHOUSE *CEASED.* (US/1055-9221) [23379700] 2277, **5276**

CDHES / COMISION DE DERECHOS HUMANOS DE EL SALVADOR (US) [12714519] **4505**

CDIAC COMMUNICATIONS (US/1053-1106) [17400792] **1421**

CDMARC BIBLIOGRAPHIC (US/1054-3996) [22876447] **413**

CDMARC NAMES (US/1041-2964) [18758700] **1174**

●CDMARC SERIALS (US/1063-8784) [26167838] **3201**

CDMARC SUBJECTS (US/1041-2956) [18543489] **3201**

CDMARC SUBJECTS (US/1041-2956) [27206939] **3201**

CDP FILE [COMPUTER FILE] / NATIONAL CENTER FOR CHRONIC DISEASE PREVENTION AND HEALTH PROMOTION (US) [25355073] **4771**

CDPRESS (AU/0376-7795) [02337070] **2683**

CDR ANNUAL REPORT *See* CDR IN **1468**

CDR IN (DK) [18060051] 5195, **1468**

CDR PROJECT PAPER (DK/0904-4698) [26490400] **72**

CDR PROJECT PAPERS (DK/0106-0805) [10884937] **2908**

CDR PROJECT PAPERS. A *See* CDR PROJECT PAPER **72**

CDR RESEARCH REPORT (DK/0108-6596) [13000696] **5195**

CDR WORKING PAPERS (DK/0904-4701) [I09044701] **5093**

CDROM DATABASES (US/0897-3296) [17461169] 3201, **1174**

CDRR NEWS (US) **5553**

CDS CONNECTION (US/0895-2485) [16521606] **3201**

CDS. CONSEIL DE DEVELOPPEMENT SOCIAL DU MONTREAL METROPOLITAIN (CN/0316-5175) [02247471] **5242**

CDS INFO PLUS (UK) **1174**

CDS REVIEW (US/0091-1666) [03960488] **1318**

●CDS ZUM AUSLEIHEN (GW) **4160**

CDWORD *See* CD WORLDLIBRARY : THE INTERACTIVE BIBLICAL LIBRARY. CD-ROM **4943**

CE COMPUTING REVIEW *CEASED.* (US/1044-8179) [19906702] **2020**

CE.D.R.E.S. DOCUMENTI (IT) [10631957] 1469, **1531**

CE FASTU? : RIVISTA DELLA SOCIETA FILOLOGICA FRIULANA "GRAZIADO I. ASCOLI." (IT) [05144155] **3273**

CE/Q MEDICAL NEWSLETTER (US/1047-6059) [20730755] **3795**

CEA ADVISOR (US/0007-8050) [02259056] **1731**

CEA CONGRESSIONAL LEDGER (US/0737-3007) [09289212] **4637**

CEA CRITIC (US/0007-8069) [01537968] **3373**

CEA CRITIC, THE (US/0007-8069) [01911525] **3273**

CEA FORUM (US/0007-8034) [01564054] **3273**

CEAL DIRECTORY (US) [13847073] **2648**

CEARA (BRAZIL : STATE). PROCURADORIA GERAL DO ESTADO *See* REVISTA DA PROCURADORIA GERAL DO ESTADO **3040**

CEARA MEDICO (BL/0101-1782) [07801533] **3562**

CEBU COMMERCIAL GUIDE (PH) [01795861] **826**

CEBU Y DERIVADOS (AG/0008-8668) [02999692] **209**

CEC CENSUS OF BUYERS IN THE CHEMICAL PROCESS INDUSTRIES (US/0190-4760) [04706049] 2009, **1601**

CECIDOLOGIA INTERNATIONALE (II/0970-5112) [07099867] **5580**

CECIL WHIG, THE (US/1046-2058) [09728296] **5686**

CECON RECORD (1983) (US/0747-9948) [10202705] **2038**

CECS NEWSLETTER *See* EXCEL **2862**

CED (DENVER, COLO.) (US/1044-2871) [19732395] **1130**

CED DIRECTORY OF ENGINEERING AND ENGINEERING TECHNOLOGY CO-OP PROGRAMS (US) [09722138] **1968**

CEDA ANNUAL REPORT (AT) [11125668] **1551**

CEDAC - CARTHAGE (TI/0330-2210) [I03302210] **265**

CEDAR COUNTY HISTORICAL SOCIETY REVIEW, THE (US/0576-9736) [03467079] **2727**

CEDAR COUNTY REPUBLICAN AND STOCKTON JOURNAL (US) [26175173] **5703**

CEDAR CREEK PILOT (US/1046-8633) [18091847] **5748**

CEDAR FALLS CITIZEN, THE (US/8750-5665) [11521467] **5669**

CEDAR HILL CHRONICLE See TODAY CEDAR HILL **5755**

CEDAR LAKE JOURNAL (US) [18373725] **5663**

CEDAR TREE, THE CEASED. (US/0738-1905) [05845137] **2442**

CEDAR VALE MESSENGER, THE (US) [09876043] **5674**

CEDAR VALLEY TIMES (VINTON, IOWA : 1971) (US/0746-5645) [10125792] **5669**

CEDARTOWN STANDARD (1950) (US/1056-8271) [18333248] **5652**

CEDEFOP NEWS (GW) [08859176] **1731**

● CEDEL EUROMONEY DIRECTORY, THE (UK) [27743742] **782**

CEDIGAZ NEWS REPORT (FR) **4253**

CEDOCLA See BOLETIN INFORMATIVO - CEDOCLA **344**

CEE NEWS (US/1045-2710) [20060617] **2038**

CEGB ABSTRACTS CEASED. (UK) [13609167] **2038**

CEGB DIGEST (UK/0374-2792) [08014022] **2038**

CEGB RESEARCH CEASED. (UK/0305-7194) [01597115] **2038**

CEGEP DE DRUMMONDVILLE See MOUTON NOIR **5790**

CEGEP-INTER (CN/0229-3390) [08028020] **1814**

CEGEP-PRESSE (CN/0706-182X) [06132816] **4637**

CEGEPROPOS CEASED. (CN/0319-681X) [01931116] **1814**

CEI (UK) **1151**

CEIBA (HO/0008-8692) [01553619] **72**

CELADE (ORGANIZATION) See BOLETIN DEMOGRAFICO - CENTRO LATINOAMERICANO DE DEMOGRAFIA **4550**

CELADE (ORGANIZATION). BANCO DE DATOS See BOLETIN DEL BANCO DE DATOS **4550**

CELAT-INFORMATION (CN/0710-197X) [08192719] 3273, **2318**

CELEBRATE CEASED. (AT) [02824043] **4943**

CELEBRATE LIFE (US) **4943**

CELEBRATE! (OTTAWA) (CN/0843-2538) [20178152] **4943**

CELEBRATION (HAGERSTOWN, MD.) (US/0887-1094) [13114858] **5057**

CELEBRATION (KANSAS CITY, MO.) (US/0094-2421) [01605470] **5027**

CELEBRATIONS TO CROSS STITCH AND CRAFT (US/1045-3814) [20082962] **5183**

CELEBRER (FR) **4343**

CELEBRER PARIS (FR/0240-4656) [I02404656] **2844**

CELEBRIANO (IT) [09649649] **384**

CELEBRITY (US/0163-8378) [04483705] **2530**

CELEBRITY DOLL PRICE GUIDE & ANNUAL (US) [12169982] **2584**

CELESTIAL MECHANICS AND DYNAMICAL ASTRONOMY (NE/0923-2958) [20751247] **394**

CELESTINESCA (US/0147-3085) [03136935] **3373**

CELIBATAIRES MAGAZINE (CN/1183-7675) [25423446] 5553, **3994**

CELJSKI ZBORNIK (XV/0576-9760) [03102076] **2683**

CELL ADHESION AND COMMUNICATION (US/1061-5385) [25354748] **532**

CELL ANALYSIS (US/0737-1233) [08438755] **533**

CELL AND CHROMOSOME RESEARCH (II/0254-2935) [10685483] 543, **533**

CELL AND TISSUE RESEARCH (GW/0302-766X) [01794057] **533**

CELL BIOCHEMISTRY AND FUNCTION (UK/0263-6484) [09500510] 533, **484**

CELL BIOLOGY AND TOXICOLOGY (PRINCETON SCIENTIFIC PUBLISHERS) (NE/0742-2091) [12617538] 3979, **533**

● CELL BIOLOGY INTERNATIONAL (UK/1065-6995) [26684328] **533**

CELL BIOLOGY INTERNATIONAL REPORTS (UK/0309-1651) [02823639] **533**

CELL BIOLOGY REVIEWS : CBR CEASED. (SP) [24914252] **533**

CELL BIOPHYSICS (US/0163-4992) [04391788] 533, **495**

CELL CALCIUM (UK/0142-8020) [12259271] 484, **3562**

CELL CALCIUM (EDINBURGH) (UK/0143-4160) [06565416] **533**

CELL (CAMBRIDGE) (US/0092-8674) [01792038] **533**

● CELL CONTACT AND COMMUNICATION (UK/1351-5314) **533**

CELL CONTACT PHENOMENA See CELL CONTACT AND COMMUNICATION **533**

CELL CONTACT PHENOMENA (UK/0142-8039) [I01428039] **533**

CELL CYCLE (UK/0263-7251) **533**

● CELL DEATH AND DIFFERENTIATION (UK/1350-9047) **451**

CELL DIFFERENTIATION SHEFFIELD (UK/0263-726X) [I0263726X] **533**

CELL GROWTH & DIFFERENTIATION (US/1044-9523) [19958252] **533**

CELL MEMBRANES (UK/0142-8047) [02254527] **533**

CELL MEMBRANES, METHODS AND REVIEWS (US/0740-784X) [09474589] **533**

CELL MOTILITY AND THE CYTOSKELETON (US/0886-1544) [12848217] **533**

CELL NUCLEUS (UK/0141-299X) [04684384] **534**

CELL PROLIFERATION (UK/0960-7722) [23197707] **534**

CELL REGULATION See MOLECULAR BIOLOGY OF THE CELL **539**

CELL SCIENCE (JA/0915-907X) [I0915907X] **451**

CELL STRUCTURE AND FUNCTION (JA/0386-7196) [02381348] **534**

CELL TRANSFORMATION (UK/0142-8063) [08890705] **534**

● CELL TRANSPLANTATION (US/0963-6897) [25644585] **3795**

● CELL VISION (US/1073-1180) [29333547] **534**

CELLE NEWSLETTER (US/0743-4979) [08883516] **2442**

CELLS AND MATERIALS (US/1051-6794) [22055813] **534**

CELLS AND MATERIALS. SUPPLEMENT (US/1060-9989) [25149778] **534**

CELLULAR & MOBILE INTERNATIONAL (US/1054-7703) [22969341] **1151**

CELLULAR AND MOLECULAR BIOLOGY (UK/0145-5680) [08769603] **534**

● CELLULAR AND MOLECULAR BIOLOGY (FR) [27137595] **534**

● CELLULAR & MOLECULAR BIOLOGY RESEARCH (US/0968-8773) [28366324] **534**

CELLULAR AND MOLECULAR MECHANISMS OF INFLAMMATION (US/1052-5882) [22329758] **484**

CELLULAR AND MOLECULAR NEUROBIOLOGY (US/0272-4340) [06842143] **534**

CELLULAR BUSINESS (US/0741-6520) [10203877] **1151**

CELLULAR CLOCKS (US/1049-0302) [21127807] **534**

CELLULAR DYNAMICS (US) [04405018] **534**

CELLULAR IMMUNOLOGY (US/0008-8749) [01553623] 534, **3667**

CELLULAR INVESTOR (US/0898-0403) [17697367] **1151**

CELLULAR MARKET FORECASTS (US/1071-779X) [28731375] **1151**

CELLULAR MARKETING (US/0890-2402) [14231573] **922**

CELLULAR MOBILE COMMUNICATIONS DIRECTORY See WIRELESS INDUSTRY DIRECTORY **1169**

CELLULAR / MOBILE COMMUNICATIONS DIRECTORY, THE (US) [28125349] **1151**

CELLULAR PEOPLE / PUBLISHED IN ASSOCIATION WITH THE INTERNATIONAL REGISTRY FOR CELLULAR PROFESSIONALS (IRCP) (US/1059-3888) [24579766] **1106**

● CELLULAR PHARMACOLOGY (UK/1351-3214) [30613188] 484, **4295**

CELLULAR PHYSIOLOGY AND BIOCHEMISTRY (SZ/1015-8987) [23603870] 484, **534**

CELLULAR POLYMERS (UK/0262-4893) [09184370] **4454**

CELLULAR SALES & MARKETING (US/0892-2683) [15140070] 922, **1151**

CELLULAR SENESCENCE AND SOMATIC CELL GENETICS (US/0190-146X) [03726147] **534**

CELLULAR SIGNALLING (UK/0898-6568) [17868798] **534**

CELLULAR TECHNOLOGY CEASED. (US/1049-507X) [21245364] **1151**

CELLULAR TELEPHONE DIRECTORY, THE (US) [17864244] **1151**

CELLULE, LA SUSPENDED. (BE/0008-8757) [01553624] **534**

CELLULOSA E CARTA (IT/0008-8765) [01553625] **4233**

CELLULOSE (UK/0969-0239) **3562**

CELLULOSE CHEMISTRY AND TECHNOLOGY (RM/0576-9787) [02988118] **1021**

CELSIUS (AT) **2604**

CELTA SOCIAL (CN/0705-9124) [04097969] **5781**

CELTIBERIA (SP/0528-3647) [02988183] **2613**

CELTICA (DUBLIN) (IE/0069-1399) [03349287] 3373, **3273**

CELULOIDE (PO/0008-8781) [04659544] **4065**

CELULOSA Y PAPEL (CL/0716-2308) [I07162308] **4233**

CELULOSE & PAPEL (BL) [19828413] **4233**

CELULOZA I KHARTIYA (BU/0204-6377) [03886364] **4233**

CELULOZA SI HIRTIE (BUCHAREST, ROMANIA : 1986) (RM) [16781230] **4233**

CEM, CHILTON'S CONTROL EQUIPMENT MASTER (US/0163-0679) [03510068] **2111**

CEMC/ENR DIRECTORY OF LAW FIRMS See DIRECTORY OF CONSTRUCTION LAW FIRMS, THE **2962**

CEMENT ABSTRACTS (II/0970-6720) [I09706720] **606**

CEMENT AMSTERDAM (NE/0008-8811) [I00088811] **606**

CEMENT & CONCRETE (II/0008-8838) [01553634] **606**

CEMENT AND CONCRETE ASSOCIATION See TECHNICAL REPORT - CEMENT AND CONCRETE ASSOCIATION **2594**

CEMENT & CONCRETE COMPOSITES (UK/0958-9465) [22171878] **606**

CEMENT AND CONCRETE RESEARCH (US/0008-8846) [01553635] **2020**

CEMENT (BOMBAY) (II/0008-8803) [11472506] **606**

CEMENT, CONCRETE AND AGGREGATES (US/0149-6123) [03528769] **606**

CEMENT-, KALK- EN OVERIGE MINERALE PRODUKTENINDUSTRIE, GLASINDUSTRIE EN -BEWERKINGSINRICHTINGEN / CENTRAAL BUREAU VOOR DE STATISTIEK, HOOFDAFDELING STATISTIEKEN VAN INDUSTRIE EN BOUWNIJVERHEID (NE/0168-4841) [11886237] **2587**

CEMENT (OTTAWA) (CN/0380-6898) [02443818] **606**

CEMENT, WAPNO, GIPS (PL/0008-8897) [09374194] **607**

CEMENT. ZAGREB (CI/0008-882X) [I00088882X] 1021, 2020, **607**

CEMENTO 1945, IL (IT/0393-6732) [I03936732] **607**

CEMENTO HORMIGON (SP/0008-8919) [09677710] **607**

CEMENTS RESEARCH PROGRESS (US/0363-8642) [02533961] **607**

● CEMETERIES OF THE U.S (US/1071-8729) [28745012] **2442**

CEMETERY BUSINESS & LEGAL GUIDE (US/0162-4237) [04157211] 2949, **2407**

CEMETERY - FUNERAL SERVICE LEGAL COMPASS (US) [25596490] **2407**

CEMETERY LEGAL COMPASS See CEMETERY - FUNERAL SERVICE LEGAL COMPASS **2407**

CEMETERY MANAGEMENT (US/0270-5281) [06434009] **2407**

CEMLA BOLETIN MENSUEL (MX/0008-9958) [03023524] **1469**

CEMOTI. CAHIERS D'ETUDES SUR LA MEDITERRANEE ORIENTALE ET LE MONDE TURCO-IRANIEN (FR/0764-9878) [I07649878] **2648**

CEMREL REPORTS (US) [08542132] **1876**

CEN

CEN GENERAL TECHNICAL REPORT (BE) **4030**

CEN MUN HAGHOI JI (KO/0253-3065) [06657398] **394**

CENAFOR *See* RELATORIO - CENAFOR **1915**

CENCRASTUS (UK) [10038167] **317**

CENELEC CATALOGUE (BE) **2038**

CENIMM; CENTRO NACIONAL DE INVESTIGACIONES METALURGICAS (SP) **4000**

CENIT (FR) **3339**

CENOBIO (SZ/0008-896X) [02529702] **5074**

CENSIS : NOTE E COMMENTI (IT) **1469**

CENSO AGROPECUARIO; VIII RECENSEAMENTO GERAL (BL) [02398096] 72, **152**

CENSO - AGRUPACION SINDICAL NACIONAL DE EMPRESAS DE FINANCIACION (SP) [02619457] **782**

CENSO DE INDUSTRIAS MANUFACTURERAS DE PUERTO RICO. CENSUS OF MANUFACTURING INDUSTRIES OF PUERTO RICO (PR) [05166935] 1658, **3476**

CENSO DE MAQUINARIA AGRICOLA (SP) [06105697] **158**

CENSO DO CALCADO RS / ASSOCIACAO COMERCIAL E INDUSTRIAL DE NOVO HAMBURGO (BL) [09544981] **1082**

CENSORSHIP NEWS (US/0749-6001) [11148902] **1106**

CENSUS AND YOU (US/1057-9656) [18054335] **4561**

CENSUS BUREAU METHODOLOGICAL RESEARCH (US/0565-0828) [02246655] **4550**

CENSUS HIGHLIGHTS *CEASED.* (US) [24357326] **5325**

CENSUS OF AGRICULTURE (1985) / CYPRUS (CY) **72**

CENSUS OF AGRICULTURE. V. 1. STATE AND COUNTY DATA (US) [03086402] **73**

CENSUS OF AGRICULTURE. V. 3. AGRICULTURAL SERVICES (US) [03086491] **73**

CENSUS OF BOARDS OF EXECUTORS AND TRUST COMPANIES (SP/0303-9226) [01798782] **782**

CENSUS OF BUILDING AND CONSTRUCTION (FIJI) (FJ) [01788369] **607**

CENSUS OF BUSINESSES, PROFESSIONS, AND TRADES, NATIONAL STATES LEBOWA / REPUBLIC OF SOUTH AFRICA, DEPARTMENT OF STATISTICS (SA) [10737978] **656**

CENSUS OF EMPLOYMENT / NATIONAL STATISTICAL OFFICE (PP) [19321227] **1658**

CENSUS OF INDUSTRIES (FJ) [17256185] **1601**

CENSUS OF LIBRARIES (NZ) [01760247] **3201**

CENSUS OF LIVESTOCK IN EUROPEAN AREAS (RH/0376-5822) [02240875] **209**

CENSUS OF LOCAL GOVERNMENTS / DEPARTMENT OF VETERAN AND COMMUNITY AFFAIRS (US) [08244256] **4717**

CENSUS OF LOCAL LAW ENFORCEMENT PERSONNEL (US) [09973903] **3160**

CENSUS OF MAINE MANUFACTURES (US/0090-7111) [01785256] **1601**

CENSUS OF MANUFACTURING ESTABLISHMENTS. DETAILS OF OPERATIONS AND SMALL AREA STATISTICS, TASMANIA / [AUSTRALIAN BUREAU OF STATISTICS, TASMANIA] (AT/0157-2156) [08433187] 3476, **3489**

CENSUS OF MINERAL INDUSTRIES (US/0082-9382) [03323992] **1438**

CENSUS OF MINING ESTABLISHMENTS: INDUSTRY CONCENTRATION STATISTICS, AUSTRALIA (AT) [06549708] 2136, **2003**

CENSUS OF POPULATION AND HOUSING (1980) (US) [09859824] **4551**

CENSUS OF PRODUCTION (ZIMBABWE. CENTRAL STATISTICAL OFFICE.) (RH) [06873274] **1551**

CENSUS OF RETAIL SALES AND SELECTED SERVICES (PP) [08459004] **952**

CENSUS OF RETAIL TRADE (US) [02698378] **952**

CENSUS OF SELECTED SERVICE INDUSTRIES (US) [02698282] **4637**

CENSUS OF STORAGE, COMMUNICATIONS, FINANCING, INSURANCE, AND BUSINESS SERVICES *See* SURVEY OF STORAGE, COMMUNICATIONS, FINANCING, INSURANCE, AND BUSINESS SERVICES **714**

CENSUS OF TOURIST ACCOMMODATION ESTABLISHMENTS, WESTERN AUSTRALIA (AT) [02833913] **2804**

CENSUS OF TRANSPORTATION (US) [02846329] **5379**

CENSUS OF U.S. CIVIL AIRCRAFT (US/0069-1437) [01136794] **16**

CENSUS OF WHOLESALE TRADE (US) [02844511] **826**

CENTAUR : HOUSE JOURNAL OF THE INDIAN ASSOCIATION OF EQUINE INTERESTS (II) [14925839] 5507, **2798**

CENTAURUS (DK/0008-8994) [02445765] **5093**

CENTED MONOGRAPH SERIES (US/0275-2751) [07106767] **2226**

CENTENNIAL REVIEW, THE (US/0162-0177) [04088161] **2844**

CENTENNIAL STATE LIBRARIES (US/0887-1116) [13132858] **3201**

CENTER (AUSTIN, TEX.) (US/8755-2019) [11240914] **294**

CENTER CITY REPORT (US/0891-1029) [07426992] **2817**

CENTER FOCUS (US/0889-0765) [09516379] **4943**

CENTER FOR ADVANCED STUDY IN THE VISUAL ARTS (U.S.) *See* CENTER RESEARCH REPORTS AND RECORD OF ACTIVITIES **347**

CENTER FOR ANALYTICAL CHEMISTRY (U.S.) *See* ANNUAL REPORT ... CENTER FOR ANALYTICAL CHEMISTRY **1013**

CENTER FOR COMMUNICATIONS MANAGEMENT, RAMSEY, N.J *See* EXECUTIVE TELECOMMUNICATION PLANNING GUIDE **1155**

CENTER FOR CONSTITUTIONAL RIGHTS (NEW YORK, N.Y.) *See* DOCKET REPORT - CENTER FOR CONSTITUTIONAL RIGHTS **3092**

CENTER FOR DISEASE CONTROL *See* FAMILY PLANNING SERVICES. ANNUAL SUMMARY **589**

CENTER FOR EDUCATIONAL INNOVATION AND TECHNOLOGY *See* INNOTECH NEWSLETTER **1752**

CENTER FOR FOREIGN STUDY *See* ACADEMIC YEAR ABROAD IN EUROPE-AFRICA-AUSTRALIA **1721**

CENTER FOR HEALTH STATISTICS (MICHIGAN) *See* MICHIGAN HEALTH STATISTICS **4810**

CENTER FOR HERMENEUTICAL STUDIES IN HELLENISTIC AND MODERN CULTURE *See* PROTOCOL OF THE COLLOQUY OF THE CENTER FOR HERMENEUTICAL STUDIES IN HELLENISTIC AND MODERN CULTURE **1079**

CENTER FOR JEWISH-CHRISTIAN LEARNING *See* PROCEEDINGS OF THE CENTER FOR JEWISH-CHRISTIAN LEARNING **4988**

CENTER FOR LIFE CYCLE SCIENCES NEWSLETTER (US) **863**

CENTER FOR MATERIALS SCIENCE (NATIONAL MEASUREMENT LABORATORY) *See* ANNUAL REPORT - CENTER FOR MATERIALS SCIENCE (NATIONAL MEASUREMENT LABORATORY) **4029**

CENTER FOR MATERIALS SCIENCE (NATIONAL MEASUREMENT LABORATORY). POLYMER SCIENCE AND STANDARDS DIVISION *See* ANNUAL REPORT / POLYMER SCIENCE AND STANDARDS DIVISION **2100**

CENTER FOR NAVAL ANALYSES *See* CENTER FOR NAVAL ANALYSES PUBLICATIONS CLEARED FOR PUBLIC RELEASE **4175**

CENTER FOR NAVAL ANALYSES PUBLICATIONS CLEARED FOR PUBLIC RELEASE (US) [22607903] **4175**

CENTER FOR POLICY RESEARCH MONOGRAPH SERIES (US/0731-809X) [07476959] **5195**

CENTER FOR PROCESS STUDIES *See* NEWSLETTER OF THE CENTER FOR PROCESS STUDIES **4982**

CENTER FOR REFORMATION RESEARCH *See* NEWSLETTER - CENTER FOR REFORMATION RESEARCH **4981**

CENTER FOR RESEARCH FOR MOTHERS AND CHILDREN (U.S.). NUTRITION AND ENDOCRINOLOGY SECTION *See* RESEARCH PROGRAMS OF THE NATIONAL INSTITUTE OF CHILD HEALTH AND HUMAN DEVELOPMENT. NUTRITION AND ENDOCRINOLOGY **4198**

CENTER FOR RESEARCH LIBRARIES (U.S.) *See* CATALOG MICROFORM / CENTER FOR RESEARCH LIBRARIES **3200**

CENTER FOR RESEARCH LIBRARIES (U.S.) *See* SAMP CATALOG : SUPPLEMENT **3247**

CENTER FOR RESEARCH LIBRARIES (U.S.) *See* FOCUS ON THE CENTER FOR RESEARCH LIBRARIES **3211**

CENTER FOR RURAL AFFAIRS NEWSLETTER (US) **73**

CENTER FOR SELF SUFFICIENCY UPDATE (US/0736-3044) **1876**

CENTER FOR SPORTS SPONSORSHIP'S SPONSOR QUEST, THE (US/0747-6817) [10810054] **4889**

CENTER FOR STRATEGIC AND INTERNATIONAL STUDIES, GEORGETOWN UNIVERSITY, THE (US/0272-2429) [06773528] **4517**

CENTER (LOUISVILLE, KY.), THE (US/0748-6464) [10989944] **384**

CENTER OF MILITARY HISTORY *See* DEPARTMENT OF THE ARMY HISTORICAL SUMMARY (WASHINGTON) **4042**

CENTER ON SOCIAL WELFARE POLICY AND LAW *See* LIBRARY BULLETIN - CENTER ON SOCIAL WELFARE POLICY AND LAW **5295**

CENTER PAPER (PRINCETON, N.J.) (US/0513-1529) [02269747] **4551**

CENTER QUARTERLY (US/0890-4634) [09569211] **4368**

CENTER RESEARCH REPORTS AND RECORD OF ACTIVITIES (US/0737-7010) [09075136] **347**

CENTER STAGE (NEW YORK) (US) **5362**

CENTERING (US) [02824282] **3461**

CENTERLINE (US) [01789609] **5439**

CENTERPOINT *CEASED.* (US/0098-924X) [03147006] **5195**

CENTERPOINT (ASIAN VEGETABLE RESEARCH AND DEVELOPMENT CENTER) (CH) [09775116] **166**

CENTERS OF CIVILIZATION SERIES (US/0069-1461) [02996757] **2613**

CENTERS; UPSCALE SPECIALTY, URBAN MIXED-USE AND FESTIVAL (US) **4835**

CENTERVIEWS (HONOLULU, HAWAII) (US/0746-1402) [09796465] **1814**

● CENTERWATCH (US) **3562**

CENTINELA (NAMPA, IDAHO), EL (US/8750-4308) [11409116] **5057**

CENTO COSE (IT) **2486**

CENTRAAL ECONOMISCH PLAN (NE) [04661493] **1551**

CENTRAALWEEKBLAD (NE) **4943**

CENTRAFRIC-PRESS (CX) [01789539] **2498**

CENTRAIS ELETRICAS DO PIAUI *See* RELATORIO - CEPISA **2079**

CENTRAL AFRICA...BUSINESS DIRECTORY *See* SADCC DIRECTORY AND TRADERS GUIDE **708**

CENTRAL AFRICAN AIRWAYS GUIDE TO THE FEDERATION OF RHODESIA AND NYASALAND (RH/0577-0394) [01127778] **16**

CENTRAL AFRICAN CHAMBER OF COMMERCE AND INDUSTRY DIRECTORY (CM) [08943762] **818**

CENTRAL AFRICAN JOURNAL OF MEDICINE (RH/0008-9176) [01553663] **3562**

CENTRAL AFRICAN ZIONIST DIGEST (RH) [02395766] **5046**

CENTRAL ALABAMA GENEALOGICAL SOCIETY : NEWSLETTER (US) [07625576] **2442**

CENTRAL ALABAMA INDEPENDENT ADVERTISER AND THE UNION-BANNER, THE (US) [12569863] **5625**

CENTRAL ALBERTA BITS & BYTES (CN/1188-2697) [25796571] **1266**

CENTRAL AMERICA AND CARIBBEAN: BASIC OIL LAWS AND CONCESSION CONTRACTS. ORIGINAL TEXTS. SUPPLEMENT (US) [06323106] **4253**

CENTRAL AMERICA NEWSPAK (US/0887-0594) [13077309] 2727, **4467**

CENTRAL AMERICA REPORT (US) **4517**

CENTRAL AMERICA REPORT (UK/0267-4130) [12608629] **4505**

CENTRAL AMERICA REPORT (GUATEMALA CITY) (GT/0254-2471) [03866165] **1551**

CENTRAL AMERICA UPDATE (CN/0823-7689) [07080678] **4467**

CENTRAL AMERICA UPDATE (ALBUQUERQUE, N.M.) (US) [16245031] 4517, **4467**

CENTRAL AMERICA UPDATE (ALBUQUERQUE, N.M.) (US/1054-8882) [23010548] **4467**

CENTRAL AMERICAN ECONOMIST HANDBOOK (UK) [16805445] **1551**

CENTRAL AMERICAN MONITOR *See* LATIN AMERICAN NEWSLINE **2512**

CENTRAL AMERICAN REFUGEE DEFENSE FUND NEWSLETTER / NATIONAL IMMIGRATION PROJECT OF THE NATIONAL LAWYERS GUILD, CENTRAL AMERICAN REFUGEE DEFENSE FUND *CEASED.* (US) [16981566] **1918**

CENTRAL AND EAST EUROPEAN TAX DIRECTORY (NE) 4717

CENTRAL & INNER ASIAN STUDIES *CEASED.* (US/0893-2301) [15465060] 2648

CENTRAL ASIA (PK) [05199764] 2648

CENTRAL ASIA AND THE CAUCASUS IN WORLD AFFAIRS (UK/0968-8689) 656

●CENTRAL ASIA BRIEF (UK/0966-3452) [26140206] 5042

CENTRAL ASIAN SURVEY (UK/0263-4937) [09805528] 2648

CENTRAL ASIATIC JOURNAL (GW/0008-9192) [01553665] 3273, 2648

CENTRAL BANK CIRCULARS AND MEMORANDA (PH/0115-2807) [01790889] 782

CENTRAL BANK OF BARBADOS *See* ANNUAL REPORT - CENTRAL BANK OF BARBADOS 1546

CENTRAL BANK OF BARBADOS. RESEARCH DEPT *See* ECONOMIC AND FINANCIAL STATISTICS 1531

CENTRAL BANK OF IRELAND *See* QUARTERLY BULLETIN - CENTRAL BANK OF IRELAND 805

CENTRAL BANK OF IRELAND. QUARTERLY STATISTICAL BULLETIN *See* QUARTERLY BULLETIN - CENTRAL BANK OF IRELAND 805

CENTRAL BANK OF LESOTHO *See* ANNUAL REPORT ... / CENTRAL BANK OF LESOTHO 1546

CENTRAL BANK OF MALTA *See* ANNUAL REPORT AND STATEMENT OF ACCOUNTS - CENTRAL BANK OF MALTA 770

CENTRAL BANK OF NIGERIA *See* MONTHLY REPORT - CENTRAL BANK OF NIGERIA, LAGOS 799

CENTRAL BANK OF SEYCHELLES *See* ANNUAL REPORT / CENTRAL BANK OF SEYCHELLES 771

CENTRAL BANK OF THE BAHAMAS *See* QUARTERLY REVIEW / THE CENTRAL BANK OF THE BAHAMAS 805

CENTRAL BANK OF THE PHILIPPINES *See* CENTRAL BANK CIRCULARS AND MEMORANDA 782

CENTRAL BANK OF THE PHILIPPINES *See* ANNUAL REPORT / CENTRAL BANK OF THE PHILIPPINES 771

CENTRAL BANK OF TRINIDAD AND TOBAGO *See* ANNUAL REPORT - CENTRAL BANK OF TRINIDAD AND TOBAGO 1546

CENTRAL BANK OF TRINIDAD AND TOBAGO *See* QUARTERLY ECONOMIC BULLETIN - CENTRAL BANK OF TRINIDAD AND TOBAGO 1579

CENTRAL BANKING (UK/0960-6319) [22974384] 782

CENTRAL BUDGET PROPOSALS - DEMOCRATIC REPUBLIC OF SUDAN, MINISTRY OF FINANCE & NATIONAL ECONOMY (SJ) [06586933] 4717

CENTRAL BUREAU FOR SATELLITE GEODESY *See* INFORMATION BULLETIN OF THE CENTRAL BUREAU FOR SATELLITE GEODESY 1407

CENTRAL BUSINESS REVIEW (US/1053-9263) [22692791] 656

CENTRAL BUTTE STAR, THE (CN/0701-0842) [03625993] 5781

CENTRAL CALIFORNIA VEGETABLE REPORT (US/0744-2351) [08126058] 2331

CENTRAL CITIES SIGHT AND SOUND (US/1058-9252) [24433890] 384

CENTRAL CITIES SOURCEBOOK, THE (US/1063-1984) [25341786] 757

CENTRAL COMMITTEE FOR CONSCIENTIOUS OBJECTORS, PHILADELPHIA *See* CCCO NEWS NOTES 4039

CENTRAL CONFERENCE OF AMERICAN RABBIS *See* CENTRAL CONFERENCE OF AMERICAN RABBIS ANNUAL CONVENTION 5046

CENTRAL CONFERENCE OF AMERICAN RABBIS ANNUAL CONVENTION (US/0069-1607) [03473164] 5046

CENTRAL COUNCIL FOR RESEARCH IN UNANI MEDICINE (INDIA) *See* ANNUAL REPORT / CENTRAL COUNCIL FOR RESEARCH IN UNANI MEDICINE 3550

CENTRAL DE COOPERATIVAS AGRARIAS DE PRODUCCION AZUCARERA DEL PERU, NO. 69 *See* MEMORIA - CENTRAL DE COOPERATIVAS AGRARIAS DE PRODUCCION AZUCARERA DEL PERU LTDA. NO. 69 1542

CENTRAL DISTRICT ALMANAC (US) 2949

CENTRAL ELECTRICITY GENERATING BOARD *See* STATISTICAL YEARBOOK 5341

CENTRAL ELECTRICITY GENERATING BOARD *See* REPORT AND ACCOUNTS - CENTRAL ELECTRICITY GENERATING BOARD (LONDON) 707

CENTRAL ELECTRICITY GENERATING BOARD. CENTRAL LIBRARY & INFORMATION SERVICES *See* CEGB ABSTRACTS 2038

CENTRAL ELECTRICITY GENERATING BOARD. INFORMATION SERVICES. DIGEST *See* CEGB DIGEST 2038

CENTRAL ELECTRICITY GENERATING BOARD. TECHNICAL INFORMATION UNIT *See* CEGB DIGEST 2038

CENTRAL EUROPE JOURNAL (GW/0008-9362) [01553678] 2514

CENTRAL EUROPEAN (UK/0962-2543) [23877182] 1633

CENTRAL EUROPEAN FINANCE AND BUSINESS (UK) 656, 782

CENTRAL EUROPEAN HISTORY (US/0008-9389) [01553679] 2683

CENTRAL FLORIDA MAGAZINE (US/8750-2852) [11248262] 2530

CENTRAL IDAHO STAR-NEWS, THE (US/0747-248X) [10664987] 5656

CENTRAL IDAHO STAR-NEWS, THE (US) [18899755] 5656

CENTRAL ILLINOIS GENEALOGICAL QUARTERLY (US/0577-0807) [05395443] 2442

CENTRAL INLAND FISHERIES RESEARCH INSTITUTE (BARRACKPORE, INDIA) *See* BULLETIN - CENTRAL INLAND FISHERIES RESEARCH INSTITUTE BARRACKPORE 2297

CENTRAL INSTITUTE OF ENGLISH AND FOREIGN LANGUAGES *See* CIEFL BULLETIN NEW SERIES 3273

CENTRAL INSTITUTE OF FISHERIES NAUTICAL & ENGINEERING TRAINING (INDIA) *See* ANNUAL REPORT - CENTRAL INSTITUTE OF FISHERIES NAUTICAL & ENGINEERING TRAINING (INDIA) 2294

CENTRAL ISLIP NEWS (1984) (US/8750-104X) [10988853] 5714

CENTRAL ISSUES IN ANTHROPOLOGY *CEASED.* (US/0739-7917) [06173915] 233

CENTRAL KENTUCKY NEWS-JOURNAL (US) [15203023] 5680

CENTRAL KENTUCKY RESEARCHER (US/0095-1439) [01794628] 2442

CENTRAL LAND COUNCIL (AUSTRALIA) *See* ANNUAL REPORT / CENTRAL LAND COUNCIL 4627

CENTRAL LATINOAMERICANA DE TRABAJADORES *See* INFORMATIVO CLAT 1679

CENTRAL LIBRARY SELECTED ACQUISITIONS RELATING TO URBAN AFFAIRS (CN/0824-6459) [10926495] 413

CENTRAL LUZON STATE UNIVERSITY *See* CLSU SCIENTIFIC JOURNAL 75

CENTRAL MINNESOTA ARTS COUNCIL *See* ANNUAL REPORT / CENTRAL MINNESOTA ARTS COUNCIL 312

CENTRAL MISSISSIPPI VALLEY EARTHQUAKE BULLETIN (US) 1404

CENTRAL MISSOURI NEWS (US/0883-7112) [12197413] 5703

CENTRAL MONTANA WAGON TRAILS (US/0883-9603) [08151613] 2442

CENTRAL NEVADA'S GLORIOUS PAST (US/0882-8792) [11946873] 2727

CENTRAL NEW JERSEY HOME NEWS, THE (US) [13854028] 5709

CENTRAL NEW YORK ENVIRONMENT (US/0275-827X) [04126371] 2162

CENTRAL NORTH CAROLINA JOURNAL (US/1050-1339) [21366028] 2530

CENTRAL OFFICE OF INFORMATION REFERENCE PAMPHLET *CEASED.* (UK/0072-5722) [01589721] 4637

CENTRAL ONTARIO REGIONAL LIBRARY SYSTEM *See* DIRECTORY - CENTRAL ONTARIO REGIONAL LIBRARY SYSTEM 3206

CENTRAL PARK (US/0273-3323) [07045907] 2844

CENTRAL PENN BUSINESS JOURNAL (US/1058-3599) [17761914] 656

CENTRAL PENTECOSTAL COLLEGE *See* CENTRAL THEMES 4943

CENTRAL POST, THE (US/8750-1392) [11036107] 5709

CENTRAL RAILWAY CHRONICLE (US/0008-9532) [02445773] 5430

CENTRAL RECORD (LANCASTER, KY.) (US) [13720405] 5680

CENTRAL RECORD (MEDFORD, N.J.) (US/0745-7030) [09385297] 5709

CENTRAL SCHOOL LAW DIGEST (US/0363-7980) [02530373] 1731, 2949

CENTRAL SOYA, INC., FORT WAYNE, IND *See* REPORT - CENTRAL SOYA, INC., FORT WAYNE IND 2627

CENTRAL ST. CROIX NEWS (US) [12181240] 5766

CENTRAL STATE BUSINESS REVIEW (US/8756-4521) [09913074] 656

CENTRAL STATES ANTHROPOLOGICAL SOCIETY *See* BULLETIN - CENTRAL STATES ANTHROPOLOGICAL SOCIETY (U.S.) 232

CENTRAL STATES ARCHAEOLOGICAL JOURNAL (US/0008-9559) [00850921] 265

CENTRAL STATES SPEECH ASSOCIATION (U.S.) *See* DIRECTORY OF MEMBERSHIP - CENTRAL STATES SPEECH ASSOCIATION 1110

CENTRAL TEXAS ARCHEOLOGIST (US/0882-3693) [11821672] 265

CENTRAL TEXAS BLUEGRASS BULLETIN (US) [21127790] 4108

CENTRAL THEMES (CN/0821-4107) [09925267] 1814, 4943

CENTRAL UNIVERSITY OF VENEZUELAU TECHNICAL BULLETINS (VE) 5093

CENTRAL VIRGINIA HERITAGE (US/1043-4895) [13513204] 2442

CENTRAL WEST END JOURNAL (US) [24435674] 5703

CENTRALBLATT FUER DAS GESAMTE FORSTWESEN (AU/0008-9583) [10552777] 2377

CENTRALE CATALOGUS VAN PERIODIEKEN EN SERIEWERKEN IN NEDERLANDSE BIBLIOTHEKEN (CCP). CUMULATIEF SUPPLEMENT (NE) [05466365] 413

CENTRALE DE BILANS (IV) [02857881] 782

CENTRALE DE L'ENSEIGNEMENT DU QUEBEC *See* DECISIONS DU CONGRES DE LA C. E. Q 1662

CENTRALE HANDICAPRAD (DENMARK) *See* DET CENTRALE HANDICAPRADS VIRKSOMHED I ... 5281

CENTRALE VIDENSKABETISKE KOMITE (DENMARK) *See* BERETNING FOR ... / DEN CENTRALE VIDENSKABETISKE KOMITE 3555

CENTRALFORBUNDET FOR BEFALSUTBILDNING *See* VERKSAMHETSBERATTELSE - CENTRALFORBUNDET FOR BEFALSUTBILDNING 4060

CENTRALIA FIRESIDE GUARD (US) [13380779] 5703

CENTRALIA SENTINEL (US/1059-8162) [24774250] 5658

CENTRALLY PLANNED ECONOMIES OUTLOOK (US/0749-6508) [11139779] 1469

CENTRE BELGE D'ETUDE DE LA CORROSION *See* TECHNICAL REPORTS 2017

CENTRE CANADIEN DE GESTION *See* ANNUAL REPORT-CANADIAN CENTRE FOR MANAGEMENT DEVELOPMENT 860

CENTRE CANADIEN DE LA TECHNOLOGIE DES MINERAUX ET DE L'ENERGIE *See* PLAN D'ENTREPRISE DE CANMET 1443

CENTRE (CHICOUTIMI) (CN/0381-8152) [02943083] 5277

CENTRE COUNTY HERITAGE (US/0577-1099) [12006252] 2727

CENTRE COUNTY LEGAL JOURNAL (US) [09875172] 2949

CENTRE CULTUREL PORTUGAIS *See* ARQUIVOS DO CENTRO CULTURAL PORTUGUES 2676

CENTRE DAILY TIMES (US/0745-483X) [09227597] 5735

CENTRE DE CREATION INDUSTRIELLE *See* RAPPORT D'ACTIVITE / CENTRE DE CREATION INDUSTRIELLE 3487

CENTRE DE CULTURE DIALOGUE ORIENTAL *See* ANNUAIRE TELEPHONIQUE - CENTRE DE CULTURE DIALOGUE ORIENTAL 5239

CENTRE DE DOCUMENTATION DE L'ARMEMENT *See* RECAPITULATIF MENSUEL DES SIGNALEMENTS D'ORIGINE CEDOCAR 5145

CENTRE DE DOCUMENTATION DE L'IPD-AOS *See* BULLETIN BIBLIOGRAPHIQUE DU FONDS DOCUMENTAIRE DU CENTRE DE DOCUMENTATION DE L'IPD-AOS / INSTITUT PANAFRICAIN POUR LE DEVELOPPEMENT, DIRECTION REGIONALE DE L'OUEST SAHEL (IPD-AOS) 1530

CENTRE DE DOCUMENTATION PAYSANNE DU PARAGUAY (BE/0771-3398) [I07713398] 4467, 1551

CENTRE DE DONNEES STELLAIRES *See* BULLETIN D'INFORMATION - CENTRE DE DONNEES STELLAIRES 394

CENTRE DE FORMATION PROFESSIONNELLE ET DE PERFECTIONNEMENT (FRANCE) *See* IGD, INITIATION GENERALE AU DROIT 2980

CENTRE — Alphabetical Title Index

CENTRE DE RECHERCHE INDUSTRIELLE DU QUEBEC See RAPPORT ANNUEL - CENTRE DE RECHERCHE INDUSTRIELLE DU QUEBEC **1623**

CENTRE DE RECHERCHES D'HISTOIRE ANCIENNE See PUBLICATION - CENTRE DE RECHERCHES D'HISTOIRE ANCIENNE **2626**

CENTRE DE RECHERCHES ET D'ETUDES OCEANOGRAPHIQUES See TRAVAUX DU CENTRE DE RECHERCHES ET D'ETUDES OCEANOGRAPHIQUES **1457**

CENTRE DE RECHERCHES ET D'ETUDES OCEANOGRAPHIQUES See CIRCULAIRES DU CENTRE DE RECHERCHES ET D'ETUDES OCEANOGRAPHIQUES. I.T **1447**

CENTRE DE RECHERCHES INDUSTRIELLES EN AFRIQUE CENTRALE See SCIENCES, TECHNIQUES, INFORMATIONS CRIAC **5154**

CENTRE DE RECHERCHES POUR LE DEVELOPPEMENT INTERNATIONAL (CANADA) See CRDI EXPLORE, LE **2908**

CENTRE DE RECHERCHES SUR LA RENAISSANCE (SERIES) (FR/0398-6772) [08920435] **2683**

CENTRE DE RECHERCHES SUR L'AMERIQUE ANGLOPHONE See ANNALES DU CENTRE DE RECHERCHES SUR L'AMERIQUE ANGLOPHONE **3362**

CENTRE DE REFLEXION SUR LE MONDE NON OCCIDENTAL. BULLETIN See HOMME ET L'HUMANITE, L' **5247**

CENTRE DE SERVICES SOCIAUX DU CENTRE DU QUEBEC See MISSION IMPOSSIBLE **5296**

CENTRE DE SOCIOLOGIE URBAINE (FRANCE) See ACTIVITE SCIENTIFIQUE DU CENTRE DE SOCIOLOGIE URBAINE, L' **5238**

CENTRE D'ENQUETES STATISTIQUES DE CAEN See ENQUETE ANNUELLE D'ENTERPRISE : MATERIEL DE MANUTENTION, MATERIEL POUR LES MINES, LA SIDERURGIE, LE GENIE CIVIL **1974**

CENTRE D'ENQUETES STATISTIQUES DE CAEN See ENQUETE ANNUELLE D'ENTREPRISE : TRAVAIL DES METAUX **4001**

CENTRE D'ESTUDIS DE LA CONCA DE BARBERA See APLEC DE TREBALLS - CENTRE D'ESTUDIS DE LA CONCA DE BARBERA **2675**

CENTRE D'ETUDE DE LA VIE POLITIQUE FRANCAISE, PARIS See SERIE : ETUDES SYNDICALES **1710**

CENTRE D'ETUDE ET DE DOCUMENTATION AFRICAINES See CAHIERS DU CEDAF, LES **5194**

CENTRE D'ETUDES DE MUSIQUE ORIENTALE See BULLETIN - CENTRE D'ETUDES DE MUSIQUE ORIENTALE **4105**

CENTRE D'ETUDES DE RECHERCHE OPERATIONNELLE, BRUSSELS See CAHIERS - CENTRE D'ETUDES DE RECHERCHE OPERATIONNELLE **1173**

CENTRE D'ETUDES DES SYSTEMES D'INFORMATION DES ADMINISTRATIONS (FRANCE) See RAPPORT D'ACTIVITE - CENTRE D'ETUDES DES SYSTEMES D'INFORMACION DES ADMINISTRATIONS (FRANCE) **3243**

CENTRE D'ETUDES ECONOMIQUES ET SOCIALES D'AFRIQUE OCCIDENTALE See C.E.S.A.O. AUJOURD'HUI, LE **5194**

CENTRE D'HISTOIRE ECONOMIQUE ET SOCIALE DE LA REGION LYONNAISE. BULLETIN DU CENTRE D'HISTOIRE ECONOMIQUE ET SOCIALE DE LA REGION LYONNAISE See BULLETIN / CENTRE PIERRE LEON D'HISTOIRE ECONOMIQUE ET SOCIALE **1549**

CENTRE D'HISTOIRE ET D'ART DE LA THUDINIE See PUBLICATIONS - ASBL CENTRE D'HISTOIRE ET D'ART DE LA THUDINIE **2626**

CENTRE D'ORGANISATION SCIENTIFIQUE DE L'ENTERPRISE See SESSIONS DE FORMATION... / COSE **886**

CENTRE FOR EAST ASIAN STUDIES OCCASIONAL PAPERS (CN/0225-2732) [04473710] **2648**

CENTRE FOR ENVIRONMENTAL STUDIES (GREAT BRITAIN) See ANNUAL REPORT - CENTRE FOR ENVIRONMENTAL STUDIES **2160**

CENTRE FOR IRRIGATION RESEARCH (AUSTRALIA) See REPORT / CSIRO CENTRE FOR IRRIGATION RESEARCH **184**

CENTRE FOR LINGUISTIC AND HISTORICAL STUDIES BY ORAL TRADITION See RAPPORT D'ACTIVITES DU ... / ORGANISATION DE L'UNITE AFRICAINE, CENTRE D'ETUDES LINGUISTIQUES ET HISTORIQUES PAR TRADITION ORALE **3314**

CENTRE FOR OVERSEAS PEST RESEARCH (GREAT BRITAIN) See MISCELLANEOUS REPORT - CENTRE FOR OVERSEAS PEST RESEARCH **109**

CENTRE FOR OVERSEAS PEST RESEARCH (GREAT BRITAIN) See REPORT - CENTRE FOR OVERSEAS PEST RESEARCH **4247**

CENTRE FOR POLICY ON AGING (LONDON, ENGLAND) See ANNUAL REPORT - CENTRE FOR POLICY ON AGING (LONDON, ENGLAND) **5178**

CENTRE FOR POLICY ON AGING (LONDON, ENGLAND). ANNUAL REPORT FOR THE YEAR ENDED 30TH SEPTEMBER . See ANNUAL REPORT - CENTRE FOR POLICY ON AGING (LONDON, ENGLAND) **5178**

CENTRE FRANCAIS DU COMMERCE EXTERIEUR. DIRECTION DES PRODUITS AGRO-ALIMENTAIRES See LEGUMES FRAIS, FRANCE: STATISTIQUES DE COMMERCE EXTERIEUR **1616**

CENTRE FRANCAIS DU COMMERCE EXTERIEUR. DIRECTION DES PRODUITS AGRO-ALIMENTAIRES See COMMERCE EXTERIEUR FRANCAIS DE PRODUITS AGRICOLES ET ALIMENTAIRES **828**

CENTRE FRANCO-ONTARIEN DE RESSOURCES EN ALPHABETISATION See REPERTOIRE DES OUTILS DE REFERENCE **423**

CENTRE INTERNATIONAL DE RECHERCHES SUR L'ANARCHISME See BULLETIN - CENTRE INTERNATIONAL DE RECHERCHES SUR L'ANARCHISME **4540**

CENTRE INTERNATIONAL D'ETUDES POETIQUES See COURRIER DU CENTRE INTERNATIONAL D'ETUDES POETIQUES **3461**

CENTRE INTERUNIVERSITAIRE DE RECHERCHE SUR LA RENAISSANCE ITALIENNE (FR/0768-1305) [07681305] **3373**

CENTRE INTERUNIVERSITAIRE D'ETUDES EUROPEENNES See BULLETIN - CENTRE INTERUNIVERSITAIRE D'ETUDES EUROPEENNES **2680**

CENTRE LETTER (BANFF) (CN/0705-6842) [04233465] **317**

CENTRE LINE (TORONTO) (CN/0702-8369) [03412338] **5409**

CENTRE LOCAL DE SERVICES COMMUNAUTAIRES SAINT-HUBERT See GAZETTE DU C. L. S. C, LA **5785**

CENTRE MEDICAL (MOULINS) (FR/0008-9826) [06931389] **3562**

CENTRE NATIONAL DE DOCUMENTATION PEDAGOGIQUE (FRANCE). SERVICE DU FILM DE RECHERCHE SCIENTIFIQUE See CATALOGUE DU SERVICE DU FILM DE RECHERCHE SCIENTIFIQUE **5092**

CENTRE NATIONAL DE LA CINEMATOGRAPHIE (FRANCE) See INFORMATIONS CNC **4072**

CENTRE NATIONAL DE LA CINEMATOGRAPHIE (FRANCE). BULLETIN D'INFORMATION See INFORMATIONS CNC **4072**

CENTRE NATIONAL DE LA RECHERCHE SCIENTIFIQUE (FRANCE) See IMAGES DE LA CHIMIE **977**

CENTRE NATIONAL DE LA RECHERCHE SCIENTIFIQUE (FRANCE) See FORMATIONS DE RECHERCHE, LES **5105**

CENTRE NATIONAL DE LA RECHERCHE SCIENTIFIQUE (FRANCE) See COLLOQUES INTERNATIONAUX DU CENTRE NATIONAL DE LA RECHERCHE SCIENTIFIQUE **234**

CENTRE NATIONAL DE LA RECHERCHE SCIENTIFIQUE (FRANCE). GROUPE DE RECHERCHES SUR L'ARMEE ROMAINE ET LES PROVINCES See CAHIERS DU GROUPE DE RECHERCHES SUR L'ARMEE ROMAINE ET LES PROVINCES **2682**

CENTRE NATIONAL D'ETUDES SPATIALES (FRANCE) See RAPPORT ANNUEL / CENTRE NATIONAL D'ETUDES SPATIALES **32**

CENTRE ON AGING NEWS (CN/0826-4694) [11895280] **5178**

CENTRE PROTESTANT D'ETUDES See BULLETIN DU CENTRE PROTESTANT D'ETUDES **5057**

CENTRE QUEBECOIS DE COORDINATION SUR LE SIDA See RAPPORT D'ACTIVITES / CENTRE QUEBECOIS DE COORDINATION SUR LE SIDA **4798**

CENTRE QUEBECOIS DE RELATIONS INTERNATIONALES See ACTIVITES DU CQRI **4514**

CENTRE REGIONAL DE DOCUMENTATION PEDAGOGIQUE DE BESANCON See CATALOGUE DISQUES **4108**

CENTRE REGIONAL DE LA SANTE ET DES SERVICES SOCIAUX. REGION 01 See JOURNAL - CONSEIL REGIONAL DE LA SANTE ET DES SERVICES SOCIAUX, REGION 01 **5291**

CENTRE REGIONAL D'ENERGIE SOLAIRE (BAMAKO, MALI) See RAPPORT D'ACTIVITIE / CENTRE REGIONAL D'ENERGIE SOLAIRE **2127**

CENTRE SCIENTIFIC ET TECHNIQUE DE LA CONSTRUCTION See CSTC REVUE **611**

CENTRE SCIENTIFIQUE ET TECHNIQUE DE LA CONSTRUCTION (BE/0770-7274) [107707274] **607**

CENTRE SCIENTIFIQUE ET TECHNIQUE DU BATIMENT (FRANCE) See CAHIERS DU CENTRE SCIENTIFIQUE ET TECHNIQUE DU BATIMENT **5092**

CENTRE STAGE MAGAZINE (CN/0380-4720) [02443249] **5362**

CENTRE TECHNIQUE FORESTIER TROPICAL DU CAMEROUN See RAPPORT ANNUEL - CENTRE TECHNIQUE FORESTIER TROPICAL DU CAMEROUN **2391**

CENTRE THIRD (CN/0712-1334) [08693686] **4889**

CENTRE UNIVERSITAIRE DE LA REUNION See CAHIERS DU CENTRE UNIVERSITAIRE DE LA REUNION **3272**

CENTRE UNIVERSITAIRE MEDITERRANEEN DE NICE See ANNALES DU CENTRE UNIVERSITAIRE MEDITERRANEEN **1089**

CENTRE VIDEO POPULAIRE DE LA RIVE-SUD See CVPOP. CENTRE VIDEO POPULAIRE DE LA RIVE-SUD **1130**

CENTREFOLD (BRANDON) (CN/0710-5851) [08774039] **2817**

CENTREGRAMME (CN/0227-3233) [10440785] **4108**

CENTRES HOSPITALIERS. GUIDE BUDGETAIRE (CN/0712-3108) [08752138] **3778**

CENTRET FOR UDVIKLINGSFORSKNING (DENMARK) See CDR IN **1468**

CENTREVILLE PRESS, THE (US) [11780029] **5625**

CENTRING SLAGELSE (DK/0106-7303) [I01067303] **4849**

CENTRO (IT) **2486**

CENTRO AGRICOLA (CU/0253-5785) [03057709] **73**

CENTRO AMERICA (GUATEMALA, GUATEMALA) (GT) [09264388] **1551**

CENTRO ARQUIDIOCESANO DE PASTORAL, LIMA See COLECCION TEMAS **4948**

CENTRO AZUCAR **SUSPENDED.** (CU/0253-5777) [07124398] **2331**

CENTRO BRASILEIRO DE PESQUISAS FISICAS See RELATORIO DAS ATIVIDADES ADMINISTRATIVAS **4419**

CENTRO BRASILEIRO DE PESQUISAS FISICAS See RELATORIO DA PRESIDENCIA **4419**

CENTRO CAMUNO DI STUDI PREISTORICI See BOLLETTINO DEL CENTRO CAMUNO DI STUDI PREISTORICI **344**

CENTRO DE DESARROLLO INDUSTRIAL DEL ECUADOR See BOLETIN INDUSTRIAL **1599**

CENTRO DE ESTUDIOS DE ESTADO Y SOCIEDAD See REPORT OF ACTIVITIES - CEDES **5215**

CENTRO DE ESTUDIOS DE POBLACION, (BUENOS AIRES, ARGENTINA) See RESENA DE ACTIVIDADES - CENEP **4559**

CENTRO DE ESTUDIOS GENEALOGICOS DE BUENOS AIRES See REVISTA DEL CENTRO DE ESTUDIOS GENEALOGICOS DE BUENOS AIRES **2470**

CENTRO DE ESTUDIOS INTERPLANETARIOS See STENDEK; SERVICIO INFORMATIVO **37**

CENTRO DE ESTUDIOS MARTIANOS (1977-) See ANUARIO DEL CENTRO DE ESTUDIOS MARTIANOS **2721**

CENTRO DE ESTUDIOS MONETARIOS LATINOAMERICANOS See CEMLA BOLETIN MENSUEL **1469**

CENTRO DE ESTUDIOS PUERTORRIQUENOS BULLETIN (US/1042-0371) [16621514] **2613**

CENTRO DE ESTUDOS AGRICOLAS (INSTITUTO BRASILEIRO DE ECONOMIA) See AGROPECUARIA : PRECOS, MEDIOS E INDICES DE ARRENDAMENTOS, VENDAS DE TERRAS, SALARIOS, SERVICOS **56**

CENTRO DE ESTUDOS DEMOGRAFICOS (PORTUGAL) See REVISTA DO CENTRO DE ESTUDOS DEMOGRAFICOS **4560**

CENTRO DE ESTUDOS NIPO-BRASILEIROS See KENKYU REPOTO - SAN PAURO JIMBUN KAGAKU KENKYUJO **2743**

Alphabetical Title Index

CERTIFIED

CENTRO DE INDUSTRIALES SIDERURGICOS (BUENOS AIRES, ARGENTINA) See BOLETIN ESTADISTICO **3999**

CENTRO DE INFORMACION DE COMUNICACIONES See CIC INFORMACION TECNICA **1151**

CENTRO DE INFORMACION Y DOCUMENTACION PARA AMERICA LATINA See DOCUMENTOS - CENTRO DE INFORMACION Y DOCUMENTACION PARA AMERICA LATINA **5326**

CENTRO DE INVESTIGACION PARA LA INTEGRACION SOCIAL See BOLETIN INFORMATIVO - CENTRO DE INVESTIGACION PARA LA INTEGRACION SOCIAL **5240**

CENTRO DE INVESTIGACIONES EDUCATIVAS See PLAN DE ACTIVIDADES - CENTRO DE INVESTIGACIONES EDUCATIVAS **1774**

CENTRO DI DOCUMENTAZIONE D'INGEGNERIA CIVILE, ARCHITETTURA E PIANIFICAZIONE TERRITORIALE See SCHEDE **2030**

CENTRO DI RICERCHE STORICHE (ROVINJ, CROATIA) See ATTI **2677**

CENTRO DI STUDI FILOLOGICI E LINGUISTICI SICILIANI See BOLLETINO - CENTRO DI STUDI FILOLOGICI E LINGUISTICI SICILIANI **3269**

CENTRO DI STUDI VICHIANI See BOLLETTINO DEL CENTRO DI STUDI VICHIANI **4342**

CENTRO DOMINICANO DE PROMOCION DE EXPORTACIONES See MEMORIA ANUAL DEL CENTRO DOMINICANO DE PROMOCION DE EXPORTACIONES **845**

CENTRO DOMINICANO DE PROMOCION DE EXPORTACIONES See INFORME DE LABORES - CENTRO DOMINICANO DE PROMOCION DE EXPORTACIONES **840**

CENTRO INTERAMERICANA DE FOTOINTERPRETACION See REVISTA CIAF **1395**

CENTRO INTERAMERICANO DE INVESTIGACION Y DOCUMENTACION SOBRE FORMACION PROFESIONAL. COMISION TECNICA See MEETING OF THE TECHNICAL COMMITTEE - CINTERFOR **1690**

CENTRO INTERNACIONAL DE AGRICULTURA TROPICAL See INFORME ANUAL - CENTRO INTERNATIONAL DE AGRICULTURA TROPICAL **96**

CENTRO ITALIANO DI STUDI SULL'ALTO MEDIOEVO See SETTIMANE DI STUDIO DEL CENTRO ITALIANO DI STUDI SULL'ALTO MEDIOEVO **2709**

CENTRO MEDICO (SP/0210-6361) [I02106361] **3562**

CENTRO NACIONAL DE PESQUISA DA SERINGUEIRA (BRAZIL) See SERINGUEIRA: RESUMOS INFORMATIVOS **186**

CENTRO NACIONAL DE RESTAURACION DE LIBROS Y DOCUMENTOS : ACTIVIDADES (SP) [07368725] **3201**

CENTRO NACIONAL DE RESTAURACION DE LIBROS Y DOCUMENTOS (SPAIN) See CENTRO NACIONAL DE RESTAURACION DE LIBROS Y DOCUMENTOS : ACTIVIDADES **3201**

CENTRO PRO UNIONE : [BOLLETTINO] (IT) [08979911] **4467**

CENTRO REGIONAL DE PESQUISAS EDUCACIONAIS DO SUDESTE. ESTUDOS E DOCUMENTOS - CENTRO REGIONAL DE PESQUISAS EDUCACIONAIS DO SUDESTE See ESTUDOS E DOCUMENTOS (UNIVERSIDAD DE SAO PAULO. FACULDADE DE EDUCACAO) **1745**

CENTRO ROSSINIANO DI STUDI, PESARO See BOLLETINO DEL CENTRO ROSSINIANO DI STUDI **4104**

CENTRO SCAVI E RICERCHE ARCHEOLOGICHE IN ASIA DELL'IS. M.E.O. E DI TORINO See REPORTS AND MEMOIRS **280**

CENTRO STUDI INVESTIMENTI SOCIALI See RAPPORTO SULLA SITUAZIONE SOCIALE DEL PAESE **5254**

CENTROAMERICA INTERNACIONAL (CR) [21800379] **5195**

CENTURY (ALBUQUERQUE) (US/0272-1082) [06753697] **3339**

CENTURY HOME (1988) (CN/0838-9330) [18314769] **294**

CENTURY PSYCHOLOGY SERIES (US/0271-9223) [06771907] **4580**

CENTZONTLE : REVISTA DE LA SOCIEDAD MEXICANA DE ORNITOLOGIA (MX) [06844155] **5580**

CEO, INTERNATIONAL STRATEGIES (US/1058-7950) [24261426] **1601**

CEO INTERVIEWS (US/0887-9168) [13415166] **1601**

CEO UPDATE (US) **656**

CEO'S REPORT ON COST CUTTING (US/1061-5997) [25377405] **939**

CEP REPORT (US/0196-9021) [03522626] **1469**

CEP RESEARCH REPORT (US/0898-4328) [17285956] **1469**

CEPA NEWSLETTER (US/8756-0550) [11463413] **1227, 1231**

CEPAL REVIEW (CL/0251-2920) [03113183] **1551**

CEPHALALGIA (NO/0333-1024) [08314843] **3829**

CEPS PAPER (UK/0962-3876) [I09623876] **4468**

CEPS PAPERS (BE) [19946509] **4517**

CERAMIC ABSTRACTS (US/0095-9960) [02445786] **2587, 2595**

CERAMIC ABSTRACTS CD-ROM (US/1056-3490) [23703147] **2587**

CERAMIC ARTS & CRAFTS (US/0009-0190) [01781677] **370, 2587**

CERAMIC ENGINEERING AND SCIENCE PROCEEDINGS (US/0196-6219) [05865854] **2587**

CERAMIC INDUSTRIES INTERNATIONAL (UK) [20190367] **2587**

CERAMIC INDUSTRY (US/0009-0220) [01553730] **2587**

CERAMIC PROJECTS (US/0009-0328) **2587**

CERAMIC REVIEW (UK/0144-1825) [00985987] **2587**

CERAMIC SCOPE *CEASED.* (US/0009-0247) [04028547] **2587**

CERAMIC SOURCE (US/8756-8187) [11689148] **2587**

CERAMIC STUDY GROUP NEWSLETTER (AT) **2587, 2772**

CERAMIC TRANSACTIONS (US/1042-1122) [18942741] **2587**

CERAMIC WORLD (US/0748-304X) [10921187] **2587**

CERAMICA ACTA (IT/1121-6093) [I11216093] **2587**

CERAMICA DE CULTURA MAYA ET AL (US/0577-3334) [01779658] **233, 265**

CERAMICA INFORMAZIONE (IT/0009-0271) [05228152] **2587**

CERAMICA ITALIANA NELL'EDILIZIA See CERAMICA PER L'EDILIZIA NTERNATIONAL **2587**

CERAMICA MADRID (SP/0210-010X) [I0210010X] **2587**

CERAMICA MENDOZA (AG/0327-0947) [I03270947] **2587**

CERAMICA PER L'ARCHITETTURA : CA (IT) [22446585] **295, 2587**

CERAMICA PER L'EDILIZIA INTERNATIONAL (IT) [07820097] **2587**

CERAMICA (SAO PAULO) (BL/0366-6913) [06432405] **2587**

CERAMICA Y CRISTAL (AG/0325-0229) [05150544] **2588**

CERAMICA Y VIDRIO See BOLETIN DE LA SOCIEDAD ESPANOLA DE CERAMICA Y VIDRIO (1983) **2586**

CERAMICANTICA FERRARA (IT/1121-6956) [I11216956] **2588**

CERAMICS AND CIVILIZATION (US/8756-8179) [11689182] **2588**

CERAMICS, HEALTH AND SAFETY (UK) [06497099] **2860**

CERAMICS INTERNATIONAL (IT/0272-8842) [06970292] **2588**

CERAMICS MAGAZINE (US/1041-1305) [18664829] **2588**

CERAMICS MONTHLY (US/0009-0328) [01553732] **2588**

CERAMICS PADDINGTON (AT/1035-1841) [I10351841] **2588**

CERAMICS (PRAHA) (XR/0862-5468) [22190725] **2588**

CERAMICS TODAY (SZ/0254-4636) [10910386] **2588**

CERAMIQUE MODERNE, LA (FR/0009-0336) [05150308] **2588**

CERAMISTE (CN/0712-8770) [08734135] **2588**

CERAMURGIA (IT/0045-6152) [02242202] **2588**

CERCETARI ARHEOLOGICE / MUZUEL NATIONAL DE ISTORIE (RM) [08885988] **265**

CERCETARI DE CONSERVARE SI RESTAURARE A PATRIMONIULUI MUZEAL / MUZEUL NATIONAL DE ISTORIE (RM) [09377373] **4086**

CERCETARI DE LINGVISTICA (RM/0373-1545) [02155652] **3273**

CERCETARI ISTORICE / MUZEUL DE ISTORIE A MOLDOVEI (RM) [06849991] **4086, 2683**

CERCETARI MARINE: RECHERCHES MARINES (RM) [03217577] **1447, 553**

CERCETARI METALURGICE. INSTITUL DE CERCETARI METALURGICE (BUCURESTI) (RM/0524-8140) [01952847] **4000**

CERCETARI NUMISMATICE (RM/0256-0844) [I02560844] **2780**

CERCULAR / COASTAL ENGINEERING RESEARCH CENTER, THE (US) [10979221] **2088**

CEREAL CHEMISTRY (US/0009-0352) [01553733] **1021**

CEREAL FOODS WORLD (US/0146-6283) [01223658] **2331**

CEREAL POLICIES REVIEW (IT) [25667478] **166**

CEREAL RESEARCH COMMUNICATIONS (HU/0133-3720) [02840881] **200**

CEREAL RUSTS AND POWDERY MILDEWS BULLETIN (NE/1013-8609) [18811374] **574, 166**

CEREALIST / THE KUSA SOCIETY, THE (US) [24271500] **200**

CEREALS & BAKERY (UK) **2331**

CEREALS AND OILSEEDS REVIEW (CN/0820-9030) [09612910] **200**

CEREBRAL CORTEX (NEW YORK, N.Y. 1991) (US/1047-3211) [20665497] **3829**

CEREBROVASCULAR AND BRAIN METABOLISM REVIEWS (US/1040-8827) [18565056] **3562**

CEREBROVASCULAR DISEASES (SZ/1015-9770) [22789090] **3702, 3829**

CEREBUS (CN/0712-7774) [08777630] **4858**

CEREDIGION (UK/0069-2263) [03005902] **2683**

CERES (ROME, ENGLISH EDITION) (IT/0009-0379) [05909949] **73**

CERETARI AGRONOMICE IN MOLDOVA (RM/0379-5837) [09519593] **73**

CEREVISIA See CEREVISIA AND BIOTECHNOLOGY **3690**

CEREVISIA AND BIOTECHNOLOGY (BE/0778-2640) [24889087] **2366**

CEREVISIA AND BIOTECHNOLOGY (BE) **3690**

CERI QUARTERLY SEIMOLOGICAL BULLETIN (US) [17998582] **1353**

CERMIN MASYARAKAT (MY) [03512006] **2502**

CERN COURIER (SZ/0304-288X) [02445796] **4446**

CERR NEWS & VIEWS (CN/1191-1719) [25883024] **1353**

CERRAHPASA MEDICAL REVIEW (TU/0254-4113) [08983811] **3562**

CERRAHPASA TIP FAKULTESI DERGISI (TU/0376-7833) [01427283] **3562**

CERTIFICATED ENGINEER (SA/0009-0409) [09840214] **1968**

CERTIFICATED PERSONNEL AND RELATED INFORMATION (US) [18422538] **1890**

CERTIFICATION OF AVERAGE RATIOS AND COMMON LEVEL RANGE FOR USE IN THE TAX YEAR ... / STATE OF NEW JERSEY, DEPARTMENT OF THE TREASURY, DIVISION OF TAXATION (US) [06433975] **4717**

CERTIFICATION OF CONSTITUTIONAL LIMITATION ON THE BONDED DEBT OF THE STATE OF WASHINGTON (US/0362-2517) [02441497] **4717**

CERTIFIED ACCOUNTANT (IE/0306-2406) [01150691] **740**

CERTIFIED COPY, THE (US/0749-5684) [03993787] **2442**

CERTIFIED ENGINEERING TECHNICIAN (US/0746-6641) [05639722] **1968**

CERTIFIED GENERAL ACCOUNTANTS' ASSOCIATION OF CANADA See NATIONAL DIRECTORY OF PUBLIC PRACTITIONERS / CGA CANADA **748**

CERTIFIED MANAGEMENT ACCOUNTANT EXAMINATION. QUESTIONS AND UNOFFICIAL ANSWERS (MONTVALE, N.J.) (US/1041-7222) [15801788] **740, 863**

CERTIFIED NEWS : A NEWSLETTER FOR CERTIFIED CLINICAL AND HEALTH & FITNESS PROFESSIONALS (US/1056-9677) [23905037] **3953**

CERTIFIED POPULATION OF TENNESSEE INCORPORATED MUNICIPALITIES (US) [10839183] **4551**

CERTIFIED PROTECTION PROFESSIONAL DIRECTORY (US/0734-9114) [08811555] **3160**

CERTIFIED PUBLIC ACCOUNTANTS AND PUBLIC ACCOUNTANTS REGISTERED TO PRACTICE IN CONNECTICUT See REGISTER OF CERTIFIED PUBLIC ACCOUNTANTS AND PUBLIC ACCOUNTANTS REGISTERED TO PRACTICE IN CONNECTICUT **750**

CERTIFIED PUBLIC HOSPITAL LIST (CN/0828-0967) [03216085] **3778**

CERTITUDES — Alphabetical Title Index

CERTITUDES (SZ) **1130**

CERVANTES (GAINESVILLE, FLA.) (US/0277-6995) [07626276] 3339, **431**

CERVANTES : REVISTA DE POESIA E INFORMACION CULTURAL (SP) **3461**

CERVELLO E FARMACI (US) 4295, **3923**

CERVEZA Y MALTA (SP/0300-4481) [01424196] **2366**

CERVIX AND THE LOWER FEMALE GENITAL TRACT, THE (IT/0393-3512) [11125196] **3758**

●CESKA A SLOVENSKA FARMACIE : CASOPIS CESKE FARMACEUTICKE SPOLECNOSTI A SLOVENSKE FARMACEUTICKE SPOLECNOSTI (XR/1210-7816) [30946634] **4295**

●CESKA GYNEKOLOGIE / CESKA LEKARSKA SPOLECNOST J EV. PURKYNE (XR) [30107902] **3758**

CESKA LITERARNI VEDA. BOHEMISTIKA (XR) [08177969] **3458**

CESKA LITERARNI VEDA : NESLOVANSKE LITERATURY (XR) [02608467] **3458**

CESKA LITERATURA (XR/0009-0468) [02053893] **3373**

CESKA MYKOLOGIE (XR/0009-0476) [03007800] **506**

●CESKA STOMATOLOGIE (XR) [30107810] **1318**

CESKE A MORAVSKOSLEZSKE ZEMEDELSKE NOVINY (XR) [24190336] **73**

CESKE DIVADLO (XR) [07502902] **5362**

CESKE HUDEBNINY A GRAMOFONOVE DESKY (XR/0323-1569) [01553760] **4108**

CESKE KNIHY (XR) [03007853] **413**

CESKOSLOVENSKA AKADEMIE VED See ROZPRAVY. RADA MATEMATICKYCH A PRIRODNICH VED **5149**

CESKOSLOVENSKA AKADEMIE VED See ZPRAVY CSAV **2525**

CESKOSLOVENSKA AKADEMIE VED See ROZPRAVY. RADA TECHNICKYCH VED **5149**

CESKOSLOVENSKA AKADEMIE VED See ROZPRAVY CESKOSLOVENSKE AKADEMIE VED. RADA SPOLECENSKYCH VED **5217**

CESKOSLOVENSKA AKADEMIE VED See INFORMACNI PRIRUCKA / CESKOSLOVENSKA AKADEMIE VED **5232**

CESKOSLOVENSKA CESTA ... (CN/0820-7488) [09796046] **2683**

CESKOSLOVENSKA DERMATOLOGIE (XR/0009-0514) [01779394] **3718**

CESKOSLOVENSKA EPIDEMIOLOGIE, MIKROBIOLOGIE, IMUNOLOGIE (XR/0009-0522) [07112256] 561, **3734**

CESKOSLOVENSKA FARMACIE (XR/0009-0530) [03043474] **4296**

CESKOSLOVENSKA FYSIOLOGIE CEASED. (XR/0009-0557) [01553767] **579**

CESKOSLOVENSKA GASTROENTEROLOGIA A VYZIVA (XR/0009-0565) [01553768] **3795**

CESKOSLOVENSKA GYNAEKOLOGIE (XR/0374-6852) [03043639] **3758**

CESKOSLOVENSKA HYGIENA (XR/0009-0573) [03024643] **561**

CESKOSLOVENSKA NARODNI RADA AMERICKA See VESTNIK **1921**

CESKOSLOVENSKA NEUROLOGIE A NEUROCHIRURGIE (XR/0301-0597) [04255480] **3829**

CESKOSLOVENSKA OFTALMOLOGIE (XR/0009-059X) [03025070] **3873**

CESKOSLOVENSKA OTOLARYNGOLOGIE (XR/0009-0603) [03025256] **3887**

CESKOSLOVENSKA PATOLOGIE (XR/0009-0611) [06365023] **3893**

CESKOSLOVENSKA PEDIATRIE (XR/0069-2328) [07614218] **3901**

CESKOSLOVENSKA PSYCHIATRIE (XR/0069-2336) [03025368] **3923**

CESKOSLOVENSKA PSYCHOLOGIE (XR/0009-062X) [01553771] **4580**

CESKOSLOVENSKA RADIOLOGIE (XR/0069-2344) [01641510] **3939**

CESKOSLOVENSKA STOMATOLOGIE (XR/0009-0654) [02259128] **1318**

CESKOSLOVENSKA BANKY / VYDAVA CESKOSLOVENSKE STATNI BANKA (XR) [24187056] **782**

CESKOSLOVENSKE VYZKUMNE ZPRAVY A DISERTACE (XR) [05733986] **5093**

CESKOSLOVENSKE ZDRAVOTNICTVI CEASED. (CS/0009-0689) [06522708] **4771**

CESKOSLOVENSKE ZEMEDELSKE MUZEUM. VEDECKE PRACE See VEDECKE PRACE ZEMEDELASKEHO MUZEA **144**

CESKOSLOVENSKO (XR) [01784924] **2784**

CESKOSLOVENSKY ARCHITEKT (XR/0009-0697) [03231314] **295**

CESKOSLOVENSKY CASOPIS PRO FYSIKU (XR/0009-0700) [09936854] **4399**

CESKOSLOVENSKY SACH CEASED. (XR/0009-0743) [04048211] **4858**

CESKOSLOVENSKY SVET (XR) [02259129] **2514**

CESKY CASOPIS HISTORICKY / CESKOSLOVENSKA AKADEMIE VED (XR/0862-6111) [22161642] **2613**

CESKY DENIK (XR) [25384949] **5799**

CESKY EXPRES See EXPRES **5799**

CESKY JAZYK A LITERATURA (XR/0009-0786) [03040615] **3373**

CESKY LID (XR/0009-0794) [02259130] **2683**

CESLOSLOVENSKY VOJAK See VECKO : B.V **4060**

CESSATIONS DE COTISATION EN ..., LES (CN) [05912866] **1658**

CESSNA OWNER MAGAZINE, THE (US/0745-3523) [09094515] **16**

C'EST-A-DIRE (MONTREAL) (CN/0577-4179) [03418540] **3273**

C'EST FACILE (IT) **1731**

C'EST MOI (CN/0823-7794) [10852339] **402**

C'EST POUR QUAND (CN/0705-3215) [04129492] **3758**

CETA ACTIVITY IN NEW YORK STATE / PREPARED BY THE STAFF OF THE NEW YORK STATE EMPLOYMENT AND TRAINING COUNCIL (SETC) (US) [10833398] **1658**

CETA ACTIVITY IN THE STATE OF MAINE, FISCAL YEAR ... / STATE EMPLOYMENT AND TRAINING COUNCIL (US) [08711595] **1658**

CETA AREA EMPLOYMENT AND UNEMPLOYMENT (US) [05163342] **1658**

CETA BULLETIN (US) [11151425] **1658**

CETA PRIME SPONSOR AGREEMENT AND TITLE I ANNUAL PLAN (SOUTH DAKOTA) (US) [05637928] **1658**

CETERIS PARIBUS (PR) [24809638] **1469**

CETIM INFORMATIONS (FR/0399-0001) [I03990001] 3476, **2111**

CETOLOGY CEASED. (US/0097-031X) [01404441] **5580**

CEUMT : LA REVISTA MUNICIPAL (AU) [01789049] **1814**

CEW, CHEMICAL ENGINEERING WORLD (II/0009-2517) [01553971] **2009**

CEYLON GEOGRAPHER, THE (CE) [01553816] **2558**

CEYLON JOURNAL OF MEDICAL SCIENCE (CE/0011-2232) [07499874] **3562**

CEYLON JOURNAL OF SCIENCE. BIOLOGICAL SCIENCES (CE/0069-2379) [01553821] **451**

CEYLON MEDICAL JOURNAL (CE/0009-0875) [01553832] **3562**

CEYLON VETERINARY JOURNAL (CE/0009-0891) [01553840] **5507**

CFA CALIFORNIA PROFESSOR (US/0279-8360) [07012105] **1890**

CFANEWS (WASHINGTON, D.C.) (US/0732-8281) [08445140] **1294**

CFAO SYNTHESE (FR) **1227**

CFB GANDER GAZETTE (CN/0828-8046) [12227631] **4039**

CFBS NEWSLETTER / CANADIAN FEDERATION OF BIOLOGICAL SOCIETIES (CN/0714-9956) [09743233] **451**

●CFC REPORT (US/1063-1615) [25904436] **5093**

CFCM REPORT (CN/1184-9827) [24690755] **4943**

CFDT AUJOURD'HUI (FR) [05085690] **1659**

CFDT MAGAZINE (FR) [03018968] **1659**

CFDT SYNDICALISME HEBDO (FR) [03080810] **1659**

●CFE BATIMENT (FR) [28004899] **2038**

●CFE INDUSTRIE (FR/1146-1497) [28004846] 4000, **2038**

CFEC REPORT (US) [11947784] **2299**

CFI, CERAMIC FORUM INTERNATIONAL (GW/0173-9913) [07014171] **2588**

CFO ALERT (US/0894-4822) [15213901] **740**

CFO'S REPORT FOR TREASURERS, FINANCIAL OFFICERS & BUSINESS MANAGERS See FINANCIAL OFFICER'S TAX & MANAGEMENT REPORT **868**

CFO'S REPORT FOR TREASURERS, FINANCIAL OFFICERS & BUSINESS MANAGERS, THE (US/1056-5469) [23737201] **656**

CFP TODAY (US/1058-4455) [24297215] **783**

CFRU PROGRESS REPORT (US/0748-1721) [10908802] **2377**

CFRU RESEARCH NOTE (US/0748-1748) [08441880] **2377**

CFS NOTEBOOK See FEDERALISM REPORT, THE **4474**

CFS REVIEW, THE (II) [11320029] **4065**

CFTC ADMINISTRATIVE REPORTER (US/0745-8452) [09274838] **826**

CFTC DATABOOK (US/0195-3591) [05201899] **894**

CFTC REPORT (US/0897-067X) [16641061] **826**

CG. CAR GRAPHIC (JA/0915-1702) [I09151702] **5409**

CGA DOMESTIC DEMAND FORECAST (CN) 4253, **4760**

CGA MAGAZINE (CN/0318-742X) [03031841] **740**

CGCR. COMPRESSED GASES AND CRYOGENICS REPORT (US/0270-0492) [06333983] **4399**

CGL REPORTER (US/0748-951X) [11036285] **2877**

CGS NEWS - CALIFORNIA GENEALOGICAL SOCIETY (US/1058-5133) [24262428] **2442**

CGS NEWSLETTER (US/1056-2095) [23582472] **2442**

CGST JOURNAL (HK) **4943**

CH-FORSCHUNG (SZ) [19074439] **5093**

CH4 ENERGIA METANO (IT/0393-0971) [I03930971] **1935**

CHA CHOSA HOKOKUSHO See CHA TOKEI NEMPO **73**

CHA TOKEI NEMPO (JA) [01797083] **73**

CHABON SIJANG YONBO (KO) [05004151] **894**

CHABOTAP (KO) [11336792] 5409, **2878**

CHAC INFO (CN/0822-8426) [11050446] 5027, **4771**

●CHAC MOL NEWSLETTER (US/1062-5283) [25660679] **2511**

CHACRA & CAMPO MODERNO (AG) [01327301] **73**

CHAD. MINISTERE DU COMMERCE ET DE L'INDUSTRIE See RAPPORT ECONOMIQUE ANNUEL - CHAD. MINISTERE DU COMMERCE ET DE L'INDUSTRIE **1580**

CHAD. SOUS-DIRECTION DE LA STATISTIQUE See BULLETIN DE STATISTIQUE (CHAD) **5324**

CHADBURN, THE (US) [05071963] **5448**

CHADONGCHA CHONOL (KO) [25039973] **5409**

CHADONGCHA SAENGHWAL (KO) [11765913] **5409**

CHAEHWAL YONGU (KO) [11276318] 5277, **4385**

CHAEMI KWAGIHYOP HOEBO (KO) [08748578] **5093**

CHAGRIN VALLEY DIRECTORY (US/0749-6834) [09314983] **2727**

CHAILLOT PAPERS (FR/1017-7566) [24210350] **4039**

CHAIN DRUG REVIEW (US/0164-9914) [04276234] **656**

CHAIN MERCHANDISER (US/0009-0921) [13350568] **952**

CHAIN-REACTION (CARLTON, VIC.) (AT/0312-1372) [16083150] **2189**

CHAIN SAW AGE & POWER EQUIPMENT TRADE See POWER EQUIPMENT TRADE **634**

CHAIN STORE AGE EXECUTIVE WITH SHOPPING CENTER AGE (US) [01193949] **952**

CHAINE LETTER See GASTRONOME (NEW YORK, N.Y.) **5071**

●CHAINON (MONTREAL. 1992) (CN/1191-1085) [25796523] **1601**

CHAINON (OTTAWA. 1983) (CN/0823-6186) [12199562] **2727**

CHAIRMAN'S REPORT - AFRICA INSTITUTE OF SOUTH AFRICA (SA) [02705212] **2638**

CHAIRMAN'S REPORT - EAST AFRICAN LIBRARY ASSOCIATION. KENYA BRANCH (KE) [01785312] **3201**

CHAIRMAN'S REPORT - NATIONAL ARTHRITIS ADVISORY BOARD (US/0196-2728) [05761111] **3804**

CHAIRMAN'S REPORT - THE ASIA SOCIETY--SEADAG (US/0361-8684) [02043635] **1601**

CHAKRA (US) 317, **3373**

CHALEUR ET CLIMATS WARMTE EN KLIMAAT (BE) [17209189] **2604**

CHALLENGE (RE) [01788125] **2277**

Alphabetical Title Index — CHANGEMENTS

CHALLENGE (US) [06161607] **5553**

CHALLENGE (BLOOMINGTON, ILL.) (US/0894-5535) [16157021] **4858**

CHALLENGE (CARTHAGE, ILL.) (US/0745-6298) [09319891] **1877**

CHALLENGE FUND JOURNAL (CN/0838-8334) [18248075] **1090**

CHALLENGE GRANTS / NATIONAL ENDOWMENT FOR THE ARTS (US/0743-3883) [04445787] **317**

CHALLENGE (HARRISBURG), THE (US/0528-7928) [02445803] **5277**

CHALLENGE II GRANTS (US) [18314858] **4637**

CHALLENGE IN EDUCATIONAL ADMINISTRATION (CN/0045-625X) [01931082] **1861**

CHALLENGE / JOURNAL OF RESEARCH ON AFRICAN-AMERICAN MEN (US) **2258**

CHALLENGE (MEMPHIS) (US) **5057**

CHALLENGE (NEW YORK, N.Y.) (US/0009-1049) [02253762] **5714**

CHALLENGE OF CONSERVATIVE BAPTIST HOME MISSIONS, THE (US/0745-2918) [02250686] **5057**

CHALLENGE OF THE '80S UPDATE *See* SPECTRUM (WHEATON, ILL.) **4999**

CHALLENGE; SUPPLEMENT OF BA-MAARAKHAH (IS) [04007264] **5047**

CHALLENGE TO CHANGE : LIBRARY APPLICATIONS OF CONCEPTS *CEASED.* (US/0276-0525) [03726785] **3201**

CHALLENGE (WASHINGTON, D.C. 1989) (US/1062-1849) [24488447] **4943**

CHALLENGE (WHITE PLAINS) (US/0577-5132) [05464845] 656, **1469**

CHALLENGER (BUFFALO, N.Y.), THE (US/1040-8886) [18572480] **5714**

CHALLENGER (NORTH VANCOUVER) (CN/0824-8427) [11802886] **1731**

CHALLENGES : LE PLUS EUROPEEN DES MAGAZINES DE L'ENTREPRISE (FR) **656**

CHALLENGES (MIDDLETOWN, CONN.) *CEASED.* (US/1058-4773) [24306904] **1061**

CHALLENGES OF THE CHANGING ECONOMY OF NEW YORK CITY (US) [03466526] **1469**

CHALLENGES (WASHINGTON, D.C. 1987) (US/1042-0088) [17357021] **656**

CHALLENGING THE LITERARY CANON (US/1056-4241) [23715008] **3373**

CHALLENGING TIMES (US) 1731, **1342**

CHALLIS MESSENGER, THE (US) [18888130] **5669**

CHAMBER DE COMMERCE ET D'INDUSTRIE DE PAU *See* SITUATION ECONOMIQUE ET PERSPECTIVES D'AVENIR **1584**

CHAMBER EXECUTIVE NETWORK, THE (US/1070-2342) [28303426] **818**

CHAMBER MUSIC AMERICA *See* MEMBERSHIP DIRECTORY / CHAMBER MUSIC AMERICA **4130**

CHAMBER MUSIC (NEW YORK, N.Y.) (US/1071-1791) [16507353] **4108**

CHAMBER NEWS - NARAYANGANJ CHAMBER OF COMMERCE & INDUSTRY (BG) [06300089] **818**

CHAMBER OF COMMERCE OF ST. JOSEPH COUNTY *See* MEMBERSHIP DIRECTORY AND BUSINESS PAGES FOR THE CHAMBER OF COMMERCE OF ST. JOSEPH COUNTY **820**

CHAMBER OF COMMERCE OF THE P. R. OF ALBANIA *See* COMMERCE EXTERIEUR ALBANAIS **819**

CHAMBER OF COMMERCE OF THE UNITED STATES OF AMERICA *See* ANALYSIS OF WORKMEN'S COMPENSATION LAWS **3144**

CHAMBER OF MINES JOURNAL (RH/0009-1162) [08077426] 1438, **2136**

CHAMBER OF MINES' NEWSLETTER (SA) [09380595] 2136, **1438**

CHAMBER OF MINES OF SOUTH AFRICA *See* REVIEW / CHAMBER OF MINES OF SOUTH AFRICA **1444**

CHAMBER OF MINES OF SOUTH AFRICA *See* PRESIDENTIAL ADDRESS / CHAMBER OF MINES OF SOUTH AFRICA **2148**

CHAMBER OF MINES OF SOUTH AFRICA *See* ANNUAL REPORT / CHAMBER OF MINES OF SOUTH AFRICA **2133**

CHAMBER OF MINES (ZIMBABWE) *See* ANNUAL REPORT / CHAMBRE OF MINES, ZIMBABWE **2133**

CHAMBER PROGRESS / DODGE CITY AREA CHAMBER OF COMMERCE, THE (US/1062-905X) [23826195] **819**

CHAMBER (WINNIPEG, MAN.) (CN/0227-6593) [08854743] **819**

CHAMBEREXECUTIVE (US/0884-8114) [12437942] **819**

CHAMBERLAIN ASSOCIATION NEWS (US/0882-987X) [11635519] **2442**

CHAMBERLAIN REGISTER, THE (US) [12813014] **5743**

CHAMBERS & PARTNERS DIRECTORY OF THE LEGAL PROFESSION (UK) **2949**

CHAMBERS HELPING CHAMBERS (US/0736-2390) [09078320] **2442**

CHAMBERS OF COMMERCE DIRECTORY, ZIMBABWE (RH) [08198159] **819**

CHAMBER'S TRADE DIRECTORY (PK) [03142640] **827**

CHAMBLEE DEKALB NEIGHBOR, THE (US/0199-7416) [06119473] **5652**

CHAMBRE BLANCHE (CN/0820-781X) [09581900] **347**

CHAMBRE DE COMMERCE, D'AGRICULTURE, D'INDUSTRIE ET D'ARTISANAT DU NIGER *See* BULLETIN DE LA CHAMBRE DE COMMERCE, D'AGRICULTURE, D'INDUSTRIE ET D'ARTISANAT DU NIGER **1549**

CHAMBRE DE COMMERCE, D'AGRICULTURE ET D'INDUSTRIE DE LA REPUBLIQUE TOGOLAISE *See* BULLETIN MENSUEL - CHAMBRE DE COMMERCE, D'AGRICULTURE ET D'INDUSTRIE DE LA REPUBLIQUE TOGOLAISE **1549**

CHAMBRE DE COMMERCE, D'AGRICULTURE ET D'INDUSTRIE DU NIGER. BULLETIN *See* BULLETIN DE LA CHAMBRE DE COMMERCE, D'AGRICULTURE, D'INDUSTRIE ET D'ARTISANAT DU NIGER **1549**

CHAMBRE DE COMMERCE, D'INDUSTRIE ET D'AGRICULTURE DE MAURITANIE *See* BULLETIN DE LA CHAMBRE DE COMMERCE D'INDUSTRIE ET AGRICULTURE DE MAURITANIE **818**

CHAMBRE DE COMMERCE, D'INDUSTRIE ET D'ARTISANAT DE LA REGION DU CAP-VERT *See* INDUSTRIE SENEGALAISE, L' **1611**

CHAMBRE DE COMMERCE, D'INDUSTRIE ET DES MINES DU CAMEROUN *See* RAPPORT ANNUEL - CHAMBRE DE COMMERCE, D'INDUSTRIE ET DES MINES DU CAMEROUN **821**

CHAMBRE DE COMMERCE, D'INDUSTRIE ET DES MINES DU CAMEROUN *See* PRINCIPALES EXPORTATIONS **849**

CHAMBRE DE COMMERCE, D'INDUSTRIE ET DES MINES DU CAMEROUN *See* COMPTE-RENDU D'ACTIVITES - CHAMBRE DE COMMERCE, D'INDUSTRIE ET DES MINES DU CAMEROUN **819**

CHAMBRE DE COMMERCE DU DISTRICT DE MONTREAL. EXERCICE *See* PROGRAMME DU ... EXERCICE - CHAMBRE DE COMMERCE DU DISTRICT DE MONTREAL **821**

CHAMBRE DE COMMERCE ET D'IDUSTRIE DE STRASBOURG *See* BILAN DES ACTIVITES ECONOMIQUES DANS LE BAS-RHIN **1548**

CHAMBRE DE COMMERCE ET D'INDUSTRIE D'ANVERS *See* BULLETIN - CHAMBRE DE COMMERCE ET D'INDUSTRIE D'ANVERS **1549**

CHAMBRE DE COMMERCE ET D'INDUSTRIE DE LA REPUBLIQUE POPULAIRE DE BENIN *See* NOTE HEBDOMADAIRE - CHAMBRE DE COMMERCE ET D'INDUSTRIE DE LA REPUBLIQUE POPULAIRE DE BENIN **1620**

CHAMBRE DE COMMERCE ET D'INDUSTRIE DE LA REUNION *See* CCIR **818**

CHAMBRE DE COMMERCE ET D'INDUSTRIE DE PARIS *See* CONTRIBUTION DES EMPLOYEURS A L'EFFORT DE CONSTRUCTION **1661**

CHAMBRE DE COMMERCE ET D'INDUSTRIE DE POINTE-A-PITRE *See* RAPPORT D'ACTIVITE / CHAMBRE DE COMMERCE ET D'INDUSTRIE DE POINTE-A-PITRE **821**

CHAMBRE DE COMMERCE FRANCO-RUSSE (FR/1241-5251) [I12415251] **819**

CHAMBRE D'INDUSTRIE DE COTE D'IVOIRE *See* PRINCIPALES ENTREPRISES IVOIRIENNES : TRAVAUX PUBLICS, GENIE-CIVIL, BATIMENT ET ACTIVITES CONNEXES **1621**

CHAMBRE D'INDUSTRIE DE COTE D'IVOIRE *See* PRINCIPALES INDUSTRIES INSTALLEES EN COTE D'IVOIRE **1579**

CHAMBRE D'INDUSTRIE DE COTE D'IVOIRE. SERVICE DOCUMENTATION *See* REVUE DE PRESSE - CHAMBRE D'INDUSTRIES DE COTE D'IVOIRE. SERVICE DOCUMENTATION **1582**

CHAMBRE NATIONALE DE COMMERCE *See* BULLETIN MENSUEL D'INFORMATION DE LA CHAMBRE NATIONALE DE COMMERCE **818**

CHAMBRE REGIONALE DE COMMERCE ET D'INDUSTRIE D'ALSACE *See* RAPPORT SUR LES ACTIVITES - CHAMBRE REGIONALE DE COMMERCE ET D'INDUSTRIE D'ALSACE **821**

CHAMBRE SYDNICALE DES CONSTRUCTEURS D'AUTOMOBILES ET DE MOTOCYCLES DE BELGIQUE ET FEDERATION BELGE DES INDUSTRIES DE L'AUTOMOBILE ET DU CYCLE REUNIES *See* EXERCICE - CHAMBRE SYNDICALE DES CONSTRUCTEURS D'AUTOMOBILES ET DE MOTOCYCLES DE BELGIQUE ET FEDERATION BELGE DES INDUSTRIES DE L'AUTOMOBILE ET DU CYCLE REUNIES **1606**

CHAMBRE SYNDICALE DES CONSTRUCTEURS DE NAVIRES ET DE MACHINES MARINE *See* CONSTRUCTION NAVALE, LA **4176**

CHAMBRES D'AGRICULTURE (FR/0396-7883) [06257181] **73**

CHAMINADE LITERARY REVIEW (US/0894-6396) [16150477] **3339**

CHAMP CHANNELS (US/0747-9840) [09680666] 4241, **5580**

CHAMPAGNE-ARDENNE, STATISTIQUE AGRICOLE (FR/0243-6884) [02243470] **73**

CHAMPAGNE ECONOMIQUE (FR) **1469**

CHAMPAGNE HORROR (CN/0847-1711) [21530582] **3373**

CHAMPAGNE VITICOLE, LA (FR) **2366**

CHAMPAIGN COUNTY GENEALOGICAL SOCIETY *See* CHAMPAIGN COUNTY GENEALOGICAL SOCIETY QUARTERLY **2442**

CHAMPAIGN COUNTY GENEALOGICAL SOCIETY QUARTERLY (US/0277-2086) [06262215] **2442**

CHAMPIGNON (GW/0009-1308) [02722111] **166**

CHAMPIGNONCULTUUR, DE (NE/0009-1316) [03041576] **166**

CHAMPION (HOUSTON, TEX.), THE (US/0744-9488) [08672365] **3105**

CHAMPION KATOWICE (PL/0867-6704) [I08676704] **2798**

CHAMPIONS (US/0892-4341) [15193030] **4858**

CHAMPIONS DU SPORT AMATEUR, LES (CN/0822-5621) [10156810] **4889**

CHAMPIONS OF FREEDOM (US/0741-3408) [02923206] **1590**

CHAMPLAIN VALLEY FIDDLERS CLUB *See* CHAMPLAIN VALLEY FIDDLERS CLUB, INC. [NEWS LETTER], THE **4108**

CHAMPLAIN VALLEY FIDDLERS CLUB, INC. [NEWS LETTER], THE (US) [04576533] **4108**

CHAMPS D'APPLICATION (CN/0317-3399) [02248185] **3373**

CHAMPS-ELYSEES (US/0886-005X) **2514**

CHAMPS-ELYSEES (NASHVILLE, TENN.) (US/0886-005X) [12674619] **3273**

CHAMPS-ELYSEES STUDY GUIDE (US) **1731**

CHAN. CONSUMER HEALTH ACTION NETWORK (US/0196-3813) [05802741] 4771, **1294**

CHAN LY (CN/0821-7688) [10450924] **5058**

CHAN NHU / VIETNAMESE-CANADIAN BUDDHIST ASSOCIATION (CN/0822-0581) [10450950] **5021**

CHANCE (NEW YORK) (US/0933-2480) [17524494] **3499**

CHANDRABHAGA (II/0970-5147) [06705796] **3373**

CHANG-CHIANG (CC) [07399819] **3373**

CHANG-CHIANG WEN I (CC) [08509452] **317**

CHANG-CHUN TI CHIH HSUEH YUAN HSUEH PAO (CN/0253-6072) [03454579] **1371**

CHANG-KENG I HSUEH TSA CHIH / CHANG-KENG CHI NIEN I YUAN / CHANG GUNG MEDICAL JOURNAL / CHANG GUNG MEMORIAL HOSPITAL (CH) [26962091] **3562**

CHANG LAO SHIH YUEH KAN (CH) [17605705] **4580**

CHANGE AGENT (US) **1912**

CHANGE : ATMOSPHERIC POLLUTION AND CLIMATE CHANGE (NE) **2226**

CHANGE EXCHANGE (US/0886-2435) [12879605] **3140**

CHANGE (NEW ROCHELLE, N.Y.) (US/0009-1383) [01553876] **1814**

●CHANGE NOTICE, THE (US/1062-0079) [25503251] **607**

CHANGEMENTS (MONTREAL) (CN/1183-2916) [25423685] **827**

CHANGES

Alphabetical Title Index

CHANGES : AN INTERNATIONAL JOURNAL OF PSYCHOLOGY AND PSYCHOTHERAPY (UK/0263-8371) [23045724] **4580**

●CHANGES (DEERFIELD BEACH, FLA.) (US/0892-1504) [26375436] **5277**

CHANGES MAGAZINE (BISBEE) (US/0093-9064) [01793160] **3374**

CHANGES (POMPANO BEACH, FLA.) *See* CHANGES (DEERFIELD BEACH, FLA.) **5277**

CHANGES (TORONTO) (CN/0316-7046) [02247802] **2530**

CHANGGENG YIXUE (CH/0255-8270) [09741320] **3562**

CHANGING CHINA : A PUBLICATION SPONSORED BY THE NORTH AMERICAN COALITION FOR CHINESE DEMOCRACY (NACCD), A *CEASED.* (US) [23477461] **4468**

CHANGING EDUCATION (AT) **1861**

CHANGING FACES, CHANGING TIMES (CN/0848-1059) [20983216] **3201**

CHANGING HOMES *CEASED.* (US/0890-4154) [14221595] **4835**

CHANGING MEDICAL MARKETS (US/1070-6771) [04651642] 3563, **922**

CHANGING MEN (US) [04029498] **3994**

CHANGING MEN (MADISON, WIS.) (US/0889-7174) [12070938] **3994**

CHANGING PUBLIC ATTITUDES ON GOVERNMENTS AND TAXES (US/0272-6017) [04530529] **4717**

CHANGING SCHOOLS (MUNCIE, IND (US/0738-9418) [06545914] **1731**

CHANGING STRUCTURE OF THE CANADIAN MINERAL INDUSTRY, THE (CN) [08783682] **1438**

CHANGING VIEWS IN SURGICAL ONCOLOGY (US/1058-4986) [24314865] **3814**

CHANGING VILLAGES / CONSORTIUM ON RURAL TECHNOLOGY (IT) [09884054] **2817**

CHANGING WORK (NEW HAVEN, CONN.) (US/0883-1416) [12157655] **1659**

CHANGJAK KWA PIPYONG (KO) [05252801] **3374**

CHANGSO MONGNOK (KO) [08933248] **1551**

CHANNEL GUIDE *CEASED.* (US/0744-6462) [08466485] **1130**

CHANNEL GUIDE (MILWAUKEE, WIS.) (US/1042-1238) [18945025] **1106**

CHANNEL ISLANDS SPECIALISED CATALOGUE OF STAMPS AND POSTAL HISTORY (UK/0142-5625) [I01425625] **2784**

CHANNEL (ONTARIO LIBRARY SERVICE, TRENT) *SUSPENDED.* (CN/0829-1152) [16219675] **3201**

CHANNEL (ST. CATHARINES) (CN/0228-8206) [08770576] **2530**

CHANNELMARKER LETTER (US/1045-2990) [20085593] **1601**

CHANNELS (CINCINNATI, OHIO) (US/0730-3556) [07994633] **1413**

CHANNELS (NEWBURY PARK, CALIF.) (US/0744-4079) [08246203] **4943**

CHANOYU QUARTERLY (KYOTO, JAPAN : 1976) (JA) [04044546] **5268**

CHANSONS D'AUJOURD'HUI *See* CHANSONS (MONTREAL. 1992) **4108**

CHANSONS D'AUJOURD'HUI (CN/0227-5023) [08071583] **4108**

CHANSONS (MONTREAL. 1992) (CN/1193-9249) [28061911] **4108**

●CHANTEH (ARLINGTON, VA.) (US/1065-7150) [26702841] **5242**

●CHANTER (MONTREAL) (CN/1192-1900) [27391246] **4109**

CHANTIER (CN/0226-6210) [06473439] **607**

CHANTIERS AMERINDIA (FR/0757-9314) [07579314] **3273**

CHANTIERS (ANJOU) *CEASED.* (CN/0825-9895) [12782170] **607**

CHANTIERS DE FRANCE (FR/0397-4650) [04116343] **607**

CHANTIERS JEUNESSE (CN/1184-9339) [24570975] **5277**

CHANUTE TRIBUNE (CHANUTE, KAN. : 1946) (US) [12141037] **5674**

CHAO CHI SHIH CHANG SHIH PIN PAI HUO TSAI KOU NIEN CHIEN / CHEN FENG-JEN PIEN (CH) [09425859] **2331**

CHAOS NETWORK, THE (US/1070-8146) [22604960] **5242**

CHAOS, SOLITONS AND FRACTALS (UK/0960-0779) [24834575] **3499**

CHAOS (WOODBURY, N.Y.) (US/1054-1500) [22771698] **4399**

CHAPBOOK MISCELLANY (US) [03028268] **3374**

CHAPEAU (CN/0228-5045) [08078734] **1541**

●CHAPEL HILL NEWS (CHAPEL HILL, N.C. 1992) (US/1070-2741) [26889790] **5723**

CHAPEL HILL NEWSPAPER *See* CHAPEL HILL NEWS (CHAPEL HILL, N.C. 1992) **5723**

CHAPEL HILL NEWSPAPER, THE (US) [09747649] **5723**

CHAPELHOW CHRONICLE AND COMMUNITY NEWS (CN/1188-2603) [25796574] **4039**

CHAPHWA CHEPUM PUMJIL PAEKSO (KO) [11402211] **827**

CHAPLAINCY TODAY (US/0895-7916) [14056663] **4943**

CHAPLEAU SENTINEL (CN/0832-2414) [16164568] **5781**

CHAPMAN ADVERTISER AND THE ENTERPRISE JOURNAL, THE (US) [11105790] **5674**

CHAPMAN CHATTER (US/0883-1181) [12067294] **2442**

CHAPTER 1 HANDBOOK (US/0737-2094) [09336917] **4717**

CHAPTER 11 REPORTER (US/0748-562X) [10208838] **3086**

CHAPTER 11 UPDATE (US/1055-9477) [23378867] **783**

CHAPTER AND RAIL NEWS AS VIEWED FROM THE OBSERVATION PLATFORM (US) [07883139] **5430**

CHAPTER ELEVEN THEORY AND PRACTICE (US) **3086**

CHAPTER NEWSLETTER - BIG BAND SOCIETY. ED WALKER CHAPTER (US/0731-4051) [08179430] **4109**

CHAPTER ONE (US/0895-3384) [16571370] 2009, **1814**

CHAPTER ONE : A NEWSLETTER FOR FRIENDS OF THE UNIVERSITY OF FLORIDA LIBRARIES (US) [23251451] **3201**

CHAPTER ONE FOR THE UNPUBLISHED WRITER IN ALL OF US (US/1056-9227) [23897175] 3374, **2918**

CHAPTER ONE IN OHIO : EDUCATION CONSOLIDATION AND IMPROVEMENT ACT ... ANNUAL EVALUATION REPORT (US) [11130246] **1731**

CHAPTERLETTER / THE BOSTON SOCIETY OF ARCHITECTS (US) [11919485] **295**

CHAPTERS (CAMBRIDGE) (US/0270-8035) [06497626] **2530**

CHAR-KOOSTA NEWS (US/0893-8970) [15699955] **4505**

CHARACTERISTICS OF COLLEGE STUDENTS, ENTERING FRESHMEN, AND TRANSFER UNDERGRADUATES : JUNIOR COLLEGE SURVEY (US) [01329711] **1815**

CHARACTERISTICS OF DOCTORAL SCIENTISTS AND ENGINEERS IN THE UNITED STATES. DETAILED STATISTICAL TABLES (US/0734-6468) [08654404] **5174**

CHARACTERISTICS OF DUAL-EARNER FAMILIES (CN/1188-1879) [25351921] **2277**

CHARACTERISTICS OF FHA SINGLE-FAMILY MORTGAGES, SELECTED SECTIONS OF NATIONAL HOUSING ACT (US/0193-1660) [06546464] **4717**

CHARACTERISTICS OF FLUID MILK SALES IN PENNSYLVANIA *See* CHARACTERISTICS OF PACKAGED FLUID MILK SALES IN PENNSYLVANIA **192**

CHARACTERISTICS OF MAJOR COLLECTIVE BARGAINING AGREEMENTS (US/0160-2934) [03658937] **1659**

CHARACTERISTICS OF NEW COURT COMMITMENTS / STATE OF NEW YORK, DEPARTMENT OF CORRECTIONAL SERVICES, DIVISION OF PROGRAM PLANNING, RESEARCH AND EVALUATION (US) [22397768] **3160**

CHARACTERISTICS OF NONPUBLIC SCHOOLS IN FLORIDA (US) [03931800] **1731**

CHARACTERISTICS OF OCCUPATIONAL INJURIES AND ILLNESSES IN ARKANSAS (US) [22438435] **2860**

CHARACTERISTICS OF PACKAGED FLUID MILK SALES IN PENNSYLVANIA (US) [08631705] **192**

CHARACTERISTICS OF PERSONS ENTERING PAROLE (US/0749-3347) [10409266] **3160**

CHARACTERISTICS OF PROFESSIONAL STAFF IN CALIFORNIA PUBLIC SCHOOLS *CEASED.* (US/0735-3650) [08732767] **1861**

CHARACTERISTICS OF REGISTERED APPRENTICES IN CALIFORNIA (US/0146-8863) [03058350] **1659**

CHARACTERISTICS OF STATE PLANS FOR AID TO FAMILIES WITH DEPENDENT CHILDREN UNDER THE SOCIAL SECURITY ACT, TITLE IV-A, AND FOR GUAM, PUERTO RICO, & VIRGIN ISLANDS (US/0149-1792) [03437421] **5277**

CHARACTERISTICS OF WASTES AND SOILS AFFECTING TRANSPORT OF RADIONUCLIDES THROUGH THE SOIL AND THEIR RELATIONSHIP TO WASTE MANAGEMENT (US) [09422573] **2226**

CHARACTERISTICS OF WORK-RELATED INJURIES AND ILLNESSES IN MAINE (US/0733-8384) [04698722] **2860**

CHARBONNAGES DE FRANCE *See* RAPPORT D'ACTIVITE / CHARBONNAGES DE FRANCE **2149**

CHARBONNAGES DE FRANCE. RAPPORT DE GESTION *See* RAPPORT D'ACTIVITE / CHARBONNAGES DE FRANCE **2149**

CHARBONNEAU CONNECTION (US/1046-5901) [20463212] **2442**

CHARCUTERIE ET GASTRONOMIE PARIS (FR/0222-0377) [I02220377] **2331**

CHARENTAIS, LE (FR) [20305646] **5800**

●CHARIHO TIMES (1993), THE (US/1069-9473) [28207494] **5741**

CHARIOT (CRAWFORDSVILLE, IND.) (US/0745-5828) [09306914] **3374**

CHARIOTEER, THE (US/0577-5574) [01553895] **3374**

CHARISMA AND CHRISTIAN LIFE (US/0895-156X) [16502324] **4943**

CHARITABLE GIFT PLANNING NEWS (US) [10468853] **4717**

CHARITABLE GIVING AND SOLICITATION (US/0278-0593) [07695088] **4335**

CHARITABLE GIVING TAX SERVICE (US) **4717**

CHARITABLE GIVING TECHNIQUES (US/1061-9461) [23951829] **4717**

●CHARITABLE ORGANIZATIONS OF THE U.S (US/1052-3979) [22283701] **4335**

CHARITABLE TRUST DIRECTORY, OFFICE OF ATTORNEY GENERAL (US/0148-3188) [03285726] **3140**

CHARITE-ANNALEN (GW/0232-7090) [17006118] **3563**

CHARITHRAM (II) [01790546] **2648**

CHARITIES DIGEST (UK/0590-9783) [03030749] **5277**

CHARITIES USA (US/0364-0760) [02591631] **5277**

CHARITON COLLECTOR, THE (US/0742-129X) [10250769] **2727**

CHARITON HERALD-PATRIOT, THE (US) [15012041] **5669**

CHARITON LEADER (CHARITON, IOWA : 1904) (US) [15012420] **5669**

CHARITON REVIEW, THE (US/0098-9452) [02242564] **3374**

CHARITY AND CHILDREN (US/0009-1723) [04032166] 5058, **5277**

CHARITY LONDON. 1983 (UK/0265-5209) [I02655209] **4335**

CHARITY TRENDS (UK) [17462269] **5277**

CHARLES BELL JOURNAL, THE (UK) **3778**

CHARLES CITY PRESS (1951) (US/1049-7242) [16116784] **5669**

CHARLES DEGARMO LECTURE OF THE SOCIETY OF PROFESSORS OF EDUCATION (US) [28196345] **1815**

CHARLES F KETTERING FOUNDATION *See* KETTERING REPORT **5207**

CHARLES FARRELL'S DANCE BUSINESS NEWSLETTER (US/0739-1994) [06933160] 656, **1311**

CHARLES LAMB BULLETIN, THE (UK/0308-0951) [01034937] **3339**

CHARLES RIVER ASSOCIATES. CRA RESEARCH REVIEW *See* CRA REVIEW, THE **1590**

CHARLES S. PIERCE SOCIETY *See* TRANSACTIONS OF THE CHARLES S. PIERCE SOCIETY **4364**

CHARLESBOURG (QUEBEC) *See* INFO-BOURG **4656**

CHARLESTON CHRONICLE (CHARLESTON, S.C.) *See* CHRONICLE (CHARLESTON, S.C.), THE **5742**

CHARLESTON DAILY MAIL (CHARLESTON, W.VA. : 1920) (US) [13060388] **5763**

CHARLESTON GAZETTE (CHARLESTON, W. VA. : 1907) (US) [09334859] **5763**

CHARLESTON MAGAZINE (US/0162-2722) [04032103] **2486**

CHARLESTON MAGAZINE, THE (UK/0963-4770) **3374**

CHARLESTON NEWSLETTER *See* CHARLESTON MAGAZINE, THE **3374**

CHARLESTON NEWSPAPER INDEX (US) [04864786] **5763**

CHARLEVOIX COURIER (US) **5691**

CHARLOTTE BUSINESS QUARTERLY (US) **656**

CHARLOTTE OBSERVER
(CHARLOTTE, N.C. : 1916) (US)
[09554626] **5723**

CHARLOTTE OBSERVER, THE (US)
[05086347] **5723**

CHARLOTTE POST, THE (US)
[17635192] **5723**

CHARLOTTE SUN HERALD
(US/1044-0399) [19655719] 5648, **5649**

CHARLOTTES, THE *SUSPENDED*.
(CN/0316-6724) [02441577] **2727**

CHARLOTTESVILLE ALBEMARLE
OBSERVER (US/0882-9322) [12058103]
5758

CHARLOTTESVILLE OBSERVER *See*
CHARLOTTESVILLE ALBEMARLE
OBSERVER **5758**

CHARLTON AUCTIONS *See*
COLLECTABLES AUCTION /
CHARLTON AUCTIONS **2772**

CHARLTON AUCTIONS *See*
JEWELLERY AUCTION / CHARLTON
AUCTIONS **2914**

CHARLTON AUCTIONS *See*
NUMISMATIC AUCTION / CHARLTON
AUCTIONS **2782**

CHARLTON AUCTIONS *See*
PHILATELIC AUCTION / CHARLTON
AUCTIONS **2786**

CHARLTON CANADA STAMP ALBUM &
STORYBOOK, THE (CN/0822-482X)
[10052135] **2784**

CHARLTON CANADIAN TRADE
DOLLAR GUIDE, THE (CN/0228-152X)
[06858698] **2780**

CHARLTON COUNTY HERALD (US)
[19704280] **5652**

CHARLTON HOCKEY CARD PRICE
GUIDE, THE (CN/1183-3033) [24571006]
2772

CHARLTON NUMISMATIC BULLETIN,
THE (CN/0703-5837) [03951151] **2780**

CHARLTON STANDARD CATALOGUE
OF CANADIAN TIRE CASH BONUS
COUPONS, THE (CN/1183-7098)
[25066614] **5379**

CHARLTON STANDARD CATALOGUE
OF ROYAL DOULTON FIGURINES, THE
(US/0228-6947) [23598607] **2772**

CHARLTON STANDARD CATALOGUE
OF THE CANADIAN NUMISMATIC
ASSOCIATION'S MEDALS AND
AWARDS, THE (CN/1183-7101)
[25066620] **2780**

CHARLTON'S STANDARD
CATALOGUE OF CANADIAN COINS
(CN/0706-0424) [08818808] **2780**

CHARME MODA (IT) **5553**

CHARNY (QUEBEC) *See* AVIS
MUNICIPAL - VILLE DE CHARNY **4631**

CHAROLAIS BANNER (CN/0824-1767)
[11816215] **209**

CHAROLAIS CONNECTION
(CN/0828-7600) [12606656] **209**

CHAROLAIS JOURNAL (US/0191-5444)
[04659507] **209**

CHAROLAIS NEWSLETTER, THE (AT)
[03210418] **209**

CHAROLAIS ROUNDUP
(CN/1184-1575) [23598650] **209**

CHARPENTE MENUISERIE
METALLIQUES SERRURERIE (FR) **607**

CHART AND QUILL (US/0737-2655)
[09306878] **2442**

CHART BOOK OF GOVERNMENTAL
DATA: ORGANIZATION, FINANCES
AND EMPLOYMENT (US/0360-2508)
[02244426] **4717**

CHART CATALOG, GREAT LAKES,
CONNECTING WATERS, NEW YORK
CANALS, LAKE WINNEBAGO,
MINNESOTA-ONTARIO BORDER
LAKES, LAKE CHAMPLAIN, INLAND
ROUTE-MICHIGAN (US) [07714632]
2580

CHART (CHICAGO. 1956)
(US/0069-2778) [01328398] **3853**

●CHART CONNECTION, THE
(US/1065-2299) [26538379] **370**

CHART LIBRARIES. CURRENCY AND
FINANCIAL FUTURES WEEKLY (UK)
783

CHART MAGAZINE (CN) **4109**

CHARTAC ACCOUNTANCY NEWS
(AT/1037-6267) [I10376267] **740**

CHARTAC PRACTICE MANAGEMENT
NEWS (AT) **656**

CHARTAC TAX PLANNING NEWS
(AT/1037-6275) [I10376275] **740**

●CHARTAC TAX PRACTICE IDEAS (AT)
740

CHARTAC TAXATION MANUAL (UK)
4717

CHARTBOOK OF FEDERAL
PROGRAMS IN AGING (US/0197-0429)
[05949485] **5277**

CHARTBOOK ON OCCUPATIONAL
INJURIES AND ILLNESSES
(US/0145-3599) [02724800] **2860**

CHARTBOOK ON PRICES, WAGES,
AND PRODUCTIVITY (US/0095-4837)
[01796507] **1590**

CHARTER OF RIGHTS DECISIONS
(CN/0821-719X) [09863988] **4505**

CHARTER OF RIGHTS NEWSLETTER
(CN/0838-4843) [19577722] **4505**

CHARTER OF THE CITY OF NEW
YORK (US) **2530**

CHARTER (SYDNEY, AUSTRALIA) (AT)
[21469092] **740**

CHARTERED ACCOUNTANT, THE
(II/0009-188X) [02067778] **740**

CHARTERED ACCOUNTANTS
STUDENTS' ASSOCIATION OF
ONTARIO *See* STUDY BINDER -
CHARTERED ACCOUNTANTS
STUDENTS' ASSOCIATION OF
ONTARIO **751**

CHARTERED ASSOCIATION OF
CERTIFIED ACCOUNTANTS (GREAT
BRITAIN) *See* LIST OF MEMBERS /
CHARTERED ASSOCIATION OF
CERTIFIED ACCOUNTANTS **747**

CHARTERED BUILDER (AT/0311-1903)
[I03111903] **607**

CHARTERED BUILDER (ASCOT, 1989)
(UK/0957-8773) [22053668] **607**

CHARTERED BUILDER : THE
NEWSPAPER OF THE CHARTERED
INSTITUTE OF BUILDING (UK)
[13733040] **607**

CHARTERED INSTITUTE OF PATENT
AGENTS (LONDON, ENG.). COUNCIL
See ANNUAL REPORT OF THE
COUNCIL OF THE CHARTERED
INSTITUTE OF PATENT AGENTS FOR
THE YEAR ENDED ... - (LONDON,
ENG.) **1301**

CHARTERED INSTITUTE OF PUBLIC
FINANCE AND ACCOUNTANCY *See*
STATISTICAL INFORMATION SERVICE
: POLICE FORCE AND REGIONAL
CRIME SQUAD STATISTICS, ACTUALS
3083

CHARTERED INSTITUTE OF PUBLIC
FINANCE AND ACCOUNTANCY *See*
RETURN OF OUTSTANDING DEBT
(ENGLAND AND WALES) **4746**

CHARTERED INSTITUTE OF PUBLIC
FINANCE AND ACCOUNTANCY *See*
STATISTICAL INFORMATION
SERVICE: PERSONAL SOCIAL
SERVICES STATISTICS ACTUALS
5267

CHARTERED INSTITUTE OF PUBLIC
FINANCE AND ACCOUNTANCY *See*
POLICE FORCE STATISTICS **3082**

CHARTERED INSTITUTE OF PUBLIC
FINANCE AND ACCOUNTANCY.
STATISTICAL INFORMATION SERVICE
See PLANNING AND DEVELOPMENT
STATISTICS. ESTIMATES **2840**

CHARTERED INSTITUTE OF
PURCHASING AND SUPPLY REPORT
ON BUSINESS (UK) **656**

CHARTERED INSURANCE INSTITUTE
See JOURNAL / CHARTERED
INSURANCE INSTITUTE, THE **2885**

CHARTERED QUANTITY SURVEYOR
CEASED. (UK/0142-5196) [06520175]
2020

CHARTERED SECRETARY (NEW
DELHI) (II/0376-7868) [01790519] **863**

CHARTERED SURVEYOR : BUILDING
AND QUANTITY SURVEYING
QUARTERLY (UK) [01789131] **607**

CHARTERED SURVEYOR : RURAL
QUARTERLY (UK) [03699250] **2020**

CHARTERED SURVEYOR : URBAN
QUARTERLY (UK/0306-3178)
[01788720] **2817**

CHARTERED SURVEYOR WEEKLY
(UK/0264-049X) [09371904] **4835**

CHARTERING MAGAZINE'S YACHT
VACATIONS (US/0890-9547)
[14574349] **5466**

CHARTES (GR) [10209888] **317**

CHARTING STEEL'S PROGRESS
(US/0569-5910) [01480090] 4000, **1601**

CHARTIST (US) **894**

●CHARTS, GRAPHS & STATS INDEX
(US/1060-1465) [24881730] **5325**

CHARYO MINJOK TONGIL (JA)
[10762794] **2648**

CHAS PIK (RU) [23226492] **5809**

CHASE ALMANAC. CANADIAN
EDITION (CN/0227-0900) [08811632]
2530

CHASE COUNTY LEADER-NEWS (US)
[09863300] **5674**

CHASE FINANCIAL QUARTERLY
(US/0730-0360) [07941441] **783**

CHASE INVESTMENT PERFORMANCE
DIGEST (US/1048-2717) [20882040]
894, **656**

CHASE'S ANNUAL EVENTS
(US/0740-5286) [09958492] **5268**

CHASKA HERALD (US) [22742204]
5695

CHASQUI : REVISTA
LATINOAMERICANA DE
COMUNICACION (EC) [29658550] **1106**

CHASQUI (SAN JOSE, COSTA RICA)
(CR) [04233579] **1815**

CHASQUI (WILLIAMSBURG, VA.)
(US/0145-8973) [01071097] **3374**

●CHASSE AU QUEBEC, PRINCIPALES
REGLES, LA (CN/1185-247X)
[24401852] **4871**

CHASSE ET LE PIEGEAGE AU
QUEBEC, PRINCIPALES REGLES, LA
See CHASSE AU QUEBEC,
PRINCIPALES REGLES, LA **4871**

CHASSE MAREE (FR) 2613, **233**

CHASSE REVUE NATIONALE CHASSE
(FR) **2772**

CHASSEUR D'IMAGES (FR/0396-8235)
[I03968235] **4368**

CHASSIS SERVICE & REPAIR.
DOMESTIC CARS (US) [11429336]
5409

CHAT (TRYON), THE (US/0009-1987)
[02445814] **5580**

CHATEAUGAY RECORD AND
FRANKLIN COUNTY DEMOCRAT (US)
[16854461] **5714**

CHATEAUGUAY (QUEBEC) *See*
BULLETIN DE CHATEAUGAY, LE
4634

CHATEAUGUAY VALLEY HISTORICAL
SOCIETY *See* CHATEAUGUAY VALLEY
HISTORICAL SOCIETY ANNUAL
JOURNAL **2727**

CHATEAUGUAY VALLEY HISTORICAL
SOCIETY ANNUAL JOURNAL
(CN/0319-1249) [02443184] **2727**

CHATEAUX DE LA LOIRE (FR)
[03076620] **5466**

CHATELAINE (EDITION FRANCAISE)
(CN/0317-2635) [01553921] **5553**

CHATELAINE (TORONTO, ONT.: 1928)
(CN/0009-1995) [01983402] **5553**

CHATELAINE'S NEW MOTHER
(CN/0708-5303) [05362589] **2277**

CHATELAINE'S NEW OTHER *See* NEW
MOTHER (1992) **2284**

CHATHAM COURIER, THE ROUGH
NOTES, THE (US/1064-4644)
[17315424] **5714**

CHATHAM HOUSE PAPERS
(UK/0143-5795) [08157618] **4517**

CHATHAM NEWS (SILER CITY, N.C.),
THE (US/1067-1773) [13142116] **5723**

CHATHAM RECORD, THE
(US/1067-1765) [11794532] **5723**

CHATHAM THIS WEEK (CN/1185-5614)
[24860886] **5781**

CHATHAM THIS WEEK (CN/1185-5614)
[25590004] **5781**

CHATSWORTH RECORD AND THE
QUEEN'S BUSH QUILL, THE
(CN/0702-7982) [03436384] **5781**

CHATSWORTH TIMES (US) [20150828]
5652

CHATTAHOCHEE NEWS *See* TWIN
CITY NEWS (CHATTAHOOCHEE, FLA.)
5651

CHATTAHOOCHEE REVIEW, THE
(US/0741-9155) [08787865] **3339**

CHATTANOOGA AND TRI-STATE
AREA DIRECTORY OF
MANUFACTURERS (US/0160-4716)
[03678716] **3476**

●CHATTANOOGA FREE PRESS (US)
5744

CHATTANOOGA LIFE & LEISURE
CEASED. (US/0888-0077) [13445892]
2486

CHATTANOOGA NEWS-FREE PRESS
(US) [12797641] **5744**

CHATTANOOGA TIMES, THE (US)
[12797991] **5744**

CHATTOOGA PRESS, THE (US)
[24799894] **5652**

CHAUCER NEWSLETTER : A
PUBLICATION OF THE NEW CHAUCER
SOCIETY, THE (US) [05105079] **3374**

CHAUCER REVIEW, THE
(US/0009-2002) [01553931] **3339**

CHAUFFAGE, VENTILATION,
CONDITIONNEMENT (FR/0009-2029)
[06350474] 1935, **2604**

CHAUSSER 1968 (FR/0151-4040)
[I01514040] **1082**

CHAUTAUQUA COUNTY
AGRICULTURAL NEWS (US)
[07126174] **73**

CHAUTAUQUAN DAILY, THE
(US/0746-0414) [08687190] **5714**

CHAWON KAEBAL YONGUSO *See*
JOSA NYENGU BOGO - JANWEN
GAIBAR NYENGUSO **2141**

CHAYON KWAHAK YONGU (KO)
[08352176] **5093**

CHAYON KWAHAK YONGUSO
HAKSUL NONMUNJIP (KO) [10340142]
5093

CHAYON POHO (KO) [10254461] **2189**

CHAYON POJON (KO) [10088810] **2189**

CHAYON POJON YONGU POGOSO
(KO) [11121994] **2189**

CHAYONMI SAENGHWAL (KO)
[11327639] **2412**

CHAYU AKADEMI *See* CHAYU AKADEMI YON'GU NONCHONG 5195

CHAYU AKADEMI YON'GU NONCHONG (KO) [04869725] 5195

CHCG PULSE (CN/1197-4729) 3853

CHE-CHIANG CHUNG I HSUEH YUAN HSUEH PAO (CC) [10571073] 3563

CHE-CHIANG HSUEH KAN. ZHEJIANGXUEKAN CHE-CHIANG SHENG SHE HUI KO HSUEH YEN CHIU SO (CC) [10673650] 5195

CHE-CHIANG LIN HSUEH YUAN HSUEH PAO (CC) [20179394] 2377

CHE-CHIANG TA HSUEH HSUEH PAO (CC) [10946635] 5093

CHE-CHIANG WEN SHIH TZU LIAO HSUAN CHI / CHUNG-KUO JEN MIN CHENG CHIH HSIEH SHANG HUI I CHE-CHIANG SHENG WEI YUAN HUI, WEN SHIH TZU LIAO YEN CHIU WEI YUAN HUI PIEN (CH) [09541831] 2648

CHE VUOI? (US/0749-906X) [11206869] 3563

CHEAP INVESTOR, THE (US/0747-7236) [10811234] 894

●CHEAP RELIEF (US/1062-9548) [25814766] 4580

CHEBOYGAN DAILY TRIBUNE (US/0746-665X) [10222412] 5691

CHECK IT OUT! (CN/1191-0887) [25882777] 3201

CHECK-LIST OF BIRDS OF THE WORLD (US) [01320981] 5616

CHECK LIST OF BRITISH OFFICIAL SERIAL PUBLICATIONS (UK/0084-8085) [03024902] 4468

CHECK UP INCONTRI (IT) 3563

CHECK-UP (SAN DIEGO, CALIF.) (US/1063-0538) [25848990] 4771

CHECKBOOK'S GUIDE TO HEALTH INSURANCE PLANS FOR FEDERAL EMPLOYEES (US/0740-3925) [08595431] 2878

CHECKLIST OF AMERICAN IMPRINTS, A (US/0361-7920) [02441053] 413

CHECKLIST OF CURRENT PERIODICALS / NATIONAL UNIVERSITY OF SINGAPORE LIBRARY (SI/0217-2070) [10940702] 413

CHECKLIST OF HUMAN RIGHTS DOCUMENTS (US/0149-5372) [02854416] 4505

CHECKLIST OF INDIANA STATE DOCUMENTS (US/0361-0284) [03264032] 413

CHECKLIST OF OFFICIAL NEW JERSEY PUBLICATIONS (US/0146-0838) [01759841] 413

CHECKLIST OF OFFICIAL NORTH CAROLINA STATE PUBLICATIONS (US/0193-9432) [05294018] 413

CHECKLIST OF OFFICIAL PENNSYLVANIA PUBLICATIONS (US/0196-1608) [02259176] 413

CHECKLIST OF OFFICIAL PUBLICATIONS OF THE STATE OF ARIZONA (US) [20674757] 3201

CHECKLIST OF OFFICIAL PUBLICATIONS OF THE STATE OF NEW YORK, A (US/0077-9296) [01644873] 413

CHECKLIST OF SOUTH CAROLINA STATE PUBLICATIONS (US) [03011196] 413

CHECKLIST OF UNIVERSITY INSTITUTIONS IN THE COMMONWEALTH (UK/1353-329) 1815

CHECKLIST : PUBLICATIONS OF CONNECTICUT STATE AGENCIES (US) [01564833] 4697

CHECKLISTS AND ILLUSTRATIVE FINANCIAL STATEMENTS FOR COLLEGES AND UNIVERSITIES (US) [24329794] 4717, 1815

CHECKLISTS AND ILLUSTRATIVE FINANCIAL STATEMENTS FOR EMPLOYEE HEALTH AND WELFARE BENEFIT PLANS (US) [25034982] 741

CHECKLISTS AND ILLUSTRATIVE FINANCIAL STATEMENTS FOR HEALTH CARE PROVIDERS (US) [24330154] 4771, 741

CHECKLISTS OF BASIC AMERICAN LEGAL PUBLICATIONS (US) [01762400] 2949

CHECKPOINT (AT) [06749999] 4943

CHECKPOINT (IRVING, TEX.) (US/0747-2080) [10631793] 5410

CHECKPOINTS FOR CHILDREN / REGIONAL INSTITUTE OF SOCIAL WELFARE RESEARCH (US) [08789042] 5277

CHECKS & CHECKING (US/1046-4956) [20427528] 741

CHED, CHEMIE EXPERIMENT + DIDAKTIK (GW/0340-3335) [02741195] 967

CHEEKTOWAGA TIMES (US) [24450941] 5714

CHEER (CN/0229-1509) [08023747] 4109

CHEER NEWS TODAY (US/0893-8091) [15650384] 4889

CHEESE MARKET NEWS (US/0891-1509) [14631738] 192

CHEESE REPORTER (US/0009-2142) [03028059] 192

●CHEF (US) [27348603] 2331

CHEF DE FORME - RESEAU PARTICIPACTION (CN/0827-3502) [11873808] 2596

CHEF DES VENTES INFOS (FR) 1469

CHEF INSTITUTIONAL (US) [04346115] 2789

CHEF MGAZINE *See* CHEF INSTITUTIONAL 2789

CHEF PARIS, LE (FR/0980-8396) [I09808396] 5070, 2789

CHEFS (SZ) [03264446] 2331

CHEIN SUTOO (KO) [09552122] 656

CHEIRON (II/0379-542X) [01512065] 5507

CHEIRON (BRESCIA, ITALY) (IT) [10111159] 2613

CHEJIANG NONGYE KEXUE (CC/0528-9017) [21991089] 73

CHEJU HANGJAENG (KO) [25160589] 2648

CHELIABINSKII ELEKTROMETLLURGICHESKII KOMBINAT *See* SBORNIK TRUDOV CHELIABINSKOGO ELEKTROMETALLURICHESKOGO KOMBINATA 4018

CHELMSFORD INDEPENDENT (US) [20481791] 5688

CHELOVEK I POLITIKA *See* NAROD I DEMOKRATIIA 4482

CHELOVEK I STIKHIIA (RU/0203-2198) [20153854] 2212

●CHELOVEK I TRUD (RU) [25701750] 1659

CHELSEA (NEW YORK, N.Y.) (US/0009-2185) [04227687] 3374

CHELSEA RECORD (CHELSEA, MASS.), THE (US/1054-6529) [20127037] 5688

CHELSEA YEAR : THE YEARBOOK OF THE ROYAL HORTICULTURAL SOCIETY, THE (UK) [19367456] 2412

CHELSEY OVERVIEW (CN/0225-7017) [06272435] 5781

CHELYS (VIOLA DA GAMBA SOCIETY) (UK/0952-8407) [03025078] 4109

CHEM 13 NEWS. CHEM 12 NEWS (CN/0703-1157) [03443621] 1890, 967

CHEM-FACTS: AMMONIA (UK) 967

CHEM-FACTS: BELGIUM (UK) 967

CHEM-FACTS: CANADA (UK) 967

CHEM-FACTS: FEDERAL REPUBLIC OF GERMANY (UK) 967

CHEM-FACTS: FRANCE (UK) 967

CHEM-FACTS: ITALY (UK) 967

CHEM-FACTS: JAPAN (UK) 967

CHEM-FACTS METHANOL (UK) 967

CHEM-FACTS: NETHERLANDS (UK) 967

CHEM-FACTS: POLYETHYLENE (UK) 967

CHEM-FACTS: POLYPROPYLENE (UK) 967

CHEM-FACTS: SCANDINAVIA (UK) 967

CHEM-FACTS: SPAIN (UK) 967

CHEM-FACTS: UNITED KINGDOM (UK) 967

CHEM INFORM (GW/0931-7597) [15729948] 967, 1011

CHEM PACKAGE (US) 3563

CHEM SOURCES INTERNATIONAL (US) [16828278] 1021

CHEM SOURCES U.S.A (US/0094-6567) [01026936] 967

CHEM TRENDS (CN/0711-3447) [08479240] 967

CHEMCYCLOPEDIA (US/0736-6019) [08960699] 1021

CHEMECOLOGY (US/0738-7776) [08918492] 2162

CHEMIA (PL/0324-9034) [06134016] 967

CHEMIA ANALITYCZNA (PL/0009-2223) [03025042] 1014

CHEMIA STOSOWANA (1971) (PL/0376-0898) [06496206] 2009

CHEMICA (FI) [04770021] 1050

CHEMICA SCRIPTA *CEASED.* (SW/0004-2056) [01774905] 967

CHEMICAL ABSTRACTS (US/0009-2258) [01553947] 967, 1011

CHEMICAL ABSTRACTS (US/0009-2258) [08279146] 967

CHEMICAL ABSTRACTS. APPLIED CHEMISTRY AND CHEMICAL ENGINEERING SECTIONS (US/0090-8363) [01337215] 1021

CHEMICAL ABSTRACTS. BIOCHEMISTRY SECTIONS (US/0009-2304) [01553948] 485

CHEMICAL ABSTRACTS. COLLECTIVE INDEX (US/0097-6474) [01337182] 1011

CHEMICAL ABSTRACTS. INDEX GUIDE (US/0093-5719) [01390050] 967

CHEMICAL ABSTRACTS. MACROMOLECULAR SECTION (US/0009-2274) [01553949] 967

CHEMICAL ABSTRACTS. ORGANIC CHEMISTRY SECTIONS (US/0009-2282) [01779661] 1040

CHEMICAL ABSTRACTS. PHYSICAL, INORGANIC, AND ANALYTICAL CHEMISTRY SECTIONS (US/0278-1832) [07742392] 968

CHEMICAL ABSTRACTS SERVICE *See* REGISTRY HANDBOOK: NUMBER SECTION. SUPPLEMENT 991

CHEMICAL ABSTRACTS SERVICE SOURCE INDEX (US/0001-0634) [02239430] 1011

CHEMICAL AGE OF INDIA (II/0009-2320) [08855822] 5093, 968

CHEMICAL ANALYSIS (US/0069-2883) [1553955] 1014

CHEMICAL AND BIOCHEMICAL ENGINEERING QUARTERLY (CI) [19478459] 2009

CHEMICAL AND CHEMICAL PRODUCTS INDUSTRIES (1986) (CN/0835-0183) [16885980] 1021

CHEMICAL & ENGINEERING NEWS (US/0009-2347) [01553956] 2009, 1022

CHEMICAL AND PETROLEUM ENGINEERING (US/0009-2355) [02445823] 4253, 2009

CHEMICAL & PHARMACEUTICAL BULLETIN (JA/0009-2363) [06067231] 968, 4296

CHEMICAL AND PHYSICAL CHARACTERISTICS OF WATER IN ESTUARIES OF TEXAS (US/0748-0075) [05974132] 5532

CHEMICAL AND PHYSICAL PROCESSES IN COMBUSTION (US/0277-1128) [07582022] 968

CHEMICAL BANK NEW YORK TRUST COMPANY *See* REPORT - CHEMICAL BANK NEW YORK TRUST COMPANY 807

CHEMICAL BULLETIN, THE (US/0009-2401) [02445825] 968

CHEMICAL BUSINESS (II/0970-3136) [27358681] 2009

CHEMICAL BUSINESS *CEASED.* (US/0731-8774) [05690436] 968

CHEMICAL BUSINESS BULLETIN. SPECIALITY CHEMICALS (UK/0267-5889) [I02675889] 968

CHEMICAL BUSINESS BULLETINS (UK) 656, 968, 727

●CHEMICAL BUSINESS NEWSBASE [ONLINE DATABASE] (UK) 656, 968, 727

CHEMICAL BUSINESS UPDATE (UK/0950-6144) [I09506144] 656, 968, 1011

CHEMICAL COMMUNICATIONS / UNIVERSITY OF STOCKHOLM (SW/0366-5607) [08518772] 968

CHEMICAL CORRESPONDENCE (JA) [10589275] 968

CHEMICAL DESIGN AUTOMATION NEWS (US/0886-6716) [12956061] 1174, 968

CHEMICAL DIGEST DELHI (II/0970-9525) [I09709525] 968

CHEMICAL ECONOMICS NEWSLETTER (US/0577-6066) [01553960] 968

CHEMICAL ENGINEER (LONDON) (UK/0302-0797) [01553961] 2009

CHEMICAL ENGINEERING AND PROCESSING (SZ/0255-2701) [11226819] 2009

CHEMICAL ENGINEERING & TECHNOLOGY (GW/0930-7516) [15579344] 2009

CHEMICAL ENGINEERING ASPECTS OF BIOMEDICINE RESEARCH STUDIES SERIES (UK/0277-4038) [07429655] 3690

●CHEMICAL ENGINEERING BUYERS GUIDE FOR ... (US) [26775401] 2009

CHEMICAL ENGINEERING CATALOG (US/0276-8429) [04218379] 2009

CHEMICAL ENGINEERING COMMUNICATIONS (US/0098-6445) [02240082] 2009

CHEMICAL ENGINEERING, CONCEPTS AND REVIEWS (US/0734-1644) [08683472] 2009

CHEMICAL ENGINEERING EDUCATION (US/0009-2479) [01151209] 1731, 2009

CHEMICAL ENGINEERING EQUIPMENT BUYERS' GUIDE (US/0272-4057) [06776598] 2009

Alphabetical Title Index — CHEMISTRY

CHEMICAL ENGINEERING IN AUSTRALIA : CEA (AT/0157-9762) [06180687] **2010**

CHEMICAL ENGINEERING IN AUSTRALIA / THE INSTITUTION OF ENGINEERS, AUSTRALIA (AT/0313-5527) [03824236] **2010**

CHEMICAL ENGINEERING JOURNAL AND THE BIOCHEMICAL ENGINEERING JOURNAL, THE (SZ/0923-0467) [10112441] **2010**

CHEMICAL ENGINEERING MONOGRAPHS (NE/0167-4188) [03158483] **2010**

CHEMICAL ENGINEERING (NEW YORK) (US/0009-2460) [01553962] 2010, **1034**

CHEMICAL ENGINEERING PROGRESS (US/0360-7275) [01929453] **2010**

CHEMICAL ENGINEERING RESEARCH & DESIGN (UK/0263-8762) [08838563] **2010**

CHEMICAL ENGINEERING RESEARCH BULLETIN (BG/0379-7678) [11351229] **2010**

CHEMICAL ENGINEERING SCIENCE (UK/0009-2509) [01553970] **2010**

CHEMICAL EQUIPMENT (US/0009-2525) [02445829] **968**

CHEMICAL ERA (II/0009-2533) [01247253] **1022**

CHEMICAL FORMULARY; A COLLECTION OF VALUABLE, TIMELY, PRACTICAL COMMERCIAL FORMULAE AND RECIPES FOR MAKING THOUSANDS OF PRODUCTS IN MANY FIELDS OF INDUSTRY, THE (US) [01519522] **1022**

CHEMICAL GEOLOGY (NE/0009-2541) [01553973] **1040**

CHEMICAL HAZARDS IN INDUSTRY (UK/0265-5721) [11925608] 2860, **2872**

●CHEMICAL HEALTH & SAFETY (US/1074-9098) [29881662] **2860**

●CHEMICAL HERITAGE (US/1066-5315) [26986704] **968**

CHEMICAL HIGHLIGHTS (US/0009-255X) [02529941] **1040**

CHEMICAL IMMUNOLOGY (SZ/1015-0145) [20639733] **3667**

CHEMICAL INDIA ANNUAL (II/0304-1166) [01797758] **2010**

CHEMICAL INDUSTRIAL UNDERTAKINGS LICENSED (II/0591-1230) [01553976] **968**

CHEMICAL INDUSTRIES (NEW YORK, N.Y. : 1979) (US/0737-8025) [08163860] **968**

CHEMICAL INDUSTRY (JA) [06263404] **1022**

CHEMICAL INDUSTRY BUYER'S GUIDE FOR SOUTHERN AFRICA (SA/0304-1174) [02240035] **1601**

CHEMICAL INDUSTRY EUROPE (UK/0960-2992) [23930584] **968**

CHEMICAL INDUSTRY INSTITUTE OF TOXICOLOGY *See* ACTIVITIES / CHEMICAL INDUSTRY INSTITUTE OF TOXICOLOGY **3978**

CHEMICAL INDUSTRY NOTES (US/0045-639X) [04032200] 968, **1011**

CHEMICAL INDUSTRY UPDATE. NORTH AMERICA *CEASED*. (US/0732-5568) [08384278] **968**

CHEMICAL INDUSTRY UPDATE. OVERSEAS *CEASED*. (US/0732-5576) [08383636] **1601**

●CHEMICAL INFORMATION ALERT (US/1064-4601) [26288831] **968**

CHEMICAL INFORMATION BULLETIN (US/0364-1910) [02255630] **968**

CHEMICAL INSIGHT (UK/0045-6403) [I00456403] **1022**

CHEMICAL MARKETING REPORTER (US/0090-0907) [00932494] **968**

CHEMICAL MATTERS (UK) [20513797] **1022**

CHEMICAL MONITOR, THE (US/1049-1015) [21135359] **1022**

CHEMICAL MUTAGENS (US/0093-6855) [02969794] **543**

CHEMICAL NEW PRODUCT DIRECTORY, THE (US/0160-6360) [03712017] **1022**

CHEMICAL OCEANOGRAPHY (US/1058-9740) [19578605] **1447**

CHEMICAL PACKAGING REVIEW, THE (US/1054-5131) [22904219] **2162**

CHEMICAL PAPERS (GW) **968**

CHEMICAL PATENTS INDEX (UK) 969, **1302**

CHEMICAL PATENTS INDEX. PLASTICS AND POLYMERS (UK) **969**

CHEMICAL PHYSICS (NE/0301-0104) [01786275] **1050**

CHEMICAL PHYSICS LETTERS (NE/0009-2614) [01553982] **1050**

CHEMICAL PHYSICS OF SOLIDS AND THEIR SURFACES (UK/0142-3401) [04991493] 969, **4399**

CHEMICAL PROCESSING AND ENGINEERING (NEW YORK) (US/0146-681X) [02117191] **2010**

CHEMICAL PROCESSING (CHICAGO, ILL.) (US/0009-2630) [03956108] **969**

CHEMICAL REFERENCE MANUAL (US/0094-6249) [01794627] **1014**

CHEMICAL REGULATION REPORTER (US/0148-7973) [03338525] 969, **2949**

CHEMICAL RESEARCH IN CHINESE UNIVERSITIES (CH) [24006257] **969**

CHEMICAL RESEARCH IN TOXICOLOGY (US/0893-228X) [15464975] **3979**

CHEMICAL RESEARCH LABORATORIES (AUSTRALIA) *See* REPORT **1029**

CHEMICAL REVIEW (US/0191-4170) [04863237] 4253, **1022**

CHEMICAL REVIEWS (US/0009-2665) [01553987] **969**

●CHEMICAL SCIENCES GRADUATE SCHOOL FINDER (US/1058-1227) [24223106] 1815, **969**

CHEMICAL SCREENING, INITIAL EVALUATIONS OF SUBSTANTIAL RISK NOTICES, SECTION 8(E) (US/0278-1824) [07631729] **4244**

CHEMICAL SENSES (UK/0379-864X) [06398320] **969**

CHEMICAL SENSOR TECHNOLOGY (JA) [19230296] **1022**

CHEMICAL SOCIETY (GREAT BRITAIN) *See* CHEMICAL SOCIETY REVIEWS **969**

CHEMICAL SOCIETY (GREAT BRITAIN) *See* ANNUAL REPORT OF COUNCIL AND ACCOUNTS - CHEMICAL SOCIETY **961**

CHEMICAL SOCIETY OF PAKISTAN *See* JOURNAL OF THE CHEMICAL SOCIETY OF PAKISTAN **982**

CHEMICAL SOCIETY REVIEWS (UK/0306-0012) [01784930] **969**

CHEMICAL SPECIATION AND BIOAVAILABILITY (UK/0954-2299) [20003212] 969, **2162**

CHEMICAL SPOTLIGHT *CEASED*. (US/0411-8871) [02749384] **969**

CHEMICAL SUBSTANCES CONTROL (US/0271-1478) [06559213] **969**

CHEMICAL TECHNOLOGY EUROPE (GW/0945-9618) [01554022] **1022**

CHEMICAL THERMODYNAMICS OF ACTINIDE ELEMENTS AND COMPOUNDS (AU) **969**

CHEMICAL TIMES & TRENDS (US/0149-2381) [03450822] **969**

CHEMICAL TITLES (US/0009-2711) [01554012] 969, **1011**

●CHEMICAL VAPOR DEPOSITION PATENTS (US/1062-8827) [25783510] **1302**

CHEMICAL WASTE LITIGATION REPORTER (US/0889-0633) [12895385] 2226, **3110**

CHEMICAL WEAPONS CONVENTION BULLETIN (US/1060-8095) [24154867] **4039**

CHEMICAL WEEK (US/0009-272X) [01554014] **1022**

CHEMICAL WEEK. EXECUTIVE EDITION (US) **969**

CHEMICAL WEEK INTERNATIONAL (US) **969**

CHEMICAL WEEKLY (II/0045-6500) [03061200] 2010, **969**

CHEMICAL WORKER, THE (US/0162-637X) [04128901] 969, **1659**

CHEMICHE VLAKNA (XO/0528-9432) [10489575] **5348**

CHEMICKE LISTY (XR/0009-2770) [06536532] **969**

CHEMICKY PRUMYSL (XR/0009-2789) [02445847] **1022**

CHEMICO-BIOLOGICAL INTERACTIONS (IE/0009-2797) [01421161] **485**

CHEMIE-ANLAGEN + VERFAHREN (GW/0009-2800) [04016735] **2010**

CHEMIE DER ERDE (GW/0009-2819) [03081657] 1371, **1438**

CHEMIE IN DER SCHULE (GW) [03663607] **969**

CHEMIE IN LABOR UND BIOTECHNIK : CLB (GW/0722-6764) [23465601] 3690, **969**

CHEMIE IN UNSERER ZEIT (GW/0009-2851) [01554021] **969**

CHEMIE, KUNSTSTOFFE AKTUELL (AU/0251-1126) [02244412] 4454, **1022**

CHEMIE MAGAZINE : MAANDBLAD VAN DE VLAAMSE CHEMISCHE VERENIGING (BE) [11119550] **969**

CHEMIE, MIKROBIOLOGIE, TECHNOLOGIE DER LEBENSMITTEL (GW/0366-7154) [01730073] **2331**

CHEMIE-TECHNIK (GW/0340-9961) [02245177] **2010**

CHEMIE UND TECHNIK IN DER LANDWIRTSCHAFT : DER RARGEBER FUER DIE GENOSSENCHAFTLICHE WARENVERMITTLUNG (GW) [06306630] **73**

CHEMIEFASERN, TEXTILINDUSTRIE (GW/0340-3343) [08942129] **5348**

CHEMIEINGENIEURTECHNIK (GW/0009-286X) [01554022] **2010**

CHEMIJA / LIETUVOS MOKSLU SKADEMIJA (LI/0235-7216) [23866018] 73, **5093**

CHEMIK (PL/0009-2886) [03989733] **1022**

CHEMIKA CHRONIKA. GENIKE EKDOSIS (GR/0366-5526) [04266194] **969**

CHEMIKER ZEITUNG (1970) *See* JOURNAL FUER PRAKTISCHE CHEMIE, CHEMIKER-ZEITUNG **979**

CHEMINDEX PLUS (UK) **4296**

CHEMINS DE FER : BULLETIN OFFICIEL (FR/0009-2924) [04129521] **5430**

CHEMISCH JAARBOEK (NE) [04795727] **969**

CHEMISCH JAARBOEKJE *See* CHEMISCH JAARBOEK **969**

CHEMISCH MAGAZINE (NE/0167-2746) [06549379] **970**

CHEMISCH WEEKBLAD. CHEMISCHE COURANT (NE/0378-1887) [02993871] **970**

CHEMISCHE BERICHTE (GW/0009-2940) [01554024] **970**

CHEMISCHE INDUSTRIE (DUSSELDORF) (GW/0009-2959) [01554025] 2011, **970**

CHEMISCHE INDUSTRIE INTERNATIONAL *CEASED*. (GW/0009-2967) [01554026] **1022**

CHEMISCHE RUNDSCHAU (SZ/0009-2983) [09959789] **970**

CHEMISCHE RUNDSCHAU ORGAN FUER FORSCHUNG, TECHNIK, FABRIKATION, HANDEL, IMPORT AND EXPORT CHEMISCHER, PHARMAZEUTISCHER UND VERWANDTER ERZEUGNISSE (SZ/0009-2983) [02445857] **970**

CHEMISCHE TECHNIK *CEASED*. (GW/0045-6519) [03084747] **2011**

CHEMIST-ANALYST (US/0095-8484) [01554034] **1014**

CHEMIST & DRUGGIST (UK/0009-3033) [01554035] **4296**

CHEMIST & DRUGGIST DIRECTORY (UK/0262-5881) [06468688] **4296**

CHEMIST & DRUGGIST DIRECTORY AND TABLET & CAPSULE IDENTIFICATION GUIDE (UK) [03085051] **4296**

CHEMIST (NEW YORK), THE (US/0009-3025) [01554031] **970**

CHEMIST NEWS, THE (US) [05379416] **970**

CHEMISTRY AND BIOCHEMISTRY OF AMINO ACIDS, PEPTIDES, AND PROTEINS *CEASED*. (US/0069-3111) [01040787] 485, **1040**

●CHEMISTRY & BIOLOGY (US/1074-5521) [29743387] 970, **451**

CHEMISTRY AND BIOLOGY OF MINERALIZED TISSUES : PROCEEDINGS OF THE SECOND INTERNATIONAL CONFERENCE ON THE CHEMISTRY AND BIOLOGY OF MINERALIZED TISSUES, THE (US) [12569138] 451, **970**

CHEMISTRY AND INDUSTRY (LONDON) (UK/0009-3068) [06183681] **970**

CHEMISTRY AND INDUSTRY [MICROFORM] (UK) [09975509] **970**

CHEMISTRY AND PHARMACOLOGY OF DRUGS (US/0737-8033) [08585452] 4296, **970**

CHEMISTRY AND PHYSICS OF CARBON (US/0069-3138) [01265930] **1035**

CHEMISTRY AND PHYSICS OF LIPIDS (IE/0009-3084) [00876631] **485**

CHEMISTRY AND TECHNOLOGY OF FUELS AND OILS (US/0009-3092) [02445864] 4253, **970**

CHEMISTRY CITATION INDEX (US/1057-6088) [24080888] 970, **1011**

CHEMISTRY EXPRESS : JOURNAL OF KINKI CHEMICAL SOCIETY, JAPAN (JA) [13385470] **970**

CHEMISTRY IN AUSTRALIA (AT/0314-4240) [03616215] **970**

CHEMISTRY IN BRITAIN (UK/0009-3106) [01554042] **970**

CHEMISTRY IN ECOLOGY (US/0275-7540) [07228323] **2212**

CHEMISTRY IN NEW ZEALAND (NZ/0110-5566) [01796348] **971**

CHEMISTRY IN SRI LANKA (CE/1012-8999) [12788450] **971**

CHEMISTRY — Alphabetical Title Index

CHEMISTRY INTERNATIONAL (UK/0193-6484) [05231749] **971**

CHEMISTRY LETTERS (JA/0366-7022) [01222426] 1050, **1040**

CHEMISTRY OF FUNCTIONAL GROUPS, THE (US) [06289994] **971**

CHEMISTRY OF HETEROCYCLIC COMPOUNDS (NEW YORK. 1965) (US/0009-3122) [01554043] **971**

CHEMISTRY OF HETEROCYCLIC COMPOUNDS, THE (US/0069-3154) [02250687] **971**

CHEMISTRY OF MATERIALS (US/0897-4756) [17512860] **971**

CHEMISTRY OF NATURAL COMPOUNDS (US/0009-3130) [01554044] **1040**

CHEMISTRY OF ORGANOMETALLIC COMPOUNDS, THE *CEASED.* (UK/0190-096X) [04625298] **1040**

CHEMISTRY OF PEPTIDES AND PROTEINS (GW/0723-6271) [12755577] **1040**

CHEMISTRY OF PLANT PROTECTION (GW/0937-2148) [13277834] **506**

CHEMISTRY REVIEW (UK/0959-8464) **971**

●CHEMISTRY REVIEWS (SZ/1071-6114) [28707350] **971**

CHEMISTRY (SPRINGFIELD) *CEASED.* (US/0163-1519) [02575951] **971**

CHEMKON : CHEMIE KONKRET, FORUM FUER UNTERRICHT UND DIDAKTIK (GW) **1022**

CHEMMATTERS (US/0736-4687) [09135366] **971**

CHEMNITZ. TECHNISCHE HOCHSCHULE, KARL-MARX-STADT *See* WISSENSCHAFTLICHE ZEITSCHRIFT **2495**

CHEMOECOLOGY (GW/0937-7409) [23228587] **971**

CHEMOMETRICS AND INTELLIGENT LABORATORY SYSTEMS (NE/0169-7439) [13352494] **971**

CHEMOMETRICS AND INTELLIGENT LABORATORY SYSTEMS : LABORATORY INFORMATION MANAGEMENT (NE/0925-5281) **1014**

CHEMORECEPTION ABSTRACTS (US/0300-1261) [01793631] 579, **477**

CHEMOSPHERE (OXFORD) (UK/0045-6535) [02845873] **2226**

CHEMOTHERAPIE-JOURNAL (GW/0940-6735) [09406735] 561, **3814**

CHEMOTHERAPY (BASEL) (SZ/0009-3157) [01554049] **3814**

CHEMOTHERAPY (TOKYO) (JA/0009-3165) [09498522] **3815**

CHEMPRESS (NE/0009-3173) [I00093173] **971**

CHEMSA *CEASED.* (SA/0379-4687) [02240829] **2011**

CHEMSPHERE (US/0577-6406) [02579881] 1551, 4253, **1022**

CHEMTECH (US/0009-2703) [01553943] **1022**

CHEMTRACTS. BIOCHEMISTRY AND MOLECULAR BIOLOGY (US/1045-2680) [20059159] **485**

CHEMTRACTS. INORGANIC CHEMISTRY (US/1051-7227) [22096319] **1036**

CHEMTRACTS. MACROMOLECULAR CHEMISTRY *CEASED.* (US/0899-7829) [18216587] **971**

CHEMTRACTS. ORGANIC CHEMISTRY (US/0895-4445) [16642153] **1041**

CHEMTRONICS *See* ADVANCED MATERIALS FOR OPTICS AND ELECTRONICS **5080**

CHEMUNG HISTORICAL JOURNAL, THE (US/0528-9599) [03467034] **2727**

CHEMUNG VALLEY REPORTER (US/1064-4091) [11191984] **5714**

CHEMUNITY (US/0743-9806) [10737769] **971**

CHENE (CN/0228-5037) [08072129] **4637**

CHENEY FREE PRESS (US) [17315741] **5760**

CHENEY SENTINEL, THE (US) [12564875] **5674**

CHENG CHIH CHIAO YU (CH) [09114120] **4468**

CHENG CHIH PING LUN (CH) [01554054] **3339**

CHENG CHIH YU FA LU (CC) [09371921] **4468**

CHENG FA LUN TAN : CHUNG-KUO CHENG FA TA HSUEH HSUEH PAO (CC) [18047371] 4468, **2949**

CHENG-KUNG TA HSUEH HSUEH PAO. JEN WEN, SHE HUI, KO CHI, I HSUEH PIEN (CH) [26164845] 3563, 5093, **2844**

CHENG MING (NAN-CHANG SHIH, CHINA) (HK) [10674717] **5229**

CHENGDU KEJI DAXUE XUEBAO (CC/0253-2263) [08863071] **5093**

CHENJI XUEBAO (CC/1000-0550) [13843220] **1371**

CHERAW CHRONICLE (US/0889-0617) [13640557] **5741**

CHERCHEURS DE LA WALLONIE : BULLETIN DE LA SOCIETE ROYALE BELGE D'ETUDES GEOLOGIQUES ET ARCHEOLOGIQUES, LES (BE) 265, **1371**

CHERNO & BIALO : CHB (BU) [24088911] **2514**

CHEROKEE COUNTY HERALD, THE (US) [12540906] **5625**

CHEROKEE DAILY TIMES (US/0747-4776) [10902064] **5669**

CHEROKEE FAMILY HISTORY (US) **2442**

CHEROKEE FAMILY RESEARCHER (US) **2443**

CHEROKEE ONE FEATHER, THE (US/0890-4448) [01554058] **2258**

CHEROKEE SCOUT *CEASED.* (US/0746-3987) [00012322] **5723**

CHEROKEE TRACER, THE (US/1073-8363) [27476775] **2443**

CHEROKEE TRIBUNE, THE (US) [19297584] **5652**

CHERRIES (ALBANY, N.Y.) (US/0193-8835) [04040485] **166**

CHERRY CIRCLE *See* CAA MAGAZINE **4889**

CHERRY UTILIZATION (US/0735-7389) [04168670] **166**

CHERRY VALLEY HISTORICAL ASSOCIATION (US) [11296223] **2727**

CHERYL WATSON'S TUNING LETTER (US) **1174**

CHESA TONGGYE YONBO (KO) [08122084] **5349**

CHESAPEAKE BAY FOUNDATION *See* ANNUAL REPORT - CHESAPEAKE BAY FOUNDATION **4162**

CHESAPEAKE BAY MAGAZINE (US/0045-656X) [03875102] **593**

CHESAPEAKE BOATMAN, THE (US/0164-808X) [04323089] **593**

CHESAPEAKE COUSINS (US/0882-1208) [11738407] **2443**

CHESHIRE ARCHAEOLOGICAL BULLETIN (UK/0307-6628) [06946590] **265**

CHESHIRE HERALD (US) [25180503] **5645**

CHESNAIE (CN/0822-6342) [10179219] **4637**

CHESOPIEAN, THE (US/0009-3300) [02393676] **265**

CHESS (UK/0009-3319) [04121317] **4858**

CHESS COLLECTOR (UK) **4858**

CHESS CORRESPONDENT, THE (US/0009-3327) [04007446] **4858**

CHESS DIGEST MAGAZINE (US/0009-3335) [04032208] **4858**

CHESS HORIZONS (US/0147-2569) [03122209] **4858**

CHESS IN INDIANA (US/1044-8888) [19932151] **4858**

CHESS LIFE (1980) (US/0197-260X) [05885790] **4858**

●CHESS (OXFORD) (UK/0964-6221) [25453995] **4858**

CHESS PRESS SYNDICATE *See* NEWS RELEASE FROM THE CHESS PRESS SYNDICATE **4864**

CHEST (US/0012-3692) [01554067] **3702**

CHEST DISEASES *See* CHEST DISEASES, THORACIC SURGERY AND TUBERCULOSIS **3949**

CHEST DISEASES (PH/0300-0974) [01778059] **3563**

CHEST DISEASES, THORACIC SURGERY AND TUBERCULOSIS (NE/0014-4193) [02441223] **3949**

CHEST SURGERY CLINICS OF NORTH AMERICA (US/1052-3359) [22252779] **3961**

CHESTER COUNTY LAW REPORTER (US) **2949**

CHESTER COUNTY PRESS (US) [18606397] **5735**

CHESTER COUNTY REPORTS (US) [02250921] **2949**

CHESTER WHITE JOURNAL (US/0009-3386) [10151791] **209**

CHESTERFIELD ADVERTISER, THE *CEASED.* (US/0889-2334) [13819786] **5742**

CHESTERTON REVIEW, THE (CN/0317-0500) [02247651] 431, **3374**

CHESTERTON TRIBUNE, THE (US) [13214066] **5663**

CHESTNUT HILL LOCAL, THE (US/0009-3394) [04032202] **5735**

CHESTNUT TREE, THE (US/0363-4493) [02465813] **2443**

CHET, CHEMIE EXPERIMENT + I.E. UND TECHNOLOGIE (GW/0342-6696) [03460970] **1023**

CHETEK ALERT, THE (US) [15076337] **5766**

CHEVAL MAGAZINE (FR) **2798**

CHEVAL (WIEN) (AU/1010-3422) [03858061] **2798**

CHEVAUX DE PENNY (FR) 2798, **1061**

CHEVRE QUEBEC (CN/0714-3621) [09137702] **209**

CHEVRE TOURS, LA (FR/0045-6608) [I00456608] **209**

CHEVROLET CAMARO SHOP MANUAL *See* SERVICE MANUAL. CAMARO **5425**

CHEVROLET HIGH PERFORMANCE *See* CHEVY HIGH PERFORMANCE **5410**

CHEVRON FOCUS *CEASED.* (US/0748-6367) [10979414] **4253**

CHEVRON, THE (CN) [02259212] **5781**

CHEVRON WORLD *CEASED.* (US/0148-3102) [02852887] **4253**

CHEVY ACTION (US/1056-2974) [23614057] **5410**

CHEVY HIGH PERFORMANCE (US/1062-192X) [25538102] **5410**

CHEWELAH INDEPENDENT, THE (US) [17365580] **5760**

CHEY-ARAP BULLETIN (US) [03085328] **2727**

CHEYAK KISUL CHONGBO (KO) [08605963] **4296**

CHEYUGIN (KO) [11763585] **4890**

CHEZ NOUS (NEW YORK) (US/0009-3424) [04032223] 1890, **3273**

CHF NEWSBRIEFS (US/1046-8196) [20414408] **2817**

CHFC REPORT (US/0739-9154) [09823195] **3778**

CHI CHE KUNG CHENG. QICHE GONGCHENG (CC) [09689705] **5410**

CHI CHE TIEN CHUAN TUNG (CC) [11613374] **5430**

CHI CHUNG YUN SHU CHI HSIEH / TI 1 CHI HSIEH KUNG YEH PU CHI CHUNG YUN SHU CHI HSIEH YEN CHIU SO (CC) [11500841] **2111**

CHI E - DOV' E ; ANNUARIO DELL'INDUSTRIA FONOGRAFICA E DELL'EDITORIA MUSICALE IN ITALIA (IT) [01788941] 4109, **5316**

CHI HSIANG HSUEH PAO (CC/0577-6619) [03859265] **1421**

CHI HSIANG HSUEH PAO (CHUNG-KUO CHI HSIANG HSUEH HUI) (CC/0894-0525) [15734445] **1421**

CHI HSIEH KUNG CHENG HSUEH PAO (US/1000-9345) [18103215] **2111**

CHI HSIEH KUNG CHENG HSUEH PAO (CC/0577-6686) [03085419] **2111**

CHI KO HSUEH, TA (US/0891-3862) [14713357] **5093**

CHI KUANG CHI SHU (CC) [19117076] **4434**

CHI KUANG YU HUNG WAI (CC/1001-5078) [21248310] **4434**

CHI-LIN TA HSUEH TZU JAN KO HSUEH HSUEH PAO (CC/0529-0279) [05355564] **5093**

CHI NAN HSUEH PAO. CHE HSUEH SHE HUI KO HSUEH PAN (CH/1000-5072) [10891162] **1815**

CHI NO KOKOGAKU (JA) [02244245] **5229**

CHI SHU CHING CHI YU KUAN LI YEN CHIU (CC) [09146884] **863**

CHI SUAN CHI KO HSUEH (CH) [10964596] **1256**

CHI TUNG WEN I / JIDONG WENYI (CC) [11455404] **317**

CHI YEH KUAN LI (CHUNG-KUO CHI YEH KUAN LI HSIEH HUI) (CH) [09301669] **863**

CHI YEH TIEN TI (CH) [01797606] **656**

CHIA HO TIEN YING (CH) [01790377] **4065**

CHIA HUA CH'IAO PAO (CN/0226-5109) [06315719] **2727**

CHIA KO LI LUN YU SHIH CHIEN (CH) [09262085] **1590**

CHIAN MUNJE (KO) [10248827] **3160**

CHIANG HAN LUN TAN (CC) [06202385] **2502**

CHIANG-HSI SHIH FAN TA HSUEH HSUEH PAO. CHE HSUEH SHE HUI KO HSUEH PAN (CC/1000-579X) [15863949] **5195**

CHIANG-HSI WEN SHIH TZU LIAO HSUAN CHI / CHENG HSIEH CHIANG-HSI SHENG WEN SHIH TZU LIAN YEN CHIU WEI YUAN HUI (CH) [08734003] **2648**

CHIANG NAN (CC) [08398751] **3374**

CHIANG SHAN TO CHIAO (CC) [04723235] **2648**

Alphabetical Title Index — CHICAGO

CHIANG-SU CHIAO YU (CC/0411-9606) [03055309] **1731**

CHIANG-SU CHIAO YU. CHUNG HSUEH PAN (CC) [11567546] **1731**

CHIANG-SU NUNG HSUEH YUAN HSUEH PAO (CC) [24019870] **73**

CHIANG-SU NUNG YEH KO HSUEH (CC) [06653715] **73**

CHIAO HSUEH TUNG HSUN (CC) [11413821] **1731**

CHIAO HSUEH TUNG HSUN. LI KO PAN (CH) [11100583] **5093**

CHIAO HSUEH YEN CHIU (CC) [11093596] **1731**

CHIAO HSUEH YU YEN CHIU. / JIAOXUE YU YANJIU (CC/0411-9630) [03060549] **1890**

CHIAO HSUEH YU YEN CHIU (TAIPEI, TAIWAN) (CH) [07120835] **1815**

CHIAO HSUEH YUEH KAN. CHUNG HSUEH LI KO PAN (CH) [11093032] **5093**

CHIAO HSUEH YUEH KAN. CHUNG HSUEH WEN KO PAN (CC) [11413963] **1731**

CHIAO HSUH YUEH KAN. HSIAO HSUEH PAN / JIAO XUE YUE KAN (CC) [11101234] **1731**

CHIAO TUNG CHIEN SHE (CH) [09668465] **5379**

CHIAO TUNG HSUEH KAN (CH) [06907440] **3160**

CHIAO TUNG PU TIEN HSIN TSUNG CHU TIEN HSIN YEN CHIU SO *See* DETAILED VALUES OF IONOSPHERIC CHARACTERISTICS AND F-PLOTS FOR CHUNG-LI **1425**

CHIAO YU HSUEH PAO (SI) [01797566] **1731**

CHIAO YU LUN WEN CHAI YAO / KUO LI TAI-WAN SHIH FAN TA HSUEH TU SHU KUAN PIEN (CH) [06124666] **1731**

CHIAO YU YEN CHIU / CHUNG YANG CHIAO YU KO HSUEH YEN CHIU SO (CC) [05461541] **1731**

CHIBA DAIGAKU ENGEI GAKUBU GAKUJUTSU KOKOKU (JA/0069-3227) [07023922] **2412**

CHIBA DAIGAKU KOGAKUBU KENKYU HOKOKU (JA/0577-6848) [09370757] 1968, **5093**

CHIBA DAIGAKU. SEIBUTSU KASSEI KENKYUJO *See* CHIBA DAIGAKU SEIBUTSU KASSEI KENKYUJO HOKOKU **561**

CHIBA DAIGAKU SEIBUTSU KASSEI KENKYUJO HOKOKU (JA) [02245382] **561**

CHIBA IGAKU ZASSHI (JA/0303-5476) [00967567] **3563**

CHIBA-KEN DANCHI ENGEI SHIKENJO *See* CHIBA-KEN DANCHI ENGEI SHIKENJO KENKYU HOKOKU **2412**

CHIBA-KEN DANCHI ENGEI SHIKENJO KENKYU HOKOKU (JA) [02246899] **2412**

CHIBA-KEN EISEI KENKYUJO KENKYU HOKOKU (JA/0386-6742) [10408285] **4771**

CHIBA-KEN GAN SENTA *See* CHIBA-KEN GAN SENTA NEMPO **3815**

CHIBA-KEN GAN SENTA NEMPO (JA) [02244329] **3815**

CHIBA-KEN (JAPAN). KANKYOBU *See* CHIBA-KEN KANKYO HAKUSHO **2226**

CHIBA-KEN KANKYO HAKUSHO (JA) [03429053] **2226**

CHIBA-KEN KOGAI KENKYUJO *See* CHIBA-KEN NO JIBAN CHINKA **2020**

CHIBA-KEN KOGAI KENKYUJO *See* CHIBA-KEN KOGAI KENKYUJO KENKYU HOKOKU **2226**

CHIBA-KEN KOGAI KENKYUJO KENKYU HOKOKU (JA) [02961146] **2226**

CHIBA-KEN NO JIBAN CHINKA (JA) [03645665] **2020**

CHIBA-KEN NOGYO SHIKENJO KENKYU HOKOKU (JA/0577-6880) [13746188] **73**

CHIBA-KEN SANGYO SHIKENJO *See* CHIBA-KEN SANGYO SHIKENJO TOKUBETSU HOKOKU **209**

CHIBA-KEN SANGYO SHIKENJO TOKUBETSU HOKOKU (JA) [06830843] **209**

CHIBA-KEN SUISAN SHIKENJO *See* GYOMU NENPO **2304**

CHIBA KENRITSU CHUO HAKUBUTSUKAN SHIZENSHI KENKYU HOKOKU (JA/0915-9452) [24610539] **4164**

CHIBA KOGYO DAIGAKU KENKYU HOKOKU. RIKO HEN (JA/0385-7026) [12483914] **5093**

CHIBA REVIEW (JA/0388-2241) [03882241] **3374**

CHIBRET INTERNATIONAL JOURNAL OF OPHTHALMOLOGY EDICION ESPANOLA (SP/0212-3940) [02123940] **3873**

CHIBRET INTERNATIONAL JOURNAL OF OPHTHALMOLOGY (ENGLISH ED.) (US/0748-9501) [11041925] **3873**

CHICAGO (US/0362-4595) [02398937] **2530**

CHICAGO ACADEMY OF SCIENCES *See* BULLETIN OF THE CHICAGO ACADEMY OF SCIENCES **5091**

CHICAGO & COOK COUNTY MARKETING DIRECTORY (US/0896-4017) [17064702] **922**

CHICAGO ANTHROPOLOGY EXCHANGE (US/8756-0011) [11455981] **233**

CHICAGO APPAREL NEWS (US/0195-0819) [05267093] **1082**

CHICAGO AREA TRANSPORTATION STUDY *See* ... TRANSPORTATION SYSTEM MANAGEMENT REPORT FOR NORTHEASTERN ILLINOIS, THE **5397**

CHICAGO. ART INSTITUTE. RYERSON LIBRARY *See* INDEX TO ART PERIODICALS. SUPPLEMENT **352**

CHICAGO ARTS & COMMUNICATION (US/1061-8864) [25159644] **317**

CHICAGO ASSOCIATION LIFE UNDERWRITERS *See* YOUR CHICAGO EXPRESS **2897**

CHICAGO ASSOCIATION LIFE UNDERWRITERS *See* YOUR CHICAGO EXPRESS **2897**

CHICAGO ASSOCIATION OF COMMERCE AND INDUSTRY. RESEARCH AND STATISTICS DIVISION *See* MAJOR EMPLOYERS, METROPOLITAN CHICAGO **691**

CHICAGO ASSOCIATION OF LAW LIBRARIES *See* CHICAGO LAW LIBRARY BULLETIN **3201**

CHICAGO BANKS (US/0361-7661) [02287367] **783**

CHICAGO BAR RECORD *CEASED.* (US/0009-3505) [01554144] **2949**

CHICAGO BEAR REPORT (US/1056-4284) [23714403] **4890**

CHICAGO BOARD OPTIONS EXCHANGE *See* MARKET STATISTICS **906**

CHICAGO BOWLER (US/0009-3513) [04032215] **4890**

CHICAGO BOWLER, INC, THE (US/1056-3547) [23667508] **4890**

CHICAGO CONSUMER (CHICAGO, ILL. : 1987) (US/0895-9064) [16854772] **1294**

CHICAGO CONTRACTORS REGISTER (US/0732-0604) [08274430] **607**

CHICAGO CREATIVE DIRECTORY, THE (US/0193-7596) [05242356] **1130**

CHICAGO CRUSADER, THE (US) [10405260] **5658**

CHICAGO DAILY LAW BULLETIN (US/0362-6148) [04582572] **2949**

CHICAGO DEFENDER (1973) (US/0745-7014) [09387279] 2258, **5659**

CHICAGO DIRECTORY *See* CU DIRECTORY **384**

CHICAGO ENTERPRISE (US/1044-0844) [15278122] **1601**

CHICAGO ENVIRONMENT, THE (US/1056-8948) [23887956] **2162**

CHICAGO FACES (US/0195-9638) [05697591] **2727**

CHICAGO FED LETTER (US/0895-0164) [16402000] **783**

CHICAGO FIRE FIGHTER *See* LOCAL 2 NEWS **2291**

CHICAGO FRUIT & VEGETABLE REPORTER (US) [06332885] **2412**

CHICAGO GALLERY NEWS (US/1046-6185) [20385782] **4086**

CHICAGO GENEALOGICAL SOCIETY *See* NEWSLETTER OF THE CHICAGO GENEALOGICAL SOCIETY **2463**

CHICAGO GENEALOGIST (US/0009-3556) [04177388] **2443**

CHICAGO HEIGHTS STAR *See* STAR (CHICAGO HEIGHTS AREA [ED.]), THE **5662**

CHICAGO HISTORY (US/0272-8540) [03109657] **2727**

CHICAGO HOSPITAL COUNCIL *See* FACTS ABOUT HOSPITALS IN METROPOLITAN CHICAGO **3780**

CHICAGO (ILL.) *See* CITY OF CHICAGO BUILDING CODE **2950**

CHICAGO (ILL.). DEPT. OF CITY PLANNING *See* URBAN RENEWAL PROGRESS REPORT **2838**

CHICAGO (ILL.). DEPT. OF DEVELOPMENT AND PLANNING *See* CAPITAL IMPROVEMENTS PROGRAM FOR CHICAGO **4716**

CHICAGO (ILL.). DEPT. OF PERSONNEL *See* PERSONNEL NEWS **4704**

CHICAGO (ILL.). DEPT. OF PUBLIC WORKS *See* PUBLIC WORKS PROGRESS **4677**

CHICAGO (ILL.). MAYOR *See* CITY OF CHICAGO ... BUDGET RECOMMENDATIONS / AS SUBMITTED TO THE CITY COUNCIL **4717**

CHICAGO (ILL.) MUNICIPAL REFERENCE LIBRARY *See* BIBLIOGRAPHY : A SELECTED BIBLIOGRAPHY OF MATERIALS IN THE CHICAGO MUNICIPAL REFERENCE LIBRARY **410**

CHICAGO (ILL.). MUNICIPAL REFERENCE LIBRARY *See* RECENT ADDITIONS / MUNICIPAL REFERENCE LIBRARY, CITY OF CHICAGO **3244**

CHICAGO INDEPENDENT BULLETIN (US) [10623242] **5659**

CHICAGO JEWISH STAR (US/1054-1365) [22770554] **5659**

●CHICAGO JOB BANK, THE (US/1072-575X) [29042203] 656, **4203**

●CHICAGO JOURNAL OF THEORETICAL COMPUTER SCIENCE (US) [29297160] **1174**

CHICAGO-KENT LAW REVIEW (US/0009-3599) [01554167] **2949**

CHICAGO LAW LIBRARY BULLETIN (US) [02254971] 2949, **3201**

CHICAGO LAWYER (US/0199-8374) [04717710] **2950**

CHICAGO LECTURES IN MATHEMATICS (US/0069-3286) [05537612] **3499**

CHICAGO MANUAL OF STYLE, THE (US) [08869087] **1082**

●CHICAGO ... MEDIA SOURCEBOOK (US/1069-2355) [27931232] **757**

CHICAGO MEDIA UPDATE (US/1058-4935) [24314785] **1106**

CHICAGO MEDICINE (US/0009-3637) [01778064] **3563**

CHICAGO MERCANTILE EXCHANGE *See* DAILY INFORMATION BULLETIN **830**

CHICAGO METRO BOOK, THE *CEASED.* (US/0145-4714) [02743989] **757**

●CHICAGO METRO MARKET MEDIA DIRECTORY (US/1058-4927) [24314808] **1106**

CHICAGO METRO NEWS *See* NEW METRO NEWS **5661**

CHICAGO. ORDINANCES, ETC *See* MUNICIPAL CODE OF CHICAGO **3012**

CHICAGO. POLISH MUSEUM OF AMERICA *See* POLISH MUSEUM OF AMERICA QUARTERLY, THE **4095**

CHICAGO POST, THE (US) [25242598] **5659**

CHICAGO PRODUCTION BIBLE (US) **4065**

CHICAGO. PUBLIC SCHOOLS *See* SELECTED SCHOOL CHARACTERISTICS. REPORT ON THE CITY-WIDE TESTING PROGRAM. REPORT ON PER PUPIL STAFFING COSTS : ELEMENTARY SCHOOLS **1783**

CHICAGO PURCHASING AGENT *See* CHICAGO PURCHASOR, THE **949**

CHICAGO PURCHASOR, THE (US/0009-367X) [04968843] **949**

CHICAGO REGIONAL MARKETING AREA *See* REPORTER - CHICAGO REGIONAL MARKETING AREA **935**

CHICAGO REPORTER, THE (US/0300-6921) [01354575] **4505**

CHICAGO REVIEW (US/0009-3696) [01554183] **3374**

CHICAGO SHIMPO, THE (US/0009-370X) [04032234] **2258**

CHICAGO SHORELAND NEWS, THE (US) [23117764] 2258, **5659**

CHICAGO SOURCEBOOK (US/1078-5949) [26756208] **757**

CHICAGO STUDIES (US/0009-3718) [01554188] **5027**

CHICAGO SUN-TIMES (US) [08800779] **5659**

CHICAGO SYMPHONY ORCHESTRA *See* PROGRAM / CHICAGO SYMPHONY ORCHESTRA **4147**

CHICAGO TALENT SOURCEBOOK (US/0734-6662) [08788249] **757**

CHICAGO THEOLOGICAL SEMINARY *See* CHICAGO THEOLOGICAL SEMINARY REGISTER, THE **4943**

CHICAGO THEOLOGICAL SEMINARY REGISTER, THE (US/0739-5124) [01587160] **4943**

CHICAGO TIMES MAGAZINE (US/0894-5640) [16138130] **2530**

CHICAGO TRANSIT AUTHORITY *See* CTA QUARTERLY **5380**

CHICAGO TRIBUNE (CHICAGO, ILL. : 1963) (US) [07960243] **5659**

CHICAGO TRIBUNE INDEX (US/0731-9045) [08265145] **5814**

CHICAGO. UNION STOCK YARD AND TRANSIT COMPANY *See* RECEIPTS AND SHIPMENTS OF LIVESTOCK FOR THE YEAR **220**

CHICAGO
Alphabetical Title Index

CHICAGO. UNIVERSITY. INDUSTRIAL RELATIONS CENTER See OCCASIONAL PAPERS - CHICAGO. UNIVERSITY. INDUSTRIAL RELATIONS CENTER **1696**

CHICAGO. UNIVERSITY. PHILIPPINE STUDIES PROGRAM See RESEARCH SERIES **2663**

CHICAGO. UNIVERSITY. PHILIPPINE STUDIES PROGRAM See TRANSCRIPT **2667**

CHICAGO UNLIMITED, INC See CU DIRECTORY **384**

CHICAGO URBAN LEAGUE See STUDIES OF THE LABOR MARKET. REPORT **1712**

CHICAGO USED CAR SELLER'S GUIDE, THE (US/1046-6142) [20463996] **5410**

CHICAGO VIDEO RESOURCE See CHICAGO PRODUCTION BIBLE **4065**

CHICAGO WEEKEND (US) [23181656] **5659**

CHICAGOLAND JOB SOURCE (US) **5659**

CHICANO DATABASE (US/1056-2516) [22740591] **2258**

CHICANO DATABASE ON CD-ROM (US/1056-2516) **2258**

CHICANO EDUCATION DIGEST (US) [03081590] 2258, **1731**

CHICANO INDEX, THE (US/1044-3487) [19783841] 2727, **2635**

CHICANO-LATINO LAW REVIEW (US/1061-8899) [24476726] **2950**

CHICANOS IN THESE TIMES (US) [17284018] **2258**

CHICKADEE (CN/0707-4611) [04879660] **1061**

CHICKASHA DAILY EXPRESS, THE (US) [15045329] **5731**

CHICKASHA STAR, THE (US) [13686103] **5731**

CHICKEN FORUM (CN/1185-1708) [24265730] **209**

CHICKEN FORUM (CN/1185-1708) [24265721] **209**

CHICKENS AND EGGS, FINAL ESTIMATES FOR ... (US) [08382805] **209**

●CHICKENS AND EGGS / NATIONAL AGRICULTURAL STATISTICS SERVICE, UNITED STATES DEPARTMENT OF AGRICULTURE (US) [29875707] **209**

CHICO ENTERPRISE-RECORD (US/0746-5548) [10129791] **5633**

CHICO TEXAN, THE (US) [17460994] **5748**

CHICOREL INDEX SERIES (US/0590-983X) [01777457] **2844**

CHICOREL INDEX TO ABSTRACTING AND INDEXING SERVICES : PERIODICALS IN HUMANITIES AND THE SOCIAL SCIENCES (US/0149-7006) [01599964] 5195, **2844**

CHICOREL INDEX TO POETRY IN ANTHOLOGIES AND COLLECTIONS IN PRINT (US/0163-5603) [03953982] **3461**

CHICOREL INDEX TO READING AND LEARNING DISABILITIES (US/0149-5496) [03487987] **1877**

CHICOREL INDEX TO SHORT STORIES IN ANTHOLOGIES AND COLLECTIONS (US/0149-4503) [03297750] **3374**

CHICOREL INDEX TO VIDEO TAPES AND CASSETTES (US/0149-5860) [03531426] **5316**

CHICOS (IT) **1731**

CHIDAE NONMUNJIP (KO) [11320296] **1319**

CHIEF CIVIL SERVICE LEADER, THE (US/0746-7761) [10261799] **5715**

CHIEF EXECUTIVE *CEASED*. (UK/0262-5865) [06408711] **863**

CHIEF EXECUTIVE (NEW YORK, N.Y. 1977) (US/0160-4724) [03681994] **863**

CHIEF EXECUTIVE OPINION (US) [21176499] **656**

CHIEF EXECUTIVES AND MEMBERS OF GOVERNING BOARDS OF ALABAMA INSTITUTIONS OF HIGHER EDUCATION (US/0094-9094) [01795326] **1815**

CHIEF EXECUTIVES COMPENSATION IN CANADA (CN/1185-524X) [25313987] **1659**

CHIEF INFORMATION OFFICER JOURNAL *CEASED*. (US/0899-0182) [17972394] **1174**

CHIEFS OF STATE AND CABINET MEMBERS OF FOREIGN GOVERNMENTS (US/0162-2951) [04124278] **4637**

CHIEFS OF STATE AND CABINET MINISTERS OF THE AMERICAN REPUBLICS (US/0250-6114) [01761477] **4637**

●CHIEFS OF STATE & CABINET OFFICERS FOR NATIONS OF THE WORLD (US/1060-2917) [24915919] **4637**

CHIEFTAIN (IROQUOIS) (CN/0821-7696) [09863916] **5782**

CHIEFTAIN, THE (US) [20850655] **5652**

CHIEH FANG CHUN HUA PAO (CC) [09103953] **4540**

CHIEH NENG CHI SHU / CHUNG-KUO KO HSUEH CHI SHU CHING PAO YEN CHIU SO CHUNG-CHING FEN SO (CH) [09198930] **2111**

CHIEH P'OU HSUEH PAO (CC/0529-1356) [03082145] **3679**

CHIEN CHIN CHOU KAN (US) [11394339] **2648**

CHIEN CHU CHIEH KOU HSUEH PAO (CC) [09146772] **2020**

CHIEN CHU CHIEH KOU / JIANZHU JIEGOU (CC) [11630569] **2020**

CHIEN CHU LI SHIH YU LI LUN / CHUNG-KUO CHIEN CHU HSUEH HUI CHIEN CHU LI SHIH HSUEH SHU WEI YUAN HUI PIEN (CH) [08909630] **295**

CHIEN CHU SHIH (TAIPEI, TAIWAN) (CH) [09764952] **295**

CHIEN HU (PARIS, FRANCE) (FR) [20475550] **2648**

CHIEN TSAI NIEN CHIEN (CH) [10712487] **2020**

CHIEN WEI (SI/0303-0857) [01797530] **2502**

CHIESA E QUARTIERE; QUADERNI DI ARCHITETTURA SACRA (IT/0529-1488) [01554201] **295**

CHIESE DI ROMA ILLUSTRATE, LE (IT) [03092954] **347**

CHIFFRES CLES DE L'ENERGIE, LES *CEASED*. (FR) [07638317] **1935**

CHIFFRES CLES DES MATIERES PREMIERES MINERALES See CHIFFRES CLES, MATIERES PREMIERES MINERALS, LES **1601**

CHIFFRES CLES, MATIERES PREMIERES MINERALS, LES (FR) [07616771] **1601**

CHIFFRES POUR L'ALSACE (FR/0395-8191) [04118921] **1531**

CHIGAKU KENKYU (JA) [03333715] **1353**

CHIGAKU KYOIKU (JA/0009-3831) [09276468] **1353**

CHIGAKU ZASSHI (JA/0022-135X) [03093004] **2558**

CHIGIANA (IT/0069-3391) [01898916] **4109**

CHIH CHIAO I SHENG TSA CHIH (CC) [01797471] **3563**

CHIH PU SHENG HUO. CHUNG-CHING (CC) [11618964] **4637**

CHIH PU SHENG HUO. KUANG-TUNG (CC) [11618828] **4637**

CHIH PU SHENG HUO. SSU-CHUAN / CHUNG KUNG SSU-CHUAN SHENG WEI TSU CHIH PU, HSUAN CHUAN PU CHU PAN (CC) [11618910] **4637**

CHIH WU FEN LEI HSUEH PAO (CC/0529-1526) [01571086] **506**

CHIH WU HSUEH CHI KAN / CHUNG-KUO KO HSUEH YUAN CHIH WU YEN CHIU SO PIEN CHI (CC) [12091223] **506**

CHIH WU HSUEH PAO (CC/0577-7496) [02445891] **506**

CHIH WU PAO HU HSUEH HUI HUI K'AN (CH/0577-750X) [01762472] 73, **506**

CHIH WU PAO HU HSUEH PAO (CC/0577-7518) [03093308] **506**

CHIH WU PING LI HSUEH PAO (CC/0412-0914) [03093383] **506**

CHIH WU SHENG LI HSUEH PAO (CC/0257-4829) [09144002] **579**

CHIH WU SHENG LI HSUEH TUNG HSUN (CC/0412-0914) [09950423] **506**

CHIH WU YEN CHIU (CC) [09296464] 534, **506**

CHIHO KOKYO DANTAI SHIKEN KENKYU KIKAN SORAN (JA) [03415487] **5093**

CHIHO ZAISEI (JA) [02639179] **4717**

CHIHUA XUEBAO (CC/0253-9837) [09120981] **1050**

CHIHUAHUAN DESERT DISCOVERY, THE (US) [06645471] **2558**

CHIIKI TOKEI TEIYO (JA) [02376504] **5325**

CHIIKIGAKU KENKYU (JA) [09848679] **2817**

CHIJIKE KANSOKUJO, KAKIOKA, JAPAN See REPORT OF THE GEOMAGNETIC AND GEOELECTRIC OBSERVATIONS **4445**

CHIJIKI KANSOKUJO YOHO (JA) [09147611] **1404**

CHIJIL HAKHOE CHI (KO/0435-4036) [08605894] **1371**

CHIKASUI GAKKAI SHI (JA/0913-4182) [16668258] **1413**

CHIKASUII NEMPYO / KENSETSUSHO KASENKYOKU HEN (JA) [08057137] **1413**

CHIKCHANGIN (KO) [09688459] **1659**

CHIKUJI KANKOBUTSU UKEIRE MOKUROKU (JA) [02399350] **413**

CHIKUSAMBUTSU SEISANHI CHOSA HOKOKU (JA) [01797116] **209**

CHIKUSAN NO KENKYU. ANIMAL HUSBANDRY (JA) [03744387] **5507**

CHIKUSAN SHIKANJO (CHIBA, JAPAN) See CHIKUSAN SHIKENJO HOKOKU **73**

CHIKUSAN SHIKENJO KENKYU HOKOKU (JA/0577-7658) [03087108] **73**

CHIKYU KAGAKU (JA/0366-6611) [07184182] **1371**

CHILD ABUSE & NEGLECT (US/0145-2134) [03475531] **5277**

CHILD ABUSE AND NEGLECT GRANTS PROGRAM (US/0195-8836) [05128654] **5277**

CHILD ABUSE AND NEGLECT PROGRAMS (US/0146-9665) [03092999] **5277**

CHILD ABUSE AND NEGLECT RESEARCH (US/0145-3025) [02363357] **5277**

CHILD ABUSE AND NEGLECT STATISTICS (US) [09524706] 5277, **5266**

CHILD ABUSE & NEGLECT [MICROFORM] (US/0145-2134) [08632473] **5277**

CHILD ABUSE, NEGLECT, AND THE FOSTER CARE SYSTEM (US/1058-5516) [21352659] **2950**

CHILD ABUSE REPORT (HARRISBURG, PA.) (US/0148-5601) [05460616] **5277**

CHILD ABUSE REVIEW (UK/0952-9136) [23912499] 4580, **5277**

CHILD ABUSE REVIEW See CHILD ABUSE REVIEW : JOURNAL OF THE BRITISH ASSOCIATION FOR THE STUDY AND PREVENTION OF CHILD ABUSE AND NEGLECT **5277**

●CHILD ABUSE REVIEW : JOURNAL OF THE BRITISH ASSOCIATION FOR THE STUDY AND PREVENTION OF CHILD ABUSE AND NEGLECT (UK) [27015296] **5277**

CHILD ADVOCACY PROGRAMS (US/0160-290X) [03636222] **3901**

CHILD ANALYSIS (US) [22712613] 5277, **4580**

CHILD AND ADOLESCENT MENTAL HEALTH CARE *CEASED*. (US/1071-2828) [28601477] 3923, **4580**

●CHILD AND ADOLESCENT PSYCHIATRIC CLINICS OF NORTH AMERICA (US/1056-4993) [23725782] **3923**

CHILD & ADOLESCENT SOCIAL WORK JOURNAL (US/0738-0151) [09495904] **5277**

CHILD AND FAMILY (US/0009-3882) [01554208] **2277**

CHILD & FAMILY BEHAVIOR THERAPY (US/0731-7107) [08234819] 3901, **4580**

CHILD AND FAMILY POLICY (US/0741-2312) [10007294] **5277**

CHILD AND MAN (UK/0009-3890) [I00093890] **1731**

CHILD AND YOUTH CARE ADMINISTRATOR / NOVA UNIVERSITY, THE (US/0899-093X) [17989502] **5277**

CHILD AND YOUTH CARE FORUM (US/1053-1890) [22471611] **5278**

CHILD AND YOUTH PSYCHIATRY, EUROPEAN PERSPECTIVES (CN) [23657428] 4580, **3923**

CHILD & YOUTH SERVICES (US/0145-935X) [03128677] **5278**

CHILD ASSESSMENT NEWS (US/1055-0518) [23065336] **4580**

CHILD CARE (CN/0838-9683) [18372173] **3901**

CHILD CARE CENTER *CEASED*. (US/0889-4558) [13897048] **5278**

CHILD CARE DIRECTORY & FAMILY RESOURCE GUIDE (DENVER METRO ED.), THE (US/1055-2448) [23124512] **2277**

CHILD CARE, HEALTH AND DEVELOPMENT (UK/0305-1862) [01953438] **3901**

CHILD CARE INFORMATION EXCHANGE (US/0164-8527) [04299013] **5278**

CHILD CARE (KITCHENER) (CN/1187-4678) [25652229] **2277**

CHILD CARE LAW FOR PRACTITIONERS IN SOCIAL WORK, HEALTH & EDUCATION (UK) **5278**

CHILD CARE LEGISLATIVE UPDATE (US) **4637**

CHILD CARE MANAGEMENT *CEASED*. (US/0890-4715) [14232524] **2277**

Alphabetical Title Index

CHILD'S

CHILD CARE REVIEW (US) [17778244] **5278**

CHILD CARE WORK (US/0741-2398) [I0107294] **5278**

CHILD CARE WORKER, THE (SA/0258-8927) [I02588927] **5242**

CHILD DEVELOPMENT (US/0009-3920) [01554210] **4580**

CHILD DEVELOPMENT ABSTRACTS AND BIBLIOGRAPHY (US/0009-3939) [06193560] 3901, 1803, **3655**

CHILD DEVELOPMENT PROGRAM EVALUATION REPORT (CALIFORNIA) (US/0364-3166) [02628629] **1731**

CHILD DEVELOPMENT STATE PLAN (PENNSYLVANIA) (US/0093-8009) [01792412] **5278**

CHILD EDUCATION (UK/0009-3947) [01782024] **1890**

CHILD FOCUS (CN/0708-997X) [05258042] **2277**

CHILD HEALTH ALERT (US/1064-4849) [11721167] **4771**

CHILD HEALTH MAGAZINE (HK) **3901**

CHILD HEALTH PLUS, HEALTH PLAN FOR KIDS : ANNUAL REPORT TO THE GOVERNOR & LEGISLATURE, CHILD HEALTH INSURANCE PLAN (US) [25763985] 5278, **2878**

CHILD LABOR MONITOR (US/1060-6661) [25053212] **1659**

CHILD LABOUR SERIES (UK) [10164014] **4505**

CHILD LANGUAGE TEACHING AND THERAPY (UK/0265-6590) [12071785] 1890, **1877**

CHILD LAW (UK) **2950**

CHILD LIFE (INDIANAPOLIS, IND. 1922) (US/0009-3971) [01554218] 4858, **1061**

CHILD NEPHROLOGY AND UROLOGY *CEASED.* (SZ/1012-6694) [19276618] **3989**

CHILD NEUROPSYCHOLOGY (NE/0929-7049) 3829, **3923**

CHILD (NEW YORK, N.Y.) (US/0894-7988) [15620838] **2277**

CHILD NURTURANCE (US/0738-4726) [08802926] **2277**

CHILD PERSONALITY AND PSYCHOPATHOLOGY (US/0093-2175) [01790811] 4580, **3901**

CHILD PROTECTION REPORT (US/0147-1260) [01318647] **4771**

CHILD PSYCHIATRY AND HUMAN DEVELOPMENT (US/0009-398X) [01465561] 4580, **3923**

CHILD PSYCHIATRY QUARTERLY *CEASED.* (II/0009-3998) [02942685] 3923, **3901**

CHILD REFERENCE BULLETIN (US/0251-5547) [07547081] **5278**

CHILD SAFETY LIBRARY NEWS (AT/1033-7660) [I10337660] **4771**

CHILD SAFETY LIBRARY NEWS *See* CHILD SAFETY NEWS **4771**

●CHILD SAFETY NEWS (AT) [I10397477] **4771**

CHILD SAFETY REVIEW (UK/0957-4107) [I09574107] **4771**

CHILD STUDY JOURNAL (US/0009-4005) [01692643] **4580**

CHILD SUPPORT AND ALIMONY ... (ADVANCE REPORT) (US) [09901658] **2278**

CHILD SUPPORT REPORT (US/0884-8076) [06413179] **3120**

CHILD THERAPY NEWS, THE (US/1072-6241) [29063542] **4580**

CHILD WELFARE (US/0009-4021) [01071435] **5278**

CHILD WELFARE LEAGUE OF AMERICA *See* ANNUAL REPORT - CHILD WELFARE LEAGUE OF AMERICA, INC **5272**

CHILD WELFARE LEAGUE OF AMERICA *See* DIRECTORY OF MEMBER AGENCIES - CHILD WELFARE LEAGUE OF AMERICA (1986) **5283**

CHILD WORKERS IN ASIA (TH) [22939011] **1061**

CHILDCARE NEWS (US) **5278**

CHILDCRAFT ANNUAL (US/0069-343X) [02253968] **1890**

CHILDHOOD (DK) 1061, **1803**

CHILDHOOD EDUCATION (US/0009-4056) [01554226] **1803**

CHILDLIFE (US) **1061**

CHILDREN & SOCIETY (UK/0951-0605) [21317957] **1061**

CHILDREN & TEENS TODAY *CEASED.* (US/0882-942X) [12032085] 4580, **5278**

CHILDREN AND THE LAW COMMITTEE NEWSLETTER (US) 2950, **5278**

CHILDREN AND WAR (UK/0956-3113) [I09563113] **5195**

●CHILDREN & YOUTH FUNDING REPORT (US/1063-892X) [26173775] **5278**

CHILDREN & YOUTH, HEALTH PROGRAMS *See* GRANT$ FOR HEALTH PROGRAMS FOR CHILDREN AND YOUTH **5286**

CHILDREN AND YOUTH SERVICES REVIEW (US/0190-7409) [04762661] **5278**

CHILDREN AUSTRALIA (AT/1035-0772) **5278**

CHILDREN FOR TODAY'S PARENT (US/0886-3792) [12923752] **2278**

CHILDREN IN CARE OR UNDER SUPERVISION ORDERS IN WALES *See* CHILDREN LOOKED AFTER BY LOCAL AUTHORITIES IN WALES / WELSH OFFICE / PLANT Y GOFELIR AM DANYNT GAN AWDURDODAU LLEOL CYMRU / Y SWYDDFA GYMREIG **5278**

CHILDREN IN CARE OR UNDER SUPERVISION, SCOTLAND (UK/0260-5473) [I02605473] **5278**

CHILDREN IN CUSTODY (US/0147-9881) [03260083] **3160**

CHILDREN IN HOSPITAL (AT/0814-9127) [I08149127] **4580**

CHILDREN IN THE TROPICS (FR/0379-2269) [03264749] 3901, **3985**

●CHILDREN LOOKED AFTER BY LOCAL AUTHORITIES IN WALES / WELSH OFFICE / PLANT Y GOFELIR AM DANYNT GAN AWDURDODAU LLEOL CYMRU / Y SWYDDFA GYMREIG (UK/0968-4050) [30597034] **5278**

CHILDREN OF THE AMERICAN REVOLUTION MAGAZINE (US) [03564209] **2443**

CHILDREN OF WORKING MOTHERS / U.S. DEPARTMENT OF LABOR, BUREAU OF LABOR STATISTICS (US) [05070579] **1659**

CHILDREN TODAY (US/0361-4336) [01159272] **5278**

CHILDREN'S ADVOCATE, THE (US/0739-425X) [09729196] **5279**

CHILDREN'S ALBUM, THE *CEASED.* (US/0749-8659) [11190043] **1061**

CHILDREN'S BIBLE STUDIES. ELEMENTARY B. STUDENT BOOK (US/0278-3746) [07789079] 1061, **5016**

CHILDREN'S BOOK BAG, THE (US/1064-0541) [22589383] 1061, **3374**

CHILDREN'S BOOK COUNCIL (NEW YORK, N.Y.) *See* CHILDREN'S BOOK SHOWCASE, THE **1061**

CHILDREN'S BOOK COUNCIL (NEW YORK, N.Y.) *See* CHILDREN'S BOOKS. AWARDS & PRIZES **1061**

CHILDREN'S BOOK NEWS (TORONTO) (CN/0705-0038) [04040009] 3374, **1061**

CHILDREN'S BOOK REVIEW INDEX (US/0147-5681) [02306438] **3339**

CHILDREN'S BOOK REVIEW (PROVO, UTAH) (US/0890-5746) [14282132] **3201**

CHILDREN'S BOOK REVIEW SERVICE *See* CHILDREN'S BOOK REVIEW SERVICE **3339**

CHILDREN'S BOOK REVIEW SERVICE (US/0090-7987) [01785977] 1061, **3339**

CHILDREN'S BOOK SHOWCASE, THE (US/0098-9371) [02242203] **1061**

CHILDREN'S BOOKS *See* BOOKS FOR KEEPS **3368**

CHILDREN'S BOOKS. AWARDS & PRIZES (US/0069-3472) [03898318] **1061**

CHILDREN'S BOOKS HISTORY SOCIETY NEWSLETTER (UK) **4827**

CHILDREN'S BOOKS IN IRELAND (IE/0791-2641) [I07912641] 3374, **4827**

CHILDREN'S BOOKS IN PRINT (LONDON, ENGLAND) (UK/0577-781X) [03096272] **4827**

CHILDREN'S BOOKS IN PRINT (NEW YORK) (US/0069-3480) [01554233] **1072**

CHILDREN'S BOOKS IN PRINT. SUBJECT GUIDE (US) [18768616] 1072, **3458**

CHILDREN'S BOOKS OF THE YEAR (UK) [06846127] **1072**

CHILDRENS BRAILLE BOOK CLUB (US) **4385**

CHILDREN'S BROADCAST INSTITUTE (CN/0824-7005) [11400832] 1061, **1130**

CHILDREN'S BULLETIN FOR NURSERY AND KINDERGARTEN TEACHERS AND LEADERS (CN/0825-2556) [12227587] **1890**

CHILDREN'S BUSINESS (US/0884-2280) [12322789] **1083**

CHILDREN'S CASES DISPOSED OF BY THE JUVENILE COURTS (US/0507-0619) [02241223] **3160**

CHILDREN'S DIGEST (INDIANAPOLIS. : 1981) (US/0272-7145) [06901337] **1061**

●CHILDREN'S ENVIRONMENTS (UK) [27372384] 4858, **1803**

CHILDREN'S ENVIRONMENTS QUARTERLY *See* CHILDREN'S ENVIRONMENTS **1803**

CHILDREN'S FICTION ON FICHE (UK/1350-4347) 3374, **1061**

CHILDREN'S FOCUS (US/0893-486X) [15602751] **1061**

CHILDREN'S FOLKLORE REVIEW, THE (US/0739-5558) [21127719] **2318**

CHILDREN'S FRIEND *See* FRIEND (SALT LAKE CITY), THE **4960**

CHILDREN'S FUN PUZZLES (1985) (US/0886-4284) [12885596] **4858**

CHILDREN'S HEALTH CARE (US/0273-9615) [07048538] **3901**

CHILDREN'S HOSPITAL QUARTERLY (US/0899-5869) [18145371] **3901**

CHILDREN'S HOUSE, CHILDREN'S WORLD (US) [12114347] **1803**

CHILDREN'S LANGUAGE (US/0163-2809) [04330173] **3273**

CHILDREN'S LEADERSHIP *CEASED.* (US/0162-461X) [01780817] **1061**

CHILDREN'S LEGAL RIGHTS JOURNAL (US/0278-7210) [05471837] **3120**

CHILDREN'S LITERARY ALMANAC (US/0093-0431) [01784486] **3374**

CHILDREN'S LITERATURE ABSTRACTS (UK/0306-2015) [01799257] 1061, 3374, **3458**

CHILDREN'S LITERATURE ASSOCIATION QUARTERLY (US/0885-0429) [05853997] 1890, **3340**

CHILDREN'S LITERATURE ASSOCIATION (U.S.). CHLA NEWSLETTER *See* CHILDREN'S LITERATURE ASSOCIATION QUARTERLY **3340**

CHILDREN'S LITERATURE AWARDS AND WINNERS (US/0749-3096) [11125939] **3374**

CHILDREN'S LITERATURE IN EDUCATION (US/0045-6713) [01021278] 1803, **3374**

CHILDREN'S LITERATURE REVIEW (US/0362-4145) [02338277] **3340**

CHILDREN'S LITERATURE (STORRS) (US/0092-8208) [01783742] 3374, **1061**

CHILDREN'S MAGAZINE GUIDE (US/0743-9873) [07934526] 1061, 3374, **3258**

CHILDREN'S MAGIC WINDOW MAGAZINE (US) **1061**

CHILDREN'S MEDIA MARKET PLACE (US/0734-8169) [04754306] **1106**

CHILDREN'S MINISTRY (US/1054-1144) [22752789] **4943**

CHILDREN'S MONITOR (US) **5279**

CHILDRENS' MYSTERY WORD (CN/0705-3819) [03900278] 1061, **4859**

CHILDREN'S NURSE (US) [18249437] **3853**

CHILDREN'S OWN (KE) [01788979] **1061**

CHILDREN'S PARADISE (HK) **1061**

CHILDREN'S PLAYMATE MAGAZINE (US/0009-4161) [07661793] **1062**

CHILDREN'S PSYCHIATRIC RESEARCH INSTITUTE *See* MONOGRAPH - CHILDREN'S PSYCHIATRIC RESEARCH INSTITUTE **3931**

CHILDREN'S SERMONS SERVICE PLUS (US/8750-1929) [11106513] **1062**

CHILDREN'S SURPRISES (US) **1062**

CHILDREN'S TRUST FUND OF PENNSYLVANIA ANNUAL REPORT, THE (US) [23737318] **5279**

CHILDREN'S VIDEO REPORT (US/0883-6922) [12229443] 4065, **1062**

CHILDREN'S VIDEO REVIEW NEWSLETTER (US/0895-2094) [16531110] 1891, **4065**

CHILDREN'S VOICE (US) [24133806] **5279**

CHILDREN'S WELFARE ASSOCIATION OF VICTORIA NEWSLETTER (AT) **5279**

CHILDREN'S WORLD (II) [27701909] 1062, **3500**

CHILDREN'S WORLD (BOSTON, MASS.) (US/0895-2221) [06365176] **1877**

CHILDREN'S WRITER (US/1060-5274) [25023289] **3374**

CHILDREN'S WRITER'S & ILLUSTRATOR'S MARKET (US/0897-9790) [17682152] **3374**

CHILDRESS INDEX, THE (US) [13661587] **5748**

CHILDRIGHT (UK/0265-1459) [13401686] 4505, **1062**

CHILD'S DOCTOR, THE (US/0882-2301) [11788504] **3902**

CHILD'S GALLERY *See* PAINTING ANNUAL **361**

CHILD'S NERVOUS SYSTEM (GW/0256-7040) [11965790] 3829, **3902**

CHILD'S — Alphabetical Title Index

CHILD'S PLAY (CHICAGO, ILL.) (US/0749-8632) [11190349] **1803**

CHILD'S PLAY (WHEELING, W. VA.) (US/1056-3709) [23672370] **377**

CHILDSCOPE (US/0882-6390) [11930764] **3902**

CHILE See LEYES ... APROBADAS BAJO LA CONSTITUCION DE 1980 **3002**

CHILE ACTION BULLETIN ON POLITICAL PRISONERS AND HUMAN RIGHTS (US) [05043081] **4505**

CHILE BUSINESS UPDATE (CN/0711-6225) [09318483] **656**

CHILE. DIRECCION DE AGRICULTURA Y PESCA See BOLETIN TECNICO - CHILE. DIRECCION DE AGRICULTURA Y PESCA **67**

CHILE. DIRECCION DE ESTADISTICA Y CENSOS See INDICE DE PRECIOS AL POR MAYOR **730**

CHILE. DIRECCION DE ESTADISTICA Y CENSOS See BOLETIN DE ESTADISTICA MINERA **2002**

CHILE. DIRECCION DE ESTADISTICA Y CENSOS See INDICE DE VENTAS NOMINALES DE COMERCIO INTERIOR **730**

CHILE ECOMOMIC REPORT (US/0884-4488) [07040058] **1551**

CHILE : ENERGIEWIRTSCHAFT (GW) [06597826] **1935**

CHILE FORESTAL (CL/0716-1190) [02696775] **2377**

CHILE NEWS (CL) [07530449] **1469**

CHILE NEWSLETTER (BERKELEY, CALIF. 1984) (US/0899-0387) [10987719] **4637**

CHILE PEPPER (US/1069-7985) [21899636] **2331**

CHILE PESQUERO (CL) [05031190] **2299**

CHILE. SERVICIO DE SEGURO SOCIAL See ESTADISTICAS (CHILE. SERVICIO DE SEGURO SOCIAL) **2897**

CHILE. UNIVERSIDAD, SANTIAGO. CENTRO DE ESTUDIOS ENTOMOLGICOS See PUBLICACIONES **5595**

CHILE. UNIVERSIDAD, SANTIAGO. CENTRO DE LA VIVIENDA Y CONSTRUCCION See INFORME **617**

CHILE. UNIVERSIDAD, SANTIAGO. DEPARTAMENTO DE GEOLOGIA See APARTADO **1365**

CHILE. UNIVERSIDAD, SANTIAGO. FACULTAD DE AGRONOMIA See PUBLICACIONES EN CIENCIAS AGRICOLAS **123**

CHILE. UNIVERSIDAD, SANTIAGO. INSTITUTO DE ECONOMIA Y PLANIFICACION See PUBLICACIONES **1514**

CHILE. UNIVERSIDAD, SANTIAGO. INSTITUTO DE EDUCACION. CENTRO DE DOCUMENTACION See ANO PEDAGOGICO **1725**

CHILE. UNIVERSIDAD, SANTIAGO. INSTITUTO DE INVESTIGACIONES ESTADISTICAS See INFORMATIVO ESTADISTICO **5329**

CHILE. UNIVERSIDAD, SANTIAGO. INSTITUTO DE PSICOLOGIA See ARCHIVOS **4575**

CHILE. UNIVERSIDAD, SANTIAGO. SEMINARIO DE DERECHO PUBLICO See PUBLICACIONES - CHILE. UNIVERSIDAD, SANTIAGO. SEMINARIO DE DERECHO PUBLICO **3033**

CHILE, WIRTSCHAFTSDATEN UND WIRTSCHAFTSDOKUMENTATION / BUNDESSTELLE FUER AUSSENHANDELSINFORMATION (GW) [10239695] **1551**

CHILEAN FORESTRY NEWS (CL) [04050821] **2377**

CHILEANS, THE (UK) [06262349] **2412, 506**

CHILKAT VALLEY NEWS (US/8750-3336) [11256589] **5629**

CHILLICOTHE BULLETIN, THE (US) [25563414] **5659**

CHILLICOTHE GAZETTE (1940) (US) [10186147] **5727**

CHILLO (KO) [10259505] **2366**

CHILLO NYUUSU (KO) [10259809] **1601**

CHILTON COUNTY NEWS (CLANTON, ALA. : 1986) (US/0888-451X) [13585582] **5625**

CHILTON FUEL INJECTION & ELECTRONIC ENGINE CONTROLS. ASIA (US/1050-1142) [21395633] **2038**

CHILTON ... MOTOR/AGE PROFESSIONAL ELECTRONIC ENGINE CONTROLS MANUAL. ASIAN See CHILTON'S DRIVEABILITY MANUAL. ASIAN **5410**

CHILTON TIMES-JOURNAL (US) [13311588] **5766**

CHILTON'S AIR CONDITIONING AND HEATING LABOR GUIDE (US/1055-5560) [23235801] **5410**

CHILTON'S AIR CONDITIONING AND HEATING MANUAL (US/1053-1114) [22456030] **5410**

CHILTON'S AUTO REPAIR MANUAL (US/0069-3634) [03700887] **5410**

CHILTON'S AUTOMOTIVE INDUSTRIES (1976) (US/0273-656X) [02928956] **5410**

CHILTON'S AUTOMOTIVE MARKETING (US/0193-3264) [05250644] **922, 5410**

●CHILTON'S CASCADE EMISSION CONTROL APPLICATION GUIDE (US/1072-7507) [29195852] **5410**

CHILTON'S CHASIS ELECTRONICS SERVICE MANUAL. ASIAN CARS AND TRUCKS (US/1056-1285) [23471414] **2038, 5410**

CHILTON'S CHASIS ELECTRONICS SERVICE MANUAL. FORD/CHRYSLER/JEEP-EAGLE CARS AND LIGHT TRUCKS See CHILTON'S CHASSIS ELECTRONIC SERVICE MANUAL. CHRYSLER **5410**

CHILTON'S CHASIS ELECTRONICS SERVICE MANUAL. FORD/CHRYSLER/JEEP-EAGLE CARS AND LIGHT TRUCKS See CHILTON'S CHASSIS ELECTRONIC SERVICE MANUAL. FORD **5410**

●CHILTON'S CHASSIS ELECTRONIC SERVICE MANUAL. CHRYSLER (US/1065-660X) [26669116] **5410**

●CHILTON'S CHASSIS ELECTRONIC SERVICE MANUAL. FORD (US/1065-6618) [26669159] **5410**

CHILTON'S CHASSIS ELECTRONICS SERVICE MANUAL. EUROPEAN (US/1056-1307) [23471434] **2038**

CHILTON'S COMMERCIAL CARRIER JOURNAL FOR PROFESSIONAL FLEET MANAGERS (US/1062-0060) [25440354] **5379**

CHILTON'S DISTRIBUTION (1986) (US/1057-9710) [13153986] **5379**

CHILTON'S DISTRIBUTION (RADNOR, PA. : 1986) See DISTRIBUTION (RADNOR, PA. 1992) **5381**

●CHILTON'S DRIVEABILITY MANUAL. ASIAN (US/1072-7469) [29195722] **5410**

●CHILTON'S DRIVEABILITY MANUAL. CHRYSLER (US/1072-7477) [29195460] **5410**

●CHILTON'S DRIVEABILITY MANUAL. EUROPEAN (US/1072-7485) [29195560] **5410**

●CHILTON'S DRIVEABILITY MANUAL. FORD (US/1072-7493) [29195595] **5410**

CHILTON'S ELECTRONIC COMPONENT NEWS (US/0193-614X) [05231990] **2038**

CHILTON'S ELECTRONIC ENGINE CONTROLS MANUAL. AUDI, BMW, JAGUAR, MERCEDES-BENZ, MERKUR, PEUGEOT, PORSCHE, SAAB, STERLING, VOLKSWAGEN, VOLVO, YUGO See CHILTON'S DRIVEABILITY MANUAL. EUROPEAN **5410**

CHILTON'S ELECTRONIC ENGINE CONTROLS MANUAL. EUROPEAN CARS AND LIGHT TRUCKS (US/1050-1134) [21395579] **5410**

CHILTON'S ELECTRONIC ENGINE CONTROLS MANUAL. FORD, CHRYSLER, JEEP-EAGLE CARS AND LIGHT TRUCKS See CHILTON'S DRIVEABILITY MANUAL. FORD **5410**

CHILTON'S ELECTRONIC ENGINE CONTROLS MANUAL. FORD, CHRYSLER, JEEP-EAGLE CARS AND LIGHT TRUCKS See CHILTON'S DRIVEABILITY MANUAL. CHRYSLER **5410**

CHILTON'S EMISSION CONTROL MANUAL (US/1053-2196) [22481020] **5410**

CHILTON'S EMISSION CONTROLS APPLICATION GUIDE (US/1053-2188) [22481058] **5410**

CHILTON'S EMISSION, DIAGNOSIS, TUNE-UP AND SERVICE MANUAL. DOMESTIC CARS AND LIGHT TRUCKS (US/1050-1169) [21395735] **5410**

CHILTON'S FOOD ENGINEERING (US/0193-323X) [04821315] **2331**

CHILTON'S FOOD ENGINEERING INTERNATIONAL (US/0148-4478) [03313143] **2331**

CHILTON'S FOOD ENGINEERING MASTER (US/0192-6098) [05034983] **2331**

CHILTON'S GEARBOX FLUID SERVICE LOCATOR (US/1055-6834) [23269527] **5410**

CHILTON'S GOING PLACES (US/0192-8023) [05061281] **5466**

CHILTON'S GUIDE TO CHASSIS ELECTRONIC CONTROLS AND POWER ACCESSORIES. IMPORT CARS AND TRUCKS (US/1053-1823) [22469291] **5410**

CHILTON'S GUIDE TO CHASSIS ELECTRONICS & POWER ACCESSORIES. FORD/CHRYSLER/JEEP/EAGLE (US/1053-1130) [22456021] **5410**

CHILTON'S GUIDE TO CHASSIS ELECTRONICS AND POWER ACCESSORIES. GENERAL MOTORS (US/1053-6302) [22599719] **5410**

●CHILTON'S GUIDE TO FUEL INJECTION AND ELECTRONIC ENGINE CONTROLS. BUICK, OLDS, PONTIAC CARS AND TRUCKS (US/1061-740X) [25455411] **5410**

●CHILTON'S GUIDE TO FUEL INJECTION AND ELECTRONIC ENGINE CONTROLS. CHEVROLET CARS AND TRUCKS (US/1061-7418) [25455493] **5411**

●CHILTON'S GUIDE TO FUEL INJECTION AND ELECTRONIC ENGINE CONTROLS. CHRYSLER CARS AND TRUCKS (US/1061-7388) [25455206] **5411**

●CHILTON'S GUIDE TO FUEL INJECTION AND ELECTRONIC ENGINE CONTROLS. FORD CARS AND TRUCKS (US/1061-7396) [25455302] **5411**

CHILTON'S GUIDE TO FUEL INJECTION AND ELECTRONIC ENGINE CONTROLS. FORD/CHRYSLER See CHILTON'S GUIDE TO FUEL INJECTION AND ELECTRONIC ENGINE CONTROLS. CHRYSLER CARS AND TRUCKS **5411**

CHILTON'S GUIDE TO FUEL INJECTION AND ELECTRONIC ENGINE CONTROLS. FORD/CHRYSLER See CHILTON'S GUIDE TO FUEL INJECTION AND ELECTRONIC ENGINE CONTROLS. FORD CARS AND TRUCKS **5411**

CHILTON'S GUIDE TO FUEL INJECTION AND ELECTRONIC ENGINE CONTROLS. GENERAL MOTORS See CHILTON'S GUIDE TO FUEL INJECTION AND ELECTRONIC ENGINE CONTROLS. CHEVROLET CARS AND TRUCKS **5411**

CHILTON'S GUIDE TO FUEL INJECTION AND ELECTRONIC ENGINE CONTROLS. GENERAL MOTORS See CHILTON'S GUIDE TO FUEL INJECTION AND ELECTRONIC ENGINE CONTROLS. BUICK, OLDS, PONTIAC CARS AND TRUCKS **5410**

CHILTON'S HARDWARE AGE (1984) (US/8755-254X) [10626803] **2810**

●CHILTON'S HEAVY DUTY TRUCK SERVICE MANUAL (US/1065-6626) [26667619] **5411**

CHILTON'S IAN (1977) (US/0193-6174) [05250601] **1968**

CHILTON'S I&CS (US/0746-2395) [09673774] **1968**

CHILTON'S I&CS See INSTRUMENTATION & CONTROL SYSTEMS: I&CS **1979**

CHILTON'S IMPO (US/8755-2523) [11276896] **3476**

CHILTON'S IMPORT LABOR GUIDE AND PARTS MANUAL (US/0742-0323) [09624853] **5411**

CHILTON'S INDUSTRIAL SAFETY & HYGIENE NEWS (US/8755-2566) [11276598] **2860**

CHILTON'S LABOR GUIDE AND PARTS MANUAL (1980) **CEASED.** (US/0749-5579) [06842674] **5411**

CHILTON'S LABOR GUIDE MANUAL (US/1060-443X) [25027953] **1659**

●CHILTON'S MEDIUM/HEAVY DUTY TRUCK SERVICE MANUAL (US/1060-4405) [25027910] **5411**

CHILTON'S MOTOR/AGE (1970) (US/0193-7022) [05702916] **5411**

CHILTON'S MOTOR/AGE ... PROFESSIONAL MECHANIC'S REFERENCE GUIDE (US/0737-2663) [09306688] **5411**

CHILTON'S MOTORCYCLE AND ATV REPAIR MANUAL (US/1050-0251) [13569189] **4081**

CHILTON'S MOTORCYCLE REPAIR MANUAL See CHILTON'S MOTORCYCLE AND ATV REPAIR MANUAL **4081**

●CHILTON'S NISSAN REPAIR MANUAL (US/1060-4413) [25027924] **5411**

CHILTON'S OWNER OPERATOR (US) [28531279] **5411**

CHILTON'S PD&D (US/0193-6182) [05231970] **1601**

CHILTON'S QUICK LUBRICATION GUIDE (US/1055-6842) [23269500] **5411**

CHILTON'S REVIEW OF OPTOMETRY (US/0147-7633) [03224955] **4215**

●CHILTON'S TRANSMISSION DIAGNOSTIC MANUAL (US/1065-6634) [26667641] **5411**

CHILTON'S TRUCK & OFF-HIGHWAY INDUSTRIES (US/0194-1410) [05363666] **5379**

CHIME NEWSLETTER, THE **CEASED.** (US/0748-738X) [10993391] **1731**

CHIMERE (SHERBROOKE) (CN/1183-3211) [24257819] **3374**

CHIMIA (SZ/0009-4293) [02059073] **1023**

CHIMIA (CK) [06927535] **971**

Alphabetical Title Index — CHINESE

CHIMICA ACTA TURCICA (TU/0379-5896) [10485649] **971**

CHIMICA E L'INDUSTRIA, LA (IT/0009-4315) [06371332] **971**

CHIMICA INORGANICA. SERVIZI DOCUMONT (IT) **1036**

CHIMICA OGGI (IT/0392-839X) [15470227] **3690**

CHIMICA : SOCIETA MERCATI PAESI. SERVIZI DOCUMONT (IT) **971**

CHIMIE (BE/0771-341X) [I0771341X] **971**

CHIMIE ACTUALITES (FR/0009-4323) [02445901] **971**

CHIMIE MAGAZINE (FR/0245-940X) [08424378] **972**

CHIMIE NOUVELLE (BE/0771-730X) [I0771730X] **972**

CHIMIE PURE ET CHIMIE APPLIQUEE. LEXIQUE (FR/0154-0327) [07087526] **3201**

CHIMIKA CHRONIKA (INTERNATIONAL EDITION) (GR/0366-693X) [01476473] **972**

CHIMO MAGAZINE (CN/0823-1354) [10595491] **2530**

CHIMO (TORONTO) (CN/0704-4909) [06511296] **5021**

CHIN JIH TI CHENG (CH) [11668921] **1469**

CHIN SHU HSUEH PAO (CC/0412-1961) [07040786] **4000**

CHIN YIN CHENG CHUAN YUEH PAO (HK) [01797562] **783**

CHINA AGRIBUSINESS REPORT (HK) **73**

CHINA AGRICULTURE YEARBOOK (CC) [13450741] **73**

CHINA AKTUELL / INSTITUT FUER ASIENKUNDE (GW/0341-6631) [03460982] **4468**

●CHINA ANALYST (CN/1189-7090) [29593035] **783**

CHINA AND CHURCH TODAY See CHINA PRAYER LETTER **5058**

CHINA AND OURSELVES (CN/0828-1602) [07073785] **4943**

CHINA AND PACIFIC RIM LETTER (US/1044-890X) [19936125] **2502**

CHINA & THE WORLD (CC) [09033590] **4517**

CHINA AND US (US/0191-3166) [04164517] **5195**

CHINA-BRITAIN TRADE REVIEW (UK/0952-9756) [17820628] 1633, **827**

CHINA BUSINESS & TRADE (US/0731-7700) [08247630] **827**

●CHINA BUSINESS MONITOR (US/1056-4500) [23712057] **656**

CHINA BUSINESS REPORT (UK/0143-9405) [05936177] **656**

CHINA BUSINESS REVIEW, THE (US/0163-7169) [03437109] 1633, **657**

CHINA CENTER OF ADVANCED SCIENCE AND TECHNOLOGY (WORLD LABORATORY) SYMPOSIUM/WORKSHOP PROCEEDINGS (UK/0894-2536) [15909837] **5093**

CHINA. CHUAN KUO JEN MIN TAI PIAO TA HUI. CHANG WU WEI YUAN HUI See CHUNG-HUA JEN MIN KUNG HO KUO CHUAN KUO JEN MIN TAI PIAO TA HUI CHANG WU WEI YUAN HUI KUNG PAO **2950**

CHINA CITY PLANNING REVIEW (CC) [15671474] **2817**

CHINA CIVIL ENGINEERING JOURNAL (CC) **2020**

CHINA COAL INDUSTRY YEARBOOK (HK/0258-3062) [09818460] **2136**

CHINA COMMERCIAL RELATIONS DIRECTORY (HK) [20243880] **657**

CHINA COURIER, THE (CC) [19611548] **5798**

CHINA CURRENT LAWS CEASED. (HK/1011-2359) [17944848] **2950**

●CHINA CURRENTS : A PHILIPPINE QUARTERLY ON CHINA CONCERNS (PH) [26939525] **2648**

CHINA DAILY INDEX (AT) [26643504] **413**

CHINA DAILY (INTERNATIONAL EDITION) (CC/0253-9543) [08008734] **5798**

CHINA DECORATOR, THE (US) [01554307] **2899**

CHINA DIGEST, THE CEASED. (US/0892-3884) [15207797] **1551**

CHINA EARTH SCIENCES CEASED. (CC) **1353**

CHINA EARTH SCIENCES CEASED. (NE/0923-6805) [22538110] **1353**

CHINA ECONOMIC NEWS (HK/1000-9094) [13297718] **1469**

CHINA ECONOMIC REPORT CEASED. (US/0196-3554) [05793714] **1469**

CHINA ECONOMIC REVIEW (US/1043-951X) [19614844] **1469**

CHINA ECONOMIC REVIEW (UK) 827, **1551**

CHINA ENERGY REPORT CEASED. (HK) [17789571] **1935**

CHINA EXCHANGE NEWS (US/0272-0086) [06567214] **5195**

CHINA FACTS & FIGURES ANNUAL (US/0190-602X) [04271068] **2502**

CHINA FAX AND TELEX DIRECTORY (HK) [27300429] 1151, **827**

CHINA GLASS & TABLEWARE (US/0009-4382) [09051265] **2588**

CHINA HANDBOOK (TAIPEI, TAIWAN) (CH) [03491346] **2502**

CHINA INFORMATION (NE/0920-203X) [17845166] **4468**

CHINA INFORMATION BULLETIN (PORTLAND, OR.) (US/1055-8047) [23346899] **2648**

CHINA : INTERNATIONAL TRADE. ANNUAL STATISTICAL SUPPLEMENT (US/0739-3512) [08796627] 827, **727**

CHINA: INTERNATIONAL TRADE (WASHINGTON, D.C. : 1980) CEASED. (US/0734-9599) [07487596] **827**

CHINA INVESTMENT GUIDE, THE CEASED. (UK) [11385944] **894**

CHINA. KUO WU YUAN See CHUNG-HUA JEN MIN KUNG HO KUO KUO WU YUAN KUNG PAO **4637**

CHINA LABOR NOTES (US) [21344297] **1659**

CHINA LAW AND PRACTICE (HK) [16780791] **2950**

CHINA LAW REPORTER (US/0891-6829) [07357165] **2950**

CHINA LAW YEARBOOK (UK) [20254996] **2950**

CHINA LETTER (US/0529-3189) [03102606] **657**

CHINA M&A AND INVESTMENT REPORTER See ASIAN M&A AND INVESTMENT DATABASE **891**

CHINA MARKET (HK) [09039998] 657, **1633**

CHINA MEDICAL ABSTRACTS (CC) [08356532] **3563**

CHINA MEDICAL REPORTER (US/0090-5003) [03105103] **3563**

●CHINA MONTHLY DATA / INSTITUTE OF ASIAN AFFAIRS (GW/0943-7533) [28383978] 1469, **4468**

●CHINA MONTHLY STATISTICS / CHINA STATISTICAL INFORMATION AND CONSULTANCY SERVICE CENTRE (CC) [26784736] **5325**

CHINA NEWS ANALYSIS (CH/0009-4404) [01554317] **2502**

CHINA NEWSLETTER (JA) [06072157] **827**

CHINA NOTES CEASED. (US/0009-4412) [01643449] **4943**

CHINA NOW (UK/0045-6764) [03123942] **2502**

CHINA. NUNG KUNG SHANG PU See NUNG KUNG SHANG PU TUNG CHI PIAO **5335**

CHINA OCEAN ENGINEERING (CC/0890-5487) [14263623] **2088**

CHINA OIL AND GAS REPORT (UK) **4253**

CHINA PAINTER, THE (US/0889-8189) [14093014] **371**

CHINA PAPER (AT/1037-4299) [I10374299] **2648**

CHINA PHILATELY (US) [08733855] **2784**

CHINA PHONE BOOK & BUSINESS DIRECTORY, THE (HK) [17604793] 1151, **827**

CHINA PICTORIAL (CC/0009-4420) [01554319] **2502**

CHINA PLASTIC & RUBBER JOURNAL (HK) 5075, **4454**

CHINA PRAYER LETTER (HK) **5058**

CHINA PRESS (US) **5715**

CHINA QUARTERLY (LONDON) (UK/0305-7410) [01554322] **2648**

CHINA REFORM (HK) [19639103] **4468**

CHINA REPORT (US) [11878785] **2502**

CHINA REPORT. AGRICULTURE (US) [05388516] **73**

CHINA REPORT (NEW DELHI) (II/0009-4455) [09354452] **5242**

CHINA REPORT (NEW DELHI) (II/0009-4455) [01554325] **2648**

CHINA REPORT. PLANT AND INSTALLATION DATA (US) [05385480] **657**

CHINA REPORT. POLITICAL, SOCIOLOGICAL AND MILITARY AFFAIRS (US/0891-351X) [05397485] **4468**

CHINA (REPUBLIC : 1949-). HSING CHENG YUAN See MONTHLY BULLETIN OF STATISTICS, THE REPUBLIC OF CHINA **5333**

CHINA (REPUBLIC). ECONOMIC RESEARCH DEPARTMENT See TAIWAN FINANCIAL STATISTICS MONTHLY **1540**

CHINA RESEARCH MONOGRAPHS / CENTER FOR CHINESE STUDIES, UNIVERSITY OF CALIFORNIA, BERKELEY (US/0069-3693) [01554331] **2648**

●CHINA REVIEW INTERNATIONAL (US/1069-5834) [28108670] **2648**

●CHINA RIGHTS FORUM (US/1068-4166) [27671002] **4505**

CHINA SCIENCE & TECHNOLOGY ABSTRACTS. SERIES II, CHEMISTRY, EARTH SCIENCE, ENERGY SOURCES CEASED. (CC) [09139692] **5093**

CHINA, SIGHTS & INSIGHTS (US) [10004748] **2649**

CHINA SOURCES. HARDWARE (CH/1012-3520) [19026888] **2810**

CHINA STATISTICAL YEARBOOK (HK/1052-9225) [20443299] **5325**

CHINA STATISTICS MONTHLY CEASED. (US/0897-7224) [17615022] **5325**

CHINA STUDY JOURNAL (UK/0956-4314) [I09564314] **4943**

CHINA TELECOM NEWSLETTER (US) **1151**

CHINA TELECOMMUNICATIONS CONSTRUCTION (HK/1017-5199) [10175199] **1130**

CHINA TELECOMMUNICATIONS CONSTRUCTION (HK/1017-5199) [I10175199] **1151**

CHINA TELEX & FAX DIRECTORY (HK) [19525348] **1151**

CHINA TELEX AND FAX DIRECTORY See CHINA FAX AND TELEX DIRECTORY **827**

CHINA TEXTILE (HK) **5349**

CHINA TODAY (CC) [20919718] **2502**

CHINA TRADE AND PRICE STATISTICS (CC) [18702861] **1469**

CHINA TRADE REPORT (HK/0009-448X) [01442933] **827**

CHINA. TSUI KAO JEN MIN FA YUAN See CHUNG-HUA JEN MIN KUNG HO KUO TSUI KAO JEN MIN FA YUAN KUNG PAO **2950**

CHINA UPDATE (OUD-HEVERLEE, BELGIUM) (BE) [09093830] **2502**

CHINA URBAN STATISTICS CEASED. (UK) [13140289] 2817, **2840**

CHINAFRICA : A MONTHLY MAGAZINE OF NEWS AND VIEWS (US) [27060570] **4540**

CHINAMAC JOURNAL (HK) **3476**

CHINA'S EXPORTS (HK) **827**

CHINA'S FOREIGN TRADE CORPORATIONS AND ORGANIZATIONS / COMPILED BY DEPARTMENT OF PUBLIC RELATIONS, CHINA COUNCIL FOR THE PROMOTION OF INTERNATIONAL TRADE (CC) [09666052] **827**

CHINA'S MILITARY : THE PLA IN ... (CH/1017-8716) [23353016] **4039**

CHINATOWN NEWS (CN/0009-4501) [01935916] **2486**

CHINDAN HAKPO (KO) [04701731] **5805**

CHINE EN CONSTRUCTION, LA (CC/0529-3294) [03561180] **607**

CHINESE AMERICA, HISTORY AND PERSPECTIVES (US/1051-7642) [19785732] **2258**

CHINESE AMERICAN FORUM (US/0895-4690) [11835877] 2258, **1731**

CHINESE ANNALS OF MATHEMATICS. SER. B (CC/0252-9599) [09914120] **3500**

CHINESE AROUND THE WORLD (HK/1011-2979) [I10112979] **4943**

CHINESE ASTRONOMY AND ASTROPHYSICS (UK/0275-1062) [07087546] **394**

CHINESE AWARENESS (US) [03126385] **2502**

CHINESE BUSINESS HISTORY (US) 1469, **657**

CHINESE-CANADIAN BULLETIN (1980) (CN/0227-874X) [06859826] **2727**

CHINESE CHEMICAL LETTERS (CH/1001-8417) **1023**

CHINESE COMPARATIST (US/1041-3928) [17545759] **3374**

CHINESE CULTURE (CH/0009-4544) [01554354] **3374**

CHINESE ECONOMIC STUDIES (US/0009-4552) [01554358] **1469**

CHINESE EDUCATION (US/0009-4560) [01554359] **1731**

●CHINESE EDUCATION AND SOCIETY (US/1061-1932) [25215594] **1731**

CHINESE — Alphabetical Title Index

●CHINESE ENVIRONMENT & DEVELOPMENT (US/1061-9534) [25495332] **2558**

CHINESE FOR AFFIRMATIVE ACTION NEWSLETTER (US/0743-2291) [10536092] **4468**

CHINESE GEOGRAPHICAL ABSTRACTS (CC) [14088791] **2558**

CHINESE GEOGRAPHY AND ENVIRONMENT See CHINESE ENVIRONMENT & DEVELOPMENT **2558**

CHINESE HISTORIANS (US/1043-643X) [19503558] **2649**

CHINESE HISTORICAL SOCIETY OF AMERICA See BULLETIN - CHINESE HISTORICAL SOCIETY OF AMERICA **2724**

CHINESE INSTITUTE OF CHEMICAL ENGINEERS See JOURNAL OF THE CHINESE INSTITUTE OF CHEMICAL ENGINEERS **2014**

CHINESE JOURNAL OF ACOUSTICS (CC) [09206133] **4452**

●CHINESE JOURNAL OF ADVANCED SOFTWARE RESEARCH (US/1074-7443) [29817758] **1284**

CHINESE JOURNAL OF AERONAUTICS (CC/1000-9361) [18575934] **16**

CHINESE JOURNAL OF ARID LAND RESEARCH (US/0898-5146) [17844507] **1353**

CHINESE JOURNAL OF AUTOMATION (US/1044-064X) [19678023] **1968**

CHINESE JOURNAL OF BIOCHEMISTRY AND BIOPHYSICS (US/0898-512X) [17835001] **495, 485**

CHINESE JOURNAL OF BIOTECHNOLOGY (US/1042-749X) [19127715] **3690**

CHINESE JOURNAL OF BOTANY (CC/1001-0718) [20378883] **506**

CHINESE JOURNAL OF CHEMISTRY (CC/1001-604X) [23028615] **972**

CHINESE JOURNAL OF CONTEMPORARY MATHEMATICS (US/0898-5111) [17834244] **3500**

CHINESE JOURNAL OF ENGINEERING THERMOPHYSICS (US/1043-8033) [19564944] **2101**

CHINESE JOURNAL OF GEOCHEMISTRY (CC/0253-486X) [14197919] **1050**

CHINESE JOURNAL OF GEOPHYSICS (US/0898-9591) [17959607] **1404**

CHINESE JOURNAL OF INFRARED AND MILLIMETER WAVES (US/0890-9903) [14514711] **4399**

CHINESE JOURNAL OF MATHEMATICS (CH/0379-7570) [03408627] **3500**

CHINESE JOURNAL OF METAL SCIENCE & TECHNOLOGY See JOURNAL OF MATERIALS SCIENCE & TECHNOLOGY **5119**

CHINESE JOURNAL OF NUMERICAL MATHEMATICS AND APPLICATIONS (US/0899-4358) [18096078] **3500**

CHINESE JOURNAL OF OCEANOLOGY AND LIMNOLOGY (CC/0254-4059) [10256375] **1447**

CHINESE JOURNAL OF PHYSICS (TAIPEI) (CH/0577-9073) [03112796] **4399**

CHINESE JOURNAL OF PHYSIOLOGICAL SCIENCES (CC/0258-6428) [I02586428] **579**

CHINESE JOURNAL OF PHYSIOLOGY, THE (CH/0304-4920) [02242131] **579**

CHINESE JOURNAL OF POLYMER SCIENCE (CC/0254-7679) [17670371] **972**

CHINESE JOURNAL OF POPULATION SCIENCE (US/1044-8403) [19916979] **4551**

CHINESE JOURNAL OF PSYCHOLOGY (CC) [12841160] **4580**

CHINESE JOURNAL OF SEMICONDUCTORS CEASED. (US/0899-9988) [18287836] **4399**

CHINESE LAW AND GOVERNMENT (US/0009-4609) [01554365] **4637, 2950**

CHINESE LITERATURE (BEIJING) (CH/0009-4617) [01554366] **3375**

CHINESE LITERATURE (MADISON) (US/0161-9705) [04071713] **3375**

CHINESE MEDICAL JOURNAL (CC/0366-6999) [01446494] **3563**

CHINESE MEDICAL SCIENCES JOURNAL (UK/1001-9294) [24546445] **3563**

●CHINESE MEDICINE AND HEALTH (US/1054-4704) [22901455] **3563**

CHINESE MUSIC (US/0192-3749) [05014767] **4109**

CHINESE OUR MISSIONS WORLD (US/1056-358X) [23703858] **4943**

CHINESE PEN (CH) [02694553] **3375**

CHINESE PHYSICS CEASED. (US/0273-429X) [07052624] **4399**

CHINESE PHYSICS LETTERS (US/0256-307X) [11950896] **4400**

CHINESE SCIENCE (US/0361-9001) [02441331] **5093**

CHINESE SCIENCE ABSTRACTS. PART A (CC/0254-5179) [09311909] **5093**

CHINESE SCIENCE ABSTRACTS. PART B (CC/0254-4903) [09311913] **5093**

CHINESE SCIENCE BULLETIN (CC/1001-6538) [21023798] **5094**

CHINESE SOCIOLOGY AND ANTHROPOLOGY (US/0009-4625) [01548629] **233, 5242**

CHINESE STUDIES IN HISTORY (US/0009-4633) [00872517] **2649**

CHINESE STUDIES IN PHILOSOPHY (US/0023-8627) [01554375] **4343**

CHINESE THEOLOGICAL REVIEW (US/0896-7660) [14869416] **4943**

CHINESE TRADE UNIONS, THE (CC/0577-9103) [02259290] **1659**

CHINESE UNIVERSITY OF HONG KONG. NEW ASIA COLLEGE See HSIN YA HSUEH SHU CHI KAN. NEW ASIA ACADEMIC BULLETIN **2847**

CHINESE YEARBOOK OF INTERNATIONAL LAW AND AFFAIRS (US/0731-0854) [08118037] **3126**

CHINETSU (JA/0385-7034) [04451478] 1935, **1353**

CHING CHA HSUEH SHU SHI KAN See CHING HSUEH TSUNG KAN. POLICE SCIENCE QUARTERLY **3160**

CHING CHENG HSUEH PAO / CHUNG YANG CHING KUAN HSUEH HSIAO (CH) [10523408] **3160**

CHING CHI HSUEH TUNG TAI (CC) [09200286] **1590**

CHING CHI JIH PAO (CC) [12230908] **5798**

CHING CHI KO HSUEH (CC) [07186103] **1469**

CHING CHI KUAN LI (CC) [05341524] **863**

CHING CHI LI LUN YU CHING CHI KUAN LI (CH) [09037823] **1590**

CHING CHI PU LIEN HO.KUANG YEH YEN CHIU SO. MRSO REPORT See M.R.S.O. REPORT **2143**

CHING CHI TI LI / CHUNG-KUO TI LI HEUEH HUI CHING CHI TI LI CHUAN YEH WEI YUAN HUI, HU-NAN SHENG CHING CHI TI LI YEN CHIU SO HO PAN (CH) [10673434] 1469, **2558**

CHING CHI TSUNG HENG (CC) [24033246] **1469**

CHING CHI WEN TI TAN SO (CC) [09031030] **1469**

CHING CHI YEN CHIU (CH) [04278382] **1590**

CHING CHI YEN CHIU (CC) [01554378] **1469**

CHING CHI YU KUAN LI YEN CHIU (CC) [10501648] **1601**

CHING FENG (ENGLISH EDITION) (HK/0009-4668) [01554379] **4943**

CHING-HAI CHIAO YU (CC) [09934840] **1732**

CHING HSIN (HK) [01790370] **2502**

CHING HSUEH TSUNG KAN. POLICE SCIENCE QUARTERLY (CH) [04533358] **3160**

CHING MING (CC) [09953397] **3375**

CHING NIEN I TAI (CC) [05585569] **2278**

CHING NIEN SHIH TAN (CC) [10620803] **3461**

CHING NIEN WEN HSUEH (CC) [10548900] **3375**

CHING PAO HSUEH KAN (CC) [11384983] **3201**

CHING TSAO MU KO (CC) [08808623] **4564, 377**

CHINGIN HIKIAGE TO NO JITTAI NI KANSURU CHOSA KEKKA HOKOKUSHO (JA) [02686295] **1659**

CHINGIN KENTO SHIRYO (JA) [02239260] **1659**

CHINGIN KETTEI NO TAME NO BUKKA TO SEIKEIHI SHIRYO (JA) [01799653] **1469**

CHINGIN ROMU SORAN (JA) [05113984] **1659**

CHINGIN SHIKI HO (JA) [01790218] **1659**

CHINHAE SANGGONG MYONGGAM (KO) [07499667] **657**

CHINOOK (CALGARY. 1993) (CN/1192-8190) [30570795] **2443**

CHINOOK OBSERVER (US/0739-9200) [09834143] **5760**

CHINOOK REGIONAL LIBRARY See PAPERBACKS BY MAIL **4831**

CHINOOK REGIONAL LIBRARY See CHINOOK REGIONAL LIBRARY DIRECTORY **3201**

CHINOOK REGIONAL LIBRARY DIRECTORY (CN/0705-2480) [04039810] **3201**

CHINOOK REPORTER (CN/0707-3860) [04746983] **5782**

CHINOPERL PAPERS (US/0193-7774) [03400918] **384, 3375**

CHIP (IT) **1174**

CHIP (GW/0170-6632) [06247645] **1266**

CHIP CHATS (US/0577-9294) [01642704] **633**

CHIP MADRID CEASED. (SP/0211-2841) [I02112841] **1174**

CHIP NEWS [COMPUTER FILE] / [COMPILED BY] STEVE ANDERSON (CL) [23603807] **4506**

CHIP OFF THE OLD BISON, A (US) [05210606] **1090**

CHIPPEWA HERALD-TELEGRAM (US/8756-2960) [08786817] **5766**

CHIPS & SHIPS (US/0591-1281) [04264123] **2727**

CHIP'S CLOSET CLEANER (US/1064-9719) [26479208] **2530**

CHIPS OFF THE WRITER'S BLOCK CATHARSIS (US/1058-6326) [24352444] **3375, 2918**

CHIRALITY (NEW YORK, N.Y.) (US/0899-0042) [18115575] **4296, 972**

CHIRI CHOSAJO. BULLETIN See BULLETIN OF THE GEOGRAPHICAL SURVEY INSTITUTE **2557**

CHIRIBOTAN (JA/0577-9316) **5094**

CHIRICU (BLOOMINGTON, IND. : 1981) (US/0277-7223) [06751900] **2613**

CHIRIGAKU HYORON (JA/0016-7444) [01554390] **2558**

CHIRIGAKUHO (JA) [01790295] **2558**

CHIRIHAK (KO) [05328125] **2558**

CHIROHEALTH (FULLERTON, CALIF.) (US/1056-8530) [23880408] **2596**

CHIRON (GW/0069-3715) [03118676] **1075**

CHIROPODY REVIEW (UK/0009-4714) **3917**

CHIROPRACTIC COLLEGE ADMISSIONS AND CURRICULUM DIRECTORY See CHIROPRACTIC COLLEGE DIRECTORY, THE **3563**

●CHIROPRACTIC COLLEGE DIRECTORY, THE (US) [26177879] **3563**

CHIROPRACTIC (FORT WAYNE, IND.) (US/0897-6058) [17564047] **3804, 4379**

CHIROPRACTIC HISTORY (US/0736-4377) [08640170] **4379**

CHIROPRACTIC JOURNAL OF AUSTRALIA (AT/1036-0913) [I10360913] **4379**

CHIROPRACTIC LEGAL UPDATE (US) **3563, 2950**

CHIROPRACTIC PRODUCTS (US/1041-2360) [18691251] **3563**

CHIROPRACTIC REPORT, THE (CN/0836-1444) [17245179] **4380**

CHIROPRACTIC RESEARCH ARCHIVES COLLECTION (CN/0824-9709) [11543861] **3563**

CHIROPRACTIC RESEARCH JOURNAL (US/0899-6938) [18185926] **4380, 3804**

CHIROPRACTIC SPORTS MEDICINE (US/0889-6976) [13999151] **3953**

●CHIROPRACTIC TECHNIQUE (US) [28577292] **3804**

CHIRURG (GW/0009-4722) [01554395] **3961**

CHIRURGIA (IT/0394-9508) **3961**

CHIRURGIA DEGLI ORGANI DI MOVIMENTO (IT/0009-4749) [01585608] **3881, 3961**

CHIRURGIA DEL PIEDE (IT/0392-0771) [I03920771] **3917**

CHIRURGIA DELLA TESTA E DEL COLLO : QUADERNI A.I.C.M.F., A.S.C.M.F.O.I (IT) [17800533] **3961**

CHIRURGIA E PATOLOGIA SPERIMENTALE. SUPPLEMENTO (IT/0412-264X) [10149387] **3961**

CHIRURGIA EPATOBILIARE SUSPENDED. (IT/0393-1471) [19261977] **3962**

CHIRURGIA GASTROENTEROLOGICA (IT/0009-4765) [03118859] **3743**

CHIRURGIA ITALIANA (IT/0009-4773) [06522793] **3962**

CHIRURGIA NARZADOW RUCHY I ORTOPEDIA POLSKA (PL/0009-479X) [01778072] **3962, 3881**

CHIRURGIA OGGI : ORGANO UFFICIALE DELLA SOCIETA EMILIANO-ROMAGNOLA DI CHIRURGIA (IT/0393-1463) [19668034] **3962**

CHIRURGIA TORACICA, LA (IT/0366-6298) [01778073] **3962**

CHIRURGIA TRIVENETA (IT/0009-4811) [06365334] **3962**

CHIRURGICA (OULU) (FI/0358-4917) [04828379] **3962**

CHIRURGIE (FR/0001-4001) [03359654] **3962**

CHIRURGIE (PARIS) (FR/0001-4001) [01554398] **3962**

CHIRURGIEN - DENTISTE DE FRANCE, LE (FR/0009-4838) [06365596] **1319**

CHIRURGISCHE GASTROENTEROLOGIE MIT INTERDISZIPLINAREN GESPRACHEN (GW/0177-9990) [14380084] **3962, 3743**

CHIRURGISCHE PRAXIS (GW/0009-4846) [06467166] **3962**

CHIRURGISCHES FORUM FUER EXPERIMENTELLE UND KLINISCHE FORSCHUNG (GW/0303-6227) [01077034] **3962**

CHIRYOGAKU (JA/0386-8109) [10287212] **4380, 3563**

CHISAGO COUNTY PRESS (US) [01554403] **5695**

CHISHITSU CHOSAJO GEPPO (JA/0016-7665) [01754184] **1371**

CHISHITSU KAISEKI IINKAI HOKOKUSHO (JA) [02971608] **2136**

CHISHOLM TRAIL, THE (US) [09988436] **2443**

CHISPA (US/0564-478X) [03531716] **5094, 1062**

CHISPAS (US) [05324898] **1106**

CHITANIUMU, JIRUKONIUMU (JA/0577-9391) [10287160] **4000**

CHITARRE (IT) **4109**

CHITRABIKSHAN (II) [03967976] **4065**

CHITTAGONG PORT AUTHORITY *See* MONTHLY BULLETIN, PORT OF CHITTAGONG **5453**

CHITTAGONG PORT AUTHORITY *See* PORT FOLIO, PORT OF CHITTAGONG **5454**

CHITTAGONG UNIVERSITY STUDIES. PART II, SCIENCE (BG/0253-5459) [09396249] **5094**

CHITTENANGO, BRIDGEPORT TIMES (US) [18932588] **5715**

CHITTY ON CONTRACTS (UK) **2950**

CHITTY'S LAW JOURNAL AND FAMILY LAW REVIEW (US/1077-8519) [30901229] **3120**

CHIU SHIH (CC/1002-4980) [20999722] **4517**

CHIU SHIH NIEN TAI (HK) [10894044] **4468**

CHIYOK SAHOE KAEBAL YONGU (KO) [11175307] **2817**

CHIZU. MAP (JA/0009-4897) [03122432] **2558**

CHIZU SENTA NYUSU (JA) [01797166] **2581**

CHLOE AMSTERDAM (NE/0168-9878) [I01689878] **3375**

CHLOR-ALKALI MARKETWIRE (US) **972**

CHLOROPLASTS (UK/0264-9640) **485, 3563**

CHMELARSTVI (XR/0577-943X) [03129223] **166**

CHO TO GA. TYO TO GA (JA) [04874535] **5606**

CHO-YANG / CHOS YANS (II) [14903288] **5021**

CHOATE ROSEMARY HALL *See* ALUMNI DIRECTORY / CHOATE ROSEMARY HALL **1097**

CHOCOLATE MANUFACTURERS ASSOCIATION OF THE UNITED STATES OF AMERICA *See* ANNUAL REPORT CMA/ACRI **2327**

CHOCOLATE NEWS *CEASED.* (UK) [07486291] **2331**

CHOCOLATE PRODUCTION *See* CONFECTIONERY PRODUCTION **2332**

CHOCOLATE SINGLES (US/0882-4460) [11858964] **2258**

CHOCOLATERIE, CONFISERIE DE FRANCE (FR/0009-4943) [04264130] **2331**

CHOCOLATIER (US/0887-591X) [12682079] **2331**

CHOCS (VILLENEUVE-SAINT-GEORGES) (FR/1157-741X) [26249406] **2154**

CHOCTAW ADVOCATE, THE (US) [12569923] **5625**

CHOCTAW COMMUNITY NEWS (US) [03974836] **5700**

CHOCTAW PLAINDEALER (US) [14515303] **5700**

CHODNICTWO (PL/0009-4919) [I00094919] **73**

CHOESIN UIHAK. THE NEW MEDICAL JOURNAL (KO) [05060152] **3563**

CHOFUKU SHOGAI KYOIKU KANKEI BUNKEN MOKUROKU (JA) [02246901] **4385, 1877**

CHOHUNG KYONGJE (KO) [07902160] **1551**

CHOICE (US/0009-4978) [01554411] **3201**

CHOICE BIBLIOGRAPHICAL ESSAY SERIES (US) [03129293] **413**

CHOICE (CHIPPENDALE, N.S.W.) (AT) [08299210] **1294**

CHOICE INDIA (II) [11779296] **5195**

CHOICE$ (RESEARCH TRIANGLE PARK, N.C.) (US/1060-3239) [24926563] **783**

CHOICES (AMES, IOWA) (US/0886-5558) [12924829] **73**

CHOICES (EVANSTON, ILL.) (US/0735-6358) [08963926] **1062**

CHOICES IN CARDIOLOGY (US/0894-5853) [16149596] **3702**

CHOICES IN RESPIRATORY MANAGEMENT *CEASED.* (US/1044-0690) [19366392] **3949**

●CHOICES (LONDON, ONT.) (CN/1188-8172) [26714736] **5279**

●CHOICES : THE HUMAN DEVELOPMENT MAGAZINE / UNDP (US) [25661448] **2908**

●CHOIR & ORGAN (UK/0968-7262) [27408274] **4109**

CHOIRS ONTARIO (CN/0822-4749) [10036561] **4109**

CHOIX: DOCUMENTATION AUDIOVISUELLE (CN/0706-2257) [05910256] **1891**

CHOIX : DOCUMENTATION IMPRIMEE (CN/0706-2249) [04239574] **3201**

CHOIX JEUNESSE : DOCUMENTATION IMPRINEE (CN/0706-2265) [04239621] **3201**

CHOKE CANYON SERIES (US) [09107003] **265**

CHOKSIPCHA PYONGWON CHI (KO) [04856471] **3563**

CHOLESTEROL AND LIPOPROTEINS (UK/0964-7597) **485**

CHOLGANG TONGGYE (KO) [09202610] **4000, 1601**

CHOLGANG TONGGYE YONBO (KO) [09292826] **4000, 1601**

CHOLTO CHARYANG KISUL ROLLING STOCK ENGINEERING (KO) [10225067] **5430**

CHOLTO TONGGYE YONBO *CEASED.* (KO) [05927583] **5430**

CHOLTO YONBO *See* CHOLTO TONGGYE YONBO **5430**

CHO'N-TRO'I (CN/0713-4002) [09246120] **5195**

CHONG / ILSONG SINYAK CHUSIK HOESA (KO) [10278890] **4296**

CHONGBO SANOP (KO) [09089569] **1174**

CHONGBU KUMAE MULCHA KAGYOK CHONGBO (KO) [07781395] **1469**

CHONGHWA (KO) [08578390] **5242**

CHONGI ANJON (KO) [10125646] **2038**

CHONGI KONGOP PYOLLAM (KO) [11799242] **1601**

CHONGI KONGSAOP TONGGYE CHARYO (KO) [10241572] **607, 632**

CHONGI TONGSIN (KO) [10061743] **1151**

CHONGMIL SABO (KO) [10392769] **1601**

CHONGNO SOJOK SINGAN SOSIK (KO) [10763737] **413**

CHON'GONGNYON HOEBO (KO) [05019112] **1551**

CHONGQING DAXUE XUEBAO (CC/0253-3626) [08694178] **5229**

CHONGSIN MUNHWA YONGU (KO) [11447006] **2649**

CHONGSIN PAKYAK YONGU (KO) [24252233] **4580, 3923**

CHONGU (KO) [09085169] **2502**

CHONGUK CHUNGSO KWANGGONGOP TONGGYE CHOSA POGOSO (KO) [08839063] **3476, 2136**

CHONGUK KAJOK POGON SILTAE CHOSA POGO (KO) [10177378] **588**

CHON'GUK KYONGJEIN YONHAPHOE *See* CHON'GONGNYON HOEBO **1551**

CHONGUK KYONGJEIN YONHAPHOE *See* CHONGYONGNYON **1551**

CHONGUK TAEHAKSAENG HAKSUL YONGU PALPYO NONMUNJI : KICHO KWAHAK PUNYA (KO) [05153923] **5094**

CHON'GUK TAEHAKSAENG HAKSUL YON'GU PALPYO NONMUNJIP: NONGSUSAN, HAEYANGHAK PUNYA (KO) [05063993] **73**

CHON'GUK TAEHAKSAENG HAKSUL YON'GU PALPYO NONMUNJIP : SAHOE KWAHAK PUNYA (KO) [05040628] **5195**

CHONGYONGNYON (KO) [04388272] **1551**

CHONJA KWAHAK (KO) [05156483] **2038**

CHONNAM JOURNAL OF MEDICAL SCIENCES (KO/1013-3968) [20566367] **3563**

CHONSON MUNHAK (KO) [09114789] **3375**

CHONTONG MUNHWA (KO) [10008316] **2649**

CHOOMIA (US) [02873062] **3461**

CHOONPA IGAKU. JAPANESE JOURNAL OF MEDICAL ULTRASONICS (JA) [04770590] **3563**

CHOOSE LIFE (WEYBURN, SASK.) (CN/0824-0663) [11825373] **2249**

CHOPPER GUIDE *See* MOTORCYCLE RIDER'S GUIDE **4082**

CHOPSKA DROGA (PL/0137-9070) [I01379070] **73**

CHORAL JOURNAL, THE (US/0009-5028) [01554417] **4109**

CHORAL MUSIC IN PRINT (US) [02251151] **4109**

CHORAL OVERTONES (US/0360-2443) [02243761] **4109**

CHORAL TONES (US/0360-2524) [02243739] **4109**

CHORALE (UK) [08244118] **4109**

CHORD AND DISCORD (US/0069-3758) [01554418] **4109**

CHOREOGRAPHY AND DANCE (SZ/0891-6381) [14940725] **1311**

●CHOREOGRAPHY AND DANCE ARCHIVE (SW/1072-9216) [29238613] **1311**

CHOREOGRAPHY AND DANCE STUDIES (SZ/1053-380X) [22521975] **1311**

CHORISTERS' GUILD *See* CHORISTERS GUILD LETTERS **4109**

CHORISTERS GUILD LETTERS (US/0412-2801) [02445911] **4109**

CHORSANGER, DER (GW) [01794335] **4109**

CHORUS! (DULUTH, GA.) (US/1044-7857) [19900658] **4109**

CHORUS (HALIFAX) (CN/0821-1108) [09743247] **4109**

CHOSA (JA) [01790303] **894, 657**

CHOSA GEPPO (JA) [01797150] **4771**

CHOSA GEPPO / NIHON GINKO CHOSA TOKEIKYOKU (JA) [22253101] **1551**

CHOSA KENKYU HOKOKU (JA) [10335058] **3375**

CHOSA KENKYU HOKOKUSHU (JA) [09047596] **607**

CHOSA KENKYU JIHO - KOKAI KUNRENJO (JA) [04654195] **4175**

CHOSA SHIRYO (JA) [01799671] **1469**

CHOSA TONGGYE WOLBO (KO) [08863402] **1551**

CHOSA WOLBO (CHUNGSO KIOP UNHAENG) *See* KIUN CHOSA WOLBO **1614**

CHOSA WOLBO (KUNGMIN UNHAENG) (KO) [07962115] **1551**

CHOSE SINBO (KO) [20397379] **4717**

CHOSEN GAKUHO (JA/0577-9766) [03129575] **2649**

CHOSEN MINSHU SHUGI JINMIN KYOWAKOKU SOSHIKIBETSU JINMEIBO (JA) [19288441] **4637**

CHOSETSU KOHO NIIGATA (JA) [07038508] **2088**

CHOSON CHUNGANG ILBO (KO) [10656234] **317**

CHOSON ILBO (MIJU PAN) (US/0743-7056) [10641497] **5715**

CHOSON KONGOP HYOPHOE PO (KO) [09201068] **4175**

CHOSON MINJUJUUI INMIN KONGHWAGUK KWAHAGWON *See* CHOSON MINJUJUUI INMIN KONGHWAGUK KWAHAGWON TONGBO **5094**

CHOSON MINJUJUUI INMIN KONGHWAGUK KWAHAGWON. CHOSON KWAHAGWON TONGBO *See* CHOSON MINJUJUUI INMIN KONGHWAGUK KWAHAGWON TONGBO **5094**

CHOSON MINJUJUUI INMIN KONGHWAGUK KWAHAGWON TONGBO (KO/0366-6662) [07190330] **5094**

CHOSON TAEHAKKYO UIDAE NONMUNJIP (KO) [12832061] **3563**

CHOTEAU ACANTHA, THE (US) [11692027] **5705**

CHOVATEL (XR) [06342648] **209**

CHOWAN HERALD, THE (US/0739-0246) [09701155] **5723**

CHOWKHAMBA SANSKRIT STUDIES (II) [04759501] **2649**

CHRIE COMMUNIQUE (US/1042-5918) [18115993] 5466, **2804**

CHRISMAN LEADER (US) [21952919] **5659**

CHRIST IN DER GEGENWART (GW/0170-5148) [I01705148] **4943**

CHRIST SEUL (FR/0750-2087) [07899461] **4943**

CHRIST TO THE WORLD (IT/0011-1465) [01554420] **4943**

CHRIST UND WELT / RHEINISCHER MERKUR (GW/0173-3028) [07880605] **5027**

CHRISTADELPHIAN ADVOCATE, THE (US/0746-8253) [10259120] **4944**

CHRISTCHURCH, N.A. UNIVERSITY OF CANTERBURY. DEPT. OF PSYCHOLOGY AND SOCIOLOGY *See* RESEARCH PROJECT **4615**

CHRISTELIJKE MUZIEKBODE, DE (NE/0009-5176) [04862363] **4109**

CHRISTEN DEMOCRATISCHE VERKENNINGEN : MAANDBLAD VAN HET WETENSCHAPPELIJK INSTITUUT VOOR HET CDA (NE) [08025483] **4517**

CHRISTENLEHRE, DIE (GE/0009-5192) [07990732] **4944**

CHRISTIAN (UK) [19094564] **4944**

CHRISTIAN ACTIVIST, THE ***CEASED***. (US/8756-9930) [10733721] **4944**

CHRISTIAN ACTIVITIES CALENDAR (MIDDLE ATLANTIC ED.) (US/0883-4210) [12143399] 4109, **4944**

●CHRISTIAN ADVOCATE (AUSTIN, TEX.) (US/1062-970X) [25823138] **4944**

CHRISTIAN ANTHROPOLOGY (US/1064-1602) [09202446] 4944, **233**

CHRISTIAN ANTI-COMMUNISM CRUSADE *See* CHRISTIAN ANTI-COMMUNISM CRUSADE **4540**

CHRISTIAN ANTI-COMMUNISM CRUSADE (US/0195-9387) [05712041] **4540**

CHRISTIAN ARENA (UK/0264-598X) [I0264598X] **4944**

CHRISTIAN ASSOCIATION FOR PSYCHOLOGICAL STUDIES *See* PROCEEDINGS OF THE ANNUAL CONVENTION - CHRISTIAN ASSOCIATION FOR PSYCHOLOGICAL STUDIES **4988**

CHRISTIAN BEACON ***SUSPENDED***. (US/0009-5265) [01776541] **4944**

CHRISTIAN BEGINNINGS (US/1058-8558) [24402471] **4944**

CHRISTIAN BIOETHICS (NE/1380-3603) 451, 2249, **4944**

CHRISTIAN BRETHREN REVIEW : THE JOURNAL OF THE CHRISTIAN BRETHREN RESEARCH FELLOWSHIP (UK/0306-7467) [08463997] **4944**

CHRISTIAN BROTHERS COLLEGE (MEMPHIS, TENN.) *See* ALUMNI DIRECTORY - CHRISTIAN BROTHERS COLLEGE (MEMPHIS, TENN.) **1098**

CHRISTIAN BROTHERS STUDIES *See* CATHOLIC SCHOOL STUDIES: A JOURNAL OF EDUCATION FOR AUSTRALIAN & NEW ZEALAND CATHOLIC SCHOOLS **1890**

CHRISTIAN BROTHERS STUDIES (AT/0312-9519) [I03129519] 4944, **1732**

CHRISTIAN CENTURY (1902), THE (US/0009-5281) [06083626] **4944**

CHRISTIAN CHALLENGE, THE (US/0890-6793) [05965577] **5058**

CHRISTIAN CHURCH (DISCIPLES OF CHRIST) *See* YEARBOOK & DIRECTORY OF THE CHRISTIAN CHURCH (DISCIPLES OF CHRIST) **5010**

CHRISTIAN COMMUNICATIONS (CN/0009-5303) [01957175] **4944**

CHRISTIAN COMMUNICATOR, THE (US/1043-1225) [19330965] **4944**

CHRISTIAN COMMUNITY : A JOURNAL FOR THE NEW AGE OF CHRISTIANITY PUBLISHED BY THE CHRISTIAN COMMUNITY IN GREAT BRITAIN, THE (UK) [09025745] **4944**

CHRISTIAN COMMUNITY (COLUMBUS), THE (US/0145-3297) [02225921] **4944**

CHRISTIAN COMMUNITY : THE MAGAZINE OF THE NATIONAL CENTRE FOR CHRISTIAN COMMUNITIES AND NETWORKS (UK) **4944**

CHRISTIAN COMPUTER NEWS (US/0882-0961) [11742859] **1174**

CHRISTIAN COMPUTING MAGAZINE (US/1063-7672) [26135867] 4944, **1174**

CHRISTIAN COMPUTING (VERSAILLES, MO.) *See* CHRISTIAN COMPUTING MAGAZINE **1174**

CHRISTIAN CONQUEST (US/0892-9300) [15294951] **4944**

●CHRISTIAN COUNSELING TODAY (US/1076-9668) [29627224] **4944**

CHRISTIAN COUNTY GENEALOGICAL SOCIETY (US/0897-408X) [17498041] **2443**

●CHRISTIAN COURIER (CN/1192-3415) [27038928] **5058**

CHRISTIAN CROSE FAMILY NEWSLETTER (US/0196-8947) [04264118] **2443**

CHRISTIAN CRUSADE (US/0195-265X) [05433933] **4944**

CHRISTIAN DEFENCE LEAGUE (AT) 4518, **2669**

CHRISTIAN DIRECTORY (TH) [05113737] **4944**

CHRISTIAN EARLY CHILDHOOD CONNECTION : METHODS AND MATERIALS FOR THE PRE-SCHOOL YEARS (US/1045-4977) [20160672] 4944, **1732**

●CHRISTIAN EDUCATION COUNSELOR (US/1072-1436) [28871542] **5058**

CHRISTIAN EDUCATION DIGEST (US/8756-1751) [11479594] 1732, **4944**

CHRISTIAN EDUCATION INFORMER, THE (US/0740-1876) [09901810] **4944**

CHRISTIAN EDUCATION JOURNAL (US/0739-8913) [09809735] 1732, **4944**

CHRISTIAN EDUCATION TODAY ***CEASED***. (US/0884-5506) [12389264] **4944**

CHRISTIAN EDUCATOR (US/0091-2867) [01786885] **4944**

CHRISTIAN EDUCATORS JOURNAL (US) [01605835] 1891, **4944**

CHRISTIAN ENDEAVOR LEADER'S MONTHLY, INTERMEDIATE NUMBER (US) [01554439] **4944**

CHRISTIAN ENDEAVOR LEADER'S MONTHLY, JUNIOR NUMBER (US) [01554440] **4945**

CHRISTIAN ENDEAVOR WORLD, THE (US/0009-5338) [01776542] **4945**

CHRISTIAN EXAMINER AND CHURCH OF IRELAND MAGAZINE, THE (IE) [11036422] **4945**

CHRISTIAN FAMILY (BLOWNTVILLE, TEX.) (US/0279-5310) [07090399] 2278, **4945**

CHRISTIAN FAMILY NEW MALDEN (UK) [I02694689] **4945**

CHRISTIAN HERALD (US/0009-5354) [02787911] 4945, **431**

CHRISTIAN HERALD (CHAPPAQUA) ***CEASED***. (US/0009-5354) [01554447] **4945**

CHRISTIAN HERALD WORTHING (UK/0953-4385) [I09534385] **5058**

CHRISTIAN HISTORY (WORCESTER, PA.) (US/0891-9666) [08540047] **4945**

CHRISTIAN HOME AND SCHOOL (US) [10004564] **2278**

●CHRISTIAN HOME JOURNAL, THE (US/1065-8386) [26757873] **4945**

CHRISTIAN INDEX (MEMPHIS, TENN.), THE (US/0744-4060) [08245965] **5058**

CHRISTIAN INDEX, THE (US) [02133549] **5058**

CHRISTIAN INFO COMMUNIGRAM (CN/0229-0219) [08063573] **4945**

CHRISTIAN INFO DIRECTORY (CN) [12178011] **4945**

CHRISTIAN INQUIRER (NATIONAL EDITION) (CN/0315-6532) [03258752] **4945**

CHRISTIAN INQUIRER (TORONTO EDITION) (CN/0315-6559) [03258755] **4945**

CHRISTIAN INSTITUTE FOR THE STUDY OF RELIGION AND SOCIETY, BANGALORE *See* RELIGION AND SOCIETY REPORT **4991**

CHRISTIAN IRELAND TODAY (US/1040-8622) [18554172] **4945**

CHRISTIAN JOURNAL (FORT WORTH, TEX.) (US/1056-3644) [08916335] **4945**

CHRISTIAN JOURNAL OF PSYCHOLOGY AND COUNSELING *See* CHRISTIAN COUNSELING TODAY **4944**

CHRISTIAN LEADER (HILLSBORO) (US/0009-5419) [04032287] **5058**

CHRISTIAN LEADERSHIP *See* LEADER (ANDERSON, IND.) **4973**

CHRISTIAN LIBRARIAN (UK/0309-4170) [11151921] **3202**

CHRISTIAN LIBRARIAN (CEDARVILLE, OHIO), THE (US/0412-3131) [01781779] 4945, **3202**

CHRISTIAN LIFE COMMUNICATOR *See* CHRISTIAN LIFE COMMUNITIES HARVEST **4945**

CHRISTIAN LIFE COMMUNITIES HARVEST (US/0739-6422) [09809274] **4945**

CHRISTIAN LIVING (ELGIN) (US/0162-9255) [04261895] **4945**

CHRISTIAN MEDICAL & DENTAL SOCIETY JOURNAL (US) [19006226] 1319, 4945, **3563**

CHRISTIAN MEDICAL ASSOCIATION OF INDIA *See* JOURNAL OF THE CHRISTIAN MEDICAL ASSOCIATION OF INDIA **3598**

CHRISTIAN MEDICAL JOURNAL OF INDIA : QUARTERLY JOURNAL OF THE CHRISTIAN MEDICAL ASSOCIATION OF INDIA (II) [18305810] **3563**

CHRISTIAN MESSENGER (GH/0009-5478) [02179930] **4945**

CHRISTIAN MINISTRY, THE (US/0033-4138) [01713914] **4945**

CHRISTIAN MISSION (US/8750-7765) [08198920] **4945**

CHRISTIAN MISSIONS IN MANY LANDS (US/0744-4052) [08244815] **4945**

CHRISTIAN MONTHLY (US/0009-5494) [01908202] **4945**

CHRISTIAN MUSIC (UK) [19743280] **4109**

CHRISTIAN MUSIC DIRECTORIES. PRINTED MUSIC, THE (US) [20397193] **4109**

CHRISTIAN NEW AGE QUARTERLY (US/0899-7292) [18201466] 4185, **4945**

CHRISTIAN NEWS FROM ISRAEL (IS/0009-5532) [01554468] **4945**

CHRISTIAN NEWS (NEW HAVEN, MO.) (US/0009-5516) [01554467] **4945**

CHRISTIAN OBSERVER (MANASSAS, VA.) (US/0899-2584) [18046396] **4945**

CHRISTIAN ORDER (UK/0009-5559) [01554471] **4945**

CHRISTIAN ORIENT (II/0258-1744) [08289796] **5039**

CHRISTIAN OUTREACH (CN/0701-0451) [03406185] **4945**

CHRISTIAN PARAPSYCHOLOGIST, THE (UK/0308-6194) [10963847] **4241**

CHRISTIAN PARENTING *See* CHRISTIAN PARENTING TODAY **2278**

CHRISTIAN PARENTING TODAY (US/1065-7215) [24281813] **2278**

CHRISTIAN PEACE CONFERENCE *See* CPC INFORMATION **4951**

CHRISTIAN PERIODICAL INDEX (US/0069-3871) [02256655] 4945, **5012**

CHRISTIAN PSYCHOLOGY FOR TODAY (US/0892-4686) [12005091] **4580**

CHRISTIAN PUZZLER *See* BIBLE PUZZLER **5056**

CHRISTIAN READER, THE (US/1064-9239) [01587649] **4945**

CHRISTIAN RENEWAL (CN/0820-7593) [10446063] **4945**

CHRISTIAN RESEARCH JOURNAL (US) **4945**

CHRISTIAN RESOURCE DIRECTORY (CN/0846-3905) [25127507] **4946**

CHRISTIAN RETAILING (US/0892-0281) [15030319] **952**

CHRISTIAN SCHOLAR'S REVIEW (US/0017-2251) [01554486] **4946**

CHRISTIAN SCIENCE HEROLD *See* KRISTEN VIDENSKABS HEROLD **4972**

CHRISTIAN SCIENCE JOURNAL, THE (US/0009-5613) [01554487] **4946**

CHRISTIAN SCIENCE MONITOR (1983), THE (US/0882-7729) [10969332] **5688**

CHRISTIAN SCIENCE MONITOR (INDEXES) (US/0578-0144) [03573167] **4946**

CHRISTIAN SCIENCE QUARTERLY (US/0009-5621) [04032300] **4946**

CHRISTIAN SCIENCE SENTINEL (US) [02445938] **4946**

●CHRISTIAN SCIENCE SENTINEL (RADIO ED.) (US/1065-1241) [26513404] **2530**

CHRISTIAN SINGLE (US/0191-4294) [04878389] **4946**

CHRISTIAN SOCIAL ACTION (WASHINGTON, D.C.) (US/0897-0459) [17374455] **4946**

CHRISTIAN SOCIAL ASSOCIATION *See* INFORMATION BULLETIN - CHRISTIAN SOCIAL ASSOCIATION **4965**

CHRISTIAN SOCIALIST, THE (UK/0009-5648) [01828637] **4540**

CHRISTIAN STANDARD (US/0009-5656) [02445939] **4946**

CHRISTIAN STATESMAN (US/0009-5664) [01554494] **4946**

CHRISTIAN STUDIES (AUSTIN, TEX.) (US/1050-4125) [21479649] **4946**

CHRISTIAN THEOLOGICAL SEMINARY *See* CHRISTIAN THEOLOGICAL SEMINARY BULLETIN **4946**

CHRISTIAN THEOLOGICAL SEMINARY BULLETIN (US/0529-472X) [01695605] **4946**

CHRISTIAN VISION (CN/0843-7602) [20493854] 347, 4946, **3375**

CHRISTIAN WEEK (CN/0835-412X) [17463529] **4946**

CHRISTIAN WOMAN (US/0009-5702) [04038493] 5553, **4946**

CHRISTIAN WORLD REPORT, THE (CN/0846-4243) [20377944] **4946**

CHRISTIAN WRITER'S SERVICE GUIDE (US/0736-7600) [09204667] **4946**

CHRISTIANISME AU VINGTIEME SIECLE, LE (FR/0009-5729) [02199898] **4946**

CHRISTIANITY & CIVILIZATION *CEASED.* (US/0278-8187) [07934498] **4946**

CHRISTIANITY AND CRISIS *CEASED.* (US/0009-5745) [01554504] **4946**

CHRISTIANITY & LITERATURE (US/0148-3331) [03128374] **4946**, **3375**

CHRISTIANITY TODAY (WASHINGTON) (US/0009-5753) [01554505] **4946**

CHRISTIANS AGAINST TERRORISM (CN/0317-0772) [02247685] **4946**

CHRISTIAN'S EXPOSITOR (US/1073-2209) [27047926] **4946**

CHRISTIANS, JEWS TODAY (CN/0225-5367) [06212951] **4946**

CHRISTIANS, JEWS TODAY (FRENCH EDITION) (CN/0225-5375) [06244670] **5047**

CHRISTIANS WRITING (AT/0729-4042) [l07294042] **3375**

CHRISTIC NEWS / THE CHRISTIC INSTITUTE OF LOS ANGELES, LA (US) [24531082] **4468**

CHRISTIE, MANSON & WOODS INTERNATIONAL INC *See* NEWS FROM CHRISTIE'S **360**

CHRISTIES CATALOGO GENERALE ASTE DI ROMA (IT) **317**

CHRISTIE'S INTERNATIONAL MAGAZINE (UK/0266-1217) [11561288] **347**

CHRISTLICH-DEMOKRATISCHE UNION DEUTSCHLANDS (GERMANY : EAST) *See* POLITISCHES JAHRBUCH DER CHRISTLICH - DEMOKRATISCHEN UNION DEUTSCHLANDS **4491**

CHRISTMAS : AN AMERICAN ANNUAL OF CHRISTMAS LITERATURE AND ART (US) [04522613] **5268**

CHRISTMAS (BIRMINGHAM, ALA.) *CEASED.* (US/1047-0328) [20583987] **5183**, **371**

CHRISTMAS IDEAS (US/0748-8106) [05763227] **371**

CHRISTMAS IDEAS FOR CHILDREN (US/0512-5901) [01791196] **371**

CHRISTMAS IS COMING! (HARDCOVER) (US/0883-9077) [12245576] **2789**, **371**

CHRISTMAS TREES (US/0199-0217) [01711451] **2377**

CHRISTMAS WITH SOUTHERN LIVING (US/0747-7791) [10407321] **371**

CHRISTO BOOK REVIEWS, EN *See* CHRISTO, EN **4946**

●CHRISTO, EN (US/1064-9751) [26480204] **4946**

CHRISTOPHER NEWS NOTES (US/8755-6901) [02530390] **4946**

CHRISTOPHER STREET (US/0146-7921) [03029084] **2793**

CHRISTOPHORUS STUTTGART (GW/0412-3417) [l04123417] **5411**

CHRISTUS (FR/0009-5834) [01714388] **5027**

CHRISTUS (MEXICO CITY, MEXICO (MX) [07768701] **4946**

●CHROMATIN *SUSPENDED.* (UK/0961-0901) [26352555] **543**

CHROMATOGRAM (SAN RAMON, CALIF.) (US/1053-8097) [16778009] **972**

CHROMATOGRAPHIA (GW/0009-5893) [00813697] **1014**

CHROMATOGRAPHIC SCIENCE (US/0069-3936) [01554523] **1014**

CHROMATOGRAPHY *CEASED.* (US/0892-8797) [15277868] **1014**

CHROMATOGRAPHY ABSTRACTS (UK/0268-6287) [13348922] **1014**

CHROMIUM (1977) (US) [05326606] **1438**

CHROMIUM REVIEW (SA/0256-0038) [10187033] **4000**

CHROMNY PRZYRODE OJCZYSTA (PL/0009-6172) [04550714] **2189**

CHROMOSOMA (GW/0009-5915) [01554525] **534**

CHROMOSOME RESEARCH (UK/0967-3849) [29186347] **3563**

CHRONIC DISEASES IN CANADA (CN/0228-8699) [07822810] **4771**, **3563**

CHRONIC PAIN LETTER (US) **3564**

CHRONICA (DAVIS) (US/0009-5931) [03407003] **2683**, **3375**

CHRONICA DERMATOLOGICA (IT/0390-5411) [06365708] **3718**

CHRONICA HORTICULTURAE (NE/0578-039X) [01554531] **2412**

CHRONICLE (US) [20761039] **5695**

CHRONICLE (ANN ARBOR) *SUSPENDED.* (US/0440-9426) [01681152] **2728**

CHRONICLE (ARMOUR, S.D.) *See* ARMOUR CHRONICLE, THE **5743**

CHRONICLE (BARTON, VT.) (US/0746-438X) [10049095] **5757**

CHRONICLE - CANADIAN FEDERATION OF UNIVERSITY WOMEN (CN/0316-330X) [03282416] **5553**

CHRONICLE CAREER INDEX (US/0276-0355) [07320838] **4203**

CHRONICLE (CHARLESTON, S.C.), THE (US/0746-1429) [09797007] **5742**

CHRONICLE (CRESWELL, OR.) (US/0739-9758) [09839545] **5733**

CHRONICLE-EXPRESS (US) [11048387] **5715**

●CHRONICLE FINANCIAL AID GUIDE (US/1063-7915) [24336937] **1815**

CHRONICLE FOUR-YEAR COLLEGE DATABOOK (US/0191-3670) [04852951] **1815**

CHRONICLE GRADUATE & PROFESSIONAL MAJORS : FINANCING GRADUATE STUDY *CEASED.* (US/0147-3905) [03717924] **1815**

CHRONICLE GUIDE TO EXTERNAL & CONTINUING EDUCATION *CEASED.* (US/0161-424X) [03880713] **1800**

CHRONICLE GUIDE TO GRADUATE & PROFESSIONAL STUDY *CEASED.* (US/0194-4045) [05366006] **1815**

CHRONICLE-HERALD, THE (CN/0828-1807) [12027101] **5782**

CHRONICLE. HOUSTON, TX (US) **5748**

CHRONICLE-INDEPENDENT (US) [25968582] **5742**

CHRONICLE (MILFORD, DEL.) (US) [16052229] **5648**

CHRONICLE-NEWS, THE (US) [22195509] **5642**

CHRONICLE OF HIGHER EDUCATION ALMANAC, THE (US/1043-7967) [18548861] **1815**

CHRONICLE OF HIGHER EDUCATION, THE (US/0009-5982) [01554535] **1815**

CHRONICLE OF LATIN AMERICAN ECONOMIC AFFAIRS (US/1054-8874) [23010451] **1469**

CHRONICLE OF PARLIAMENTARY ELECTIONS (SZ/0302-2498) [01792858] **4637**

CHRONICLE OF PHILANTHROPY, THE (US/1040-676X) [18498690] **4335**

CHRONICLE OF THE AARON BURR ASSOCIATION, THE (US/0001-3048) [05309236] **2728**

CHRONICLE OF THE CATHOLIC CHURCH IN LITHUANIA (CHICAGO, ILL.), THE (US/0730-7349) [07952661] **5027**

CHRONICLE OF THE EARLY AMERICAN INDUSTRIES ASSOCIATION, INC, THE (US/0012-8147) [08981346] **5094**

CHRONICLE OF THE HORSE, THE (US/0009-5990) [01642499] **2798**

CHRONICLE OF THE OMAHA DISTRICT DENTAL SOCIETY *See* CHRONICLE (OMAHA, NEB.), THE **4188**

CHRONICLE OF THE U.S. CLASSIC POSTAL ISSUES, THE (US/0009-6008) [04032554] **2784**

CHRONICLE OF UNITED NATIONS DOCUMENT SERVICE, THE (US) [10572123] **4518**

CHRONICLE (OMAHA, NEB.), THE (US/0030-2201) [03973898] **4188**

CHRONICLE / SOCIETY OF WINE EDUCATORS (US/8756-2286) [11511794] **2366**

CHRONICLE STUDENT AID ANNUAL *See* CHRONICLE FINANCIAL AID GUIDE **1815**

CHRONICLE SUMMARY REPORT *CEASED.* (US/0193-1601) [04964469] **1815**

CHRONICLE-TELEGRAM, THE (US) [10932283] **5727**

CHRONICLE, THE (US) [27905831] **5645**

CHRONICLE, THE (US) [23026349] **5230**

CHRONICLE, THE (US) [22107864] **5760**

CHRONICLE TRIBUNE (MARION, IND.) (US) [15151064] **5663**

CHRONICLE TWO-YEAR COLLEGE DATABOOK (US/0191-3662) [04852869] **1815**

CHRONICLE VOCATIONAL SCHOOL MANUAL (US/0276-0371) [07320922] **1912**

CHRONICLES OF OKLAHOMA (US/0009-6024) [01554537] **2728**

CHRONICLES OF SMITH COUNTY, TEXAS (US/0578-0462) [05274202] **2728**

CHRONICLES (PHILADELPHIA, PA.) (US/0893-2921) [15495876] **2443**

CHRONICLES (ROCKFORD, ILL.) (US/0887-5731) [13313430] **2844**

CHRONIK DER FINANZ- UND WAHRUNGSPOLITIK (GW) [02630687] **4717**

CHRONIQUE DE LA RECHERCHE MINIERE (FR/0182-564X) [04203746] **2136**, **1371**

CHRONIQUE DE L'U.G.G.I (FR/0047-1259) [01605824] **1404**

CHRONIQUE D'EGYPTE (BE/0009-6067) [01554541] **265**

CHRONIQUE DES ECRITS EN COURS, LA (FR) [07889539] **3375**

CHRONIQUE DES NATIONS UNIES (INT/1013-5235) [l10135235] **3126**

CHRONIQUE DES RELATIONS EXTERIEURES DU CANADA (CN/0847-1304) [20985516] **4518**

CHRONIQUE DES RELATIONS EXTERIEURES DU CANADA (CN/0847-1304) [20985507] **4518**

CHRONIQUE FEMINISTE (BE) [14154389] **5553**

CHRONIQUE HYPOTHECAIRE / COMPAGNIE D'ASSURANCE D'HYPOTHEQUES DU CANADA (CN/0712-2756) [08818821] **783**

CHRONIQUE / INSTITUT CATHOLIQUE DE TOULOUSE (FR/0495-9396) [05243928] **1732**

CHRONIQUE INTERNATIONALE PARIS (FR/1145-1408) [I11451408] **1470**

CHRONIQUE JUDICIAIRE D'HAITI, LA (HT) [08747153] **3126**

CHRONIQUE (LAC BEAUPORT) (CN/0712-7464) [08724016] **5782**

CHRONIQUE (QUEBEC) (CN/0706-3431) [08302624] **2481**

CHRONIQUES D'ACTUALITE DE LA S.E.D.E.I.S *See* CHRONIQUES DE LA S.E.D.E.I.S **1470**

CHRONIQUES D'ART SACRE (FR/0246-1331) [I02461331] **347**

CHRONIQUES DE LA DROUINERIE, LES (CN/0711-0359) [08422662] **2443**

●CHRONIQUES DE LA S.E.D.E.I.S (FR) [25394382] **5195**, **1470**

CHRONIQUES DES FOUILLES ET DECOUVERTES ARCHEOLOGIQUES EN GRECE EN (GR) [17377199] **265**

CHRONIQUES DU PROTECTEUR DU CITOYEN (CN/1188-0856) [25796707] **4637**

CHRONIQUES - GRET (FR/1168-1209) [I11681209] **5094**

CHRONIQUES ITALIENNES (FR/0766-4257) [14268628] **3273**

CHRONIQUEUR DE L'ILE, LE (CN/0823-6097) [09819056] **2728**

CHRONOBIOLOGIA (IT/0390-0037) [01038392] **3795**

CHRONOBIOLOGY INTERNATIONAL (UK/0742-0528) [10259604] **451**

CHRONOLOG (PALO ALTO, CALIF.) (US/0163-3732) [04365669] **3202**

CHRONOLOGICAL INDEX / CONSEIL DU PATRONAT DU QUEBEC (CN/0822-5478) [10440924] **413**

CHRONOLOGICAL SUMMARY OF OREGON'S UNEMPLOYMENT INSURANCE PROGRAM FROM THE BEGINNING OF THE OPERATION TO DATE / PREPARED BY RESEARCH & STATISTICS SECTION (US) [10774977] **2878**

CHRONOLOGICAL TABLE OF THE STATUTES (UK) [01152470] **2950**

CHRONOLOGIES OF MAJOR DEVELOPMENTS IN SELECTED AREAS OF FOREIGN AFFAIRS (CUMULATIVE EDITION) (US/0278-8365) [07878996] **4518**

CHRONOLOGY OF AFRICAN-AMERICAN HISTORY (US) **2613**

CHRONOLOGY OF AMERICAN AEROSPACE EVENTS, A (US) [04128964] **16**

CHRONOS (WALTHAM, MASS.) (US/0733-6470) [08612687] **5242**

CHRONOSTRATIGRAPHIE UND NEOSTRATOTYPEN (GW/0578-0578) [04082034] **1353**

CHROSTWAITE'S PENNSYLVANIA MUNICIPAL LAW REPORTER (US) [06335857] **2950**

●CHRYSALIS CONNECTION (CN/1191-3339) [26497788] **5279**

CHRYSALIS (NEW YORK, N.Y.) (US/0888-9384) [13230019] **4343**

CHRYSANTHEMUM (US/0090-5771) [04104804] **2412**

CHRYSLER / AMC COLLISION ESTIMATING GUIDE (US) **5411**

CHRYSLER CUP CANADIAN HOCKEY LEAGUE EAST-WEST ALL-STAR CHALLENGE OFFICIAL GUIDE (CN/1191-4009) [26497599] **4890**

CHRYSLER MUSEUM *See* CHRYSLER MUSEUM, THE **4086**

CHRYSLER MUSEUM, THE (US/0270-7926) [06473737] **4086**

CHRYSLER POWER (US/0885-663X) [12708170] **1968**

CHRYSOSTOM : QUARTERLY BULLETIN OF THE SOCIETY OF ST JOHN CHRYSOSTOM (UK/0529-5025) [01947584] **4946**

CHRZESCIJANIE (PL) [11435251] **5027**

CHRZESCIJANIN W SWIECIE (PL) [03635055] **5027**

CHTENIIA PAMIATI A.F. IOFFE / AKADEMIIA NAUK SSSR, ORDENA LENINA FIZIKO-TEKHNICHESKII INSTITUT IMENI A.F. IOFFE (RU) [11199549] **4400**

CHTENIIA PAMIATI AKADEMIKA A. N. ZAVARITSKOGO (RU) [06802865] **1372**

CHU FENG / CHUNG-KUO MIN CHIEN WEN I YEN CHIU HUI HU-NAN FEN HUI (CH) [10652687] 2318, **3375**

CHU JEN (CC) [08517923] **3375**

CHU PAN CHIA TSA CHIH (CH) [01797538] **413**

CHU PAN JEN / CHUNG-HUA MIN KUO TU SHU CHU PAN SHIH YEH HSIEH HUI (CH) [24979674] **4813**

CHU PAN SHIH LIAO (CH) [10631824] **4813**

CHU PEN (CC) [06576900] **3375**

CHU PEN YUAN TI (CH) [09141687] **3375**

CHU-SHIKOKU STUDIES IN AMERICAN LITERATURE (JA/0388-0176) [I03880176] **3375**

CHU TAN (CH) [09424639] **5362**

CHUAN CHI WEN HSUEH (CH/0578-0705) [02259142] 3375, **431**

CHUAN HSI LU *See* TUNG WU CHE HSUEH CHUAN HSI LU / TUNG WU TA HSUEH **4364**

CHUAN HSUEH PAO (US/0898-5138) [17844442] **543**

CHUAN KUO HSIN SHU MU (CC/0578-073X) [03133964] 4828, **4821**

CHUAN MIN CHENG CHIH CHI KAN (CH) [10652421] **4468**

CHUAN PO KUNG CHENG (CH) [09220412] **4175**

CHUANG TSO (KUEI-YANG SHIH, CHINA) (CC) [09039005] **431**

CHUBU DAIGAKU KOGAKUBU KIYO (JA/0910-8629) [12640168] 5094, **1968**

CHUBU SAENGHWAL (KO) [05071603] **2502**

CHUBUKEN NO MIRAIZO (JA) [04265359] **2817**

CHUBUN KENKYU (JA/0578-0780) [01554551] **1551**

CHUCHE UIHAK (KO) [09313623] **3564**

CHUCHOTERIES (CN/0825-8449) [12740250] **1861**

CHUGAN HANGUK (KO) [07962350] **2502**

CHUGAN KIDOKKYO (KO) [08252376] **4947**

CHUGAN KWANGGO (US/0279-9758) [07511038] **5634**

CHUGAN KYONGJE (KO) [04771804] **1551**

CHUGAN MAEGYONG (KO) [11768036] **1551**

CHUGAN SUUN NYUSU (KO) [08029876] **783**

CHUGOKU (JA/0578-0918) [01554553] **2649**

CHUGOKU BUNGAKU KENKYU (WASEDA DAIGAKU. CHUGOKU BUNGAKKAI) (JA/0385-0919) [07625079] **3375**

CHUGOKU BUNGAKUHO (JA/0578-0934) [01554554] **3375**

CHUGOKU CHIIKI TSUSHO SANGYO TOKEI NEMPO (JA) [08534993] **1551**

CHUGOKU GEPPO (JA) [05433762] **2649**

CHUGOKU KEIZAI KANKEI SHUYO RONSETSU SHU (JA) [06663371] **1551**

CHUGOKU KENKYU GEPPO (JA/0910-4348) [01554559] **5195**

CHUGOKU KOGYO GIJUTSU (JA) [01797380] **5094**

CHUGOKU KOGYO GIJUTSU SHIKENJO *See* CHUGOKU KOGYO GIJUTSU SHIKENJO NEMPO **5094**

CHUGOKU KOGYO GIJUTSU SHIKENJO *See* CHUGOKU KOGYO GIJUTSU SHIKENJO HOKOKU **1968**

CHUGOKU KOGYO GIJUTSU SHIKENJO *See* CHUGOKU KOGYO GIJUTSU **5094**

CHUGOKU KOGYO GIJUTSU SHIKENJO HOKOKU (JA) [04473297] **1968**

CHUGOKU KOGYO GIJUTSU SHIKENJO NEMPO (JA) [02245317] **5094**

CHUGOKU MONDAI (JA/0285-8282) [09463122] **1551**

CHUGOKU NOGYO SHIKENJO KENKYU HOKOKU (JA/0913-4239) [I09134239] **73**

CHUGOKU SHIKOKU NOGYO JOSEI HOKOKU (JA) [02823933] **74**

CHUGOKU TSUSAN TOKEI NEMPO *See* CHUGOKU CHIIKI TSUSHO SANGYO TOKEI NEMPO **1551**

CHUGOKUBUN CHOSENBUN TOSHO MOKUROKU (CH) [08542771] **413**

CHUGOKUGO CHOSENGO TOSHO SOKUHO (JA/0001-4532) [04183042] **413**

CHUIL HAKKYO KYOSA UI POT (KO) [09494687] **4947**

CHUKAI JIDOSHA ROPPO (JA) [05158780] **2950**

CHUKAI SHIN KYOIKU ROPPO (JA) [02805949] **1732**

CHUKEN HOKOKU (JA) [03426664] **4000**

CHUKHYOP CHOSA KYEBO (KO) [09458490] **209**

CHUKSAN CHINHUNG (KO) [07898002] **209**

CHULALONGKORN LAW REVIEW (TH) [10648579] **2950**

CHULPAN MUNHWA (KO/0009-6245) [03757823] **4828**

CHUM (SEOUL, KOREA) (KO) [10112871] **1311**

CHUMOKU HATSUMEI NO SENTEI (JA) [04625748] **1303**

CHUN CHIU (HK/0578-1175) [02259144] **2502**

CHUN CHUNG WEN HUA (CC) [08998343] **2502**

CHUN FENG (SHEN-YANG SHIH, CHINA) (CC) [11521311] **3375**

CHUN FENG WEN I TSUNG KAN *See* CHUN FENG (SHEN-YANG SHIH, CHINA) **3375**

CHUNG-CHOU HSUEH KAN (CH) [10673569] **5230**

CHUNG CHUAN CHI KAN (CH) [07036831] **4175**

CHUNG FU HSUAN CHI (CH) [11327383] **3375**

CHUNG HSI I CHIEH HO TSA CHIH *See* CHUNG-KUO CHUNG HSI I CHIEH HO TSA CHIH **3564**

CHUNG HSUEH CHENG CHIH KO CHIAO HSUEH (CC) [11100742] **4468**

CHUNG HSUEH SHENG (HK) [02245534] **1090**

CHUNG-HUA CHAN LUEH HSUEH KAN (CH) [10063005] **4039**

CHUNG-HUA CH'I KUAN I CHIH TSA CHIH (CC/0254-1785) [08322854] **3564**

CHUNG-HUA CHI KUNG / CHUAN KUO CHUNG I HSUEH HUI CHI KUNG KO YEN HUI CHU PAN (CC/1000-4610) [11510909] **4380**

CHUNG-HUA ERH KO TSA CHI. / ZHONGHUA ERKE ZAZHI / CHINESE JOURNAL OF PEDIATRICS (CC/0578-1310) [03112783] **3902**

CHUNG-HUA FANG SHE HSUEH TSA CHIH (CC/0529-5661) [10298254] **3939**

CHUNG-HUA FU CHAN KO TSA CHIH (CC/0529-567X) [03112760] **3758**

CHUNG-HUA HSIN HSUEH KUAN PING TSA CHIH (CC/0253-3758) [05827901] **3702**

CHUNG-HUA HSUEH PAO (CH) [01797612] **2649**

CHUNG-HUA JEN MIN KUNG HO KUO CHUAN KUO JEN MIN TAI PIAO TA HUI CHANG WU WEI YUAN HUI KUNG PAO (CC) [08472558] **2950**

CHUNG-HUA JEN MIN KUNG HO KUO KUO WU YUAN KUNG PAO (CC) [07130138] **4637**

CHUNG-HUA JEN MIN KUNG HO KUO TSUI KAO JEN MIN FA YUAN KUNG PAO (CC/1002-4611) [20292278] **2950**

CHUNG-HUA KO HSUEH HUA PAO (CC) [08526903] **5094**

CHUNG-HUA MIN KUO CHI CHI SHE PEI HSUAN LU (CH) [08073148] **2111**

CHUNG-HUA MIN KUO CHI CHI YU TIEN KUNG CHI TSAI NIEN CHIEN (CH) [02458497] **2111**

CHUNG-HUA MIN KUO CHI YEH MING JEN LU (CH) [08269342] **657**

CHUNG-HUA MIN KUO CHING CHI NIEN CHIEN (CH) [03305959] **1470**

CHUNG HUA MIN KUO KUNG SHANG MING LU *See* TAIWAN BUYERS' GUIDE **3488**

CHUNG-HUA MIN KUO ... LAN I NIEN CHIEN / LAN HUA SHIH CHIEH TSA CHIH SHE CHU PIEN (CH) [10814457] **2412**

CHUNG-HUA MIN KUO MIN I TSE YEN HSIEH HUI *See* CHUNG-HUA MIN KUO MIN I TSE YEN HUI PIEN **5242**

CHUNG-HUA MIN KUO MIN I TSE YEN HUI PIEN (CH) [03397799] **5242**

CHUNG-HUA MIN KUO SHOU I HSUEH HUI *See* ZHONGHUA MINGUO SHOUYI XUEHUI ZAZHI **5528**

CHUNG-HUA MIN KUO TI YU HSUEH CHIN HUI *See* CHUNG-HUA MIN KUO TI YU HSIEH CHIN HUI CHI KAN **4890**

CHUNG-HUA MIN KUO TI YU HSUEH CHIN HUI CHI KAN (CH) [03368099] **4890**

CHUNG-HUA MIN KUO TU SHU LIEN HO MU LU / KUO LI CHUNG YANG TU SHU KUAN PIEN (CH) [08272255] **413**

CHUNG-HUA NEI KO TSA CHIH (CC/0578-1426) [03112740] **3564**

CHUNG-HUA NUNG YEH YEN CHIU (CH/0376-477X) [02600887] **74**

CHUNG-HUA PI FU KO TSA CHIH (CC/0412-4030) [03112725] **3718**

CHUNG-HUA PING LI HSUEH TSA CHIH (CC/0529-5807) [03131657] **3893**

CHUNG-HUA SHANG YEH (CH) [25913708] **827**

CHUNG-HUA SHEN CHING CHING SHEN K'O TSA CHIH (CC/0412-4057) [I04124057] **3829**

CHUNG-HUA SHIH HSUEH (CH) [10920511] **3461**

CHUNG-HUA WAI KAO TSA CHIH (CC/0529-5815) [01778079] **3962**

CHUNG-HUA YEN K'O TSA CHIH (CC/0412-4081) [03131725] **3873**

CHUNG I TSA CHIH (CC/0529-5858) [03131748] **3564**

CHUNG I YAO HSUEH PAO (CC) [08631781] **3564**

CHUNG JIH WEN HUA (CH) [09364168] **2649**

CHUNG-JUO YIN MU *CEASED.* (CC/0577-893X) [04099833] **4065**

CHUNG KUNG YEN CHIU STUDIES ON CHINESE COMMUNISM (CH/0014-9667) [06059735] **4540**

CHUNG KUNG YUAN SHIH TZU LIAO HSUAN CHI. TSUNG HO LEI / CHUNG KUNG YEN CHIU TSA CHIH SHE PIEN YIN (CH) [10861177] **4637**

CHUNG-KUO CHA YEH (CC) [11384835] **166**

CHUNG-KUO CHE HSUEH (CC) [06873924] **4343**

CHUNG-KUO CHE HSUEH SHIH YEN CHIU (CC) [10945741] **4343**

CHUNG-KUO CHENG SHIH CHIEN SHE NIEN CHIEN ZHONG GUO CHENG SHI JIAN SHE NIAN JIAN / "CHUNG-KUO CHENG SHIH CHIEN SHE NIEN CHIEN" PIEN WEI HUI (CC) [21930034] **2817**

CHUNG-KUO CHENG SHIH TUNG CHI NIEN CHIEN (CC) [17723884] **5325**

CHUNG-KUO CHI HUA SHENG YU NIEN CHIEN (CC) [18821489] **588**

CHUNG-KUO CHI YEH (HK) [11434117] **827**

CHUNG-KUO CHIAO TUNG NIEN CHIEN (CC) [17723761] **5439**

CHUNG-KUO CHIEN CHU FA CHAN (HK) [11464781] **607**

CHUNG-KUO CHIEN CHU TSAI LIAO NIEN CHIEN (CH) [09301358] **607**

CHUNG-KUO CHIH LIANG KUAN LI / CHUNG-KUO CHIH LIANG KUAN LI HSIEH HUI CHU PAN (CC) [10552974] **3476**

CHUNG-KUO CHIN JUNG (CC) [02259336] **783**

CHUNG-KUO CHIN JUNG NIEN CHIEN. ALMANAC OF CHINA'S FINANCE AND BANKING / CHUNG-KUO CHIN JUNG HSUEH HUI PIEN (CC) [20216471] **783**

CHUNG-KUO CHING CHI NIEN CHIEN (HK) [08393846] **1551**

CHUNG-KUO CHING CHI / THE CHINA ECONOMIST (CH/0529-5920) [03131810] **1470**

CHUNG-KUO CHING CHI WEN TI (CH/1000-4181) [09201425] **1551**

CHUNG-KUO CHING NIEN (PEKING, CHINA : 1948) (CH) [09215924] **4540**

CHUNG-KUO CHU KOU SHANG PIN HUI PIEN (HK) [06413786] **827**

CHUNG-KUO CHUAN LI YU SHANG PIAO (HK) [12210467] **1303**

● CHUNG-KUO CHUNG HSI I CHIEH HO TSA CHIH (CC/1003-5370) [26123843] **3564**

CHUNG-KUO ERH TUNG (CC/0412-4154) [03132354] 3375, **1062**

CHUNG-KUO FA LU NIEN CHIEN / LAW YEAR BOOK OF CHINA (CC) [19119655] **2950**

CHUNG-KUO FU NU / ZHONGGUO FUNU (CC/0529-603X) [01554607] **5553**

CHUNG-KUO HAI KUAN TUNG CHI (HK) [10470918] 827, **727**

CHUNG-KUO HAI YUN (HK) [10308177] **5448**

CHUNG-KUO HO TSO NIEN PAO. CO-OPERATIVE YEARBOOK REPUBLIC OF CHINA (CH) [03752166] **1541, 1470**

CHUNG-KUO HSIAO SHUO NIEN CHIEN (CC) **3375**

CHUNG-KUO HSIEN TAI WEN HSUEH YEN CHIU TSUNG KAN / KAO HSIAO CHUNG-KUO HSIEN TAI WEN HSUEH YEN CHIU HUI [HO] PEI-CHING CHU PAN SHE HO PIEN (CC) [06955899] **3375**

CHUNG-KUO HSIN WEN NIEN CHIEN (CC) [09999197] **2918**

CHUNG-KUO HSU MU HSUEH HUI HUI CHIH (HK) [02643607] **209**

CHUNG-KUO HSU MU HUEH HI *See* CHUNG-KUO HSU MU HSUEH HUI HUI CHIH **209**

CHUNG-KUO HSUEH SHU NIEN KAN (CH) [03744783] **2649**

CHUNG-KUO HSUEN HUI, T'AI-PEI *See* JOURNAL OF THE CHINA SOCIETY **5232**

CHUNG-KUO HUA HSUEH HUI, TAIPEI *See* JOURNAL OF THE CHINESE CHEMICAL SOCIETY (TAIPEI) **982**

CHUNG-KUO JEN KUO TUNG CHI NIEN CHIEN (CC) [21881169] **4551**

CHUNG-KUO JEN WU NIEN CHIEN (CC) **2502**

CHUNG-KUO KO CHI SHIH LIAO (CC) [09221468] **5094**

CHUNG-KUO KO HSUEH YUAN HUA NAN CHIH WU YEN CHIU SO CHI KAN / CHUNG-KUO KO HSUEH YUAN HUA NAN CHIH WU YEN CHIU SO (CC) [12278304] **506**

CHUNG-KUO KO HSUEH YUAN. TA CHI WU LI YEN CHIU SO *See* ANNUAL REPORT / INSTITUTE OF ATMOSPHERIC PHYSICS, ACADEMIA SINICA **1420**

CHUNG-KUO KUANG PO TIEN SHIH (CC) [11437441] **1130**

CHUNG-KUO KUNG CH'ENG HSUEH KAN (CH/0253-3839) [04680759] **1968**

CHUNG-KUO KUO CHI FA NIEN KAN / CHUNG-KUO KUO CHI FA HSUEH HUI PIEN CHI (CC) [10929876] **3126**

CHUNG-KUO KUO CHI SHU / ZHONG GUO GUOSHU (CC) [08732910] **2412**

CHUNG-KUO LI SHIH HSUEH NIEN CHIEN (CC) [07480125] **2502**

CHUNG-KUO LI SHIH TI LI LUN TSUNG / CHIH NIEN-HAI CHU PIEN (CC) [08818718] **2649**

CHUNG-KUO LIN YEH / ZHONGGUO LINYE / FORESTRY OF CHINA (CC/0529-6315) [03132555] **2377**

CHUNG-KUO LUN TAN *CEASED.* (CH) [03757988] **2502**

CHUNG-KUO MA TSO (CC) [11613482] **166**

CHUNG-KUO MIEN HUA (CC) [11384720] **166**

CHUNG-KUO NIEN CHIEN (CC) [08574980] **2502**

CHUNG-KUO NUNG MIN CHAN CHENG SHIH YEN CHIU CHI KAN (CC) [06875048] **2649**

CHUNG-KUO NUNG YEH HUA HSUEH HUI *See* CHUNG-KUO NUNG YEH HUA HSUEH. HUI CHIH **972**

CHUNG-KUO NUNG YEH HUA HSUEH. HUI CHIH (CH/0578-1736) [03132629] **972**

CHUNG-KUO NUNG YEH KO HSUEH (CC/0578-1752) [01554615] **74**

CHUNG-KUO PAI KO NIEN CHIEN (CC) [07232978] **2649**

CHUNG-KUO PAN HUA NIEN CHIEN / CHUNG-KUO PAN HUA NIEN CHIEN PIEN CHI WEI YUAN HUI PIEN (CH) [11135346] **377**

CHUNG-KUO PIEN CHIANG SHIH TI YEN CHIU (CC/1002-6800) [27990143] **2683**

CHUNG-KUO SHANG YEH NIEN CHIEN (CC) [21428719] **827**

CHUNG-KUO SHAO NIEN PAO (CC) [05578461] **5798**

CHUNG-KUO SHE HUI CHING CHI SHIH LUN TSUNG / SHAN-HSI SHENG SHE HUI KO HSUEH YEN CHIU SO PIEN (CH) [09332319] **1551**

CHUNG-KUO SHE HUI CHING CHI SHIH YEN CHIU (CH) [10501562] **2649**

CHUNG-KUO SHE HUI HSUEH NIEN CHIEN (CC) **5195**

CHUNG-KUO SHE HUI KO HSUEH (CC) [06656677] **5195**

CHUNG-KUO SHE HUI PAO HSIEN HSUEH HUI *See* SHE HUI PAO HSIEN NIEN KAN **5307**

CHUNG-KUO SHENG WU I HSUEH KUNG CHENG HSUEH PAO (CH/0258-8021) [10248620] **3564**

CHUNG-KUO SHIH PIN (CC) [11578007] **2789**

CHUNG-KUO SHIH PIN KUNG YEH NIEN CHIEN (CC) [16634016] **2331**

CHUNG-KUO SHIH YEN CHIU (CC) [05436424] **2649**

CHUNG-KUO SHIH YU (HK) [14162489] **4253**

CHUNG-KUO SHIH YUNG CHUN (CC) [17682589] **574**

CHUNG-KUO SHU-HUA (HK/0529-6463) [03131066] **377**

CHUNG-KUO SHU MU CHI KAN (CH) [08069365] **413**

CHUNG-KUO SHUI CHAN (CH/0529-6471) [12329154] **2299**

CHUNG-KUO SHUI LI (CC) [19609212] **5532**

CHUNG-KUO SHUI TU PAO CHIH (CC) [10553711] **166**

CHUNG-KUO SHUI WU (CC) [12863686] **4717**

CHUNG-KUO TA LU YEN CHIU (KUO LI CHENG CHIH TA HSUEH. KUO CHI KUAN HSI YEN CHIU CHUNG HSIN) (CH) [14037454] **4518**

CHUNG-KUO TI CHIH HSUEH HUI (TAIPEI, TAIWAN) CHUNG-KUO TI CHIH HSUEH HUI HUI KAN *See* JOURNAL OF THE GEOLOGICAL SOCIETY OF CHINA **1385**

CHUNG-KUO TI CHIH KO HSUEH YUAN YUAN PAO. KUANG CHUANG *See* KUANGCHUANG DIZHI KEXUEYUAN, KUANGCHUANG DIZHI YANJIUSUO SUOKAN **1386**

CHUNG-KUO TI CHIH KO HSUEH YUAN YUAN PAO. KUANG CHUANG TI CHIH YEN CHIU SO FEN KAN *See* KUANGCHUANG DIZHI KEXUEYUAN, KUANGCHUANG DIZHI YANJIUSUO SUOKAN **1386**

CHUNG-KUO TIEN YING NIEN CHIEN / CHUNG-KUO TIEN YING CHIA HSIEH HUI PIEN TSUAN (CC) [09179105] **4065**

CHUNG-KUO TSAO YUAN (CH) [09680376] **451**

CHUNG-KUO TU SHU KUAN HSUEH PAO (CC/1001-8667) [23921554] **3202**

CHUNG-KUO TUI WAI CHING CHI MAO I NIEN CHIEN (HK) [20118927] 1633, **827**

CHUNG-KUO TUI WAI CHING CHI MAO I NIEN CHIEN (HK) [12131445] 827, **1551**

CHUNG-KUO TUI WAI MAO I (CC/0009-4498) [02681972] **827**

CHUNG-KUO TUNG CHI YUEH PAO. ENGLISH. CHINA STATISTICS MONTHLY *See* CHINA MONTHLY STATISTICS / CHINA STATISTICAL INFORMATION AND CONSULTANCY SERVICE CENTRE **5325**

CHUNG-KUO WEN CHE YEN CHIU CHI KAN (CH/1017-6462) [24451557] 4343, **3375**

CHUNG-KUO WEN HSUEH YEN CHIU *CEASED.* (CH) [17476010] **3375**

CHUNG-KUO WEN I NIEN CHIEN (US) [04237541] **3375**

CHUNG-KUO WEN TZU (CHUNG-KUO WEN TZU PIEN CHI WEI YUAN HUI) (US) [09843311] 265, **3273**

CHUNG-KUO WU TZU LIU TUNG (CC) [20743041] **1601**

CHUNG-KUO YIN YUEH NIEN CHIEN / CHUNG-KUO I SHU YEN CHIU YUAN YIN YUEH YEN CHIU SO PIEN (CC) [18812309] **4109**

CHUNG-KUO YU EN (JEN MIN CHIAO YU CHU PAN SHE) (CC/0578-1949) [01554629] **3273**

CHUNG-KUO YU KAN (CH) [10616861] **2785**

CHUNG-KUO YU LIAO (CC) [18631488] **167**

CHUNG-KUO YU YIN-NI (CH) [09350887] **2649**

CHUNG-KYO YU WEN (TAIPEI, TAIWAN) (CH/0578-1930) [02259358] **3273**

CHUNG PAO YUEH KAN (HK) [06652286] **2502**

CHUNG PIEN HSIAO SHUO NIEN PIEN (CH) [09554428] **3375**

CHUNG SHAN (CH) [09038327] **657**

CHUNG-SHAN HSUEH SHU LUN TSUNG (CH) [08965068] **2649**

CHUNG-SHAN TA HSUEH (CANTON, CHINA) *See* CHUNG-SHAN TA HSUEH HSUEH PAO. CHE HSUEH SHE HUI KO HSUEH PAN **5195**

CHUNG-SHAN TA HSUEH HSUEH PAO. CHE HSUEH SHE HUI KO HSUEH PAN (CC/0412-443X) [01797571] **5195**

CHUNG-SO YONGU (KO) [08507053] **2649**

CHUNG TUNG KO KUO MAO I MING LU (CH) [10820893] **827**

CHUNG WAI HUA PAO (HK/0010-9568) [02256723] **2502**

CHUNG WAI WEN HSUEH (CH) [01797546] **3375**

CHUNG WEN FA LU LUN WEN SO YIN / SHENG TSE-LIANG PIEN (CH) [07706892] **2950**

CHUNG WEN HSUEH HSI (HK) [02322446] 3273, **3376**

CHUNG YANG JIH PAO / CENTRAL DAILY NEWS (CH) [16769006] **5798**

CHUNG YANG MIN TSU HSUEH YUAN HSUEH PAO *See* CHUNG YANG MIN TSU TA HSUEH HSUEH PAO / ZHONGYANG MINZU DAXUE XUEBAO **2258**

CHUNG YANG MIN TSU HSUEH YUAN HSUEH PAO / ZHONGYANG MINZU XUEYUAN XUEBAO (CC) [10890020] **2258**

●CHUNG YANG MIN TSU TA HSUEH HSUEH PAO / ZHONGYANG MINZU DAXUE XUEBAO (CC/1000-8667) [30639409] **2258**

CHUNG YANG YEN CHIU YUAN. CHIH WU YEN CHIU SO *See* BOTANICAL BULLETIN OF ACADEMIA SINICA **503**

CHUNG YANG YEN CHIU YUAN. CHIN TAI SHIH YEN CHIU SO *See* CHUNG YANG YEN CHIU YUAN CHIN TAI SHIH YEN CHIU SO CHI KAN **2649**

CHUNG YANG YEN CHIU YUAN CHIN TAI SHIH YEN CHIU SO CHI KAN (CC) [02239291] **2649**

CHUNG YANG YEN CHIU YUAN. HUA HSUEH UEN CHIU SO *See* BULLETIN OF THE INSTITUTE OF CHEMISTRY, ACADEMIA SINICA **963**

CHUNG YANG YEN CHIU YUAN. SHU HSUEH YEN CHIU SO *See* BULLETIN OF THE INSTITUTE OF MATHEMATICS, ACADEMIA SINICA **3498**

CHUNG YANG YEN CHIU YUAN TUNG WU YEN CHUI SO CHI KAN (CH/0001-3943) [02256859] **5580**

CHUNG YANG YEN CHIU YUAN. WU LI YEN CHIU SO *See* ANNUAL REPORT OF THE INSTITUTE OF PHYSICS, ACADEMIA SINICA **4397**

CHUNG YANG YIN HANG *See* ANNUAL REPORT / THE CENTRAL BANK OF CHINA **772**

CHUNG YANG YIN HANG *See* REPORT - CHUNG YANG YIN HANG **807**

CHUNG YANG YIN HANG CHI KAN / CHUNG YANG YIN HANG CHING CHI YEN CHIU CHU PIEN (CH) [10248207] **783**

CHUNG YANG YIN YUEH HSUEH YUAN HSUEH PAO (CC) [09242681] **657**

CHUNG YUAN HUA HSUEH. CHEM (CH) [07030153] **972**

CHUNG YUAN WEN WU (CC) [08867917] **2649**

CHUNGANG CHODAL (KO) [05230595] **4468**

CHUNGARA (CL/0716-1182) [05244964] **266**

CHUNGBUK YONGAM (KO) [01790353] **2649**

CHUNGDUNG KYOYUK UI KISU (KO) [01790354] **1732**

CHUNGGUK KYONGJE SOKPO (HK/1013-5375) [I10135375] **1470**

CHUNGGUK MUNHAK (KO) [04852190] **3376**

CHUNGKWON CHOSA WOLBO. MONTHLY REVIEW (KO) [04973361] **894**

CHUNGKWON HAKHOE CHI (KO) [08044831] **894**

CHUNGKWON KAMDOGWON *See* CHUNGKWON CHOSA WOLBO. MONTHLY REVIEW **894**

CHUNGKWON KUMYUNG (KO) [09087202] **894**

CHUNGKWON TUJA SINTAK (KO) [10077157] **894**

CHUNGNAM KWAHAK YONGUJI / CHAYON KWAHAK YONGUSO (KO) [10175588] **5094**

CHUNGNAM UIDAE CHAPCHI (KO) [13694380] **3564**

CHUNGSO KIOP CHONGBO MONGNOK (KO) [10303665] **5094**

CHUNGSO KIOP. HAEOE KYONGGONGOP (KO) [04360219] **657**

CHUNGSO KIOP KYONGYONG KISUL CHONGBO (KO) [10326379] **657**

CHUNGSO KIOP SONGGONG SARYEJIP (KO) [11479749] **657**

CHUNGSO KIOP UNHAENG *See* ANNUAL REPORT - MEDIUM INDUSTRY BANK **771**

CHUO CHA USHIRIKA (MOSHI, TANZANIA) *See* PROSPECTUS - CO-OPERATIVE COLLEGE, MOSHI **1843**

CHUO DAIGAKU RIKOGAKUBU KIYO (JA) [01790117] **5094**

CHUO DAIGAKU, TOKYO BUNGAKUBU *See* KIYO - CHUO DAIGAKU BUNGAKUBU **5232**

CHUO DAIGAKU, TOKYO. FACULTY OF SCIENCE AND ENGINEERING See BULLETIN - CHUO DAIGAKU, TOKYO. FACULTY OF SCIENCE AND ENGINEERING **1967**

CHUO DAIGAKU, TOKYO. RIKOGAKUBU See CHUO DAIGAKU RIKOGAKUBU KIYO **5094**

CHUO KEIBA NENKAN (JA) [02244904] 4890, **2798**

CHUO KIKUU CHA DAR ES SALAAM See DAR ES SALAAM UNIVERSITY LAW JOURNAL **2959**

CHUO KIKUU CHA DAR ES SALAAM. DAR ES SALAAM UNIVERSITY LAW JOURNAL See UNIVERSITY OF DAR ES SALAAM LAW JOURNAL **3068**

CHUO KIKUU CHA DAR ES SALAAM. INSTITUTE OF RESOURCE ASSESSMENT See ANNUAL REPORT / INSTITUTE OF RESOURCE ASSESSMENT **1597**

CHUO KORON KEIEI MONDAI (JA) [09181617] **1601**

CHUO-KORON KEIEI MONDAI (JA) [01590504] **863**

CHUO KORON / THE CENTRAL REVIEW (JA) [03760507] **2503**

CHUOKORON (JA/0529-6838) [01554651] **5195**

CHUONG VIET (US) [03659148] 1732, **5027**

CHURCH ADMINISTRATION (US/0412-4553) [01776556] **4947**

CHURCH ADVOCATE (FINDLAY, OHIO), THE (US/0009-630X) [04785567] **4947**

CHURCH ALERT (SZ) [04426114] **4947**

CHURCH AND CLERGY FINANCE **CEASED.** (US/0045-6861) [01776557] **783**

CHURCH AND SOCIETY (NEW YORK) (US/0037-7805) [01554654] **4947**

CHURCH AND STATE (US/0009-6334) [06026430] 4947, **4468**

CHURCH & SYNAGOGUE LIBRARIES (US/0009-6342) [01715672] 4947, **3202**

CHURCH BUSINESS (CN/1183-2339) [25882984] **4947**

CHURCH BYTES (US/0884-7193) [12433895] 1174, **4947**

CHURCH EDUCATOR (US/0164-5625) [04405606] **4947**

CHURCH GROWTH (KO) **4947**

CHURCH GROWTH DIGEST (UK/0268-7658) [I02687658] **4947**

CHURCH GROWTH JOURNAL (US) **4947**

CHURCH GROWTH TODAY (US) **4947**

CHURCH HERALD, THE (US/0009-6393) [04038524] **4947**

CHURCH HERITAGE (AT/0156-224X) [I0156224X] **4947**

CHURCH HISTORY (US/0009-6407) [01554659] **4947**

CHURCH LAW & TAX REPORT (US) [18475611] 4947, **2950**

CHURCH MANAGEMENT (US/0009-6431) [01696978] **4947**

CHURCH MEDIA LIBRARY MAGAZINE (US/0884-6197) [12401867] **3202**

CHURCH MINISTRIES WORKER **CEASED.** (US/0888-0255) [13448736] **4947**

CHURCH MISSIONARY SOCIETY See CMS NEWS-LETTER **4948**

CHURCH MONUMENTS (UK/0268-7518) [16787771] **4947**

CHURCH MUSIC QUARTERLY (UK/0307-6334) [03027885] 4947, **4109**

CHURCH MUSIC REPORT : TCMR, THE (US/1071-9903) [22400883] 4947, **4109**

CHURCH MUSICIAN, THE (US/0009-6466) [01607606] 4947, **4109**

CHURCH (NEW YORK, N.Y.) (US/0883-5667) [12173723] **4947**

CHURCH OBSERVER (UK/0009-6482) [03296100] **4947**

CHURCH OF ENGLAND. GENERAL SYNOD See CHURCH OF ENGLAND YEAR BOOK, THE **4947**

CHURCH OF ENGLAND NEWSPAPER : CEN (UK/0964-816X) [09237119] **2514**

CHURCH OF ENGLAND YEAR BOOK, THE (UK/0069-3987) [10191758] **4947**

CHURCH OF GOD MISSIONS (US/0009-6504) [04038535] **4947**

CHURCH OF IRELAND GAZETTE, THE (IE) [14366860] **4947**

CHURCH OF JESUS CHRIST OF LATTER-DAY SAINTS. GENEALOGICAL DEPT See RESEARCH PAPERS : SERIES C - THE GENEALOGICAL DEPARTMENT OF THE CHURCH OF JESUS CHRIST OF LATTER-DAY SAINTS **2470**

CHURCH OF SCOTLAND See YEAR BOOK ... (... YEAR OF ISSUE) / THE CHURCH OF SCOTLAND **5010**

CHURCH OF THE PROVINCE OF SOUTHERN AFRICA See CLERICAL DIRECTORY / CHURCH OF THE PROVINCE OF SOUTHERN AFRICA **4948**

CHURCH PIANIST, THE (US/0890-9032) [14444358] **4110**

CHURCH PROGRAMS FOR MIDDLERS & JUNIORS (US/0273-5059) [07062569] **4947**

CHURCH PROGRAMS FOR PRESCHOOLERS See PRESCHOOL CHILDREN'S CHURCH TEACHER GUIDE **4987**

CHURCH PROGRAMS FOR PRIMARIES (US/0273-5113) [07062010] **4947**

CHURCH QUARTERLY See A.M.E. ZION QUARTERLY REVIEW, THE **5054**

CHURCH RECREATION MAGAZINE **CEASED.** (US/0162-4652) [02980576] 4947, **4849**

CHURCH RESOURCE DIRECTORY (US) [08798985] **4947**

CHURCH SCENE (MELBOURNE, AUSTRALIA) (AT/0009-6563) [14366934] **4948**

CHURCH SECRETARYS COMMUNIQUE (US) **4203**

CHURCH SECRETARY'S SWAP SHOP, THE **CEASED.** (US/0738-6885) [09659766] **4948**

CHURCH TEACHERS **CEASED.** (US/0164-6451) [01590220] **4948**

CHURCH TIMES, THE (US) [04345719] **4948**

CHURCH WOMAN, THE (US/0009-6598) [01554679] 5553, **4948**

CHURCH WORLD (US/0009-6601) [04038541] **5027**

CHURCH WORSHIP (US/1063-9187) [26181918] **4948**

CHURCHMAN (LONDON. 1879) (UK/0009-661X) [01714467] **4948**

CHURCHSCAPE (UK/0262-4966) [I02624966] **295**

CHURYU KONGOP (KO) [10265621] **2366**

CHUSHO KIGYO GIJUTSU JITTAI CHOSA: GIJUTSU KAIHATSU KADAI HOKOKUSHO (JA) [03125051] **5094**

CHUSHO KIGYO KANKEI BUNKEN SAKUIN (JA) [06873194] **4947**

CHUSHO KIGYO KANKEI SHIRYO RISUTO. HOKOKUSHO HEN (JA) [10903874] **657**

CHUSHO KIGYO KEIEI BUNSEKI (JA/0412-4715) [03137019] **863**

CHUSHO KIGYO KINYU KOKO See GYOMU HOKOKUSHO **678**

CHUSHO KIGYO NO CHINGIN JIJO (JA) [02245378] **1659**

CHUSHO KIGYO SHINKO JIGYODAN See CHUSHO KIGYO GIJUTSU JITTAI CHOSA: GIJUTSU KAIHATSU KADAI HOKOKUSHO **5094**

CHUSHO KIGYO SHINKO JIGYODAN See GYOKAI JITTAI CHOSA HOKOKUSHO **678**

CHUSHO KIGYO SHINKO JIGYODAN See GIJUTSU RENKAN CHOSA KENKYU HOKOKUSHO **4003**

CHUSIK (KO) [07959990] **894**

CHUTAEK KUMYUNG (KO) [04473711] **2817**

CHUTANZO TO NETSUSHORI (JA/0387-0502) [10308258] **4000**

CHUTO KENKYU (JA) [15514150] **2768**

CHUTO KIHO (JA) [05578701] **2649**

CHUTO SOGO KENKYU (JA) [03713907] **2649**

CHUVASHSKII IAZYK, LITERATURA I FOLKLOR (RU) [02902663] **3273**

CHYANKUTI (NP) [02239614] **3376**

CIA PUBLICATIONS RELEASED TO THE PUBLIC THROUGH LIBRARY OF CONGRESS DOCEX (US/0190-7794) [08822405] **4638**

CIA WORLD FACTBOOK. CD-ROM (US) **4468**

CIAK SI GIRA (IT) [14995051] 1130, **4065**

CIAO (IT) **1732**

CIAO 2001 (IT) **2950**

CIAO (MONTREAL) (CN/0382-8557) [02370132] **2258**

CIAT INTERNATIONAL (CK) [09838094] **74**

CIB : EDIFICI INTELLIGENTI (IT) **2020**

CIBA FOUNDATION SYMPOSIUM (NE/0300-5208) [01770716] **485**

CIBEDO BEITRAEGE ZUM GESPRACH ZWISCHEN CHRISTEN UND MUSLIMEN (GW) [16949509] **5042**

CIBOLA COUNTY BEACON (US/1071-3506) [22148246] **5712**

CIC (MX) [08695711] **2020**

CIC INFORMA (SP/0211-9919) [I02119919] **607**

CIC INFORMACION TECNICA **SUSPENDED.** (CU) [01783968] **1151**

CICERO LIFE (US) [27238105] **5659**

CICERONE (MIAMI) (US/0193-4244) [05182573] **5466**

CICIM : REVUE POUR LE CINEMA FRANCAISE (GW) **4065**

CICINDELA (US/0590-6334) [01554695] **5580**

CICLO DE CONFERENCIAS (AG) [01785662] **5094**

CIC'S SCHOOL DIRECTORY. ALABAMA (US) [07448576] **1732**

CIC'S SCHOOL DIRECTORY. ARKANSAS (US) [06388789] **1732**

CIC'S SCHOOL DIRECTORY. DISTRICT OF COLUMBIA (US) [08634066] **1732**

CIC'S SCHOOL DIRECTORY. FLORIDA (US) [06407453] **1891**

CIC'S SCHOOL DIRECTORY. IDAHO (US/0743-8184) [08232298] **1891**

CIC'S SCHOOL DIRECTORY. IDAHO See MARKET DATA RETRIEVAL'S CIC SCHOOL DIRECTORY. IDAHO **1762**

CIC'S SCHOOL DIRECTORY. INDIANA (US) [06638978] **1732**

CIC'S SCHOOL DIRECTORY. MAINE See MARKET DATA RETRIEVAL'S CIC SCHOOL DIRECTORY. MAINE **1762**

CIC'S SCHOOL DIRECTORY. MASSACHUSETTS See MARKET DATA RETRIEVAL'S CIC SCHOOL DIRECTORY. MASSACHUSETTS **1762**

CIC'S SCHOOL DIRECTORY. MINNESOTA See MARKET DATA RETRIEVAL'S CIC SCHOOL DIRECTORY. MINNESOTA **1762**

CIC'S SCHOOL DIRECTORY. MISSISSIPPI (US) [07336400] **1891**

CIC'S SCHOOL DIRECTORY. NEW HAMPSHIRE See MARKET DATA RETRIEVAL'S CIC SCHOOL DIRECTORY. NEW HAMPSHIRE **1763**

CIC'S SCHOOL DIRECTORY. NORTH CAROLINA (US) [08327006] **1891**

CIC'S SCHOOL DIRECTORY. PENNSYLVANIA See MARKET DATA RETRIEVAL'S CIC SCHOOL DIRECTORY. PENNSYLVANIA **1763**

CIC'S SCHOOL DIRECTORY. RHODE ISLAND See MARKET DATA RETRIEVAL'S CIC SCHOOL DIRECTORY. RHODE ISLAND **1763**

CIC'S SCHOOL DIRECTORY. VERMONT See MARKET DATA RETRIEVAL'S CIC SCHOOL DIRECTORY. VERMONT **1763**

CIC'S SCHOOL DIRECTORY. WISCONSIN (US) [05766625] **1891**

CICS UPDATE (UK) **1278**

CID : ELECTRONICA Y PROCESO DE DATOS EN CUBA (CU) [10231952] **1174**

CIDA / CENTRE INTERNATIONAL DE DOCUMENTATION ARACHNOLOGIQUE (FR) **5580**

CIDADE DE EVORA, A (PO/0871-1992) [06567933] **2844**

CIDEM EXPRESS (CN/1183-0409) [23598328] **1470**

CIE NATIONAL NEWS (CN/0826-0206) [11807833] **1935**

CIEFL BULLETIN NEW SERIES (II/0970-8340) [03383572] **3273**

●CIEL BLEU (SAINT-EDOUARD) (CN/1191-3851) [26497526] **4890**

CIEL ET ESPACE REVUE (FR/0373-9139) [I03739139] **394**

CIEL ET TERRE (BE/0009-6709) [02067716] 1404, **394**

CIEL VARIABLE :LE MANIFESTE DU TEMPS (CN/0831-3091) [16056783] 4368, **347**

CIENCIA AGRONOMICA (BL/0045-6888) [02969227] **74**

CIENCIA AGROPECUARIA (MX) [24026091] **74**

CIENCIA AL DIA (VE/0529-7281) [01799510] **5094**

CIENCIA & INDUSTRIA FARMACEUTICA **CEASED.** (SP/0210-0819) [11110534] **4296**

CIENCIA BIOLOGICA. B, ECOLOGIA E SISTEMATICA (PO/0870-1695) [I08701695] **2212**

CIENCIA BIOLOGICA. MOLECULAR AND CELLULAR BIOLOGY (PO) [08699663] **534**

CIENCIA DA INFORMACAO (BL/0100-1965) [02989944] **3202**

CIENCIA DEL SUELO (AG/0326-3169) [10447003] **1353**

CIENCIA E CULTURA (SAO PAULO) (BL/0009-6725) [02992970] **5094**

6110

CIENCIA E FILOSOFIA (BL) [06453715] **4343**

CIENCIA E INVESTIGACION (AG/0009-6733) [02445961] **5094**

CIENCIA E INVESTIGACION AGRARIA (CL/0304-5609) [02403413] **74**

CIENCIA E INVESTIGACION FORESTAL (CH/0716-5994) [20287991] **2377**

CIENCIA E NATURA (BL/0100-8307) [09520466] **5094**

CIENCIA E PRATICA (BL/0100-3267) [03723020] 972, **74**

CIENCIA E TECNICA VITIVINICOLA (PO/0254-0223) [12742277] **5094**

CIENCIA E TECNOLOGIA DE ALIMENTOS (BL/0101-2061) [09536241] **4188**

CIENCIA FORESTAL *SUSPENDED.* (MX/0185-2418) [03134320] **2377**

CIENCIA HOJE : REVISAT DE DIVULGACAO CIENTIFICA DA SOCIEDADE BRASILEIRA PARA O PROGRESSO DA CIENCIA (BL/0101-8515) [09961894] 2844, **5094**

CIENCIA INTERAMERICANA *SUSPENDED.* (US/0009-675X) [02445962] **5094**

CIENCIA MEDICA (SP/0212-6052) [02126052] **3564**

CIENCIA (MEXICO CITY, MEXICO) (MX/0185-075X) [01554696] **5094**

CIENCIA PEDIATRIKA (MADRID, SPAIN : 1986) (SP) [18898960] **3902**

CIENCIA PESQUERA / DIRECCION GENERAL DEL INSTITUTO NACIONAL DE LA PESCA (MX/0185-0334) [14912921] **2299**

CIENCIA PHARMACEUTICA (SP) **4296**

CIENCIA PHARMACEUTICA (SP/1131-5253) [28446595] **3740**

CIENCIA POLITICA (CK) [13791032] **4518**

CIENCIA RURAL : REVISTA CIENTIFICA DO CENTRO DE CIENCIAS RURAIS DA UNIVERSIDADE FEDERAL DE SANTA MARIA (BL/0103-8478) [27140358] **74**

CIENCIA TOMISTA (SP/0210-0398) [01774675] **5027**

CIENCIA VETERINARIA JABOTICABAL (BL/0103-006X) [I0103006X] **5507**

CIENCIA Y DESARROLLO (MX/0185-0008) [03896153] **5094**

CIENCIA Y NATURALEZA (EC/0009-6768) [01554700] **5094**

CIENCIA Y TECHNICA EN LA AGRICULTURA. VETERINARIA (CU/0253-5750) [09332789] **5507**

CIENCIA Y TECNICA EN LA AGRICULTURA (CU) [07070812] **74**

CIENCIA Y TECNICA EN LA AGRICULTURA. ARROZ (CU) [07905443] **2331**

CIENCIA Y TECNICA EN LA AGRICULTURA (CENTRO DE INFORMACION Y DOCUMENTACION AGROPECUARIO) (CU) [09966943] **74**

CIENCIA Y TECNICA EN LA AGRICULTURA (CENTRO DE INFORMACION Y DOCUMENTACION AGROPECUARIO) (CU) [09967539] **74**

CIENCIA Y TECNICA EN LA AGRICULTURA. CITRICOS Y OTROS FRUTALES (CU) [09967081] 2331, **167**

CIENCIA Y TECNICA EN LA AGRICULTURA. GANADO PORCINO (CU/0259-2932) [09967349] 74, 5580, **5094**

CIENCIA Y TECNICA EN LA AGRICULTURA. HORTALIZAS, PAPAS, GRANOS Y FIBRAS (CU) [14171598] **74**

CIENCIA Y TECNICA EN LA AGRICULTURA. MECANIZACION DE LA AGRICULTURA (CU/1010-2000) [07905149] **74**

CIENCIA Y TECNICA EN LA AGRICULTURA. PASTOS Y FORRAJES (CU/0259-2924) [09967463] **74**

CIENCIA Y TECNICA EN LA AGRICULTURA. RIEGO Y DRENAJE (CU/1013-9850) [08858128] 167, **2088**

CIENCIA Y TECNICA EN LA AGRICULTURA. TABACO (CU/1013-9869) [09966975] **5372**

CIENCIA Y TECNOLOGIA DEL MAR / COMITE OCEANOGRAFICO NACIONAL (CL/0716-2006) [05910783] **1447**

CIENCIAS ADMINISTRATIVAS (AG/0009-6784) [04797237] **4638**

CIENCIAS AMBIENTALES (CR) [15482343] **2212**

CIENCIAS BIOLOGICAS (CU/0138-7154) [04691965] **451**

CIENCIAS DE LA INFORMACION *SUSPENDED.* (CU/0864-4659) [27693845] **3202**

CIENCIAS DE LA SALUD : ORGANO DE DIFUSION CIENTIFICA DE LA FACULTAD DE CIENCIAS DE LA SALUD, UNIVERSIDAD AUTONOMA DE SANTO DOMINGO (DR) [19462754] **3564**

CIENCIAS DE LA TIERRA Y DEL ESPACIO (CU/0253-5637) [07556538] **1353**

CIENCIAS ECONOMICAS (BL) [02241822] **1590**

CIENCIAS HUMANAS (BL) [04813977] **5195**

CIENCIAS (MADRID), LAS (SP/0009-6776) [03264843] **5095**

CIENCIAS MARINAS (MX/0185-3880) [04308479] **553**

CIENCIAS MEDICAS (BL) [01123371] **3564**

CIENCIAS MEDICAS (NITEROI) (BL/0101-4501) [10550000] **3564**

CIENCIAS TECHNICAS. ARQUITECTURA Y URBANISMO *See* ARQUITECTURA Y URBANISMO **292**

CIENCIAS TECNICAS. INGENIERIA HIDRAULICA *See* INGENIERIA HIDRAULICA (LA HABANA) **2091**

CIENCIAS TECNICAS. TRANSPORTE Y VIAS DE COMUNICACION *See* TRANSPORTE Y VIAS DE COMUNICACION **5397**

CIENCIAS VETERINARIAS (HEREDIA) (CR/0250-5649) [07055592] **5507**

CIENCIAS Y TECNICA EN LA AGRICULTURA. PROTECCION DE PLANTAS (CU/1010-1578) [07905282] **74**

CIENTIFICA (JABOTICABAL) (BL/0100-0039) [02890696] 74, **5507**

CIERVO, EL (SP/0045-6896) [01280357] **4948**

CIFA OCCASIONAL PAPER (IT) [03794590] **2299**

●CIFAR'S GLOBAL COMPANY HANDBOOK (US/1060-8710) [25084212] **657**

CIFRAO; REVISTA DE ECONOMIA E NEGOCIOS (BL) [01787883] **827**

CIFRAS (CK/0120-5331) [I01205331] **5799**

●CIGAR AFICIONADO (US/1063-7885) [26139401] **5372**

CIGGT REPORT (CN/0383-2449) [03213136] **5430**

CII : CONSTRUCTION INDUSTRY INTERNATIONAL (UK) [21400920] **607**

CIIG REVIEW (UK/0309-5347) [I03095347] **607**

CIIR ANNUAL REVIEW (UK) [17343205] **4948**

CIIR JUSTICE PAPERS (UK/1010-1845) [I10101845] **4518**

CIIR NEWS (UK/1010-1853) [I10101853] **4518**

●CIJE ON DISC (US/1073-1113) [29333736] 1732, **1793**

CIJL BULLETIN *See* CIJL YEARBOOK **2950**

●CIJL YEARBOOK (SZ) [26273226] **2950**

CIM BULLETIN (CN/0317-0926) [02340677] **2136**

CIM DIRECTORY (CN/0068-9009) [23302793] **2136**

CIM-MANAGEMENT (GW/0179-2679) [I01792679] **1174**

CIM-PRAXIS (GW/0931-3125) [I09313125] 3476, **1218**

CIM STRATEGIES (US/0748-9250) [11026459] **3476**

CIM TECHNOLOGY : CASA/SME'S MAGAZINE OF COMPUTERS IN DESIGN AND MANUFACTURING *CEASED.* (US) [11617145] **1231**

CIMADE INFORMATION (FR/0181-4788) [I01814788] **4468**

CIMAISE (FR/0009-6830) [01554704] 295, **347**

CIMAL (SP/0210-119X) [07980274] **317**

CIMARRON REVIEW (US/0009-6849) [01554705] **3461**

CIMBEBASIA : JOURNAL OF THE STATE MUSEUM, WINDHOEK (SX/1012-4926) [20362322] **5095**

CIMBEBASIA. MEMOIR (SX/0578-2724) [03145275] **2638**

CIMBRA (SP/0210-0479) [I02100479] **295**

CIMENTS, BETONS, PLATRES, CHAUX (FR/0397-006X) [03006971] 3476, **607**

CIMI NEWS (CN/1189-461X) [25718631] 1240, **4086**

CIMLINC TECHNICAL UPDATE *CEASED.* (US/0896-3444) [17007124] **5095**

CIMMYT REPORT ON MAIZE IMPROVEMENT (MX/0304-548X) [11980936] **74**

CIMMYT REPORT ON WHEAT IMPROVEMENT (MX/0304-5439) [02532506] **200**

CIMMYT REVIEW (MX/0304-5463) [02171783] **167**

CINA (IT/0529-7451) [01554706] **2503**

CINA, LA (CC/1000-9310) [I10009310] **827**

CINA : OFFICIAL JOURNAL OF THE CANADIAN INTRAVENOUS NURSES ASSOCIATION (CN) **3853**

CINAHL NEWS (US) [15322826] **3853**

●CINAHL (PEABODY, MASS.) (US) [29354755] 3853, **3655**

CINCINNATI (US/0009-689X) [04038548] **2530**

CINCINNATI BENGALS REPORT, THE (US/0746-1127) [10341261] **4890**

CINCINNATI BUSINESS COURIER (US/0882-8881) [10783002] **657**

CINCINNATI DENTAL SOCIETY BULLETIN (1979) (US/0894-0975) [15351595] **1319**

CINCINNATI ENQUIRER (CINCINNATI, OHIO : 1872) (US) [12065651] **5727**

CINCINNATI FRESH FRUIT AND VEGETABLE REPORT (US/0744-4095) [08249157] **167**

CINCINNATI JUDAICA REVIEW (US/1066-2863) [22340592] **5047**

CINCINNATI MAGAZINE (US/0746-8210) [10305190] **5466**

CINCINNATI MEDICINE (US/0163-0075) [04284688] **3564**

CINCINNATI. (OHIO). CITY PLANNING COMMISSION *See* ANNUAL REPORT - CINCINNATI CITY PLANNING COMMISSION **2814**

CINCINNATI POETRY REVIEW (US) [02880929] **3461**

CINCINNATI POST (CINCINNATI, OHIO : 1974) (US) [17672784] **5727**

CINCINNATI PURCHASOR (US/0009-6903) [05523006] **949**

CINCINNATI ROMANCE REVIEW (US/0883-9816) [12224943] **3376**

CINCINNATI SYMPHONY ORCHESTRA *See* YEAR BOOK - CINCINNATI SYMPHONY ORCHESTRA **4159**

CINCINNATI SYMPHONY ORCHESTRA *See* HANDBOOK TO THE SEASON / CINCINNATI SYMPHONY ORCHESTRA **4120**

CINCO DIAS (SP) **5810**

CINCOM (US/0742-3632) [05039166] **1106**

CINDA (AU) [01554735] 4446, **4426**

CINE AL DIA (VE/0009-692X) [05111264] **4065**

CINE & MEDIA (BE/1016-9660) 3994, **1106**

CINE ARGENTINO (AG) [06511701] **4065**

CINE BULLES (CN/0820-8921) [09818972] **4065**

CINE CUBANO *SUSPENDED.* (CU/0009-6946) [02259400] **4065**

CINE-FICHES DE GRAND ANGLE, LES (BE/0773-2279) [I07732279] **4065**

CINE NEWS (SI) [03348254] **4368**

CINE TELE REVUE (FR) [20143573] **4065**

CINE Y MAS (SP) **4065**

CINEACTION! (CN/0826-9866) [12734662] **4065**

CINEASTE (NEW YORK, N.Y.) (US/0009-7004) [01780823] **4066**

CINECORRIERE (IT) **4066**

CINEDOSSIER (AT/0813-1600) [I08131600] **4066**

CINEFAN (US/0095-1447) [01796246] **4066**

CINEFANTASTIQUE (US/0145-6032) [02757769] **4066**

CINEFEX (US/0198-1056) [06178827] **4066**

CINEFOCUS (US/1059-0900) [24491310] **4066**

CINEFORUM (IT/0009-7039) [02612559] **4066**

CINEGRAM (US/0145-3483) [02728513] **4066**

CINEMA (FR/0045-6926) [01770717] **4066**

CINEMA 19 (FR) **4066**

CINEMA AU QUEBEC, REPERTOIRE, LE (CN/0225-3151) [06035222] **4066**

CINEMA BLUE (US/0743-8389) [10681651] **2486**

CINEMA D'OGGI (IT/0392-9981) [I03929981] **4066**

CINEMA E CINEMA *CEASED.* (IT) [04675441] **4066**

CINEMA IN INDIA *CEASED.* (II) [15926676] **4066**

CINEMA JOURNAL (US/0009-7101) [02244743] **4066**

CINEMA — Alphabetical Title Index

CINEMA NUOVO (IT/0009-711X) [02259402] **4066**

CINEMA ONE (UK/0578-2988) [03209595] **4066**

CINEMA ORGAN (UK) [02243645] **4110**

CINEMA ORGAN SOCIETY *See* CINEMA ORGAN SOCIETY : NEWSLETTER **5230**

CINEMA ORGAN SOCIETY : NEWSLETTER (UK) [20334809] **5230**

CINEMA PAPERS (AT/0311-3639) [08024821] **4066**

CINEMA (PORTO, PORTUGAL) (PO) [10137717] **4066**

CINEMA PRATIQUE (FR/0009-7128) [03157335] **4066**

CINEMA SOCIETA (IT/0009-7152) [03157392] 5242, **4066**

CINEMA STUDIO (IT) [24488448] **4066**

CINEMA SUD (IT) **4066**

CINEMA TECHNOLOGY (UK) [18535915] **4066**

CINEMA THE WORLD OVER (PK) [02378535] **4066**

CINEMA TV TODAY (UK) [03157458] **4066**

CINEMA (ZURICH, SWITZERLAND) (SZ/1010-3627) [02859779] **4066**

CINEMABOOK (US/0363-9665) [02567857] **4066**

CINEMACABRE *CEASED.* (US/0198-1064) [06294300] **4066**

CINEMACTION (FR/0243-4504) [13384706] **4066**

CINEMAG (CN/0709-5635) [05720218] **4066**

CINEMAGIC (NEW YORK, N.Y.) *CEASED.* (US/0090-3000) [07695186] **4067**

CINEMANTICS (UK) [03157496] **4871**

CINEMART (HK) **2486**

CINEMAS (UK) [08197124] **4067**

CINEMAS (MONTREAL) (CN/1181-6945) [23238248] **4067**

●CINEMATHEQUE : REVUE SEMESTRIELLE D'ESTHETIQUE ET D'HISTOIRE DU CINEMA (FR) [26738388] **4067**

CINEMATOGRAPH (US/0886-6570) [12966160] **317**

CINEMATOGRAPHE, LE (CN/1188-3162) [25796413] **4067**

CINEMAYA (II) [19234070] **4067**

CINEMONKEY (US/0162-0126) [04082345] **4067**

CINESIOLOGIE (FR/0009-7209) [100097209] **3804**

CINEVUE (US/0895-805X) [14000688] 4067, **4368**

CINFAC BIBLIOGRAPHIC REVIEW. SUPPLEMENT (US) [05779751] **4061**

●CINFOLINK DIRECTORY OF INFORMATION SERVICES IN CHINA (CN) [28797208] **3202**

CINQUIEME SAISON (FR/0529-777X) [03158260] **3340**

CINTAMANI (II) [02245571] **5040**

CINTAREA ROMANIEI / REVISTA EDITATA DE CONSILIUL CULTURII SE EDUCATIEI SOCIALISTE *CEASED.* (RM) [07883070] **317**

CINTERFOR (ORGANIZATION) *See* BOLETIN CINTERFOR, OIT **1911**

CINTRAFOR NEWS (US) **2377**

CIO (FRAMINGHAM, MASS.) (US/0894-9301) [16315402] **863**

CIO LETTER, THE *CEASED.* (US/0891-4044) [14757832] **657**

CIOMS CALENDAR (SZ/0379-8100) [04706435] **3564**

CIP CIRCULAR (ENGLISH ED.) (PE/0256-8632) [05237085] **167**

CIP. COVJEK I PROSTOR (CI/0011-0728) [00110728] **295**

CIPA (UK) **1303**

CIPA GUIDE TO THE PATENTS ACTS (UK) **1303**

CIR NEWS / THE COMMITTEE OF INTERNS AND RESIDENTS (US) [08099460] **3564**

CIRA NEWSLETTER (CN/0710-555X) [08777513] **1659**

CIRA PAPER (US/0737-5352) [09404481] **1421**

CIRCA 76 (CN/0383-7890) [03230475] **250**

CIRCA (BELFAST, NORTHERN IRELAND) (UK/0263-9475) [09983837] **347**

CIRCA. CONFLITS INTERNATIONAUX, LES REGIONS ET LE CANADA (CN/0822-8418) [10768409] **4518**

CIRCAEA : BULLETIN OF THE ASSOCIATION FOR ENVIRONMENTAL ARCHAEOLOGY (UK/0268-425X) [17854185] **266**

CIRCE: CAHIERS DU CENTRE DE RECHERCHE SUR L'IMAGINAIRE (FR/0529-7788) [01152790] **4580**

CIRCLE; A PERIODICAL OF REVERSIBLE POETRY (US) [02880962] **3461**

CIRCLE-A-WORD PUZZLES (US/0194-3146) [05397474] **4859**

CIRCLE K (US/0745-1962) [08924432] **1090**

CIRCLE K MAGAZINE *See* CIRCLE K **1090**

CIRCLE (MINNEAPOLIS, MINN.), THE (US/1067-5639) [03175584] **2258**

CIRCLE TRACK (US/1052-9624) [22417780] **4890**

CIRCLEVILLE HERALD (1883 : DAILY) (US) [11696360] **5727**

●CIRCO CRIOLLO : PUBLICACION DE LA ESCUELA DE CIRCO CRIOLLO DE BUENOS AIRES (AG) [28487148] 4859, **384**

CIRCOLAZIONE STRADALE *See* CODICE DELLA STRADA **5379**

CIRCOLAZIONE STRADALE (IT/1120-4141) [11204141] **5379**

CIRCUIT CELLAR INK (US/0896-8985) [17329217] 1264, **1227**

CIRCUIT EQUIPMENT TRADER MAGAZINE *See* CIRCUIT NEWS MAGAZINE **2038**

CIRCUIT FERME (INSTITUT TECCART) (CN/0822-5516) [10092633] **4400**

CIRCUIT (FREDERICTON) (CN/0715-4828) [09344804] **3691**

CIRCUIT INDUSTRIEL (CN/0843-2651) [20125605] **3476**

CIRCUIT (MONTREAL) (CN/0821-1876) [10105717] **3273**

●CIRCUIT (MONTREAL. 1991) (CN/1183-1693) [24256532] **4110**

CIRCUIT NEWS (US/1058-9317) [24443957] **2038**

CIRCUIT NEWS ASSEMBLY (US/1058-9325) [24443862] **2038**

CIRCUIT NEWS (JERICHO) (US/0164-5447) [04576367] **2038**

●CIRCUIT NEWS MAGAZINE (US/1058-9333) [24443643] **2038**

CIRCUIT NEWSLETTER FOR THE CANBERRA MATHEMATICAL ASSOCIATION (AT) **3500**

CIRCUIT RIDER (COLORADO SPRINGS, COLO.), THE (US/1057-8102) [24123276] **4948**

CIRCUIT RIDER (FRANKFORT, KY.), THE (US/0898-0330) [13913613] **2728**

CIRCUIT RIDER (NASHVILLE), THE (US/0146-9924) [03092658] **5058**

CIRCUIT RIDER (SPRINGFIELD, ILL.), THE (US/0741-8264) [03919804] **2443**

CIRCUIT (TORONTO. 1977) (CN/0711-1355) [09099710] **1541**

CIRCUIT WORLD (UK/0305-6120) [04305483] **2038**

CIRCUITREE MAGAZINE (US) **2038**

CIRCUITS (IV) [01787887] **2038**

CIRCUITS ASSEMBLY (US/1054-0407) [22724210] **2038**

CIRCUITS CULTURE PARIS (FR/0751-6037) [07516037] **167**

CIRCUITS, SYSTEMS, AND SIGNAL PROCESSING (US/0278-081X) [07712205] **2039**

CIRCULAIRE AUX PRETRES ET AUTRES AGENTS DE PASTORALE (CN/0227-552X) [08071576] **5027**

CIRCULAIRE D'INFORMATION (CG) [01787970] **819**

CIRCULAIRE D'INFORMATION - FEDERATION NATIONALE DES CHAMBRES DE COMMERCE, D'INDUSTRIE ET D'AGRICULTURE DU CONGO *See* CIRCULAIRE D'INFORMATION **819**

CIRCULAIRE HEBDOMADAIRE DE L'IFRB / UNION INTERNATIONALE DES TELECOMMUNICATIONS, COMITE INTERNATIONAL D'ENREGISTREMENT DES FREQUENCES, IFRB (SW) [15001000] **1151**

CIRCULAIRES DE LA FEDERATION NATIONALE DES PROMOTEURS-CONSTRUCTEURS (FR/0294-7390) [I02947390] **4296**

CIRCULAIRES DU CENTRE DE RECHERCHES ET D'ETUDES OCEANOGRAPHIQUES. I.T (FR/0528-4651) [01125222] **1447**

CIRCULAR (US/0161-2670) [21548650] **1372**

CIRCULAR (ALABAMA AGRICULTURAL EXPERIMENT STATION) (US) [15719912] **74**

CIRCULAR - ASSOCIATION OF AMERICAN RAILROADS, MECHANICAL DIVISION (US/0148-723X) [03354473] **5430**

CIRCULAR - CENTRAL BUREAU FOR ASTRONOMICAL TELEGRAMS, INTERNATIONAL ASTRONOMICAL UNION (US/0081-0304) [01078311] **394**

CIRCULAR - COPYRIGHT OFFICE (US/0082-9692) [01375745] **1303**

CIRCULAR - ENGINEERING EXPERIMENT STATION, OREGON STATE UNIVERSITY (US/0160-3647) [01761388] **1968**

CIRCULAR FARMACEUTICA (SP/0366-6425) [06925450] **4296**

CIRCULAR (FLORIDA COOPERATIVE EXTENSION SERVICE) (US/0099-7676) [08809430] **1541**

CIRCULAR - FUNDACAO INSTITUTO AGRONOMICO DO PARANA (BL/0100-3356) [03966916] **74**

CIRCULAR / GEOLOGICAL SURVEY OF ALABAMA (US/0097-3149) [01478902] **1372**

CIRCULAR - ILLINOIS NATURAL HISTORY SURVEY (US/0073-4926) [01277967] **4164**

CIRCULAR - ILLINOIS STATE GEOLOGICAL SURVEY (US/0073-506X) [10958060] 1438, **2136**

CIRCULAR (INGEOMINAS) (CK/0120-1743) [07494848] **1372**

CIRCULAR / LONDON RICE BROKERS' ASSOCIATION (UK) [06389683] **167**

CIRCULAR - LOUISIANA AGRICULTURAL EXPERIMENT STATION (US/0889-7506) [03996200] **74**

CIRCULAR / NATIONAL AUDUBON SOCIETY (US) [01606448] **5617**

CIRCULAR - NEW JERSEY DEPARTMENT OF AGRICULTURE (US/0275-0600) [05205435] **74**

CIRCULAR (NEW YORK STATE MUSEUM : 1981) (US) [11378024] **2189**

CIRCULAR (OKLAHOMA GEOLOGICAL SURVEY) (US/0078-4397) [01688273] **1372**

CIRCULAR / SOUTH DAKOTA GEOLOGICAL SURVEY (US/0085-6487) [09749219] **1372**

CIRCULAR - STATE OF HAWAII, DEPARTMENT OF LAND AND NATURAL RESOURCES, DIVISION OF WATER AND LAND DEVELOPMENT (US/0438-7619) [01148518] **1413**

CIRCULAR TECNICA (BL/0101-1847) [13340416] **2377**

CIRCULAR TECNICA (CENTRO NACIONAL DE PESQUISA DE ARROZ E FEIJAO) (BL) [07870556] **167**

CIRCULAR TECNICA - CENTRO NACIONAL DE PESQUISA DE TRIGO (BL/0100-8625) [I01008625] **200**

CIRCULAR TECNICA - EMPA-MT (BL/0102-3691) [I01023691] **74**

CIRCULAR TECNICA - EMPAER (BL/0101-9678) [I01019678] **74**

CIRCULAR TECNICA / EMPRESA GOIANA DE PESQUISA AGROPECUARIA (BL/0100-3003) [09386998] **74**

CIRCULAR TECNICA - UNIDADE DE EXECUCAO DE PESQUISA DE AMBITO ESTADUAL DE DOURADOS (BL/0100-6886) [I01006886] **167**

CIRCULAR - UNIVERSITY OF FLORIDA. AGRICULTURAL EXPERIMENT STATIONS (US/0734-8452) [01394893] **74**

CIRCULAR - UNIVERSITY OF GEORGIA. COLLEGE OF AGRICULTURE (US) [01434397] **75**

CIRCULAR / UTAH GEOLOGICAL AND MINERAL SURVEY (US/0097-2924) [01639413] **1372**

CIRCULAR - WEST VIRGINIA GEOLOGICAL AND ECONOMIC SURVEY (US) [07001305] 4253, **1372**

CIRCULAR / WEST VIRGINIA UNIVERSITY AGRICULTURAL AND FORESTRY EXPERIMENT STATION (US/0889-8065) [08748450] **75**

CIRCULARS OF THE AGRICULTURAL REFINANCE AND DEVELOPMENT CORPORATION FROM ... (II) [08945951] 783, **75**

CIRCULARS - SOUTH AFRICAN ASTRONOMICAL OBSERVATORY (SA/0376-7884) [20240543] **394**

CIRCUL'ART (CN/0711-6179) [08489314] **384**

CIRCULATION ET METABOLISME DU CERVEAU (FR/0264-6900) [20293960] **3564**

CIRCULATION IDEA SERVICE (US/1051-8983) [22147016] **4813**

CIRCULATION MANAGEMENT (SPRINGFIELD, OR.) (US/0888-8191) [13727388] **2918**

CIRCULATION (NEW YORK, N.Y.) (US/0009-7322) [01554748] **3702**

CIRCULATION RESEARCH (US/0009-7330) [00856122] **3702**

CIRCULATION RESEARCH (US/0009-7330) [09838230] **3702**

CIRCULATION ROUTIERE: FAITS ET CHIFFRES, LA (FR) [02241874] **5439**

CIRCULATION. SUPPLEMENT (US) [01781871] **3702**

CIRCULATION (WILMETTE, ILL.) (US/0569-6704) [01005578] 757, **922**

CIRCULATION. [MICROFICHE] (US) **3702**

CIRCULATORY SHOCK (US/0092-6213) [01793413] 3795, **3702**

CIRCULATORY SHOCK. SUPPLEMENT (US/0193-7545) [05162203] **3702**

CIRCULO - CIRCULO DE CULTURA PANAMERICANO (US/0009-7349) [02259408] **3376**

CIRCULO POETICO (US) [01947855] **3461**

CIRCUMPOLAR NOTES (CN/1191-1255) [25883155] **5095**

CIRCUMPOLAR NOTES / CIRCUMPOLAR AND SCIENTIFIC AFFAIRS DIRECTORATE, NORTHERN AFFAIRS PROGRAM, DEPARTMENT OF INDIAN AFFAIRS AND NORTHERN DEVELOPMENT (CN/1191-1255) [25883153] **5095**

CIRCUS (NEW YORK, N.Y. 1979) (US/0009-7365) [05396968] **4110**

CIRCUS REPORT, THE (US/0889-5996) [14102930] **4849**

CIRCUS ROCK IMMORTALS (US/0740-7858) [09991872] **4110**

CIRDAP STUDY SERIES (BG) [10465463] **2817**

CIRES, CAHIERS IVOIRIENS DE RECHERCHE ECONOMIQUE ET SOCIALE (IV/1011-839X) [02805761] **1551**

CIRP ANNALS (SZ/0007-8506) [04447337] **2111**

CIRPON, REVISTA DE INVESTIGACION (AG/0326-3789) [13362667] **5606**

CIRUGIA DE URGENCIA **SUSPENDED.** (SP/0213-5353) [I02153353] 3962, **3723**

CIRUGIA DEL URUGUAY (UY/0009-7381) [04336971] **3962**

CIRUGIA ESPANOLA (SP/0009-739X) [11111016] **3962**

CIRUGIA, GINECOLOGIA Y UROLOGIA **See** CIRUGIA ESPANOLA **3962**

CIRUGIA PEDIATRICA : ORGANO OFICIAL DE LA SOCIEDAD ESPANOLA DE CIRUGIA PEDIATRICA (SP) [19022042] **3902**

CIRUGIA PLASTICA IBERO-LATINOAMERICANA (SP/0376-7892) [01924855] **3962**

CIRUGIA Y CIRUJANOS (MX/0009-7411) [01554753] **3962**

CIS : CHROMOSOME INFORMATION SERVICE (JA/0574-9549) [06267349] **451**

CIS DOCUMENTACAO / CENTRO DE INFORMACOES SIDERURGICAS (BL/0103-0078) [11266016] **4000**

CIS FEDERAL REGISTER INDEX (US/0741-2878) [10139759] **4697**

CIS HILINCIWEG (GW) [03690660] **2683**

CIS INDEX TO PUBLICATIONS OF THE UNITED STATES CONGRESS (US/0007-8514) [01564780] 4638, **4697**

CIS LAW REPRINTS. CRIMINAL LAW SERIES : THE SUPREME COURT OF THE UNITED STATES PETITIONS AND BRIEFS (US) [12119561] **3105**

CIS LAW REPRINTS. LABOR LAW SERIES : THE SUPREME COURT OF THE UNITED STATES PETITIONS AND BRIEFS (US) [11609714] **3145**

CIS LAW REPRINTS. SECURITIES REGULATION SERIES : THE SUPREME COURT OF THE UNITED STATES PETITIONS AND BRIEFS (US) [15131400] **2950**

CIS LAW REPRINTS. TAX SERIES : THE SUPREME COURT OF THE UNITED STATES PETITIONS AND BRIEFS (US) [11639149] **4717**

CIS LAW REPRINTS. TRADE REGULATION SERIES : THE SUPREME COURT OF THE UNITED STATES PETITIONS AND BRIEFS (US) [11990916] **3097**

CIS TODAY **See** RUSSIA & CIS TODAY / COMPILED BY THE RFE/AL RESEARCH INSTITUTE MONITORING UNIT **2707**

CIS TODAY **See** CIS TODAY / COMPILED BY RFE/RL RESEARCH INSTITUTE MONITORING UNIT **1130**

●CIS TODAY / COMPILED BY RFE/RL RESEARCH INSTITUTE MONITORING UNIT (RU) [25487089] **1130**

CISA WORKING PAPER (LOS ANGELES, CALIF. : 1985) (US/0897-4705) [12627083] **4518**

CISCO PRESS, THE (US) [14049747] **5748**

CISEM INFORMAZIONI (IT) **1732**

CISILUTE (CN/0704-7282) [04039513] **5782**

CISLA PRO KAZDEHO (XR/0578-3208) [03144584] **5325**

CISLENNYE METODY V DINAMIKE RAZREZENNYH GAZOV (RU/0302-6086) [01792831] **4427**

CISM JOURNAL (CN/0841-8233) [18133410] **2581**

●CISSM PAPERS (US/1065-6391) [26661623] **4518**

CISSNA PARK NEWS, THE (US) [24396683] **5659**

CIST LICNI DOHODAK PO RADNIKU ZA ODREENA ZANIMANJA (YU) [11016882] **1659**

CISTERCIAN FATHERS SERIES (US) [03144611] **5027**

CISTERCIAN STUDIES QUARTERLY (US/1062-6549) [25357253] **5027**

CISTI NEWS (CN/0715-8661) [09960158] **3202**

CIT REAL ESTATE REPORT (US/0743-5630) [10608136] **4835**

CIT TASK FORCE REPORT (AT/1032-3007) [18708840] **5095**

CITADEL SCENE, THE (CN/0317-364X) [02248118] **5363**

CITADEL THEATRE **See** CITADEL SCENE, THE **5363**

CITADELS NEWS **CEASED.** (CN/0846-3492) [25066817] **4890**

CITADIN DE LA GARDEUR (CN/0712-2888) [08808338] **4638**

CITAS LATINOAMERICANAS EN CIENCIAS SOCIALES Y HUMANIDADES : CLASE (MX/0185-0903) [21572527] 2844, **5195**

CITATION (CHICAGO, ILL.) (US/0009-7446) [01554755] **2950**

●CITATIONS FOR SERIAL LITERATURE (US/1061-7434) [25450773] **3202**

CITATOR OF THE DECISIONS OF THE OCCUPATIONAL SAFETY AND HEALTH REVIEW COMMISSION (US/0271-2873) [06577135] **2860**

CITE (HOUSTON, TEX.) (US/8755-0415) [10370551] **295**

CITE LIBRE (1991) (CN/1183-7144) [25313981] **5466**

CITEAUX, COMMENTARII CISTERCIENSES (BE/0774-4919) [02099069] 2683, **5027**

CITEPHILE (CN/0823-616X) [09859866] **5279**

CITES NOUVELLES (CN/0319-5198) [02442296] **5782**

CITHARA (US/0009-7527) [01774678] **4948**

CITIES & VILLAGES (US/0009-7535) [04063238] **4638**

CITIES (LONDON, ENGLAND) (UK/0264-2751) [09930206] **2817**

CITIES OF THE UNITED STATES (US/0899-6075) [18150793] **4638**

CITIES OF THE WORLD (US/0889-2741) [10953007] **5466**

CITIS CD-ROM (IE) 2020, **607**

CITIZEN (US) 2278, **4468**

CITIZEN ACTION (II) [23938020] **2950**

CITIZEN-ADVERTISER, THE (US) [13555239] **5680**

CITIZEN ADVOCACY FORUM (US/1071-2321) [28578105] **5279**

CITIZEN AGENDA (US/1040-1024) [18320725] **3110**

CITIZEN AIRMAN (US/0887-9680) [13302442] 16, **4039**

CITIZEN (AMERICAN FORK, UTAH) (US/8750-4677) [11459523] **5756**

CITIZEN (AUBURN, N.Y.), THE (US/0738-7520) [09672166] **5715**

CITIZEN. CAPITAL IDEAS, THE (CN/0712-1075) [08651975] **5782**

CITIZEN (DENVER), THE (US/0009-7543) [04127562] **4702**

CITIZEN GEORGIAN, THE (US/0883-7007) [12185748] **5652**

CITIZEN (HAMTRAMCK, MICH.), THE (US/1042-6906) [09428424] **5691**

CITIZEN (JAY, OKLA.) (US/0745-7561) [09468991] **5731**

CITIZEN NEWS (US/0191-5134) [05011098] **5645**

CITIZEN NEWS (US) **5742**

CITIZEN NEWS-RECORD (COUNTY ED.), THE (US) **5723**

CITIZEN NEWS-RECORD (ROBBINS ED.), THE (US/0886-3261) [12869432] **5723**

CITIZEN OF MORRIS COUNTY, THE (US) [11721990] **5709**

CITIZEN PARTICIPATION AND VOLUNTARY ACTION ABSTRACTS (US/0360-5698) [01877309] **5279**

CITIZEN PARTICIPATION (CLEVELAND, OHIO) (US/1055-7814) [23237177] **4717**

CITIZEN PARTICIPATION (MEDFORD) **SUSPENDED.** (US/0198-8468) [05928128] **4468**

CITIZEN-PATRIOT, THE (US) [08782332] **5674**

CITIZEN RECORD (US) [10204138] **5686**

CITIZEN (SAINT JOHN, N.B.) (CN/0829-9269) [13563865] **5782**

CITIZEN-STANDARD, THE (US/1053-489X) [18650265] **5735**

CITIZEN-STATESMAN (US/0746-7745) [10262005] **5744**

CITIZEN-TIMES, THE (US) [14195447] **5680**

CITIZEN TRIBUNE (US) **5744**

CITIZEN VOICE & TIMES (US) [11837237] **5680**

CITIZENS' BAND (UK) **1130**

CITIZENS' BUSINESS (US) [03146238] **657**

CITIZENS FOR LAW AND ORDER **See** CLO NEWS **3160**

CITIZENS' GUIDE TO LOCAL GOVERNMENT (OLYMPIA, WASH.) (US) [09883211] **4638**

●CITIZENS HEALTH ALERT (US/1062-1245) [25528958] **4771**

CITIZENS' HOUSING AND PLANNING COUNCIL OF NEW YORK **See** REPORT **2833**

CITIZENS JOURNAL (ATLANTA, TEX.) (US) [13868428] **5748**

CITIZENS LAW ADVISOR (US/0270-8299) [06503433] **2950**

CITIZENS LEAGUE RESEARCH INSTITUTE REPORTS (US) **4638**

CITIZENS MEDIA DIRECTORY **See** TELE-TIPS LONG DISTANCE RATE COMPARISON CHART **1164**

CITIZENS ON CYCLES (ASSOCIATION) **See** BULLETIN - LE MONDE BICYCLETTE **428**

CITIZENS RESEARCH COUNCIL OF MICHIGAN **See** PUBLIC EDUCATION IN MICHIGAN; BACKGROUND PAPER **1775**

CITIZENS RESEARCH COUNCIL OF MICHIGAN **See** COUNCIL COMMENTS **4641**

CITIZENS' RESEARCH FOUNDATION **See** STUDY - CITIZENS' RESEARCH FOUNDATION **5160**

CITIZENSHIP DAY AND CONSTITUTION WEEK GUIDE (US) [02242594] **1918**

CITL MEMBERSHIP DIRECTORY (CN/1184-7840) [24367946] **5379**

CITOLOGIA : REVISTA OFICIAL DE LE SOCIEDAD ESPANOLA DE CITOLOGIA, EN COLABORACION CON LAS SOCIEDADES LATINOAMERICANAS DE CITOLOGIA (SP/0210-1130) [14690879] **535**

CITOLOGIJA I GENETIKA (KIEV) (UN/0564-3783) [10161225] **543**

CITOYEN (CAP-SANTE) (CN/0712-4228) [08716902] **4638**

CITOYEN (COWANSVILLE) (CN/0822-8957) [10638734] **5782**

CITOYEN (NORMETAL) (CN/0229-3943) [08323942] **5782**

CITRA FILM (IO) [08479647] **4067**

CITRANA (NP/0303-2930) [01790451] **2503**

CITROGRAPH (FRESNO, CALIF.) (US/0009-7578) [01771245] **167**

CITRUS AND SUB-TROPICAL FRUIT JOURNAL, THE **CEASED.** (SA/0257-2095) [02403458] **167**

CITRUS AND SUBTROPICAL FRUIT RESEARCH INSTITUTE **See** INLIGHTINSBULLETIN - NAVORSINGSINSTITUUT VIR SITRUS EN SUBTROPIESE VRUGTE **174**

CITRUS COUNTY CHRONICLE **CEASED.** (US) [15802799] 5648, **5649**

CITRUS DEED REPORT (US) **4835**

CITRUS DIGEST (US/0749-4475) [10343511] **1601**

CITRUS FRUIT INDUSTRY STATISTICAL BULLETIN (US/0362-014X) [02441351] 2331, **2362**

CITRUS FRUITS (1976) (US/0883-2870) [03191281] **167**

CITRUS INDUSTRY (BARTOW, FLA. : 1982), THE (US) [11475411] **2331**

CITT NEWS (CN/0227-5708) [10036702] **5379**

CITT NEWSLETTER (CN/1185-1627) [24265771] **5363**

CITTA DI VITA (IT/0009-7632) [07013216] **4948**

CITTA E SOCIETA (IT/0009-7640) [03148448] **2817**

CITTA FUTURA, LA (IT) [03246862] **4540**

CITTA NUOVA, LA (IT) [15377883] **4468**

CITY — Alphabetical Title Index

CITY AND COUNTRY AMERICAN ELSEWHEN ALMANAC, THE (US/0147-6270) [03208056] **2530**

CITY & COUNTRY CLUB LIFE (US/0897-4926) [17514732] **2530**

CITY & COUNTRY HOME *CEASED.* (CN/0715-5689) [09387051] **2904**

CITY AND REGIONAL MAGAZINE DIRECTORY (US/0192-5040) [03904964] **2918**

CITY & SOCIETY (US/0893-0465) [15328645] **2818**

CITY & STATE (CHICAGO, ILL.) (US/0885-940X) [11930690] **4717**

CITY & STATE DIRECTORIES IN PRINT *CEASED.* (US/1043-8939) [19596012] **1924**

CITY AND SUBURBAN TRAVEL *SUSPENDED.* (US/0045-6985) [02259419] **5466**

CITY & TOWN (NORTH LITTLE ROCK, ARK.) (US/0193-8371) [03862739] **4638**

CITY CRIES (UK) [10964068] **4948**

CITY EMPLOYMENT (US/0091-9209) [01788013] **4638**

CITY EMPLOYMENT (US) [02532735] **1659, 4702**

CITY FISCAL CONDITIONS IN ... (WASHINGTON, D.C. : 1986) (US) [14065436] **4717**

CITY GOVERNMENT FINANCES (US/0082-9439) [01796776] **4717**

CITY GUIDE (NEW YORK, N.Y.) (US/1043-3937) [19408690] **5466**

CITY GUIDE (NEW YORK, N.Y.) *See* OFFICIAL CITY GUIDE **5487**

CITY HALL DIGEST (US/0190-0005) [03775561] **4638**

●CITY JOURNAL (NEW YORK, N.Y.), THE (US/1060-8540) [25172204] **4468**

CITY LIGHTS REVIEW (US/1045-1943) [16943310] **3376**

CITY LIMITS (US/0199-0330) [05159232] **5279, 2818**

CITY LIVING (US/0899-0948) [17989129] **2531**

CITY MAGAZINE (WINNIPEG) (CN/0822-790X) [10259244] **4638**

CITY NEWSPAPER (US) [05685007] **5715**

CITY OF BALTIMORE ANNUAL REPORT (US) [06073704] **4638**

CITY OF CHICAGO ... BUDGET RECOMMENDATIONS / AS SUBMITTED TO THE CITY COUNCIL (US) [09285904] **4717**

CITY OF CHICAGO BUILDING CODE (US) [03810122] **607, 2950**

CITY OF CHICAGO/HSA *See* ANNUAL REPORT - CITY OF CHICAGO/HSA **4765**

CITY OF COTE SAINT-LUC HOUSEHOLDER'S DIRECTORY (CN/0318-2339) [02441945] **2558**

CITY OF LETHBRIDGE INFORMATION DIRECTORY (CN) [16859110] **2558**

CITY OF LONDON LAW REVIEW *CEASED.* (UK/0306-9788) [02253841] **2950**

CITY OF LONDON PHONOGRAPH AND GRAMOPHONE SOCIETY *See* HILLANDALE NEWS, THE **4121**

CITY OF LONDON, THE (UK) [01790921] **5466**

CITY OF LOS ANGELES BUILDING CODE (US) [07270759] **607, 2950**

CITY OF LOS ANGELES PLANNING AND ZONING CODE : CHAPTER 1 OF THE LOS ANGELES MUNICIPAL CODE (US) [07270704] **2818**

CITY OF ROCHESTER BUDGET (US/0361-0578) [01908739] **4717**

CITY OF TORONTO INDUSTRIAL DIRECTORY (CN/0828-6280) [12069300] **1601**

CITY ON A HILL (US/0273-7736) [06909559] **1090**

CITY OPERA SPOTLIGHT (US/0737-8009) [09448640] **4110**

CITY PAGES (US/0744-0456) [08027766] **317**

CITY PAPER (US/0195-0843) [05267286] **5686**

CITY PAPER (BALTIMORE, MD.) (US/0740-3410) [09930226] **5686**

CITY PARENT (CN) **4849**

CITY POPULATION ESTIMATES - GEORGIA. STATE DATA CENTER (US/0362-3904) [02299547] **4551**

CITY RECORD (US) [06655056] **4638**

CITY RECORD (CLEVELAND), THE (US/0196-8327) [01901045] **4638**

CITY RECORD, THE (US) [06185968] **4638**

CITY (SAN FRANCISCO, CALIF. 1989), THE (US/1051-3183) [21924692] **2531**

CITY SPORTS MONTHLY *See* METRO SPORTS MAGAZINE **4904**

CITY SUN, THE (US/8750-2720) [10868443] **5715**

CITY WATCH : A RESEARCH BULLETIN OF THE INSTITUTE OF GLOBAL URBAN STUDIES (US) **5242**

CITYBUSINESS (NEW YORK, N.Y.) (US/8756-6249) [11640437] **657**

CITYSCAPE (US/0097-7195) [01799232] **2728**

CITYSCOPE - BRISBANE EDITION (AT) **4835**

CITYSCOPE - CANBERRA (AT) **4835**

CITYSCOPE - GOLD COAST EDITION (AT) **4835**

CITYSCOPE - SPRING HILL EDITION (AT) **4835**

CIUDAD DE DIOS, LA (SP/0009-7756) [05468077] **4948**

CIUDAD Y TERRITORIO (SP) [03151401] **2818, 4638**

●CIUDAD Y TERRITORIO--ESTUDIOS TERRITORIALES (SP) [30578220] **2818**

CIVANANA PUJA MALAR (II) [08756341] **4948**

CIVIC AFFAIRS (II/0009-7772) [01604121] **4638**

CIVIC AFFAIRS (TORONTO) (CN/0045-7027) [01950396] **4638**

CIVIC ARTS REVIEW, THE (US/1047-2169) [20123503] **5242**

CIVIC CENTER NEWSOURCE (US/1067-4357) [24641993] **5634**

CIVIC CINEMA (US/0489-8850) [02079831] **4638**

CIVIC HEALTH OCCASIONAL PAPER (US/0896-2359) [16968065] **4771, 3667**

CIVIC PUBLIC WORKS (CN/0829-772X) [05756229] **4760**

CIVIC TRUST *See* CIVIC TRUST AWARDS **295**

CIVIC TRUST AWARD *See* CIVIC TRUST AWARDS **295**

CIVIC TRUST AWARDS (UK) [07937813] **295**

CIVICA STAZIONE IDROBIOLOGICA DI MILANO *See* QUADERNI DELLA CIVICA STAZIONE IDROBIOLOGICA DI MILANO **471**

CIVICI MUSEI DI STORIA ED ARTE DI TRIESTE *See* ATTI DEI CIVICI MUSEI DI STORIA ED ARTE **4084**

CIVIELE TECHNIEK (NE) 2088, **1968**

CIVIL (SW) [24941719] 4039, **4580**

CIVIL AFFAIRS JOURNAL AND NEWSLETTER (US/0045-7035) [03146717] **4638**

CIVIL AIR PATROL NEWS (US/0009-7810) [04041033] **16**

CIVIL AIRCRAFT AND AIRCRAFT ENGINES (US) [22423176] **16**

CIVIL AIRCRAFT FORECAST (US) **16**

CIVIL & MILITARY LAW JOURNAL (II/0045-7043) [01554794] **3182**

CIVIL AND STRUCTURAL ENGINEERING ABSTRACTS *CEASED.* (US/1063-7338) [26133815] 2020, **2003**

CIVIL AVIATION STATISTICS OF THE WORLD (CN) [04961590] **41**

CIVIL AVIATION TRAINING : CAT (UK/0960-9024) [25529821] **16**

CIVIL CAUSE (BS) [01785774] **2950**

CIVIL CODE (CALIFORNIA) (US) [04650358] **3089**

CIVIL ENGINEER IN SOUTH AFRICA *See* CIVIL ENGINEERING : MAGAZINE OF THE SOUTH AFRICAN INSTITUTION OF CIVIL ENGINEERS / SIVIELE INGENIEURSWESE **2021**

CIVIL ENGINEER IN SOUTH AFRICA *See* JOURNAL OF THE SOUTH AFRICAN INSTITUTION OF CIVIL ENGINEERS / JOERNAAL VAN DIE SUID-AFRIKAANSE INSTITUUT VAN SIVIELE INGENIEURS **2026**

CIVIL ENGINEER IN SOUTH AFRICA, THE (SA/0009-7845) [02259430] **2020**

CIVIL ENGINEERING, CONSTRUCTION & PUBLIC WORKS JOURNAL (II) [02246137] **2020**

CIVIL ENGINEERING CONTRACTOR (SA/0009-7888) [l00097888] **2020**

CIVIL ENGINEERING EDUCATION (US/0884-1926) [05842731] **2020**

CIVIL ENGINEERING IN JAPAN (JA/0578-3747) [02259431] **2020**

●CIVIL ENGINEERING : MAGAZINE OF THE SOUTH AFRICAN INSTITUTION OF CIVIL ENGINEERS / SIVIELE INGENIEURSWESE (SA/1021-2000) [28012032] **2021**

CIVIL ENGINEERING (NEW YORK, N.Y. 1979) (US/0195-3664) [05389262] **2021**

CIVIL ENGINEERING (NEW YORK, N.Y. 1983) (US/0885-7024) [10480594] **2021**

CIVIL ENGINEERING NEWS (MARIETTA, GA.) (US/1051-9629) [22160411] **2021**

CIVIL ENGINEERING / NTIS *See* NTIS ALERT. CIVIL ENGINEERING **2028**

CIVIL ENGINEERING PRACTICE (US/0886-9685) [13048334] **2021**

CIVIL ENGINEERING REPORT SERIES (US/0095-1692) [01796170] **2021**

CIVIL ENGINEERING STUDIES. CONSTRUCTION MATERIALS RESEARCH SERIES (US/1058-9929) [24456455] **2021**

CIVIL ENGINEERING STUDIES. GEOTECHNICAL RESEARCH SERIES (US/0734-9971) [08903964] **2021**

CIVIL ENGINEERING SURVEYOR (UK/0266-139X) [l0266139X] **2021**

CIVIL ENGINEERING SYSTEMS (UK/0263-0257) [10142450] **2021**

●CIVIL ENGINEERING YEOVILLE (SA/1021-2000) [I10212000] **2021**

●CIVIL ENGINEERS AUSTRALIA (AT) [28566997] **1968**

CIVIL JUSTICE QUARTERLY (UK/0261-9261) [08512318] **3089**

CIVIL LAW OPINIONS OF THE JUDGE ADVOCATE GENERAL, UNITED STATES AIR FORCE (US/0748-7657) [09663347] **3089**

CIVIL LIBERTIES (US/0045-7051) [04041074] **5760**

CIVIL LIBERTIES ALERT : A LEGISLATIVE NEWSLETTER OF THE AMERICAN CIVIL LIBERTIES UNION/WASHINGTON OFFICE (US) [03919338] **4506**

CIVIL LIBERTIES IN TEXAS *SUSPENDED.* (US/0749-3061) [10547640] **4506**

CIVIL LIBERTIES (NEW YORK, N.Y.) (US/0009-790X) [01554799] **4506**

CIVIL LIST OF GAZETTED EMPLOYEES UNDER THE GOVERNMENT OF MEGHALAYA, AS ON 1ST JANUARY ... (II) [10214621] **4638**

CIVIL LITIGATION REPORTER (US/0199-0802) [05366622] **3089**

CIVIL PRACTICE ANNUAL OF NEW YORK (US) [01606511] **3089**

CIVIL PRACTICE LAW & RULES OF THE STATE OF NEW YORK : CPLR (US) [08782477] **3089**

CIVIL PROCEDURE (US/0099-1244) [02239707] **3089**

CIVIL PROTECTION (UK/0961-2564) [l09612564] **1072**

CIVIL RICO LITIGATION REPORTER (US) [15649734] **3097**

CIVIL RICO REPORT (US/0884-0032) [12144317] 3097, **3089**

CIVIL RIGHTS (US) [12208295] **4506**

CIVIL RIGHTS & CIVIL LIBERTIES LITIGATION : A GUIDE TO [SECTION SYMBOL] 1983 / SHELDON H. NAHMOD (US) [09484966] **4506**

CIVIL RIGHTS DIRECTORY (US/0360-1587) [02239734] **4506**

CIVIL RIGHTS EMPLOYMENT REPORTER *See* FAIR EMPLOYMENT REPORT **1669**

CIVIL RIGHTS LITIGATION AND ATTORNEY FEES ANNUAL HANDBOOK (US/0887-1191) [13043364] **4506**

CIVIL RIGHTS MONITOR (US) [13746572] **4506**

CIVIL RIGHTS MONITOR (US/1063-9454) [13746562] **2613**

CIVIL RIGHTS UPDATE (US/0893-0473) [03655242] **4506**

CIVIL RIGHTS (VANCOUVER) (CN/0824-7552) [11463182] **4506**

CIVIL SERVANT, THE (NR/0331-085X) [02240430] **4702**

CIVIL SERVICE COURT DIGEST, THE (US/0272-006X) [06212620] **4702**

CIVIL SERVICE POETRY (UK) [04260487] **3461**

CIVIL SERVICE REPORTER (QUEZON CITY) (PH/0300-3620) [01440327] **4702**

CIVIL SEVICE YEAR BOOK, THE (UK) [01793318] **4638**

CIVIL WAR (BERRYVILLE, VA.) (US/0897-6015) [17562051] **2728**

CIVIL WAR CHRONICLES (US/1070-3756) [28119643] **2728**

CIVIL WAR COLLECTORS' DEALER DIRECTORY, THE (US/0094-1182) [01794046] 2772, **250**

CIVIL WAR HISTORY (US/0009-8078) [01554809] **2728**

CIVIL WAR NEWS, THE (US/1053-1181) [19582427] **2728**

CIVIL WAR REGIMENTS (US/1055-3266) [23152974] **2728**

CIVIL WAR ROUND TABLE DIGEST (US/0009-8086) [03146903] **2728**

CIVIL WAR SERIALS & BIBLIOGRAPHY (US/1059-4302) [23936892] **2728**

CIVIL WAR TIMES ILLUSTRATED (US/0009-8094) [01554811] **2728**

Alphabetical Title Index — CLASSIC

CIVIL WAR TOKEN JOURNAL, THE (US) [18827259] **2780**

CIVIL WORKS WATER RESOURCES DEVELOPMENT PROGRAM (US) [06289137] **5532**

CIVILIAN-BASED DEFENSE (US/0886-6015) [12953190] **4039**

CIVILIAN LABOR FORCE, EMPLOYMENT, UNEMPLOYMENT AND UNEMPLOYMENT RATE (US/0145-4137) [02732578] **1659**

CIVILIAN LABOR FORCE ESTIMATES FOR NORTH CAROLINA (US) [13773621] **1659**

CIVILIAN MANPOWER STATISTICS (US/0882-8857) [07849813] **4039**, **4061**

CIVILISATIONS (BE/0009-8140) [01554814] **234**, **5242**

CIVILISATIONS ET SOCIETES (FR/0069-4290) [03209569] **5268**

CIVILITA DEL BERE (IT/0390-1572) [I03901572] **2366**

CIVILITA VENEZIANA. FONTI E TESTI. SERIE TERZA : LETTERE, MUSICA E TEATRO (IT/0578-4034) [03176167] **2683**

CIVILTA CATTOLICA, LA (IT/0009-8167) [01774680] **5027**

CIVILTA CIBERNETICA *SUSPENDED*. (SM/0258-5308) [I02585308] **5095**

CIVILTA CLASSICA E CRISTIANA *CEASED*. (IT/0392-8632) [07829601] **3273**

CIVILTA DELLA CAMPANIA (IT) [02504305] **2683**

CIVILTA MANTOVANA *CEASED*. (IT/0391-7479) [04071488] **2683**

CIVILTA PADANA (IT) [20708759] **2683**

CIVILTA VENEZIANA. FONTI E TESTI. SER. 1 : FONTI E DOCUMENTI PER LA STORIA DELL'ARTE VENETA (IT/0069-4355) [01554816] **347**

CIVILTA VENEZIANA. SAGGI (IT/0069-4371) [03209093] **5268**

CIVILTA VENEZIANA. STUDI (IT/0069-438X) [03545674] **2683**

CIVIS MUNDI (NE/0030-3283) [05248639] **4540**

CIVITAN MAGAZINE, THE (US/0194-5785) [04853124] **5230**

CIVITAS (SZ) [04071928] **1090**

CIVITAS (IT/0009-8191) [06085274] **4468**

CIVITAS (MADRID, SPAIN) (SP) [21577559] **3145**

CIVITAS. REVISTA ESPANOLA DE DERECHO ADMINISTRATIVO (SP/0210-8461) [05373552] **3092**

CIVITAS. REVISTA ESPANOLA DE DERECHO DEL TRABAJO (SP/0212-6095) [I02126095] **2951**

CIZI JAZYKY VE SKOLE (XR) [06141232] **1732**

CJ EUROPE (US/1059-2423) [24516294] **3160**

CJ INTERNATIONAL (US/0882-0244) [11777838] **3105**, **3160**

●CJ MANAGEMENT & TRAINING DIGEST (US) **3160**

C:JET (US/0198-6554) [03428587] **2918**

CJO : CANADIAN JOURNAL OF OPTOMETRY (CN/0834-2245) [16349238] **4215**

CKS YAPAN YABANC ZIYARETCILER ANKETI (TU) [20370887] **5466**

CLA HANDBOOK AND MEMBERSHIP DIRECTORY / CATHOLIC LIBRARY ASSOCIATION (US) [02068998] **3202**

CLA JOURNAL (US/0007-8549) [02445986] **3376**, **3273**

CLACKAMAS COUNTY REVIEW, THE (US/0746-0260) [09694254] **5733**

CLACKAMAS LEGACY (US/1047-4358) [20698558] **2443**

CLACKMANNAN DISTRICT OFFICIAL GUIDE (UK) [12229768] **2558**

CLADISTICS (US/0748-3007) [10921118] **451**

CLAFLIN REVIEW, THE (US/0895-5182) [15188553] **1090**

CLAIBORNE PROGRESS (US) [14983145] **5744**

CLAIMANTS UNDER THREAT (UK/0265-1866) [I02651866] **1225**

CLAIMS ADMINISTRATION DIGEST COURT DECISIONS *See* CLAIMS ADMINISTRATION, INSURANCE, TORT COURT DECISIONS DIGEST **2878**

CLAIMS ADMINISTRATION, INSURANCE, TORT COURT DECISIONS DIGEST (US/0743-3840) [10534975] **2878**

CLAIMS ADMINISTRATION, WORKERS' COMPENSATION COURT DECISIONS DIGEST (US/0743-3859) [10535857] **2878**

CLAIMS COLLECTION HANDBOOK (US) [05780937] **2818**

CLAIMS FORUM (US/0364-3603) [02640295] **827**, **2951**

CLAIMS MANAGEMENT (US) **3086**

CLAIMS (SEATTLE, WASH.) (US/0895-7991) [16909630] **2878**

CLAIMS TERM LISTS (US) **972**

CLAIR FOYER *See* FAMILLE MAGAZINE **2279**

CLAIRLIEU : TIJDSCHRIFT GEWIJD AAN DE GESCHIEDENIS DER KRUISHEREN (BE) [05064146] **4948**, **2683**

CLAIRON (MONTREAL) (CN/0710-099X) [08601794] **5016**

CLAIRVOYANT (MONTREAL) (CN/0843-0578) [20125656] **4385**

CLALLAM COUNTY GENEALOGICAL SOCIETY BULLETIN (US) **2443**

CLAMOR / COMMITTEE FOR THE DEFENSE OF HUMAN RIGHTS IN THE SOUTHERN CONE, SAO PAULO'S ARCHDIOCESAN PASTORAL COMMISSION FOR HUMAN RIGHTS AND THE MARGINALIZED (BL) [14281700] **4506**

CLAMOR (LAREDO, TEX.) (US/0894-1904) [15866649] **2531**

CLAN. CARIBBEAN LABORATORY ACTION NEWS (JM/1018-9041) [I10189041] **3564**

CLAN CHATTER (US/0731-3845) [08161114] **2443**

CLAN DIGGER (US/8755-3635) [11269006] **2443**

CLAN MACNEIL ASSOCIATION OF AMERICA *See* GALLEY (HARRISONBURG, VA.), THE **2449**

CLANCI I GRADA ZA KULTURNU ISTORIJU ISTOCNE BOSNE (BN) [06164110] **2684**

CLANDESTINE CONFIDENTIAL *CEASED*. (US) **1130**

CLANDIGGER (EDMONTON) (CN/0226-2436) [08023753] **2443**

CLANTON ADVERTISER, THE (US/1050-2084) [21214781] **5625**

CLAO JOURNAL, THE (US/0733-8902) [08652706] **3873**

CLAREMONT DAILY PROGRESS (US) [12100119] **5731**

CLARENCE COURIER (CLARENCE, MO. : 1946 (US) [18976348] **5703**

CLARENDON NEWS (1990), THE (US/1048-8170) [21027358] **5748**

CLARIDAD (SANTURCE, P.R.) (PR/0279-313X) [04990208] **3376**

CLARIN, BUENOS AIRES. INDICE (AG) [02240738] **5814**, **5777**

CLARIN : REVISTA DE CULTURA (SP) **3461**

CLARINDA, IOWA HERALD-JOURNAL, THE (US) [15728262] **5669**

CLARINET AND SAXOPHONE (UK) [07594857] **4110**

CLARINET & SAXOPHONE SOCIETY (GREAT BRITAIN) *See* YEAR BOOK & REGISTER OF MEMBERS / CLARINET AND SAXOPHONE SOCIETY **4159**

CLARINET (POCATELLO, IDAHO), THE (US/0361-5553) [02381020] **4110**

CLARINETTE MAGAZINE (FR/0761-9553) [11508278] **4110**

CLARINETWORK *CEASED*. (US/0733-3544) [08561577] **4110**

CLARION (US) [01554822] **1090**

CLARION CALL (SAN FRANCISCO, CALIF.), THE (US/0896-8071) [17291723] **4948**

CLARION (CAPREOL) (CN/0316-0211) [02624114] **5782**

CLARION-LEDGER, JACKSON DAILY NEWS, THE (US/0746-3421) [08058499] **5700**

CLARION-LEDGER, THE (US/0744-9526) [08674244] **5700**

CLARION (MILLTOWN, IND.) (US) [12198922] **5663**

CLARION (NEW YORK, 1971), THE (US/0197-6850) [04279936] **347**

CLARION (NEW YORK. 1972) (US/0191-8079) [04080825] **1815**

CLARION NEWS (US) [29431225] **5663**

CLARION NEWS, THE (US) [02259441] **5735**

CLARION TECH JOURNAL, THE (US/1044-4750) [19795269] **5095**

●CLARISWORKS JOURNAL (US/1059-6542) [24656669] **1174**

CLARK CLARION, THE (US/0883-2692) [04328186] **2443**

CLARK COUNTY CLIPPER (ASHLAND, KAN. : 1976) (US) [10085900] **5674**

CLARK COUNTY FARM BUREAU NEWS (MARTINSVILLE, ILL.) (US/0746-4533) [10050035] **75**

CLARK COUNTY GENEALOGICAL SOCIETY *See* C.C.G.S. NEWSLETTER **2441**

CLARK COUNTY HISTORY (US/0090-449X) [01785087] **2728**

CLARK COUNTY JOURNAL (US) [11330549] **5663**

CLARK COUNTY KIN (US) [17671813] **2443**

CLARK COUNTY PRESS (NEILLSVILLE, WIS. : 1938) (US) [13143729] **5766**

CLARKE BURTON NEWS ANALYSIS (US/1051-0915) [21815255] **1240**

CLARKE BURTON REPORT (US/1048-4620) [20954523] **1106**

CLARKE COUNTY DEMOCRAT, THE (US) [10957705] **5625**

CLARKE COUNTY TRIBUNE, THE (US) [16260914] **5700**

CLARKE COURIER (BERRYVILLE, VA.) (US) [11704653] **5758**

●CLARK'S BANK DEPOSITS AND PAYMENTS MONTHLY (US/1063-2220) [25931285] **783**

CLARK'S DIRECTORY OF SOUTHERN HOSPITALS (US/0069-4428) [02441496] **3778**

CLARK'S GUIDE TO AMERICA'S ANTIQUE SHOPS (US/0272-0175) [06715937] **250**

CLARKSBURG EXPONENT, THE (US) [12818751] **5763**

CLARKSBURG TELEGRAM (CLARKSBURG, W.VA. : DAILY) (US) [12819626] **5763**

CLARKSDALE PRESS REGISTER, THE (US) [15003806] **5700**

CLARKSON TETRAULT REGULATORY REPORTER *See* MCCARTHY TETRAULT REGULATORY REPORTER **1160**

CLARKSTON HERALD (CLARKSTON, WASH. : 1973) (US) [16993010] **5760**

CLARKSVILLE STAR, THE (US) [10860561] **5669**

CLARKSVILLE TIMES, THE (US/1040-2489) [10151683] **5748**

CLAROSCURO (CK) [05670071] **4087**

CLASS ACT (US) **1732**

CLASS ACTION REPORTS (US/0746-7168) [02083856] **2951**

CLASS/BRAND QTR$ (US/8756-1212) [08161891] **757**

CLASS / CANADIAN LADIES ASSOCIATION OF SHOOTING SPORTS (CN/0713-052X) [08584577] **5553**, **4890**

CLASS I FREIGHT RAILROADS SELECTED EARNINGS DATA / INTERSTATE COMMERCE COMMISSION, BUREAU OF ACCOUNTS (US) [10760194] **5430**

CLASS (MILAN, ITALY) (IT) [15188459] **1470**, **657**

CLASS (NEW YORK, N.Y.) (US/0747-3826) [10786281] **2486**

CLASS OF ... EMPLOYMENT REPORT AND SALARY SURVEY (US/0882-5025) [11859159] **1659**

CLASS RACEHORSES OF AUSTRALIA AND NEW ZEALAND (AT/0814-2513) [I08142513] **2798**

CLASS STRUGGLE (US) [04346136] **4540**

CLASS UPDATE (US/1056-0904) [23461545] **3202**

CLASSIC (US) [05742180] **2798**

●CLASSIC AMUSEMENTS (US/1066-6281) [27017932] **2772**

CLASSIC & MOTORCYCLE MECHANICS (UK) **4081**

CLASSIC AND SPORTSCAR (UK) **5411**

CLASSIC AUTO RESTORER (US/1042-5683) [19084687] **5411**

CLASSIC BIKE (UK/0142-890X) [I0142890X] **1294**

CLASSIC CAR (US/0009-8310) [04042079] **250**, **2772**, **5411**

CLASSIC CAR BIMONTHLY (US/0740-4794) [08037594] **250**, **5411**

CLASSIC CAR CLUB OF AMERICA *See* HANDBOOK AND DIRECTORY - CLASSIC CAR CLUB OF AMERICA **5416**

CLASSIC CAR DIGEST (US) **2772**, **5411**

●CLASSIC CD (U.S. ED.) (US/1070-4574) [23366459] **4110**

CLASSIC COLLECTOR, THE (US/0093-1918) [01791777] **347**

CLASSIC CROSSWORD PUZZLES (US/0199-5588) [05987157] **4859**

CLASSIC CYCLE REVIEW (US/1054-3147) [22841335] **4948**

CLASSIC FILM/VIDEO IMAGES *See* CLASSIC IMAGES **4067**

CLASSIC IMAGES (US/0275-8423) [07236510] **4067**

CLASSIC

CLASSIC MG YEARBOOK, THE (US/0098-2741) [02239680] **5411**

CLASSIC MOTOR CYCLE, THE (UK/0263-0850) [08018350] **5379**

CLASSIC RACER (UK) **4849**

CLASSIC TOY TRAINS (US/0895-0997) [16455991] **2772**

CLASSICA ET MEDIAEVALIA (DK) [01770718] 2684, **1075**

CLASSICAL *SUSPENDED.* (AT) **4110**

CLASSICAL ACCORDIONIST (US) **4110**

CLASSICAL AND MEDIEVAL LITERATURE CRITICISM (US/0896-0011) [16885265] **3376**

CLASSICAL AND MODERN LITERATURE (US/0197-2227) [05986688] 3340, **1075**

CLASSICAL AND QUANTUM GRAVITY (UK/0264-9381) [10389833] **4400**

CLASSICAL ANTIQUITY (US/0278-6656) [07870789] **1075**

CLASSICAL ASSOCIATION *See* PROCEEDINGS OF THE CLASSICAL ASSOCIATION **3312**

CLASSICAL ASSOCIATION OF NEW ENGLAND *See* BULLETIN / CLASSICAL ASSOCIATION OF NEW ENGLAND **1075**

CLASSICAL BULLETIN (ST. LOUIS, MO.), THE (US/0009-8337) [01554841] **1075**

CLASSICAL CALLIOPE (US/0271-1966) [06568005] **1062**

CLASSICAL CATALOGUE (UK/0961-5237) [23290349] 4110, **5316**

CLASSICAL FORUM (US) [01713875] **1075**

CLASSICAL GUITAR (UK/0950-429X) [09957235] 4110, **1075**

CLASSICAL JOURNAL (CLASSICAL ASSOCIATION OF THE MIDDLE WEST AND SOUTH), THE (US/0009-8353) [01554844] **1075**

CLASSICAL MUSIC (UK) [06184154] **4110**

CLASSICAL MUSIC MAGAZINE (MISSISSAUGA) (CN/1185-9717) [24333475] **4110**

CLASSICAL NUMISMATIC REVIEW (US) [23667486] **2780**

CLASSICAL OUTLOOK, THE (US/0009-8361) [01554847] **1075**

CLASSICAL PHILOLOGY (US/0009-837X) [01166972] **1075**

CLASSICAL QUARTERLY (UK/0009-8388) [01166978] **1075**

CLASSICAL RAG (SILVER SPRING, MD.) (US/0736-5632) [09135086] **2531**

CLASSICAL REVIEW (UK/0009-840X) [01554850] **1076**

●CLASSICAL RUSSIA (US/1070-9711) [28523019] **1076**

CLASSICAL STUDIES (ODENSE) (DK) [01772317] **1076**

CLASSICAL WORLD, THE (US/0009-8418) [01554851] **1076**

CLASSICI URANIA (IT/1120-4966) [11204966] **5074**

CLASSICO GIALLO (IT) **3461**

CLASSICS CHRONICLE (US/1070-7557) [28475302] **3376**

CLASSICS IN EDUCATION (US/0069-4495) [01554852] **1732**

CLASSICS IN PSYCHOANALYSIS *CEASED.* (US/0735-0341) [10304488] **4581**

CLASSICS OF WESTERN SPIRITUALITY (US) [05429032] **4948**

CLASSIFICATION: A CLASSIFICATION SCHEME FOR THE INSPEC DATABASE /INSPEC (UK) [23729058] **3202**

CLASSIFICATION AND HANDBOOK OF DAHLIAS (XXU) [14693698] **2412**

CLASSIFICATION AND PAY PLAN - (TALLAHASSEE) DIVISION OF PERSONNEL (US/0092-0142) [01788291] **4638**

CLASSIFICATION, ASSETS AND LOCATION OF REGISTERED INVESTMENT COMPANIES UNDER THE INVESTMENT COMPANY ACT OF 1940 (US/0192-5997) [04745810] **894**

CLASSIFICATION AUTOMATIQUE ET PERCEPTION PAR ORDINATEUR (FR) **1174**

CLASSIFICATION CANADIENNE DESCRIPTIVE DES PROFESSIONS (CN) [05700624] **4203**

CLASSIFICATION NUMBERS AND INDEXES (US) [04169424] **2818**

CLASSIFICATION PLAN AND SALARY SCHEDULE (US) [04765870] **4638**

CLASSIFIED BUSINESS DIRECTORY OF THE STATE OF CONNECTICUT (US/0069-4517) [03563272] **657**

CLASSIFIED DIRECTORY OF MEMBERS - LAHORE CHAMBER OF COMMERCE & INDUSTRY *CEASED.* (PK) [02246802] **819**

CLASSIFIED DIRECTORY OF WISCONSIN MANUFACTURERS *CEASED.* (US/0069-4525) [04359483] **3476**

CLASSIFIED ELEMENTARY SCHOOLS AND APPROVED KINDERGARTENS (WEST VIRGINIA. DIVISION OF INSTRUCTIONAL LEARNING SYSTEMS : 1981) (US) [09886743] **1732**

CLASSIFIED INDEX OF DECISIONS OF THE REGIONAL DIRECTORS OF THE NATIONAL LABOR RELATIONS BOARD IN REPRESENTATION PROCEEDINGS (US/0190-4310) [03929444] **3145**

CLASSIFIED INDEX OF DISPOSITIONS OF ULP CHARGES BY THE GENERAL COUNSEL OF THE NATIONAL LABOR RELATIONS BOARD (US/0147-7250) [03220240] **1659**

CLASSIFIED INDEX OF NATIONAL LABOR RELATIONS BOARD DECISIONS AND RELATED COURT DECISIONS *SUSPENDED.* (US/0092-4962) [01789332] **3145**

CLASSIFIED INDEX, TRULY AGREED TO AND FINALLY PASSED HOUSE AND SENATE BILLS (US) [06109569] **2951**

CLASSIFIED TRADE DIRECTORY OF MEMBERS (LEEDS CHAMBER OF COMMERCE) (UK) [06698099] **819**

CLASSIQUES AFRICAINS (FR/0578-459X) [03157983] **3376**

CLASSIQUES FRANCAIS DU MOYEN-AGE (FR/0755-1959) [01554855] **1076**

CLASSMATE (CN/0315-906X) [01980122] 2844, **1732**

CLASSROOM (AT/0727-1255) [07271255] 1222, **1891**

CLASSROOM COMPUTING (AT/0726-2132) [07262132] 1891, **1222**

CLASSROOM PRACTICES IN TEACHING ENGLISH (US/0550-5755) [06036362] 1891, **3273**

CLAT NEWS (VE) [12681826] **1659**

CLAT REPORT (US/0257-7151) [12746967] **1659**

CLAUDE MONTEFIORE LECTURES *CEASED.* (UK) [20716777] **5047**

CLAUDEL STUDIES (US/0090-1237) [01784780] 431, **3376**

CLAUDIA *CEASED.* (MX/0009-8515) [06924717] **2531**

CLAUSTHALER GEOLOGISCHE ABHANDLUNGEN (GW/0009-8523) [03160497] **1372**

CLAUSTHALER TEKTONISCHE HEFTE (GW/0069-4584) [03159275] **1353**

CLAUSTRO (MX) [09429785] **2728**

CLAVE DE SOL (CK) [01786042] **3376**

CLAVE (HAVANA, CUBA) (CU) [17280517] **4110**

CLAVIER (US/0009-854X) [01554858] **4110**

CLAVIER'S PIANO EXPLORER (US/0279-0858) [07518779] **4110**

CLAY CENTER DISPATCH (1930) (US) [10129696] **5675**

CLAY CITY TIMES, THE (US) [14447214] **5680**

CLAY COUNTY FREE PRESS (US) [12768375] **5763**

CLAY COUNTY LEADER, THE (US) [14265334] **5748**

CLAY MINERALS (UK/0009-8558) [04431169] **1438**

CLAY RESEARCH (II/0255-7193) [10387593] **1353**

CLAY RESOURCES BULLETIN (US/0069-4592) [01696721] **2137**

CLAY SCIENCE (JA/0009-8574) [01554865] **1353**

CLAY TIMES-JOURNAL, THE (US/1053-9123) [22413044] **5625**

CLAYMORE (CONVENT STATION), THE (US/0163-9943) [04553758] **2728**

CLAYS AND CLAY MINERALS (US/0009-8604) [02244738] **1438**

CLAYS IN ... (US) [05512594] **1438**

CLAYTON COMPLETIONS FORECAST *See* CLAYTON COMPLETIONS REPORT **2818**

●CLAYTON COMPLETIONS REPORT (CN/1193-6517) [27202858] **2818**

CLAYTON CONSUMER REPORT (CN/1183-7446) [24623600] **1294**

CLAYTON COUNTY REGISTER, THE (US) [15465447] **5669**

CLAYTON-FILLMORE REPORT, THE (US/1047-6083) [20730965] 1551, **4835**

CLAYTON HOUSING FORECAST (CN/1183-8442) [25796341] **2818**

CLAYTON HOUSING REPORT (CN/1183-8434) [25423612] **2818**

CLAYTON NEIGHBOR, THE (US/0192-074X) [04997741] **5652**

CLAYTON NEWS (US) [26057377] **5723**

CLAYTON RECORD, THE (US) [11793798] **5626**

CLAYTON SUN (US/0199-7270) [06105378] **5652**

CLAYTON TRIBUNE, THE (US) [19096936] **5652**

CLAYWORKER (UK) [02485358] **607**

CLC TODAY *CEASED.* (CN/0848-7448) [23658949] **1659**

CLE BULLETIN (US/0148-4346) [03308746] **2951**

CLE JOURNAL AND REGISTER, THE (US) [17389361] 1815, **2951**

CLE TV: THE LAWYERS' VIDEO MAGAZINE (US) [20443072] **2951**

CLEAN AIR (UK/0300-5143) [02445996] **2226**

●CLEAN AIR ACT COMPLIANCE GUIDE UPDATE (US/1074-7729) [29825200] **3110**

●CLEAN AIR AND ENVIRONMENTAL PROTECTION (UK) [26513749] **2163**

CLEAN AIR (HEIDELBERG) (AT/0009-8647) [06402560] **2226**

CLEAN AIR NEWSLETTER (US) **2163**

CLEAN AIR PERMITS (US/1070-0099) [28227952] **2951**

CLEAN COAL TECHNOLOGIES (US/0896-517X) [17197524] 1023, **1935**

CLEAN CURRENTS / HALIFAX HARBOUR CLEANUP INC (CN/1187-3612) [25127931] **2226**

CLEAN FUEL VEHICLE WEEK (US/1059-2202) [24514572] **4253**

CLEAN FUELS REPORT, THE (US/1051-3116) [20865531] 1935, **4253**

CLEAN WATER ACTION NEWS (US/0277-8467) [07641627] **5532**

CLEAN WATER REPORT (US/0009-8620) [02445999] 2226, **5532**

CLEAN WATER (WASHINGTON) (US/0092-9433) [01788589] 2226, **5532**

CLEAN WATERS FOR OHIO (US/0529-9268) [03161327] **2190**

CLEAN YIELD, THE (US/0882-3820) [11828835] **895**

CLEANERS AND DYERS ADVERTISER *See* AMERICAN DRYCLEANER **5347**

CLEANFAX (COLUMBUS, OHIO) (US/1042-6442) [19099181] **5349**

CLEANING AND CARING FOR BOOKS (UK) [10682764] **4828**

CLEANING & MAINTENANCE (UK) **5349**

CLEANING AND RESTORATION (US/0886-9901) [13132019] 1023, **5349**

CLEANING BUSINESS (US) **657**

CLEANING INDUSTRY YEARBOOK (UK/0961-4729) [I09614729] **5349**

CLEANING MAINTENANCE AND BIG BUILDING MANAGEMENT (UK/0143-0963) [07009825] **607**

CLEANING MANAGEMENT *See* CLEANING MANAGEMENT MAGAZINE **863**

CLEANING MANAGEMENT MAGAZINE (US/1051-5720) [18250034] **863**

CLEANROOMS (FLEMINGTON, N.J.) (US/1043-8017) [19568566] **2860**

CLEAR LAKE COURIER (US) [12812895] **5743**

CLEAR PURPOSE, COMPLETE COMMITMENT (US) [08943219] **3202**

CLEAR TRACK (US/0193-3477) [05177825] **5430**

CLEARFIELD CHRONICLE, THE (US) [16830103] **5669**

CLEARING (US) **2163**

CLEARING & SETTLEMENT (UK/0964-671X) [I0964671X] **783**

CLEARING (ELIZABETHTOWN, N. Y.), THE (US/1054-8998) [23009201] **2818**

CLEARING HOUSE (MENASHA, WIS.) (US/0009-8655) [04220688] **1732**

CLEARING UP (US/0738-2332) [09548195] **4760**

CLEARING UP. CALIFORNIA ENERGY MARKETS (US/1044-2022) [19715162] **1601**

CLEARINGHOUSE ADELL *See* CLEARINGHOUSE ADELL'S CATALOG OF ADULT EDUCATION PROJECTS **1800**

CLEARINGHOUSE ADELL'S CATALOG OF ADULT EDUCATION PROJECTS (US/0191-4561) [04790094] **1800**

CLEARINGHOUSE BULLETIN / CARRYING CAPACITY NETWORK (US/1066-5404) [26991020] **2163**

●CLEARINGHOUSE DIRECTORY, THE (US/1053-0460) [22441490] **1924**

CLEARINGHOUSE FOR FEDERAL SCIENTIFIC AND TECHNICAL INFORMATION (U.S.) *See* PB - U.S. CLEARINGHOUSE FOR FEDERAL SCIENTIFIC AND TECHNICAL INFORMATION **5137**

CLEARINGHOUSE REVIEW (US/0009-868X) [01483611] **3179**

CLEARWATER NAVIGATOR (US/0747-2218) [10635219] **2226**

CLEARWATER TIMES (CLEARWATER, KAN. : 1963) (US) [12759389] **5675**

CLEARWATER TRIBUNE (US) [13205793] **5656**

CLEARWATERS (US/0164-2030) [03483933] **5532**

CLEARY NEWS (US/0883-7716) [12225058] **2443**

CLEBURNE COUNTY HISTORICAL SOCIETY JOURNAL (US/0740-5987) [04164227] **2728**

CLEBURNE NEWS (HEFLIN, ALA.) (US) [12590376] **5626**

CLEBURNE TIMES-REVIEW (US) [14091798] **5748**

CLEC. CARIB-LATIN ENERGY CONSULTANT (TR/0253-0538) [03107888] **1935**

CLEF, LA (CN) **2951**

CLEFS C.E.A (FR/0298-6248) [14262307] **4446**

CLEFT PALATE-CRANIOFACIAL JOURNAL (US/1055-6656) [23093057] **3962**, **3564**

CLEIRPPA INFOS PARIS (FR/1146-2965) [11462965] **3750**

CLEM LABINE'S TRADITIONAL BUILDING (US/0898-0284) [17692812] **295**

CLEMENTS' ENCYCLOPEDIA OF WORLD GOVERNMENTS (US/0145-9686) [02811397] **4468**

CLEMENTS' ENCYCLOPEDIA OF WORLD GOVERNMENTS. BIANNUAL SUPPLEMENT (US/0733-0286) [03297962] **4468**

CLEMSON UNIVERSITY *See* ANNOUNCEMENTS ... RECORD - CLEMSON UNIVERSITY **1808**

CLEMSON UNIVERSITY. DEPT. OF FORESTRY *See* DEPARTMENT OF FORESTRY TECHNICAL PAPER **2378**

CLEMSON UNIVERSITY. WATER RESOURCES RESEARCH INSTITUTE *See* REPORT - WATER RESOURCES RESEARCH INSTITUTE, CLEMSON UNIVERSITY **5538**

CLENEXCHANGE (MILFORD, OHIO : 1984) (US) [11409846] **3202**

CLEO (AT/0310-1797) [I03101797] **5553**

CLEO-SCHRIFTEN (BE/0250-7692) [I02507692] **75**

●CLERGY FOCUS (US/1061-527X) [25343722] **4948**

CLERGY JOURNAL (US) [01988309] **4948**

CLERGY MALPRACTICE ALERT *SUSPENDED*. (US/0893-3596) [15515107] **4948**, **2951**

CLERICAL DIRECTORY / CHURCH OF THE PROVINCE OF SOUTHERN AFRICA (SA) [21601080] **4948**

CLERICAL OFFICERS AND TYPISTS LISTS (HK/0376-7914) [02242228] **4638**

CLERK & LINDSELL ON TORTS (UK) **2951**

CLERK OF WORKS (UK/0020-2789) [08828770] **607**

CLERMONT SUN (BATAVIA, OHIO : 1854) (US) [09842286] **5727**

CLEVELAND ADVOCATE (CLEVELAND, TEX.), THE (US/0746-7125) [10221778] **5748**

CLEVELAND AREA METROPOLITAN LIBRARY SYSTEM *See* CAMLS NEWS **3199**

CLEVELAND BAR JOURNAL (1968) (US/0160-1598) [03610578] **2951**

CLEVELAND BUSINESS REVIEW (US/0164-453X) [04723539] **657**

CLEVELAND CLINIC JOURNAL OF MEDICINE (US/0891-1150) [14576751] **3564**

CLEVELAND DAILY BANNER (US) [17636484] **5744**

CLEVELAND EAST SUBURBAN DIRECTORY (CUYAHOGA COUNTY, OHIO) (US) [04794792] **2558**

CLEVELAND ENGINEERING (US/0009-8809) [04040873] **1968**

CLEVELAND ENTERPRISE (CLEVELAND, OHIO. 1991) (US/1059-3055) [24384731] **657**, **1601**

CLEVELAND JEWISH NEWS, THE (US/0009-8825) [01967206] **5727**

CLEVELAND MAGAZINE (US/0160-8533) [03776028] **2486**

CLEVELAND-MARSHALL LAW NOTES (US/0145-1545) [02703247] **2951**

●CLEVELAND METRO EAST MARKETING DIRECTORY (US) [23379983] **657**

●CLEVELAND METRO WEST MARKETING DIRECTORY (US) [23380010] **657**

CLEVELAND MUSEUM OF ART *See* BULLETIN OF THE CLEVELAND MUSEUM OF ART, THE **345**

●CLEVELAND NOW (US/1062-1431) [25532009] **2531**

CLEVELAND (OHIO) *See* CITY RECORD (CLEVELAND), THE **4638**

CLEVELAND ORCHESTRA *See* CLEVELAND ORCHESTRA AT SEVERANCE HALL, THE **4110**

CLEVELAND ORCHESTRA AT SEVERANCE HALL, THE (US) [10356583] **4110**

CLEVELAND PARENT (US/1060-8222) [25080035] **2278**

CLEVELAND PHYSICIAN (US) [06116178] **3564**

CLEVELAND STATE LAW REVIEW (US/0009-8876) [01798161] **2951**

CLI REPORT (CN) [01787683] **2190**

CLIA LOSS PREVENTION BULLETIN / CANADIAN LAWYERS INSURANCE ASSOCIATION (CN/1186-8694) [24623621] **2951**

CLIC QUARTERLY *CEASED*. (US/0736-0045) [08874717] **863**, **3202**

CLICHES (FR) [10690164] **4368**

CLICK LONDON. 1973 (UK/0142-1042) [I01421042] **3273**

CLIENT *See* TQS : TOTAL QUALITY SALES **767**

CLIENT COUNSELING UPDATE : CCU (US/0276-752X) [07079087] **2951**

CLIENT (MONTREAL) (CN/1183-9236) [25066723] **863**

CLIENT SERVER (UK/0964-8844) [I09648844] **1174**

CLIENT/SERVER COMPUTING (US/1059-3470) [24569804] **1174**

CLIENT SERVER REPORT, THE *CEASED*. (US/1056-7844) [23852726] **1174**

●CLIENT/SERVER TODAY (US) **1174**

CLIENTS MONTHLY ALERT (US) **741**

CLIFTON RECORD, THE (US) [14108857] **5748**

CLIJ (SP/0214-4123) [I02144123] **1062**, **3376**

CLIMAT (MONTREAL) (CN/0715-9897) [10008023] **1421**

CLIMATE ALERT (US/1071-328X) [18574673] **1421**

CLIMATE ANALYSIS CENTER (U.S.) *See* DAILY WEATHER MAPS. WEEKLY SERIES / NATIONAL OCEANIC AND ATMOSPHERIC ADMINISTRATION, NATIONAL WEATHER SERVICE, NATIONAL METEOROLOGICAL CENTER, CLIMATE ANALYSIS CENTER **1424**

CLIMATE CONTROL (II/0009-8930) [01554916] **2604**

CLIMATE DIAGNOSTICS BULLETIN (US/1048-6747) [11459457] **1421**

CLIMATE DYNAMICS (GW/0930-7575) [14770228] **1421**

CLIMATE MONITOR *SUSPENDED*. (UK/0140-458X) [03985399] **1422**

CLIMATE OF ALBERTA WITH DATA FOR YUKON AND NORTHWEST TERRITORIES, REPORT (CN/0383-3593) [02246722] **1422**

CLIMATE OF TROPICAL AFRICA (FR) **1422**

CLIMATE RESEARCH (GW/0936-577X) [22630859] **1422**

CLIMATIC ATLAS OF EUROPE (SZ) [01770172] **1422**

CLIMATIC CHANGE (NE/0165-0009) [03045407] **1422**

CLIMATIC DATA SHEETS (CN) [03251436] **1422**

CLIMATIC PERSPECTIVES (CN/0225-5707) [06132913] **1422**

CLIMATOGRAPHY OF THE UNITED STATES (US/0565-4564) [05104966] **1422**

CLIMATOLOGIA (SAO PAULO, BRAZIL) (BL) [02414739] **1422**

CLIMATOLOGICAL BULLETIN (MONTREAL) (CN/0541-6256) [01589923] **1422**

CLIMATOLOGICAL DATA. ALABAMA (US/0145-0050) [04506505] **1422**

CLIMATOLOGICAL DATA. ALASKA (US/0364-5762) [04506619] **1422**

CLIMATOLOGICAL DATA, ANNUAL SUMMARY. NEBRASKA (US) [06128504] **1422**

CLIMATOLOGICAL DATA, ANNUAL SUMMARY. NEW ENGLAND (US) [06128067] **1422**

CLIMATOLOGICAL DATA, ANNUAL SUMMARY. SOUTH DAKOTA (US) [06158312] **1422**

CLIMATOLOGICAL DATA. ARIZONA (US/0145-0387) [04506663] **1422**

CLIMATOLOGICAL DATA. ARKANSAS (US/0364-605X) [04506684] **1422**

CLIMATOLOGICAL DATA. CALIFORNIA (US/0145-0069) [04506704] **1422**

CLIMATOLOGICAL DATA. COLORADO (US/0145-0506) [04506722] **1422**

CLIMATOLOGICAL DATA. FLORIDA (US/0145-0484) [04506739] **1422**

CLIMATOLOGICAL DATA FOR AMUNDSEN-SCOTT, ANTARCTICA (US/0148-5628) [03322627] **1422**

CLIMATOLOGICAL DATA FOR JAKARTA OBSERVATORY (IO) [04169170] **1422**

CLIMATOLOGICAL DATA. GEORGIA (US/0145-0492) [04506768] **1422**

CLIMATOLOGICAL DATA. HAWAII AND PACIFIC (US/0095-4373) [04506836] **1422**

CLIMATOLOGICAL DATA. IDAHO (US/0145-0514) [04506848] **1422**

CLIMATOLOGICAL DATA. ILLINOIS (US/0145-0522) [04506862] **1423**

CLIMATOLOGICAL DATA. INDIANA (US/0145-0530) [04506933] **1423**

CLIMATOLOGICAL DATA. IOWA (US/0145-0468) [04506946] **1423**

CLIMATOLOGICAL DATA. KANSAS (US/0145-0417) [04506957] **1423**

CLIMATOLOGICAL DATA. KENTUCKY (US/0145-0433) [04507008] **1423**

CLIMATOLOGICAL DATA. LOUISIANA (US/0145-0409) [04507018] **1423**

CLIMATOLOGICAL DATA. MARYLAND AND DELAWARE (US/0145-0549) [04507029] **1423**

CLIMATOLOGICAL DATA. MICHIGAN (US/0145-045X) [04507039] **1423**

CLIMATOLOGICAL DATA. MINNESOTA (US/0145-0476) [04507054] **1423**

CLIMATOLOGICAL DATA. MISSISSIPPI (US/0145-0425) [04507068] **1423**

CLIMATOLOGICAL DATA. MISSOURI (US/0364-6068) [04507090] **1423**

CLIMATOLOGICAL DATA. MONTANA (US/0145-0395) [04507129] **1423**

CLIMATOLOGICAL DATA. NEBRASKA (US/0145-0441) [04507138] **1423**

CLIMATOLOGICAL DATA. NEVADA (US/0364-5312) [04507148] **1423**

CLIMATOLOGICAL DATA. NEW ENGLAND (US/0364-5339) [04507155] **1423**

CLIMATOLOGICAL DATA. NEW JERSEY (US/0364-5614) [04507166] **1423**

CLIMATOLOGICAL DATA. NEW MEXICO (US/0364-5622) [04507178] **1423**

CLIMATOLOGICAL DATA. NEW YORK (US/0364-5606) [04507194] **1423**

CLIMATOLOGICAL DATA. NORTH CAROLINA (US/0145-0794) [04507203] **1423**

CLIMATOLOGICAL DATA. NORTH DAKOTA (US/0364-5029) [04507223] **1423**

CLIMATOLOGICAL DATA. OHIO (US/0364-5584) [04507228] **1423**

CLIMATOLOGICAL DATA. OKLAHOMA (US/0364-4960) [04507239] **1423**

CLIMATOLOGICAL DATA. OREGON (US/0364-5851) [04507396] **1423**

CLIMATOLOGICAL DATA. PENNSYLVANIA (US/0364-5843) [04507490] **1423**

CLIMATOLOGICAL DATA. PUERTO RICO AND VIRGIN ISLANDS (US/0500-4780) [04507528] **1423**

CLIMATOLOGICAL DATA. SOUTH CAROLINA (US/0364-5037) [04507552] **1424**

CLIMATOLOGICAL DATA. SOUTH DAKOTA (US/0364-5045) [04507661] **1424**

CLIMATOLOGICAL DATA. TENNESSEE (US/0364-5010) [04507691] **1424**

CLIMATOLOGICAL DATA. TEXAS (US/0364-6041) [04507712] **1424**

CLIMATOLOGICAL DATA. UTAH (US/0364-5592) [04507732] **1424**

CLIMATOLOGICAL DATA. VIRGINIA (US/0364-5630) [04507751] **1424**

CLIMATOLOGICAL DATA. WASHINGTON (US/0364-5320) [04507787] **1424**

CLIMATOLOGICAL DATA. WEST VIRGINIA (US/0364-5371) [04507812] **1424**

CLIMATOLOGICAL DATA. WISCONSIN (US/0364-5304) [04507839] **1424**

CLIMATOLOGICAL DATA. WYOMING (US/0364-5002) [04507889] **1424**

CLIMATOLOGICAL — Alphabetical Title Index

CLIMATOLOGICAL STUDIES (DOWNSVIEW) (CN/0068-7715) [02603610] **1424**

CLIMBER AND HILL WALKER (UK/0955-3045) [I09553045] 4871, **4849**

CLIMBING (ASPEN, COLO.) (US/0045-7159) [04040888] 4890, **4871**

CLIN-ALERT (US/0069-4770) [01554917] 4296, **3564**

CLIN D'OEIL - CENTRE HOSPITALIER DES BOIS-FRANCS (CN/0821-2252) [09428103] **5279**

CLIN D'OEIL (VILLE MONT-ROYAL) (CN/0711-0340) [08555780] 1083, **402**

CLINCH VALLEY NEWS, THE (US/8750-1171) [11000710] **5758**

CLINCH VALLEY TIMES (US) **5758**

CLINICA (UK/0144-7777) [08649895] **3564**

CLINICA & TERAPIA CARDIOVASCOLARE (IT/0392-1344) [16410036] **3703**

CLINICA ANESTESIOLOGICA *CEASED.* (SP/0210-4660) [I02104660] **3565**

CLINICA CARDIOVASCULAR (SP/0212-1808) [17193811] **3703**

CLINICA CHIMICA ACTA (NE/0009-8981) [02259463] 3893, **972**

CLINICA CHIRURGICA DEL NORD AMERICA, LA (IT) **3962**

CLINICA DIETOLOGICA, LA (IT/0392-7318) [08424883] **4188**

CLINICA E INVESTIGACION EN ARTERIOSCLEROSIS (SP) [26050203] **3703**

CLINICA E INVESTIGACION EN GINECOLOGIA Y OBSTETRICIA (SP/0210-573X) [08060397] **3758**

CLINICA E LABORATORIO (ROMA) (IT/0391-2035) [05731931] **3565**

CLINICA EUROPEA *CEASED.* (IT/0009-9007) [03226669] **3565**

CLINICA GINECOLOGICA, LA (IT/0529-9608) [01362141] **3758**

CLINICA MEDICA DEL NORD AMERICA (IT) **3778**

CLINICA OCULISTICA E PATOLOGIA OCULARE (IT/0391-8998) [I03918998] **3893**

CLINICA ODONTOIATRICA DEL NORD AMERICA (IT/0393-7593) **1319**

CLINICA PEDIATRICA *SUSPENDED.* (IT/0009-9058) [03180185] **3902**

CLINICA RURAL (SP/0210-7945) [I02107945] **3565**

CLINICA TERAPEUTICA, LA *CEASED.* (IT/0009-9074) [01554922] **3565**

CLINICA VETERINARIA; RASSEGNA DI POLIZIA SANITARIA E DI IGIENE *SUSPENDED.* (IT/0009-9082) [01554923] **5508**

CLINICA Y ANALISIS GRUPAL (SP/0210-0657) [04295977] **4581**

CLINICAL ABSTRACTS/CURRENT THERAPEUTIC FINDINGS (US/1043-3031) [19379418] **4296**

●CLINICAL ADVANCES IN CARDIO-RESPIRATORY CARE (US/1073-1644) [29350485] 3703, **3949**

CLINICAL ADVANCES IN GASTROENTEROLOGY (US/1046-7165) [20496784] **3743**

CLINICAL ALLERGY AND IMMUNOLOGY SERIES (US) **3667**

CLINICAL ALLERGY. SUPPLEMENT (UK/0263-4848) [08891820] **3667**

CLINICAL ANATOMY (NEW YORK, N.Y.) (US/0897-3806) [17469528] **3679**

CLINICAL ANATOMY (NORWALK, CONN.) (US/0891-2238) [14642375] **3565**

●CLINICAL AND APPLIED THROMBOSIS / HEMOSTATIS (US) **3703**

CLINICAL AND BIOCHEMICAL ANALYSIS (US/0095-4861) [01160526] 1014, **485**

●CLINICAL AND DIAGNOSTIC LABORATORY IMMUNOLOGY (CD-ROM) (US/1071-4138) [28638641] **3667**

●CLINICAL AND DIAGNOSTIC LABORATORY IMMUNOLOGY (PRINT) (US/1071-412X) [28638632] **3667**

●CLINICAL AND DIAGNOSTIC VIROLOGY (NE/0928-0197) [28707312] **561**

CLINICAL AND EXPERIMENTAL ALLERGY (UK/0954-7894) [19251541] **3667**

CLINICAL AND EXPERIMENTAL DERMATOLOGY (UK/0307-6938) [02163925] **3718**

●CLINICAL AND EXPERIMENTAL HYPERTENSION (1993) (US/1064-1963) [26226768] 3796, **3703**

CLINICAL AND EXPERIMENTAL HYPERTENSION. PART A, THEORY AND PRACTICE (US/0730-0077) [07939555] **3703**

CLINICAL AND EXPERIMENTAL HYPERTENSION. PART B, HYPERTENSION IN PREGNANCY (US/0730-0085) [07939493] 3703, **3758**

CLINICAL AND EXPERIMENTAL IMMUNOLOGY (UK/0009-9104) [01554926] **3667**

●CLINICAL AND EXPERIMENTAL METABOLISM (UK/1072-1630) [28873325] **3668**

CLINICAL & EXPERIMENTAL METASTASIS (UK/0262-0898) [09776900] **3815**

CLINICAL AND EXPERIMENTAL NEUROLOGY (US/0196-6383) [05748485] **3830**

CLINICAL AND EXPERIMENTAL NUTRITION (US/0888-7748) [10551089] **4188**

CLINICAL AND EXPERIMENTAL OBSTETRICS & GYNECOLOGY (IT/0390-6663) [03995609] **3758**

CLINICAL AND EXPERIMENTAL OPTOMETRY (AT/0816-4622) [13770921] **4215**

CLINICAL AND EXPERIMENTAL PHARMACOLOGY & PHYSIOLOGY (AT/0305-1870) [00972372] 579, **4296**

CLINICAL AND EXPERIMENTAL PHARMACOLOGY & PHYSIOLOGY. SUPPLEMENT (UK/0143-9294) [01402412] **4296**

CLINICAL AND EXPERIMENTAL RHEUMATOLOGY (IT/0392-856X) [09404208] **3565**

CLINICAL AND INVESTIGATIVE MEDICINE (UK/0147-958X) [03711976] **3565**

CLINICAL AND LABORATORY HAEMATOLOGY (UK/0141-9854) [05735199] **3771**

CLINICAL AND LABORATORY HAEMATOLOGY. SUPPLEMENT (UK/0960-3964) [I09603964] **3771**

CLINICAL AND SCIENTIFIC SESSIONS (US/0197-6958) [06069878] **3853**

CLINICAL APHASIOLOGY (US/0195-7015) [05536150] **3830**

CLINICAL APPROACHES TO PROBLEMS OF CHILDHOOD (US/0069-4797) [02259464] **3902**

CLINICAL ASPECTS OF BIOMEDICINE (NE) [25962586] **3565**

CLINICAL AUTONOMIC RESEARCH : OFFICIAL JOURNAL OF THE CLINICAL AUTONOMIC RESEARCH SOCIETY (UK/0959-9851) [23835817] **3565**

CLINICAL BIOCHEMIST REVIEWS (AT/0159-8090) [08944059] **485**

CLINICAL BIOCHEMISTRY (NE) [01787185] **485**

CLINICAL BIOCHEMISTRY (GW) [20103132] **485**

CLINICAL BIOCHEMISTRY (NEW YORK, N.Y.) (US/0009-9120) [01554928] **485**

CLINICAL BIOCHEMISTRY REVIEWS (ELMSFORD, N.Y.) *CEASED.* (US/0272-9881) [15076029] **485**

CLINICAL BIOFEEDBACK AND HEALTH *CEASED.* (CN/0827-1038) [12227851] **4581**

CLINICAL BIOMECHANICS (US/0191-7870) [04896285] **3917**

CLINICAL BIOMECHANICS (BRISTOL) (UK/0268-0033) [13991445] **3565**

CLINICAL BIOTECHNOLOGY *CEASED.* (US/1046-3305) [20379398] **3691**

CLINICAL CANCER LETTER, THE (US/0164-985X) [04274503] **3815**

CLINICAL CARDIOLOGY ALERT (US/0741-4218) [09846287] **3703**

CLINICAL CARDIOLOGY (LOS ALTOS , CALIF.) (US/0891-2092) [09654354] **3703**

CLINICAL CARDIOLOGY (MAHWAH, N.J.) (US/0160-9289) [03792174] **3703**

CLINICAL CHEMICA (OULU) (FI/0358-4879) [04788391] 485, **3565**

CLINICAL CHEMISTRY AND ENZYMOLOGY COMMUNICATIONS (SZ/0892-2187) [15122518] **972**

CLINICAL CHEMISTRY (BALTIMORE, MD.) (US/0009-9147) [01554929] 4296, **972**

CLINICAL CHEMISTRY (CHICAGO, ILL.) (US/1056-599X) [23743382] **972**

CLINICAL CHEMISTRY LOOKOUT *CEASED.* (NE) [12202412] **972**

CLINICAL CHEMISTRY NEWS (US/0161-9640) [04285761] **972**

CLINICAL CHEMISTRY NEWSLETTER (IT/0392-5803) [09399402] **972**

CLINICAL CHEMISTRY (REFERENCE EDITION) (US/0009-9147) [09763559] **972**

CLINICAL CHIROPRACTIC REPORT *CEASED.* (US/1053-072X) [22448291] **4380**

CLINICAL CONNECTION, THE (US/0890-409X) [14221504] 1877, **4385**

CLINICAL CONSULTATIONS IN OBSTETRICS AND GYNECOLOGY (US/1043-0660) [19290655] **3758**

CLINICAL CYTOGENETICS (UK/0260-5872) [I02605872] **535**

●CLINICAL DATA MANAGEMENT (US/1073-6379) [29533797] **863**

CLINICAL DECISIONS IN OBSTETRICS AND GYNECOLOGY *CEASED.* (US/0892-7081) [15239753] **3758**

CLINICAL DENTAL BRIEFING *CEASED.* (US/1057-5480) [24055455] **1319**

CLINICAL DENTISTRY (US/0093-8769) [04253242] **1319**

CLINICAL DENTISTRY IN HEALTH AND DISEASE (UK) [20103758] **1319**

CLINICAL DERMATOLOGY (US/1053-9697) [04223410] **3718**

CLINICAL DIABETES (US/0891-8929) [10035927] **3726**

CLINICAL DIAGNOSIS BY LABORATORY METHODS; A WORKING MANUAL OF CLINICAL PATHOLOGY (US) [01554930] **3565**

CLINICAL DIGEST SERIES. DERMATOLOGY (US/1043-2604) [19365273] **3718**

CLINICAL DISORDERS ON PEDIATRIC NUTRITION (US/0733-933X) [08691654] 3902, **4188**

CLINICAL DYSMORPHOLOGY (UK/0962-8827) [25517748] **451**

CLINICAL ECOLOGY (US/0735-9306) [09092108] **3565**

CLINICAL ECOLOGY See ENVIRONMENTAL MEDICINE **3574**

CLINICAL EEG ELECTROENCEPHALOGRAPHY (US/0009-9155) [01554931] **3830**

CLINICAL ELECTIVES FOR MEDICAL AND DENTAL STUDENTS AT THE NATIONAL INSTITUTES OF HEALTH (US) [09607675] 1815, **4771**

●CLINICAL ENDOCRINOLOGY (NEW YORK, N.Y.,1992) (US/1059-0471) [24464636] **3727**

CLINICAL ENDOCRINOLOGY (OXFORD) (UK/0300-0664) [01644247] **3727**

CLINICAL ENGINEERING INFORMATION SERVICE (US/0277-0393) [02905652] **3691**

CLINICAL ENZYMOLOGY SYMPOSIA (IT/0392-1905) [05022306] **451**

CLINICAL EXERCISES IN INTERNAL MEDICINE (US/0164-0852) [04551805] **3796**

CLINICAL EYE AND VISION CARE (US/0953-4431) [20225907] **3873**

CLINICAL GENETICS (DK/0009-9163) [01554932] **543**

CLINICAL GERONTOLOGIST (US/0731-7115) [08236085] 5178, **3750**

CLINICAL GINECOLOGICA (BARCELONA, SPAIN) (SP) [18526338] **3758**

CLINICAL HEMORHEOLOGY (US/0271-5198) [06633771] **3771**

CLINICAL HEMOSTASIS REVIEW (US/0894-1025) [15351710] 3771, **3565**

CLINICAL IMAGING (US/0899-7071) [18185958] **3939**

CLINICAL IMMUNOLOGY AND IMMUNOPATHOLOGY (US/0090-1229) [01784768] **3668**

●CLINICAL IMMUNOLOGY DIGEST (US/1061-6969) [25405948] **3668**

CLINICAL IMMUNOLOGY NEWSLETTER (US/0197-1859) [05983915] **3668**

●CLINICAL IMMUNOTHERAPEUTICS (NZ/1172-7039) 3668, **4296**

CLINICAL INFANT REPORTS (US/0735-2530) [08804639] **4581**

●CLINICAL INFECTIOUS DISEASES (US/1058-4838) [24308833] **3712**

CLINICAL INSTRUMENT SYSTEMS : CIS (US/0730-7578) [07965113] **3691**

CLINICAL INTENSIVE CARE : INTERNATIONAL JOURNAL OF CRITICAL & CORONARY CARE MEDICINE (UK/0956-3075) [23110547] **3703**

CLINICAL INVESTIGATION (GW) **3796**

●CLINICAL INVESTIGATOR NEWS (US/1068-1191) [27448347] **3565**

CLINICAL INVESTIGATOR, THE (GW/0941-0198) [25647053] **3565**

CLINICAL JOURNAL (MANHASSET) (US/0366-6743) [04561695] **3565**

CLINICAL JOURNAL OF PAIN, THE (US/0749-8047) [11198567] **3565**

CLINICAL JOURNAL OF SPORT MEDICINE (US/1050-642X) [21569253] **3953**

CLINICAL JOURNAL OF TRADITIONAL CHINESE MEDICINE. CHUI RINSHO (JA) **3565**

CLINICAL KINESIOLOGY (US/0896-9620) [17349432] 4385, **4380**

CLINICAL LAB LETTER (US/0197-8454) [06151597] **3893**

CLINICAL LAB PRODUCTS
(US/0192-1282) [04963928] **3565**

CLINICAL LABORATORY
INTERNATIONAL (BE) **3565**

CLINICAL LABORATORY
MANAGEMENT REVIEW
(US/0888-7950) [13720381] **4771**

CLINICAL LABORATORY PRODUCT
COMPARISON SYSTEM (US)
[15811744] **3565**

CLINICAL LABORATORY REFERENCE
(US/0093-8076) [01791816] **3566**

CLINICAL LABORATORY SCIENCE
(US/0894-959X) [16360620] **3566**

CLINICAL LASER MONTHLY *CEASED.*
(US/0746-469X) [10062208] **3566**

CLINICAL LAW REVIEW : A JOURNAL
OF LAWYERING AND LEGAL
EDUCATION (US) **2951**

CLINICAL LINGUISTICS & PHONETICS
(UK/0269-9206) [14814635] **3274**

CLINICAL MANAGEMENT : THE
MAGAZINE OF THE AMERICAN
PHYSICAL THERAPY ASSOCIATION
(US) [21399470] **4380**

CLINICAL MATERIALS (UK/0267-6605)
[12968283] **3566**

CLINICAL MEDICAL ETHICS (NE)
[24732161] **2249**

CLINICAL MEDICINE (WINNETKA.
1940) *CEASED.* (US/0412-7994)
[01554934] **3566**

CLINICAL MICROBIOLOGY AND
INFECTIOUS DISEASES
(CN/1198-743X) **3712, 561**

CLINICAL MICROBIOLOGY
NEWSLETTER (US/0196-4399)
[05094855] **561**

●CLINICAL MICROBIOLOGY REPORTS
(US/1062-8150) [25756422] **3712**

CLINICAL MICROBIOLOGY REVIEWS
(US/0893-8512) [15671495] **561**

CLINICAL MICROBIOLOGY UPDATE
PROGRAMME (AT/0728-4837)
[28551970] **561**

CLINICAL NEPHROLOGY
(GW/0301-0430) [01747233] **3989**

CLINICAL NEUROLOGY AND
NEUROSURGERY (NE/0303-8467)
[01188204] **3962, 3830**

CLINICAL NEUROPATHOLOGY
(GW/0722-5091) [08528798] **3894**

CLINICAL NEUROPHARMACOLOGY
(US/0362-5664) [02278021] **4296**

CLINICAL NEUROPHYSIOLOGY
UPDATES (NE/0923-084X) [20857429]
3830

CLINICAL NEUROPSYCHOLOGIST,
THE (NE/0920-1637) [16264653] **4581,
3830**

●CLINICAL NEUROSCIENCE (NEW
YORK, N.Y.) (US/1065-6766) [26676964]
3830

CLINICAL NEUROSURGERY
(US/0069-4827) [01564776] **3830, 3962**

CLINICAL NUCLEAR MEDICINE
(US/0363-9762) [02512675] **3940, 3847**

CLINICAL NURSE SPECIALIST
(US/0887-6274) [13304036] **3853**

●CLINICAL NURSING RESEARCH
(US/1054-7738) [22969428] **3853**

CLINICAL NUTRITION (UK/0261-5614)
[09599419] **4188**

CLINICAL NUTRITION IN HEALTH AND
DISEASE (US) **4189**

CLINICAL NUTRITION (PHILADELPHIA,
PA.) (US/1050-5008) [11042503] **4189**

CLINICAL OBSTETRICS AND
GYNECOLOGY (US/0009-9201)
[01784397] **3759**

CLINICAL ONCOLOGY : A JOURNAL
OF THE ROYAL COLLEGE OF
RADIOLOGISTS (UK/0936-6555)
[21232301] **3815**

CLINICAL ONCOLOGY ALERT
(US/0886-7186) [12965824] **3815**

CLINICAL OPHTHALMOLOGY UPDATE
(US/0883-0320) [12047099] **3873**

CLINICAL ORAL IMPLANTS
RESEARCH (DK/0905-7161) [23657396]
1319

CLINICAL ORTHOPAEDICS AND
RELATED RESEARCH (US/0009-921X)
[01554937] **3881**

CLINICAL OTOLARYNGOLOGY AND
ALLIED SCIENCES (UK/0307-7772)
[02883045] **3887**

CLINICAL OUTCOMES : MANAGING
PATIENTS AND THE TOTAL COST OF
CARE (US) [26853955] **3778**

CLINICAL PEDIATRIC
ENDOCRINOLOGY (JA/0918-5739)
[I09185739] **3727**

CLINICAL PEDIATRICS (US/0009-9228)
[00879341] **3902**

CLINICAL PEDIATRICS, MATERNAL
AND CHILD HEALTH (US/0193-9742)
[05279690] **3902**

CLINICAL PEDIATRICS (NEW YORK.
1985) (US/0883-7198) [11040046] **3902**

●CLINICAL PERFORMANCE AND
QUALITY HEALTH CARE
(US/1063-0279) [25844360] **3566**

CLINICAL PHARMACOKINETICS
(US/0312-5963) [02280673] **4296**

CLINICAL PHARMACOKINETICS.
DRUG DATA HANDBOOK *CEASED.*
(NZ/0114-0892) [19601228] **4296**

CLINICAL PHARMACOLOGY
(GW/0937-0978) [22814267] **4296**

CLINICAL PHARMACOLOGY AND
THERAPEUTICS (US/0009-9236)
[01554939] **4297**

CLINICAL PHARMACOLOGY AND
TOXICOLOGY CONSULTANT *CEASED.*
(US/0898-6037) [14231665] **4297**

CLINICAL PHARMACOLOGY (NEW
YORK, N.Y.) (US/0892-001X) [09769813]
4297

CLINICAL PHARMACY (US/0278-2677)
[07760648] **4297**

CLINICAL PHYSICS AND
PHYSIOLOGICAL MEASUREMENT
(UK/0143-0815) [06827724] **3691, 4400**

CLINICAL PHYSICS AND
PHYSIOLOGICAL MEASURMENT *See*
PHYSIOLOGICAL MEASUREMENT
3695

CLINICAL PHYSIOLOGY (OXFORD)
(UK/0144-5979) [07865432] **579**

●CLINICAL PRACTICE GUIDELINE (US)
[26320545] **3566**

●CLINICAL PRACTICE GUIDELINES
(US/1066-677X) [27025290] **3566**

CLINICAL PRACTICE OF
GYNECOLOGY *SUSPENDED.*
(US/1043-3198) [19411542] **3759**

CLINICAL PREVENTIVE DENTISTRY
(US/0163-9633) [04540620] **1319**

CLINICAL PROGRAMS FOR
MENTALLY RETARDED CHILDREN
(US/0501-798X) [04159442] **5279, 3902**

CLINICAL PSYCHIATRY NEWS
(US/0270-6644) [02255267] **3923**

●CLINICAL PSYCHOLOGY AND
PSYCHOTHERAPY (UK/1063-3995)
[26001147] **4581**

CLINICAL PSYCHOLOGY REVIEW
(US/0272-7358) [06910269] **4581**

CLINICAL PSYCHOLOGY : SCIENCE
AND PRACTICE (US/0969-5893) **4581**

●CLINICAL PULMONARY MEDICINE
(US/1068-0640) [27422440] **3703**

CLINICAL RADIOLOGY (UK/0009-9260)
[01554941] **3940**

CLINICAL RC MANAGER
(US/0896-5765) [17215752] **3778**

CLINICAL REHABILITATION
(US/0269-2155) [16399115] **4380**

CLINICAL RESEARCH (US/0009-9279)
[01554942] **3566**

●CLINICAL RESEARCH AND
REGULATORY AFFAIRS
(US/1060-1333) [24877793] **4297**

CLINICAL RESEARCH ASSOCIATES
NEWSLETTER (US) [07902682] **3566**

CLINICAL RESEARCH PRACTICES
AND DRUG REGULATORY AFFAIRS
See CLINICAL RESEARCH AND
REGULATORY AFFAIRS **4297**

CLINICAL REVIEWS IN ALLERGY
(US/0731-8235) [08261670] **3668**

CLINICAL RHEUMATOLOGY
(BE/0770-3198) [08661865] **3804**

CLINICAL SCIENCE (1979)
(UK/0143-5221) [04596879] **485**

CLINICAL SOCIAL WORK JOURNAL
(US/0091-1674) [01786884] **3923, 5279**

CLINICAL SOCIOLOGY ASSOCIATION
See REGISTRY OF MEMBERS -
CLINICAL SOCIOLOGY ASSOCIATION
5255

CLINICAL SOCIOLOGY REVIEW
CEASED. (US/0730-840X) [08072976]
5242

CLINICAL SPORTS MEDICINE
CEASED. (UK/0953-9875) [20289624]
3953

CLINICAL STUDIES (US) [01772840]
3566

CLINICAL SUPERVISOR, THE
(US/0732-5223) [08374673] **4581**

CLINICAL SURGERY INTERNATIONAL
(UK/0263-4422) [07212002] **3962**

CLINICAL SYMPOSIA (1957)
(US/0009-9295) [01642384] **3566**

CLINICAL SYMPOSIA ... ANNUAL
CEASED. (US) [17830855] **3566**

CLINICAL THERAPEUTICS
(US/0149-2918) [03313358] **4297**

CLINICAL THERMOLOGY (US) **3566**

CLINICAL TRANSPLANTATION
(DK/0902-0063) [16743589] **3566**

CLINICAL TRANSPLANTS
(US/0890-9016) [14450491] **3962**

CLINICAL TRENDS IN UROLOGY
CEASED. (US/0091-1682) [01830586]
3989

CLINICAL TRIALS (US/1061-608X)
[25378636] **3740**

CLINICAL TRIALS AND
META-ANALYSIS *CEASED.*
(NE/0927-5401) [26467398] **4297**

CLINICAL TRIALS JOURNAL *See*
CLINICAL TRIALS AND
META-ANALYSIS **4297**

●CLINICAL TRIALS MONITOR :
MONTHLY MONITORING OF CLINICAL
TRIALS OF HUMAN
PHARMACEUTICALS (US) [29065600]
3740

CLINICAL ULTRASOUND REVIEW
(US/0275-4541) [07117834] **3796**

CLINICAL UPDATE (US/0882-6617)
[11980552] **3566**

CLINICAL UPDATE IN NEPHROLOGY
(US/0883-0339) [12047141] **3796**

CLINICAL UPDATE IN PEDIATRICS
(US/0883-0290) [12046813] **3902**

CLINICAL UPDATE. SPORTS
MEDICINE *CEASED.* (US/0740-7238)
[09991422] **3953**

CLINICAL VISION SCIENCES
(US/0887-6169) [13307264] **3566**

CLINICAS DE MEDICINA DEPORTIVA
(SP) **3566**

CLINICAS ODONTOLOGICAS DE
NORTEAMERICA (SP) **1319**

CLINICAS
OTORRINOLARINGOLOGICAS DE
NORTEAMERICA (SP) **3887**

CLINICAS PEDIATRICAS DE
NORTEAMERICA (SP) **3902**

CLINICAS QUIRURGICAS DE
NORTEAMERICA (SP) **3962**

CLINICIAN IN MANAGEMENT
(UK/0965-5751) [I09655751] **863, 3913**

CLINICIAN (MACCLESFIELD,
ENGLAND) (UK/0264-6404) [19585048]
4297

CLINICIAN REVIEWS (US/1052-0627)
[22173556] **3566**

CLINICIAN'S MANUAL ON
HYPERLIPIDEMIA (US/0961-7787)
[22411320] **3703**

CLINICIAN'S RESEARCH DIGEST
(US/8756-3207) [11545367] **4581**

CLINICIEN (CN/0832-9184) [16309204]
3566

CLINICS IN APPLIED NUTRITION
CEASED. (US/1053-0452) [22441041]
4189

CLINICS IN CHEST MEDICINE
(US/0272-5231) [05433901] **3566**

CLINICS IN COMMUNICATION
DISORDERS (US/1054-8505)
[22994143] **3887**

CLINICS IN DERMATOLOGY
(US/0738-081X) [09508305] **3718**

CLINICS IN DEVELOPMENTAL
MEDICINE (UK/0069-4835) [01554950]
3830

CLINICS IN DIAGNOSTIC
ULTRASOUND (US/0193-743X)
[05162352] **3566**

CLINICS IN EMERGENCY MEDICINE
CEASED. (US/0733-4354) [07804815]
3723

CLINICS IN GERIATRIC MEDICINE
(US/0749-0690) [11077910] **3750**

CLINICS IN LABORATORY MEDICINE
(US/0272-2712) [06829971] **3566**

CLINICS IN PERINATOLOGY
(US/0095-5108) [01162647] **3759**

CLINICS IN PLASTIC SURGERY
(US/0094-1298) [00962944] **3962**

CLINICS IN PODIATRIC MEDICINE AND
SURGERY (US/0891-8422) [13324960]
3917

CLINICS IN SPORTS MEDICINE
(US/0278-5919) [07845187] **3953**

CLINIGUIDE TO RHEUMATOLOGY
(US/1055-9361) [23369232] **3804**

CLINIMED (CN/0825-3005) [11360557]
3567

CLINIQUE OPHTALMOLOGIQUE
PARIS, LA (FR/0009-9368) [I00099368]
3873

CLINMED-CD (US) **3567**

CLINS D'OEIL DE DIEU (CN/0823-9614)
[11762362] **4948**

CLINTON ADVERTISER (CLINTON,
IOWA) *See* CLINTON HERALD, THE
5669

CLINTON CHRONICLE (CLINTON,
S.C.), THE (US/0893-035X) [13640682]
5742

CLINTON COUNTY HISTORICAL
SOCIETY (US) **2613**

CLINTON COUNTY NEWS (US)
[25302799] **5659**

CLINTON COUNTY NEWS (US)
[14200778] **5691**

CLINTON COURIER (CLINTON, N.Y.)
(US) [04772540] **5715**

CLINTON　　　　　　　　　　　Alphabetical Title Index

CLINTON DAILY DEMOCRAT, THE (US) [13433334] **5703**

CLINTON DAILY HERALD *See* CLINTON HERALD, THE **5669**

CLINTON DAILY ITEM (US) [19907170] **5688**

CLINTON DAILY JOURNAL (US) [21654281] **5659**

CLINTON DAILY NEWS (US) [28322612] **5731**

CLINTON EYE, THE (US) [13493702] **5703**

CLINTON HERALD, THE (US) [15512315] **5669**

CLINTON MONTHLY, THE *CEASED*. (US/1075-1130) [29931324] **4468**

CLINTON NEWS-RECORD. MICROFORM (CN/0834-6151) [16274423] **5782**

CLINTON RECORDER (US) [25862412] **5645**

CLINTON TOPPER, THE (US) [12993851] **5766**

CLINTONVILLE TRIBUNE-GAZETTE (US/0749-7024) [11165409] **5766**

CLIO BIBLIOGRAPHY SERIES (US) [03550223] **413**

CLIO (FORT WAYNE, IND.) (US/0884-2043) [01776005] **3376**

CLIO MEDICA (NE/0366-676X) [01554954] **3567**

CLIO NOTIZIE *CEASED*. (IT) [24868162] **5553**

CLIO (SANTO DOMINGO) (DR/0009-9376) [01641178] **2844**

CLIP ART QUARTERLY (US) 757, **347**

CLIPBOARD (CN/1189-0657) [25314214] **4771**

●CLIPPER ADVISOR (US/1068-0675) [27422483] **1284**

CLIPPER (BASEL), THE (SZ/1012-9707) [24385381] **2331**

CLIPPER CREATIVE ART SERVICE (US) **347**

CLIPPER (LOS ANGELES, CALIF.) *See* PAN AM CLIPPER **31**

CLIPPER STUDIES IN THE AMERICAN THEATER (US/0748-237X) [10910815] **5363**

CLIPPING SERVICE (CN/1182-6665) [23231519] **5279**

CLIPS / CONGRESSIONAL INSTITUTE FOR THE FUTURE (US) **5195**

CLIS OBSERVER (II/0970-0943) [11928367] **3202**

CLL JOURNAL : COMPUTER-ASSISTED ENGLISH LANGUAGE LEARNING JOURNAL (US/1049-9059) [21347143] 1222, **3274**

CLLI'S COMMERCIAL PROPERTY LAW DIGESTS *CEASED*. (US/1058-8485) [24404189] **2951**

CLM, CONSUMER LAW MONTHLY (US) [03940608] **2951**

CLO NEWS (US/0164-4815) [04749803] **3160**

CLOAK AND DAGGER (1990) *CEASED*. (US/1053-7627) [22636379] **377**

CLOCKMAKER (HINCKLEY) (UK/0961-5032) [I09615032] **2772**

CLOCKS (UK) [10034424] **2916**

CLOCKS (UK) [24582778] **2916**

CLOCKWATCH REVIEW (US/0740-9311) [10047741] **317**

CLOGHER RECORD (IE) [07903198] **2684**

CLOSED-END FUND DIGEST (US) **895**

CLOSED END FUNDS ONFLOPPY (US) [30377995] **783**

CLOSED LOOP (MINNEAPOLIS, MINN.) (US/0739-036X) [04363055] **2111**

CLOSELY HELD BUSINESS, THE (US) [23360199] **3118**

CLOSING THE GAP (US/0886-1935) [12894951] 1266, **1877**

CLOSING THE GAP RESOURCE DIRECTORY (US) [19279425] 1266, **1877**

CLOTH DIRECTORY (UK) 5349, **1083**

CLOTH DOLL, THE (US/8755-2655) [11258539] **371**

CLOTHING AND TEXTILE ARTS INDEX, THE (US/0887-2937) [12046991] 5349, **1083**

CLOTHING AND TEXTILES RESEARCH JOURNAL (US/0887-302X) [09746357] 1083, **5349**

CLOTHING INDUSTRIES (CN/0835-006X) [18121063] **1083**

CLOTHING INSTITUTE *See* CLOTHING INSTITUTE YEAR BOOK & MEMBERSHIP REGISTER, THE **1083**

CLOTHING INSTITUTE YEAR BOOK & MEMBERSHIP REGISTER, THE (UK/0307-8515) [02242310] **1083**

CLOUD FAMILY JOURNAL (US/0883-0940) [11849373] **2443**

CLOVER COMPARATIVE COST CHART FOR ONLINE FILES *See* ONLINE FILES **1275**

CLOVER HERALD (US) [29377543] **5742**

CLOVER NEWSPAPER INDEX (UK/0952-9950) [I09529950] **5811**

CLOVERDALE WEEKLY REVEILLE (US) [13042233] **5634**

CLOVIS INDEPENDENT (CLOVIS, CALIF. 1946), THE (US/1068-5944) [26657405] **5634**

CLOVIS NEWS-JOURNAL (US) [11302139] **5712**

CLR REPORTS (US/0892-0605) [15071166] **3202**

CLS BULLETIN / PUBLISHED BY THE COUNCIL FOR THE LIBERATION OF SURINAME (NE) [15210282] **4506**

●CLS MARKET PLACE (US/1061-6020) [25377336] **657**

CLSC EXPRESS (CN/0838-4347) [19027279] **5279**

CLSU SCIENTIFIC JOURNAL (PH/0115-0405) [04027204] **75**

CLUB AUTOMOBILE QUEBEC *See* GUIDE DE ROUTE **5478**

CLUB DES AMIS DE GILLES VILLENEUVE *See* CLUB DES AMIS DE GILLES VILLENEUVE INC **4890**

CLUB DES AMIS DE GILLES VILLENEUVE INC (CN/0228-4839) [08063937] **4890**

CLUB DES ORNITHOLOGUES DU QUEBEC *See* LISTE DES MEMBRES DU CLUB DES ORNITHOLOGUES DE SIC QUEBEC **5618**

CLUB INDUSTRY (US/0747-8283) [10811366] 657, **2596**

CLUB INFORMATIONS NANTERRE (FR/1161-1804) [I11611804] **1968**

CLUB INTERNATIONAL (NEWTOWN, CONN.) (US/0747-0819) [10534890] 5187, **3994**

CLUB LIVING (US/0160-6166) [03724994] **4890**

CLUB MANAGEMENT (US/0009-9589) [05267407] **5230**

CLUB MANAGEMENT IN AUSTRALIA (AT/0045-7205) [I00457205] **5230**

CLUB (NEWTOWN, CONN.) (US/0747-0827) [10534855] **5230**

CLUB REGIONAL DE L'ENTREPRENEURSHIP, LE (CN/0840-9145) [19924441] **864**

CLUBHOUSE (BERRIEN SPRINGS, MICH.) (US/1071-4073) [28638561] 1062, **4948**

CLUBS IN TOWN AND COUNTRY (US/0438-6256) [07525823] **5230**

CLUES (BOWLING GREEN, OHIO) (US/0742-4248) [07540087] **5074**

CLUES (LINCOLN) (US/0149-1725) [02251153] **2728**

CLUJUL MEDICAL (RM) [03157461] **3567**

CLUMBER SPANIEL CORRESPONDENCE (AT) **4286**

CLUTCH (FRANKFORT, KY.) (US/1061-737X) [25426145] 3461, **3340**

CLUW NEWS (US/0199-8919) [06269058] 5553, **1659**

CLYDE ENTERPRISE (CLYDE, OHIO : 1881) (US) [11944487] **5727**

CLYDE JOURNAL (US) [16963411] **5748**

CLYDE REPUBLICAN (CLYDE, KAN. : 1986) (US) [14064085] **5675**

CLYDEBANK POST (UK) **5811**

CM BULLETIN (US/0738-5099) [09616897] **4638**

CM : CANADIAN MATERIALS FOR SCHOOLS AND LIBRARIES (CN/0821-1450) [06583908] 1732, **3376**

CM. CONTROLLER-MAGAZIN 1988 (GW/0939-0359) [I09390359] **1590**

CMA MATTERS (US/1050-9887) [21587577] **4110**

CMA : THE MANAGEMENT ACCOUNTING MAGAZINE (CN/0831-3881) [12822299] **741**

CMAJ. CANADIAN MEDICAL ASSOCIATION JOURNAL (CN/0820-3946) [12748813] **3567**

CMBC ALUMNI BULLETIN (CN/0823-2725) [10051976] 5058, **1101**

CMBH CRIMINAL BEHAVIOUR AND MENTAL HEALTH (UK/0957-9664) [I09579664] 4581, **3160**

CMC MEMBERSHIP DIRECTORY (CN) **757**

CMC NEWS (US/0738-8845) [09694082] **1174**

CMC YEARBOOK (CN/1184-0420) [23598131] **5058**

CMEA NEWS (US/0007-8638) [01537991] **4110**

CMFRI BULLETIN (II/0378-2387) [03061338] **2299**

CMG PROCEEDINGS (US) **1174**

CMG TRANSACTIONS (US) **1174**

CMHA FOCUS (CN/0715-5654) [09448357] **5279**

CMI RESEARCH (CN/0712-2918) [08808182] **827**

CMI NEWS LETTER (BE) [03183564] **3180**

CMI NEWSLETTER AND YEARBOOK (NO) **3180**

CMIP PUBLICATIONS (US) **2649**

CMJ CANADA (CN/1188-1518) [25652257] 1130, **4110**

CMJ NEW MUSIC MONTHLY (US) **4110**

CMJ NEW MUSIC REPORT (US/0890-0795) [13920492] **4110**

CMJ, PROGRESSIVE MEDIA *See* CMJ NEW MUSIC REPORT **4110**

CML ARMY CHEMICAL REVIEW (US/0899-7047) [17010444] **4039**

CMLEA *See* CMLEA JOURNAL **3202**

CMLEA JOURNAL (US/0196-3309) [03789113] **3202**

●CMM : CANADIAN MEDIA MAG (CN/1191-2707) [26497735] **4443**

CMM, CONFECTIONERY MANUFACTURE AND MARKETING (UK/0007-8654) [10523198] 922, **3477**

CMN *See* CANNATA REPORT **4211**

CMN. COMMON MARKET NEWS (UK/0300-4406) [01141020] **1470**

CMN OFFICE MACHINE NEWS (US/0889-5880) [14088980] **4211**

CMOS BULLETIN SCMO (CN) **1353**

CMRI QUARTERLY REVIEW (US) **2137**

CMRR REPORT (US/0888-7381) [11595994] **5316**

CMS NEWS-LETTER (UK) [05986832] **4948**

●CMS NOTES (CN/1193-9273) [28061904] **3500**

CMS PROCEEDINGS (US/1053-9794) [12621486] **4110**

CMU JOURNAL OF SCIENCE (PH/0116-7847) [24685549] 75, **5095**

CN LINES (US/1061-9739) **5430**

CNA TODAY (CN/1188-1887) [25589897] **3854**

CNA TODAY (CN/1188-1887) [25589895] **3854**

CNC INFO (FR) [23018749] **4067**

CNC STATISTIQUES / CENTRE NATIONAL DE LA CINEMATOGRAPHIE (FR) [07477266] 4067, **4080**

CNC WEST (US/0747-3362) [10748985] 4000, **3477**

CNEA / REPUBLICA ARGENTINA, COMISION NACIONAL DE ENERGIA ATOMICA (AG/0325-1403) [19549762] **4446**

CNIDAIRES FOSSILES : BULLETIN DE LIAISON *See* FOSSIL CNIDARIA **1376**

CNL/REVIEW OF BOOKS (US) **3340**

CNL/WORLD REPORT 1985 (US) **3376**

CNPF LA REVUE DES ENTREPRISES (FR) [08626167] **922**

CNPQ BOLETIM (BL) [04015527] **5095**

CNRS PETROLE ET GAZ *CEASED*. (FR) **4253**

CNRS PETROLE ET GAZ. INDEX CUMULATIF (FR) **4253**

●CNS DRUGS : THE CLINICAL REVIEW OF DRUGS AND THERAPEUICS IN PSYCHIATRY AND NEUROLOGY (NZ/1172-7047) 3923, 3830, **4297**

CNSW NEWSLETTER (US/0164-7032) [04390411] **3989**

CNY BUSINESS JOURNAL, THE (US/1050-3005) [21174751] **657**

CO-EXISTENCE (DORDRECHT) (NE/0587-5994) [01554971] **4518**

CO-OP CONSUMERS (DK) [06636998] **1294**

CO-OP NORTH (CN/0822-7438) [10398389] **1541**

CO-OP SOURCE DIRECTORY (US/0736-0878) [08060383] **757**

CO-OP UPDATE (ST. JOHN'S) (CN/0714-3281) [09021872] **1541**

CO-OPERATEUR AGRICOLE, LE (CN/0315-1204) [01983480] **75**

CO-OPERATIVE ASSOCIATIONS IN NOVA SCOTIA (CN/0318-3955) [02241172] **1541**

CO-OPERATORS' PLATFORM (UK/0032-1370) [19756679] **4468**

CO-OPERATORS' YEAR BOOK (UK) [09033391] **2137**

CO-OPSERVATIONS (CN/0226-8531) [07857921] **1541**

CO-ORD. TRANSPORT INDUSTRIES RESEARCH COUNCIL OF AUSTRALIA *See* QUARTERLY BULLETIN **5390**

CO-WORKER (US/0891-0723) [14562311] **1659**

COA BULLETIN (CN/0832-0128) [15287398] **3881**

COA REVIEW *CEASED.* (US/0738-1395) [09529149] **1342**

COACH AND BUS OPERATIONS (UK) **5379**

COACH AND BUS WEEK (UK/0953-8240) **5411**

COACHEN (NE) **4890**

COACHES' CORNER, THE (US) [20543565] **2918**

COACHES REPORT (US) **1855**

COACHING CLINIC, THE (US/0009-9880) [01554988] **4890**

COACHING CLINIC'S BASKETBALL COACH (US/1053-1904) [22471607] **4890**

COACHING DIRECTOR (AT/0814-7752) [I08147752] **4890**

COACHING : MEN'S ATHLETICS (US/0146-1265) [02865788] **4890**

COACHING VOLLEYBALL (US/0894-4237) [16074296] **4890**

COACHING WOMEN'S BASKETBALL (US/0894-4245) [16074276] **4890**

COAL ABSTRACTS *CEASED.* (UK/0309-4979) [04576510] 1935, **1961**

COAL AGE LIBRARY OF OPERATING HANDBOOKS (US/0197-6354) [03695197] **2137**

COAL AND COKE STATISTICS (CN/0380-6847) [02585706] 2137, **2003**

COAL AND ENERGY QUARTERLY (UK/0306-8544) [02200792] **1935**

COAL & MINING REVIEW (II/0376-7493) [02246000] **2137**

COAL & SYNFUELS TECHNOLOGY (US/0883-9735) [12267531] **1023**

COAL ASH MARKET REPORT *CEASED.* (US/0891-7957) [15000374] **1602**

COAL-BASED GAS STREAM CLEANUP PROGRAM ... SUMMARY PROGRAM PLAN (US) [25596003] **1023**

COAL CALENDAR *CEASED.* (UK/0143-6287) [06208823] **1935**

COAL (CHICAGO, ILL. : 1988) (US/1040-7820) [17616326] **2137**

COAL CITY COURANT, THE (US) [23624728] **5659**

COAL CITY REVIEW (US/1062-5011) [23851102] **3376**

COAL CONSUMERS ASSOCIATION OF INDIA *See* C.C.A.I. MONTHLY NEWSLETTER **1294**

COAL CONVERSION (US/0195-413X) [05876684] **1023**

COAL CONVERSION AND UTILIZATION. TECHNICAL REPORT (US/0146-3691) [C2921803] **972**

COAL CONVERSION SYSTEMS TECHNICAL DATA BOOK (US) [04507644] **1935**

COAL DATA (US/0145-417X) [02732705] **1935**

COAL DEMONSTRATION PLANTS. TECHNICAL REPORT (US/0146-3683) [02921924] **972**

COAL (DENVER) (US/0160-5941) [02356083] **2137**

COAL ECONOMY IN ... - LUXEMBOURG, THE (LU) [19329474] **1602**

COAL FOCUS / THE COAL ASSOCIATION OF CANADA (CN/0821-7068) [09816176] 1602, **2137**

COAL INDUSTRY IN EUROPE (FR/0473-3177) [01205301] **1602**

COAL INFORMATION / INTERNATIONAL ENERGY AGENCY (FR) [14080044] **1935**

COAL INTERNATIONAL (REDHILL, SURREY, ENGLAND) (UK/0264-9799) [09507392] **1438**

COAL JOURNAL (AT/0815-6883) [I08156883] **2137**

COAL LAW & REGULATION / [PATRICK C. MCGINLEY, DONALD VISH, EDITORS] *CEASED.* (US) [09751946] 2137, **2951**

COAL MINE DIRECTORY *See* COAL MINE DIRECTORY, UNITED STATES AND CANADA **2137**

COAL MINE DIRECTORY, UNITED STATES AND CANADA (US/1045-6430) [02303294] **2137**

COAL MINES - (GREAT BRITAIN) (UK) [07038353] **2137**

COAL MINING AND QUARRYING (US/0190-7867) [02851753] **2137**

COAL MINING INDUSTRY IN ..., THE (LU) [19349957] **1602**

COAL MINING TECHNOLOGY, ECONOMICS, AND POLICY (US/0748-1993) [10899775] **2137**

COAL OUTLOOK (US/0162-2714) [04147258] **1935**

COAL OUTLOOK'S PRODUCTIVITY REPORT *See* PRODUCTIVITY REPORT FOR ALL PRODUCERS BY STATE, COUNTY, & TYPE MINING **2148**

COAL PATROL (US) [03172054] **1935**

COAL-- PENNSYLVANIA ANTHRACITE *See* COAL PRODUCTION **2137**

COAL PEOPLE (US/0748-6073) [10972542] **2728**

COAL PLANNER (US/0734-7243) [08788026] 1438, **2137**

COAL PREPARATION (NEW YORK, N.Y.) (US/0734-9343) [08829100] **2137**

COAL PROCESSING TECHNOLOGY (US/0147-1708) [03044711] **2137**

COAL PRODUCTION (US/0736-4504) [08643799] **2137**

COAL PRODUCTION & TRANSPORTATION : ANNUAL CONFERENCE (US/0199-977X) [03758990] **1602**

COAL REVIEW (LEXINGTON) (US/0191-4103) [04863288] **2137**

COAL SCIENCE AND TECHNOLOGY (NE/0167-9449) [08804575] **2137**

COAL SERVICE REFERENCE MANUAL (US/0195-3672) [05391401] **1602**

COAL SITUATION, THE (US/0737-6499) [06899332] **1935**

COAL STATISTICS INTERNATIONAL (US/0276-1890) [07254949] **1438**

COAL TRANSPORTATION REPORT (US/0732-8397) [08444026] **5379**

COAL TRANSPORTATION STATISTICS (US/1046-9486) [19832311] **1439**

COAL VALLEY NEWS (US/0745-7111) [09395264] **5763**

COAL VOICE (US/1049-0574) [21133889] **1439**

COAL WEEK (US/0149-578X) [02673891] **2137**

COAL WEEK INTERNATIONAL (US/0272-0205) [06758638] 827, **1439**

COALDAT MARKETING REPORT. PRODUCING DISTRICT FORMAT (1988) (US/1043-1845) [19320594] **1935**

COALDAT MARKETING REPORT. SUPPLIER FORMAT (1988) (US/1043-0474) [19255403] **1935**

COALDAT MARKETING REPORT. UTILITY FORMAT (US/0895-2361) [16518996] **1935**

COALFIELD PROGRESS, THE (US/0889-3330) [13866557] **5758**

COALGATE RECORD-REGISTER, THE (US) [13645882] **5731**

COALINGA RECORD (US) [26577780] **5634**

COALITION CLOSE-UP (US/0730-1251) [07952723] **4518**

COALITION OF UNIONS NEWSLETTER (CN/1186-8325) [24623517] **1659**

COALTRANS INTERNATIONAL (UK) [15102037] **2137**

COALTRANS WORCESTER PARK (UK/0269-381X) [I0269381X] 2137, **1935**

COARSE ANGLING (UK) [I1354263X] **2299**

COAST & COUNTRY *CEASED.* (US/0897-4640) [17503234] **2531**

COAST BUSINESS (US/1060-3417) [24940198] **657**

COAST GUARD LETTER (US/1055-8373) [23352475] **4175**

COAST INSTITUTE OF TECHNOLOGY *See* PROGRESS REPORT - COAST INSTITUTE OF TECHNOLOGY **5142**

COAST MARINE & TRANSPORTATION DIRECTORY (US) [03172067] **5379**

COAST TO COAST COUNTRY (CN/0826-3140) [11085026] **4110**

COAST WATCH (US/0194-5742) [04844651] 2190, **1448**

COASTAL AND ESTUARINE SCIENCES (US/0733-9569) [07956322] 1448, **2212**

COASTAL AND ESTUARINE STUDIES (US/0938-0949) [20881224] **1968**

COASTAL BEND APARTMENT & RENTAL GUIDE (US/0748-2019) [10908339] **4835**

COASTAL COURIER (CN/0707-6916) [04875792] **5782**

COASTAL COURIER (HINESVILLE, GA.), THE (US/1047-6636) [19405761] **5653**

COASTAL CRUISING (US/0897-750X) [17610840] **4890**

COASTAL ENGINEERING (AMSTERDAM) (NE/0378-3839) [03236994] **1968**

COASTAL ENGINEERING IN JAPAN (JA/0578-5634) [02080364] **2088**

COASTAL ENGINEERING RESEARCH CENTER (U.S.) *See* TECHNICAL PAPER - U.S. ARMY, CORPS OF ENGINEERS, COASTAL ENGINEERING RESEARCH CENTER **1998**

COASTAL ENGINEERING RESEARCH CENTER (U.S.) *See* MISCELLANEOUS REPORT - U.S. ARMY, CORPS OF ENGINEERS, COASTAL ENGINEERING RESEARCH CENTER **2093**

COASTAL ENGINEERING RESEARCH CENTER (U.S.) *See* TECHNICAL REPORT - COASTAL ENGINEERING RESEARCH CENTER (U.S.) **1998**

COASTAL ENGINEERING TECHNICAL AID (US/0271-6690) [03778055] **1448**

COASTAL JOURNAL (US/0192-4524) [05043706] **5685**

COASTAL MANAGEMENT (US/0892-0753) [15075137] **2190**

COASTAL NEWS (DESTIN, FLA.) (US/1058-1065) [24220500] **5466**

COASTAL OBSERVER (PAWLEYS ISLAND, S.C.) (US/8750-3425) [11270239] **5742**

COASTAL PLAINS CENTER FOR MARINE DEVELOPMENT SERVICES *See* PUBLICATION - COASTAL PLAINS CENTER FOR MARINE DEVELOPMENT SERVICES **1455**

COASTAL PLAINS FARMER. ALABAMA, FLORIDA ED (US/0737-1756) [09336993] **75**

COASTAL PLAINS FARMER NORTH CAROLINA, VIRGINIA ED (US/0737-1748) [09337518] **75**

COASTAL RESEARCH (US/0271-5376) [02990117] 2190, **1353**

COASTAL STUDIES BULLETIN. LOUISIANA STATE UNIVERSITY (US/0375-684X) [01079678] **1448**

COASTAL TIMES, THE (US) [28283855] **5742**

COASTAL ZONE MANAGEMENT (US/0045-723X) [03174877] **4253**

COASTER, THE (CN/0707-2325) [04754968] **5782**

COASTER WORLD *See* ROLLERCOASTER! MAGAZINE **4865**

COASTGUARD (UK) [04082673] **4175**

COASTLAND TIMES, THE (US/1069-4722) [13142070] **5723**

COASTLINE (AT/0311-4805) [I03114805] **5742**

COASTLINES (SANTA BARBARA, CALIF.) (US/0279-1862) [07607041] **1101**

COASTLINES (STONY BROOK, N.Y.) (US/1062-3442) [04357447] **2299**

COASTLINES (SURREY) (CN/1184-7581) [24368209] **3376**

COASTWISE TRADE REPORT (PH) [02436545] **827**

COAT OF ARMS, THE (UK/0010-003X) [03529331] **2443**

COATES ART REVIEW: IMPRESSIONISM. CD-ROM (US) **347**

COATING (SZ/0590-8450) [04082758] 2101, **2011**

COATINGS (CN/0225-6363) [06034824] **4223**

COATINGS, DYES & PIGMENTS (US/1041-9144) [12795522] **4223**

COATNEY/COURTNEY EXCHANGE (US) **2443**

COBALT + COBALT ABSTRACTS (ENGLISH ED.) *SUSPENDED.* (US/0376-7450) [01798685] **1023**

COBBLESTONE (US/0199-5197) [05962536] **1062**

COBOL INFORMATION BULLETIN (US) [04626468] **1278**

COBOUW (NE/0010-0064) **607**

COBURGER LANDESSTIFTUNG *See* JAHRBUCH DER COBURGER LANDESSTIFTUNG **2693**

COBWEB : NEWSLETTER OF THE DES PLAINES HISTORICAL SOCIETY (US) [04552945] **2728**

COCHRANE TIMES (CN/0319-745X) [02442953] **5782**

COCK-A-DOODLE WAKE UP WORLD (US/0735-8628) [09052229] **4948**

COCKPIT (LANCASTER, CALIF.) (US/0742-1508) [09208639] **16**

COCKRELL CONNECTION, THE (US/0891-5296) [14906661] **2443**

COCKSHAW'S CONSTRUCTION LABOR NEWS & OPINION (US/0094-0372) [01398624] **607**

COCKTAIL MOLOTOV, LE (CN/0228-9067) [07817517] **1090**

COCOA GROWERS' BULLETIN (UK/0045-7256) [04026715] **167**

COCOA / WORLD MARKETS AND TRADE (US) **75**

COCOMUNITY — Alphabetical Title Index

COCOMUNITY NEWSLETTER (IO/0215-1502) [05285114] **75**

COCONUT BULLETIN (LUNUWILA, SRI LANKA) (CE/0255-4119) [11743668] **167**

COCONUT FARMERS BULLETIN, THE (PH/0115-1541) [09301589] **167**

COCONUT STATISTICS / COMPILED AND EXPANDED BY UCAP RESEARCH DEPARTMENT (PH) [08933065] 167, **152**

COCONUT TELEGRAPH (HO) **2511**

COCOS : JOURNAL OF THE COCONUT RESEARCH INSTITUTE OF SRI LANKA (CE/0255-4100) [12816144] **167**

COCUK EDEBIYAT YLLG (TU) [17652981] **1062**

COCUK SAGLIGI VE HASTALIKLARI DERGISI (TU/0010-0161) [01588396] **4771**

CODA MAGAZINE (CN/0820-926X) [08893658] **4110**

CODASYL COBOL JOURNAL OF DEVELOPMENT (US/0591-0218) [04328371] **1278**

CODATA *See* CODATA NEWSLETTER **5095**

CODATA *See* CODATA BULLETIN **5095**

CODATA BULLETIN *CEASED.* (US/0366-757X) [02520398] **5095**

CODATA NEWSLETTER (GW/0538-6918) [02520384] **5095**

CODE ADMINISTRATIF (FR) [05910325] **3092**

CODE & SYMBOL (US/0362-4455) [02826884] **864**

CODE BOOK CONNECTION (US) **1815**

CODE CIVIL (FR) [05929964] **3089**

CODE CRIMINEL, L.R.C. (1985), CH. C-46, ET LOIS CONNEXES (CN/1184-7476) [24256640] **2951**

CODE DE LA SANTE PUBLIQUE (FR) **4771**

CODE DE L'URBANISME (FR) [06037511] **2818**

CODE DE PROCEDURE CIVILE DU QUEBEC, L.R.Q. C-25, ET LOIS ET REGLEMENTS CONNEXES (CN/1184-7514) [24256649] **2951**

CODE DE PROCEDURE CIVILE (EDITIONS THEMIS) (CN/1184-7506) [24256646] **2951**

CODE DES LOYERS ET DE LA COPROPRIETE (FR) [06052995] **2818**

CODE DU TRAVAIL DU QUEBEC ET REGLEMENTS (CN/0836-3935) [16891456] 3145, **1659**

CODE FISCAL LUXEMBOURGEOIS. MISE A JOUR (LU) **4718**

CODE GENERAL DES IMPOTS ET ANNEXES AVEC ANNOTATIONS ET RENVOIS (FR) [06053020] 4718, **827**

CODE MUNICIPAL FD DU QUEBEC (CN/0842-5698) [19573964] **4638**

CODE NAME DIRECTORY. INTERNATIONAL *SUSPENDED.* (US/0883-2803) [10626484] **4039**

CODE NAME DIRECTORY. US *SUSPENDED.* (US/0882-7621) [10137255] **4039**

CODE NEWS (CLEVELAND, OHIO) (US/0735-9330) [08504473] **608**

CODE OF COLORADO REGULATIONS. LIMITED EDITION (US) **4639**

CODE OF COLORADO REGULATIONS. REGULAR EDITION (US) **4639**

CODE OF FEDERAL REGULATIONS (US) [02786662] **4639**

CODE OF FEDERAL REGULATIONS. 7, AGRICULTURE (US) [07515004] 75, **2951**

CODE OF FEDERAL REGULATIONS. 10, ENERGY (US) [06506744] 2190, **1935**

CODE OF FEDERAL REGULATIONS. 16, COMMERCIAL PRACTICES (US) [07439179] 827, **2951**

CODE OF FEDERAL REGULATIONS. 18, CONSERVATION OF POWER AND WATER RESOURCES (US) [07220398] **3110**

CODE OF FEDERAL REGULATIONS. 20, EMPLOYEES BENEFITS (US) [07439298] **3145**

CODE OF FEDERAL REGULATIONS. 21, FOOD AND DRUGS (US) [07862848] 2331, **2951**

CODE OF FEDERAL REGULATIONS. 23, HIGHWAYS (US) [07858740] 5439, **2951**

CODE OF FEDERAL REGULATIONS. 24, HOUSING AND URBAN DEVELOPMENT (US) [07607526] 2818, **2951**

CODE OF FEDERAL REGULATIONS. 25, INDIANS (US) [07562265] **2258**

CODE OF FEDERAL REGULATIONS. 26, INTERNAL REVENUE (US) [07514430] 4718, **2951**

CODE OF FEDERAL REGULATIONS. 27, ALCOHOL, TOBACCO PRODUCTS AND FIREARMS (US) [06724266] **2951**

CODE OF FEDERAL REGULATIONS. 29, LABOR (US) [06273972] **3145**

CODE OF FEDERAL REGULATIONS. 30, MINERAL RESOURCES (US/0276-8445) [07263068] 1439, **2952**

CODE OF FEDERAL REGULATIONS. 31, MONEY AND FINANCE, TREASURY (US) [07220656] 4718, **2952**

CODE OF FEDERAL REGULATIONS. 33, NAVIGATION AND NAVIGABLE WATERS (US) [07561911] **3180**

CODE OF FEDERAL REGULATIONS. 37, PATENTS, TRADEMARKS, AND COPYRIGHTS (US) [07288624] **1303**

CODE OF FEDERAL REGULATIONS. 40, PROTECTION OF ENVIRONMENT (US/0271-4094) [06565630] **2163**

CODE OF FEDERAL REGULATIONS. 42, PUBLIC HEALTH (US) [05531338] 4771, **2952**

CODE OF FEDERAL REGULATIONS. 44, EMERGENCY MANAGEMENT AND ASSISTANCE (US) [07530091] 1073, **2952**

CODE OF FEDERAL REGULATIONS. 46, SHIPPING (US) [07510980] **3180**

CODE OF FEDERAL REGULATIONS. 47, TELECOMMUNICATIONS (US) [07526720] 1151, **2952**

CODE OF FEDERAL REGULATIONS. 48, FEDERAL ACQUISITION REGULATIONS SYSTEM (US) [11580527] **4718**

CODE OF FEDERAL REGULATIONS. 49, TRANSPORTATION (US) [07220683] 5379, **2952**

CODE OF FEDERAL REGULATIONS. 50, WILDLIFE AND FISHERIES (US) [05955164] **3110**

CODE OF FEDERAL REGULATIONS. CFR INDEX AND FINDING AIDS (US/0276-6906) [04828101] **2952**

CODE OF FEDERAL REGULATIONS INDEX (US/0000-1058) [17564267] **3079**

CODE OF FEDERAL REGULATIONS. LSA, LIST OF CFR SECTIONS AFFECTED (US) [04509194] **2952**

CODE OF FEDERAL REGULATIONS. N.1, GENERAL PROVISIONS (US) [07878464] **2952**

CODE OF FEDERAL REGULATIONS. N.13, BUSINESS CREDIT AND ASSISTANCE (US) [07864777] **657**

● CODE OF FEDERAL REGULATIONS UPDATE. 21 CFR, DRUGS AND MEDICAL DEVICES (US/1066-3703) [26936664] 3567, **4297**

CODE OF GEORGIA: ANNOTATED (US) **2952**

CODE OF GEORGIA, UNANNOTATED EDITION *CEASED.* (US) [01751075] **2952**

CODE OF LAWS OF SOUTH CAROLINA; ANNOTATED (US) [01642446] **2952**

CODE OF THE CITY OF DETROIT, MICHIGAN (US) [01566318] **4639**

CODE ONE (US/1071-3816) [24396692] **16**

CODE PENAL (FR) [05929782] **3105**

CODE PERMANENT ENVIRONNEMENT ET NUISANCES (FR/0397-6416) [I03976416] **2163**

CODE RURAL; CODE FORESTIER - (FRANCE) (FR) [06072703] **2952**

CODEH : [BOLETIN] / COMITE PARA LA DEFENSA DE LOS DERECHOS HUMANOS EN HONDURAS (HO) [16138003] **4506**

CODEPU FIFTH REGION BOLETIN (US) 4518, **4506**

CODES DE LA SANTE PUBLIQUE DE LA FAMILLE ET DE L'AIDE SOCIALE (FR) [06044802] **5279**

CODES DE LA SECURITE SOCIALE ET DE LA MUTUALITE, MUTUALITE SOCIALE AGRICOLE (FR) [14447539] **5279**

CODESRIA BULLETIN (SG/0850-8712) [16720153] **5195**

CODICE ANALISI DI BILANCIO E CONTABILI (IT) **741**

CODICE BILANCIO E CONTABILITA D'ESERCIZIO (IT) **741**

CODICE CONDOMINIO (IT) **2021**

CODICE DEGLI ALCOLI (IT) **973**

CODICE DEI TRIBUTI LOCALI (IT) **783**

CODICE DELL EDILIZIA LOCAZIONI CONDOMINIO (IT) **2021**

CODICE DELLA GIURISPRUDENZA (IT) **2952**

CODICE DELLA GIURISPRUDENZA PREVIDENZIALE (IT) **2952**

● CODICE DELLA STRADA (IT/1121-6840) [I11216840] **5379**

CODICE DELLE LEGGI E DEI REGOLAMENTI DELLA REGIONE VENETO (IT) **4639**

CODICE DELLE LOCAZIONE (IT) **2818**

CODICE DI PROCEDURA E CONTENZIOSO TRIBUTARIO : 4 RIFORMA TRIBUTARIA (IT) **741**

CODICE D'ITALIA. TESTO VIGENTE. SCHEDE DI AGGIORNAMENTO (IT) **2952**

CODICE IMPOSTE DIRETTE : 4 CODICI RIFORMA TRIBUTARIA (IT) **741**

CODICE INTERNAL AUDITING *CEASED.* (IT) **741**

CODICE IVA : 4 CODICI RIFORMA TRIBUTARIA (IT) **741**

CODICES ARABICI ANTIQUI (GW) [08044457] **2649**

CODICES MANUSCRIPTI (AU) [02246558] **413**

CODICINI MORONI (IT) **1470**

CODIFICACION DE NORMAS DE TRANSITO Y TRANSPORTES - (COLOMBIA) (CK) [03734179] **5379**

CODIFICATION OF PRESIDENTIAL PROCLAMATIONS AND EXECUTIVE ORDERS (US/0191-4839) [04826797] **2952**

CODING CLINIC FOR ICD-9-CM (US/0742-9800) [10481317] **3778**

CODO A CODO (AG) [23825021] **3340**

CODY ENTERPRISE, THE (US/0747-2498) [10663037] **5772**

COENOSES (IT/0393-9154) [19977335] **2212**

COENZYMES AND COFACTORS (US/0892-256X) [15134901] **1041**

COEUR ATOUT (CN/0712-6042) [09336580] **5187**

COEUR ET SANTE PARIS (FR/0335-5306) [I03355306] 2596, **3567**

COFAQ'TUALITE : BULLETIN DE LIAISON DE LA CONFEDERATION DES ORGANISMES FAMILIAUX DU QUEBEC (CN/0834-2121) [16083908] **5279**

COFFEE & COCOA INTERNATIONAL (UK/0262-5938) [07581415] **2366**

COFFEE BREAK (US/0191-9210) [04959616] **2531**

COFFEE INTERNATIONAL (UK/0309-331X) [03570275] **2366**

COFFEE INTERNATIONAL DIRECTORY : CID (UK) [09653659] **2366**

COFFEE STATISTICS (II/0536-7093) [01752778] **152**

COFFEEVILLE COURIER, THE (US) [15003926] **5700**

COFFEY COUNTY FOOTPRINTS (US) **2443**

COFFEY COUNTY REPORTER, THE (US) [10226855] **5675**

COFFEY COUNTY TODAY (US/0745-838X) [09497165] **5675**

COFFEY COUSINS' CLEARINGHOUSE (US/0749-758X) [11145293] **2443**

COFFEYVILLE JOURNAL (COFFEYVILLE, KAN. : 1964) (US/0746-8202) [10305230] **5675**

COFFIN CORNER: OFFICIAL NEWSLETTER/MAGAZINE OF P.F.R.A, THE (US) [12392050] **4890**

COFIEC *See* COFIEC INFORME ANUAL **783**

COFIEC INFORME ANUAL (EC) [01796319] **783**

COG NOTES. MONTHLY PROGRESS REPORT (US) [03190315] **4639**

COGEL BLUE BOOK (US/1060-5045) [23040988] 2249, **4639**

COGEL GUARDIAN *See* GUARDIAN (LEXINGTON, KY.), THE **2250**

COGENERATION (US/0884-7339) [11741181] **2112**

● COGENERATION AND COMPETITIVE POWER JOURNAL (US/1066-8683) [27075057] 2604, **2039**

COGENERATION AND RESOURCE RECOVERY (US) **2039**

COGENERATION & RESOURCE RECOVERY (US) **1935**

COGENERATION AND SMALL POWER MONTHLY *See* COGENERATION AND RESOURCE RECOVERY **2039**

COGENERATION JOURNAL *See* COGENERATION AND COMPETITIVE POWER JOURNAL **2039**

COGENERATION JOURNAL, THE (US/0883-5985) [12174451] **4400**

COGENERATION LETTER, THE (US/0749-5617) [11171940] **1935**

COGENERATION WORLD *See* COGENERATION & RESOURCE RECOVERY **1935**

COGEODATA *See* COGEODATA NEWSLETTER **1372**

COGEODATA NEWSLETTER (CN/0381-5609) [03291567] **1372**

COGITARE See MIND MATTERS **4604**

COGITO (BRISTOL, ENGLAND) (UK/0950-8864) [19510391] **4344**

COGITO DARMSTADT (GW/0178-8728) [I01788728] 1106, **1175**

COGNITION (SZ/0010-0277) [00963652] **4581**

COGNITION AND COMPUTING (US) **1222**

COGNITION & EMOTION (UK/0269-9931) [15584579] **4581**

COGNITION AND INSTRUCTION (US/0737-0008) [09290300] **1891**

COGNITION AND LITERACY (US) **1732**

COGNITION (SCARBOROUGH) (CN/0227-0781) [09137747] **167**

COGNITIVA MADRID (SP/0214-3550) [I02143550] **4581**

●COGNITIVE AND BEHAVIORAL PRACTICE (US) **4581**

●COGNITIVE BRAIN RESEARCH (NE/0926-6410) [26247816] 4581, **3830**

COGNITIVE DEVELOPMENT (US/0885-2014) [12603626] **4581**

COGNITIVE LINGUISTICS (GW/0936-5907) [21589219] **3274**

COGNITIVE NEUROPSYCHOLOGY (UK/0264-3294) [10691303] **4581**

COGNITIVE PSYCHOLOGY (US/0010-0285) [01411264] **4581**

COGNITIVE SCIENCE (US/0364-0213) [02973264] **1212**

COGNITIVE SYSTEMS (NE/0256-663X) [I0256663X] **4581**

COGNITIVE THEORY *CEASED.* (US/0163-2035) [04300654] **4581**

COGNITIVE THERAPY AND RESEARCH (US/0147-5916) [03119600] **4581**

COGNIZER REPORT (US/1057-8374) [24124551] **1175**

COGNIZER REPORT (US) 1250, **1212**

COGNOTES (US/0738-4319) [09602814] **3202**

COHASSET MARINER (US) [26471898] **5688**

COHOCTON JOURNAL, THE (US/1064-4954) [26406683] **2613**

COHSE JOURNAL (UK) [21049727] **1659**

COI. COUNTERTRADE AND OFFSET INTELLIGENCE (UK/0950-916X) [I0950916X] **827**

COIFFBEC (CN/0228-7021) [07802414] **402**

COIFFURE (NE) **402**

COIFFURE DE PARIS ARTS & COIFFURE (US) **403**

COIFFURE DE PARIS, LA (FR) [10805960] **402**

COIFFURE DU CANADA (CN/0226-1383) [06273109] **403**

COIFFURE ET STYLES PARIS (FR/1161-899X) [I1161899X] **403**

COIFFURE Q : INTERNATIONAL HAIR MAGAZINE (UK) **403**

COIMBATORE, INDIA (CITY). SUGARCANE BREEDING INSTITUTE *See* ANNUAL REPORT - SUGARCANE BREEDING INSTITUTE **163**

COIMBRA. BIBLIOTECA MUNICIPAL *See* ARQUIVO COIMBRAO (BOLETIM DA BIBLIOTECA MUNICIPAL) **3192**

COIMBRA. UNIVERSIDADE. CENTRO DE ESTUDOS GEOGRAFICOS *See* BOLETIM - COIMBRA. UNIVERSIDADE. CENTRO DE ESTUDOS GEOGRAFICOS **1074**

COIMBRA. UNIVERSIDADE. FACULDADE DE CIENCIAS *See* REVISTA DA FACULDADE DE CIENCIAS **5147**

COIMBRA. UNIVERSIDADE. INSTITUTO DE FARMACOLOGIA E TERAPEUTICA EXPERIMENTAL *See* ARQUIVOS **4292**

COIN DEALER NEWSLETTER, THE (US/1062-8169) [19948655] **2780**

COIN HOARDS (UK) [03620862] **2780**

COIN INDEXED CHECKLIST TO COLORADO STATE PUBLICATIONS (US) [03298942] **4468**

COIN MAGAZINE (US) **2780**

COIN MONTHLY (UK) **2780**

COIN NEWS (HINDHEAD, ENGLAND) (UK/0955-4386) [20676228] **2780**

COIN PRICES (US/0010-0412) [04040937] **2780**

COIN SLOT (LUZERNE, PA.), THE (US/0745-8533) [08506943] **250**

COIN WORLD (US/0010-0447) [01555023] **2780**

COIN WORLD ALMANAC (US/0361-0845) [02369616] **2780**

... COIN WORLD GUIDE TO U.S. COINS, PRICES, AND VALUE TRENDS, THE (US/1047-8000) [19271277] **2780**

COIN YEARBOOK (UK/0307-6571) [01794065] **2780**

COINAGE (US/0010-0455) [01641265] **2780**

COINAGE MAGAZINE'S GOLD & SILVER (US/0270-4625) [06409059] **2780**

COINAGE OF THE AMERICAS CONFERENCE *See* PROCEEDINGS / COINAGE OF THE AMERICAS CONFERENCE **2783**

COINS (IOLA, WIS.) (US/0010-0471) [06933087] **2780**

COINS MARKET VALUES (UK) [07979329] **2780**

COIR *CEASED.* (II/0530-0495) [03178122] **5349**

COKEMAKING INTERNATIONAL (GW/0937-9258) [I09379258] **2137**

COKER COLLEGE *See* ALUMNI DIRECTORY / COKER COLLEGE **1098**

COL BLANC *CEASED.* (CN/0227-6046) [08072141] **1659**

COLABORACION INTERNACIONAL (CU) [16288529] **1470**

COLADA (SP/0010-0544) [11110031] **4000**

COLBY FREE PRESS AND THE PRAIRIE DRUMMER, THE (US) [12732714] **5675**

COLBY QUARTERLY (US/1050-5873) [21399403] **3376**

COLCHESTER COUNTY, NOVA SCOTIA, TRAVEL GUIDE (CN/0828-7651) [12199514] **5466**

COLD-DRILL MAGAZINE (US/0890-0086) [14116191] **3376**

COLD REGIONS SCIENCE AND TECHNOLOGY (NE/0165-232X) [05392089] **1968**

COLD REGIONS TECHNICAL DIGEST (US) [12155694] **1968**

COLD SPRING HARBOR LABORATORY *See* ANNUAL REPORT / COLD SPRING HARBOR LABORATORY **442**

COLD SPRING HARBOR MONOGRAPH SERIES (US/0270-1847) [05350933] **451**

COLD SPRING HARBOR, NEW YORK. LABORATORY OF QUANTITATIVE BIOLOGY *See* ABSTRACTS OF PAPERS PRESENTED AT ... MEETINGS - LABORATORY OF QUNATITATIVE BIOLOGY **439**

COLD SPRING HARBOR, NEW YORK. LABORATORY OF QUANTITATIVE BIOLOGY *See* ANNUAL REPORT - COLD SPRING HARBOR, NEW YORK. LABORATORY OF QUANTITATIVE BIOLOGY **442**

COLD SPRING HARBOR SYMPOSIA ON QUANTITATIVE BIOLOGY (US/0091-7451) [01280332] **451**

COLD STORAGE (US/0091-1267) [07119275] **167**

COLD STORAGE / STATE OF NEW YORK, DEPARTMENT OF AGRICULTURE AND MARKETS (US) [05016354] **2604**

COLDWATER DAILY REPORTER (US/0745-6794) [09399135] **5691**

COLDWATER JOURNAL, THE (CN/0711-2181) [08649637] **5782**

COLE CHRONICLE (US/0887-1264) [13105373] **2443**

COLE PAPERS, THE (US/1062-6727) [25695467] **2918**

COLECAO CLE (BL/0103-3247) [I01033247] **5095**

COLECAO DOS AUTORES CELEBRES DA LITERATURA BRASILEIRA (BL) **3376**

COLECAO RODOLFO GARCIA (BL) [09519650] **413**

COLECCIO HISTORICA (SP) [01644982] **2684**

COLECCION ANTROPOLOGIA E HISTORIA / ADMINISTRACION DEL PATRIMONIO CULTURAL (SP) [13680047] **234**

COLECCION BASICA ARAGONESA (SP) [07634999] **2514**

COLECCION BREVE (MX) [02418256] **234**

COLECCION CIENCIAS SOCIALES (VE/0505-172X) [01486214] **5195**

COLECCION DE DOCUMENTOS PARA LA HISTORIA DEL COMERCIO EXTERIOR DE MEXICO (MX/0587-8160) [03164821] **1551**

COLECCION ESPACIO Y FORMA (VE/0505-1762) [01489370] **2818**

COLECCION ESTUDIOS CIEPLAN (CL/0716-0631) [06175141] **1552**

COLECCION FILOLOGICA (SP/0436-2888) [01454453] **3274**

COLECCION INI (MX) [10410668] **234**

COLECCION JUVENIL MC (SP) 1732, **2278**

COLECCION METODOLOGICA; PUBLICACION (AG) [05330413] **1590**

COLECCION RELACIONES DE TRABAJO (VE) [29231333] **1660**

COLECCION SEP-INI (MX) [03554617] **234**

COLECCION TAMESIS. SERIA A : MONOGRAFIAS (UK/0587-9914) [03165128] **2514**

COLECCION TEATRO (SP/0587-9957) [03165254] **5363**

COLECCION TEMAS (CK) [03032274] **4948**

COLECCION TESIS DOCTORALES (VE/0505-1827) [01496822] **4344**

COLECTANEA DE JURISPRUDENCIA CANONICA (SP) [02901166] **2952**

COLECTIA DE HOTARIRI ALE CONSILIULUI DE MINISTRI SI ALTE ACTE NORMATIVE (RM) [07730505] **4639**

COLEGIO BRASILEIRO DE CIRURGIOES *See* REVISTA DO COLEGIO BRASILEIRO DE CIRURGIOES **3973**

COLEGIO DE ABAGADOS DE ZARAGOZA *See* LISTA DE LOS SENORES QUE FORMAN LOS EXPRESADOS COLEGIOS **3141**

COLEGIO DE INGENIERNOS CIVILES DE MEXICO *See* CIC **2020**

COLEGIO DE MEXICO *See* JORNADAS **5205**

COLEGIO DE MEXICO *See* BOLETIN SEMESTRAL - COLEGIO DE MEXICO **1089**

COLEGIO NACIONAL (MEXICO) *See* MEMORIA DE EL COLEGIO NACIONAL **1835**

COLEGIO OFICIAL DE APAREJADORES Y ARQUITECTOS TECNICOS DEL CENTRO DE ESPANA *See* LISTIN DE COLEGIADOS - COLEGIO OFICIAL DE APAREJADORES Y ARQUITECTOS TECNICOS DEL CENTRO DE ESPANA **302**

●COLEGIOS : THE NEWSLETTER ON THE HISTORY OF IDEAS IN COLONIAL LATIN AMERICA (US) [26408856] **2728**

COLEMAN COUNTY CHRONICLE (US) [14091796] **5766**

COLEMAN GUIDE TO CAMPING & THE GREAT OUTDOORS (US/0734-7251) [08787504] **4871**

COLEMAN OUTDOOR ANNUAL *See* COLEMAN GUIDE TO CAMPING & THE GREAT OUTDOORS **4871**

COLEMANIA (BANGALORE) (II/0970-3292) [08311784] **5607**

COLEOPTERISTS' BULLETIN, THE (US/0010-065X) [01555042] **5580**

COLE'S REGISTER OF BRITISH ANTIQUARIAN & SECONDHAND BOOKDEALERS (UK) [18145670] **4828**

COLETANEA DE RESOLUCOES DO CONSELHO DELIBERATIVO. COLETANEA DE ATOS DA PRESIDENCIA (BL) [02649225] **2952**

COLETANEA DO INSTITUTO DE TECNOLOGIA DE ALIMENTOS (BL/0100-350X) [01788632] **2331**

COLFAX MESSENGER, THE (US) [13194760] **5766**

COLIBRI (MX) [06912709] **1924**

COLIN WILSON STUDIES (US) **431**

COLLABORATION (HIGH FALLS) (US/0164-1522) [04588110] 4948, **4344**

COLLABORATIVE COMPUTING (UK/0968-2082) **1175**

COLLABORATIVE STUDY ON CEREBRAL PALSY, MENTAL RETARDATION, & OTHER NEUROLOGICAL & SENSORY DISORDERS OF INFANCY & CHILDHOOD (US/0361-3267) [02040145] **3830**

COLLAGE (CN) [04754572] **4087**

COLLAGE (CAMP HILL, PA.) (US/0883-2781) [12056444] **4760**

COLLAGE (WHEELING, ILL.) (US/0745-2810) [09047977] **2531**

COLLANA DEL CENTENARIO (IT) [13392390] **3477**

COLLANA DI AGGIORNAMENTI IN ANESTESIA E RIANIMAZIONE (IT/0390-6310) [02670688] **3682**

COLLANA DI SAGGI E TESTI. SEZIONE SESTA, STORIA DELL'ARTE (IT) [09158618] **347**

COLLANA DI STUDI CICERONIANI (IT/0588-0750) [03165072] **2684**

COLLANA DI STUDI CLASSICI (IT/0588-0777) [03165079] **1076**

COLLANA
Alphabetical Title Index

COLLANA DI STUDI DI STORIA E POLITICA AFRICANA (IT/0530-6442) [03165097] **2498**

COLLANA DI STUDI E DOCUMENTAZIONE *CEASED.* (IT/0573-2697) [03296831] **1602**

COLLANA DI STUDI PALESTRINIANI (IT/0069-5211) [03165118] **4110**

COLLANA DI STUDI SULLA PUBBLICITA (IT/0413-4028) [03165124] **4813**

COLLANA DOCUMENTAZIONE STATISTICA E NOTIZIARIO STATISTICO REGIONALE (IT) **5325**

COLLANA STORICA (IT/0418-727X) [04753721] **2684**

COLLEAGUE (US) [05462303] **4582**

COLLEAGUE (US) [17826789] **1815**

COLLECCION BIBLIOGRAFICA - ACADEMIA NACIONAL DE LA HISTORIA, DEPARTAMENTO DE INVESTIGACIONES (VE) [03247047] **2635**

COLLECCION LEGISLATIVA DEL MINISTERIO DE DEFENSA. AÑO 1988 (SP/0213-3156) **4039**

COLLECT, I (US/1056-4527) [23719176] **2772**

COLLECTABLE OLD ADVERTISING (US/0091-0473) [01783401] **757**

COLLECTABLES AUCTION (CN/0822-4927) [10007990] **2772**

COLLECTABLES AUCTION / CHARLTON AUCTIONS (CN/0822-4889) [10007948] **2772**

COLLECTANEA BOTANICA (SP/0010-0730) [02350827] **507**

COLLECTANEA CISTERCIENSIA (BE) [03296921] **5027**

COLLECTANEA FRANCISCANA (IT/0010-0749) [01771258] **5027**

COLLECTANEA HIBERNICA (IE/0530-7058) [02446049] **2684**

COLLECTANEA INSTITUTI ANTHROPOS (GW) [01716702] **234**

COLLECTANEA MARITIMA (BE) 4175, 2684, **1448**

COLLECTANEA MATHEMATICA (BARCELONA) (SP/0010-0757) [03400637] **3500**

COLLECTANEA THEOLOGICA (PL/0137-6985) [04746304] **5028**

COLLECTED ALGORITHMS FROM ACM (US) [03561539] 3500, **1175**

COLLECTED ALGORITHMS FROM ACM. SUPPLEMENT (US/0149-1989) [03451055] **1175**

COLLECTED LETTERS / CORRESPONDENCE SOCIETY OF SURGEONS (US/0162-6477) [04200048] **3962**

COLLECTED LETTERS OF THE INTERNATIONAL CORRESPONDENCE SOCIETY OF OBSTETRICIANS, GYNECOLOGISTS (US/0443-9058) [04200008] **3759**

COLLECTED PAPERS - FLORIDA. UNIVERSITY, GAINESVILLE. COLLEGE OF MEDICINE. DEPARTMENT OF PHYSIOLOGY (US) [01400628] **579**

COLLECTED PAPERS FROM THE NATIONAL CANCER RESEARCH INSTITUTE (JA/0077-3662) [01183685] **3815**

COLLECTED PAPERS ON SOUTH ASIA (UK/0141-0156) [03835029] **2649**

COLLECTED REPRINTS - ATMOSPHERIC PHYSICS AND CHEMISTRY LABORATORY (US) [02707585] 973, **4400**

COLLECTED REPRINTS - NATIONAL OCEAN SURVEY (US/0361-2805) [02246047] **1448**

COLLECTED REPRINTS (SOUTHWEST FISHERIES CENTER) (US) [08450159] 1448, **2299**

COLLECTED REPRINTS - UNIVERSITY OF GEORGIA MARINE INSTITUTE (US/0072-1328) [01280203] **553**

COLLECTED REPRINTS - WATER RESOURCES RESEARCH CENTER, UNIVERSITY OF HAWAII *CEASED.* (US) [05666046] **5532**

COLLECTED REPRINTS - WEATHER MODIFICATION PROGRAM OFFICE (US/0147-8702) [03246377] **1424**

COLLECTED SEMINAR PAPERS / UNIVERSITY OF LONDON, INSTITUTE OF COMMONWEALTH STUDIES (UK/0076-0773) [02321780] 3376, **5195**

COLLECTED STUDIES IN CRIMINOLOGICAL RESEARCH (FR) [03424296] **3160**

COLLECTED WORKS ON CARDIO-PULMONARY DISEASES (US/0069-5319) [01564013] **3703**

COLLECTIBLE AUTOMOBILE (US/0742-812X) [10487008] **5411**

COLLECTIBLE NEWSPAPERS (US/1076-4356) [13591323] **2772**

COLLECTIBLE TRUCKS (US) [25718250] 2772, **5411**

COLLECTIBLES CANADA (CN) **250**

●COLLECTIBLES, COUNTRY & AMERICANA (US/1073-8142) [29534960] **2772**

COLLECTIBLES MARKET GUIDE & PRICE INDEX TO LIMITED EDITION PLATES, FIGURINES, BELLS, GRAPHICS, STEINS, AND DOLLS *See* COLLECTORS' INFORMATION BUREAU'S COLLECTIBLES MARKET GUIDE & PRICE INDEX **2772**

COLLECTIF PAROLES (CN/0710-5002) [08651905] **2728**

●COLLECTING TOYS (US/1068-347X) [27364300] 2772, **2584**

COLLECTION AGENCY ACT WITH RULES AND REGULATIONS - (CALIFORNIA) (US) [06857370] **2952**

COLLECTION AGENCY DIRECTORY (US/1058-983X) [24452594] **1602**

COLLECTION AGENCY REPORT (US/1052-4029) [22283901] 783, **658**

COLLECTION ANALYSE DES NOUVEAUX PROGRAMMES (CN/0820-747X) [09457088] **1891**

COLLECTION BUILDING (US/0160-4953) [03691824] **3202**

COLLECTION COLLOQUES ET SEMINAIRES. INSTITUT FRANCAIS DU PETROLE (FR/0073-8360) [07530527] **4253**

COLLECTION CONTACTOLOGIA (GW/0934-215X) [20929773] **3873**

COLLECTION CXP CATALOGUES DE PROGICIELS (FR/0985-0791) [I09850791] **1284**

COLLECTION - (DAKAR) (FR/0418-2901) [01565826] **2638**

COLLECTION DE DOCUMENTS INEDITS SUR L'HISTOIRE DE FRANCE. SERIE IN-8 (FR/0588-1773) [01639606] **2684**

COLLECTION DE GRAMMAIRES (FR) [02716226] **3274**

COLLECTION DE LA DIRECTION DES ETUDES ET RECHERCHES D'ELECTRICITE DE FRANCE (FR/0399-4198) [16694124] **2039**

COLLECTION DE L'ECOLE FRANCAISE DE ROME (IT) [01567346] **1076**

COLLECTION DE MEDECINE LEGALE ET DE TOXICOLOGIE MEDICALE (FR/0398-9119) [04633638] **3740**

COLLECTION DE MONOGRAPHIES DE MEDECINE DU TRAVAIL (FR/0248-742X) [17301524] **2860**

COLLECTION DE RELATIONS INTERNATIONALES (NE) [03170983] **4518**

COLLECTION DE TRAVAUX DE L'ACADEMIE INTERNATIONALE D'HISTOIRE DES SCIENCES (FR) [01460672] **5095**

COLLECTION D'ECOLOGIE (FR/0335-7473) [01326897] **2212**

COLLECTION DES DICTIONNAIRES TECHNIQUES (FR/0530-7678) [03179322] 1372, **4253**

COLLECTION DES MELANGES DE LA BIBLIOTHEQUE DE LA SORBONNE (FR) [15259362] **3202**

COLLECTION DES UNIVERSITES DE FRANCE (FR/0184-7155) [08329065] **1815**

COLLECTION D'ESTHETIQUE (FR/0588-1757) [03179370] **2844**

COLLECTION D'ETUDES ANCIENNES (FR) **2613**

COLLECTION DU BICENTENAIRE DE LA REVOLUTION FRANCAISE *CEASED.* (FR) [15001038] **2684**

COLLECTION DU DEPARTEMENT D'ECONOMIQUE (CN/0318-6334) [02442065] **75**

COLLECTION ECOLOGIE APPLIQUEE ET SCIENCES DE L'ENVIRONNEMENT (FR) [07324054] **2226**

COLLECTION ENCRE (CN/0228-0337) [07295223] **3376**

COLLECTION ENSEIGNEMENT DES SCIENCES (FR/0768-0341) [12366024] **5095**

COLLECTION ESSAIS SUR L'HISTOIRE DU PROTESTANTISME FRANCAIS (BE/0530-7848) [03179536] **5058**

COLLECTION FORUM (OTTAWA) (CN/0831-4985) [13407069] **4165**

COLLECTION IDEES (FR/0530-8089) [03183468] **4344**

COLLECTION LATOMUS (BE) [01564024] 3274, **1076**

COLLECTION "LES GRANDS PROBLEMES DE LA BIOLOGIE." (FR/0588-2206) [03183521] **451**

COLLECTION LETTRES MEDIEVALES (FR) [12871780] **5195**

COLLECTION MANAGEMENT (US/0146-2679) [03492312] **3202**

COLLECTION MONOGRAPHIQUE RODOPI EN LITTERATURE FRANCAISE CONTEMPORAINE (NE/0169-0078) [01690078] **3376**

COLLECTION NORDICANA (CN/0078-1053) [01781288] 234, **451**

COLLECTION OF CZECHOSLOVAK CHEMICAL COMMUNICATIONS (UK/0010-0765) [01564026] **973**

COLLECTION OF LEGAL OPINIONS, A (US/0361-6673) [02246700] **3110**

COLLECTION OF TALKS OF HISTORICAL INTEREST, A (CN/0828-7597) [12204293] **2728**

COLLECTION ORGANISATION PEDAGOGIQUE (CN/0820-7860) [09547370] **1861**

COLLECTION PALEO-QUEBEC (CN/0821-3801) [02167100] **266**

COLLECTION RECHERCHES GERMANIQUES (FR) [18680700] **3376**

COLLECTION "SCIENCES SOCIALES DU TRAVAIL." (FR/0588-2478) [03188637] **5196**

COLLECTION SEPTIEME ART 7 ART (FR) **347**

COLLECTION STENDHALIENNE (SZ/0530-9220) [03188660] **3376**

COLLECTION - UNIVERSITE DE LYON II. CENTRE D'HISTOIRE DU CATHOLICISME (FR) [01515056] **5028**

COLLECTION UPDATE (CN/0226-3300) [06461671] **3203**

COLLECTIONS (BUFFALO) (US/0160-0664) [03596890] **4165**

COLLECTIONS (COLUMBIA, S.C.) (US/1046-2252) [19994091] 317, **4087**

COLLECTIONS DE STATISTIQUE AGRICOLE. ETUDE (FR) [03149528] **75**

COLLECTIONS FOR A HISTORY OF STAFFORDSHIRE (UK) [01715079] **2684**

COLLECTIONS / GEORGIA HISTORICAL SOCIETY (US/0733-7760) [01771998] **2728**

COLLECTIONS - MALONE SOCIETY, LONDON (UK) [01909297] **3376**

COLLECTIONS (NEWARK, DEL.) (US/8755-3473) [11274777] **3203**

COLLECTIONS OF THE MASSACHUSETTS HISTORICAL SOCIETY (US/1046-1396) [01756821] **2728**

COLLECTIONS OF THE ROYAL NOVA SCOTIA HISTORICAL SOCIETY (CN/1193-9451) [28061952] **2728**

COLLECTIONS (PHILADELPHIA, PA.) (US/0275-8091) [07223619] 5553, **3567**

●COLLECTIONS SERVICES NEWS (US/1065-5859) [26639514] **3203**

COLLECTIVE BARGAINING HANDBOOK (CN/0710-5193) [08534492] **939**

COLLECTIVE BARGAINING IN HIGHER EDUCATION AND THE PROFESSIONS (US/0738-1913) [08712254] 939, **1815**

●COLLECTIVE BARGAINING IN NEW BRUNSWICK (CN/1193-3437) [27019058] **1660**

COLLECTIVE BARGAINING NEGOTIATIONS AND CONTRACTS (US/0010-079X) [01537825] **3145**

COLLECTIVE BARGAINING REVIEW (CN/0010-0803) [01552851] **1660**

COLLECTIVE BARGAINING SETTLEMENTS IN NEW YORK STATE (US) [05080707] **1660**

COLLECTIVE BARGAINING SETTLEMENTS IN ONTARIO 1985 (CN/0829-7800) [I08297800] **1660**

COLLECTIVE BARGAINING : STATISTICS IN EDUCATION (CN/0700-5121) [03403153] 1732, **1793**

COLLECTIVE CATALOGUE BELGIUM : CCB. CD-ROM (BE) **413**

COLLECTIVE VOLUME OF SCIENTIFIC PAPERS. RECUEIL DE DOCUMENTS SCIENTIFIQUES. COLECCION DE DOCUMENTOS CIENTIFICOS (SP) [06031963] **2299**

COLLECTIVITES EXPRESS (FR/0010-0811) [I00100811] **5279**

COLLECTIVITES EXPRESS *See* COLLECTIVITES HOTELLERIE ET RESTAURATION PARIS **5279**

COLLECTIVITES HOTELLERIE ET RESTAURATION PARIS (FR/1242-2126) [I12422126] **5279**

COLLECTOR CAR NEWS (US/0888-1944) [13501069] 5411, **2772**

COLLECTOR EDITIONS (US/0733-2130) [08537989] **2772**

COLLECTOR (HUNTER, N.Y.), THE (US/1071-4162) [05521123] **2772**

COLLECTOR MAGAZINE & PRICE GUIDE (US) **250**

COLLECTOR (MINNEAPOLIS, MINN.) (US/0010-082X) [06598776] **783**

COLLECTORS' AUCTION (BALTIMORE) (US/0093-1047) [01788434] **4087**

COLLECTORS BULLETIN (CANTON, ILL.) (US/1048-0951) [20850042] **2780**

COLLECTOR'S CAR (UK) [06484753] 5411, **2772**

COLLECTORS' CHRONICLE, THE (CN/1183-2185) [25066710] **2772**

COLLECTORS CLASSICS (UK) [05418124] **2772**

COLLECTORS CLUB (NEW YORK, N.Y.) See COLLECTORS CLUB PHILATELIST, THE **2785**

COLLECTORS CLUB PHILATELIST, THE (US/0010-0838) [01564036] **2785**

COLLECTOR'S EDITIONS REVIEW See COLLECTORS PHOTOGRAPHY **4368**

●COLLECTORS' INFORMATION BUREAU'S COLLECTIBLES MARKET GUIDE & PRICE INDEX (US/1068-4808) [27542449] **2772**

COLLECTORS' JOURNAL OF ANCIENT ART (US/0885-2995) [07040839] 2781, **347**

COLLECTORS JOURNAL (VINTON) (US/0164-6915) [04413851] **5669**

COLLECTORS' MARKETPLACE DIRECTORY. NEW YORK CITY DESIGN (US/0735-9357) [08251131] **2772**

COLLECTORS MART (US/0744-9879) [08697407] **250**

COLLECTORS NEWS & THE ANTIQUE REPORTER (US/0162-1033) [02250975] **250**

COLLECTORS PHOTOGRAPHY (US/0896-9043) [17338556] **4368**

COLLECTORS' SHOWCASE (SAN DIEGO, CALIF.) (US/0744-5989) [08437762] 2772, **250**

●COLLECTOR'S SOURCE (US/1066-3649) [26923170] **2772**

COLLECTORS WORLD (STAFFORD, STAFFORDSHIRE) (UK) [11296352] **2773**

COLLECTRIX *CEASED.* (US/0738-9981) [09692833] **250**

COLLEGAMENTO (SZ) [01564039] **4297**

COLLEGE ADMINISTRATOR AND THE COURTS, THE (US/0192-1371) [04952645] 1815, **2952**

COLLEGE ADMISSIONS DATA HANDBOOK. MID-WEST REGION (US/0738-9574) [08090249] **1815**

COLLEGE ADMISSIONS DATA HANDBOOK. NORTHEAST REGION (US/0738-9566) [08881037] **1815**

COLLEGE ADMISSIONS DATA HANDBOOK. SOUTHEAST REGION (US/0738-9590) [08011288] **1815**

COLLEGE ADMISSIONS DATA HANDBOOK. WEST REGION (US/0738-9582) [08877081] **1816**

COLLEGE ADMISSIONS DATA SERVICE See COLLEGE ADMISSIONS DATA HANDBOOK. WEST REGION **1816**

COLLEGE ADMISSIONS DATA SERVICE See COLLEGE ADMISSIONS DATA HANDBOOK. NORTHEAST REGION **1815**

COLLEGE ADMISSIONS INDEX OF MAJORS & SPORTS (US) [16937312] **1855**

COLLEGE & JR. TENNIS See COLLEGE AND JUNIOR TENNIS **4890**

COLLEGE AND JUNIOR TENNIS (US/0279-1153) [07565479] **4890**

COLLEGE AND PRO BASKETBALL TIMES See BASKETBALL TIMES **4887**

COLLEGE & RESEARCH LIBRARIES (US/0010-0870) [02354797] **3203**

●COLLEGE & UNDERGRADUATE LIBRARIES (US/1069-1316) [27942488] **3203**

COLLEGE AND UNIVERSITY (US/0010-0889) [06168802] **1816**

COLLEGE AND UNIVERSITY ADMISSIONS AND ENROLLMENT, NEW YORK STATE (US/0147-5894) [03195748] **1816**

COLLEGE & UNIVERSITY EMPLOYEES, NEW YORK STATE (US) [11327822] **1861**

COLLEGE BAND DIRECTORS NATIONAL ASSOCIATION JOURNAL (US/0742-8480) [10466792] **4110**

COLLEGE BLUE BOOK. DEGREES OFFERED BY COLLEGES AND SUBJECTS, THE (US) [05388903] **1816**

COLLEGE BLUE BOOK. NARRATIVE DESCRIPTIONS, THE (US) [08508402] **1816**

COLLEGE BLUE BOOK. TABULAR DATA, THE (US) [05653189] **1816**

COLLEGE BOARD NEWS (US/0530-9581) [02255270] **1816**

COLLEGE BOARD REVIEW, THE (US/0010-0951) [01564050] **1816**

COLLEGE BOUND (EVANSTON, ILL.) (US/1068-7912) [27803138] **1816**

COLLEGE BROADCASTER (US/1055-0461) [21338707] 2039, **1130**

COLLEGE CATALOG COLLECTION [MICROFORM] (US) [18267299] **1816**

COLLEGE CHEMISTRY FACULTIES (US/0588-2699) [04675312] 1816, **973**

COLLEGE COMMENT (THUNDER BAY) (CN/0700-3668) [03279363] **1816**

COLLEGE COMPOSITION AND COMMUNICATION (US/0010-096X) [01564051] 3274, **1816**

COLLEGE CORNER NEWS (US) [12849738] **5663**

COLLEGE COST BOOK, THE (US/0270-8493) [06505271] **1816**

COLLEGE CREDIT RECOMMENDATIONS : THE DIRECTORY OF THE NATIONAL PROGRAM ON NONCOLLEGIATE SPONSORED INSTRUCTION (US) [13244186] **1912**

COLLEGE DE FRANCE See ANNUAIRE DU COLLEGE DE FRANCE **1809**

COLLEGE DE LA GASPESIE See ANNUAIRE - CEGEP DE LA GASPESIE ET DES ILES **1809**

COLLEGE DE L'ASSOMPTION. BIBLIOTHEQUE See LISTE DES NOUVEAUTES - COLLEGE DE L'ASSOMPTION. BIBLIOTHEQUE DU COLLEGIAL **3228**

COLLEGE DE L'ASSOMPTION. BIBLIOTHEQUE See REGARD SUR LA BIBLIOTHEQUE DU COLLEGE DE L'ASSOMPTION **3244**

COLLEGE DE MAISONNEUVE. BIBLIOTHEQUE See PERIODIQUES - BIBLIOTHEQUE. CEGEP DE MAISONNEUVE **422**

COLLEGE DU VIEUX MONTREAL. ASSOCIATION DES PARENTS See BULLETIN DE L'ASSOCIATION DE PARENTS DU COLLEGE VIEUX MONTREAL **1812**

COLLEGE ENGLISH (US/0010-0994) [01564053] 1816, **3274**

COLLEGE ENGLISH ASSOCIATION See CEA FORUM **3273**

COLLEGE ENTRANCE EXAMINATION BOARD See ANNUAL MEETING PROCEEDINGS - COLLEGE ENTRANCE EXAMINATION BOARD **1809**

COLLEGE ENTRANCE EXAMINATION BOARD See NEED ANALYSIS REQUIREMENTS, PLUS THE COMPLETE CSS CODE LIST **1837**

COLLEGE ENTRANCE EXAMINATION BOARD See COLLEGE PLACEMENT AND CREDIT BY EXAMINATION **1816**

COLLEGE ENTRANCE EXAMINATION BOARD See COLLEGE HANDBOOK, THE **1816**

COLLEGE ENTRANCE EXAMINATION BOARD. ADMISSIONS TESTING PROGRAM See GUIDE TO THE ADMISSIONS TESTING PROGRAM **1827**

COLLEGE ENTRANCE EXAMINATION BOARD. COLLEGE SCHOLARSHIP SERVICE See COLLEGE COST BOOK, THE **1816**

COLLEGE ENTRANCE EXAMINATION BOARD. COLLEGE SCHOLARSHIP SERVICE See C.S.S. NEED ANALYSIS **1813**

COLLEGE FACTS CHART (US/0069-5688) [01796285] **1816**

COLLEGE FINANCIAL AID EMERGENCY KIT / JOYCE LAIN KENNEDY & HERM DAVIS, THE (US) [14767476] **1816**

COLLEGE FINANCIAL AID STRATEGIES (US) **1816**

COLLEGE FINANCIAL FACTS (US/1046-8501) [20610043] **1816**

COLLEGE FOOTBALL MODERN RECORD BOOK (US/0092-881X) [01783400] **4890**

COLLEGE FOOTBALL TODAY (US/1059-4825) [24639487] **4890**

COLLEGE GRADUATES APPOINTED BY IRS (US) [05069645] 1816, **4718**

COLLEGE GRANTS FROM UNCLE SAM (US) [08042680] **1816**

COLLEGE HANDBOOK, THE (US/0069-5653) [01564057] **1816**

COLLEGE HELP NEWSLETTER See PIP COLLEGE "HELPS" NEWSLETTER **1883**

COLLEGE HOCKEY (US/1061-6357) [25298865] **4890**

COLLEGE HOCKEY MAGAZINE See U.S. COLLEGE HOCKEY MAGAZINE **4927**

COLLEGE JEAN-DE-BREBEUF. BIBLIOTHEQUE DU PAVILLON LALEMANT See GUIDE DE LA BIBLIOTHEQUE DU CENTRE AUDIO-VISUEL - COLLEGE JEAN-DE-BREBEUF **3212**

COLLEGE LANGUAGE ASSOCIATION (U.S.) See CLA JOURNAL **3273**

COLLEGE LAW BULLETIN (US/0010-101X) [01564061] **2952**

COLLEGE LAW DIGEST (US/0045-737X) [01605515] **2952**

COLLEGE LITERATURE (US/0093-3139) [01791774] **3376**

COLLEGE LOANS FROM UNCLE SAM (US) [08003855] **1816**

●COLLEGE MANAGEMENT TODAY (UK/0966-6907) 1816, **864**

COLLEGE MARIE-VICTORIN. CENTRE DE DOCUMENTATION See BIBLIO SERVICE **1727**

●COLLEGE MARKETING ANNUAL (US/1065-0369) [26492076] 922, **1816**

COLLEGE MATHEMATICS JOURNAL, THE (US/0746-8342) [10310554] **3500**

COLLEGE MEDIA DIRECTORY, THE (US/1046-4255) [20019735] **1816**

COLLEGE MEDIA REVIEW (US/0739-1056) [09703341] **2918**

COLLEGE MONTHLY (US/0094-6613) [01795163] **1816**

COLLEGE MONTMORENCY See MONTMORENCY **1836**

COLLEGE MUSIC SOCIETY See CMS PROCEEDINGS **4110**

COLLEGE MUSIC SOCIETY See NEWSLETTER - COLLEGE MUSIC SOCIETY **4141**

COLLEGE MUSIC SYMPOSIUM (US/0069-5696) [01022678] **4110**

COLLEGE NEWSPAPER DIRECTORY AND RATE BOOK (US) [09362952] **1090**

COLLEGE OF AGRICULTURE ALUMNI DIRECTORY / UNIVERSITY OF KENTUCKY (US) [23927126] **1101**

COLLEGE OF AGRICULTURE, NAGPUR See MAGAZINE - COLLEGE OF AGRICULTURE, NAGPUR **106**

COLLEGE OF AMERICAN PATHOLOGISTS SURVEYS (US) **3894**

COLLEGE OF AMERICAN PATHOLOGISTS SURVEYS. ASHI. CAP HISTORCOMPATIBILTY (US) **3894**

COLLEGE OF ENGINEERING, TRIVANDRUM, INDIA See MAGAZINE - COLLEGE OF ENGINEERING, TRIVANDRUM, INDIA **1985**

COLLEGE OF PHYSICIANS AND SURGEONS OF ALBERTA See MEDICAL DIRECTORY - COLLEGE OF PHYSICIANS AND SURGEONS OF ALBERTA **3915**

COLLEGE OF PHYSICIANS AND SURGEONS OF BRITISH COLUMBIA See MEDICAL DIRECTORY (VANCOUVER) **3915**

COLLEGE OF PHYSICIANS AND SURGEONS OF MANITOBA See LIST OF MEDICAL PRACTITIONERS CURRENTLY LICENSED TO PRACTISE IN THE PROVINCE / THE COLLEGE OF PHYSICIANS AND SURGEONS OF MANITOBA **3914**

COLLEGE OF PHYSICIANS OF PHILADELPHIA See TRANSACTIONS & STUDIES OF THE COLLEGE OF PHYSICIANS OF PHILADELPHIA **3647**

COLLEGE OF SCIENCE ALUMNI DIRECTORY, THE PENNSYLVANIA STATE UNIVERSITY (US/0740-462X) [09936923] 5095, **1101**

COLLEGE OF THE VIRGIN ISLANDS. AGRICULTURAL EXPERIMENT STATION See REPORT / COLLEGE OF THE VIRGIN ISLANDS. AGRICULTURAL EXPERIMENT STATION **125**

COLLEGE OF VETERINARIANS OF ONTARIO See DIRECTORY / COLLEGE OF VETERINARIANS OF ONTARIO. [DISKETTE] **5509**

COLLEGE OF WILLIAM & MARY ANNUAL TAX CONFERENCE : [PAPERS] (US) [15559283] **4718**

COLLEGE PLACEMENT AND CREDIT BY EXAMINATION (US/0364-2208) [02626915] **1816**

COLLEGE PLACEMENT COUNCIL See CPC SALARY SURVEY FOR REGION MAPA **1819**

COLLEGE PLACEMENT COUNCIL See CPC SALARY SURVEY FOR REGION MCPA **4203**

COLLEGE PLACEMENT COUNCIL See CPC SALARY SURVEY **4203**

COLLEGE PLACEMENT COUNCIL DIRECTORY (US/1076-1799) [27373742] 4203, **1817**

COLLEGE PLACER, THE (US) [17377441] **5760**

●COLLEGE PLANNING QUARTERLY (US/1071-3751) [28626366] **1732**

COLLEGE PLANNING QUARTERLY (US) 1817, **1090**

COLLEGE PLANNING/SEARCH BOOK (US/0147-8826) [03247069] **1817**

COLLEGE POETRY REVIEW *SUSPENDED.* (US) [02223164] **3340**

COLLEGE PRESS SERVICE (US/0010-1125) [05731947] **5659**

COLLEGE RECRUITING REPORT (US/0361-5057) [02246351] **1660**

COLLEGE REVIEW (DENVER, COLO.), THE (US/0742-8057) [10442781] **3567**

COLLEGE

●COLLEGE SPORTS (RUTHERFORD, N.J.) (US/1065-8270) [26755844] **4890**

COLLEGE STORE EXECUTIVE (US/0010-1141) [05078391] 949, **922**

COLLEGE STORE JOURNAL, THE (US/0010-115X) [05165500] **1817**

COLLEGE STUDENT AFFAIRS JOURNAL, THE (US/0888-210X) [08624699] **1817**

COLLEGE STUDENT AND THE COURTS, THE (US/0145-1472) [02702677] **2952**

COLLEGE STUDENT JOURNAL (US/0146-3934) [01564072] **1817**

COLLEGE TEACHING (US/8756-7555) [11658781] **1817**

COLLEGE THEOLOGY SOCIETY *See* PROCEEDINGS **4988**

COLLEGE UNION & ON-CAMPUS HOSPITALITY (US/0887-431X) [13230687] 1817, **1090**

COLLEGE WOMAN (BURBANK, CALIF.) **SUSPENDED.** (US/0885-937X) [12797742] 5553, **1817**

COLLEGES AND UNIVERSITIES. FINANCE (US) [20510843] **1817**

COLLEGES AND UNIVERSITIES. TEACHERS PREPARED (US) [19990162] **1891**

COLLEGIATE BASEBALL (US/0530-9751) [06106137] **4890**

COLLEGIATE BASEBALL DIGEST *See* COLLEGIATE BASEBALL **4890**

●COLLEGIATE JOURNAL, THE (US/1061-8767) [25482408] **4771**

COLLEGIATE MICROCOMPUTER **CEASED.** (US/0731-4213) [08178824] 1817, **1266**

COLLEGIATE QUARTERLY (US/0744-2939) [08166074] **5058**

COLLEGIATE SPORTS REPORT (US/0748-9668) [11055333] **4890**

COLLEGIATE TRENDS (RIDGEWOOD, N.J.) (US/1065-0296) [26489593] **1817**

COLLEGIO REGIONALE LOMBARDO DEGLI ARCHITETTI *See* ATTI - COLLEGIO REGIONALE LOMBARDO DEGLI ARCHITETTI **292**

COLLEGIUM ANTROPOLOGICUM (CI/0350-6134) [06287861] **234**

COLLEGIUM CAROLINUM *See* VEROFFENTLICHUNGEN **2714**

COLLEGIUM MEDIEVALE (NO/0801-9282) [19117775] **2613**

COLLETTIVITA CONVIVENZE (IT/1120-639X) [I1120639X] **4771**

COLLEZIONI DONNA (IT) **1083**

COLLEZIONISTA *See* COLLEZIONISTA FRANCOBOLLI, IL **377**

COLLEZIONISTA FRANCOBOLLI, IL (IT) [11464350] **377**

COLLIE & SHETLAND SHEEPDOG REVIEW *See* COLLIE REVIEW **4286**

COLLIE REVIEW (US/0744-0731) [08014581] **4286**

COLLIER BANKRUPTCY CASES (US/0099-1848) [02241453] **3086**

COLLIER BANKRUPTCY MANUAL (US) [01564085] **3086**

COLLIER COUNTY STAR NEWS, THE (US/0191-7323) [04960681] 5648, **5649**

COLLIER ON BANKRUPTCY (US) [01564086] **3086**

COLLIERVILLE HERALD, THE (US) [19026081] **5744**

COLLIERY GUARDIAN (UK/0010-1281) [01564089] 1372, **2137**

COLLIN CHRONICLES (US/1060-0949) [09604463] **2443**

COLLIN COUNTY COMMERCIAL RECORD (US/0745-5909) [09306244] **5748**

COLLINGWOOD CONNECTION, THE (CN/1182-9095) [23242460] **5782**

COLLINGWOOD LIFE & PICTORIAL (CN/1186-1193) [24267093] **2728**

COLLINGWOOD TIMES, THE (CN/0710-0078) [08292867] **5782**

COLLINS BAY CON. T. A. C. T (CN/0225-0535) [06082707] **3160**

COLLINSVILLE HERALD (COLLINSVILLE, ILL.), THE (US/0883-6574) [08807973] **5659**

COLLISION (US/0739-7437) [09801891] **5411**

COLLISION ESTIMATING GUIDE DOMESTIC (US) [18981217] **5411**

COLLISION ESTIMATING GUIDE, DOMESTIC OLDER MODELS (US/0883-3117) [12060830] **5411**

COLLISION ESTIMATING GUIDE. EARLY MODELS (US) [13083241] **5412**

COLLISION ESTIMATING GUIDE. FORD MOTOR CO (US) **5412**

COLLISION ESTIMATING GUIDE IMPORTED (US/0735-858X) [08978120] **5412**

COLLISION ESTIMATING GUIDE, IMPORTED OLDER MODELS (US/0735-7826) [08965302] **5412**

COLLNET (CN/0833-0980) [16728504] **3203**

COLLOID AND POLYMER SCIENCE (GW/0303-402X) [01403275] **1050**

●COLLOID JOURNAL OF THE RUSSIAN ACADEMY OF SCIENCES (US/1061-933X) [25489792] **5095**

COLLOID JOURNAL OF THE USSR *See* COLLOID JOURNAL OF THE RUSSIAN ACADEMY OF SCIENCES **5095**

COLLOIDS AND SURFACES (NE/0166-6622) [06547068] **1051**

●COLLOIDS AND SURFACES. A, PHYSICOCHEMICAL AND ENGINEERING ASPECTS (NE/0927-7757) [27826255] **1051**

●COLLOIDS AND SURFACES B: BIOINTERFACES (NE/0927-7765) [28276639] **1051**

COLLOQUE DE METALLURGIE (FR/0069-5807) [11334962] **4000**

COLLOQUE SCIENTIFIQUE INTERNATIONAL SUR LE CAFE : [PROCEEDINGS] (SZ) [27050857] 2366, **75**

COLLOQUES DE L'INRA, LES (FR/0293-1915) [09832529] **75**

COLLOQUES INTERNATIONAUX DU CENTRE NATIONAL DE LA RECHERCHE SCIENTIFIQUE (FR/0366-7634) [01570008] **234**

COLLOQUES SCIENTIFIQUES / LES FLORALIES INTERNATIONALES DE MONTREAL (CN/0710-572X) [08920515] **75**

COLLOQUI DEL SODALIZIO (IT/0394-2961) [I03942961] **347**

COLLOQUIA GERMANICA (SZ/0010-1338) [01564093] **3274**

COLLOQUIA MATHEMATICA (NE) [04991575] **3500**

COLLOQUIUM (AT/0588-3237) [01776568] **4948**

COLLOQUIUM DER GESELLSCHAFT FUER BIOLOGISCHE CHEMIE (GW/0366-5887) [07513369] **485**

COLLOQUIUM GEOGRAPHICUM (GW/0588-3253) [03200662] **2558**

COLLOQUIUM - GESELLSCHAFT FUR BIOLOGISCHE CHEMIE (GW) [01751177] **973**

COLLOQUIUM HELVETICUM (SZ/0179-3780) [13470292] **3376**

COLLOQUIUM MATHEMATICUM (PL/0010-1354) [01564095] **3500**

COLLOQUIUM PUBLICATIONS / AMERICAN MATHEMATICAL SOCIETY (US/0065-9258) [07229913] **3500**

COLO-PROCTOLOGY, INTERNATIONAL EDITION (GW/0174-2450) [09632171] **3962**

COLOGNE. UNIVERSITAT. INSTITUT FUR VERKEHRSWISSENSCHAFT *See* FORSCHUNGSBERICHTE DES INSTITUTS FUR VERKEHRSWISSENSCHAFT AN DER UNIVERSITAT ZU KOLN **1824**

COLOGNE. UNIVERSITAT. SEMINAR FUER ALLGEMEINE UND INDUSTRIELLE BETRIEBSWIRTSCHAFTSLEHRE *See* ABHANDLUNGEN AUS DEM INDUSTRIESEMINAR DER UNIVERSITAT ZU KOLN **1806**

COLOGNE WALLRAF-RICHARTZ-MUSEUM *See* KATALOGE **355**

COLOGNE. WALLRAF-RICHARTZ MUSEUM *See* KLEINE SCHRIFTEN **4090**

COLOMBIA *See* IMPUESTOS SUCESORIALES; REGIMEN LEGAL TRIBUTARIO **2980**

COLOMBIA *See* IMPUESTO A LA RENTA; REGIMEN LEGAL TRIBUTARIO **4731**

COLOMBIA A SU ALCANCE (CK) [01792740] **5466**

COLOMBIA. ARCHIVO NACIONAL *See* REVISTA DEL ARCHIVO NACIONAL **2483**

COLOMBIA, CIENCIA Y TECNOLOGIA (CK/0120-4335) [11055280] **5095**

COLOMBIA. CONTRALORIA GENERAL DE LA REPUBLICA. DIVISION DE CONTROL INTERNO Y ANALISIS FINANCIERO *See* GOBIERNOS DEPARTAMENTALES : EJECUCION PRESUPUESTAL **4727**

COLOMBIA. DEPARTAMENTO ADMINISTRATIVO NACIONAL DE ESTADISTICA *See* INDICE DE PRECIOS AL CONSUMIDOR **1495**

COLOMBIA. DEPARTAMENTO ADMINISTRATIVO NACIONAL DE ESTADISTICA *See* ENCUESTA AGROPECUARIA NACIONAL **81**

COLOMBIA. DEPARTAMENTO NACIONAL DE PLANEACION *See* MEMORIA / DEPARTAMENTO NACIONAL DE PLANEACION **1574**

COLOMBIA. DIRECCION GENERAL DEL PRESUPUESTO *See* DECRETO DEL PRESUPUESTO GENERAL DE LA NACION **4720**

COLOMBIA. DIRECCION GENERAL DEL PRESUPUESTO *See* PROYECTO DE PRESUPUESTO. SECTOR CENTRAL **3032**

COLOMBIA. FUERZAS DE POLICIA. REVISTA *See* REVISTA POLICIA NACIONAL DE COLOMBIA **3175**

COLOMBIA. INSTITUTO CARO Y CUERVO *See* PUBLICACIONES. SERIES MINOR **3312**

COLOMBIA. INSTITUTO CARO Y CUERVO *See* PUBLICACIONES. SERIE BIBLIOGRAFICA **423**

COLOMBIA MEDICA : CM (CK/0120-8322) [21125928] **3567**

COLOMBIA. MINISTERIO DE AGRICULTURA *See* SERIE DE PLANEAMIENTO **1583**

COLOMBIA. MINISTERIO DE AGRICULTURA *See* GANADERIA **211**

COLOMBIA. MINISTERIO DE AGRICULTURA *See* SERIE INSTRUMENTOS DE POLITICA AGRARIA **133**

COLOMBIA. MINISTERIO DE MINAS Y ENERGIA *See* MEMORIAS AL CONGRESO NACIONAL / REPUBLICA DE COLOMBIA, MINISTERIO DE MINAS Y ENERGIA **2144**

COLOMBIA. POLICIA NACIONAL *See* REVISTA POLICIA NACIONAL DE COLOMBIA **3175**

COLOMBIA, PROYECTO DE PRESUPUESTO *See* PROYECTO DE PRESUPUESTO. SECTOR CENTRAL **3032**

COLOMBIA. SUPERINTENDENCIA DE NOTARIADO Y REGISTRO *See* INFOLIOS **2982**

COLOMBIA. UNIVERSIDAD LIBRE, PEREIRA. CENTRO DE INVESTIGACIONES *See* BOLETIN - UNIVERSIDAD LIBRE, SECCIONAL DE PEREIRA, CENTRO DE INVESTIGACIONES **5089**

COLOMBIEN, LE **CEASED.** (CN) [02510083] **5230**

COLOMBO, CEYLON. FISHERIES RESEARCH STATION *See* BULLETIN - COLOMBO, CEYLON. FISHERIES RESEARCH STATION **2297**

COLOMBO PLAN BUREAU *See* PROGRESS OF THE COLOMBO PLAN **2911**

COLOMBO PLAN FOR COOPERATIVE ECONOMIC & SOCIAL DEVELOPMENT IN ASIA & THE PACIFIC : PROCEEDINGS & CONCLUSIONS OF THE CONSULTATIVE COMMITTEE MEETING, THE (AT) [08448043] **1552**

COLON AND RECTAL SURGERY OUTLOOK (US/0894-8062) [16259319] **3962**

COLONIA ROMANICA (GW/0930-8555) [18094037] **295**

COLONIAL ECHO (US) [05842114] **1090**

COLONIAL HOMES (US/0195-1416) [05306121] 2899, **295**

●COLONIAL LATIN AMERICAN HISTORICAL REVIEW (US/1063-5769) [26074858] **2728**

COLONIAL LAWYER, THE *See* WILLIAM AND MARY BILL OF RIGHTS JOURNAL, THE **3075**

COLONIAL NEWSLETTER (HUNTSVILLE), THE (US/0010-1443) [04108132] **2781**

COLONIAL RECORDS OF THE STATE OF GEORGIA / COMPILED AND PUBLISHED UNDER THE AUTHORITY OF THE LEGISLATURE **CEASED.** (US) [01564123] **2481**

COLONIAL WATERBIRDS (US/0738-6028) [09152304] **5617**

COLONIAL WILLIAMSBURG ARCHAEOLOGICAL SERIES (US/0069-5971) [05178392] **266**

COLONIAL WILLIAMSBURG FOUNDATION *See* PRESIDENTS REPORT - COLONIAL WILLIAMSBURG FOUNDATION, THE **5235**

COLONIAL WILLIAMSBURG INTERPRETER, THE (US/0883-2749) [09527809] **2729**

COLONIALISM IN AFRICA **CEASED.** (UK) **2638**

COLONY OF NORTH BORNEO ANNUAL REPORT (MY) [01185712] **1552**

COLONY VISITOR (US/0149-9149) [03574443] **2729**

COLOQUIO : ARTES (PO/0870-3841) [03611474] **317**

COLOQUIO/CIENCIAS (PO/0870-7650) [18633910] **5095**

COLOQUIO (CONGRESO JUDIO LATINOAMERICANO) (AG) [06368102] **5047**

Alphabetical Title Index

COLORADO

COLOQUIO DE ESTUDOS LUSO-BRASILEIROS *See* ANAIS - COLOQUIO DE ESTUDOS LUSO-BRASILEIROS **2720**

COLOQUIO : LETRAS (PO/0010-1451) [02078821] **3376**

COLOR (ATLANTA, GA.) (US/1059-5007) [24607885] **2258**

COLOR BUSINESS REPORT (US/1055-3339) [23156751] **1231**

COLOR DESKTOP PUBLISHING PRODUCTS MONTHLY (US/1058-3580) [24271630] **1263**

●COLOR LIFE (US/1064-8070) [26407759] **2794**

COLOR PUBLISHING (US/1055-9701) [23380235] **1263, 4813**

COLOR RESEARCH AND APPLICATION (US/0361-2317) [02247114] **5095**

COLOR TELEVISION RECEIVERS : QUARTERLY PROFITS AND CAPACITY AND CERTAIN ANNUAL EXPENDITURES OF U.S. PRODUCERS, QUARTERLY PRICES, ORDERS, AND INVENTORIES OF IMPORTERS (US) [08701159] **1602**

COLOR WHEEL (US/1053-1831) [22469305] **3377**

COLOR XEROX ANNUAL (US/0748-4399) [10935693] **377**

COLORADO AGRIBUSINESS ROUNDUP (US/0732-7226) [08210621] **75**

COLORADO AIR QUALITY REPORT TO THE PUBLIC (US) [11748140] **16**

COLORADO BANKRUPTCY COURT REPORTER, THE (US/1048-3683) [20927428] **2952**

COLORADO BEVERAGE ANALYST (US/0010-1516) [05034699] **2366**

COLORADO BLUEGRASS MUSIC SOCIETY *See* C.B.M.S. NEWSLETTER **4106**

COLORADO BUSINESS (US) [08338552] **658**

COLORADO BUSINESS MAGAZINE : CBM (US/0898-6363) [13909372] **658**

COLORADO CITY RECORD (US) [14109178] **5748**

COLORADO CITY RETAIL SALES BY STANDARD INDUSTRIAL CLASSIFICATION (US/0732-071X) [08275553] **952**

COLORADO CIVIL LIBERTIES (US/0413-7949) [04067241] **4506**

COLORADO. CIVIL RIGHTS COMMISSION *See* ACTIVITIES REPORT - COLORADO. CIVIL RIGHTS COMMISSION **4503**

COLORADO COLLEGE MUSIC PRESS *See* SERIES A. MASTERWORKS OF YESTERDAY **4152**

COLORADO COLLEGE STUDIES (1958), THE (US/0588-4934) [01564183] **1817**

●COLORADO COMPUTER RESOURCES (US/1062-4791) [25636616] **1175**

COLORADO CONNOISSEUR, THE *CEASED.* (US/0896-3177) [16998574] **2331**

COLORADO CONSTRUCTION INDUSTRY REFERENCE BOOK (US/0162-6744) [04179217] **608**

COLORADO COUNTRY LIFE (US) [06502808] **4760**

COLORADO COUNTY AND CITY RETAIL SALES BY STANDARD INDUSTRIAL CLASSIFICATION *See* COLORADO CITY RETAIL SALES BY STANDARD INDUSTRIAL CLASSIFICATION **952**

COLORADO COUNTY AND CITY RETAIL SALES BY STANDARD INDUSTRIAL CLASSIFICATION *See* COLORADO STATE AND COUNTY RETAIL SALES BY STANDARD INDUSTRIAL CLASSIFICATION (ANNUAL) **953**

COLORADO COUNTY CITIZEN, THE (US) [14109175] **5748**

COLORADO CPA NEWSACCOUNT (US) **741**

COLORADO DENTAL ASSOCIATION *See* JOURNAL - COLORADO DENTAL ASSOCIATION **1326**

COLORADO. DEPT. OF CORRECTIONS *See* ANNUAL REPORT / COLORADO DEPARTMENT OF CORRECTIONS **3157**

COLORADO. DEPT. OF EDUCATION. MANAGEMENT AND INFORMATION SERVICES *See* FINANCIAL INFORMATION, COLORADO SCHOOL DISTRICTS **1864**

COLORADO. DEPT. OF HEALTH. WATER QUALITY CONTROL DIVISION *See* REPORT TO THE COLORADO WATER QUALITY CONTROL COMMISSION **5538**

COLORADO. DEPT. OF HIGHWAYS *See* EXPENDITURE REPORT - STATE OF COLORADO, DEPARTMENT OF HIGHWAYS **5440**

COLORADO. DEPT. OF HIGHWAYS *See* ANNUAL REPORT - COLORADO. DEPT. OF HIGHWAYS **5438**

COLORADO. DEPT. OF HIGHWAYS. EXPENDITURE REPORT *See* ANNUAL REPORT - COLORADO. DEPT. OF HIGHWAYS **5438**

COLORADO. DEPT. OF SOCIAL SERVICES. RESEARCH AND STATISTICS SECTION *See* RESEARCH REPORT AFDC **5306**

COLORADO. DEPT. OF THE TREASURY *See* STATE TREASURER'S ANNUAL REPORT (COLORADO) **4750**

COLORADO. DIVISION OF ACCOUNTS AND CONTROL *See* FINANCIAL STATEMENTS, STATE OF COLORADO, STATE CONTROLLER **4726**

COLORADO. DIVISION OF HIGHWAY SAFETY *See* STATE OF COLORADO ANNUAL HIGHWAY SAFETY WORK PROGRAM **5444**

COLORADO. DIVISION OF MINES *See* COAL (DENVER) **2137**

COLORADO. DIVISION OF PLANT INDUSTRY *See* ANNUAL REPORT / DIVISION OF PLANT INDUSTRY **2409**

COLORADO. DIVISION OF PROPERTY TAXATION *See* SALES RATIO STUDY; RESIDENTIAL AND COMMERCIAL PROPERTIES **4747**

COLORADO. DIVISION OF WILDLIFE *See* SPECIAL REPORT / COLORADO DIVISION OF WILDLIFE **2205**

COLORADO. DIVISION OF WILDLIFE *See* DIVISION REPORT / COLORADO DIVISION OF WILDLIFE **2191**

COLORADO EDITOR (US/0162-0010) [02098043] **2918**

COLORADO EDUCATION & LIBRARY DIRECTORY (US) [22975025] **3203, 1732**

COLORADO EDUCATION DIRECTORY (US/0588-4349) [02310827] **1732**

COLORADO EDUCATION REVIEW (US/0010-1575) [02103138] **1732**

●COLORADO EMPLOYMENT LAW LETTER (US/1059-504X) [24609743] **3145**

COLORADO ENERGY FOCUS (US) [07846356] **1935**

COLORADO ENGINEER, THE (US/0010-1583) [02259537] **1732, 1968**

●COLORADO ENVIRONMENTAL COMPLIANCE UPDATE (US/1072-057X) [28855555] **3110**

COLORADO ENVIRONMENTAL REPORT, THE (US/0891-3463) [13528255] **2226, 2190**

COLORADO EPISCOPALIAN, THE (US/0883-6728) [09679362] **5058**

COLORADO FEVER (US/0740-9109) [08457382] **5466**

COLORADO FIELD ORNITHOLOGISTS *See* C.F.O. JOURNAL **5616**

COLORADO FIELD ORNITHOLOGISTS' JOURNAL (US/1066-7342) [25361257] **5617**

COLORADO GENEALOGIST, THE (US/0010-1613) [02620889] **2443**

COLORADO. GENERAL ASSEMBLY *See* DIGEST OF BILLS ENACTED BY THE GENERAL ASSEMBLY **2961**

COLORADO. GENERAL ASSEMBLY. LEGISLATIVE AUDIT COMMITTEE *See* ANNUAL REPORT - LEGISLATIVE AUDIT COMMITTEE. (COLORADO) **4710**

COLORADO. GENERAL ASSEMBLY. LEGISLATIVE COUNCIL *See* COLORADO LEGISLATIVE COUNCIL RECOMMENDATIONS **2952**

COLORADO. GENERAL ASSEMBLY. STATUTORY REVISION COMMITTEE *See* REPORT OF FINDINGS AND RECOMMENDATIONS / STATUTORY REVISION COMMITTEE (COLORADO) **3038**

COLORADO GEOLOGICAL SURVEY *See* COLORADO GEOLOGICAL SURVEY OPEN-FILE REPORT **1372**

COLORADO GEOLOGICAL SURVEY OPEN-FILE REPORT (US/0271-888X) [06701029] **1372**

COLORADO. GOVERNOR *See* GOVERNOR'S BUDGET **4729**

COLORADO GREEN (US/0195-0045) [05188832] **2412**

COLORADO GUIDE TO GOVERNMENT (US) **1602, 827**

●COLORADO HEALTH CARE IN PERSPECTIVE (US/1065-4089) [26604743] **4771**

COLORADO HERITAGE (US/0272-9377) [06966345] **2729**

COLORADO HIGH TECHNOLOGY DIRECTORY (US/0883-8208) [11663563] **5095**

COLORADO HISTORY NEWS (US/0895-0083) [16387660] **2729**

COLORADO HOMES & LIFESTYLES (US/0272-6904) [06901285] **2531, 2904**

COLORADO IN PERSPECTIVE (US/1065-5352) [26628325] **5325**

COLORADO INSURANCE INDUSTRY STATISTICAL REPORT (US/0277-9595) [07498960] **2878, 2897**

COLORADO JOB FINDER (US) **4203**

COLORADO JOURNAL OF HEALTH, PHYSICAL EDUCATION, RECREATION, AND DANCE (US) [06794196] **1855**

COLORADO JOURNAL OF INTERNATIONAL ENVIRONMENTAL LAW AND POLICY (US/1050-0391) [21379882] **3110**

COLORADO JOURNAL OF PHARMACY, THE *CEASED.* (US/0010-163X) [01471856] **4297**

COLORADO LABOR ADVOCATE (US/0190-8235) [04753200] **5642**

COLORADO LAWYER (US/0363-7867) [02038795] **2952**

COLORADO LEGISLATIVE ALMANAC (US/0277-3708) [07542949] **4468**

COLORADO LEGISLATIVE COUNCIL RECOMMENDATIONS (US) [05398026] **2952**

COLORADO LIBRARIES (US/0147-9733) [03108275] **3203**

COLORADO MEDICAL SOCIETY *See* COLORADO MEDICINE. DIRECTORY OF PHYSICIANS **2878**

COLORADO MEDICAL SOCIETY PHYSICIAN'S RESOURCE BOOK (US) **3913**

COLORADO MEDICINE (1980) (US/0199-7343) [05994166] **3567**

COLORADO MEDICINE. DIRECTORY OF PHYSICIANS (US/0743-5037) [08686121] **3913, 2878**

COLORADO MEDICINE PHYSICIANS'S DIRECTORY *See* COLORADO MEDICAL SOCIETY PHYSICIAN'S RESOURCE BOOK **3913**

COLORADO MONTHLY LOCAL CLIMATOLOGICAL DATA MICROFORM (US) [10827797] **1424**

COLORADO MUNICIPALITIES (US/0010-1664) [01564191] **4639**

COLORADO MUSIC EDUCATOR (US/0010-1672) [04040971] **4111**

COLORADO-NORTH REVIEW *CEASED.* (US/0194-0589) [04455867] **3377**

COLORADO NURSE (1985) (US/8750-846X) [11853226] **3854**

COLORADO. OFFICE OF HEALTH PROTECTION *See* ANNUAL WORK PLAN ... FOR THE OFFICE OF HEALTH PROTECTION, COLORADO DEPARTMENT OF HEALTH **4767**

COLORADO. OFFICE OF STATE PLANNING AND BUDGETING *See* ANNUAL CAPITAL INVESTMENT BUDGET - COLORADO. OFFICE OF STATE PLANNING AND BUDGETING **890**

COLORADO. OFFICE OF THE STATE COURT ADMINISTRATOR *See* ANNUAL REPORT OF THE COLORADO JUDICIARY **3139**

COLORADO OUTDOOR JOURNAL *CEASED.* (US/0891-3145) [14756898] **4871**

COLORADO OUTDOORS (US/0010-1699) [01564193] **4871, 2190**

COLORADO POTATO GROWER (US/0279-389X) [03229115] **167**

●COLORADO PRIVATE ELEMENTARY AND SECONDARY SCHOOLS (US/1061-0294) [25161204] **1732**

COLORADO PROSPECTOR (US/0010-1702) [04040978] **5196, 2729**

COLORADO RAIL ANNUAL (US) **5430**

COLORADO RANCHER AND FARMER (US/0010-1729) [04040991] **75**

●COLORADO REAL ESTATE JOURNAL (US/1060-4383) [25028016] **4835**

COLORADO REGISTER. AIR QUALITY CONTROL COMMISSION (US) **4639**

COLORADO REGISTER. LIMITED EDITION (US) **4639**

COLORADO REGISTER. REGULAR EDITION (US) **4639**

COLORADO REPORTER COLORADO CASES REPORTED IN PACIFIC REPORTER, SECOND SERIES (US/0744-9828) [08690616] **2952**

COLORADO RETAIL SALES (US) **953**

COLORADO REVIEW (1985) (US/1046-3348) [12603424] **3340**

COLORADO RIVER ASSOCIATION *See* NEWSLETTER - COLORADO RIVER ASSOCIATION **4876**

COLORADO SCHOOL OF MINES QUARTERLY (US/0163-9153) [04536476] **2137**

●COLORADO SCHOOL OF MINES QUARTERLY REVIEW OF ENGINEERING, SCIENCE, EDUCATION AND RESEARCH (US/1068-2937) [25760173] **2137**

COLORADO
Alphabetical Title Index

COLORADO SKI INDUSTRY CHARACTERISTICS AND FINANCIAL ANALYSIS (US/0898-4603) [13737203] 4849, **4890**

COLORADO SPORTS MONTHLY (US/8755-8653) [11423391] **4891**

COLORADO SPRINGS BUSINESS JOURNAL, THE (US/1062-810X) [25762063] **658**

COLORADO SPRINGS GAZETTE-TELEGRAPH (US) [08814329] **5642**

COLORADO STATE AND COUNTY RETAIL SALES BY STANDARD INDUSTRIAL CLASSIFICATION (US) [04066922] **953**

COLORADO STATE AND COUNTY RETAIL SALES BY STANDARD INDUSTRIAL CLASSIFICATION (ANNUAL) (US/0732-1015) [08269251] **953**

COLORADO STATE UNIVERSITY *See* WATER MANAGEMENT TECHNICAL REPORT **5543**

COLORADO. STATE UNIVERSITY, FORT COLLINS *See* FLUID MECHANICS PAPERS **2089**

COLORADO STATE UNIVERSITY. RANGE SCIENCE DEPT *See* RANGE SCIENCE SERIES (FORT COLLINS, COLO.) **124**

COLORADO STATE UNIVERSITY. WATER MANAGEMENT RESEARCH PROJECT *See* ANNUAL PROGRESS REPORT - WATER MANAGEMENT RESEARCH PROJECT **5529**

COLORADO STATESMAN, THE (US) [06352561] **5642**

COLORADO. SUPREME COURT *See* STATE OF THE COLORADO JUDICIARY, THE **3143**

COLORADO TAX PROFILE STUDY (US) [04239746] **4718**

COLORADO TAXPAYER REPORT, A (US) [05279255] 741, **4718**

COLORADO TRIAL LAWYERS ASSOCIATION *See* TRIAL TALK **3066**

COLORADO. UNIVERSITY. BUSINESS RESEARCH DIVISION *See* COLORADO STATE AND COUNTY RETAIL SALES BY STANDARD INDUSTRIAL CLASSIFICATION **953**

COLORADO WATER RESOURCES CIRCULAR (US/0092-2684) [01789487] **5532**

COLORADO WEST SALARY SURVEY (US/0275-942X) [07235473] **1660**

COLORADO WHEAT GROWER (US/1078-5612) [31120421] **167**

COLORADO WHO'S WHO (US/0882-004X) [11663549] **431**

COLORADO WILDLIFE RESEARCH REVIEW (US/0276-8992) [06634827] **4871**

COLORADO WOMAN (US/1042-9549) [17993921] **5553**

●COLORADO WOMEN'S YELLOW PAGES (US/1071-1880) [28565102] **5553**

COLORADO-WYOMING ACADEMY OF SCIENCE *See* JOURNAL OF THE COLORADO-WYOMING ACADEMY OF SCIENCE, THE **5175**

COLORADO ZIP+4 STATE DIRECTORY (US) [11535675] **1144**

COLORBAT LAB PRO (US/1055-0704) [23067952] **847**

COLOUR INDEX. ADDITIONS & AMENDMENTS (UK) **1023**

COLOURAGE (II/0010-1826) [01564207] **5349**

COLOURAGE ANNUAL (II/0588-5108) [01771266] **5349**

COLOURIST (OTTAWA) (CN/0843-3607) [19763688] **4400**

COLS BLEUS (FR) [02241068] **4175**

COLSTON PAPERS (UK/0069-6277) [03258164] 5095, **1817**

COLT AMERICAN HANDGUNNING ANNUAL (US/0364-071X) [02579852] **4891**

COLT ARCHAEOLOGICAL INSTITUTE *See* MONOGRAPH SERIES - COLT ARCHAEOLOGICAL INSTITUTE **275**

COLTELLO DI DELFO (IT) **295**

COLTIVATORE : SETTIMANALE DELLA CONFEDERAZIONE NAZIONALE DEI COLTIVATORI DIRETTI, IL (IT) [08982293] **75**

COLTON CLARION (US/0896-9590) [17349568] **2443**

COLTSFOOT (US/0279-4969) [07912543] **507**

COLTURE PROTETTE (IT/0390-0444) [01950047] **2412**

COLUMBA / THE MIDWEST REVIEW OF BOOKS (US) **3377**

COLUMBAN FATHERS MISSIONS *See* COLUMBAN MISSION **4948**

COLUMBAN MISSION (US/0095-4438) [01789998] **4948**

COLUMBIA, A MAGAZINE OF POETRY AND PROSE (US/0161-486X) [03938457] 3461, **3377**

COLUMBIA BASIN HERALD (US/1041-1658) [18670398] **5760**

COLUMBIA BASIN NEWS (US) [17164688] **5760**

COLUMBIA BIOLOGICAL SERIES (US/0069-6285) [01564211] **452**

COLUMBIA BROADCASTING SYSTEM, INC. CBS RECORDS DIVISION *See* CBS MAIN ALPHABETICAL & NUMERICAL CATALOGUE **4108**

COLUMBIA BUSINESS LAW REVIEW (US/0898-0721) [15081194] **3097**

COLUMBIA COLLEGE (COLUMBIA, S.C.) *See* ALUMNAE DIRECTORY - COLUMBIA COLLEGE (COLUMBIA, S.C.) **1096**

COLUMBIA COLLEGE (COLUMBIA UNIVERSITY) *See* ALUMNI DIRECTORY - COLUMBIA COLLEGE (COLUMBIA UNIVERSITY) **1098**

●COLUMBIA COUNTY INDEPENDENT, THE (US) [25569282] **5715**

COLUMBIA DAILY NEWS (US) [13048674] **5735**

COLUMBIA DAILY SPECTATOR (US) **1090**

COLUMBIA DAILY TRIBUNE (US) [13380852] **5703**

●COLUMBIA DOCUMENTS OF ARCHITECTURE AND THEORY (US/1065-304X) [26569982] 152, **295**

COLUMBIA ESSAYS ON MODERN WRITERS (US/0069-6315) [01564216] **3377**

COLUMBIA FILM VIEW (US) [19842116] **4067**

COLUMBIA FLIER (US/0192-7841) [05077238] **5686**

COLUMBIA GORGE MAGAZINE *See* COLUMBIA GORGE VISITOR & RECREATION GUIDE (1992) **4849**

●COLUMBIA GORGE VISITOR & RECREATION GUIDE (1992) (US/1063-763X) [26134874] **4849**

●COLUMBIA HEIGHTS BUSINESS NEWS (US/1062-273X) [25567981] **658**

COLUMBIA HUMAN RIGHTS LAW REVIEW (US/0090-7944) [01785348] 2953, **4506**

COLUMBIA JESTER, THE (US) [06368266] **1090**

COLUMBIA JOURNAL OF ENVIRONMENTAL LAW (US/0098-4582) [02241525] **3110**

COLUMBIA JOURNAL OF GENDER AND LAW (US/1062-6220) [24786087] 5553, **2953**

COLUMBIA JOURNAL OF LAW AND SOCIAL PROBLEMS (US/0010-1923) [01564225] 5196, **2953**

COLUMBIA JOURNAL OF TRANSNATIONAL LAW (US/0010-1931) [00825065] **3126**

COLUMBIA JOURNAL OF WORLD BUSINESS, THE (US/0022-5428) [01564227] **658**

COLUMBIA LAW ALUMNI BULLETIN (NEW YORK, N.Y. : 1980) (US) [07132397] 2953, **1101**

COLUMBIA LAW REVIEW (US/0010-1958) [01564231] **2953**

COLUMBIA LAW SCHOOL NEWS (US) [02254978] 1817, **2953**

COLUMBIA LIBRARY COLUMNS (US/0010-1966) [01564233] 5196, **2844**

COLUMBIA, LUZERNE, WYOMING FARM AND HOME NEWS *See* SEVEN COUNTY FARM AND HOME NEWS **134**

COLUMBIA MAGAZINE (COLUMBIA, MD.) (US/0889-2342) [13825522] **2531**

COLUMBIA MISSOURIAN (US/0747-1874) [10632065] **5703**

COLUMBIA (NEW HAVEN) (US/0010-1869) [01564210] **5028**

COLUMBIA (NEW YORK, N.Y. 1978) (US/0162-3893) [04163593] **1090**

COLUMBIA NEWS-TIMES, THE (US/1053-7511) [19462482] **5653**

COLUMBIA REVIEW *CEASED.* (US/0010-1982) [02916907] **3340**

COLUMBIA (RHINEBECK, N.Y.), THE (US/8755-2914) [11276837] **2443**

COLUMBIA RIVER WATER MANAGEMENT GROUP *See* COLUMBIA RIVER WATER MANAGEMENT REPORT **2088**

COLUMBIA RIVER WATER MANAGEMENT REPORT (US/0360-6864) [02243936] **2088**

COLUMBIA SPECTATOR (US) [02250807] **5715**

COLUMBIA STUDIES IN ARCHAEOLOGY AND ETHNOLOGY (US) [01771267] 234, **266**

COLUMBIA STUDIES IN ECONOMICS (US/0069-6331) [01564236] **1470**

COLUMBIA STUDIES IN PHILOSOPHY (US/0098-9436) [01625817] **4344**

COLUMBIA STUDIES IN THE CLASSICAL TRADITION (NE) [05729928] **1076**

COLUMBIA (TACOMA, WASH.) (US/0892-3094) [15149263] **2729**

COLUMBIA UNIVERSITY BIOLOGICAL SERIES *See* COLUMBIA BIOLOGICAL SERIES **452**

COLUMBIA UNIVERSITY. CENTER OF ISRAEL AND JEWISH STUDIES *See* COLUMBIA UNIVERSITY STUDIES IN JEWISH HISTORY, CULTURE, AND INSTITUTIONS **5047**

COLUMBIA UNIVERSITY. CONSERVATION OF HUMAN RESOURCES PROJECT *See* REPORT - COLUMBIA UNIVERSITY. CONSERVATION OF HUMAN RESOURCES PROJECT **1094**

COLUMBIA UNIVERSITY. COUNCIL FOR RESEARCH IN THE SOCIAL SCIENCES *See* BIBLIOGRAPHY : PUBLICATIONS RESULTING FROM COUNCIL SUPPORT **5227**

COLUMBIA UNIVERSITY. LEGISLATIVE DRAFTING RESEARCH FUND *See* CONSTITUTIONS OF THE UNITED STATES, NATIONAL AND STATE **3092**

COLUMBIA UNIVERSITY. LIBRARIES *See* NOTES ON SELECTED ACQUISITIONS **3237**

COLUMBIA UNIVERSITY. LIBRARIES. LAW LIBRARY *See* DICTIONARY CATALOG OF THE COLUMBIA UNIVERSITY LAW LIBRARY. SUPPLEMENT **3206**

COLUMBIA UNIVERSITY. RADIOLOGICAL RESEARCH LABORATORY *See* RADIATION PHYSICS, BIOPHYSICS AND RADIATION BIOLOGY **4440**

COLUMBIA UNIVERSITY. SCHOOL OF INTERNATIONAL AFFAIRS *See* REPORT ON PUBLICATIONS OF THE SCHOOL OF INTERNATIONAL AFFAIRS AND THE REGIONAL INSTITUTES **4533**

COLUMBIA UNIVERSITY. SOUTHERN ASIAN INSTITUTE *See* OCCASIONAL BIBLIOGRAPHICAL PAPERS **421**

COLUMBIA UNIVERSITY STUDIES IN INTERNATIONAL ORGANIZATION (US/0069-6358) [01564262] **1817**

COLUMBIA UNIVERSITY STUDIES IN JEWISH HISTORY, CULTURE, AND INSTITUTIONS (US/0069-6366) [01781289] **5047**

COLUMBIA UNIVERSITY STUDIES IN LIBRARY SERVICE (US/0069-6374) [01564263] **3203**

COLUMBIA-VLA JOURNAL OF LAW & THE ARTS (US/0888-4226) [13162259] 317, **2953**

COLUMBIAN-PROGRESS, THE (US/1044-9922) [15004748] **5700**

COLUMBIAN (VANCOUVER, WASH.) (US/1043-4151) [15644994] **5760**

COLUMBIANA (US/0893-276X) [15474403] **2531**

COLUMBINE FAX DIRECTORY (US/1043-545X) [19483624] **1151**

COLUMBUS 92 (IT) [17857568] **2684**

COLUMBUS AND CENTRAL OHIO HISTORIAN (US/0882-7761) [10769939] **2729**

COLUMBUS ART (US/0892-6328) [07771887] **348**

COLUMBUS COMPUTER XCHANGE (US/0742-3519) [10309344] **1175**

COLUMBUS DAILY ADVOCATE (US/8756-6044) [12558880] **5675**

COLUMBUS DISPATCH, THE (US) [08736947] **5727**

COLUMBUS FREEPRESS (COLUMBUS, OHIO : 1976) *See* FREE PRESS (COLUMBUS, OHIO), THE **2920**

COLUMBUS GAZETTE (COLUMBUS JUNCTION, IOWA), THE (US/0747-2889) [10692864] **5669**

COLUMBUS HERALD (COLUMBUS, IND. : WEEKLY) (US) [12159196] **5663**

COLUMBUS JOURNAL-REPUBLICAN (COLUMBUS, WIS. : 1971) (US) [13303680] **5766**

COLUMBUS LEDGER-ENQUIRER (US/0898-3860) [17797136] **5653**

COLUMBUS MAGAZINE (US/0740-2171) [09888985] **2729**

COLUMBUS TIMES, THE (US) [19534602] 2258, **5653**

COLUMNS (FAIRMONT), THE (US/0010-2091) [05226302] **1090**

COLUMNS (MADISON) (US/0196-1306) [05752586] **2729**

COLUSA COUNTY FARMER, THE (US/0746-3871) [10010626] **5634**

COLUSA COUNTY SUN HERALD (US/0897-8743) [17646314] **5634**

COM 3 (AT) **1222**

COM-AND, COMPUTER AUDIT NEWS DEVELOPMENTS (US/0738-4270) [09602769] 1175, **741**

COMANCHE CHIEF, THE (US) [11974064] **5748**

COMBAT (UK) [06724425] **4540**

COMBAT AND SURVIVAL MAGAZINE (UK/0955-9841) [I09559841] **4039**

COMBAT CREW *See* COMBAT EDGE, THE **16**

COMBAT CREW / STRATEGIC AIR COMMAND (US/0010-213X) [02062777] **4039**

COMBAT DATA SUBSCRIPTION SERVICE (US/0098-7956) [02242323] **4039**

●COMBAT EDGE, THE (US/1063-8970) [26180148] **4039**, **16**

COMBAT HANDGUNS (US/1043-7584) [19549768] **4039**

COMBAT NATIONAL, LE (RE) [02241952] **2638**

COMBAT NATURE PERIGUEUX (FR/0184-7473) [I01847473] **2163**

COMBAT WEAPONS *CEASED.* (US/0887-2546) [13153383] **4039**

COMBINATICNS (US/0145-899X) [02988195] **4368**

COMBINATORICA (BUDAPEST. 1981) (NE/0209-9683) [07743727] **3500**

●COMBINATORICS, PROBABILITY & COMPUTING : CPC (UK/0963-5483) [26286529] **1175**, **3500**

COMBINE FACTS *CEASED.* (US/0148-6470) [03340880] **158**

COMBINED ANNUAL REPORTS FOR FISCAL YEAR ... (US) [14919423] **3160**

COMBINED CUMULATIVE INDEX TO OBSTETRICS AND GYNECOLOGY (US/0884-8092) [12438244] **3759**, **3655**

COMBINED CUMULATIVE INDEX TO PEDIATRICS (US/0190-4981) [04728204] **39C2**, **3655**

COMBINED INDEX FOR THE JOURNALS SULPHUR, NITROGEN AND PHOSPHORUS & POTASSIUM *CEASED.* (UK) [03338008] **1023**

COMBINED PROCEEDINGS / INTERNATIONAL PLANT PROPAGATORS' SOCIETY (US/0538-9143) [04455713] **75**, **2412**

COMBINED PROCEEDINGS - INTERNATIONAL PLANT PROPAGATORS' SOCIETY (US/0538-9143) [01753678] **2412**

COMBINED ROSTERS OF CERTIFIED PUBLIC ACCOUNTS, PUBLIC ACCOUNTANTS, AND ACCOUNTANTS AUTHORIZED TO CONDUCT MUNICIPAL AUDITS LICENSED OREGON AS OF ... (US) [10771551] **741**

●COMBO (EVANSTON, ILL.) (US/1078-389X) [31062833] **2773**, **4859**

COMBONI MISSIONS (US/0279-3652) [07816527] **4949**

COMBROAD (UK/0951-0826) [03614956] **1130**

COMBUSTIBLES MINERAUX SOIDES, APPROVISIONNEMENT DE LA CONSOMMATION FRANCAISE (FR) [09485968] **827**

COMBUSTION AND FLAME (US/0010-2180) [01564277] **1051**

COMBUSTION, EXPLOSION, AND SHOCK WAVES (US/0010-5082) [01564276] **1051**

COMBUSTION INSTITUTE. EASTERN SECTION. FALL TECHNICAL MEETING *See* CHEMICAL AND PHYSICAL PROCESSES IN COMBUSTION **968**

COMBUSTION (NEW YORK, N.Y. : 1989) (US/1040-2756) [18367240] **2112**

COMBUSTION RESEARCH (US) [06663084] **1935**

COMBUSTION SCIENCE AND TECHNOLOGY (US/0010-2202) [01564278] **1051**

COMBUSTION SCIENCE AND TECHNOLOGY BOOK SERIES (US/0883-5519) [09523802] **1051**

COMCAR REVIEW (CN/1185-9326) [25423401] **5380**

COMCISE (AT/0817-5837) [I08175837] **1470**

COME-ALL-YE (HATBORO, PA.) (US/0736-6132) [05840527] **2319**

COME AND SEE (CN/0316-3040) [02247220] **5016**

COME BACK SAFELY (US) **5380**

COME FLY WITH US (US/0094-839X) [01795801] **16**

COME FOR TO SING (US/0270-4609) [06408765] **4111**

COMECON REPORTS (US/0142-0763) [05458441] **1470**

COMEDIANTES (ASSOCIATION) *See* BULLETIN OF THE COMEDIANTES **3370**

COMEDIE FRANCAISE (FR) **5363**

COMEDY (US/0272-7404) [06896602] **3377**

COMENTARIO SOCIOLOGICO (SP) [06956020] **5242**

COMENTARIOS BIBLIOGRAFICOS AMERICANOS (UY/0301-6579) [01792384] **3340**

COMENTARIOS ECONOMICOS DE ACTUALIDAD : BOLETIN INFORMATIVO DEL CENTRO DE INVESTIGACION Y CONSULTORIA (BO) [12062013] **1470**

COMENTARIOS SOBRE LA SITUACION ECONOMICA (CL) [03083851] **1552**

COMER Y BEBER (SP) **2331**

COMERCIALIZACION EXTERNA DEL CAFE MEXICANO EN EL CICLO ... / INSTITUTO MEXICANO DEL CAFE, LA (MX) [09054707] **2331**

COMERCIALIZACION HORTOFRUTICOLA (SP) **75**

COMERCIO (PE) **2486**

COMERCIO (MX) [28941068] **828**

COMERCIO E INDUSTRIA DE LA MADERA (SP/1131-8694) [I11318694] **633**

COMERCIO E INDUSTRIA (SAN SALVADOR, EL SALVADOR) (ES) [11912679] **828**

COMERCIO, EL (EC) [04554480] **5800**

COMERCIO EXTERIOR (MX/0185-0601) [02445206] **1633**, **828**

COMERCIO EXTERIOR : IBCE, INSTITUTO BOLIVIANO DE COMERCIO EXTERIOR (BO) [25727769] **828**

COMERCIO EXTERIOR (LA PAZ) (BO/0520-4712) [01224472] **828**

COMERCIO EXTERIOR, SISTEMA DE PREFERENCIAS ARANCELARIAS GENERALIZADAS (SPG). IMPORTACIONES (LU) [19968027] **828**

COMERCIO (FEDERACAO DE COMERCIO DO ESTADO DE MINAS GERAIS) (BL) [07917286] **828**

COMERCIO (TORONTO. 1982) (CN/0824-5800) [10768288] **5782**

COMFORTABLE LIVING AND QUEENSLAND HOMES./FOR AUSTRALIA (AT) **295**, **2899**

COMIC ART COLLECTION *See* COMIC ART STUDIES **377**

●COMIC ART STUDIES (US/1062-6964) [25698369] **377**

COMIC BOOK COLLECTOR (US/1063-7982) [26139946] **2773**, **4859**

COMIC BOOKS, PAPERBACKS, MAGAZINES *CEASED.* (US/0747-5225) [10733109] **413**

COMIC PRESS NEWS (US) **4468**, **4859**

COMIC READER, THE (US/0747-3575) [04454668] **1062**

COMIC RELIEF (US/1055-9639) [23378299] **4859**

COMIC TALE EASY READER (US/0748-2264) [10906120] **1062**

COMICS BUYER'S GUIDE PRICE GUIDE *CEASED.* (US/1053-8704) [22683379] **4859**

COMICS BUYER'S GUIDE, THE (US/0745-4570) [09185196] **4859**

COMICS FEATURE (US/0199-7459) [06125944] **4859**

COMICS JOURNAL, THE (US/0194-7869) [04521305] **377**

COMICS MANIFESTO, THE (US/1055-7164) [23274935] **4859**

●COMICS RETAILER (US/1059-9401) [24833360] **2773**

COMICS SCENE (US/1053-0398) [11062177] **4859**

●COMICS VALUES ANNUAL (US/1062-4503) [25624163] **2773**, **4849**

COMISIA NATIONALA A REPUBLICII SOCIALISTE ROMANIA PENTRU UNESCO *See* REVUE - LA COMMISSION NATIONALE DE LA REPUBLIQUE SOCIALISTE DE ROUMANIE. JOURNAL - THE NATIONAL COMMISSION OF THE SOCIALIST REPUBLIC OF ROMANIA **4684**

COMISIA NATIONALA A REPUBLICII SOCIALISTE ROMANIA PENTRU UNESCO. BULLETIN DE LA COMMISSION NATIONALE DE LA REPUBLIQUE SOCIALISTE DE ROUMANIE POUR L'UNESCO *See* REVUE - LA COMMISSION NATIONALE DE LA REPUBLIQUE SOCIALISTE DE ROUMANIE. JOURNAL - THE NATIONAL COMMISSION OF THE SOCIALIST REPUBLIC OF ROMANIA **4684**

COMISION CHILENA DEL COBRE *See* MEMORIA ANUAL / COMISION CHILENA DEL COBRE **4008**

COMISION COORDINADORA DE LA INDUSTRIA SIDERURGICA *See* BOLETIN - COMISION COORDINADORA DE LA INDUSTRIA SIDERURGICA **1599**

COMISION COORDINADORA DEL SISTEMA NACIONAL DE SERVICIOS DE BIBLIOTECAS E INFORMACION HUMANISTICA *See* REVISTA DEL SINASBI **3246**

COMISION DE INTEGRACION ELECTRICA REGIONAL *See* BOLETIN - COMISION DE INTEGRACION ELECTRICA REGIONAL **4633**

COMISION DE INTEGRACION ELECTRICA REGIONAL. SUBCOMITE DE DISTRIBUCION DE ENERGIA ELECTRICA *See* REUNION **2079**

COMISION DE INTEGRACION ELECTRICA REGIONAL SUBCOMITE DE DISTRIBUCION ENERGIA ELECTRICA *See* INFORME - COMISION DE INTEGRACION ELECTRICA REGIONAL. SUBCOMITE DE DISTRIBUCION ENERGIA ELECTRICA **2064**

COMISION EJECUTIVA HIDROELECTRUCA DEL RIO LEMPA *See* INFORME ANUAL - COMISION EJECUTIVA HIDROELECTRICA DEL RIO LEMPA **1612**

COMISION NACIONAL DE INVESTIGACION CIENTIFICA Y TECNOLOGICA *See* SERIE "INFORMACION Y DOCUMENTACION" **5157**

COMISSAO ESTADUAL DE PLANEJAMENTO AGRICOLA DE SERGIPE *See* ANALISE DO SETOR AGROPECUARIO DE SERGIPE **58**

COMISSAO GOIANA DE FOLCLORE *See* BOLETIM - COMISSAO GOIANA DE FOLCLORE **2318**

COMITATUS (US/0069-6412) [02534142] **3377**

COMITE CENTRAL DES ARMATEURS DE FRANCE, PARIS *See* MARINE MARCHANDE EN ..., LA **5452**

COMITE CONSULTATIF POUR LES ETALONS DE MESURE DES RAYONNEMENTS IONISANTS : RAPPORT (FR/0255-3147) [07468949] **4030**

COMITE DE INVESTIGACIONES TECNOLOGICAS DE CHILE *See* INTEC **5114**

COMITE DE LA RECHERCHE AGRONOMIQUE DE HAUTE-VOLTA *See* SECTEURS D'EXPERIMENTATION DE BOBO-DIOULASSO ET DE OUAGADOUGOU : CAMPAGNE COTONNIERE **185**

COMITE DEPARTEMENTAL DE DEFENSE CONTRE L'ALCOOLISME DE LA REUNION *See* COMPTE-RENDU D'ACTIVITES / COMITE DEPARTEMENTAL DE DEFENSE CONTRE L'ALCOOLISME DE LA REUNION **3160**

COMITE D'EXPANSION DE LA METROPOLE NORD *See* ACTIVITES - COMITE D'EXPANSION DE LA METROPOLE NORD **2813**

COMITE EURO-INTERNATIONAL DU BETON *See* BULLETIN D'INFORMATION - COMITE EURO-INTERNATIONAL DU BETON **605**

COMITE FRANCAIS DE CARTOGRAPHIE *See* BULLETIN DU COMITE FRANCAIS DE CARTOGRAPHIE **2581**

COMITE FRANCAIS DE DROIT INTERNATIONAL PRIVE *See* TRAVAUX DU COMITE FRANCAIS DE DROIT INTERNATIONAL PRIVE **3137**

COMITE FRANCAIS DE LUTTE CONTRE LES MAUVAISES HERBES *See* COMPTE RENDU DE LA CONFERENCE DU COLUMA **76**

COMITE INTERNATIONAL DES POIDS ET MESURES. COMITE CONSULTATIF DE PHOTOMETRIE ET RADIOMETRIE *See* RAPPORT AU COMITE INTERNATIONAL DES POIDS ET MESURES **4032**

COMITE INTERNATIONAL DES POIDS ET MESURES. COMITE CONSULTATIF D'ELECTRICITE *See* COMITE INTERNATIONAL DES POIDS ET MESURES, COMITE CONSULTATIF D'ELECTRICITE. RAPPORT **4030**

COMITE INTERNATIONAL DES POIDS ET MESURES, COMITE CONSULTATIF D'ELECTRICITE. RAPPORT (FR) [04306579] **4030**

COMITE INTERNATIONAL DES POIDS ET MESURES. COMITE CONSULTATIF DES UNITES *See* COMITE INTERNATIONAL DES POIDS ET MESURES, COMITE CONSULTATIF DES UNITES. RAPPORT **4030**

COMITE INTERNATIONAL DES POIDS ET MESURES, COMITE CONSULTATIF DES UNITES. RAPPORT (FR) [04251085] **4030**

COMITE INTERNATIONAL DES POIDS ET MESURES. COMITE CONSULTATIF POUR LES ETALONS DE MESURE DES RAYONNEMENTS IONISANTS *See* COMITE CONSULTATIF POUR LES ETALONS DE MESURE DES RAYONNEMENTS IONISANTS : RAPPORT **4030**

COMITE INTERNATIONAL DES POIDS ET MESURES. COMITE CONSULTATIF POUR LES ETALONS DE MESURE DES RAYONNEMENTS IONISANTS. SECTION II *See* REUNION - COMITE INTERNATIONAL DES POIDS ET MESURES, COMITE CONSULTATIF POUR LES ETALONS DE MESURE DES RAYONNEMENTS IONISANTS, SECTION II **4451**

COMITE INTERNATIONAL DES POIDS ET MESURES. COMITE CONSULTATIF POUR LES ETALONS DE MESURE DES RAYONNEMENTS IONISANTS. SECTION III *See* REUNION - COMITE INTERNATIONAL DES POIDS ET MESURES, COMITE CONSULTATIF POUR LES ETALONS DE MESURE DES RAYONNEMENTS IONISANTS, SECTION III **4032**

COMITE NATIONAL DE LA POMME DE TERRE *See* RAPPORT STATISTIQUE - COMITE NATIONAL DE LA POMME DE TERRE **2355**

COMITE PROFESSIONEL DU PETROLE *See* CPDP BULLETIN MENSUEL **4254**

COMITE PROFESSIONNEL DU PETROLE, PARIS *See* STATISTIQUES F. O. A. : DISTRIBUTION DES FUELS-OILS **4284**

COMITETUL NATIONAL PENTRU LITERATURA COMPARATA *See* SYNTHESIS (BUCURESTI) **3444**

COMITEXTIL. BULLETIN (BE) [05356403] **5349**

COMLA NEWSLETTER (JM/0378-1070) [02360775] **3203**

COMLINE (US/8755-4143) [11299649] **3203**

COMLINE INDUSTRIAL REPORT SERIES. ROBOTICS (UK) **1212**

COMLINE NEWS SERVICE (JA) **3691**

COMM - EUROPEAN REGIONAL CLEARING HOUSE FOR COMMUNITY WORK *SUSPENDED.* (BE/0773-0357) [I07730357] **5279**

COMMACK NEWS (US/0746-7508) [10253698] **5715**

COMMAND (DENVER, COLO.) (US/0010-2474) [01716775] 4949, **4039**

COMMAND HISTORY - UNITED STATES. NAVAL FACILITIES ENGINEERING COMMAND (US/0740-6029) [08660454] **4175**

COMMAND MAGAZINE (SAN LUIS OBISPO, CALIF.) (US/1059-5651) [22456702] **4039**

COMMAND POST (US/0191-7439) [04947811] **5659**

COMMANDER (TACOMA, WASH.) (US/0746-3197) [09796122] **1175**

COMME LES AUTRES (FR) **4385**

COMMEMORATIVE SERIES (US) [05163818] **2729**

COMMENT CA MARCHE (CN) [04130056] **5095**

COMMENT (DON MILLS) (CN/0382-7038) [02319758] **2878**

COMMENT LONDON. 1971 (UK/0308-7093) [I03087093] **4518**

COMMENTAIRE DES PRINCIPAUX RESULTATS TOURISTIQUES POUR L'ANNEE ... / OFFICE DEPARTEMENTAL DU TOURISME DE LA MARTINIQUE (MQ) [18804499] **5466**

COMMENTAIRE (JULLIARD) (FR/0180-8214) [06724574] **3377**

COMMENTAIRE SUR LA TPS (CN/1183-3343) [23599105] **4718**

COMMENTARI DELL'ATENEO DI BRESCIA (IT/0375-6181) [I03756181] **2844**

COMMENTARI; RIVISTA DI CRITICA E STORIA DELL'ARTE (IT/0586-6391) [03287974] **348**

COMMENTARIES (US/0147-6696) [03213463] **2953**

COMMENTARII MATHEMATICI HELVETICI (SZ/0010-2571) [01564292] **3500**

COMMENTARII MATHEMATICI UNIVERSITATIS SANCTI PAULI (JA/0010-258X) [03821058] **3500**

COMMENTARY (NEW YORK) (US/0010-2601) [01564295] **5047**

COMMENTARY (SINGAPORE) (SI/0084-8956) [04011471] **2503**

COMMENTATIONES HUMANARUM LITTERARUM (FI/0069-6587) [01587127] **3274**

COMMENTATIONES MATHEMATICAE UNIVERSITATIS CAROLINAE (XR/0010-2628) [01639653] **3500**

COMMENTATIONES PHYSICO-MATHEMATICAE ET CHEMICO-MEDICAE (FI/0788-5717) [23247632] 3500, **4400**

COMMENTATIONES SCIENTIARUM SOCIALIUM (FI/0355-256X) [06445054] **5196**

COMMENTATOR (US) [02254980] **2953**

COMMENTS (US) [05778094] **783**

COMMENTS FROM THE FRIENDS (US/1063-7575) [26143594] **4949**

COMMENTS ON ARGENTINE TRADE (BUENOS AIRES, ARGENTINA : 1985) (AG) [13791019] **828**

COMMENTS ON ASTROPHYSICS (US/0146-2970) [02917602] 4400, **394**

COMMENTS ON ATOMIC AND MOLECULAR PHYSICS (UK/0010-2687) [00813488] **4446**

COMMENTS ON CURRENT WORLD AFFAIRS (US) [03299612] **4518**

COMMENTS ON DEVELOPMENTAL NEUROBIOLOGY *CEASED.* (US/0896-5099) [17197694] 452, **3830**

COMMENTS ON ETYMOLOGY (US/0740-0330) [03299655] **3274**

COMMENTS ON MODERN BIOLOGY. PART D. COMMENTS ON DEVELOPMENTAL NEUROBIOLOGY *See* PERSPECTIVES ON DEVELOPMENTAL NEUROBIOLOGY **468**

COMMENTS ON MODERN CHEMISTRY. PART A, COMMENTS ON INORGANIC CHEMISTRY (UK/0260-3594) [07680688] **1036**

COMMENTS ON MODERN CHEMISTRY. PART B, COMMENTS ON AGRICULTURAL AND FOOD CHEMISTRY (UK/0892-2101) [15117815] **1041**

COMMENTS ON MODERN PHYSICS. PART B, COMMENTS ON CONDENSED MATTER PHYSICS (UK/0885-4483) [12640345] **4400**

COMMENTS ON MOLECULAR AND CELLULAR BIOPHYSICS (US/0143-8123) [07193380] 495, **535**

COMMENTS ON NUCLEAR AND PARTICLE PHYSICS (US/0010-2709) [01643668] **4446**

COMMENTS ON PLASMA PHYSICS AND CONTROLLED FUSION (US/0374-2806) [01798292] **4400**

COMMENTS ON THEORETICAL BIOLOGY (UK/0894-8550) [16270296] **452**

COMMENTS ON TOXICOLOGY (UK/0886-5140) [12900259] **3980**

COMMERCE (RH) [05769484] **828**

COMMERCE (II/0010-275X) [01775723] **828**

COMMERCE BUSINESS DAILY (US/0095-3423) [04506910] **949**

COMMERCE BUSINESS DIRECTORIES REDDITCH ED (UK/0964-8585) [I09648585] **658**

COMMERCE CLEARING HOUSE *See* FOOD DRUG COSMETIC LAW REPORTS (RX EDITION) **3100**

COMMERCE CLEARING HOUSE *See* FEDERAL EXCISE TAX REPORTS **4723**

COMMERCE CLEARING HOUSE *See* PRODUCTS LIABILITY REPORTS **3032**

COMMERCE CLEARING HOUSE *See* UNITED STATES EXCISE TAX GUIDE **4757**

COMMERCE CLEARING HOUSE *See* GUIDEBOOK TO FAIR EMPLOYMENT PRACTICES **3148**

COMMERCE CLEARING HOUSE *See* ACCOUNTING ARTICLES **725**

COMMERCE CLEARING HOUSE *See* LABOR ARBITRATION AWARDS **1683**

COMMERCE CLEARING HOUSE *See* FEDERAL CARRIERS CASES (CHICAGO) **2969**

COMMERCE CLEARING HOUSE *See* COPYRIGHT LAW REPORTER **1303**

COMMERCE CLEARING HOUSE *See* GUIDEBOOK TO PENNSYLVANIA TAXES **4730**

COMMERCE CLEARING HOUSE *See* IRS LETTER RULINGS **4734**

COMMERCE CLEARING HOUSE *See* GUIDEBOOK TO NEW JERSEY TAXES **4730**

COMMERCE CLEARING HOUSE *See* NUCLEAR REGULATION REPORTS **3115**

COMMERCE CLEARING HOUSE *See* BRITISH TAX GUIDE **4714**

COMMERCE CLEARING HOUSE *See* INTERNAL REVENUE MANUAL; AUDIT **4732**

COMMERCE CLEARING HOUSE *See* U.S. TAX CASES **4757**

COMMERCE CLEARING HOUSE *See* FEDERAL TAX ARTICLES: INCOME, ESTATE, GIFT, EXCISE, EMPLOYMENT TAXES **4724**

COMMERCE CLEARING HOUSE *See* COMPLIANCE GUIDE FOR PLAN ADMINISTRATORS **1660**

COMMERCE CLEARING HOUSE AUSTRALIA LIMITED *See* AUSTRALIAN TAX CASES **4712**

COMMERCE CREDIT INDEX, THE (CN/0383-9729) [03258711] **828**

COMMERCE DE GROS (FRANCE. DIRECTION DU COMMERCE INTERIEUR) (FR) [10678739] **828**

COMMERCE DIGEST (BOSTON) (US/0465-1499) [01789163] **828**

COMMERCE DU CANADA: EXPORTATIONS PAR MERCHANDISES (CN) [01773819] **828**

COMMERCE ET COOPERATION PARIS (FR/0222-6618) [I02226618] **828**

COMMERCE EXTERIEUR ALBANAIS *CEASED.* (AA) [06522302] **819**

COMMERCE EXTERIEUR DE L'U.E.B.L. AVEC LES PAYS D'AFRIQUE, LE (BE) [01783821] **828**

COMMERCE EXTERIEUR DE L'U.E.B.L. AVEC LES PAYS D'AMERIQUE LATINE, LE (BE) [01783814] **828**

COMMERCE EXTERIEUR DE L'U.E.B.L. AVEC LES PAYS DE L'A.E.L.E, LE (BE) [01790368] **828**

COMMERCE EXTERIEUR DE L'U.E.B.L. AVEC LES PAYS DE L'EST, LE (BE) [01800212] **828**

COMMERCE EXTERIEUR DE L'U. L'U.E.B.L. AVEC LES PAYS INDUSTRIALISES (AUTRES QUE LES PAYS DE LA C.E.E. ET DE L'A.E.L.E.), LE (BE) [01799949] **828**

COMMERCE EXTERIEUR DE L'UNION ECONOMIQUE BELGO-LUXEMBOURGEOISE, LE (BE) [02239246] **828**

COMMERCE EXTERIEUR DES REGIONS PROVENCE, ALPES, COTE D'AZUR ET CORSE, LE (FR) [04819484] **828**

COMMERCE EXTERIEUR DU LIVRE POUR L'ANNEE ... D'APRES LES STATISTIQUES DOUANIERES, LE (FR) [20373523] **4813**

COMMERCE EXTERIEUR FRANCAIS DE PRODUITS AGRICOLES ET ALIMENTAIRES (FR) [07004298] **828**

COMMERCE (HACKENSACK, N.Y.) (US/0745-077X) [08802048] **658**

COMMERCE IN FRANCE (FR/0010-2849) [01564350] **828**

COMMERCE INTERNATIONAL *CEASED.* (UK/0010-2733) [02404562] **828**

COMMERCE INTERNATIONAL DU QUEBEC (CN/0820-0025) [11619905] **1633**

COMMERCE JOURNAL (COMMERCE, TEX.) (US) [14198271] **5748**

COMMERCE LEADING INDICATOR, THE (CN/0383-9699) [03261981] **828**

COMMERCE (MANILA, PHILIPPINES) (PH/0010-2776) [03638687] **828**

COMMERCE MONCTON (1981) (CN/0227-079X) [08562607] **828**

COMMERCE NEWS (CN/0704-8017) [05787766] **819**

COMMERCE NEWS, THE (US) [20590487] **5653**

COMMERCE PUBLICATIONS UPDATE *CEASED.* (US/1057-9672) [06504692] **828**

COMMERCE (RED DEER) (CN/1187-4651) [25796343] **828**

COMMERCE RIVE-SUD (CN/0823-6658) [09985983] **828**

COMMERCE YEARBOOK OF PORTS, SHIPPING AND SHIPBUILDING (II) [02241565] **5448**

COMMERCE YEARBOOK OF ROAD TRANSPORT (II) [11682832] **5380**

COMMERCIAL ACTIVITIES INVENTORY REPORT AND FIVE-YEAR REVIEW SCHEDULE / DEPARTMENT OF DEFENSE (US/0736-1807) [08788922] **4039**

COMMERCIAL AGRICULTURE IN ZIMBABWE *CEASED.* (RH) [12671889] **75**

COMMERCIAL AIRCRAFT FLEETS (US/0270-5249) [04701981] **16**

COMMERCIAL AND FINANCIAL CHRONICLE (1978), THE (US/0163-2876) [04339621] **895**

COMMERCIAL AND INDUSTRIAL FLOORSPACE STATISTICS, WALES *CEASED.* (UK/0262-5334) [10214446] **5325**

COMMERCIAL AND INDUSTRIAL REGISTER OF SOUTHERN AFRICA, THE (SA) [22696391] **1602**

COMMERCIAL APPEAL, THE (US/0745-4856) [09227552] **5744**

COMMERCIAL ARCHITECTURE (JA) **295**

COMMERCIAL AVIATION NEWS *CEASED.* (US/1063-8598) [26180000] **16**

COMMERCIAL AVIATION REPORT (UK) **16**

COMMERCIAL BANKING PRODUCTS SURVEY. BUSINESS CHEQUE ACCOUNTS (AT/1038-6505) **783**

COMMERCIAL BANKING PRODUCTS SURVEY. COMMERCIAL LOANS (AT/1038-6491) **783**

COMMERCIAL BAR, THE (US/0098-4957) [02241745] **2953**

COMMERCIAL BUILDING VALUATION GUIDE (US) [17850981] **608**

COMMERCIAL BUYERS GUIDE FOR ALASKA (US) [25139705] **953**

COMMERCIAL BUYERS GUIDE : PUERTO RICO, VIRGIN ISLANDS, THE (PR/0198-9650) [06263081] 922, **949**

COMMERCIAL CARPET DIGEST (US/0890-0027) [14222392] **5349**

Alphabetical Title Index — COMMISSION

COMMERCIAL DIRECTORY OF MALAYSIA, THE (MY) [07289472] **828**

COMMERCIAL DISPUTE RESOLUTION JOURNAL (AT) **2953**

COMMERCIAL DIVER AND UNDERWATER CONTRACTOR (UK) **4891**

COMMERCIAL FERTILIZER AND PLANT FOOD INDUSTRY (US) [01564380] **167**

COMMERCIAL FINANCE AUSTRALIA (AT/1031-0193) [I10310193] **783, 727**

COMMERCIAL FINANCE, FACTORING, AND OTHER ASSET-BASED LENDING (US/0732-1023) [07131146] **3086**

COMMERCIAL FISH FARMER (US) [03247312] **2299**

COMMERCIAL FISHERIES NEWS (US/0273-6713) [06800129] **2299**

COMMERCIAL FISHING *CEASED.* (UK/0143-652X) [02562532] **2299**

COMMERCIAL FISHING *CEASED.* (NZ/0110-1730) [02099060] **2299**

COMMERCIAL FOOD PATENTS, U.S (US/0275-7184) [01191651] **2332**

COMMERCIAL GAS MARKET SURVEY (US) [12102788] **4253**

COMMERCIAL GROWER WEEKLY (UK) [08159875] **167**

COMMERCIAL INFORMATION *See* YUGOSLAVIA EXPORT **858**

COMMERCIAL INSOLVENCY REPORTER (CN/0832-7688) [17661642] **3086**

COMMERCIAL INVESTMENT REAL ESTATE JOURNAL (US/0887-4778) [13274791] **4835**

COMMERCIAL LAW ADVISER (US) [27951113] **783**

COMMERCIAL LAW ANNUAL (US) [24025701] **2953**

COMMERCIAL LAW BULLETIN (CHICAGO, ILL.) (US/0888-8000) [13083953] **3097**

COMMERCIAL LAW DIGEST *CEASED.* (CN/0832-235X) [16870274] **3097**

COMMERCIAL LAW. GOLD BOOK. BENDER PAMPHLET EDITION. NEW YORK UNIFORM COMMERCIAL CODE, GENERAL OBLIGATIONS LAW (US/0277-3643) [07542728] **3097**

COMMERCIAL LAW JOURNAL (US/0010-3055) [01564375] **3098**

COMMERCIAL LAW QUARTERLY (AT/0819-4262) [I08194262] **2953**

COMMERCIAL LAWS OF EUROPE (UK/0141-7258) [04669763] **3098**

COMMERCIAL LAWS OF THE WORLD. CLASS C (US) **3126**

COMMERCIAL LEASE LAW INSIDER (US/0736-0517) [09059399] **4835, 2953**

COMMERCIAL LEASES (UK) **895**

COMMERCIAL LEASING LAW & STRATEGY (US/0898-5634) [17850534] **4835, 2953**

COMMERCIAL LENDING NEWSLETTER (US) [06418445] **783**

COMMERCIAL LENDING REVIEW (US/0886-8204) [13027041] **783**

●COMMERCIAL LIBRARY PUBLICATIONS LIST / UNITED STATES DEPARTMENT OF STATE LIBRARY (US) [24768501] 3203, **1924**

COMMERCIAL MOTOR, THE (UK/0010-3063) [08755198] **5412**

COMMERCIAL NEWS (US/0192-5253) [05085649] **5715**

COMMERCIAL-NEWS (DANVILLE, ILL.), THE (US/0742-8286) [08807652] **5659**

COMMERCIAL NEWS FOR THE FOREIGN SERVICE *See* COMMERCIAL NEWS USA **829**

COMMERCIAL NEWS INTERNATIONAL (US/0885-7989) [12736380] **5634**

COMMERCIAL NEWS USA (US/0161-9772) [03831918] **829**

COMMERCIAL NEWS USA. ANNUAL DIRECTORY (US/0738-0992) [09432870] **829**

COMMERCIAL OPERATORS (US) [02240369] **2299**

COMMERCIAL PHOTO (JA) **4368**

COMMERCIAL PHOTOGRAPHY IN AUSTRALIA (AT/1037-6992) [I10376992] **4368**

COMMERCIAL PRICE LIST FOR STILL PHOTOGRAPHS (CN/0709-6771) [07314547] **4368**

COMMERCIAL PRICE LIST - N.F.B. PHOTOTHEQUE (CN/0709-678X) [05697335] **4067**

COMMERCIAL PROPERTY NEWS (US/1043-1675) [19330815] **4835**

COMMERCIAL REAL ESTATE BROKERS DIRECTORY, THE (US/0882-7664) [11962533] **4835**

COMMERCIAL REAL ESTATE LEASES (US/0192-3897) [04998088] **4835**

●COMMERCIAL REAL ESTATE PROPERTY DIRECTORY (US/1062-5879) [25677726] **4836**

COMMERCIAL RECORD (SOUTH WINDSOR, CT.), THE (US/0010-3098) [04042152] **4836**

COMMERCIAL RENOVATION *CEASED.* (US/0747-0134) [10466872] **608**

COMMERCIAL-REVIEW (PORTLAND, IND. : DAILY : 1922) (US) [13177689] **5663**

COMMERCIAL REVIEW (PORTLAND, OR.) (US/0010-3101) [11189112] **75**

COMMERCIAL TELEVISION AND RADIO YEAR BOOK (UK/0306-7718) [01796426] **1130**

●COMMERCIAL TRAILER BLUE BOOK (US/1058-3076) [24258329] **949**

COMMERCIAL TRANSPORT (SA) [05228378] 829, **5380**

COMMERCIAL TRANSPORT AND FREIGHT *See* COMMERCIAL TRANSPORT **5380**

COMMERCIAL VEGETABLE PRODUCTION RECOMMENDATIONS (US) [05425198] **4244**

COMMERCIO (IT) [08828307] **829**

COMMERCIO CARTOLERIA E CANCELLERIA (IT) **829**

COMMERCIO ESTERO CINESE (IT) **1633**

COMMERCIO INTERNAZIONALE (IT) **829**

COMMERICAL LAWS OF THE WORLD. BERMUDA (US) **2953**

COMMINITY CRIME PREVENTION DIGEST *See* COMMUNITY POLICING DIGEST **3160**

COMMISARYMAN 1 & C *See* COMMISSARYMAN 1 & C **4175**

COMMISSAIRE A L'INFORMATION ET A LA PROTECTION DE LA VIE PRIVEE/ONTARIO *See* PERSPECTIVES / COMMISSAIRE A L'INFORMATION ET A LA PROTECTION DE LA VIE PRIVEE/ONTARIO **4673**

COMMISSAIRE D'ECOLES (CN/0228-7684) [08323961] **1861**

COMMISSARYMAN 1 & C (US/0097-9910) [03140814] **4175**

COMMISSIE INDUSTRIEVESTIGING GRONINGEN *See* JAARVERSLAG / COMMISSIE INDUSTRIEVESTIGING GRONINGEN **1613**

COMMISSION D'APPEL EN MATIERE DE LESIONS PROFESSIONNELLES *See* JURISELECTION (QUEBEC) **2990**

COMMISSION DE LA FONCTION PUBLIQUE DU CANADA *See* DIRECTIONS - PUBLIC SERVICE COMMISSION OF CANADA **4643**

COMMISSION DE LA FONCTION PUBLIQUE DU QUEBEC. COMITES D'APPEL DE LA FONCTION PUBLIQUE *See* RECUEIL DES DECISIONS / COMITES D'APPEL DE LA FONCTION PUBLIQUE **4679**

COMMISSION DE LA SANTE MENTALE DU NOUVEAU-BUNSWICK *See* ANNUAL REPORT / MENTAL HEALTH COMMISSION OF NEW BRUNSWICK **4766**

COMMISSION DE L'ENSEIGNEMENT SUPERIEUR DES PROVINCES MARITIMES *See* PLAN FINANCIER - COMMISSION DE L'ENSEIGNEMENT SUPERIEUR DES PROVINCES MARITIMES **803**

COMMISSION DE PROTECTION DU TERRITOIRE AGRICOLE DU QUEBEC *See* RAPPORT ANNUEL / COMMISSION DE PROTECTION DU TERRITOIRE AGRICOLE DU QUEBEC **2203**

COMMISSION DE TRANSPORT DE LA RIVE SUD DE MONTREAL *See* REFLET **5391**

COMMISSION DES ANTIQUITES DU DEPARTEMENT DE LA COTE-D'OR *See* MEMOIRES DE LA COMMISSION DES ANTIQUITES DU DEPARTEMENT DE LA COTE-D'OR **2850**

COMMISSION DES ASSURANCES DE L'ONTARIO *See* ANNUAL REPORT - ONTARIO INSURANCE COMMISSION **2873**

COMMISSION DES ECOLES CATHOLIQUES DE MONTREAL *See* ECOLES SECONDAIRES DE LA CECM, LES **1737**

COMMISSION DES SERVICES JURIDIQUES *See* RAPPORT ANNUEL - COMMISSION DES SERVICES JURIDIQUES **3034**

COMMISSION D'INITIATIVE ET DE DEVELOPPEMENT ECONOMIQUES DE MONTREAL *See* CIDEM EXPRESS **1470**

COMMISSION FOR THE GEOLOGICAL MAP OF THE WORLD *See* BULLETIN - COMMISSION DE LA CARTE GEOLOGIQUE DU MONDE **1368**

COMMISSION GEOLOGIQUE DU CANADA *See* INFORMATION CIRCULAR - GEOLOGICAL SURVEY OF CANADA (1990) **1382**

COMMISSION INTERNATIONALE TECHNIQUE DE SUCRERIE *See* COMPTES-RENDUS DE LA ASSEMBLEE GENERALE DE LA COMMISSION INTERNATIONALE TECHNIQUE DE SUCRERIE **2332**

COMMISSION INTERNATIONALE TECHNIQUE DE SUCRERIE *See* COMPTES-RENDUS DE L' ASSEMBLEE GENERALE DE LA COMMISSION INTERNATIONALE TECHNIQUE DE SUCRERIE **5096**

COMMISSION MUNICIPALE DU QUEBEC *See* RAPPORT ANNUEL / COMMISSION MUNICIPALE DU QUEBEC **4678**

COMMISSION OF THE EUROPEAN COMMUNITIES *See* DIRECTORY OF THE COMMISSION OF THE EUROPEAN COMMUNITIES **3127**

COMMISSION OF THE EUROPEAN COMMUNITIES *See* AGRICULTURAL SITUATION IN THE COMMUNITY; REPORT, THE **52**

COMMISSION OF THE EUROPEAN COMMUNITIES *See* FINANCIAL REPORT - COMMISSION OF THE EUROPEAN COMMUNITIES **4725**

COMMISSION OF THE EUROPEAN COMMUNITIES *See* BULLETIN DES COMMUNAUTES EUROPEENNES **1466**

COMMISSION OF THE EUROPEAN COMMUNITIES *See* GENERAL REPORT ON THE ACTIVITIES OF THE COMMUNITIES **1492**

COMMISSION OF THE EUROPEAN COMMUNITIES *See* REPORT ON COMPETITION POLICY **3038**

COMMISSION OF THE EUROPEAN COMMUNITIES *See* DOCUMENTS - COMMISSION OF THE EUROPEAN COMMUNITIES **4645**

COMMISSION OF THE EUROPEAN COMMUNITIES *See* COMMUNITY BUDGET : THE FACTS AND FIGURES, THE **4718**

COMMISSION OF THE EUROPEAN COMMUNITIES *See* DIRECTORY OF THE EUROPEAN COMMISSION **3127**

COMMISSION OF THE EUROPEAN COMMUNITIES. DIRECTORATE-GENERAL FOR ECONOMIC AND FINANCIAL AFFAIRS *See* RESULTATERNE AF KONJUNKTURUNDERSGELSEN HOS VIRKSOMHEDSLEDERE I FLLESSKABET **1581**

COMMISSION OF THE EUROPEAN COMMUNITIES. DIRECTORATE-GENERAL FOR SCIENCE, RESEARCH, AND DEVELOPMENT *See* COMMUNITY'S RESEARCH AND DEVELOPMENT PROGRAMME ON DECOMMISSIONING OF NUCLEAR POWER PLANTS. ANNUAL PROGRESS REPORT, THE **4772**

COMMISSION OF THE EUROPEAN COMMUNITIES. DIRECTORY OF THE COMMISSION OF THE EUROPEAN COMMUNITIES *See* DIRECTORY OF THE EUROPEAN COMMISSION **3127**

COMMISSION OF THE EUROPEAN COMMUNITIES HEALTH SERVICES RESEARCH SERIES (UK/0953-1084) [16410297] **4771**

COMMISSION ON AUDIT JOURNAL (PH) [07366231] **4718**

COMMISSION ON BEHAVIORAL AND SOCIAL SCIENCES AND EDUCATION (NATIONAL RESEARCH COUNCIL) *See* CBASSE NEWSLETTER **5195**

COMMISSION ON INSURANCE TERMINOLOGY *See* BULLETIN. COMMISSION ON INSURANCE TERMINOLOGY **2876**

COMMISSION ON ORE-FORMING FLUIDS IN INCLUSIONS *See* FLUID INCLUSION RESEARCH **1439**

COMMISSION ON PROFESSIONAL AND HOSPITAL ACTIVITIES *See* LENGTH OF STAY IN PAS HOSPITALS, UNITED STATES, EASTERN REGION **3788**

COMMISSION REGIONALE SARRE, LORRAINE, LUXEMBOURG, RHENANIE-PALATINAT *See* DONNEES ECONOMIQUES DES REGIONS FRONTALIEERES SAAR-LOR-LUX **1555**

COMMISSION SCOLAIRE L'ISLET-SUD *See* EFFECTIFS HUMAINS - COMMISSION SCOLAIRE L'ISLET-SUD **1743**

COMMISSION SCOLAIRE REGIONALE DE L'ESTRIE *See* ANNUAIRE GENERALE - COMMISSION SCOLAIRE REGIONALE DE L'ESTRIE **1860**

COMMISSION SCOLAIRE REGIONALE LOUIS-FRECHETTE *See* ANNUAIRE / COMMISSION SCOLAIRE REGIONALE LOIS-FRECHETTE **1724**

COMMISSION, THE (US/0010-3179) [01605114] **4949**

COMMISSION Alphabetical Title Index

COMMISSION TO STUDY THE ORGANIZATION OF PEACE See REPORT OF THE COMMISSION TO STUDY THE ORGANIZATION OF PEACE **4533**

COMMISSIONE ARCHEOLOGICA COMUNALE DI ROMA See BULLETTINO DELLA COMMISSIONE ARCHEOLOGICA COMUNALE DI ROMA **265**

COMMISSIONE TRIBUTARIA CENTRALE (IT) **741**

COMMISSIONED CORPS BULLETIN (US) [19504287] **4771**

COMMISSIONED OFFICERS ASSOCIATION OF THE UNITED STATES PUBLIC HEALTH SERVICE See C.O.A. BULLETIN **4770**

COMMISSIONER'S REPORT ON THE EDUCATION PROFESSIONS (US/0148-5415) [03276778] **1891**

COMMITMENT PLUS (US/0884-934X) [12531456] **864**

COMMITMENTS OF TRADERS CEASED. (US) **829**

COMMITMENTS TO JAILS See JAIL COMMITMENTS AND CONFINEMENTS **3166**

COMMITTEE AGAINST REPRESSION IN THE PACIFIC AND ASIA See CARPA BULLETIN **4505**

COMMITTEE BULLETIN (AT) **4639**

COMMITTEE FOR COORDINATION OF JOINT PROSPECTING FOR MINERAL RESOURCES IN ASIAN OFFSHORE AREAS (CCOP) See TECHNICAL PUBLICATION - COMMITTEE FOR COORDINATION OF JOINT PROSPECTING FOR MINERAL RESOURCES IN ASIAN OFFSHORE AREAS (CCOP) **1445**

COMMITTEE FOR ECONOMIC DEVELOPMENT See C. E. D. PRESS REACTION **1467**

COMMITTEE FOR ECONOMIC DEVELOPMENT See PROBLEMS OF UNITED STATES ECONOMIC DEVELOPMENT **1513**

COMMITTEE FOR ECONOMIC DEVELOPMENT OF AUSTRALIA See P SERIES - COMMITTEE FOR ECONOMIC DEVELOPMENT OF AUSTRALIA **1511**

COMMITTEE FOR ECONOMIC DEVELOPMENT OF AUSTRALIA See SUPPLEMENTARY PAPER - COMMITTEE FOR ECONOMIC DEVELOPMENT OF AUSTRALIA **1523**

COMMITTEE FOR ECONOMIC DEVELOPMENT OF AUSTRALIA See CEDA ANNUAL REPORT **1551**

COMMITTEE HANDBOOK - AICPA (US/0147-5673) [03197737] **741**

COMMITTEE OF PROVINCIAL GEOLOGISTS (CANADA) See PROVINCIAL GEOLOGISTS JOURNAL **1392**

COMMITTEE OF VICE-CHANCELLORS AND PRINCIPALS OF THE UNIVERSITIES OF THE UNITED KINGDOM See COMPENDIUM OF UNIVERSITY ENTRANCE REQUIREMENTS FOR FIRST DEGREE COURSES IN THE UNITED KINGDOM, A **1818**

COMMITTEE ON EAST ASIAN LIBRARIES BULLETIN (US/0148-6225) [03337580] **3203**

●COMMITTEE ON EAST ASIAN LIBRARIES DIRECTORY (US/1067-0580) [27128444] **2613**

COMMITTEE ON TAXATION, RESOURCES AND ECONOMIC DEVELOPMENT See PUBLICATIONS - COMMITTEE ON TAXATION, RESOURCES AND ECONOMIC DEVELOPMENT **4743**

COMMITTEE PAPER (UK) [03640903] **167**

COMMITTEE REPORT / LAWYERS' COMMITTEE FOR CIVIL RIGHTS UNDER LAW (US/0730-9988) [17165723] **4506**

COMMITTEE REPORTS - LOCAL GOVERNMENT LAW SECTION OF THE AMERICAN BAR ASSOCIATION (US/0587-2936) [01784541] **4639**, **2953**

COMMITTEE REPORTS PUBLISHED BY HMSO INDEXED BY CHAIRMAN (UK/0267-2146) [13297614] **4639**

●COMMLAW CONSPECTUS (US/1068-5871) [27716160] **2953**

COMMODEX (US/0279-0939) [07533929] **829**

COMMODITIES LAW LETTER (US/0277-2930) [07529743] **2953**

COMMODITIES LITIGATION REPORTER (US/0887-784X) [12622297] **895**

COMMODITIES (WASHINGTON, D.C.) (US/1071-250X) [28596949] **4000**

COMMODITY BULLETIN SERIES (IT) [01681136] **1602**

COMMODITY CREDIT CORPORATION See ANNUAL REPORT FOR FISCAL YEAR ... / COMMODITY CREDIT CORPORATION **60**

COMMODITY CREDIT CORPORATION See REVIEW OF THE COMMODITY CREDIT CORPORATION'S FINANCIAL STATEMENTS **809**

COMMODITY CREDIT CORPORATION See REPORT OF FINANCIAL CONDITION AND OPERATIONS OF THE COMMODITY CREDIT CORPORATION / UNITED STATES DEPARTMENT OF AGRICULTURE, COMMODITY CREDIT CORPORATION **807**

COMMODITY CREDIT CORPORATION CHARTS / UNITED STATES DEPARTMENT OF AGRICULTURE, PRODUCTION AND MARKETING ADMINISTRATION (US) [01298325] **75**

COMMODITY CREDIT CORPORATION. REPORT OF FINANCIAL CONDITION AND OPERATIONS See REPORT OF FINANCIAL CONDITION AND OPERATIONS OF THE COMMODITY CREDIT CORPORATION / UNITED STATES DEPARTMENT OF AGRICULTURE, COMMODITY CREDIT CORPORATION **807**

COMMODITY PERSPECTIVE (US/0730-7217) [08024475] **895**

COMMODITY POLICY STUDIES / FOOD AND AGRICULTURE ORGANIZATION OF THE UNITED NATIONS (IT) [01099387] **75**

COMMODITY REFERENCE SERIES (IT/0071-6952) [01225023] **1602**

COMMODITY REVIEW AND OUTLOOK (IT) [09856998] **75**

COMMODITY STATISTICAL BULLETIN (AT/0817-685X) [17375767] **75**

COMMODITY TRADE AND PRICE TRENDS (US/0251-401X) [04994437] **829**

COMMODITY WEEK (UK) **1470**

COMMODITY YEAR BOOK STATISTICAL SUPPLEMENT (US) [18305586] **658**

COMMODORE COMPUTING (UK) **1175**

COMMODORE FORCE CEASED. (UK) 4859, **1244**

COMMODORE INFO (NE) **1175**

COMMODORE USER See CU AMIGA **1181**

COMMON BOUNDARY, THE (US/0885-8500) [12759594] 4949, **4582**

COMMON CARRIER DOMESTIC FACILITIES APPLICATIONS (US) [06731601] **1106**

COMMON CARRIER PUBLIC MOBILE SERVICES INFORMATION (US) [06730943] **1106**

COMMON CARRIER RULES (US) **1130**

COMMON CARRIER SERVICES INFORMATION (US) [03457235] **1106**

COMMON CARRIER WEEK (US/0743-4812) [10597656] **1151**

COMMON CAUSE (AT) [05805293] 2138, **1660**

COMMON CAUSE/COLORADO (US/1042-3966) [19032797] **2531**

COMMON CAUSE MAGAZINE (US/0884-6537) [10806617] **4469**

COMMON CONCERN (US) **5196**

COMMON FOCUS (US) [07941294] **4582**

COMMON GROUND (UK/0010-325X) [01645147] **4949**

COMMON GROUND (ARLINGTON, VA.) (US/0885-6133) [11932378] **4639**

COMMON GROUND (CHARLOTTETOWN) (CN/0715-478X) [09332341] **5553**

COMMON GROUND (DES MOINES, IOWA) (US/0746-5114) [10101386] 2531, **5028**

COMMON GROUND. (OTTAWA) (CN/1189-6892) [29534200] **1732**

COMMON GROUND (REGINA) (CN/0838-8032) [18243138] **1660**

COMMON GROUND (VANCOUVER) (CN/0824-0698) [11847620] **3774**

●COMMON KNOWLEDGE (US/0961-754X) [25986603] **2844**

COMMON LAW LAWYER, THE (US/0160-659X) [03718430] **2953**

COMMON LIVES, LESBIAN LIVES (US/0891-6969) [08234014] **2794**

COMMON LOT (US/1049-9962) [02870192] **5058**

COMMON MARKET LAW REPORTS (UK/0588-7445) [02259601] **2953**

COMMON MARKET LAW REVIEW (NE/0165-0750) [02133371] **2953**

COMMON SENSE (AT) **2510**

COMMON SENSE; A MONTHLY MAGAZINE DEVOTED TO THE INTERESTS OF THE NORTHWEST (US) [01564418] **2486**

COMMON SENSE ABOUT AIDS (US) 3712, **3668**

COMMON SENSE ECONOMICS CEASED. (CN/0319-7549) [01980307] 1732, **1470**

COMMON SENSE (GALENDA BAY) CEASED. (CN/0709-4191) [05694545] **2226**

●COMMON-SENSE GUIDE TO AMERICAN COLLEGES, THE (US/1065-0571) [26495072] **1817**

COMMON SENSE NEGOTIATIONS (US) [18537167] **658**

COMMON SENSE ON ENERGY AND OUR ENVIRONMENT (US/1052-6331) [22339051] 2163, **1935**

COMMON SENSE PEST CONTROL QUARTERLY (US/8756-7881) [11656818] **4244**

COMMON SENSE (PORTSMOUTH) (US/0197-7377) [06108896] **4469**

COMMON USAGE DRUG SCHEDULE (CN/0707-1035) [04631679] **4297**

COMMON WEALTH, THE (US) [06316277] **1732**

COMMONS (HARRISONBURG, VA.), THE (US/1059-5015) [24609667] **1090**

COMMONWEAL (US/0010-3330) [01564424] **2531**

COMMONWEALTH (CC) **658**

COMMONWEALTH (FR/0395-6989) [03279552] **3377**

COMMONWEALTH AGRICULTURAL BUREAUX See CAB ANNUAL REPORT **70**

COMMONWEALTH ASSOCIATION OF SCIENTIFIC AGRICULTURAL SOCIETIES See C A S A S NEWS **70**

COMMONWEALTH BILLS TABLE AND ASSOCIATED MATERIAL (AT/1036-9589) [10369589] **2953**

COMMONWEALTH BROADCASTING ASSOCIATION See HANDBOOK - COMMONWEALTH BROADCASTING ASSOCIATION **1132**

COMMONWEALTH BROADCASTING ASSOCIATION See WHO'S WHO - COMMONWEALTH BROADCASTING ASSOCIATION **1143**

COMMONWEALTH BUREAU OF AGRICULTURAL ECONOMICS See ANNOTATED BIBLIOGRAPHY. SERIES B - COMMONWEALTH BUREAU OF AGRICULTURAL ECONOMICS **151**

COMMONWEALTH CODE OF THE NORTHERN MARIANA ISLANDS (NW) [10297060] **2953**

COMMONWEALTH COURT REPORTS (US) [01714338] **2953**

COMMONWEALTH CURRENTS (UK/0141-8513) [04340173] **2908**

COMMONWEALTH ESSAYS & STUDIES (FR) **3377**

COMMONWEALTH FORESTRY HANDBOOK, THE (UK) [08437213] **2377**

COMMONWEALTH FORESTRY REVIEW, THE (UK/0010-3381) [09885318] 2190, **2399**

COMMONWEALTH FOUNDATION (BRITISH COMMONWEALTH) See REPORT - THE COMMONWEALTH FOUNDATION **1707**

COMMONWEALTH GOVERNMENT DIRECTORY (AT) [03837990] **4639**

COMMONWEALTH IN WORLD TRADE, THE (UK/0308-4884) [02243011] **829**

COMMONWEALTH INSTITUTE OF BIOLOGICAL CONTROL See REPORT OF WORK CARRIED OUT **471**

COMMONWEALTH INSTITUTE OF ENTOMOLOGY See BULLETIN OF ENTOMOLOGICAL RESEARCH **5606**

COMMONWEALTH INSTITUTE OF ENTOMOLOGY, LONDON See DISTRIBUTION MAPS OF PESTS. SERIES A (AGRICULTURAL) **79**

COMMONWEALTH-JOURNAL (SOMERSET, KY.), THE (US/0899-1839) [14286854] **5680**

COMMONWEALTH LAW BULLETIN (UK/0305-0718) [01799322] **2953**

COMMONWEALTH LAW REPORTS, THE (AT/0069-7133) [01518742] **2953**

COMMONWEALTH LETTERS (US/0893-9136) [15710953] **1470**

COMMONWEALTH MINING AND METALLURGICAL CONGRESS See PROCEEDINGS - COMMONWEALTH MINING AND METALLURGICAL CONGRESS **2148**

COMMONWEALTH MINISTERS REFERENCE BOOK, THE (UK) [20765089] **4639**

COMMONWEALTH MYCOLOGICAL INSTITUTE (GREAT BRITAIN) See BIBLIOGRAPHY OF SYSTEMATIC MYCOLOGY **574**

COMMONWEALTH NOVEL IN ENGLISH (US/0732-6734) [08318281] **3340**

COMMONWEALTH OF AUSTRALIA GAZETTE See AUSTRALIAN GOVERNMENT GAZETTE **4631**

COMMONWEALTH OF AUSTRALIA GAZETTE. BUSINESS (AT/0819-7091) [I08197091] **658**

COMMONWEALTH OF AUSTRALIA GAZETTE. GOVERNMENT NOTICES (AT/0819-7105) [I08197105] **4639**

COMMONWEALTH OF AUSTRALIA GAZETTE. PERIODIC (AT) [04294999] **2954**

COMMONWEALTH OF AUSTRALIA GAZETTE. PUBLIC SERVICE (AT) [04008157] **2954**

COMMONWEALTH OF AUSTRALIA GAZETTE. PURCHASING AND DISPOSALS (AT/0815-9017) [I08159017] **949**

COMMONWEALTH OF AUSTRALIA GAZETTE. TARIFF CONCESSIONS (AT/0813-8389) [I08138389] **829**

COMMONWEALTH OF AUSTRALIA NATIONAL REPORT (AT) [01785627] **2581**

COMMONWEALTH OF DOMINICA CONSOLIDATED INDEX OF STATUTES AND SUBSIDIARY LEGISLATION TO ... (BB) [13894367] **3126**

●COMMONWEALTH OF INDEPENDENT STATES AND THE MIDDLE EAST (IS/0334-4142) [26100796] **4518**

COMMONWEALTH PAPERS (UK/0076-0765) [02321799] **1090**

COMMONWEALTH PARLIAMENTARY ASSOCIATION. CANADIAN REGIONAL CONFERENCE *See* SUMMARY REPORT ... CANADIAN REGIONAL CONFERENCE. COMMONWEALTH PARLIAMENTARY ASSOCIATION **4497**

COMMONWEALTH PAYMENTS TO OR FOR VICTORIA (AT) [20686586] **2908**

COMMONWEALTH QUARTERLY (II/1013-9877) [03790780] **3377**

COMMONWEALTH RECORD (AT) [04975082] **4639**

COMMONWEALTH (SAN FRANCISCO), THE (US/0010-3349) [01564427] **2531**

COMMONWEALTH SCIENTIFIC & INDUSTRIAL RESEARCH ORGANISATION. DIVISION OF HORTICULTURE. REPORT (AT/0069-7435) **2412**

COMMONWEALTH SCIENTIFIC AND INDUSTRIAL RESEARCH ORGANIZATION (AUSTRALIA) *See* CSIRO DIRECTORY **5097**

COMMONWEALTH SCIENTIFIC AND INDUSTRIAL RESEARCH ORGANIZATION (AUSTRALIA). CSIRO RESEARCH PROGRAM *See* DIRECTORY OF CSIRO RESEARCH PROGRAMS / COMPILED BY THE SCIENCE COMMUNICATION UNIT, BUREAU OF SCIENTIFIC SERVICES **5100**

COMMONWEALTH SCIENTIFIC AND INDUSTRIAL RESEARCH ORGANIZATION (AUSTRALIA). DIVISION OF ANIMAL PRODUCTION *See* RESEARCH REPORT - CSIRO DIVISION OF ANIMAL PRODUCTION **220**

COMMONWEALTH SCIENTIFIC AND INDUSTRIAL RESEARCH ORGANIZATION (AUSTRALIA). DIVISION OF BUILDING RESEARCH *See* BUILDING RESEARCH **604**

COMMONWEALTH SCIENTIFIC AND INDUSTRIAL RESEARCH ORGANIZATION (AUSTRALIA). DIVISION OF BUILDING RESEARCH *See* SHEET - CSIRO, DIVISION OF BUILDING RESEARCH **627**

COMMONWEALTH SCIENTIFIC AND INDUSTRIAL RESEARCH ORGANIZATION (AUSTRALIA). DIVISION OF CHEMICAL AND WOOD TECHNOLOGY *See* RESEARCH REVIEW / DIVISION OF CHEMICAL AND WOOD TECHNOLOGY **991**

COMMONWEALTH SCIENTIFIC AND INDUSTRIAL RESEARCH ORGANIZATION (AUSTRALIA). DIVISION OF ENTOMOLOGY *See* BIENNIAL REPORT / DIVISION OF ENTOMOLOGY, CSIRO **5606**

COMMONWEALTH SCIENTIFIC AND INDUSTRIAL RESEARCH ORGANIZATION (AUSTRALIA). DIVISION OF ENVIRONMENTAL MECHANICS *See* REPORT - DIVISION OF ENVIRONMENTAL MECHANICS. CSIRO (CANBERRA) **2181**

COMMONWEALTH SCIENTIFIC AND INDUSTRIAL RESEARCH ORGANIZATION (AUSTRALIA). DIVISION OF FOOD RESEARCH *See* REPORT OF RESEARCH / COMMONWEALTH SCIENTIFIC AND INDUSTRIAL RESEARCH ORGANIZATION, AUSTRALIA, DIVISION OF FOOD RESEARCH **2355**

COMMONWEALTH SCIENTIFIC AND INDUSTRIAL RESEARCH ORGANIZATION (AUSTRALIA). DIVISION OF FOREST RESEARCH *See* BIENNIAL REPORT / CSIRO DIVISION OF FOREST RESEARCH **2376**

COMMONWEALTH SCIENTIFIC AND INDUSTRIAL RESEARCH ORGANIZATION (AUSTRALIA). DIVISION OF GROUNDWATER RESEARCH *See* GROUNDWATER RESEARCH / CSIRO, [DIVISION OF GROUNDWATER RESEARCH] **5534**

COMMONWEALTH SCIENTIFIC AND INDUSTRIAL RESEARCH ORGANIZATION (AUSTRALIA). DIVISION OF HORTICULTURAL RESEARCH *See* REPORT / DIVISION OF HORTICULTURAL RESEARCH **2430**

COMMONWEALTH SCIENTIFIC AND INDUSTRIAL RESEARCH ORGANIZATION (AUSTRALIA). DIVISION OF HUMAN NUTRITION *See* REPORT / CSIRO, DIVISION OF HUMAN NUTRITION **4198**

COMMONWEALTH SCIENTIFIC AND INDUSTRIAL RESEARCH ORGANIZATION (AUSTRALIA). DIVISION OF MANUFACTURING TECHNOLOGY *See* RESEARCH REPORT ... / DIVISION OF MANUFACTURING TECHNOLOGY, COMMONWEALTH SCIENTIFIC AND INDUSTRIAL RESEARCH ORGANIZATION **3487**

COMMONWEALTH SCIENTIFIC AND INDUSTRIAL RESEARCH ORGANIZATION (AUSTRALIA). DIVISION OF MECHANICAL ENGINEERING *See* DIVISIONAL REPORT - CSIRO DIVISION OF MECHANICAL ENGINEERING OF THE INSTITUTE OF INDUSTRIAL TECHNOLOGY **2113**

COMMONWEALTH SCIENTIFIC AND INDUSTRIAL RESEARCH ORGANIZATION (AUSTRALIA). DIVISION OF OCEANOGRAPHY *See* RESEARCH REPORT / CSIRO DIVISION OF OCEANOGRAPHY **1456**

COMMONWEALTH SCIENTIFIC AND INDUSTRIAL RESEARCH ORGANIZATION (AUSTRALIA). DIVISION OF PLANT INDUSTRY *See* REPORT / CSIRO DIVISION OF PLANT INDUSTRY **526**

COMMONWEALTH SCIENTIFIC AND INDUSTRIAL RESEARCH ORGANIZATION (AUSTRALIA). DIVISION OF PROTEIN CHEMISTRY *See* BIENNIAL REPORT / DIVISION OF PROTEIN CHEMISTRY, INSTITUTE OF INDUSTRIAL TECHNOLOGY **962**

COMMONWEALTH SCIENTIFIC AND INDUSTRIAL RESEARCH ORGANIZATION (AUSTRALIA). DIVISION OF RADIOPHYSICS *See* BIENNIAL REPORT / CSIRO, DIVISION OF RADIOPHYSICS **4398**

COMMONWEALTH SCIENTIFIC AND INDUSTRIAL RESEARCH ORGANIZATION (AUSTRALIA). DIVISION OF SOILS *See* ANNUAL REPORT - CSIRO DIVISION OF SOILS (1987) **162**

COMMONWEALTH SCIENTIFIC AND INDUSTRIAL RESEARCH ORGANIZATION (AUSTRALIA). DIVISION OF TROPICAL CROPS AND PASTURES *See* BIENNIAL RESEARCH REPORT **66**

COMMONWEALTH SCIENTIFIC AND INDUSTRIAL RESEARCH ORGANIZATION (AUSTRALIA). DIVISION OF WILDLIFE AND ECOLOGY *See* BIENNIAL REPORT / DIVISION OF WILDLIFE AND ECOLOGY **5578**

COMMONWEALTH SCIENTIFIC AND INDUSTRIAL RESEARCH ORGANIZATION (AUSTRALIA). GRAIN QUALITY RESEARCH LABORATORY *See* REPORT FOR THE YEAR ... **203**

COMMONWEALTH SCIENTIFIC AND INDUSTRIAL RESEARCH ORGANIZATION (AUSTRALIA). SCIENCE COMMUNICATION UNIT *See* DIRECTORY OF CSIRO RESEARCH PROGRAMS / COMPILED BY THE SCIENCE COMMUNICATION UNIT, BUREAU OF SCIENTIFIC SERVICES **5100**

COMMONWEALTH SCIENTIFIC AND INDUSTRIAL RESEARCH ORGANIZATION (AUSTRALIA). WHEAT RESEARCH UNIT *See* BIENNIAL REPORT / WHEAT RESEARCH UNIT **200**

COMMONWEALTH SCIENTIFIC AND INDUSTRIAL RESEARCH ORGANIZATION (AUSTRALIA). WHEAT RESEARCH UNIT. ANNUAL REPORT *See* BIENNIAL REPORT / WHEAT RESEARCH UNIT **200**

COMMONWEALTH SCIENTIFIC AND INDUSTRIAL RESEARCH ORGANIZATION (AUSTRALIA). WHEAT RESEARCH UNIT. REPORT FOR THE YEAR. *See* REPORT FOR THE YEAR ... **203**

COMMONWEALTH SCIENTIFIC AND INDUSTRIAL RESEARCH ORGANIZATION (AUSTRIA). DIVISION OF FOOD RESEARCH *See* REPORT OF RESEARCH - DIVISION OF FOOD RESEARCH **2355**

COMMONWEALTH SCIENTIFIC AND INDUSTRIAL RESEARCH ORGANIZATION. DIVISION OF APPLIED MINERALOGY *See* DIVISION OF APPLIED MINERALOGY TECHNICAL PAPER **1439**

COMMONWEALTH SCIENTIFIC AND INDUSTRIAL RESEARCH ORGANIZATION. DIVISION OF APPLIED ORGANIC CHEMISTRY *See* RESEARCH REPORT - DIVISION OF APPLIED ORGANIC CHEMISTRY **1047**

COMMONWEALTH SCIENTIFIC AND INDUSTRIAL RESEARCH ORGANIZATION. DIVISION OF FOREST PRODUCTS *See* PROGRAM OF RESEARCH **2391**

COMMONWEALTH SCIENTIFIC AND INDUSTRIAL RESEARCH ORGANIZATION. DIVISION OF PLANT INDUSTRY *See* DIVISION OF PLANT INDUSTRY TECHNICAL PAPER **1413**

COMMONWEALTH SCIENTIFIC AND INDUSTRIAL RESEARCH ORGANIZATION. WOOL RESEARCH LABORATORIES *See* CSIRO TEXTILE NEWS **5350**

COMMONWEALTH SECRETARIAT *See* DAIRY PRODUCE; A REVIEW OF PRODUCTION, TRADE, CONSUMPTION AND PRICES RELATING TO BUTTER, CHEESE, CONDENSED MILK, MILK POWDER, CASEIN, EGGS AND EGG PRODUCTS **194**

COMMONWEALTH SECRETARIAT *See* COMMONWEALTH IN WORLD TRADE, THE **829**

COMMONWEALTH SECRETARIAT *See* REPORT TO THE HEADS OF GOVERNMENT BY THE COMMONWEALTH SECRETARY-GENERAL **4682**

COMMONWEALTH SERIES, THE (US) [03561412] **1817**

COMMONWEALTH TAXATION BOARD OF REVIEW DECISIONS. NEW SERIES (AT) [01518762] 4718, **2954**

COMMONWEALTH TEACHING SERVICE *See* ANNUAL REPORT - COMMONWEALTH TEACHING SERVICE **1649**

COMMONWEALTH, THE (US) [18898725] **5703**

COMMONWEALTH UNIVERSITIES YEARBOOK (UK/0069-7745) [03688319] **1817**

COMMONWEALTH YEARBOOK, THE (UK/0952-8083) [15708740] **4639**

COMMUNAL SOCIETIES (US/0739-1250) [08736924] **5242**

COMMUNAUTE CHRETIENNE (CN/0010-3454) [01715110] **4949**

COMMUNAUTE ECONOMIQUE DU BETAIL ET DE LA VIANDE. SECRETARIAT EXECUTIF *See* REVUE TRIMESTRIELLE D'INFORMATION TECHNIQUE ET ECONOMIQUE **220**

COMMUNAUTE EUROPEENNE INFORMATIONS (FR/0223-3053) [I02233053] **1470**

COMMUNAUTES AFRICAINES : REVUE TRIMESTRIELLE (CM) [24186994] **2818**

COMMUNAUTES EDUCATIVES (FR) **1732**

COMMUNAUTES ET LITURGIES *CEASED.* (BE) [02251591] **4949**

COMMUNES (UK) [03319276] **4540**

COMMUNIC-ACTION (VICTORIAVILLE) (CN/0846-5347) [20985335] **1106**

COMMUNICABLE DISEASE NEWSLETTER (US) [01780545] **4771**

COMMUNICABLE DISEASE STATISTICS / OFFICE OF POPULATION CENSUSES AND SURVEYS [AND] COMMUNICABLE DISEASE SURVEILLANCE CENTRE OF THE PUBLIC HEALTH LABORATORY SERVICE (UK) [07556533] 3712, **3655**

COMMUNICANTES (CN/0706-3644) [12064662] **4949**

COMMUNICARE *CEASED.* (US/0279-1196) [07565000] **4949**

COMMUNICATE FOR THE TELECOMMUNICATION USER *See* COMMUNICATE (HIGH WYCOMBE) **1151**

COMMUNICATE (HIGH WYCOMBE) (UK/0264-4509) [24565471] **1151**

COMMUNICATE (KAMLOOPS) (CN/0384-661X) [02653704] **4949**

COMMUNICATEUR, LE (CN/0700-5261) [03402777] **1106**

COMMUNICATEUR (OTTAWA) *CEASED.* (CN/0822-8396) [10638886] **1151**

COMMUNICATIE (BE/0771-7342) [I07717342] **1106**

COMMUNICATIE TECHNIEK & MANAGEMENT (NE) **1106**

COMMUNICATIEF (NE) **1106**

COMMUNICATING FOR HEALTH SERIES (US) [25786639] **4772**

COMMUNICATING NURSING RESEARCH (US/0160-1652) [03369719] **3854**

COMMUNICATING TOGETHER (CN/0822-0638) [10036685] **1106**

COMMUNICATIO (SA) [05520921] **1106**

COMMUNICATIO SOCIALIS (GW/0010-3497) [10422187] **1106**

COMMUNICATIO SOCIALIS YEARBOOK (II/0970-0382) [09340555] **4949**

COMMUNICATION *CEASED.* (US/0305-4233) [02243555] **1106**

COMMUNICATION ABSTRACTS (US/0162-2811) [03812396] 1106, **1124**

COMMUNICATION — Alphabetical Title Index

COMMUNICATION & COMPUTER NEWS *CEASED.* (US/1057-0071) [23907050] 1175, **1106**

COMMUNICATION AND CYBERNETICS *CEASED.* (GW/0340-0034) [01069749] **1250**

●COMMUNICATION AND LANGUAGE INTERVENTION SERIES (US) [24944591] 1106, 3567, **4385**

COMMUNICATION ARTS (US/0010-3519) [01798163] **377**

COMMUNICATION BOOKNOTES (US/0748-657X) [08701864] **1125**

COMMUNICATION BRIEFINGS (US/0730-7799) [08078855] **757**

COMMUNICATION - CANADIAN CO-ORDINATING COUNCIL ON DEAFNESS *CEASED.* (CN/0228-5401) [08010261] **4385**

COMMUNICATION CB NEWS (FR) **1106**

COMMUNICATION (COMMUNICATION ASSOCIATION OF THE PACIFIC) (US) [06201625] **1106**

COMMUNICATION DIGEST (BE) **1106**

COMMUNICATION EDGE, THE (US/1053-0169) [22435317] **1106**

COMMUNICATION EDUCATION (US/0363-4523) [02076115] 1891, **1106**

COMMUNICATION ET INFORMATION (CN/0382-7798) [02775637] **1106**

COMMUNICATION ET LANGAGES PARIS (FR/0336-1500) [I03361500] **3274**

COMMUNICATION GRAPHICS (US/0272-0930) [04096909] **377**

COMMUNICATION - INSTITUTE OF CHARTERED ACCOUNTANTS OF BRITISH COLUMBIA (CN/0834-0188) [16308739] **741**

COMMUNICATION - INTERNATIONAL SKATING UNION (SZ) [03741682] **4891**

COMMUNICATION (LIGUE INTERNATIONALE CONTRE LA CONCURRENCE D'ELOYALE) *See* REVUE INTERNATIONALE DE LA CONCURRENCE **3103**

COMMUNICATION LINES *See* INFORMATION TECHNOLOGY DIGEST/ INFORMATION TECHNOLOGY DIVISION, UNIVERSITY OF MICHIGAN **1268**

COMMUNICATION LONDON. 1967 (UK/0045-7663) [I00457663] **3923**

COMMUNICATION MONOGRAPHS (US/0363-7751) [02313630] **1107**

COMMUNICATION NEWS (AT/0819-9817) [I08199817] **1107**

COMMUNICATION / NTIS *See* NTIS ALERT. COMMUNICATION **1118**

COMMUNICATION OPTIONS (US/8755-8955) [11464770] **864**

COMMUNICATION OUTLOOK (US/0161-4126) [03935971] 4385, **1107**

COMMUNICATION-PARENTS (CN/0822-5613) [10156839] **1861**

COMMUNICATION PNEU (FR) **1107**

COMMUNICATION QUARTERLY (US/0146-3373) [02193441] **1107**

COMMUNICATION QUARTERLY (EAST LANSING) *CEASED.* (US/0274-6530) [04331955] **1891**

COMMUNICATION REPORTS (PULLMAN, WASH.) (US/0893-4215) [15513023] **1107**

COMMUNICATION RESEARCH (US/0093-6502) [01792462] **1107**

COMMUNICATION RESEARCH REPORTS (US/0882-4096) [11855065] **1107**

COMMUNICATION RESEARCH TRENDS (US/0144-6061) [07990591] **1107**

COMMUNICATION REVUE QUEBECOISE DES RECHERCHES ET DES PRATIQUES EN COMMUNICATION (CN) **1107**

●COMMUNICATION SERIALS (US/1041-7893) [18846633] 3203, **1107**

COMMUNICATION STOCKS AND THE TSE 300 (CN/1186-0294) [24265542] **895**

COMMUNICATION STUDIES (US/1051-0974) [20705944] **1107**

COMMUNICATION TECHNOLOGY IMPACT (UK/0142-5854) [10434171] **1152**

COMMUNICATION / THE INSTITUTION OF GAS ENGINEERS (UK/0367-7850) [10318348] **1968**

COMMUNICATION THEORY (US/1050-3293) [21463248] **1107**

COMMUNICATION THEORY IN THE CAUSE OF MAN (US/0162-8216) [04244941] **234**

COMMUNICATION - UNIVERSITY OF ZAMBIA. INSTITUTE FOR AFRICAN STUDIES (ZA) [01517671] **1107**

COMMUNICATION WORLD (SAN FRANCISCO, CALIF.) *CEASED.* (US/0744-7612) [10897719] **1107**

COMMUNICATION YEARBOOK (US/0147-4642) [03176048] **1107**

COMMUNICATIONES ARCHEOLOGICAE HUNGARIAE (HU) [10137845] **266**

COMMUNICATIONES INSTITUTI FORESTALIS CECHOSLOVENIAE (XR/0507-5548) [01769312] **2377**

COMMUNICATIONES - PONTIFICIA COMMISSIO CODICI IURIS CANONICI RECOGNOSCENDO (VC/0393-0327) [02251592] **2954**

COMMUNICATIONS (UK) **1107**

COMMUNICATIONS (US) **1107**

COMMUNICATIONS AFRICA (UK) **1107**

COMMUNICATIONS - AMNISTIE INTERNATIONALE, SECTION CANADIENNE (CN/0226-3556) [06512009] **3126**

COMMUNICATIONS AND CLERICAL SKILLS PROGRAM; SCHEDULE OF COURSES (US) [04057733] 4203, **1912**

COMMUNICATIONS & COGNITION (BE/0378-0880) [02558344] **1108**

COMMUNICATIONS & STRATEGIES MONTPELLIER (FR/1157-8637) [I11578637] **1175**

COMMUNICATIONS AND THE LAW (US/0162-9093) [04252472] 1108, **2954**

COMMUNICATIONS BUSINESS AND FINANCE (US) 1152, **658**

COMMUNICATIONS CONCEPTS (US/0741-0069) [10068081] **1108**

COMMUNICATIONS DAILY (US/0277-0679) [07494339] **1152**

COMMUNICATIONS DE LA FACULTE DES SCIENCES DE L'UNIVERSITE D'ANKARA. SERIES AB1S, MATHEMATICS AND STATISTICS (TU) [19910409] 5325, **3500**

COMMUNICATIONS DE LA FACULTE DES SCIENCES DE L'UNIVERSITE D'ANKARA. SERIES AB2S, AB3S, PHYSICS, ENGINEERING PHYSICS AND ASTRONOMY (TU) [18925258] 394, **4400**

COMMUNICATIONS DE LA FACULTE DES SCIENCES DE L'UNIVERSITE D'ANKARA. SERIES B, CHEMISTRY AND CHEMICAL ENGINEERING (TU) [20002287] **973**

COMMUNICATIONS D'ENTERPRISE (FR) **1108**

COMMUNICATIONS D'ENTREPRISE (FR) **658**

COMMUNICATIONS DIRECTORY & YEARBOOK (IE) [01788721] **1108**

COMMUNICATIONS ENGINEERING INTERNATIONAL *See* CEI **1151**

COMMUNICATIONS (ENGLEWOOD. 1964) (US/0010-356X) [02255643] **1152**

COMMUNICATIONS FOR BETTER LIVING (US/8755-9579) [11465005] **3203**

COMMUNICATIONS FROM THE INTERNATIONAL BRECHT SOCIETY (US/0740-8943) [03431399] 5363, **3377**

COMMUNICATIONS FROM THE KAMERLINGH ONNES LABORATORY OF THE UNIVERSITY OF LEIDEN (NE) [08118837] **4400**

COMMUNICATIONS IN ALGEBRA (US/0092-7872) [01791702] **3500**

COMMUNICATIONS IN APPLIED CELL BIOLOGY (JA/0913-8188) [I09138188] **452**

COMMUNICATIONS IN APPLIED NUMERICAL METHODS (UK/0748-8025) [11011263] 1968, **3500**

COMMUNICATIONS IN LABORATORY MEDICINE *CEASED.* (UK/0267-3320) [12824227] 486, **3567**

COMMUNICATIONS IN MATHEMATICAL PHYSICS (GW/0010-3616) [01564493] 3501, **4400**

●COMMUNICATIONS IN NUMERICAL METHODS IN ENGINEERING (UK/1069-8299) [27388966] 1968, **3501**

COMMUNICATIONS IN PARTIAL DIFFERENTIAL EQUATIONS (US/0360-5302) [02459551] **3501**

●COMMUNICATIONS IN RELIABILITY, MAINTAINABILITY, AND SUPPORTABILITY (US/1072-3757) [28920106] **1968**

COMMUNICATIONS IN SOIL SCIENCE AND PLANT ANALYSIS (US/0010-3624) [01564494] **167**

COMMUNICATIONS IN STATISTICS : SIMULATION AND COMPUTATION (US/0361-0918) [02540877] 5325, **1282**

COMMUNICATIONS IN STATISTICS : STOCHASTIC MODELS (US/0882-0287) [11716959] **5325**

COMMUNICATIONS IN STATISTICS : THEORY AND METHODS (US/0361-0926) [02364002] **3501**

COMMUNICATIONS IN THEORETICAL PHYSICS (CC/0253-6102) [08505716] **4400**

COMMUNICATIONS - INSTITUT PROFESSIONNEL DE LA FONCTION PUBLIQUE DU CANADA (CN/0820-7658) [09543130] **1108**

COMMUNICATIONS INTERNATIONAL (UK/0305-2109) [02441329] **1152**

COMMUNICATIONS LAW (1982) (US/0898-2457) [09078569] 1108, **2954**

COMMUNICATIONS LAW BULLETIN (AT/0727-1301) [08512751] **1108**

COMMUNICATIONS LAWYER : PUBLICATION OF THE FORUM COMMITTEE ON COMMUNICATIONS LAW, AMERICAN BAR ASSOCIATION (US/0737-7622) [09214931] 1108, **2954**

COMMUNICATIONS MANAGEMENT (UK) **864**

COMMUNICATIONS MANAGER (US) **1108**

COMMUNICATIONS MIDDLE EAST AFRICA (UK/0961-7590) [I09617590] **1108**

COMMUNICATIONS NETWORK SERVICES (UK) **1108**

COMMUNICATIONS NEWS (GENEVA, ILL.) (US/0010-3632) [01564496] **1108**

COMMUNICATIONS NEWSLETTER *See* TELECOMEUROPA/ COMMUNICATIONS NEWSLETTER **1123**

COMMUNICATIONS OF CHINESE AND ORIENTAL LANGUAGES INFORMATION PROCESSING SOCIETY (SI) **3274**

COMMUNICATIONS OF THE ACM (US/0001-0782) [01514517] **1175**

COMMUNICATIONS OF THE DUBLIN INSTITUTE FOR ADVANCED STUDIES. SERIES A (IE/0070-7414) [01697441] 4400, **3501**

COMMUNICATIONS OF THE DUBLIN INSTITUTE FOR ADVANCED STUDIES. SERIES D. GEOPHYSICAL BULLETIN *CEASED.* (IE/0070-7422) [01697463] **1404**

COMMUNICATIONS OF THE GEOLOGICAL SURVEY OF NAMIBIA / DEPARTMENT OF ECONOMIC AFFAIRS (SX) [23157747] **1372**

COMMUNICATIONS OF THE WORKSHOP FOR SCIENTIFIC LINGUISTICS (US/1061-4710) [25314556] **3274**

COMMUNICATIONS ON HYDRAULIC AND GEOTECHNICAL ENGINEERING (NE/0169-6548) [01696548] **2088**

COMMUNICATIONS ON PURE AND APPLIED MATHEMATICS (US/0010-3640) [06232835] **3501**

COMMUNICATIONS (OTTAWA) (CN/0380-0334) [02441187] **1152**

COMMUNICATIONS (PARIS. 1962) (FR/0588-8018) [03319819] **1108**

COMMUNICATIONS QUARTERLY (US/1053-9433) [22696110] **1152**

COMMUNICATIONS REGULATION (US) **1152**

COMMUNICATIONS REPORT. SYDNEY (AT/1035-6959) [I10356959] **1152**

COMMUNICATIONS (SANKT AUGUSTIN) (GW/0341-2059) [04236669] **1108**

COMMUNICATIONS SATELLITE CORPORATION *See* COMSAT TECHNICAL REVIEW **1152**

COMMUNICATIONS: SERIES C BIOLOGY AND GEOLOGICAL ENGINEERING (TU/0256-7865) [18893101] 1969, **452**

●COMMUNICATIONS SERIES. COMMUNICATIONS NETWORKING SERVICES (US) [25308955] 1240, **1152**

●COMMUNICATIONS SERIES. VOICE NETWORKING SYSTEMS (US) [25308980] **1152**

COMMUNICATIONS STANDARDS REVIEW (US/1064-3907) [26273644] **829**

COMMUNICATIONS TECHNOLOGY (US/0884-2272) [12317702] **1130**

COMMUNICATIONS WORKERS OF AMERICA *See* CWA NEWS **1662**

COMMUNICATIONS WORLD *CEASED.* (US/0095-4063) [01795853] **1130**

COMMUNICATIONSWEEK INTERNATIONAL (US/1042-6086) [19092637] **1108**

COMMUNICATIONSWEEK (MANHASSET, N.Y.) (US/0746-8121) [10304255] **1152**

COMMUNICATOR (US/0745-3671) [09104112] **1108**

COMMUNICATOR (ARLINGTON, VA. 1981) (US/0745-2233) [07903692] **1861**

COMMUNICATOR (CHICAGO, ILL. : 1981), THE (US/0277-8955) [07667368] **3203**

COMMUNICATOR (EDMONTON) (CN/0319-3454) [02442841] **1732**

●COMMUNICATOR (NASHVILLE, TENN., 1992), THE (US/1061-4133) [25301655] **4949**

COMMUNICATOR (NORTHWEST COMMUNICATION ASSOCIATION), THE (US/0193-5437) [04051706] **1108**

COMMUNICATOR OF PHI DELTA CHI FRATERNITY, THE (US/0746-3979) [07093762] 4297, **5230**

COMMUNICATOR (SPRINGHILL) *CEASED.* (CN/0381-095X) [03222692] **3160**

COMMUNICATOR (ST. JOHN'S) (CN/0707-9133) [04955035] 1660, **4639**

COMMUNICATOR, THE (PK) [03298589] **1108**

COMMUNICATOR (VANCOUVER) (CN/0702-7990) [03412158] **2918**

COMMUNICATOR (WASHINGTON, D.C. 1988) (US/1041-7117) [18830227] **2918**

COMMUNICATOR'S JOURNAL (US/0737-3244) [09343096] **1108**

COMMUNICO (US/1044-7202) [19877348] **5230**

COMMUNIO (UK) **4949**

COMMUNIO (SEVILLA) (SP/0010-3705) [03944629] **4949**

COMMUNIO (SPOKANE, WASH.) (US/0094-2065) [01794100] **4949**

COMMUNION (FR/0042-370X) [01782031] **5028**

COMMUNION, EN (CN/0847-2939) [22425661] **5028**

COMMUNION ET DIACONIE WATTRELOS (FR/0224-0254) [I02240254] **4949**

●COMMUNIQUE - ASSOCIATION CANADIENNE DE TELEVISION PAR CABLE (1992) (CN/1192-5035) [28061885] **1130**

COMMUNIQUE - ASSOCIATION FOR PRESERVATION TECHNOLOGY (US/0319-4558) [02443267] **295**

COMMUNIQUE / CALIFORNIA GOVERNOR'S COMMITTEE FOR EMPLOYMENT OF DISABLED PERSONS (US) [23751855] **4385**

COMMUNIQUE - CANADIAN ASSOCIATION OF HOUSING AND RENEWAL OFFICIALS (CN/0711-480X) [08569973] **2818**

COMMUNIQUE - CANADIAN AUTOMOBILE ASSOCIATION (CN/0380-6987) [02583277] **5412**

COMMUNIQUE - CANADIAN CABLE TELEVISION ASSOCIATION 1992 (CN/1193-5898) [I11935898] **1130**

COMMUNIQUE / CANADIAN COMMUNICATION ASSOCIATION (CN/0821-4379) [09562926] **1108**

COMMUNIQUE / CANADIAN DENTAL ASSOCIATION (CN/0710-5614) [08777540] **1319**

COMMUNIQUE - CDA (CN/0711-8112) [08605186] **4189**

COMMUNIQUE - CHILDREN'S AID SOCIETY OF OTTAWA (CN/0319-7468) [02130515] **5279**

COMMUNIQUE (COLUMBUS, OHIO) (US/1043-0695) [19292263] **4949**

COMMUNIQUE - CONSEIL DE LA JEUNESSE SCIENTIFIQUE (CN/0317-8803) [02441635] **5095**

COMMUNIQUE / GANNETT CENTER FOR MEDIA STUDIES (US) [17870621] **2918**

COMMUNIQUE HEBDOMADAIRE (INSTITUT NATIONAL DE STATISTIQUE (BELGIUM) : 1963) *See* COMMUNIQUE HEBDOMADAIRE (INSTITUT NATIONAL DE STATISTIQUE (BELGIUM) : 1982) **5325**

COMMUNIQUE HEBDOMADAIRE (INSTITUT NATIONAL DE STATISTIQUE (BELGIUM) : 1982) (BE/0771-0364) [09865863] **5325**

COMMUNIQUE HEBROMADAIRE (INSTITUT NATIONAL DE STATISTIQUE (BELGIUM) : 1982) (BE/0771-0410) [09866424] **5325**

COMMUNIQUE / HUMAN FACTORS ASSOCIATION OF CANADA (CN/0712-936X) [09606627] **2860**

COMMUNIQUE - INTERMET (CN/0315-5900) [02443024] **5242**

COMMUNIQUE (KENT) (US/0164-775X) [04254243] **4582**

COMMUNIQUE (LAW SOCIETY OF MANITOBA) (CN/0824-2186) [10052122] **2954**

COMMUNIQUE - LEARNING DISABILITIES ASSOCIATION OF ONTARIO (CN/0843-2236) [19746988] **1877**

COMMUNIQUE - MANITOBA DIVISION, CANADIAN CANCER SOCIETY (CN/0707-5995) [04678114] **3815**

COMMUNIQUE (MILWAUKEE, WIS.), THE (US/0887-4557) [08301887] **3854**

COMMUNIQUE / NATIONAL ASSOCIATION FOR GIFTED CHILDREN (US/0884-3643) [10134775] **1877**

COMMUNIQUE - NATIONAL BOARD. ASSOCIATION OF ADMINISTRATIVE ASSISTANTS (CN/0384-9066) [11377350] **658**

COMMUNIQUE NATIONAL DE LA SCRP (CN/0710-071X) [08828251] **757**

COMMUNIQUE / ORDER OF THE INDIAN WARS (US) **2729**

COMMUNIQUE (OVERSEAS DEVELOPMENT COUNCIL) (US/0273-2181) [05717774] **2908**

COMMUNIQUE (RICHMOND, VA) (US) 4772, **1319**

COMMUNIQUE - SASKATCHEWAN POWER CORPORATION (CN/0713-3030) [08752150] **1602**

COMMUNIQUE - SOCIETE D'ARCHITECTURE DE MONTREAL (CN/0700-4389) [03291434] **295**

COMMUNIQUE - SOCIETE D'ARTHRITE (CN/0824-4154) [10440885] **3804**

COMMUNIQUE / SOCIETE D'ARTHRITE DU CANADA *See* ARTHRO EXPRESS **3803**

COMMUNIQUE - SOCIETY FOR INTERCULTURAL EDUCATION, TRAINING AND RESEARCH (US/0276-1386) [04406385] **1733**

COMMUNIQUE - SYNCHRO SWIM CANADA (CN/0226-8701) [06859966] **4891**

COMMUNIQUE / THE FREEDOM FORUM MEDIA STUDY CENTER (US) **1108**

COMMUNIQUE / THE INSTITUTE FOR THE STUDY OF WOMEN (CN/0821-2589) [09428181] **5553**

COMMUNIQUER (FR) **1108**

COMMUNIS SCRIPTURA (US/0730-6970) [08039225] **2954**

COMMUNISME (PARIS, FRANCE : 1982) (FR/0751-3496) [08769905] **4540**

●COMMUNIST AND POST-COMMUNIST STUDIES (UK/0967-067X) [28136245] **4540**

COMMUNIST ECONOMIES AND ECONOMIC TRANSFORMATION (UK) [23888130] **1633**

COMMUNIST LEAGUE (GT. BRIT.) *See* COMBAT **4540**

COMMUNIST LEAGUE (GT. BRIT.) *See* COMPASS **4469**

COMMUNIST PROGRAM : ORGAN OF THE INTERNATIONAL COMMUNIST PARTY (FR) [04265813] **4541**

COMMUNIST STATES AND DEVELOPING COUNTRIES, AID AND TRADE (US/0148-2998) [01268147] **4541**

COMMUNISTE (MONTREAL) (CN/0709-3845) [05585570] **4541**

COMMUNITIES (LOUISA) (US/0199-9346) [03130385] **2818**

COMMUNITIES PARTICIPATING IN THE NATIONAL FLOOD INSURANCE PROGRAM (US) [03113625] **2878**

COMMUNITY ACTIVITIES (SALEM) (US/0145-353X) [02728565] **4039**

COMMUNITY AFFAIRS QUARTERLY (US/0743-1864) [10238691] **2818**

COMMUNITY (ALEXANDRIA, VA. : 1982) *CEASED.* (US/0736-2099) [09060027] **5279**

COMMUNITY ALTERNATIVES (US/1052-7656) [20702742] **5279**

COMMUNITY & JUNIOR COLLEGE LIBRARIES (US/0276-3915) [07374686] **3203**

COMMUNITY AND THE BANK (US/0162-363X) [04141062] **783**

COMMUNITY ANIMAL CONTROL *CEASED.* (US/0278-2863) [07765881] **226**

COMMUNITY ASSOCIATION LAW REPORTER (US/0190-1192) [04620896] **2954**

COMMUNITY BANK MARKETING / BANK MARKETING ASSOCIATION (US/1055-4947) [23193600] 922, **783**

COMMUNITY BANK PRESIDENT, THE (US/0276-0908) [07309005] **783**

COMMUNITY BASED REHABILITATION NEWS : CBR (UK) **4385**

COMMUNITY BROADSHEET, THE (UK) [19957310] **4949**

COMMUNITY BUDGET : THE FACTS AND FIGURES, THE (LU) [18884740] **4718**

COMMUNITY/BUSINESS PROFILE, TERRITORY OF GUAM (GU) [08379064] **1552**

●COMMUNITY CABLE LETTER (US/1074-3936) [29695514] **1152**

COMMUNITY CARE (US) [10631517] **5279**

COMMUNITY CARE (UK/0307-5508) [04122016] **5279**

●COMMUNITY CARE BULLETIN (UK) **5279**

COMMUNITY CARE MANAGEMENT & PLANNING (UK/0968-9249) **4639**

COMMUNITY CHANGE (US/0896-9159) [17332210] **2818**

COMMUNITY COLLEGE CAPSULES (US/0892-5453) [15246606] **1817**

COMMUNITY COLLEGE FINANCES (US/0147-3808) [03155131] **1817**

COMMUNITY COLLEGE HUMANIST, THE (US/0739-473X) [09741148] **2844**

COMMUNITY COLLEGE HUMANITIES REVIEW, THE (US/0748-0741) [10896080] **2844**

●COMMUNITY COLLEGE JOURNAL (US/1067-1803) [26820067] **1817**

●COMMUNITY COLLEGE JOURNAL OF RESEARCH AND PRACTICE (US/1066-8926) [27083345] **1817**

COMMUNITY COLLEGE JOURNALIST : OFFICIAL PUBLICATION OF THE COMMUNITY COLLEGE JOURNALISM ASSOCIATION (US) [10679256] **2918**

COMMUNITY COLLEGE REVIEW (US/0091-5521) [00932486] **1817**

COMMUNITY COLLEGE SOCIAL SCIENCE ASSOCIATION (U.S.) *See* CCSSA NEWSLETTER **5195**

COMMUNITY COLLEGE WEEK (US/1041-5726) [18804328] **1817**

COMMUNITY COUNCIL OF GREATER NEW YORK. BUDGET STANDARD SERVICE *See* ANNUAL PRICE SURVEY: FAMILY BUDGET COSTS **1462**

COMMUNITY CRIER, THE (US/0193-077X) [05142800] **5691**

COMMUNITY CRIME PREVENTION DIGEST (US/0889-5767) [06794061] **3160**

COMMUNITY DENTAL HEALTH (UK/0265-539X) [11535575] **1319**

COMMUNITY DENTISTRY AND ORAL EPIDEMIOLOGY (DK/0301-5661) [01780835] 3734, **1319**

COMMUNITY DESIGN CENTERS : PROFILE (US/0145-1855) [02702622] **295**

COMMUNITY DEVELOPMENT BLOCK GRANT PROGRAM. DIRECTORY OF ALLOCATIONS FOR FISCAL YEARS ... (US/0363-1613) [02428353] **2818**

COMMUNITY DEVELOPMENT DIGEST (WASHINGTON) (US/0094-2324) [02275493] **2818**

COMMUNITY DEVELOPMENT EVALUATION SERIES (US) [01784855] **2818**

COMMUNITY DEVELOPMENT EXECUTIVE *See* CHAMBER EXECUTIVE NETWORK, THE **818**

COMMUNITY DEVELOPMENT EXECUTIVE, THE (US/0747-7503) [10786381] **819**

COMMUNITY DEVELOPMENT (GUELPH) (CN/0823-6062) [09819008] **2818**

COMMUNITY DEVELOPMENT JOURNAL (UK/0010-3802) [01714942] **5242**

COMMUNITY DEVELOPMENT REPORTER (US) 2954, **2818**

COMMUNITY DIGEST (VANCOUVER) (CN/0826-4260) [11193120] **2531**

COMMUNITY: EAST AFRICAN COMMUNITY MONTHLY MAGAZINE, THE (TZ/0588-8387) [03638729] **2498**

COMMUNITY ECONOMIC REPORTER *See* SOUTHERN COMMUNITIES **2836**

COMMUNITY ECONOMICS (GREENFIELD, MASS.) (US/1045-4322) [20123235] **2818**

COMMUNITY EDUCATION (US/0097-7438) [01798275] **1891**

COMMUNITY EDUCATION JOURNAL (US/0045-7736) [01564520] **1733**

COMMUNITY EDUCATION NEWSLETTER (AT/0156-2878) [I01562878] **1733**

COMMUNITY EDUCATION RESEARCH DIGEST (US/1041-4827) [15277278] **1733**

COMMUNITY EDUCATION SERIES (CN/0317-3585) [02248138] **3105**

COMMUNITY EYE HEALTH (UK/0953-6833) [20103860] **3873**

COMMUNITY FOCUS *See* COMMUNITY (ALEXANDRIA, VA. : 1982) **5279**

COMMUNITY HEALTH BULLETIN (AT/0312-6579) [04186547] **4772**

COMMUNITY HEALTH FUNDING REPORT (US/1052-6552) [22343701] 4772, **5280**

COMMUNITY HEALTH INSTITUTE CLEARINGHOUSE NEWS, THE (US/0191-3972) [04814392] **4772**

COMMUNITY HERALD (MONONA, WIS.), THE (US/0745-6646) [09354879] **5766**

COMMUNITY INITIATIVES (CN/1185-3107) [24368135] **1817**

COMMUNITY

COMMUNITY INTEGRATION : THE NEWSLETTER OF THE REHABILITATION RESEARCH AND TRAINING CENTER ON COMMUNITY INTEGRATION OF PERSONS WITH TRAUMATIC BRAIN INJURY, AT THE STATE UNIVERSITY OF NEW YORK AT BUFFALO (US) [23437612] **3567**

COMMUNITY ISSUES (LEXINGTON, KY.) (US) [08844540] **2531**

COMMUNITY JOBS (US/0195-1157) [05291016] **1660**

COMMUNITY JOURNAL-PRESS (US) [19866660] **5727**

COMMUNITY/JUNIOR COLLEGE See COMMUNITY COLLEGE JOURNAL OF RESEARCH AND PRACTICE **1817**

COMMUNITY/JUNIOR COLLEGE (US/0277-6774) [07625585] **1817**

COMMUNITY LEADERS OF AMERICA (1981) (US/0741-4161) [08748110] **431**

COMMUNITY LIVING (UK/0951-9815) [I09519815] **5280**

COMMUNITY LIVING OF FLORIDA (US) **4639**

COMMUNITY MARKETS CANADA See CMC MEMBERSHIP DIRECTORY **757**

COMMUNITY MARKETS CANADA : THE COMPREHENSIVE GUIDE TO THE LATEST COMMUNITY NEWSPAPER MARKET DATA (CN/0229-1630) [07857952] **757**

COMMUNITY MARKETS / FINANCIAL TIMES (UK) [06284914] **658**

COMMUNITY MATRIX FOR DEVELOPMENT PROJECTS (US) [06441969] **2818**

COMMUNITY MENTAL HEALTH IN NEW ZEALAND (NZ/0112-3599) [13039150] **5280**

COMMUNITY MENTAL HEALTH JOURNAL (US/0010-3853) [01564527] **5280**

COMMUNITY MENTAL HEALTH JOURNAL. MONOGRAPH SERIES *CEASED.* (US/0069-7850) [01778104] **4772**

●COMMUNITY MOVES (NZ/1171-8587) [I1718587] **4385**

COMMUNITY NEWS (BROWNS MILLS, N.J.), THE (US/0745-8150) [09480555] **5709**

COMMUNITY NEWS - WELSH OFFICE OF THE EUROPEAN COMMUNITIES (UK/0140-1084) [I01401084] **4639**

COMMUNITY OUTLOOK (UK/0262-8759) [04126495] **3854**

COMMUNITY PHARMACY LONDON (UK/0960-376X) [I0960376X] **4297**

COMMUNITY PLANNING ASSOCIATION OF CANADA See CPAC BOOKSHOPPE **2819**

COMMUNITY PLANNING ASSOCIATION OF CANADA See C P A C REVIEW **2816**

●COMMUNITY POLICING DIGEST (US) **3160**

COMMUNITY PRESS (US) [23905495] **5727**

COMMUNITY PRESS (MILLBROOK, ALA.) (US/0739-9219) [09237874] **5626**

COMMUNITY PROFILE, STETTLER (CN/1185-5800) [25066625] **1470**

COMMUNITY PSYCHIATRIC NURSING JOURNAL See MENTAL HEALTH NURSING **3861**

COMMUNITY PSYCHIATRIC NURSING JOURNAL (UK/0265-7007) [I02657007] **3923, 3854**

COMMUNITY PSYCHIATRIC PRACTICE (CN) **3923**

COMMUNITY PUBLICATION ADVERTISING SOURCE (US) [30506295] **757**

COMMUNITY PUBLICATION RATES AND DATA (US/0162-8887) [03777043] **757**

COMMUNITY PUBLICATION SOURCE (US/1071-4650) [28643492] **757**

COMMUNITY PUBLICATIONS RATES AND DATA See COMMUNITY PUBLICATION SOURCE **757**

COMMUNITY QUARTERLY (AT/0814-401X) [I0814401X] **2818**

COMMUNITY RADIO NEWS (US) **1130**

COMMUNITY RECREATION COUNCIL OF WESTERN AUSTRALIA See ANNUAL REPORT - COMMUNITY RECREATION COUNCIL OF WESTERN AUSTRALIA **4848**

COMMUNITY REFLECTION (CN/0710-0086) [08192589] **5782**

COMMUNITY RELATIONS REPORT (BARTLESVILLE, OKLA.), THE (US/0736-7147) [09206097] **757**

COMMUNITY REVIEW (NEW BRUNSWICK) (US/0163-8475) [05868858] **1818**

COMMUNITY SCENE (CN/1185-5347) [25067049] **5280**

COMMUNITY SERVICE (UK) **5280**

COMMUNITY SERVICE BUSINESS (US/0747-6086) [10756328] **5196**

COMMUNITY SERVICE NEWSLETTER (US/0277-6189) [03076534] **2818**

COMMUNITY SERVICES CATALYST (US/0739-9227) [03334057] **1800**

COMMUNITY SOCIAL SERVICES ACT ... EFFECTIVENESS REPORT (US) [09387820] **5280**

COMMUNITY STORYTELLERS QUARTERLY NEWSLETTER, THE *CEASED.* (US/0892-1598) [13176861] **5268**

COMMUNITY, TECHNICAL, AND JUNIOR COLLEGE JOURNAL (US/0884-7169) [12438461] **1818**

COMMUNITY TELEVISION REVIEW : CTR (US) [10524161] **1130**

COMMUNITY TRANSPORTATION REPORTER : CTR (US/0895-4437) [15299757] **5380**

COMMUNITY UPO (US/0277-464X) [05313629] **2818**

COMMUNITY WORK *CEASED.* (UK/0307-6067) [02240711] **5280**

COMMUNITY'S RESEARCH AND DEVELOPMENT PROGRAMME ON DECOMMISSIONING OF NUCLEAR POWER PLANTS. ANNUAL PROGRESS REPORT, THE (BE) [14557386] **4772**

COMMUTATION & ELECTRONIQUE (FR/0010-3926) [03333126] **1108**

COMMUTATION & TRANSMISSION (FR/0242-1283) [06946294] **1152**

COMMUTED RATE SCHEDULE (US) [26988059] **5380**

COMMUTED RATE SCHEDULE FOR TRANSPORTATION OF HOUSEHOLD GOODS (US) [04617095] **5380**

COMMUTER AIR CARRIER TRAFFIC STATISTICS (US/0270-448X) [05157479] **41**

COMMUTER AIR INTERNATIONAL (US/1054-7436) [21989245] **16, 5380**

COMMUTER (COLLEGE PARK, MD.), THE (US/0734-3817) [08543810] **5380**

COMMUTER / REGIONAL AIRLINE NEWS (US/1040-5402) [11455560] **5380**

COMMUTER / REGIONAL AIRLINE NEWS INTERNATIONAL (US/1056-0254) [23601215] **5380, 16**

COMMUTER WORLD (UK/0265-4504) [10442868] **16**

COMP-TECH FEDERAL REGISTER, THE (US) **829**

COMPACT BANKRUPTCY CODE & RULES (US) **3086**

COMPACT CAMBRIDGE LIFE SCIENCES COLLECTION [COMPUTER FILE] (US) [22233024] **452, 5095**

COMPACT CAMBRIDGE MEDLINE [COMPUTER FILE] (US) [14263633] **3203, 3567**

COMPACT (CHICAGO, ILL.) *CEASED.* (US/0895-7118) [16787404] **5280**

COMPACT D/SEC (US/1062-8525) [22143418] **658**

COMPACT DISC BUYERS' GUIDE (US) [14639781] **5316**

COMPACT DISC NEWS (US/0895-3902) [16619687] **1175**

COMPACT FRUIT TREE (US) [04356408] **168**

COMPACT: LA REVUE DU DISQUE LASER (FR) **4111**

COMPADRES DE SANTO ANTONIO MISSIONS NATIONAL PARK NEWSLETTER, LOS (US) **4706**

COMPAGNA (IT) [01789187] **5553**

COMPAGNIE DES AGENTS DE CHANGE DE PARIS See COTE OFFICIELLE **895**

COMPAGNIE DES AGENTS DE CHANGE DE PARIS. CHAMBRE SYNDICALE. BULLETIN DE LA COTE See COTE OFFICIELLE **895**

COMPAGNIE DES CHEMINS DE FER KINSHASA-DILOLO-LUBUMBASHI See RAPPORT ANNUEL **5436**

COMPAGNIE EUROPEENNE ET D'OUTRE-MER See COMPAGNIE EUROPEENNE ET D'OUTRE-MER. RAPPORTS **1552**

COMPAGNIE EUROPEENNE ET D'OUTRE-MER. RAPPORTS (BE) [02241937] **1552**

COMPAGNIE FINANCIERE DE SUEZ See REPORT & ACCOUNTS TO BE SUBMITTED AT THE ANNUAL GENERAL MEETING OF SHAREHOLDERS **5455**

COMPAGNIE FRANCAISE DES PETROLES See NOTES ET MEMOIRES - COMPAGNIE FRANCAISE DES PETROLES **1390**

COMPAGNIE GENERALE D'ELECTRICITE See ANNUAL REPORT / COMPAGNIE GENERALE D'ELECTRICITE **1597**

COMPAGNIE NATIONALE DU RHONE See DONZERE MONDRAGON **1664**

COMPAGNIES, SOCIETES COMMERCIALES ET FAILLITE See COMPAGNIES, SOCIETES PAR ACTIONS ET FAILLITE **3089**

●COMPAGNIES, SOCIETES PAR ACTIONS ET FAILLITE (CN/1187-2861) [25066880] **3098, 3089**

COMPAGNONNAGE: ORGANE DES COMPAGNONS DU DEVOIR (FR) **5242**

COMPAK (AT) **1733**

COMPANHIA BRASILEIRA DE ARMAZENAMENTO See ARMAZENAGEM **63**

COMPANHIA DE ELECTRICIDADE DE PERNAMBUCO See RELATORIO CELPE **1624**

COMPANHIA DE ELETRICIDADE DE CERA See BOLETIM ESTATISTICO ANUAL - COMPANHIA DE ELETRICIDADE DE CEARA **4696**

COMPANHIA DE HABITACAO DO ESTADO DE SANTA CATARINA See RELATORIO DAS ATIVIDADES DA COMPANHIA DE HABITACAO DO ESTADO DE SANTA CATARINA **2833**

COMPANHIA DE SANEAMENTO DE MINAS GERAIS See RELATORIO DE GESTAO / COMPANHIA DE SANEAMENTO DE MINAS GERAIS **2241**

COMPANHIA DE SANEAMENTO DE MINAS GERAIS. RELATORIO - COMPANHIA DE SANEAMENTO DE MINAS GERAIS See RELATORIO DE GESTAO / COMPANHIA DE SANEAMENTO DE MINAS GERAIS **2241**

COMPANHIA ENERGETICA DE SAO PAULO See BOLETIM ESTATISTICO - CESP **1599**

COMPANHIA ESTADUAL DE TECNOLOGIA DE SANEAMENTO BASICO E DE DEFESA DO MEIO AMBIENTE See RELATORIO ANUAL DA DIRETORIA - CETESB **2241**

COMPANHIA PAULISTA DE FORCA E LUZ See BOLETIM ESTATISTICO - COMPANHIA PAULISTA DE FORCA E LUZ **4696**

COMPANHIA SIDERURGICA NACIONAL See DIRECTORS' ANNUAL REPORT **1604**

COMPANHIA VALE DO RIO DOCE See CVRD REVISTA **1970**

COMPANIA ENTRERRIANA DE TELEFONOS See GUIA DE ABONADOS : PARANA, VICTORIA, GUALEGUAY **1112**

COMPANIES AND SECURITIES BULLETIN (AT) **658**

COMPANIES AND THEIR BRANDS (US/1047-6393) [20739956] **1303**

COMPANIES HANDBOOK OF THE KUALA LUMPUR STOCK EXCHANGE BERHAD See ANNUAL COMPANIES HANDBOOK / THE KUALA LUMPUR STOCK EXCHANGE **890**

COMPANIES HOLDING BOILER AND PRESSURE VESSEL CERTIFICATES OF AUTHORIZATION FOR USE OF CODE SYMBOL STAMPS (US/0148-6594) [03340945] **2112**

COMPANIES HOLDING NUCLEAR CERTIFICATES OF AUTHORIZATION (US/0272-6777) [06879596] **2154**

COMPANIES HOUSE DIRECTORY OF COMPANIES. MICROFICHE (UK) **658**

COMPANIES INTERNATIONAL [COMPUTER FILE] (US) **658**

COMPANIES - IRELAND. DEPT. OF INDUSTRY, COMMERCE AND TOURISM (IE) [08521629] **1602**

COMPANIES PARTICIPATING IN THE DEPARTMENT OF DEFENSE SUBCONTRACTING PROGRAM (US/1057-9222) [09126730] **4039**

COMPANION (US) [01586142] **4385**

COMPANION (TORONTO) (CN/0010-3985) [02617001] **5028**

COMPANY (UK/0141-1144) [I01411144] **5553**

COMPANY ACCOUNTANT (UK/0954-8106) [22856842] **741**

COMPANY ADMINISTRATION (UK) **864**

COMPANY AND SECURITIES LAW JOURNAL (AT/0729-2775) [12207679] **3098**

COMPANY CAR (UK/0267-8519) [I02678519] **5412**

COMPANY CAR (UK/0267-8519) **5380**

COMPANY (CHICAGO, ILL.) (US/0886-1293) [10212613] **4949**

COMPANY GUIDE FOR BUSINESS IN EUROPE (NE) **658**

COMPANY INFORMATION (UK/0967-635X) **658**

COMPANY LAW DIGEST (NEW DELHI, INDIA) (II) [10228148] **3098**

COMPANY LAW JOURNAL. ANNUAL REVIEW, THE (II/0970-3640) [17304741] **3098**

COMPANY LAW JOURNAL (NEW DELHI, INDIA) (II) [10987816] **3098**

●COMPANY LAW MONITOR (UK) [I09693831] **3098**

COMPANY LAWYER, THE (UK/0144-1027) [06334283] **3098**

COMPANY LIQUIDITY / CENTRAL STATISTICAL OFFICE (UK) [24100996] **658**

COMPANY NEWS AND NOTES (II/0010-4027) [01564543] **3098**

COMPANY RECOGNITION STUDY. RETAILER EDITION (US/0275-7486) [07188279] **1969**

COMPANY SECRETARY'S FACTBOOK (UK) **658**

COMPANY SECRETARY'S REVIEW (UK/0309-703X) [08375846] **3098**

COMPANY THESAURUS / PREDICASTS, INC CEASED. (US/0739-1862) [07228199] **1602**

COMPARABLE WORTH PROJECT NEWSLETTER CEASED. (US/0278-4122) [07799768] **658**

COMPARAISON (IT/0942-8917) **3377**

COMPARAISONS INTERPROVINCIALES DU FINANCEMENT DES UNIVERSITES : ... RAPPORT DU COMITE TRIPARTITE SUR LES COMPARAISONS INTERPROVINCIALES (CN/1184-9444) [24623954] **1818**

COMPARATIO : REVUE INTERNATIONAL DE LITTERATURE COMPAREE See COMPARAISON **3377**

COMPARATIST, THE (US/0195-7678) [03256483] **3377**

COMPARATISTICA (IT) [22760127] **3377**

COMPARATIVE AND INTERNATIONAL EDUCATION SOCIETY See C I E S NEWSLETTER **1729**

COMPARATIVE AND INTERNATIONAL EDUCATION SOCIETY OF CANADA See NEWSLETTER - COMPARATIVE AND INTERNATIONAL EDUCATION SOCIETY OF CANADA (1975) **1768**

COMPARATIVE AND INTERNATIONAL LAW JOURNAL OF SOUTHERN AFRICA, THE (SA/0010-4051) [01564546] **3126**

COMPARATIVE ANNUITY REPORT: MONTHLY NEWSLETTER (US) **895**

COMPARATIVE ASIAN STUDIES (NE) [20021038] **2649**

COMPARATIVE BIOCHEMISTRY AND PHYSIOLOGY. A, COMPARATIVE PHYSIOLOGY (UK/0300-9629) [01237399] 486, **579**

●COMPARATIVE BIOCHEMISTRY AND PHYSIOLOGY. B, BIOCHEMISTRY & MOLECULAR BIOLOGY : CBP (UK) [29987816] 579, **486**

COMPARATIVE BIOCHEMISTRY AND PHYSIOLOGY. B, COMPARATIVE BIOCHEMISTRY (UK/0305-0491) [01237378] 579, **486**

COMPARATIVE BIOCHEMISTRY AND PHYSIOLOGY. C, COMPARATIVE PHARMACOLOGY AND TOXICOLOGY (UK/0742-8413) [09476479] 3980, **4297**

●COMPARATIVE BIOCHEMISTRY AND PHYSIOLOGY. C, PHARMACOLOGY, TOXICOLOGY & ENDOCRINOLOGY : CBP (UK) [29986792] 579, **486**

COMPARATIVE CIVILIZATIONS REVIEW (US/0733-4540) [08397577] 2844, **5196**

COMPARATIVE CLIMATIC DATA FOR THE UNITED STATES (US/0195-8259) [05629209] **1424**

COMPARATIVE COSTS AND STAFFING REPORT FOR COLLEGE AND UNIVERSITY FACILITIES (US/0742-7476) [10428146] **1862**

COMPARATIVE CRITICISM (UK/0144-7564) [06119311] **3340**

●COMPARATIVE CULTURES AND LITERATURE (US/1070-955X) [28521396] **3377**

COMPARATIVE DRAMA (US/0010-4078) [01564550] **5363**

COMPARATIVE ECONOMIC STUDIES (US/0888-7233) [11980420] **1470**

COMPARATIVE EDUCATION (UK/0305-0068) [01564551] **1733**

COMPARATIVE EDUCATION REVIEW (US/0010-4086) [01564552] **1733**

COMPARATIVE FINANCIAL CONDITION OF COMMERCIAL BANKS IN PUERTO RICO (PR) [02243751] **783**

COMPARATIVE GUIDE TO AMERICAN COLLEGES : FOR STUDENTS, PARENTS, AND COUNSELORS (US/0090-8053) [01238611] **1818**

COMPARATIVE GUIDE TO JUNIOR AND TWO-YEAR COMMUNITY COLLEGES (US) [03307101] **1818**

COMPARATIVE HAEMATOLOGY INTERNATIONAL (UK/0938-7714) [23835773] **3771**

COMPARATIVE IMMUNOLOGY, MICROBIOLOGY AND INFECTIOUS DISEASES (UK/0147-9571) [04172813] 5508, 3668, **561**

●COMPARATIVE INDUSTRIAL RELATIONS NEWSLETTER (CN) [29865362] **1660**

COMPARATIVE JURIDICAL REVIEW (US/0069-7893) [01564554] **2954**

COMPARATIVE LABOR LAW JOURNAL (US/1043-5255) [15052461] **3145**

COMPARATIVE LAW SERIES (UK/0068-2160) [01537255] **3126**

COMPARATIVE LAW YEARBOOK OF INTERNATIONAL BUSINESS (UK) [23042514] **3098**

COMPARATIVE LITERATURE (US/0010-4124) [01564555] **3377**

●COMPARATIVE LITERATURE AND FILM STUDIES (US/0899-9902) [18283509] 4067, **3377**

COMPARATIVE LITERATURE IN CANADA (CN/0045-7795) [02483476] **3377**

COMPARATIVE LITERATURE STUDIES (URBANA) (US/0010-4132) [01326039] **3377**

COMPARATIVE MEDICINE CEASED. (US/1058-2401) [24251345] 452, **5508**

COMPARATIVE MOTOR VEHICLE TRAFFIC ACCIDENT STATISTICS IN CITIES OF 5,000 POPULATION AND OVER / STATE OF ILLINOIS, DEPARTMENT OF PUBLIC WORKS AND BUILDINGS, DIVISION OF HIGHWAYS, BUREAU OF TRAFFIC (US) [06183081] **5400**

COMPARATIVE PATHOBIOLOGY (US/0161-6935) [03978333] **3894**

COMPARATIVE PATHOLOGY BULLETIN (US/1041-116X) [01564559] **3894**

COMPARATIVE PHYSIOLOGY See MOLECULAR COMPARATIVE PHYSIOLOGY **584**

COMPARATIVE PHYSIOLOGY AND ECOLOGY CEASED. (II/0379-0436) [02789484] 2212, **579**

COMPARATIVE PHYSIOLOGY : CELLULAR AND MOLECULAR APPROACH TO COMPARATIVE PHYSIOLOGY (SZ/1015-1702) [21455980] **579**

COMPARATIVE PHYSIOLOGY OF THERMOREGULATION CEASED. (US) [01781167] **579**

COMPARATIVE POLITICAL ECONOMY AND PUBLIC POLICY SERIES (US/0272-166X) [06077668] **1470**

COMPARATIVE POLITICAL STUDIES (US/0010-4140) [01564560] **4469**

COMPARATIVE POLITICS (US/0010-4159) [01564561] **4469**

COMPARATIVE POLITICS (GUILFORD, CONN.) (US/0741-7233) [09374421] **4469**

COMPARATIVE RECEIPTS AND SHIPMENTS OF LIVE STOCK FOR MONTHS ENDING ... / OKLAHOMA NATIONAL STOCK YARDS CO (US) [06583359] **209**

COMPARATIVE REPORT OF LOCAL GOVERNMENT REVENUES AND EXPENDITURES, YEAR ENDED JUNE 30, ... (US/0737-3392) [08864787] **4718**

COMPARATIVE ROMANCE LINGUISTICS NEWSLETTER (US/0010-4167) [02626462] **3274**

COMPARATIVE SOCIAL RESEARCH (US/0195-6310) [05276076] **5242**

COMPARATIVE STATE POLITICS (US/1047-1006) [20395647] **4469**

COMPARATIVE STATEMENT OF ASSETS, LIABILITIES, AND CAPITAL ACCOUNTS OF ALASKA BANKS AS OF ... / COMPILED ... BY THE DIVISION OF BANKING, SECURITIES, SMALL LOANS, AND CORPORATIONS (US) [08403268] **784**

COMPARATIVE STATISTICS OF INDUSTRIAL AND OFFICE REAL ESTATE MARKETS (US/1066-0933) [23859978] **4836**

COMPARATIVE STRATEGY (US/0149-5933) [04233180] **4518**

COMPARATIVE STUDIES IN BEHAVIORAL SCIENCE (US/0190-1079) [04629288] **4582**

COMPARATIVE STUDIES IN SOCIETY AND HISTORY (UK/0010-4175) [01564563] **5196**

COMPARATIVE SUMMARY OF WATER BORNE FOREIGN COMMERCE WITH GRAPHIC CHARTS (US) [24561328] **5448**

COMPARATIVE URBAN AND COMMUNITY RESEARCH (US/0892-5569) [15214341] **5196**

COMPARE (UK/0305-7925) [04030265] **1891**

COMPARISON OF COMPENSATION PAID SCIENTISTS AND ENGINEERS IN RESEARCH AND DEVELOPMENT (US/0743-7692) [05114542] 5095, **1660**

COMPARISON OF STATE UNEMPLOYMENT INSURANCE LAWS (US) [23817763] **2878**

COMPARISON OF THE YOUTH AUTHORITY'S INSTITUTION AND PAROLE POPULATIONS (US) [17530120] **3160**

COMPARISON REPORT ON ENGINEERING DOCUMENT MANAGEMENT (EDMS) SYSTEMS (US/1056-182X) [23526039] **1969**

COMPASS (UK) [06724414] **4469**

COMPASS & TAPE (US/1074-5696) [11459108] **2581**

COMPASS KENSINGTON (AT/1036-9686) [I10369686] **4949**

COMPASS PATHFINDER (US/1056-1943) [23528733] **3962**

COMPASS (ROME, ITALY) (IT) [08323292] **2908**

COMPASS ROSE (US/0742-8928) [10517997] **658**

COMPASS SPORT/THE ORIENTEER (UK/0263-6697) [I02636697] **4891**

COMPASS (SYRACUSE, N.Y.) (US/1054-9056) [23010984] **5412**

COMPASS, THE (US/0894-802X) [11985680] **1353**

COMPASS THEOLOGY REVIEW (AT) [05145895] **4949**

COMPASS (TORONTO) (CN/0715-8777) [09804090] **4949**

COMPATIBLES PC MAGAZINE (FR) **1266**

COMPCON : PROCEEDINGS (US) [08269986] **1175**

COMPEL (IE/0332-1649) [09636637] **2039**

COMPENDEX PLUS (US/1063-8709) [20439095] 1969, **2003**

COMPENDIA (UK/0950-6756) [03811483] 3377, **3274**

COMPENDIA RHEUMATOLOGICA (SZ/0379-7996) [04747149] **3567**

COMPENDIO DE ESTADISTICAS SOCIALES / ESTADO LIBRE ASOCIADO DE PUERTO RICO, OFICINA DEL GOBERNADOR, JUNTA DE PLANIFICACION (PR) [07486404] **5325**

COMPENDIO DELLA LEGISLAZIONE ITALIAN SULL'AIUTO PUBBLICO ALLO SVILUPPO (IT) **4469**

COMPENDIO STATISTICO ITALIANO (IT/0301-8628) [01792718] **5325**

COMPENDIO TEORICO Y PRACTICO - ALALC (AG) [08578240] 4718, **829**

COMPENDIUM (US/0517-127X) [03499334] **1319**

COMPENDIUM DE INVESTIGACIONES CLINICAS LATINOAMERICANAS (MX/0185-1934) [08619461] **3567**

COMPENDIUM - DEUTSCHE GESELLSCHAFT FUER MINERALOLWISSENSCHAFT UND KOHLECHEMIE E.V (GW/0341-6852) [02684441] **4253**

COMPENDIUM NEWSLETTER, THE (US/0198-9103) [06260120] 2212, **2190**

COMPENDIUM (NEWTOWN, PA.) (US/0894-1009) [15351626] **1319**

COMPENDIUM OF ADVANCED COURSES IN COLLEGES OF FURTHER AND HIGHER EDUCATION, A (UK) [05391099] **1912**

COMPENDIUM OF ADVANCED COURSES IN TECHNICAL COLLEGES See COMPENDIUM OF ADVANCED COURSES IN COLLEGES OF FURTHER AND HIGHER EDUCATION, A **1912**

COMPENDIUM OF CASE NOTES OF THE OMBUDSMEN (NZ) [20443142] **4639**

COMPENDIUM OF COMMERCIAL FINANCE LAW (US) **784**

COMPENDIUM OF COMMUNITY PROVISIONS ON SOCIAL SECURITY / COMMISSION OF THE EUROPEAN COMMUNITIES (BE) [10857608] **5280**

COMPENDIUM OF COMPENSATORY ACTIVITIES (US) [01786024] **1733**

COMPENDIUM OF COPYRIGHT OFFICE PRACTICES (US) [02784587] **1303**

COMPENDIUM OF DRUG & PATIENT INFORMATION (US/8756-9582) [12894037] **3759**

COMPENDIUM OF DRUG THERAPY (US/8756-9523) [20180142] **3796**

COMPENDIUM OF HUMAN SETTLEMENTS STATISTICS / DEPARTMENT OF INTERNATIONAL ECONOMICS AND SOCIAL AFFAIRS, STATISTICAL OFFICE RECUEIL DES STATISTIQUES DES ETABLISSEMENTS HUMAINS / DEPARTEMENT DES AFFAIRES ECONOMIQUES ET SOCIALES INTERNATIONALES, BUREAU DE STATISTIQUE (US) [13084156] 2819, **2840**

COMPENDIUM OF INFORMATION - SCOTTISH UNIVERSITIES COUNCIL ON ENTRANCE (UK) [07180900] **1818**

COMPENDIUM OF LAWS AND JURISPRUDENCE OF THE REPUBLIC OF LEBANON (SY) [01786913] **2954**

COMPENDIUM OF LAWS OF THE FEDERATION OF ARAB REPUBLICS (SY) [01788346] **2954**

COMPENDIUM — Alphabetical Title Index

COMPENDIUM OF LOCAL GOVERNMENT AREA STATISTICS / AUSTRALIAN BUREAU OF STATISTICS, TASMANIAN OFFICE (AT/0157-2067) [09662753] **4697**

COMPENDIUM OF MUNICIPAL STATISTICS *See* COMPENDIUM OF LOCAL GOVERNMENT AREA STATISTICS / AUSTRALIAN BUREAU OF STATISTICS, TASMANIAN OFFICE **4697**

COMPENDIUM OF ORGANIC SYNTHETIC METHODS (US/0149-9378) [03580803] **1041**

COMPENDIUM OF PROJECTS AS OF 31 DECEMBER ... (US) [20988674] **1633**

COMPENDIUM OF PUBLICLY AVAILABLE REPORTS ON PROCUREMENT AND FINANCIAL ASSISTANCE AWARDS - (DEPT OF ENERGY) (US) [04629472] 4639, **1935**

COMPENDIUM OF RESEARCH CONTRACTS AND REPORTS - (DEPT. OF HOUSING AND URBAN DEVELOPMENT) (US/0097-7810) [01798238] **2819**

COMPENDIUM OF RESEARCH REPORTS (US/0272-5800) [05625450] **2819**

COMPENDIUM OF SAFETY DATA SHEETS FOR RESEARCH AND INDUSTRIAL CHEMICALS (GW) **973**

COMPENDIUM OF TECHNICAL PAPERS : INSTITUTE OF TRANSPORTATION ENGINEERS ... ANNUAL MEETING (US/0743-1570) [04334463] **5439**

COMPENDIUM OF TEXAS COLLEGES AND FINANCIAL AID CALENDAR FOR HIGH SCHOOL SENIORS, A (US) [05744356] **1818**

COMPENDIUM OF TOURISM STATISTICS (SP) [15666615] **5466**

COMPENDIUM OF UNIVERSITY ENTRANCE REQUIREMENTS FOR FIRST DEGREE COURSES IN THE UNITED KINGDOM, A (UK/0571-625X) [01796316] **1818**

COMPENDIUM OF VETERINARY PRODUCTS (US/1195-6038) [23932926] **5508**

COMPENDIUM ON CONTINUING EDUCATION FOR THE PRACTICING VETERINARIAN, THE (US/0193-1903) [05160973] **5508**

COMPENDIUM VOOR DE JAARREKENING (NE) **741**

●COMPENSATION & BENEFITS ALERT (US/1061-1576) [25194459] **658**

COMPENSATION & BENEFITS MANAGEMENT (US/0748-061X) [10874002] **864**

COMPENSATION & BENEFITS MANAGERS LETTER (US) **864**

COMPENSATION & BENEFITS REPORT (US/0738-1034) [09499536] 5280, **1660**

COMPENSATION AND BENEFITS REVIEW (US/0886-3687) [12595484] **1660**

COMPENSATION AND WORKING CONDITIONS (US/1059-0722) [23898753] **1660**

COMPENSATION FOCUS (CN/0846-2895) [25066941] **4639**

COMPENSATION FOCUS (CN/0846-2895) [25066944] **4639**

COMPENSATION INSTITUTE *See* GEOGRAPHIC SALARY DIFFERENTIALS **1675**

COMPENSATION INSTITUTE *See* EXECUTIVE COMPENSATION REPORT FOR SMALL TO MEDIUM SIZED COMPANIES **674**

COMPENSATION MIRROR (ZA) [03496820] 2878, **1660**

COMPENSATION REPORT, MANAGEMENT EMPLOYEES IN HOSPITAL & NURSING HOME MANAGEMENT COMPANIES (US/0742-5937) [10381772] 3778, **939**

COMPENSATION REPORT ON HOSPITAL-BASED AND GROUP PRACTICE PHYSICIANS *See* PHYSICIAN SALARY SURVEY REPORT, HOSPITAL-BASED AND GROUP PRACTICE **3916**

COMPENSATION SURVEY FOR CHICAGO AREA HOSPITALS / CHICAGO HOSPITAL COUNCIL (US) [10980557] **3778**

COMPENSATION (WASHINGTON, D.C. : 1982) (US/0732-5282) [08370349] 2878, **1660**

●COMPETENCY (UK/1351-5802) [I13515802] **2860**

COMPETITION ANGLER (US/1047-1669) [20617873] **4871**

COMPETITION LAW IN THE EUROPEAN COMMUNITIES (UK) [06122085] **3098**

COMPETITION PLUS (US/1064-055X) [26210225] **5412**

COMPETITION POLICY IN OECD COUNTRIES (FR) [13807092] **3098**

COMPETITION RULES FOR ATHLETICS / ATHLETICS CONGRESS USA (US) [09982834] **4891**

COMPETITIONHOTLINE (US) [24189581] 2819, **295**

COMPETITIONS (LOUISVILLE, KY.) (US/1058-6539) [24189567] **295**

COMPETITIONS, SUMMARIES, PROJECTS, TRIALS (CN/0228-2232) [07298455] **75**

COMPETITIVE ADVANCES. MATERIALS AND PROCESSES (US) **5095**

COMPETITIVE ADVANTAGE, THE (US/0886-1994) [12850089] **757**

COMPETITIVE ANALYSIS : OHIO (US/0361-4743) [02246563] **784**

COMPETITIVE ANALYSIS: OKLAHOMA (US/0361-4891) [02246561] **784**

COMPETITIVE ANALYSIS: PENNSYLVANIA (US/0361-4786) [02246564] **784**

COMPETITIVE ANALYSIS : VIRGINIA (US/0361-4778) [02246562] **784**

COMPETITIVE BRAND CUMULATIVE (US/0010-4272) [01792188] **757**

COMPETITIVE EDGE (BEVERLY HILLS, CALIF.) (US/0897-3881) [17486079] **659**

COMPETITIVE GRADE FINDER FOR THE PAPER AND GRAPHIC ARTS INDUSTRIES, THE (US) [12759858] 377, **4233**

COMPETITIVE GRADE FINDER FOR THE PAPER INDUSTRY, THE (US) [02997144] **4233**

COMPETITIVE INTELLIGENCE REVIEW (US/1058-0247) [22401672] **659**

COMPETITIVE INTELLIGENCER (US/1040-9645) [18595554] **659**

COMPETITIVE MATERIALS SERVICE (US/0738-1824) [09523755] **829**

COMPETITIVENESS REVIEW (US/1059-5422) [24623967] 234, **5242**

COMPETITORS AND COMPETITION OF THE U.S. POSTAL SERVICE (US/0882-8970) [11770580] **1144**

COMPFLASH (US/0147-1570) [03113835] **1660**

COMPILATION DES REFERENCES UNIVERSITAIRES (FR) **3203**

COMPILATION OF ABSTRACTS OF DISSERTATIONS, THESES, AND RESEARCH PAPERS SUBMITTED BY CANDIDATES FOR DEGREES *See* COMPILATION OF ABSTRACTS OF THESES SUBMITTED BY CANDIDATES FOR DEGREES **5095**

COMPILATION OF ABSTRACTS OF THESES SUBMITTED BY CANDIDATES FOR DEGREES (US/0736-1769) [09030790] **5095**

COMPILATION OF GAO'S WORK ON TAX ADMINISTRATION ACTIVITIES (US/0741-9260) [08896968] 4639, 4718, **741**

COMPILATION OF LAW RELATING TO THE PRACTICE OF VETERINARY MEDICINE AND SURGERY (US/0362-5532) [02341758] 5508, **2954**

COMPILATION OF LAWS RELATING TO THE PRACTICE OF VETERINARY MEDICINE AND SURGERY, WITH RULES AND REGULATIONS, GENERAL PROVISIONS OF THE BUSINESS AND PROFESSIONS CODE, INCLUDING THE CONSUMER AFFAIRS ACT, AND EXCERPTS FROM THE GOVERNMENT CODE *See* COMPILATION OF LAWS RELATING TO THE PRACTICE OF VETERINARY MEDICINE, SURGERY AND ANIMAL HEALTH TECHNOLOGY WITH RULES AND REGULATIONS, GENERAL PROVISIONS OF THE BUSINESS AND PROFESSIONS CODE, INCLUDING THE CONSUMER AFFAIRS **5508**

COMPILATION OF LAWS RELATING TO THE PRACTICE OF VETERINARY MEDICINE, SURGERY AND ANIMAL HEALTH TECHNOLOGY WITH RULES AND REGULATIONS, GENERAL PROVISIONS OF THE BUSINESS AND PROFESSIONS CODE, INCLUDING THE CONSUMER AFFAIRS (US) [12159765] **5508**

COMPILATION OF MEAT AND POULTRY ISPECTION ISUANCES / UNITED STATES DEPARTMENT OF AGRICULTURE, FOOD SAFETY AND INSPECTION SERVICE (US) [10806897] **209**

COMPILATION OF PRESIDENTIAL DECREES - (PHILIPPINES) (PH/0115-2203) [05790604] **2954**

COMPILATION OF SCHOOL DISTRICT AND COUNTY ... REVENUE LIMITS COMPUTED BY COUNTY SUPERINTENDENTS OF SCHOOLS / PREPARED BY THE BUREAU OF SCHOOL APPORTIONMENTS AND REPORTS, A (US) [05761379] **1862**

COMPILATION OF STATE AND FEDERAL PRIVACY LAWS (US/0882-9136) [05096895] **2954**

COMPILER, THE (US/0742-2784) [10304406] 2400, **1175**

COMPILER, THE (US/1059-6569) [05375294] **3160**

COMPLEAT GOLFER (SA/1015-8014) [I10158014] **4891**

COMPLEAT LAWYER, THE (US/0741-9066) [10232149] **2954**

COMPLEAT MOTHER, THE (CN/0829-8564) [13541463] **3759**

COMPLEMENT PROFILES *CEASED*. (SZ) [28011316] **3668**

COMPLEMENTARY MEDICAL RESEARCH (UK/0268-4055) [20818218] **5096**

COMPLEMENTARY MEDICINE INDEX : CURRENT AWARENESS TOPICS SERVICES (UK/0950-6667) [17383150] **3567**

COMPLEMENTARY THERAPIES IN MEDICINE (UK/0965-2299) [28041224] **3567**

●COMPLEMENTARY THERAPIES IN NURSING AND MIDWIFERY (UK/1353-6117) 3854, **3567**

COMPLETE ANTIQUES PRICE LIST *See* KOVELS' COMPLETE ANTIQUES PRICE LIST, THE **251**

COMPLETE BASEBALL RECORD BOOK, THE (US/0885-9183) [12769919] **4891**

COMPLETE BOOK OF AUTOPISTOLS : BUYER'S GUIDE (US/1058-3823) [24282365] **4891**

COMPLETE BOOK OF TAX DEDUCTIONS *CEASED*. (US/0743-2224) [10549066] **4718**

COMPLETE BUYER'S GUIDE TO STEREO/HI-FI EQUIPMENT, THE (US/0270-627X) [06463290] **5316**

COMPLETE CAR (UK) [I13520245] **5412**

COMPLETE CAR BUYER'S GUIDE, THE (US/1060-8400) [23035886] **5412**

COMPLETE CAR COST GUIDE, THE (US/1045-2206) [16917376] **5412**

COMPLETE CATALOG - LIBRARY OF CONGRESS. CATALOGING DISTRIBUTION SERVICE, THE (US/1058-5257) [23273691] **3203**

COMPLETE CATALOGUE FROM KENYA LITERATURE BUREAU (KE) [06337117] **413**

●COMPLETE DIRECTORY FOR PEOPLE WITH DISABILITIES, THE (US/1063-0023) [25215332] **4385**

COMPLETE DIRECTORY OF LARGE PRINT BOOKS & SERIALS, THE (US/0000-1120) [17681313] **4828**

COMPLETE DRUG REFERENCE, THE (US/1063-6498) [23070944] **4297**

●COMPLETE GUIDE TO .38/.357 (US/1072-8457) [29212048] **4891**

●COMPLETE GUIDE TO 9MM (US/1059-5783) [24639126] 4039, **4871**

●COMPLETE GUIDE TO 45'S (US/1059-5716) [24638941] **4891**

COMPLETE GUIDE TO AMERICAN POCKET WATCHES, THE (US/0730-2924) [08042858] **2916**

COMPLETE GUIDE TO AMERICA'S NATIONAL PARKS : THE OFFICIAL VISITOR'S GUIDE OF THE NATIONAL PARK FOUNDATION, THE (US) [13639237] **5466**

COMPLETE GUIDE TO FLORIDA FOUNDATIONS, THE (US/1070-7840) [13084524] **4335**

COMPLETE GUIDE TO HAZARDOUS MATERIALS ENFORCEMENT AND LIABILITY (CN) **2226**

COMPLETE GUIDE TO SPECIAL INTEREST VIDEOS, THE (US/1061-4850) [24263154] **4368**

COMPLETE HANDBOOK OF COLLEGE FOOTBALL, THE (US/0149-0168) [03406912] **4891**

COMPLETE HANDBOOK OF PRO BASKETBALL, THE (US) [02936470] **4891**

COMPLETE HANDBOOK OF PRO FOOTBALL, THE (US/0361-2988) [02246435] **4891**

COMPLETE HANDBOOK OF SOCCER, THE (US/0363-6046) [02506420] **4891**

COMPLETE HANDBOOK OF THE OLYMPIC GAMES, THE (US/0749-9248) [11173134] **4891**

COMPLETE HANDBOOK OF THE OLYMPIC WINTER GAMES, THE (US) [10961442] **4891**

COMPLETE HOCKEY BOOK (US/1052-7133) [22754891] **4891**

COMPLETE INCOME TAX GUIDE, THE (US/0090-7219) [01785704] **4718**

COMPLETE INTELLIGENCE DIGEST SERVICE (UK) **4469**

COMPLETE LIBRARIES GROUP USER MANUAL (US) **1175**

●COMPLETE MEMBERSHIP DIRECTORY OF THE INTERACTIVE MULTIMEDIA ASSOCIATION, THE (US/1051-2721) [21915837] **1222**

COMPLETE MORNING OF BABY & TODDLER PROGRAMS See BABY & TODDLER TEACHER GUIDE **4937**

COMPLETE SUPER BOWL BOOK, THE (US/1071-8958) [23662023] **4891**

COMPLETE UNITED STATES JEWISH TRAVEL GUIDE (US) 5047, **5466**

COMPLEX HUMAN BEHAVIOR (US/0271-9193) [06771876] **4582**

COMPLEX SYSTEMS (US/0891-2513) [14687206] **3501**

COMPLEX VARIABLES THEORY AND APPLICATION (US/0278-1077) [07712246] **3501**

COMPLEXE NBR (CN/1182-6436) [23265288] **2088**

COMPLEXITY: AN INTERNATIONAL JOURNAL OF COMPLEX AND ADAPTIVE SYSTEMS *CEASED.* (UK/0964-1816) **5096**

●COMPLEXITY (NEW YORK, N.Y.) (US/1076-2787) [30446118] **3501**

COMPLIANCE ALERT (US) 2954, **784**

COMPLIANCE ENGINEERING (US/0898-3577) [15579321] **1152**

COMPLIANCE GUIDE FOR PLAN ADMINISTRATORS (US/0274-8304) [02534539] **1660**

COMPLIANCE GUIDE TO ELECTRONIC HEALTH RECORDS (US) **741**

COMPLIANCE STRATEGIES REVIEW (US) **5380**

COMPLIANCE WITH TITLE VI OF THE CIVIL RIGHTS ACT: ANNUAL REPORT (US) [05912088] **1818**

COMPLICATIONS IN ORTHOPEDICS (US/0887-1736) [13117848] **3881**

COMPLICATIONS IN SURGERY (US/1053-749X) [22621345] **3963**

COMPOLUX (IT) **2039**

COMPONENT ACCEPTANCE DIRECTORY, PLASTICS PROGRAM (CN/1186-2300) [24401500] **4454**

COMPORTEMENT HUMAIN (CN/0832-929X) [I0832929X] **4582**

COMPORTEMENTS (FR/0769-7996) [16986637] **580**

COMPOSER NEWS (US/0894-5950) [16146048] **4111**

COMPOSER/USA (US) [08131696] **4111**

COMPOSERS, AUTHORS AND PUBLISHERS ASSOCIATION OF CANADA See MEMBERSHIP LIST / CAPAC **4130**

COMPOSERS' FORUM (U.S.) See DIRECTORY / COMPOSERS' FORUM, INC, THE **4114**

COMPOSERS WEST (CN/0709-8219) [06141420] **4111**

COMPOSICION ARQUITECTONICA / FUNDACION FAUSTINO ORBEGOZO EIZAGUIRRE, INSTITUTO DE ARTE Y HUMANIDADES (SP/0214-4832) [20554798] **295**

COMPOSITAE NEWSLETTER (SW/0284-8422) [19110148] **4165**

COMPOSITE FINANCIAL STATEMENTS OF THE S & P 400 AND SELECTED INDUSTRY GROUPS, THE (US) [11295535] **784**

COMPOSITE INDEXES OF LEADING, COINCIDENT, AND LAGGING INDICATORS (US) [18431640] **1470**

COMPOSITE INTERFACES (NE/0927-6440) **973**

COMPOSITE MATERIALS (US/0095-4497) [02969164] **973**

COMPOSITE MATERIALS SERIES (NE) [15003440] **973**

COMPOSITE POLYMERS (UK/0952-6919) [18150515] 1969, **4454**

COMPOSITE STRUCTURES (UK/0263-8223) [10281251] **2101**

COMPOSITES (UK/0010-4361) [03347128] **2101**

COMPOSITES & ADHESIVES NEWSLETTER, THE (US/0888-1227) [13506147] 4454, **1023**

COMPOSITES ENGINEERING (US/0961-9526) [24527124] **2101**

COMPOSITES ET NOUVEAUX MATERIAUX (FR/0763-0018) [I07630018] **4454**

COMPOSITES IN MANUFACTURING (US/1040-5054) [17985006] **3477**

COMPOSITES INDUSTRY MONTHLY (US/1058-904X) [24424186] **1969**

COMPOSITES MANUFACTURING (UK/0956-7143) [21630668] 3477, **2101**

COMPOSITES PARIS (FR/0754-0876) [I07540876] **4454**

COMPOSITES REPORT / FIBERGLAS CANADA INC (CN/1187-1261) [25066883] **4454**

COMPOSITES SCIENCE AND TECHNOLOGY (UK/0266-3538) [11723630] **2101**

COMPOSITEUR CANADIEN (CN/0008-3259) [02578699] **4111**

COMPOSITIO MATHEMATICA (NE/0010-437X) [01564581] **3501**

COMPOSITION AND TEACHING (US) [07458259] **1891**

COMPOSITION CHRONICLE (US/0897-263X) [17452154] 1891, **3377**

COMPOSITION OF THE WMO (SZ) [03234602] **1424**

●COMPOSITION STUDIES : FRESHMAN ENGLISH NEWS (US) [26049621] 3377, **3274**

●COMPOST SCIENCE & UTILIZATION (US/1065-657X) [26666632] **2226**

COMPOSTELLANUM (SP/0573-2018) [I05732018] **5028**

COMPOUNDINGS (US/1042-508X) [19080829] **4253**

COMPRARE OGGI (IT) **829**

COMPREHENSIVE ANNUAL, FINANCIAL REPORT (US) [19418523] **4639**

COMPREHENSIVE ANNUAL FINANCIAL REPORT / CITY OF PHILADELPHIA, PENNSYLVANIA (US) [10938006] **4718**

COMPREHENSIVE ANNUAL FINANCIAL REPORT, COUNTY OF LOS ANGELES (US) [09312472] **4718**

COMPREHENSIVE ANNUAL FINANCIAL REPORT FOR THE FISCAL YEAR ENDED JUNE 30 ... / STATE OF UTAH (US) [10268326] **4718**

COMPREHENSIVE ANNUAL FINANCIAL REPORT FOR THE YEAR ENDED ... - COMPTROLLER'S OFFICE, COMPTROLLER OF THE TREASURY OF MARYLAND (US) [09449359] **4718**

COMPREHENSIVE ANNUAL FINANCIAL REPORT FOR THE YEAR ENDED JUNE 30, ... (MINNESOTA) (US) [10271350] **4718**

COMPREHENSIVE ANNUAL FINANCIAL REPORT FOR THE YEAR ENDED JUNE 30 ... / STATE OF ILLINOIS. TEACHERS' RETIREMENT SYSTEM (US) [17564489] **1891**

COMPREHENSIVE ANNUAL FINANCIAL REPORT MONTGOMERY COUNTY, MARYLAND (US) [10805572] **4718**

COMPREHENSIVE ANNUAL FINANCIAL REPORT OF THE COMPTROLLER FOR THE YEAR ENDED JUNE 30 ... - NEW YORK STATE (US) [15010436] **4718**

COMPREHENSIVE ANNUAL FINANCIAL REPORT OF THE HIGHWAY PATROLMENS' RETIREMENT FUND FOR THE FISCAL YEAR ENDING JUNE 30 ... - (MINNESOTA) (US) [07482048] 4639, **3160**

COMPREHENSIVE ANNUAL FINANCIAL REPORT, STATE OF MISSOURI (US) [09118617] **4718**

COMPREHENSIVE ANNUAL SERVICES PROGRAM PLAN - (ARKANSAS) (US) [04840657] **5280**

COMPREHENSIVE ANNUAL SERVICES PROGRAM PLAN - (NEVADA) (US) [06271940] **5280**

COMPREHENSIVE BIBLE STUDY (US/0162-962X) [04288480] **5016**

COMPREHENSIVE BIOCHEMISTRY (NE/0069-8032) [02251166] **486**

COMPREHENSIVE CHEMICAL KINETICS (NE/0069-8040) [02288215] **973**

COMPREHENSIVE CRIMINAL JUSTICE PLAN, CRIMINAL JUSTICE PROGRAMS (US/0098-5740) [02241041] **3160**

COMPREHENSIVE DATABASE OF US CHEMICAL PATENTS TAPES (US) **973**

COMPREHENSIVE DIRECTORY OF SPORTS ADDRESSES See SPORTS ADDRESS BIBLE **4922**

COMPREHENSIVE DISSERTATION INDEX (US) [05623069] **3567**

COMPREHENSIVE DISSERTATION INDEX. SUPPLEMENT (US/0361-6657) [02247094] **414**

COMPREHENSIVE EDUCATION *SUSPENDED.* (UK/0588-9278) [04479279] **1733**

COMPREHENSIVE EMPLOYMENT AND TRAINING PLAN, ANNUAL PLAN. BALANCE OF STATE / STATE OF ALASKA, CETA DIVISION (US) [08374339] **1660**

COMPREHENSIVE EMPLOYMENT & TRAINING PROGRAMS IN ALASKA (US) [06808701] **1660**

COMPREHENSIVE ENDOCRINOLOGY (US/0160-242X) [03646220] **3727**

COMPREHENSIVE ENVIRONMENT, HEALTH, AND SAFETY PROGRAM REPORT (US/0192-270X) [04836697] 2163, **4772**

COMPREHENSIVE FACILITIES INVENTORY REPORT (HARTFORD) (US/0094-3525) [01794044] **1818**

COMPREHENSIVE HEALTH PLANNING ASSOCIATION FOR THE METROPOLITAN PORTLAND AREA See PHYSICIAN MANPOWER IN OREGON DATA BOOK **3916**

COMPREHENSIVE IMMUNOLOGY *CEASED.* (US/0149-1148) [03321098] **3668**

COMPREHENSIVE INDEX, CALIFORNIA CODE OF REGULATIONS (US/0897-7852) [17624980] **3079**

COMPREHENSIVE INDEX OF PUBLICATIONS OF THE AMERICAN ASSOCIATION OF PETROLEUM GEOLOGISTS (US) [01479400] **4253**

COMPREHENSIVE LAW ENFORCEMENT AND CRIMINAL JUSTICE PLAN AND ACTION GRANT APPLICATION (US) [04764719] **3160**

COMPREHENSIVE LISTING OF AERIAL PHOTOGRAPHY (US) [02156646] **2558**

COMPREHENSIVE MANAGEMENT REPORT (US) [21897594] **741**

COMPREHENSIVE MANPOWER PLAN (US/0091-066X) [01786489] **1660**

COMPREHENSIVE MANPOWER PLAN AND GRANT APPLICATION (US/0148-7140) [03356826] **1660**

COMPREHENSIVE MANUALS IN RADIOLOGY (US/0172-4843) [08449754] **3940**

COMPREHENSIVE MEDLINE/EBSCO CD-ROM (US/1040-4074) [18438363] 3203, **3567**

COMPREHENSIVE MENTAL HEALTH CARE (US/1051-7782) [22121540] 3923, **4582**

COMPREHENSIVE PLAN FOR CRIMINAL JUSTICE (US/0093-8912) [02242004] **3160**

COMPREHENSIVE PLAN FOR EMERGENCY MEDICAL SERVICES (US) [08679635] **3723**

COMPREHENSIVE PSYCHIATRY (US/0010-440X) [01564585] **3923**

COMPREHENSIVE PSYCHOTHERAPY (US/0275-7222) [06100979] **3923**

COMPREHENSIVE PUBLICATION LIST - MINISTRY OF FORESTS AND LANDS (VICTORIA) (CN/0839-8585) [18335457] **2378**

COMPREHENSIVE SERVICES PROGRAM PLAN (US) [08226306] **5280**

●COMPREHENSIVE STATE PLAN AND HUMAN SERVICES PLAN FOR THE PREVENTION/INTERVENTION/TREATMENT OF ALCOHOLISM AND OTHER DRUG DEPENDENCY FOR FISCAL YEARS, A (US) [18794498] **1342**

COMPREHENSIVE STATE PLAN FOR ALCOHOLISM AND SUBSTANCE ABUSE SERVICES See COMPREHENSIVE STATE PLAN AND HUMAN SERVICES PLAN FOR THE PREVENTION/INTERVENTION/TREATMENT OF ALCOHOLISM AND OTHER DRUG DEPENDENCY FOR FISCAL YEARS, A **1342**

COMPREHENSIVE STATE PLAN FOR DRUG ABUSE CONTROL (VIRGINIA) (US/0361-9176) [10130808] **1342**

COMPREHENSIVE THERAPY (US/0098-8243) [02242426] **3567**

COMPRENDRE (IT/0010-4418) [02386752] **5242**

COMPRESSED AIR (1965) (US/0010-4426) [01564586] **1602**

COMPTE GENERAL DE L'ADMINISTRATION DE LA JUSTICE PENALE / MINISTERE DE LA JUSTICE (FR) [09834078] 3160, **3079**

COMPTE RENDU ANALYTIQUE - REPUBLIQUE DU ZAIRE, CONSEIL LEGISLATIF NATIONAL (BE/0376-7531) [02240100] **4639**

COMPTE RENDU ANNUEL DES TRAVAUX / OENOLOGIE EQUIPEMENTS VINICOLES (FR) **168**

COMPTE RENDU ANNUEL DES TRAVAUX / VITICULTURE EQUIPEMENTS VITICOLES (FR) **168**

COMPTE RENDU - ASSOCIATION PROFESSIONNELLE DES BANQUES, COMITE D'ETUDES TECHNIQUES ET DE NORMALISATION BANCAIRE (FR) [03188425] **784**

COMPTE RENDU D'ACTIVITE See RAPPORT D'ACTIVITE / CHAMBRE DE COMMERCE ET D'INDUSTRIE DE POINTE-A-PITRE **821**

COMPTE RENDU D'ACTIVITE - EDF, DIRECTION DE LA DISTRIBUTION (FR) [04967293] **4640**

COMPTE-RENDU D'ACTIVITES - CHAMBRE DE COMMERCE, D'INDUSTRIE ET DES MINES DU CAMEROUN (CM) [02713299] **819**

COMPTE-RENDU D'ACTIVITES / COMITE DEPARTEMENTAL DE DEFENSE CONTRE L'ALCOOLISME DE LA REUNION (RE) [09866187] **3160**

COMPTE RENDU DE LA CONFERENCE DU COLUMA (FR) [03499196] **76**

COMPTE RENDU DE LA SITUATION ECONOMIQUE (CN) [01784540] **1552**

COMPTE RENDU DES ESSAIS (FR) [25088299] 2332, **76**

COMPTE RENDU DES RECHERCHES (STATION DAMELIORATION DES PLANTES, GEMBLOUX) (BE/0379-184X) [08419243] **76**

COMPTE RENDU DES SEANCES DE LA SOCIETE DE BIOGEOGRAPHIE (FR/0037-9018) [02450631] **2558**

COMPTE RENDU DES TRAVAUX EFFECTUES EN ... / INSTITUT TECHNIQUE DE LA BETTERAVE, ITB (FR/0373-305X) [11741156] **168**

COMPTE RENDU DU COLLOQUE DE L'INSTITUT INTERNATIONAL DE LA POTASSE (SZ/0074-7491) [07124726] **1023**

COMPTE RENDU / PRESENTE A MONSIEUR LE PRESIDENT DE LA REPUBLIQUE AU NOM DU CONSEIL GENERAL DE LA BANQUE DE FRANCE (FR) [03337965] **784**

COMPTE RENDU SOMMAIRE DES SEANCES DE LA SOCIETE GEOLOGIQUE DE FRANCE (FR/0037-9417) [01765828] **1372**

COMPTES ANNUELS DES ETABLISSEMENTS DE CREDIT (FR) [18456590] **784**

COMPTES DE LA NATION, LES (FR) [24020258] **1470**

COMPTES DE L'AGRICULTURE, LES (FR) [04209105] **76**

COMPTES DE L'EXERCICE / SOCIETE NATIONALE INDUSTRIELLE AEROSPATIALE (FR) [09613555] **17**

COMPTES DE RESULTATS D'EXECUTION DU BUDGET / MINISTERE DE L'ECONOMIE ET DU PLAN, SOCIETE DE DEVELOPPEMENT DU NKAM (CM) [07118459] **784**

COMPTES ECONOMIQUES DE LA GUADELOUPE (FR) [03353104] **1552**

COMPTES ECONOMIQUES NATIONAUX DU RWANDA / REPUBLIQUE RWANDAISE, MINISTERE DU PLAN, DIRECTION GENERALE DE LA STATISTIQUE, BUREAU DE LA COMPTABILITE NATIONALE (RW) [06700893] **1552**

COMPTES ET RATIOS DES SOCIETES (FR) [20541431] **659**

COMPTES-RENDUS DE L' ASSEMBLEE GENERALE DE LA COMMISSION INTERNATIONALE TECHNIQUE DE SUCRERIE (BE/0254-5128) [09832204] **5096**

COMPTES-RENDUS DE LA ASSEMBLEE GENERALE DE LA COMMISSION INTERNATIONALE TECHNIQUE DE SUCRERIE (BE) [04102470] **2332**

COMPTES RENDUS DE LA CONFERENCE - UNION INTERNATIONALE DE CHIMIE PURE ET APPLIQUE (SP/0074-9508) [04527867] **973**

COMPTES RENDUS DE L'ACADEMIE BULGARE DES SCIENCES *See* DOKLADI NA BULGARSKATA AKADEMIIA NA NAUKITE **5101**

COMPTES RENDUS DE L'ACADEMIE D'AGRICULTURE DE FRANCE (FR/0989-6988) [18240779] **76**

COMPTES RENDUS DE L'ACADEMIE DES SCIENCES (FR/0762-0969) [10907890] **5096**

COMPTES RENDUS DE L'ACADEMIE DES SCIENCES. SERIE I, MATHEMATIQUE (FR/0764-4442) [10662852] **3501**

●COMPTES RENDUS DE L'ACADEMIE DES SCIENCES. SERIE II, MECANIQUE, PHYSIQUE, CHIMIE, ASTRONOMIE (FR) [29905619] 394, **4400**

COMPTES RENDUS DE L'ACADEMIE DES SCIENCES. SERIE II, MECANIQUE, PHYSIQUE, CHIMIE, SCIENCES DE L'UNIVERS, SCIENCES DE LA TERRE (FR/0764-4450) [10662601] **5096**

●COMPTES RENDUS DE L'ACADEMIE DES SCIENCES. SERIE II, SCIENCES DE LA TERRE ET DES PLANETES EARTH & PLANETARY SCIENCES (FR) [29905472] **4400**

COMPTES RENDUS DE L'ACADEMIE DES SCIENCES. SERIE III, SCIENCES DE LA VIE (FR/0764-4469) [10662893] **5096**

COMPTES RENDUS DE THERAPEUTIQUE ET DE PHARMACOLOGIE CLINIQUE (FR/0293-9908) [09449766] **4297**

COMPTES RENDUS DES SEANCES - ACADEMIE DES INSCRIPTIONS & BELLES-LETTRES (FR/0065-0536) [01460646] **2844**

COMPTES RENDUS DES SEANCES DE LA SOCIETE DE BIOLOGIE ET DES SES FILIALES (FR/0037-9026) [02256271] **452**

COMPTES RENDUS DES TRAVAUX DES COLLOQUES (FR/0223-6335) 1969, **4400**

COMPTES RENDUS MATHEMATIQUES DE L'ACADEMIE DES SCIENCES (CN/0706-1994) [04960487] **3501**

COMPTES RENDUS, PROCES-VERBAUX, MEMOIRES - MEMOIRES - ASSOCIATION BRETONNE ET UNION REGIONALISTE BRETONNE (FR) [03494992] **2684**

COMPTROLLER GENERAL'S ANNUAL REPORT (US) [15291147] **4718**

COMPTROLLER GENERAL'S PROCUREMENT DECISIONS (US/0095-2117) [01794939] **949**

COMPTROLLER'S MANUAL FOR REPRESENTATIVES IN TRUSTS : REGULATIONS, INSTRUCTIONS, OPINIONS (US) [01545855] **784**

COMPTROLLER'S REPORT OF COOK COUNTY (US) [04302288] **4640**

COMPU-FAX (US/0195-8526) [05659847] **1175**

COMPU-INFO *See* COMPUTER-SPECS **1178**

COMPU-MARK DIRECTORY OF U.S. TRADEMARKS *See* DIRECTORY OF U.S. TRADEMARKS, THE **1303**

COMPU-MART (RICHARDSON, TEX.) (US/1072-3544) [28916199] **1236**

COMPU-MGR TELE-MGR (US) 1152, **1175**

COMPUMATH CITATION INDEX : CMCI (US/0730-6199) [08036058] 3501, **3542**

COMPUSCUOLA (IT) **1862**

COMPUSERVE MAGAZINE (US/1058-8965) [21142093] **1240**

COMPUT-A-CAL *CEASED.* (US/0742-5686) [10365754] 5096, **5174**

COMPUTA (JM) **1175**

COMPUTABLE (NE) [06897276] **1256**

COMPUTATIONAL COMPLEXITY (SZ/1016-3328) [24441333] 1175, **3501**

●COMPUTATIONAL ECONOMICS (NE/0927-7099) [27735320] 1175, **1470**

COMPUTATIONAL FLUID DYNAMICS (NEW YORK, N.Y.) (US/1055-677X) [23272362] **1175**

COMPUTATIONAL GEOMETRY (NE/0925-7721) [I09257721] **3501**

COMPUTATIONAL INTELLIGENCE (CN/0824-7935) [12073389] 1282, **1212**

COMPUTATIONAL LINGUISTICS (ASSOCIATION FOR COMPUTATIONAL LINGUISTICS) (US/0891-2017) [11322424] 3274, **1175**

●COMPUTATIONAL MATERIALS SCIENCE (NE/0927-0256) [27704267] **2101**

●COMPUTATIONAL MATHEMATICS AND MATHEMATICAL PHYSICS (UK/0965-5425) [25625195] **3501**

COMPUTATIONAL MATHEMATICS AND MODELING (US/1046-283X) [20373234] **3501**

COMPUTATIONAL MECHANICS (GW/0178-7675) [14220227] **2112**

COMPUTATIONAL MECHANICS ADVANCES (SZ/0927-7951) [29297179] **2112**

COMPUTATIONAL MUSICOLOGY NEWSLETTER (US/0093-0253) [01791666] **4111**

COMPUTATIONAL OPTIMIZATION AND APPLICATIONS (NE/0926-6003) **3502**

COMPUTATIONAL POLYMER SCIENCE (US/1052-0643) [22173714] **4454**

COMPUTATIONAL SEISMOLOGY *CEASED.* (US/0733-5792) [07199640] **1404**

●COMPUTATIONAL STATISTICS (GW) [25620039] 5325, **3502**

COMPUTATIONAL STATISTICS & DATA ANALYSIS (NE/0167-9473) [09415738] **3502**

COMPUTATIONAL STATISTICS QUARTERLY *See* COMPUTATIONAL STATISTICS **3502**

COMPUTATIONAL TECHNIQUES (US) [09550770] **3502**

COMPUTE (GREENSBORO) *CEASED.* (US/0194-357X) [05391833] **1266**

COMPUTEK (CN/0827-262X) [12151060] **1266**

COMPUTER ABSTRACTS (UK/0010-4469) [04763423] 1175, **1208**

COMPUTER ABSTRACTS ON DISKETTE (US) 1175, **1208**

COMPUTER ABSTRACTS ON MICROFICHE (US) [20638629] **1175**

COMPUTER AGE. EFTS *CEASED.* (US) [09658277] **1175**

COMPUTER AIDED DESIGN (UK/0010-4485) [02250813] **1231**

COMPUTER-AIDED DESIGN, ENGINEERING, AND DRAFTING *CEASED.* (US/0742-5716) [10366261] 1228, **1231**

COMPUTER AIDED DESIGN. FRENCH EDITION (FR/0991-1960) **1231**

COMPUTER AIDED DESIGN OF DIGITAL SYSTEMS (US/0191-2305) [04705477] **1232**

COMPUTER AIDED DESIGN REPORT (US/0276-749X) [07405983] **1232**

COMPUTER-AIDED ENGINEERING (US/0733-3536) [08539421] **1228**

COMPUTER AIDED ENGINEERING REVIEW (US) [18028241] **2039**

COMPUTER AIDED ENGINEERING SERIES (US) **1969**

COMPUTER AIDED GEOMETRIC DESIGN (NE/0167-8396) [11160704] 1228, **1232**

COMPUTER-AIDED PROCESS CONTROL ABSTRACTS (UK/0955-4319) [20579190] **1232**

COMPUTER AIDED SELLING (US/8756-8780) [11692659] 1175, **659**

COMPUTER AND COMMUNICATIONS BUYER (US/0272-4553) [06847015] **1244**

COMPUTER & CONTROL ABSTRACTS (UK/0036-8113) [04263628] **1208**

COMPUTER & ELECTRONICS GRADUATE, THE *CEASED.* (US/0882-200X) [11788030] 2039, **4203**

●COMPUTER AND INFORMATION SYSTEMS ABSTRACTS (US) [28259972] 1256, **1208**

COMPUTER AND INFORMATION SYSTEMS ABSTRACTS JOURNAL (US/0191-9776) [03781271] 1176, **1208**

COMPUTER & NETWORK LAN (JA) **1240**

COMPUTER & OFFICE ELECTRONICS RETAILER (US) **953**

COMPUTER & OFFICE PRODUCT EVALUATIONS *CEASED.* (US/1051-0680) [21720113] 4211, **1176**

COMPUTER & TELECOM INDUSTRY UPDATE (CN/1182-9052) [23599120] **4211**

COMPUTER & VIDEO GAMES (UK/0261-3697) [I02613697] **1230**

COMPUTER & VIDEOGIOCHI (IT) **4859**

COMPUTER APPLICATIONS (UK/0308-4221) [03356690] 1176, **5096**

●COMPUTER APPLICATIONS IN ENGINEERING EDUCATION (US/1061-3773) [25277404] **1969**

COMPUTER APPLICATIONS IN THE BIOSCIENCES (UK/0266-7061) [11875762] 3691, **1176**

COMPUTER ARCHITECTURE NEWS (US/0163-5964) [02259651] **1232**

●COMPUTER ARTIST (US/1063-312X) [25970635] **1232**

COMPUTER ASAP [ONLINE DATABASE] (US) 1176, **1208**

COMPUTER-ASIA SOFTWARE GUIDE (HK) [11049232] **1176**

COMPUTER-ASSISTED COMPOSITION JOURNAL, THE (US/1047-2452) [15021452] **1292**

COMPUTER ASSISTED LANGUAGE LEARNING (UK/0958-8221) [23721154] **3274**

●COMPUTER ASSISTED REHABILITATION THERAPY (US/1062-9734) [25826729] **1176**

COMPUTER AUDIT UPDATE (UK/0960-2593) [I09602593] **1256**

COMPUTER BOOK REVIEW (US/0737-0334) [09287683] 4813, **1176**

COMPUTER BOOKBASE *CEASED.* (US/0740-2015) [09927525] **1256**

COMPUTER BULLETIN (UK/0010-4531) [01564593] **1256**

COMPUTER BUSINESS (LOS ANGELES, CALIF.) (US/0732-8346) [04732733] 1236, **1208**

COMPUTER BUSINESS REVIEW (UK) **1176**

COMPUTER BUYER'S GUIDE AND HANDBOOK (US/0738-9213) [09692971] 1244, **1266**

COMPUTER BUYING GUIDE (US/0882-7818) [11319765] 1236, **1266**

COMPUTER BUYING WORLD (US/1057-9982) [24176405] **1244**

COMPUTER CASES *CEASED.* (US/1060-9040) [22283713] **1176**

COMPUTER COMMENTARY (AT) **1176**

COMPUTER COMMUNICATION REVIEW (US/0146-4833) [02681898] **1240**

COMPUTER COMMUNICATIONS (UK/0140-3664) [04537318] **1240**

COMPUTER COMPENDIUM (US/1058-2606) [24234019] **1176**

COMPUTER CONFERENCE ANALYSIS NEWSLETTER, THE (US/1071-2216) [20432827] **1236**

COMPUTER CONTENTS *CEASED.* (US/0747-0193) [09678155] 1176, **1208**

COMPUTER CONTRACTOR (UK) **1236**

COMPUTER CONTROL QUARTERLY *See* INFORMATION MANAGEMENT & COMPUTER SECURITY **1188**

COMPUTER COUNSEL (US/1044-1794) [19351471] 2954, **864**

COMPUTER CRAFTSMAN JOURNAL (US) [10756274] **1176**

Alphabetical Title Index — COMPUTER

COMPUTER DAILY **CEASED.** (US/1042-7090) [15581592] **1176**

COMPUTER DATA STORAGE NEWSLETTER (FR/0988-3452) [I09883452] 1264, **1276**

COMPUTER DATABASE [ONLINE DATABASE] (US) 1176, **1208**

COMPUTER DEALER NEWS (1990) (CN/1184-2369) [24256417] **1236**

●COMPUTER DEALER NEWS SOURCE GUIDE (CN/1193-1272) [26715176] **1236**

COMPUTER DESIGN (WINCHESTER) (US/0010-4566) [01564597] **1176**

COMPUTER DIRECT MARKETING RREPORT *See* COMPUTER MARKETING & DISTRIBUTION REPORT **864**

COMPUTER DIRECTORY AND BUYERS' GUIDE, THE (US/0734-0583) [03926828] **1244**

COMPUTER-DISABILITY NEWS **CEASED.** (US) [12316796] **4386**

COMPUTER DISPLAY REVIEW, THE **CEASED.** (US/0010-4582) [01564599] **1264**

COMPUTER DOWNLOAD (AT/0818-1748) [I08181748] **1222**

COMPUTER (DURANGO, COLO.) (US/0883-4881) [12099810] **1236**

COMPUTER ECONOMIC$ REPORT (US/0739-0874) [08223863] **1256**

COMPUTER ECONOMIC$ REPORT (INTERNATIONAL ED.) (US/1054-5026) [22902783] **1176**

COMPUTER ECONOMICS SOURCEBOOK (US/0890-4308) [14223908] 1470, **1256**

COMPUTER EDUCATION (UK/0010-4590) [02251593] **1222**

COMPUTER ENTERTAINER **CEASED.** (US/0890-2143) [14192197] **1230**

●COMPUTER FINANCE (UK/0966-7849) [I09667849] **1236**

COMPUTER FORUM (SZ) **1176**

COMPUTER FRAUD & SECURITY BULLETIN (NE/0142-0496) [05688772] **1225**

●COMPUTER FREEBIE$ (US/1062-3647) [25598309] **1176**

COMPUTER GAMES (US/0748-4461) [10932403] 4859, **1230**

COMPUTER GAMES STRATEGY PLUS (US) **1230**

COMPUTER GAMING WORLD (US/0744-6667) [08482876] **1230**

COMPUTER GRAFICA E DESKTOP PUBLISHING (IT) **1263**

COMPUTER GRAPHICS (US/0097-8930) [01799521] **1232**

COMPUTER GRAPHICS DIRECTORY *See* COMPUTER GRAPHICS WORLD BUYERS GUIDE **1232**

COMPUTER GRAPHICS FORUM : A JOURNAL OF THE EUROPEAN ASSOCIATION FOR COMPUTER GRAPHICS (NE/0167-7055) [09957826] **1232**

COMPUTER GRAPHICS MARKETPLACE **CEASED.** (US/0278-2774) [07760496] **1232**

COMPUTER GRAPHICS NEWS (WASHINGTON, D.C.) (US/0276-2811) [07331680] **1232**

●COMPUTER GRAPHICS PROCEEDINGS, ANNUAL CONFERENCE SERIES (US/1069-529X) [28087946] **1232**

COMPUTER GRAPHICS WORLD (US/0271-4159) [06606082] **1232**

COMPUTER GRAPHICS WORLD BUYERS GUIDE (US/0895-2760) [15535001] **1232**

COMPUTER GUIDE (US/0743-457X) [10224560] 1266, **1273**

COMPUTER HOT LINE (US/0192-6349) [05060909] **1176**

COMPUTER IMAGES (UK) **1232**

COMPUTER IMAGES (US/1042-1130) [18968190] 1176, **377**

COMPUTER INDUSTRY ADVERTISING & MARKETING FORECAST (US) [16074448] 1176, **757**

COMPUTER INDUSTRY ALMANAC (US/0893-0791) [15340180] **1176**

COMPUTER INDUSTRY FORECASTS (1987) (US/0894-6213) [16148080] 1244, **1236**

COMPUTER INDUSTRY GUIDE (UK/0955-2111) [I09552111] **1176**

COMPUTER INDUSTRY LITIGATION REPORTER (US/0740-1469) [09882954] 1236, **1303**

COMPUTER INDUSTRY REPORT (US/0889-082X) [13584787] **1256**

COMPUTER INDUSTRY UPDATE (US/0744-0081) [07982084] 1236, **1208**

COMPUTER INFO (NE) **1176**

●COMPUTER INFO (US/1061-6403) [25384672] **1176**

COMPUTER INFORMATION REVIEW (US/0895-6588) [13564143] **1176**

COMPUTER INSTRUCTOR, THE (US/8755-5816) [11423345] **1222**

COMPUTER-INTEGRATED MANUFACTURING SYSTEMS (UK/0951-5240) [18201536] 3477, **1228**

COMPUTER JOURNAL (UK/0010-4620) [01564600] **1176**

COMPUTER JOURNAL (KALISPELL, MONT.) (US/0748-9331) [11036571] **1177**

COMPUTER LANGUAGE (US/0749-2839) [11110074] 1278, 1284, **1218**

COMPUTER LANGUAGES (US/0096-0551) [02246698] **1278**

COMPUTER LAW & PRACTICE *See* TOLLEY'S COMPUTER LAW AND PRACTICE **1227**

COMPUTER LAW AND SECURITY REPORT, THE (UK) [14114834] **1225**

COMPUTER LAW AND TAX REPORT (US/0361-7203) [02247071] 1177, 4718, **2954**

COMPUTER LAW ANNUAL **CEASED.** (US/0883-6019) [12174246] 1177, 1303, **2954**

COMPUTER LAW FORMS HANDBOOK (US/0894-1858) [15862039] 1177, **2954**

COMPUTER/LAW JOURNAL (US/0164-8756) [04182920] 1177, **2954**

COMPUTER LAW MONITOR, THE (US/0741-8809) [10232957] 1177, **2954**

COMPUTER LAW NEWSLETTER **CEASED.** (US) [07125954] 1177, **2954**

COMPUTER LAW REPORTER (US/0739-7771) [08643146] 1225, **2954**

COMPUTER LAW SERIES (NE) **2954**

COMPUTER LAW STRATEGIST (US/0747-8933) [10828720] 1177, **2954**

COMPUTER LAW (TORONTO) (CN/0824-4790) [11283978] 1177, **2955**

COMPUTER LAWYER, THE (US/0742-1192) [10292308] 1177, **2955**

COMPUTER LETTER (US) 784, **5096**

●COMPUTER LIFE (US/1076-9862) [30660941] **1177**

COMPUTER LITERACY NEWSLETTER (US) **1177**

COMPUTER LITERATURE INDEX (US/0270-4846) [06321339] 1256, **1208**

COMPUTER LIVING, NEW YORK (US/8750-4375) [11401088] **1177**

COMPUTER (LONG BEACH, CALIF.) (US/0018-9162) [02240099] **1266**

COMPUTER MANAGEMENT **CEASED.** (UK/0010-4639) [10249386] **1253**

COMPUTER MARKETING & DISTRIBUTION REPORT **CEASED.** (US/1071-2488) [28595233] **864**

COMPUTER MARKETING NEWSLETTER, THE **CEASED.** (US/0886-7194) [12962331] 922, **1244**

COMPUTER METHODS AND PROGRAMS IN BIOMEDICINE (NE/0169-2607) [12146309] 1212, 1279, **3691**

COMPUTER METHODS IN APPLIED MECHANICS AND ENGINEERING (NE/0045-7825) [01777463] 1969, **1256**

COMPUTER MUSIC JOURNAL (US/0148-9267) [03393019] **1240**

COMPUTER NETWORKS AND ISDN SYSTEMS (NE/0169-7552) [12119244] 1246, **1240**

COMPUTER NETWORKS FOR RESEARCH IN EUROPE (NE) **1240**

COMPUTER NEWS INTERNATIONAL (US/1050-396X) [21475083] **1177**

COMPUTER NEWS OF SAN DIEGO (US/0738-5900) [09631725] **1177**

COMPUTER OPTICS **CEASED.** (UK/0955-355X) [21708662] **1177**

COMPUTER PAPER (BRITISH COLUMBIA ED.) (CN/0840-3929) [19109355] **1177**

●COMPUTER PARTNER LEADS (US/1064-7007) [26459761] **1177**

COMPUTER PERIODICALS INDEX (US/0888-1987) [13385325] **1266**

COMPUTER PERIPHERALS REVIEW (US/0149-5054) [03503064] **1264**

COMPUTER PERSONLICH (GW/0722-0987) [I07220987] **1177**

COMPUTER PERSONNEL (US/0160-2497) [02681883] **1279**

COMPUTER PHYSICS COMMUNICATIONS (NE/0010-4655) [00966945] 1279, **4400**

COMPUTER PICTURES (US/0883-5683) [09470312] **1232**

COMPUTER POST (CN/1194-305X) [28166189] 659, **1177**

COMPUTER PRICE GUIDE (US/0045-7841) [08325505] 1264, **1244**

COMPUTER PRICE WATCH (US/1052-3502) [16369250] **1244**

COMPUTER PROCESSING OF CHINESE & ORIENTAL LANGUAGES (US/0715-9048) [10552053] 1177, 3203, **3274**

COMPUTER PRODUCT NEWS (BE) **1244**

COMPUTER PRODUCTS **CEASED.** (US/0161-6862) [03992856] **1244**

COMPUTER PROTOCOLS (US/0899-126X) [18000829] **1177**

COMPUTER PUBLICITY NEWS **CEASED.** (US/0276-9972) [07466525] **758**

COMPUTER PUBLISHERS & PUBLICATIONS (US/0740-4085) [09935623] **1236**

COMPUTER PUBLISHING & ADVERTISING REPORT (US/0740-6231) [09983784] 758, **1177**

COMPUTER PUBLISHING MAGAZINE **CEASED.** (US/1054-0415) [22724731] **1177**

COMPUTER RAMBLINGS (US/0899-3025) [15741739] 76, **1266**

COMPUTER-READABLE DATA BASES (US/0271-4477) [05758648] **1236**

COMPUTER REPORT (JA) **1177**

COMPUTER REPORT & THE PC STREET PRICE INDEX (US/1063-8369) [26166371] **1246**

COMPUTER RESELLER NEWS (US/0893-8377) [15512744] 953, **1244**

COMPUTER RESELLER SOURCES **CEASED.** (US/1060-1376) [24881804] **1177**

COMPUTER RETAIL WEEK (US/1066-7598) [27045911] **1244**

COMPUTER RETAILERS' GUIDE (US/0748-8610) [11025531] 1284, **1266**

COMPUTER REVIEW (US/0093-416X) [01792367] **1264**

COMPUTER REVIEW INDEX (US/1040-5003) [14994028] 1279, **1208**

COMPUTER SCIENCE AND APPLIED MATHEMATICS (US/0884-2027) [03370787] 1177, **3502**

COMPUTER SCIENCE AND COMPUTER ENGINEERING (US) **1228**

COMPUTER SCIENCE AND INFORMATICS (II/0254-7813) [10526878] 1257, **1177**

COMPUTER SCIENCE AND SCIENTIFIC COMPUTING (US) **1177**

COMPUTER SCIENCE EDUCATION (US/0899-3408) [18066652] **1177**

COMPUTER SCIENCE IN ECONOMICS AND MANAGEMENT (NE/0921-2736) [18409670] **1177**

COMPUTER SCIENCE LIBRARY. OPERATING AND PROGRAMMING SYSTEMS SERIES, THE (US) [09678160] **1177**

●COMPUTER SCIENCE SYLLABUS (US/1065-2078) [26529236] **1177**

COMPUTER SCIENCE. VERY LARGE SCALE INTEGRATION (US/1053-9808) [16998294] 2039, **1177**

COMPUTER SECURITY (US) [05460132] **1257**

COMPUTER SECURITY ALERT (US/0742-0633) [10255541] **1226**

COMPUTER SECURITY, AUDITING AND CONTROLS (US/0738-4262) [04418699] **1226**

COMPUTER SECURITY DIGEST (US/0882-1453) [11794603] **1226**

COMPUTER SECURITY INSTITUTE (US) [09024944] **1226**

COMPUTER SECURITY JOURNAL (US/0277-0865) [07480018] **1226**

●COMPUTER SECURITY PRODUCTS BUYERS GUIDE (US) [26202861] **1226**

COMPUTER SELECT (US/1062-8509) [24116850] **1284**

COMPUTER SERVICES REPORT *See* COMPUTER SOFTWARE & SERVICES REPORT **1236**

COMPUTER SHOPPER (US/0886-0556) [11762456] **1244**

COMPUTER SHOPPER'S PC CLONES (US/0895-7398) [16774235] **1177**

COMPUTER SOFTWARE (US/1041-7133) [11152209] **1226**

COMPUTER SOFTWARE AND CHIPS : PROTECTION AND MARKETING (US) [12443990] 1246, **1226**

COMPUTER SOFTWARE & SERVICES REPORT **CEASED.** (US) **1236**

COMPUTER SOFTWARE ENGINEERING SERIES (US/0888-2088) [13519352] **1178**

COMPUTER SOFTWARE/HARDWARE INDEX (US/0882-5629) [11823219] 1264, **1284**

COMPUTER + SOFTWARE NEWS **CEASED.** (US/0745-5291) [09266621] **1245**

COMPUTER-SPECS — Alphabetical Title Index

COMPUTER-SPECS (US) **1178**

COMPUTER SPEECH & LANGUAGE (UK/0885-2308) [12597555] 1178, **3274**

COMPUTER STANDARDS & INTERFACES (SZ/0920-5489) [14523660] **1178**

COMPUTER STUDIES NEWSLETTER (CN/0319-6216) [02442872] **1257**

●COMPUTER SUPPORTED COOPERATIVE WORK : CSCW : AN INTERNATIONAL JOURNAL (NE/0925-9724) [26914585] 1241, **1232**

COMPUTER SURVEY (UK/0010-4760) [00876578] **1236**

COMPUTER SWEDEN (SW/0280-9982) [02809982] **1178**

COMPUTER SYSTEMS *CEASED.* (UK/0264-4193) [09004545] **1246**

COMPUTER SYSTEMS EUROPE (UK/0957-2945) [24959368] **1246**

COMPUTER SYSTEMS JOURNAL (US/0887-5553) [13306465] **1178**

COMPUTER SYSTEMS SCIENCE AND ENGINEERING (UK/0267-6192) [13045431] **1228**

COMPUTER TALK *CEASED.* (UK) [14106930] **1178**

COMPUTER TAPE OUTLOOK. HALF-INCH PRODUCTS / BY ROBERT C. ABRAHAM AND RAYMOND C. FREEMAN, JR (US/1059-7018) [24459756] **1236**

COMPUTER TECHNOLOGY REVIEW (US/0278-9647) [07901859] **1246**

●COMPUTER TELEPHONY (US/1072-1711) [28873566] **1178**

COMPUTER TERMINALS REVIEW (US/0147-9415) [02804798] **1264**

COMPUTER TRADE SHOW WORLD (US) **1178**

COMPUTER TRADE WEEKLY (UK) **1178**

COMPUTER UND RECHT (KOLN) (GW/0179-1990) [13412097] 1178, **2955**

COMPUTER USE IN SOCIAL SERVICES NETWORK : NEWSLETTER (US/0889-6194) [09692535] 5280, **1178**

COMPUTER USER'S LEGAL REPORTER, THE *SUSPENDED.* (US/8756-2642) [11383148] 1178, **2955**

COMPUTER USER'S SURVIVAL MAGAZINE, THE (US/1053-3834) [22521905] **1178**

COMPUTER USERS' YEAR BOOK (UK/0268-6821) [02686821] **1245**

●COMPUTER VIRUS DEVELOPMENTS QUARTERLY (US/1065-8246) [26755522] **1178**

●COMPUTER VISION AND IMAGE UNDERSTANDING (US) **1232**

COMPUTER WEEK (SA/0254-2188) [02542188] **1178**

COMPUTER WEEKLY (UK/0010-4787) [10180291] **1178**

COMPUTER WORKSTATIONS (US/0899-9783) [18284294] **1241**

COMPUTER YEARBOOK (HK) [03287278] **1178**

COMPUTER YEARBOOK (DETROIT) (US/0163-4003) [01131843] **1257**

COMPUTERCRAFT (HICKSVILLE, N.Y.) (US/1055-5072) [23194074] **1266**

COMPUTERGRAM INTERNATIONAL (UK/0268-716X) [02687160X] **1178**

●COMPUTERGRAM WEEKLY (UK/0969-2053) [109692053] **1178**

COMPUTERITER (US/8756-7911) [11694391] 2918, **1266**

COMPUTERIZATION AND NETWORKING OF MATERIALS DATABASES (US/1050-8112) [21616101] **1178**

COMPUTERIZED DIRECTORY OF NEW BUSINESSES (US/0896-0402) [16898858] **659**

COMPUTERIZED DRAFTING AND DESIGN NEWSLETTER (US/0748-660X) [10991931] 295, 1228, **1232**

COMPUTERIZED ENGINE CONTROLS. IMPORTED CARS & TRUCKS (US) [17311696] **5412**

COMPUTERIZED INVESTING (US/0734-4597) [08755335] **895**

COMPUTERIZED MANUFACTURING (US/0746-3405) [09934098] 1245, 3477, **1236**

COMPUTERIZED MEDICAL IMAGING AND GRAPHICS (US/0895-6111) [16702127] **3940**

COMPUTERIZED SERIALS SYSTEMS SERIES (US/0095-0130) [01000219] **3203**

COMPUTERIZED SURNAME MAGAZINE (US/0743-7919) [09176537] 1178, **2443**

COMPUTERRECHT (BE/0771-7784) [107717784] **1178**

COMPUTERS AND ARTIFICIAL INTELLIGENCE (XO) [15504720] 1232, **1212**

COMPUTERS AND BIOMEDICAL RESEARCH (US/0010-4809) [01564611] 1178, **3691**

COMPUTERS AND BUSINESS EQUIPMENT (US) 1178, **4211**

COMPUTERS & CHEMICAL ENGINEERING (UK/0098-1354) [01455819] 1178, **2011**

COMPUTERS & CHEMISTRY (UK/0097-8485) [01351124] 1178, **973**

COMPUTERS & COMMUNICATIONS (UK) 1152, 1236, **1266**

●COMPUTERS & COMMUNICATIONS IN AFRICA (UK) [28163526] **1178**

COMPUTERS AND COMPOSITION (US/8755-4615) [11313310] **1222**

COMPUTERS AND COMPUTING INFORMATION RESOURCES DIRECTORY (US/0894-8941) [15255480] 1257, **1241**

COMPUTERS & EDUCATION (US/0360-1315) [02477101] **1222**

COMPUTERS & ELECTRICAL ENGINEERING (US/0045-7906) [01788239] 2039, **1228**

COMPUTERS AND ELECTRONICS IN AGRICULTURE (NE/0168-1699) [11310518] **76**

COMPUTERS & FLUIDS (UK/0045-7930) [01786276] **2088**

COMPUTERS & GEOLOGY (US/0271-0420) [06258289] **1372**

COMPUTERS & GEOSCIENCES (UK/0098-3004) [02246148] 1353, **1178**

COMPUTERS AND GEOTECHNICS (US/0266-352X) [12730135] **1372**

COMPUTERS & GRAPHICS (US) [08012091] **1178**

COMPUTERS & GRAPHICS (US/0097-8493) [02246027] **1232**

COMPUTERS & INDUSTRIAL ENGINEERING (US/0360-8352) [03722153] **2097**

COMPUTERS AND LAW (UK/0140-3249) [05504418] 2955, **1178**

COMPUTERS AND LAW SYDNEY (AT/0811-7225) [108117225] 2955, **1178**

COMPUTERS AND MATH SERIES (US/0888-2193) [13528193] 3502, **1179**

COMPUTERS & MATHEMATICS WITH APPLICATIONS (1987) (UK/0898-1221) [15719402] **1179**

COMPUTERS & MEDICINE (US/0163-0547) [02259658] 3568, **1179**

COMPUTERS & MINING (US/1068-4425) [17468903] **2138**

COMPUTERS AND OFFICE AND ACCOUNTING MACHINES (US/0744-0170) [06176663] 4211, **1602**

COMPUTERS & OPERATIONS RESEARCH (US/0305-0548) [01793974] **1179**

COMPUTERS AND PEOPLE (US/0361-1442) [02246637] **1218**

COMPUTERS AND PROGRAMMING (US/0279-070X) [07506868] **1279**

COMPUTERS & SECURITY (UK/0167-4048) [09108475] **1226**

COMPUTERS & SOCIETY (US/0095-2737) [01796437] 5196, **1179**

COMPUTERS & SOFTWARE - EXPORT LICENSING CONTROLS (US) 1179, **829**

COMPUTERS & STRUCTURES (UK/0045-7949) [00816337] **1228**

COMPUTERS AND THE HISTORY OF ART (SZ/1048-6798) [21015776] 1179, **348**

COMPUTERS AND THE HUMANITIES (NE/0010-4817) [01564613] 1222, **2844**

COMPUTERS CLOSING THE GAP FOR THE HANDICAPPED *See* CLOSING THE GAP **1877**

COMPUTERS, CONTROL & INFORMATION THEORY / NTIS *See* NTIS ALERT. COMPUTERS, CONTROL & INFORMATION THEORY **1197**

COMPUTERS (CROYDON) (UK/0588-9448) [02240672] **1236**

COMPUTERS, ENVIRONMENT AND URBAN SYSTEMS (US/0198-9715) [06287967] **2819**

COMPUTERS (GREENWICH, CONN.) (US/0737-4313) [07897735] 1266, **1273**

COMPUTERS IN ACCOUNTING (US/0883-1866) [11730401] 1179, **741**

COMPUTERS IN AFRICA (UK/0953-3257) **1179**

COMPUTERS IN AFRICA & TELECOMS UPDATE *See* COMPUTERS & COMMUNICATIONS IN AFRICA **1178**

COMPUTERS IN BIOLOGY AND MEDICINE (US/0010-4825) [01564614] **3691**

COMPUTERS IN BIOMEDICAL RESEARCH (US/0573-2107) [03449677] **3568**

COMPUTERS IN CARDIOLOGY (US/0276-6574) [02453337] **3703**

COMPUTERS IN CHEMICAL EDUCATION NEWSLETTER (US/8756-8829) [08855915] 1179, **973**

COMPUTERS IN CHEMISTRY AND INSTRUMENTATION (US/0146-7115) [01624398] **1023**

COMPUTERS IN DEFENSE *CEASED.* (UK) 4039, **1179**

COMPUTERS IN EDUCATION (GUILFORD, CONN.) (US) [12429238] 1179, **1733**

COMPUTERS IN EDUCATION JOURNAL (US/1069-3769) [24933604] **1179**

COMPUTERS IN EDUCATION SERIES (US/0888-2177) [13527265] 1733, **1179**

COMPUTERS IN EDUCATION (TORONTO, ONT.) *CEASED.* (CN/0823-9940) [11802958] 1891, **1222**

COMPUTERS IN ENGINEERING (US/1065-3201) [24918634] 1179, **1969**

COMPUTERS IN EUROPE (UK) [01783754] **1179**

COMPUTERS IN GENEALOGY (UK/0263-3248) [10591552] 1279, 1292, 2443, **1266**

COMPUTERS IN HEALTHCARE (US/0745-1075) [08822646] 3778, **1179**

COMPUTERS IN HOSPITALS (US/0274-631X) [06463996] **1179**

COMPUTERS IN HR MANAGEMENT *CEASED.* (US/1047-6458) [20769656] **1179**

COMPUTERS IN HUMAN BEHAVIOR (US/0747-5632) [10746756] 1179, **4582**

COMPUTERS IN HUMAN SERVICES (US/0740-445X) [09960892] 5280, **1179**

COMPUTERS IN INDUSTRY (NE/0166-3615) [06180257] **1228**

COMPUTERS IN LIBRARIES (US/1041-7915) [18848244] 1273, **3203**

COMPUTERS IN LIFE SCIENCE EDUCATION *CEASED.* (US/0742-3233) [10304461] **1222**

COMPUTERS IN MUSIC RESEARCH (US/1046-1744) [20347129] **4111**

COMPUTERS IN NURSING (US/0736-8593) [09231528] 1179, **3854**

COMPUTERS IN PHYSICS (US/0894-1866) [15862616] 1179, **4401**

COMPUTERS IN PSYCHIATRY/PSYCHOLOGY (US/0738-3614) [09051330] 1179, 4582, **3923**

COMPUTERS IN SCHOOL LIBRARIES (CN/1188-6331) [26244892] 1179, **3203**

COMPUTERS IN THE SCHOOLS (US/0738-0569) [09500831] 1891, **1222**

COMPUTERS-R-DIGITAL (US/0741-5893) [10252087] **1179**

COMPUTERS TODAY (II/0970-0129) [13030315] **1179**

COMPUTERTALK FOR THE PHARMACIST (US/0736-3893) [08780771] 1266, **4297**

COMPUTERWHAT? (US/0886-4225) [12885392] **1179**

COMPUTERWOCHE (GW/0170-5121) [11980167] **1179**

COMPUTERWORLD (US/0010-4841) [02259660] 1266, **1236**

COMPUTERWORLD CANADA *CEASED.* (CN/0826-1547) [11734482] **1236**

COMPUTERWORLD ESPANA (SP) **1180**

COMPUTERWORLD ITALIA (IT/0392-8845) [103928845] **1180**

COMPUTERWORLD NEDERLAND *CEASED.* (NE/0922-954X) [I0922954X] **1180**

COMPUTERWORLD SINGAPORE *CEASED.* (SI/0217-8362) [102178362] **1180**

COMPUTE'S APPLE APPLICATIONS *CEASED.* (US/0895-9595) [16866134] **1180**

COMPUTE!'S ATARI ST DISK & MAGAZINE *CEASED.* (US/0888-8442) [13735826] **1180**

COMPUTE!S PC MAGAZINE (US/0893-8261) [15649694] **1180**

COMPUTE!'S PC SOFTWARE BUYER'S GUIDE (US) [18511053] **1284**

COMPUTHINK WINDOWS WATCHER, THE (US/1054-0784) [22842350] **1180**

COMPUTING (AU/0010-485X) [01564616] **1257**

COMPUTING & COMMUNICATIONS DECISIONS (UK) 1109, **1180**

COMPUTING AND COMMUNICATIONS LAW AND PROTECTION REPORT (US) **1226**

COMPUTING & COMMUNICATIONS NEWSLETTER (CN/1188-3383) [25882970] 1109, **1180**

COMPUTING & COMMUNICATIONS NEWSLETTER (CN/1184-7557) [24279932] 1109, **1180**

Alphabetical Title Index — CONCILIUM

COMPUTING AND COMMUNICATIONS PROTECTION (US/0749-1484) [25263389] **1226**

COMPUTING & CONTROL ENGINEERING JOURNAL (UK/0956-3385) [22967366] 1219, **1228**

●COMPUTING AND SOFTWARE DESIGN CAREER DIRECTORY (US/1070-728X) [28514018] **1236**

COMPUTING AND THE CLASSICS (US/8756-596X) [11689754] **1222**

COMPUTING ARCHIVE (US/1053-7856) [22646001] **1180**

COMPUTING CANADA (CN/0319-0161) [02442084] **1257**

COMPUTING, COMMUNICATIONS & MEDIA TREND MONITOR (UK/0954-7479) [09547479] 1109, **1180**

COMPUTING DECISIONS / NATIONAL COMPUTING CENTRE (UK/0266-268X) [14993370] **1180**

COMPUTING EQUIPMENT *CEASED.* (UK/0266-4283) [I02664283] **1180**

COMPUTING IN MUSICOLOGY (US/1057-9478) [21202412] **1240**

COMPUTING INFORMATION DIRECTORY (US/0887-1175) [12321068] 659, **727**

COMPUTING JOURNAL ABSTRACTS (UK/0309-8885) [14522005] 1180, **1208**

COMPUTING (LONDON. 1980) (UK/0144-3097) [06025925] **1237**

COMPUTING NEWS / YORK UNIVERSITY (CN/0226-9201) [09145788] **1180**

COMPUTING NOW! (CN/0823-6437) [09938301] 1266, **1273**

COMPUTING PHYSICIAN (US/0737-8556) [09469122] **3568**

COMPUTING REPORT IN SCIENCE AND ENGINEERING (US/0010-4876) [01564619] 1257, 1969, **5096**

COMPUTING RESEARCH NEWS (US/1069-384X) [21133481] **1180**

COMPUTING RESOURCES FOR THE PROFESSIONAL *CEASED.* (US/0276-5756) [07391536] 1266, **659**

COMPUTING REVIEWS (US/0010-4884) [01564620] 1257, **1208**

COMPUTING STRATEGY SERVICE (US) **1241**

COMPUTING STUDIES (CN/0380-9501) [03245048] **1257**

COMPUTING SYSTEMS (US/0895-6340) [16735694] **1279**

COMPUTING SYSTEMS IN ENGINEERING (US/0956-0521) [22501084] **1969**

COMPUTING TEACHER, THE (US/0278-9175) [35810231] 1891, **1222**

COMPUTING TODAY (LONDON) (UK/0142-7210) [10121297] **1266**

COMSAT TECHNICAL REVIEW (US/0095-9669) [01429664] **1152**

COMSERVANT, THE (CN/0319-4523) [02442818] **5280**

COMSTOCK'S (US) **659**

COMTEC CABLE TELEVISION VIEWERS GUIDE (US/0744-3269) [08186200] **1130**

COMUN (SP) [07432519] **348**

COMUNE, LA (IT) [01787971] **5230**

COMUNI D'EUROPA (IT/0010-4973) [03567689] **4640**

COMUNI D'ITALIA (IT/0394-8277) [I03948277] **4640**

COMUNICACAO (BL) [03353625] **1109**

COMUNICACAO E SOCIEDADE (BL) [07095411] **1109**

COMUNICACION (VE) [03475017] **5242**

COMUNICACION PSIQUIATRICA (SP/0210-1424) [05529504] **3923**

COMUNICACION Y CULTURA *SUSPENDED.* (AG) [08059558] 2918, **1109**

COMUNICACION Y CULTURA EN AMERICA LATINA (MX) [17289270] **1109**

COMUNICACION Y SOCIEDAD (SP/0214-0039) [I02140039] 2918, **1109**

COMUNICACIONES (CU) [03006338] 1180, **1109**

COMUNICACIONES ANTROPOLOGICAS DEL MUSEO DE HISTORIA NATURAL DE MONTEVIDEO (UY/0077-1244) [02264338] 4165, **4087**

COMUNICACIONES BIOLOGICAS (AG/0326-1956) [09832156] **452**

COMUNICACIONES (CORAL GABLES, FLA.) (US/0748-3104) [10926945] 1180, **1152**

COMUNICACIONES I.N.I.A. SERIE ECONOMIA (SP/0214-0322) [18547310] **76**

COMUNICACIONES I.N.I.A. SERIE GENERAL (SP/0210-3311) [04138753] **76**

COMUNICACIONES I.N.I.A. SERIE RECURSOS NATURALES (SP/0210-3338) [09179505] 4165, **76**

COMUNICACIONES I.N.I.A. SERIE TECNOLOGIA *See* COMUNICACIONES I.N.I.A. SERIE TECNOLOGIA AGRARIA **76**

COMUNICACIONES I.N.I.A. SERIE TECNOLOGIA AGRARIA (SP/0210-2560) [07953555] **76**

COMUNICACIONES PRESENTADAS A LAS ... JORNADAS DEL COMITE ESPANOL DE LA DETERGENCIA (SP/0212-7466) [10528870] **1023**

COMUNICACIONES UROLOGICAS (SP/0211-528X) [I0211528X] **3796**

COMUNICACIONES ZOOLOGICAS DEL MUSEO DE HISTORIA NATURAL DE MONTEVIDEO (UY/0027-0113) [01730977] **5581**

COMUNICACOES CIENTIFICAS DA FACULDADE DE MEDICINA VETERINARIA E ZOOTECNIA DA UNIVERSIDADE DE SAO PAULO (BL/0100-3313) [04788501] **5508**

COMUNICACOES DO INSTITUTO DE INVESTIGACAO CIENTIFICA TROPICAL, SERIE DE CIENCIAS AGRARIAS (PO) **76**

COMUNICACOES DO INSTITUTO DE INVESTIGACAO CIENTIFICA TROPICAL, SERIE DE CIENCIAS BIOLOGICAS (PO/0871-1755) **452**

COMUNICACOES DO INSTITUTO DE INVESTIGACAO CIENTIFICA TROPICAL, SERIE DE CIENCIAS ETNOLOGICAS E ETNOMUSEOLOGICAS (PO/0871-178X) 4087, **2258**

COMUNICACOES DO INSTITUTO DE INVESTIGACAO CIENTIFICA TROPICAL, SERIE DE CIENCIAS HISTORICAS, ECONOMICAS E SOCIOLOGICAS (PO/0871-1771) 5196, **1470**

COMUNICACOES - INSTITUTO DE INVESTIGACAO CIENTIFICA TROPICAL. SERIE DE CIENCIAS DA TERRA (PO/0871-1798) [I08711798] **1354**

COMUNICACOES - INSTITUTO DE INVESTIGACAO CIENTIFICA TROPICAL. SERIE DE CIENCIAS DE ENGENHARIA GEOGRAFICA (PO/0871-1747) [I08711747] **2559**

COMUNICADO MENSAL DA CONFERENCIA NACIONAL DOS BISPOS DO BRASIL (BL) [03350558] **5028**

COMUNICADO TECNICO (CENTRO DE PESQUISA AGROPECUARIA DO TROPICO SEMI-ARIDO) (BL/0100-6061) [08608911] **76**

COMUNICADO TECNICO - CENTRO DE TECNOLOGIA AGRICOLA E ALIMENTAR (BL/0101-5508) [I01015508] 2332, **76**

COMUNICADO TECNICO (CENTRO NACIONAL DE PESQUISA DE MANDIOCA E FRUTICULTURA (BRAZIL)) (BL/0100-8854) [08537520] **2412**

COMUNICADO TECNICO - EMCAPA (BL/0101-7683) [I01017683] **76**

COMUNICADO TECNICO - EMPRESA BRASILEIRA DE PESQUISA AGROPECUARIA, UNIDADE DE EXECUCAO DE PESQUISA DE AMBITO ESTADUAL, MANAUS (BL) [05529435] **76**

COMUNICADO TECNICO - EMPRESA DE PESQUISA AGROPECUARIA DO ESTADO DO RIO DE JANEIRO (BL/0100-896X) [04590033] **76**

COMUNICADO TECNICO - EMPRESA GOIANA DE PESQUISA AGROPECUARIA (BL) [06725136] **76**

COMUNICADO TECNICO - UEPAE DE DOURADOS (BL/0100-8617) [I01008617] **168**

COMUNICADO TECNICO - UNIDADE DE EXECUCAO DE PESQUISA DE AMBITO TERRITORIAL DE PORTO VELLIO (BL/0100-8765) [I01008765] **168**

COMUNICADOR, EL (HO) [08537818] **1152**

COMUNICARE (IT) **758**

COMUNICAZIONE (IT) [02403544] **348**

COMUNICAZIONI E STUDI *CEASED.* (IT) [01757465] **2955**

COMUNICAZIONI SOCIALI (IT/0392-8667) [06127874] **1109**

COMUNICO : THE NATIONAL MAGAZINE FOR MEMBERS OF UNICO (US) [25111811] **2258**

COMUNIDAD (US) [04928310] **2531**

COMUNIDAD (ASOCIACION MUTUAL ISRAELITA ARGENTINA) (AG) [08026457] **2258**

COMUNIDAD ESCOLAR : PERIODICO SEMANAL DE INFORMACION IDUCATIVA (SP) [25573462] **1733**

COMUNIDAD INFORMATICA / SECRETARIA DE PROGRAMACION Y PRESUPUESTO, COORDINACION GENERAL DEL SISTEMA NACIONAL DE INFORMACION (MX) [08191070] **1257**

COMUNIDAD Y DROGAS (SP/0213-5884) [I02135884] **3568**

COMUNIDADE (HULL) (CN/0382-8794) [03202348] **5782**

COMUNIDADES EUROPEAS (SP) [19910511] **2955**

COMUNIDADES Y CULTURAS PERUANAS (PE) [02459000] **1733**

COMUNIMEF (MX) [04459513] 1470, **784**

COMUNITA (IT/0010-504X) [02218203] **3340**

COMUNITA INTERNAZIONALE (IT/0010-5066) [01564624] **4518**

COMUNITA (MONTREAL) (CN/0712-5070) [09128342] **2729**

COMUNIUNEA ROMANEASCA (US/0197-1441) [01316385] 2258, **3377**

CON-TEKST (WAGENINGEN) *See* INZET AMSTERDAM **2910**

CON TEXT MAGAZINE (BE) 5349, **1083**

CONA JOURNAL (CN/0708-6474) [05376112] **3854**

CONAN THE BARBARIAN *CEASED.* (US/0273-0782) [04633827] **4859**

CONAN THE KING *CEASED.* (US/0746-8237) [10305131] **4859**

CONCENTRATION AND FOREIGN CONTROL IN RETAIL AND WHOLESALE TRADE IN CANADA / STATISTICS CANADA, FINANCIAL FLOWS AND MULTINATIONAL ENTERPRISES DIVISION, MERCHANDISING AND SERVICES DIVISION (CN) [11984423] **829**

CONCEPT (ISLAMABAD, PAKISTAN) (PK) [07810867] 5042, **2649**

CONCEPT NEWS (II/0970-6437) [I09706437] **5196**

CONCEPTIONS SOUTHWEST (US/1048-8790) [05729864] **317**

CONCEPTS AND TECHNIQUES IN MODERN GEOGRAPHY (UK/0306-6142) [05544358] **2559**

CONCEPTS FOR TRAFFIC SAFETY (US/0588-9715) [01714721] 4772, **5439**

CONCEPTS IN IMMUNOPATHOLOGY (SW/0255-7983) [11603088] **3668**

CONCEPTS IN MAGNETIC RESONANCE (US/1043-7347) [19542716] **4443**

CONCEPTS IN NEUROSCIENCE *CEASED.* (SI/0129-0568) [22178171] **3830**

CONCEPTS IN PEDIATRIC NEUROSURGERY (SZ/0251-2068) [07605570] 3830, **3902**

CONCEPTUS (AU/0010-5155) [05725524] **4344**

CONCERN LONDON (UK/0591-017X) [I0591017X] **2278**

CONCERN (NEW WESTMINSTER) (CN/0229-2661) [08443933] **4772**

CONCERN (REGINA) (CN/0836-7310) [17759160] **3854**

CONCERNED CANADIAN (CN/0704-5522) [03890235] **2531**

CONCERNED : THE OFFICIAL PUBLICATION OF THE CONTEMPORARY SOCIAL PROBLEMS SPECIAL INTEREST SECTION, AMERICAN ASSOCIATION OF LAW LIBRARIES (US) [10180542] **5196**

CONCERNING CARS (US) **5412**

CONCERNS (DON MILLS) (CN/0045-799X) [01980968] **1342**

CONCERT MAGAZINE (WALPOLE, MASS.) (US/0277-9560) [07655336] **4111**

CONCERT NOTES; CARL FISCHER NEWSLETTER (US) [01788343] **4111**

CONCERTACTION (CN/0226-5729) [06511190] **5280**

CONCERTI PUBBLICI / RTSI, RADIOTELEVISIONE DELLA SVIZZERA ITALIANA, RETE 2 (SZ) [19318263] **1130**

CONCERTINA & SQUEEZEBOX (US) [16320460] **4111**

●CONCERTINO MILANO (IT/1121-6875) [I11216875] **2845**

CONCERTO : DAS MAGAZIN FUER ALTE MUSIK (GW) [11128619] **4111**

CONCERTO VOCALE (GW) **4111**

CONCH REPUBLIC MAGAZINE (US/1055-4149) [23167850] **2531**

CONCH REVIEW OF BOOKS, THE *SUSPENDED.* (US/0092-7708) [01789922] **3340**

CONCHO HERALD, THE (US) [14370242] **5748**

CONCHO RIVER REVIEW (US/1048-9568) [17446948] **3377**

CONCILIUM (IT) **4949**

CONCILIUM (PL) [04601194] **5028**

CONCILIUM (ENGLISH LANGUAGE EDITION) (UK/0010-5236) [05811311] **4949**

CONCILIUM
Alphabetical Title Index

CONCILIUM (MADRID) (SP/0210-1041) [09403306] **4949**

CONCILIUM (PARIS, FRANCE) (FR) [08570770] **5028**

CONCILIUM TRIDENTINUM (GW) **5028**

CONCISE STATISTICAL YEARBOOK OF POLAND (PL) [04999721] **5325**

CONCORD BUSINESS (US) **659**

CONCORD JOURNAL (US) [19985913] **5688**

CONCORD MONITOR (CONCORD, N.H. : 1970) (US) [10828908] **5708**

CONCORD REVIEW, THE (US/0895-0539) [16415030] **2614**

CONCORDES (EQUIPE DE FOOTBALL) See PROSPECTUS - CONCORDES **4913**

CONCORDES (FOOTBALL TEAM) See GUIDE MEDIA - CONCORDES **4897**

CONCORDIA COMMENTATOR (US/0162-7929) [04232555] **4949, 4828**

CONCORDIA HISTORICAL INSTITUTE See CONCORDIA HISTORICAL INSTITUTE QUARTERLY **5058**

CONCORDIA HISTORICAL INSTITUTE QUARTERLY (US/0010-5260) [01564643] **2729, 5058**

CONCORDIA JOURNAL (US/0145-7233) [02250319] **4949**

CONCORDIA PUBLISHING HOUSE See CPH COMMENTATOR **4813**

CONCORDIA SENTINEL, THE (US) [15152017] **5683**

CONCORDIA THEOLOGICAL QUARTERLY (US/0038-8610) [02813609] **4949**

CONCORDIA UNIVERSITY. LIBRARIES See LIBRARY OWNER'S MANUAL (1980) **3226**

CONCORDIA UNIVERSITY MAGAZINE (CN/0706-1005) [05761755] **1090**

CONCORDIAN, THE (US) [01564648] **1091**

CONCOURS LITTERAIRE (CN/0822-546X) [10199152] **3377**

CONCOURS MEDICAL (FR/0010-5309) [01564649] **3568**

CONCRETE ABSTRACTS (US/0045-8007) [02239468] **608, 2021, 2003**

CONCRETE FORUM (UK) **608**

CONCRETE HERALD, THE (US) [14574917] **5760**

CONCRETE INDUSTRY BULLETIN (US/0010-535X) [03465943] **608**

CONCRETE INTERNATIONAL (US/0162-4075) [04163061] **608**

CONCRETE INTERNATIONAL (US) [22789332] **608**

CONCRETE JOHANNESBURG (SA/0379-9824) [I03799824] **608**

CONCRETE LIBRARY INTERNATIONAL / JAPAN SOCIETY OF CIVIL ENGINEERS (JA) [12645293] **2021**

CONCRETE (LONDON) (UK/0010-5317) [01564651] **2021**

CONCRETE PIPE INDUSTRY STATISTICS (US/0360-2877) [02243705] **608, 632**

CONCRETE PIPE NEWS (US) [01564657] **608**

CONCRETE PLANT AND PRODUCTION (UK/0264-0236) [09360479] **608**

CONCRETE PRODUCTS (1975) (US/0010-5368) [05366114] **608**

CONCRETE PRODUCTS MANUFACTURERS (PRELIMINARY ED.) (CN/0708-6199) [05072353] **3477**

CONCRETE PUMPING (US) **608**

CONCRETE QUARTERLY **CEASED.** (UK/0010-5376) [03383021] **608**

CONCRETE ROADS (JA) **608**

CONCRETE ... SOURCEBOOK (US/0749-9191) [11164222] **1969**

CONCRETE TECHNOLOGY TODAY (US) 2021, **608**

CONCRETE TRADER See ABERDEEN'S CONCRETE TRADER **597**

CONCRETE TRADER, THE (US/1040-5321) [18441149] **608**

CONCRETE YEAR BOOK, THE (UK/0069-8288) [05042145] **608**

CONCURRENCY (CHICHESTER, ENGLAND) (UK/1040-3108) [18371988] **1180**

●CONCURRENT ENGINEERING : RESEARCH AND APPLICATIONS (UK/1063-293X) [25961600] **1969**

CONDE NAST'S TRAVELER (US/0893-9683) [15716404] **5466**

CONDEMNATION PROCEDURES AND TECHNIQUES, FORMS (US) [01764479] **3140**

CONDENSED CPA TAX REVIEW (US/0192-3854) [04998687] **741, 2955**

CONDENSED MATTER AND MATERIALS COMMUNICATIONS (US/1067-6147) [27313254] **1041, 1031**

CONDENSED MATTER NEWS (US/1056-7046) [23824202] **4401**

CONDENSED MATTER THEORIES (US/0893-861X) [20866033] **4401**

CONDENSER (TONGAAT, SOUTH AFRICA) (SA) [07695438] **659**

CONDITION MONITOR (UK/0268-8050) [26471520] **2112**

CONDITION MONITORING AND DIAGNOSTIC TECHNOLOGY (UK) [I09577661] **1969**

CONDITION OF EDUCATION, THE (US/0098-4752) [02241465] **1733**

CONDITIONING FOR CYCLING **CEASED.** (US/1057-6908) [24097649] **4891**

CONDITIONS DE LOGEMENT DES MENAGES EN ... / REPUBLIQUE FRANCAISE, MINISTERE DE L'ECONOMIE ET DES FINANCES, INSTITUT NATIONAL DE LA STATISTIQUE ET DES ETUDES ECONOMIQUES, LES (FR) [11076790] **2819**

CONDITIONS DE TRAVAIL CONTENUES DANS LES CONVENTIONS COLLECTIVES AU QUEBEC (CN/0228-0922) [10534301] **1661**

CONDITIONS DE TRAVAIL / MINISTERE DU TRAVAIL, DE L'EMPLOI ET DE LA FORMATION PROFESSIONNELLE, CONSEIL SUPERIEUR DE LA PREVENTION DES RISQUES PROFESSIONNELS (FR) [20957591] **1661**

CONDITIONS OF WORK DIGEST (SZ/0257-3512) [14351500] **1661**

CONDIZIONAMENTO DELL'ARIA See CONDIZIONAMENTO DELL'ARIA, RISCALDAMENTO, REFRIGERAZIONE **2604**

CONDIZIONAMENTO DELL'ARIA, RISCALDAMENTO, REFRIGERAZIONE (IT/0373-7772) [08244374] **2604**

CONDO SALES REPORT (US/8750-1236) [11005294] **4836**

●CONDO VACATIONING (US/1062-9653) [25820782] **4849**

CONDOMINIUM LAW AND PRACTICE, FORMS (US) [01764480] **3140**

CONDOMINIUM LIVING OF FLORIDA See COMMUNITY LIVING OF FLORIDA **4639**

CONDOMINIUM (TORONTO. 1989) (CN/0849-6714) [21486688] **4836**

CONDOMINIUM WORLD (US/0095-487X) [01798105] **2819**

CONDON LECTURES (US/0069-8296) [01564660] **1818**

CONDOR (LOS ANGELES, CALIF.), THE (US/0010-5422) [06135996] **5617**

CONDUCTEUR AVERTI (CN/0228-9083) [08143603] **5412**

CONEJO VALLEY BUSINESS (US/0364-8230) [02677117] **659**

CONEXION (UY) [26707431] **1470**

CONFECTIE (NE/0010-5449) [01794881] **5349, 1602**

CONFECTIE & TRICOTAGE See CONTEXT MAGAZINE **1083**

CONFECTION 2000 NOUVELLES TECHNIQUES DE L'HABILLEMENT (FR/0245-5781) [I02455781] **1083**

CONFECTIONER (1989), THE (US/1047-8345) [20790302] **2332**

CONFECTIONERY PRODUCTION (UK/0010-5473) [04293542] **2332**

CONFECTIONNEURS A FORFAIT DU QUEBEC, LES (CN/1187-5879) [25468468] **1602**

CONFEDERACION COLOMBIANA DE CAMARAS DE COMERCIO See INDICADORES ECONOMICOS **790**

CONFEDERACION DE CAMARAS INDUSTRIALES (MX) [03019312] **1552**

CONFEDERACION DE CAMARAS INDUSTRIALES DE LOS ESTADOS UNIDOS MEX See CONFEDERACION DE CAMARAS INDUSTRIALES **1552**

CONFEDERACION ESPANOLA DE CAJAS DE AHORROS. DIRECCION DE ESTUDIOS SOCIALES See COMENTARIO SOCIOLOGICO **5242**

CONFEDERACION GENERAL DE LA INDUSTRIA See MEMORIA Y BALANCE GENERAL **1574**

CONFEDERATE CHRONICLES OF TENNESSEE (US/0895-9455) [15694612] **2729**

CONFEDERATE HISTORICAL INSTITUTE JOURNAL (US/0734-3671) [07377314] **2614**

CONFEDERATE VETERAN (MURFREESBORO, TENN.) (US/0890-2216) [12607022] **2729**

CONFEDERATION DES SYNDICATS NATIONAUX. CONGRES See PROCES-VERBAL DU CONGRES DE LA CSN (1978) **1703**

CONFEDERATION FRANCAISE DEMOCRATIQUE DU TRAVAIL See CFDT SYNDICALISME HEBDO **1659**

CONFEDERATION FRANCAISE DEMOCRATIQUE DU TRAVAIL See CFDT MAGAZINE **1659**

CONFEDERATION FRANCAISE DEMOCRATIQUE DU TRAVAIL See CADRES CFDT **1657**

CONFEDERATION OF AUSTRALIAN CRITICAL CARE NURSES JOURNAL See AUSTRALIAN CRITICAL CARE : OFFICIAL JOURNAL OF THE CONFEDERATION OF AUSTRALIAN CRITICAL CARE NURSES **3851**

CONFEDERATION OF BRITISH INDUSTRY See CBI EDUCATION & TRAINING BULLETIN **1912**

CONFEDERAZIONE GENERALE DELL'INDUSTRIA ITALIANA See COLLANA DI STUDI E DOCUMENTAZIONE **1602**

CONFEDERAZIONE GENERALE DELL'INDUSTRIA ITALIANA. DIREZIONE CENTRALE RAPPORTI INTERNI See GUIDE ORGANIZZATIVA / CONFINDUSTRIA, DIREZIONE CENTRALE RAPPORTI INTERNI **1608**

CONFERENCE & COMMON ROOM (UK/0265-4458) [I02654458] **1733**

CONFERENCE & INCENTIVE TRAVEL (UK/0965-125X) [I0965125X] **5467**

CONFERENCE AND WORKSHOP SERIES - QUEENSLAND DEPARTMENT OF PRIMARY INDUSTRIES (AT/0728-067X) [I0728067X] **1602**

CONFERENCE - AUSTRALASIAN CORROSION ASSOCIATION (AT/0729-2341) [08746398] **2011**

CONFERENCE BLUE BOOK (UK/0260-2431) [I02602431] **5467**

CONFERENCE BLUE BOOK (UK) **5467, 2804**

CONFERENCE BOARD See ANNUAL REPORT / THE CONFERENCE BOARD **1462**

CONFERENCE BOARD See TOP EXECUTIVE COMPENSATION **716**

CONFERENCE BOARD See QUARTERLY BUSINESS REVIEW **706**

CONFERENCE BOARD BRIEFING See CONFERENCE BOARD'S MEMBERSHIP UPDATE, THE **864**

CONFERENCE BOARD BRIEFING, THE (US/0899-6741) [18180780] **864**

CONFERENCE BOARD. MONTHLY BUSINESS See QUARTERLY BUSINESS REVIEW **706**

CONFERENCE BOARD OF THE ASSOCIATED RESEARCH COUNCILS. COMMITTEE ON INTERNATIONAL EXCHANGE OF PERSONS See UNITED STATES GOVERNMENT GRANTS UNDER THE FULBRIGHT-HAYS ACT : UNIVERSITY LECTURING, ADVANCED RESEARCH **4692**

CONFERENCE BOARD OF THE MATHEMATICAL SCIENCES See CBMS-NSF REGIONAL CONFERENCE SERIES IN APPLIED MATHEMATICS **3499**

●CONFERENCE BOARD'S MEMBERSHIP UPDATE, THE (US/1072-0235) [28865433] **864**

CONFERENCE BRIEFS - UNITED STATES. NATIONAL BUREAU OF STANDARDS (US) [03455486] **5096**

CONFERENCE FOR MUNICIPAL CLERKS, RUTGERS UNIVERSITY See PROCEEDINGS OF THE ANNUAL CONFERENCE FOR MUNICIPAL CLERKS **4675**

CONFERENCE GREEN BOOK (UK) [I02602199] **5467, 2804**

CONFERENCE - INTERNATIONAL SOLAR ENERGY SOCIETY UK SECTION (UK/0306-7874) [10972148] **295, 1936**

CONFERENCE NOTES - AMERICAN INDUSTRIAL DEVELOPMENT COUNCIL, INC (US/0195-5942) [05452322] **1602**

CONFERENCE OF CONSULTING ACTUARIES. MEETING See PROCEEDINGS / CONFERENCE OF CONSULTING ACTUARIES, THE **2890**

CONFERENCE OF GUIDANCE PERSONNEL IN OCCUPATIONAL EDUCATION See PROCEEDINGS, ANNUAL CONFERENCE OF GUIDANCE PERSONNEL IN OCCUPATIONAL EDUCATION **1915**

CONFERENCE OF MENNONITES IN CANADA See CMC YEARBOOK **5058**

CONFERENCE OF PRESIDING OFFICERS AND CLERKS OF THE PARLIAMENTS OF AUSTRALIA, FIJI, NAURU, PAPUA NEW GUINEA AND WESTERN SAMOA (AT/0311-9513) [02239888] **4640**

CONFERENCE ON APPLIED CRYSTALLOGRAPHY. PROCEEDINGS (PL/0208-8584) [08179214] **1031**

CONFERENCE ON CLAY MINERALOGY AND PETROLOGY (XR) [06831281] **1458, 1439**

CONFERENCE ON DATA SYSTEMS LANGUAGES. PROGRAMMING LANGUAGE COMMITTEE See CODASYL COBOL JOURNAL OF DEVELOPMENT **1278**

CONFERENCE ON PRECISION ELECTROMAGNETIC MEASUREMENT (US) **4401**

CONFERENCE ON RELIABILITY AND MAINTAINABILITY (US) **1969**

CONFERENCE ON TAX PLANNING FOR 501(C)(3) ORGANIZATIONS : [PROCEEDINGS] / NEW YORK UNIVERSITY (US) [19987356] **4718**

CONFERENCE PAPER [PREPRINTS] (US) [02751541] **2039**

CONFERENCE PAPERS ANNUAL INDEX (US/0194-0546) [05292752] **5096**

CONFERENCE PAPERS INDEX (US/0162-704X) [03837820] 1969, **5096**

CONFERENCE PAPERS QUARTERLY INDEX (US/0194-0740) [05321732] **414**

CONFERENCE PROCEEDINGS / ANNUAL ADVANCED RESEARCH TECHNIQUES FORUM (US/1052-6838) [22349841] **829**

CONFERENCE PROCEEDINGS / ANTEC (US) [16638617] 1969, **4454**

CONFERENCE PROCEEDINGS (ARTHRITIS AND RHEUMATISM COUNCIL FOR RESEARCH IN GREAT BRITAIN AND THE COMMONWEALTH) (UK) [19347762] **3804**

CONFERENCE PROCEEDINGS / AUTOFACT (US/1063-5432) [11037701] **3477**

CONFERENCE PROCEEDINGS / CANADIAN MATHEMATICAL SOCIETY (CN/0731-1036) [08117734] **3502**

CONFERENCE PROCEEDINGS / IEEE INTERNATIONAL CONFERENCE ON SYSTEMS, MAN, AND CYBERNETICS (US/1062-922X) [21479523] **1250**

CONFERENCE PROCEEDINGS - IEEE PACIFIC RIM CONFERENCE ON COMMUNICATIONS, COMPUTERS AND SIGNAL PROCESSING (US/0893-4266) [15515609] **1152**

CONFERENCE PROCEEDINGS / INSTITUTE OF MARINE ENGINEERS (UK) 5448, **1969**

CONFERENCE PROCEEDINGS - INTERNATIONAL SOCIETY FOR MUSIC EDUCATION (UK) 1733, **4111**

CONFERENCE PROCEEDINGS / ISTFA ..., INTERNATIONAL SYMPOSIUM FOR TESTING AND FAILURE ANALYSIS (US) [19029350] **2039**

CONFERENCE PROCEEDINGS / LOS ALAMOS SCIENTIFIC LABORATORY (US/0731-308X) [08152134] **5096**

CONFERENCE PROCEEDINGS - SOCIETY FOR THE ADVANCEMENT OF GIFTED EDUCATION. CONFERENCE (CN/1184-8448) [24265940] **1877**

CONFERENCE PROCEEDINGS - WESTERN FORESTRY COUNCIL (U.S.) CONFERENCE (US/0749-2111) [10297291] **2378**

CONFERENCE PUBLICATIONS OF THE INSTITUTE OF MECHANICAL ENGINEERS (US) **2112**

CONFERENCE RECORD / ASILOMAR CONFERENCE ON SIGNALS, SYSTEMS & COMPUTERS (US/1058-6393) [16620517] **2039**

CONFERENCE RECORD / IEEE GLOBAL TELECOMMUNICATIONS CONFERENCE & EXHIBITION (US/1054-5921) [19080921] **1152**

CONFERENCE RECORD - IEEE INTERNATIONAL CONFERENCE ON COMMUNICATIONS (US/1044-4556) [10771622] **1152**

CONFERENCE RECORD / IEEE MILITARY COMMUNICATIONS CONFERENCE (US) [16709928] **4039**

CONFERENCE RECORD - INDUSTRIAL & COMMERCIAL POWER SYSTEM TECHNICAL CONFERENCE (US) [07014868] 2039, **2097**

CONFERENCE RECORD OF ... ANNUAL PULP AND PAPER INDUSTRY TECHNICAL CONFERENCE (US/1041-7249) [14171282] **4233**

CONFERENCE RECORD OF IEEE INTERNATIONAL SYMPOSIUM ON ELECTRICAL INSULATION (US/0164-2006) [04610739] **2039**

CONFERENCE RECORD OF ... INTERNATIONAL DISPLAY RESEARCH CONFERENCE (US) [09037184] **2039**

CONFERENCE RECORD OF THE ... ANNUAL ACM SYMPOSIUM ON PRINCIPLES OF PROGRAMMING LANGUAGES (US/0730-8566) [09940867] **1279**

CONFERENCE RECORD OF THE ... IEEE PHOTOVOLTAIC SPECIALISTS CONFERENCE (US/0160-8371) [08145880] **2039**

CONFERENCE RELIGIEUSE CANADIENNE See BULLETIN - CONFERENCE RELIGIEUSE CANADIENNE **4940**

CONFERENCE REPORT ON COTTON INSECT RESEARCH AND CONTROL See ANNUAL CONFERENCE REPORT ON COTTON INSECT RESEARCH AND CONTROL **4244**

CONFERENCE REPORT - PRIMARY ELEMENTARY TEACHERS ASSOCIATION (CN/0826-516X) [11377388] **1862**

CONFERENCE REPORTS (UK) [07538989] **507**

CONFERENCE REPORTS : ENGINEERING, TECHNOLOGY AND APPLIED SCIENCES (UK) [03435439] **2021**

CONFERENCE SERIES - AUSTRALASIAN INSTITUTE OF MINING AND METALLURGY (AT/0728-7178) [05273919] 4000, **2138**

CONFERENCE SERIES / AUSTRALIAN WATER RESOURCES COUNCIL (AT/0725-4695) [07664316] **5532**

CONFERENCE SERIES - FEDERAL RESERVE BANK OF BOSTON (US/0361-8714) [01355692] **784**

CONFERENCE SUMMARY REPORT - AVIATION REVIEW CONFERENCE (US/0360-5175) [02243908] **17**

CONFERENCE TRANSACTIONS - BRITISH ARCHAEOLOGICAL ASSOCIATION (UK/0144-0179) [07748317] **266**

CONFERENCE WITH THE DIRECTORS OF THE NATIONAL RECLAMATION ASSOCIATION (US/0499-0021) [01183623] **2088**

CONFERENCES & EXHIBITIONS INTERNATIONAL (UK/0260-8316) [08268806] **5096**

CONFERENCES D'ACTUALITES SCIENTIFIQUES ET INDUSTRIELLES See ACTUALITES SCIENTIFIQUES ET INDUSTRIELLES **5080**

CONFERENCES + EXHIBITIONS See CONFERENCES & EXHIBITIONS INTERNATIONAL **5096**

CONFERENCIA NACIONAL DOS BISPOS DO BRASIL. SECRETARIADO REGIONAL LESTE 2 See BOLETIM INFORMATIVO - CONFERENCIA NACIONAL DOS BISPOS DO BRASIL, SECRETARIADO REGIONAL LESTE 2 **5024**

CONFERENCIER (MONTREAL) **CEASED.** (CN/0822-4137) [09816146] **4640**

CONFERENZE DEL SEMINARIO DI MATEMATICA DELL'UNIVERSITA DI BARI (IT/0374-2113) [02541215] **3502**

CONFETTI (ELK GROVE VILLAGE, ILL.) **CEASED.** (US/0897-5973) [17560221] **1109**

CONFEZIONE (IT/0393-4888) [I03934888] **5553**

CONFIDENCES (MONTREAL. 1972) (CN/0317-3607) [02248113] **5187**

CONFIDENCIAL ECONOMICO NE See CONFIDENCIAL ECONOMICO NORDESTE **1470**

CONFIDENCIAL ECONOMICO NORDESTE (BL) [05667338] 4469, **1470**

CONFIDENTIAL BULLETIN (HOOSIER STATE PRESS ASSOCIATION) See INDIANA PUBLISHER, THE **4815**

CONFIDENTIAL REPORT FOR ATTORNEYS (US/0890-3034) [14199897] **2955**

CONFIDENTIAL, REPORT FROM ZURICH (US/0885-9043) [12774481] **1470**

CONFIDENZE (IT) **5553**

●CONFIGURATIONS (BALTIMORE, MD.) (US/1063-1801) [25911023] **5096**

CONFINIA CEPHALALGICA (IT/1122-0279) [I11220279] **3568**

CONFIRMADO See ANALISIS-CONFIRMADO **2551**

CONFLICT See STUDIES IN CONFLICT AND TERRORISM **5263**

CONFLICT AND CONSCIOUSNESS (US/0899-9910) [18283549] **5242**

CONFLICT INTERNATIONAL (UK/0963-1674) [I09631674] **4518**

CONFLICT MANAGEMENT AND PEACE SCIENCE (US/0738-8942) [08055590] **4518**

CONFLICT QUARTERLY (CN/0227-1311) [07817333] **4518**

CONFLICT STUDIES (UK/0069-8792) [03112088] **4518**

CONFLICTS OF LAW (US/0099-0418) [02246632] **2955**

CONFLUENCE (BELPRE, OHIO) (US/1055-7334) [23283350] **3340**

CONFLUENCE (FORT SIMPSON) (CN/0228-0515) [06959015] **5782**

CONFLUENCE (WASHINGTON) (US/0090-3175) [01784929] **1733**

CONFLUENCIA (BL) [24992921] **3377**

CONFLUENCIA (GREELEY, COLO.) (US/0888-6091) [13657913] **5196**

CONFLUENTS (FR/0154-5639) [14970888] **2614**

CONFORT MENAGER (FR/0761-5779) [I07615779] **758**

CONFORTIQUE MAGAZINE (FR) **2486**

CONFRATERNITAS (TORONTO) (CN/1180-0682) [24368318] **4949**

CONFRONTACIONES PSIQUIATRICAS (SP) **3923**

CONFRONTATION/CHANGE LITERARY REVIEW (US/0363-9460) [02547354] **5196**

CONFRONTATION (SOUTHAMPTON, N.Y.) (US/0010-5716) [00876671] **3377**

CONFRONTATIONS PSYCHIATRIQUES PARIS (FR/0153-9329) [I01539329] **3923**

CONFRONTI (IT) **3340**

CONFRONTI (IT) **4950**

CONFRUCTA **CEASED.** (GW/0177-7440) [02573309] **2366**

CONFRUCTA (GW/0016-2213) [09370259] **2332**

CONGENITAL ANOMALIES (JA/0914-3505) [21439506] **543**

CONGENITAL MALFORMATIONS SURVEILLANCE (US/0092-5594) [01792916] **3759**

CONGIUNTURA ESTERA (IT) [06589662] **1602**

CONGIUNTURA ITALIANA (IT/0010-5759) [03434981] **1552**

CONGO (BRAZZAVILLE) See JOURNAL OFFICIEL DE LA REPUBLIQUE POPULAIRE DU CONGO **2990**

CONGO (BRAZZAVILLE). DIRECTION DE LA STATISTIQUE ET DE LA COMPTABILITE ECONOMIQUE See BULLETIN MENSUEL DES STATISTIQUES - DIRECTION DE LA STATISTIQUE ET DE LA COMPTABILITE ECONOMIQUE (CONGO (BRAZZAVILLE)) **5324**

CONGO (BRAZZAVILLE). SERVICE DE LA STATISTIQUE. BULLETIN MENSUEL DE STATISTIQUE See BULLETIN MENSUEL DES STATISTIQUES - DIRECTION DE LA STATISTIQUE ET DE LA COMPTABILITE ECONOMIQUE (CONGO (BRAZZAVILLE)) **5324**

CONGREGATION, THE (US/0361-8862) [01564754] **5058**

CONGREGATIONAL JOURNAL **CEASED.** (US/0361-2376) [01990585] **5058**

CONGREGATIONAL LIBRARY (BOSTON, MASS.) See BULLETIN OF THE CONGREGATIONAL LIBRARY **3198**

CONGREGATIONALIST (BELOIT), THE (US/0010-5856) [02446149] **4950**

CONGREGATIONS ALBAN JOURNAL (US) **4950**

CONGRES (FR) **4640**

CONGRES ANNUEL - CONSEIL CANADIEN DA LA SECURITE (CN/0700-6659) [03348601] **4772**

CONGRES ARCHEOLOGIQUE DE FRANCE (FR/0069-8881) [06079331] **266**

CONGRES - ASSOCIATION DE PLANIFICATION FISCALE ET FINANCIERE (CN/0848-2489) [20777788] **3118**

CONGRES DES RELATIONS INDUSTRIELLES DE L'UNIVERSITE LAVAL See CONGRES DES RELATIONS INDUSTRIELLES DE L'UNIVERSITE LAVAL **1661**

CONGRES DES RELATIONS INDUSTRIELLES DE L'UNIVERSITE LAVAL (CN/0319-2482) [02670900] **1661**

CONGRES DU TRAVAIL DU CANADA See MEMOIRE PRESENTE AU GOUVERNEMENT DU CANADA PAR LE CONGRES DU TRAVAIL DU CANADA **1618**

CONGRES DU TRAVAIL DU CANADA. ASSEMBLEE STATUTAIRE See PROCES-VERBAL - CONGRES DU TRAVAIL DU CANADA, ASSEMBLEE STATUTAIRE **1703**

CONGRES - ENTRAIDE MISSIONNAIRE (CN/0821-1752) [09766468] **4950**

CONGRES JUIF CANADIEN RAPPORT INTERIMAIRE (CN/0710-0418) [08078858] **2258**

CONGRES NATIONAL DES SOCIETES SAVANTES See ACTES DU ... CONGRES NATIONAL DES SOCIETES SAVANTES. SECTION DES SCIENCES **5080**

CONGRESISTA, EL (DR) [03262577] **4640**

CONGRESO INTERNACIONAL DE LITERATURA IBEROAMERICANA See MEMORIA DEL CONGRESO INTERNACIONAL DE LITERATURA IBEROAMERICANA **3347**

CONGRESS AND HEALTH (US/0195-9840) [05671485] 4640, **4772**

CONGRESS AND THE NATION (US/1047-1324) [01421109] 2955, **4469**

CONGRESS & THE PRESIDENCY (US/0734-3469) [08373939] **4469**

CONGRESS AT YOUR FINGERTIPS (US) **4640**

CONGRESS — Alphabetical Title Index

CONGRESS BULLETIN - INDIAN NATIONAL CONGRESS (II/0019-6010) [01681112] **2649**

CONGRESS HIGHLIGHTS (US) [13686225] **4706**

CONGRESS IN PRINT (US/0193-4627) [05259558] **4640**

CONGRESS MARCHES AHEAD (II/0376-5776) [01790629] **4640**

CONGRESS MONTHLY (1985) (US/0887-0764) [12433266] **2258**

CONGRESS NEWS (SPRINGFIELD, ILL.) *See* DISPATCH CONGRESS NEWS **2731**

CONGRESS OF ASTROLOGICAL ORGANIZATIONS *See* CAO TIMES **390**

CONGRESS OF MICRONESIA BIBLIOGRAPHY (TI) [02805267] **4697**

CONGRESS OF RACIAL EQUALITY *See* CORE **4506**

CONGRESS OF THE UNIVERSITIES OF THE COMMONWEALTH *See* REPORT OF PROCEEDINGS OF THE CONGRESS OF THE UNIVERSITIES OF THE COMMONWEALTH **1844**

CONGRESS ON RESEARCH IN DANCE *See* CORD NEWSLETTER **1311**

CONGRESS ... PROCEEDINGS - FEDERATION DES SPORTS DU CANADA (CN/0229-5156) [08555835] **4891**

CONGRESS PUBLICATIONS (SZ) **2021**

CONGRESS REPORT / CONGRESS (SZ) [18826345] **2021**

CONGRESSIONAL AWARD FOUNDATION (U.S.) *See* ANNUAL REPORT - CONGRESSIONAL AWARD FOUNDATION (U.S.) **4627**

CONGRESSIONAL BUDGET REQUEST (US/0198-0351) [04837750] **1936**

CONGRESSIONAL DIGEST, THE (US/0010-5899) [06183469] **4469**

CONGRESSIONAL DISTRICT ATLAS (US/0090-8061) [01768235] 4640, **2559**

CONGRESSIONAL DISTRICT BUSINESS PATTERNS (US/0275-746X) [07227812] 659, **1470**

CONGRESSIONAL INFORMATION BUREAU (US/1062-6506) [19454951] **4175**

CONGRESSIONAL INFORMATION SERVICE *See* CIS INDEX TO PUBLICATIONS OF THE UNITED STATES CONGRESS **4697**

CONGRESSIONAL INSIGHT *CEASED.* (US/0196-0784) [03460202] **4469**

CONGRESSIONAL MASTERFILE 2 (US/1064-4679) [20137004] 4640, **2955**

CONGRESSIONAL PRESENTATION, FISCAL YEAR *CEASED.* (US/0276-6469) [07126125] **4518**

CONGRESSIONAL PRESENTATION / UNITED STATES TRADE AND DEVELOPMENT PROGRAM (US/0742-3012) [09617968] **1552**

CONGRESSIONAL QUARTERLY ALMANAC (US/0095-6007) [01564784] 4469, **4640**

CONGRESSIONAL QUARTERLY WEEKLY REPORT (US/0010-5910) [02103060] **4469**

CONGRESSIONAL QUARTERLY'S POLITICS IN AMERICA (US/1064-6809) [20310704] **4469**

CONGRESSIONAL RECORD (DAILY ED.) *CEASED.* (US/0363-7239) [02437919] 4640, **2955**

CONGRESSIONAL RECORD INDEX (US/0364-7544) [02428236] 4640, **2955**

CONGRESSIONAL RECORD (PERMANENT ED.) (US/0883-1947) [05058415] **2955**

CONGRESSIONAL RECORD [COMPUTER FILE] : PROCEEDINGS AND DEBATES OF THE ... CONGRESS (US) [22840665] 4640, **2955**

CONGRESSIONAL STAFF DIRECTORY (US/0589-3178) [01239097] **4640**

CONGRESSIONAL STAFF DIRECTORY. ADVANCE LOCATOR FOR CAPITOL HILL (US/0069-8938) [02652345] **4640**

CONGRESSIONAL YELLOW BOOK (QUARTERLY ED.) (US/0191-1422) [03838743] 4640, **1924**

CONGRESSO NACIONAL DE PREVENCAO DE ACIDENTES DO TRABALHO *See* ANAIS DO CONPAT **2858**

CONGRESSO (ROME, ITALY) (IT) [19796820] **4640**

CONGRESSO (TORONTO) (CN/0705-6885) [04098015] **2729**

CONGRESSUS NUMERANTIUM (CN/0384-9864) [08270976] **3502**

CONIGLICOLTURA (IT/0010-5929) [03720252] **209**

CONIMBRIGA (PO) [02259726] **2684**

CONJOINT DIRECTORY OF AMERICAN ACADEMY OF OTOLARYNGOLOGY-HEAD AND NECK SURGERY, AND AMERICAN ACADEMY OF FACIAL PLASTIC AND RECONSTRUCTIVE SURGERY, AND AMERICAN NEUROTOLOGY SOCIETY, AND AMERICAN RHINOLOGIC SOCIETY, AND AMERICAN SOCIETY OF OPHTHALMOLOGIC AND OTOLARYNGOLOGIC ALLERGY (US/0734-0710) [08659455] 3963, **3887**

CONJONCTION (HT/0304-5757) [03009058] **2729**

CONJONCTURE (FR) [06269415] **1552**

CONJONCTURE; BULLETIN D'INFORMATION ECONOMIQUE (TI) [01798964] **1552**

CONJONCTURE CANADIENNE (CN/0834-3152) [16458639] **784**

CONJONCTURE DES AFFAIRES (CN/0714-7635) [09387063] **1470**

CONJONCTURE ET PREVISION / REPUBLIQUE FRANCAISE, MINISTERE DE L'ECONOMIE, DES FINANCES ET DU BUDGET (FR/1140-5228) [23746185] **1552**

CONJONCTURES (MONTREAL) (CN/0838-8881) [18314922] **5242**

CONJUNCTIONS (NEW YORK, N.Y.) (US/0278-2324) [07753878] **3340**

CONJUNCTUURTEST (NL/0166-9087) [06382555] **1552**

CONJUNTURA AGRICOLA (BL) [02244553] **76**

CONJUNTURA ECONOMICA (BL/0010-5945) [16015370] 784, **1471**

CONJUNTURA SOCIAL (BL) [06720587] **5280**

CONKLIN'S GUIDE (US/1045-5175) [20135600] **317**

CONN-CEPT VIII. CONNECTICUT'S PROGRAMMING FOR THE GIFTED AND TALENTED : A SAMPLE LIST AND DIRECTORY OF STATE APPROVED PROGRAMS FOR THE GIFTED AND TALENTED (US) [05638849] **1877**

CONN CORPORATION *See* CONNCHORD **4111**

CONNAISSANCE DE LA CHASSE (FR) [03568614] **4891**

CONNAISSANCE DE LA VIGNE ET DU VIN *See* JOURNAL INTERNATIONAL DES SCIENCES DE LA VIGNE ET DU VIN **175**

CONNAISSANCE DE L'EURE (FR/1142-5067) [11425067] **2845**

CONNAISSANCE DES ARTS, PLAISIR DE FRANCE (FR/0395-5907) [06406926] **348**

CONNAISSANCE DES TEMPS (FR/0181-3048) [11800430] **4175**

CONNAISSANCE ET VIE (CN/0709-9347) [06264948] **2614**

CONNAISSANCEG DES PERES DE L'EGGLISE (FR) **4950**

CONNAISSONS NOS VOISINS (CN/0713-3111) [08818734] **5467**

CONNCHORD (US/0010-6038) [01777466] **4111**

CONNEAUTVILLE COURIER (CONNEAUTVILLE, PA. : 1871) (US/8750-0590) [10209112] **5735**

CONNECT (UK) [21967831] **1180**

●CONNECT (ANN ARBOR, MICH.) (US/1070-0994) [28278056] **1180**

CONNECT (BRATTLEBORO, VT.) (US/1041-682X) [18824673] **1733**

CONNECT. BRUNSWICK (AT/0158-4995) [01584995] **1733**

CONNECT (SUISUN, CALIF.) *CEASED.* (US/0896-0666) [16899620] **3203**

CONNECT: UNESCO-UNEP ENVIRONMENTAL EDUCATION NEWSLETTER (FR/0250-4499) [02629321] **2163**

CONNECTICARD ANNUAL STATISTICAL REPORT (US) [10468238] 3204, **3258**

CONNECTICUT *See* WORKERS' COMPENSATION LAW OF THE STATE OF CONNECTICUT **3155**

CONNECTICUT *See* PUBLIC AND SPECIAL ACTS **3032**

CONNECTICUT *See* CONNECTICUT MAGAZINE (FAIRFIELD, CONN.) **2531**

CONNECTICUT *See* GENERAL STATUTES OF CONNECTICUT **2973**

CONNECTICUT *See* LAWS RELATING TO STATE BANKS AND TRUST COMPANIES, SAVINGS BANKS, INDUSTRIAL BANKS, SAVINGS BANK LIFE INSURANCE, BUILDING OR SAVINGS AND LOAN ASSOCIATIONS **3087**

CONNECTICUT *See* STATUTES GOVERNING MUNICIPAL PLANNING AND ZONING **3059**

CONNECTICUT ACADEMY OF ARTS AND SCIENCES *See* MEMOIRS OF THE CONNECTICUT ACADEMY OF ARTS AND SCIENCES **2850**

CONNECTICUT. ADVISORY COUNCIL ON VOCATIONAL AND CAREER EDUCATION *See* VOCATIONAL EDUCATION EVALUATION REPORT **1917**

CONNECTICUT AIR QUALITY SUMMARY (US/0147-3557) [03146104] **2226**

CONNECTICUT ANCESTRY (US/0197-2103) [04429325] **2444**

CONNECTICUT ANNUAL STATE PLAN FOR THE ADMINISTRATION OF VOCATIONAL EDUCATION : ACCOUNTABILITY REPORT (US) [05762534] **1912**

CONNECTICUT ANTIQUARIAN, THE *CEASED.* (US/0010-6054) [08932459] 250, **2729**

CONNECTICUT. APPELLATE COURT *See* CONNECTICUT APPELLATE REPORTS **2955**

CONNECTICUT APPELLATE REPORTS (US) [11168126] **2955**

CONNECTICUT AREA LABOR TRENDS IN EMPLOYMENT AND UNEMPLOYMENT *See* CONNECTICUT LABOR SITUATION / CONNECTICUT LABOR DEPARTMENT, EMPLOYMENT SECURITY DIVISION **1661**

CONNECTICUT ASSESSMENT OF EDUCATIONAL PROGRESS. ART AND MUSIC. / PREPARED FOR CONNECTICUT STATE DEPARTMENT OF EDUCATION, BUREAU OF RESEARCH, PLANNING, AND EVALUATION; PREPARED BY NATIONAL EVALUATION SYSTEMS, INC (US) [08684997] 4111, **348**

CONNECTICUT. AUDITORS OF PUBLIC ACCOUNTS *See* REPORT ON OFFICE OF THE LIEUTENANT GOVERNOR - CONNECTICUT **4682**

CONNECTICUT. AUDITORS OF PUBLIC ACCOUNTS *See* REPORT ON DEPARTMENT OF SOCIAL SERVICES **5305**

CONNECTICUT. AUDITORS OF PUBLIC ACCOUNTS *See* REPORT ON DEPARTMENT OF VETERANS' AFFAIRS FOR THE FISCAL YEARS ENDED JUNE 30 **4055**

CONNECTICUT. AUDITORS OF PUBLIC ACCOUNTS *See* REPORT ON STATE COMPTROLLER - CONNECTICUT **4746**

CONNECTICUT. AUDITORS OF PUBLIC ACCOUNTS *See* REPORT ON DEPARTMENT OF ECONOMIC DEVELOPMENT AND CONNECTICUT DEVELOPMENT AUTHORITY FOR FISCAL YEARS ENDED JUNE 30 ... **1581**

CONNECTICUT. AUDITORS OF PUBLIC ACCOUNTS *See* REPORT ON STATE ELECTIONS COMMISSION - CONNECTICUT **4682**

CONNECTICUT. AUDITORS PF PUBLIC ACCOUNTS *See* REPORT ON DEPARTMENT OF HEALTH, OFFICE OF MENTAL RETARDATION, NORTH CENTRAL REGIONAL CENTER **5305**

CONNECTICUT BAR JOURNAL (US/0010-6070) [01564848] **2955**

CONNECTICUT BEVERAGE JOURNAL (US/0744-1843) [08092038] **2366**

CONNECTICUT BEVERAGE JOURNAL AND BLUE BOOK *See* CONNECTICUT BEVERAGE JOURNAL **2366**

CONNECTICUT. BOARD OF EDUCATION *See* CONNECTICUT ANNUAL STATE PLAN FOR THE ADMINISTRATION OF VOCATIONAL EDUCATION : ACCOUNTABILITY REPORT **1912**

CONNECTICUT. BOARD OF EDUCATION *See* ANNUAL REPORT OF PROGRAMS AND EVALUATIONS OF THE CONNECTICUT STATE BOARD OF EDUCATION **1725**

CONNECTICUT. BUREAU OF COMMUNITY AND ADULT EDUCATION *See* CONNECTICUT STATE PLAN FOR CAREER EDUCATION **1912**

CONNECTICUT BUSINESS AND INDUSTRY ASSOCIATION *See* CBIA NEWS **656**

CONNECTICUT BUSINESS TIMES *See* BUSINESS TIMES (EAST HARTFORD, CONN.), THE **653**

CONNECTICUT. CIRCUIT COURT. APPELLATE DIVISION *See* CONNECTICUT CIRCUIT COURT REPORTS. CASES ARGUED AND DETERMINED IN THE APPELLATE DIVISION OF THE CIRCUIT COURT, AND MEMORANDA FILED IN THE CIRCUIT COURT OF THE STATE OF CONNECTICUT **3140**

CONNECTICUT CIRCUIT COURT REPORTS. CASES ARGUED AND DETERMINED IN THE APPELLATE DIVISION OF THE CIRCUIT COURT, AND MEMORANDA FILED IN THE CIRCUIT COURT OF THE STATE OF CONNECTICUT (US/0589-3577) [01564796] **3140**

CONNECTICUT COLLEGE ALUMNI MAGAZINE, THE (US) [03660843] **1101**

CONNECTICUT COLLEGE MAGAZINE (US/1060-5134) [25014599] **1091**

Alphabetical Title Index — CONNECTICUT

CONNECTICUT. COMMISSION FOR HIGHER EDUCATION See BUDGET RECOMMENDATIONS FOR THE CONNECTICUT SYSTEM OF HIGHER EDUCATION **1812**

CONNECTICUT. COMMISSION FOR HIGHER EDUCATION See COMPREHENSIVE FACILITIES INVENTORY REPORT (HARTFORD) **1818**

CONNECTICUT. COMMISSION ON HOSPITALS AND HEALTH CARE See ANNUAL REPORT TO THE GOVERNOR AND GENERAL ASSEMBLY - STATE OF CONNECTICUT, COMMISSION ON HOSPITALS & HEALTH CARE **3776**

CONNECTICUT. COUNCIL ON ENVIRONMENTAL QUALITY See CONNECTICUT ENVIRONMENT REVIEW : THE ANNUAL REPORT OF THE COUNCIL ON ENVIRONMENTAL QUALITY **2163**

CONNECTICUT CPA QUARTERLY *CEASED.* (US/0884-2817) [08381660] **741**

CONNECTICUT. DEPT. OF ADMINISTRATIVE SERVICES See CONNECTICUT DIGEST OF ADMINISTRATIVE REPORTS TO THE GOVERNOR **4469**

CONNECTICUT. DEPT. OF AGING See PROPOSED CONNECTICUT STATE PLAN ON AGING **5302**

CONNECTICUT. DEPT. OF CORRECTION See FIVE YEAR PLAN / CONNECTICUT DEPARTMENT OF CORRECTION **3164**

CONNECTICUT. DEPT. OF ENVIRONMENTAL PROTECTION See CONNECTICUT AIR QUALITY SUMMARY **2226**

CONNECTICUT. DEPT. OF HUMAN RESOURCES See CONNECTICUT TITLE XX COMPREHENSIVE ANNUAL SERVICES PROGRAM PLAN **5280**

CONNECTICUT. DEPT. OF TRANSPORTATION See CONNECTICUT MASTER TRANSPORTATION PLAN **5380**

CONNECTICUT. DEPT. OF TRANSPORTATION. OFFICE OF RESEARCH See SUMMARY OF ACTIVITIES, OFFICE OF RESEARCH **5393**

CONNECTICUT. DEPT. ON AGING See LEGISLATIVE SUMMARY - CONNECTICUT. DEPT. ON AGING **3002**

CONNECTICUT. DEPT. ON AGING See ANNUAL REPORT - DEPARTMENT ON AGING (CONNECTICUT) **5272**

CONNECTICUT DIGEST OF ADMINISTRATIVE REPORTS TO THE GOVERNOR (US/0277-5700) [06416994] **4469**

CONNECTICUT. DIVISION OF PUBLIC UTILITY CONTROL See REPORT OF THE DIVISION OF PUBLIC UTILITY CONTROL (CONNECTICUT) **4681**

CONNECTICUT ECONOMIC INDICATORS AND EMPLOYMENT, WAGES, HOURS IN CONNECTICUT See CONNECTICUT LABOR SITUATION / CONNECTICUT LABOR DEPARTMENT, EMPLOYMENT SECURITY DIVISION **1661**

CONNECTICUT EDUCATION ASSOCIATION See EDUCATIONAL FINANCE, CONNECTICUT **1863**

CONNECTICUT EDUCATION ASSOCIATION See LOCAL SCHOOL EXPENDITURES **1866**

CONNECTICUT EDUCATION DIRECTORY (US) [03582736] **1733**

●CONNECTICUT EMPLOYMENT LAW LETTER (US/1064-4903) [26294524] **3145**

CONNECTICUT. EMPLOYMENT SECURITY DIVISION. OFFICE OF RESEARCH AND INFORMATION See ANNUAL PLANNING INFORMATION FOR BRISTOL-NEW BRITAIN SERVICE DELIVERY AREA, PLANNING YEAR ... **1646**

CONNECTICUT ENGLISH JOURNAL (US/0893-0376) [03583095] **1891**

CONNECTICUT ENVIRONMENT *CEASED.* (US/1040-9203) [18575470] **2163**

CONNECTICUT ENVIRONMENT REVIEW : THE ANNUAL REPORT OF THE COUNCIL ON ENVIRONMENTAL QUALITY (US) [17930172] **2163**

●CONNECTICUT ENVIRONMENTAL COMPLIANCE UPDATE (US/1064-2382) [26238176] 2163, **2955**

CONNECTICUT FAMILY LAW CITATIONS : A REFERENCE GUIDE TO CONNECTICUT FAMILY LAW DECISIONS (US) [12959602] **3120**

CONNECTICUT FAMILY LAW JOURNAL, THE (US/0737-920X) [09469853] **3120**

CONNECTICUT FIRESIDE *CEASED.* (US/0300-8258) [01331167] **2531**

CONNECTICUT FOUNDATION DIRECTORY (US/0734-4694) [08250352] **4335**

CONNECTICUT. GENERAL ASSEMBLY. OFFICE OF FISCAL ANALYSIS See STATE BUDGET - OFFICE OF FISCAL ANALYSIS (HARTFORD) **4749**

CONNECTICUT. GENERAL ASSEMBLY. OFFICE OF LEGISLATIVE RESEARCH See SUMMARY OF PUBLIC ACTS (HARTFORD) **3061**

CONNECTICUT. GOVERNOR See GOVERNOR'S ... BUDGET IN-BRIEF **4729**

CONNECTICUT GREENHOUSE NEWSLETTER (US) [01182990] **2412**

CONNECTICUT. HEALTH AND EDUCATIONAL FACILITIES AUTHORITY See ANNUAL REPORT - STATE OF CONNECTICUT HEALTH & EDUCATIONAL FACILITIES AUTHORITY **3776**

CONNECTICUT HEALTH CARE (US/0889-8707) [09250841] **3778**

●CONNECTICUT HEALTH CARE IN PERSPECTIVE (US/1065-4097) [26604828] **4772**

CONNECTICUT HISTORICAL SOCIETY See ANNUAL REPORT OF THE CONNECTICUT HISTORICAL SOCIETY, THE **2720**

CONNECTICUT HISTORICAL SOCIETY BULLETIN, THE (US/0885-4831) [10104749] **2729**

CONNECTICUT HISTORY (US) [03723566] **2729**

CONNECTICUT IN PERSPECTIVE (US/1065-5360) [26628387] **5325**

CONNECTICUT INSURANCE LAW REVIEW, THE (US/0742-924X) [10446216] 2878, **2955**

CONNECTICUT JOURNAL OF INTERNATIONAL LAW (US/0897-1218) [13662858] **3126**

CONNECTICUT. JUDICIAL DEPT See BIENNIAL REPORT OF THE CONNECTICUT JUDICIAL DEPARTMENT **3139**

CONNECTICUT. JUDICIAL REVIEW COUNCIL See REPORT / CONNECTICUT, JUDICIAL REVIEW COUNCIL **3142**

CONNECTICUT JUSTICE COMMISSION See ANNUAL REPORT - CONNECTICUT JUSTICE COMMISSION **3157**

CONNECTICUT JUSTICE COMMISSION See FUNDING REPORT - CONNECTICUT JUSTICE COMMISSION **3165**

CONNECTICUT. LABOR DEPT See OCCUPATIONAL INJURIES AND ILLNESSES IN CONNECTICUT **2866**

CONNECTICUT LABOR SITUATION / CONNECTICUT LABOR DEPARTMENT, EMPLOYMENT SECURITY DIVISION (US/0414-5798) [03477321] **1661**

CONNECTICUT LAW JOURNAL (US/8750-0973) [01564860] **2955**

CONNECTICUT LAW REVIEW (US/0010-6151) [01564861] **2955**

CONNECTICUT LAW TRIBUNE, THE (US/0198-0289) [06157735] **2955**

CONNECTICUT LEAGUE OF HISTORICAL SOCIETIES, INC See LEAGUE BULLETIN **2744**

CONNECTICUT LEGAL DIRECTORY, THE (US/0195-6809) [04911532] **2955**

CONNECTICUT LEGISLATIVE GUIDE / COMPILED BY OFFICE OF LEGISLATIVE MANAGEMENT (US) [12072543] **4640**

CONNECTICUT LIBRARIES (1954-) (US/0010-616X) [02251172] **3204**

CONNECTICUT MAGAZINE (FAIRFIELD, CONN.) (US/0889-7670) [14056846] **2531**

CONNECTICUT MANUFACTURING DIRECTORY (US/0099-0124) [02242949] **3477**

CONNECTICUT MARKET BULLETIN (US/0161-5858) [03970246] **76**

CONNECTICUT MARKET DATA (US/0573-665X) [03775204] 1471, **1531**

CONNECTICUT MASTER TRANSPORTATION PLAN (US/0090-8460) [01783764] **5380**

CONNECTICUT MEDICINE (US/0010-6178) [01564865] **3568**

CONNECTICUT NEWS HANDBOOK (US/0277-5956) [07592374] **2918**

CONNECTICUT NINTH-GRADE PROFICIENCY TEST, SCHOOL YEAR ... ADMINISTERED ... SUMMARY REPORT (US) [08559466] **1862**

CONNECTICUT. NURSING HOME OMBUDSMEN OFFICE See ANNUAL REPORT - NURSING HOME OMBUDSMEN OFFICE **3776**

CONNECTICUT NURSING NEWS (1980) (US/0278-4092) [07819960] **3854**

CONNECTICUT NUTMEGGER, THE (US/0045-8120) [04428851] **2444**

CONNECTICUT OCCUPATIONAL INJURY AND ILLNESS SURVEY (US) [24996831] **2860**

CONNECTICUT. OFFICE OF LABOR RELATIONS See ANNUAL REPORT - CONNECTICUT OFFICE OF LABOR RELATIONS **1649**

CONNECTICUT. OFFICE OF PROTECTION AND ADVOCACY FOR HANDICAPPED AND DEVELOPMENTALLY DISABLED PERSONS See ANNUAL PROGRESS REPORT TO THE GOVERNOR AND TO THE JOINT COMMITTEE ON HUMAN SERVICES OF THE ... CONNECTICUT GENERAL ASSEMBLY FROM OFFICE AND BOARD OF PROTECTION AND ADVOCACY FOR HANDICAPPED AND DEVELOPMENTALLY DISABLED PERSONS **4383**

CONNECTICUT. OFFICE OF THE BANK COMMISSIONER See LIST OF LEGAL INVESTMENTS FOR SAVINGS BANKS IN CONNECTICUT **905**

CONNECTICUT. OFFICE OF VETERANS AFFAIRS FOR EDUCATION See RESEARCH MONOGRAPH - CONNECTICUT OFFICE OF VETERANS AFFAIRS FOR EDUCATION **4055**

CONNECTICUT POETRY REVIEW, THE (US/0277-7770) [07638852] **3461**

●CONNECTICUT POST (BRIDGEPORT, CONN.) (US/1070-874X) [26273432] **5645**

CONNECTICUT PRESERVATION (US/0884-7053) [05870747] **295**

CONNECTICUT PROBATE LAW JOURNAL, THE (US/0897-1234) [12731861] **2955**

CONNECTICUT REAL ESTATE LAW JOURNAL, THE (US) [09484609] 4836, **2955**

CONNECTICUT REVIEW (NEW BRITAIN) (US/0010-6216) [01564867] **2729**

CONNECTICUT, RHODE ISLAND DIRECTORY OF MANUFACTURERS (US/0193-5909) [05214990] **3477**

CONNECTICUT RIVER VALLEY COVERED BRIDGE SOCIETY See BULLETIN - CONNECTICUT RIVER VALLEY COVERED BRIDGE SOCIETY **2019**

CONNECTICUT SCHOOL OF LAW ANNUAL (US/0749-131X) [11056837] 1733, **2955**

CONNECTICUT. SECRETARY OF THE STATE See REGISTER AND MANUAL - STAGE OF CONNECTICUT **4679**

CONNECTICUT. STATE BOARD OF REGISTRATION FOR PROFESSIONAL ENGINEERS AND LAND SURVEYORS See ROSTER OF REGISTERED PROFESSIONAL ENGINEERS AND LAND SURVEYORS **2030**

CONNECTICUT STATE DENTAL ASSOCIATION See JOURNAL - CONNECTICUT STATE DENTAL ASSOCIATION, THE **1326**

CONNECTICUT STATE ETHICS COMMISSION See ANNUAL REPORT TO THE GOVERNOR **4464**

CONNECTICUT STATE LIBRARY See ANNUAL REPORT OF THE CONNECTICUT STATE LIBRARY **3191**

CONNECTICUT STATE LIBRARY. DEPT. OF PLANNING AND RESEARCH See LIBRARY SERVICES AND CONSTRUCTION ACT ANNUAL PROGRAM **3227**

CONNECTICUT STATE PLAN FOR CAREER EDUCATION (US) [04838074] 4203, **1912**

CONNECTICUT. SUPERIOR COURT. FAMILY DIVISION See ANNUAL REPORT, FISCAL YEAR ... / STATE OF CONNECTICUT, SUPERIOR COURT, FAMILY DIVISION **3119**

CONNECTICUT SUPERIOR COURT REPORTS (US/1052-6714) [16172816] **2955**

CONNECTICUT TECHNOLOGY DIRECTORY (US/1046-9672) [20576781] **5096**

CONNECTICUT TECHNOLOGY RESOURCE GUIDE (US/1055-7342) [23283146] **5096**

CONNECTICUT TITLE XX COMPREHENSIVE ANNUAL SERVICES PROGRAM PLAN (US) [06622776] **5280**

CONNECTICUT TRAVELER (US/0746-8636) [10351747] **5467**

CONNECTICUT WALK BOOK (US/0092-5764) [01782327] **4871**

CONNECTICUT WARBLER, THE (US) [10964329] 5617, **4165**

CONNECTICUT WATER RESOURCES BULLETIN (US/0589-400X) [01186897] **5532**

CONNECTICUT. WATER RESOURCES COMMISSION. CONNECTICUT WATER RESOURCES BULLETIN See CONNECTICUT WATER RESOURCES BULLETIN **5532**

CONNECTICUT WEEKLY AGRICULTURAL REPORT (US/1059-8723) [24798742] **76**

CONNECTICUT WOODLANDS (US/0010-6259) [01642604] **2163**

CONNECTICUT

CONNECTICUT. WORKERS' COMPENSATION COMMISSION. COMPENSATION REVIEW DIVISION *See* CONNECTICUT WORKER'S COMPENSATION REVIEW OPINIONS **3145**

CONNECTICUT WORKER'S COMPENSATION REVIEW OPINIONS (US/0732-0833) [08301947] **3145**

CONNECTICUT'S PRIVATE MENTAL HOSPITALS : INPATIENT STATISTICS FOR YEAR ENDING ... / PREPARED BY STATISTICS SECTION, CONNECTICUT STATE DEPARTMENT OF MENTAL HEALTH (US) [07515411] **3778, 3655**

●CONNECTION - ALBERTA. STUDENT PROGRAMS AND EVALUATION DIVISION (CN/1193-2759) [26776085] **1891**

CONNECTION (ATLANTA, GA. 1983), THE (US/0746-9233) [10418317] **784**

CONNECTION (BOSTON, MASS.) (US/0895-6405) [13800257] **1818**

CONNECTION (NORTH CANTON, OHIO) *See* PROGRAMMER'S PROVANTAGE COMPUTER PRODUCTS BUYER'S GUIDE **1281**

CONNECTION SCIENCE (UK/0954-0091) [20640930] **1212**

CONNECTION TECHNOLOGY (US/8756-4076) [11558384] **5096**

CONNECTION, THE (US/1045-7445) [20191736] **1266, 1279**

CONNECTIONS (US) [17347976] **5280**

CONNECTIONS (US/1044-7652) [19889753] **5467**

●CONNECTIONS (ASSOCIATION OF AMERICAN COLLEGES) (US/1064-8755) [26442794] **1091**

CONNECTIONS (EDMONTON) (CN/0701-0400) [03400166] **2190**

CONNECTIONS (FULLERTON, CALIF.) *CEASED.* (US/0894-170X) [15965386] **1180**

CONNECTIONS (GRIMSBY) (CN/1186-1509) [24368027] **784**

CONNECTIONS JOURNAL (CN/0714-8550) [09145857] **2190**

CONNECTIONS (MINNEAPOLIS, MINN. 1993) (US/1070-8154) [28474755] **4386**

CONNECTIONS (NEW YORK, N.Y.) (US/0272-6513) [06887429] **1062**

CONNECTIONS - ONTARIO. MINISTRY OF CULTURE AND COMMUNICATIONS (CN/1180-2014) [22716508] **3204**

CONNECTIONS (POINTE CLAIRE) (CN/0707-7130) [04955189] **2444**

CONNECTIONS (PROVIDENCE, R.I.) (US/1051-6700) [22044032] **1276**

CONNECTIONS (TORONTO) (CN/0226-1766) [08770470] **5242**

CONNECTIONS (WILLOWDALE) (CN/0825-2696) [11245883] **1602**

CONNECTIUCT. GOVERNOR *See* EXECUTIVE ORDER **2968**

CONNECTIVE ISSUES (US/8756-9086) [11693956] **543, 3568**

CONNECTIVE TISSUE DISEASES / LE MALATTIE DEL TESSUTO CONNETTIVO (IT) [11535111] **3804**

CONNECTIVE TISSUE RESEARCH (US/0300-8207) [02036211] **580**

CONNECTIVE TISSUE TOKYO. 1989 (JA/0916-572X) [l0916572X] **3568**

CONNECTOR SPECIFIER (US/1078-1528) [31004088] **1180**

CONNERSVILLE NEWS-EXAMINER (US) [12891209] **5663**

CONNEXION (UK) [25667663] **659**

CONNEXION (US) [02256051] **1818**

CONNEXIONS (ASSOCIATION CANADIENNE DE L'ELECTRICITE) (CN/0848-984X) [21680678] **2039, 1936**

Alphabetical Title Index

CONNEXIONS (CUPERTINO, CALIF.) (US/0894-5926) [16146197] **1241**

CONNEXIONS DIGEST, THE (CN/0845-874X) [20776594] **5242**

CONNEXIONS (MANASSAS, VA.) (US/1058-6806) [24536923] **1241**

CONNEXIONS (OAKLAND, CALIF.) (US/0886-7062) [08015674] **5553**

CONNEXIONS (PARIS) (FR/0337-3126) [04431478] **4582**

CONNIE DATA SUMMARIES (US/0145-5907) [02765376] **2226**

CONNOISSEUR, THE *CEASED.* (UK/0010-6275) [01564870] **348**

CONNOISSEURS' GUIDE TO CALIFORNIA WINE (US/0161-6668) [03993978] **2366**

CONNOLLY REPORT, THE (CN/0823-6216) [10664631] **895**

CONN'S CURRENT THERAPY (US/8755-8823) [10480383] **3796**

CONOCO (US/0884-7045) [02259745] **4253**

CONOCO (WILMINGTON, DEL.) *CEASED.* (US/0883-4318) [12183332] **1602**

CONOMIKES MEDICARE HOTLINE (US) [28895934] **3568**

CONOMIKES REPORTS ON MEDICAL PRACTICE MANAGEMENT : AN INFORMATION SERVICE OF CONOMIKES ASSOCIATES, INC (US/0890-4383) [14233496] **3568**

CONOSCERE I FATTI (IT) [19964705] **2486**

CONOVER-MAST PURCHASING DIRECTORY (1973). CONOVER-MAST PURCHASING DIRECTORY *See* U.S. INDUSTRIAL DIRECTORY **1630**

CONQUISTADORES. ALUMNOS (US/0731-2717) [08157286] **5058**

CONQUISTADORES. MAESTROS (US/0731-2725) [08157396] **5058**

CONQUISTE DEL LAVORO (IT/0010-6348) [03757895] **1661**

CONRAD GREBEL REVIEW, THE (CN/0829-044X) [12628911] **4950**

CONRADIAN : THE JOURNAL OF THE JOSEPH CONRAD SOCIETY (U.K.), THE (UK) [07982428] **431, 3378**

CONRADIANA (US/0010-6356) [00816360] **3340, 431**

CONROE DAILY COURIER (US) [15101866] **5748**

CONSCIENCE AND LIBERTY : INTERNATIONAL JOURNAL OF RELIGIOUS FREEDOM (UK) **4950**

CONSCIENCE CANADA NEWSLETTER (CN/0823-8669) [11856767] **4519, 4718**

CONSCIENCE ET LIBERTE (SZ) [02285476] **4469, 4950**

CONSCIENCE (WASHINGTON, D.C.) (US/0740-6835) [10008502] **588**

CONSCIOUSNESS (AT) **4241**

●CONSCIOUSNESS AND COGNITION (US/1053-8100) [22646776] **4582**

CONSCIOUSNESS AND SELF-REGULATION (US/0146-5457) [02949985] **4582**

CONSECRATED LIFE (ENGLISH ED.) (US/0884-7010) [05794709] **4950**

CONSEIL CANADIEN DE LA SECURITE *See* CONGRES ANNUEL - CONSEIL CANADIEN DA LA SECURITE **4772**

CONSEIL CANADIEN DES INGENIEURS *See* CCI NOUVELLES **1967**

CONSEIL CANADIEN DES MINISTRES DE L'ENVIRONNEMENT *See* ANNUAL REPORT - CANADIAN COUNCIL OF MINISTERS OF THE ENVIRONMENT **5272**

CONSEIL DE DEVELOPPEMENT SOCIAL DU MONTREAL METROPOLITAIN *See* CDS. CONSEIL DE DEVELOPPEMENT SOCIAL DU MONTREAL METROPOLITAIN **5242**

CONSEIL DE LA JEUNESSE SCIENTIFIQUE *See* BULLETIN DE LIAISON DU CONSEIL DE LA JEUNESSE SCIENTIFIQUE **5090**

CONSEIL DE LA JEUNESSE SCIENTIFIQUE *See* COMMUNIQUE - CONSEIL DE LA JEUNESSE SCIENTIFIQUE **5095**

CONSEIL DE LA RADIODIFFUSION ET DES TELECOMMUNICATIONS CANADIENNES *See* TETE-A-TETE (OTTAWA. 1991) **1141**

CONSEIL DE LA SANTE ET DES SERVICES SOCIAUX, REGION SAGUENAY-LAC-ST-JEAN (QUEBEC) *See* CENTRE (CHICOUTIMI) **5277**

CONSEIL DES ARTS DU NOUVEAU-BRUNSWICK *See* ANNUAL REPORT - NEW BRUNSWICK ARTS BOARD **313**

CONSEIL DES MINISTRES DE L'EDUCATION, CANADA *See* ANNUAL REPORT - COUNCIL OF MINISTERS OF EDUCATION, CANADA **1725**

CONSEIL DU PATRONAT DU QUEBEC *See* REPERTOIRE DES ASSOCIATIONS PATRONALES QUEBECOISES **1706**

CONSEIL DU PATRONAT DU QUEBEC *See* CHRONOLOGICAL INDEX / CONSEIL DU PATRONAT DU QUEBEC **413**

CONSEIL DU PATRONAT DU QUEBEC *See* INDEX CHRONOLOGIQUE / INDEX CHRONOLOGIQUE - CONSEIL DU PATRONAT DU QUEBEC **1678**

CONSEIL DU PATRONAT DU QUEBEC (CN/0228-1511) [06859227] **1661**

CONSEIL DU PATRONAT DU QUEBEC *See* BULLETIN SUR LES RELATIONS DU TRAVAIL (EDITION ANGLAISE) **1657**

CONSEIL DU PATRONAT DU QUEBEC *See* CONSEIL DU PATRONAT DU QUEBEC ET SES MEMBRES AFFILIEES, LE **1661**

CONSEIL DU PATRONAT DU QUEBEC ET SES MEMBRES AFFILIEES, LE (CN/0714-8453) [09086763] **1661**

CONSEIL INFORMATIQUE A LA DIRECTION GENERALE, LE *See* INFORMATIQUE ET STRATEGIE D'ENTREPRISE **5113**

CONSEIL INFORMATIQUE A LA DIRECTION GENERALE, LE (FR/1156-4903) [I11564903] **5096**

CONSEIL NATIONAL DE RECHERCHES DU CANADA. DIVISION DES RECHERCHES SUR LE BATIMENT *See* BULLETIN DE RECHERCHES DE LA DIVISION DES RECHERCHES SUR LE BATIMENT **605**

CONSEIL NATIONAL DU CREDIT (FRANCE) *See* RAPPORT ANNUEL - CONSEIL NATIONAL DU CREDIT **4744**

CONSEIL REGIONAL DE DEVELOPPEMENT DE L'OUTAOUAIS *See* BULLETIN D'INFORMATION - CONSEIL REGIONAL DE DEVELOPPEMENT DE L'OUTAOUAIS (07) **1466**

CONSEIL REGIONAL DE LA SANTE ET DES SERVICES SOCIAUX DE L'OUTAOUAIS (QUEBEC) *See* RAPPORT ANNUEL - CONSEIL REGIONAL DE LA SANTE ET DES SERVICES SOCIAUX DE L'OUTAOUAIS **4798**

CONSEIL REGIONAL DE LA SANTE ET DES SERVICES SOCIAUX, SAGUENAY-LAC-SAINT-JEAN (QUEBEC) LE CENTRE *See* EPICENTRE (CHICOUTIMI) **4646**

CONSEIL SCOLAIRE DE L'ILE DE MONTREAL *See* REPERTOIRE DES BIENS A STATUT PARTICULIER **4846**

CONSEIL SCOLAIRE DE L'ILE DE MONTREAL *See* REPERTOIRE DES ECOLES - CONSEIL SCOLAIRE DE L'ILE DE MONTREAL **1778**

CONSEILLER COMPTABLE, LE (CG) [02241608] **4718**

CONSEJO DE RECURSOS MINERALES (MEXICO) *See* CRM, BOLETIN DE INFORMACION : ORGANO DE COMUNICACION INTERNO **2138**

CONSEJO SUPERIOR DE INVESTIGACIONES CIENTIFICAS (SPAIN) *See* MEMORIA - CONSEJO SUPERIOR DE INVESTIGACIONES CIENTIFICAS **5128**

CONSELHO DE DESENVOLVIMENTO INDUSTRIAL (BRAZIL). SECRETARIA EXECUTIVA *See* RELATORIO ANUAL / MINISTERIO DA INDUSTRIA E DO COMERCIO, CONSELHO DE DESENVOLVIMENTO INDUSTRIAL, SECRETARIA EXECUTIVA **4679**

CONSELHO DE NAO-FERROSOS E DE SIDERURGIA (BRAZIL) *See* RELATORIO - CONSELHO DE NAO-FERROSOS E DE SIDERURGIA **1624**

CONSELHO DE REITORES DAS UNIVERSIDADES BRASILEIRAS *See* RELATORIO DA GESTAO / CONSELHO DE REITORES DAS UNIVERSIDADES BRASILEIRAS **1843**

CONSELHO DE REITORES DAS UNIVERSIDADES BRASILEIRAS *See* RELATORIO DE ATIVIDADES / CONSELHO DE REITORES DAS UNIVERSIDADES BRASILEIRAS **1844**

CONSELHO DE REITORES DAS UNIVERSIDADES BRASILEIRAS. RELATORIO DA GESTAO *See* RELATORIO DE ATIVIDADES / CONSELHO DE REITORES DAS UNIVERSIDADES BRASILEIRAS **1844**

CONSELHO FEDERAL DE CULTURA (BRAZIL) *See* BOLETIM - CONSELHO FEDERAL DE CULTURA **5229**

CONSELHO NACIONAL DE DESENVOLVIMENTO CIENTIFICO E TECNOLOGICO *See* CNPQ BOLETIM **5095**

CONSENSUS AND REVIEW OF THE LATEST ISSUES OF RECORDED CLASSICAL MUSIC *See* NEW CONSENSUS AND REVIEW OF THE LATEST ISSUES OF RECORDED CLASSICAL MUSIC, THE **4140**

CONSENSUS (BROOKLYN) (US/0090-0842) [01784679] **659**

CONSENSUS (CHICAGO, ILL.) (US/0740-3461) [09910263] **4040**

CONSENSUS DEVELOPMENT CONFERENCE SUMMARIES (US/0737-4674) [07514627] **3568**

CONSENSUS FORECASTS (UK/0957-0950) [27798440] **1634, 1471**

CONSENSUS (OTTAWA) (CN/0380-1314) [03421694] **4030**

CONSENSUS (TORONTO. 1975) (CN/0381-7385) [03209929] **1552**

CONSENSUS (WINNIPEG) (CN/0317-1493) [02247942] **4950**

CONSENT MANUAL (SACRAMENTO, CALIF.) (US/1071-5320) [14640643] **3778**

CONSEQUENCE (COTONOU) (DM/0377-6824) [01796450] **4344**

CONSER (US/0163-8610) [04470247] **3204**

CONSER MICROFICHE (US/0707-3747) [05279340] **3204**

CONSER PROGRAM *See* CDMARC SERIALS **3201**

CONSER PROGRAM *See* CONSERLINE (WASHINGTON, D.C.) **3204**

CONSER TABLES *CEASED.* (US/0190-3608) [04694522] **3204**

Alphabetical Title Index — CONSTRUCTION

●CONSERLINE (WASHINGTON, D.C.) (US/1072-611X) [29049140] **3204**

CONSERVA (SA/0258-3313) [15729190] **2163**

CONSERVATION (CN/0702-732X) [03425239] **2190**

CONSERVATION ADMINISTRATION NEWS (US/0192-2912) [04993144] **3204**

●CONSERVATION AND MANAGEMENT OF ARCHAEOLOGICAL SITES (UK/1350-5033) **266**

CONSERVATION ASSESSMENT PROGRAM, GRANT APPLICATION AND INFORMATION (US) [24728497] **317, 4718, 4087**

CONSERVATION AUTHORITY DIRECTORY (CN/1183-773X) [24986884] **2190**

CONSERVATION BIOLOGY (US/0888-8892) [13740815] **2212, 2190**

CONSERVATION BULLETIN (UK/0953-8674) [I09538674] **4087**

CONSERVATION COMMENT (CN/0381-4610) [03193215] **2190**

CONSERVATION COMMISSION OF THE NORTHERN TERRITORY *See* ANNUAL REPORT FOR YEAR ENDING 30 JUNE ... CONSERVATION COMMISSION OF THE NORTHERN TERRITORY **2186**

CONSERVATION COURT DIGEST, THE (US/0589-4468) [01564880] **2190**

CONSERVATION DIRECTORY (US/0069-911X) [00971464] **2190**

CONSERVATION FEDERATION OF MISSOURI *See* MISSOURI WILDLIFE **2218**

CONSERVATION GUIDES (IT) **2190**

CONSERVATION IMPACT (US/1056-9707) [17222054] **168**

CONSERVATION IN KANSAS (US/0094-1670) [01792537] **2190**

CONSERVATION INFORMATION NETWORK *See* NETWORK NEWS / CONSERVATION INFORMATION NETWORK **359**

CONSERVATION MICRO NEWS (UK) [19763642] **5096**

CONSERVATION NEWS (II) [06691572] **2481**

CONSERVATION NEWS (LONDON) (UK/0309-2224) [07787815] **4087**

CONSERVATION NOTE (WASHINGTON) (US/0069-9128) [01363198] **2190**

CONSERVATION NOW (UK) **2190**

CONSERVATION OF CULTURAL PROPERTY IN INDIA (II/0376-7965) [01797704] **2190**

CONSERVATION RESEARCH REPORT (US/0565-2421) [01640250] **2190**

CONSERVATION RESTAURATION (FR/0765-5428) [17641114] **348**

CONSERVATION RESTAURATION DES BIENS CULTURELS PARIS (FR/1157-688X) [I1157688X] **4087, 348**

CONSERVATION (SACRAMENTO) (US/0362-0328) [02441474] **2190**

CONSERVATION : THE GCI NEWSLETTER (US) [25038844] **348**

CONSERVATION UPDATE : NEWSLETTER OF THE CONSERVATION UNIT, MUSEUMS & GALLERIES COMMISSION (UK/0958-1847) [21224129] **348**

CONSERVATIONEWS (US) [07560580] **4828**

CONSERVATIONIST (SUDBURY) (CN/0319-4914) [01950654] **2191**

CONSERVATIONIST, THE (US/0010-650X) [01564888] **2190**

CONSERVATIVE (CARROLLTON, MISS.) (US) [15009945] **5700**

CONSERVATIVE CHRONICLE (US/0888-7403) [13718568] **2531**

CONSERVATIVE JUDAISM (US/0010-6542) [01786187] **5047**

CONSERVATIVE NEWSLINE *CEASED.* (UK) [09292670] **4469**

CONSERVATIVE REVIEW (WASHINGTON, D.C.) (US/1047-5990) [20730287] **1471**

CONSERVATOIRE ROYAL DE MUSIQUE DE BRUXELLES. MUSEE INSTRUMENTAL *See* BRUSSELS MUSEUM OF MUSICAL INSTRUMENTS BULLETIN, THE **4105**

CONSERVATOR (LONDON) (UK/0140-0096) [04025925] **348**

CONSIDERATIONS (CN/0709-6461) [06025860] **4344**

CONSIGLIO DI STATO (IT/0010-6569) [I00106569] **4640**

CONSIGNA (CK) [09138818] **4469**

CONSILIUM CEDIP PRACTICUM (GW/0932-3791) [11926953] **4298**

CONSOLATA MISSIONARIES (CN/0826-7499) [11825525] **4950**

CONSOLIDATED ANNUAL REPORT FOR THE YEAR ENDING DECEMBER 31 ... / DEPARTMENT OF COMMERCE, BANKING DIVISION (US) [08713818] **784**

CONSOLIDATED ANNUAL REPORT OF ILLINOIS STATE CHARTERED CREDIT UNIONS (US) [06493259] **784**

CONSOLIDATED DEVELOPMENT DIRECTORY (US/0362-7586) [02337106] **2819**

CONSOLIDATED FEDERAL FUNDS REPORT. VOLUME I, COUNTY AREAS (US) [10681892] **5280**

CONSOLIDATED FEDERAL FUNDS REPORT. VOLUME II, SUBCOUNTY AREAS (US/0747-5764) [10681827] **4640**

CONSOLIDATED FINANCE AND REVENUE ACCOUNTS OF ZILLA PARISHADS AND PANCHAYAT SAMITIS IN THE STATE OF MAHARASHTRA (II) [06494978] **4718**

CONSOLIDATED INDEX OF ARMY PUBLICATIONS AND BLANK FORMS [COMPUTER FILE] (US) [28096005] **4040**

CONSOLIDATED INDEX OF ARMY PUBLICATIONS AND BLANK FORMS [MICROFORM] (US) [09991780] **4040**

CONSOLIDATED INDEX TO GOVERNMENT PUBLICATIONS (UK) [01640390] **4640**

CONSOLIDATED PLAN. APPENDICES / MISSOURI DEPARTMENT OF MENTAL HEALTH (US/0732-2658) [08309042] **4772**

CONSOLIDATED PLAN / MISSOURI DEPARTMENT OF MENTAL HEALTH (US/0732-264X) [08309006] **4772**

CONSOLIDATED RETURNS TAX REPORT *CEASED.* (US/1047-8949) [20807894] **2955**

CONSOLIDATED REVENUE FUND : SUMMARY OF ESTIMATED EXPENDITURE (INCLUDING EXPENDITURE RESERVED BY LAW) AND ESTIMATED REVENUE (AT) [01787543] **4718**

CONSOLIDATED STANDARDS MANUAL FOR CHILD, ADOLESCENT, AND ADULT PSYCHIATRIC, ALCOHOLISM, AND DRUG ABUSE FACILITIES (US) [07907556] **3778**

CONSOLIDATED TAX RETURNS (US/0148-009X) [03260303] **4718**

CONSOLIDATED TREATIES & INTERNATIONAL AGREEMENTS. CURRENT DOCUMENT SERVICE, EUROPEAN COMMUNITY (US/1059-8561) [24787518] **4519**

CONSOMMATEUR CANADIEN, LE *CEASED.* (CN/0315-1867) [01852125] **1294**

CONSOMMATION (MONTREAL) (CN/1184-1869) [23686553] **4719**

CONSOMMATIONS D'ENERGIE DANS LE COMMERCE DE DETAIL ET LES SERVICES A CARACTERE COMMERCIAL EN ..., LES (FR) [19076004] **1936**

CONSORT (DOLMETSCH FOUNDATION), THE (UK/0268-9111) [02133575] **4111**

CONSORT (HALIFAX) (CN/0823-8278) [11431437] **4111**

CONSORTIUM DIRECTORY (US/0091-701X) [01787864] **1818**

CONSORTIUM FOR COMPARATIVE LEGISLATIVE STUDIES *See* PUBLICATIONS OF THE CONSORTIUM FOR COMPARATIVE LEGISLATIVE STUDIES **3033**

CONSORTIUM NEWS / HEALTH SCIENCES CONSORTIUM (US) [17360053] **1800, 3913**

CONSORTIUM OF RHODE ISLAND ACADEMIC AND RESEARCH LIBRARIES *See* NEWSLETTER - CONSORTIUM OF RHODE ISLAND ACADEMIC AND RESEARCH LIBRARIES **3235**

CONSORTIUM OF TELEVISION ARCHIVISTS *See* COTA NEWSLETTER **1130**

CONSORTIUM ON REVOLUTIONARY EUROPE, 1750-1850 *See* PROCEEDINGS - CONSORTIUM ON REVOLUTIONARY EUROPE **2703**

CONSORTIUM ON REVOLUTIONARY EUROPE PROCEEDINGS *See* SELECTED PAPERS **2709**

CONSORZIO DI CREDITO PER LE OPERE PUBBLICHE *See* FINANCIAL STATEMENTS / CONSORZIO DI CREDITO PER LE OPERE PUBBLICHE **4726**

CONSPECT, ROMANIA IN 30 DE ZILE (RM) [24459377] **2684**

CONSTABLE (PH/0414-6883) [02438871] **3161**

CONSTELLATION / MIDDLE ATLANTIC PLANETARIUM SOCIETY (US/0278-5021) [07817613] **394**

CONSTELLATIONS : AN INTERNATIONAL JOURNAL OF CRITICAL AND DEMOCRATIC THEORY (UK/1351-0487) **4469**

CONSTITUTION, BY-LAWS AND REGULATIONS - INVESTMENT DEALERS' ASSOCIATION OF CANADA (CN/0711-4877) [08559606] **895**

CONSTITUTION, BY-LAWS, REGULATIONS, HISTORY / CANADIAN AMATEUR HOCKEY ASSOCIATION (CN/0834-3055) [16386351] **4891**

CONSTITUTION, JEFFERSON'S MANUAL, AND RULES OF THE HOUSE OF REPRESENTATIVES OF THE UNITED STATES (US/0195-5888) [03163759] **4640**

CONSTITUTION OF THE UNITED STATES, JEFFERSON'S MANUAL, THE RULES OF THE HOUSE OF REPRESENTATIVES, AND A DIGEST AND MANUAL OF THE RULES AND PRACTICE OF THE HOUSE OF REPRESENTATIVES *See* CONSTITUTION, JEFFERSON'S MANUAL, AND RULES OF THE HOUSE OF REPRESENTATIVES OF THE UNITED STATES **4640**

CONSTITUTION - ONTARIO FEDERATION OF LABOUR (CN/0318-4196) [02441993] **1661**

CONSTITUTION-TRIBUNE (CHILLICOTHE, MO. : 1985) (US) [19822816] **5703**

CONSTITUTIONAL AND PARLIAMENTARY INFORMATION (SZ/0010-6623) [01139174] **4469, 3092**

CONSTITUTIONAL COMMENTARY (US/0742-7115) [10415979] **3092**

CONSTITUTIONAL FORUM (CN/0847-3889) [24934084] **3092**

CONSTITUTIONAL LAW (US/0098-7638) [02239703] **3092**

CONSTITUTIONAL LAW JOURNAL / SETON HALL LAW SCHOOL (US) [23095105] **3092**

CONSTITUTIONAL POLITICAL ECONOMY (US/1043-4062) [19451550] **1471, 3092**

CONSTITUTIONAL REFORM : THE QUARTERLY REVIEW *CEASED.* (UK/0269-2511) [15809170] **3092**

CONSTITUTIONALLY SPEAKING (CN) [10978517] **2259, 2956**

CONSTITUTIONS OF DEPENDENCIES AND SPECIAL SOVEREIGNTIES (US) [06399007] **4470**

CONSTITUTIONS OF THE UNITED STATES, NATIONAL AND STATE (US/0572-8274) [02534106] **3092**

CONSTRUCAO HOJE (BL) [06535600] **2021**

CONSTRUCAO MODERNA *See* CONSTRUCAO HOJE **2021**

CONSTRUCCION Y TECNOLOGIA (MX/0187-7895) [19870811] **608**

CONSTRUCT IN STEEL (AT/1030-2581) [19370572] **4000, 608**

CONSTRUCTEUR (NE/0010-6658) [10345050] **2112**

CONSTRUCTIA DE MASINI (RM/0573-7419) [09284097] **2112**

CONSTRUCTIEWERKPLAATSEN, EXCL. TANK-, RESERVOIR- EN PIJPLEIDINGBOUW / CENTRAAL BUREAU VOOR DE STATISTIEK, HOOFDAFDELING STATISTIEK VAN INDUSTRIE EN BOUWNIJVERHEID (NE/0168-3225) [10283098] **1552**

CONSTRUCTIEWERKPLAATSEN, EXCL. TANK-, RESERVOIR- EN PIJPLEIDINGBOUW PRODUKTIESTATISTIEKEN *See* CONSTRUCTIEWERKPLAATSEN, EXCL. TANK-, RESERVOIR- EN PIJPLEIDINGBOUW / CENTRAAL BUREAU VOOR DE STATISTIEK, HOOFDAFDELING STATISTIEK VAN INDUSTRIE EN BOUWNIJVERHEID **1552**

CONSTRUCTII (RM/0373-7748) [07583346] **608**

CONSTRUCTION (BE) **608**

CONSTRUCTION ALBERTA NEWS (CN/0700-9178) [03304230] **608**

CONSTRUCTION & BUILDING MATERIALS (UK/0950-0618) [17615532] **608**

CONSTRUCTION AND DESIGN LAW DIGEST (US/8755-7568) [11366408] **608, 2956**

CONSTRUCTION AND ENGINEERING, ZIMBABWE (RH) [21140703] **1969**

CONSTRUCTION & SURETY LAW DIVISION NEWSLETTER (US/0148-933X) [03400461] **608, 2956**

CONSTRUCTION (ARLINGTON) (US/0010-6704) [06794897] **608**

CONSTRUCTION ASSOCIATION OF MONTREAL AND THE PROVINCE OF QUEBEC *See* NEWSLETTER. LABOUR RELATIONS. CONSTRUCTION ASSOCIATION OF MONTREAL AND THE PROVINCE OF QUEBEC **1695**

CONSTRUCTION — Alphabetical Title Index

CONSTRUCTION ASSOCIATION OF MONTREAL AND THE PROVINCE OF QUEBEC *See* NEWSLETTER. SAFETY. CONSTRUCTION ASSOCIATION OF MONTREAL AND THE PROVINCE OF QUEBEC **622**

CONSTRUCTION ATLANTIC (CN/0714-3133) [09145929] **608**

CONSTRUCTION BOXSCORE PLUS / SOFTWARE (US) **608**

CONSTRUCTION BRIEFINGS (US/0162-3176) [04187094] **608**

CONSTRUCTION BRIEFINGS COLLECTION, THE (US/0747-5233) [10573697] **609**

CONSTRUCTION BULLETIN (US/0010-6720) [01564900] **609**

CONSTRUCTION BUSINESS REVIEW (US/1059-406X) [24606782] **609**

CONSTRUCTION CANADA (CN/0228-8788) [07817268] **609**

CONSTRUCTION CLAIMS CITATOR, THE (US/0742-0889) [10236583] **609**

CONSTRUCTION CLAIMS MONTHLY (US/0272-4561) [06846983] **609**

CONSTRUCTION CLAIMS TRAINING GUIDE *CEASED*. (US/0899-5982) [18238144] **609**

CONSTRUCTION COMPLAINTS (US) [03116735] **609**

CONSTRUCTION COMPUTING (UK/0264-6854) [15864163] **1180**

CONSTRUCTION CONTRACT MODIFICATIONS; COURSE MANUAL (US) [05108350] **609, 2956**

CONSTRUCTION CONTRACTOR, THE (US/0146-9479) [03057427] **609**

CONSTRUCTION CONTRACTS AND LITIGATION (US) [15741944] **609, 2956**

CONSTRUCTION DIGEST (US/0194-2476) [05348052] **609**

CONSTRUCTION DIMENSIONS (US/0194-8903) [05081887] **609**

CONSTRUCTION EMPLOYMENT GUIDE IN THE NATIONAL AND INTERNATIONAL FIELD (US/0161-3405) [03902856] **609**

CONSTRUCTION EQUIPMENT (1970) (US/0192-3978) [05005234] **609**

CONSTRUCTION EQUIPMENT DISTRIBUTION (US/0010-6755) [01796729] **609**

CONSTRUCTION EQUIPMENT, OPERATION AND MAINTENANCE *CEASED*. (US/0010-6771) [04434085] **609**

CONSTRUCTION HISTORY : JOURNAL OF THE CONSTRUCTION HISTORY GROUP (UK/0267-7768) [13019433] **609**

CONSTRUCTION IN CANADA (ANNUAL ED.) (CN/0527-4974) [02442556] **609, 632**

CONSTRUCTION IN HAWAII (US/0069-9187) [02536644] **609**

CONSTRUCTION INDEX (US/0892-2047) [15116855] **295, 609, 632**

CONSTRUCTION INDUSTRY ANNUAL FINANCIAL SURVEY (US) **609**

CONSTRUCTION INDUSTRY EMPLOYMENT LAW (CN/0827-4614) [13231875] **609, 3145**

CONSTRUCTION INDUSTRY IN IRELAND : REVIEW OF ... AND OUTLOOK FOR (IE) [17929794] **609**

CONSTRUCTION INDUSTRY LAW LETTER (UK/0269-0039) [02690039] **2956**

CONSTRUCTION INDUSTRY LITIGATION REPORTER *See* ASBESTOS PROPERTY LITIGATION REPORTER **599**

CONSTRUCTION INDUSTRY RESEARCH AND INFORMATION ASSOCIATION. UNDERWATER ENGINEERING GROUP *See* REPORT - CIRIA UNDERWATER ENGINEERING GROUP **1994**

CONSTRUCTION INDUSTRY THESAURUS UPDATE SERVICE (UK) **609**

CONSTRUCTION INJURY LIABILITY MONTHLY (US/1050-4060) [21477606] **4772, 609**

CONSTRUCTION LABOR NEWS (US/0161-990X) [04078219] **609, 1661**

CONSTRUCTION LABOR RATE TRENDS AND OUTLOOK (US/0272-8478) [06930099] **1661**

CONSTRUCTION LABOR REPORT (US/0010-6836) [03463805] **609, 1661**

CONSTRUCTION LABOR RESEARCH COUNCIL (U.S.) *See* CONSTRUCTION LABOR RATE TRENDS AND OUTLOOK **1661**

CONSTRUCTION LAW JOURNAL (UK/0267-2359) [14125910] **609**

CONSTRUCTION LAW LETTER (CN/0827-3480) [11847614] **609, 2956**

CONSTRUCTION LAW REPORTS (CN/0824-2593) [10638858] **609, 2956**

CONSTRUCTION LAW REPORTS (LONDON, ENGLAND) (UK/0950-3889) [18484243] **609, 2956**

CONSTRUCTION LAWYER, THE (US/0272-0116) [06208347] **609, 2956**

CONSTRUCTION LITIGATION LAW BULLETIN (US) [17925224] **609, 2956**

CONSTRUCTION LITIGATION REPORTER (US/0279-1102) [06987574] **609, 2956**

CONSTRUCTION (LONDON, 1977) (UK/0142-0410) [04144062] **609**

CONSTRUCTION MANAGEMENT AND ECONOMICS (UK/0144-6193) [11601942] **610**

●CONSTRUCTION MANAGEMENT JOURNAL (US/1056-7801) [23880581] **610**

CONSTRUCTION MANITOBA (CN/0832-5804) [17846535] **610**

CONSTRUCTION MATERIALS INVENTORY / KANSAS DEPARTMENT OF TRANSPORTATION, BUREAU OF MATERIALS & RESEARCH, BUREAU OF TRANSPORTATION PLANNING (US) [10827611] **2021**

CONSTRUCTION MATERIALS SPECIFIER, THE (CN/0316-1064) [03436697] **610**

CONSTRUCTION METALLIQUE (FR/0045-8198) [03779148] **4000**

CONSTRUCTION MODERNE (FR) [24062857] **295**

CONSTRUCTION NAVALE, LA (FR) [02241633] **4176**

CONSTRUCTION NEWS (UK/0010-6860) [00106860] **610**

CONSTRUCTION NEWS (LITTLE ROCK) (US/0160-5607) [02446165] **610**

CONSTRUCTION NEWS MAGAZINE (UK/0306-3232) [03063232] **610**

CONSTRUCTION NEWS WEST (US/0892-3337) [15236341] **610**

CONSTRUCTION NORTHWEST (CN/1182-9818) [23598132] **610**

CONSTRUCTION NOTEBOOK NEWS (US) **610**

CONSTRUCTION PAPERS (UK/0144-8587) [09983960] **610**

CONSTRUCTION PLANT & EQUIPMENT ANNUAL (UK) [04164698] **610**

CONSTRUCTION PLANT & EQUIPMENT INTERNATIONAL ANNUAL (UK/0142-0550) [07154134] **610**

CONSTRUCTION PRICE STATISTICS (QUARTERLY ED.) (CN/0833-238X) [15561709] **610, 632**

CONSTRUCTION PRODUCT AND SERVICE (CN) **610**

●CONSTRUCTION PRODUCTS (US/1070-4531) [27847357] **610**

CONSTRUCTION PROGRAMS / SOUTH DAKOTA DEPARTMENT OF TRANSPORTATION (US) [08308709] **610**

CONSTRUCTION PROJECT NEWS. GREATER DETROIT EDITION (US/0746-8377) [10311037] **610**

CONSTRUCTION REFERENCES *CEASED*. (UK/0306-0152) [03639542] **632**

●CONSTRUCTION REPAIR (UK/0967-0726) [26485773] **610**

CONSTRUCTION REPORTS. C45, HOUSING UNITES AUTHORIZED FOR DEMOLITION IN PERMIT-ISSUING PLACES (US) [03306089] **2819**

CONSTRUCTION REPORTS: NEW ONE-FAMILY HOMES SOLD AND FOR SALE (US/0363-8537) [01713878] **2819**

CONSTRUCTION REPORTS: VALUE OF NEW CONSTRUCTION PUT IN PLACE (US/0363-8294) [01715318] **610**

CONSTRUCTION REVIEW (US/0010-6917) [01564905] **610**

CONSTRUCTION REVIEW, THE (SI) [01789628] **610**

CONSTRUCTION SAFETY JOURNAL (CN/0704-6766) [03887235] **2860, 610**

CONSTRUCTION SAFETY MANUAL (UK) **610**

CONSTRUCTION SIGHTLINES *CEASED*. (CN/0708-1073) [05018155] **610**

CONSTRUCTION SPECIFIER, THE (US/0010-6925) [01564906] **610**

CONSTRUCTION STATISTICS YEARBOOK (US) [11938670] **610, 632**

CONSTRUCTION SUPERVISION & SAFETY LETTER *CEASED*. (US/0744-7167) [08507661] **2860, 610**

CONSTRUCTION TIMES, THE (SI) [03469919] **611**

CONSTRUCTION TODAY (UK/0268-5507) [12167144] **2021**

CONSTRUCTION TYPE PLYWOOD (CN/0708-6229) [05257763] **2400**

CONSTRUCTION WEEKLY (UK) [19567786] **611, 2021**

CONSTRUCTIONAL LAW (UK/0963-6706) [09636706] **2956**

CONSTRUCTIONAL REVIEW (AT/0010-695X) [03882266] **611**

CONSTRUCTIONEER (US/0010-6968) [02446168] **611**

CONSTRUCTIONS (US/0898-8609) [10979677] **3378**

CONSTRUCTIS (UK) **611**

CONSTRUCTIVE APPROXIMATION (US/0176-4276) [11768028] **3502**

CONSTRUCTIVE CITIZEN PARTICIPATION (CN/0319-2385) [01949696] **5242**

CONSTRUCTIVE CRITICISM (US/1052-8164) [22397780] **317, 4582**

CONSTRUCTOR (WASHINGTON) (US/0162-6191) [02642359] **611**

CONSTRUIRE ENSEMBLE / CESAO (UV) [07413042] **2819**

CONSTRUIRE (QUEBEC) (CN/0833-0239) [16687606] **611**

CONSU/STATS I. CD-ROM (US) **1294**

CONSULAR AND TRADE REPRESENTATIVES IN AUSTRALIA *See* CONSULAR, TRADE, AND OTHER OFFICIAL REPRESENTATIVES IN AUSTRALIA / DEPARTMENT OF FOREIGN AFFAIRS **3126**

CONSULAR LIST AND LIST OF INTERNATIONAL ORGANIZATIONS (BR) [05790532] **4519**

CONSULAR LIST / DEPARTMENT OF FOREIGN AFFAIRS AND TRADE (AT) [29002061] **3126**

CONSULAR POSTS, OFFICIALLY RECOGNIZED REPRESENTATIVES AND BODIES ESTABLISHED UNDER THE SINO-BRITISH JOINT DECLARATION / HONG KONG (HK) [23235877] **3126**

CONSULAR, TRADE, AND OTHER OFFICIAL REPRESENTATIVES IN AUSTRALIA *See* CONSULAR LIST / DEPARTMENT OF FOREIGN AFFAIRS AND TRADE **3126**

CONSULAR, TRADE, AND OTHER OFFICIAL REPRESENTATIVES IN AUSTRALIA / DEPARTMENT OF FOREIGN AFFAIRS (AT) [13707174] **3126**

CONSULENTE IMMOBILIARE (IT/0010-7050) [00107050] **2819**

CONSULENZA (IT) **4640**

CONSULTA MADRID. 1983 (SP/1131-4184) [11314184] **3568**

CONSULTANT - ASSOCIATION OF CONSULTING FORESTERS OF AMERICA, THE (US/0010-7085) [01564912] **2378**

CONSULTANT COMPENDIUM (US) **784**

CONSULTANT (HACKENSACK) (US/0010-7069) [01133190] **3568**

CONSULTANT (MONTREAL. 1974) (CN/0712-9890) [08828193] **1969**

CONSULTANT PHARMACIST, THE (US/0888-5109) [13623012] **4298**

CONSULTANT PRACTICE (US/0748-1837) [10909108] **864**

CONSULTANT, THE (US) [06651597] **2191, 2378**

CONSULTANTS AND CONSULTING ORGANIZATIONS DIRECTORY (US/0196-1292) [05672292] **659**

CONSULTANTS & CONSULTING ORGANIZATIONS DIRECTORY. SUPPLEMENT (US) [23702837] **659**

CONSULTANTS NEWS (US/0045-8201) [03007211] **659**

CONSULTATIONS EN CARDIOLOGIE (CN/1181-9049) [24256400] **3703**

CONSULTATIONS IN LAPORASCOPIC SURGERY *See* VIDEOSCOPIC SURGERY **3977**

●CONSULTATIONS PREBUDGETAIRES/ COMITE PERMANENT DES FINANCES ET DES AFFAIRES ECONOMIQUES (CN) [25608115] **4719**

CONSULTING ENGINEERS OF ONTARIO *See* DIRECTORY / CONSULTING ENGINEERS OF ONTARIO **1970**

CONSULTING ENGINEERS WHO'S WHO & YEAR BOOK, THE (UK) [03036913] **1969, 431**

CONSULTING OPPORTUNITIES JOURNAL (US/0273-4613) [07054794] **659**

●CONSULTING PSYCHOLOGY JOURNAL (US/1065-9293) [26795812] **4582**

CONSULTING SERVICES (US/1064-2811) [07424894] **973**

CONSULTING-SPECIFYING ENGINEER (US/0892-5046) [15127428] **2097**

CONSULTOR (AG) [05672006] **5380**

CONSUMENTENGIDS (NE/0165-6775) [01656775] **1294**

Alphabetical Title Index — CONTACT

CONSUMER ACTION (US) [01642327] **1294**

CONSUMER ACTION CANBERRA (AT/1036-1162) [I10361162] **1294**

CONSUMER ACTION NEWS / CONSUMER ACTION (US/1071-1783) [27993247] **829**

CONSUMER ADVANTAGE INSIDERS VEHICLE MARKET DIGEST (US/1045-8956) [20284549] **5412**

CONSUMER AFFAIRS LETTER, THE (US/0270-0999) [06343773] **1294**

CONSUMER ALERT (US) [01564915] **1294**

CONSUMER ALERT COMMENTS (US/0740-4964) [09966244] **1294**

CONSUMER ANALYSIS (MILWAUKEE, WIS.) (US/0735-178X) [04309572] **1552**

CONSUMER ANALYSIS OF THE GREATER MILWAUKEE MARKET *See* CONSUMER ANALYSIS (MILWAUKEE, WIS.) **1552**

CONSUMER AND COMMUNITY AFFAIRS HANDBOOK / BOARD OF GOVERNORS OF THE FEDERAL RESERVE SYSTEM (US) [13463892] **3086**

●CONSUMER ASIA (UK) **829**

CONSUMER BANKRUPTCY NEWS (US/1058-3963) [24292330] **784, 2956**

●CONSUMER BANKRUPTCY NEWS DESK BOOK (US/1068-1906) [27464535] **2956**

CONSUMER BRIEF (UK) **2332**

CONSUMER BUSINESS REVIEW (US/0148-3072) [03285265] **1552**

CONSUMER BUYING GUIDE : BEST BUYS & DISCOUNT PRICES *See* BEST BUYS & DISCOUNT PRICES **1293**

CONSUMER BUYING GUIDE (SKOKIE, ILL.) (US) [18009733] **2789, 1294**

CONSUMER CHOICE (IE/0790-486X) [14513297] **1294**

CONSUMER CLOSE-UPS (US) [09166519] **1294**

CONSUMER COMPLAINT GUIDE (US/0160-2225) [01042912] **1294**

CONSUMER CONFIDENCE SURVEY (US/1046-1876) [17408765] **1294**

CONSUMER CREDIT AND OTHER RETAIL BANKING DEVELOPMENTS (US) [13777833] **3086**

CONSUMER CREDIT AND TRUTH-IN-LENDING COMPLIANCE REPORT (US/0300-6034) [01331145] **1294, 2956**

CONSUMER CURRENTS (MY/0128-1143) [I01281143] **1294**

CONSUMER DEBTORS AND THE BANKRUPTCY CODE (US/0732-863X) [08398681] **3086**

CONSUMER DIGEST / COOPERATIVE EXTENSION ASSOCIATION OF SUFFOLK COUNTY (US) [09551261] **1295**

CONSUMER ELECTRONICS & APPLIANCE NEWS. SOUTHERN CALIFORNIA *See* RETAILER NEWS **957**

CONSUMER ELECTRONICS BUYER'S GUIDE *CEASED.* (US/1056-7372) [23835097] **2039**

●CONSUMER ELECTRONICS EDGE, THE (US/1065-7223) [26708699] **2039**

CONSUMER ELECTRONICS PRODUCT NEWS (US/0097-8329) [01799252] **2039**

CONSUMER EUROPE (UK/0308-4353) [03443662] **922**

CONSUMER EXPENDITURE STATISTICS (NZ/1170-747X) [25357255] **1471**

CONSUMER FEDERATION OF AMERICA *See* NEWS - CONSUMER FEDERATION OF AMERICA **1298**

CONSUMER FEDERATION OF AMERICA (US/0276-1270) [07303956] **1295**

CONSUMER FINANCE LAW BULLETIN (US) [01564926] **3086**

CONSUMER FINANCE LAW QUARTERLY REPORT (US/0883-4555) [11439980] **3086**

CONSUMER FINANCE NEWSLETTER (US) [04659163] **784**

CONSUMER FOOD BULLETIN (CN/0317-2058) [02247950] **2332**

CONSUMER GUIDE : AUTO (US/0097-8337) [01799364] **5412**

CONSUMER GUIDE : CARS (US/0364-0809) [02591520] **5412, 1295**

CONSUMER GUIDE PHOTOGRAPHIC EQUIPMENT TEST REPORTS (US/0091-4576) [01783768] **4368**

CONSUMER GUIDE TO HOME ENERGY SAVINGS (US/1052-9179) [22409985] **1295, 2810**

CONSUMER GUIDES (KAPUSKASING) (CN/0317-381X) [02248122] **5782**

CONSUMER HEALTH (US/0736-010X) [09068756] **4772**

CONSUMER HEALTH & NUTRITION INDEX (US/0883-1963) [12089049] **4189, 4200**

●CONSUMER HEALTH SAFETY DIGEST (US/1058-0387) [24184512] **4772**

CONSUMER INFORMATION APPLIANCE (US/1054-4909) [22903126] **1295**

CONSUMER INFORMATION CATALOG, THE (US) [03458485] **1295**

CONSUMER INFORMATION SERIES (WASHINGTON. 1971) (US/0190-2938) [02251896] **1295**

CONSUMER LAW JOURNAL (UK) **2956**

CONSUMER LENDING REPORT *CEASED.* (US/0891-558X) [14968319] **1295**

CONSUMER MAGAZINE AND AGRI-MEDIA RATES AND DATA *See* CONSUMER MAGAZINE & AGRI-MEDIA SOURCE **1295**

CONSUMER MAGAZINE AND AGRI-MEDIA RATES AND DATA / SRDS (US/0746-2522) [09898150] **758**

●CONSUMER MAGAZINE & AGRI-MEDIA SOURCE (US/1071-4537) [28642280] **1109, 1295**

CONSUMER MAGAZINE AND FARM PUBLICATION RATES AND DATA (US/0038-9595) [01766424] **758**

CONSUMER MAGAZINE PROFILES (US) **1295**

CONSUMER MAGAZINES DIGEST : NUTRITION AND FOOD-RELATED HEALTH TOPICS (US/1044-6516) [19861205] **4189**

CONSUMER MARKETS SERVICE (US/0734-4341) [08731218] **1295**

CONSUMER MEDIA TECH (US/1055-0666) [23067612] **1109**

●CONSUMER MULTIMEDIA REPORT (US/1067-7887) [27348983] **1152**

CONSUMER PHARMACIST, THE (US/0738-0615) [09504039] **4298**

CONSUMER POLICY IN OECD COUNTRIES (FR) [12842587] **1295**

CONSUMER POLICY REVIEW (UK) [24159014] **1295**

CONSUMER PRICE INDEX (AT) [03492453] **1531**

CONSUMER PRICE INDEX (NEWS) (US) [07556726] **1661, 1531**

CONSUMER PRICE INDEX (OTTAWA) (CN/0703-9352) [02248908] **1471**

CONSUMER PRICE INDEXES (PORT MORESBY, PAPUA NEW GUINEA) (PP) [14095711] **1590**

CONSUMER PRICE INDICATORS FOR VIRGINIA METROPOLITAN AREAS (US) [05929539] **1552**

CONSUMER PRICE INDICES, ANNUAL REVIEW (JM) [01789457] **1295**

CONSUMER PRICE INDICES (KINGSTON, JAMAICA) (JM) [05044090] **1471**

CONSUMER PRICES AND PRICE INDEXES (CN/0380-691X) [02585585] **1471**

●CONSUMER PRODUCT AND MANUFACTURER RATINGS (US/1068-4158) [27670634] **3477**

CONSUMER PRODUCT HAZARD INDEX (US/0147-3360) [03144394] **1295, 4772**

CONSUMER PRODUCT LITIGATION REPORTER (US/1052-9632) [22416777] **1295, 2956**

CONSUMER PROTECTION NEWSLETTER (US/0191-8567) [04915374] **1295, 2956**

CONSUMER PROTECTION REPORT (US/0362-157X) [03150535] **1295**

CONSUMER PROTECTION REPORT / NATIONAL ASSOCIATION OF ATTORNEYS GENERAL (US) [08085714] **2956, 1295**

CONSUMER REFERENCE DISC (US/1053-1424) [22461266] **1295**

CONSUMER REPORTS (US/0010-7174) [01564931] **1295**

CONSUMER REPORTS HEALTH LETTER (US/1044-3193) [19751252] **4772**

CONSUMER REPORTS ON CD-ROM (ADVANCED USER'S ED.) (US/1053-1416) [22461246] **1295, 1471**

CONSUMER REPORTS ON CD-ROM (BEGINNER'S ED.) (US/1053-1408) [22461215] **1295, 1471**

CONSUMER REPORTS ON HEALTH (US/1058-0832) [24202835] **2596, 1295**

●CONSUMER REPORTS TRAVEL BUYING GUIDE (US/1060-1511) [24883449] **1295, 5467**

CONSUMER REPORTS TRAVEL LETTER (US/0887-8439) [13171335] **5467, 1295**

CONSUMER SOFTWARE NEWS (US/8756-730X) [11638092] **1237, 1245, 1284**

CONSUMER SOURCEBOOK (US/0738-0518) [04055328] **1295**

CONSUMER SOUTH AMERICA (UK) **829**

CONSUMER SURVEYS. INTERIM REPORT (AT/0313-7732) [I03137732] **1296**

CONSUMER TRENDS (US) [04715597] **784**

CONSUMER USA (UK/0952-9543) [19280019] **1296**

CONSUMERISM (BOCA RATON) (US/0273-2475) [06004012] **1296**

CONSUMERS DIGEST (CHICAGO, ILL.) (US/0010-7182) [01607834] **1296**

CONSUMERS DIRECTORY OF CERTIFIED EFFICIENCY RATINGS FOR RESIDENTIAL HEATING AND WATER HEATING EQUIPMENT (US/1048-3330) [17965521] **2604**

CONSUMERS' FORUM (PH/0117-0171) [I01170171] **1296**

CONSUMERS GUIDE *See* SEARS **1299**

CONSUMERS INDEX TO PRODUCT EVALUATIONS AND INFORMATION SOURCES (US/0094-0534) [03672857] **1296, 1300**

CONSUMERS INFORMATION GUIDE (US) **1296**

CONSUMER'S REGISTER OF AMERICAN BUSINESS, THE *CEASED.* (US/0098-7344) [02242383] **659**

CONSUMERS REPORTS NEWS DIGEST *CEASED.* (US/1047-4048) [20686614] **1296**

CONSUMERS' RESEARCH MAGAZINE (US/0095-2222) [01788281] **1296**

CONSUMERS' RESEARCH MAGAZINE. HANDBOOK OF BUYING ISSUE (US/0069-9241) [03697240] **1296**

CONSUMING INTEREST. CHIPPENDALE (AT/0728-3008) [I07283008] **1296**

CONSUMING PASSIONS (US/0741-7748) [10203657] **4189**

CONSUMPTION (US/0010-7204) [02916078] **3378**

CONSUMPTION OF CONTAINERS AND OTHER PACKAGING SUPPLIES BY THE MANUFACTURING INDUSTRIES (CN/0576-0186) [01787237] **4218**

CONTABILITA DI MAGAZZINO (IT) **741**

CONTACT (UK/0589-5014) [05954235] **939**

CONTACT (CN) [06167163] **1969, 5096**

CONTACT (UK) **4386**

CONTACT (UK/0573-777X) [01781872] **5196, 4950**

CONTACT : A BI-MONTHLY PUBLICATION OF THE CHRISTIAN MEDICAL COMMISSION, WORLD COUNCIL OF CHURCHES (SZ) [03635989] **3568**

CONTACT : A NEWSLETTER AND NETWORKING TOOL FOR THE GESTALT COMMUNITY (US) [23364059] **4582**

CONTACT-ACADIE (CN/0820-8301) [09929622] **2729**

CONTACT - ALBERTA POTTERS' ASSOCIATION (1992) (CN/1194-6377) [29790183] **2588**

CONTACT & URGENCES 92 (FR/0296-1350) [I02961350] **3723**

CONTACT - ASSOCIATION CANADIENNE DES PROFESSIONNELS DE LA VENTE (CN/1193-7521) [I11937521] **659**

CONTACT - ASSOCIATION DE SPINA-BIFIDA ET D'HYDROCEPHALIE DU QUEBEC (CN/1195-6925) [30099221] **4335**

CONTACT - ASSOCIATION OF REGISTRARS OF THE UNIVERSITIES AND COLLEGES OF CANADA (CN/0822-7632) [10620195] **1818**

CONTACT (ASSOCIATION OF TEACHERS OF ENGLISH AS A SECOND LANGUAGE OF ONTARIO) (CN/0227-2938) [06757559] **3274**

CONTACT (BRITISH COLUMBIA HOSPITAL/HOMEBOUND TEACHERS' ASSOCIATION) (CN/0226-1456) [06273136] **1877**

CONTACT C I L (CN/0384-8701) [02678456] **1602**

CONTACT - CANADIAN COUNCIL FOR INTERNATIONAL COOPERATION (CN/0832-140X) [15465669] **4519**

CONTACT / CANADIAN COUNCIL FOR NATIVE BUSINESS (CN/1184-8839) [24368463] **864**

CONTACT - CANADIAN ELECTROACOUSTIC COMMUNITY (CN/0838-3340) [19604034] **2039**

CONTACT - CANADIAN PROFESSIONAL SALES ASSOCIATION (CN/1193-7513) [27272178] **659**

CONTACT — Alphabetical Title Index

CONTACT - CEGEP DE CHICOUTIMI (CN/1188-0686) [25882856] **1818**

CONTACT / COMITE NATIONAL MIXTE DE L'ACCP & SCF *CEASED.* (CN/0822-2592) [11074928] **3161**

CONTACT DERMATITIS (DK/0105-1873) [02254536] **3718**

CONTACT (DON MILLS) (CN/0703-119X) [03781505] **4836**

CONTACT II (US/0197-6796) [04121680] **3461**

CONTACT (KEMPTVILLE COLLEGE OF AGRICULTURAL TECHNOLOGY) (CN/0228-1759) [06778104] **76**

CONTACT LENS FORUM (US/0363-1621) [02430973] **4215**

CONTACT LENS JOURNAL (US/0096-2716) [01240986] **3873**

CONTACT LENS JOURNAL (THORNTON HEATH, SURREY), THE (UK/0306-9575) [04239817] **4215**

CONTACT LENS MEDICAL SEMINAR (US/0591-0307) [01639968] **3873**

CONTACT LENS SPECTRUM (US/0885-9175) [12769696] **4215**

CONTACT LENS UPDATE (US/0885-9264) [10269843] **3873**

CONTACT-LINSE, DIE (GW) [05119198] **4215**

CONTACT MAGAZINE (CALGARY) (CN/0843-1981) [19931732] **2588**

CONTACT MAGAZINE (CALGARY, ALTA.) *See* CONTACT - ALBERTA POTTERS' ASSOCIATION (1992) **2588**

CONTACT (MONTREAL. 1976) (CN/0701-0818) [03402787] **5187**

CONTACT (MONTREAL. 1977) (CN/0703-5780) [03979893] **1661**

CONTACT - NATIONAL ASSOCIATION OF FREE WILL BAPTISTS (US/0573-7796) [09821564] **5058**

CONTACT - NEW BRUNSWICK. DEPT. OF EDUCATION *CEASED.* (CN/1182-9869) [23659146] **1733**

●CONTACT - ONTARIO EQUESTRIAN FEDERATION (CN/1187-9327) [26497732] **2798**

CONTACT / PLENTY CANADA (CN/1182-9028) [23599128] **5097**

CONTACT QUARTERLY (US/0198-9634) [06263027] **1311**

CONTACT /REVUE OFFICIELLE DE L ASSOCIATION QUEBECOICE DES ARCHIVISTES MEDICALES (CN) **3655**

CONTACT SANTE (FR) **4772**

CONTACT (SOCIETE DE RELATIONS D'AFFAIRES, ECOLE DES HAUTES ETUDES COMMERCIALES. 1981) (CN/0713-5009) [09156960] **659**

CONTACT (ST-ANACLET DE LESSARD) (CN/0820-0084) [09631154] **4640**

CONTACT (TEMISCAMING) (CN/0821-2341) [09506596] **2531**

CONTACT (TORONTO. 1972) *CEASED.* (CN/0319-7379) [01983021] **4386**

CONTACT - UNIVERSITE SIMON FRASER. FACULTE D'EDUCATION *CEASED.* (CN/0714-3192) [10676869] 1733, **3275**

CONTACT WEST ISLAND (CN/0226-9074) [08045949] **5782**

CONTACTOLOGIA (GW/0936-1235) [23526766] **3873**

CONTACTOLOGIA-BUECHEREI (GW/0724-6226) [10865951] **4215**

CONTACTOLOGIA. DEUTSCHE AUSGABE (GW/0171-9599) [06565673] **4215**

CONTACTOLOGIA ED. FRANCAISE (GW/0171-9602) [01719602] **3873**

●CONTACTS AND COURSES, WHO'S WHO IN CANADIAN PLACEMENT (CN/1193-5073) [26969404] **1818**

CONTACTS IN AGRICULTURE (NZ) [07040083] **76**

CONTACTS INFLUENTIAL *See* CONTACTS INFLUENTIAL. SOUTH ORANGE COUNTY **660**

CONTACTS INFLUENTIAL. ATLANTA, GEORGIA (US/8756-1298) [06315208] **659**

CONTACTS INFLUENTIAL. CALGARY : CI (CN) [11406781] **659**

CONTACTS INFLUENTIAL. CENTRAL ORANGE COUNTY (US/8756-0747) [11436670] **659**

CONTACTS INFLUENTIAL. COLORADO FRONT RANGE (US/0748-3295) [09309248] **660**

CONTACTS INFLUENTIAL. DALLAS, DALLAS COUNTY, TEXAS (US/0743-2623) [10523843] **660**

CONTACTS INFLUENTIAL. DENVER (US/0743-1007) [10270689] **660**

CONTACTS INFLUENTIAL. EAST BAY (US/0743-2682) [10512114] **660**

CONTACTS INFLUENTIAL. EDMONTON : CI (CN) [10917477] **660**

CONTACTS INFLUENTIAL. FORT WORTH, TEXAS, TARRANT COUNTY (US/0884-9722) [11511510] **660**

CONTACTS INFLUENTIAL. KANSAS CITY *See* KANSAS CITY METRO BUSINESS DIRECTORY **688**

CONTACTS INFLUENTIAL. LOS ANGELES COUNTY, LAX (US/0749-8365) [11165871] **660**

CONTACTS INFLUENTIAL. LOS ANGELES COUNTY, LONG BEACH METRO (US/8756-5889) [11710198] **660**

CONTACTS INFLUENTIAL. LOS ANGELES COUNTY, SOUTH BAY (US/0748-4429) [10928787] **660**

CONTACTS INFLUENTIAL. LOS ANGELES COUNTY, SOUTHEAST L.A. : CI (US/8756-0119) [11406855] **660**

CONTACTS INFLUENTIAL. METROPOLITAN TORONTO EAST : CI (CN) [10512043] **660**

CONTACTS INFLUENTIAL. METROPOLITAN TORONTO WEST : CI (CN) [10512073] **660**

CONTACTS INFLUENTIAL. NORTH ORANGE COUNTY (US/8756-064X) [11434988] **660**

CONTACTS INFLUENTIAL. PHOENIX *See* CONTACTS INFLUENTIAL. PHOENIX, ARIZONA **660**

CONTACTS INFLUENTIAL. PHOENIX, ARIZONA (US/0743-1813) [10518345] **660**

CONTACTS INFLUENTIAL. PORTLAND, OREGON (US/0743-2674) [10523971] **660**

CONTACTS INFLUENTIAL. SAN FRANCISCO, CALIFORNIA (US/0743-2690) [10518284] **660**

CONTACTS INFLUENTIAL. SOUTH BAY (US/8756-5803) [10704047] **660**

CONTACTS INFLUENTIAL. SOUTH CENTRAL KANSAS (US/8756-5838) [11541393] **660**

CONTACTS INFLUENTIAL. SOUTH ORANGE COUNTY (US/8756-0976) [11434904] **660**

CONTACTS INFLUENTIAL. SOUTH SAN DIEGO COUNTY (US/0743-2712) [10512155] **660**

CONTACTS INFLUENTIAL. TACOMA AND OLYMPIA (US/8756-0682) [11437362] **660**

CONTACTS INFLUENTIAL. TAMPA BAY (US/0748-4437) [09595184] **660**

CONTACTS INFLUENTIAL. WASHINGTON, D.C (US/0743-264X) [08446208] **660**

CONTACTS; REVUE FRANCAISE DE L'ORTHODOXIE (FR/0045-8325) [03521093] **4950**

CONTADURIA UNIVERSIDAD DE ANTIOQUIA (CK/0120-4203) [10365106] **741**

CONTAGENS DE TRAFEGO: TEMPORADA DE VERAO (BL) [04838365] **5439**

CONTAGIOUS MAGAZINE (AT) **1062**

CONTAINER & PACKAGING RECYCLING UPDATE (US/1070-8057) [28473048] **2226**

CONTAINER MANAGEMENT (UK/0269-7726) [20881733] **5448**

CONTAINER NEWS (US/0010-7360) [01789258] **5380**

CONTAINERISATION (UK) **864**

CONTAINERISATION INTERNATIONAL (UK/0010-7379) [03601838] **864**

CONTAINERISATION INTERNATIONAL WORLD DIRECTORY OF LINER SHIPPING AGENTS (UK/0951-5879) [I09515879] **829**

CONTAINERISATION INTERNATIONAL YEARBOOK (UK) [00944759] **1969**

CONTAINERS (FR) 5380, **4218**

CONTAMINACION AMBIENTAL (CK) [04892538] **2226**

●CONTAMINATION ALERT (US/1061-866X) [25484840] **4772**

CONTAMINATION CONTROL ABSTRACTS (UK/0952-1542) [I09521542] 2226, **2183**

CONTATTO ELETTRICO (IT/1120-2351) [I11202351] **1936**

CONTAX *CEASED.* (UK) [14933633] **4215**

CONTEMPO (BIRMINGHAM, ALA.) (US/0162-1971) [04117742] **4950**

CONTEMPORANEA *CEASED.* (IT/0394-428X) [21954453] **384**

CONTEMPORANUL IDEEA EUROPEANA (RM) [23353892] **2514**

CONTEMPORARY ACCOUNTING RESEARCH (CN/0823-9150) [13027638] **742**

CONTEMPORARY AFFAIRS (II) [18676582] **2649**

CONTEMPORARY AFFAIRS (TORONTO) *SUSPENDED.* (CN/0384-9333) [01564950] **4519**

CONTEMPORARY AMERICAN PAINTING AND SCULPTURE (US/0069-9365) [05705442] **348**

CONTEMPORARY ANALYSIS IN EDUCATION SERIES *CEASED.* (UK) [14580633] **1891**

CONTEMPORARY APPROACHES TO IBSEN : PROCEEDINGS OF THE INTERNATIONAL IBSEN SEMINARY (NO) [06458991] 2684, **3340**

CONTEMPORARY ART (UK) **317**

CONTEMPORARY AUSTRIAN STUDIES (US) **2514**

CONTEMPORARY AUTHORS (US/0010-7468) [01564953] 3378, **431**

CONTEMPORARY AUTHORS AUTOBIOGRAPHY SERIES (US/0748-0636) [10881327] 3378, **431**

CONTEMPORARY AUTHORS. NEW REVISION SERIES (US/0275-7176) [06921683] **414**

●CONTEMPORARY BLACK BIOGRAPHY (US/1058-1316) [24225462] **2259**

CONTEMPORARY BRITAIN : AN ANNUAL REVIEW (UK/0957-5960) [22257838] **2684**

CONTEMPORARY BRITISH PHILOSOPHY : PERSONAL STATEMENTS (UK) [04697568] **4344**

CONTEMPORARY CHRISTIAN MUSIC (1986) (US/1049-3379) [17938622] 4950, **4111**

CONTEMPORARY COMPOSERS (US) **4111**

CONTEMPORARY CONCEPTS IN PHYSICS (US/0272-2488) [06796825] **4401**

CONTEMPORARY DIAGNOSTIC RADIOLOGY (US/0149-9009) [03579147] **3940**

CONTEMPORARY DIALYSIS & NEPHROLOGY (US/0899-837X) [18236486] **3989**

CONTEMPORARY DOLL MAGAZINE (US/1052-486X) [22401456] **2773**

CONTEMPORARY DRAMATISTS (UK/1050-3919) [04083136] 5363, **431**

CONTEMPORARY DRUG PROBLEMS (US/0091-4509) [01786889] **1342**

CONTEMPORARY ECONOMIC ANALYSIS (UK) [07034637] **1590**

●CONTEMPORARY ECONOMIC POLICY (US/1074-3529) [29716982] **1471**

CONTEMPORARY ECONOMIC PROBLEMS (1987) (US/0892-3981) [15187306] **1552**

CONTEMPORARY EDUCATION (US/0010-7476) [01564957] **1891**

CONTEMPORARY EDUCATIONAL PSYCHOLOGY (US/0361-476X) [02246972] 1733, **4582**

CONTEMPORARY ENDOCRINOLOGY (US/0196-8653) [05857729] **3727**

CONTEMPORARY ERGONOMICS : PROCEEDINGS OF THE ERGONOMICS SOCIETY'S ANNUAL CONFERENCE (UK/0267-4718) [14516098] **1969**

CONTEMPORARY ETHNOGRAPHIC STUDIES (US) **5243**

CONTEMPORARY EUROPEAN AFFAIRS *CEASED.* (UK/0955-3843) [20727031] **1552**

●CONTEMPORARY EUROPEAN HISTORY (UK/0960-7773) [25706166] **2684**

CONTEMPORARY FAMILY THERAPY (US/0892-2764) [13511530] 4582, **2278**

CONTEMPORARY FRENCH CIVILIZATION (US/0147-9156) [03234085] **2684**

CONTEMPORARY GERIATRIC MEDICINE (US/0748-2760) [09632206] **3750**

CONTEMPORARY GERMAN PHILOSOPHY *CEASED.* (US/0740-719X) [09544741] **4344**

●CONTEMPORARY GERONTOLOGY (US/1069-0840) [27921510] **3750**

CONTEMPORARY GRAPHIC ARTISTS *SUSPENDED.* (US/0885-8462) [12761188] **377**

CONTEMPORARY HEALTH JOURNAL (US/0882-4479) [10633752] **4772**

CONTEMPORARY HEMATOLOGY/ONCOLOGY (US/0197-3649) [05996645] 3815, **3771**

CONTEMPORARY HYPNOSIS : THE JOURNAL OF THE BRITISH SOCIETY OF EXPERIMENTAL AND CLINICAL HYPNOSIS (UK/0960-5290) [23667161] **2857**

CONTEMPORARY INTERNAL MEDICINE (US/1042-9646) [19259410] **3796**

CONTEMPORARY ISSUES (AT/0155-2171) [I01552171] **1733**

CONTEMPORARY ISSUES IN CLINICAL BIOCHEMISTRY (UK/0265-6701) [12700624] **486**

Alphabetical Title Index — CONTINUATION

CONTEMPORARY ISSUES IN CLINICAL IMMUNOLOGY AND ALLERGY (UK) [08585503] **3668**

CONTEMPORARY ISSUES IN CLINICAL NUTRITION (US/0736-4369) [08691911] **4189**

CONTEMPORARY ISSUES IN CLINICAL ONCOLOGY (US/0892-0079) [09605778] **3815**

CONTEMPORARY ISSUES IN COMPUTED TOMOGRAPHY (UK) [10182683] **3940**

CONTEMPORARY ISSUES IN FETAL AND NEONATAL MEDICINE (US/0893-8822) [12163656] 3902, **3759**

CONTEMPORARY ISSUES IN INFECTIOUS DISEASES (US/0888-7756) [10106238] **3712**

CONTEMPORARY ISSUES IN NEPHROLOGY (US/0161-9934) [04078276] **3989**

CONTEMPORARY ISSUES IN NUCLEAR IMAGING (US/0895-996X) [12444627] **3847**

CONTEMPORARY ISSUES IN OPHTHALMOLOGY (UK/0888-7691) [11244656] **3873**

CONTEMPORARY ISSUES IN SMALL ANIMAL PRACTICE (US/0891-9747) [11254636] **5508**

CONTEMPORARY JAPANESE PRINTS (JA) [10243142] **377**

CONTEMPORARY JEWRY (US/0147-1694) [03111427] **2259**

CONTEMPORARY LEGEND : THE JOURNAL OF THE INTERNATIONAL SOCIETY FOR CONTEMPORARY LEGEND RESEARCH (UK/0963-8334) [25363838] **2319**

CONTEMPORARY LITERATURE (US/0010-7484) [02244753] **3378**

CONTEMPORARY LONGTERM CARE (US/8750-9652) [11965066] **5280**

CONTEMPORARY MANAGEMENT IN INTERNAL MEDICINE *SUSPENDED.* (US/1050-9607) [21722524] **3796**

CONTEMPORARY MANAGEMENT IN OBSTETRICS AND GYNECOLOGY *CEASED.* (US/1050-9615) [21722585] **3759**

CONTEMPORARY MATHEMATICS (AMERICAN MATHEMATICAL SOCIETY) (US/0271-4132) [06646888] **3502**

CONTEMPORARY MUSIC ALMANAC (US/0196-6200) [05864313] **4111**

CONTEMPORARY MUSIC FORUM (US/1065-4712) [26612469] **4111**

CONTEMPORARY MUSIC REVIEW (UK/0749-4467) [11128997] **4111**

CONTEMPORARY MUSIC STUDIES (SZ/0891-5415) [14907393] **4111**

CONTEMPORARY MUSICIANS (US/1044-2197) [19730669] **4111**

CONTEMPORARY NEPHROLOGY (US/0278-1700) [07099822] **3989**

CONTEMPORARY NEUROLOGY SERIES (US/0069-9446) [02250819] **3830**

CONTEMPORARY NEUROLOGY SYMPOSIA (US/0069-9454) [01564965] **3830**

CONTEMPORARY NEUROSURGERY (US/0163-2108) [04317352] **3963**

CONTEMPORARY NOVELISTS (UK) [04086362] **3378**

●CONTEMPORARY NURSE : A JOURNAL FOR THE AUSTRALIAN NURSING PROFESSION (AT/1037-6178) [26350877] **3854**

CONTEMPORARY NUTRITION (US/0198-0009) [06168654] **4189**

CONTEMPORARY OB/GYN (US/0090-3159) [01784935] **3759**

CONTEMPORARY ONCOLOGY (US/1061-0383) [25162617] **3815**

●CONTEMPORARY ORGANIC SYNTHESIS (UK/1350-4894) **1041**

CONTEMPORARY ORTHOPAEDICS (US/0194-8458) [05057206] **3881**

CONTEMPORARY PACIFIC, THE (US/1043-898X) [19596864] **2510**

CONTEMPORARY PEDIATRICS (MONTVALE, N.J.) (US/8750-0507) [10956598] **3902**

CONTEMPORARY PERSPECTIVES IN REHABILITATION (US/1040-2217) [13388504] **3568**

CONTEMPORARY PHILOSOPHY (BOULDER, COLO.) (US/0732-4944) [04980204] **4344**

CONTEMPORARY PHYSICS (UK/0010-7514) [01564967] **4401**

CONTEMPORARY POETS (UK) [04086293] **3461**

CONTEMPORARY POETS OF AMERICA (US/0734-4260) [06245255] **3461**

CONTEMPORARY POLICY ISSUES (US/0735-0007) [08854805] **1471**

CONTEMPORARY PRAISE (US/1046-3801) [20403022] **5058**

CONTEMPORARY PROBLEMS IN CARDIOLOGY (US/0093-5166) [01780548] **3703**

CONTEMPORARY PROBLEMS OF CHILDHOOD (US/0147-1082) [04121184] 5280, **4582**

CONTEMPORARY PSYCHIATRY (NEW YORK, N.Y.) *CEASED.* (US/0277-8041) [07646208] **3923**

CONTEMPORARY PSYCHOANALYSIS (US/0010-7530) [01564972] **3923**

CONTEMPORARY PSYCHOLOGY (US/0010-7549) [01564973] **4582**

CONTEMPORARY PSYCHOLOGY SERIES (UK) [25193419] **4582**

CONTEMPORARY PSYCHOTHERAPY REVIEW (US/0737-9544) [09485507] **3924**

CONTEMPORARY PUBLIC HEALTH ISSUES (US) [25963379] 4772, **3740**

CONTEMPORARY RECORD : THE JOURNAL OF THE INSTITUTE OF CONTEMPORARY BRITISH HISTORY (UK/0950-9224) [16835480] **2684**

CONTEMPORARY RELIGIOUS MOVEMENTS (US/0190-0986) [04625313] **4950**

CONTEMPORARY REVIEW (LONDON, ENGLAND) (UK/0010-7565) [01564974] **2486**

CONTEMPORARY REVIEWS IN OBSTETRICS AND GYNAECOLOGY (UK/0953-9182) [19743789] **3759**

CONTEMPORARY SECURITY POLICY (UK) **4519**

CONTEMPORARY SENIORHEALTH (US) **5178**

CONTEMPORARY SHOWCASE (FESTIVAL) *See* CONTEMPORARY SHOWCASE. SYLLABUS **4111**

CONTEMPORARY SHOWCASE. SYLLABUS (CN/0316-893X) [02247352] **4111**

CONTEMPORARY SOCIAL ISSUES (SANTA CRUZ, CALIF.) (US/0887-3569) [13195731] **5227**

CONTEMPORARY SOCIAL PROBLEMS (US) [07261923] **5196**

CONTEMPORARY SOCIAL SCIENCES (II) [01784126] **5196**

CONTEMPORARY SOCIAL WORK EDUCATION (AT/0313-6124) [05400076] 1877, **5280**

CONTEMPORARY SOCIOLOGY (WASHINGTON) (US/0094-3061) [00958948] **5243**

●CONTEMPORARY SOUTH ASIA (UK/0958-4935) [26135792] **2503**

CONTEMPORARY SOUTHEAST ASIA (SI/0129-797X) [05526448] **2649**

CONTEMPORARY SSOCIAL PSYCHOLOGY (US/1041-3030) [18726830] 5196, **4582**

CONTEMPORARY STUDIES IN APPLIED BEHAVIORAL SCIENCE (US) [11013825] **4582**

CONTEMPORARY STUDIES IN ECONOMIC AND FINANCIAL ANALYSIS (US) **1471**

CONTEMPORARY STUDIES IN ECONOMIC AND FINANCIAL ANALYSIS (US) [05032054] **1471**

CONTEMPORARY STUDIES IN PHILOSOPHY AND THE HUMAN SCIENCES (US) **4344**

CONTEMPORARY STUDIES IN SOCIOLOGY (US) [10790407] **5243**

CONTEMPORARY SURGERY (US/0045-8341) [01640923] **3963**

CONTEMPORARY THEATER STUDIES (SZ/1049-6513) [21269825] **5363**

CONTEMPORARY THEATRE, FILM, AND TELEVISION (US/0749-064X) [11078702] **384**

●CONTEMPORARY THEATRE REVIEW (SZ/1048-6801) [21015542] **5363**

CONTEMPORARY TIMES (US/1071-2917) [28604698] **864**

●CONTEMPORARY TOPICS IN ENTOMOLOGY (US) [25578216] **5607**

CONTEMPORARY TOPICS IN IMMUNOBIOLOGY (US/0093-4054) [01800148] **3668**

CONTEMPORARY TOPICS IN INFORMATION TRANSFER (NE) [09880865] 1180, **2039**

●CONTEMPORARY TOPICS IN LABORATORY ANIMAL SCIENCE (US/1060-0558) [24857273] **5508**

CONTEMPORARY TOPICS IN MOLECULAR IMMUNOLOGY (US/0090-8800) [01790060] **3668**

CONTEMPORARY TOPICS IN POLYMER SCIENCE (US/0160-6727) [03736209] **1041**

CONTEMPORARY TOPICS IN PURE AND APPLIED CONDENSED MATTER SCIENCE (UK/1043-3996) [19451021] **5097**

●CONTEMPORARY URBAN STUDIES (US/1065-7002) [26683709] **2819**

CONTEMPORARY UROLOGY (US/1042-2250) [18976684] **3989**

CONTEMPORARY UROLOGY (MISSISSAUGA) (CN/1185-2526) [24367996] **3989**

CONTEMPORARY VERSE TWO (CN/0831-9502) [12788368] **3461**

CONTEMPORARY WALES : AN ANNUAL REVIEW OF ECONOMIC AND SOCIAL RESEARCH (UK/0951-4937) [17591375] 5196, **1471**

CONTEMPORARY WRITINGS ON LONG TERM CARE PHARMACY (US/0892-1865) [04372989] **4298**

CONTENIDO (MX/0010-7581) [01564977] **2531**

CONTENT *See* MEDIA **2922**

CONTENT FOR CANADIAN JOURNALISTS (1984) (CN/0045-835X) [15236068] **2918**

CONTENTA RELIGIONUM (FI/0782-7342) [07827342] **4950**

CONTENTION (BLOOMINGTON, IND.) (US/1056-1072) [23466888] **5196**

CONTENTS OF CURRENT JOURNALS (UK) **728**

CONTENTS OF RECENT ECONOMICS JOURNALS *CEASED.* (UK) [03989952] 1471, **1531**

CONTENTS PAGES IN EDUCATION (UK/0265-9220) [14389741] 1733, **1794**

CONTENTS PAGES IN MANAGEMENT (UK/0306-3224) [I03063224] 864, **728**

CONTENUTI (IT/0010-762X) [04442855] **3378**

CONTEST AND LOTTERY NEWS (CN/0710-6297) [08401530] **4640**

CONTEST BUSTER (US/0898-3747) [17795603] **2531**

CONTEST HOTLINE (US/0195-9735) [05739649] **4859**

CONTEST NEWS-LETTER (US/0894-0207) [12010531] **758**

CONTEXT (PH) [02410061] **758**

CONTEXT (CHICAGO. 1969) (US/0361-8854) [01776577] **4950**

CONTEXTO BOLETIM (BL) [02241946] 1471, **660**

CONTI DEGLI ITALIANI : COMPENDIO DELLA VITA ECONOMICA NAZIONALE / ISTITUTO CENTRALE DI STATISTICA, I (IT) [07700317] **1531**

CONTI ECONOMICI TRIMESTRALI (IT) **1471**

CONTINENT (FR) [02576712] **3378**

CONTINENT CENDRARS (SZ) [16989641] **3378**

CONTINENTAL BANK JOURNAL OF APPLIED CORPORATE FINANCE (US/0898-4484) [17813766] **784**

CONTINENTAL BIRDLIFE (US/0270-2894) [05469389] **5617**

CONTINENTAL COMMENTS (US/0573-8164) [06999073] **5412**

CONTINENTAL DIRECTORY NMF. STANDARD POINT LOCATION CODES SPLC (US/0363-9983) [02549424] **5400**

CONTINENTAL DRIFTER (US/0743-3107) [10548578] **3378**

CONTINENTAL FILM & VIDEO REVIEW (UK) [07621585] **4067**

CONTINENTAL FRANCHISE REVIEW (US/0045-8376) [05259010] **660**

CONTINENTAL HANDBOOK & GUIDE TO WESTERN EUROPE (UK/0589-5413) [03783681] **5412**

CONTINENTAL HOMEWARES *CEASED.* (GW) [11350771] 2904, **2588**

CONTINENTAL HOTEL GUIDE (UK) [18172762] **2804**

CONTINENTAL MODELLER (UK/0955-1298) [I09551298] **2773**

CONTINENTAL NEWS-REVIEW, THE (US) [10529550] **5727**

CONTINENTAL OIL COMPANY *See* CONOCO **4253**

CONTINENTAL REFLECTIONS (CN/0226-8949) [08045886] **4950**

CONTINENTAL SHELF RESEARCH (UK/0278-4343) [07821866] **1354**

CONTINENTALER STAHLMARKT *See* STAHL MARKT **1627**

CONTINGENCIES (WASHINGTON, D.C.) (US/1048-9851) [21101923] **2878**

CONTINGENCY PLANNING & RECOVERY JOURNAL : CPR-J (US/0899-4595) [18114368] **1226**

CONTINGENT FOREIGN LIABILITIES OF THE UNITED STATES GOVERNMENT (US/0162-6779) [06229691] **4719**

CONTINUATION EDUCATION (CALIFORNIA CONTINUATION EDUCATION ASSOCIATION : 1979) (US) [07334539] **1800**

CONTINUING CARE (US/1057-428X) [18355082] **5280**

●CONTINUING CARE CONNECTION : LINKING LONG-TERM, HOME AND COMMUNITY CARE SYSTEMS (US) [30017684] 3568, **5280**

CONTINUING CARE RESOURCES (CN/0824-1384) [12606707] 3750, **3778**

CONTINUING EDUCATION FOR HEALTH CARE PROVIDERS (US/0160-6980) [03693718] 3568, **1800**

CONTINUING EDUCATION IN NURSING, A DIRECTORY (CN/1183-7985) [24690436] **3854**

CONTINUING EDUCATION IN NURSING, A DIRECTORY (CN/1183-7985) [24690440] **3854**

CONTINUING EDUCATION IN ORTHOPAEDIC SURGERY. SOUND RECORDING (US/0193-2349) [08913592] 3881, **3568**

CONTINUING EDUCATION LECTURES (US/0148-1010) [03267259] 1818, **3568**

CONTINUING EDUCATION / OFFICE OF CONTINUING EDUCATION (US) [24421002] **1800**

CONTINUING EDUCATION (TORONTO) (CN/0318-5141) [02442119] **4298**

CONTINUING ENGINEERING STUDIES SERIES. MONOGRAPHS (US/0069-9551) [01564987] **1969**

CONTINUING HIGHER EDUCATION REVIEW (US/0893-0384) [15335320] **1818**

●CONTINUING MEDICAL EDUCATION DIRECTORY / AMERICAN MEDICAL ASSOCIATION (US) [26714408] 3568, **1924**

CONTINUING THE CONVERSATION *CEASED.* (US/0889-468X) [14083500] 4582, **4344**

CONTINUITA E SCUOLA (IT) **1924**

CONTINUITE (CN/0714-9476) [09547438] 295, **348**

CONTINUITY (US/0277-1446) [07223869] **2614**

CONTINUITY AND CHANGE (UK/0268-4160) [13551705] **5243**

CONTINUO (CN/0705-6656) [04097904] **4111**

CONTINUO (BRISBANE, QLD.) (AT/0310-6802) [14914420] 1818, **4112**

CONTINUOUS COUNT TRAFFIC DATA (US) [04910085] **5439**

CONTINUOUS IMPROVEMENT (US/1071-2240) [28576922] **3477**

●CONTINUOUS JOURNEY (US/1065-3406) [26577048] 1661, **864**

CONTINUOUS SAMPLE SURVEY OF POPULATION (TR/0564-2612) [02092964] **4551**

CONTINUOUS WAGE AND BENEFIT HISTORY (US/0361-9400) [02441308] 2878, **1661**

CONTINUOUS WAGE AND BENEFIT HISTORY REPORT IN UNEMPLOYMENT INSURANCE *See* CONTINUOUS WAGE AND BENEFIT HISTORY **1661**

CONTINUUM (US) [23077402] **2614**

CONTINUUM (DOWNSVIEW) (CN/0381-0925) [02505820] **2956**

CONTINUUM (L. D. PANKEY INSTITUTE) (US/0195-6043) [05509562] **1319**

CONTINUUM MECHANICS AND THERMODYNAMICS (GW/0935-1175) [20792872] **2112**

CONTINUUM (MONTREAL) (CN/0226-6385) [06515865] **5782**

CONTINUUM (MT. LAWLEY, W.A.) (AT/1030-4312) [16998366] 384, **4067**

CONTOTERZISTA, IL (IT) **158**

CONTOURS BANGKOK (TH/0857-491X) [I0857491X] **4506**

CONTOURS (OTTAWA) (CN/0848-7952) [23249059] **2559**

●CONTRA COSTA COUNTY COMMERCE AND INDUSTRY DIRECTORY (US/1059-7093) [24681244] **829**

CONTRA COSTA COUNTY POPULAR STREET ATLAS (CENSUS TRACT ED.) (US/0733-6845) [08641639] **2559**

CONTRA COSTA TIMES (US/0192-0235) [05005293] **5634**

CONTRA MUNDUM (US/1070-9495) [26334563] **4950**

CONTRABAND (US/0888-7586) [06579160] **5683**

CONTRACAMPO (SP) [08187546] **4067**

CONTRACEPTION, FERTILITE, SEXUALITE (FR/1157-8181) [28711839] **588**

CONTRACEPTION (STONEHAM) (US/0010-7824) [01564991] **588**

CONTRACEPTIVE TECHNOLOGY (US/0091-9721) [03537573] **588**

CONTRACEPTIVE TECHNOLOGY UPDATE (US/0274-726X) [06537532] **588**

CONTRACT AND CAPTIVE ELECTRONIC MANUFACTURING AND PRINTED CIRCUIT PRODUCTION (US/1053-1017) [20974790] **2039**

CONTRACT AUDIT MANUAL (US) [05931897] **4040**

CONTRACT BRIDGE BULLETIN *See* BULLETIN - AMERICAN CONTRACT BRIDGE LEAGUE (1993), THE **4858**

CONTRACT BRIDGE BULLETIN, THE (US/0010-7840) [01564992] **4859**

CONTRACT CLEANING *See* BUILDING SERVICES CONTRACTOR **604**

CONTRACT DESIGN (US/1053-5632) [22579294] **2904**

CONTRACT EMPLOYMENT WEEKLY (US/1063-9268) [25104421] **4203**

CONTRACT ENGINEER *See* CONTRACT EMPLOYMENT WEEKLY **4203**

CONTRACT FURNITURE BUYER'S GUIDE (US/0883-9360) [12257468] 949, **4211**

CONTRACT HEALTHCARE *CEASED.* (US/0891-5059) [14874627] **3568**

CONTRACT JOURNAL (SUTTON) (UK/0010-7859) [04207353] **611**

CONTRACT MANAGEMENT (US/0190-3063) [04659922] 4640, **2956**

CONTRACT SERIES. REPORTS IN CONTRACT ARCHAEOLOGY (US) [07798126] **266**

CONTRACTING BUSINESS (US/0279-4071) [07833285] **2604**

CONTRACTING DMS INTELLIGENCE *See* CONTRACTING INTELLIGENCE **4640**

CONTRACTING FOR SERVICES; COURSE MANUAL (US/0195-9247) [05687897] **3146**

CONTRACTING INTELLIGENCE (US/1041-7427) [11889058] **4640**

CONTRACTING PARTIES TO THE GENERAL AGREEMENT ON TARIFFS AND TRADE *See* GATT BIBLIOGRAPHY, 1947-1953; THE TEXT OF THE GATT, SELECTED GATT PUBLICATIONS, A CHRONOLOGICAL LIST OF REFERENCES TO THE GATT. SUPPLEMENT **729**

CONTRACTIONS (US) [02786806] **17**

CONTRACTOR BUSINESS REPORT (US/0271-5511) [06645310] **660**

CONTRACTOR (NEWTON, MASS.) (US/0897-7135) [17616691] 611, **2604**

CONTRACTOR REPORT - TRANSPORT AND ROAD RESEARCH LABORATORY (UK/0266-7045) [I02667045] **611**

CONTRACTOR'S BUSINESS MANAGEMENT REPORT (US/1058-9260) [24433905] **864**

CONTRACTOR'S CONFERENCE OF THE ARTIFICIAL KIDNEY PROGRAM OF THE NATIONAL INSTITUTE OF ARTHRITIS AND METABOLIC DISEASES. ANNUAL CONTRACTOR'S CONFERENCE *See* PROCEEDINGS - ANNUAL CONTRACTOR'S CONFERENCE OF THE ARTIFICIAL KIDNEY PROGRAM OF THE NATIONAL INSTITUTE OF ARTHRITIS, METABOLISM, AND DIGESTIVE DISEASES **3800**

CONTRACTORS DATA REPORT : NATIONWIDE TABULATED BID RESULTS (US) [08984674] **660**

CONTRACTORS GUIDE (LOMBARD, ILL.) (US/0273-5954) [07449162] **611**

CONTRACTORS HOT LINE EQUIPMENT ESTIMATOR (US/0279-5566) [07099271] **611**

CONTRACTORS JOURNAL, THE (US/1058-7780) [24384385] **611**

CONTRACTORS MANAGEMENT JOURNAL (US) 611, **295**

CONTRACTOR'S PRICING GUIDE. FRAMING AND ROUGH CARPENTRY (US) [29584504] **611**

●CONTRACTOR'S PRICING GUIDE. RESIDENTIAL DETAILED COSTS (US/1074-0481) [29585128] **611**

●CONTRACTOR'S PRICING GUIDE. RESIDENTIAL SQUARE FOOT COSTS (US/1074-049X) [29585164] **611**

CONTRACTS (US/0098-762X) [02239702] **2956**

CONTRADDIZIONE, LA (IT) **4470**

CONTRADICTIONS BRUXELLES (BE/0770-8521) [I07708521] 4470, **1471**

CONTRAGATE ALERT / THE CHRISTIC INSTITUTE (US) [16719443] **4470**

CONTRAPONTO (BL) [03501588] **5196**

CONTRARY INVESTOR FOLLOW-UP, THE (US/0740-0306) [09856350] **895**

CONTRARY INVESTOR, THE (US/0010-793X) [06063845] **895**

CONTRASTES (PARIS) (FR/0247-915X) [11846171] **3275**

CONTRATTAZIONE COLLETTIVA (IT) **1661**

CONTRATTO E IMPRESA (IT) [18459800] **3098**

CONTRECHAMPS *CEASED.* (FR) [11394008] **4112**

CONTREE / RAAD VIR GEESTESWETENSKAPLIKE NAVORSING, INSTITUUT VIR GESKIEDENISNAVORSING,AFDELING STREEKGESKIEDENIS (SA/0379-9867) [08487002] **2638**

CONTRETEMPS (MONTREAL) (CN/0829-240X) [13364650] **2212**

CONTRIBUCION HISTORICA (CL) [10319155] **2729**

CONTRIBUCION - INSTITUTO ECUATORIANO DE CIENCIAS NATURALES (EC/0480-8029) [01437447] **5097**

CONTRIBUCIONES CIENTIFICAS DEL INSTITUTO ANTARTICO ARGENTINO (AG) [05654002] **5097**

CONTRIBUCIONES CIENTIFICAS DEL INSTITUTO ARGENTINO DE OCEANOGRAFIA (AG/0325-6367) [08746281] **1448**

CONTRIBUCIONES CIENTIFICAS Y TECNOLOGICAS / UNIVERSIDAD TECNICA DEL ESTADO (CH) [10518515] **5097**

CONTRIBUCIONES : PUBLICACION TRIMESTRAL DEL CENTRO INTERDISCIPLINARIO DE ESTUDIOS SOBRE EL DESARROLLO LATINOAMERICANO (AG/0326-4068) [10862344] **1634**

CONTRIBUTI DEL CENTRO LINCEO INTERDISCIPLINAIRE BENIAMINO SEGRE (IT/0394-0705) [I03940705] **3502**

CONTRIBUTI DEL CENTRO LINCEO INTERDISCIPLINARE DI SCIENZE E LORO APPLICAZIONI (IT/0391-8041) [04800599] **3502**

CONTRIBUTI DELL'ISTITUTO DI FILOLOGIA MODERNA : SERIE INGLESE (IT) [03332955] **3378**

CONTRIBUTI DELL'ISTITUTO DI FILOLOGIA MODERNA. SERIE ITALIANA (IT) [07922338] 3275, **3378**

CONTRIBUTII BOTANICE (RM/0069-9616) [10121106] **507**

CONTRIBUTION (CALIFORNIA WATER RESOURCES CENTER) (US/0575-4941) [14998681] 5532, **1413**

CONTRIBUTION DES EMPLOYEURS A L'EFFORT DE CONSTRUCTION (FR) [05756566] **1661**

CONTRIBUTION - FLORIDA DEPARTMENT OF NATURAL RESOURCES MARINE RESEARCH LABORATORY (US) [01398005] 452, **1448**

CONTRIBUTION - INSTITUT D'ASTRONOMIE ET DE GEOPHYSIQUE GEORGES LEMAITRE. MEDEDELINGEN VAN HET ASTRONOMISCH INSTITUUT VAN DE KATHOLIEKE UNIVERSITEIT LEUVEN (BE/0537-7560) [04940961] 1404, **394**

CONTRIBUTION - NEW ZEALAND OCEANOGRAPHIC INSTITUTE (NZ/0511-4470) [01122455] **1448**

CONTRIBUTION (PAMLICO MARINE LABORATORY) (US) [05242885] 554, **1448**

CONTRIBUTION - SUOMEN TIEDESEURA. PARASITOLOGIAN LAITOS (FI) [01785781] **452**

CONTRIBUTION - UNIVERSITY OF MARYLAND, NATURAL RESOURCES INSTITUTE (US/0097-0832) [01417653] **2191**

CONTRIBUTION - VIRGINIA INSTITUTE OF MARINE SCIENCE (US/0083-6400) [01359286] **554**

CONTRIBUTIONS A L'ETUDE DES SCIENCES DE L'HOMME (CN/0589-5820) [03884012] **5097**

CONTRIBUTIONS. ANTHROPOLOGY AND HISTORY (US) [02253547] **234**

CONTRIBUTIONS - BROOKLYN BOTANIC GARDEN (US) [01537439] **507**

CONTRIBUTIONS DE LA STATION BIOLOGIQUE DU ST-LAURENT A TROIS-PISTOLES, P. Q., CANADA (CN) [01347794] **452**

CONTRIBUTIONS DE L'INSTITUT DE BIOLOGIE DE L'UNIVERSITE DE MONTREAL (1948) (CN) [01410501] **5581**

CONTRIBUTIONS FROM THE BERMUDA BIOLOGICAL STATION FOR RESEARCH (BM) [02386364] 1448, **2226**

CONTRIBUTIONS FROM THE LABORATORY OF VERTEBRATE BIOLOGY (US/0096-0411) [01405971] **452**

CONTRIBUTIONS FROM THE MUSEUM OF PALEONTOLOGY (US/0097-3556) [07897097] **4226**

CONTRIBUTIONS FROM THE NEW YORK BOTANICAL GARDEN (US/0736-0509) [05375405] **507**

CONTRIBUTIONS FROM THE UNIVERSITY OF KANSAS HERBARIUM (US/0735-3669) [08501906] **507**

CONTRIBUTIONS FROM THE UNIVERSITY OF MICHIGAN HERBARIUM (US/0091-1860) [01757325] **507**

CONTRIBUTIONS IN AFRO-AMERICAN AND AFRICAN STUDIES (US/0069-9624) [02957030] 2259, **2638**

CONTRIBUTIONS IN AMERICAN HISTORY (US/0084-9219) [03623319] **2729**

CONTRIBUTIONS IN AMERICAN STUDIES (US/0084-9227) [02255650] **2729**

CONTRIBUTIONS IN ANTHROPOLOGY AND HISTORY (US/0737-6448) [07163794] 2614, **234**

CONTRIBUTIONS IN ANTHROPOLOGY (PORTALES, N.M.) (US/0070-8232) [02694667] 266, **234**

CONTRIBUTIONS IN ASIAN STUDIES (US/1053-1866) [22469360] **2649**

CONTRIBUTIONS IN BIOLOGY AND GEOLOGY (US/0160-5313) [02256435] 1372, **452**

CONTRIBUTIONS IN BLACK STUDIES (US/0196-9099) [05251281] 5196, **2845**

CONTRIBUTIONS IN COMPARATIVE COLONIAL STUDIES (US/0163-3813) [04372645] **2729**

CONTRIBUTIONS IN CRIMINOLOGY AND PENOLOGY (US/0732-4464) [08357645] **3161**

CONTRIBUTIONS IN DRAMA AND THEATRE STUDIES (US/0163-3821) [04372623] 384, **5363**

CONTRIBUTIONS IN ECONOMICS AND ECONOMIC HISTORY (US/0084-9235) [01906322] **1552**

CONTRIBUTIONS IN ETHNIC STUDIES (US/0196-7088) [05876906] **2259**

CONTRIBUTIONS IN FAMILY STUDIES (US/0147-1023) [03562075] **2278**

CONTRIBUTIONS IN INTERCULTURAL AND COMPARATIVE STUDIES (US/0147-1031) [02918861] **2845**

CONTRIBUTIONS IN LATIN AMERICAN STUDIES (US/1054-6790) [22937371] **2729**

CONTRIBUTIONS IN LIBRARIANSHIP AND INFORMATION SCIENCE (US/0084-9243) [01908432] **3204**

CONTRIBUTIONS IN MARINE SCIENCE (US/0082-3449) [01565005] **1448**

CONTRIBUTIONS IN MEDICAL STUDIES (US/0886-8220) [13000717] **3568**

CONTRIBUTIONS IN MILITARY HISTORY *See* CONTRIBUTIONS IN MILITARY STUDIES **4040**

CONTRIBUTIONS IN MILITARY STUDIES (US/0883-6884) [12183547] **4040**

CONTRIBUTIONS IN OCEANOGRAPHY (US/0069-9640) [01223649] 1424, **1448**

CONTRIBUTIONS IN PHILOSOPHY (US/0084-926X) [02957435] **4344**

CONTRIBUTIONS IN POLITICAL SCIENCE (US/0147-1066) [03877272] **4470**

CONTRIBUTIONS IN PSYCHOLOGY (US/0736-2714) [09095091] **4582**

CONTRIBUTIONS IN SCIENCE (LOS ANGELES, CALIF.) (US/0459-8113) [01266175] **4165**

CONTRIBUTIONS IN SOCIOLOGY (US/0084-9278) [01565006] **5243**

CONTRIBUTIONS IN WOMEN'S STUDIES (US/0147-104X) [03877174] **5553**

CONTRIBUTIONS OF THE AMERICAN ENTOMOLOGICAL INSTITUTE (US/0569-4450) [01479817] **5607**

CONTRIBUTIONS OF THE ECONOMIC GEOLOGY RESEARCH UNIT (AT/0816-780X) [0816780X] **1372**

CONTRIBUTIONS OF THE GEOPHYSICAL INSTITUTE OF THE SLOVAK AKADEMY OF SCIENCES. SERIES OF METEOROLOGY (XO/0231-9004) [04738166] **1424**

CONTRIBUTIONS OF THE GREAT BASIN FOUNDATION *CEASED.* (US/0890-9172) [14578645] **5532**

CONTRIBUTIONS OF THE INSTITUTE OF METEOROLOGY AND CLIMATOLOGY OF THE SLOVAK ACADEMY OF SCIENCES (XO) [02611851] **1424**

CONTRIBUTIONS OF THE UCLA CENTER FOR MEDIEVAL AND RENAISSANCE STUDIES (US) [06764556] **1076**

CONTRIBUTIONS OF THE UNIVERSITY OF CALIFORNIA ARCHAEOLOGICAL RESEARCH FACILITY (US/0068-5933) [01087514] **266**

CONTRIBUTIONS SERIES - AMERICAN ASSOCIATION OF STRATIGRAPHIC PALYNOLOGISTS (US/0160-8843) [03782960] 4226, **1372**

CONTRIBUTIONS - THE DOVE MARINE LABORATORY (UK/0545-803X) [01321234] **554**

CONTRIBUTIONS TO AFRICAN AMERICAN LITERATURE AND AFRICAN STUDIES (US/1051-2853) [21920287] 2639, **3378**

CONTRIBUTIONS TO ATMOSPHERIC PHYSICS (GW/0303-4186) [03416825] **1424**

CONTRIBUTIONS TO CALIFORNIA ARCHAEOLOGY *CEASED.* (US/0573-8547) [02536089] **266**

CONTRIBUTIONS TO CELLULAR AND MOLECULAR ENDOCRINOLOGY (US/1055-7229) [23280166] **535**

CONTRIBUTIONS TO ECONOMIC ANALYSIS (NE/0573-8555) [01565010] **1471**

CONTRIBUTIONS TO EPIDEMIOLOGY AND BIOSTATISTICS (SZ/0377-3574) [04633885] **3734**

CONTRIBUTIONS TO GENERAL ALGEBRA (AU/1011-8918) [I10118918] **3502**

CONTRIBUTIONS TO GEOLOGY (LARAMIE) (US/0010-7980) [01565011] **1372**

CONTRIBUTIONS TO GYNECOLOGY AND OBSTETRICS (SZ/0304-4246) [02802257] **3759**

CONTRIBUTIONS TO HUMAN DEVELOPMENT (SZ/0301-4193) [00972511] **4583**

CONTRIBUTIONS TO HUMAN HISTORY *CEASED.* (CN/0832-8609) [15643426] **234**

CONTRIBUTIONS TO INDIAN SOCIOLOGY. NEW SERIES (US/0069-9667) [01641283] **5243**

CONTRIBUTIONS TO LIBRARIANSHIP (US/0145-8485) [02862060] **3204**

CONTRIBUTIONS TO LIBRARY SCIENCE. BIBLIOTEEKUNDIGE HYDRAES (SA) [06635288] **3204**

CONTRIBUTIONS TO MARINE SCIENCE (MENAI BRIDGE) (UK) [01387474] **554**

CONTRIBUTIONS TO MEDICAL PSYCHOLOGY (UK/0191-2488) [03643444] **4583**

CONTRIBUTIONS TO MICROBIOLOGY AND IMMUNOLOGY (SZ/0301-3081) [01641028] **3668**

CONTRIBUTIONS TO MINERALOGY AND PETROLOGY (GW/0010-7999) [01565013] 1458, **1439**

CONTRIBUTIONS TO MUSIC EDUCATION (US/0190-4922) [01036344] 1733, **4112**

CONTRIBUTIONS TO NEPALESE STUDIES (NP/0376-7574) [02241836] **2650**

CONTRIBUTIONS TO NEPHROLOGY (SZ/0302-5144) [01857043] **3989**

CONTRIBUTIONS TO PLASMA PHYSICS (1988) (GW/0863-1042) [18189493] **4401**

CONTRIBUTIONS TO POLITICAL ECONOMY (UK/0277-5921) [07611475] **1590**

CONTRIBUTIONS TO PRIMATOLOGY (SZ/0092-4016) [01585552] **5581**

CONTRIBUTIONS TO SEDIMENTOLOGY (GW/0343-4125) [01716801] **1372**

CONTRIBUTIONS TO SOUTH ASIAN STUDIES (II/0257-1404) [05788918] **2650**

CONTRIBUTIONS TO SOUTHEAST ASIAN ETHNOGRAPHY (SI/0217-2992) [09211802] **234**

CONTRIBUTIONS TO THE GEOLOGY OF THE NORTHWEST TERRITORIES (CN/0833-2614) [12025653] **1372**

CONTRIBUTIONS TO THE STUDY OF AGING (US/0732-085X) [08301686] **3750**

CONTRIBUTIONS TO THE STUDY OF ANTHROPOLOGY (US/0890-9377) [14470770] **234**

●CONTRIBUTIONS TO THE STUDY OF ART AND ARCHITECTURE (US/1058-9120) [24426164] 295, **348**

CONTRIBUTIONS TO THE STUDY OF CHILDHOOD AND YOUTH (US/0273-124X) [07004250] **4583**

CONTRIBUTIONS TO THE STUDY OF EDUCATION (US/0196-707X) [05876844] **1733**

CONTRIBUTIONS TO THE STUDY OF MASS MEDIA AND COMMUNICATIONS (US/0732-4456) [08357695] **1109**

CONTRIBUTIONS TO THE STUDY OF MUSIC AND DANCE (US/0193-9041) [05267798] 1311, **4112**

CONTRIBUTIONS TO THE STUDY OF POPULAR CULTURE (US/0198-9871) [06289969] **5243**

CONTRIBUTIONS TO THE STUDY OF RELIGION (US/0196-7053) [05876778] **4950**

CONTRIBUTIONS TO THE STUDY OF SCIENCE FICTION AND FANTASY (US/0193-6875) [05251683] **3378**

CONTRIBUTIONS TO THE STUDY OF WORLD LITERATURE (US/0738-9345) [09674520] **3378**

CONTRIBUTIONS TO VERTEBRATE EVOLUTION *CEASED.* (SZ/0376-4230) [02841955] **5581**

CONTRIBUTIONS - UNIVERSITY OF PUERTO RICO, DEPARTMENT OF MARINE SCIENCES (PR) [01394052] **554**

CONTROL AND COMPUTERS (US/0730-9538) [07832483] **1219**

CONTROL AND CYBERNETICS (PL/0324-8569) [01787161] 1219, **1250**

CONTROL AND DYNAMIC SYSTEMS (US/0090-5267) [01785707] **1969**

CONTROL & INSTRUMENTATION (UK/0010-8022) [01565018] 2112, **1219**

CONTROL AND SALE OF ALCOHOLIC BEVERAGES IN CANADA, THE *SUSPENDED.* (CN/0705-4319) [02249277] **2366**

CONTROL AND SYSTEMS THEORY *CEASED.* (US/0734-1695) [03299019] **2039**

CONTROL (CHICAGO, ILL.) (US/1049-5541) [20622302] **3477**

CONTROL CIBERNETICA Y AUTOMATIZACION (CU/1013-2287) [04204021] 1219, **1250**

CONTROL DATA CORPORATION. INSTITUTE FOR ADVANCED TECHNOLOGY *See* CATALOG OF PROFESSIONAL DEVELOPMENT SEMINARS / INSTITUTE FOR ADVANCED TECHNOLOGY, CONTROL DATA CORPORATION **5092**

CONTROL DE CALIDAD ASISTENCIAL *CEASED.* (SP/0213-8328) [I02138328] **3568**

CONTROL ENGINEERING (US/0010-8049) [01565020] **1219**

●CONTROL ENGINEERING PRACTICE (UK/0967-0661) [27750834] **2163**

CONTROL MAGAZINE (UK) [04087155] **348**

CONTROL OF BANKING (US/0197-7172) [08514731] **3086**

CONTROL OF COMMUNICABLE DISEASES IN MAN (US/8755-4046) [11284411] **3713**

CONTROL OF WASTE AND WATER POLLUTION FROM COAL-FIRED POWER PLANTS; B.R & D REPORT (US) [04941078] **2227**

CONTROL OF WASTE AND WATER POLLUTION FROM POWER PLANT FLUE GAS CLEANING SYSTEMS (US/0278-2995) [03013657] **2227**

CONTROL REVUE (SZ) [02950256] **2112**

CONTROL SYSTEMS TONBRIDGE (UK/0266-2493) [I02662493] **1180**

CONTROL THEORY AND ADVANCED TECHNOLOGY (JA/0911-0704) [12964970] **1180**

CONTROL THEORY AND APPLICATIONS STUDIES SERIES (UK) [07748294] **5097**

CONTROLLED CLINICAL TRIALS (US/0197-2456) [06001006] **3568**

CONTROLLED DRUG BIOAVAILABILITY (US/0888-773X) [09639865] **4298**

CONTROLLED SUBSTANCES HANDBOOK (US) [02256409] **4298**

CONTROLLED SUBSTANCES QUARTERLY (US) [02313298] **2956**

CONTROLLER (SZ/0010-8073) [08295581] **17**

CONTROLLERS INSTITUTE OF AMERICA. MEMBER DIRECTORY *See* MEMBER DIRECTORY - FINANCIAL EXECUTIVES INSTITUTE **693**

CONTROLLERS MAGAZINE (NE) 742, **660**

CONTROLLERS QUARTERLY, THE (US/8756-5684) [11636286] **1471**

CONTROLLER'S REPORT (NEW YORK, N.Y.) (US/0895-2787) [16545424] **864**

CONTROLLER'S TAX REPORT (US) **742**

CONTROLLERS' UPDATE, THE (US/8756-5676) [11636116] **784**

CONTROLLI NUMERICI E MACCHINE *See* CONTROLLI NUMERICI MACCHINE A CN ROBOT INDUSTRIALI **2112**

CONTROLLI NUMERICI MACCHINE A CN ROBOT INDUSTRIALI (IT) [04449394] **2112**

CONTROLLING (GW/0935-0381) [I09350381] **1181**

CONTROLS DIGEST (US/1067-3121) [27189546] **1181**

CONTROSPAZIO (IT) [03813751] **296**

CONVENIENCE STORE (UK) **953**

CONVENIENCE STORE INDUSTRY'S COMPENSATION SURVEY REPORT FOR ..., THE (US/0742-5848) [10357927] **1661**

CONVENIENCE STORE NEWS (US/0194-8733) [05067169] **660**

CONVENIENCE   Alphabetical Title Index

CONVENIENCE STORE PEOPLE (US/1057-0411) [23916336] **864**

CONVENIENT AUTOMOTIVE SERVICES RETAILER (US/0895-1047) [16469552] **5412**

CONVENING CIRCULAR AND SYNOD JOURNAL FOR THE ... SESSION OF SYNOD (CN/0826-0621) [10935169] **4950**

CONVENTION ON INTERNATIONAL TRADE IN ENDANGERED SPECIES OF WILD FAUNA AND FLORA (US/0193-6999) [05038798] **2191**

CONVENTION REPORT - C U P E (CN/0380-7789) [02585145] **1661**

CONVENTION REPORT / CANADA EMPLOYMENT AND IMMIGRATION UNION (CN) [11856723] **1661**

CONVENTION REPORTER (US/0882-5319) [11859903] **3568**

CONVENTIONS & MEETINGS CANADA (1981) (CN/0226-8922) [07817136] **2804**

● CONVERGE (SUNNYVALE, CALIF.) (US/1072-9224) [29238645] **1109**

CONVERGENCE (FRIBOURG) *CEASED.* (SZ/0010-8154) [01779399] **5028**

CONVERGENCE (TORONTO) (CN/0010-8146) [01565024] **1800**

CONVERGENCE (WASHINGTON, D.C.) *SUSPENDED.* (US/1046-6231) [13617582] **4506**

CONVERGENT WORLD *See* UNISYS WORLD OPEN SYSTEMS NEWS **1206**

CONVERSE BASKETBALL YEARBOOK (US) [05031473] **4891**

CONVERSION PLANNER, THE (US) [05319182] **4506**

CONVERTED FLEXIBLE PACKAGING PRODUCTS (US/0364-1783) [02547109] **4218**

CONVERTER (UK/0010-8189) [02446193] **4233**

CONVERTING MAGAZINE (US/0746-7141) [10221832] **1602**

CONVERTING TODAY (UK/0264-715X) [I0264715X] **2039**

CONVEYANCER AND PROPERTY LAWYER, THE (UK/0010-8200) [01565027] **2956**

CONVEYING MATERIAL CATALOGUE (SZ) **414**

CONVORBIRI LITERARE (RM) [04442225] **3340**

CONVOY (US) [04845325] **1661**

CONVULSIVE THERAPY (US/0749-8055) [11198516] **3568**

CONWAY COUNTY PETIT JEAN COUNTRY HEADLIGHT (US) [24103537] **5631**

COOK CO., ILL. OFFICE OF THE COMPTROLLER *See* COMPTROLLER'S REPORT OF COOK COUNTY **4640**

COOK COUNTY JURY VERDICT REPORTER (US) **3089**

COOK ISLANDS. LEGISLATIVE ASSEMBLY *See* PAPERS PRESENTED AND ORDER PAPERS - COOK ISLANDS. LEGISLATIVE ASSEMBLY **4486**

COOK ISLANDS. LEGISLATIVE ASSEMBLY *See* PAPERS AND ORDER PAPERS PRESENTED : OFFICIAL REPORT / PARLIAMENT OF THE COOK ISLANDS **4486**

COOK ISLANDS. PARLIAMENT *See* PAPERS AND ORDER PAPERS PRESENTED : OFFICIAL REPORT / PARLIAMENT OF THE COOK ISLANDS **4486**

COOK POLITICAL REPORT (US) **4470**

COOK REPORT ON INTERNET, NREN, THE (US/1071-6327) [28693379] **1181**

COOKBOOK COLLECTOR, THE (US/1055-8071) [23346731] **2332**

COOKBOOK DIGEST (US/0010-826X) [03904499] **2789**

● COOKBOOK REVIEW, THE (US/1060-7765) [25060710] **2789**

● COOKBOOK (STEUBEN, ME.) (US/1061-0537) [25173972] **2332**

COOKEIA : SERIES OF MISCELLANEOUS PUBLICATIONS IN THE HUMAN SCIENCES BY THE NATIONAL MUSEUMS AND MONUMENTS OF ZIMBABWE (RH/0250-2992) [12288618] 234, **2639**

COOKING CONNECTION (US) **2789**

COOKING CONTEST NEWSLETTER, THE (US/1061-4729) [25314390] 2789, **2332**

COOKING EDGE, THE (US/1040-1903) [18340879] **2332**

COOKING FOR PROFIT (US/0091-861X) [01565038] 5070, **2332**

COOKING LIGHT (SOUTHERN LIVING, INC.) (US/0886-4446) [12889339] **4189**

COOKING SCHOOL ALTERNATIVE NEWSLETTER (US) **2332**

● COOK'S ILLUSTRATED (US/1068-2821) [27552930] **2789**

COOK'S INDEX (US/0731-8634) [08260498] **2789**

COOKSTOVE NEWS *CEASED.* (US/0882-3561) [11823458] **5097**

COOLIA (NE/0525-6097) [04069618] **452**

COOMBE LODGE REPORT (UK/0305-8441) [I03058441] **1818**

COON RAPIDS HERALD (US) [01565040] **5695**

COOPER MONOGRAPHS ON ENGLISH AND AMERICAN LANGUAGE AND LITERATURE, THE (SZ/0069-9780) [08570024] 3275, **3378**

COOPER REVIEW (US) [14148322] **5748**

COOPERATION AND CONFLICT (NO/0010-8367) [01565046] **4470**

COOPERATION CENTRE FOR SCIENTIFIC RESEARCH RELATIVE TO TOBACCO *See* BULLETIN D'INFORMATION. INFORMATION BULLETIN **5372**

COOPERATION (JEFFERSON CITY) (US/0192-4842) [05081361] **3569**

COOPERATION SOUTH / UNITED NATIONS DEVELOPMENT PROGRAMME (US) [12169008] **5097**

COOPERATIVA AGRICOLA GENERAL PUEYRREDON *See* MEMORIA Y BALANCE GENERAL **108**

COOPERATIVA CENTRAL DOS PRODUTORES DE ACUCAR E ALCOOL DO ESTADO DE SAO PAULO. DIVISOA ECONOMICA *See* CUSTOS DE PRODUCAO E PERSPECTIVAS DA AGROINDUSTRIA DO ACUCAR E DO ALCOOL **2366**

COOPERATIVE ACCOUNTABILITY PROJECT *See* REPORT - COOPERATIVE ACCOUNTABILITY PROJECT **1869**

COOPERATIVE ACCOUNTANT, THE (US/0010-8391) [03101481] **742**

COOPERATIVE ADVERTISING PLANS FOR YELLOW PAGES (US/0883-4857) [12010022] **758**

COOPERATIVE BUSINESS JOURNAL *See* NCBA COOPERATIVE BUSINESS JOURNAL **697**

● COOPERATIVE CATALOGING NEWS (US/1060-8621) [25079305] **3204**

COOPERATIVE CHILDREN'S BOOK CENTER, MADISON, WIS *See* CCBC : COOPERATIVE CHILDREN'S BOOK CENTER CIRCULAR **4827**

COOPERATIVE EDUCATION QUARTERLY (US/0190-4655) [04696313] **1733**

COOPERATIVE ENERGY (CN/0226-952X) [08649821] 1541, **1936**

COOPERATIVE FARMER (US/0010-8448) [04336425] **76**

COOPERATIVE FORECASTING. TECHNICAL REPORT (US/1043-7800) [19550104] **1471**

COOPERATIVE FOREST GENETICS RESEARCH PROGRAM (US/0071-6146) [01416260] **2378**

COOPERATIVE GAMES NEWSLETTER (CN/0229-9852) [08439973] **4859**

COOPERATIVE GROCER (US) **2332**

COOPERATIVE HOUSING JOURNAL (US/0589-6355) [01511555] **2819**

COOPERATIVE HOUSING LAW AND PRACTICE, FORMS (US) [01764481] **2819**

COOPERATIVE INFORMATION REPORT (US/0742-9487) [05739468] 1541, **76**

COOPERATIVE NATIONAL PARK RESOURCES STUDIES UNIT, UNIVERSITY OF HAWAII *See* TECHNICAL REPORT - COOPERATIVE NATIONAL PARK RESOURCES STUDIES UNIT, UNIVERSITY OF HAWAII AT MANOA **2206**

COOPERATIVE PARTNERS (US/0896-9426) [17342967] **192**

COOPERATIVE PERSPECTIVE (II/0302-7767) [01790545] **1541**

COOPERATIVE RESEARCH REPORT - INTERNATIONAL COUNCIL FOR THE EXPLORATION OF THE SEA (1972) (DK/0105-3213) [04402390] **1448**

COOPERATIVE SUGAR / NATIONAL FEDERATION OF COOPERATIVE SUGAR FACTORIES LTD (II) [12170070] 829, **2332**

COOPERATIVE TECHNOLOGY RD&D REPORT (US/1062-5399) [25651678] **5097**

COOPERATIVEMENT VOTRE (CN/0227-535X) [08010325] **1541**

COOPERATIVES ET DEVELOPPEMENT (CN/0712-2748) [15997781] **1542**

COOPERATIVISMO E ECONOMIA SOCIAL (SP/1130-2682) [I11302682] **1471**

COOPERAZIONE (IT/0393-3059) [18355073] **2908**

COOPERAZIONE *CEASED.* (IT/0391-674X) [I0391674X] **2908**

COOPERAZIONE ECONOMICA NEI PAESI DEL COMECON (IT) **1542**

COOPERAZIONE EDUCATIVA (IT) [04627063] **1733**

COOPERAZIONE IN AGROCOLTURA (IT) **76**

COOPERAZIONE ITALIANA, LA (IT) [05988785] **1542**

COOPERTIVA CENTRAL DOS PRODUTORES DE ACUCAR E ALCOOL DO ESTADO DE SAO PAULO. DEPARTAMENTO TECNICO *See* BOLETIM TECNICO COPERSUCAR **165**

COOPRIX INFORMATION (1983) (CN/0822-6598) [10339676] **1296**

COORDINATING AGENCY FOR SUPPLIER EVALUATION *See* CASE REGISTER **949**

COORDINATING COUNCIL OF LITERARY MAGAZINES *See* CCLM NEWSLETTER **3373**

COORDINATION CHEMISTRY REVIEWS (SZ/0010-8545) [01565057] **1051**

COORDINATION DIRECTORY OF STATE AND FEDERAL AGENCY WATER AND LAND RESOURCES OFFICIALS (US/0363-8170) [02550390] **2191**

COOS COUNTY DEMOCRAT, THE (US) [21551242] **5708**

COOS GENEALOGICAL BULLETIN *CEASED.* (US/0591-2083) [04459907] **2444**

COOS GENEALOGICAL FORUM *See* COOS GENEALOGICAL BULLETIN **2444**

COOTIE COURIER (US) [21096763] **5230**

COPAINS (NEW YORK, N.Y.) (US/1055-1220) [23086172] **2531**

COPE (PE) [03675398] **2551**

COPEIA (US/0045-8511) [01565060] **5581**

COPENHAGEN DISCUSSION PAPERS (DK/0904-8626) [I09048626] **2503**

COPENHAGEN. KONGELIGE BIBLIOTEK *See* UDVALGSLISTE OVER ORKESTERMATERIALE **4157**

COPENHAGEN PAPERS IN EAST AND SOUTHEAST ASIAN STUDIES (DK/0903-2703) [18869455] **5243**

COPENHAGEN POLITICAL STUDIES ABSTRACTS (DK) [10599929] 4470, **4502**

COPENHAGEN. POLYTEKNISK L'REANSTALT. LABORATORIET FOR ELEKTRONIK *See* BERETNING FRA LABORATORIET FOR ELEKTRONIK, DANMARKS TEKNISKE HJSKOLE **2036**

COPENHAGEN. SOCIAL- OG SUNDHEDSFORVALTNINGEN *See* BERETNING - SOCIAL- OG SUNDHEDSFORVALTNINGEN I KBENHAVN **5274**

COPENHAGEN. STADSLGEEMBEDET *See* SUNDHEDSTILSTANDEN I KBENHAVN; STADSLGENS ARSBERETNING **4804**

COPENHAGEN STUDIES IN LANGUAGE (DK) [24273234] **3275**

COPENHAGEN. UNIVERSITET. DRAMATISK BIBLIOTEK *See* ACCESSIONSKATALOG FOR DRAMATISK BIBLIOTEK **3187**

COPENHAGEN WORKING PAPERS IN LINGUISTICS (DK/0906-7639) [25563430] **3275**

COPIA (IT) **4211**

COPIAH COUNTY COURIER (US) [15247768] **5700**

COPIER (US) **4211**

COPIER REVIEW (US/0899-6164) [12436512] **4211**

COPIER SPECIFICATION GUIDE (US/1050-978X) [20832298] **4211**

COPIER USER *See* WHAT TO BUY **4214**

COPIERS OF THE WORLD (GW) **4211**

COPING (FRANKLIN, TENN.) (US/1043-8637) [16836832] **3815**

● COPING NEWSLETTER (US/1061-4117) [25305620] **5553**

COPNIP LIST (US/0007-8816) [01565082] **4298**

COPPER AND COPPER ALLOY MILL PRODUCTS (UK) **4000**

COPPER & COPPER ALLOYS COMPUTER FILE / COPPER DEVELOPMENT ASSOCIATION (UK) [24537280] **4000**

COPPER (BOR, SERBIA) (YU/0350-6142) [11233040] **4000**

COPPER ENAMELING (US/0009-0328) **2588**

Alphabetical Title Index — CORNERSTONE

`COPPER INDUSTRY ANNUAL SUPPLEMENT / U.S. DEPARTMENT OF THE INTERIOR, BUREAU OF MINES (US) [09313414] 4000, 2138, **2003**

COPPER JOURNAL, THE (US/1055-7776) [23297915] **1602**

COPPER METAL SERVICE (UK) **4000**

COPPER-NICKEL ALLOYS / COMPUTER FILE NICKEL DEVELOPMENT INSTITUTE. ALUMINIUM BRONZE ALLOYS / THE ALUMINIUM BRONZE ADVISORY SERVICE (UK) [24537282] **4000**

COPPER STATE BULLETIN (US/0098-4841) [02240914] **2444**

COPPER STUDIES (US/0091-2204) [01786620] **4000**

COPPER VALLEY VIEWS (US/0740-963X) [10064879] **5629**

COPRED PEACE CHRONICLE (US) **4506**

COPTIC CHURCH REVIEW (US/0273-3269) [06970380] **5039**

COPTIC STUDIES (NE) [12209206] 3275, **2768**

COPY EDITOR (US/1049-3190) [21203067] **4813**

COPY MAGAZINE (US/0897-9405) [17671139] **4211**

COPY TECHNOLOGY REVIEW (US) [08963635] **5097**

COPYCAT MAGAZINE (US/0886-5612) [12932191] **1891**

COPYRIGHT BOARD CANADA *See* BULLETIN - COPYRIGHT BOARD CANADA **1302**

COPYRIGHT BULLETIN : QUARTERLY REVIEW / UNESCO (FR/0010-8634) [01768107] **1303**

COPYRIGHT (GENEVA) (SZ/0010-8626) [01565090] **1303**

COPYRIGHT LAW DECISIONS *CEASED.* (US) [08155172] **1303**

COPYRIGHT LAW JOURNAL, THE (US/0884-4437) [10898636] **1303**

COPYRIGHT LAW REPORTER (US) [04380288] **1303**

COPYRIGHT LAW SYMPOSIUM (US/0069-9950) [01565092] **1303**

COPYRIGHT LAWS AND TREATIES OF THE WORLD (US/0069-9969) [01768100] **1303**

COPYRIGHT MANAGEMENT CIRCLE (US/0884-1306) [12174987] **1303**

COPYRIGHT REPORTER (AT/0725-0509) [107250509] **1303**

COPYRIGHT WORLD (UK/0950-2505) [20160310] **1303**

COQUILLE, LA (CN/0318-4374) [02248410] **4950**

COR ET VASA (ENGLISH ED.) (XR/0010-8650) [01586468] **3703**

CORACLE (GLASGOW, STRATHCLYDE) (UK) [09049224] **5280**

CORAJE CHICANO, EL (US) [05806029] **2259**

CORAL GABLES CONFERENCE ON FUNDAMENTAL INTERACTIONS AT HIGH ENERGY. PROCEEDINGS (US/0069-9977) [02397110] **1936**

CORAL REEF NEWSLETTER (US/0278-324X) [02200768] 452, **1448**

CORAL REEFS (GW/0722-4028) [08755866] **1448**

CORANTO (LOS ANGELES, CALIF.) *CEASED.* (US/0010-8669) [01565095] **4828**

CORAPORTER (US/0749-1298) [11055083] **1918**

CORAX (GW) [06525985] **5617**

CORAZON Y SALUD (SP) **3703**

CORBEL FORMS MANUAL (US) **5178**

CORCORAN (WASHINGTON, D.C.) (US/1059-8472) [24785140] 4087, **348**

CORD. COCONUT RESEARCH & DEVELOPMENT (IO/0215-1162) [102151162] **168**

CORD (HAMILTON) (CN/0225-7033) [06272473] **5280**

CORD NEWSLETTER (US/0734-4856) [08530503] **1311**

CORD SPORTFACTS FISHERMAN ANNUAL (US/0590-8817) [01794637] **2299**

CORD SPORTFACTS HOCKEY GUIDE (US/0591-0374) [01793032] **4891**

CORD SPORTFACTS HUNTING (US/0092-8216) [01791298] 4891, **4871**

CORD SPORTFACTS PRO FOOTBALL GUIDE (US/0197-7105) [06076287] **4891**

CORD (ST. BONAVENTURE, N.Y.), THE (US/0010-8685) [01645869] **5028**

CORDAGE NEWS (US/1063-746X) [26146109] **5349**

CORDELE DISPATCH AND THE WILCOX COUNTY CHRONICLE, THE (US) [19539249] **5653**

CORDELL'S BUILDING COST GUIDE. COMMERCIAL AND INDUSTRIAL. NEW SOUTH WALES (AT/0816-8903) [108168903] **611**

CORDELL'S BUILDING COST GUIDE. COMMERCIAL AND INDUSTRIAL. QUEENSLAND (AT/0816-8865) [108168865] **611**

CORDELL'S BUILDING COST GUIDE. COMMERCIAL AND INDUSTRIAL. VICTORIA (AT/0816-8830) [108168830] **611**

CORDELL'S BUILDING COST GUIDE. COMMERCIAL, INDUSTRIAL AND HOUSING. WESTERN AUSTRALIA (AT/0817-4210) [108174210] **611**

CORDELL'S BUILDING COST GUIDE. HOUSING, NEW CONSTRUCTION. NEW SOUTH WALES (AT/0816-8822) [108168822] **611**

CORDELL'S BUILDING COST GUIDE. HOUSING, NEW CONSTRUCTION. QUEENSLAND (AT/0816-8792) [108168792] **611**

CORDELL'S BUILDING COST GUIDE. HOUSING, NEW CONSTRUCTION. VICTORIA (AT/0816-8806) [108168806] **611**

CORDIAAL (NE) **3703**

CORDIALITY (US) **2486**

CORDOVA TIMES, THE (US/1048-8766) [02683912] **5629**

CORDUBA / MUSEO ARQUEOLOGICO PROVINCIAL (SP/0211-2078) [09405630] **2684**

CORDULIA *SUSPENDED.* (CN/0700-4966) [03403122] **5581**

CORE (US/0300-743X) [01450010] **4506**

CORE ANALYTE *CEASED.* (US/1058-1936) [24238484] **973**

CORE ARBORETUM BULLETIN (US) [03765825] **76**

CORE CHEMISTRY *See* CORE ANALYTE **973**

CORE. COATINGS, REGULATIONS AND THE ENVIRONMENT (UK/0967-2508) [109672508] 2227, **4226**

CORE. COLLECTED ORIGINAL RESOURCES IN EDUCATION (UK/0308-6909) [03250843] **1734**

CORE DISCUSSION PAPERS (BE) [03813860] **1471**

CORE JOURNALS EN ALERGIA E INMUNOLOGIA (SP/0214-3755) [102143755] **3668**

CORE JOURNALS EN ANESTESIOLOGIA (SP/0214-9370) [102149370] **3682**

CORE JOURNALS EN ENFERMEDADES PULMONARES (SP/1130-0965) [111300965] **3949**

CORE JOURNALS IN CARDIOLOGY (NE/0165-9405) [08149111] **3703**

CORE JOURNALS IN CLINICAL NEUROLOGY (NE/0165-1056) [09038636] **3830**

CORE JOURNALS IN CLINICAL PHARMACOLOGY (NE/0167-8965) [10583018] **3569**

CORE JOURNALS IN DERMATOLOGY (NE/0167-5796) [18305566] **3718**

CORE JOURNALS IN GASTROENTEROLOGY (NE/0165-8719) [08411602] **3743**

CORE JOURNALS IN OBSTETRICS/GYNECOLOGY (NE/0376-5059) [04029215] **3759**

CORE JOURNALS IN OPHTHALMOLOGY (NE/0165-1005) [18305774] **3873**

CORE JOURNALS IN PEDIATRICS (NE/0376-5040) [04108365] **3902**

CORE-LATOR *See* CORE **4506**

CORE MEDLINE/EBSCO CD-ROM (US/1040-4066) [18438314] 3204, **3569**

CORE (NORTH YORK) (CN/1183-1944) [24266802] 1891, **1818**

CORE TEACHER (US/0045-8538) [09222333] **1891**

●COREL MAGAZINE (US/1063-7591) [26143508] **1233**

CORELATION MAGAZINE (US) **1284**

CORELLA (AT/0155-0438) [03811291] **5617**

CORINTH : RESULTS OF EXCAVATIONS CONDUCTED BY THE AMERICAN SCHOOL OF CLASSICAL STUDIES AT ATHENS (US) [01480710] **1076**

CORINTHIAN HORSE SPORT (CN/0829-2930) [24256680] **2798**

CORMORANT NEWS BULLETIN, THE (US/0045-8554) [03018558] **5412**

CORMOSEA BULLETIN (US/0734-449X) [04844230] 2650, **3204**

CORN FOR GRAIN : HARVESTING, HANDLING AND DRYING METHODS / IOWA CROP AND LIVESTOCK REPORTING SERVICE (US) [06140626] **200**

CORN GROWER (US/0279-4217) [07833322] **168**

CORN ROW WIDTH, CORN PLANT POPULATION AND SOYBEAN ROW SPACING AND VARIETIES / IOWA CROP AND LIVESTOCK REPORTING SERVICE (US) [06204061] **168**

CORNEA (US/0277-3740) [07580301] **3873**

CORNELL ALUMNI NEWS (US/1058-3467) [03457846] **1101**

CORNELL ALUMNI NEWS *See* CORNELL MAGAZINE **1101**

CORNELL AND LAKE HOLCOMBE COURIER, THE (US/0885-078X) [12565570] **5766**

CORNELL CHRONICLE (US/0747-4628) [04762901] **1091**

CORNELL COLLEGE (MOUNT VERNON, IOWA) *See* ALUMNI DIRECTORY - CORNELL COLLEGE (MOUNT VERNON, IOWA) **1098**

CORNELL COOPERATIVE EXTENSION AGRICULTURAL NEWS (US/1049-7021) [21289731] **76**

CORNELL COUNTRYMAN (US/0010-8782) [01565108] **77**

CORNELL DAILY SUN (US) [04310936] **5715**

CORNELL DESKBOOK (US/0276-1920) [04232929] **1818**

CORNELL EAST ASIA SERIES (US/1050-2955) [21454771] 5196, 2650, **2503**

CORNELL ENGINEER, THE (US/0010-8790) [02446207] **1969**

●CORNELL FOCUS (US/1067-585X) [26707756] **77**

CORNELL HOTEL AND RESTAURANT ADMINISTRATION QUARTERLY, THE (US/0010-8804) [01565109] 5070, **2804**

CORNELL INTERNATIONAL AGRICULTURE BULLETIN (US/0363-8693) [01253400] **77**

CORNELL INTERNATIONAL LAW JOURNAL (US/0010-8812) [01565112] **3126**

CORNELL INTERNATIONAL NUTRITION MONOGRAPH SERIES (US/0198-9510) [05019465] **4189**

CORNELL JOURNAL OF ARCHITECTURE, THE *CEASED.* (US/0731-5384) [08063600] **296**

CORNELL LAW FORUM (ITHACA, N.Y. : 1974) (US/0010-8839) [01794043] **2956**

CORNELL LAW REVIEW (US/0010-8847) [01565116] **2956**

●CORNELL MAGAZINE (US/1070-2733) [28321144] **1101**

CORNELL PLANTATIONS, THE *SUSPENDED.* (US/0010-8863) [01565119] **1818**

●CORNELL/SMITHERS REPORT ON WORKPLACE SUBSTANCE ABUSE POLICY (US) [25235068] **1342**

CORNELL STUDIES IN CIVIL LIBERTY (US) [01565127] **4506**

CORNELL STUDIES IN CLASSICAL PHILOLOGY (US) [03644833] **3275**

CORNELL UNIVERSITY *See* CORNELL STUDIES IN CIVIL LIBERTY **4506**

CORNELL UNIVERSITY. CORNELL PLANTATIONS *See* CORNELL PLANTATIONS, THE **1818**

CORNELL UNIVERSITY. LIBRARIES *See* JOHN M. ECHOLS COLLECTION ON SOUTHEAST ASIA ACCESSIONS LIST, THE **2496**

CORNELL UNIVERSITY. NEW YORK STATE SCHOOL OF INDUSTRIAL AND LABOR RELATIONS *See* ILR PAPERBACK **1677**

CORNELL UNIVERSITY. PROGRAM IN URBAN AND REGIONAL STUDIES *See* OCCASIONAL PAPER - PROGRAM IN URBAN AND REGIONAL STUDIES **2829**

CORNELL UNIVERSITY. WATER RESOURCES AND MARINE SCIENCES CENTER *See* TECHNICAL REPORT - CORNELL UNIVERSITY WATER RESOURCES AND MARINE SCIENCES CENTER **5540**

CORNELL UNIVERSITY. WATER RESOURCES AND MARINE SCIENCES CENTER *See* PUBLICATION - CORNELL UNIVERSITY WATER RESOURCES AND MARINE SCIENCES CENTER **5538**

CORNELL VETERINARIAN. SUPPLEMENT *CEASED.* (US/0589-7432) [01780550] **5508**

CORNELL VETERINARIAN, THE *CEASED.* (US/0010-8901) [01565146] **5508**

CORNELL WORKING PAPERS IN LINGUISTICS (US/0888-3122) [08091082] **3275**

CORNER BROOK WESTERN STAR (CN) **5782**

CORNERSTONE (CHICAGO, ILL.) (US/0275-2743) [07106672] **4950**

CORNERSTONE

CORNERSTONE CLUES (US/0739-0904) [07820814] **2444**

●CORNERSTONE (NEW PROVIDENCE, N.J.), THE (US/0000-1392) [25732025] **3204**

CORNERSTONE (SAN ANTONIO, TEX.), THE (US/0883-6108) [12171222] **4950**

CORNING OBSERVER, THE (US) [27053211] **5634**

CORNING RESEARCH (US/0589-7483) [I05897483] **2588**

CORNISH ARCHAEOLOGY (UK/0070-024X) [I0070024X] **266**

CORNSILK (US/0731-8375) [08252216] **2444**

CORNSTALK GAZETTE (AT/0818-7339) [I08187339] 2319, **384**

CORNWALL FAMILY HISTORY SOCIETY *See* JOURNAL / CORNWALL FAMILY HISTORY SOCIETY **2455**

CORNWALL LOCAL (CORNWALL, N.Y. : 1923) (US) [12246250] **5715**

CORNWALL, ONTARIO CITY DIRECTORY (CN/0229-1991) [07966544] **2559**

CORO, DIRECTORIO DE ACTIVIDADES ECONOMICAS (VE) [05158288] **1471**

COROLLA LONDINIENSIS (NE) [10009999] **3275**

CORONA (BOZEMAN) (US/0270-6687) [06491695] 317, **3378**

CORONA-NORCO INDEPENDENT (US/0745-3930) [09120607] **5634**

CORONARY ARTERY DISEASE (US/0954-6928) [21162492] **3703**

CORONARY CLUB BULLETIN, THE (US/8755-5271) [11387342] **3703**

●CORONER (SAINTE-FOY) (CN/1191-3959) [26715052] **4772**

CORONICA, LA (US/0193-3892) [03660718] **3275**

CORPIQ VOUS INFORME (CN/0712-9564) [08858468] **4836**

CORPO CLIP (CN/0843-140X) [19768992] **3204**

CORPORACION ANDINA DE FOMENTO *See* MEMORIA / CORPORACION ANDINA DE FOMENTO **798**

CORPORACION DE INVESTIGACIONES ECONOMICAS PARA LATINOAMERICA *See* INFORME DE ACTIVIDADES / CORPORACION DE INVESTIGACIONES ECONOMICAS PARA LATINOAMERICA **1495**

CORPORACION FINANCIERA NACIONAL (ECUADOR) *See* MEMORIA - CORPORACION FINANCIERA NACIONAL **798**

CORPORACION NACIONAL DE TURISMO DE COLOMBIA *See* BOLETIN DE INVESTIGACIONES E INFORMACION TURISTICA **5465**

CORPORATE 500. THE DIRECTORY OF CORPORATE PHILANTHROPY (US/0197-937X) [06162222] **4335**

CORPORATE 1000 YELLOW BOOK *See* CORPORATE YELLOW BOOK **1924**

CORPORATE ACCOUNTING INTERNATIONAL (US/0791-2471) [21487798] **742**

CORPORATE ACQUISITIONS, MERGERS, AND DIVESTITURES (US/0737-4046) [09365262] **3098**

CORPORATE ANALYST, THE (US/1041-3871) [18767169] **3098**

CORPORATE & BUSINESS LAW JOURNAL (AT) [20709482] **3098**

●CORPORATE AND FOUNDATION GRANTS (US/1061-1274) [25184543] 5280, **660**

CORPORATE & INCENTIVE TRAVEL (US/0739-1587) [09699058] 5467, **661**

CORPORATE AND OFFICE DESIGN (AT) **296**

CORPORATE AND PERSONAL TAXATION IN THE ARAB WORLD (US/0160-4732) [03674498] 4719, **3098**

CORPORATE ANTI-TAKEOVER DEFENSES (US/0897-6740) [17592645] **661**

CORPORATE ARTNEWS *SUSPENDED.* (US/8755-2582) [11145497] **348**

CORPORATE AUTHOR AUTHORITY LIST (US/0741-3270) [10107439] **3204**

CORPORATE BOARD, THE (US/0746-8652) [10352183] **661**

CORPORATE BOND RECORD, THE (CN/0831-9774) [15287317] **661**

CORPORATE BRIEFING (UK/0950-6209) [20923674] **2956**

CORPORATE BUYERS OF DESIGN SERVICES USA (US/0145-3017) [02722234] 922, **296**

CORPORATE CAPITAL TRANSACTIONS ALERT (US/0731-4604) [07163669] **4719**

CORPORATE CAPITAL TRANSACTIONS COORDINATOR (US/0731-650X) [08224843] 3098, **742**

CORPORATE CASHFLOW (US/1040-0311) [17976195] **784**

CORPORATE CLEVELAND *CEASED.* (US/1055-5978) [23190996] **661**

CORPORATE COMMUNICATIONS TECHNOLOGY (US/0734-9262) [09801116] **661**

CORPORATE COMPUTING *CEASED.* (US/1065-8610) [26775234] **1241**

CORPORATE CONDUCT QUARTERLY (US/1061-8775) [25482336] **2957**

CORPORATE CONSUMER FORUM TRENDLETTER (US) 661, **2789**

CORPORATE CONTRIBUTIONS (US) [23026715] **661**

CORPORATE CONTROL ALERT (US/0743-0272) [10489776] **895**

CORPORATE CONTROLLER *CEASED.* (US/0899-0174) [17972367] **661**

CORPORATE COUNSEL REVIEW (US/0886-327X) [04911507] **3098**

CORPORATE COUNSEL : STATE BAR SECTION REPORT (US) [04008826] **3098**

CORPORATE COUNSEL, THE (US/0193-4880) [05092063] **3098**

CORPORATE COUNSEL'S ANNUAL (US/0589-784X) [01565160] **3098**

CORPORATE COUNSEL'S COMMERCIAL LAW ADVISER *See* COMMERCIAL LAW ADVISER **783**

CORPORATE COUNSEL'S INTERNATIONAL ADVISER (US/0898-9907) [13338036] 3098, **3126**

CORPORATE COUNSEL'S MONITOR (US/0898-9923) [16014991] **3098**

CORPORATE COUNSEL'S QUARTERLY (US/0897-1617) [11663019] **3098**

CORPORATE COVER (UK) **2878**

CORPORATE CRIMINAL LIABILITY REPORTER *CEASED.* (US/0892-4848) [15307494] **3098**

CORPORATE DATA EXCHANGE, INC *See* CDE STOCK OWNERSHIP DIRECTORY: TRANSPORTATION INDUSTRY **5379**

CORPORATE DATA EXCHANGE, INC *See* CDE STOCK OWNERSHIP DIRECTORY : AGRIBUSINESS **656**

CORPORATE DATABASE [COMPUTER FILE] / DATEXT (US) [13843870] **661**

CORPORATE DETROIT (US/1062-368X) [23076868] **661**

CORPORATE DIRECTORS' COMPENSATION (US/0885-1360) [11601171] **661**

CORPORATE DIRECTORY OF NIGERIA'S BESTSELLERS (NR/0795-1477) [22169162] **661**

CORPORATE DIRECTORY OF U.S. PUBLIC COMPANIES, THE (US/1059-7964) [23232053] **661**

CORPORATE DIRECTORY, THE (US/1044-3525) [19114375] **661**

CORPORATE EFT REPORT (US/0272-0299) [06743595] **784**

CORPORATE ENVIRONMENTAL OFFICER MAGAZINE (US/1055-7865) [23309637] **2163**

CORPORATE ETHICS MONITOR, THE (CN/0841-1956) [19995512] **661**

CORPORATE EXAMINER, THE (US/0361-2309) [02030905] **661**

CORPORATE EXECUTIVE, THE (US) [05229644] **3098**

CORPORATE EXPLORATION STRATEGIES (CN) 661, **2138**

CORPORATE FEDERAL INCOME TAX SPECIMEN RETURNS COMPLETELY FILLED OUT FOR FILING IN (US) [19284434] **661**

CORPORATE FINANCE (US/0894-6817) [15567184] **784**

CORPORATE FINANCE AND TREASURY MANAGEMENT (UK) [11798044] **661**

CORPORATE FINANCE BLUEBOOK *See* AMERICA'S CORPORATE FINANCE DIRECTORY **769**

CORPORATE FINANCE BLUEBOOK, THE (US/0740-2546) [09636201] 661, **784**

CORPORATE FINANCE LETTER (US/0882-3073) [11810411] **785**

CORPORATE FINANCE (LONDON) (UK/0958-2053) [17005593] **785**

CORPORATE FINANCE (NEW YORK, N.Y. 1991) (US/1057-8056) [23813833] **785**

CORPORATE FINANCE SOURCEBOOK, THE (US/0163-3031) [04342877] **785**

CORPORATE FINANCING WEEK - INSTITUTIONAL INVESTOR (FIRM) (US/1064-1912) [21710357] **785**

CORPORATE FOUNDATION PROFILES (US) [10112731] 661, **4335**

●CORPORATE FUNDERS OPERATING IN MISSOURI (US/1061-4273) [25306433] **661**

CORPORATE GIVING DIRECTORY (US/1055-0623) [22571684] **4335**

CORPORATE GIVING WATCH (US/0747-8003) [08123791] 661, **5280**

●CORPORATE GIVING YELLOW PAGES (1992) (US/1058-689X) [24366812] 661, **5281**

CORPORATE GOVERNANCE (UK/0964-8410) **864**

●CORPORATE GOVERNANCE ADVISOR, THE (US/1067-6163) [27296820] **3099**

CORPORATE GOVERNANCE SERVICE. VOTING RESULTS (US/1052-8342) [18176296] **895**

CORPORATE GROWTH REPORT, THE (US/1050-320X) [20620901] **661**

CORPORATE HEALTH PROMOTION TODAY *CEASED.* (US/1061-172X) [25198772] **4772**

CORPORATE INSURANCE IN CANADA *See* CANADIAN INSURANCE **2877**

Alphabetical Title Index

CORPORATE INSURANCE LAW BULLETIN *See* RISK MANAGER LAW BULLETIN **2892**

CORPORATE INTELLIGENCE (US/1047-4854) [20701295] **661**

CORPORATE JOBS OUTLOOK! (US/0892-5232) [15264885] **4203**

CORPORATE LEGAL LETTER *See* COMPANY LAW MONITOR **3098**

CORPORATE LEGAL LETTER, THE (UK) [06253185] **3099**

CORPORATE LEGAL TIMES (US) [24874596] **3099**

●CORPORATE LIBRARY UPDATE (US/1061-5288) [25343778] **3204**

CORPORATE LOCATION (UK) **895**

CORPORATE MANAGEMENT (SYDNEY) *See* JOURNAL OF CORPORATE MANAGEMENT, THE **3101**

CORPORATE MANAGEMENT TAX CONFERENCE *See* CORPORATE MANAGEMENT TAX CONFERENCE **4719**

CORPORATE MANAGEMENT TAX CONFERENCE (CN/0070-0282) [02441981] **4719**

CORPORATE MEETING PLANNERS DIRECTORY (US) **864**

CORPORATE MEETINGS AND INCENTIVES (US/0745-1636) [08891349] 661, **5467**

CORPORATE MONEY (UK/0951-3639) [I09513639] **785**

CORPORATE MONTHLY (US/0889-941X) [12111469] **661**

CORPORATE OFFICERS & DIRECTORS LIABILITY LITIGATION REPORTER (US/0887-7793) [13368097] **3099**

CORPORATE, PARTNERSHIP, ESTATE AND GIFT TAXATION (US/0742-7824) [10438157] **4719**

CORPORATE PHILANTHROPY IN NEW ENGLAND. VOLUME 3, MAINE (US) [17062145] **4335**

CORPORATE PHILANTHROPY IN NEW ENGLAND. VOLUME 4, VERMONT (US) [17062077] **4335**

CORPORATE PHILANTHROPY IN RHODE ISLAND (US/1051-6514) [20718342] **4335**

CORPORATE PHILANTHROPY REPORT (US/0885-8365) [12756032] **4335**

CORPORATE PLAN SUMMARY, CAPITAL BUDGET SUMMARY, OPERATING BUDGET SUMMARY (CN/1187-4546) [25314269] **5097**

CORPORATE PLANNING IDEAS (US/0589-7904) [02660360] **661**

CORPORATE PLANNING JOURNAL *See* LOCAL GOVERNMENT POLICY MAKING **4663**

CORPORATE PRACTICE COMMENTATOR (US/0010-8995) [01565164] **3099**

CORPORATE PRACTICE SERIES (US/0162-5691) [04177937] **3099**

CORPORATE PRACTICE SERIES. BNA'S CORPORATE COUNSEL WEEKLY (US/0886-0475) [12818095] **3099**

CORPORATE PROFILES / BUSINESS DAY (PH) [10843300] **662**

CORPORATE PSYCHOLOGY (US/1055-7873) [23310044] **4583**

CORPORATE PUBLIC ISSUES AND THEIR MANAGEMENT (US/0730-5192) [06023281] **662**

CORPORATE REAL ESTATE EXECUTIVE (US/1042-9115) [19252009] **4836**

CORPORATE REGISTER See ARTHUR ANDERSEN CORPORATE REGISTER, THE **639**

CORPORATE REGISTER, THE (UK) [25224503] **662**

CORPORATE REPORT FACT BOOK (US/0589-7920) [01565168] **895**

CORPORATE REPORT MINNESOTA (US/0279-5299) [07090661] **662**

CORPORATE REPORT WISCONSIN (US/0890-4278) [12795345] 728, **662**

CORPORATE REPORTS ON FILE *SUSPENDED.* (US/0091-4975) [01787750] **895**

CORPORATE RESTRUCTURING (UK) **662**

CORPORATE RISK MANAGEMENT *CEASED.* (US/1046-5626) [20487417] **662**

CORPORATE SECUIRTY DIGEST See SECURITY DIRECTOR'S DIGEST **3176**

CORPORATE SECURITY (NEW YORK, N.Y.) (US/1040-4201) [07352446] **5176**

CORPORATE SECURITY'S TECHNOLOGY ALERT (US) **1152**

CORPORATE SHOWCASE (US/0742-9975) [10191687] 4368, **377**

CORPORATE SYNDICATE PERSONNEL (US) **662**

CORPORATE SYSTEMS (US/0362-501X) [02293927] **864**

●CORPORATE TAX PLANNING (US/1188-7834) [27996789] **4719**

CORPORATE TAX RETURN HANDBOOK *CEASED.* (CN/0824-314X) [10199157] **4719**

CORPORATE TAXATION *CEASED.* (US/0898-798X) [17912458] **785**

CORPORATE TAXATION FOR LATIN AMERICA (NE) [10892789] 662, **4719**

CORPORATE TAXATION IN LATIN AMERICA See TAXATION IN LATIN AMERICA **4755**

CORPORATE TAXATION IN LATIN AMERICA See TAXATION IN LATIN AMERICA. SUPPLEMENT **4755**

CORPORATE TAXES, A WORLDWIDE SUMMARY (US) [07069154] **4719**

CORPORATE TECHNOLOGY DIRECTORY (US/0887-1930) [13133812] **3477**

CORPORATE TIMES (US/0882-4681) [11909553] **1602**

CORPORATE TRAVEL (US/0882-8709) [12014255] 662, **5467**

CORPORATE TRENDTRAC *CEASED.* (US/1041-1712) [18670941] **662**

CORPORATE VIDEO See TELEVISUAL **1141**

CORPORATE VIEW, MINNESOTA, A (US/0747-6701) [10762130] **662**

●CORPORATE YELLOW BOOK (US/1058-2908) [24255597] 662, **1924**

CORPORATION DES BIBLIOTHECAIRES PROFESSIONNELS DU QUEBEC See RAPPORT ANNUEL - CORPORATION DES BIBLIOTHECAIRES PROFESSIONNELS DU QUEBEC **3243**

CORPORATION DES METIERS D'ART DU QUEBEC EN ESTRIE See CATALOGUE-REPERTOIRE DES CREATEURS-CONCEPTEURS **317**

CORPORATION FINANCE AND NEW ISSUE WEEKLY (US) [01786022] **895**

CORPORATION FRANCHISE TAX. NUMBER OF CORPORATIONS AND REPORTED TAX LIABILITY BY TAX BASE (COLUMBUS, OHIO: 1981) (US) [10621566] **4719**

CORPORATION FRANCHISE TAX. NUMBER OF MANUFACTURING CORPORATIONS AND REPORTED TAX LIABILITY BY TAX BASE / OHIO DEPARTMENT OF TAXATION (US) [08364373] **4719**

CORPORATION JOURNAL, THE (US/0045-8597) [01565169] **3099**

CORPORATION LAW AND TAX REPORT (1975) *CEASED.* (US/0147-1619) [03116965] 4719, **3099**

CORPORATION LAWS OF OHIO (US) [24113862] **3099**

CORPORATION OF FOREIGN BONDHOLDERS, LONDON See ANNUAL REPORT OF THE COUNCIL OF THE CORPORATION OF FOREIGN BONDHOLDERS **891**

CORPORATION OF TRANSLATORS AND INTERPRETERS OF NEW BRUNSWICK See REPERTOIRE / CORPORATION DES TRADUCTEURS, TRADUCTRICES, TERMINOLOGUES ET INTERPRETES DU NOUVEAU-BRUNSWICK **3315**

CORPORATION OF TRANSLATORS, TERMINOLOGISTS AND INTERPRETERS OF NEW BRUNSWICK See REPERTOIRE / CORPORATION DES TRADUCTEURS, TRADUCTRICES, TERMINOLOGUES ET INTERPRETES DU NOUVEAU-BRUNSWICK **3315**

CORPORATION PROFESSIONNELLE DES COMPTABLES EN ADMINISTRATION INDUSTRIELLE DU QUEBEC See RAPPORT ANNUEL / CORPORATION PROFESSIONNELLE DES COMPTABLES EN ADMINISTRATION INDUSTRIELLE DU QUEBEC **750**

CORPORATION PROFESSIONNELLE DES DIETETISTES DU QUEBEC See REPERTOIRE DES MEMBRES - CORPORATION PROFESSIONNELLE DES DIETETISTES DU QUEBEC **4198**

CORPORATION PROFESSIONNELLE DES DIETETISTES DU QUEBEC See BULLETIN - CORPORATION PROFESSIONNELLE DES DIETETISTES DU QUEBEC **4188**

CORPORATION PROFESSIONNELLE DES MEDECINS DU QUEBEC See BULLETIN - CORPORATION PROFESSIONNELLE DES MEDECINS DU QUEBEC **3559**

CORPORATION PROFESSIONNELLE DES PHYSIOTHERAPEUTES DU QUEBEC See RAPPORT ANNUEL / LA CORPORATION PROFESSIONNELLE DES PHYSIOTHERAPEUTES DU QUEBEC **4382**

CORPORATION PROFESSIONNELLE DES URBANISTES DU QUEBEC See GUIDE DES RESSOURCES PROFESSIONNELLES EN URBANISME **2823**

CORPORATION PROFESSIONNELLE DES URBANISTES DU QUEBEC See ANNUAIRE / CORPORATION PROFESSIONNELLE DES URBANISTES DU QUEBEC **2814**

CORPORATION TAXATION STATISTICS (OTTAWA) (CN/0576-0119) [01793757] 4719, **4697**

CORPORATION TRUST COMPANY JOURNAL See CORPORATION JOURNAL, THE **3099**

CORPORATIONS (US/0099-1236) [02239701] **3099**

●CORPS REPORT, THE (US/1069-2657) [27965885] **2088**

CORPTECH DIRECTORY (US) **662**

CORPUS ADMINISTRATIVE INDEX (CN/0703-7384) [107037384] **4640**

CORPUS ALMANAC & CANADIAN SOURCEBOOK (CN/0823-1133) [09580308] **1924**

CORPUS ANTIQUITATUM AMERICANENSIUM. ITALIA (IT) [09492403] **2259**

CORPUS CATHOLICORUM (GW/0070-0320) [06845200] **5028**

CORPUS CHEMICAL REPORT See CAMFORD CHEMICAL REPORT **966**

CORPUS CHEMICAL REPORT (CN/0228-653X) [08091609] **1023**

CORPUS CHRISTI CALLER-TIMES (US/0894-5365) [15805360] **5748**

CORPUS CHRISTI GEOLOGICAL SOCIETY See BULLETIN - CORPUS CHRISTI GEOLOGICAL SOCIETY **1368**

CORPUS CHRISTI MAGAZINE (1984) (US/8750-5460) [11502106] **662**

CORPUS CHRISTIANORUM. CLAVIS PATRUM GRAECORUM *CEASED.* (BE) [06839068] 3378, **4950**

CORPUS CHRISTIANORUM. CONTINUATIO MEDIAEVALIS (BE) [03521187] 2614, **4950**

CORPUS CHRISTIANORUM. INITIA (BE) [05581758] **4950**

CORPUS CHRISTIANORUM. SERIES APOCRYPHORUM (BE) [10689710] **4950**

CORPUS CHRISTIANORUM: SERIES GRAECA (BE) [04378781] **4950**

CORPUS CHRISTIANORUM. SERIES LATINA (BE) [01565173] **4951**

CORPUS DER MINOISCHEN UND MYKENISCHEN SIEGEL (GW/0589-8021) [03653006] **266**

CORPUS FONTIUM HISTORIAE BYZANTINAE (GW/0589-8048) [04479865] **2684**

CORPUS HISPANORUM DE PACE (SP/0589-8056) [01643593] **2729**

CORPUS INSCRIPTIONUM LATINARUM, CONSILIO ET AUCTORIATE ACADEMIAE LITTERARUM REGIAE BORUSSICAE EDITUM (GW) [01565177] **3378**

CORPUS MEDICORUM GRAECORUM (GW/0070-0347) [07750582] **3569**

CORPUS MENSURABILIS MUSICAE (IT/0070-0363) [01908338] **4112**

CORPUS OF EARLY KEYBOARD MUSIC (GW/0070-0371) [01889881] **4112**

CORPUS PHILOSOPHORUM DANICORUM MEDII AEVI (DK/0589-8080) [03643392] **4344**

CORPUS SCRIPTORUM CHRISTIANORUM ORIENTALIUM (FR) [04759080] **4951**

CORPUS SCRIPTORUM DE MUSICA (GW/0070-0460) [01889910] **4112**

CORPUS SCRIPTORUM ECCLESIASTICORUM LATINORUM (AU) [01565180] **4951**

CORPUS VASORUM ANTIQUORUM. GREAT BRITAIN (UK) [04970223] **2684**

CORPUS VASORUM ANTIQUORUM. ITALIA (IT) [05667208] 2588, **4087**

CORPUS VASORUM ANTIQUORUM. POLOGNE (PL) [05667198] **2588**

CORPUS WORKERS' COMPENSATION HANDBOOK (CN/1182-610X) [23237335] 1661, **2878**

CORRECTIONAL ASSOCIATION OF NEW YORK See ANNUAL REPORT TO THE LEGISLATURE - CORRECTIONAL ASSOCIATION OF NEW YORK **3157**

CORRECTIONAL COMPASS; OFFICIAL NEWSLETTER (US) [01372102] **3161**

CORRECTIONAL EDUCATION ASSOCIATION (U.S.) See MEMBERSHIP UPDATE / CORRECTIONAL EDUCATION ASSOCIATION **3169**

CORRECTIONAL LITERATURE PUBLISHED IN CANADA (CN/0070-0509) [02248098] **3161**

CORRECTIONAL POPULATIONS IN THE UNITED STATES / U.S. DEPT. OF JUSTICE, BUREAU OF JUSTICE STATISTICS (US) [17766488] 3161, **3079**

CORRECTIONAL SERVICES NEWS (US/0196-2353) [03987806] **3161**

●CORRECTIONS ALERT (US/1075-203X) [29962936] **3161**

CORRECTIONS COMPENDIUM (US/0738-8144) [03852025] **5281**

CORRECTIONS COURT DIGEST, THE (US/0360-196X) [02243371] **2957**

CORRECTIONS DIGEST (US) [01565192] **3161**

CORRECTIONS, STATE OF RHODE ISLAND (US/0364-1716) [02618549] **3161**

CORRECTIONS TODAY (US/0190-2563) [04676827] **3161**

CORRECTIONS YEARBOOK, THE (US/0273-4230) [07052649] **3161**

CORRECTIVE AND SOCIAL PSYCHIATRY AND JOURNAL OF BEHAVIOR TECHNOLOGY METHODS AND THERAPY (US/0093-1551) [01791643] 4583, **3924**

CORREIO DA UNESCO, O (BL) 1734, 5097, **317**

CORREIOS E TELECOMUNICACOES DE PORTUGAL See ANUARIO ESTATISTICO - CORREIOS E TELECOMUNICACOES DE PORTUGAL **1124**

CORREIOS E TELECOMUNICACOES DE PORTUGAL See LISTA DAS ESTACOES E POSTOS, CORREIO **1145**

CORRELATION (UK/0260-8790) [08811589] **390**

CORRELATION, TEXTILE, AND APPAREL CATEGORIES WITH TARIFF SCHEDULES OF THE UNITED STATES ANNOTATED / PREPARED BY INTERNATIONAL AGREEMENTS AND MONITORING DIVISION (US) [06374647] **1083**

CORRELATIVE NEUROANATOMY (EAST NORWALK, CONN.) (US/1042-0398) [18398226] **3830**

CORREO BACTERIOLOGICO (SP) **3569**

CORREO DE LOS ANDES (CK/0120-1395) [07086026] **1818**

CORREO, EL (FR/0304-310X) [07531750] **2845**

CORRESPONDANCE DE LA PRESSE (FR) **2918**

CORRESPONDANCE DE LA PUBLICITE (FR) **758**

CORRESPONDANCE ECONOMIQUE (FR) **1471**

CORRESPONDANCE INTERNATIONALE (MONTREAL) (CN/0229-1185) [08469790] **4541**

CORRESPONDANCES (SILLERY) (CN/0707-8935) [05257191] **2213**

CORRESPONDENCE CHESS (UK) [04154387] **4859**

CORRESPONDENCE OF JOHN LOCKE (UK) **4344**

CORRESPONDENCE SOCIETY OF SURGEONS See COLLECTED LETTERS / CORRESPONDENCE SOCIETY OF SURGEONS **3962**

CORRESPONDENT BANKING (US/0277-1454) [07496129] **785**

CORRIDOR REAL ESTATE JOURNAL, THE (US/1048-7948) [21022724] **4836**

CORRIERE ADRIATICO (IT) **5804**

CORRIERE DEI TRASPORTI (IT) **5380**

CORRIERE DEL GIORNO PUGLIA E LUCANIA (IT) **5804**

CORRIERE DEL MEDICO
(IT/0390-8798) [I03908798] **3569**

CORRIERE DELLA SERA (IT)
[01565202] **5804**

CORRIERE DELLA VALLE D'AOSTA (IT)
5804

CORRIERE DI CHIERI E DINTORNI (IT)
2486

CORRIERE DI NOVARA (IT) **5804**

CORRIERE DI ROMA, IL (IT) **2486**

CORRIERE DI SALUZZO (IT) **2486**

CORRIERE EUROPEO (IT) **1634**

CORRIERE GIURIDICO (IT) **2957**

CORRIERE MERCANTILE (IT) **5448**

CORRIERE TERMO IDRO SANITARIO, IL (IT/0393-9723) [I03939723] **2604**

CORRIERE TRIBUTARIO, IL (IT) **742**

CORRIERE UNESCO (IT/0304-3134) [I03043134] **234**

CORRIERE VINICOLO, IL (IT) [03992844] **168**

CORRISPONDENZE (IT) [20441003] **2845**

CORROSAO E PROTECCAO DE MATERIALS (PO/0870-1164) [10931015] **2101**

CORROSION ABSTRACTS (US/0010-9339) [00946176] 2011, 2101, **2003**

CORROSION & COATINGS SOUTH AFRICA (SA/0377-8711) [03528215] 2101, **2011**

CORROSION AUSTRALASIA (AT/0155-6002) [03856624] 2101, **2011**

CORROSION ENGINEERING (NEW YORK, N.Y.) (US/0892-4228) [30832382] **2011**

CORROSION (HOUSTON, TEX.) (US/0010-9312) [01565203] 2101, **2011**

CORROSION PREVENTION AND CONTROL (UK/0010-9371) [02446215] 2101, **2011**

CORROSION PREVENTION/INHIBITION DIGEST (US/0364-3301) [02625606] 2101, **2011**

CORROSION REVIEWS (IS/0048-7538) [13502983] **2011**

CORROSION SCIENCE (UK/0010-938X) [01565206] 2101, **2011**

CORROSION SCIENCE [MICROFORM] (US/0010-938X) [23301893] **2011**

CORROSION TECHNOLOGY (US) [21615546] **1969**

CORROSION Y PROTECCION (SP/0045-8678) [03585867] 2102, **2012**

CORRUGATED BOXES AND WRAPPERS (CN/0380-7037) [02443794] **4218**

CORRUPTION AND REFORM (NE/0169-7528) [14117024] **4470**

CORRY JOURNAL (US) [14978670] **5735**

CORSAN See RELATORIO DA DIRETORIA - CORSAN **2241**

CORSE (FR) [03042817] **5467**

CORSETERIA Y LENCERIA (SP) **1083**

CORSI DI CULTURA SULL'ARTE RAVENNATE E BIZANTINA (IT/0392-5269) [I03925269] **318**

CORSICANA DAILY SUN (US/8750-2518) [11173414] **5748**

CORSO DI CULTURA SULL'ARTE RAVENNATE E BIZANTINA : [CONFERENZE] (IT) [04289236] **348**

CORTEX (IT/0010-9452) [02116577] **3830**

CORTEZ SENTINEL, THE (US) [03526686] **5642**

CORTICA (PO/0870-1059) [03960231] **1602**

CORTLAND COUNTY CONNECTION (US/1043-5557) [19493590] **77**

CORTLAND DEMOCRAT (1877), THE (US/0745-9823) [09650364] **5715**

CORTLAND STANDARD (US) [17629201] **5715**

CORTO CIRCUITO CEASED. (FR) [22465911] **4067**

CORVALLIS GAZETTE-TIMES (US/0746-3995) [10012551] **5733**

CORVETTE FEVER MAGAZINE (US/0195-1661) [05322697] **5412**

CORVETTE QUARTERLY (US/0897-4179) [17494459] **5412**

CORVETTE SERVICE MANUAL (US) [18484877] **5412**

CORVETTE SHOP MANUAL See CORVETTE SERVICE MANUAL **5412**

CORYDON DEMOCRAT (CORYDON, IND. : 1880) (US) [12562758] **5663**

CORYELL KIN (US/0748-3309) [10916132] **2444**

CORYELL NEWSLETTER (US/0883-7600) [07620551] **2444**

COSA VISTA, LA (IT/0393-9162) [17864601] **4067**

COSAS (CL) [10732656] 2512, **4640**

COSMATOM (UK) [01799244] **394**

COSMATOM (UK/0143-926X) [I0143926X] **4401**

COSMEP NEWSLETTER (1981) (US/1064-4482) [07583790] **4813**

COSMESI IN FARMACIA (IT) **4298**

COSMETIC BENCH REFERENCE (US/1069-1448) [09883467] **403**

COSMETIC DENTISTRY FOR GPS See GP (ATLANTA, GA.) **1324**

COSMETIC INSIDER'S REPORT (US/0275-4681) [07139412] **403**

COSMETIC NEWS : CN (IT) [15469994] **403**

COSMETIC RESEARCH / TOILETRIES AND HAIR CARE. USA NEWS (FR) **403**

COSMETIC SCIENCE AND TECHNOLOGY SERIES (US/0887-6541) [11889038] **403**

COSMETIC, TOILETRY AND FRAGRANCE ASSOCIATION See CTFA COSMETIC JOURNAL **403**

COSMETIC WORLD (US/0589-8447) [04249690] **403**

COSMETIC WORLD NEWS (UK/0305-0319) [02771510] **403**

COSMETICA DISTRIBUTION LEVALLOIS-PERRET (FR/1150-1677) [I11501677] **403**

COSMETICS AEROSOLS & TOILETRIES IN AUSTRALIA (AT/0817-637X) [24578748] **403**

COSMETICS AND TOILETRIES (US/0361-4387) [02076293] **403**

COSMETICS & TOILETRIES (IT) [14766513] **403**

COSMETICS & TOILETRIES & HOUSEHOLD PRODUCTS MARKETING NEWS IN JAPAN (JA) **403**

COSMETICS AND TOILETRIES MANUFACTURERS AND SUPPLIERS (UK) **403**

COSMETICS (DON MILLS) (CN/0315-1301) [01985704] **403**

COSMETICS HANDBOOK (CN/0316-9871) [02247558] **403**

COSMETICS INTERNATIONAL (UK) [23721846] **403**

COSMETIQUE NEWS PARIS (FR/0980-0875) [I09800875] **403**

COSMIC AND SUBATOMIC PHYSICS REPORT (SW/0348-9329) [11472330] **4401**

COSMIC RESEARCH (US/0010-9525) [01565215] 395, **1404**

COSMIC SOFTWARE CATALOG (US/1043-9935) [10941131] 1212, 1279, **1228**

COSMICA : AREA STUDIES (JA) [03610248] **2503**

COSMOGLOTTA (SAINT GALL, SWITZERLAND) (SZ) [13483391] **3275**

COSMOPOLITAN (NE) 403, 2596, **5554**

COSMOPOLITAN (1952) (US/0010-9541) [01770745] 403, 1083, **5554**

COSMOPOLITAN AUSTRALIAN EDITION (AT/0310-2076) [I03102076] 403, 1083, **5554**

COSMOPOLITAN CONTACT (US/0010-955X) [02920899] **4541**

COSMOPOLITAN. (ENGLAND EDITION) (UK) 403, 2596, **5554**

COSMOPOLITAN LIVING (US/0195-7953) [05664401] **2789**

COSMOPOLITAN (PARIS) (FR/1161-2258) [26619003] 403, 2596, **5554**

COSMOS (UK/0269-8773) [17787863] **2319**

COSMOS CLUB (WASHINGTON, D.C.) See BULLETIN - COSMOS CLUB (WASHINGTON, D.C.) **5229**

COSMOS (WASHINGTON, D.C.) (US/1058-2029) [24136947] **5230**

COSPAR See COSPAR INFORMATION BULLETIN **17**

COSPAR INFORMATION BULLETIN (UK/0045-8732) [01909486] **17**

COSSA WASHINGTON UPDATE (US/0749-4394) [11177271] **5196**

COSSMHO REPORTER, THE (US) [04459704] **2259**

COST AND PRODUCTION SURVEY REPORT See COST SURVEY (1992) **3778**

COST AND QUALITY OF FUELS FOR ELECTRIC UTILITY PLANTS (ANNUAL) (US/0743-6815) [09906185] **2039**

● COST CONTROLLER, THE (US/1063-2735) [25955943] **864**

COST EFFECTIVENESS RESOURCE PERSONNEL DIRECTORY (US/0735-6188) [08938135] **3569**

COST ENGINEER (UK/0010-9606) [10527557] **864**

COST ENGINEERING (US) [08587222] **1969**

COST ENGINEERING (MORGANTOWN. 1980) (US/0274-9696) [06755189] **1969**

COST ENGINEERS HANDBOOK (NE) **1970**

COST FORECASTING SERVICE APPLICATIONS BULLETIN (US/0730-2436) [07940498] **611**

COST OF CLEAN AIR AND CLEAN WATER, THE (US/0275-0384) [06045831] **2227**

COST OF DOING BUSINESS : CORPORATIONS (US/0574-1831) [03646355] **662**

COST OF DOING BUSINESS, PARTNERSHIPS & PROPRIETORSHIPS (US/0574-1831) [03923201] **662**

COST OF FOOD AT HOME ESTIMATED FOR FOOD PLANS AT THREE COST LEVELS. WESTERN REGION (US) [06622449] **2332**

COST OF FOOD AT HOME FOR FOOD PLANS AT FOUR COST LEVELS. U.S. AVERAGE (US) [06664358] **2332**

COST OF LIVING DIFFERENTIALS See GEOGRAPHIC COST OF LIVING DIFFERENTIALS : LARGE CITIES **1492**

COST OF LIVING INDEX (AMERICAN CHAMBER OF COMMERCE RESEARCHERS ASSOCIATION) See ACCRA COST OF LIVING INDEX **1460**

COST OF LIVING INDEX (LOUISVILLE, KY.) (US/1048-2830) [18541739] **1471**

COST OF LIVING NEWS (US/0743-2569) [10455180] **1552**

COST OF PRODUCING MILK ON N.C. GRADE A DAIRY FARMS, THE (US/0737-6324) [06152842] **192**

COST OF SOCIAL SECURITY. LE COUT DE LA SECURITE SOCIALE. EL COSTO DE LA SEGURIDAD SOCIAL, THE (SZ/0538-8295) [01714319] **5281**

COST OF STORING AND HANDLING COTTON AT PUBLIC STORAGE FACILITIES (US/0092-9530) [01783440] **77**

COST OF TRANSPORTING FREIGHT BY CLASS I AND CLASS II MOTOR COMMON CARRIERS OF GENERAL COMMODITIES, BY REGIONS OR TERRITORIES (US) [01606301] **5380**

COST OF TRANSPORTING FREIGHT BY CLASS I AND CLASS II MOTOR COMMON CARRIERS OF GENERAL COMMODITIES. CENTRAL REGION (US) [17742561] 5380, **829**

COST OF TRANSPORTING FREIGHT BY CLASS I AND CLASS II MOTOR COMMON CARRIERS OF GENERAL COMMODITIES. EASTERN-CENTRAL TERRITORY (US/0499-6909) [05845324] 5380, **829**

COST OF TRANSPORTING FREIGHT BY CLASS I AND CLASS II MOTOR COMMON CARRIERS OF GENERAL COMMODITIES : MIDDLE ATLANTIC REGION, SOUTHERN (INTRA) REGION, EAST-SOUTH TERRITORY, SOUTH-CENTRAL TERRITORY (US) [04081959] 5380, **829**

COST OF TRANSPORTING FREIGHT BY CLASS I AND CLASS II MOTOR COMMON CARRIERS OF GENERAL COMMODITIES. TRANSCONTINENTAL TERRITORY, ROCKY MOUNTAIN REGION, MIDDLEWEST REGION, SOUTHWEST REGION, PACIFIC REGION (US) [03331981] 5380, **829**

COST OF TRANSPORTING FREIGHT BY CLASS I MOTOR COMMON CARRIERS OF GENERAL COMMODITIES. EASTERN-CENTRAL TERRITORY See COST OF TRANSPORTING FREIGHT BY CLASS I AND CLASS II MOTOR COMMON CARRIERS OF GENERAL COMMODITIES. EASTERN-CENTRAL TERRITORY **829**

COST OF TRANSPORTING FREIGHT; CLASS I AND CLASS II MOTOR COMMON CARRIERS OF GENERAL COMMODITIES. NEW ENGLAND REGION - GROUP I, NEW ENGLAND REGION- GROUP II, CENTRAL REGION, EASTERN CENTRAL TERRITORY (US) [06694291] 5380, **830**

● COST SURVEY (1992) (US/1064-4571) [26288042] **3778**

COSTA MESA NEWS (US/0195-0126) [05213254] **5634**

COSTA RICA. ARCHIVO NACIONAL See REVISTA DEL ARCHIVO NACIONAL **2483**

COSTA RICA, ENERGIEWIRTSCHAFT / BUNDESSTELLE FUR AUSSENHANDELSINFORMATION (GW) [07696649] **1936**

COSTA RICA, PANORAMA ECONOMICO EN ... Y PERSPECTIVAS PARA . See PANORAMA ECONOMICO DE COSTA RICA / MINISTERIO DE PLANIFICACION NACIONAL Y POLITICA ECONOMICA, DIRECCION DE POLITICA ECONOMICA Y SOCIAL **1511**

COSTA RICA, PANORAMA ECONOMICO EN ... Y PERSPECTIVAS PARA ... / MINISTERIO DE PLANIFICACION NACIONAL Y POLITICA ECONOMICA, DIRECCION DE PLANIFICACION GLOBAL, DEPARTAMENTO DE ANALISIS ECONOMICO (CR) [22612156] **1472**

COSTA RICA REPORT (US/0276-4644) [07370610] **2512**

COSTA RICA WIRTSCHAFTSDATEN / BUNDESSTELLE FUR AUSSENHANDELSINFORMATION (GW) [07473168] **1552**

COSTERUS (NE/0165-9618) [03603003] 3378, **3275**

COSTOS Y GESTION (AG/0327-5345) [I03275345] **662**

COSTRUIRE IN LATERIZIO (IT/0394-1590) [I03941590] 611, **296**

COSTRUIRE MILANO (IT/1121-6336) [I11216336] **611**

COSTRUIRE PER ABITARE (IT) [09446337] **611**

COSTRUTTORE EDILE DELLA MARCA TREVIGIANA (IT) **2021**

COSTRUTTORI ITALIANI NEL MONDO (IT/0589-8765) [I05898765] **2021**

COSTRUZIONI (IT/0010-9665) [I00109665] **611**

COSTRUZIONI METALLICHE (IT/0010-9673) [10341081] **611**

COSTRUZIONI STRADE CANTIERI (IT/0393-8220) [I03938220] **2022**

COSTS AND MARGINS IN BANKING. STATISTICAL SUPPLEMENTS (US) 785, **728**

COSTS AND RETURNS FOR RICE, SOUTHWEST LOUISIANA RICE AREA (US) [03956799] **168**

COSTS AND RETURNS FROM VEGETABLE CROPS IN FLORIDA, WITH COMPARISONS (US/0149-0613) [03425969] **168**

COSTS OF FOODS PURCHASED BY USDA AND LOCAL SCHOOL SYSTEMS (US/0098-8294) [02172439] **1862**

COSTUME (UK/0590-8876) [02070784] 2614, **1083**

COSTUME SOCIETY OF AMERICA *See* BIBLIOGRAPHY - COSTUME SOCIETY OF AMERICA **1088**

COTA NEWSLETTER (US/0271-3438) [05388146] **1130**

COTE 100 (CN/0849-5793) [21325772] **895**

COTE DE L'ATLANTIQUE (FR) [03502002] **2684**

COTE DE L'ATLANTIQUE DE LA LOIRE AUX PYRENEES *See* COTE DE L'ATLANTIQUE **2684**

COTE DESFOSSES *See* TRIBUNE PARIS. 1992, LA **855**

COTE DESFOSSES (FR/0750-0424) [07500424] **5800**

COTE D'IVOIRE (FR) [01795566] **1552**

COTE D'IVOIRE : ANNUAIRE INTERNATIONAL, LA (IV) [02418956] **4640**

COTE D'IVOIRE EN CHIFFRES, LA (IV) [02744259] **5326**

COTE D'IVOIRE SELECTION (FR) [08867010] **1472**

COTE OFFICIELLE (FR/0220-6358) [04815173] **895**

COTEAU REVIEW *CEASED.* (CN/0836-4915) [17235846] **5782**

COTECFLASH (SP/0376-7590) [01785980] **4368**

COTH REPORT (US/0146-2814) [02883864] **3778**

COTIDIANO, EL (MX/0186-1840) [15616007] **1661**

COTLOOK DAILY (UK) **5349**

COTLOOK PRISCOPE (UK) **5349**

COTON ET FIBRES TROPICALES *CEASED.* (FR/0010-9711) [03938825] **2413**

COTTAGE CONNECTION, THE (US) **662**

COTTAGE GROVE SENTINEL (US) **5733**

COTTAGE LIFE (CN/0838-2395) [20183836] 2531, **4849**

COTTAGER MAGAZINE, THE (CN/0226-0344) [06516230] **2819**

●COTTAGER (VICTORIA BEACH. MANITOBA ED.) (CN/1188-0163) [26497574] **384**

COTTON *See* COTTON, REVIEW OF THE WORLD SITUATION **1603**

COTTON AND GENERAL ECONOMIC REVIEW *See* COTTON OUTLOOK **5349**

COTTON AND TROPICAL FIBRES ABSTRACTS *See* COTTON AND TROPICAL FIBRES ABSTRACTS BIBLIOGRAPHY **152**

COTTON AND TROPICAL FIBRES ABSTRACTS BIBLIOGRAPHY (UK) 168, **152**

COTTON COUNTS ITS CUSTOMERS (US) [06769427] **5349**

COTTON CROP LETTER (US) [06713829] **168**

COTTON DIGEST INTERNATIONAL, THE (US/0090-2462) [04369023] **5349**

COTTON FARMING (US/0746-8385) [03613800] **168**

COTTON FIBER AND PROCESSING RESULTS *See* COTTON FIBER AND PROCESSING TEST RESULTS **5349**

COTTON FIBER AND PROCESSING TEST RESULTS (US/0566-5469) [01799482] 3477, **5349**

COTTON GIN AND OIL MILL PRESS, THE (US/0010-9800) [05577612] **5349**

COTTON GINNINGS (A.20) *See* COTTON GINNINGS. A10 **168**

COTTON GINNINGS. A10 (US/0093-4313) [01768240] **168**

COTTON GINNINGS IN THE UNITED STATES (US/0093-433X) [01795775] **168**

COTTON GROWER (US/0194-9772) [05168284] **168**

COTTON INTERNATIONAL (US/0070-0673) [01798553] **5349**

COTTON: MONTHLY REVIEW OF THE WORLD SITUATION (US) [07000858] 168, **5349**

COTTON OUTLOOK (UK) [06725796] **5349**

COTTON PRICE STATISTICS (US/0010-9827) [02259845] 168, **152**

COTTON QUALITY CROP (US/0098-7026) [02242160] 168, **5350**

COTTON QUALITY. SUPPLY, DISAPPEARANCE, CARRY-OVER (US) [02240981] 5350, **168**

●COTTON QUARTERLY, THE (US/1063-5084) [26057103] **3378**

COTTON, REVIEW OF THE WORLD SITUATION (US/0010-9754) [18997788] **1603**

COTTON TECHNOLOGICAL RESEARCH LABORATORY *See* TECHNOLOGICAL REPORT - COTTON TECHNOLOGICAL RESEARCH LABORATORY **189**

●COTTON, WORLD MARKETS & TRADE / UNITED STATES DEPARTMENT OF AGRICULTURE, FOREIGN AGRICULTURAL SERVICE (US) [29824798] **77**

COTTON : WORLD STATISTICS (US) [07633915] **5360**

COTTONSEED QUALITY (US/0565-2014) [02242161] **168**

COTTONSEED VARIETIES PLANTED (US/0498-1987) [02240938] **168**

COTTONWOOD CHRONICLE (US) [18945459] **5656**

COTTONWOOD COUNTY CITIZEN AND THE WINDOM REPORTER. [MICROFILM] (US) [01565232] **5695**

COTTONWOOD (LAWRENCE, KAN.) (US/0147-149X) [10971751] **3378**

COTTONWOOD MONTHLY *See* CLASS ACT **1732**

COUGAR REPORT, THE (US/0747-3656) [10774818] **1091**

COULICOU (CN/0822-7098) [11147618] **1062**

COUNCIL CHRONICLE (URBANA, ILL.), THE (US/1057-4190) [24033615] 3275, **1803**

COUNCIL COLUMNS / COUNCIL ON FOUNDATIONS (US) [19953256] **4335**

COUNCIL COMMENTS (US) [01554774] **4641**

COUNCIL FOR AGRICULTURAL SCIENCE AND TECHNOLOGY *See* SPECIAL PUBLICATION - COUNCIL FOR AGRICULTURAL SCIENCE AND TECHNOLOGY **137**

COUNCIL FOR AGRICULTURAL SCIENCE AND TECHNOLOGY PUBLICATIONS SUBSCRIPTION (US) **5097**

COUNCIL FOR BASIC EDUCATION *See* BASIC EDUCATION (WASHINGTON, D.C.) **1727**

COUNCIL FOR BRITISH ARCHAEOLOGY, LONDON *See* REPORT - COUNCIL FOR BRITISH ARCHAEOLOGY **280**

COUNCIL FOR FRANCO-ONTARIAN EDUCATION *See* REPORT OF THE COUNCIL FOR FRANCO-ONTARIAN EDUCATION **1778**

COUNCIL FOR HUMAN RIGHTS IN LATIN AMERICA NEWSLETTER, THE (US) [12714479] **4506**

COUNCIL FOR MINERAL TECHNOLOGY (SOUTH AFRICA) *See* ANNUAL REPORT / COUNCIL FOR MINERAL TECHNOLOGY **2133**

COUNCIL FOR MUTUAL ECONOMIC ASSISTANCE *See* COUNCIL FOR MUTUAL ECONOMIC ASSISTANCE **1472**

COUNCIL FOR MUTUAL ECONOMIC ASSISTANCE *See* STANDARTY SEV I REKOMENDATSII SEV PO STANDARTIZATSII: UKAZATEL **4032**

COUNCIL FOR MUTUAL ECONOMIC ASSISTANCE (RU/0303-8696) [01794664] **1472**

COUNCIL FOR NATIONAL ACADEMIC AWARDS (GREAT BRITAIN) *See* ANNUAL REPORT / COUNCIL FOR NATIONAL ACADEMIC AWARDS **1725**

COUNCIL FOR NATIONAL ACADEMIC AWARDS (GREAT BRITAIN) *See* DIRECTORY OF FIRST DEGREE COURSES **1912**

COUNCIL FOR NATIONAL ACADEMIC AWARDS (GREAT BRITAIN). COMPENDIUM OF DEGREE COURSES *See* DIRECTORY OF FIRST DEGREE COURSES **1912**

COUNCIL FOR PERIODICAL DISTRIBUTORS ASSOCIATIONS *See* CPDA NEWS **1303**

COUNCIL FOR RESEARCH IN MUSIC EDUCATION *See* BULLETIN - COUNCIL FOR RESEARCH IN MUSIC EDUCATION **4105**

COUNCIL FOR TOBACCO RESEARCH--U.S.A *See* REPORT OF THE COUNCIL FOR TOBACCO RESEARCH--U.S.A., INC **5373**

COUNCIL GROVE REPUBLICAN (COUNCIL GROVE, KAN. : DAILY) (US) [12141264] **5675**

COUNCIL NOTES (US) [02256534] **2819**

COUNCIL NOTES - INDIANA FAMILY HEALTH COUNCIL, INC (US/0146-1117) [02860298] **3569**

COUNCIL OF BETTER BUSINESS BUREAUS *See* ANNUAL REPORT - COUNCIL OF BETTER BUSINESS BUREAUS **1293**

COUNCIL OF EUROPE *See* PUBLICATIONS / COUNCIL OF EUROPE **4532**

COUNCIL OF EUROPE *See* PRESS COMMUNIQUE **4512**

COUNCIL OF EUROPE *See* FUTURE FOR OUR PAST / COUNCIL OF EUROPE, A **299**

COUNCIL OF EUROPE. COMMITTEE OF MINISTERS *See* RECOMMENDATIONS AND RESOLUTIONS / COUNCIL OF EUROPE, COMMITTEE OF MINISTERS **3036**

COUNCIL OF EUROPE. CONSULTATION ASSEMBLY. RESOLUTION *See* RESOLUTION - PARLIAMENTARY ASSEMBLY OF THE COUNCIL OF EUROPE **4683**

COUNCIL OF EUROPE. COUNCIL FOR CULTURAL CO-OPERATION *See* EDUCATION IN EUROPE. SECTION 2. GENERAL AND TECHNICAL EDUCATION **1739**

COUNCIL OF EUROPE. DIRECTORATE OF HUMAN RIGHTS *See* EUROPEAN CONVENTION ON HUMAN RIGHTS; COLLECTION OF DECISIONS OF NATIONAL COURTS REFERRING TO THE CONVENTION **4507**

COUNCIL OF EUROPE. DIRECTORATE OF LEGAL AFFAIRS *See* INFORMATION BULLETIN ON LEGAL ACTIVITIES WITHIN THE COUNCIL OF EUROPE AND IN MEMBER STATES **3129**

COUNCIL OF EUROPE. PARLIAMENTARY ASSEMBLY *See* ORDERS OF DAY. MINUTES OF PROCEEDINGS - COUNCIL OF EUROPE. PARLIAMENT ASSEMBLY **4671**

COUNCIL OF EUROPE. PARLIAMENTARY ASSEMBLY *See* TEXTS ADOPTED BY THE ASSEMBLY - COUNCIL OF EUROPE. PARLIAMENTARY ASSEMBLY **4690**

COUNCIL OF EUROPE. PARLIAMENTARY ASSEMBLY *See* DOC. - COUNCIL OF EUROPE, PARLIAMENTARY ASSEMBLY **3127**

COUNCIL OF EUROPE. PARLIAMENTARY ASSEMBLY *See* OFFICIAL REPORT OF DEBATES - COUNCIL OF EUROPE, PARLIAMENTARY ASSEMBLY **4671**

COUNCIL OF EUROPE. PARLIAMENTARY ASSEMBLY *See* MINUTES OF PROCEEDINGS - COUNCIL OF EUROPE, PARLIAMENTARY ASSEMBLY **4666**

COUNCIL OF EUROPE. PARLIAMENTARY ASSEMBLY *See* DOCUMENTS, WORKING PAPERS - COUNCIL OF EUROPE, PARLIAMENTARY ASSEMBLY **3127**

COUNCIL OF EUROPE. PARLIAMENTARY ASSEMBLY *See* RESOLUTION - PARLIAMENTARY ASSEMBLY OF THE COUNCIL OF EUROPE **4683**

COUNCIL OF GENEALOGY COLUMNISTS NEWSLETTER (US/1046-641X) [20479359] **2444**

COUNCIL OF GRADUATE SCHOOLS IN THE UNITED STATES *See* PROCEEDINGS OF THE ANNUAL MEETING **1842**

COUNCIL OF LEGAL EDUCATION (ZAMBIA) *See* ACCOUNTS FOR THE YEAR ENDED 31ST DECEMBER ... : AUDITOR-GENERAL'S REPORT / REPUBLIC OF ZAMBIA, THE COUNCIL OF LEGAL EDUCATION **4708**

COUNCIL OF LOGISTICS MANAGEMENT (U.S.). CONFERENCE *See* ANNUAL CONFERENCE - COUNCIL OF LOGISTICS MANAGEMENT (U.S.) **860**

COUNCIL OF MARITIME PREMIERS *See* ANNUAL REPORT - COUNCIL OF MARITIME PREMIERS **4515**

COUNCIL OF OUTDOOR EDUCATORS OF QUEBEC *See* C. O. E. Q. JOURNAL, THE **1729**

COUNCIL OF PETROLEUM ACCOUNTANTS SOCIETIES (U.S.) *See* DIRECTORY OF LIMITED MEMBERS / COUNCIL OF PETROLEUM ACCOUNTANTS SOCIETIES **743**

COUNCIL OF PETROLEUM ACCOUNTANTS SOCIETIES (U.S.) *See* DIRECTORY / COUNCIL OF PETROLEUM ACCOUNTANTS SOCIETIES **742**

COUNCIL OF SCIENTIFIC & INDUSTRIAL RESEARCH (INDIA) *See* CSIR HANDBOOK **5097**

COUNCIL OF SOCIAL AND HEALTH AGENCIES OF SAN FRANCISCO *See* LOOKOUT, THE **2519**

COUNCIL OF SOCIAL SERVICE OF NEW SOUTH WALES *See* NCOSS NEWS **5297**

COUNCIL OF STATE GOVERNMENTS *See* ANNUAL REPORT / THE COUNCIL OF STATE GOVERNMENTS **4629**

COUNCIL OF STATE GOVERNMENTS. ORGANIZATIONAL PLANNING AND COORDINATING COMMITTEE. SUBCOMMITTEE ON INFORMATION POLICY *See* DIRECTORY OF STATE INFORMATION POLICY ORGANIZATIONS / THE COUNCIL OF STATE GOVERNMENTS, [ORGANIZATIONAL PLANNING AND COORDINATING COMMITTEE (OPACC), SUBCOMMITTEE ON INFORMATION POLICY] **4644**

COUNCIL OF TEACHING HOSPITALS. MEMBERSHIP DIRECTORY (1989) *See* AAMC DIRECTORY OF AMERICAN MEDICAL EDUCATION **1806**

COUNCIL OF TEACHING HOSPITALS SURVEY OF HOUSESTAFF STIPENDS, BENEFITS, AND FUNDING / PREPARED BY: ASSOCIATION OF AMERICAN MEDICAL COLLEGES, DIVISION OF CLINICAL SERVICES (US) [23008241] **3778**

COUNCIL OF THE EUROPEAN COMMUNITIES *See* CONSOLIDATED TREATIES & INTERNATIONAL AGREEMENTS. CURRENT DOCUMENT SERVICE, EUROPEAN COMMUNITY **4519**

COUNCIL OF THE EUROPEAN COMMUNITIES. LIBRARIES-DOCUMENTATION *See* FORTEGNELSE OVER NYERHVERVELSER / RADET FOR DE EUROPAEISKE FAELLESSKABER, BIBLIOTEKER-DOKUMENTATION **416**

COUNCIL ON BLACK MINNESOTANS *See* LEGISLATIVE REPORT - COUNCIL ON BLACK MINNESOTANS **3002**

COUNCIL ON ECONOMIC PRIORITIES *See* OCCASIONAL PAPER - COUNCIL ON ECONOMIC PRIORITIES **1509**

COUNCIL ON ECONOMIC PRIORITIES *See* CEP REPORT **1469**

COUNCIL ON FOREIGN RELATIONS *See* ANNUAL REPORT - COUNCIL ON FOREIGN RELATIONS, INC **4515**

COUNCIL ON LEGAL EDUCATION FOR PROFESSIONAL RESPONSIBILITY *See* REPORT - COUNCIL ON LEGAL EDUCATION FOR PROFESSIONAL RESPONSIBILITY **3037**

COUNCIL ON SOCIAL WORK EDUCATION *See* SUMMARY INFORMATION ON MASTER OF SOCIAL WORK PROGRAMS **5312**

COUNCIL ON UNDERGRADUATE RESEARCH NEWSLETTER (US/0890-8273) [14404557] **1818**

COUNCIL PAPER - ECONOMIC PLANNING ADVISORY COUNCIL (AT/0816-4991) [I08164991] **1472**

COUNCIL SPOTLIGHT BOOKNOTES (US/0740-1183) [09872467] **4502**

COUNCILS, COMMITTEES & BOARDS (UK) [05952208] **4641**

COUNCILS WEST (AT) **4641**

COUNSEL : THE JOURNAL OF THE BAR OF ENGLAND & WALES (UK/0268-3784) [13783462] **2957**

COUNSELING AND HUMAN DEVELOPMENT (US/0193-7375) [03393635] **5281**

COUNSELING AND VALUES (US/0160-7960) [01565311] **4583**

COUNSELING CLIENTS IN THE ENTERTAINMENT INDUSTRY (US/0271-2385) [04975218] **2957**

COUNSELING INTERVIEWER, THE (US/0160-6794) [03728077] **4583**

COUNSELING PSYCHOLOGIST, THE (US/0011-0000) [01565312] **4583**

●COUNSELING TODAY (US) **4583**

COUNSELLING (UK/0264-9977) [I02649977] **4583**

COUNSELLING PSYCHOLOGY QUARTERLY (UK/0951-5070) [18582175] **4583**

COUNSELLING : THE JOURNAL OF THE BRITISH ASSOCIATION FOR COUNSELLING (UK) [15356894] **4583**, **5281**

COUNSELOR (US/0011-0027) [04043820] **758**

COUNSELOR (ARLINGTON, VA.), THE (US/1047-7314) [12619221] **5281**, **1342**

COUNSELOR EDUCATION AND SUPERVISION (US/0011-0035) [01565314] **1892**, **1877**

COUNSELOR EDUCATION DIRECTORY. PERSONNEL AND PROGRAMS *See* COUNSELOR PREPARATION **1877**

COUNSELOR PREPARATION (US/0271-5368) [06631180] **1877**

COUNTDOWN 1992 (BE) [22447813] **2957**

COUNTDOWN (ATHENS, OHIO) (US/0746-8830) [10413026] **17**

COUNTDOWN / JUVENILE DIABETES FOUNDATION INTERNATIONAL (US/1070-9282) [28492878] **3727**

COUNTED THREAD (US/0164-3460) [04626558] **5183**

COUNTER-TERRORISM (US/0887-6398) [13313527] **5196**

COUNTERFEITS AND FORGERIES (NE) **785**

COUNTERMAN (US/0739-3695) [09718567] **5412**

COUNTERPOINT (AT) **2810**

COUNTERPOINT CLASSICAL RECORD REVIEW (CN/0709-7166) [05840752] **5316**, **4112**

COUNTERPOINT (WASHINGTON, D.C.) (US/1053-1386) [15062127] **1877**

COUNTERPOINT'S BASIC CLASSICAL RECORD LIBRARY GUIDE (CN/0709-7158) [05840977] **5316**, **4112**

COUNTERPROOF (US/0275-7516) [07188380] **377**

●COUNTERTERRORISM & SECURITY REPORT (US/1064-9093) [26459664] **4519**

COUNTERTRADE & BARTER INTERNATIONAL (US/0743-250X) [10538599] **830**

COUNTERTRADE OUTLOOK (US/0743-0396) [10501480] **830**

COUNTERTRADE UPDATE EASTERN EUROPE (SZ) **830**

COUNTRIES OF THE WORLD AND THEIR LEADERS YEARBOOK (US/0196-2809) [05782973] **2559**

COUNTRY (US) [03678482] **2486**

COUNTRY ACCENTS (US/0894-4083) [16081580] **2899**

COUNTRY ALMANAC (NEW YORK, N.Y.) (US/1058-3734) [24282027] **1924**

COUNTRY ALMANAC, THE (US/0192-0111) [04999157] **5634**

COUNTRY AMERICA (US/1043-4488) [19480869] **4112**

COUNTRY ANALYSIS OF EXTERNAL TRADE (NZ) [04359392] **830**

COUNTRY & WESTERN NEWS SCENE *See* COUNTRYSIDE (BLAINE) **4112**

COUNTRY CHRONICLE, THE (US/0742-4566) [08633428] **5766**

COUNTRY COLLECTIBLES (US/1071-8036) [28733339] **371**

COUNTRY CONNECTION (NORTH BATTLEFORD) (CN/1192-9974) [23598186] **5782**

COUNTRY CONNECTION, THE (US/0746-4789) [10063259] **5731**

COUNTRY COOKING *CEASED.* (US) [10794890] **2789**

COUNTRY COURIER (HINCKLEY, ILL.) (US/1061-3218) [25252173] **5659**

COUNTRY CRAFTS (US/0731-5376) [08179079] **371**

COUNTRY DANCE AND SONG (US/0070-1262) [03597435] **1311**

COUNTRY DANCE & SONG SOCIETY NEWS (US/1070-8251) [13673377] **1311**

COUNTRY DATA FORECASTS (US) **2531**

COUNTRY DATABASE *CEASED.* (US/0890-4952) [16048309] **4470**

COUNTRY DECORATING IDEAS (US/0731-2164) [08145046] **2899**

COUNTRY DEMOGRAPHIC PROFILES (US/0360-8514) [01245673] **4551**

COUNTRY EXTRA (US/1052-8849) [08448579] **2531**

COUNTRY FACTS *CEASED.* (US/0889-5007) [13990600] **1472**

●COUNTRY FEVER (US/1066-0453) [26777003] **4112**

COUNTRY FOLK ART MAGAZINE (US/1047-4625) [20702393] **318**

●COUNTRY FOLKS GROWER (US/1065-1756) [26520173] **77**

COUNTRY FORECASTS (US/1041-3553) [18731942] **1472**

COUNTRY GALLERY (US/1053-2277) [22482501] **371**

COUNTRY GENTLEMEN'S MAGAZINE, THE (UK) [04865808] **2486**

COUNTRY (GREENDALE, WIS.) (US/0895-0377) [15608824] **2531**

COUNTRY GUIDE (CN/0011-0140) [01565324] **77**

COUNTRY HANDCRAFTS (US/0745-3116) [09055075] **371**

COUNTRY HERITAGE (US/0733-8759) [08631121] **4112**

COUNTRY HOME (US/0737-3740) [09364452] **2899**

COUNTRY HOMES AND INTERIORS (UK/0951-3019) [25106067] **2899**

●COUNTRY INNS AND BACK ROADS. CALIFORNIA (US/1060-3786) [24956092] **5467**

COUNTRY INNS AND BACK ROADS (CONTINENTAL EUROPE ED.) *CEASED.* (US/0893-1291) [15356708] **5467**, **2804**

●COUNTRY INNS AND BACK ROADS. NEW ENGLAND (US/1060-3778) [24956071] **5467**

COUNTRY INNS AND BACK ROADS. NORTH AMERICA (US/1042-6248) [12650288] **2804**

COUNTRY INNS AND BACKROADS. BRITAIN AND IRELAND (US/0893-1186) [12440171] **2804**

COUNTRY INNS, BED & BREAKFAST (US/0898-560X) [17574482] **2804**

COUNTRY INNS GAZETTE (US/0892-4481) [15194020] **2805**

COUNTRY JOURNAL (HARRISBURG, PA.) (US/0898-6355) [14276946] **2531**

COUNTRY LABOR MARKET AND ECONOMIC PROFILES (US) **1661**

COUNTRY LANDOWNER : JOURNAL OF THE COUNTRY LANDOWNERS' ASSOCIATION (UK) [06742570] **77**

COUNTRY LIFE (UK/0045-8856) [01565327] **2514**

COUNTRY LIFE IN BRITISH COLUMBIA (CN/0011-0183) [01565328] **77**

COUNTRY LIVING COUNTRY KITCHENS (US) **2899**

COUNTRY LIVING. (ENGLAND EDITION) (UK) **2899**

COUNTRY LIVING (NEW YORK, N.Y.) (US/0732-2569) [08316132] **2789**

COUNTRY MARKET SURVEY : CMS (US) [03457128] **830**

COUNTRY MUSIC (US/0090-4007) [01785014] **4112**

COUNTRY MUSIC BOOKING GUIDE (US/0360-8131) [02244906] **4112**

COUNTRY MUSIC CITY NEWS (US/1066-3312) [26919653] **4112**

COUNTRY MUSIC EXPLORER (US/0360-8697) [02244934] **4112**

COUNTRY MUSIC NEWS (OTTAWA) (CN/0714-8356) [09106476] **4112**

COUNTRY MUSIC NEWS (TURBOTVILLE, PA.) (US/0098-9037) [02242570] **4112**

COUNTRY MUSIC NEWSLETTER, THE (AT) [01791498] **4112**

COUNTRY MUSIC PEOPLE (UK/0591-2237) [02243760] **4112**

COUNTRY MUSIC REVIEW (UK) [03236629] **4112**

COUNTRY MUSIC ROUND UP (UK/0140-5721) [101405721] **4112**

COUNTRY MUSIC TIMES (AT) [01788820] **4112**

COUNTRY MUSIC WORLD (US/0094-1344) [01793972] **4112**

COUNTRY MUSICAL TRAILS LESS TRAVELED (US) **4112**

COUNTRY NEWS (US/0746-3251) [09930415] **2531**

COUNTRY PLACE (US/0095-5558) [02240765] **77**

COUNTRY PRESS (US/0745-9920) [09668401] **5642**

COUNTRY PROFILE. ALGERIA / EIU, THE ECONOMIST INTELLIGENCE UNIT (UK) [14585116] **1552**

COUNTRY PROFILE. ANGOLA, SAO TOME & PRINCIPE *See* COUNTRY PROFILE. CONGO, SAO TOME AND PRINCIPE, GUINEA-BISSAU, CAPE VERDE / THE ECONOMIST INTELLIGENCE UNIT **1552**

COUNTRY PROFILE. CONGO *See* COUNTRY PROFILE. CONGO, SAO TOME AND PRINCIPE, GUINEA-BISSAU, CAPE VERDE / THE ECONOMIST INTELLIGENCE UNIT **1552**

● COUNTRY PROFILE. CONGO, SAO TOME AND PRINCIPE, GUINEA-BISSAU, CAPE VERDE / THE ECONOMIST INTELLIGENCE UNIT (UK/1352-0849) [30352315] **1552**

COUNTRY PROFILE. COTE D'IVOIRE *See* COUNTRY PROFILE. COTE D'IVOIRE, MALI / THE ECONOMIST INTELLIGENCE UNIT **1552**

COUNTRY PROFILE. COTE D'IVOIRE / EIU, THE ECONOMIST INTELLIGENCE UNIT (UK) [19062253] **1552**

● COUNTRY PROFILE. COTE D'IVOIRE, MALI / THE ECONOMIST INTELLIGENCE UNIT (UK) [28284419] **1552**

● COUNTRY PROFILE. CYPRUS, MALTA / EIU, THE ECONOMIST INTELLIGENCE UNIT (UK) [28911194] **1553**

COUNTRY PROFILE. DENMARK, ICELAND (UK/0269-5138) [14281655] **1553**

COUNTRY PROFILE. EAST GERMANY *See* COUNTRY PROFILE. GERMANY/ THE ECONOMIST INTELLIGENCE UNIT **1553**

COUNTRY PROFILE. GAMBIA, GUINEA-BISSAU, CAPE VERDE *See* COUNTRY PROFILE. CONGO, SAO TOME AND PRINCIPE, GUINEA-BISSAU, CAPE VERDE / THE ECONOMIST INTELLIGENCE UNIT **1552**

COUNTRY PROFILE. GAMBIA, GUINEA-BISSAU, CAPE VERDE *See* COUNTRY PROFILE. THE GAMBIA, MAURITANIA / EIU, THE ECONOMIST INTELLIGENCE UNIT **1554**

● COUNTRY PROFILE. GERMANY/ THE ECONOMIST INTELLIGENCE UNIT (UK) [24181911] **1553**

COUNTRY PROFILE. GUINEA, MALI, MAURITANIA *See* COUNTRY PROFILE. COTE D'IVOIRE, MALI / THE ECONOMIST INTELLIGENCE UNIT **1552**

COUNTRY PROFILE. GUINEA, MALI, MAURITANIA *See* COUNTRY PROFILE. GUINEA, SIERRA LEONE, LIBERIA / THE ECONOMIST INTELLIGENCE UNIT **1553**

COUNTRY PROFILE. GUINEA, MALI, MAURITANIA *See* COUNTRY PROFILE. THE GAMBIA, MAURITANIA / EIU, THE ECONOMIST INTELLIGENCE UNIT **1554**

● COUNTRY PROFILE. GUINEA, SIERRA LEONE, LIBERIA / THE ECONOMIST INTELLIGENCE UNIT (UK) [28236242] **1553**

COUNTRY PROFILE. GUYANA, BARBADOS, WINDWARD & LEEWARD ISLANDS *See* COUNTRY PROFILE. GUYANA, WINDWARD & LEEWARD ISLANDS / EIU, THE ECONOMIST INTELLIGENCE UNIT **1553**

● COUNTRY PROFILE. GUYANA, WINDWARD & LEEWARD ISLANDS / EIU, THE ECONOMIST INTELLIGENCE UNIT (UK) [29214903] **1553**

COUNTRY PROFILE. HONG KONG, MACAU (UK) [14627489] **1553**

COUNTRY PROFILE. IRAN (UK/0269-5960) [13802413] **1553**

COUNTRY PROFILE. LEBANON, CYPRUS *See* COUNTRY PROFILE. LEBANON, CYPRUS, MALTA / EIU, THE ECONOMIST INTELLIGENCE UNIT **1553**

COUNTRY PROFILE. LEBANON, CYPRUS *See* COUNTRY PROFILE. CYPRUS, MALTA / EIU, THE ECONOMIST INTELLIGENCE UNIT **1553**

COUNTRY PROFILE. LEBANON, CYPRUS / EIU, THE ECONOMIST INTELLIGENCE UNIT (UK/0269-7351) [14174566] **1553**

● COUNTRY PROFILE. LEBANON / EIU, THE ECONOMIST INTELLIGENCE UNIT (UK) [29307258] **1553**

COUNTRY PROFILE. MADAGASCAR, COMOROS (UK/0269-736X) [14578441] **1553**

COUNTRY PROFILE. MADAGASCAR, COMOROS *See* COUNTRY PROFILE. MADAGASCAR / THE ECONOMIST INTELLIGENCE UNIT **1553**

COUNTRY PROFILE. MADAGASCAR, COMOROS *See* COUNTRY PROFILE. TANZANIA, COMOROS / THE ECONOMIST INTELLIGENCE UNIT **1554**

● COUNTRY PROFILE. MADAGASCAR / THE ECONOMIST INTELLIGENCE UNIT (UK) [28284293] **1553**

COUNTRY PROFILE. MALAYSIA, BRUNEI (UK/0269-5588) [15056642] **1553**

COUNTRY PROFILE. MALTA *See* COUNTRY PROFILE. CYPRUS, MALTA / EIU, THE ECONOMIST INTELLIGENCE UNIT **1553**

COUNTRY PROFILE. MAURITIUS, SEYCHELLES (UK/0269-7378) [14562236] **1553**

COUNTRY PROFILE. MOZAMBIQUE (UK/0269-7017) [13769731] **1553**

COUNTRY PROFILE. OMAN, YEMEN / EIU, THE ECONOMIST INTELLIGENCE UNIT (UK) [22730465] **1553**

COUNTRY PROFILE. SAUDI ARABIA (UK/0269-6355) [14220351] **1553**

● COUNTRY PROFILE. SENEGAL/ THE ECONOMIST INTELLIGENCE UNIT (UK) [25207481] **1553**

COUNTRY PROFILE.SENEGAL, THE GAMBIA, GUINEA-BISSAU, CAPE VERDE *See* COUNTRY PROFILE. SENEGAL/ THE ECONOMIST INTELLIGENCE UNIT **1553**

COUNTRY PROFILE. SENEGAL, THE GAMBIA, GUINEA-BISSAU, CAPE VERDE *See* COUNTRY PROFILE. THE GAMBIA, GUINEA-BISSAU, CAPE VERDE **1554**

COUNTRY PROFILE. SIERRA LEONE, LIBERIA *See* COUNTRY PROFILE. GUINEA, SIERRA LEONE, LIBERIA / THE ECONOMIST INTELLIGENCE UNIT **1553**

COUNTRY PROFILE. SINGAPORE (UK/0269-7041) [14700417] **1553**

COUNTRY PROFILE. SRI LANKA (UK/0269-5073) [14173662] **1553**

COUNTRY PROFILE. TANZANIA (UK/0269-6630) [13769704] **1553**

COUNTRY PROFILE. TANZANIA *See* COUNTRY PROFILE. TANZANIA, COMOROS / THE ECONOMIST INTELLIGENCE UNIT **1554**

● COUNTRY PROFILE. TANZANIA, COMOROS / THE ECONOMIST INTELLIGENCE UNIT (UK) [28756831] **1554**

COUNTRY PROFILE. THE GAMBIA, GUINEA-BISSAU, CAPE VERDE (UK/0968-2422) [25207448] **1554**

● COUNTRY PROFILE. THE GAMBIA, MAURITANIA / EIU, THE ECONOMIST INTELLIGENCE UNIT (UK/1352-0938) [29786996] **1554**

COUNTRY PROFILE. UNITED ARAB EMIRATES (UK/0269-6606) [15078923] **1554**

COUNTRY PROFILE. USA (UK/0269-8005) [14054104] **1554**

COUNTRY PROFILE. WEST GERMANY *See* COUNTRY PROFILE. GERMANY/ THE ECONOMIST INTELLIGENCE UNIT **1553**

COUNTRY PROFILES (US/0097-305X) [01439918] **4551**

COUNTRY RECORDING VOICE (US/0092-4059) [01789773] **4112**

COUNTRY REPORT. ALGERIA / EIU, THE ECONOMIST INTELLIGENCE UNIT (UK) [13910517] **2498**

COUNTRY REPORT. ANGOLA, SAO TOME & PRINCIPE (UK) [13679470] **1554**

● COUNTRY REPORT. ANGOLA / THE ECONOMIST INTELLIGENCE UNIT (UK) [27864393] **1472**

COUNTRY REPORT. ARGENTINA (UK/0269-4212) [13679216] **1472**

COUNTRY REPORT. AUSTRALIA / EIU, THE ECONOMIST INTELLIGENCE UNIT (UK) [13769481] **1472**

COUNTRY REPORT. AUSTRIA (UK/0269-5170) [13910662] **1472**

COUNTRY REPORT. BAHRAIN, QATAR / THE ECONOMIST INTELLIGENCE UNIT (UK) [23025437] **1472**

● COUNTRY REPORT. BALTIC REPUBLICS: ESTONIA, LATVIA, LITHUANIA / THE ECONOMIST INTELLIGENCE UNIT (UK) [28535890] **1472**

COUNTRY REPORT. BALTIC REPUBLICS: LITHUANIA, LATVIA, ESTONIA *See* COUNTRY REPORT. BALTIC REPUBLICS: ESTONIA, LATVIA, LITHUANIA / THE ECONOMIST INTELLIGENCE UNIT **1472**

COUNTRY REPORT. BANGLADESH (UK/0269-431X) [13685183] **1472**

COUNTRY REPORT. BELGIUM, LUXEMBOURG (UK/0269-4158) [13688433] **1472**

● COUNTRY REPORT. BOSNIA-HERCEGOVINA, CROATIA, MACEDONIA, SERBIA-MONTENEGRO, SLOVENIA / THE ECONOMIST INTELLIGENCE UNIT (UK) [27930089] **1472**

COUNTRY REPORT. BRAZIL (UK/0269-5731) [14055692] **1472**

COUNTRY REPORT. CAMEROON, CAR, CHAD (UK/0269-4336) [13730383] **1472**

COUNTRY REPORT. CANADA (UK/0269-4166) [13691374] **1472**

COUNTRY REPORT. CHILE (UK/0269-5197) [13721581] **1473**

● COUNTRY REPORT. CHINA, MONGOLIA / THE ECONOMIST INTELLIGENCE UNIT (UK) [27875913] **1473**

COUNTRY REPORT. CHINA, NORTH KOREA *CEASED*. (UK/0269-6231) [14075187] **1473**

COUNTRY REPORT. COLOMBIA (UK/0269-7157) [13769384] **1473**

COUNTRY REPORT. COMMONWEALTH OF INDEPENDENT STATES *See* COUNTRY REPORT. RUSSIA / EIU, THE ECONOMIST INTELLIGENCE UNIT **1476**

COUNTRY REPORT. COMMONWEALTH OF INDEPENDENT STATES / THE ECONOMIST INTELLIGENCE UNIT (UK) [25745377] **1473**

COUNTRY REPORT. CONGO, GABON, EQUATORIAL GUINEA *See* COUNTRY REPORT. GABON, EQUATORIAL GUINEA / THE ECONOMIST INTELLIGENCE UNIT **1473**

COUNTRY REPORT. CONGO, GABON, EQUATORIAL GUINEA *See* COUNTRY REPORT. CONGO, SAO TOME & PRINCIPE, GUINEA-BISSAU, CAPE VERDE / THE ECONOMIST INTELLIGENCE UNIT **1473**

● COUNTRY REPORT. CONGO, SAO TOME & PRINCIPE, GUINEA-BISSAU, CAPE VERDE / THE ECONOMIST INTELLIGENCE UNIT (UK) [27870076] **1473**

● COUNTRY REPORT. COSTA RICA, PANAMA / THE ECONOMIST INTELLIGENCE UNIT (UK) [27455156] **1473**

COUNTRY REPORT. CUBA, DOMINICAN REPUBLIC, HAITI, PUERTO RICO (UK/0269-5251) [13802302] **1473**

● COUNTRY REPORT. CYPRUS, MALTA / THE ECONOMIST INTELLIGENCE UNIT (UK) [27749517] **1473**

● COUNTRY REPORT. CZECH REPUBLIC AND SLOVAKIA / THE ECONOMIST INTELLIGENCE UNIT (UK) [27536794] **1473**

COUNTRY REPORT. CZECHOSLOVAKIA *See* COUNTRY REPORT. CZECH REPUBLIC AND SLOVAKIA / THE ECONOMIST INTELLIGENCE UNIT **1473**

COUNTRY REPORT. DENMARK, ICELAND (UK/0269-574X) [13806509] **1473**

COUNTRY REPORT. ECUADOR (UK/0269-7165) [13733245] **1473**

COUNTRY REPORT. EGYPT (UK/0269-526X) [13980060] **1473**

COUNTRY REPORT. FINLAND / EIU, THE ECONOMIST INTELLIGENCE UNIT (UK) [13805966] **1473**

COUNTRY REPORT. FRANCE (UK/0269-5286) [14055530] **1473**

● COUNTRY REPORT. GABON, EQUATORIAL GUINEA / THE ECONOMIST INTELLIGENCE UNIT (UK) [27870569] **1473**

COUNTRY REPORT. GERMANY / THE ECONOMIST INTELLIGENCE UNIT (UK) [23597808] **1473**

COUNTRY REPORT. GHANA, SIERRA LEONE, LIBERIA *See* COUNTRY REPORT. GHANA / THE ECONOMIST INTELLIGENCE UNIT **1474**

COUNTRY REPORT. GHANA, SIERRA LEONE, LIBERIA *See* COUNTRY REPORT. GUINEA, SIERRA LEONE, LIBERIA / THE ECONOMIST INTELLIGENCE UNIT **1474**

● COUNTRY REPORT. GHANA / THE ECONOMIST INTELLIGENCE UNIT (UK) [27722274] **1474**

COUNTRY REPORT. GREECE (UK/0269-591X) [13729560] **1474**

COUNTRY REPORT. GUATEMALA, EL SALVADOR, HONDURAS *See* COUNTRY REPORT. NICARAGUA, HONDURAS / ECONOMIST INTELLIGENCE UNIT **1475**

COUNTRY REPORT. GUATEMALA, EL SALVADOR, HONDURAS *See* COUNTRY REPORT. GUATEMALA, EL SALVADOR / THE ECONOMIST INTELLIGENCE UNIT **1474**

● COUNTRY REPORT. GUATEMALA, EL SALVADOR / THE ECONOMIST INTELLIGENCE UNIT (UK) [27712526] **1474**

COUNTRY REPORT. GUINEA, MALI, MAURITANIA *See* COUNTRY REPORT. GUINEA, SIERRA LEONE, LIBERIA / THE ECONOMIST INTELLIGENCE UNIT **1474**

COUNTRY REPORT. GUINEA, MALI, MAURITANIA *See* COUNTRY REPORT. SENEGAL, THE GAMBIA, MAURITANIA / THE ECONOMIST INTELLIGENCE UNIT **1476**

● COUNTRY REPORT. GUINEA, SIERRA LEONE, LIBERIA / THE ECONOMIST INTELLIGENCE UNIT (UK) [27688579] **1474**

COUNTRY REPORT. HONG KONG, MACAU (UK/0269-6762) [14075105] **1474**

COUNTRY

COUNTRY REPORT. HUNGARY (UK/0269-4301) [13729613] **1474**

COUNTRY REPORT. INDIA, NEPAL (UK/0269-5294) [13721646] **1474**

COUNTRY REPORT. INDOCHINA: VIETNAM, LAOS, CAMBODIA (UK/0269-5677) [13878763] **1474**

COUNTRY REPORT. INDONESIA (UK/0269-5413) [13877862] **1474**

COUNTRY REPORT. IRAN (UK/0269-5448) [13802291] **1474**

COUNTRY REPORT. IRAQ (UK/0269-5502) [13685372] **1474**

COUNTRY REPORT. IRELAND (UK/0269-5278) [13729440] **1474**

COUNTRY REPORT. ISRAEL *See* COUNTRY REPORT. ISRAEL, THE OCCUPIED TERRITORIES / EIU, THE ECONOMIST INTELLIGENCE UNIT **1474**

COUNTRY REPORT. ISRAEL / EIU, THE ECONOMIST INTELLIGENCE UNIT (UK) [13730444] **1474**

●COUNTRY REPORT. ISRAEL, THE OCCUPIED TERRITORIES / EIU, THE ECONOMIST INTELLIGENCE UNIT (UK/1353-3142) [29766515] **1474**

COUNTRY REPORT. ITALY (UK/0269-5421) [14055628] **1474**

COUNTRY REPORT. JAMAICA, BELIZE, BAHAMAS, BERMUDA *See* COUNTRY REPORT. JAMAICA, BELIZE, BAHAMAS, BERMUDA, BARBADOS / THE ECONOMIST INTELLIGENCE UNIT **1474**

●COUNTRY REPORT. JAMAICA, BELIZE, BAHAMAS, BERMUDA, BARBADOS / THE ECONOMIST INTELLIGENCE UNIT (UK) [27859659] **1474**

COUNTRY REPORT. JAPAN (UK/0269-6681) [13863802] **1474**

COUNTRY REPORT. JORDAN (UK/0269-722X) [13769539] **1475**

COUNTRY REPORT. KENYA (UK/0269-4239) [13680120] **1475**

COUNTRY REPORT. KUWAIT (UK/0269-5715) [14038624] **1475**

COUNTRY REPORT. LEBANON, CYPRUS *See* COUNTRY REPORT. LEBANON / THE ECONOMIST INTELLIGENCE UNIT **1475**

COUNTRY REPORT. LEBANON, CYPRUS *CEASED.* (UK/0269-5693) [13689103] **1554**

COUNTRY REPORT. LEBANON, CYPRUS *See* COUNTRY REPORT. CYPRUS, MALTA / THE ECONOMIST INTELLIGENCE UNIT **1473**

●COUNTRY REPORT. LEBANON / THE ECONOMIST INTELLIGENCE UNIT (UK) [27697855] **1475**

COUNTRY REPORT. LIBYA / EIU, THE ECONOMIST INTELLIGENCE UNIT (UK) [13679602] **1475**

COUNTRY REPORT. MADAGASCAR, MAURITIUS, SEYCHELLES, COMOROS *See* COUNTRY REPORT. TANZANIA, COMOROS / THE ECONOMIST INTELLIGENCE UNIT **1477**

COUNTRY REPORT. MADAGASCAR, MAURITIUS, SEYCHELLES, COMOROS *CEASED.* (UK/0269-5154) [13810762] **1475**

COUNTRY REPORT. MADAGASCAR, MAURITIUS, SEYCHELLES, COMOROS *See* COUNTRY REPORT. MAURITIUS, MADAGASCAR, SEYCHELLES / THE ECONOMIST INTELLIGENCE UNIT **1475**

COUNTRY REPORT. MALAYSIA, BRUNEI (UK/0269-6703) [13979945] **1475**

●COUNTRY REPORT. MAURITIUS, MADAGASCAR, SEYCHELLES / THE ECONOMIST INTELLIGENCE UNIT (UK) [27673441] **1475**

COUNTRY REPORT. MEXICO (UK/0269-5936) [13689376] **1475**

COUNTRY REPORT. MOROCCO (UK/0269-6126) [13827176] **1475**

●COUNTRY REPORT. MOZAMBIQUE, MALAWI / THE ECONOMIST INTELLIGENCE UNIT (UK) [27859720] **1475**

COUNTRY REPORT. NAMIBIA, BOTSWANA, LESOTHO, SWAZILAND (UK/0269-6746) [14079093] **1475**

COUNTRY REPORT. NETHERLANDS (UK/0269-6134) [13800571] **1475**

COUNTRY REPORT. NEW ZEALAND (UK/0269-7114) [13878530] **1475**

COUNTRY REPORT. NICARAGUA, COSTA RICA, PANAMA *See* COUNTRY REPORT. COSTA RICA, PANAMA / THE ECONOMIST INTELLIGENCE UNIT **1473**

COUNTRY REPORT. NICARAGUA, COSTA RICA, PANAMA *See* COUNTRY REPORT. NICARAGUA, HONDURAS / ECONOMIST INTELLIGENCE UNIT **1475**

●COUNTRY REPORT. NICARAGUA, HONDURAS / ECONOMIST INTELLIGENCE UNIT (UK) [27583274] **1475**

COUNTRY REPORT. NIGERIA (UK/0269-4204) [13877944] **1475**

COUNTRY REPORT. NORWAY / EIU, THE ECONOMIST INTELLIGENCE UNIT (UK) [13679387] **1475**

COUNTRY REPORT. OMAN, YEMEN / THE ECONOMIST INTELLIGENCE UNIT (UK) [23709394] **1476**

COUNTRY REPORT. PACIFIC ISLANDS: PAPUA NEW GUINEA, FIJI, SOLOMON ISLANDS, WESTERN SAMOA, VANUATU, TONGA (UK/0269-7122) [14074089] **1476**

COUNTRY REPORT. PAKISTAN, AFGHANISTAN (UK/0269-7173) [13810978] **1476**

COUNTRY REPORT. PERU, BOLIVIA (UK/0269-543X) [14075333] **1476**

COUNTRY REPORT. PHILIPPINES (UK/0269-428X) [13679280] **1476**

COUNTRY REPORT. POLAND (UK/0269-6193) [13769782] **1476**

COUNTRY REPORT. PORTUGAL (UK/0269-5456) [13980359] **1476**

COUNTRY REPORT. ROMANIA, BULGARIA, ALBANIA (UK/0269-5669) [13910609] **1476**

●COUNTRY REPORT. RUSSIA / EIU, THE ECONOMIST INTELLIGENCE UNIT (UK) [27878134] **1476**

COUNTRY REPORT. SAUDI ARABIA (UK/0269-6215) [13733138] **1476**

COUNTRY REPORT. SENEGAL, THE GAMBIA, GUINEA-BISSAU, CAPE VERDE *See* COUNTRY REPORT. CONGO, SAO TOME & PRINCIPE, GUINEA-BISSAU, CAPE VERDE / THE ECONOMIST INTELLIGENCE UNIT **1473**

COUNTRY REPORT. SENEGAL, THE GAMBIA, GUINEA-BISSAU, CAPE VERDE *See* COUNTRY REPORT. SENEGAL, THE GAMBIA, MAURITANIA / THE ECONOMIST INTELLIGENCE UNIT **1476**

●COUNTRY REPORT. SENEGAL, THE GAMBIA, MAURITANIA / THE ECONOMIST INTELLIGENCE UNIT (UK) [27711958] **1476**

COUNTRY REPORT. SINGAPORE (UK/0269-6711) [13979657] **1476**

COUNTRY REPORT. SOUTH AFRICA (UK/0269-6738) [13770272] **1476**

COUNTRY REPORT. SOUTH KOREA (UK/0269-669X) [13985621] **1476**

●COUNTRY REPORT. SOUTH KOREA, NORTH KOREA / THE ECONOMIST INTELLIGENCE UNIT (UK) [27721888] **1476**

COUNTRY REPORT. SPAIN (UK/0269-4263) [13679332] **1476**

COUNTRY REPORT. SRI LANKA (UK/0269-4174) [13681475] **1476**

COUNTRY REPORT. SUDAN (UK/0269-6150) [13980207] **1477**

COUNTRY REPORT. SWEDEN (UK/0269-6142) [13706322] **1477**

COUNTRY REPORT. SWITZERLAND (UK/0269-6169) [13729676] **1477**

COUNTRY REPORT. SYRIA (UK/0269-7211) [13730196] **1477**

COUNTRY REPORT. TAIWAN (UK/0269-672X) [13770363] **1477**

●COUNTRY REPORT. TANZANIA, COMOROS / THE ECONOMIST INTELLIGENCE UNIT (UK) [27828698] **1477**

COUNTRY REPORT. TANZANIA, MOZAMBIQUE (UK/0269-6630) [13769667] **1477**

COUNTRY REPORT. TANZANIA, MOZAMBIQUE *See* COUNTRY REPORT. MOZAMBIQUE, MALAWI / THE ECONOMIST INTELLIGENCE UNIT **1475**

COUNTRY REPORT. TANZANIA, MOZAMBIQUE *See* COUNTRY REPORT. TANZANIA, COMOROS / THE ECONOMIST INTELLIGENCE UNIT **1477**

COUNTRY REPORT. THAILAND, BURMA *See* COUNTRY REPORT. THAILAND, MYANMAR (BURMA) / THE ECONOMIST INTELLIGENCE UNIT **1477**

●COUNTRY REPORT. THAILAND, MYANMAR (BURMA) / THE ECONOMIST INTELLIGENCE UNIT (UK) [27181323] **1477**

COUNTRY REPORT. TOGO, NIGER, BENIN, BURKINA (UK/0269-7262) [14075251] **1477**

●COUNTRY REPORT. TRINIDAD AND TOBAGO, GUYANA, WINDWARD AND LEEWARD ISLANDS, SURINAME, NETHERLANDS ANTILLES, ARUBA / THE ECONOMIST INTELLIGENCE UNIT (UK) [27864608] **1477**

COUNTRY REPORT. TRINIDAD, TOBAGO, GUYANA, BARBADOS, WINDWARD & LEEWARD ISLANDS *CEASED.* (UK/0269-7149) [14079418] **1477**

COUNTRY REPORT. TUNISIA, MALTA *See* COUNTRY REPORT. CYPRUS, MALTA / THE ECONOMIST INTELLIGENCE UNIT **1473**

COUNTRY REPORT. TUNISIA, MALTA *See* COUNTRY REPORT. TUNISIA / THE ECONOMIST INTELLIGENCE UNIT **1477**

●COUNTRY REPORT. TUNISIA / THE ECONOMIST INTELLIGENCE UNIT (UK) [27743192] **1477**

COUNTRY REPORT. TURKEY (UK/0269-5464) [13910706] **1477**

COUNTRY REPORT. UGANDA, ETHIOPIA, SOMALIA, DJIBOUTI *See* COUNTRY REPORT. UGANDA, RWANDA, BURUNDI / EIU, THE ECONOMIST INTELLIGENCE UNIT **1477**

●COUNTRY REPORT. UGANDA, RWANDA, BURUNDI / EIU, THE ECONOMIST INTELLIGENCE UNIT (UK) [27930827] **1477**

COUNTRY REPORT. UNITED ARAB EMIRATES (UK/0269-5162) [13979843] **1477**

COUNTRY REPORT. UNITED KINGDOM (UK/0269-5472) [14038532] **1477**

●COUNTRY REPORT. UNITED STATES OF AMERICA / EIU, THE ECONOMIST INTELLIGENCE UNIT (UK) [31164214] **1554**

COUNTRY REPORT. URUGUAY, PARAGUAY (UK/0269-6177) [13878628] **1478**

COUNTRY REPORT. USA *See* COUNTRY REPORT. UNITED STATES OF AMERICA / EIU, THE ECONOMIST INTELLIGENCE UNIT **1554**

COUNTRY REPORT. USA (UK/0269-6185) [14054134] **1554**

COUNTRY REPORT. USSR *See* COUNTRY REPORT. COMMONWEALTH OF INDEPENDENT STATES / THE ECONOMIST INTELLIGENCE UNIT **1473**

COUNTRY REPORT. VENEZUELA, SURINAME, NETHERLANDS ANTILLES *See* COUNTRY REPORT. VENEZUELA / THE ECONOMIST INTELLIGENCE UNIT **1478**

COUNTRY REPORT. VENEZUELA, SURINAME, NETHERLANDS ANTILLES *See* COUNTRY REPORT. TRINIDAD AND TOBAGO, GUYANA, WINDWARD AND LEEWARD ISLANDS, SURINAME, NETHERLANDS ANTILLES, ARUBA / THE ECONOMIST INTELLIGENCE UNIT **1477**

●COUNTRY REPORT. VENEZUELA / THE ECONOMIST INTELLIGENCE UNIT (UK) [27531982] **1478**

COUNTRY REPORT. YUGOSLAV REPUBLICS *See* COUNTRY REPORT. BOSNIA-HERCEGOVINA, CROATIA, MACEDONIA, SERBIA-MONTENEGRO, SLOVENIA / THE ECONOMIST INTELLIGENCE UNIT **1472**

COUNTRY REPORT. ZAIRE, RWANDA, BURUNDI *See* COUNTRY REPORT. UGANDA, RWANDA, BURUNDI / EIU, THE ECONOMIST INTELLIGENCE UNIT **1477**

COUNTRY REPORT. ZAIRE, RWANDA, BURUNDI *See* COUNTRY REPORT. ZAMBIA, ZAIRE / THE ECONOMIST INTELLIGENCE UNIT **1478**

COUNTRY REPORT. ZAMBIA *See* COUNTRY REPORT. ZAMBIA, ZAIRE / THE ECONOMIST INTELLIGENCE UNIT **1478**

●COUNTRY REPORT. ZAMBIA, ZAIRE / THE ECONOMIST INTELLIGENCE UNIT (UK) [27868387] **1478**

COUNTRY REPORT. ZIMBABWE, MALAWI *See* COUNTRY REPORT. MOZAMBIQUE, MALAWI / THE ECONOMIST INTELLIGENCE UNIT **1475**

COUNTRY REPORT. ZIMBABWE, MALAWI *See* COUNTRY REPORT. ZIMBABWE / THE ECONOMIST INTELLIGENCE UNIT **1478**

●COUNTRY REPORT. ZIMBABWE / THE ECONOMIST INTELLIGENCE UNIT (UK) [27697718] **1478**

COUNTRY REPORTS (UK) **662**

COUNTRY REPORTS ON HUMAN RIGHTS PRACTICES (US/0198-9669) [06026722] **4506**

COUNTRY ROADS MAGAZINE (CARP) *CEASED.* (CN/1185-975X) [25423670] **2729**

COUNTRY ROADS (VANCOUVER) (CN/1185-3387) [24368286] **77**

COUNTRY SAMPLER (US/1047-3955) [20689894] **2899**

COUNTRY SAMPLER : NORTH AMERICAN FOLK ART (US/0272-7889) [06909779] **371**

●COUNTRY SAMPLER'S WEST (US/1066-7245) [27033859] **2899**

COUNTRY SHOPPER, THE (US/0192-1126) [05019933] **5715**

COUNTRY-SIDE (UK/0011-023X) [I0011023X] 4165, **2213**

COUNTRY SIDE MAGAZINE **CEASED.** (CN/0849-0635) [22103266] **2789**

COUNTRY SONG ROUNDUP (US/0011-0248) [01716166] **4112**

COUNTRY SONG ROUNDUP. SPECIAL (US/0277-3554) [07537262] **4112**

COUNTRY SOUNDS OF THE SOUTHWEST (US/0147-5738) [03198058] **4112**

COUNTRY SQUIRE (US/0092-0991) [01788821] **4112**

COUNTRY STANDARD **CEASED.** (UK/0011-0256) [03992860] **77**

COUNTRY STYLE MONTHLY (US/0364-0078) [02586299] **4112**

COUNTRY TIMES (US/0744-8627) [08601921] **5695**

COUNTRY TIMES AND LANDSCAPE (UK/0954-7843) [19008990] **2413, 296**

COUNTRY TIMES (THORNHILL) (CN/0821-7971) [09981897] **4112**

COUNTRY TODAY, THE (US/0192-9658) [05142535] **5766**

COUNTRY (TORONTO) (CN/1180-8047) [22135054] **4112**

COUNTRY VACATIONS IN ALBERTA (CN/0229-5229) [09021573] **5467, 4849**

COUNTRY VICTORIAN ACCENTS (US/1053-9980) [22718889] **2899**

COUNTRY VICTORIAN DECORATING & LIFESTYLE (US/1071-0256) [28536041] **2899**

COUNTRY WAYS (US) **2729**

COUNTRY WOMAN (US/0892-8525) [15272003] **5554**

COUNTRY WOOD PROJECTS (US/1058-3769) [24282090] **371**

COUNTRY WORLD (US) [05397216] **2486**

COUNTRYMAN, THE (UK/0011-0272) [01565331] **2514**

COUNTRYMARK (US/0885-8152) [12754515] **168**

●COUNTRYPLACE (BIRMINGHAM, ALA.) (US/1061-3560) [25264052] **2531**

COUNTRYSIDE AND SMALL STOCK JOURNAL (1985) (US/8750-7595) [11738170] **209**

COUNTRYSIDE BANKING (PH) [03652595] **785**

COUNTRYSIDE (BARRINGTON, ILL.) (US/1054-7940) [22971711] **5659**

COUNTRYSIDE (BLAINE) (US/0098-4566) [02240790] **4112**

COUNTRYSIDE COMMISSION NEWS (UK/0264-8822) [I02648822] **4641**

COUNTRYSIDE (NEW YORK, N.Y. 1990) **CEASED.** (US/1061-6349) [23870865] **2486**

COUNTRYWIDE ANNUAL YEARBOOK (US/0092-5454) [01788567] **4113**

COUNTRYWOMAN, THE (UK) [04859361] **5554**

COUNTY AGENT, THE (US/0164-3932) [04347432] **77**

COUNTY AGENTS (US/0739-4330) [09753002] **4641, 77**

COUNTY AND CITY COMPENDIUM. CD-ROM (US) **4551**

COUNTY AND CITY DATA BOOK (US/0082-9455) [01184940] **2819, 2840**

COUNTY & CITY DATA BOOK (CD-ROM ED.) (US/1057-8781) [23844464] **5326**

●COUNTY AND CITY EXTRA (US/1059-9096) [24807687] **5326**

COUNTY AND CITY STATISTICS ANNUAL CD-ROM (US) **5326**

COUNTY AND CITY STATISTICS CD-ROM (US) **2819, 2840**

COUNTY AND MUNICIPAL RECREATION AND PARK SERVICES STUDY (MARYLAND) (US) [10811003] **4849**

COUNTY & MUNICIPAL YEAR BOOK FOR SCOTLAND *See* SCOTLANDS REGIONS **4685**

COUNTY ASSESSMENT STATUS REPORT (SALEM) (US/0093-0768) [01786916] **4719**

COUNTY BAR UPDATE (US/0279-9626) [07391003] **2957**

COUNTY BUSINESS PATTERNS (US) [02475762] **662**

COUNTY BUSINESS PATTERNS, ALABAMA (US) [07536775] **662**

COUNTY BUSINESS PATTERNS, LOUISIANA (US) [07567041] **662**

COUNTY BUSINESS PATTERNS, MINNESOTA (US) [06996547] **662**

COUNTY BUSINESS PATTERNS, NEVADA (US) [07589504] **662**

COUNTY BUSINESS PATTERNS, RHODE ISLAND (US) [07567135] **662**

COUNTY BUSINESS PATTERNS, UTAH (US) [07589438] **662**

COUNTY BUSINESS PATTERNS, WYOMING (US) [07589774] **662**

COUNTY BUSINESS PATTERNS [COMPUTER FILE] (US) [23018656] **1554**

COUNTY-CITY PLUS. CD-ROM (US) **4551**

COUNTY COMMENT (US/1049-7838) [21264736] **4641**

COUNTY COMMISSIONER (MONTGOMERY), THE (US/0199-2546) [05739466] **4641**

COUNTY COURIER (US/0590-0107) [04011360] **2729**

COUNTY COURT PRACTICE, THE (UK) [01565337] **2957**

COUNTY EMPLOYMENT PATTERNS (US) [06857920] **1661**

COUNTY ESTIMATES OF FEED GRAIN (US) **77**

COUNTY ESTIMATES OF SOYBEAN AND WHEAT (US) **77**

COUNTY EXECUTIVE DIRECTORY (US/0742-1702) [10270974] **4641**

COUNTY GOVERNMENT EMPLOYMENT (US/0193-5593) [02200215] **4641, 1661**

COUNTY GOVERNMENT FINANCES (US/0098-678X) [02240336] **4719**

COUNTY GROWER (CN/0823-6887) [10032172] **77**

COUNTY INFORMATION SERVICE (US/0743-4197) [10566521] **4641**

COUNTY JUDGES' AND COMMISSIONERS' CONFERENCE *See* PROCEEDINGS - COUNTY JUDGES' AND COMMISSIONERS' CONFERENCE **4675**

COUNTY KILDARE ARCHAEOLOGICAL SOCIETY *See* JOURNAL OF THE COUNTY KILDARE ARCHAEOLOGICAL SOCIETY **272**

COUNTY LEDGER-PRESS, THE (US/0749-7237) [11166986] **5766**

COUNTY LIFE (READING) (US/0164-5927) [04522339] **2531**

COUNTY LINE (US/0888-2851) [13533384] **2444**

COUNTY LINE (PANAMA CITY, FLA.), THE (US/0888-2851) [13533394] **2444**

COUNTY LINE, THE (US) [05468812] **3204**

COUNTY LINES (ALBERT LEA, MINN.) (US/8755-9099) [11449763] **1542**

COUNTY LINES (PRINCETON, IND.) (US/1070-4922) [28384377] **2444**

COUNTY MAGAZINE (BLOOMFIELD. 1983) (CN/0826-3035) [15231554] **2729**

●COUNTY NEIGHBORS (PUNXSUTAWNEY, PA.) (US/1065-268X) [26562710] **5735**

COUNTY NEIGHBOURS (CN/0715-545X) [09543095] **5782**

COUNTY OF ALLEGHENY BUDGET FOR OPERATING DEPARTMENTS, THE (US/0090-2829) [01784858] **4719**

COUNTY OFFICERS / STATE OF ILLINOIS (US) [05012802] **4641**

COUNTY PRESS (LAPEER, MICH.) (US/8750-4561) [11460192] **5691**

COUNTY PROGRESS (US/0011-0353) [03488233] **4641**

COUNTY RECREATION & PARK SERVICES STUDY (NORTH CAROLINA) (US/0360-4667) [02243929] **4706**

COUNTY REPORT - CALIFORNIA. DIVISION OF MINES AND GEOLOGY (US/0575-3104) [01604522] **1372**

COUNTY REPORT / KENTUCKY GEOLOGICAL SURVEY (US/0075-5567) [07583462] **1372**

COUNTY SEAT SCRAPS (US/1058-2703) [18616522] **2444**

COUNTY STATE AID HIGHWAY APPORTIONMENT DATA *See* CSAH APPORTIONMENT DATA **5380**

COUNTY UNDIVIDED LOCAL GOVERNMENT REVENUE ASSISTANCE FUNDS. AMOUNTS DISTRIBUTED WITHIN COUNTIES BY COUNTY BUDGET COMMISSIONS, BY SUBDIVISION OR SUBDIVISION CLASS, CALENDAR YEAR ... / OHIO DEPARTMENT OF TAXATION (US) [23741820] **4719**

COUNTY VETERAN POPULATION (US/0194-0511) [05292740] **4034**

COUNTY VIEWPOINT (US/0279-8867) [07333848] **4641**

COUNTYLINE, THE (US) [16959069] **5727**

COUNTYWIDE ANNUAL PLAN REVIEW / FAIRFAX COUNTY, VA. OFFICE OF COMPREHENSIVE PLANNING (US/0149-5208) [03500242] **2819**

COUP DE POUCE (MONTREAL) (CN/0822-3033) [10926559] **5554**

COUP D'OEIL GRANDVILLIERS (FR/0987-0113) [I09870113] **3874**

COUP D'OEIL (NAPIERVILLE) (CN/0710-3786) [08713431] **5782**

COUP D'OEIL SUR L'HALTEROPHILIE (CN/0287-6909) [08072080] **4891**

COUP D'OEIL (VICTORIAVILLE) (CN/0715-8238) [11559870] **1818**

COUPLE ET FAMILLE (CN/0384-5281) [02547741] **2278**

COUPLES (BOSTON, MASS.) (US/1054-0296) [22715262] **2794**

COUPLES (NEW YORK) (US/0092-3893) [01789656] **2278**

COURAGE (GW) [04259699] **5554**

COURANT (US/01536928] **5725**

COURANT (ANN ARBOR, MICH.) (US) [10614326] **4113**

COURANT, LE (CN/0712-3086) [08808257] **3830**

COURANT (MONTREAL) (CN/0712-4570) [09590495] **4871**

COURANTS PARIS. 1990 (FR/1146-5786) [I11465786] **5532**

COURIER. AFRICA-CARIBBEAN-PACIFIC-EUROPEAN COMMUNITIES, THE (CY/1013-7335) [I10137335] **1554**

COURIER (BROCKTON, MASS.), THE (US/1062-8371) [11492180] **4859**

COURIER (BRUSSELS) (BE/0378-3480) [03648209] **1554**

COURIER (CANADA. CANADIAN FORCES BASE (COLD LAKE, ALTA.)) (CN/0045-8872) [10832013] **5782**

COURIER DEMOCRAT (US/0745-6956) [09383954] **5631**

COURIER (EDMONTON) (CN/0318-0220) [02324400] **3275**

COURIER-EXPRESS (DUBOIS, PA. : 1964) (US/8750-4049) [11382835] **5735**

COURIER-GAZETTE (MCKINNEY, TEX.) (US) [17391983] **5748**

COURIER-GAZETTE, THE (US) [09352226] **5685**

COURIER HERALD, THE (US) [21946736] **5653**

COURIER JOURNAL (US) [20213547] **5703**

COURIER JOURNAL (JUPITER, FLA.), THE (US/0896-0283) [16886002] **5648, 5649**

COURIER-JOURNAL (LOUISVILLE, KY. : KENTUCKY ED.) (US) [12068359] **5680**

COURIER (LEXINGTON, KY.) (US/0279-4489) [07883586] **5467**

COURIER (MIDDLETOWN, N.J.), THE (US/0891-7272) [15011463] **5709**

COURIER (MONTREAL) (CN/0383-0330) [02743237] **3989**

COURIER NETWORK (CN/0828-6345) [12045324] **830**

COURIER NEWS (US/0746-9527) [10407266] **5631**

COURIER-NEWS (BRIDGEWATER, N.J.) (US/0895-8785) [14093085] **5709**

COURIER-OBSERVER (US) **5715**

COURIER OF HISTORICAL EVENTS (US) **2444, 2614**

COURIER (ORLEANS) (CN/0316-0262) [02247312] **5782**

COURIER (PLANT CITY, FL) (US) **5648, 5649**

COURIER PLUS (US) **1924**

COURIER-POST (CHERRY HILL, N.J.) (US/1050-432X) [12230254] **5709**

COURIER-PRESS (US) [13370549] **5766**

COURIER-STANDARD-ENTERPRISE (US/0738-7709) [09671533] **5715**

COURIER (SYRACUSE) (US/0011-0418) [01791244] **3204**

COURIER, THE (US) [25104014] **5715**

COURIER, THE (US) [07918343] **5629**

COURIER, THE (US) [20363922] **5727**

COURIER, THE (US) [21180218] **5708**

●COURIER, THE (US) [28096605] **5659**

COURIER-TIMES, THE (US) [25618541] **5723**

COURIER-TIMES, THE (US) [13223204] **5663**

COURIER (TORONTO) (CN/0319-8383) [01986734] **3204**

COURIER-TRIBUNE (SENECA, KAN.) (US) [11986271] **5675**

COURIER-TRIBUNE, THE (US) [13168530] **5723**

COURIER (WASHINGTON, D.C.) **CEASED.** (US) [04453372] **4849**

COURIER-WEDGE, THE (US) [13286589] **5766**

COURIER WEEKEND (CN/0707-4905) [04746957] **5782**

COURRIER AGRIROYAL (CN/0822-7144) [10440805] **785, 77**

COURRIER AUSTRALIEN (AT/0011-0442) **2486**

COURRIER Alphabetical Title Index

COURRIER AVICOLE, LE (FR/0011-0450) [06746364] **77**

COURRIER CERN (SZ) [07083985] **4446**

COURRIER DE GAND, LE (BE/0770-9021) [I07709021] **5778**

COURRIER DE GRAND'MERE, LE (CN/0228-6645) [07802357] **5782**

COURRIER DE L'A.C.A.T. / ACTION DES CHRETIENS POUR L'ABOLITION DE LA TORTURE (FR) [28096879] **4506**

COURRIER DE L'A.C.I (FR/0395-9112) [I03959112] **5028**

COURRIER DE LA MONETIQUE ET DE LA CARTE A MEMOIRE, LE (FR/0757-8768) [I07578768] **830**

COURRIER DE LA NATURE, LE (FR) [04327950] **2191**

COURRIER DE LA PLANETE PARIS (FR/1161-8043) [I11618043] **5097**

COURRIER DE LA SCLEROSE EN PLAQUES, LE (FR/0290-5736) [I02905736] **3569**

COURRIER DE L'EDUCATION NATIONALE. ANNUAIRE STATISTIQUE (LU) [19481119] 1734, **1794**

COURRIER DE L'ENSEIGNEMENT INDIVIDUALISE A TOUTES LES ANIMATRICES ET A TOUS LES ANIMATEURS DU 2E CYCLE DE L'ELEMENTAIRE, LE (CN/0380-9757) [03202155] **3275**

COURRIER DE LOTBINIERE, LE (CN/0226-9139) [08045805] **5782**

COURRIER DE L'UNESCO, LE (INT/0304-3118) [I03043118] **2908**

COURRIER DE PAUL DEHEME, LE (FR) **1734**

COURRIER DE PORTNEUF, LE (CN/0228-6297) [07802270] **5782**

COURRIER DE ST. HYACINTHE, LE (CN) **5782**

COURRIER DES FAMILLES, LE (CN/0702-0376) [04631865] **5412**

COURRIER DES METIERS D'ART, LE (FR/0399-6921) [08971305] **348**

COURRIER DES PAYS DE L'EST (FR/0590-0239) [02259875] **1478**

COURRIER DIPLOMATIQUE DE L'OCEAN INDIEN (MG) [03048600] **2684**

COURRIER DU BOIS, LE (BE/0770-111X) [I0770111X] **633**

COURRIER DU CENTRE INTERNATIONAL D'ETUDES POETIQUES (BE/0577-1757) [03029187] **3461**

COURRIER DU CNRS, LE (FR/0153-985X) [04012259] **5097**

COURRIER DU MEUBLE PARIS, LE (FR/0751-6320) [I07516320] **2904**

COURRIER DU SURVENANT, LE (CN/0710-4561) [08828228] **5782**

COURRIER EUROPEEN DE L'ENTREPRISE PARIS, LE (FR/1143-4325) [I11434325] **830**

COURRIER EXPRESS DE VAUDREUIL-SOULANGES, LE (CN/0710-9938) [08330475] **5782**

COURRIER FRANCAIS (1991) (CN/1184-8677) [24368475] **3275**

COURRIER FRONTENAC (CN/0704-0474) [04039712] **5782**

COURRIER HEBDOMADAIRE DU C.R.I.S.P (BE/0577-148X) [02673720] **5196**

COURRIER INTERNATIONAL PARIS (FR/1154-516X) [I1154516X] **2486**

COURRIER LAURENTIDES (EDITION EST) (CN/0829-2442) [13191914] **5782**

COURRIER - O.C.C, LE (FR/0249-9975) [I02499975] **5467**

COURRIER P.R.H. MONTREAL (CN/0821-0101) [09666902] **4583**

COURRIER PEDAGOGIQUE, 1ER CYCLE DE L'ELEMENTAIRE (CN/0380-9714) [03202152] **1734**

COURRIER PROFESSIONNEL PARIS, LE (FR/1140-7581) [I11407581] **1144**

COURRIER ROUMAIN (MONTREAL) (CN/0827-4045) [12178018] **5196**

COURRIER SAINT-HUBERT (CN/0712-6794) [09379012] **5783**

COURRIER (SOCIETE D'HISTOIRE DES FRANCO-COLOMBIENS) (CN/0840-9536) [20367606] **2730**

COURS DE PERFECTIONNEMENT DU NOTARIAT (CN/0316-1234) [02731803] **3089**

COURSE ANNOUNCEMENT - DIVISION OF TRAINING. NATIONAL INSTITUTE FOR OCCUPATIONAL SAFETY AND HEALTH (US/0093-5093) [01792336] **2861**

COURSE CATALOG / NATIONAL FIRE ACADEMY (US) [09869587] **2288**

COURSE DATA REPORT (US) [10785796] **1734**

COURSE TRENDS (US) [16949617] **1734**

COURSE TRENDS IN ADULT LEARNING *See* COURSE TRENDS **1734**

COURSES AND LECTURES / INTERNATIONAL CENTRE FOR MECHANICAL SCIENCES (IT/0254-1971) [07257649] **2112**

COURSES ET ELEVAGE (FR) [03992865] **4891**

COURSES FOR FOREIGNERS IN SPAIN (SP) [06921479] **3275**

COURSES HANDBOOK - THE OPEN UNIVERSITY (UK) [02366185] **1818**

COURT COMMENTARIES (US/0731-7972) [07560377] **3140**

COURT DECISIONS AND LEGAL OPINIONS (SEATTLE) (US/0093-3023) [01787462] **2957**

COURT DECISIONS RELATING TO THE NATIONAL LABOR RELATIONS ACT (US/0083-2219) [01606251] **3146**

COURT EXCELLENCE (US) **2957**

COURT JUDGEMENT REPORT (NEW BRUNSWICK ED.) (CN/0706-7178) [04079975] **2957**

COURT MANAGEMENT & ADMINISTRATION REPORT (US/1063-0821) [22647890] **2957**

COURT MANAGER, THE (US/1046-249X) [12921721] **3140**

COURT NEWS (US) [06576176] **3140**

COURT NEWS (US) [22974379] **2957**

COURT OF JUSTICE OF THE EUROPEAN COMMUNITIES *See* PROCEEDINGS OF THE COURT OF JUSTICE AND OF THE COURT OF FIRST INSTANCE OF THE EUROPEAN COMMUNITIES **3031**

COURT OF JUSTICE OF THE EUROPEAN COMMUNITIES *See* RECUEIL DE LA JURISPRUDENCE DE LA COUR **3036**

COURT OF JUSTICE OF THE EUROPEAN COMMUNITIES. DIRECTION RECHERCHE, DOCUMENTATION, ET BIBLIOTHEQUE *See* NOTES / COUR DE JUSTICE DES COMMUNANTES EUROPEENES, DIRECTION RECHERCHE, DOCUMENTATION ET BIBLIOTHEQUE **3019**

COURT PRACTICE INSTITUTE *See* NEWSLETTER - COURT PRACTICE INSTITUTE **3142**

COURT REPORTER *See* ALASKA COURT SYSTEM NEWSLETTER **3138**

COURT REVIEW (US/0011-0647) [03101384] **3140**

COURT RULES FOR NORTHERN CALIFORNIA *See* NORTHERN CALIFORNIA COURT RULES **3142**

COURT STATISTICS, TASMANIA / AUSTRALIAN BUREAU OF STATISTICS (AT) [08055734] 2957, **3079**

COURTAGE IMMOBILIER, LE (CN/0706-1811) [06133209] **2191**

COURTAULD INSTITUTE ILLUSTRATION ARCHIVES. ARCHIVE 4, LATE 18TH & 19TH CENTURY SCULPTURE IN THE BRITISH ISLES (UK/0307-8086) [03998285] 296, **2481**

COURTENAY AND COMOX (CN/0383-6118) [03219808] **2559**

COURTHOUSE JOURNAL, THE (US) [09509262] **4641**

COURTLINK (VANCOUVER) (CN/1180-1468) [23598749] **2957**

COURTNEY CHRONICLE (US/0882-8806) [11956192] **2444**

COURTROOM MEDICINE (US/0590-0301) [01565363] 3569, **2957**

COURTS & CLE BULLETIN / THE MISSOURI BAR (US/0544-4993) [05059191] **2957**

COURTS OF SUMMARY JURISDICTION, SOUTH AUSTRALIA (AT) [19461658] **3161**

COUSHATTA CITIZEN, THE (US) [16402259] **5683**

COUSINS ET COUSINES (US/0740-3046) [04299364] **2444**

COUTS DES FACTEURS EN COTE D'IVOIRE (IV) [02246944] **1590**

COUTTS LIBRARY SERVICES. CURRENT CANADIAN BOOKS (CN/0316-9448) [02247453] 3204, **414**

COVENANT COMPANION (US/0011-0671) [01565366] **5058**

COVENANT DISCIPLESHIP QUARTERLY (US/1052-3790) [17784486] **4951**

COVENANT QUARTERLY, THE (US/0361-0934) [01714050] **4951**

COVENANTER WITNESS (US/0749-4319) [02446225] **4951**

COVENTRY EVENING TELEGRAPH YEAR BOOK AND WHO'S WHO (UK) [01787863] **431**

COVER NOTE SYDNEY (AT/0312-6757) [I03126757] **2878**

COVER STORY INDEX, THE (US/1054-433X) [22851444] **2532**

COVER-TO-COVER WITH CASPR (US/1059-1362) [24487023] **3204**

COVERAGE (CHAMPAIGN, ILL.), THE (US/8755-7444) [11480384] **2878**

COVERED BRIDGE TOPICS (US) [01565368] **2022**

COVERED EMPLOYMENT AND WAGES IN SOUTH CAROLINA (US) [23710966] **1661**

COVERED EMPLOYMENT AND WAGES : QUARTERLY REPORT (US) [04737871] **1661**

COVERED WAGON, THE (US/0574-3680) [02242921] **2730**

COVERTACTION INFORMATION BULLETIN (US/0275-309X) [07115253] **4519**

● COVERTACTION QUARTERLY (US/1067-7232) [27258758] **1073**

COVINGTON LEADER, THE (US) [19249780] **5745**

COVINGTON NEWS (COVINGTON, GA.), THE (US/1049-4936) [19585310] **5653**

COW COUNTRY (US/0279-8204) [06746980] **209**

COW IN THE ROAD *SUSPENDED.* (US/0887-9427) [13421039] **318**

COWAN CLAN UNITED *See* NEWSLETTER - COWAN CLAN UNITED **2463**

COWBOY MAGAZINE (US/1053-2633) [22496568] **2532**

COWDEN REFLECTOR *See* BEECHER CITY JOURNAL **5658**

COWETA COUNTY GENEALOGICAL SOCIETY *See* COWETA COUNTY GENEALOGICAL SOCIETY MAGAZINE **2444**

COWETA COUNTY GENEALOGICAL SOCIETY MAGAZINE (US/0736-2404) [09078284] **2444**

COWETA COURIER (US) **2444**

COWICHAN NEWS (CN/0703-9220) [03960106] **5783**

COWLEY COUNTY REPORTER, THE (US) [10444620] **5675**

COWLITZ HISTORICAL QUARTERLY (US/8756-0542) [03646252] **2730**

COWRIE (CC) [12544036] **3378**

COYOTE (TUCSON, ARIZ.) (US/0737-0466) [08413482] **2332**

COYUNTURA ANDINA (CK) [03746252] **1554**

COYUNTURA ECONOMICA (CK/0120-3576) [01133880] **1554**

COYUNTURA ENERGETICA (SP/0211-2213) [09366185] **1936**

COYUNTURA INDUSTRIAL, REGION VALENCIANA (SP) [03579331] **1554**

COYUNTURA INDUSTRIAL REGIONAL (SPAIN) (SP) [01795920] **1603**

CP RAIL NEWS *See* CP RAIL SYSTEM NEWS **5430**

● CP RAIL SYSTEM NEWS (CN/1189-363X) [25883098] **5430**

CP + T INTERNATIONAL CASTING PLANT AND TECHNOLOGY (GW/0177-1469) [I01771469] **4000**

CPA COMPREHENSIVE EXAM REVIEW (US) [24104504] **742**

CPA COMPUTER REPORT (US/0745-1342) [08859835] 1181, **742**

CPA DIGEST (US/0741-3610) [08938015] **742**

CPA EXAMINATION REVIEW (US/0743-815X) [04233972] **742**

CPA EXAMINATION REVIEW. AUDITING (US/0749-9485) [09984015] **742**

CPA EXAMINATION REVIEW. THEORY AND PRACTICE (US/0743-3794) [10471015] **742**

CPA FIRM PRACTICE MANUAL *See* PUBLIC ACCOUNTING PRACTICE MANUAL **750**

CPA FREEWHEELER (CN/0824-7226) [11377352] **4386**

CPA JOURNAL (1975), THE (US/0732-8435) [03342314] **742**

CPA LETTER, THE (US/0094-792X) [01794977] **742**

CPA MANAGING PARTNER REPORT (US/0894-1815) [15866784] **742**

CPA MARKETING REPORT (US/0279-1021) [07537878] 742, **922**

CPA PERSONNEL REPORT (US/0745-0877) [08809506] 742, **939**

CPA PROFIT REPORT (US/1047-5834) [20738482] **742**

● CPA SOFTWARE NEWS, THE (US/1068-8285) [27826520] 1285, **662**

CPAC BOOKSHOPPE (CN/0317-0780) [02247698] **2819**

CPA'S PC NETWORK ADVISOR (US/1059-4590) [24600322] **1241**

CPB REPORT (US) [04761420] **1130**

CPC ANNUAL *See* PLANNING JOB CHOICES **4208**

CPC ANNUAL *See* JOB CHOICES ... IN SCIENCE & ENGINEERING **4205**

CPC ANNUAL *See* PLANNING JOB CHOICES (TWO-YEAR COLLEGE ED.) **4208**

CPC ANNUAL *See* JOB CHOICES ... IN HEALTHCARE **4205**

CPC ANNUAL *See* JOB CHOICES ... IN BUSINESS **4205**

CPC ANNUAL, THE (US/0749-7474) [09887531] **4203**

CPC EAST COAST REPORT, THE (US/8750-5568) [11514158] 1153, **4254**

CPC INFORMATION (XR) [03011489] **4951**

CPC NATIONAL DIRECTORY (US/8755-8378) [11412448] 4203, **1818**

CPC PETRONEWS (US/8750-5584) [11514500] **4254**

CPC SALARY SURVEY (US/0196-1004) [02104147] **4203**

CPC SALARY SURVEY FOR REGION MAPA (US/0272-2186) [06805441] **1819**

CPC SALARY SURVEY FOR REGION MCPA (US/0272-2216) [06805754] **4203**

CPCU JOURNAL (US/0162-2706) [03919962] **2878**

CPCU NEWS (US/0007-8883) [03981321] **2878**

CPD NOTES / HEADQUARTERS, COMMUNITY PLANNING AND DEVELOPMENT (US) [24883609] **2819**

CPDA NEWS (US/0590-711X) [02981549] **1303**

CPDP BULLETIN MENSUEL (FR) [04228887] **4254**

CPE NEWSLETTER (US/1013-4689) [18787016] **1877**

CPE STRATEGIES (US/0747-9050) [10839257] **1153**

CPER BULLETIN (US) [03921693] **1661**

CPF IMMERSION REGISTRY, THE (CN/0829-1020) [12648569] **3275**

CPF ONTARIO (CN/0832-1310) [15367849] **3275**

CPH COMMENTATOR (US/0007-8905) [01776975] **4813**

CPI (BALTIMORE, MD.) (US/0897-8751) [04587319] **5412**

CPI DETAILED REPORT (US/0095-926X) [02251913] **1590**

CPI DIGEST (US/0891-1886) [11535153] **973**

CPI NATIONAL REPORT (US/0740-7947) [10025047] **4583**

CPI PURCHASING (US/0746-9012) [10383423] 949, **1023**

CPIV RAPIDINFO (BE) **1109**

CPJ : CANADIAN PHARMACEUTICAL JOURNAL (CN/0828-6914) [12199466] **4298**

CPJ UPDATE (US/1056-8093) [14270053] **4506**

CPJ UPDATE *See* DANGEROUS ASSIGNMENTS **4507**

CPL BIBLIOGRAPHY (US/0743-1635) [04900311] 2819, **2840**

CPL NEWSLETTER / COUNCIL OF PLANNING LIBRARIANS (US) [02830662] **3204**

CPN. CRIME PREVENTION NEWS (UK/0961-0286) [I09610286] **3161**

CPNEWS (SACRAMENTO, CALIF.) (US/1058-4595) [24298385] **2596**

CPOA TRAINING BULLETIN (US) **3161**

CPR, CAIRO PRESS REVIEW (US) [04349963] **2486**

CPR POPULATION RESEARCH (US/0190-7190) [02671172] **4551**

CPRS CROSS-REFERENCE LIST (CN/0229-3870) [08071436] **758**

CPRS NATIONAL NEWSLETTER (CN/0710-0701) [08828253] **758**

CPS. CANADIAN POWER & SAIL *See* CANADIAN BOATING **592**

●CPS EXPRESS (US/1062-2535) [25566167] **2957**

CPSR NEWSLETTER, THE (US) [20063730] **1181**

CPST OCCASSIONAL PAPERS *CEASED.* (US) **5097**

CPU JOURNAL (1981) (CN/0711-1053) [08478777] **1661**

CPU NEWS : JOURNAL OF THE COMMONWEALTH PRESS UNION (UK) [24144686] **2918**

CPU : QUARTERLY OF THE COMMONWEALTH PRESS UNION (UK) [10746712] **2918**

CPU REVIEW (US/1056-1838) [23526090] **1091**

CQ (US/0007-893X) [01537996] **1130**

CQ AMATEUR RADIO ... ANTENNA BUYER'S GUIDE *See* CQ AMATEUR RADIO ... BEGINNER'S GUIDE TO AMATEUR RADIO **1130**

CQ AMATEUR RADIO ... BEGINNER'S GUIDE TO AMATEUR RADIO (US/1068-848X) [27827541] **1130**

CQ AMATEUR RADIO ... BUYER'S GUIDE (US/1040-1369) [18333155] **1130**

CQ. CONNECTICUT QUARTERLY (US/0270-5702) [05704142] **3378**

CQ, CONTEMPORARY QUARTERLY *SUSPENDED.* (US/0162-7201) [04221926] **3462**

CQ-DL (GW) [I0178269X] **1109**

... CQ GUIDE TO CURRENT AMERICAN GOVERNMENT, THE (US/0196-612X) [02055163] **4641**

CQ RESEARCHER, THE (US/1056-2036) [23535710] **4470**

CRA BULLETIN (US/1058-5931) [24335826] **4641**

CRA REVIEW, THE (US/0889-7395) [14066549] **1590**

CRAB CREEK REVIEW (US/0738-7008) [09651022] **2532**

CRAB, THE (US/0300-7561) [01565371] **3204**

CRABB NEWSLETTER, THE (US/1061-1088) [25054553] **2444**

CRACKED (US/0883-6361) [12178537] **2532**

CRACKED MAGAZINE *See* CRACKED **2532**

CRACKER CRUMBS (US) [13495297] **2444**

●CRACKING THE ACT (US/1059-101X) [24479731] **1819**

●CRACKING THE GRE (US/1062-5534) [25663169] **1819**

CRACKING THE SYSTEM. GRE *See* CRACKING THE GRE **1819**

CRACKNELL'S LAW STUDENT'S COMPANION (UK/0590-0441) [04024743] **2957**

CRADAT INFORMATIONS : BULLETIN DU CENTRE REGIONAL AFRICAIN D'ADMINISTRATION DU TRAVAIL (CM) [09968121] **3146**

CRADLE CLUB MAGAZINE (CN/0225-2708) [06859344] **2278**

CRADLE ROLL PROGRAM HELPS (US/0163-8688) [04520529] 1892, **5058**

CRAFT & DECORATING (AT/1030-9713) [I10309713] **371**

CRAFT & NEEDLEWORK AGE (US/0887-9818) [13434719] **5183**

CRAFT ARTS (AT) [12203795] **371**

CRAFT CONNECTION (US/1067-8328) [02250330] **371**

CRAFT CONNECTION, THE (CN/1193-3208) [I11933208] **371**

CRAFT CONTACTS (1983) (CN/0823-2148) [10036589] **371**

CRAFT DIGEST (US) 371, **2773**

CRAFT FACTOR (CN/0228-7498) [08091222] **371**

CRAFT HISTORY (UK/0953-931X) [19616435] **371**

CRAFT INTERNATIONAL (US/1044-4009) [07688264] **371**

CRAFT RANGE (US/0199-5200) [05962593] **371**

CRAFT SCHOOL (CN/0712-2659) [08867751] **371**

CRAFT SHOW DIGEST (US/0882-7486) [11962881] **371**

CRAFT SHOWS IN ONTARIO *See* ANNUAL CRAFT SHOWS IN ONTARIO / CRAFT RESOURCE CENTRE **370**

CRAFT SUPPLY DIRECTORY (US) [08273533] **2584**

CRAFT SUPPLY MAGAZINE (US/1059-8766) [24798775] **371**

CRAFT VICTORIA (AT/0158-7048) [I01587048] **371**

CRAFTNEWS (TORONTO) (CN/0319-7832) [02729175] **371**

CRAFTRENDS *See* CRAFTRENDS SEW BUSINESS **5183**

CRAFTRENDS SEW BUSINESS (US) **5183**

CRAFTS & SEWING *CEASED.* (US/0092-4180) [01789830] 5183, **371**

CRAFTS COUNCIL (SZ) [15988462] **371**

CRAFTS (CRAFTS ADVISORY COMMITTEE) (UK/0306-610X) [02240657] **371**

CRAFTS 'N THINGS (US/0146-6607) [02987677] **371**

CRAFTS (PEORIA, ILL.) (US/0148-9127) [03504120] **371**

CRAFTS PLUS (CN/0833-8337) [15152508] **371**

CRAFTS RELATED NEWSLETTERS, PERIODICALS, AND PUBLICATIONS ETC (US/1053-2013) [22473866] **372**

CRAFTS REPORT, THE (US/0160-7650) [03763022] **372**

CRAFTWORKS FOR THE HOME (US/0891-0588) [14561015] **372**

CRAG AND CANYON (CN/0701-3558) [03039930] **4871**

CRAIG-LINKS (US) [08646218] **2444**

CRAIGHEAD COUNTY HISTORICAL QUARTERLY, THE (US/0574-377X) [03853359] **2730**

CRAIGHEAD'S COUNTRY REPORTS (US) **5467**

●CRAIGHEAD'S INTERNATIONAL BUSINESS, TRAVEL, AND RELOCATION GUIDE TO 71 COUNTRIES (US/1058-3904) [24291302] 662, **5467**

CRAIGHEAD'S INTERNATIONAL EXECUTIVE TRAVEL AND RELOCATION SERVICE (US) 662, **5467**

CRAIN'S CHICAGO BUSINESS (US/0149-6956) [03535526] **662**

CRAIN'S CLEVELAND BUSINESS (US/0197-2375) [06002153] **663**

CRAIN'S DETROIT BUSINESS (US/0882-1992) [11793300] **663**

CRAIN'S NEW YORK BUSINESS (US/8756-789X) [11620213] **1478**

CRAIN'S TIRE BUSINESS (US/0746-9071) [10382221] **663**

CRANBERRIES (PORTLAND) (US/0011-0787) [01565377] **168**

CRANBERRIES (WASHINGTON) (US/0196-884X) [04023113] **168**

CRANBROOK INSTITUTE OF SCIENCE *See* YEAR IN REVIEW - CRANBROOK INSTITUTE OF SCIENCE **4097**

CRANBROOK'S RESPONSE (CN/0708-0239) [04784078] **5783**

CRANBURY PRESS, THE (US/1061-5563) [11837268] **5709**

CRANE LIBRARY *See* CRANE LIBRARY W.I.P **3204**

CRANE LIBRARY *See* WIP FUN **3256**

CRANE LIBRARY NEWS (CN/0316-7372) [12045289] **3204**

CRANE LIBRARY NEWS SUBSTITUTE (CN/0827-3766) [12045286] **3204**

CRANE LIBRARY UPDATE (CN/0228-9571) [08070916] **3204**

CRANE LIBRARY W.I.P (CN/0228-9555) [09357704] **3204**

CRANE NEWS (CRANE, TEX. : 1945)- (US) [15127762] **5748**

CRANES TODAY (UK/0307-0018) [05248028] **2112**

CRANFORD CHRONICLE (1979) (US) [12130686] **5709**

CRANIO (US/0886-9634) [11620880] 3881, **3569**

CRANIO CLINICS INTERNATIONAL (US/1050-009X) [21369743] **3569**

CRANIOFACIAL GROWTH SERIES (US/0162-7279) [04183917] 1319, **3569**

●CRANK (PHILADELPHIA, PA.) (US/1076-9102) [30637689] **4113**

CRANSTON HERALD (US) [26044290] **5741**

CRANWELLS BUILDING SUPPLIES (NZ) **611**

CRAPOUILLOT, LE (FR) [01565385] **3340**

CRAS (DK/0105-0583) [01794181] **348**

CRAWFORD COUNTY INDEPENDENT AND THE KICKAPOO SCOUT (US) [13511397] **5766**

CRAWFORD COUNTY IOWA GENEALOGICAL SOCIETY (US/1059-0374) [24462485] **2444**

CRAWFORD COUNTY LEGAL JOURNAL (US/0574-3869) [01565387] **2957**

CRAWFORD DIRECTORY OF CITY CONNECTIONS (UK) **785**

CRAWFORD'S DIRECTORY OF CITY CONNECTIONS (UK/0953-8089) [I09538089] **4641**

CRAY CHANNELS (US) [11452191] **1181**

CRAY RESEARCH, INC *See* CRAY CHANNELS **1181**

CRAZYHORSE (LITTLE ROCK, ARK.) (US/0011-0841) [01695421] **3462**

CRB COMMODITY YEAR BOOK (US/1046-8226) [12359407] 1478, **830**

CRB FUTURES MARKET SERVICE (US/1057-4883) [23956291] **895**

CRC HANDBOOK OF CHEMICAL SYNONYMS AND TRADE NAMES (US) [04260030] **973**

CRC HANDBOOK OF CHEMISTRY AND PHYSICS (US/0147-6262) [03208084] 4401, **973**

CRC — Alphabetical Title Index

CRC HANDBOOK OF CLINICAL ENGINEERING (US/0734-1407) [07295690] **3691**

CRC HANDBOOK OF MICROBIOLOGY *CEASED.* (US) [06719728] **561**

CRC HANDBOOK SERIES IN NUTRITION AND FOOD. SECTION G : DIETS, CULTURE MEDIA, FOOD SUPPLEMENTS *CEASED.* (US/0191-1368) [04735872] **4189**

CRC STANDARD MATHEMATICAL TABLES AND FORMULAE (US) [24025033] **3502**

CRC SUBSYSTEM HANDBOOK (US) [04169539] **1661**

CRCS NEWSLETTER / CENTRE FOR RESEARCH ON CULTURE AND SOCIETY, CARLETON UNIVERSITY (CN/1183-479X) [25423195] **5243**

CRD NEWS / COMMITTEE FOR THE RIGHTS OF THE DISABLED (US/0749-3177) [10622855] **4386**, **4506**

CRDI EXPLORE, LE (CN/0380-1438) [02248950] **2908**

CREACTION *CEASED.* (SZ/1011-9019) [18129668] **1819**

CREAM CITY REVIEW (US/0884-3457) [08152164] **3340**

CREATE: JOURNAL OF THE CREATIVE AND EXPRESSIVE ARTS THERAPIES EXCHANGE (CN/1186-0391) [24266283] **4583**

●CREATEURS QUEBECOIS (CN/1193-1140) [26497609] **372**

●CREATEURS QUEBECOIS (CN/1193-1140) [26497610] **372**

CREATING EXCELLENCE (US/1045-7011) [09641483] **663**

●CREATING QUALITY K-12 (US/1070-5341) [28399545] **1862**

CREATION/EVOLUTION (US/0738-6001) [07940439] **543**

CREATION EX NIHILO (AT/0819-1530) [08191530] 5097, **4951**

CREATION EX NIHILO TECHNICAL JOURNAL (AT/1036-2916) [I10362916] **4951**

CREATION MAGAZINE (FR/0765-9911) [I07659911] **758**

CREATION RESEARCH QUARTERLY (US/0092-9166) [01791775] **5097**

CREATION RESEARCH SOCIETY *See* CREATION RESEARCH QUARTERLY **5097**

CREATION SCIENCE DIALOGUE (CN/0229-253X) [07865718] 4951, **5097**

CREATION SOCIAL SCIENCE AND HUMANITIES QUARTERLY *CEASED.* (US/0740-3399) [04820102] 2845, **5196**

CREATION SPIRITUALITY (US/1053-9891) [22715305] **4951**

CREATIONS CANNES LA BOCCA (FR/0293-0196) [I02930196] **5097**

CREATIONS TISSUS (FR/0336-7274) [I03367274] **1083**

CREATIVE (US/0737-5883) [09425363] 922, **758**

CREATIVE ARTISTS PUBLIC SERVICE PROGRAM *See* CATALOG OF NEW YORK STATE VISUAL ARTISTS SELECTED FOR THE CREATIVE ARTISTS PUBLIC SERVICE PROGRAM, A **347**

CREATIVE ARTS (HAMILTON) (CN/0820-7909) [09467709] **318**

CREATIVE BLACK BOOK (PORTFOLIO ED.), THE (US/0740-283X) [09906480] **758**

CREATIVE BLACK BOOK (PRODUCER'S ED.), THE (US/0889-6372) [13979388] **758**

CREATIVE BLACK BOOK, THE (US/0738-9000) [04429295] **758**

CREATIVE BUSINESS (US/1073-8444) [29539342] **663**

CREATIVE CAMERA (UK/0011-0876) [01792886] **4368**

CREATIVE CHILD AND ADULT QUARTERLY, THE (US/0884-4291) [04316797] **1877**

CREATIVE CLASSROOM (US/0887-042X) [13622374] **1892**

CREATIVE COMPUTING BUYER'S GUIDE TO PERSONAL COMPUTERS, PERIPHERALS, AND ELECTRONIC GAMES (US/0735-6668) [08774594] 1230, **1266**

CREATIVE COMPUTING SOFTWARE BUYER'S GUIDE (US/0734-3361) [08720659] 1285, **1237**

CREATIVE CONSERVATION *CEASED.* (UK) 2163, **2191**

CREATIVE COOK'S DIGEST, THE (US/0279-9847) [07411259] **2789**

CREATIVE CRAFTS & MINIATURES *See* CRAFTS 'N THINGS **371**

●CREATIVE EXHIBITING TECHNIQUES (US/1070-826X) [26406973] **758**

CREATIVE FAMILY LIVING *See* FAMILY LIFE TODAY **2279**

CREATIVE FORECASTING (US/1052-2573) [22227275] **5281**

CREATIVE FORUM (II) [18676927] **3378**

CREATIVE GUITAR INTERNATIONAL (US/0092-8887) [01791802] **4113**

CREATIVE HANDBOOK, THE (UK) [09296466] **377**

CREATIVE HELP FOR DAILY LIVING *See* PLUS (PAWLING, N.Y.) **4986**

CREATIVE INTERFACE, THE (US/0070-1459) [01211398] **4470**

CREATIVE KIDS (US/0892-9599) [14369800] **1062**

CREATIVE LIVING (MILWAUKEE, WIS.) (US/0893-3022) [15501182] **2532**

CREATIVE LIVING TODAY (US/8755-884X) [11459245] **4583**

CREATIVE LOAFING (1978) (US/0889-8685) [06661238] **5653**

CREATIVE MANAGEMENT (NEW YORK, N.Y.) (US/1040-421X) [07285496] **864**

CREATIVE NEEDLE (US/0887-2384) [13151064] **5183**

CREATIVE NURSING (US) **3854**

CREATIVE OHIO (US/0741-6504) [10243873] **372**

●CREATIVE OUTLETS (US/1062-8207) [25760448] **1603**

CREATIVE PRODUCTS NEWS *CEASED.* (US/0273-9240) [07039830] **1603**

CREATIVE QUILTING (US/0887-3690) [13196628] **5183**

CREATIVE READING (US/1059-0676) [24469498] **3378**

CREATIVE REAL ESTATE MAGAZINE (US/0194-7222) [04964871] **4836**

CREATIVE REVIEW LONDON. 1980 (UK/0262-1037) [I02621037] 785, **922**

CREATIVE REVIEW (LONDON, ENGLAND) (UK) [10910455] 949, **922**

CREATIVE SALES MANAGER (US/8750-9555) [11951918] **864**

CREATIVE SECRETARY (US/0276-5845) [01782033] **663**

CREATIVE SIGNS & DISPLAYS *See* CREATIVE **758**

CREATIVE SOURCE AUSTRALIA (AT/0726-3589) [12325335] 377, **4368**

CREATIVE TAX PLANNING FOR REAL ESTATE TRANSACTIONS (US/0732-751X) [08394575] **4836**

CREATIVE THINKING HELPER (US) **1734**

CREATIVE TRAINING TECHNIQUES (US/1053-170X) [18353641] **939**

CREATIVE TRANSFORMATION (US/1062-4708) [25184064] **4951**

CREATIVE WOMAN (PARK FOREST SOUTH, ILL.), THE (US/0736-4733) [08809365] 3378, **5554**

CREATIVE WORD PROCESSING IN THE CLASSROOM *See* WRITING NOTEBOOK **1292**

CREATIVE WORD PROCESSING IN THE CLASSROOM : CWP (US/0749-2537) [11119335] 1222, 1892, **1292**

CREATIVE WORLD (US/0360-7135) [02244882] **4113**

CREATIVI E FORNITORI (IT) **758**

CREATIVITY (US/0097-6075) [01790885] **758**

●CREATIVITY AND INNOVATION MANAGEMENT (UK/0963-1690) [25652186] **864**

CREATIVITY IN ACTION (US/0093-5263) [01345335] **4583**

CREATIVITY IN ORGANIC SYNTHESIS (UK) [01491141] **1041**

CREATIVITY RESEARCH JOURNAL (US/1040-0419) [18299247] **5196**

CREATOR (WICHITA, KAN.) (US/1045-0815) [17931225] **4113**

CREDIT & COLLECTION CLINIC (US/0746-293X) [08369891] **785**

CREDIT & COLLECTION MANAGEMENT BULLETIN (US/1048-275X) [20905603] **663**

CREDIT & COLLECTION MANAGERS' LETTER (US/1060-2739) [24901096] **785**

●CREDIT & FINANCE (US/1055-8225) [23352045] **785**

CREDIT CARD INSIDER REPORT, THE (US/1062-1008) [25526063] **785**

CREDIT CARD MANAGEMENT (US/0896-9329) [17339946] **785**

●CREDIT CARD MANAGEMENT EUROPE (US) **785**

CREDIT CARD NEWS (US) **785**

CREDIT CODE LETTER, THE (US/0738-6877) [07562909] 785, **1296**

CREDIT COMMERCIAL DE FRANCE *See* ANNUAL REPORT / CREDIT COMMERCIAL DE FRANCE **771**

CREDIT COMMUNAL DE BELGIQUE *See* BULLETIN TRIMESTRIEL **4715**

CREDIT COMMUNAL DE BELGIQUE. BULLETIN TRIMESTRIEL *See* BULLETIN DU CREDIT COMMUNAL **780**

CREDIT CONTROL (UK/0143-5329) [I01435329] 939, **785**

CREDIT DECISIONS (US/0748-6030) [10974581] **785**

CREDIT INSURANCE NEWSLETTER, THE (US/1054-1063) [22748272] **2878**

CREDIT LYONNAIS. CONSEIL D'ADMINISTRATION *See* RAPPORT DU CONSEIL D'ADMINISTRATION - CREDIT LYONNAIS **806**

CREDIT LYONNAIS. RAPPORT *See* RAPPORT DU CONSEIL D'ADMINISTRATION - CREDIT LYONNAIS **806**

CREDIT MANAGEMENT (UK/0265-2099) [23245685] **785**

CREDIT MANAGEMENT (UK) **785**

CREDIT MANUAL OF COMMERCIAL LAWS (US/0070-1467) [01565400] **3099**

CREDIT MANUAL OF COMMERCIAL LAWS WITH DIARY *See* CREDIT MANUAL OF COMMERCIAL LAWS **3099**

CREDIT REPORT MAGAZINE : CR : A PUBLICATION OF THE NATIONAL CONSUMER ADVOCATE ASSOCIATION (US/1055-9981) [23441816] **1296**

CREDIT RISK MANAGEMENT REPORT (US/1054-5069) [22902757] **785**

CREDIT SUISSE *See* BULLETIN - CREDIT SUISSE (ENGLISH ED.) **780**

CREDIT UNION $50 MILLION YEARBOOK (US/1061-3676) [25059007] **785**

CREDIT UNION DIRECTOR (US/1040-9246) [18610038] **785**

CREDIT UNION DIRECTORS NEWSLETTER (US/1058-1561) [24231157] **785**

CREDIT UNION DIRECTORY (US/0196-3678) [05316182] **786**

CREDIT UNION DIRECTORY AND BUYERS' GUIDE (US/0092-4954) [01784459] **786**

CREDIT UNION EXECUTIVE (MADISON, WIS. 1989) (US/1053-6744) [21989201] **786**

CREDIT UNION FINANCIAL PROFILES (US/1043-1888) [15110026] **786**

●CREDIT UNION LEGAL LETTER (US/1062-807X) [25749945] **2957**

CREDIT UNION MAGAZINE (US/0011-1066) [01565402] **786**

CREDIT UNION MANAGEMENT (US/0273-9267) [07040196] 865, **786**

CREDIT UNION MANAGER NEWSLETTER (US/1068-2120) **786**

CREDIT UNION NATIONAL ASSOCIATION *See* CUNA NATIONAL MEMBER SURVEY **786**

CREDIT UNION NATIONAL ASSOCIATION *See* YEARBOOK - CREDIT UNION NATIONAL ASSOCIATION **817**

CREDIT UNION NEWS (US/0199-9311) [06301491] 786, **1542**

CREDIT UNION NEWSWATCH (US/0889-5597) [13979234] **786**

CREDIT UNION REPORT (US/0894-752X) [08443936] **786**

CREDIT UNION TECHNOLOGY (US/1054-7304) [22944775] **786**

CREDIT UNION TIMES (US/1058-7764) [24369905] **786**

CREDIT UNION WAY (CN/0829-2175) [06769782] **786**

CREDIT (WASHINGTON) *CEASED.* (US/0097-8345) [01799250] **786**

CREDIT WORLD, THE (US/0011-1074) [01565405] **786**

CREDITO E COOPERAZIONE : RIVISTA DELLE CASSE RURALI ED ARTIGIANE (IT) [21223431] **786**

CREDITO ITALIANO *See* REPORT AND ACCOUNTS - CREDITO ITALIANO **807**

CREDITOPICS *See* BROADCAST CABLE FINANCIAL JOURNAL & CREDITOPICS **1127**

CREDITWEEK INTERNATIONAL RATINGS GUIDE *See* STANDARD & POOR'S RATINGS HANDBOOK **915**

CREDO (NO) [01696120] **4951**

CREEL FAMILY QUARTERLY *CEASED.* (US/0361-820X) [02246864] **2278**

CREEM *See* CREEM (NEW YORK, N.Y.) **4113**

CREEM CLOSEUP (US/0737-1918) [09300969] **4113**

●CREEM (NEW YORK, N.Y.) *SUSPENDED.* (US/0011-1147) [25265451] **4113**

Alphabetical Title Index — CRIS

CREEPING BENT (US/8756-0291) [11455401] **3462**

CREER (AG) [04378243] **4951**

CREEZ! *See* CREEZ! LOISIRS CLICHY **865**

CREEZ! (FR/0248-1855) [I02481855] **663**

CREEZ! LOISIRS CLICHY (FR/1168-6448) [I11686448] **865**

CREIGHTON LAW REVIEW (US/0011-1155) [01565409] **2957**

CREIGHTON PREPARATORY SCHOOL *See* ALUMNI DIRECTORY / CREIGHTON PREPARATORY SCHOOL **1098**

CREMATION SOCIETY OF GREAT BRITAIN AND THE INTERNATIONAL CREMATION FEDERATION *See* PHAROS **5269**

CREOLE LANGUAGE LIBRARY (NE/0920-9026) [I09209026] **3275**

CREPE COOKBOOK FOR DINNERS & DESSERTS (US/0145-7012) [02782341] **2789**

● CRESCENDO & JAZZ MUSIC (UK/0962-7472) [24245016] **4113**

CRESCENDO (CHARLOTTETOWN) (CN/0225-9370) [08323953] **4113**

CRESCENT INTERNATIONAL (CN/0705-3754) [03956565] **4470**

CRESCENT-NEWS (US) [20727200] **5727**

CRESCENT REVIEW, THE (US/0749-2871) [10821407] **2532**

CRESCERE CON LA MUSICA (IT) **4113**

CRESSET (VALPARAISO), THE (US/0011-1198) [01565413] **3340**

CRESSON & GALLITZIN MAINLINER, THE (US/0745-7499) [09424522] **5735**

CRESTLINE ADVOCATE (CRESTLINE, OHIO : 1869) (US) [10529490] **5727**

CRESTLINE COURIER-NEWS (US/1058-5737) [24330781] **5634**

CRESTON NEWS ADVERTISER (CRESTON, IOWA : 1928 : DAILY) (US) [13956808] **5669**

CRETACEOUS RESEARCH (UK/0195-6671) [05585552] **4226**

CREW REPORTS (BE/0772-8867) [I07728867] **5554**

CREWE, BURKEVILLE JOURNAL, THE (US/8755-9463) [11429842] **5758**

CRI ABSTRACTS (II) [08368303] 611, **2022**

CRI COMMUNICATIONS UPDATE SERVICE (US/0271-4795) [06618360] **1109**

CRI (INSTITUTE) *See* CRI COMMUNICATIONS UPDATE SERVICE **1109**

CRIB : CHEMOTHERAPY RESEARCH BULLETIN (US/0577-6392) [06878544] **4298**

CRICKET (LA SALLE) (US/0090-6034) [01785236] **1062**

CRICKET LIFE INTERNATIONAL (US/0956-5620) **4891**

CRICKETER *CEASED.* (AT) **4891**

CRICKETER INTERNATIONAL (UK/0266-7398) [I02667398] **4891**

CRICKETER QUARTERLY FACTS AND FIGURES (UK/0266-7401) [I02667401] **4891**

CRICKETERS' WHO'S WHO, THE (UK) [13889768] **4850**

CRIE : CENTRO REGIONAL DE INFORMACIONES ECUMENICAS, A.C (MX) [09446080] **4951**

CRIEE (CN/0227-0803) [08330433] **2532**

CRIM. COMMITTAL (BS) [01785775] **3105**

CRIME AND DELINQUENCY (US/0011-1287) [01565415] **3161**

CRIME & DETECTION *See* CRIMINOLOGIST, THE **3163**

CRIME AND ITS VICTIMS IN HONG KONG : A REPORT ON THE CRIME VICTIMIZATION SURVEY CONDUCTED IN ... BY THE CENSUS & STATISTICS DEPARTMENT, HONG KONG GOVERNMENT (HK) [19320700] **3161**

CRIME AND JUSTICE ANNUAL REPORT (US) [13783276] 3161, **3079**

CRIME AND JUSTICE BULLETIN (AT/1030-1046) [I10301046] **3161**

CRIME AND JUSTICE (CHICAGO, ILL.) (US/0192-3234) [05015066] **3161**

CRIME AND JUVENILE DELINQUENCY : A BIBLIOGRAPHIC GUIDE TO THE DOCUMENTS UPDATE (US) [05820005] **3079**

CRIME BEAT (US/1058-529X) [24324785] **3161**

● CRIME BUSTER (VANCOUVER) (CN/1191-386X) [26497525] **3161**

CRIME CONTROL DIGEST (US/0011-1295) [02112297] **3161**

CRIME IN ARKANSAS (US) [08365162] 3161, **3079**

CRIME IN COLORADO / COLORADO BUREAU OF INVESTIGATION (US) [04071085] 3161, **3079**

CRIME IN CONNECTICUT (US) [09938616] 3161, **3079**

CRIME IN FLORIDA (US) [08644836] 3161, **3080**

CRIME IN HAWAII (US/0146-9029) [03094963] 3161, **3080**

CRIME IN LOUISIANA (US) [03660882] 3161, **3080**

CRIME IN MAINE (ANNUAL) (US/0148-6292) [03340996] 3161, **3080**

CRIME IN MONTANA (US/0160-7103) [03471030] 3161, **3080**

CRIME IN SOUTH CAROLINA (US) [03751774] 3161, **3080**

CRIME IN TEXAS (US) [04903855] 3161, **3080**

CRIME LABORATORY DIGEST (US/0743-1872) [10541356] 3161, **3080**

CRIME, LAW, AND SOCIAL CHANGE (NE/0925-4994) [23185905] 5243, **3161**

CRIME PREVENTION AND CRIMINAL JUSTICE NEWSLETTER, U.N (AU) [10939698] **3162**

● CRIME PREVENTION FUNDING NEWS (US/1069-1324) [27942527] **3162**

CRIME PREVENTION REVIEW (US/0093-044X) [01791770] **3162**

● CRIME PREVENTION STUDIES (US/1065-7029) [26684508] **3162**

CRIME PREVENTION TECHNOLOGY (UK/0269-4905) [13615507] **3162**

● CRIME STATE RANKINGS (US) [30018989] 3162, **3080**

CRIME TO COURT (US) 1800, **3162**

CRIME VICTIMS DIGEST *See* COMMUNITY POLICING DIGEST **3160**

CRIMES AGAINST BUSINESS (US/0192-706X) [05108261] **3162**

CRIMINAL APPEAL REPORTS (SENTENCING), THE (UK/0144-3321) [06780592] **3105**

CRIMINAL APPEAL REPORTS, THE (UK/0070-1521) [02617568] **3105**

CRIMINAL DEFENSE NEWSLETTER (US/0731-082X) [05632224] **3105**

CRIMINAL DIVISION (US/0747-8542) [10789921] **3105**

CRIMINAL INJURIES COMPENSATION (CN/0833-5737) [16641955] 2957, **3080**

CRIMINAL JUSTICE ABSTRACTS (US/0146-9177) [02859642] 3162, **3080**

CRIMINAL JUSTICE AND BEHAVIOR (US/0093-8548) [01793415] 3162, **4583**

CRIMINAL JUSTICE AND THE PUBLIC (US/0160-9688) [03794583] **3162**

CRIMINAL JUSTICE CAREER DIGEST (US/0278-5277) [07823058] **4203**

CRIMINAL JUSTICE (CHICAGO, ILL. 1986) (US/0887-7785) [13348735] **3162**

CRIMINAL JUSTICE COMPREHENSIVE PLAN (US/0091-9128) [01788516] **3162**

CRIMINAL JUSTICE DIGEST *See* CJ MANAGEMENT & TRAINING DIGEST **3160**

CRIMINAL JUSTICE ETHICS (US/0731-129X) [08127732] 3162, **2249**

CRIMINAL JUSTICE EXPENDITURE AND EMPLOYMENT / OFFICE OF THE ATTORNEY GENERAL, KANSAS BUREAU OF INVESTIGATION, STATISTICAL ANALYSIS CENTER (US) [09187782] **3140**

CRIMINAL JUSTICE (GUILFORD, CONN.) (US/0272-3816) [06536611] **3162**

CRIMINAL JUSTICE HISTORY (US/0194-0953) [06887463] **3162**

CRIMINAL JUSTICE IN SOUTH DAKOTA (US/0361-7378) [02441322] **3162**

CRIMINAL JUSTICE ISSUES (US) [04163216] **4506**

CRIMINAL JUSTICE JOURNAL (SAN DIEGO, CALIF.) (US/0145-4226) [02636249] **3162**

CRIMINAL JUSTICE MONOGRAPH (US) [02255281] **3162**

CRIMINAL JUSTICE NEWSLETTER (BLOOMINGTON) (US/0095-7496) [01796502] **3162**

CRIMINAL JUSTICE NEWSLETTER (NEW YORK, N.Y.) (US/0045-9038) [01784779] **3105**

CRIMINAL JUSTICE NEWSLETTER (SPRINGFIELD) (US/0098-7670) [02242005] **3162**

CRIMINAL JUSTICE PACKAGE (UK) **3162**

CRIMINAL JUSTICE PERIODICAL INDEX (US/0145-5818) [02192329] 3162, **3080**

CRIMINAL JUSTICE PLAN FOR NEW JERSEY. APPLICANTS GUIDE *CEASED.* (US) [04454254] **3162**

CRIMINAL JUSTICE POLICY REVIEW (US/0887-4034) [13188392] **3162**

CRIMINAL JUSTICE PROFILE. ALAMEDA COUNTY (US) [07703557] **3162**

CRIMINAL JUSTICE PROFILE. ALPINE COUNTY (US) [07713132] **3162**

CRIMINAL JUSTICE QUARTERLY, THE *SUSPENDED.* (US/0092-3907) [01786655] **3105**

CRIMINAL JUSTICE REVIEW (ATLANTA, GA.) (US/0734-0168) [02313761] **3162**

CRIMINAL LAW (US) [02718894] **3106**

CRIMINAL LAW BULLETIN (US/0011-1317) [01565430] **3106**

CRIMINAL LAW COMMENTATOR (NEW YORK) (US/0093-4674) [01336701] **3106**

CRIMINAL LAW DIGEST (US) [01641931] **3106**

CRIMINAL LAW DIGEST. SUPPLEMENT (TORONTO 1982) (CN/0824-7544) [11422242] **3106**

CRIMINAL LAW FORUM (US/1046-8374) [20501549] **3106**

CRIMINAL LAW JOURNAL (II/0011-1325) [01565433] **3106**

CRIMINAL LAW JOURNAL (AT/0314-1160) [04027630] **3106**

CRIMINAL LAW (LOS ANGELES, CALIF.) (US/0098-8049) [02239705] **3106**

CRIMINAL LAW NEWSLETTER (SAN JOSE, CALIF.) (US/0888-7012) [13728287] **3106**

CRIMINAL LAW OUTLINE (US/0145-7322) [02805022] **3106**

CRIMINAL LAW QUARTERLY (TORONTO) (CN/0011-1333) [01565435] **3106**

CRIMINAL LAW REPORTER, THE (US/0011-1341) [01565436] **3106**

CRIMINAL LAW REVIEW (LONDON, ENGLAND) (UK/0011-135X) [01565437] **3106**

CRIMINAL LAW REVIEW (NEW YORK, N.Y. : 1979) (US/0192-3323) [05014984] **3106**

CRIMINAL LAWYER, THE (UK/0956-7429) [I09567429] **3106**

CRIMINAL PROCEDURE (US/0099-1228) [02239706] **3106**

CRIMINAL PROCEDURE HANDBOOK (US/0743-4626) [10587027] **3106**

CRIMINAL REPORTS (CN/0383-9494) [01565442] **3106**

CRIMINAL REPORTS FOURTH SERIES (CN/0703-4687) [23763628] **3106**

CRIMINAL STATISTICS, ENGLAND AND WALES (UK) [01751468] **3080**

CRIMINAL STATISTICS, ENGLAND AND WALES. SUPPLEMENTARY TABLES. VOL. 1, PROCEEDINGS IN MAGISTRATES' COURTS (UK) [08297249] 3162, **3080**

CRIMINAL STATISTICS, ENGLAND AND WALES. SUPPLEMENTARY TABLES. VOL. 3, TABLES BY POLICE FORCE AREAS AND SOME COURT AREAS (UK) [08299499] 3162, **3080**

CRIMINAL TRIAL MANUAL, CALIFORNIA. SUPPLEMENT (US/0732-0930) [08316486] **3106**

CRIMINAL TRIAL MANUAL. MARYLAND (US/0732-7293) [08413116] **3106**

CRIMINAL TRIAL MANUAL. NEW JERSEY (US/0732-7285) [08419618] **3106**

CRIMINALITEIT EN STRAFRECHTSPELEGING (NE/0168-9029) [12564420] 3162, **3080**

CRIMINOLOGIE (MONTREAL) (CN/0316-0041) [02441618] **3162**

CRIMINOLOGIE (MONTREAL) (CN/0316-0041) [02243923] **3163**

CRIMINOLOGIST (COLUMBUS), THE (US/0164-0240) [04556881] **3163**

CRIMINOLOGIST, THE (UK/0011-1376) [04049454] **3163**

CRIMINOLOGY & PENOLOGY ABSTRACTS *See* CRIMINOLOGY, PENOLOGY AND POLICE SCIENCE ABSTRACTS **3080**

CRIMINOLOGY AUSTRALIA : QUARTERLY JOURNAL OF THE AUSTRALIAN INSTITUTE OF CRIMINOLOGY (AT/1033-4777) [24896430] **3163**

CRIMINOLOGY (BEVERLY HILLS) (US/0011-1384) [01565445] **3163**

● CRIMINOLOGY, PENOLOGY AND POLICE SCIENCE ABSTRACTS (NE/0928-8759) [26907118] 3163, **3080**

CRIMMER'S (US/0363-292X) [02438103] **318**

CRIS / ICAR *See* AGRISEARCH [COMPUTER FILE] : CRIS, SIS-SPAAR, ICAR, ARRIP, AGREP **54**

CRISIS

● CRISIS INTERVENTION AND TIME-LIMITED TREATMENT (US/1064-5136) [26320514] **5281**

CRISIS (NEW YORK, N.Y.), THE (US/0011-1422) [01565450] **2259**

CRISIS (NOTRE DAME, IND.) (US) [14288189] **5028**

CRISIS (TORONTO) (CN/0227-5910) [08443942] **4583**

CRISOL NANTERRE (FR/0764-7611) [07647611] **663**

CRISP THESAURUS (US/1046-8692) [19675857] **3204**

"CRISS-CROSS" MONTREAL METROPOLITAIN (CN/1187-2608) [25423761] **5467**

"CRISS-CROSS" MONTREAL METROPOLITAIN (CN/1187-2608) [25423766] **5467**

CRISTALLO / CENTRO DI CULTURA DELL'ALTO ADIGE, IL (IT/0011-1449) [10347235] **3340**

CRISTIANESIMO NELLA STORIA (IT/0393-3598) [07543045] **4951**

CRISTIANISMO Y SOCIEDAD (BUENOS AIRES) (AG/0326-5633) [02259924] **4951**

CRISWELL THEOLOGICAL REVIEW (US/0892-5712) [15220533] **4951**

CRIT (US/0277-6863) [04597325] **296**

CRITERIO (AG/0011-1473) [01713626] **5028**

CRITERION (CHICAGO) (US/0590-0980) [01607530] 1091, **4951**

CRITERIOS HOY (VE) [24362667] **4951**

CRITIC; A CATHOLIC REVIEW OF BOOKS AND THE ARTS, THE (US/0011-149X) [01565456] **5028**

CRITIC (NEW YORK) *SUSPENDED.* (UK/0090-9831) [01785349] **4067**

CRITIC, THE (US/0011-149X) [02813544] 318, **3340**

CRITICA & UTOPIA (AG) [06020835] **3275**

CRITICA D'ARTE *CEASED.* (IT/0011-1511) [01565463] **348**

CRITICA DEL DIRITTO (IT/0390-0657) [04558958] **2957**

CRITICA GIUDIZIARIA (IT) [03699181] **2957**

CRITICA HISPANICA (US/0278-7261) [05380402] 3340, **3275**

CRITICA (LA JOLLA, CALIF.) (US/8755-3325) [11127556] **5243**

CRITICA LETTERARIA (IT/0390-0142) [02240786] **3378**

CRITICA MARXISTA (IT/0011-152X) [03662733] **4541**

CRITICA; REVISTA HISPANOAMERICANA DE FILOSOFIA (MX/0011-1503) [03112075] **4344**

CRITICA SOCIAL (BL) [02467935] **5281**

CRITICA SOCIALE (IT/0011-1538) [03653601] **4541**

CRITICA SOCIOLOGICA, LA (IT/0011-1546) [03637300] **5243**

CRITICAL ARTS (SA/0256-0046) [07936723] **1109**

CRITICAL BIBLIOGRAPHY OF FRENCH LITERATURE, A (US) [02727280] 3378, **3458**

CRITICAL CARE (US/0270-7462) [06460750] **3569**

● CRITICAL CARE ALERT (US/1067-9502) [27386033] **3569**

CRITICAL CARE CLINICS (US/0749-0704) [11078407] **3779**

● CRITICAL CARE MANAGEMENT (US/1070-4523) [28367020] **3569**

CRITICAL CARE MEDICINE (US/0090-3493) [01789720] **3723**

CRITICAL CARE NURSE (US/0279-5442) [07092948] **3854**

CRITICAL CARE NURSING CLINICS OF NORTH AMERICA (US/0899-5885) [18145596] **3854**

CRITICAL CARE NURSING QUARTERLY (US/0887-9303) [13448769] **3854**

CRITICAL CARE OUTLOOK *CEASED.* (US/0892-3930) [15181967] **3569**

CRITICAL DIGEST (US/0045-9070) [01565464] **5363**

CRITICAL ESSAYS ON AMERICAN LITERATURE (US) [08615866] **3378**

CRITICAL ESSAYS ON BRITISH LITERATURE (US) **3378**

CRITICAL ESSAYS ON WORLD LITERATURE (US) 3340, **3378**

CRITICAL GUIDE TO CATHOLIC REFERENCE BOOKS (US) [19124014] 1924, **5028**

CRITICAL GUIDES TO FRENCH TEXTS (UK) [09184824] **3378**

CRITICAL GUIDES TO SPANISH TEXTS (UK) [13133344] **3378**

CRITICAL HEALTH (SA) **3724**

CRITICAL INQUIRY (US/0093-1896) [02241746] **318**

CRITICAL ISCHAEMIA (UK/0956-2257) [I09562257] **3569**

CRITICAL ISSUES (WASHINGTON DC) (US/0363-6283) [02662303] **5197**

CRITICAL LEGAL ISSUES (US/1056-389X) [15742320] **2957**

CRITICAL MASS (BERKELEY, CA) *CEASED.* (US/0890-3654) [13672316] **4951**

CRITICAL MASS (HALIFAX) (CN/1180-193X) [23238173] 3379, **3462**

CRITICAL MATERIALS REGISTER *See* MICHIGAN CRITICAL MATERIALS REGISTER **2236**

CRITICAL MATRIX (US/1066-288X) [13313631] **5554**

CRITICAL PATH PROCESSING TERMINAL OPERATING PROCEDURES (US) [03775504] **2819**

CRITICAL PEDAGOGY NETWORK (AT) 5197, **1734**

CRITICAL PERSPECTIVES (US) [16116956] **318**

CRITICAL PERSPECTIVES ON ACCOUNTING (UK/1045-2354) [20049939] **742**

CRITICAL PERSPECTIVES ON CONTEMPORARY PSYCHOLOGY (US/0276-5330) [06767928] **4583**

CRITICAL PUBLIC HEALTH (UK/0958-1596) [I09581596] **4772**

CRITICAL QUARTERLY, THE (UK/0011-1562) [01565465] **3379**

CRITICAL REPORTS ON APPLIED CHEMISTRY (UK/0263-5917) [07267435] **973**

CRITICAL REVIEW (MELBOURNE), THE (AT/0070-1548) [02259929] **3340**

CRITICAL REVIEW (NEW YORK, N.Y.) (US/0891-3811) [14714365] **4470**

CRITICAL REVIEW OF BOOKS IN RELIGION (US/0894-8860) [16287050] **3340**

CRITICAL REVIEWS IN ANALYTICAL CHEMISTRY (US/1040-8347) [15335326] **1014**

CRITICAL REVIEWS IN BIOCHEMISTRY AND MOLECULAR BIOLOGY (US/1040-9238) [18575830] 452, **486**

CRITICAL REVIEWS IN BIOMEDICAL ENGINEERING (US/0278-940X) [07921410] **3691**

CRITICAL REVIEWS IN BIOTECHNOLOGY (US/0738-8551) [09660505] **3691**

CRITICAL REVIEWS IN CLINICAL LABORATORY SCIENCES (US/1040-8363) [01151594] **3894**

CRITICAL REVIEWS IN DIAGNOSTIC IMAGING (US/1040-8371) [12330600] **3940**

CRITICAL REVIEWS IN ENVIRONMENTAL CONTROL (US/1040-838X) [15335207] **2163**

● CRITICAL REVIEWS IN ENVIRONMENTAL SCIENCE AND TECHNOLOGY (US/1064-3389) [26251154] **2163**

CRITICAL REVIEWS IN EUKARYOTIC GENE EXPRESSION (US/1045-4403) [20114919] **486**

CRITICAL REVIEWS IN FOOD SCIENCE AND NUTRITION (US/1040-8398) [12330732] 4189, **2332**

CRITICAL REVIEWS IN IMMUNOLOGY (US/1040-8401) [18553639] **3668**

CRITICAL REVIEWS IN MICROBIOLOGY (US/1040-841X) [01422432] **561**

● CRITICAL REVIEWS IN MULTIPHASE SCIENCE AND TECHNOLOGY (US/1065-2388) [26535604] **5097**

CRITICAL REVIEWS IN NEUROBIOLOGY (US/0892-0915) [15076105] **3569**

CRITICAL REVIEWS IN NEUROSURGERY : CR (GW/0939-0146) [23835676] 3830, **3963**

CRITICAL REVIEWS IN ONCOGENESIS (US/0893-9675) [15716210] **3815**

CRITICAL REVIEWS IN ONCOLOGY/HEMATOLOGY (US/1040-8428) [12331173] 3771, **3815**

CRITICAL REVIEWS IN ORAL BIOLOGY AND MEDICINE (US/1045-4411) [20114961] **1319**

CRITICAL REVIEWS IN PHARMACOLOGY *CEASED.* (US/1069-4110) [28034085] **4298**

CRITICAL REVIEWS IN PHYSICAL AND REHABILITATION MEDICINE (US/0896-2960) [16994961] 3569, **507**

CRITICAL REVIEWS IN PLANT SCIENCES (US/0735-2689) [08901777] 2413, **507**

CRITICAL REVIEWS IN POULTRY BIOLOGY *See* POULTRY SCIENCE REVIEWS **218**

CRITICAL REVIEWS IN SOLID STATE AND MATERIALS SCIENCES (US/1040-8436) [07969290] **4401**

CRITICAL REVIEWS IN SURFACE CHEMISTRY (US/1049-9407) [21357477] **1051**

CRITICAL REVIEWS IN THERAPEUTIC DRUG CARRIER SYSTEMS (US/0743-4863) [10588544] **4298**

CRITICAL REVIEWS IN TOXICOLOGY (US/1040-8444) [01342710] **3980**

CRITICAL REVIEWS IN TROPICAL MEDICINE (US/0737-609X) [08750944] **3985**

CRITICAL SOCIOLOGY (US/0896-9205) [17335079] **5243**

CRITICAL STUDIES (AMSTERDAM, THE NETHERLANDS) (NE) [20696333] 3340, **3379**

CRITICAL STUDIES IN MASS COMMUNICATION (US/0739-3180) [09716729] **1109**

CRITICAL SURVEY (UK/0011-1570) [20102503] **3379**

CRITICAL TEXTS *SUSPENDED.* (US/0730-2304) [07973214] 5197, **3341**

CRITICAL THEORY (NE/0920-3060) [12753971] **3275**

CRITICAS DE LA ECONOMIA POLITICA *SUSPENDED.* (MX) [03827729] **1478**

CRITICISM (DETROIT) (US/0011-1589) [01565471] **2845**

CRITICON (FR) [06373698] **3379**

CRITIQUE (FR/0011-1600) [01565474] **3341**

CRITIQUE - BOLINGBROKE SOCIETY (US/0011-1619) [01565475] **3341**

CRITIQUE (CLANDEBOYE) (CN/0821-5561) [09688366] **4067**

CRITIQUE COMMUNISTE (FR) [06285782] **4541**

CRITIQUE (GLASGOW) (UK/0301-7605) [01792678] **4470**

CRITIQUE (LONDON) (UK/0954-7487) [19577189] **3205**

CRITIQUE OF ANTHROPOLOGY (UK/0308-275X) [02805710] **234**

CRITIQUE REGIONALE (BE/0770-0075) [15586366] **5243**

CRITIQUE SOCIALISTE (FR/0045-9089) [04567125] **4470**

CRITIQUES (MELBOURNE, VIC.) (AT) [19273188] **296**

CRITTENDEN HARD-TO-FINANCE DEALS *See* CRITTENDEN REPORT REAL ESTATE FINANCING **4836**

CRITTENDEN INCOME PROPERTY DEALS (US/0888-9147) [13034289] **4836**

CRITTENDEN INSURANCE MARKETS, COMMERCIAL LINES (US/0899-6350) [15024420] **2878**

CRITTENDEN MORTGAGE DIRECTORY (US/0271-3942) [06606066] **786**

CRITTENDEN PRESS, THE (US) [14183519] **5680**

CRITTENDEN REAL ESTATE BUYERS (US/0888-9139) [13039071] **4836**

CRITTENDEN REPORT REAL ESTATE FINANCING (US/0736-0339) [06675737] **4836**

CRIV SHEET, THE (US) [18602399] 2957, **3205**

CRM, BOLETIN DE INFORMACION : ORGANO DE COMUNICACION INTERNO (MX/0187-8565) [07510642] **2138**

● CRM MONOGRAPH SERIES / CENTRE DE RECHERCHES MATHEMATIQUES (US/1065-8599) [26779152] **3502**

● CRM PROCEEDINGS & LECTURE NOTES (US/1065-8580) [26779041] **3502**

CRNA (US/1048-2687) [20881699] 3854, **3682**

CROATIAN MEDICAL JOURNAL (CI/0353-9504) [I03539504] **3569**

CROATICA (CI) [03699334] **3379**

CROATICA CHEMICA ACTA (CI/0011-1643) [06396261] **973**

CROC (CN/0226-6083) [06511166] **3379**

CROC CLASSIQUE (CN/1183-8159) [25652188] **318**

CROCEVIA MERANO (IT/0394-6088) [I03946088] **4641**

● CROCHET DIGEST (US/1074-1798) [29614699] **5183**

CROCHET FANTASY (US/8750-8877) [11885359] **5183**

CROCHET PATTERNS BY HERRSCHNERS (US/0894-5659) [16138157] **5183**

CROCHET TODAY FASHIONS *See* CROCHET WORLD SPECIAL **5183**

CROCHET WORLD (US/0164-7962) [04355050] **5183**

CROCHET WORLD SPECIAL (US/1057-7076) [24101448] **5183**

CROCKER ART MUSEUM *See* ARTLETTER / CROCKER ART MUSEUM **342**

CROCKER COMMUNICATION RESOURCES NEWSLETTER (US/1042-217X) [18976067] 865, **663**

CROCKETT CO. SENTINEL, TRI-CO. NEWS, CROCKETT TIMES, THE (US/0746-0309) [09693542] **5745**

CROES LETTER, THE (US/1056-3377) [23667289] **372**

CROIRE AUJOURD'HUI (FR/0223-4734) [06693823] **5028**

CROISSANCE (FR) [22197307] **4519**

CROITRE (CN/0712-2292) [08737668] **4951**

CROIX, LA (DM) [01788613] **4951**

CROIX-ROUGE LIBANAISE *See* BULLETIN / CROIX-ROUGE LIBANAISE **4769**

CRONACHE DI CHIMICA (IT/0574-4741) [03048863] **973**

CRONACHE ECONOMICHE *SUSPENDED.* (IT/0011-1775) [04563531] 663, **1478**

CRONACHE ERCOLANESI (IT/0391-1535) [03637338] **3275**

CRONACHE FARMACEUTICHE (IT/0011-1783) [11446896] **4298**

CRONACHE PARLAMENTARI SICILIANE (IT) **4641**

CRONER'S EMPLOYMENT LAW (UK) **3146**

CRONER'S EUROPE (UK) **663**

CRONER'S EXPORT DIGEST (UK) [14122628] **830**

CRONER'S HEALTH & SAFETY AT WORK (UK/0967-8344) [I09678344] **2861**

CRONER'S MODEL BUSINESS CONTRACTS (UK) **663**

CRONER'S OFFICE COMPANION (UK) **4211**

CRONER'S PREMISES MANAGEMENT (UK/0967-621X) [I09676621X] **865**

CRONER'S REFERENCE BOOK FOR EMPLOYERS (UK/0070-1580) [19637077] **939**

CRONER'S REFERENCE BOOK FOR EXPORTERS (UK/0070-1599) [07584116] **830**

CRONER'S REFERENCE BOOK FOR IMPORTERS (UK/0070-1602) [17402462] 1924, **830**

CRONER'S REFERENCE BOOK FOR THE SELF EMPLOYED & SMALLER BUSINESS (UK) **663**

CRONER'S REFERENCE BOOK FOR VALUE ADDED TAX (UK) **4719**

CRONER'S ROAD TRANSPORT OPERATION (OF GOODS VEHICLES IN THE UNITED KINGDOM AND ON THE CONTINENT OF EUROPE) (UK/0070-1610) [00455964] **5380**

CRONER'S SUBSTANCES HAZARDOUS TO HEALTH (UK) **2227**

CRONICA DE INFORMACION LABORAL (SP) **1662**

CRONICA DE LA GUERRA ESPANOLA (AG/0590-1154) [04043911] **2730**

CRONICA GENERAL DEL URUGUAY (UY) [06515702] **2730**

CRONICA TRIBUTARIA / MINISTERIO DE HACIENDA, INSTITUTO ESTUDIOS FISCALES (SP) [17609957] **4719**

CROOKSTON TIMES (US) [01775733] **5695**

CROP AND LIVESTOCK ANNUAL SUMMARY (US/0743-6572) [02742122] **77**

CROP AND LIVESTOCK SERIES (US) [05392209] **77**

CROP AND WEATHER REPORT (CN/0701-7065) [03564892] 1424, **168**

CROP CONDITION REPORT : A REPORT COMMENTING ON CROP CONDITIONS TRIBUTARY TO ELEVATORS IN MINNESOTA, NORTH DAKOTA, AND SOUTH DAKOTA, BASED PRIMARILY ON MANAGERS' AND SUPERINTENDENTS' REPORTS DATED ... (US) [06777493] **169**

CROP IMPROVEMENT (II/0256-0933) [03785545] **169**

CROP PHYSIOLOGY ABSTRACTS (UK/0306-7556) [01967820] 169, **152**

CROP PRODUCTION / IOWA CROP AND LIVESTOCK REPORTING SERVICE (US) [06525248] **169**

CROP PRODUCTION SCIENCE (SW/1100-1186) [19645181] **169**

CROP PRODUCTION. SMALL GRAINS, ... ANNUAL SUMMARY AND .. CROP WINTER WHEAT AND RYE SEEDINGS (US) [10616770] **169**

CROP PRODUCTION (WASHINGTON, D.C.) (US/0363-8561) [01768298] **169**

CROP PROTECTION BULLETIN *CEASED.* (AT/1033-3967) [I10333967] **169**

CROP PROTECTION DIRECTORY UNITED KINGDOM ED (UK/0953-2463) [I09532463] **169**

CROP PROTECTION (GUILDFORD, SURREY) (UK/0261-2194) [08641877] 4244, **169**

CROP PROTECTION IN NORTHERN BRITAIN (UK/0260-485X) [17234755] **169**

CROP PROTECTION MONTHLY (UK) **169**

CROP PROTECTION NEWSLETTER (CN/0225-5774) [06133166] **169**

CROP PROTECTION RESEARCH (US/0733-2068) [08107540] 169, **4244**

CROP REPORT (AT) **77**

CROP REPORT / ALBERTA WHEAT POOL (CN) [06777874] **169**

CROP REPORT / SASKATCHEWAN WHEAT POOL (CN/0843-6894) [20983208] **169**

CROP RESEARCH (HISAR) (II/0970-4884) [20900442] **169**

CROP RESEARCH NEWS (NZ/0110-1978) [02235079] **169**

CROP SCIENCE (US/0011-183X) [01565498] **169**

CROP VALUES (WASHINGTON, D.C.) (US/0884-2329) [10254862] **169**

CROPS AND LIVESTOCK SERIES / SOUTH CAROLINA CROPS REPORTING SERVICE *See* CROP AND LIVESTOCK SERIES **77**

CROPS AND PASTURES, TASMANIA / AUSTRALIAN BUREAU OF STATISTICS (AT/0519-5357) [08312465] **169**

CROPS AND PASTURES, WESTERN AUSTRALIA *See* SUMMARY OF CROPS, WESTERN AUSTRALIA **157**

CROPS / IOWA *See* IOWA CROP REPORT **175**

CROPS (TOPEKA, KAN.) (US/0279-9405) [04078173] **169**

CROPS, WESTERN AUSTRALIA *See* SUMMARY OF CROPS, WESTERN AUSTRALIA **157**

CROQUILOU *CEASED.* (FR) **1062**

CROQUIS (SP/0212-5633) [14627990] **296**

CROSBY COUNTY NEWS AND THE CROSBYTON REVIEW (US) [15681035] **5748**

CROSBY VOICE : NEWSLETTER OF THE VICTORIAN BING CROSBY SOCIETY, THE (AT) [12534808] **4113**

CROSBYTON REVIEW, THE (US) [14077650] **5748**

CROSS & COCKADE GREAT BRITAIN JOURNAL (UK) [04227905] 2614, **4040**

CROSS-CANADA COMMENT (CN/0319-843X) [01994471] **663**

CROSS COUNTRY (CN/0318-6075) [01619667] **3462**

CROSS-COUNTRY CONNECTION, THE *CEASED.* (CN/0842-5205) [19568652] **5783**

CROSS COUNTRY JOURNAL (US/0746-083X) [09734930] **4892**

CROSS COUNTRY SKIER (US/0278-9213) [07900362] **4892**

CROSS COUNTRY STITCHING (US/1063-9950) [20803620] **5183**

CROSS COUNTY GENEALOGICAL PUBLICATION (US/0883-1009) [10727978] **2444**

CROSS-CULTURAL PSYCHOLOGY BULLETIN (CN/0710-068X) [08103096] **4583**

●CROSS-CULTURAL RESEARCH (US/1069-3971) [28013395] **5197**

CROSS-CULTURAL RESEARCH AND METHODOLOGY SERIES (US/0271-9177) [06771319] **5197**

CROSS CURRENT (UK/0260-6313) [12071255] 4951, **1734**

CROSS CURRENTS (US/0011-1953) [01565510] **4951**

CROSS CURRENTS (US) [06056162] 2259, **2650**

CROSS CURRENTS *SUSPENDED.* (JA/0289-1239) [06342278] **3275**

CROSS CURRENTS (ANN ARBOR, MICH.) *CEASED.* (US/0748-0164) [09579579] 3379, **3275**

CROSS PLAINS REVIEW (CROSS PLAINS, TEX.) (US) [14077599] **5748**

CROSS POINT (US/1064-4490) [18936145] **4951**

CROSS RHYTHMS (UK) **4113**

CROSS SECTION (AT) **3502**

CROSS SECTION (II) [01797749] **830**

CROSS SECTIONS (RICHMOND, VA.) (US/0747-5543) [10756139] **786**

CROSS STITCH (AT/1037-339X) 2773, **5183**

CROSS STITCH & COUNTRY CRAFTS (US/0886-6600) [12966173] **5183**

CROSS STITCH AUSTRALIA (AT) **5183**

CROSS STITCH! MAGAZINE (US/1056-7542) [23845549] **372**

CROSS-STITCH QUICK & EASY (US/1048-3969) [20942600] **372**

CROSS STITCHER, THE (US/1055-2871) [23133554] **5183**

CROSS TIMBERS REVIEW *CEASED.* (US/0890-8885) [10864168] **2845**

CROSSCURRENTS (US) [14198649] **3462**

CROSSCURRENTS (JA) [05845339] **2650**

CROSSCURRENTS (NEW BRUNSWICK, N.J.) (US/1053-9778) [17610987] **234**

CROSSCURRENTS (SASKATOON) (CN/0704-6588) [03887227] 4470, **318**

CROSSCURRENTS (WESTLAKE VILLAGE, CALIF.) (US/0739-2354) [09098889] **3379**

CROSSE CITY BUSINESS, LA (US) [11731928] **663**

CROSSFACE, THE (US/0273-9135) [07015020] **4892**

CROSSFIELD CHRONICLE (CN/0822-8299) [10441472] **5783**

CROSSLINK, THE (US) [05291427] **5281**

CROSSOSOMA (US/0891-9100) [10870069] **507**

CROSSROAD TRAILS (US/0735-6196) [08252735] **2444**

CROSSROADS (DE KALB, ILL.) (US/0741-2037) [09588010] **2503**

CROSSROADS (OAKLAND, CALIF.) (US/1051-0575) [21815449] **4470**

CROSSROADS (SHOAL LAKE, MAN.) (CN) [09951432] **5783**

CROSSROADS (SPRINGDALE, ARK.) (US/1044-5544) [18269621] **5281**

●CROSSROADS (SUNNYVALE, CALIF.) (US/1065-6863) [26679375] **4951**

●CROSSROADS (UNIVERSITY, MISS.) (US/1065-9110) [26790790] **2730**

CROSSSTITCH SAMPLER (US/1054-1551) [22769541] **5183**

CROSSTALK AND ANGLICAN JOURNAL EPISCOPAL (CN/0845-4795) [20243838] **5058**

CROSSTIES (US/0097-4536) [01565511] **2378**

CROSSVILLE CHRONICLE (US) [12846719] **5745**

●CROSSWORD CHALLENGE (US/1065-2922) [26572170] **4859**

CROSSWORD TREAT (US/0194-3154) [05396029] **4859**

CROSSWORD VARIETIES (US/0194-3162) [05430237] **4859**

CROSSWORDS GALORE (US/0743-7005) [10650071] **4859**

CROSSWORDS TO RELAX WITH (US/1058-4781) [24309352] **4859**

CROSSWORDS (WALNUT CREEK, CALIF.) (US/1061-6519) [25387573] 4892, **4081**

CROSSWORLD (LONDON, ONT.) (CN/0225-3992) [06045661] **2908**

CROTON REVIEW (US/0741-6210) [04459567] **3379**

CROWLEY POST-SIGNAL, THE (US) [12758846] **5683**

CROWLEY REVIEW (US/1041-3081) [17795880] **2332**

CROWN (CH) **2503**

CROWN JEWELS OF THE WIRE (US/0884-7983) [12434608] **1153**

CROWN LONDON (UK/0045-9127) [I00459127] **3275**

CROWN OFFICE DIGEST (UK) **2957**

CROWN POINT REGISTER, THE (US) [11021804] **5663**

CROWN ZELLERBACH CORPORATION. CENTRAL RESEARCH *See* FORESTRY RESEARCH NOTE (CAMAS) **2382**

CROWNED WITH THORNS (JA/0911-7482) [I09117482] **4506**

CROWN'S NEWSLETTER (CN/0319-8510) [01994704] **3106**

CROW'S (US) [22620708] **2378**

CROW'S BUYER'S & SELLER'S GUIDE TO THE FOREST PRODUCTS INDUSTRIES (US) [10597268] **2400**

CROW'S PLYWOOD GUIDE (US) [01487540] **2400**

CROW'S WEEKLY MARKET REPORT OF LUMBER & PANEL PRODUCTS (US) [23114128] **2400**

CRP NOTIZIE **SUSPENDED.** (IT) **4772**

CRREL BENCHNOTES : U.S. ARMY CORPS OF ENGINEERS INFORMATION EXCHANGE BULLETIN (US) [02977171] **1970**

CRREL REPORT (US/0501-5782) [02452700] **5097**

CRS PUBLICATIONS' CAREER OPPORTUNITY INDEX (EAST-SOUTH-CENTRAL) (US/0897-909X) [17662129] **4203**

CRS PUBLICATIONS' CAREER OPPORTUNITY INDEX (WESTERN) (US/0898-218X) [17755944] **4203**

CRS REVIEW **CEASED.** (US/1045-9170) [19371798] **4470**

CRSCL NEWSLETTER (CN/0820-8247) [10036602] **3341**

CRSP DAILY EXCESS RETURNS FILE (US/1052-3456) [12882164] **895**

CRSP INDICES FILES (US/1054-4437) [18804931] **895**

CRSS DE QUEBEC (QUEBEC) *See* RAPPORT ANNUEL - CONSEIL REGIONAL DE LA SANTE ET DES SERVICES SOCIAUX DE QUEBEC **5303**

CRSSS 09 (CN/0701-8967) [08045916] **5281**

CRU ENERGY MONITOR *See* OIL MARKET TRENDS **4269**

CRU METAL MONITOR (UK) **4000**

CRUCIBLE (UK/0011-2100) [04562666] **4951**

CRUCIBLE (MERCEDES, TEX.), THE (US/8756-1247) [11477691] **4951**

CRUCIBLE (TORONTO) (CN/0381-8047) [02585353] 1892, **5097**

CRUCIBLE (WILSON, N.C.) (US/0888-4730) [08186348] **3379**

CRUCIFERAE NEWSLETTER (UK/0263-9459) [09165374] 2413, **77**

CRUDE OIL AND GAS NOMINATIONS (US) **4254**

CRUDE OIL NOMINATIONS AND PURCHASES BY DISTRICT (US) **4254**

CRUDE PETROLEUM AND NATURAL GAS INDUSTRY (CN/0068-7103) [02324130] **4254**

CRUDE PETROLEUM AND NATURAL GAS PRODUCTION (CN/0702-6846) [02248924] **4254**

CRUISE DIGEST (US/0886-5604) [11713590] **5467**

CRUISE DIGEST REPORTS *See* PORTHOLE (DEERFIELD BEACH, FLA.) **5489**

CRUISE INDUSTRY NEWS (ANNUAL) (US/1047-3378) [20666716] **5467**

CRUISE INDUSTRY NEWS (NEWSLETTER) (US/0893-1240) [15364426] **5467**

CRUISE INDUSTRY NEWS QUARTERLY, THE (US/0893-1240) [25641788] 5448, **5467**

CRUISE MAGAZINE (US/0897-5078) [16466963] **5467**

CRUISE TRAVEL MAGAZINE (US/0199-5111) [05952448] **5467**

CRUISE VACATIONS *See* CRUISES & TOURS **5467**

CRUISER (1985), THE (US/0897-313X) [12905255] **2378**

●CRUISES & TOURS (US/1060-0086) [24877827] **5467**

CRUISING AROUND THE WORLD (US/0744-6004) [08423987] **5467**

CRUISING HELMSMAN (AT/0812-4086) [08124086] **593**

CRUISING WORLD (US/0098-3519) [02241702] **593**

CRUSADER (CENTERVILLE, IND.) (US) [13053256] **5663**

CRUSADER (MEMPHIS) (US/0011-2151) [02897465] **5058**

CRUSADER'S ALMANAC, THE (US) [04633232] **1924**

CRUSTACEANA (NE/0011-216X) [01565523] **5581**

CRUSTACEANA. SUPPLEMENT **CEASED.** (NE/0167-6563) [04087226] **5581**

CRUX (CN/0011-2186) [10135705] **4951**

CRUX MATHEMATICORUM (CN/0705-0348) [04039779] **3502**

CRUX OF THE NEWS (US/0591-2296) [06875530] **4952**

CRUX (PRETORIA) (SA/0250-0035) [05916056] 1892, **3275**

CRYO LETTERS (UK/0143-2044) [06888267] 477, **452**

CRYOBIOLOGY (US/0011-2240) [00890697] **452**

CRYOGAS INTERNATIONAL (US/1052-0139) [22166404] 1023, 4401, **2112**

CRYOGENICS (GUILFORD) (UK/0011-2275) [01565530] **4401**

CRYONICS (RIVERSIDE, CALIF.) (US/1054-4305) [22473860] **3569**

CRYPTIC SCHOLAR, THE (US/1062-6182) [25357256] **611**

CRYPTOGAMIC BOTANY (GW/0935-2147) [20292265] **507**

CRYPTOGAMIC STUDIES (GW/0931-4113) [19340263] **507**

CRYPTOGAMICA HELVETICA (SW/0257-9421) [13618744] **507**

CRYPTOGAMIE. ALGOLOGIE (FR/0181-1568) [06852829] **452**

CRYPTOGAMIE. BRYOLOGIE, LICHENOLOGIE (FR/0181-1576) [06404341] **507**

CRYPTOGAMIE. MYCOLOGIE (1979) (FR/0181-1584) [06596406] 452, **507**

CRYPTOGRAPHY MAGAZINE (US/0732-5495) [08407509] 4859, **2773**

CRYPTOLOG (US/0740-7602) [09983261] **4176**

CRYPTOLOGIA (US/0161-1194) [02935836] **1226**

CRYPTOSYSTEMS JOURNAL (US/0899-8159) [18231633] **1181**

CRYPTOZOOLOGY (US/0736-7023) [09306748] 4241, **5581**

CRYSTAL MIRROR (US/0097-7209) [01799320] 4344, **5021**

●CRYSTAL MOUNTAIN MINING QUARTERLY (US/1062-8797) [25783324] **1439**

CRYSTAL RESEARCH AND TECHNOLOGY (1979) (GW/0232-1300) [05159520] **1031**

CRYSTAL ROBBINSDALE POSTNEWS (US) [22188355] **5695**

●CRYSTALLOGRAPHY REPORTS (US/1063-7745) [26141038] **1031**

CRYSTALLOGRAPHY REVIEWS (US/0889-311X) [13855436] **1031**

CRYSTALS (GW/0172-5076) [04683991] **1032**

CSA FRATERNAL LIFE (SOCIETY) *See* CSA JOURNAL, THE **5230**

CSA JOURNAL *See* CSA JOURNAL, THE **5230**

CSA JOURNAL, THE (US/0195-9050) [12404886] **5230**

CSA NEUROSCIENCES ABSTRACTS (US/0141-7711) [09271323] 3830, **3656**

●CSAH APPORTIONMENT DATA (US) [29508791] **5380**

●CSAP PREVENTION PIPELINE / CENTER FOR SUBSTANCE ABUSE PREVENTION, THE (US) [27089627] **1342**

CSAS NEWSLETTER (CN/0714-8240) [09086721] **209**

CSCC NEWS (CN/0826-1024) [10845357] **973**

●CSD BULLETIN (SA) [30826323] **5197**

CSE REPORT (US/0575-4550) [01552511] **1819**

CSELT TECHNICAL REPORTS (IT/0393-2648) [14414900] **1153**

CSFM JOURNAL (US) [19781166] **2288**

CSG BACKGROUNDER / COUNCIL OF STATE GOVERNMENTS **CEASED.** (US) [09092259] **4641**

CSI FEDERAL REGISTER ABSTRACTS (MASTER EDITION) **CEASED.** (US/0738-646X) [09635822] **4641**

CSIA DISCUSSION PAPER (US) [23899064] **4519**

CSIA NEWS (US/0897-120X) [16669730] **4519**

CSIA STUDIES IN INTERNATIONAL SECURITY (US) [24919098] **4519**

CSIO COMMUNICATIONS (II/0304-9841) [11012518] **5097**

CSIR ANNUAL REPORT (SA) [06180986] **5097**

CSIR HANDBOOK (II) [09317198] **5097**

CSIR RESEARCH REPORT (SA/0584-2840) [02077128] **611**

CSIRO ABSTRACTS **CEASED.** (AT/0007-912X) [01538000] **5097**

CSIRO DIRECTORY (AT) [01814844] **5097**

CSIRO DIVISION OF ATMOSPHERIC RESEARCH RESEARCH REPORT (AT/0817-0576) [17965186] **1424**

CSIRO DIVISION OF ENTOMOLOGY REPORT (AT/0726-6588) [09113421] **5581**

CSIRO INDEX **CEASED.** (AT/0311-5836) [04971329] **5097**

CSIRO MARINE LABORATORIES *See* REPORT - CSIRO MARINE LABORATORIES **2311**

CSIRO RANGELANDS RESEARCH (AT) [09749190] 5508, **2191**

CSIRO SPACE INDUSTRY NEWS (AT/1037-5759) [I10375759] **17**

CSIRO TEXTILE NEWS (AT/0312-5211) [04255754] **5350**

CSIRO TEXTILE PHYSICS (AT) [13515344] **5350**

CSIRO WATER RESOURCES SERIES (AT/1032-1403) [22202602] **5532**

CSIRONET (ORGANIZATION : AUSTRALIA) *See* ANNUAL REPORT / CSIRONET **1170**

CSIS AFRICA NOTES (US/0736-9506) [09262925] **2499**

CSKW MEDEDELINGEN (BE) **5197**

CSL (NEW YORK, N.Y.) (US/0883-9980) [08321538] **3379**

CSLI LECTURE NOTES (US) [14700786] **3502**

CSM'S ... EQUIPMENT BUYERS' GUIDE FOR THE FOOD INDUSTRY (US/0277-1268) [07438365] **2332**

CSN. CONVENIENCE STORE NEWS *See* CONVENIENCE STORE NEWS **660**

CSNI REPORT (US/0254-3427) [06399723] **2154**

CSO BUSINESS BULLETINS (UK) **663**

CSONGRAD MEGYEI KONYVTAROS (HU/0133-705X) [I0133705X] **3205**

CSP. CRITICAL SOCIAL POLICY (UK/0261-0183) [09136744] **4541**

CSP DIRECTORY OF SUPPLIERS OF EDUCATIONAL FOREIGN LANGUAGE MATERIALS (US/0162-5977) [04185264] **1892**

CSPP BOLETIN (CK) [13723129] **4507**

CSR ADVISOR, THE (US/1044-9884) [19964113] **2878**

CSR HOTLINE (US/0894-6418) [16158455] **1153**

●CSRO. CANADIAN SPINAL RESEARCH ORGANIZATION (CN/1193-7343) [27203173] **3569**

CSSA SPECIAL PUBLICATION - CROP SCIENCE SOCIETY OF AMERICA (US/0895-9978) [10128371] **169**

CSSE CONTACT (CN/0713-3421) [09084916] **2861**

CSSR BULLETIN (US) **4952**

CSSR DIRECTORY OF DEPARTMENTS OF RELIGIOUS STUDIES IN NORTH AMERICA (US) **4952**

CSSR ZDRAVOTNICTVI (XR/0514-2431) [05433932] **4772**

CSSS DIGEST : CENTER FOR THE STUDY OF SPORT IN SOCIETY **CEASED.** (US) [22517683] **4892**

CSSS NEWSLETTER (CN/0845-308X) [20365569] **170**

CSSSC MONOGRAPH (II) [08444000] **5197**

CST TECHNOLOGY TRANSACTIONS (AT) **5097**

CSTC REVUE (FR) [04050701] **611**

CSU COLLEGE YEAR REPORT (US) [23088056] **1819**

C'T (GW/0724-8679) [I07248679] **1181**

CT DEC INFORMATION (FR) **2112**

CT INFOS PARIS (FR/1165-4651) [I11654651] **2332**

CTA ACTION (1986) (US/0896-7326) [17283179] **1862**

CTA QUARTERLY (US/0361-2791) [02155464] **5380**

CTBA INFO (FR) **2400**

CTC BULLETIN : OCCASIONAL BULLETIN OF THE COMMISSION ON THEOLOGICAL CONCERNS, CHRISTIAN CONFERENCE OF ASIA (SI) [08338043] **4952**

CTC NEWSLETTER (AT/1038-2062) [I10382062] **663**

CTC REPORTER *See* TRANSNATIONAL CORPORATIONS **716**

CTD POCKET GUIDE, THE (CN/0713-813X) [08996142] **2781**

●CTDNEWS (PHILADELPHIA, PA.) (US/1062-6743) [25692539] **3569**

CTFA COSMETIC JOURNAL (US/0090-0591) [01538003] **403**

CTFA ... INTERNATIONAL BUYERS' GUIDE (US/1058-4080) [24250350] **403**

CTHULHU CALLS (US) [02536268] **3379**

CTI JOURNAL (US) **2112**

CTI PLUS [COMPUTER FILE] (UK) 5098, **5174**

CTISS FILE (UK/0959-3004) [I09593004] **1222**

CTN LONDON (UK/0955-2758) [I09552758] **663**

CTNS BULLETIN (US/0889-8243) [12366234] **5098**

CTOSIAN (US) **1245**

CTT NEWS & REPORTS *See* CAPITAL TAXES NEWS AND REPORTS **4717**

Alphabetical Title Index

CTVD, CINEMA, TV DIGEST (US/0007-9219) [02058605] 4067, **1109**

● CTVRTLETNIK KRESTANSKE VEDY. BIBLICKE LEKCE (US/1061-673X) [25404281] **5016**

CU AMIGA (UK) **1181**

CU DIRECTORY (US/0363-745X) [02533665] **384**

CU IN CHICAGO (US/8750-6114) [11589775] **2532**

CUADERNO DE ACTUALIZACION TECNICA - ESTACION EXPERIMENTAL AGROPECUARIA MANFREDI (AG/0327-4950) [I03274950] **77**

CUADERNO DE DERECHO INTERNACIONAL PRIVADO (UY) [04508247] **3126**

CUADERNO LITERARIO AZOR (SP) [02578787] **3379**

CUADERNOS (CK) [01786443] **1478**

CUADERNOS AFRO-AMERICANOS (PE) [02243958] **2259**

CUADERNOS AMERICANOS (MX/0011-2356) [01565536] **2730**

CUADERNOS (CENTRO DE INFORMACION Y DOCUMENTACION AFRICANAS (MADRID, SPAIN)) (SP) [19930880] **2639**

CUADERNOS COLOMBIANOS (CK/0302-3087) [01793588] **2551**

CUADERNOS DE ACCION SOCIAL *CEASED.* (SP/0213-5612) **5197**

CUADERNOS DE ACTUALIDAD INTERNACIONAL (VE/0798-0841) [I07980841] **5197**

CUADERNOS DE ALDEEU (US/0740-0632) [09869507] **3205**

CUADERNOS DE ALGEBRA (SP) [14922776] **3502**

CUADERNOS DE ANTROPOLOGIA (CIUDAD DE GUATEMALA) (GT/0590-160X) [01472349] **234**

CUADERNOS DE ARAGON (SP/0590-1626) [04093260] **2684**

CUADERNOS DE ARQUITECTURA MESOAMERICANA (MX/0185-5131) [12883050] **296**

CUADERNOS DE ARQUITECTURA VIRREINAL (MX/0185-8572) [20807429] **296**

CUADERNOS DE ARTE COLONIAL (SP/0213-6716) [16134356] **348**

CUADERNOS DE ARTE DE LA UNIVERSIDAD DE GRANADA (SP/0210-962X) [02620250] **318**

CUADERNOS DE ARTE E ICONOGRAFIA / FUNDACION UNIVERSITARIA ESPAÑOLA, SEMINARIO DE ARTE MARQUES DE LOZOYA (SP) [19052799] **348**

CUADERNOS DE BIBLIOGRAFIA ESPAÑOLA. SERIE A : DERECHO (SP) [01794888] **3080**

CUADERNOS DE BIOESTADISTICA Y SUS APLICACIONES INFORMATICAS (SP) **3569**

CUADERNOS DE CIDAMO (MX) [22783453] **1662**

CUADERNOS DE COMUNICACION & INFORMACION (PE) [06502043] **1109**

● CUADERNOS DE DIFUSION / ESCUELA DE ADMINISTRACION DE NEGOCIOS PARA GRADUADOS, ESAN (PE) [26790897] **865**

CUADERNOS DE ECONOMIA (SP/0210-0266) [02390730] **1554**

CUADERNOS DE ECONOMIA (SANTIAGO) (CL/0716-0046) [01589906] 5243, **1478**

CUADERNOS DE ECONOMIA SOCIAL (AG/0325-9757) [06382199] **1478**

CUADERNOS DE EDUCACION *SUSPENDED.* (VE) [03105140] **1734**

CUADERNOS DE ESTUDIOS BORJANOS (SP) [06020772] **2684**

CUADERNOS DE ESTUDIOS CASPOLINOS / GRUPO CULTURAL CASPOLINO, INSTITUCION FERNANDO EL CATOLICO (SP/0211-7649) [19756995] **2684**

CUADERNOS DE ESTUDIOS GALLEGOS *CEASED.* (SP/0210-847X) [02067860] **2684**

CUADERNOS DE ETNOLOGIA Y ETNOGRAFIA DE NAVARRA (SP/0590-1871) [06083831] **234**

CUADERNOS DE FAMILIA (AG) [08998273] **3120**

CUADERNOS DE FARMACIA (SP) **4298**

CUADERNOS DE FILOLOGIA CLASICA (SP) [03672097] **3275**

CUADERNOS DE FILOLOGIA CLASICA. ESTUDIOS LATINOS / FACULTAD DE FILOLGIA, DEPARTAMENTO DE FILOLOGIA LATINA, UNIVERSIDAD COMPLUTENSE DE MADRID (SP) [27535994] **1076**

CUADERNOS DE FILOLOGIA. II, STUDIA LINGUISTICA HISPANICA (SP/0214-6746) [08369920] **3276**

CUADERNOS DE FILOLOGIA. III, LITERATURAS, ANALISIS (SP/0214-6738) [08369860] **3379**

CUADERNOS DE FILOSOFIA (CL) [03641612] **4344**

CUADERNOS DE FILOSOFIA LATINOAMERICANA / ORGANO DE DIVULGACION DE LA FACULTAD DE FILOSOFIA Y EL CENTRO DE ENSEÑANZA DESESCOLARIZADA DE LA UNIVERSIDAD SANTO TOMAS (CK/0120-8462) [10378555] **4344**

CUADERNOS DE FILOSOFIA Y LETRAS (CK/0120-0992) [08706136] 3379, **4344**

CUADERNOS DE FITOPATOLOGIA (SP) **507**

CUADERNOS DE HISTORIA CONTEMPORANEA (SP/0214-400X) [22578091] **2614**

CUADERNOS DE HISTORIA DE ESPAÑA (AG/0325-1195) [01565544] **2684**

CUADERNOS DE HISTORIA DEL ARTE (AG/0070-1688) [I00701688] **348**

CUADERNOS DE HISTORIA EECONOMICA DE CATALUÑA (SP/0045-9186) [02827533] **1554**

CUADERNOS DE HISTORIA MODERNA (SP/0214-4018) [22578087] **2614**

CUADERNOS DE HISTORIA (SANTIAGO, CHILE) (CL) [09353964] **2614**

CUADERNOS DE INFORMACION ECONOMICA (SP) **1554**

CUADERNOS DE INVESTIGACION FILOLOGICA (SP/0211-0547) [05764904] 3379, **3276**

CUADERNOS DE INVESTIGACION HISTORICA (SP/0210-6272) [04980974] **2684**

CUADERNOS DE INVESTIGACION HISTORICA (GW) [11299480] **2614**

CUADERNOS DE INVESTIGACION HISTORICA BROCAR (SP/0214-4670) [I02144670] **2614**

CUADERNOS DE LA BIBLIOTECA ISLAMICA "FELIX MARIA PAREJA" (SP/0213-6465) [I02136465] **414**

CUADERNOS DE LA CONSEJERIA DE TRABAJO Y SEGURIDAD SOCIAL DE SANTA CRUZ DE TENERIFE (SP) **4772**

CUADERNOS DE LA FACULTAD DE HUMANIDADES (PR) [06136368] **2845**

CUADERNOS DE MARCHA (UY) [13720010] **2551**

CUADERNOS DE MEDICINA PSICOSOMATICA (SP/1132-0273) [I11320273] **3759**

CUADERNOS DE NUESTRA AMERICA (CU) [12169552] 5197, **4470**

CUADERNOS DE ORIENTACION "ESTUDIAR PARA LUCHAR". SERIE ESTUDIOS E INVESTIGACIONES (UY) [24157275] **1662**

CUADERNOS DE PEDAGOGIA (SP/0210-0630) [I02100630] **1734**

CUADERNOS DE POETICA (DR/0257-6457) [11406532] **3379**

CUADERNOS DE POSTGRADO : PUBLICACIONES DE LA UNIVERSIDAD AUTONOMA DE SANTO DOMINGO (DR) [11268714] **5363**

CUADERNOS DE PREHISTORIA DE LA UNIVERSIDAD DE GRANADA (SP) [05281162] **234**

CUADERNOS DE PREHISTORIA Y ARQUEOLOGIA CASTELLONENSES (SP/0212-1824) [12720186] **266**

CUADERNOS DE PSICOLOGIA (BARCELONA, SPAIN) (SP/0211-3481) [11013547] **4583**

CUADERNOS DE SECCION. MEDICINA / SOCIEDAD ES ESTUDIOS VASCOS (SP) [19261629] **3894**

CUADERNOS DE SECCION. MUSICA / EUSKO-IKASKUNTZA, SOCIEDAD DE ESTUDIOS VASCOS (SP/0213-0815) [15259809] **4113**

CUADERNOS DE SEMIOTICA (UY) [05394530] **4344**

CUADERNOS DE TEATRO CLASICO (SP/0214-1388) [20401908] **5363**

CUADERNOS DE TEOLOGIA (AG) [06780383] **4952**

CUADERNOS DE TRADUCCION E INTERPRETACION (SP/0212-0550) [10054634] **3276**

CUADERNOS DEL BANCO NACIONAL DE PANAMA (PN) [02242423] **786**

CUADERNOS DEL CENDES (VE) [13056427] **1478**

CUADERNOS DEL CLAEH (UY) [13032880] **5197**

CUADERNOS DEL SUR (AG/0070-1769) [02259969] **2730**

CUADERNOS DEL TERCER MUNDO (UY) [03495310] **1554**

CUADERNOS DO LABORATORIO XEOLOXICO DE LAXE (SP/0213-4497) [I02134497] **2559**

CUADERNOS ECONOMICOS DE I.C.E (SP) [06484759] **1478**

CUADERNOS FORMACION CONTINUADA. AEFA (SP) **3569**

CUADERNOS GEOGRAFICOS DEL SUR (CL) [04254173] **2559**

CUADERNOS HISPANOAMERICANOS (SP/0011-250X) [01565548] **2514**

CUADERNOS JURIDICOS (DR) [04338393] **2957**

CUADERNOS JURIDICOS (CL) [05201640] **2957**

CUADERNOS NACIONALES (AG) [01794766] **1554**

CUADERNOS OCEANOGRAFICOS (VE/0590-3351) [01611984] 554, **1448**

CUADERNOS PARA INVESTIGACION DE LA LITERATURA HISPANICA (SP/0210-0061) [04927145] **3379**

CUADERNOS POLITICOS *SUSPENDED.* (MX) [02243187] **5197**

CUADERNOS PREHISPANICOS (MX) [05725312] **2730**

CUADERNOS REFORMA (SP) **4470**

CUADERNOS SALMANTINOS DE FILOSOFIA (SP) [02767069] **4344**

CUADERNOS SIGMUND FREUD (AG) [03101642] **4583**

CUADERNOS VALENCIANOS DE HISTORIA DE LA MEDICINA Y DE LA CIENCIA (SP) [04557197] **3569**

CUADERNOS - VENEZUELA. UNIVERSIDAD CENTRAL, CARACAS. ESCUELA DE PERIODISMO (VE/0506-6131) [01489215] **3205**

CUB CLUES (US/0889-437X) [13997145] **17**

CUBA AZUCAR (CU/0590-2916) [02259982] **2332**

CUBA BUSINESS (UK/0951-4708) [17275895] **663**

CUBA. DIRECCION GENERAL DE NORMAS *See* NORMA CUBANA **155**

CUBA, ECONOMIA PLANIFICADA (CU/0864-1420) [14815434] **1478**

CUBA. FISCALIA GENERAL DE LA REPUBLICA *See* REVISTA JURIDICA **3042**

CUBA FOREIGN TRADE (CU) [07107386] 1634, **663**

CUBA FREE PRESS, THE (US) [20179213] **5703**

CUBA, HALF-YEARLY ECONOMIC REPORT (CU/0138-7766) [27403900] **1478**

CUBA HISTORICAL SOCIETY (N.Y.) *See* NEWSLETTER - CUBA HISTORICAL SOCIETY, THE **2749**

CUBA, INFORME ECONOMICO TRIMESTRAL (CU) [11047322] **1478**

CUBA INTERNACIONAL *SUSPENDED.* (CU/0011-2593) [01565557] **2486**

CUBA PATRIOT AND FREE PRESS (US/0746-9969) [10453262] **5715**

● CUBA REPORT, THE (US/1062-0672) [25517044] **2614**

CUBA SOCIALISTA (HAVANA, CUBA : 1981) (CU) [08560375] **4541**

CUBA TABACO (CU) [06643427] **5372**

CUBA UPDATE (US/0196-0830) [09476874] **4541**

CUBAN CHRONOLOGY (US/0195-8135) [05624286] **4519**

CUBAN HERITAGE *SUSPENDED.* (US/0894-2714) [15925337] **5197**

CUBAN JOURNAL OF AGRICULTURAL SCIENCE *SUSPENDED.* (CU/0253-5815) [04142557] **77**

CUBAN STUDIES (US/0361-4441) [01665872] **2730**

CUCINA BELLA E BUONA (IT) **5554**

CUCINA ITALIANA (IT) **2486**

CUCURBIT GENETICS COOPERATIVE *See* REPORT / CUCURBIT GENETICS COOPERATIVE **184**

CUDAHY REMINDER-ENTERPRISE (CUDAHY, WIS. : 1984) (US) [13013159] **5766**

CUDZIE JAZYKY (XO) [05512409] **3276**

CUE (HOLLAND PATENT), THE (US/0197-7962) [04574271] **5363**

CUE MAGAZINE (US/1064-2579) [26241480] **4850**

CUE OF THETA ALPHA PHI *See* CUE (HOLLAND PATENT), THE **5363**

CUE SHEET, THE (US/0888-9015) [13769635] 4067, **4113**

CUE TRACK (CN/0229-1533) [07821218] 5316, **4113**

CUE (VANCOUVER) (CN/0712-2519) [08898803] 1892, **1222**

CUED ECONOMIC DEVELOPMENTS (US/8755-8718) [10748360] **1603**

CUED SPEECH ANNUAL (US/1041-6226) [12617590] **3276**

CUED SPEECH CENTER LINES (US/1041-6196) [16395483] **4386**

CUED — Alphabetical Title Index

CUED SPEECH JOURNAL (US/1059-8243) [23097233] **4386**

CUED SPEECH NEWS (US/0888-9112) [13787270] **4386**

CUENTA Y RAZON (SP/0211-1381) [07855745] **2514**

CUENTAS DEL SECTOR AGRARIO (SP) [04299208] **77**

CUENTAS MONETARIAS See CUENTAS MONETARIAS DEL SISTEMA BANCARIO NACIONAL / [BANCO CENTRAL DE COSTA RICA] **786**

CUENTAS MONETARIAS / BANCO CENTRAL DE COSTA RICA, DIVISION ECONOMICA, DEPARTAMENTO MONETARIO (CR) [27551260] **786**

CUENTAS MONETARIAS DEL SISTEMA BANCARIO NACIONAL / [BANCO CENTRAL DE COSTA RICA] (CR) [28124293] **786**

CUENTOS PARA OIR (UY) [06083940] **3379**

CUERO RECORD, THE (US/1062-1202) [14178923] **5748**

CUESTION SOCIAL (MEXICO CITY, MEXICO : 1985) (MX/0186-5617) [18994939] **5281**

CUESTIONARIO (AG) [02757970] **2730**

CUICUILCO (MX/0185-1659) [08072061] **234**

CUIR, LE (FR) **3183**

CUISINE ACTUELLE (FR/0989-3091) [I09893091] **2789**

CUISINE AUCKLAND (NZ/0113-1206) [I01131206] **2789**

CUISINE COLLECTIVE (FR/0045-9208) [04579121] **2332**

CUISINE DE AAZ (FR) **2332**

CUISINE ET VINS DE FRANCE (1975) (FR/0337-8810) [02584255] **2366**

CUISINEWS (FR) **2332**

CUKORIPAR (US) [05316938] **2332**

CULINARY & FINE ARTS NEWS CEASED. (US/0734-7073) [08901249] **318**

CULINARY INSTITUTE OF AMERICA See ALUMNI DIRECTORY - CULINARY INSTITUTE OF AMERICA **1098**

CULINARY TRENDS (US/1057-3453) [23984621] **2332**

CULLMAN TIMES, THE (US) [11779773] **5626**

CULLMAN TRIBUNE, THE (US/0739-523X) [09764740] **5626**

CULOT, LE (CN/0704-7142) [04039551] **1734**

CULPEPER STAR-EXPONENT (1988) (US/0899-4803) [18103326] **5758**

CULPEPPER LETTER, THE (US/8750-3697) [11349084] 1245, **1285**

CULT OBSERVER, THE (US/0892-340X) [13337958] **5268**

CULTIC STUDIES JOURNAL (US/0748-6499) [11001534] **5243**

CULTIVADOR MODERNO, EL (SP) [03744621] **77**

CULTIVAR (FR/0045-9216) [01079224] **170**

CULTIVAR 1989 (FR/1143-7405) [I11437405] **77**

CULTIVATOR (STATE ARBORETUM OF UTAH) (US) [07324799] **2413**

CULTIVOS TROPICALES (CU/0258-5936) [02585936] **77**

CULTIVOS TROPICALES : CT. INSTITUTO DE CIENCIA AGRICOLA, CUBA (CU) [10353405] **170**

CULTURA & LIBRI (IT/0393-9707) [23099061] **2514**

CULTURA ATESINA (IT/0392-1506) [I03921506] **318**

CULTURA BIBLICA (SP) [01774697] **5016**

CULTURA DE GUATEMALA (GT) [06754553] **2512**

CULTURA E FE (BL) [06870588] **4952**

CULTURA E NATURA (IT) **5243**

CULTURA E SCUOLA (IT/0011-2771) [01785508] **1734**

CULTURA, LA (IT) [03881762] **2845**

CULTURA LUDENS (US/0882-3049) [11804777] **5197**

CULTURA NEL MONDO, LA (IT/0011-2798) [03694768] **2486**

CULTURA NEOLATINA (IT/0391-5654) [01228234] 3379, **3276**

CULTURAL AFFAIRS NEWS (US) [25167101] **318**

CULTURAL & PUBLISHING BUREAU See DIGEST OF KUWAIT OFFICIAL GAZETTE **2961**

CULTURAL ANTHROPOLOGY (US/0886-7356) [12964171] **234**

CULTURAL CRITIQUE (US/0882-4371) [11836154] **5197**

CULTURAL DIGEST, THE (II) [03391725] **318**

CULTURAL DIVERSITY AT WORK (US/1070-3160) [25030387] 2259, **1662**

CULTURAL DYNAMICS CEASED. (NE/0921-3740) [18077250] 4344, **5243**

CULTURAL EVENTS - NATIONAL LIBRARY OF CANADA (CN/1186-9348) [25351911] **318**

CULTURAL FUTURES RESEARCH SUSPENDED. (US/0748-772X) [09750999] **234**

CULTURAL GUIDE (OTTAWA) (CN/0229-0154) [08070874] **318**

CULTURAL INFORMATION SERVICE (US/0097-952X) [01799457] **4952**

CULTURAL POLICY (FR) **4470**

CULTURAL RESOURCE SERIES (US) [05502813] **2191**

CULTURAL RESOURCE SERIES (UNITED STATES. BUREAU OF LAND MANAGEMENT. NEVADA STATE OFFICE (US) [06190105] **2191**

CULTURAL RESOURCES SERIES (DENVER) (US/0271-633X) [05905722] **2191**

●CULTURAL STUDIES FROM BIRMINGHAM (UK) [26147452] **2845**

CULTURAL STUDIES (LONDON, ENGLAND) (UK/0950-2386) [17011286] **5197**

CULTURAL SURVIVAL QUARTERLY (US/0740-3291) [09935688] 2259, **4507**

CULTURAL SURVIVAL REPORT (US) [16728177] 234, **5243**

CULTURAL TRENDS (UK/0954-8963) [19984090] **318**

CULTURAL VISTAS (US/1048-8650) [21072363] **2845**

CULTURAL WATCHDOG NEWSLETTER, THE (US) [08946450] **3341**

CULTURAMA (CN/0824-3077) [10179241] **318**

CULTURE & AGRICULTURE (US/1048-4876) [08675078] 5243, **78**

CULTURE & HISTORY (US/0195-2714) [05437157] **2730**

CULTURE & HISTORY (COPENHAGEN) (DK/0902-7521) [18770634] 234, **2614**

CULTURE AND LIFE (RU) [01565575] **4519**

CULTURE AND POLICY / ICPS (AT/1033-8713) [24228787] **2845**

CULTURE & TRADITION (CN/0701-0184) [03406353] 234, **2319**

CULTURE ET COMMUNICATION (FR) [06653820] **348**

CULTURE, ETHNICITY, AND NATION (US/0888-8779) [13739447] **5197**

CULTURE KHMERE (FR) [09380536] 2684, **234**

CULTURE, MEDICINE AND PSYCHIATRY (NE/0165-005X) [03375343] 234, **3924**

CULTURE MUSICALI : SEMESTRALE DELLA SOCIETA ITALIANA DI ETNOMUSICOLOGIA (IT) [09330684] **4113**

CULTURE POPULAIRE ALBANAISE (AA/0257-6074) [17668834] **5268**

CULTURE (QUEBEC. 1981) (CN/0229-009X) [26088459] **234**

CULTURE SERVICE BULLETIN CEASED. (CN/1183-9155) [26666408] **318**

CULTURE TECHNIQUE (FR/0223-4386) [10942691] **5098**

CULTURED DAIRY PRODUCTS JOURNAL OF THE AMERICAN CULTURED DAIRY PRODUCTS INSTITUTE (US/0045-9259) [02847789] **192**

CULTUREEL JAARBOEK STAD ANTWERPEN (BE) [13439765] **318**

●CULTUREFRONT (NEW YORK, N.Y.) (US/1063-634X) [26043448] **2845**

CULTUREN (NE/0920-1327) [18595201] **2684**

CULTURES AU ZAIRE ET EN AFRIQUE (CG/0302-5640) [01792628] **234**

CULTURES CANADA : NEWSLETTER OF THE CANADIAN CONSULTATIVE COUNCIL ON MULTICULTURALISM (CN/0710-8559) [08341186] **5243**

CULTURES DU CANADA FRANCAIS (CN/0825-2777) [17237059] **2730**

CULTURES ET CONFLITS (FR/1157-996X) [24524235] 4040, **4519**

CULTURES INTERNATIONAL (CN/1185-9938) [25590061] **5243**

CULTURES INTERNATIONAL (CN/1185-9938) [25590063] **5243**

CULTURGRAMS (US) **2559**

CULTUUR EN MIGRATIE (BE) **5243**

CUMANIA (HU/0133-6088) [02568206] **2684**

CUMBERLAND ADVOCATE (US/0748-965X) [11041997] **5766**

CUMBERLAND COUNTY (KY.). FISCAL COURT See REPORT OF THE AUDITOR OF PUBLIC ACCOUNTS. AUDIT EXAMINATIONS OF THE CUMBERLAND COUNTY FISCAL COURT, FISCAL YEAR ENDED JUNE 30 ... CUMBERLAND COUNTY CLERK, CALENDAR YEAR ... **4745**

CUMBERLAND COUNTY NEWS, THE (US) [14205258] **5680**

CUMBERLAND FLAG, THE (US/0011-2968) [04043948] **4952**

CUMBERLAND JOURNAL (US/0195-7848) [05664451] **318**

CUMBERLAND LAW REVIEW (US/0360-8298) [02244588] **2957**

CUMBERLAND LAWYER, THE (US/0590-3378) [02254992] **2957**

CUMBERLAND NEWS (BURKESVILLE, KY.) See CUMBERLAND COUNTY NEWS, THE **5680**

CUMBERLAND POETRY REVIEW (US/0731-7980) [08236356] **3462**

CUMBERLAND PRESBYTERIAN, THE (US/0011-2976) [02260010] **5058**

CUMBERLAND SEMINARIAN, THE (US/0590-3386) [01776581] **4952**

CUMBERLAND TIMES-LAW (US) [19073771] **5686**

CUMBERLANDS (PIKEVILLE. 1977) (US/0163-1209) [04222402] **3379**

CUMBRIA (UK/0590-3394) [03640236] **2514**

CUMHURIYET (TU) [06674946] **5811**

CUMITECH (US/0160-1660) [02253186] **561**

CUMTUX : CLATSOP COUNTY HISTORICAL SOCIETY QUARTERLY (US) [10576551] **2730**

CUMULATED ABRIDGED INDEX MEDICUS (US/0090-1377) [02254993] 3569, **3656**

CUMULATED ANNOTATIONS / CLEARINGHOUSE ON HEALTH INDEXES (US/0145-1294) [02670089] **4809**

CUMULATED INDEX MEDICUS (US/0090-1423) [01565584] 3569, **3656**

CUMULATED INDEX TO THE U.S. DEPARTMENT OF STATE PAPERS RELATING TO THE FOREIGN RELATIONS OF THE UNITED STATES, THE (US/0198-7070) [06210567] **4641**

CUMULATIF DES REFERENCES PEDAGOGIQUES (CN/0319-5481) [02443048] **1794**

CUMULATIVE BOOK INDEX. CD-ROM (US/0011-300X) 4821, **3458**

CUMULATIVE BOOK INDEX, THE (US/0011-300X) [01565587] **3458**

CUMULATIVE DOCUMENT ACCESSION LIST (US/0360-7488) [02244019] **414**

CUMULATIVE INDEX - FOOD MARKETING INSTITUTE, INFORMATION SERVICE (US/0270-0352) [04683939] **2332**

CUMULATIVE INDEX OF HOSPITAL LITERATURE (US/0517-2160) [01777832] **3779**

CUMULATIVE INDEX OF SAE TECHNICAL PAPERS (US/0742-2350) [06094450] **5412**

CUMULATIVE INDEX OF THE JOURNAL OF THE AIR POLLUTION CONTROL ASSOCIATION (US) [06494162] **2227**

CUMULATIVE INDEX TO NURSING & ALLIED HEALTH LITERATURE (US/0146-5554) [02892848] 3854, **3656**

CUMULATIVE INDEX TO NURSING & ALLIED HEALTH LITERATURE. [MICROFICHE] (US) 3854, **3656**

CUMULATIVE LIST OF ORGANIZATIONS DESCRIBED IN SECTION 170 (C) OF THE INTERNAL REVENUE CODE OF 1954 (US/0499-6453) [02457127] **4719**

CUMULATIVE RECORDS - EXPORT-IMPORT BANK OF THE UNITED STATES (US/0098-8359) [02242249] **786**

CUMULUS (WOOD MOUNTAIN) (CN/1188-1631) [25652258] **3462**

CUNA NATIONAL MEMBER SURVEY (US/0195-8674) [05651929] **786**

CUNEIFORM TEXTS FROM NIMRUD (UK) [04758261] **266**

CUNEO PROVINCIA GRANDE (IT) [04762261] **5467**

CUNI SCIENCES LEMPDES (FR/0984-7847) [I09847847] **209**

CUNICULTURAL (SP/0210-1912) [I02101912] **210**

CUNICULTURE (PARIS) (FR/0152-3058) [I01523058] **210**

Alphabetical Title Index

CURRENT

CUNNINGHAMIA : ECOLOGICAL CONTRIBUTIONS FROM THE NATIONAL HERBARIUM OF NEW SOUTH WALES (AT/0727-9620) [08146218] 2213, **507**

CUNY-INDUSTRY FORUM SERIES, THE (US/0882-4509) [11837358] **1819**

CUOIO, PELLI, MATERIE CONCIANTI (IT/0011-3034) [02446270] **3183**

CUORE, IL (IT) [19484967] 3963, **3704**

CUPA JOURNAL (WASHINGTON, D.C.: 1987) (US/1046-9508) [17316267] 1819, **939**

CUPA NEWS (WASHINGTON D.C. : 1987) (US/0892-7855) [15259638] 939, **1819**

CURA ANIMARUM (US/0893-0198) [11659748] **3569**

CURA REPORTER (US) [01757988] **2819**

CURACAO TRADE AND INDUSTRY DIRECTORY (NA) [02441509] **830**

CURACAO TRADE DIRECTORY *See* CURACAO TRADE AND INDUSTRY DIRECTORY **830**

CURACAO TRADE INFORMATION GUIDE (NE) [15321365] **830**

CURARE (GW/0344-8622) [05735244] **3924**

CURATIONIS (PRETORIA) (SA/0379-8577) [04825308] **3854**

CURATOR (NEW YORK, N.Y.) (US/0011-3069) [01565592] 4165, **4087**

CURIOSPRESS INTERNATIONAL (FR/0398-8074) [01794256] **4813**

CURLEW, THE *CEASED.* (CN/0011-3093) [02358812] **4165**

CURLEY (US/1049-0396) [21113906] **3379**

CURLING CANADA (CN/0828-9034) [13207828] 2596, **4892**

CURRENCIES & CREDIT MARKETS (GW) **786**

CURRENCY *CEASED.* (AT/0314-7320) [03147320] **5281**

CURRENCY COMPETITION (US/0731-3551) [08173782] **786**

CURRENCY CONFIDENTIAL *CEASED.* (UK/0141-1047) **786**

CURRENCY FORECASTERS DIGEST (US) **1478**

CURRENCY FORECASTING SERVICE (UK/0142-4823) [05790218] 786, **895**

CURRENCY PROFILES (UK/0143-0769) [05927083] **786**

CURRENCY QUARTERLY *CEASED.* (UK) **786**

CURRENT ACCOUNTING LAW & PRACTICE (UK) [02422830] **742**

CURRENT ACCOUNTING LITERATURE (UK) [03048719] **742**

CURRENT ACCOUNTING LITERATURE; A SUPPLEMENT (UK) [06437243] **742**

●CURRENT ADVANCES IN APPLIED MICROBIOLOGY & BIOTECHNOLOGY (UK/0964-8712) [25255616] 561, 3691, **477**

CURRENT ADVANCES IN BIOCHEMISTRY *See* CURRENT ADVANCES IN PROTEIN BIOCHEMISTRY **478**

CURRENT ADVANCES IN BIOCHEMISTRY *See* CURRENT ADVANCES IN PROTEIN CHEMISTRY **478**

CURRENT ADVANCES IN CANCER RESEARCH (UK/0895-9803) [16883762] 3815, **3656**

CURRENT ADVANCES IN CELL AND DEVELOPMENTAL BIOLOGY (UK/0741-1626) [10093961] 535, **477**

CURRENT ADVANCES IN CLINICAL CHEMISTRY (UK/0885-1980) [12603240] 974, **1011**

CURRENT ADVANCES IN ECOLOGICAL & ENVIRONMENTAL SCIENCES (UK/0955-6648) [19112124] 2227, **2183**

●CURRENT ADVANCES IN ENDOCRINOLOGY AND METABOLISM (UK/0964-8720) [25063714] 3727, **3656**

CURRENT ADVANCES IN GENETICS & MOLECULAR BIOLOGY (UK/0741-1642) [10094224] 543, **477**

CURRENT ADVANCES IN IMMUNOLOGY *See* CURRENT ADVANCES IN IMMUNOLOGY & INFECTIOUS DISEASES **3656**

●CURRENT ADVANCES IN IMMUNOLOGY & INFECTIOUS DISEASES (UK/0964-8747) [25213826] 3668, **3656**

CURRENT ADVANCES IN MICROBIOLOGY *See* CURRENT ADVANCES IN APPLIED MICROBIOLOGY & BIOTECHNOLOGY **477**

CURRENT ADVANCES IN NEUROSCIENCE (UK/0741-1677) [10094412] 3830, **3656**

CURRENT ADVANCES IN PHARMACOLOGY & TOXICOLOGY *See* CURRENT ADVANCES IN TOXICOLOGY **3656**

CURRENT ADVANCES IN PHYSIOLOGY *See* CURRENT ADVANCES IN ENDOCRINOLOGY AND METABOLISM **3656**

CURRENT ADVANCES IN PLANT SCIENCE (UK/0306-4484) [01786742] **507**

●CURRENT ADVANCES IN PROTEIN BIOCHEMISTRY (UK/0965-0504) [25191743] 486, **478**

●CURRENT ADVANCES IN PROTEIN CHEMISTRY (UK/0965-0504) [25255753] 486, **478**

●CURRENT ADVANCES IN TOXICOLOGY (UK/0965-0512) [25236565] 3980, **3656**

CURRENT AFFAIRS BULLETIN (AT/0011-3182) [01565598] **4470**

CURRENT AFFAIRS TRANSLATIONS - ANTARA (IO) [02762923] **2650**

CURRENT AFRICAN DIRECTORIES (UK) [04820927] 2499, **3205**

CURRENT AGRICULTURE (II/0254-1092) [03862120] **78**

CURRENT AIDS LITERATURE (UK/0952-8075) [17060323] 3713, **3668**

CURRENT AIRCRAFT PRICES (SZ) [10536441] **17**

CURRENT ALTERNATIVE ENERGY RESEARCH AND DEVELOPMENT IN ILLINOIS (US/0883-2943) [10172100] **1936**

CURRENT ANAESTHESIA AND CRITICAL CARE (UK/0953-7112) [21591728] **3963**

CURRENT ANALYSIS (US/0736-606X) [09200951] **830**

CURRENT & CHOICE (CN/0705-2499) [04039747] **414**

CURRENT ANTARCTIC LITERATURE (US/0096-879X) [03491447] **2559**

CURRENT ANTHROPOLOGY (US/0011-3204) [01565600] **234**

CURRENT APPROACHES TO AFRICAN LINGUISTICS (NE) [10708673] **3276**

CURRENT ARCHAEOLOGY (UK/0011-3212) [03672481] **266**

CURRENT AUSTRALIAN AND NEW ZEALAND LEGAL LITERATURE INDEX *CEASED.* (AT) [01789701] **2957**

CURRENT AUSTRALIAN HEALTH SERIALS (AT/0727-2545) [05732139] **3656**

●CURRENT AWARENESS ABSTRACTS (UK) [25352295] **3205**

CURRENT AWARENESS BULLETIN (LONDON, ENGLAND) *See* CURRENT AWARENESS ABSTRACTS **3205**

CURRENT AWARENESS IN BIOLOGICAL SCIENCES (UK/0733-4443) [08584740] 452, **478**

CURRENT AWARENESS IN BIOTECHNOLOGY (US/0735-956X) [09030581] **3691**

CURRENT AWARENESS IN PARTICLE TECHNOLOGY / PUBLISHED AND COMPILED BY: PARTICLE SCIENCE AND TECHNOLOGY INFORMATION SERVICE, UNIVERSITY OF TECHNOLOGY, LOUGHBOROUGH, GREAT BRITAIN (UK/0376-4842) [06598052] **5098**

CURRENT AWARENESS PROFILE ON QUANTUM CHEMISTRY (US/0145-6814) [02766678] **974**

CURRENT AWARENESS SERVICE (CAMBRIDGE, MASS.) (US/0882-3677) [11822415] **3205**

CURRENT BASEBALL PUBLICATIONS (US) 4892, **4856**

CURRENT BIBLIOGRAPHICAL INFORMATION / DAG HAMMARSKJOLD LIBRARY *CEASED.* (US/0041-7343) [01776737] **4502**

CURRENT BIBLIOGRAPHIES IN MEDICINE (US/1052-9063) [17913615] **3656**

CURRENT BIBLIOGRAPHY ON AFRICAN AFFAIRS, A (US/0011-3255) [01565605] **2635**

CURRENT BIOGRAPHY (US/0011-3344) [02446272] **431**

CURRENT BIOGRAPHY YEARBOOK (US/0084-9499) [04423830] **432**

CURRENT BIOLOGY (UK/0960-9822) [23593628] **452**

CURRENT BIOTECHNOLOGY (UK/0960-5037) [23854566] 3691, **3656**

●CURRENT BOOKS MAGAZINE (US/1063-9012) [26174669] **3341**

CURRENT BRITISH DIRECTORIES (UK/0070-1858) [01565607] 1478, **663**

CURRENT BRITISH FOREIGN POLICY (US) [00579921] **4519**

CURRENT BRITISH JOURNALS (UK) [08603704] **3258**

CURRENT BUSINESS REPORTS. ADVANCE MONTHLY RETAIL SALES (US/0190-5988) [01714084] **953**

CURRENT BUSINESS REPORTS. BR, MONTHLY RETAIL TRADE, SALES AND INVENTORIES (US/0739-5361) [07815899] **953**

CURRENT BUSINESS REPORTS. COMBINED ANNUAL AND REVISED MONTHLY RETAIL TRADE (US) [28123960] **953**

CURRENT BUSINESS REPORTS. COMBINED ANNUAL AND REVISED MONTHLY WHOLESALE TRADE (US) [28090104] **830**

CURRENT BUSINESS REPORTS. MONTHLY WHOLESALE TRADE, SALES, AND INVENTORIES (US/0363-8553) [02532948] **663**

CURRENT BUSINESS REPORTS: MONTHLY WHOLESALE TRADE, SALES AND INVENTORIES (US) [02252207] 830, **663**

CURRENT BUSINESS REPORTS. RETAIL TRADE, ANNUAL SALES, YEAR-END INVENTORIES, PURCHASES, GROSS MARGIN, AND ACCOUNTS RECEIVABLE, BY KIND OF RETAIL STORE *See* CURRENT BUSINESS REPORTS. COMBINED ANNUAL AND REVISED MONTHLY RETAIL TRADE **953**

CURRENT BUSINESS REPORTS. REVISED MONTHLY RETAIL SALES AND INVENTORIES *See* CURRENT BUSINESS REPORTS. COMBINED ANNUAL AND REVISED MONTHLY RETAIL TRADE **953**

CURRENT BUSINESS REPORTS. REVISED MONTHLY WHOLESALE TRADE, SALES AND INVENTORIES (US/0741-7268) [08852927] **830**

CURRENT BUSINESS REPORTS. WHOLESALE TRADE, ANNUAL SALES AND YEAR-END INVENTORIES, PURCHASES, AND GROSS MARGIN ESTIMATES OF MERCHANT WHOLESALERS (US) [14642861] **830**

●CURRENT CANCER THERAPEUTICS (US/1074-2816) [29665953] **3815**

CURRENT CARDIOLOGY *CEASED.* (US/0163-9501) [04543900] **3704**

CURRENT CARDIOVASCULAR PATENTS. CARDIOVASCULAR FAST-ALERT *CEASED.* (UK/0957-0462) [20706666] **3704**

CURRENT CAREER AND OCCUPATIONAL LITERATURE (US/0161-0562) [03818336] **4203**

CURRENT CATALOG PROOF SHEETS, SEMIWEEKLY PROOF *CEASED.* (US) [01472303] **3205**

CURRENT CENTRAL LEGISLATION (II) [12157645] **2957**

CURRENT CHARGES FOR SELECTED HOSPITAL SERVICES ... / STATE OF FLORIDA, HOSPITAL COST CONTAINMENT BOARD (US) [08575379] **3779**

CURRENT CHEMICAL REACTIONS (US/0163-6278) [04419332] 974, **1011**

●CURRENT CLINICAL CANCER (UK/0969-692X) **3815**

CURRENT CLINICAL PRACTICE SERIES (NE/0168-6917) [09811319] **3570**

CURRENT COINS OF THE WORLD (US/0070-1882) [01783391] **2781**

CURRENT COMEDY FOR SPEAKERS (US) [19830564] **384**

CURRENT COMMERCIAL CASES (SA/1019-2530) [I10192530] **2499**

CURRENT COMMUNICATIONS IN CELL & MOLECULAR BIOLOGY (US/1063-8806) [23730791] **535**

CURRENT COMMUNICATIONS IN MOLECULAR BIOLOGY (US/0737-3708) [09364490] 1109, **452**

CURRENT CONCEPTS IN ALLERGY AND CLINICAL IMMUNOLOGY *CEASED.* (US/0736-4350) [03527242] **3668**

CURRENT CONCEPTS IN COMMUNITY PHARMACY (US) **4298**

CURRENT CONCEPTS IN GASTROENTEROLOGY *SUSPENDED.* (US/0363-6526) [02531822] **3743**

CURRENT CONCEPTS IN NUTRITION (US/0090-0443) [01777704] **4189**

CURRENT CONCEPTS IN ONCOLOGY *SUSPENDED.* (US/0199-4697) [05904284] **3815**

CURRENT CONCEPTS IN ONCOLOGY (SP) **3570**

CURRENT CONCEPTS IN ORTHOPAEDIC SURGERY (US) **3881**

CURRENT CONCEPTS IN PSYCHIATRY (US/0360-7569) [02246085] **3924**

CURRENT CONCEPTS IN RADIOLOGY (US/0149-2454) [03455661] **3940**

CURRENT CONCEPTS IN SKIN DISORDERS (US/0199-8757) [06235473] **3718**

CURRENT CONDITIONS & PROBLEMS IN THE CONSTRUCTION INDUSTRY (JA) [05167531] **612**

CURRENT

CURRENT CONSTRUCTION COSTS (US/0161-7257) [04007371] **612**

CURRENT CONSTRUCTION REPORTS. C20, HOUSING STARTS (US/0896-6761) [17245452] 612, **2819**

CURRENT CONSTRUCTION REPORTS. C21, NEW RESIDENTIAL CONSTRUCTION IN SELECTED METROPOLITAN STATISTICAL AREAS (US/0896-6737) [17244942] 612, **2819**

CURRENT CONSTRUCTION REPORTS. C22, HOUSING COMPLETIONS (US/0896-6702) [17244478] **612**

CURRENT CONSTRUCTION REPORTS. C25, NEW ONE-FAMILY HOUSES SOLD /U.S. DEPT. OF COMMERCE, BUREAU OF THE CENSUS [AND] U.S. DEPT. OF HOUSING AND URBAN DEVELOPMENT (US) [24163121] **2819**

CURRENT CONSTRUCTION REPORTS. C40, HOUSING UNITS AUTHORIZED BY BUILDING PERMITS (US/0896-9221) [17335507] **612**

CURRENT CONSTRUCTION REPORTS. C50, EXPENDITURES FOR RESIDENTIAL IMPROVEMENTS AND REPAIRS (US) [24006272] **612**

CURRENT CONTENTS AFRICA *CEASED.* (UK/0721-5207) [05383526] 2486, **2496**

CURRENT CONTENTS. AGRICULTURE, BIOLOGY, & ENVIRONMENTAL SCIENCES (US/0090-0508) [01787045] 78, 452, **152**

●CURRENT CONTENTS. AGRICULTURE, BIOLOGY & ENVIRONMENTAL SCIENCES (CD-ROM VERSION) (US/1073-1245) [29335091] 78, 452, **152**

CURRENT CONTENTS. ARTS & HUMANITIES (US/0163-3155) [04359443] 318, 2845, **334**

CURRENT CONTENTS. CLINICAL MEDICINE (US/0891-3358) [14709694] 3570, **3656**

●CURRENT CONTENTS. CLINICAL MEDICINE (CD-ROM VERSION) (US/1073-1237) [29335041] 3570, **3656**

CURRENT CONTENTS. COMPUMATH (US/0276-220X) [07378812] 1181, **3502**

CURRENT CONTENTS. ENGINEERING, TECHNOLOGY & APPLIED SCIENCES (US/0095-7917) [01190418] 1970, 5098, **2003**

CURRENT CONTENTS. HEALTH SERVICES ADMINISTRATION *CEASED.* (US/0893-5165) [15555683] **4772**

CURRENT CONTENTS IN FOLKLORE *See* CURRENT FOLKLORE **2319**

CURRENT CONTENTS. LIFE SCIENCES (US/0011-3409) [01715088] 5098, **5174**

●CURRENT CONTENTS. LIFE SCIENCES (CD-ROM VERSION) (US/1073-1229) [29335001] 5098, **5174**

CURRENT CONTENTS OF ACADEMIC JOURNALS IN JAPAN. THE HUMANITIES AND SOCIAL SCIENCES (JA/0386-7293) [08521181] 5197, **2845**

CURRENT CONTENTS OF PERIODICALS ON THE MIDDLE EAST (IS/0333-9858) [07936376] **2650**

CURRENT CONTENTS ON DISKETTE. AGRICULTURE, BIOLOGY & ENVIRONMENTAL SCIENCES (US/1062-3167) [21480418] 78, **152**

CURRENT CONTENTS ON DISKETTE. CLINICAL MEDICINE (US/1062-3159) [25585321] 3570, **3656**

CURRENT CONTENTS ON DISKETTE. ENGINEERING, TECHNOLOGY & APPLIED SCIENCES (US/1062-3132) [25585591] 5098, **1970**

CURRENT CONTENTS ON DISKETTE. LIFE SCIENCES. J600 (US/1062-3078) [25577765] 5098, **5174**

CURRENT CONTENTS ON DISKETTE. LIFE SCIENCES. J1200 (US/1062-3027) [25574906] 5098, **5174**

CURRENT CONTENTS ON DISKETTE. PHYSICAL, CHEMICAL & EARTH SCIENCES (US/1062-1180) [21142449] 1354, **1362**

CURRENT CONTENTS ON DISKETTE. SOCIAL & BEHAVIORAL SCIENCES (US/1062-3140) [25585504] 5197, **5197**

CURRENT CONTENTS ON DISKETTE WITH ABSTRACTS. AGRICULTURE, BIOLOGY & ENVIRONMENTAL SCIENCES (US/1062-3124) [25601529] 78, 452, **152**

CURRENT CONTENTS ON DISKETTE WITH ABSTRACTS. CLINICAL MEDICINE (US/1062-3116) [25585669] 3570, **3656**

CURRENT CONTENTS ON DISKETTE WITH ABSTRACTS. LIFE SCIENCES (US/1062-3108) [25585777] 5098, **5174**

CURRENT CONTENTS ON DISKETTE WITH ABSTRACTS. PHYSICAL, CHEMICAL & EARTH SCIENCES (US/1062-3094) [25585920] 1354, **1362**

CURRENT CONTENTS. PHYSICAL, CHEMICAL & EARTH SCIENCES (US/0163-2574) [04336878] **1362**

●CURRENT CONTENTS. PHYSICAL, CHEMICAL & EARTH SCIENCES (CD-ROM VERSION) (US/1073-1253) [29335134] **1362**

CURRENT CONTENTS SEARCH (US) **2487**

CURRENT CONTENTS. SOCIAL & BEHAVIORAL SCIENCES (US/0092-6361) [01565614] 5197, 4583, **5227**

CURRENT DEFERRALS (US/1047-1065) [20607421] **1662**

CURRENT DEVELOPMENTS IN ANTHROPOLOGICAL GENETICS (US/0748-7819) [06820155] 235, 4551, **544**

CURRENT DEVELOPMENTS IN BANKRUPTCY AND REORGANIZATION (US/0883-055X) [07019457] **3086**

CURRENT DEVELOPMENTS IN COMPUTER SOFTWARE PROTECTION (US) [24244751] **1226**

CURRENT DEVELOPMENTS IN COPYRIGHT LAW (US/0733-0243) [04279222] **1303**

CURRENT DIAGNOSTIC PATHOLOGY (UK/0968-6053) 3894, **3570**

CURRENT DIAGNOSTIC PEDIATRICS (GW/0172-1232) [04272650] **3902**

CURRENT DIALOGUE (SZ) [07342032] **4952**

●CURRENT DIGEST OF THE POST-SOVIET PRESS, THE (US/1067-7542) [25330684] 4470, **4502**

CURRENT DIGEST OF THE SOVIET PRESS *See* CURRENT DIGEST OF THE POST-SOVIET PRESS, THE **4502**

CURRENT DIGEST OF THE SOVIET PRESS, THE (US/0011-3425) [01565621] **4470**

●CURRENT DIRECTIONS IN PSYCHOLOGICAL SCIENCE : A JOURNAL OF THE AMERICAN PSYCHOLOGICAL SOCIETY (US/0963-7214) [25768799] **4583**

CURRENT DIVIDEND RECORD (US) [23066651] **895**

●CURRENT DRUG THERAPY (US/1065-7630) [26725806] **4298**

CURRENT ECONOMIC ANALYSIS (OTTAWA) (CN/0228-5819) [07674280] **1478**

CURRENT ECONOMIC STATISTICS (FJ) [02430381] 1478, **1531**

CURRENT EMERGENCY DIAGNOSIS & TREATMENT (US/0894-2293) [10138321] **3724**

CURRENT EMERGENCY THERAPY (US/0739-8573) [09820506] **3724**

●CURRENT EMPLOYMENT (US/1055-8292) [23352393] **4203**

CURRENT ENERGY PATENTS *CEASED.* (US/0273-298X) [07038010] **1936**

CURRENT ESTIMATES - CITY OF WINNIPEG (CN/0317-9664) [05018635] **4719**

CURRENT ESTIMATES FROM THE NATIONAL HEALTH INTERVIEW SURVEY, UNITED STATES (US/0891-4591) [08981427] **4772**

CURRENT EUROPE FOR EUROPE (UK) [I09648518] **1478**

CURRENT EUROPEAN ANAESTHESIOLOGY (UK/0883-4490) [12141677] **3682**

CURRENT EUROPEAN DIRECTORIES (UK) [04224864] **1924**

CURRENT EVENTS DIGEST (PH) [08441919] 5197, **1734**

CURRENT EVENTS (MIDDLETOWN) (US/0011-3492) [02250335] **1734**

CURRENT EVENTS SWEEPSTAKES (US/0739-1145) [09712278] **2730**

CURRENT EXPENSE DISBURSEMENTS BY SOURCE OF FUNDS (US/0090-4317) [01784958] **1862**

CURRENT EYE RESEARCH (UK/0271-3683) [06629649] **3874**

CURRENT FARM ECONOMICS (1984) (US/0030-1701) [15293994] **170**

CURRENT FEDERAL AID RESEARCH REPORT. FISH (US/0882-763X) [08074652] **2299**

CURRENT FEDERAL AID RESEARCH REPORT. WILDLIFE (US) [07966932] **2191**

●CURRENT FOLKLORE (UK) [I09661603] **2319**

CURRENT GASTROENTEROLOGY (US/0198-8085) [06230926] **3743**

CURRENT GENETICS (GW/0172-8083) [06203326] **544**

CURRENT GEOGRAPHICAL PUBLICATIONS (US/0011-3514) [01479917] 1354, 2559, **2580**

CURRENT GEOLOGICAL AND GEOPHYSICAL STUDIES IN MONTANA / STATE OF MONTANA, BUREAU OF MINES AND GEOLOGY (US/0092-9565) [01784603] **1354**

CURRENT GEOLOGICAL RESEARCH IN WEST VIRGINIA (US/0093-240X) [04240013] **1372**

CURRENT HEALTH *See* CURRENT HEALTH 2 **4772**

CURRENT HEALTH 1 (US/0199-820X) [06190101] **4772**

CURRENT HEALTH 2 (US/0163-156X) [04309220] **4772**

CURRENT HEMATOLOGY AND ONCOLOGY (US/0739-4810) [09745740] 3815, **3771**

CURRENT HEPATOLOGY (US/0198-8093) [06230893] **3796**

CURRENT HISTORY (1941) (US/0011-3530) [01565627] **2614**

CURRENT HOUSING REPORTS. H-111, HOUSING VACANCIES AND HOMEOWNERSHIP (US) [18076594] **2820**

CURRENT HOUSING REPORTS. H-111, HOUSING VACANCIES AND HOMEOWNERSHIP, ANNUAL STATISTICS (US) [18077172] **2820**

CURRENT HOUSING REPORTS. H-131, CHARACTERISTICS OF APARTMENTS COMPLETED (US) [02703294] **2820**

CURRENT HOUSING REPORTS. H-150, AMERICAN HOUSING SURVEY FOR THE UNITED STATES IN ... (US/1048-7565) [19600672] **2820**

CURRENT HOUSING REPORTS. H-170, AMERICAN HOUSING SURVEY FOR THE CHICAGO METROPOLITAN AREA IN ... (US) [22369062] **2820**

CURRENT HOUSING REPORTS. H-170, AMERICAN HOUSING SURVEY FOR THE HARTFORD METROPOLITAN AREA IN ... (US) [22369018] **2861**

CURRENT HOUSING REPORTS. H-170, AMERICAN HOUSING SURVEY FOR THE MIAMI-FT. LAUDERDALE METROPOLITAN AREA IN ... (US) [21387743] **2861**

CURRENT HOUSING REPORTS. H-170, AMERICAN HOUSING SURVEY FOR THE NEW ORLEANS METROPOLITAN AREA IN ... (US) [21281097] **2861**

CURRENT HOUSING REPORTS. H-170, AMERICAN HOUSING SURVEY FOR THE PORTLAND METROPOLITAN AREA IN ... (US) [21388732] **2820**

CURRENT HOUSING REPORTS. H-170, ANNUAL HOUSING SURVEY, HONOLULU, HAWAII, STANDARD METROPOLITAN STATISTICAL AREA. HOUSING CHARACTERISTICS FOR SELECTED METROPOLITAN AREAS (US) [12055090] 2820, **2840**

CURRENT HOUSING REPORTS. H-170, ANNUAL HOUSING SURVEY, HOUSTON, TEX., STANDARD METROPOLITAN STATISTICAL AREA. HOUSING CHARACTERISTICS FOR SELECTED METROPOLITAN AREAS (US) [12055057] 2820, **2840**

CURRENT HOUSING REPORTS. H-170, ANNUAL HOUSING SURVEY, LOUISVILLE, KY.-IND. STANDARD METROPOLITAN STATISTICAL AREA. HOUSING CHARACTERISTICS FOR SELECTED METROPOLITAN AREAS (US) [10381826] 2820, **2840**

CURRENT HOUSING REPORTS. H-170, ANNUAL HOUSING SURVEY, NEW YORK, NY., STANDARD METROPOLITAN STATISTICAL AREA. HOUSING CHARACTERISTICS FOR SELECTED METROPOLITAN AREAS (US) [10326790] 2820, **2840**

CURRENT HOUSING REPORTS. H-170, ANNUAL HOUSING SURVEY, ORLANDO, FLA., STANDARD METROPOLITAN STATISTICAL AREA. HOUSING CHARACTERISTICS FOR SELECTED METROPOLITAN AREAS (US) [08342172] **2820**

CURRENT HOUSING REPORTS. H-170, ANNUAL HOUSING SURVEY, RALEIGH, N.C., STANDARD METROPOLITAN STATISTICAL AREA. HOUSING CHARACTERISTICS FOR SELECTED METROPOLITAN AREAS (US) [10164549] **2820**

CURRENT HOUSING REPORTS. H-170, ANNUAL HOUSING SURVEY, SACRAMENTO, CALIF., STANDARD METROPOLITAN STATISTICAL AREA. HOUSING CHARACTERISTICS FOR SELECTED METROPOLITAN AREA (US) [10480348] 2820, **2840**

CURRENT HOUSING REPORTS. H-170, ANNUAL HOUSING SURVEY, SEATTLE-EVERETT, WASH., STANDARD METROPOLITAN STATISTICAL AREA. HOUSING CHARACTERISTICS FOR SELECTED METROPOLITAN AREAS (US) [10330753] **2820**

CURRENT HOUSING REPORTS. H-170, ANNUAL HOUSING SURVEY, ST. LOUIS, MO-ILL., STANDARD METROPOLITAN STATISTICAL AREA. HOUSING CHARACTERISTICS FOR SELECTED METROPOLITAN AREAS (US) [10463727] 2820, **2840**

CURRENT HOUSING REPORTS. H171, SUPPLEMENT TO THE AMERICAN HOUSING SURVEY FOR SELECTED METROPOLITAN AREAS IN ... (US) [24579595] **2820**

CURRENT IMAGING See IMAGING : AN INTERNATIONAL JOURNAL OF CLINICO-RADIOLOGICAL PRACTICE **3942**

CURRENT INDEX OF COMPUTER LITERATURE (US/0748-898X) [10814397] **1181**

CURRENT INDEX TO COMMONWEALTH LEGAL PERIODICALS (CN/0382-5027) [02624802] **2957**

CURRENT INDEX TO JOURNALS IN EDUCATION (US/0011-3565) [01565633] 1734, **1794**

CURRENT INDEX TO JOURNALS IN EDUCATION. SEMIANNUAL CUMULATION (US) [06747414] **1734**

CURRENT INDEX TO JOURNALS IN SCIENCE & TECHNOLOGY, BIOLOGY, AGRICULTURE, PHARMACY (KO) 78, 4298, **452**

CURRENT INDEX TO LEGAL PERIODICALS (SEATTLE, WASH.) (US/0898-9451) [01565634] 2957, **3080**

CURRENT INDEX TO STATISTICS (US/0364-1228) [02593972] 3502, **3542**

CURRENT INDONESIAN STUDIES IN THE NETHERLANDS (NE) [05199866] **2730**

CURRENT INDUSTRIAL REPORTS. ELECTRONIC BULLETIN BOARD (US) **2040**

CURRENT INDUSTRIAL REPORTS. FATS AND OILS-OILSEED CRUSHINGS See CURRENT INDUSTRIAL REPORTS. M20J, FATS AND OILS-OILSEED CRUSHINGS / U.S. DEPARTMENT OF COMMERCE, ECONOMICS AND STATISTICS ADMINISTRATION, BUREAU OF THE CENSUS **1603**

CURRENT INDUSTRIAL REPORTS. FATS AND OILS, PRODUCTION, CONSUMPTION, AND STOCKS See CURRENT INDUSTRIAL REPORTS. FATS AND OILS, PRODUCTION, CONSUMPTION, AND STOCKS / U.S. DEPT. OF COMMERCE, ECONOMICS AND STATISTICS ADMINISTRATION, BUREAU OF THE CENSUS **1603**

CURRENT INDUSTRIAL REPORTS. FATS AND OILS, PRODUCTION, CONSUMPTION, AND STOCKS / U.S. DEPT. OF COMMERCE, ECONOMICS AND STATISTICS ADMINISTRATION, BUREAU OF THE CENSUS (US) [25616338] **1603**

CURRENT INDUSTRIAL REPORTS : FOOTWEAR (US) [04053616] **1603**

CURRENT INDUSTRIAL REPORTS. M20J, FATS AND OILS-OILSEED CRUSHINGS / U.S. DEPARTMENT OF COMMERCE, ECONOMICS AND STATISTICS ADMINISTRATION, BUREAU OF THE CENSUS (US) [25609525] **1603**

CURRENT INDUSTRIAL REPORTS. M22P, CONSUMPTION ON THE COTTON SYSTEM AND STOCKS See CURRENT INDUSTRIAL REPORTS. M22P, CONSUMPTION ON THE COTTON SYSTEM AND STOCKS [COMPUTER FILE] **170**

CURRENT INDUSTRIAL REPORTS. M22P, CONSUMPTION ON THE COTTON SYSTEM AND STOCKS / U.S. DEPARTMENT OF COMMERCE, ECONOMICS AND STATISTICS ADMINISTRATION, BUREAU OF THE CENSUS (US) [25609727] 5350, **170**

CURRENT INDUSTRIAL REPORTS. M22P, CONSUMPTION ON THE COTTON SYSTEM AND STOCKS [COMPUTER FILE] (US) **170**

CURRENT INDUSTRIAL REPORTS. M33-3, CONSUMPTION ON THE COTTON SYSTEM, SUMMARY FOR COTTON SEASON ... / U.S. DEPARTMENT OF COMMERCE, BUREAU OF THE CENSUS (US) [09672748] **1603**

CURRENT INDUSTRIAL REPORTS. M33-3, INVENTORIES OF STEEL MILL SHAPES See CURRENT INDUSTRIAL REPORTS. M33J, INVENTORIES OF STEEL PRODUCING MILLS **1603**

CURRENT INDUSTRIAL REPORTS. M33J, INVENTORIES OF STEEL PRODUCING MILLS (US) [16106463] **1603**

CURRENT INDUSTRIAL REPORTS. M37G, CIVIL AIRCRAFT AND AIRCRAFT ENGINES (EXCEPT MILITARY) See CIVIL AIRCRAFT AND AIRCRAFT ENGINES **16**

CURRENT INDUSTRIAL REPORTS. MA-26B, SELECTED OFFICE SUPPLIES AND ACCESSORIES / U.S. DEPARTMENT OF COMMERCE, BUREAU OF THE CENSUS (US) [09672190] 4211, **1603**

CURRENT INDUSTRIAL REPORTS. MA-27A, BUSINESS FORMS, BINDERS, CARBON PAPER, AND INKED RIBBONS / U.S. DEPARTMENT OF COMMERCE, BUREAU OF THE CENSUS (US) [08072094] 4211, **1603**

CURRENT INDUSTRIAL REPORTS. MA-28B, SULFURIC ACID / U.S. DEPARTMENT OF COMMERCE, BUREAU OF THE CENSUS (US) [03246209] **974**

CURRENT INDUSTRIAL REPORTS. MA-28C, INDUSTRIAL GASES / U.S. DEPARTMENT OF COMMERCE, BUREAU OF THE CENSUS (US) [05960561] **4254**

CURRENT INDUSTRIAL REPORTS. MA-30B, RUBBER AND PLASTICS HOSE AND BELTING (US) [03048542] **5075**

CURRENT INDUSTRIAL REPORTS. MA-30D, SHIPMENTS OF SELECTED PLASTICS PRODUCTS / U.S. DEPARTMENT OF COMMERCE, BUREAU OF THE CENSUS (US) [03056807] 1603, **4454**

CURRENT INDUSTRIAL REPORTS. MA-32J, GLASS FIBERS CEASED. (US) [18515838] 1603, **2588**

CURRENT INDUSTRIAL REPORTS. MA-34N, SELECTED HEATING EQUIPMENT / U.S. DEPARTMENT OF COMMERCE, BUREAU OF THE CENSUS (US) [03057346] **2604**

CURRENT INDUSTRIAL REPORTS. MA-35N, FLUID POWER PRODUCTS, INCLUDING AEROSPACE / U.S. DEPARTMENT OF COMMERCE, BUREAU OF THE CENSUS (US) [09672965] **1603**

CURRENT INDUSTRIAL REPORTS. MA-36E, ELECTRIC HOUSEWARES AND FANS CEASED. (US) [03060370] **2811**

CURRENT INDUSTRIAL REPORTS. MA-36M, RADIO AND TELEVISION RECEIVERS, PHONOGRAPHS, AND RELATED EQUIPMENT / U.S. DEPT. OF COMMERCE, BUREAU OF THE CENSUS (US) [05717140] **2040**

CURRENT INDUSTRIAL REPORTS. MA26A, PULP, PAPER, AND BOARD (US) [09608044] **4233**

CURRENT INDUSTRIAL REPORTS. MA28F, PAINT AND ALLIED PRODUCTS (US) [09553086] **4223**

CURRENT INDUSTRIAL REPORTS. MA31A, FOOTWEAR (US) [09672796] 1083, **3477**

CURRENT INDUSTRIAL REPORTS. MA33E, NONFERROUS CASTINGS / U.S. DEPARTMENT OF COMMERCE, BUREAU OF THE CENSUS (US) [10739419] 4000, **1603**

CURRENT INDUSTRIAL REPORTS. MA37D, AEROSPACE INDUSTRY ORDERS, SALES, AND BACKLOG (US) [12843842] **1603**

CURRENT INDUSTRIAL REPORTS. MQ20J, FATS AND OILS-OILSEED CRUSHINGS (US) [23822105] **1603**

CURRENT INDUSTRIAL REPORTS. MQ22P, CONSUMPTION ON THE COTTON SYSTEM AND STOCKS (US) [23906567] **5350**

CURRENT INDUSTRIAL REPORTS. MQ28A, INORGANIC CHEMICALS / U.S. DEPARTMENT OF COMMERCE, ECONOMICS AND STATISTICS ADMINISTRATION, BUREAU OF THE CENSUS (US) [23957074] **1023**

CURRENT INDUSTRIAL REPORTS. MQ28B, FERTILIZER MATERIALS / U.S. DEPARTMENT OF COMMERCE, ECONOMICS AND STATISTICS ADMINISTRATION, BUREAU OF THE CENSUS (US) [23906335] **78**

CURRENT INDUSTRIAL REPORTS. MQ28F, PAINT, VARNISH, AND LACQUER (US) [23887210] **4223**

CURRENT INDUSTRIAL REPORTS. MQ28F PAINT, VARNISH, LACQUER (COMPUTER FILE) (US) **4223**

CURRENT INDUSTRIAL REPORTS. MQ32D, CLAY CONSTRUCTION PRODUCTS (US) [23906436] **612**

CURRENT INDUSTRIAL REPORTS. MQ34E PLUMBING See CURRENT INDUSTRIAL REPORTS. MQ34E PLUMBING FIXTURES (COMPUTER FILE) **2604**

CURRENT INDUSTRIAL REPORTS. MQ34E PLUMBING FIXTURES (COMPUTER FILE) (US) **2604**

CURRENT INDUSTRIAL REPORTS. MQ36C, FLOURESCENT LAMPS BALLASTS See FLUORESCENT LAMP BALLASTS **2055**

CURRENT INFORMATION IN THE CONSTRUCTION INDUSTRY CEASED. (UK) [04424822] 296, **612**

CURRENT INFORMATION TECHNOLOGY RESOURCE REQUIREMENTS OF THE FEDERAL GOVERNMENT (US) [23747041] **4641**

CURRENT INQUIRY INTO LANGUAGE AND LINGUISTICS CEASED. (CN) [01781296] **3276**

CURRENT INQUIRY INTO LANGUAGE, LINGUISTICS, AND HUMAN COMMUNICATIONS (CN) [11945018] **3276**

CURRENT INTERESTS OF THE FORD FOUNDATION (US/0162-5780) [04174712] **5281**

CURRENT ISSUE OUTLINE (US/0734-9661) [06492410] **1448**

CURRENT ISSUES AND RESEARCH IN ADVERTISING See JOURNAL OF CURRENT ISSUES AND RESEARCH IN ADVERTISING **761**

CURRENT ISSUES IN BANK AUDITING (US) **787**

CURRENT ISSUES IN CATHOLIC HIGHER EDUCATION (US) [07391147] **1819**

CURRENT ISSUES IN CLINICAL PSYCHOLOGY (US/0741-9724) [09562229] **4584**

CURRENT ISSUES IN CRIMINAL JUSTICE (AT/1034-5329) [22523034] **3163**

CURRENT ISSUES IN EUROPEAN SOCIAL PSYCHOLOGY (UK/0264-4517) [10523413] **4584**

CURRENT ISSUES IN EXERCISE SCIENCE CEASED. (US/1055-1352) [23092104] **2596**

CURRENT ISSUES IN INTERNATIONAL SHIP FINANCE (US/0883-0517) [11145156] **2957**

●CURRENT ISSUES IN MIDDLE LEVEL EDUCATION (US/1059-7107) [24681291] **1734**

CURRENT ISSUES IN MUSIC EDUCATION (US) [01565636] **4113**

CURRENT ISSUES IN PSYCHOANALYTIC PRACTICE (US) [21237037] **4584**

●CURRENT ISSUES IN PUBLIC HEALTH (US/1076-7762) [30609011] **4773**

CURRENT ISSUES IN THE AMERICAN ECONOMY (US/0270-3246) [06379982] **1478**

CURRENT ISSUES (WASHINGTON) (US/0161-6641) [03980286] **4470**

CURRENT JAPANESE PERIODICALS FOR ... (JA) [08120205] 3205, **4821**

CURRENT JOBS FOR GRADUATES (US/1054-7762) [22978668] **4203**

CURRENT LAW CASE CITATOR (UK) [01784791] **2958**

CURRENT LAW CITATOR (UK) [01565642] **2958**

CURRENT LAW INDEX (US/0196-1780) [05756625] 2958, **3080**

CURRENT LAW LEGISLATION CITATOR (UK) [14158740] **2958**

CURRENT LAW MONTHLY DIGEST (UK) [23156630] **2958**

CURRENT LAW, PART A (UK) **2958**

CURRENT LAW, PART B (UK) **2958**

CURRENT LAW, PART C (UK) **2958**

CURRENT LAW STATUTES ANNOTATED (UK) [06536534] **2958**

●CURRENT LAW WEEK (UK) **2958**

CURRENT LC SUBJECT HEADINGS IN THE FIELD OF RELIGION / PUBLISHED BY THE BIBLIOGRAPHIC SYSTEMS COMMITTEE OF THE AMERICAN THEOLOGICAL LIBRARY ASSOCIATION CEASED. (US) [10685741] 3205, **4952**

CURRENT LEATHER LITERATURE See LEATHER SCIENCE ABSTRACTS : LESA **3185**

CURRENT LEGAL FORMS (US) [01605223] **2958**

CURRENT LEGAL PROBLEMS (UK/0070-1998) [01565648] **2958**

CURRENT LEGAL SOCIOLOGY (SP/1017-4559) [I10174559] **5243**

CURRENT LEGAL THEORY : INTERNATIONAL JOURNAL FOR DOCUMENTATION ON LEGAL THEORY (BE/0772-1668) [11135148] **2958**

CURRENT LITERATURE IN FAMILY PLANNING (US/0092-6000) [03101337] 2278, **2287**

CURRENT LITERATURE IN NEPHROLOGY CEASED. (US/0743-8036) [10675331] **3989**

CURRENT LITERATURE IN TRAFFIC AND TRANSPORTATION (US/0011-3654) [01565654] **5380**

CURRENT LITERATURE ON OCCUPATIONAL PENSIONS (UK) **1662**

CURRENT LITERATURE ON SCIENCE OF SCIENCE (II) [04240144] 5098, **5174**

CURRENT LITERATURE REVIEW IN OBSTETRICS & GYNECOLOGY (US/0733-8643) [08672907] **3759**

CURRENT LOCAL, THE (US) [13663584] **5703**

CURRENT (LONDON, ENGLAND) (UK/0142-1050) [08774825] **2514**

CURRENT MATERIAL HIGHLIGHTS FOR UNIFORM COMMERCIAL CODE REPORTING SERVICE See UCC BULLETIN **3067**

CURRENT MATHEMATICAL PUBLICATIONS (US/0361-4794) [02246076] 3502, **3542**

CURRENT MEDICAL DIAGNOSIS & TREATMENT (US/0092-8682) [01791712] **3570**

CURRENT MEDICAL LITERATURE. ANAESTHESIOLOGY / THE ROYAL SOCIETY OF MEDICINE (UK/0269-6959) [24732576] **3682**

CURRENT — Alphabetical Title Index

CURRENT MEDICAL LITERATURE. BREAST AND PROSTRATE CANCER/THE ROYAL SOCIETY OF MEDICINE (UK/0953-6787) [24172649] **3759**

CURRENT MEDICAL LITERATURE-BREAST CANCER (UK/0956-6511) [22328869] **3759**

CURRENT MEDICAL LITERATURE-CARDIOVASCULAR MEDICINE (UK) [23110537] **3704**

CURRENT MEDICAL LITERATURE. DIABETES (UK/0265-797X) [I0265797X] **3727**

CURRENT MEDICAL LITERATURE. GASTROENTEROLOGY / THE ROYAL SOCIETY OF MEDICINE (UK/0263-2659) [24172640] **3743**

CURRENT MEDICAL LITERATURE. GENERAL PRACTICE / THE ROYAL SOCIETY OF MEDICINE *CEASED.* (UK/0958-9376) [24379855] **3737**

CURRENT MEDICAL LITERATURE-GERIATRICS (UK/0953-2501) [23730723] **3750**

CURRENT MEDICAL LITERATURE. GROWTH AND GROWTH FACTORS (UK/0269-185X) [I0269185X] **3570**

CURRENT MEDICAL LITERATURE / HOSPITAL PHARMACY (UK/0958-9384) [I09589384] **4298**

CURRENT MEDICAL LITERATURE-INFECTIOUS DISEASES (UK/0951-9602) **3980**

CURRENT MEDICAL LITERATURE / NEPHROLOGY AND UROLOGY (UK/0951-9629) [I09519629] **3989**

CURRENT MEDICAL LITERATURE. NEUROLOGY (UK/0267-0445) [I02670445] **3830**

CURRENT MEDICAL LITERATURE / OPHTHALMOLOGY (UK/0963-0112) [I09630112] **3874**

CURRENT MEDICAL LITERATURE ORTHOPAEDICS (UK/0952-7494) [I09527494] **3881**

CURRENT MEDICAL LITERATURE / PAEDIATRICS (UK/0951-9610) [I09519610] **3902**

CURRENT MEDICAL LITERATURE. PAEDIATRICS / THE ROYAL SOCIETY OF MEDICINE (UK/0951-9610) [29573759] **3902**

CURRENT MEDICAL LITERATURE. RADIOLOGY (UK/0955-1476) [I09551476] **3940**

CURRENT MEDICAL LITERATURE / REVERSIBLE OBSTRUCTIVE AIRWAYS DISEASE (UK/0950-8724) [I09508724] 3796, **3949**

CURRENT MEDICAL LITERATURE. RHEUMATOLOGY (UK/0261-3360) [I02613360] **3804**

CURRENT MEDICAL LITERATURE. THROMBOSIS (UK/0961-2246) [I09612246] 3796, **3771**

CURRENT MEDICAL PRACTICE (II/0011-3700) [01565657] **3963**

CURRENT MEDICAL RESEARCH AND OPINION (UK/0300-7995) [01778119] **3570**

CURRENT MEDICAL RESEARCH AND OPINION SUPPLEMENT (UK/0141-9951) [I01419951] **3570**

CURRENT MEDICINE (US/0734-9939) [08851163] **3570**

CURRENT METHODS IN CELLULAR NEUROBIOLOGY (US/0738-0720) [09508209] **452**

CURRENT MICROBIOLOGY (US/0343-8651) [03876758] **561**

CURRENT MILITARY & POLITICAL LITERATURE *CEASED.* (UK/0954-3589) [19871634] 4040, **4061**

CURRENT MUNICIPAL PROBLEMS (CUMULATION) (US/0161-5122) [03357580] **4641**

CURRENT MUSICOLOGY (US/0011-3735) [01565661] **4113**

CURRENT NEMATOLOGY (II/0971-0116) [25396198] **507**

CURRENT NEPHROLOGY (US/0148-4265) [03301068] **3989**

CURRENT NEUROLOGY (US/0161-780X) [04026196] **3831**

CURRENT (NEW YORK) (US/0011-3131) [01565595] **2487**

CURRENT NEWS ON FILE (US/1058-8124) [24383695] **2532**

CURRENT NEWS. SUPPLEMENT (US) [20043454] **4040**

CURRENT NOTES (US/8750-1937) [11098629] **1181**

CURRENT OBSTETRIC & GYNECOLOGIC DIAGNOSIS & TREATMENT (US/0197-582X) [05967147] **3759**

CURRENT OBSTETRIC MEDICINE (US/1051-077X) [21798596] **3759**

CURRENT OBSTETRICS AND GYNAECOLOGY (UK/0957-5847) [23835748] **3759**

CURRENT OCULAR THERAPY (US) [12687855] **3874**

CURRENT ONCOLOGY (US/0743-930X) [10713867] **3815**

CURRENT OPINION (US/0090-824X) [01785990] **5244**

CURRENT OPINION IN ANAESTHESIOLOGY (UK/0952-7907) [18187359] **3682**

CURRENT OPINION IN BIOTECHNOLOGY (UK/0958-1669) [22926384] **3691**

CURRENT OPINION IN CARDIOLOGY (UK/0268-4705) [14037285] **3704**

CURRENT OPINION IN CELL BIOLOGY (US/0955-0674) [19865265] **535**

●CURRENT OPINION IN COSMETIC DENTISTRY (US/1065-6278) [26659233] **1319**

CURRENT OPINION IN CRITICAL CARE (UK/1070-5295) [28398632] **3570**

CURRENT OPINION IN DENTISTRY (US/1046-0764) [20323470] **1319**

●CURRENT OPINION IN ENDOCRINOLOGY & DIABETES (US/1068-3097) [27644545] **3727**

CURRENT OPINION IN GASTROENTEROLOGY (UK/0267-1379) [12389567] **3744**

●CURRENT OPINION IN GENERAL SURGERY (US/1065-6243) [26659169] **3963**

CURRENT OPINION IN GENETICS AND DEVELOPMENT (UK/0959-437X) [24242182] **544**

●CURRENT OPINION IN HEMATOLOGY (US/1065-6251) [26659188] **3771**

CURRENT OPINION IN IMMUNOLOGY (US/0952-7915) [18609859] **3668**

CURRENT OPINION IN INFECTIOUS DISEASES (UK/0951-7375) [18109134] **3713**

CURRENT OPINION IN INVESTIGATIONAL DRUGS (UK/0967-8298) [29185898] **4298**

CURRENT OPINION IN LIPIDOLOGY (UK/0957-9672) [21681965] **3704**

●CURRENT OPINION IN NEPHROLOGY AND HYPERTENSION (US/1062-4821) [25637631] **3989**

CURRENT OPINION IN NEUROBIOLOGY (UK/0959-4388) [24206417] 3831, **453**

●CURRENT OPINION IN NEUROLOGY (US/1350-7540) [29188477] **3831**

CURRENT OPINION IN NEUROLOGY AND NEUROSURGERY (UK/0951-7383) [18131956] **3831**

CURRENT OPINION IN OBSTETRICS & GYNECOLOGY (US/1040-872X) [18553569] **3759**

CURRENT OPINION IN ONCOLOGY (US/1040-8746) [18553648] **3815**

CURRENT OPINION IN OPHTHALMOLOGY (US/1040-8738) [18553607] **3874**

●CURRENT OPINION IN ORTHODONTICS AND PEDODONTICS (US) **1319**

CURRENT OPINION IN ORTHOPAEDICS (US/1041-9918) [18882167] **3881**

●CURRENT OPINION IN OTOLARYNGOLOGY & HEAD AND NECK SURGERY (US/1068-9508) [27866824] 3963, **3887**

CURRENT OPINION IN PEDIATRICS (US/1040-8703) [18553476] **3902**

CURRENT OPINION IN PERIDONTOLOGY (US) **1319**

●CURRENT OPINION IN PERIODONTOLOGY (UK/1065-626X) [26659216] **1319**

CURRENT OPINION IN PSYCHIATRY (UK/0951-7367) [18170121] **3924**

●CURRENT OPINION IN PULMONARY MEDICINE (US/1070-5287) [28398600] **3570**

CURRENT OPINION IN RADIOLOGY *CEASED.* (US/1040-869X) [18553447] **3940**

CURRENT OPINION IN RHEUMATOLOGY (US/1040-8711) [18553510] **3804**

CURRENT OPINION IN STRUCTURAL BIOLOGY (UK/0959-440X) [23812553] **453**

●CURRENT OPINION IN SURGICAL INFECTIONS (UK/0969-8868) [30471668] **3963**

CURRENT OPINION IN THERAPEUTIC PATENTS (US) **3570**

CURRENT OPINION IN THERAPEUTIC PATENTS (UK) [23664270] **1303**

CURRENT OPINION IN UROLOGY (UK/0963-0643) [25047329] **3989**

CURRENT ORNITHOLOGY (US/0742-390X) [10181578] **5617**

CURRENT ORTHOPAEDICS (UK/0268-0890) [17593696] **3881**

CURRENT PACKAGING ABSTRACTS (PISCATAWAY, N.J.) *SUSPENDED.* (US/0890-4227) [12131213] **4218**

CURRENT PAEDIATRICS (UK/0957-5839) [23835735] **3902**

CURRENT PAPERS IN ELECTRICAL & ELECTRONICS ENGINEERING (UK/0011-3778) [00923903] 2040, **2003**

CURRENT PAPERS IN PHYSICS (UK/0011-3786) [00825105] 4401, **4426**

CURRENT PAPERS ON COMPUTERS & CONTROL (UK/0011-3794) [00923911] 1181, **1208**

CURRENT PEDIATRIC DIAGNOSIS & TREATMENT (US/0093-8556) [02254834] **3903**

CURRENT PEDIATRIC THERAPY *See* GELLIS & KAGAN'S CURRENT PEDIATRIC THERAPY **3903**

CURRENT PERSPECTIVES IN NURSING MANAGEMENT (US) [05255811] **3855**

CURRENT PERSPECTIVES IN SOCIAL THEORY (US/0278-1204) [07063117] **5244**

CURRENT PERSPECTIVES ON AGING AND THE LIFE CYCLE (US/1040-2608) [13477092] **2278**

CURRENT PHYSICS INDEX (US/0098-9819) [02242886] 4401, **4426**

CURRENT PLANT SCIENCE AND BIOTECHNOLOGY IN AGRICULTURE (NE/0924-1949) [14575293] 3691, **507**

●CURRENT POLITICS AND ECONOMICS OF CHINA (US) 1554, **4470**

CURRENT POLITICS AND ECONOMICS OF EUROPE (US/1057-2309) [23983717] 1554, **4470**

CURRENT POLITICS AND ECONOMICS OF JAPAN (US/1056-7593) [23841336] 1554, **4470**

CURRENT POLITICS AND ECONOMICS OF RUSSIA (US/1061-9186) [25488858] 1554, **4470**

●CURRENT POLITICS AND ECONOMICS OF THE MIDDLE EAST (US) 1554, **4471**

CURRENT POLITICS AND ECONOMICS OF THE UNITED STATES (US) 1554, **4471**

CURRENT POPULATION REPORTS : FARM POPULATION. SERIES P-27 (US) [02156125] **4551**

CURRENT POPULATION REPORTS. SER. P-25, POPULATION ESTIMATES AND PROJECTIONS (US/0738-453X) [02244269] **4551**

CURRENT POPULATION REPORTS. SERIES P-20, POPULATION CHARACTERISTICS (US/0363-6836) [01768314] **4551**

CURRENT POPULATION REPORTS. SERIES P-23, SPECIAL STUDIES (US/0498-8485) [02504301] **4551**

CURRENT POPULATION REPORTS. SERIES P-25, POPULATION ESTIMATES *See* CURRENT POPULATION REPORTS. SER. P-25, POPULATION ESTIMATES AND PROJECTIONS **4551**

CURRENT POPULATION REPORTS. SERIES P-28, SPECIAL CENSUSES (US/0270-6660) [06432855] **4551**

CURRENT POPULATION REPORTS. SERIES P-60, CONSUMER INCOME (US/0730-4803) [04738786] 4551, **1478**

CURRENT POPULATION REPORTS. SERIES P-70, HOUSEHOLD ECONOMIC STUDIES (US/0886-5698) [11567017] **4551**

CURRENT POPULATION SURVEY ... ANNUAL DEMOGRAPHIC FILES [COMPUTER FILE] (US) [24817052] **1662**

CURRENT PRACTICE IN GERONTOLOGICAL NURSING (US) [05255788] **3855**

CURRENT PRACTICE IN NURSING CARE OF THE ADULT (US/0190-6771) [05365621] **3855**

CURRENT PRACTICE IN OBSTETRIC AND GYNECOLOGIC NURSING (US/0361-9249) [02145258] **3760**

CURRENT PRACTICE IN SURGERY (UK/0952-0627) [20293992] **3963**

CURRENT PRACTICES IN GEOTECHNICAL ENGINEERING (II/0253-5122) [12984482] **2022**

CURRENT PRESCRIBING (US/0097-8620) [01812627] **4298**

CURRENT PRIMATE REFERENCES (US/0590-4102) [01332411] 5098, **5174**

CURRENT PROBLEMS / COMMITTEE ON SAFETY OF MEDICINES (UK) [27429843] **3570**

CURRENT PROBLEMS IN ANESTHESIA AND CRITICAL CARE MEDICINE (US/0147-197X) [03636061] **3963**

CURRENT PROBLEMS IN CANCER (US/0147-0272) [03054021] **3815**

CURRENT PROBLEMS IN CARDIOLOGY (US/0146-2806) [02883137] **3704**

CURRENT PROBLEMS IN CLINICAL BIOCHEMISTRY **CEASED**. (SZ/0300-1725) [05019228] **486**

CURRENT PROBLEMS IN DERMATOLOGY (SZ/0070-2064) [01776017] **3718**

CURRENT PROBLEMS IN DERMATOLOGY (CHICAGO, ILL.) (US/1040-0486) [18300806] **3719**

CURRENT PROBLEMS IN DIAGNOSTIC RADIOLOGY (US/0363-0188) [02309024] **3940**

CURRENT PROBLEMS IN EPILEPSY (UK/0950-4591) [11925472] **3831**

CURRENT PROBLEMS IN FEDERAL CIVIL PRACTICE (US/0748-7592) [04701527] **3089**

CURRENT PROBLEMS IN NEUROLOGY (UK/0268-6252) [19676248] **3831**

CURRENT PROBLEMS IN OBSTETRICS, GYNECOLOGY AND FERTILITY (US/8756-0410) [11454555] **3760**

CURRENT PROBLEMS IN PEDIATRICS (ENGLISH ED.) (US/0045-9380) [01565666] **3903**

CURRENT PROBLEMS IN SURGERY (US/0011-3840) [01565668] **3963**

CURRENT PROBLEMS IN UROLOGY **CEASED**. (US/1046-5111) [20431457] **3989**

CURRENT PROBLEMS IN UROLOGY **CEASED**. (US/1052-4010) [22283853] **3989**

CURRENT PROJECTS - SWEDISH COUNCIL FOR BUILDING RESEARCH (SW) [03249327] **612**

CURRENT PROTOCOLS IN MOLECULAR BIOLOGY (US) **453**

CURRENT PSYCHOLOGY (NEW BRUNSWICK, N.J.) (US/1046-1310) [18767012] **4584**

CURRENT PUBLICATIONS FROM THE FOREST, WILDLIFE AND RANGE EXPERIMENT STATION (US/0748-1616) [10909299] 2191, **2378**

CURRENT PUBLICATIONS IN LEGAL AND RELATED FIELDS (US/0011-3859) [01565672] **3080**

CURRENT PUBLICATIONS / NEW ZEALAND AGRICULTURAL ENGINEERING INSTITUTE (NZ/0111-8234) [09116827] **158**

CURRENT PULMONOLOGY (US/0163-7800) [04474573] **3704**

CURRENT RADIOLOGY (US/0161-7818) [04026235] **3940**

CURRENT REFERENCES IN FISH RESEARCH (US/0739-540X) [03944574] 2299, **2317**

CURRENT RESEARCH FOR THE INFORMATION PROFESSION **CEASED**. (UK/0268-7372) [13081473] **3205**

CURRENT RESEARCH - GEOLOGICAL SURVEY OF CANADA (CN/0704-2884) [03980545] **1372**

CURRENT RESEARCH IN BRITAIN. BIOLOGICAL SCIENCES (UK/0267-1956) [13468602] **453**

CURRENT RESEARCH IN BRITAIN. PHYSICAL SCIENCES (UK/0267-1948) [13482649] **414**

CURRENT RESEARCH IN BRITAIN. SOCIAL SCIENCES (UK/0267-1964) [13467376] **5197**

CURRENT RESEARCH IN BRITAIN. THE HUMANITIES (UK/0267-1972) [13467378] **2845**

CURRENT RESEARCH IN FILM **CEASED**. (US/0748-8580) [11018239] **4067**

CURRENT RESEARCH IN FRENCH STUDIES AT UNIVERSITIES & POLYTECHNICS IN THE UNITED KINGDOM & IRELAND (UK/0957-4751) [18894547] **3276**

●CURRENT RESEARCH IN FRENCH STUDIES AT UNIVERSITIES IN THE UNITED KINGDOM & IRELAND (UK/1350-9209) [30757624] **3276**

CURRENT RESEARCH IN LIBRARY & INFORMATION SCIENCE (UK/0263-9254) [09471344] **3205**

CURRENT RESEARCH IN OPHTHALMIC ELECTRON MICROSCOPY (GW/0173-7082) [06589217] **3874**

CURRENT RESEARCH IN SOCIAL SECURITY (SZ/0379-0290) [04251298] **5281**

CURRENT RESEARCH IN THE NETHERLANDS : MATHEMATICS, PHYSICS, GEOLOGY, ASTRONOMY (NE) [03231834] **5098**

CURRENT RESEARCH IN THE NETHERLANDS : TECHNOLOGICAL SCIENCES (NE) [07536388] **5098**

CURRENT RESEARCH IN THE PLEISTOCENE (US/8755-898X) [11447416] 4226, **235**

CURRENT RESEARCH (MAKHON HA-GEOLOGI (ISRAEL)) (IS/0333-6425) [08245683] **1373**

CURRENT RESEARCH - NEWFOUNDLAND. GEOLOGICAL SURVEY BRANCH (CN/0843-4972) [23659521] **1439**

CURRENT RESEARCH ON MEDICINAL & AROMATIC PLANTS (II/0253-7125) [08223965] **2413**

CURRENT RESEARCH ON OCCUPATIONS AND PROFESSIONS (US) [17021823] **4203**

CURRENT RESEARCH PROJECTS (SW) [04610810] **5197**

CURRENT RESEARCH REPORTER (II/0256-6885) [13416743] **78**

CURRENT RESEARCH - THE SWEDISH INSTITUTE OF INTERNATIONAL AFFAIRS (SW) [07348874] **4502**

CURRENT RESEARCH - UNIVERSITY OF AGRICULTURAL SCIENCES (II/0253-7133) [03309563] **78**

CURRENT RESEARCH UPDATES IN HUMAN SEXUALITY (US/0748-0679) [10873283] **5187**

CURRENT RESEARCH UPDATES. OBSTETRICS & GYNECOLOGY (US/0882-2441) [11794117] 3760, **3657**

●CURRENT REVIEW OF CEREBROVASCULAR DISEASE (US/1068-2252) [27477136] **3570**

●CURRENT REVIEW OF MAGNETIC RESONANCE IMAGING (US/1072-8392) [29210063] **3570**

●CURRENT REVIEW OF PAIN (US/1069-5850) [28122941] **3570**

●CURRENT REVIEW OF SPORTS MEDICINE (US/1069-5842) [28122919] **3953**

CURRENT REVIEWS FOR NURSE ANESTHETISTS (US/0164-310X) [04612008] **3855**

CURRENT REVIEWS FOR POST ANESTHESIA CARE NURSES (US/0896-1182) [15233999] 3963, **3855**

CURRENT REVIEWS IN BIOMEDICINE (US/0167-7209) [08196470] **3570**

CURRENT REVIEWS IN CLINICAL ANESTHESIA (US/0891-9917) [10883047] **3682**

CURRENT (RICHMOND) (CN/0828-7902) [12227642] **2299**

CURRENT SCIENCE (II/0011-3891) [01565678] **5098**

CURRENT SCIENCE (MIDDLETOWN) (US/0011-3905) [04043994] **5098**

CURRENT SENTENCING PRACTICE NEWS (UK/0964-8461) [I09648461] **2958**

CURRENT SEPARATIONS (US/0891-0006) [07939293] **1051**

CURRENT SERIALS RECEIVED (US/0959-4914) [13246882] **3205**

CURRENT SOCIOLOGY (PARIS, FRANCE) (UK/0011-3921) [01565681] **5244**

CURRENT SOUTH AFRICAN PERIODICALS. HUIDIGE SUID-AFRIKAANSE TYDSKRIFTE (SA) [06352279] **414**

CURRENT SOVIET POLICIES (US/0590-3890) [02070580] **4541**

CURRENT STATUS OF LEGISLATION IN THE HOUSE OF COMMONS AND SENATE OF CANADA (CN/0846-085X) [24256966] **4471**

CURRENT STATUS OF MODERN THERAPY (US/0192-7736) [05022327] **4298**

CURRENT STUDIES IN HEMATOLOGY AND BLOOD TRANSFUSION (SZ/0258-0330) [13104419] **3771**

CURRENT STUDIES IN LIBRARIANSHIP (US/0742-8227) [03409249] **3205**

CURRENT STUDIES IN LINGUISTICS SERIES (US) [20226927] **3276**

CURRENT SURGERY (US/0149-7944) [03556097] **3963**

CURRENT SURGICAL DIAGNOSIS & TREATMENT (US/0894-2277) [05461407] **3963**

CURRENT SURGICAL PRACTICE (UK/0141-3368) [03494837] **3963**

CURRENT SURGICAL THERAPY (US/0835-3689) [11088726] **3963**

CURRENT SWEDEN / THE SWEDISH INSTITUTE (SW/1101-6345) [04155553] **2514**

●CURRENT SWEDISH ARCHAEOLOGY (SW/1102-7355) [28173336] **266**

CURRENT SWEDISH RESEARCH ON LATIN AMERICA (SW) [19735918] **2551**

CURRENT TAX INTELLIGENCE (UK) [11936799] **4719**

CURRENT TAX REPORTER (II) [01784208] **4719**

●CURRENT TECHNIQUES IN ARTHROSCOPY (US/1068-4107) [27667851] **3963**

●CURRENT TECHNIQUES IN INTERVENTIONAL RADIOLOGY (US/1068-3879) [27667774] **3940**

CURRENT TECHNIQUES IN SMALL ANIMAL SURGERY (US) [02142502] **5508**

●CURRENT TECHNIQUES IN SURGERY (US/1065-0717) [26506267] **3963**

CURRENT TECHNOLOGY INDEX : CTI (UK/0260-6593) [07378113] 5098, **5174**

CURRENT, THE (II/0011-3123) [04581241] **2503**

CURRENT THEMES IN TROPICAL SCIENCE (UK/0742-2725) [10296052] **5098**

CURRENT THERAPEUTIC RESEARCH (US/0011-393X) [01565683] 3570, **4298**

CURRENT THERAPEUTICS (AT/0311-905X) [01160367] **4298**

CURRENT THERAPY IN INFECTIOUS DISEASE (CN/0899-3947) [11180730] **3713**

CURRENT THERAPY IN INTERNAL MEDICINE (US/0899-6865) [11126881] **3796**

CURRENT THERAPY IN NEUROLOGICAL SURGERY (CN/0899-3963) [12444634] **3831**

CURRENT THERAPY IN SPORTS MEDICINE (US/0831-8670) [12577990] **3954**

CURRENT THERAPY NEWSLETTER (US/0893-763X) [15640331] **3570**

CURRENT THERAPY OF INFERTILITY (US/0899-3882) [09065718] **3760**

CURRENT THOUGHTS AND TRENDS (US/1054-8688) [22337683] 4952, **5012**

CURRENT TITLES IN DENTISTRY (DK/0903-3483) [17959401] 1319, **1338**

CURRENT TITLES IN ELECTROCHEMISTRY (II/0300-4376) [01439961] 1034, **1011**

CURRENT TITLES IN SPELEOLOGY (UK) [03639605] **1354**

CURRENT TOPICS IN AIDS (UK/0898-5871) [16522379] 4773, **3669**

CURRENT TOPICS IN ANAESTHESIA (UK/0144-8684) [05978382] **3682**

CURRENT TOPICS IN ANTHROPOLOGY (US) [00826191] **235**

CURRENT TOPICS IN BIOENERGETICS (US/0070-2129) [01320760] **453**

CURRENT TOPICS IN CELLULAR REGULATION (US/0070-2137) [01565690] **535**

CURRENT TOPICS IN CHINESE SCIENCE. SECTION A, PHYSICS (US/0732-4383) [08357224] **4401**

CURRENT TOPICS IN CHINESE SCIENCE. SECTION B, CHEMISTRY (US/0732-4391) [08357254] **974**

CURRENT TOPICS IN CHINESE SCIENCE. SECTION D, BIOLOGY (US/0732-4413) [08357313] **453**

CURRENT TOPICS IN CHINESE SCIENCE. SECTION E, ASTRONOMY (UK/0732-4421) [08357375] **395**

CURRENT TOPICS IN CHINESE SCIENCE. SECTION F, EARTH SCIENCE (US/0732-443X) [08357482] **1354**

CURRENT TOPICS IN CHINESE SCIENCE. SECTION G, MEDICAL SCIENCE (US/0732-4448) [08357542] **3570**

CURRENT TOPICS IN DEVELOPMENTAL BIOLOGY (US/0070-2153) [01424326] **453**

CURRENT TOPICS IN EARLY CHILDHOOD EDUCATION (US/0363-8332) [03147125] **1803**

CURRENT TOPICS IN EXPERIMENTAL ENDOCRINOLOGY (US/0091-7397) [01770754] **3727**

CURRENT TOPICS IN HEMATOLOGY (US/0190-1486) [04653148] **3771**

CURRENT TOPICS IN HUMAN INTELLIGENCE (US/8755-0040) [11241680] **4584**

CURRENT TOPICS IN IMMUNOLOGY (US) [03197903] **3669**

CURRENT TOPICS IN INFECTION **CEASED**. (UK) [07418127] **3713**

CURRENT TOPICS IN INFECTIOUS DISEASES AND CLINICAL MICROBIOLOGY (GW/0937-2156) [19808395] **3713**

CURRENT TOPICS IN MATERIALS SCIENCE **SUSPENDED**. (US/0165-1854) [04128160] **2022**

CURRENT TOPICS IN MEDICAL MYCOLOGY (US/0177-4204) [12276388] **574**

CURRENT TOPICS IN MEMBRANES (US/1063-5823) [24814151] **535**

CURRENT TOPICS IN MICROBIOLOGY AND IMMUNOLOGY (GW/0070-217X) [01565694] **3669**

CURRENT TOPICS IN NEUROBIOLOGY (US/0093-4747) [01038015] **3831**

CURRENT

CURRENT TOPICS IN NEUROENDOCRINOLOGY (GW/0723-1229) [08353562] **3727**

CURRENT TOPICS IN NUTRITION AND DISEASE (US/0191-2453) [03547035] **4189**

CURRENT TOPICS IN NUTRITIONAL SCIENCES (GW/0340-1960) [01356396] **4189**

CURRENT TOPICS IN PATHOLOGY (GW/0070-2188) [01565695] **3894**

CURRENT TOPICS IN PHOTOVOLTAICS (UK/1053-122X) [12814640] **4401**

CURRENT TOPICS IN PLANT BIOCHEMISTRY AND PHYSIOLOGY : PROCEEDINGS OF THE ... PLANT BIOCHEMISTRY AND PHYSIOLOGY SYMPOSIUM HELD AT THE UNIVERSITY OF MISSOURI--COLUMBIA (US) [09930899] **507**

CURRENT TOPICS IN PULMONARY PHARMACOLOGY AND TOXICOLOGY (US/0890-1449) [14158264] 3949, **3980**

CURRENT TOPICS IN REPRODUCTIVE ENDOCRINOLOGY (UK/0742-3616) [09069123] **3727**

CURRENT TOPICS IN RESEARCH ON SYNAPSES (US/0747-5454) [10749285] **580**

CURRENT TOPICS OF CONTEMPORARY THOUGHT (US/0275-9098) [03647892] **5098**

CURRENT TOXICOLOGY (US/1069-4587) [28050688] **3980**

CURRENT TRAVEL AND TOURISM INDICATORS (SP) [22245011] **5467**

CURRENT TREATY INDEX (US/0731-8189) [08261448] 4519, **3080**

CURRENT TREND REVIEW (US/0362-4269) [02289638] **5326**

CURRENT TRENDS IN GEOLOGY (II) [06451355] **1373**

CURRENT TRENDS IN LIFE SCIENCES (II/0378-7540) [07087481] 2213, **507**

CURRENT TRENDS IN LIMNOLOGY (II) [24118923] **453**

CURRENT TRENDS IN UROLOGY **CEASED.** (US/0731-5910) [07851209] **3989**

CURRENT TURKISH THOUGHT (TU) [05295203] **2685**

CURRENT VETERINARY THERAPY (US/0070-2218) [01202155] **5508**

CURRENT WAGE DEVELOPMENTS (US) [01768199] **1662**

CURRENT (WASHINGTON, D.C. : 1980) (US/0739-991X) [06758682] **1153**

CURRENT WORK IN THE HISTORY OF MEDICINE (UK/0011-3999) [01565701] **3570**

CURRENT WORLD AFFAIRS (US/1050-4850) [21389872] **4040**

CURRENT WORLD LEADERS (US/0192-6802) [04217990] 5197, **4519**

CURRENTLY (TORONTO) (CN/0384-9627) [04875785] **4087**

CURRENTS (CALGARY) (CN/1186-8783) [24262623] **1181**

CURRENTS / CANADA-ASIA WORKING GROUP (CN/0820-3296) [16580140] **4507**

CURRENTS (CHAPEL HILL, N.C.) (US/0882-7915) [11895550] 2332, **4189**

CURRENTS IN AFFECTIVE ILLNESS (US/8750-8699) [10640917] 3570, **4584**

CURRENTS IN ALCOHOLISM (US/0161-8504) [04042003] **1342**

CURRENTS IN COMPARATIVE ROMANCE LANGUAGES AND LITERATURES (US/0893-5963) [15600291] **3379**

CURRENTS IN EMERGENCY CARDIAC CARE (US/1054-917X) [23019917] **3704**

CURRENTS IN SCIENCE, TECHNOLOGY AND SOCIETY (US) **5098**

CURRENTS IN THEOLOGY AND MISSION (US/0098-2113) [01448947] **4952**

CURRENTS IN TOXICOLOGY AND THERAPY (IT) **3980**

CURRENTS (PHILADELPHIA) (US/0146-874X) [03058148] **5281**

CURRENTS (TORONTO) (CN/0715-7045) [09666843] 4471, **5244**

CURRENTS (WASHINGTON, D.C. 1983) (US/0748-478X) [10153689] **1819**

CURRICULA IN THE ATMOSPHERIC AND OCEANOGRAPHIC SCIENCES (US) [03751475] **1424**

CURRICULUM (VE) [03296408] **1892**

CURRICULUM AND TEACHING (AT/0726-416X) [14039876] 1892, **1734**

CURRICULUM CONCERNS : NEWSLETTER OF ACSA (AT/0814-3641) [17275773] 1892, **1734**

CURRICULUM DIGEST - CURRICULUM DEVELOPMENT CENTRE (AT/0725-8488) [I07258488] **1892**

CURRICULUM (DRIFFIELD) (UK/0143-8689) [I01438689] **1892**

CURRICULUM EXCHANGE (AT/0727-6826) [I07276826] **1892**

CURRICULUM INQUIRY (US/0362-6784) [02670036] **1892**

CURRICULUM JOURNAL (UK/0958-5176) [I09585176] **1892**

CURRICULUM PERSPECTIVES (AT/0159-7868) [11240496] **1892**

CURRICULUM PLANS (US/0160-0885) [03611810] **5059**

CURRICULUM PRODUCT NEWS : CPN (US/1063-3375) [17931515] **1892**

CURRICULUM REPORT (US/0547-4205) [02446287] **1892**

CURRICULUM RESOURCES (CN/0714-6124) [09074997] **3379**

CURRICULUM REVIEW (US/0147-2453) [02272853] **1892**

CURRICULUM SERIES (CN/0078-4923) [05931213] **1892**

●CURRICULUM STUDIES (UK/0965-9757) [28600819] **1892**

CURRICULUM THEORY NETWORK *See* CURRICULUM THEORY NETWORK **1892**

CURRICULUM THEORY NETWORK (CN/0011-4049) [01565710] **1892**

CURRICULUM UPDATE (ALEXANDRIA, VA.) (US/0734-0044) [07332671] **1892**

CURRITUCK COUNTY HISTORICAL SOCIETY. YEARBOOK COMMITTEE *See* JOURNAL OF CURRITUCK COUNTY HISTORICAL SOCIETY, THE **2741**

CURRRENT INDUSTRIAL REPORTS. MQ28F PAINT, VARNISH, LACQUER *See* CURRENT INDUSTRIAL REPORTS. MQ28F PAINT, VARNISH, LACQUER (COMPUTER FILE) **4223**

CURRY COUNTY ECHOES (US) [05840556] **2730**

CURSOR (MX) [19029270] **1257**

CURTIN UNIVERSITY OF TECHNOLOGY *See* ANNUAL REPORT / CURTIN UNIVERSITY OF TECHNOLOGY **5084**

CURTIS'S BOTANICAL MAGAZINE (UK) **508**

CUSANUS GESELLSCHAFT, VEREINIGUNG ZUR FORDERUNG DER CUSANUSFORSCHUN *See* MITTEILUNGEN UND FORSCHUNGSBEITRAGE DER CUSANUS-GESELLSCHAFT **4353**

CUSANUS-GESELLSCHAFT, VEREINIGUNG ZUR FORDERUNG DER CUSANUSFORSCHUNG *See* BUCHREIHE DER CUSANUS-GESELLSCHAFT **5024**

CUSHING ACADEMY *See* ALUMNI DIRECTORY / CUSHING ACADEMY **1098**

CUSHING CITIZEN, THE (US) [13646009] **5731**

CUSHMAN FOUNDATION FOR FORAMINIFERAL RESEARCH *See* SPECIAL PUBLICATION - CUSHMAN FOUNDATION FOR FORAMINIFERAL RESEARCH **5597**

CUSO FORUM (OTTAWA, ONT. : 1980) **SUSPENDED.** (CN/0823-5740) [08458445] **1634**

CUSSCO NEWSLETTER (CN/0823-3918) [12204335] **4773**

CUSSNEWS (CN/0316-6791) [02247896] **5244**

●CUSTOM & CLASSIC TRUCKS (US/1073-4732) [29410951] **5412**

CUSTOM APPLICATOR (US/0011-4111) [05321189] **170**

CUSTOM BIKE CHOPPERS (US/0745-0567) [08412291] **4081**

CUSTOM BUILDER (US/0895-2493) [16520871] **612**

CUSTOM CAR (UK/0591-2334) [I05912334] **5412**

CUSTOM CHEMICAL SYNTHESIS SERVICES IN OTHER EUROPEAN COUNTRIES (UK) **974**

CUSTOM HOME (US/1055-3479) [23157810] **296**

●CUSTOM HOME PLANS (US/1065-8157) [26751273] **612**

CUSTOM HOMES (US/0194-3324) [05391253] **612**

●CUSTOM PAINT & BODY (US/1059-5732) [24638981] **5412**

CUSTOM RODDER (US/1076-3678) [30468476] **5412**

CUSTOM TAILOR, THE (US/1071-1147) [28552928] 1603, **1479**

CUSTOM WOODWORKING BUSINESS (US/1058-403X) [24262904] **634**

CUSTOMER COMMUNICATOR, THE (US/0145-8450) [02785971] **663**

CUSTOMER INFORMATION - BRITISH COLUMBIA. PURCHASING COMMISSION (CN/1187-0265) [24986830] **949**

... CUSTOMER SERVICE MANAGER'S GUIDE, THE (US/1061-9119) [25454541] **865**

CUSTOMER SERVICE MANAGER'S LETTER (US) **865**

CUSTOMER SERVICE MANAGER'S LETTER (US/1068-154X) [19952733] **663**

CUSTOMER SERVICE NEWSLETTER (US/0145-8442) [02786037] **865**

CUSTOMER SERVICE POSTING (US) **663**

CUSTOMER SERVICE REPORT **CEASED.** (US/1046-252X) [20367160] **865**

CUSTOMS AND EXCISE FEDERATION *See* JOURNAL OF H.M. CUSTOMS AND EXCISE, THE **4704**

CUSTOMS AND EXCISE TARIFF OF IRELAND (IE) [14522716] **2958**

CUSTOMS BULLETIN *See* CUSTOMS BULLETIN AND DECISIONS **2958**

CUSTOMS BULLETIN AND DECISIONS (US/0162-6442) [03200705] **2958**

CUSTOMS RECORD (US/1063-7443) [18119466] **3126**

CUSTOMS REGULATIONS OF THE UNITED STATES (US) [02784214] **2958**

CUSTOMS TODAY (US/0897-1609) [09845834] **4719**

CUSTOS (SA) [01784912] **4706**

CUSTOS DE PRODUCAO E PERSPECTIVAS DA AGROINDUSTRIA DO ACUCAR E DO ALCOOL (BL) [05045119] **2366**

CUT BANK PIONEER PRESS (US) [11982522] **5705**

CUTBANK (US/0734-9963) [02536303] **3379**

CUTIS (NEW YORK, N.Y.) (US/0011-4162) [01770756] 3713, **3719**

CUTT : CORNELL UNIVERSITY TURFGRASS TIMES (US) [23819122] **2413**

CUTTER RADAR PROJECT NEWSLETTER (US) [03454510] **4040**

CUTTER, THE (US/0274-8851) [06668021] 403, **663**

CUTTIN' HOSS CHATTER *See* CUTTING HORSE **2798**

CUTTING EDGE - AMERICAN MEDICAL RECORDS ASSOCIATION (US) **3570**

CUTTING EDGE (NEW ROCHELLE, N.Y.) (US/0885-999X) [15578483] **1734**

CUTTING EDGE, THE **CEASED.** (US/1049-4839) [21238197] **2487**

CUTTING HORSE (US/1061-3986) [25302405] **2798**

CUTTING HORSE CHATTER (US) **2798**

CUTTING TOOL ENGINEERING (US/0011-4189) [01565724] **4000**

CUTTINGTON RESEARCH JOURNAL (LB) [10032214] 5098, **3341**

CUTW VOICE (US/0745-3302) [09068334] **1662**

CUU QUOC (MICROFICHE) (VM/0574-8070) [03647909] **5813**

CUVANTUL ROMANESC (US/0705-8365) [02623012] **2259**

CUYAHOGA CRIMINAL DEFENSE LAWYERS ASSOCIATION NEWSLETTER (US/0882-9853) [11378629] **3106**

CUYAHOGA REVIEW **CEASED.** (US/0737-139X) [09328453] **3379**

CUYO : ANUARIO DE FILOSOFIA ARGENTINA Y AMERICANA (AG) [15814153] **4344**

CV GUIDE TO THE ARTS (UK/0969-1189) [I09691189] **372**

CV : JOURNAL OF ART AND CRAFTS (UK/0954-1608) [20717354] **372**

CV (NEW YORK, N.Y.) **CEASED.** (US/1042-3672) [19027202] **4203**

CV NEWS LETTER (IT/0308-2237) [08971266] **1479**

●CVA NEWSLETTER / COMMISSION ON VISUAL ANTHROPOLOGY (GW) [26016561] 4067, 4368, **235**

CVA REVIEW (CN/0846-8648) [20834116] 235, **4067**

CVC VIDEO REPORT (US/0743-2402) [10548504] **2040**

CVETOVODSTVO (RU/0041-4905) [04141405] **2413**

CVGIP : GRAPHICAL MODELS & IMAGE PROCESSING *See* GRAPHICAL MODELS AND IMAGE PROCESSING **1233**

CVGIP. GRAPHICAL MODELS AND IMAGE PROCESSING (US/1049-9652) [21359200] **1233**

CVGIP. IMAGE UNDERSTANDING (US/1049-9660) [21359231] **1233**

CVO UPDATE (CN/0849-2395) [23231274] **5508**

CVPOP. CENTRE VIDEO POPULAIRE DE LA RIVE-SUD (CN/0710-1562) [08144051] **1130**

CVQ *See* CMM : CANADIAN MEDIA MAG **4443**

CVR HOTEL GUIDE TO SOUTHERN AFRICA, THE (SA) [08595744] **2805**

CVRD REVISTA (BL/0102-9541) [09500104] **1970**

CW/PS SPECIAL STUDY (US/0730-9058) [08079061] **4040**

CWA NEWS (US/0007-9227) [01963615] 1153, **1662**

CWI MONOGRAPHS (NE/0169-4669) [01694669] **3502**

CWI QUARTERLY (NE) [19217524] **3503**

CWI SYLLABUS (NE) [14260727] **3503**

CWI TRACT / CENTRUM VOOR WISKUNDE EN INFORMATICA (NE) [11418652] 1181, **3503**

CWRU - CASE WESTERN RESERVE UNIVERSITY (US/1042-9220) [19045121] **1091**

CYANOSIS (SANTA ROSA, CALIF.) (US/1057-3577) [24020487] **318**

CYBEREDGE JOURNAL (US/1061-3099) [25237906] **1181**

CYBERNETIC (FAIRFAX, VA.) (US/0883-4202) [12141823] **1250**

CYBERNETICA (BE/0011-4227) [02446289] **1250**

CYBERNETICS ABSTRACTS / SCIENTIFIC INFORMATION CONSULTANTS LIMITED, LONDON, ENGLAND *CEASED.* (UK/0011-4243) [01565729] **1250**

CYBERNETICS AND SYSTEMS (US/0196-9722) [05930760] **1250**

CYBERNETICS AND SYSTEMS ANALYSIS (US/1060-0396) [24858378] **1251**

CYBERSUIT ARKADYNE *CEASED.* (CN/1188-7710) [26714746] **377**

CYBIUM (FR/0399-0974) [01492885] **2299**

CYCLE CANADA (CN/0319-2822) [01989275] **4081**

CYCLE GUIDE ROAD TEST ANNUAL (US/0590-4641) [01794690] **4081**

CYCLE GUIDE'S MOTORCYCLE ACCESSORIES GUIDE (US/0090-4775) [01785240] **4081**

CYCLE INDUSTRY (UK) 4892, **1603**

CYCLE NEWS EAST (US/0274-7502) [06546430] **428**

CYCLE PROJECTIONS (US/1055-1700) [23102153] 1479, 4836, **787**

CYCLE STREET AND TOURING GUIDE (US/0272-8923) [06446207] **4081**

CYCLE TOURING & CAMPAIGNING (UK) [19639620] **428**

CYCLE TRADER (UK) **428**

CYCLE WORLD (US/0011-4286) [01565731] **4081**

CYCLE WORLD TEST ANNUAL & BUYER'S GUIDE (US/0270-2746) [04956341] **4081**

CYCLES ET TENDANCES (CN/0822-8205) [30097760] **1590**

CYCLES (PITTSBURGH) (US/0011-4294) [02113095] 5197, **5098**

CYCLES THEN AND NOW (CN/1187-7367) [25652136] **787**

CYCLIC AMP (SHEFFIELD, ENGLAND) (UK/0142-8055) [18839643] **486**

CYCLICAL INVESTING QUARTERLY REPORT (US) **895**

CYCLING SCIENCE (US/1049-8990) [I10498990] 4892, **428**

CYCLING U.S.A (US/0274-4813) [06346449] **428**

CYCLING WEEKLY (UK/0951-5852) [I09515852] **428**

CYCLING WORLD (UK/0143-0238) [I01430238] **4892**

CYCLO-FLAME (US/0011-4359) [02942894] **3379**

CYCLO NOUVELLES (CN/0383-9664) [03235754] **429**

CYCLODEXTRIN NEWS (HU/0951-256X) [I0951256X] **1041**

CYCLONE (II) [03117268] **2650**

CYCLOPEDIA OF INSURANCE IN THE UNITED STATES (US) [01565733] **2878**

CYCLOTOURISME ORGANE OFFICIEL DE LA FEDERATION FRANCAISE DE CYCLOTOURISME (FR) **429**

CYCNOS (FR) [17603325] **3379**

CYCON COMMUNICATIONS' COMPUTER PR UPDATE (US/0893-5947) [15638794] **758**

CYGNUS (II) [07040352] **3379**

CYLA QUARTERLY (US/8750-944X) [11945615] **2958**

CYLCHGRAWN LLYFRGELL GENEDLAETHOL CYMRU (UK/0011-4421) [02269327] **3205**

CYNEGETICUS (US/0160-2543) [03645664] **4892**

CYNOMAG (CN/0317-1965) [02247946] **4286**

CYNTHIANA ARGUS, THE (US) [14517512] **5663**

CYNTHIANA DEMOCRAT, THE (US) [11064933] **5680**

CYPRIS (US/0886-3806) [12920900] **4226**

CYPRUS. HYPOURGEION OIKONOMIKON *See* EXPLANATORY NOTE ON THE ... BUDGET / MINISTRY OF FINANCE, CYPRUS, AN **4723**

CYPRUS JOURNAL OF ECONOMICS, THE (CY/1013-3224) [21399493] **1479**

CYPRUS ORNITHOLOGICAL SOCIETY *See* ANNUAL REPORT - CYPRUS ORNITHOLOGICAL SOCIETY **5614**

CYPRUS PORTS AUTHORITY *See* ANNUAL REPORT - CYPRUS PORTS AUTHORITY **5447**

CYPRUS REVIEW, THE (CY/1015-2881) [I10152881] 1479, **4471**

CYPRUS REVIEW, THE (CY) [20470816] 1555, 4519, **5197**

CYPRUS. STATISTICS AND RESEARCH DEPT *See* STATISTICAL ABSTRACT - STATISTICS AND RESEARCH DEPARTMENT (NICOSIA) **5340**

CYPRUS. TMEMA ARCHAIOTETON *See* ANNUAL REPORT OF THE DEPARTMENT OF ANTIQUITIES FOR THE YEAR ... / REPUBLIC OF CYPRUS, MINISTRY OF COMMUNICATIONS WORKS **255**

CYPRUS. TMEMA TACHYDROMEION *See* ANNUAL REPORT OF THE DEPARTMENT OF POSTAL SERVICES (CYPRUS) **1144**

CYPRUS TO-DAY (CY/0045-9429) [03693956] **2650**

CYRANO'S JOURNAL (US/0740-5405) [09449835] **1109**

CYRILLOMETHODIANUM (GR) [04219366] **2614**

CYSTIC FIBROSIS CLUB ABSTRACTS (US/0070-2455) [01644185] **3570**

CYSTIC FIBROSIS CLUB. MEETING *See* CYSTIC FIBROSIS CLUB ABSTRACTS **3570**

CYSTIC FIBROSIS FOUNDATION *See* REPORT OF THE PATIENT REGISTRY **3801**

CYSTIC FIBROSIS FOUNDATION *See* CYSTIC FIBROSIS FOUNDATION ANNUAL REPORT FOR THE FISCAL YEAR ... **3804**

CYSTIC FIBROSIS FOUNDATION ANNUAL REPORT FOR THE FISCAL YEAR ... (US) [08857478] **3804**

CYSTIC FIBROSIS FOUNDATION. RESEARCH PROGRAM *See* GAP CONFERENCE REPORT / RESEARCH PROGRAM, CYSTIC FIBROSIS FOUNDATION **3578**

CYSTIC FIBROSIS (NATIONAL INSTITUTE OF ARTHRITIS, DIABETES, AND DIGESTIVE AND KIDNEY DISEASES (U.S.)) (US) [07895724] **3570**

CYTOBIOS (UK/0011-4529) [01565747] **535**

CYTOGENETICS AND CELL GENETICS (SZ/0301-0171) [01787030] 535, **544**

CYTOKINE (PHILADELPHIA, PA.) (US/1043-4666) [19480996] **453**

CYTOKINES (SZ/1013-9982) [20224555] **535**

CYTOLOGIA (JA/0011-4545) [01565749] **535**

CYTOLOGY AND GENETICS (US/0095-4527) [01159194] 544, **535**

CYTOMETRY (NEW YORK, N.Y.) (US/0196-4763) [05855268] **535**

CYTOMETRY. SUPPLEMENT (US/1046-7386) [16310808] **535**

●CYTOPATHOLOGY ANNUAL (US/1069-045X) [24897304] **535**

CYTOPATHOLOGY (OXFORD) (UK/0956-5507) [22155184] **535**

CYTOSKELETON SHEFFIELD (UK/0268-1625) [I02681625] 486, **3570**

CYTOTECHNOLOGISTS BULLETIN *See* ASC BULLETIN **532**

CYTOTECHNOLOGY (DORDRECHT) (NE/0920-9069) [17645742] 544, 3691, **535**

CZARNY PAS (PL/0867-3993) [I08673993] **4892**

CZAS (PL) [03160244] **2514**

CZAS KRAKOWSKI (PL/0867-0374) [I08670374] **5807**

CZASOPISMO GEOGRAFICZNE : KWARTALNIK ZRZESZENIA POL. NAUCZYCIELI GEOGRAFJI, TOWARZYSTWA GEOGRAFICZNEGO WE LWOWIE I TOWARZYSTWA GEOGRAFICZNEGO W POZNANIU (PL/0045-9453) [30425572] **2559**

CZASOPISMO PRAWNO-HISTORYCZNE (PL/0070-2471) [04289745] **2958**

CZASOPISMO STOMATOLOGICZNE (PL/0011-4553) [04319115] **1319**

CZECH & SLOVAK MARKETS (XR) **663**

●CZECH BUSINESS AND TRADE (XR) [30128082] **830**

CZECH FOREIGN TRADE (XR/1210-5546) [28137858] **663**

●CZECH MYCOLOGY (XR) [29981966] **574**

CZECH REPUBLIC. MINISTERSTVO SKOLSTVI, MLADEZE A TELOVYCHOVY *See* VESTNIK MINISTERSTVA SKOLSTVI, MLADEZE A TELOVYCHOVY CESKE REPUBLIKY **1886**

CZECH SOCIALIST REPUBLIC, (CZECHOSLOVAKIA) *See* USTREDNI VESTNIK CESKE SOCIALISTICKE REPUBLIKY **3070**

CZECH SOCIALIST REPUBLIC (CZECHOSLOVAKIA). MINISTERSTVO SKOLSTVI, MLADEZE A TELOVYCHOVY. VESTNIK MINISTERSTVA SKOLSTVI, MLADEZE A TELOVYCHOVY A MINISTERSTVA KULTURY CESKE SOCIALISTICKE REPUBLIKY *See* VESTNIK MINISTERSTVA SKOLSTVI, MLADEZE A TELOVYCHOVY CESKE REPUBLIKY **1886**

CZECH SOCIALIST REPUBLIC, (CZECHOSLOVAKIA). MINISTERSTVO STAVEBNICTVI *See* ZPRAVODAJ MINISTERSTVA STAVEBNICTVI CESKE SOCIALISTICKE REPUBLIKY **632**

CZECHOSLOVAK AND CENTRAL EUROPEAN JOURNAL (US/1056-005X) [23076969] **2685**

CZECHOSLOVAK BIBLIOGRAPHY ON EPIDEMIOLOGY AND MICROBIOLOGY (XR/0139-598X) [04788593] 561, **3734**

CZECHOSLOVAK BIBLIOGRAPHY ON INDUSTRIAL HYGIENE AND OCCUPATIONAL DISEASES (XR/0302-4288) [01789489] **2872**

CZECHOSLOVAK ECONOMIC DIGEST *CEASED.* (CS/0045-9461) [02260062] **1479**

CZECHOSLOVAK ECONOMIC PAPERS (CS/0590-5001) [01565752] **1479**

CZECHOSLOVAK FILM, THE *CEASED.* (XR/0011-4588) [02158358] **4067**

CZECHOSLOVAK FOREIGN TRADE (CS/0011-460X) [01565753] **830**

CZECHOSLOVAK HEAVY INDUSTRY *See* CZECHOSLOVAK INDUSTRY **5098**

CZECHOSLOVAK INDUSTRIAL DESIGN (XR) [04323315] **2097**

●CZECHOSLOVAK INDUSTRY (XR) [28154044] **5098**

CZECHOSLOVAK JOURNAL OF PHYSICS (XR/0011-4626) [02260065] **4401**

CZECHOSLOVAK LIFE (CS/0011-4634) [02446298] **2514**

CZECHOSLOVAK MARKET (XR) 1479, **664**

CZECHOSLOVAK MATHEMATICAL JOURNAL (XR/0011-4642) [02916944] **3503**

CZECHOSLOVAK MOTOR REVIEW (XR/0011-4650) [I00114650] **5380**

CZECHOSLOVAK NATIONAL ASSOCIATION OF CANADA. VANCOUVER BRANCH *See* ZPRAVODAJ - CESKOSLOVENSKE NARODNI SDRUZENI V KANADE, ODBOCKA VANCOUVER **2550**

CZECHOSLOVAK REPUBLIC. MINISTERSTVO ZEMDELSTVI, LESNIHO A VODNIHO HOSPODARSTVI. USTAV VEDECKO-TECHNICKYCH INFORMACI *See* LESNICTVI **2387**

CZECHOSLOVAK SOCIETY OF ARTS AND SCIENCES IN AMERICA *See* ZPRAVY - SVU **2857**

CZECHOSLOVAK *See* ZBIERKA ZAKONOV, CESKOSLOVENSKA SOCIALISTICKA REPUBLIKA **4549**

CZECHOSLOVAKIA. FEDERALNI MINISTERSTVO DOPRAVY *See* VESTNIK DOPRAVY **5399**

CZECHOSLOVAKIA. FEDERALNI MINISTERSTVO PRO TECHNICKY A INVESTICNI ROZVOJ *See* ZPRAVODAJ - FEDERALNI MINISTERSTVO PRO TECHNICKY A INVESTICNI ROZVOJ, MINISTERSTVO VYSTAVBY A TECHNIKY CSR, MINISTERSTVO VYSTAVBY A TECHNIKY SSR **5173**

CZECHOSLOVAKIA. FEDERALNI SHROMAZDENI *See* ZPRAVA O SPOLECNE SCHUZI SNEMOVNY LIDU A SNEMOVNY NARODU / FEDERALNI SHROMAZDENI CESKOLOVENSKE SOCIALISTICKE REPUBLIKY **4696**

CZECHOSLOVAKIA — Alphabetical Title Index

CZECHOSLOVAKIA. FEDERALNI SHROMAZDENI See ZPRAVA O SCHUZI SNEMOVNY NARODU / FEDERALNI SHROMAZDENI CESKOLOVENSKE SOCIALISTICKE REPUBLIKY **4501**

●CZECHOSLOVAKIA, MAJOR BUSINESSES / DUN & BRADSTREET INTERNATIONAL (UK/0964-0401) [26570865] **664**

CZECHOSLOVAKIA. URAD PRO NORMALIZACI A MERENI See SEZNAM PLATNYCH CESKOSLOVENSKYCH STATNICH A OBOROVYCH NOREM **5157**

CZESKOSLOVENSKA GYNEKOLOGIE See CESKA GYNEKOLOGIE / CESKA LEKARSKA SPOLECNOST J EV. PURKYNE **3758**

CZI REGISTER AND BUYER'S GUIDE, THE (RH) [07397782] **949**

CZYNNI ZAWODOWO W GOSPODARCE NARODOWEJ (PL) [04657094] **1662**

D.A.C. NEWS (US/0011-4707) [04047369] 3994, **4892**

D A D ARCHITECTURES (FR) **296**

D.A. DIFESA AMBIENTALE *CEASED.* (IT/0392-8950) [11603066] **2213**

D.A.E. RESEARCH REPORT (US/0886-4861) [09497372] **78**

D.A.I.R.S. AND SYSTEMS FOR INSTRUCTION (US/0012-2009) [01548054] **1892**

D A : RIVISTA D'ARCHITETTURA (IT) **296**

D.A.T.A.'S MICROWAVE TUBE *CEASED.* (US/0097-3564) [01440077] **2040**

●D & B EUROPA (UK) [26926162] **664**

D & B REPORTS *CEASED.* (US/0746-6110) [05454221] **664**

D & J RITCHIE LTD See SALE - D & J RITCHIE **364**

D.C. CIRCUIT HANDBOOK (US/0270-0506) [06325379] **2958**

D.C. CODE UPDATER (US/0740-1744) [08365843] **2958**

D.C. DIRECTORY OF NATIVE AMERICAN FEDERAL AND PRIVATE PROGRAMS / NATIVE AMERICAN-PHILANTHROPIC NEWS SERVICE (US) [09462413] **4335**

D.C. GAZETTE (US/0011-7153) [02260154] **2532**

D/C : NATIONAL NEWSLETTER FOR STATE ADMINISTERED DEFERRED COMPENSATION PROGRAMS (US) [07331983] 4641, **1662**

D.C. TRACTS (US/1041-469X) [18774791] **3804**

D.C. ZONING NEWS, THE (US/1056-7739) [23765472] **2820**

D (DALLAS. 1978) *CEASED.* (US/0164-8292) [04314768] **2532**

D. DIETRICH ASSOCIATES See EXECUTIVE COMPENSATION ANALYSIS OF PROFESSIONAL SERVICES' FIRMS **1668**

D.E.R. ... PANORAMA (FR/0767-4635) [18602809] **2040**

D.H. LAWRENCE REVIEW, THE (US/0011-4936) [00816394] **3341**

D.I.N. NEWSERVICE *CEASED.* (US/0739-4683) [09743498] **1342**

D-J-M ENZYME REPORT (US/0731-4027) [08178930] 3570, **453**

D-LIST (US/0196-4143) [06325267] **4298**

D.O., DIARIO OFICIAL, ESTADO DO RIO DE JANEIRO. PARTE I (BL) [03096693] **2958**

D.O., DIARIO OFICIAL, ESTADO DO RIO DE JANEIRO. PARTE II (BL) [04887693] **4471**

D.O., DIARIO OFICIAL, ESTADO DO RIO DE JANEIRO. PARTE III (BL) [03097510] **2958**

D.O., DIARIO OFICIAL, ESTADO DO RIO DE JANEIRO. PARTE IV (BL) [02481668] **2958**

D.O., DIARIO OFICIAL, ESTADO DO RIO DE JANEIRO. PARTE V (BL) [02470095] **2958**

D.O. LEITURA (BL) [15990942] **3379**

D O R L S TECHNICAL SERVICES COMMITTEE'S INFORMATION EXCHANGE (CN/0703-1688) [03680513] **3205**

D.O.T.C. NEWS (1983) (CN/0822-6261) [10179119] **5783**

D PROJECT (US/0198-9308) [06268104] **2532**

D.S (DICTIONNAIRE DE SPIRITUALITE) (FR/0336-8106) [I03368106] **5028**

D. S. I. R. DISCUSSION PAPER (NZ/0110-5221) [09751842] **5098**

D-U-N-S ACCOUNT IDENTIFICATION SERVICE See DUN'S BUSINESS IDENTIFICATION SERVICE [MICROFORM] **669**

DA, DATA ASIA See DATA ASIA **1555**

D'A PALMA DE MALLORCA (SP/1130-3794) [I11303794] **296**

●DA UPDATE (US/1062-5569) [25662838] **1319**

DA VINCI (CN/0315-9914) [02247430] **3462**

DA&DSM MONITOR (US/1064-0886) [26223896] **4760**

DAAT (IS/0334-2336) [06360178] 4344, **5047**

DABAU (US) **1062**

DACAS : DRUG ABUSE CURRENT AWARENESS SYSTEM (US/0091-424X) [01065341] **1342**

DACCA UNIVERSITY STUDIES. PART A, THE (BG/1013-543X) [11674036] 5197, 2845, **318**

DACCA UNIVERSITY STUDIES. PART B, THE (BG/0259-7365) [13257838] **5098**

DACCA UNIVERSITY STUDIES, THE (BG/0011-5223) [01549569] **1819**

DACHAUER HEFTE (GW/0257-9472) [15368889] **2685**

DACHAUER HEFTER (GW/0934-361X) [19576258] **2685**

DACHDECKER-HANDWERK, DAS (GW/0012-124X) [04596286] **612**

DACIA (RM/0070-251X) [02260072] 2685, **266**

DACOROMANIA (GW) [02243880] **2685**

DACOTAH TERRITORY (US/0084-9529) [01565782] **3462**

DACS ANNOTATED BIBLIOGRAPHY. ANNUAL SUPPLEMENT, THE (US/0882-7613) [10342772] **1362**

DACTYLUS / DEPT. OF SPANISH AND PORTUGUESE & THE CENTER FOR MEXICAN AMERICAN STUDIES (US) [11049820] 3379, **3276**

DAD (US) 3994, **2278**

DADA SURREALISM (US/0084-9537) [01565784] 3379, **318**

DADE STREET ATLAS (US) **1924**

DADES BALEARS / CONSELL GENERAL INTERINSULAR, CONSELLERIA D'ECONOMIA I HISENDA (SP) [09171353] **5326**

DADEVILLE RECORD, THE (US/0739-9677) [09228382] **5626**

DADOS E IDEIAS *CEASED.* (BL) [02244195] 1257, **1237**

DADOS ESTATISTICOS DA MOVIMENTACAO DE CARGA E PASSAGEIROS (BL) [01787227] **5400**

DADOS ESTATISTICOS : PRODUTOS AGRO PECUARIOS SAIDOS DE MATO GROSSO (BL) [01794833] 78, **152**

DADOS ESTATISTICOS - SECRETARIA DE EDUCACAO E CULTURA, INSTITUTO DE INFORMATICA (BL) [03469732] 1734, **1794**

DADOS (RIO DE JANEIRO) (BL/0011-5258) [01556194] **5197**

DADSWELL FAMILY BULLETIN (CN/0824-7730) [11895302] **2444**

DADZIS (LV) [02241798] **3379**

DAEDALUS (CAMBRIDGE) (US/0011-5266) [01565785] 5197, **5098**

DAEDALUS LIBRARY, THE (US/0070-2536) [01556226] **3205**

DAEHAN HWAHAK HWOEJEE (KO/0418-2472) [09641987] **974**

DAFFODIL JOURNAL, THE (US/0011-5290) [03977416] **2413**

DAFFODILS (UK) [01787052] **2413**

DAFTAR JENIS BIDANG USAHA SEKTOR INDUSTRI (IO) [10523836] **895**

DAFTAR PENERBITAN PENERBITAN BIRO PUSAT STATISTIK (IO) [02864736] **5326**

DAFTAR PERBANDINGAN KONTROLE PENGOLAHAN KELAPA SAWIT (IO) [02125714] **4254**

DAFTAR PERUSAHAAN DAGANG/JASA YANG IZINNYA DITERBITKAN (IO) [01795351] **664**

DAFTAR TAMBAHAN KOLEKSI MIKROFIS (IO) [06280861] **2650**

DAFTAR TAMBAHAN KOLEKSI PERPUSTAKAAN LEKNAS (IO) [02173750] **1531**

DAG HAMMARSKJOLD LIBRARY See CURRENT BIBLIOGRAPHICAL INFORMATION / DAG HAMMARSKJOLD LIBRARY **4502**

DAGANG & INDUSTRI (IO) [22992954] **1603**

DAGENS INDUSTRI (SW/0346-640X) [08294726] **664**

DAGENS NRINGSLIV [MICROFORM] (NO) [25517112] **5807**

DAGENS NYHETER (SW) [01565787] **5811**

DAGESTANSKII NAUCHNYI TSENTR AN SSSR, INSTITUT GEOLOGII : [TRUDY] (RU) [29924573] **1373**

DAI CIVICI MUSEI D'ARTE E DI STORIA DI BRESCIA. STUDI E NOTIZIE (IT/0394-5219) [18913127] **348**

DAI DAMU / LARGE DAMS (JA/0011-5347) [10474619] **2088**

DAI HAN SENG RI HAK HUI See DAI HAN SENG RI HAK HUI JI **580**

DAI HAN SENG RI HAK HUI JI (KO/0300-4015) [01421187] **580**

DAI NIHON SUISANKAI See FISHERIES OF JAPAN **2302**

DAI NIHON SUISANKAI. JAPAN'S FISHERY INDUSTRY See FISHERIES OF JAPAN **2302**

DAIBYAKURENGE (JA) [02243277] **5021**

DAIDALOS (GW/0721-4235) [08343763] **296**

DAIDZHEST (BU/0861-1033) [23034486] **2514**

DAIGAKU KENKYU NOTO (JA) [02246453] **1819**

DAIGAKU KIJUN KYOKAI See KAIHO - DAIGAKU KIJUN KYOKAI **1833**

DAIGAKU NYUSHI FORAMU (JA/0288-2493) [11809333] **1819**

DAIGAKU TO GAKUSEI / MOMBUSHO DAIGAKUKYOKU GALISEOLA HEN (JA) [08982151] **1734**

DAIGAKU TOSHOKAN KANKYU (JA) [02441481] **3205**

DAIGAKU TOSHOKAN KYORYOKU NYUSU (JA/0388-5623) [08981704] **3205**

DAIGES MALAYSIA (MY) [10773549] **2503**

DAIHAN GUMSOG HAGHOI JI (KO/0253-3847) [05344576] **4000**

DAIHAN GWANSANHAG HOI JI (KO/0379-7511) [05367356] 1439, **2138**

DAIHAN JAIHWAR NUIHAG HOIJI (KO/0379-752X) [04767346] **4380**

DAIHAN MISAINMUR HAGHOI JI (KO/0253-3162) [09257456] **561**

DAIICHI YAKKA DAIGAKU KENKYU NENPO. THE ANNUAL REPORT OF THE DAIICHI COLLEGE OF PHARMACEUTICAL SCIENCES (JA) [05778513] **4298**

DAILIES (CN/0838-9365) [18371771] **895**

DAILY ADVOCATE (GREENVILLE, OHIO : 1978) (US) [17278100] **5727**

DAILY ADVOCATE (VICTORIA, TEX. : 1897) See VICTORIA ADVOCATE (VICTORIA, TEX. : DAILY) **5755**

DAILY ALVA REVIEW-COURIER See ALVA REVIEW-COURIER, THE **5731**

DAILY AMERICAN REPUBLIC (US/1061-7116) [21580378] **5703**

DAILY AMERICAN (SOMERSET, PA.), THE (US/8750-247X) [11175159] **5735**

DAILY ARDMOREITE, THE (US/1065-7894) [12101538] **5731**

DAILY ARGUS (WHITE PLAINS, N.Y.), THE (US/1060-4723) [10089215] **5715**

DAILY ASTORIAN, THE (US/0739-5078) [09748406] **5733**

DAILY BANNER, THE (US) [18778410] **5686**

DAILY BREAD (US/0092-7147) [01791286] **4952**

DAILY BULLETIN (BROWNWOOD, TEX.) See BROWNWOOD BULLETIN **5747**

DAILY BULLETIN - EUROPE, AGENCE INTERNATIONALE D'INFORMATION POUR LA PRESSE (LU/0423-6394) [05719096] **2514**

DAILY BULLETIN / INSTITUTE OF GOVERNMENT, UNIVERSITY OF NORTH CAROLINA AT CHAPEL HILL (US) [04511542] **4641**

DAILY CALIFORNIAN (US/1050-2300) [04370719] **5634**

DAILY CAMERA (BOULDER, COLO. : 1973) (US) [20078553] **5642**

DAILY CAPITAL NEWS (US) [10271291] **5703**

DAILY CHALLENGE (US/0746-8865) [10378434] **5715**

DAILY CHIEF-UNION, THE (US) [16994060] **5727**

DAILY CITIZEN (BEAVER DAM, WIS. : 1971) (US/0749-1379) [11093825] **5766**

DAILY CITIZEN, THE (US) [24476804] **5631**

DAILY CLAY COUNTY ADVOCATE-PRESS, THE (US) [15061942] **5659**

DAILY CLINTONIAN, THE (US) [14768845] **5663**

DAILY COMET, THE (US) [17497532] **5683**

DAILY COMMERCE (US/0279-4195) [07833119] 4836, **830**

DAILY

DAILY COMMERCIAL (LEESBURG LAKE/SUMTER EDITION) (US/0896-1042) [16913137] **5648, 5649**

DAILY COMMERCIAL NEWS AND CONSTRUCTION RECORD (CN/0317-3178) [02358847] **612**

DAILY COMMERCIAL RECORD (US/0889-2431) [13826633] **5748**

DAILY COMMERCIAL RECORDER, THE (US/8750-734X) [11711054] **5748**

DAILY CONSTRUCTION SERVICE (US/0011-5401) [04047434] **612**

DAILY CORINTHIAN, THE (US) [14963599] **5700**

DAILY COUGAR, THE (US) [10236216] **1091**

DAILY COURIER (CONNELLSVILLE, PA.) (US) [16317423] **5735**

DAILY COURIER-OBSERVER (US) [21361780] **5715**

DAILY COURT REVIEW (US/0740-1949) [09926425] **2958**

DAILY DEMOCRAT. DAVIS EDITION (US) [05773271] **5634**

DAILY DEMOCRAT (WOODLAND, CALIF.) (US/0747-1890) [10623496] **5634**

DAILY DEPOSITORY SHIPPING LIST (US/0145-0646) [02600177] **5448**

DAILY DIGEST (UNITED STATES. FEDERAL COMMUNICATIONS COMMISSION) (US/1071-3212) [16582608] **1153**

DAILY DISPATCH (MOLINE, ILL.) (US/8750-7552) [11741621] **5659**

DAILY DUNKLIN DEMOCRAT, THE (US/1047-7160) [20613810] **5703**

DAILY EASTERN NEWS, THE (US/0894-1599) [06748578] **1091**

●DAILY ENVIRONMENT REPORT (US/1060-2976) [24918135] **3110**

DAILY EVENING ITEM (US/8750-8249) [11822610] **5688**

DAILY EXAMINER (PETERBOROUGH, ONT. : 1891) *See* PETERBOROUGH EXAMINER (DAILY ED.) **5792**

DAILY EXPRESS (LONDON, ENGLAND) (UK) [04363424] **5811**

DAILY FACTS, THE (US) [13042885] **5634**

DAILY FAVORITE, THE (US) [14049690] **5749**

DAILY FREEMAN-JOURNAL, THE (US) [12619435] **5669**

DAILY FREEMAN (KINGSTON, N.Y. 1969), THE (US/0746-4932) [11656221] **5715**

DAILY GAS PRICE INDEX (US) **4254**

DAILY GATE CITY (KEOKUK, IOWA : 1957) (US) [13038966] **5669**

DAILY GAZETTE (1990), THE (US/1050-0340) [20836106] **5715**

DAILY GAZETTE NEWSPAPER (US) **5659**

DAILY GLEANER (CN) [01557174] **5783**

DAILY GLOBE (WORTHINGTON, MINN.) (US/1045-487X) [20121543] **5695**

●DAILY GRAPHIC (GH) [29663380] **5802**

DAILY GRAPHIC (PORTAGE LA PRAIRIE. 1954) (CN/0832-4298) [16851901] **5783**

DAILY GRAPHS. AMERICAN/OTC STOCK EXCHANGE *See* DAILY GRAPHS. NASDAQ (OTC)/AMERICAN STOCK EXCHANGE **895**

DAILY GRAPHS. NASDAQ (OTC)/AMERICAN STOCK EXCHANGE (US/1067-9375) [26061584] **895**

DAILY GRAPHS. NEW YORK STOCK EXCHANGE (US) [18209012] **896**

DAILY GRAPHS OPTION GUIDE WEEKLY (US) **787, 896**

DAILY GRAPHS. STOCK OPTION GUIDE (US/0195-2021) [03813839] **787, 896**

DAILY GUIDEPOSTS (US/0190-5457) [04701111] **4952**

DAILY HAMPSHIRE GAZETTE (US/0739-3504) [09725082] **5688**

DAILY HERALD (PROVO, UTAH. 1939), THE (US/0891-2777) [14221549] **5756**

DAILY HERALD, THE (US) [19249328] **5745**

DAILY HERALD, THE (US) [19000377] **5728**

DAILY HOME (US/1059-6461) [11779720] **5626**

DAILY ILLINI (CHAMPAIGN-URBANA, ILL.), THE (US/8750-6769) [11682576] **5659**

DAILY INDEPENDENT (ASHLAND, KY), THE (US/0744-6837) [08500395] **5680**

DAILY INDEPENDENT (CORONA, CALIF.) *See* CORONA-NORCO INDEPENDENT **5634**

DAILY INDEX *See* MINERAL WELLS INDEX **5752**

DAILY INFORMATION BULLETIN (US) [05986750] **830**

DAILY INTER LAKE, THE (US) [12318410] **5705**

DAILY IOWAN, THE (US) [02260093] **5669**

DAILY ITEM (SUNBURY, PA.) (US) [13365086] **5735**

DAILY ITEM (WHITE PLAINS, N.Y.), THE (US/1060-4553) [11071958] **5715**

DAILY JAPAN DIGEST, THE (US/1060-2240) [23066636] **664, 4471**

DAILY JEFFERSON COUNTY UNION (FORT ATKINSON, WIS. : 1969) (US) [11990590] **5766**

DAILY JEFFERSONIAN (CAMBRIDGE, OHIO) (US) [11181839] **5728**

DAILY JOURNAL (US) [20807828] **5695**

DAILY JOURNAL DIRECTORY OF ATTORNEYS : LOS ANGELES AND ORANGE COUNTIES, THE (US) [16636136] **2958**

DAILY JOURNAL (ELIZABETH, N.J.) *CEASED.* (US) [13647471] **5709**

DAILY JOURNAL (FRANKLIN, IND.) (US) [11793729] **5663**

DAILY JOURNAL, THE (US) [22408315] **5695**

DAILY JOURNAL (WHEATON, ILL.) *See* JOURNAL, THE **5660**

DAILY LABOR REPORT (WASHINGTON, D.C. : 1948) (US/0418-2693) [01292043] **1662**

DAILY LEADER (BROOKHAVEN, MISS.) (US) [14867948] **5700**

DAILY LEDGER (ANTIOCH, CALIF.) (US/0746-7370) [10247052] **5634**

DAILY LEDGER, POST DISPATCH (US/1054-8459) [22999195] **5634**

DAILY LEGISLATIVE REPORT (US/0277-4917) [05341106] **4641**

DAILY LIST / HMSO BOOKS (UK/0263-743X) [13233861] **4697**

DAILY LOCAL NEWS (WEST CHESTER) (US/0163-3082) [02260094] **5735**

DAILY MAIL BOOK OF HOME PLANS (UK) [06235157] **296**

DAILY MAIL (HAGERSTOWN, MD.) (US) [09623540] **5686**

DAILY MAIL (LONDON, ENGLAND) (UK) [16310567] **5812**

DAILY MARKET REPORT - NEW YORK COFFEE AND SUGAR EXCHANGE (US) [04940628] **2332**

DAILY MESSENGER (CANANDAIGUA, N.Y.) (US) [10768064] **5715**

DAILY MESSENGER (UNION CITY, TENN.) (US/0745-5534) [09287347] **5745**

DAILY MIDWAY DRILLER (US/0745-5364) [09276608] **5634**

DAILY MINER & NEWS (CN) **5783**

DAILY MINING GAZETTE, THE (US) [09940134] **5691**

DAILY MIRROR (LONDON, ENGLAND) (UK) [04364531] **5812**

DAILY MOUNTAIN EAGLE (US/0893-0759) [11793723] **5626**

DAILY MUNGER OILOGRAM (US/0276-5934) [07387619] **4254**

DAILY NEWS (VI) [01557259] **2487**

DAILY NEWS (US) [17463740] **5683**

DAILY NEWS (US) [24672439] **5653**

DAILY NEWS BUDAPEST (HU/0133-0306) [01330306] **5802**

DAILY NEWS (GREENVILLE, MICH.), THE (US/0899-6342) [18176486] **5691**

DAILY NEWS HALIFAX-DARTMOUTH EDITION (CN/0715-4321) [09149647] **5783**

DAILY NEWS (HAVRE, MONT.), THE (US/1046-1590) [13744440] **5705**

DAILY NEWS (HUNTINGDON, PA.) (US) [14397803] **5736**

DAILY NEWS JOURNAL (MURFREESBORO, TENN.), THE (US/0745-2683) [09008844] **5745**

DAILY NEWS LEADER, THE (US/0747-2501) [10662899] **5758**

DAILY NEWS (LEBANON, PA.), THE (US/0746-8563) [10339582] **5736**

DAILY NEWS (LONGVIEW, WASH.), THE (US/0889-0005) [13781223] **5760**

DAILY NEWS (MCKEESPORT, PA.) (US) [02263934] **5736**

DAILY NEWS-MERCURY, THE (US) [26471037] **5688**

DAILY NEWS (MIDDLESBORO, KY. 1981) (US/1041-7095) [14395566] **5680**

DAILY NEWS (NEW YORK, N.Y. : 1920) (US) [09541172] **5715**

DAILY NEWS-PRESS. (CASTLE ROCK, COLO. : 1987) (US/1067-4241) [21261584] **5642**

DAILY NEWS (PULLMAN, WASH.) (US/0883-5748) [12156167] **5760**

DAILY NEWS (RED BLUFF, CALIF.) (US) [13042897] **5634**

DAILY NEWS (RHINELANDER, WIS. : 1968), THE (US/0746-5866) [10133332] **5766**

DAILY NEWS-TELEGRAM *See* SULPHUR SPRINGS NEWS-TELEGRAM **5755**

DAILY NEWS, THE (US) [01565796] **5725**

DAILY NEWS, THE (US) [09659012] **5715**

DAILY NEWS (WHITTIER, CALIF.) *See* WHITTIER DAILY NEWS **5641**

DAILY NEWS (WHITTIER, CALIF.), THE (US/0746-6188) [10164236] **5634**

DAILY NONPAREIL (1976), THE (US/1046-1833) [12895103] **5669**

DAILY NORWEGIAN PRESS DIGEST (NO) **830**

DAILY OF THE UNIVERSITY OF WASHINGTON, THE (US) [19464732] **5760**

DAILY OIL NEWS DIGEST (UK) **4254**

DAILY PALM BEACH NEWS, THE (US) [13998478] **5648, 5649**

DAILY PLAINSMAN *See* HURON DAILY PLAINSMAN **5743**

DAILY PLANET ALMANAC, THE (US/0148-5369) [03336432] **390**

DAILY POST (LIVERPOOL, ENG. : 1978) (UK) [17867657] **5812**

DAILY PRAYER REMINDER (CN/0227-096X) [08375619] **4952**

DAILY PRESS (1988) (US/1042-8496) [19227667] **5634**

DAILY PRESS AND DAKOTIAN *See* YANKTON DAILY PRESS & DAKOTAN **5744**

DAILY PRESS (ASHLAND, WIS.), THE (US/1050-4095) [14403096] **5766**

DAILY PRESS (ESCANABA, MICH.) (US) [09671025] **5691**

DAILY PRESS (NEWPORT NEWS, VA.) (US) [07529015] **5758**

DAILY PRESS (SAINT MARYS, PA.) (US) [15088856] **5736**

DAILY PROGRESS (CHARLOTTESVILLE, VA.), THE (US/0746-0430) [09701919] **5758**

DAILY RACING FORM (US) [04506540] **2798**

DAILY RATES UPDATE (AT) **787**

DAILY RECORD (1989) (US/1054-3457) [21616740] **5642**

DAILY RECORD & THE KANSAS CITY DAILY NEWS PRESS (US) **5703**

DAILY RECORD (ELLENSBURG, WASH.) (US) [17308766] **5760**

DAILY RECORD (NEW ORLEANS), THE (US/0194-5327) [04796008] **5683**

DAILY RECORD (PARSIPPANY, N.J.) (US) [12777527] **5710**

DAILY RECORD, THE (US) [09117118] **5686**

DAILY RECORD (WOOSTER, OHIO), THE (US/0892-8215) [15295902] **5728**

DAILY RECORDER, THE (US/0197-8055) [06126338] **2958**

DAILY REFLECTOR (GREENVILLE, N.C.) (US/1060-6130) [13338961] **5723**

DAILY REGISTER (OELWEIN, IOWA) (US/1074-4487) [29710992] **5669**

DAILY REGISTER (PORTAGE, WIS.) (US/0747-2927) [10698517] **5766**

DAILY REPORT (BAKERSFIELD, CALIF.), THE (US/0276-5926) [07389300] **2958**

DAILY REPORT CARD (US) [25660879] **1734**

●DAILY REPORT. CENTRAL EURASIA / FOREIGN BROADCAST INFORMATION SERVICE (US) [25110324] **1130**

●DAILY REPORT. CENTRAL EURASIA. INDEX (US/1062-9939) [25602260] **1130**

DAILY REPORT. CHINA (US/0892-015X) [07522935] **2650**

DAILY REPORT. EAST ASIA (US/0898-347X) [16076306] **2503**

DAILY REPORT. EAST ASIA. INDEX (US/1045-2192) [17345486] **1130**

DAILY REPORT. EASTERN EUROPE. INDEX (US/0731-4116) [17450468] **1131**

DAILY REPORT FOR EXECUTIVES (US/0148-8155) [03382146] **664**

DAILY REPORT. LATIN AMERICA (US/0899-0913) [01113413] **1131**

DAILY REPORT. LATIN AMERICA. INDEX (US/0278-1360) [05366388] **1131**

DAILY REPORT. NEAR EAST & SOUTH ASIA (US/0898-3402) [16076319] **1131**

DAILY Alphabetical Title Index

DAILY REPORT. NEAR EAST & SOUTH ASIA. INDEX (US/1046-0691) [16987811] **1131**

DAILY REPORT. SOVIET UNION *See* FBIS REPORT. SOVIET UNION. REPUBLIC AFFAIRS **1132**

DAILY REPORT. SOVIET UNION *See* DAILY REPORT. CENTRAL EURASIA / FOREIGN BROADCAST INFORMATION SERVICE **1130**

DAILY REPORT. SOVIET UNION / FOREIGN BROADCAST INFORMATION SERVICE (US/0565-5560) [01113404] **1131**

DAILY REPORT. SOVIET UNION. INDEX *See* DAILY REPORT. CENTRAL EURASIA. INDEX **1130**

DAILY REPORT. SUB-SAHARAN AFRICA. INDEX (1989) (US/1046-0713) [20323806] **1131**

DAILY REPORT. USSR & EAST EUROPE *See* DAILY REPORT. SOVIET UNION / FOREIGN BROADCAST INFORMATION SERVICE **1131**

DAILY REPORT. WEST EUROPE (US/0898-3496) [16076318] **2515**

DAILY REPORT. WEST EUROPE. INDEX / FOREIGN BROADCAST INFORMATION SERVICE (US) [17544688] **1131**

DAILY REPORTER (COLUMBUS, OHIO) (US/0011-5487) [08178118] **5728**

DAILY REPORTER (SIOUX CITY), THE (US/0360-9510) [02242397] **2958**

DAILY REPORTER (SPENCER, IOWA), THE (US/0746-0872) [09735460] **5669**

DAILY REPORTER, THE (US) [12574696] **5675**

DAILY REPORTER (TUCSON, ARIZ.) *See* DAILY TERRITORIAL, THE **5630**

DAILY REPUBLIC (FAIRFIELD, CALIF.) (US/0746-5858) [10133416] **5634**

DAILY REVIEW, THE (US) [17734626] **5683**

DAILY REVIEW, THE (US) [27514679] **5634**

DAILY REVIEW (TOWANDA, PA.) (US) [13547564] **5736**

DAILY SENTINEL (GRAND JUNCTION, COLO.) (US) [11217358] **5642**

DAILY SENTINEL (NACOGDOCHES, TEX.: 1900) (US) [13695089] **5749**

DAILY SENTINEL (POMEROY, OHIO) (US) [16933050] **5728**

DAILY SENTINEL (ROME, N.Y.) (US) [14082459] **5715**

DAILY SENTINEL (SCOTTSBORO, ALA.) (US) [11827103] **5626**

DAILY SENTINEL (SITKA, ALASKA) (US) [02701902] **5629**

DAILY SENTINEL-STAR, THE (US/1066-7512) [15216930] **5700**

DAILY SIFTINGS HERALD, THE (US) [23816895] **5631**

DAILY SOUTHERNER (US) [13168613] **5723**

DAILY SPARKS TRIBUNE, THE (US/0899-9538) [18277040] **5707**

DAILY SPECTRUM (CEDAR CITY, UTAH), THE (US/0747-0010) [10453147] **5756**

DAILY SPECTRUM (SAINT GEORGE, UTAH), THE (US/0745-6611) [11739934] **5756**

DAILY SPOT COTTON QUOTATIONS / UNITED STATES DEPARTMENT OF AGRICULTURE, AGRICULTURAL MARKETING SERVICE, COTTON DIVISION (US) [03455256] 5350, **170**

DAILY STANDARD (CELINA, OHIO : 1905) (US) [17359155] **5728**

DAILY STAR (ONEONTA, NEW YORK) (US) [05283755] **5715**

DAILY STATEMENT OF THE UNITED STATES TREASURY *See* DAILY TREASURY STATEMENT **787**

DAILY / STATISTICS CANADA, THE (CN/0827-0465) [13563284] **4697**

DAILY STOCK PRICE RECORD. AMERICAN STOCK EXCHANGE (US/0737-4127) [01776215] **896**

● DAILY STOCK PRICE RECORD. NASDAQ (US/1072-3846) [28249539] **896**

DAILY STOCK PRICE RECORD. NEW YORK STOCK EXCHANGE (US/0737-4119) [01624443] **896**

DAILY STOCK PRICE RECORD. OVER-THE-COUNTER (US/0737-4100) [00946163] **896**

DAILY SUBSISTANCE ALLOWANCE RATES (US/1014-9600) 2805, **1634**

DAILY SUN-NEWS (US/1046-1612) [14767540] **5760**

DAILY TARGUM, THE (US) [15814709] **5710**

DAILY TAX REPORT (WASHINGTON) (US/0092-6884) [02256507] 4719, **2958**

DAILY TELEGRAM (MECHANICSBURG, OHIO) *See* TELEGRAM (MECHANICSBURG, OHIO) **5730**

DAILY TELEGRAM, THE (US) **5766**

DAILY TELEGRAPH (LONDON, ENGLAND : 1969) (UK) [06412514] **5812**

DAILY TERRITORIAL, THE (US/0743-8397) [10681831] **5630**

DAILY TEXAN, THE (US) [12033646] **5749**

DAILY TIMES (MW) [29046421] **5806**

DAILY TIMES (NR) [05537138] **5807**

DAILY TIMES (US) [30024527] **5712**

DAILY TIMES-CALL (US) [20551713] **5642**

DAILY TIMES-LEADER (WEST POINT, MISS.) (US) [16568050] **5700**

DAILY TIMES-NEWS, THE (US) [11388600] **5723**

DAILY TIMES (PRIMOS, PA.) (US) [14941743] **5736**

DAILY TIMES (SALISBURY, MD.) (US) [09958506] **5686**

DAILY TIMES, THE (US) [25758209] **5659**

DAILY TIMES, THE (US) [27828027] **5772**

DAILY TREASURY STATEMENT (US/0145-0239) [02611865] **787**

DAILY TRIBUNE (AMES, IOWA), THE (US/0893-7915) [15503577] **5669**

DAILY TRIBUNE (BAY CITY, TEX.) (US) [13987788] **5749**

DAILY TRIBUNE (MOUNT CLEMENS, MICH.) (US/1041-9977) [15217591] **5691**

DAILY TRIBUNE (MT. PLEASANT, TEX.) (US) [16734870] **5749**

DAILY TRIBUNE NEWS (CARTERSVILLE, GA.), THE (US/1049-6750) [20398154] **5653**

DAILY TRIBUNE (WISCONSIN RAPIDS, WIS.) (US) [15220377] **5766**

DAILY UNION (JUNCTION CITY, KAN.) (US/0745-743X) [09420312] **5675**

DAILY VARIETY (US/0011-5509) [02536362] 5363, **4067**

DAILY WASHINGTON LAW REPORTER, THE (US/1066-6095) [10211824] **2958**

DAILY WEATHER MAPS. WEEKLY SERIES / NATIONAL OCEANIC AND ATMOSPHERIC ADMINISTRATION, NATIONAL WEATHER SERVICE, NATIONAL METEOROLOGICAL CENTER, CLIMATE ANALYSIS CENTER (US) [13571612] **1424**

DAILY WORD (US/0011-5525) [01775549] **4952**

DAILY WORLD (ABERDEEN, WASH.) (US/0740-3135) [09939554] **5760**

DAILY WORLD (HELENA, ARK.), THE (US/8750-5274) [11478034] **5631**

DAILY YOMIURI (JA) **5805**

DAINIKA AVAJA (II) [08352691] **2650**

DAINIKA BAMLA (ANNUAL) (BG) [08756857] **3379**

DAIRY CATTLE (CN/0821-7440) [09809077] **210**

DAIRY CATTLE FEEDING AND MANAGEMENT (US) [01558783] **210**

DAIRY. CENTRAL ED *See* DAIRY (SAINT PAUL, MINN.) **194**

DAIRY CONTACT (CN/0383-6207) [03222198] **193**

DAIRY COUNCIL DIGEST (US/0011-5568) [01759176] 4189, **193**

DAIRY ECONOMICS RESEARCH REPORT (AT/1032-9552) [I10329552] **193**

DAIRY EXPORTER (NZ/0111-915X) [09012835] **193**

DAIRY FARMER (IPSWICH, SUFFOLK) (UK/0011-5576) [12423871] **193**

DAIRY FARMER (LONDON, ONT.) (CN/1182-8900) [23599049] **193**

DAIRY FIELD (1991) (US/1055-0607) [23066271] **193**

DAIRY, FOOD AND ENVIRONMENTAL SANITATION (US/1043-3546) [19412933] **2333**

DAIRY FOODS (US/0888-0050) [13336024] **193**

DAIRY FOODS NEWSLETTER (US/1057-2619) [23990648] **193**

DAIRY GOAT GAZETTE (1977) (CN/0708-6164) [05071999] **193**

DAIRY GOAT JOURNAL (US/0011-5592) [05325643] 210, **193**

DAIRY GUIDE. NEW DELHI (II/0970-3438) [I09703438] **193**

DAIRY HERD MANAGEMENT (US/0011-5614) [01565813] **193**

DAIRY INDIA (II) [10568773] 193, **152**

DAIRY INDUSTRIES INTERNATIONAL (UK/0308-8197) [02246759] **193**

DAIRY INDUSTRY LEADER (AT) [11585617] **193**

DAIRY INDUSTRY NEWSLETTER (UK/0956-8131) [I09568131] **193**

DAIRY INDUSTRY NEWSLETTER (US) [05841745] **193**

DAIRY INDUSTRY NEWSLETTER (ARLINGTON, VA. : 1975) *See* DAIRY FOODS NEWSLETTER **193**

● DAIRY, LIVESTOCK, AND POULTRY. DAIRY, WORLD MARKETS AND TRADE / UNITED STATES DEPARTMENT OF AGRICULTURE, FOREIGN AGRICULTURAL SERVICE (US) [30521215] **193**

DAIRY, LIVESTOCK, AND POULTRY, U.S. TRADE AND PROSPECTS (US) [15603940] **3503**

● DAIRY, LIVESTOCK AND POULTRY, U.S. TRADE AND PROSPECTS / UNITED STATES DEPARTMENT OF AGRICULTURE, FOREIGN AGRICULTURAL SERVICE (US) [30506368] 210, **193**

DAIRY MARKET NEWS (US/0744-1282) [04532667] **193**

DAIRY MARKET STATISTICS, ANNUAL SUMMARY (US/0098-6690) [02242104] 193, **152**

DAIRY MARKETS WEEKLY (UK/0957-8625) [I09578625] **193**

DAIRY MONTHLY IMPORTS / UNITED STATES DEPARTMENT OF AGRICULTURE, FOREIGN AGRICULTURAL SERVICE (US) [23160480] **193**

DAIRY PACKAGING NEWSLETTER (FR) [07075103] 4218, **193**

DAIRY PLANTS SURVEYED AND APPROVED FOR USDA GRADING SERVICE (US/0565-2049) [04306325] **193**

DAIRY PRODUCE; A REVIEW OF PRODUCTION, TRADE, CONSUMPTION AND PRICES RELATING TO BUTTER, CHEESE, CONDENSED MILK, MILK POWDER, CASEIN, EGGS AND EGG PRODUCTS (UK/0069-7699) [04255079] **194**

DAIRY PRODUCTS ... SUMMARY / UNITED STATES DEPARTMENT OF AGRICULTURE, STATISTICAL REPORTING SERVICE, CROP REPORTING BOARD (US) [10829175] **194**

DAIRY PRODUCTS (WASHINGTON, D.C.) (US/0093-1446) [01780464] **194**

DAIRY RESEARCH REPORT (GUELPH) (CN/1182-5480) [22926974] **194**

DAIRY REVIEW, THE (CN/0300-0753) [02443455] 194, **152**

DAIRY (SAINT PAUL, MINN.) *CEASED.* (US/0883-007X) [11224448] **194**

DAIRY SCIENCE ABSTRACTS (UK/0011-5681) [01565820] 194, **153**

DAIRY SCIENCE EXTENSION LEAFLET (US/0578-4875) [01554889] **194**

DAIRY SCIENCE HANDBOOK *CEASED.* (US/0418-2804) [03321914] **194**

DAIRY SITUATION AND OUTLOOK REPORT / AGRICULTURAL MARKETING AUTHORITY (RH) [12540189] **194**

DAIRY. WESTERN ED *See* DAIRY (SAINT PAUL, MINN.) **194**

DAIRY WORLD (MILLBURY, MASS.) (US/0736-4962) [09069470] **194**

DAIRYMAN (ARMADALE), THE (AT) [01581119] **194**

DAIRYMAN (CORONA), THE (US/0011-572X) [01714198] **194**

DAIRYMEN'S DIGEST (MORNING GLORY FARMS ED.) (US/0894-1653) [15814450] **194**

DAIRYMEN'S DIGEST. NORTH CENTRAL REGION EDITION (US/0745-9033) [01782043] **194**

DAIRYNEWS (PEARL RIVER, N.Y.) (US/0011-5738) [06687108] **194**

DAISY SHOOTING ANNUAL (US/0362-7160) [02327429] **4871**

DAITA (US/1051-7685) [22121405] **3669**

DAITA *See* AIDS THERAPIES **3664**

DAITO BUNKA DAIGAKU HOGAKKAI *See* DAITO HOGAKU **2959**

DAITO BUNKA DAIGAKU KIYO. JINBUN KAGAKU (JA/0386-1082) [I03861082] **2845**

DAITO HOGAKU (JA) [02652521] **2959**

DAITOSHIKEN YORAN: SHUTOKEN KINKI-KEN CHUBU-KEN (JA) [02639123] **2820**

DAIWA FISHING ANNUAL (US/0145-613X) [02762402] **2299**

DAIYAMONDO GENDAI EIGO NO KISO CHISHIKI (JA/0303-0512) [01797231] **3276**

DAIYAMONDO KABUKA GURAFU (JA) [01790289] **896**

Alphabetical Title Index — DANGEROUS

DAIYAMONDO KABUSHIKI TOSHIBAN (JA) [06830259] **896**

DAIYAMONDO KIGYO RANKINGU (JA) [05841753] **664**

DAIZU TANPAKUSHITSU EIYO KENKYUKAI KAISHI (JA) [10308553] **4189**

DAK TAR (II/0011-5762) [03785067] **1144**

DAKAR. UNIVERSITE. CENTRE DE HAUTES ETUDES AFRO-IBERO-AMERICAIN *See* PUBLICATION - DAKAR. UNIVERSITE. CENTRE DE HAUTES ETUDES AFRO-IBERO-AMERICAINES **1843**

DAKAR. UNIVERSITE. CENTRE DE RECHERCHES, D'ETUDES ET DE DOCUMENTATION SUR LES INSTITUTIONS ET LA LEGISLATION AFRICAINES *See* COLLECTION - (DAKAR) **2638**

DAKAR. UNIVERSITE. SECTION DE LANGUES ET LITTERATURES *See* PUBLICATIONS - DAKAR. UNIVERSITE. SECTION DE LANGUES ET LITTERATURES **3312**

DAKOTA COUNTRY (US/0194-5769) [04853221] **4871**

DAKOTA COUNTY GENEALOGIST, THE (US/1044-6524) [17755786] **2444**

DAKOTA COUNTY TRIBUNE (US/8750-2895) [01565831] **5695**

DAKOTA FAMILY (US/0199-7122) [06098802] **78**

DAKOTA FARMER, THE (US/0198-6171) [06112712] **78**

DAKOTA OUTDOORS (US/1041-1968) [18675871] **4871**

DAKOTA SCIENTIST, THE (US) [02252323] **5725**

DAKOTA STUDENT, THE (US/0274-9262) [02252324] **1819**

DAKOTA TERRITORY (US/0045-9518) [04792349] **2444**

DAKSHINESIA (II) [02239590] **2650**

DAKWAH (MY/0126-5938) [04535627] **5042**

DALARNAS MUSEUMS SERIE AV RAPPORTER (SW/0348-2863) [11846078] **2820**

DALE NEWS, THE (US) [14584061] **5663**

DALGETY FARMERS' ANNUAL WOOL DIGEST (AT) [11782210] 5350, **5360**

DALHART DAILY TEXAN, THE (US) [14351862] **5749**

DALHOUSIE DENTAL JOURNAL (CN/0418-3010) [02247263] **1320**

DALHOUSIE FRENCH STUDIES (CN/0711-8813) [06010558] **3379**

DALHOUSIE GAZETTE, THE (CN/0011-5819) [03335938] **1091**

●DALHOUSIE JOURNAL OF LEGAL STUDIES (CN/1188-4258) [27725120] **2959**

DALHOUSIE LAW JOURNAL (CN/0317-1663) [01697289] **2959**

DALHOUSIE NEWS (HALIFAX) (CN/0845-8677) [20659304] **1091**

DALHOUSIE REVIEW, THE (CN/0011-5827) [01565841] **3380**

DALHOUSIE UNIVERSITY *See* DALHOUSIE NEWS (HALIFAX) **1091**

DALHOUSIE UNIVERSITY. SCHOOL OF LIBRARY AND INFORMATION STUDIES *See* NEWSLETTER - DALHOUSIE UNIVERSITY. SCHOOL OF LIBRARY AND INFORMATION STUDIES **3235**

DALHOUSIE UNIVERSITY, SCHOOL OF LIBRARY AND INFORMATION STUDIES SERIES (US/1048-471X) [21074335] **3205**

DALIBRARY (US/1053-7848) [22646029] **1233**

DALIL AL-HUKUMAH WA-AL-QITA AL-AMM FI JUMHURIYAT MISR AL-ARABIYAH (TS) [04562204] **4641**

DALIL AL-KUWAYT AL-YAWM / WIZARAT AL-TAKHTIT, MARKAZ AL-KUWAYT LIL-MALUMAT WA-AL-MIKRUFILM (KU) [07365250] **2959**

DALIL AL-MAARID WA-AL-ASWAQ AL-DAWLIYAH / IDAD DAIRAT AL-ILAM, AL-GHURFAH AL-TIJARIYAH AL-SINAIYAH, AL-RIYAD AL-MAMLAKAH AL-ARABIYAH AL-SAUDIYAH (SU) [07484045] **5099**

DALIL AL-MUSADDIRIN FI JUMHURIYAT MISR AL-ARABIYAH / AL-ITTIHAD AL-AMM LIL-GHURAF AL-TIJARIYAH AL-MISRIYAH (UA) [07211526] **830**

DALIL AL-QITAAT AL-INTAJIYAH WA-AL-SHARIKAT (UA) [04680205] **830**

DALIL AL-SINIMA AL-ARABIYAH (UA) [07511631] **4067**

DALIL AL-TAAWUN AL-IQTISADI (SJ) [11760963] **1479**

DALJE (YU) [09200994] **3276**

DALLAS APPAREL NEWS (US/0279-4888) [07909924] **1083**

DALLAS BUSINESS JOURNAL (US/0899-4129) [18042695] **664**

DALLAS COUNTY BUSINESS GUIDE, THE (US/0192-2009) [03906410] **664**

DALLAS COUNTY NEWS (ADEL, IOWA) (US) [11131178] **5669**

DALLAS COWBOYS OFFICIAL WEEKLY (US/0745-0370) [08741871] **4892**

DALLAS-FORT WORTH HOME GARDEN *CEASED.* (US/0161-8741) [08518079] **2789**

●DALLAS/FORT WORTH REAL ESTATE FINANCE SOURCEBOOK (US/1071-5134) [28658872] **4836**

DALLAS-FT. WORTH HOME GARDEN *See* DALLAS-FORT WORTH HOME GARDEN **2789**

DALLAS HISTORICAL SOCIETY *See* REPORT / DALLAS HISTORICAL SOCIETY **2627**

DALLAS MEDICAL JOURNAL (US/0011-586X) [01777937] **3570**

DALLAS MORNING NEWS, THE (US) [09475176] **5749**

DALLAS NEW ERA, THE (US/8750-1376) [11008666] **5653**

DALLAS OBSERVER (US/0732-0299) [07095491] **384**

DALLAS OPERA MAGAZINE, THE (US/0731-8529) [08064694] **4113**

DALLAS ORNAMENTAL CROPS MARKET NEWS (US/0273-8619) [06229763] **170**

DALLAS PERSPECTIVE (US/0897-3938) [17487043] **1479**

DALLAS POST, THE (US) [15814992] **5736**

DALLAS POST TRIBUNE, THE (JS/0746-7303) [10247179] **5749**

DALLAS QUARTERLY, THE (US/0890-8125) [11930621] **2444**

DALLAS. SOUTHERN METHODIST UNIVERSITY. CASUALTY AND PROPERTY INSURANCE INSTITUTE *See* LECTURES - DALLAS. SOUTHERN METHODIST UNIVERSITY. CASUALTY AND PROPERTY INSURANCE INSTITUTE **2886**

DALLAS. SOUTHERN METHODIST UNIVERSITY. SCHOOL OF LAW *See* SMU LAW SCHOOL STUDY, AN **3056**

DALLAS WEEKLY POST *See* DALLAS POST, THE **5736**

DALLAS WEEKLY, THE (US/0885-1271) [08294783] **5749**

DALLASFED DISTRICT HIGHLIGHTS (US/0739-7720) [08885953] **787**

DALLES CHRONICLE, THE (US/0747-3443) [10767022] **5733**

DALMENY REVIEW (CN/0225-7025) [06272453] **5783**

DALMO'MA (US/0191-7722) [02943155] **3462**

DALTON TRANSACTIONS (UK/0300-9246) [01034240] 1051, **1036**

DALTON'S NEW YORK METROPOLITAN DIRECTORY (US/1052-6609) [11088123] **664**

DALTON'S PHILADELPHIA METROPOLITAN DIRECTORY (US/1053-685X) [13734764] 1603, **664**

DALU ZAZHI TEKAN (CH/0494-4445) [I04944445] 266, **2650**

DAM ENGINEERING (UK/0958-9341) [21260077] **2088**

DAMAGE ANALYSIS AND FUNDAMENTAL SIC STUDIES (US) [05247725] **830**

DAMASCUS COURIER-GAZETTE, THE (US) [19401712] **5686**

DAMASCUS ECONOMIC LETTER (SY) [04598126] **1479**

DAMASZENER MITTEILUNGEN (GW/0176-2354) [10592772] **266**

DAMILICA (II/0376-8090) [02245641] **2650**

DAMMING THE SOLID WASTE STREAM : THE BEGINNING OF SOURCE REDUCTION IN MINNESOTA (US/0361-3569) [02246150] **2227**

DAMPF & REISE, UBERSEEISCHE BAHNEN (SZ/0933-7598) [19707928] **5431**

DAMS WITHIN JURISDICTION OF THE STATE OF CALIFORNIA (US/0591-0722) [06720554] **2088**

DAN CHUA (US/0747-2315) [05150921] **5028**

DAN MIL (DK) [01787703] **4040**

DAN-QUYEN *CEASED.* (CN/0229-673X) [08071067] **2650**

DAN SHA *CEASED.* (CN/0833-3831) [15731271] **5783**

DANA (DANMARKS FISKERI- OG HAVUNDERSGELSER) (DK/0106-553X) [06303159] 2299, **554**

DANAS (ZAGREB, CROATIA : 1982) (CI) [08716270] **2515**

DANCE/AMERICA (US/0045-9577) [05296642] **1311**

DANCE AND DANCERS (UK/0011-5983) [01565856] **1311**

DANCE AND MOVEMENT ANALYSIS NEWSLETTER (US) **2319**

DANCE AUSTRALIA (AT) [12800354] **1311**

DANCE BOOK FORUM (US/0271-9940) [06740274] **1311**

DANCE COMPANY GRANTS / NATIONAL ENDOWMENT FOR THE ARTS (US) [08152407] **1311**

DANCE CONNECTION (CN/0838-1313) [19816763] **1311**

DANCE DIMENSIONS (US) [04408703] **1312**

DANCE GAZETTE (UK/0306-0128) [I03060128] **1312**

DANCE IN CANADA *SUSPENDED.* (CN/0317-9737) [02441681] **1312**

DANCE INK (US/1047-823X) [20809299] 1314, **1312**

●DANCE INTERNATIONAL (VANCOUVER) (CN/1189-9816) [28712256] **1312**

DANCE LIFE (US) [04531281] **1312**

DANCE (LONDON, ENGLAND : 1986) (UK) [16552968] **1312**

DANCE MAGAZINE (US/0011-6009) [05580983] **1312**

DANCE MATTERS (UK) **1312**

DANCE/MOVEMENT THERAPY ABSTRACTS (US/1064-7538) [26388272] **1312**

DANCE MUSIC REPORT *CEASED.* (US/0883-1122) [10593658] **4113**

DANCE (NEW YORK, N.Y. 1980) (US/0190-7220) [04738085] **1312**

DANCE (NEW YORK, N.Y. 1988) (US/0894-4849) [16115389] **1312**

DANCE NEWS WELLINGTON (NZ/0112-4951) [I01124951] **1312**

●DANCE NOW (UK/0966-6346) [26430089] **1312**

DANCE PAGES MAGAZINE (US/1064-6183) [24225987] **1312**

DANCE PROGRAM, THE (US) [04878256] **1312**

DANCE RESEARCH (UK/0264-2875) [11948703] **1312**

DANCE RESEARCH JOURNAL (US/0149-7677) [02255660] **1312**

DANCE STUDIES (UK) [04862900] **1312**

DANCE TEACHER (UK) [13613762] **1312**

DANCE TEACHER NOW (US/0199-1795) [05695178] **1312**

DANCE THEATRE JOURNAL (UK/0264-9160) [11264626] **1312**

DANCE (WASHINGTON, D.C. : 1986) (US) [11976707] **1312**

DANCEBAG (NORMAN, OKLA.) *CEASED.* (US/1041-5564) [18799836] 1062, **1312**

●DANCEHALL (TORONTO) (CN/1183-4048) [24368648] **4113**

DANCEMAGAZINE COLLEGE GUIDE (US/0193-1202) [05116356] 1819, **1312**

●DANCEVIEW (US) [26458154] **1312**

DANCING TIMES (UK/0011-605X) [02623442] **1312**

DANCING USA (US/1053-5454) [22577104] **1313**

DANCSCENE (US/0745-3949) [09120536] **1313**

DANDELION (CN/0383-9575) [02909321] **3380**

DANDELION, THE (US) [03522854] **4541**

DANDENONG VALLEY LIBRARIES REPORTER (AT/0818-9056) [08189056] **3205**

D&O BOOK (US) **2959**

DANEMARK, ENERGIEWIRTSCHAFT / BUNDESSTELLE FUR AUSSENHANDELSINFORMATION (GW) [07681615] **1936**

DANEMARK, FAROER UND GRONLAND, WIRTSCHAFT IN ZAHLEN UND WIRTSCHAFTSDOKUMENTATION / BUNDESSTELLE FUR AUSSENHANDELSINFORMATION (GW) [09363529] **1555**

DANEMARK : WIRTSCHAFTLICHE ENTWICKLUNG (GW) [05140611] **1555**

DANGDAI YIXUE (CH/0258-3291) [03904150] **3570**

DANGEROUS AND/OR UNUSUAL OCCURRENCES (CN/0225-9990) [06180422] **2861**

DANGEROUS ASSIGNMENTS (US/1073-841X) [29539548] **4507**

DANGEROUS GOODS : NEWSLETTER (CN/0710-0914) [08091154] **5380**

DANGEROUS — Alphabetical Title Index

DANGEROUS GOODS REGULATIONS (CN/0256-3223) [08633400] 5380, **4773**

DANGEROUS PROPERTIES OF INDUSTRIAL MATERIALS REPORT (US/0270-3777) [06399945] **2861**

DANGEROUS SUBSTANCES & AMENDMENTS (UK) [10538736] **2227**

DANIA POLYGLOTTA (DK/0070-2714) [03910750] **3458**

DANIDA *See* DENMARK'S DEVELOPMENT ASSISTANCE **1555**

DANIEL BLUM'S OPERA WORLD (US/0418-3290) [04361850] **4113**

DANIEL WEBSTER COLLEGE *See* ALUMNI DIRECTORY / DANIEL WEBSTER COLLEGE, NEAI **1098**

DANIELS COUNTY LEADER (US) [14137795] **5705**

DANISH FILMS (DK) [02471800] **4067**

DANISH HANDCRAFT GUILD (DK/0416-6817) [01607709] **5183**

DANISH HYDRAULICS (DK/0109-5110) [07699304] **2088**

DANISH JOURNAL (DK/0011-6084) [01565870] **2685**

DANISH MEDICAL BULLETIN *CEASED*. (DK/0011-6092) [01565872] **3570**

DANISH REVIEW OF GAME BIOLOGY (DK/0374-7344) [01290817] 2213, **5581**

DANISH YEARBOOK OF PHILOSOPHY (DK/0070-2749) [01565875] **4344**

DANIZDAT (DK) [10377745] **4507**

DANMARK-AMERIKA FONDET *See* ARSBERETNING - DENMARK-AMERIKA FONDET **2721**

DANMARK I SPEJLET (DK/0903-7837) [19797093] **3380**

DANMARK I TAL (DK/0107-7139) [19687222] **5326**

DANMARK TEKNISKE HJSKOLES. INSTITUTE OF HYDRODYNAMICS AND HYDRAULIC ENGINEERING *See* PROGRESS REPORT - INSTITUTE OF HYDRODYNAMICS AND HYDRAULIC ENGINEERING (LYNGBY) **2095**

DANMARKS BIBLIOTEKSSKOLE *See* BERETNING FOR UNDERVISNINGSARET ... / DANMARKS BIBLIOTEKSSKOLE **3194**

DANMARKS KIRKER (DK) [03917781] **4952**

DANMARKS KLIMA (DK/0904-3101) [20052875] **1424**

DANMARKS PDAGOGISKE INSTITUT *See* BERETNING - DANMARKS PAEDAGOGISKE INSTITUT **1889**

DANMARKS STATISTIK. STATISTISKE EFTERRETNINGER *See* STATISTISKE EFTERRETNINGER. INDUSTRI OG ENERGI / DANMARKS STATISTIK **1540**

DANMARKS TEKNISKE HJSKOLE. LABORATORIET FOR HALVLEDERTEKNIK *See* ARSBERETNING / LABORATORY FOR SEMICONDUCTOR TECHNOLOGY **2036**

DANMARKS VAREINDFRSEL OG -UDFRSEL (DK/0070-2781) [03695578] **830**

DANS LA MELEE (CN/0700-513X) [03519926] **1662**

DANS LE VENT (FR) **4386**

DANSALAN QUARTERLY *CEASED*. (PH) [06103657] 235, **2650**

DANSALAN RESEARCH CENTER. BIBLIOGRAPHICAL BULLETIN *See* DANSALAN QUARTERLY **2650**

DANSALAN RESEARCH CENTER. OCCASIONAL PAPERS *See* DANSALAN QUARTERLY **2650**

DANSALAN RESEARCH CENTER. RESEARCH BULLETIN *See* DANSALAN QUARTERLY **2650**

DANSER (FR/0755-7639) [I07557639] **1313**

DANSK AARBOG FOR MUSIKFORSKNING (DK/0416-6884) [01792025] **4113**

DANSK AMATRMUSIK (DK) [01788832] **4113**

DANSK ARTIKELINDEKS (DK/0106-147X) [08325590] **414**

DANSK AUDIOLOGOPDI (DK/0105-7200) [I01057200] **3887**

DANSK BOGFORTEGNELSE *CEASED*. (DK) [01565885] **414**

DANSK ELFORSYNING (DK) [04791136] 2040, **2003**

DANSK FORENET SUDAN MISSION *See* UNDER AFRIKAS SOL **5006**

DANSK GEOLOGISK FORENING *See* ARSSKRIFT - DANSK GEOLOGISK FORENING **1366**

DANSK GEOLOGISK FORENING *See* BULLETIN OF THE GEOLOGICAL SOCIETY OF DENMARK **1370**

DANSK GRAFIA (DK) [04815350] 378, **4564**

DANSK ILLUSTRERET SKIBSLISTE (DK) [06738093] **5448**

DANSK INGENIRFORENING VOLDGIFTSRET *See* KENDELSER OM FAST EJENDOM **2992**

DANSK INSTITUT FOR PRVNING OG JUSTERING *See* ARSBERETNING / DANTEST **4029**

DANSK KEMI (DK/0011-6335) [10453146] **974**

DANSK KONOMISK BIBLIOGRAFI (DK/0106-0767) [12252950] **1479**

DANSK MASKINHANDLERFORENING *See* HANDBOG - DANSK MASKINHANDLERFORENING **159**

DANSK MONSTERTIDENDE (DK/0903-8825) [I09038825] **1303**

DANSK MUSIKFORTEGNELSE (DK) [04428679] **4113**

DANSK NAUTISK ALMANAK *See* NAUTISK ALMANAK **397**

DANSK OKONOMI (DK) [04443315] **1479**

DANSK ORGELAARBOG (DK/0107-4857) [10268772] **4113**

DANSK ORNITHOLOGISK FORENING *See* SKAGEN FUGELSTATION **5620**

DANSK ORNITHOLOGISK FORENINGS TIDSSKRIFT (DK/0011-6394) [02250982] **5617**

DANSK PAEDAGOGISK TIDSSKRIFT (DK/0011-6408) [01565900] **1734**

DANSK PELSDYRAVL (DK/0011-6424) [06977996] **3183**

DANSK PERIODICAFORTEGNELSE. SUPPLEMENT (DK/0084-9596) [01028148] **414**

DANSK PLAST (DK) [01784583] **4454**

DANSK SELSKAB FOR BYGNINGSSTATIK *See* BYGNINGSSTATISKE MEDDELELSER **2020**

DANSK SKOVBRUGS TIDSSKRIFT : DST (DK) [20666032] **2378**

DANSK SOCIOLOGI (DK/0905-5908) [23196501] **5244**

DANSK TEOLOGISK TIDSSKRIFT (DK/0105-3191) [01774703] **4952**

DANSK UDSYN (DK/0106-4622) [03653036] **2685**

DANSK VETERINAERTIDSSKRIFT (DK/0106-6854) [02253058] **5508**

DANSKE FYSIOTERAPEUTER (DK/0105-0648) [02214776] **4380**

DANSKE GEOGRAFISKE SELSKAB *See* KULTURGEOGRAFISKE SKRIFTER **2567**

DANSKE INFORMATIONSBASER (DK/0903-1871) [19694001] **1181**

DANSKE MAGAZIN (DK) [04446803] **3380**

DANSKE MALERMESTRE (DK/0905-6440) [23158361] **4223**

DANSKE PIONEER, DEN (US/0747-3869) [09665848] **5659**

DANSKE STUDIER (DK/0106-4525) [01565916] 2319, **3341**

DANTE SOCIETY OF AMERICA *See* DANTE STUDIES, WITH THE ANNUAL REPORT OF THE DANTE SOCIETY **3380**

DANTE STUDIES, WITH THE ANNUAL REPORT OF THE DANTE SOCIETY (US/0070-2862) [02240452] **3380**

DANTEC INFORMATION (DK/0900-5579) [12983224] **2040**

DANVERS HISTORICAL SOCIETY *See* HISTORICAL COLLECTIONS OF THE DANVERS HISTORICAL SOCIETY **2737**

DANVILLE COMMERCIAL-NEWS *See* COMMERCIAL-NEWS (DANVILLE, ILL.), THE **5659**

DANVILLE NEWS (DANVILLE, PA.) (US) [14688952] **5736**

DANVILLE REGISTER, THE (US/0744-3242) [08186332] **5758**

DAOYU JIKAN (SI/0303-0954) [01797555] **3380**

DAPHNIS (SZ/0300-693X) [01075509] **3380**

DAQI KEXUE (CC/0254-0002) [03637701] **1424**

DAR ES SALAAM UNIVERSITY LAW JOURNAL (TZ) [04486028] **2959**

DARBININKAS (US/0011-6637) [02254542] **2259**

D'ARCHITECTURES : D'A (FR/1145-0835) [26429716] **296**

DARE (US/0418-3789) [01548148] **2487**

DAREDEVIL (US/0279-8271) [07292899] **4859**

DARI DE SEAMA ALE SEDINTELOR. 2, ZACAMINTE *See* ROMANIAN JOURNAL OF MINERAL DEPOSITS **1396**

DARI DE SEAMA ALE SEDINTELOR. 3, PALEONTOLOGIE *See* ROMANIAN JOURNAL OF PALEONTOLOGY **4230**

DARI DE SEAMA ALE SEDINTELOR - INSTITUTUL DE GEOLOGIE SI GEOFIZICA. 4, STRATIGRAFIE (RM/0254-7309) [05185835] **1373**

DARI DE SEAMA ALE SEDINTELOR - INSTITUTUL DE GEOLOGIE SI GEOFIZICA. 5, TECTONICA SI GEOLOGIE REGIONALA (RM/0253-1798) [05185857] **1373**

DARIEN HISTORICAL SOCIETY *See* DARIEN HISTORICAL SOCIETY ANNUAL, THE **2730**

DARIEN HISTORICAL SOCIETY ANNUAL, THE (US/0415-0368) [03776806] **2730**

DARIEN NEWS-REVIEW (US/0744-3862) [08246589] **5645**

DARIEN NEWS, THE (US) [19503514] **5653**

DARIUS MILHAUD SOCIETY NEWSLETTER, THE (US/0898-1558) [17735629] **4113**

DARK CRIMES (US) [24140335] **3380**

DARK SHADOWS ANNOUNCEMENT, THE (US) **1131**

●DARK SHADOWS (WHEELING, W. VA.) (US/1060-684X) [25052316] **348**

DARKE COUNTY KINDLING (US) **2444**

DARKHAWK (NEW YORK, N.Y.) (US/1056-3830) [23527244] **4859**

DARKNERVE (US) [18248214] **4241**

DARKROOM & CREATIVE CAMERA TECHNIQUES (US) [11823585] **4368**

DARMA PUTRA (IO) [05734030] **2503**

DARMSTADT CONCRETE : ANNUAL JOURNAL ON CONCRETE AND CONCRETE STRUCTURES (GW/0931-1181) [17245635] **612**

DARMSTADTER BEITRAEGE ZUR NEUEN MUSIK (GW/0418-3878) [01625772] **4113**

DARMSTADTER ECHO (GW) [11985531] **5801**

DARMSTADTER ZEITUNG (GW) [20981055] **5801**

D'ARS (IT) [04611582] 296, **348**

DARSE CUENTA (BO) [25774522] **4344**

DARSHAI AZ MAKTAB-I ISLAM (IR) [11105119] **5042**

DARSHANA INTERNATIONAL (II/0011-6734) [04533036] 4952, **4344**

DARSTELLUNGEN UND QUELLEN ZUR GESCHICHTE DER DEUTSCHEN EINHEITSBEWEGUNG IM NEUNZEHNTEN UND ZWANZIGSTEN JAHRHUNDERT (GW/0418-3886) [01565941] **2685**

DARSTELLUNGEN ZUR AUSWARTIGEN POLITIK (GW/0418-3894) [01626095] **4519**

D'ART (SP/0211-0768) [I02110768] **349**

DARTMOUTH ALUMNI MAGAZINE (US) [04719181] **1101**

DARTMOUTH BUSINESS DIRECTORY (CN/0827-2786) [11734450] **664**

DARTMOUTH BUSINESS NEWS (CN/0824-2682) [10082732] **664**

DARTMOUTH COLLEGE. LIBRARY *See* DARTMOUTH COLLEGE LIBRARY BULLETIN **3205**

DARTMOUTH COLLEGE LIBRARY BULLETIN (US/0011-6750) [01565942] **3205**

DARTMOUTH REVIEW, THE (US) [15377824] **1091**

DARTMOUTH, THE (US/0199-9931) [06311027] **1091**

DARTNELL OFFICE ADMINISTRATION HANDBOOK, THE *CEASED*. (US/0418-4025) [01608705] **865**

DARTNELL SALES MANAGER'S HANDBOOK, THE (US) [03422217] **664**

●DARTNELL'S ... SALES FORCE COMPENSATION SURVEY (US/1070-9207) [27209420] **1662**

DARTS WORLD (UK/0140-6000) [13206706] 4850, **4892**

DARWINIANA (AG/0011-6793) [01608938] **508**

DAS AUDIOVISUELLE ARCHIV : INFORMATIONSBLATT DER ARBEITSGEMEINSCHAFT AUDIOVISUELLER ARCHIVE OSTERREICHS (AU) [19864773] **2481**

DASEIN (US/0011-6807) [02943427] **318**

DASEINSANALYSE (BASEL) (SZ/0254-6221) [10567143] **3924**

DAT WAS DE TOESTAND IN DE WERELD (NE) [02564236] **2614**

DATA-ACQUISITION DATABOOK (US/0882-2433) [11766710] **2040**

DATA & KNOWLEDGE ENGINEERING (NE/0169-023X) [12392467] 1257, **1253**

DATA ARCHIVE BULLETIN / SSRC (UK/0307-1391) [08581688] **2481**

DATA ASIA (PH) [08093616] **1555**

Alphabetical Title Index

DATAMEX.

DATA BANK : A PUBLICATION OF THE NATIONAL ORIENTATION DIRECTORS ASSOCIATION (US) [09444571] **1862**

DATA BANKS (US/8756-5439) [11538652] **4254**

DATA BASE (US/0095-0033) [02240015] 664, **1257**

DATA BASE ALERT (US/0737-951X) [09481621] 1237, **1253**

DATA BASE DIRECTORY (US/0749-6680) [11166469] **1253**

DATA BASE MANAGEMENT (MILWAUKEE, WIS.) *See* DATA MANAGEMENT REVIEW **1253**

DATA BASE MANAGEMENT (WILWAUKEE, WIS.) (US/1066-5498) [27001729] **1253**

DATA BASE NEWSLETTER (PRINCETON, N.J.) (US/0735-3677) [05460006] **1253**

DATA BASE PRODUCT REPORTS / MIC (US/0740-6800) [09940046] 1266, **1253**

DATA BASED ADVISOR (US/0740-5200) [09973022] **1253**

DATA BOOK (US) [25501461] **5326**

DATA BOOK OF SOCIAL STUDIES MATERIALS AND RESOURCES *CEASED.* (US/0747-4857) [06394125] **5197**

DATA BOOK ON ILLINOIS HIGHER EDUCATION (US/0098-5279) [02241411] **1819**

DATA BOOK, OPERATING BANKS AND BRANCHES (US) [11056816] **787**

DATA BROADCASTING REPORT *CEASED.* (US/0882-5726) [11893500] **1131**

DATA CAPTURE CASE STUDIES AND TECHNOLOGY (US/1054-5468) [22918494] **5099**

DATA CATALOGUE - WORLD DATA CENTER C2 FOR GEOMAGNETISM (JA) [05059739] **4443**

DATA CHANNELS (US/0093-7290) [00928264] **1257**

DATA (CHICAGO, ILL.) (US/0276-4784) [07370399] **1734**

DATA/COMM INDUSTRY REPORT *CEASED.* (US/0149-9556) [03593500] **1257**

DATA COMMUNICATIONS (US/0363-6399) [01919240] **1241**

DATA COMMUNICATIONS INTERNATIONAL (US) **1241**

DATA-DATA IKLIM DI INDONESIA (IO) [04507755] **1425**

DATA DIGEST ON IOWA POSTSECONDARY INSTITUTIONS (US) [03582370] **1819**

DATA DISPENSER (US/1040-8924) [18572372] **1819**

DATA ENGINEERING / INTERNATIONAL CONFERENCE ON DATA ENGINEERING (US) [11269468] **2040**

DATA ENTRY/DATA CONVERSION SERVICES DIRECTORY *CEASED.* (US/1057-2554) [23747747] **1181**

DATA ENTRY SERVICES DIRECTORY (US/0899-4579) [18098845] **1257**

DATA EXTRACT (AT) **2510**

DATA FROM THE CLIENT ORIENTED DATA ACQUISITION PROCESS. ANNUAL DATA (US/0196-4879) [04597295] **1342**

DATA FROM THE CLIENT ORIENTED DATA ACQUISITION PROCESS. SMSA STATISTICS (US/0161-5033) [03906821] 1342, **1350**

DATA FROM THE CLIENT ORIENTED DATA ACQUISITION PROCESS. STATE OFFICIALS (US/0161-4967) [03496888] 1342, **1350**

DATA FROM THE CLIENT ORIENTED DATA ACQUISITION PROCESS. TREND REPORT (US/0197-0259) [04485995] **1342**

DATA FROM THE DRUG ABUSE WARNING NETWORK. SEMIANNUAL REPORT (US/0884-2132) [12202784] **1342**

DATA IN SCIENCE AND TECHNOLOGY (US) **5099**

DATA INDIA (II/0377-6832) [01797778] **2650**

DATA INFORMER *See* LESKOS INFO POWER **3223**

DATA INFORMER, THE (US) [12811951] **3205**

DATA JURIDICA (NE) [01789445] **2959**

DATA (KBENHAVN. 1971) (DK/0105-9912) [01787826] **1257**

DATA KREDIT PERBANKAN (IO/0302-2013) [01790680] **787**

● DATA MANAGEMENT REVIEW (US/1067-3717) [27195276] **1253**

DATA MANAGER (IT) **865**

DATA NETWORKING / DATAPRO (US) [24366763] **1241**

DATA NEWS (BE) **1181**

DATA ON EARNED DEGREES CONFERRED BY INSTITUTIONS OF HIGHER EDUCATION BY RACE, ETHNICITY AND SEX (US/0271-8561) [04887171] 2259, **1819**

DATA ON IOWA'S AREA SCHOOLS AND PUBLIC JUNIOR COLLEGE (US/0092-3761) [01789444] **1819**

DATA ON VIETNAM ERA VETERANS (US/0882-9837) [05855559] 4040, **4062**

DATA PAPERS ON PAPUA NEW GUINEA LANGUAGES (PP) [18128342] **3276**

DATA PRESS (AU) [02461530] **1257**

DATA PROCESSING (UK/0011-684X) [03667435] **1257**

DATA PROCESSING AND COMMUNICATIONS SECURITY *See* COMPUTING AND COMMUNICATIONS PROTECTION **1226**

DATA PROCESSING & COMMUNICATIONS SECURITY (US/0749-1484) [10421913] 1226, **1257**

DATA PROCESSING ANNUAL REPORT AND LONG-RANGE PLAN FOR FISCAL YEARS ... / STATE OF LOUISIANA (US) [08224349] **4641**

DATA PROCESSING AUDITING REPORT *CEASED.* (US/0735-3863) [08913604] **3571**

DATA PROCESSING DIGEST (US/0011-6858) [01565955] 1257, **1209**

DATA PROCESSING IN ALASKA (US/0192-3986) [04993858] **1257**

DATA PROCESSING MANAGER'S BULLETIN (US/1065-7177) [26704968] 1257, **865**

DATA PROCESSING SURVEY. OREGON CITIES / BUREAU OF GOVERNMENTAL RESEARCH AND SERVICE, SCHOOL OF COMMUNITY SERVICE AND PUBLIC AFFAIRS, UNIVERSITY OF OREGON, IN COOPERATION WITH THE LEAGUE OF OREGON CITIES AND ASSOCIATION OF OREGON COUNTIES (US) [11312267] **1257**

DATA PRODUCT NEWS (TORONTO) *CEASED.* (CN/0226-6091) [06511124] **1245**

DATA RECORD. RECUEIL DE DONNEES STATISTIQUES. COLECCION DE DATOS ESTADISTICOS (SP) [04915054] **2299**

DATA REPORT (GW/0374-289X) [06306078] **1257**

DATA REPORT, HIGH ALTITUDE METEOROLOGICAL DATA. INTERNATIONAL DELAYED DATA ISSUE (US/0149-807X) [03415624] **1425**

DATA REPORT OF HYDROGRAPHIC OBSERVATIONS (JA/0910-9102) [20818324] **1354**

DATA REPORT OF HYDROGRAPHIC OBSERVATIONS. SERIES OF OCEANOGRAPHY (JA) [01796989] **1448**

DATA REPORT ON PROGRAMS FOR THE HANDICAPPED (US/0145-8132) [02793526] **1877**

DATA REPORT - U.S. DEPARTMENT OF COMMERCE, NATIONAL OCEANIC AND ATMOSPHERIC ADMINISTRATION NATIONAL MARINE FISHERIES SERVICE (US/0098-0765) [01799556] **2300**

DATA RESOURCE MANAGEMENT *CEASED.* (US/1053-5594) [22375189] **865**

DATA RESOURCES, INC *See* INSURANCE SERVICE: REGIONAL REVIEW **2884**

DATA RESOURCES, INC *See* DRI INDUSTRY FINANCIAL SERVICES: ANNUAL LONG-TERM REVIEW **788**

DATA RESOURCES, INC *See* DRI ENERGY BULLETIN **1936**

DATA RESOURCES, INC *See* DRI-FACS : REFERENCE GUIDE TO U.S. WEEKLY BANKING STATISTICS **728**

DATA RESOURCES, INC *See* COAL REVIEW (LEXINGTON) **2137**

DATA RESOURCES, INC *See* CHEMICAL REVIEW **1022**

DATA RESOURCES, INC *See* STEEL MILL PRODUCTS (LEXINGTON) **1628**

DATA RESOURCES, INC *See* DRI INDUSTRY FINANCIAL SERVICE **788**

DATA RESOURCES, INC *See* DRI-FACS, FINANCIAL AND CREDIT STATISTICS INFORMATION SERVICE : APPLIED REPORTS AND GRAPHICS LIBRARY **728**

DATA RESOURCES, INC *See* STATE & AREA FORECASTING SERVICE **1522**

DATA RESOURCES, INC *See* PULP & PAPER REVIEW **4238**

DATA RESOURCES, INC. COAL SERVICE *See* COAL SERVICE REFERENCE MANUAL **1602**

DATA RESOURCES, INC. TRANSPORTATION SERVICE *See* TRANSPORTATION MONITORING REPORT **5396**

DATA RESOURCES MODEL OF CANADIAN ENERGY MARKETS, THE (CN/0823-9584) [11559750] **1936**

DATA RESOURCES OF CANADA *See* CANADIAN PROPERTY AND CASUALTY INSURANCE SERVICE : QUARTERLY REPORT **2877**

DATA RESOURCES REVIEW OF THE U.S. ECONOMY *See* REVIEW OF THE U.S. ECONOMY **1518**

DATA RESOURCES SERIES (US) [05953486] **664**

DATA RESOURCES U.S. LONG-TERM REVIEW *See* U.S. LONG-TERM REVIEW **1540**

DATA : REVISTA DEL INSTITUTO DE ESTUDIOS ANDINOS Y AMAZONICOS (BO) [25645346] **2730**

DATA SCOPE (OAKVILLE) (CN/0228-9512) [07857909] **1603**

DATA SECURITY DIGEST EMMELOORD (NE/0924-6711) [I09246711] **1226**

DATA SECURITY LETTER (US/1065-9986) [26823088] **1181**

DATA SOURCES (US/0744-1673) [07857144] **1237**

DATA-STAR NEWS *See* NEWS / RADIOSUISSE SERVICES **1197**

DATA STORAGE REPORT (NE) [13369796] **1181**

DATA STORAGE REPORT (UK/0267-5447) [I02675447] **1257**

● DATA STORAGE / TECHNOLOGY & MANUFACTURE OF STORAGE DEVICES (US) **1257**

DATA-TEK SEMICONDUCTOR PRICE GUIDE (US/0739-1013) [09821463] **2040**

DATA TRAINING *CEASED.* (US/0884-2604) [10079186] **1257**

DATA USER EDUCATION & TRAINING ACTIVITIES (US/0147-7064) [03215691] **5326**

DATA USERS GUIDE - GEOLOGICAL SURVEY (U.S.) (US/1061-8759) [25482266] **1373**

DATABASE AND NETWORK JOURNAL (UK/0265-4490) [09822161] 1241, **1253**

DATABASE CANADA (CN/0840-7797) [23598383] **1253**

DATABASE PROGRAMMING & DESIGN (US/0895-4518) [16644178] 1279, **1253**

DATABASE REVIEW (US/1042-2595) [18978285] **1253**

DATABASE SEARCH AIDS *CEASED.* (US) **1253**

DATABASE SEARCHER (US/0891-6713) [14960538] 1276, **1253**

DATABASE SEARCHSHEETS (US) **664**

DATABASE (WESTON) (US/0162-4105) [04172284] **1253**

DATABASES ONLINE (US/0275-9152) [07250649] 1274, **1253**

DATABOOK - U.S. DEPT. OF HEALTH, EDUCATION, AND WELFARE, NATIONAL INSTITUTE OF EDUCATION, DISSEMINATION AND RESOURCES GROUP, R & D SYSTEM SUPPORT DIVISION (US/0146-857X) [03046950] **1892**

DATACOM (GW/0176-3288) [I01763288] **1296**

DATACOM READER SERVICE (US/0886-2400) [10690084] **1237**

DATACOM : THE JOURNAL OF INTERCONNECTION AND NETWORKING (UK) **1241**

DATACOMM & DISTRIBUTED PROCESSING REPORT *See* DISTRIBUTED PROCESSING PRODUCT REPORTS **1183**

DATACOMMS BOOK, THE (UK/0959-6429) [I09596429] **1257**

DATACOMMUNICATOR (CN/0712-3302) [08932733] **1153**

DATADISK. [ECONOMIC, FINANCIAL, CONSUMER, PRODUCTION AND RETAIL] COMPUTER FILE (US) [25950442] 787, 923, **1479**

DATADISK. [EQUITIES] COMPUTER FILE (US) [25949624] **896**

DATAEASE DIALOGUE (US) **1181**

DATAFONDI (IT) **896**

DATAGUIDE (US/0270-9872) [06435878] **1237**

DATALINE (DALLAS, TEX.) (US/8755-2361) [09932757] **2959**

DATALINK *SUSPENDED.* (UK) [13742728] **664**

DATAMARKNADEN (SW) [01799525] **1237**

DATAMATION (US/0011-6963) [00945019] **1258**

DATAMATION [MICROFORM] (US/0011-6963) [04517739] **2097**

DATAMEX. WESTERN HEMISPHERE (US/0091-9160) [01787892] **5468**

DATAPAC — Alphabetical Title Index

DATAPAC CARIBBEAN (JM) [11508573] 787, **923**

DATAPRO 70 *CEASED*. (US/0045-9704) [01781513] **1258**

DATAPRO BANKNEWS *CEASED*. (US/0730-7497) [08055411] **1258**, **787**

DATAPRO BROADBAND NETWORKING (US) 664, **1109**

DATAPRO COMPETITIVE EDGE IN COMMUNICATIONS, THE (US/1052-6226) [22338867] **1109**

DATAPRO COMPUTER SYSTEMS SERIES / OVERVIEWS (US) **1246**

DATAPRO COMPUTER SYSTEMS SERIES / PERIPHERALS (US) **1246**

DATAPRO COMPUTER SYSTEMS SERIES / SOFTWARE (US) 1285, **1246**

DATAPRO COMPUTER SYSTEMS SERIES / SYSTEMS (US) **1246**

DATAPRO CORPORATE SOFTWARE & SOLUTIONS / INTERNATIONAL EDITION (UK) **1181**

DATAPRO DESKTOP SOFTWARE & SOLUTIONS / INTERNATIONAL EDITION (UK) 1285, **1181**

DATAPRO DIRECTORY OF MICROCOMPUTER HARDWARE (US) [15228476] 1264, **1266**

DATAPRO DIRECTORY OF MICROCOMPUTER SOFTWARE (US/0730-8795) [07636998] **1237**

DATAPRO DIRECTORY OF SOFTWARE (US/0730-8779) [02613825] **1285**

DATAPRO ENTERPRISE SYSTEMS / INTERNATIONAL EDITION (UK) **1181**

DATAPRO INFORMATION MANAGEMENT & WORKFLOW (US) **1181**

DATAPRO INTERNATIONAL NETWORK SERIES (UK) **1241**

DATAPRO LAN INTERNETWORKING (US) 664, **1109**

DATAPRO LOCAL AREA NETWORKS (US) **1109**

DATAPRO MANAGEMENT OF APPLICATIONS SOFTWARE (US/8756-6516) [11626205] **1254**

DATAPRO MANAGEMENT OF INTERNATIONAL TELECOMMUNICATIONS (UK) **1153**

DATAPRO MANAGEMENT OF MICROCOMPUTER SYSTEMS (US/8750-6858) [11637493] 1266, **1274**

DATAPRO MANAGEMENT OF OFFICE AUTOMATION *CEASED*. (US/8750-6416) [11553671] **4211**

DATAPRO MANAGEMENT OF TELECOMMUNICATIONS *See* MANAGING VOICE NETWORKS **1159**

DATAPRO MANAGING DATA NETWORKS (US) [24416048] **1241**

DATAPRO MANAGING INFORMATION TECHNOLOGY (US) [24400799] **1258**

DATAPRO MASTER INDEX [COMPUTER FILE] (US) [18596195] **1181**

DATAPRO MIDRANGE SYSTEMS / INTERNATIONAL EDITION (UK) **1181**

DATAPRO MININEWS. INTERNATIONAL EDITION (US/0730-7500) [08054721] **1258**

DATAPRO NETWORK MANAGEMENT (US) **1109**

DATAPRO NETWORK MANAGEMENT INFORMATION SERVICES (US) **1109**

DATAPRO NETWORK MANAGEMENT SYSTEMS (US) **1109**

DATAPRO NEWSCOM. INTERNATIONAL EDITION *CEASED*. (US/0730-7519) [08054622] **1258**

DATAPRO OFFICE PRODUCTS EVALUATION SERVICE *CEASED*. (US/0898-4468) [17667034] **4211**

DATAPRO PERIPHERALS / INTERNATIONAL EDITION (UK) **1181**

DATAPRO REPORTS ON BANKING AUTOMATION (US/0730-8809) [08089971] 1258, **787**

DATAPRO REPORTS ON DOCUMENT IMAGING SYSTEMS (US) [21617190] **1181**

DATAPRO REPORTS ON ELECTRONIC PUBLISHING *See* WORKGROUP COMPUTING SERIES. INFORMATION DELIVERY / DATAPRO **1263**

DATAPRO REPORTS ON ELECTRONIC PUBLISHING *See* WORKGROUP COMPUTING SERIES. MULTIMEDIA SOLUTIONS / DATAPRO **1263**

DATAPRO REPORTS ON ELECTRONIC PUBLISHING SYSTEMS (US) [14563363] **1181**

DATAPRO REPORTS ON INFORMATION SECURITY (US) 1226, **1246**

DATAPRO REPORTS ON INTERNATIONAL COMMUNICATIONS SOFTWARE (UK) **1285**

DATAPRO REPORTS ON INTERNATIONAL TELECOMMUNICATIONS (UK) **1109**

DATAPRO REPORTS ON INTERNATIONAL TELECOMMUNICATIONS (UK) **1153**

DATAPRO REPORTS ON MICROCOMPUTERS (US/0741-2541) [10138627] **1267**

DATAPRO REPORTS ON MINICOMPUTERS (US/0275-0813) [01639524] **1274**

DATAPRO REPORTS ON MINICOMPUTERS. INTERNATIONAL EDITION (US/0730-7055) [08090585] **1274**

DATAPRO REPORTS ON OFFICE AUTOMATION *CEASED*. (US) [10658547] 1219, **1258**

DATAPRO REPORTS ON OFFICE SYSTEMS (US/0277-4984) [02360629] **4211**

DATAPRO REPORTS ON RETAIL AUTOMATION (US/0730-8817) [08090174] 664, **1258**

DATAPRO REPORTS ON TELECOMMUNICATIONS *See* COMMUNICATIONS SERIES. COMMUNICATIONS NETWORKING SERVICES **1152**

DATAPRO REPORTS ON TELECOMMUNICATIONS *See* COMMUNICATIONS SERIES. VOICE NETWORKING SYSTEMS **1152**

DATAPRO REPORTS ON UNIX SYSTEMS & SOFTWARE (US) 1285, **1246**

DATAPRO RESEARCH CORPORATION *See* DATAPRO REPORTS ON MINICOMPUTERS **1274**

DATAPRO SOFTWARE FINDER (COMPLETE ED.) (US/1052-195X) [22214329] **1285**

DATAPRO SOFTWARE FINDER (MICROCOMPUTER ED.) (US/1052-1941) [22214309] 1267, **1285**

DATAPRO SOFTWARE FINDER (MID-RANGE/MAINFRAME ED.) (US/1052-1968) [22214388] **1285**

DATAPRO SOFTWARE NEWS *CEASED*. (US/0730-7381) [08057429] 1285, **1258**

DATAPRO WORKGROUP COMPUTING SERIES / DEVELOPMENT TOOLS (US) **1181**

DATAPRO WORKGROUP COMPUTING SERIES / DISTRIBUTED DATABASES (US) **1254**

DATAPRO WORKGROUP COMPUTING SERIES / STRATEGIES & LAN SERVICES (US) **1181**

DATAPRO WORKSTATIONS & SERVERS / ISSUES (US) **1246**

DATAPRO WORKSTATIONS & SERVERS / SYSTEMS (US) **1246**

DATAPRO WORKSTATIONS / INTERNATIONAL EDITION (UK) **1181**

DATAQUEST : DQ (II) [16703673] 1285, **1267**

DATASPORT (AT/0817-1440) [08171440] **4892**

DATATRENDS REPORT ON DEC *See* TERRY SHANNON ON DEC **1205**

DATATRENDS REPORT ON DEC AND IBM *See* DATATRENDS REPORT ON DEC, THE **1237**

DATATRENDS REPORT ON DEC AND IBM, THE (US) [22200237] **1181**

DATATRENDS REPORT ON DEC, THE (US/1064-377X) [25468383] **1237**

DATCH INFORMATION *See* NEWSLETTER - DANISH CENTRE FOR TECHNICAL AIDS FOR REHABILITATION AND EDUCATION **1882**

DATE PALM JOURNAL, THE (IQ/0252-3353) [09201095] **170**

DATEK IMAGING SUPPLIES MONTHLY, THE (US/1050-6993) [17985160] **4564**

DATEK PRINTER DATABASE SERVICE (US/0739-4519) [09736203] 1245, **1258**

DATELINE HYPERTENSION (US/0747-6124) [10763704] **3704**

DATELINE NAMIBIA (US) [10976839] **4952**

DATELINE : NRPA (US) [05840347] **2191**

DATELINE TURKEY (TU) **2503**

DATEN DES GESUNDHEITSWESENS (GW/0172-3723) [05626949] 4773, **4809**

DATEN UND DOKUMENTE ZUM UMWELTSCHUTZ *CEASED*. (GW/0170-608X) [04637028] **2191**

DATEN ZUR LAGE DER ARBEITNEHMER IM SAARLAND / ARBEITSKAMMER DES SAARLANDES (GW) [10292010] 1479, **1662**

DATEN ZUR SOZIALSTRUKTUR: DIE MATERIELLE LEBENSSICHERUNG (GW) [05623125] 5281, **1479**

DATEN ZUR UMWELT (GW) [05507918] **2227**

DATENSCHUTZ-BERATER (GW/0170-7256) [01707256] **1226**

DATENSCHUTZ-NACHRICHTEN (GW/0173-7767) [01737767] **4507**

DATENSCHUTZ UND DATENSICHERUNG (GW) [07357029] **2959**

DATENVERARBEITUNG IN STEUER, WIRTSCHAFT UND RECHT *See* DATENVERARBEITUNG, STEUER, WIRTSCHAFT, RECHT : DSWR : ORGAN DER DATEV **664**

DATENVERARBEITUNG, STEUER, WIRTSCHAFT, RECHT : DSWR : ORGAN DER DATEV (GW) [08048398] **664**

DATES & DEADLINES (US) **664**

DATES OF LATEST EDITIONS. AIRPORT OBSTRUCTION CHARTS (US) [20273351] **17**

DATI E TARIFFE PUBBLICITARIE (IT) **758**

DATI STATISTICI SUL COMMERCIO ESTERO : IMPORTAZIONI ED ESPORTAZIONI PER PAESI, TAVOLA 3 (IT) **2614**

DATOS - SOCIEDAD PRIVADA MUNICIPAL TRANSPORTES DE BARCELONA (SP/0376-8112) [01796449] **5380**

DATUTOP, DEPARTMENT OF ARCHITECTURE, TAMPERE UNIVERSITY OF TECHNOLOGY OCCASIONAL PAPERS (FI/0359-7105) [11586336] 2820, **296**

DATZ : AQUARIEN TERRARIEN (GW/0941-8393) [19891274] **2773**

DATZ PHILATELIC INDEX OF UNITED STATES POSTAGE STAMPS (US/0146-4728) [02993552] **2785**

DAUGAVA (LV/0207-4001) [05345343] **3380**

DAUGAVAS VANAGU MENESRAKSTS (CN/0418-4297) [01780113] **2845**

DAUGHTERS OF SARAH (US/0739-1749) [02254361] 5554, **4952**

DAUGHTERS OF THE AMERICAN REVOLUTION *See* DAUGHTERS OF THE AMERICAN REVOLUTION MAGAZINE **2730**

DAUGHTERS OF THE AMERICAN REVOLUTION. CONTINENTAL CONGRESS *See* PROCEEDINGS OF THE ... CONTINENTAL CONGRESS OF THE NATIONAL SOCIETY OF THE DAUGHTERS OF THE AMERICAN REVOLUTION **2755**

DAUGHTERS OF THE AMERICAN REVOLUTION MAGAZINE (US/0011-7013) [01565978] 2444, **2730**

DAUGHTERS OF THE REPUBLIC OF TEXAS *See* PROCEEDINGS OF THE ANNUAL CONVENTION OF THE DAUGHTERS OF THE REPUBLIC OF TEXAS **2755**

DAUPHIN (BE/0773-0292) [l07730292] **1062**

DAUPHIN COUNTY REPORTS (US) [01565980] **2959**

DAUPHINE LIBERE, LE (FR) [20815242] **5800**

DAV MAGAZINE (1985) (US/0885-6400) [12680503] **5281**

DAVAI (IT) **1734**

DAVANTAGE (CN/0703-6485) [05018226] **4952**

DAVANTAGE (POINTE-CLAIRE) (CN/0705-7032) [04097992] **5244**

DAVE CAMPBELL'S ARKANSAS FOOTBALL (US/0147-1295) [03096206] **4892**

DAVE CAMPBELL'S TEXAS FOOTBALL (US/0147-1287) [03096247] **4892**

DAVE HEEREN'S BASKETBALL ABSTRACT (US/1051-1849) [21885223] **4892**

DAVENPORT NEWSLETTER, THE (US/0736-2633) [09085273] **2444**

DAVID ANTHONY KRAFTS COMICS INTERVIEW (US/1052-5548) [11911378] **4859**

DAVID CHANDLER'S AGE OF NAPOLEON *CEASED*. (US) [17624235] **2685**

DAVID DUNLAP DOINGS, THE (CN/0713-5904) [09606652] **395**

DAVID FIELD ALL-WORLD MINIATURE SHEET CATALOGUE (UK/0308-549X) [01792344] **2785**

DAVID H. BOWEN'S SOFTWARE SUCCESS (US/0896-4386) [17157123] **1181**

DAVID INGRAM'S THE ULTIMATE YEAR ROUND TAX GUIDE (CN/1184-0323) [23302735] **4719**

DAVID LORD'S WORLD OF CRICKET (AT/0311-0435) [01792687] **4859**

DAVID Y GOLIATH : BOLETIN CLACSO *SUSPENDED*. (AG/0325-0431) [07588938] **2551**

DAVIE COUNTY ENTERPRISE-RECORD (US) [13168632] **5723**

DAVIESS COUNTY HISTORICAL QUARTERLY, THE (US/0882-2395) [10927376] **2730**

DAVIS' ANTHOLOGY OF NEWSPAPER VERSE (US) [04352372] **3462**

DAVIS COUNTY CLIPPER (US) [11930754] **5756**

DAVIS ENTERPRISE (US) [26709961] **5634**

DAVIS ON EXECUTIVE COMPENSATION **CEASED.** (CN/1183-4676) [24280020] **1662**

DAVIS REVIEW **SUSPENDED.** (US/0893-3510) [15493772] **1603**

DAVIS WORKING PAPERS IN LINGUISTICS **SUSPENDED.** (US) [13316578] **3276**

DAVISON INDEX, THE (US/0192-4516) [05044048] **5691**

DAVISON'S "SALESMAN'S BOOK." (US/0363-5252) [02114096] **5350**

DAVISON'S TEXTILE "BLUE BOOK" (US/0070-2951) [01565986] **5350**

DAVISON'S TEXTILE BLUE BOOK. EUROPE (US) [26979094] **5350**

DAVISON'S TEXTILE BLUE BOOK : UNITED STATES AND CANADA (US) [05346819] **5350**

DAVISON'S TEXTILE BUYERS GUIDE (1980) (US/0734-4708) [06526616] **5350**

DAVKA (US/0011-7048) [02314699] **2650**

DAWN (PK) [04478014] **2503**

DAWN : A HERALD OF CHRIST'S PRESENCE, THE (US) [08322601] **5016**

DAWN (HONESDALE, PA.) **CEASED.** (US/0277-4461) [07564513] **4185**

DAWRIYAT MALUMAT / TASDURU AN MARKAZ TADRIB MALAKAT MAHW AL-UMMIYAH WA-TALIM AL-KIBAR, TARABULUS (LY) [07654252] **1734**

DAWSON AND HIND (CN/0703-6507) [03412332] **4087**

DAWSON COUNTY GENEALOGICAL NEWSLETTER (US/0893-5408) [15578923] **2445**

DAWSON SENTINEL (US) [20389360] **5695**

DAWSON SPRINGS PROGRESS, THE (US) [14107102] **5680**

DAWSON'S LOCAL PINK PAGES. BANKSTOWN (AT/0813-4057) [I08134057] **1924**

DAWSON'S LOCAL PINK PAGES. BLACKTOWN (AT/0812-1176) [I08121176] **1924**

DAWSON'S LOCAL PINK PAGES. BRISBANE WATERS (AT/1034-4888) [I10344888] **1924**

DAWSON'S LOCAL PINK PAGES. CRONULLA-SUTHERLAND (AT/0813-4049) [I08134049] **1924**

DAWSON'S LOCAL PINK PAGES. EASTERN SUBURBS (AT/0810-4670) [I08104670] **1924**

DAWSON'S LOCAL PINK PAGES. FAIRFIELD (AT/0812-5643) [I08125643] **1924**

DAWSONS LOCAL PINK PAGES. HILLS DISTRICT (AT/0810-2643) [I08102643] **1924**

DAWSON'S LOCAL PINK PAGES. KU-RING-GAI (AT/0811-479X) [I08111479X] **1924**

DAWSON'S LOCAL PINK PAGES. LIVERPOOL (AT/0811-7276) [I08117276] **1924**

DAWSON'S LOCAL PINK PAGES. LOWER NORTH SHORE (AT/0811-0360) [I08110360] **1924**

DAWSON'S LOCAL PINK PAGES. MACARTHUR (AT/1034-4896) [I10344896] **1924**

DAWSON'S LOCAL PINK PAGES. MANLY-WARRINGAH (AT/0812-7050) [I08127050] **1924**

DAWSON'S LOCAL PINK PAGES. NEWCASTLE (AT/1034-4918) [I10344918] **1924**

DAWSON'S LOCAL PINK PAGES. NORTHERN DISTRICTS (AT/0810-4689) [I08104689] **1924**

DAWSON'S LOCAL PINK PAGES. PARRAMATTA AND HOLROYD (AT/0813-4030) [I08134030] **1925**

DAWSON'S LOCAL PINK PAGES. PENRITH AND LOWER BLUE MOUNTAINS (AT/0814-1770) [I08141770] **1925**

DAWSONS LOCAL PINK PAGES. RYDE, HUNTERS HILL (AT/0810-2465) [I08102465] **1925**

DAWSON'S LOCAL PINK PAGES. ST. GEORGE (AT/1034-490X) [I1034490X] **1925**

DAWSON'S LOCAL PINK PAGES. WOLLONGONG (AT/1034-4926) [I10344926] **1925**

DAX MONEY-MAKER (US/0147-1112) [03099047] **664**

DAXUE HUAXUE (CC/1000-8438) [21663566] **974**

DAY & NIGHT IN UPSTATE NEW YORK : THE TRAVEL AND ENTERTAINMENT MAGAZINE (US) [08516829] **5468**

DAY CARE & CHILD DEVELOPMENT REPORTS **See** DAY CARE INFORMATION SERVICE **5281**

DAY CARE AND EARLY EDUCATION (US/0092-4199) [01789785] **1803**

DAY CARE AND EARLY EDUCATION. [MICROFILM] (US/0092-4199) [06326169] **1803**

DAY CARE CENTRES AND NURSERY SCHOOLS HAMILTON-WENTWORTH (CN/0711-7930) [08559638] **5281**

DAY CARE FOR CHILDREN (KITCHENER) (CN/0821-4360) [09523803] **5281**

DAY CARE INFORMATION SERVICE (US) [08518959] **5281**

DAY CARE JOURNAL **CEASED.** (US/0732-7889) [08425499] **5281**

DAY CARE (TORONTO) (CN/0384-1537) [03284806] **5281**

DAY CARE U.S.A. NEWSLETTER, THE (US) [08254159] **1803**

DAY (NEW LONDON, CONN.), THE (US/0744-0499) [08012330] **5645**

DAY RESEARCHER (US/0743-216X) [10549110] **2445**

DAYANANDA SANDESA (II) [02245575] **4952**

DAYBREAK (HIGHLAND (HOWARD COUNTY, MD.)) (US) [17863449] **2259**

DAYCLEAN (GY) [24123197] **1662**

DAYIG U-MIDGEH BE-YISRAEL (.S/0011-7110) [02949433] **2300**

DAYLILY JOURNAL, THE (US/0744-0219) [07870721] **2413**

DAYTIME SERIAL NEWSLETTER (US/0164-8306) [03522893] **1131**

DAYTIME TV (US/0011-7129) [C1786473] **1131**

DAYTON **SUSPENDED.** (US/0199-9214) [06290317] **2730**

DAYTON ART INSTITUTE **See** BULLETIN / THE DAYTON ART INSTITUTE **346**

DAYTON ART INSTITUTE **See** BULLETIN - DAYTON ART INSTITUTE **345**

DAYTON BUSINESS JOURNAL **See** DAYTON-SPRINGFIELD BUSINESS LIFE **664**

DAYTON BUSINESS REPORTER (US/1063-3413) [25983334] **664**

DAYTON DAILY NEWS (DAYTON, OHIO : 1987) (US/0897-0920) [17396173] **5728**

DAYTON REVIEW (DAYTON, IOWA) (US) [14398217] **5669**

DAYTON-SPRINGFIELD BUSINESS LIFE (US) **664**

DAYTON U.S.A **See** DAYTON **2730**

DAZE INC, THE (US/0895-3961) [12182643] **2588**

DAZZLE (CN/0706-6449) [04678074] **1083, 403**

DB (NE) [04427960] **1603**

DB; DEINE BAHN (GW) [01788338] **5431**

DB. DEUTSCHE BAUZEITUNG (1981) (GW/0721-1902) [08182647] **296**

DB THE SOUND ENGINEERING MAGAZINE (US) [21216848] **4452**

DB2 FOR THE COBOL PROGRAMMER (US) **1182**

DB2 JOURNAL **See** RELATIONAL DATABASE JOURNAL **1255**

DB2 UPDATE (UK) **1254**

● DBASE ADVISOR (US) [29176729] **1254**

DBJR (GW) [17969335] **5197**

DBMS (REDWOOD CITY, CALIF.) (US/1041-5173) [18478492] **1254**

DBPH NEWSLETTER (US/0737-6235) [09426400] **4386, 3205**

DBS NEWS **CEASED.** (US/0733-9739) [08675480] **664, 1153**

DBS REPORT, THE (US/1054-0814) [22743825] **1109**

DBZ-DEUTSCHE BAUZEITSCHRIFT (GW/0011-4782) [01566348] **296**

DBZ. DEUTSCHE BRIEFMARKEN-ZEITUNG (GW/0931-4393) [I09314393] **2773**

DBZ, NEUE DEUTSCHE BAUERNZEITUNG (GW/0548-2739) [02343082] **78**

D+C. DEVELOPMENT AND COOPERATION (ENGLISH EDITION) (GW/0723-6980) [05723321] **1555**

DC RULES OF PROFESSIONAL CONDUCT (US) **2959**

DCA NEWS (US) [09041082] **1313**

DCAA CONTRACT AUDIT MANUAL (US/1058-076X) [20586058] **4040**

DCAS MANAGEMENT SYNOPSIS EXECUTIVE SUMMARY (US/0148-3293) [03297151] **4040**

DCAS MANUFACTURING COST CONTROL DIGEST (US/0099-1961) [02171969] **3477**

DCMEA NEWSLETTER (US) **4113**

● DCQFORUM (SILVER SPRING, MD.) (US/1071-5975) [28691511] **612**

DCS NEWSLETTER (CN/0225-4034) [19027309] **2040**

DDH. DAS DACHDECKER-HANDWERK (GW/0172-1003) [I01721003] **612**

DDM JOURNAL : A QUARTERLY PUBLICATION OF THE PHILIPPINE DENTAL FOUNDATION, INC, THE (PH) [24245968] **1320**

DDR-LITERATUR ... IM GESPRACH (GW/0233-1594) [14056437] **3380**

DDR-PERIODICA (GW) [03575883] **3458**

DDR-PUBLIKATIONEN ZUR IMPERIALISMUSFORSCHUNG, AUSWAHLBIBLIOGRAPHIE (GW) [01789764] **4502**

DDR - REVUE; MAGAZINE AUS DER DEUTSCHEN DEMOKRATISCHEN REPUBLIK **CEASED.** (GW/0414-8894) [03786624] **2515**

DDR-STUDIEN (US/0882-7095) [11935707] **2685**

DDR VERKEHR (SZ/0011-4820) [04508840] **5380**

DDZ. DER DEUTSCHE ZOLLBEAMTE (GW) [06550032] **4719**

DE HAEN NEW PRODUCT SURVEY (US) [03441342] **4299**

DE HAEN'S DRUG PRODUCT INDEX. INTERNATIONAL **CEASED.** (US) [19376795] **4299**

DE. JOURNAL OF DENTAL ENGINEERING (JA/0385-0129) [10262250] **1320**

DE LLOYD / LE LLOYD (BE) **5381**

DE PAUL LAW REVIEW (US/0011-7188) [01566000] **2959**

DE PERE JOURNAL (US/0748-6219) [10990072] **5766**

DE QUEEN BEE (US) [20069354] **5631**

DE SMET NEWS, THE (US) [12813263] **5743**

DEACON (US/0045-9771) [01606096] **5059**

DEACON DIGEST (US/8750-7749) [11747021] **4952**

DEAD OF NIGHT (US/1049-0892) [21132977] **3462, 2319**

DEAD SEA DISCOVERIES (NE/0929-0761) **2768, 4952**

DEADLINE (US) 1970, **1285**

DEADLINE (CHICAGO, ILL.) (US/0738-2901) [09559596] **4519, 2918**

DEADLINES (HAWLEY, MASS.) (US/0889-1931) [13812276] **296**

DEADLY IMPULSE (US/1045-2923) [20078930] **3380**

● DEAF CANADA (CN/1195-3349) [29342349] **4386**

DEAF CANADIAN ADVOCATE **See** SOURDS DU CANADA **4393**

DEAF CANADIAN ADVOCATE (CN/0841-9116) [16402801] **4386**

DEAF CANADIAN ADVOCATE **See** DEAF CANADA **4386**

DEAF CATHOLIC, THE (US/0045-978X) [08077036] **5028**

DEAF LIFE (US/0898-719X) [17887154] **4386**

DEAF SPORTS REVIEW (US/1059-3063) [24562335] **4892**

DEAF USA (US/0898-5480) [17846839] **4386**

DEALER PROGRESS (US/1043-3104) [19365008] **78**

DEALERNEWS (1987) (US/0893-2522) [15472053] **4081**

DEALER'S AND TRAPPER'S LISTING BOOK (US/0276-2803) [07320052] **3183**

DEALERSCOPE MERCHANDISING (US/0888-4501) [13585752] **2811, 953**

● DEALERSCOPE MERCHANDISING GOLDBOOK (US/1064-6280) [26345067] **2811**

DEALING WITH TECHNOLOGY (UK) **5099**

DEALMAKERS (BELLE MEAD, N.J.), THE (US/1055-0771) [23068582] **953, 4836**

DEAN AND DIRECTOR (US/0730-2444) [07992643] **1862**

DEAN ARCHAEOLOGY (UK/0954-8874) [23601292] **266**

DEAN BURGON NEWS, THE (US) [09764681] **5230**

DEAR COLLEAGUE (ST. CATHARINES, ONT.) (CN/0714-3869) [09029924] **1862**

DEARBORN COUNTY REGISTER (LAWRENCEBURG, INC. : 1954) (US) [11620794] **5663**

DEARBORN TIMES-HERALD (US/0193-0230) [05144555] **5691**

DEATH & DYING (BOCA RATON, FLA.) (US/0273-2483) [06027935] **4344**

DEATH ROW U.S.A (US) **3163**

DEATH STUDIES (US/0748-1187) [10890428] 2249, **4584**

DEATH VALLEY GATEWAY GAZETTE (US/0746-7419) [10241391] **5707**

DEATHLOK (US/1059-0773) [24470746] **378**

DEATHS, AUSTRALIA (AT) [09289159] 4551, **4561**

DEATHS, QUEENSLAND (AT/0816-0465) [108160465] 4551, **4561**

DEATHS REPORT / REPUBLIC OF TRINIDAD & TOBAGO, CENTRAL STATISTICAL OFFICE (TR) [20862997] **4551**

DEATHS, TASMANIA (AT/0814-8155) [17109344] 4809, **4561**

DEBAT, LE (FR/0246-2346) [07155102] **2845**

DEBATE AGRARIO (PE) [17835292] **78**

DEBATE & [I.E. E] CRITICA (BL) [02240977] **5197**

DEBATE, EL *CEASED*. (PR) [20495512] **5808**

DEBATE ISSUES (US/0886-1803) [03522920] **1734**

DEBATE LABORAL : REVISTA AMERICANA E ITALIANA DE DERECHO DEL TRABAJO (CR) [20437985] **3146**

DEBATE (LIMA, PERU) (PE) [09631308] **4471**

DEBATES AND PROCEEDINGS - LEGISLATIVE ASSEMBLY OF MANITOBA (CN/0542-5492) [02443881] **4641**

DEBATES AND PROCEEDINGS - NOVA SCOTIA HOUSE OF ASSEMBLY (CN/0707-8315) [02249743] **4641**

DEBATES EN SOCIOLOGIA (PE) [08425869] **5244**

DEBATES IN CLINICAL SURGERY (US/1040-1733) [18339178] **3963**

DEBATES OF PARLIAMENT / REPUBLIC OF SOUTH AFRICA (SA) [18128480] **4641**

DEBATES OF THE NATIONAL ASSEMBLY (SA) [04998437] **4471**

DEBATES OF THE SENATE (CN) [02885859] **4471**

DEBATES : OFFICIAL REPORT - PROVINCIAL ASSEMBLY OF SIND (PK/0376-8120) [01796012] **4471**

DEBATS DE L'ASSEMBLEE LEGISLATIVE DU QUEBEC (CN/0709-3616) [04040410] **4642**

DEBATS (VALENCIA, SPAIN) (SP) [10708850] **2515**

DEBATTE OXFORD (UK/0965-156X) [I0965156X] **2845**

DEBATTE VAN DIE PRESIDENTSRAAD (SA) [18504049] **4642**

DEBATTE VAN DIE ... SESSIE VAN DIE WETGEWENDE VERGADERING VAN DIE KAVANGO (SA) [19223639] **4642**

DEBATTE VAN DIE STAANDE KOMITEE VOOR BEGROTINGSWETSONTWERP (SA) [06868360] **4642**

DEBATTE VAN STAANDE KOMITEES / REPUBLIEK VAN SUID-AFRIKA, VOLKSRAAD (SA) [08268945] **4471**

DEBIT BALANCES, WEST VIRGINIA'S UNEMPLOYMENT COMPENSATION LAW (US) [03954900] **1662**

DEBIT CARD DIRECTORY (US) **742**

DEBITS AND DEPOSIT TURNOVER AT COMMERCIAL BANKS (US/0731-0536) [05062091] **787**

DEBIUTY POETYCKIE ... ANTOLOGIA (PL) [19992808] **3462**

DEBONAIR (II) [03214063] **2503**

DEBRECENI DERI MUZEUM EVKONYVE, A (HU/0418-4513) [05198329] **4087**

DEBRETT'S DISTINGUISHED PEOPLE OF TODAY *See* DEBRETT'S PEOPLE OF TODAY **432**

DEBRETT'S PEERAGE AND BARONETAGE (UK) [07124287] **2445**

DEBRETT'S PEOPLE OF TODAY (UK) [24992865] **432**

●DEBROUILLARDS (MONTREAL) (CN/1187-8681) [26497499] **1062**

DEBT-EQUITY SWAP HANDBOOK (US) **787**

DEBTOR & CREDITOR. BENDER PAMPHLET EDITION (US/0147-3719) [03148333] **2959**

DEC COMPUTING (UK/0950-5482) [24819978] **1182**

DEC DIRECT SOFTWARE (IT) **1285**

DEC PROFESSIONAL, THE (US/0744-9216) [08656402] **1246**

DEC USER (UK/0263-6530) [I02636530] **1182**

DECA DIMENSIONS (US/1060-6106) [24877621] **1912**

DECADE (US/0162-7139) [04215802] **318**

DECADE OF EDUCATION FINANCE (CN/0827-0090) [13119261] 1734, **1794**

DECANTER (LONDON. 1985) (UK/0954-4240) [18905159] **2366**

DECATUR DAILY (1927) (US) [12275234] **5626**

DECATUR DAILY DEMOCRAT (US/0894-2307) [11287192] **5663**

DECATUR DEKALB NEIGHBOR, THE (US/0199-6010) [06034434] **5653**

DECATUR-DEKALB NEWS/ERA (US) [19946163] **5653**

DECATUR GENEALOGICAL SOCIETY *See* CENTRAL ILLINOIS GENEALOGICAL QUARTERLY **2442**

DECCAN GEOGRAPHER (II/0011-7269) [I00117269] **2559**

DECDIRECT NOW (US) **1182**

DECEMBER (US/0070-3141) [03902847] **3380**

DECEMBER ROSE *SUSPENDED*. (US/0748-1195) [10890521] **5178**

DECENCY REPORTER / CHILDREN'S LEGAL FOUNDATION (US) [23076639] 4507, **2959**

DECENNIAL INDEX ... : INDEX OF AUTHORS IN PROCEEDINGS, PHILOSOPHICAL TRANSACTIONS, AND BIOGRAPHICAL MEMOIRS (UK) [05635569] **432**

DECENNIE 2 [I.E. DEUX] (IV) [01788046] **2639**

DECENTRALISATION BOARD ANNUAL REPORT (SA) [25259999] **2639**

DECHEMA BIOTECHNOLOGY CONFERENCES (GW/0934-3792) [27638135] **3691**

DECHEMA CORROSION HANDBOOK (UK) **2012**

DECHEMA MONOGRAPHIEN (GW/0070-315X) [01699340] **974**

DECHENIANA (GW/0366-872X) [06130264] **4165**

DECIDUOUS FRUIT GROWER, THE (SA/0302-7074) [08332802] **2413**

DECIMA QUARTERLY REPORT (CN/0823-0080) [09808969] **2730**

DECIMAL (FR) [06292598] 1479, **1531**

DECISION ADOPTED BY THE INTERNATIONAL TROPICAL TIMBER COUNCIL (SZ) [20970894] **2378**

DECISION (CALCUTTA) (II/0304-0941) [01798790] **865**

DECISION (CANADIAN ED.) (CN/0820-9057) [09822990] **4952**

DECISION INFORMATIQUE (FR) **1182**

DECISION LINE (US/0732-6823) [03972073] **664**

DECISION MICRO PARIS (FR/1148-4675) [I11484675] **5099**

DECISION (NORTH AMERICA ED.) (US/0011-7307) [00929428] **4952**

DECISION OF THE UMPIRE (CN/0822-367X) [11463629] **3146**

DECISION RESEARCH SCIENCES *See* DEPOSIT HISTORY AND PROJECTIONS **787**

DECISION SANTE NEUILLY-SUR-SEINE (FR/1157-6197) [I11576197] **2596**

DECISION SCIENCES (US/0011-7315) [01566025] **664**

DECISION SCIENCES INSTITUTE. MEETING *See* PROCEEDINGS OF THE ANNUAL MEETING OF THE DECISION SCIENCES INSTITUTE **882**

DECISION SUPPORT SYSTEMS (NE/0167-9236) [11804282] **865**

DECISION - TRIBUNAL CANADIEN DU COMMERCE EXTERIEUR (CN/1182-5316) [23242689] **2959**

DECISIONES DE PUERTO RICO (US) [04586239] **2959**

DECISIONES DEL TRIBUNAL SUPREMO DE PUERTO RICO [COMPUTER FILE] (PR) [23558221] **2959**

DECISIONES SEU SENTENTIAE (VC) [01782022] **5028**

DECISIONS (US) [01641714] **1662**

DECISIONS AND ORDERS OF THE NATIONAL LABOR RELATIONS BOARD (US) [01768562] **3146**

DECISIONS AND ORDERS OF THE NEW YORK STATE LABOR RELATIONS BOARD (US) [01643953] **3146**

DECISIONS AND REPORTS - EUROPEAN COMMISSION OF HUMAN RIGHTS (FR/0379-8461) [02256075] **4507**

DECISIONS DE LA COMMISSION DES AFFAIRES SOCIALES (CN/0702-9683) [17640966] **4642**

DECISIONS DISCIPLINAIRES CONCERNANT LES CORPORATIONS PROFESSIONNELLES (CN/0702-9578) [18773710] **665**

DECISIONS DU CONGRES DE LA C. E. Q (CN/0317-221X) [02248320] **1662**

DECISIONS - FEDERAL MINE SAFETY AND HEALTH REVIEW COMMISSION (US/0193-7987) [05043907] **2861**

DECISIONS IN COMPUTER MANAGEMENT (US) [01923822] **1237**

●DECISIONS MEDIAS (FR/1165-8606) [I11658606] 2918, **1109**

DECISIONS - MEDICAL RESEARCH COUNCIL (CANADA) (CN/1180-5358) [23248097] **3571**

DECISIONS OF THE COMPTROLLER GENERAL OF THE UNITED STATES *CEASED*. (US) [05308060] **4719**

DECISIONS OF THE DEPARTMENT OF THE INTERIOR (MONTHLY) (US/0011-7331) [02786449] **4642**

DECISIONS OF THE FEDERAL LABOR RELATIONS AUTHORITY (US/0278-7695) [07582079] **3146**

DECISIONS OF THE FEDERAL MARITIME COMMISSION (US) [00929110] **3180**

DECISIONS OF THE HAWAII LABOR RELATIONS BOARD (US) **1662**

DECISIONS OF THE HAWAII PUBLIC EMPLOYMENT RELATIONS BOARD (US) [06175389] **1662**

DECISIONS OF THE MARITIME SUBSIDY BOARD, MARITIME ADMINISTRATION, DEPARTMENT OF COMMERCE (US) [09898875] **3180**

DECISIONS OF THE OCCUPATIONAL SAFETY AND HEALTH REVIEW BOARD (US) [04848733] 2861, **2959**

DECISIONS OF THE OFFICE OF ADMINISTRATIVE LAW JUDGES AND OFFICE OF ADMINISTRATIVE APPEALS (US/1057-5812) [16519737] **3092**

DECISIONS OF THE PUBLIC UTILITIES COMMISSION OF THE STATE OF CALIFORNIA (US) [08224744] **4760**

DECISIONS OF THE UNITED STATES COURTS INVOLVING COPYRIGHT (US/0070-3176) [00975912] **1303**

DECISIONS OF THE UNITED STATES DEPARTMENT OF THE INTERIOR (US/0193-5070) [01768358] **4642**

DECISIONS OF THE UNITED STATES MERIT SYSTEMS PROTECTION BOARD (US/0731-4450) [07301848] **4702**

DECISIONS ON GEOGRAPHIC NAMES IN THE UNITED STATES (US/0363-6828) [01768178] **2559**

DECISIONS - WISCONSIN TAX APPEALS COMMISSION (US) [05437890] **4719**

DECISIONS - WORKERS COMPENSATION BOARD (VICTORIA) (AT) [05094962] **3146**

DECISOES DE TRIBUNAIS FISCAIS : IMPOSTO DE RENDA (BL) [03097697] **4720**

DECKS AWASH (CN/0317-7076) [09389556] **2487**

DECLARATION (INDEPENDENCE, VA.), THE (US/1064-4172) [26282319] **5758**

DECLASSIFIED DOCUMENTS CATALOG, THE (US/1046-4239) [13316543] **414**

●DECLENCHEUR (MALARTIC) (CN/1188-3359) [25796548] **1603**

DECODEUR, LE (CN/0383-1515) [03199570] **1819**

DECOLLETAGE (FR) **1083**

DECOR (ST. LOUIS) (US/0011-7358) [04055298] **349**

DECORAH JOURNAL (US) [15309169] **5669**

DECORAH PUBLIC OPINION (DECORAH, IOWA : 1954) (US) [15175361] **5669**

DECORATING CONTRACTOR ANNUAL DIRECTORY (UK) **2899**

DECORATING DIGEST *See* DECORATING DIGEST CRAFT AND HOME PROJECTS **372**

DECORATING DIGEST CRAFT AND HOME PROJECTS (US/1064-3095) [26248682] **372**

DECORATING RETAILER (US/0011-7404) [05120019] **2899**

DECORATING WITH ART & ANTIQUES CEASED. (US) [22607144] **2899**

DECORATION CHEZ-SOI (CN/0705-1093) [03960169] **2899**

DECORATION JET SET AMBIANCE (CN/0828-4946) [12045238] **2899**

DECORATIVE ARTIST'S WORKBOOK (US/0893-1097) [15355764] **372**

DECORATIVE ARTS DIGEST (US/0888-076X) [13460347] **372**

●DECORATIVE ARTS PAINTING (US/1067-0068) [27118566] **372**

DECORATIVE ARTS SOCIETY 1890-1940 See NEWSLETTER / DECORATIVE ARTS SOCIETY 1890-1940 **374**

DECORATIVE ARTS SOCIETY NEWSLETTER, THE (US/0884-4011) [04785982] **372**

DECORATIVE RUG, THE (US/1045-8816) [20279162] **2904**

DECORATOR (GLENS FALLS, N.Y.), THE (US/0277-1160) [04347995] **372**

DECORMAG (CN/0315-047X) [01994780] **2899**

DECOUVERTES ARCHEOLOGIQUES EN TOURNUGEOIS (FR/0290-1188) [02901188] **266**

DECOY MAGAZINE (US/1055-0364) [23063381] 4871, **2773**

DECRETO DEL PRESUPUESTO GENERAL DE LA NACION (CK) [26227897] **4720**

DECRETOS-LEYES Y LEYES DE LA REPUBLICA DE NICARAGUA (NQ) [18461160] **2959**

DECUBITUS (CHICAGO, ILL.) (US/0898-1655) [17693273] **3571**

DED BRIEF (GW) [02559040] **2908**

DEDALE (BE) [02809058] **3380**

DEDALO (IT) **2614**

DEE JAY AND RADIO MONTHLY (UK) [01791361] 4113, **1131**

DEEP FOCUS : A FILM QUARTERLY (II) [20720373] **4067**

DEEP-SEA RESEARCH. PART A. OCEANOGRAPHIC RESEARCH PAPERS (UK/0198-0149) [04764804] 1448, **1362**

DEEP-SEA RESEARCH. PART B. OCEANOGRAPHIC LITERATURE REVIEW (UK/0198-0254) [04764857] 1448, **1362**

●DEEP-SEA RESEARCH. PART I, OCEANOGRAPHIC RESEARCH PAPERS (UK/0967-0637) [27162204] **1448**

●DEEP-SEA RESEARCH. PART II, TOPICAL STUDIES IN OCEANOGRAPHY (UK/0967-0645) [27162205] **1448**

DEEP-SEA RESEARCH. SUPPLEMENTS (UK) [24338412] **1373**

DEEP SKY CEASED. (US/0735-3073) [08904729] **395**

DEEP SOUTH GENEALOGICAL QUARTERLY (US/0418-4904) [01689234] 432, **2445**

DEER (UK/0141-4259) [04538455] **226**

DEER AND DEER HUNTING (US/0164-7318) [04377973] **4871**

DEER CREEK PILOT (ROLLING FORK, MISS. : 1886) (US) [15152071] **5700**

DEER FARMER, THE (NZ/0110-7992) [06430357] **210**

DEER FARMING INVERNESS (UK/0957-0276) [I09570276] **5581**

DEER PARK BROADCASTER (US) [17445891] **5749**

DEER SPORTSMAN (US/0362-1952) [02303164] **4871**

DEERFARMING ANNUAL See DEER FARMER, THE **210**

DEERFIELD LIFE (US/0192-0073) [05079398] **5659**

DEFAMATION & DISPARAGEMENT (US/1047-8515) [20794256] **2959**

DEFAULTED BONDS NEWSLETTER (US/1057-7521) [21450311] **896**

DEFAZET. DEUTSCHE FARBEN-ZEITSCHRIFT (GW/0012-009X) [03718181] **4223**

DEFECT ACTION SHEETS (UK) [13154556] **612**

DEFEKTOLOGIJA (RU/0130-3074) [02462801] 4386, **1877**

DEFEKTOSKOPIIA (RU/0130-3082) [04539205] **1970**

DEFENCE CONSTRUCTION (1951) LIMITED See ANNUAL REPORT - DEFENCE CONSTRUCTION (1951) LIMITED **4035**

DEFENCE ECONOMICS (SZ/1043-0717) [19292504] 1334, **4040**

DEFENCE (ETON) (UK/0142-6184) [04624148] **4040**

DEFENCE FOR CHILDREN INTERNATIONAL. INFORMATION AND DOCUMENTATION SERVICE See INTERNATIONAL CHILDREN S RIGHTS MONITOR **4477**

DEFENCE HELICOPTER (UK/0963-116X) [24202331] 4040, **17**

DEFENCE HELICOPTER WORLD (UK/0263-5062) [09930133] 4040, **17**

DEFENCE INDUSTRY AND AEROSPACE REPORT (AT/1033-2898) [I10332898] 17, **4040**

DEFENCE INDUSTRY DIGEST (UK/0260-408X) **4040**

DEFENCE JOURNAL (PK) [02245647] **4040**

DEFENCE (OTTAWA. 1971) (CN/0383-4638) [02242740] **4040**

DEFENCE REVIEW (NZ) [06932571] **4040**

DEFENCE SYSTEMS INTERNATIONAL : THE INTERNATIONAL REVIEW OF LAND SYSTEMS (UK) [18426113] **4040**

DEFENCE SYSTEMS MODERNISATION (UK/0953-4970) [I09534970] **4040**

DEFENDER (COLUMBUS), THE (US/0270-3432) [06380039] **3106**

DEFENDER (DES MOINES, IOWA), THE (US/0744-186X) [08117103] **4507**

DEFENDER (NAIROBI) (KE/0379-5071) [03826103] **4773**

DEFENDER NEWSLETTER (US/0011-751X) [01566044] **2959**

DEFENDER NORTH MELBOURNE (AT/0811-6407) [I08116407] **3179**

DEFENDERS (US/0162-6337) [03103168] **2191**

DEFENSA DEL MARXISMO, EN (AG) [25363693] **4541**

DEFENSA MADRID (SP/0211-3732) [I02113732] **17**

DEFENSE (FR) **4040**

DEFENSE ACQUISITION CIRCULAR (US) [04507519] **4040**

●DEFENSE ACQUISITION REPORT (US/1072-2386) [28893443] **4040**

DEFENSE ACTIVE CEASED. (FR) **4040**

DEFENSE/AEROSPACE COMPANY CONTRACT QUARTERLY (US/0733-8082) [08645091] **17**

DEFENSE ANALYSIS (UK/0743-0175) [10490881] **4040**

DEFENSE & AEROSPACE AGENCIES BRIEFING (US) 4041, **17**

DEFENSE & AEROSPACE COMPANIES (US) **4041**

DEFENSE & AEROSPACE COMPANIES BRIEFING (US) 4041, **17**

DEFENSE & AEROSPACE ELECTRONICS (US/1056-747X) [23835683] 17, 4041, **2040**

DEFENSE & ARMEMENT HERACLES CEASED. (FR) [16260362] **4041**

DEFENSE & ECONOMY WORLD REPORT See INTERNATIONAL OBSERVER (WASHINGTON, D.C.) **2620**

DEFENSE & ECONOMY : WORLD REPORT AND SURVEY (US/0364-9008) [10976726] 1479, **4519**

DEFENSE & FOREIGN AFFAIRS (US/0277-4933) [07095461] **4041**

DEFENSE & FOREIGN AFFAIRS HANDBOOK (US/0160-5836) [02588314] **4041**

DEFENSE & FOREIGN AFFAIRS WEEKLY CEASED. (US/0884-4054) [08852640] 4519, **4041**

DEFENSE & FOREIGN AFFAIRS' WEEKLY REPORT ON STRATEGIC AFRICAN AFFAIRS (US/0193-9181) [05267169] **4519**

DEFENSE & INDUSTRY WORLD REPORT (US/0893-8199) [15667279] **4041**

DEFENSE & TECHNOLOGIE INTERNATIONAL PARIS (FR/1155-3480) [I11553480] **4041**

DEFENSE (ARLINGTON, VA.) (US/0737-1217) [05901778] **4041**

DEFENSE (BOCA RATON) (US/0273-2491) [06099265] **4041**

DEFENSE BUSINESS (US/0364-9008) [02701308] **4041**

DEFENSE BUSINESS BRIEFING (US) 665, **4041**

DEFENSE CLEANUP (US/1052-0635) [22173642] 4041, **2227**

DEFENSE COMMUNICATION STUDY, THE (US/0741-3602) [10151431] **4041**

DEFENSE CONTRACT AUDIT MANUAL (US) [03454742] **4041**

●DEFENSE CONTRACT AWARDS (US/1062-0613) [25517212] **4041**

DEFENSE CONTRACTING AGENCY AUDIT MANUAL (US) **4642**

DEFENSE CONTRACTING AGENCY AUDIT MANUAL / DISKETTE (US) **4041**

●DEFENSE CONVERSION (US/1065-8653) [26782617] **4041**

DEFENSE COUNSEL JOURNAL (US/0895-0016) [15181996] **3089**

DEFENSE DAILY (US/0889-0404) [08970659] **4041**

DEFENSE ELECTRONICS (US/0278-3479) [07618583] 4041, **2040**

DEFENSE INTEGRATED DATA SYSTEMS DIDS PROCEDURES MANUAL. VOL. 4, ITEM IDENTIFICATION (US) [10262200] **4041**

●DEFENSE INTELLIGENCE JOURNAL (US/1061-6845) [25404473] **4041**

●DEFENSE / INTERNATIONAL DEFENSE REVIEW (UK) [25612959] **4041**

DEFENSE ISSUES (US) [13446978] **4041**

DEFENSE LATIN AMERICA (UK/0261-233X) [07391314] **4041**

DEFENSE LAW JOURNAL (US/0011-7587) [01566052] **2959**

DEFENSE MAGAZINE (BE) [03200625] **4041**

DEFENSE MANUAL (US/0191-877X) [04939257] 3163, **3089**

DEFENSE MAPPING AGENCY. AEROSPACE CENTER. TECHNICAL TRANSLATION BRANCH See DMAAC TECHNICAL TRANSLATIONS LIST **4043**

DEFENSE MAPPING AGENCY. HYDROGRAPHIC CENTER See SAILING DIRECTIONS (ENROUTE) FOR NOVA SCOTIA, AND THE ST. LAWRENCE **5392**

DEFENSE MAPPING AGENCY HYDROGRAPHIC CENTER See SAILING DIRECTIONS (ENROUTE) FOR NEWFOUNDLAND, LABRADOR AND HUDSON BAY **5455**

DEFENSE MARKETING INTERNATIONAL (US/1044-3975) [19769417] **4041**

DEFENSE MEDIA REVIEW (US/0893-0619) [15337625] **4041**

DEFENSE MERGERS & ACQUISITIONS (US/1064-3583) [26267568] **665**

DEFENSE MONITOR, THE (US/0195-6450) [02250340] **4041**

DEFENSE NATIONALE (FR/0336-1489) [01786060] **4041**

DEFENSE NEWS (SPRINGFIELD, VA.) (US/0884-139X) [12308008] **4041**

DEFENSE ORGANIZATION SERVICE (US/1064-7147) [24771260] **4042**

DEFENSE RDT & E/O & M BUDGETS (US) [13081727] **4042**

DEFENSE SCIENCE JOURNAL (II/0011-748X) [01699394] **4042**

DEFENSE STANDARDIZATION AND SPECIFICATION PROGRAM, POLICIES, PROCEDURES, AND INSTRUCTIONS (US) [04872444] **4042**

DEFENSE SURVEY & DIRECTORY (US/0099-166X) [01689496] **4042**

DEFENSE SYSTEMS MANAGEMENT COLLEGE See CATALOG **4039**

DEFENSE TECHNOLOGY BUSINESS (US/1048-4612) [20954425] **4042**

DEFENSE TRANSPORTATION JOURNAL (US/0011-7625) [03662854] 5381, **4042**

DEFENSE WEEK (US/0273-3188) [07049022] **4042**

DEFENSOR CHIEFTAIN (US/0011-7633) [04049023] **5712**

DEFENSOR LEGIS; ORGAN FOR FINLANDS ADVOKAT-FORBUND (FI) [01566056] **2959**

DEFESA NACIONAL, A (BL) [04358862] **4042**

DEFI (CN/0831-4640) [14639406] **3205**

DEFI (CN/0709-2148) [08003180] **4386**

DEFI-A.C.L (CN/0835-0337) [16656328] 3380, **318**

DEFI (OTTAWA) (CN/0826-273X) [11085186] **5783**

DEFI-SANTE (CN/0848-9068) [21486672] 4189, **2596**

DEFI-SCIENCE (CN/0714-4032) [09050454] **1091**

DEFINED CONTRIBUTION NEWS (US) **896**

DEFINED CONTRIBUTION PLAN INVESTING (US) **896**

●DEFINED PROVIDENCE (US/1066-2197) [26904693] **3462**

DEFINIZIONI CRITICHE (IT/0415-1747) [04561904] **349**

DEFOREST TIMES-TRIBUNE (US/8755-8971) [11427143] **5767**

DEFORMACION METALICA (SP/0210-685X) [I0210685X] **4000**

DEGRE Alphabetical Title Index

DEGRE SECOND *CEASED*. (US/0148-561X) [03321356] **3341**

DEGREE COURSE GUIDES (UK) [03225491] 1912, **1819**

DEGREE COURSE OFFERS (UK/0306-5812) [01826603] **1819**

DEGREES AND OTHER AWARDS CONFERRED IN VIRGINIA / STATE COUNCIL OF HIGHER EDUCATION FOR VIRGINIA (US) [10616239] **1819**

DEGREES AND OTHER FORMAL AWARDS CONFERRED, KENTUCKY COLLEGES AND UNIVERSITIES / KENTUCKY CENTER FOR EDUCATION STATISTICS (US) [06177767] **1819**

DEGRES (BE/0376-8163) [01793600] **3276**

DEHAEN'S NEW PRODUCT SURVEY. MONTHLY SUPPLEMENT (US) [13341495] **4299**

DEI DELITTI E DELLE PENE (IT) [10840908] **3163**

DEIATELNOST KPSS PO RAZVITIIU SOTSIALISTICHESKOI KULTURY (RU) [05829227] **1734**

DEISTVIE PROIZVODSTVENNYKH FAKTOROV NA ORGANIZM I MERY ZASHCHITY (RU) [02987073] **2861**

DEJINY A SOUCASNOST (XR/0418-5129) [04559449] **2614**

DEJINY VED A TECHNIKY (XR/0300-4414) [01423026] **5099**

DEKADNO AGROMETEOROLOSKO POROCILO / HIDROMETEOROLOSKI ZAVOD SR SLOVENIJE, AGROMETEOROLOSKI ODDELEK (YU) [24434556] **78**

DEKALB COUNTY HERITAGE (US/8755-8459) [04621304] **2614**

DEKORATIVNOE ISKUSSTVO / UCHREDITELI SKH SSSR (RU/0130-3031) [25420151] **372**

DEL-CHEM BULLETIN, THE (US/0095-8387) [01431426] **974**

DEL-MAR-VA HEARTLAND (US) [04620222] 4871, **78**

DEL RIO NEWS-HERALD (US) [13658036] **5749**

DELAND SUN NEWS (US) [01699451] 5648, **5649**

DELANEY REPORT ON R.R.S.P.'S, THE *CEASED*. (CN/0821-7491) [09809088] **1662**

DELANEY REPORT, THE (US/1070-7409) [28460496] **865**

DELANEY'S SONG BOOK (US) [18724692] **4113**

DELANO RECORD (US/1074-410X) [12904804] **5634**

DELAP'S F & SF REVIEW (US/0161-7931) [01941700] **3380**

DELAVAN ENTERPRISE (1992), THE (US/1064-4539) [26287593] **5767**

DELAVAN ENTERPRISE AND THE DELAVAN REPUBLICAN *See* DELAVAN ENTERPRISE (1992), THE **5767**

DELAVAN ENTERPRISE AND THE DELAVAN REPUBLICAN, THE (US/0899-7616) [15112060] **5767**

DELAVAN TIMES, THE (US) [16822190] **5659**

DELAVCI V ZDRUZENEM DELU IN SAMOSTOJNEM OSEBNEM DELU, PRIPRAVNIKI TER FLUKTUACIJA DELAVCEV (XV) [06872675] **1662**

DELAVCI V ZDRUZENEM DELU / ZAVOD SR SLOVENIJE ZA STATISTIKO (XV) [11310784] **5326**

DELAWARE ACADEMY OF SCIENCE *See* TRANSACTIONS OF THE DELAWARE ACADEMY OF SCIENCE **5166**

DELAWARE AGRICULTURAL STATISTICS / PREPARED BY DELAWARE CROP REPORTING SERVICE (US) [13102420] 78, **153**

DELAWARE BUSINESS DIRECTORY (US/1048-7085) [21011982] **665**

DELAWARE BUSINESS REVIEW (US/1061-4605) [24393440] **665**

DELAWARE CASE NAMES CITATOR (US) **2959**

DELAWARE COAST PRESS (US/0740-2023) [09891874] **5647**

DELAWARE CONSERVATIONIST (GW/0045-9852) [01683433] **2191**

DELAWARE CORPORATE LITIGATION REPORTER (US/1042-5756) [15151198] **3099**

DELAWARE CORPORATION LAW UPDATE (EXECUTIVE EDITION) (US/0884-1683) [12322898] **3099**

● DELAWARE COUNTY GENEALOGIST (US/1062-6468) [25505400] **2445**

DELAWARE COUNTY NEWS *See* GROVE SUN, THE **5732**

DELAWARE COUNTY TIMES (US/0745-0206) [08433977] **5715**

DELAWARE. DEFERRED COMPENSATION COUNCIL *See* STATE OF DELAWARE DEFERRED COMPENSATION COUNCIL'S ANNUAL REPORT FOR THE FISCAL YEAR ENDED JUNE 30 ... **4688**

DELAWARE. DEPT. OF PUBLIC INSTRUCTION *See* EDUCATIONAL PERSONNEL IN DELAWARE PUBLIC SCHOOLS **1863**

DELAWARE. DEPT. OF PUBLIC INSTRUCTION *See* DROPOUT REPORT : DELAWARE PUBLIC SCHOOLS **1737**

DELAWARE. DEPT. OF PUBLIC INSTRUCTION. DIVISION OF PLANNING, RESEARCH, AND EVALUATION *See* SUMMARY OF SCHOOL REFERENDA IN DELAWARE **1873**

DELAWARE DIRECTORY OF COMMERCE AND INDUSTRY (US/0272-8117) [06928422] **1603**

DELAWARE DIVISION OF LIBRARIES NEWSLETTER, THE (USUS/1058-6644) [24351051] **3205**

DELAWARE. DIVISION OF SOCIAL SERVICES *See* ANNUAL REPORT OF THE DIVISION OF SOCIAL SERVICES OF THE DEPARTMENT OF HEALTH AND SOCIAL SERVICES **5272**

DELAWARE GAZETTE (DELAWARE, OHIO 1932), THE (US/1064-2013) [18143442] **5728**

DELAWARE GENEALOGICAL SOCIETY JOURNAL (US/0731-3896) [07644570] **2445**

DELAWARE GENEALOGIST, THE (US/1065-4887) [18003949] **2445**

DELAWARE GEOLOGICAL SURVEY *See* GEOLOGIC MAP SERIES **1377**

DELAWARE. GOVERNOR *See* BUDGET MESSAGE **4714**

● DELAWARE HEALTH CARE IN PERSPECTIVE (US/1065-4100) [26604870] **4773**

DELAWARE HISTORY (GW/0011-7765) [01566099] **2730**

DELAWARE IN PERSPECTIVE (US/1065-5379) [26628415] **5326**

DELAWARE JOURNAL OF CORPORATE LAW, THE (US/0364-9490) [02696675] **3099**

DELAWARE LAW MONTHLY, THE (US/0193-4007) [05174418] **2959**

DELAWARE LAWYER (US/0735-6595) [08538514] **2959**

DELAWARE LEGISLATIVE ROSTER (US) 4642, **4697**

DELAWARE MEDICAL JOURNAL (US/0011-7781) [01776018] **3571**

DELAWARE. OFFICE OF THE GOVERNOR *See* FINANCIAL SUMMARY - DELAWARE. OFFICE OF THE GOVERNOR **4726**

DELAWARE PHARMACIST (US/0418-5420) [01701789] **4299**

DELAWARE RACING COMMISSION *See* ANNUAL REPORT OF THE DELAWARE RACING COMMISSION TO THE GOVERNOR OF THE STATE OF DELAWARE **2797**

DELAWARE RIVER BASIN COMMISSION *See* ANNUAL REPORT / DELAWARE RIVER BASIN COMMISSION **5529**

DELAWARE SEA GRANT REPORTER (GW) [09505441] **554**

DELAWARE. STATE BOARD OF EDUCATION *See* REPORT OF EDUCATION STATISTICS **1796**

DELAWARE STATE NEWS AND MARYLAND STATE NEWS (US/0745-8096) [09477022] **5647**

DELAWARE THOROUGHBRED RACING COMMISSION *See* ANNUAL REPORT OF THE DELAWARE THOROUGHBRED RACING COMMISSION TO THE GOVERNOR OF THE STATE OF DELAWARE **2797**

DELAWARE TODAY (WILMINGTON, DEL. : 1983) (US) [14584229] **2532**

DELAWARE TURNPIKE ADMINISTRATION *See* DELAWARE TURNPIKE ANNUAL REPORT **5439**

DELAWARE TURNPIKE ANNUAL REPORT (US) [11428844] **5439**

DELAWARE VALLEY GUIDE TO TRANSPORTATION (US/0277-1136) [04220426] **5381**

DELAWARE VALLEY NEWS (US) [12190576] **5710**

DELAWARE VALLEY RAIL PASSENGER, THE (US) **5431**

DELAWARE VALLEY TRANSPORTATION FACTS & FACILITIES *See* DELAWARE VALLEY GUIDE TO TRANSPORTATION **5381**

DELAY LETTER, THE (US/1064-6531) [26365174] **923**

DELECTUS SEMINUM ET SPORARUM QUAE HORTUS BOTANICUS MONTIS-REGII PRO MUTUA COMMUTATIONE OFFERT (CN/0318-059X) [02443054] **508**

DELECTUS SEMINUM FRUCTUM, SPORARUM ... QUEM PRO MUTUA COMMUTATIONE HORTUS BOTANICUS UNIVERSITATIS OSLOENSIS OFFERT *See* INDEX SEMINUM **2420**

DELEGACIJE OSNOVNIH SAMOUPRAVNIH ORGANIZACIJA I ZAJEDNICA I SKUPSTINE DRUSTVENO-POLITICKIH ZAJEDNICA (YU) [06793009] **4697**

DELEGATION ARCHEOLOGIQUE FRANCAISE EN IRAN *See* CAHIERS DE LA DAFI **265**

DELEK, HEVRAT HA-DELEK HA-YISREELIT *See* ANNUAL REPORT - DELEK, THE ISRAEL FUEL CORPORATION **4250**

DELFINO ROMA, IL (IT/1121-0311) [I11210311] **2487**

DELFT INTEGRAAL (NE) [I0920508X] **5099**

DELFT PROGRESS REPORT *CEASED*. (NE/0304-985X) [03183051] **2022**

DELHI, INSTITUTE OF APPLIED MANPOWER RESEARCH *See* I.A.M.R. REPORT **1677**

DELHI LAW REVIEW (II) [01566109] **2959**

DELHI. NATIONAL MUSEUM OF INDIA *See* BULLETIN - NATIONAL MUSEUM, NEW DELHI **4086**

DELHI NEWS RECORD (CN) **5783**

DELHI PRESS (US/1058-0298) [17937726] **5728**

DELHI. PUBLIC LIBRARY *See* REPORT - DELHI. PUBLIC LIBRARY **3245**

DELHI (UNION TER.). BUREAU OF ECONOMICS AND STATISTICS *See* SANKHYIKIYA PUSTIKA **1538**

DELI NEWS (US/0011-7862) [04968661] **2333**

DELIBERATIONS DE L'ASSOCIATION DENTAIRE CANADIENNE (CN/0380-9307) [03222623] **1320**

DELIBERATIONS DU CONGRES - ASSOCIATION CANADIENNE DU PERSONNEL ADMINISTRATIF UNIVERSITAIRE (CN/0383-6231) [03284634] 939, **1819**

DELIBROS : REVISTA PROFESIONAL DEL LIBRO (SP) [20253287] **4813**

DELICHON URBICA (UK/0142-7938) [13310169] **2445**

DELICIOUS! (US) [21179800] **4189**

DELICIOUS MAGAZINE (US) 2596, **2333**

DELIKT EN DELINKWENT (NE) [02239765] **3106**

DELINCUENCIA VALENCIA (SP/0214-6908) [I02146908] **5244**

DELINEAVIT ET SCULPSIT (NE/0923-9790) [21585546] **378**

● DELITO Y SOCIEDAD (AG) [27995729] **3163**

DELIUS SOCIETY *See* DELIUS SOCIETY JOURNAL, THE **4113**

DELIUS SOCIETY JOURNAL, THE (UK/0306-0373) [02550356] **4113**

DELL CHAMPION CROSSWORD PUZZLES (US/0747-590X) [10764077] **4859**

DELL CHAMPION VARIETY PUZZLES (US/0747-5888) [10764346] **4859**

DELL CROSSWORD ANNUAL *See* DELL CROSSWORD SPECIAL **4859**

DELL CROSSWORD PUZZLES (US/0274-6301) [06464032] **4859**

DELL CROSSWORD SPECIAL (US/0747-5896) [10763931] **4859**

DELL CROSSWORDS AND VARIETY PUZZLES (US/0747-5934) [10764248] **4859**

DELL EASY FAST 'N' FUN CROSSWORDS (US/1059-3985) [24582417] **4860**

DELL LOGIC PUZZLES (US/1058-3343) [24269453] **4860**

DELL MATH PUZZLES AND LOGIC PROBLEMS (US/1070-4078) [28359215] **4860**

DELL OFFICIAL CROSSWORD PUZZLES (US/0274-6239) [06463804] **4860**

DELL OFFICIAL WORD SEARCH PUZZLES (US/0747-5926) [10764161] **4860**

DELL PENCIL PUZZLES & WORD GAMES (US/0274-6220) [06463783] **4860**

DELL POCKET CROSSWORD PUZZLES (US/0274-6425) [06492175] **4860**

DELLBOOK OF SUPERWINNERS, THE (US/0732-457X) [08336298] **4892**

DELMARVA BROILER CHICKS (US) [03816715] **210**

DELMARVA FARMER, THE (US/0194-2964) [05369901] **78**

DELMARVA NEWS *See* WAVE **5647**

DELMARVA ORNITHOLOGICAL SOCIETY See DELMARVA ORNITHOLOGIST **5617**

DELMARVA ORNITHOLOGIST (US) [04741689] **5617**

DELO (BEOGRAD) *CEASED.* (YU/0011-7935) [01688926] **3380**

DELOS (US/0011-7951) [06106684] **3462**

DELOVAIA ZHIZN (RU) [25001878] **1555**

●DELOVIE LYUDI (FR) [25491186] **787**

DELOVOI MIR (RU) [24843419] **5809**

DELPHI, THE (US) [13149118] 3163, **5281**

DELPHIN (GW) [04634956] 2845, **318**

DELPHOS REPUBLICAN, THE (US) [12282338] **5675**

DELTA (PL) [01794501] 4401, **3503**

DELTA ATLAS (US) [11914744] **5728**

DELTA AUSTRALIA (AT) **3503**

DELTA COUNCIL NEWS, THE (US/1051-7936) [07058622] **78**

DELTA COUNTY INDEPENDENT (US/0891-9704) [11154056] **5642**

DELTA DEMOCRAT-TIMES, THE (US) [04582164] **5700**

DELTA EPSILON SIGMA JOURNAL (US/0745-0958) [08808394] **5230**

DELTA FARM PRESS (US/0011-8036) [04049038] **78**

DELTA KAPPA GAMMA BULLETIN, THE (US/0011-8044) [01566125] **1734**

DELTA KAPPA GAMMA SOCIETY See DELTA KAPPA GAMMA BULLETIN, THE **1734**

DELTA OPTIMIST, THE (CN/0710-1422) [08436396] **5783**

DELTA (PALMERSTON NORTH) (NZ/0419-9855) [04430107] **1735**

DELTA PI EPSILON See DELTA PI EPSILON RAPID READER **1735**

DELTA PI EPSILON See NEEDED RESEARCH IN BUSINESS EDUCATION **697**

DELTA PI EPSILON See DELTA PI EPSILON JOURNAL **665**

DELTA PI EPSILON JOURNAL (US/0011-8052) [01566126] 5230, **665**

DELTA PI EPSILON RAPID READER (US/0160-3949) [03674843] **1735**

DELTA PI EPSILON SERVICE BULLETIN (US/0160-3957) [03674806] **1735**

DELTA PRIMATE REPORT (US/0418-5978) [01702112] **5508**

DELTA REPORT, THE (CN/0710-1856) [08205701] **1153**

DELTA SIGMA DELTA See DESMOS OF DELTA SIGMA DELTA **1819**

DELTA WEEKLY (US/0746-0538) [09715833] **5700**

DELTA ZETA LAMP See LAMP OF DELTA ZETA, THE **1834**

DELTA ZETA SORORITY See ALUMNAE DIRECTORY / DELTA ZETA SORORITY **1096**

DELTA ZETA SORORITY See LAMP OF DELTA ZETA, THE **1834**

DELTAMBIENTE *SUSPENDED.* (IT) **2213**

DELTIO EMPORIKOU KAI VIOMECHANIKOU EPIMELETERIOU THESSALONIKES (GR) [19451031] **1555**

DELTIO PHOROLOGIKES NOMOTHESIAS (GR) [12124816] **4720**

DELTION (GR) [09065510] **4042**

DELTION AUTOKINETIKES NOMOTHESIAS KAI NOMOLOGIAS (GR) [02241398] **2959**

DELTION BIBLIKON MELETON (GR/1012-2311) [03340655] **5016**

DELTION DIOIKESEOS EPICHEIRESEON (GR) [01792020] **665**

DELTION ELLENIKES MIKROBIOLOGIKES ETAIREIAS (GR/0438-9573) [I04389573] **562**

DELTION ELLENIKIS MATHEMATIKIS ETAIREIAS (GR) **3503**

DELTION HRISTIANIKES ARHAIOLOGIKES ETAIREIAS (GR/1105-5758) [I11055758] **266**

DELTION STATISTIKE DEMASION OIKONOMIKON (GR/0256-3592) [05154408] 4720, **4697**

DELTION TES HELLENIKES KTENIATRIKES HETAIREIAS. PERIODOS B (GR/0437-2085) [00974825] **5508**

DELTION TES HELLENIKES MATHEMATIKES HETAIREIAS (GR/0373-1391) [06155033] **3503**

DELTION TES HISTORIKES KAI ETHNOLOGIKES HETAIREIAS TES HELLADOS (GR/1012-229X) [01589596] **2319**

DEMAIN L'AFRIQUE (FR/0152-2981) [05119468] **2639**

DEMAND SIDE MONTHLY (US) 2040, **4760**

DEMAND-SIDE REPORT (US) **1479**

DEMAND-SIDE TECHNOLOGY REPORT (US) **5099**

DEMARCHE, LA (CN/0707-5510) [04875714] **384**

DEMENTIA (BASEL, SWITZERLAND) (SZ/1013-7424) [22154943] **3831**

●DEMENTIA REVIEWS (US/1066-5056) [26970864] 4584, **3924**

DEMEURE HISTORIQUE (FR) **296**

DEMEURE HISTORIQUE PARIS, LA (FR/0998-5956) [I09985956] **296**

DEMEURES & CHATEAUX (FR/0291-1191) [I02911191] 4836, **296**

DEMING HEADLIGHT (1956) (US/0738-8349) [26252857] **5712**

DEMOCRACIA 76 I.E. SETENTA E SEIS (PO) [03647456] **4642**

DEMOCRACY IN ACTION (SA/1017-0243) [I10170243] **4471**

DEMOCRACY INTERNATIONAL *CEASED.* (UK/1011-1778) [19224272] **4471**

DEMOCRAT AND CHRONICLE (US) [05757784] **5715**

DEMOCRAT (EMMETSBURG, IOWA) (US/1042-119X) [16513737] **5669**

DEMOCRAT HERALD (BAKER, OR.) (US/8756-6419) [11627579] **5733**

DEMOCRAT-LEADER (FAYETTE, MO.) (US/0746-9934) [10454498] **5703**

DEMOCRAT-NEWS (FREDERICKTOWN, MO.) (US) [13433563] **5703**

DEMOCRAT-REPORTER, THE (US) [11800888] **5626**

DEMOCRAT-TRIBUNE (MINERAL POINT, WIS.) (US) [14991319] **5767**

DEMOCRAT-UNION, THE (US) [19255258] **5745**

DEMOCRAT (VANCOUVER) (CN/0070-3346) [01988032] **4471**

DEMOCRATE, LE (SG) [02557453] **4471**

DEMOCRATE (PARTI NOUVEAU DEMOCRATIQUE DU QUEBEC) (CN/0228-488X) [08439985] **4471**

DEMOCRATIC FOCUS, THE (US/0094-7903) [01794871] **4471**

DEMOCRATIC JOURNALIST, THE (XR/0011-8214) [01691229] **2918**

DEMOCRATIC LEFT (US/0164-3207) [04614931] **4471**

DEMOCRATIC PARTY. YEAR BOOK (US/0147-6769) [03213448] **4471**

DEMOCRATIC REVIEW (WASHINGTON) (US/0363-1834) [01145870] **4471**

DEMOCRATIC WOMEN (CN/0828-654X) [12097944] **5554**

DEMOCRATIC WORLD (II/0301-9047) [01784257] **1591**

DEMOCRATIZATION (UK) **4471**

DEMOCRATS (WASHINGTON, D.C.) (US/1051-1679) [21343021] **4471**

DEMOCRAZIA DIRETTA (IT) [19690469] **4471**

DEMOCRAZIA E DIRITTO (IT/0416-9565) [I04169565] **2959**

DEMOGRAFIA (HU/0011-8249) [01688464] **4551**

DEMOGRAFICHESKIE ISSLEDOVANIIA / ACADEMIIA NAUK UKRAINSKOI SSR, INSTITUT EKONOMIKI (UN) [19473748] **4551**

DEMOGRAFIE (XR/0011-8265) [01688374] **4551**

DEMOGRAFISCHE DATA VOOR SURINAME (SR) [19465698] **1591**

DEMOGRAFISCHE GEGEVENS (NE) [02421470] **5326**

DEMOGRAPHIC AND INCOME STATISTICS FOR POSTAL AREAS, CANADA *CEASED.* (CN/0840-8491) [21103877] **5326**

DEMOGRAPHIC BULLETIN (TORONTO) (CN/0702-0031) [04801305] **4551**

DEMOGRAPHIC MONOGRAPHS (US/0275-9594) [04645086] **4552**

DEMOGRAPHIC PROFILES, SOCIOECONOMIC PROFILES, AND PER CAPITA INCOMES OF THE RESIDENT POPULATIONS OF WASHINGTON STATE SCHOOL DISTRICTS (US) [04370410] 1735, **4552**

DEMOGRAPHIC REPORT, HEW (US/0148-6284) [03341158] **4552**

DEMOGRAPHIC REVIEW OF THE MALTESE ISLANDS / CENTRAL OFFICE OF STATISTICS, MALTA (MM) [12335115] **4561**

DEMOGRAPHIC STATISTICS (JM) [01789456] **4561**

DEMOGRAPHIC TRENDS (NZ/0113-3667) [20547573] **4552**

DEMOGRAPHIC YEARBOOK (US/0082-8041) [01168223] 4552, **4561**

DEMOGRAPHISCHE INFORMATIONEN / HRSG. VOM INSTITUT FUER DEMOGRAPHIE, OSTERREICHISCHE AKADEMIE DER WISSENSCHAFTEN (AU) [11046754] **4552**

DEMOGRAPHY (US/0070-3370) [01566147] **4552**

DEMOGRAPHY INDIA (II/0970-454X) [01790481] **4552**

DEMOGRAPHY, QUEENSLAND (AT/1036-2649) [I10362649] 4552, **4561**

DEMOGRAPHY, SOUTH AUSTRALIA (AT/1036-2657) [I10362657] 4552, **4561**

DEMOKRATICHESKII ZHURNALIST (RU) [03867906] **2918**

DEMOKRATIE UND RECHT (KOLN) (GW/0340-8590) [04621482] **2959**

DEMOKRATISCHE GEMEINDE (GW) [19638252] **4642**

DEMOKRATISCHE VOLKSREPUBLIK JEMEN: ENERGIEWIRTSCHAFT (GW) [06345900] **1936**

DEMOKRATISCHE VOLKSREPUBLIK JEMEN, WIRTSCHAFTLICHE ENTWICKLUNG / BUNDESSTELLE FUER AUSSENHANDELSINFORMATION (GW) [10931591] **1555**

DEMOKRATISCHE VOLKSREPUBLIK JEMEN, WIRTSCHAFTSDATEN / BUNDESTELLE FUR AUSSENHANDELSINFORMATION (GW) [09345934] **1555**

DEMOKRATISHCHES VOLKSBLATT (AU) [12594560] **5777**

DEMOKRATSIIA (BU) [25097260] **5779**

DEMOKRATYCHNA UKRAINA (UN) [25178724] **5811**

DEMOLITION AGE (US/0362-7772) [02337817] **612**

DEMONSTRATIO MATHEMATICA (PL/0420-1213) [04636764] **3503**

DEMOPOLIS TIMES, THE (US) [12743271] **5626**

DEMOSCOOP L'ECHO DE SOFREXPER See RELOCALISER : LA LETRE DE LA MOBILITE-DEMOSCOOP **946**

DEMPA DIGEST (JA/0288-6103) [10553894] **2040**

DEMPA SHIMBUN (JA) [04681460] **5805**

DEMPSEY CANADIAN LETTER, THE (US/0893-3758) [16220418] **2532**

DEN POEZII (LENINGRAD) (RU/0418-6176) [01642906] **3462**

DENDROCHRONOLOGIA / ISTITUTO ITALIANO DI DENDROCRONOLOGIA (IT) [10467518] **1373**

DENDROFLORA (NE/0374-7247) [01566153] **2413**

●DENDRON : AN INTERNATIONAL BIOMEDICAL JOURNAL FOR RESEARCH IN NEUROSCIENCE *SUSPENDED.* (UK/0961-0898) [27196713] **3831**

DENDRONATURA / ASSOCIAZIONE FORRESTALE DEL TRENTINO (IT) [08236797] **2378**

DENEUVE (SAN FRANCISCO, CALIF.) (US/1062-6247) [25378445] **2794**

DENGEN KAIHATSU NO GAIYO (JA) [02245369] **2040**

DENGI I KREDIT (RU/0130-3090) [05230477] **787**

DENHAM SPRINGS AND LIVINGSTON PARISH NEWS (US/0164-9027) [04232703] **5683**

DENHAMWOOD, INC See FASTFACTS EUROPEAN HOTEL LOCATOR **2805**

DENISON DAILY HERALD See DENISON HERALD (DENISON, TEX.) **5749**

DENISON HERALD (DENISON, TEX.) (US) [14289584] **5749**

DENISON REVIEW, THE (US) [11166125] **5669**

DENISON UNIVERSITY See DENISON UNIVERSITY ALUMNI DIRECTORY **1101**

DENISON UNIVERSITY ALUMNI DIRECTORY (US) [03815665] **1101**

DENKBEELD (NE) 4584, **3750**

DENKI GAKKAI RONBUNSHI. A, KISO ZAIRYO (JA/0385-4205) [11197139] **2040**

DENKI GAKKAI RONBUNSHI. B, ENERUGI, DENKI KIKI, DENRYOKU (JA/0385-4213) [11197154] **2040**

DENKI GAKKAI RONBUNSHI. C, EREKUTORONIKUSU, JOHO KOGAKU, SHISUTEMU (JA/0385-4221) [11197164] **2040**

DENKI GAKKAI RONBUNSHI. D, SANGYO OYO BUMONSHI (JA/0913-6339) [I09136339] **2040**

DENKI GAKKAI ZASSHI (JA) [10308996] **2040**

DENKI GIJUTSU: ELECTRICAL TECHNICS (JA) **2040**

DENKI JIGYO YORAN (JA) [01797295] **2040**

DENKI KAGAKU OYOBI KOGYO BUTSURI KAGAKU (JA/0366-9297) [09519607] **1034**

DENKI KYOKAI ZASSHI (JA/0387-0758) [15862193] **2040**

DENKI-SEIKO (JA/0011-8389) [09284135] **4001**

DENKI TSUSHIN DAIGAKU GAKUHO (JA/0493-4253) [10262937] **1109**

DENKMAELER DER TONKUNST IN BAYERN. NEUE FOLGE (GW) **4114**

DENKMALER DER MUSIK IN SALZBURG / HERAUSGEGEBEN VOM INSTITUT FUER MUSIKWISSENSCHAFT AN DER UNIVERSITAT SALZBURG (GW) [04164027] **4114**

DENKMALER DER TONKUNST IN OSTERREICH (AU) [01682419] **4114**

DENKMALER RHEINISCHER MUSIK (GW/0416-9816) [04609788] **4114**

●DENKMALPFLEGE, DIE (GW/0947-031X) [31484921] 349, **296**

DENKMALPFLEGE IN BADEN-WURTTEMBERG (GW) [01785806] **349**

DENKMALPFLEGE INFORMATIONEN. AUSGABE D (GW) [19643157] **296**

DENKSCHRIFTEN DER SCHWEIZERISCHEN ADAKEMIE DER NATURWISSENSCHAFTEN DSANW (SZ) **5099**

DENKSCHRIFTEN DER SCHWEIZERISCHEN NATURFORSCHENDEN GESELLSCHAFT (SZ/0366-970X) [07236315] **5099**

DENKSCHRIFTEN DER SCHWEIZERISCHEN NATURFORSCHENDEN GESELLSCHAFT DNSG *See* DENKSCHRIFTEN DER SCHWEIZERISCHEN ADAKEMIE DER NATURWISSENSCHAFTEN DSANW **5099**

DENKSCHRIFTEN - OESTERREICHISCHE AKADEMIE DER WISSENSCHAFTEN, MATHEMATISCH-NATURWISSENSCH AFTLICHE KLASSE (AU/0379-0207) [11288069] **3503**

DENMARK *See* GOVERNMENT FINANCES IN DENMARK **4728**

DENMARK *See* ADMINISTRATIONSDEPARTEMENTET : ARSBERETNING **4461**

DENMARK. BOLIGMINISTERIET *See* BYGGE - OG BOLIGPOLITISKE UDVIKLING (DENMARK), DEN **606**

DENMARK. DANMARKS STATISTIK *See* DETAILPRISER **5326**

DENMARK. DANMARKS STATISTIK *See* STATISTISK ARBOG **5343**

DENMARK. DIREKTORATET FOR ERHVERVSUDDANNELSERNE *See* ARSBERETNING **1910**

DENMARK. DIREKTORATET FOR KRIMINALFORSORGEN *See* FAENGSELSVASENET **3164**

DENMARK. DIREKTORATET FOR STATENS SKIBSTILSYN *See* SKIBSTILSYNETS MEDDELELSER / STATENS SKIBSTILSYN **4183**

DENMARK. DIREKTORATET FOR STATENS SKIBSTILSYN. MEDDELELSER *See* SKIBSTILSYNETS MEDDELELSER / STATENS SKIBSTILSYN **4183**

DENMARK. DIREKTORATET FOR TOLDVAESENET *See* TOLDVAESENET **4756**

DENMARK. FINANSMINISTERIET *See* ECONOMIC SURVEY OF DENMARK **1485**

DENMARK. FLLESRADET VEDRRENDE MINERALSKE RASTOFFER I GRNLAND *See* BERETNING FOR PERIODEN ... / FRA FLLESRADET VEDRRENDE MINERALSKE RASTOFFER I GRNLAND **2135**

DENMARK. FORBRUGERSTYRELSEN *See* ARSBERETNING / FORBRUGERSTYRELSEN **1293**

DENMARK. FRAKVANDSDIREKTORATET *See* EFTERRETNINGER FOR SOFARENDE **4176**

DENMARK. GENERALDIREKTRATET FOR STATSBANERNE *See* KREPLAN **5432**

DENMARK. JUSTERVSENET *See* ARSBERETNING - JUSTERVSENET **4029**

DENMARK PRESS (DENMARK, WIS. : 1953) (US) [13103608] **5767**

DENMARK QUARTERLY REVIEW (DK/0011-8427) [03700789] 4471, **1555**

DENMARK REVIEW (DK/0418-6745) [01566202] **665**

DENMARK. RIGSBIBLIOTEKAREMBEDET *See* ACCESSIONSKATALOG - DENMARK. RIGSBIBLIOTEKAREMBEDET **3187**

DENMARK. SIKKERHEDS- OG NEDRUSTNINGSPOLITISKE UDVALG *See* ARSBERETNING **4037**

DENMARK. STATENS FORSGSVIRKSOMHED I PLANTEKULTUR *See* TIDSSKRIFT FOR PLANTEAVL **189**

DENMARK. STATENS HUSDYRBRUGSFORSG *See* BERETNING FRA STATENS HUSDYRBRUGSFORSG **65**

DENMARK. STATENS ISTJENESTE *See* ISBERETNING **1415**

DENMARK. STATENS PLANTEAVLSUDVALG *See* STATENS PLANTEAVLSUDVALG BERETNING / UDARBEJDET AF INFORMATIONSTJENESTEN **188**

DENMARK. STATENS REGNSKABSDIREKTORAT *See* ANNUAL REPORT - DENMARK. STATENS REGNSKABSDIREKTORAT **4710**

DENMARK. STATSSKATTEDIREKTORATET *See* LIGNINGSVEJLEDNINGEN. SELSKABER / STATSSKATTEDIREKTORATET, LIGNINGSAFDELINGEN, SELSKABSSKATTEKONTORET **4736**

DENMARK. STATSSKATTEDIREKTORATET *See* MEDDELELSER FRA STATSSKATTEDIREKTORATET OG LIGNINGSRADET **4737**

DENMARK. TEATERRÍADET *See* TEATERRAADETS INDSTILLINGER, FORSLAG OG KONKLUSIONER **5369**

DENMARK. TEKNOLOGIRADET. SEKRETARIATET *See* STATSTILSKUD TIL PRODUKTUDVIKLING **1627**

DENMARK. UDENRIGSMINISTERIET *See* UDENRIGSMINISTERIETS TIDSSKRIFT: NYT FRA EKSPORTMARKEDERNE **856**

DENMARK'S DEVELOPMENT ASSISTANCE (DK) [01790006] **1555**

DENNI HLASATEL (US/0744-6586) [08496749] **5659**

DENNING LAW JOURNAL, THE (UK/0269-1922) [15924219] **2959**

DENNISON MANUFACTURING COMPANY *See* ANNUAL REPORT - DENNISON MANUFACTURING COMPANY **3475**

DENPUN KAGAKU (JA/0021-5406) [06182568] **2333**

DENRYOKU DOBOKU (JA/0386-2895) [10451539] **2022**

DENRYOKU JUKYU NO GAIYO (JA) [01797064] **4760**

DENSHI GIJUTSU SOGO KENKYUJO CHOSA HOKOKU (JA/0366-9084) [08190485] **2040**

DENSHI GIJUTSU SOGO KENKYUJO HOKOKURUI ICHIRAN (JA) [01797157] **2040**

DENSHI GIJUTSU SOGO KENKYUJO IHO (JA/0366-9092) [09787089] **2041**

DENSHI GIJUTSU SOGO KENKYUJO KENKYU HOKOKU (JA/0366-9106) [03688964] **2041**

DENSHI GIJUTSU SOGO KENKYUJO YORAN (JA/0301-9845) [01797151] **2041**

DENSHI IGAKU / MEDICAL ELECTRONICS (JA) [10309037] 2041, **3571**

DENSHI JOHO TSUSHIN GAKKAI RONBUNSHI. A (JA/0913-5707) [17780517] **2041**

DENSHI JOHO TSUSHIN GAKKAI RONBUNSHI. B (JA) [17780540] **2041**

DENSHI JOHO TSUSHIN GAKKAI RONBUNSHI. C (JA) [17780558] **2041**

DENSHI JOHO TSUSHIN GAKKAI RONBUNSHI. D (JA/0374-468X) [17793608] **2041**

DENSHI JOHO TSUSHIN GAKKAI SHI (JA/0373-6121) [17793635] **1153**

DENSHI KENBIKYO (1974) (JA) [02428211] **572**

DENSHI KOGYO GEPPO (JA) [11931656] **2041**

DENSHI KOGYO KANKEI KAISHA MEIBO (JA) [02477041] **1603**

DENSHI SHASHIN GAKKAISHI (JA/0387-916X) [11596959] **4368**

DENSHI TOKYO (JA/0285-1903) [08273751] **2041**

DENSHI TSUSHIN GAKKAI. DENSHI TSUSHIN GAKKAI ROMBUNSHI (JA/0413-6869) [04704267] **2041**

DENSHI TSUSHIN NO GENJO TO TEMBO (JA) [01797302] **1153**

DENSHI ZAIRYO (JA/0387-0774) [I03870774] **2041**

DENT POUR DENT (CN/0227-5538) [08071551] **1320**

DENTAL ABSTRACTS (CHICAGO) (US/0011-8486) [01566204] 1320, **1338**

DENTAL ADMISSION TESTING PROGRAM REPORT (US/0161-7540) [04000195] **1320**

DENTAL ADVISOR (US/0748-4666) [10958664] **1320**

DENTAL ADVISOR PLUS, THE (US/1054-5425) [22917937] **1320**

DENTAL ANAESTHESIA AND SEDATION *SUSPENDED.* (AT/0311-0699) [04588853] 3963, **1320**

DENTAL ANNUAL (BRISTOL, ENGLAND) (UK/0266-6073) [11165131] **1320**

DENTAL ASEPSIS REVIEW (US/0733-9836) [08622101] **1320**

DENTAL ASSISTANT JOURNAL *See* DENTAL ASSISTANT : JOURNAL OF THE AMERICAN DENTAL ASSISTANTS ASSOCIATION, THE **1320**

●DENTAL ASSISTANT : JOURNAL OF THE AMERICAN DENTAL ASSISTANTS ASSOCIATION, THE (US) [30637881] **1320**

DENTAL CADMOS (IT/0011-8524) [04685652] **1320**

DENTAL CLINICS OF NORTH AMERICA (US/0011-8532) [01566208] **1320**

DENTAL COMPUTER NEWSLETTER (US/0738-9744) [09697774] 1267, **1320**

DENTAL CORPS INTERNATIONAL (GW) **1320**

DENTAL DIMENSIONS (US/0191-2542) [04687212] **1320**

DENTAL-ECHO (GW/0011-8575) [02260229] **1320**

DENTAL ECONOMICS (PITTSBURGH. 1968) (US/0011-8583) [02246749] 665, **1320**

DENTAL EDUCATION REGISTER (CN/0315-2669) [02247987] **1320**

DENTAL EQUIP. GUIA DE EQUIPAMIENTO DENTAL (SP) **1320**

DENTAL FLASH (IT/0393-067X) [20423319] **1320**

DENTAL GRADUATE *See* DENTALPRACTICE **1322**

DENTAL GUIDE (CN) [07599052] **1320**

DENTAL GUIDE (CN/0070-3656) [02441872] **1320**

DENTAL HAIJIN (JA) **1320**

DENTAL HEALTH (LONDON, ENGLAND) (UK/0011-8605) [02251604] **1320**

DENTAL HISTORIAN (UK/0958-6687) [13341556] **1320**

DENTAL HYGIENE NEWS (ROCHESTER, N.Y.) (US/0882-9543) [12011467] **1321**

DENTAL IMAGES (US/0070-3664) [04899975] **1321**

DENTAL IMPLANTOLOGY UPDATE (US/1062-0346) [24844920] **1321**

DENTAL JOURNAL OF MALAYSIA (MY/0126-8023) [02370083] **1321**

DENTAL LAB PRODUCTS (US/0146-9738) [03064245] **1321**

DENTAL-LABOR, DAS (GW/0011-8656) [I00118656] **1321**

DENTAL-LABOR. LABORATOIRE DENTAIRE. DENTAL LABORATORY, DAS (GW) [07613243] **1321**

DENTAL LABORATORY NOTTINGHAM (UK/0957-5138) [I09575138] **1321**

DENTAL MATERIALS (DK/0109-5641) [11776187] **1321**

DENTAL MATERIALS JOURNAL (JA/0287-4547) [10108229] **1321**

DENTAL OFFICE (US/1049-4871) [20534839] **1321**

DENTAL OUTLOOK. SHIKAI TENBO (JA) **1321**

DENTAL OUTLOOK, THE *SUSPENDED.* (AT/0418-694X) [02670783] **1321**

DENTAL PRACTICE (EWELL) (UK/0011-8710) [04019703] **1321**

DENTAL PRACTICE MANAGEMENT (DON MILLS, ONT.) (CN/0827-1305) [12905670] 665, **1321**

DENTAL PRACTITIONERS' FORMULARY (UK) [20062305] **1321**

DENTAL PRODUCTS REPORT (US/0011-8737) [05152019] **1321**

DENTAL RADIOGRAPHY AND PHOTOGRAPHY *CEASED.* (US/0045-9941) [01566230] **1321**

DENTAL REFLECTIONS (US/0149-2853) [03417865] **1321**

DENTAL RESEARCH IN THE UNITED STATES AND OTHER COUNTRIES (US/0147-264X) [03952069] **1321**

DENTAL-REVUE (SZ/0255-6928) [13678076] **1321**

DENTAL SPECTRUM (OTTAWA) (CN/0227-8529) [07295241] **1321**

●DENTAL STUDY CLUB (CN/1183-9996) [26715089] **1321**

DENTAL SUMMARIES (SA) **1321**

DENTAL TEAMWORK (US/0895-318X) [16567149] **1321**

DENTAL TECHNICIAN (UK/0011-8796) [02251607] **1321**

DENTAL UPDATE (UK/0305-5000) [04562049] **1321**

DENTAL WORLD / FDI (UK/0965-9986) [25278221] **1322**

DENTALETTER, THE (CN/0822-1596) [10199144] **1322**

DENTALPRACTICE *CEASED.* (US/0199-736X) [07340680] **1322**

DENTEKSA (SA/0259-563X) [I0259563X] **1322**

DENTIST (WACO, TEX.) *CEASED.* (US/0887-5669) [12918278] **1322**

DENTISTA MODERNO, IL (IT) [16920741] **1322**

DENTISTRY (CHICAGO, ILL.) (US/0277-3635) [07483630] **1322**

DENTISTRY (HAMILTON, ONT.) (CN/1057-1418) [23854895] **1322**

DENTISTRY IN JAPAN (JA/0070-3737) [02260300] **1322**

DENTISTRY TODAY (US/8750-2186) [11135332] **1322**

DENTISTS REGISTER, THE (UK) [01698428] **1322**

DENTO MAXILLO FACIAL RADIOLOGY (UK/0250-832X) [02428238] 3940, **1322**

DENTON RECORD-CHRONICLE (US) [14198299] **5749**

DENTURO + (CN/0714-7619) [09336562] **1322**

DENUNCIA (WASHINGTON, D.C.) (US/0740-882X) [10027557] **4471**

DENVER BUSINESS *SUSPENDED.* (US/0746-2964) [09923558] **665**

DENVER BUSINESS JOURNAL, THE (US/0893-7745) [15123620] **665**

DENVER DOWNTOWN DIRECTORY, THE (US/0736-7562) [09204733] **665**

DENVER HEALTH & WELFARE PLANS SURVEY (US) [08224881] **1662**

DENVER HERALD DISPATCH (US/0898-1701) [16769796] **5642**

DENVER JOURNAL OF INTERNATIONAL LAW AND POLICY (US/0196-2035) [01566256] **3126**

DENVER MAGAZINE, THE *SUSPENDED.* (US/0161-4886) [03939510] **2532**

DENVER METROPOLITAN MEDIA DIRECTORY (US/0196-8491) [05913632] **1110**

DENVER OIL & GAS INDUSTRY SURVEY (US) [12153130] **4254**

DENVER POST (1901) (US) [08789877] **5642**

DENVER POST INDEX (1987), THE (US/0893-2441) [15477266] **5691**

DENVER QUARTERLY (US/0011-8869) [01566260] 3458, **3380**

DENVER REGIONAL COUNCIL OF GOVERNMENTS *See* COG NOTES. MONTHLY PROGRESS REPORT **4639**

DENVER. UNIVERSITY. GRADUATE SCHOOL OF LIBRARIANSHIP *See* STUDIES IN LIBRARIANSHIP **3251**

DENVER UNIVERSITY LAW REVIEW (US/0883-9409) [11990038] **2959**

DENVER WESTERNERS MONTHLY ROUNDUP *See* DENVER WESTERNERS ROUNDUP, THE **2730**

DENVER WESTERNERS ROUNDUP, THE (US/0278-7970) [07872605] **2730**

DEO (UK) 4952, **4114**

DEOSNEWS (UNIVERSITY PARK, PA.) (US/1062-9416) [25334182] **1735**

DEPARTEMENTSNYTT (SW) [02620811] **1591**

DEPARTMENT AND SPECIALTY STORE MERCHANDISING AND OPERATING RESULTS (US/0271-5015) [06296901] **953**

DEPARTMENT CHAIR, THE (US/1049-3255) [21206821] **1862**

DEPARTMENT OF AGRICULTURAL EDUCATION REPORT (US/0090-7391) [03146064] **78**

DEPARTMENT OF DEFENSE FACT BOOK (US/1049-8672) [08084587] **4042**

DEPARTMENT OF DEFENSE SUPPLEMENT / DISKETTE (US) **4042**

●DEPARTMENT OF EDUCATION REPORTS / NATIONAL CENTER FOR EDUCATION INFORMATION (US) [27289761] **1735**

DEPARTMENT OF ENERGY FY ... OBLIGATIONS AND COSTS BY STATE (US) [09163904] **1936**

DEPARTMENT OF ENERGY PRESS RELEASES *CEASED.* (UK) **1936**

DEPARTMENT OF ENERGY RED BOOK (US/0275-3014) [07124572] **1936**

DEPARTMENT OF ENERGY SOLAR ENERGY OBJECTIVES (US) [06269500] **1936**

DEPARTMENT OF FORESTRY TECHNICAL PAPER (US/0193-8223) [03639624] **2378**

DEPARTMENT OF GEOGRAPHY PUBLICATION SERIES (CN/0843-7378) [07407650] **2559**

DEPARTMENT OF HEALTH AND SOCIAL SERVICES QUARTERLY MAGAZINE (US) [03244169] **5281**

DEPARTMENT OF HOUSING AND URBAN DEVELOPMENT ANNUAL REPORT TO CONGRESS ON INDIAN AND ALASKA NATIVE HOUSING AND COMMUNITY DEVELOPMENT PROGRAMS (US/0271-1753) [06369257] **2820**

DEPARTMENT OF INDUSTRY, TRADE AND TOURISM AND LOTTERIES FUNDED PROGRAMS, FITNESS AND SPORT DIRECTORATES, SUPPLEMENTARY INFORMATION FOR LEGISLATIVE REVIEW, ... EXPENDITURE ESTIMATES (CN/1184-9347) [24571412] **4720**

DEPARTMENT OF JUSTICE FINANCIAL LITIGATION ANNUAL REPORT (US) [25575648] **2959**

DEPARTMENT OF NATURAL RESOURCES GEOLOGICAL SURVEY GUIDEBOOK (US) [01307595] **2191**

DEPARTMENT OF NATURAL RESOURCES GEOLOGICAL SURVEY SPECIAL REPORT (US) [08229952] 1373, **2191**

DEPARTMENT OF REVENUE ANNUAL REPORT (ARIZONA) (US) [08754568] **4642**

DEPARTMENT OF STATE PLANNING PUBLICATION *CEASED.* (US) [20738751] **4642**

DEPARTMENT OF STATE PUBLICATION. BACKGROUND NOTES SERIES (US/1049-5517) [07437325] **2559**

DEPARTMENT OF THE ARMY HISTORICAL SUMMARY (WASHINGTON) (US/0092-7880) [02243790] **4042**

DEPARTMENT OF THE NAVY SUPPLEMENT / DISKETTE (US) 4042, **4176**

DEPARTMENT OF TRANSPORTATION, STATE OF RHODE ISLAND (US/0148-298X) [03282852] **5381**

DEPARTMENT OF VETERANS AFFAIRS PUBLICATIONS INDEX (US) [19387997] **4042**

DEPARTMENT PROJECTIONS OF CAPITAL NEEDS FOR THE FIVE YEAR CAL PERIOD . *See* CAPITAL IMPROVEMENT PROGRAM, FISCAL YEARS ... / STATE OF MARYLAND, DEPARTMENT OF STATE PLANNING **4716**

DEPARTMENT PUBLICATIONS - STATE OF CALIFORNIA, RESOURCES AGENCY, DEPARTMENT OF WATER RESOURCES (US/0360-3946) [02243931] **5532**

DEPARTMENT STORE ECONOMIST (US) [02255663] **665**

DEPARTMENT STORE INVENTORY PRICE INDEXES / U.S. DEPARTMENT OF LABOR, BUREAU OF LABOR STATISTICS (US/0498-7284) [04682645] **953**

DEPARTMENT STORE MONTHLY SALES, BY PROVINCE AND METROPOLITAN AREA (ENGLISH EDITION 1991) (CN/1183-7888) [25590071] **953**

DEPARTMENT STORE MONTHLY SALES, BY PROVINCE AND METROPOLITAN AREA (FRENCH EDITION 1991) (CN/1183-7888) [25590072] **953**

DEPARTMENT STORE SALES AND STOCKS (CN/0380-7045) [02443796] **953**

DEPARTMENTAL EXPENDITURE ESTIMATES SUPPLEMENT GUIDELINES *CEASED.* (CN/1184-7999) [24280643] **4720**

DEPARTMENTAL INFORMATION REPORT (US) [25528318] **78**

DEPARTMENTAL SERIES - DEPARTMENT OF AGRONOMY AND SOILS, AGRICULTURAL EXPERIMENT STATION, AUBURN UNIVERSITY (US) [03367778] **78**

DEPARTMENTAL WORKING PAPER - CARLETON UNIVERSITY. DEPARTMENT OF SOCIOLOGY AND ANTHROPOLOGY (CN/0822-6733) [10224928] 5244, **235**

DEPAUL BUSINESS LAW JOURNAL (US/1049-6122) [20064809] **3099**

DEPECHE (CN/0831-0467) [13770069] **1662**

DEPECHE DU MIDI TOULOUSE, LA (FR/0181-7981) [I01817981] **5800**

DEPECHE, LA (FR) **1110**

●DEPECHE MAC (CN/1191-0755) [25652398] **1182**

DEPECHE MODE GRAND PUBLIC (FR) **1083**

DEPECHE-TPS : BULLETIN MENSUEL DE TPS CANADA-QUEBEC (CN/1183-4420) [24368316] **4720**

DEPENDENCY (US) [12637588] **5281**

DEPENSES OBLIGATOIRES DE SANTE, STATISTIQUES DEPARTEMENTALES / MINISTERE DE LA SANTE ET DE LA SECURITE SOCIALE, DIRECTION GENERALE DE LA SANTE, BUREAU DES AFFAIRES GENERALES, LES (FR) [08041367] **3571**

DEPEW BEE (US/0746-4460) [10049365] **5716**

DEPONIROVANNYE RUKOPISI / GOSUDARSTVENNYI KOMITET SSSR PO NAUKE I TEKHNIKE, AKADEMIIA NAUK SSSR, VSESOIUZNYI INSTITUT NAUCHNOI I TEKHNICHESKOI INFORMATSII, SEKTOR TEORII I METODIKI DEPONIROVANIIA NAUCHNYKH RABOT (RU/0135-0617) [08355883] **5099**

DEPORT TIMES, THE (US) [14175398] **5749**

DEPORTE, EL (CU) [02454704] **4892**

DEPOSIT HISTORY AND PROJECTIONS (US) [06293004] **787**

DEPOSIT INSURANCE CORPORATION *See* ANNUAL REPORT: DIRECTORS' REPORT, BALANCE SHEET AND ACCOUNTS **2873**

●DEPOT MILITAIRE (US/1064-2153) [26232147] **4042**

DEPRECIATION AND CAPITAL PLANNING (US) [18661398] **2960**

DEPRECIATION : FOR USE IN PREPARING ... RETURNS (US) [23264933] **4720**

DEPREM ARASTRMA ENSTITUSU *See* DEPREM ARASTRMA ENSTITUSU BULTENI **1373**

DEPREM ARASTRMA ENSTITUSU BULTENI (TU) [01798003] **1373**

DEPRESSION GLASS NATIONAL MARKET APPRAISAL REPORT, THE (US/0274-5577) [06407400] **2588**

●DEPRESSION (NEW YORK, N.Y.) (US/1062-6417) [25688777] 3924, **4584**

DEPTH NEWS INDONESIA (IO/0376-8201) [01797925] **1479**

DEPUTAZIONE DI STORIA PATRIA PER LA CALABRIA *See* COLLANA STORICA **2684**

DEPUTAZIONE DI STORIA PATRIA PER LE ANTICHE PROVINCIE MODENESI *See* ATTI E MEMORIE - DEPUTAZIONE DI STORIA PATRIA PER LE ANTICHE PROVINCIE MODENESI **2677**

DEPUTAZIONE DI STORIA PATRIA PER L'UMBRIA, PERUGIA *See* BOLLETTINO DELLA DEPUTAZIONE DI STORIA PATRIA PER L'UMBRIA **4633**

DEQ FLASH RULES. LEVEL THREE (US) **2163**

DEQUINCY NEWS, THE (US) [17545393] **5683**

DER-PE RELATORIO / GOVERNO DO ESTADO DE PERNAMBUCO, SECRETARIA DOS TRANSPORTES, ENERGIA E COMUNICACOES, DEPARTAMENTO DE ESTRADAS DE RODAGEM (BL) [10253835] **5439**

DERAP WORKING PAPERS (NO/0800-2045) [I08002045] **2821**

DERBY EVENING TELEGRAPH (UK) [17645774] **5812**

DERBY (NORMAN, OKLA.) *CEASED.* (US/0199-5928) [06027153] 4892, **2798**

DERBYSHIRE ARCHAEOLOGICAL JOURNAL, THE (UK/0070-3788) [03823266] **266**

DERECHO (CK) [01793302] **2960**

DERECHO (CK) [25389749] **2960**

DERECHO A LA INFANCIA (CL/0716-7865) [24060971] **5281**

DERECHO COMPARADO (AG) [03858001] **2960**

DERECHO DEL TRABAJO; REVISTA CRITICA MENSUAL DE JURISPRUDENCIA, DOCTRINA Y LEGISLACION (AG) [04637353] **3146**

DERECHO FINANCIERO (CK) [02278803] 831, **2960**

DERECHO LABORAL; REVISTA DE DOCTRINA, JURISPRUDENCIA E INFORMACIONES SOCIALES (UY) [01692421] **3146**

DERECHO
Alphabetical Title Index

DERECHO PESQUERO / [ACADEMIA INTERNACIONAL DE DERECHO PESQUERO] (MX) [08950607] **2960**

DERECHO SOCIAL (PY) [07019811] **3146**

DERECHO Y REFORMA AGRARIA; REVISTA (VE/0304-2820) [02398468] 78, **2960**

DERECHOS DEL PUEBLO / COMISION ECUMENICA DE DERECHOS HUMANOS, LOS (EC) [13557426] **4507**

DERECHOS HUMANOS EN CHILE / ARZOBISPADO DE SANTIAGO, VICARIA DE LA SOLIDARIDAD (CL) [19745106] **4507**

DERECHOS HUMANOS EN NICARAGUA (NQ) [19700485] **4507**

DERECHOS HUMANOS : TRIBUNA INFORMATIVA / ASOCIACION PRO DERECHOS HUMANOS (SP) [10288618] **4507**

DERECHOS SOCIALES (PE) [01798653] **3146**

DEREK JOHANSEN'S RECOMMENDED HOTELS IN GREAT BRITAIN (UK) **2805**

DEREVOOBRABATYVAJUSCAJA PROMYSLENNOST (RU/0011-9008) [04695495] **634**

DERHECHOS HUMANOS / ACADEMIA MEXICANA DE DERECHOS HUMANOS (MX) [22577410] **4507**

DERIVATION AND TABULATION ASSOCIATES, INC See RELAY MINIATURE AND SUBMINIATURE D.A.T.A. BOOK **2079**

DERIVATION AND TABULATION ASSOCIATES, INC See SEMICONDUCTOR HEAT SINK, SOCKET & ASSOCIATED HARDWARE D.A.T.A. BOOK **2080**

DERIVATION AND TABULATION ASSOCIATES, INC See TRANSISTOR D.A.T.A. BOOK **2085**

DERIVATION AND TABULATION ASSOCIATES, INC See D.A.T.A.'S MICROWAVE TUBE **2040**

DERIVATIVES IN FUND MANAGEMENT (UK) **787**

DERIVATIVES REVIEW (US) **787**

●DERIVATIVES WEEK (US/1075-2412) [25652930] **787**

DERIVE URBAINE, LA (CN/0702-8830) [03439478] **384**

DERMASCOPE (DALLAS, TEX.) (US/1075-055X) [23721869] **403**

DERMATO SELECTIEF (NE) 3571, **5099**

DERMATOLOGIA (MX/0185-4038) [I01854038] **3719**

DERMATOLOGIA CLINICA (IT/0392-1395) [16986191] **3719**

DERMATOLOGIA OGGI (IT/0394-2503) [I03942503] **3719**

DERMATOLOGIA REVISTA MEXICANA (MX) **3719**

DERMATOLOGIC CAPSULE & COMMENT (US/0741-7489) [08163013] **3719**

DERMATOLOGIC CLINICS (US/0733-8635) [08649114] **3719**

●DERMATOLOGIC SURGERY (US/1076-0512) [30376574] 3963, **3719**

DERMATOLOGICA See DERMATOLOGY (BASEL) **3719**

DERMATOLOGIE MALADIES SEXUELLEMENT TRANSMISSIBLES. E73 (FR) **3719**

DERMATOLOGIE PRATIQUE (FR/0982-8567) [I09828567] **3719**

DERMATOLOGIJA I VENEROLOGIJA (BU/0417-0792) [03824998] **3719**

DERMATOLOGISCHE MONATSSCHRIFT (GW/0011-9083) [01566270] **3719**

DERMATOLOGIST'S COMPENDIUM OF DRUG THERAPY, THE (US/0276-430X) [07361790] **3719**

DERMATOLOGY & ALLERGY (US/0273-2254) [06988653] 3669, **3719**

●DERMATOLOGY (BASEL) (SZ/1018-8665) [25275441] **3719**

DERMATOLOGY (BIENNIAL) (US/1051-8258) [22135233] **3719**

DERMATOLOGY DIGEST (1979) (US/0198-6643) [06074297] **3719**

DERMATOLOGY IN PRACTICE (LONDON) (UK/0262-5504) [09487684] **3719**

DERMATOLOGY (NEW YORK, N.Y.) (US/0742-3217) [08916678] **3719**

DERMATOLOGY NURSING (US/1060-3441) [21801234] **3719**

DERMATOLOGY TIMES (US/0196-6197) [05865816] **3719**

DERMATOLOGY UPDATE (US/0163-1691) [04307119] **3719**

●DERMATON (GW) **3720**

●DERMATOPATHOLOGY: PRACTICAL & CONCEPTUAL (US/1078-4454) **3720**

DERMATOSEN IN BERUF UND UMWELT (GW/0343-2432) [04161293] **3720**

DERMO TIME (IT) **3720**

DERMOFARMACIA (IT/0303-8890) [01219656] **3720**

DERRICK (OIL CITY, PA.) (US) [02260315] **5736**

DERROTERO ARGENTINO (AG) [06365716] **4176**

DERRY NEWS, THE (US) [22333588] **5708**

DERWENT BIOTECHNOLOGY ABSTRACTS (UK/0262-5318) [08986444] **3691**

DES CHANTIERS ET DES HOMMES (CN/0820-778X) [10681050] **612**

DES LITIGATION REPORTER (US/0276-5675) [07391371] 4299, **2960**

DES LIVRES ET DES JEUNES (CN/0706-795X) [10682040] **3380**

DES MOINES BUSINESS RECORD (US/1068-6681) [27757283] **665**

DES MOINES COUNTY GENEALOGICAL SOCIETY (US/0736-3931) [09089238] **2445**

DES MOINES COUNTY NEWS (US) [18702775] **5669**

DES MOINES REGISTER, THE (US) [01566275] **5669**

DES MOTS ET DES GENS (SAINT-LAURENT) (CN/0846-0140) [24256466] **4642**

DES MOTS ET DES GENS (SAINT-LAURENT) (CN/0846-0140) [24256466] **4642**

DES (NORWALK, CONN. 1984) (US/0884-6324) [11474009] **2112**

DES PLAINES EDITION OF THE TIMES (US/0895-0148) [16399236] **5659**

DES PLAINES TIMES See DES PLAINES EDITION OF THE TIMES **5659**

DESALINATION (NE/0011-9164) [01566278] **5532**

DESALINATION AND RECYCLING ABSTRACTS CEASED. (IS/0011-9172) [13309206] 2163, **2184**

DESARROLLO DEL MERCADO DE LOS FERTILIZANTES NITROGENADOS EN ESPANA (SP) [06431947] **78**

DESARROLLO ECONOMICO (BUENOS AIRES) (AG/0046-001X) [01566279] **5198**

DESARROLLO INDOAMERICANO (CK/0418-7547) [05690640] **2730**

DESARROLLO NACIONAL (US/0279-2958) [07747181] **5099**

DESARROLLO Y MODERNIZACION (AG/0325-5824) [04681667] **1555**

DESARROLLO Y SOCIEDAD CEASED. (CK/0120-3584) [04975286] **1555**

DESCANT (FORT WORTH, TEX.) (US/0011-9210) [01566280] 3380, **1091**

DESCANT (TORONTO) (CN/0382-909X) [02380621] **3380**

DESCENDER, THE (US/0420-0063) [04650236] **2445**

DESCENT (SYDNEY) (AT/0084-9731) [04649741] **2445**

DESCENT WELLS (UK/0046-0036) [I00460036] **1373**

DESCO See MEMORIA - DESCO **5209**

DESCRIPTION AND ANALYSIS OF CONTEMPORARY STANDARD RUSSIAN (NE/0070-3826) [01692854] **3276**

DESCRIPTIONS OF FUNGI & BACTERIA (UK) **453**

DESCRIPTIONS OF PLANT VIRUSES (UK) [01692904] **508**

DESCRIPTIVE REPORT OF ACTIVITIES IN THE FIELDS OF AGRICULTURE, TRADES AND INDUSTRY, VOCATIONAL & GENERAL HOME ECONOMICS, OCCUPATIONAL INFORMATION AND GUIDANCE, DISTRIBUTIVE EDUCATION, AND INDUSTRIAL ARTS (US) [06301788] **1912**

DESCRIPTIVE REPORT OF PROGRAM ACTIVITIES FOR VOCATIONAL EDUCATION (US/0090-6743) [01785226] **1912**

DESCRIPTIVE REPORT OF PROGRAM ACTIVITIES FOR VOCATIONAL EDUCATION (OKLAHOMA CITY) (US/0360-5736) [02244490] **1912**

DESCRIPTOR FREQUENCY LIST (US/0884-7819) [12411776] **3205**

DESEMPENHO DA ECONOMIA DE PERNAMBUCO (BL) [04342130] 1555, **1531**

DESEMPENHO DAS FINANCAS PUBLICAS DE PERNAMBUCO (BL) [05459007] **4720**

DESEMPENHO DO SETOR AGROPECUARIO DO RIO GRANDE DO SUL / GOVERNO DO ESTADO DO RIO GRANDE DO SUL, SECRETARIA DA AGRICULTURA, DEPARTAMENTO DE PLANEJAMENTO AGRICOLA (BL) [11696339] **78**

DESENVOLVIMENTO DO ORCAMENTO DA DESPESA FIXADA PARA O ANO ECONOMICO (PO) [02240650] **4042**

DESERET NEWS CHURCH ALMANAC (US/0093-786X) [01793136] **5059**

DESERET NEWS (SALT LAKE CITY, UTAH : 1964) (US/0745-4724) [09198605] **5756**

DESERT BIGHORN COUNCIL See TRANSACTIONS - DESERT BIGHORN COUNCIL **2207**

DESERT BOTANICAL GARDEN (ARIZ.) See ANNUAL REPORT / DESERT BOTANICAL GARDEN **499**

DESERT CALL See FOREFRONT CO **4959**

DESERT CALL / SPIRITUAL LIFE INSTITUTE (US/0011-9229) [08920279] **4953**

DESERT FISHES COUNCIL (U.S.) See PROCEEDINGS OF THE DESERT FISHES COUNCIL **2310**

DESERT LIFE CEASED. (US) **4871**

DESERT PLANTS (US/0734-3434) [05527161] **508**

DESERT POST (US/0745-5585) [09286022] **5634**

DESERT TORTOISE COUNCIL See PROCEEDINGS OF SYMPOSIUM - DESERT TORTOISE COUNCIL **5595**

DESERT TRAIL, THE (US/0746-5599) [10127273] **5634**

DESERTIFICATION CONTROL (KE/0379-2455) [12319640] **2227**

DESEZONIRANE CASOVNE VRSTE SR SLOVENIJE (XV) [06977694] **1662**

DESFILE (BL) [05201018] **2789**

DESIDOC BULLETIN (II/0970-8154) [22719575] **1110**

DESIGN SUSPENDED. (II/0011-9261) [01774298] **296**

DESIGN & APPLIED ARTS INDEX (UK/0953-0681) [17985545] 378, **334**

DESIGN AND CONTROL OF CONCRETE MIXTURES (US/0190-6755) [02193347] **612**

DESIGN & ELEKTRONIK (GW/0933-8667) [I09338667] **2041**

DESIGN AND INDUSTRIES ASSOCIATION (GREAT BRITAIN) See DIA YEARBOOK **2163**

DESIGN & TECHNOLOGY TEACHING (UK/0958-3017) [I09583017] **5099**

DESIGN ARTS (NEW YORK, N.Y.) (US/0278-1522) [06837561] **318**

DESIGN AUTOMATION FOR EMBEDDED SYSTEMS (NE/0929-5585) **1219**

DESIGN (BERGAMO) (IT/0304-033X) [01795755] **372**

DESIGN BOOK REVIEW (US/0737-5344) [09361004] **296**

DESIGN COST AND DATA (US/1054-3163) [22263771] **297**

DESIGN DK (DK) [26137152] **297**

DESIGN E HABITAT (IT) [01799076] **297**

DESIGN ENGINEERING (LONDON, ENGLAND) (UK/0308-8448) [06237037] **1970**

DESIGN ENGINEERING (TORONTO) (CN/0011-9342) [01566292] **1970**

DESIGN FIRM DIRECTORY (ENVIRONMENTAL AND INTERIOR DESIGN ED.) (US/0891-5997) [14923630] **2899**

●DESIGN FIRM MANAGEMENT & ADMINISTRATION REPORT (US/1057-2864) [23997147] **865**

DESIGN FOR ARTS & EDUCATION See ARTS EDUCATION POLICY REVIEW **314**

DESIGN FOR ARTS IN EDUCATION (US/0732-0973) [05004435] 1735, **318**

DESIGN FOR LEADERSHIP (US/1051-8193) [22134396] **1862**

DESIGN FOR MANUFACTURING NEWSLETTER (US) **3477**

DESIGN FROM DENMARK See DESIGN FROM SCANDINAVIA **372**

DESIGN FROM SCANDINAVIA (DK/0108-0695) [01788285] **372**

DESIGN IN FINLAND (FI/0418-7717) [09025526] **2899**

DESIGN IN STEEL (US/0418-7679) [01612148] **4001**

DESIGN INDEX ... FOR THE CORPORATE MANAGER, THE CEASED. (SZ) [24788379] **378**

DESIGN INDUSTRIE (FR) [04817192] **2097**

DESIGN/INTERNATIONAL REVIEW (IT) [14233097] **297**

DESIGN ISSUES (US/0747-9360) [10836452] **297**

DESIGN JOURNAL **SUSPENDED.** (KO) **349**

DESIGN JOURNAL (CHICAGO ILL.) *See* AMERICAN CENTER FOR DESIGN JOURNAL **287**

DESIGN (LONDON) **CEASED.** (UK/0011-9245) [01160420] **2097**

DESIGN MANAGEMENT (US/1042-8534) [19230509] **865**

DESIGN MANAGEMENT JOURNAL (US/1045-7194) [20214126] **1970**

●DESIGN METHODS (US/1067-9359) [25107759] **297**

DESIGN METHODS AND THEORIES *See* DESIGN METHODS **297**

DESIGN NEWS (US/0011-9407) [01566297] **2097**

DESIGN NEWS (JA/0385-3462) [06568331] **2097**

DESIGN NEWS (UK) **1970**

DESIGN NEWS SPECIFIER'S ANNUAL DIRECTORY (US) [01793593] **2097**

DESIGN PROCESSES NEWSLETTER (US/1046-980X) [17388452] **2097**

DESIGN PRODUCTS & APPLICATIONS (UK) [08203416] **2097**

DESIGN QUARTERLY JAPAN (JA) [23373137] **297**

DESIGN QUARTERLY (MINNEAPOLIS, MINN.) (US/0011-9415) [01566298] **2097, 297**

DESIGN REPORT (GW) **319**

DESIGN SOLUTIONS (US/0277-3538) [07537179] **2899, 297**

DESIGN STATEMENTS / AMERICAN CENTER FOR DESIGN (US) [27798147] **1233**

DESIGN STUDIES (UK/0142-694X) [05523939] **2097**

DESIGN SYSTEMS STRATEGIES **CEASED.** (US/0895-6790) [16729070] **1233**

DESIGN TECHNOLOGIES **CEASED.** (US/1066-7504) [26782757] **378, 2097**

DESIGN TECHNOLOGY TEACHING (UK) [21913969] **372**

DESIGN TIMES (US/1041-0422) [18614888] **2899**

DESIGN / U.S. DEPARTMENT OF THE INTERIOR, HERITAGE CONSERVATION AND RECREATION SERVICE (US) [02401162] **4706**

DESIGN (WASHINGTON, D.C., 1980) (US/1050-9224) [09667091] **2918**

DESIGN WEEK (UK/0950-3676) **297, 2899**

DESIGN WITH FLOWERS **CEASED.** (US/1043-9145) [19601374] **372**

DESIGN WORLD (AT/0810-6029) [10190384] **2900, 297**

DESIGNATED AIRSPACE HANDBOOK (CN) **17**

DESIGNATORS FOR AIRCRAFT OPERATING AGENCIES, AERONAUTICAL AUTHORITIES AND SERVICES / INDICATIFS DES EXPLOITANTS D'AERONEF ET DES ADMINISTRATIONS ET SERVICES AERONAUTIQUES / DESIGNADORES DE EMPRESAS EXPLOTADORAS DE AERONAVES, DE ENTIDADES OFICIALES Y DE SERVICIOS AERONAUTICOS (CN) [06324070] **17**

DESIGNER HOME PLANS (US) [16412309] **297**

DESIGNERS' COLLECTION HOME PLANS (US/0897-6228) [17571586] **297**

DESIGNERS DIGEST MAGAZINE (GW) [21371680] **2097, 378**

DESIGNERS' JOURNAL **CEASED.** (UK/0264-8148) [11489887] **297**

DESIGNERS WEST **CEASED.** (US/0192-1487) [04087182] **2900**

DESIGNERS WEST RESOURCE DIRECTORY (US) [01787518] **2900**

DESIGNERS WORKSHOP (JA) **297**

DESIGNERS WORLD **CEASED.** (US/1057-8277) [24124902] **2900**

DESIGNFAX (US/0163-6669) [04431086] **2097**

DESIGNING **CEASED.** (UK) [14253635] **2900**

DESIGNINK **CEASED.** (AU/1035-0500) [10350500] **2900, 297**

DESIGNNET (AUSTIN, TEX.) **CEASED.** (US/1061-1118) [25161927] **1233**

●DESIGNNETWORK'S WORKSTATION REPORT (US) [28305442] **4211**

DESIGNS, CODES AND CRYPTOGRAPHY (NE/0925-1022) [24133394] **2041**

DESIGNSOURCE (1989) (US/1046-6223) [20348578] **612**

DESK REFERENCE (US) [11674723] **3917**

DESK-REFERENCE DIRECTORY (CN/0711-3331) [08767191] **1603, 4892**

DESKBOOK ENCYCLOPEDIA OF AMERICAN SCHOOL LAW (US/1058-4919) [07678359] **1862, 2960**

DESKTOP BANK DIRECTORY, THE (US) [13430757] **787**

DESKTOP COMMUNICATIONS (US/1050-1800) [21419834] **1182**

DESKTOP MAGAZINE (AT/1037-7603) [I10377603] **1233**

DESKTOP MARKETING ALERT (US/1062-0842) [25518902] **923**

DESKTOP PUBLISHER (US) **1263**

DESKTOP PUBLISHING AND OFFICE AUTOMATION BUYER'S GUIDE AND HANDBOOK (US/0890-7226) [16222657] **1263**

DESKTOP PUBLISHING COMMENTARY (UK/0957-3178) [I09573178] **4813**

DESKTOP PUBLISHING DIGEST (US/1040-8932) [18572379] **4813**

●DESLINDES : REVISTA DE LA BIBLIOTECA NACIONAL (UY/0797-6402) [27408789] **3380**

DESMOS OF DELTA SIGMA DELTA (US/0011-9474) [02260323] **1819**

DESOTO COUNTY TRIBUNE, THE (US) [15253848] **5700**

DESOTO NEWS-ADVERTISER (US/0747-0428) [10498929] **5749**

DESOTO PLUME (US) **2614**

DESOTO TIMES (1981) (US/1064-4784) [17576873] **5700**

DESPACHOS PUBLICOS (CK) [09021760] **4642**

DESPATCH (UK/0046-0079) [03672547] **2685, 4042**

DESPENCER, LE (US/0749-5633) [10554094] **2445**

DESPORTO (TORONTO, ONT.) (CN/0229-7906) [08099103] **4892**

DESSAUER'S JOURNAL (US) **4519**

DESSERTS! (BERNE, IND.) (US/1072-639X) [29147591] **2333**

DESSOUS MODE INTERNATIONAL (FR/0981-1842) [I09811842] **1083**

DESTAQUES (BL) [02483262] **1603**

●DESTINATION DISCOVERY (US/1065-1535) [26516362] **2532**

DESTINATION INTEGRATION (CN/1186-8953) [24690522] **5281**

DESTINATION INTEGRATION (CN/1186-8953) [24690527] **5281**

●DESTINATION OF SHIPMENTS OF WESTERN U.S. SOFTWOOD LUMBER BY STATE, EXCEPT REDWOOD LUMBER (US) [30445365] **2400**

DESTINATION OF SHIPMENTS OF WESTERN WOOD SPECIES BY STATE *See* DESTINATION OF SHIPMENTS OF WESTERN U.S. SOFTWOOD LUMBER BY STATE, EXCEPT REDWOOD LUMBER **2400**

DESTINATION (TORONTO, ONT.) (CN/0229-2130) [08070861] **5468**

DESTINATIONS (CN) [13841500] **5468**

DESTINATIONS (US/0279-8468) [07331142] **5381**

DESTINATIONS (13-30 CORPORATION) *See* DESTINATIONS (KNOXVILLE, TENN.) **5468**

DESTINATIONS (KNOXVILLE, TENN.) (US/0275-8024) [07184546] **5468**

DESTINY (CN/0225-9796) [06272859] **4953**

DET BASTA UR READER'S DIGEST (SW/0005-3856) [01519015] **2515**

DET BESTA FRA READER'S DIGEST (NO) [01779569] **2515**

DET CENTRALE HANDICAPRADS VIRKSOMHED I ... (DK) [10153868] **5281**

DET FORSTLIGE FORSOEGSVAESEN I DANMARK : BERETNINGER UTGIVNE VED DEN FORSTLIGE FORSOEGSKOMMISSION **CEASED.** (DK/0367-2174) [04610031] **2378**

DETA TSUSHIN (JA/0285-9394) [I02859394] **1258**

DETAIL (MUNCHEN) (GW/0011-9571) [01566304] **297**

DETAILED AGRICULTURE BUDGET (II) [03347991] **78**

DETAILED CIVIL BUDGET ESTIMATES. GOVERNMENT OF WEST BENGAL (II/0376-821X) [06170224] **4720**

DETAILED DEMAND FOR GRANTS OF EDUCATION DEPARTMENT. GOVERNMENT OF JAMMU AND KASHMIR (II/0303-8653) [01797794] **1735**

DETAILED DEMAND FOR GRANTS OF FOOD SUPPLIES AND TRANSPORT DEPARTMENT. GOVERNMENT OF JAMMU AND KASHMIR (II/0303-8645) [01797784] **4642**

DETAILED DEMAND FOR GRANTS OF HOUSING AND URBAN DEVELOPMENT DEPARTMENT (II/0376-8260) [01797789] **4720, 2821**

DETAILED DEMAND FOR GRANTS OF INDUSTRIES & COMMERCE DEPARTMENT. GOVERNMENT OF JAMMU AND KASHMIR (II/0303-8629) [01797793] **4720, 831**

DETAILED DEMAND FOR GRANTS OF LABOUR AND SOCIAL WELFARE DEPARTMENT (II/0376-8279) [01797782] **5281, 4720, 1662**

DETAILED DEMAND FOR GRANTS OF LADAKH AFFAIR DEPARTMENT. GOVERNMENT OF JAMMU AND KASHMIR (II/0303-8637) [01797781] **4720, 1479**

DETAILED DEMAND FOR GRANTS OF LAW DEPARTMENT (II/0376-8287) [01797783] **2960**

DETAILED DEMAND FOR GRANTS OF PLANNING DEPARTMENT (II/0376-8295) [01797786] **4720, 1479**

DETAILED DEMAND FOR GRANTS OF REVENUE DEPARTMENT FOR ... (II) [22246541] **4720**

DETAILED DEMAND FOR GRANTS OF REVENUE, RELIEF, AND EMPLOYMENT DEPARTMENT FOR . *See* DETAILED DEMAND FOR GRANTS OF REVENUE DEPARTMENT FOR ... **4720**

DETAILED DEMAND FOR GRANTS OF WORKS DEPARTMENT. GOVERNMENT OF JAMMU AND KASHMIR (II/0303-948X) [01797792] **4720**

DETAILED DIAGNOSES AND SURGICAL PROCEDURES FOR PATIENTS DISCHARGED FROM SHORT-STAY HOSPITALS, UNITED STATES (US) [08775614] **3963**

DETAILED ESTIMATES OF IRRIGATION, ELECTRICITY AND PUBLIC WORKS FOR ... (II) [07069069] **2088, 2041**

DETAILED ESTIMATES OF REVENUE OF THE PUNJAB GOVERNMENT FOR THE YEAR ... (II) [05358247] **4642, 4720**

DETAILED IRRIGATION BUDGET (II/0570-0345) [07069113] **2088, 4720**

DETAILED IRRIGATION BUDGET FOR THE YEAR ... - TAMIL NADU (INDIA) (II) [07069175] **2088**

DETAILED LISTING OF REAL PROPERTY OWNED BY THE UNITED STATES AND USED BY CIVIL AGENCIES THROUGHOUT THE WORLD AS OF ... (US) [07913183] **4642**

DETAILED LISTING OF REAL PROPERTY OWNED BY THE UNITED STATES AND USED BY THE DEPARTMENT OF DEFENSE FOR MILITARY FUNCTIONS THROUGHOUT THE WORLD AS OF SEPTEMBER 30 ... (US) [09384902] **4042**

DETAILED MORTALITY STATISTICS, ALABAMA (US/0732-9830) [05719288] **4552**

DETAILED MORTALITY STATISTICS, SOUTH CAROLINA (US/8755-2744) [07297405] **5326**

DETAILED SURFACE WATER QUALITY DATA. ALBERTA, MANITOBA, NORTHWEST TERRITORIES, AND SASKATCHEWAN (CN) [12096659] **5532**

DETAILED TECHNICAL PLAN FOR THE GREAT LAKES ENVIRONMENTAL RESEARCH LABORATORY (US) [06162126] **2163**

DETAILED VALUES OF IONOSPHERIC CHARACTERISTICS AND F-PLOTS FOR CHUNG-LI (CH) [01797602] **1425**

DETAILHANDEL IN BLOEMEN, PLANTEN EN TUINBENODIGDHEDEN, DIEREN EN DIERBENODIGDHEDEN / CENTRAAL BUREAU VOOR DE STATISTIEK, HOOFDAFDELING STATISTIEKEN VAN BIENNENLANDSE HANDEL EN DIENSTVERLENING (NE/0923-0203) [10406902] **2435**

DETAILHANDEL MAGAZINE (NE/0168-0021) [I01680021] **831**

DETAILLANT, LE (CN/0383-6762) [03284983] **4254**

DETAILPRISER (DK/0417-0164) [03816774] **5326**

DETAILS (NEW YORK, N.Y.) (US/0740-4921) [09953684] **3995**

DETAILS OF WORKS FOR DEMANDS 39, ROADS AND BRIDGES AND 52, CAPITAL OUTLAY ON ROADS AND BRIDGES FOR THE YEAR ... (II) [10090225] **5440**

DETALI MASIN (KIEV) (UN/0130-3066) [02998624] **2112**

DETECTION, DIAGNOSIS, AND THERAPY, AND PRE-CLINICAL BIOLOGY OF BREAST CANCER, THE (US) [03458139] **3815**

DETECTION, DIAGNOSIS, AND THERAPY OF LUNG CANCER, THE (US) [03457829] **3815**

DETEKTYW — Alphabetical Title Index

DETEKTYW (PL/0860-4436) [I08604436] **4860**

DETENTION REPORTER (US/0742-552X) [10379683] **3163**

DETERMINATIONS OF THE NATIONAL MEDIATION BOARD (US/0270-4196) [06275291] **3146**

DETERMINATIONS OF THE NEW YORK STATE COMMISSION ON JUDICIAL CONDUCT (US) [08337186] **3140**

DETROIT *See* CODE OF THE CITY OF DETROIT, MICHIGAN **4639**

DETROIT ATHLETIC CLUB *See* D.A.C. NEWS **4892**

DETROIT AUTOMOTIVE SERVICES. NEW CAR INVOICE GUIDE (US/8755-6936) [11352060] **5412**

DETROIT. CITY PLAN COMMISSION *See* URBAN RENEWAL SERIES - DETROIT. CITY PLAN COMMISSION **2838**

DETROIT COLLEGE OF LAW *See* DETROIT COLLEGE OF LAW ALUMNI NEWS **1101**

DETROIT COLLEGE OF LAW ALUMNI NEWS (US) [05424243] 2960, **1101**

DETROIT COLLEGE OF LAW REVIEW (US/0099-135X) [02243392] **2960**

DETROIT DENTAL BULLETIN (US/0011-9601) [02260326] **1322**

DETROIT FREE PRESS (DETROIT, MICH., 1858) (US/1055-2758) [10345127] **5691**

DETROIT INSTITUTE OF ARTS *See* BULLETIN OF THE DETROIT INSTITUTE OF ARTS **345**

DETROIT LABOR MARKET REVIEW *See* DETROIT'S LABOR MARKET NEWS **1662**

DETROIT LABOR NEWS (US/1072-1525) [28873960] **1662**

DETROIT LABOR TRENDS *See* LABOR TRENDS (SOUTHFIELD, MICH.) **1685**

DETROIT LAKES TRIBUNE (US) [01566328] **5695**

DETROIT LAWYER, THE (US/0011-9652) [06715421] **2960**

DETROIT LEGAL NEWS (DAILY ED.) (US/0739-9480) [09973069] **2960**

DETROIT MARINE HISTORIAN (US) [01566332] **5448**

DETROIT MEDICAL NEWS (US/0098-471X) [01469988] **3571**

DETROIT METRO TIMES *See* METRO TIMES (DETROIT, MICH.), THE **5692**

DETROIT METROPOLITAN AREA REGIONAL PLANNING COMMISSION *See* SHOPPING CENTERS IN THE DETROIT REGION **2835**

DETROIT. METROPOLITAN AREA REGIONAL PLANNING COMMISSION *See* REPORT - DETROIT. METROPOLITAN AREA REGIONAL PLANNING COMMISSION **307**

DETROIT. METROPOLITAN AREA REGIONAL PLANNING COMMISSION *See* URBAN ENVIRONMENT STUDY; PUBLICATION **2183**

DETROIT (MICH.). CITY PLANNING COMMISSION *See* BI-ANNUAL REPORT / DETROIT CITY PLANNING COMMISSION **2816**

DETROIT (MICH.) HUMAN RIGHTS DEPT *See* ANNUAL REPORT - CITY OF DETROIT, HUMAN RIGHTS DEPT **4504**

DETROIT MONOGRAPHS IN MUSICOLOGY (US) [01698617] **4114**

DETROIT MONTHLY (US/0888-0867) [13066827] **2532**

DETROIT NEWS (DETROIT, MICH.), THE (US/1055-2715) [09611687] **5691**

DETROIT NEWS INDEX, THE (US/0893-2433) [15559375] 5691, **5814**

DETROIT. PUBLIC LIBRARY. MUNICIPAL REFERENCE LIBRARY *See* MRL BULLETIN **3232**

DETROIT STUDIES IN MUSIC BIBLIOGRAPHY (US/0070-3885) [01566335] 4114, **4160**

DETROITER, THE (US/0011-9709) [05323528] **819**

●DETROIT'S LABOR MARKET NEWS (US) [25953384] **1662**

DETSKAIA LITERATURA (RU/0418-7946) [04880202] 1062, **3380**

DETSKAYA LITERATURA (RU) **3380**

●DETWILER DIRECTORY OF MEDICAL MARKET SOURCES, THE (US/1058-2797) [24252214] **3571**

DEUDA EXTERNA LATINOAMERICANA : CUADERNOS (PE) [25691635] **2908**

DEUKALION : PERIODIKE EKDOSE TOU KENTROU PHILOSOPHIKON EREUNON (GR) [04658500] **4344**

DEUS LOCI *SUSPENDED.* (CN/0707-9141) [08415773] **3380**

DEUTSCH ALS FREMDSPRACHE (GW/0011-9741) [01566337] **3276**

DEUTSCH-AMERIKANISCHE GESCHAFTSBEZIEHUNGEN (GW/0932-2973) [16502133] **665**

DEUTSCH BAUERN-KORRESPOONDENZ (GW/0343-3846) [07085547] **78**

DEUTSCH - BRASILIANISCHE HEFTE. CADERNOS GERMANO - BRASILEIROS (GW) [04659323] **2551**

DEUTSCH-CHINESISCHES FORUM (GW) **1634**

DEUTSCH-SLAWISCHE FORSCHUNGEN ZUR NAMENKUNDE UND SIEDLUNGSGESCHICHTE (GW/0070-3893) [01566340] **3276**

DEUTSCHAMERIKANER (CHICAGO), DER (US/0273-5261) [05522616] **2532**

DEUTSCHE AKADEMIE DER LANDWIRTSCHAFTSWISSENSCHAFTEN *See* ARCHIV FUER ZUCHTUNGSFORSCHUNG **5085**

DEUTSCHE AKADEMIE DER LANDWIRTSCHAFTSWISSENSCHAFTEN *See* WISSENSCHAFTLICHE ABHANDLUNGEN **146**

DEUTSCHE AKADEMIE DER LANDWIRTSCHAFTSWISSENSCHAFTEN, BERLIN *See* GRUNDLAGEN ZUR PFLANZENQUARANTAENE **173**

DEUTSCHE AKADEMIE DER LANDWIRTSCHAFTSWISSENSCHAFTEN, BERLIN STITUT FUR TIERZUCHTFORSCHUNG DUMMERSTORF *See* JAHRESBERICHT **98**

DEUTSCHE AKADEMIE DER LANDWIRTSCHAFTSWISSENSCHAFTEN ZU BERLIN *See* FELDWIRTSCHAFT **86**

DEUTSCHE AKADEMIE FUER SPRACHE UND DICHTUNG *See* JAHRBUCH - DEUTSCHE AKADEMIE FUER SPRACHE UND DICHTUNG (DARMSTADT) **3398**

DEUTSCHE AKADEMIE FUR STADTEBAU UND LANDESPLANUNG *See* SCHRIFTENREIHE **2835**

DEUTSCHE AKADEMIE FUR STADTEBAU UND LANDESPLANUNG *See* MITTEILUNGEN - DEUTSCHE AKADEMIE FUER STADTEBAU UND LANDESPLANUNG **2828**

DEUTSCHE ANNALEN (GW) [01785034] **432**

DEUTSCHE APOTHEKER, DER (GW/0366-8622) [03683387] **4299**

DEUTSCHE APOTHEKER-ZEITUNG (GW/0011-9857) [I00119857] **4299**

DEUTSCHE APOTHEKER-ZEITUNG, VEREINIGT MIT SUDDEUTSCHE APOTHEKER-ZEITUNG (GW) [01721937] **4299**

DEUTSCHE ARCHITEKTUR (GE/0011-9865) [04870314] **311**

DEUTSCHE AUSGLEICHSBANK *See* DEUTSCHE AUSGLEICHSBANK **787**

DEUTSCHE AUSGLEICHSBANK (GW/0931-2471) [16826175] **787**

DEUTSCHE AUSSENPOLITIK (GW/0011-9881) [02260335] **4519**

DEUTSCHE BACKERZEITUNG (GW/0046-0117) [I00460117] **2333**

DEUTSCHE-BANK-BULLETIN ENGLISCHE AUSGABE (GW/0722-3250) [08874090] **787**

DEUTSCHE BAUMSCHULE (GW/0011-992X) [02446361] 2378, **2413**

DEUTSCHE BIBLIOGRAPHIE : MUSIKALIEN-VERZEICHNIS (GW) [03346402] **4160**

DEUTSCHE BIBLIOGRAPHIE. ZEITSCHRIFTEN-VERZEICHNIS (GW/0170-1002) [01570072] **414**

DEUTSCHE BIBLIOTHEK (GW) [01724433] **3206**

DEUTSCHE BODENKUNDLICHE GESELLSCHAFT *See* MITTEILUNGEN DER DEUTSCHEN BODENKUNDLICHE GESELLSCHAFT **178**

DEUTSCHE BOERSE *See* ANNUAL REPORT **891**

DEUTSCHE BRIEFMARKEN REVUE / SD SAMMLER DIENST (GW) **2785**

DEUTSCHE BUCHER (NE) [04157481] **4828**

DEUTSCHE BUHNE, DIE (GW) [04254291] **5363**

DEUTSCHE BUNDESBAHN *See* KURSBUCH - DEUTSCHE BUNDESBAHN **5432**

DEUTSCHE BUNDESBANK *See* STATISTISCHE BEIHEFTE ZU DEN MONATSBERICHTEN DER DEUTSCHEN BUNDESBANK. REIHE 5, DIE WAHRUNGEN DER WELT **813**

DEUTSCHE BUNDESBANK *See* REPORT OF THE DEUTSCHE BUNDESBANK FOR THE YEAR **808**

DEUTSCHE BUNDESBANK *See* STATISTISCHE BEIHEFTE ZU DEN MONATSBERICHTEN DER DEUTSCHEN BUNDESBANK. REIHE 1 : BANKENSTATISTIK NACH BANKENGRUPPEN **734**

DEUTSCHE BUNDESBANK *See* STATISTISCHE BEIHEFTE ZU DEN MONATSBERICHTEN DER DEUTSCHEN BUNDESBANK. REIHE 2 : WERTPAPIERSTATISTIK **1539**

DEUTSCHE BUNDESBANK *See* STATISTISCHE BEIHEFTE ZU DEN MONATSBERICHTEN DER DEUTSCHEN BUNDESBANK. REIHE 4 : SAISONBEREINIGTE WIRTSCHAFTSZAHLEN **1539**

DEUTSCHE BUNDESBANK *See* STATISTISCHE BEIHEFTE ZU DEN MONATSBERICHTEN DER DEUTSCHEN BUNDESBANK. REIHE 3 : ZAHLUNGSBILANZSTATISTIK **5343**

DEUTSCHE BUNSENGESELLSCHAFT FUR PHYSIKALISCHE CHEMIC *See* BERICHTE DER BUNSENGESELLSCHAFT FUER PHYSIKALISCHE CHEMIE **1050**

DEUTSCHE DROGISTEN ZEITUNG (GW) [03992913] **4299**

DEUTSCHE ENTOMOLOGISCHE ZEITSCHRIFT (GW/0012-0073) [01591757] **5607**

DEUTSCHE FORSCHUNGS- UND VERSUCHSANSTALT FUR LUFT- UND RAUMFAHRT. BEREICH WISSENSCHAFTLICH-TECHNISCHE BETRIEBSEINRICHTUNGEN *See* WISSENSCHAFTLICH-TECHNISCHER BERICHT / BEREICH WISSENSCHAFTLICH-TECHNISCHE BETRIEBSEINRICHTUNGEN **40**

DEUTSCHE FORSCHUNGSGEMEINSCHAFT *See* JAHRESBERICHT. BD. 2, PROGRAMME UND PROJEKTE **5232**

DEUTSCHE FORSCHUNGSGEMEINSCHAFT (1951-) *See* MEXIKO-PROJEKT DER DEUTSCHEN FORSCHUNGSGEMEINSCHAFT, DAS **2746**

DEUTSCHE FORSCHUNGSGEMEINSCHAFT (FOUNDED 1949). SENATSKOMMISSION FUER HUMANISMUS-FORSCHUNG *See* VEROFFENTLICHUNGEN DER SENATSKOMMISSION FUER HUMANISMUS-FORSCHUNG **2714**

DEUTSCHE FORSCHUNGSGEMEINSCHAFT. KOMMISSION FUR GEOWISSENSCHAFTLICHE GEMEINSCHAFTSFORSCHUNG *See* GEOWISSENSCHAFTEN (BOPPARD) **1381**

DEUTSCHE GARTNERPOST (GW/0940-2454) [25181419] **2413**

DEUTSCHE GEMMOLOGISCHE GESELLSCHAFT *See* ZEITSCHRIFT DER DEUTSCHEN GEMMOLOGISCHEN GESELLSCHAFT **2915**

DEUTSCHE GENOSSENSCHAFTSKASSE *See* BERICHT - DEUTSCHE GENOSSENSCHAFTSKASSE **1464**

DEUTSCHE GEOLOGISCHE GESELLSCHAFT *See* ZEITSCHRIFT DER DEUTSCHEN GEOLOGISCHEN GESELLSCHAFT **1401**

DEUTSCHE GESELLSCHAFT FUER AUSWAERTIGE POLITIK *See* JAHRESBERICHT - DEUTSCHE GESELLSCHAFT FUER AUSWAERTIGE POLITIK **4526**

DEUTSCHE GESELLSCHAFT FUER VOLKSKUNDE *See* DGV INFORMATIONEN **2319**

DEUTSCHE GESELLSCHAFT FUR CHIRURGIE. KONGRESS *See* LANGENBECKS ARCHIV FEUR CHIRURGIE. SUPPLEMENT. KONGRESSBAND **3969**

DEUTSCHE GESELLSCHAFT FUR ERNAHRUNG *See* ERNAHRUNGSBERICHT **4190**

DEUTSCHE GESELLSCHAFT FUR HERPETOLOGIE UND TERRARIENKUNDE *See* STADTGRUPPEN- UND MITGLIEDERVERZEICHNIS / DEUTSCHE GESELLSCHAFT FUER HERPETOLOGIE UND TERRARIENKUNDE E.V., DGHT **2523**

DEUTSCHE GESELLSCHAFT FUR HERPETOLOGIE UND TERRARIENKUNDE *See* MITGLIEDER-VERZEICHNIS MIT UBERSICHT DER ARBEITS-, LANDES-, REGIONAL- UND STADTGRUPPEN / DEUTSCHE GESELLSCHAFT FUER HERPETOLOGIE UND TERRARIENKUNDE E.V **3617**

DEUTSCHE GESELLSCHAFT FUR HERPETOLOGIE UND TERRARIENKUNDE. STADTGRUPPEN- UND MITGLIEDERVERZEICHNIS *See* MITGLIEDER-VERZEICHNIS MIT UBERSICHT DER ARBEITS-, LANDES-, REGIONAL- UND STADTGRUPPEN / DEUTSCHE GESELLSCHAFT FUER HERPETOLOGIE UND TERRARIENKUNDE E.V **3617**

DEUTSCHE

DEUTSCHE GESELLSCHAFT FUR INNERE MEDIZIN See MITGLIEDER DER DEUTSCHEN GESELLSCHAFT FUR INNERE MEDIZIN **3617**

DEUTSCHE GESELLSCHAFT FUR LASERMEDIZIN. TAGUNG See VERHANDLUNGSBERICHT DER DEUTSCHEN GESELLSCHAFT FUR LASERMEDIZIN E.V. / ... TAGUNG **3649**

DEUTSCHE GESELLSCHAFT FUR LUFT- UND RAUMFAHRT See JAHRBUCH. DEUTSCHE GESELLSCHAFT FUER LUFT- UND RAUMFAHRT **25**

DEUTSCHE GESELLSCHAFT FUR MINERALOLWISSENSCHAFT UND KOHLECHEMIE See COMPENDIUM - DEUTSCHE GESELLSCHAFT FUER MINERALOLWISSENSCHAFT UND KOHLECHEMIE E.V **4253**

DEUTSCHE GESELLSCHAFT FUR MUSIK DES ORIENTS See MITTEILUNGEN DER DEUTSCHEN GESELLSCHAFT FUER MUSIK DES ORIENTS **4131**

DEUTSCHE GESELLSCHAFT FUR RHEUMATOLOGIE See VERHANDLUNGEN DER DEUTSCHEN GESELLSCHAFT FUER RHEUMATOLOGIE **3807**

DEUTSCHE GESELLSCHAFT FUR VOLKSKUNDE. KOMMISSION FUR OSTDEUTSCHE VOLKSKUNDE See SCHRIFTENREIHE - DEUTSCHE GESELLSCHAFT FUR VOLKSKUNDE. KOMMISSION FUR OSTDEUTSCHE VOLKSKUNDE **2324**

DEUTSCHE GEWAESSERKUNDLICHE MITTEILUNGEN (GW/0012-0235) [01633497] **5532**

DEUTSCHE HEBE- UND FORDERTECHNIK (GW/0012-0278) [02446372] **5099**

DEUTSCHE HUGENOTT, DER (GW/0012-0294) [04301511] **5059**

DEUTSCHE HYDROGRAPHISCHE ZEITSCHRIFT (GW/0012-0308) [01633636] **1354**

DEUTSCHE INGENIEURSCHULE See NEUE HOCHSCHULE, DIE **1914**

DEUTSCHE JUGEND (GW/0012-0332) [05199530] **5282**

DEUTSCHE KATHOLIK IN KANADA, DER (CN/0381-8950) [02585407] **5028**

DEUTSCHE KERAMISCHE GESELLSCHAFT See SONDERHEFT - DEUTSCHE KERAMISCHE GESELLSCHAFT **2594**

DEUTSCHE KINOTECHNISCHE GESELLSCHAFT See FILM UND FARBE **4070**

DEUTSCHE KRANKENPFLEGEZEITSCHRIFT (GW/0012-074X) [08716132] **3855**

DEUTSCHE KUNST UND DENKMALPFLEGE (GW/0012-0375) [04069726] 349, **297**

DEUTSCHE LEBENSMITTEL-EINZELHANDEL IM SPIEGEL DER STATISTIK, DER (GW/0720-1206) [I07201206] **2333**

DEUTSCHE LEBENSMITTEL-RUNDSCHAU (GW/0012-0413) [03683245] 1023, **2333**

DEUTSCHE LEHRER IM AUSLAND (GW/0418-8802) [04895358] **3276**

DEUTSCHE LEHRERZEITUNG (SZ) [06095880] **1735**

DEUTSCHE LITERATURZEITUNG CEASED. (GE/0012-043X) [01566414] **3380**

DEUTSCHE LUFTHANSA (1953-) See CALENDAR OF EVENTS. TRADE FAIRS AND EXHIBITIONS **5092**

DEUTSCHE LUFTHANSA (1953-) See GESCHAFTSBERICHT / DEUTSCHE LUFTHANSA AKTIENGESELLSCHAFT **22**

DEUTSCHE LUFTHANSA (1953-). JAHRESBERICHT See GESCHAFTSBERICHT / DEUTSCHE LUFTHANSA AKTIENGESELLSCHAFT **22**

DEUTSCHE MALERBLATT, DAS (GW/0012-0448) [11603354] **4223**

DEUTSCHE MATHEMATIKER-VEREINIGUNG See JAHRESBERICHT DER DEUTSCHEN MATHEMATIKER-VEREINIGUNG **3511**

DEUTSCHE MEDIZIN (GW/0178-3351) **3571**

DEUTSCHE MEDIZINISCHE WOCHENSCHRIFT (GW/0012-0472) [01566417] **3571**

DEUTSCHE MILCHWIRTSCHAFT (HILDESHEIM) (GW/0012-0480) [04687561] **194**

DEUTSCHE MONATSHEFTE (BERG (STARNBERG, GERMANY) : 1982) (GW/0023-2211) [08842526] **2515**

DEUTSCHE MORGENLANDISCHE GESELLSCHAFT See ABHANDLUNGEN FUER DIE KUNDE DES MORGENLANDES / HRSG. VON DER DEUTSCHEN MORGENLANDISCHEN GESELLSCHAFT **3260**

DEUTSCHE MUSIKBIBLIOGRAPHIE CEASED. (GE/0012-0502) [01566427] **4114**

DEUTSCHE NATION IN GESCHICHTE UND GEGENWART See DEUTSCHLAND IN GESCHICHTE UND GEGENWART **2685**

●DEUTSCHE NATIONALBIBLIOGRAPHIE UND BIBLIOGRAPHIE DER IM AUSLAND ERSCHIENEN DEUTSCHSPRACHIGEN VEROFFENTLICHUNGEN. REIHE T, MUSIKTONTRAGER MONATLICHES VERZEICHNIS (GW/0939-0642) [23575867] **4114**

DEUTSCHE NATIONALBIBLIOGRAPHIE UND BIBLIOGRAPHIE DER IM AUSLAND ERSCHIENEN DEUTSCHSPRACHIGEN VEROFFENTLICHUNGEN (GW/0939-0588) [23459934] **414**

DEUTSCHE NATIONALBIBLIOGRAPHIE UND BIBLIOGRAPHIE DER IM AUSLAND ERSCHIENEN DEUTSCHSPRACHIGEN VEROFFENTLICHUNGEN. MONOGRAPHIEN UND PERIODIKA DES VERLAGSBUCHHANDELS UND AUSSERHALB DES VERLAGSBUCHHANDELS. WOCHENTLICHES VERZEICHNIS. WOCHENREGISTER ZU REIHE A UND REIHE B / BEARBEITER UND HERAUSGEBER, DIE DEUTSCHE BIBLIOTHEK (GW/0939-0480) [23284960] **414**

DEUTSCHE NATIONALBIBLIOGRAPHIE UND BIBLIOGRAPHIE DER IM AUSLAND ERSCHIENEN DEUTSCHSPRACHIGEN VEROFFENTLICHUNGEN. REIHE B, MONOGRAPHIEN UND PERIODIKA AUSSERHALB DES VERLAGSBUCHHANDELS. WOCHENTLICHES VERZEICHNIS / BEARBEITER UND HERAUSGEBER, DIE DEUTSCHE BIBLIOTHEK (GW/0939-043X) [23132331] **414**

DEUTSCHE NATIONALBIBLIOGRAPHIE UND BIBLIOGRAPHIE DER IM AUSLAND ERSCHIENEN DEUTSCHSPRACHIGEN VEROFFENTLICHUNGEN. REIHE C, KARTEN, VIERTELJAHRLICHES VERZEICHNIS / BEARBEITER UND HERAUSGEBER, DIE DEUTSCHE BIBLIOTHEK (GW/0939-0553) [23853403] **4813**

DEUTSCHE NATIONALBIBLIOGRAPHIE UND BIBLIOGRAPHIE DER IM AUSLAND ERSCHIENENEN DEUTSCHSPRACHIGEN VEROFFENTLICHUNGEN. REIHE D, MONOGRAPHIEN UND PERIODIKA -- HALBJAHRESVERZEICHNIS (GW/0940-2721) [25469604] **4813**

DEUTSCHE NATIONALBIBLIOGRAPHIE UND BIBLIOGRAPHIE DER IM AUSLAND ERSCHIENENEN DEUTSCHSPRACHIGEN VEROFFENTLICHUNGEN. REIHE E, MONOGRAPHIEN UND PERIODIKA -- FUNFJAHRESVERZEICHNIS / BEARBEITER UND HERAUSGEBER: DIE DEUTSCHE BIBLIOTHEK (GW/0942-4318) [27307480] **414**

DEUTSCHE NATIONALBIBLIOGRAPHIE UND BIBLIOGRAPHIE DER IM AUSLAND ERSCHIENENEN DEUTSCHSPRACHIGEN VEROFFENTLICHUNGEN. REIHE N, VORANKUNDIGUNGEN MONOGRAPHIEN UND PERIODIKA (CIP). WOCHENTLICHES VERZEICHNIS / BEARBEITER UND HERAUSGEBER, DIE DEUTSCHE BIBLIOTHEK (GW/0939-0634) [23361432] **414**

DEUTSCHE NATIONALBIBLIOGRAPHIE UND BIBLIOGRAPHIE DES IM AUSLAND ERSCHIENENEN DEUTSCHSPRACHIGEN VEROFFENTLICHUNGEN. REIGE A. ESCHIENENE (GW/0939-0421) [23132339] **414**

DEUTSCHE NATIONALBIBLIOGRAPHIE WOECHENTLICHES VERZEICHNIS NORMALAUSGABE. AUSGABE I (GW) **414**

DEUTSCHE NEUDRUCKE. REIHE: BAROCK (GW/0418-8926) [01931835] **3380**

DEUTSCHE NEUDRUCKE. REIHE: TEXTE DES 19. JAHRHUNDERT (GW/0418-8950) [05013952] **3380**

DEUTSCHE OPTIKERZEITUNG (GW/0344-7103) [04263116] 4215, **3874**

DEUTSCHE ORIENT-GESELLSCHAFT See MITGLIEDER-VERZEICHNIS / DEUTSCHE ORIENT-GESELLSCHAFT **2659**

DEUTSCHE ORIENT-GESELLSCHAFT See ABHANDLUNGEN DER DEUTSCHEN ORIENT-GESELLSCHAFT **253**

DEUTSCHE ORIENT-GESELLSCHAFT See MITTEILUNGEN DER DEUTSCHEN ORIENT-GESELLSCHAFT ZU BERLIN **2659**

DEUTSCHE PELZTIERZUCHTER, DER CEASED. (GW/0012-0553) [03996583] **5581**

DEUTSCHE POLIZEI (GW/0012-057X) [04692789] **3163**

DEUTSCHE PRESSE (TORONTO. GERMAN ED.) (CN/0839-2676) [24256993] **5783**

DEUTSCHE RECHTSPRECHUNG AUF DEM GEBIETE DES INTERNATIONALEN PRIVATRECHTS, DIE (GW) [01566439] **3127**

DEUTSCHE REICHBAHN (EAST GERMANY) See KURSBUCH: INTERNATIONALER + I.E. UND BINNENVERKEHR **5432**

DEUTSCHE REIHE FUR AUSLANDER. REIHE C : ERGANZUNGSHEFTE ZU GRAMMATISCHEN FRAGEN (GW/0418-8993) [04996396] **3276**

DEUTSCHE RENTENVERSICHERUNG (GW/0012-0618) [10130061] **2878**

DEUTSCHE RICHTERZEITUNG (GW) [01566442] **2960**

DEUTSCHE SCHACHZEITUNG / ORGAN FUR DAS GESAMMTE SCHACHLEBEN (GW/0012-0669) [04038215] **4860**

DEUTSCHE SCHILLERGESELLSCHAFT See JAHRBUCH DER DEUTSCHEN SCHILLERGESELLSCHAFT **3398**

DEUTSCHE SCHRIFT, DIE (GW) [02514313] **3276**

DEUTSCHE SCHULE, DIE (GW/0012-0731) [00120731] **1735**

DEUTSCHE SCHWARZBUNTE (GW/0343-3145) [03473803] **210**

DEUTSCHE SHAKESPEARE-GESELLSCHAFT WEST See JAHRBUCH - DEUTSCHE SHAKESPEARE-GESELLSCHAFT WEST **3398**

DEUTSCHE SPORTHOCHSCHULE KOLN See FORSCHUNGSBERICHT / DEUTSCHE SPORTHOCHSCHULE KOLN **4872**

DEUTSCHE SPRACHE (GW/0340-9341) [01798326] **3276**

DEUTSCHE SPRACHE IN EUROPA UND UBERSEE (GW/0170-3153) [04996946] **3276**

DEUTSCHE STEUER-ZEITUNG (GW/0724-5637) [06609507] **4720**

DEUTSCHE STIFTUNG FUR INTERNATIONALE ENTWICKLUNG See DOKUMENT - DEUTSCHE STIFTUNG FUR INTERNATIONALE ENTWICKLUNG **1555**

DEUTSCHE STOMATOLOGIE CEASED. (GW/0863-4904) [22926366] **1322**

DEUTSCHE STUDIEN (SCHLOSS BLECKEDE) (GW/0012-0812) [01566451] **2515**

DEUTSCHE TEXTE DES MITTELALTERS (GW/0070-4334) [01566453] **3380**

DEUTSCHE UBERSEEISCHE BANK, HAMBURG See WIRTSCHAFTSBERICHT UBER DIE LATEINAMERIKANISCHEN LAENDER SOWIE SPANIEN UND PORTUGAL **1589**

DEUTSCHE UNIVERSITATSZEITUNG (GW) [01647154] **1820**

DEUTSCHE UNIVERSITATSZEITUNG VEREINIGT MIT HOCHSCHUL-DIENST BONN, DIE (GW/0012-088X) [01647216] **5801**

DEUTSCHE VIERTELJAHRSSCHRIFT FUER LITERATURWISSENSCHAFT UND GEISTESGESCHICHTE (GW/0012-0936) [01777481] **3380**

DEUTSCHE VOLKS-ZEITUNG (FR) [21009722] **5800**

DEUTSCHE WAHLERGESELLSCHAFT See SCHRIFTEN **4495**

DEUTSCHE WEINBAU (GW/0012-0979) [04687937] **2366**

DEUTSCHE WEINBAU, DER (GW) [04708591] **2366**

DEUTSCHE WOCHEN-ZEITUNG (GW) [01793175] **2515**

DEUTSCHE ZAHN-, MUND-, UND KIEFERHEILKUNDE MIT ZENTRALBLATT (GW/0940-855X) [24097673] **1322**

DEUTSCHE ZAHNAERZTLICHE ZEITSCHRIFT (GW/0012-1029) [04974109] **1322**

DEUTSCHE ZEITSCHRIFT FUER AKUPUNKTUR : DZA (GW) [11472194] **3571**

DEUTSCHE ZEITSCHRIFT FUER BIOLOGISCHE VETERINAR-MEDIZIN (GW/0179-714X) [16750682] **5508**

DEUTSCHE ZEITSCHRIFT FUER BIOLOGISCHE ZAHNMEDIZIN : BZM (GW) [27143449] **1322**

DEUTSCHE
Alphabetical Title Index

DEUTSCHE ZEITSCHRIFT FUER MUND-, KIEFER- UND GESICHTS-CHIRURGIE (GW/0343-3137) [05423442] **3963**

DEUTSCHE ZEITSCHRIFT FUER ONKOLOGIE (GW/0931-0037) [21080575] **3816**

DEUTSCHE ZEITSCHRIFT FUER PHILOSOPHIE (GW/0012-1045) [01566472] **4344**

DEUTSCHE ZEITSCHRIFT FUER SPORTMEDIZIN (GW/0344-5925) [04218956] 1855, **3954**

DEUTSCHE ZEITSCHRIFT FUER WIRTSCHAFTSRECHT (GW/0940-1555) [26347244] **2960**

DEUTSCHE ZOOLOGISCHE GESELLSCHAFT *See* VERHANDLUNGEN DER DEUTSCHEN ZOOLOGISCHEN GESELLSCHAFT **5599**

DEUTSCHE ZUCKERRUEBENZEITUNG (GW) **194**

DEUTSCHER BIBLIOTHEKSVERBAND (GERMAN : WEST). ARBEITSSTELLE FUR DAS BIBLIOTHEKSWESEN *See* ARBEITSBERICHT - ARBEITSSTELLE FUR DAS BIBLIOTHEKSWESEN **3191**

DEUTSCHER BIBLIOTHEKSVERBAND (GERMANY : WEST). ARBEITSSTELLE FUR DAS BIBLIOTHEKSWESEN *See* STATISTIK DER KOMMUNALEN OFFENTLICHEN BIBLIOTHEKEN DER BUNDESREPUBLIK, REGIONALSTATISTIK **3260**

DEUTSCHER BUCHEREIVERBAND. ARBEITSSTELLE FUR DAS BUCHEREIWESEN *See* ZEITSCHRIFTENDIENST **3257**

DEUTSCHER DRUCKER STUTTGART (GW/0012-1096) [I00121096] **4233**

DEUTSCHER ENTWICKLUNGSDIENST *See* DED BRIEF **2908**

DEUTSCHER FACHHOCHSCHULFUHRER (GW) [01787705] **1912**

DEUTSCHER FORSCHUNGSDIENST. GERMAN RESEARCH SERVICE (GW/0722-0839) [07165638] **5099**

DEUTSCHER FORSCHUNGSDIENST. GERMAN RESEARCH SERVICE. SPECIAL SCIENCE REPORTS (GW/0933-7814) [I09337814] **5099**

DEUTSCHER GARTENBAU (GW) [05001952] **2413**

DEUTSCHER GEOGRAPHENTAG *See* VERHANDLUNGEN DES DEUTSCHEN GEOGRAPHENTAGES **2578**

DEUTSCHER GERMANISTENVERBAND *See* MITTEILUNGEN DES DEUTSCHEN GERMANISTENVERBANDES **1764**

DEUTSCHER INDUSTRIE- UND HANDELSTAG *See* BERICHT - DEUTSCHER INDUSTRIE- UND HANDELSTAG **1599**

DEUTSCHER INDUSTRIE- UND HANDELSTAG. TATIGKEITSBERICHT *See* BERICHT - DEUTSCHER INDUSTRIE- UND HANDELSTAG **1599**

DEUTSCHER KURIER (GW) [01785740] **4471**

DEUTSCHER KUSTEN-ALMANACH (GW) [02242733] **395**

DEUTSCHER MUSIKRAT *See* MUSIKFORUM : REFERATE UND INFORMATIONEN DES DEUTSCHEN MUSIKRATES **4138**

DEUTSCHER STADTE-UND GEMEINDEBUND *See* SCHRIFTENREIHE DES DEUTSCHEN STADTE- UND GEMEINDEBUNDES **4685**

DEUTSCHER VERBAND FUR WOHNUNGSWESEN, STADTEBAU UND RAUMPLANUNG *See* DV MITTEILUNGEN **2821**

DEUTSCHER VEREIN FUER OFFENTLICHE AND PRIVATE FURSORGE *See* NACHRICHTENDIENST **5297**

DEUTSCHER VEREIN ZUR ERFORSCHUNG PALASTINAS *See* ZEITSCHRIFT DES DEUTSCHEN PALASTINA-VEREINS (1953) **2634**

DEUTSCHER WETTERDIENST *See* BERICHTE DES DEUTSCHEN WETTERDIENST **1420**

DEUTSCHES ADELSBLATT (GW/0012-1193) [07496120] **2445**

DEUTSCHES ALLGEMEINES SONNTAGSBLATT (GW) [06229461] **5801**

DEUTSCHES ARCHAOLOGISCHES INSTITUT *See* VERZEICHNIS DER MITGLIEDER / DEUTSCHES ARCHAOLOGISCHES INSTITUT **285**

DEUTSCHES ARCHAOLOGISCHES INSTITUT. ABTEILUNG KAIRO *See* ABHANDLUNGEN. KOPTISCHE REIHE **253**

DEUTSCHES ARCHAOLOGISCHES INSTITUT. ABTEILUNG KAIRO *See* MITTEILUNGEN DES DEUTSCHEN ARCHAOLOGISCHEN INSTITUTS **275**

DEUTSCHES ARCHAOLOGISCHES INSTITUT. ABTEILUNG KAIRO *See* ABHANDLUNGEN. ISLAMISCHE REIHE **253**

DEUTSCHES ARCHAOLOGISCHES INSTITUT. ATHENISCHE ABTEILUNG *See* MITTEILUNGEN DES DEUTSCHEN ARCHAOLOGISCHEN INSTITUTS, ATHENISCHE ABTEILUNG **275**

DEUTSCHES ARCHAOLOGISCHES INSTITUT. ROMISCH-GERMANISCHE KOMMISSION *See* GERMANISCHE DENKMALER DER VOLKERWANDERUNGSZEIT. SERIES B. DIE FRANKISCHEN ALTERTUMER DES RHEINLANDES **269**

DEUTSCHES ARCHAOLOGISCHES INSTITUT. ROMISCH-GERMANISCHE KOMMISSION *See* BERICHT DER ROMISCH-GERMANISCHEN KOMMISSION **261**

DEUTSCHES ARCHAOLOGISCHES INSTITUT. ROMISCHE ABTEILUNG *See* MITTEILUNGEN DES DEUTSCHEN ARCHAEOLOGISCHEN INSTITUTS, ROEMISCHE ABTEILUNG **275**

DEUTSCHES ARCHITEKTENBLATT. AUSGABE BADEN-WURTTEMBERG (GW/0012-1215) [04678477] 612, **297**

DEUTSCHES ARCHIV FUER ERFORSCHUNG DES MITTELALTERS (GW/0012-1223) [01566509] **2685**

DEUTSCHES ARZTEBLATT (GW/0012-1207) [01777947] **3571**

DEUTSCHES ARZTEBLATT AUSG. C (GW/0176-3695) [I01763695] **3571**

DEUTSCHES BIBLIOTHEKSADRESSBUCH (GW) [03518902] **3206**

●DEUTSCHES BIENEN JOURNAL (GW/0943-2914) [27704883] **78**

DEUTSCHES BUNDES-ADRESSBUCH BEZUGSQUELLENTEIL *See* EINKAUFS-1X1 DER DEUTSCHEN INDUSTRIE **832**

DEUTSCHES BUNDES-ADRESSBUCH. BUND, LANDER UND GEMEINDEN (GW) [13113147] **665**

DEUTSCHES BUNDES-ADRESSBUCH. INDUSTRIE, GROSS UND AUSSENHANDEL, DIENSTLEISTUNGEN, ORGANISATIONEN *See* DEUTSCHES BUNDES-ADRESSBUCH. BUND, LANDER UND GEMEINDEN **665**

DEUTSCHES BUNDESBAHN-ADRESSBUCH. TEIL 2 : GLEISANSCHLUSSBESITZER UND-MITBENUTZER (GW) [03383759] **5431**

DEUTSCHES DANTE - JAHRBUCH (GW/0070-444X) [01067784] **3380**

DEUTSCHES GEWASSERKUNDLICHES JAHRBUCH. RHEINGEBIET *See* DEUTSCHES GEWASSERKUNDLICHES JAHRBUCH. RHEINGEBIET. TEIL III, MITTEL- UND NIEDERRHEIN MIT IJSSELGEBIET **5532**

DEUTSCHES GEWASSERKUNDLICHES JAHRBUCH. RHEINGEBIET. TEIL III, MITTEL- UND NIEDERRHEIN MIT IJSSELGEBIET (GW/0170-9976) [12235066] **5532**

DEUTSCHES HISTORISCHES INSTITUT, LONDON *See* VEROFFENTLICHUNGEN DES DEUTSCHEN HISTORISCHEN INSTITUTS IN LONDON **2714**

DEUTSCHES HUDROGRAPHISCHES INSTITUT *See* JACHTFUNKDIENST MITTELMEER FUR NICHTAUSRUSTUNGSPFLICHTIGE SCHIFFE **4177**

DEUTSCHES HYDROGRAPHISCHES INSTITUT *See* JACHTFUNKDIENST NORD- UND OSTSEE FUR NICHTAUSRUSTUNGSPFLICHTIGE SCHIFFE **4177**

DEUTSCHES IMKER JOURNAL *See* DEUTSCHES BIENEN JOURNAL **78**

DEUTSCHES INDUSTRIEINSTITUT, COLOGNE *See* KONZERTIERTE AKTION; BERICHT UEBER DIE ERFAHRUNGEN SEIT IHREM BESTEHEN **1502**

DEUTSCHES INDUSTRIEINSTITUT, COLOGNE. KONZERTIERTE AKTION; BERICHT UEBER DIE ERFAHRUNGEN SEIT IHREM BESTEHEN *See* KONZERTIERTE AKTION; BERICHT UEBER DIE ERFAHRUNGEN SEIT IHREM BESTEHEN **1502**

DEUTSCHES INSTITUT FUR INTERNATIONALE PADGOGISCHE FORSCHUNG *See* BERICHT - DEUTSCHES INSTITUT FUR INTERNATIONALE PADAGOGISCHE FORSCHUNG **1889**

DEUTSCHES INSTITUT FUR WIRTSCHAFTSFORSCHUNG *See* WOCHENBERICHT - DEUTSCHES INSTITUT FUER WIRTSCHAFTSFORSCHUNG **1589**

DEUTSCHES LITERATUR LEXIKON (SZ) **3381**

DEUTSCHES METEOROLOGISCHES JAHRBUCH, BUNDESREPUBLIK (GW/0417-3562) [05072999] **1425**

DEUTSCHES METEOROLOGISCHES JAHRBUCH, BUNDESREPUBLIK DEUTSCHLAND (GW/0724-7125) [10096773] **1425**

DEUTSCHES MOZARTFEST DER DEUTSCHEN MOZART-GESELLSCHAFT (GW/0418-8896) [03864682] **4114**

DEUTSCHES MUNZPREIS-JAHRBUCH (GW) [04289382] **2781**

DEUTSCHES RECHT (GW) [19737632] **2960**

DEUTSCHES ROTES KREUZ DER DEUTSCHEN DEMOKRATISCHEN REPUBLIK (SZ) [04306391] **5282**

DEUTSCHES SCHIFFAHRTSARCHIV (GW) [05313365] **5448**

DEUTSCHES SPORTECHO AUSGABE A (GW/0323-8628) [I03238628] **4892**

DEUTSCHES SPORTECHO AUSGABE B (GW/0232-4814) [I02324814] **4892**

DEUTSCHES SPRACHARCHIV *See* MONUMENTA GERMANIAE ACUSTICA **3304**

DEUTSCHES STEUERRECHT (GW/0012-1347) [I00121347] 2960, **4720**

DEUTSCHES TIERARZTEBLATT (GW/0340-1898) [03115196] **5508**

DEUTSCHES VERWALTUNGSBLATT (GW/0012-1363) [05095810] **2960**

DEUTSCHES VOLKSBLATT (VIENNA, AUSTRIA : WEEKLY) (AU) [20305917] **5778**

DEUTSCHES WOERTERBUCH (GW) **1925**

DEUTSCHLAND (GW) **2515**

DEUTSCHLAND (GW) [03075156] **2685**

DEUTSCHLAND ARCHIV (GW/0012-1428) [01566525] **4471**

DEUTSCHLAND IN GESCHICHTE UND GEGENWART (GW) [01788785] **2685**

DEUTSCHLAND NACHRICHTEN (US) [21347134] **2515**

DEUTSCHOSTERREICHISCHE TAGES-ZEITUNG (AU) [20308739] **5778**

DEUTSCHSPRACHIGE MYKOLOGISCHE GESELLSCHAFT *See* WISSENSCHAFTLICHE TAGUNG; VORTRAGE **530**

DEUTSCHSPRACHIGE ZEITSCHRIFTEN (GW/0419-005X) [03733211] **414**

DEUTSCHUNTERRICHT (GW/0012-1460) [01652332] 3276, **3381**

DEUTSCHUNTERRICHT (STUTTGART) (GW/0340-2258) [01566529] **3276**

DEVA NAGARA (II) [01784234] **2503**

DEVELOP (CUPERTINO, CALIF.) (US/1047-0735) [20591599] **1182**

●DEVELOPERS AND BUILDERS NEWS (US/1062-5348) [25652142] **2821**

DEVELOPING COUNTRY COURIER, THE (US/0160-8037) [03765043] 1634, **4471**

DEVELOPING ECONOMIES, THE (JA/0012-1533) [01883903] **5198**

DEVELOPING EDUCATION **CEASED**. (AT/0310-5709) [I03105709] **1735**

DEVELOPING INDIA (II) [11579229] **1555**

DEVELOPING METROS (UK) [12264501] **5431**

●DEVELOPING NATIONS (US/1057-9206) [24170582] **1634**

DEVELOPING NATIONS MONOGRAPH SERIES (US) [01653428] **1555**

DEVELOPING WORLD : A U F S READINGS (US/0066-1090) [05113250] **2908**

●DEVELOPING YOUR CREATIVE WRITING STYLE AND LEARNING THE CRAFT OF WRITING (US/1061-6039) [25377311] 2919, 3462, **3381**

DEVELOPMENT (NZ) [06909657] **2908**

DEVELOPMENT ADMINISTRATION JOURNAL (PH) [09405990] **4642**

DEVELOPMENT AND CHANGE (UK/0012-155X) [01192612] **5198**

DEVELOPMENT AND FOREIGN POLICY REPORT (US/8756-7466) [11640564] **4519**

DEVELOPMENT & INTERNATIONAL COOPERATION (XV) [25315939] **2908**

DEVELOPMENT AND MATERIALS BULLETIN (UK) [01566534] **612**

DEVELOPMENT AND PSYCHOPATHOLOGY (US/0954-5794) [19716359] **4584**

DEVELOPMENT & SOCIO-ECONOMIC PROGRESS (UA) [04209218] **1555**

DEVELOPMENT ANTHROPOLOGY NETWORK (US/8756-0488) [11463672] 235, **2908**

DEVELOPMENT ASSISTANCE PROGRAMS OF U. S. NON-PROFIT ORGANIZATIONS IN EL SALVADOR (US/0146-0617) [02871916] **2908**

DEVELOPMENT BANK OF SEYCHELLES *See* ANNUAL REPORT / DEVELOPMENT BANK OF SEYCHELLES **771**

DEVELOPMENTS

DEVELOPMENT BIBLIOGRAPHIES (UK/0955-0569) [l09550569] **415**

DEVELOPMENT BUSINESS (US) [11989479] **665**

DEVELOPMENT (CAMBRIDGE) (UK/0950-1991) [15088415] **541**

DEVELOPMENT / CANADIAN INTERNATIONAL DEVELOPMENT AGENCY (CN/0828-0584) [12570675] **1555**

DEVELOPMENT CO-OPERATION EFFORTS AND POLICIES OF THE MEMBERS OF THE DEVELOPMENT ASSISTANCE COMMITTEE; REVIEW (FR) [01785851] **2908**

DEVELOPMENT COMMUNICATION REPORT (US/0192-1312) [04964722] 2908, **1110**

DEVELOPMENT COOPERATION (FR) **2909**

DEVELOPMENT DIALOGUE (SW/0345-2328) [01785483] **1634**

DEVELOPMENT DISCUSSION PAPER (US) [06292749] **1555**

DEVELOPMENT DOSSIER (AT/0815-9424) [l08159424] **1918**

DEVELOPMENT DOSSIER / ACFOA (AT) [14352285] **2909**

DEVELOPMENT EDUCATION EXCHANGE PAPERS : DEEP (IT/1020-0339) [12296492] **1735**

DEVELOPMENT FORUM - UNITED NATIONS **CEASED.** (US/0251-6632) [01487492] **1479**

DEVELOPMENT, GROWTH & DIFFERENTIATION (JA/0012-1592) [01566536] **541**

DEVELOPMENT HOTLINE (IT) **2909**

DEVELOPMENT IN AGING (US/0734-3213) [03582309] **5178**

DEVELOPMENT IN PRACTICE (UK/0961-4524) [23888138] **2909**

DEVELOPMENT JOURNAL (LONDON) (UK/0957-4115) [21325127] **4642**

DEVELOPMENT NEWS (UK) **665**

DEVELOPMENT OF STATE COMMERCIAL BANKS IN INDONESIA, THE (IO) [11701102] **787**

DEVELOPMENT OF THE OIL AND GAS RESOURCES OF THE UNITED KINGDOM (UK) [05519186] **4254**

DEVELOPMENT ORIENTED RESEARCH IN AGRICULTURE (NE) **78**

DEVELOPMENT PLAN - BRITISH SOLOMON ISLANDS PROTECTORATE (BP) [03318295] **1555**

DEVELOPMENT POLICY AND ADMINISTRATION REVIEW **CEASED.** (II) [02713617] **4642**

DEVELOPMENT POLICY REVIEW (UK/0950-6764) [09691139] **2909**

... DEVELOPMENT REPORT CARD FOR THE STATES, THE (US/1053-3672) [20619094] **1555**

DEVELOPMENT (ROME) (IT/1011-6370) [04910508] **2909**

DEVELOPMENT SERIES (US) [02396010] **2821**

DEVELOPMENT SERIES (ALBUQUERQUE, N.M.) (US) [07336537] **1479**

DEVELOPMENT SOUTHERN AFRICA (SANDTON, SOUTH AFRICA) (SA) [11231936] **2909**

DEVELOPMENT STUDIES (UK/0486-0837) [01770914] 2088, **170**

DEVELOPMENT. SUPPLEMENT (UK) [24559381] **541**

DEVELOPMENTAL AND CELL BIOLOGY (UK/0951-0818) [06031870] **536**

DEVELOPMENTAL AND COMPARATIVE IMMUNOLOGY (US/0145-305X) [02712411] **3669**

DEVELOPMENTAL BIOLOGY (US/0012-1606) [01718504] **453**

●DEVELOPMENTAL BRAIN DYSFUNCTION (SZ/1019-5815) [28226715] **3831**

DEVELOPMENTAL BRAIN RESEARCH (NE/0165-3806) [19645066] **3831**

DEVELOPMENTAL CLINICAL PSYCHOLOGY AND PSYCHIATRY (US/0892-8150) [13713115] 3924, **4584**

DEVELOPMENTAL DISABILITIES BULLETIN (CN/1184-0412) [23251628] **4386**

DEVELOPMENTAL DISABILITIES SPECIAL INTEREST SECTION NEWSLETTER (US/0279-4098) [07841216] **1877**

DEVELOPMENTAL DISABILITIES STATE PLAN (US) [06072459] **5282**

●DEVELOPMENTAL DYNAMICS (US/1058-8388) [24403911] **3679**

DEVELOPMENTAL GENETICS (US/0192-253X) [05002659] **544**

DEVELOPMENTAL IMMUNOLOGY (SZ/1044-6672) [19863675] **3669**

DEVELOPMENTAL MEDICINE & CHILD NEUROLOGY (UK/0012-1622) [01566540] 3903, 3831, **3657**

DEVELOPMENTAL MEDICINE AND CHILD NEUROLOGY. SUPPLEMENT (UK/0419-0238) [01713974] **3831**

DEVELOPMENTAL NEUROPSYCHOLOGY (US/8756-5641) [11594037] **3571**

DEVELOPMENTAL NEUROSCIENCE (SZ/0378-5866) [04262003] **3831**

DEVELOPMENTAL PHARMACOLOGY AND THERAPEUTICS **CEASED.** (SZ/0379-8305) [06261418] 3760, **4299**

DEVELOPMENTAL PHYSIOPATHOLOGY & CLINICS (IT) **3894**

DEVELOPMENTAL POLICY STUDIES **CEASED.** (US/1066-9477) [25213607] **5326**

DEVELOPMENTAL PSYCHOBIOLOGY (US/0012-1630) [00913788] 4584, **453**

DEVELOPMENTAL PSYCHOLOGY (US/0012-1649) [01566542] **4584**

DEVELOPMENTAL REVIEW (US/0273-2297) [07033929] **4584**

DEVELOPMENTAL STUDIES AND LABORATORY INVESTIGATIONS CONDUCTED BY VETERINARY SERVICES DIAGNOSTIC LABORATORIES (US/0361-9745) [02441162] **5508**

DEVELOPMENTS (EDMONTON) (CN/0714-1017) [09089101] **1342**

DEVELOPMENTS IN ADHESIVES (UK/0262-1576) [07938309] **2012**

DEVELOPMENTS IN AGRICULTURAL AND MANAGED FOREST ECOLOGY (NE/0166-2287) [01957546] **2213**

DEVELOPMENTS IN AGRICULTURAL ECONOMICS (NE/0926-5589) [09710078] 1479, **79**

DEVELOPMENTS IN AGRICULTURAL ENGINEERING (NE/0167-4137) [07571003] **79**

DEVELOPMENTS IN ANIMAL AND VETERINARY SCIENCES (NE/0167-5168) [04737618] **5509**

DEVELOPMENTS IN APPLIED EARTH SCIENCES (NE) [08571603] **1354**

DEVELOPMENTS IN AQUACULTURE AND FISHERIES SCIENCE (NE/0167-9309) [02902656] **2300**

DEVELOPMENTS IN ATMOSPHERIC SCIENCE (US/0167-5117) [03332352] **1425**

DEVELOPMENTS IN BIOCHEMISTRY (NL/0165-1714) [04112491] **486**

DEVELOPMENTS IN BIOENERGETICS AND BIOMEMBRANES (NE/0166-0861) [03806130] **453**

DEVELOPMENTS IN BIOLOGICAL STANDARDIZATION (SZ/0301-5149) [00983297] **453**

DEVELOPMENTS IN BLOCK COPOLYMERS (UK/0264-8393) [09591615] **1041**

DEVELOPMENTS IN BOUNDARY ELEMENT METHODS (UK) [08514596] **3503**

DEVELOPMENTS IN CANCER RESEARCH (US/0163-6146) [04415861] **3816**

DEVELOPMENTS IN CARDIOLOGY (US/1046-6959) [20495823] **3704**

DEVELOPMENTS IN CARDIOVASCULAR MEDICINE (NE/0166-9842) [05348607] **3704**

DEVELOPMENTS IN CELL BIOLOGY (US/0165-2265) [04088411] **536**

DEVELOPMENTS IN CIVIL AND FOUNDATION ENGINEERING (NE/0924-5308) [l09245308] **2022**

DEVELOPMENTS IN CLINICAL BIOCHEMISTRY (NE/0167-4978) [05908795] **486**

DEVELOPMENTS IN CORPORATE, BANKING, AND SECURITIES LAW (US/0093-1829) [01786923] 3086, **3099**

DEVELOPMENTS IN CROP SCIENCE (NE/0378-519X) [03287764] **170**

DEVELOPMENTS IN CRYSTALLINE POLYMERS (UK/0263-6204) [08732392] **1032**

DEVELOPMENTS IN DAIRY CHEMISTRY (UK/0264-8407) [09480076] 974, **194**

DEVELOPMENTS IN ECONOMIC GEOLOGY (NE/0168-6178) [04810373] 1479, **1373**

DEVELOPMENTS IN ENDOCRINOLOGY (THE HAGUE) **CEASED.** (US/0167-6334) [08962676] **3727**

DEVELOPMENTS IN ENGLISH LANGUAGE TEACHING (UK) **1735**

DEVELOPMENTS IN ENVIRONMENTAL CONTROL AND PUBLIC HEALTH (UK/0260-0862) [06432974] **4773**

DEVELOPMENTS IN ENVIRONMENTAL MODELLING (NE/0167-8892) [08527417] **2163**

DEVELOPMENTS IN FLOW MEASUREMENT (UK) [08867133] **2088**

DEVELOPMENTS IN FOOD COLOURS... (UK/0262-1606) [07642075] **2333**

DEVELOPMENTS IN FOOD MICROBIOLOGY (UK/0264-2670) [08472161] **562**

DEVELOPMENTS IN FOOD PACKAGING (UK/0263-3752) [07619164] 2333, **4218**

DEVELOPMENTS IN FOOD PRESERVATION (UK/0263-4376) [09134960] **2333**

DEVELOPMENTS IN FOOD PRESERVATIVES (UK/0263-3728) [08392493] **2333**

DEVELOPMENTS IN FOOD PROTEINS (UK/0263-4708) [09098738] **2333**

DEVELOPMENTS IN FOOD SCIENCE (NE/0167-4501) [04753910] **2333**

DEVELOPMENTS IN FRACTURE MECHANICS (UK) [07902328] **1970**

DEVELOPMENTS IN GENETICS (NE/0167-6458) [05918649] **544**

DEVELOPMENTS IN GEOCHEMISTRY (NE/0921-3198) [04472915] 1373, **974**

DEVELOPMENTS IN GEOMATHEMATICS (US) [02418288] **1373**

DEVELOPMENTS IN GEOPHYSICAL EXPLORATION METHODS (UK/0264-844X) [06522963] **1404**

DEVELOPMENTS IN GEOTECHNICAL ENGINEERING (NE/0165-1250) [01608069] **1970**

DEVELOPMENTS IN GEOTECTONICS (NE/0419-0254) [01566544] **1373**

●DEVELOPMENTS IN HEALTH ECONOMICS AND PUBLIC POLICY (NE) [26105519] 1479, **4773**

DEVELOPMENTS IN HEMATOLOGY AND IMMUNOLOGY (NE/0167-8418) [08411619] 3669, **3771**

DEVELOPMENTS IN HUMAN SERVICES **CEASED.** (US/0092-5470) [01790988] **5282**

DEVELOPMENTS IN IMMUNOLOGY **CEASED.** (US/0163-5921) [04415936] **3669**

DEVELOPMENTS IN INDUSTRIAL MICROBIOLOGY **CEASED.** (US/0070-4563) [01425924] **562**

DEVELOPMENTS IN INTERNATIONAL LAW (NE) [09723121] **3127**

DEVELOPMENTS IN IONIC POLYMERS (UK/0264-7982) [09592840] **1041**

DEVELOPMENTS IN LANDSCAPE MANAGEMENT AND URBAN PLANNING (NE) [02158886] **2413**

DEVELOPMENTS IN MARINE BIOLOGY (US/0163-6995) [04445705] 1448, **453**

DEVELOPMENTS IN MARKETING SCIENCE (US/0149-7421) [03547721] **923**

DEVELOPMENTS IN MEAT SCIENCE (UK/0144-8811) [06972838] **2333**

DEVELOPMENTS IN MENTAL HEALTH LAW (US/1063-9977) [07121238] 4773, **2960**

DEVELOPMENTS IN MINERAL PROCESSING (NE/0167-4528) [03399213] **1439**

DEVELOPMENTS IN MOLECULAR AND CELLULAR BIOCHEMISTRY (NE/0167-9023) [08182027] **486**

DEVELOPMENTS IN MOLECULAR VIROLOGY (NE/0167-8256) [08634365] **562**

DEVELOPMENTS IN NANOTECHNOLOGY (UK/1053-7465) [22620406] **5099**

DEVELOPMENTS IN NEPHROLOGY (US/0167-8205) [08097177] **3989**

DEVELOPMENTS IN NEUROSCIENCE **CEASED.** (NE/0165-7003) [04321600] **3831**

DEVELOPMENTS IN NUCLEAR MEDICINE (US/0167-9074) [08566617] **3848**

DEVELOPMENTS IN NUTRITION AND METABOLISM (NE/0167-6504) [06008323] **4189**

DEVELOPMENTS IN OBSTETRICS AND GYNECOLOGY **CEASED.** (US/0167-8302) [10698264] **3760**

DEVELOPMENTS IN ONCOLOGY (NE/0167-4927) [06132670] **3816**

DEVELOPMENTS IN OPHTHALMOLOGY (SZ/0250-3751) [06988675] **3874**

DEVELOPMENTS IN ORIENTED POLYMERS (UK/0264-3022) [09312445] **1041**

DEVELOPMENTS IN PALEONTOLOGY AND STRATIGRAPHY (NE/0920-5446) [04815077] **4227**

DEVELOPMENTS IN PERINATAL MEDICINE **CEASED.** (NE/0167-6385) [08182073] **3760**

DEVELOPMENTS — Alphabetical Title Index

DEVELOPMENTS IN PETROLEUM GEOLOGY (UK/0260-4248) [07078134] 1373, **4254**

DEVELOPMENTS IN PETROLEUM SCIENCE (NE/0376-7361) [02418283] **4254**

DEVELOPMENTS IN PETROLOGY (NE/0167-2894) [01654193] **1458**

DEVELOPMENTS IN PLANT GENETICS AND BREEDING (US/0168-7972) [10386454] **508**

DEVELOPMENTS IN PLASTICS TECHNOLOGY (UK) [09459603] **4454**

DEVELOPMENTS IN POLYMER DEGRADATION (UK/0260-4310) [07398809] **1041**

DEVELOPMENTS IN POLYMER STABILISATION (UK/0262-155X) [06972843] **4454**

DEVELOPMENTS IN POLYMERISATION (UK/0260-4337) [05583148] **974**

DEVELOPMENTS IN PRECAMBRIAN GEOLOGY (NE/0166-2635) [05020070] **1373**

DEVELOPMENTS IN PRESSURE VESSEL TECHNOLOGY (UK/0266-156X) [06972805] **3477**

DEVELOPMENTS IN PSYCHIATRY (NE/0166-2481) [05199920] **3924**

DEVELOPMENTS IN REINFORCED PLASTICS (UK/0260-9185) [07119220] **4454**

DEVELOPMENTS IN RUBBER AND RUBBER COMPOSITES (UK/0262-1592) [06984960] **5075**

DEVELOPMENTS IN SEDIMENTOLOGY (NE/0070-4571) [01566547] **1373**

DEVELOPMENTS IN SOCIOLOGY (UK/0956-9359) [I09569359] **5244**

DEVELOPMENTS IN SOIL SCIENCE (NE/0166-0918) [01654295] **170**

DEVELOPMENTS IN SOLAR SYSTEM AND SPACE SCIENCE (NE/0167-5834) [05882541] **395**

DEVELOPMENTS IN SOLID EARTH GEOPHYSICS (NE/0419-0297) [01566548] **1404**

DEVELOPMENTS IN STRUCTURAL GEOLOGY (NE) [18209129] **1373**

DEVELOPMENTS IN SWEETENERS (UK/0950-6438) [06972831] **2333**

DEVELOPMENTS IN THE EUROPEAN COMMUNITIES (DUBLIN) (IE/0302-7465) [01792256] **1555**

DEVELOPMENTS IN THE QUARK THEORY OF HADRONS (US) [06838197] **4401**

DEVELOPMENTS IN THIN-WALLED STRUCTURES (UK) [09312439] **2022**

DEVELOPMENTS IN TOXICOLOGY AND ENVIRONMENTAL SCIENCE (NE/0165-2214) [03825321] 2163, **3980**

DEVELOPMENTS IN VETERINARY VIROLOGY *CEASED.* (US/0924-5359) [15173573] **5509**

DEVELOPMENTS IN VOLCANOLOGY (NE) [10504225] **1404**

DEVELOPMENTS IN WATER SCIENCE (NE/0167-5648) [04827403] **1413**

DEVELOPMENTS IN WATER TREATMENT (UK/0263-3736) [07664862] 1023, **5532**

DEVELOPPEMENT CULTUREL. LIVRES ET ARTICLES PARUS EN ... / MINISTERE DE LA CULTURE ET DE LA COMMUNICATION, SERVICE DES ETUDES ET RECHERCHES (FR) [07828800] **415**

DEVELOPPEMENT ET SANTE (FR/0396-8014) [I03968014] **4773**

DEVELOPPEMENT PERSONNEL (FR/0985-3766) [I09853766] **1110**

DEVELOPPEMENT SOCIAL EN PERSPECTIVES (CN/0822-7128) [10451195] **5282**

DEVELOPPEURS LEVALLOIS-PERRET (FR/1145-2099) [I11452099] **4836**

DEVENIR (SZ) **3571**

DEVEREUX PAPERS, THE (US) [01785537] **1110**

DEVEREUX SCHOOLS FORUM *See* FORUM (DEVON) **1747**

DEVIANCE ET SOCIETE (SZ/0378-7931) [04893637] **4584**

DEVIANT BEHAVIOR (US/0163-9625) [04540788] 5244, **4584**

DEVICE TECHNIQUES (US/0273-3137) [07049517] **3571**

DEVICES & DIAGNOSTICS LETTER (US/0098-7573) [01591229] **3571**

DEVIL'S ARTISAN, THE (CN/0225-7874) [06858823] **4564**

DEVIL'S BOX (US/0092-0789) [01788801] **4114**

DEVIL'S MILLHOPPER, THE (US/0733-9615) [07915291] **3462**

DEVIL'S RIVER NEWS (US) [14362901] **5749**

DEVINDEX AFRICA / UNITED NATIONS, ECONOMIC COMMISSION FOR AFRICA (ET) [08595361] **1479**

DEVINE NEWS, THE (US) [14257132] **5749**

DEVLET GELIRLERI BULTENI *See* BUTCE GELIRLERI YLLG **4716**

DEVLET ISTATISTIK ENSTITUSU (TURKEY). ANNUAIRE STATISTIQUE *See* TURKIYE ISTATISTIK YLL. STATISTICAL YEARBOOK OF TURKEY **5345**

DEVOIR (MONTREAL, QUEBEC) (CN) [01566553] **5783**

DEVON & CORNWALL NOTES & QUERIES (UK/0012-1681) [01566554] **2685**

DEVON AND CORNWALL RECORD SOCIETY *See* ANNUAL GENERAL MEETING / DEVON AND CORNWALL RECORD SOCIETY **5228**

DEVON AND CORNWALL RECORD SOCIETY. ANNUAL REPORT *See* ANNUAL GENERAL MEETING / DEVON AND CORNWALL RECORD SOCIETY **5228**

DEVON DISPATCH, THE (CN/0710-5495) [08716776] **5783**

DEVON HISTORIAN, THE (UK/0305-8549) [04670476] **2614**

DEVONIAN GAS SHALES TECHNOLOGY REVIEW *See* GAS SHALES TECHNOLOGY REVIEW **4258**

DEVONSHIRE ASSOCIATION FOR THE ADVANCEMENT OF SCIENCE, LITERATURE AND ART *See* REPORT AND TRANSACTIONS - THE DEVONSHIRE ASSOCIATION FOR THE ADVANCEMENT OF SCIENCE, LITERATURE AND ART **329**

DEVOTEE (US/0197-7784) [06002143] **4114**

DEVOTIONAL SPEECHES OF THE YEAR (US/0160-6654) [03721904] **5059**

DEWAN MASHARAKAT *See* DEWAN MASYARAKAT **5198**

DEWAN MASYARAKAT (MY) [02244094] **5198**

DEWAN PEMAKAI JASA ANGKUTAN LAUT INDONESIA *See* LAPORAN TAHUNAN - DEPALINDO **5451**

DEWAN SASTERA (MY/0126-5059) [07615947] **3381**

DEWEY DECIMAL CLASSIFICATION ADDITIONS, NOTES, AND DECISIONS (US/0191-3646) [04796681] **3206**

DEWITT COUNTY GENEALOGICAL QUARTERLY (US/0890-4456) [04671100] **2445**

DEWITT POLYMER SERVICE (US) 923, **4454**

DEXTER LEADER, THE (US) [12248586] **5691**

DFW, DOKUMENTATION, INFORMATION *CEASED.* (GW/0373-8825) [02260470] **3206**

DFZ WIRTSCHAFTSMAGAZINE *See* HANDEL, DER **838**

DG BANK *See* DG BANK MITTEILUNGEN **787**

DG BANK MITTEILUNGEN (GW) [02610685] **787**

DG REVIEW *CEASED.* (US/1050-9127) [17432973] **1182**

DGA NEWS (US/1075-6116) [23722120] 1662, **4067**

DGF INFORMACAO (PO/0871-5440) [I08715440] **508**

DGS, DEUTSCHE GEFLUGELWIRTSCHAFT UND SCHWEINEPRODUKTION (GW/0340-3858) [04480204] **210**

DGV INFORMATIONEN (GW) [01789282] 235, **2319**

DHA UNDRO NEWS / UNITED NATIONS, DEPT. OF HUMANITARIAN AFFAIRS (SZ) [27185265] **4519**

DHAKA COURIER (BG) [19250607] **2503**

● DHAKA UNIVERSITY JOURNAL OF SCIENCE, THE (BG/1022-2502) [29980023] **5099**

DHAKA UNIVERSITY STUDIES. PART B *See* DHAKA UNIVERSITY JOURNAL OF SCIENCE, THE **5099**

DHARANA : MUKHAPATRA, SVATANTRA VIDYARTHI YUNIYANA JANA-PRASASANA KYAMPASA (NP) [08768086] **1735**

DHARMA MARGA (II) [09100849] **5040**

DHARMA WARTA (IO) [02458605] **3163**

DHARMASENA (IO) [01797887] **4042**

DHEW OBLIGATIONS TO INSTITUTIONS OF HIGHER EDUCATION AND OTHER NONPROFIT ORGANIZATIONS (US/0147-6912) [02432058] **1820**

DHF. DEUTSCHE HEBE- UND FORDERTECHNIK (GW/0723-7901) [I07237901] **2102**

DHSS OFFICIAL TAX CONTRIBUTIONS (UK) **4720**

DHZ MARKT (NE) **2811**

DHZ VAKHANDEL (NE) 612, **2900**

DI. DECISIONS INFORMATION (CN/0318-6377) [01794822] **1662**

DI, DRINKS INTERNATIONAL (UK) [01791136] **2366**

DIA LATINOAMERICANO, EL (MX) [23845832] **2532**

DIA LONDON (UK/0950-8473) [I09508473] **1479**

DIA MEDICO, EL (AG/0012-1762) [06523644] **3571**

DIA YEARBOOK (UK) [04187157] **2163**

DIABC (NE) 4189, **3571**

DIABETE & METABOLISME (FR/0338-1684) [02044762] **3727**

DIABETE ET NUTRITION (FR/0012-1789) [I00121789] **3727**

DIABETE MILANO, IL (IT/0394-901X) [I0394901X] **4519**

DIABETES (CARACAS) (VE/0378-6277) [03176250] **3727**

DIABETES CARE (US/0149-5992) [03524314] **3727**

DIABETES CONSULTANT (US/1055-8322) [23352989] **3727**

DIABETES CONTENTS (UK) [I09518487] **3727**

DIABETES COUNTDOWN *See* COUNTDOWN / JUVENILE DIABETES FOUNDATION INTERNATIONAL **3727**

DIABETES DATELINE : THE NDIC BULLETIN (US) [06608056] **3727**

DIABETES DIALOGUE (CN/0703-5764) [03979830] **3727**

DIABETES EDUCATOR, THE (US/0145-7217) [02776215] **3727**

DIABETES FORECAST (US/0095-8301) [01798678] **3727**

DIABETES IN THE NEWS (1987) (US/0893-5939) [15587986] 1296, **3728**

DIABETES MELLITUS (UK/0263-7294) [02637294] 486, **3728**

DIABETES/METABOLISM REVIEWS (US/0742-4221) [10330259] **3728**

DIABETES (NEW YORK, N.Y.) (US/0012-1797) [01566563] **3728**

DIABETES NEWS DIGEST *SUSPENDED.* (US/1048-5597) [20972299] **3728**

DIABETES NEWS ED. ESPANOLA (SP/0213-5787) [I02135787] **3728**

DIABETES, NUTRITION & METABOLISM (IT/0394-3402) [I03943402] **4189**

DIABETES PATIENT (US/0895-0644) [16438400] **3728**

DIABETES, PREVENTION AND THERAPY (UK/1056-053X) [23456334] **3728**

DIABETES RESEARCH AND CLINICAL PRACTICE (NE/0168-8227) [12187252] **3728**

DIABETES RESEARCH AND CLINICAL PRACTICE (NE/0168-8227) [14380094] **3728**

DIABETES RESEARCH (EDINBURGH, LOTHIAN) (UK/0256-5985) [11702144] **3728**

● DIABETES REVIEWS (ALEXANDRIA, VA.) (US/1066-9442) [27096587] **3728**

DIABETES SELF-MANAGEMENT (US/0741-6253) [10187046] **3728**

DIABETES SPECTRUM (US/1040-9165) [18574215] **3728**

DIABETES. [MICROFICHE] (US) **3728**

DIABETIC DIARY *SUSPENDED.* (US/8755-8858) [11425224] **5282**

DIABETIC MEDICINE (UK/0742-3071) [10315661] **3728**

DIABETIC TRAVELER, THE (US/0899-2398) [18045360] 3728, **5468**

DIABETOLOGIA (GW/0012-186X) [01566567] **3728**

DIABETOLOGIA CROATICA (CI/0351-0042) [04166124] **3728**

DIABETOLOGIE-INFORMATIONEN (GW/0171-8045) [05826787] **3728**

DIABLO BUSINESS (US/1055-7431) [23289042] **665**

DIABOLO TOULOUSE (FR/0987-1209) [I09871209] **3341**

DIACHRONICA (GW/0176-4225) [11422862] **3277**

DIACRITICS (US/0300-7162) [00832096] **3341**

DIADORA (CI/0417-4046) [03815570] **266**

DIAGNOSE & LABOR (GW/0178-8345) [14960903] **3571**

DIAGNOSIS AND TREATMENT OF HODGKIN'S DISEASE (US) [03457688] **3816**

DIAGNOSIS AND TREATMENT OF SARCOMAS AND RELATED TUMORS (US) [03458342] **3816**

DIAGNOSIS MILANO *CEASED.* (IT/1120-7108) [I11207108] **3571**

DIAGNOSIS (ORADELL, N.J.) *CEASED.* (US/0163-3228) [04349856] **3571**

●DIAGNOSTIC AND THERAPEUTIC ENDOSCOPY (SZ/1070-3608) [28352865] **3571**

DIAGNOSTIC CYTOPATHOLOGY (US/8755-1039) [11276508] **536**

DIAGNOSTIC DIALOG (US/0198-6627) [06174852] 3571, **974**

DIAGNOSTIC ENGINEERING : NEWSLETTER OF THE INSTITUTION OF DIAGNOSTIC ENGINEERS (UK/0269-0225) [12653586] **1970**

DIAGNOSTIC IMAGING INTERNATIONAL (US/0898-2473) [17762730] **3940**

DIAGNOSTIC IMAGING (SAN FRANCISCO, CALIF.) (US/0194-2514) [05365753] 3848, **3940**

DIAGNOSTIC IMAGING SCAN (US) **3940**

DIAGNOSTIC MICROBIOLOGY AND INFECTIOUS DISEASE (US/0732-8893) [08463683] 3713, **562**

DIAGNOSTIC MOLECULAR PATHOLOGY (US/1052-9551) [22418103] **3894**

●DIAGNOSTIC NUTRITION NETWORK (US/1065-7746) [26732969] **4189**

DIAGNOSTIC ONCOLOGY (SZ/1013-8129) [22267360] **3816**

DIAGNOSTIC RADIOLOGY (1982) (US/1042-7872) [13187141] **3940**

DIAGNOSTIC RADIOLOGY SERIES (NEW YORK, N.Y.) (US/0742-8383) [09892693] **3940**

DIAGNOSTIC TUMOUR BIBLIOGRAPHIES (UK) [08857069] **3657**

DIAGNOSTICA (GOTTINGEN) (GW/0012-1924) [01663289] **4585**

DIAGNOSTICA PER IMMAGINI (IT) [12111840] **3941**

DIAGNOSTICS BUSINESS (UK/0954-1837) [I09541837] **665**

DIAGNOSTICS INTELLIGENCE (US/1054-9609) [23034602] **3571**

DIAGNOSTIK (GW/0340-5680) [02900406] **3571**

DIAGNOSTIQUE (US/0737-2477) [07325631] **1735**

DIAGNOSTYKJA LABORATORYJNA (PL/0012-1932) [11465900] **3571**

DIAGONAL (FR) [04151384] **2821**

DIAGONAL PROGRESS (DIAGONAL, IOWA : 1979) (US) [14075861] **5669**

DIAGONAL : ZEITSCHRIFT DER UNIVERSITAT-GESAMTHOCHSCHULE -SIEGEN (GW) [24170542] **1091**

DIAGRAMMES (FR/0224-3911) [06525243] **3503**

DIAKONEO (NEW ORLEANS, LA.) (US/1070-7875) [12071272] **4953**

DIAKONIA (BRONX, N.Y.) (US/0012-1959) [01566571] **5039**

DIAKONIA (MAINZ, GERMANY : 1972) (GW/0341-9592) [05426208] **4953**

DIAKONIA MAS TES BASILEIAS (KANADE EKDOSIS) (CN/0382-7933) [03409810] **4953**

DIAKONIA TES BASILEIAS (CN/0316-6864) [02247750] **4953**

DIAKONIE (GW/0341-826X) [03721671] **4953**

DIAKRISIS (GW/0174-5506) [I01745506] **4953**

DIAL-A-FAX DIRECTORY (US/1046-7262) [20468705] **1153**

DIAL : DIFFUSION DE L'INFORMATION SUR L'AMERIQUE LATINE (FR) **2731**

DIAL ELECTRICAL ELECTRONICS SALES CONTACTS (UK) **2041**

DIAL ENGINEERING SALES CONTACTS (UK) **2112**

DIAL IN *See* OPAC DIRECTORY **1198**

DIAL IN (US/1047-3424) [20667531] **3206**

DIAL. WNET/THIRTEEN (COMPOSITE ED.) *CEASED.* (US/0884-2078) [11275666] **1131**

DIALECT (CN/0383-8528) [03279123] **5282**

DIALECTES DE WALLONIE, LES (BE/0773-7688) [02246513] **3277**

DIALECTICA (SZ/0012-2017) [01592034] **4345**

DIALECTICAL ANTHROPOLOGY (NE/0304-4092) [01926226] **235**

DIALEKTIK (GW/0939-5512) [25267581] **4345**

DIALISI OGGI (IT) **3796**

DIALOG (IO) [05764831] **2503**

DIALOG (EDMONTON) (CN/0842-8336) [19272215] **4386**

DIALOG (MOSCOW, R.S.F.S.R.) (RU/0236-0942) [21067718] **4541**

DIALOG ONDISC. ERIC [COMPUTER FILE] (US) [18196225] **1735**

DIALOG ONDISC. PHILOSOPHER'S INDEX [COMPUTER FILE] (US) [23872855] **4345**

DIALOG (ST. PAUL) (US/0012-2033) [01566581] **4953**

DIALOG (WARSAW, POLAND) (PL/0012-2041) [01566582] **3381**

DIALOGANDO : BOLETIN INFORMATIVO DE LA VICARIA DE PASTORAL OBRERA DE SANTIAGO-CHILE (CL) [08945089] 1663, **4953**

DIALOGHI DI ARCHEOLOGIA (IT/0392-8535) [03799006] **266**

DIALOGO (CN/0826-2187) [11197144] **2731**

DIALOGO / DIALOGUE (IT) **2487**

DIALOGO ECUMENICO (SP/0210-2870) [07027586] **4953**

DIALOGO FILOSOFICO (SP/0213-1196) [I02131196] **4345**

DIALOGO IBEROAMERICANO (SP) [08780749] **2731**

DIALOGO INDIGENA MISIONERO : DIM (PY) [10177595] **2259**

DIALOGO SOCIAL *SUSPENDED.* (PN/0046-0206) [03181460] 5244, **2614**

DIALOGO TEOLOGICO (US) [04011957] **5059**

DIALOGOS (UK) 3381, **3277**

DIALOGOS (PR/0012-2122) [02323262] **4345**

DIALOGOS HISPANICOS DE AMSTERDAM (NE/0167-8744) [10265868] **3277**

DIALOGUE (IT) **2487**

DIALOGUE & ALLIANCE (US/0891-5881) [14918922] **4953**

DIALOGUE AND HUMANISM (PL) [23872818] **4345**

DIALOGUE - ANGLICAN CHURCH OF CANADA. DIOCESE OF ONTARIO (CN/1184-6283) [24266573] **4953**

DIALOGUE (BRAILLE ED.) (US/1069-6865) [28163431] 4395, **4386**

DIALOGUE (CANADIAN CHAMBER OF COMMERCE. EDITION FRANCAISE) (CN/0702-7877) [03412173] **819**

DIALOGUE - CANADIAN INSTITUTE OF CHARTERED ACCOUNTANTS (CN/0045-4982) [10392572] **742**

DIALOGUE - CANADIAN PHILOSOPHICAL ASSOCIATION (CN/0012-2173) [00919134] **4345**

DIALOGUE (CASSETTE ED.) (US/1069-6873) [28163507] **4386**

DIALOGUE (COLOMBO, SRI LANKA) (CE/0012-2181) [01776587] **5021**

DIALOGUE - COUNCIL OF MINISTERS OF EDUCATION (CN/0715-7037) [09925326] **3277**

DIALOGUE - FONDATION ASIE PACIFIQUE DU CANADA (CN/1184-8758) [24368391] **4519**

DIALOGUE FOR ENGINEERS & GEOSCIENTISTS (CN/1184-1737) [23599058] **1970**

DIALOGUE IMMERSION (CN/0824-4189) [11355545] **3277**

DIALOGUE IN INSTRUMENTAL MUSIC EDUCATION (US/0147-7544) [03228782] **4114**

DIALOGUE : JOURNAL OF ADDIS ABABA UNIVERSITY MAIN CAMPUS TEACHERS ASSOCIATION (US) [04728969] 4953, **1820**

DIALOGUE (LARGE PRINT ED.) (US/1069-6857) [11652748] **4386**

DIALOGUE (LOS ANGELES) (US/0012-2157) [01566589] **5059**

DIALOGUE - MANITOBA TELEPHONE SYSTEM (CN/0710-2313) [08286310] **1153**

DIALOGUE (MILWAUKEE, WIS.) (US/0012-2246) [01664331] **4345**

DIALOGUE (MUNROE FALLS, OHIO) (US/0279-568X) [04730991] **319**

DIALOGUE ON DIARRHOEA (UK/0950-0235) [16811341] **3796**

DIALOGUE ON LIBERTY (US/0276-4563) [02509192] **4471**

DIALOGUE PARIS. 196? (FR/0242-8962) [I02428962] **5244**

DIALOGUE (PORT-AU-PRINCE, HAITI) (HT) [10435962] **2731**

DIALOGUE (WASHINGTON, D.C.) (KO) [10827153] **4642**

DIALOGUE (WASHINGTON, D.C. : ENGLISH ED.) (US/0272-7692) [06901559] **1110**

DIALOGUES D'HISTOIRE ANCIENNE (FR/0755-7256) [03265144] **2614**

DIALOGUES ET CULTURES (CN/0226-6881) [08882673] 1735, **3277**

DIALOGUES IN PEDIATRIC MANAGEMENT (US/8755-2701) [11276950] **3903**

DIALOGUES IN PEDIATRIC UROLOGY (US/0164-9507) [04249720] 3989, **3903**

DIALYSIS & TRANSPLANTATION (US/0090-2934) [01777952] **3571**

DIAMANT (BE) **2914**

DIAMANT-, GOUD- EN ZILVERVERWERKENDE INDUSTRIE, SIERADENINDUSTRIE (NE/0920-5578) [16817595] 1604, **2914**

DIAMANTAIRE (UK) **2914**

DIAMOND AND RELATED MATERIALS (NE/0925-9635) [26490791] **4001**

DIAMOND DEPOSITIONS, SCIENCE AND TECHNOLOGY (US/1051-9084) [22147752] 1041, **1023**

DIAMOND DUDS (US/1058-711X) [24362058] **319**

DIAMOND FILMS AND TECHNOLOGY (JA/0917-4540) [27215101] **4001**

DIAMOND INDUSTRIA (JA/0385-7360) [14262331] **5099**

DIAMOND INSIGHT (US/0954-5581) [20010897] **2914**

DIAMOND INTELLIGENCE BRIEFS (SZ) **665**

DIAMOND INTERNATIONAL (UK/0957-0446) [20818805] **2914**

DIAMOND JAPAN BUSINESS DIRECTORY *See* DIAMOND'S JAPAN BUSINESS DIRECTORY **665**

DIAMOND LEAD COMPANY *See* DIAMOND'S JAPAN BUSINESS DIRECTORY **665**

DIAMOND LIFE BULLETINS *See* ADVANCED SALES REFERENCE SERVICE **2872**

DIAMOND NEWS & S.A. JEWELLER (SA) [05078508] **2914**

DIAMOND REGISTRY *See* DIAMOND REGISTRY BULLETIN, THE **2914**

DIAMOND REGISTRY BULLETIN, THE (US/0199-9753) [06297295] **2914**

DIAMOND RESEARCH (UK) [05358819] **2138**

DIAMOND TRAIL NEWS (US) [12573198] **5669**

DIAMOND WORLD (II) [04694002] **2914**

DIAMOND WORLD REVIEW (IS) [03262751] **2914**

DIAMONDBACK, THE (US) [14403262] **5686**

DIAMOND'S JAPAN BUSINESS DIRECTORY (JA) [02243876] 896, **665**

DIAN (KOTA BHARU) (MY/0302-8887) [01793162] **2503**

DIANCHI (CC/1001-1579) [I10011579] **5099**

DIANDU YU HUANBAO (CC/1000-4742) [21722460] 2227, **2041**

DIANOIA, ANUARIO DE FILOSOFIA (MX) [08678070] **4345**

DIANOIA (CAMROSE) (CN/1192-1854) [27165171] **1820**

DIANZIXUE YU TANCE JISHU, HE (CC/0258-0934) [I02580934] 4446, **2041**

DIAPASON (FR) [31049180] 5316, **4114**

DIAPASON (CHICAGO), THE (US/0012-2378) [01566598] **4114**

DIAPASON HARMONIE (FR/0765-5983) [18717228] 5316, **4114**

DIAPAZON (RU) [25695486] **3381**

DIARI DE SESSIONS DEL PARLAMENT DE CATALUNYA (NL) [08227312] **4471**

DIARI OFICIAL DE LA GENERALITAT DE CATALUNYA (SP) [07890270] **2960**

DIARI OFICIAL DE LA GENERALITAT DE CATALUNYA (SP) [07890345] **5810**

DIARIO DA JUSTICA DO ESTADO DE MATO GROSSO (BL) [07120944] **2960**

DIARIO DA REPUBLICA (SF) [07758838] **2960**

DIARIO DA REPUBLICA (PO) [03383690] **2960**

DIARIO DE CENTRO AMERICA (GT) [02341285] **2960**

DIARIO DE CONGRESOS MEDICOS (SP) **3572**

DIARIO DE HOY. REPERTORIO, EL (ES) [06243739] **5800**

DIARIO Alphabetical Title Index

DIARIO DE NOTICIAS (LISBON, PORTUGAL) (PO) [14347785] **5808**

DIARIO DO GOVERNO *See* DIARIO DA REPUBLICA **2960**

DIARIO ECONOMICO (PO/0872-1696) [l08721696] **1479**

DIARIO LA PRENSA, EL (US) [01664928] **2259**

DIARIO, LA PRENSA, EL (US/0742-9428) [10480104] **5716**

DIARIO LAS AMERICAS (US/0744-3234) [01774712] 5648, **5649**

DIARIO LATINO (ES) [20990817] **5800**

DIARIO OFICIAL DO ESTADO DO RIO DE JANEIRO. PARTE I *See* D.O., DIARIO OFICIAL, ESTADO DO RIO DE JANEIRO. PARTE I **2958**

DIARIO OFICIAL DO ESTADO DO RIO DE JANEIRO. PARTE II *See* D.O., DIARIO OFICIAL, ESTADO DO RIO DE JANEIRO. PARTE II **4471**

DIARIO OFICIAL DO ESTADO DO RIO DE JANEIRO. PARTE III *See* D.O., DIARIO OFICIAL, ESTADO DO RIO DE JANEIRO. PARTE III **2958**

DIARIO OFICIAL DO MUNICIPIO (BL) [12310280] **2960**

DIARIO OFICIAL, ESTADO DE SAO PAULO: DIARIO DA JUSTICA (BL) [04015519] **2960**

DIARIO OFICIAL, ESTADO DE SAO PAULO : INEDITORIAIS (BL) [04027426] **2960**

DIARIO OFICIAL, ESTADO DE SAO PAULO. PODER JUDICIARIO (BL) [08272658] **2960**

DIARIO OFICIAL: INDUSTRIA & [I.E. E] COMERCIO (BL) [04378946] **1555**

DIARIST'S JOURNAL (US) **3381**

DIARKES KODIX NAUTERGATIKES & NAUTILIAKES NOMOTHESIAS / EKDIDETAI KAI DIEUTHYNETAI HYPO TOU INSTITOUTOU ERGATIKON MELETON, SYNTASSETAI HYOP EPITROPES EIDIKON (GR) [12151685] 4176, **3180**

DIARY / CANADIANS FOR HEALTH RESEARCH (CN/1181-7720) [25066473] 3924, **4773**

DIARY OF SOCIAL LEGISLATION AND POLICY (AT/0725-2455) [13176497] **5282**

DIARY OF THE CORPORATION OF THE CITY OF GLASGOW & C (UK) [02356999] **4642**

●DIASPORA (MAGNOLIA, ARK.) (US/1062-6972) [25698583] 2259, **3381**

DIASPORA (NEW YORK, N.Y.) (US/1044-2057) [19720920] **5198**

DIASTEMA (SA/0419-0955) [04146420] **1322**

DIATOM RESEARCH (UK/0269-249X) [15245081] **508**

DIAVAZO (GR) [10750883] **415**

DIBLUMASI (JIDDAH, SAUDI ARABIA) (SU) [10235887] **4520**

DIBRUGARH UNIVERSITY. DEPT. OF ANTHROPOLOGY *See* BULLETIN OF THE DEPARTMENT OF ANTHROPOLOGY, DIBRUGARH UNIVERSITY, THE **233**

DICCIONARIO HISTORICO DE LA LENGUA ESPANOLA (SP) [06164821] **3277**

DICENGXUE ZAZHI (CC/0253-4959) [04885523] **1373**

DICHTER UBER IHRE DICHTUNGEN *CEASED*. (GW) [01665145] **3462**

DICINE (MX) [12096005] **4067**

DICK DAVIS DIGEST (US/0890-0957) [12029761] **896**

DICK DOCUMENTS (US) [15682713] **2445**

DICK VINOCUR'S FOOTPRINTS (US/1063-9276) [26184131] 378, **4564**

DICK VITALE'S BASKETBALL (US/1054-2213) [13998465] **4892**

DICKENS QUARTERLY (US/0742-5473) [10362455] **3381**

DICKENS STUDIES ANNUAL (US/0084-9812) [01624299] **3381**

DICKENS' UNIVERSE (US/1054-8777) [23004450] **3381**

DICKENSIAN, THE (UK/0012-2440) [00936752] **3381**

DICKENSON STAR, THE (US/0746-584X) [10133529] **5758**

DICKEY COUNTY LEADER (US) [01566608] **5725**

DICKINSON ALUMNUS *See* DICKINSON MAGAZINE **1091**

DICKINSON COLLEGE *See* ALUMNI DIRECTORY / DICKINSON COLLEGE **1098**

DICKINSON COLLEGE. DIRECTORY OF ALUMNI *See* ALUMNI DIRECTORY / DICKINSON COLLEGE **1098**

DICKINSON DIGGINGS : THE QUARTERLY PUBLICATION OF THE DICKINSON COUNTY GENEALOGICAL SOCIETY (US) [10074748] **2445**

●DICKINSON JOURNAL OF ENVIRONMENTAL LAW & POLICY (US/1063-7419) [26146383] **2960**

DICKINSON JOURNAL OF INTERNATIONAL LAW (US/0887-283X) [11761337] **3127**

DICKINSON LAW REVIEW (US/0012-2459) [01566607] **2960**

DICKINSON MAGAZINE (US/0271-9134) [06690881] **1091**

DICKINSON PRESS (DICKINSON, N.D. 1942), THE (US/1049-6718) [01566609] **5725**

DICKINSON STUDIES *CEASED*. (US/0164-1492) [04430845] **3462**

DICKINSON'S FDA (US/0885-159X) [12578917] 4299, 2333, **4642**

DICKINSON'S FDA INSPECTION (US) **4773**

DICKINSON'S FDA INSPECTION (US/1063-2433) [25936801] 4299, 2333, **4642**

●DICKINSON'S FDA REVIEW (US/1073-4414) [29407746] 4299, 2333, **4642**

DICKINSON'S PHARMACY (US/1063-2441) [25418947] **4299**

DICKINSON'S PSAO (US/0889-5953) [13990272] 4299, **665**

DICKSON COUNTY HERALD *See* DICKSON HERALD, THE **5745**

DICKSON HERALD DEATH NOTICES (US) [16938677] **2445**

DICKSON HERALD, THE (US/0747-041X) [10498885] **5745**

DICKSON MOUNDS MUSEUM *See* DICKSON MOUNDS MUSEUM ANTHROPOLOGICAL STUDIES **235**

DICKSON MOUNDS MUSEUM ANTHROPOLOGICAL STUDIES (US/0095-2907) [01424063] **235**

DICP *See* ANNALS OF PHARMACOTHERAPY, THE **4291**

DICTA (US/0419-1110) [05151538] **1820**

DICTA: A LAWYER'S MAGAZINE (US) [04945106] **2960**

DICTA : HARVARD LAW SCHOOL MAGAZINE (US) [09681069] **2960**

DICTA / NEWSLETTER FOR ATTORNEYS OF SAN DIEGO COUNTY (US/0417-4569) [05151706] **2960**

DICTIONARIES (US/0197-6745) [06076984] **3277**

DICTIONARIUM MUSICUM (NE/0419-1129) [01667210] **4114**

DICTIONARY CATALOG OF OFFICIAL PUBLICATIONS OF THE STATE OF NEW YORK (US) [03030679] **4697**

DICTIONARY CATALOG OF THE COLUMBIA UNIVERSITY LAW LIBRARY. SUPPLEMENT (US/0098-7395) [02242324] 2960, **3206**

DICTIONARY CATALOG OF THE JEWISH COLLECTION. SUPPLEMENT (US/0360-3261) [02484015] **415**

DICTIONARY ENCYCLOPEDIA HANDBOOK REVIEW (US/0270-3750) [06399809] **1925**

DICTIONARY OF CANADIAN BIOGRAPHY (CN/0070-4717) [01566617] **432**

DICTIONARY OF CONTEMPORARY QUOTATIONS (US/0360-215X) [02414700] **3381**

DICTIONARY OF INTERNATIONAL BIOGRAPHY (UK) [22684597] **432**

DICTIONARY OF LITERARY BIOGRAPHY (US) [08098645] **3381**

DICTIONARY OF LITERARY BIOGRAPHY YEARBOOK (US/0731-7867) [08000229] 3381, **432**

DICTIONARY OF OCCUPATIONAL TITLES (US) [07537146] **4203**

DICTIONARY OF ORGANIC COMPOUNDS (US) [02252834] **1041**

DICTIONARY OF PERFUMES (FR) **403**

DICTIONARY OF SCIENTIFIC BIOGRAPHY (US) [01605836] **432**

DICTIONARY OF SKIN CARE PRODUCTS (FR) **403**

DICTIONARY OF THE DEFENSE INDUSTRY (US/0734-1008) [07301477] **4042**

DICTIONNAIRE BIOGRAPHIQUE DU CANADA (CN/0420-0446) [02489252] **432**

DICTIONNAIRE DE BIOGRAPHIE FRANCAISE (FR/0415-8091) **432**

DICTIONNAIRE DE LA BIBLE. SUPPLEMENT (FR) [06310514] **5016**

DICTIONNAIRE DE L'INDUSTRIE FRANCAISE (FR) **665**

DICTIONNAIRE D'HISTOIRE ET GEOGRAPHIE ECCLESIASTIQUES (FR) [02258193] **2559**

DICTIONNAIRE DU MARCHE COMMUN (FR) **3127**

DICTIONNAIRE PERMANENT. CONSTRUCTION (FR) **2487**

DICTIONNAIRE PERMANENT DROIT EUROPEEN DES AFFAIRES (FR/0998-4313) [l09984313] **2960**

DICTIONNAIRE PERMANENT FISCAL (FR) [08039961] **4642**

DICTIONNAIRE PERMANENT / SECURITE ET CONDITIONS DE TRAVAIL (FR) **1663**

DICTIONNAIRE VIDAL (FR/0419-1153) [05898432] **4299**

DIDAKOMETRY AND SOCIOMETRY (SW/0345-2360) [l03452360] **3277**

DIDAKTIEF (NE) [09507605] **1735**

DIDAKTIKA RUSTINY A JINYCH CIZICH JAZYKU (XR) [21101684] **3277**

DIDASCALIA (ROSARIO, SANTA FE, ARGENTINA) (AG) [09236877] **5028**

DIDASCALIES : CAHIERS OCCASIONNELS DE L'ENSEMBLE THEATRAL MOBILE (BE) [11466104] 3341, **5363**

DIDASCO (CN/0715-9609) [10634808] **1735**

DIDASKALIA (LISBOA) (PO/0253-1674) [01791100] **4953**

DIDASKALIA (OTTERBURNE) (CN/0847-1266) [21497050] **4953**

DIDATTICA DELLE SCIENZE E INFORMATICA NELLA SCUOLA (IT) **1862**

DIDATTICA SCIENTIFICA, LA (IT) [01786739] **5099**

DIDEROT STUDIES (SZ/0070-4806) [01226561] **3381**

DIDSBURY BOOSTER AND MOUNTAIN VIEW COUNTY NEWS (CN/0316-683X) [02247751] **5783**

DIE CASTING ENGINEER (US/0012-253X) [01566622] **2102**

DIE CASTING INDUSTRY BLUE BOOK (US/1056-6090) [23747239] **1604**

DIE CASTING MANAGEMENT (US/0745-449X) [09175966] 865, **3477**

DIEBOLD-MANAGEMENT-REPORT (GW/0341-3683) [l03413683] **665**

DIECIOCHO (US/0163-0415) [04267875] **3381**

DIEHARD (BOSTON, MASS.) (US/0896-7970) [17291426] **2773**

DIELECTRICS & EI NEWS BULLETIN (SW) **2041**

DIELEKTRIKI I POLUPROVODNIKI (UN) [01796545] **4443**

DIELEKTRYCZNE I OPTYCZNE ASPEKTY ODDZIAYWAN MIEDZYCZASTECZKOWYCH (PL/0137-1053) [03303462] **1051**

DIEMAKING STAMPING & EDMING (US) 3477, **2112**

DIEMEX-WHARTON MEXICAN PROJECT, THE (US/8755-0113) [11198410] **1555**

DIEMEX-WHARTON. PROYECTO AUTOMOTRIZ. PROYECCIONES PREVIAS A LA JUNTA (US/8755-0881) [11188517] **5412**

DIEN AN NGI VIET (CN) [24321811] **2259**

DIEN AN TH O *CEASED*. (US/0885-1255) [12573091] **5758**

DIEN DAN NGUOI VIET (FR) **2614**

DIENSPLIG (SA/0250-0280) [12085456] **4042**

DIENST FUER GESELLSCHAFTSPOLITIK (GW) **4471**

DIENST GRONDWATERVERKENNING TNO *See* JAARVERSLAG / DIENST GRONDWATERVERKENNING TNO **1415**

DIENSTLEISTUNGS UND BEHORDEN-COMPASS (AU) [04694307] **665**

DIEPZEE (NE/0921-6111) [l09216111] **3462**

DIESEL & GAS TURBINE CATALOG *See* DIESEL & GAS TURBINE WORLDWIDE CATALOG (1992) **2112**

DIESEL & GAS TURBINE PROGRESS WORLDWIDE *See* DIESEL & GAS TURBINE WORLDWIDE **2112**

DIESEL & GAS TURBINE WORLDWIDE (US/0278-5994) [07823621] **2112**

●DIESEL & GAS TURBINE WORLDWIDE CATALOG (1992) (US/1070-4884) [26117904] **2112**

DIESEL CAR (UK/0956-3806) [l09563806] **5412**

DIESEL CAR DIGEST *CEASED*. (US/0160-7065) [03731903] **5413**

DIESEL ENGINEERING HANDBOOK (US) [01667881] **2112**

DIESEL FUEL DIRECTORY (US/0272-3611) [06797193] **5413**

Alphabetical Title Index — DIGESTS

DIESEL PROGRESS ENGINES & DRIVES (US/1040-8878) [18506003] **2112**

DIET & EXERCISE (US/0163-0334) [04287659] **2596**

DIET AND HEALTH MAGAZINE (US/1048-8391) [21052283] **4189**

●DIET BUSINE$$ BULLETIN, THE (US/1062-9289) [25812073] **4189**

●DIETARY MANAGER (US/1062-1121) [25527426] **4189**

DIETETIC CURRENTS (US/0890-7803) [03985457] **4189**

DIETETIQUE EN ACTION (CN/0834-3160) [16459137] **4189**

DIETETIQUE ET MEDICINE (FR/0769-1793) [07691793] **4189**

DIETETIQUE (MONTREAL) (CN/0701-1350) [03412147] **4190**

DIETITIANS IN NUTRITION SUPPORT : [NEWSLETTER] *See* SUPPORT LINE (CHICAGO, ILL.) **4199**

DIETSCHE WARANDE EN BELFORT (BE/0012-2645) [01566628] **3381**

DIEU EST AMOUR SAINT-CENERE (FR/0180-9288) [01809288] **5028**

DIEZ MINUTOS (SP) **5198**

DIFESA DEL POPOLO (IT) **4471**

DIFESA DELLE PIANTE (IT/0391-4119) [03914119] **508**

DIFESA OGGI (IT/1120-1657) [11201657] **4042**

DIFESA PENALE, LA (IT) [12197851] **3106**

DIFESA SOCIALE (IT/0012-2653) [01777953] 2878, **4773**

DIFFERENCES (FR) **1735**

DIFFERENCES (BLOOMINGTON, IND.) (US/1040-7391) [18507940] **5554**

DIFFERENCES PARIS. 1980 (FR/0247-9095) [02479095] **4471**

DIFFERENCIALNAJA GEOMETRIJA (RU/0130-3198) [02641459] **3503**

DIFFERENDS COMMERCIAUX ENTRE LE CANADA ET LES ETATS-UNIS (CN/1185-9687) [25467975] **831**

●DIFFERENT DRUMMER MAGAZINE (US/1075-1653) [29452077] **2378**

DIFFERENT DRUMMER (TOMS RIVER, N.J.), A (US/0162-8739) [04252400] **3381**

DIFFERENTIA (FLUSHING, N.Y.) (US/0890-4294) [14223608] **4345**

DIFFERENTIAL AND INTEGRAL EQUATIONS (US/0893-4983) [15555206] **3503**

DIFFERENTIAL EQUATIONS (US/0012-2661) [01566629] **3503**

DIFFERENTIAL GEOMETRICAL METHODS IN MATHEMATICAL PHYSICS (GW/0720-485X) [05994462] **4401**

DIFFERENTIAL GEOMETRY AND APPLICATIONS *CEASED.* (US/1053-0517) [22439992] **3503**

DIFFERENTIAL GEOMETRY AND ITS APPLICATIONS (NE/0926-2245) [24621552] **3503**

DIFFERENTIAL THERMAL ANALYSIS (UK) [02255289] **1051**

DIFFERENTIATION (LONDON) (GW/0301-4681) [02240102] **536**

DIFFERENTSIALNYE URAVNENIJA (RJAZAN) (RU/0320-104X) [02621548] **3503**

DIFFUSION AND DEFECT DATA. [PT. A], DEFECT AND DIFFUSION FORUM (SZ/1012-0386) [18285596] **1051**

DIFFUSION AND DEFECT DATA. [PT. B], SOLID STATE PHENOMENA : SSP (LH/1012-0394) [18452655] **1051**

DIFFUSION BECANCOUR (CN/0836-5369) [17314124] **974**

DIFFUSION DES PROGRAMMES AUDIOVISUELS, LA (BE) 5316, **4368**

DIFUSION FISCAL *See* REVISTA DIFUSION FISCAL **4747**

DIG (TORONTO) (CN/0710-0493) [08078863] **2249**

DIGEST (US) [01784740] **4067**

DIGEST AND DECISIONS OF THE EMPLOYEES' COMPENSATION APPEALS BOARD (US) [16702590] **3146**

DIGEST - ANTENNAS AND PROPAGATION SOCIETY SYMPOSIUM (US/1064-3125) [24778651] 2041, **5099**

DIGEST - BRITISH CATTLE BREEDERS' CLUB (UK/0521-0097) [03834922] **210**

DIGEST BUSINESS & LAW JOURNAL (CN/0315-811X) [01996024] **3099**

DIGEST DE LA CONSTRUCTION AU CANADA (CN/0701-5267) [02603737] **612**

DIGEST FOR EDUCATIONAL & TRAINING (UK) **1912**

DIGEST FOR HOME FURNISHERS (US/1053-4571) [01782047] **2905**

DIGEST FOR REPORTERS (US/0364-2658) [02549754] **170**

DIGEST, HOUSE AND SENATE BILLS AND RESOLUTIONS (SOUTH CAROLINA) (US) [06172678] **2960**

DIGEST - INTERNATIONAL GEOSCIENCE AND REMOTE SENSING SYMPOSIUM (IGARSS) (US) [07928872] **1354**

DIGEST : LLOYD'S LAW REPORTS (UK) [03718711] **3180**

DIGEST OF ACTS OF THE GENERAL ASSEMBLY OF VIRGINIA (US) [07643321] **2961**

DIGEST OF ADVISORY OPINIONS (US) [06976447] 4642, **2249**

DIGEST OF AGRICULTURAL CENSUS STATISTICS, UNITED KINGDOM / MINISTRY OF AGRICULTURE, FISHERIES AND FOOD ... [ET AL.], THE (UK) [27522549] 79, **153**

DIGEST OF ANNUAL STATISTICS - HONG KONG TOURIST ASSOCIATION. RESEARCH DEPT *See* STATISTICAL REVIEW OF TOURISM, HONG KONG, A **5500**

DIGEST OF BALANCE SHEETS (UK) [04071284] **787**

DIGEST OF BENEFIT ENTITLEMENT PRINCIPLES (CN) [01553003] 2878, **1663**

DIGEST OF BILLS ENACTED BY THE GENERAL ASSEMBLY (US/0160-1377) [03621701] **2961**

DIGEST OF BILLS PASSED BY THE ... LEGISLATURE (US) [11196833] **2961**

DIGEST OF CHIROPRACTIC ECONOMICS, THE (US/0415-8407) [05049593] **3572**

DIGEST OF CITY LAWS (SEATTLE, WASH.) (US/0090-175X) [01784656] **2961**

DIGEST OF COMMISSION POLICIES AND COURT DECISIONS. WATER AND SEWER (US) [07703586] **2961**

DIGEST OF COUNCIL BILLS - WISCONSIN. LEGISLATIVE COUNCIL (US/0272-832X) [06928692] **2961**

DIGEST OF COURT DECISIONS (NEW YORK, N.Y.) (US/0516-9011) [04819752] **2961**

DIGEST OF DECISIONS (US) **939**

DIGEST OF DECISIONS OF THE COURT (KE) [07601527] **2961**

DIGEST OF ENACTMENTS, GENERAL ASSEMBLY (US/0160-0915) [03611724] **2961**

DIGEST OF ENVIRONMENTAL LAW (US) [25525574] 2163, **2961**

DIGEST OF ENVIRONMENTAL PROTECTION AND WATER STATISTICS / DEPARTMENT OF THE ENVIRONMENT (UK) [18203161] **2227**

DIGEST OF GENERAL LAWS ENACTED BY THE REGULAR SESSION AND SPECIAL SESSION OF THE FLORIDA LEGISLATURE (US) [06597581] **2961**

DIGEST OF GERIATRICS *CEASED.* (US/1056-1951) [23528768] **3750**

DIGEST OF INFORMATION AND PATENT REVIEW (UK) [05180310] **2588**

DIGEST OF INFORMATION ON FUSES PROTECTIVE AND SWITCHING DEVICES (UK) **2041**

DIGEST OF INVESTMENT ADVICES, THE (US/0012-2742) [04049207] 1479, **896**

DIGEST OF JAPANESE INDUSTRY & TECHNOLOGY : DJIT (JA) [09380460] **5099**

DIGEST OF KUWAIT OFFICIAL GAZETTE (KU) [07036901] **2961**

DIGEST OF MOTOR LAWS (US/0093-4062) [01792717] 5381, **2961**

DIGEST OF MUNICIPAL & PLANNING LAW, THE (CN/1181-9006) [23598122] **2961**

DIGEST OF NEUROLOGY AND PSYCHIATRY (US/0012-2769) [06698998] 3924, **3831**

DIGEST OF OFFICIAL OPINIONS - ATTORNEY GENERAL (LITTLE ROCK) (US/0364-0817) [02591598] **3140**

DIGEST OF OFFICIAL OPINIONS - ATTORNEY GENERAL (TALLAHASSEE) (US/0092-0843) [01788027] **3140**

DIGEST OF OPINIONS OF THE ATTORNEY GENERAL (US/0012-2777) [03208493] **3140**

DIGEST OF OREGON LAWS (US/0095-1161) [01783757] **2961**

DIGEST OF PAPERS - INTERNATIONAL SYMPOSIUM ON FAULT-TOLERANT COMPUTING (1979) (US/0731-3071) [04013616] **1182**

DIGEST OF POLYMER DEVELOPMENTS. SER. 3, STYRENICS AND ACRYLICS (US/1075-2013) [29967446] **2012**

DIGEST OF PUBLIC GENERAL BILLS AND RESOLUTIONS *CEASED.* (US/0012-2785) [02554382] **4642**

DIGEST OF REPORT - TRANSPORT AND ROAD RESEARCH LABORATORY (UK/0269-8196) [03554959] **5440**

DIGEST OF RICO INVESTIGATIONS (US/0276-0150) [07133029] **2961**

DIGEST OF SELECTED REPORTS - UNITED WAY OF AMERICA *CEASED.* (US/0146-9088) [03058167] **5282**

DIGEST OF SIGNIFICANT CLASSIFICATION DECISIONS AND OPINIONS (US/0276-3567) [07333432] **939**

DIGEST OF SOFTWARE REVIEWS : EDUCATION, THE (US/0749-9302) [09453878] 1223, **1285**

DIGEST OF STATE LAND SALES REGULATIONS, THE (US/0739-6368) [09801241] **4836**

DIGEST OF STATE LEGISLATION AND RULE MAKING ACTIVITIES / PREPARED BY NEW YORK STATE DEPARTMENT OF COMMERCE IN COOPERATION WITH NEW YORK STATE DEPARTMENT OF STATE (US) [25294320] **665**

DIGEST OF STATISTICS (INTERNATIONAL CIVIL AVIATION ORGANIZATION) (CN) [06936858] **41**

DIGEST OF STATISTICS - INTERNATIONAL CIVIL AVIATION ORGANIZATION. SERIES AT, AIRPORT TRAFFIC (INT/0074-2422) [00742422] **17**

DIGEST OF STATISTICS - INTERNATIONAL CIVIL AVIATION ORGANIZATION. SERIES FP, FLEET-PERSONNEL (INT/0074-2449) [00742449] **17**

DIGEST OF STATISTICS - INTERNATIONAL CIVIL AVIATION ORGANIZATION. SERIES R, CIVIL AIRCRAFT ON REGISTER (INT/0074-2457) [00742457] **17**

DIGEST OF TECHNICAL INFORMATION (US/0882-1143) [11364642] **1153**

DIGEST OF TECHNICAL PAPERS (US/0097-966X) [01799368] **2041**

DIGEST OF TECHNICAL PAPERS / IEEE INTERNATIONAL CONFERENCE ON CONSUMER ELECTRONICS (US/0747-668X) [08777098] **2041**

DIGEST OF TECHNICAL PAPERS / IEEE INTERNATIONAL SOLID-STATE CIRCUITS CONFERENCE (US/0193-6530) [02675897] **2041**

DIGEST OF TECHNICAL PAPERS / SYMPOSIUM ON VLSI TECHNOLOGY (US/0743-1562) [08313250] **2041**

DIGEST OF TOURISM STATISTICS / BARBADOS STATISTICAL SERVICE (BB) [08091349] **5500**

DIGEST OF TOURIST STATISTICS (UK) [03529726] **5468**

DIGEST OF UNITED KINGDOM ENERGY STATISTICS (UK/0307-0603) [02241803] 1936, **1961**

DIGEST OF UNITED STATES PRACTICE IN INTERNATIONAL LAW (US/0095-3369) [04916863] **3127**

DIGEST OF WELSH STATISTICS (UK) [01566645] **1479**

DIGEST ON GAY RIGHTS (CN/0229-0812) [08028268] **4507**

DIGEST - TEXAS. DEPT. OF PUBLIC SAFETY. DIVISION OF DISASTER EMERGENCY SERVICES, THE (US) [05285161] **4773**

DIGEST - UNIVERSITY OF PENNSYLVANIA. DEPT. OF FOLKLORE AND FOLKLIFE, THE (US/0737-7703) [09234884] 235, **2333**

DIGESTER *See* DIGESTER, OVER THE SPILLWAY, THE **2227**

DIGESTER, OVER THE SPILLWAY, THE (US) [04731022] **2227**

DIGESTION (SZ/0012-2823) [01566646] **3744**

DIGESTIVE DISEASES (US) [05758425] **3744**

DIGESTIVE DISEASES AND SCIENCES (US/0163-2116) [04317782] **3744**

DIGESTIVE DISEASES (BASEL) (SZ/0257-2753) [13877772] **3744**

DIGESTIVE ENDOSCOPY : OFFICIAL JOURNAL OF THE JAPAN GASTROENTEROLOGICAL ENDOSCOPY SOCIETY (JA/0915-5635) [23045533] **3744**

DIGESTIVE SURGERY (SZ/0253-4886) [11354687] 3744, **3963**

DIGESTO ECONOMICO / SOB OS AUSPICIOS DA ASSOCIACAO COMERCIAL DE SAO PAULO E DA FEDERACAO DO COMERCIO DO ESTADO DE SAO PAULO (BL) [05828861] **1479**

DIGESTO NOTARIAL (AG) [05078467] **4720**

DIGESTS OF DECISIONS OF THE COMPTROLLER GENERAL OF THE UNITED STATES (US) [21953125] **4720**

DIGGER'S Alphabetical Title Index

DIGGER'S DIGEST (YUBA CITY, CALIF. : 1980), THE **CEASED.** (US/0740-9079) [10026174] **2445**

DIGHTON HERALD (DIGHTON, KAN. : 1916) (US) [11704927] **5675**

DIGITAL AERONAUTICAL CHART SUPPLEMENT. SECTION 7, STANDARD INSTRUMENT DEPARTURES (US) [16992620] **17**

DIGITAL & AUDIO/VIDEO DISCONTINUED DEVICES **CEASED.** (US/8755-738X) [11378404] **5316**

DIGITAL DESKTOP REVIEW (US/1048-4639) [20954672] **1182**

DIGITAL DIRECTIONS REPORT (US/1047-1693) [20617633] **1246, 1258**

DIGITAL EQUIPMENT COMPUTER USERS SOCIETY **See** PROCEEDINGS OF THE DIGITAL EQUIPMENT COMPUTER USERS SOCIETY **1200**

DIGITAL EVOLUTION MAGAZINE (CN/1181-7917) [24266752] **4368, 1131**

DIGITAL GAMES REVIEW (US/1059-5457) [24654183] **4860**

DIGITAL INFORMATION GROUP'S INFORMATION INDUSTRY BULLETIN (US/1059-0080) [24418337] **3206**

DIGITAL MEDIA (US) **1233**

DIGITAL MEDIA (US/1056-7038) [23820003] **2113**

●DIGITAL NEWS & REVIEW (US/1065-7452) [26710736] **1246**

DIGITAL NEWS (BOSTON, MASS.) (US/0891-9860) [15049764] **1182**

DIGITAL NEWS (BOSTON, MASS.) **See** DIGITAL NEWS & REVIEW **1246**

DIGITAL PROCESSES **SUSPENDED.** (SZ/0301-4184) [03398825] **2042**

DIGITAL PUBLISHING (US/0884-0881) [12307561] **4813**

DIGITAL REVIEW (NEW YORK, N.Y.) **See** DIGITAL NEWS & REVIEW **1246**

DIGITAL REVIEW (NEW YORK, N.Y.) (US/0739-4314) [09734850] **1267**

DIGITAL SIGNAL PROCESSING (US/1051-2004) [21889588] **1182**

DIGITAL SYSTEM DESIGN SERIES (US/0888-2118) [13519435] **1182**

●DIGITAL SYSTEMS JOURNAL (US/1067-7224) [27189658] **1279, 1182**

DIGITAL TECHNICAL JOURNAL (US/0898-901X) [15467755] **2113**

●DIGITAL UNIX NEWS (US/1074-8911) [29870524] **1182**

DIGITALE BILDDIAGNOSTIK (GW/0724-7591) [11227360] **3941**

DIGITAL'S RDB WORLD **CEASED.** (US/1059-9991) [24842506] **1182**

DIGNIDAD (US) [24112766] **1663**

DIGNITY (US/0147-1139) [03087880] **5187**

DIGO KAPELLEN (BE/0775-8251) [I07758251] **1892**

DIJALEKTIKA (YU/0419-1439) [05237399] **5099**

DIKAIO KAI POLITIKE (THESSALONIKE, GREECE : 1982) (GR) [10768642] **3127**

DIKGANG TSA GOMPIENO (BS) **5779**

●DIKOBRAZ (XR) [28329833] **4860**

DIKTA (US/0363-5414) [02470956] **4386, 3206**

DILI ZHISHI (CC/0257-019X) [02106071] **2559**

DILIMAN REVIEW, THE (PH/0012-2858) [01777498] **319, 5198**

DILLON HERALD, THE (US) [13622262] **5742**

DILTHEY-JAHRBUCH FUER PHILOSOPHIE UND GESCHICHTE DER GEISTESWISSENSCHAFTEN (GW) [10625449] **2614**

DIMANCHE EN PAROISSE (FR) **4953**

DIMANCHE ET FETE (CN/0317-2198) [02247943] **4953**

DIMANCHES BIOLOGIQUES DE LARIBOISIERE ... (FR/1169-0356) [I11690356] **453**

DIME NOVEL ROUND-UP (1953) (US/0012-2874) [04995603] **3381**

DIMENSAO (BL) [02480467] **1735**

DIMENSION (US/0162-6825) [04206341] **4953**

●DIMENSIONP2S (KILGORE, TEX.) (US/1072-7655) [29197611] **3381**

DIMENSION; CONTEMPORARY GERMAN ARTS AND LETTERS **CEASED.** (US/0012-2882) [01566650] **3381**

DIMENSIONAL STONE (US/0883-0258) [12037286] **613**

DIMENSIONI E PROBLEMI DELLA RICERCA STORICA : RIVISTA DEL DIPARTIMENTO DI STUDI STORICI DAL MEDIOEVO ALL'ETA CONTEMPORANEA DELL'UNIVERSITA "LA SAPIENZA" DI ROMA (IT) [20831969] **2614**

DIMENSIONS (CN/0839-1300) [18805432] **865**

DIMENSIONS (CN/0836-5059) [17241052] **4241**

DIMENSIONS (US) [05510154] **1101**

DIMENSIONS ... (US) [04122407] **3163**

DIMENSIONS ECONOMIQUES DE LA BOURGOGNE (FR) [06288415] **5227**

DIMENSIONS (EXXON CORPORATION) (US/0732-4758) [08336335] **1604**

DIMENSIONS (HULL) (CN/0705-0666) [03900303] **1820**

DIMENSIONS IN HEALTH SERVICE **See** LEADERSHIP IN HEALTH SERVICES **3787**

DIMENSIONS (LITTLE ROCK, ARK. 1973) (US/0160-6425) [03431443] **1892**

DIMENSIONS (MONTREAL) (CN/0709-2334) [06316034] **1735**

DIMENSIONS (NEW YORK, N.Y.) (US/0882-1240) [11768415] **2685**

DIMENSIONS OF CRITICAL CARE NURSING (US/0730-4625) [08005218] **3855**

●DIMENSIONS OF EARLY CHILDHOOD (US/0160-6425) [26066787] **1803**

DIMENSIONS OF INTERNATIONAL EDUCATION (US) [04047671] **1735**

DIMENSIONS OF THE INDEPENDENT SECTOR **See** NONPROFIT ALMANAC **5299**

DIMENSIONS (WINONA, MINN.) (US/1057-4506) [24037319] **1182**

DIMS. DRUG INDEX FOR MALAYSIA & SINGAPORE (HK) [03917149] **4299**

DIN-ANZEIGER FUER TECHNISCHE REGELN (GW/0723-7685) [I07237685] **4030**

DIN : CATALOG OF THE GERMAN INSTITUTE OF STANDARDS (GW) **4030**

DIN-KATALOG FUER TECHNISCHE REGELN (GW/0722-9313) [I07229313] **5099**

DIN-MITTEILUNGEN + ELEKTRONORM (GW/0722-2912) [I07222912] **4030**

DIN O DANISH (PK) [01695640] **5042**

DINAMIKA I PROCHNOST GORNYKH MASHIN (RU) [02703470] **2138**

DINAMIKA I TOCHNOST FUNKTSIONIROVANIA TEPLOMEKHANICHESKIKH SISTEM (RU) [05734483] **2113**

DINAMIKA SISTEM (RU/0130-318X) [05926272] **3503**

DINAMIS (AG) [01787889] **2731**

DINAR (KU) [07633098] **787**

DINE ISRAEL (IS/0070-4903) [01566655] **2259, 3089**

DINERO (SP) **1479**

DINES LETTER (US) [01670759] **896**

DINGHY SAILING (UK/0307-3017) [01785449] **593**

DINNY'S CALGARY DIGEST (CN/0046-029X) [01996087] **5581**

●DINOSAUR REVIEW (BOULDER, COLO.), THE (US/1060-4006) [24960286] **1062, 4227**

DINOSAURIAN WHO'S-WHO (CN/0315-0801) [02362904] **432**

DINTERIA (SA/0012-3013) [04794864] **508**

DINUBA SENTINEL (US/0745-6654) [09352967] **5634**

DIO (BALTIMORE, MD.) (US/1041-5440) [18798426] **395**

DIOCESAN POST (CN/0846-3301) [25314117] **5059**

DIOCESE OF FOND DU LAC **See** FOND DU LAC CLARION, THE **5767**

DIODEN (GW) [03353985] **2042**

DIOGENE (EDITION FRANCAISE) (FR/0419-1633) [04713491] **4345, 2845**

DIOGENES : ANUARIO CRITICO DEL TEATRO LATINOAMERICANO (AG) [17167960] **5363**

DIOGENES (ENGLISH ED.) (IT/0392-1921) [01592604] **2845, 4345**

DIONGA (CG) [01786034] **2639**

DIONISO (IT) [02260385] **5363**

DIONYSIUS (CN/0705-1085) [03798512] **4345, 1076**

DIONYSOS (SUPERIOR, WISC.) (US/1044-4149) [19783445] **1350, 1342**

DIOTIMA (GR/1010-7363) [02246664] **4345**

DIOZESE HILDESHEIM IN VERGANGENHEIT UND GEGENWART, DIE (GW/0341-9975) [02245129] **5028**

DIPCO (IT) **1479**

DIPINTI DEL XIX SECOLO. CATALOGO E LISTINO (IT) **319**

DIPLOMACIA EN ACCION (UY) [25836849] **4520**

DIPLOMACY (KO) [03315117] **4520**

DIPLOMACY AND STATECRAFT (UK/0959-2296) [22548326] **4520**

DIPLOMAT (LONDON, ENGLAND), THE (UK) [13621597] **4520**

DIPLOMATE DIRECTORY **See** DIRECTORY OF DIPLOMATES / AMERICAN BOARD OF FAMILY PRACTICE **3737**

DIPLOMATIC AND CONSULAR DIRECTORY (LILONGWE, MALAWI) (MW) [10069721] **4520**

DIPLOMATIC AND CONSULAR LIST (BB) [17239577] **831**

DIPLOMATIC AND CONSULAR LIST (ZOMBA, MALAWI) **See** DIPLOMATIC AND CONSULAR DIRECTORY (LILONGWE, MALAWI) **4520**

DIPLOMATIC, CONSULAR AND OTHER REPRESENTATION IN THE DEMOCRATIC SOCIALIST REPUBLIC OF SRI LANKA (CE) [06494739] **3127**

DIPLOMATIC, CONSULAR, AND OTHER REPRESENTATIVES IN CANADA (CN/0825-6683) [10740640] **4642**

DIPLOMATIC CORPS AND CONSULAR, TRADE, AND OTHER FOREIGN REPRESENTATIVES IN PAKISTAN / MINISTRY OF FOREIGN AFFAIRS (PK) [08391706] **4520**

DIPLOMATIC CORPS. MINISTRY OF EXTERNAL AFFAIRS (KINGSTON) (JM/0376-8384) [01794919] **4520**

DIPLOMATIC HISTORY (US/0145-2096) [02693658] **2731**

DIPLOMATIC LIST AND LIST OF REPRESENTATIVES OF INTERNATIONAL ORGANIZATIONS / DEPARTMENT OF FOREIGN AFFAIRS AND TRADE (AT) [20506710] **4643**

DIPLOMATIC LIST (INDIA) (II) [05194264] **4643**

DIPLOMATIC LIST (WASHINGTON) (US/0012-3099) [01768336] **3127**

DIPLOMATIC PRESS DIRECTORY OF THE REPUBLIC OF CYPRUS INCLUDING TRADE INDEX AND BIOGRAPHICAL SECTION (UK/0417-5131) [05204551] **432, 4520**

DIPLOMATIC PRESS SUDAN TRADE DIRECTORY, THE (UK/0082-5735) [01566665] **831**

DIPLOMATIC RECORD, THE (US/1052-0309) [22169376] **4471**

DIPLOMATIC REGISTER AND DESK REFERENCE (US/0736-0959) [09031153] **3127**

DIPLOMATIC SERVICE LIST (GREAT BRITAIN), THE (UK/0419-1714) [01566667] **4471**

DIPLOMATIC WORLD BULLETIN AND DELEGATES WORLD BULLETIN, THE (US/0363-8200) [02530758] **4520**

●DIPLOMATICHESKII VESTNIK (RU) [25929432] **3127**

DIPLOMAT'S ANNUAL, THE (UK/0070-4962) [01566668] **4472**

DIPLOMES - UNIVERSITE DE MONTREAL (CN/0228-9636) [07817456] **1820**

DIPPY. DIRECT INPUT PHOTOTYPESETTING NEWSLETTER (US) [05814771] **4564**

DIQIU HUAXUE (CC/0379-1726) [02093785] **974, 1373**

DIQIU WULIXUE BAO (CC/0001-5733) [02098160] **1404**

DIRASAT AFRIQIYAH (UA) [07625954] **2639**

DIRASAT DAWLIYAH (TI) [11047222] **4520**

DIRASAT KURDIYAH (FR/0765-1074) [11994345] **2768**

DIRASAT. SERIES B, PURE AND APPLIED SCIENCES (JO) [23980935] **5099**

DIRASAT SUKKANIYAH (UA) [04449869] **4552**

DIRASAT THAQAFIYAH (US) [25387590] **5244**

DIRE **See** NOUVEAU DIRE, LE **1620**

DIRE PARIS. 1988 (FR/1015-2512) [I10152512] **4472**

DIRECCION (KANSAS CITY, MO.) **See** HERALDO DE SANTIDAD (1992), EL **4962**

DIRECCION (KANSAS CITY, MO.) (US/1047-6318) [20742586] **4953**

DIRECCION Y PROGRESO (SP/0210-0908) [I02100908] **665**

DIRECCIONES DE TANDIL (AG) [01799163] **831**

DIRECT ACCESS (CALGARY) (CN/0843-5979) [19930130] **4386**

Alphabetical Title Index — **DIRECTORY**

DIRECT (BUFFALO, N.Y.) (US/1057-4182) [24033554] **2532**

DIRECT CONTRACTING & HOSPITAL MANAGED CARE (US/1057-0098) [23907282] **3779**

DIRECT DEPOSIT MARKETING (US) [17884278] **787**

●DIRECT-FED MICROBIAL, ENZYME & FORAGE ADDITIVE COMPENDIUM (US) [28131376] **79**

DIRECT FROM CUBA (CU) [01566672] **2512**

DIRECT INVESTMENT IN NORTH AMERICA (UK) **896**

DIRECT INVESTMENT LAW REPORT (US/0270-4552) [06429732] **3127**

DIRECT LABOUR ORGANISATIONS STATISTICS ... ACTUALS / CIPFA, STATISTICAL INFORMATION SERVICE (UK) [10880332] 1663, **1531**

DIRECT LEVIES ON GAMING IN NEVADA (US/0093-8823) [01792432] 4860, **4720**

DIRECT LINE (US) [01566673] **2512**

DIRECT LINE (SASKATOON) (CN/1185-0213) [23598317] **1153**

DIRECT LOAN PROGRAM FOR THE ELDERLY OR HANDICAPPED (US) [03116413] 5178, 4386, **5282**

DIRECT MAGAZINE (US) **923**

DIRECT MAIL LIST RATES AND DATA (US/0419-182X) [02250576] **758**

DIRECT MARKETING (US/0012-3188) [02104882] **923**

DIRECT MARKETING INTERNATIONAL (UK) **923**

●DIRECT MARKETING LIST SOURCE (US/1071-4561) [28642447] **923**

DIRECT MARKETING MARKET PLACE, THE (US/0192-3137) [05015170] 923, **728**

DIRECT MARKETING NEWS DIGEST (US/0197-1875) [05985667] **923**

DIRECT MARKETING NEWS (MARKHAM) (CN/1187-7111) [26066711] **923**

DIRECT RESPONSE (UK/0952-9764) [l09529764] **923**

DIRECT RESPONSE MARKETING TO SCHOOLS *See* SCHOOL MARKETING NEWSLETTER **936**

DIRECT RESPONSE MARKETING TO SCHOOLS NEWSLETTER (US/0882-701X) [11929967] **923**

DIRECT RESPONSE SPECIALIST (US) **2532**

DIRECT SELLING IN CANADA (CN/0590-5702) [02443705] **923**

DIRECT (STAMFORD, CONN.) (US/1046-4174) [20316133] **923**

DIRECT TAXES BULLETIN *CEASED.* (II) [01752784] **4720**

DIRECTEUR D'ASSOCIATION (CN/0839-1629) [18805630] **665**

DIRECTIEVE THERAPIE (NE) [06194760] **3924**

DIRECTION (US/0092-7449) [01789838] **5381**

DIRECTION DES RESSOURCES EDUCATIVES FRANCAISES EN ACTION, LA (CN/1191-145X) [25883306] **1735**

DIRECTION ET GESTION DES ENTREPRISES (FR/0012-320X) [04710035] **665**

DIRECTION INFORMATIQUE (CN/0842-1951) [19271758] **1182**

DIRECTION (LONDON, ENGLAND) (UK) [13686427] **349**

DIRECTION (LONDON, ENGLAND) *See* XYZ DIRECTION **369**

DIRECTION OF TRADE STATISTICS (ELECTRONIC ED.) *CEASED.* (US/1017-2734) [13172206] **831**

DIRECTION OF TRADE STATISTICS - INTERNATIONAL MONETARY FUND (MONTHLY EDITION) (US/0252-306X) [07154584] 831, **728**

DIRECTION OF TRADE STATISTICS. YEARBOOK - INTERNATIONAL MONETARY FUND (US/0252-3019) [07866916] 831, **728**

DIRECTION (WINNIPEG) (US/0384-8515) [01586804] **4953**

DIRECTIONARY OF THE DEFENSE INDUSTRY INCLUDING NATO AND WARSAW PACT COUNTRIES (US/0734-1008) [21494210] **4042**

DIRECTIONS : A NEWSLETTER FROM EBSCO PUBLISHING *SUSPENDED.* (US/0897-9499) [17679707] **3206**

DIRECTIONS AT RIDER COLLEGE (US/0279-408X) [07833486] **1101**

DIRECTIONS (AUSTIN, TEX.) *CEASED.* (US/0742-678X) [10416655] **1237**

DIRECTIONS - B.C. HYDRO (CN/1181-9367) [23659164] **4643**

DIRECTIONS - BRITISH COLUMBIA PREMIER'S ADVISORY COUNCIL FOR PERSONS WITH DISABILITIES (CN/1182-4441) [23259499] **4386**

DIRECTIONS (BROOKLINE, MASS.) (US) [10462106] 1820, **4953**

DIRECTIONS (EVANSTON, ILL.) (US) [28996171] **1110**

DIRECTIONS FOR PENNSYLVANIA SINGLES! (US/1058-4188) [24298598] 3995, **5554**

DIRECTIONS; HUMAN RESOURCES DIRECTORY OF SAN DIEGO-IMPERIAL COUNTIES & TIJUANA (US) [05434164] **5282**

DIRECTIONS IN APPLIED NUTRITION *CEASED.* (US/0888-286X) [13521103] **4190**

DIRECTIONS IN FAITH (US/0885-4335) [12680139] **4953**

DIRECTIONS IN GOVERNMENT (AT/1030-391X) [1030391X] **4472**

DIRECTIONS IN MENTAL HEALTH COUNSELING (US/1062-0788) [25518795] **4585**

DIRECTIONS IN ONCOLOGY (US/0883-0312) [12047002] **3816**

DIRECTIONS IN PSYCHIATRY (US/0891-3870) [11603127] **3924**

DIRECTIONS (KANSAS CITY, MO.) (US/0732-7498) [08435174] **3572**

DIRECTIONS (NEW YORK, N.Y. 1975) (US/0360-473X) [02244719] **3206**

DIRECTIONS (NEW YORK, N.Y. : 1985) *CEASED.* (US/0883-9727) [12269863] **923**

DIRECTIONS - ONTARIO ASSOCIATION FOR COMMUNITY LIVING (CN/0836-6160) [17526767] **4386**

DIRECTIONS - ONTARIO COUNCIL OF TEACHERS OF ENGLISH (CN/1184-2717) [24257167] **3381**

DIRECTIONS - PUBLIC SERVICE COMMISSION OF CANADA (CN/0848-6859) [22928291] **4643**

DIRECTIONS - PUBLIC SERVICE COMMISSION OF CANADA (CN/0848-6859) [22928291] **4643**

DIRECTIONS SUVA (FJ/1011-5846) [l0115846] 1735, **3206**

DIRECTIONS (TORONTO. 1981) (CN/0711-0561) [08861995] **1820**

DIRECTOIRE. NEW YORK METROPOLITAN ED., INCLUDING SUBURBAN DESIGNER RESOURCES, LE (US/0749-4556) [11108578] **2905**

DIRECTOR (LONDON. 1935) (UK/0012-3242) [09907489] **666**

DIRECTOR (MADISON, WIS.), THE (US/0199-3186) [05062183] **2407**

DIRECTOR, THE (II/0012-3250) [03908872] **665**

DIRECTORIES AND ASSOCIATIONS OF THE BOOK TRADE AND LIBRARIANSHIP (US) [05244455] **4828**

DIRECTORIES IN PRINT (US/0899-353X) [18075722] **415**

DIRECTORIES IN PRINT. SUPPLEMENT (US) [19790096] **415**

DIRECTORIES OF HAWAII (US/0094-209X) [01794154] **2559**

DIRECTORIO, ARTE Y ARTISTAS DE COLOMBIA *See* FORMA Y COLOR COLOMBIA **350**

DIRECTORIO COLOMBIANO DE UNIDADES DE INFORMACION (CK) [03717968] **3206**

DIRECTORIO COMERCIAL E INDUSTRIAL DE EL SALVADOR. EL SALVADOR'S COMMERCIAL AND INDUSTRIAL DIRECTORY (ES) [05912195] 666, **1604**

DIRECTORIO DE DESPACHOS PUBLICOS (CK) [02244998] **4643**

DIRECTORIO DE ESTABLECIMIENTOS INDUSTRIALES DE PRIMERA Y SEGUNDA CATEGORIA (BO) [06893603] **1604**

DIRECTORIO DE INSTITUCIONES FINANCIERAS (CK) [05223486] **787**

DIRECTORIO DE LA EXPORTACION CHILENA *See* EXPORT DIRECTORY CHILE **834**

DIRECTORIO DE LA INDUSTRIA DE LAS ARTES GRAFICAS (MX) [03790849] **378**

DIRECTORIO DE LA INDUSTRIA TURISTICA DE EL SALVADOR (ES) [07986958] **5468**

DIRECTORIO DE LA INDUSTRIA Y COMERCIO DE CENTROAMERICA Y PANAMA (CR) [02703668] **1604**

DIRECTORIO DE MEDIOS (MX) [01790050] **1110**

DIRECTORIO DE MIEMBROS - SOCIEDAD INTERAMERICANA DE PSICOLOGIA (US/0149-4368) [03488052] **4585**

DIRECTORIO DE PERIODISTAS PROFESIONALES DE COLOMBIA (CK) [05453169] **2919**

DIRECTORIO DE SOCIOS / CAMARA DE COMERCIO AMERICANA EN ESPANA (SP) [09104548] **819**

DIRECTORIO DEL ABOGADO (PE) [02906202] **2961**

DIRECTORIO FINANCIERO NACIONAL (CK/0120-0755) [01798276] **787**

DIRECTORIO INDUSTRIAL AZUCARERO (VE) [01785381] **2333**

DIRECTORIO INDUSTRIAL, CENTROAMERICA-PANAMA (GT) [02246888] **1604**

DIRECTORIO INDUSTRIAL DE LATINO AMERICA (MX) [03566178] **1604**

DIRECTORIO INDUSTRIAL U.S.A (US/0094-5595) [01794819] **1604**

DIRECTORIO INDUSTRIAL Y COMERCIAL DE HONDURAS (HO/0331-0639) [09395140] **1604**

DIRECTORIO LATINOAMERICANO DE INSTITUCIONES FINANCIERAS DE DESARROLLO (PE) [03123304] **787**

DIRECTORIO MEDICO PANAMENO (PN/0417-5433) [01682434] **3913**

DIRECTORIO MINERO NACIONAL (CK) [04718251] **2138**

DIRECTORIO MPM : MEDIOS AUDIO/VISUALES; INFORMACION Y TARIFAS (MX) [02173842] **758**

DIRECTORIO MUSICAL VENEZOLANO / DIVISION DE MUSICA Y FONOTECA (VE) [08578607] **4114**

DIRECTORIO NACIONAL DE CURSOS DE POSTGRADO (VE) [02241690] **1820**

DIRECTORIO ONCOLOGICO LATINOAMERICANO / FLASCA, FEDERACION LATINOAMERICANA DE SOCIEDADES DE CANCEROLOGIA (AG) [15688912] **3816**

DIRECTORIO POSTAL DE PANAMA (PN) [09332734] **1144**

DIRECTORIO PROFESIONAL HISPANO (US/0147-5657) [03197666] **1663**

DIRECTORIO PROVISIONAL DE EXPORTADORES / MINISTERIO DE COMERCIO EXTERIOR (NQ) [08784328] **831**

DIRECTORIO TELEX (SAN SALVADOR, EL SALVADOR) (ES) [12096068] **1153**

DIRECTORIO TURISTICO / DEPARTAMENTO DE ASUNTOS ECONOMICOS, DIVISION DE COMERCIO INTERNACIONAL Y TURISMO *CEASED.* (US) [11099760] **5468**

DIRECTORS & BOARDS (US/0364-9156) [02694117] **865**

DIRECTORS' ANNUAL REPORT (BL) [02417049] **1604**

DIRECTOR'S ANNUAL REPORT / TANZANIA BUREAU OF STANDARDS *See* ANNUAL REPORT / TANZANIA BUREAU OF STANDARDS **4029**

DIRECTORS DIGEST (CHICAGO, ILL.) (US) [13108971] **787**

DIRECTOR'S DIGEST PORTFOLIO (II) [11031447] **1555**

DIRECTORS ENCYCLOPEDIA OF NEWSPAPERS, THE (US/0270-7543) [06465953] **1925**

DIRECTORS GUILD OF AMERICA *See* DIRECTORY OF MEMBERS - DIRECTORS GUILD OF AMERICA **4068**

DIRECTORS GUILD OF GREAT BRITAIN *See* DIRECTORY OF MEMBERS / DIRECTORS GUILD OF GREAT BRITAIN **4068**

DIRECTORS' REPORT AND ACCOUNTS / BRITISH GAS (UK) [27419479] **4254**

DIRECTORS' REPORT AND FINANCIAL STATEMENT (IS) [01792844] **787**

DIRECTORS' REPORT - AUSTRALIAN MINES AND METALS ASSOCIATION (AT) [02351494] 4001, **2138**

DIRECTOR'S REPORT FOR THE ARNOLD ARBORETUM, THE (US/8755-1799) [10603423] **508**

DIRECTOR'S REPORT - PAPANICOLAOU CANCER RESEARCH INSTITUTE AT MIAMI FLORIDA (US/0090-7359) [01785267] **3816**

DIRECTORSHIP (WESTPORT) (US/0193-4279) [06395420] **865**

DIRECTORY (US) [13433975] **742**

●DIRECTORY (US) [24888652] **5100**

DIRECTORY (US/0543-2774) [02255069] 3572, **3206**

DIRECTORY - ACADEMY OF ACCOUNTING HISTORIANS (US/1054-3619) [21951688] **742**

DIRECTORY - AGRICULTURAL COMMUNICATORS IN EDUCATION (U.S.) (US/8755-5972) [11341208] **79**

DIRECTORY AKOMODASI JAWA, BALI DAN SUMATERA UTARA (IO) [02785017] **2805**

DIRECTORY / AMATEUR ATHLETIC UNION OF THE UNITED STATES (US) [05105109] **4892**

DIRECTORY - AMERICAN ACADEMY OF DERMATOLOGY (US/0278-9000) [07901302] **3720**

DIRECTORY — Alphabetical Title Index

DIRECTORY / AMERICAN BAR ASSOCIATION (US/1046-0349) [01479463] **2961**

DIRECTORY / AMERICAN CHAMBER OF COMMERCE IN ITALY (IT) [10607086] **819**

DIRECTORY / AMERICAN COLLEGE OF HEALTHCARE EXECUTIVES (US) [13449676] **3779**

DIRECTORY / AMERICAN COUNCIL OF INDEPENDENT LABORATORIES, INC (US) [09058318] **5100**

DIRECTORY - AMERICAN ELECTRONICS ASSOCIATION (US/0890-1244) [04199026] **2042**

DIRECTORY - AMERICAN GROUP PRACTICE ASSOCIATION (US/0098-2377) [01403078] **3779**

DIRECTORY / AMERICAN GROUP PSYCHOTHERAPY ASSOCIATION (US/0733-2920) [08543922] **3924**

DIRECTORY / AMERICAN HOLISTIC MEDICAL ASSOCIATION AND FOUNDATION (US) [22893148] **3913**

DIRECTORY / AMERICAN MUSICOLOGICAL SOCIETY (US) [15481365] **4114**

DIRECTORY - AMERICAN PUBLIC WORKS ASSOCIATION (US/0360-6899) [02642305] **4760**

DIRECTORY - AMERICAN RECOVERY ASSOCIATION, INC (US/0149-5216) [03500198] **666**

DIRECTORY - AMERICAN SOCIETY FOR CLINICAL PHARMACOLOGY AND THERAPEUTICS (US/0191-2550) [04797306] **4299**

DIRECTORY / AMERICAN SOCIETY OF COMMERCIAL LABORATORIES *See* DIRECTORY / AMERICAN COUNCIL OF INDEPENDENT LABORATORIES, INC **5100**

DIRECTORY / AMERICAN SOCIETY OF JOURNALISTS AND AUTHORS (US/0278-8829) [05226865] **2919**

DIRECTORY - AMERICAN WATER WORKS ASSOCIATION, ONTARIO SECTION (CN/0704-7878) [03797426] **4760**, **5532**

DIRECTORY & ADVERTISING RATE BOOK (US) [08731061] **758**

DIRECTORY & CALENDAR / IAAF (UK) [23451330] **4892**

DIRECTORY & CONSUMER GUIDE - BETTER BUSINESS BUREAU GREATER TORONTO (CN/0225-2686) [06184805] **1296**

DIRECTORY AND GUIDE - BUILDING CONSTRUCTION EMPLOYERS' ASSOCIATION OF CHICAGO, INC (US/0190-4787) [04701178] **613**, **2961**

DIRECTORY & GUIDE - FLORIDA INSTITUTE OF CONSULTING ENGINEERS (US/0742-3381) [09439523] **1970**

DIRECTORY & HANDBOOK / STATE BAR OF GEORGIA (US) [23292062] **2961**

DIRECTORY AND INDEX OF STANDARDS (CN) [17538012] **4030**

DIRECTORY AND LISTING OF PAINTINGS AS SHOWN IN THE MAGAZINE "ANTIQUES", A (US/0747-4997) [10772674] **349**

DIRECTORY AND NEWSLETTER - FORESTRY ALUMNI ASSOCIATION, UNIVERSITY OF TORONTO (CN/0705-1875) [03963631] **2378**, **1101**

DIRECTORY AND REGISTER / ROLLS-ROYCE OWNERS' CLUB (US/0485-3695) [08341607] **5413**

DIRECTORY AND REPORT / CARPET AND RUG INSTITUTE (US/0069-0740) [01788458] **5350**

DIRECTORY & RESOURCE GUIDE / UNITED SYNAGOGUE OF AMERICA (US) [24868165] **5047**

DIRECTORY AND RULES OF GENERAL APPLICATION, CERTIFIED PUBLIC ACCOUNTANTS AND PUBLIC ACCOUNTANTS OF OKLAHOMA REGISTERED IN ACCORDANCE WITH OKLAHOMA STATUTES AND RULES *See* DIRECTORY OF CERTIFIED PUBLIC ACCOUNTANTS AND PUBLIC ACCOUNTANTS OF OKLAHOMA **743**

DIRECTORY & SERVICES GUIDE - CANADIAN ASSOCIATION OF WAREHOUSING AND DISTRIBUTION SERVICES (CN/1184-1796) [23686538] **1604**

DIRECTORY & SERVICES GUIDE - CANADIAN ASSOCIATION OF WAREHOUSING AND DISTRIBUTION SERVICES (CN/1184-1796) [23686541] **1604**

DIRECTORY AND STATISTICS OF OREGON LIBRARIES (US/0162-0290) [03931759] **3206**

DIRECTORY AND YEAR BOOK OF AMERICAN BUSINESS IN IRELAND (IE) [10990381] **666**

DIRECTORY AND YEARBOOK - HUMAN FACTORS SOCIETY (US/0270-5311) [03672849] **1970**

DIRECTORY : AREAWIDE PLANNING ORGANIZATIONS, STATE OF IOWA (US/0363-0013) [04404565] **2821**

DIRECTORY / ART LIBRARIES SOCIETY (UK/0305-7380) [15360605] **3206**, **349**

DIRECTORY - ASSOCIATION OF ACADEMIC HEALTH CENTERS (U.S.) (US/0276-6590) [07367767] **3779**

DIRECTORY / ASSOCIATION OF AMERICAN UNIVERSITY PRESSES (US/0739-3024) [01843276] **4813**

DIRECTORY - ASSOCIATION OF HALFWAY HOUSE ALCOHOLISM PROGRAMS OF NORTH AMERICA (US/0145-2401) [02716528] **1342**

DIRECTORY / ASSOCIATION OF JESUIT COLLEGES AND UNIVERSITIES JESUIT SECONDARY EDUCATION ASSOCIATION (US/1053-8941) [05296459] **1820**

... DIRECTORY. ASSOCIATIONS. EAST NORTH CENTRAL REGION, THE (US/1058-7985) [24345992] **5230**

DIRECTORY. ASSOCIATIONS. MOUNTAIN REGION *See* DIRECTORY. ASSOCIATIONS. WESTERN REGION **1604**

... DIRECTORY. ASSOCIATIONS. MOUNTAIN REGION, THE (US/1058-8027) [24356233] **5230**

... DIRECTORY. ASSOCIATIONS. NORTH EAST REGION, THE (US/1058-7977) [24345632] **1604**

DIRECTORY. ASSOCIATIONS. PACIFIC REGION *See* DIRECTORY. ASSOCIATIONS. WESTERN REGION **1604**

... DIRECTORY. ASSOCIATIONS. SOUTH ATLANTIC REGION, THE (US/1058-8000) [24350321] **5230**

DIRECTORY. ASSOCIATIONS. SOUTH CENTRAL REGION *See* DIRECTORY. ASSOCIATIONS. WESTERN REGION **1604**

... DIRECTORY. ASSOCIATIONS. SOUTH CENTRAL REGION, THE (US/1058-8019) [24350357] **5230**

DIRECTORY. ASSOCIATIONS. WEST NORTH CENTRAL REGION *See* DIRECTORY. ASSOCIATIONS. WESTERN REGION **1604**

... DIRECTORY. ASSOCIATIONS. WEST NORTH CENTRAL REGION, THE (US/1058-7993) [24346041] **5230**

●DIRECTORY. ASSOCIATIONS. WESTERN REGION (US/1063-5475) [25976678] **1604**

DIRECTORY. AUTOMOBILE DEALERS, NEW (US) [17616206] **5413**

DIRECTORY, AVIATION MEDICAL EXAMINERS (US) [05825703] **3572**

DIRECTORY : BANKS AND FINANCIAL INSTITUTIONS (US) [04023242] **787**

DIRECTORY - BELGIAN AMERICAN CHAMBER OF COMMERCE IN THE UNITED STATES, INC, THE (US/0196-7622) [03874689] **819**

DIRECTORY - BRITISH COLUMBIA MOTOR TRANSPORT ASSOCIATION (CN/0714-8658) [09313015] **5381**

DIRECTORY / BROOKHAVEN NATIONAL LABORATORY (US) [08595247] **5100**

DIRECTORY/BUYERS' GUIDE AND DAILY PLANNER (CN/1184-0439) [23599116] **819**

DIRECTORY, CALIFORNIA CAMPAIGN CONTRIBUTORS (US/0731-7263) [08239236] **4472**

DIRECTORY / CAMBRIDGE & DISTRICT CHAMBER OF COMMERCE & INDUSTRY (UK) [11294890] **819**

DIRECTORY - CANADIAN ASSOCIATION OF GEOGRAPHERS (CN/0707-3844) [04678128] **2559**

DIRECTORY / CANADIAN ASSOCIATION OF LAW LIBRARIES (CN/0821-4638) [09562844] **2961**, **3206**

DIRECTORY - CANADIAN ASSOCIATION OF PATHOLOGISTS (CN/0712-1997) [08808192] **3894**

DIRECTORY / CANADIAN GAS ASSOCIATION (CN/0229-1142) [07869976] **4254**, **4760**

DIRECTORY - CANADIAN INTERUNIVERSITY ATHLETIC UNION (CN/0706-697X) [05527537] **4892**

DIRECTORY - CANADIAN LIFE AND HEALTH INSURANCE ASSOCIATION (CN/0710-2429) [08261056] **2878**

DIRECTORY - CANADIAN PAYMENTS ASSOCIATION (CN/0822-7152) [10441153] **787**

DIRECTORY - CANADIAN RELIGIOUS CONFERENCE (CN/0705-3118) [03827548] **4953**

DIRECTORY - CANADIAN ROOFING CONTRACTORS' ASSOCIATION (CN/0228-1619) [06859760] **613**

DIRECTORY / CANADIAN SOCIETY FOR RENAISSANCE STUDIES (CN/0822-6369) [10199148] **2685**

DIRECTORY / CANADIAN SOCIETY OF ZOOLOGISTS (CN/1187-7286) [25652148] **5581**

DIRECTORY - CANADIAN STAMP DEALERS' ASSOCIATION (CN/0827-2034) [11559826] **2785**

DIRECTORY - CANADIAN TESTING ASSOCIATION (CN/0703-1742) [05787508] **865**

DIRECTORY - CENTRAL ONTARIO REGIONAL LIBRARY SYSTEM (CN/0702-8350) [03418042] **3206**

DIRECTORY, CERTIFIED APPLIANCES AND ACCESSORIES (US/0732-1252) [05836813] **2811**

DIRECTORY. CLASSIFIED TRADE INDEX (NAIROBI) (KE/0376-8422) [02241898] **831**

DIRECTORY / COLLEGE OF VETERINARIANS OF ONTARIO. [DISKETTE] (CN/1193-7998) [27649129] **5509**

●DIRECTORY (COLLEGE PLACEMENT COUNCIL) (US/1077-0771) [30694158] **1820**

DIRECTORY : COMMUNITY DEVELOPMENT EDUCATION AND TRAINING PROGRAMS THROUGHOUT THE WORLD (US/0362-4366) [02306783] **5244**

DIRECTORY / COMPOSERS' FORUM, INC, THE (US) [10015529] **4114**

DIRECTORY / CONSULTING ENGINEERS OF ONTARIO (CN/0833-305X) [15644978] **1970**

DIRECTORY / COUNCIL OF PETROLEUM ACCOUNTANTS SOCIETIES (US) [08575485] **4254**, **742**

DIRECTORY - COUNCIL OF SCOTTISH CLAN ASSOCIATIONS (US/0747-6434) [07635242] **2731**

DIRECTORY - COUNCIL OF SPECIALISTS IN PSYCHIATRIC AND MENTAL HEALTH NURSING (US/0272-5940) [06803511] **3924**, **3855**

DIRECTORY DE EXPORTADORES (PN) [21281013] **831**

DIRECTORY : DIOCESAN AGENCIES OF CATHOLIC CHARITIES, UNITED STATES, PUERTO RICO, AND CANADA (US/0091-1003) [01786016] **5282**

●DIRECTORY / EASTERN KENTUCKY UNIVERSITY, NATIONAL ALUMNI ASSOCIATION (US) [29920020] **1101**

DIRECTORY : EASTERN ONTARIO, POSTAL CODE (CN) [01791463] **1144**

DIRECTORY / ECOLOGICAL SOCIETY OF AMERICA (US) [19407148] **2213**

●DIRECTORY / ECONOMIC DEVELOPERS ASSOCIATION OF CANADA (CN/1193-7912) [27649094] **1479**

DIRECTORY / ENGINEERING EMPLOYERS' FEDERATION (UK/0141-7592) [17466487] **1970**

DIRECTORY / ESOMAR (NE) [18474676] **923**

DIRECTORY / EUROPEAN ASSOCIATION OF DISTANCE TEACHING UNIVERSITIES (UK) [19575076] **1735**

DIRECTORY - EUROPEAN COIL COATING ASSOCIATION (UK) [01794376] **4001**

DIRECTORY - FEDERAL COMMUNICATIONS BAR ASSOCIATION (US/0093-1780) [01786138] **2961**

DIRECTORY : FLORIDA PORTS AND WATERWAYS (US/0091-8458) [01786662] **5448**

DIRECTORY FOR EXCEPTIONAL CHILDREN, THE (US/0070-5012) [01682880] **1877**

DIRECTORY FOR MEMBERS - SOCIETY OF MOTION PICTURE AND TELEVISION ENGINEERS, INC (US/0364-8788) [02675792] **4067**

DIRECTORY FOR THE EASTERN ASSOCIATION OF STUDENT FINANCIAL AID ADMINISTRATORS (US/0091-7168) [01786953] **1820**

DIRECTORY FOR THE ILLINOIS PUBLIC COMMUNITY COLLEGE SYSTEM (US) [06521467] **1820**

DIRECTORY FOR THE NATIONAL BLOOD EXCHANGE : A PROGRAM OF THE AMERICAN ASSOCIATION OF BLOOD BANKS (US) [18820861] **3771**

DIRECTORY FOR ZAMBIA, MALAW, BOTSWANA AND ADJACENT TERRITORIES, THE (ZA) [03746369] **2639**

DIRECTORY, FOREST SERVICE *See* FOREST SERVICE ORGANIZATIONAL DIRECTORY **2381**

DIRECTORY / FORUM COMMITTEE ON COMMUNICATIONS LAW (US/0731-8766) [08243435] **1110**, **2961**

DIRECTORY - FORUM COMMITTEE ON FRANCHISING (US/0272-1198) [06744685] **3099**

DIRECTORY - FORUM COMMITTEE ON HEALTH LAW, AMERICAN BAR ASSOCIATION (US/0271-0196) [06518283] **2961**

DIRECTORY - FORUM COMMITTEE ON THE CONSTRUCTION INDUSTRY, AMERICAN BAR ASSOCIATION (US/0273-5180) [06646830] **613**, **2961**

Alphabetical Title Index — DIRECTORY

DIRECTORY - FORUM COMMITTEE ON THE ENTERTAINMENT AND SPORTS INDUSTRIES (US/0273-5172) [07056788] 4892, **2961**

DIRECTORY, HANDBOOK - CALIFORNIA STATE PSYCHOLOGICAL ASSOCIATION (US/0193-7561) [05242576] **4585**

DIRECTORY: HOME CENTERS & HARDWARE CHAINS, AUTO SUPPLY CHAINS *See* DIRECTORY OF HOME CENTER OPERATORS & HARDWARE CHAINS **2811**

DIRECTORY - HOME ECONOMISTS IN BUSINESS, SECTION OF THE AMERICAN HOME ECONOMICS ASSOCIATION (US/0569-5058) [02017886] **2789**

DIRECTORY. HOSPITAL EQUIPMENT & SUPPLIES (US/0884-3368) [12325289] **3779**

DIRECTORY HOTEL, LOSMEN DAN PENGINAPAN (IO) [02441183] **2805**

DIRECTORY HOTEL PARIWISATA & TRAVEL BUREAU (IO/0304-1484) [02240308] 5468, **2805**

DIRECTORY - INDEPENDENT CANADIAN BUSINESSMEN ASSOCIATION OF BRITISH COLUMBIA (CN/0225-9583) [06295671] **666**

DIRECTORY INDUSTRY MARKET REPORT (US) **923**

DIRECTORY - INTERNATIONAL ASSOCIATION OF LAW LIBRARIES (GW/0376-8430) [02242334] 3206, **2961**

DIRECTORY - INTERNATIONAL REAL ESTATE FEDERATION (FR) [07916423] **4836**

DIRECTORY - INTERNATIONAL TEXTILE MANUFACTURERS FEDERATION (SZ) [08038292] **5350**

DIRECTORY, INTERNSHIP AND POSTDOCTORAL PROGRAMS IN PROFESSIONAL PSYCHOLOGY *See* APPIC DIRECTORY **4574**

DIRECTORY, INTERNSHIP PROGRAMS IN PROFESSIONAL PSYCHOLOGY (INCLUDING POST-DOCTORAL TRAINING PROGRAMS) (US) [05031578] **4585**

DIRECTORY, INTERSTATE OIL AND GAS COMPACT COMMISSION AND STATE OIL & GAS AGENCIES (US) [28763019] **4254**

DIRECTORY - INTERSTATE OIL COMPACT COMMISSION (US/8755-5956) [01753809] **4254**

DIRECTORY, INVESTOR-OWNED HOSPITALS, RESIDENTIAL TREATMENT FACILITIES AND CENTERS, HOSPITAL MANAGEMENT COMPANIES, HEALTH SYSTEMS (US/1059-7220) [22969242] **3779**

DIRECTORY, IOWA MANUFACTURERS, A BUYER'S GUIDE *See* DIRECTORY OF IOWA MANUFACTURERS **3477**

DIRECTORY, JAPANESE-AFFILIATED COMPANIES IN USA & CANADA (JA) [19842043] **666**

●DIRECTORY, JUVENILE & ADULT CORRECTIONAL DEPARTMENTS, INSTITUTIONS, AGENCIES & PAROLING AUTHORITIES / AMERICAN CORRECTIONAL ASSOCIATION (US/1071-3530) [28621620] **3163**

DIRECTORY : JUVENILE AND ADULT CORRECTIONAL DEPARTMENTS, INSTITUTIONS, AGENCIES AND PAROLING AUTHORITIES, UNITED STATES AND CANADA (US) [07546267] **3163**

DIRECTORY : KOREA ELECTRONICS MANUFACTURERS (KO/0376-8449) [02240681] **3477**

DIRECTORY - LAKE ONTARIO REGIONAL LIBRARY SYSTEM (CN/0315-2774) [02248229] **3206**

DIRECTORY / LIBRARY OF CONGRESS (US) [07621067] **3206**

DIRECTORY: LICENSED & CERTIFIED HEALTH CARE FACILITIES (US/0363-2563) [02456702] **3779**

DIRECTORY, LICENSED HOSPITALS AND AMBULATORY SURGICAL TREATMENT CENTERS IN TENNESSEE (US/0272-0892) [06671038] **3779**

DIRECTORY: LICENSED HOSPITALS AND RELATED INSTITUTIONS *See* DIRECTORY: LICENSED & CERTIFIED HEALTH CARE FACILITIES **3779**

DIRECTORY, LICENSED REAL ESTATE BROKERS AND SALES ASSOCIATES (US/0730-7357) [08040413] **4836**

DIRECTORY LISTING CURRICULUMS OFFERED IN THE COMMUNITY COLLEGES OF PENNSYLVANIA (US/0092-8526) [01789504] **1820**

DIRECTORY - LOUISIANA STATE BOARD OF EXAMINERS FOR SPEECH PATHOLOGY AND AUDIOLOGY (US) [06525770] **3887**

DIRECTORY: LUTHERAN CHURCHES IN CANADA (CN/0316-800X) [01783553] **5059**

DIRECTORY / MANITOBA DENTAL ASSOCIATION (CN/0711-2238) [08555802] **1322**

DIRECTORY MARKETPLACE (US/0894-346X) [16001710] **415**

DIRECTORY, MARYLAND PUBLIC AND INDEPENDENT COLLEGES AND UNIVERSITIES (US) [10787895] **1820**

DIRECTORY - MASSACHUSETTS DEPARTMENT OF FOOD AND AGRICULTURE (US/0145-661X) [02771459] **79**

DIRECTORY, MEMBER LIBRARIES, GEORGIAN BAY REGIONAL LIBRARY SYSTEM (CN/0380-8068) [02585197] **3206**

DIRECTORY, MEMBERS AND ASSOCIATE MEMBERS - AMERICAN APPAREL MANUFACTURERS ASSOCIATION (1983) (US/0738-520X) [09469217] **1083**

DIRECTORY / MENNONITE CONFERENCE OF EASTERN CANADA (CN/1182-1701) [22285039] **5059**

DIRECTORY: MUNICIPAL AND COUNTY OFFICIALS IN COLORADO *See* DIRECTORY OF MUNICIPAL AND COUNTY OFFICIALS IN COLORADO / COLORADO MUNICIPAL LEAGUE **4644**

●DIRECTORY / NATIONAL ASIAN PACIFIC AMERICAN BAR ASSOCIATION (US) [26329767] **2961**

DIRECTORY / NATIONAL ASSOCIATION OF SCHOOLS OF ART AND DESIGN (US) [10042357] **319**

DIRECTORY - NATIONAL ASSOCIATION OF SCHOOLS OF MUSIC (US/0547-4175) [01789396] **4114**

DIRECTORY - NATIONAL BAND ASSOCIATION (US/0196-9757) [05917098] **4114**

DIRECTORY - NATIONAL COUNCIL OF SAVINGS INSTITUTIONS (U.S.) *CEASED.* (US/0882-1941) [10650927] **788**

DIRECTORY - NATIONAL FLUID POWER ASSOCIATION (US/0145-3866) [02729152] 3477, **2113**

DIRECTORY (NATIONAL LEGAL AID AND DEFENDER ASSOCIATION). DIRECTORY *See* ... DIRECTORY OF LEGAL AID AND DEFENDER OFFICES IN THE UNITED STATES, THE **3179**

DIRECTORY - NATIONAL RESEARCH COUNCIL (U.S.). FOOD AND NUTRITION BOARD (1982) (US/0898-4905) [15136615] **4190**

DIRECTORY : NEW JERSEY AGRICULTURAL ORGANIZATIONS (US/0095-5205) [01796292] **79**

DIRECTORY, NON-OPERATING LIBRARY BOARDS / GEORGIAN BAY REGIONAL LIBRARY SYSTEMS (CN/0712-9777) [08794427] **3206**

DIRECTORY : NORTH DAKOTA CITY OFFICIALS (US/0090-1989) [01784742] **4643**

DIRECTORY - NORTHWESTERN ONTARIO REGION, MINISTRY OF EDUCATION (CN/0228-3441) [06966086] **1735**

DIRECTORY. OCCUPATIONAL PROGRAMS - CANADIAN ADDICTIONS FOUNDATION (CN/0705-5587) [04079875] **1343**

DIRECTORY, OCCUPATIONAL SAFETY AND HEALTH LEGISLATION IN CANADA (CN/0703-6426) [04590098] 2861, **2961**

DIRECTORY OF AAAS FELLOWS (US) [07084542] **5100**

DIRECTORY OF ACCREDITED AND RECOGNIZED PRACTITIONERS OF INTERPRETING & TRANSLATING (AT) **3277**

DIRECTORY OF ACCREDITED CAMPS (CN/0316-1226) [02593608] **4871**

DIRECTORY OF ACCREDITED INSTITUTIONS, CANDIDATES FOR ACCREDITATION (US/0882-6870) [11828789] **1820**

DIRECTORY OF ACTIVE MINES IN ARIZONA (US/0273-0553) [04691287] **2138**

DIRECTORY OF ADDRESSES - FEDERATION INTERNATIONALE DE FOOTBALL ASSOCIATION (SZ) [02952377] **4892**

DIRECTORY OF ADMINISTRATIVE SERVICES (US/0149-337X) [24521758] **4643**

DIRECTORY OF ADMINISTRATORS OF COMMUNITY, TECHNICAL, AND JUNIOR COLLEGES (US/8756-4254) [11367503] **1820**

DIRECTORY OF ADULT DAY CARE CENTERS (US/0195-9859) [04781940] **5282**

●DIRECTORY OF AFRICAN AND AFRICAN-AMERICAN STUDIES IN THE UNITED STATES (US) [30486268] 2639, **2259**

DIRECTORY OF AFRICAN & AFRO-AMERICAN STUDIES IN THE UNITED STATES *See* DIRECTORY OF AFRICAN AND AFRICAN-AMERICAN STUDIES IN THE UNITED STATES **2259**

DIRECTORY OF AFRICAN STATISTICIANS / ECONOMIC COMMISSION FOR AFRICA (ET) [10969294] **5326**

DIRECTORY OF AGENCIES : U.S. VOLUNTARY, INTERNATIONAL VOLUNTARY, INTERGOVERNMENTAL *CEASED.* (US) [05526386] **5282**

DIRECTORY OF AGENTS BEING TESTED FOR CARCINOGENICITY (FR) [23465265] **3816**

DIRECTORY OF AGRICULTURAL CO-OPERATIVES IN THE UNITED KINGDOM (UK) [22470873] **79**

DIRECTORY OF AIA FIRMS IN MASSACHUSETTS, THE (US) [22572346] **297**

DIRECTORY OF AIDS RELATED PERIODICALS (US) [20929989] **3669**

DIRECTORY OF AIR QUALITY MONITORING SITES (US/0093-5476) [01792337] **2227**

DIRECTORY OF ALABAMA HEALTH SCIENCE LIBRARIES AND HANDBOOK OF THE ALABAMA HEALTH LIBRARIES ASSOCIATION (US/0889-4671) [13897625] **3206**

DIRECTORY OF ALBERTA GOVERNMENT LIBRARIES (CN/0382-3482) [03230506] **3206**

DIRECTORY OF ALCOHOLISM COUNCILS IN AMERICA (US/0148-9771) [03403386] **1343**

DIRECTORY OF ALTERNATIVE AND RADICAL PUBLICATIONS (US) **4813**

DIRECTORY OF ALTERNATIVE MEDIA PERIODICALS *See* DIRECTORY OF ALTERNATIVE PERIODICALS (BRIGHTON) **415**

DIRECTORY OF ALTERNATIVE PERIODICALS (BRIGHTON) (UK/0302-3303) [01793236] **415**

DIRECTORY OF ALUMNI - NATIONAL SCHOLARSHIP CENTER (PHILIPPINES) (PH) [11314185] **1101**

DIRECTORY OF ALUMNI / PENNSYLVANIA STATE UNIVERSITY, COLLEGE OF EARTH AND MINERAL SCIENCES (US/0739-1331) [09647862] **1101**

DIRECTORY OF AMERICAN BUSINESS IN AUSTRIA (AU) [03233757] **666**

DIRECTORY OF AMERICAN BUSINESS IN HONG KONG (HK) [10244823] **666**

DIRECTORY OF AMERICAN BUSINESS IN MALAYSIA (MY/0127-2179) [09351350] **666**

DIRECTORY OF AMERICAN EMPLOYMENT AGENCIES (CN) **4203**

DIRECTORY OF AMERICAN FIRMS OPERATING IN FOREIGN COUNTRIES (US/0070-5071) [01239899] **666**

DIRECTORY OF AMERICAN FULBRIGHT SCHOLARS : UNIVERSITY LECTURING & ADVANCED RESEARCH ABROAD (US/0883-0975) [09405605] **1820**

DIRECTORY OF AMERICAN INDIAN LAW ATTORNEYS (US/1055-8519) [23359615] 2259, **2961**

DIRECTORY OF AMERICAN PHILOSOPHERS (US/0070-508X) [01566685] **4345**

DIRECTORY OF AMERICAN POETS AND FICTION WRITERS, A (US/0734-0605) [06747640] **3381**

DIRECTORY OF AMERICAN RESEARCH AND TECHNOLOGY (US/0886-0076) [12789089] **5174**

DIRECTORY OF AMERICAN YOUTH ORGANIZATIONS (US/1044-4440) [18396423] **1062**

DIRECTORY OF ANIMAL DISEASE DIAGNOSTIC LABORATORIES (US/0146-1621) [02878566] **5509**

DIRECTORY OF APPROVED PROVIDERS OF TRAINING IN THE IDENTIFICATION AND REPORTING OF CHILD ABUSE AND INFORMATION PERTAINING TO EXEMPTIONS (US) [25777205] **5282**

DIRECTORY OF AQUARIUM SPECIALISTS (US/0098-4469) [02240446] **2300**

DIRECTORY OF ARCHITECTURAL FIRMS (US/0363-4531) [02464949] **297**

DIRECTORY OF AREA WAGE SURVEYS (US/0566-7801) [02338650] **1663**

DIRECTORY OF ARIZONA CRIMINAL AND CIVIL JUSTICE AGENCIES AND DIGEST OF RELATED INFORMATION (US) [24691892] **3163**

DIRECTORY OF ARKANSAS MANUFACTURERS (US) [13775246] **1604**

DIRECTORY OF ART AND DESIGN FACULTIES IN COLLEGES AND UNIVERSITIES, U.S. AND CANADA (US/0897-3989) [17022436] 378, **349**

DIRECTORY OF ARTISTS / BRITISH ASSOCIATION OF CONCERT AGENTS (UK) [15060130] **319**

DIRECTORY OF ARTISTS USING SCIENCE AND TECHNOLOGY (US/1067-8506) [23018298] **349**

DIRECTORY Alphabetical Title Index

DIRECTORY OF ARTS LIBRARIES AND RESOURCE COLLECTIONS IN AUSTRALIA (AT/0811-6253) [10702364] 319, **3206**

DIRECTORY OF ARTS ORGANIZATIONS IN MISSISSIPPI (US/0098-4477) [02241291] **319**

DIRECTORY OF ASIAN HIGH TECH COMPANIES IN THE UNITED STATES (US/1044-4734) [19796290] **5100**

DIRECTORY OF ASSOCIATIONS IN CANADA (CN/0316-0734) [02244957] **5230**

DIRECTORY OF ATA MEMBERS (US) [16504418] **2785**

DIRECTORY OF AUSTRALIAN ACADEMIC AND RESEARCH LIBRARIES (AT) [20927928] **3206**

DIRECTORY OF AUSTRALIAN ASSOCIATIONS (NZ) [04837204] **5230**

DIRECTORY OF AUSTRALIAN COMPOSERS (AT/0815-5232) [I08155232] **4114**

DIRECTORY OF AUSTRALIAN PUBLIC LIBRARIES (AT/0729-4271) [10757472] **3206**

DIRECTORY OF AUTO AFTERMARKET SUPPLIERS (US/0736-0452) [09068830] **5413**

DIRECTORY OF BANK ECONOMISTS (US) [04990874] **788**

DIRECTORY OF BANKING INSTRUCTORS (US/0092-4717) [01789864] **788**

DIRECTORY OF BAR ACTIVITIES (US/0273-494X) [07047550] **2961**

DIRECTORY OF BAR ASSOCIATIONS (US/8756-1565) [09482888] **2961**

DIRECTORY OF BARRIER-FREE BUILDING PRODUCTS (CN/0848-8134) [21190797] 4386, **297**

DIRECTORY OF BARTER ASSOCIATIONS AND ORGANIZATIONS BASED IN NEW HAMPSHIRE (US) [09100638] **666**

DIRECTORY OF BILINGUAL SPEECH-LANGUAGE PATHOLOGISTS AND AUDIOLOGISTS (US/0743-5096) [09328678] 3277, **4386**

DIRECTORY OF BIOMEDICAL AND HEALTH CARE GRANTS (US/0883-5330) [12148371] 4773, **3572**

DIRECTORY OF BIOMEDICAL ETHICS ORGANIZATIONS / AHA (US) [19489057] 2249, **3572**

DIRECTORY OF BLACK FILM/TV TECHNICIANS & ARTISTS, WEST COAST (US/0277-1500) [07407134] **4067**

DIRECTORY OF BLOOD ESTABLISHMENTS REGISTERED UNDER SECTION 510 OF THE FOOD, DRUG, AND COSMETIC ACT (US/0163-6065) [03133264] **5282**

DIRECTORY OF BOOK, CATALOG, AND MAGAZINE PRINTERS (US/0895-139X) [16512010] **4564**

DIRECTORY OF BOOK PRINTERS (US) [23157437] **4564**

DIRECTORY OF BRITISH ASSOCIATIONS & ASSOCIATIONS IN IRELAND (UK/0309-5487) [03059592] **5230**

DIRECTORY OF BRITISH BRASS BANDS (UK) [04550876] **4114**

●DIRECTORY OF BRITISH POLITICAL ORGANISATIONS UPDATING SERVICE (UK) **4472**

DIRECTORY OF BROADCAST EXECUTIVES (TORONTO) (CN/0419-2273) [01798209] **1131**

DIRECTORY OF BUILDERS AND CONTRACTORS (II) **613**

DIRECTORY OF BUSINESS AND FINANCIAL SERVICES (US) [02239060] **666**

DIRECTORY OF BUSINESS AND INDUSTRY, FAIRFAX COUNTY, VIRGINIA (US) [04784964] **1604**

DIRECTORY OF BUSINESS ASSOCIATIONS IN THE STATE OF WASHINGTON *See* DIRECTORY OF WASHINGTON BUSINESS ASSOCIATIONS **667**

DIRECTORY OF BUSINESS CAPITAL SOURCES (US/0734-6832) [08791821] **896**

●DIRECTORY OF BUYOUT FINANCING SOURCES (US/1066-9736) [25514736] **788**

●DIRECTORY OF CALIFORNIA LICENSED CONTRACTORS (NORTHERN ED.) (US/1063-1232) [25881606] 2022, **613**

●DIRECTORY OF CALIFORNIA LICENSED CONTRACTORS (SOUTHERN ED.) (US/1063-1240) [25881633] **613**

DIRECTORY OF CAMPUS MINISTRY (US/0070-5209) [01787952] **4953**

DIRECTORY OF CANADIAN ARCHIVES (CN/0711-0413) [07906023] **2481**

DIRECTORY OF CANADIAN CHARTERED ACCOUNTANTS (CN/0527-9275) [01787919] **743**

DIRECTORY OF CANADIAN DENTAL ASSOCIATION (CN/1184-6194) [23599102] **1322**

DIRECTORY OF CANADIAN DENTAL ASSOCIATION (CN/1184-6194) [23599100] **1322**

DIRECTORY OF CANADIAN EDUCATION & TRAINING PROGRAMS IN AQUACULTURE RELATED FIELDS (CN/1182-5758) [23302744] **554**

DIRECTORY OF CANADIAN ENVIRONMENTAL EXPERTS (CN/0704-1497) [05694168] **2163**

DIRECTORY OF CANADIAN MAP COLLECTIONS (CN/0070-5217) [02802283] **2559**

DIRECTORY OF CANADIAN MARINE OILSPILL SPECIALISTS (CN/1189-3273) [25264171] **2227**

DIRECTORY OF CANADIAN MUSEUMS AND RELATED INSTITUTIONS (CN/0714-2188) [08977582] **4087**

DIRECTORY OF CANADIAN ORCHESTRAS AND YOUTH ORCHESTRAS *See* CANADIAN ORCHESTRAS AND YOUTH ORCHESTRAS DIRECTORY **4107**

DIRECTORY OF CANADIAN ORCHESTRAS AND YOUTH ORCHESTRAS / ANNUAIRE CANADIEN DES ORCHESTRES ET ORCHESTRES DES JEUNES (CN/0705-6249) [04079675] **4114**

●DIRECTORY OF CANADIAN REHABILITATION SERVICES (CN/1191-1514) [25882882] **4386**

DIRECTORY OF CANADIAN SCHOLARS AND UNIVERSITIES INTERESTED IN LATIN AMERICAN STUDIES (CN/0382-9073) [03245034] **2731**

DIRECTORY OF CANADIAN THEATRE SCHOOLS, A (CN/0709-8421) [06131749] **5363**

DIRECTORY OF CANADIAN UNIVERSITIES (CN/0706-2338) [04129930] **1820**

DIRECTORY OF CANADIANISTS IN ALBERTA (CN/1185-3417) [24368275] **2731**

DIRECTORY OF CARDAMOM PLANTERS (II) [02357648] **170**

DIRECTORY OF CE, PHOTOGRAPHY & MAJOR APPLIANCE RETAILERS & DISTRIBUTORS *See* DIRECTORY OF CONSUMER ELECTRONICS, PHOTOGRAPHY & MAJOR APPLIANCE RETAILERS & DISTRIBUTORS **953**

DIRECTORY OF CERTIFICATES OF AUTHORIZATION HOLDERS AUTHORIZED TO PRACTISE PROFESSIONAL ENGINEERING IN THE PROVINCE OF ONTARIO (CN/0712-7499) [08581164] **1970**

DIRECTORY OF CERTIFIED NURSES (US) [04634725] **3855**

DIRECTORY OF CERTIFIED PETROLEUM GEOLOGISTS (US/0272-1309) [01606867] 4254, **1373**

DIRECTORY OF CERTIFIED PSYCHIATRISTS AND NEUROLOGISTS (US/0196-6421) [05113910] 3913, 3831, **3924**

DIRECTORY OF CERTIFIED PUBLIC ACCOUNTANTS AND PUBLIC ACCOUNTANTS OF OKLAHOMA (US/0361-4115) [02246337] **743**

DIRECTORY OF CERTIFIED UNITARY AIR-CONDITIONERS, UNITARY AIR-SOURCE HEAT PUMPS, SOUND-RATED OUTDOOR UNITARY EQUIPMENT (US/1047-7497) [19901370] **2604**

DIRECTORY OF CHAIN RESTAURANT OPERATORS (US/0411-7085) [04091121] **5070**

DIRECTORY OF CHAMBERS OF COMMERCE IN TEXAS *CEASED.* (US/0737-5573) [08920677] **819**

DIRECTORY OF CHARITABLE ORGANIZATIONS AND TRUSTS REGISTERED WITH THE OFFICE OF ATTORNEY GENERAL (OLYMPIA) *See* CHARITABLE TRUST DIRECTORY, OFFICE OF ATTORNEY GENERAL **3140**

DIRECTORY OF CHEMICAL DEPENDENCY PROGRAMS IN MINNESOTA (US/0734-0192) [08648232] **1343**

DIRECTORY OF CHEMICAL ENGINEERING RESEARCH IN CANADIAN UNIVERSITIES (1979) (CN/0709-3438) [05585600] **2012**

DIRECTORY OF CHEMICAL PRODUCERS, CANADA (US/1045-5256) [20061187] **1023**

DIRECTORY OF CHEMICAL PRODUCERS OF ASIA AND AUSTRALASIA (US/0362-3785) [02311822] **1023**

DIRECTORY OF CHEMICAL PRODUCERS : UNITED STATES OF AMERICA (US/0012-3277) [01246805] **1023**

DIRECTORY OF CHEMICAL PRODUCERS, WESTERN EUROPE (US) [05039379] **1023**

DIRECTORY OF CHILD CARE CENTERS (US/0147-4405) [03163228] **5282**

DIRECTORY OF CHINESE OFFICIALS AND ORGANIZATIONS (US) [15305557] **4643**

DIRECTORY OF CITY POLICY OFFICIALS (US/1046-2686) [12899120] **4643**

DIRECTORY OF CLINICAL FELLOWSHIPS IN MEDICINE : UNITED STATES AND CANADA (US/0161-5793) [03947444] **3572**

DIRECTORY OF CLINICAL LABORATORIES, CLINICAL LABORATORY PERSONNEL (US/0095-3725) [01791198] **3894**

DIRECTORY OF CLUB OFFICERS (US/0736-637X) [08984612] **1101**

DIRECTORY OF COLLECTION STRENGTHS IN VICTORIAN LIBRARIES (AT) [16958431] **3206**

DIRECTORY OF COLLEGE & UNIVERSITY FOODSERVICE (US/1048-4663) [20961265] **1820**

DIRECTORY OF COLLEGE SEMINARS AND SHORT COURSES IN ENGINEERING AND MANAGEMENT (US/0278-1182) [07715346] **1820**

DIRECTORY OF COLLEGES OFFERING COURSES AND DEGREES BY MAIL (US/0196-4704) [05815088] **1820**

DIRECTORY OF COLORADO LIBRARIES ... & LIBRARY STATISTICS / COLORADO DEPARTMENT OF EDUCATION (US) [09988330] **3206**

DIRECTORY OF COLORADO MANUFACTURERS (US/0084-9898) [01330168] **3477**

DIRECTORY OF COMMERCE AND INDUSTRY, STATE OF DELAWARE *See* DELAWARE DIRECTORY OF COMMERCE AND INDUSTRY **1603**

DIRECTORY OF COMMERCIAL CENTRAL AIR CONDITIONERS / PREPARED BY THE NEW YORK STATE ENERGY OFFICE ; PREPARED FOR CENTRAL HUDSON GAS & ELECTRIC ... [ET. AL.] (US) [25907613] **2604**

DIRECTORY OF COMMUNICATORS IN AGRICULTURE (US) [01788146] **79**

DIRECTORY OF COMMUNITY-BASED MENTAL RETARDATION SERVICES (US/0096-3054) [01798669] **5282**

DIRECTORY OF COMMUNITY CARE FACILITIES (US/0361-6282) [02246928] **5282**

DIRECTORY OF COMMUNITY (HAMILTON) (CN/0316-1099) [02247734] **5282**

DIRECTORY OF COMMUNITY LEGISLATION IN FORCE AND OTHER ACTS OF THE COMMUNITY INSTITUTIONS (LU) [12205168] **3127**

DIRECTORY OF COMMUNITY NEWSPAPERS *See* NATIONAL DIRECTORY OF COMMUNITY NEWSPAPERS (1992) **5697**

DIRECTORY OF COMMUNITY SERVICES FOR HAMILTON-WENTWORTH (CN/0826-7391) [11868869] **5282**

DIRECTORY OF COMMUNITY SERVICES FOR WATERLOO REGION (CN/0713-4681) [08967811] **5282**

DIRECTORY OF COMMUNITY SERVICES IN MARYLAND (US/0070-5306) [01788009] **5282**

DIRECTORY OF COMMUNITY SERVICES IN METROPOLITAN TORONTO (CN/0315-0631) [08534478] **5282**

DIRECTORY OF COMMUNITY SERVICES IN REGIONAL NIAGARA (CN/0823-6046) [09809053] **5282**

DIRECTORY OF COMMUNITY SERVICES (NEW WESTMINSTER) (CN/0381-629X) [02627474] **5282**

DIRECTORY OF COMMUNITY SERVICES (NEW YORK PUBLIC LIBRARY) (US) [06973852] **5282**

DIRECTORY OF COMMUNITY SERVICES, OTTAWA-CARLETON (CN/0705-7075) [04233153] **5282**

DIRECTORY OF COMMUNITY SERVICES (SUDBURY) (CN/0709-0749) [05375404] **5282**

DIRECTORY OF COMPANIES OFFERING DIVIDEND REINVESTMENT PLANS (US/1045-0041) [10848579] **896**

DIRECTORY OF COMPUTER AND HIGH TECHNOLOGY GRANTS (US/1070-3950) [28357849] **1182**

DIRECTORY OF COMPUTER & SOFTWARE RETAILERS (TAMPA, FLA.) (US/1066-9698) [26910830] **1237**

DIRECTORY OF COMPUTER & SOFTWARE STOREFRONT DEALERS (US/0738-839X) [16949556] **1182**

DIRECTORY OF COMPUTER DEALERS. INTERNATIONAL EDITION (US/0277-3694) [07542820] **1237**

DIRECTORY OF COMPUTER EDUCATION AND RESEARCH (US) [04701829] **1182**

DIRECTORY OF COMPUTER PROGRAMS AVAILABLE FROM COSMIC See COSMIC SOFTWARE CATALOG **1228**

DIRECTORY OF COMPUTER SOFTWARE See DIRECTORY OF U.S. GOVERNMENT SOFTWARE FOR MAINFRAMES AND MICROCOMPUTERS **1285**

DIRECTORY OF COMPUTER SOFTWARE, A (US/0748-1543) [09789329] 1237, **1285**

DIRECTORY OF COMPUTER SOFTWARE APPLICATIONS. ATMOSPHERIC SCIENCES, A (US) [04520992] 5100, **1182**

DIRECTORY OF COMPUTER SOFTWARE APPLICATIONS. ENERGY, A (US) [04016616] 1936, **1285**

DIRECTORY OF COMPUTER SOFTWARE APPLICATIONS. ENVIRONMENTAL POLLUTION & CONTROL, A (US) [06843315] 2227, **1182**

DIRECTORY OF COMPUTER SOFTWARE APPLICATIONS. MARINE ENGINEERING, A (US) [05150156] 1970, **1285**

DIRECTORY OF COMPUTER SOFTWARE APPLICATIONS. TRANSPORTATION, A (US) [04179649] 5381, **1285**

DIRECTORY OF COMPUTERIZED INFORMATION IN SCIENCE AND TECHNOLOGY (US/0070-5330) [01640703] **5100**

●DIRECTORY OF CONNECTICUT AND RHODE ISLAND HIGH TECHNOLOGY COMPANIES, THE (US/1061-334X) [25070391] **1604**

DIRECTORY OF CONNECTICUT MANUFACTURING AND MECHANICAL ESTABLISHMENTS See CONNECTICUT MANUFACTURING DIRECTORY **3477**

DIRECTORY OF CONSTITUENT ORGANIZATIONS (US/0161-2298) [03861953] **2259**

●DIRECTORY OF CONSTRUCTION LAW FIRMS, THE (US/1056-8735) [23882492] **2962**

DIRECTORY OF CONSULTANTS IN BIOTECHNOLOGY, THE (US/0882-6005) [11900697] **3691**

DIRECTORY OF CONSULTANTS IN ELECTRONICS, THE (US/0882-6064) [11900627] **2042**

DIRECTORY OF CONSULTANTS IN ENVIRONMENTAL SCIENCE, THE (US/0882-6048) [11901974] 79, **2163**

DIRECTORY OF CONSULTANTS IN LASERS AND PHYSICS, THE (US/0882-6056) [11900573] **4401**

DIRECTORY OF CONSULTANTS IN PLASTICS AND CHEMICALS, THE (US/0882-6021) [11901890] 1024, **4454**

DIRECTORY OF CONSULTING SPECIALISTS (US/0090-4945) [01785200] **865**

DIRECTORY OF CONSUMER ELECTRONICS, PHOTOGRAPHY & MAJOR APPLIANCE RETAILERS & DISTRIBUTORS (US) [18269808] **953**

DIRECTORY OF CONTINUING EDUCATION OPPORTUNITIES IN NEW YORK CITY (US/0094-095X) [01793816] **1800**

DIRECTORY OF CONTRACT SERVICE FIRMS (US/0148-1819) [03276621] **1970**

DIRECTORY OF CONVENTIONS See DIRECTORY OF CONVENTIONS. CENTRAL CONVENTION GUIDE **758**

DIRECTORY OF CONVENTIONS See DIRECTORY OF CONVENTIONS. NORTHEAST & MID-ATLANTIC CONVENTION GUIDE **758**

DIRECTORY OF CONVENTIONS See DIRECTORY OF CONVENTIONS. SOUTHEAST CONVENTION GUIDE **758**

DIRECTORY OF CONVENTIONS See DIRECTORY OF CONVENTIONS. WEST CONVENTION GUIDE **758**

●DIRECTORY OF CONVENTIONS. CENTRAL CONVENTION GUIDE (US/1076-786X) [30610890] **758**

●DIRECTORY OF CONVENTIONS. NORTHEAST & MID-ATLANTIC CONVENTION GUIDE (US/1076-7878) [30610958] **758**

●DIRECTORY OF CONVENTIONS. SOUTHEAST CONVENTION GUIDE (US/1076-7843) [30610815] **758**

●DIRECTORY OF CONVENTIONS. WEST CONVENTION GUIDE (US/1076-7851) [30610859] **758**

DIRECTORY OF COOPERATING AGENCIES (US/8755-7118) [04617944] **5283**

DIRECTORY OF CORPORATE AFFILIATIONS / INTERNATIONAL (US) **666**

DIRECTORY OF CORPORATE AFFILIATIONS / U.S. PRIVATE (US) **666**

DIRECTORY OF CORPORATE AFFILIATIONS / U.S. PUBLIC (US) **666**

●DIRECTORY OF CORPORATE AND FOUNDATION GIVERS, THE (US) [25109041] 666, **5283**

DIRECTORY OF CORPORATE MEMBER FIRMS AND MEMBER-ASSOCIATIONS / CANADIAN CONSTRUCTION ASSOCIATION (CN/0847-9720) [20778375] **613**

DIRECTORY OF CORPORATE URBAN AFFAIRS OFFICERS (US/0090-4066) [01785052] **1604**

DIRECTORY OF COUNSELING SERVICES (US/0094-7512) [01786137] **1912**

DIRECTORY OF COUNTY OFFICIALS (ANNAPOLIS, MD.) (US) [11414736] **4643**

DIRECTORY OF CRIMINAL JUSTICE AGENCIES IN ARIZONA (US) [05790270] **3163**

DIRECTORY OF CROSS-CULTURAL RESEARCH AND RESEARCHERS (US/0093-6251) [05390763] **5198**

DIRECTORY OF CSIRO RESEARCH PROGRAMS / COMPILED BY THE SCIENCE COMMUNICATION UNIT, BUREAU OF SCIENTIFIC SERVICES (AT/0727-6753) [10362168] **5100**

DIRECTORY OF CURRENT RESEARCH / NATIONAL UNIVERSITY OF SINGAPORE (SI) [10597389] **5100**

DIRECTORY OF CZECHOSLOVAK OFFICIALS / DIRECTORATE OF INTELLIGENCE (US) [13230591] **4643**

DIRECTORY OF DANCE COMPANIES (US/0363-972X) [02589213] **1313**

DIRECTORY OF DANCE FACULTIES IN COLLEGES AND UNIVERSITIES, U.S. AND CANADA (US/0898-4735) [16849697] **1313**

DIRECTORY OF DATA FILES (US) [06085221] **4643**

DIRECTORY OF DCAA OFFICES (US/1058-0158) [07505305] **4643**

DIRECTORY OF DEFENSE ELECTRONIC PRODUCTS AND SERVICES : UNITED STATES SUPPLIERS, THE (US) [02441106] 2042, **4042**

DIRECTORY OF DELAWARE LIBRARIES, A (US/0730-5222) [08036467] **3207**

DIRECTORY OF DELAWARE SCHOOLS See EDUCATIONAL DIRECTORY **1741**

DIRECTORY OF DENTAL EDUCATORS CEASED. (US/0090-0141) [03957195] **1322**

DIRECTORY OF DENTAL EDUCATORS (WASHINGTON, D.C. : 1983) (US/0882-1860) [09623427] **1322**

DIRECTORY OF DEPARTMENT OF VETERANS AFFAIRS FACILITIES (US) [24999190] **4042**

DIRECTORY OF DEPARTMENT STORES (US/0419-2508) [03718970] **953**

DIRECTORY OF DEPARTMENT STORES, MAIL ORDER FIRMS (US) [16799175] **953**

DIRECTORY OF DESIGNATED MEMBERS - APPRAISAL INSTITUTE OF CANADA (CN/0316-9839) [02247562] **4836**

DIRECTORY OF DIESEL FUEL STATIONS COAST TO COAST, A (US/0360-9987) [02245152] **4254**

DIRECTORY OF DIETETIC PROGRAMS : ACCREDITED AND APPROVED (US) [07852777] **4190**

DIRECTORY OF DIOCESAN AGENCIES OF CATHOLIC CHARITIES IN THE UNITED STATES AND CANADA See DIRECTORY : DIOCESAN AGENCIES OF CATHOLIC CHARITIES, UNITED STATES, PUERTO RICO, AND CANADA **5282**

DIRECTORY OF DIPLOMATES (US) [05667013] **3881**

DIRECTORY OF DIPLOMATES / AMERICAN BOARD OF FAMILY PRACTICE (US/1055-3487) [23158607] **3737**

DIRECTORY OF DIRECTORS IN THE CITY OF NEW YORK AND TRI-STATE AREA (US) [08601849] **865**

DIRECTORY OF DIRECTORS, THE (UK/0070-5438) [02472519] **865**

DIRECTORY OF DIRECTORS (TORONTO) (CN/0071-5042) [02248175] **432**

DIRECTORY OF DIRECTORS. [EXECUTIVES OF CANADA] (CN/0071-5042) [01714867] **728**

DIRECTORY OF DIRECTORY PUBLISHERS (US/1053-4210) [22529049] **4813**

DIRECTORY OF DISABILITY MEDIA IN CANADA (CN/1187-7219) [25652135] **4386**

DIRECTORY OF DISCOUNT DEPARTMENT STORES (NEW YORK, N.Y. : 1988) (US/0897-5442) [17537992] **953**

DIRECTORY OF DISTINGUISHED AMERICANS, THE (US/0742-3349) [10294741] **432**

DIRECTORY OF DISTRIBUTORS (US/8755-3821) [11129566] **831**

●DIRECTORY OF DOCTORAL PROGRAMS IN THEATRE STUDIES IN THE U.S.A. AND CANADA (US) [25556349] **5363**

DIRECTORY OF DOCTORS OF OSTEOPATHY LICENSED AND REGISTERED IN TENNESSEE (US/0149-3760) [03472241] **3572**

DIRECTORY OF DRUG INFORMATION AND TREATMENT ORGANIZATIONS (US/0361-1493) [02241246] **1343**

DIRECTORY OF DRUG STORE & HBA CHAINS INCLUDES DRUG WHOLESALERS See DIRECTORY OF DRUG STORES & HBC CHAINS **4299**

●DIRECTORY OF DRUG STORES & HBC CHAINS (US) [25858900] **4299**

DIRECTORY OF ECONOMIC DEVELOPMENT DISTRICTS AND AREA GRANTEES (US) [04537435] **1555**

DIRECTORY OF ECONOMIC RESEARCH IN MISSISSIPPI (US/0094-1433) [05703698] **1479**

DIRECTORY OF EDUCATION (TORONTO) (CN/0316-8549) [04520923] **1735**

DIRECTORY OF EDUCATIONAL INSTITUTIONS ACCREDITED BY THE ACCREDITING COMMISSION OF THE ASSOCIATION OF INDEPENDENT COLLEGES AND SCHOOLS (US/0733-2858) [07271773] **1820**

DIRECTORY OF EDUCATIONAL INSTITUTIONS AND APPRENTICESHIP AND OTHER ON- THE-JOB TRAINING FACILITIES APPROVED BY THE WEST VIRGINIA DEPARTMENT OF EDUCATION FOR VETERANS EDUCATIONAL BENEFITS UNDER PUBLIC LAW 96-466 (US) [11293226] **1912**

DIRECTORY OF EDUCATIONAL INSTITUTIONS IN OGUN STATE, A (NR) [05199423] **1735**

DIRECTORY OF EDUCATIONAL INSTITUTIONS, RAJASTHAN (II/0420-0586) [01566694] **1735**

DIRECTORY OF EDUCATIONAL OPPORTUNITIES IN GEORGIA (US/0419-2559) [01788006] **1912**

DIRECTORY OF EDUCATIONAL PROGRAMS (US/0275-9357) [07234788] **1735**

DIRECTORY OF EDUCATIONAL PROGRAMS (NEW YORK, N.Y. : 1984) (US) [11354556] 2042, **4452**

DIRECTORY OF EDUCATIONAL SOFTWARE FOR NURSING (US) [15503626] 1285, **3855**

DIRECTORY OF EDUCATIONAL SPECIALISTS (US) [01781688] **1735**

DIRECTORY OF ELECTRIC LIGHT AND POWER COMPANIES See ELECTRIC GENERATING AND DISTRIBUTING COMPANIES **2043**

DIRECTORY OF ELECTRONIC JOURNALS, NEWSLETTERS, AND ACADEMIC DISCUSSION LISTS (US/1057-1337) [23952084] **4813**

DIRECTORY OF ELECTRONIC SERVICES AND COMMUNICATION NETWORKS (AT/1322-350X) **2042**

DIRECTORY OF ELEMENTARY AND SECONDARY SCHOOL DISTRICTS, AND SCHOOLS IN SELECTED SCHOOL DISTRICTS (US) [04964344] **1735**

DIRECTORY OF EMPLOYEE LEASING FIRMS, A (US/1056-6112) [23747501] **1663**

DIRECTORY OF ENERGY DATA COLLECTION FORMS / ENERGY INFORMATION ADMINISTRATION, OFFICE OF STATISTICAL STANDARDS (US) [13138046] **1936**

●DIRECTORY OF ENGINEERING AND ENGINEERING TECHNOLOGY UNDERGRADUATE PROGRAMS (US/1057-5286) [24048508] **1970**

DIRECTORY OF ENGINEERING DOCUMENT SOURCES (US/1044-8829) [06462723] **3207**

●DIRECTORY OF ENGINEERING GRADUATE STUDIES & RESEARCH (US/1067-9022) [26934603] **1970**

DIRECTORY OF ENGINEERING SOCIETIES AND RELATED ORGANIZATIONS See INTERNATIONAL DIRECTORY OF ENGINEERING SOCIETIES AND RELATED ORGANIZATIONS **1979**

DIRECTORY OF ENGINEERING UNITS IN PAKISTAN (PK/0376-8473) [02245934] **2113**

DIRECTORY OF ENGINEERS AND LAND SURVEYORS REGISTERED IN SOUTH CAROLINA (US) [01788121] **1970**

DIRECTORY OF ENVIRONMENTAL CONSULTANTS (US) [01785778] 1971, **2163**

DIRECTORY

Alphabetical Title Index

●DIRECTORY OF ENVIRONMENTAL GROUPS IN THE NEWLY INDEPENDENT STATES AND BALTIC NATIONS, THE (US/1053-7880) [22646607] **2163**

DIRECTORY OF ENVIRONMENTAL ORGANIZATIONS (LOS ANGELES) (US/0270-1111) [06340292] 2191, **2213**

DIRECTORY OF ERIC INFORMATION SERVICE PROVIDERS (US) [14923688] **1736**

DIRECTORY OF EUROPEAN INDUSTRIAL & TRADE ASSOCIATIONS (UK/0952-3626) [14278837] **1604**

DIRECTORY OF EUROPEAN PROFESSIONAL & LEARNED SOCIETIES (UK) [19732742] **5230**

DIRECTORY OF EUROPEAN RETAILERS (UK) [14059901] **953**

DIRECTORY OF EVALUATION TRAINING (US/0277-0873) [07480064] **5283**

DIRECTORY OF EXECUTIVE RECRUITERS (US/0090-6484) [20364677] **939**

DIRECTORY OF EXECUTIVE RECRUITERS (CORPORATE ED.), THE (US/1059-163X) [20682255] **939**

DIRECTORY OF EXECUTIVE RECRUITERS (STANDARD ED.) (US/0090-6484) [01785773] **940**

DIRECTORY OF EXPANDED ROLE PROGRAMS FOR REGISTERED NURSES, A (US) [04598701] **3855**

DIRECTORY OF EXPERTS AND CONSULTANTS IN SCIENCE AND ENGINEERING (US/0892-1660) [15097944] **5100**

DIRECTORY OF EXPORTERS (PK) [05118919] **831**

DIRECTORY OF FACILITIES AND SERVICES FOR LEARNING DISABLED (US) [07526030] **1877**

DIRECTORY OF FACILITIES OBLIGATED TO PROVIDE UNCOMPENSATED SERVICES BY STATE AND CITY (US/8755-593X) [11334372] 5283, **3779**

DIRECTORY OF FACULTY CONTRACTS AND BARGAINING AGENTS IN INSTITUTIONS OF HIGHER EDUCATION (US/0276-7805) [04239238] 1820, **1663**

DIRECTORY OF FACULTY, PROFESSIONAL AND ADMINISTRATIVE STAFF, AND STIDEMTS *See* DIRECTORY OF STUDENTS - HARVARD UNIVERSITY **1821**

DIRECTORY OF FAMILY PRACTICE RESIDENCY PROGRAMS (US/0897-182X) [06476931] **3737**

DIRECTORY OF FEDERAL AGENCY EDUCATION DATA TAPES (US) [06359630] **1736**

DIRECTORY OF FEDERAL & STATE BUSINESS ASSISTANCE / PREPARED BY THE CENTER FOR UTILIZATION OF FEDERAL TECHNOLOGY, NATIONAL TECHNICAL INFORMATION SERVICE, U.S. DEPARTMENT OF COMMERCE (US) [14633208] **666**

DIRECTORY OF FEDERAL AND STATE PROGRAMS FOR THE ... SCHOOL YEAR (US) [19603113] **1736**

DIRECTORY OF FEDERAL AUDIT AND INSPECTOR GENERAL ORGANIZATIONS (US) [06344214] **743**

DIRECTORY OF FEDERAL DROUGHT ASSISTANCE (US/0148-5091) [03315102] **79**

DIRECTORY OF FEDERAL GOVERNMENT SCIENTIFIC & TECHNOLOGICAL ESTABLISHMENTS (CN/0829-6030) [14698410] **5100**

DIRECTORY OF FEDERAL HEALTH/MEDICINE GRANTS AND CONTRACTS PROGRAMS (US/0744-0804) [05047756] 4773, **3572**

DIRECTORY OF FEDERAL LABORATORY & TECHNOLOGY RESOURCES (US/0891-8333) [13421336] **5100**

DIRECTORY OF FEDERAL PROGRAMS ADMINISTERED BY THE NEW JERSEY DEPARTMENT OF EDUCATION, A (US/0145-4374) [02740204] **1862**

DIRECTORY OF FEDERAL STATISTICAL DATA FILES (US/0731-3594) [08157023] 3207, **3258**

DIRECTORY OF FEDERALLY SPONSORED TRAINING MATERIALS (US) **666**

DIRECTORY OF FIELD CONTACTS FOR THE COORDINATION OF THE USE OF RADIO FREQUENCIES (US/0198-6422) [01727148] **1153**

DIRECTORY OF FILM LIBRARIES IN NORTH AMERICA (US) [05283564] 3207, **4068**

DIRECTORY OF FINANCIAL AIDS FOR MINORITIES (US/0738-4122) [09599894] **1821**

DIRECTORY OF FINANCIAL AIDS FOR WOMEN (US/0732-5215) [08380964] **1821**

DIRECTORY OF FINANCIAL INSTITUTIONS (MONETARY AUTHORITY OF SINGAPORE (SI) [06742624] **788**

DIRECTORY OF FINE ART REPRESENTATIVES & CORPORATIONS COLLECTING ART (US/1053-2854) [22212318] **349**

DIRECTORY OF FIRMS AND CORPORATIONS AUTHORIZED TO PRACTISE PROFESSIONAL ENGINEERING IN THE PROVINCE OF ONTARIO (CN/0316-8123) [02247178] **1971**

DIRECTORY OF FIRST DEGREE COURSES *CEASED*. (UK) [03437071] **1912**

DIRECTORY OF FLORIDA INDUSTRIES (US) [01308604] **666**

DIRECTORY OF FLORIDA INDUSTRIES (US) [06875266] **923**

DIRECTORY OF FLORIDA MANUFACTURERS *See* DIRECTORY OF FLORIDA INDUSTRIES **923**

DIRECTORY OF FLORIDA SAVINGS ASSOCIATIONS (US) [23660854] **788**

DIRECTORY OF FOOD SERVICE DISTRIBUTORS (BUSINESS GUIDES, INC.) (US/0271-7662) [06661917] **2333**

DIRECTORY OF FOOTWEAR & RELATED ACCESSORIES BUYERS (US/1057-7610) [24090849] **1083**

DIRECTORY OF FOREIGN FIRMS OPERATING IN THE UNITED STATES (US/0070-5543) [04365267] **666**

DIRECTORY OF FOREIGN INVESTMENT IN THE U.S (US/1050-8694) [21664233] **896**

DIRECTORY OF FOREIGN MANUFACTURERS IN THE UNITED STATES (US/1052-0031) [04704612] **3477**

DIRECTORY OF FOREST INDUSTRIES IN MALAYSIA (MY) [02658563] 2378, **2400**

DIRECTORY OF FORESTRY AND NATURAL RESOURCES COMPUTER SOFTWARE (US/1053-8453) [21141317] 2378, **1182**

DIRECTORY OF FOUNDATIONS OF THE GREATER WASHINGTON AREA (US/0884-9056) [11696929] **4335**

DIRECTORY OF FRANCHISING ORGANIZATIONS (US/0070-556X) [03646332] **954**

DIRECTORY OF FRANCHISING ORGANIZATIONS AND A GUIDE TO FRANCHISING *See* DIRECTORY OF FRANCHISING ORGANIZATIONS **954**

DIRECTORY OF FREE PROGRAMS, PERFORMING TALENT AND ATTRACTIONS, THE (US/0736-7759) [09205837] 4335, **384**

DIRECTORY OF FRENCH VIDEOTEX DATABASES FOR COMPANIES (FR/1164-0642) [I11640642] **1254**

DIRECTORY OF FULL-TIME COUNTY AND URBAN HEALTH DEPARTMENTS, A (US/0197-0704) [04086240] **4773**

DIRECTORY OF FULL YEAR HEAD START PROGRAMS (US/0092-6078) [01788123] **1736**

DIRECTORY OF FUNDED PROJECTS (US/0193-9084) [05254781] **1821**

DIRECTORY OF FURTHER EDUCATION (UK) [01788088] **1800**

DIRECTORY OF GALLERIES FOR THE FINE ARTIST (US/1048-3438) [22298494] **4087**

DIRECTORY OF GENERAL MERCHANDISE VARIETY CHAINS & SPECIALTY STORES (US/0741-6903) [10176587] **954**

DIRECTORY OF GEORGIA MUNICIPAL OFFICIALS (US/0419-2699) [01788578] **4702**

●DIRECTORY OF GEOSCIENCE DEPARTMENTS (US) [27863236] **1373**

DIRECTORY OF GEOSCIENCE DEPARTMENTS, NORTH AMERICA (US) [209077413] **1373**

DIRECTORY OF GERIATRIC PUBLICATIONS, THE (US/0745-) [20939569] **3750**

DIRECTORY OF GOVERNMENT AGENCIES SAFEGUARDING CONSUMER AND ENVIRONMENT (US/0070-5586) [01172830] 1296, **4643**

DIRECTORY OF GOVERNMENT AND PUBLIC SECTOR IN A.R.E (UA) [06524222] 831, **4643**

DIRECTORY OF GOVERNMENT OFFICIALS. FEDERAL, STATE, COUNTY, CITY, TOWNSHIP AND SPECIAL DISTRICT OFFICIALS IN NORTH DAKOTA (US/0736-6183) [08938143] **4643**

DIRECTORY OF GOVERNMENTS IN METROPOLITAN TORONTO (CN/0084-9944) [02442036] **4643**

DIRECTORY OF GRADUATE MEDICAL EDUCATION PROGRAMS (US/0892-0109) [15058481] **3572**

DIRECTORY OF GRADUATE PROGRAMS IN ENGINEERING *See* DIRECTORY OF ENGINEERING GRADUATE STUDIES & RESEARCH **1970**

DIRECTORY OF GRADUATE RESEARCH (US/0193-5011) [05229212] **974**

DIRECTORY OF GRADUATE STUDIES (US) **4953**

DIRECTORY OF GRANT-MAKING TRUSTS (UK) [07600586] **4335**

DIRECTORY OF GRANTS FOR FOREIGN STUDY AND RESEARCH IN LAW (US/1056-9626) [23913853] **1821**

DIRECTORY OF GRANTS FOR ORGANIZATIONS SERVING PEOPLE WITH DISABILITIES (US) [28604966] 5283, **4387**

DIRECTORY OF GRANTS IN THE HUMANITIES (US/0887-0551) [13072233] **2845**

DIRECTORY OF HALFWAY HOUSES AND GROUP HOMES FOR TROUBLED CHILDREN (US/0149-0788) [03415890] **5283**

DIRECTORY OF HARDLINES DISTRIBUTORS (US/0882-536X) [16078597] **2811**

DIRECTORY OF HAZARDOUS WASTE SERVICES (CN/1194-2355) [18385261] **2227**

DIRECTORY OF HEALTH CARE FACILITIES (US/0098-6135) [01484174] **3779**

DIRECTORY OF HEALTH CARE FACILITIES AND APPROVED SCHOOLS OF NURSING *See* DIRECTORY OF HEALTH CARE FACILITIES **3779**

DIRECTORY OF HEALTH CARE GROUP PURCHASING ORGANIZATIONS (US/1064-8496) [17246306] **3779**

DIRECTORY OF HEALTH SCIENCES LIBRARIES IN THE UNITED STATES (US/0095-7925) [01214941] 3572, **3207**

DIRECTORY OF HEALTH SERVICE ORGANIZATIONS (US) **2596**

DIRECTORY OF HEALTH, WELFARE AND RECREATION SERVICES FOR GREATER DALLAS (US) [04363098] **5283**

DIRECTORY OF HELICOPTER OPERATORS IN THE UNITED STATES, CANADA, MEXICO, AND PUERTO RICO (US/0741-0166) [10048961] **17**

DIRECTORY OF HIGH SCHOOL COACHES *See* NATIONAL DIRECTORY OF HIGH SCHOOL COACHES, THE **4906**

●DIRECTORY OF HIGH VOLUME INDEPENDENT DRUG STORES (US/1054-3082) [22841200] **831**

DIRECTORY OF HIGH-VOLUME INDEPENDENT RESTAURANTS (US/0888-0166) [13448516] **5070**

DIRECTORY OF HIGHER EDUCATION (US/0094-8322) [01794973] **1821**

DIRECTORY OF HIGHER EDUCATION COURSES (AT) [05594191] **1821**

DIRECTORY OF HIGHER EDUCATION INSTITUTIONS / COMMISSION OF THE EUROPEAN COMMUNITIES (LU) [12394139] **1821**

DIRECTORY OF HIGHER EDUCATION INSTITUTIONS IN MISSOURI (US/0196-9307) [05223142] **1821**

DIRECTORY OF HIGHER EDUCATION NURSING COURSES (AT) [I08125856] **3855**

●DIRECTORY OF HISPANIC EXPERTS, THE (US/1074-9667) [29894372] **2731**

DIRECTORY OF HISTORIANS OF LATIN AMERICAN ART (US/0196-8475) [05899599] **349**

DIRECTORY OF HISTORICAL ORGANIZATIONS IN THE UNITED STATES AND CANADA (US/1045-456X) [20115225] **4087**

DIRECTORY OF HISTORICAL SOCIETIES OF NEW JERSEY (US) [01783689] **2731**

DIRECTORY OF HISTORY DEPARTMENTS AND ORGANIZATIONS IN THE UNITED STATES AND CANADA (US) [22613105] **2615**

DIRECTORY OF HOME CENTER OPERATORS & HARDWARE CHAINS (US/0272-0167) [06716450] **2811**

DIRECTORY OF HOME CENTERS (US/0093-8718) [01792303] **2811**

DIRECTORY OF HOME FURNISHINGS RETAILERS (US/0888-0158) [13448579] **2905**

DIRECTORY OF HONG KONG INDUSTRIES (HK) [03575405] **1604**

DIRECTORY OF HOSPITAL PERSONNEL, THE (US/0885-9671) [12797284] **3779**

DIRECTORY OF HOSPITALITY EDUCATORS (US/0742-3306) [10292511] 865, **2805**

DIRECTORY OF HOSPITALS IN INDIA (II) [09507820] **3779**

●DIRECTORY OF HOTEL & MOTEL COMPANIES (US) [25585365] **2805**

Alphabetical Title Index — DIRECTORY

DIRECTORY OF HOTEL & MOTEL SYSTEMS (US) [04757499] **2805**

DIRECTORY OF HOTEL SYSTEMS *See* DIRECTORY OF HOTEL & MOTEL SYSTEMS **2805**

DIRECTORY OF HOTELS IN KENYA (KE) [05671486] **2805**

DIRECTORY OF HOUSING CO-OPERATIVES (CN/0226-8558) [07857923] 2821, **1542**

DIRECTORY OF HOUSING RELATED STATISTICS (AT/1032-0865) [I10320865] **2840**

DIRECTORY OF HUMAN RESOURCE SERVICES & PRODUCTS, THE (US/0732-4723) [08336509] **666**

DIRECTORY OF HUMAN SERVICE ORGANIZATIONS (US/0364-4766) [02657925] **5283**

DIRECTORY OF HUMAN SERVICES IN THE KALAMAZOO AREA (US) [06094586] **5283**

DIRECTORY OF HUNGARIAN RESEARCH INSTITUTIONS (HU) [03262065] **5100**

DIRECTORY OF ILLINOIS NONPUBLIC SCHOOLS (US) [21489458] **1736**

●DIRECTORY OF ILLINOIS POLITICAL LEADERS (US/1058-2657) [23229567] **4643**

DIRECTORY OF ILLINOIS VISUAL ARTISTS (US/0277-0164) [06340246] **349**

DIRECTORY OF INCENTIVE TRAVEL INTERNATIONAL (US/0732-6572) [08381727] **5468**

DIRECTORY OF INDEPENDENT HOSPITALS AND HEALTH SERVICES, THE (UK/0260-8820) [16958423] **3779**

DIRECTORY OF INDEPENDENT IBM PERSONAL COMPUTER HARDWARE AND SOFTWARE, THE (US/0735-617X) [08955842] **1182**

DIRECTORY OF INDEPENDENT SECONDARY SCHOOLS OF AUSTRALIA (AT) **1736**

DIRECTORY OF INDIAN ECONOMIC JOURNALS (II) [06248788] **1479**

DIRECTORY OF INDIAN ENGINEERING EXPORTERS (II) [01790446] **831**

DIRECTORY OF INDIAN SCIENTIFIC PERIODICALS (II/0419-2745) [03857403] **5174**

DIRECTORY OF INDIANA LOCAL AND REGIONAL PLANNING AND DEVELOPMENT COMMISSIONS, A (US) [04738131] **2821**

DIRECTORY OF INDONESIAN IMPORTERS (SI) [06408400] **831**

DIRECTORY OF INDONESIAN IMPORTERS & EXPORTERS (SI) **831**

DIRECTORY OF INDUSTRIAL DESIGNERS (US/0897-0432) [16620058] **2098**

DIRECTORY OF INDUSTRIAL ESTABLISHMENTS (TZ) [01786424] **1604**

DIRECTORY OF INDUSTRIAL HEAT PROCESSING AND COMBUSTION EQUIPMENT. UNITED STATES MANUFACTURERS, THE (US/0738-0887) [06193040] 1971, **613**

DIRECTORY OF INDUSTRIAL HEATING AND COMBUSTION EQUIPMENT. UNITED STATES MANUFACTURERS *See* DIRECTORY OF INDUSTRIAL HEAT PROCESSING AND COMBUSTION EQUIPMENT. UNITED STATES MANUFACTURERS, THE **613**

DIRECTORY OF INDUSTRIAL LABORATORIES IN ISRAEL (IS) [11897542] **5100**

DIRECTORY OF INDUSTRIAL RELATIONS LIBRARIES IN CANADA (CN/0225-5472) [06132712] **3207**

DIRECTORY OF INDUSTRIAL UNITS (II) [05691212] **1604**

DIRECTORY OF INDUSTRY DATA SOURCES. THE UNITED STATES OF AMERICA AND CANADA (US/0278-0119) [07684832] **1531**

DIRECTORY OF INDUSTRY DATA SOURCES. WESTERN EUROPE (US/0732-7358) [08422965] **1604**

DIRECTORY OF INFORMATION AGE NEWSLETTERS (US/0742-6755) [10413620] **1237**

DIRECTORY OF INFORMATION AND REFERRAL SERVICES IN THE UNITED STATES AND CANADA (US/0749-050X) [10485375] **5283**

DIRECTORY OF INFORMATION MANAGEMENT SOFTWARE FOR LIBRARIES, INFORMATION CENTERS, RECORD CENTERS (US) [10393340] 1182, **3207**

DIRECTORY OF INPATIENT FACILITIES FOR THE MENTALLY RETARDED (US/0147-3921) [03147809] 3924, **3779**

DIRECTORY OF INSTITUTE/COMPONENT OFFICERS (US/1054-2000) [16170365] **297**

DIRECTORY OF INSTITUTIONS OF ORIENTAL STUDIES IN OVERSEAS COUNTRIES (II/0377-6948) [01795890] **2650**

DIRECTORY OF INSTITUTIONS - ONTARIO. FREEDOM OF INFORMATION AND PRIVACY BRANCH (CN/0845-096X) [25351966] **4643**

DIRECTORY OF INSTRUCTIONAL PROGRAMS (K-8). LANGUAGE ARTS (US) [22160143] 1892, **1803**

DIRECTORY OF INSTRUCTIONAL PROGRAMS (K-8). READING (US) [22160195] **1803**

DIRECTORY OF INSTRUCTIONAL PROGRAMS (K-8). SCIENCE/HEALTH (US) [22160051] **1892**

DIRECTORY OF INSTRUCTIONAL PROGRAMS (K-8). SPELLING/HANDWRITING (US) [22160006] **1803**

DIRECTORY OF INSURANCE BROKERS AND CLAIMS ASSESSORS *See* DIRECTORY OF INSURANCE BROKERS, LOSS ADJUSTORS AND CLAIMS ASSESSORS, THE **2878**

DIRECTORY OF INSURANCE BROKERS, LOSS ADJUSTORS AND CLAIMS ASSESSORS, THE (UK) [01791155] **2878**

DIRECTORY OF INSURANCE COMPANIES LICENSED IN NEW YORK STATE (US) [05037873] **2878**

DIRECTORY OF INSURANCE COMPANIES (SANTA FE, N.M.) (US/0732-1767) [04786463] **2878**

●DIRECTORY OF INTELLECTUAL PROPERTY ATTORNEYS (US/1064-0355) [26196454] 1303, **2962**

DIRECTORY OF INTELLECTUAL PROPERTY LAWYERS AND PATENT AGENTS *See* DIRECTORY OF INTELLECTUAL PROPERTY ATTORNEYS **2962**

DIRECTORY OF INTERCULTURAL EDUCATION NEWSLETTERS (US/0278-4084) [07972720] **1736**

DIRECTORY OF INTERNATIONAL CORPORATE GIVING IN AMERICA (US/1046-4263) [18903009] **4335**

DIRECTORY OF INTERNATIONAL FILM AND VIDEO FESTIVALS (UK/0268-5256) [12962178] **4068**

DIRECTORY OF INTERNATIONAL STANDARDIZING BODIES / REPERTOIRE DES ORGANISMES INTERNATIONAUX A ACTIVITES NORMATIVES (SZ) [06096776] **4030**

DIRECTORY OF INTERNSHIP AND RESIDENCIES MATCHING PROGRAM FOR ... / PREPARED BY THE AMERICAN ASSOCIATION OF VETERINARY CLINICIANS (US) [09023666] 1821, **5509**

DIRECTORY OF INTERPRETERS FOR THE DEAF IN TEXAS (US/0741-8140) [09673251] **5283**

DIRECTORY OF IOWA MANUFACTURERS (US/0095-4446) [01783342] **3477**

DIRECTORY OF IOWA MUNICIPALITIES (US/0363-1842) [02429377] **4643**

DIRECTORY OF IRANIAN NEWSPAPERS (IR) [05462028] 5814, **5803**

DIRECTORY OF IRANIAN PERIODICALS (IR/0084-9960) [01316056] **415**

DIRECTORY OF ISRAEL, THE (IS) [06849097] **831**

DIRECTORY OF JAPANESE HEALTHCARE INDUSTRY (US) **3572**

DIRECTORY OF JAPANESE PUBLISHING INDUSTRY (JA) **4814**

DIRECTORY OF JAPANESE SCIENTIFIC PERIODICALS (JA/0916-1198) [01566708] **5174**

DIRECTORY OF JAPANESE TECHNICAL RESOURCES IN THE UNITED STATES (US) [18737273] **5100**

DIRECTORY OF JEWISH FAMILY & CHILDREN'S AGENCIES (US/0271-0277) [06215105] 2259, **5283**

DIRECTORY OF JOBS & CAREERS ABROAD (UK/0143-3482) [I01433482] **4203**

DIRECTORY OF KANSAS MANUFACTURERS AND THEIR PRODUCTS (US/0070-5721) [03685107] **3477**

DIRECTORY OF KANSAS PUBLIC OFFICIALS (US/0196-7681) [03502084] **4643**

DIRECTORY OF KEY CONTACTS AND SERVICES / COMMERCE DEPARTMENT (US) [06829718] **831**

DIRECTORY OF KOREAN ELECTRONICS EXPORTERS (KO) [07215747] **831**

DIRECTORY OF KOREAN PHYSICIANS: DISTRICT OF COLUMBIA, MARYLAND, AND VIRGINIA (US/0271-9851) [06704621] **3913**

DIRECTORY OF LABOR MARKET AND OCCUPATIONAL INFORMATION (US) [08045305] **1663**

DIRECTORY OF LABOR MARKET INFORMATION (US/0190-3217) [04675355] **1663**

DIRECTORY OF LABOR MARKET INFORMATION (COLUMBIA, S.C.) (US) [08674795] **1663**

DIRECTORY OF LABOR MARKET INFORMATION REPORTS AND PUBLICATIONS (US/0149-4961) [03434766] **1663**

DIRECTORY OF LABOUR ORGANIZATIONS IN CANADA (CN/0711-1703) [07003976] **1663**

DIRECTORY OF LABOUR ORGANIZATIONS IN NEW BRUNSWICK (CN/0840-3651) [04232871] **1663**

DIRECTORY OF LATIN AMERICANISTS (US/0091-3235) [01786350] **2512**

DIRECTORY OF LAW ENFORCEMENT AND CRIMINAL JUSTICE EDUCATION *CEASED.* (US/0097-6083) [01798468] **3163**

DIRECTORY OF LAW ENFORCEMENT PROFESSORS (US) [01788087] **3163**

DIRECTORY OF LAW LIBRARIES (US) [01566713] 2962, **3207**

DIRECTORY OF LAW TEACHERS (MONTREAL) (CN/0383-8358) [02592229] **2962**

DIRECTORY OF LAWYER REFERRAL SERVICES (1976) (US/1045-3342) [11413413] **2962**

DIRECTORY OF LEADING PRIVATE COMPANIES, INCLUDING CORPORATE AFFILIATIONS (US/1066-9779) [25399229] **666**

DIRECTORY OF LEADING US EXPORT MANAGEMENT COMPANIES (US) **831**

DIRECTORY OF LEARNING RESOURCES FOR READING (US) [05306198] **1892**

... DIRECTORY OF LEGAL AID AND DEFENDER OFFICES IN THE UNITED STATES, THE (US/0276-5365) [07097783] **3179**

DIRECTORY OF LEGAL EMPLOYERS (1985) (US/0882-5033) [11102300] **2962**

DIRECTORY OF LEGISLATIVE LEADERS (US/1051-4988) [12006335] **4643**

DIRECTORY OF LEGISLATIVE LOBBYISTS / STATE OF KANSAS (US) [08421446] **4643**

DIRECTORY OF LENDING & LEASING INSTITUTIONS (US/0734-6840) [08789313] **788**

DIRECTORY OF LIBRARIES AND ARCHIVAL INSTITUTIONS IN PRINCE EDWARD ISLAND (CN/0715-1624) [08674339] 2481, **3207**

DIRECTORY OF LIBRARIES AND INFORMATION SOURCES *See* DIRECTORY OF LIBRARIES AND INFORMATION SOURCES IN THE PHILADELPHIA AREA **3207**

DIRECTORY OF LIBRARIES AND INFORMATION SOURCES IN THE PHILADELPHIA AREA (US/0278-5684) [03780412] **3207**

DIRECTORY OF LIBRARIES IN MANITOBA (CN/0317-8536) [02240929] **3207**

DIRECTORY OF LIBRARIES IN NEWFOUNDLAND AND LABRADOR (CN/0317-2465) [02248026] **3207**

DIRECTORY OF LIBRARY AND INFORMATION CONSULTANTS IN METROPOLITAN WASHINGTON (US/0743-4995) [09679804] **3207**

DIRECTORY OF LIBRARY & INFORMATION PROFESSIONALS (US/0894-7031) [16167386] **3207**

●DIRECTORY OF LIBRARY AUTOMATION SOFTWARE, SYSTEMS, AND SERVICES (US/1071-264X) [27371602] 1285, **3207**

DIRECTORY OF LIBRARY REPROGRAPHIC SERVICES (US/0160-6077) [02320367] **3207**

DIRECTORY OF LIBRARY SYSTEMS IN NEW YORK STATE, A (US) [03059690] **3207**

DIRECTORY OF LICENSED AUCTIONEERS, APPRENTICE AUCTIONEERS, AND FIRMS ENGAGED IN THE AUCTION BUSINESS IN NORTH CAROLINA (US) [06506656] **954**

DIRECTORY OF LICENSED REAL ESTATE APPRAISERS (US/0361-4980) [02246904] **4836**

DIRECTORY OF LICENSED YACHT AND SHIP BROKERS AND SALESMEN *See* DIRECTORY OF LICENSED YACHT AND SHIP BROKERS AND SALESPERSONS **593**

DIRECTORY OF LICENSED YACHT AND SHIP BROKERS AND SALESPERSONS (US) [09559932] **593**

DIRECTORY OF LICENSEES - OREGON STATE BOARD OF RADIOLOGIC TECHNOLOGY (US) [07200118] **3941**

DIRECTORY
Alphabetical Title Index

DIRECTORY OF LICENSEES / TEXAS STATE BOARD OF PUBLIC ACCOUNTANCY (US/0731-2415) [07862814] **743**

DIRECTORY OF LICENSES (US) [06976451] **4380**

DIRECTORY OF LICENTIATES, REGULATIONS, AND REGISTRATION LAW / ARKANSAS STATE MEDICAL BOARD (US) [15348488] **3913**

DIRECTORY OF LIMITED MEMBERS / COUNCIL OF PETROLEUM ACCOUNTANTS SOCIETIES (US) [08575424] **4254, 743**

DIRECTORY OF LITERARY MAGAZINES (US/0884-6006) [11733470] **3381**

DIRECTORY OF LOCAL CHIEF EXECUTIVES *See* DIRECTORY OF CITY POLICY OFFICIALS **4643**

DIRECTORY OF LOCAL HOUSING AUTHORITIES (US/0098-1095) [01799456] **2821**

DIRECTORY OF LONDON PUBLIC LIBRARIES (UK/0419-2915) [05461861] **3207**

DIRECTORY OF LONG TERM CARE CENTRES IN CANADA (CN/0226-5419) [06299019] **3779**

DIRECTORY OF LOUISIANA CITIES, TOWNS AND VILLAGES *See* LOUISIANA DIRECTORY OF CITIES, TOWNS, AND VILLAGES **2745**

●DIRECTORY OF MAILING LIST COMPANIES (US) [24484121] **1144, 666**

DIRECTORY OF MAILING LIST HOUSES *See* DIRECTORY OF MAILING LIST COMPANIES **666**

DIRECTORY OF MAILING LIST HOUSES *See* DIRECTORY OF MAILING LISTS COMPANIES **758**

DIRECTORY OF MAILING LISTS COMPANIES (US) **758**

DIRECTORY OF MAINE INDUSTRIAL EDUCATION TEACHERS (US) [07817220] **372**

DIRECTORY OF MAINE LABOR ORGANIZATIONS (US) [07014806] **1663**

DIRECTORY OF MAJOR MAILERS & WHAT THEY MAIL (US/1045-6201) [20174725] **923**

DIRECTORY OF MAJOR MALLS (US/0732-5983) [08377308] **4836, 954**

DIRECTORY OF MAJOR U.S. CORPORATIONS INVOLVED IN AGRIBUSINESS (US) [02960729] **2333, 79**

DIRECTORY OF MANAGEMENT CONSULTANTS (US/0743-6890) [04630098] **865**

DIRECTORY OF MANAGEMENT CONSULTANTS IN THE UK (UK/0268-375X) [11569740] **865**

DIRECTORY OF MANUFACTURERS OF LUMBER, PLYWOOD, AND BUILDING MATERIALS ... MADE IN B.C (CN) [06229681] **2400**

DIRECTORY OF MANUFACTURERS, STATE OF HAWAII (US/0190-3047) [03689409] **3477**

DIRECTORY OF MANUFACTURING INDUSTRIES OF ROCHESTER AND MONROE COUNTY, NEW YORK : INFORMATION AS SUPPLIED BY THE FIRMS LISTED, OR COMPILED FROM AVAILABLE SOURCES (US) [05663812] **3478**

DIRECTORY OF MARKETING INFORMATION COMPANIES : FEATURING THE BEST 100 (US) [22885446] **923**

DIRECTORY OF MARYLAND MUNICIPAL OFFICIALS (US/0415-9659) [04707650] **4702**

DIRECTORY OF MASTER GARDENING PROGRAMS IN THE UNITED STATES AND CANADA (US/1054-9161) [23018914] **2413**

DIRECTORY OF MASTERCARD AND VISA CREDIT CARD SOURCES, THE (US/1061-3358) [24662750] **788**

DIRECTORY OF MEDICAL AND HEALTH CARE LIBRARIES IN THE UNITED KINGDOM AND REPUBLIC OF IRELAND (UK) [10089047] **3572, 3207**

DIRECTORY OF MEDICAL COMPUTER SYSTEMS (US) [12115766] **3572, 1182**

DIRECTORY OF MEDICAL FACILITIES. REGION VIII, DENVER (US/0894-1114) [11778869] **3779**

DIRECTORY OF MEDICAL INSTITUTIONS CONDUCTING RESEARCH AND SERVICES FOR PERSONS WITH THE MARFAN SYNDROME AND RELATED CONNECTIVE TISSUE DISORDERS (US) **3572**

DIRECTORY OF MEDICAL LIBRARIES IN THE BRITISH ISLES *See* DIRECTORY OF MEDICAL AND HEALTH CARE LIBRARIES IN THE UNITED KINGDOM AND REPUBLIC OF IRELAND **3207**

DIRECTORY OF MEDICAL PRACTICE POSITIONS (US) [24783689] **3572**

DIRECTORY OF MEDICAL REHABILITATION PROGRAMS (US/1063-1712) [21556860] **3572**

DIRECTORY OF MEDICAL SCHOOLS WORLDWIDE (US/0160-6468) [03714883] **3572, 1821**

DIRECTORY OF MEDICAL SPECIALISTS (US/0070-5829) [01740128] **3913**

DIRECTORY OF MEDICAL VIDEO PROGRAMS, THE (US) [22361910] **3572**

DIRECTORY OF MEMBER AGENCIES - CHILD WELFARE LEAGUE OF AMERICA (1986) (US/1042-9042) [14154379] **5283**

DIRECTORY OF MEMBER AGENCIES IN THE UNITED STATES AND CANADA (US/1045-1684) [16119190] **5283**

DIRECTORY OF MEMBER ARCHIVES (UK) [06892948] **5230, 5316**

DIRECTORY OF MEMBERS (US) [05296014] **3964**

DIRECTORY OF MEMBERS (AT) [01787004] **2962**

DIRECTORY OF MEMBERS / AMERICAN ASSOCIATION FOR CANCER RESEARCH (US/0277-3414) [07516931] **3816**

●DIRECTORY OF MEMBERS / AMERICAN ASSOCIATION OF COLLEGES FOR TEACHER EDUCATION (US) [30927771] **1862**

DIRECTORY OF MEMBERS / AMERICAN ASSOCIATION OF HOMES FOR THE AGING (US) [10637127] **5178, 5283**

DIRECTORY OF MEMBERS - AMERICAN FEDERATION OF CLINICAL ONCOLOGIC SOCIETIES (US) [04060872] **3816**

DIRECTORY OF MEMBERS - AMERICAN PHILOLOGICAL ASSOCIATION (US/0044-779X) [01793522] **3277**

DIRECTORY OF MEMBERS / AMERICAN POLITICAL SCIENCE ASSOCIATION (US) [23728560] **4472**

DIRECTORY OF MEMBERS - AMERICAN SOCIETY FOR MICROBIOLOGY (US/0196-8254) [04636823] **562**

DIRECTORY OF MEMBERS - AMERICAN STATISTICAL ASSOCIATION; BIOMETRIC SOCIETY. EASTERN NORTH AMERICAN REGION. BIOMETRIC SOCIETY. WESTERN NORTH AMERICAN REGION (US/0740-7181) [08757942] **5326**

DIRECTORY OF MEMBERS AND BUYERS GUIDE / INDIAN ARTS & CRAFTS ASSOCIATION (US) [12058445] **372**

DIRECTORY OF MEMBERS AND CONSTITUTION *See* IASSW DIRECTORY **5289**

DIRECTORY OF MEMBERS AND FRIENDS / RSCM (US) [09955910] **4114**

DIRECTORY OF MEMBERS & MUSEUMS (US/0197-9949) [06137750] **4114**

DIRECTORY OF MEMBERS - APPRAISAL INSTITUTE (U.S.) (US/1061-1673) [23540704] **4836**

DIRECTORY OF MEMBERS / ASSOCIATION OF CANADIAN UNIVERSITY PRESSES (CN/0711-3056) [08469657] **4814**

DIRECTORY OF MEMBERS - AUSTRALIAN BOOK PUBLISHERS ASSOCIATION (AT) [09965525] **4828**

DIRECTORY OF MEMBERS - CALIFORNIA SOCIETY, CERTIFIED PUBLIC ACCOUNTANTS (US/0364-5703) [02665696] **743**

DIRECTORY OF MEMBERS / CANADIAN LIBRARY ASSOCIATION (CN/0846-2038) [24005973] **3207**

DIRECTORY OF MEMBERS - DIRECTORS GUILD OF AMERICA (US/0419-2052) [02251189] **4068**

DIRECTORY OF MEMBERS / DIRECTORS GUILD OF GREAT BRITAIN (UK) [11404952] **4068**

DIRECTORY OF MEMBERS - ELECTROCHEMICAL SOCIETY (US/0735-8687) [08982080] **1051**

DIRECTORY OF MEMBERS - FEDERATION OF INDIAN PUBLISHERS (II) [10559978] **4814**

DIRECTORY OF MEMBERS' FIRMS - SOUTH AFRICAN ASSOCIATION OF CONSULTING ENGINEERS (SA) [01786845] **1971**

DIRECTORY OF MEMBERS - FREELANCE EDITORS' ASSOCIATION OF CANADA (CN/0226-9031) [07966284] **4814**

DIRECTORY OF MEMBERS / INSTITUTE OF CHARTERED FINANCIAL ANALYSTS *See* MEMBERSHIP DIRECTORY **906**

DIRECTORY OF MEMBERS - INSTITUTE OF MANAGEMENT CONSULTANTS (US/0097-6547) [01799599] **865**

DIRECTORY OF MEMBERS - INTERNATIONAL ASSOCIATION OF SURVEY STATISTICIANS (FR) [02401132] **5326**

DIRECTORY OF MEMBERS - INTERNATIONAL BAR ASSOCIATION, SECTION ON BUSINESS LAW (UK) [03249606] **3099**

DIRECTORY OF MEMBERS / LOS ANGELES COUNTY MEDICAL ASSOCIATION (US) [05671700] **3913**

DIRECTORY OF MEMBERS, LOT EXCHANGE, MAUSOLEUM CRYPT EXCHANGE, DOLLAR CREDIT PLANS (US/0272-2674) [05916890] **2407**

DIRECTORY OF MEMBERS - MUNICIPAL FINANCE OFFICERS ASSOCIATION (US/0148-1762) [03276507] **4720**

DIRECTORY OF MEMBERS - NATIONAL SOFT DRINK ASSOCIATION (US/0278-050X) [07681963] **2366**

DIRECTORY OF MEMBERS, NEW YORK STATE LEGISLATURE, AND MEMBERS OF CONGRESS (US/0415-9675) [02241675] **4643**

●DIRECTORY OF MEMBERS OF THE ASSOCIATION OF TRANSLATORS AND INTERPRETERS OF ONTARIO (CN/1188-102X) [27165199] **3277**

●DIRECTORY OF MEMBERS OF THE ASSOCIATION OF TRANSLATORS AND INTERPRETERS OF ONTARIO (CN/1188-102X) [27165201] **3277**

DIRECTORY OF MEMBERS, OFFICERS, COMMITTEES - AMERICAN VACUUM SOCIETY (US/0360-8794) [02244593] **2113**

DIRECTORY OF MEMBERS - PERIODICAL WRITERS ASSOCIATION OF CANADA (CN/0833-9821) [15466163] **4814, 2919**

DIRECTORY OF MEMBERS - PUNJAB HARYANA & DELHI CHAMBER OF COMMERCE AND INDUSTRY (II/0376-8511) [02245609] **819**

DIRECTORY OF MEMBERS - QUEBEC ASSOCIATION OF SCHOOL ADMINISTRATORS (CN/0702-729X) [03412107] **1862**

DIRECTORY OF MEMBERS' RESEARCH. SUPPLEMENT / OXFORDSHIRE FAMILY HISTORY SOCIETY (UK) [11735944] **2445**

DIRECTORY OF MEMBERS / SOCIETY OF AMERICAN TRAVEL WRITERS (US/0277-5301) [07578109] **5468**

DIRECTORY OF MEMBERS - STATE BAR OF ARIZONA (US/0099-1643) [02242467] **2962**

●DIRECTORY OF MEMBERS / THE AMERICAN SOCIOLOGICAL ASSOCIATION (US) [26565716] **5244**

DIRECTORY OF MEMBERS / THE BIBLIOGRAPHICAL SOCIETY OF CANADA (CN/0826-8541) [09073195] **415**

DIRECTORY OF MEMBERS / THE CANADIAN HISTORICAL ASSOCIATION (CN/1183-9260) [25589793] **2731**

DIRECTORY OF MEMBERS / THE CANADIAN HISTORICAL ASSOCIATION (CN/1183-9260) [25589794] **2731**

DIRECTORY OF MEMBERS / THE INSTITUTE (US/0569-5821) [01480078] **4836**

DIRECTORY OF MEMBERS / THE MANUSCRIPT SOCIETY (US/0742-373X) [10269858] **2773**

DIRECTORY OF MEMBERS / THE NATIONAL ASSOCIATION OF REAL ESTATE INVESTMENT TRUSTS, INC (US/0731-8553) [07874532] **896, 4836**

DIRECTORY OF MEMBERS - VEHICLE BUILDERS & REPAIRERS ASSOCIATION (UK) [08674612] **5413**

DIRECTORY OF MEMBERS / ZETA PSI FRATERNITY OF NORTH AMERICA (US) [18095284] **1821**

DIRECTORY OF MEMBERSHIP - CENTRAL STATES SPEECH ASSOCIATION (US/0577-098X) [02064846] **1110**

DIRECTORY OF MEMBERSHIP - FLORIDA COUNCIL OF TEACHERS OF ENGLISH (US/0426-5688) [01385121] **1892, 3277**

DIRECTORY OF MEMBERSHIP OF THE AMERICAN ANIMAL HOSPITAL ASSOCIATION (US) [07497907] **5509**

DIRECTORY OF MEN'S & BOYS' WEAR SPECIALTY STORES (US/0277-9625) [07667789] **3995, 1083**

DIRECTORY OF MENTAL HEALTH AND ALCOHOLISM PROGRAMS IN MARYLAND (US/0361-9516) [02441258] **1343, 4773**

DIRECTORY OF MENTAL HEALTH AND MENTAL RETARDATION SERVICES FOR TEXAS See DIRECTORY OF SERVICES - TEXAS DEPARTMENT OF MENTAL HEALTH AND MENTAL RETARDATION **5283**

DIRECTORY OF MENTAL HEALTH SERVICES IN ILLINOIS *CEASED.* (US/0361-8455) [02246905] **4773**

DIRECTORY OF MERGERS & ACQUISITIONS IN CANADA (CN/1186-6047) [24367949] **666**

DIRECTORY OF METROPOLITAN PLANNING ORGANIZATIONS AND STATE TRANSPORTATION AGENCIES (US) [06633306] **5381**

DIRECTORY OF MICHIGAN MUNICIPAL OFFICIALS (US/0148-7442) [03367597] **4643**

DIRECTORY OF MICROCOMPUTER SOFTWARE IN THE HUMAN SERVICES, A (US/0892-9262) [12317732] 5283, **1285**

DIRECTORY OF MINE SUPPLY HOUSES, DISTRIBUTORS AND SALES AGENTS (US/0417-612X) [05538062] **2138**

DIRECTORY OF MINES PERSONNEL (CN/0383-1779) [03202287] **2138**

DIRECTORY OF MINING PROGRAMS (US/0884-917X) [12442851] **2138**

DIRECTORY OF MINISTERIAL ADVISERS AND ASSISTANTS (AT/1035-3062) [I10353062] **4697**

DIRECTORY OF MINNESOTA CITY OFFICIALS (US/0890-1651) [12036664] **4643**

DIRECTORY OF MINNESOTA'S AREA MENTAL HEALTH, MENTAL RETARDATION, INEBRIETY PROGRAMS (US/0095-4888) [01788557] **4773**

DIRECTORY OF MINORITY OWNED BUSINESSES AND WOMEN OWNED BUSINESSES / KANSAS DEPARTMENT OF COMMERCE (US) [18768511] **667**

DIRECTORY OF MINORITY OWNED BUSINESSES IN TEXAS (US/0094-8004) [01794974] **667**

DIRECTORY OF MISSISSIPPI ELECTIVE OFFICIALS (US/0540-3820) [01758353] **4643**

DIRECTORY OF MISSOURI LIBRARIES (US/0092-4067) [03575847] **3207**

DIRECTORY OF MISSOURI MUNICIPAL OFFICIALS (US) **4644**

DIRECTORY OF MISSOURI'S REGIONAL PLANNING SYSTEM, A (US/0090-7812) [01785809] **2821**

DIRECTORY OF MONTANA BROADCASTERS (US) [02539023] **1131**

●DIRECTORY OF MULTIMEDIA EQUIPMENT, SOFTWARE, AND SERVICES / ICIA (US) [26485562] 1285, **1153**

DIRECTORY OF MUNICIPAL AND COUNTY OFFICIALS IN COLORADO / COLORADO MUNICIPAL LEAGUE (US) [08860998] **4644**

DIRECTORY OF MUNICIPAL AND PROVINCIAL HERITAGE PROPERTY IN SASKATCHEWAN (1990) (CN/1184-6070) [23659476] **2615**

DIRECTORY OF MUNICIPAL AUTHORITIES IN PENNSYLVANIA (US/0361-6924) [02441317] **4644**

DIRECTORY OF MUNICIPAL OFFICIALS OF NEW MEXICO (US) [01787203] **4644**

DIRECTORY OF MUSIC FACULTIES IN COLLEGES AND UNIVERSITIES, U.S. AND CANADA (US/0098-664X) [02242067] **4114**

DIRECTORY OF MUTUAL FUNDS / INVESTMENT COMPANY INSTITUTE (US/1062-1857) [23371369] **896**

DIRECTORY OF NATIONAL AND INTERNATIONAL UNIONS AND ASSOCIATIONS WITH EXCLUSIVE RECOGNITION IN THE FEDERAL SERVICE (US/0097-8639) [01799220] **1663**

DIRECTORY OF NATIONAL DEFENSE EXECUTIVE RESERVISTS ON ASSIGNMENT TO OFFICE OF SECRETARY OF TRANSPORTATION, U.S. DEPARTMENT OF TRANSPORTATION (US) [04550182] **5381**

DIRECTORY OF NATIONAL ENVIRONMENTAL ORGANIZATIONS (US/1040-1555) [18335926] 2191, **2164**

DIRECTORY OF NATIONAL HELPLINES (US/1067-4217) [20458825] **1296**

DIRECTORY OF NATIONAL SOURCES OF DATA ON BLACKS IN HIGHER EDUCATION (US/0364-6955) [02667500] 2259, **1821**

DIRECTORY OF NATIVE COMMUNITIES AND ORGANIZATIONS IN ONTARIO (CN/0227-1109) [06562568] **2259**

●DIRECTORY OF NATIVE HAWAIIAN-OWNED BUSINESSES, THE (US/1063-0856) [25862655] **667**

DIRECTORY OF NATURAL GAS COMPANY OPERATIONS See NATURAL GAS UTILITY DIRECTORY **4761**

DIRECTORY OF NATURAL GAS COMPANY OPERATIONS (CN/1193-1345) [26715132] 4254, **4760**

DIRECTORY OF NATURAL GAS VEHICLE REFUELING STATIONS, PRODUCTS, AND SERVICES (US/1059-0072) [23886541] **5413**

DIRECTORY OF NEW AND EMERGING FOUNDATIONS (US) [19690135] **4335**

DIRECTORY OF NEW BRUNSWICK LIBRARIES (CN/0713-6358) [08932719] **3207**

DIRECTORY OF NEW ENGLAND MANUFACTURERS (US/0889-0382) [03685282] **3478**

DIRECTORY OF NEW ENGLAND SKI TOURING CENTERS, A (US/0270-3815) [06382543] 5468, **4892**

DIRECTORY OF NEW JERSEY CERTIFIED NURSERIES AND PLANT DEALERS (US/8756-0178) [11116038] **2413**

DIRECTORY OF NEW JERSEY MAYORS (US) [17240391] **4644**

●DIRECTORY OF NEW MEXICO MANUFACTURERS (1991) (US/1057-4565) [21063640] **1604**

DIRECTORY OF NIGHTCLUBS, HOTELS, THEATRES, LOUNGES & DISCOTHEQUES (US/0194-178X) [05344182] 4850, **5363**

DIRECTORY OF NON-FACULTY BARGAINING AGENTS IN INSTITUTIONS OF HIGHER EDUCATION (US/1054-7568) [22967974] 1821, **1663**

DIRECTORY OF NONPUBLIC SCHOOLS AND ADMINISTRATORS, NEW YORK STATE (US) [03927846] **1862**

DIRECTORY OF NORTH AMERICAN FAIRS AND EXPOSITIONS (US) [03947193] **4860**

DIRECTORY OF NORTH AMERICAN FAIRS, FESTIVALS, AND EXPOSITIONS (US) [13370727] **4860**

●DIRECTORY OF NORTH AMERICAN GUIDE AND CHARTERBOAT SERVICES (US/1048-1370) [20859527] **593**

DIRECTORY OF NORTH AMERICAN MILITARY AVIATION COMMUNICATIONS, VHF/UHF. CENTRAL (US/1055-579X) [22964993] 4042, **18**

DIRECTORY OF NORTH AMERICAN MILITARY AVIATION COMMUNICATIONS, VHF/UHF. NORTHEASTERN (US/1055-582X) [22959721] 4042, **18**

DIRECTORY OF NORTH AMERICAN MILITARY AVIATION COMMUNICATIONS, VHF/UHF. SOUTHEASTERN (US/1055-5803) [22965223] 1110, **18**

DIRECTORY OF NORTH AMERICAN MILITARY AVIATION COMMUNICATIONS, VHF/UHF. WESTERN (US/1055-5811) [22968007] **18**

●DIRECTORY OF NORTH CAROLINA MANUFACTURING FIRMS (US) [25684089] **667**

DIRECTORY OF NORTH DAKOTA MANUFACTURERS & FOOD PROCESSORS (US) [24784842] **3478**

DIRECTORY OF NORTH DAKOTA MUNICIPAL OFFICIALS See DIRECTORY : NORTH DAKOTA CITY OFFICIALS **4643**

DIRECTORY OF NURSERYMEN AND OTHERS LICENSED TO SELL NURSERY STOCK IN CALIFORNIA See DIRECTORY OF NURSERYMEN AND OTHERS LICENSED TO SELL NURSERY STOCK IN CALIFORNIA, AND SUMMARY OF LAWS AND REGULATIONS **2413**

DIRECTORY OF NURSERYMEN AND OTHERS LICENSED TO SELL NURSERY STOCK IN CALIFORNIA, AND SUMMARY OF LAWS AND REGULATIONS (US/0099-1589) [02242392] **2413**

DIRECTORY OF NURSING HOME ADMINISTRATORS LICENSED AND REGISTERED IN TENNESSEE (US/0191-2879) [04796306] **3779**

DIRECTORY OF NURSING HOMES IN THE UNITED STATES, U.S. TERRITORIES, AND CANADA See MODERN NURSING HOME DIRECTORY OF NURSING HOMES IN THE UNITED STATES, U.S. POSSESSIONS AND CANADA **3789**

DIRECTORY OF NURSING HOMES (PHOENIX, ARIZ.) (US/0888-7624) [12186951] **5178**

DIRECTORY OF O.C.U.L. LIBRARIES (CN/0822-935X) [10680958] **3207**

DIRECTORY OF OBSOLETE SECURITIES (US/0085-0551) [03300138] **896**

DIRECTORY OF OCEAN SHIPPING SERVICES (CN/0845-3039) [20365017] **5448**

DIRECTORY OF OFFICERS, COUNCIL, AND COMMITTEES (US/0147-1325) [03149233] **2962**

DIRECTORY OF OFFICIAL ARCHITECTURE & PLANNING (UK) [02740352] **297**

DIRECTORY OF OFFICIALS AND STAFF / AMERICAN MEDICAL ASSOCIATION (US) [27537867] 3913, **1925**

DIRECTORY OF OIL REFINERIES (US/0889-597X) [04382021] **4254**

DIRECTORY OF OKLAHOMA (US/0095-0920) [01796243] **4644**

DIRECTORY OF OKLAHOMA AIRPORTS (US/0094-5390) [01792085] **18**

DIRECTORY OF OKLAHOMA'S CITY AND TOWN OFFICIALS (US/0099-197X) [02246654] **4644**

DIRECTORY OF OMBUDSMEN AND INTERNATIONAL OMBUDSMAN OFFICES (CN/0849-391X) [23237458] **4644**

DIRECTORY OF ON-GOING RESEARCH IN CANCER EPIDEMIOLOGY (FR) [03785076] 3734, **3816**

DIRECTORY OF ON-GOING RESEARCH IN SMOKING AND HEALTH (US/0070-6000) [07362454] **4773**

DIRECTORY OF ONLINE DATABASES (US/0193-6840) [05231731] 1274, **3207**

DIRECTORY OF ONLINE HEALTHCARE DATABASES, THE *CEASED.* (US/0892-2756) [13118707] 1183, **3572**

DIRECTORY OF ONTARIO MUSEUMS (CN) [11256497] **4087**

DIRECTORY OF OPERATING LIBRARIES / GEORGIAN BAY REGIONAL LIBRARY SYSTEM (CN/0712-9785) [08794430] **3207**

DIRECTORY OF OPERATING SMALL BUSINESS INVESTMENT COMPANIES (US/0736-2129) [05389122] **896**

DIRECTORY OF OPPORTUNITIES IN INTERNATIONAL LAW (US/0148-7345) [03352175] **3127**

DIRECTORY OF OREGON MANUFACTURERS (US/0070-6027) [03830320] **3478**

DIRECTORY OF ORGANIZATIONS AND INDIVIDUALS PROFESSIONALLY ENGAGED IN GOVERNMENTAL RESEARCH AND RELATED ACTIVITIES (US/0072-520X) [01751361] **4472**

DIRECTORY OF ORGANIZATIONS CONCERNED WITH ENVIRONMENTAL RESEARCH (US) [01169419] **2164**

DIRECTORY OF ORGANIZATIONS IN EDUCATIONAL MANAGEMENT (US/1044-0453) [19481856] **1736**

DIRECTORY OF ORGANIZATIONS INTERESTED IN THE HANDICAPPED (US) [04228798] **4387**

DIRECTORY OF ORGANIZATIONS PROMOTING EQUAL EMPLOYMENT OPPORTUNITIES FOR WOMEN, CALIFORNIA (US) [02994912] 5554, **1663**

DIRECTORY OF ORGANIZATIONS WORKING FOR WOMEN'S EDUCATIONAL EQUITY (US/0272-1864) [06753022] 5554, **1736**

DIRECTORY OF OUTPLACEMENT FIRMS (US/0735-3707) [06596255] **940**

DIRECTORY OF OVERSEAS SUMMER JOBS (UK) [11553528] **4203**

DIRECTORY OF OWNERSHIP LINKS IN THE LEAD AND ZINC INDUSTRY (UK) **4001**

●DIRECTORY OF PACKAGING SOURCES (US/1071-9571) [28774852] **4218**

●DIRECTORY OF PANAMANIAN BUSINESSES, ASSOCIATIONS AND ORGANIZATIONS IN THE UNITED STATES (US/1064-9018) [26458774] **2731**

DIRECTORY OF PARA-MEDICAL INSTITUTIONS OF INDIA (II/0253-7656) [06512915] **3572**

DIRECTORY OF PATHOLOGY TRAINING PROGRAMS IN THE UNITED STATES AND CANADA (US) [20698828] **3894**

DIRECTORY OF PENSION FUNDS AND THEIR INVESTMENT MANAGERS (US/0736-6051) [09090647] **896**

DIRECTORY OF PERIODICALS ONLINE (US) [12267858] 1183, **3207**

DIRECTORY OF PERIODICALS ONLINE. SCIENCE & TECHNOLOGY : INDEXED, ABSTRACTED & FULL TEXT (US/0884-0911) [24860749] **3258**

DIRECTORY OF PERIODICALS ONLINE. VOL. 2, MEDICINE & SOCIAL SCIENCE (US) [12300895] 3207, **3258**

DIRECTORY OF PERMITS, STATE OF ALASKA (US) [05763962] **4644**

DIRECTORY OF PERSONAL IMAGE CONSULTANTS (US/0163-6537) [04426320] **758**

DIRECTORY

Alphabetical Title Index

DIRECTORY OF PERSONNEL OF UNITED NATIONS ORGANIZATIONS AND THE INTERNATIONAL MONETARY FUND IN THE DEMOCRATIC REPUBLIC OF THE SUDAN (SJ) [07113275] **4520**

DIRECTORY OF-- PERSONNEL RESPONSIBLE FOR RADIOLOGICAL HEALTH PROGRAMS (US/0149-8304) [03075149] **4773**

DIRECTORY OF PHYSICAL THERAPISTS AND PHYSICAL THERAPISTS ASSISTANTS LICENSED AND REGISTERED IN TENNESSEE (US/0162-5543) [04158820] **4380**

DIRECTORY OF PHYSICAL THERAPISTS REGISTERED IN TENNESSEE *See* DIRECTORY OF PHYSICAL THERAPISTS AND PHYSICAL THERAPISTS ASSISTANTS LICENSED AND REGISTERED IN TENNESSEE **4380**

●DIRECTORY OF PHYSICIANS IN THE UNITED STATES / AMERICAN MEDICAL ASSOCIATION (US) [26669646] 3913, **1925**

●DIRECTORY OF PLANT BIOTECHNOLOGY COMPANIES IN USA/ BY FORE (US/1060-4200) [24990807] 3691, **508**

DIRECTORY OF POETRY PUBLISHERS (US) [12744102] 1925, **3462**

●DIRECTORY OF POLITICAL NEWSLETTERS (1994) (US/1071-796X) [28731598] **4472**

DIRECTORY OF POLITICAL PERIODICALS (US/1057-0578) [23926255] 4644, **5675**

DIRECTORY OF PORTABLE DATABASES (US/1045-8352) [20268699] **1183**

DIRECTORY OF POST-PRIMARY INSTITUTIONS IN THE EAST-CENTRAL STATE OF NIGERIA (NR/0331-0299) [02241731] **1736**

DIRECTORY OF POSTGRADUATE STUDY (US) **1821**

DIRECTORY OF POSTSECONDARY EDUCATIONAL INSTITUTIONS IN ALASKA (US/0147-9113) [03245653] **1821**

DIRECTORY OF POSTSECONDARY EDUCATIONAL RESOURCES IN ALASKA (US) [21568894] **1821**

DIRECTORY OF POSTSECONDARY INSTITUTIONS (US/0898-2317) [15610434] **1821**

DIRECTORY OF POSTSECONDARY OCCUPATIONAL EDUCATION OPPORTUNITIES IN LOUISIANA (US/0149-6697) [03520775] **1912**

DIRECTORY OF PRECEPTORSHIP PROGRAMS IN THE HEALTH PROFESSIONS, A (US/0162-9387) [04233483] **4773**

DIRECTORY OF PREVENTIVE MEDICINE RESIDENCY PROGRAMS IN THE UNITED STATES AND CANADA (US) [09553441] **3572**

... DIRECTORY OF PRIVATE BAR INVOLVEMENT PROGRAMS, THE (US) [12077195] **3179**

DIRECTORY OF PRIVATE ELEMENTARY SCHOOLS AND HIGH SCHOOLS IN CALIFORNIA THAT HAVE COMPLIED WITH EDUCATION CODE SECTION 29009.5 (US/0092-2404) [01783472] **1736**

DIRECTORY OF PRIVATE SCHOOLS AND INSTITUTIONS IN KENYA (KE) [04079548] **1736**

DIRECTORY OF PRIVATE SCHOOLS IN NEW YORK STATE (US/0095-828X) [01798721] 1912, **1736**

DIRECTORY OF PRIVATE TRADE, TECHNICAL, AND ART SCHOOLS (TRENTON) (US/0092-4202) [01789435] **1912**

DIRECTORY OF PRODUCTS AND MANUFACTURERS, NEW BRUNSWICK, CANADA (CN/0845-6208) [20211821] **3478**

DIRECTORY OF PRODUCTS AND MANUFACTURERS (SAINT JOHN, N.B.) (CN/0843-2511) [19898719] **3478**

DIRECTORY OF PROFESSIONAL ENGINEERS OF ONTARIO (CN/0701-1814) [03409843] **1971**

DIRECTORY OF PROFESSIONAL GENEALOGISTS (US/1055-6710) [23228985] **2445**

DIRECTORY OF PROFESSIONAL GENEALOGISTS AND RELATED SERVICES (US/0272-3387) [06213176] **2445**

DIRECTORY OF PROFESSIONAL PERSONNEL (US) [03860115] **1821**

DIRECTORY OF PROFESSIONAL RELOCATION AND REAL ESTATE SERVICES (US) [25648232] **4836**

DIRECTORY OF PROFESSIONAL WORKERS IN STATE AGRICULTURAL EXPERIMENT STATIONS AND OTHER COOPERATING STATE INSTITUTIONS (US/0732-8524) [07537305] **79**

DIRECTORY OF PROGRAMS AND SERVICES FOR OLDER ADULTS : STATE OF OREGON BY COUNTIES (US/0090-5658) [01785582] **5283**

DIRECTORY OF PROGRAMS IN LINGUISTICS IN THE UNITED STATES & CANADA (US/0898-8528) [09721313] **3277**

DIRECTORY OF PROGRAMS IN RUSSIAN, EURASIAN, AND EAST EUROPEAN STUDIES (US) [30406083] **2685**

DIRECTORY OF PROGRAMS IN SOVIET AND EAST EUROPEAN STUDIES *See* DIRECTORY OF PROGRAMS IN RUSSIAN, EURASIAN, AND EAST EUROPEAN STUDIES **2685**

DIRECTORY OF PROGRAMS IN SOVIET & EAST EUROPEAN STUDIES (US/0889-9487) [14104760] **2685**

DIRECTORY OF PROGRAMS IN STATISTICS AND RELATED AREAS IN CANADIAN UNIVERSITIES / STATISTICAL SOCIETY OF CANADA (CN/0229-0081) [07857809] **3503**

DIRECTORY OF PROVIDERS OF FAMILY PLANNING AND ABORTION SERVICES (US/0148-6322) [03341080] **588**

DIRECTORY OF PSYCHIATRY RESIDENCY TRAINING PROGRAMS (US/0740-8250) [08684748] **3924**

DIRECTORY OF PSYCHOLOGISTS AND PSYCHOLOGICAL EXAMINERS LICENSED AND REGISTERED IN TENNESSEE (US/0732-1333) [04953709] **4585**

DIRECTORY OF PSYCHOSOCIAL INVESTIGATORS (US/0361-3771) [02246301] **4585**

●DIRECTORY OF PUBLIC COMPANIES IN CANADA (CN/1183-6814) [24650054] **667**

●DIRECTORY OF PUBLIC DATABASES PRODUCED BY THE INSTITUTIONS OF THE EUROPEAN COMMUNITIES / OFFICE FOR OFFICIAL PUBLICATIONS OF THE EUROPEAN COMMUNITIES (LU) [27522351] **1237**

DIRECTORY OF PUBLIC EDUCATION, STATE OF MARYLAND (US/0361-8919) [02441345] **1862**

DIRECTORY OF PUBLIC ELEMENTARY AND SECONDARY EDUCATION AGENCIES (US/1041-6331) [16903389] **1736**

DIRECTORY OF PUBLIC ENTERPRISES IN INDIA (II/0376-8546) [02245594] **1604**

DIRECTORY OF PUBLIC HOUSING AGENCIES (US/0160-4856) [02976172] **2821**

DIRECTORY OF PUBLIC LIBRARY SERVICES IN VICTORIA (AT) [03475619] **3207**

DIRECTORY OF PUBLIC LIBRARY SERVICES, WESTERN AUSTRALIA (AT) [09163579] **3208**

DIRECTORY OF PUBLIC SCHOOLS (US) [01767263] **1736**

DIRECTORY OF PUBLIC SCHOOLS AND ADMINISTRATORS NEW YORK STATE (US) [03819135] **1862**

DIRECTORY OF PUBLICATIONS RESOURCES (US/1062-8010) [23747054] **4814**

DIRECTORY OF PUBLISHED PROCEEDINGS *See* DIRECTORY OF PUBLISHED PROCEEDINGS. SERIES - SCIENCE/ENGINEERING/MEDICINE/TECHNOLOGY **5174**

DIRECTORY OF PUBLISHED PROCEEDINGS. SERIES MLS, MEDICAL/LIFE SCIENCES (US/1060-1759) [24080941] **3572**

DIRECTORY OF PUBLISHED PROCEEDINGS. SERIES PCE : POLLUTION CONTROL/ECOLOGY (US/0093-5816) [01793434] 2213, **2227**

DIRECTORY OF PUBLISHED PROCEEDINGS. SERIES - SCIENCE/ENGINEERING/MEDICINE/TECHNOLOGY (US) [01483054] **5174**

DIRECTORY OF PUBLISHED PROCEEDINGS. SERIES SEMT, SCIENCE/ENGINEERING/MEDICINE/TECHNOLOGY. ANNUAL CUMULATIVE VOLUME / INTERDOK (US/0419-3350) [02612914] 1971, 3572, **5100**

DIRECTORY OF PUBLISHED PROCEEDINGS. SERIES SEMT SCIENCE/ENGINEERING/MEDICINE/TECHNOLOGY. CUMULATED INDEX SUPPLEMENT (US) [03885379] 1971, 3572, **5100**

DIRECTORY OF PUBLISHED PROCEEDINGS. SERIES SSH: SOCIAL SCIENCES/HUMANITIES (US/0012-3307) [01783334] **5227**

●DIRECTORY OF PUBLISHING. CONTINENTAL EUROPE (UK) [24834445] 4828, **4814**

●DIRECTORY OF PUBLISHING. UNITED KINGDOM, COMMONWEALTH AND OVERSEAS (UK) [25016578] **4814**

DIRECTORY OF QUARRIES AND PITS (UK) [01786174] **2138**

DIRECTORY OF QUARRIES, CLAYWORKS, SAND AND GRAVEL PITS, ETC *See* DIRECTORY OF QUARRIES AND PITS **2138**

DIRECTORY OF RECOGNIZED ACCREDITING BODIES (US) [21570842] **1821**

DIRECTORY OF RECREATIONAL MARINE PRODUCT DEALERS (US/1048-4671) [20961274] **593**

DIRECTORY OF REGIONAL COUNCILS IN THE UNITED STATES (US) [20395142] **4644**

DIRECTORY OF REGIONAL SOCIAL WELFARE ACTIVITIES (ET) [01485750] **5283**

DIRECTORY OF REGISTERED ARCHITECTS, PROFESSIONAL ENGINEERS, LAND SURVEYORS, AND ARCHITECTURAL, ENGINEERING AND LAND SURVEYING CORPORATIONS (US) [04943565] **298**

DIRECTORY OF REGISTERED FACTORIES IN THE PUNJAB (PK) [03699019] **1604**

DIRECTORY OF REGISTERED INVESTMENT ADVISORS (US/1059-7433) [15220063] **896**

DIRECTORY OF REGISTERED LICENSEES, BOARD OF MEDICAL EXAMINERS OF THE STATE OF OREGON (US) [07048073] **3913**

DIRECTORY OF REGISTERED LICENTIATES IN NORTH DAKOTA (US) [08202697] **3913**

DIRECTORY OF REGISTERED PROFESSIONAL ARCHITECTS, ENGINEERS, AND LAND SURVEYORS (VI/0732-782X) [08405228] 2022, **298**

DIRECTORY OF REGULAR ARMY OFFICERS *See* OFFICIAL DIRECTORY / U.S. ARMY CORPS OF ENGINEERS **4053**

DIRECTORY OF REGULATED LOAN COMPANIES, PAWNBROKERS, INSURANCE PREMIUM FINANCE COMPANIES (US/0145-3521) [02728685] **788**

DIRECTORY OF RELIGION BROADCASTING (1982/83), THE (US/0731-0331) [08098075] 1131, **4953**

DIRECTORY OF RESEARCH GRANTS (US/0146-7336) [02341825] **1821**

DIRECTORY OF RESEARCH INSTITUTES IN ISRAEL (IS) [09876040] **5100**

DIRECTORY OF RESEARCH INSTITUTIONS IN THAILAND (TH) [02365061] **5100**

DIRECTORY OF RESEARCH PERSONNEL (IS) [02243884] **940**

●DIRECTORY OF RESEARCH / RESEARCH BRANCH / ANNUAIRE DE LA RECHERCHE / DIRECTION GENERALE DE LA RECHERCHE (CN) [27230878] **79**

DIRECTORY OF RESEARCH WHICH IS BEING CONDUCTED BY KENYATTA UNIVERSITY COLLEGE STAFF, A (KE) [03826870] **1821**

DIRECTORY OF RESEARCH WORKERS IN AGRICULTURE AND ALLIED SCIENCES (UK/0962-0036) [l09620036] 79, **153**

DIRECTORY OF RESIDENTIAL CENTRAL AIR CONDITIONERS / PREPARED BY THE NEW YORK STATE ENERGY OFFICE ; PREPARED FOR CENTRAL HUDSON GAS & ELECTRIC ... [ET. AL.] (US) [25907671] **2604**

DIRECTORY OF RESIDENTIAL FACILITIES FOR EMOTIONALLY HANDICAPPED CHILDREN AND YOUTH *CEASED.* (US/8756-2170) [17592599] 3903, **3924**

DIRECTORY OF RESOURCE ORGANIZATIONS AND MEDIA SERVING MINORITY COMMUNITIES IN CONNECTICUT (US/0362-9562) [02380055] 5283, **1663**

DIRECTORY OF RESOURCES (US) **1083**

DIRECTORY OF RESOURCES FOR OLDER PEOPLE IN NEW HAMPSHIRE (US/0094-1441) [01793759] **5283**

DIRECTORY OF RESOURCES FOR SENIOR CITIZENS OF OTTAWA-CARLETON (CN/0824-5398) [10676944] **5283**

DIRECTORY OF RESTAURANT AND FAST FOOD CHAINS IN CANADA (CN/0227-4302) [07817426] **5070**

DIRECTORY OF RETAIL CHAINS IN CANADA (CN/0225-9443) [06244415] **954**

DIRECTORY OF RETAILER OWNED COOPERATIVES, WHOLESALER SPONSORED VOLUNTARIES, WHOLESALE GROCERS, SERVICES MERCHANDISERS (US/0277-1969) [07512131] 954, **1604**

●DIRECTORY OF RETIREMENT FACILITIES, THE (US/1053-6825) [27334357] **5179**

DIRECTORY OF RIBA MEMBERS *See* RIBA MEMBERS **308**

DIRECTORY OF RURAL HEALTH CARE PROGRAMS (US/0270-9953) [06513312] **4773**

DIRECTORY OF SAN FRANCISCO ATTORNEYS (US/0092-9174) [01789454] **2962**

Alphabetical Title Index — DIRECTORY

DIRECTORY OF SCHOOLS AND ESTABLISHMENTS APPROVED FOR VETERANS TRAINING (US/0146-2431) [02914786] **1736**

DIRECTORY OF SCHOOLS OFFERING LIBRARY SCIENCE (PH) [05591614] **3208**

DIRECTORY OF SCIENTIFIC & TECHNICAL ASSOCIATIONS IN ISRAEL (IS/0334-2824) [05253402] **5100**

DIRECTORY OF SCIENTIFIC AND TECHNICAL PERSONNEL OF SRI LANKA (CE) [02980409] **5100**

DIRECTORY OF SCIENTIFIC AND TECHNICAL SOCIETIES IN SOUTH AFRICA (SA) [04341859] **5100**

DIRECTORY OF SCIENTIFIC RESEARCH INSTITUTIONS IN INDIA, THE (II/0419-3482) [01566735] **5100**

DIRECTORY OF SCIENTIFIC RESOURCES IN GEORGIA (US/0417-6480) [01783050] **5100**

DIRECTORY OF SCOTTISH SPORTS (UK) [07037877] **4892**

DIRECTORY OF SEASONAL/HOLIDAY CRAFT BOUTIQUES (US/1043-9722) [19638064] **5268**

DIRECTORY OF SECONDARY SCHOOLS *See* MAINE EDUCATIONAL DIRECTORY **1762**

DIRECTORY OF SECONDARY SCHOOLS AND TERTIARY INSTITUTIONS (NZ) [09087041] **1736**

DIRECTORY OF SECURITY ANALYST SOCIETIES, ANALYST SPLINTER GROUPS, STOCKBROKER CLUBS (US/0160-404X) [03672515] **896**

DIRECTORY OF SELECTED RESEARCH & POLICY CENTERS WORKING ON WOMEN'S ISSUES, A *CEASED.* (US/1052-7737) [17601834] **5554**

DIRECTORY OF SENIOR CENTERS AND CLUBS (US/0098-2709) [02241299] **5179**

DIRECTORY OF SERVICES (US) [24046944] **5283**

DIRECTORY OF SERVICES (CN/1184-1753) [23599046] **5283**

DIRECTORY OF SERVICES, ARKANSAS MENTAL HEALTH SERVICES (US) [08848732] **4773**

DIRECTORY OF SERVICES FOR BLIND AND VISUALLY IMPAIRED PERSONS IN THE UNITED STATES (US/0899-2533) [18055271] **4387**

DIRECTORY OF SERVICES FOR MIGRANT FAMILIES (US/0362-7179) [02327382] **5283**

DIRECTORY OF SERVICES - TEXAS DEPARTMENT OF MENTAL HEALTH AND MENTAL RETARDATION (US/0164-0550) [04523118] **5283**

DIRECTORY OF SHOPPING CENTERS IN THE UNITED STATES (US/0037-4210) [03532761] **954**

DIRECTORY OF SINGLE-UNIT SUPERMARKET OPERATORS (US/0896-2162) [16955360] **831, 2333**

DIRECTORY OF SMALL PRESS & MAGAZINE EDITORS & PUBLISHERS, THE (US/0277-1519) [06855355] **4814**

DIRECTORY OF SMALL SCALE INDUSTRIAL UNITS EMPLOYING FIVE OR MORE PERSONS IN THE UNORGANISED SECTOR IN HARYANA (II/0376-8570) [01797715] **1663**

DIRECTORY OF SOCIAL SERVICE ADMINISTRATORS OF LOCAL MUNICIPALITIES (CN/0226-0905) [06270549] **5283**

DIRECTORY OF SOCIAL SERVICES. OTTAWA-CARLETON (CN/0318-9686) [09907026] **5283**

DIRECTORY OF SOCIAL WELFARE ACTIVITIES IN AFRICA (ET) [03634928] **5283**

DIRECTORY OF SOLAR ENERGY RESEARCH ACTIVITIES IN THE UNITED STATES (US/0273-1525) [06591171] 2113, **1936**

●DIRECTORY OF SOURCES FOR EDITORS, REPORTERS & RESEARCHERS, THE (CN/1197-5148) [30013304] **2919**

DIRECTORY OF SOUTH AFRICAN ASSOCIATIONS (SA) **1925**

DIRECTORY OF SOUTH AFRICAN ASSOCIATIONS (SA) [24610423] **5230**

DIRECTORY OF SOUTH CAROLINA PORT SERVICES (US/0732-5975) [08376208] **5448**

DIRECTORY OF SOUTH CAROLINA SCHOOLS (US/0190-6283) [03896419] **1736**

DIRECTORY OF SOUTH DAKOTA REGISTERED NURSES AND LICENSED PRACTICAL NURSES (US) [01788712] **3855**

DIRECTORY OF SOUTH DAKOTA STATE LICENSES, PERMITS, FEES, AND INFORMATION (US) [25292916] **4644**

●DIRECTORY OF SOUTHEAST ASIAN ACADEMIC & SPECIAL LIBRARIES (TH) [27325522] **3208**

DIRECTORY OF SOUTHERN BAPTIST CHURCHES (US/0740-9915) [08873765] **5059**

DIRECTORY OF SOVIET OFFICIALS. NATIONAL ORGANIZATIONS (US/0742-2830) [10217931] **4644**

DIRECTORY OF SOVIET OFFICIALS. REPUBLIC ORGANIZATIONS (US/0743-5371) [08802488] **4644**

DIRECTORY OF SOVIET OFFICIALS. SCIENCE AND EDUCATION / DIRECTORATE OF INTELLIGENCE (US) [08855839] **4644**

DIRECTORY OF SPARC-BASED HARDWARE PRODUCTS & COMPANIES (US/1065-187X) [26522478] **1264**

DIRECTORY OF SPECIAL LIBRARIES AND INFORMATION CENTERS (US/0731-633X) [03449105] **3208**

DIRECTORY OF SPECIAL LIBRARIES AND INFORMATION CENTERS IN TEXAS (US/0741-4536) [09105612] **3208**

DIRECTORY OF SPECIAL LIBRARIES IN THE MONTREAL AREA (CN/0319-2563) [02443179] **3208**

DIRECTORY OF SPECIAL PROGRAMS FOR MINORITY GROUP MEMBERS; CAREER INFORMATION SERVICES, EMPLOYMENT SKILLS BANKS, FINANCIAL AID (US/0093-9501) [01784495] **5283**

DIRECTORY OF SPECIAL PURPOSE FACILITIES FOR THE EDUCATION OF THE HANDICAPPED (US/0731-289X) [08138968] **1878**

DIRECTORY OF SPECIFIC LEARNING DISABILITY SERVICES (US/0092-2455) [01788362] 4387, **1878**

DIRECTORY OF SPIRITUALIST ORGANIZATIONS IN CANADA (CN/1187-7227) [25652147] **4953**

DIRECTORY OF SPOKEN-VOICE AUDIO-CASSETTES (US) [04365839] 5316, **4115**

DIRECTORY OF STANDARD MULTI-MODAL CARRIER AND TARIFF AGENT'S CODES. SCAC AND STAC (US) **5381**

DIRECTORY OF STANDARDS LABORATORIES (US) [04889714] **4030**

DIRECTORY OF STANDARDS LABORATORIES IN THE UNITED STATES *See* DIRECTORY OF STANDARDS LABORATORIES **4030**

DIRECTORY OF STATE AGENCIES, COUNCILS OF GOVERNMENTS, UNIVERSITIES AND COLLEGES, TECHNICAL COLLEGES, AND ASSOCIATIONS, A (US) [09004582] **4644**

DIRECTORY OF STATE AND PUBLIC LIBRARY SERVICES IN QUEENSLAND (AT/0314-9307) [16500439] **3208**

●DIRECTORY OF STATE BAR PUBLIC SERVICE ACTIVITIES AND PROGRAMS (US/1062-0133) [25504572] 2962, **4644**

DIRECTORY OF STATE CORPORATIONS (CE) [03208974] **1604**

DIRECTORY OF STATE, COUNTY, AND FEDERAL OFFICIALS (US/0440-4947) [01794151] **4644**

DIRECTORY OF STATE COURT CLERKS AND COUNTY COURTHOUSES (US/1042-4172) [19037975] **4644**

DIRECTORY OF STATE EDUCATION AGENCIES (US/0897-4462) [11000929] **1736**

DIRECTORY OF STATE INFORMATION POLICY ORGANIZATIONS / THE COUNCIL OF STATE GOVERNMENTS, [ORGANIZATIONAL PLANNING AND COORDINATING COMMITTEE (OPACC), SUBCOMMITTEE ON INFORMATION POLICY] (US) [25063169] **4644**

DIRECTORY OF STATE, REGIONAL AND COMMERCIAL ORGANIZATIONS (US/0098-5368) [02241752] 5230, **831**

DIRECTORY OF STATE - USDA RURAL DEVELOPMENT COMMITTEES (US/0091-7672) [01787936] **5198**

DIRECTORY OF STATISTICAL MICROCOMPUTER SOFTWARE (US) [13020135] 3503, **1267**

●DIRECTORY OF STATISTICS IN CANADA (CN/1193-7580) [26776949] **5326**

DIRECTORY OF STUDENTS - HARVARD UNIVERSITY (US/0145-6539) [03124880] **1821**

DIRECTORY OF SUBSPECIALTY FELLOWSHIP TRAINING PROGRAMS (US/0192-8104) [05066127] **3572**

●DIRECTORY OF SUBSTANCE ABUSE ORGANIZATIONS IN CANADA (CN/1188-4886) [25883081] 5284, **1343**

●DIRECTORY OF SUBSTANCE ABUSE ORGANIZATIONS IN CANADA (CN/1188-4886) [25883084] **1343**

DIRECTORY OF SUICIDE PREVENTION/CRISIS INTERVENTION AGENCIES IN THE UNITED STATES : SUPPLEMENT (US) [04274450] **4345**

DIRECTORY OF SUMMER CHAMBER MUSIC WORKSHOPS, SCHOOLS & FESTIVALS, A (US) [06352224] **4115**

DIRECTORY OF SUPERMARKET, GROCERY, AND CONVENIENCE STORE CHAINS (US/0196-1845) [02207316] **2333**

DIRECTORY OF SUPPLIERS - INTERNATIONAL MAP DEALERS ASSOCIATION (US) **2559**

DIRECTORY OF SURNAMES - ONTARIO GENEALOGICAL SOCIETY (CN/0823-7891) [11046459] **2445**

DIRECTORY OF TAIWAN SCHOLARS (US/1048-2350) [19091777] **5198**

DIRECTORY OF TEACHERS OF LIBRARY SCIENCE IN THE PHILIPPINES (PH) [04288979] **3208**

DIRECTORY OF TELEFACSIMILE SITES IN NORTH AMERICAN LIBRARIES (US/1049-7218) [19494839] **1153**

DIRECTORY OF TENNESSEE COUNTY OFFICIALS (US/0160-0273) [03590325] **4644**

DIRECTORY OF TENNESSEE MANUFACTURERS (US/0070-6450) [10356222] **3478**

DIRECTORY OF TERTIARY EXTERNAL COURSES IN AUSTRALIA (AT/0818-0687) [08180687] **1736**

DIRECTORY OF TEXAS AIRPORTS *See* TEXAS AIRPORT DIRECTORY **37**

DIRECTORY OF TEXAS FOUNDATIONS (US) [04947326] **4335**

DIRECTORY OF TEXAS MANUFACTURERS / BUREAU OF BUSINESS RESEARCH, UNIVERSITY OF TEXAS (US) [01566743] **3478**

DIRECTORY OF TEXAS WHOLESALERS (US/1049-6076) [20645630] **831**

DIRECTORY OF THE AGRICULTURAL RESEARCH SERVICE (US/0196-3511) [01435620] **79**

DIRECTORY OF THE AMERICAN BAPTIST CHURCHES IN THE U.S.A (US/0091-9381) [01788645] **5059**

DIRECTORY OF THE AMERICAN OPTOMETRIC ASSOCIATION (US/0091-4258) [05437092] **4215**

DIRECTORY OF THE AMERICAN PSYCHOLOGICAL ASSOCIATION (1978) (US/0196-6545) [04171465] 4585, **1925**

DIRECTORY OF THE AMERICAN SOCIETY OF PLANT PHYSIOLOGISTS (US/0271-9789) [05293504] **508**

DIRECTORY OF THE ARTS (OTTAWA) (CN/0832-865X) [17527059] **319**

DIRECTORY OF THE ASSOCIATION OF PROFESSIONAL ENGINEERS AND GEOSCIENTISTS OF THE PROVINCE OF BRITISH COLUMBIA (CN/1187-2306) [25313989] **1971**

DIRECTORY OF THE BUSINESS RESEARCH ADVISORY COUNCIL TO THE BUREAU OF LABOR STATISTICS (US) [04160624] 1663, **1531**

DIRECTORY OF THE CANADIAN ASSOCIATION OF UNIVERSITY SCHOOLS OF MUSIC (CN/0317-2155) [02247880] **4115**

DIRECTORY OF THE CANADIAN BOTANICAL ASSOCIATION & CANADIAN SOCIETY OF PLANT PHYSIOLOGISTS (CN/0824-1996) [11895315] **508**

DIRECTORY OF THE CANADIAN PSYCHOLOGICAL ASSOCIATION (CN/0068-9475) [10220653] **4585**

DIRECTORY OF THE CANNING, FREEZING, PRESERVING INDUSTRIES, THE (US/0419-3717) [02256509] **2333**

DIRECTORY OF THE COMMISSION OF THE EUROPEAN COMMUNITIES (BE/0591-1745) [01775727] **3127**

●DIRECTORY OF THE EUROPEAN COMMISSION (LU) [30459085] **3127**

DIRECTORY OF THE FOREST PRODUCTS INDUSTRY (US/0070-6477) [01077185] **2400**

DIRECTORY OF THE FOREST PRODUCTS INDUSTRY (US/1063-9985) [03875942] **2400**

DIRECTORY OF THE IRON AND STEEL WORKS OF THE UNITED STATES AND CANADA / AMERICAN IRON AND STEEL INSTITUTE (US) [01480091] **4001**

DIRECTORY OF THE LABOR RESEARCH ADVISORY COUNCIL TO THE BUREAU OF LABOR STATISTICS (US/0091-9497) [01788608] **1663**

DIRECTORY OF THE LEADING FIRMS IN THE JOB PLATING AND ENAMELING INDUSTRY (US/0092-6418) [01788430] **4001**

●DIRECTORY OF THE MAJOR INDIANA FOUNDATIONS, THE (US) [24149620] **4335**

DIRECTORY OF THE MINERAL INDUSTRY IN VIRGINIA (US/0419-3776) [02282380] **1439**

DIRECTORY Alphabetical Title Index

DIRECTORY OF THE NATIONAL ASSOCIATION OF ADVISORS FOR THE HEALTH PROFESSIONS (US/1043-6669) [19006552] 1912, **3913**

DIRECTORY OF THE NEW MEXICO BENCH AND BAR (US/8756-1611) [06216241] **2962**

DIRECTORY OF THE OFFICERS, BOARD OF MANAGERS, COMMITTEES AND SECTIONS AFFILIATED AND COOPERATING ORGANIZATIONS (US/0363-4930) [02468041] **2962**

DIRECTORY OF THE OVERSEAS PRESS CLUB OF AMERICA AND AMERICAN CORRESPONDENTS OVERSEAS *See* MEMBERSHIP DIRECTORY AND AMERICAN CORRESPONDENTS OVERSEAS **2922**

DIRECTORY OF THE PUBLIC AQUARIA OF THE WORLD (US/0085-0039) [01788354] **5581**

DIRECTORY OF THE REFRACTORIES INDUSTRY (US) [23011374] **1024**

DIRECTORY OF THE REPUBLIC OF SENEGAL (SG/0376-8627) [01786409] **4644**

DIRECTORY OF THE RESEARCH ESTABLISHMENTS IN PAKISTAN (PK) [03218201] **5100**

DIRECTORY OF THE STATE AND COUNTY OFFICIALS OF NORTH CAROLINA (US) [01760535] **4697**

DIRECTORY OF THE STATE AND COUNTY OFFICIALS OF NORTH CAROLINA AND MEMBERS OF THE GENERAL ASSEMBLY *See* DIRECTORY OF THE STATE AND COUNTY OFFICIALS OF NORTH CAROLINA **4697**

DIRECTORY OF THE TRANSPORTATION RESEARCH BOARD (US/0360-5078) [02243803] **5381**

DIRECTORY OF THE UNITED NATIONS ORGANIZATION AND SPECIALIZED AGENCIES IN IRAQ (IQ/0303-1594) [01792541] **3127**

DIRECTORY OF THE WINE INDUSTRY IN NORTH AMERICA *See* WINES & VINES. BUYER'S GUIDE ISSUE **2373**

●DIRECTORY OF THE WOOD PRODUCTS INDUSTRY (1992) (US/1064-749X) [26388012] **2400**

DIRECTORY OF THEATRE FACULTIES IN COLLEGES AND UNIVERSITIES, U.S. AND CANADA (US/1041-7273) [16751853] **5363**

DIRECTORY OF THEATRE TRAINING PROGRAMS (US/1041-5211) [17408262] **5363**

DIRECTORY OF TOURISM STATISTICS (AT/1036-2606) [I10362606] **5500**

DIRECTORY OF TOXICOLOGY TESTING INSTITUTIONS IN THE UNITED STATES *CEASED.* (US/0892-1881) [10236014] **3980**

DIRECTORY OF TRADE AND INDUSTRIAL EDUCATION : SOUTH CAROLINA (US/0146-5341) [02971987] **1912**

DIRECTORY OF TRADE & INDUSTRY (PK) [21337930] **1605**

DIRECTORY OF TRADITIONAL MUSIC (US/0893-3065) [15477966] **4115**

DIRECTORY OF TRAVEL INFORMATION SOURCES FOR THE PACIFIC ISLANDS (US) [18559123] **5468**

DIRECTORY OF TRUST INSTITUTIONS (US/0093-951X) [01794127] **788**

... DIRECTORY OF U.S. CORPORATIONS, THE *CEASED.* (US/0894-4997) [10361626] **667**

DIRECTORY OF U.S. FIRMS AND ORGANIZATIONS IN INDONESIA (IO/0149-7553) [03534940] **1605**

DIRECTORY OF U.S. FLEXOGRAPHIC PACKAGING SOURCES *See* DIRECTORY OF PACKAGING SOURCES **4218**

DIRECTORY OF U.S. GOVERNMENT AUDIOVISUAL PERSONNEL (US/0098-1109) [02239306] **4644**

DIRECTORY OF U.S. GOVERNMENT INVENTIONS, THE (US) [24689242] **1303**

●DIRECTORY OF U.S. GOVERNMENT SOFTWARE FOR MAINFRAMES AND MICROCOMPUTERS (US/1063-9748) [25473394] **1285**

DIRECTORY OF U.S. HOSPITALS (US/1062-1946) [24681572] **3780**

DIRECTORY OF U.S. LABOR ORGANIZATIONS (US/0734-6786) [08788821] **1663**

DIRECTORY OF U.S.S.R. MINISTRY OF DEFENSE AND ARMED FORCES OFFICIALS (US/0096-9990) [01798707] **4042**

●DIRECTORY OF U.S. TRADEMARKS, THE (US/1042-0665) [25027655] **1303**

DIRECTORY OF U.S. TRAVEL AGENTS (CN) [23288348] **5468**

DIRECTORY OF UK SPACE CAPABILITIES (UK) [19695732] **18**

DIRECTORY OF UNDERGRADUATE POLITICAL SCIENCE FACULTY (US/0884-5859) [12160439] **4472**

DIRECTORY OF UNIONS AND ASSOCIATIONS WITH EXCLUSIVE RECOGNITION IN THE FEDERAL SERVICE (US/0193-385X) [05165937] **1663**

DIRECTORY OF UNIT TRUSTS (UK) [01788446] **896**

DIRECTORY OF UNITED NATIONS PERSONNEL IN FIJI, KIRIBATI, NAURU, SOLOMON ISLANDS, TONGA, TUVALU, VANUATU, FEDERATED STATES OF MICRONESIA, MARSHALL ISLANDS, PALAU *See* UNITED NATIONS TELEPHONE DIRECTORY. FIJI, FEDERATED STATES OF MICRONESIA, KIRIBATI, MARSHALL ISLANDS, NAURU, SOLOMON ISLANDS, TONGA, TUVALU, VANUATU AND PACIFIC REGIONAL PROGRAMMES **1168**

DIRECTORY OF UNITED NATIONS SERIAL PUBLICATIONS (US/1011-2952) [18792404] **3208**

DIRECTORY OF UNITED STATES CEMETERIES (US/0095-1862) [01796181] **2407**

DIRECTORY OF UNITED STATES EXPORTERS (US/1057-6878) [22915789] **831**

DIRECTORY OF UNITED STATES IMPORTERS (1991) (US/1057-5111) [22915785] **831**

DIRECTORY OF UNITED STATES PROBATION AND PRETRIAL SERVICES OFFICERS (US) [20654959] **2962**

DIRECTORY OF UNITED STATES TRADITIONAL AND ALTERNATIVE COLLEGES AND UNIVERSITIES (US/0882-7745) [10613848] **1821**

DIRECTORY OF UNUSUAL MAJORS (US) **1821**

DIRECTORY OF USSR FOREIGN TRADE ORGANIZATIONS AND OFFICIALS (US/0742-9118) [02627301] **831**

DIRECTORY OF USSR MINISTRY OF FOREIGN AFFAIRS OFFICIALS (US/0191-8621) [02197572] **3127**

... DIRECTORY OF VARS, THE (US/0884-8300) [12437564] **1245**

●DIRECTORY OF VIDEO, COMPUTER, AND AUDIO-VISUAL PRODUCTS, THE (US/0884-2124) [27092187] **1893**

DIRECTORY OF VIDEO RETAILERS (US/1053-9069) [22688205] **1131**

DIRECTORY OF VIRGINIA PROPRIETARY SCHOOLS (US) [11502499] **1912**

DIRECTORY OF VIRGINIA'S POSTSECONDARY EDUCATION AND TRAINING OPPORTUNITIES (US/0148-0782) [03266075] **1821**

DIRECTORY OF VOLUNTARY AGENCIES (US/0743-9725) [10190568] 1918, **5284**

DIRECTORY OF WASHINGTON BUSINESS ASSOCIATIONS (US/0098-5635) [02240931] **667**

DIRECTORY OF WASHINGTON CREATIVE SERVICES (US/0191-3719) [04848906] **319**

DIRECTORY OF WATER RESOURCES EXPERTISE (US/0364-9296) [02693734] **5532**

DIRECTORY OF WIRE COMPANIES OF NORTH AMERICA (US/1048-373X) [11555435] **2113**

DIRECTORY OF WOMEN ENTREPRENEURS, THE *CEASED.* (US/1042-2420) [18364714] 5554, **667**

DIRECTORY OF WOMEN HISTORIANS (US/1048-4418) [04651888] 5554, **2615**

DIRECTORY OF WOMEN IN BUSINESS PROFESSIONS & MANAGEMENT (AT) **5554**

DIRECTORY OF WOMEN IN SPORTS BUSINESS, THE (US) [24289021] 667, 5554, **4892**

DIRECTORY OF WOMEN IN THE MATHEMATICAL SCIENCES (US/0732-5967) [08376147] 5554, **3503**

DIRECTORY OF WOMEN MATHEMATICIANS *See* DIRECTORY OF WOMEN IN THE MATHEMATICAL SCIENCES **3503**

DIRECTORY OF WOMEN-OWNED BUSINESSES. WASHINGTON-BALTIMORE METROPOLITAN AREA (US/0147-4553) [03173353] 5560, **688**

DIRECTORY OF WOMEN'S & CHILDREN'S WEAR SPECIALTY STORES (US/0277-9617) [07667722] **1083**

DIRECTORY OF WOMEN'S HEALTH CARE CENTERS / EDITED AND COMPILED BY THE ORYX PRESS IN COOPERATION WITH THE NATIONAL ASSOCIATION OF WOMEN'S HEALTH PROFESSIONALS *CEASED.* (US) [21591524] **3760**

DIRECTORY OF WOMEN'S MEDIA (US/1040-1156) [17912267] **5554**

DIRECTORY OF WOOL, HOSIERY & FABRICS (II) [01784209] **5350**

DIRECTORY OF WORD PROCESSING MANAGEMENT (US/0278-9663) [07799475] 866, **1292**

DIRECTORY OF WORLD CHEMICAL PRODUCERS (US/0196-0555) [05729795] **1024**

DIRECTORY OF WORLD LEADERS & FACTBOOK (US/1043-2043) [19339039] **4472**

●DIRECTORY OF WORLD MANUFACTURED FIBER PRODUCERS (US/1062-9343) [25812185] **1605**

DIRECTORY / ONTARIO AMATEUR FOOTBALL ASSOCIATION (CN/0713-6781) [08916626] **4892**

DIRECTORY / ONTARIO LIBRARY SERVICE, RIDEAU (CN/0831-3148) [14954965] **3208**

DIRECTORY. ONTARIO POSTAL REGION. POSTAL CODE (CN/0317-4271) [01794580] **1144**

DIRECTORY - ONTARIO PSYCHOLOGICAL ASSOCIATION (CN/0316-7569) [02247839] **4585**

DIRECTORY / ORGANIZATION OF AMERICAN STATES (US/0250-6211) [01761479] **4644**

DIRECTORY, ORGANIZATIONS OFFERING LITERACY TRAINING COURSES (IR) [04691429] **1736**

DIRECTORY - OUTDOOR WRITERS ASSOCIATION OF AMERICA (US/0195-6124) [05510205] **2919**

DIRECTORY - PARENT COOPERATIVE PRESCHOOLS INTERNATIONAL (CN) [02511660] **1803**

DIRECTORY - PERSEKUTUAN PEKILAND-PEKILANG MALAYSIA (MY/0126-9801) [09583924] **3478**

DIRECTORY PERUSAHAAN BIS (ANTAR PROPINSI) (IO/0126-4613) [07242926] **5381**

DIRECTORY. POSTAL CODE (CN/0835-4693) [16971862] **1144**

DIRECTORY, PROCEEDINGS, AND HANDBOOK (US/1071-8966) [28619312] **5100**

DIRECTORY, PROFESSIONAL REAL ESTATE MANAGEMENT WHO'S WHO (US/0161-3154) [03888334] **4837**

DIRECTORY : PROGRAMS IN PUBLIC AFFAIRS AND ADMINISTRATION (US) [04702782] **4644**

DIRECTORY / SECTION OF TORT AND INSURANCE PRACTICE (US/0732-9857) [08484445] 2879, **2962**

DIRECTORY, SERVICES FOR VICTIMS OF CRIME (CN) [19824268] 5284, **3163**

DIRECTORY - SINGAPORE INDIAN CHAMBER OF COMMERCE (SI/0376-8635) [01799030] **819**

DIRECTORY (SOUTH CAROLINA STATE BOARD OF ENGINEERING EXAMINERS) *See* DIRECTORY / SOUTH CAROLINA STATE BOARD OF REGISTRATION FOR PROFESSIONAL ENGINEERS AND LAND SURVEYORS **1971**

DIRECTORY / SOUTH CAROLINA STATE BOARD OF REGISTRATION FOR PROFESSIONAL ENGINEERS AND LAND SURVEYORS (US) [10712660] **1971**

DIRECTORY - SOUTH DAKOTA REAL ESTATE BOARD (US/0731-9525) [07489527] **4837**

DIRECTORY / SPECTROSCOPY SOCIETY OF CANADA (CN/0709-8448) [06131689] 974, **4401**

DIRECTORY - SPORTS FEDERATION OF CANADA (CN/0229-3161) [08071833] **4893**

DIRECTORY - STATE BAR OF GEORGIA (US/1067-4861) [06382504] **2962**

DIRECTORY - STATE BOARD OF ACCOUNTANCY, STATE OF FLORIDA (US) [06661465] **743**

DIRECTORY - STATE BOARD OF MEDICAL EXAMINERS OF SOUTH CAROLINA (US/0194-0554) [05292715] **3914**

DIRECTORY STRATEGIES (US) **4814**

DIRECTORY: SUB-STATE PLANNING DISTRICTS IN OKLAHOMA (US/0094-5994) [01794387] **2821**

DIRECTORY. SWIMMING POOL DEALERS & CONTRACTORS (US/0884-3481) [12328599] **613**

DIRECTORY / TEXAS LIBRARY ASSOCIATION (US) [11952976] **3208**

DIRECTORY - TEXAS OSTEOPATHIC MEDICAL ASSOCIATION (US/0196-6340) [05838368] **3572**

DIRECTORY / THE AMERICAN CHAMBER OF COMMERCE IN FRANCE (FR) [09063064] **819**

DIRECTORY / THE ASSOCIATED CHURCH PRESS (US/0066-8710) [03151982] **4953**

DIRECTORY / THE AUSTRALASIAN INSTITUTE OF MINING AND METALLURGY (AT) [15670885] **4001**

Alphabetical Title Index — DISCO

DIRECTORY - THE NEW YORK SOCIETY OF CLINICAL PSYCHOLOGISTS, INC (US/0545-6371) [05587045] **4585**

DIRECTORY / THE YOUNG LAWYERS DIVISION OF THE AMERICAN BAR ASSOCIATION (US/0731-6496) [08204456] **2962**

DIRECTORY TO THE FURNISHING TRADE (UK/0070-6604) [I00706604] **2905**

DIRECTORY / TOY TRAIN OPERATING SOCIETY (US/0732-9873) [08484283] 5431, **2584**

DIRECTORY TRADE-COMMERCE AND LOCAL MANUFACTURERS *See* DIRECTORY. CLASSIFIED TRADE INDEX (NAIROBI) **831**

DIRECTORY - U. S. COAST GUARD ACADEMY ALUMNI ASSOCIATION (US) [05178467] 4176, **1101**

DIRECTORY (UNITARIAN UNIVERSALIST ASSOCIATION : 1965) (US/0503-2636) [10233390] **5059**

DIRECTORY, UNITED WAY AFFILIATED INFORMATION AND REFERRAL SERVICES (US/0731-9509) [08264814] **5284**

DIRECTORY: UNIVERSITIES AND INSTITUTES OFFERING LITERACY TRAINING PROGRAMMES (IR) [04222617] **1736**

DIRECTORY / VIRGINIA HIGH SCHOOL LEAGUE, INC (US) [10419022] **1736**

DIRECTORY / WESTCOASTS WOMEN'S NETWORK *CEASED.* (CN/0836-4192) [16888339] **5554**

DIRECTORY WORLD (US) **4814**

DIRECTORY WORLD (US) **4814**

DIREITO ADMINISTRATIVO (COIMBRA, PORTUGAL) (PO) [08038341] **3092**

DIREITO E AVESSO : BOLETIM DA NOVA ESCOLA JURIDICA BRASILEIRA (BL) [10552858] **2962**

DIREITO TRIBUTARIO (BL) [01798902] 4720, **2962**

DIREITO TRIBUTARIO ATUAL (BL) [09204832] **4720**

DIREKTOR (YU/0419-3903) [01701264] **866**

DIREKTORI PERUSAHAAN TRUK (ANTAR PROPINSI) DI JAWA (IO/0216-700X) [11477453] **5381**

DIRES (CN/0820-0890) [09929477] **5198**

DIRETORIO LITURGICO (BL) [04987849] **5028**

DIRETTORE COMMERCIALE, IL (IT/0012-3323) [I00123323] **759**

DIREZIONE DEL PERSONALE (IT) **940**

DIREZIONE E CONSULENZA AZIENDALE (IT) **866**

DIRIGENTE INDUSTRIAL (BL/0012-3366) [05174942] **866**

DIRIGENTE RURAL, O *CEASED.* (BL/0012-3374) [07215251] **79**

DIRIGENTI DI SCUOLA (IT) **1893**

DIRIGENZA BANCARIA (IT) **788**

DIRIGIDO POR ... (SP) **2845**

DIRITTO AEREO *SUSPENDED.* (IT/0012-3390) [05332417] 18, **2962**

DIRITTO AMMINISTRATIVO : RIVISTA TRIMESTRALE (IT) **2962**

DIRITTO & PRACTICA DEL LAVORO ORO (IT) **2962**

DIRITTO & PRATICA DEL LAVORO / IPSOA (IT/1120-7965) [12886294] **3146**

DIRITTO COMUNITARIO E DEGLI SCAMBI INTERNAZIONALI (IT/0391-6111) [03226469] **2962**

DIRITTO DEGLI ITALIANI, IL (IT) [07020351] **2962**

DIRITTO DEL COMMERCIO INTERNAZIONALE (IT) [21321466] **2962**

DIRITTO DEL LAVORO (IT/0012-3404) [01566752] **3146**

DIRITTO DELLA BANCA E MERCATO FINANZIARIO (IT) **788**

DIRITTO DELLA REGIONE, IL (IT) **2962**

DIRITTO DELLE RADIODIFFUSIONI E DELLE TELECOMUNICAZIONI, IL (IT) [04880933] 1153, **2962**

DIRITTO DELLE RELAZIONI INDUSTRIALI : RIVISTA DELLA ASSOCIAZIONE LAVORO E RICERCHE, ALAR (IT) [26289215] **3146**

DIRITTO DELL'ECONOMIA, IL (IT) [24602608] **2962**

DIRITTO DELL'IMPRESA (IT) [10661014] **2962**

DIRITTO DELL'INFORMAZIONE E DELL'INFORMATICA / RIVISTA QUADRIMESTRALE PROMOSSA DAL CENTRO DI INIZIATIVA GIURIDICA PIERO CALAMANDREI, IL (IT) [15064457] **2962**

DIRITTO DI AUTORE, IL (IT/0012-3420) [01566753] **1304**

DIRITTO DI FAMIGLIA E DELLE PERSONE (IT) [02244459] **3120**

DIRITTO E GIURISPRUDENZA (IT) [01566755] **2963**

DIRITTO E PRACTICA NELL'ASSICURAZIONE *See* DIRITTO ED ECONOMIA DELL'ASSICURAZIONE **2963**

DIRITTO E PRATICA NELL ASSICURAZIONE (IT) **2963**

DIRITTO E PRATICA TRIBUTARIA (IT) **743**

DIRITTO E PRATICA TRIBUTARIA (IT/0012-3447) [I00123447] **2963**

DIRITTO E SOCIETA (IT) [01794427] **2963**

DIRITTO E TECNICA DELLA CIRCOLAZIONE STRADALE E ASSICURAZIONE OBBLIGATORIA DI RCA (IT) 2879, 5440, **2963**

DIRITTO ECCLESIASTICO E RASSEGNA DI DIRITTO MATRIMONIALE *See* DIRITTO ECCLESIASTICO, IL **2963**

DIRITTO ECCLESIASTICO E RASSEGNA DI DIRITTO MATRIMONIALE, IL (IT/0012-3455) [05703090] 5028, **2963**

DIRITTO ECCLESIASTICO, IL (IT) **2963**

DIRITTO ED ECONOMIA (IT/0394-8366) [I03948366] 2963, **1479**

●DIRITTO ED ECONOMIA DELL'ASSICURAZIONE (IT) 2879, **2963**

DIRITTO FALLIMENTARE E DELLE SOCIETA COMMERCIALI (IT/0391-5239) [I03915239] **2963**

DIRITTO INDUSTRIALE, IL (IT) **1605**

DIRITTO MARITTIMO (IT/0012-348X) [I0012348X] **3180**

DIRITTO PROCESSUALE AMMINISTRATIVO (IT/0393-1315) [19560702] 4644, **2963**

DIRITTO SANITARIO MODERNO (IT/0416-024X) [I0416024X] **4773**

●DIRIZHABL (RU) [26820045] **3381**

DIRKZWAGER'S GUIDE TO THE NEW WATERWAY, ROTTERDAM AND DORDRECHT *See* DIRKZWAGER'S GUIDE TO THE NEW WATERWAY, ROTTERDAM, DORDRECHT, EUROPOORT, AND BOTLEK **5448**

DIRKZWAGER'S GUIDE TO THE NEW WATERWAY, ROTTERDAM, DORDRECHT, EUROPOORT, AND BOTLEK (NE) [01792090] **5448**

DIRT BIKE (US/0364-1546) [02604687] **4081**

DIRT BIKE RIDER (UK/0262-5628) [I02625628] **4081**

DIRT BIKE RIDER. GRAND PRIX SPECIAL (UK/0969-1650) [I09691650] **4081**

●DIRT (NEW YORK, N.Y.) (US/1061-8481) [25480494] **3995**

DIRT RIDER (US/0735-4355) [08964756] **4081**

DIRT WHEELS (US/1060-4804) [25006216] **4893**

DIRT WHEELS MAGAZINE (US/0745-0192) [08720786] **4893**

DIRTY LINEN (US/1047-4315) [20697477] **4115**

DIRVA (US) [10111574] **5728**

DIS COLLECTOR (CHESWOLD, DEL. : 1981) (US/0731-843X) [08224667] **4115**

DIS HEKIMLIGI YUKSEK OKULU BULTENI (TU/0254-5462) [07538844] **1322**

DIS POLITIKA (TU) [05289597] **4520**

DISABILITIES AND IMPAIRMENTS (II/0970-356X) [I0970356X] **4387**

DISABILITY AND CHRONIC DISEASE QUARTERLY *See* DISABILITY STUDIES QUARTERLY : DSQ **4387**

●DISABILITY AND REHABILITATION (UK/0963-8288) [25415346] **4387**

DISABILITY & SOCIETY (UK) **4387**

DISABILITY COMPLIANCE BULLETIN (US) [23436341] **4387**

DISABILITY DIGEST *SUSPENDED.* (CN/1183-9678) [25351920] **5284**

●DISABILITY FUNDING NEWS (US/1069-1359) [27944435] **5284**

DISABILITY, HANDICAP & SOCIETY (UK/0267-4645) [13564218] 4387, **5284**

DISABILITY ISSUES (US/1063-9373) [26181602] **4387**

DISABILITY NEWS (UK/0964-010X) [I0964010X] **4387**

DISABILITY NEWSLETTER (US/0195-4482) [05452891] **2879**

DISABILITY NOW (UK/0049-1840) **4387**

DISABILITY RAG, THE (US/0749-8586) [10401605] **4387**

DISABILITY STATISTICS REPORT / NATIONAL INSTITUTE ON DISABILITY AND REHABILITATION RESEARCH (US) [24800349] **4387**

DISABILITY STUDIES QUARTERLY : DSQ (US/1041-5718) [16269357] **4387**

DISABILITY TODAY (ST. CATHARINES) (CN/1186-9666) [24860231] **4387**

DISABLED AND AGED PERSONS AUSTRALIA ... PRELIMINARY RESULTS (AT/1032-2396) [I10322396] 4387, **4395**

DISABLED OUTDOORS (US) **4387**

DISABLED OUTDOORS MAGAZINE (US/1067-098X) [27135309] 4893, **4387**

DISADVANTAGED STUDENT GRANT ANNUAL REPORT FOR FY ... (US) [10089003] **1821**

DISAM JOURNAL OF INTERNATIONAL SECURITY ASSISTANCE MANAGEMENT, THE (US) [10358682] **2909**

DISAM NEWSLETTER *See* DISAM JOURNAL OF INTERNATIONAL SECURITY ASSISTANCE MANAGEMENT, THE **2909**

DISARMAMENT CAMPAIGNS (NE) [12658608] **4043**

DISARMAMENT NEWS & INTERNATIONAL VIEWS (US/0363-3721) [02454803] **4520**

DISARMAMENT NEWS & VIEWS *See* DISARMAMENT NEWS & INTERNATIONAL VIEWS **4520**

DISARMAMENT. STUDY SERIES (US) [07843556] **4043**

DISARMAMENT TIMES (US/0259-3629) [04522056] **4043**

DISARMAMENT - UNITED NATIONS (US/0251-9518) [03971541] **4520**

DISASTER MANAGEMENT (UK/0961-1428) [I09611428] **1073**

DISASTER MEDICINE (PHILADELPHIA, PA.) (US/0736-8070) [09228546] **3724**

DISASTER PREPAREDNESS IN THE AMERICAS. AMERICAN SANITARY BUREAU (US/0251-4494) [07507020] **4773**

DISASTER PREVENTION AND MANAGEMENT (UK) **1226**

DISASTER RECOVERY JOURNAL (US) [12394370] **5284**

DISASTERS (UK/0361-3666) [02933132] **5284**

DISC *SUSPENDED.* (US/1052-4053) [22284090] **1183**

DISC AND THAT (US/0092-0436) [01788881] **4115**

DISC GOLF JOURNAL (US/1055-4785) [23189681] **4893**

DISC JOKIES (CN/0702-892X) [03439491] **1131**

DISC SPORTS *CEASED.* (US/0747-9956) [10858005] **4893**

DISCERNER (US/0416-0274) [01776590] **4954**

DISCERNING TRAVELER, THE (US/0898-6231) [17863627] **5468**

DISCERNMENT (US) **2249**

DISCHARGE PLANNING UPDATE (US/0276-4652) [07423597] **3780**

DISCHARGES FROM STATE MENTAL HEALTH FACILITIES FISCAL YEAR ... / PREPARED BY DATA SERVICES DIVISION, DEPARTMENT OF MENTAL HEALTH/RETARDATION (US) [07480356] **4773**

DISCIPLE (ST. LOUIS, MO.) (US/0092-8372) [01791378] **5059**

DISCIPLES THEOLOGICAL DIGEST, THE (US/0888-1111) [13492620] **4954**

DISCIPLESHIP JOURNAL (US/0273-5865) [07082459] **4954**

DISCIPLESHIP TRAINING (US/1047-9449) [20818912] **4954**

DISCIPLIANA (1960) (US/0732-9881) [08090077] **4954**

DISCIPLINA DEL COMMERCIO *CEASED.* (IT) **831**

DISCIPLINA SCAMBI CON L ESTERO (IT) **1634**

DISCIPLINE & GRIEVANCES FOR SUPERVISORS, LOCAL, STATE, AND FEDERAL GOVERNMENT (US) [11638520] **4644**

DISCIPLINE AND GRIEVANCES. WHITE COLLAR EDITION (US/0271-3462) [06583526] **940**

●DISCIPLINE NETWORK (ELEMENTARY SCHOOL ED.) (US/1073-6123) [29487100] **1736**

●DISCIPLINE NETWORK (MIDDLE/HIGH SCHOOL ED.) (US/1073-6107) [29487032] **1736**

DISCIPULOS RESPONSABLES *CEASED.* (US/1052-3804) [22271694] **4954**

DISCLOSURE (CHICAGO) (US/0196-8203) [05338390] 2821, **1296**

DISCLOSURE RECORD (US/0094-2561) [01788432] 896, **788**

DISCLOSURES (US) **743**

DISCO 45 (UK) [01788745] 5316, **4115**

DISCO FEVER (CN/0706-7763) [05359851] 5316, **4115**

DISCO-MAGAZIN — Alphabetical Title Index

● DISCO-MAGAZIN (GW) [27903306] 384, **4115**

DISCOGRAPHIES (WESTPORT) (US/0192-334X) [05320044] **4115**

DISCOTECA ALTA FEDELTA (IT) [01789041] **5316**

DISCOTECA ALTO FEDELTA *See* DISCOTECA HI-FI **5316**

DISCOTECA HI-FI *SUSPENDED.* (IT) [05467070] 4115, **5316**

DISCOTHEQUE MAGAZINE (US/0195-6728) [05529025] **1313**

DISCOUNT AND WHOLESALE PRINTING NEWSLETTER (US/1053-3699) [22518428] **4564**

DISCOUNT MERCHANDISER, THE (US/0012-3579) [00912574] **954**

DISCOUNT STORE NEWS (US/0012-3587) [00936780] **954**

DISCOURS ET DECLARATIONS DU PRESIDENT DE LA REPUBLIQUE FRANCAISE (FR/0396-5988) [04629056] **4644**

DISCOURS ET ENTRETIENS - PRESIDENCE DE LA REPUBLIQUE (RW) [04109955] **4644**

DISCOURS PSYCHANALYTIQUE, LE (FR) **3924**

DISCOURS SOCIAL (MONTREAL) (CN/0842-1420) [19450790] **3381**

DISCOURSE (UK/0159-6306) [09595059] **1736**

DISCOURSE & SOCIETY (UK/0957-9265) [22106916] **5198**

DISCOURSE PROCESSES (US/0163-853X) [04095368] **3277**

DISCOURSES IN MATHEMATICS AND ITS APPLICATIONS (US) [25821389] **3503**

DISCOVER AMERICA SALES GUIDE (US/0419-4071) [04304954] **5468**

DISCOVER (CHICAGO, ILL.) (US/0274-7529) [06560726] **5101**

DISCOVER COSTA RICA (US) **5468**

DISCOVER GUATEMALA (US) **5468**

DISCOVER INDIA (HK) **5468**

DISCOVER MID-AMERICA (US) **2532**

DISCOVER RENO/TAHOE (US/0148-7884) [03475307] **2532**

DISCOVER SOUTHWEST WISCONSIN'S HIDDEN VALLEYS (US/0738-8071) [09692918] **5468**

DISCOVER THE BIBLE (CN/0018-912X) [01640164] **5016**

DISCOVER WILLIAMSBURG (US) [06533866] **5468**

... DISCOVERAMERICARD DIRECTORY OF CITIES & HOTELS, THE (US/0277-8416) [07556708] **2805**

DISCOVERIES IN PHARMACOLOGY (US) [10386410] **4299**

DISCOVERIES (PORT TOWNSEND, WASH.) (US/0896-8322) [17303721] 4115, **2773**

DISCOVERING ALBERTA (CN/1186-7787) [24571315] **5468**

DISCOVERING AND EXPLORING NEW JERSEY'S FISHING STREAMS (US/1058-5761) [24333412] **4871**

DISCOVERING ART HISTORY (US) **349**

● DISCOVERING AUTHORS (US/1066-7792) [27046084] **3381**

DISCOVERING ETHIOPIA (ET) [04374647] **5468**

DISCOVERY AND INNOVATION (KE/1015-079X) [19891920] **5101**

DISCOVERY (AUSTIN) (US/0197-4947) [03814024] **2532**

DISCOVERY (BIRMINGHAM, ALA.) (US/0162-198X) [04117761] **5059**

DISCOVERY CHANNEL *See* DESTINATION DISCOVERY **2532**

DISCOVERY CHANNEL, THE (US/0890-8540) [14405192] **1153**

DISCOVERY FIVE HUNDRED : NEWSLETTER OF THE INTERNATIONAL COLUMBIAN QUINCENTENARY ALLIANCE LTD (US/0899-8329) [18264504] **2731**

DISCOVERY (NEW HAVEN, CONN.) (US/0012-3625) [01566763] 4165, **4087**

● DISCOVERY NEWS (CN/1191-4297) [26776108] **3478**

DISCOVERY (SKOKIE, ILL.) (US/0012-3641) [03880857] **5468**

DISCOVERY (VANCOUVER. 1972) (CN/0319-8480) [01996115] **2191**

DISCOVERY (VICTORIA) (CN/0822-5796) [10156778] **4087**

DISCOVERY YMCA (US) [12089682] 2596, **4850**

DISCRETE & COMPUTATIONAL GEOMETRY (US/0179-5376) [12986080] **3503**

DISCRETE APPLIED MATHEMATICS (NE) [20639870] **3503**

DISCRETE EVENT DYNAMIC SYSTEMS (US/0924-6703) [24132389] **1282**

DISCRETE MATHEMATICS (NE/0012-365X) [01566766] **3504**

DISCRETE MATHEMATICS AND APPLICATIONS (NE/0924-9265) [24864491] **3504**

DISCRETE SEMICONDUCTORS. DIODES (US/1040-0249) [18316932] **2042**

DISCRETE SEMICONDUCTORS. DIRECT ALTERNATE SOURCES (US/1043-6367) [19501574] **2042**

DISCRETE SEMICONDUCTORS. OPTOELECTRONICS (US/1040-0907) [18316968] **2042**

DISCRETE SEMICONDUCTORS. POWER SEMICONDUCTORS (US/1040-0214) [18316772] **4401**

DISCRETE SEMICONDUCTORS. SUGGESTED REPLACEMENT ALTERNATE SOURCES *See* DISCRETE SEMICONDUCTORS. SUGGESTED REPLACEMENTS **2042**

● DISCRETE SEMICONDUCTORS. SUGGESTED REPLACEMENTS (US/1058-8566) [24403278] **2042**

DISCRETE SEMICONDUCTORS. SURFACE-MOUNTED DISCRETE SEMICONDUCTORS (US/1040-0230) [30859059] **1971**

DISCRETE SEMICONDUCTORS. SURFACE-MOUNTED DISCRETES *See* DISCRETE SEMICONDUCTORS. SURFACE-MOUNTED DISCRETE SEMICONDUCTORS **1971**

DISCRETE SEMICONDUCTORS. THYRISTORS (US/1040-0222) [18316865] **4402**

DISCRETE SEMICONDUCTORS. TRANSISTORS (US/1040-0230) [18316900] **4402**

DISCURSO (PY/0737-8742) [25304604] **3381**

DISCURSO LITERARIO (PY/0737-8742) [09468253] **3382**

DISCURSO (SEVILLE, SPAIN) (SP) [18095309] **1110**

DISCUS NEWS LETTER (US/0162-5993) [02251193] **2366**

DISCUSION (AG) [04082594] **1555**

DISCUSSION PAPER (UK) [10462474] **79**

DISCUSSION PAPER (NZ) [10348069] **2413**

DISCUSSION PAPER (AT) [27332475] **1480**

DISCUSSION PAPER (AT) [05977362] **1480**

DISCUSSION PAPER - AGRIBUSINESS & ECONOMICS RESEARCH UNIT, LINCOLN COLLEGE (NZ/0113-4507) [I01134507] 1480, **79**

DISCUSSION PAPER - AGRICULTURAL ADMINISTRATION, RESEARCH AND EXTENSION, NETWORK (UK/0951-1873) [09511873] **79**

DISCUSSION PAPER (AUSTRALIAN BUREAU OF AGRICULTURAL AND RESOURCE ECONOMICS) *See* ABARE RESEARCH REPORT **42**

DISCUSSION PAPER - CENTER FOR ECONOMIC RESEARCH (NE/0924-7815) [I09247815] **1591**

DISCUSSION PAPER - CENTER FOR LATIN AMERICA IN THE UNIVERSITY OF WISCONSIN, MILWAUKEE (US/0146-258X) [02902949] **1821**

DISCUSSION PAPER - CENTER FOR RESEARCH ON ECONOMIC DEVELOPMENT, THE UNIVERSITY OF MICHIGAN (US/0580-6062) [06188881] **1480**

DISCUSSION PAPER - ECONOMIC COUNCIL OF CANADA (CN/0225-8013) [02248434] **1480**

DISCUSSION PAPER - ECONOMICS RESEARCH CENTRE (UK/0956-7895) [I09567895] **1591**

DISCUSSION PAPER - IFC (US/1012-8069) [18391221] **2909**

DISCUSSION PAPER IN NATURAL RESOURCE ECONOMICS / DEPARTMENT OF AGRICULTURAL ECONOMICS AND FARM MANAGEMENT, MASSEY UNIVERSITY (NZ/0110-2044) [10471328] **79**

DISCUSSION PAPER - INSTITUTE FOR ECONOMIC RESEARCH. QUEEN'S UNIVERSITY. KINGSTON, ONTARIO (CN/0316-5078) [02588383] **1480**

DISCUSSION PAPER (JOINT CENTRE ON MODERN EAST ASIA) (CN/0713-8180) [08996175] **2650**

DISCUSSION PAPER PROGRAM / CASUALTY ACTUARIAL SOCIETY (US/1046-6444) [17933439] **2879**

DISCUSSION PAPER SERIES / CENTRE FOR ECONOMIC POLICY RESEARCH (UK/0265-8003) [16403299] **1480**

DISCUSSION PAPER SERIES - DEPARTMENT OF GEOGRAPHY, SYRACUSE UNIVERSITY (US/0363-6038) [02480727] **2559**

DISCUSSION PAPER SERIES - FACULTY OF BUSINESS ADMINISTRATION. SIMON FRASER UNIVERSITY (CN/0824-4146) [10611117] **1480**

DISCUSSION PAPER SERIES - ONTARIO ECONOMIC COUNCIL (CN/0702-0643) [03883158] **1480**

DISCUSSION PAPER SERIES (UNIVERSITY OF CALGARY. DEPT. OF ECONOMICS) (CN/0709-0870) [05375371] **1480**

DISCUSSION PAPER SERIES - UNIVERSITY OF LEEDS. SCHOOL OF BUSINESS AND ECONOMIC STUDIES (UK/0956-1110) [I09561110] **79**

DISCUSSION PAPER - SIMON FRASER UNIVERSITY, DEPARTMENT OF GEOGRAPHY (CN/0823-3039) [10057378] **2559**

DISCUSSION PAPER - SPECIAL COMMITTEE ON CRIMINAL JUSTICE (US) [03766437] **3163**

DISCUSSION PAPER / UNITED NATIONS RESEARCH INSTITUTE FOR SOCIAL DEVELOPMENT (SZ/1012-6511) [18398125] **1480**

DISCUSSION PAPER (UNIVERSITY OF BRITISH COLUMBIA. DEPT. OF ECONOMICS) (CN/0317-0144) [02247659] **1480**

DISCUSSION PAPER - UNIVERSITY OF TORONTO, DEPARTMENT OF GEOGRAPHY (CN/0317-9893) [02441659] **2559**

DISCUSSION PAPERS - AUSTRALIAN NATIONAL UNIVERSITY, CENTRE FOR ECONOMIC POLICY RESEARCH (AT/0725-430X) [I0725430X] **1480**

DISCUSSION PAPERS / ECONOMIC COMMISSION FOR EUROPE (US/1014-9066) [26165076] **1480**

● DISCUSSION PAPERS / HELSINKI SCHOOL OF ECONOMICS, DEPARTMENT OF ECONOMICS (FI/1235-2209) [26464530] **1480**

DISCUSSION PAPERS IN GEOLINGUISTICS (UK/0262-9291) [08714538] **2559**

DISCUSSION / STUDIES OF THE ECONOMIC COMMISSION FOR EUROPE (SZ) **1480**

DISCUSSIONES MATHEMATICAE (PL) [04375171] **3504**

DISCUSSIONS AND CLOSURES OF ABSTRACTED PAPERS FROM THE WINTER MEETING (US/0270-3807) [06368099] **2042**

DISCUSSIONS IN DIETETICS *CEASED.* (US/1065-4666) [26613822] **4190**

DISCUSSIONS IN NEUROSCIENCES (SZ/0254-8852) [10661555] **3831**

DISCUSSIONS ON TEACHING *CEASED.* (US/0277-2736) [05467918] **2615**

DISEASE-A-MONTH (US/0011-5029) [01565772] **3572**

DISEASE CONTROL NEWSLETTER (US) [02256704] **4773**

DISEASE INFORMATION (FR/1012-5329) [18825222] **5509**

DISEASE MARKERS (UK/0278-0240) [07684066] **3713**

DISEASE SURVEILLANCE *See* BC HEALTH AND DISEASE SURVEILLANCE **4768**

DISEASES OF AQUATIC ORGANISMS (GW/0177-5103) [13369805] **554**

DISEASES OF THE COLON & RECTUM (US/0012-3706) [01566768] 3964, **3744**

DISEASES OF THE ESOPHAGUS : OFFICIAL JOURNAL OF THE INTERNATIONAL SOCIETY FOR DISEASES OF THE ESOPHAGUS / I.S.D.E (IT/1120-8694) [18466687] **3887**

DISEASES OF THE LIVER AND BILIARY SYSTEM (US) **3796**

DISEGNI E PROPOSTE DI LEGGE, RELAZIONI (IT) [05314606] **4472**

DISEGNO DI LEGGE (IT) [16781879] **4645**

DISEGNO MAGAZINE *SUSPENDED.* (IT) 1228, **1233**

DISENPLUS (MONTREAL) (CN/1182-946X) [23598081] 4585, **3924**

DISINFESTAZIONE (IT) **2963**

DISKRETNAIA MATEMATIKA (RU/0234-0860) [19862884] **1183**

DISKURS : STUDIEN ZU KINDHEIT, JUGEND, FAMILIE UND GESELLSCHAFT (GW/0937-9614) [24111744] **2278**

DISKUSI (MY/0126-5180) [05725469] **2503**

DISKUSSION DEUTSCH (GW/0342-1589) [03685967] 1893, **3277**

DISKUSSIONS (GUELPH) (CN/1180-338X) [23598495] 5509, **1183**

DISKUSSIONSBEITRAGE - UNIVERSITAT KIEL, INSTITUT FUER AGRARPOLITIK UND MARKTLEHRE (GW/0178-3335) [I01783335] **79**

DISKWORLD FOR THE MACINTOSH (US/0899-4838) [18115818] **1285**

DISMISSAL AND EMPLOYMENT LAW DIGEST (CN/0831-2516) [15645086] **3146**

DISNEY ADVENTURES (US/1050-2491) [21431041] **1062**

DISNEY BABIES OUT & AROUND / DISNEY (US/1053-6272) [22590307] **1062**

DISNEY CHANNEL MAGAZINE, THE (US/0747-4644) [10895644] **1131**

DISNEY MAGAZINE (US/0362-1960) [02380349] **1063**

DISNEY NEWS (US/0095-7178) [01798515] 5468, **4850**

DISNEY'S CHIP'N'DALE RESCUE RANGERS (US/1050-2599) [21432977] **1063**

DISNEY'S DUCKTALES (US/1044-0720) [19022167] **1063**

DISNEY'S DUCKTALES *CEASED.* (US/1044-0720) [21431534] **1063**

DISNEY'S TALE SPIN (US/1055-4203) [23169154] **1063**

DISNEY'S YEAR BOOK (US/0273-1274) [07037298] **1063**

DISORDERS OF HUMAN COMMUNICATION *CEASED.* (AU/0173-170X) [07480440] 4387, **3887**

DISP (SZ) [08571030] **2022**

●DISPATCH (US) [29812892] **2731**

DISPATCH CENTER MANAGEMENT (US/1068-2023) [27469295] **1153**

DISPATCH CENTER MANGEMENT *See* PUBLIC SAFETY ON-LINE **1162**

DISPATCH - COLUMBIA UNIVERSITY. CENTER FOR AMERICAN CULTURE STUDIES, THE (US/1046-2341) [18702757] **2731**

DISPATCH CONGRESS NEWS *See* DISPATCH/NEWS (SPRINGFIELD, ILL.) **2731**

DISPATCH CONGRESS NEWS (US/1065-0636) [26280970] **2731**

DISPATCH (COOKEVILLE, TENN.) (US/8750-7528) [11731024] **5745**

DISPATCH FROM THE ILLINOIS STATE HISTORICAL SOCIETY *See* DISPATCH CONGRESS NEWS **2731**

DISPATCH (GLASGOW, SCOTLAND) (UK) [13177506] **4043**

DISPATCH (LEXINGTON), THE *CEASED.* (US/0163-3090) [04342886] **5723**

DISPATCH MONTHLY (US) **4773**

●DISPATCH/NEWS (SPRINGFIELD, ILL.) (US/1069-451X) [28048180] **2731**

DISPATCH-NEWS, THE (US) [13640210] **5742**

DISPATCH (OLYMPIA, WASH.) (US) [14512969] **1936**

DISPATCH (ROCKVILLE, MD.) (US/0743-7269) [10658120] 667, **5381**

DISPATCH (SPRINGFIELD, ILLINOIS) (US/0419-4187) [01566770] **2731**

DISPATCHER, THE (US/0012-3765) [05284373] **1663**

DISPENSING OPTICS (UK/0954-3201) [13771977] **4215**

DISPLAY (DK/0107-7481) [I01077481] **1241**

DISPLAY & DESIGN IDEAS (US/1049-9176) [21358489] **759**

DISPLAY AND IMAGING TECHNOLOGY (US/0733-2386) [08542784] **1971**

DISPLAY DEVICE : ELECTRONIC DISPLAY DEVICE AND APPLICATION TECHNOLOGY (JA) [22636473] **1183**

DISPLAYS (UK/0141-9382) [05212865] 1233, **1228**

DISPO (AU) [03680931] **667**

DISPOSABLES AND NONWOVENS (UK/0012-3811) [05521324] **5350**

DISPOSITIO (US/0734-0591) [02483477] **3382**

DISPOSITIONS DES REGIMES ET LES COTISANTS EN ..., LES (CN) [06189468] 2879, **1663**

DISPUTATIONES RHENO-TRAJECTINAE (NE/0083-4998) [01560022] **3277**

DISPUTE RESOLUTION FORUM (US) [10271121] **2963**

●DISPUTE RESOLUTION JOURNAL (US/1074-8105) [29630772] **2963**

DISPUTE RESOLUTION PAPERS SERIES (US/0741-3793) [10137907] **2963**

DISPUTE RESOLUTION PROGRAM DIRECTORY (US/0731-4833) [07225726] **2963**

DISPUTE RESOLUTION RESOURCE DIRECTORY (US/0741-8442) [10222135] **2963**

DISPUTED PATERNITY PROCEEDINGS (US) [02383351] **2963**

DISQUISITIONES MATHEMATICAE HUNGARICAE (HU) [01781317] **3504**

DISSENT (NEW YORK) (US/0012-3846) [00935678] **4541**

DISSERTATION ABSTRACTS INTERNATIONAL (US/0419-4217) [01566777] **415**

DISSERTATION ABSTRACTS INTERNATIONAL. A, THE HUMANITIES AND SOCIAL SCIENCES (US/0419-4209) [01566776] 5198, **2845**

DISSERTATION ABSTRACTS INTERNATIONAL. A, THE HUMANITIES AND SOCIAL SCIENCES. B, THE SCIENCES AND ENGINEERING. CUMULATED AUTHOR INDEX (MICROFORM) (US) [09455987] 5101, **5227**

DISSERTATION ABSTRACTS INTERNATIONAL. C, WORLDWIDE (US/1042-7279) [19132490] **1821**

DISSERTATION ABSTRACTS ONDISC [COMPUTER FILE] (US) [20167130] **415**

DISSERTATIONEN DER UNIVERSITAT FUER BODENKULTUR IN WIEN (AU/0256-4246) [I02564246] **79**

DISSERTATIONEN DER UNIVERSITAT WIEN (AU/0419-4225) [01632470] 2846, **5101**

DISSERTATIONEN ZUR KUNSTGESCHICHTE (GW/0935-7114) [16066516] **319**

DISSERTATIONES AD HISTORIAM RELIGIONUM PERTINENTES (NE/0419-4233) [01566778] **4954**

DISSERTATIONES BOTANICAE (GW/0070-6728) [04027094] **508**

DISSERTATIONES SLAVICAE. SECTIO HISTORIAE LITTERARUM (HU) [14403720] **3382**

DISSOCIATION (SMYRNA, GA.) (US/0896-2863) [16978375] **4585**

DISSONANZ (SW) [12148317] **4115**

DISTAFF, A CRITICAL-LITERARY QUARTERLY, THE (US/0012-3889) [01633011] **1091**

DISTANCE EDUCATION (AT/0158-7919) [10166083] **1736**

DISTANCE EDUCATION AND TECHNOLOGY NEWSLETTER (US/1064-2439) [26246191] **1736**

DISTANCES ROUTIERES (CN/0714-2153) [08964037] **5440**

●DISTANT CROSSROADS (US) **2445**

DISTILLED SPIRITS COUNCIL OF THE U.S *See* DISCUS NEWS LETTER **2366**

DISTILLED SPIRITS COUNCIL OF THE U.S *See* RETAIL OUTLETS FOR THE SALE OF DISTILLED SPIRITS **957**

DISTILLERS FEED RESEARCH COUNCIL *See* PROCEEDINGS - DISTILLERS FEED RESEARCH COUNCIL CONFERENCE **121**

DISTINGUISHED HOME PLANS. HOMES FOR SLOPING SITES (US/0897-6236) [13801599] **298**

DISTINGUISHED LECTURERS SERIES (US/0196-9684) [03597487] **3382**

DISTRENDS (US/0891-2807) [14771074] **1605**

DISTRESSED REAL ESTATE LAW ALERT *CEASED.* (US/0892-4198) [15187792] 4837, **3086**

DISTRIBUCION ACTUALIDAD (SP) **923**

DISTRIBUTED AND PARALLEL DATABASES (US/0926-8782) **1254**

DISTRIBUTED COMPUTING (GW/0178-2770) [13296607] 1241, **1258**

●DISTRIBUTED COMPUTING MONITOR (US/1068-6266) [26327832] **1241**

DISTRIBUTED PROCESSING PRODUCT REPORTS (US/0888-4129) [13576170] **1183**

DISTRIBUTED SYSTEMS ENGINEERING JOURNAL (UK) **1228**

DISTRIBUTION BUSINESS (UK/0953-7147) [I09537147] **954**

DISTRIBUTION CENTER MANAGEMENT (US/0894-7651) [13723578] **866**

DISTRIBUTION D'AUJOURD'HUI (BE/0012-3935) [I00123935] **3478**

DISTRIBUTION DEVELOPMENTS (UK/0305-0378) [I03050378] **2042**

DISTRIBUTION MAINZ (GW/0342-1635) [I03421635] 949, **923**

DISTRIBUTION MANAGEMENT *CEASED.* (US/0737-0903) [09341740] 949, **923**

DISTRIBUTION MAPS OF PESTS. SERIES A (AGRICULTURAL) (UK/0588-778X) [04840501] **79**

DISTRIBUTION MAPS OF PLANT DISEASES (UK/0012-396X) [05984948] **508**

DISTRIBUTION OF DENTISTS IN THE UNITED STATES BY REGION AND STATE (US) [10641100] **1322**

DISTRIBUTION OF HIGH SCHOOL GRADUATES (US/0098-423X) [02241460] **1736**

DISTRIBUTION OF MOTOR VEHICLE REGISTRATION FEES AND FUEL TAXES TO OHIO CITIES (US/0145-1782) [02704783] **5413**

DISTRIBUTION OF OCCUPATIONAL EMPLOYMENT IN STATES AND AREAS BY RACE AND SEX (US/0270-8469) [06325731] **1663**

DISTRIBUTION OF STATE FOUNDATION AID TO NEW HAMPSHIRE SCHOOL DISTRICTS (US/0550-7960) [01797999] **1862**

DISTRIBUTION OF STEEL CASTINGS SALES BY END USE OF PRODUCT (US/0360-2001) [02441063] 4001, **923**

●DISTRIBUTION (RADNOR, PA. 1992) (US/1066-8489) [26668174] **5381**

DISTRIBUTION REPORT OF INTANGIBLE PERSONAL PROPERTY TAX COLLECTIONS AND SPECIAL ALLOCATIONS (US) [17469257] **4720**

DISTRIBUTIQUE (FR) **1183**

DISTRIBUTIVE WORKER, THE (US/0012-3986) [04049316] **1663**

DISTRIBUTOR SALES *CEASED.* (US/1048-8774) [21057919] **5695**

DISTRIBUTOR'S & WHOLESALER'S ADVISOR, THE (US/1043-7118) [19537368] **866**

DISTRIBUTORS LINK (US) **923**

DISTRIBUTORS OF ELECTRONIC PARTS (US/0160-0842) [03601148] **2042**

DISTRIBUZIONE E COOPERAZIONE (IT) [04233350] **1605**

DISTRICT AND PRECINCT BOUNDARIES, STATE OF HAWAII (US/0361-9508) [02441073] **4472**

DISTRICT ATTORNEY NEWSLETTER (NEW YORK, N.Y.) (US) [12395860] **3106**

DISTRICT COUNCIL JOURNAL (US/0748-1179) [09696969] 2963, **4645**

DISTRICT COUNCILS REVIEW (UK/0306-3240) [03943361] **4645**

DISTRICT COUNCILS SUMMARY OF STATEMENTS OF ACCOUNTS - (NORTHERN IRELAND) (IE) [03460355] **4720**

DISTRICT COURT AND BMC ADVANCE SHEETS (US) **2963**

DISTRICT COURT REPORTS (NZ/0111-4239) [19367067] **2963**

DISTRICT ENERGY (US) [30841926] **2604**

DISTRICT EXPORT COUNCILS MEMBERSHIP DIRECTORY (US) [06703575] **831**

DISTRICT HEATING AND COOLING (US/0885-6621) [12611048] **2604**

DISTRICT HEATING INTERNATIONAL (GW/0933-6540) [I09336540] **2604**

DISTRICT INCOME OF KERALA (II) [06105170] **1480**

DISTRICT MEMOIR / GEOLOGICAL SURVEY OF WEST MALAYSIA (MY) [04199912] **1373**

DISTRICT OF COLUMBIA *See* EXECUTIVE BUDGET - DISTRICT OF COLUMBIA **4722**

DISTRICT OF COLUMBIA. AIR & WATER MONITORING DIVISION *See* ANNUAL REPORT ON THE QUALITY OF THE AIR IN WASHINGTON, D.C **2224**

DISTRICT OF COLUMBIA BAR *See* BAR REPORT **2940**

DISTRICT OF COLUMBIA. BOARD OF COMMISSIONERS *See* DISTRICT OF COLUMBIA REGISTER **4645**

DISTRICT OF COLUMBIA CASE NAMES CITATOR (US) **2963**

DISTRICT OF COLUMBIA CODE ENCYCLOPEDIA (US) [01566797] **2963**

DISTRICT OF COLUMBIA COURT RULES ANNOTATED (US/0747-6949) [08512305] **3140**

DISTRICT OF COLUMBIA COURT RULES SERVICE (US) **3140**

DISTRICT OF COLUMBIA. DEPT. OF MANPOWER. DIVISION OF MANPOWER REPORTS AND ANALYSIS *See* ANNUAL PLANNING REPORT, DISTRICT OF COLUMBIA **1648**

DISTRICT OF COLUMBIA. EMPLOYMENT AND TRAINING SERVICES ADVISORY COUNCIL *See* ANNUAL EMPLOYMENT AND TRAINING REPORT TO THE MAYOR, DISTRICT OF COLUMBIA / EMPLOYMENT AND TRAINING SERVICES ADVISORY COUNCIL **1645**

●DISTRICT OF COLUMBIA LAW REVIEW (US/1063-8601) [26179949] **2963**

DISTRICT

DISTRICT OF COLUMBIA. MANPOWER SERVICES PLANNING ADVISORY COUNCIL See ANNUAL REPORT TO THE MAYOR OF THE DISTRICT OF COLUMBIA **1650**

DISTRICT OF COLUMBIA. OFFICE OF HUMAN RIGHTS See CASE ENFORCEMENT REPORT / DISTRICT OF COLUMBIA, OFFICE OF HUMAN RIGHTS **4505**

DISTRICT OF COLUMBIA. OFFICE OF THE AUDITOR See ANNUAL REPORT ON DEPOSITORY ACTIVITIES, FY ... / OFFICE OF THE DISTRICT OF COLUMBIA AUDITOR **4710**

DISTRICT OF COLUMBIA. OFFICE ON AGING See DISTRICT OF COLUMBIA PLAN ON AGING **5179**

DISTRICT OF COLUMBIA PLAN ON AGING (US) [08419820] **5179**

DISTRICT OF COLUMBIA. PUBLIC DEFENDER SERVICE. BOARD OF TRUSTEES See REPORT / DISTRICT OF COLUMBIA. PUBLIC DEFENDER SERVICE. BOARD OF TRUSTEES **3037**

DISTRICT OF COLUMBIA REAL ESTATE REPORTER (US/0738-6931) [09670756] **4837**

DISTRICT OF COLUMBIA REGISTER (US/0419-439X) [02862928] **4645**

DISTRICT OF COLUMBIA VIRGINIA ZIP+4 STATE DIRECTORY (US) [11544105] **1144**

DISTRICT STATISTICAL HANDBOOK - (INDIA) (II/0523-3456) [01532925] **5326**

DISTRITO FEDERAL, BRAZIL See LEGISLACAO DO DISTRITO FEDERAL **3001**

DISTRITO FEDERAL (BRAZIL). COORDENACAO DO SISTEMA DE ORCAMENTO See PROJETO DE LEI ORCAMENTARIA ANUAL - COORDENACAO DO SISTEMA DE ORCAMENTO **804**

DISTRITO FEDERAL (BRAZIL). TRIBUNAL DE CONTAS See REVISTA DO TRIBUNAL DE CONTAS DO DISTRITO FEDERAL **4747**

DISTRITO FEDERAL (VENEZUELA). CONTRALORIA MUNICIPAL See INFORME - DISTRITO FEDERAL (VENEZUELA). CONTRALORIA MUNICIPAL **4732**

DITCHLEY NEWSLETTER, THE (UK/0262-8015) [08244982] **5198**

●DIVADELNI NOVINY (XR) [26265328] **5363**

DIVADLO (XR) [06473027] **5363**

DIVE TRAINING (US/1061-3323) [25217145] **4893**

DIVER (UK) [03886905] **4893**

DIVER DOWN (CN/0700-3994) [03250960] **4893**

DIVER MAGAZINE (CN/0706-5132) [05018623] 2773, **4893**

DIVER (PORTLAND CONN.), THE (US/0273-8589) [06996998] **4893**

DIVER'S ALMANAC (US/8755-5573) [11326836] **4893**

DIVERS FREE PRESS (CN/0846-0477) [23598407] **4893**

DIVERSION (TITUSVILLE) (US/0363-4825) [02251194] 3914, **4850**

DIVERSITY (US/0744-8163) [08501748] **508**

●DIVERSITY & DIVISION (US/1064-7430) [26387593] **5244**

DIVERSITY EAST MELBOURNE (AT/0812-0102) [I08120102] **5244**

DIVERSITY (WASHINGTON, D.C.) See DIVERSITY & DIVISION **5244**

DIVIDEND (US/0046-0400) [02688018] **667**

DIVIDEND RECORD (CN/0046-0419) [02418106] 788, **4720**

DIVIDEND REINVESTMENT PLANS (US/1052-5092) [22201169] **896**

DIVIDENDE (CN/0828-5292) [12035571] **831**

DIVIDENDS FROM WOOD RESEARCH (US/0748-1276) [02854562] **2378**

DIVINE LIFE, THE (II) [22532936] 5040, **4185**

●DIVING & SNORKELING QUARTERLY (US/1062-1210) [25523891] **4893**

●DIVING (BLOOMSBURG, PA.) (US/1063-0767) [25851073] **4893**

DIVING WORLD (VAN NUYS, CALIF.) (US/1042-1343) [18945504] 4850, **4893**

DIVINITAS (VC/0012-4222) [01640582] **4954**

DIVISION OF APPLIED GEOMECHANICS TECHNICAL PAPER (AT/0374-4957) [02250652] **1971**

DIVISION OF APPLIED MINERALOGY TECHNICAL PAPER (AT) [01678114] **1439**

DIVISION OF ENVIRONMENTAL CONTROL TECHNOLOGY PROGRAM (US/0197-2731) [04167545] **2227**

DIVISION OF FISH AND GAME (US) [01522525] **2191**

DIVISION OF FORESTRY IN THE CALIFORNIA CONSERVATION CAMP PROGRAM, THE (US) [01434542] **2378**

DIVISION OF PLANT INDUSTRY TECHNICAL PAPER (AT/0069-7567) [01201573] **1413**

DIVISION OF SOILS DIVISIONAL REPORT (AT/0725-8526) [15720005] **170**

DIVISION OF SOILS DIVISIONAL REPORT (AT/0705-2332) [03832075] **170**

DIVISION OF WILDLIFE AND RANGELANDS RESEARCH TECHNICAL PAPER (AT/0812-2237) [11465054] **2191**

DIVISION REPORT / COLORADO DIVISION OF WILDLIFE (US/0276-0231) [02745157] **2191**

DIVISIONAL NOTE (UK) 79, **1971**

DIVISIONAL NOTE - NATIONAL INSTITUTE OF AGRICULTURAL ENGINEERING (UK/0267-5471) [02675471] 1971, **79**

DIVISIONAL REPORT - CSIRO DIVISION OF FOREST RESEARCH (AT) [04225227] **2378**

DIVISIONAL REPORT - CSIRO DIVISION OF MECHANICAL ENGINEERING OF THE INSTITUTE OF INDUSTRIAL TECHNOLOGY (AT) [06597023] **2113**

DIVISIONS CEASED. (US/0192-6128) [05032641] **4115**

DIVITIAE MUSICAE ARTIS (NE) **4115**

DIVORCE LITIGATION (US/1050-141X) [19655451] **3120**

DIVORCE TAXATION (US/0730-6555) [08030726] **3120**

DIVORCES AUSTRALIA / AUSTRALIAN BUREAU OF STATISTICS (AT) [08165319] 2278, **2287**

DIVULGACIA IMPOSITIVA (AG) [06221273] **4720**

DIVULGACION LEGISLATIVA (CU) **2963**

DIVULGACION TRIBUTARIA (CL/0417-7371) [01635247] **4720**

DIVUS THOMAS: COMMENTARIUM DE PHILOSOPHIA ET THEOLOGIA (IT/0012-4257) [01696824] 4345, **4954**

DIVYAJYOTIH (II) [01800220] **5041**

Alphabetical Title Index

DIWAN AL-MAWANI AL-QAWMIYAH See BULLETIN ANNUEL DES STATISTIQUES - REPUBLIQUE TUNISIENNE, OFFICE DES PORTS NATIONAUX **5448**

DIWEN WULI XUEBAO (CC/1000-3258) [21979941] **4402**

DIX, LES See CAHIERS DES DIX **2725**

DIX-HUITIEME SIECLE (FR/0070-6760) [01604517] **2615**

DIX-NEUVIEME SIECLE : BULLETIN DE LA SOCIETE DES ETUDES ROMANTIQUES (FR) [12739747] **3382**

DIX-SEPTIEME SIECLE (FR/0012-4273) [02269738] **2685**

DIXIE CONTRACTOR, THE (US/0012-4281) [01618212] 613, **2022**

DIXIE GUN WORKS See MUZZLELOADERS' ANNUAL **3485**

DIXIE GUN WORKS BLACKPOWDER ANNUAL (US/0737-0105) [07897703] **3478**

DIXIE LOGGER AND LUMBERMAN MAGAZINE (US/0046-0435) [01646611] **2400**

DIXIE LUMBERMAN (US/0417-741X) [01646958] **2400**

DIXIE NEWS (US) [12352681] **5680**

DIXON ARNETT'S CALIFORNIA COMMENT FROM WASHINGTON, DC (US/1055-159X) [23096395] **4472**

DIXON GALLERY AND GARDENS See NEWSLETTER - DIXON GALLERY AND GARDENS **4094**

DIXON TELEGRAPH (DIXON, ILL. : 1985) (US/0889-4612) [14074047] **5659**

DIXON TRIBUNE, THE (US/0739-0181) [09689477] **5634**

DIXSON LIBRARY REPORT (AT/0728-6481) [I07286481] **3208**

DIY SUPERSTORE (UK/0951-7812) [I09517812] **2333**

DIY WEEK (UK) [18723117] **2811**

DIYARUNA WA-AL-ALAM (QA) [04681466] **1555**

DIZHEN DIZHI (CC/0253-4967) [06661272] **1404**

DIZHEN XUEBAO CEASED. (CC/0253-3782) [05912718] **1404**

DIZHI KEXUE (CC/0563-5020) [01570984] **1373**

DIZHIXUE BAO (CC/0001-5717) [06674907] **1373**

DIZIONARIO BIBLIOGRAFICO DELLE RIVISTE GIURIDICHE ITALIANE (IT/0419-4632) [01566813] **3080**

DIZIONARIO BIOGRAFICO DEGLI ITALIANI. INDICE (IT) [06340130] **432**

DIZIONARIO ENCICLOPEDICO D'INFORMAZIONI, IL (IT) [04258470] **1925**

DIZIONARIO EPIGRAFICO DI ANTICHITA ROMANE (IT) **2615**

DIZIONARIO GIURIDICO (IT) **2963**

DJ TIMES (US/1045-9693) [20309053] **1131**

DJAWAL IDI (AT/0314-7797) [I03147797] **1803**

DJEICH : REVUE DE L'ARMEE NATIONALE POPULAIRE, EL (AE/0419-4799) [03531321] **4043**

DJF BLADET (DK) [09479099] **2963**

DJF HANDBOGEN (DK/0108-3627) [11009439] **3146**

DJURNAL PERPUSTAKAAN (IO) [01798499] **3208**

DK NEWSLETTER (II) [03367979] **415**

DLA BULLETIN (OAKLAND, CALIF.) (US/0272-037X) [06743658] **3208**

DLG MITTEILUNGEN AGRAR-INFORM (GW) [25810031] **79**

DLI BULLETIN See BLI BULLETIN **1655**

DLR-NACHRICHTEN : MITTEILUNGSBLATT DER DEUTSCHEN FORSCHUNGSANSTALT FUER LUFT- UND RAUMFAHRT (GW/0937-0420) [21218474] **18**

DLW-NACHRICHTEN (GW/0172-2867) [I01722867] **613**

DM (GW/0416-5551) [I04165551] **4030**

DM & S ADP PLAN (US/8756-5447) [11540651] 4043, **3573**

DM. DECISIONS MEDIAS See DECISIONS MEDIAS **1109**

DM. JAHRBUCH (GW) [06427253] **1296**

DM-M DATABASE MAGAZINE (NE) **1183**

DM-MAGAZINE See ADFO DIRECT MAGAZINE **920**

DM NEWS (US/0194-3588) [05391700] **923**

DMA AERONAUTICAL CHART BULLETIN See DMA AERONAUTICAL CHART MONTHLY BULLETIN **18**

DMA AERONAUTICAL CHART MONTHLY BULLETIN (US/0278-1956) [07726927] **18**

DMA AERONAUTICAL CHART UPDATING MANUAL, CHUM (US/0195-3702) [05385523] **18**

DMA DANCE MUSIC AUTHORITY (US) 1313, **4115**

DMA MATTERS (US/0883-6256) [12211464] **923**

DMAAC TECHNICAL TRANSLATIONS LIST (US/0095-0742) [01795428] **4043**

DMS WORLD HELICOPTER INVENTORY & FORECAST (US/1050-8910) [19943681] **18**

DMS WORLD MISSILES FORECAST (US/1047-8760) [20783158] **4043**

DMSG AKTIV (GW/0177-8293) [I01778293] **4387**

DMSP SSM/I BRIGHTNESS TEMPERATURE GRIDS. POLAR REGIONS [COMPUTER FILE] / NATIONAL SNOW AND ICE DATA CENTER (US) [23122467] **4434**

DMT. DANSK MUSIK TIDSSKRIFT (DK/0106-5629) [06752065] **4115**

DMZ, LEBENSMITTELINDUSTRIE UND MILCHWIRTSCHAFT (GW/0938-9369) [24785426] **2334**

DNA AND CELL BIOLOGY (US/1044-5498) [19827838] **544**

DNA PROBES (UK/0266-6308) [I02666308] **453**

DNA REPORTER (US) [20880642] **3855**

DNA SEQUENCE (SZ/1042-5179) [19075340] **453**

DNA SHEFFIELD (UK/0142-8640) [I01428640] 486, **3573**

DNA - UNITED STATES. DEFENSE NUCLEAR AGENCY (US/0277-8203) [07668936] **4446**

DNAG CUSTOMER NEWSLETTER (US) [13490155] **1374**

DNC ECONOMIC SURVEY (NO) [20794250] **788**

DNC OIL NOW (NO/0800-2355) [07410413] **4254**

DNEVNAIA ZVEZDA; VOSTOCHNYI ALMANAKH (RU) [02243658] **3382**

DNI JOURNAL (US/0883-6698) [12212768] **4773**

DNIAS ANNUAL REPORT + 1 (JA/0303-5514) [01796988] **5101**

DNIPRO (UN/0130-321X) [02069577] **3382**

Alphabetical Title Index — DOCUMENTOS

DNR PERFORMANCE REPORT (PH) [04045818] **2191**

DNZ INTERNATIONAL (GW/0011-507X) [04713627] **5350**

DO IT (AT/0727-971X) [I0727971X] 384 5363, **2615**

DO IT YOURSELF *CEASED*. (UK/0012-4370) [I00124370] **613**

DO-IT-YOURSELF PROJECTS (US/0278-7474) [07862778] **372**

DO-IT-YOURSELF RETAILING (US/0889-2989) [13832614] **2811**

DO RE MI PARIS (FR/1158-4270) [I11584270] **1063**

DO, THE (US/0011-5088) [04975590] **3573**

DOAR, HA- (US/0017-6524) [05372484] 2259, **5047**

DOBERMAN QUARTERLY (US/1045-1757) [20034389] **4286**

DOBOKU GAKKAI *See* DOBOKU GAKKAI RONBUN HOKOKUSHU **2022**

DOBOKU GAKKAI RONBUN HOKOKUSHU (JA/0385-5392) [08270769] **2022**

DOBOKU GAKKAI SHI (JA/0021-468X) [10118916] **2022**

DOBOKU SEKO (JA/0387-0790) [12040816] **2022**

DOBUTSU BUNRUI GAKKAI SHI (JA/0287-0223) [10958032] **5581**

DOBUTSU IYAKUHIN KENSAGO NEMPO (JA/0388-7421) [06712603] **5509**

DOBUTSU SHINRIGAKU NENPO (JA/0003-5130) [02257563] **4585**

DOBUTSU TO DOBUTSUEN. ANIMALS AND ZOOS (JA) [04774406] **5581**

DOC. - C.C.I.R (SZ) [03323917] **1153**

DOC. - COUNCIL OF EUROPE, PARLIAMENTARY ASSEMBLY (FR) [02242994] **3127**

DOC IFE PROFILS (FR) **1936**

DOC ITALIA / ISTITUTO NAZIONAL DELL'INFORMAZIONE (IT) [05184422] **5230**

DOCENCIA (MX) [05324260] **1821**

DOCENT EDUCATOR (US) **1893**

DOCK AND HARBOUR AUTHORITY (UK/0012-4419) [01619495] **5449**

●DOCKET : A JOURNAL OF THE INTERNATIONAL HUMAN RIGHTS LAW GROUP (US) [30945961] **4507**

DOCKET REPORT - CENTER FOR CONSTITUTIONAL RIGHTS (US/0148-5997) [02708978] **3092**

DOCKET SERIES (US/0078-317X) [01566824] **2963**

DOCKET SHEET / SUPREME COURT OF THE UNITED STATES, THE (US) [05856005] **2963**

DOCKET (ST. PAUL, MINN.) (US/0739-3210) [06938230] **2963**

DOCKET, THE (US/0895-1659) [12271799] **2963**

DOCKLANDS NEWS (UK/0264-9691) [I02649691] 4850, 4893, **667**

DOCKS (FR) **593**

DOCPAL RESUMENES SOBRE POBLACION EN AMERICA LATINA (CL/0378-5378) [04200519] **4552**

DOCS TODAY (US) [17190014] **3163**

DOCTOR COMMUNIS (VC/0012-4443) [02069883] **5028**

DOCTOR GUILDFORD (UK/0046-0451) [I00460451] **3737**

DOCTOR (MILAN, ITALY) *CEASED*. (IT) [18713496] **3954**

DOCTOR NUTRIZIONE *CEASED*. (IT) [I11205954] **3573**

DOCTOR PEDIATRIA *SUSPENDED*. (IT/0394-7238) [I03947238] **3903**

DOCTOR STRANGE, SORCERER SUPREME (US/1044-7172) [18837931] **372**

●DOCTOR VETERINARIAN BOARD REVIEW (US/1057-9605) [24171830] **5509**

●DOCTOR VETERINARIAN QUICK REVIEW (US/1057-9591) [24171893] **5509**

DOCTORAL DISSERTATIONS IN HISTORY (US/0145-9929) [02429011] **2615**

DOCTORAL DISSERTATIONS IN MUSICOLOGY (PHILADELPHIA, PA. : 1984) (US) [13387851] **4115**

DOCTORAL DISSERTATIONS ON ASIA (US/0098-4485) [02241413] 1822, **2650**

DOCTOR'S FINANCIAL REPORT (US) 3914, **788**

DOCTOR'S OFFICE, THE (US/0733-2262) [08538469] 667, **3914**

DOCTOR'S REVIEW (CN/0821-5758) [09658255] **4850**

DOCTRINA PENAL *SUSPENDED*. (AG) [08201276] **3107**

DOCTRINA Y LEGISLACION ADUANERA (UY) [04631674] **2963**

DOCTRINE AND LIFE (IE/0012-446X) [01566828] **4954**

DOCTRINE JURIDIQUE BELGE (PE) [24148837] **2963**

DOCUMENT - AFRIKA BARAZA (US/1052-8512) [17361651] **2639**

DOCUMENT DE TRAVAIL - UNIVERSITE D'OTTAWA. FACULTE D'ADMINISTRATION (CN/0824-4316) [10392244] 4645, **667**

DOCUMENT DELIVERY WORLD *CEASED*. (US/1067-0815) [27130393] **1183**

DOCUMENT IMAGE AUTOMATION (US/1054-9692) [23035230] 3208, **1277**

DOCUMENT IMAGE AUTOMATION UPDATE (US/1054-9706) [23035387] 3208, **1277**

●DOCUMENT IMAGING REPORT (US) [28555595] 2042, **1183**

●DOCUMENT MANAGEMENT & WINDOWS IMAGING (US/1071-8567) [27856799] **1258**

●DOCUMENT MANAGEMENT : NNIEUWSBRIEF VOOR DOCUMENTAIRE INFORMATIEKUNDE / INSTITUUT VOOR TOEGEPASTE INFORMATICA (NE) [26514582] **866**

DOCUMENT MANAGEMENT (SCOTTSDALE, ARIZ.) (US/1057-0365) [23913879] **1258**

DOCUMENT MANAGEMENT TECHNOLOGY (US/1051-2217) [21893712] **1258**

DOCUMENT MANAGEMENT TECHNOLOGY SOURCEBOOK *CEASED*. (US/1054-4615) [22895298] **1971**

DOCUMENT OF MINISTRY FOR FOREIGN AFFAIRS, FINNISH INTERNATIONAL DEVELOPMENT AGENCY (FI/0780-9212) [19766034] **2909**

DOCUMENT RETRIEVAL INDEX (US/0364-5754) [01619584] **3163**

DOCUMENT SUPPLY NEWS (UK/0952-892X) [17361616] **3208**

DOCUMENT - SWEDISH COUNCIL FOR BUILDING RESEARCH (SW/0347-0962) [10044114] **2821**

DOCUMENTA (PE) [01788988] **2300**

DOCUMENTA (BL) [02239909] 1737, **2963**

DOCUMENTA MUSICOLOGICA *See* DOCUMENTA MUSICOLOGICA. 1. REIHE. DRUCKSCHRIFTEN-FAKSIMILES **4115**

DOCUMENTA MUSICOLOGICA. 1. REIHE. DRUCKSCHRIFTEN-FAKSIMILES (GW/0419-5205) [05357530] **4115**

DOCUMENTA MUSICOLOGICA. 2. REIHE: HANDSCHRIFTEN-FAKSIMILES (GW/0417-805X) [01566831] **4115**

DOCUMENTA OPHTHALMOLOGICA (NE/0012-4486) [01566832] **3874**

DOCUMENTA OPHTHALMOLOGICA. PROCEEDINGS SERIES (NE/0303-6405) [01090171] **3874**

DOCUMENTACAO AMAZONICA : CATALOGO COLETIVO (BL) [02441335] **5101**

DOCUMENTACION ADMINISTRATIVA (SP/0012-4494) [02070308] **4645**

DOCUMENTACION JURIDICA (SP) [02242023] **2963**

DOCUMENTACION SOCIAL (SP) [04720307] **5198**

DOCUMENTACION SOCIAL CATOLICA LATINOAMERICANA : DOCLA / INSTITUTO LATINOAMERICANO DE DOCTRINA Y ESTUDIOS SOCIALES (CL) [05060033] **5198**

DOCUMENTAIRE EN EUROPE, LE (BE) **4068**

DOCUMENTALISTE (PARIS) (FR/0012-4508) [04720228] **3208**

DOCUMENTARIO DA VIDA RURAL (BL/0417-8254) [01649359] **79**

DOCUMENTARY EDITING (US/0196-7134) [10685677] 4814, **2919**

DOCUMENTARY HISTORY OF THE FIRST FEDERAL CONGRESS OF THE UNITED STATES OF AMERICA, MARCH 4, 1789-MARCH 3, 1791 (US) [01653767] **4472**

DOCUMENTATIEBLAD (NE) [05295699] **415**

DOCUMENTATIEBLAD / LEIDEN AFRIKA-STUDIECENTRUM (NE) [09697965] 5198, 2846, **5227**

DOCUMENTATIEBLAD WERKGROEP ACHTTIENDE EEUW (NE/0166-6304) [06401652] **319**

DOCUMENTATION AND INFORMATION CENTER FOR INDIGENOUS AFFAIRS IN THE AMAZON REGION *See* AMAZIND BULLETIN **2718**

DOCUMENTATION BIBLIOTECOLOGICA (AG) [01620003] **3208**

DOCUMENTATION BULLETIN (VAIKUNTHBHAI MEHTA SMARAK TRUST, DOCUMENTATION CENTRE-CUM-REFERENCE LIBRARY) (II) [07428511] **5101**

DOCUMENTATION CATHOLIQUE, LA (FR/0012-4613) [01774714] **5028**

DOCUMENTATION CENTRE CATALOGUE (SZ) [15233964] **1737**

DOCUMENTATION CENTRE FOR EDUCATION IN EUROPE *See* EUDISED R & D BULLETIN **1745**

DOCUMENTATION DU MINISTERE DE L'ENERGIE ET DES RESSOURCES, REPERTOIRE (CN/0824-3689) [09725285] 2191, **1555**

DOCUMENTATION ET BIBLIOTHEQUES (CN/0315-2340) [01786818] **3208**

DOCUMENTATION ET INFORMATION PROTESTANTES : DIP (CG) [08733392] **5059**

DOCUMENTATION IN PUBLIC ADMINISTRATION (II/0377-7081) [01797735] **4645**

DOCUMENTATION - INTERNATIONAL MARITIME COMMITTEE (BE/0538-8643) [02844999] **4176**

DOCUMENTATION JURIDIQUE ETRANGERE (BE) [01566838] **3127**

DOCUMENTATION, LIBRARIES, AND ARCHIVES : BIBLIOGRAPHIES AND REFERENCE WORKS (FR) [01649303] **2478**

DOCUMENTATION MATHEMATIQUE (FR/0417-8300) [05774164] **3504**

DOCUMENTATION ON BOOKS / INTERNATIONAL UNIVERSITY CONTACT FOR MANAGEMENT EDUCATION. LITERATURE SERVICE (BE) [02446802] 3208, **866**

DOCUMENTATION ON FOREIGN TRADE (II) [01790447] **1634**

DOCUMENTATION ORGANIQUE (FR) **2963**

DOCUMENTATION PAR L'IMAGE, LA (FR/0046-0478) [I00460478] 1737, **5101**

DOCUMENTATION PHOTOGRAPHIQUE, LA (FR/0419-5361) [02623843] **4368**

DOCUMENTATION-REFUGIES (FR/0984-8541) [19564539] **4472**

DOCUMENTATION REFUGIES PARIS (FR/0984-8541) [I09848541] **1918**

DOCUMENTATION SERVICE BULLETIN (II/0376-8651) [05544103] **5198**

DOCUMENTATION - SNCB, DIRECTION DU PERSONNEL ET DES SERVICES SOCIAUX (BE) [07207780] **5431**

DOCUMENTATION TECHNIQUE - COMMISSION DE LA FONCTION PUBLIQUE DU QUEBEC (CN/0712-0451) [08878417] **4645**

DOCUMENTATION TOURISTIQUE (FR) [07102177] 4850, **5468**

DOCUMENTAZIONE DOGANALE VALUTARIA E DEGLI SCAMBI CON L'ESTERO (IT) **1634**

DOCUMENTI (IT) **3341**

DOCUMENTI COM + CES: QUESTIONI SOCIALI (IT) **1634**

DOCUMENTI DI ARCHITETTURA ARMENA (IT/0420-0810) [01001099] **298**

DOCUMENTI SULLE ARTI DEL LIBRO (IT/0070-6906) [04898250] **4828**

DOCUMENTO ABRIL (BL) [02244895] **2515**

DOCUMENTO DE TRABAJO / INSTITUTO TORCUATO DI TELLA, CENTRO DE INVESTIGACIONES SOCIALES (AG/0325-8483) [01753301] 5198, **1663**

DOCUMENTO DE TRABAJO. SERIE RELACIONES INTERNACIONALES Y POLITICA EXTERIOR / FLACSO, PROGRAMA CHILE (CL) [23535679] **4520**

DOCUMENTOS A (SP/1130-4936) [23945042] **2685**

DOCUMENTOS - CENTRO DE INFORMACION Y DOCUMENTACION PARA AMERICA LATINA (VE/0577-2567) [03023661] **5326**

DOCUMENTOS (CENTRO DE PESQUISA AGROPECUARIA DO TROPICO SEMI-ARIDO) (BL/0100-9729) [08598118] **79**

DOCUMENTOS - CENTRO NACIONAL DE PESQUISA DE COCO (BL/0102-9185) [I01029185] **80**

DOCUMENTOS (CENTRO NACIONAL DE PESQUISA DE GADO DE CORTE (BRAZIL)) (BL/0100-9443) [14208931] **210**

DOCUMENTOS - CENTRO NACIONAL DE PESQUISA DE TRIGO (BL/0101-6644) [I01016644] **200**

DOCUMENTOS

Alphabetical Title Index

DOCUMENTOS DDT / EMBRAPA, DEPARTAMENTO DE DIFUSAO DE TECNOLOGIA AND CENTRONACIONAL DE PESQUISA DE SOJA (BL) [08537532] **80**

DOCUMENTOS DE ARQUITECTURA ALMERIA (SP/0214-9249) [I02149249] **298**

DOCUMENTOS DE DERECHO SOCIAL (SZ/1014-703X) **1664**

DOCUMENTOS DE TRABAJO (UNIVERSIDAD DE COSTA RICA, INSTITUTO DE INVESTIGACIONES EN CIENCIAS ECONOMICAS) (CR) [08354105] **1664**

DOCUMENTOS - EMCAPA (BL/0101-8949) [19549462] **80**

DOCUMENTOS / EMPA-MT (BL/0102-2423) [26512922] **80**

DOCUMENTOS / EMPRESA BRASILEIRA DE PESQUISA AGROPECUARIA, VINCULADA AO MINISTERIO DA AGRICULTURA, CENTRO NACIONAL DE PESQUISA DE SOJA (BL/0101-5494) [13340505] 2334, **170**

DOCUMENTOS - EMPRESA CATARINENSE DE PESQUISA AGROPECUARIA 1978- (BL/0100-8986) [07973500] **80**

DOCUMENTOS / UEPAE DOURADOS (BL/0102-5651) [26512945] **80**

DOCUMENTS - B.R.G.M (FR/0221-2536) [05201798] **1439**

DOCUMENTS - COMMISSION OF THE EUROPEAN COMMUNITIES (LU/0254-1475) [10312156] **4645**

DOCUMENTS D'ACTUALITE INTERNATIONALE (FR/0338-4454) [24324789] **1634**

DOCUMENTS D'ANALISI GEOGRAFICA / [PUBLICACIONS DEL DEPARTAMENT DE GEOGRAFIA, UNIVERSITAT AUTONOMA DE BARCELONA] (SP/0212-1573) [10442018] **2560**

DOCUMENTS D'ARCHEOLOGIE MERIDIONALE (FR/0184-1068) [05911964] **266**

DOCUMENTS D'ARCHEOLOGIE MERIDIONALE. NUMERO SPECIAL, SERIE METHODES ET TECHNIQUES (FR/0249-8316) [08828455] **266**

DOCUMENTS DE CARTOGRAPHIE ECOLOGIQUE (FR/0335-5330) [06711999] **2213**

DOCUMENTS DE DROIT SOCIAL - BUREAU INTERNATIONAL DU TRAVAIL (SZ/1014-7063) [I10147063] **2963**

DOCUMENTS DE LINGUISTIQUE QUANTITATIVE (FR/0085-4786) [01657322] **3277**

DOCUMENTS DE PRESSE MENSUELS : ARTS PLASTIQUES (CN/0710-9350) [08193027] **319**

DOCUMENTS DE RECHERCHES EN MEDECINE GENERALE (FR/0767-1407) [16920916] **3737**

DOCUMENTS DES LABORATOIRES DE GEOLOGIE, LYON (FR/0750-6635) [11174106] **1374**

DOCUMENTS D'HISTOIRE MAGHREBINE (FR) [01780854] **2685**

DOCUMENTS D'INFORMATION ET DE GESTION (FR/0223-5625) [I02235625] **866**

DOCUMENTS, ETUDES ET REPERTOIRES (FR/0073-8212) [02024413] 2639, **267**

DOCUMENTS EXPERIENCES (FR) **4954**

DOCUMENTS HISTORIQUES - SOCIETE HISTORIQUE DU NOUVEL-ONTARIO (CN/0700-6039) [10669701] **2731**

DOCUMENTS IN AMERICAN HISTORY (US) [01657539] **2731**

DOCUMENTS - INTERNATIONAL DAIRY FEDERATION (BE) [09141706] **194**

DOCUMENTS JURIDIQUES INTERNATIONAUX (CN/0714-931X) [10007984] **3127**

DOCUMENTS LIST (US/0379-8127) [02141817] **4502**

DOCUMENTS OF MODERN ARCHITECTURE (US/0419-5671) [01657729] **298**

DOCUMENTS OF THE INTERNATIONAL LABOUR CONFERENCE (US) **1664**

DOCUMENTS ON BIOLOGY (US) [01772856] **454**

DOCUMENTS ON BRITISH POLICY OVERSEAS. SERIES 1 (UK) [10648170] **4645**

DOCUMENTS ON CANADIAN EXTERNAL RELATIONS (CN) [01552813] **4520**

DOCUMENTS ON DISARMAMENT (US/0082-8785) [01966148] **4043**

DOCUMENTS PEDAGOGIQUES (FR) [02734132] **3277**

DOCUMENTS POUR LE MEDECIN DU TRAVAIL (FR/0339-6517) [I03396517] **2861**

DOCUMENTS POUR SERVIR A L'HISTOIRE DE L'AFRIQUE EQUATORIALE FRANCAISE. DEUXIEME SERIE: BRAZZA ET LA FONDATION DU CONGO FRANCAIS (FR/0419-5779) [01566849] **2639**

DOCUMENTS SCIENTIFIQUES (SZ) [20857424] 3903, **4190**

DOCUMENTS STRASBOURG (FR/0151-0827) [01510827] **2615**

DOCUMENTS SUR L'ESPERANTO (NE/0165-2621) [I01652621] **3277**

DOCUMENTS TO THE PEOPLE (US/0270-5095) [02683281] **3208**

DOCUMENTS - VIRGINIA HISTORICAL SOCIETY (US/0083-6389) [01555709] **2731**

DOCUMENTS, WORKING PAPERS - COUNCIL OF EUROPE, PARLIAMENTARY ASSEMBLY (FR/0252-0656) [03281462] **3127**

DOD DIRECTORY OF CONTRACT ADMINISTRATION SERVICES COMPONENTS (US/0095-4349) [01796742] **4043**

DOD STATISTICAL REPORT ON THE MILITARY RETIREMENT SYSTEM / OFFICE OF ACTUARY, DEFENSE MANPOWER DATA CENTER (US) [08466512] 4043, **4062**

DODD DIGGINGS (US/0736-2854) [09103337] **2445**

DODGE BUILDING COST AND SPECIFICATION DIGEST (US) [02539116] **613**

DODGE BUILDING COST CALCULATOR & VALUATION GUIDE (US) [05576737] **613**

DODGE CENTER STAR-RECORD (US) [01566854] **5695**

DODGE CITY AREA CHAMBER OF COMMERCE See CHAMBER PROGRESS / DODGE CITY AREA CHAMBER OF COMMERCE, THE **819**

DODGE CITY DAILY GLOBE, THE (US/0889-3489) [11242643] **5675**

DODGE COUNTY INDEPENDENT (US) [01566856] **5695**

DODGE COUNTY INDEPENDENT-NEWS, THE (US) [14402658] **5767**

DODGE REMODEL AND RETROFIT COST DATA See REPAIR & REMODEL QUARTERLY **4846**

DODGE REMODELING & RETROFIT COST DATA (US/1053-3001) [15028975] **613**

DODGE REPORTS (US) [17758774] **613**

DODGE/SWEET'S CONSTRUCTION OUTLOOK / MCGRAW-HILL CONSTRUCTION INFORMATION GROUP (US) [06464822] **613**

DODO (TRINITY) (UK/0265-5640) [04559185] **5581**

DODONAEUS (BE/0774-6318) [I07746318] **2846**

DOD'S EUROPEAN COMPANION See EUROPEAN COMPANION, THE **4521**

DOD'S HISTORY OF PARLIAMENT (UK) [24625097] **2685**

DOD'S PARLIAMENTARY COMPANION (UK/0070-7007) [05862249] **4645**

DOD'S REPORT (UK/0956-0580) [I09560580] **1605**

DOE/ER (UNITED STATES. DEPT. OF ENERGY. OFFICE OF ENERGY RESEARCH) (US/0270-6512) [06032820] **1936**

DOE/ET (US) [05914805] **5101**

DOE HET VEILIG (BE/0773-6231) [I07736231] **2861**

DOE NEW TECHNOLOGY (US/1058-9767) [24451183] **1936**

DOE NEWS / U.S. DEPARTMENT OF ENERGY (US) [07512562] **1936**

DOE STATE & LOCAL ASSISTANCE PROGRAMS (US/0730-3025) [07979127] **1936**

DOE TELEPHONE DIRECTORY (US) [04102978] 1936, **4645**

DOE THIS MONTH (US/1057-5782) [10434778] **1936**

DOEDSARSAKER. HOVEDTABELLER (NO/0550-032X) [01199246] **4561**

DOEHETZELF (NE) 2900, **2773**

DOELMATIG BEDRIJFSBEHEER See DB **1603**

DOFASCO (TORONTO) (CN/1186-8635) [24571119] **788**

DOG FANCY (LOS ANGELES, CALIF.) (US/0892-6522) [13617547] **4286**

DOG INDUSTRY NEWSLETTER (US/1074-777X) [28159287] **4286**

DOG RIVER REVIEW (US/0749-260X) [10902696] **3382**

DOG SPORTS (US/0279-4144) [07833558] 4893, **4286**

DOG SPORTS MAGAZINE See DOG SPORTS **4286**

DOG WATCH (STUDIO CITY, CALIF.) (US/1062-0699) [25424376] **4286**

DOG WATCH, THE (AT) [04748644] **4176**

DOG WORLD (US/0012-4893) [01566865] **4286**

DOG WORLD (UK) **4286**

DOGA BILIM DERGISI. SERI A See DOGA BILIM DERGISI. SERI A2, BIYOLOJI **454**

DOGA BILIM DERGISI. SERI A2, BIYOLOJI (TU) [16775152] **454**

DOGA BILIM DERGISI. SERI B, MUHENDISLIK VE CEVRE (TU) [16775148] **1971**

DOGA BILIM DERGISI. SERI D1, VETERINERLIK VE HAYVANCILIK (TU/1011-0925) [16775128] **5509**

DOGA BILIM DERGISI. SERI D2, TARIM V ORMANCILIK (TU/1011-0917) [16775144] 2378, **80**

DOGA. TURK BIYOLOJI DERGISI (TU/1010-7576) [16264741] **454**

DOGA. TURK BOTANIK DERGISI (TU/1011-0887) [I10110887] **508**

DOGA. TURK KIMYA DERGISI (TU/1010-7614) [16244553] **974**

DOGA. TURK TARIM VE ORMANCLK DERGISI (TU/1010-7649) [16775105] 2378, **80**

DOGA. TURK TIP VE ECZACILIK DERGISI (TU/1010-7584) [I10107584] 4299, **3573**

DOGA. TURK VETERINERLIK VE HAYVANCILIK (TU/1010-7592) [I10107592] **5509**

DOGA. TURK ZOOLOJI DERGISI (TU) [16775089] **5581**

DOGA. TURKISH JOURNAL OF PHYSICS (TU/1010-7630) [24202369] **4402**

DOGA. TURKISH JOURNAL OF VETERINARY AND ANIMAL SCIENCES (TU/1010-7649) [16775102] **5509**

DOGAR MONTHLY GENERAL KNOWLEDGE DIGEST (II) [07901512] **4520**

DOGAR'S MONTHLY GENERAL KNOWLEDGE DIGEST See DOGAR MONTHLY GENERAL KNOWLEDGE DIGEST **4520**

DOGE (FR) **667**

DOGS IN CANADA (CN/0012-4915) [01997006] **4286**

DOGSOLDIER (SPOKANE) (US/0094-3118) [01794258] **3382**

DOHNER FAMILY NEWSLETTER (US/0736-2412) [09078268] **2445**

DOHO DAIGAKU RONSO (JA) [02724580] **5021**

DOHO GAKKAI See DOHO DAIGAKU RONSO **5021**

DOIG'S DIGEST (CN/0827-4290) [13769957] **4254**

DOING BUSINESS ABROAD. JOYNER'S GUIDE TO OFFICIAL WASHINGTON (US/0163-0210) [02312460] **667**

DOING BUSINESS IN AUSTRALIA (US) [06636197] **667**

DOING BUSINESS IN AUSTRIA (US) [09179905] **667**

DOING BUSINESS IN BAHRAIN (US) [08660255] **667**

DOING BUSINESS IN BARBADOS (US) [06995272] **667**

DOING BUSINESS IN BELGIUM (NEW YORK, N.Y. 1978) (US/1057-3828) [06865907] **667**

DOING BUSINESS IN BERMUDA (US) [05527116] **667**

DOING BUSINESS IN BOLIVIA (US) [11715482] **667**

DOING BUSINESS IN CANADA (US/0734-4422) [08659918] **667**

DOING BUSINESS IN CENTRAL AMERICA (US) [07593600] **667**

DOING BUSINESS IN CYPRUS (US/1059-1265) [12534039] **667**

DOING BUSINESS IN CZECHOSLOVAKIA (US) [24316090] 897, **2964**

DOING BUSINESS IN DENMARK (US) [09368536] **667**

DOING BUSINESS IN EASTERN EUROPE (US) [09185553] **667**

DOING BUSINESS IN ECUADOR (US) [07471632] **667**

DOING BUSINESS IN FIJI (US) [07881411] **667**

DOING BUSINESS IN FINLAND (US) [06991868] **667**

DOING BUSINESS IN FRANCE (US) [06870359] **667**

DOING BUSINESS IN GERMANY (US/1049-4057) [06865948] **667**

DOING BUSINESS IN GREECE (US) [06637568] **668**

DOING BUSINESS IN HAWAII (US) [06637479] **668**

DOING BUSINESS IN HONG KONG (US) [06865873] **668**

DOING BUSINESS IN INDIA (US/1057-3844) [07434163] **668**

DOING BUSINESS IN INDONESIA (US) [06637034] **668**

DOING BUSINESS IN IRELAND / DELOITTE HASKINS & SELLS INTERNATIONAL (US) [21064323] **668**

DOING BUSINESS IN ITALY (US) [06636880] **668**

DOING BUSINESS IN JAMAICA (US) [07592452] **668**

DOING BUSINESS IN JAPAN (1975) (US/1057-3925) [06637397] **668**

DOING BUSINESS IN KENYA (US/1047-9953) [14176406] **668**

DOING BUSINESS IN KOREA (US) [10150093] **668**

DOING BUSINESS IN KUWAIT (US) [07593550] **668**

DOING BUSINESS IN LUXEMBOURG (US) [09416310] **668**

DOING BUSINESS IN MALAWI (US) [11579483] **668**

DOING BUSINESS IN MALTA (US) [09695261] **668**

DOING BUSINESS IN MOROCCO (US) [06636843] **668**

DOING BUSINESS IN NEW ZEALAND (US) [07859385] **668**

DOING BUSINESS IN NIGERIA (US) [08777910] **668**

DOING BUSINESS IN NORTHERN IRELAND (US) [06546087] **668**

DOING BUSINESS IN NORWAY (US) [08689914] **668**

DOING BUSINESS IN PANAMA (US) [06865838] **668**

DOING BUSINESS IN PAPUA NEW GUINEA (US) [06359697] **668**

DOING BUSINESS IN PARAGUAY (US/1062-8029) [08657498] **668**

DOING BUSINESS IN PERU (US) [06870332] **668**

DOING BUSINESS IN PORTUGAL (US) [07785074] **668**

DOING BUSINESS IN PUERTO RICO (US) [08656683] **668**

DOING BUSINESS IN QATAR (US) [09900700] **668**

DOING BUSINESS IN SENEGAL (US/1054-6839) [08662183] **668**

DOING BUSINESS IN SINGAPORE (US/1057-3909) [07592535] **668**

DOING BUSINESS IN SOUTH AFRICA (US/1057-3801) [06450861] **668**

DOING BUSINESS IN SPAIN (NEW YORK, N.Y. 1980) (US/1057-3887) [06636309] **668**

DOING BUSINESS IN SWEDEN (US/1059-1281) [06834279] **668**

DOING BUSINESS IN SWITZERLAND (US) [06637112] **668**

DOING BUSINESS IN TAIWAN (US) [06663926] **668**

DOING BUSINESS IN THE BAHAMAS (US) [06446147] **668**

DOING BUSINESS IN THE CAYMAN ISLANDS (US) [06839607] **668**

DOING BUSINESS IN THE CHANNEL ISLANDS (US) [07711375] **668**

DOING BUSINESS IN THE DOMINICAN REPUBLIC (US) [07593144] **668**

DOING BUSINESS IN THE EUROPEAN COMMUNITY (US) [24450269] 897, 4720, **2964**

DOING BUSINESS IN THE ISLE OF MAN (US) [23996688] 897, **2964**

DOING BUSINESS IN THE NETHERLANDS ANTILLES (US/1049-4081) [06870316] **668**

DOING BUSINESS IN THE NETHERLANDS (NEW YORK, N.Y. 1980) (US/1059-2849) [06865891] **668**

DOING BUSINESS IN THE NEW HEBRIDES (US) [08657291] **669**

DOING BUSINESS IN THE PEOPLE'S REPUBLIC OF CHINA (US/1059-2857) [06548083] **669**

DOING BUSINESS IN THE PHILIPPINES (US) [07592604] **669**

DOING BUSINESS IN THE REPUBLIC OF IRELAND (US) [07471618] **669**

●DOING BUSINESS IN THE RUSSIAN FEDERATION (US/1078-5108) [30373292] **2964**

DOING BUSINESS IN THE UNION OF SOVIET SOCIALIST REPUBLICS *See* DOING BUSINESS IN THE RUSSIAN FEDERATION **2964**

DOING BUSINESS IN THE UNITED ARAB EMIRATES (US) [07592875] **669**

DOING BUSINESS IN THE UNITED KINGDOM (US) [06839208] **669**

DOING BUSINESS IN THE UNITED KINGDOM. SUPPLEMENT (US) [16891207] **669**

DOING BUSINESS IN THE UNITED STATES (NEW YORK, N.Y. 1980) (US/1057-8684) [06995251] **669**

DOING BUSINESS IN TRINIDAD AND TOBAGO (US) [06726891] **669**

DOING BUSINESS IN TURKEY (US) [12739911] **669**

DOING BUSINESS IN URUGUAY (US) [06637162] **669**

DOING BUSINESS IN VENEZUELA (US) [07593734] **669**

DOING BUSINESS IN WESTERN SAMOA (US) [06843592] **669**

DOING BUSINESS IN ZIMBABWE (US/1057-381X) [11569108] **669**

DOING BUSINESS WITH THE USSR (UK/1044-1093) [19683767] **669**

DOING RIGHT THINGS RIGHT (US/1070-678X) [28452155] **669**

DOJ ALERT, THE (US/1056-2230) [23587424] **3140**

DOJIN NYUSU (JA/0385-1516) [05910370] **1014**

DOJO ARTS MARTIAUX *CEASED*. (FR) **4893**

DOKKYO JOURNAL OF MEDICAL SCIENCES (JA/0385-5023) [02134195] **3573**

DOKLADHOI AKADEMIAI FANHOI RSS TOCIKISTON (TA/0002-3469) [05725541] 454, 4402, **3504**

DOKLADHOI AKADEMIIAI ILMHOI JUMHURII TOJIKISTON / DOKLADY AKADEMII NAUK RESPUBLIKI TADZHIKISTAN (TA) [28475929] **5101**

DOKLADI NA BULGARSKATA AKADEMIIA NA NAUKITE (BU) [24944350] **5101**

DOKLADY (BU/0587-2650) [01777626] **80**

DOKLADY AKADEMII NAUK (US) **1024**

●DOKLADY AKADEMII NAUK BELARUSI (BW) [26126157] **5101**

DOKLADY AKADEMII NAUK BSSR *See* DOKLADY AKADEMII NAUK BELARUSI **5101**

●DOKLADY AKADEMII NAUK / ROSSIISKAIA AKADEMIIA NAUK (RU/0869-5652) [26002128] **5101**

DOKLADY AKADEMII NAUK SSSR (RU/0002-3264) [01478791] **1354**

DOKLADY AKADEMII NAUK TADZHIKSKOÊI SSR *See* DOKLADHOI AKADEMIIAI ILMHOI JUMHURII TOJIKISTON / DOKLADY AKADEMII NAUK RESPUBLIKI TADZHIKISTAN **5101**

DOKLADY AKADEMII NAUK UKRAINSKOI SSR. SERIIA A, FIZIKO-MATEMATICHESKIE I TEKHNICHESKIE NAUKI (UN) [20666719] 4402, **3504**

DOKLADY AKADEMII NAUK UKRAINSKOI SSR. SERIIA B, GEOLOGICHESKIE, KHIMICHESKIE I BIOLOGICHESKIE NAUKI (UN/0201-8454) [10566079] **5101**

DOKLADY AKADEMII NAUK UZSSR *See* UZBEKISTON RESPUBLIKASI FANLAR AKADEMIIASINING MABRUZALARI **5168**

DOKLADY / AKADEMIIA NAUK AZERBAIDZHANA (AJ) [27990355] **5101**

DOKLADY / AKADEMIIA NAUK AZERBAIDZHANSKOI SSR (AJ/0002-3078) [02829658] **5101**

DOKLADY. BIOCHEMISTRY (US/0012-4958) [01478785] **486**

DOKLADY. BIOLOGICAL SCIENCES (US/0012-4966) [02254790] **454**

DOKLADY. BIOPHYSICS (US/0012-4974) [01478787] **495**

DOKLADY. BOTANICAL SCIENCES (US/0012-4982) [01478789] **508**

DOKLADY. CHEMISTRY (US/0012-5008) [01913541] **974**

DOKLADY I SOOBSCENIJA INSTITUTA ISTORII (RU/0568-5796) [05688113] **2615**

DOKLADY. MATHEMATICS (US/1064-5624) [26328383] **3504**

●DOKLADY MATHEMATICS (RU) **3504**

DOKLADY NA EZHEGODNOM CHTENII PAMIATI N. A. KHOLODKOVSKOGO (RU) [05543034] **5581**

DOKLADY. PHYSICAL CHEMISTRY (US/0012-5016) [07436211] **1051**

DOKLADY. PHYSICAL CHEMISTRY (US/0012-5016) [02053030] **1051**

●DOKLADY ROSSIISKOI AKADEMII SELSKOKHOZIAISTVENNYKH NAUK (RU) [26961063] **80**

DOKLADY VSESOIUZNOI AKADEMII SELSKOKHOZIAISTVENNYKH NAUK IMENI V.I. LENINA *See* DOKLADY ROSSIISKOI AKADEMII SELSKOKHOZIAISTVENNYKH NAUK **80**

DOKLADY VSESOIUZNOI ORDENA LENINA I ORDENA TRUDOVOGO KRASNOGO ZNAMENI AKADEMII SELSKOKHOZIAISTVENNYKH NAUK IMENI V. I LENINA (RU) [11862303] **80**

DOKLADY VSESOUZNOJ ORDENA LENINA AKADEMII SELSKOHOZAJSTVENNYH NAUK IM. V.I. LENINA (RU/0042-9244) [01769308] **80**

DOKTORSAVHANDLINGAR VID CHALMERS TEKNISKA HOGSKOLA (SW/0366-8746) [02399559] **5101**

DOKUMENT - DEUTSCHE STIFTUNG FUR INTERNATIONALE ENTWICKLUNG (GW) [02510010] **1555**

DOKUMENTAAL (NE) 3382, **3277**

DOKUMENTACJA GEOGRAFICZNA (PL/0012-5032) [03942913] **2560**

DOKUMENTACNI SLUZBA *See* OBCHOD VE SVETE **848**

DOKUMENTATION ARBEITSMEDIZIN (GW/0340-3238) [04741893] **3796**

DOKUMENTATION DEUTSCHSPRACHIGER VERLAGE (GW) [06219114] **4814**

DOKUMENTATION FUER UMWELTSCHUTZ UND LANDESPFLEGE (GW/0026-6957) [01476475] **2191**

DOKUMENTATION : MEDIZIN IM UMWELTSCHUTZ (GW/0342-0795) [04997812] **3573**

DOKUMENTATION NATUR UND LANDSCHAFT (GW/0936-0948) [24425235] **2191**

DOKUMENTATION OSTMITTELEUROPA (GW/0340-3297) [02241890] **2685**

DOKUMENTATION STRASSE (GW/0012-5148) [I00125148] 1971, **2003**

DOKUMENTATION WASSER ABFALL (GW) **5532**

DOKUMENTATION WESTEUROPA (GW) [23208112] **2685**

DOKUMENTATION. WETTBEWERB, PANORAMA, KINDERFILMFEST / INTERNATIONALE FILMFESTSPIELE BERLIN (GW/0724-7117) [19770386] **4068**

DOKUMENTATIONEN DES STADTARCHIVS NEUSS (GW/0933-0321) [19470811] **4087**

DOKUMENTATIONS-LEITSTELLE MODERNER ORIENT (DEUTSCHES ORIENT-INSTITUT) *See* KURZDARSTELLUNG DER DOKUMENTATIONS-LEITSTELLE MODERNER ORIENT UND TATIGKEITSBERICHT **3222**

DOKUMENTATIONSDIENST AFRIKA. AUSGEWAHLTE NEUERE LITERATUR (GW/0342-040X) [08972647] 5244, **2496**

DOKUMENTATIONSDIENST LATEINAMERIKA. AUSGEWAHLTE NEUERE LITERATUR (GW/0342-037X) [01784825] **5198**

DOKUMENTE DER MODERNEN ARCHITEKTUR *CEASED*. (GW/0419-5981) [01667764] **298**

DOKUMENTE - INSTITUT FUER INTERNATIONALE ANGELEGENHEITEN DER UNIVERSITAT HAMBURG *CEASED*. (GW) [03264329] **3127**

DOKUMENTE (KOLN) (GW/0012-5172) [02446433] **5198**

DOKUMENTE ZUR DEUTSCHLANDPOLITIK (GW/0070-7031) [08042842] **2685**

DOLCIANI MATHEMATICAL EXPOSITIONS, THE (US/0884-4461) [01781788] **3504**

DOLENTIUM HOMINUM : JOURNAL OF THE PONTIFICAL COUNCIL FOR PASTORAL ASSISTANCE TO HEALTH CARE WORKERS (IT) **5244**

DOLL & TOY (UK) [12187658] **2773**

DOLL & TOY COLLECTOR (LONDON) *CEASED*. (CN/0840-3813) [19461903] **2773**

DOLL ARTISTRY *CEASED*. (US/1052-0805) [22177012] **2773**

DOLL CASTLE NEWS (US/0363-7972) [02541796] **372**

DOLL COLLECTOR'S PRICE GUIDE (US/1072-6381) [29147444] **5183**

DOLL CRAFTER (US/0746-9624) [10426329] **372**

DOLL DESIGNS *CEASED*. (US/1050-4796) [21498538] **372**

DOLL NEWS (US/0191-460X) [04902240] **2773**

DOLL READER (US/0744-0901) [02252973] 2773, **2584**

DOLL TALK FOR COLLECTORS *CEASED*. (US/0012-5229) [01566869] **2773**

DOLL TIMES (US) [08204992] **2584**

DOLL WORLD (BERNE, IND.) (US/1066-4726) [26948892] **372**

DOLLAR Alphabetical Title Index

DOLLAR LINES (US/1045-4578) [20116219] **1605**

DOLLAR WISE GUIDE TO ENGLAND (US) [02539148] **5468**

DOLLAR WISE GUIDE TO ENGLAND AND SCOTLAND / BY STANLEY HAGGART AND DARWIN PORTER (US) [04736365] **5468**

DOLLAR$ENSE (LOS ANGELES) (US/0194-8490) [05057256] **788, 1296**

DOLLARS & CENTS OF SHOPPING CENTERS, THE (US/0070-704X) [01768864] **4837**

DOLLARS...AND DECISIONS (US) [01662411] **1296**

DOLLARS & SENSE (CHICAGO, ILL.) (US/0884-5611) [06744947] **2259, 669**

DOLLARS & SENSE (SOMERVILLE, MASS.) (US/0012-5245) [01185225] **3341, 1480**

DOLLARS & SENSE (WASHINGTON, D.C. 1979) (US/0745-9092) [09509374] **4720**

DOLLS (US/0733-2238) [08534883] **372**

DOLLS AND DOLLS HOUSES (US) [20815637] **373**

DOLLS IN MINIATURE : THE MAGAZINE (US/1058-157X) [24231270] **2773**

DOLLY (AT/0811-7179) [I08117179] **1063**

DOLMETSCH FOUNDATION, HASLEMERE, ENGLAND *See* BULLETIN - DOLMETSCH FOUNDATION **4106**

DOLOR (SP/0214-0659) [I02140659] **3573**

DOLOR & INFLAMACION : FARMACOTERAPIA, INVESTIGACION Y CLINICA MEDICA / PATROCINADA POR LIGA REUMATOLOGICA ESPANOLA (LIRE) (SP/0214-1485) [25714460] **3804**

DOLORES STAR (US/0889-5155) [11176410] **5642**

DOLPHIN (ARRHUS, DENMARK) (DK/0106-4487) [09613926] **3382**

DOLPHIN DIGEST (US/0744-3226) [08189990] **4893**

DOLPHIN LOG (US/8756-6362) [08300470] **1063, 1448**

DOLPHIN UPDATE (CN/1185-1783) [24280690] **5449**

DOM (PL/0209-147X) [19506906] **319**

DOM I WNETRZE (PL/0867-2105) [I08672105] **2900**

DOM POLITICHESKOGO PROSVESHCHENIIA MK I MGK KPSS *See* PRIMERNYE TEMATIKA I PLANY TEORETICHESKIKH SEMINAROV **4545**

DOMA INFORMATIONSDIENST : FEINBEARBEITUNG (GW) **2113**

DOMA INFORMATIONSDIENST : NEUE WERKSTOFFE FUER DEN MASCHINEN UND ANLAGENBAU (GW) **2113**

DOMANKONCERNEN (SW) [18236788] **2378**

DOMANVERKET *See* DOMANKONCERNEN **2378**

● DOMES (MILWAUKEE, WIS.) (US/1060-4367) [25028067] **3208, 2768**

DOMESTIC AFFAIRS (US/1060-0655) [24296110] **4472**

DOMESTIC AIR SERVICE INSTRUCTIONS (US) [06582851] **1144**

DOMESTIC & FOREIGN TRUCK & VAN PRICES NEW AND USED *See* PACE BUYER'S GUIDES. DOMESTIC & FOREIGN TRUCK, VAN, 4X4 PRICES, NEW & USED **5422**

DOMESTIC AND IMPORTED EARLY MODEL ESTIMATING GUIDE (US) **5413**

DOMESTIC AND IMPORTED VEHICLES TOWING MANUAL (US/0735-0333) [08855076] **5413**

DOMESTIC AND INTERNATIONAL COMMERCIAL LOAN CHARGE-OFFS (US/0192-7639) [04449567] **788**

DOMESTIC ANIMAL ENDOCRINOLOGY (US/0739-7240) [09834328] **5509, 3728**

DOMESTIC BASE FACTORS REPORT (US/0192-1150) [04952388] **4043**

DOMESTIC CAR AND LIGHT TRUCK TRANSMISSION MANUAL (US) **5413**

DOMESTIC CARS REPAIR MANUAL MECHANICAL PARTS AND LABOR ESTIMATING MANUAL (US) **5413**

DOMESTIC CARS SERVICE & REPAIR (US/1041-4290) [16143032] **5413**

DOMESTIC CARS SERVICE AND REPAIR MANUAL. ELECTRICAL (US) **5413**

DOMESTIC CARS SERVICE AND REPAIR MANUAL. ELECTRICAL COMPONENT LOCATOR (US) **5413**

DOMESTIC CARS SERVICE AND REPAIR MANUAL. ENGINE PERFORMANCE (US) **5413**

DOMESTIC CARS SERVICE AND REPAIR MANUAL. HEATING AND AIR CONDITIONING (US) **5413**

DOMESTIC LIGHT TRUCKS AND VANS SERVICE AND REPAIR *See* MITCHELL DOMESTIC LIGHT TRUCKS AND VANS SERVICE AND REPAIR **5387**

DOMESTIC LIGHT TRUCKS AND VANS SERVICE AND REPAIR MANUAL. ANNUAL DATA ENGINE PERFORMANCE / ELECTRICAL / MECHANICAL (US) **5413**

DOMESTIC LIGHT TRUCKS AND VANS SERVICE AND REPAIR MANUAL ELECTRICAL (US) **5413**

DOMESTIC LIGHT TRUCKS AND VANS SERVICE AND REPAIR MANUAL ENGINE PERFORMANCE (US) **5413**

DOMESTIC MAIL MANUAL (US/1058-0867) [05153904] **1144**

DOMESTIC MERGER YEARBOOK *See* ... US MERGER YEARBOOK, THE **717**

DOMESTIC TRANSMISSIONS, SERVICE & REPAIR (US) [07626187] **5413**

DOMESTIC TRAVEL IN VICTORIA (AT) [10137362] **5468**

DOMESTIC TRAVEL IN WESTERN AUSTRALIA (AT) [16458601] **5468**

DOMESTIC VEHICLES TOWING MANUAL *See* DOMESTIC AND IMPORTED VEHICLES TOWING MANUAL **5413**

DOMESTIC VIOLENCE LAW BULLETIN *CEASED.* (US/0895-8858) [16850607] **3120**

DOMESTIC VIOLENCE MONOGRAPH SERIES / NATIONAL CLEARINGHOUSE ON DOMESTIC VIOLENCE (US) [07300132] **2278**

DOMESTIC WATERBORNE TRADE OF THE UNITED STATES (US) [02568959] **831**

DOMINGUEZIA (AG) [08085003] **508**

DOMINICA, WIRTSCHAFTSDATEN / BUNDESSTELLE FUER AUSSENHANDELSINFORMATION (GW) [11460648] **1555**

DOMINICAINS. PROVINCE CANADIENNE DE SAINT-DOMINIQUE *See* ANNUAIRE / FRERES PRECHEURS, PROVINCE SAINT-DOMINIQUE DU CANADA **4935**

DOMINICAN REPUBLIC *See* GACETA OFICIAL - REPUBLICA DOMINICANA **2973**

DOMINICAN REPUBLIC. BOLETIN OFICIAL *See* GACETA OFICIAL - REPUBLICA DOMINICANA **2973**

DOMINICAN REPUBLIC. CAMARA DE CUENTAS *See* BOLETIN DE LA CAMARA DE CUENTAS Y DEL TRIBUNAL SUPERIOR ADMINISTRATIVO **4713**

DOMINICAN REPUBLIC. DEPARTAMENTO DE ECONOMIA AGROPECUARIA *See* BOLETIN INFORMATIVO DE PRECIOS Y MERCADOS **67**

DOMINICAN REPUBLIC. DIRECCION GENERAL DE ESTADISTICA *See* BOLETIN DE DIVULGACIONES **4163**

DOMINICAN REPUBLIC, THE (US) [01625741] **2532**

DOMINIKANISCHE REPUBLIK, WIRTSCHAFTSDATEN / BUNDESSTELLE FUER AUSSENHANDELSINFORMATION (GW) [10931528] **1555**

DOMINION LAW REPORTS (CN/0012-5350) [06300974] **3089**

DOMINION LAW REPORTS. FOURTH SERIES, INDEX, ANNOTATIONS, TABLE OF CASES (CN/0836-5768) [12776453] **2964**

DOMINION POST (US) [13118992] **5763**

DOMINION TAX CASES (CN/0046-0567) [02442993] **4721**

DOMINION (TORONTO) (CN/0827-2395) [11734398] **5059**

DOMODOMO : FIJI MUSEUM QUARTERLY *SUSPENDED.* (FJ) [09632727] **4087**

DOMOSTROI (RU) [27365465] **5809**

DOMOTIQUE NEWS PARIS (FR/0989-8107) [I09898107] **5101**

DOMUS (IT/0012-5377) [02108210] **298, 2900**

DOMUS MAZZINIANA *See* BOLLETTINO DELLA DOMUS MAZZINIANA **2679**

DOMYAKU KOKA (JA/0386-2682) [I03862682] **3704**

DON (RU/0130-3562) [02260480] **3382**

DON BALON (SP) **4893**

DON CLEARY'S RECORD COLLECTORS DIRECTORY (US/0197-2626) [05970434] **2773, 5316**

DON KORN'S BREAKTHROUGH INVESTING *CEASED.* (US/1046-8315) [20553512] **897**

DON LARSON'S BUSINESS NEWSLETTER (US/0894-1882) [10254586] **669**

● DON THE BEAR SERIES (US/1062-1385) [25531949] **3382, 1063**

DONALD R. MORRIS NEWSLETTER (US/1053-5829) [22590617] **4520**

DONALDSON, LUFKIN & JENRETTE, INC *See* ELECTRIC UTILITY STATISTICAL REFERENCE **2003**

DONALDSON, LUFKIN & JENRETTE SECURITIES CORPORATION *See* RELATIVE VALUE ANALYSIS **912**

DONALDSON, LUFKIN & JENRETTE SECURITIES CORPORATION *See* EXPANSION SURVEY, RETAIL TRADE INDUSTRY **954**

DONALDSONVILLE CHIEF (DONALDSONVILLE, LA. : 1871) (US) [12597940] **5683**

DONAUSCHWABISCHE FORSCHUNGS- UND LEHRERBLATTER (GW) [06340896] **2685**

DONAUSCHWABISCHE LEHRERBLATTER (GW) [03176000] **1737**

DONAUZEITUNG (AU) [20070910] **5778**

DONBAS : LITERATURNO-KHUDOZHNII TA HROMADS'KO-POLITYCHNYI ZHURNAL SPILKY PYSMENNYKIV UKRAINY (UN/0321-1363) [05525615] **2138**

DONBASS *See* DONBAS : LITERATURNO-KHUDOZHNII TA HROMADS'KO-POLITYCHNYI ZHURNAL SPILKY PYSMENNYKIV UKRAINY **2138**

DONCASTER AND DISTRICT ORNITHOLOGICAL SOCIETY *See* REPORT ON THE BIRDS OF THE DONCASTER DISTRICT **5620**

DONDEVIVIR : REVISTA DE PROPIEDADES (CL) [08380246] **2821**

DONEGAL ANNUAL (IE/0416-2773) [03835957] **2685**

DONEN (JA) [04214808] **2154**

DONG BANG HAK CHI (KO) [01566896] **1737**

DONGBEI GONGXUEYUAN XUEBAO (CC/0253-4258) [09152187] **5101**

DONGBEI NONGXUEYUAN XUEBAO (CC/0253-228X) [08863494] **80**

DONGHAI HAIYANG (CC/1001-909X) [I1001909X] **554**

DONGNAN DAXUE XUEBAO (CC/1001-0505) [I10010505] **1971, 5101**

DONGWU FENLEI XUEBAO (CC/1000-0739) [07024636] **5581**

DONGWUXUE JIKAN (CC/1000-1786) [08854981] **5581**

DONGWUXUE YANJIU (CC/0254-5853) [08249288] **5582**

DONGWUXUE ZAZHI (CC/0250-3263) [02583408] **5582**

DONIZETTI SOCIETY *See* NEWSLETTER - THE DONIZETTI SOCIETY **5234**

DONIZETTI SOCIETY JOURNAL (UK/0307-1448) [02241020] **4115**

DONKEY DIGEST (AT/1031-6280) **5582**

● DONKEY TALK (US/1062-3426) [25589884] **1063, 4954**

DONNA & BAMBINI (IT) **1083**

DONNA (DOWNSVIEW) (CN/0225-4786) [06053895] **5554**

DONNA. INTERNATIONAL EDITION (IT) **5554**

DONNA MODERNA (IT) **5554**

DONNA PIU *See* MARIE CLAIRE (ITALIAN EDITION) **5561**

DONNE PARLEMENTO E SOCIETA (IT) **4472**

DONNEES BUDGETAIRES RELATIVES A L'EDUCATION NATIONALE (FR) [03095503] **1862**

DONNEES ECONOMIQUES DES REGIONS FRONTALIEERES SAAR-LOR-LUX (GW) [06258356] **1555**

DONNEES SOCIALES (FR/0758-6531) [03903976] **5244**

DONNEES STATISTIQUES DU LIMOUSIN (FR/0395-8280) [06268059] **5326**

DONNEES SUR LA POPULATION ACTIVE : QUEBEC, ONTARIO ET CANADA (CN/0715-1055) [09184926] **5326**

DONNELLEY SEC HANDBOOK (US/0273-3633) [07028466] **3099**

DONNELLSON STAR, THE (US) [14278667] **5670**

DONOGHUE'S MONEY FUND DIRECTORY *See* IBC/DONOGHUE'S MONEY FUND DIRECTORY **900**

DONOGHUE'S MONEYLETTER (US/0197-7083) [06099451] **788, 897**

DONOR BRIEFING *CEASED.* (US/0886-9359) [13041340] **5284**

Alphabetical Title Index — DOWN

DONOSY (WASHINGTON, D.C.) (US/1059-4027) [24602131] **2487**

DONT ACTE (CN/0381-1875) [05842147] **669**

DON'T MISS OUT (US/0277-6987) [05661178] **1822**

DONUM DEI (ENGLISH ED.) (CN/0318-0123) [02539136] **4954**

DONZERE MONDRAGON (FR) [02210244] **1664**

●DOODY'S HEALTH SCIENCES BOOK REVIEW JOURNAL (US/1071-7560) [28762004] **5101**

DOOM PATROL, THE (US) [17288019] **4860**

DOON PRESS (US) [16747611] **5670**

DOOPSGEZIND JAARBOEKJE (NE) [10129957] **4954**

DOOR COUNTY ADVOCATE (US/0749-7180) [11167199] **5767**

DOOR (EL CAJON, CALIF.) (US/1044-7512) [19357555] **4954**

DOORS AND HARDWARE (US/0361-5294) [02246674] **613**

DOPOVIDI AKADEMII NAUK UKRAINY. MATEMATYKA, PRYRODOZNAVSTVO, TEKHNICHNI NAUKY : NAUKOVYI HURNAL PREZYDII AN UKRAINY (UN) [25910220] **3504**

DORAVILLE DEKALB NEIGHBOR, THE (US/0199-7289) [06105568] **5653**

DORAVILLE NEIGHBOR *See* DORAVILLE DEKALB NEIGHBOR, THE **5653**

DORCHESTER COUNTY GENEALOGICAL MAGAZINE, THE (US/8755-2353) [11216515] **2445**

DORCHESTER EAGLE-RECORD (US) [27969769] **5742**

DOREM AFRIKE (SA) [01800240] **2259**

DORIS LESSING NEWSLETTER (US/0882-486X) [03702602] **3382**

DORITSU MIGISHI KOTARO BIJUTSUKAN HO (JA) [06913398] **349**

DORLAND'S ILLUSTRATED MEDICAL DICTIONARY (US) [04802975] **3573**

DORLAND'S POCKET MEDICAL DICTIONARY (US) [05528410] **3573**

DORLS TECHNICAL SERVICES COMMITTEE *See* D O R L S TECHNICAL SERVICES COMMITTEE'S INFORMATION EXCHANGE **3205**

DORM (US/0743-2860) [10546147] **1091**

DORNIER-POST (GW/0012-5563) [10492801] **18**

DOROT (US/0886-2796) [12893391] **2445**

DOROTHEUM. KUNSTABTEILUNG *See* KUNSTAUKTION **356**

DOROTHEUM. KUNSTABTEILUNG *See* KUNSTVERSTEIGERUNG **356**

●DOROTHY KAMM'S PORCELAIN COLLECTOR'S COMPANION (US/1065-7789) [26734153] **2773**

DOROTHY L. SAYERS HISTORICAL AND LITERARY SOCIETY. CONVENTION *See* PROCEEDINGS OF THE ... CONVENTION **3425**

DORS OPENERS (US) [14923735] **5284, 4387**

●DORSANEO & SOULES' TEXAS CODES AND RULES. CIVIL LITIGATION (US) [26948813] **2964**

DORSANEO'S TEXAS CODES AND RULES. CIVIL LITIGATION (US/1064-7368) [25258376] **2964**

DORSET HORN AND POLL DORSET SHEEP BREEDERS' ASSOCIATION *See* FLOCK BOOK OF DORSET HORN AND POLL DORSET SHEEP, THE **211**

DORSET NATURAL HISTORY AND ARCHAEOLOGICAL SOCIETY *See* PROCEEDINGS - DORSET NATURAL HISTORY AND ARCHAEOLOGICAL SOCIETY **4170**

DORSEY DREAMS (US/0742-0846) [10237358] **2445**

DORTMUND. INSTITUT FUR WASSERFORSCHUNG *See* VEROFFENTLICHUNGEN DES INSTITUTS FUER WASSERFORSCHUNG GMBH DORTMUND UND DER HYDROLOGISCHEN ABTEILUNG DER DORTMUNDER STADTWERKE AG **5541**

DORTMUNDER BEITRAGE ZUR ZEITUNGSFORSCHUNG (GW/0417-9994) [03010180] **2919**

DORYOKURO KAKUNENRYO KAIHATSU JIGYODAN *See* DONEN **2154**

DO'S AND DON'TS IN ADVERTISING (US) **1296**

DOS EXTRA (GW/0934-2842) [I09342842] **1183**

DOS INTERNATIONAL (GW/0933-1557) [I09331557] **1183**

DOS RESOURCE GUIDE (US/1056-7364) [23835154] **1202**

DOS SPECIAL (NE) [I09294929] **1183**

DOS USER'S JOURNAL *CEASED.* (US/1063-2271) [25933930] **1292**

●DOS-WIN SPECIAL (NE/0929-5011) [I09295011] **1183**

DOS WORLD (US) **1207**

DOSENTENKURSUS (SA) [02864764] **1822**

DOSHISHA AMERIKA KENKYU (JA/0420-0918) [11188946] **2615**

DOSHISHA DAIGAKU *See* DOSHISHA DAIGAKU RIKOGAKU KENKYU HOKOKU **5102**

DOSHISHA DAIGAKU. DAIGAKUIN *See* DOSHISHA DAIGAKU DAIGAKUIN SHOGAKU RONSHU **1556**

DOSHISHA DAIGAKU DAIGAKUIN SHOGAKU RONSHU (JA) [06592389] **1556**

DOSHISHA DAIGAKU EIGO EIBUNGAKU KENKYU (JA/0286-1291) [06418649] **3277**

DOSHISHA DAIGAKU RIKOGAKU KENKYU HOKOKU (JA/0036-8172) [02446438] 1971, **5102**

DOSHISHA DANSO (JA) [08964612] **1822**

DOSHISHA GAIKOKU BUNGAKU KENKYU (JA) [01790307] **3382**

DOSHISHA KOKUBUNGAKU (JA) [08690847] **3382**

DOSHISHA LITERATURE (JA/0046-063X) [05638520] **3382**

DOSHKOLNOE VOSPITANIE (RU/0012-561X) [01566911] **1737**

DOSSIER AMBIENTE (IT) **2213**

DOSSIER CASA (IT) **2905**

DOSSIER DE L'ART (FR) [25807604] **349**

DOSSIER DE L'EUROPE (LU/0379-3109) [I03793109] **1480**

DOSSIER DU CENTRE NATIONAL D'INFORMATION SUR LE MEDICAMENT HOSPITALIER (FR/0223-5242) [I02235242] **4299**

DOSSIER ECONOMIQUE (SALE, MOROCCO) *See* DOSSIER SOCIO-POLITIQUE **4472**

DOSSIER HERTOGENBOSCH (NE/0925-1057) [I09251057] **1480**

DOSSIER - INSTITUTE DE RECHERCHE EN EXPLORATION MINERALE (CN/0714-4865) [09074904] **2138**

DOSSIER. L'UFFICIO TECNICO (IT/0394-8315) [I03948315] **298**

DOSSIER POELES A BOIS (CN/0822-5877) [10220660] **2604**

DOSSIER SOCIO-POLITIQUE (MR) [11476449] **4472**

DOSSIER (WASHINGTON, D.C.) *CEASED.* (US/0891-5741) [14347840] **2532**

DOSSIER - WOMEN LIVING UNDER MUSLIM LAWS (PK/1018-1342) [I10181342] 4507, **5554**

DOSSIERS (FR) **1110**

DOSSIERS ARCHEOLOGIQUES, HISTORIQUES ET CULTURELS DU NORD ET DU PAS-DE-CALAIS (FR/0150-0104) [I01500104] 267, **2685**

DOSSIERS BREVETS... CENTRE DU DROIT DE L'ENTREPRISE (FR/0992-8421) [I09928421] **1304**

DOSSIERS CSN (1980 OCT.) (CN/0821-4433) [09551417] **1664**

DOSSIERS D'ARCHEOLOGIE, LES (FR) [20123314] **267**

DOSSIERS DE LA BIBLE, LES (FR/0761-7267) [12071072] **4954**

DOSSIERS DE L'AUDIOVISUEL (FR/0767-4775) [14442486] **3278**

DOSSIERS DE L'ECONOMIE LORRAINE, LES (FR) [04889259] **1556**

DOSSIERS DE L'ELEVAGE, LES *SUSPENDED.* (FR/0150-0112) [04400124] **5509**

DOSSIERS DE L'HISTOIRE (FR/0419-683X) [01682247] **2615**

DOSSIERS DE L'OUTRE-MER : BULLETIN D'INFORMATION DU CENADDOM, LES (FR/0337-4084) [13073723] 4645, **1556**

DOSSIERS DU CANARD, LES (FR/0292-5354) [10806690] **4472**

DOSSIERS DU CENTRE REGIONAL ARCHEOLOGIQUE D'ALET, LES (FR/0399-6662) [03969660] **267**

DOSSIERS DU CEPED, LES (FR/0993-6165) [22205088] **4552**

DOSSIERS DU MARKETING DIRECT, LES (FR/0769-5918) [I07695918] **923**

DOSSIERS ET DEBATS - INSTITUT INTERNATIONAL D'ADMINISTRATION PUBLIQUE (FR/1152-5096) [I11525096] **4645**

DOSSIERS ET DOCUMENTS - INSTITUT FRANCAIS D'ARCHITECTURE (FR/0759-9048) [10976337] **298**

DOSSIERS POUR L'ANIMATION BIBLIQUE (FR) [08999215] **5016**

DOSSIERS STATISTIQUES DU TRAVAIL ET DE L'EMPLOI (FR) [11860247] **1664**

DOSSIERS TECHNIQUES PAUL HUET. ELECTRICITE ELECTRONIQUE (FR) **2042**

DOSSIERS TECHNIQUES PAUL HUET / HYDRAULIQUE PNEUMATIQUE (FR) **2088**

DOSSIERS TECHNIQUES PAUL HUET / MECANIQUE (FR) **2113**

DOSSIERS TECHNIQUES PAUL HUET / TRANSMISSION MECANIQUE (FR) **2113**

DOSTOEVSKY STUDIES : JOURNAL OF THE INTERNATIONAL DOSTOEVSKY SOCIETY (AU/1013-2309) [07475685] **3382**

DOTHAN EAGLE, THE (US/0745-855X) [09512126] **5626**

DOTOKU TO KYOIKU (JA) [09262414] 2249, **1737**

DOUBLE FEATURE (LETHBRIDGE) (CN/0824-278X) [10061631] **2278**

DOUBLE-GUN JOURNAL, THE (US/1050-2262) [21427658] **4893**

DOUBLE LIAISON (FR/0012-5709) [02446440] 349, **4223**

DOUBLE LIAISON-CHIMIE DES PEINTURES (FR/0012-5709) [02252143] **4223**

DOUBLE PAGE (FR/0240-8392) [09630323] **4369**

DOUBLE PLATINUM CIRCUS (US/0198-8654) [06229655] **4115**

DOUBLE REED, THE (US/0741-7659) [04026787] **4115**

DOUBLE TALK (US/0889-8804) [14137503] **2789**

DOUBLE TRESSURE : JOURNAL OF THE HERALDRY SOCIETY OF SCOTLAND, THE (UK/0141-237X) [07528723] **2445**

DOUGHTY TREE, THE (US/0897-3350) [09005126] **2446**

DOUGLAS COUNTY GAZETTE *See* DOUGLAS COUNTY POST-GAZETTE **5706**

DOUGLAS COUNTY PIONEER (US/0895-7444) [16786196] **2446**

DOUGLAS COUNTY POST-GAZETTE (US/0746-1437) [09796943] **5706**

DOUGLAS COUNTY SENTINEL (US) [19717829] **5653**

DOUGLAS DAILY DISPATCH (US) [10309567] **5630**

DOUGLAS ENTERPRISE, THE (US) [19332322] **5653**

DOUGLAS NEIGHBOR, THE (US/0192-0758) [04997691] **5653**

DOUGLAS TRAILS AND TRACES (US/0741-6954) [10176574] **2446**

DOULEUR ET ANALGESIE (SZ/1011-288X) [I1011288X] **3573**

DOUSOU SHUANGYUEKAN (HK/0301-9489) [01797507] **2503**

DOVE MARINE LABORATORY *See* CONTRIBUTIONS - THE DOVE MARINE LABORATORY **554**

DOVE MILANO (IT/1121-1792) [I11211792] **5468**

DOVER POST (US/0191-5037) [04934974] **5647**

DOW, JONES & CO *See* DOW JONES STOCK OPTIONS HANDBOOK, THE **897**

DOW JONES STOCK OPTIONS HANDBOOK, THE (US/0147-5649) [03197648] **897**

DOW THEORY FORECASTS (US/0300-7324) [01774716] **897**

DOWLINE (US/1052-3545) [10012311] **788**

DOWN BEAT (US/0012-5768) [02260489] **4115**

DOWN EAST (US/0012-5776) [01683246] **5468**

DOWN HOME (CN/0703-458X) [03645208] **4115**

DOWN HOME (BIRMINGHAM) (US/0273-9186) [07025171] **5468**

DOWN MEMORY LANE (LAKELAND, FLA.) *CEASED.* (US/1061-5474) [25349419] **2532**

DOWN SOUTH (US/0416-3184) [03518625] **2731**

DOWN SYNDROME NEWS / THE NEWSLETTER OF THE NATIONAL DOWN SYNDROME CONGRESS (US/0161-0716) [12395902] **544**

DOWN SYNDROME PAPERS AND ABSTRACTS FOR PROFESSIONALS (US) **3831**

DOWN — Alphabetical Title Index

DOWN SYNDROME TODAY (US) **4387**

●DOWN THE ROAD (US/1072-4656) [29019503] **4203**

DOWN TO EARTH (US/0012-5792) [01566919] **80**

●DOWN TO EARTH : SCIENCE AND ENVIRONMENT FORTNIGHTLY (II) [28743337] **2164**

DOWN UNDER QUILTS (AT/1033-4513) [I10334513] **5183**

DOWNEAST ANCESTRY (US/0891-0960) [05536541] **2446**

DOWNLINK : SATELLITE & CABLE INDUSTRY NEWS (UK/0960-3352) **1153**

DOWNRIVER NEWS-HERALD, THE (US/0194-7303) [04978994] **5691**

DOWNS NEWS AND TIMES, THE (US) [12258558] **5675**

DOWN'S SYNDROME (US/0149-7162) [03589817] **544**

DOWNS SYNDROME ASSOCIATION OF NEW SOUTH WALES NEWSLETTER (AT) **4387**

DOWN'S SYNDROME NEWS (US/0161-0716) [03825645] **544**

DOWNSIDE REVIEW, THE (UK/0012-5806) [01566922] 5029, **3382**

DOWNSTATE SERIES OF RESEARCH IN PSYCHIATRY AND PSYCHOLOGY, THE (US/0162-2315) [04108486] 4585, **3924**

DOWNTOWN ACTION (CN/0701-0796) [03403202] **1556**

DOWNTOWN IDEA EXCHANGE (US/0012-5822) [02255298] **669**

DOWNTOWN NEWS (US) **5634**

DOWNTOWN PLANNING & DEVELOPMENT ANNUAL (US/0145-1715) [03015463] 669, **2821**

DOWNTOWN PROMOTION REPORTER (US/0363-2830) [02404239] 669, **759**

DOWNTOWNER (TORONTO) (CN/0710-1619) [08489201] **5783**

DOXA, ISTITUTO PER LE RICERCHE STATISTICHE E L'ANALISI DELL'OPINIONE PUBBLICA, MILAN See BOLLETTINO DELLA DOXA **5240**

DOXOLOGY (US/0748-4682) [10821617] **4954**

DP BUDGET (US/0890-4316) [13314606] **1258**

DP BUDGET See IS BUDGET **1260**

DP, DANSK PRESSE (DK) [03768004] **2515**

DP DIRECTORY (US/0730-6806) [08044810] **1258**

DP MARKET FACTS *CEASED.* (CN/0711-7884) [09106511] **1258**

DPI YELLOW PAGES (US/0360-4357) [02156459] **5284**

DPN: DESIGN PRODUCT NEWS (CN/0319-8413) [01994737] **1971**

DPW. DEUTSCHE PAPIERWIRTSCHAFT (GW/0070-4296) [11311448] **4233**

DPWT TIMES, THE (CN/0843-2716) [20026697] **4387**

DQR STUDIES IN LITERATURE (NE/0921-2507) [13468724] **3382**

●DR. ATKINS' HEALTH REVELATIONS (US/1073-8169) [29535537] 4190, **3573**

DR. C.S. LOVETT'S MARANATHA FAMILY MINI-MAGAZINE (US/8750-4901) [11484919] **4954**

DR, DE REBUS See REBUS, DE **3035**

DR. DOBB'S JOURNAL (1989) (US/1044-789X) [19901592] **1267**

DR. FOX'S NEW HEALTH JOURNAL (US/1043-8165) [19566970] **4774**

DR. JULIAN WHITAKER'S HEALTH & HEALING (US/1057-9273) [24168017] **2596**

DR. MCBIRNIE'S NEWSLETTER (US) [11894588] **4472**

DR. S. RADHAKRISHNAN INSTITUTE FOR ADVANCED STUDY IN PHILOSOPHY See UNIVERSITY OF MADRAS. CENTRE OF ADVANCED STUDY IN PHILOSOPHY. YEAR BOOK **4364**

DR : THE FASHION BUSINESS (UK) [19114923] **1083**

DR. WILLIAM CAMPBELL DOUGLASS' SECOND OPINION (US/1068-2953) [27597305] **3573**

DR. WILLIAMS'S LIBRARY See BULLETIN OF DR. WILLIAMS'S LIBRARY **4941**

DRAFT ANNUAL PLAN - GOVERNMENT OF NAGALAND, PLANNING AND COORDINATION DEPT (II) [06266399] **1605**

DRAFT FACTS FOR GRADUATES AND GRADUATE STUDENTS (US/0420-0942) [01788018] **4043**

DRAFT, FULL DESIGNATION RENEWAL APPLICATION (US) [05748123] **3573**

DRAFT HEALTH SYSTEMS PLAN FOR SOUTH CAROLINA HEALTH SERVICE AREA III (US) [04231037] **4774**

DRAFT HORSE JOURNAL, THE (US/0012-5865) [03815213] **2798**

●DRAFT INTENDED USE PLAN, PROJECT PRIORITY SYSTEM, PROJECT PRIORITY LIST, FEDERAL FISCAL YEAR: NEW YORK STATE REVOLVING FUND FOR WATER POLLUTION CONTROL (US) [24209479] **2227**

DRAFTING CONSTRUCTION CONTRACTS AND HANDLING CONSTRUCTION LITIGATION (US) 613, **2964**

DRAG RACING WORLD / AMERICAN HOT ROD ASSOCIATION, AHRA (US/0747-4148) [10833341] **4893**

DRAG RULES (US/0277-4771) [07566269] **4893**

DRAGER REVIEW (GW/0366-9610) [03117168] **1664**

DRAGOCO REPORT (FLAVORS EDITION. ENGLISH) (US/0012-5881) [01566925] **4299**

DRAGON (LAKE GENEVA, WIS.) See DRAGON MAGAZINE **4860**

DRAGON (LAKE GENEVA, WIS.) (US/0279-6848) [07189350] **4860**

DRAGON LODE, THE (US) **3382**

DRAGON MAGAZINE (US/1062-2098) [25539091] **4860**

DRAGONFLIES (US/0190-7093) [04737912] **4585**

DRAGONFLY (PORTLAND) (US/0364-359X) [02636780] 3462, **3382**

●DRAGONS' QUEST, THE (US/1065-8181) [26751696] **4241**

DRAGON'S TEETH (US) [18393476] **3382**

DRAHT (GW/0012-5911) [02446446] **4001**

DRAHT-WELT (GW/0012-592X) [I0012592X] **4001**

DRAHTHERSTELLUNG UND BEARBEITUNG, DRAHTERZEUGNISSE (GW/0303-2507) [01784571] **3478**

DRAIN ENTERPRISE (US) **5733**

DRAINAGE CONTRACTOR (CN) [03184765] **80**

DRAKE LAW REVIEW (US/0012-5938) [01566926] **2964**

DRAKE UPDATE (US) **1091**

DRAMA *CEASED.* (UK/0012-5946) [04378369] **5363**

DRAMA BROADSHEET (UK/0261-1651) [I02611651] **5363**

DRAMA CRITICISM (DETROIT, MICH. : 1991) (US/1056-4349) [23711365] **5363**

DRAMA IN EDUCATION (UK) [01138522] 1737, **384**

DRAMA INFORMER, THE (YU/0353-0701) [19785781] **5363**

DRAMA-LOGUE (US/0272-2720) [06830013] **5364**

DRAMA/THEATRE TEACHER, THE (US/1046-5022) [20281012] **5364**

DRAMATHERAPY (NEWSLETTER) (UK) [13844932] **5364**

DRAMATHERAPY : THE JOURNAL OF THE BRITISH ASSOCIATION OF DRAMATHERAPY (UK) [07982284] **5364**

DRAMATICS (US/0012-5989) [04126949] **384**

DRAMATISTS GUILD QUARTERLY, THE (US/0012-6004) [01566942] **5364**

DRAMATISTS SOURCEBOOK (US/0733-1606) [08172952] **5364**

DRAPERIES & WINDOW COVERINGS (US/0279-4918) [07910156] **2905**

DRAUDZES VESTIS (CN/0701-0214) [03406223] **4954**

DRAUGAS (US) [09426502] **5659**

DRAUGHTING & DESIGN (UK/0951-5704) [I09515704] 1971, **1183**

DRAWING (NEW YORK, N.Y. 1979) (US/0191-6963) [04913358] **349**

DRC REPORTS See DANSALAN QUARTERLY **2650**

DREADSTAR (US/8750-3271) [11257017] **4860**

DREAM (SAN DIEGO, CALIF.) (US/1057-8366) [24124463] **2532**

DREAMING (NEW YORK, N.Y.) (US/1053-0797) [22447901] 5244, 4585, **580**

DREAMS & VISIONS (CN/0843-445X) [20881008] 4954, **3382**

DREAMWEAVER MAGAZINE (CN/0823-2180) [09981889] **4585**

DREDGING + PORT CONSTRUCTION. SERIES II (UK/0264-4835) [10571636] **613**

DREDGING RESEARCH (US) [18517466] **2088**

DREI (STUTTGART, GERMANY : 1948) (GW/0012-6063) [04759775] 5198, **2846**

DREISER STUDIES (US/0896-6362) [16507765] **3382**

DREISSENA POLYMORPHA INFORMATION REVIEW (US/1065-8408) [23460109] **5582**

DREPTUL / UNIUNEA JURISTILOR DEMOCRATI DIN ROMANIA (RM) [23435465] **2964**

DRESDEN ENTERPRISE AND SHARON TRIBUNE (US) [19248670] **5745**

DRESDEN. STAATLICHES MUSEUM FUER VOLKERKUNDE See ABHANDLUNGEN UND BERICHTE DES STAATLICHEN MUSEUMS FUER VOLKERKUNDE, DRESDEN **4083**

DRESDEN. STAATLICHES MUSEUM FUR TIERKUNDE See ZOOLOGISCHE ABHANDLUNGEN / STAATLICHES MUSEUM FUER TIERKUNDE IN DRESDEN **5602**

DRESDENER KUNSTBLATTER (GW/0323-4088) [07135179] **349**

DRESS (US/0361-2112) [02246361] **1083**

DRESSAGE AND COMBINED TRAINING See DRESSAGE & CT **2798**

DRESSAGE & CT (US/0147-796X) [03231014] **2798**

DRESSMAKING (JA/0012-611X) [02319485] **1083**

DREVARSKY VYSKUM (XO/0012-6136) [03997041] **2400**

DREVO (XR/0012-6144) [07293866] **634**

DREW (US/0889-0153) [13812334] **1822**

DREW GATEWAY, THE *CEASED.* (US/0012-6152) [01714158] **4954**

DREXEL INSULATION REPORT (US) 2042, **613**

DREXEL POLYMER NOTES (US/8756-4572) [11565028] **4454**

DREXEL TECHNICAL JOURNAL (US/0012-6179) [01688329] **5102**

DRG MONITOR *CEASED.* (US/0741-6512) [10243901] **3573**

DRH COMMUNICATIONS QUARTERLY, THE (CN/0848-7642) [23238113] 669, **1110**

DRI ENERGY BULLETIN (US/0147-5665) [03197689] **1936**

DRI EUROPEAN REVIEW See EUROPEAN REVIEW (LEXINGTON, MASS.) **1560**

DRI-FACS, FINANCIAL AND CREDIT STATISTICS INFORMATION SERVICE : APPLIED REPORTS AND GRAPHICS LIBRARY (US/0271-1931) [06549388] 788, **728**

DRI-FACS : REFERENCE GUIDE TO U.S. WEEKLY BANKING STATISTICS (US/0271-3470) [06598039] 788, **728**

DRI INDUSTRY FINANCIAL SERVICE (US/0197-1654) [05961728] **788**

DRI INDUSTRY FINANCIAL SERVICES: ANNUAL LONG-TERM REVIEW (US/0271-4868) [06502439] **788**

DRI INSURANCE SERVICE QUARTERLY REVIEW See INSURANCE SERVICE QUARTERLY REVIEW **2884**

DRI MONTHLY FINANCIAL FORECASTS AND ANALYSES FIXED INCOME INVESTMENT SERVICE (US/0735-8962) [08981020] 897, **788**

DRIED FRUITS RESEARCH COUNCIL (AUSTRALIA) See ANNUAL REPORT / DRIED FRUITS RESEARCH COUNCIL **2327**

DRIEMAANDELIJKSE BLADEN (NE) [05283328] 2319, **3278**

DRIJARKARA (IO) [01798627] **4345**

DRILLING ACTIVITY REPORT (CN/0228-5630) [08752008] **4254**

DRILLING AND LAND REPORT (CN/0407-212X) [03979676] **1374**

DRILLING CONTRACTOR (US/0046-0702) [01688379] **4254**

DRILLING NEWS (UK/0955-7369) **4255**

DRILLING WEEKLY (UK) **4255**

DRINKERS, DRINKING AND ALCOHOL-RELATED MORTALITY AND HOSPITALIZATIONS (US/0273-1657) [06989261] **1343**

DRINKING AND DRUG PRACTICES SURVEYOR, THE *SUSPENDED.* (US/0363-0811) [02364945] **1343**

DRINKING DRIVER ACCIDENT SUMMARY See SUMMARY OF ACCIDENTS INVOLVING THE DRINKING DRIVER **5445**

DRINKING/DRIVING LAW LETTER (US/0730-2568) [07980444] 1343, **2964**

●DRINKING, DRUGS & DRIVING (US/1062-3337) [25603987] **1343**

DRINKING WATER & BACKFLOW PREVENTION (US/1055-2782) [23131265] **5533**

Alphabetical Title Index — DRUG

DRINKING WATER RESEARCH : AN UPDATE FROM THE AWWA RESEARCH FOUNDATION (US/1055-9140) [23377216] **5533**

DRINKS FILE (UK/0966-4661) [I09664661] **2366**

DRIP/TRICKLE IRRIGATION (US/0276-8232) [03494766] **170**

DRIPPING SPRINGS DISPATCH, THE (US/0746-603X) [10157039] **5749**

DRIPPS' INTRODUCTION TO ANESTHESIA (US/1058-1200) [24222171] **3682**

DRIS CATALOG OF SUPPORT SERVICES (US/0883-0606) [08293919] **4043**

DRITA (AA) [10075644] **5777**

DRITTO E GIURISPRUDENZA See DIRITTO E GIURISPRUDENZA **2963**

DRIVE (BE) **5381**

DRIVE (US/0899-6717) [17376909] **5440**

DRIVE SAFELY (US) **5440**

DRIVER/EDUCATION (TORONTO) (CN/1183-7314) [24690734] 1893, **5413**

DRIVER LICENSING LAWS ANNOTATED. SUPPLEMENT (US/0740-9788) [09239478] **2964**

●DRIVER (MIAMI, FLA.) (US/1062-9394) [25812161] 923, **4893**

DRIVERS AND CONTROLS (UK/0950-5490) [I09505490] **1971**

DRIVERS AND RIDERS LICENCES / BUREAU OF STATISTICS (PP) [08816523] **5413**

DRIVERS AND RIDERS LICENSES ISSUED See DRIVERS AND RIDERS LICENCES / BUREAU OF STATISTICS **5413**

DRIVERS LICENSES (US/0097-8655) [01799077] **5381**

DRIVING WHEEL (US/0095-3717) [01796276] **4115**

DROCHAID (CN/0703-1491) [03781950] **2259**

DROGMISSBRUK (SW/0349-1773) [12619533] **1343**

DROIT ADMINISTRATIF (FR) [01566954] **4645**

DROIT & LIBERTE : ORGANE MENSUEL DE MOUVEMENT CONTER LE RACISME, L'ANTISEMITISME, ET POUR LA PAIX *CEASED.* (FR/0012-6411) [12786888] **4507**

DROIT D'AUTEUR (SZ) **1304**

DROIT DE LA COMMUNAUTE ECONOMIQUE EUROPEENNE (BE) **3127**

DROIT DE LA PRESSE (FR) **2919**

DROIT DE L'INFORMATIQUE ET DES TELECOMS (FR/0991-2738) [20105434] 2964, **1153**

DROIT DES AFFAIRES EN GRANDE BRETAGNE (FR) **2964**

DROIT DES AFFAIRES PAR PAYS (FR) **2964**

DROIT DES AFFAIRES REGIME DES SOCIETES (FR) **2964**

DROIT DES ENTREPRISES. ASSURANCES (FR) **2964**

DROIT DISCIPLINAIRE EXPRESS (CN/0835-9636) [19841162] **2964**

DROIT DU TRAVAIL EXPRESS (CN/0712-9300) [09273074] **3146**

DROIT ET AFFAIRES INTERNATIONAL (FR/0184-5926) [I01845926] **2964**

DROIT ET CULTURES : CAHIERS DU CENTRE DE RECHERCHE DE L'U.E.R. DE SCIENCES JURIDIQUES (FR/0247-9788) [10617185] **3127**

DROIT ET CULTURES / REVUE SEMESTRIELLE ANTHROPOLOGIE ET D'HISTOIRE (FR) 2964, **235**

DROIT ET PRATIQUE DU COMMERCE INTERNATIONAL (US/0335-5047) [02243128] **831**

DROIT ET SOCIETE (FR/0769-3362) [12832369] **2964**

DROIT INTERNATIONAL PRIVE : TRAVAUX DU COMITE FRANCAIS DE DROIT INTERNATIONAL PRIVE (FR) [10114942] **3089**

DROIT MARITIME FRANCAIS, LE (FR/0012-642X) [01566959] **3180**

DROIT OUVRIER, LE (FR/0222-4194) [01566960] **3146**

DROIT POLONAIS CONTEMPORAIN *SUSPENDED.* (PL/0070-7325) [01566961] **2964**

DROIT POPULAIRE, LE (CN/0384-6008) [03279095] **5198**

DROIT SOCIAL (FR/0012-6438) [01566962] **3146**

DROITS DE LA PERSONNE. BULLETIN D'INFORMATION SUR LA RECHERCHE ET L'ENSEIGNEMENT (CN/0826-7766) [12168382] **4507**

DROITS DE L'HOMME SANS FRONTIERES (BE/0776-0256) [I07760256] **4507**

DROITS ET LIBERTES EN SYRIE (SZ/0257-1676) [I02571676] **4507**

DROITS : REVUE FRANCAISE DE THEORIE JURIDIQUE (FR) [13592226] **2964**

DROOD REVIEW OF MYSTERY, THE (US/0893-0252) [15340100] **5074**

DROPOUT RATE BY SCHOOL DISTRICT (US) [06175594] 1737, **1794**

DROPOUT REPORT : DELAWARE PUBLIC SCHOOLS (US/0094-0860) [01793465] **1737**

DROSOPHILA INFORMATION SERVICE (US/0070-7333) [01566964] **454**

DROSTE-JAHRBUCH / IM AUFTRAG DER ANNETTE VON DROSTE-GESELLSCHAFT (GW) [16676111] **2515**

DROVER'S JOURNAL (SHAWNEE MISSION, KAN.) (US/0012-6454) [01775324] **210**

DRP BULLETIN (KO/0011-5134) [04590682] **4472**

DRUCK PRINT (GW/0012-6462) [02104355] **4564**

DRUCKINDUSTRIE (ST. GALLEN) (SZ/0046-0737) [04597831] **4564**

DRUCKLUFTTECHNIK (MAINZ) (GW/0723-7537) [09926659] **5102**

DRUCKSACHE - BUNDESRAT (GW/0720-2946) [05854730] **4472**

DRUCKSPIEGEL, DER (GW/0012-6500) [02446458] **4564**

DRUCKWELT (GW/0012-6519) [03603938] **4564**

DRUG ABUSE & ALCOHOLISM NEWSLETTER (US/0160-0028) [02998704] **1343**

DRUG ABUSE CURRENT AWARENESS BULLETIN (UK) **1343**

DRUG ABUSE PREVENTION PLAN (US) [06511376] **1343**

DRUG ABUSE PREVENTION REPORT (US/0091-5025) [01787259] **1343**

DRUG ABUSE SERVICES RESEARCH SERIES / NATIONAL INSTITUTE ON DRUG ABUSE (US) [24771316] **1343**

DRUG ABUSE / THE SWEDISH COUNCIL FOR INFORMATION ON ALCOHOL AND OTHER DRUGS (CAN) ; NATIONAL DIRECTORATE FOR THE PREVENTION OF ALCOHOL AND DRUG PROBLEMS (SW/0283-8117) [23662431] **1343**

DRUG ABUSE UPDATE (US/0739-6562) [08885890] **1343**

DRUG, ALCOHOL, AND OTHER ADDICTIONS (US/1067-814X) [20123753] **1343**

DRUG ALERTS FOR INTERNAL MEDICINE See PRIMARY CARE MEDICINE DRUG ALERTS **4325**

DRUG AND ALCOHOL DEPENDENCE (SZ/0376-8716) [01847307] **1343**

DRUG AND ALCOHOL REVIEW (UK/0959-5236) [22741790] **1343**

DRUG AND CHEMICAL TOXICOLOGY (NEW YORK, N.Y. 1978) (US/0148-0545) [03500584] **3980**

DRUG AND CHEMICAL TOXICOLOGY (NEW YORK, N.Y. 1984) (US/0888-8337) [11100491] **3980**

DRUG & COSMETIC INDUSTRY (US/0012-6527) [01566972] 403, **4299**

●DRUG & CRIME PREVENTION FUNDING NEWS (US/1076-1519) [30414829] 1343, **4774**

DRUG AND DEVICE RECALL BULLETIN (US/8756-5935) [11770712] **4299**

DRUG & MARKET DEVELOPMENT (US/1053-1564) [22465297] **4299**

DRUG AND THERAPEUTICS BULLETIN (UK/0012-6543) [01566973] **4299**

DRUG AND THERAPEUTICS BULLETIN. (ITALIAN EDITION) (UK) **4299**

●DRUG DELIVERY (US/1071-7544) [28717175] **4299**

DRUG DELIVERY SYSTEM (JA/0913-5006) [I09135006] **4300**

●DRUG DEMAND REDUCTION NETWORK: A SUPPLEMENT TO THE LECC/VICTIM-WITNESS NETWORK NEWS/ U.S. DEPARTMENT OF JUSTICE, EXECTUVE OFFICE FOR UNITED STATES ATTORNEYS (US) [25645487] **3163**

DRUG DESIGN AND DISCOVERY (SZ/1055-9612) [23375430] **4300**

DRUG DETECTION REPORT (US/1055-6281) [23245222] **3163**

DRUG DEVELOPMENT AND INDUSTRIAL PHARMACY (US/0363-9045) [02855103] **4300**

DRUG DEVELOPMENT RESEARCH (US/0272-4391) [06841222] **4300**

DRUG ENFORCEMENT REPORT (NEW YORK, N.Y.) (US/0894-1300) [11652169] **1343**

DRUG EVALUATIONS ANNUAL : DE / PREPARED BY THE DEPARTMENT OF DRUGS, DIVISION OF DRUGS AND TOXICOLOGY, AMERICAN MEDICAL ASSOCIATION (US) [23001229] **4300**

DRUG FACT SHEET (CN/1184-695X) [24986815] **4300**

DRUG FACTS AND COMPARISONS (US/0277-9714) [07667512] **4300**

DRUG FATE AND METABOLISM (US/0160-6697) [03685717] **4300**

DRUG FILE UPDATE (CN) [27766274] **4893**

DRUG FILES, THE (US/0892-2373) [15127811] **4300**

DRUG FREE WORKPLACE REPORT (US) **1343**

●DRUG GMP REPORT (US/1061-2335) [25219041] **4300**

DRUG INDEX (TORONTO) (CN/0317-2627) [02248069] **4300**

DRUG-INDUCED DISORDERS (NE/0921-2582) [12008358] **4300**

DRUG INFORMATION JOURNAL (US/0092-8615) [02245968] **4300**

DRUG INTERACTION FACTS / THE MEDIPHOR EDITORIAL GROUP, DIVISION OF CLINICAL PHARMACOLOGY, STANFORD UNIVERSITY SCHOOL OF MEDICINE (US) [10007411] **4300**

DRUG INTERACTION PROGRAM FOR IBM-PC AND COMPATIBLES (US/1041-5041) [18789891] **4300**

DRUG INTERACTIONS AND SIDE EFFECT INDEX See PDR GUIDE TO DRUG INTERACTIONS, SIDE EFFECTS, INDICATIONS **4319**

DRUG INTERACTIONS AND SIDE EFFECTS INDEX (US/1044-7083) [17887549] **4300**

DRUG INTERACTIONS AND SIDE EFFECTS SYSTEM (US/1055-0186) [23060328] **4300**

DRUG INTERACTIONS NEWSLETTER (US/0271-8707) [06699692] **4300**

DRUG INVESTIGATION (NZ/0114-2402) [21115138] **4300**

DRUG LAUNCHES (UK) **4300**

DRUG LAW REPORT (US/0734-6166) [08774109] 1343, **2964**

DRUG LICENSE OPPORTUNITIES (UK) [10531244] **4300**

DRUG MERCHANDISING (CN/0012-6586) [02393292] **4300**

DRUG METABOLISM AND DISPOSITION (US/0090-9556) [01784380] **4300**

DRUG METABOLISM AND DRUG INTERACTIONS (UK/0792-5077) [19276640] **3796**

DRUG METABOLISM NEWSLETTER (US/0199-7912) [06159386] **4301**

DRUG METABOLISM REVIEWS (SOFTCOVER ED.) (US/0360-2532) [03384085] **4301**

DRUG NEWS & PERSPECTIVES (SP/0214-0934) [17985509] **4301**

DRUG NEWSLETTER (ST. LOUIS, MO.) (US/0731-5163) [08209389] **4301**

DRUG-NUTRIENT INTERACTIONS *CEASED.* (US/0272-3530) [06822305] **4301**

DRUG PROTOCOL *SUSPENDED.* (CN/0836-6314) [18758945] **4301**

●DRUG RESISTANCE WEEKLY (US) **4301**

DRUG SAFETY (NZ/0114-5916) [21000223] 3980, **4301**

DRUG STORE MARKET GUIDE (US/0277-3716) [07539819] 954, **4301**

DRUG STORE NEWS (US/0191-7587) [04597490] **4301**

DRUG STORE NEWS FOR THE PHARMACIST (US/1055-2952) [23132914] **4301**

DRUG STORE NEWS, INSIDE PHARMACY (US/0891-9828) [15050142] **4301**

DRUG STORE NEWS. REFERENCE FOR PHARMACY PRACTICE (US) [05694156] **4301**

DRUG TARGETING (UK/0952-0317) [I09520317] **4301**

DRUG TARGETING AND DELIVERY (US/1058-241X) [24251355] 454, **3573**

DRUG TARIFF (UK/0962-3582) [I09623582] **4721**

DRUG THERAPEUTICS (US/0163-1705) [04307097] **4301**

DRUG THERAPY (NEW YORK, N.Y.) *CEASED.* (US/0001-7094) [01691124] **3573**

DRUG — Alphabetical Title Index

DRUG THERAPY TOPICS (US/0882-6684) [11910697] **4301**

DRUG THERAPY (WALTHAM, MASS.) (US/1055-2057) [23118115] **4301**

DRUG TOPICS (US/0012-6616) [01566986] **4301**

DRUG TOPICS RED BOOK (US) [05695350] **4301**

DRUG TOPICS REDBOOK UPDATE (US/0731-8596) [08152399] **4301**

DRUG USE AMONG AMERICAN HIGH SCHOOL STUDENTS (US) [04013659] **1343**

DRUG UTILIZATION IN THE U.S (US/0897-1757) [09040130] **4302**

DRUG UTILIZATION REVIEW *CEASED.* (US/0884-8521) [12492026] **4302**

DRUGLINK INFORMATION LETTER (UK/0305-4349) [08654604] **1343**

DRUGLINK LONDON (UK/0957-3100) [I09573100] **1344**

DRUGS & AGING (NZ/1170-229X) [23110687] 3750, **4302**

DRUGS & DEVICES (CN/0823-7786) [10768341] **4302**

DRUGS AND DRUG ABUSE EDUCATION NEWSLETTER, (1982) (US/0744-2823) [08166867] **1344**

DRUGS AND PHARMACEUTICALS, CURRENT HIGHLIGHTS (R & D) (II/0250-6912) [08269815] **4302**

DRUGS AND PHARMACEUTICALS. INDUSTRY HIGHLIGHTS (II/0250-6920) [I02506920] **4302**

DRUGS & SOCIETY (NEW YORK, N.Y.) (US/8756-8233) [11664155] **1344**

DRUGS AND THE PHARMACEUTICAL SCIENCES (US/0360-2583) [01832469] **4302**

DRUGS AND THERAPEUTICS FOR MARITIME PRACTITIONERS (CN/0705-291X) [04079722] **4302**

●DRUGS & THERAPY PERSPECTIVES : FOR RATIONAL DRUG SELECTION AND USE (NZ/1172-0360) [29573587] **4302**

DRUGS (BOCA RATON) (US/0273-2505) [01165905] **1344**

●DRUGS : EDUCATION, PREVENTION AND POLICY (UK/0968-7637) 1878, **1344**

DRUGS: EDUCATION, PREVENTION AND POLICY (UK) **1344**

●DRUGS IN DEVELOPMENT (US/1066-7008) [27032847] **4302**

DRUGS IN PEDIATRICS (CN/0824-703X) [11096354] **3903**

DRUGS IN PREGNANCY AND LACTATION (US/0897-6112) [17567211] **4302**

DRUGS IN PSYCHIATRY (POINTE-CLAIRE) (CN/0824-7102) [11197166] 3924, **4302**

DRUGS IN RESEARCH (US/0739-8824) [09529134] **4302**

●DRUGS IN SPORTS (CN/1188-0260) [25582687] 4893, **1344**

DRUGS IN THE WORKPLACE (US/1040-4228) [18407172] **1344**

DRUGS MADE IN GERMANY (GW/0012-6683) [01691846] **4302**

DRUGS (NEW YORK, N.Y.) (US/0012-6667) [01566990] **4302**

DRUGS NEWS (SP) **4302**

DRUGS OF CHOICE FROM THE MEDICAL LETTER (US/1065-6596) [05091784] **4302**

DRUGS OF THE FUTURE (SP/0377-8282) [02462947] **4302**

DRUGS PREVENTION INITIATIVE PROGRESS REPORT / HOME OFFICE ; [PREPARED BY THE HOME OFFICE CENTRAL DRUGS PREVENTION UNIT] (UK/0964-8313) [25681973] **4302**

DRUGS UNDER EXPERIMENTAL AND CLINICAL RESEARCH (SP/0378-6501) [03994253] **4302**

DRUM (US/0899-5443) [05272074] 319, **3382**

DRUM CALL, THE (CM) [08358320] **4954**

DRUM CORPS NEWS *CEASED.* (US/0012-6748) [04074161] **4115**

DRUM CORPS REVIEW (US/0094-3649) [01793696] **4115**

DRUM CORPS WORLD (MADISON) (US/0164-3223) [04618263] **4115**

DRUM. EAST AFRICAN EDITION (KE/0419-7690) [01799029] **2278**

DRUM MAJOR (US) [01566995] 1313, **4115**

DRUMHELLER MAIL (CN/0714-637X) [I0714637X] **5783**

DRUMHELLER SUN, THE (CN/0709-0595) [05360194] **5783**

DRUMMER (SAN FRANCISCO, CALIF.) (US/1055-7415) [14913221] **2794**

DRUMS & DRUMMING (US/1052-3324) [22252293] **4115**

DRUSTVENA POLJOPRIVREDNA GAZDINSTVA (YU) [01785887] **80**

DRUSTVENE ZANATSKE ORGANIZACIJE (YU) [01789033] 669, **728**

DRUSTVENI PROIZVOD I NARODNI DOHODAK (YU) [01784848] **1556**

DRUSTVENI PROIZVOD I NARODNI DOHODAK NEPOLJOPRIVREDNIH DJELATNOSTI INDIVIDUALNOG SEKTORA PRIVREDE / SOCIJALISTICKA REPUBLIKA HRVATSKA, REPUBLICKI ZAVOD ZA STATISTIKU SR HRVATSKE (CI) [10827055] **1556**

DRUSTVENI PROIZVOD I NARODNI DOHODAK ... POLJOPRIVREDE INDIVIDUALNOG SEKTORA / SOCIJALISTICKA REPUBLIKA HRVATSKA, REPUBLICKI ZAVOD ZA STATISTIKU (CI) [09873550] **1605**

DRUSTVENI RACUNI TERITORIJE REPUBLIKE VAN TERITORIJA AUTONOMNIH POKRAJINA / SOCIJALISTICKA REPUBLIKA SRBIJA, REPUBLICKI ZAVOD ZA STATISTIKU (YU) [07534790] **1556**

DRUSTVO ISTORICARA BOSNE I HERCEGOVINE *See* GODISNJAK DRUSTVA ISTORICARA BOSNE I HERCEGOVINE **2689**

DRUZBA NARODOV (RU/0012-6756) [04886519] **3341**

DRUZBENA PREHRANA (XV) [06507265] **2334**

DRUZBENI PROIZVOD IN NARODNI DOHODEK V SR SLOVENIJI (XV) [09872770] **1480**

DRUZHBA (IOSHKAR-OLA, R.S.F.S.R.) (RU/0135-7832) [09601006] **3382**

DRVNA INDUSTRIJA (CI/0012-6772) [03744966] **2400**

DRY CARGO MARKET REPORT FOR WEEK ENDING NOON (UK) **831**

DRY CRIK REVIEW (US/1062-3612) [23949105] **3462**

DRYCLEANER NEWS (US/0012-6802) [04935592] **5350**

DRYDEN THEATRE, CURTIS THEATRE AT THE INTERNATIONAL MUSEUM OF PHOTOGRAPHY AT GEORGE EASTMAN HOUSE : [SCHEDULE OF EVENTS] (US/1055-3878) [23161965] **4369**

DRYDOCK (UK/0143-5000) [07321550] **5449**

DRYING TECHNOLOGY (US/0737-3937) [09359396] **1024**

DS (ROME, ITALY) (IT) [12046024] **349**

DS TICARET ISTATISTIKLERI (TU) [10946462] 832, **728**

DS TICARET YLLK ISTASTISTIK *See* DS TICARET ISTATISTIKLERI **728**

D'SANTE (BE) **3573**

DSF JOURNAL (GW) [02610665] **2685**

DSI-RAIL ROUTING SUPPLEMENT, THE (US/0883-1831) [11834002] **5431**

DSIR BULLETIN *CEASED.* (NZ/0077-961X) [07407692] **5102**

DSIR INFORMATION SERIES (NZ/0077-9636) [04266049] **5102**

DSM LETTER (US) **2042**

DST (MILANO, ITALY : 1988) (IT/1120-2505) [21964093] **2022**

DTEXPERT *SUSPENDED.* (US/0894-1742) [15681583] **4721**

DTI QA REGISTER (UK/0958-8574) [I09588574] **1605**

DTW. DEUTSCHE TIERAERZTLICHE WOCHENSCHRIFT (GW/0341-6593) [03418218] **5509**

DU (SZ/0012-6837) [03836381] **2515**

DU PONT CONTEXT (US/0300-7138) [01776983] **1605**

DU PONT MAGAZINE (US/0095-8808) [01567105] **1024**

DU PONT REGISTRY (US/0890-362X) [14255217] **1971**

DU PONT TODAY (US) [04846160] **669**

DU UND DAS TIER (GW) [05731397] **4286**

DUAH HA-DIREKTORYON U-MAAZAN (IS) [01792843] **788**

DUAL SPORTER (US) **4081**

DUALISMO (MX/0185-237X) [03825535] **1591**

DUBAI ANNUAL TRADE REVIEW (UK) [05224791] **832**

DUBLIN HISTORICAL RECORD (IE/0012-6861) [02070353] **2685**

DUBLIN. INSTITUTE FOR ADVANCED STUDIES. SCHOOL OF COSMIC PHYSICS *See* COMMUNICATIONS OF THE DUBLIN INSTITUTE FOR ADVANCED STUDIES. SERIES D. GEOPHYSICAL BULLETIN **1404**

DUBLIN. NATIONAL LIBRARY OF IRELAND. COUNCIL OF TRUSTEES *See* REPORT - DUBLIN. NATIONAL LIBRARY OF IRELAND. COUNCIL OF TRUSTEES **3245**

DUBLIN NEWS (US) [13289580] **5728**

DUBLIN PROGRESS (DUBLIN, TEX. : 1923) (US) [16998157] **5749**

DUBLIN UNIVERSITY LAW JOURNAL (IE/0332-3250) [06606909] **2964**

DUBLIN VILLAGER (US/0191-7927) [04938648] **5728**

DUBUQUE LEADER, THE (US/0012-6918) [04074178] **5670**

DUC HOC (VM) [01796511] **4302**

DUC ME HANG CUU GIUP (VM) [01795250] **4954**

DUCKBURG TIMES, THE (US/0887-2155) [08038464] **2532**

DUCKS OLD TIME JOURNAL (US) **2615**

DUCKS UNLIMITED (US/0012-6950) [01774718] **2191**

DUCTILE IRON PIPE NEWS (US) [03157939] **4001**

DUDE RANCHER (US/0012-6969) [01567010] **2532**

DUDHERI (II) [08714285] **3382**

DUDLEY GENEALOGICAL REVIEW, THE (US/0090-483X) [01785109] **2446**

DUE CULTURE, LE (IT) [20081366] **2515**

DUEMILA (IT) **2487**

DUGDALE SOCIETY *See* OCCASIONAL PAPERS - DUGDALE SOCIETY **5234**

DUGDALE SOCIETY *See* PUBLICATIONS OF THE DUGDALE SOCIETY **3426**

DUGNAD (NO/0332-5784) [15161379] **235**

DUISBURGER FORSCHUNGEN (GW/0419-8026) [03822308] **2685**

DUKE ENDOWMENT *See* ANNUAL REPORT OF THE DUKE ENDOWMENT **4334**

DUKE ENVIRONMENTAL LAW & POLICY FORUM (US/1064-3958) [24821016] 2164, **2964**

DUKE JOURNAL OF COMPARATIVE & INTERNATIONAL LAW (US/1053-6736) [22605280] **3127**

DUKE JOURNAL OF GENDER LAW & POLICY (US) **2964**

DUKE JOURNAL OF POLITICS (US) [12182988] **4472**

DUKE LAW JOURNAL (US/0012-7086) [01567016] **2964**

DUKE LAW MAGAZINE (US) [09137961] 1822, **2964**

DUKE MATHEMATICAL JOURNAL (US/0012-7094) [01567017] **3504**

DUKE POLICY NEWS (US/8755-3899) [07927357] **4645**

DUKE UNIVERSITY *See* PUBLICATIONS OF THE FACULTY **1869**

DULCIMER PLAYER NEWS, THE (US/0098-3527) [02241526] **4115**

DULUTH BUDGETEER, THE (US) [01567035] **5695**

DULUTH BUSINESS INDICATORS (US/0419-814X) [01567036] **669**

DULUTH NEWS-TRIBUNE (1987), THE (US/0896-9418) [17221576] **5695**

DULUTHIAN, THE (US/0012-7116) [01567083] **832**

DULWICH CENTRE NEWSLETTER (AT/1030-2883) [I10302883] **4585**

DUMAS CLARION, THE (US) [22066170] **5631**

DUMB OX, THE (US) [04410707] **319**

DUMBARTON OAKS *See* DUMBARTON OAKS **2685**

DUMBARTON OAKS (US/0197-9159) [06187603] **2685**

DUMBARTON OAKS PAPERS (US/0070-7546) [01567085] **2650**

DUMBARTON OAKS STUDIES (US/0070-7554) [01567086] **2532**

DUMFRIES AND GALLOWAY COURIER *CEASED.* (CN/0959-793X) [23598930] **2919**

DUMONT FOTO (GW) [04851530] **4369**

DUMP DIGGERS GAZETTE (US) [09093685] **250**

DUN & BRADSTREET COMMENTS ON THE ECONOMY (US/1063-0635) [21576786] **1480**

DUN & BRADSTREET EXPORT DOCUMENTATION DIGEST (US/0149-8126) [03562258] **832**

DUN AND BRADSTREET, INC *See* D & B REPORTS **664**

DUN AND BRADSTREET, INC *See* COST OF DOING BUSINESS, PARTNERSHIPS & PROPRIETORSHIPS **662**

DUN AND BRADSTREET, INC *See* DUN'S CENSUS OF AMERICAN BUSINESS **728**

DUN AND BRADSTREET, INC. BUSINESS ECONOMICS DIVISION *See* DUN & BRADSTREET'S KEY BUSINESS RATIOS **669**

DUN AND BRADSTREET, INC. BUSINESS ECONOMICS DIVISION *See* NEWS FROM DUN & BRADSTREET, INC. BUSINESS ECONOMICS DIVISION. WEEKLY FAILURES **1508**

DUN AND BRADSTREET INTERNATIONAL *See* DUN & BRADSTREET EXPORT DOCUMENTATION DIGEST **832**

DUN & BRADSTREET RECORD OF BUSINESS CLOSINGS. MONTHLY BUSINESS FAILURES *See* MONTHLY BUSINESS FAILURES / THE DUN & BRADSTREET CORPORATION **696**

DUN & BRADSTREET REFERENCE BOOK OF AMERICAN BUSINESS, THE (US) [24045560] **669**

DUN & BRADSTREET REFERENCE BOOK OF TRANSPORTATION (US/0093-9528) [01793978] **5381**

DUN & BRADSTREET'S GUIDE TO YOUR INVESTMENTS (US/0098-2466) [02239424] **897**

●DUN & BRADSTREET'S KEY BUSINESS DIRECTORY OF LATIN AMERICA (US/1069-3041) [27972660] **669**

DUN & BRADSTREET'S KEY BUSINESS RATIOS (US/0270-7713) [06166343] **669**

DUNAKANYAR (HU/0139-0252) [I01390252] **4850**

DUNCAN'S RADIO MARKET GUIDE (US/0743-7498) [10331842] **1131**

DUNCANVILLE SUBURBAN (US/0888-1960) [13509594] **5749**

DUNDALK EAGLE, THE (US) [20432047] **5686**

DUNDEE OBSERVER (DUNDEE, N.Y. : 1971) (US) [14121206] **5716**

DUNE BUGGIES AND HOT VWS (US/0012-7132) [04074201] **4893**, **5413**

DUNGEMITTELVERSORGUNG (GW) [07302305] **170**

DUNGEON (LAKE GENEVA, WISC.) (US/0890-7102) [14363880] **4860**

DUNGEON MASTER (US) **2794**

DUNHILL LIABILITY LOSS REPORT (CN/0706-8964) [04518970] **2964**

DUNHILL PERSONAL INJURY AND DEATH REPORTS (CN/1180-9647) [23295979] **2964**

DUNIA MARITIM (IO) [01798535] **5449**

DUNIA PENDIDIKAN (IO) [03409116] **1737**

DUNKIRK EVENING OBSERVER (US) [18788152] **5716**

DUNLAP REPORTER (DUNLAP, IOWA : 1913) (US) [12888350] **5670**

DUNN COUNTY NEWS, THE (US) [07464878] **5767**

DUNN REPORT, ELECTRONIC PUBLISHING & PREPRESS PUBLISHING NEWS & VIEWS (US/0741-6547) [10200591] **4814**

DUN'S 5000 SURVEY (US) **669**

DUN'S ASIA / PACIFIC KEY BUSINESS ENTERPRISES (US/1050-5172) [21510291] **669**

DUN'S BUSINESS IDENTIFICATION SERVICE [MICROFORM] (US) [07992635] **669**

DUN'S BUSINESS RANKINGS (US/0734-2845) [08752733] **669**

DUN'S CENSUS OF AMERICAN BUSINESS (US/0196-8610) [05703349] **669**, **728**

DUN'S CONSULTANTS DIRECTORY (US/0884-3724) [12365580] **866**

DUN'S DIRECTORY OF SERVICE COMPANIES (US/1040-6395) [18477525] **1605**

DUNS EUROPA (UK/0957-5812) [20592188] **669**

DUN'S GUIDE TO GROUP INSURANCE PLANS (US) [16940580] **2879**

●DUN'S HEALTHCARE REFERENCE BOOK (US/1062-1679) [24391285] **3780**

DUN'S INDUSTRIAL GUIDE, THE METALWORKING DIRECTORY (US/0278-8799) [07579185] **4001**

DUN'S LATIN AMERICA'S TOP 25,000 *CEASED.* (US/0742-9649) [10485277] **669**

DUN'S PROSPECT FINDER. ARKANSAS, LOUISIANA, OKLAHOMA, TEXAS (US/0740-6924) [09973333] **1556**

DUN'S REFERENCE BOOK OF TRANSPORTATION *See* DUN & BRADSTREET REFERENCE BOOK OF TRANSPORTATION **5381**

DUN'S REGIONAL BUSINESS DIRECTORY. CENTRAL INDIANA (US/1061-1126) [22993898] **669**

DUN'S REGIONAL BUSINESS DIRECTORY. CHARLOTTE/GREENSBORO AREA (US/1061-1134) [22775410] **669**

●DUN'S REGIONAL BUSINESS DIRECTORY. COLUMBUS AREA (US/1061-0758) [24384710] **670**

●DUN'S REGIONAL BUSINESS DIRECTORY. GEORGIA (EXCLUDING ATLANTA) AREA (US/1061-1207) [24632207] **1605**

DUN'S REGIONAL BUSINESS DIRECTORY. MICHIGAN METROS (EXCLUDING DETROIT) AREA (US/1061-1177) [22605588] **670**

DUN'S REGIONAL BUSINESS DIRECTORY. NORTHERN CALIFORNIA (US/1061-1185) [22783833] **670**

DUN'S REGIONAL BUSINESS DIRECTORY. NORTHERN NEW YORK STATE AREA (US/1061-0804) [24159972] **670**

DUN'S REGIONAL BUSINESS DIRECTORY. OKLAHOMA/ARKANSAS AREA (US/1061-0790) [24655528] **670**

DUN'S REGIONAL BUSINESS DIRECTORY. ORLANDO/JACKSONVILLE AREA (US/1061-1193) [22575164] **670**

DUN'S REGIONAL BUSINESS DIRECTORY. SAN ANTONIO AREA (US/1061-0812) [24859143] **670**

DUN'S REGIONAL BUSINESS DIRECTORY. ST. LOUIS AREA (US/1061-1355) [22619579] **670**

●DUN'S REGIONAL BUSINESS DIRECTORY. TENNESSEE METROS AREA (US/1061-0731) [24652328] **670**

DUN'S REGIONAL DIRECTORY OF SERVICE COMPANIES. TORONTO (CN/1185-4073) [24571064] **670**

DUNS'S GUIDE TO HEALTHCARE COMPANIES *See* DUN'S HEALTHCARE REFERENCE BOOK **3780**

DUNWOODY DEKALB NEIGHBOR, THE (US/0199-7408) [06119550] **5653**

DUNYA AL-ARAB (CY) [11780426] **2650**

DUNYA AL-MUJTAMA (LE) [05468539] **2650**

DUODECIM (FI/0012-7183) [01777964] **3573**

DUODECIMAL BULLETIN, THE (US/0046-0826) [01567102] **3504**

DUPAGE *SUSPENDED.* (US/0891-7159) [15004564] **2731**

DUPAGE CONSERVATIONIST, THE (US/0278-0909) [07699764] **2191**

DUPLEX BIJOUX (SP) **2914**

DUPLEX PLANET, THE (US/0882-2549) [11537753] **3382**

DUQUESNE LAW REVIEW (US/0093-3058) [01792094] **2964**

DUQUESNE STUDIES. LANGUAGE AND LITERATURE SERIES (US) [05279533] 3278, **3382**

DUQUESNE STUDIES. PHILOLOGICAL SERIES (US/0070-7694) [01567109] **3278**

DUQUESNE STUDIES. PSYCHOLOGICAL SERIES (US/0070-7716) [01567110] **4585**

DUQUESNE UNIVERSITY *See* ESPRIT DU DUC / DUQUESNE UNIVERSITY, L' **1823**

DUQUETTE'S SHOW CAR QUARTERLY (US/0748-3341) [10941355] **5413**

DURABILITY OF BUILDING MATERIALS *CEASED.* (NE/0167-3890) [08419552] **613**

DURANGO HERALD, THE (US) [14441678] **5642**

DURBAN MUSEUM *See* DURBAN MUSEUM NOVITATES **4165**

DURBAN MUSEUM NOVITATES (SA/0012-723X) [01627724] **4165**

DURBAN, NATAL. CITY TREASURER *See* FINANCIAL STATEMENTS - CITY TREASURER **4725**

DURBAN, NATAL. OCEANOGRAPHIC RESEARCH INSTITUTE *See* INVESTIGATIONAL REPORT - OCEANOGRAPHIC RESEARCH INSTITUTE (DURBAN) **555**

DURBIN ASSOCIATES *See* DURBIN DATA SHEETS **378**

DURBIN DATA SHEETS (US/0197-470X) [06032522] **4564**, **378**

DURHAM ARCHAEOLOGICAL JOURNAL (UK/0265-8038) [10958143] **267**

DURHAM MEDIEVAL TEXTS (UK/0955-0666) [I09550666] **3382**

DURHAM MODERN LANGUAGE SERIES (UK/0955-6427) [I09556427] **3278**

DURHAM RECORD, THE (US/0739-9618) [09839608] **2731**

DURHAM SPECTRUM AND RECREATION (CN/0821-5847) [09670603] **5783**

DURHAM TODAY (CN/0701-0974) [03406317] **832**

DURHAM UNIVERSITY JOURNAL, THE (UK/0012-7280) [01707754] **1822**

DURKHEIM STUDIES (US) [22902398] **5244**

DUROC NEWS (US/0012-7299) [08206864] **210**

DUSHANBE. INSTITUT ISTORII PARTII *See* MATERIALY PO ISTORII KOMMUNISTICHESKOI PARTII TADZHIKISTANA **4481**

DUSSELDORFER GEOGRAPHISCHE SCHRIFTEN (GW) [04062124] **2560**

DUSSELDORFER NACHRICHTEN (GW) [20980956] **5801**

DUST (BIG COVE TANNERY, PA.) (US/0749-940X) [11292544] **432**

DUSTY DOG CHAPBOOK SERIES (US/1052-4789) [22294464] **3462**

DUSTY TIMES (US/8750-1732) [11081838] **4893**

DUTA RIMBA / PERUM PERHUTANI (IO/0126-1118) [08426411] **2378**

DUTCH & FLEMISH ETCHINGS, ENGRAVINGS AND WOODCUTS (NE) **349**

DUTCH BIRDING (NE/0167-2878) [06513438] **5582**

DUTCH COMPANY YEARBOOK (NE) [19300014] **670**

DUTCH CROSSING (UK/0309-6564) [09838591] 3278, **3382**

DUTCH FILM (NE) [04750613] **4068**

DUTCH HARBOR FISHERMAN (US) **5629**

DUTCH STUDIES (NE/0376-8686) [01794624] 3278, **2686**

DUTCHESS COUNTY HISTORICAL SOCIETY *See* YEAR BOOK / DUTCHESS COUNTY HISTORICAL SOCIETY **2766**

DUTCHESS, THE (US/0735-6242) [03989853] **2446**

DUTY-FREE NEWS INTERNATIONAL (UK) **832**

DUZ, UNIVERSITATS-ZEITUNG : DAS DEUTSCHE HOCHSCHULMAGAZIN (GW/0724-147X) [10621714] **1822**

DV MITTEILUNGEN (GW) [05033680] **2821**

DV [I.E. DATENVERARBEITUNG]-MAGAZIN (GW) [04581481] **670**

DVADTSAT DVA (IS) [05579476] **3382**

DVGW-NACHRICHTEN (GW/0724-7605) [I07247605] 5533, **4255**

DVGW-SCHRIFTENREIHE: WASSER (GW) [02015342] **1413**

DVIGATELI VNUTRENNOGO SGORANIJA (OMSK) (RU/0320-1074) [02998769] **5413**

DVIVEDI'S ANNUAL DIGEST FOR MADHYA PRADESH (II) [01567135] **2964**

DVM (US/0012-7337) [01409668] **5509**

DVM MANAGEMENT CONSULTANTS' REPORTS (US) [15923608] **5509**

DVS-BERICHTE (GW/0418-9639) [03553933] **4027**

DVW HESSEN MITTEILUNGEN (GW/0173-6290) [09461572] **2022**

DVZ DEUTSCHE VERKEHRS-ZEITUNG (GW/0342-166X) [08210788] **5381**

DW DOKUMENTATION WASSER (GW/0012-5156) [05284123] **5533**

DW : DROGISTEN WEEKBLAD (NE) **403**

DWARF CONIFER NOTES (US) [07767433] **2413**

DWB (BE/0012-2645) [18773152] **3383**

DWELLING CONSTRUCTION UNDER THE UNIFORM BUILDING CODE (US) [02949150] 613, **2965**

DWELLING CONSTRUCTION UNDER THE UNIFORM MECHANICAL CODE (US/1055-4505) [23175850] **613**

DWF (IT) [14269077] **5554**

DWI JOURNAL (US/0889-0234) [13576661] 1344, **2965**

DWJ, DEUTSCHES WAFFEN-JOURNAL (GW) [04296250] 2773, **4893**

DX BULLETIN, THE (US/0279-8077) [07267440] **1154**

DX MAGAZINE, THE (US/1043-4208) [19484194] **1154**

DX NEWS (US/0737-1659) [09314339] 1131, **2773**

DYERSVILLE COMMERCIAL (US) [10891451] **5670**

DYES AND PIGMENTS (UK/0143-7208) [07477148] **4223**

DYMAT JOURNAL (FR) **4402**

DYNAMIC ASPECTS OF HOST-PARASITE RELATIONSHIPS (US/0091-049X) [02759513] **454**

DYNAMIC — Alphabetical Title Index

DYNAMIC BUSINESS : A PUBLICATION OF THE SMALLER MANUFACTURER'S COUNCIL (US/0279-4039) [07823773] **670**

DYNAMIC MASS SPECTROMETRY (UK/0367-0007) [01781790] **1014**

DYNAMIC (NEW YORK, N.Y.) (US/0741-0263) [10103851] 5244, **4472**

● DYNAMIC NUTRITION RESEARCH (SZ) [28709374] **4190**

DYNAMIC PREACHING (US/1044-0178) [19647532] **4954**

DYNAMIC SELLING (US) **670**

DYNAMIC SUPERVISION (US/0012-7396) [01620378] **670**

DYNAMIC SUPERVISION IN THE HOSPITAL *CEASED.* (US) [12436530] **3780**

● DYNAMIC SYSTEMS AND APPLICATIONS (US/1056-2176) [23600456] **3504**

DYNAMICA (SA) [02760106] **670**

DYNAMICS (BE) **670**

DYNAMICS AND CONTROL (US/0925-4668) [23750077] **2113**

DYNAMICS AND STABILITY OF SYSTEMS (UK/0268-1110) [14106767] **1246**

DYNAMICS OF ATMOSPHERES AND OCEANS (NE/0377-0265) [02998215] **1449**

DYNAMICS OF POPULATION AND FAMILY WELFARE (II) [09668617] **588**

DYNAMICS OF THE CHAIN RESTAURANT MARKET (US) [06516545] **5070**

DYNAMICS REPORTED (GW) [18386786] **3504**

DYNAMIK IM HANDEL 1982 (GW/0722-6950) [I07226950] 866, **2334**

DYNAMIS (GRANADA) (SP/0211-9536) [09135133] **3573**

DYNAMISCHE PSYCHIATRIE (GW/0012-740X) [02260529] **3924**

DYNAMITE (NEW YORK) (US/0163-3562) [03403856] **1063**

DYNAMITRON-TANDEM-LABORATORIUM (BOCHUM, GERMANY) *See* JAHRESBERICHT - DYNAMITRON-TANDEM-LABORATORIUM, BOCHUM **4448**

DYNAMO (VANCOUVER) (CN/1185-8788) [25423239] **4893**

DYNIX DATALINE (US/8756-2294) [11511753] **3208**

DYSART REPORTER, THE (US) [15924213] **5670**

● DYSLEXIA (CHICHESTER, ENGLAND) (UK/1076-9242) [30641425] **1878**

DYSLEXIA REVIEW (UK/0308-6275) [08673144] **3573**

DYSMORPHOLOGY AND CLINICAL GENETICS *CEASED.* (US/0893-6633) [15610023] **4387**

DYSPHAGIA (US/0179-051X) [13162964] **3887**

DYSPONENDA PUBLIKACJI (PL) [01783806] **415**

DZIALKOWIEC (PL/0137-7930) [03997105] **2413**

DZIAOWY KATALOG NOWOSCI (PL) [01789667] **415**

DZIEJE NAJNOWSZE (PL/0419-8824) [01620567] **2615**

DZIENNIK BALTYCKI (PL/0137-9062) [I01379062] **5807**

DZIENNIK LODZKI 1980 (PL/0208-7707) [I02087707] **5807**

DZIENNIK LUBELSKI (PL/0867-5090) [I08675090] **5807**

DZIENNIK POLSKI (PL/0137-9089) [I01379089] **5807**

DZIENNIK TARYF I ZARZADEN KOLEJOWYCH. WYDAWNICTWO MINISTERSTWA KOMUNIKACJI (PL) [06678996] **5431**

DZIENNIK URZEDOWY CEN (PL/0137-5849) [11462948] **1591**

DZIENNIK URZEDOWY GOWNEGO KOMITETU KULTURY FIZYCZNEJ I SPORTU (PL/0137-6187) [11462975] 4893, **2596**

DZIENNIK URZEDOWY GOWNEGO KOMITETU KULTURY FIZYCZNEJ I TURYSTYKI *See* DZIENNIK URZEDOWY GOWNEGO KOMITETU KULTURY FIZYCZNEJ I SPORTU **2596**

DZIENNIK URZEDOWY MINISTERSTWA OSWIATY I WYCHOWANIA (PL) [02240004] **1862**

DZIENNIK URZEDOWY MINISTERSTWA PRACY, PAC I SPRAW SOCJALNYCH (PL) [01798436] **3146**

DZIENNIK URZEDOWY MINISTERSTWA ROLNICTWA, LESNICTWA I GOSPODARKI ZYWNOSCIOWEJ (PL) [20286748] **80**

DZIENNIK URZEDOWY WOJEWODZTWA SZCZECINSKIEGO (PL) [19966345] **5807**

DZIENNIK WIECZORNY (PL/0137-9046) [I01379046] **5807**

DZIENNIK ZACHODNI (PL/0137-9038) [I01379038] **5807**

DZIENNIK ZWIAZKOWY (US/0742-6615) [09357895] **5660**

DZIMTENES BALSS (GW) [21021538] **5801**

DZIS WARSZAWA (PL/0867-3608) [I08673608] **2515**

DZVIN : CHASOPYS SPILKY PYSMENNYKIV UKRAINY (UN/0868-4790) [21181672] **3383**

E A UPDATE SUMMARY (CN/0708-7292) [05590562] **2164**

E AKROPOLIS (CN/0713-8539) [09046687] **5783**

E & MJ INTERNATIONAL DIRECTORY OF MINING (US) [07718456] **2138**

E-DIVISION SEMIANNUAL REPORT (US) [06609471] **1936**

E I C, ELECTRONIQUE, INDUSTRIELLE & COMMERCIALE (CN/0226-7748) [06512313] 3478, **2056**

E.I.T.D. ELECTRONIC INDUSTRY TELEPHONE DIRECTORY (US/0422-9053) [01794233] **1605**

E-LAB (US/0739-4233) [07411450] **1936**

E/MJ INTERNATIONAL DIRECTORY MINING ACTIVITY DIGEST (US/0149-5275) [02620536] **2138**

E/MJ LIBRARY OF OPERATING HANDBOOKS (US/0732-2763) [04406836] **2138**

E NEW YORKE (US/0742-4728) [10412634] **2532**

E (NORWALK, CONN.) (US/1046-8021) [20535392] **2164**

E-NOTES : QUARTERLY NEWSLETTER OF THE INTERNATIONAL INSTITUTE FOR ENERGY CONSERVATION (US) [25910301] **1937**

E.P.A.'S IRIS CHEMICAL INFORMATION DATABASE [COMPUTER FILE] (US) [27751192] **2164**

E.P.S. 1 (FR/0245-8977) [I02458977] **2596**

E.R.B.IVORE (CN/0071-1071) [08405152] **3383**

E-R-C DIRECTORY OF EMPLOYEE RELOCATION REAL ESTATE SERVICES (US) [12005876] **4837**

E.R.M. JOURNAAL (NE/0921-5131) [I09215131] **2042**

E.T.A. HOFFMANN-GESELLSCHAFT. MITTEILUNGEN DER E.T.A. HOFFMANN-GESELLSCHAFT E.V *See* E.T.A. HOFFMANN-JAHRBUCH : MITTEILUNGEN DER E.T.A. HOFFMANN-GESELLSCHAFT **3462**

● E.T.A. HOFFMANN-JAHRBUCH : MITTEILUNGEN DER E.T.A. HOFFMANN-GESELLSCHAFT (GW/0944-5277) [29932509] **3462**

E.T. IDEAS (US/1053-1912) [22471407] **1737**

E-Z TELEPHONE DIRECTORY OF BROKERS AND BANKS, THE (US/0739-554X) [09780631] **788**

EA, BESTAMMELSER OM REDOVISNING, BOKFORING, REVISION, UPPHANDLING, ARKIVVARD M.M (SW) [03507902] **743**

EA JOURNAL (AT) **3278**

EAA EXPERIMENTER (US/0894-1289) [15808268] **18**

● EAA SPORT AVIATION FOR KIDS (US/1070-566X) [27099560] 1063, **18**

EAAP PUBLICATION (NE/0259-322X) [25070066] **210**

EACROTANAL INFORMATION *CEASED.* (TZ) [08333682] 3278, **235**

EADI BULLETIN (SZ) [05105336] **2515**

EADI EAST TRADE DIRECTORY (SP) [01788768] **832**

EAE *See* ETHNIC AMERICAN EXPERIENCE **2260**

EAE (RENTON, WASH.), THE (US/1053-7457) [22621617] **2259**

EAE SERVICES, RESULTATS DETAILLEES. PROMOTION, LOCATION, SOCIETES IMMOBILIERES EN ... (FR) [20313842] **788**

EAF JOURNAL (CN/0831-3318) [15466417] 1822, **1862**

EAGAN CHRONICLE *See* CHRONICLE **5695**

EAGLE (US) [18435663] **5626**

EAGLE (AUBURN, ALA.) *See* LEE COUNTY EAGLE, THE **5627**

EAGLE BUTTE NEWS (US) [12813225] **5743**

EAGLE (CAMBRIDGE, N.Y.), THE (US/0745-9831) [09658272] **5716**

EAGLE GROVE EAGLE AND GOLDFIELD CHRONICLE (US) [18026067] **5670**

● EAGLE : INFORMATION FOR CALIFORNIA VETERANS FROM THE CALIFORNIA EMPLOYMENT DEVELOPMENT DEPARTMENT, THE (US) [26322444] 1664, **4043**

EAGLE LAKE HEADLIGHT (US) [14184951] **5749**

EAGLE NEWSPAPERS (US) **5756**

EAGLE PASS NEWS-GUIDE (US) [08564752] **5749**

EAGLE, THE (US) **3163**

EAGLE TIMES (US) [21554463] **5708**

EAGLE (UNITED STATES FIELD HOCKEY ASSOCIATION, INC.), THE *SUSPENDED.* (US/0162-5144) [01567171] **4893**

EAGLES (NEW MARKET, FREDERICK COUNTY, MD.) (US/1042-1785) [18951781] **373**

EAGLET, THE (US/0732-1007) [08316337] **2446**

EAGLEVIEW POST, THE (CN/0821-2171) [09428073] **5783**

EAGLEVIEW : THE STAFF MAGAZINE OF BARCLAYS BANK PLC MAURITIUS (MF) [24344191] **788**

EALS NEWSLETTER : THE NEWSLETTER OF THE EAST ASIAN LEGAL STUDIES PROGRAM AT HARVARD LAW SCHOOL (US) [24149608] **2965**

E&P ENVIRONMENT (US/1054-6464) [22927227] **1439**

● E&P HEALTH, SAFETY AND ENVIRONMENT (US/1067-1013) [27132369] **4255**

EANHS BULLETIN (KE/0374-7387) [03295214] **4165**

EANS REPORT (EMPIRE AIR NAVIGATION SCHOOL (GREAT BRITAIN)) (UK) [18796983] **4176**

EAP DIGEST (US/0273-8910) [07009461] 940, **1344**

EAP DIGEST ANNUAL *SUSPENDED.* (US) [11146458] **1664**

EAR AND HEARING (US/0196-0202) [05731857] **3887**

EAR CLINICS INTERNATIONAL (US/0739-733X) [08248091] **3887**

EAR. EDINBURGH ARCHITECTURAL RESEARCH (UK/0140-5039) [06887600] **298**

EAR FALLS ECHO, THE (CN/0702-9020) [03564285] **5783**

EAR (NEW YORK, N.Y.) *CEASED.* (US/0893-9500) [12335055] 384, **4115**

EAR, NOSE & THROAT JOURNAL (US/0145-5613) [02454369] **3887**

EAR RESEARCH INSTITUTE *See* PROGRESS REPORT - EAR RESEARCH INSTITUTE **3891**

EARLITEEN-JUNIOR PROGRAM HELPS (US/0163-8769) [04520616] 1893, **5059**

EARLITEEN (TEACHER'S ED.) (US/8755-2175) [11281987] 1063, **5016**

EARLY AMERICAN INDUSTRIES ASSOCIATION *See* DIRECTORY **5100**

EARLY AMERICAN LIFE (US/0012-8155) [01775554] **2731**

EARLY AMERICAN LIFE. YEARBOOK (US/0094-7083) [01794745] **2731**

EARLY AMERICAN LITERATURE (US/0012-8163) [03141118] **3341**

EARLY BIRD (ARCANUM, OHIO) (US) [17278013] **5728**

EARLY CHILD DEVELOPMENT AND CARE (UK/0300-4430) [01772625] **2278**

EARLY CHILDHOOD EDUCATION (CN/0012-8171) [01998533] **1737**

EARLY CHILDHOOD EDUCATION COUNCIL (MAN.) *See* NEWSLETTER - EARLY CHILDHOOD EDUCATION COUNCIL **1768**

EARLY CHILDHOOD EDUCATION (GUILFORD) (US/0272-4456) [06821107] **1803**

EARLY CHILDHOOD LAW AND POLICY REPORTER (US/1055-4157) [23167894] **2965**

EARLY CHILDHOOD LEVEL D (US) **1803**

EARLY CHILDHOOD NEWS (US) **1803**

EARLY CHILDHOOD REPORTER (US/1058-6482) [24347279] 1803, **1878**

EARLY CHILDHOOD RESEARCH QUARTERLY (US/0885-2006) [12603670] **1803**

EARLY CHINA (US/0362-5028) [02292773] **2650**

EARLY COUNTY NEWS (BLAKELY, GA. : 1859) (US) [12367738] **5653**

EARLY DANCE DIRECTORY (UK) [20408681] **1313**

EARLY DAYS (AT/0312-6145) [01794563] **2669**

Alphabetical Title Index — EAST

●EARLY DEVELOPMENT AND PARENTING (UK/1057-3593) [24020627] 4585, **1803**

EARLY DRAMA, ART, AND MUSIC MONOGRAPH SERIES (US) [06398709] 3341, **319**

EARLY DRAMA, ART, AND MUSIC REFERENCE SERIES (US/1059-1168) [06406668] **319**

EARLY DRAMA, ART, AND MUSIC REVIEW, THE (US/1048-9401) [20788857] 2686, **319**

EARLY EDUCATION AND DEVELOPMENT (US/1040-9289) [18578031] **1737**

EARLY ENGLISH CHURCH MUSIC (UK/0424-0359) [04364403] **4116**

EARLY ENGLISH TEXT SOCIETY (PUBLICATION) (UK/0070-7872) [01567182] **3383**

EARLY ENGLISH TEXT SOCIETY : PUBLICATIONS (UK) [22187609] **3383**

EARLY ENGLISH TEXT SOCIETY (SERIES). ORIGINAL SERIES *See* EARLY ENGLISH TEXT SOCIETY : PUBLICATIONS **3383**

EARLY GEORGIA (US/0422-0374) [01567184] 2731, **267**

EARLY INTERVENTION (US/1058-8396) [15102458] **5284**

EARLY KEYBOARD JOURNAL (US/0899-8132) [09837764] **4116**

EARLY KEYBOARD STUDIES NEWSLETTER (US/0882-0201) [11763819] **4116**

EARLY MAN *SUSPENDED.* (US/0197-9930) [06137845] **267**

EARLY MAN NEWS (GW/0174-4224) [05025895] **4227**

EARLY MEDIEVAL EUROPE (UK/0963-9462) [27836677] **2686**

EARLY MODERN HISTORY (UK/0962-0648) [I09620648] **2686**

EARLY MORN AFRICAN VIOLET GROUP INC NEWSLETTER (AT) **508**

EARLY MUSIC (UK/0306-1078) [01642878] **4116**

EARLY MUSIC HISTORY (UK/0261-1279) [08595852] **4116**

EARLY MUSIC NEWS (UK) [04763741] **4116**

EARLY MUSIC THEORY IN THE LOW COUNTRIES (NE) [01567185] **4116**

EARLY NORRLAND (SW) **2686**

●EARLY PREGNANCY: BIOLOGY AND MEDICINE (UK/1354-4195) **3760**

EARLY SITES RESEARCH SOCIETY *See* WORK REPORTS - EARLY SITES RESEARCH SOCIETY **5237**

EARLY SITES RESEARCH SOCIETY *See* BULLETIN - EARLY SITES RESEARCH SOCIETY **5229**

EARLY WARNING FORECAST (US/0733-0138) [08507622] **1480**

EARLY WARNING REPORT (US/0193-3655) [05186677] **670**

EARNEST CHRISTIAN (US) **4954**

EARNINGS FORECASTER (US/1073-631X) [15741417] **897**

EARNINGS GUIDE (NEW YORK, N.Y.) (US/1064-7678) [24818524] **897**

EARNINGS OF MEN AND WOMEN (CN/0829-6235) [11931645] 1664, **1531**

EARNINGS POWER (AT) **670**

EARNSHAW'S INFANTS-GIRLS-BOYS WEAR REVIEW (US/0161-2786) [03876760] **1083**

EARTH AND MINERAL SCIENCES (US/0026-4539) [01567192] **1354**

EARTH AND PLANETARY SCIENCE LETTERS (NE/0012-821X) [01567193] 395, **1374**

EARTH & TIDE (CN/0228-572X) [08028098] **2731**

●EARTH BOUND (US/1064-4970) [26346200] **3462**

EARTH CARE ANNUAL (US/1054-0067) [21344222] **4185**

EARTH CHANGES REPORT, THE (US/1058-8981) [24423633] **4185**

EARTH ENERGY (US/0731-4930) [07665663] **1937**

EARTH FIRST! (1991) (US/1055-8411) [23363671] 2184, **2164**

●EARTH FORUM (US/1062-9076) [25805778] **2213**

EARTH GARDEN (AT/0310-222x) [03300305] **5244**

EARTH IN SPACE (US/1040-3124) [18372790] **1404**

EARTH ISLAND JOURNAL (US/1041-0406) [15290410] **2164**

EARTH JOURNAL (BOULDER, COLO.) (US/1059-6488) [24655349] **2164**

EARTH MATTERS *See* COMMON GROUND (DES MOINES, IOWA) **5028**

EARTH, MOON, AND PLANETS (NE/0167-9295) [10610068] **395**

EARTH NOTES (US) [25485899] **2164**

●EARTH OBSERVATION MAGAZINE (US) [28558664] **1354**

EARTH OBSERVATION QUARTERLY (FR/0256-596X) [I0256596X] **1354**

EARTH RESOURCES LABORATORY (U.S.) *See* RESEARCH AND TECHNOLOGY ANNUAL REPORT **5146**

EARTH RESOURCES TECHNOLOGY SATELLITE: NON-U.S. STANDARD CATALOG *See* LANDSAT NON-U.S. STANDARD CATALOG **27**

EARTH RESOURCES TECHNOLOGY SATELLITE: U.S. STANDARD CATALOG *See* LANDSAT U.S. STANDARD CATALOG **27**

EARTH SATELLITE CATALOG (US/1061-5067) [25236249] **18**

EARTH SCIENCE AND RELATED INFORMATION (AT/0311-3531) [I03113531] **1354**

EARTH SCIENCE BULLETIN (US/0012-8236) [02250850] **1354**

EARTH SCIENCE CONSERVATION (UK/0142-2324) [05054403] **2192**

EARTH SCIENCE INVESTIGATIONS, UNITED STATES ANTARCTIC RESEARCH PROGRAM (USARP) (US) [06312351] **1354**

EARTH SCIENCE OPPORTUNITIES (US/1058-0425) [24185776] **1354**

EARTH-SCIENCE REVIEWS (NE/0012-8252) [01567198] **1374**

EARTH SCIENCE SERIES (JS/0531-8874) [01282209] **1354**

EARTH SCIENCES AT ANU (AT/1032-5999) [I10325999] **1354**

EARTH SCIENCES (DUBLIN, OHIO) (US/0899-5168) [18119166] 1374, **1355**

EARTH SCIENCES HISTORY (US/0736-623X) [09185224] **1355**

EARTH SHELTER LIVING NEWSLETTER (US) [14954582] **613**

●EARTH SPACE REVIEW (US/1060-1848) [24883641] **1355**

EARTH SUMMIT UPDATE (US/1066-9175) [24773538] **2164**

EARTH SURFACE PROCESSES AND LANDFORMS (UK/0197-9337) [06160332] **1374**

●EARTH (WAUKESHA, WIS.) (US/1056-148X) [23440374] **1355**

EARTH WORDS (OTTAWA) (CN/0847-9933) [20873258] **2227**

EARTH WORK (US/1060-5053) [23590410] **2192**

EARTHBEAT (CN) 4507, **2909**

EARTHBOND (US/0098-9479) [02242899] **2965**

EARTHCARE NORTHWEST (US/0732-684X) [08148045] **2192**

EARTHKEEPER MAGAZINE (CN/1181-7828) [23296330] **2164**

EARTHKEEPING ONTARIO (CN/1183-630X) [23716146] 4954, **80**

EARTHLETTER (US/1059-2253) [24571785] **5284**

EARTHLINES (UK/0968-4425) **2164**

EARTHQUAKE ENGINEERING & STRUCTURAL DYNAMICS (UK/0098-8847) [01785750] **2022**

EARTHQUAKE ENGINEERING - EUROPEAN SYMPOSIUM ON EARTHQUAKE ENGINEERING (UK/1012-9243) [07194418] **2022**

EARTHQUAKE ENGINEERING RESEARCH INSTITUTE *See* NEWSLETTER - EARTHQUAKE ENGINEERING RESEARCH INSTITUTE **1409**

EARTHQUAKE RESEARCH IN CHINA (US/0891-4176) [14766370] **1374**

EARTHQUAKE SPECTRA (US/8755-2930) [11276736] **2022**

EARTHQUAKES & VOLCANOES (US/0894-7163) [15041297] **1404**

EARTHQUEST (BOULDER, COLO.) (US/1041-5483) [16666960] **1355**

EARTH'S DAUGHTERS (US/0163-0989) [02260537] **3383**

EARTHTONE (US/0194-5386) [08466776] **80**

EARTHWATCH (BELMONT, MASS.) (US/8750-0183) [10916823] **2560**

EARTHWATCH OREGON (US/0890-1201) [08637012] **2164**

EARTHWISE *CEASED.* (US) **2164**

EARTHWORD (US) **2164**

EASING THE PAIN OF THE MEETINGS EPIDEMIC (UK) **866**

EASLEY PROGRESS, THE (US) [27776266] **5742**

EAST AFRICA JOURNAL OF EVANGELICAL THEOLOGY (KE/1018-8975) [09586090] **4954**

EAST AFRICA NATURAL HISTORY SOCIETY *See* EANHS BULLETIN **4165**

EAST AFRICAN AGRICULTURAL AND FORESTRY JOURNAL (KE/0012-8325) [01567202] 2378, **80**

EAST AFRICAN CERTIFICATE OF EDUCATION : REGULATIONS AND SYLLABUSES (UG/0376-9151) [02240086] **1862**

EAST AFRICAN COMMUNITY *See* ESTIMATES OF RECURRENT EXPENDITURE OF THE EAST AFRICAN COMMUNITY **4722**

EAST AFRICAN COMMUNITY *See* ESTIMATES OF CAPITAL EXPENDITURE OF THE EAST AFRICAN COMMUNITY **4721**

EAST AFRICAN COMMUNITY. COMMON MARKET AND ECONOMIC AFFAIRS SECRETARIAT *See* REVIEW OF ECONOMIC INTEGRATION ACTIVITIES WITHIN THE EAST AFRICAN COMMUNITY **1581**

EAST AFRICAN COMMUNITY. EAST AFRICAN CUSTOMS AND EXCISE DEPT *See* ABRIDGED TRADE STATISTICS FOR TANZANIA, UGANDA, AND KENYA **725**

EAST AFRICAN EXAMINATIONS COUNCIL *See* EAST AFRICAN CERTIFICATE OF EDUCATION : REGULATIONS AND SYLLABUSES **1862**

EAST AFRICAN EXAMINATIONS COUNCIL *See* REGULATIONS AND SYLLABUSES : BUSINESS EDUCATION SINGLE SUBJECT AND GROUP CERTIFICATE EXAMINATIONS **706**

EAST AFRICAN GEOGRAPHICAL REVIEW, THE (UG/0070-7961) [00832989] **2560**

EAST AFRICAN LIBRARY ASSOCIATION. KENYA BRANCH *See* CHAIRMAN'S REPORT - EAST AFRICAN LIBRARY ASSOCIATION. KENYA BRANCH **3201**

EAST AFRICAN LITERATURE BUREAU *See* OCCASIONAL PAPERS ON COMMUNITY DEVELOPMENT - EAST AFRICAN LITERATURE BUREAU **2829**

EAST AFRICAN LITERATURE BUREAU. COMPLETE CATALOGUE *See* COMPLETE CATALOGUE FROM KENYA LITERATURE BUREAU **413**

EAST AFRICAN MEDICAL JOURNAL, THE (KE/0012-835X) [01567213] **3573**

EAST AFRICAN NEWSLETTER ON OCCUPATIONAL HEALTH AND SAFETY (FI/0783-6201) [I07836201] **4774**

EAST AFRICAN RAILWAYS CORPORATION *See* ESTIMATES OF REVENUE AND EXPEDITURE - EAST AFRICAN RAILWAYS CORPORATION **5400**

EAST ALLEN COURIER (US) [15587998] **5663**

EAST AND WEST (ROME, ITALY) (IT/0012-8376) [01567218] 267, **349**

EAST ANGLIAN ARCHAEOLOGY (UK) [04140863] **267**

EAST ANGLIAN BIBLIOGRAPHY / THE LIBRARY ASSOCIATION, EASTERN BRANCH, THE (UK/0046-0958) [17374085] **415**

EAST ASIA AND THE WESTERN PACIFIC (US/1043-2140) [11177071] **2650**

EAST ASIA EXPRESS *CEASED.* (UK/0961-2793) [I09612793] **670**

EAST ASIA (FRANKFURT AM MAIN, GERMANY) (GW/0723-8398) [10006551] **1556**

EAST ASIA MILLIONS (ROBESONIA) (US/0012-8406) [03866583] **4954**

EAST ASIA QUARTERLY (CH) [01567220] **4541**

EAST ASIA SERIES (US/0066-0957) [02294365] **2503**

EAST ASIAN BUSINESS INTELLIGENCE (US/0888-580X) [13662580] **923**

EAST ASIAN CIVILIZATIONS (GW) [09781533] **2650**

EAST ASIAN EXECUTIVE REPORTS (US/0272-1589) [06751578] 3127, **3099**

EAST ASIAN HISTORY (AT/1036-6008) [25637578] **2650**

EAST ASIAN INVESTMENT IN U.S. AND CANADIAN REAL ESTATE DIRECTORY (US/1053-0339) [22438145] **4837**

EAST ASIAN PASTORAL REVIEW (PH/0116-0257) [05897153] **4954**

EAST ASIAN TERTIARY (HK) **1374**

EAST AURORA BEE (US/0898-2945) [17781733] **5716**

EAST BALTIMORE GUIDE, THE (US) [18710439] **5686**

EAST BAY GENEALOGICAL SOCIETY (OAKLAND, CALIF.) *See* LIVE OAK (OAKLAND, CALIF. 1982), THE **2458**

EAST
Alphabetical Title Index

EAST CAROLINA MANUSCRIPT COLLECTION BULLETIN (US/0360-5191) [02243583] **415**

EAST CAROLINA UNIVERSITY PUBLICATIONS IN HISTORY (US/0070-8089) [08253422] **2615**

EAST CENTRAL EUROPE (US/0094-3037) [02287430] **2846**

EAST CENTRAL STATE (NIGERIA) See OFFICIAL GAZETTE - EAST CENTRAL STATE OF NIGERIA **3021**

EAST CENTRAL STATE (NIGERIA). MINISTRY OF CO-OPERATIVES See ANNUAL REPORT / EAST-CENTRAL STATE OF NIGERIA, MINISTRY OF CO-OPERATIVES **1541**

EAST CHICAGO GLOBE (US) [15503990] **5663**

EAST COAST ANGLER (US/0899-0506) [17978699] **2300**

EAST COAST OFFSHORE (CN/0823-1788) [10105626] **4255**

EAST COAST ROCKER (US) 319, **4116**

EAST COBB NEIGHBOR, THE (US/0191-5029) [04934612] **5653**

EAST COUNTY CHRONICLE (US) [20546330] **5656**

EAST DUBUQUE REGISTER (US) [14195762] **5660**

EAST END ENVIRONMENT (US) [07368635] **2164**

EAST EUROPE SUSPENDED. (US/0012-8430) [01567224] **2686**

EAST EUROPE AGRICULTURE & FOOD (UK) **80**

●EAST EUROPE & THE REPUBLICS (US/1060-6157) [25097666] **1480**

EAST EUROPE AND USSR AGRICULTURE & FOOD See EAST EUROPE AGRICULTURE & FOOD **80**

EAST EUROPE BUSINESS FOCUS CEASED. (UK/0959-9010) [I09599010] **670**

EAST EUROPE REPORT. SCIENTIFIC AFFAIRS (US) [05393267] **5102**

EAST EUROPE/SOVIET UNION EXECUTIVE GUIDE See EAST/WEST EXECUTIVE GUIDE **832**

EAST EUROPEAN BANKER (IE/0791-3931) **788**

EAST EUROPEAN BUSINESS INFORMATION (UK/0966-7970) **670**

EAST EUROPEAN BUSINESS LAW (UK) **3099**

EAST EUROPEAN BUSINESS LAW / FINANCIAL TIMES (UK) [26939809] 2965, **670**

●EAST EUROPEAN CONSTITUTIONAL REVIEW (US) [25783148] **4472**

EAST EUROPEAN INDUSTRIAL MONITORING SERVICE. OIL AND GAS (UK) 974, **4255**

EAST EUROPEAN INDUSTRIAL MONITORING SERVICE. PETROCHEMICALS (UK) 1605, **832**

EAST EUROPEAN INSURANCE REPORT (UK/0965-9676) [I09659676] **2879**

●EAST EUROPEAN INVESTMENT MAGAZINE (US/1063-4029) [26001431] **897**

EAST EUROPEAN INVESTMENT MONTHLY See EAST EUROPEAN INVESTMENT MAGAZINE **897**

●EAST EUROPEAN JEWISH AFFAIRS (UK) [26679362] **5047**

EAST EUROPEAN LANGUAGES AND LITERATURES (UK) [09869803] 3383, **3278**

EAST EUROPEAN MARKETS (UK/0262-0456) [09190890] **897**

EAST EUROPEAN POLITICS AND SOCIETIES : EEPS (US) [25723194] **4472**

EAST EUROPEAN QUARTERLY (US/0012-8449) [01567227] **2686**

EAST EUROPEAN REPORTER (UK/0267-808X) [12926553] **2686**

EAST EUROPEAN STATISTICS SERVICE (BE) [06834580] 1480, **1531**

EAST GEORGIAN BAY HISTORICAL JOURNAL (CN/0710-1279) [08581267] **2731**

EAST GREENWICH PENDULUM, THE (US) [25969060] **5741**

EAST HAMPTON STAR, THE (US) [04954053] **5716**

EAST HARTFORD GAZETTE, THE (US/8750-9156) [11909820] **5645**

EAST KENTUCKIAN, THE (US/0424-107X) [05511462] **2446**

EAST LAKES GEOGRAPHER, THE (US/0070-8127) [01567232] **2560**

EAST LAUDERDALE NEWS (US) [15233238] **5626**

EAST LONDON RECORD (UK/0141-6286) [08737914] **2686**

EAST MIDLAND ARCHAEOLOGICAL BULLETIN (UK) [05774732] **267**

EAST MIDLAND GEOGRAPHER (UK/0012-8481) [01567235] **2560**

EAST MIDLANDS BIBLIOGRAPHY (UK/0029-2885) [06232503] **415**

EAST OF SCOTLAND COLLEGE OF AGRICULTURE See PUBLICATION - THE SCOTTISH AGRICULTURAL COLLEGES **123**

EAST ORANGE RECORD (US) [10773940] **5710**

EAST OREGONIAN (US) **5733**

EAST PROVIDENCE POST (US) [12869117] **5741**

EAST RIDING ARCHAEOLOGIST : A JOURNAL OF THE EAST RIDING ARCHAEOLOGICAL SOCIETY (UK/0012-852X) [02287480] **267**

EAST ROCHESTER POST-HERALD (US/1053-7619) [08074713] **5716**

EAST ROCKAWAY LYNNBROOK OBSERVER (US/0746-2093) [09865055] **5716**

EAST SIDE HERALD INDIANAPOLIS, IND.) (US) [16364499] **5663**

EAST ST. LOUIS MONITOR (US/0046-0966) [22355725] **5660**

EAST TENNESSEE HISTORICAL SOCIETY See NEWSLINE **2750**

EAST TENNESSEE ROOTS (US/0885-4025) [10922367] **2446**

EAST TENNESSEE TODAY (US/1045-2559) [20085671] **866**

EAST TENNESSEE'S WEEKEND JOURNAL (US) **5745**

EAST TEXAS BANNER (US) **5749**

EAST TEXAS FAMILY RECORDS (US/0272-4405) [06466521] **2446**

EAST TEXAS HISTORICAL JOURNAL (US/0424-1444) [02313483] **2732**

EAST TEXAS MEDICINE (US/1050-6675) [21579625] **3573**

EAST TIMOR NEWS : BULLETIN OF THE EAST TIMOR NEWS AGENCY (AT/0314-2825) [03885021] **4507**

EAST (TOKYO, JAPAN) (JA/0012-8295) [01387796] **2650**

EAST TROY NEWS, THE (US/0749-5943) [11177319] **5767**

EAST WEST SUSPENDED. (US/0745-0494) [08767394] **2532**

EAST-WEST (IT) **2487**

●EAST/WEST BUSINESS & TRADE (US/1065-6790) [26700545] **832**

EAST/WEST BUSINESS REPORT See EAST/WEST EXECUTIVE GUIDE **832**

EAST-WEST CENTER VIEWS (US/1055-9795) [23436669] **1822**

EAST-WEST COMMERCIAL RELATIONS SERIES (CN/0318-1316) [02441807] **4520**

EAST/WEST EDUCATION (US/0899-0247) [13996557] **1737**

EAST WEST EDUCATION : EWE (KO) [08026246] **1737**

EAST-WEST EUROPEAN ECONOMIC INTERACTION (AT/0170-0243) [08694238] **1480**

●EAST/WEST EXECUTIVE GUIDE (US/1067-635X) [25406296] **832**

EAST-WEST FILM JOURNAL CEASED. (US/0891-6780) [14978918] **4068**

EAST WEST FORTNIGHTLY BULLETIN (BE/0012-8570) [09190940] **1634**

EAST-WEST JOINT VENTURE NEWS (US) 670, **2965**

EAST-WEST JOINT VENTURES NEWS (INT/1014-6911) [I10146911] **670**

EAST-WEST JOURNAL OF NUMERICAL MATHEMATICS (NE/0928-0200) [28557160] **3504**

EAST-WEST POPULATION INSTITUTE See PAPERS OF THE EAST-WEST POPULATION INSTITUTE **4556**

EAST-WEST POPULATION INSTITUTE See ANNUAL REPORT - EAST-WEST POPULATION INSTITUTE **4549**

EAST-WEST S.P.R.L See EAST EUROPEAN STATISTICS SERVICE **1531**

EAST/WEST TECHNOLOGY DIGEST CEASED. (US/0145-1421) [02672619] **5102**

EAST WEST TRADE INFORMATION BULLETIN (AU/0376-9186) [02441118] **832**

EAST-WEST TRADE, WORLD MARKETS (US/0195-7503) [05578330] **832**

EASTER SCHOOL IN AGRICULTURAL SCIENCE See PROCEEDINGS OF THE EASTER SCHOOL IN AGRICULTURAL SCIENCE, UNIVERSITY OF NOTTINGHAM **122**

EASTER SEALER (CN/0844-5559) [20160289] **5284**

EASTERN AFRICA ECONOMIC REVIEW (KE/1011-4750) [01567270] **1480**

EASTERN AFRICA JOURNAL OF RURAL DEVELOPMENT (UG/0377-7103) [01795158] **80**

EASTERN AFRICA LAW REVIEW (TZ/0012-8678) [01567272] **2965**

EASTERN AND SOUTHERN AFRICAN MANAGEMENT INSTITUTE See ANNUAL REPORT AND REPORT OF ... TRAINING PROGRAMME - EASTERN AND SOUTHERN AFRICAN MANAGEMENT INSTITUTE **5550**

EASTERN ANTHROPOLOGIST, THE (II/0012-8686) [01567273] **235**

EASTERN ARCTIC ICE, THE SEASONAL OUTLOOK (US/0567-0020) [02239733] **1413**

EASTERN ARKANSAS WEEKLY SHOPPING GUIDE (US/0744-690X) [08515782] **1296**

EASTERN ART REPORT : FORTNIGHTLY SURVEY OF THE ARTS OF THE MIDDLE EAST, SOUTH ASIA, CHINA & JAPAN (UK/0269-8404) [21286533] **349**

EASTERN ASSOCIATION OF STUDENT FINANCIAL AID ADMINISTRATORS See DIRECTORY FOR THE EASTERN ASSOCIATION OF STUDENT FINANCIAL AID ADMINISTRATORS **1820**

EASTERN BASKETBALL (US/0195-0223) [05217803] **4893**

EASTERN BLOC CHEMICALS CEASED. (UK) 4255, **974**

EASTERN BLOC ENERGY (UK/0954-2981) [I09542981] **1937**

EASTERN BUDDHIST, THE (JA/0012-8708) [01771007] **5021**

EASTERN BUSINESS MAGAZINE (SW/0346-8186) [03107147] **670**

EASTERN CAMPGROUND DIRECTORY: AREAS IN THE EASTERN UNITED STATES AND CANADA See EASTERN CAMPING & TRAILERING AREAS IN EASTERN UNITED STATES AND CANADA **4871**

EASTERN CAMPING & TRAILERING AREAS IN EASTERN UNITED STATES AND CANADA (US) [05243093] **4871**

EASTERN CANADA CAMPING (US/0363-2091) [02435024] **4871**

EASTERN CANADA TOUR BOOK See TOUR BOOK: ATLANTIC PROVINCES AND QUEBEC **5492**

EASTERN CHALLENGE (US/0898-9346) [01642794] **4954**

EASTERN COLLEGE FOOTBALL MAGAZINE (US/0896-8233) [17297353] **4893**

EASTERN COLLEGE HOCKEY MAGAZINE See COLLEGE HOCKEY **4890**

EASTERN COMPUTING FARMER (US/0748-9897) [11047376] **80**

EASTERN DAILY PRESS (UK/0307-0956) [I03070956] **5812**

EASTERN ECONOMIC JOURNAL (US/0094-5056) [01794414] **1480**

EASTERN ENVIRONMENTAL RADIATION FACILITY (U.S.) See ANNUAL REPORT OF THE EASTERN ENVIRONMENTAL RADIATION FACILITY, U. S. ENVIRONMENTAL PROTECTION AGENCY **2161**

●EASTERN EUROPE ANALYST (US/0965-0350) [27204701] **1481**

●EASTERN EUROPE AND THE COMMONWEALTH OF INDEPENDENT STATES (UK/0962-1040) [25733336] **1925**

EASTERN EUROPE FINANCE (US/1060-2518) [24851587] **832**

EASTERN EUROPE MARKETS (UK) **897**

EASTERN EUROPE NEWSLETTER (UK/0950-7450) [17366188] **2515**

EASTERN EUROPE ON FILE (US/1053-4679) [22533912] **2686**

EASTERN EUROPEAN AND SOVIET ADVANCED MATERIALS REPORT, THE (US/1053-1270) [22469631] **1971**

EASTERN EUROPEAN & SOVIET TELECOM REPORT (US/1054-6499) [22927599] **1154**

EASTERN EUROPEAN ECONOMICS (US/0012-8775) [01567282] **1481**

EASTERN EUROPEAN ENERGY REPORT (US/1054-1608) [22771239] **1937**

EASTERN EUROPEAN OPPORTUNITIES (HK) **670**

●EASTERN EXPRESS (OMAHA, NEB.) (US/1064-3486) [26343179] **3208**

EASTERN FINANCIAL TIMES (US/0161-6110) [04278681] **788**

EASTERN GAZETTE (1985), THE (US/8750-961X) [12373146] **5685**

EASTERN GERMANY; A HANDBOOK (GW) [01437861] **2686**

EASTERN GREAT LAKES SALES GUIDE TO HIGH-TECH COMPANIES (US/1040-0559) [18304531] **5102**

EASTERN HILLS JOURNAL-PRESS (US) [17937630] **5728**

EASTERN ITASCAN, THE (US) [01567284] **5695**

EASTERN JOURNAL OF PRACTICAL THEOLOGY (CN) **5059**

EASTERN KENTUCKY UNIVERSITY *See* EASTERN KENTUCKY UNIVERSITY ALUMNI DIRECTORY **1102**

EASTERN KENTUCKY UNIVERSITY ALUMNI DIRECTORY (US/0278-8780) [07862675] **1102**

EASTERN KENTUCKY UNIVERSITY. EASTERN KENTUCKY UNIVERSITY ALUMNI DIRECTORY *See* DIRECTORY / EASTERN KENTUCKY UNIVERSITY, NATIONAL ALUMNI ASSOCIATION **1101**

EASTERN KENTUCKY UNIVERSITY. NATIONAL ALUMNI ASSOCIATION *See* DIRECTORY / EASTERN KENTUCKY UNIVERSITY, NATIONAL ALUMNI ASSOCIATION **1101**

EASTERN LAW REPORTS (II) [09791830] **2965**

EASTERN METALS REVIEW, THE (II/0012-8856) [02326117] **4001**

EASTERN MINERAL LAW FOUNDATION (U.S.). ANNUAL INSTITUTE *See* PROCEEDINGS OF THE ANNUAL INSTITUTE - EASTERN MINERAL LAW FOUNDATION (U.S.). ANNUAL INSTITUTE **3031**

EASTERN NEWS (MISSISSAUGA) (CN/0226-5117) [06315798] **5783**

EASTERN NUTRITION CONFERENCE PROCEEDINGS (CN) **200**

EASTERN OFFSHORE NEWS (CN/0710-5142) [07586895] **4255**

EASTERN PACKING NEWS *See* NATIONAL PACKING NEWS **2351**

EASTERN PHARMACIST (II/0012-8872) [01567291] **4302**

EASTERN PURCHASING JOURNAL *See* MATERIALS-MANAGEMENT JOURNAL OF INDIA **692**

EASTERN REVIEW (NEW YORK, N.Y.) *CEASED.* (US/0898-1744) [17737731] **415**

EASTERN SHORE COURIER (US) [11855250] **5626**

EASTERN SHORE ECHO (CN/0707-6908) [04784154] **5783**

EASTERN STAR (CN/0381-9604) [02942915] **2732**

EASTERN STATES ARCHEOLOGICAL FEDERATION (U.S.). MEETING *See* BULLETIN - EASTERN STATES ARCHEOLOGICAL FEDERATION (U.S.). MEETING **263**

EASTERN STATES CONFERENCE ON LINGUISTICS *See* PROCEEDINGS OF THE ... EASTERN STATES CONFERENCE ON LINGUISTICS **3312**

EASTERN TRAVEL SALES GUIDE (US/0739-4780) [09726482] **5468**

EASTERN VIRGINIA MEDICAL SCHOOL, NORFOLK, VA. MOORMAN MEMORIAL LIBRARY *See* SERIAL PUBLICATIONS CURRENTLY RECEIVED AND ON ORDER - EASTERN VIRGINIA MEDICAL SCHOOL, NORFOLK, VA. MOORMAN MEMORIAL LIBRARY **3249**

EASTERN/WESTERN QUARTER HORSE JOURNAL *CEASED.* (US/0191-7714) [05066115] **2798**

EASTERN WOODS & WATERS (CN/0827-8911) [15127788] **4871**

EASTERN WORKER (PK/0012-8953) [01774722] **1664**

EASTERN WORLD (UK/0012-8961) [01567301] **2650**

EASTERN ZONE NEWSLETTER - ONTARIO ASSOCIATION OF ARCHERS (CN/0228-2348) [06860000] **4893**

EASTLAND TELEGRAM (EASTLAND, TEX. : 1953) (US) [14091298] **5749**

EASTMAIN 1 HYDROELECTRIC DEVELOPMENT (CN/1186-690X) [24402177] **1481**

EASTMAN KODAK COMPANY *See* HERE'S HOW (NEW YORK) **4370**

EASTMAN KODAK COMPANY. RESEARCH LABORATORIES *See* SCIENTIFIC PUBLICATIONS FROM EASTMAN KODAK LABORATORIES **4376**

EASTMAN NOTES (US/0147-345X) [03145137] **4116**

EASTMAN ORGANIC CHEMICAL BULLETIN (US/0096-221X) [01385425] **1041**

EASTMAN SCHOOL OF MUSIC *See* EASTMAN NOTES **4116**

EASTSIDE MESSENGER (US/0891-2300) [14703776] **5728**

EASTSIDE PARENT (US/1065-2655) [26558607] **2278**

EASTSIDE SUN (US) **5634**

EASTWEST (BROOKLINE, MASS. : 1986) *See* EASTWEST NATURAL HEALTH **2596**

EASTWEST MARKETS (US/0147-8397) [03231519] **832**

EASTWEST NATURAL HEALTH (US/1061-4664) [25120655] **2596**

EASTWORD (HALIFAX) (CN/1187-3531) [25589913] **3383**

EASY ACT (US) **1183**

EASY & FUN WORD SEEK PUZZLES (US/1062-323X) [25586476] **4860**

●EASY APPROACH (US/1076-0814) [30385152] **1183**

EASY COMPUTING (US/0885-0305) [16167754] **1183**

EASY HOME COMPUTER (US/0747-3931) [10786573] **1267**

EASY LISTENING (UK) [01789851] **4116**

EASY LIVING GUIDE : THE ORIGINAL GUIDE FOR THE COMMUNITIES OF NEW WESTMINSTER, COQUITLAM, PORT MOODY, BURNABY (CN/0821-7394) [09981915] **2487**

EASY LIVING (SURREY-DELTA ED. 1991) (CN/1183-5591) [25066839] **2532**

●EASY MONEY (WESTPORT, CONN.) (US/1072-9356) [29241836] **670**

EASY READER (US/0194-6412) [04904952] **5634**

EASY-TO-BUILD WOOD PROJECTS (US/1058-3807) [24282292] **634**

EASYRIDERS (US/0046-0990) [03731529] **4081**

EASYRIDERS IN THE WIND *See* IN THE WIND (ANGOURA HILLS, CALIF.) **4081**

EASYRIDERS PRESENTS BIKER *See* BIKER (AGOURA HILLS, CALIF.) **4080**

EATERN AIZONA COURIER (US) **5630**

EATING AWARENESS & SELF ENHANCEMENT NEWSLETTER (US/1064-4121) [26294721] **2597**

EATING DISORDERS (UK/1351-5276) 486, **3573**

●EATING DISORDERS (US/1064-0266) [26191047] **3924, 4585**

EATING DISORDERS DIGEST (US/0891-6977) [14973722] **4190, 4774**

EATING DISORDERS REVIEW (CHICHESTER, ENGLAND) (UK/1067-1633) [27153876] **4585**

EATING DISORDERS REVIEW (CHICHESTER, ENGLAND) *See* EUROPEAN EATING DISORDERS REVIEW **4586**

EATING DISORDERS REVIEW (VAN NUYS, CALIF.) (US/1048-6984) [21016281] **4190**

EATING WELL (US/1046-1639) [20339034] **4190**

EATON COUNTY NEWSCHRONICLE (US/0747-4156) [10833286] **5692**

EATON COUNTY QUEST (US) **2446**

EAU CLAIRE COUNTY BUYER'S GUIDE (US/8750-6009) [11581707] **1296**

EAU DU QUEBEC *See* SCIENCES ET TECHNIQUES DE L'EAU **1418**

EAU, L'INDUSTRIE, LES NUISANCES, L' (FR/0755-5016) [10076494] **5533, 2227**

EAU VIVE, L' (CN/0046-1016) [02442827] **5783**

EAWARUDO (JA) [10781307] **18**

EBA NEWSLETTER (FR/0987-2507) [109872507] **788**

EBARA-INFIRUKO JIHO (JA/0385-096X) [10286946] **1971**

EBARA JIHO (JA/0385-3004) [02246273] **1971**

EBARA SEISAKUJO *See* EBARA JIHO **1971**

EBAUCHES (SAINT-FELIX-DE-KINGSEY) (CN/1183-0786) [23242539] **3383**

EBERT, ROGER. ROGER EBERT'S MOVIE HOME COMPANION *See* ROGER EBERT'S VIDEO COMPANION **4077**

EBONY (US/0012-9011) [01567306] **2259**

EBONY JR *CEASED.* (US/0091-8660) [01787757] **1063**

EBONY MAN (US/0884-4879) [12412637] **3995**

EBRI ISSUE BRIEF (US/0887-137X) [12259277] **1664**

EBRI QUARTERLY PENSION INVESTMENT REPORT (US/0889-4396) [13882328] **897**

EBSCO BUGLE (US) [05731751] **670**

EBSCO BULLETIN OF SERIALS CHANGES (US/0360-0637) [02246447] **415**

EBSCO CD-ROM HANDBOOK. CD-ROM *CEASED.* (US) **3208**

EBSCO INDUSTRIES *See* EBSCO BULLETIN OF SERIALS CHANGES **415**

EBU REVIEW. TECHNICAL *See* EBU TECHNICAL REVIEW **1110**

●EBU TECHNICAL REVIEW (SZ/1019-6587) [26655408] **1110**

EC BRIEF (US/1049-6459) [21269461] **2965**

EC CLASSICS (US) [13013511] **4850**

EC CORPORATE TAX LAW (NE) 4721, **3099**

EC DAIRY FACTS & FIGURES (UK) [25400851] **194**

EC ELECTRONICS COMPONENTS EUROPE (UK) [01788598] **2042**

EC ENERGY MONTHLY (UK/0957-3666) [109573666] **1937**

EC ENVIRONMENTAL POLICY MONITOR (UK) **2164**

EC FINANCIAL INDUSTRY MONITOR (IE/0956-3261) [21487729] **788**

EC FOOD LAW (UK/0965-0717) [109650717] 2334, **2965**

EC INDUSTRIAL REPORT (US/1054-4003) [22876558] **1481**

EC NEWS (AT/0811-5842) [I08115842] **1481**

EC NEWSLETTER (IT) **1481**

EC NEWSLETTER - DELEGATION OF THE COMMISSION OF THE EUROPEAN COMMUNITIES (CN/0835-8451) [18047444] **1634**

EC PACKAGING REPORT (UK/0967-7852) [I09677852] **80**

EC - UNIVERSITY OF ARKANSAS, FAYETTEVILLE. COOPERATIVE EXTENSION SERVICE (US/1057-1949) [12812018] **80**

EC UPDATE (US/0749-5749) [09743929] **670**

EC UPDATE (UK) **2515**

ECA (ES/0014-1445) [01681642] **5198**

ECA JOURNAL *See* CATHOLIC ANCESTOR **2442**

ECA MAGAZINE (US/0896-3169) [17004930] **1971**

ECAM ANNUAL REPORT *See* ANNUAL REPORT AND REVIEW OF ACTIVITIES FOR THE YEAR / THE EMPLOYERS' CONSULTATIVE ASSOCIATION OF MALAWI **938**

ECB NEWSLETTER (US/0895-6928) [16747766] **2192**

ECCLES NURSERIES *See* SPRING ... PRICE LIST - ECCLES NURSERIES **2432**

ECCLESIA MADRID (SP/0012-9038) [I00129038] **5029**

ECCLESIA ORANS (IT/1010-3872) [16837231] **4954**

ECCLESIASTICAL COURT DIGEST, THE (US/0424-2068) [01567311] **2965**

ECCLESIASTICAL LAW JOURNAL : THE JOURNAL OF THE ECCLESIASTICAL LAW SOCIETY (UK/0956-618X) [19730536] **2965**

ECCSSA JOURNAL, THE (US/0896-1360) [16920004] **5198**

ECCTIS 2000 : THE UK COURSES INFORMATION SERVICE ON CD-ROM (UK) **1822**

ECD. ENERGY CONSERVATION DIGEST (US/0270-823X) [04945669] **1937**

ECHANGE DE DOCUMENTS INFORMATISES AU CANADA (CN/1186-8449) [24571106] **866**

ECHANGE DU YWCA QUEBEC, L' (CN/1186-0189) [24266217] **5554**

ECHANGE (EDMONTON) (CN/0831-5825) [15466904] **3278**

ECHANGE (NORANDA) (CN/0706-5205) [04631824] **3208**

ECHANGE TRAVAIL PARIS *CEASED.* (FR/0240-396X) [I0240396X] **1664**

ECHANGER POUR MIEUX FAIRE (CN/1185-1635) [24265746] **4850**

ECHANGES (FR) [28123516] **4955**

ECHANGES, BOURSES, VOYAGES (CN/0844-7357) [20019942] **1737**

ECHANGES DE L'A.E.L.E, LES (SZ) [03261373] **832**

ECHANGES - ECOLE DES HAUTES ETUDES COMMERCIALES, MONTREAL, QUEBEC (CN/1184-7239) [24266848] **671**

ECHANGES (FRANCE. AMBASSADE (TUNISIA). SERVICE CULTUREL) (TI/0330-2601) [08823920] **2639**

ECHANGES INTERNATIONAUX ET DEVELOPPEMENT (FR) [05724487] 1634, **832**

ECHANGES SANTE SOCIAL (FR) **2597**

ECHAPPEMENT (FR) **5102**

ECHEC + (CN/0825-0049) [11355548] 1230, **4860**

ECHINODERM NEWSLETTER *See* ECHINODERMS NEWSLETTER, THE **5582**

ECHINODERM STUDIES (NE) [09873340] **5582**

ECHINODERMS NEWSLETTER, THE (US/0735-7494) [05455278] **5582**

ECHO (SZ/0012-9143) [01567313] 2909, **1893**

ECHO (CN/1182-3100) [22570093] **5783**

ECHO (US) [06841480] **1822**

ECHO ABITIBIEN (CN/0844-0905) [19451567] **5783**

ECHO D'AFRIQUE (QUEBEC) (CN/0318-4382) [02442029] **2639**

ECHO DE LA COUR (CN/0227-1141) [07294876] **2965**

ECHO DE LA PRESSE (PARIS, FRANCE) (FR) [19453083] **2919**

ECHO DE L'AFRIQUE, L' (FR/0150-3146) [01503146] **4472**

ECHO DE MONNOIR (CN/0821-9869) [10852366] **2732**

ECHO DES BASQUES (CN/0228-5908) [07849838] **2446**

ECHO DES BOIS, L' (BE) [03997154] **2400**

ECHO DES CANTONS (CN/0706-7402) [04955195] **2732**

ECHO DES FRONTIERES, L' (CN/0823-5503) [10386314] **5783**

ECHO DES RECHERCHES, L' (FR/0012-9283) [05705221] 2042, **1154**

ECHO DES VOYAGES, L' (CN/0228-667X) [07821007] **5469**

ECHO DNIA (PL/0137-902X) [0137902X] **5807**

ECHO DU TRANSPORT, L' (CN/0705-7040) [04098002] **5381**

ECHO (HUMBLE, TEX.) (US/0746-7184) [10222333] **5749**

ECHO : JOURNAL DU SYNDICAT PROFESSIONNEL DES INGENIEURS DE L'HYDRO-QUEBEC, L' (CN/0713-5688) [08916677] **1664**

ECHO KRAKOWA (PL/0137-9011) [01379011] **5807**

ECHO MUNICIPAL (CN/0713-8024) [09054358] **4645**

ECHO NOTRE-DAME (CN/0227-5457) [08045845] **2732**

ECHO (OTTAWA) (CN/0382-7194) [02740450] **5284**

ECHO (OTTAWA. 1977) (CN/0821-7785) [10082545] **4302**

ECHO PILOT (US) [13048440] **5736**

ECHO : QUOTIDIEN DE L'ECONOMIE ET DE LA BOURSE, L' (BE) **1481**

ECHO-X (CN/0820-6295) [09519493] **3941**

ECHOCARDIOGRAPHY (MOUNT KISCO, N.Y.) (US/0742-2822) [10304666] **3704**

ECHOES (SZ) 5244, **4955**

ECHOES (BLAINE, ME.) (US/1043-3341) [19256633] **2732**

ECHOES (COLUMBUS) (US/0012-933X) [01567321] **2732**

ECHOES FROM TIANANMEN (HK) [20181216] **4507**

●ECHOES (MEDICINE HAT) (CN/1193-0748) [26714702] **4955**

ECHOES OF HISTORY (US/0046-1091) [02243715] **2732**

ECHOES OF PEACE (JA/0287-2145) [02872145] 4507, **2249**

ECHOS DE LA REPUBLIQUE DE CHINE (CH) [06729796] **2503**

ECHOS DE L'EXPORTATION PARIS, LES (FR/1148-1757) [11481757] **832**

ECHOS DU CENTRE INTERNATIONAL D'ETUDES PEDAGOGIQUES DE SEVRES (FR/0154-5280) [01545280] **2686**

ECHOS DU MONDE CLASSIQUE (CN/0012-9356) [08919448] **267**

ECHOS DU MONDE / COSMOS EN BRAILLE (FR) **4387**

ECHOS DU MONDE / ETOILE EN BRAILLE (FR) **4387**

ECHOS GENEALOGIQUES (CN/0828-8151) [13490310] **2446**

ECHOS PARIS. 1928, LES (FR/0153-4831) [01534831] **1737**

ECHOS PHILATELIQUES (CN/0707-7203) [07966590] **2785**

ECIA CHARTER 2, ANNUAL EVALUATION REPORT (US) [22937153] **1737**

ECLAIR, L' (MG) [06893241] **2639**

ECLAT (FR/0268-109X) **3278**

ECLECTIC BUDGET (US) [07841814] **4721**

ECLECTIC THEOSOPHIST, THE (US/0890-8117) [11764396] **4955**

ECLETICA QUIMICA (BL/0100-4670) [08395148] **1737**

ECLIPSE-NEWS-REVIEW, THE (US) [16107135] **5670**

ECLOGAE GEOLOGICAE HELVETIAE (SZ/0012-9402) [01567335] **1374**

ECLOSION, L' (CN/0319-1710) [02442210] **5783**

ECLUSE, L' (CN/0710-1708) [08205815] **5783**

ECM POST-REVIEW, THE (US/0891-0731) [14631896] **5695**

ECMA FOLDING CARTON BULLETIN ENGLISH ED (NE/0924-9303) [09249303] **4233**

ECMI NEWSLETTER (FI/1013-9338) [10139338] **3504**

ECN CHEMSCOPE (UK/0952-8377) [08901188] **974**

ECN. EUROPEAN CHEMICAL NEWS (UK/0014-2875) [02320546] 1556, **974**

ECO (MX) [02241556] **2732**

ECO (CK/0012-9410) [01827677] **3383**

ECO 3 (FR/0247-8277) [07914977] **2227**

ECO ALERT / CONSERVATION COUNCIL (CN/0833-448X) [16081694] **2192**

ECO CUOIO : DELLE INDUSTRIE E DEI COMMERCI DEL CUOIO E DELLE CALZATURE (IT) **3183**

ECO D ARTE MODERNA (IT) **349**

ECO DE AFRICA *See* ECO DE AFRICA Y DE OTROS CONTINENTES **4955**

ECO DE AFRICA Y DE OTROS CONTINENTES (SP) [08101186] **4955**

ECO DE VIRGINIA, EL (US) [24947807] **2259**

ECO DEI VIGILI DEL FUOCO (IT) **2288**

ECO DEL CHISONE (IT) **2487**

ECO DI BERGAMO (IT) **5804**

ECO DI BIELLA (IT) **5804**

ECO E NOTIZIARIO DELL ECOLOGIA **SUSPENDED**. (IT) [29625682] **2213**

ECO FORUM : NEWSLETTER OF THE SOUTH DAKOTA RESOURCES COALITION (US) [19062357] **2213**

ECO-IDEAS *See* NATURALIST (DANVILLE, VT.), THE **2199**

ECO/LOG. CANADIAN POLLUTION LEGISLATION (CN/0704-4062) [07044062] **2227**

ECO/LOG WEEK (CN/0315-0380) [01999062] **2227**

ECO LOGIC (US) **2213**

ECO MODEL (IT) **2213**

●ECO : PUBLICACAO DA POS-GRADUACAO DA ESCOLA DE COMUNICACAO DA UNIVERSIDADE FEDERAL DO RIO DE JANEIRO (BL) [27763428] **1110**

ECO TRAVELER (US) **5469**

ECOCARDIOGRAFIA (IT) **3704**

ECODATE (AT) 1591, **1481**

ECODECISION (MONTREAL) (CN/1183-2355) [24279924] **2192**

ECODECISION (MONTREAL) (CN/1183-2355) [24279923] **2192**

ECODOC : REVUE BIBLIOGRAPHIQUE BIMESTRIELLE PUBLIEE PAR LE RESEAU D'INFORMATION EN ECONOMIE GENERALE (FR/0292-1782) [07800831] **1531**

ECOFORUM ENGLISH EDITION (SA/0250-9989) [02509989] **2164**

●ECOGRAPHY (DK/0906-7590) [25696039] **2213**

ECOINDICATEUR DE LA BANQUE ROYALE (CN/0319-1877) [02442255] **1556**

ECOL NEWS (US) [01567340] **2164**

ECOLE (IT) **2213**

ECOLE DES LETTRES / PREMIER CYCLE, L' (FR) **1737**

ECOLE DES PARENTS (FR/0626-2238) **1737**

ECOLE DES PARENTS, L' (FR/0424-2238) [04242238] 1737, **2278**

ECOLE FRANCAISE D'ATHENES *See* ETUDES CRETOISES **2687**

ECOLE FRANCAISE D'ATHENES *See* FOUILLES DE DELPHES **268**

ECOLE FRANCAISE D'ATHENES *See* ETUDES CHYPRIOTES **2515**

ECOLE FRANCAISE D'ATHENES *See* EXPLORATION ARCHEOLOGIQUE DE DELOS FAITE PAR L'ECOLE FRANCAISE D'ATHENES **268**

ECOLE FRANCAISE DE ROME *See* COLLECTION DE L'ECOLE FRANCAISE DE ROME **1076**

ECOLE MATERNELLE FRANCAISE, L' (FR/0012-9585) [00129585] **1737**

ECOLE NATIONAL SUPERIEURE DES BIBLIOTHEQUES (FRANCE) *See* ESEIGNEMENTS PROFESSIONNELS, LES **3209**

ECOLE NATIONALE D'ADMINISTRATION PUBLIQUE (QUEBEC) *See* ENAP, CARREFOUR UNVERSITAIRE DE L'ADMINISTRATION PUBLIQUE, PLAN DE DEVELOPMENT **4646**

ECOLE NATIONALE SUPERIEURE DE TECHNIQUES AVANCEES *See* RAPPORT D'ACTIVITES SUR LES RECHERCHES A L'ENSTA **5144**

ECOLE NORMALE SUPERIEURE (FRANCE) *See* ANNALES SCIENTIFIQUES DE L'ECOLE NORMALE SUPERIEURE **3493**

ECOLE POLYTECHNIQUE (FRANCE) *See* LABORATOIRES ET CENTRES DE RECHERCHE : RAPPORT D'ACTIVITE / ECOLE POLYTECHNIQUE **5125**

ECOLES SECONDAIRES DE LA CECM, LES (CN/1184-6186) [24266541] 5029, **1737**

ECOLES SECONDAIRES, LES (CG) [01796517] **1737**

ECOLOGIA AUSTRAL (AG/0327-5477) [03275477] **2213**

ECOLOGIA DELLA MENTE (IT) [18581960] **3925**

ECOLOGIA E DESENVOLVIMENTO (BL) [24170162] **2227**

ECOLOGIA EN BOLIVIA : REVISTA DEL INSTITUTO DE ECOLOGIA (BO) [10616673] 2192, **2213**

ECOLOGIA (MADRID) (SP/0214-0896) [21289428] **2213**

ECOLOGIA MEDITERRANEA (FR/0153-8756) [08951575] 508, **2213**

ECOLOGICAL ABSTRACTS (UK/0305-196X) [01794982] 2213, **2184**

ECOLOGICAL APPLICATIONS (US/1051-0761) [21798547] **2213**

ECOLOGICAL BULLETINS (SW/0346-6868) [01906919] **2213**

ECOLOGICAL ECONOMICS (NE/0921-8009) [19769548] **2213**

●ECOLOGICAL ENGINEERING (NE/0925-8574) [25901239] 2213, **1971**

ECOLOGICAL ENTOMOLOGY (UK/0307-6946) [02218142] 2214, **5607**

ECOLOGICAL ILLNESS LAW REPORT **SUSPENDED**. (US/8755-9013) [10703519] **3110**

ECOLOGICAL LAND CLASSIFICATION SERIES (CN/0823-406X) [07465003] **2214**

ECOLOGICAL MODELLING (NE/0304-3800) [02242959] **2214**

ECOLOGICAL MONOGRAPHS (US/0012-9615) [01567355] **2214**

ECOLOGICAL PSYCHOLOGY (US/1040-7413) [18508007] 2214, **4585**

ECOLOGICAL RESEARCH (JA/0912-3814) [14198895] **2214**

ECOLOGICAL RESEARCH SERIES (US/1052-2468) [01731691] **2214**

ECOLOGICAL SOCIETY OF AMERICA *See* DIRECTORY / ECOLOGICAL SOCIETY OF AMERICA **2213**

ECOLOGICAL SOCIETY OF AUSTRALIA BULLETIN (AT) **2214**

ECOLOGICAL STUDIES (GW/0070-8356) [01645889] **2214**

ECOLOGIE (FR) **2214**

ECOLOGIST (1979) (UK/0261-3131) [05226399] **2214**

ECOLOGY ABSTRACTS (US/0143-3296) [06028595] 2214, **2184**

ECOLOGY AND FARMING : INTERNATIONAL IFOAM MAGAZINE (GW) [24477793] 2214, **81**

ECOLOGY, ECONOMY & ENVIRONMENT (NE) [25565659] **2214**

ECOLOGY (HOUSTON) (US/0361-2600) [02245958] **2214**

ECOLOGY INTERNATIONAL (US) [20542895] **2214**

ECOLOGY LAW QUARTERLY (US/0046-1121) [01567362] **3110**

ECOLOGY OF FOOD AND NUTRITION (US/0367-0244) [01285522] **4190**

●ECOLOGY OF FRESHWATER FISH (DK/0906-6691) [28186890] **2300**

ECOLOGY (TEMPE) (US/0012-9658) [02006581] **2214**

ECOLOGY USA (HOUSTON) (US/0098-6615) [02240746] **2214**

ECOMINE (FR/0246-0971) [02460971] **1355**

ECON/STATS I. CD-ROM (US) 1481, **1531**

ECONEWS (ARCATA, CALIF.) (US/0885-7237) [12717215] **2192**

ECONLIT [COMPUTER FILE] (US) [25360493] 1481, **1531**

ECONOMIC

ECONOCAST (US/0889-6151) [13997110] **2164**

ECONOCLAST (HOUSTON, TEX.), THE (US/0890-166X) [14174563] **1481**

ECONOMETRIC INVESTING (US/8756-4602) [11567036] **897**

ECONOMETRIC REVIEWS (US/0747-4938) [10728049] **1481**

ECONOMETRIC SOCIETY PUBLICATION (UK) [09566989] **5230**

ECONOMETRIC THEORY (US/0266-4666) [12406910] **1591**

ECONOMETRICA (US/0012-9682) [01567366] **1481**

ECONOMIA (FR/0151-5055) [02461306] **1556**

ECONOMIA & LAVORO (1967) (IT/0012-978X) [06038533] **1481**

ECONOMIA & MANAGEMENT (IT/1120-5032) [I11205032] **1481**

ECONOMIA AZIENDALE : FOUR MONTHLY REVIEW OF THE ACCADEMIA ITALIANA DI ECONOMIA AZIENDALE (IT) [09330617] **1591**

ECONOMIA BRASILEIRA, A (BL) [01823535] **1556**

ECONOMIA BRASILEIRA E SUAS PERSPECTIVAS, A (BL/0424-2386) [01567369] 671, **1481**

ECONOMIA COLOMBIANA, LA (CK) [05323151] **1556**

ECONOMIA CULTURA (IT) **1481**

ECONOMIA DE AMERICA LATINA ***CEASED.*** (MX) [04682141] **1556**

ECONOMIA DELLE FONTI DI ENERGIA (IT) [02634831] **1937**

ECONOMIA DELLE SCELTE PUBBLICHE / JOURNAL OF PUBLIC FINANCE AND PUBLIC CHOICE (IT) [11932382] **4721**

ECONOMIA E AMBIENTE (IT) **2214**

ECONOMIA E BANCA (IT/0393-9243) [I03939243] 788, **1481**

ECONOMIA E CREDITO (IT/0012-9771) [I00129771] 788, **1481**

ECONOMIA E DIRITTO DEL TERZIARIO (IT) [26286708] **4760**

ECONOMIA E POLITICA INDUSTRIALE (IT/0391-2078) [12948764] **1591**

ECONOMIA E SOCIALISMO (PO) [02608622] **1556**

ECONOMIA E SOCIOLOGIA (PO/0390-5330) [04661687] **5198**

ECONOMIA E STORIA (IT) [19756351] **1556**

ECONOMIA I CREDITO; PALERMO (IT) **1481**

ECONOMIA INFORMA (MX/0185-0849) [02589964] **1481**

ECONOMIA INTERNACIONAL (SP) [20005789] **1634**

ECONOMIA INTERNAZIONALE (IT/0012-981X) [01615299] **1634**

ECONOMIA ITALIANA (CENTRO STUDI DI POLITICA ECONOMICA (TURIN, ITALY) (IT) [07781337] **1556**

ECONOMIA ITALIANA (ROME, ITALY) (IT) [13726325] **1481**

ECONOMIA (LIMA) (PE/0254-4415) [08659550] **1556**

ECONOMIA (LISBOA) (PO/0870-3531) [05184228] **1481**

ECONOMIA MARCHE (IT/0391-5271) [04589846] **1556**

ECONOMIA MEXICANA EN GRAFICAS, LA (MX) [06740488] **1556**

ECONOMIA MEXICANA (MEXICO CITY, MEXICO) (MX) [06452284] **1556**

ECONOMIA MONTANA (IT) [03997136] **1481**

ECONOMIA MONTANA ROMA (IT/0012-9836) [I00129836] 2164, 2378, **2214**

ECONOMIA NACIONAL (MX) [09603392] **1481**

ECONOMIA POLITICA (IT) [12444409] **1481**

ECONOMIA PUBBLICA (IT/0390-6140) [01618450] **1605**

ECONOMIA (QUITO) (EC/0012-9704) [02978175] **1481**

ECONOMIA SOCIETA E ISTITUZIONI (IT) [21960031] **1481**

ECONOMIA, TEORIA Y PRACTICA (MX) [11341560] **1481**

ECONOMIA TRENTINA (IT) [22142318] **1481**

ECONOMIA Y CIENCIAS SOCIALES (VE/0012-9895) [01496416] **5199**

ECONOMIA Y SOCIOLOGIA DEL TRABAJO (SP) [20175269] **1664**

ECONOMIA Y TRABAJO EN CHILE (CL) [24415595] **1664**

ECONOMIC ABSTRACT OF ALABAMA (US) [01478924] **1481**

ECONOMIC ADVISOR (TORONTO) (CN/1186-1053) [24266199] **1556**

ECONOMIC AFFAIRS (CALCUTTA) (II/0424-2513) [01774314] **1482**

ECONOMIC AFFAIRS (LONDON, ENGLAND) (UK/0265-0665) [10219247] **1482**

ECONOMIC AGE (II) [02476607] **1556**

ECONOMIC ANALYSIS (US) [12709652] **4255**

ECONOMIC ANALYSIS AND POLICY (AT/0313-5926) [02291594] **1591**

ECONOMIC ANALYSIS AND WORKERS' MANAGEMENT (YU/0351-286X) [02337142] 1664, **866**

ECONOMIC ANALYSIS OF BRITISH COLUMBIA (CN/0824-3980) [10386270] **1482**

ECONOMIC ANALYSIS OF NORTH AMERICAN SKI AREAS *See* ECONOMIC ANALYSIS OF UNITED STATES SKI AREAS **4893**

●ECONOMIC ANALYSIS OF UNITED STATES SKI AREAS (US/1070-9231) [27550878] 4850, **4893**

ECONOMIC ANALYSIS SERIES FOR SCREENING PROPOSED TIMBER MANAGEMENT PROJECTS / U.S. DEPARTMENT OF THE INTERIOR, BUREAU OF LAND MANAGEMENT, AN (US) [11576759] **2378**

ECONOMIC AND COMMERCIAL INFORMATION, BELGIUM (BE) [26877251] **1482**

ECONOMIC AND COMMERCIAL NEWS ***CEASED.*** (II) [02256069] **832**

ECONOMIC AND DEMOGRAPHIC ALMANAC OF WASHINGTON COUNTIES AND CITIES (US/1050-8627) [21654123] 1482, **4552**

ECONOMIC & ENERGY INDICATORS / NATIONAL FOREIGN ASSESSMENT CENTER ***CEASED.*** (US) [07156455] 1937, **1556**

ECONOMIC AND FINANCIAL COMPUTING (UK/0962-2780) [25044827] 788, **1482**

ECONOMIC AND FINANCIAL INFORMATION OF THE REPUBLIC OF PANAMA BANCO NACIONAL DE PANAMA (US) [10007018] **1482**

ECONOMIC AND FINANCIAL OUTLOOK (CN/0225-5952) [06213001] **1556**

ECONOMIC AND FINANCIAL PROSPECTS (SZ/0256-3525) [09401041] 1482, **788**

ECONOMIC AND FINANCIAL REPORT OF THE FINANCE LAW FOR THE FINANCIAL YEAR (US) [07816982] **1556**

ECONOMIC AND FINANCIAL STATISTICS (BB/0378-178X) [03028144] 789, 1556, **1531**

ECONOMIC AND FINANCIAL STATISTICS REVIEW (SJ) [03428659] 1556, **1532**

●ECONOMIC AND FISCAL REFERENCE TABLES (CN) [28933893] **4721**

ECONOMIC AND FUNCTIONAL CLASSIFICATION OF THE MANIPUR GOVERNMENT BUDGET, AN (II) [01797712] **4721**

ECONOMIC AND INDUSTRIAL DEMOCRACY (UK/0143-831X) [05879831] **1664**

ECONOMIC AND LABOUR RELATIONS REVIEW : ELRR, THE (AT/1035-3046) [27697724] **2861**

ECONOMIC AND POLITICAL WEEKLY (II/0012-9976) [01567377] 4472, **1556**

ECONOMIC & SHIPPING REVIEW (IO) [06337631] **5449**

ECONOMIC AND SOCIAL COMMITTEE OF THE EUROPEAN COMMUNITIES *See* BULLETIN / ECONOMIC AND SOCIAL COMMITTEE OF THE EUROPEAN COMMUNITIES **1549**

ECONOMIC AND SOCIAL HISTORY IN THE NETHERLANDS (NE/0925-1669) [22877647] **1556**

ECONOMIC AND SOCIAL INDICATORS-TURKEY (US) [02239326] **1556**

ECONOMIC AND SOCIAL ISSUES (US/0886-5345) [02684774] **81**

ECONOMIC AND SOCIAL PROGRESS IN LATIN AMERICA (US/0095-2850) [01796358] **1556**

ECONOMIC AND SOCIAL RESEARCH COUNCIL (GREAT BRITAIN) *See* RESEARCH SUPPORTED BY THE ECONOMIC AND SOCIAL RESEARCH COUNCIL **5215**

ECONOMIC AND SOCIAL RESEARCH INSTITUTE. COUNCIL *See* ANNUAL REPORT FOR THE YEAR ENDED 31 DECEMBER **1462**

ECONOMIC AND SOCIAL REVIEW, THE (IE/0012-9984) [01567378] 1556, **5199**

ECONOMIC AND SOCIAL STUDIES (UK) [01645481] 5199, **1482**

ECONOMIC AND SOCIAL SURVEY OF ASIA AND THE PACIFIC (TH) [02538563] **5199**

ECONOMIC & STATISTICAL BULLETIN (II/0570-0388) [01644309] **1532**

ECONOMIC AWARENESS (UK/0953-4997) [I09534997] **1482**

ECONOMIC BOOKS : CURRENT SELECTIONS ***CEASED.*** (US/0093-2485) [01781254] 671, **1482**

ECONOMIC BOTANY (US/0013-0001) [01567380] **508**

ECONOMIC BULLETIN (NO/0029-1676) [02603512] **1482**

ECONOMIC BULLETIN / BANCO DE ESPANA (SP) [23059878] **1482**

ECONOMIC BULLETIN (BERLIN) (UK/0343-754X) [03008805] **1556**

ECONOMIC BULLETIN FOR ASIA AND THE PACIFIC (US) [02169163] **1482**

ECONOMIC BULLETIN FOR EUROPE (UK/0041-638X) [01567385] **1634**

ECONOMIC BULLETIN - NATIONAL BANK OF EGYPT (UA/0304-274X) [01665239] **789**

ECONOMIC BULLETIN - SINGAPORE INTERNATIONAL CHAMBER OF COMMERCE (SI/0037-5659) [02024279] **819**

ECONOMIC BULLETIN, THE (MY) [02659858] **1556**

ECONOMIC BULLETIN (VIENNA) *See* LANDERBANK ECONOMIC BULLETIN **1502**

ECONOMIC CENSUS. 1987. CD-ROM (US) **671**

ECONOMIC CENSUSES : MANUFACTURING ESTABLISHMENTS *See* CENSUS OF MANUFACTURING ESTABLISHMENTS. DETAILS OF OPERATIONS AND SMALL AREA STATISTICS, TASMANIA / [AUSTRALIAN BUREAU OF STATISTICS, TASMANIA] **3489**

ECONOMIC COMMENTARY (CLEVELAND) (US/0428-1276) [02167157] **1482**

ECONOMIC COMMISSION FOR EUROPE. PRESS RELEASES (SZ) **1482**

ECONOMIC COMPUTATION AND ECONOMIC CYBERNETICS STUDIES AND RESEARCH (RM/0424-267X) [01567388] **1251**

ECONOMIC CONDITIONS IN NEW HAMPSHIRE LOCAL OFFICE AREAS (US/0091-5033) [01787481] **1664**

ECONOMIC COOPERATION SERIES (US/0083-0062) [01169130] **1482**

ECONOMIC COUNCIL OF CANADA *See* ANNUAL REVIEW - ECONOMIC COUNCIL OF CANADA **1463**

ECONOMIC COUNCIL OF CANADA *See* DISCUSSION PAPER - ECONOMIC COUNCIL OF CANADA **1480**

ECONOMIC CRIME DIGEST (US/0362-0697) [02441350] **3163**

ECONOMIC CRIME PROJECT NEWSLETTER *See* ECONOMIC CRIME DIGEST **3163**

●ECONOMIC DESIGN (NE) [I09285040] **1482**

ECONOMIC DEVELOPER (US/1041-9969) [18898183] **1482**

ECONOMIC DEVELOPERS ASSOCIATION OF CANADA *See* DIRECTORY / ECONOMIC DEVELOPERS ASSOCIATION OF CANADA **1479**

ECONOMIC DEVELOPMENT ABROAD (US/1054-0903) [16829529] **2821**

ECONOMIC DEVELOPMENT AND CULTURAL CHANGE (US/0013-0079) [01567393] 5244, **1482**

ECONOMIC DEVELOPMENT AND LAW CENTER REPORT (US/0731-6941) [05360186] **1556**

ECONOMIC DEVELOPMENT BRIEFS (US/0891-7000) [14961681] **1557**

ECONOMIC DEVELOPMENT COMMENTARY (US/8755-8629) [07529586] **1557**

●ECONOMIC DEVELOPMENT DIGEST (WASHINGTON, D.C.) (US/1060-5339) [25035546] **1482**

ECONOMIC DEVELOPMENT MONITOR (US/1054-6936) [22939729] **1482**

ECONOMIC DEVELOPMENT PROJECTS IN THE ARAB WORLD AND IRAN (US/0160-3167) [03644875] **1557**

ECONOMIC DEVELOPMENT QUARTERLY (US/0891-2424) [14687499] **1483**

ECONOMIC DEVELOPMENT REVIEW (SCHILLER PARK, ILL.) (US/0742-3713) [10310708] 1605, **1483**

ECONOMIC DEVELOPMENT TECHNICAL INFORMATION PAPER *See* INFORMATION DOCUMENT (SOUTH PACIFIC COMMISSION) **2620**

ECONOMIC DEVELOPMENTS IN THE MIDDLE EAST (US) [09721862] **1483**

ECONOMIC DIALOGUE TURKEY (TU) [13047177] **1557**

ECONOMIC — Alphabetical Title Index

ECONOMIC DIGEST (XR) [01791129] **671**

ECONOMIC EDUCATION BULLETIN (GREAT BARRINGTON) (US/0424-2769) [02250348] **789**

ECONOMIC EDUCATION EXPERIENCES OF ENTERPRISING TEACHERS (US/0070-8534) [01783086] 1893, **5199**

ECONOMIC EYE (JA/0389-0503) [06957604] **1557**

ECONOMIC FACT BOOK (DETROIT, MICH.) (US/0898-0829) [15989052] 819, **1483**

ECONOMIC, FINANCIAL, AND SOCIAL INFORMATION CONCERNING THE REPUBLIC OF PANAMA See ECONOMIC AND FINANCIAL INFORMATION OF THE REPUBLIC OF PANAMA BANCO NACIONAL DE PANAMA **1482**

ECONOMIC FORECASTS (NE/0169-1767) [11759767] **1557**

ECONOMIC FORUM MINORITY BUSINESS REVIEW (US) 2259, **671**

ECONOMIC GEOGRAPHY (US/0013-0095) [01567395] 2560, **1483**

ECONOMIC GEOLOGY AND THE BULLETIN OF THE SOCIETY OF ECONOMIC GEOLOGISTS (US/0361-0128) [02006844] **1374**

ECONOMIC GEOLOGY (MONTPELIER, VT.) (US/0531-8262) [01696091] 1483, **1374**

ECONOMIC GEOLOGY REPORT (ALBERTA RESEARCH COUNCIL) (CN) [03439967] 1483, **1374**

ECONOMIC GEOLOGY REPORT (OTTAWA) (CN/0317-445X) [02248485] 1439, **1374**

ECONOMIC GROWTH AND LEAD AND ZINC CONSUMPTION (UK) **4001**

ECONOMIC HANDBOOK OF THE MACHINE TOOL INDUSTRY (US/0070-8550) [01788561] **2113**

ECONOMIC HISTORY REVIEW, THE (UK/0013-0117) [01883400] **1557**

●ECONOMIC HOME OWNER, THE (US/1055-8284) [23352349] **2821**

ECONOMIC IMPACT ANALYSIS PROGRAM, THE ANNUAL REPORT (US/8755-7053) [08177723] **2192**

ECONOMIC IMPACT (WASHINGTON, D.C.) *CEASED.* (US/0886-8085) [13017355] **1557**

ECONOMIC INDICATORS (US) [22977507] **1483**

ECONOMIC INDICATORS (CHARLESTON, W. VA.) (US/0278-8381) [07877923] **1557**

ECONOMIC INDICATORS; EAST-CENTRAL STATE - (NIGERIA) (NR) [01997756] **1557**

ECONOMIC INDICATORS, FORECASTS FOR COMPANY PLANNING (UK/0263-7065) [I02637065] **1483**

ECONOMIC INDICATORS / NATIONAL STATISTICAL OFFICE, PAPUA, NEW GUINEA (PP) [09501994] **1557**

ECONOMIC INDICATORS OF THE FARM SECTOR. COSTS OF PRODUCTION. LIVESTOCK AND DAIRY (US) [22856232] **194**

ECONOMIC INDICATORS OF THE FARM SECTOR. COSTS OF PRODUCTION. MAJOR FIELD CROPS (US/1057-7890) [22839200] **170**

ECONOMIC INDICATORS OF THE FARM SECTOR. NATIONAL FINANCIAL SUMMARY (US/0895-2051) [13177546] **81**

ECONOMIC INDICATORS OF THE FARM SECTOR. PRODUCTION AND EFFICIENCY STATISTICS (US/0747-9492) [08055037] 81, 1483, **153**

ECONOMIC INDICATORS OF THE FARM SECTOR. STATE FINANCIAL SUMMARY (US) [13431168] 1483, **81**

ECONOMIC INDICATORS / REPUBLIC OF TRINIDAD & TOBAGO, CENTRAL STATISTICAL OFFICE (TR) [23993775] **1557**

ECONOMIC INDICATORS (WASHINGTON, D.C.) (US/0013-0125) [01567401] **1557**

ECONOMIC INFORMATION ON ARGENTINA (AG/0325-2388) [03467489] **1483**

ECONOMIC INFORMATION REPORT (GAINESVILLE, FLA.) (US/0886-4845) [02728413] **81**

ECONOMIC INQUIRY (US/0095-2583) [01794536] **1483**

ECONOMIC INTELLIGENCE REVIEW (UK) [I13501070] **1483**

ECONOMIC INVESTIGATION (FJ) [08704817] **1439**

ECONOMIC JOURNAL (LONDON) (UK/0013-0133) [01567402] **1483**

ECONOMIC JOURNAL OF HOKKAIDO UNIVERSITY (JA/0916-4650) [22858244] **1483**

ECONOMIC JOURNAL OF NEPAL, THE (NP) [06937631] **1557**

ECONOMIC JUSTICE REPORT (CN/0849-3391) [23230575] **1557**

ECONOMIC LEAFLETS (US/0013-0141) [01569435] **1483**

ECONOMIC LEAFLETS. - FLORIDA. UNIVERSITY, GAINESVILLE. BUREAU OF ECONOMIC AND BUSINESS RESEARCH (US) [01330215] **1557**

ECONOMIC LITERATURE INDEX (US) 1483, **1532**

ECONOMIC MODELLING (UK/0264-9993) [10479785] **1591**

ECONOMIC MONTHLY (SI) **1483**

ECONOMIC NEWS FROM ITALY *CEASED.* (US/0739-5566) [06642262] 789, **1557**

ECONOMIC NEWS OF BULGARIA (BU/0205-1400) [02260602] **1483**

ECONOMIC OPPORTUNITY REPORT (US/0013-0206) [05016236] **5284**

ECONOMIC OUTLOOK FOR INDUSTRIAL COUNTRIES (CN/1183-6296) [24279927] **1557**

ECONOMIC OUTLOOK FOR NEW JERSEY / ECONOMIC POLICY COUNCIL (US) [07301699] **1557**

ECONOMIC OUTLOOK (LONDON. 1977) (UK/0140-489X) [06245235] 671, **1483**

ECONOMIC PANORAMA BANCOMER (MX) [07349426] **1557**

ECONOMIC PAPER (RALEIGH) (US/0097-2290) [01306572] 1374, **1483**

ECONOMIC PAPERS (PL/0324-864X) [05734626] **1484**

ECONOMIC PAPERS / THE ECONOMIC SOCIETY OF AUSTRALIA (AT) [09997335] **1484**

ECONOMIC PERSPECTIVES (1989) (US/1048-115X) [19003481] **789**

ECONOMIC PERSPECTIVES. AGRICULTURAL CREDIT OUTLOOK (US/1048-7573) [18097625] 81, **1484**

ECONOMIC PERSPECTIVES (CHUR) (US/0142-5900) [05035367] **1484**

ECONOMIC PERSPECTIVES (WASHINGTON, D.C.) (US) [06401556] **1484**

ECONOMIC PLANNING IN FREE SOCIETIES (CN/1191-3576) [25612961] 1484, **81**

ECONOMIC PLANNING JOURNAL IN FREE SOCIETIES FOR AGRICULTURE AND RELATED INDUSTRIES (CN/1191-3576) [01567406] 1484, **81**

ECONOMIC POISONS ... REPORT (BISMARCK, N.D.) (US/0749-3312) [11082294] **2413**

ECONOMIC POLICY (UK/0266-4658) [13365818] **1484**

ECONOMIC POLICY ISSUES *CEASED.* (US/0884-4852) [07308306] 1484, **4721**

ECONOMIC POLICY PAPERS (NEW YORK, N.Y.) (US) [10635971] **1484**

ECONOMIC PROGRESS REPORT (UK/0262-5067) [02673142] **1557**

ECONOMIC QUALITY CONTROL (GW/0940-5151) [I09405151] **1484**

ECONOMIC QUARTERLY (GE) [04627012] **1484**

●ECONOMIC QUARTERLY / FEDERAL RESERVE BANK OF RICHMOND (US/1069-7225) [28103472] **1484**

ECONOMIC RECORD, THE (AT/0013-0249) [01567410] **1484**

ECONOMIC REFERENCE TABLES See ECONOMIC AND FISCAL REFERENCE TABLES **4721**

ECONOMIC REFORM TODAY (US/1058-661X) [24368096] **1484**

ECONOMIC REFORM (TORONTO) (CN/1187-080X) [25066843] **1484**

ECONOMIC REGULATIONS. PT. 214. TERMS, CHARTERS, AND LIMITATIONS OF FOREIGN AIR CARRIER PERMITS AUTHORIZING CHARTER TRANSPORTATION ONLY (US) [03835959] **18**

ECONOMIC REPORT (ALBUQUERQUE, N.M.), THE (US/0738-7210) [09711427] 789, **1484**

ECONOMIC REPORT - CENTRAL BANK OF KUWAIT (KU) [04545045] **789**

ECONOMIC REPORT - MALAYSIA. KEMENTERIAN KEWANGAN (MY) [03401246] **1557**

ECONOMIC REPORT OF THE GOVERNOR (LANSING) (US/0196-5980) [01624162] 4721, **1484**

ECONOMIC REPORT OF THE GOVERNOR / STATE OF NEW JERSEY, GOVERNOR (US) [09190718] **1557**

ECONOMIC REPORT OF THE PRESIDENT; HEARINGS BEFORE THE JOINT ECONOMIC COMMITTEE, CONGRESS OF THE UNITED STATES (US) [03160302] **1557**

ECONOMIC REPORT OF THE PRESIDENT TRANSMITTED TO THE CONGRESS (US/0193-1180) [01193149] **1484**

ECONOMIC REPORT, THE STATE OF SOUTH CAROLINA (US/0145-3637) [02724785] **1558**

ECONOMIC REPORT - TURKIYE IS BANKAS A.S (TU/0376-9275) [01798004] 671, **1484**

●ECONOMIC REPORTER (HK) [28058104] **1484**

ECONOMIC RESEARCH JOURNAL (PH/0424-2904) [01567411] **1484**

ECONOMIC RESEARCH OF INTEREST TO AGRICULTURE / UNIVERSITY OF CALIFORNIA, DIVISION OF AGRICULTURAL SCIENCES, AGRICULTURAL EXPERIMENT STATION (US/0527-0936) [03110131] **153**

ECONOMIC RESEARCH REPORT (SAN FRANCISCO, CALIF.) (US/0735-6145) [06903510] **2366**

ECONOMIC RESEARCH SERIES (JA/0441-0025) [02231136] **1484**

ECONOMIC REVIEW (AT) [07974385] **1484**

ECONOMIC REVIEW (BG) [03260912] **1558**

ECONOMIC REVIEW AND ANNUAL PLAN (ZA) [15068258] **1484**

ECONOMIC REVIEW AND OUTLOOK (IE) [05112875] **1558**

ECONOMIC REVIEW AND OUTLOOK (SQ) [15492308] **1484**

ECONOMIC REVIEW (ATLANTA, GA.) (US/0732-1813) [03107655] **789**

ECONOMIC REVIEW (CLEVELAND) (US/0013-0281) [02112462] **1484**

ECONOMIC REVIEW (COLOMBO) (CE/0259-9775) [02246798] **1484**

ECONOMIC REVIEW (CYPRUS POPULAR BANK) (CY/0254-3214) [29342385] **1484**

ECONOMIC REVIEW (DEDDINGTON) (UK/0265-0290) [13107724] **1485**

ECONOMIC REVIEW / FEDERAL RESERVE BANK OF SAN FRANCISCO (US) [26628989] **1485**

ECONOMIC REVIEW (JAKARTA, INDONESIA) (IO/0216-7107) [14705791] **1558**

ECONOMIC REVIEW (JERUSALEM) (IS/0334-441X) [02329076] **1485**

ECONOMIC REVIEW - KANSALLIS-OSAKE-PANKKI (FI/0022-8419) [01782733] **1558**

ECONOMIC REVIEW (KANSAS CITY) (US/0161-2387) [03778781] **1485**

ECONOMIC REVIEW (KARACHI) (PK/0531-8955) [01774317] **1558**

ECONOMIC REVIEW OF THE ARAB WORLD (LE/0013-032X) [02291615] **1485**

ECONOMIC REVIEW OF TRAVEL IN AMERICA, THE (US/0733-642X) [08617004] 1485, **5469**

ECONOMIC REVIEW (REGINA. 1980) (CN/0824-2828) [10156769] **1485**

ECONOMIC REVIEW (RICHMOND, VA.) (US/0094-6893) [01794851] **1485**

ECONOMIC REVIEW (SAN FRANCISCO) (US/0363-0021) [02590214] **1558**

ECONOMIC REVIEW (TAIPEI, TAIWAN) (CH/0013-029X) [03132550] 671, **1485**

ECONOMIC REVIEW (WEST BENGAL, INDIA) (II/0511-5272) [01605664] **1558**

ECONOMIC ROUND-UP / AUSTRALIA, THE TREASURY (AT) [18138989] **4721**

ECONOMIC SITUATION IN THE FEDERAL REPUBLIC OF GERMANY, THE (GW/0431-6045) [03151076] **1485**

ECONOMIC STABILIZATION PROGRAM (US/0091-8342) [01788061] **1485**

ECONOMIC STATISTICS QUARTERLY / CENTRAL BANK OF ICELAND (IC) [06932666] 1485, **1532**

ECONOMIC STATISTICS REPORT (CN/1184-9231) [24296400] **1485**

ECONOMIC STATISTICS YEARBOOK (KO/0440-2588) [01605265] **728**

ECONOMIC STUDIES (CALCUTTA, INDIA) (II/0013-0362) [01607809] **1558**

ECONOMIC STUDIES : UN ECONOMIC COMMISSION FOR EUROPE See OCCASIONAL STUDIES OF THE ECONOMIC COMMISSION FOR EUROPE **1638**

ECONOMIC STUDIES / UNITED NATIONS ECONOMIC COMMISSION FOR EUROPE (US/1014-4994) [21181374] **1485**

ECONOMIC SUMMARY OF EXTENSION TECHNICAL BULLETIN NO. ... / UNIVERSITY OF ARKANSAS COOPERATIVE EXTENSION SERVICE, AN (US) [24661344] **81**

ECONOMIC SURVEY (UK) [03735283] **4828**

ECONOMY

ECONOMIC SURVEY / CENTRAL BUREAU OF STATISTICS OF NORWAY (NO/0801-8324) [23665529] **1485**

ECONOMIC SURVEY ... FINLAND (FI) [11680883] **1485**

ECONOMIC SURVEY OF AFRICA (US/0070-8682) [01768045] **1485**

ECONOMIC SURVEY OF DENMARK (DK) [01566165] **1485**

ECONOMIC SURVEY OF EUROPE (US/0070-8712) [01696134] **1485**

ECONOMIC SURVEY OF HARYANA (II) [01604711] **1558**

ECONOMIC SURVEY OF JAPAN (JA/0021-4833) [01179466] **1558**

ECONOMIC SURVEY OF LATIN AMERICA AND THE CARIBBEAN / ECONOMIC COMMISSION FOR LATIN AMERICA AND THE CARIBBEAN (CL/0257-2184) [11734519] **1485**

ECONOMIC SURVEY OF LIBERIA (LB/0303-853X) [01798398] **1558**

ECONOMIC SURVEY OF NEW ZEALAND WHEATGROWERS : FINANCIAL ANALYSIS, AN (NZ) [06841367] **81**

ECONOMIC SURVEY OF SINGAPORE (SI/0376-8791) [02245659] **1558**

ECONOMIC SURVEY OF THE ... KOREAN ECONOMY (KO/0454-3653) [01181187] **1558**

ECONOMIC SURVEY - UNITED REPUBLIC OF TANZANIA (TZ/0300-1741) [01784801] **1558**

ECONOMIC SURVEYS BY THE OECD. JAPAN *See* OECD ECONOMIC SURVEYS: JAPAN **1510**

ECONOMIC SURVEYS: PORTUGAL *See* OECD ECONOMIC SURVEYS : PORTUGAL **1576**

ECONOMIC SYSTEMS (GW/0939-3625) [24118150] **1558**

ECONOMIC SYSTEMS RESEARCH (UK/0953-5314) [20337274] **1485**

ECONOMIC THEORY (GW/0938-2259) [23524949] **1591**

ECONOMIC TIMES (UK) **671**

ECONOMIC TIMES ANNUAL, THE (II) [01790403] **1558**

ECONOMIC TIMES (NEW YORK, N.Y.) (US/1050-0200) [21370724] **1485**

ECONOMIC TIMES, THE (NP) [25585858] **1485**

ECONOMIC TRENDS (US) [12376230] **3780**

ECONOMIC TRENDS (BG) [05226443] **1558**

ECONOMIC TRENDS (CLEVELAND, OHIO) (US/0748-2922) [10625526] **1485**

ECONOMIC TRENDS IN COLOR (1978) (US/0270-6814) [04151404] **1485**

● ECONOMIC TRENDS IN EASTERN EUROPE (HU/1216-1829) [I12161829] **1558**

ECONOMIC TRENDS IN EASTERN EUROPE AND THE WORLD ECONOMY *See* ECONOMIC TRENDS IN EASTERN EUROPE **1558**

ECONOMIC TRENDS IN HUNGARY (HU) **1558**

ECONOMIC TRENDS (LONDON) (UK/0013-0400) [01567420] **1485**

ECONOMIC TRENDS (NEW DELHI) (II/0014-9470) [01645278] **1591**

ECONOMIC UPDATE (US) [05198554] **1485**

ECONOMIC UPDATE - DOMINION SECURITIES AMES. ECONOMICS (CN/0824-3425) [10398386] **1558**

ECONOMIC UPDATE ULTIMO (AT/1034-747X) [I1034747X] **1486**

ECONOMIC WORLD (PK) [02240267] **1486**

ECONOMIC WORLD DIRECTORY OF JAPANESE COMPANIES IN USA *CEASED*. (US/0163-4682) [04030745] **832**

ECONOMIC WORLD (LOS ANGELES) *CEASED*. (US/0164-3525) [02251614] **832, 1486**

ECONOMICA (IO) [06771938] **1486**

ECONOMICA (AG/0013-0419) [02326547] **1486**

ECONOMICA (FI) [05304284] **1486**

ECONOMICA (LONDON) (UK/0013-0427) [01567422] **1486**

ECONOMICS (AT) **1486**

ECONOMICS AND BUSINESS EDUCATION (UK/0969-2509) [27989550] **1486**

ECONOMICS AND PHILOSOPHY (UK/0266-2671) [12425827] **4345, 1486**

ECONOMICS & POLITICS (OXFORD, ENGLAND) (UK/0954-1985) [20157198] **4472, 1486**

ECONOMICS AND RELATED DISCIPLINES / INTERNATIONAL CURRENT AWARENESS SERVICES *CEASED*. (UK/0960-152X) [23856022] **1486**

ECONOMICS AND RURAL WELFARE RESEARCH REPORT (IE/0332-0251) [01795391] **81**

ECONOMICS AND SOCIETY SERIES (UK) [08235087] **1486**

ECONOMICS (BOCA RATON, FLA.) (US/1058-1758) [24233488] **1486**

ECONOMICS BRANCH PUBLICATION (CN) [02069567] **1486, 81**

ECONOMICS CLASSICS - OLD AND RARE BOOKS ON ECONOMICS (US) **1486**

ECONOMICS (DUSHKIN PUBLISHING GROUP) (US) [06534480] **1486**

ECONOMICS : ENCYCLOPEDIA (US/0090-4422) [01783679] **1486**

ECONOMICS FOR KIDS (US) 1893, **1486**

ECONOMICS ILLUSTRATED (US) **1486**

ECONOMICS LETTERS (NE/0165-1765) [04596608] **1486**

ECONOMICS (LONDON) (UK/0300-4287) [01425598] **1486**

ECONOMICS MONITOR (AT) **1486**

ECONOMICS OF AGRICULTURAL PRODUCTION AND FARM MANAGEMENT IN PUNJAB (II) [05157005] **1486, 81**

ECONOMICS OF CONFEDERATION (CN/1183-899X) [25882887] **1486**

ECONOMICS OF EDUCATION REVIEW (US/0272-7757) [06933446] **1737**

ECONOMICS OF INNOVATION AND NEW TECHNOLOGY (SZ/1043-8599) [19583017] **5102**

ECONOMICS OF MARINE RESOURCES (US/0424-3110) [01179820] **2192**

ECONOMICS OF MILK PRODUCTION IN ALBERTA (CN/0226-3947) [06860948] **194**

ECONOMICS OF PLANNING (NE/0013-0451) [06678671] **1558**

ECONOMICS OF TRANSITION, THE (UK/0967-0750) [29189453] **1486**

ECONOMICS SERIES- FLORIDA. UNIVERSITY, GAINESVILLE. AGRICULTURAL EXTENSION SERVICE (US/0428-6782) [01313003] **81**

ECONOMICS, STATISTICS, COOPERATIVES; PROGRAM RESULTS AND PLANS (US) [05855685] **1486, 1532**

ECONOMICS : TEXT (US/0090-4430) [01783680] **1591**

ECONOMICS (TUBINGEN) (GW/0341-616X) [04610532] **1487**

ECONOMICUS (BG) [06076922] **1487**

ECONOMIE ALGERIENNE, L' (FR) [06502915] **1558**

ECONOMIE AND GESTION AGRO-ALIMENTAIRE (FR/0981-8715) [I09818715] **1487, 81**

ECONOMIE & PREVISION (FR/0249-4744) [08641792] **1487**

ECONOMIE APPLIQUEE (SZ/0013-0494) [01567425] **1591**

ECONOMIE DE L'ENERGIE (FR/0046-1202) [04950063] **1961**

ECONOMIE DU CENTRE-EST, L' (FR/0153-4459) [03675050] **1558**

ECONOMIE DU TOURISME, L' (FR/0753-311X) [12873724] **5469**

ECONOMIE ELECTRIQUE, L' (FR/0013-0508) [01785831] **2042**

● ECONOMIE ET AFFAIRES AU QUEBEC (CN/1188-4304) [27019088] **671**

ECONOMIE ET COMPTABILITE (FR) [06803445] **1487**

ECONOMIE ET FINANCES AGRICOLES (FR/0070-8798) [25831333] **1487, 81**

ECONOMIE ET HUMANISME (FR/0245-9132) [01567426] **1634**

ECONOMIE ET POLITIQUE (PARIS. 1954) (FR/0424-3218) [01616834] **1487**

ECONOMIE ET SOCIALISME (FR/0424-3226) [01833917] **4541, 1487**

ECONOMIE ET STATISTIQUE (FR/0336-1454) [05158531] **1487, 1532**

ECONOMIE FAMILIALE HOME ECONOMICS, L' (FR/0397-8389) [05109934] **2789**

ECONOMIE FAMILIALE, L' (FR) [02245682] **2789**

ECONOMIE GABONAISE, L' (FR) [05135286] **1558**

ECONOMIE, GEOGRAPHIE (FR) [02242223] **1558**

● ECONOMIE INTERNATIONALE : LA REVUE DU CEPII (FR) [28689628] **1634**

ECONOMIE IVOIRIENNE, L' (FR) [01783829] **1487**

ECONOMIE IVOIRIENNE, L' (IV) [04015626] **1558**

ECONOMIE, L' (FR/0013-0478) [06472724] **1558**

ECONOMIE PAPETIERE (FR/0247-3372) [I02473372] **1487**

ECONOMIE PROSPECTIVE INTERNATIONALE (FR/0242-7818) [09843871] **1634**

ECONOMIE PROSPECTIVE INTERNATIONALE *See* ECONOMIE INTERNATIONALE : LA REVUE DU CEPII **1634**

ECONOMIE RURALE (FR/0013-0559) [01567429] **1487**

ECONOMIE SENEGALAISE, L' (FR) [01783815] **1559**

ECONOMIES ET SOCIETES (FR/0013-0567) [02260616] **5244, 1487**

ECONOMIQUE (MONTREAL) (CN/0820-8816) [09631120] **1487**

ECONOMISCH BEELD (NE/0924-073X) [20957166] **1591, 1559**

ECONOMISCH- EN SOCIAAL-HISTORISCH JAARBOEK (NE/0167-7942) [01567430] **1559**

ECONOMISCH EN SOCIAAL TIJDSCHRIFT (BE/0013-0575) [02294400] **1487, 671**

ECONOMISCH INSTITUUT VOOR HET MIDDEN- EN KLEINBEDRIJF *See* BEDRIJFSGEGEVENS VOOR DE DETAILHANDEL IN UURWERKEN EN GGOUDEN EN ZILVEREN WWERKEN **2913**

ECONOMISCH INSTITUUT VOOR HET MIDDEN- EN KLEINBEDRIJF *See* BEDRIJFSGEGEVENS VOOR DE DETAILHANDEL IN KOFFERS EN LEDERWAREN **3183**

ECONOMISCH INSTITUUT VOOR HET MIDDEN- EN KLEINBEDRIJF *See* EIM MEDEDELINGEN, DE **954**

ECONOMISCH INSTITUUT VOOR HET MIDDEN- EN KLEINBEDRIJF *See* BEDRIJFSGEGEVENS VOOR HET SLAGERSBEDRIJF, BEDRIFJSRESULTATEN IN- EN VERKOOPBELEID, VESTIGINGSPLAATS EN RESULTAAT **1548**

ECONOMISCH PROFIEL NEDERLANDSE ANTILLEN (NE) [17883925] **1559**

ECONOMISCH RAPPORT (BE) [23835569] **1487**

ECONOMISCH-STATISTISCHE BERICHTEN (NE/0013-0583) [01567432] **1559**

ECONOMIST ANNUAL INDEX *See* ECONOMIST QUARTERLY INDEX, THE **1532**

ECONOMIST BOOK OF VITAL WORLD STATISTICS, THE (UK) **5326**

ECONOMIST. BRIEF, THE (UK/0422-3586) [01891598] **1559**

ECONOMIST, DE (NE/0013-063X) [02210758] **1559**

ECONOMIST DESK DIARY (UK) **1487**

ECONOMIST INTELLIGENCE UNIT (GREAT BRITAIN) *See* WORLD OUTLOOK / EIU **1527**

ECONOMIST INTELLIGENCE UNIT, LTD., LONDON, THE *See* EIU WORLD COMMODITY OUTLOOK: INDUSTRIAL RAW MATERIALS **1605**

ECONOMIST (LONDON) (UK/0013-0613) [01081684] **1559**

ECONOMIST QUARTERLY INDEX, THE (UK) **1487, 1532**

ECONOMISTA MADRID. 1886, EL (SP/0013-0656) [I00130656] **1487**

ECONOMISTA MEXICANO, EL (MX) [06039433] **1559**

ECONOMISTAS (MADRID, SPAIN) (SP/0212-4386) [17361683] **1487**

ECONOMISTE DU TIERS MONDE, L' (FR/0223-5978) [02686176] **1559**

ECONOMISTE (QUEBEC) (CN/0381-0828) [04129268] **1559**

ECONOMISTS', SOCIOLOGISTS' AND STATISTICANS' ASSOCIATION *See* ESSA BULLETIN **1668**

ECONOMY AND FINANCES, PUERTO RICO (PR) [01785683] **4721, 1487**

ECONOMY AND SOCIETY (UK/0308-5147) [01682349] **5199**

ECONOMY & TRADE (II) [11009054] **832**

● ECONOMY AT A GLANCE, THE (US/1063-1208) [25866721] **1487**

ECONOMY BULLETINS (UK) **1487**

ECONOMY HOME PLANS FOR TODAY! (US/0278-2650) [07751855] **298**

ECONOMY SPECTATOR (US) [01567441] **1487**

ECONOMY SURVEY (PK) [12289345] **1487**

ECONOMY WIDE CENSUS (NZ/0114-6912) [I01146912] **613**

ECONOMY — Alphabetical Title Index

ECONOMY WIDE CENSUS : AGRICULTURAL SERVICES, FORESTRY AND FISHING (NZ) **1605**

ECONOSCOPE (CN/0712-2012) [08777685] **1487**

ECONOSCOPE VIEW, THE (US/0193-6468) [05232626] **1559**

ECONOTRACK (NR) [10866914] **1559**

ECOPECHE *See* FRANCE ECOPECHE **2216**

ECORIO (BL/0104-0030) [I01040030] **2164**

ECOS (AT/0311-4546) [04119971] **2227**

ECOS (UK/0143-9073) [10206542] **2192**

ECOS BRITISH ASSOCIATION OF NATURE CONSERVATIONISTS (UK/0143-9073) [I01439073] **2192**

ECOS CRISTOFOROS (US/0882-3707) [11832888] **4955**

●ECOS (LEXINGTON, KY.) (US/1071-8478) [28740411] **2192**

ECOSOURCE *CEASED.* (CN/1181-9707) [24368190] 671, **2164**

ECOSSISTEMA / FACULDADE DE AGRONOMIA E ZOOTECNIA "MANOEL CARLOS GONCALVES." (BL/0100-4107) [02863771] **81**

●ECOSYSTEM HEALTH AND MEDICINE (US/1076-2825) [30446070] **3573**

ECOSYSTEMS OF THE WORLD (NE) [03719301] **454**

ECOTASS (ENGLISH EDITION) *CEASED.* (SZ/0733-5989) [08777618] **1487**

ECOTOXICOLOGY AND ENVIRONMENTAL SAFETY (US/0147-6513) [03702909] 2227, **2214**

●ECOTOXICOLOGY LONDON (UK/0963-9292) [I09639292] 974, **2215**

ECOTREKS (CN) **5469**

●ECOTRENDS (US) **1487**

ECOTROPICOS : REVISTA DE LA SOCIEDAD VENEZOLANA DE ECOLOGIA (VE/1012-1692) [18403425] 454, **2215**

ECOZOO (CN/1184-1877) [23284054] 4165, **5582**

ECP REPORT (US/0364-3840) [02323991] 2192, **1937**

ECQUID NOVI (SA/0256-0054) [09250794] **2919**

ECRAN FANTASTIQUE, L' (FR) [09001967] **4068**

ECRAN (PARIS, FRANCE) *See* REVUE DU CINEMA (PARIS. 1969) **4077**

ECRIRE (MONTREAL) (CN/0711-5474) [08720698] **3383**

ECRITIQUE (CN/0226-6253) [06473540] **3462**

●ECRITIQUE (IOWA CITY, IOWA) (US/1061-1479) [25191223] 3341, **3383**

ECRITOIRE (MONTREAL) (CN/0229-7043) [08767021] **3383**

ECRITS DE PARIS (FR/0013-0710) [05507814] **2515**

ECRITS DE PARIS (FR/0013-0710) [01617327] **4472**

ECRITS DU CANADA FRANCAIS (CN/0013-0729) [02247669] **3383**

ECRITS SUR LE CINEMA (SUPPLEMENT) (CN/0822-6350) [10199273] **4068**

ECRITURE FRANCAISE DANS LE MONDE *CEASED.* (CN/0228-5791) [07822704] **3383**

ECRITURES / UNIVERSITE DE PARIS X, UNIVERSITE DE YAOUNDE (FR) [16799791] **3383**

ECS MARINE FINANCIAL YEAR BOOK (UK) [12588359] **5449**

ECTACOM (AT/0813-9423) [I08139423] **1487**

ECU REPORT, THE (US/0744-7183) [08507898] **1822**

ECU SME INFORMAZIONI (LU) **832**

ECUADOR : ENERGIEWIRTSCHAFT (GW) [05725457] **1937**

ECUADOR, WIRTSCHAFTSDATEN UND WIRTSCHAFTSDOKUMENTATION / BUNDESSTELLE FUR AUSSENHANDELSINFORMATION (GW) [07720698] **1559**

ECUADOR, WIRTSCHAFTSSTRUKTUR / BUNDESSTELLE FUR AUSSENHANDELSINFORMATION (GW) [09363494] **1559**

ECUM BULLETIN *SUSPENDED.* (UK/0263-662X) [10964048] **4955**

●ECUMENE (UK/0967-4608) [29304269] **2560**

ECUMENICAL DIRECTORY OF RETREAT AND CONFERENCE CENTERS (US/0361-2236) [02246254] **4955**

ECUMENICAL REVIEW, THE (SZ/0013-0796) [01567448] **4955**

ECUMENICAL TRENDS (US/0360-9073) [01776986] **4955**

ECUMENISM (CN/0383-431X) [09365652] **4955**

ECUNEWS : ECUMENICAL NEWS SERVICE OF THE SOUTH AFRICAN COUNCIL OF CHURCHES (SA) [09712883] **4955**

ECYM. ENDOCRINOLOGIA CLINICA Y METABOLISMO (SP/0212-0348) [I02120348] **3729**

ED (US) [19231745] 1737, **1154**

ED MANAGEMENT (US/1044-9167) [19948388] 3780, **3724**

ED-TECH REVIEW (US/1065-6901) [26678042] 1737, **1223**

EDAD DE ORO (MADRID, SPAIN) (SP) [11358713] **3383**

EDAV. EDUCAZIONE AUDIOVISIVA (IT/0393-098X) [I0393098X] **1737**

EDC TODAY (CN/0839-9549) [19217501] **832**

EDCAL (US/0740-0357) [07878917] **1737**

EDDA (NO/0013-0818) [01567451] **3341**

EDDY-CURRENT INSPECTION FOR STEAM GENERATOR TUBING PROGRAM ANNUAL PROGRESS REPORT FOR PERIOD ENDING ... / OAK RIDGE NATIONAL LABORATORY, METALS AND CERAMICS DIVISION (US) [08352884] **2154**

EDDY-CURRENT INSPECTION FOR STEAM GENERATOR TUBING PROGRAM QUARTERLY PROGRESS REPORT FOR PERIOD ENDING ... / OAK RIDGE NATIONAL LABORATORY, METALS AND CERAMICS DIVISION (US) [08455004] **1971**

EDDYVILLE TRIBUNE, THE (US) [13913312] **5670**

EDEBIYAT: JOURNAL OF MIDDLE EASTERN LITERATURES (US) 2768, **3383**

EDEBIYAT (PHILADELPHIA, PA.) (SZ/0364-6505) [02667511] **3383**

EDEKA HANDELSRUNDSCHAU (GW) 1487, **671**

EDELL HEALTH LETTER, THE *CEASED.* (US/0896-6613) [17242320] **3573**

EDELSTEIN PRO FOOTBALL LETTER, THE (US/0891-7329) [15011473] **4894**

EDEN ECHO, THE (US) [14091000] **5749**

EDESIPAR (HU/0013-0842) [02309429] **2334**

EDF LETTER (US/0163-2566) [03210407] 2227, **2192**

EDGE (HACKETTSTOWN, N.J.) (US/1063-8431) [26149688] **1241**

EDGE (MORRISTOWN, N.J.) *CEASED.* (US/0890-9563) [14562064] **1154**

EDGE, THE (UK) [24282325] **1063**

EDGEBROOK EDITION OF THE TIMES REVIEW (US/0895-0105) [16402294] **5660**

EDGEFIELD ADVERTISER (US) [10722626] **5742**

EDGELEY MAIL, THE (US) [01567456] **5725**

EDGERTON EARTH, THE (US) [10245177] **5728**

EDGERTON ENTERPRISE (US) [01567457] **5695**

EDGERTON REPORTER, THE (US) [14581467] **5767**

EDGEWATER TRIBUNE (US/0745-774X) [09444963] **5642**

EDGEWOOD ENTERPRISE (US) [14185047] **5749**

EDI ANALYSIS (UK/0958-5052) [I09585052] **866**

EDI (DALLAS, TEX.) *SUSPENDED.* (US/1045-5698) [20141231] 671, **1258**

EDI DEVELOPMENT POLICY CASE SERIES. ANALYTICAL CASE STUDIES (US/1013-333X) [18757840] **1487**

EDI DEVELOPMENT POLICY CASE SERIES. TEACHING CASES (US/1013-3348) [18757889] **1487**

EDI DIRECTORY *See* WHO'S WHO IN ELECTRONIC COMMERCE **1207**

EDI EXECUTIVE (US) **671**

EDI FORUM (US/1048-3047) [19523350] **671**

EDI IN FINANCE (UK/0960-4634) [I09604634] **5102**

EDI LAW REVIEW, THE (UK/0929-2233) **2965**

EDI MONTHLY REPORT (US/1062-645X) [25690210] **4645**

EDI NEWS (US/0894-9212) [16314368] **1183**

EDI POLICY SEMINAR REPORT, AN (US/1042-490X) [17995077] **1487**

EDI RESEARCH AUSTRALIA (AT/1034-8360) [I10348360] **1183**

EDI SEMINAR PAPER, AN (US/1013-2015) [18615828] **1487**

EDI UPDATE LONDON (UK/0954-6154) [I09546154] **4721**

EDI WORLD (US/1055-0399) [23026431] **2042**

EDI YELLOW PAGES INTERNATIONAL (US) **1183**

EDIBLE NUT MARKET REPORT (UK/0951-1547) [I09511547] **170**

EDIBLE NUT STATISTICS (UK) [07495939] **2334**

EDICESA NEWS / ECUMENICAL DOCUMENTATION AND INFORMATION CENTRE FOR EASTERN AND SOUTHERN AFRICA (RH) [21139600] **4955**

EDICIONES (VE/0506-5992) [01486797] **3208**

EDICIONES BIBLIOTECA JOSE AGUSTIN ARANGO CH. BOLETIN CULTURAL (PN) [09812144] **3209**

EDICIONES CICERONE *See* GUIA DE TURISMO : REPUBLICA ARGENTINA **5478**

EDICOES CADERNOS CULTURAIS (BL) [02477150] **349**

EDIFICACION CRISTIANA (SP) **4955**

EDILIZIA (IT) **2022**

EDILIZIA-EX PREFABBRICAZIONE (IT) **2022**

EDILIZIA POPOLARE (IT/0422-5619) [02323807] **2821**

EDILIZIA RESIDENZIALE PUBBLICA NOTIZ ANIACAP (IT) **2821**

EDILIZIA SCOLASTICA E CULTURALE (IT) [28474970] **2821**

EDIMED (IT) **4302**

EDINBURGH ANTHROPOLOGY (UK/0953-2919) [18269419] **235**

EDINBURGH BIBLIOGRAPHICAL SOCIETY *See* EDINBURGH BIBLIOGRAPHICAL SOCIETY TRANSACTIONS **415**

EDINBURGH BIBLIOGRAPHICAL SOCIETY TRANSACTIONS (UK/0140-7082) [01567477] **415**

EDINBURGH DENTAL HOSPITAL GAZETTE (UK/0013-0907) [01297481] **1322**

EDINBURGH INFORMATION TECHNOLOGY SERIES (UK) [19559203] **5102**

EDINBURGH JOURNAL OF BOTANY (UK/0960-4286) [21684344] **508**

EDINBURGH MATHEMATICAL SOCIETY *See* PROCEEDINGS OF THE EDINBURGH MATHEMATICAL SOCIETY **3528**

EDINBURGH REVIEW (EDINBURGH : 1985) (UK/0267-6672) [11835472] **3383**

EDINBURGH REVIEW OF THEOLOGY AND RELIGION (UK/1354-991X) **4955**

EDINBURGH. ROYAL OBSERVATORY *See* PUBLICATIONS - EDINBURGH. ROYAL OBSERVATORY **398**

EDINBURGH SCHOOL OF AGRICULTURE *See* ANNUAL REVIEW / THE EDINBURGH SCHOOL OF AGRICULTURE **62**

EDINBURGH STUDIES IN THE ENGLISH LANGUAGE (UK) [18103942] **3383**

EDINBURGH WORKING PAPERS IN APPLIED LINGUISTICS (UK/0959-2253) [23888139] **3278**

EDIOS (CN/0707-2287) [04677974] **4345**

EDISON ELECTRIC INSTITUTE *See* EXECUTIVE COMPENSATION SURVEY (PRINCETON, N.J.) **1668**

EDISON ELECTRIC INSTITUTE. ELECTRIC POWER SURVEY COMMITTEE *See* POST-SUMMER ELECTRIC POWER SURVEY **1953**

EDISON ELECTRIC INSTITUTE. TASK FORCE ON RECREATION USE AND RESOURCE MANAGEMENT. NATIONAL CONFERENCE *See* NATIONAL CONFERENCE TASK FORCE ON RECREATION USE AND RESOURCE MANAGEMENT / EDISON ELECTRIC INSTITUTE **4852**

EDISON-NORWOOD EDITION OF THE TIMES REVIEW (US/0895-0091) [16402270] **5660**

EDISON TIMES (US) [27209497] **1937**

EDITED PROCEEDINGS ... INTERNATIONAL GALVANIZING CONFERENCE (UK/0444-0013) [10690552] **974**

EDITEUR OFFICIEL DU QUEBEC *See* CATALOGUE DE L'EDITEUR OFFICIEL DU QUEBEC **4813**

EDITEURS ET DIFFUSEURS DE LANGUE FRANCAISE, LES (FR/0245-1875) [09210828] **4814**

EDITING HISTORY (US/0883-3532) [12122540] **4814**

EDITIO (GW/0931-3079) [17166153] **3341**

Alphabetical Title Index — EDUCATION

EDITION ANNUELLE : AVIS AUX NAVIGATEURS (CN) [03681412] **4176**

EDITION ARCHIV DER DEUTSCHEN JUGENDBEWEGUNG (GW) [17851338] **2481**

EDITION PHONOGRAPHIQUE D'APRES LE DEPOT LEGAL *See* EDITION PHONOGRAPHIQUE EN FRANCE D'APRES LE DEPOT LEGAL / BIBLIOTHEQUE NATIONALE, DEPARTMENT DE LA PHONOTHEQUE NATIONALE ET DE L'AUDIOVISUEL, L' **5316**

EDITION PHONOGRAPHIQUE EN FRANCE D'APRES LE DEPOT LEGAL / BIBLIOTHEQUE NATIONALE, DEPARTMENT DE LA PHONOTHEQUE NATIONALE ET DE L'AUDIOVISUEL, L' (FR) [20402168] **5316**

EDITION QUEBECOISE (CN/0704-5999) [03887222] **5070**

EDITION SPECIALE (CN/0383-803X) [03233076] **5783**

EDITION SPECIALE - CHASSE-GALERIE (CN/0227-6402) [08010208] **319**

●EDITIONS AVIS DE RECHERCHE, LES (CN/1188-6145) [26497746] **5284**

EDITIONS CATALOG (US/0277-8394) [07616002] **319**

●EDITIONS / ORSTOM (FR) [26654610] **415**

EDITIONS SR (CN) [11607926] **4955**

EDITOR & PUBLISHER (US/0013-094X) [01567511] 2919, **4814**

EDITOR & PUBLISHER (US) [01090729] **924**

EDITOR & PUBLISHER INTERNATIONAL YEAR BOOK (US/0424-4923) [02210361] **2919**

EDITOR & PUBLISHER. SYNDICATE DIRECTORY (US) [04018793] **2919**

EDITOR, EL (US) [04303143] **5749**

EDITORE, L' (IT) [06307780] **4814**

EDITORIAL EXCELLENCE (US/0736-1785) [09030518] **2919**

EDITORIAL EYE, THE (US/0193-7383) [05173509] **4814**

EDITORIALS ON FILE (US/0013-0966) [01088779] **4472**

EDITOR'S CHOICE (UK) [03524265] **3462**

EDITOR'S CHOICE CLIP ART QUARTERLY (US/0889-0528) [13818549] **378**

EDITOR'S DIGEST (US) 2919, **4814**

EDITOR'S FORUM (KANSAS CITY, MO.) (US/0746-3014) [09927598] **2919**

EDITORS' NOTES *CEASED.* (US/0888-3173) [09656560] **2919**

EDITORS ONLY (US/0735-8490) [09047674] **2919**

EDITOR'S WORKSHOP NEWSLETTER (US/0883-8569) [12256830] **2919**

EDIZILIA E INDUSTRIALIZZAZIONE *See* EDILIZIA-EX PREFABBRICAZIONE **2022**

EDIZIONI PER LA CONSERVAZIONE (IT/1120-1819) [20667143] 1304, **4828**

EDM DIGEST *See* DIEMAKING STAMPING & EDMING **2112**

EDMANDS & HIER POLICE LAW SERVICE (US) [16646870] **3164**

EDMOND EVENING SUN, THE (US) [27970269] **5731**

EDMONTON AND ALBERTA BUSINESS (CN/0712-4546) [09000576] **671**

EDMONTON & AREA AIRPORT BUSINESS DIRECTORY *See* EDMONTON & AREA AVIATION BUSINESS DIRECTORY **5381**

●EDMONTON & AREA AVIATION BUSINESS DIRECTORY (CN/1183-7861) [25882763] **5381**

EDMONTON AREA SERIES REPORT (CN/0703-8763) [05375208] **4552**

EDMONTON ART GALLERY *See* OUTLOOK - EDMONTON ART GALLERY **361**

EDMONTON AUTISM SOCIETY UPDATE (CN) 4387, **3831**

EDMONTON BULLET, THE (CN/0822-8108) [10441376] **319**

EDMONTON COMMERCE AND INDUSTRY (CN/0702-7435) [03436356] **832**

EDMONTON CULTURE VULTURE, THE (CN/0380-5123) [02578247] **384**

EDMONTON FACTS (CN/1187-3957) [25314122] **2732**

●EDMONTON JEWISH LIFE (CN/1189-3281) [25796426] **5783**

EDMONTON JOURNAL (CN) [19116483] **5783**

EDMONTON REPORT ON ECONOMIC DEVELOPMENT, THE (CN/0824-409X) [10595661] **1559**

EDMONTON SUN, THE (CN/0705-405X) [03944187] **5783**

EDMORE HERALD (US/8750-5444) [11491530] **5725**

●EDMS COMPARISON REPORT (US/1061-9550) [25495156] **1971**

EDMS JOURNAL (US/1058-0379) [24198991] **1183**

EDMUND PUBLICATIONS CORPORATION (WEST HEMPSTEAD, N.Y.) *See* EDMUND'S UNITED STATES COIN PRICES **2781**

EDMUND'S CAR SAVVY (US/1047-076X) [12814743] **5413**

EDMUND'S ECONOMY CAR BUYING GUIDE (US/0732-5835) [08299762] **5413**

EDMUND'S ... IMPORT CAR PRICES (US/1048-9738) [02096420] **5413**

EDMUND'S NEW CAR PRICES (US/1047-0751) [01715770] **5413**

EDMUND'S NEW CARS AMERICAN AND IMPORTS (UK) **5413**

EDMUND'S PRESENTS ... CAR SAVVY (US/1055-2200) [23125488] **5414**

EDMUND'S PRESENTS ... CAR, VAN & TRUCK PREVIEW (US/1055-2197) [23125444] **5414**

EDMUND'S PRESENTS ... ECONOMY CAR BUYING GUIDE (US/1055-2170) [23125185] 1296, **5414**

EDMUND'S PRESENTS ... MUSCLE CAR BUYER'S GUIDE (US/1055-2219) [23125525] **5414**

EDMUND'S PRESENTS ... NEW CAR PRICE ANNUAL (US/1055-2189) [23125405] **5414**

EDMUND'S UNITED STATES COIN PRICES (US/0270-8949) [06499042] **2781**

EDMUND'S USED CAR PRICES (US/0424-5059) [01605211] 1296, **5414**

●EDMUND'S VAN, PICKUP, SPORT UTILITY (US/1077-2111) [30643815] **5414**

EDN (US/0012-7515) [02623794] **2042**

●EDN ASIA (US) **2042**

EDN CAREER NEWS (US) [11543316] **2042**

EDN; ELECTRONIC ENGINEER'S DESIGN MAGAZINE (US/0012-7515) [01567149] **2042**

EDN NEWS (US) **2042**

EDN PRODUCTS AND CAREERS (US) **2042**

EDNA CONNELLY'S DIESEL FUEL AND TRUCK STOP GUIDE *See* DIESEL FUEL DIRECTORY **5413**

EDNA SUN, THE (US) [12168889] **5675**

EDO JIDAI BUNGAKUSHI / RYUMONSHA HEN (JA) [08775541] 2650, **3383**

EDON COMMERCIAL (US) [10529555] **5728**

EDP AUDITOR JOURNAL *See* IS AUDIT & CONTROL JOURNAL **1260**

EDP AUDITOR JOURNAL, THE (US/0885-0445) [11905359] **1258**

EDP TELEMATICA NOTIZIE *See* INFORMATION AND TECHNOLOGY **5113**

EDP WEEKLY (US) [16522416] 1267, **1237**

EDPACS (US/0736-6981) [02574271] **1226**

EDPRESS MEMBERSHIP ROSTER (US) [06097895] **1737**

EDRA; PROCEEDINGS OF THE ANNUAL ENVIRONMENTAL DESIGN RESEARCH ASSOCIATION CONFERENCE (US/0531-9293) [00923890] **298**

EDS MAGAZINE : OFFICIAL JOURNAL OF THE E.E.C. DENTAL STUDENTS COMMITTEE (GW/0937-7654) [25786312] **1323**

EDUCA (UK/0141-8459) [I01418459] **1912**

EDUCACAO & [I.E. E] SOCIEDADE (BL) [05141068] 5244, **1737**

EDUCACAO BRASILEIRA (BL) [06029316] **1737**

EDUCACAO E REALIDADE (BL) [04988978] **1737**

EDUCACION (PR/0013-1067) [05818245] **1737**

EDUCACION EN LA REPUBLICA ARGENTINA, LA (AG) [02240985] **1737**

EDUCACION FISICA, CHILE / UNIVERSIDAD DE CHILE, FACULTAD DE EDUCACION, DEPARTAMENTO DE EDUCACION FISCA, DEPORTES Y RECREACION (CL/0716-0518) [07787924] **1855**

EDUCACION HOY (CK/0120-8446) [01617397] **1737**

EDUCACION HOY : REVISTA DE LA CONFEDERACION INTERAMERICANA DE EDUCACION CATOLICA, CIEC (CL) [27763352] **1738**

EDUCACION, LA (US/0013-1059) [02302023] **1737**

EDUCACION (LIMA) (PE) [01619494] **1738**

EDUCACION (LIMA, PERU) (PE) [10105935] **4955**

EDUCACION MEDICA Y SALUD (US/0013-1091) [01567518] 1738, **3573**

EDUCACION OBRERA (SZ/0378-5564) [I03785564] **1664**

EDUCACION PARA LA SALUD (AG) [05692027] **1738**

EDUCACION POPULAR PARA EL DESARROLLO (BO) [01785294] **1738**

EDUCACION Y DERECHOS HUMANOS : CUADERNOS PARA DOCENTES : PUBLICACION DEL SERVICIO PAZ Y JUSTICIA (URUGUAY) (UY) [23096532] **4507**

EDUCACION Y PLANEAMIENTO (GT) [01786218] **1738**

EDUCADORES (SP) [18772369] **1738**

EDUCADORES; REVISTA LATINOAMERICANA DE EDUCACION (AG/0422-6399) [06445621] **1794**

EDUCAMUS (SA/0250-152X) [04058973] **1738**

EDUCARE LONDON (UK/0141-7282) [I01417282] 4387, **1878**

EDUCARE (PRETORIA) (SA/0256-8829) [01855600] **1738**

EDUCATED CONSUMER (CN/0821-512X) [09603031] **1296**

EDUCATED TRAVELER, THE (US/1052-0597) [22173337] **5469**

EDUCATING ABLE LEARNERS, DISCOVERING & NURTURING TALENT *CEASED.* (US/0896-9574) [17349776] **1878**

EDUCATING AT-RISK YOUTH (US/1040-0729) [18306712] **5284**

EDUCATING AWAY FROM HOME (IS) **1738**

EDUCATING EXCEPTIONAL CHILDREN (US/0198-7518) [05460219] **1878**

EDUCATION (US) **1738**

EDUCATION (AT) [02650975] **1738**

EDUCATION 3-13 (UK/0300-4279) [01425648] **1804**

EDUCATION ACTION WAGGA WAGGA *CEASED.* (AT/1034-6740) [I10346740] **1738**

●EDUCATION AFTER SIXTEEN (UK/0965-2396) [I09652396] **1738**

EDUCATION ALTERNATIVES (AT/1037-5104) **1738**

EDUCATION & AGEING (UK) **3750**

EDUCATION & COMPUTING *CEASED.* (NE/0167-9287) [12289868] 1893, **1223**

EDUCATION AND HEALTH : JOURNAL OF THE HEA SCHOOLS HEALTH EDUCATION UNIT, UNIVERSITY OF EXETER (UK/0265-1602) [18322446] **1855**

EDUCATION & MANAGEMENT LE PERREUX-SUR-MARNE (FR/0997-721X) [I0997721X] **1738**

EDUCATION & PEDAGOGIES *CEASED.* (FR) [21124303] **1738**

EDUCATION & SOCIAL SCIENCE (UK/0424-5318) [01199696] 5199, **1738**

EDUCATION & SOCIETY (II) [22354661] **1738**

EDUCATION AND SOCIETY IN THE MIDDLE AGES AND RENAISSANCE (NE/0926-6070) [I09266070] **2615**

EDUCATION AND SOCIETY (MELBOURNE) (AT/0726-2655) [09909897] 5244, **1738**

EDUCATION AND TECHNOLOGY (US/1069-4749) [28056704] 5102, **1738**

EDUCATION AND THE LAW (UK/0953-9964) [I09539964] 2965, **1738**

EDUCATION AND THE LAW (UK) [12907483] **1862**

EDUCATION AND TRAINING (SZ) **4774**

EDUCATION & TRAINING (BRADFORD) (UK/0040-0912) [01567531] **1912**

EDUCATION AND TRAINING IN MENTAL RETARDATION (US/1042-9859) [15995665] **1878**

●EDUCATION AND TRAINING IN MENTAL RETARDATION AND DEVELOPMENTAL DISABILITIES (US) [30016773] **1878**

EDUCATION & TREATMENT OF CHILDREN (US/0748-8491) [03768586] **1893**

EDUCATION AND URBAN SOCIETY (US/0013-1245) [01567533] **1738**

EDUCATION AT ISSUE (US/0278-6575) [07853301] **1862**

EDUCATION AUSTRALIA ANNANDALE (AT/1031-444X) [I031444X] **1738**

EDUCATION AUTHORITIES DIRECTORY AND ANNUAL, THE (UK/0070-9131) [01567534] **1862**

EDUCATION — Alphabetical Title Index

EDUCATION BIBLIOGRAPHY (PP) [08679495] **1794**

EDUCATION BRIEFING PAPER (US) [03768445] **1738**

EDUCATION BULLETIN COUNCIL FOR BRITISH ARCHAEOLOGY (UK/0952-9748) [I09529748] **267**

EDUCATION CANADA (CN/0013-1253) [02246125] **1738**

EDUCATION CAPITAL (AT/0314-3902) [I03143902] **1738**

EDUCATION (CHULA VISTA) (US/0013-1172) [01567521] **1738**

EDUCATION CODE / STATE OF CALIFORNIA (US) [09139805] **1738**

EDUCATION COMMISSION OF THE STATES *See* REPORT - EDUCATION COMMISSION OF THE STATES **1844**

EDUCATION COMPAREE (FR/0339-5456) [I03395456] **1739**

EDUCATION DAILY (US/0013-1261) [01567543] **1739**

EDUCATION DEVELOPMENT CENTER *See* REPORT - EDUCATION DEVELOPMENT CENTER **1778**

EDUCATION DIGEST, THE (US/0013-127X) [01567544] **1739**

EDUCATION DIRECTORY. STATE EDUCATION AGENCY OFFICIALS (US/0148-9887) [03125846] **1863**

●EDUCATION ECONOMICS (UK/0964-5292) 1488, **1739**

EDUCATION ECONOMIE (PARIS) (FR/0990-5413) [I09905413] **1591**

EDUCATION (EDINBURGH) (UK/0013-1164) [01713907] **1863**

EDUCATION ENFANTINE, L' (FR/0013-1288) [I00131288] **1739**

●EDUCATION ET FORMATION AU QUEBEC (CN/1192-3318) [31000998] **1739**

EDUCATION ET FORMATIONS / REALISTE PAR LA SOUS-DIRECTION DES ENQUETES STATISTIQUES ET DES ETUDES DU SERVICE DE L'INFORMATIQUE DE GESTION ET DES STATISTIQUES (S.I.G.E.S.) DU MINISTERE DE L'EDUCATION NATIONALE (FR/0294-0868) [11110910] **1739**

EDUCATION ET FRANCOPHONIE (CN/0849-1089) [22185468] **1739**

EDUCATION FOR BUSINESS AND MANAGEMENT IN THE REGION (UK) [07746063] 1739, **866**

EDUCATION FOR ENTERPRISE BULLETIN (UK) **1739**

EDUCATION FOR INFORMATION (NE/0167-8329) [09768302] **1739**

EDUCATION FOR LIBRARIANSHIP, AUSTRALIA *See* EDUCATION FOR LIBRARY AND INFORMATION SERVICES, AUSTRALIA **3209**

●EDUCATION FOR LIBRARY AND INFORMATION SERVICES, AUSTRALIA (AT) [28881951] 1822, **3209**

EDUCATION FORUM (TORONTO. 1988) (CN/0840-9269) [20443642] **1893**

EDUCATION FORWARD (US/0746-309X) [09875266] **1863**

EDUCATION FUNDING MODEL, THE (CN/1188-0481) [25127896] **1739**

EDUCATION FUNDING NEWS (US/0273-4443) [05967063] **1739**

EDUCATION GRANTS ALERT (US/1056-2656) [23612286] **1739**

EDUCATION (GUILFORD) (US/0272-5010) [06548137] **1893**

EDUCATION (HORSHAM, PA.) (US/1059-0854) [24476657] **1739**

EDUCATION IN ALASKA (US) [05186905] **1739**

EDUCATION IN ... : ANNUAL REPORT SUMMARY OF THE PERMANENT SECRETARY (LO) [20029158] **1739**

EDUCATION IN CANADA (CN/0706-3679) [04520985] 1739, **1794**

EDUCATION IN CHEMISTRY (UK/0013-1350) [01567546] 1893, **974**

EDUCATION IN EUROPE. SECTION 2. GENERAL AND TECHNICAL EDUCATION (FR/0589-9427) [01565256] **1739**

EDUCATION IN EUROPE. SECTION IV. GENERAL / COUNCIL FOR CULTURAL CO-OPERATION OF THE COUNCIL OF EUROPE (FR/0589-9443) [01565258] **1739**

EDUCATION IN FOCUS (US/1049-7250) [21286168] **1739**

EDUCATION IN ISLAM (US/1053-2951) [22503925] **5042**

EDUCATION IN KENYA (KE) [07824317] **1739**

EDUCATION IN KOREA / PREPARED BY THE CENTRAL EDUCATION RESEARCH INSTITUTE (KO) [04850614] **1739**

EDUCATION IN OECD COUNTRIES (FR) [21130418] **1739**

EDUCATION IN SCIENCE (UK/0013-1377) [08264906] **5102**

EDUCATION IN THE DEVELOPING COUNTRIES OF THE COMMONWEALTH : RESEARCH REGISTER (UK) [01788658] **1739**

EDUCATION IN THE NORTH (UK/0424-5512) [06413734] **1739**

EDUCATION IN THE PUBLIC EYE : THE NATIONAL PRESS REVIEW OF COMMUNITY ISSUES IN EDUCATION *CEASED.* (US/1055-0860) [23070633] **1739**

EDUCATION IN WASHINGTON (US/0094-3606) [01794112] **1739**

EDUCATION INDEX (US/0013-1385) [01567550] 1739, **1794**

EDUCATION INDEX. CD-ROM (US/0013-1385) **1794**

EDUCATION INTERFACE GUIDE TO VOLUNTARY SUPPORT (US/1048-3004) [20910961] **1739**

EDUCATION INTERFACE NATIONAL GUIDE TO EDUCATOR EMPOWERMENT (US/1056-1005) [23466574] **1739**

EDUCATION INTERFACE SERIES (US/1052-8261) [22393242] **1740**

●EDUCATION INTERNATIONAL (BE) **1740**

●EDUCATION INVESTOR, THE (US/1069-9988) [28297810] **1740**

EDUCATION : KEY TO CONSERVATION (US/0589-4476) [01326010] **2192**

EDUCATION, L' (FR/0013-1423) [02242377] **1738**

EDUCATION LAW AND THE PUBLIC SCHOOLS. BULLETIN AND UPDATE SUBSCRIPTION SERVICE (US/0196-6715) [05874156] **1863**

EDUCATION LAW BULLETIN *SUSPENDED.* (US/0276-718X) [06576619] **1863**

EDUCATION LAW CENTER *See* ELC **2965**

EDUCATION LAW JOURNAL (CN/0838-2875) [18910540] 1740, **2965**

EDUCATION LEADER (VANCOUVER) (CN/0843-1779) [19758793] **1740**

EDUCATION LIBRARIES (US/0148-1061) [03783240] 1740, **3209**

EDUCATION LIBRARIES JOURNAL (UK/0957-9575) [19563226] 1740, **3209**

EDUCATION LIBRARY [COMPUTER FILE] (US) [22284869] **1740**

EDUCATION LINKS (AT/0814-6802) [I08146802] **1740**

EDUCATION LITERATURE REVIEW (US/1045-0734) [20001915] **1740**

EDUCATION MARKET IN CANADA, THE (CN/0317-2740) [02441730] **1740**

EDUCATION MATERIALS IN LIBRARIES (US/0895-5514) [16670119] **3209**

EDUCATION MILLE-ILES (CN/0712-9688) [08867835] **1863**

EDUCATION MONITOR (US/1041-9462) [18888313] **1740**

EDUCATION MONITOR MELBOURNE (AT/1033-4890) [I10334890] **1740**

EDUCATION MUSICALE, L' (FR/0013-1415) [07429247] 1740, **4116**

EDUCATION NEWSLETTER (SZ/0013-144X) [01714220] **4955**

EDUCATION NEWSLETTER / EDUCATION FAITS NOUVEAUX (FR) [24147233] **1740**

EDUCATION NOVA SCOTIA (CN/0382-1110) [03022491] **1740**

EDUCATION OF THE HANDICAPPED (US/0194-2255) [03659075] **1878**

EDUCATION OF WHITES IN THE REPUBLIC OF SOUTH AFRICA, THE (SA) [06822716] **1740**

EDUCATION ON THE MOVE (FR) [07358263] **1740**

EDUCATION OUVRIERE (SZ/0378-5572) [I03785572] **1664**

EDUCATION PAR LE JEU ET L'ENVIRONNEMENT, L' *CEASED.* (FR/0246-4438) [I02464438] **1740**

EDUCATION PERMANENTE (FR/0339-7513) [11538795] **1800**

EDUCATION POLICY PROCESS AT STATE LEVEL : AN AUSTRALIA-UNITED STATES COMPARATIVE STUDY, THE (AT) [08619392] **1740**

EDUCATION QUARTERLY, THE *CEASED.* (II/0013-1482) [01567557] **1740**

●EDUCATION REFORM DIGEST (US/1068-2406) [27483075] **1740**

EDUCATION, RENSEIGNEMENTS STATISTIQUES *See* EDUCATION STATISTICS (FREDERICTON) **1740**

EDUCATION REPORTS (WASHINGTON, D.C.) *See* DEPARTMENT OF EDUCATION REPORTS / NATIONAL CENTER FOR EDUCATION INFORMATION **1735**

EDUCATION REPORTS (WASHINGTON, D.C.) (US/1041-6447) [17762125] **1740**

EDUCATION, RESEARCH AND PERSPECTIVES (AT/0311-2543) [01781520] **1822**

EDUCATION RURALE (FR/0395-7691) [I03957691] **1740**

EDUCATION SAN DIEGO COUNTY (US) [05911695] **1740**

EDUCATION SECTION REVIEW - BRITISH PSYCHOLOGICAL SOCIETY (UK/0262-4087) [I02624087] **4585**

EDUCATION SPECIAL INTEREST SECTION NEWSLETTER (US/1059-0595) [24466943] **1878**

EDUCATION, STATISTICAL INFORMATION *See* EDUCATION STATISTICS (FREDERICTON) **1740**

EDUCATION STATISTICS BULLETIN *CEASED.* (CN/0826-8258) [11506221] **1740**

EDUCATION STATISTICS ... ESTIMATES / CIPFA, STATISTICAL INFORMATION SERVICE (UK/0307-0514) [07934633] 1740, **1794**

EDUCATION STATISTICS FOR THE UNITED KINGDOM (UK) [02062870] 1740, **1794**

●EDUCATION STATISTICS (FREDERICTON) (CN/1187-841X) [26290917] **1740**

●EDUCATION STATISTICS (FREDERICTON) (CN/1187-841X) [26290910] **1740**

EDUCATION STATISTICS - (SWAZILAND) (SQ) [04795867] 1740, **1794**

EDUCATION TECHNOLOGY NEWS (US/1061-5008) [24515233] 1740, **1223**

EDUCATION TODAY (UK/0013-1547) [02280091] **1740**

EDUCATION TODAY (TORONTO) (CN/0843-5081) [20665315] **1740**

EDUCATION-TRIBUNE LIBRE (BE/0773-7394) [I07737394] **1741**

EDUCATION (TUBINGEN, GERMANY) (GW/0341-6178) [04610540] **1741**

EDUCATION U.S.A (US/0013-1571) [01567562] **1741**

EDUCATION UPDATE (CHICAGO, ILL.) (US/0731-941X) [08278614] 1741, **1323**

EDUCATION WEEK (US/0277-4232) [07579948] **1741**

EDUCATION. WHITES / REPUBLIC OF SOUTH AFRICA, DEPARTMENT OF STATISTICS (SA/0258-7831) [08560925] 2260, **1741**

EDUCATION WITH PRODUCTION (BS) [09754115] **1741**

EDUCATION YEAR BOOK (UK/0143-5469) [05175695] **1741**

EDUCATIONAL ABSTRACT (TS) [05189847] **1741**

●EDUCATIONAL ACTION RESEARCH (UK/0965-0792) [28651775] **1741**

EDUCATIONAL ADMINISTRATION ABSTRACTS (US/0013-1601) [01567563] 1863, **1794**

EDUCATIONAL ADMINISTRATION AND HISTORY. MONOGRAPH (UK/0140-0428) [I01400428] **1863**

EDUCATIONAL ADMINISTRATION AND POLICY REVIEW (AT) **1863**

EDUCATIONAL ADMINISTRATION QUARTERLY (US/0013-161X) [01567565] **1863**

EDUCATIONAL ADMINISTRATION REVIEW (AT/0812-9746) [I08129746] **1863**

EDUCATIONAL ADMINISTRATOR MELBOURNE (AT/0310-8767) [I03108767] **1863**

EDUCATIONAL AND BUSINESS SOFTWARE, RELATED PRODUCTS, HOME, SCHOOL, AND OFFICE FOR ATARI (US/0740-6886) [10025226] 1237, 1245, **1285**

EDUCATIONAL AND BUSINESS SOFTWARE, RELATED PRODUCTS-HOME, SCHOOL, AND OFFICE FOR, TRS-80 (US/0740-6894) [10025251] 1237, 1245, **1285**

EDUCATIONAL AND CHILD PSYCHOLOGY (UK/0267-1611) [12349976] **4585**

EDUCATIONAL AND PSYCHOLOGICAL INTERACTIONS (SW/0070-9263) [01880151] 4585, **1741**

EDUCATIONAL AND PSYCHOLOGICAL MEASUREMENT (US/1013-1644) [01567567] 1741, **4585**

EDUCATIONAL AND TRAINING TECHNOLOGY INTERNATIONAL *See* INNOVATIONS IN EDUCATION AND TRAINING TECHNOLOGY INTERNATIONAL **1753**

EDUCATIONAL & TRAINING TECHNOLOGY INTERNATIONAL : ETTI (UK/0954-7304) [19317361] **1741**

EDUCAZIONE

●EDUCATIONAL ASSESSMENT (US/1062-7197) [25704962] **1741**

EDUCATIONAL ASSESSMENT PROGRAM MINIMUM BASIC SKILLS TESTS STATE REPORT (US) [05206553] **1863**

EDUCATIONAL BULLETIN - FISH COMMISSION OF OREGON (US/0471-8208) [01440732] **2300**

EDUCATIONAL CHANGE (US/0748-0806) [10895651] **1741**

EDUCATIONAL COMMENT (US) [01567571] **1741**

EDUCATIONAL COMMISSION FOR FOREIGN MEDICAL GRADUATES *See* ANNUAL REPORT - EDUCATIONAL COMMISSION FOR FOREIGN MEDICAL GRADUATES **3550**

EDUCATIONAL COMPUTING AND TECHNOLOGY (UK) [22688615] **1223**

EDUCATIONAL CONSIDERATIONS (US/0146-9282) [03064190] **1913**

EDUCATIONAL DIGEST. BUYERS' GUIDE, DIRECTORY OF SUPPLIERS (CN) [02443250] **1741**

EDUCATIONAL DIGEST (TORONTO) (CN/0046-1482) [01695773] **1741**

EDUCATIONAL DIRECTORY (US) [05259474] **1741**

EDUCATIONAL DIRECTORY (US) [08725608] **1741**

EDUCATIONAL DIRECTORY OF MISSISSIPPI SCHOOLS (US/0363-874X) [02546447] **1741**

EDUCATIONAL DIRECTORY OF NORTH CAROLINA *See* NORTH CAROLINA EDUCATION DIRECTORY **1769**

EDUCATIONAL DIRECTORY. STATE & DISTRICT OFFICES (HONOLULU) (US/0092-1777) [01784626] **1741**

EDUCATIONAL ENQUIRY (AT/0155-2341) [I01552341] **1741**

EDUCATIONAL EXCHANGE OF GREATER BOSTON *See* EDUCATIONAL OPPORTUNITIES OF GREATER BOSTON **1800**

EDUCATIONAL FACILITY PLANNER (US/1059-7417) [19528254] **1863**

EDUCATIONAL FILM & VIDEO LOCATOR OF THE CONSORTIUM OF COLLEGE AND UNIVERSITY MEDIA CENTERS AND R. R. BOWKER (US/0000-135X) [21318968] 1893, **4068**

EDUCATIONAL FINANCE, CONNECTICUT (US/0360-0807) [02243675] **1863**

EDUCATIONAL FORUM (WEST LAFAYETTE, IND.), THE (US/0013-1725) [01567583] **1741**

EDUCATIONAL FOUNDATIONS (ANN ARBOR, MICH.) (US/1047-8248) [15389620] **1741**

EDUCATIONAL FREEDOM (US/0013-1741) [09637308] 1741, **2965**

EDUCATIONAL GERONTOLOGY (US/0360-1277) [02441469] **1800**

EDUCATIONAL GUIDE : TECHNICAL INSTITUTES, COMMUNITY COLLEGES (US) [01790009] **1913**

EDUCATIONAL HISTORIAN, THE (AT/1038-1775) [I10381775] 2615, **1741**

EDUCATIONAL HORIZONS (US/0013-175X) [03067681] **1741**

EDUCATIONAL INDIA (II/0013-1768) [01567587] **1742**

EDUCATIONAL INNOVATION AND INFORMATION (SZ) [14197292] **1742**

EDUCATIONAL IRM QUARTERLY (US/1055-8683) [23360572] **1223**

EDUCATIONAL LEADERSHIP : JOURNAL OF THE ASSOCIATION FOR SUPERVISION AND CURRICULUM DEVELOPMENT (US/0013-1784) [02576039] **1742**

EDUCATIONAL LEAFLET (US/0739-4195) [06399771] **1374**

EDUCATIONAL MANAGEMENT & ADMINISTRATION : JOURNAL OF THE BRITISH EDUCATIONAL MANAGEMENT AND ADMINISTRATION SOCIETY (UK/0263-211X) [08491453] **1863**

EDUCATIONAL MARKETER (US/0013-1806) **1742**

EDUCATIONAL MARKETER YELLOW PAGES (US/0195-5896) [03526497] **4564**

EDUCATIONAL MEASUREMENT, ISSUES AND PRACTICE (US/0731-1745) [08128374] **1893**

EDUCATIONAL MEDIA AND TECHNOLOGY YEARBOOK (US/8755-2094) [11279741] **1893**

EDUCATIONAL MICRO REVIEW (US/0735-2565) [08901422] 1893, **1223**

EDUCATIONAL OASIS (US/0892-2853) [15145298] **1893**

EDUCATIONAL OPPORTUNITIES OF GREATER BOSTON (US/0361-0985) [02244756] **1800**

EDUCATIONAL OPPORTUNITIES THROUGH FEDERAL ASSISTANCE PROGRAMS - (OHIO) (US) [02419922] 4387, **1742**

EDUCATIONAL OPPORTUNITY PROGRAM NOTES (US/0098-9827) [02486162] **1878**

EDUCATIONAL PERSONNEL IN DELAWARE PUBLIC SCHOOLS (USUS/0093-0008) [01789441] **1863**

EDUCATIONAL PERSPECTIVES (US/0013-1849) [01567599] **1742**

EDUCATIONAL PHILOSOPHY AND THEORY (AT/0013-1857) [01567600] **1893**

EDUCATIONAL PLANNING (US/0315-9388) [02247296] **1742**

EDUCATIONAL POLICY (LOS ALTOS, CALIF.) (US/0895-9048) [15342052] **1742**

EDUCATIONAL PRESS ASSOCIATION OF AMERICA *See* EDPRESS MEMBERSHIP ROSTER **1737**

EDUCATIONAL PROGRAMS THAT WORK (SAN FRANCISCO, CALIF.) (US/0198-9049) [06061198] **1742**

EDUCATIONAL PSYCHOLOGIST (US/0046-1520) [02243019] **4586**

EDUCATIONAL PSYCHOLOGY (DORCHESTER-ON-THAMES) (UK/0144-3410) [07530248] 1742, **4586**

EDUCATIONAL PSYCHOLOGY GUILFORD, CONN (US/0731-1141) [08093116] 1742, **4586**

EDUCATIONAL PSYCHOLOGY IN PRACTICE (UK/0266-7363) [13769505] 1742, **4586**

EDUCATIONAL PSYCHOLOGY REVIEW (US/1040-726X) [18516146] **4586**

EDUCATIONAL RANKINGS ANNUAL (US/1053-1378) [22460513] **1822**

EDUCATIONAL RECORD, THE (US/0013-1873) [01567604] **1822**

EDUCATIONAL RECORDS BUREAU *See* SPRING TESTING PROGRAM IN INDEPENDENT SCHOOLS AND SUPPLEMENTARY STUDIES **1784**

EDUCATIONAL RECORDS BUREAU *See* BULLETIN - EDUCATIONAL RECORDS BUREAU **1729**

EDUCATIONAL RECORDS BUREAU, NEW YORK. COMMITTEE ON SCHOOL AND COLLEGE RELATIONS *See* REPORT - EDUCATIONAL RECORDS BUREAU, NEW YORK. COMMITTEE ON SCHOOL AND COLLEGE RELATIONS **1844**

EDUCATIONAL REQUIREMENTS AND SCHOOLS OF STUDY FOR HEALTH CAREERS (CN/0318-9503) [02441961] 1742, **3914**

EDUCATIONAL RESEARCH AND EVALUATION (NE/1380-3611) **1742**

EDUCATIONAL RESEARCH - GREAT BRITAIN. SCOTTISH EDUCATION DEPT (UK) [03265957] **1893**

EDUCATIONAL RESEARCH IN AUSTRIA (AU) [03501091] **1742**

EDUCATIONAL RESEARCH IN BRITAIN (UK) [03422439] **1742**

EDUCATIONAL RESEARCH IN SWEDEN (SW) [02414980] **1742**

EDUCATIONAL RESEARCH INSTITUTE OF BRITISH COLUMBIA *See* REPORTS LIST - EDUCATIONAL RESEARCH INSTITUTE OF BRITISH COLUMBIA **1778**

EDUCATIONAL RESEARCH NEWSLETTER (US/1052-5122) [22295794] **1742**

EDUCATIONAL RESEARCH QUARTERLY (US/0196-5042) [02191274] **1742**

EDUCATIONAL RESEARCH SERVICE (ARLINGTON, VA.) *See* SALARIES SCHEDULED FOR ADMINISTRATIVE AND SUPERVISORY PERSONNEL IN PUBLIC SCHOOLS **1870**

EDUCATIONAL RESEARCH SERVICE (ARLINGTON, VA.) *See* ERS RESEARCH MEMO **1745**

EDUCATIONAL RESEARCH (WINDSOR) (UK/0013-1881) [01567607] **1742**

EDUCATIONAL RESEARCHER (WASHINGTON, D.C. : 1972) (US/0013-189X) [01775556] **1742**

EDUCATIONAL RESOURCES INFORMATION CENTER *See* THESAURUS OF ERIC DESCRIPTORS. SUPPLEMENT **1929**

EDUCATIONAL RESOURCES INFORMATION CENTER CLEARINGHOUSE (US/0737-1578) [08604358] **1893**

EDUCATIONAL REVIEW (BIRMINGHAM) (UK/0013-1911) [08291359] **1742**

EDUCATIONAL SERIES - NORTH DAKOTA GEOLOGICAL SURVEY (US/0091-9004) [02253472] **1374**

EDUCATIONAL SERIES ON CHINESE MEDICINE (US/0888-7640) [11129306] **3573**

EDUCATIONAL SOFTWARE PC COMPATIBILITY GUIDE, THE (US/0892-2527) [15134271] **1285**

EDUCATIONAL SOFTWARE SELECTOR, THE (US/8755-5107) [10521082] 1743, **1285**

EDUCATIONAL STANDARDS IN JAPAN *CEASED.* (JA) [01786148] **1743**

EDUCATIONAL STATISTICS : DISTRICT-WISE (IS) [01695443] **1794**

EDUCATIONAL STUDIES (UK/0305-5698) [02714667] **1743**

EDUCATIONAL STUDIES (AMES) (US/0013-1946) [01567620] **1743**

EDUCATIONAL STUDIES (AMES) (US) [01567612] **1822**

EDUCATIONAL STUDIES IN MATHEMATICS (NE/0013-1954) [01567621] 3504, **1743**

EDUCATIONAL TECHNOLOGY (US/0013-1962) [01567622] **1893**

EDUCATIONAL TECHNOLOGY ABSTRACTS (UK/0266-3368) [11982617] 1893, **1794**

EDUCATIONAL TECHNOLOGY RESEARCH (JA) [13145180] **1743**

EDUCATIONAL TECHNOLOGY RESEARCH AND DEVELOPMENT (US/1042-1629) [18956055] **1743**

●EDUCATIONAL TECHNOLOGY REVIEW (US) 1743, **1223**

EDUCATIONAL TESTING SERVICE *See* ETS DEVELOPMENTS **1745**

EDUCATIONAL TESTING SERVICE *See* GUIDE TO THE USE OF THE GRADUATE RECORD EXAMINATIONS **1827**

EDUCATIONAL THEATRE NEWS *CEASED.* (US/0013-1997) [02254170] **5364**

EDUCATIONAL THEORY (US/0013-2004) [01567631] **1743**

EDUCATIONAL TIMES *See* EDUCATION TODAY **1740**

EDUCATIONAL TRENDS, THE (II/0531-8351) [06410747] **1743**

EDUCATIONAL YEARBOOK (UK) [02441311] 1223, **1893**

EDUCATIONEWS (ALBANY, N.Y.) (US/0899-7330) [18198622] **1743**

EDUCATION'S FEDERAL FUNDING ALERT (US/0195-9700) [05739764] **1743**

EDUCATORE (IT) **1743**

EDUCATORS' ADVOCATE (US/0013-2047) [01567634] **1743**

EDUCATORS GRADE GUIDE TO FREE TEACHING AIDS (US/0070-9387) [01567636] **1893**

EDUCATORS GUIDE TO FREE AUDIO AND VIDEO MATERIALS *See* EDUCATORS GUIDE TO FREE VIDEOTAPES **1743**

EDUCATORS GUIDE TO FREE FILMS (US/0070-9395) [01048582] **1893**

EDUCATORS GUIDE TO FREE FILMSTRIPS AND SLIDES (US/1044-5943) [16221769] **1893**

EDUCATORS GUIDE TO FREE GUIDANCE MATERIALS (US/0070-9417) [01567639] **1913**

EDUCATORS GUIDE TO FREE HEALTH, PHYSICAL EDUCATION AND RECREATION MATERIALS (US) [01064332] 1894, **1855**

EDUCATORS GUIDE TO FREE HOME ECONOMICS AND CONSUMER EDUCATION MATERIALS (US) [24293755] **2789**

EDUCATORS GUIDE TO FREE SCIENCE MATERIALS / COMPILED AND EDITED BY MARY H. SATERSTROM (US/0070-9425) [01567641] 5102, **1894**

EDUCATORS GUIDE TO FREE SOCIAL STUDIES MATERIALS / COMPILED AND EDITED BY PATRICIA H. SUTTLES AND STEVEN A. SUTTLES (US/0070-9433) [01567642] **1894**

●EDUCATORS GUIDE TO FREE VIDEOTAPES (US/1068-9206) [26326488] **1743**

EDUCATORS INDEX OF FREE MATERIALS (US) [05376516] **1743**

EDUCATOR'S INTERNATIONAL GUIDE TO FREE & LOW COST HEALTH AUDIO-VISUAL TEACHING AIDS (US) [04909735] **4774**

EDUCATORS' NOTEBOOK (CN/1181-9480) [24256957] **1743**

●EDUCATORS' TECH EXCHANGE : AN EDUTECH PUBLICATION FOR THE ACADEMIC COMPUTING COMMUNITY (US/1065-9447) [28796838] **1223**

EDUCATOR'S WORLD (US/0531-836X) [01788971] **1743**

EDUCAZIONE E SCUOLA (IT) **1863**

EDUCAZIONE SANITARIA E PROMOZIONE DELLA SALUTE (IT) [19643136] **4774**

EDUCO (CN/0712-810X) [08861826] **1863**

EDUCOM REVIEW (US/1045-9146) [19588058] 1183, **1822**

●EDULAW FOR CANADIAN SCHOOLS (CN/1193-7319) [27203168] **1743**

EDULAW SCHOOL NEWSLETTER (CN/0849-4800) [21201193] **2965**

EDUNEUF (OTTAWA) (CN/1187-7669) [25796419] **3855**

EDUQ : BIBLIOGRAPHIE ANALYTIQUE SUR L'EDUCATION AU QUEBEC (CN/0712-4635) [09074977] 1743, **1794**

EDUT (IS) [17592913] 5047, **2615**

EDUTEC (MX) [03930925] **1894**

EDUTECH REPORT, THE (US/0883-1327) [12119686] 1894, **1223**

EDV RECHT (GW) **2965**

EDWARD C. ARMSTRONG MONOGRAPHS ON MEDIEVAL LITERATURE, THE (US/1054-0636) [08878927] **3383**

EDWARD SAPIR MONOGRAPH SERIES IN LANGUAGE, CULTURE, AND COGNITION (US/0163-3848) [04149468] **3278**

EDWARD WILLIAMS WEEKLY, THE (US/0747-170X) [10617243] **5716**

EDWARDIAN (LEWISTON, N.Y.) (US/1048-8596) [21068144] **1091**

EDWARDS JOURNAL, THE (US/0743-8591) [10394861] **2446**

EE PRODUCT NEWS (US/0899-952X) [18237648] **2042**

EEA NEWS (SZ) **832**

EEC COMPETITION LAW HANDBOOK (UK) **2965**

EEC FOOD LEGISLATION MANUAL (UK) **2334**

EEC NEWSLETTER (NE/0925-4641) [I09254641] **3127**

EEC SHIPPING (UK/0141-4585) [04340755] **5449**

EEG-EMG (GW) [05275930] **3574**

EEG-LABOR, DAS (GW/0170-8287) [05910516] **3831**

EEI WASHINGTON LETTER (US/0737-349X) [09354999] **1937**

EEO ANNUAL REPORT - AUSTRALIAN INDUSTRY DEVELOPMENT CORPORATION (AT/1033-596X) [I1033596X] **1605**

EEO REPORT, THE *CEASED.* (US/0276-5853) [07389321] **940**

EEO REVIEW, THE (US/0148-6934) [03354436] **1664**

EEO TRENDS AND ISSUES (US/0740-204X) [09926698] **1664**

EEO YEARBOOK (US/0147-5339) [03189639] **4043**

EEOC COMPLIANCE MANUAL (COMMERCE CLEARING HOUSE EDITION) (US) [02369728] **671**

EEPA NEWS BULLETIN (US/0889-0854) [13789655] 1937, **2043**

EERI SPECIAL REPORT (US) **1404**

EESTI HAAL (UK) [19094395] **5812**

EESTI NSV RIIKLIK ETNOGRAAFIAMUUSEUM *See* AASTARAAMAT **227**

EESTI POLLUMAJANDUSE AKADEEMIA TEADUSLIKE TOODE KOGUMIK (ER/0422-7212) [08625549] **81**

EESTI TEADUSTE AKADEEMIA TOIMETISED (ER) [22233947] **975**

EESTI TEADUSTE AKADEEMIA TOIMETISED. BIOLOOGIA (ER) [22233987] **454**

EESTI TEADUSTE AKADEEMIA TOIMETISED. FUUSIKA, MATEMAATIKA (ER) [22233964] **4402**

EESTI TEADUSTE AKADEEMIA TOIMETISED. GEOLOOGIA (ER/0201-8136) [22233895] **1374**

EESTI TEADUSTE AKADEEMIA TOIMETISED. OKOLOOGIA (ER/0868-5894) [24149713] **2215**

EESTI TEADUSTE AKADEEMIA TOIMETISED. UHISKONNATEADUSED (ER) [24958514] **5199**

EF-AVISEN (BE) [13392186] 5199, **2260**

EF NEWS / EUROPEAN FOUNDATION FOR THE IMPROVEMENT OF LIVING AND WORKING CONDITIONS (IE/0258-1965) [14191574] **1664**

EFAC BULLETIN (UK/0951-1105) [I09511105] **4955**

EFCE PUBLICATION SERIES (UK) [08987665] **2012**

EFEMERIDES ASTRONOMICAS (SP) [04587628] **4176**

EFFECTIF ETUDIANT - UNIVERSITE DE MONCTON (CN/1191-1239) [25882749] **1822**

●EFFECTIF SCOLAIRE ..., MANUEL D'OPERATIONS DES SYSTEMES INFORMATIQUES (DCS) (CN/1187-9130) [26498125] **1743**

EFFECTIFS DES COLLECTIVITES TERRITORIALES AU 31 DECEMBRE, LES (FR) [19059857] **4645**

EFFECTIFS HUMAINS - COMMISSION SCOLAIRE L'ISLET-SUD (CN/0226-9023) [07805850] **1743**

EFFECTIFS SCOLAIRES EN FORMATION PROFESSIONNELLE ..., MANUEL D'OPERATIONS DES SYSTEMES INFORMATIQUES *See* EFFECTIF SCOLAIRE ..., MANUEL D'OPERATIONS DES SYSTEMES INFORMATIQUES (DCS) **1743**

EFFECTIVE ADVERTISING (US/0749-2316) [11336722] **759**

EFFECTIVE BUSINESS WRITING (US) **671**

EFFECTIVE EXHIBITING : A PRACTICAL GUIDE (US) [18313175] **759**

EFFECTIVE MANAGER, THE *See* EXECUTIVE UPDATE NEWSLETTER **674**

●EFFECTIVE SCHOOL PRACTICES (US/1068-7378) [27784943] **1894**

EFFECTIVE SPECIAL SERVICES MANAGEMENT (US/0890-4790) [14256375] **866**

EFFECTOR ONLINE (US/1062-9424) [25812430] **1110**

EFFECTS OF US CORPORATE FOREIGN INVESTMENT : A SPECIAL RESEARCH STUDY UNDERTAKEN BY BUSINESS INTERNATIONAL CORPORATION, THE *See* FOREIGN INVESTORS' HANDBOOK : MAKING SUCCESSFUL US INVESTMENTS, THE **899**

EFFEKTIVITETSKONTROL I MJOLKPRODUKTIONEN, RESULTAT OCH ANALYS (SW) [05906346] **194**

EFFICIENCY AND ECONOMY REVIEW (NZ) [05144853] **1605**

EFFLUENT (CN/0701-0222) [03399937] **2088**

EFIR (RU/0131-694X) [24101741] **1131**

EFL GAZETTE, THE (UK/0732-5819) [08383488] **3278**

EFM. EURO FLEXO MAGAZINE (NE/0921-383X) [I0921383X] **4564**

EFOC, FIBER OPTICS & COMMUNICATIONS PROCEEDINGS (US/0731-0633) [08124199] **5102**

EFRYDIAU ATHRONYDDOL (UK) [19238349] **4345**

EFTA BULLETIN (SZ/0012-7655) [02076392] **832**

EFTA BULLETIN *See* EEA NEWS **832**

EFTA TRADE LES ECHANGES DE L'AELE (SZ/0531-4119) [01568451] **832**

EFTERRETNINGER FOR SOFARENDE (DK) [05181551] **4176**

EFTHINI (GR) **2515**

EG-AGRARPREISINDIZES. VORSCHATZUNG DER EG-AGRARPREISINDIZES (OUTPUT AND INPUT) FUR ... (LU) [20032527] **81**

EG-INDIZES DER EINKAUFSPREISE LANDWIRTSCHAFTLICHER BETRIEBSMITTEL (LU) [05050207] **81**

EGALE, L' (CN/0384-062X) [03258632] **2965**

EGALITE (MONCTON) (CN/0226-6873) [08070804] 2260, **4472**

EGATIKA NEA (CN/0710-0272) [08185758] **5784**

EGBAKOKU (DM) [05719880] **2639**

EGE COGRAFYA DERGISI / [EGE UNIVERSITESI, EDEBIYAT FAKULTESI, COGRAFYA BOLUMU] (TU) [15238441] **2560**

EGE TIP DERGISI (TU/1016-9113) [10169113] **3574**

EGE UNIVERSITESI FEN FAKULTESI DERGISI. SERI A (TU/0254-5527) [09951497] **5102**

EGE UNIVERSITESI MUHENDISLIK FAKULTESI DERGISI. SERI E, UYGULAMAL ISTATISTIK (TU) [20553302] **3504**

EGE UNIVERSITESI. ZIRAAT FAKULTESI *See* ZIRRAT FAKULTESI DERGISI. SERI: A **149**

EGE UNIVERSITESI ZIRAAT FAKULTESI DERGISI (TU/1018-8851) [I0188851] **81**

EGESZSEGNEVELES. EDUCATIO SANITARIA (HU) [04216277] **4774**

EGESZSEGUEGYI FELVILAGOSITAS *See* EGESZSEGNEVELES. EDUCATIO SANITARIA **4774**

EGG HARBOR NEWS, THE (US/0746-7036) [10221532] **5710**

EGG INDUSTRY (MOUNT MORRIS, ILL. : 1987) (US/0896-2804) [16899029] **210**

EGG MARKET NEWS REPORT (CHICAGO, ILL.) (US/0744-303X) [08166721] **210**

EGG MARKETING GUIDE (US/0148-9828) [03403846] **2334**

EGG PRODUCER, THE (CN/0821-4689) [09562884] **210**

EGG PRODUCTS (US/0145-3904) [02600891] **210**

EGGS, CHICKENS AND TURKEYS (US/0093-013X) [01768299] **210**

EGGS, CHICKENS AND TURKEYS *See* CHICKENS AND EGGS / NATIONAL AGRICULTURAL STATISTICS SERVICE, UNITED STATES DEPARTMENT OF AGRICULTURE **209**

EGITTO E VICINO ORIENTE (IT) [05271765] **2650**

EGLISE CANADIENNE, L' (CN/0013-2322) [02370727] **4955**

EGLISE CATHOLIQUE. ARCHIDIOCESE DE MONTREAL *See* ANNUAIRE : L'EGLISE DE MONTREAL **5023**

EGLISE CATHOLIQUE. ARCHIDIOCESE DE SHERBROOKE *See* ANNUAIRE - ARCHIDIOCESE DE SHERBROOKE (1977) **5023**

EGLISE CATHOLIQUE. ARCHIDIOCESE D'OTTAWA. ARCHEVEQUE (1967- : PLOURDE) *See* LETTRES MANUSCRITES OU COMMUNIQUES PUBLIES DANS L'ARCHIDIOCESE D'OTTAWA **5031**

EGLISE CATHOLIQUE. DIOCESE DE CHICOUTIMI *See* EGLISE DE CHICOUTIMI ... ANNUAIRE DIOCESAIN **5029**

EGLISE CATHOLIQUE. DIOCESE DE NICOLET *See* EGLISE DE NICOLET, ANNUAIRE **5029**

EGLISE CATHOLIQUE. DIOCESE DE SAINTE-ANNE-DE-LA-POCATIERE *See* SUPPLEMENT / DIOCESE DE SAINTE-ANNE-DE-LA-POCATIERE **5037**

EGLISE CATHOLIQUE. DIOCESE DE TROIS-RIVIERES. EVEQUE (1975- : NOEL) *See* CIRCULAIRE AUX PRETRES ET AUTRES AGENTS DE PASTORALE **5027**

EGLISE DE CHICOUTIMI ... ANNUAIRE DIOCESAIN (CN/0710-6238) [08091632] **5029**

EGLISE DE NICOLET, ANNUAIRE (CN/0838-6226) [21094693] **5029**

EGLISE DE SAINT-JEROME (CN/1184-1990) [23686625] **5029**

EGLISE DE TROIS--RIVIERES (CN/0227-6364) [08010228] **5029**

EGLISE DE TROIS-RIVIERES. DOCUMENT (CN/0227-6372) [08010225] **5029**

EGLISE, EN (CN/0317-851X) [02370294] **4955**

EGLISE ET THEOLOGIE (CN/0013-2349) [05719083] **4955**

EGLISE QUI CHANTE *CEASED.* (FR/0013-2357) [01639318] **4116**

EGMAGAZIN (GW/0343-6667) [07465898] **1634**

EGO KIDS MAGAZINE (CN) **1083**

EGO (SAN FRANCISCO) (US/0148-5822) [03337645] **2532**

EGON-RONAY-BMC GUIDE TO HOTELS, RESTAURANTS, PUBS AND INNS *See* EGON RONAY'S GUIDE TO HOTELS, RESTAURANTS, PUBS, INNS IN GREAT BRITAIN AND IRELAND AND LONDON PENSIONS **2805**

EGON RONAY'S GUIDE TO HOTELS, RESTAURANTS, PUBS, INNS IN GREAT BRITAIN AND IRELAND AND LONDON PENSIONS (UK) [01794128] **2805**

EGON RONAY'S TWA GUIDE ... TO GOOD RESTAURANTS IN 35 EUROPEAN BUSINESS CITIES (US/0882-0376) [11657552] **5070**

EGREGIOUS STEAMBOAT JOURNAL, THE (US/1058-3556) [24278193] **4176**

EGRETTA : VOGELKUNDLICHE NACHRICHTEN AUS OSTERREICH (AU/0013-2373) [02925565] **4165**

EGYPT. AL-MAJALIS AL-QAWMIYAH AL-MUTAKHASSISAH. AL-AMANAH AL-AMMAH *See* SPECIALISED NATIONAL COUNCILS' MAGAZINE, THE **5223**

EGYPT. DEPARTEMENT DU PROTOCOLE *See* LISTE DIPLOMATIQUE - DEPARTEMENT DU PROTOCOLE **3132**

EGYPT EXPLORATION SOCIETY *See* REPORT - EGYPT EXPLORATION SOCIETY **2642**

EGYPT INVESTMENT & BUSINESS DIRECTORY (UA) [12218688] **897**

EGYPT. MASLAHAT AL-ATHAR *See* SUPPLEMENT AUX ANNALES DU SERVICE DES ANTIQUTES DE L'EQYPTE **283**

EGYPT NEWSLETTER (UK/0142-9310) [05910751] **4520**

EGYPT. SERVICE DES ANTIQUITES *See* ANNALES DU SERVICE DES ANTIQUITES DE L'EGYPTE **255**

EGYPT THEN AND NOW (US/0736-945X) [09250056] **2768**

EGYPTE CONTEMPORAINE, L' (UA/0013-239X) [01567665] 3127, **1488**

EGYPTE/MONDE ARABE
(UA/0752-4412) [22770424] 5244, **4472**

EGYPTIAN ARCHAEOLOGY :
BULLETIN OF THE EGYPT
EXPLORATION SOCIETY (UK)
[24692122] **267**

EGYPTIAN BULLETIN, THE (UK)
[11081614] **2639**

EGYPTIAN COMPANIES DIRECTORY,
PUBLIC & PRIVATE SECTORS (UA)
[03974177] **832**

EGYPTIAN COMPUTER JOURNAL,
THE (UA/0377-7154) [02350110] **1258**

EGYPTIAN DENTAL JOURNAL (UA)
[06333967] **1323**

EGYPTIAN GAZETTE, THE (UA)
[11612222] **5800**

EGYPTIAN HOTEL GUIDE (UA)
[08149629] **2805**

EGYPTIAN JOURNAL OF ANIMAL
PRODUCTION (UA/0302-4520)
[02923270] **210**

EGYPTIAN JOURNAL OF
BILHARZIASIS (UA/0301-8849)
[01941494] **3796**

EGYPTIAN JOURNAL OF CHEMISTRY
(UA/0367-0422) [01793876] **975**

EGYPTIAN JOURNAL OF DAIRY
SCIENCE (UA/0378-2700) [02748951]
2334

EGYPTIAN JOURNAL OF FOOD
SCIENCE (UA/0301-8571) [01790797]
2334

EGYPTIAN JOURNAL OF
HORTICULTURE (UA/0301-8164)
[01390204] **2413**

EGYPTIAN JOURNAL OF
MICROBIOLOGY (UA/0301-8172)
[02253061] **562**

EGYPTIAN JOURNAL OF
PHARMACEUTICAL SCIENCES
(UA/0301-5068) [01793232] **4302**

EGYPTIAN JOURNAL OF PHYSICS
(UA/0376-8724) [01794148] **4402**

EGYPTIAN JOURNAL OF
PHYSIOLOGICAL SCIENCES / EDITED
BY THE EGYPTIAN PHYSIOLOGICAL
SCIENCES SOCIETY (UA) [13335380]
580, **454**

EGYPTIAN JOURNAL OF
PHYTOPATHOLOGY *SUSPENDED.*
(UA/0301-8180) [01390185] **509**

EGYPTIAN JOURNAL OF SOIL
SCIENCE (UA/0302-6701) [01793879]
170

EGYPTIAN JOURNAL OF VETERINARY
SCIENCE (UA/0301-8199) [02256073]
5509

EGYPTIAN ORTHOPEDIC JOURNAL
(UA/0013-242X) [01714168] **3881**

EGYPTIAN PAEDIATRIC
ASSOCIATION *See* GAZETTE OF THE
EGYPTIAN PAEDIATRIC
ASSOCIATION **3903**

EGYPTIAN POPULATION AND FAMILY
PLANNING REVIEW, THE (UA)
[05652270] 588, **4552**

EGYPTIAN VETERINARY MEDICAL
ASSOCIATION *See* JOURNAL OF THE
EGYPTIAN VETERINARY MEDICAL
ASSOCIATION **5513**

EGYPTOLOGICAL SEMINAR OF NEW
YORK *See* BULLETIN OF THE
EGYPTOLOGICAL SEMINAR **264**

EH & S DIGEST *CEASED.*
(US/1065-1993) [26524154] **2164**

EHA-B : ANNUAL PROGRAM PLAN
AMENDMENT FOR PART B OF THE
EDUCATION OF THE HANDICAPPED
ACT AS AMENDED BY PUBLIC LAW
94-142 (US) [04872986] **1878**

EHBO VOORPOST VAN DE DOKTER
(NE/0166-008X) [04551983] **3574**

EHIME DAIGAKU KIYO. DAI 3-BU,
KOGAKU *See* EHIME DAIGAKU
KOGAKUBU KIYO **2022**

EHIME DAIGAKU KOGAKUBU KIYO
(JA/0285-6107) [09181792] **2022**

EHIME DAIGAKU KYOIKU GAKUBU
KIYO. DAI 3-BU, SHIZEN KAGAKU (JA)
[08909610] **5102**

EHIME DAIGAKU. NOGAKUBU *See*
EHIME DAIGAKU NOGAKUBU KIYO **81**

EHIME DAIGAKU NOGAKUBU
ENSHURIN HOKOKU (JA/0424-6845)
[I04246845] **2378**

EHIME DAIGAKU NOGAKUBU KIYO
(JA/0424-6829) [02413362] **81**

EHIME-KEN CHIKUSAN SHIKENJO
KENKYU HOKOKU (JA/0389-2859)
[10314567] **81**

EHIME KENRITSU HAKUBUTSUKAN
See EHIME KENRITSU
HAKUBUTSUKAN KENKYU HOKOKU
4165

EHIME KENRITSU HAKUBUTSUKAN
KENKYU HOKOKU (JA) [04715045]
4165

EHOKOLOLONINGOMWA
LYOMTYEKINDJAYI
LYOOLEKENENGA EPANGELO
LYOWAMBO NODHOMALELO
GIILONGO MOWAMBO MOLWEENDO
LWOMUMVO GWEMBO ... (SA)
[04557073] **4721**

EHS LAW BULLETIN SERIES, JAPAN
(JA) [01642136] **2965**

EI DIGEST (US/1042-251X) [18977445]
2227

EI ENVIRONMENTAL SERVICES
DIRECTORY (US/1053-475X)
[22537464] **2227**

EI PAGE ONE [COMPUTER FILE] (US)
[27667690] 1971, **2003**

● EI THESAURUS (US) [27188608] **1999**

EI VOCABULARY *See* EI THESAURUS
1999

EIA DATA INDEX / U.S. DEPARTMENT
OF ENERGY, ENERGY INFORMATION
ADMINISTRATION, OFFICE OF
ENERGY INFORMATION SERVICES
(US) [07181609] **1937**

EIA ELECTRONICS MULTIMEDIA
HANDBOOK (US/0360-1757) [02172052]
2043

EIA GUIDE (US) [01793783] 2043, **949**

EIA PUBLICATIONS DIRECTORY / U.S.
DEPARTMENT OF ENERGY, ENERGY
INFORMATION ADMINISTRATION,
OFFICE OF ENERGY INFORMATION
SERVICES (US) [04943360] **1937**

EIB-INFORMATION / EUROPEAN
INVESTMENT BANK (LU/0250-3891)
[16102636] **897**

EIBUNGAKU SHICHO (JA/0910-500X)
[I0910500X] **3383**

EIBUNGAKU TO EIGOGAKU (JA)
[10050987] **3383**

EICHSFELDER HEIMATHEFTE (GW)
[06782868] **2686**

EICOSANOIDS *CEASED.*
(GW/0934-9820) [19560545] **3729**

EIDIKAI MELETAI EPI TES GEOLOGIAS
TES ELLADOS (ATHENAI)
(GW/0434-6238) [06657171] **1355**

EIDIKON PEIRAMATIKON
ERGASTERION (SERIES) (GR)
[19560297] **832**

EIDO ELECTA : EE : REVISTA
MEDITERRANEA DI RADIOLOGIA E
DIAGNOSTICA PER IMMAGINI (IT)
[25963254] **3941**

EIDON (AG) [05242421] **3925**

EIDOS (ASOLO, ITALY) (IT) [18430560]
319

EIDOS (CAZENOVIA) (US/0271-9819)
[03692431] **2732**

EIFAC OCCASIONAL PAPER (IT)
[04911844] **2300**

EIFAC TECHNICAL PAPER
(IT/0532-940X) [01973113] **2300**

EIGA MOKUROKU (JA) [08134764]
4068

EIGAKUSHI KENKYU / NIHON
EIGAKUSHI GAKKAI (JA) [09125718]
3278

EIGEN HUIS & INTERIEUR (NE) **2905**

EIGHT PEAK INDEX OF MASS
SPECTRA (UK) **975**

EIGHTEEN NINETIES SOCIETY *See*
JOURNAL OF THE EIGHTEEN
NINETIES SOCIETY **3400**

EIGHTEENTH-CENTURY FICTION
(DOWNSVIEW, ONT.) (CN/0840-6286)
[18885323] **3383**

EIGHTEENTH-CENTURY IRELAND (IE)
[15216573] **2686**

EIGHTEENTH-CENTURY LIFE
(US/0098-2601) [02241293] **5268**

EIGHTEENTH CENTURY (LUBBOCK),
THE (US/0193-5380) [04895874] **2686**

EIGHTEENTH-CENTURY STUDIES
(US/0013-2586) [01567675] **319**

EIGHTEENTH CENTURY STUDIES
NEWS CIRCULAR (US/0013-2586) **2615**

EIGHTEENTH CENTURY, THE
(US/0161-0996) [03834722] 2615, **2635**

EIGO EIBUNGAKU KENKYU
HIROSHIMA. 1954 (JA/0288-2876)
[I02882876] 3383, **3278**

EIGO EIBUNGAKU KENKYU (TOKYO.
1976) (JA/0388-2519) [10347002] 3383,
3278

EIGO EIBUNGAKU RONSO (JA)
[02676049] **3278**

EIGO KYOIKU. THE ENGLISH
TEACHERS' MAGAZINE (JA)
[06575253] **3278**

EIGO SEINEN. THE RISING
GENERATION (JA) [06593840] **2846**

EIGSE (IE/0013-2608) [01567157] 3383,
3278

EIGSE CHEOL TIRE (IE/0332-298X)
[01796371] 4116, **4160**

EIJINGU (JA/0288-3619) [10790798]
5179

EIKENBURG & STILES' TEXAS
ENVIRONMENTAL LAW LETTER
(US/1056-7585) [23841338] 2164, **2965**

● EILRICH FAMILY SNAPSHOTS
(US/1061-690X) [25406244] **2446**

EIM MEDEDELINGEN, DE (NE)
[03924800] **954**

EINBECKER JAHRBUCH
(GW/0934-7887) [I09347887] **2686**

EINFUHR NACH HESSEN, DIE (GW)
[05063646] 832, **728**

EINFUHR NORDRHEIN-WESTFALEN
See EINFUHR
NORDRHEIN-WESTFALENS, DIE **832**

EINFUHR
NORDRHEIN-WESTFALENS, DIE (GW)
[01795925] **832**

EINFUHRUNG IN DIE PERIKOPEN (AU)
5029

EINGEFUHRTE MOTORFAHRZEUGE
(SZ) [01794516] 832, **5414**

EINHEIT DER
GESELLSCHAFTSWISSENSCHAFTEN,
DIE (GW/0424-6985) [02384665] **5199**

EINKAEUFER (SZ) **949**

EINKAUFS-1X1 DER DEUTSCHEN
INDUSTRIE (GW/0343-5881) [08878725]
832

EINSTEIN QUARTERLY, THE
(US/0724-6706) [09648258] 454, **3574**

EINTRACHT HARMONY (US)
[13812857] **2515**

EINWOHNER-ADRESSBUCH DER
STADT FREIBERG IM BREISGAU *See*
EINWOHNER-ADRESSBUCH
FREIBURG IM BREISGAU **4645**

EINWOHNER-ADRESSBUCH DES
LANDKREISES
BREISGAU-HOCHSCHWARZWALD.
BD. 3, TITISEE-NEUSTADT UND
HOCHSCHWARZWALD (GW)
[11312518] **2686**

EINWOHNER-ADRESSBUCH
FREIBURG IM BREISGAU (GW)
[16752557] **4645**

EINWOHNERBUCH DER STADTE
LORRACH UND WEIL AM RHEIN (GW)
[06258584] **2686**

EINWOHNERBUCH OBERNDORF AM
NECKAR, EPFENDORF,
FLUORN-WINZELN (GW) [03618744]
2686

EINWOHNERBUCH RAVENSBURG,
WEINGARTEN, AULENDORF, BAD
WALDSEE, BAIENFURT, BAINDT,
BERG, BERGATREUTE, FRONREUTE,
GRUNKRAUT, SCHLIER, VOGT,
WOLPERTSWENDE (GW) [03427642]
2686

EIRE-IRELAND (ST. PAUL)
(US/0013-2683) [01567683] **3341**

EIRENE; STUDIA GRAECA ET LATINA
(XR/0046-1628) [02260699] **1076**

EIS (US/0364-1074) [05290543] **2164**

EIS CONFERENCE REPORT *CEASED.*
(US) [28360966] **1183**

EIS CUMULATIVE (US/0190-0250)
[04219699] **2164**

EIS ... DIRECTORY (US/0732-2445)
[08316218] **3734**

EISEGETIKE EKTHESE
OIKONOMIKOU ETOUS ...
HYPOURGOU OIKONOMIKON (GR)
[20020215] **4721**

EISEI DOBUTSU (JA/0424-7086)
[03762185] 5509, **5607**

EISEI GYOSEI GYOMU HOKOKU (JA)
[02243937] **4774**

EISEI KAGAKU (JA/0013-273X)
[09348533] **975**

EISEI SHIKENJO HOKOKU
(JA/0077-4715) [02899647] **4774**

EISENBAHN INGENIEUR KALENDER
(GW/0071-0075) [17571940] 1971, **5431**

EISENBAHNER *See* DB; DEINE BAHN
5431

EISENBAHNFACHMANN *See* DB;
DEINE BAHN **5431**

EISENBAHNINGENIEUR, DER
(GW/0013-2810) [08454752] **5431**

EISENHOWER CONSORTIUM
BULLETIN (US/0363-8685) [02320881]
2378

EISENHOWER CONSORTIUM FOR
WESTERN ENVIRONMENTAL
FORESTRY RESEARCH *See*
EISENHOWER CONSORTIUM
BULLETIN **2378**

EISHI JOHO (JA) [08124270] **3980**

EISMA 'S VAKPERS (NE/0920-2099)
[I09202099] **4223**

EISS YEARBOOK / ANNUAIRE EISS
(NE) [07436547] 2879, **5284**

EISZEITALTER UND GEGENWART
(GW/0424-7116) [01567686] **1374**

EITF ABSTRACTS (US/1055-3746)
[21571174] **743**

EIU SPECIAL REPORT (UK) [06133400]
1559

EIU WORLD COMMODITY OUTLOOK:
INDUSTRIAL RAW MATERIALS
CEASED. (UK) [04827539] **1605**

EIYO-GAKU ZASSHI (JA/0021-5147)
[04551019] **4190**

EIZO

Alphabetical Title Index

EIZO JOHO MEDIKARU. IMAGE TECHNOLOGY & INFORMATION DISPLAY. MEDICINE (JA) **3574**

EIZO NENKAN (JA) [01797335] **4068**

EJAG NEWS MAGAZINE, THE (US/0199-5804) [06012089] 2773, **5414**

EJECUCION DE PRESUPUESTOS DE AYUNTAMIENTOS Y CONCEJOS DE NAVARRA (SP) [20961433] **4721**

EJECUTIVOS DE FINANZAS (MX) [04746495] **1488**

EJENDOMS- OG SELSKABSBESKATNINGEN I SKATTEARET. *See* SKATTER OG AFGIFTER **4748**

EJERCITO (SP) **4043**

EJERCITO, EL (EC) [06324649] **4043**

EJERCITO MADRID (SP/0013-2918) [I00132918] **4043**

EJHP, EUROPEAN JOURNAL OF HOSPITAL PHARMACY (GW/0992-4663) [14776016] 3780, **4302**

EJOURNAL (ALBANY, N.Y.) (US/1054-1055) [22748096] **1183**

EKALAKA EAGLE (EKALAKA, MONT. : 1923) (US) [11887680] **5705**

EKATA (CN/0715-3902) [09157018] **2532**

EKHO. : EKOLOGIIA, KHOZIAISTVO, OKRUZHAIUSHCHAIA SREDA (RU) [23114690] **2192**

EKHO; LITERATURNYI ZHURNAL (FR) [04993735] **3383**

EKHO PLANETY (RU/0234-1670) [20983512] **4520**

EKISTIC INDEX OF PERIODICALS (GR) [13500532] **2821**

EKISTICS (GR/0013-2942) [02446600] **2821**

EKKLESIA KAI THEOLOGIA : EKKLESIASTIKE KAI THEOLOGIKE EPETERIS TES HIERAS ARCHIEPISKOPES THYATEIRON KAI MEGALES VRETANNIAS (GR) [07910085] **5039**

EKKLESIASTIKOS PHAROS (ET) [01590048] **5039**

EKLITRA / ASSOCIATION CULTURELLE PICARDE (FR/0424-7175) [02298017] **2515**

EKO (RU) [19559494] **866**

EKOLOGIA BRATISLAVA / ECOLOGY BRATISLAVA (XO) [30990160] **2215**

EKOLOGIA CSFR *See* EKOLOGIA BRATISLAVA / ECOLOGY BRATISLAVA **2215**

EKOLOGIA CSFR / ECOLOGY CSFR (XO/0862-9129) [25182363] **2215**

EKOLOGIA POLSKA (1970) (PL/0420-9036) [01535400] **2215**

EKOLOGIA (SOFIA) (BU/0204-7675) [02659486] **2215**

EKOLOGICHESKAIA I EKSPERIMENTALNAIA PARAZITOLOGIIA (RU/0136-9121) [02618213] **5582**

EKOLOGIIA I ZASHCHITA LESA : MEZHVUZOVSKII SBORNIK NAUCHNYKH TRUDOV / LENINGRADSKAIA LESOTEKHNICHESKAIA AKADEMIIA IMENI S.M. KIROVA (RU/0134-4978) [09707960] 2378, **2215**

EKOLOGIIA MORIA / AKADEMIIA NAUK UKRAINSKOI SSR, INSTITUT BIOLOGII IUZHNYKH MOREI IM. A.O. KOVALEVSKOGO (UN) [07063103] 2215, **554**

EKOLOGIJA (RU/0367-0597) [02156757] 4165, **2215**

EKOLOGIJA (YU/0531-9110) [02916908] **2215**

EKOLOGIJA / LIETUVOS MOKSLU AKADEMIJA / EKOLOGIIA / LITOVSKAIA AKADEMIIA NAUK / ECOLOGY / THE LITHUANIAN ACADEMY OF SCIENCES (LI/0235-7224) [23278318] **2215**

EKONOM (XR) [25238580] **866**

EKONOMI DAN KEUANGAN INDONESIA (IO/0126-155X) [02038875] **1488**

EKONOMI DAN PEMBANGUNAN (IO) [04766113] **1559**

EKONOMI SUMATERA UTARA (IO/0377-7162) [01783522] **1559**

EKONOMIA (PL) [04177449] **1591**

EKONOMIA I ORGANIZACJA (PL) [04690889] **1488**

EKONOMIAZ (SP/0213-3865) [16895366] **1559**

EKONOMICHESKAIA GEOGRAFIIA: RESPUBLIKANSKII MEZHVEDOMSTVENNYI NAUCHNYI SBORNIK (UN) [03926471] **1559**

EKONOMICHESKIE NAUKI (RU) [02319640] 1488, **671**

EKONOMICHESKIE PROBLEMY LESNOI, DEREVOOBRABATYVAIUSHCHEI PROMYSHLENNOSTI I LESNOGO KHOZIAISTVA (RU) [08118323] **2378**

EKONOMICHESKIE VOPROSY RAZVITIIA SELSKOGO KHOZIAISTVA BSSR (BW) [02239316] **81**

EKONOMICKO-MATEMATICKY OBZOR *CEASED*. (CS/0013-3027) [02298004] 3504, **1591**

EKONOMICKY CASOPIS (XO/0013-3035) [02297985] **1488**

EKONOMIK PANORAMA (TU) **1488**

EKONOMIKA (US/0474-2974) [02690071] **1559**

EKONOMIKA I MATEMATICHESKIE METODY (RU/0424-7388) [02080949] 3504, **1591**

EKONOMIKA I ORGANIZACJA PRZEDSIEBIORSTWA (PL/0860-6846) [17864419] **1605**

EKONOMIKA I ZHIZN (RU) [20860124] **1488**

EKONOMIKA I ZHIZN (UZ/0013-3051) [02697373] **5813**

EKONOMIKA POL'NOHOSPODARSTVA *See* AGROEKONOMIKA **55**

EKONOMIKA PRACE (XO) [09212745] **1488**

EKONOMIKA PROIZVODNJE HRANE (YU) [03339087] **1559**

EKONOMIKA SELSKOKHOZIAISTVENNYKH I PERERABATYVAIUSHCHIKH PREOPRIIATII (RU/0235-2494) [18083914] **81**

EKONOMIKA SOVESTKOI UKRAINY (UN) [08012133] **2686**

EKONOMIKA STROITELSTVA (RU/0013-3116) [02308304] **613**

EKONOMIKA UGOLNOI PROMYSHLENNOSTI (RU) [01788846] **2138**

EKONOMIKA UKRAINY (UN) [25974512] **1488**

EKONOMIKO-MATEMATICHESKIE MODELI / AKADEMIIA NAUK SSSR, TSENTRALNYI EKONOMIKO-MATEMATICHESKII INSTITUT (RU) [02319443] **1591**

EKONOMISKA SAMFUNDETS TIDSKRIFT (FI/0013-3183) [02302169] **1488**

EKONOMISKA UTSIKTER I NORDEN (DK) [19651277] **1488**

EKONOMISKAS INFORMACIJAS APSTRADES MEHANIZACIJA (LV) [02468248] 1259, **743**

EKONOMIST (RU) [24940333] **1488**

EKONOMIST : ORGAN DRUSTVA EKONOMISTA SRBIJE (CI/0013-3191) [02302211] **1488**

EKONOMISTA (PL) [04266979] **832**

EKONOMISUTO TOKYO. 1946 (JA/0013-0621) [I00130621] **1488**

EKONOMSKA POLITIKA (YU/0013-3248) [02298134] 1488, **671**

EKONOMSKI PREGLED (CI/0424-7558) [02297952] **1591**

EKOTASS (DEUTSCHE AUSGABE) (FR/0733-5997) [08777541] **1488**

EKRAN (RU/0868-9024) [23658400] **4068**

EKRAN I STSENA (RU) [21072457] **4068**

EKSEKUTIF (IO) [06907511] **671**

EKSPERIMENTALNA MEDITSINA I MORFOLOGIIA (BU/0367-0643) [07599647] **3574**

●EKSPERIMENTALNAIA I KLINICHESKAIA FARMAKOLOGIIA (RU/0869-2092) [26237699] **4303**

EKSPERIMENTALNAIA MEDITSINA (LV) [05635525] **3574**

EKSPERIMENTALNAIA VODNAIA TOKSIKOLOGIIA / AKADEMIIA NAUK LATVIISKOI SSR, INSTITUT BIOLOGII (LV/0367-0724) [10494485] **4244**

EKSPERIMENTALNAJA ONKOLOGIJA (UN/0204-3564) [06927556] **3816**

EKSPERIMENTALNOE ISSLEDOVANIE LICHNOSTI I TEMPERAMENTA (RU) [01791315] **4586**

EKSPERIMENTINE BIOLOGIJA *See* BIOLOGIJA / BIOLOGY / BIOLOGIIA **446**

EKSPONEN (IO/0302-8577) [01792419] **2503**

EKSPOR (INDONESIA. BIRO PUSAT STATISTIK) (IO) [07429101] **832**

EKSPORT AKTUELT / FRA NORGES EKSPORTRAD (NO/0800-6733) [11610302] **833**

EKSPORT KOEBENHAVN (DK/0900-3177) [I09003177] **833**

EKSPORTKREDITRADET (DENMARK) *See* BERETNING FOR FINANSARET ... **778**

EKSPRES (IO/0531-9145) [02245668] **2503**

EKSPRESS-SHAKHMATY : NAUCHNO-METODICHESKII ZHURNAL (RU) [24152968] **4860**

EKSTRAKTSIIA, IONNYI OBMEN (RU/0132-2354) [03084583] **1052**

EKT : ELEKTROIZOLACNA A KABLOVA TECHNIKA / VYZKUMNY USTAV KABLOV A IZOLANTOV V BRATISLAVE (XO) [24894275] **2043**

EKTHESE GIA TIS KAIRIKES SYNTHEKES STEN KYPRO STO HYDROMETEOROLOGIKO ETOS ... / KYPRIAKE DEMOKRATIA, HYPOURGEIO GEORGIAS KAI PHYSIKON PORON, METEOROLOGIKE HYPERESIA (CY) [24480663] **1425**

EKTHESIS PEPRAGMEN VIOTECHNIKON EPIMELETERION ATHENON (GR) [02241545] **833**

●EL & P U.S. ELECTRIC UTILITY INDUSTRY DIRECTORY (US/1058-2479) [24243973] 2035, **4759**

EL CHICANO (COLTON, CALIF.) (US/0893-3502) [03544542] **5634**

EL DORADO (US/0095-165X) [01793158] **235**

EL DORADO GAZETTE, GEORGETOWN GAZETTE & TOWN CRIER (US/8750-6289) [11630184] **5634**

EL DORADO NEWS-TIMES (US) [22913830] **5631**

EL DORADO TIMES, THE (US/1053-9999) [09822022] **5675**

●EL-E-PHANT (US) **3383**

EL-HI TEXTBOOKS AND SERIALS IN PRINT (US/0000-0825) [11882287] **1794**

EL HOGAR CRISTIANO (US/0018-3229) [07005195] **4955**

EL PASO ARCHAEOLOGICAL SOCIETY *See* EL PASO ARCHAEOLOGY **267**

EL PASO ARCHAEOLOGY (US/0013-4023) [08626166] **267**

EL PASO CO., TEX. AUDITOR'S OFFICE *See* AUDITOR'S ANNUAL REPORT OF EL PASO COUNTY, TEXAS **4712**

EL PASO COUNTY HISTORICAL SOCIETY (EL PASO CO., TEX.) *See* MEMBERSHIP DIRECTORY / EL PASO COUNTY HISTORICAL SOCIETY **2746**

EL PASO ECONOMIC REVIEW (1983), THE *CEASED.* (US/8750-6033) [11580773] **1488**

EL PASO HERALD-POST (US/0746-360X) [09978583] **5749**

EL PASO SUN (US) [15672919] **5749**

EL PASO TIMES (EL PASO, TEX. : 1921) (US) [08564831] **5749**

EL SALVADOR CHRONOLOGY (US) [24933883] **4507**

EL SALVADOR: ENERGIEWIRTSCHAFT (GW) [05136348] **1937**

EL SALVADOR PROCESO (ES) [11191645] **2732**

EL SALVADOR, REFUGEES IN CRISIS / SHARE - SALVADOREAN HUMANITARIAN AID, RESEARCH, AND EDUCATION FOUNDATION (US) [11018581] **1918**

EL SALVADOR: WIRTSCHAFTLICHE ENTWICKLUNG (GW) [02519749] **1559**

EL SALVADOR, WIRTSCHAFTSDATEN / BUNDESSTELLE FUER AUSSENHANDELSINFORMATION (GW) [10931681] **1559**

EL SOL (SALINAS, CALIF.) (US/1064-1998) [12260357] **5635**

EL TELEGRAPH (AT) 2260, **5777**

ELAEIS (MY/0128-1828) [20684429] **5102**

ELAN (DEVENTER, NETHERLANDS) (NE/0167-3939) [14511619] **866**

ELAN (HAUTERIVE) (CN/0701-1709) [03409819] **1091**

ELAN (NEW YORK, N.Y.) (US/0733-5288) [08598276] **2532**

ELAN RHONE-ALPES (FR) [23473555] **2560**

EL&P ELECTRIC UTILITY INDUSTRY SOFTWARE DIRECTORY (US/1058-2460) [24243718] **2043**

●EL&P U.S. ELECTRIC UTILITY INDUSTRY SOFTWARE DIRECTORY (US/1069-0557) [27479814] 1183, **2043**

ELASTICA (IT) **5075**

ELASTOMERICS *CEASED.* (US/0146-0706) [02847549] **5075**

ELASTOMERICS NEWS-LOG (US/0146-0714) [02847616] **5075**

ELASTOMERS (US) [07418666] 5075, **4455**

ELATUSTUKI (FI) [06785624] **5284**

ELAVAN KUVAN VUOSIKIRJA (FI/0785-9015) [19496036] **4068**

ELBA CLIPPER, THE (US) [12604538] **5626**

ELECTRICIDADE

ELBERT ROGERS' WASHINGTON STATE SCORE (US/0736-881X) [07625351] **2532**

ELBERTON STAR, THE (US) [23242473] **5653**

ELC (US/0364-118X) [02594375] 1743, **2965**

ELDER CHURCHMAN, THE (US/0360-6120) [01901896] **4955**

ELDER STATESMAN See TODAY'S TIMES **5182**

ELDER STATESMAN, THE (CN/0013-4074) [23302782] **5179**

ELDER UPDATE (US/1060-4545) [24995569] 1296, **5179**

ELDER VOICES (US) 3750, **2260**

ELDERLAW REPORT, THE (US/1047-7055) [20300306] 5179, **2965**

●ELDERLY CARE (UK) [27835803] **3855**

ELDERLY HEALTH SERVICES LETTER (US/0891-9275) [15042392] **5284**

ELDERLY POPULATION: ESTIMATES BY COUNTY, THE (US/0190-3896) [04160472] **4552**

ELDERS WEEKLY (AT) **210**

ELDERSONG (US) 5179, **4116**

ELDORA HERALD-LEDGER, THE (US) [13818464] **5670**

ELECTED LEADER (US/0884-7142) [12414752] **866**

ELECTION ADMINISTRATION REPORTS (US/0145-8124) [02804134] 2965, **4472**

ELECTION ARCHIVES AND INTERNATIONAL POLITICS (II) [20482658] 3092, **4645**

ELECTION CENTER REPORTS (US/1067-9774) [27427051] **4473**

ELECTION FINANCING FACT BOOK (US) [07936922] **4645**

ELECTION RESULTS AND STATISTICS / STATE OF OKLAHOMA (US) [07958432] **4502**

ELECTION RESULTS DATABOOK FOR CUYAHOGA COUNTY (US/0362-6903) [02316132] **4645**

ELECTIONS CANADA See REPORT OF THE CHIEF ELECTORAL OFFICER OF CANADA **4493**

ELECTIVE AND APPOINTIVE STATE OFFICERS, STATE OF MICHIGAN (US/0363-2571) [02455549] **4645**

ELECTORAL BOUNDARIES COMMISSION FOR THE PROVINCE OF ALBERTA (CANADA) See INTERIM REPORT OF THE ELECTORAL BOUNDARIES COMMISSION OF THE PROVINCE OF ALBERTA **4477**

ELECTORAL STUDIES (UK/0261-3794) [08912191] **4645**

ELECTRA (PARIS. 1948) (FR/0424-7701) [I04247701] **2043**

ELECTRE BIBLIO FRENCH BOOKS IN PRINT. CD-ROM (FR) **415**

ELECTRIC AND HYBRID VEHICLES PROGRAM (US) [10712730] **5381**

ELECTRIC CONSUMER (US/0745-4651) [09188791] **1937**

ELECTRIC ENERGY SYSTEMS (US/0896-5196) [17197431] **1937**

ELECTRIC GENERATING AND DISTRIBUTING COMPANIES (US/1054-3260) [22106066] **2043**

ELECTRIC GENERATION AND TRANSMISSION FACILITIES IN OHIO, SITE INFORMATION / COMPILED ... BY THE PUBLIC UTILITIES COMMISSION OF OHIO, DIVISION OF FORECASTING AND THE OHIO POWER SITING BOARD (US) [24018014] **4760**

ELECTRIC LAMPS (ANNUAL) (US/0273-4400) [06937525] **2043**

ELECTRIC LAMPS, LIGHT BULBS, AND TUBES (CN/0828-1777) [13816751] **3478**

ELECTRIC LIGHT & POWER (US/0013-4120) [01567703] **2043**

ELECTRIC LIGHTING FIXTURES CEASED. (US/0740-1698) [03145803] **2043**

ELECTRIC LINES CEASED. (US/0895-2116) [16512392] **2043**

ELECTRIC LIVING JOURNAL : ELECTRICAL ASSOCIATION FOR WOMEN (UK/0262-8279) [12026359] **2811**

ELECTRIC MACHINES AND POWER SYSTEMS (US/0731-356X) [08175504] **2043**

ELECTRIC OUTPUT (US/0277-1616) [04352309] **2043**

ELECTRIC PERSPECTIVES (US/0364-474X) [02390088] **2043**

ELECTRIC POWER ALERT (US) **2043**

ELECTRIC POWER ANNUAL (US/0736-9352) [09121513] 2043, **2003**

ELECTRIC POWER IN ASIA AND THE PACIFIC (US) [04836331] **2043**

ELECTRIC POWER IN KOREA / KOREA ELECTRIC POWER CORPORATION (KO) [09359087] **2043**

ELECTRIC POWER MONTHLY (US/0732-2305) [07056394] **2043**

ELECTRIC POWER RESEARCH INSTITUTE See EPRI JOURNAL **2053**

●ELECTRIC POWER STATISTICS. ANNUAL STATISTICS (CN/1198-4848) [30592729] 1937, **1962**

ELECTRIC POWER STATISTICS (OTTAWA. MONTHLY ED.) (CN/0380-0229) [02443575] 4760, **4697**

ELECTRIC POWER STATISTICS. VOLUME 1. ANNUAL ELECTRIC POWER SURVEY OF CAPABILITY AND LOAD (CN/0380-951X) [01785194] 1937, **1962**

ELECTRIC POWER STATISTICS. VOLUME 3. INVENTORY OF PRIME MOVER AND ELECTRIC GENERATING EQUIPMENT (CN/0702-6609) [02443587] 1937, **1962**

ELECTRIC POWER STATISTICS. VOLUME II, ANNUAL STATISTICS See ELECTRIC POWER STATISTICS. ANNUAL STATISTICS **1962**

ELECTRIC POWER SUPPLY AND DEMAND (US/0737-1845) [09297022] **2043**

ELECTRIC POWER SUPPLY AND DEMAND FOR THE CONTIGUOUS UNITED STATES CEASED. (US/0735-9446) [04710400] **2043**

ELECTRIC POWER SURVEY (TOKYO, JAPAN) (JA) [11950788] **2044**

ELECTRIC POWER SYSTEMS RESEARCH (SZ/0378-7796) [03700049] **2044**

ELECTRIC POWER TRENDS (US) [26148701] **2044**

ELECTRIC PROPULSION (CN/0831-6899) [16386319] **2044**

ELECTRIC RATE BOOK (US) 1937, **4760**

ELECTRIC RD&D CEASED. (US/0895-1853) [16512104] **2044**

ELECTRIC SALES AND REVENUE (US) [23185370] **2044**

ELECTRIC TROLLING MOTOR REPAIR FOR MR. & MS. FIX-IT (US/1057-0187) [23915269] **593**

ELECTRIC UTILITY BUSINESS (US/0894-3788) [16067096] **4760**

ELECTRIC UTILITY FORECASTING IN NEW JERSEY (US/0737-2701) [09313452] **2044**

ELECTRIC UTILITY GENERATION PLANBOOK, THE (US/0270-0743) [05192448] **2044**

ELECTRIC UTILITY INDUSTRY REVIEW (US/0747-4881) [10698779] **1605**

ELECTRIC UTILITY STATISTICAL REFERENCE (US/0190-1729) [04633239] 2044, **2003**

ELECTRIC UTILITY WEEK (US/0736-413X) [09121112] **2044**

●ELECTRIC UTILITY WEEK'S DEMAND-SIDE REPORT (US/1065-8696) [26784198] **4761**

ELECTRIC VEHICLE DEVELOPMENTS SUSPENDED. (UK/0141-9811) [05781360] **5381**

●ELECTRIC VEHICLE DIGEST (US/1064-1254) [26210456] **5414**

ELECTRIC VEHICLE NEWS MELBOURNE (AT/0818-8491) [I08188491] 2044, **5414**

ELECTRIC VEHICLE PROGRESS (US/0190-4175) [04710467] **2044**

ELECTRICAL ACCIDENT INVESTIGATION HANDBOOK SUSPENDED. (US/0732-5665) [08384617] **2861**

ELECTRICAL ADVERTISER (US) **2044**

ELECTRICAL & ELECTRONIC ENGINEERING SOCIETY See ELECTSO, ELECTRICAL & ELECTRONIC ENGINEERING SOCIETY'S MAGAZINE, THE **2051**

ELECTRICAL AND ELECTRONIC PRODUCTS INDUSTRIES (CN/0835-0159) [18701062] **2044**

ELECTRICAL & ELECTRONICS ABSTRACTS (UK/0036-8105) [02579898] 2044, **2003**

ELECTRICAL APPARATUS (US/0190-1370) [03570778] **2044**

ELECTRICAL APPLIANCE AND UTILIZATION EQUIPMENT DIRECTORY (US) [04204237] **2811**

ELECTRICAL BLUE BOOK, THE (CN/0149-6174) [03509577] **2044**

ELECTRICAL BUSINESS (CN/0013-4244) [02002530] **2044**

ELECTRICAL CODE WATCH (US/1057-0241) [23915351] **2044**

●ELECTRICAL COMMUNICATION (FR/1242-0565) [28512106] **1154**

ELECTRICAL COMMUNICATION (US/0013-4252) [01567710] **1154**

ELECTRICAL COMPONENT LOCATOR. DOMESTIC CARS, LIGHT TRUCKS & VANS, IMPORTED CARS & TRUCKS (US/0743-6076) [10012340] **5414**

ELECTRICAL COMPONENT LOCATOR. IMPORTED CARS & TRUCKS / MITCHELL (US) [10321973] **5414**

ELECTRICAL CONSTRUCTION AND MAINTENANCE (US/0013-4260) [07104983] **2044**

ELECTRICAL CONSTRUCTION ESTIMATOR (US/1041-729X) [12696656] **2044**

ELECTRICAL CONSTRUCTION MATERIALS DIRECTORY (US) [04206121] **2044**

ELECTRICAL CONTACTS (US/1062-6808) [14958160] **2044**

ELECTRICAL CONTRACTOR (UK/0308-7174) [18679824] **2044**

ELECTRICAL CONTRACTOR (WASHINGTON) (US/0033-5118) [02244861] **2044**

ELECTRICAL CONTRACTORS ASSOCIATION OF ONTARIO See ONTARIO ELECTRICAL CONTRACTOR, THE **2074**

ELECTRICAL DESIGN AND INSTALLATION SUSPENDED. (US/1058-4218) [24201491] **4761**

ELECTRICAL DESIGN & MFG (US/1065-7436) [26712783] **2044**

ELECTRICAL DESIGN : BUILDING ELECTRICAL SERVICES & LIGHTING (UK) **2044**

ELECTRICAL DISTRIBUTOR See TED : THE ELECTRICAL DISTRIBUTORS MAGAZINE **2084**

ELECTRICAL DISTRIBUTOR, THE (US/0422-8707) [05077391] **2044**

ELECTRICAL ENGINEER (CHIPPENDALE, N.S.W.) (AT) [08304195] **2044**

ELECTRICAL ENGINEERING AND ELECTRONICS (US/0891-6225) [08893012] **2045**

ELECTRICAL ENGINEERING COMMUNICATIONS AND SIGNAL PROCESSING (US/0888-2134) [13519481] **2045**

ELECTRICAL ENGINEERING IN JAPAN (US/0424-7760) [21415733] **2045**

ELECTRICAL ENGINEERING RESEARCH ABSTRACTS. CANADIAN UNIVERSITIES (CN/0070-9662) [02578389] **2045**

ELECTRICAL EQUIPMENT LONDON (UK/0013-4317) [I00134317] **2045**

ELECTRICAL EQUIPMENT NEWS (CN/0013-4333) [20776927] **2045**

ELECTRICAL INDIA (II/0013-435X) [09327834] **2045**

ELECTRICAL INDUSTRY SOFTWARE DIRECTORY See EL&P ELECTRIC UTILITY INDUSTRY SOFTWARE DIRECTORY **2043**

ELECTRICAL MANUFACTURING (LIBERTYVILLE, ILL.) See ELECTRICAL DESIGN & MFG **2044**

ELECTRICAL MANUFACTURING (LIBERTYVILLE, ILL.) (US/0895-3716) [16573883] **3478**

ELECTRICAL MARKETING (US/0149-5771) [03527161] 613, **2045**

ELECTRICAL OVERSTRESS/ELECTROSTATIC DISCHARGE SYMPOSIUM PROCEEDINGS (US/0739-5159) [07366665] **2154**

ELECTRICAL PRACTICE (US/0094-9434) [01795693] **2045**

ELECTRICAL PRODUCTS TUNBRIDGE WELLS, KENT (UK/0260-1656) [I02601656] **2045**

ELECTRICAL PRODUCTS YEARBOOK (US/0093-3236) [01792084] **2045**

ELECTRICAL RETAILING (UK/0074-8714) **2045**

ELECTRICAL REVIEW (UK) 1183, **2045**

ELECTRICAL TECHNOLOGY (UK/0965-5433) [26833422] **2045**

ELECTRICAL TIMES (UK/0013-4414) [06354145] **2045**

ELECTRICAL TRADE CONTRACTORS (CN/0835-104X) [16518796] **613**

ELECTRICAL WHOLESALER (UK/0013-4422) [I00134422] **2045**

ELECTRICAL WHOLESALING (US/0013-4430) [05625706] **2045**

ELECTRICAL WORLD (US/0013-4457) [01567724] **2045**

ELECTRICAL WORLD DIRECTORY OF ELECTRIC UTILITIES (US) [02270731] **2045**

ELECTRICAL WORLD DIRECTORY OF ELECTRIC UTILITIES IN LATIN AMERICA, BERMUDA AND THE CARIBBEAN ISLANDS (US/0092-2501) [01788817] **4761**

ELECTRICIAN'S GUIDE (US/0164-2804) [04603089] **2045**

ELECTRICIDADE (PO/0870-5364) [16781401] **2045**

ELECTRICIEN
Alphabetical Title Index

ELECTRICIEN INDUSTRIEL, L' (FR) [02243407] **2045**

ELECTRICITE *SUSPENDED.* (BE/0013-4481) [11445226] **2045**

ELECTRICITE DE FRANCE *See* STATISTIQUES ELECTRICITE **2082**

ELECTRICITE DE FRANCE. DIRECTION DE LA DISTRIBUTION *See* COMPTE RENDU D'ACTIVITE - EDF, DIRECTION DE LA DISTRIBUTION **4640**

ELECTRICITE DE FRANCE. DIRECTION DES AFFAIRES EXTERIEURES ET DE LA COOPERATION *See* RAPPORT D'ACTIVITE - ELECTRICITE DE FRANCE, DIRECTION DES AFFAIRES EXTERIEURES ET DE LA COOPERATION **2078**

ELECTRICITE DE FRANCE. DIRECTION DES ETUDES ET RECHERCHES *See* RAPPORT D'ACTIVITE - ELECTRICITE DE FRANCE, DIRECTION DES ETUDES ET RECHERCHES **2078**

ELECTRICITE DE FRANCE. DIRECTION DES ETUDES ET RECHERCHES *See* BULLETIN DE LA DIRECTION DES ETUDES ET RECHERCHES, ELECTRICITE DE FRANCE - SERIE C. MATHEMATIQUES, INFORMATIQUE **3497**

ELECTRICITE DE FRANCE. DIRECTION DES ETUDES ET RECHERCHES. QUELQUES FAITS MARQUANTS *See* FAITS MARQUANTS **2054**

ELECTRICITE DE FRANCE. DIRECTION REGIONALE POUR LED DEPARTEMENTS D'OUTRE-MER *See* RESULTATS / ELECTRICITE DE FRANCE, DIRECTION REGIONALE POUR LES DEPARTEMENTS D'OUTRE-MER **2079**

ELECTRICITE DE FRANCE. DIVISION TECHNIQUE GENERALE *See* RAPPORT D'ACTIVITE / DIVISION TECHNIQUE GENERALE **2078**

ELECTRICITE DE FRANCE. DIVISION TECHNIQUE GENERALE. ACTIVITE *See* RAPPORT D'ACTIVITE / DIVISION TECHNIQUE GENERALE **2078**

ELECTRICITY AND GAS, AUSTRALIA (AT/1037-9886) [4283, **1962**

ELECTRICITY AND GAS ESTABLISHMENTS DETAILS OF OPERATIONS, AUSTRALIA, STATES AND TERRITORIES *See* ELECTRICITY AND GAS, AUSTRALIA **1962**

●ELECTRICITY AUSTRALIA / ESAA (AT) [26565714] **2045**

ELECTRICITY CONSERVATION QUARTERLY (II/0970-2318) [I09702318] **1937**

ELECTRICITY COUNCIL *See* ANNUAL REPORT / THE ELECTRICITY COUNCIL **4696**

●ELECTRICITY DAILY REPORT, THE (US/1070-8928) [28490378] **1488**

ELECTRICITY INTERNATIONAL (UK/0955-5439) [28093542] **2045**

ELECTRICITY JOURNAL, THE (US/1040-6190) [18461995] **4761**

ELECTRICITY POOL PRICES AND BID PRICES : DEMAND DATA MONTHLY FIGURES. DISKETTE (UK) **2046**

ELECTRICITY SALES STATISTICS (MONTHLY) (US/0364-0124) [04159441] 2046, **2003**

ELECTRICITY SUPPLY & DEMAND FOR ... THE REGIONAL RELIABILITY COUNCILS OF THE NORTH AMERICAN ELECTRIC RELIABILITY COUNCIL (US/1046-3186) [14951054] 2046, **4761**

ELECTRICITY SUPPLY ASSOCIATION OF AUSTRALIA *See* ELECTRICITY SUPPLY INDUSTRY IN AUSTRALIA **2046**

ELECTRICITY SUPPLY COMMISSION OF MALAWI *See* ANNUAL REPORT AND STATEMENT OF ACCOUNTS FOR THE YEAR ENDED ... / ELECTRICITY SUPPLY COMMISSION OF MALAWI **2035**

ELECTRICITY SUPPLY INDUSTRY IN AUSTRALIA (AT/0312-8393) [02243288] **2046**

ELECTRICITY SUPPLY INDUSTRY IN QUEENSLAND, FINANCIAL REPORT, THE (AT/0725-3125) [11101337] **2046**

ELECTRICITY TODAY (PICKERING) (CN/0843-7343) [19925409] 1937, **2046**

ELECTRICITY WEEK (AT/1032-5565) [I10325565] **2046**

ELECTRICS (UK) [01785472] **2046**

ELECTRO *See* ELECTRO ANNUAIRE **2046**

●ELECTRO- AND MAGNETOBIOLOGY (US/1061-9526) [25493361] 4443, **454**

ELECTRO ANNUAIRE (FR) [07080928] **2046**

ELECTRO MANUFACTURING (US/1041-052X) [18619182] **3478**

ELECTRO OPTICS (UK/0013-4589) [11446644] **4434**

ELECTRO-OPTICS SERIES (US/0148-9046) [03400498] **1972**

ELECTROACOUSTIC MUSIC (UK) [11589085] **4116**

ELECTROACOUSTIQUE (BE/0422-888X) [02321704] **4452**

ELECTROANALYSIS (NEW YORK, N.Y.) (US/1040-0397) [18298896] 2046, **1014**

ELECTROANALYTICAL CHEMISTRY (US/0070-9778) [01567734] **1014**

ELECTROCHEMICAL INDUSTRIES AND TECHNOLOGY (US/0191-782X) [04968586] **1024**

ELECTROCHEMICAL INDUSTRY (US/0361-2686) [02038225] 4001, **1034**

ELECTROCHEMICAL SCIENCE AND TECHNOLOGY OF POLYMERS (UK/0963-5637) [I09635637] 2046, **975**

ELECTROCHEMICAL SOCIETY *See* DIRECTORY OF MEMBERS - ELECTROCHEMICAL SOCIETY **1051**

●ELECTROCHEMICAL SOCIETY INTERFACE, THE (US/1064-8208) [26409155] **975**

ELECTROCHEMISTRY & ELECTROCHEMICAL ENGINEERING (US/0733-6691) [08644745] **1034**

ELECTROCHIMICA ACTA (UK/0013-4686) [01567741] **1034**

ELECTROCOMPONENT SCIENCE MONOGRAPHS (US/0275-7230) [07219347] **2046**

ELECTRODIAGNOSTIC-THERAPIE (BE/0424-8120) [I04248120] **3574**

ELECTROENCEPHALOGRAPHY AND CLINICAL NEUROPHYSIOLOGY (IE/0013-4694) [01567742] **3831**

ELECTROENCEPHALOGRAPHY AND CLINICAL NEUROPHYSIOLOGY/ ELECTROMYOGRAPHY AND MOTOR CONTROL (IE/0924-980X) **3832**

ELECTROENCEPHALOGRAPHY AND CLINICAL NEUROPHYSIOLOGY EVOKED POTENTIALS (IE/0168-5597) [I01685597] **580**

ELECTROENCEPHALOGRAPHY AND CLINICAL NEUROPHYSIOLOGY. SUPPLEMENT (NE/0424-8155) [01587999] **3832**

ELECTROLYTE SOLUTIONS BULLETIN (UK) **2046**

ELECTROMAGNETIC METROLOGY CURRENT AWARENESS SERVICE (US/0046-1709) [01788883] **4443**

ELECTROMAGNETIC NEWS REPORT (US/0270-4935) [06450703] **2046**

ELECTROMAGNETICS (US/0272-6343) [06887276] **2046**

ELECTROMAGNETICS NEWS (UK) 2046, **4443**

●ELECTROMAGNETOEFFECT (COMMACK, N.Y.) (US/1069-4595) [28050664] 4443, **2046**

ELECTROMEDICA (GW/0013-4724) [01567743] **3941**

ELECTROMEDICA. DEUTSCHE AUSGABE (GW/0340-5389) [I03405389] **3941**

ELECTROMYOGRAPHY AND CLINICAL NEUROPHYSIOLOGY (BE/0301-150X) [02246609] 3832, **3796**

ELECTRON DISPLAY WORLD (US/0742-1532) [10294645] **2046**

ELECTRON MICROSCOPY ABSTRACTS (UK/0306-9869) [01786693] **454**

ELECTRON MICROSCOPY AND X-RAY APPLICATIONS TO ENVIRONMENTAL AND OCCUPATIONAL HEALTH ANALYSIS (US/0275-2204) [07113285] 4774, **3941**

ELECTRON MICROSCOPY IN BIOLOGY (US/0275-5262) [07147421] **572**

ELECTRON MICROSCOPY IN BIOLOGY AND MEDICINE (US/0923-0475) [12788279] 3574, **454**

ELECTRON MICROSCOPY IN HUMAN MEDICINE (US/0271-1877) [04458960] **3574**

ELECTRON MICROSCOPY REVIEWS (US/0892-0354) [15063309] **572**

ELECTRON MICROSCOPY SOCIETY OF AMERICA *See* EMSA BULLETIN **572**

ELECTRON MICROSCOPY SOCIETY OF AMERICA. MEETING *See* PROCEEDINGS, ... ANNUAL MEETING, ELECTRON MICROSCOPY SOCIETY OF AMERICA **573**

ELECTRON SPIN RESONANCE (UK/0305-9758) [01783706] 1052, **1015**

ELECTRON SPIN RESONANCE SPECTROSCOPY ABSTRACTS (UK/0301-7575) [01788890] **4443**

ELECTRON TECHNOLOGY (PL/0070-9816) [01995161] **2046**

ELECTRON (WILLOUGHBY, OHIO), THE (US/0740-1922) [09927752] 5102, **5728**

ELECTRONIC AGE (TORONTO) *CEASED.* (CN/0824-6912) [11073600] **2046**

ELECTRONIC ANBAR (UK) **671**

ELECTRONIC AND ELECTRICAL ENGINEERING (UK/0965-030X) [I0965030X] **2046**

ELECTRONIC & ELECTRICAL ENGINEERING RESEARCH STUDIES. LINES AND CABLES FOR POWER TRANSMISSION SERIES (UK) [13356925] **2046**

ELECTRONIC APPLICATION NEWS (II/0013-4813) [01567746] **2046**

ELECTRONIC ATLAS NEWSLETTER, THE (US/1053-0924) [22454127] 2560, **1183**

ELECTRONIC BULLETIN BOARD (US) **1559**

ELECTRONIC BUSINESS (US/0163-6197) [03523180] 671, **2046**

ELECTRONIC BUSINESS ASIA (HK) [26187861] **2046**

●ELECTRONIC BUSINESS BUYER (US/1073-1059) [28834258] 949, **2046**

ELECTRONIC BUSINESS FORECAST (US/0736-5705) [09165272] **2046**

ELECTRONIC BUYERS' NEWS (US/0164-6362) [04444289] **2046**

ELECTRONIC BUYERS' NEWS HANDBOOK & DIRECTORY *CEASED.* (US) [14755773] **2047**

ELECTRONIC CERAMICS (JA) **2588**

ELECTRONIC CHEMICALS NEWS (US/0886-5671) [12929442] 2012, **2047**

●ELECTRONIC CLAIMS PROCESSING REPORT (US/1071-8524) [28740747] **671**

ELECTRONIC COMBAT REPORT *See* INSIDE DEFENSE ELECTRONICS WEEKLY REPORT **4046**

ELECTRONIC COMPONENTS (US) **2047**

ELECTRONIC COMPONENTS (HK) [23013136] **2047**

ELECTRONIC COMPONENTS & APPLICATIONS *CEASED.* (NE/0141-6219) [04597216] **2047**

ELECTRONIC COMPONENTS - EXPORT LICENSING CONTROLS (US) 2047, **833**

ELECTRONIC COMPOSITION & IMAGING (CN/0838-9535) [18371799] **1263**

ELECTRONIC DATA PROCESSING SALARY SURVEY (US/0193-7979) [05242892] 1259, **1664**

ELECTRONIC DESIGN (US/0013-4872) [01567748] **2047**

ELECTRONIC DESIGN'S GOLD BOOK *CEASED.* (US/0738-0399) [01284496] **2047**

ELECTRONIC DIRECTORY & CLASSIFIED REPORT *See* ELECTRONIC MARKETPLACE REPORT **2047**

ELECTRONIC DISPLAY NEWS *CEASED.* (US/0890-8699) [14470727] **2047**

●ELECTRONIC DISSEMINATION PARTNERSHIPS (CN/1194-3750) [28277576] **4645**

ELECTRONIC DOCUMENT MANAGEMENT SYSTEMS JOURNAL (US/1067-7003) [27322925] **1183**

●ELECTRONIC DOCUMENTS (UK/0965-2035) [25937869] **5102**

ELECTRONIC DOCUMENTS NEWS BULLETIN *CEASED.* (UK) [26106263] **1183**

●ELECTRONIC EDUCATION REPORT (US) **1822**

ELECTRONIC ENGINEERING (UK/0013-4902) [01567749] **2047**

ELECTRONIC ENGINEERING TIMES (US/0192-1541) [02253857] **2047**

ELECTRONIC ENGINEERS MASTER *See* ELECTRONIC ENGINEERS MASTER CATALOG **2047**

ELECTRONIC ENGINEERS MASTER CATALOG (US/0732-9016) [08456506] **2047**

ELECTRONIC ENTERTAINMENT (US/0746-2999) [09927681] **4850**

ELECTRONIC FIELD ENGINEER, THE (US/0164-3762) [04693153] **2047**

ELECTRONIC FUEL INJECTION, DIAGNOSIS & TESTING (US/0741-6334) [09568764] **5414**

●ELECTRONIC GAMES (US/1063-8326) [26174312] **4860**

ELECTRONIC GAMING MONTHLY (US/1058-918X) [23857173] **4860**

ELECTRONIC GAMING RETAIL NEWS (US/1060-4677) [24999055] **4860**

●ELECTRONIC GREEN JOURNAL (US/1076-7975) [30613816] **2165**

ELECTRONIC HEALTH RECORDS REPORT (US) **743**

ELECTRONIC HOUSE (US/0886-6643) [12955427] **1267**

Alphabetical Title Index — ELEGANT

ELECTRONIC HOUSE / INTELLIGENCE REPORT (US) **1212**

ELECTRONIC IMAGING REPORT (US/1057-0942) [23948763] 2047, **1183**

ELECTRONIC INDUSTRIES ASSOCIATION *See* EIA ELECTRONICS MULTIMEDIA HANDBOOK **2043**

ELECTRONIC INDUSTRIES ASSOCIATION *See* TRADE DIRECTORY, MEMBERSHIP LIST - ELECTRONIC INDUSTRIES ASSOCIATION **2084**

ELECTRONIC INDUSTRIES ASSOCIATION. ENGINEERING DEPARTMENT *See* INDEX OF EIA & JEDEC STANDARDS & ENGINEERING PUBLICATIONS **2064**

ELECTRONIC INDUSTRIES ASSOCIATION. MEMBERSHIP LIST *See* TRADE DIRECTORY, MEMBERSHIP LIST - ELECTRONIC INDUSTRIES ASSOCIATION **2084**

ELECTRONIC INDUSTRY MANUFACTURERS REPRESENTATIVES LOCATOR (US/0735-3316) [08760173] 2047, **3478**

ELECTRONIC INDUSTRY OUTLOOK (US) 924, **2047**

● ELECTRONIC INFORMATION REPORT (US) [30308400] **1154**

ELECTRONIC JOURNAL OF THE ASTRONOMICAL SOCIETY OF THE ATLANTIC [ELECTRONIC JOURNAL], THE (US) [25984424] **395**

ELECTRONIC LEARNING (US/0278-3258) [07788019] **1223**

ELECTRONIC LIBRARY (UK/0264-0473) [09172203] 1274, **3209**

ELECTRONIC MAIL & MICRO SYSTEMS (US/8756-2537) [11493012] **1154**

ELECTRONIC MAIL EXECUTIVES DIRECTORY (US/0735-2379) [06860415] **1144**

ELECTRONIC MAP CABINET (US) 1184, **2560**

ELECTRONIC MARKET DATA BOOK (US/0270-0093) [02326010] 1154, **2047**

ELECTRONIC MARKET TRENDS (US/0886-8506) [12570471] **2047**

● ELECTRONIC MARKETPLACE REPORT (US/1071-247X) [28595166] **2047**

ELECTRONIC MATERIALS (UK) **2047**

ELECTRONIC MATERIALS AND PROCESSING (UK/0957-9737) [I09579737] **2047**

ELECTRONIC MATERIALS TECHNOLOGY NEWS (US/1045-0955) [20020677] **2047**

ELECTRONIC MEDIA (US/0745-0311) [08734139] **1131**

ELECTRONIC MESSAGING DIRECTORY & BUYER'S GUIDE *SUSPENDED.* (US) [24096746] **1110**

ELECTRONIC MESSAGING NEWS (US/1044-9892) [19964167] 2047, **1110**

● ELECTRONIC MESSAGING UPDATE (US/1072-1959) [28883820] 1184, **1110**

ELECTRONIC MODELING (US/0275-9136) [07250525] **2047**

ELECTRONIC MUSIC EDUCATOR (US/1044-3150) [18542783] 4116, **1240**

ELECTRONIC MUSICIAN (US/0884-4720) [12382684] **4116**

ELECTRONIC NETWORKING (US/1051-4805) [21975128] 1247, **1241**

ELECTRONIC NETWORKING *See* INTERNET RESEARCH **1242**

ELECTRONIC NEW PRODUCT DIRECTORY, THE (US/0197-2685) [05963327] **2047**

ELECTRONIC NEWS (AT) **2047**

ELECTRONIC NEWS (1991) (US/1061-6624) [25014408] **2047**

ELECTRONIC NEWS FINANCIAL FACT BOOK & DIRECTORY *See* FAIRCHILD'S ELECTRONICS INDUSTRY FINANCIAL DIRECTORY **2054**

ELECTRONIC PACKAGING AND PRODUCTION (US/0013-4945) [01385321] **2048**

ELECTRONIC PACKAGING TECHNOLOGY (JA/0911-3053) [I09113053] **4218**

ELECTRONIC PARTS & MATERIALS. DENSHI ZAIRYO (JA) **2048**

ELECTRONIC PAYMENTS INTERNATIONAL (US/0954-0393) [21493898] **671**

ELECTRONIC PHOTOGRAPHY NEWS (US/0896-0976) [16910156] **4369**

ELECTRONIC PRODUCT DESIGN (UK/0263-1474) [11541582] **2048**

ELECTRONIC PRODUCT NEWS (BE) **2048**

ELECTRONIC PRODUCT NEWS ASIA (BE) **2048**

ELECTRONIC PRODUCT REVIEW (UK/0269-3216) [24579239] **2048**

ELECTRONIC PRODUCTS (1981) (US/0013-4953) [09417600] **2048**

ELECTRONIC PRODUCTS AND TECHNOLOGY (CN/0708-4366) [16849622] **2048**

ELECTRONIC PROPERTIES OF MATERIALS; A GUIDE TO THE LITERATURE (US) [02256725] **2048**

ELECTRONIC PUBLIC INFORMATION NEWSLETTER (US/1057-834X) [24124398] **4645**

ELECTRONIC PUBLISHING (UK/0894-3982) [16068581] **4814**

ELECTRONIC PUBLISHING (US) 4564, **1263**

ELECTRONIC PUBLISHING DIGEST (US) **1263**

ELECTRONIC REPRESENTATIVES DIRECTORY (US/0887-4336) [08357217] **2048**

ELECTRONIC RETAILING (NEW YORK, N.Y.) *CEASED.* (US/0730-1189) [07963846] **2048**

ELECTRONIC SERVICES UPDATE (US) **2048**

ELECTRONIC SERVICING & TECHNOLOGY (US/0278-9922) [07955456] **2048**

ELECTRONIC SHOPPING NEWS (US/0893-0333) [15322271] **1154**

● ELECTRONIC SIMULATION (US/1063-1100) [25866625] **2048**

ELECTRONIC SOURCE BOOK FOR SOUTHERN CALIFORNIA, THE (US/8755-1527) [11214202] **2048**

ELECTRONIC STRUCTURE AND MAGNETISM OF INORGANIC COMPOUNDS *CEASED.* (UK/0305-9766) [01588780] 1052, **1036**

ELECTRONIC SWEET'S (US/1062-9580) [25857172] 2022, **614**

ELECTRONIC SYSTEMS FORECAST (US) **2048**

ELECTRONIC SYSTEMS INFORMATION BULLETIN (US/0895-8742) [09845780] **2048**

ELECTRONIC TECHNOLOGY (LONDON) *CEASED.* (UK/0141-061X) [04326685] **2048**

ELECTRONIC TRADER (UK) **2048**

ELECTRONIC TRENDS INTERNATIONAL (US/0013-5011) [08301586] **2048**

ELECTRONIC WARFARE DIGEST (US/0884-4828) [08466440] 2048, **4043**

ELECTRONIC WARFARE FORECAST (US) 2048, **4043**

ELECTRONIC WORLD NEWS *CEASED.* (US/1045-6627) [20187452] **2048**

ELECTRONICA & COMUNICACIONES MAGAZINE (SP/1130-6971) [I11306971] **1110**

ELECTRONICA HOY (SP/0213-0400) **2048**

ELECTRONICS (1985) (US/0883-4989) [12141064] **2048**

ELECTRONICS & COMMUNICATIONS ABSTRACTS *CEASED.* (UK/0013-5119) [01567759] **2049**

● ELECTRONICS AND COMMUNICATIONS ABSTRACTS (US/1069-5303) [28036948] 1154, 2049, **2003**

ELECTRONICS & COMMUNICATIONS ABSTRACTS JOURNAL *See* ELECTRONICS AND COMMUNICATIONS ABSTRACTS **2003**

ELECTRONICS AND COMMUNICATIONS ABSTRACTS JOURNAL (RIVERDALE, MD.) (US/0361-3313) [02051533] 1154, 2049, **2003**

ELECTRONICS & COMMUNICATIONS ENGINEERING JOURNAL (UK/0954-0695) [18902512] **2049**

ELECTRONICS & COMMUNICATIONS IN JAPAN. PART 1, COMMUNICATIONS (US/8756-6621) [12281484] **2049**

ELECTRONICS & COMMUNICATIONS IN JAPAN. PART 2, ELECTRONICS (US/8756-663X) [12281453] **2049**

ELECTRONICS AND COMMUNICATIONS IN JAPAN. PART 3, FUNDAMENTAL ELECTRONIC SCIENCE (US/1042-0967) [18940276] **2049**

ELECTRONICS AUSTRALIA WITH ETI (AT/1036-0212) [I10360212] **2049**

ELECTRONICS BUYERS' GUIDE *CEASED.* (US/0090-5291) [01785501] **2049**

ELECTRONICS COMMUNICATOR (CN/0046-1733) [02002617] **2049**

ELECTRONICS DISTRIBUTION TODAY *CEASED.* (US/0898-7149) [16914627] 954, **2049**

ELECTRONICS EDUCATION (LONDON) (UK/0957-2953) [I09572953] **2049**

ELECTRONICS HANDBOOK (US/0897-7631) [17616708] **2049**

ELECTRONICS IN MANUFACTURING QUARTERLY (US) **3478**

ELECTRONICS INFORMATION & PLANNING (II/0304-9876) [02381439] **2049**

ELECTRONICS INSIGHT *CEASED.* (US/0733-1614) [08527080] **2049**

ELECTRONICS INTERNATIONAL (US/0149-5542) [03529361] **2049**

ELECTRONICS INTERNATIONAL CHINA REPORT (CC) 924, **2049**

ELECTRONICS KOREA (KO) [09227185] 1605, **2049**

ELECTRONICS LETTERS (UK/0013-5194) [01567764] 1110, **2049**

ELECTRONICS MANAGEMENT (UK) [01793121] **2049**

ELECTRONICS MANUFACTURE & TEST (UK/0265-301X) [I0265301X] **2049**

● ELECTRONICS MANUFACTURERS DIRECTORY (US/1060-2100) [24886461] **3478**

ELECTRONICS MONTHLY *See* EVERYDAY WITH PRACTICAL ELECTRONICS **2054**

● ELECTRONICS NOW (US/1067-9294) [25968771] **2050**

ELECTRONICS PRODUCT NEWS *CEASED.* (CN/0826-2179) [11050372] **2050**

ELECTRONICS PURCHASING (US/0889-0196) [13805283] 949, **2050**

ELECTRONICS RESEARCH CENTRES (UK) **2050**

ELECTRONICS RETAILING *CEASED.* (US/0149-9203) [03574452] 2050, **954**

ELECTRONICS SHOWCASE (UK/0269-2309) [I02692309] **2050**

ELECTRONICS SOURCE BOOK FOR SOUTH ATLANTIC, THE (US) [17853233] **2050**

ELECTRONICS SOURCE BOOK. SOUTHWEST, THE (US) [18575313] **2050**

ELECTRONICS TIMES (UK) [14407849] **2050**

ELECTRONICS TODAY BOMBAY (II/0374-3063) [I03743063] **2050**

ELECTRONICS TODAY INTERNATIONAL (UK/0811-0727) [01785207] **2050**

ELECTRONICS WEEKLY (UK/0013-5224) [01567766] **2050**

ELECTRONICS WORLD (LAKE ZURICH, ILL.) (US/1042-3508) [19017375] **2050**

ELECTRONICS WORLD + WIRELESS WORLD (UK/0959-8332) [20557634] **2050**

ELECTRONIQUE (FR) **2050**

ELECTRONIQUE EUROPE 2000 PARIS *CEASED.* (FR/0994-1894) [I09941894] **2050**

ELECTRONIQUE FRANCAISE, L' (FR) [01791336] **2050**

ELECTRONIQUE INTERNATIONAL HEBDO PARIS (FR/1157-4445) [I11574445] **2050**

ELECTRONIQUE PARIS. 1990 (FR/1157-1152) [I11571152] **2050**

ELECTRONIQUE PRATIQUE (FR) [04221053] **2050**

ELECTRONIQUE RADIO PLANS PARIS (FR/1144-5742) [I11445742] 1131, **2050**

ELECTRONIQUE TECHNIQUES ET INDUSTRIES (FR) [11181675] **2050**

ELECTRONOTES (US/0160-1148) [02314904] **4116**

ELECTROPHORESIS (GW/0173-0835) [07297725] **1015**

ELECTROPHYSIOLOGICAL APPROACH TO THE DIAGNOSIS OF ARRHYTHMIAS, AN (US/1053-8437) [22652716] **3704**

ELECTROSOURCE : PRODUCT REFERENCE GUIDE AND TELEPHONE DIRECTORY (CN/0826-192X) [11147658] 1605, **2050**

ELECTROTECHNICA, ELECTRONICA, AUTOMATICA. AUTOMATICA SI ELECTRONICA (RM/0254-2242) [02939351] **2050**

ELECTROTECHNOLOGY (LONDON) (UK/0306-8552) [10478319] **2050**

ELECTROTECHNOLOGY (SPRINGFIELD, VA.) (US/0163-1462) [02575980] **2050**

ELECTROTEHNICA, ELECTRONICA, AUTOMATICA. ELECTROTEHNICA *CEASED.* (RM/0376-4745) [02244434] **2051**

ELECTSO, ELECTRICAL & ELECTRONIC ENGINEERING SOCIETY'S MAGAZINE, THE (SI) [02239654] **2051**

ELEGANCE (SZ) [01567769] **1084**

ELEGANCE (NE) 404, **5554**

ELEGANCE (HK) **404**

ELEGANT BRIDE (US) **2278**

ELEGANT

ELEGANT (MONTREAL) (CN/0821-4182) [09547413] **1084**

ELEGANTISSIMA (IT) **5554**

ELEKTOR (SP) **5199**

ELEKTOR AACHEN (GW/0932-5468) [I09325468] **2051**

ELEKTOR ELECTRONICS (UK/0268-4519) [14407954] **2051**

ELEKTOR ELECTRONICS USA *CEASED.* (US/1051-5690) [21990687] 1972, **4402**

ELEKTRICESKAJA I TEPLOVOZNAJA TJAGA (RU/0422-9274) [10410262] 2051, **5431**

ELEKTRICESTVO (RU/0013-5380) [02689962] **2051**

ELEKTRICHESKIE STANTSII (RU/0201-4564) [02446652] **2051**

ELEKTRIE (GW/0013-5399) [08335732] **2051**

ELEKTRISCHE BAHNEN (GW/0013-5437) [02446655] **5431**

ELEKTRISCHE ENERGIE-TECHNIK (GW/0170-2033) [I01702033] 2051, 3478, **1937**

ELEKTRIZITATSWIRTSCHAFT (GW/0013-5496) [02446657] **2051**

ELEKTRO (NO/0013-550X) [03220739] **2051**

ELEKTRO (XR) [25822161] **2051**

ELEKTRO-ANZEIGER (GW/0013-5518) [10478287] **2051**

ELEKTRO AUTOMATION (GW) **2051**

ELEKTRO MAGAZINE EDITIE DETAIL (NE/0925-5397) [I09255397] **2051**

ELEKTRO-NEUHEITEN *See* ELEKTRO-VERKAUF + ELEKTRO NEUHEITEN **2051**

ELEKTRO-VERKAUF + ELEKTRO NEUHEITEN (GW) [02241899] **2051**

ELEKTROFACH, DAS (GW/0424-8562) [I04248562] **2051**

ELEKTROHANDEL HEIDELBERG (GW/0013-5542) [I00135542] **2051**

ELEKTROHIMIA (RU/0424-8570) [02365157] **2051**

ELEKTROKHIMIA. ENGLISH. RUSSIAN ELECTROCHEMISTRY *See* RUSSIAN JOURNAL OF ELECTROCHEMISTRY **1035**

ELEKTROMAGAZINE. INSTALLATIE (NE) **2051**

ELEKTROMEISTER + DEUTSCHES ELEKTROHANDWERK (GW/0012-1258) [10473416] **2051**

ELEKTRON INTERNATIONAL (AU/0374-3098) [10475665] **1110**

ELEKTRONENMIKROSKOPIE : MITTEILUNGEN DER DEUTSCHEN GESELLSCHAFT FUER ELEKTRONENMIKROSKOPIE E.V (GW/0936-6911) [27143538] **572**

ELEKTRONICA (NE/0168-7840) [I01687840] **2051**

ELEKTRONICA + I.E. EN ELEKTROTECHNIEK (NE/0165-7062) [02246934] **2051**

ELEKTRONIK ENTWICKLUNG (GW/0172-6153) [08466460] **2051**

ELEKTRONIK HEUTE (GW/0171-4198) [05199600] **2051**

ELEKTRONIK (MUNCHEN) (GW/0013-5658) [03795256] **2051**

ELEKTRONIK-PRODUKTION & PRUFTECHNIK (GW/0172-6250) [I01726250] 1605, **2051**

ELEKTRONIK VARLDEN (SW/0033-7749) [10157325] **2052**

ELEKTRONIKA (PL/0033-2089) [10475423] **2052**

ELEKTRONIKA (RU) [06492956] **2052**

ELEKTRONIKAI ES HRADASTECHNIKAI SZAKIRODALMI TAJEKOZTATO (HU/0231-066X) [I0231066X] 1154, **2052**

ELEKTRONIKAS UN SKAITLOSANAS TEHNIKAS INSTITUTS (LATVIJAS PSR ZINATNU AKADEMIJA) *See* RASPOZNAVANIE OBRAZOV **2078**

ELEKTRONIKER (SZ/0531-9218) [09591605] **2052**

ELEKTRONIKINDUSTRIE (GW/0374-3144) [10408558] **2052**

ELEKTRONIKJOURNAL (GW/0013-5674) [I00135674] **2052**

ELEKTRONIKPRAXIS (GW/0341-5589) [I03415589] **2052**

ELEKTRONIKTIDNINGEN (SW/1102-7495) [I11027495] **2052**

ELEKTRONNAJA OBRABOTKA MATERIALOV (MV/0013-5739) [07024610] **2052**

ELEKTRONNOE MODELIROVANIE (UN/0204-3572) [07037707] 3504, **1259**

ELEKTRONNOE MODELIROVANIE. ENGLISH *See* ELECTRONIC SIMULATION **2048**

ELEKTROSVIAZ (MOSKVA. 1934) (RU/0013-5771) [09484612] 2052, **1154**

ELEKTROTECHNICKY CASOPIS (XO/0013-578X) [10523790] **2052**

ELEKTROTECHNICKY OBZOR (CS/0013-5798) [02446663] **2052**

ELEKTROTECHNIK (GW/0013-581X) [10473764] **2052**

ELEKTROTECHNIK : MESICNIK PRO VYCHOVU ELEKTROTECHNIKU (CS) [06362901] **2052**

ELEKTROTECHNIK (PRAGUE, CZECHOSLOVAKIA) *See* ELEKTRO **2051**

ELEKTROTECHNIK UND INFORMATIONSTECHNIK : E&I (AU/0932-383X) [17899784] **2052**

ELEKTROTECHNIKA (HU/0367-0708) [02446665] **2052**

ELEKTROTECHNIKAI SZAKIRODALMI TAJEKOZTATO (HU/0231-0783) [I02310783] **2052**

ELEKTROTEHNIKA (ZAGREB) (CI/0013-5844) [10766021] **2052**

ELEKTROTEHNISKI VESTNIK (YU/0013-5852) [I00135852] **2052**

ELEKTROTEKHNIKA (MOSKVA, 1963) (RU/0013-5860) [09296319] **2052**

ELEKTROWARME INTERNATIONAL. EDITION A : ELEKTOWARME IM TECHNISCHEN AUSBAU (GW/0174-6189) [02446670] **2604**

ELEKTROWARME INTERNATIONAL. EDITION B : INDUSTRIELLE ELEKTROWARME (GW/0340-3521) [02446671] **2605**

ELEKTRYKA (PL/0459-682X) [02957730] **2052**

ELEKTUUR (NE/0013-5895) [I00135895] **2052**

ELELMISZERVIZSGALATI KOZLEMENYEK (HU/0422-9576) [01290602] **2334**

ELEMENTA (SW/0013-5933) [I00135933] **4345**

ELEMENTA AD FONTIUM EDITIONES (IT/0070-9972) [01567775] **2686**

ELEMENTA THEOLOGIAE (GW/0724-4452) [14160267] **4955**

●ELEMENTA (YVERDON, SWITZERLAND) (US/1064-6663) [26368387] 2686, **3278**

ELEMENTARY ECONOMIST, THE (US/0891-1010) [07852664] 1894, **1488**

●ELEMENTARY MODULE SERIES (US/1058-2754) [24256055] **3504**

ELEMENTARY SCHOOL GUIDANCE AND COUNSELING (US/0013-5976) [01343041] **1878**

●ELEMENTARY SCHOOL JOURNAL (US) **1743**

ELEMENTARY SCHOOL JOURNAL. MICROFORM, THE (US/0013-5984) [07240337] **1743**

ELEMENTARY SCHOOL LIBRARY COLLECTION, THE (US) [04755651] **3209**

ELEMENTARY-SECONDARY SCHOOL ENROLMENT (CN/0704-6596) [02243126] 1744, **1794**

ELEMENTARY TEACHERS' GUIDE TO FREE CURRICULUM MATERIALS (US/0070-9980) [05164217] **1894**

ELEMENTE DER MATHEMATIK (SZ/0013-6018) [01567783] **3504**

ELEMENTE DER MATHEMATIK VOM HOHEREN STANDPUNKT AUS (SZ/0422-9622) [06311563] **3504**

ELEMENTS (MIDLAND) (US/0098-1710) [02241466] **1605**

ELEMENTS (WASHINGTON), THE (US/0193-4651) [02243731] **2192**

ELENCHUS OF BIBLICA (IT) [18503110] **4955**

ELENCO DEI PROTESTI CAMBIARI E DEI FALLIMENTI IN PROVINCIA DI BARI NEL MESA DI *See* ELENCO DEI PROTESTI CAMBIARI ELEVATI E DEI FALLIMENTI DICHIARATI IN PROVINCIA DI BARI NELLA ... **2965**

ELENCO DEI PROTESTI CAMBIARI ELEVATI E DEI FALLIMENTI DICHIARATI IN PROVINCIA DI BARI NELLA ... (IT) [22253841] **2965**

ELENCO DEI QUOTIDIANI E PERIODICI ITALIANI (IT/0519-198X) [03384496] **415**

ELENCO UFFICIALE DEI PROTESTI CAMBIARI. ROMA (IT) **2965**

ELENCO UFFICIALE DEI PROTESTI CAMBIARI. VERCELLI (IT) **2965**

ELEPAIO (US/0013-6069) [01751882] **2192**

ELEPHANT (DETROIT, MICH.) (US/0737-108X) [09285948] 4165, **5582**

ELEPHANT NEWSLETTER *See* ELEPHANT (DETROIT, MICH.) **5582**

ELET ES IRODALOM (HU/0424-8848) [01567785] **2515**

ELETRICIDADE MODERNA (SAO PAULO) (BL/0100-2104) [01786468] **2052**

ELETTRAUTO *See* NUOVA ELETTRAUTO **2074**

ELETTRIFICAZIONE (IT/0013-6093) [06855078] **2052**

ELETTRODOMESTICA (IT) **2052**

ELETTROMEDICALI *See* TECNOLOGIE BIOMEDICHE **3793**

ELETTRONICA E TELECOMUNICAZIONI (IT/0013-6123) [10514154] 1154, **2052**

ELETTRONICA OGGI (IT/0391-6391) [08295585] **2052**

ELETTROTECNICA, L' (IT/0013-6131) [02446673] **2053**

ELEUTHERIA (OTTAWA) (CN/0843-8064) [20493899] **4345**

ELEVAGE BOVIN, L' (FR) [12429137] **210**

ELEVAGE INSEMINATION (FR/0422-9703) [03997284] **210**

ELEVAGE OVIN (FR) **210**

ELEVAGES BELGES, LES (BE) [03536246] **210**

ELEVATOR WORLD (US/0013-6158) [02446674] **2113**

ELEVATOR WORLD SOURCE, THE (US) [11421386] 1605, **2113**

ELEVATORI MODERNI *See* ELEVATORI MODERNI : SOLLEVAMENTO E TRASPORTO A FUNE **5381**

ELEVATORI MODERNI : SOLLEVAMENTO E TRASPORTO A FUNE (IT/1121-7995) [I11217995] **5381**

ELEVES, LES (FR) [03095419] **1744**

ELEVEUR DE LAPINS, L' (FR) [04801069] **210**

ELEX (NE) **2053**

ELEZIONE DELLA CAMERA DEI DEPUTATI / REPUBBLICA ITALIANA, ISTITUTO CENTRALE DI STATISTICA - MINISTERO DELL'INTERNO (IT) [07154605] **4645**

ELF-AQUITAINE (COMPANY) *See* BULLETIN DES CENTRES DE RECHERCHES EXPLORATION-PRODUCTION ELF-AQUITAINE **1369**

$ELF-RELIANT (US/0745-7170) [09405955] **833**

ELF (TONAWANDA, N.Y.) (US/1054-3376) [22847464] **3341**

ELFENBEINKUSTE : ENERGIEWIRTSCHAFT (GW) [05063946] **1937**

ELFENBEINKUSTE : WIRTSCHAFTLICHE ENTWICKLUNG (GW) [06359706] **1559**

ELFENBEINKUSTE, WIRTSCHAFTSDATEN UND WIRTSCHAFTSDOKUMENTATION / BUNDESSTELLE FUER AUSSENHANDELSINFORMATION (GW) [10931541] **1559**

ELFQUEST (US/0887-9745) [12713726] **4860**

ELGAR SOCIETY *See* ELGAR SOCIETY JOURNAL, THE **5230**

ELGAR SOCIETY JOURNAL, THE (UK) [05055707] **5230**

ELGIN COURIER-NEWS, THE (US) [17165571] **5660**

ELH (US/0013-8304) [01567158] **3342**

ELIN-ZEITSCHRIFT (AU/0302-2560) [09349363] **1972**

ELINKEINOELAMAN TUTKIMUSLAITOS (FINLAND) *See* SUHDANNE **1586**

ELINTARVIKETEOLLISUUS (FI/0785-0522) [19489109] **2334**

ELISHA MITCHELL SCIENTIFIC SOCIETY, CHAPEL HILL, N.C *See* JOURNAL OF THE ELISHA MITCHELL SCIENTIFIC SOCIETY **5120**

ELITE CMA (CN/0847-1568) [21201105] **743**

ELITE : IL MENSILE DELLA DONNA CHE SCEGLIE *CEASED.* (IT) **5554**

ELITE (MONTREAL) (CN/0319-3187) [02442290] **2532**

ELITE SPORTIVE QUEBECOISE, L' (CN/0229-7450) [08071503] **4894**

ELITES AFRICAINES, LES (FR) [07353376] **432**

ELIZABETH RIVER TUNNEL SYSTEM, NORFOLK, VIRGINIA, CONSULTING ENGINEERS ... ANNUAL REPORT (US) [09507860] **2088**

ELIZABETHAN & RENAISSANCE STUDIES (AU) [01871267] **3383**

ELIZABETHAN CLUB SERIES, THE (US) [01567795] **5230**

●ELIZABETHAN REVIEW, THE (US/1066-7059) [27032704] **3384**

ELIZABETHAN THEATRE, THE (CN/0317-4964) [05242787] **5364**

ELIZABETHTOWN CHRONICLE (ELIZABETHTOWN, PA. : 1989) (US) [19241905] **5736**

ELK CITY DAILY NEWS, THE (US) [12101783] **5732**

ELK HORN-KIMBALLTON REVIEW (US) [16830111] **5670**

ELK ISLAND TRIANGLE, THE (CN/0704-0229) [03791116] **5784**

ELK POINT LAKELAND REVIEW (CN/0828-7759) [12199535] **5784**

ELK POINT REFLECTIONS (CN/0226-6350) [06472452] **5784**

ELK POINT SENTINEL (CN/0226-6369) [06473492] **5784**

ELK RIVER REVIEW (US/1059-4876) [24617998] **3384**

ELK VALLEY TIMES OBSERVER AND NEWS, THE (US/0747-3761) [10787837] **5745**

ELKHART TRUTH, THE (US/0746-7516) [08808036] **5663**

ELKHORN INDEPENDENT (ELKHORN, WIS. : 1892) (US) [15118364] **5767**

ELKLAND JOURNAL (ELKLAND, PA. : 1956) (US) [13206770] **5736**

ELKO DAILY FREE PRESS (US) [13457689] **5707**

ELKO INDEPENDENT (1915) (US) [14163651] **5707**

ELKS MAGAZINE, THE (US/0013-6263) [02628646] **5231**

ELKTON RECORD, THE (US/0899-966X) [12813163] **5743**

ELLE (NE) 404, 1084, **5554**

ELLE (AUSTRALIAN EDITION) (AT) 404, 1084, **5555**

ELLE DECOR (US/1046-1957) [20347333] **2900**

ELLE DECORATION (UK) **2900**

ELLE DECORATION BRITISH ED (UK/0957-8943) [I09578943] **2900**

ELLE DECORATION NEUILLY-SUR-SEINE (FR/0988-1476) [I09881476] **2900**

ELLE ED. ITALIANA (IT/1120-4397) [I11204397] 404, 1084, **5555**

ELLE (MUNICH, GERMANY) (GW/0935-462X) [19560620] 404, 1084, **5555**

ELLE (NEUILLY-SUR-SEINE, FRANCE) (FR/0013-6298) [01606382] 1084, **5555**

ELLE (NEW YORK, N.Y.) (US/0888-0808) [13460888] 404, 1084, **5555**

ELLE QUEBEC (CN/0843-6363) [21679982] 5555, **404**

ELLE (SPANISH EDITION) (SP) **5555**

ELLEN GLASGOW NEWSLETTER, THE (US/0160-7545) [02300212] **3384**

ELLENCO UFFICIALE PROTESTI CAMBIARI VALLE D AOSTA (IT) **819**

ELLENIKA NEA (LONDON, ONT.) (CN/0821-7270) [10027622] **5784**

ELLENIKA (THESSALONIKE) (GR/0013-6336) [04855742] **3278**

ELLENIKE GASTROENTEROLOGIA (GR/1012-0424) [I10120424] **3744**

ELLENIKE KTENIATRIKE *CEASED.* (GR/0018-0068) [01091080] **5509**

ELLENOKANADIKA CHRONIKA (CN/0820-7801) [09519488] **5784**

ELLENOKANADIKON VEMA (CN/0046-6387) [02442962] **5784**

ELLENVILLE JOURNAL, THE (US) [09723640] **5716**

ELLENVILLE PRESS, THE (US) [09723988] **5716**

ELLERY QUEEN *See* ELLERY QUEEN'S MYSTERY MAGAZINE **5074**

ELLERY QUEEN'S MYSTERY MAGAZINE (US/1054-8122) [21068253] **5074**

ELLERY QUEEN'S PRIME CRIMES (US/0748-1101) [10346099] **5074**

ELLINWOOD LEADER (US) [09580139] **5675**

ELLIOTT WAVE COMMODITY LETTER, THE (US/0742-891X) [10474560] **897**

ELLIOTT WAVE THEORIST, THE (US/0742-5252) [10382417] **897**

ELLIPSE (CN/0046-1830) [01780150] **3384**

ELLIPSIS (LOS GATOS, CALIF.) (US/1040-1644) [18337098] **3384**

ELLIS COUNTY STAR, THE (US) [11144752] **5675**

ELLIS COUSINS NEWSLETTER, THE (US/0740-1477) [09460144] **2446**

ELLIS (ENGLISH EDITION) (NE/0256-4467) [12872333] **2965**

ELLIS HORWOOD SERIES IN ANALYTICAL CHEMISTRY (UK/0272-6467) [07049497] **1015**

ELLIS HORWOOD SERIES IN CHEMICAL SCIENCE (UK/0276-9700) [07507301] **975**

ELLIS HORWOOD SERIES IN COMPUTERS AND THEIR APPLICATIONS, THE *CEASED.* (UK/0271-6135) [06684256] **1184**

ELLIS HORWOOD SERIES IN MATHEMATICS & ITS APPLICATIONS (UK/0271-6151) [06682186] **3504**

ELLIS ISLAND GUIDE (US) **5469**

ELLIS ISLAND SERIES (US/0892-922X) [15294046] **1918**

ELLIS REVIEW (ELLIS, KAN. : 1930) (US) [11139424] **5675**

ELLSWORTH AMERICAN (US) [10378660] **5685**

ELLSWORTH REPORTER (US) [08776082] **5675**

ELLWOOD CITY LEDGER (US) [02260731] **5736**

ELM GROVE ELM LEAVES (US) [13090363] **5767**

●ELMIRA INDEPENDENT (CN/1194-1030) [27725152] **5784**

ELMONT HERALD (US/1070-7328) [28460741] **5716**

ELMWOOD ARGUS, THE (US) [12985530] **5767**

ELNA NEWSLETTER *See* ESPERANTOUSA **3280**

ELOIZES (CN/0228-0124) [07970414] **3384**

ELORA SENTINEL, THE (CN/1184-1060) [23237360] **5784**

ELOS (BL) [06835273] **3278**

ELRAD (GW/0170-1827) [01701827] **2053**

ELS MONOGRAPH SERIES (CN/0829-7681) [04238684] **3342**

ELSEVIER (NE) [16735125] **5381**

ELSEVIER OCEANOGRAPHY SERIES (NE/0422-9894) [01941666] **1449**

ELSEVIERS MAGAZINE. MICROFORM (US/0013-6395) [14172437] **2487**

ELSKAPER (NO/0800-1235) [21467349] **5449**

ELSNERS HANDBUCH FUR STADTISCHEN INGENIEURBAU (GW) [01791808] **2228**

ELT FORUM JOURNAL OF ENGLISH STUDIES (II/0970-048X) [06034467] **3278**

ELT JOURNAL (UK/0951-0893) [07909551] 1894, **3278**

ELTA INFORMATION BULLETIN / OF THE SUPREME COMMITTEE FOR LIBERATION OF LITHUANIA (US) [15095645] **4541**

ELTEKNIK (1989) *See* ELEKTRONIKTIDNINGEN **2052**

ELTEKNIK MED AKTUELL ELEKTRONIK (SW/0346-6310) [04198117] 1110, **2053**

ELTERN (GW) [06563135] **2278**

ELVIS COSTELLO INFORMATION SERVICE (NE) **4116**

ELVIS MONTHLY (UK/0013-6484) [I00136484] **4116**

ELY DAILY TIMES (1961) (US) [14170145] **5707**

ELY ECHO (US/0746-7087) [10221153] **5695**

ELYTRON (SP/0214-1353) [19110377] **5582**

EM; ECONOMIA DE MOCAMBIQUE (MZ/0012-9755) [01791622] **1488**

EMA. ELEKTRISCHE MASCHINEN (GW/0013-5445) [I00135445] **2053**

EMA, ELEKTRISCHE MASCHINEN (GW) [06832475] **2053**

EMAJL *See* EMAJL-KERAMIKA-STAKLO **2588**

EMAJL-KERAMIKA-STAKLO (CI/0350-3607) [03005294] **2588**

EMAKEELE SELTS *See* EMAKEELE SELTSI AASTARAAMAT **3278**

EMAKEELE SELTSI AASTARAAMAT (ER/0422-9967) [01868187] **3278**

EMANCIPATIERAAD (NETHERLANDS) *See* ADVIESBRIEVEN EN- NOTA'S VAN DE EMANCIPATIERAAD **4503**

EMAP MONITOR / ENVIRONMENTAL MONITORING AND ASSESSMENT PROGRAM (US) [24149656] **2192**

EMBALAGEM (RIO DE JANEIRO) (BL/0013-6530) [01793669] **4218**

EMBALLAGE DIGEST (FR/0013-6557) [I00136557] **4218**

EMBALLAGE MODERNE *See* CARTONNAGES EMBALLAGES MODERNES **4218**

EMBALLAGES (FR/0013-6573) [08492342] **4218**

EMBALLAGES MAGAZINE (FR/0754-0590) [I07540590] **4233**

●EMBASE LIST OF JOURNALS INDEXED (NE) [28083905] 3574, **3657**

EMBASE [ONLINE DATABASE] (NE) 3574, **3657**

EMBASSY (UK) [01786175] **4520**

EMBASSY REPORT (AFRICA ED.) (US/0883-1815) [12089670] **4520**

EMBASSY REPORT (ASIA & OCEANIA ED.) (US/0883-1823) [12089591] **4520**

EMBASSY REPORT (ED. : AUSTRALIA, CANADA, JAPAN NEW ZEALAND, SCANDINAVIA & WESTERN EUROPE) (US/0883-1807) [12089482] **4520**

EMBASSY REPORT (LATIN AMERICA & CARIBBEAN ED.) (US/0882-9683) [12090290] **4520**

EMBASSY REPORT (MIDDLE EAST ED.) (US/0883-1793) [12090123] **4520**

EMBEDDED COMPUTER TRENDS (US/1069-4021) [28032011] **1184**

EMBEDDED SYSTEMS PROGRAMMING (US/1040-3272) [18377460] **1228**

EMBER (MARKHAM) (CN/0846-3298) [25066283] **2260**

EMBERS (GUILFORD, CONN.) (US/0731-0382) [08097698] **3462**

EMBLEMATICA (US/0885-968X) [12795693] 349, **3384**

EMBO JOURNAL (UK/0261-4189) [08335096] **454**

EMBOUTEILLAGE, CONDITIONNEMENT (FR/0397-8079) [03689716] **4219**

EMBOUTEILLEUR QUEBECOIS (EDITION ANGLAISE) (CN/0705-8578) [04677984] **2366**

EMBOUTEILLEUR QUEBECOIS, L' (CN/0705-6761) [04954968] **2366**

EMBROIDERY (UK/0013-6611) [02539451] **5184**

EMBRYO TRANSFER NEWSLETTER (US) [12086129] **3760**

EMC. EDUCATIONAL MEDIA SPECIAL INTEREST COUNCIL (CN/0824-782X) [11856786] **3209**

EMC INSTANTANES CHIRURGICAUX (FR) **3964**

EMC TECHNOLOGY *CEASED.* (US/1055-6230) [22622983] **2053**

EMC TECHNOLOGY ... ANTHOLOGY (US/0748-108X) [10862658] **2053**

EMC TEST & DESIGN (US/1054-5816) [22919312] **2053**

EME DOS (SP/0210-2145) [I02102145] **614**

EME EME; ESTUDIOS DOMINICANOS (DR) [01786337] **5029**

EMENTARIO DE JURISPRUDENCIA DO TRIBUNAL DE JUSTICA DO ESTADO DO RIO DE JANEIRO (BL) [08458913] **2965**

EMENTARIO DO TIT (BL) [02172718] **2965**

EMENTARO DA LEGISLACAO ESTADUAL (BL) [05114093] **2965**

EMEQ, HA- (IS/0303-1497) [01784351] **5047**

EMERALD CITY COMIX AND STORIES (US/1042-9166) [19257401] **3384**

EMERALD OF SIGMA PI *See* EMERALD OF SIGMA PI FRATERNITY, INTERNATIONAL, THE **1822**

EMERALD OF SIGMA PI FRATERNITY, INTERNATIONAL, THE (US/1074-5289) [11768348] **1822**

EMERGE (NEW YORK, N.Y.) (US/0899-1154) [17994033] **2533**

EMERGENCIAS (SP) **3724**

EMERGENCY (US/0162-5942) [04111889] **4774**

●EMERGENCY (UK) [29538937] **1073**

●EMERGENCY AND OFFICE PEDIATRICS (US/1073-7782) [29527191] **3903**

EMERGENCY BIOLOGICS LOCATIONS ... WASHINGTON STATE / DEPARTMENT OF HEALTH, DIVISION OF HEALTH INFORMATION, COMMUNICABLE DISEASE EPIDEMIOLOGY SECTION (US) [25669212] 4774, **454**

EMERGENCY CARE QUARTERLY *CEASED.* (US/8755-8467) [11412121] **3724**

EMERGENCY DEPARTMENT LAW (US/1042-2978) [19003640] 3574, **2965**

EMERGENCY LEGAL BRIEFINGS (US) **3740**

EMERGENCY LIBRARIAN (US/0315-8888) [01780152] **3209**

EMERGENCY MANAGEMENT OF HAZARDOUS MATERIALS INCIDENTS (US) 2288, **2861**

EMERGENCY MANAGEMENT TODAY : AN INFORMATION SERVICE OF EMERGENCY MANAGEMENT INFORMATION SERVICES (US/0747-9085) [10839305] 2861, **1073**

EMERGENCY — Alphabetical Title Index

EMERGENCY MEDICAL SERVICES RESEARCH METHODOLOGY WORKSHOP (US/0193-7448) [05218059] **3724**

EMERGENCY MEDICAL TECHNICIAN LEGAL BULLETIN (US/0884-4836) [11123337] **3724**

EMERGENCY MEDICAL UPDATE (US/1064-5934) [17545651] **3724**

EMERGENCY MEDICINE (US/0013-6654) [01102081] **3724**

EMERGENCY MEDICINE CLINICS OF NORTH AMERICA (US/0733-8627) [08649213] **3724**

EMERGENCY MEDICINE (GLENDALE, CALIF.) (US/0748-8947) [11299949] **3574**

EMERGENCY MEDICINE NEWS (US/1054-0725) [20120870] **3724**

EMERGENCY MEDICINE OBSERVER (US/0887-7343) [13338255] **3724**

EMERGENCY MEDICINE REPORTS (US/0746-2506) [09881608] **3724**

●EMERGENCY NURSE : THE JOURNAL OF THE RCN ACCIDENT AND EMERGENCY NURSING ASSOCIATION (UK) [26501548] **3724, 3855**

EMERGENCY PEDIATRICS (US/1044-3797) [19764782] **3903**

EMERGENCY PHYSICIAN REPORT (US/1040-7901) [18530522] **3574**

EMERGENCY PREHOSPITAL MEDICINE (CN/0836-7272) [17743255] **3724**

EMERGENCY PREPAREDNESS DIGEST (CN/0837-5771) [15637552] **1073**

EMERGENCY PREPAREDNESS NEWS (US/0275-3782) [06185394] **1073**

●EMERGENCY RADIOLOGY (US/1070-3004) [28314333] **3941**

●EMERGENCY SERVICES SOURCEBOOK (US/1066-0348) [26831791] **2165, 2215, 4774**

EMERGING FOOD R & D REPORT (US/1050-2688) [21433663] **2334**

●EMERGING ISSUES IN BIOMEDICAL POLICY (US/1062-3175) [25121413] **3574**

●EMERGING MARKETS ANALYST (CN/1199-0597) [30377382] **671**

EMERGING MARKETS WEEK (US) **897**

EMERGING PATTERNS OF WORK AND COMMUNICATIONS IN AN INFORMATION AGE (US/0882-3316) [11808667] **5244**

●EMERGING PHARMACEUTICALS (US/1061-6098) [25378669] **4303**

EMERGING STOCK MARKETS FACTBOOK (US/1012-8115) [18181722] **897**

EMERGING TECHNOLOGIES (ALEXANDRIA, VA.) (US/1040-2802) [18365961] **4043**

EMERGING TECHNOLOGY (US) [11303524] **5102**

●EMERGING TECHNOLOGY (AMERICAN SOCIETY OF CIVIL ENGINEERS) (US/1075-0495) [29927201] **5102, 2023**

EMERGING TRENDS (US/0889-8936) [04550678] **4955**

EMERGING TRENDS IN REAL ESTATE (US/0898-4050) [08208317] **4837**

EMERITA (SP/0013-6662) [01567825] **1076**

EMERSON'S AUDITOR CHANGE REPORT *CEASED*. (US/1060-8168) [25073130] **743**

EMERSON'S DIRECTORY OF LEADING U.S. ACCOUNTING FIRMS (US) [19247858] **743**

EMERSON'S PROFESSIONAL SERVICES REVIEW : PSR (US/1060-8729) [21982413] **743**

EMERY COUNTY PROGRESS (1977) (US/0747-2129) [10633128] **5756**

EMERY ENTERPRISE (US) [12813130] **5743**

●EMF HEALTH & SAFETY DIGEST (US/1062-5526) [25663422] **4774**

●EMF HEALTH REPORT (US/1070-4027) [28358443] **454**

EMF KEEPTRACK (US/1059-6631) [24660842] **1937, 2966**

●EMF, STUDIES IN EARLY MODERN FRANCE (US/1064-5020) [26319751] **2686**

EMI. EDUCATIONAL MEDIA INTERNATIONAL (UK/0952-3987) [01567595] **1894**

EMIE BULLETIN (US/0737-9021) [09477747] **2260, 3209**

EMIGRE (BERKELEY, CALIF.) (US/1045-3717) [16977449] **378**

●EMILY DICKINSON JOURNAL, THE (US/1059-6879) [24679809] **3384**

EMILY P. BISSELL HOSPITAL *See* ANNUAL STATISTICAL REPORT / EMILY P. BISSELL HOSPITAL **3654**

EMIRATES MEDICAL JOURNAL (TS/0250-6882) [06980957] **3574**

EMISSARY, THE (US) [05019245] **3832**

EMISSION CONTROL APPLICATIONS GUIDE (US) [19732488] **5414**

EMMA (GW) [04250372] **5555**

EMMANATIONS (US/0734-6158) [08815582] **1744**

EMMANUEL (NEW YORK, N.Y.) (US/0013-6719) [01774729] **4955**

EMMAUS JOURNAL, THE (US) **5016**

EMMONS COUNTY RECORD (US) [01567833] **5725**

EMMS. ELECTRONIC MAIL & MESSAGE SYSTEMS *See* ELECTRONIC MAIL & MICRO SYSTEMS **1154**

EMMY (US/0164-3495) [04629234] **1131**

EMO OUTLOOK (CN/0849-3308) [23263811] **4645**

EMORY ALUMNUS, THE (US/0162-5349) [04173141] **1102**

EMORY AND HENRY COLLEGE *See* ALUMNI DIRECTORY / EMORY & HENRY COLLEGE **1098**

EMORY INTERNATIONAL LAW REVIEW (US/1052-2840) [21493134] **3128**

EMORY LAW JOURNAL (US/0094-4076) [01793671] **2966**

EMORY MAGAZINE (US/0013-6727) [04074395] **1822**

EMORY STUDIES IN EARLY CHRISTIANITY (US/1043-5816) [19491070] **4956**

EMORY VICO STUDIES (US/0883-6000) [12174321] **4345**

EMOTION (US) [05826585] **4586**

EMOTIONAL FIRST AID *SUSPENDED*. (US/0739-828X) [11567619] **4586**

EMOTIONS AND BEHAVIOR MONOGRAPHS (US/0734-9890) [08856575] **4586**

EMP NEWSLETTER (KU/0258-9672) [16177066] **1110**

EMPATHIC PARENTING (CN/0825-7531) [12280844] **5284**

EMPHASIS (LIMA, OHIO) (US/1053-9743) [01780154] **4956**

EMPHASIS, NURSING (US/0886-7143) [12752747] **3855**

EMPIRE CLUB OF CANADA *See* ADDRESSES **1103**

EMPIRE FORESTRY HANDBOOK *See* COMMONWEALTH FORESTRY HANDBOOK, THE **2377**

EMPIRE STATE ARCHITECT (US/0013-6751) [02320509] **298**

EMPIRE STATE FARMER (US/0886-9693) [13084072] **81**

EMPIRE STATE FOOD SERVICE NEWS (US) [11108389] **2334**

EMPIRE STATE GEOGRAM (US/0013-676X) [03182793] **1375**

EMPIRE STATE MASON (US/0013-6794) [04074409] **5231**

EMPIRE STATE REPORT (1982) (US/0747-0711) [08541622] **4645**

EMPIRE STATE SURVEYOR (US) [06686631] **2023**

EMPIRICAL ECONOMICS (AU/0377-7332) [03680014] **1488**

EMPIRICAL STUDIES OF PSYCHOANALYTICAL THEORIES (US/0743-071X) [09316682] **3925**

EMPIRICAL STUDIES OF THE ARTS (US/0276-2374) [07342535] **319**

EMPIRISCHE LITERATURWISSENSCHAFT (GW) [06082264] **3384**

EMPIRISCHE PADAGOGIK (GW/0931-5020) [I09315020] **1744**

EMPLEO, HORAS Y SALARIOS EN LAS INDUSTRIAS MANUFACTURERAS DE PUERTO RICO. EMPLOYMENT, HOURS AND EARNINGS IN THE MANUFACTURING INDUSTRIES IN PUERTO RICO (PR) [07513077] **1664**

EMPLEO, HORAS Y SALARIOS EN LOS ESTABLECIMIENTOS MANUFACTUREROS PROMOVIDOD POR LA ADMINISTRACION DE FOMENTO ECONOMICO O LA COMPANIA DE FOMENTO INDUSTRIAL DE PUERTO RICO (PR/0091-9233) [01788193] **1664**

EMPLEO Y DESEMPLEO EN PUERTO RICO / DEPARTAMENTO DEL TRABAJO (PR) [07563563] **1664**

EMPLOI AU QUEBEC (CN/0837-2470) [18126543] **1664**

EMPLOI-AVENIR (CN/0833-7209) [17847039] **4204**

EMPLOI SALARIE PAR REGION AU 31 DECEMBRE (FR) [09819197] **1664**

EMPLOYED WAGE AND SALARY EARNERS (AT) [03693609] **1665**

EMPLOYEE ASSISTANCE (US) **940, 1665**

EMPLOYEE ASSISTANCE PROFESSIONAL REPORT (US/1061-7728) [25455969] **1665**

EMPLOYEE ASSISTANCE PROGRAM MANAGEMENT LETTER (US/0896-0941) [16912771] **866**

EMPLOYEE ASSISTANCE PROGRAM UPDATE *CEASED*. (US/0891-3196) [14756842] **866**

EMPLOYEE ASSISTANCE QUARTERLY (US/0749-0003) [11047417] **1665, 2861**

EMPLOYEE BENEFIT ISSUES (US/1048-2814) [20541236] **1665**

EMPLOYEE BENEFIT NEWS (US/1044-6265) [19854617] **1665**

EMPLOYEE BENEFIT NOTES (US/0887-1388) [12259239] **1665**

EMPLOYEE BENEFIT PLAN REVIEW (US/0013-6808) [01567840] **2879**

EMPLOYEE BENEFIT PLANS UNDER ERISA (US/0882-5580) [11613611] **3146**

EMPLOYEE BENEFITS (US/0194-3499) [05382596] **1665**

EMPLOYEE BENEFITS AND PERSONNEL PRACTICES SURVEY. MINNESOTA, NEW ENGLAND, NEW YORK, AND UNASSIGNED (US/0277-2256) [07511143] **1665**

EMPLOYEE BENEFITS AND PERSONNEL PRACTICES SURVEY. SAN FRANCISCO BAY AREA, NORTHWEST, COLORADO, ARIZONA, AND TEXAS (US/0277-1276) [07344878] **940**

EMPLOYEE BENEFITS AND PERSONNEL PRACTICES SURVEY. SOUTHERN CALIFORNIA (US/0277-2213) [07511189] **1665**

EMPLOYEE BENEFITS CASES (US/0273-236X) [07033880] **3146**

EMPLOYEE BENEFITS COMPLIANCE COORDINATOR (US/0273-768X) [05177372] **940**

●EMPLOYEE BENEFITS COUNSELOR (US/1068-4204) [27671173] **1488, 1665**

EMPLOYEE BENEFITS FOR NONPROFITS (US/8756-4971) [12353663] **1665**

EMPLOYEE BENEFITS HANDBOOK. UPDATE WITH CUMULATIVE INDEX (US) [10169551] **940**

EMPLOYEE BENEFITS IN MEDIUM AND LARGE FIRMS (US/0748-2663) [08740050] **1665**

EMPLOYEE BENEFITS IN MEDIUM AND LARGE PRIVATE ESTABLISHMENTS / U.S. DEPARTMENT OF LABOR, BUREAU OF LABOR STATISTICS (US) [28352805] **1665**

EMPLOYEE BENEFITS IN STATE AND LOCAL GOVERNMENTS (US) [18455126] **4645, 1665**

EMPLOYEE BENEFITS JOURNAL (US/0361-4050) [02246992] **1665**

EMPLOYEE BENEFITS MANAGEMENT DIRECTIONS (US) [21570843] **940**

EMPLOYEE BENEFITS REPORT *CEASED*. (US/0884-478X) [11395726] **1665**

EMPLOYEE BENEFITS UNIT 1 (UK) **1665**

EMPLOYEE COMMUNICATION (US/0885-7202) [12717418] **1110**

EMPLOYEE COMPENSATION IN THE PRIVATE NONFARM ECONOMY (US/0091-8261) [01787579] **1665**

EMPLOYEE COUNSELLING TODAY (UK/0933-8217) [23165641] **4586**

EMPLOYEE DEVELOPMENT BULLETIN (UK) **940**

EMPLOYEE EMPLOYER FEDERAL EMPLOYMENT TAX GUIDE (US/0278-8039) [07870591] **3146**

EMPLOYEE HEALTH & FITNESS (US/0199-6304) [06065938] **1665**

EMPLOYEE OWNERSHIP REPORT, THE (US/0899-8833) [15536285] **671**

EMPLOYEE OWNERSHIP RESOURCE GUIDE (US) [15220210] **671**

EMPLOYEE PROBLEM SOLVER (US) **3146**

EMPLOYEE RELATIONS (UK/0142-5455) [05291920] **940**

EMPLOYEE RELATIONS AND HUMAN RESOURCES BULLETIN *See* EMPLOYEE RELATIONS BULLETIN (NEW YORK, N.Y.) **1665**

EMPLOYEE RELATIONS BULLETIN (NEW YORK, N.Y.) (US/8756-3231) [09968300] **940, 1665**

EMPLOYEE RELATIONS IN ACTION (US/0013-6824) [03349600] **1665**

EMPLOYEE RELATIONS LAW JOURNAL (US/0098-8898) [02242810] **3146**

EMPLOYEE RELATIONS REPORT (RICHMOND, VA.) *CEASED*. (US/0735-4738) [08948321] **1665**

EMPLOYEE RELOCATION COUNCIL See ROSTER OF MEMBERSHIP AND RESOURCE GUIDE / EMPLOYEE RELOCATION COUNCIL **1929**

EMPLOYEE RESPONSIBILITIES AND RIGHTS JOURNAL (US/0892-7545) [15255588] **3147**

EMPLOYEE RETIREMENT INCOME SECURITY ACT : REPORT TO CONGRESS (US/0271-1567) [04820141] **3147**

EMPLOYEE SECURITY CONNECTION (US/0894-2080) [15871288] **940**

EMPLOYEE SERVICES MANAGEMENT (US/0744-3676) [08148769] 4850, **940**

EMPLOYEE TERMINATIONS LAW BULLETIN (1991) (US/1063-097X) [25816649] 2966, **1665**

EMPLOYEE TESTING & THE LAW (US/0889-5422) [13918260] **3147**

EMPLOYEES IN COLLEGES AND UNIVERSITIES, NEW YORK STATE See COLLEGE & UNIVERSITY EMPLOYEES, NEW YORK STATE **1861**

EMPLOYER-EMPLOYEE ALCOHOLISM ADVISOR (US/8755-8181) [11456462] **1344**

EMPLOYERS' CONSULTATIVE ASSOCIATION OF MALAWI See ANNUAL REPORT AND REVIEW OF ACTIVITIES FOR THE YEAR / THE EMPLOYERS' CONSULTATIVE ASSOCIATION OF MALAWI **938**

EMPLOYER'S GUIDE TO AUDITING PERSONNEL AND EMPLOYMENT PRACTICES (US) [18962727] **940**

EMPLOYER'S GUIDE TO LAW SCHOOLS (US/8755-0695) [10762758] **2966**

EMPLOYERS' GUIDE TO WORKERS' COMPENSATION AND SAFE EMPLOYMENT LAWS OF OREGON (US/0360-9456) [02245101] **3147**

EMPLOYERS' HEALTH COSTS SAVINGS LETTER (US/0740-9087) [10038089] 2879, **3574**

EMPLOYERS' HUMAN RIGHTS & EQUITY REPORT (CN/1183-8485) [25882795] **1665**

EMPLOYERS NEGOTIATING SERVICE *CEASED.* (US/0898-2139) [10044898] **4646**

EMPLOYERS' REVIEW, THE (AT) [10144493] **1665**

EMPLOYMENT, ADJUSTMENT, AND INDUSTRIALISATION (SZ/0257-3415) [15180664] **1666**

EMPLOYMENT AFFAIRS REPORT (UK/0267-5374) [I02675374] **1666**

EMPLOYMENT ALERT (US/0882-6250) [11170992] **3147**

EMPLOYMENT AND EARNINGS (1969) (US/0013-6840) [02610713] **1666**

EMPLOYMENT AND EARNINGS IN THE MOUNTAIN-PLAINS REGION / U.S. DEPARTMENT OF LABOR, BUREAU OF LABOR STATISTICS (US) [06390228] **1666**

EMPLOYMENT AND EARNINGS REPORT FOR ALASKA AND ... CENSUS AREAS (US/1063-3782) [24601599] **1666**

EMPLOYMENT AND EARNINGS TRENDS; ANNUAL SUMMARY (WEST VIRGINIA) (US) [06716568] 1666, **1532**

●EMPLOYMENT AND EARNINGS / U.S. DEPARTMENT OF LABOR, BUREAU OF LABOR STATISTICS (US) [26738442] **1666**

EMPLOYMENT AND IMMIGRATION REVIEW : ONTARIO (CN/0700-0847) [03439765] **1666**

EMPLOYMENT AND PAY ROLLS IN FLORIDA COVERED BY THE UNEMPLOYMENT COMPENSATION LAW (US) [01315541] **1666**

EMPLOYMENT AND PAYROLLS IN WASHINGTON STATE BY COUNTY AND BY INDUSTRY (US) [06588228] **1666**

●EMPLOYMENT AND TRAINING PARTNERSHIP : A PUBLICATION OF THE STATE JOB TRAINING COORDINATING COUNCIL, THE (US) [26142860] 4204, **1913**

EMPLOYMENT AND TRAINING REPORT TO THE GOVERNOR - ILLINOIS GOVERNOR'S ADVISORY COUNCIL ON MANPOWER (US) [03997686] **1666**

EMPLOYMENT AND TRAINING REPORTER (US/0146-9673) [03093513] 1913, **4204**

EMPLOYMENT AND TRENDS AS OF ... (US/1058-0859) [14146204] **4702**

EMPLOYMENT AND UNEMPLOYMENT (US) [07833312] **1666**

EMPLOYMENT AND UNEMPLOYMENT TRENDS (US/0190-1419) [04626173] **1666**

EMPLOYMENT AND WAGES (SQ) [04161598] **1666**

EMPLOYMENT AND WAGES COVERED BY WISCONSIN'S U. C. LAW (US/0510-6222) [02743635] **3147**

EMPLOYMENT-AT-WILL REPORTER (US/0745-9653) [09614232] **3147**

EMPLOYMENT BULLETIN (AMERICAN SOCIOLOGICAL ASSOCIATION : 1976) (US/0194-3642) [04579978] 5244, **4204**

EMPLOYMENT BULLETIN AND IR DIGEST (UK/0267-8314) [I02678314] **1666**

EMPLOYMENT BULLETIN - CANADA LAW BOOK INC (CN/1183-3076) [24690897] **3147**

EMPLOYMENT BULLETIN (TORONTO. 1971) (CN/0315-3525) [02586197] **1666**

EMPLOYMENT CASE LAW INDEX (UK) **3147**

EMPLOYMENT COORDINATOR (US) [11002642] **940**

EMPLOYMENT DIGEST See PERSONNEL IN PRACTICE **945**

EMPLOYMENT DISCRIMINATION (US) [02353029] **1666**

EMPLOYMENT DISCRIMINATION DIGEST (US/0148-107X) [03834801] **3147**

EMPLOYMENT, EARNINGS AND HOURS (CN/0380-6936) [04678173] **1666**

EMPLOYMENT, EARNINGS AND HOURS (CN/0380-6936) [04632180] 1666, **1532**

EMPLOYMENT EQUITY REPORTER See LANCASTER'S EMPLOYMENT EQUITY REPORTER **1687**

EMPLOYMENT EQUITY REVIEW, THE (CN/1183-1804) [24623496] **1666**

EMPLOYMENT GAZETTE (UK/0264-7052) [06433112] **1666**

EMPLOYMENT GUIDE : [REFERENCE SECTION] (US) [13141630] **1666**

EMPLOYMENT HEALTH LAW & BENEFITS (US/1050-1193) [19232241] **3147**

EMPLOYMENT, HOURS, AND EARNINGS, STATES AND AREAS / U.S. DEPARTMENT OF LABOR, BUREAU OF LABOR STATISTICS (US) [10672299] **1666**

EMPLOYMENT, HOURS, AND EARNINGS, UNITED STATES (US/1047-059X) [12000403] **1666**

EMPLOYMENT IN NEW YORK STATE (US) [23677155] **1666**

EMPLOYMENT IN STATE GOVERNMENT; A STATISTICAL SURVEY BY ETHNIC ORIGIN AND SEX (US) [04116605] **1666**

EMPLOYMENT INFORMATION IN THE MATHEMATICAL SCIENCES (US/0163-3287) [04349935] 3505, **1666**

EMPLOYMENT INJURIES QUEENSLAND (AT) [19697059] 2861, **2872**

EMPLOYMENT INJURIES, TASMANIA (AT/1033-6133) [20975654] 2861, **2872**

EMPLOYMENT INSTITUTE ECONOMIC REPORT (UK) **1666**

EMPLOYMENT LAW CITATIONS (US) **3147**

EMPLOYMENT LAW COUNSELOR (US/1052-2964) [22249036] **3147**

EMPLOYMENT LAW LINE (UK) **2966**

●EMPLOYMENT LAW NEWS (UK) **3147**

EMPLOYMENT LAW REPORT (ROSEMOUNT, MINN.) (US/1058-1308) [24226066] **3147**

EMPLOYMENT LAW REPORT, THE (CN/0228-5266) [08260927] **3147**

●EMPLOYMENT LAW STRATEGIST (US/1069-7829) [28152827] **3147**

EMPLOYMENT LAW UPDATE (US/0270-2479) [06363741] **3147**

EMPLOYMENT LAW UPDATE (EVANSVILLE, IND.) (US/0890-9253) [14472230] **3147**

EMPLOYMENT LEADER (CN) **4204**

EMPLOYMENT LITIGATION REPORTER (US/1055-6249) [23227144] **3147**

EMPLOYMENT MARKETPLACE (US) 1184, **4204**

EMPLOYMENT OBSERVATORY. POLICIES (NE) [25816518] **1667**

EMPLOYMENT OBSERVATORY. TRENDS (BE) [25637612] **1667**

EMPLOYMENT OF DISABLED AND VIETNAM ERA VETERANS IN THE FEDERAL GOVERNMENT (US/0362-5788) [02306594] **4702**

EMPLOYMENT OPPORTUNITIES (ATHLETICS) (US/1044-9574) [19960736] **4894**

EMPLOYMENT OPPORTUNITIES HANDBOOK CANADA. WESTERN EDITION (CN/0316-8964) [02247325] **4204**

EMPLOYMENT OPPORTUNITIES / UNITED STATES ENVIRONMENTAL PROTECTION AGENCY, PERSONNEL MANAGEMENT DIVISION (US/0747-8186) [10794621] 2228, **940**

●EMPLOYMENT OPPORTUNITIES, USA (US/1076-4798) [30487953] 1667, **4204**

EMPLOYMENT OUTLOOK (FR) [26847950] **1667**

EMPLOYMENT PRACTICES DECISIONS *CEASED.* (US/0149-6255) [02163851] **3147**

EMPLOYMENT RELATIONS BULLETIN (US/0746-9683) [08777858] **3147**

EMPLOYMENT RELATIONS TODAY (US/0745-7790) [09444794] **1667**

EMPLOYMENT REVIEW (US/0013-6883) [02242225] **1667**

EMPLOYMENT SECURITY ACT (INDIANA) See INDIANA EMPLOYMENT SECURITY ACT **1678**

EMPLOYMENT SECURITY COMMISSION OF WYOMING. RESEARCH AND ANALYSIS SECTION See FARM LABOR REPORT (CASPER) **1669**

EMPLOYMENT SECURITY COMMISSION OF WYOMING. RESEARCH AND ANALYSIS SECTION See ANNUAL PLANNING REPORT, STATE OF WYOMING **1648**

EMPLOYMENT SECURITY LOCAL OFFICE OPERATIONS ANNUAL (US) [09285557] **1667**

EMPLOYMENT SECURITY STATISTICAL BULLETIN (US/0735-3286) [06181778] 1667, 2879, **1532**

EMPLOYMENT SITUATION. UNITED DEPARTMENT OF LABOR (US) [02549806] **1667**

EMPLOYMENT TRENDS (ALBANY, N.Y.) (US) [05046815] **1667**

EMPORIA GAZETTE (EMPORIA, KAN. : 1899) (US) [11946256] **5675**

EMPORIA STATE RESEARCH STUDIES, THE (US/0424-9399) [01567844] **1744**

EMPORIKE TRAPEZA TES HELLADOS See REPORT OF THE CHAIRMAN OF THE BOARD OF DIRECTORS - EMPORIKE TRAPEZA TES HELLADOS **807**

EMPOWERING BLACK MANAGERS (UK) 2260, **866**

EMPOWERMENT IN ORGANIZATIONS (UK/0968-4891) **866**

EMPOWERMENT! (WASHINGTON, D.C.) (US/1062-5259) [23228200] **4473**

EMPRESA BRASILEIRA DE PERQUISA AGROPECUARIA. UNIDADE DE EXECUCAO DE PERQUISA DE AMBITO ESTADUAL DE BRASILIA See BATATINHA : RESUMOS INFORMATIVOS **2410**

EMPRESA BRASILEIRA DE PESQUISA AGROPECUARIA. UNIDADE DE EXECUCAO DE PESQUISA DE AMBITO ESTADUAL DE MANAUS See COMUNICADO TECNICO - EMPRESA BRASILEIRA DE PESQUISA AGROPECUARIA, UNIDADE DE EXECUCAO DE PESQUISA DE AMBITO ESTADUAL, MANAUS **76**

EMPRESA BRASILEIRA DE PLANEJAMENTO DE TRANSPORTES See RELATORIO DAS ATIVIDADES - EMPRESA BRASILEIRA DE PLANEJAMENTO DE TRANSPORTES **5391**

EMPRESA DE PESQUISA AGROPECUARIA DO CEARA See RELATORIO ANUAL DE PESQUISA. HORTICULTURA / EMPRESA DE PESQUISA AGROPECUARIA DO CEARA **2430**

EMPRESA DE PESQUISA AGROPECUARIA DO ESTADO DO RIO DE JANEIRO See COMUNICADO TECNICO - EMPRESA DE PESQUISA AGROPECUARIA DO ESTADO DO RIO DE JANEIRO **76**

EMPRESA DE TURISMO DA BAHIA See RELATORIO - EMPRESA DE TURISMO DA BAHIA **5490**

EMPRESA GOIANA DE PESQUISA AGROPECUARIA See COMUNICADO TECNICO - EMPRESA GOIANA DE PESQUISA AGROPECUARIA **76**

EMPRESA NACIONAL DE FUNDICIONES (BOLIVIA) See MEMORIA - EMPRESA NACIONAL DE FUNDICIONES **4008**

EMPRESA NACIONAL DE MINERIA See ANNUAL REPORT / ENAMI, EMPRESA NACIONAL DE MINERIA **2133**

EMPRESA NACIONAL DE TELECOMUNICACIONES See GUIA TELEFONICA : SAN SALVADOR DE JUJUY **1156**

EMPRESS CHINCHILLA BREEDER (1974) (US/0094-3282) [04157434] **3183**

EMPURIES (SP) [21061034] **267**

EMR; ACTIVITIES OF THE SCIENCE AND TECHNOLOGY SECTOR (CN) [02167602] 1375, **1937**

EMR ON-LINE (US) **3724**

EMS COMMUNICATOR (US/0275-0716) [07078187] **3724**

EMS INSIDER (US) **3724**

EMS LEADER, THE *CEASED.* (US/0897-0297) [17390484] **3724**

EMS MEDICAL ADVISOR (US) **3574**

EMSA BULLETIN (US/0146-6119) [03007500] **572**

EMTP NEWS *CEASED*. (BE) **2053**

EMTP NEWSLETTER *See* EMTP NEWS **2053**

EMTREE THESAURUS (NE) [24048400] **1925**

EMU (AT/0158-4197) [01567848] **5617**

EMU TODAY & TOMORROW (US/1062-6034) [25681196] **5509**, **5582**

EMULSION POLYMERISATION (UK/0143-7151) [06121452] **975**

EMULSION POLYMERISATION AND POLYMER EMULSIONS (UK/0955-2804) **4223**

EN PASSANT, POETRY (US/0271-5023) [06617846] **3468**

EN PASSANT POETRY QUARTERLY *See* EN PASSANT, POETRY **3468**

EN ROUTE TECHNOLOGY (US/1057-5618) [24059204] **1184**

EN-TROPHY INSTITUTE *See* EN-TROPHY INSTITUTE REVIEW **4190**

EN-TROPHY INSTITUTE FOR ADVANCED STUDY *See* EN-TROPHY INSTITUTE REVIEW **4190**

EN-TROPHY INSTITUTE REVIEW (CN/0707-2406) [04966224] **4190**

ENABLE EXCHANGE NEWSLETTER (US/0892-5496) [15246882] **1184**

●ENABLE SUBSCRIPTION PLAN (US) **1285**

ENACT (II/0013-6980) [01774320] **5364**

ENAP, CARREFOUR UNVERSITAIRE DE L'ADMINISTRATION PUBLIQUE, PLAN DE DEVELOPMENT (CN/1180-1271) [23295844] **4646**

ENA'S NURSING SCAN IN EMERGENCY CARE (US/1056-7062) [23825346] **3724**, **3855**

ENBI TO PORIMA (JA/0367-021X) [10263248] **4455**

ENCAN - FRASER BROS. LTD (CN/0822-7683) [10611241] **349**

ENCEPHALARTOS (SA/1012-9987) [I10129987] **2413**

ENCEPHALE (FR/0013-7006) [01350713] **3925**, **3832**

ENCEPHALITIS SURVEILLANCE (US/0191-6955) [04909111] **3832**

ENCHANTMENT (US/0046-1946) [04074454] **2533**

ENCHORIA (GW/0340-627X) [01852497] **3278**

ENCICLOPEDIA DEL DIRITTO (IT) [01567851] **2966**

ENCICLOPEDIA PER I COMUNI E GLI ALTRI ENTI LOCALI (IT) **4646**

ENCICLOPEDIA UNIVERSAL ILUSTRADA EUROPEO-AMERICANA. SUPLEMENTO ANUAL (SP) [05295628] **1925**

ENCLITIC (US/0193-5798) [03741606] **3342**

ENCOLOGY (II/0970-1753) [14289484] **2192**, **2215**

ENCOMIA (US/0363-4841) [02479293] **3342**

ENCONTRO NACIONAL DE ECONOMIA *See* ENCONTRO NACIONAL DE ECONOMIA **1559**

ENCONTRO NACIONAL DE ECONOMIA (BL) [07022452] **1559**

ENCORE (US/0071-0164) [01781299] **5364**

ENCORE AMERICAN & WORLDWIDE NEWS (US/0161-6536) [03043465] **2260**

ENCORE DIRECTORY, THE (AT) [24385465] **4068**

ENCORE (EDMONTON) (CN/0712-631X) [09223287] **4116**

ENCORE MANLY (AT/0815-2063) [I08152063] **4068**

ENCORE! (NEW YORK, N.Y. 1991) (US/1055-1239) [23086206] **2533**

ENCOUNTER (INDIANAPOLIS) (US/0013-7081) [01567853] **4956**

ENCOUNTER : THE CHALLENGING WORLD OF NEWS (US) **1063**

ENCOUNTERS (ALBUQUERQUE, N.M.) *CEASED.* (US/1049-5665) [21129123] **2732**

ENCOUNTERS (ST. PAUL, MINN.) *CEASED.* (US/0273-5717) [07082585] **4087**, **5102**

ENCUENTRO (NQ) [01792972] **2732**

ENCUENTRO (BUENOS AIRES, ARGENTINA) (AG) [09338209] **1744**

ENCUENTRO (LIMA, PERU) (PE) [06912795] **2551**

ENCUENTRO VENEZOLANO DE ENTOMOLOGIA *See* ACTAS Y TRABAJOS DEL ... ENCUENTRO VENEZOLANO DE ENTOMOLOGIA **5574**

ENCUESTA AGRICOLA NACIONAL *See* ENCUESTA AGROPECUARIA NACIONAL **81**

ENCUESTA AGROPECUARIA NACIONAL (CK) [06039239] **81**

ENCUESTA ANUAL DE COMERCIO INTERNO (EC) [01785959] **833**

ENCUESTA ANUAL DE MANUFACTURA Y MINERIA / REPUBLICA DEL ECUADOR, INSTITUTO NACIONAL DE ESTADISTICA Y CENSOS (EC) [05984234] **2138**

ENCUESTA ANUAL DE RESTAURANTES, HOTELES Y SERVICIOS (EC) [03431707] **1559**

ENCUESTA DE EDIFICACIONES (PERMISOS DE CONSTRUCCION) (EC) [01783808] **614**

ENCUESTA DE POBLACION ACTIVA (SP) [02416182] **4552**

ENCUESTA INDUSTRIAL (EC) [25880941] **1605**

ENCUESTA INDUSTRIAL. RESULTADOS REGIONALES. REGION DE LOS ANDES / REPUBLICA DE VENEZUELA, PRESIDENCIA DE LA REPUBLICA, OFICINA CENTRAL DE ESTADISTICA E INFORMATICA (VE) [08152447] **1605**

ENCUESTA NACIONAL DEL EMPLEO, GRAN SANTIAGO (SP) [04845745] **1667**

ENCUESTA NACIONAL DEL EMPLEO. REGION METROPOLITANA *See* ENCUESTA NACIONAL DEL EMPLEO, GRAN SANTIAGO **1667**

ENCUESTA SOBRE POBLACION ACTIVA *See* ENCUESTA DE POBLACION ACTIVA **4552**

ENCUESTAS DE COYUNTURA (BOLIVIA) (BO) [05309733] **1488**

ENCUESTAS DE COYUNTURA. SERIE 1 : EVOLUCION DE LA ACTIVIDAD INDUSTRIAL (AG) [01793752] **1560**

ENCUESTAS DE COYUNTURA. SERIE 2 : LA SITUACION FINANCIERA DE LA INDUSTRIA MANUFACTURERA (AG) [01783827] **1605**

ENCYCLIA (US/0196-9110) [04295051] **5199**, **5102**

ENCYCLOPAEDIA BRITANNICA EDUCATIONAL CORPORATION *See* CATALOG OF BRITANNICA FILMS **4065**

ENCYCLOPAEDIA JUDAICA YEAR BOOK (IS/0303-7819) [01161685] **5047**

ENCYCLOPAEDIA OF AUSTRALIAN PLANTS (AT) **509**

ENCYCLOPAEDIA OF ISLAM. NEW ED., PREPARED BY A NUMBER OF LEADING ORIENTALISTS. EDITED BY AN EDITORIAL COMMITTEE CONSISTING OF H.A.R. GIBB [AND OTHERS], THE (NE) [08577120] **5042**

ENCYCLOPAEDIA OF MATHEMATICS (NE) [16755499] **3505**

ENCYCLOPEDIA OF ARBITRATION LAW (UK) **3180**

ENCYCLOPEDIA OF ASSOCIATIONS (US/0071-0202) [01223579] **1925**

ENCYCLOPEDIA OF ASSOCIATIONS CD-ROM (US/1070-2318) [28299945] **1925**

ENCYCLOPEDIA OF ASSOCIATIONS. INTERNATIONAL ORGANIZATIONS (US/1041-0023) [18606162] **1925**

ENCYCLOPEDIA OF ASSOCIATIONS. REGIONAL, STATE, AND LOCAL ORGANIZATIONS (US/0894-2846) [15973678] **5231**

ENCYCLOPEDIA OF BUSINESS INFORMATION SOURCES (US/0071-0210) [01451840] **671**

ENCYCLOPEDIA OF CAREERS AND VOCATIONAL GUIDANCE, THE (US) [08760587] **4204**

ENCYCLOPEDIA OF CHEMICAL TECHNOLOGY (US) [01264868] **1024**

ENCYCLOPEDIA OF CONSUMER LAW (UK) **2966**

ENCYCLOPEDIA OF EDUCATION, THE (US) [01567855] **1744**

ENCYCLOPEDIA OF FLUID POWER STANDARDS. VOL. A : COMMUNICATIONS, INCLUDING GRAPHIC SYMBOLS AND METRIC UNITS (US) **2088**

ENCYCLOPEDIA OF FLUID POWER STANDARDS. VOL. B : PRESSURE RATING (US) **2089**

ENCYCLOPEDIA OF FLUID POWER STANDARDS. VOL. C : PUMPS, MOTORS, POWER UNITS & RESERVOIRS (US) **2089**

ENCYCLOPEDIA OF FLUID POWER STANDARDS. VOL. D : FILTRATION AND CONTAMINATION (US) **2089**

ENCYCLOPEDIA OF FLUID POWER STANDARDS. VOL. E : CONDUCTORS AND ASSOCIATED PRODUCTS (US) **2089**

ENCYCLOPEDIA OF FLUID POWER STANDARDS. VOL. F : CONTROL PRODUCTS/PNEUMATIC SYSTEMS (US) **2089**

ENCYCLOPEDIA OF FLUID POWER STANDARDS. VOL. G : CYLINDERS AND ACCUMULATORS (US) **2089**

ENCYCLOPEDIA OF FLUID POWER STANDARDS. VOL. I : TESTING (US) **2089**

ENCYCLOPEDIA OF FLUID POWER STANDARDS. VOL. J : BIBLIOGRAPHIES (US) **2089**, **2004**

ENCYCLOPEDIA OF FORMS AND PRECEDENTS OTHER THAN COURT FORMS (UK) [01567858] **1925**

ENCYCLOPEDIA OF GEORGIA LAW (US) **2966**

ENCYCLOPEDIA OF GOVERNMENTAL ADVISORY ORGANIZATIONS (US/0092-8380) [02239511] **4646**

ENCYCLOPEDIA OF HEALTH & SAFETY AT WORK (UK) **2861**

ENCYCLOPEDIA OF HEALTH INFORMATION SOURCES (US) **2597**

ENCYCLOPEDIA OF HIGHWAY LAW AND PRACTICE (UK/0142-2952) [I01422952] **5440**, **2966**

ENCYCLOPEDIA OF INDUSTRIAL CHEMICAL ANALYSIS (US) [01567859] **975**

ENCYCLOPEDIA OF LIBRARY AND INFORMATION SCIENCE (US) [04380549] **3209**

ENCYCLOPEDIA OF LIBRARY AND INFORMATION SCIENCE. SUPPLEMENT (US) [09874605] **3209**

ENCYCLOPEDIA OF MATERIALS SCIENCE AND ENGINEERING *CEASED.* (UK) **2102**

ENCYCLOPEDIA OF MATHEMATICS AND ITS APPLICATIONS (US/0953-4806) [03980645] **3505**

ENCYCLOPEDIA OF MEDICAL ORGANIZATIONS AND AGENCIES (US/0743-4510) [09833030] **3574**

ENCYCLOPEDIA OF OCCULTISM & PARAPSYCHOLOGY (US/0731-7840) [08262489] **4241**

ENCYCLOPEDIA OF PHYSICAL SCIENCE AND TECHNOLOGY. YEARBOOK *CEASED.* (US/0898-9842) [17963379] **5103**

ENCYCLOPEDIA OF PLANNING LAW AND PRACTICE (UK) [02802141] **2821**, **2966**

ENCYCLOPEDIA OF PLANT PHYSIOLOGY. NEW SERIES (GW) [02078356] **509**

ENCYCLOPEDIA OF SOCIAL WORK (US/0071-0237) [02260751] **5284**

ENCYCLOPEDIA OF U.K. AND EUROPEAN PATENT LAW (UK/0142-2987) [I01422987] **2966**

ENCYCLOPEDIA OF VALUE ADDED TAX *CEASED.* (UK) **1925**

ENCYCLOPEDIA OF WORLD PROBLEMS AND HUMAN POTENTIAL / EDITED BY UNION OF INTERNATIONAL ASSOCIATIONS (GW/0304-0089) [14337441] **1925**

ENCYCLOPEDIE ARTISTIQUE (CN/0316-0076) [10165736] **1131**

ENCYCLOPEDIE DU CHEF DE PROJET INFORMATIQUE, L' *See* TECHNIQUES ET MANAGEMENT DES PROJETS INFORMATIQUES **5162**

ENCYCLOPEDIE ENTOMOLOGIQUE PARIS (FR/0301-4282) [I03014282] **5582**

ENCYCLOPEDIE JURIDIQUE (FR) [01567869] **2966**

ENCYCLOPEDIE MEDICO-CHIRURGICALE : KINESITHERAPIE. REEDUCATION FONCTIONNELLE (FR) **3964**

ENCYCLOPEDIE MEDICO CHIRURGICALE. MEDECINE GENERALE & SPECIALITES. DERMATOLOGIE (FR) **3720**

ENCYCLOPEDIE MEDICO CHIRURGICALE: MEDECINE GENERALE AND SPECIALITES. OBSTETRIQUE (FR) **3760**

ENCYCLOPEDIE MEDICO CHIRURGICALE / MEDECINE GENERALE & SPECIALITES. OPHTHALMOLOGIE (FR) **3874**

ENCYCLOPEDIE MEDICO CHIRURGICALE. MEDECINE GENERALE & SPECIALITES. POUMON PLEVRE (FR) **3949**

ENCYCLOPEDIE MEDICO-CHIRURGICALE : MEDECINE GENERALE ET SPECIALITES. ANESTHESIE ET REANIMATION (FR) **3682**, **3964**

ENCYCLOPEDIE MEDICO-CHIRURGICALE : MEDECINE GENERALE ET SPECIALITES. COEUR VAISSEAUX (FR) **3704**, **3964**

ENCYCLOPEDIE MEDICO-CHIRURGICALE : RADIODIAGNOSTIC I-VI (FR) **3964**

ENCYCLOPEDIE MEDICO CHIRURGICALE / TECHNIQUES CHIRURGICALES. GYNECOLOGIE (FR) **3760**

Alphabetical Title Index — ENERGY

ENCYCLOPEDIE MEDICO CHIRURGICALE / TECHNIQUES CHIRURGICALES. UROLOGIE (FR) **3989**

END OF YEAR REPORT - NORTHWEST FEDERAL REGIONAL COUNCIL (US/0147-4294) [03162633] **4646**

END OF YEAR REPORT. REGIONAL PROGRAM PLANS ASSESSMENT (US/0147-7587) [03230630] 2228, **4646**

END PAPERS (UK/0262-7922) [08438897] **4473**

●END PAPERS (ARLINGTON, VA.) (US/1063-8938) [26173763] **4828**

END-STAGE RENAL DISEASE ANNUAL REPORT TO CONGRESS (US/0275-2298) [07082570] **3989**

END-USER COMPUTING MANAGEMENT (US) **1267**

ENDAI NAIYO SHOROKU, NIHON KETSUGO SOSHIKI GAKKAI SOKAI (JA) [05590507] **3574**

ENDANGERED FAECES (US/0145-5494) [02761186] **3384**

ENDANGERED SPECIES TECHNICAL BULLETIN (US/0145-9236) [02584686] **2165**

ENDANGERED SPECIES UPDATE (US) [17338120] 226, **2192**

ENDEAVOUR (AT) [05229364] **3384**

ENDEAVOUR (NEW SERIES) (UK/0160-9327) [01567873] **5103**

ENDERCOS DOS SENHORES SENADORES (BRAZIL) (BL) [05055194] **4473**

ENDERECOS DOS SENHORES DEPUTADOS E GUIA TELEFONICO DA CAMARA DOS DEPUTADOS (BL) [02244816] **4646**

ENDLESS VACATION - RESORT CONDOMINIUMS INTERNATIONAL, THE (US/0279-4853) [07909464] **5469**

ENDLESS VACATION (VACATION HORIZONS INTERNATIONAL) *See* ENDLESS VACATION - RESORT CONDOMINIUMS INTERNATIONAL, THE **5469**

●ENDO : REVUE FRANCAISE D'ENDODONTIE : PUBLICATION OFFICIELLE DE LA SOCIETE FRANCAISE D'ENDODONTIE (FR) [26585646] **1323**

●ENDOCRINE JOURNAL (JA/0918-8959) [28096305] **3729**

ENDOCRINE PATHOLOGY (US/1046-3976) [20400707] **3729**

ENDOCRINE PATHOLOGY UPDATE (US/1043-9986) [19643275] **3729**

ENDOCRINE PHYSIOLOGY (US/0732-6262) [02560882] **3729**

ENDOCRINE REGULATIONS (BRATISLAVA) (XO/1210-0668) [24270847] **3729**

ENDOCRINE-RELATED CANCER (UK) **3729**

ENDOCRINE RESEARCH (US/0743-5800) [10613076] **3729**

ENDOCRINE REVIEWS (US/0163-769X) [04470843] **3729**

ENDOCRINE SOCIETY - ANNUAL MEETING, PROGRAM AND ABSTRACTS, THE (US) [02908810] **3729**

ENDOCRINE SOCIETY. MEETING *See* ENDOCRINE SOCIETY - ANNUAL MEETING, PROGRAM AND ABSTRACTS, THE **3729**

ENDOCRINOLOGIA (BARCELONA) (SP/0211-2299) [10309867] **3729**

ENDOCRINOLOGIA JAPONICA (JA/0013-7219) [01567878] **3729**

ENDOCRINOLOGIE *See* ROMANIAN JOURNAL OF ENDOCRINOLOGY / SPONSOR [SIC] BY THE ACADEMY OF MEDICAL SCIENCES **3733**

ENDOCRINOLOGIE HUMAINE ET EXPERIMENTALE ENDOCRINOPATHIES. E64 (FR) **3729**

ENDOCRINOLOGIST (BALTIMORE, MD.), THE (US/1051-2144) [21915299] **3729**

ENDOCRINOLOGIST, THE (US/1051-2144) [21519299] **3729**

ENDOCRINOLOGY (UK/0307-157X) [01380301] **3729**

ENDOCRINOLOGY AND METABOLISM CLINICS OF NORTH AMERICA (US/0889-8529) [14091804] **3729**

●ENDOCRINOLOGY AND METABOLISM (LONDON, ENG.) (UK/1074-939X) [29887584] **3729**

ENDOCRINOLOGY AND METABOLISM SERIES (UK/0264-0767) [08015921] **3729**

ENDOCRINOLOGY (PHILADELPHIA) (US/0013-7227) [01567879] **3730**

ENDOCURIETHERAPY / HYPERTHERMIA ONCOLOGY (US/8756-1689) [11481690] **3816**

ENDOCYTOBIOSIS AND CELL RESEARCH (GW/0256-1514) [13029120] **536**

ENDODONCIA : ORGANO DE LA ASOCIACION ESPANOLA DE ENDODONCIA (SP) [23265800] **1323**

ENDODONTIC BIBLIOGRAPHY (US/0730-1308) [05969705] **1338**

ENDODONTIC REPORT, THE (US/0899-8973) [17728081] **1323**

ENDODONTICS & DENTAL TRAUMATOLOGY (DK/0109-2502) [11804935] **1323**

ENDODONTICS FOR GPS *See* GP (ATLANTA, GA.) **1324**

ENDODONTIE (GW/0940-9505) [I09409505] **1323**

ENDOMETRIOSIS ASSOCIATION NEWSLETTER (US/0897-1870) [17427288] **3760**

ENDOMETRIUM (US/0145-9937) [02829813] **3760**

ENDOSCOPIC SURGERY AND ALLIED TECHNOLOGIES (GW/0942-6027) **3964**

ENDOSCOPY (GW/0013-726X) [01604468] **3744**

ENDOSCOPY REVIEW (US/8756-968X) [11804704] **3744**

ENDOSKOPIE HEUTE (GW/0933-811X) [25711348] **3574**

ENDOSURGERY (IT/1122-8695) **3964**

ENDOTHELIUM (UK/0957-3518) **454**

●ENDOTHELIUM (NEW YORK, N.Y.) (US/1062-3329) [25587529] **536**

ENDS REPORT (UK) [23018513] **2228**

ENDURO (COMPTON) (US/0092-6272) [01791164] **4081**

ENERCOM (US) [10417698] **1937**

ENERGETICA (RM/0423-1082) [10513609] **1937**

ENERGETICHESKOE STROITELSTVO ZA RUBEZHOM : ORGAN MINISTERSTVA ENERGETIKI I ELEKTROTEKHNICHESKOI PROMYSHLENNOSTI (RU/0131-1328) [10967537] **1937**

ENERGETICOS (MX) [06829629] **1937**

ENERGETIK (MOSKVA) (RU/0013-7278) [06845887] **2053**

ENERGETIKA (LI/0235-7208) [24303418] **2053**

ENERGETIKA (XR/0375-8842) [02336705] **2113**

ENERGETIKA I ELEKTRIFIKACIA KIEV (UN/0424-9879) [I04249879] **2053**

ENERGETIKA (SOFIJA) (BU/0324-1521) [11208495] **2053**

ENERGETSKI BILANS SFR JUGOSLAVIJE (YU) [09652934] **2113**

ENERGETYKA (PL/0013-7294) [10212404] **1938**

ENERGI INDONESIA (SI/0126-2696) [09190631] **1938**

ENERGIA (BL) [07037860] **1938**

ENERGIA (IT) [09883247] **1938**

ENERGIA E INDUSTRIA (VE/0378-9578) [01786551] **1972**

ENERGIA E MATERIE PRIME (IT) [06299700] **1938**

ENERGIA ED ECONOMIA (IT) **1488**

ENERGIA ELETTRICA (IT/0013-7308) [03701002] **2053**

ENERGIA ES ATOMTECHNIKA (HU/0013-7316) [10212087] **1938**

ENERGIA MADRID (SP/0210-2056) [I02102056] **1938**

ENERGIA NUCLEAR E AGRICULTURA (BL/0100-3593) [06062203] 81, **2154**

ENERGIA NUCLEAR (MADRID) *SUSPENDED.* (SP/0013-7324) [02320533] **2155**

ENERGIA NUCLEARE (MILANO) (IT/0013-7332) [02320535] 1938, **2155**

ENERGIA NUCLEARE (ROME, ITALY) (IT) [12796871] **2155**

ENERGIAGAZDALKODAS (HU/0021-0757) [09305247] **1938**

ENERGIAIPARI ES ENERGIAGAZDALKODASI SZAKIRODALMI TAJEKOZTATO (HU/0231-0678) [I02310678] **1938**

ENERGIAN TUOTANTO JA VESIHUOLTO (FI/0786-0021) [19543506] 5533, **1938**

ENERGIATALOUDELLINEN YHDISTYS (FINLAND) *See* VERKSAMHETSBERATTELSE / ENERGIEKONOMISKA FORENINGEN **1960**

ENERGIATALOUDELLISEEN KOBJAUSTOIMINTAAN VUONNA ... MYONNETTAVAT AVUSTUKSET (FI) [19037358] **4646**

ENERGIATILASTOT / KAUPPA- JA TEOLLISUUSMINISTERIO, ENERGIAOSASTO (FI/0785-3165) [09725316] **1938**

ENERGIE (FR) **1938**

ENERGIE ALTERNATIVE HTE (IT/0391-5360) [07616142] **5103**

ENERGIE AU QUEBEC EN PRIMEUR, L' (CN/0844-7152) [19984985] **1938**

ENERGIE CONSULENT (NE) **1938**

ENERGIE DANS LES SECTEURS ECONOMIQUES, L' (FR) [12087310] **1938**

ENERGIE DIALOG (GW) **1938**

ENERGIE ET PROGRES (CG) [01787690] **2053**

ENERGIE FLUIDE ET LUBRIFICATION (FR) **1938**

ENERGIE FLUIDE, L'AIR INDUSTRIEL (FR/0336-9811) [07964526] **1938**

ENERGIE. LEXIQUE (FR/0154-0335) [07087690] **3209**

ENERGIE (MUNCHEN) (GW/0013-7359) [02446694] **2113**

ENERGIE (PFAFFHAUSEN) (SZ/0304-2065) [02240506] **1938**

ENERGIE PLUS (FR/0292-1731) [I02921731] **1938**

ENERGIE SPEKTRUM (GW/0179-9932) [16505491] **1938**

ENERGIE. T230 (FR) **1938**

ENERGIEANWENDUNG (GW/0013-7405) **1938**

ENERGIEBILANZEN DER BUNDESREPUBLIK DEUTSCHLAND (GW) **1938**

ENERGIESPECTRUM (NE/0165-2117) [03209376] **2113**

ENERGIETECHNIK (GW/0013-7421) [06341202] **1938**

ENERGIMAGASINET (SW/0348-9493) [I03489493] **1938**

ENERGIOVERSIGT (DK/0106-0244) [11935625] **1938**

ENERGISTATISTISK ARBOG. JAHRBUCH ENERGIESTATISTIK. ENERGY STATISTICS YEARBOOK (LU) [06496422] **1962**

ENERGOEXPORT (RU) [07037383] **2113**

ENERGY ALBERTA (CN/0833-3505) [13050383] **1938**

ENERGY ALERT (TORONTO) (CN/0835-5266) [17883760] **1938**

ENERGY ALTERNATIVES (AT/0813-5215) [I08135215] **1938**

ENERGY ANALECTS (CN/0315-1654) [01805302] **1938**

ENERGY ANALYSIS (US) [12642964] **1938**

ENERGY ANALYST (US/0748-5972) [10980115] **1938**

ENERGY ANALYST (SILVER SPRING, MD.) (US/1045-5728) [20333866] **1938**

ENERGY AND BUILDINGS (SZ/0378-7788) [03648888] 1938, **614**

ENERGY AND CHARACTER (UK/0013-7472) [01677894] **4586**

ENERGY & CONSCIOUSNESS (US/1050-5326) [21533562] **1939**

ENERGY & EDUCATION *CEASED.* (US/0891-0979) [08654728] 1744, **1939**

ENERGY AND ENGINEERING SCIENCE SERIES (UK/1042-1939) [18979240] **4402**

ENERGY & ENVIRONMENT (UK/0958-305X) [21187549] **1939**

ENERGY AND ENVIRONMENT ANNUAL REPORT (US/0147-8850) [03247392] 2165, **1939**

ENERGY & FUEL USERS' JOURNAL (II/0039-0828) [24527368] **1939**

ENERGY & FUELS (US/0887-0624) [13076751] **1939**

ENERGY & NUCLEAR SCIENCES INTERNATIONAL WHO'S WHO (UK) [16964432] 1939, **4446**

ENERGY AND TECHNOLOGY REVIEW (US/0884-5050) [04110972] **1939**

ENERGY ASIA (HK/0253-0783) [09454257] **1939**

ENERGY BALANCE (FR) **1939**

ENERGY BALANCES OF OECD COUNTRIES ... AND MAIN SERIES FROM 1960 BILANS ENERGETIQUES DES PAYS DE L'OCDE ... ET SERIES PRINCIPALES DEPUIS 1960 (FR) [18492240] **1939**

ENERGY BALANCES OF OECD COUNTRIES. BILANS ENERGETIQUES DES PAYS DE L'OCDE (FR) [05341485] **1939**

ENERGY BOOKS QUARTERLY *CEASED.* (US/0892-5461) [15214034] **1962**

ENERGY BUSINESS (US/0886-8514) [13022194] **1939**

ENERGY CLEARINGHOUSE (US/0273-3102) [06646714] **1939**

ENERGY CONSERVATION ANNUAL REPORT (US/0147-4359) [03162865] **1939**

ENERGY CONSERVATION BULLETIN (WASHINGTON, D.C.) (US/0747-9638) [10650553] **1939**

ENERGY — Alphabetical Title Index

ENERGY CONSERVATION IN THE INTERNATIONAL ENERGY AGENCY; REVIEW (FR) [05836867] **1939**

ENERGY CONSERVATION NEWS (US/0161-6595) [03988283] **1939**

ENERGY CONSERVATION PROGRAM GUIDE FOR INDUSTRY AND COMMERCE, EPIC (US) [02575908] **1939**

ENERGY CONSERVATION RESOURCE DIRECTORY (US) [09379768] **1939**

ENERGY CONSERVATION UPDATE (US/0162-1475) [04102771] **1939**

ENERGY CONVERSION AND MANAGEMENT (UK/0196-8904) [05918231] **1939**

ENERGY COST CUTTER, THE **SUSPENDED.** (US/0277-6103) [07604587] **1939**

ENERGY CREDIT PROGRAM / OHIO DEPARTMENT OF TAXATION (US) [07440763] **5284**

ENERGY DAILY, THE (US/0364-5274) [03011226] **1939**

ENERGY DATA BASE. SUBJECT THESAURUS, PERMUTED LISTING (US) [09010640] **1939**

ENERGY DESIGN UPDATE (US/0741-3629) [10139346] **1939**

ENERGY DEVELOPMENT AND DEMONSTRATION PROGRAM : YEAR END REPORT (US) [08608494] **1940**

ENERGY DEVELOPMENTS (GW/0342-5665) [03187947] **1940**

ENERGY DEVELOPMENTS (NEW YORK, N.Y. 1957) (US/0013-7502) [10468090] **1940**

ENERGY DIGEST (UK/0367-1119) [02446696] **1940**

ENERGY ECONOMICS (UK/0140-9883) [04802525] 1488, **1940**

ENERGY, ECONOMICS AND CLIMATE CHANGE (US/1059-5813) [24640346] 1488, **1940**

ENERGY ECONOMICS RESEARCH LTD See OIL & ENERGY TRENDS **4268**

ENERGY ECONOMIST (UK/0262-7108) [10907649] **1940**

ENERGY ENGINEERING : JOURNAL OF THE ASSOCIATION OF ENERGY ENGINEERS (US/0199-8595) [06007496] **1940**

ENERGY ENTS (US) [07020516] **1940**

ENERGY ENVIRONMENT MONITOR (II/0970-3446) [I09703446] **1940**

ENERGY EQUIPMENT (US) **1940**

ENERGY EXPLORATION & EXPLOITATION (UK/0144-5987) [08290613] **1940**

ENERGY FORUM (PHILIPPINE NATIONAL OIL COMPANY) (PH) [08933512] **1940**

ENERGY FROM BIOMASS AND WASTES (US/0277-7851) [07633780] 1940, **4255**

ENERGY IN EUROPE (LU/0256-6141) [12377952] **1940**

ENERGY IN JAPAN (JA/0919-6080) [04734489] **1940**

ENERGY IN WORLD AGRICULTURE (NE/0921-9757) [15797699] **81**

ENERGY INDUSTRIES COUNCIL (GREAT BRITAIN) See CATALOGUE : BRITISH SUPPLIERS TO THE OIL, GAS, PETROCHEMICAL, AND PROCESS INDUSTRIES / ENERGY INDUSTRIES COUNCIL **4253**

ENERGY INFORMATION ABSTRACTS **CEASED.** (US/0147-6521) [02139978] 1940, **1962**

ENERGY INFORMATION ABSTRACTS ANNUAL **CEASED.** (US/0739-3679) [07346257] 1940, **1962**

ENERGY INFORMATION ADELAIDE (AT/0729-3739) [I07293739] **1940**

ENERGY INFORMER (US) **1940**

ENERGY JOURNAL (CAMBRIDGE, MASS.) (US/0195-6574) [05585856] **1940**

ENERGY LAW JOURNAL (US/0270-9163) [06515402] 1940, **2966**

ENERGY LEGISLATIVE SERVICE (US/0149-5550) [03523190] **2966**

ENERGY LIBRARY (US/1049-7420) [21356478] **1940**

ENERGY MANAGEMENT (OTTAWA, ONT.) (CN/0821-4913) [09631114] **1940**

ENERGY MANAGEMENT : QUARTERLY JOURNAL OF NATIONAL PRODUCTIVITY COUNCIL (II/0970-289X) [24118818] **1940**

ENERGY MANAGEMENT TECHNOLOGY **CEASED.** (US/0745-984X) [09658290] **5103**

ENERGY MARKET UPDATE (CN/1183-7179) [25607910] **1941**

ENERGY NEWS (OTTAWA. 1982) (CN/0823-1478) [09938390] **1941**

ENERGY NEWSBRIEF, THE (US/1059-289X) [24536143] **1941**

ENERGY NEWSLETTER INDEX **CEASED.** (US/0276-1858) [07331879] **1941**

ENERGY / NTIS See NTIS ALERT. ENERGY **1951**

ENERGY OPPORTUNITIES (II/0970-1583) [I09701583] **1941**

ENERGY (OXFORD) (UK/0360-5442) [02235570] **1941**

ENERGY PERFORMANCE REVIEW (US/0748-9145) [11008835] **1605**

ENERGY POLICY (UK/0301-4215) [01792125] **1941**

ENERGY POLICY STUDIES (NEWARK, DEL.) (US/0882-3537) [11515347] **1941**

ENERGY, POWER, AND ENVIRONMENT (US) [06434497] 2165, **1941**

ENERGY PRICES AND TAXES (FR/0256-2332) [11552273] **1941**

ENERGY PROCESSING CANADA (CN/0319-5759) [01870723] **1941**

ENERGY PROJECTIONS (US) **897**

ENERGY-RELATED MANPOWER (US/0740-3496) [09801557] **1941**

ENERGY REPORT (US) [12189992] **1941**

ENERGY REPORT (ARLINGTON, VA.) (US/0888-8183) [13724626] **1941**

ENERGY REPORT : ENERGY POLICY & TECHNOLOGY NEWS BULLETIN (UK) [13799059] **1941**

ENERGY REPORT - TEXAS. COMPTROLLER'S OFFICE (US/0196-7754) [04020302] **1941**

ENERGY RESEARCH (NE/0167-692X) [07345047] **1941**

ENERGY RESEARCH ABSTRACTS (US/0160-3604) [03568399] 1941, **1962**

ENERGY RESEARCH AND TECHNOLOGY (US/0360-1609) [02321885] **1941**

ENERGY RESEARCH PROGRAM OF THE U.S. DEPARTMENT OF THE INTERIOR (US/0098-518X) [02239729] **1941**

ENERGY RESEARCH PROGRAMS (US/0195-699X) [05625542] **1941**

ENERGY RESOURCE NOTES (US/0270-0115) [06327315] **1941**

ENERGY RESOURCES (US) **1941**

ENERGY RESOURCES (DENVER) (US/0149-6263) [03509113] **1941**

ENERGY RESOURCES DEVELOPMENT IN THE PHILIPPINES (PH) [06507285] **1941**

ENERGY RESOURCES SERIES (US/0270-1294) [03702323] **1942**

ENERGY REVIEW (ALBANY, N.Y.) (US/0749-6362) [08593009] **1942**

ENERGY REVIEW (LEXINGTON) (US/0147-9660) [03252145] **1942**

ENERGY REVIEW (SANTA BARBARA) (US/0094-8063) [01794986] **1942**

ENERGY SOURCES (US/0090-8312) [01793046] **1942**

ENERGY (STAMFORD, CONN. 1975) (US/0149-9386) [02246438] **1942**

ENERGY STATISTICS (CHICAGO, ILL.) **CEASED.** (US/0739-3075) [04450906] 1942, **1962**

●ENERGY STATISTICS HANDBOOK (CN/1188-665X) [25796851] **1942**

●ENERGY STATISTICS HANDBOOK (CN/1188-665X) [25796853] **1942**

ENERGY STATISTICS (INTERNATIONAL ENERGY AGENCY) (FR) [04708261] **1942**

ENERGY STATISTICS OF OECD COUNTRIES / INTERNATIONAL ENERGY AGENCY (FR) [21892511] **1962**

ENERGY STATISTICS REPORT FOR FISCAL YEAR (AS) [12034191] **1942**

ENERGY STATISTICS SOURCEBOOK (US/0889-5260) [13913939] 1942, 4255, **1962**

ENERGY STATISTICS YEARBOOK (UNITED NATIONS. STATISTICAL OFFICE) (US) [10977518] 1942, **1962**

ENERGY STATUS REPORT (US/0731-0927) [05112241] **1942**

ENERGY STORAGE SYSTEMS (US/0896-5145) [17197405] **1942**

ENERGY STUDIES (AUSTIN, TEX.) (US/0743-829X) [02898443] **1942**

ENERGY STUDIES REVIEW (CN/0843-4379) [20977535] **1942**

ENERGY TODAY (US/0093-500X) [01792198] **1942**

ENERGY TRENDS (UK/0308-1222) [02321936] **1942**

ENERGY UNLIMITED **CEASED.** (US/0279-621X) [07120319] **1942**

ENERGY UPDATE (ENERGY, MINES AND RESOURCES CANADA) (CN/0713-9144) [05733436] **1942**

ENERGY USE, STATE OFFICE BUILDINGS (US) [09317431] **1942**

ENERGY USER NEWS (US/0162-9131) [02902484] 2192, **1942**

ENERGY UTILITIES (UK/0959-0196) [I09590196] 1942, **1488**

ENERGY WATCH (SACRAMENTO, CALIF.) (US/0887-610X) [07159189] **1942**

ENERGY WEST (SAN CLEMENTE, CALIF.) (US/0894-4180) [14973756] **1942**

ENERGY WHO'S WHO DIRECTORY, THE (US) [22541072] **1942**

ENERGY WORLD (UK/0307-7942) [01790007] **1943**

ENERGY YEAR BOOK (PK) [06348594] **1943**

ENERGYGRAMS (OAK RIDGE, TENN.) (US/0731-6291) [08225628] **1943**

ENERGYLETTERS (CORAL GABLES, FLA.) (US/1049-9296) [21354913] **1943**

ENERGYTALK (US) [08363294] **1943**

ENERGYTRENDS (CN/0848-9114) [21485473] **1943**

ENERMARK NEWS (CN/1182-6371) [23263338] **954**

ENERPRESSE (FR/0153-9442) [I01539442] **1943**

ENERUGI FORAMU (JA/0388-5267) [I03885267] **1943**

ENERUGI HENKAN GIJUTSU (JA/0288-5417) [09485771] **1943**

ENERUGI SEISAN JUKYU TOKEI GEPPO / [HENSHU] TSUSHO SANGYO [SHO] DAIJIN KAMBO CHOSA TOKEIBU (JA) [08223780] **1943**

ENERUGI TOKEI GEPPO (JA) [02958433] 833, **4255**

ENERUGI TOKEI NEMPO. YEARBOOK OF COAL, PETROLEUM AND COKE STATISTICS (JA) [04315119] 1943, **1962**

ENERUGI (TOKYO. 1968) (JA/0285-5437) [08402150] **1943**

ENFANCE (FR/0013-7545) [01567885] **4586**

ENFANCE ET LA MODE, L' (FR/0046-1962) [I00461962] **1084**

ENFANCE MAJUSCULE PARIS (FR/1164-8589) [I11648589] **3164**

ENFANT **CEASED.** (BE) [09390824] **1063**

ENFANT D'ABORD, L' (FR/0399-4988) [I03994988] **3903**

ENFANT EN MILIEU TROPICAL, L' (FR/0013-7561) [04446692] 3986, **3903**

ENFANTS MAGAZINE PARIS (FR/0397-4820) [I03974820] **1063**

ENFERMEDADES DEL TORAX (SP/0423-121X) [09335483] **3574**

ENFERMEDADES INFECCIOSAS Y MICROBIOLOGIA CLINICA (SP/0213-005X) [23360851] 562, **3713**

ENFERMERA AL DIA (MX/0185-0970) [07612393] **3855**

ENFERMERIA CIENTIFICA (SP/0211-9005) [26349883] **3855**

ENFERMERIA INTEGRAL (SP) **3855**

ENFIELD PRESS (1984), THE (US/8750-3123) [11219035] **5645**

ENFO (TH/0125-1783) [I01251783] **2165**

ENFO (US/0276-9956) [05170059] **2165**

ENFOQUES EN ATENCION PRIMARIA (CL/0716-2774) [24466624] **3574**

ENFORCEMENT ACTIONS (US/1056-9030) [20033200] **2155**

ENGANCE NEWSLETTER (CN/0823-8693) [11431386] **5555**

ENGARRAFADOR MODERNO (BL/0100-7947) [08381284] **2334**

ENGEI GAKKAI (JAPAN) See ENGEI GAKKAI ZASSHI **2413**

ENGEI GAKKAI ZASSHI (JA/0013-7626) [02923285] **2413**

ENGEI SHINCHISHIKI. HANA NO GO (JA) [27773958] **2414**

ENGEI SHINCHISHIKI. HANA TO MIDORI NO JOHOSHI See ENGEI SHINCHISHIKI. HANA NO GO **2414**

●ENGEI SHINCHISHIKI. YASAI GO (JA) [27774496] **82**

ENGEI SHINCHISHIKI. YASAI SAIBAI NO SAISHIN JOHOSHI See ENGEI SHINCHISHIKI. YASAI GO **82**

ENGEKIGAKU / HENSHU WASEDA DAIGKU ENGEKI GAKKAI (JA) [08724002] 4068, **5364**

ENGELHARDTIA (US) [03087572] **5582**

ENGELSMAN'S GENERAL CONSTRUCTION COST GUIDE (US/0270-1626) [06108408] **614**

ENGENHARIA See ENGENHARIA NA INDUSTRIA (SAO PAULO) **5103**

ENGENHARIA AGRICOLA (BL/0100-6916) [06239346] 1972, **82**

ENGENHARIA DE HOJE (BL) [03198439] **1972**

ENGENHARIA NA INDUSTRIA (SAO PAULO) (BL/0100-0608) [02242442] **5103**

ENGINE POWER PERSPECTIVE (US/1056-4063) [23719631] **2113**

ENGINEER (CE) [01788889] **1972**

ENGINEER (FORT BELVOIR), THE (US/0046-1989) [01567892] 4043, **1972**

ENGINEER (HALIFAX) (CN/0849-2913) [23231197] **1972**

ENGINEER (LONDON) (UK/0013-7758) [01567893] **1972**

ENGINEER OF CALIFORNIA (US/0277-1233) [04362723] **1972**

ENGINEERED MATERIALS ABSTRACTS (US/0951-9998) [13764326] 2102, **2004**

ENGINEERED SYSTEMS (US/0891-9976) [11080933] **2113**

ENGINEERING ANALYSIS WITH BOUNDARY ELEMENTS (UK/0955-7997) [20118698] **1972**

ENGINEERING & AUTOMATION (GW/0931-6221) [23879442] **1972**

ENGINEERING AND MINING JOURNAL (1926) (US/0095-8948) [04694005] **2138**

ENGINEERING AND RESEARCH CENTER (U.S.) *See* ACTIVE NAMES OF BUREAU PROJECTS AND MAJOR STRUCTURES **2087**

ENGINEERING & SCIENCE (US/0013-7812) [02260757] 5103, **1972**

ENGINEERING AND TECHNOLOGY DEGREES (US/0071-0393) [02245999] **1972**

ENGINEERING AND TECHNOLOGY ENROLLMENTS (US/0278-8985) [06347159] **1972**

ENGINEERING AND TECHNOLOGY GRADUATES (US/0092-2994) [01784507] **5103**

ENGINEERING APPLICATIONS OF ARTIFICIAL INTELLIGENCE (UK/0952-1976) [18173101] 1219, **1212**

ENGINEERING APPLICATIONS OF COMPUTATIONAL HYDRAULICS (UK/8756-6796) [11585538] **2089**

ENGINEERING ASPECTS OF MAGNETOHYDRODYNAMICS *See* PROCEEDINGS OF THE ... SYMPOSIUM ON ENGINEERING ASPECTS OF MAGNETOHYDRODYNAMICS **1992**

ENGINEERING AUTOMATION REPORT (US) 1247, **1219**

●ENGINEERING AUTOMATION REPORT (US/1065-6952) [26682303] 1264, 1285, **1972**

ENGINEERING COMPUTERS (UK/0263-4759) [12867595] **1184**

ENGINEERING CONFERENCE (US/0271-9959) [04187751] **4233**

ENGINEERING CONSTRUCTION & ARCHITECTURAL MANAGEMENT (UK/0969-9988) 298, **2023**

ENGINEERING DEGREES *See* ENGINEERING AND TECHNOLOGY DEGREES **1972**

ENGINEERING DEPARTMENT MANAGEMENT & ADMINISTRATION REPORT (US/1055-0526) [23069468] **866**

ENGINEERING DESIGN (II) [01790452] **1972**

ENGINEERING DESIGN GRAPHICS JOURNAL (US/0046-2012) [01567899] **1972**

ENGINEERING DESIGN GUIDES *CEASED.* (UK/0141-5573) [03970447] **1972**

ENGINEERING DESIGNER (UK/0013-7898) [01774731] **2098**

ENGINEERING DIGEST (TORONTO) *SUSPENDED.* (CN/0013-7901) [02006434] **1972**

ENGINEERING DIMENSIONS (CN/0820-8190) [09457247] 671, **1972**

●ENGINEERING DOCUMENTATION ADVISOR, THE (US/1062-8800) [25780517] **1973**

ENGINEERING ECONOMIC TRENDS / ENGINEERING EMPLOYERS' FEDERATION (UK) [20346364] **1973**

ENGINEERING ECONOMIST, THE (US/0013-791X) [01716582] **1973**

ENGINEERING EDGE (AT) **1973**

ENGINEERING EDUCATION *See* JOURNAL OF ENGINEERING EDUCATION (WASHINGTON, D.C.) **1982**

ENGINEERING EMPLOYERS' FEDERATION *See* DIRECTORY / ENGINEERING EMPLOYERS' FEDERATION **1970**

ENGINEERING EXTENSION DIVISION SERIES (US) [15648029] **1973**

ENGINEERING FAILURE ANALYSIS (UK) **1973**

ENGINEERING FORUM (TORONTO) (CN/0701-080X) [03402982] **1973**

ENGINEERING FRACTURE MECHANICS (US/0013-7944) [01567903] 2098, **2102**

ENGINEERING GEOLOGY (JA) 1973, **1375**

ENGINEERING GEOLOGY (NE/0013-7952) [01567904] 1375, **1973**

ENGINEERING GEOLOGY SPECIAL PUBLICATION / GEOLOGICAL SOCIETY OF LONDON (UK) [14145635] **2138**

ENGINEERING GEOLOGY SPECIALIST GROUP PAPERS (AT/0728-7224) [I07287224] 1973, **1375**

ENGINEERING HORIZONS (VAN NUYS, CALIF.) (US/1040-1679) [15124918] **1973**

ENGINEERING IN MINIATURE (UK/0955-7644) [I09557644] **2773**

ENGINEERING INDEX ANNUAL (US/0360-8557) [05118578] 1973, **2004**

ENGINEERING INDEX BIOENGINEERING AND BIOTECHNOLOGY ABSTRACTS (US/1041-2913) [18721209] 3692, **2004**

ENGINEERING INDEX ENERGY ABSTRACTS (US/0093-8408) [01385299] 1943, 1973, **2004**

ENGINEERING INDEX, INC *See* PIE, PUBLICATIONS INDEXED FOR ENGINEERING **1990**

ENGINEERING INDEX, INC. PIE, PUBLICATIONS INDEXED FOR ENGINEERING *See* PUBLICATIONS IN ENGINEERING : PIE : PUBLICATIONS ABSTRACTED AND INDEXED IN THE ... ENGINEERING INFORMATION DATABASES **1992**

ENGINEERING INDEX MONTHLY (US/0742-1974) [10285948] 1973, **2004**

ENGINEERING INDUSTRIES REVIEW *CEASED.* (UK) [01789731] **1973**

ENGINEERING INDUSTRY IN JAPAN (JA) [01791132] **1973**

ENGINEERING INTERNATIONAL (US/0896-1735) [16940559] **2023**

ENGINEERING JOURNAL (NEW YORK) (US/0013-8029) [01567912] **614**

ENGINEERING KNOW-HOW IN ENGINE DESIGN (US/0489-5606) [01782669] 5414, **2113**

ENGINEERING LASERS *CEASED.* (UK) **1973**

ENGINEERING LITERATURE GUIDES (US/0882-861X) [12003651] **1973**

ENGINEERING (LONDON) *CEASED.* (UK/0013-7782) [01567895] **1973**

ENGINEERING MANAGEMENT CONFERENCE (US) **2053**

ENGINEERING MANAGEMENT JOURNAL (UK/0960-7919) [23883791] **1973**

ENGINEERING MANPOWER BULLETIN (US/0013-8037) [02260760] **1973**

ENGINEERING MATERIALS *CEASED.* (UK/0967-7003) **1973**

ENGINEERING MATERIALS SERIES (US) **1973**

ENGINEERING NEWS (CALCUTTA) (II/0376-8872) [02246024] **1973**

ENGINEERING OPTICS : AN INSTITUTE OF PHYSICS JOURNAL *CEASED.* (UK/0952-8911) [19252768] **1973**

ENGINEERING OPTIMIZATION (UK/0305-215X) [02241619] **1973**

ENGINEERING OUTLOOK (US/0013-8088) [01567917] **1973**

ENGINEERING PAPERS *CEASED.* (UK) [20304567] **2023**

ENGINEERING PLASTICS (UK/0952-6900) [19055037] **4455**

ENGINEERING PLASTICS GUIDE (UK) [03062684] **4455**

ENGINEERING REPORT (SZ) **1974**

ENGINEERING RESEARCH CENTRES : A WORLD DIRECTORY OF ORGANIZATIONS & PROGRAMMES (UK) **1974**

ENGINEERING RESEARCH HIGHLIGHTS (US/0149-0605) [03416054] **1974**

ENGINEERING RESEARCH REPORT *See* REPORT - BROWN UNIVERSITY. DIVISION OF ENGINEERING **1993**

ENGINEERING SALARIES : SPECIAL INDUSTRY REPORT *See* ENGINEERS' SALARIES : SPECIAL INDUSTRY REPORT **1974**

ENGINEERING SALARIES SURVEY / PREPARED BY D. DIETRICH ASSOCIATES, INC (US) [29693713] 1667, **1974**

●ENGINEERING SCIENCE AND EDUCATION JOURNAL (UK/0963-7346) [26628688] **1974**

ENGINEERING SCIENCES DATA UNIT, LTD *See* INDEX - ENGINEERING SCIENCES DATA UNIT **1977**

ENGINEERING SCIENCES DATA UNIT : SUBSERIES AERODYNAMICS (UK) **1974**

ENGINEERING SCIENCES DATA UNIT : SUBSERIES FLUID MECHANICS INTERNAL FLOW (UK) **2089**

ENGINEERING SCIENCES DATA UNIT. SUBSERIES PERFORMANCE AND REVISION SERVICE (UK) **1974**

ENGINEERING SCIENCES DATA UNIT. SUBSERIES TRANSONIC AERODYNAMICS AND REVISION SERVICE (UK) **1974**

ENGINEERING, SCIENTIFIC AND TECHNICAL SALARY SURVEY (US/0093-5735) [01792169] **1974**

ENGINEERING SERVICES LABORATORY (U.S.) *See* ESL-TR (UNITED STATES. AIR FORCE. AIR FORCE ENGINEERING AND SERVICES CENTER. ENGINEERING AND SERVICES LABORATORY) **5103**

ENGINEERING SERVICES MANAGEMENT (UK/0951-7871) [I09517871] **1974**

ENGINEERING SOCIETIES LIBRARY *See* PERIODICALS CURRENTLY RECEIVED **2006**

ENGINEERING SOCIETIES LIBRARY. ACQUISITIONS DEPT *See* SELECTED ACQUISITIONS - ENGINEERING SOCIETIES LIBRARY. ACQUISITIONS DEPT **1996**

ENGINEERING STRUCTURES (UK/0141-0296) [04509038] **2023**

ENGINEERING TECHNICAL PUBLICATIONS *See* TECHNICAL REPORT - UNIVERSITY OF GUELPH, SCHOOL OF ENGINEERING **1998**

ENGINEERING TECHNOLOGY (US) [08913017] **1974**

ENGINEERING ; THE NEWSLETTER OF ENGINEERING AT CLEMSON UNIVERSITY (US) [04021215] **1974**

ENGINEERING TIMES (WASHINGTON, D.C.) (US/0195-6876) [05584971] **1974**

ENGINEERING TRANSACTIONS (PL) **1974**

ENGINEERING TROUBLESHOOTING (US) [08730709] **1974**

ENGINEERING WITH COMPUTERS (US/0177-0667) [11308430] 1233, **1974**

●ENGINEERING WORKFORCE BULLETIN / EWC AAES (US) [28171379] **1974**

ENGINEERING WORLD (LONDON, ENGLAND) (UK) [21570945] **1974**

ENGINEERS AND ENGINES MAGAZINE (US/0013-8142) [04074526] **158**

●ENGINEERS AUSTRALIA (AT) [28542552] **1974**

ENGINEERS AUSTRALIA (AT/1032-1195) [18494791] **1974**

ENGINEERS' CLUB OF ST. LOUIS *See* JOURNAL OF THE ENGINEERS' CLUB OF ST. LOUIS. A MONTHLY PERIODICAL DEVOTED TO THE INTERESTS OF THE ENGINEERING PROFESSION IN ST. LOUIS **1983**

ENGINEER'S DIGEST (WILLOW GROVE) (US/0199-0101) [06803016] **1974**

ENGINEERS JOINT COUNCIL. ENGINEERING MANPOWER COMMISSION *See* ENGINEERING AND TECHNOLOGY GRADUATES **5103**

ENGINEERS' SALARIES : SPECIAL INDUSTRY REPORT (US/0071-0415) [05852436] **1974**

ENGLAND DEMOCRAT, THE (US) [25119925] **5631**

ENGLAND'S FINEST LOGIC PROBLEMS (US/1062-2950) [25571180] **4860**

ENGLERA (GW/0170-4818) [07070890] **509**

ENGLEWOOD HERALD, THE (US/1058-9899) [24238877] **5642**

ENGLEWOOD SUN TIMES *See* SUN HERALD (ENGLEWOOD ED.) **5651**

ENGLISCH (GW/0013-8185) [06571529] **3278**

ENGLISCH AMERIKANISCHE STUDIEN (GW/0172-1992) [06661928] **3384**

ENGLISH (UK) [06153060] **3384**

ENGLISH. A NEW LANGUAGE (AT/0425-0435) [01567931] **3278**

ENGLISH ACADEMY REVIEW, THE (SA) [12229289] **3384**

ENGLISH ALIVE (SA) [06482354] **2487**

ENGLISH AND AMERICAN STUDIES IN GERMAN; SUMMARIES OF THESES AND MONOGRAPHS (GW) [01567933] 3384, **3278**

ENGLISH & MEDIA MAGAZINE, THE (UK) 1110, **3278**

ENGLISH ASSOCIATION (GREAT BRITAIN) *See* ESSAYS AND STUDIES (LONDON) **3385**

ENGLISH — Alphabetical Title Index

ENGLISH AUDIO REVIEWS ENGLISH ED (FR/1141-5134) [I11415134] **3692**

ENGLISH DAILY BULLETIN *See* SUNA **2644**

ENGLISH DANCE AND SONG (UK/0013-8231) [01567940] **384**

ENGLISH EDUCATION (US/0007-8204) [01567942] 3278, **1894**

ENGLISH FOR SPECIFIC PURPOSES (NEW YORK, N.Y.) (US/0889-4906) [13909329] **3278**

ENGLISH GENEALOGICAL HELPER (US/0361-7157) [02247064] **2446**

ENGLISH GOETHE SOCIETY *See* PAPERS READ BEFORE THE SOCIETY **3422**

ENGLISH HERITAGE MONITOR (UK/0260-0420) [I02600420] 2686, **2515**

ENGLISH HISTORICAL REVIEW, THE (UK/0013-8266) [02207424] **2615**

ENGLISH IN AFRICA (SA/0376-8902) [02241051] **3384**

ENGLISH IN AOTEAROA (NZ/0113-7867) [I01137867] **1894**

ENGLISH IN AUSTRALIA (AT/0155-2147) [10468596] 1894, **3279**

ENGLISH IN EDUCATION (UK/0425-0494) [00809712] 1894, **3279**

ENGLISH JOURNAL (US/0013-8274) [01325886] 3279, **1894**

ENGLISH LANGUAGE AND ORIENTATION PROGRAMS IN THE UNITED STATES (US/0071-0601) [06719767] **3279**

ENGLISH LANGUAGE NOTES (US/0013-8282) [01567963] **3342**

ENGLISH LANGUAGE RESEARCH JOURNAL *CEASED.* (UK/0265-847X) [10495525] **1294**

ENGLISH LANGUAGE TEACHING DOCUMENTS *See* DEVELOPMENTS IN ENGLISH LANGUAGE TEACHING **1735**

ENGLISH LANGUAGE TEACHING DOCUMENTS *See* REVIEW IN ENGLISH LANGUAGE TEACHING **1779**

ENGLISH LANGUAGE TEACHING JOURNAL (US/0307-8337) [11824007] **3279**

ENGLISH LEADERSHIP QUARTERLY (US/1054-1578) [22770035] 3279, **1863**

ENGLISH LINGUISTICS : JOURNAL OF THE ENGLISH LINGUISTIC SOCIETY OF JAPAN (JA) [19580839] **3279**

ENGLISH LITERARY RENAISSANCE (US/0013-8312) [01000078] **3342**

ENGLISH LITERATURE IN TRANSITION, 1880-1920 (US/0013-8339) [01567967] **3342**

ENGLISH (LONDON) (UK/0013-8215) [01567932] **3384**

ENGLISH MAGAZINE *See* ENGLISH & MEDIA MAGAZINE, THE **3278**

ENGLISH MANUSCRIPT STUDIES, 1100-1700 (US) [19601261] **3384**

ENGLISH MISCELLANY *SUSPENDED.* (IT/0425-0575) [01567969] **3384**

ENGLISH NEWS (US) [05050242] **1744**

ENGLISH NOVEL EXPLICATION. SUPPLEMENT (US) [07963341] **3384**

ENGLISH PAGES (BE/0771-1034) [I07711034] **3209**

ENGLISH PLACE-NAME SOCIETY *See* PUBLICATIONS - ENGLISH PLACE-NAME SOCIETY **2574**

ENGLISH PLACE-NAME SOCIETY *See* JOURNAL - THE ENGLISH PLACE-NAME SOCIETY **2695**

ENGLISH QUARTERLY, THE (CN/0013-8355) [02006448] **1894**

ENGLISH RECORD, THE (US/0013-8363) [02446724] **1744**

ENGLISH REVIEW OXFORD (UK/0955-8950) [I09558950] **3279**

ENGLISH RIDER (CN/1182-9958) [23598350] **2798**

ENGLISH STUDIES (NE/0013-838X) [01567978] **3384**

ENGLISH STUDIES IN AFRICA (SA/0013-8398) [01567979] **3384**

ENGLISH STUDIES SERIES (UK) [05883086] 3384, **3279**

ENGLISH STUDIES. TRANSLATION SUPPLEMENT (NE) [05517924] **3279**

ENGLISH TEACHERS ASSOCIATION NEWSLETTER (AT) **1894**

ENGLISH TEACHERS ASSOCIATION OF NEW SOUTH WALES *See* TEACHING OF ENGLISH **1907**

ENGLISH TEACHERS' JOURNAL (ISRAEL) / MINISTRY OF EDUCATION AND CULTURE, PEDAGOGICAL SECRETARIAT (IS/0333-533X) [15789096] **3279**

ENGLISH TEACHING GUIDANCE *See* ENGLISH TEACHERS' JOURNAL (ISRAEL) / MINISTRY OF EDUCATION AND CULTURE, PEDAGOGICAL SECRETARIAT **3279**

ENGLISH TODAY (UK/0266-0784) [11908022] **3279**

ENGLISH TOURIST BOARD *See* ANNUAL REPORT - ENGLISH TOURIST BOARD **5461**

ENGLISH TRANSLATIONS OF GERMAN STANDARDS CATALOGUE / ISSUED BY DIN DEUTSCHES INSTITUT FUER NORMUNG E.V (GW/0936-0530) [18617510] **4030**

ENGLISH TRANSLATIONS OF SELECTED TAXONOMIC PAPERS IN NEMATOLOGY (US) [11607656] **5582**

ENGLISH USAGE IN SOUTHERN AFRICA (SA/0046-2098) [01968712] **3279**

ENGLISH WESTERNERS' TALLY SHEET (UK/0013-841X) [02539557] **2732**

ENGLISH WHITE PAPER / SOCIAL & LIBERAL DEMOCRATS (UK) [21015975] **4473**

ENGLISH WORLD-WIDE (NE/0172-8865) [08101614] **3279**

ENGRAVERS JOURNAL, THE (US/0099-0043) [02242809] 4001, **4564**

ENHANCED ENERGY RECOVERY NEWS (US/0271-7085) [06680428] **1943**

ENHANCED OIL-RECOVERY FIELD REPORTS *CEASED.* (US/0160-337X) [03486171] **4255**

ENHANCED SERVICES OUTLOOK *See* INFORMATION NETWORKS **1113**

ENI GROUP IN ..., THE (IT) [21056004] **4255**

ENID MORNING NEWS, THE (US) [12101153] **5732**

ENIGMA VARIATIONS NEWS *SUSPENDED.* (UK/0951-2721) [I09512721] 3164, **4043**

ENITHARMON PRESS GISSING SERIES (UK) [06673827] **2487**

ENJEU - ENJEU ET ENVIRONNEMENT JEUNESSE (CN/0833-8000) [15992732] **2215**

ENJEUX (FR/0223-4866) [07185490] **4030**

ENJEUX NAMUR (BE/0771-6532) [I07716532] **1894**

ENJINE! ENJINE! (US/0362-2487) [02441471] **2288**

ENLACE (AMERICAN ASSOCIATION OF TEACHERS OF SPANISH AND PORTUGUESE) (US) [15860910] **1744**

ENLACE (MEXICO CITY, MEXICO : 1980) (MX) [09391577] **1744**

ENLACE (WASHINGTON, D.C. 1991) (US/1059-6402) [24652170] **1488**

ENLB, EMERGENCY NURSE LEGAL BULLETIN (US/0098-1516) [01389251] **3855**

●ENLIGHTENED EATING NEWSLETTER (US) **2597**

ENLIGHTENMENT AND DISSENT (UK/0262-7612) [08780129] **4473**

ENNAANIN ETTO (XE/1061-4435) [25325203] **2615**

ENNAKKOTIEDOT KORKEAKOULUISSA SUORITETUISTA TUTKINNOISTA JA HYVAKSYTYISTA TOHTORINVAITOSKIRJOISTA (FI/0355-2268) [03942747] **1822**

ENNAKKOTIEDOT SUORITETUISTA KORKEAKOULUTUTKINNOISTA JA HYVAKSYTYISTA VAITOSKIRJOISTA (FI) [03304684] **1894**

ENNAKKOTIETOJA ORKEAKOULUOPISKELIHAIM LUKUMAARASTA (FI) [03352506] **1822**

ENNAKKOTIETOJA TEOLLISUUDESTA / TILASTOKESKUS (FI/0785-4218) [20920948] **5326**

ENNAKKOTIETOJA TUTKIMUS- JA KEHIITTAMISTOIMINNASTA SUOMESSA (FI) [02242801] **1560**

●ENNEIGRAM EDUCATOR (US) 5029, **4586**

ENNEMI, L' (FR) [07317839] **319**

ENNIS DAILY NEWS, THE (US/8755-9056) [11449958] **5749**

ENNIS WEEKLY LOCAL, THE (US) [14201421] **5749**

ENNUI (CN/0228-1244) [06858710] **319**

ENOCH PRATT FREE LIBRARY, BALTIMORE *See* STAFF REPORTER **3251**

ENOJI YONGU (KO) [08998191] **1943**

ENONCES DE PRINCIPE - ASSOCIATION CANADIENNE DES AUTOMOBILISTES (CN/0225-9222) [06183730] **5414**

ENOTECNICO, L' (IT/0392-176X) [I0392176X] **5103**

ENOTRIA (IT) [01214658] **2367**

ENQUETE ANNUELLE DE BRANCHE. INGENIERIE, ETUDES ET CONSEILS / MINISTERE DE L'INDUSTRIE ET DE LA RECHERCHE, SERVICE D'ETUDE DES STRATEGIES ET DES STATISTIQUES INDUSTRIELLES (FR/0244-7118) [12120038] 1974, **2004**

ENQUETE ANNUELLE D'ENTERPRISE : MATERIEL DE MANUTENTION, MATERIEL POUR LES MINES, LA SIDERURGIE, LE GENIE CIVIL (FR) [06831231] **1974**

ENQUETE ANNUELLE D'ENTREPRISE. LES ENTREPRISES DE PUBLICITE EN ... (FR) [10052591] **759**

ENQUETE ANNUELLE D'ENTREPRISE. PREMIERS RESULTATS PAR SECTEUR D'ENTREPRISES (FR) [07961937] **1560**

ENQUETE ANNUELLE D'ENTREPRISE. TEXTILES, HABILLEMENT, CUIR, PAPIER, BOIS, INDUSTRIES DIVERSES / MINISTERE DE L'INDUSTRIE, STISI, DIRECTION GENERALE DES STRATEGIES INDUSTRIELLES, SERVICE DU TRAITEMENT DE L'INFORMATION ET DES STATISTIQUES INDUSTRIELLES, CENTRE D'ENQUETES STATISTIQUES DE CAEN (FR) [10225452] **1560**

ENQUETE ANNUELLE D'ENTREPRISE : TRAVAIL DES METAUX (FR) [06840115] **4001**

ENQUETE ANNUELLE D'ENTREPRISES (FR) [20955521] **5381**

ENQUETE PAR SONDAGE SUR LES PRODUCTIONS DE CEREALES DANS L'OISE (FR) [02622554] **170**

ENQUETE PERMANENTE SUR L'UTILISATION DES VEHICULES DE TRANSPORT EN COMMUN DE PERSONNES EN ... / DEPARTEMENT DES STATISTIQUES DES TRANSPORTS (FR) [07393344] **5381**

ENQUETE-SALAIRES (1981) (CN/0711-5318) [08781384] **1667**

ENQUETE SOCIO-ECONOMIQUE (BE) [05109573] **4562**

ENQUETE SUR L'EMPLOI (FR) [05672315] **1667**

ENQUETE SUR L'EMPLOI ET LA REMUNERATION (CN/0842-2192) [02601107] **1667**

ENQUETES DU MUSEE DE LA VIE WALLONNE (BE/0773-4980) [04250842] **2615**

ENQUETES ET DOCUMENTS / CENTRE DE RECHERCHES SUR L'HISTOIRE DU MONDE ATLANTIQUE, UNIVERSITE DE NANTES (FR/0983-2424) [13474031] **2686**

ENQUETES ET DOCUMENTS D'HISTOIRE AFRICAINE (BE) [03967852] **2639**

ENQUIRER-GAZETTE, THE (US) [20058651] **5686**

ENR (US/0891-9526) [15041368] **1975**

ENR DIRECTORY OF CONTRACTORS *See* ENR DIRECTORY OF CONTRACTORS. WEST REGION **614**

ENR DIRECTORY OF CONTRACTORS *See* ENR DIRECTORY OF CONTRACTORS. MIDWEST REGION **614**

ENR DIRECTORY OF CONTRACTORS *See* ENR DIRECTORY OF CONTRACTORS. SOUTH REGION **614**

●ENR DIRECTORY OF CONTRACTORS. MIDWEST REGION (US/1065-2205) [25224396] **614**

●ENR DIRECTORY OF CONTRACTORS. SOUTH REGION (US/1065-2213) [25257913] **614**

●ENR DIRECTORY OF CONTRACTORS. WEST REGION (US/1065-2183) [25257842] **614**

ENR DIRECTORY OF DESIGN FIRMS (US/0098-6305) [02167338] 614, **1975**

ENRAHONAR (SP/0211-402X) [08106658] **4345**

ENRICH! (US) **671**

ENROLLMENT AND STAFF IN CALIFORNIA'S PRIVATE ELEMENTARY SCHOOLS AND HIGH SCHOOLS (US) [07699096] **1863**

ENROLLMENT IN CALIFORNIA'S PRIVATE ELEMENTARY SCHOOLS AND HIGH SCHOOLS (US) [05922963] **1744**

ENROLLMENT IN FLORIDA'S INSTITUTIONS OF HIGHER LEARNING (US) [01329086] **1822**

ENROLLMENT INFORMATION & PLAN COMPARISON CHART FOR CSRS/FERS ANNUITANTS *See* FEHB GUIDE FOR CSRS/FERS ANNUITANTS **2880**

ENROLLMENT INFORMATION & PLAN COMPARISON CHART. OPEN SEASON FOR FEDERAL CIVILIAN EMPLOYEES *See* FEHB GUIDE. OPEN SEASON FOR FEDERAL CIVILIAN EMPLOYEES / FEDERAL EMPLOYEES HEALTH BENEFITS PROGRAM **2880**

ENROLLMENT INFORMATION & PLAN COMPARISON CHART. OPEN SEASON FOR FEDERAL CIVILIAN EMPLOYEES *See* FEHB GUIDE. OPEN SEASON FOR FEDERAL CIVILIAN EMPLOYEES / FEDERAL EMPLOYEES HEALTH BENEFITS PROGRAM (LARGE PRINT EDITION) **2880**

ENROLLMENT INFORMATION & PLAN COMPARISON CHART. OPEN SEASON FOR FEDERAL CIVILIAN EMPLOYEES IN POSITIONS OUTSIDE THE CONTINENTAL UNITED STATES See FEHB GUIDE. OPEN SEASON FOR FEDERAL CIVILIAN EMPLOYEES IN POSITIONS OUTSIDE THE CONTINENTAL UNITED STATES / FEDERAL EMPLOYEES HEALTH BENEFITS PROGRAM **2880**

ENROLLMENT INFORMATION & PLAN COMPARISON CHART. OPEN SEASON FOR INDIVIDUALS ELIGIBLE TO ENROLL FOR TEMPORARY CONTINUATION OF COVERAGE, COVERAGE UNDER THE SPOUSE EQUITY LAW OR SIMILAR STATUTES PROVDING COVERAGE TO FORMER SPOUSES See FEHB GUIDE. OPEN SEASON FOR INDIVIDUALS ELIGIBLE TO ENROLL FOR TEMPORARY CONTINUATION OF COVERAGE, COVERAGE UNDER THE SPOUSE EQUITY LAW OR SIMILAR STATUTES PROVIDING COVERAGE TO FORMER SPOUSES / FEDERAL EMPLOYEES HEALTH BENEFITS PROGRAM **2880**

ENROLLMENT INFORMATION & PLAN COMPARISON CHART. OPEN SEASON FOR INDIVIDUALS RECEIVING COMPENSATION FROM THE OFFICE OF WORKERS' COMPENSATION PROGRAMS (OWCP) See FEHB GUIDE. OPEN SEASON FOR INDIVIDUALS RECEIVING COMPENSATION FROM THE OFFICE OF WORKERS' COMPENSATION PROGRAMS (OWCP) **2880**

ENROLLMENT INFORMATION & PLAN COMPARISON CHART. OPEN SEASON FOR RETIREMENT SYSTEMS PARTICIPATING IN THE FEDERAL EMPLOYEES HEALTH BENEFITS PROGRAM See FEHB GUIDE. OPEN SEASON FOR RETIREMENT SYSTEMS PARTICIPATING IN THE FEDERAL EMPLOYEES HEALTH BENEFITS PROGRAM **2880**

ENROLLMENT INFORMATION & PLAN COMPARISON CHART. OPEN SEASON FOR UNITED STATES POSTAL SERVICE EMPLOYEES See FEHB GUIDE. OPEN SEASON FOR UNITED STATES POSTAL SERVICE EMPLOYEES / FEDERAL EMPLOYEES HEALTH BENEFITS PROGRAM **2880**

ENROLLMENT OF CHILDREN IN EDUCATIONALLY HANDICAPPED PROGRAMS IN EXCESS OF LEGAL LIMITATION (US/0145-2193) [02711730] **1878**

ENROLLMENT REPORT (US) [05039802] **1822**

ENROLLMENT REPORT OF APPRENTICES IN CALIFORNIA PUBLIC SECONDARY AND ADULT SCHOOLS AND COMMUNITY COLLEGES (US/0099-2178) [02243671] **1913**

ENROLLMENTS IN EDUCATIONAL PROGRAMS OPERATED BY THE DEPARTMENT OF HEALTH AND SOCIAL SERVICES, THE DEPARTMENT OF CORRECTION, AND THE DEPARTMENT OF SERVICES FOR CHILDREN, YOUTH, AND THEIR FAMILIES (US) [15046197] 5284, **1878**

ENROUTE (CN/0703-0312) [02442418] 5469, **2533**

ENROUTE HIGH ALTITUDE, U.S (US) [04508563] **18**

ENROUTE HIGH ALTITUDE CHARTS (CN) **18**

ENROUTE LOW ALTITUDE CHARTS (CN) **18**

ENSAIOS FEE (BL/0101-1723) [09962059] **1488**

ENSAYOS ECIEL (BL/0102-0617) [02386650] **1488**

ENSAYOS ECONOMICOS (AG/0325-3937) [03930156] **1591**

ENSAYOS SOBRE POLITICA ECONOMICA : DOCUMENTOS DE TRABAJO (CK) [09152030] **1560**

ENSEIGNANTS (MONTREAL) (CN/0046-2101) [19339106] **1744**

ENSEIGNEMENT (FR) **1744**

ENSEIGNEMENT DES SCIENCES See COLLECTION ENSEIGNEMENT DES SCIENCES **5095**

ENSEIGNEMENT DU RUSSE, L' (FR/0300-2608) [06678489] **3279**

ENSEIGNEMENT ET GESTION (PARIS) (FR/0765-7579) [06678009] **866**

ENSEIGNEMENT ET LA PEDAGOGIE EN ROUMANIE, L' (RM) [06140579] **1744**

ENSEIGNEMENT MATHEMATIQUE (FR/0013-8584) [02100735] 1744, **3505**

ENSEIGNEMENT MUSICAL (FR) [09331457] **4116**

ENSEIGNEMENT PHILOSOPHIQUE, L' (FR/0986-1653) [I09861653] **4365**

●ENSEIGNEMENT SUPERIEUR & RECHERCHE PARIS (FR/1248-2722) [I12482722] **1605**

ENSEIGNEMENT TECHNIQUE PARIS. 1938, L' (FR/0184-6906) [I01846906] **1894**

ENSEIGNEMENTS TECHNIQUES: TECHNIQUE INDUSTRIELLES See TECHNIQUES INDUSTRIELLES **3488**

ENSEMBLE (CN/0842-8409) [19451391] **4956**

ENSEMBLE (IT/0997-0274) [I09970274] **1744**

ENSEMBLE (US) **384**

●ENSEMBLE - CONFERENCE BOARD OF CANADA. NATIONAL BUSINESS AND EDUCATION CENTRE (CN/1188-8482) [26714901] 671, **1744**

ENSEMBLE D'AQUARELLES ET DE DESSINS DE MAITRES SUISSES ET FRANCAIS DU XIXE ET DU XXE SIECLE, UN (FR) [05285276] **349**

ENSEMBLE (LACHINE) (CN/0705-5005) [04079630] **3780**

ENSEMBLE (SANTA ANA, CALIF.) (US/1054-4690) [22895454] **5364**

ENSEMBLES DER DEUTSCHEN DEMOKRATISCHEN REPUBLIK (GW) [02441485] **384**

ENSENANZA DE LAS CIENCIAS (SP/0212-4521) [I02124521] **5103**

ENSENANZA DE LAS CIENCIAS : REVISTA DE INVESTIGACION Y EXPERIENCIAS DIDACTICAS (SP) **1894**

ENSENANZA E INVESTIGACION EN PSICOLOGIA (MX/0185-1594) [05082278] **4586**

ENSHO (JA/0389-4290) [10314742] **3574**

ENSIGN CLASS ASSOCIATION See YEARBOOK - ENSIGN CLASS ASSOCIATION **4931**

ENSIGN (SALT LAKE CITY, UTAH) (US/0884-1136) [12229153] **5059**

ENSIGN (SAN MATEO, CALIF.), THE (US/0744-3129) [08178072] **593**

ENSKILDA FORSAKRINGSANSTALTER See ENSKILDA FORSAKRINGSFORETAG **2897**

ENSKILDA FORSAKRINGSFORETAG (SW) [13429047] 2879, **2897**

●ENTDECKEN SIE BRITISCH KOLUMBIEN, KANADA (CN/1189-4911) [26715021] **5469**

ENTE NAZIONALE IDROCARBURI See ENI GROUP IN ..., THE **4255**

ENTE OTTAWA MEDIEVALE DI ORTE (SERIES) (IT) [20475645] **2615**

ENTE RASSEGNE MUSICALI N.S. DI LORETO (IT) [12199700] **4116**

ENTENDRE (CN/0318-9139) [02441912] **4387**

ENTENTE EUROPEENNE POUR L'ENVIRONNEMENT PARIS **CEASED**. (FR/1143-4627) [I11434627] **2192**

ENTER WARSZAWA (PL) [I08674566] **1184**

ENTEROVIRUS SURVEILLANCE (US/0734-3531) [08610171] **3574**

ENTERPRISE (US) **2487**

ENTERPRISE (CN/0013-8657) [01776594] **2533**

ENTERPRISE (SA) [29608566] **671**

ENTERPRISE AND DEVELOPMENT / UNITED STATES COUNCIL FOR INTERNATIONAL BUSINESS (US) [09690820] **672**

ENTERPRISE AND DISPATCH (US) [21028931] **5695**

ENTERPRISE (BOARDMAN, OR.), THE (US/0747-4067) [10810468] **5733**

ENTERPRISE (BRISTOL, N.H.) See RECORD ENTERPRISE (PLYMOUTH, N.H.), THE **5709**

ENTERPRISE (BROCKTON, MASS.) (US/0744-2114) [08117025] **5688**

ENTERPRISE COMMUNICATIONS (US) **1110**

ENTERPRISE-COURIER (US) [19983638] **5703**

ENTERPRISE DSI INFODISK (US) **1184**

ENTERPRISE (FALMOUTH, MASS.), THE (US/0747-0142) [10473846] **5688**

ENTERPRISE FARMING **CEASED**. (UK) **82**

ENTERPRISE INTEGRATION STRATEGIES (US) **3478**

ENTERPRISE-JOURNAL (MCCOMB, MISS.) (US) [15648876] **5700**

ENTERPRISE LEDGER (ENTERPRISE, ALA. : 1977) (US) [12593888] **5626**

ENTERPRISE NEWS (PIXLEY, CALIF.) **CEASED.** (US/0888-0212) [13449573] **5635**

ENTERPRISE-PILOT See RECORD PILOT **5720**

ENTERPRISE (PONCHATOULA, LA.) (US/0889-0684) [13789782] **5683**

ENTERPRISE (REGINA, SASK.) (CN/0829-3473) [16080658] **1488**

ENTERPRISE (SPRING CITY, TN) **CEASED.** (US/0889-2830) [13842319] **5745**

ENTERPRISE SYSTEMS JOURNAL (US/1053-6566) [22636586] **1184**

ENTERPRISE, THE (US) [07909065] **5686**

ENTERPRISE-TOCSIN, THE (US) [15273338] **5700**

ENTERPRISE ULSTER (CORPORATION) See REPORT AND STATEMENT OF ACCOUNTS - ENTERPRISE ULSTER **1706**

ENTERPRISE (VANCOUVER) (CN/0319-8626) [02006483] **1542**

ENTERPRISE WEST (CN/0709-8138) [06021359] **866**

ENTERPRISE (WHITE SALMON, WASH.) (US) [13091594] **5760**

ENTERPRISER OTTAWA (CN/0709-6828) [11100267] **1606**

ENTERTAINMENT & ARTS MANAGEMENT (UK/0143-8980) [11101319] **5364**

ENTERTAINMENT AND MEDIA LAW REPORTS (UK) **2966**

ENTERTAINMENT AND SPORTS LAWYER : PUBLICATION OF THE FORUM COMMITTEE ON THE ENTERTAINMENT AND SPORTS INDUSTRIES, THE (US/0732-1880) [08320374] 384, 4894, **2966**

ENTERTAINMENT ATLANTA : YOUR HOUR-BY-HOUR GUIDE TO ENTERTAINMENT ATLANTA (US/1057-3720) [24024472] **319**

ENTERTAINMENT EMPLOYMENT NETWORK (US/1055-1131) [23077741] 384, **1667**

ENTERTAINMENT EMPLOYMENT WEEKLY (US/1055-114X) [23077706] 384, **1667**

ENTERTAINMENT INDUSTRY DIRECTORY, THE (US/0271-8014) [06672137] **384**

ENTERTAINMENT INDUSTRY OUTLOOK (US) **319**

ENTERTAINMENT LAW & FINANCE (US/0883-2455) [11939470] 384, **2966**

ENTERTAINMENT LAW REPORTER (US/0270-3831) [05108098] 384, **2966**

ENTERTAINMENT LAW REVIEW (UK/0959-3799) [I09593799] **2966**

ENTERTAINMENT LITIGATION REPORTER (US/1047-4137) [20679999] **2966**

ENTERTAINMENT MAGAZINE, THE (US/0883-1890) [12210770] **4850**

ENTERTAINMENT MARKETING LETTER (US/1048-5112) [20961423] 319, **924**

ENTERTAINMENT, PUBLISHING AND THE ARTS HANDBOOK (US/0739-1897) [09698073] **385**

ENTERTAINMENT WEEKLY (US/1049-0434) [21114137] **385**

ENTI PUBBLICI (IT) **4646**

ENTOMOFAUNA (AU/0250-4413) [07706538] **5582**

ENTOMOLOGIA EXPERIMENTALIS ET APPLICATA (NE/0013-8703) [01568001] **5607**

ENTOMOLOGIA GENERALIS (GW/0171-8177) [04670608] **5607**

ENTOMOLOGIA HELLENICA (GR/0254-5381) [13566187] **5582**

ENTOMOLOGICA (IT/0425-1016) [02945117] **5607**

ENTOMOLOGICA BASILIENSIA (SZ/0253-2484) [02900493] **5607**

ENTOMOLOGICA FENNICA (FI/0785-8760) [22576975] **5607**

ENTOMOLOGICA SCANDINAVICA (DK/0013-8711) [01568004] **5607**

ENTOMOLOGICAL NEWS (US/0013-872X) [02044369] **5607**

ENTOMOLOGICAL RESEARCH BULLETIN (KO) [23448908] **5607**

ENTOMOLOGICAL REVIEW (US/0013-8738) [01568009] **5607**

ENTOMOLOGICAL REVIEW OF JAPAN, THE (JA) [02945145] **5582**

ENTOMOLOGICAL SOCIETY OF ALBERTA See PROCEEDINGS OF THE ANNUAL MEETING OF THE ENTOMOLOGICAL SOCIETY OF ALBERTA **5612**

ENTOMOLOGICAL SOCIETY OF AMERICA See ANNALS OF THE ENTOMOLOGICAL SOCIETY OF AMERICA **5605**

ENTOMOLOGICAL SOCIETY OF BRITISH COLUMBIA See JOURNAL OF THE ENTOMOLOGICAL SOCIETY OF BRITISH COLUMBIA **5611**

ENTOMOLOGICAL SOCIETY OF CANADA (1951-) See BULLETIN - ENTOMOLOGICAL SOCIETY OF CANADA **5579**

ENTOMOLOGICAL — Alphabetical Title Index

ENTOMOLOGICAL SOCIETY OF MANITOBA See PROCEEDINGS OF THE ENTOMOLOGICAL SOCIETY OF MANITOBA **5613**

ENTOMOLOGICAL SOCIETY OF NEW ZEALAND See BULLETIN - ENTOMOLOGICAL SOCIETY OF NEW ZEALAND **5579**

ENTOMOLOGICAL SOCIETY OF ONTARIO See PROCEEDINGS OF THE ENTOMOLOGICAL SOCIETY OF ONTARIO **5595**

ENTOMOLOGICAL SOCIETY OF SOUTHERN AFRICA. JOURNAL OF THE ENTOMOLOGICAL SOCIETY OF SOUTHERN AFRICA See AFRICAN ENTOMOLOGY **5605**

ENTOMOLOGICAL SOCIETY OF WASHINGTON See PROCEEDINGS OF THE ENTOMOLOGICAL SOCIETY OF WASHINGTON **5595**

ENTOMOLOGICESKOE OBOZRENIE (RU/0367-1445) [07619241] **5582**

ENTOMOLOGICHESKIE ISSLEVDOVANIIA NA DALNEM VOSTOKE (RU) [10762149] **5582**

ENTOMOLOGIE ET PHYTOPATHOLOGIE APPLIQUEES (IR/0013-8800) [01780160] 509, **5582**

ENTOMOLOGISCHE ABHANDLUNGEN (GW/0373-8981) [05349894] **5607**

ENTOMOLOGISCHE BERICHTE LUZERN : MITTEILUNGEN DER ENTOMOLOGISCHEN GESELLSCHAFT LUZERN (SZ) [09101544] **5607**

ENTOMOLOGISCHE BERICHTEN (NE/0013-8827) [01345338] **5582**

ENTOMOLOGISCHE BLATTER FUER BIOLOGIE UND SYSTEMATIK DER KAFER (GW/0013-8835) [10522226] **5582**

ENTOMOLOGISCHE GESELLSCHAFT BASEL See MITTEILUNGEN DER ENTOMOLOGISCHEN GESELLSCHAFT BASEL **5612**

ENTOMOLOGISCHE MITTEILUNGEN AUS DEM ZOOLOGISCHEN MUSEUM HAMBURG (GW/0044-5223) [03251784] **5582**

ENTOMOLOGISCHE NACHRICHTEN UND BERICHTE (GW/0232-5535) [09495362] **5582**

ENTOMOLOGISCHE ZEITSCHRIFT MIT INSEKTENBOERSE (GW/0020-1839) [11875774] **5582**

ENTOMOLOGISK TIDSKRIFT / ENTOMOLOGISKA FORENINGEN I STOCKHOLM (SW/0013-886X) [01030570] **5608**

ENTOMOLOGISKE MEDDELELSER (DK/0013-8851) [01568046] **5608**

ENTOMOLOGIST, THE (UK/0013-8878) [07322611] **5608**

ENTOMOLOGISTE, L' (FR/0013-8886) [01568048] **5608**

ENTOMOLOGIST'S GAZETTE (UK/0013-8894) [01568051] **5608**

ENTOMOLOGIST'S MONTHLY MAGAZINE, THE (UK/0013-8908) [01568052] **5608**

ENTOMOLOGIST'S RECORD AND JOURNAL OF VARIATION, THE (UK/0013-8916) [01568053] **5582**

ENTOMOLOGY ABSTRACTS (US/0013-8924) [01568055] 5608, **5604**

ENTOMOLOGY BRANCH INSECT PEST BULLETIN (AT) [01159215] **4244**

ENTOMOLOGY CIRCULAR (US/0013-8932) [01939283] **5583**

ENTOMON (II/0377-9335) [02811620] **5608**

ENTOMOPHAGA (FR/0013-8959) [01568057] **4244**

ENTONCES (VE) [04648734] **2551**

ENTOPATH NEWS, THE (UK) [21112736] **2378**

ENTOPURAIJU (KO) [11772433] **672**

ENTOURAGE (DOWNSVIEW, ONT.) (CN/0829-8815) [13494298] **5284**

ENTRAIDE COOP (CN/0820-795X) [09467697] **1542**

ENTRAIDE GENEALOGIQUE (CN/0226-6245) [06473549] **2446**

ENTRAIDE MISSIONNAIRE, INC See BULLETIN DE L'ENTRAIDE MISSIONNAIRE **4941**

ENTRAIDE MISSIONNAIRE, INC. CONGRES See CONGRES - ENTRAIDE MISSIONNAIRE **4950**

ENTRAIDE SOCIALE, L' (CN/0711-4567) [08534437] **5784**

ENTRAINEMENTS & SYSTEMES (FR/0765-006X) [l0765006X] **2113**

ENTRAINEUR, L' CEASED. (CN/0828-4954) [12035490] **4894**

ENTRANCE REQUIREMENTS FOR DIPLOMA SCHOOLS OF NURSING AND SCHOOLS OF PRACTICAL NURSING (CN/0710-2976) [08378966] **3855**

ENTRE GENS D'ICI (CN/0713-049X) [08720381] 4721, **1744**

ENTRE-GENS, L' (CN/0704-6146) [04746895] **1542**

ENTRE LE POUCE ET L'INDEX (CN/0833-9880) [15466477] **3574**

ENTRE-NOUS - ASSOCIATION CANADIENNE DE LA DYSTROPHIE MUSCULAIRE (CN/1183-2738) [25423229] **4388**

ENTRE NOUS GENS DE BERNIERES (CN/0712-967X) [08890921] **4646**

ENTRE NOUS, LES MARTIN (CN/0711-1789) [08818729] **2446**

ENTRE NOUS (MONTREAL, QUEBEC : 1981) (CN) [10392112] **4116**

ENTRE NOUS (OTTAWA) (CN/0319-1788) [02442219] **1744**

ENTRE-NOUS - SOCIETE DES ELEVEURS DE BOVINS CANADIENS (CN/0709-8510) [06284774] **210**

ENTRE NOUS (TROIS-RIVIERES) (CN/0705-0631) [04518873] **5199**

ENTRE PARENTHESES (CN/0714-8674) [09099672] **1744**

ENTREFILET (CN/0228-071X) [07313556] **4894**

ENTREFILET (POINTE CLAIRE) (CN/0826-4546) [11193167] **2334**

ENTREFILETS (CN/0710-6211) [08124507] **4646**

ENTRELINEAS (US/0013-9017) [04914020] **298**

ENTRELLES, L' (CN/0225-5545) [06131645] **5555**

ENTRELLES (ORGANISATION) See ENTRELLES, L' **5555**

ENTREMETTEUR (CN/0225-3569) [08439980] **5784**

ENTREMISE, L' (CN/0709-4256) [06315934] **1744**

ENTREPASADOS : REVISTA DE HISTORIA (AG/0327-649X) [26142203] **2732**

ENTREPRENDRE : REVUE MENSUELLE DE LA CHAMBRE DE COMMERCE DE BRUXELLES (BE) [07312608] **833**

ENTREPRENEUR (US/0364-7218) [02658562] **672**

ENTREPRENEUR MAGAZINE (BERTRIX) (BE/0775-7239) [l07757239] **672**

● ENTREPRENEUR NEWSLETTER (US/1073-046X) [29296972] **672**

ENTREPRENEUR POTCHEFSTROOM (SA/0259-5559) [l02595559] **672**

ENTREPRENEUR (SANTA MONICA, CALIF.) (US/0163-3341) [04026654] **672**

ENTREPRENEURIAL COUPLES (US/1054-4046) [22877156] **672**

ENTREPRENEURIAL ECONOMY REVIEW, THE CEASED. (US/0899-7721) [18212104] **1488**

ENTREPRENEURIAL MANAGER'S NEWSLETTER (US/0272-0396) [06743723] **672**

ENTREPRENEURIAL WOMAN (US/1051-2624) [21317007] 672, **5555**

ENTREPRENEURSHIP AND REGIONAL DEVELOPMENT (UK/0898-5626) [17850595] **672**

● ENTREPRENEURSHIP, INNOVATION AND CHANGE (US/1059-0137) [24458830] **672**

ENTREPRENEURSHIP THEORY AND PRACTICE (US/1042-2587) [18894013] **672**

ENTREPRISE (FR) **1489**

ENTREPRISE 1951, L' (BE/0777-6357) [l07776357] **2605**

ENTREPRISE/A POUR AFFAIRES See ENTREPRISE, L' **672**

ENTREPRISE A POUR AFFAIRES ECONOMIQUES, L' (FR) **1489**

ENTREPRISE / A POUR AFFAIRES, L' (FR/1164-7027) [25843765] **672**

ENTREPRISE & CARRIERES PARIS (FR/0995-4945) [l09954945] 672, **1489**

ENTREPRISE ET LE DROIT, L' (BE/0772-5310) [07725310] **2966**

ENTREPRISE ET L'HOMME (BE) [05428760] 672, **2249**

ENTREPRISE EUROPEENNE, L' (FR) [02240012] **1606**

● ENTREPRISE, L' (FR) [29674825] **672**

ENTREPRISE (MONTREAL) (CN/0702-455X) [03053924] **672**

ENTREPRISE NETWORKING (US) **672**

ENTREPRISE (QUEBEC) (CN/0705-0542) [03980064] **866**

ENTREPRISES FORMATION (FR/0765-5762) [12881871] 1913, **4204**

ENTRETIENS D'ORAISON (CN) [02247364] **4956**

ENTRETIENS SUR L'ANTIQUITE CLASSIQUE (SZ/0071-0822) [01568059] **1076**

● ENTREZ (BETHESDA, MD.) (US/1065-707X) [26699312] **3692**

ENTREZ. REFERENCES (US/1072-3072) [28899099] **486**

ENTROPIE (FR/0013-9084) [02300547] 4430, **1975**

ENTRY (ANN ARBOR, MICH.) (US/0886-845X) [13026938] **4369**

ENTSCHEIDUNGEN DER OBERLANDESGERICHTE IN ZIVILSACHEN EINSCHLIESSLICH DER FREIWILLIGEN GERICHTSBARKEIT (GW/0425-1288) [l04251288] **2966**

ENTSCHEIDUNGEN DER OBERVERWALTUNGSGERICHTE FUER DAS LAND NORDRHEIN-WESTFALEN IN MUENSTER SOWIE FUER DIE LANDER NIEDERSACHSEN UND SCHLESWIG-HOLSTEIN IN LUENEBURG (GW/0340-8779) [l03408779] **2966**

ENTSCHEIDUNGEN DES BUNDESARBEITSGERICHTS (GW/0433-7050) [01586751] **3147**

ENTSCHEIDUNGEN DES BUNDESGERICHTSHOFES IN ZIVILSACHEN (GW) [01751146] **2966**

ENTSCHEIDUNGEN DES BUNDESPATENTGERICHTS (GW/0423-250X) [l0423250X] **2966**

ENTSCHEIDUNGEN DES BUNDESVERFASSUNGSGERICHTS (GW/0433-7646) [01751151] **2966**

ENTSCHEIDUNGEN DES BUNDESVERWALTUNGSGERICHT (GW/0013-9106) [01751152] **2966**

ENTSCHEIDUNGEN DES PREUSSISCHEN OBERVERWALTUNGSGERICHTS. HRSG. VON JEBENS ... UND VON MEYEREN (GE) [01775905] **2966**

ENTSCHEIDUNGEN IN ARBEITSRECHTSSACHEN (GW) [05725526] **2966**

ENTSORGUNGSPRAXIS (GW/0724-6870) [l07246870] **2165**

ENTWICKLUNG + LANDLICHER RAUM (GW/0343-6462) [l03436462] **82**

ENTWICKLUNGSLANDER-STUDIEN / DEUTSCHE STIFTUNG FUER ENTWICKLUNGSLANDER (GW) [02044679] **415**

ENTWICKLUNGSPOLITIK; JAHRESBERICHT (GW) [06870506] **1560**

ENU NO KUNI (JA) [04346029] **2650**

ENUMCLAW COURIER-HERALD (US) [17216165] **5760**

ENVIO (NQ/0259-4374) [11655285] **2732**

ENVIOS (US/0091-522X) [01787415] **3384**

ENVIRO (SW/1101-7341) [24083735] **2228**

ENVIRO/ENERGYLINE ABSTRACTS PLUS See ENVIRONMENT ABSTRACTS [COMPUTER FILE] **2184**

ENVIRO/ENERGYLINE ABSTRACTS PLUS (US/1076-6464) [25719546] **2184**

ENVIROACTION : ENVIRONMENTAL DIGEST OF THE NATIONAL WILDLIFE FEDERATION (US) [23353445] **3110**

ENVIROBUSINESS REPORT (US/1059-390X) [24581947] 672, **2165**

ENVIROFAX (US) **2165**

ENVIROLINE (CALGARY) (CN/0847-4524) [21485566] **2165**

ENVIROLINE (FINDLAY, OHIO) (US/1072-2416) [28893406] 5381, **2165**

ENVIROLINE USER'S MANUAL CEASED. (US/0270-0751) [05192425] **2228**

ENVIRON (FORT COLLINS, COLO.) (US/0883-9719) [12267432] **5199**

ENVIRONEWS SHREWSBURY (UK/0962-4740) [l09624740] **2165**

ENVIRONMENT ABSTRACTS (US/0093-3287) [01792323] 2165, **2184**

ENVIRONMENT ABSTRACTS ANNUAL (US/0000-1198) [07298964] 2165, **2184**

● ENVIRONMENT ABSTRACTS [COMPUTER FILE] (US) [30117125] 2192, **2184**

ENVIRONMENT & ART LETTER (US/1040-6611) [18492936] **349**

ENVIRONMENT AND BEHAVIOR (US/0013-9165) [01568065] 5244, **2215**

● ENVIRONMENT & DEVELOPMENT / APA, AMERICAN PLANNING ASSOCIATION (US/1066-954X) [25403680] 4837, **2165**

ENVIRONMENT & ECOLOGY (II/0970-0420) [15242176] 82, **454**

ENVIRONMENT & INDUSTRY DIGEST (UK/0958-2126) [l09582126] **2192**

ENVIRONMENT AND INDUSTRY DIGEST NEWSLETTER See ENVIRONMENT, TECHNOLOGY AND INDUSTRY **2166**

ENVIRONMENTAL

ENVIRONMENT & PLANNING A (UK/0308-518X) [01945034] **2821**

ENVIRONMENT AND PLANNING. B, PLANNING & DESIGN (UK/0265-8135) [10070935] **2821**

ENVIRONMENT AND PLANNING. C, GOVERNMENT & POLICY (UK/0263-774X) [09343642] **4646**

ENVIRONMENT AND PLANNING. D, SOCIETY & SPACE (UK/0263-7758) [09432992] **5199**

ENVIRONMENT & PUBLIC SAFETY TODAY (CN/1182-9745) [23659144] **4774**

ENVIRONMENT & REGION (BG) [08407016] **1560**

ENVIRONMENT AND URBANIZATION (UK/0956-2478) [22223760] **2165**

ENVIRONMENT BRAZIL (UK) **2165**

ENVIRONMENT BUSINESS (UK/0959-7042) [22935414] **2165**

●ENVIRONMENT BUSINESS MAGAZINE (UK/1352-8882) [31048608] 3478, **2228**

●ENVIRONMENT CONNECTIONS (US/1064-7422) [26387342] **2165**

ENVIRONMENT COUNCIL OF ALBERTA *See* BULLETIN - ENVIRONMENT COUNCIL OF ALBERTA **2162**

ENVIRONMENT COUNCIL OF CANADA. PUBLIC ADVISORY COMMITTEE ON THE ENVIRONMENT *See* PROCEEDINGS OF THE ANNUAL JOINT MEETING OF THE PUBLIC ADVISORY COMMITTEE ON THE ENVIRONMENT AND THE ENVIRONMENT COUNCIL OF ALBERTA **2239**

ENVIRONMENT DAILY (ARLINGTON, VA.) *CEASED.* (US/1058-3955) [24291253] **2165**

ENVIRONMENT DIGEST (UK/0951-5100) [I09515100] **2165**

●ENVIRONMENT ENCYCLOPEDIA AND DIRECTORY, THE (UK) 2165, **1925**

ENVIRONMENT FILM REVIEW *CEASED.* (US/0090-0486) [01783673] **2165**

ENVIRONMENT (GUILFORD) (US/0272-9008) [06635613] **2165**

ENVIRONMENT HAWAII (US/1050-3285) [21463126] **2165**

ENVIRONMENT, HEALTH & SAFETY MANAGEMENT (US/1053-9190) [22690090] **4774**

ENVIRONMENT INFORMATION BULLETIN (UK/0964-5322) [I09645322] **2165**

ENVIRONMENT INSTITUTE OF AUSTRALIA NEWSLETTER (AT/1030-1429) [I10301429] **2165**

ENVIRONMENT INTERNATIONAL (UK/0160-4120) [04079573] 4774, **2165**

ENVIRONMENT LAW BRIEF (UK) **2966**

ENVIRONMENT LIBRARY (US/1049-7404) [21356864] **2165**

ENVIRONMENT LIBRARY ACQUISITIONS LIST - NEW BRUNSWICK. DEPT. OF THE ENVIRONMENT. LIBRARY (CN/1182-8935) [23264739] **3209**

ENVIRONMENT MATTERS (UK) [22926262] **2165**

ENVIRONMENT MATTERS (INTERNATIONAL) (UK/0966-9272) [I09669272] **2166**

ENVIRONMENT MONTHLY, THE (US/0013-919X) [01568069] **2166**

ENVIRONMENT NEWS (BOSTON) *CEASED.* (US/0364-1317) [02529765] **2166**

ENVIRONMENT NEWS DIGEST (US) **2166**

ENVIRONMENT PROTECTION ENGINEERING (PL/0324-8828) [02441314] **2166**

ENVIRONMENT REPORTER (US/0013-9211) [01568071] **3111**

ENVIRONMENT REPORTER. CURRENT DEVELOPMENTS (US) [01537828] **2166**

ENVIRONMENT REPORTER. DECISIONS (US) [01537829] **2166**

ENVIRONMENT RISK (UK/0965-3813) [25367115] **2166**

ENVIRONMENT, SAFETY, HEALTH AT DOE FACILITIES (US/0738-3746) [09014933] **2861**

ENVIRONMENT (ST. LOUIS) (US/0013-9157) [02246130] **2228**

ENVIRONMENT (ST. LOUIS) (US/0013-9157) [05454541] **2215**

ENVIRONMENT SYSTEMS & INDUSTRIES (CN/0705-9272) [04233227] 1975, **614**

ENVIRONMENT, TECHNOLOGY AND INDUSTRY *CEASED.* (UK/0965-0482) [I09650482] **2166**

ENVIRONMENT TODAY (US/1054-7517) [21947700] **2166**

ENVIRONMENT UPDATE (CANADA. ENVIRONMENT CANADA) (CN/0714-9263) [09170547] **2228**

ENVIRONMENT VICTORIA (AT/0727-5366) [I07275366] **2192**

ENVIRONMENT VIEWS (CN/0701-9637) [04080410] **2166**

ENVIRONMENT WATCH. EAST EUROPE, RUSSIA & EURASIA (US/1063-5955) [26077385] **2166**

ENVIRONMENT WATCH- EAST EUROPE, RUSSIA & EURASIA *See* EAST/WEST EXECUTIVE GUIDE **832**

ENVIRONMENT WATCH. LATIN AMERICA (US/1060-1414) [24881253] **672**

●ENVIRONMENT WATCH. WESTERN EUROPE (US/1066-6001) [27007210] **672**

ENVIRONMENT WEEK (US/1041-8105) [18851780] **2166**

ENVIRONMENTAL ACTION (WASHINGTON, D.C.) (US/0013-922X) [00920324] **2166**

●ENVIRONMENTAL AND ECOLOGICAL STATISTICS (UK/1352-8505) 5326, **2215**

ENVIRONMENTAL AND ENERGY STUDY SPECIAL REPORTS (US) 1943, **2166**

ENVIRONMENTAL AND ENGINEERING GEOSCIENCE (US) **1375**

ENVIRONMENTAL AND EXPERIMENTAL BOTANY (UK/0098-8472) [01619613] **509**

ENVIRONMENTAL AND HEALTH CONTROLS ON LEAD (UK) **2166**

ENVIRONMENTAL & LAND USE AADMINISTRATIVE LAW REPORTER ER FALR (US/1044-7695) [19890856] **3111**

ENVIRONMENTAL AND MOLECULAR MUTAGENESIS (US/0893-6692) [15615950] **544**

ENVIRONMENTAL AND PLANNING LAW JOURNAL (AT/0813-300X) [11467147] **3111**

ENVIRONMENTAL AND RESOURCE ASSESSMENT PROGRAM; PROGRAM SUMMARY (US) [04168221] **2192**

ENVIRONMENTAL AND RESOURCE ECONOMICS (NE/0924-6460) [24441715] 1489, **2166**

ENVIRONMENTAL AND URBAN ISSUES (US/1044-033X) [17730417] 2166, **2821**

ENVIRONMENTAL & WASTE MANAGEMENT WORLD *CEASED.* (CN/0835-3778) [19916078] **2228**

ENVIRONMENTAL APPROVALS IN CANADA : PRACTICE AND PROCEDURE (CN) **3111**

ENVIRONMENTAL ASSESSMENT. ELECTRIC HYBRID VEHICLE RESEARCH, DEVELOPMENT AND DEMONSTRATION PROGRAM (US/0197-1956) [04877229] **2228**

ENVIRONMENTAL ASSESSMENT OF THE ALASKAN CONTINENTAL SHELF. ANNUAL REPORTS OF PRINCIPAL INVESTIGATORS FOR THE YEAR ENDING ... (US/0748-1527) [05721406] 4255, **2166**

ENVIRONMENTAL ASSESSMENT OF THE ALASKAN CONTINENTAL SHELF. FINAL REPORTS OF PRINCIPAL INVESTIGATORS. PHYSICAL SCIENCE STUDIES (US/0891-1053) [08516713] **2166**

ENVIRONMENTAL AUDIT ADVISER (US/0742-6062) [10384346] **2192**

ENVIRONMENTAL BIOLOGY (US/0094-7237) [02923195] 2228, **454**

ENVIRONMENTAL BIOLOGY OF FISHES (NE/0378-1909) [02986368] 2166, **2300**

●ENVIRONMENTAL BUILDING NEWS : A NEWSLETTER ON ENVIRONMENTALLY SUSTAINABLE DESIGN & CONSTRUCTION (US/1062-3957) [25610681] 2166, **614**

ENVIRONMENTAL BUSINESS JOURNAL (US/1045-8611) [20274528] **2166**

ENVIRONMENTAL BUYERS' GUIDE (US/1068-4980) [22605922] **2228**

ENVIRONMENTAL CARCINOGENESIS REVIEWS (US/0882-8164) [11984725] **3816**

●ENVIRONMENTAL CAREER DIRECTORY (US/1072-1835) [28866449] **2167**

●ENVIRONMENTAL CHANGE (US/1065-8548) [26778110] **2167**

ENVIRONMENTAL CHEMISTRY (UK/0305-7712) [02241862] **975**

ENVIRONMENTAL CLAIMS JOURNAL (US/1040-6026) [18474513] **3111**

ENVIRONMENTAL COMMUNICATOR (US/1072-1029) [28865000] **2167**

ENVIRONMENTAL COMPLIANCE. A NATIONAL SIMPLIFIED GUIDE (CN) **2228**

ENVIRONMENTAL COMPLIANCE AND LITIGATION STRATEGY (US) [29491813] **3111**

ENVIRONMENTAL COMPLIANCE CALIFORNIA. INCLUDES UPDATES (CN) **2228**

ENVIRONMENTAL COMPLIANCE (MADISON, CONN.) (US/1066-2553) [26910191] **3111**

ENVIRONMENTAL COMPLIANCE REPORT, THE (CN/1187-0125) [24860660] **3111**

ENVIRONMENTAL CONSERVATION (SZ/0376-8929) [02239976] **2193**

ENVIRONMENTAL CONSERVATION LIBRARY OF MINNESOTA *See* ECOL NEWS **2164**

ENVIRONMENTAL CONTRACT OPPORTUNITY REPORT, THE (US/1061-155X) [25193679] **2167**

ENVIRONMENTAL CONTRACTOR MAGAZINE (US/1047-336X) [20666987] 4774, **614**

ENVIRONMENTAL CONTROL NEWS FOR SOUTHERN INDUSTRY (US/0013-9238) [02763830] **2167**

ENVIRONMENTAL CONTROL TECHNOLOGY ACTIVITIES OF THE DEPARTMENT OF ENERGY (US/0192-8856) [04167680] **2167**

ENVIRONMENTAL COUNSELOR, THE (US/1041-3863) [18764784] **3111**

ENVIRONMENTAL DEFENSE FUND *See* ANNUAL REPORT - ENVIRONMENTAL DEFENSE FUND **2160**

ENVIRONMENTAL DEFENSE FUND, INC *See* EDF LETTER **2192**

ENVIRONMENTAL DESIGN RESEARCH ASSOCIATION *See* EDRA; PROCEEDINGS OF THE ANNUAL ENVIRONMENTAL DESIGN RESEARCH ASSOCIATION CONFERENCE **298**

ENVIRONMENTAL DESIGN (ROME, ITALY) (IT/0393-5183) [13019779] **298**

ENVIRONMENTAL DEVELOPMENT PLAN. BIOMASS ENERGY SYSTEMS (US) [05779379] 1943, 2228, **2167**

ENVIRONMENTAL DEVELOPMENT PLAN. COAL LIQUEFACTION (US) [06829762] **2228**

ENVIRONMENTAL DEVELOPMENT PLAN. DECONTAMINATION AND DECOMMISSIONING (US) [05329659] **2228**

ENVIRONMENTAL DEVELOPMENT PLAN (EDP). DIRECT COMBUSTION PROGRAM (US) [04020204] **1943**

ENVIRONMENTAL DEVELOPMENT PLAN (EDP). ELECTRIC ENERGY SYSTEMS (US) [04173128] **2053**

ENVIRONMENTAL DEVELOPMENT PLAN (EDP). ENERGY STORAGE SYSTEMS (US) [04020789] **1943**

ENVIRONMENTAL DEVELOPMENT PLAN (EDP). ENHANCED GAS RECOVERY (US) [04167526] **4255**

ENVIRONMENTAL DEVELOPMENT PLAN (EDP). INDUSTRIAL ENERGY CONSERVATION (US) [04021198] **1943**

ENVIRONMENTAL DEVELOPMENT PLAN (EDP). WIND ENERGY CONVERSION (US) [04020108] **1943**

ENVIRONMENTAL DEVELOPMENT PLAN. INDUSTRIAL PROGRAMS (US) [05329750] **1943**

ENVIRONMENTAL DEVELOPMENT PLAN. OCEAN THERMAL ENERGY CONVERSION (US) [05455987] **1943**

ENVIRONMENTAL DEVELOPMENT PLAN. SOLAR HEATING AND COOLING OF BUILDINGS (US) [05807158] 614, **1943**

ENVIRONMENTAL DEVELOPMENT PLAN. URANIUM MINING, MILLING, AND CONVERSION (US) [05418405] **2167**

ENVIRONMENTAL DEVELOPMENT PLAN. WIND ENERGY CONVERSION (US) [05303732] **1943**

ENVIRONMENTAL DIGEST (CN/1183-6466) [25423710] **2167**

ENVIRONMENTAL DIGEST FOR WALES / WELSH OFFICE / CRYNHOAD O YSTADEGAU'R AMGYLCHEDD / Y SWYDDFA GYMREIG (UK/0267-310X) [15042788] **2167**

ENVIRONMENTAL DIGEST (OWEN SOUND) (CN/1183-8795) [25066663] **2228**

●ENVIRONMENTAL DISCOVERY (US/1062-4961) [25641728] **2167**

ENVIRONMENTAL EDUCATION AND INFORMATION (UK/0144-9281) [08850512] 2215, **2167**

●ENVIRONMENTAL EDUCATION RESEARCH (UK/1350-4622) 1744, **2167**

ENVIRONMENTAL EFFECTS OF DREDGING : INFORMATION EXCHANGE BULLETIN / U.S. ARMY CORPS OF ENGINEERS, WATERWAYS EXPERIMENT STATION (US) [10353538] **2228**

●ENVIRONMENTAL ENCYCLOPEDIA (US/1072-5083) [28989383] **2167**

ENVIRONMENTAL — Alphabetical Title Index

ENVIRONMENTAL ENGINEERING ABSTRACTS *CEASED*. (US/1063-7346) [26133826] 1975, 2167, **2184**

ENVIRONMENTAL ENGINEERING & POLLUTION CONTROL (US/0732-7188) [08416443] **2228**

ENVIRONMENTAL ENGINEERING (BURY SAINT EDMUNDS, ENG. : 1988) (UK/0954-5824) [18659264] 2228, **1975**

●ENVIRONMENTAL ENGINEERING (NEW YORK, N.Y.) (US/1056-7054) [23825670] 2228, **2167**

ENVIRONMENTAL ENTOMOLOGY (US/0046-225X) [01229150] **5608**

ENVIRONMENTAL ETHICS (US/0163-4275) [04372676] **2167**

●ENVIRONMENTAL EXECUTIVE DIRECTORY (US/1067-7208) [27209933] **2167**

ENVIRONMENTAL FINANCE (US/0735-5394) [08707571] 2228, **4721**

ENVIRONMENTAL FINANCE (NEW YORK, N.Y.) *CEASED*. (US/1054-8017) [22973202] **2167**

ENVIRONMENTAL FORUM (WASHINGTON, D.C.), THE (US/0731-5732) [08227987] **3111**

ENVIRONMENTAL GEOCHEMISTRY AND HEALTH (UK/0269-4042) [12269097] **2167**

●ENVIRONMENTAL GEOLOGY (US) [28348142] **1375**

ENVIRONMENTAL GEOLOGY AND WATER SCIENCES (US/0177-5146) [11314132] **1375**

ENVIRONMENTAL GEOLOGY (COLORADO GEOLOGICAL SURVEY) (US/0360-7674) [02244650] **1375**

ENVIRONMENTAL GEOLOGY (MONTPELIER, VT.) (US/0071-0857) [02321943] **1375**

ENVIRONMENTAL GEOLOGY NOTES (US/0073-5086) [01752615] **1375**

ENVIRONMENTAL GEOLOGY SERIES (LAWRENCE) (US/0197-1778) [04444354] **1375**

ENVIRONMENTAL GEOLOGY SERIES (NASHVILLE) (US/0362-8175) [02067700] **1375**

ENVIRONMENTAL GEOSCIENCES (US) 1355, **2167**

ENVIRONMENTAL HEALTH AND CHEMICAL SAFETY (SZ) **4774**

ENVIRONMENTAL HEALTH BULLETIN (WASHINGTON, D.C.) *CEASED*. (US/0897-6422) [17594851] **4774**

ENVIRONMENTAL HEALTH (COPENHAGEN) (DK/1011-4173) [20042335] **2167**

ENVIRONMENTAL HEALTH CRITERIA (SZ/0250-863X) [03201366] **4774**

ENVIRONMENTAL HEALTH LETTER (US/0196-0598) [01568082] **2228**

ENVIRONMENTAL HEALTH (LONDON) (UK/0013-9270) [10031648] **2822**

ENVIRONMENTAL HEALTH PERSPECTIVES (US/0091-6765) [01727134] **4774**

ENVIRONMENTAL HEALTH PERSPECTIVES. SUPPLEMENTS (US/1078-0475) [28638184] **2597**

ENVIRONMENTAL HEALTH REVIEW (CN/0319-6771) [01917175] **4774**

ENVIRONMENTAL HEALTH REVIEW, AUSTRALIA : THE OFFICIAL JOURNAL OF THE AUSTRALIAN INSTITUTE OF ENVIRONMENTAL HEALTH (AT/0818-5670) [27348853] **2167**

ENVIRONMENTAL HISTORY REVIEW : EHR (US/1053-4180) [22195612] **2228**

ENVIRONMENTAL HOTLINE (US/1040-1725) [18339225] **2171**

ENVIRONMENTAL IMPACT (UK) **2167**

ENVIRONMENTAL IMPACT ASSESSMENT REVIEW (US/0195-9255) [05701894] **2167**

ENVIRONMENTAL IMPACT NEWS (US/0148-8317) [02488756] **2168**

ENVIRONMENTAL INDEX, THE *CEASED*. (US/1061-9755) [25497373] **2168**

ENVIRONMENTAL INTERPRETATION : THE BULLETIN OF THE CENTRE FOR ENVIRONMENTAL INTERPRETATION (UK) [21325040] **2168**

ENVIRONMENTAL ISSUES NEWSLETTER (UK) **2168**

●ENVIRONMENTAL ISSUES REPORT (US/1061-3935) [25285339] **2168**

ENVIRONMENTAL LAB (US/1042-5209) [19075577] **5103**

ENVIRONMENTAL LAW ALERT (CN/0847-2068) [21201013] **3111**

●ENVIRONMENTAL LAW AND MANAGEMENT (UK/1067-6058) [27313517] **3111**

ENVIRONMENTAL LAW AND PRACTICE (US) [06587174] **3111**

ENVIRONMENTAL LAW ANTHOLOGY (US/1054-8297) [22979290] **3111**

ENVIRONMENTAL LAW CITATIONS (US) **3111**

ENVIRONMENTAL LAW HANDBOOK (US/0147-7714) [03225071] **3111**

ENVIRONMENTAL LAW INSTITUTE. STATE AND LOCAL ENERGY CONSERVATION PROJECT *See* ECP REPORT **1937**

ENVIRONMENTAL LAW JOURNAL OF OHIO (US/1045-599X) [20156082] **3111**

●ENVIRONMENTAL LAW NEWS (SAN FRANCISCO, CALIF.) (US/1064-2129) [26234403] **3111**

ENVIRONMENTAL LAW NEWSLETTER (US/0163-545X) [04393717] **3111**

ENVIRONMENTAL LAW (PORTLAND, ORE.) (US/0046-2276) [01568088] **3111**

ENVIRONMENTAL LAW REPORTER (US/0046-2284) [01568089] **3111**

ENVIRONMENTAL LAW REPORTER SYDNEY (AT/1035-6150) [I10356150] **3111**

ENVIRONMENTAL LAW REPORTS (UK) **3111**

ENVIRONMENTAL LAW SECTION JOURNAL (US/8756-9280) [11657488] **3111**

ENVIRONMENTAL LAW SYMPOSIUM (US) [07868752] **3112**

ENVIRONMENTAL LAW (WASHINGTON D.C.) (US/0748-8769) [03961441] **3112**

ENVIRONMENTAL LEGISLATION (US) [01568090] **3112**

ENVIRONMENTAL LEGISLATION REPORTER *CEASED*. (US/0362-5400) [02294669] **3112**

ENVIRONMENTAL LIABILITY (UK) **3112**

ENVIRONMENTAL LIABILITY REPORT, THE *CEASED*. (US/1043-2698) [19403273] **2168**

ENVIRONMENTAL MANAGEMENT (UK) **2168**

ENVIRONMENTAL MANAGEMENT ABSTRACTS (RU/0234-7059) [17437326] **2193**

ENVIRONMENTAL MANAGEMENT AND HEALTH (UK/0956-6163) [22504901] **2168**

ENVIRONMENTAL MANAGEMENT (DENVER, COLO.) (US/1051-2837) [21915222] **2228**

ENVIRONMENTAL MANAGEMENT (NEW YORK) (US/0364-152X) [02566256] **2168**

ENVIRONMENTAL MANAGEMENT NEWS (US/0893-3413) [13431096] **2168**

ENVIRONMENTAL MANAGEMENT / PA (US) 2168, **2228**

ENVIRONMENTAL MANAGEMENT REVIEW (ROCKVILLE, MD.) (US/1041-8172) [18853111] **3112**

ENVIRONMENTAL MANAGER (US/1043-786X) [19563096] **2228**

ENVIRONMENTAL MANAGER (AT) **2168**

ENVIRONMENTAL MANAGER'S COMPLIANCE ADVISOR, THE (US/0887-9753) [12715508] **3112**

ENVIRONMENTAL MANAGERS' SAFETY GUIDE (CN) **4775**

ENVIRONMENTAL MEDICINE (US) **3574**

ENVIRONMENTAL MEDICINE : ANNUAL REPORT OF THE RESEARCH INSTITUTE OF ENVIRONMENTAL MEDICINE, NAGOYA UNIVERSITY (JA/0287-0517) [09137308] 2168, **3574**

ENVIRONMENTAL MONITORING AND ASSESSMENT (NE/0167-6369) [07589096] 2229, **2168**

ENVIRONMENTAL MONITORING AND ASSESSMENT PROGRAM *See* EMAP MONITOR / ENVIRONMENTAL MONITORING AND ASSESSMENT PROGRAM **2192**

ENVIRONMENTAL MONITORING AND ECOLOGICAL STUDIES PROGRAM (US) [01405907] 2215, **2168**

ENVIRONMENTAL MONITORING AT MAJOR U.S. ENERGY RESEARCH & DEVELOPMENT ADMINISTRATION CONTRACTOR SITES (US/0148-6004) [03080915] 1943, **2168**

ENVIRONMENTAL MONITORING REPORT, UNITED STATES DEPARTMENT OF ENERGY, PADUCAH GASEOUS DIFFUSION PLANT (US) [04926073] 2168, **1943**

ENVIRONMENTAL MUTAGENS AND CARCINOGENS (KO) [14943474] **2168**

ENVIRONMENTAL NEWS (NZ) [10437559] **2229**

ENVIRONMENTAL NEWSLINE (US) **2168**

ENVIRONMENTAL NOTICE BULLETIN (US/0740-5847) [09316557] **2229**

ENVIRONMENTAL NUTRITION (US/0893-4452) [14637573] **4190**

ENVIRONMENTAL OPPORTUNITIES (US/0736-9603) [09271328] 2215, **2193**

ENVIRONMENTAL OUTLOOK (US/1051-1229) [21867381] **2229**

ENVIRONMENTAL OUTLOOK (SEATTLE, WASH.) (US/0899-9511) [04421464] **2168**

ENVIRONMENTAL PARTNERS FUND (CANADA) *See* PEOPLE OF ACTION **2179**

ENVIRONMENTAL PERIODICALS BIBLIOGRAPHY (US/0145-3815) [02933579] 2168, **2184**

ENVIRONMENTAL PERIODICALS BIBLIOGRAPHY ON CD-ROM (US/1053-1440) [22461337] 2168, **2184**

ENVIRONMENTAL PHYSICIAN, THE (US/1062-3736) [25601661] **3574**

ENVIRONMENTAL POLICY AND LAW (SZ/0378-777X) [02245680] **3112**

ENVIRONMENTAL POLICY AND PRACTICE (UK/0961-9356) [I09619356] **2168**

ENVIRONMENTAL POLICY REVIEW (IS/0792-0032) [17367064] **2168**

●ENVIRONMENTAL POLITICS (UK/0964-4016) [26490878] **2168**

ENVIRONMENTAL POLLUTION (1987) (UK/0269-7491) [15211864] **2229**

ENVIRONMENTAL POLLUTION & CONTROL / NTIS *See* NTIS ALERT. ENVIRONMENTAL POLLUTION & CONTROL **2237**

ENVIRONMENTAL PROFESSIONAL, THE (US/0191-5398) [04901489] **2169**

ENVIRONMENTAL PROGRAM ADMINISTRATORS (US/0099-2275) [02243320] **2169**

ENVIRONMENTAL PROGRESS (US/0278-4491) [07816827] **2229**

ENVIRONMENTAL PROTECTION AGENCY PLANNING AND BUDGETING GUIDANCE (US) [04161847] **2229**

ENVIRONMENTAL PROTECTION BULLETIN (UK/0957-9052) 2012, **2229**

ENVIRONMENTAL PROTECTION NEWS (US/1057-171X) [23987649] **2169**

ENVIRONMENTAL PROTECTION SURVEY (UK) [03734635] **2169**

ENVIRONMENTAL PROTECTION TECHNOLOGY (UK/0966-4904) [I09664904] 5103, **2169**

ENVIRONMENTAL PROTECTION : THE LEGAL FRAMEWORK / FRANK F. SKILLERN (US) [09788172] **3112**

ENVIRONMENTAL PROTECTION (WACO, TEX.) (US/1057-4298) [24035120] **2169**

ENVIRONMENTAL PROTECTION WEEK (US/1050-7124) [21578214] **2169**

ENVIRONMENTAL QUALITY AND SAFETY (GW/0300-824X) [02329775] **2169**

ENVIRONMENTAL QUALITY SERIES (US) [03689815] **2169**

ENVIRONMENTAL QUALITY (WASHINGTON) (US/0095-2044) [01797988] **2169**

ENVIRONMENTAL RADIOACTIVITY ANNUAL REPORT (NZ/0110-9944) [04594674] **2229**

●ENVIRONMENTAL RADON PROGRAM, SUMMARIES OF RESEARCH IN FY ... / ENVIRONMENTAL SCIENCES DIVISION, OFFICE OF HEALTH AND ENVIRONMENTAL RESEARCH [AND] OFFICE OF ENERGY RESEARCH, DEPARTMENT OF ENERGY (US) [28354448] **1943**

ENVIRONMENTAL REGISTER (US) **2169**

ENVIRONMENTAL REGULATION (US/1055-7598) [23302519] **2169**

ENVIRONMENTAL REGULATORY ADVISOR (US/1056-3164) [23660383] **3112**

●ENVIRONMENTAL REMEDIATION TECHNOLOGY (US/1071-538X) [28660381] **2169**

ENVIRONMENTAL REPORT CLAYTON (AT/0314-9781) [I03149781] **2169**

ENVIRONMENTAL REPORTER (US) [25896913] **2169**

ENVIRONMENTAL RESEARCH (SW) [01788028] **2169**

ENVIRONMENTAL RESEARCH BULLETIN (AT/0156-6245) [I01566245] **2169**

ENVIRONMENTAL RESEARCH CENTER PAPERS (JA/0286-5408) [09627535] 1425, **1404**

ENVIRONMENTAL RESEARCH LABORATORIES (U.S.) *See* PROGRAMS AND PLANS / ENVIRONMENTAL RESEARCH LABORATORIES **5142**

ENVIRONMENTAL RESEARCH LABORATORIES (U.S.). WEATHER MODIFICATION PROGRAM OFFICE *See* COLLECTED REPRINTS - WEATHER MODIFICATION PROGRAM OFFICE **1424**

ENVIRONMENTAL RESEARCH (NEW YORK, N.Y.) (US/0013-9351) [00859838] **2169**

ENVIRONMENTAL RESEARCH NEWSLETTER (IT) **2215**

ENVIRONMENTAL RESEARCH NOTE (AT/0156-7268) [I01567268] **2169**

●ENVIRONMENTAL REVIEWS (CN/1181-8700) [28453746] **2215**

ENVIRONMENTAL RIGHTS AND REMEDIES. CUMULATIVE SUPPLEMENT (US) [09331656] **3112**

ENVIRONMENTAL RISK WATCH *CEASED*. (US/1062-0834) [25518975] **2169**

ENVIRONMENTAL SAFETY ALERT (US/1060-8648) [25079818] **2229**

ENVIRONMENTAL SANITATION REVIEWS (TH/0125-5088) [10865296] **5533**

●ENVIRONMENTAL SATELLITE DATA RESEARCH (US/1065-6588) [26666666] **2169**

ENVIRONMENTAL SCIENCE & ENGINEERING (AURORA) (CN/0835-605X) [18910250] 2169, **1975**

ENVIRONMENTAL SCIENCE AND POLLUTION SERIES (US) **2169**

ENVIRONMENTAL SCIENCE & TECHNOLOGY (US/0013-936X) [01568096] **2169**

ENVIRONMENTAL SCIENCE & TECHNOLOGY MICROFORM (US/0013-936X) [07426593] **2169**

ENVIRONMENTAL SCIENCE AND TECHNOLOGY (NEW YORK) (US/0194-0287) [05395188] **2170**

ENVIRONMENTAL SCIENCE AND TECHNOLOGY SERIES (US) [04851152] **2170**

ENVIRONMENTAL SCIENCE, HOKKAIDO : JOURNAL OF THE GRADUATE SCHOOL OF ENVIRONMENTAL SCIENCE, HOKKAIDO UNIVERSITY, SAPPORO (JA) [13165449] **2170**

ENVIRONMENTAL SCIENCE RESEARCH (US/0090-0427) [01781323] **2170**

●ENVIRONMENTAL SCIENCE REVIEW (US/1071-8923) [28761049] **2170**

ENVIRONMENTAL SCIENCES. AN INTERNATIONAL JOURNAL ON ENVIRONMENTAL PHYSIOLOGY AND TOXICOLOGY (US) **2170**

ENVIRONMENTAL SEED PRODUCERS, INC *See* PRICE LIST / ENVIRONMENTAL SEED PRODUCERS, INC **2428**

ENVIRONMENTAL SOFTWARE (UK/0266-9838) [13802510] 1282, 1286, **2170**

ENVIRONMENTAL SOFTWARE DIRECTORY (US/1043-9056) [19609654] 1286, **2170**

ENVIRONMENTAL SOFTWARE REPORT (US/1043-2884) [19403319] 1286, **2170**

●ENVIRONMENTAL SOLUTIONS (US/1077-2537) [30604069] **2229**

ENVIRONMENTAL SPECTRUM (US/0013-9386) [01568099] **2170**

ENVIRONMENTAL STATUTES (US/0736-573X) [08104724] **3112**

ENVIRONMENTAL STRATEGY & PLANNING : BULLETIN OF THE COMMISSION ON ENVIRONMENTAL STRATEGY AND PLANNING OF THE WORLD CONSERVATION UNION (US/1017-4648) [22913232] **2193**

ENVIRONMENTAL STUDIES (CN/0706-1072) [09151773] **2170**

ENVIRONMENTAL SURVEILLANCE AT LOS ALAMOS DURING ... / ENVIRONMENTAL SURVEILLANCE GROUP (US) [05980202] **2170**

ENVIRONMENTAL SURVEILLANCE REPORT FOR THE INEL RADIOACTIVE WASTE MANAGEMENT COMPLEX (US) [08675948] **2229**

ENVIRONMENTAL TECHNOLOGY (UK/0959-3330) [21455443] **2170**

ENVIRONMENTAL TECHNOLOGY AND PRODUCT PROFILES (US) **2170**

●ENVIRONMENTAL TESTING & ANALYSIS (US/1068-7432) [27788949] **2170**

ENVIRONMENTAL TOPICS (UK/1046-5294) [20437069] **2170**

ENVIRONMENTAL TOXICOLOGY AND CHEMISTRY (US/0730-7268) [08047857] **2229**

ENVIRONMENTAL TOXICOLOGY AND WATER QUALITY (US/1053-4725) [22537100] **3980**

ENVIRONMENTAL TOXICOLOGY NEWSLETTER / COOPERATIVE EXTENSION, UNIVERSITY OF CALIFORNIA (US/1061-7787) [21963848] 2229, **2170**

ENVIRONMENTAL TOXIN SERIES (GW/0935-0209) [17361064] **2229**

●ENVIRONMENTAL TRADE EVENT PREVIEW (US/1065-3570) [26593432] **2170**

ENVIRONMENTAL UPDATE / NEBRASKA DEPARTMENT OF ENVIRONMENTAL CONTROL (US) [13842243] **2170**

●ENVIRONMENTAL UPDATE (NEW YORK, N.Y.) (US/1064-816X) [26408593] **2170**

●ENVIRONMENTAL VALUES (UK/0963-2719) [25598903] **2170**

●ENVIRONMENTAL VIEWPOINTS (US/1063-116X) [25866534] **2170**

ENVIRONMENTAL WASTE MANAGEMENT *CEASED*. (US/1049-4715) [21233439] **2229**

ENVIRONMENTAL WATCH (CHICAGO, ILL.) *CEASED*. (US/1049-8877) [21343417] 2193, **4837**

ENVIRONMENTALICA (XR) [19893256] **2229**

ENVIRONMENTALIST, THE (UK/0251-1088) [07686509] **2193**

ENVIRONMENTS (CN/0711-6780) [08558124] **2822**

●ENVIRONMETRICS (LONDON, ONT.) (UK/1180-4009) [24330152] **2170**

ENVIRONNEMENT (BE) [12007386] **2171**

ENVIRONNEMENT ACTUALITE *SUSPENDED*. (FR) **2171**

ENVIRONNEMENT & TECHNIQUE (FR/0986-2943) [I09862943] 5103, **2171**

ENVIRONNEMENT : BULLETIN DE DOCUMENTATION, L' (FR) [02758227] **2193**

ENVIRONNEMENT (MONTREAL) (CN/0709-8847) [06034786] 2229, **2184**

ENVIRONNEMENT PLUS (CN/0711-5806) [08655460] **2171**

●ENVIRONNEMENT (QUEBEC) (CN/1192-4578) [28396020] **2171**

ENVIRONS (DAVIS) (US/0193-6387) [05225494] **3112**

ENVIRONTECH (OAKLAND GARDENS, N.Y.) (US/1053-8852) [22684393] **2171**

ENVIROSOURCE (HULL. ED. FRANCAISE) (CN/1183-420X) [25590171] **2171**

ENVIROSOURCE (HULL. ENGLISH ED.) (CN/1183-4196) [25590172] **4646**

ENVIROSOUTH *SUSPENDED*. (US/0272-1120) [04737080] **2171**

ENVISIONEERING (US/1055-9892) [23445293] **1975**

ENVOI (UK/0013-9394) [03243518] **3462**

ENVOI (MONTREAL) (CN/0823-1834) [11073592] **4894**

ENVOI (NEW YORK, N.Y.) (US/0897-4888) [17514733] **3384**

ENVOL (MONTREAL. 1978) (CN/0707-7165) [04875775] **5617**

ENVOY INTERNATIONAL (ASHFORD, KENT : 1981) (UK/0140-2935) [07786557] **4520**

ENVOY (PITTSBURGH) (US/0013-9408) [01568102] **4956**

ENYO SOKOBIKIAMI GYOGYO HOKUYO TENKANSEN GYOJOBETSU GYOKAKU TOKEI NEMPO (JA) [03200030] **2300**

ENYO SUISAN KENKYUJO *See* KENKYU HOKOKU **2307**

ENYO : SUISAN KENKYUJO NYUSU (JA) [09387119] **2300**

ENZYKLOPAEDIE DES MAERCHENS (GW) 1925, **476**

ENZYME (SZ/0013-9432) [01568103] 580, **486**

ENZYME AND MICROBIAL TECHNOLOGY (UK/0141-0229) [04815338] **3692**

●ENZYME & PROTEIN (SZ/1019-6773) [28960311] 487, **580**

ENZYME ENGINEERING (US/0094-8500) [00972541] **3692**

ENZYME ENGINEERING AND BIOTECHNOLOGY (US) **3692**

ENZYME REGULATION (UK/0142-8071) [I01428071] **487**

ENZYMES & REAGENTS FOR MOLECULAR BIOLOGY (US) [19112300] **454**

ENZYMES, THE (US/0423-2607) [02254810] **487**

ENZYMOLOGY *CEASED*. (US/0146-8049) [01950951] **487**

EO NEWS (IT/0394-6681) [I03946681] **2053**

EOHSI INFOLETTER (US) [28968109] 2861, **2171**

EOQ QUALITY (INT/1018-5925) [I10185925] **1606**

EOQ QUALITY *See* EUROPEAN QUALITY. : THE OFFICIAL JOURNAL OF THE EUROPEAN ORGANIZATION FOR QUALITY **1606**

EOS (NE) **5103**

EOS (PL/0012-7825) [02260791] **3279**

EOS (MADRID) (SP/0013-9440) [01568106] **5608**

EOS REFERENCE HANDBOOK / NASA, GODDARD SPACE FLIGHT CENTER (US) [24513270] **1355**

EOS (ROMA) (IT/0392-6699) [12194795] 4303, **3669**

EOS (WASHINGTON, D.C.) (US/0096-3941) [02246774] **1404**

EOSAT LANDSAT APPLICATION NOTES (US/0896-7083) [15029376] **1110**

EOSAT LANDSAT DATA USER NOTES (US/0896-7091) [15029380] **1355**

EOTU (US) **3384**

EOTVOS LORAND TUDOMANYEGYETEM *See* ANNALES UNIVERSITATIS SCIENTIARUM BUDAPESTINENSIS DE ROLANDO EOTVOS NOMINATAE. SECTIO LINGUISTICA **3265**

EOTVOS LORAND TUDOMANYEGYETEM *See* ANNALES UNIVERSITATIS SCIENTIARUM BUDAPESTINENSIS DE ROLANDO EOTVOS NOMINATAE. SECTIO GEOGRAPHICA **2554**

EOTVOS LORAND TUDOMANYEGYETEM *See* ANNALES UNIVERSITATIS SCIENTIARUM BUDAPENTINENSIS DE ROLANDO EOTVOS NOMINATAE. SECTIO PHILOLOGICA MODERNA **3264**

EOTVOS LORAND TUDOMANYEGYETEM *See* ANNALES UNIVERSITATIS SCIENTIARUM BUDAPESTINENSIS DE ROLANDO EOTVOS NOMINATAE. SECTIO PHILOSOPHICA ET SOCIOLOGICA **4341**

EOTVOS LORAND TUDOMANYEGYETEM *See* ANNALES UNIVERSITATIS SCIENTIARUM BUDAPESTINENSIS DE ROLANDO EOTVOS NOMINATAE. SECTIO MATHEMATICA **3493**

EOTVOS LORAND TUDOMANYEGYETEM *See* ANNALES UNIVERSITATIS SCIENTIARUM BUDAPESTINENSIS DE ROLANDO EOTVOS NOMINATAE. SECTIO HISTORICA **2841**

EP. EXPRESS POZNANSKI (PL/0137-9100) [I01379100] **5808**

EP NEWS (BE/0250-5754) [05746882] **4646**

EP NEWS SERVICE (US/8750-7064) [09777858] **4956**

EPA ACTIVITIES UNDER THE RESOURCE CONSERVATION AND RECOVERY ACT OF 1976 (US/0161-8490) [03899915] **2193**

EPA ADMINISTRATIVE LAW REPORTER (US) [27457657] 2171, **3112**

EPA AND THE ACADEMIC COMMUNITY, PARTNERS IN RESEARCH SOLICITATION FOR GRANT PROPOSALS (US) [06696135] **2229**

EPA BULLETIN (NATIONAL INSTITUTE OF EDUCATIONAL PLANNING AND ADMINISTRATION (INDIA)) (II) [07988918] **1863**

EPA CITIZEN'S BULLETIN (US) [01567162] **2171**

EPA COMPENDIUM OF REGISTERED PESTICIDES. VOLUME 1. HERBICIDES AND PLANT REGULATORS (US/1040-1512) [02784829] **4244**

EPA COMPENDIUM OF REGISTERED PESTICIDES. VOLUME 2. FUNGICIDES AND NEMATICIDES (US/1040-1520) [02784791] **4244**

EPA COMPENDIUM OF REGISTERED PESTICIDES. VOLUME 3. INSECTICIDES, ACARICIDES, MOLLUSCICIDES AND ANTIFOULING COMPOUNDS (US) [02784964] **4244**

EPA COMPENDIUM OF REGISTERED PESTICIDES. VOLUME 4. RODENTICIDES AND MAMMAL, BIRD AND FISH TOXICANTS (US) [02784821] **4244**

EPA COMPENDIUM OF REGISTERED PESTICIDES. VOLUME 5. DISINFECTANTS (US) [02784747] **4244**

EPA JOURNAL (US/0145-1189) [02663078] **2171**

EPA PROGRAM STATUS REPORT, OIL SHALE (US/0732-8257) [05380709] 1439, **2229**

EPA PUBLICATIONS (US/0192-5008) [04965670] **2229**

EPA PUBLICATIONS BIBLIOGRAPHY (US/0196-0091) [03806538] **2184**

EPA REVIEW (AT/1035-0233) [I10350233] **2171**

●EPA WATCH (US/1065-920X) [26793628] **2171**

●EPARGNE & FINANCE PARIS (FR/1157-6472) [I11576472] **1591**

EPATOLOGIA E MALATTIE DEL RICAMBIO *CEASED*. (IT) [18582043] **3796**

Alphabetical Title Index

EPC PUBLICATION (UK/0267-5994) [17251194] **4775**

EPD CONGRESS (US) **2102**

EPD FILM (GW) [10782883] **4068**

EPE (UK/0963-5920) **2053**

EPETERIS (CY/0071-0954) [01792208] **2650**

EPETERIS ETAIREIAS BUZANTINON SPOUDON (GR/0253-391X) [01644310] **2686**

EPETERIS TES HETAIREIAS ELEIAKON MELETON (GR) [11870919] **2686**

EPETERIS TOU KENTROU EREUNES TES HELLENIKES LAOGRAPHIAS (GR) [08234052] **2319**

EPHEMERA NANCY (FR/0992-4922) [I09924922] **2686**

EPHEMERE, L' (FR/0013-9483) [01568108] **3342**

EPHEMERIDES IURIS CANONICI (IT/0013-9491) [01680751] **5029**

EPHEMERIDES LITURGICAE (IT/0013-9505) [01624303] **4956**

EPHEMERIDES MARIOLOGICAE (SP/0425-1466) [01585835] **4956**

EPHEMERIDES THEOLOGICAE LOVANIENSES (BE/0013-9513) [01568110] **4956**

EPHEMERIS HELLENON NOMIKON (GR) [10497733] **2967**

EPHRAIM ENTERPRISE (EPHRAIM, UTAH : 1981) (US) [12799513] **5756**

EPHRATA REVIEW, THE (US) [13048657] **5736**

EPI. EQUIPOS PRODUCTOS INDUSTRIALES (SP/1130-9571) [I11309571] **1606**

EPI-LOG (DUNLAP, TENN.) (US/1058-109X) [24221327] **1131**

EPI NEWSLETTER (US/0251-4710) [06174891] **3713**

EPI NOTES (US) [15691380] **3713**

EPI / REVUE TRIMESTRIELLE DE L'ASSOCIATION ENSEIGNMENT PUBLIC ET INFORMATIQUE (FR/0758-590X) **1744**

EPIC EVENTS (US) [19009371] **3279**

EPIC ILLUSTRATED (US/0279-246X) [07678816] **4860**

EPICA BOOK, ... EUROPEAN ADVERTISING ANNUAL (SZ) [19409634] **378**

●EPICENTRE (CHICOUTIMI) (CN/1192-5019) [27996964] **4646**

EPICIER (MONTREAL) *CEASED.* (CN/0013-9521) [01988122] **2334**

EPIDEMIOLOGIA E PREVENZIONE (IT) [19169994] **3734**

●EPIDEMIOLOGIA E PSICHIATRIA SOCIALE (IT/1121-189X) [I1121189X] 3925, **3734**

EPIDEMIOLOGIC REVIEWS (US/0193-936X) [05273707] **3734**

EPIDEMIOLOGICAL BULLETIN - PAN AMERICAN HEALTH ORGANIZATION (US/0256-1859) [06692437] **3734**

EPIDEMIOLOGICAL COMMENTS (SA) [06796235] **3734**

EPIDEMIOLOGIE ET SANTE ANIMALE : BULLETIN DE L'ASSOCIATION POUR L'ETUDE DE L'EPIDEMIOLOGIE DES MALADIES ANIMALES (FR) [10298033] 5509, **4775**

EPIDEMIOLOGIIA, MIKROBIOLOGIIA, I INFEKTSIOZNI BOLESTI (BU) [07599943] 3734, **562**

EPIDEMIOLOGY AND INFECTION (UK/0950-2688) [15218155] 3734, **3713**

EPIDEMIOLOGY (CAMBRIDGE, MASS.) (US/1044-3983) [19769281] **3734**

EPIDEMIOLOGY MONITOR, THE (US/0744-0898) [08026980] 3735, **4775**

EPIEGRAM (1988) (US/1046-1493) [17969827] 1286, **1241**

EPIGRAFIKA VOSTAKA (RU/0131-1344) [01568117] **267**

EPIGRAPHIC SOCIETY OCCASIONAL PAPERS, THE (US/1061-5938) [23593643] 3279, **267**

EPIGRAPHICA (FAENZA) (IT/0013-9572) [01568119] **267**

EPIGRAPHISCHE STUDIEN (GW/0071-0989) [01568120] **1076**

EPILEPSIA (COPENHAGEN) (NE/0013-9580) [01568121] **3832**

EPILEPSIES (FR) **3575**

EPILEPSY (UK/0141-965X) [05109899] **3832**

EPILEPSY ADVANCES IN CLINICAL EXPERIMENTAL RESEARCH (US/0894-6590) [13405605] **3832**

EPILEPSY RESEARCH (NE/0920-1211) [15022074] **3832**

EPILEPSY RESEARCH. SUPPLEMENT (NE/0922-9833) [20224739] **3575**

EPILEPSY USA (US/1060-9369) [25070517] **3832**

EPILOGE (GR) [01795242] **1560**

EPILOGES (MONTREAL) (CN/0827-3774) [11895344] **2487**

EPILOGUE (HALIFAX, N.S.) (CN/0836-088X) [19105388] 2481, **3209**

EPIPHANY (US) **4956**

EPISCOPAL CHURCH ANNUAL, THE (US/0071-1012) [05790871] **5059**

EPISCOPAL CHURCH. DIOCESE OF BETHLEHEM *See* JOURNAL OF THE ANNUAL CONVENTION - EPISCOPAL CHURCH. DIOCESE OF BETHLEHEM **5062**

EPISCOPAL CHURCH. DIOCESE OF LOS ANGELES *See* EPISCOPAL NEWS, THE **4956**

EPISCOPAL CLERICAL DIRECTORY (US) [03820186] **5059**

EPISCOPAL LIFE (US/1050-0057) [21369399] **5059**

EPISCOPAL NEWS, THE (US/0195-0681) [05252651] **4956**

EPISCOPAL RECORDER (US/0013-9610) [02587775] **5059**

EPISCOPAL TEACHER (US/0895-0830) [16687854] **5059**

EPISCOPAL WOMEN'S HISTORY PROJECT, THE (US/0749-9574) [09298081] 5555, **5059**

EPISKEPSIS (FRENCH ED.) (SZ) [09982455] **5039**

EPISODES (US) **2533**

EPISODES (CN/0705-3797) [04130038] **1375**

EPISTEME NS : REVISTA DEL INSTITUTE DI FILOSOFIA (VE) [09602637] **4345**

EPISTEMOLOGIA (IT) [05426607] **5103**

EPISTEMOLOGIE SOCIOLOGIQUE (FR/0013-9645) [06225561] **235**

EPISTEMONIKE EPETERIS TES ODONTIATRIKES SCHOLES TOU PANEPISTEMIOU ATHENON (GR/0376-8775) [01351247] **1323**

EPISTEMONIKE EPETERIS TES PHILOSOPHIKES SCHOLES (GR) [10766309] **3279**

EPISTEMONIKE SKEPSE (GR) [13924539] **5199**

EPISTOLODIDAKTIKA (UK) [16787032] **1744**

EPISUTEME. EPISTEME (JA) [03209434] **5231**

EPITAPH (GW/0340-0603) [01798862] **3384**

EPITHELIA *CEASED.* (UK/0269-4565) [17464432] **5583**

●EPITHELIAL CELL BIOLOGY (UK/0940-9912) [25715971] **536**

EPITHEORESE KLINIKES FARMAKOKINETIKES ELLENIKE EKD (GR) [I10116575] **4303**

EPITHEORESE KLINIKES FARMAKOLOGIAS KAI FARMAKOKINETIKES INTERNATIONAL ED (GR/1011-6583) [I10116583] **4303**

EPITHEORESE KYPRIAKOU DIKAIOU (CY/0254-6396) [12137282] **2967**

EPITHEORESE TON EUROPAIKON KOINOTETON (GR) [11505214] **5199**

EPITHEORESE ZOOTEHNIKES EPISTEMES (GR/1105-2651) [I11052651] **5583**

EPITHEORESIS KOINONIKON EREUNON (GR/0013-9696) [01791565] **5199**

EPITHEORESIS NAUTILIAKOU DIKAIOU (GR) [01796423] **3181**

EPITOANYAG (HU/0013-970X) [07786226] 2588, **614**

EPITOIPARI ARAK ALAKULASA, AZ (HU) [01785428] **614**

EPJOURNAL (UK/0954-3244) [10514214] 2053, **4814**

EPLB. EMERGENCY PHYSICIAN LEGAL BULLETIN (US/0098-1524) [01389109] 3914, 3740, **3724**

EPOCA (MILANO) (IT/0013-9718) [01718813] **2515**

EPOCH (CROYDON) (UK/0301-0643) [01786660] **5244**

EPOCH (ITHACA) (US/0145-1391) [01568135] **3384**

EPOCHE (GW) [03226899] **2515**

EPOCHE (LOS ANGELES) (US/0149-3043) [03337588] **4956**

EPOPTEIA (GR) [10255820] **4345**

EPOS / UNIVERSIDAD NACIONAL DE EDUCACION A DISTANCIA, FACULTAD DE FILOLOGIA (SP/0213-201X) [23994503] **3279**

EPPO PUBLICATIONS. SERIES B (FR/0071-2396) [02917071] **509**

EPPO PUBLICATIONS. SERIES C (FR/0374-7565) [I03747565] **509**

EPR ANNUAL REVIEW (US) 672, **1943**

EPR QUARTERLY REVIEW (US) 672, **1943**

EPRDF NEWS BULLETIN (US) [24951155] **4473**

EPRI JOURNAL (US/0362-3416) [02218183] **2053**

EPS, ECUMENICAL PRESS SERVICE (SZ) [06727764] **4956**

EPS. EDUCATION PHYSIQUE ET SPORT (FR/0245-8969) [I02458969] **4894**

EPSCC NEWSLETTER (US/0737-3449) [09352744] **4894**

EPSIG NEWS (US/1042-3737) [19029569] **2053**

EPSILON (DK/0902-5162) [17683579] **3279**

EPSON WORLD (US/8755-1047) [11280241] **1184**

EPSONCONNECTION (US/8750-622X) [11559179] **1184**

●EPSTEIN-BARR VIRUS REPORT (UK) **3575**

EPTA BULLETIN (BE) [10967753] **5059**

EPURE (FR/0758-489X) [I0758489X] **2053**

EPWORTH REVIEW (UK/0308-0382) [03093809] **5059**

EQ (CUPERTINO, CALIF.) (US/1050-7868) [21590466] **4116**

EQB MONITOR (US) [03597504] **2230**

EQL REPORT (US/0149-3094) [03463426] **2230**

EQUAL EMPLOYMENT COMPLIANCE UPDATE (US/0160-435X) [03678143] **3147**

EQUAL EMPLOYMENT OPPORTUNITY COMMISSION AFFIRMATIVE ACTION PLAN (US/0149-8320) [03130912] **1667**

EQUAL EMPLOYMENT OPPORTUNITY COMPLIANCE (US/0161-4541) [03915751] **3147**

EQUAL EMPLOYMENT OPPORTUNITY IN THE FEDERAL COURTS (US/0735-9187) [08506032] **3147**

EQUAL EMPLOYMENT OPPORTUNITY REPORT. MINORITIES AND WOMEN IN APPRENTICESHIP PROGRAMS AND REFERRAL UNIONS (US/0741-2479) [06727625] **1667**

EQUAL EMPLOYMENT OPPORTUNITY YEARLY REPORT (AT) [20976446] **1667**

EQUAL MEANS (US/1059-164X) [24486755] **5555**

EQUAL OPPORTUNITIES INTERNATIONAL (UK/0261-0159) [08979483] 4507, **1667**

EQUAL OPPORTUNITIES REVIEW (UK) [14689443] **4507**

EQUAL OPPORTUNITIES REVIEW. DISCRIMINATION CASE LAW DIGEST (UK/0957-882X) [22878049] **3148**

EQUAL OPPORTUNITY (US/0071-1039) [01568141] 2260, **1822**

EQUAL OPPORTUNITY ASSESSMENT AND AFFIRMATIVE ACTION PLAN (US/0148-4303) [03305015] **1323**

EQUAL OPPORTUNITY IN EMPLOYMENT / OFFICE OF PERSONNEL MANAGEMENT, LIBRARY (US) [05947087] **1667**

EQUAL OPPORTUNITY IN HOUSING (US/0745-4821) [03470664] **2822**

EQUAL OPPORTUNITY NEWSLETTER (AT/0813-5363) [I08135363] **1744**

EQUAL OPPORTUNITY REPORT USDA PROGRAMS (US/0146-2938) [02575656] **1667**

EQUAL PLAY *SUSPENDED.* (US/0740-2201) [09889150] **5555**

●EQUAL TIME (MENTOR, OHIO) (US/1063-0589) [25848840] **5555**

EQUALS ADELAIDE (AT/0729-1809) [I07291809] **1744**

EQUATOR (SAN FRANCISCO, CALIF.) *CEASED.* (US/0890-5681) [14291581] **2533**

EQUATOR (SAN FRANCISCO, CALIF. 1991), THE (US/1043-0687) [19292560] **4346**

EQUESTRIAN TRAILS (US/0013-9831) [04013522] **2798**

EQUI (UK) [11008729] **2798**

EQUILIBRIUM (WASHINGTON, D.C.) (US/0090-7871) [01785741] 1591, **4552**

EQUINE ATHLETE, THE (US/1047-8620) [19247176] **2798**

EQUINE BUSINESS JOURNAL (US/1054-9323) [22526603] **1084**

EQUINE IMAGES (US/1044-0224) [19572092] **373**

EQUINE PRACTICE (US/0162-8941) [04251564] **2798**

EQUINE VETERINARY DATA (US/0739-9065) [06702504] 5509, **2798**

EQUINE VETERINARY EDUCATION (UK/0957-7734) [21207859] **2798**

EQUINE VETERINARY JOURNAL (UK/0425-1644) [01568146] **5509**

EQUINEWS (CN/0828-864X) [12846968] **2799**

EQUINOX (CAMDEN EAST) (CN/0710-9911) [08569837] **2560**

EQUINOXE (NANTES) (FR/0765-5320) [12739055] **455**

EQUIP-AFRIC (FR) [06907297] **614**

EQUIP-AFRIQUE (FR/0184-9697) [08418992] **1975**

EQUIPE DE LUNDI (FR) **4850**

EQUIPE. PARIS, L' (FR/0153-1069) [I01531069] **4894**

EQUIPEMENT DES MENAGES EN BIENS DURABLES AU DEBUT DE ..., L' (FR) [09842367] **1560**

EQUIPEMENT DES MENAGES, L' (FR) [02650149] **1489**

EQUIPEMENT ENERGETIQUE DES LOGEMENTS NEUFS, L' (FR) [12174604] 1943, **2822**

EQUIPEMENT ET METHODES (CN/0700-432X) [03412015] **614**

EQUIPH (SP) **5103**

EQUIPMENT & TECHNOLOGY INTERNATIONAL (US/0098-5376) [02241506] **5103**

EQUIPMENT, CORROSION, AND CORROSION PROTECTION (UK/0938-5807) **2012**

EQUIPMENT, CORROSION, AND CORROSION PROTECTION (UK/0938-5207) **2012**

EQUIPMENT DIRECTORY OF AUDIO-VISUAL, COMPUTER AND VIDEO PRODUCTS *See* EQUIPMENT DIRECTORY OF VIDEO, COMPUTER, AND AUDIO-VISUAL PRODUCTS, THE **1184**

EQUIPMENT DIRECTORY OF VIDEO, COMPUTER, AND AUDIO-VISUAL PRODUCTS *See* DIRECTORY OF VIDEO, COMPUTER, AND AUDIO-VISUAL PRODUCTS, THE **1893**

EQUIPMENT DIRECTORY OF VIDEO, COMPUTER, AND AUDIO-VISUAL PRODUCTS, THE (US) [24370613] 1110, **1184**

EQUIPMENT FORECAST, AN (US) **4043**

EQUIPMENT JOURNAL (CN/0710-2720) [08415819] **2114**

EQUIPMENT LEASING (US/0194-3839) [05105876] **2967**

EQUIPMENT LEASING & ASSET BASED BORROWING REPORT INCLUDING CURRENT RATES AND SOURCES *CEASED.* (US/1051-6573) [22036707] **866**

EQUIPMENT MANAGEMENT (US/0733-3056) [08560093] **1975**

EQUIPMENT RULES (US) **1154**

EQUIPMENT TODAY (US/0891-141X) [14584358] **614**

EQUIPMENT WORLD (US/1057-7262) [23227470] **5103**

EQUIPOS PRODUCTOS ELECTRONICOS (SP) **2053**

EQUIPPING YOUTH (US/0196-0911) [05752796] **1063**

EQUITABLE DISTRIBUTION JOURNAL (US/0743-247X) [10538530] **2967**

EQUITIES (NEW YORK, N.Y.) (US/1053-2544) [22460911] **897**

EQUITY AND CHOICE (US/0882-3863) [11828583] **1744**

EQUITY & EXCELLENCE (US/0894-0681) [15037564] **1744**

EQUITY & EXCELLENCE *See* EQUITY & EXCELLENCE IN EDUCATION **1744**

●EQUITY & EXCELLENCE IN EDUCATION (US/1066-5684) [26997551] **1744**

EQUITY INTERNATIONAL (UK) **897**

EQUITY NEWS (US/0092-4520) [01789089] **385**

EQUITY NEWSLETTER (TORONTO) (CN/1181-974X) [24266765] **4388**

EQUITY (TORONTO. 1986) (CN/0832-9370) [16642185] 3179, **4507**

EQUITY (VANCOUVER) (CN/0823-6801) [10032159] **672**

EQUITYMAN (PH) [01966279] **897**

EQUIVALENCES (BE/0751-9532) [09089263] **3279**

EQUIVALENCIAS (SP) [10054490] 3384, **3462**

EQUUS (US/0149-0672) [03450654] **2799**

ER NEWS : ENERGY RESEARCH (US) [25220552] **1943**

ERA, ELEKTRICITETENS RATIONELLA ANVANDNING (SW) [02446746] **2054**

ERA ELETTRONICA (IT) **2054**

ERA, L' (IT) [03528252] **319**

ERA SOCIALISTA *CEASED.* (RM) [01790982] **4541**

ERA SOLAR (SP/0212-4157) [I02124157] **1943**

ERANOS (SW/0013-9947) [01568151] **1076**

ERANOS (NE) [03833990] 4241, **4185**

ERANOS LECTURES (US/0743-586X) [10613908] **4586**

ERASME (FR/0425-1687) [01966083] **3384**

ERASMUS (NE/0013-9955) [01568153] **4821**

ERASMUS AND LINGUA ACTION II DIRECTORY / EUROPEAN COMMUNITY ACTION SCHEME FOR THE MOBILITY OF UNIVERSITY STUDENTS (LU) [24042774] **1822**

ERASMUS IN ENGLISH *CEASED.* (CN/0071-1063) [01956845] **4346**

ERASMUS OF ROTTERDAM SOCIETY YEARBOOK (US/0276-2854) [07339327] **1076**

ERASMUS (ORGANIZATION) *See* ERASMUS AND LINGUA ACTION II DIRECTORY / EUROPEAN COMMUNITY ACTION SCHEME FOR THE MOBILITY OF UNIVERSITY STUDENTS **1822**

ERASMUS STUDIES (CN) [01961845] **2615**

ERATOSTHENES THESSALONIKE (GR/1011-6656) [I10116656] **2560**

ERBA D'ARNO (IT) [17702089] 3385, **319**

ERBA D'ARNO (IT/0394-5618) [I03945618] 267, **2615**

ERBE DEUTSCHER MUSIK. SONDERREIHE / HERAUSGEGEBEN IM AUFTRAGE DES STAATLICHEN INSTITUTS FUER MUSIKFORSCHUNG, DAS (GW/0425-1695) [04541509] **4116**

ERBE UND AUFTRAG (BEURON) (GW/0013-9963) [07115885] **5029**

ERBORISTERIA DOMANI (IT) **509**

ERCB ST (CN) [11413212] **4255**

ERCILLA (CL/0013-9971) [01568155] **2551**

ERDBEBEN IN DER BUNDESREPUBLIK DEUTSCHLAND (GW) [14629137] **1404**

ERDE (GW/0013-9998) [01568156] **2560**

ERDEM : ATATURK KULTUR MERKEZI DERGISI (TU) [13493222] **2651**

ERDESZETI ES FAIPARI TUDOMANYOS KOZLEMENYEK (HU/0209-9306) [08358148] **2379**

ERDESZETI KUTATASOK (HU/0521-3851) [I05213851] **82**

ERDESZETI LAPOK : AZ ORSZAGOS ERDESZETI EGYESULET LAPJA (HU/1215-0389) [28352832] **2379**

ERDKUNDE (GW/0014-0015) [01568161] 2560, **1375**

ERDO *See* ERDESZETI LAPOK : AZ ORSZAGOS ERDESZETI EGYESULET LAPJA **2379**

ERDO, AZ (HU/0014-0031) [03745269] **2379**

ERDOGAZDASAG ES FAIPAR (HU/0014-0066) [07667355] **2400**

ERDOL & KOHLE, ERDGAS, PETROCHEMIE (GW/0014-0058) [02408200] **4255**

ERDOL, ERDGAS, KOHLE (GW/0179-3187) [13568050] **4255**

ERDOL-INFORMATIONSDIENST (GW/0343-6705) [I03436705] 4255, **672**

ERDSTALL, DER (GW) [03712866] **267**

ERDWISSENSCHAFTLICHE FORSCHUNG (GW/0170-3188) [01961238] **2560**

ERE ATLANTEENNE (CN/0225-543X) [09046641] **4241**

EREKUTORONIKUSU (JA/0421-3513) [10314761] **2054**

ERES MAGAZINE (US) **5555**

ERETRIA (SZ/0425-1768) [01568164] **267**

ERETZ MAGAZINE (IS) [15139825] 4956, **267**

ERFAHRUNG UND DENKEN (GW) [01568166] **1744**

ERFAHRUNGSAUSTAUSCH UBER ERDARBEITEN IM STRASSENBAU (GW) [02550806] **5440**

ERFAHRUNGSHEILKUNDE (GW/0014-0082) [03505972] **3575**

ERFGOED VAN INDUSTRIE EN TECHNIEK (NE/0927-3026) [I09273026] 267, **2686**

ERFRISCHUNGSGETRANK, DAS (GW/0342-2232) [I03422232] **2367**

ERFTVERBAND (GERMANY) *See* JAHRESBERICHT **5535**

ERGA NOTICIAS (SP) **3575**

ERGAENZUNGSBAENDE ZUM REALLEXIKON DER GERMANISCHEN ALTERTUMSKUNDE (GW) [17664508] **1076**

ERGANZUNGSHEFT ZU PETERMANNS GEOGRAPHSCHISCHEN MITTEILUNGEN (GW) [01714238] **2560**

ERGEBNIS DER FORDERUNGSMASSNAHMEN AUF GRUND DES FLUCHTLINGSSIEDLUNGSGESETZES UND DES BUNDESVERTRIEBENENGESEZES ZUGUNSTEN DER VERTRIEBENEN UND GEFLUCHTETEN LANDWIRTE VOM (GW) [20506300] **1608**

ERGEBNIS DER WASSER- UND WATVOGELZAHLUNGEN ... IN NIEDERSACHSEN UND AN DER WESTKUSTE VON SCHLESWIG-HOLSTEIN (GW) [11707815] **5617**

ERGEBNISSE DER AEROLOGISCHEN UND BODENNAHEN OZONMESSUNGEN (GW) [04447300] 2171, **1425**

ERGEBNISSE DER BEOBACHTUNGEN AM ERDMAGNETISCHEN OBSERVATORIUM FURSTENFELDBRUCK IM JAHRE (GW/0343-7493) [19036243] **4443**

ERGEBNISSE DER CHIRURGISCHEN ONKOLOGIE (GW/0720-3462) [07787967] **3816**

ERGEBNISSE DER ERDMAGNETISCHEN BEOBACHTUNGEN IM JAHRE . *See* ERGEBNISSE DER BEOBACHTUNGEN AM ERDMAGNETISCHEN OBSERVATORIUM FURSTENFELDBRUCK IM JAHRE **4443**

ERGEBNISSE DER GASTROENTEROLOGIE (GW/0174-1616) [06370448] **3744**

ERGEBNISSE DER INNEREN MEDIZIN UND KINDERHEILKUNDE (GW/0071-111X) [01568171] 3903, **3796**

ERGEBNISSE DER INTERNISTISCHEN ONKOLOGIE (GW/0932-3279) [13678292] **3816**

ERGEBNISSE DER LIMNOLOGIE (GW/0071-1128) [01568178] **1413**

ERGEBNISSE DER MATHEMATIK UND IHRER GRENZGEBIETE (GW/0071-1136) [01568179] **3505**

ERGEBNISSE UND METHODEN MODERNER SPRACHWISSENSCHAFT (GW) [13073242] **5199**

ERGO-MED (GW/0170-2327) [05081248] **3575**

ERGODIC THEORY AND DYNAMICAL SYSTEMS (UK/0143-3857) [07780897] **3505**

ERGOGENIC AIDS IN SPORTS (UK) **3954**

ERGON TES ARCHAILOGIKES HETAIRIAS (GW) **267**

ERGONOMIA (HU/0014-0120) [I00140120] **82**

ERGONOMIA WROCAW (PL/0137-4990) [I01374990] **2114**

ERGONOMICS (UK/0014-0139) [01568187] **1251**

ERGONOMICS ABSTRACTS (UK/0046-2446) [01423137] 1251, **1209**

ERGONOMICS AUSTRALIA (AT/1033-1875) [I10331875] **2114**

●ERGONOMICS IN DESIGN (US/1064-8046) [26407446] **1975**

ERGONOMICS SOCIETY (GREAT BRITAIN). CONFERENCE *See* CONTEMPORARY ERGONOMICS : PROCEEDINGS OF THE ERGONOMICS SOCIETY'S ANNUAL CONFERENCE **1969**

ERGONOMIST (UK/0268-5639) [I02685639] **2114**

ERGOTHERAPIE (AU) **1251**

ERGOTHERAPIE & REHABILITATION (GW) **1878**

ERH SHIH I SHIH CHI (HK/1017-5725) [23259880] **2651**

ERH TUNG TU SHU YU CHIAO YU TSA CHIH (CH) [09266476] 1745, **1063**

ERH TUNG WEN HSUEH HSUAN KAN (CH) [09198445] **3385**

ERH TUNG WEN HSUEH YEN CHIU (CC) [05578502] **3385**

ERHEBUNG DER LAND- UND FORSTWIRTSCHAFTLICHEN ARBEITSKRAFTE (AU) [02483739] 1667, **1532**

ERHVERVSHISTORISK AARBOG; MEDDELELSER FRA ERHVERVSARKIVET (DK/0071-1152) [01568188] **2686**

ERIA, EL (SP) **3385**

ERIC ABSTRACTS (US) [02849927] 1863, **1794**

ERIC (BOSTON, MASS.)
(US/1062-5577) [15535905] **1745**

ERIC CLEARINGHOUSE ON EDUCATIONAL MANAGEMENT *See* ERIC ABSTRACTS **1794**

ERIC DESCRIPTOR AND IDENTIFIER USAGE REPORT (US) [05356795] **3209**

ERIC (DUBLIN, OHIO) (US/0894-3699) [18466778] **1745**

ERIC HIGHER EDUCATION RESEARCH CURRENTS (US) [01568198] **1823**

●ERIC IDENTIFIER AUTHORITY LIST (US/1062-0508) [25514296] **1745, 1795**

ERIC IDENTIFIER AUTHORITY LIST. ALPHABETICAL DISPLAY (US) [07589903] **1745**

ERIC IDENTIFIER AUTHORITY LIST. CATEGORY DISPLAY (US) [09762826] **1237**

●ERIC (PEABODY, MASS.) (US/1065-6537) [26666892] **1745**

ERIC PROCESSING AND REFERENCE FACILITY *See* INTERCHANGE - ERIC PROCESSING AND REFERENCE FACILITY **3217**

ERIC/SMEAC MATHEMATICS EDUCATION DIGEST / ERIC CLEARINGHOUSE FOR SCIENCE, MATHEMATICS, AND ENVIRONMENTAL EDUCATION (US) [12275125] **3505**

ERICSSON REVIEW (ENGLISH EDITION) (SW/0014-0171) [07367435] **1154**

ERIE DAILY TIMES, THE (US) [13000386] **5736**

ERIE RECORD (ERIE, KAN. : 1904) (US) [12169728] **5675**

ERIGENIA (US/8755-2000) [09565772] **2193, 509**

ERINDALE COLLEGE. LIBRARY *See* SERIALS LIST / ERINDALE COLLEGE LIBRARY **424**

ERINDALE REVIEW (CN/0828-7686) [12199550] **3385**

●ERISA AND BENEFITS LAW JOURNAL (US/1068-3542) [26702486] **1667**

ERISA BENEFIT FUNDS. DIRECTORY OF PENSION FUNDS, DETROIT AREA *See* FINANCIAL DIRECTORY OF PENSION FUNDS. MICHIGAN, DETROIT CITY PROPER **1671**

ERISA BENEFIT FUNDS. DIRECTORY OF PENSION FUNDS, NORTHERN OHIO *See* FINANCIAL DIRECTORY OF PENSION FUNDS. OHIO, NORTHERN, CLEVELAND AREA **1673**

ERISA BENEFIT FUNDS. DIRECTORY OF PENSION FUNDS, STATE OF GEORGIA *See* FINANCIAL DIRECTORY OF PENSION FUNDS. GEORGIA, EXCLUDING ATLANTA AREA **1670**

ERISA BENEFIT FUNDS. DIRECTORY OF PENSION FUNDS, STATE OF KENTUCKY *See* FINANCIAL DIRECTORY OF PENSION FUNDS. KENTUCKY **1671**

ERISA BENEFIT FUNDS. DIRECTORY OF PENSION FUNDS. STATE OF MINNESOTA *See* FINANCIAL DIRECTORY OF PENSION FUNDS. MINNESOTA (EXCLUDING MINNEAPOLIS-ST. PAUL AREA) **1671**

ERISA BENEFIT FUNDS. DIRECTORY OF PENSIONS, SOUTHERN OHIO *See* FINANCIAL DIRECTORY OF PENSION FUNDS. OHIO, SOUTHERN, EXCLUDING CINCINNATI AREA (COLUMBUS, DAYTON, ATHENS & OTHERS) **1673**

ERISA BENEFIT FUNDS. DIRECTORY OF PENSIONS, SOUTHERN OHIO *See* FINANCIAL DIRECTORY OF PENSION FUNDS. OHIO, SOUTHERN, CINCINNATI AREA **1673**

ERISA BENEFIT FUNDS. FINANCIAL DIRECTORY OF PENSION FUNDS, DISTRICT OF COLUMBIA *See* FINANCIAL DIRECTORY OF PENSION FUNDS. DISTRICT OF COLUMBIA **1670**

ERISA BENEFIT FUNDS. FINANCIAL DIRECTORY OF PENSION FUNDS, EASTERN MISSOURI *See* FINANCIAL DIRECTORY OF PENSION FUNDS. MISSOURI, EASTERN. ST. LOUIS, JEFFERSON CITY & OTHERS **1672**

ERISA BENEFIT FUNDS. FINANCIAL DIRECTORY OF PENSION FUNDS, EASTERN PENNSYLVANIA, EXCLUDING PHILADELPHIA AREA *See* FINANCIAL DIRECTORY OF PENSION FUNDS. PENNSYLVANIA, EASTERN, EXCLUDING PHILADELPHIA AREA. HARRISBURG, WILKESBARRE & OTHERS **1673**

ERISA BENEFIT FUNDS. FINANCIAL DIRECTORY OF PENSION FUNDS, EASTERN PENNSYLVANIA, PHILADELPHIA AREA *See* FINANCIAL DIRECTORY OF PENSION FUNDS. PENNSYLVANIA, EASTERN, PHILADELPHIA CITY PROPER **1673**

ERISA BENEFIT FUNDS. FINANCIAL DIRECTORY OF PENSION FUNDS, NORTH CAROLINA, EASTERN *See* FINANCIAL DIRECTORY OF PENSION FUNDS. NORTH CAROLINA, EASTERN. RALEIGH, FAYETTEVILLE, WILMINGTON & OTHERS **1673**

ERISA BENEFIT FUNDS. FINANCIAL DIRECTORY OF PENSION FUNDS, NORTH CAROLINA, WESTERN *See* FINANCIAL DIRECTORY OF PENSION FUNDS. NORTH CAROLINA, WESTERN. WINSTON-SALEM, LEXINGTON, GREENSBORO, CHARLOTTE & OTHERS **1673**

ERISA BENEFIT FUNDS. FINANCIAL DIRECTORY OF PENSION FUNDS, NORTHERN CALIFORNIA, EXCLUDING SAN FRANCISCO *See* FINANCIAL DIRECTORY OF PENSION FUNDS. CALIFORNIA, NORTHERN, EXCLUDING SAN FRANCISCO. OAKLAND, SAN JOSE, FRESNO & OTHERS **1670**

ERISA BENEFIT FUNDS. FINANCIAL DIRECTORY OF PENSION FUNDS, NORTHERN CONNECTICUT *See* FINANCIAL DIRECTORY OF PENSION FUNDS. CONNECTICUT, NORTHERN. HARTFORD, WILLIMANTIC, WATERBURY & OTHERS **1670**

ERISA BENEFIT FUNDS. FINANCIAL DIRECTORY OF PENSION FUNDS, NORTHERN FLORIDA *See* FINANCIAL DIRECTORY OF PENSION FUNDS. FLORIDA, NORTHERN. JACKSONVILLE, TALLAHASSEE, GAINESVILLE & OTHERS **1670**

ERISA BENEFIT FUNDS. FINANCIAL DIRECTORY OF PENSION FUNDS, NORTHERN INDIANA *See* FINANCIAL DIRECTORY OF PENSION FUNDS. INDIANA, NORTHERN. SOUTH BEND, FT. WAYNE, MUNCIE & OTHERS **1671**

ERISA BENEFIT FUNDS. FINANCIAL DIRECTORY OF PENSION FUNDS, NORTHERN VIRGINIA *See* FINANCIAL DIRECTORY OF PENSION FUNDS. VIRGINIA, NORTHERN. (ARLINGTON, WINCHESTER, HARRISONBURG & OTHERS) **1674**

ERISA BENEFIT FUNDS. FINANCIAL DIRECTORY OF PENSION FUNDS, SOUTHERN CALIFORNIA, LOS ANGELES PROPER *See* FINANCIAL DIRECTORY OF PENSION FUNDS. CALIFORNIA, SOUTHERN. LOS ANGELES CITY PROPER **1670**

ERISA BENEFIT FUNDS. FINANCIAL DIRECTORY OF PENSION FUNDS, SOUTHERN CONNECTICUT *See* FINANCIAL DIRECTORY OF PENSION FUNDS. CONNECTICUT, SOUTHERN. STAMFORD, NEW HAVEN, NEW LONDON & OTHERS **1670**

ERISA BENEFIT FUNDS. FINANCIAL DIRECTORY OF PENSION FUNDS, SOUTHERN FLORIDA *See* FINANCIAL DIRECTORY OF PENSION FUNDS. FLORIDA, SOUTHERN. WEST PALM BEACH, MIAMI, FT. MYER & OTHERS **1670**

ERISA BENEFIT FUNDS. FINANCIAL DIRECTORY OF PENSION FUNDS, SOUTHERN INDIANA *See* FINANCIAL DIRECTORY OF PENSION FUNDS. INDIANA, SOUTHERN (INDIANAPOLIS, TERRE HAUTE, EVANSVILLE & OTHERS) **1671**

ERISA BENEFIT FUNDS. FINANCIAL DIRECTORY OF PENSION FUNDS, SOUTHERN NEW JERSEY *See* FINANCIAL DIRECTORY OF PENSION FUNDS. NEW JERSEY, SOUTHERN. TRENTON, CAMDEN, ATLANTIC CITY & OTHERS **1672**

ERISA BENEFIT FUNDS. FINANCIAL DIRECTORY OF PENSION FUNDS, STATE OF ALABAMA *See* FINANCIAL DIRECTORY OF PENSION FUNDS. ALABAMA **1669**

ERISA BENEFIT FUNDS. FINANCIAL DIRECTORY OF PENSION FUNDS, STATE OF ALASKA *See* FINANCIAL DIRECTORY OF PENSION FUNDS. ALASKA **1669**

ERISA BENEFIT FUNDS. FINANCIAL DIRECTORY OF PENSION FUNDS, STATE OF ARIZONA *See* FINANCIAL DIRECTORY OF PENSION FUNDS. ARIZONA **1669**

ERISA BENEFIT FUNDS. FINANCIAL DIRECTORY OF PENSION FUNDS, STATE OF ARKANSAS *See* FINANCIAL DIRECTORY OF PENSION FUNDS. ARKANSAS **1669**

ERISA BENEFIT FUNDS. FINANCIAL DIRECTORY OF PENSION FUNDS, STATE OF COLORADO *See* FINANCIAL DIRECTORY OF PENSION FUNDS. COLORADO **1670**

ERISA BENEFIT FUNDS. FINANCIAL DIRECTORY OF PENSION FUNDS, STATE OF GEORGIA, ATLANTA AREA *See* FINANCIAL DIRECTORY OF PENSION FUNDS. GEORGIA, ATLANTA AREA **1670**

ERISA BENEFIT FUNDS. FINANCIAL DIRECTORY OF PENSION FUNDS, STATE OF IDAHO *See* FINANCIAL DIRECTORY OF PENSION FUNDS. IDAHO **1670**

ERISA BENEFIT FUNDS. FINANCIAL DIRECTORY OF PENSION FUNDS, STATE OF ILLINOIS, CHICAGO PROPER *See* FINANCIAL DIRECTORY OF PENSION FUNDS. ILLINOIS, CHICAGO CITY PROPER **1670**

ERISA BENEFIT FUNDS. FINANCIAL DIRECTORY OF PENSION FUNDS, STATE OF IOWA *See* FINANCIAL DIRECTORY OF PENSION FUNDS. IOWA **1671**

ERISA BENEFIT FUNDS. FINANCIAL DIRECTORY OF PENSION FUNDS, STATE OF LOUISIANA *See* FINANCIAL DIRECTORY OF PENSION FUNDS. LOUISIANA **1671**

ERISA BENEFIT FUNDS. FINANCIAL DIRECTORY OF PENSION FUNDS, STATE OF MAINE *See* FINANCIAL DIRECTORY OF PENSION FUNDS. MAINE **1671**

ERISA BENEFIT FUNDS. FINANCIAL DIRECTORY OF PENSION FUNDS, STATE OF MASSACHUSETTS, EXCLUDING BOSTON AREA *See* FINANCIAL DIRECTORY OF PENSION FUNDS. MASSACHUSETTS, EXCLUDING BOSTON & SUBURBS. WORCESTER, SPRINGFIELD, PITTSFIELD & OTHERS **1671**

ERISA BENEFIT FUNDS. FINANCIAL DIRECTORY OF PENSION FUNDS, STATE OF MINNESOTA, MINNEAPOLIS-ST. PAUL AREA *See* FINANCIAL DIRECTORY OF PENSION FUNDS. MINNESOTA, MINNEAPOLIS-ST. PAUL AREA **1672**

ERISA BENEFIT FUNDS. FINANCIAL DIRECTORY OF PENSION FUNDS. STATE OF MISSISSIPPI *See* FINANCIAL DIRECTORY OF PENSION FUNDS. MISSISSIPPI **1672**

ERISA BENEFIT FUNDS. FINANCIAL DIRECTORY OF PENSION FUNDS, STATE OF MONTANA *See* FINANCIAL DIRECTORY OF PENSION FUNDS. MONTANA **1672**

ERISA BENEFIT FUNDS. FINANCIAL DIRECTORY OF PENSION FUNDS, STATE OF NEBRASKA *See* FINANCIAL DIRECTORY OF PENSION FUNDS. NEBRASKA **1672**

ERISA BENEFIT FUNDS. FINANCIAL DIRECTORY OF PENSION FUNDS, STATE OF NEVADA *See* FINANCIAL DIRECTORY OF PENSION FUNDS. NEVADA **1672**

ERISA BENEFIT FUNDS. FINANCIAL DIRECTORY OF PENSION FUNDS, STATE OF NEW HAMPSHIRE *See* FINANCIAL DIRECTORY OF PENSION FUNDS. NEW HAMPSHIRE **1672**

ERISA BENEFIT FUNDS. FINANCIAL DIRECTORY OF PENSION FUNDS, STATE OF NEW YORK, BROOKLYN, S.I., BRONX, QUEENS, L.I *See* FINANCIAL DIRECTORY OF PENSION FUNDS. NEW YORK. BROOKLYN, S.I., BRONX, QUEENS **1672**

ERISA BENEFIT FUNDS. FINANCIAL DIRECTORY OF PENSION FUNDS, STATE OF NEW YORK, EASTERN UPSTATE *See* FINANCIAL DIRECTORY OF PENSION FUNDS. NEW YORK, EASTERN UPSTATE. POUGHKEEPSIE, ALBANY, GLENS FALLS & OTHERS **1672**

ERISA BENEFIT FUNDS. FINANCIAL DIRECTORY OF PENSION FUNDS, STATE OF NEW YORK MANHATTAN-DOWNTOWN WALL ST. TO 40 ST.) *See* FINANCIAL DIRECTORY OF PENSION FUNDS. NEW YORK, MANHATTAN-DOWNTOWN. WALL ST. TO 40 ST **1672**

ERISA BENEFIT FUNDS. FINANCIAL DIRECTORY OF PENSION FUNDS, STATE OF NEW YORK, MANHATTAN-MIDTOWN (41 ST. TO 50 ST.) *See* FINANCIAL DIRECTORY OF PENSION FUNDS. NEW YORK, MANHATTAN-MIDTOWN, 41 ST. TO 50 ST **1672**

ERISA BENEFIT FUNDS. FINANCIAL DIRECTORY OF PENSION FUNDS, STATE OF NEW YORK, MANHATTAN-UPTOWN (51 ST. TO HARLEM RIVER) *See* FINANCIAL DIRECTORY OF PENSION FUNDS. NEW YORK, MANHATTAN-UPTOWN. 51 ST. TO HARLEM RIVER **1672**

ERISA BENEFIT FUNDS. FINANCIAL DIRECTORY OF PENSION FUNDS, STATE OF NEW YORK, WESTERN UPSTATE *See* FINANCIAL DIRECTORY OF PENSION FUNDS. NEW YORK, WESTERN UPSTATE. ROCHESTER, BUFFALO, ELMIRA & OTHERS **1672**

ERISA BENEFIT FUNDS. FINANCIAL DIRECTORY OF PENSION FUNDS, STATE OF NORTH DAKOTA *See* FINANCIAL DIRECTORY OF PENSION FUNDS. NORTH DAKOTA **1673**

ERISA BENEFIT FUNDS. FINANCIAL DIRECTORY OF PENSION FUNDS, STATE OF OREGON *See* FINANCIAL DIRECTORY OF PENSION FUNDS. OREGON **1673**

ERISA BENEFIT FUNDS. FINANCIAL DIRECTORY OF PENSION FUNDS. STATE OF RHODE ISLAND *See* FINANCIAL DIRECTORY OF PENSION FUNDS. RHODE ISLAND **1673**

ERISA BENEFIT FUNDS. FINANCIAL DIRECTORY OF PENSION FUNDS, STATE OF SOUTH DAKOTA *See* FINANCIAL DIRECTORY OF PENSION FUNDS. SOUTH DAKOTA **1673**

ERISA BENEFIT FUNDS. FINANCIAL DIRECTORY OF PENSION FUNDS, STATE OF TENNESSEE *See* FINANCIAL DIRECTORY OF PENSION FUNDS. TENNESSEE **1673**

ERISA BENEFIT FUNDS. FINANCIAL DIRECTORY OF PENSION FUNDS, STATE OF UTAH *See* FINANCIAL DIRECTORY OF PENSION FUNDS. UTAH **1674**

Alphabetical Title Index — ESPACIO

ERISA BENEFIT FUNDS. FINANCIAL DIRECTORY OF PENSION FUNDS, STATE OF VERMONT *See* FINANCIAL DIRECTORY OF PENSION FUNDS. VERMONT **1674**

ERISA BENEFIT FUNDS. FINANCIAL DIRECTORY OF PENSION FUNDS, STATE OF WISCONSIN, EXCLUDING MILWAUKEE AREA *See* FINANCIAL DIRECTORY OF PENSION FUNDS. WISCONSIN, SOUTHERN, EXCLUDING MILWAUKEE AREA. MADISON, LACROSSE, OSHKOSH & OTHERS **1674**

ERISA BENEFIT FUNDS. FINANCIAL DIRECTORY OF PENSION FUNDS, WESTERN MISSOURI *See* FINANCIAL DIRECTORY OF PENSION FUNDS. MISSOURI, WESTERN. KANSAS CITY, ST. JOSEPH, SPRINGFIELD & OTHERS **1672**

ERISA BENEFIT FUNDS. FINANCIAL DIRECTORY OF PENSION FUNDS, WESTERN PENNSYLVANIA, EXCLUDING PITTSBURGH AREA *See* FINANCIAL DIRECTORY OF PENSION FUNDS. PENNSYLVANIA, WESTERN, EXCLUDING PITTSBURGH AREA. ERIE, NEW CASTLE, GREENSBURG & OTHERS **1673**

ERISA BENEFIT FUNDS. FINANCIAL DIRECTORY OF PENSION FUNDS. WESTERN PENNSYLVANIA, PITTSBURGH AREAA41 *See* FINANCIAL DIRECTORY OF PENSION FUNDS. PENNSYLVANIA, WESTERN (PITTSBURGH AREA) **1673**

ERISA BENEFITS FUNDS. DIRECTORY OF PENSION FUNDS, STATE OF MICHIGAN, EXCLUDING DETROIT AREA *See* FINANCIAL DIRECTORY OF PENSION FUNDS. MICHIGAN, SOUTHERN, EXCLUDING DETROIT & SUBURBS (FLINT, GRAND RAPIDS, KALAMAZOO & OTHERS) **1671**

ERISA CITATOR (US/0883-3052) [12114674] **1667**

ERISA LITIGATION REPORTER (US/1055-5307) [23199241] **3148**

ERISA NEWSLETTER, THE (US/8755-5379) [11348230] **1667**

ERISA RED BOOK OF PENSION FUNDS, THE (US) [14291724] **897**

ERISA TOP 25,000 COMPANIES : THE RED BOOK OF PENSION FUNDS (US/1068-6304) [22949367] **672**

ERISA UPDATE, THE (US/0194-4959) [04785336] **1667**

ERIU (IE/0332-0758) [01967360] **3279**

ERKENNTNIS (NE/0165-0106) [02243440] **4346**

ERKRANKUNGEN DER ZOOTIERE : VERHANDLUNGSBERICHT DES INTERNATIONALEN SYMPOSIUMS UEBER DIE ERKRANKUNGEN DER ZOOTIERE *CEASED.* (GW/0863-2332) [04814773] **5509**

ERLANGER BEITRAEGE ZUR SPRACH UND KUNSTWISSENSCHAFT (GW/0425-2268) [01949946] **1076**

ERLANGER GEOLOGISCHE ABHANDLUNGEN (GW/0071-1160) [06289494] **1375**

ERLANGER GEOLOGISCHE HANDLUNGEN (GW) [06210085] **1375**

ERMLANDBUCH (GW) [02470076] **2515**

ERN. EXECUTIVE RECRUITER NEWS (US/0271-0781) [06538507] **940**

ERNAHRUNG (VIENNA, AUSTRIA) (AU/0250-1554) [06435391] **4190**

ERNAHRUNGS- UMSCHAU (GW/0014-021X) [02916970] **4190**

ERNAHRUNGS-UMSCHAU 1977 (GW/0174-0008) [01740008] **2334**

ERNAHRUNGSBERICHT (GW) [04508229] **4190**

ERNAHRUNGSFORSCHUNG (GW/0071-1179) [01098316] **4190**

ERNAHRUNGSWIRTSCHAFT (GW) [03997403] 2367, **2334**

● ERNEST & YOUNG NEW YORK, NEW JERSEY, CONNECTICUT STATE TAX GUIDE, THE (US/1065-7312) [26714113] **4721**

ERNEST BECKER (US/1059-3551) [24577479] 4346, **3925**

ERNST & ERNST *See* NATIONAL TAX TRAINING PROGRAM : TAX PRACTICE FUNDAMENTALS FOR NONTAX PROFESSIONALS **3102**

ERNST & WHINNEY *See* TAX NOTES **4753**

ERNST & YOUNG RESOURCE GUIDE TO GLOBAL MARKETS, THE (US/1059-3098) [23011746] **1634**

● ERNST & YOUNG TAX GUIDE, THE (US/1059-809X) [24773286] **4721**

ERNST & YOUNG'S ARTHUR YOUNG TAX GUIDE *See* ERNST & YOUNG TAX GUIDE, THE **4721**

ERNST & YOUNG'S OIL AND GAS FEDERAL INCOME TAXATION (US/1055-5781) [22529134] **4255**

ERNST & YOUNG'S TAX-SAVING STRATEGIES / ERNST & YOUNG (US/1058-6342) [22997374] **4721**

EROTIC ART BY LIVING ARTISTS (US/0899-4005) [18082620] **349**

EROZIJA (YU) [03012781] **82**

ERRL PUBLICATION (US/0361-9524) [02441094] 1024, **82**

ERROR TRENDS (US) **2781**

ERS (US/0082-9730) [03917191] **82**

ERS RESEARCH MEMO (US/0098-1257) [01798594] **1745**

ERS SPECIAL REPORT (US/0731-4957) [07320804] **1745**

ERS SPECTRUM (US) [15270459] **1863**

● ERS UPDATE (HONOLULU, HAWAII) (US/1065-5085) [26621661] **1668**

ERSKINE ECHO, THE (US) [01568213] **5695**

ERU PRESS INDEX (PK) [09871988] **5807**

ERWACHSENENBILDUNG IN OESTERREICH (AU) [05300497] **1800**

ERWERBSOBSTBAU (GW/0014-0309) [03997431] **170**

ERWERBUNGEN, GESCHENKE UND LEIHGABEN (GW) [04872377] **4087**

ERWIN RECORD, THE (US) [19036521] **5745**

ERYTHROCYTES (UK/0268-808X) [I0142808X] **536**

ERZIEHUNG UND UNTERRICHT (AU/0014-0325) [I00140325] **1745**

ERZIEHUNG UND UNTERRICHT (GW/0014-0325) **1745**

ERZIEHUNG UND WISSENSCHAFT (GW/0342-0671) [05376019] 5103, **1745**

ERZMETALL (GW/0044-2658) [06568613] **4001**

ES (IT) [02714641] **2515**

ES. ELEKTRONIKSCHAU (AU/0254-4318) [I02544318] **1132**

ESA BULLETIN (FR/0376-4265) [02908353] **18**

ESA DIRECTORY OF OFFICES / U.S. DEPARTMENT OF LABOR, EMPLOYMENT STANDARDS ADMINISTRATION (US) [06023252] **1668**

ESA FLGEFORSKNING (DK) [10204522] **395**

ESA IUE NEWSLETTER (SP) [08481400] **395**

ESA JOURNAL (FR/0379-2285) [04168646] **18**

ESA NEWSLETTER - ENTOMOLOGICAL SOCIETY OF AMERICA (US/0273-7353) [03728350] **5608**

ESA SP (FR/0379-6566) [11059078] **18**

ESAKIA (JA/0071-1268) [02945095] **5608**

ESAO PROCEEDINGS / EUROPEAN SOCIETY FOR ARTIFICIAL ORGANS (UK/0952-3391) [11135491] **3575**

ESARS QUARTERLY SUMMARY OF LOCAL OFFICE ACTIVITIES (US) [07865882] **1668**

ESARS SUMMARY OF LOCAL OFFICE ACTIVITIES *See* ESARS QUARTERLY SUMMARY OF LOCAL OFFICE ACTIVITIES **1668**

● ESC! (DEKALB, ILL.) (US/1065-4844) [26618343] **3385**

ESCALE (QUEBEC) (CN/0822-4056) [11825354] **4176**

ESCAMBIA COUNTY HISTORICAL QUARTERLY (US) 2446, **2615**

ESCANDALAR (US) [04284063] **320**

ESCAP AGRICULTURE DIVISION, ARSAP/FADINAP, REGIONAL INFORMATION SUPPORT SERVICE (RISS) (TH/0252-354X) [18853954] 170, **153**

ESCAP REMOTE SENSING NEWSLETTER (TH/0257-6384) [I02576384] **1355**

ESCAPE (SALT LAKE CITY, UTAH) (US/0745-6182) [09399096] **5469**

ESCAPE TO THE MINNESOTA GOOD TIMES *CEASED.* (US/0740-9648) [07866277] **2533**

ESCARGOT FOLK?, L' (FR) [03530715] **4116**

ESCARGOT, L' (FR) [02717125] **4116**

ESCENA (NQ) [23906616] **5364**

ESCENA LATINOAMERICANA, LA *SUSPENDED.* (AG/0840-5891) [20785252] **5364**

ESCOLA PARA PROFESSORES (BL) [01787524] **1745**

ESCOLA SUPERIOR DE AGRICULTURA "LUIZ DE QUEIROZ." *See* ANAIS DA ESCOLA SUPERIOR DE AGRICULTURA LUIZ DE QUEIROZ **4161**

ESCOLA SUPERIOR DE AGRICULTURA "LUIZ DE QUEIROZ." INSTITUTO DE PESQUISAS E ESTUDOS FLORESTAIA *See* IPEF, INSTITUTO DE PESQUISAS E ESTUDOS FLORESTAIS **2385**

ESCOLIOSIS (SP) **3804**

ESCONDIDO NEWS-REPORTER (US/1067-4365) [27235522] **5635**

ESCRIBANO, EL (US/0014-0376) [04412105] 267, **2732**

ESCRIME (FR/0153-4661) [09352701] **4894**

ESCRIME FRANCAISE *See* ESCRIME **4894**

ESCRITA (BL/0102-6615) [02459139] **3385**

ESCRITOS (CK) [04080594] **2846**

ESCRITOS DE FILOSOFIA / C.ACADEMIA NACIONAL DE CIENCIAS, CENTRO DE ESTUDIOS FILOSOFICOS (AG/0325-4933) [06257513] **4346**

ESCRITOS DEL VEDAT (SP/0210-3133) [02864500] **4956**

ESCRITURA (CARACAS) (VE/1011-7989) [03337987] **3342**

ESCUELA DE ENFERMERIA (SP) **3855**

ESCUELA DE FARMACIA. ORGANO DE LA FACULTAD DE C.C.N.N. FARMACIA (GT) [01568220] **4303**

ESCUELA MEDICA (SP/0212-0283) [I02120283] **4775**

ESCUELA NACIONAL DE CIENCIAS BIOLOGICAS DEL IPN *See* BOLETIN BIBLIOGRAFICO DE LA ESCUELA NACIONAL DE CIENCIAS BIOLOGICOS **449**

ESD TECHNOLOGY (US/1043-982X) [18363698] **1975**

ESEA TITLE 1 PROJECTS, FINAL REPORT (US) [06125279] **1745**

ESEIGNEMENTS PROFESSIONNELS, LES (FR) [01796460] **3209**

ESELSOHR (AU) [01791510] **3385**

ESF COMMUNICATIONS (FR/0293-082X) [15646945] **2171**

ESIC MARKET (SP/0212-1867) [I02121867] 759, **1489**

ESKIMO; COUNTRY, INHABITANTS, CATHOLIC MISSIONS (CN/0318-7551) [06870182] **5029**

ESL-TR (UNITED STATES. AIR FORCE. AIR FORCE ENGINEERING AND SERVICES CENTER. ENGINEERING AND SERVICES LABORATORY) (US/0197-8543) [06150018] 18, **5103**

ESN INFORMATION BULLETIN (UK) [17369360] **5103**

ESOMAR *See* DIRECTORY / ESOMAR **923**

ESOMAR *See* PROCEEDINGS OF THE ANNUAL CONFERENCE : ESOMAR **5336**

ESOMAR MARKETING RESEARCH MONOGRAPH SERIES (NE) **924**

ESOMAR SEMINARS-CONFERENCE SYMPOSIA PUBLICATIONS (NE) **924**

ESOPE : BI-MENSUEL SOCIAL, POLITIQUE, ECONOMIQUE / PUBLIE AVEC LA COLLABORATION DE LA S.E.D.D.E.S (FR/0421-4226) [08313495] **1489**

ESOPO, L' (IT/0392-9752) [06382755] **415**

ESP, ECONOMY SOCIETY POLICY (JA) [01799686] **2822**

ESPACE BUREAU PARIS (FR/1148-5566) [I11485566] **4211**

ESPACE GEOGRAPHIQUE (FR/0046-2497) [01036068] **2560**

ESPACE INFORMATION (FR) **5103**

ESPACE (MONTREAL) (CN/0821-9222) [09925413] **349**

● ESPACE MONTREAL (ENGLISH EDITION 1992) (CN/1188-5831) [26497856] **1489**

● ESPACE MONTREAL (FRENCH EDITION 1992) (CN/1188-5831) [26497858] **1489**

ESPACE POPULATIONS SOCIETES (FR/0755-7809) [11909726] **4552**

ESPACE SOCIAL EUROPEEN PARIS (FR/0999-7822) [I09997822] **5244**

ESPACES DE SAINT-JOHN PERSE (FR) [07419220] **3385**

ESPACES ET RESSOURCES MARITIMES (FR/0988-2022) [I09882022] **5449**

ESPACES ET SOCIETES (FR/0014-0481) [01677758] 2822, **298**

ESPACES LATINO-AMERICAINS (FR/1168-1179) [11681179] 2260, **4473**

ESPACES PARIS. 1970 (FR/0336-1446) [I03361446] **5469**

ESPACES VERTS (CN/0846-5339) [20781860] **2414**

ESPACIO (PE) [06450325] **2822**

ESPACIO
Alphabetical Title Index

ESPACIO, TIEMPO Y FORMA. SERIE 7, HISTORIA DEL ARTE : REVISTA DE LA FACULTAD DE GEOGRAFIA E HISTORIA / UNIVERSIDAD NACIONAL DE EDUCACION A DISTANCIA (SP/1130-0124) [25192037] 298, **349**

ESPACO & DEBATES (BL) [08951432] **2822**

ESPANA AGRICOLA Y GANADERA (SP) [18436604] 210, **2300**

ESPANA AL DIA (SP) [01784580] **1489**

ESPANA CONTEMPORANEA : EC (SP/0214-1396) [17928130] **3385**

ESPANA, PANORAMICA SOCIAL (SP) [02416569] **5244**

ESPANA, PORTUGAL (FR) [02225701] **5469**

ESPANOL ACTUAL (SP/0425-2772) [02260818] **3279**

ESPANOL EN AUSTRALIA (AT) **3279**

ESPANOLES, LOS (SP) [01792341] **432**

ESPANSIONE (IT) **866**

ESPECIALLY FOR SENIORS **CEASED.** (CN/0705-9418) [04784014] **5179**

ESPERANTO (NE/0014-0635) [11327644] **3279**

ESPERANTO DOCUMENTS (NE/0165-2575) [04289291] **3279**

ESPERANTO - DOKUMENTOJ (NE/0165-2524) [I01652524] **3279**

ESPERANTOUSA (US/1056-0297) [23447059] **3280**

ESPERIA (IT) [17154446] **3342**

ESPERIENZE LETTERARIE (IT/0392-3495) [04054251] **3385**

ESPIAL CANADIAN DATA BASE DIRECTORY, THE (CN/0834-3888) [15726178] 1277, **1259**

ESPIONAGE MAGAZINE (US/8756-8535) [11667267] **5074**

ESPIRAL (CK/0014-0708) [02387129] **349**

ESPIRITO SANTO (BRAZIL : STATE). SECRETARIA DE ADMINISTRACAO **See** RELATORIO DE ATIVIDADES - SECRETARIA DE ADMINISTRACAO DO ESTADO DO ESPIRITO SANTO **4679**

ESPIRITO SANTO (BRAZIL : STATE). SECRETARIA DE ESTADO DA EDUCACAO **See** PLANO ESTADUAL DE EDUCACAO **1774**

ESPIRITU (SP/0014-0716) [09080319] **4346**

ESPLUMOIR, L' (CN/0706-0556) [04955161] **3462**

ESPMENA BULLETIN (SU/1011-7997) [08277438] **3280**

ESPOIR (FR) [01688704] **1668**

ESPOIR (LASALLE) (CN/1193-6886) [24292272] **4473**

ESPOON KAUPUNGIN TILASTOLLINEN VUOSIKIRJA (FI/0357-6825) [09668385] **5327**

ESPRESSIONI IN VETRINA (IT) **833**

ESPRESSO, L' (IT/0423-4243) [01568229] **2487**

ESPRESSO SERA (IT) **5804**

ESPRIT CREATEUR, L' (US/0014-0767) [01568231] **3342**

ESPRIT DE CORPS, CANADIAN MILITARY THEN & NOW (CN/1194-2266) [27898477] **4043**

ESPRIT DU DUC / DUQUESNE UNIVERSITY, L' (US) [10411064] **1823**

ESPRIT ET VIE (FR/0014-0775) [05653769] **4956**

ESPRIT (PARIS, 1932-) (FR/0014-0759) [01568230] **2515**

ESQ (US/0093-8297) [01567166] **3385**

ESQUIMALT STAR, THE (CN/0821-0403) [09674438] **5784**

ESQUIRE (1979) (US/0194-9535) [05154955] **2533**

ESQUIRE SPORTSMAN (US) **4894**

ESQUISSES (MONTREAL) (CN/1182-5510) [22769120] **298**

ESQUIVE (MONTREAL, QUEBEC) (CN/0823-793X) [10862245] **4894**

ESRA NEWSLETTER (LU/1010-8149) [I10108149] **1668**

ESSA BULLETIN (CN/0710-1996) [08419043] **1668**

ESSA PROFESSIONAL PAPER **See** NOAA PROFESSIONAL PAPER **1453**

ESSAIS ET TRAVAUX - GRENOBLE. UNIVERSITE (FR/0434-6629) [01508849] **1823**

ESSAY AND GENERAL LITERATURE INDEX (US/0014-083X) [02004165] **3458**

ESSAY AND GENERAL LITERATURE INDEX. CD-ROM (US/0014-083X) **3458**

ESSAY PROOF JOURNAL, THE (US/0014-0848) [01568239] **1144**

ESSAYS AND MONOGRAPHS IN COLORADO HISTORY (US/0899-0409) [12119130] **2732**

ESSAYS AND REPORTS - LUTHERAN HISTORICAL CONFERENCE (US/0090-3817) [01783644] **5059**

ESSAYS AND STUDIES BY THE FACULTY OF HIROSHIMA JOGAKUIN COLLEGE (JA/0374-8057) [10813547] **1823**

ESSAYS AND STUDIES (LONDON) (UK) [01567935] **3385**

ESSAYS AND STUDIES (LONDON, ENGLAND : 1950) (UK/0071-1357) [05341381] 3280, **3385**

ESSAYS BY DIVERS HANDS (UK/0080-4584) [01607974] **3385**

ESSAYS IN ARTS AND SCIENCES (US/0361-5634) [01955831] **2846**

ESSAYS IN BIOCHEMISTRY (UK/0071-1365) [01568241] **487**

ESSAYS IN COGNITIVE PSYCHOLOGY (UK/0959-4779) [I09594779] **5245**

ESSAYS IN CRITICISM (UK/0014-0856) [01568243] **3385**

ESSAYS IN ECONOMIC AND BUSINESS HISTORY : SELECTED PAPERS FROM THE ECONOMIC AND BUSINESS HISTORICAL SOCIETY (US/0896-226X) [12001765] **1560**

ESSAYS IN FRENCH LITERATURE (AT/0071-139X) [01774740] **3385**

ESSAYS IN GRAHAM GREENE (US/0738-0763) [09508021] **3385**

ESSAYS IN HISTORY **CEASED.** (US/0071-1411) [02104541] **2615**

ESSAYS IN HISTORY (ARLINGTON) (US/0272-0337) [05996085] **2615**

ESSAYS IN LITERATURE (US/0094-5404) [01645163] **3342**

ESSAYS IN NEUROCHEMISTRY AND NEUROPHARMACOLOGY (UK/0147-0205) [03054333] 975, 4303, **3832**

ESSAYS IN POETICS (UK/0308-888X) [04093998] **3385**

ESSAYS IN PUBLIC WORKS HISTORY (US/1047-5257) [03764139] **5245**

ESSAYS IN THEATRE (CN/0821-4425) [09523761] **5364**

ESSAYS ON CANADIAN WRITING (CN/0316-0300) [02247614] **3385**

ESSAYS ON FANTASTIC LITERATURE (US/0891-9593) [15048287] **3385**

ESSAYS ON MUSIC IN AFRICA (GW) [18762141] **4116**

ESSE (CN/0831-859X) [15226735] **349**

ESSECOME (IT) **5103**

ESSECOME (IT/0394-8625) [I03948625] **3164**

ESSEN & TRINKEN (GW/0721-9776) [I07219776] **2334**

ESSENCE (US/0014-0880) [01568247] **5555**

ESSENCE EXPRESS (CN/0844-8698) [20241165] **833**

ESSENTIAL GUIDE TO PRESCRIPTION DRUGS, THE (US/0894-7058) [15608737] **4303**

ESSENTIAL MOLECULAR BIOLOGY (US) [25396108] **455**

ESSENTIAL NEWS (US/1059-0633) [24469538] **5630**

ESSENTIEL (SAINT-LAURENT) (CN/0842-4624) [19579697] **5555**

ESSENZE E DERIVATI AGRUMARI (IT/0014-0902) [07676905] **1024**

ESSEX ARCHAEOLOGY AND HISTORY : THE TRANSACTIONS OF THE ESSEX ARCHAEOLOGICAL SOCIETY (UK/0308-3462) [02319614] 267, **2686**

ESSEX COUNTRYSIDE (UK/0014-0910) [01667427] **2515**

ESSEX FAMILY HISTORIAN, THE (UK/0140-7503) [10690380] **2446**

ESSEX FREE PRESS (CN) **5784**

ESSEX GENEALOGIST, THE (US/0279-067X) [07490738] **2446**

ESSEX INDEPENDENT, THE (US) [16830083] **5670**

ESSEX INSTITUTE **See** ESSEX INSTITUTE HISTORICAL COLLECTIONS **2732**

ESSEX INSTITUTE HISTORICAL COLLECTIONS (US) [01568256] **2732**

ESSEX JOURNAL (UK/0014-0961) [01681567] 267, **2686**

ESSEX RECUSANT **CEASED.** (UK/0423-4456) [02000608] **5029**

ESSEX SUCCULENT REVIEW (UK) [03997534] 2773, **2414**

ESSEX UNION LIST OF SERIALS : EULOS (UK) [08261710] **415**

ESSO INFORMATIONS (FR) [02241224] **1606**

ESSO MAGAZINE (UK/0014-1011) [10449221] **4255**

ESSO NORTH (CN/0823-7751) [10785479] **4255**

ESSO SOCIETE ANONYME FRANCAISE **See** ESSO INFORMATIONS **1606**

ESSOR FRANCAIS DU COMMERCE EXTERIEUR **See** ESSOR FRANCAIS DU COMMERCE INTERNATIONAL **833**

●ESSOR FRANCAIS DU COMMERCE INTERNATIONAL (FR) [29233862] **833**

ESSOR HEBDOMADAIRE **See** ESSOR, L' **2639**

ESSOR, L' (ML) [06289682] **2639**

ESSOR RURAL (UV) [02470507] **2822**

EST AGRICOLE ET VITICOLE, L' (FR) [07717451] **82**

EST & OUEST **CEASED.** (FR/0014-1267) [01688367] **4541**

EST & OUEST : BULLETIN DE L'ASSOCIATION D'ETUDES ET D'INFORMATIONS POLITIQUES INTERNATIONALES **CEASED.** (FR/0014-1267) [08911041] **4520**

EST EUROPEEN, L' (FR/0014-1097) [01780163] **2686**

EST MEDECINE (FR/0248-9643) [09118398] **3575**

EST-OVEST (IT/0046-256X) [11980551] **4473**

ESTABLISHING AN OFFICE IN HONG KONG (HK) **672**

ESTABLISHMENT AND PRODUCTS LICENSED UNDER SECTION 351 OF THE PUBLIC HEALTH SERVICES ACT / U.S. DEPARTMENT OF HEALTH AND HUMAN SERVICES, PUBLIC HEALTH SERVICE, FOOD AND DRUG ADMINISTRATION (US) [07536243] **4775**

ESTABLISHMENT REGISTER, INDUSTRIAL CLASS (BS) [19133740] **4646**

ESTABLISHMENTS HOLDING U.S. VETERINARY LICENSES TO PRODUCE BIOLOGICAL PRODUCTS **See** VETERINARY BIOLOGICAL PRODUCTS. LICENSEES **5525**

ESTACION EXPERIMENTAL DE AULA DEI **See** ANALES DE LA ESTACION EXPERIMENTAL DE AULA DEI **58**

ESTACION EXPERIMENTAL REGIONAL AGROPECUARIA BALCARCE **See** BOLETIN TECNICO - ESTACION EXPERIMENTAL REGIONAL AGROPECUARIA BALCARCE **68**

ESTADISTICA (US/0014-1135) [01568264] **5327**

ESTADISTICA DE CRIMINALIDAD (CK) [02514249] 3164, **3080**

ESTADISTICA DE ESTABLECIMIENTOS SANITARIOS CON REGIMEN DE INTERNADO (SP/0210-4598) [04030931] **3780**

ESTADISTICA DEL SUICIDIO EN ESPANA (SP) [05395636] **5327**

ESTADISTICA EDUCATIVA (AG) [01785966] 1745, **1795**

ESTADISTICA ESPANOLA (SP/0014-1151) [01688516] **5327**

ESTADISTICA - MINISTERIO DE ALIMENTACION DIRECCION GENERAL DE INFORMATICA Y ESTADISTICA (PE) [03269478] 82, **153**

ESTADISTICA - OSE (UY) [02240865] **5533**

ESTADISTICA PANAMENA; BOLETIN SEMANAL (PN) [07571176] **5327**

ESTADISTICA PANAMENA. SERIE H.2 : INFORMACION AGROPECUARIA, PRECIOS PAGADOS POR EL PRODUCTOR AGROPECUARIO (PN) [02871683] 82, **153**

ESTADISTICA PANAMENA. SERIE K. 1: ANUARIO DE COMERCIO EXTERIOR **See** ESTADISTICA PANAMENA. SERIE K : ANUARIO DE COMERCIO EXTERIOR **833**

ESTADISTICA PANAMENA. SERIE K : ANUARIO DE COMERCIO EXTERIOR (PN) [01203200] **833**

ESTADISTICA PANAMENA. SITUACION ECONOMICA, SECCION 331 : ANUARIO DE COMERCIO EXTERIOR (PN) [04703052] 833, 1634, **728**

ESTADISTICA Y ACTUARIADO (VE) [03300993] 2879, **2897**

ESTADISTICAS AGROPECUARIAS (UY) [06924227] **5327**

ESTADISTICAS AGROPECUARIAS CONTINUAS (GT) [15067390] **210**

ESTADISTICAS (CHILE. SERVICIO DE SEGURO SOCIAL) (CL/0577-8174) [02259263] 2879, **2897**

ESTADISTICAS DE LA EDUCACION (AG) [02380605] 1745, **1795**

ESTADISTICAS DEL COMERCIO EXTERIOR DE VENEZUELA; IMPORTACION: ARTICULO Y PAIS (VE) [05107782] 833, **728**

ESTADISTICAS FINANCIERAS INTERNACIONALES / FONDO MONETARIO INTERNACIONAL (US/0252-3078) [08119726] **728**

Alphabetical Title Index — ESTIMATES

ESTADISTICAS HOSPITALARIAS *See* ANUARIO DE ESTADISTICAS HOSPITALARIAS **3776**

ESTADISTICAS INDUSTRIALES (BO) [03594911] 1606, **1532**

ESTADISTICAS JUDICIALES DE ESPANA (SP/0561-4473) [03244071] 2967, **3080**

ESTADISTICAS SOCIOECONOMICAS, PUERTO RICO / JUNTA DE PLANIFICACION, AREA DE ANALISIS Y ASESORAMIENTO ECONOMICO, NEGOCIADO DE ANALISIS Y PROYECCIONES ECONOMICAS (PR) [07466576] 1560, **1532**

ESTADISTICO DE ENCUESTAS (SP/0214-3240) [I02143240] **5327**

ESTADO & SOCIEDAD (BO) [15134169] **5199**

ESTADO DA PARAIBA, ANUARIO ESTATISTICO (BL) [09500028] **5327**

ESTADO DE SAO PAULO (BL) [02407296] **5779**

ESTADO DO RIO DE JANEIRO : INDICADORES ECONOMICOS (BL) [02556361] **1560**

ESTADO DO RIO : INDUSTRIA & I.E.E. COMERCIO (BL) [01787115] **1606**

ESTAMPILLE, L'OBJET D'ART, L' (FR/0998-8041) [21801958] **320**

ESTATE & FINANCIAL PLANNERS ALERT *See* ESTATE PLANNER'S ALERT (1994) **3118**

ESTATE & FINANCIAL PLANNERS ALERT (US/1044-7911) [19903926] **3118**

●ESTATE PLANNER'S ALERT (1994) (US/1076-819X) [30010895] **3118**

ESTATE PLANNERS QUARTERLY (US/0423-4596) [06175344] **3118**

ESTATE PLANNING & CALIFORNIA PROBATE REPORTER (US/0273-7027) [06852708] **3118**

ESTATE PLANNING & TAXATION COORDINATOR (US/0195-1238) [05293401] 4721, **3118**

ESTATE PLANNING CHECKLISTS AND FORMS (US/0014-1224) [04075030] **3118**

ESTATE PLANNING (ENGLEWOOD CLIFFS, N.J.) (US/0014-1216) [02660405] **3118**

ESTATE PLANNING (LOS ANGELES, CALIF.) (US/0278-4009) [07800487] **3118**

ESTATE PLANNING REVIEW (US/0098-2873) [01799578] **3118**

ESTATE PLANNING (TAMPA) (US/0094-1794) [01793979] **3118**

ESTATE TAX TECHNIQUES (US) [01642003] **3118**

ESTATES & TRUSTS JOURNAL (CN/0840-7886) [18954042] **3118**

ESTATES & TRUSTS REPORTS (CN/0706-5655) [03946754] **3118**

ESTATES GAZETTE (UK/0014-1240) [I00141240] **4837**

ESTATES GAZETTE. DIGEST OF LAND AND PROPERTY CASES (UK) [08152953] **2967**

ESTATES TIMES (UK/0014-1259) [I00141259] **4837**

ESTATISTICA BASICA DE ARRECADACAO (BL) [06765943] **4721**

ESTATISTICA DA ACTIVIDADE MINEIRA NO ESTADO DE ANGOLA (AO/0301-6552) [01792314] 2138, **2004**

ESTATISTICA DO CULTO CATOLICO (BL) [02741097] **5029**

ESTATISTICA / EMPRESA DE PORTOS DO BRASIL S/A, PORTOBRAS, ADMINISTRACAO DO PORTO DO RECIFE, SETOR COMERCIAL, SUB-SETOR DE CONTROLE E ESTATISTICA (BL) [08297874] **5400**

ESTATISTICA INDUSTRIAL (LISBOA) (PO/0079-418X) [01183289] **1532**

ESTATISTICAS DA EDUCACAO NACIONAL (BL) [02613063] 1745, **1795**

ESTATISTICAS DA ORGANIZACAO CORPORATIVA E PREVIDENCIA : CONTINENTE E ILHAS ADJACENTES (PO) [02471290] **5284**

ESTATISTICAS DA SAUDE. ASSISTENCIA MEDICO-SANITARIA (BL/0101-3033) [08914280] **3780**

ESTATISTICAS DE MORTALIDADE, BRASIL / MINISTERIO DA SAUDE, SECRETARIA NACIONAL DE ACOES BASICAS DE SAUDE, DIVISAO NACIONAL DE EPIDEMIOLOGIA (BL) [10024994] **4552**

ESTATISTICAS DO COMERCIO EXTERNO (AO) [01786981] 833, **728**

ESTATISTICAS DO TURISMO (PO/0377-2306) [05627153] **5500**

ESTATUTOS Y REGLAMENTO / FONDO MONETARIO INTERNACIONAL *CEASED*. (US/0250-7323) [07585549] **1489**

ESTES PARK TRAIL-GAZETTE, THE (US) [23156197] **5642**

ESTES TRAILS (US/0737-481X) [09367350] **2446**

ESTETIKA (XR/0014-1291) [02302050] **320**

ESTEVAN MERCURY (CN) **5784**

ESTHERVILLE DAILY NEWS (US/0747-0754) [10535225] **5670**

ESTHETIC DENTISTRY UPDATE (PHILADELPHIA, PA.) (US/1045-9812) [20306049] **1323**

ESTHETICA (PARIS, 1989) *CEASED*. (FR/1142-2599) [I11422599] **404**

ESTHETICA PROFESSIONNEL *CEASED*. (FR) [I11465794] **404**

ESTIMACION DE LA PRODUCCION AGRICOLA EN LOS DISTRITOS DE RIEGO (MX) [08920729] **82**

ESTIMATE OF EXPENDITURE IN RESPECT OF WHICH A VOTE-ON-ACCOUNT IS REQUIRED (II) [01784165] **4721**

ESTIMATE OF THE ADDITIONAL EXPENDITURE TO BE DEFRAYED FROM REVENUE AND LOAN ACCOUNTS (SA) [01788309] 4646, **4721**

ESTIMATE OF THE ADDITIONAL EXPENDITURE TO BE DEFRAYED FROM STATE REVENUE ACCOUNT. BEGROTING VAN DIE ADDISIONALE UITGAWES WAT UIT STAATSINKOMSTEREKENING (SA) [06127710] **4721**

ESTIMATE, THE (US/1043-1667) **4520**

ESTIMATED 25% PAYMENTS TO BE MADE TO COUNTIES IN FISCAL YEAR ... FROM GOVERNMENT OWNED LANDS ADMINISTERED BY THE FOREST SERVICE / U.S. DEPT. OF AGRICULTURE, FOREST SERVICE (US) [08276976] **2379**

ESTIMATED CIVILIAN LABOR FORCE. MONTGOMERY, ALABAMA STANDARD METROPOLITAN STATISTICAL AREA, MONTGOMERY, AUTAUGA & ELMORE COUNTIES (US) [10903552] **1668**

ESTIMATED GRADE AND STAPLE OF UPLAND COTTON GINNED IN THE UNITED STATES (US) [03455201] **171**

ESTIMATED INTERNAL MIGRATION BULLETIN (PORT OF SPAIN) (TR/0303-4410) [01794032] **4552**

ESTIMATED OIL AND GAS RESERVES, SOUTHERN CALIFORNIA OUTER CONTINENTAL SHELF / UNITED STATES DEPARTMENT OF THE INTERIOR, GEOLOGICAL SURVEY (US) [05766576] **4255**

ESTIMATED POTENTIAL LABOR SUPPLY FOR INDUSTRIAL EXPANSION IN ARKANSAS *See* POTENTIAL LABOR SUPPLY, ARKANSAS **1702**

ESTIMATED POUNDAGE EQUIVALENTS (CN) [04629061] **5350**

ESTIMATED RESIDENT POPULATION BY AGE AND SEX IN STATISTICAL LOCAL AREAS, WESTERN AUSTRALIA / AUSTRALIAN BUREAU OF STATISTICS (AT) [22135819] 4552, **4562**

ESTIMATED RESIDENT POPULATION BY COUNTRY OF BIRTH, AGE AND SEX, AUSTRALIA / AUSTRALIAN BUREAU OF STATISTICS (AT/1030-9179) [26089482] **4552**

ESTIMATED RESIDENT POPULATION BY MARITAL STATUS, AGE AND SEX, AUSTRALIA (AT/1030-8989) [26522741] **4552**

ESTIMATED RESIDENT POPULATION BY SEX AND AGE, STATES AND TERRITORIES OF AUSTRALIA (AT/0810-0039) [13750301] **4552**

ESTIMATED RESIDENT POPULATION IN LOCAL GOVERNMENT AREAS / AUSTRALIAN BUREAU OF STATISTICS, SOUTH AUSTRALIAN OFFICE (AT) [08917603] 4553, **4562**

ESTIMATED WORLD REQUIREMENTS OF NARCOTIC DRUGS AND ESTIMATES OF WORLD PRODUCTION OF OPIUM (US/0566-764X) [01753647] **1344**

ESTIMATES, HIGHLIGHTS - TREASURY BOARD (CN) [02244139] **4721**

ESTIMATES OF ADDITIONAL EXPENDITURE - DEPARTMENT OF POSTS AND TELECOMMUNICATIONS (SA) [06545354] **1154**

ESTIMATES OF CAPITAL EXPENDITURE OF THE EAST AFRICAN COMMUNITY (TZ) [03511927] **4721**

ESTIMATES OF EMPLOYEES BY PROVINCE AND INDUSTRY (CUMULATED EDITION) (CN/0702-0961) [01792920] 1668, **1532**

ESTIMATES OF EMPLOYMENT, HOURS, AND EARNINGS IN NONAGRICULTURAL ESTABLISHMENTS: DECATUR STANDARD METROPOLITAN STATISTICAL AREA (US/0091-4517) [01786857] **1668**

ESTIMATES OF EMPLOYMENT, HOURS, AND EARNINGS IN NONAGRICULTURAL ESTABLISHMENTS. SPRINGFIELD STANDARD METROPOLITAN STATISTICAL AREA (US/0091-4355) [01786854] **1668**

ESTIMATES OF EXPENDITURE (ALBERTA. TREASURY DEPT.) (CN) [03258258] **4721**

ESTIMATES OF EXPENDITURE : CAPITAL ACCOUNT AND SUMMARY OF AMOUNTS TO BE VOTED (ALBERTA) (CN) [01786894] **4721**

ESTIMATES OF EXPENDITURE FOR THE YEAR ENDING JUNE 30 - ZIMBABWE (RH) [06155818] **4721**

ESTIMATES OF EXPENDITURE : INCOME ACCOUNT (CN) [01786895] **4721**

ESTIMATES OF EXPENDITURE. SUPPLEMENTARY INFORMATION. RECONCILIATION OF HISTORICAL DATA (CN/0713-0872) [02537809] **4722**

ESTIMATES OF EXPENDITURE (TRINIDAD AND TOBAGO) (TR) [05202367] **4722**

ESTIMATES OF GROSS DOMESTIC PRODUCT (HK) [05204786] **1560**

ESTIMATES OF INCOME & EXPENDITURE (SA) [02349758] **4722**

ESTIMATES OF LABOUR INCOME (OTTAWA) (CN/0318-9007) [06853654] 1668, **1532**

ESTIMATES OF PROVINCIAL REVENUE TO BE COLLECTED AND EXPENDITURE TO BE DEFRAYED FROM THE PROVINCIAL REVENUE FUND DURING THE YEAR ... / REPUBLIC OF SOUTH AFRICA, PROVINCE OF THE CAPE OF GOOD HOPE (SA) [09869497] **4722**

ESTIMATES OF RECURRENT EXPENDITURE OF THE EAST AFRICAN COMMUNITY (TZ) [03511673] **4722**

ESTIMATES OF RECURRENT EXPENDITURE OF THE GOVERNMENT OF KENYA (KE/0453-5855) [02226922] 4722, **4646**

ESTIMATES OF RECURRENT REVENUE AND EXPENDITURE (BS) [01786635] **4722**

ESTIMATES OF RECURRENT REVENUE, EXPENDITURE & LOCAL CONTRIBUTION TO CAPITAL BUDGET / GOVERNMENT OF ANGUILLA (AM) [20639284] **4722**

ESTIMATES OF REVENUE AND EXPEDITURE - EAST AFRICAN RAILWAYS CORPORATION (KE) [03648325] **5400**

ESTIMATES OF REVENUE AND EXPENDITURE (BS) [01786686] **4722**

ESTIMATES OF REVENUE AND EXPENDITURE - DEPARTMENT OF POSTS AND TELECOMMUNICATIONS (SA) [04897697] **1145**

ESTIMATES OF SCHOOL STATISTICS (US/0077-4278) [04131183] 1745, **1795**

ESTIMATES OF THE GOVERNMENT - KANO. NIGERIA (STATE) (NR) [01785625] **4722**

ESTIMATES OF THE GOVERNMENT OF NIGER STATE OF NIGERIA (NR) [27767589] **4646**

ESTIMATES OF THE GOVERNMENT OF NOVA SCOTIA (CN/0383-4786) [02241537] **4722**

ESTIMATES OF THE MILITARY GOVERNMENT OF NIGER STATE OF NIGERIA / NIGER STATE OF NIGERIA (NR) [19052486] **4646**

ESTIMATES OF THE PROBABLE WAYS AND MEANS AND EXPENDITURE OF THE GOVERNMENT OF QUEENSLAND (AT) [01785343] **4722**

ESTIMATES. PART I, THE GOVERNMENT EXPENDITURE PLAN (CN) [11980248] **4722**

ESTIMATES. PART III, AGRICULTURE CANADA (CN) [10443715] **82**

ESTIMATES. PART III, ATOMIC ENERGY CONTROL BOARD (CN) [10443973] **1560**

ESTIMATES. PART III, AUDITOR GENERAL OF CANADA (CN) [10817525] 4722, **4646**

ESTIMATES. PART III, CANADA LABOUR RELATIONS BOARD (CN) [10445122] **3148**

ESTIMATES. PART III, CANADIAN ADVISORY COUNCIL ON THE STATUS OF WOMEN (CN) [10817487] **5555**

ESTIMATES. PART III, CANADIAN HUMAN RIGHTS COMMISSION (CN) [10443491] **4507**

ESTIMATES. PART III, CANADIAN INTERGOVERNMENTAL CONFERENCE SECRETARIAT (CN) [10817364] **4646**

ESTIMATES. PART III, CANADIAN INTERNATIONAL DEVELOPMENT AGENCY (CN) [10817291] **1560**

ESTIMATES — Alphabetical Title Index

ESTIMATES. PART III CANADIAN INTERNATIONAL TRADE TRIBUNAL (CN) [19961458] **833**

ESTIMATES. PART III, CANADIAN RADIO-TELEVISION AND TELECOMMUNICATIONS COMMISSION (CN) [10444977] **1154**

ESTIMATES. PART III, CANADIAN TRANSPORTATION ACCIDENT AND INVESTIGATION SAFETY BOARD. EXPENDITURE PLAN *See* ESTIMATES. PART III, TRANSPORTATION SAFETY BOARD OF CANADA. EXPENDITURE PLAN **4646**

ESTIMATES. PART III, CONSUMER AND CORPORATE AFFAIRS EXPENDITURE PLAN (CN) [10446326] 1560, **4646**

ESTIMATES. PART III, CORRECTIONAL SERVICE CANADA (CN) [10444416] **3164**

ESTIMATES. PART III, DEPARTMENT OF COMMUNICATIONS (CN) [12183057] **1154**

ESTIMATES. PART III, DEPARTMENT OF FINANCE CANADA (CN) [10817735] **4722**

●ESTIMATES. PART III, DEPARTMENT OF FOREIGN AFFAIRS AND INTERNATIONAL TRADE (CN) [31069921] **4722**

ESTIMATES. PART III, DEPARTMENT OF JUSTICE CANADA, CANADIAN UNITY INFORMATION OFFICE PROGRAM (CN) [10443851] **2967**

ESTIMATES. PART III, ECONOMIC COUNCIL OF CANADA (CN) [10442974] 1560, **4646**

ESTIMATES. PART III, EMPLOYMENT AND IMMIGRATION CANADA (CN) [10446559] **1668**

ESTIMATES. PART III, ENERGY, MINES AND RESOURCES CANADA (CN) [11920393] **2138**

ESTIMATES. PART III, ENERGY, MINES AND RESOURCES CANADA, MINERALS AND EARTH SCIENCES PROGRAM (CN) [10444363] **2114**

ESTIMATES. PART III, ENVIRONMENT CANADA (CN) [10847704] **1560**

ESTIMATES. PART III, ENVIRONMENT CANADA, PARKS CANADA PROGRAM (CN) [10445341] **2193**

ESTIMATES. PART III, EXTERNAL AFFAIRS AND INTERNATIONAL TRADE CANADA. EXPENDITURE PLAN (CN) [23110834] **4722**

ESTIMATES. PART III, FEDERAL COURT OF CANADA (CN) [10444218] **2967**

ESTIMATES. PART III, FISHERIES AND OCEANS (CN) [10817865] **2300**

ESTIMATES. PART III, HEALTH AND WELFARE CANADA (CN) [10847663] **4775**

ESTIMATES. PART III, HEALTH AND WELFARE CANADA, HEALTH AND SOCIAL SERVICES PROGRAM, INCOME SECURITY PROGRAM, FITNESS AND AMATEUR SPORT PROGRAM (CN) [10444251] **5285**

ESTIMATES. PART III, IMMIGRATION APPEAL BOARD (CN) [10443142] **1918**

ESTIMATES. PART III, INDIAN AND NORTHERN AFFAIRS CANADA (CN) [11921114] **2732**

ESTIMATES. PART III, INDIAN AND NORTHERN AFFAIRS CANADA AND CANADIAN POLAR COMMISSION (CN) [29905276] **2260**

ESTIMATES. PART III, INDUSTRY, SCIENCE AND TECHNOLOGY CANADA. EXPENDITURE PLAN (CN) [23110900] **1606**

ESTIMATES. PART III, INVESTMENT CANADA (CN) [13726427] **897**

ESTIMATES. PART III, LAW REFORM COMMISSION OF CANADA (CN) [10446511] **2967**

ESTIMATES. PART III, MEDICAL RESEARCH COUNCIL (CN) [10446635] **3575**

ESTIMATES. PART III, MINISTRY OF STATE, ECONOMIC AND REGIONAL DEVELOPMENT (CN) [10818043] **1560**

ESTIMATES. PART III, NATIONAL ARCHIVES OF CANADA (CN) [18536596] **2481**

ESTIMATES. PART III, NATIONAL DEFENCE (CN) [10817889] **4043**

ESTIMATES. PART III, NATIONAL ENERGY BOARD (CN) [10443342] **1943**

ESTIMATES. PART III, NATIONAL FILM BOARD (CN) [10445268] **4068**

ESTIMATES. PART III, NATIONAL LIBRARY OF CANADA (CN) [10443258] **3209**

ESTIMATES. PART III, NATIONAL MUSEUMS OF CANADA (CN) [10817772] **4087**

ESTIMATES. PART III, NATIONAL PAROLE BOARD (CN) [10446802] **3164**

ESTIMATES. PART III, NATIONAL RESEARCH COUNCIL CANADA (CN) [10817580] 5103, **4646**

ESTIMATES. PART III, NATIONAL TRANSPORTATION AGENCY OF CANADA (CN) [19942543] **5381**

●ESTIMATES. PART III, NATURAL RESOURCES CANADA (CN) [31093425] **2193**

ESTIMATES. PART III, NATURAL SCIENCES AND ENGINEERING RESEARCH COUNCIL OF CANADA (CN) [10443614] **5103**

ESTIMATES. PART III, NORTHERN PIPELINE AGENCY (CN) [10446967] **1560**

ESTIMATES. PART III, OFFICE OF THE CHIEF ELECTORAL OFFICER (CN) [11919957] **4646**

ESTIMATES. PART III, OFFICE OF THE COMMISSIONER OF OFFICIAL LANGUAGES (CN) [10446759] **3280**

ESTIMATES. PART III, PRIVY COUNCIL OFFICE (CN) [10817692] **4646**

ESTIMATES. PART III, PUBLIC SERVICE COMMISSION OF CANADA (CN) [10444031] **4646**

ESTIMATES. PART III, PUBLIC SERVICE STAFF RELATIONS BOARD (CN) [10444093] 4646, **1668**

ESTIMATES. PART III, RESTRICTIVE TRADE PRACTICES COMMISSION OF CANADA (CN) [10444918] **2967**

ESTIMATES. PART III, REVENUE CANADA, CUSTOMS AND EXCISE (CN) [10817907] **4722**

ESTIMATES. PART III, REVENUE CANADA, TAXATION (CN) [10444074] **4722**

ESTIMATES. PART III, ROYAL CANADIAN MOUNTED POLICE (CN) [10817930] **3164**

ESTIMATES. PART III, SCIENCE COUNCIL OF CANADA (CN) [10443703] **5103**

ESTIMATES. PART III, SECRETARY OF STATE, OFFICIAL LANGUAGES PROGRAM (CN) [10443992] **3280**

ESTIMATES. PART III, SOCIAL SCIENCES AND HUMANITIES RESEARCH COUNCIL (CN) [10443840] **5199**

ESTIMATES. PART III, SOLICITOR GENERAL CANADA (CN) [10817978] **2967**

ESTIMATES. PART III, STATUS OF WOMEN CANADA (CN) [10940515] **5555**

ESTIMATES. PART III, SUPPLY AND SERVICES CANADA (CN) [10446673] **4646**

ESTIMATES. PART III, SUPREME COURT OF CANADA (CN) [10444884] **2967**

ESTIMATES. PART III, TARIFF BOARD (CN) [10445068] **2967**

ESTIMATES. PART III, TAX REVIEW BOARD (CN) [10443055] 4722, **2967**

ESTIMATES. PART III, TRANSPORT CANADA (CN) [10817838] **5381**

●ESTIMATES. PART III, TRANSPORTATION SAFETY BOARD OF CANADA. EXPENDITURE PLAN (CN) [25908342] **4646**

ESTIMATES. PART III, TREASURY BOARD OF CANADA, COMPTROLLER GENERAL (CN) [10817805] **743**

ESTIMATES. PART III, VETERANS AFFAIRS CANADA (CN) [10446850] **4043**

ESTIMATES. PART III, WESTERN ECONOMIC DIVERSIFICATION CANADA (CN) [19976802] **1489**

ESTIMATES - PROVINCE OF BRITISH COLUMBIA (CN/0712-4597) [08556776] **4722**

ESTIMATES SUPPLEMENT GUIDELINES *See* DEPARTMENTAL EXPENDITURE ESTIMATES SUPPLEMENT GUIDELINES **4720**

ESTIMATING INFORMATION SERVICE (UK/0308-8073) [03088073] **614**

ESTIMATION AND TRACKING : PRINCIPLES AND TECHNIQUES (US/1057-8390) [24124636] **3505**

ESTIMATOR (HUNTSVILLE, ALA.) *See* NATIONAL ESTIMATOR **2889**

ESTIMATOR'S HANDBOOK (US) [03257170] **614**

ESTIMULACION CARDIACA (SP/0210-9697) [I02109697] **3704**

ESTO ES VENEZUELA (VE) [05324858] **2732**

ESTONIAN LEARNED SOCIETY IN AMERICA *See* YEARBOOK OF THE ESTONIAN LEARNED SOCIETY IN AMERICA **1854**

ESTONIAN PAPERS IN PHONETICS. PUBLIKATTSII ESTONSKIKH FONETISTOV (ER) [03739383] **3280**

ESTRATEGIA *CEASED.* (MX) [02302199] **4473**

ESTRATEGIA (AG/0046-2578) [01688799] **4043**

ESTRATEGIA ECONOMICA Y FINANCIERA (CK/0121-4802) [04306658] **1489**

ESTRELLA DE PANAMA, LA (PN) [12528362] **5807**

ESTRENO (US/0097-8663) [02300200] **5364**

ESTUAIRE (CN/0700-365X) [03304235] **3462**

ESTUAIRE GENEALOGIQUE, L' (CN/0824-4936) [12064724] **2446**

ESTUARIES (US/0160-8347) [03703760] **554**

ESTUARIES AND COASTAL WATERS OF THE BRITISH ISLES : A BIBLIOGRAPHY OF RECENT SCIENTIFIC PAPERS (UK/0309-3964) [08286462] **554**

ESTUARINE, COASTAL AND SHELF SCIENCE (UK/0272-7714) [06929198] **1449**

ESTUDIO AGUSTINIANO (SP) **4956**

ESTUDIO ECONOMICO DE AMERICA LATINA Y EL CARIBE / COMISION ECONOMICA PARA AMERICA LATINA Y EL CARIBE (CL/0252-2217) [12686425] **1489**

ESTUDIOS (SP) **1745**

ESTUDIOS AGROPECUARIOS DE LA FAO (US) [01379486] **82**

ESTUDIOS ARQUEOLOGICOS (AG) [02240080] **267**

ESTUDIOS CLASICOS (MADRID) (SP/0014-1453) [09305409] **1076**

ESTUDIOS DE ARQUEOLOGIA ALAVESA / DIPUTACION FORAL DE ALAVA, CONSEJO DE CULTURA (SP/0425-3507) [02310487] **267**

ESTUDIOS DE ASIA & AFRICA (MX/0185-0164) [01926210] **2503**

ESTUDIOS DE CIENCIAS Y LETRAS : REVISTA DEL INSTITUTO DE FILOSOFIA, CIENCIAS Y LETRAS (UY) [09678135] **4346**

ESTUDIOS DE CULTURA MAYA *CEASED.* (MX/0185-5271) [01568280] **2732**

ESTUDIOS DE CULTURA NAHUATL (MX/0071-1675) [01568281] **2732**

ESTUDIOS DE DERECHO (CK/0014-1461) [01568282] **2967**

ESTUDIOS DE DEUSTO (SP/0423-4847) [05281156] **2967**

ESTUDIOS DE ECONOMIA (CL) [02350448] **1591**

ESTUDIOS DE FILOSOFIA Y RELIGIONES DEL ORIENTE (AG) [05352224] **4346**

ESTUDIOS DE HISTORIA MODERNA Y CONTEMPORANEA DE MEXICO (MX/0185-2620) [01568284] **2615**

ESTUDIOS DE HISTORIA NOVOHISPANA (MX/0185-2523) [01771954] **2732**

ESTUDIOS DE HISTORIA Y DE ARQUEOLOGIA MEDIEVALES (SP/0212-9515) [10789160] **2687**

ESTUDIOS DE LA SEGURIDAD SOCIAL / AISS (AG/0379-0266) [16678753] **1668**

ESTUDIOS DE LINGUISTICA (SP/0212-7636) [11996508] **3280**

ESTUDIOS DE LINGUISTICA APLICADA (MX/0185-2647) [I01852647] **3280**

ESTUDIOS DE PREHISTORIA Y ARQUEOLOGIA MADRILENAS (SP/0213-0246) [12494879] **267**

ESTUDIOS DE PSICOLOGIA (SP/0210-9395) [07612696] **4586**

ESTUDIOS DE RONDA Y SU SERRANIA (SP) [18761769] **2687**

ESTUDIOS DEL DESARROLLO (INT/1013-4069) [I10134069] **5199**

ESTUDIOS DEMOGRAFICOS Y URBANOS (MX/0186-7210) [15570681] **4553**

ESTUDIOS - DEPARTAMENTO DE HISTORIA MODERNA, UNIVERSIDAD DE ZARAGOZA (SP/0211-3759) [05764405] **2615**

ESTUDIOS E INFORMES DE LA CEPAL (CL) [09306900] **2909**

ESTUDIOS ECLESIASTICOS (SP/0210-1610) [01776405] **5029**

ESTUDIOS ECUMENICOS (MX) [04428710] **2615**

ESTUDIOS EMPRESARIALES (SP/0425-3698) [02383308] **866**

ESTUDIOS FILOLOGICOS (CL/0071-1713) [01771955] 3385, **3280**

ESTUDIOS FILOSOFICOS (VE) [04901150] **4346**

ESTUDIOS FILOSOFICOS (VALLADOLID) (SP/0210-6086) [05262650] **4346**

ESTUDIOS FRANCISCANOS (SP) [09817308] **5327**

ESTUDIOS FRONTERIZOS : REVISTA DEL INSTITUTO DE INVESTIGACIONES SOCIALES (MX) [12875931] **1560**

ESTUDIOS GEOGRAFICOS (SP/0014-1496) [02255682] **2560**

Alphabetical Title Index — ETHNIC

ESTUDIOS GEOOGICOS (MADRID) (SP/0367-0449) [02446766] **1375**

ESTUDIOS HUMANISTICOS. FILOLOGIA (SP/0213-1382) [16676233] **3280**

ESTUDIOS HUMANISTICOS. GEOGRAFIA, HISTORIA, ARTE (SP) [16676234] **2846**

ESTUDIOS - INSTITUTO DE ESTUDIO ECONOMICOS SOBRE LA REALIDAD ARGENTINA Y LATINOAMERICANA *SUSPENDED.* (AG/0325-6928) [05323094] **1489**

ESTUDIOS INTERDISCIPLINARIOS (AG) [01793012] **5103**

ESTUDIOS INTERNACIONALES (MX) [05774725] **4520**

ESTUDIOS INTERNACIONALES (CL/0716-0240) [01568286] **4473**

ESTUDIOS LATINOAMERICANOS / POLSKA AKADEMIA NAUK, INSTYTUT HISTORII (PL/0137-3080) [02300454] **2551**

ESTUDIOS MADRID (SP/0210-0525) [I02100525] **3385**

ESTUDIOS MARIANOS (SP) [06094518] **4956**

ESTUDIOS MIGRATORIOS LATINOAMERICANOS (AG/0326-7458) [13979159] **2732**

ESTUDIOS NORTEAMERICANOS (CL/0716-1468) [20718184] **2732**

ESTUDIOS PARAGUAYOS (PY/0251-2483) [02240497] **2732**

ESTUDIOS POLITICOS (MEXICO CITY, MEXICO) (MX/0185-1616) [03307455] **4473**

ESTUDIOS PUBLICOS (SP) [09631322] **1560**

ESTUDIOS ROMANICOS (SP) [04930091] **3280**

ESTUDIOS RURALES LATINOAMERICANAS (CK/0120-0747) [04218692] **82**

ESTUDIOS SEGOVIANOS (SP/0210-7260) [06593693] **2687**

ESTUDIOS SOCIALES (MX) [23752502] **5199**

ESTUDIOS SOCIALES CENTROAMERICANOS *SUSPENDED.* (CR/0303-9676) [01667701] **5245**

ESTUDIOS SOCIALES SANTA FE (AG/0327-4934) [I03274934] **5199**

ESTUDIOS SOCIALES (SANTIAGO, CHILE) (CL/0716-0321) [01097198] **5199**

ESTUDIOS SOCIALES (SANTO DOMINGO) (DR/1017-0596) [02260851] **5199**

ESTUDIOS SOCIOLOGICOS (MX/0185-4186) [I01854186] **5245**

ESTUDIOS TERRITORIALES (SP/0211-6871) [09636243] **2822**

ESTUDIOS TRINITARIOS (SP/0210-0363) [I02100363] **4956**

ESTUDIOS TURISTICOS (SP/0423-5037) [I04235037] **5469**

ESTUDIOS Y DOCUMENTOS (SP/0504-9806) [01466451] **4346**

ESTUDIS BALEARICS (SP) [09776197] **2687**

ESTUDIS D'HISTORIA AGRARIA (SP/0210-4830) [04903677] **82**

ESTUDIS D'HISTORIA CONTEMPORANIA DEL PAIS VALENCIA (SP/0210-8704) [11706922] **2687**

ESTUDIS ESCENICS (SP/0212-3819) [10628066] **5364**

ESTUDO GERAL (BL) [01796425] **2551**

ESTUDOS ANGLO-AMERICANOS (BL/0102-4906) [06354235] 3385, **3280**

ESTUDOS AVANCADOS (BL/0103-4014) [19281445] **2732**

ESTUDOS BIBLICOS (BL) [13385423] **4956**

ESTUDOS DE ANTROPOLOGIA CULTURAL (PO/0425-3906) [01963279] **235**

ESTUDOS DE ANTROPOLOGIA CULTURAL E SOCIAL (PO/0870-4457) [I08704457] **235**

ESTUDOS DE CASTELO BRANCO (PO/0870-6344) [01667569] **2615**

ESTUDOS DE DIREITO PUBLICO : EDP (BL) [10153408] **2967**

ESTUDOS DE HISTORIA E CARTOGRAFIA ANTIGA. MEMORIAS (PO/0870-5879) [I08705879] **2615**

ESTUDOS E DOCUMENTOS (UNIVERSIDADE DE SAO PAULO. FACULDADE DE EDUCACAO) (BL) [03278231] **1745**

ESTUDOS ECONOMICOS - INSTITUTO DE PESQUISAS ECONOMICAS (BL/0101-4161) [01787671] **1592**

ESTUDOS, ENSAIOS E DOCUMENTOS (PORTUGAL. JUNTA DE INVESTIGACOES CIENTIFICAS DO ULTRAMAR) (PO/0870-001X) [09516758] **5103**

ESTUDOS FEMINISTAS (BL/0104-026X) [27392733] **5555**

ESTUDOS HISTORICOS (BL) 5199, 3385, **2732**

ESTUDOS IBERO-AMERICANOS (BL/0101-4064) [02364984] **2687**

ESTUDOS ITALIANOS EM PORTUGAL (PO/0870-8584) [01967647] 2260, **2687**

ESTUDOS LEGISLATIVOS (BL) [01791915] **4647**

ESTUDOS MATEMATICA E INFORMATICA, INSTITUTO GULBENKIAN DE CIENCIA (PO/0251-4230) [11224693] 3505, **1259**

ESTUDOS PORTUGUESES E AFRICANOS : EPA (BL/0103-1821) [10742352] **3385**

ESTUDOS TEOLOGICOS (BL/0101-3130) [07512332] **4956**

ESTUDOS UNIVERSITARIOS (BL) [01787222] **2846**

ESWAU HUPPEDAY (US/0747-5810) [10519797] **2446**

ET AL (US/0425-4090) [01568294] **5245**

ET. ENERGIEWIRTSCHAFTLICHE TAGESFRAGEN (GW/0720-6240) [I07206240] 2054, 4255, **1944**

ET LA LUMIERE FUT (FR) **4388**

ET-MOL (IS) [03097455] **2651**

ETA EVOLUTIVA (FIRENZE) (IT/0392-0658) [05045261] **3903**

ETA SIGMA GAMMAN *See* HEALTH EDUCATOR : JOURNAL OF ETA SIGMA GAMMA **4779**

ETA SIGMA GAMMAN, THE (US/8756-5943) [07453052] **4775**

ETA VERDE, L' (IT/0394-0276) [I03940276] 1913, **2215**

ETABLISSEMENTS SCOLAIRES PUBLICS ET PRIVES, LES (FR) [03095569] **1745**

ETAIT DEUX FOIS, IL (CN/0823-6844) [10061821] **2278**

ETAPE EN ETAPE (CN/0844-6237) [19861298] **2481**

ETAT DE L'ENVIRONNEMENT (PARIS, FRANCE) (FR) [04739035] **3112**

ETAT DES FORETS AU CANADA, RAPPORT AU PARLEMENT, L' (CN/1183-3548) [24623835] **2379**

ETAT DES PERMIS ACCORDES AUX COMPAGNIES ETRANGERES *See* PERMIS ACCORDES AUX COMPAGNIES ETRANGERES **4740**

ETAT DU MONDE (CN/0712-1180) [08569903] **4520**

ETAT DU MONDE, L' (FR) [08298895] **1560**

ETATS FINANCIERS DES ENTREPRISES DU GOUVERNEMENT DU QUEBEC (1988) (CN/0848-3663) [19644247] 672, **1489**

ETATS-UNIS (FR) [18493196] **5469**

ETC (US/0014-164X) [01435639] **3280**

ETC / EXECUTIVE TRAVEL COLLECTION (US) **4116**

ETC (MONTREAL) (CN/0835-7641) [18242466] **350**

ETCETERA (US) **250**

ETCHEMIN DE ST-ROMUALD, L' (CN/0711-4761) [08700947] **5784**

ETERNAUTA (IT) **2487**

ETERNIT ARGENTINA S.A *See* MEMORIA Y ESTADOS CONTABLES / ETERNIT ARGENTINA S.A **693**

ETESIA EKTHESIS PEPRAGMENON - HYPERESIA POLITIKES AEROPORIAS (GR) [01798155] **18**

ETHELBERT ECHO (CN/0712-2624) [08867624] **5784**

ETHICA (RIMOUSKI) (CN/0840-9935) [19995408] **2249**

ETHICAL CURRENTS (US) 3575, **2249**

ETHICAL HUMANIST, THE (US/0362-0859) [02111033] **2249**

ETHICAL INVESTOR *CEASED.* (US/0895-9145) [16854962] **897**

ETHICAL ISSUES IN MEDICINE *CEASED.* (US) [15373779] 3575, **2249**

ETHICAL MANAGEMENT (US/1058-6571) [24350396] **2249**

ETHICAL TABLET & CAPSULE HANDBOOK (AT/0157-9509) [06588185] **4303**

ETHICS (US/0014-1704) [01568301] **2250**

ETHICS & BEHAVIOR (US/1050-8422) [21653741] **2250**

ETHICS & INTERNATIONAL AFFAIRS (US/0892-6794) [15234487] **4520**

ETHICS & LOBBYING (US/1068-3526) [25796937] 4647, **2250**

ETHICS & MEDICINE : A CHRISTIAN PERSPECTIVE ON ISSUES IN BIOETHICS (UK/0266-688X) [14999387] 2250, **3575**

ETHICS & MEDICS (US/1071-3778) [04302981] 2250, **3575**

ETHICS & POLICY (US/1065-0113) [05254200] **2250**

●ETHICS & PSYCHOTHERAPY (US/1064-8771) [26442822] 3925, **2250**

ETHICS (BOCA RATON) (US/0273-2513) [06027686] **2250**

ETHICS, EASIER SAID THAN DONE (US/0897-0106) [17368639] **2250**

ETHICS IN GOVERNMENT REPORTER (US/0279-2869) [07016853] 4473, **2250**

ETHICS IN-SERVICE (CN/0824-5622) [11054238] **2250**

ETHICS RESOURCE CENTER REPORT (US/0748-5344) [10961876] **2250**

●ETHICS ROUNDTABLE (US/1064-5438) [26326374] **2250**

ETHIK IN DER MEDIZIN (GW/0935-7335) [I09357335] 3575, **2250**

ETHIK UND SOZIALWISSENSCHAFTEN (GW/0937-938X) [23246516] 5199, **2250**

ETHIKOS (US/0895-5026) [16642206] 672, **2250**

ETHIOPIA *See* NEGARIT GAZETA **3014**

ETHIOPIA. CENTRAL STATISTICAL OFFICE *See* STATISTICAL ABSTRACT - ETHIOPIA. CENTRAL STATISTICAL OFFICE **5339**

ETHIOPIA. YAERSA MINISTER. EXTENSION AND PROJECT IMPLEMENTATION DEPT *See* WORK PROGRAMME AND BUDGET **146**

ETHIOPIA. YAERSA MINISTER. EXTENSION AND PROJECT IMPLEMENTATION DEPT *See* ANNUAL REPORT - ETHIOPIA. YAERSA MINISTER. EXTENSION AND PROJECT IMPLEMENTATION DEPT **60**

ETHIOPIA. YAKABTERBATANA YASEGA BORD *See* ANNUAL REPORT - PROVISIONAL MILITARY GOVERNMENT OF SOCIALIST ETHIOPIA, LIVESTOCK AND MEAT BOARD **206**

ETHIOPIAN ART AND CULTURE CODEX / THE ETHIOPIAN ART AND CULTURE CHRONICLES SOCIETY, THE (US/1048-812X) [21066970] **2639**

●ETHIOPIAN BUSINESS MAGAZINE (US/1062-3639) [25596434] **672**

ETHIOPIAN CHAMBER OF COMMERCE *See* ANNUAL REPORT - ETHIOPIAN CHAMBER OF COMMERCE **818**

●ETHIOPIAN (CHANTILLY, VA.), THE (US/1060-6149) [25044391] **2499**

ETHIOPIAN HERALD, THE (ET) [12004437] **5800**

ETHIOPIAN JEWRY REPORT (CN/0827-8687) [08965535] **5047**

ETHIOPIAN JOURNAL OF AFRICAN STUDIES YA ITYOPYA YA AFRIQA QAND TENATENA MERMARA MASHET (ET) [10201412] **2639**

ETHIOPIAN JOURNAL OF AGRICULTURAL SCIENCES (ET/0257-2605) [I02572605] **82**

ETHIOPIAN JOURNAL OF HEALTH DEVELOPMENT, THE (ET) [21022759] 3575, **4775**

ETHIOPIAN MANUSCRIPT MICROFILM LIBRARY *See* BULLETIN OF ETHIOPIAN MANUSCRIPTS **412**

ETHIOPIAN MEDICAL JOURNAL (ET/0014-1755) [01777978] **3575**

ETHIOPIAN PUBLICATIONS (ET/0071-1772) [02349312] **416**

ETHIOPIAN REVIEW (US/1056-2354) [23592410] **2639**

ETHIOPIAN TRADE JOURNAL (ET/0014-1763) [02260858] **833**

ETHIOPIA'S DEVELOPMENT CURRENT ABSTRACTS / SEDOC-ETHIOPIA (ET) [09723426] 1489, **1532**

ETHIOPIQUES (SG/0850-2005) [03076661] **2639**

ETHIQUE (FR/1151-5422) [24692130] 5103, **2250**

●ETHNIC AMERICAN EXPERIENCE (US/1069-1170) [27929601] **2260**

ETHNIC AND CULTURAL DIRECTORY (CN/0384-0441) [03222687] **2260**

ETHNIC AND RACIAL STUDIES (UK/0141-9870) [04013828] **2260**

ETHNIC BROADCASTING IN AUSTRALIA (AT) [07495486] 2260, **1132**

ETHNIC CLOUT (CN/0823-7107) [10199134] **759**

ETHNIC COMMUNITIES' REFERENCE YEARBOOK (AT/1035-1094) [I10351094] **2260**

ETHNIC DIRECTORY (CN/0705-3177) [03797363] **2260**

ETHNIC

ETHNIC DIRECTORY OF ALASKA, HAWAII, OREGON AND WASHINGTON (CN) [03698915] **2260**

ETHNIC DIRECTORY OF CALIFORNIA (CN) [03738868] **2260**

ETHNIC DIRECTORY OF WINDSOR & ESSEX COUNTY (CN/0703-8348) [03680933] **2260**

ETHNIC FORUM (US/0278-9078) [07286679] **2260**

ETHNIC GROUPS (US/0308-6860) [02370759] **2260**

ETHNIC INFORMATION SOURCES OF THE UNITED STATES (US/0738-1719) [09536958] **2260**

ETHNIC MINORITIES & EMPLOYMENT (UK) [03060588] 2260, **1668**

ETHNIC MINORITY AFFAIRS DIRECTORY (US/0095-0548) [01794017] 1823, **2260**

ETHNIC NEWS WATCH [COMPUTER FILE] (US) [26167049] **2260**

●ETHNIC NEWSWATCH [COMPUTER FILE] (US) [26231007] **2260**

ETHNIC RACIAL BROTHERHOOD (1982) (US/0736-6086) [09164329] **2260**

ETHNIC REPORTER (CLAREMONT, CALIF.), THE (US/0893-7362) [13767053] **2260**

ETHNIC SCENE (CN/0317-3011) [02248187] **2260**

ETHNIC SCHOOLS IN FOCUS (AT/1035-3682) [I10353682] 2260, **1745**

ETHNIC STUDIES REPORT (CE) [12987362] **235**

ETHNIC TECHNOLOGY NOTES (US/0071-1799) [01966796] 267, **235**

ETHNIC WOMAN, THE (US/0897-4683) [05237243] 5555, **2260**

ETHNICITY & DISEASE (US/1049-510X) [21245181] **3735**

ETHNICITY AND PUBLIC POLICY SERIES (US) [13099695] **2260**

ETHNIE FRANCAISE : REVUE TRIMESTRIELLE DE LA FONDATION CHARLES PLISNIER, L' (BE/0014-178X) [19946707] **2260**

ETHNIES **CEASED.** (US/0073-4667) [01982305] **2261**

ETHNIKE BIBLIOTHEKE (GR) [01773162] 2261, **3209**

ETHNIKE STATISTIKE HYPERESIA TES HELLADOS **See** STATISTIKE TOU DELOTHENTOS EISODEMATOS PHYSIKON PROSOPON KAI TES PHOROLOGIAS AUTOU **1539**

ETHNIKE STATISTIKE HYPERESIA TES HELLADOS **See** STATISTIKE DEMOSION OIKONOMIKON **4750**

ETHNIKE TRAPEZA TES HELLADOS **See** NATIONAL BANK OF GREECE REPORT **800**

ETHNIKON KENTRON KOINONIKON EREUNON **See** PROGRAMMA DRASTERIOTETOS **5254**

ETHNIKOS KERUX (US) [06836811] **5716**

ETHNOARTS INDEX (US/0893-0120) [15313640] 320, **334**

ETHNOBOTANY : JOURNAL OF SOCIETY OF ETHNOBOTANISTS (II) [24404240] **509**

ETHNOGRAPHIA (BUDAPEST. 1949) (HU/0014-1798) [09478002] **235**

ETHNOGRAPHIE, L' (FR) [01285410] **235**

ETHNOGRAPHISCH-ARCHAOLOGISCHE ZEITSCHRIFT : EAZ (GW/0012-7477) [01685195] 235, **267**

ETHNOGRAPHY MONOGRAPH (CN) [01781795] **235**

ETHNOHISTORY (US/0014-1801) [01568314] **2261**

ETHNOLOGIA EUROPAEA (DK/0425-4597) [02300716] **235**

ETHNOLOGIA FENNICA (FI/0355-1776) [07394933] **235**

ETHNOLOGIA FLANDRICA (BE/0774-3297) [17789338] **2319**

ETHNOLOGIA SCANDINAVICA (SW/0348-9698) [00963944] **2319**

ETHNOLOGICA (RM) [06950343] **235**

ETHNOLOGIE FRANCAISE (FR/0046-2616) [01687956] 2319, **2261**

ETHNOLOGUE (US/0364-9288) [02693922] **3280**

ETHNOLOGY (US/0014-1828) [01568323] **235**

ETHNOMUSICOLOGY (US/0014-1836) [04184114] **4117**

●ETHNOMUSICOLOGY AND SYSTEMATIC MUSICOLOGY AT UCLA (US) [24190337] **4117**

ETHNOMUSICOLOGY AT UCLA (US/0749-4033) [10487810] 2261, **4117**

ETHNOMUSICOLOGY RESEARCH DIGEST (US/1054-1624) [22771154] **4117**

ETHNOS (SW/0014-1844) [01568325] 267, **236**

ETHNOZOOTECHNIE (FR) [08832893] **5583**

ETHOLOGY (GW/0179-1613) [13189290] 4586, **5583**

ETHOLOGY AND SOCIOBIOLOGY (US/0162-3095) [04148763] **4586**

ETHOLOGY, ECOLOGY & EVOLUTION (IT/0394-9370) [20334991] 2215, **5583**

ETHOS (US/0091-2131) [01786694] 236, **4586**

ETHOS (FR) [01798309] **3385**

ETHOS (AT) 5199, 1894, **1745**

ETHOS PAPERS (AT/1034-4128) [I10344128] 5199, **1894**

ETICA (AG) [25736571] **2250**

ETICA DEGLI AFFARI (IT) **833**

ETIENNE GILSON SERIES, THE (CN/0708-319X) [08426350] **4346**

ETIMOLOGIURI ZIEBANI / SAKARTVELOS SSR MECNIEREBATA AKADEMIA, ENATMECNIEREBIS INITITUTI (GS) [24445917] **3280**

ETINCELLE (LAVAL) (CN/0226-9783) [08861885] **5285**

ETLIK VETERINER MIKROBIYOLOJI DERGISI (TU/1016-3573) [20307992] 562, **5510**

ETLIK VETERINER MIKROBIYOLOJI ENSITITUSU DERGISI (TU/0259-272X) [06483126] **5510**

ETNIA (AG/0046-2632) [01568327] **236**

ETNIE **SUSPENDED.** (IT) [11612992] **2261**

●ETNOFOLK : REVISTA DEL COMITE DEPARTAMENTAL DE ETNOGRAFIA Y FOLKLORE (BO) [28308828] **2319**

ETNOGRAFIA ESPANOLA (SP/0211-772X) [12330764] **236**

ETNOGRAFIA POLSKA (PL/0071-1861) [02302220] **236**

ETNOGRAFIA SALVADORENA (ES) [02952048] **236**

ETNOGRAFSKI INSTITUT (SRPSKA AKADEMIJA NAUKA I UMETNOSTI) **See** ZBORNIK RADOVA ETNOGRAFSKOG INSTITUTA **248**

ETNOLOGISKA STUDIER (SW) [01751342] **236**

ETNOLOSKA ISTRAZIVANJA / ETNOGRAFSKI MUZEJ U ZAGREBU (CI/0351-4323) [09120974] **236**

Alphabetical Title Index

ETNOS (LUBLIN, POLAND) (PL) [19905120] **4956**

ETOILE DE L'OUTAOUAIS-ST-LAURENT, L' (CN/0319-4124) [02442846] **5784**

ETOILE DU MATIN (CN/0712-2667) [08790890] **5016**

ETOLOGIA (SP/1130-3204) [23467785] **5583**

ETR (GW/0013-2845) [10410252] 2114, **5431**

ETS DEVELOPMENTS (US/0046-1547) [01617603] **1745**

ETS JOURNAL MONITOR **CEASED.** (US) **1745**

ETTELAAT (IR) [01588253] **5803**

ETTORE MAJORANA INTERNATIONAL SCIENCE SERIES : PHYSICAL SCIENCE (US/0270-188X) [06312270] **5103**

ETUDE FAO : ALIMENTATION ET NUTRITION / ORGANISATION DES NATIONS UNIES POUR L'ALIMENTATION ET L'AGRICULTURE **SUSPENDED.** (IT) [08249072] **4190**

ETUDES (FR/0520-0121) [02513455] **2687**

ETUDES & EXPERIMENTATION EN FORMATION CONTINUE (FR) **1745**

ETUDES ANGLAISES (FR/0014-195X) [01568334] **3342**

ETUDES ANGLO-AMERICAINES (FR) [15319453] **3385**

ETUDES BALKANIQUES (BU/0324-1645) [02083595] **2687**

ETUDES BAUDELAIREINNES. BIBLIOGRAPHIE (SZ) [09486191] 3342, **3462**

ETUDES BYZANTINES ET POST-BYZANTINES (RM) [08030907] **2687**

ETUDES CANADIENNES (FR/0153-1700) [06166575] **2732**

ETUDES CELTIQUES (FR/0373-1928) [01568335] 3280, **3336**

ETUDES CHYPRIOTES (FR/0424-2246) [01956843] **2515**

ETUDES CINEMATOGRAPHIQUES (FR/0014-1992) [01568336] **4068**

ETUDES CLASSIQUES (NAMUR, BELGIUM) (BE/0014-200X) [01568337] **1076**

ETUDES CORSES (FR/0338-361X) [01963850] **2846**

ETUDES CREOLES (CN/0708-2398) [09220704] **3280**

ETUDES CRETOISES (FR) [01567341] **2687**

ETUDES DANUBIENNES (FR/0769-3656) [13001684] **2687**

ETUDES D'ARCHEOLOGIE CLASSIQUE (FR/0425-4813) [01911457] **267**

ETUDES DE LA REVUE DU LOUVRE ET DES MUSEES DE FRANCE (FR/0248-3351) [I02483351] **4087**

ETUDES DE LETTRES (SZ/0014-2026) [01568339] **3385**

ETUDES DE LINGUISTIQUE APPLIQUEE (FR/0071-190X) [01783004] **3280**

ETUDES DE LOGIQUE JURIDIQUE (BE) [03153550] **2967**

ETUDES DE PHILOSOPHIE MEDIEVALE (FR/0249-7921) [01568343] **4346**

ETUDES DE PSYCHOLOGIE ET DE PHILOSOPHIE (FR) [06598113] 4586, **4346**

ETUDES DE RADIO TELEVISION **SUSPENDED.** (BE) **1132**

ETUDES DE TRANSPORT EN ..., LES (FR) [09139433] **5382**

ETUDES DES GITES MINERAUX DE LA FRANCE (FR) [01332418] **2138**

ETUDES D'HISTOIRE RELIGIEUSE (CN/1193-199X) [I1193199X] **2616**

ETUDES DROMOISES (FR/0240-3994) [I02403994] **350**

ETUDES ECONOMIQUES DE L'O C D E : CANADA (FR/0378-0376) [03278987] **1489**

ETUDES ET DOCUMENTS - CONSEIL D'ETAT (FR) [01570020] **3093**

ETUDES ET DOCUMENTS DU CERCLE ROYAL D'HISTOIRE ET D'ARCHEOLOGIE D'ATH ET DE LA REGION (BE/0771-5692) [I07715692] 267, **2687**

ETUDES ET DOCUMENTS - INSTITUT DE RELATIONS INTERNATIONALES (CH/0256-5552) [I02565552] **4521**

ETUDES ET MEMOIRES (FR/0078-9585) [02734556] 4850, **5469**

ETUDES ET RECHERCHES (SZ) **5285**

ETUDES ET RECHERCHES ARCHEOLOGIQUES DE L'UNIVERSITE DE LIEGE (BE/0777-2173) [I07772173] **268**

ETUDES ET STATISTIQUES - BANQUE DES ETATS DE L'AFRIQUE CENTRALE (CM/0014-2069) [01787552] **728**

ETUDES ET SYNTHESES DE L'I.E.M.V.T (FR/0297-4444) [I02974444] 210, **5510**

ETUDES ET TRAVAUX (SZ/0073-859X) [01443070] **1823**

ETUDES ET TRAVAUX - CENTRE D'ARCHEOLOGIE MEDITERRANEENNE DE L'ACADEMIE POLONAISE DES SCIENCES (PL/0079-3566) [I00793566] **268**

ETUDES ET TRAVAUX SUR CENDRARS (FR/0766-4214) [17992114] **3575**

ETUDES FINNO-OUGRIENNES (FR) [01787716] **3280**

ETUDES FRANCAISES (MONTREAL) (CN/0014-2085) [01781853] **3385**

ETUDES GERMANIQUES (FR/0014-2115) [01568352] **3280**

ETUDES HAGUENOVIENNES (FR/0085-0322) [01837692] 268, **2687**

ETUDES HELLENIQUES (CN/0824-8621) [10857700] **2687**

ETUDES HISTORIQUES HONGROISES (HU/0237-30301) [102370301] **2687**

ETUDES INDO-EUROPEENNES (FR/0750-3547) [11912838] **2515**

ETUDES INTERNATIONALES (QUEBEC) (CN/0014-2123) [06366119] **4521**

ETUDES INTERNATIONALES (QUEBEC) (CN/0014-2123) [01677841] **4473**

ETUDES INUIT (CN/0701-1008) [03887274] 2261, **2687**

ETUDES IRLANDAISES (FR/0183-973X) [03390007] **2687**

ETUDES LAWRENCIENNES NANTERRE (FR/0994-5490) [I09945490] 2687, **3386**

ETUDES LINGUISTIQUES (NG/0255-0393) [06563856] **3280**

ETUDES LINGUISTIQUES (PARIS) (FR/0071-2124) [01966181] **3280**

ETUDES LITTERAIRES FRANCAISES (GW) [08969875] **3386**

ETUDES LITTERAIRES (UNIVERSITE LAVAL) (CN/0014-214X) [01568358] **3386**

ETUDES MALIENNES (ML) [01795973] **2639**

EUROPA

ETUDES MONGOLES ET SIBERIENNES (FR/0766-5075) [25066615] **2687**

ETUDES MUSULMANES (FR/0531-1888) [01568359] 4346, **5042**

ETUDES NAPOLEONIENNES : BULLETIN HISTORIQUE DE LA SOCIETE DE SAUVEGARDE DU CHATEAU IMPERIAL DE PONT-DE-BRIQUES (FR) [12259704] **2687**

ETUDES NORMANDES (FR/0014-2158) [01718367] **2687**

ETUDES (PARIS. 1897) (FR/0014-1941) [01568332] **2846**

ETUDES PHENOMENOLOGIQUES (BE) [12876393] **4346**

ETUDES PHILOSOPHIQUES (FR/0395-7632) [01580607] **4346**

ETUDES POLITIQUES *CEASED*. (SZ) [01798291] **4521**

ETUDES PREHISTORIQUES ET HISTORIQUES DES PAYS DE LA LOIRE (FR) [26515228] **236**

ETUDES PREHISTORIQUES ORGNAC L'AVEN (FR/0049-111X) [I0049111X] **268**

ETUDES PRELIMINAIRES AUX RELIGIONS ORIENTALES DANS L'EMPIRE ROMAIN (NE/0531-1950) [01714016] **4956**

ETUDES PROUSTIENNES (FR) [02316286] **3386**

ETUDES QUATERNAIRES LANGUEDOCIENNES (FR) [08937844] 1375, **4227**

ETUDES QUATERNAIRES. MEMOIRE (FR/0768-3650) [08971448] 4227, **1375**

ETUDES REBELAISIENNES (SZ/0531-1969) [01696847] **3386**

ETUDES ROMANES DE LUND (SW) [01568362] 3386, **3280**

ETUDES ROMANES (ODENSE) (DK) [01772318] **3280**

ETUDES RURALES (FR/0014-2182) [09037966] **5245**

ETUDES RWANDAISES. SERIE LETTRES ET SCIENCES HUMAINES / UNIVERSITE NATIONALE DU RWANDA (RW) [21884204] **3575**

ETUDES SLAVES (QUEBEC) (CN/0318-0808) [02442945] **2687**

ETUDES SOCIOCRITIQUES. CO-TEXTES (FR/0249-6356) [I02496356] **5245**

ETUDES STATISTIQUES (BRUSSELS, BELGIUM) (BE/0522-7585) [03424319] **5327**

ETUDES STATISTIQUES ET ECONOMETRIQUES *See* ETUDES STATISTIQUES (BRUSSELS, BELGIUM) **5327**

ETUDES SUR LA PRESSE AU XVIIIE I.E. DIX-HUITIEME (FR) [05757484] **1823**

ETUDES SUR LE FUTURISME ET LES AVANT-GARDES (CN/0226-9635) [24368140] **3386**

ETUDES SUR LE JUDAISME MEDIEVAL (NE) [01977913] **5047**

ETUDES SUR LE XVIIIE SIECLE (BE) [02813302] **2687**

ETUDES SUR L'EGYPTE ET LE SOUDAN ANCIENS (FR) [03739714] **2639**

ETUDES TELECOM PARIS (FR/0999-582X) [I0999582X] **1154**

ETUDES THEOLOGIQUES ET RELIGIEUSES (FR/0014-2239) [01780167] **4956**

ETUDES TOGOLAISES (TG/0531-2051) [01118747] **2639**

ETUDES TOULOISES (FR/0395-238X) [I0395238X] **2687**

ETUDES TSIGANES (FR/0014-2247) [02078947] **4553**

ETUDES VAUCLUSIENNES (FR/0153-9221) [17349853] **2846**

ETUDIANT (FR) **1745**

ETV NEWSLETTER (US/0012-8023) [00903958] **1745**

ETYKA (PL/0014-2263) [02310518] **2250**

ETYKA, ESTETYKA I TEORIIA KULTURY / MINISTERSTVO VYSHCHOI I SEREDNOI SPETSIALNOI OSVITY URSR, KYIVSKYI ORDENA LENINA I ORDENA ZHOVTNEVOI REVOLIUTSII DERZHAVNYI UNIVERSYTET IM. T.H. SHEVCHENKA (UN/0868-5045) [24336643] **2250**

ETZ. ELEKROTECHNISCHE ZEITSCHRIFT (BERLIN, WEST) (GW/0170-1711) [16769106] **2054**

EUCHARISTIC MINISTER (US/0743-524X) [10609773] **5029**

EUCLIDES (GRONINGEN, NETHERLANDS) (NE/0165-0394) [08778599] 5103, **3505**

EUDISED R & D BULLETIN (FR) [05524195] **1745**

EUDORA WELTY NEWSLETTER (US/0146-7220) [03008418] **3386**

EUFAULA TRIBUNE, THE (US) [12291270] **5626**

EUGENE O'NEILL REVIEW, THE (US/1040-9483) [18587572] **3386**

EUHEMER *See* PRZEGLAD RELIGIOZNAWCZY **4988**

EUI WORKING PAPER. ECO / ECONOMICS DEPT., EUROPEAN UNIVERSITY INSTITUTE (IT) [23155931] **1489**

EUI WORKING PAPER. HEC / DEPARTMENT OF HISTORY AND CIVILIZATION, EUROPEAN UNIVERSITY INSTITUTE (IT) [23166695] **2616**

EUI WORKING PAPER. LAW / DEPARTMENT OF LAW, EUROPEAN UNIVERSITY INSTITUTE (IT) [23762036] **2967**

EUI WORKING PAPER. SPS / DEPARTMENT OF POLITICAL AND SOCIAL SCIENCES, EUROPEAN UNIVERSITY INSTITUTE (IT) [23762018] 4473, **5199**

EULAR BULLETIN. MONOGRAPH SERIES (SZ/0253-0333) [05778555] **3804**

EUNTES DOCETE (IT) [05996516] **4956**

EUPHONY (US/0277-898X) [07645157] **2054**

EUPHORBIA JOURNAL, THE (US/0737-8823) [09481653] **2414**

EUPHORIA ET CACOPHORIA (JA) [02989438] **3720**

EUPHORION (GW/0014-2328) [01568372] **3386**

EUPHORION. BEIHEFTE (GW/0531-2167) [01568373] **3386**

EUPHORION (HEIDELBERG, GERMANY) (GW/0014-2328) [06300463] **3386**

EUPHYTICA (NE/0014-2336) [01568375] **509**

●EUR-OP NEWS DEUTSCHE AUSG (LU/1021-1667) [I10211667] 4521, **1489**

EUR PUBLICATION (LU) **4521**

EUR RAPPORT - COMMUNAUTE EUROPEENNE DE L'ENERGIE ATOMIQUE (BE/0423-6734) [I04236734] **1944**

EUR REPORT (LU) **4521**

EURAIL GUIDE (US/0085-0330) [01783658] 5469, **5431**

EURASIAN LANGUAGE ARCHIVES (US/0898-0454) [17697281] **3280**

●EURASIAN SOIL SCIENCE (US/1064-2293) [26271640] 1975, **1355**

●EURASIAN STUDIES YEARBOOK (US) [28480162] **3280**

EURE (CL/0250-7161) [01789953] **2822**

EUREKA (BECKENHAM) (UK/0261-2097) [21134022] 2102, **2098**

EUREKA HERALD, THE (US) [11713218] **5675**

EUREKA : INNOVATIVE ENGINEERING DESIGN (UK) [25218808] **1975**

EUREKA NEWS (BE/1022-7059) [I10227059] **5103**

EUREKA REPORTER, THE (US) [12935972] **5756**

EUREKA REVIEW *CEASED*. (US/0363-1850) [02430510] **3342**

EUREKA SENTINEL (EUREKA, NEV. : 1902) (US) [13787902] **5707**

EUREKA : THE ARCHIMEDEANS' JOURNAL (UK/0071-2248) [01568379] **3505**

EUREM ... : PROCEEDINGS OF THE ... EUROPEAN CONGRESS ON ELECTRON MICROSCOPY (UK) [20702681] **572**

EURIDICA (NE) **3128**

EURO (IT) [07112968] **2515**

EURO AFRICA INTERNATIONAL LTD *See* EURO AFRICA'S REVIEW OF THE NAIROBI PROPERTY MARKET **4837**

EURO AFRICA'S REVIEW OF THE NAIROBI PROPERTY MARKET (KE) [07038922] **4837**

EURO-AMERICAN QUARTERLY (US/0887-3100) [13207500] **4473**

EURO CABLE TV PROGRAMMING (US/1053-8313) [22651762] **1110**

EURO COOPERATION; ECONOMIC STUDIES ON EUROPE (FR) [01792170] **1560**

EURO COOPERAZIONE (IT) [03454802] **1489**

EURO COURSES. HEALTH PHYSICS AND RADIATION PROTECTION (NE) [25180468] **2861**

EURO-EAST TELECOMMUNICATIONS (US) **1154**

EURO FILE MUSIC INDUSTRY DIRECTORY (NE) **4117**

EURO-FOCUS RATINGEN (GW/0936-1928) [I09361928] **4215**

EURO HOLLAND TRADE (NE) **833**

EURO P.V (FR/0245-8438) [102458438] **833**

EURO POP BOOK PARIS (FR/1154-5399) [I11545399] **2515**

EURO PRINTER (GW/0938-1236) 867, **4564**

EURO VIANDE (FR) **2334**

●EURO WHO'S WHO: WHO'S WHO IN THE EUROPEAN COMMUNITIES AND IN THE OTHER EUROPEAN ORGANIZATIONS (BE) [24188289] 5231, **432**

EUROBIOLOGISTE, L' (FR) [20945790] **455**

EUROBUSINESS (LONDON) (UK/0953-0711) [19055000] **672**

EUROCARNI (IT/0394-2910) [I03942910] **2334**

EUROCAT - COMPLETE CATALOGUE OF EC PUBLICATIONS AND DOCUMENTS (UK) **4814**

●EUROCAT [COMPUTER FILE] (LU/1021-7789) [30346682] **416**

EUROCHEM MONITOR (UK/0967-7844) **82**

EUROCHEM MONITOR UPDATES (UK) **82**

EUROCRIMINOLOGY / INSTITUTE OF CRIME PROBLEMS (PL/0860-3723) [22669634] **3164**

EURODATA FOUNDATION VOICEBOOK (UK) [17626390] **1154**

EURODIENCE (FR) **385**

EURODIRECTORY (US) **759**

EUROFACH ELECTRONICA (SP/0211-2973) [I02112973] **2054**

EUROFILE RADIO INDUSTRY DIRECTORY (NE) **1132**

EUROFISH REPORT (UK/1040-8720) [12903232] **2300**

EUROFOOD (UK/0955-5404) **2334**

EUROFOOD MONITOR (UK/0960-7943) **2334**

EUROFOOD MONITOR UPDATES (UK) **82**

EUROFRUIT (UK) [02451954] **2414**

EUROGIDS (BE) [15477552] **673**

EUROHEALTH HANDBOOK (US/0094-9361) [01076081] **3780**

EUROIL (NO/0802-9474) [22500704] **4255**

EUROINFORMAZIONI (IT) **1668**

EUROLETTRE PARIS (FR) [I11417528] 673, **82**

EUROLINK AGE BULLETIN (UK) **4521**

EUROMARKET DIRECTORY *CEASED*. (UK) [09719273] **1634**

EUROMARKET LETTER & REPORT (UK) **673**

EUROMARKETING : THE WEEKLY EUROPEAN NEWS BULLETIN FROM ADVERTISING AGE (UK/0952-3820) [16988379] **759**

EUROMASKE: THE EUROPEAN THEATRE QUARTERLY (XV/0353-7161) [22977475] **5364**

EUROMATERIALS (GW/0946-0470) **2102**

EUROMONEY TREASURY REPORT *See* TREASURY MANAGER **814**

EUROMONITOR BOOK READERSHIP SURVEY, THE (UK) [07827637] **4828**

EUROP (FR) [08730751] 1918, **1489**

EUROP PRODUCTION (GW/0065-003X) [02338931] **833**

EUROP PRODUCTION (GW) [02110396] **1634**

EUROPA 1992 (US/1049-9040) [21347068] **833**

EUROPA-ARCHIV (GW/0014-2476) [02199809] **4521**

EUROPA BIRKNER (GW) [04761941] **4233**

EUROPA CAMPING + CARAVANING (GW) [07407590] **4871**

EUROPA CHEMIE (GW/0014-2484) [06674165] 975, **2012**

EUROPA DELLA CEE (IT) **1634**

EUROPA DES CAPITALES (BE) [01794922] **2822**

EUROPA DOMANI (IT/0390-2102) [11828963] **833**

EUROPA E LA CEE, L' *CEASED*. (IT) **4521**

EUROPA ETHNICA (AU/0014-2492) [07466138] 4507, **2261**

EUROPA FACILE (IT) [01787219] **2516**

EUROPA FORUM LUXEMBOURG (LU/1016-572X) [I1016572X] **4521**

EUROPA MANAGEMENT *See* REPERTORIO COMMERCIALE **707**

EUROPA MEDICOPHYSICA (IT/0014-2573) [I00142573] **3575**

EUROPA — Alphabetical Title Index

EUROPA (NEW YORK, N.Y.) (US/0277-0423) [07495284] **2687**

EUROPA REGIONAAL CUIJK (NE/0928-0758) [I09280758] **673**

EUROPA RITROVATA : BIMESTRALE DELL'ISCOS SULL'EUROPA CENTRALE E DELL'EST, L' *CEASED.* (IT) [24775697] **4521**

EUROPA STAR (SZ/0014-2603) [I00142603] **2914, 2916**

EUROPA TRANSPORT. KONJUNKTURERHEBUNG *CEASED.* (BE/0252-239X) [09750871] **5382**

EUROPA VAN MORGEN (NE) **673**

EUROPA WORLD YEAR BOOK, THE (UK/0956-2273) [19757085] **4473**

EUROPABREVET (NO) **1606**

EUROPAEISCHE GRUNDRECHTE - ZEITSCHRIFT (GW/0341-9800) [03286131] **4507**

EUROPAEISCHE RUNDSCHAU (AU/0304-2782) [01787985] **1489, 4521**

EUROPAEISCHE SICHERHEIT. KAMPFTRUPPEN EDITION (GW) **4043**

EUROPAEISCHE WEHRKUNDE. AUSGABE A *See* EUROPAEISCHE SICHERHEIT. KAMPFTRUPPEN EDITION **4043**

EUROPAFORUM : MENSILE DI ECONOMIA E DIRITTO COMUNITARIO (IT) [23467278] **1489**

EUROPAGES (FR) [18409375] **833**

EUROPAISCHE GEMEINSCHAFT, FORSCHUNGSPOLITIK UND FORSCHUNGSPRAXIS / BUNDESSTELLE FUR AUSSENHANDELSINFORMATION (GW) [09962646] **5103, 1606**

EUROPAISCHE HOCHSCHULSCHRIFTEN. REIHE 6, PSYCHOLOGIE (GW/0531-7347) [05998869] **4586**

EUROPAISCHE IDEEN (GW) [05593743] **2687**

EUROPAISCHE INTEGRATION AUSWAHLBIBLIOGRAPHIE (GW) [05692096] **673, 4473**

EUROPAISCHE INTEGRATION : MITTEILUNGEN DES ARBEITSKREISES EUROPAISCHE INTEGRATION (GW) [12307959] **1635**

EUROPAISCHE PARLAMENT. DAS *See* EUROPA FORUM LUXEMBOURG **4521**

EUROPAISCHE SAGEN (GW/0531-2450) [01969309] **4957**

EUROPAISCHE SICHERHEIT (GW/0940-4171) [23299602] **4043**

EUROPAISCHE STADTKULTUR (US/0893-6862) [15626187] **5200**

EUROPAISCHE ZEITSCHRIFT FUER WIRTSCHAFTSRECHT : EUZW (GW/0937-7204) [22218218] **833, 2967**

EUROPAISCHE ZEITUNG (GW) [06267166] **4473**

EUROPAISCHER WETTERBERICHT (GW/0341-2970) [I03412970] **1425**

EUROPAISCHES PATENTBLATT (GW/0170-9305) [I01709305] **1304**

EUROPAMARKT : MILCH (GW) [01299956] **194**

EUROPAMARKT: MILCH BUTTER KASE (GW) **194**

EUROPAPOKAL (GW) [03218560] **4894**

EUROPARECHT (GW/0531-2485) [01568397] **2967**

EUROPAWAHL (GW) [20414178] **4473**

EUROPE (BE) **2516**

EUROPE (FR/0014-2751) [01933600] **3342**

EUROPE '92, LES QUATRE VENTS *See* QUATRE VENTS (OTTAWA) **884**

EUROPE 92 (PORT WASHINGTON, N.Y.) (US/1065-1055) [22700817] **2967**

EUROPE 1992 *CEASED.* (US/1041-6145) [18809981] **1489**

EUROPE 1992 AND BEYOND (MINNEAPOLIS, MINN.) (US/1054-8335) [22979418] **833**

EUROPE 2000 YEOVIL (UK/0959-9584) [I09599584] **2687**

EUROPE, AGENCE INTERNATIONALE D'INFORMATION POUR LA PRESSE *See* DAILY BULLETIN - EUROPE, AGENCE INTERNATIONAL D'INFORMATION POUR LA PRESSE **2514**

EUROPE, AGENCE INTERNATIONALE D'INFORMATION POUR LA PRESSE *See* EUROPE BRIEF NOTES **4647**

EUROPE / AGENCE INTERNATIONALE D'INFORMATION POUR LA PRESSE, AGENCE EUROPE (BE) [21345772] **2516**

EUROPE AND LATIN AMERICA (UK) [06987944] **4521**

● EUROPE-ASIA STUDIES (UK/0966-8136) [27447826] **2651, 2687**

EUROPE ASIA STUDIES (UK) **4541**

EUROPE : BASIC OIL LAWS AND CONCESSION CONTRACTS. ORIGINAL TEXTS. SUPPLEMENT (US/0093-5018) [01792047] **4256, 2967**

EUROPE BRIEF NOTES *CEASED.* (US/0423-6378) [05690864] **4647**

● EUROPE BUSINESS TRAVEL ORGANIZER, THE (CN/1191-4238) [26497682] **673**

EUROPE DRUG & DEVICE REPORT (US/1056-179X) [23525840] **4303**

EUROPE ECHECS (FR/0014-2794) [I00142794] **4860**

EUROPE EN FORMATION, L' (FR/0014-2808) [01804694] **4521**

EUROPE ENERGY (BE) **1944**

EUROPE ENTREPRISES (BE) **2516**

EUROPE ENVIRONMENT (BE/0778-7928) [21139066] **2171**

EUROPE IN FIGURES (LU) [20750345] **4697**

EUROPE INFORMATION. EXTERNAL RELATIONS / COMMISSION OF THE EUROPEAN COMMUNITIES, SPOKESMAN'S GROUP, AND DIRECTORATE-GENERAL FOR INFORMATION (BE) [09568162] **4521**

EUROPE OIL-TELEGRAM (GW/0014-2824) [I00142824] **4256**

EUROPE. OUTREMER *See* OUTREMER (PARIS, FRANCE : 1982) **2500**

EUROPE PLURILINGUE (FR/1161-8884) [I11618884] **2487**

EUROPE REPORT, THE (US/0274-8037) [06598696] **2516**

EUROPE REVIEW (UK/0269-3852) [13473404] **4473**

EUROPE SANS FRONTIERES (UK) **673**

EUROPE (WASHINGTON, D.C.) (US/0191-4545) [04621187] **4521, 833**

EUROPE'92, LES QUATRE VENTS (CN/1181-652X) [23242844] **867**

EUROPE 500 *See* EUROPEAN TOP 500 / FINANCIAL TIMES **673**

EUROPEAN ACCESS (UK/0264-7362) [12210301] **4473**

EUROPEAN ACCOMMODATIONS DIRECTORY (US/0146-5171) [02973092] **2805**

● EUROPEAN ACCOUNTANCY YEARBOOK (UK/0963-0538) [26156443] **743**

EUROPEAN ACCOUNTANT DUBLIN (IE/0791-3664) [I07913664] **743**

EUROPEAN ACCOUNTING : A PUBLICATION OF THE EUROPEAN ACCOUNTING ASSOCIATION (BE) [22399530] **743**

EUROPEAN ACCOUNTING FOCUS (UK/0955-4882) [I09554882] **743**

● EUROPEAN ACCOUNTING REVIEW (UK/0963-8180) [26430199] **743**

EUROPEAN ADDICTION RESEARCH (SZ/1022-6877) **1344**

EUROPEAN ADHESIVES AND SEALANTS (UK/0264-9047) [I02649047] **1052, 4223**

EUROPEAN ADVERTISING & MEDIA FORECAST (UK) **759**

EUROPEAN ADVERTISING & MEDIA FORECAST, THE (UK/0951-7758) [I09517758] **759**

EUROPEAN ADVERTISING, MARKETING, AND MEDIA DATA (UK) [22161342] **759**

EUROPEAN AFFAIRS (FR) [12572976] **2516**

EUROPEAN AGREEMENT CONCERNING THE INTERNATIONAL CARRIAGE OF DANGEROUS GOODS BY ROAD (UK) **5382, 2230**

EUROPEAN AGRIBUSINESS (UK/1350-4460) **82**

EUROPEAN AND AMERICAN PAINTING, SCULPTURE AND DECORATIVE ARTS (CN/0826-9726) **320**

EUROPEAN AND MEDITERRANEAN PLANT PROTECTION ORGANISATION *See* BULLETIN OEPP **165**

EUROPEAN AND MEDITERRANEAN PLANT PROTECTION ORGANIZATION *See* EPPO PUBLICATIONS. SERIES B **509**

EUROPEAN & MIDDLE EAST TAX REPORT, THE (UK/0141-1047) [05790119] **4722**

EUROPEAN APPLIED RESEARCH REPORTS. ENVIRONMENT AND NATURAL RESOURCES SECTION *CEASED.* (UK/0272-4626) [06842394] **2171**

EUROPEAN APPLIED RESEARCH REPORTS. NUCLEAR SCIENCE AND TECHNOLOGY SECTION (SZ/0379-4229) [07243547] **2155**

EUROPEAN ARCHIVES OF BIOLOGY (BE/0777-0553) [20335057] **455**

EUROPEAN ARCHIVES OF OTO-RHINO-LARYNGOLOGY (GW/0937-4477) [21114907] **3888**

● EUROPEAN ARCHIVES OF OTO-RHINO-LARYNGOLOGY. SUPPLEMENT (GW/0934-2400) [26585748] **3888**

EUROPEAN ARCHIVES OF PSYCHIATRY AND CLINICAL NEUROSCIENCE (GW/0940-1334) [22696524] **3832, 3925**

EUROPEAN ASPHALT MAGAZINE (GW/0941-5092) [I09415092] **614**

EUROPEAN ASSOCIATION FOR JAPANESE STUDIES *See* BULLETIN OF THE EUROPEAN ASSOCIATION FOR JAPANESE STUDIES **2502**

EUROPEAN ASSOCIATION FOR POTATO RESEARCH *See* PROCEEDINGS OF THE TRIENNIAL CONFERENCE **183**

EUROPEAN ASSOCIATION OF DEVELOPMENT RESEARCH AND TRAINING INSTITUTES *See* EADI BULLETIN **2515**

EUROPEAN ASSOCIATION OF DISTANCE TEACHING UNIVERSITIES *See* DIRECTORY / EUROPEAN ASSOCIATION OF DISTANCE TEACHING UNIVERSITIES **1735**

EUROPEAN AUTOMOTIVE BULLETIN (US) **5414**

EUROPEAN BAKER (UK) **2334**

EUROPEAN BIBLIOGRAPHY OF SOVIET, EAST EUROPEAN AND SLAVONIC STUDIES (UK/0140-492X) [03953056] **2635**

EUROPEAN BIOGRAPHICAL DIRECTORY (BE) [21416093] **432**

EUROPEAN BIOPHYSICS JOURNAL (GW/0175-7571) [11035862] **495**

EUROPEAN BIOTECHNOLOGY INFORMATION SERVICE (NE) [25448134] **3692**

EUROPEAN BIOTECHNOLOGY NEWSLETTER (PARIS) (FR/0765-2046) [14907259] **3692**

EUROPEAN BOOKSELLER (UK/0958-3866) [I09583866] **4815, 4828**

EUROPEAN BROADCASTING UNION *See* LISTE DES STATIONS DE TELEVISION. ZONE EUROPEENNE **1134**

EUROPEAN BROADCASTING UNION *See* MONOGRAPH: LEGAL AND ADMINISTRATIVE SERIES **3011**

EUROPEAN BULLETIN (LEXINGTON, MASS.) (US/8755-4283) [06931716] **1560**

EUROPEAN BUREAU OF ADULT EDUCATION NEWSLETTER (NE) **1745**

EUROPEAN BUSINESS & ECONOMIC DIGEST (UK/1352-4518) **1489, 673**

EUROPEAN BUSINESS AND INDUSTRY (GW) [14926784] **673**

EUROPEAN BUSINESS GUIDE (BN) [02278108] **673**

EUROPEAN BUSINESS INFORMATION (UK) **673**

EUROPEAN BUSINESS INFORMATION SOURCEBOOK (UK/0964-8550) **673**

EUROPEAN BUSINESS INTELLIGENCE BRIEFING (UK/0957-0039) [I09570039] **673**

EUROPEAN BUSINESS JOURNAL (UK/0955-808X) [I0955808X] **673**

EUROPEAN BUSINESS LAW REVIEW (UK/0959-6941) [22768458] **3099**

EUROPEAN BUSINESS LETTER *CEASED.* (US/1061-6543) [23027457] **833**

EUROPEAN BUSINESS REVIEW (UK/0955-534X) [20443619] **4521, 673**

● EUROPEAN BUSINESS SERVICES DIRECTORY (US/1063-5718) [26067392] **673**

EUROPEAN CABLE/PAY TV (US/1050-3579) [21473428] **1110**

EUROPEAN CABLE / PAY TV FINANCIAL DATABOOK (US) **673, 1110**

EUROPEAN CANCER NEWS (NE/0921-3732) [18305689] **3816**

EUROPEAN CAR (US/1056-8476) [23880804] **5414**

EUROPEAN CELLULAR *CEASED.* (UK/1056-2281) [23670953] **1154**

EUROPEAN CELLULAR/MOBILE COMMUNICATIONS DIRECTORY (US) **1155**

EUROPEAN CENTRE FOR THE DEVELOPMENT OF VOCATIONAL TRAINING *See* ANNUAL REPORT ... / CEDEFOP **1910**

EUROPEAN CHEMICAL BUYER'S GUIDE (UK) [04450537] **1024**

● EUROPEAN CHILD AND ADOLESCENT PSYCHIATRY (CN) [26585556] **3925**

● EUROPEAN CHILD & ADOLESCENT PSYCHIATRY. SUPPLEMENT (CN) [26671900] **4586, 3925**

EUROPEAN CHRISTIAN BOOKSELLER (UK) **4828**

EUROPEAN CLINICAL LABORATORY (US/1047-5354) [20106376] **3575**

Alphabetical Title Index

EUROPEAN

EUROPEAN COAL AND STEEL COMMUNITY. HIGH AUTHORITY *See* REPORT ON THE SITUATION OF THE COMMUNITY **1625**

EUROPEAN COATINGS JOURNAL (GW/0930-3847) [I09303847] **4223**

EUROPEAN COIL COATING ASSOCIATION *See* DIRECTORY - EUROPEAN COIL COATING ASSOCIATION **4001**

EUROPEAN COLLISION ESTIMATING GUIDE (US) **5414**

EUROPEAN COMMERCIAL CASES (UK/0141-7266) [04669758] **3100**

EUROPEAN COMMISSION OF HUMAN RIGHTS *See* ANNUAL REVIEW - EUROPEAN COMMISSION OF HUMAN RIGHTS **4504**

EUROPEAN COMMISSION OF HUMAN RIGHTS *See* DECISIONS AND REPORTS - EUROPEAN COMMISSION OF HUMAN RIGHTS **4507**

EUROPEAN COMMUNICATIONS (UK/0955-4041) [I09554041] **1111**

EUROPEAN COMMUNITIES (US) [16933098] **1635, 897**

●EUROPEAN COMMUNITIES ENCYCLOPEDIA & DIRECTORY (UK) [24310537] **1925**

EUROPEAN COMMUNITIES LEGISLATION : CURRENT STATUS (UK/0950-7361) [18489860] **3128**

EUROPEAN COMMUNITY BUSINESS LAW. HANDBOOK (US/1065-6235) [26656534] **3100**

●EUROPEAN COMMUNITY BUSINESS LAW. SOURCEBOOK (US/1065-6227) [26656519] **3100**

EUROPEAN COMMUNITY : FACTS AND FIGURES, THE (UK) [02244033] **5327**

EUROPEAN COMMUNITY (SYRACUSE, N.Y.), THE (US/1045-3857) [20086166] **1489**

EUROPEAN COMPANIES (UK/0071-2582) [01977781] **673**

●EUROPEAN COMPANION, THE (UK) [25790018] **4521**

EUROPEAN COMPETITION LAW REVIEW : ECLR (UK/0144-3054) [07090338] **3100**

EUROPEAN CONFEDERATION OF AGRICULTURE. SECRETARIAT GENERAL *See* BULLETIN D'INFORMATIONS CEA / SECRETARIAT GENERAL **69**

EUROPEAN CONFEDERATION OF AGRICULTURE. SECRETARIAT GENERAL. BULLETIN D'INFORMATION *See* BULLETIN D'INFORMATIONS CEA / SECRETARIAT GENERAL **69**

EUROPEAN CONFERENCE ON MICROCIRCULATION *See* EUROPEAN CONFERENCE ON MICROCIRCULATION **3575**

EUROPEAN CONFERENCE ON MICROCIRCULATION *CEASED*. (SZ/0071-2655) [02075382] **3575**

EUROPEAN CONSORTIUM FOR POLITICAL RESEARCH NEWS (UK) **4473**

EUROPEAN CONSTRUCTION DOCUMENTS (UK) **614**

●EUROPEAN CONSULTANTS DIRECTORY (US/1060-1880) [24884530] **673**

EUROPEAN CONTINENTAL SHELF GUIDE (UK) [10916232] **4256**

EUROPEAN CONTRIBUTIONS TO AMERICAN STUDIES (NE) [13926104] **4521**

EUROPEAN CONVENTION ON HUMAN RIGHTS; COLLECTION OF DECISIONS OF NATIONAL COURTS REFERRING TO THE CONVENTION (FR) [01565261] **4507**

EUROPEAN CONVENTIONS AND AGREEMENTS (FR) [13179819] **4521**

EUROPEAN COSMETIC MARKETS (UK) **404**

EUROPEAN COUNCIL OF INTERNATIONAL SCHOOLS *See* INTERNATIONAL SCHOOLS DIRECTORY / ECIS, THE **1754**

EUROPEAN COURT OF HUMAN RIGHTS *See* PUBLICATIONS DE LA COUR EUROPEENNE DES DROITS DE L'HOMME SERIE A, ARRETS ET DECISIONS **3134**

EUROPEAN CUPS (UK) **4894**

●EUROPEAN CURRENT LAW : MONTHLY DIGEST (UK/0964-0037) [25211982] **2967**

EUROPEAN CYTOKINE NETWORK (FR/1148-5493) [22982437] **536**

EUROPEAN DAIRY MAGAZINE (GW/0936-6318) [23193803] **194**

EUROPEAN DESIGN DIRECTORY (UK) [02241974] **2114**

EUROPEAN DIRECTORY OF AGROCHEMICAL PRODUCTS (UK) [12951572] **4245**

●EUROPEAN DIRECTORY OF CONSUMER BRANDS AND THEIR OWNERS, THE (UK) [25978275] **673**

EUROPEAN DIRECTORY OF CONSUMER MARKET REPORTS AND SURVEYS (UK) **924**

EUROPEAN DIRECTORY OF MARKETING INFORMATION SOURCES (UK/0950-656X) [17495086] **924**

EUROPEAN DIRECTORY OF NON-OFFICIAL STATISTICAL SOURCES (UK/0953-0258) [18514328] **5327**

EUROPEAN EARTHQUAKE ENGINEERING (IT/0394-5103) [19406900] **2023**

●EUROPEAN EATING DISORDERS REVIEW (UK/1072-4133) [28941641] **4586**

EUROPEAN ECONOMIC COMMUNITY. SAVINGS BANK GROUP *See* REPORT - SAVINGS BANKS GROUP OF THE EEC **808**

EUROPEAN ECONOMIC REVIEW (NE/0014-2921) [01568446] **1489**

EUROPEAN ECONOMIES IN GRAPHS AND FIGURES / IFO, THE (GW/0175-8330) [23124126] **1489**

EUROPEAN ECONOMY (LU/0379-0991) [04878020] **1489**

●EUROPEAN ECONOMY. REPORTS AND STUDIES (LU) [28479758] **1489**

EUROPEAN ECONOMY. SPECIAL EDITION *See* EUROPEAN ECONOMY. REPORTS AND STUDIES **1489**

EUROPEAN ECONOMY. SPECIAL EDITION / COMMISSION OF THE EUROPEAN COMMUNITIES (LU) [24385836] **1490**

EUROPEAN ECONOMY. SUPPLEMENT A, RECENT ECONOMIC TRENDS / COMMISSION OF THE ECONOMIC COMMUNITIES, DIRECTORATE-GENERAL FOR ECONOMIC AND FINANCIAL AFFAIRS (LU/0379-2056) [05343906] **1490**

EUROPEAN ECONOMY. SUPPLEMENT B, BUSINESS AND CONSUMER SURVEY RESULTS (LU/0379-2110) [12727029] **1490**

EUROPEAN EDUCATION (US/1056-4934) [23725446] **1745**

EUROPEAN EDUCATION YEARBOOK (UK) [24478903] **1823**

EUROPEAN ELECTRICAL APPLIANCES MARKETING DIRECTORY (UK/0952-956X) [I09529856X] **2054**

EUROPEAN ELECTRO-OPTICS *CEASED*. (US/1057-4956) [24021631] **4434**

EUROPEAN EMPLOYMENT DIRECTORY, THE (US) [24493328] **1668**

EUROPEAN ENERGY PROFILE (UK/0261-7374) [07969194] **1635**

EUROPEAN ENERGY REPORT (UK) [06660825] **1944**

EUROPEAN ENVIRONMENT LAW (UK/1353-3525) **3112**

●EUROPEAN ENVIRONMENTAL BUSINESS NEWS, THE (US/1060-3573) [24946235] **2171**

●EUROPEAN ENVIRONMENTAL LAW REVIEW (UK/0966-1646) [I09661646] **3112**

EUROPEAN ENVIRONMENTAL YEARBOOK (UK) **2171**

EUROPEAN FACULTY DIRECTORY (UK/1053-640X) [22600940] **1823**

EUROPEAN FERTILIZER REVIEW (UK) **82**

EUROPEAN FILE *CEASED*. (BE/0379-3133) [05211930] **2516**

EUROPEAN FILMFILE (UK) **4068**

EUROPEAN FINANCIAL SERVICES LAW (UK/1350-4741) **2967**

EUROPEAN FOOD AND DRINK REVIEW (UK/0955-4416) [I09554416] **2334**

EUROPEAN FOOTBALL BOOK, THE (UK) [01789085] **4894**

EUROPEAN FORUM FOR MANAGEMENT DEVELOPMENT / EFMD (BE) [24363918] **867**

EUROPEAN FOUNDATION FOR THE IMPROVEMENT OF LIVING AND WORKING CONDITIONS *See* PROGRAMME OF WORK **1704**

EUROPEAN FOUNDATION FOR THE IMPROVEMENT OF LIVING AND WORKING CONDITIONS *See* ANNUAL REPORT / EUROPEAN FOUNDATION FOR THE IMPROVEMENT OF LIVING AND WORKING CONDITIONS **1649**

EUROPEAN FREE TRADE ASSOCIATION *See* ECHANGES DE L'A.E.L.E, LES **832**

EUROPEAN FREE TRADE ASSOCIATION *See* ANNUAL REPORT OF THE EUROPEAN FREE TRADE ASSOCIATION **823**

EUROPEAN FREE TRADE ASSOCIATION *See* EFTA TRADE LES ECHANGES DE L'AELE **832**

EUROPEAN FREIGHT MANAGEMENT (UK) **5382**

EUROPEAN GAY REVIEW, THE (UK) [16930288] **5200**

EUROPEAN GAZETTE (UK) [01786952] **2516**

EUROPEAN GENERATING SET DIRECTORY (UK/0905-2233) **2054**

EUROPEAN GOURMET: THE GRAND DINING TOUR OF EUROPE, THE (US) **5469, 2334**

EUROPEAN GRADUATE RECRUITMENT NEWS (UK) **1823, 4204**

EUROPEAN HANDBOOK (UK/0966-4858) [I09664858] **673**

EUROPEAN HEART JOURNAL (UK/0195-668X) [05585193] **3704**

EUROPEAN HISTORY QUARTERLY (UK/0265-6914) [10535838] **2687**

EUROPEAN HOME VIDEO (US/1055-2839) [23133092] **1111**

EUROPEAN HUMAN RIGHTS REPORTS (UK/0260-4868) [05083508] **4508**

EUROPEAN ILLUSTRATION *CEASED*. (UK) [01196134] **378**

EUROPEAN INDUSTRIAL & COMMERCIAL REVIEW (UK) [02556177] **1606**

EUROPEAN INDUSTRIAL RELATIONS REVIEW (UK/0309-7234) [02545070] **940, 1668**

EUROPEAN INFORMATION BULLETIN (UK) [12352016] **1668**

EUROPEAN INFORMATION SERVICE (UK/0261-2747) [I02612747] **2516**

EUROPEAN INLAND FISHERIES ADVISORY COMMISSION *See* EIFAC OCCASIONAL PAPER **2300**

EUROPEAN INSIGHT (BE) **2516**

EUROPEAN INSURANCE MARKET (UK) **2879**

EUROPEAN INSURANCE MARKET (UK/0960-0981) [I09600981] **2879**

EUROPEAN INSURANCE STRATEGIES (UK) **2879**

EUROPEAN INTELLECTUAL PROPERTY REVIEW (UK/0142-0461) [06256132] **1304**

EUROPEAN INVESTMENT BANK *See* ANNUAL REPORT - EUROPEAN INVESTMENT BANK **891**

EUROPEAN INVESTMENT BANKING REPORT *See* INTERNATIONAL INVESTMENT & BANKING REPORT **792**

EUROPEAN INVESTMENT IN U.S. AND CANADIAN REAL ESTATE DIRECTORY (US/1049-8508) [21324070] **4837**

EUROPEAN JOURNAL FOR FLUID POWER, OIL-HYDRAULICS AND PNEUMATICS (GW/0937-8243) **2089**

EUROPEAN JOURNAL FOR HIGH ABILITY (CN/0937-4450) **1878**

●EUROPEAN JOURNAL OF AGRONOMY (FR/1161-0301) [26441571] **171**

EUROPEAN JOURNAL OF ANAESTHESIOLOGY (UK/0265-0215) [11092625] **3682**

EUROPEAN JOURNAL OF ANAESTHESIOLOGY. SUPPLEMENT (UK/0952-1941) [17346767] **3682**

EUROPEAN JOURNAL OF APPLIED MATHEMATICS (UK/0956-7925) [21383830] **3505**

EUROPEAN JOURNAL OF APPLIED PHYSIOLOGY AND OCCUPATIONAL PHYSIOLOGY (GW/0301-5548) [01793760] **580**

EUROPEAN JOURNAL OF BASIC AND APPLIED HISTOCHEMISTRY *See* EUROPEAN JOURNAL OF HISTOCHEMISTRY : EJH **975**

EUROPEAN JOURNAL OF BIOCHEMISTRY (GW/0014-2956) [01568454] **487**

EUROPEAN JOURNAL OF CANCER (1990) (UK/0959-8049) [21363349] **3816**

EUROPEAN JOURNAL OF CANCER CARE / THE OFFICIAL JOURNAL OF THE EUROPEAN ONCOLOGY NURSING SOCIETY (UK/0961-5423) [25449441] **3817, 3855**

EUROPEAN JOURNAL OF CANCER (OXFORD, ENGLAND : 1990) *See* EUROPEAN JOURNAL OF CANCER. PART B : ORAL ONCOLOGY **3817**

●EUROPEAN JOURNAL OF CANCER. PART B : ORAL ONCOLOGY (UK/0964-1955) [26282387] **3817**

EUROPEAN JOURNAL OF CANCER PREVENTION (UK/0959-8278) [26408704] **3817**

EUROPEAN JOURNAL OF CARDIAC PACING AND ELECTROPHYSIOLOGY (GW/0939-6780) [25047165] **3704**

EUROPEAN JOURNAL OF CARDIO-THORACIC SURGERY : OFFICIAL JOURNAL OF THE EUROPEAN ASSOCIATION FOR CARDIO-THORACIC SURGERY (GW/1010-7940) [17726302] **3964**

EUROPEAN — Alphabetical Title Index

EUROPEAN JOURNAL OF CELL BIOLOGY (GW/0171-9335) [05045176] **536**

EUROPEAN JOURNAL OF CELL BIOLOGY. SUPPLEMENT (GW/0724-5130) [09705204] **536**

EUROPEAN JOURNAL OF CHIROPRACTIC (UK/0263-9114) [09299556] **3575**

EUROPEAN JOURNAL OF CLINICAL CHEMISTRY AND CLINICAL BIOCHEMISTRY (GW/0939-4974) [23467023] **487**

EUROPEAN JOURNAL OF CLINICAL INVESTIGATION (GW/0014-2972) [02243336] **3575**

EUROPEAN JOURNAL OF CLINICAL INVESTIGATION SUPPLEMENT (UK/0960-135X) [I0960135X] **3575**

EUROPEAN JOURNAL OF CLINICAL MICROBIOLOGY & INFECTIOUS DISEASES (GW/0934-9723) [17800606] 3713, **562**

EUROPEAN JOURNAL OF CLINICAL NUTRITION (UK/0954-3007) [17616551] **4190**

EUROPEAN JOURNAL OF CLINICAL PHARMACOLOGY (GW/0031-6970) [01568457] **4303**

EUROPEAN JOURNAL OF COGNITIVE PSYCHOLOGY, THE (UK/0954-1446) [20288251] **4586**

EUROPEAN JOURNAL OF COMBINATORICS (UK/0195-6698) [05585232] **3505**

EUROPEAN JOURNAL OF COMMUNICATION (LONDON) (UK/0267-3231) [13312226] **1111**

EUROPEAN JOURNAL OF DERMATOLOGY : EJD (FR/1167-1122) [25786339] **3720**

EUROPEAN JOURNAL OF DEVELOPMENT RESEARCH, THE (UK/0957-8811) [22465929] **2909**

●EUROPEAN JOURNAL OF DISORDERS OF COMMUNICATION (UK/0963-7273) [25647838] 3280, **1111**

EUROPEAN JOURNAL OF DRUG METABOLISM AND PHARMACOKINETICS (FR/0398-7639) [02181264] **4303**

EUROPEAN JOURNAL OF EDUCATION (UK/0141-8211) [05257132] **1745**

EUROPEAN JOURNAL OF EMERGENCY MEDICINE (UK/1969-9546) **3575**

●EUROPEAN JOURNAL OF ENDOCRINOLOGY / EUROPEAN FEDERATION OF ENDOCRINE SOCIETIES (NO/0804-4643) [29970781] **3730**

EUROPEAN JOURNAL OF ENGINEERING EDUCATION (UK/0304-3797) [02881393] **1975**

●EUROPEAN JOURNAL OF ENTOMOLOGY (XR/1210-5759) [28143038] **5608**

EUROPEAN JOURNAL OF EPIDEMIOLOGY (NE/0392-2990) 3713, **3735**

EUROPEAN JOURNAL OF EPIDEMIOLOGY (IT/0393-2990) [12670884] **3735**

●EUROPEAN JOURNAL OF EXPERIMENTAL MUSCULOSKELETAL RESEARCH (NO/0803-5288) [26850523] **3804**

EUROPEAN JOURNAL OF FOOT AND ANKLE SURGERY (IT/1122-8660) **3964**

EUROPEAN JOURNAL OF FOREST PATHOLOGY (GW/0300-1237) [01643880] **2379**

EUROPEAN JOURNAL OF GASTROENTEROLOGY & HEPATOLOGY (UK/0954-691X) [20609040] **3744**

●EUROPEAN JOURNAL OF GERONTOLOGY : THE JOURNAL OF THE EUROPEAN REGION OF THE INTERNATIONAL ASSOCIATION OF GERONTOLOGY *SUSPENDED.* (SP) [25047232] **3750**

EUROPEAN JOURNAL OF GYNAECOLOGICAL ONCOLOGY (IT/0392-2936) [07236962] 3760, **3817**

EUROPEAN JOURNAL OF HAEMATOLOGY (DK/0902-4441) [15468015] **3771**

EUROPEAN JOURNAL OF HAEMATOLOGY. SUPPLEMENTUM (DK/0902-4506) [15468034] **3771**

EUROPEAN JOURNAL OF HEALTH LAW (NE/0929-0273) 3575, **2967**

●EUROPEAN JOURNAL OF HISTOCHEMISTRY : EJH (IT) [25963230] **975**

●EUROPEAN JOURNAL OF HUMAN GENETICS : EJHG (SZ/1018-4813) [27638318] **544**

EUROPEAN JOURNAL OF IMMUNOGENETICS : OFFICIAL JOURNAL OF THE BRITISH SOCIETY FOR HISTOCOMPATABILITY AND IMMUNOGENETICS (UK/0960-7420) [23535118] **3669**

EUROPEAN JOURNAL OF IMMUNOLOGY (GW/0014-2980) [01568458] **3669**

EUROPEAN JOURNAL OF IMPLANT AND REFRACTIVE SURGERY, THE (FR/0955-3681) [16986501] **3874**

EUROPEAN JOURNAL OF INFORMATION SYSTEMS (UK/0960-085X) [25195210] **1184**

EUROPEAN JOURNAL OF INTERCULTURAL STUDIES (UK/0952-391X) [25209150] 5245, **2261**

EUROPEAN JOURNAL OF INTERNAL MEDICINE (UK/0953-6205) [21307570] **3796**

EUROPEAN JOURNAL OF INTERNATIONAL AFFAIRS, THE *SUSPENDED.* (IT/0394-6444) [20674759] **4473**

EUROPEAN JOURNAL OF INTERNATIONAL LAW (IT/0938-5428) [23282487] **3128**

EUROPEAN JOURNAL OF LAW AND ECONOMICS (US/0929-1261) 1490, **2967**

EUROPEAN JOURNAL OF MARKETING (UK/0309-0566) [00974094] **924**

EUROPEAN JOURNAL OF MECHANICAL ENGINEERING (BE/0777-2734) [I07772734] **2114**

EUROPEAN JOURNAL OF MECHANICS. A. SOLIDS (FR/0997-7538) [19528048] **4427**

EUROPEAN JOURNAL OF MECHANICS. B. FLUIDS (FR/0997-7546) [19538423] **4402**

EUROPEAN JOURNAL OF MEDICINAL CHEMISTRY (FR/0223-5234) [02255316] 975, **3575**

●EUROPEAN JOURNAL OF MEDICINE (FR/1165-0478) [26585675] **3575**

EUROPEAN JOURNAL OF MINERALOGY (STUTTGART) (GW/0935-1221) [19563867] **1439**

EUROPEAN JOURNAL OF MORPHOLOGY (NE/0924-3860) [22150994] 5583, **3679**

EUROPEAN JOURNAL OF NEUROLOGY (UK/1351-5101) **3832**

EUROPEAN JOURNAL OF NEUROSCIENCE, THE (UK/0953-816X) [19991225] **3832**

EUROPEAN JOURNAL OF NON-DESTRUCTIVE TESTING *See* INSIGHT (NORTHAMPTON) **2102**

EUROPEAN JOURNAL OF NON-DESTRUCTIVE TESTING, THE (UK/0957-767X) [I0957767X] **5104**

EUROPEAN JOURNAL OF NUCLEAR MEDICINE (GW/0340-6997) [02502280] **3848**

EUROPEAN JOURNAL OF OPERATIONAL RESEARCH (NE/0377-2217) [03231916] **5104**

EUROPEAN JOURNAL OF OPHTHALMOLOGY (IT/1120-6721) [23602757] **3874**

●EUROPEAN JOURNAL OF ORIENTAL MEDICINE (UK) **3575**

EUROPEAN JOURNAL OF ORTHODONTICS (UK/0141-5387) [05307606] **1323**

EUROPEAN JOURNAL OF PAIN, THE (GW/0939-6365) [I09396365] **3575**

EUROPEAN JOURNAL OF PARAPSYCHOLOGY (NE) [14154613] **4241**

EUROPEAN JOURNAL OF PEDIATRIC SURGERY : OFFICIAL JOURNAL OF AUSTRIAN ASSOCIATION OF PEDIATRIC SURGERY ... ZEITSCHRIFT FUER KINDERCHIRURGIE (GW/0939-7248) [23456761] 3903, **3964**

EUROPEAN JOURNAL OF PEDIATRICS (GW/0340-6199) [02016047] **3903**

EUROPEAN JOURNAL OF PERSONALITY (UK/0890-2070) [14173673] **4587**

●EUROPEAN JOURNAL OF PHARMACEUTICAL SCIENCES (NE/0928-0987) [28704641] **4303**

EUROPEAN JOURNAL OF PHARMACEUTICS AND BIOPHARMACEUTICS : OFFICIAL JOURNAL OF ARBEITSGEMEINSCHAFT FUER PHARMAZEUTISCHE VERFAHRENSTECHNIK E.V (GW/0939-6411) [24147951] **4303**

EUROPEAN JOURNAL OF PHARMACOLOGY (NE/0014-2999) [01568459] **4303**

●EUROPEAN JOURNAL OF PHARMACOLOGY : ENVIRONMENTAL TOXICOLOGY AND PHARMACOLOGY SECTION (NE/0926-6917) [25906667] **4303**

EUROPEAN JOURNAL OF PHARMACOLOGY. MOLECULAR PHARMACOLOGY SECTION (NE/0922-4106) [19496243] **4303**

EUROPEAN JOURNAL OF PHILOSOPHY (UK/0966-8373) **4346**

●EUROPEAN JOURNAL OF PHYCOLOGY (UK/0967-0262) [27861903] **509**

EUROPEAN JOURNAL OF PHYSICAL MEDICINE & REHABILITATION (AU/1017-6721) [25545679] **4380**

EUROPEAN JOURNAL OF PHYSICS (UK/0143-0807) [06568770] **4402**

EUROPEAN JOURNAL OF PLANT PATHOLOGY (NE/0929-1873) **509**

EUROPEAN JOURNAL OF PLASTIC SURGERY (GW/0930-343X) [14396455] **3964**

EUROPEAN JOURNAL OF POLITICAL ECONOMY (NE) [21278236] **1560**

EUROPEAN JOURNAL OF POLITICAL RESEARCH (NE/0304-4130) [01794225] **4473**

EUROPEAN JOURNAL OF POPULATION (NE/0168-6577) [11885330] **4553**

EUROPEAN JOURNAL OF PROTISTOLOGY (GW/0932-4739) [17422663] **562**

EUROPEAN JOURNAL OF PSYCHIATRY, THE (SP/0213-6163) [16410082] **3925**

EUROPEAN JOURNAL OF PSYCHOLOGICAL ASSESSMENT (GW/1015-5759) **4587**

EUROPEAN JOURNAL OF PSYCHOLOGY OF EDUCATION (PO/0256-2928) [21054570] 4587, **1878**

EUROPEAN JOURNAL OF PUBLIC HEALTH (SW/1101-1262) [25627514] 3735, **4775**

EUROPEAN JOURNAL OF PURCHASING AND SUPPLY MANAGEMENT (UK/0969-7012) **949**

EUROPEAN JOURNAL OF RADIOLOGY (GW/0720-048X) [07808542] **3941**

EUROPEAN JOURNAL OF RHEUMATOLOGY AND INFLAMMATION (ENGLISH EDITION) (UK/0140-1610) [04557228] **3804**

EUROPEAN JOURNAL OF SERIALS LIBRARIANSHIP (US/1048-5287) [20968424] **3209**

EUROPEAN JOURNAL OF SOCIAL PSYCHOLOGY (UK/0046-2772) [01804759] 4587, **5245**

●EUROPEAN JOURNAL OF SOIL BIOLOGY (FR/1164-5563) [28056567] 455, 2171, **171**

●EUROPEAN JOURNAL OF SOIL SCIENCE (UK/1351-0754) [30313977] **171**

EUROPEAN JOURNAL OF SOLID STATE AND INORGANIC CHEMISTRY (FR/0992-4361) [18493390] **1036**

EUROPEAN JOURNAL OF SPECIAL NEEDS EDUCATION (UK/0885-6257) [12681898] **1878**

EUROPEAN JOURNAL OF SURGERY. SUPPLEMENT / ACTA CHIRURGICA. SUPPLEMENT, THE (SW) [24525884] **3964**

EUROPEAN JOURNAL OF SURGERY, THE (SW/1102-4151) [23657406] **3964**

EUROPEAN JOURNAL OF SURGICAL ONCOLOGY (UK/0748-7983) [11011097] **3817**

EUROPEAN JOURNAL OF TEACHER EDUCATION (UK/0261-9768) [09258527] **1894**

●EUROPEAN JOURNAL OF THE HISTORY OF ECONOMIC THOUGHT, THE (UK/0967-2567) **1560**

EUROPEAN JOURNAL OF THEOLOGY (UK/0960-2720) **4957**

EUROPEAN JOURNAL OF ULTRASOUND (IE/0929-8266) **3941**

EUROPEAN JOURNAL OF VASCULAR SURGERY (UK/0950-821X) [16530303] **3964**

●EUROPEAN JOURNAL OF WOMEN'S STUDIES, THE (US/1350-5068) [30758367] **5555**

●EUROPEAN JOURNAL ON CRIMINAL POLICY AND RESEARCH (NE/0928-1371) [I09281371] **3164**

EUROPEAN JOYCE STUDIES (NE) [20845372] **3386**

EUROPEAN JUDAISM (UK/0014-3006) [02309096] **5047**

EUROPEAN LAW DIGEST *See* EUROPEAN CURRENT LAW : MONTHLY DIGEST **2967**

●EUROPEAN LAW JOURNAL (UK) **2967**

EUROPEAN LAW REVIEW (UK/0307-5400) [02142791] **2967**

EUROPEAN LONG-TERM REVIEW / DATA RESOURCES, INC (US) [10351589] **1560**

EUROPEAN MAC PROFESSIONAL *SUSPENDED.* (SP) **1237**

EUROPEAN MACHINING (UK/0966-002X) [I0966002X] **2114**

EUROPEAN MANAGEMENT JOURNAL (UK/0263-2373) [09596039] **867**

EUROPEAN MARKET & MEDIA FACT *CEASED.* (UK/0966-8608) [I09668608] **1490**

EUROPEAN

EUROPEAN MARKETING DATA AND STATISTICS (UK/0071-2930) [01969204] 673, **728**

EUROPEAN MARKETING POCKET BOOK (UK/0966-7717) [I09667717] **924**

EUROPEAN MASTER'S DEGREES IN MANAGEMENT (NE) [25778360] 867, **1823**

EUROPEAN MATHEMATICAL NEWSLETTER (GW) [08037502] **3505**

EUROPEAN MEDIA BULLETIN (UK/0962-8312) [I09628312] **1132**

EUROPEAN MEDIA BUSINESS & FINANCE (US/1071-1570) [28561537] 1111, **673**

EUROPEAN METALWORKING MANUAL (GW) **4001**

● EUROPEAN MICROBIOLOGY (US/1064-4725) [26294051] **562**

EUROPEAN MICROSCOPY AND ANALYSIS (UK/0958-1952) [I09581952] **572**

EUROPEAN MICROSCOPY & ANALYSIS (UK) **572**

EUROPEAN MICROWAVE CONFERENCE; CONFERENCE PROCEEDINGS (UK) [05428128] **2054**

EUROPEAN MINIATURE ELECTRONIC COMPONENTS AND ASSEMBLIES DATA : INCLUDING SIX-LANGUAGE GLOSSARIES OF ELECTRONIC COMPONENT AND MICROELECTRONICS TERMS (UK) [09080180] **2054**

EUROPEAN MONITOR NEWSLETTER (US) **1237**

EUROPEAN MONOGRAPHS IN SOCIAL PSYCHOLOGY (UK/0892-7286) [01775335] **4587**

EUROPEAN MOTOR BUSINESS (UK/0267-8233) [15022406] **5414**

EUROPEAN NEUROLOGY (SZ/0014-3022) [01568463] **3832**

EUROPEAN NEUROPSYCHOPHARMACOLOGY : THE JOURNAL OF THE EUROPEAN COLLEGE OF NEUROPSYCHOPHARMACOLOGY (NE/0924-977X) [24317986] 3925, 4303, **3832**

EUROPEAN NEWSLETTER ON QUALITY ASSURANCE (NE/0920-2153) [I09202153] **3780**

EUROPEAN OFFICE FURNITURE (GW) [20413253] **4211**

EUROPEAN OFFSHORE OIL & GAS (UK) [13161585] **4256**

EUROPEAN OFFSHORE PETROLEUM NEWSLETTER (NO/0332-5210) [I03325210] **4256**

EUROPEAN ORGANIZATION FOR NUCLEAR RESEARCH *See* ANNUAL REPORT OF THE EUROPEAN ORGANIZATION FOR NUCLEAR RESEARCH **4446**

EUROPEAN ORGANIZATION FOR RESEARCH ON TREATMENT OF CANCER *See* MONOGRAPH SERIES OF THE EUROPEAN ORGANIZATION FOR RESEARCH ON TREATMENT OF CANCER **3821**

EUROPEAN PACKAGING (GW/0966-4734) [I09664734] **4219**

EUROPEAN PACKAGING MAGAZINE (HEUSENSTAMM, GERMANY) (GW) [13494374] **4219**

EUROPEAN PACKAGING NEWSLETTER AND WORLD REPORT (FR/1052-2131) [12426452] **4219**

EUROPEAN PAINT AND RESIN NEWS (UK/0266-7800) [I02667800] **4223**

EUROPEAN PAPERMAKER (SW) **4233**

EUROPEAN PARLIAMENT *See* LIST OF WORKING DOCUMENTS **4662**

EUROPEAN PARLIAMENT *See* EUROPEAN PARLIAMENT DIGEST **4647**

EUROPEAN PARLIAMENT *See* LISTE OVER MDEDOKUMENTER **3132**

EUROPEAN PARLIAMENT *See* BULLETIN - EUROPEAN PARLIAMENT **3125**

EUROPEAN PARLIAMENT *See* SITTINGS - EUROPEAN PARLIAMENT, THE **4686**

EUROPEAN PARLIAMENT DIGEST (US/0095-7607) [01798568] **4647**

EUROPEAN PATENT OFFICE REPORTS (UK/0269-0802) [13770039] **1304**

EUROPEAN PETROLEUM DIRECTORY (US/0275-3871) [06114188] **4256**

EUROPEAN PHARMACOPOEIA (FR) **4303**

EUROPEAN PHOTOGRAPHY (GOTTINGEN, GERMANY) (GW/0172-7028) [07466750] **4369**

EUROPEAN PHYSICAL SOCIETY *See* EUROPHYSICS CONFERENCE ABSTRACTS **4402**

● EUROPEAN PLANNING STUDIES (UK/0965-4313) [28143254] **2822**

EUROPEAN PLASTICS DIRECTORY (UK) [22577533] **4455**

EUROPEAN PLASTICS NEWS (UK/0306-3534) [01794623] **4455**

EUROPEAN POLYMER JOURNAL (UK/0014-3057) [01568467] **1041**

EUROPEAN POLYMERS PAINT COLOUR JOURNAL (UK/0963-8474) [22903182] **4223**

EUROPEAN POWER NEWS (UK/0261-8214) [24681513] 2054, **1944**

● EUROPEAN PRODUCTION ENGINEERING : EPE (GW/0940-2470) [26622824] **1975**

EUROPEAN PSYCHIATRY (FR/0924-9338) [24466861] **3925**

● EUROPEAN PUBLIC LAW (NE/1354-3725) **2967**

EUROPEAN PUBLICATIONS CATALOGUE (CN/0847-4583) [23247988] **614**

● EUROPEAN QUALITY. : THE OFFICIAL JOURNAL OF THE EUROPEAN ORGANIZATION FOR QUALITY (UK/0969-059X) [29674160] **1606**

EUROPEAN RACEHORSE, THE (UK/0260-7468) [09139663] **2799**

EUROPEAN RADIO (US/1050-0561) [21389624] **1111**

EUROPEAN RADIOLOGY (GW/0938-7994) [24914338] **3941**

EUROPEAN REFINERY REPORT (FR) **4256**

EUROPEAN REFINING ACTIVITY (FR) **4001**

EUROPEAN REGIONAL PLANNING STUDY SERIES (FR) [05192405] **2516**

EUROPEAN REGISTER OF RESEARCH ON VISUAL IMPAIRMENT (US/0098-0986) [01371922] **4388**

EUROPEAN REPORT (BE) [03997603] **1635**

EUROPEAN RESEARCH CENTRES (UK) [09123359] **5104**

EUROPEAN RESEARCH IN REGIONAL SCIENCE (UK/0960-6130) **5104**

EUROPEAN RESEARCH LIBRARIES COOPERATION : THE LIBER QUARTERLY (AU/1018-0826) [24934058] **3209**

EUROPEAN RESPIRATORY JOURNAL. SUPPLEMENT, THE (DK/0904-1850) [18929065] **3949**

EUROPEAN RESPIRATORY JOURNAL, THE (DK/0903-1936) [17450139] **3949**

EUROPEAN RESPIRATORY REVIEW : AN OFFICIAL JOURNAL OF THE EUROPEAN RESPIRATORY SOCIETY (DK/0905-9180) [24317979] **3949**

EUROPEAN RETAIL (UK) **954**

● EUROPEAN REVIEW (CHICHESTER, ENGLAND) (UK/1062-7987) [25744730] **1745**

EUROPEAN REVIEW (LEXINGTON, MASS.) (US/0276-7430) [07389935] **1560**

EUROPEAN REVIEW OF AGRICULTURAL ECONOMICS (NE/0165-1587) [01916834] 1490, **82**

EUROPEAN REVIEW OF APPLIED PYCHOLOGY / REVUE EUROPEENNE DE PSYCHOLOGIE APPLIQUEE (FR) [24161014] **4587**

● EUROPEAN REVIEW OF HISTORY (UK/1350-7486) **2687**

EUROPEAN REVIEW OF NATIVE AMERICAN STUDIES (GW/0238-1486) [17421023] **2261**

EUROPEAN REVIEW OF PRIVATE LAW (NE/0928-9801) [29733161] **2967**

EUROPEAN REVIEW OF SOCIAL PSYCHOLOGY (UK/1046-3283) [20379243] **5245**

EUROPEAN ROMANTIC REVIEW (US/1050-9585) [21722456] **3386**

EUROPEAN RUBBER DIRECTORY (UK/0306-414X) [01795537] **5075**

EUROPEAN RUBBER JOURNAL (LONDON, ENGLAND : 1982) (UK/0266-4151) [08538292] **5075**

EUROPEAN SATELLITE DIRECTORY (US) **1155**

EUROPEAN SCIENCE EDITING : BULLETIN OF THE EUROPEAN ASSOCIATION OF SCIENCE EDITORS (UK/0309-4715) [13154588] **4815**

EUROPEAN SCIENCE FOUNDATION *See* ANNUAL REPORT / EUROPEAN SCIENCE FOUNDATION **5084**

● EUROPEAN SECURITY (UK/0966-2839) [28735331] **4521**

EUROPEAN SECURITY STUDIES (UK) [14711347] **4043**

EUROPEAN SEMICONDUCTOR (UK/0957-5685) [24575817] **2054**

EUROPEAN SOCIETY FOR ARTIFICIAL ORGANS. MEETING *See* ESAO PROCEEDINGS / EUROPEAN SOCIETY FOR ARTIFICIAL ORGANS **3575**

EUROPEAN SOCIOLOGICAL REVIEW (UK/0266-7215) [13105813] **5245**

EUROPEAN SOURCES OF SCIENTIFIC AND TECHNICAL INFORMATION (UK) [10419473] **5104**

EUROPEAN SPACE AGENCY *See* ESA BULLETIN **18**

EUROPEAN SPACE AGENCY. SPACE SCIENCE DEPT *See* REPORT ON THE ACTIVITIES OF SPACE SCIENCE DEPARTMENT IN ... **399**

EUROPEAN SPACE DIRECTORY (FR/0765-0574) [15311810] **18**

EUROPEAN SPACE REPORT (GW/0940-0842) [I09400842] **18**

● EUROPEAN SPINE JOURNAL : OFFICIAL PUBLICATION OF THE EUROPEAN SPINE SOCIETY, THE EUROPEAN SPINAL DEFORMITY SOCIETY, AND THE EUROPEAN SECTION OF THE CERVICAL SPINE RESEARCH SOCIETY (GW/0940-6719) [27638222] **3964**

EUROPEAN SPONSORSHIP NEWSLETTER PARIS, THE **SUSPENDED.** (FR/0995-2721) [I09952721] **1635**

EUROPEAN STEEL REVIEW (UK) **4001**

EUROPEAN STUDIES (DK/0906-0308) [23340230] **2687**

EUROPEAN STUDIES JOURNAL, THE (US/0894-6337) [11829613] **2687**

EUROPEAN STUDIES NEWSLETTER (US/0046-2802) [01804194] **2687**

EUROPEAN SUPPLIES BULLETIN / FISHERY ECONOMICS RESEARCH UNIT, WHITE FISH AUTHORITY (UK/0142-937X) [07368554] 2334, **2300**

EUROPEAN SURFACE TREATMENT (UK/0967-9650) [I09679650] **2114**

EUROPEAN SURGICAL RESEARCH (SZ/0014-312X) [01568474] **3964**

EUROPEAN SYNCHROTON RADIATION FACILITY (FR) [13357801] **4434**

EUROPEAN TABLEWARE BUYERS GUIDE (UK/0264-5041) [10602132] **2589**

EUROPEAN TAX HANDBOOK (NE/0925-9759) [23070945] **4722**

EUROPEAN TAXATION (NE/0014-3138) [01568475] **4722**

EUROPEAN TAXATION. SUPPLEMENTARY SERVICE (NE/0531-4577) [06564588] **4722**

EUROPEAN TELECOMMUNICATIONS (US/8756-4459) [11558219] **1155**

EUROPEAN TIMES (SP) **2688**

● EUROPEAN TOP 500 / FINANCIAL TIMES (UK) [26249019] **673**

● EUROPEAN TRADE UNION INFORMATION BULLETIN (UK) [30091666] **1668**

EUROPEAN TRANSACTIONS ON ELECTRICAL POWER ENGINEERING (GW/0939-3072) [24446248] **2054**

EUROPEAN TRANSACTIONS ON TELECOMMUNICATIONS AND RELATED TECHNOLOGIES (IT/1120-3862) [21898075] **1155**

EUROPEAN TRANSPORT LAW (BE/0014-3154) [06857578] 5382, **2967**

EUROPEAN TRAVEL & LIFE (US/0882-7737) [11986444] **5469**

EUROPEAN TREATY SERIES (FR/0070-105X) [01568478] **4473**

EUROPEAN TRENDS (UK/0014-3162) [01803834] **1635**

EUROPEAN TV SPORTS (US/1050-298X) [21455698] **1111**

EUROPEAN UNIVERSITY INSTITUTE *See* REPORT OF ACTIVITIES / EUROPEAN UNIVERSITY INSTITUTE **1844**

EUROPEAN URBAN AND REGIONAL STUDIES (UK/0969-7764) 2516, **2822**

EUROPEAN UROLOGY (SZ/0302-2838) [01809591] **3989**

EUROPEAN UROLOGY UPDATE SERIES (UK/0968-7645) [I09687645] **3990**

EUROPEAN VENTURE CAPITAL JOURNAL : EUROPEAN VCJ (UK/0954-1675) [23059386] **1490**

EUROPEAN VIDEO JOURNAL OF CARDIOLOGY, THE (NE/0928-0529) **3704**

EUROPEAN WATER POLLUTION CONTROL : OFFICIAL PUBLICATION OF THE EUROPEAN WATER POLLUTION CONTROL ASSOCIATION (EWPCA) (NE/0925-5060) [24603066] **5533**

EUROPEAN WEEKLY MARKET SURVEY / MLC (UK) [08455471] **211**

EUROPEAN WHOLESALERS AND DISTRIBUTORS DIRECTORY **CEASED.** (US/1063-8288) [26174713] **1606**

EUROPEAN WORK AND ORGANISATIONAL PSYCHOLOGIST, THE (UK/0960-2003) [24364760] **4587**

EUROPEAN — Alphabetical Title Index

EUROPEAN YEARBOOK IN THE SOCIOLOGY OF LAW (IT) [20337947] **5245**

EUROPEEN, L' (BE/0531-4631) [01828004] **2516**

EUROPEMARKT: DIE MARKTE FUR SCHLACHTRINDER UND SCHWEINE WESTEUROPAS See ZMP MARKTBERICHT: SCHLACHTVIEH **224**

EUROPEO MILANO, L' (IT/0014-3189) [I00143189] **2516**

EUROPE'S 15,000 LARGEST COMPANIES DIE 15,000 GROSSTEN UNTERNEHMEN EUROPAS LES 15,000 PLUS GRANDES SOCIETES DE L'EUROPE (UK/0800-0638) [11987804] **673**

EUROPE'S WONDERFUL LITTLE HOTELS AND INNS (US) [05187272] **2805**

EUROPHYSICS CONFERENCE ABSTRACTS (SZ/0378-2271) [01978663] **4402**

EUROPHYSICS LETTERS (FR/0295-5075) [13098554] **4402**

EUROPHYSICS NEWS (SZ/0531-7479) [03226819] **4402**

EUROPLASTICS YEARBOOK (UK) [01788532] **4455**

EUROPROPERTY LONDON (UK/0961-9712) [I09619712] **897**

EUROSAFETY (UK) **4775**

EUROSCAMBI (IT) **833**

● EUROSCOPE INC (US/1060-9105) [25105934] **4647**

● EUROSERIALS (BINGHAMTON, N.Y.) (US/1069-4641) [28050270] **3209**

EUROSLOT OLDHAM (UK/0966-0259) [I09660259] **4860**

EUROSOCIAL NEWSLETTER (AU) [29458408] **5285**

EUROSTAMPA (IT) **4815**

EUROSTAT. AGRICULTURAL PRICES. PRICE INDICES AND ABSOLUTE PRICES. QUARTERLY STATISTICS (LU/1015-9924) [I10159924] **153**

EUROSTAT CATALOGUE : PUBLICATIONS AND ELECTRONIC SERVICES (LU) [19452961] **5327**

EUROSTAT, GENERAL GOVERNMENT ACCOUNTS AND STATISTICS (LU/0255-3953) [06700685] **4722**, **4697**

EUROSTAT. REGNSKABER. LANDBRUG, SKOVBRUG, ENHEDSVRDIER (LU/0257-5264) [05394300] **82**

EUROSTATISTIK, DATEN ZUR KONJUNKTURANALYSE / STATISTISCHES AMT DER EUROPAISCHEN GEMEINSCHAFTEN (LU/0252-8266) [08977368] 1490, **1532**

EUROSTRATEGIE (BE) [19692917] **4043**

EUROTAX (BE) **833**

EUROTAX AUTOVETTURE (IT) **833**

EUROTAX DUE RUOTE (IT) **5414**

EUROTAX FUORISTRADA (IT) **833**

EUROTAX NAUTICA (IT) **833**

EUROTAX VEICOLI INDUSTRIALI (IT) **743**

EUROTECH FORUM JOURNAL (BE/0775-2903) [I07752903] **5104**

EUROTECHNOLOGY (UK/0959-7735) **5104**

● EUROWATCH: ECONOMICS, POLICY, AND LAW IN THE NEW EUROPE (US) [25258649] **2688**

EUSKAL HERRIKO AGINTARITZAREN ALDIZKARIA / BOLETIN OFICIAL DEL PAIS VASCO (SP) [10686824] **2968**

EUSKAL HERRIKO POETAK (SP) **3386**

EUSKARIEN (QUEBEC) (CN/1195-5015) [29874073] 4165, **2193**

EUTAW MIRROR See GREENE COUNTY DEMOCRAT (EUTAW, ALA.), THE **5626**

EUTHANASIA REVIEW, THE CEASED. (US/0884-2981) [12359074] **2250**

EUTHYNE (GR/0302-1041) [01793247] **2516**

● EUTOPIA (IT/1121-1628) [29233773] **268**

EUTOPIAS CEASED. (US/0213-246X) [13103325] **3281**

EV CIRCUIT - ELECTRIC VEHICLE CLUB OF OTTAWA (CN/0837-3752) [18243069] **2054**

EVA BRATISLAVA (XO/0139-8717) [I01398717] 5555, **1084**

EVA (MILAN, ITALY) (IT) [20950552] **5555**

EVALUACION PSICOLOGICA (SP) [14372239] **4587**

EVALUATING AND BUYING A FRANCHISE (US) [15282669] **673**

EVALUATING TAX SHELTER OFFERINGS (US/0749-2529) [06416532] **4722**

EVALUATING YOUR FIRM'S INJURY & ILLNESS RECORD. CONSTRUCTION INDUSTRIES (US/0743-6149) [10200674] **1668**

EVALUATION AND PROGRAM PLANNING (US/0149-7189) [03547275] **5285**

EVALUATION & RESEARCH IN EDUCATION (UK/0950-0790) [16961931] **1745**

EVALUATION & THE HEALTH PROFESSIONS (US/0163-2787) [03945887] **3576**

EVALUATION COMMENT (US/0575-4577) [02260923] 5245, **1746**

EVALUATION EN ACTION, L' (CN/1188-245X) [25796362] **1746**

EVALUATION ENGINEERING (US/0149-0370) [03427108] **2054**

EVALUATION OF THE URBAN HOMESTEADING DEMONSTRATION PROGRAM, ANNUAL REPORT (US/0161-9535) [04060778] **2822**

EVALUATION PRACTICE (US/0886-1633) [12847616] **5200**

EVALUATION REPORT / GOA, DAMAN AND DIU (INDIA). DIRECTORATE OF PLANNING, STATISTICS AND EVALUATION (II) [01790400] **1561**

EVALUATION REPORT OF VOCATIONAL AND TECHNICAL EDUCATION IN SOUTH CAROLINA / BY THE SOUTH CAROLINA ADVISORY COUNCIL ON VOCATIONAL AND TECHNICAL EDUCATION (US) [13210413] **1913**

EVALUATION REPORT - PRAIRIE AGRICULTURAL MACHINERY INSTITUTE (CN/0383-3445) [05791059] **158**

EVALUATION REPORT - PRAIRIE AGRICULTURAL MACHINERY INSTITUTE (CN/0383-3445) [09273083] 82, **2114**

EVALUATION REPORT : REPORT OF THE EXECUTIVE DIRECTOR (KE/0259-2940) [15313223] **2193**

EVALUATION RESULTS FOR ... WORLD BANK (US/1019-4363) [22496652] **1561**

EVALUATION REVIEW (US/0193-841X) [05267706] **5245**

EVALUATION : TITLE I (US) [04599062] **1746**

EVALUATIONS OF DRUG INTERACTIONS (US/0090-6654) [01786376] **4303**

EVALUATOR (RIVER FOREST, ILL.) (US/8756-775X) [11653081] 250, **320**

EVANGEL : QUARTERLY REVIEW OF BIBLICAL, PRACTICAL AND CONTEMPORARY THEOLOGY (UK/0265-4547) **4957**

EVANGEL (WINONA LAKE) (US/0162-1890) [04118074] **4957**

EVANGELICAL ALLIANCE MISSION See TEAM TORIZONS **5002**

EVANGELICAL BAPTIST (CN/0014-3324) [01776408] **5059**

EVANGELICAL BEACON AND EVANGELIST See EVANGELICAL BEACON, THE **4957**

EVANGELICAL BEACON, THE (US/0014-3332) [01695151] **4957**

EVANGELICAL FREE CHURCH OF AMERICA See YEARBOOK AND MINUTES OF THE ANNUAL CONFERENCE - EVANGELICAL FREE CHURCH OF AMERICA **5069**

EVANGELICAL FREE CHURCH OF AMERICA See YEARBOOK / EVANGELICAL FREE CHURCH OF AMERICA **5069**

EVANGELICAL FREE CHURCH OF AMERICA See YEARBOOK / EVANGELICAL FREE CHURCH OF AMERICA **5069**

EVANGELICAL FRIEND CEASED. (US/0014-3340) [04075041] **4957**

EVANGELICAL JOURNAL (US/0741-1758) [10090050] **4957**

EVANGELICAL LIBRARY BULLETIN (UK) **3209**

EVANGELICAL LUTHERAN CHURCH IN AMERICA See YEARBOOK / EVANGELICAL LUTHERAN CHURCH IN AMERICA **5069**

EVANGELICAL MAGAZINE OF WALES (UK/0421-8094) [I04218094] **4957**

EVANGELICAL METHODIST, THE (US/0745-8495) [08551297] **5060**

EVANGELICAL MISSIONS QUARTERLY (US/0014-3359) [01783538] **4957**

EVANGELICAL MORMON OUTREACH QUARTERLY, THE (US/1065-4852) [26618797] **4957**

EVANGELICAL PHILOSOPHICAL SOCIETY See BULLETIN OF THE EVANGELICAL PHILOSOPHICAL SOCIETY **4343**

EVANGELICAL QUARTERLY (UK/0014-3367) [01568492] **4957**

EVANGELICAL REVIEW OF THEOLOGY (II/0144-8153) [04283366] **4957**

EVANGELICAL STUDIES BULLETIN (US/0890-703X) [10511474] **4957**

EVANGELICAL SUNDAY SCHOOL TEACHER'S GUIDE, THE (US/0731-0463) [08097737] **4957**

EVANGELICAL THEOLOGICAL SOCIETY See JOURNAL OF THE EVANGELICAL THEOLOGICAL SOCIETY **4970**

EVANGELICAL TIMES (UK) **5060**

EVANGELICAL VISITOR (US/0745-0486) [02446809] **4957**

EVANGELIKALE MISSIOLOGIE (GW/0177-8706) [I01778706] **4957**

EVANGELISCHE ERZIEHER, DER (GW/0014-3413) [06152284] **4957**

EVANGELISCHE INFORMATION : NACHRICHTENSPIEGEL DES EVANGELISCHEN PRESSEDIENSTES (GW) [07086868] **4957**

EVANGELISCHE KIRCHE IM RHEINLAND See KIRCHLICHES AMTSBLATT DER EVANGELISCHEN KIRCHE IM RHEINLAND **4972**

EVANGELISCHE KOMMENTARE (GW/0300-4236) [01641882] **4957**

EVANGELISCHE THEOLOGIE (GW/0014-3502) [01776415] **4957**

EVANGELISCHER BUND. KONFESSIONSKUNDLICHES INSTITUT See MD, MATERIALDIENST DES KONFESSIONSKUNDLICHEN INSTITUTS **4976**

EVANGELISCHES GEMEINDEBLATT FUER WUERTTEMBERG / [IM AUFTRAG VON LANDESBISCHOF D. WURM HERAUSGEGEBEN VON DER EVANG. GESELLSCHAFT IN STUTTGART] (GW) [07974031] **4957**

EVANGELISM (MEQUON, WIS.) (US/0890-667X) [14338959] **4957**

EVANGELIST (ALBANY, N.Y.), THE (US/0738-8489) [09698091] **5029**

EVANGELIUM / GOSPEL / EUAGGELION CEASED. (GW) [09034404] **4957**

EVANGELIUM UND WISSENSCHAFT (GW/0934-0769) [09340769] **4957**

EVANGELIZE (MINNEAPOLIS, MINN.) (US/0745-4074) [01568505] **5060**

EVANGELIZING TODAY'S CHILD (US/0891-3846) [01780874] **4958**

EVANS-NOVAK POLITICAL REPORT (US/0014-3650) [07411627] **4473**

EVANS REPORT (CN/1180-3711) [21480039] **1184**

EVANSIA (US/0747-9859) [10863619] **509**

EVANSTON REVIEW, THE (US/1044-7733) [08807426] **5660**

EVANSVILLE COURIER, THE (US) [09201480] **5663**

EVANSVILLE PRESS (US/0896-6249) [08810009] **5664**

EVASION (CN/0381-8349) [02588136] **5469**

EVEIL, L' (CN/0383-6274) [02909515] **1746**

EVEIL (SAINT-EUSTACHE) (CN/0384-7845) [03412276] **5784**

EVELYN WAUGH NEWSLETTER AND STUDIES (US/1058-8272) [22330531] 3342, **432**

EVENEMENT DU JEUDI, L' (FR/0765-412X) [14516015] **2733**

EVENEMENT EUROPEEN, L' (FR) [18279874] **4541**

EVENING BULLETIN (PROVIDENCE, R.I.) (US) [09378311] **5741**

EVENING CHRONICLE (OLDHAM) (UK/0968-3623) [I09683623] **5812**

EVENING CITIZEN (LACONIA, N.H.), THE (US/8750-6386) [11643383] **5708**

EVENING HERALD (BRADENTON, FLORIDA) See BRADENTON HERALD, THE **5649**

EVENING HERALD (SANFORD, FLA.) See SANFORD HERALD (SANFORD, FLA.) **5651**

EVENING HERALD (SHEHANDOAH, PA. : 1969) (US/1055-8403) [13619233] **5736**

EVENING INDEPENDENT (SAINT PETERSBURG, FLA.) See ST. PETERSBURG TIMES **5651**

EVENING JOURNAL (LUBBOCK, TEX.) (US/0745-547X) [09288705] **5749**

EVENING JOURNAL, THE (US) [12698698] **5763**

EVENING LEADER (SAINT MARYS, OHIO) (US/0745-5550) [09286248] **5728**

EVENING NEWS (HARRISBURG, PA.), THE (US/0887-7939) [12249588] **5736**

EVENING NEWS (JEFFERSONVILLE, IND. : 1924) (US) [11330360] **5664**

EVENING NEWS (NORWICH. 1991) (UK/0964-4946) [I09644946] **5812**

Alphabetical Title Index   EXCELSIOR

EVENING NEWS (SAULT SAINTE MARIE, MICH.) (US) [17191079] **5692**

EVENING OBSERVER (DUNKIRK, N.Y. : 1904) *See* DUNKIRK EVENING OBSERVER **5716**

EVENING OBSERVER, THE (US) [15730496] **5716**

EVENING PATRIOT (CN) **5784**

EVENING REVIEW, THE (US) [17655632] **5728**

EVENING SENTINEL (SHENANDOAH, IOWA) (US) [15728665] **5670**

EVENING STAR (AUBURN, IND.) (US) [15698269] **5664**

EVENING SUN (BALTIMORE, MD.) (US) [07909798] **5686**

EVENING SUN (NORWICH, N.Y.) (US/0747-0355) [10498810] **5716**

EVENING TELEGRAM (HERKIMER, N.Y.) (US) [11233532] **5716**

EVENING TELEGRAM (ROCKY MOUNT, N.C.) (US/0738-5137) [09612383] **5723**

EVENING TELEGRAM (SUPERIOR, WIS. : 1922) (US) [14815954] **5767**

EVENING TIMES (US) [17375077] **5631**

EVENING TIMES (LITTLE FALLS, N.Y.), THE (US) [11192226] **5716**

EVENING TIMES (PAWTUCKET, R.I. : 1978) *See* TIMES (PAWTUCKET, R.I.), THE **5741**

EVENING TIMES (PAWTUCKET, R.I. : 1978) (US) [12432448] **5741**

EVENING TIMES (SAYRE, PA.) (US/0746-4843) [10078889] **5736**

EVENING TIMES (WEST PALM BEACH, FLA.), THE (US/8750-5339) [11484663] 5648, **5649**

EVENING TRIBUNE (HORNELL, N.Y. : 1934) (US) [11992425] **5716**

EVENING WORLD (BLOOMFIELD, IND.) (US) [14204709] **5664**

EVENING WORLD (SPENCER, IND.) (US/0745-7227) [09400682] **5664**

EVENSONGS, THE (CH) [01790385] **5231**

EVENT (NEW WESTMINSTER) (CN/0315-3770) [01804576] **3386**

EVENT (NEW YORK), THE (US/0271-9649) [06695212] **2616**

EVENTS (BEIRUT) (LE/0252-9459) [02607372] **2651**

●EVENTS USA (US/1066-6346) [26903694] **4850**

EVEREADY BATTERY ENGINEERING DATA / UNION CARBIDE (US) [10608839] **2012**

EVEREST REVIEW (SP/0376-9100) [02245618] **1561**

EVEREST WORLD, THE (US) [09954379] **5675**

EVERFOTO (SP) [02242171] **4369**

EVERGREEN (US) [05896793] **3386**

EVERGREEN (CHELTENHAM, ENGLAND) (UK) [12360255] **2516**

EVERGREEN CHRONICLES, THE (US/1043-3333) [18317677] 2796, **2794**

EVERGREEN COURANT, THE (US) [11809530] **5626**

EVERGREEN (PEECHI, INDIA) (II/0254-6426) [12058624] **2379**

EVERGREEN STATE FILM & VIDEO INDEX, THE (US/0737-0113) [09265775] **1132**

EVERLASTING NATION, THE (US/0423-8699) [04409344] **4958**

EVERMAN TIMES (US) [17796534] **5749**

●EVERTON'S GENEALOGICAL HELPER (US/1016-6359) [25307643] **2446**

EVERYBODY'S MONEY (US/0423-8710) [01568533] **1296**

EVERYDAY ELECTRONIC *See* EVERYDAY WITH PRACTICAL ELECTRONICS **2054**

EVERYDAY ELECTRONICS (UK/0262-3617) [I02623617] **2054**

●EVERYDAY TLC (US/1077-5544) [30834648] **1894**

EVERYDAY WITH PRACTICAL ELECTRONICS (UK) **2054**

EVERYMAN'S SCIENCE (II/0531-495X) [I0531495X] **5104**

EVERYONE'S BACKYARD (US/0749-3940) [11124261] **2171**

EVERYONE'S UNITED NATIONS (US/0251-690X) [06104926] **3128**

EVERYTHING NATURAL (US/0889-8421) [14086263] **2790**

EVERYTHING'S ARCHIE *CEASED.* (US/0745-7766) [09444564] **4860**

EVERYWOMAN'S ALMANAC (CN/0319-7530) [02442920] **5555**

EVE'S WEEKLY *SUSPENDED.* (II) [01696337] **5555**

EVIDENCE (US) [02239697] **2968**

EVIDENTIA *CEASED.* (US/0161-3138) [03888541] **3148**

EVM, EICH- UND VERMESSUNGSMAGAZIN (AU) [06722346] **2023**

EVOCATIONS CREMIEU (FR/1149-2031) [11492031] **2688**

EVOLUTION (US/0014-3820) [01568544] **544**

EVOLUTION (MONTREAL) (CN/0701-4686) [03128134] **2487**

EVOLUTION PSYCHIATRIQUE, L' (FR/0014-3855) [02260936] **3925**

●EVOLUTIONARY ANTHROPOLOGY / ISSUES, NEWS AND REVIEWS (US/1060-1538) [24883421] **236**

EVOLUTIONARY BIOLOGY (US/0071-3260) [01568546] 236, **544**

EVOLUTIONARY BLUES (US/0730-0247) [07917075] **4521**

●EVOLUTIONARY COMPUTATION (US/1063-6560) [26104051] **1247**

EVOLUTIONARY ECOLOGY (UK/0269-7653) [15249218] **2216**

EVOLUTIONARY THEORY & REVIEW (US) [25023875] **236**

EVOLUTIONARY TRENDS IN PLANTS (UK/1011-3258) [15607044] **509**

EVOLUZIONE AGRICOLA; MENSILE DI ATTUALITA E TECNICA ZOOAGRICOLA (IT) [03997621] **82**

EVOLUZIONE DEI SETTORI INDUSTRIALI NEL ... / CONFINDUSTRIA, CENTRO STUDI (IT) [16800922] **1606**

EVREI I EVREISKII NAROD. MATERIALY IZ SOVETSKOI PECHATI *CEASED.* (IS/0334-4436) [13323840] 2261, **5047**

EVREISKII ZHURNAL (GW/0939-5369) [25223662] **5047**

EW DESIGN ENGINEERS' HANDBOOK (US/0895-7541) [16784835] **1975**

EW DESIGN ENGINEERS' HANDBOOK & MANUFACTURERS DIRECTORY (US/1069-708X) [28136554] 2054, **4043**

EW. ERNAHRUNGSWIRTSCHAFT (GW/0179-8812) [I01798812] 2367, **2334**

●EW REFERENCE & SOURCE GUIDE (US) [29680231] 2054, **4043**

EWGS BULLETIN (US/0738-5234) [09477057] **2446**

EWING EXCHANGE (US/0892-2144) [15122204] **2446**

EWOKS (US/0888-0743) [13118303] **4860**

●EWP UPDATE, THE (US/1062-3787) [25602734] **1155**

EX AUDITU (US/0883-0053) [12032714] **4958**

EX AUDITU : AN ANNUAL OF THE FREDERICK NEUMANN SYMPOSIUM ON THEOLOGICAL INTERPRETATION SCRIPTURE *See* EX AUDITU : AN INTERNATIONAL JOURNAL OF THEOLOGICAL INTERPRETATION OF SCRIPTURE **4958**

EX AUDITU : AN INTERNATIONAL JOURNAL OF THEOLOGICAL INTERPRETATION OF SCRIPTURE (US) **4958**

EX-CBI ROUNDUP (US/0014-388X) [02385653] 4044, **2733**

EX LIBRIS (OTTAWA) (CN/0226-9791) [08268289] **3210**

EX LIBRIS (PORTSMOUTH, N.H.) (US/1042-6647) [19043339] **3386**

EX LONDON (UK/0956-0122) [I09560122] 5469, **18**

EX MAGAZINE (GW/0176-0920) [10498540] **2054**

EX NIHILO TECHNICAL JOURNAL (AT/0814-6764) [16179795] **4958**

EX PARTE PRESENTATIONS IN INFORMAL RULEMAKINGS (US) [06756228] **1111**

EX TEMPORE (CN/0276-6795) [07397325] **4117**

EXAKT (GW/0340-0220) [01796459] **5104**

EXALTATION (US/1046-3798) [20402854] **4958**

EXAME (1983) (BL) [10049319] **673**

EXAMENS ET LES DIPLOMES, LES (FR) [02362541] **1913**

EXAMINATION OF FINANCIAL STATEMENTS, INTER-AMERICAN FOUNDATION (US/0094-5609) [01794199] 743, **4722**

EXAMINATION OF FINANCIAL STATEMENTS OF OVERSEAS PRIVATE INVESTMENT CORPORATION (US/0094-470X) [01793920] **897**

EXAMINATION OF FINANCIAL STATEMENTS OF STUDENT LOAN INSURANCE FUND (US/0098-7646) [02239461] **1823**

EXAMINATION OF FINANCIAL STATEMENTS OF THE PENNSYLVANIA AVENUE DEVELOPMENT CORPORATION (US/0098-6798) [02242071] 2822, **4647**

EXAMINATION OF FINANCIAL STATEMENTS OF THE PENSION BENEFIT GUARANTY CORPORATION (US/0193-4325) [05182580] **1668**

EXAMINATION OF FINANCIAL STATEMENTS, THE GOVERNMENT NATIONAL MORTGAGE ASSOCIATION, THE FEDERAL NATIONAL MORTGAGE ASSOCIATION *See* GOVERNMENT NATIONAL MORTGAGE ASSOCIATION EXAMINATION OF FINANCIAL STATEMENTS **789**

EXAMINATION OF FISCAL ... PRESIDENTIAL AND VICE PRESIDENTIAL CERTIFIED EXPENDITURES (US/0272-7013) [06885553] **4647**

EXAMINATION OF THE FINANCIAL STATEMENTS OF FHA INSURANCE OPERATIONS (US/0273-026X) [06968661] **2879**

EXAMINATION OF THE NATIONAL CONSUMER COOPERATIVE BANK'S FINANCIAL STATEMENTS FOR THE FISCAL YEAR ENDED ..., AND THE QUARTER ENDED ... - COMPTROLLER GENERAL OF THE UNITED STATES (US) [09573101] **1542**

EXAMINATION OF THE PANAMA CANAL COMMISSION'S FINANCIAL STATEMENTS (US/0743-7404) [10192088] **5449**

EXAMINATION OF THE PANAMA CANAL COMMISSION'S FISCAL YEAR ... FINANCIAL STATEMENTS AND TREATY-RELATED ISSUES. SUMMARY (US) [08904174] **743**

EXAMINATION OF THE RURAL TELEPHONE BANK'S FINANCIAL STATEMENTS (US/0096-9893) [01798718] 1155, **743**

EXAMINATION OF UNITED STATES RAILWAY ASSOCIATION'S FINANCIAL STATEMENTS (US/0272-7021) [06885478] **5431**

EXAMINER (BARRIE) (CN/0839-4164) [18450753] **5784**

EXAMINER, THE (US) [28205230] **5703**

EXAMINING COURT DECISIONS AND OPINIONS OF THE ATTORNEY GENERAL CONSTRUING ALASKA STATUTES (US) [09436849] **3140**

EXAMS AND ANSWERS: BUSINESS ARITHMETIC *See* BARRON'S REGENTS EXAMS AND ANSWERS : BUSINESS MATHEMATICS **642**

EXAMS AND ANSWERS: ELEMENTARY ALGEBRA *See* BARRON'S REGENTS EXAMS AND ANSWERS, 9TH YEAR MATHEMATICS, ELEMENTARY ALGEBRA **3496**

EXAMS AND ANSWERS: SPANISH THREE YEARS *See* BARRON'S REGENTS EXAMS AND ANSWERS : SPANISH LEVEL 3, COMPREHENSIVE SPANISH **3268**

EXAMS AND ANSWERS: TENTH YEAR MATHEMATICS *See* BARRON'S REGENTS EXAMS AND ANSWERS: 10TH YEAR MATHEMATICS **3496**

EXCALIBUR (US/1045-1366) [20021281] **4860**

EXCALIBUR (DOWNSVIEW, ONT.) (CN/0823-1915) [11734390] **5784**

EXCAVACIONES ARQUEOLOGICAS EN ESPANA (SP/0071-3279) [01775560] **268**

EXCAVATING CONTRACTOR *SUSPENDED.* (US/0014-3995) [01568559] **614**

EXCAVATIONS AND SURVEYS IN ISRAEL (IS/0334-1607) [11437560] **268**

EXCAVATIONS AT CARTHAGE (US) [04553594] **268**

EXCAVATIONS AT THE ATHENIAN AGORA: PICTURE BOOK (US/0569-7425) [01242088] **268**

EXCEL *SUSPENDED.* (AT/0817-4792) [13998227] **3954**

EXCEL (US) **2862**

EXCEL (SAN FRANCISCO, CALIF.) (US/0893-5017) [15597544] **5200**

EXCELENCIA (BL) [24635353] **2733**

EXCELLENCE IN ECOLOGY (GW/0932-2205) [17938302] **2216**

EXCELLENCE IN HIGHWAY DESIGN (US/0882-4258) [11704877] **2023**

EXCELLENCE IN TEACHING *CEASED.* (US/0740-9893) [10063690] **1894**

EXCELLENCE (LOUISVILLE, KY.) (US/0886-9812) [12854051] **1286**

EXCELLENCE (ROSS, CALIF.) (US/0896-0798) [16905549] **5414**

EXCELSA (RH/0301-441X) [01791038] **509**

EXCELSIOR (MX) [01568561] **5806**

EXCELSIOR Alphabetical Title Index

EXCELSIOR (QUEBEC) (CN/0381-1913) [03279127] **1091**

EXCEPTIONAL CHILD EDUCATION RESOURCES (US/0160-4309) [03429088] 1878, **1795**

EXCEPTIONAL CHILDREN (US/0014-4029) [01568566] **1878**

EXCEPTIONAL HUMAN EXPERIENCE (US/1053-4768) [22537637] 4241, **4243**

EXCEPTIONAL PARENT, THE (US/0046-9157) [00974895] **2278**

EXCEPTIONALITY EDUCATION CANADA (CN/1183-322X) [24570863] **1879**

EXCEPTIONALITY : THE OFFICIAL JOURNAL OF THE DIVISION FOR RESEARCH OF THE COUNCIL FOR EXCEPTIONAL CHILDREN (US/0936-2835) [21193047] **1879**

EXCERPTA BOTANICA. SECTIO A. TAXONOMICA ET CHOROLOGICA (GW/0014-4037) [01568568] **509**

EXCERPTA BOTANICA. SECTIO B. SOCIOLOGICA (GW/0014-4045) [01568569] **5245**

EXCERPTA INDONESICA (NE/0046-0885) [01967125] **5227**

EXCERPTA INFORMATICA (NE/0169-5509) [I01695509] **1219**

EXCERPTA MEDICA. SECTION 1. ANATOMY, ANTHROPOLOGY, EMBRYOLOGY AND HISTOLOGY (NE/0014-4053) [01568572] 3576, **3657**

EXCERPTA MEDICA. SECTION 2A. PHYSIOLOGY (NE/0367-1089) [01778954] 580, **478**

EXCERPTA MEDICA. SECTION 3. ENDOCRINOLOGY (NE/0014-407X) [05103720] 3730, **3657**

EXCERPTA MEDICA. SECTION 4. MICROBIOLOGY *See* EXCERPTA MEDICA. SECTION 4. MICROBIOLOGY, BACTERIOLOGY, MYCOLOGY, PARASITOLOGY, AND VIROLOGY **3657**

●EXCERPTA MEDICA. SECTION 4. MICROBIOLOGY, BACTERIOLOGY, MYCOLOGY, PARASITOLOGY, AND VIROLOGY (NE) [25571295] 562, **3657**

EXCERPTA MEDICA. SECTION 5. GENERAL PATHOLOGY AND PATHOLOGICAL ANATOMY (NE/0014-4096) [01568610] 3894, 3679, **3657**

EXCERPTA MEDICA. SECTION 6. INTERNAL MEDICINE (NE/0014-410X) [01568602] 3796, **3657**

EXCERPTA MEDICA. SECTION 7. PEDIATRICS AND PEDIATRIC SURGERY (NE/0373-6512) [01640144] 3903, **3657**

EXCERPTA MEDICA. SECTION 8. NEUROLOGY AND NEUROSURGERY (NE/0014-4126) [01568604] 3832, **3657**

EXCERPTA MEDICA. SECTION 9. SURGERY (NE/0014-4134) [01568605] 3964, **3657**

EXCERPTA MEDICA. SECTION 10. OBSTETRICS AND GYNECOLOGY (NE/0014-4142) [01568573] 3760, **3657**

EXCERPTA MEDICA. SECTION 11. OTO-, RHINO-, LARYNGOLOGY (NE/0014-4150) [02277550] **3888**

EXCERPTA MEDICA. SECTION 12. OPHTHALMOLOGY (NE/0014-4169) [01568575] 3874, **3658**

EXCERPTA MEDICA. SECTION 13. DERMATOLOGY AND VENEREOLOGY (NE/0014-4177) [01568576] 3720, **3658**

EXCERPTA MEDICA. SECTION 14. RADIOLOGY (NE/0014-4185) [01568577] 3941, **3658**

EXCERPTA MEDICA. SECTION 16. CANCER (NE/0014-4207) [01568579] 3817, **3658**

EXCERPTA MEDICA. SECTION 17. PUBLIC HEALTH, SOCIAL MEDICINE AND EPIDEMIOLOGY (NE) [17802293] 4775, 3735, **3658**

EXCERPTA MEDICA. SECTION 18. CARDIOVASCULAR DISEASES AND CARDIOVASCULAR SURGERY (NE/0014-4223) [01568581] 3704, **3658**

EXCERPTA MEDICA. SECTION 19. REHABILITATION AND PHYSICAL MEDICINE (NE/0014-4231) [01568582] 4380, **3658**

EXCERPTA MEDICA. SECTION 20. GERONTOLOGY AND GERIATRICS (NE/0014-424X) [01568583] 3750, **3658**

EXCERPTA MEDICA. SECTION 21. DEVELOPMENTAL BIOLOGY AND TERATOLOGY (NE/0014-4258) [01568584] **3658**

EXCERPTA MEDICA. SECTION 22. HUMAN GENETICS (NE/0014-4266) [02262053] 545, **3658**

EXCERPTA MEDICA. SECTION 23. NUCLEAR MEDICINE (NE/0014-4274) [01568586] 3848, **3658**

EXCERPTA MEDICA. SECTION 24. ANESTHESIOLOGY (NE/0014-4282) [01568587] 3683, **3658**

EXCERPTA MEDICA. SECTION 25. HEMATOLOGY (NE/0014-4290) [01568588] 3771, **3658**

EXCERPTA MEDICA. SECTION 26. IMMUNOLOGY, SEROLOGY AND TRANSPLANTATION (NE/0014-4304) [01568589] 3669, **3658**

EXCERPTA MEDICA. SECTION 27. BIOPHYSICS, BIOENGINEERING AND MEDICAL INSTRUMENTATION (NE/0014-4312) [01568590] 495, **3658**

EXCERPTA MEDICA. SECTION 28. UROLOGY AND NEPHROLOGY (NE/0014-4320) [01568591] 3990, **3658**

EXCERPTA MEDICA. SECTION 29. CLINICAL BIOCHEMISTRY (NE/0300-5372) [01642550] 487, 1011, **478**

●EXCERPTA MEDICA. SECTION 30. CLINICAL AND EXPERIMENTAL PHARMACOLOGY (NE) [25584794] 4303, 3576, **3658**

EXCERPTA MEDICA. SECTION 30. PHARMACOLOGY *See* EXCERPTA MEDICA. SECTION 30. CLINICAL AND EXPERIMENTAL PHARMACOLOGY **3658**

EXCERPTA MEDICA. SECTION 32. PSYCHIATRY (NE/0014-4363) [01568595] 3925, **3659**

EXCERPTA MEDICA. SECTION 35. OCCUPATIONAL HEALTH AND INDUSTRIAL MEDICINE (NE/0014-4398) [03667831] 2862, **2872**

EXCERPTA MEDICA. SECTION 36. HEALTH POLICY, ECONOMICS, AND MANAGEMENT (NE) [17937190] 3780, **3659**

EXCERPTA MEDICA. SECTION 37. DRUG LITERATURE INDEX *CEASED*. (NE/0167-9171) [08538006] 4304, **3659**

EXCERPTA MEDICA. SECTION 38. ADVERSE REACTIONS TITLES (NE/0167-9090) [07245091] 4304, **3659**

EXCERPTA MEDICA. SECTION 40. DRUG DEPENDENCE, ALCOHOL ABUSE, AND ALCOHOLISM (NE/0304-4041) [17994190] 1344, **3659**

EXCERPTA MEDICA. SECTION 46. ENVIRONMENTAL HEALTH AND POLLUTION CONTROL (NE/0300-5194) [01778965] 2171, **3659**

EXCERPTA MEDICA. SECTION 49. FORENSIC SCIENCE ABSTRACTS (NE/0031-0743) [02246687] **3740**

EXCERPTA MEDICA. SECTION 50. EPILEPSY ABSTRACTS (NE/0303-8459) [09395080] 3832, **3659**

EXCERPTA MEDICA. SECTION 52. TOXICOLOGY (NE/0167-8353) [09340517] 3980, **3659**

EXCERPTA MEDICA. SECTION 65. CANCER IMMUNOLOGY. LITERATURE INDEX (NE/0304-3789) [01856364] 3817, **3659**

EXCERPTA MEDICA. SECTION 130. CLINICAL PHARMACOLOGY *See* EXCERPTA MEDICA. SECTION 30. CLINICAL AND EXPERIMENTAL PHARMACOLOGY **3658**

EXCESS EXPRESS (US/0740-1388) [09939060] 867, **2879**

EXCHANGE (NE/0166-2740) [04283393] **4958**

EXCHANGE (ALEXANDRIA, VA.) (US/1046-1485) [19273112] **2193**

EXCHANGE & COMMISSARY NEWS (US/0014-4452) [05143283] **4044**

EXCHANGE & MART NORTH/MIDLAND ED (UK/0965-9269) [I09659269] **5812**

EXCHANGE BOOK (YOUNGSTOWN, ARIZ.) (US/0890-9911) [14576731] **5469**

EXCHANGE (COLUMBIA) (US/0145-4072) [02733041] **385**

EXCHANGE (FORT WORTH, TEX.) (US/0888-5648) [13657571] **3914**

EXCHANGE (KITCHENER) (CN/0824-457X) [10522275] **833**

EXCHANGE LILYFIELD (AT/1033-2014) [I10332014] **673**

EXCHANGE (PROVO) (US/0146-4000) [02934409] **1091**

EXCHANGE (TORONTO) (CN/0700-7949) [03291503] **5060**

EXCHANGE (TUSCALOOSA, ALA.) (US/1042-4083) [19036818] **1746**

EXCHANGITE, THE (US/0014-4487) [04075045] **5231**

EXCISE NEWS (CN/0708-9031) [03233206] **2968**

EXCITEMENT & FASCINATION OF SCIENCE, THE (US) **5104**

EXCLUSIVE (OTTAWA) (CN/1187-3183) [25313939] **5469**

●EXCLUSIVELY MALLS : CHICAGO'S METROPOLITAN MALL RESOURCE AND REFERENCE DIRECTORY (US/1058-577X) [24333380] **954**

EXE (UK/0268-6872) [21427823] **1184**

EXEC-U-TARY, THE (US/0894-5748) [16146843] **673**

EXECUTION AND CONTROL SYSTEMS *CEASED*. (US/0736-8305) [09231189] 1247, **1228**

EXECUTION DES DECISIONS DES JURIDICTIONS ADMINISTRATIVES (FR) [21537724] **4647**

EXECUTION DES PROJECTS FINANCES PAR LE PROGRAMME DE COOPERATION BELGO-RWANDAIS (RW) [04200597] **1561**

EXECUTIVE ACCOUNTANT (UK) **743**

EXECUTIVE ACTION REPORT (US/1043-3082) [19336831] **3100**

EXECUTIVE AIDS WATCH (US/0885-6168) [12681689] **673**

EXECUTIVE AIR GUIDE (US/0746-9446) [10406876] **18**

EXECUTIVE ALERT (US) **4647**

EXECUTIVE : AN ACADEMY OF MANAGEMENT PUBLICATION, THE (US) [21073923] **867**

EXECUTIVE AND OWNERSHIP REPORT. CLASS I & II MOTOR CARRIERS OF PROPERTY (US/0883-7473) [12153449] **673**

EXECUTIVE BIO-PICTORIAL DIRECTORY, THE *See* PRESIDENT'S TEAM **4674**

EXECUTIVE BRIEFING (US) **867**

EXECUTIVE BRIEFING, CASE (US/1053-1599) [22465809] 1286, **1228**

EXECUTIVE BRIEFING (NEW YORK, N.Y.) (US/0898-7912) [13238686] **867**

●EXECUTIVE BUDGET AND FINANCIAL PLAN / TRIBOROUGH BRIDGE AND TUNNEL AUTHORITY (US) [27091160] **4722**

EXECUTIVE BUDGET / COMMONWEALTH OF VIRGINIA (US) [08577947] **4722**

EXECUTIVE BUDGET - DISTRICT OF COLUMBIA (US/0738-3258) [09549161] **4722**

EXECUTIVE BUDGET : EDUCATIONAL FUNDS - ALABAMA (US) [03939149] **1746**

EXECUTIVE BUDGET FOR FISCAL YEAR ... / STATE OF IDAHO (US) [19637469] **4722**

EXECUTIVE BUDGET MESSAGE / STATE OF WISCONSIN (US) [11199093] **4723**

EXECUTIVE BUDGET POLICY ISSUE PAPERS (US) [04847453] **4647**

EXECUTIVE BUDGET RECOMMENDATIONS *See* GOVERNOR'S BUDGET **4729**

EXECUTIVE BUDGET / STATE OF ARIZONA (US) [05012671] **4723**

EXECUTIVE BUDGET / STATE OF NEBRASKA ; SUBMITTED TO THE ... SESSION OF THE LEGISLATURE BY ... GOVERNOR ; PREPARED BY ... TAX COMMISSIONER AND BUDGET DIRECTOR (US) [01759554] **4723**

EXECUTIVE CAPITAL BUDGET AND CAPITAL PROGRAM - NEW YORK CITY (US) [04863320] **4723**

EXECUTIVE CAPITAL CONSTRUCTION BUDGET (US/0090-841X) [01786003] **4723**

EXECUTIVE COMMITTEE MEETING - INTERNATIONAL UNION OF FOOD AND ALLIED WORKERS' ASSOCIATIONS. EXECUTIVE COMMITTEE (SZ) [06134863] **1668**

EXECUTIVE COMMUNICATIONS *CEASED*. (US/0892-3299) [15159786] **1111**

EXECUTIVE COMPANION (UK) **674**

EXECUTIVE COMPENSATION (US/0733-3412) [04232891] **674**

EXECUTIVE COMPENSATION ANALYSIS OF PROFESSIONAL SERVICES' FIRMS (US/0148-7353) [03352080] **1668**

EXECUTIVE COMPENSATION & TAXATION COORDINATOR (US/0273-7612) [06909226] 4723, **2968**

EXECUTIVE COMPENSATION IN RETAILING (US) **954**

EXECUTIVE COMPENSATION IN THE HIGH-TECHNOLOGY INDUSTRIES (US/0164-2812) [04598357] **1668**

EXECUTIVE COMPENSATION REPORT FOR SMALL TO MEDIUM SIZED COMPANIES (US/0270-1561) [06322121] **674**

EXECUTIVE COMPENSATION REPORT (PARAMUS, N.J.) (US/8756-2111) [11491272] **1668**

EXECUTIVE COMPENSATION REPORTS (ALEXANDRIA, VA.) (US/0738-6982) [09651141] **940**

EXECUTIVE COMPENSATION SURVEY (PRINCETON, N.J.) (US/0741-3424) [10115470] 4647, **1668**

EXECUTIVE COMPENSATION ... SURVEY RESULTS (US/0743-6130) [10614024] **1668**

EXECUTIVE COMPUTING (US/0741-0050) [11256439] 1247, **1237**

EXECUTIVE COUNSELOR (US) [06122216] **867**

Alphabetical Title Index   **EXPERIENCE**

EXECUTIVE DEPT. PERSONNEL DIVISION. COMPENSATION PLAN *See* REPRESENTABLE COMPENSATION PLAN - OREGON. EXECUTIVE DEPT. PERSONNEL DIVISION. OPERATIONS AND DEVELOPMENT UNIT **4683**

EXECUTIVE DEVELOPMENT (UK) **867**

●EXECUTIVE DIRECTIONS (US) [29492728] **674**

EXECUTIVE DIRECTORY OF THE U.S. PHARMACEUTICAL INDUSTRY (US/0071-3309) [02757381] **4304**

EXECUTIVE EDGE (US/1048-2954) [20912346] **2597**

EXECUTIVE EDGE (US/0733-9291) [08672223] **674**

EXECUTIVE EDUCATOR, THE (US/0161-9500) [04067801] **1863**

EXECUTIVE EXCELLENCE (US/8756-2308) [11520319] **867**

EXECUTIVE FEMALE, THE (US/0199-2880) [05757390] 5555, **867**

EXECUTIVE FLIGHT PLANNER. AMERICAS *CEASED*. (US/1055-4858) [23193861] **5469**

EXECUTIVE GAS INDUSTRY STATISTICS (US) [13789320] **4256**

EXECUTIVE GRAPEVINE : EG, THE (UK) [17463781] **674**

EXECUTIVE HEALTH'S GOOD HEALTH REPORT (US/1071-8680) [25064259] 4775, **2597**

EXECUTIVE (HONG KONG EDITION) (HK) [11102708] **674**

EXECUTIVE HOUSEKEEPING TODAY (US/0738-6583) [09636718] **2790**

EXECUTIVE INTELLIGENCE REVIEW (US/0273-6314) [03057911] **1490**

EXECUTIVE INVESTMENT LETTER, THE (US/0896-6494) [17238098] **897**

EXECUTIVE JEWELER *CEASED*. (US/0273-5423) [07065170] **2914**

EXECUTIVE LETTER (DALLAS) (US/0193-8150) [05266981] **867**

EXECUTIVE MANAGEMENT AND MOTIVATION (US/0735-4746) [08936900] **867**

EXECUTIVE NOTES ON ENVIRONMENT AND DEVELOPMENT : INFORMATION BULLETIN PREPARED JOINTLY BY THE ENVIRONMENT AND HUMAN SETTLEMENTS DIVISION AND THE INFORMATION SERVICE OF THE ECONOMIC COMMISSION FOR LATIN AMERICA AND THE CARIBBEAN, ECLAC (CL) [26408825] 2171, **1490**

EXECUTIVE OFFICE FOR U.S. ATTORNEYS *See* STATISTICAL REPORT - EXECUTIVE OFFICE FOR U.S. ATTORNEYS **3083**

EXECUTIVE ORDER (US) [05157547] **2968**

EXECUTIVE ORDER / EXECUTIVE DEPARTMENT, STATE OF CALIFORNIA (US) [08491146] **2968**

EXECUTIVE ORDER - VIRGINIA (US) [05116250] **2968**

EXECUTIVE PC LETTER, THE (US/0882-6463) [11991096] **867**

EXECUTIVE PERSONNEL IN THE FEDERAL SERVICE (US/0149-502X) [04029208] **4647**

EXECUTIVE PERSPECTIVE (US/0191-2135) [04815945] **1237**

EXECUTIVE PHARMACY REPORT (US/1065-7118) [26699913] **4304**

EXECUTIVE PROGRAM: EXECUTIVE BUDGET *See* EXECUTIVE BUDGET FOR FISCAL YEAR ... / STATE OF IDAHO **4722**

EXECUTIVE REPORT, DATA FROM THE NATIONAL DRUG ABUSE TREATMENT UTILIZATION SURVEY (NDATUS) (US/0161-5068) [03905991] **1344**

EXECUTIVE REPORT ON CUSTOMER SATISFACTION (US/1064-8623) [26432964] **867**

EXECUTIVE REPORT ON LARGE CORPORATE PENSION PLANS (US) [11645618] **1668**

EXECUTIVE REPORT ON MANAGED CARE, THE (US/0898-9753) [17965400] **940**

EXECUTIVE REPORT (PITTSBURGH, PA.) (US/0279-1382) [07578413] **674**

EXECUTIVE SECRETARY (UK/0955-6230) **619**

EXECUTIVE SECRETARY BRADFORD (UK/0955-6230) [I09556230] **4204**

EXECUTIVE SPEAKER, THE (US/0271-3659) [06636477] **867**

EXECUTIVE SPEECHES (DAYTON, OHIO) (US/0888-4110) [13566838] **674**

EXECUTIVE STRATEGIES (NEW YORK, N.Y.) (US/1042-0657) [18785200] **867**

EXECUTIVE SUMMARY *See* NONWOVENS INDUSTRY EXECUTIVE REPORT **5354**

●EXECUTIVE SUMMARY OF CALIFORNIA EDUCATION (US/1065-5115) [26621698] **1746**

EXECUTIVE SUMMARY OF THE KANSAS JUDICIAL BRANCH / OFFICE OF JUDICIAL ADMINISTRATION, AN (US) [11214784] **3140**

EXECUTIVE SYSTEMS INTERNATIONAL NEWSLETTER (UK/0968-8803) [I09688803] **674**

EXECUTIVE TELECOMMUNICATION PLANNING GUIDE (US) [09911675] **1155**

EXECUTIVE, THE (US) [05810953] **4204**

EXECUTIVE UPDATE NEWSLETTER *CEASED*. (US) **674**

EXECUTIVE WEALTH ADVISORY (US/0195-0746) [05259185] **674**

EXECUTIVE'S HANDBOOK ON POLITICAL CONTRIBUTIONS (US/0738-4297) [09193022] **4473**

EXECUTIVES' INVESTMENT REACTIONS TO TAX PROPOSALS AFFECTING SAVINGS AND INVESTMENT (US) **898**

EXECUTIVE'S MANUAL OF PERSONAL SECRETARIES, THE (US/1052-2336) [22222939] **4211**

EXECUTIVES ON THE MOVE (US/1044-2243) [19746312] **867**

EXECUTIVE'S TAX REPORT (US/1063-0481) [17976903] **743**

EXECUTIVE'S TAX REPORT (US/1063-0481) [17979603] **4723**

EXECUTIVES TAX REPORT & WHAT'S HAPPENING IN TAXATION *See* EXECUTIVE'S TAX REPORT **4723**

EXEDRA : THE JOURNAL OF THE SCHOOL OF ARCHITECTURE, DEAKIN UNIVERSITY (AT) [23877716] **298**

EXEGESIS (PR) [16521609] **2503**

EXEGETICAL RESOURCE (US/0744-0448) [08027698] **5016**

EXEMPLA MUSICA NEERLANDICA (NE) [20243041] **4117**

EXEMPLARIA (BINGHAMTON, N.Y.) (US/1041-2573) [18695585] **3386**

●EXEMPLARIA HISPANICA (JS/1062-4511) [25625167] **2733**

EXEMPLARY PRACTICES IN EDUCATION : EPIE *CEASED*. (US/1061-4745) [25314127] **1746**

EXEMPT ORGANIZATION TAX REVIEW, THE (US/0899-3831) [18091286] **4723**

EXEMPT SALARY SURVEY (US/0736-4482) [09114587] **1668**

EXERCICE - CHAMBRE SYNDICALE DES CONSTRUCTEURS D'AUTOMOBILES ET DE MOTOCYCLES DE BELGIQUE ET FEDERATION BELGE DES INDUSTRIES DE L'AUTOMOBILE ET DU CYCLE REUNIES (BE) [01795623] 5414, **1606**

EXERCISE AND SPORT SCIENCES REVIEWS (US/0091-6331) [01783628] **3954**

EXERCISE EXCHANGE (US/0531-531X) [01568620] **1894**

EXERCISE FOR MEN ONLY (US/0882-4657) [11886802] **2597**

●EXERCISE IMMUNOLOGY REVIEW (US) **3669**

EXERCISE PHYSIOLOGY (NEW YORK, N.Y.) (US/0748-3155) [10920747] 580, 2597, **3954**

EXERCISE STANDARDS & MALPRACTICE REPORTER, THE (US/0891-0278) [14545903] **2968**

EXERCISES IN DENTAL RADIOLOGY (MICROFICHE) (US) [05040527] 3941, **1323**

EXETASIS (US/0163-7282) [03375874] **3386**

EXETER (US/0195-0207) [05217759] **1091**

EXETER HISPANIC TEXTS (UK) [01983278] **2261**

EXETER LINGUISTIC STUDIES (UK/0309-4375) [13220520] **3281**

EXETER MIDDLE EAST POLITICS (UK) [17556752] **4473**

EXETER NEWS-LETTER (1867), THE (US/0886-3962) [10891809] **5708**

EXETER STUDIES IN AMERICAN AND COMMONWEALTH ARTS (UK) [18886538] **320**

EXETER TIMES-ADVOCATE (CN) **5784**

EXETER WORKING PAPERS IN BRITISH BOOK TRADE HISTORY. SPECIAL SERIES (UK) [19224244] **4828**

EXHAUST AND UNDERCAR (AT/1030-2077) [I10302077] **5414**

EXHAUST NEWS (US/0192-7469) [05105559] **5104**

EXHIBIT BUILDER (US/0887-6878) [13317428] **1606**

EXHIBIT BUILDER QUARTERLY (US/0740-6762) [09986412] **867**

EXHIBIT BUILDER SOURCE BOOK DIRECTORY (US) **674**

EXHIBIT REVIEW, THE (US/1046-2872) [20376140] **759**

EXHIBITION BULLETIN (UK/0014-4649) [I00144649] **759**

EXHIBITION DIRECTORY (US/1056-1579) [06684338] **350**

EXHIBITION MANAGEMENT (UK) 674, **759**

EXHIBITIONS 'ROUND THE WORLD (CH) [11027959] **759**

EXHIBITOR'S HANDBOOK, THE (UK/0260-1508) [08584636] **759**

EXHIBITS DIRECTORY - ASSOCIATION OF AMERICAN PUBLISHERS (US/0147-0310) [03075769] **4815**

EXIL (TROIS- RIVIERES) (CN/0315-4165) [02007005] **5364**

EXILE LONDON (UK/0958-3971) [I09583971] **1918**

EXILE (PASADENA, CALIF.) (US/0743-9849) [10701984] **4474**

EXILE (TORONTO) (CN/0380-6596) [01781464] **3386**

EXILFORSCHUNG (GW) [10472026] **5245**

EXISTING HOME SALES (US/0161-5882) [03890566] **4837**

EXIT (GLENMONT) (US/0195-3516) [05463662] **3386**

EXKIES 'S-GRAVENHAGE (NE/0928-4109) [I09284109] **350**

EXOTIC CARS QUARTERLY (US/1054-8084) [22975512] **5414**

EXPANDED ACADEMIC INDEX [COMPUTER FILE] (US) 2487, **2496**

EXPANDING HORIZONS FOR THE FUTURE OF FLORIDA THROUGH EDUCATION, REPORT (US) [01420885] **1746**

EXPANDING HORIZONS, PSYCHIATRIC RESEARCH BULLETIN (CN/1183-6342) [24986840] **3925**

EXPANSAO (BL) [01785979] **867**

EXPANSE (BALTIMORE, MD.) (US/1070-6844) [28451819] **3386**

EXPANSION (MX) [05189922] 674, **4647**

EXPANSION (SP) **5810**

EXPANSION (SA) [02441276] **1606**

EXPANSION ARTS (US/0160-0087) [02924560] **320**

EXPANSION COMERCIAL (SP/0212-7350) [I02127350] **833**

EXPANSION DES CITES ET VILLES (CN/0318-5125) [02442068] **2822**

EXPANSION MANAGEMENT (US/1073-8355) [23162389] **674**

EXPANSION MANAGEMENT REVIEW, L' (FR) **867**

EXPANSION SURVEY, RETAIL TRADE INDUSTRY (US/0161-2581) [03874069] **954**

EXPATRIATE OBSERVER (US) **940**

EXPEDICIONARIO, O (BL) [06792396] **2616**

EXPEDITION (US/0014-4738) [01568625] 236, **268**

EXPENDITURE ON EDUCATION, AUSTRALIA (AT) [06073242] 1746, **1795**

EXPENDITURE REPORT - STATE OF COLORADO, DEPARTMENT OF HIGHWAYS (US/0146-7506) [03018856] **5440**

EXPENDITURES FOR STAFF DEVELOPMENT AND TRAINING ACTIVITIES (US/0095-6813) [01798102] 1668, **5285**

EXPENDITURES OF GENERAL REVENUE SHARING AND ANTIRECESSION FISCAL ASSISTANCE FUNDS (US/0197-2529) [05277930] **4723**

EXPENDITURES REPORT OF THE MASSACHUSETTS REHABILITATION COMMISSION (US/0095-8050) [01798439] **1668**

EXPENSE ANALYSIS, CONDOMINIUMS, COOPERATIVES, & PLANNED UNIT DEVELOPMENTS (US/0191-2208) [04800563] 2822, **4837**

EXPENSES AND APPROPRIATIONS OF THE MISSISSIPPI LEGISLATURE (US/0363-0919) [02409020] **2968**

EXPENSES OF SALES REPRESENTATIVES, TAX TREATMENT (CN/0824-3131) [10157016] **674**

EXPENSIVE (UK) [18368949] **3386**

EXPERIENCE BY STATE (BY LINE). LIFE/HEALTH. REPORT FORMAT, ACCIDENT & HEALTH LINES, FIVE YEAR STUDY (US) [22392751] **2879**

EXPERIENCE BY STATE (BY LINE). LIFE/HEALTH. REPORT FORMAT, ACCIDENT & HEALTH LINES, ONE YEAR STUDY (US) [22355470] **2879**

EXPERIENCE

EXPERIENCE BY STATE (BY LINE). LIFE/HEALTH. REPORT FORMAT, LIFE LINE, FIVE YEAR STUDY (US) [22392875] **2879**

EXPERIENCE BY STATE (BY LINE). LIFE/HEALTH. REPORT FORMAT, LIFE LINES ONE YEAR STUDY (US) [22356147] **2879**

EXPERIENCE BY STATE (BY LINE). PROPERTY/CASUALTY. REPORT FORMAT A8, FIVE YEAR STUDY (US) [22369538] **2879**

EXPERIENCE BY STATE (BY LINE). REPORT FORMAT, A5, TWO YEAR STUDY. PROPERTY/CASUALTY (US) [22356681] **2879**

EXPERIENCE BY STATE (BY LINE). REPORT FORMAT, A6, TWO YEAR STUDY. PROPERTY/CASUALTY (US) [22400280] **2879**

EXPERIENCE BY STATE (BY LINE). REPORT FORMAT, A7, FIVE YEAR STUDY. PROPERTY/CASUALTY (US) [22400626] **2879**

EXPERIENCE OF FEDERAL AGENCIES UNDER THE PROGRAM OF SELF-INSURING FIDELITY LOSSES PURSUANT TO PUBLIC LAW 92-310 (US/0098-6402) [03149447] **2879**

EXPERIENCE OF THE SOVIET COMMUNIST PARTY (RU) [10461454] **4541**

EXPERIENCE : THE MAGAZINE OF THE SENIOR LAWYERS DIVISION, AMERICAN BAR ASSOCIATION (US/1054-3473) [22718936] 5179, **2968**

EXPERIENCE THE WILLAMETTE NATIONAL FOREST (US) [22965073] 4706, **2379**

EXPERIENCE TRILLIUM : THE OFFICIAL PUBLICATION OF TRILLIUM TERMINAL 3 - TORONTO, CANADA (CN/1183-6423) [24690671] **5382**

EXPERIENCED PROFESSIONAL (US) **4204**

EXPERIENTIA (SZ/0014-4754) [01327195] **5104**

EXPERIENTIA OPHTHALMOLOGICA (PO/0253-0643) [07915221] **3874**

EXPERIENTIAL EDUCATION (US/0739-2338) [05344916] **1746**

EXPERIMENT (US/0014-4770) [03247732] **3463**

EXPERIMENT STATION BULLETIN / MAINE AGRICULTURAL EXPERIMENT STATION, UNIVERSITY OF MAINE AT ORONO (US/0734-9548) [12609264] **82**

EXPERIMENTAL AGING RESEARCH (US/0361-073X) [01950825] **3750**

EXPERIMENTAL AGRICULTURE (UK/0014-4797) [01568630] **82**

EXPERIMENTAL AIRCRAFT ASSOCIATION. ANTIQUE CLASSIC DIVISION (US) **18**

EXPERIMENTAL & APPLIED ACAROLOGY (NE/0168-8162) [12482559] **5583**

EXPERIMENTAL AND CLINICAL ENDOCRINOLOGY (GW/0232-7384) [09358429] **3730**

EXPERIMENTAL AND CLINICAL GASTROENTEROLOGY (US/0353-9245) [25047340] **3744**

EXPERIMENTAL AND CLINICAL IMMUNOGENETICS (SZ/0254-9670) [10902421] **3669**

EXPERIMENTAL AND CLINICAL PSYCHIATRY (US/0272-6408) [06096612] **3925**

●EXPERIMENTAL AND CLINICAL PSYCHOPHARMACOLOGY (US/1064-1297) [26210441] 4304, **4587**

EXPERIMENTAL AND MOLECULAR PATHOLOGY (US/0014-4800) [01568631] **3894**

EXPERIMENTAL AND TOXICOLOGIC PATHOLOGY : OFFICIAL JOURNAL OF THE GESELLSCHAFT FUR TOXIKOLOGISCHE PATHOLOGIE (GW/0940-2993) [25828770] 3894, **3980**

EXPERIMENTAL ASTRONOMY (NE/0922-6435) [20297628] **395**

EXPERIMENTAL BRAIN RESEARCH (GW/0014-4819) [03262584] **3832**

EXPERIMENTAL BRAIN RESEARCH SERIES (GW/0932-4011) [14981918] **3833**

EXPERIMENTAL CELL RESEARCH (US/0014-4827) [01568634] **536**

●EXPERIMENTAL DERMATOLOGY (DK/0906-6705) [I09066705] **3720**

EXPERIMENTAL EDUCATION PROGRAMS FOR HANDICAPPED CHILDREN (US/0362-8779) [02378871] **1879**

EXPERIMENTAL EDUCATION PROGRAMS IN SPECIAL EDUCATION (US/0146-342X) [02920219] **1879**

EXPERIMENTAL EYE RESEARCH (UK/0014-4835) [01568636] **3874**

EXPERIMENTAL GENETICS (II) [16744415] **545**

EXPERIMENTAL GERONTOLOGY (UK/0531-5565) [01568637] **3751**

EXPERIMENTAL HEAT TRANSFER (UK/0891-6152) [14928000] **4430**

EXPERIMENTAL HEMATOLOGY (US/0301-472X) [01260939] **3771**

EXPERIMENTAL LUNG RESEARCH (US/0190-2148) [04692740] **3949**

EXPERIMENTAL MAGNETISM (UK/0271-1869) [06569559] **4443**

●EXPERIMENTAL MATHEMATICS (US/1058-6458) [24346305] **3505**

EXPERIMENTAL MECHANICS (US/0014-4851) [01568641] **4427**

EXPERIMENTAL MUSICAL INSTRUMENTS (US/0883-0754) [12054864] **4117**

EXPERIMENTAL MYCOLOGY (US/0147-5975) [02924841] **574**

EXPERIMENTAL NEPHROLOGY (SZ/1018-7782) [I10187782] **3990**

EXPERIMENTAL NEUROLOGY (US/0014-4886) [01568644] **3833**

EXPERIMENTAL PARASITOLOGY (US/0014-4894) [01568645] **562**

EXPERIMENTAL PATHOLOGY (1981) (GW/0232-1513) [07485985] **3894**

EXPERIMENTAL PHYCOLOGY (US) **455**

EXPERIMENTAL PHYSIOLOGY (UK/0958-0670) [20954666] **580**

●EXPERIMENTAL ROCKET FLYER (US/1062-8576) [25771859] **18**

EXPERIMENTAL TECHNIQUES (WESTPORT, CONN.) (US/0732-8818) [07492412] **2114**

EXPERIMENTAL THERMAL AND FLUID SCIENCE (US/0894-1777) [15814360] 4430, **4427**

EXPERIMENTAL YACHT SOCIETY See EXPERIMENTAL YACHT SOCIETY JOURNAL **4176**

EXPERIMENTAL YACHT SOCIETY JOURNAL (US/0149-239X) [03450905] **4176**

EXPERIMENTELLE TECHNIK DER PHYSIK (GW/0014-4924) [02304142] **4402**

EXPERIMENTELLE UND KLINISCHE HYPNOSE : ZEITSCHRIFT DER DEUTSCHEN GESELLSCHAFT FUER HYPNOSE (GW/0933-1093) [24372615] **2858**

EXPERIMENTS IN FLUIDS (GW/0723-4864) [09519940] **2089**

EXPERIODICA (SZ/0014-4932) [02260960] **2516**

EXPERT AND THE LAW, THE (US/0737-8726) [09456131] 3740, **2968**

EXPERT COMMITTEE ON WEEDS. EASTERN SECTION See RESEARCH REPORT - EXPERT COMMITTEE ON WEEDS. EASTERN CANADA SECTION **127**

EXPERT COMMITTEE ON WEEDS. WESTERN CANADA See RESEARCH REPORT - EXPERT COMMITTEE ON WEEDS. WESTERN CANADA SECTION **127**

EXPERT (LOUISVILLE, KY.) (US/0896-7725) [17286860] 1237, **1267**

EXPERT OPINION ON THERAPEUTIC PATENTS (UK) 4304, **1304**

EXPERT SYSTEMS (UK/0266-4720) [11395090] 1223, **1212**

EXPERT SYSTEMS AI IN BUSINESS CEASED. (UK) [16650508] **1212**

EXPERT SYSTEMS APPLICATIONS (UK) **1184**

EXPERT SYSTEMS FOR INFORMATION MANAGEMENT (UK/0953-5551) [19001009] **1212**

EXPERT SYSTEMS REVIEW FOR BUSINESS & ACCOUNTING See INTERNATIONAL JOURNAL OF INTELLIGENT SYSTEMS IN ACCOUNTING, FINANCE & MANAGEMENT **745**

EXPERT SYSTEMS USER (UK) [15873070] **1212**

EXPERT SYSTEMS WITH APPLICATIONS (US/0957-4174) [21492026] **1212**

EXPERT WITNESS JOURNAL (US/0277-0555) [07472813] **2968**

EXPERTEASE See DATAEASE DIALOGUE **1181**

EXPERTEASE (FEDERAL WAY, WASH.) (US/1047-7705) [20789963] **1184**

EXPIRING LEGISLATION WITH BUDGETARY IMPACT / COMMITTEE ON THE BUDGET, U.S. HOUSE OF REPRESENTATIVES (US) [05116124] **4723**

EXPLANATION [OF] INDIVIDUAL FEDERAL INCOME TAX RETURN See INDIVIDUALS' FILLED-IN TAX RETURN FORMS **4732**

EXPLANATORY MEMORANDUM AND STATISTICAL SUPPLEMENT, PAKISTAN RAILWAY BUDGET (PK) [03256960] **5400**

EXPLANATORY MEMORANDUM ON THE BUDGET AND ECONOMIC SURVEY See EXPLANATORY MEMORANDUM ON THE BUDGET (ISLAMABAD) **4723**

EXPLANATORY MEMORANDUM ON THE BUDGET (ISLAMABAD) (PK/0304-0933) [02240535] **4723**

EXPLANATORY MEMORANDUM ON THE BUDGET OF THE GOVERNMENT OF NAGALAND FOR ... (II) [07387354] **4723**

EXPLANATORY MEMORANDUM ON THE BUDGET OF THE GOVERNMENT OF WEST BENGAL (II/0511-5280) [01640979] **4723**

EXPLANATORY NOTE ON THE ... BUDGET / MINISTRY OF FINANCE, CYPRUS, AN (CY) [06873813] **4723**

EXPLANATORY NOTES OF THE BRUSSELS NOMENCLATURE See EXPLANATORY NOTES TO THE HARMONIZED SYSTEM **833**

EXPLANATORY NOTES TO THE HARMONIZED SYSTEM (BE) 2968, **833**

EXPLICACION DE TEXTOS LITERARIOS (US/0361-9621) [01568653] **3386**

EXPLICATOR, THE (US/0014-4940) [01327211] **3386**

EXPLOR (EVANSTON, ILL.) (US/0362-0867) [02108630] **4958**

EXPLORATEUR (MONTREAL) (CN/1183-4307) [25127469] **1323**

EXPLORATION AND ECONOMICS OF THE PETROLEUM INDUSTRY (US/0537-9741) [03295322] 1490, **4256**

●EXPLORATION AND MINING GEOLOGY : JOURNAL OF THE GEOLOGICAL SOCIETY OF CIM (UK/0964-1823) [25702249] 1375, **2138**

EXPLORATION AND PRODUCTION THESAURUS (US/0894-9204) [15247882] **3210**

EXPLORATION ARCHEOLOGIQUE DE DELOS FAITE PAR L'ECOLE FRANCAISE D'ATHENES (FR) [01567344] **268**

EXPLORATION, DEVELOPMENT AND CAPITAL EXPENDITURES FOR MINING AND PETROLEUM AND NATURAL GAS WELLS, INTENTIONS (CN/0833-0034) [16503680] **4256**

EXPLORATION GEOPHYSICS (US/0071-3473) [01886937] **1405**

EXPLORATION GEOPHYSICS (MELBOURNE) (AT/0812-3985) [11329079] **4402**

EXPLORATION IN BRITISH COLUMBIA (CN/0823-2059) [04065305] **2139**

EXPLORATION INTERNATIONAL NEWS (UK/0960-9989) [I09609989] **4256**

EXPLORATION (NORMAL, ILL.) (US/0097-806X) [01799210] 5469, **3387**

EXPLORATION (SANTA FE, N.M.) CEASED. (US/0277-089X) [04381170] **236**

EXPLORATIONS (PK/0014-4975) [01771966] **3281**

EXPLORATIONS (DAYTON, OHIO) (US/0889-8693) [10195427] **4958**

EXPLORATIONS IN ECONOMIC HISTORY (US/0014-4983) [01568657] **1561**

EXPLORATIONS IN ETHNIC STUDIES (US/0730-904X) [04009870] **2261**

EXPLORATIONS IN KNOWLEDGE (UK/0261-1376) [11699405] **4346**

EXPLORATIONS IN MUSIC LIBRARIANSHIP CEASED. (US) [06691165] 4117, **3210**

EXPLORATIONS IN RENAISSANCE CULTURE (US/0098-2474) [02239679] **2846**

EXPLORATIONS IN SIGHTS AND SOUNDS (US/0733-3323) [08260306] **2261**

EXPLORATIONS IN SOCIOLOGY (UK/0954-3082) [I09543082] **5245**

●EXPLORATIONS (LA JOLLA, CALIF.) (US/1075-2560) [29983513] **1449**

EXPLORATIONS (ORONO, ME.) CEASED. (US) [13751582] **5104**

EXPLORATIONS. SPECIAL SERIES (US/1043-2493) [18179527] **2846**

EXPLORATORIUM See EXPLORATORIUM QUARTERLY **4087**

EXPLORATORIUM QUARTERLY (US/0889-8197) [14092954] 4402, **4087**

EXPLORE (CALGARY) (CN/0714-816X) [09106488] **4871**

EXPLORE (LAWRENCE, KAN.) (US/0741-8493) [09597311] **1823**

EXPLORER (FALLS CHURCH, VA.), THE (US/0894-7929) [16263068] **1323**

EXPLORER KNIFE JOURNAL (US/1067-3202) [27178866] 2773, **4894**

EXPLORER (MERCED, CALIF.), THE (US/1055-6621) [23293153] **2560**

Alphabetical Title Index — EXTENSION

EXPLORER NEWS (US/0895-8521) [16824695] **2560**

EXPLORER, THE (US/0014-5009) [01568659] **4165**

EXPLORERS JOURNAL (US/0014-5025) [01568660] 2560, **5104**

EXPLORING 1 FOR LEADERS (US/0745-0346) [08737725] **5060**

EXPLORING A FOR LEADERS *See* EXPLORING 1 FOR LEADERS **5060**

EXPLORING B (US/0162-4431) [04165470] **5060**

EXPLORING BOOKS *CEASED.* (US/1065-6960) [26682394] **3210**

EXPLORING CAREERS (US) [20220894] **1669**

●EXPLORING MAGAZINE (US) 4402, **4087**

EXPLORING THE BIBLE. AGES 8-12. PACKET (US/0149-8584) [03569681] **5016**

EXPLOSIFS *CEASED.* (BE/0367-1526) [02446822] **1024**

EXPLOSIONSSCHUTZ-RICHTLINIEN (GW) **2862**

EXPLOSIVE SAFETY AND CONTROL IN CANADA (CN/0848-5712) [22928206] 1944, **2012**

EXPLOSIVES AND PYROTECHNICS (US/0014-505X) [02446823] 2102, **2012**

EXPLOSIVES ENGINEERING (UK/0952-3960) [17004253] 2102, **2012**

EXPLOSIVES INCIDENTS REPORT (US) [15248397] **3164**

EXPO NEWS (FR/0757-4223) [I07574223] **834**

EXPO (WAUCONDA, ILL.) (US/1046-3925) [20398555] **867**

EXPONENT II (US) [15672873] **4958**

EXPORRE (IT) **4087**

EXPORT ADMINISTRATION REGULATIONS (US) [19033993] 834, **2968**

EXPORT BY PENNSYLVANIA MANUFACTURERS (US/0556-3585) [02242997] **834**

EXPORT CANADA (CN/0708-1332) [04879587] **834**

EXPORT COMMUNICATIONS : EC (US/1058-2533) [24242347] **834**

EXPORT CONTACT LIST SERVICES (US) [06481478] **834**

EXPORT CONTROL NEWS (US/0896-0682) [16899410] **834**

●EXPORT DENMARK : KONGERIGET DANMARKS HANDELS- OG EKSPORTKALENDER (DK) [29880394] **834**

EXPORT DEVELOPMENT CORPORATION (CANADA) *See* ANNUAL REPORT - EXPORT DEVELOPMENT CORPORATION **822**

EXPORT DEVELOPMENT CORPORATION (CANADA) *See* INFORMATION CIRCULAR - EXPORT DEVELOPMENT CORPORATION **840**

EXPORT DEVELOPMENT CORPORATION (CANADA) *See* STATISTICAL REVIEW - EXPORT DEVELOPMENT CORPORATION **852**

EXPORT DIRECTOR INTERNATIONAL (UK) [18218736] **834**

EXPORT DIRECTORY CHILE (CL) [05337483] **834**

EXPORT DIRECTORY OF BRAZIL (BL) [04029503] **834**

EXPORT DIRECTORY OF CHILE. GUIA CHILENA DE LA EXPORTACION (CL) [04663573] **834**

EXPORT DIRECTORY OF NEPAL (NP) [03265176] **834**

EXPORT EN ESPANOL (US/1065-6677) [26670422] 834, **2811**

EXPORT FACILITIES, POLICIES, AND PROCEDURES (PK) [10862429] **834**

EXPORT FINANCE (UK) [18170709] 834, **2879**

EXPORT GAZETTE (II/0970-6186) [I09706186] **834**

EXPORT GAZETTE (II) [03519527] **834**

EXPORT GRAFICAS USA (US/0741-7160) [10197840] 4565, **378**

EXPORT GRAFICS USA (US/0147-409X) [03160360] 378, **834**

EXPORT GUIDE TO EUROPE, THE *CEASED.* (US/0269-7777) [15025508] **834**

EXPORT HANDBOOK SYDNEY (AT/0312-3774) [I03123774] **674**

EXPORT HONG KONG (HK) [06310855] **834**

EXPORT-IMPORT BANK OF THE UNITED STATES *See* CUMULATIVE RECORDS - EXPORT-IMPORT BANK OF THE UNITED STATES **786**

EXPORT-IMPORT MARKETS (PR/0270-5184) [06415841] **834**

EXPORT INTERNATIONAL (HK) [04970029] **834**

EXPORT LEADS (US/1064-1513) [26226218] **834**

EXPORT MAILING LIST SERVICE; SIC RECORD COUNT, FTI PROFILE (US) [04977501] **834**

EXPORT MARKET. ENGINEERING ED *See* EXPORT MARKT. ENGINEERING **1975**

EXPORT MARKETS FOR U.S. GRAIN AND PRODUCTS *CEASED.* (US/0896-0216) [15361541] **83**

EXPORT MARKETS FOR U.S. GRAIN AND PRODUCTS *See* GRAIN, WORLD MARKETS AND TRADE **202**

EXPORT MARKT. ENGINEERING (GW) [08340820] **1975**

EXPORT (NEW YORK, N.Y.) (US/0014-519X) [07887086] 834, **2811**

EXPORT NEWS (OTTAWA) (CN/0713-0341) [08924115] **834**

EXPORT PAYMENTS INSURANCE CORPORATION *See* ANNUAL REPORT - EXPORT PAYMENTS INSURANCE CORPORATION **2873**

EXPORT POLICIES, REBATES, PROCEDURES, RULES AND NOTIFICATIONS (PK) [21577371] **834**

EXPORT POLYGRAPH INTERNATIONAL (GW/0344-2039) [10073804] **378**

EXPORT-POLYGRAPH INTERNATIONAL 1990 (GW/0937-9924) [I09379924] **4565**

EXPORT PRICE INDEXES (PORT MORESBY, PAPUA NEW GUINEA) (PP) [05936914] **1490**

EXPORT PROMOTION COUNCIL FOR FINISHED LEATHER & LEATHER MANUFACTURES *See* LEXPORT **3185**

EXPORT RECEIPTS (PR) [03039284] **834**

EXPORT REPORT - WESTERN WOOD PRODUCTS ASSOCIATION (US/0730-5176) [08043233] 834, **2400**

EXPORT SALES AND MARKETING MANUAL (US/1054-8327) [21209843] 924, **834**

EXPORT TAX REPORT (US) **4723**

EXPORT TIMES (NEW DELHI), THE (II/0257-8018) [02240184] **834**

EXPORT TODAY (US/0882-4711) [11854683] **834**

EXPORT TRADE CONTROL HAND-BOOK OF POLICY AND PROCEDURE (II) [03254025] **834**

EXPORT TRADE REPORTER (US/0278-1646) [07750400] **834**

EXPORT TRADE TODAY (ENGINEERING EDITION) (GW) [10867453] 835, **3478**

EXPORT YELLOW PAGES, THE (US/1055-8365) [23352905] **835**

EXPORTACION (AG) [05636578] **835**

EXPORTACOES (BL) [10936693] **835**

EXPORTADOR *See* EXPORT EN ESPANOL **2811**

EXPORTADOR DOMINICANO, EL (DR) [03260219] **835**

EXPORTADOR, EL (US/0279-456X) [07887241] **835**

EXPORTATEUR CONGOLAIS : REVUE TRIMESTRIELLE DU CENTRE CONGOLAIS DU COMMERCE EXTERIEUR, L' (CF) [10675096] **835**

EXPORTATIONS NOUVELLES (CN/0713-0368) [08924120] **835**

EXPORTER (NEW YORK, N.Y.), THE (US/0736-9239) [09264308] **835**

EXPORTERS (CR) [22123426] **835**

EXPORTERS' ENCYCLOPAEDIA, (1982) (US/8755-013X) [08723525] **835**

EXPORTERS GUIDE (PR) [03901373] **835**

EXPORTERS GUIDE & KEY BUSINESS DIRECTORY - CARIBBEAN & LATIN AMERICA. GUIA DEL EXPORTADOR Y DIRECTOR DE EMPRESAS CLAVES - CARIBE Y AMERICA LATINA (PR) [05242449] **835**

EXPORTERS' REGISTER, PHILIPPINES / MINISTRY OF TRADE, PHILIPPINES (PH) [08937749] **835**

●EXPORTERS RESOURCES DIRECTORY (US/1062-3191) [25585332] **835**

EXPORTING COMPUTERS WITHOUT A VALIDATED LICENSE (US) 1184, **835**

EXPORTMARKTEN, OESO-LANDEN/OOST-EUROPA (NE/0014-5211) [10156822] **835**

EXPORTS BY COUNTRIES (OTTAWA) (CN/1181-6724) [02442602] **835**

EXPORTS BY PENNSYLVANIA MANUFACTURERS *See* EXPORT BY PENNSYLVANIA MANUFACTURERS **834**

EXPORTS, MERCHANDISE TRADE, H.S. BASED (CN/0844-8361) [20189529] **835**

EXPORTS OF CANADIAN GRAIN AND WHEAT FLOUR (CN/0832-6215) [07815865] **200**

EXPORTS OF THE REPUBLIC OF CHINA (CH) [01793166] **835**

EXPORTS UNDER THE CONCESSIONAL SALES PROGRAM : B.TITLE I, PUBLIC LAW 480 (US) [08458469] 83, **2968**

●EXPOSE: THE VISUAL ARTS MAGAZINE (US/1063-1321) [25895764] **350**

EXPOSITIONES MATHEMATICAE (GW/0723-0869) [09363140] **3505**

EXPOSITOR BIBLICO. MAESTROS DE ADOLESCENTES-JOVENES-ADULTOS , EL (US/0014-5238) [08148517] **4958**

EXPOSITORY TIMES, THE (UK/0014-5246) [01568670] **5016**

EXPOSURE DRAFT (STAMFORD, CONN. 1974) (US/0885-9116) [02630137] **743**

EXPOSURE (NEW YORK, N.Y.) (US/0098-8863) [02242622] **4369**

EXPOSURE (SASKATOON) (CN/1180-3568) [24368353] **2334**

EXPOSURE (WASHINGTON, D.C.) (US/0277-5220) [07582828] **455**

EXPOVISIE (NE) 759, **674**

●EXPRES (XR) [25864204] **5799**

EXPRESS (BANGOR, MICH.), THE (US/0747-4113) [10810964] **5692**

●EXPRESS (CHICAGO, ILL.) (US/1063-0570) [25848887] **5660**

EXPRESS (DRUMMONDVILLE) (CN/0713-5483) [08902984] **5784**

EXPRESS EQUESTRE (CN/0822-7330) [10398415] **2799**

EXPRESS ILUSTROWANY (PL/0137-9097) [I01379097] **5808**

EXPRESS INTERNATIONAL (PARIS, FRANCE) (FR) [17388034] **2516**

EXPRESS (LOCK HAVEN, PA. : 1971) (US) [12375104] **5736**

EXPRESS (MECHANICVILLE, N.Y.) (US/0746-6080) [10143389] **5716**

EXPRESS-NEWS (SAN ANTONIO, TEX.) *See* SAN ANTONIO EXPRESS-NEWS **5754**

EXPRESS (PARIS), L' (FR/0014-5270) [01327248] **2516**

EXPRESS PLUS (CN/1183-4323) [24256998] **5784**

EXPRESS-TIMES, THE (US/1062-3620) [24821639] **5736**

EXPRESS WIECZORNY (PL) [12004516] **5808**

EXPRESSION : BULLETIN DE L'ASSOCIATION DES JURISTES D'EXPRESSION FRANCAISE DE L'ONTARIO (AJEFO), L' (CN/1183-6792) [24690488] **2968**

EXPRESSION (OTTAWA) (CN/0822-8213) [11250590] **5285**

EXPRESSION (WINNIPEG, DEUTSCHE AUSG.) (CN/0824-474X) [10517704] **4958**

EXPRESSION (WINNIPEG. ENGLISH ED.) (CN/0824-4731) [10517714] **4958**

EXPRESSO (PO) [05176704] 1490, **674**

EXQUISITE CORPSE (US/0740-7823) [10025381] **3463**

EXS (SZ) [25388608] **5104**

EXTEL HANDBOOK OF MARKET LEADERS (UK) [03466505] **835**

EXTEL STATISTICAL SERVICES *See* EXTEL HANDBOOK OF MARKET LEADERS **835**

EXTENDED ABSTRACTS AND PROGRAM - BIENNIAL CONFERENCE ON CARBON (US/0160-7464) [03744519] **1975**

EXTENDED ABSTRACTS - ELECTROCHEMICAL SOCIETY (US/0160-4619) [03721976] **1034**

EXTENDED ABSTRACTS / MATERIALS RESEARCH SOCIETY (US/1048-5090) [18966440] **2102**

EXTENDED ABSTRACTS OF THE CONFERENCE ON SOLID STATE DEVICES AND MATERIALS (JA) [10956427] 5104, **975**

EXTENSION BULLETIN (ASIAN AND PACIFIC COUNCIL. FOOD & FERTILIZER TECHNOLOGY CENTER) (CH) [01641205] **83**

EXTENSION BULLETIN - DEPARTMENT OF AGRICULTURAL ECONOMICS AND FARM MANAGEMENT FACULTY OF AGRICULTURE. UNIVERSITY OF MANITOBA (CN/0316-8808) [02247370] **83**

EXTENSION BULLETIN - MICHIGAN. STATE UNIVERSITY, EAST LANSING. COOPERATIVE EXTENSION SERVICE (US) [04764908] **83**

EXTENSION — Alphabetical Title Index

EXTENSION BULLETIN - WASHINGTON STATE UNIVERSITY. COOPERATIVE EXTENSION (US/0748-125X) [09668859] **83**

EXTENSION CONNECTION *See* AGRICULTURAL NEWS (HAMDEN, N.Y.) **50**

EXTENSION ENGINEERING IN KANSAS; R (US) [05626076] **1542**

EXTENSION INFORMATION BULLETIN (CN/0703-9166) [03979884] **83**

EXTENSION NEWS *See* CORNELL COOPERATIVE EXTENSION AGRICULTURAL NEWS **76**

EXTENSION NEWS & ADVISOR (US/1061-4613) [23276278] **83**

EXTENSION (TORONTO) (CN/1183-9163) [25589887] **378**

EXTENSIONS AND CORRECTIONS TO THE UDC (SZ) [11628170] **3210**

EXTENSIONS (YPSILANTI, MICH.) (US/0892-5135) [15347297] **1746**

EXTERIORS *CEASED.* (US/0886-5949) [12931450] **298, 614**

●EXTERNADISTA : REVISTA DE LA UNIVERSIDAD EXTERNADO DE COLOMBIA (CK/0121-6279) [28061396] **5200, 2968**

EXTERNADO (UNIVERSIDAD EXTERNADO DE COLOMBIA) (CK) [08538107] **2968**

EXTERNADO (UNIVERSIDAD EXTERNADO DE COLOMBIA) *See* EXTERNADISTA : REVISTA DE LA UNIVERSIDAD EXTERNADO DE COLOMBIA **2968**

EXTERNAL AFFAIRS SERVICE LIST (MM) [09340941] **2968**

EXTERNAL DEBT STATISTICS (FR/1015-4159) [15503306] **1532**

EXTERNAL PUBLIC DEBT *See* WORLD DEBT TABLES **1540**

EXTERNAL RESEARCH STUDY (US) [04058367] **4647**

●EXTERNAL TRADE AND BALANCE OF PAYMENTS (LU) [25321480] **728**

EXTERNAL TRADE (LUXEMBOURG, LUXEMBOURG) *See* EXTERNAL TRADE AND BALANCE OF PAYMENTS **728**

EXTERNAL TRADE OF LIBERIA : EXPORTS (LB/0376-9097) [01798578] **835**

EXTERNAL TRADE STATISTICS (SAN JUAN) (PR/0091-5386) [01787638] **835, 728**

EXTERNAL TRADE STATISTICS, SRI LANKA (CE) [09991065] **835, 728**

EXTERNAL TRADE ... THROUGH BRITISH COLUMBIA CUSTOMS PORTS (CN) [06965616] **835**

●EXTRA!, EXTRA! (GREENSBURG, PA.) (US/1062-7715) [25735924] **4647**

EXTRA! EXTRA! NEWSPAPERS ACROSS CANADA (CN/1187-0664) [24570928] **5784**

EXTRA INCOME NEWS NEWSLETTER (US/0899-8485) [18237183] **674**

●EXTRA INNINGS (US/1072-0510) [28855273] **4894, 1855**

EXTRA !NCOME (US/0888-367X) [13577046] **674**

EXTRA! (NEW YORK, N.Y. 1987) (US/0895-2310) [16641891] **2919**

EXTRA PAY FOR EXTRA SERVICES IN NEW JERSEY SCHOOL DISTRICTS (US/0149-6190) [03509540] **1863**

EXTRA PHARMACOPOEIA, THE (UK) [01770847] **4304**

EXTRA TO THE ONTARIO WELFARE REPORTER (CN/0821-3356) [10330456] **5285**

EXTRA VERSE (UK/0531-6243) [03250143] **3463**

EXTRABLATT (AU) [04725210] **2516**

EXTRACELLULAR MATRIX (UK/0268-1617) [I02681617] **495, 536**

EXTRACTA ORTHOPAEDICA (GW/0344-5046) [09396799] **3881**

EXTRACTA UROLOGICA (GW/0344-5038) [05109015] **3990**

EXTRAMURAL RESEARCH PROGRAMS SUPPORTED BY THE FOOD AND DRUG ADMINISTRATION (US/0149-9742) [03582152] **3576**

EXTRAORDINARY CONTRACTUAL RELIEF REPORTER (US/0162-3184) [04156224] **674**

EXTRAPOLATION (US/0014-5483) [01568678] **3342**

EXTRUSION COMMUNIQUE (UK/0958-0549) [I09580549] **2334**

EXTRUSION DIGEST (US/0276-0819) [07318142] **4455**

EXXON CORPORATION *See* DIMENSIONS (EXXON CORPORATION) **1604**

EXXON CORPORATION *See* WORLD ENERGY OUTLOOK **1961**

EXXON EDUCATION FOUNDATION *See* EXXON EDUCATION FOUNDATION REPORT **1746**

EXXON EDUCATION FOUNDATION REPORT (US/0148-608X) [03334498] **1746**

EXXON TRAVEL CLUB MEXICO VACATION TRAVEL GUIDE (US/0270-8434) [06299549] **2805**

EXXON TRAVEL CLUB TRAVEL GUIDE. CANADA (US/0884-1802) [09435449] **5469**

EXXON TRAVEL CLUB TRAVEL GUIDE. CENTRAL USA (US/0743-6467) [09275084] **5469**

EYAS, THE *CEASED.* (US/0736-5470) [05230670] **2193**

EYE (DOWNSVIEW. 1979) (CN/0708-5974) [05362553] **2616**

EYE (LONDON, ENGLAND) (UK/0950-222X) [15260106] **3874**

EYE OPENER (YORKTON) (CN/0229-5520) [08324004] **5784**

EYE SPY (CN/0381-7423) [03258445] **3164**

EYE : THE INTERNATIONAL REVIEW OF GRAPHIC DESIGN (UK/0960-779X) [24494240] **378**

●EYEBALL (ST. LOUIS, MO.) (US/1063-9675) [26182960] **3387**

EYEBEAM (AUSTIN, TEX.) (US/1055-162X) [23096941] **350**

EYECARE BUSINESS (US/0885-9167) [12769743] **4215**

EYELINE (AT) [I08188734] **373**

EYEPIECE (US/0146-7662) [03012669] **395**

EYEPIECE (UK/0950-737X) [I0950737X] **4369**

E+Z, ENTWICKLUNG UND ZUSAMMENARBEIT (GW/0721-2178) [06341408] **1490**

EZHEGODNIK (RU/0201-9280) [04298897] **4227**

EZHEGODNIK / AKADEMIIA NAUK SSSR, URALSKII NAUCHNYI TSENTR, INSTITUT GEOLOGII I GEOKHIMII IM. AKAD. A. N. ZAVARITSKOGO (RU) [01795965] **1375**

EZHEGODNIK KNIGI SSSR (RU/0201-6354) [06477902] **3387**

EZHEGODNIK PAMIATNYKH MUZYKALNYKH DAT I SOBYTII (RU) [04298273] **4117**

EZHEGODNIK VSESOIUZNOGO PALEONTOLOGICHESKOGO OBSHCHESTVA (RU) [09721920] **4227**

●EZHEKVARTALNIK KHRISTIANSKOI NAUKI. BIBLEISKIE UROKI (US/1061-6721) [25404146] **5016**

EZIK I LITERATURA (BU/0324-1270) [02078088] **3281**

EZSEARCH-MINING (US) **2139**

F A E M (US/0429-9310) [01368191] **1746**

F.A.R.O.G. FORUM JOURNAL BILINGUE (US/0741-577X) [06881976] **5200**

F.A.S. PUBLIC INTEREST REPORT (US/0092-9824) [04294285] **5104**

F & B MARKETPLACE (US/1040-7537) [18516888] **2334, 2367, 924**

F & M / ORGAN DER VDI/VDE-GESELLSCHAFT MIKRO- UND FEINWERKTECHNIK (GW) [26332871] **5104**

F & S. FILTRIEREN UND SEPARIEREN (GW/0933-5927) [I09335927] **2012**

●F & S INDEX UNITED STATES (US) [28317797] **674**

F & W, FUHREN UND WIRTSCHAFTEN IM KRANKENHAUS (GW/0175-4548) [11135981] **3780**

F.C.C. WEEK (US/0738-5714) [08325328] **1111**

F C N, FLOOR COVERING NEWS (CN/0319-616X) [02864960] **2905**

●F-D-C REPORTS. NONPRESCRIPTION PHARMACEUTICALS AND NUTRITIONALS (US/1068-5316) [27695607] **4304**

F.H.A. HOMES (US/0091-4932) [01787244] **2822**

F H A TRENDS OF HOME MORTGAGE CHARACTERISTICS (US) [01639321] **2822**

F.I.B.A. RULES CASEBOOK (CN/0712-5585) [09201181] **4894**

F.I.D. NEWS BULLETIN (NE/0014-5874) [01284485] **3210**

F.I.S.C.A.L. DIRECTORY, FEE-BASED INFORMATION SERVICE CENTERS IN ACADEMIC LIBRARIES (US) [19667097] **3210**

F.J., REVISTA DE LA FACULTAD DE JURISPRUDENCIA Y CIENCIAS SOCIALES (SP) [03641588] **2968**

F.O.C. REVIEW (US/1041-8164) [18898175] **3387**

F. O. LICHT'S INTERNATIONAL SUGAR AND SWEETENER REPORT (GW/0940-8541) [I09408541] **83**

F.O. LICHT'S INTERNATIONAL SUGAR AND SWEETENER REPORT / WORLD SUGAR BALANCES (GW) [26910111] **171**

F. PAUL PACULT'S SPIRIT JOURNAL (US/1055-8993) [23374758] **2367**

F R I MONTHLY PORTFOLIO (US/0014-6137) [01782068] **4335**

F.S.U. REPORTS (US/0427-8518) [01346904] **1823**

F. SCOTT FITZGERALD SOCIETY NEWSLETTER (US) [26571663] **3387**

F.T.C. STATISTICAL REPORT ON MERGERS AND ACQUISITIONS *See* STATISTICAL REPORT ON MERGERS AND ACQUISITIONS **1539**

F.W. DODGE CONSTRUCTION OUTLOOK *See* DODGE/SWEET'S CONSTRUCTION OUTLOOK / MCGRAW-HILL CONSTRUCTION INFORMATION GROUP **613**

F.Y.E.O (US/0738-4203) [09595187] **4044**

FA CHIH HSUEH KAN (CH) [03947806] **2968**

FA HSUEH TSA CHIH (CC) [18807200] **2968**

FA HSUEH YEN CHIU (CC) [05461552] **2968**

FAA AVIATION FORECASTS (US/0276-9212) [04341789] **19**

FAA AVIATION NEWS (1987) (US/1057-9648) [15582182] **19**

FAA AVIATION SAFETY JOURNAL (US/1056-2761) [23170539] **19**

FAA HORIZONS (US/0427-8011) [01368150] **19**

FAA OFFICE OF AVIATION MEDICINE REPORTS (US) **3576**

FAA STATISTICAL HANDBOOK OF AVIATION / FEDERAL AVIATION AGENCY (US/0566-9618) [02707503] **19**

FAB GUIDE (UK/0043-2245) [10522571] **4027**

FABIAN NEWSLETTER (AT/0949-138X) **4474**

FABIAN PAMPHLET / FABIAN SOCIETY (UK/0307-7523) [23436535] **1490**

FABIAN REVIEW (UK) [23271808] **4541**

FABIAN SOCIETY (GREAT BRITAIN) *See* FABIAN TRACT **4474**

FABIAN TRACT (UK/0307-7535) [01347029] **4474**

FABIS (SY/0255-6448) [08354139] **171**

FABRERIES (CN/0318-6725) [02442117] **5608**

FABRIC INTELLIGENCE : THE INTERNATIONAL FABRIC DIRECTORY (UK) [21998493] **5350**

FABRICANTS DE PRODUITS ELECTRIQUES ET ELECTRONIQUES AU QUEBEC, REPERTOIRE, LES (CN/0846-9105) [23263498] **2054**

FABRICATED METAL PRODUCTS INDUSTRIES (CN/0835-0124) [17365536] **4001**

FABRICATIONS : THE JOURNAL OF THE SOCIETY OF ARCHITECTURAL HISTORIANS, AUSTRALIA & NEW ZEALAND (AT/1033-1867) **298**

FABRICATOR (ROCKFORD, ILL.) (US/0888-0301) [13449104] **3478**

FABRICNEWS (US/0733-1843) [07150441] **5350**

FABRICS & ARCHITECTURE (US/1045-0483) [20005884] **5350, 298**

FABRICS-FASHIONS (US/0097-2495) [01798394] **5350**

FABRIEKEN VAN MACHINES EN APPARATEN VOOR HOUT- EN MEUBELINDUSTRIE, TEXTIEL- EN KLEDINGINDUSTRIE, WASSERIJEN EN CHEMISCHE REINIGING, LEDER- EN LEDERVERWERKENDE INDUSTRIE, PAPIER- EN GRAFISCHE INDUSTRIE / CENTRAAL BUREAU VOOR DE STATISTIEK, HOOFDAFDELING STATISTIEKEN VAN INDUSTRIE EN BOUWNIJVERHEID (NE/0168-3527) [10339658] **2114**

FABRIEKEN VAN TANDWIELEN, LAGERS EN ANDERE DRIJFWERKELEMENTEN / CENTRAAL BUREAU VOOR DE STATISTIEK, HOOFDAFDELING STATISTIEKEN VAN INDUSTRIE EN BOUWNIJVERHEID I.E. STATISTIEKEN VAN INDUSTRIE EN BOUWNIJVERHEID (NE/0168-4949) [10339521] **1606**

FABRIK *CEASED.* (GW) [28835030] **5104**

FABRIK OG BOLIG (DK/0106-3324) [I01063324] **2688**

FABRIMETAL (BE/0377-9084) [I03779084] **3478**

FABULA (GW/0014-6242) [01568717] **2319**

FABULA (LILLE, FRANCE) (FR/0755-0960) [09916606] **3387**

FABULOUS MEXICO - WHERE EVERYTHING COSTS LESS (US/0429-9639) [01351493] **5469**

FABULOUS MUSTANGS & EXOTIC FORDS *CEASED.* (US/0885-4750) [12641967] **5414**

FAC, FORTSCHRITTE DER ANTIMIKROBIELLEN UND ANTINEOPLASTISCHEN CHEMOTHERAPIE (GW/0722-7566) [12700429] **3817**

FACCC BULLETIN (US) **1091**

FACE A LA JUSTICE (CN/0710-1090) [08296962] **3164**

FACE AU RISQUE (FR/0014-6269) [I00146269] **5200**

FACE (LONDON, ENGLAND) (UK/0263-1210) [17459622] **4117**

●FACE (MALIBU, CALIF.) (US/1064-7953) [26393938] **2533**

FACE (SAO PAULO, BRAZIL) (BL/0103-1562) [19211856] **3281**

FACE TO FACE (NEW YORK) *SUSPENDED.* (US/0361-6061) [02012491] **4958**

FACEPLATE (US/1040-807X) [18541789] **4176**

FACES (PETERBOROUGH, N.H.) (US/0749-1387) [11079252] **1063**

FACES ROCKS *SUSPENDED.* (US/0882-2921) [11652553] **4117**

FACET BOOKS. BIBLICAL SERIES (US/0071-3597) [01350346] **5016**

FACET BOOKS. SOCIAL ETHICS SERIES (US/0071-3619) [01350398] **2250**

FACET TALK (AT/1035-0977) [I10350977] **2773**

FACETS (CHICAGO, ILL.) (US/0163-0512) [03305638] **3737**

FACETS FEATURES (US/0736-3745) [09103878] **4068**

FACETS OF FRESHWATER (US) [01568718] **5533**

FACHBERICHTE HUTTENPRAXIS METALLWEITERVERARBEITUNG (GW/0340-8043) [10522397] **4001**

FACHBLATT FUR SELBSTBEDIENUNG (GW) [06483382] **5104**

FACHHEFTE. CHEMIGRAPHIE, LITHOGRAPHIE UND TIEFDRUCK (SZ/0367-1933) [09947177] **4565**

FACHHEFTE GRAFISCHE INDUSTRIE, BULLETIN TECHNIQUE (SZ) [25743568] **1606**

FACHLITERATUR ZUM BUCH- UND BIBLIOTHEKSWESEN (GW) [03267078] **4821**

FACHMEDIEN GESUNDHEIT 1989 (GW/0937-8898) [I09378898] **3576**

FACHSERI D. INDUSTRIE UND HANDWERK : REIHE 1. BESCHAFTIGUNG UND UMSATZ, BRENNSTOFF- UND ENERGIEVERSORGUNG DER INDUSTRIE (GW/0446-0995) [01128252] **1606**

FACHSERIE C, UNTERNEHMEN UND ARBEITSSTATTEN. REIHE 1, DIE KOSTENSTRUKTUR IN DER WIRTSCHAFT, VI, GASTGEWERBE *See* UNTERNEHMAN UND ARBEITSSTATTEN. REIHE 1.4, KOSTENSTRUKTUR IM GASTGEWERBE / HERAUSGEBER STATISTISCHES BUNDESAMT **2809**

FACHSPRACHE (AU) [07531190] **3281**

FACHSPRACHE (AU/0251-1207) [07531192] **3281**

FACHSPRACHE 1990 (AU/1017-3285) [I10173285] **3281**

FACHTAGUNG UBER PROGRAMMIERSPRACHEN (US) [01790805] **1279**

FACHVORTRAGE DES WVAO-JAHRESKONGRESSES, DIE (GW) [05460142] **4215**

FACHWORTERBUCHER UND LEXIKA (GW) [01586169] **1925**

FACIAL ORTHOPEDICS AND TEMPOROMANDIBULAR ARTHROLOGY *SUSPENDED.* (US/0749-0399) [11052846] **3881**

FACIAL PLASTIC SURGERY (US/0736-6825) [09181795] **3964**

●FACIAL PLASTIC SURGERY CLINICS OF NORTH AMERICA (US/1064-7406) [26387272] **3965**

FACIES (GW/0172-9179) [06818923] 1375, **4227**

FACILITATION; INTERNATIONAL STANDARDS AND RECOMMENDED PRACTICES. ANNEX 9 TO THE CONVENTION ON INTERNATIONAL CIVIL AVIATION (CN) [01753446] **19**

FACILITIES (BRADFORD, WEST YORKSHIRE, ENGLAND) (UK/0263-2772) [19682942] 867, **3478**

FACILITIES DESIGN & MANAGEMENT (US/0279-4438) [07868243] **2900**

FACILITIES DEVELOPMENT CORPORATION (N.Y.) *See* REPORT TO THE GOVERNOR - NEW YORK STATE FACILITIES DEVELOPMENT CORPORATION **4799**

FACILITIES DIRECTORY (US) [06866115] **4706**

FACILITIES INVENTORY & UTILIZATION STUDY (US/0148-8368) [03381238] **1746**

FACILITIES INVENTORY OF INSTITUTIONS OF HIGHER EDUCATION IN OREGON (US/0090-1075) [01784676] **1823**

FACILITIES MANAGEMENT (UK) 2862, **1606**

FACILITIES MANAGER : THE OFFICIAL PUBLICATION OF THE ASSOCIATION OF PHYSICAL PLANT ADMINISTRATORS OF UNIVERSITIES AND COLLEGES (US/0882-7249) [11985961] 1823, **867**

FACILITIES PLANNING NEWS (US/1045-7089) [14267842] **298**

FACILITY FAST FACTS (US/1059-4035) [24603052] **759**

FACILITY ISSUES (US/1040-5828) [18474124] **867**

FACILITY MANAGEMENT JOURNAL : A PUBLICATION OF THE INTERNATIONAL FACILITY MANAGEMENT ASSOCIATION (US/1059-3667) [24473851] **867**

FACILITY MANAGEMENT MAGAZINE (NE) **868**

FACILITY MANAGER (US/0888-0085) [13445915] **868**

FACILITY STRATEGIES *CEASED.* (JS/1054-9196) [23020747] **1155**

FACKFORENINGSRORELSEN *See* LO I.E. LANDSORGANISATIONEN I SVERIGE TIDNINGEN **1572**

FACLIA (UK) [03415497] **2516**

FACS *See* JOURNAL OF MUTUAL FUND SERVICES, THE **904**

FACS OF THE WEEK *See* MUTUAL FUND MARKET NEWS **908**

FACS OF THE WEEK (US/1056-2540) [23591367] **898**

FACS SHEET (CN/0710-5878) [08713511] **2790**

FACSIMILE & VOICE SERVICES (US) **1155**

FACSIMILE OF DUTCH SONGBOOKS (NE) [16447545] **4117**

FACSIMILE REPRINTS IN THE HISTORY OF SCIENCE (US/0429-9809) [01351573] **5104**

FACSIMILES IN COLLOTYPE OF IRISH MANUSCRIPTS (IE) [01362398] **4828**

FACSIMILES OF EARLY BIOGRAPHIES (NE) [01351660] **432**

FACSIMILIA MUSICA NEERLANDICA (NE) [06568917] **4117**

FACT BOOK (JA) [24002856] **5431**

FACT BOOK : ALABAMA INSTITUTIONS OF HIGHER EDUCATION, UNIVERSITIES AND COLLEGES (US/0095-0637) [01794927] **1823**

FACT BOOK / AMERICAN STOCK EXCHANGE (US) [12292923] **898**

FACT BOOK AND REPORT OF THE WEST VIRGINIA STATE SYSTEM OF HIGHER EDUCATION (US/0093-8831) [01793292] **1823**

FACT BOOK / ATHABASCA UNIVERSITY (CN/0820-8328) [09796201] **1823**

FACT BOOK (HANGUK CHUNGKWON KORAESO) (KO) [07421581] **898**

FACT BOOK / NATIONAL INSTITUTE OF NEUROLOGICAL AND COMMUNICATIVE DISORDERS AND STROKE (US/0278-2502) [05952495] **3833**

FACT BOOK - NAVAL RESEARCH LABORATORY (U.S.) (US/0739-3229) [09697689] **4176**

FACT BOOK - NEW YORK STOCK EXCHANGE (US/8756-6788) [03805583] **898**

FACT BOOK, NON-LIFE INSURANCE IN JAPAN (JA) [06507594] **2879**

FACT BOOK OF AGRICULTURE (US) [23748075] **83**

FACT BOOK ON HIGHER EDUCATION (NEW YORK, N.Y.) *SUSPENDED.* (US) [11295066] **1823**

FACT BOOK - SASKATCHEWAN ROUGHRIDERS, FOOTBALL TEAM (CN/1184-6208) [24266554] **4894**

FACT BOOK / SECURITIES INDUSTRY ASSOCIATION ; PRODUCED BY SIA RESEARCH DEPARTMENT (US) [24307912] **898**

FACT BOOK (STATE COUNCIL OF HIGHER EDUCATION IN VIRGINIA) (US/0734-4759) [08405400] **1823**

FACT BOOK (STOCK EXCHANGE OF SINGAPORE) (SI) [07063065] **898**

FACT BOOK : TABLES AND CHARTS ON THE NEW YORK METROPOLITAN REGION (US) [04649011] **5327**

FACT BOOK - TOKYO SHOKEN TORIHIKIJO (JA) [09906605] **728**

FACT FINDER (CHICAGO, ILL.), THE (US/0014-651X) [04075092] **4474**

FACT FINDER (JAMESTOWN, N.Y.), THE (US/1053-2331) [21995369] **940**

FACT SHEET - ACADEMIC COLLECTIVE BARGAINING INFORMATION SERVICE (US/0891-2785) [10025766] **1669**

FACT SHEET BOOKLET (US/0098-7964) [02241655] **5285**

FACT SHEET - FOOD ANIMAL CONCERNS TRUST (US/0882-3022) [11805905] **226**

FACT SHEET (NORWAY. OLJE OG ENERGIDEPARTEMENTET) (NO/0800-7683) [09238309] **4256**

FACT SHEET / SENIORS ADVISORY COUNCIL FOR ALBERTA (CN/0848-6778) [23455444] **5179**

FACT SHEETS / NORTH DAKOTA INDIAN AFFAIRS COMMISSION (US) [07718054] **2733**

FACTA UNIVERSITATIS. SERIES, MATHEMATICS AND INFORMATICS (YU/0352-9665) [19101336] **3505**

FACTBOOK AND MEMBERSHIP DIRECTORY / MORTGAGE INSURANCE COMPANIES OF AMERICA (US) [23661844] **2879**

FACTBOOK - BUREAU OF HIGHER AND CONTINUING EDUCATION (US/0194-4142) [04828669] **1823**

FACTBOOK ON PUBLIC HIGHER EDUCATION IN LOUISIANA (US) [03303644] **1823**

FACTFINDER FOR THE NATION (US/0193-8762) [04026191] **4553**

FACTORS AFFECTING ECONOMIC CONDITIONS IN REAL ESTATE (AT) [28157478] **1561**

FACTORY EQUIPMENT NEWS (UK/0014-6579) **3479**

FACTORY MANAGEMENT (NEW YORK) (US/0146-3314) [02857470] **868**

FACTORY OUTLET NEWSLETTER, THE (US/0146-2857) [02902199] **1296**

FACTORY OUTLET SHOPPING GUIDE. WASHINGTON, D.C., MARYLAND, VIRGINIA, DELAWARE (US/0146-2873) [02901263] **1296**

FACTORY SALES OF ELECTRIC STORAGE BATTERIES (CN/0380-7061) [02586142] **2054**

FACTOTUM (LONDON, ENGLAND) (UK/0141-3635) [04623217] **3210**

FACTS (US) [22378223] 4775, **5440**

FACTS ABOUT ALASKA (1990) (US/1051-5623) [21990374] **2533**

FACTS ABOUT ALASKA (BOTHELL, WASH.) *See* ALASKA ALMANAC : FACTS ABOUT ALASKA, THE **2527**

FACTS ABOUT COAL (US) [09381417] **2139**

FACTS ABOUT HOSPITALS IN METROPOLITAN CHICAGO (US) [06535953] **3780**

FACTS ABOUT KOREA (KO) [01295987] **2651**

FACTS ABOUT NURSING (US/0071-3651) [02585590] **3855**

FACTS ABOUT STORE DEVELOPMENT (US/0732-233X) [07866259] **2334**

FACTS ABOUT TVA OPERATIONS (US) [01228768] **5245**

FACTS AND COMPARISONS, INC., SAINT LOUIS *See* FACTS AND COMPARISONS (MONTHLY ED.) **4304**

FACTS AND COMPARISONS (MONTHLY ED.) (US/0014-6617) [01568736] **4304**

FACTS & FEATURES / ONTARIO RESEARCH FOUNDATION (CN/0710-6092) [08751874] **5104**

FACTS AND FIGURES (UK) **3210**

FACTS AND FIGURES (II) [01790483] **1561**

FACTS AND FIGURES. AUSTRALIAN DENTISTRY (AT/0157-4094) [03719684] **1323**

FACTS AND FIGURES : MINING IN CANADA (CN/0316-2281) [02443279] **2139**

FACTS AND FIGURES (MONTEDISON GROUP) (IT) [09294866] **675**

FACTS AND FIGURES - NATIONAL COUNCIL OF INDEPENDENT SCHOOLS (AT/0811-6458) [I08116458] **1863**

FACTS AND FIGURES: NEW MEXICO EMPLOYERS, INDUSTRY, SIZE, AND LOCATION (US) [05778377] **1669**

FACTS AND FIGURES OF THE AUTOMOBILE INDUSTRY (CN) [01280012] **5400**

FACTS AND FIGURES OF THE AUTOMOTIVE INDUSTRY (ANNUAL EDITION) (CN/0316-3504) [02247379] **5401**

FACTS Alphabetical Title Index

FACTS & FIGURES OF THE U.S. PLASTICS INDUSTRY (US/0741-0859) [08983865] **4455**

FACTS AND FIGURES ON FOOTWEAR (US/0362-3890) [02298383] **1084**

FACTS AND FIGURES ON GOVERNMENT FINANCE (US/0071-3678) [04052798] **4723**

FACTS & FIGURES ON NEW ZEALAND AGRICULTURE (NZ) [05017693] **83**

FACTS AND FINDINGS (US) **2968**

FACTS AND FINDINGS (US/0736-2269) [09064593] **2446**

FACTS AND REPORTS (NE/0046-3116) [01780879] **2639**

● FACTS AND RESEARCH IN GERONTOLOGY (US) [26704864] **3751**

FACTS AND TRENDS (VANCOUVER) (CN/0429-9949) [09747512] **1669**

FACTS AT YOUR FINGERTIPS (US/0196-6294) [05094639] **4775**

FACTS FILE (II/0046-3132) [01790608] **1561**

FACTS FOR INDUSTRY. M77C, GLASS CONTAINERS *See* GLASS CONTAINERS (WASHINGTON) **2589**

FACTS FOR YOU (II) [05822332] **1561**

● FACTS NEW ZEALAND (NZ) [26626935] **5327**

FACTS OF THE GENERAL INSURANCE INDUSTRY IN CANADA (CN/0319-1826) [02443040] **2880**

FACTS ON FILE (US/0014-6641) [01568745] **2616**

FACTS ON FILE FIVE-YEAR INDEX (US/0427-9026) [07050403] **2616**

FACTS ON FILE NEWS DIGEST CD-ROM *CEASED.* (US/1062-9572) [25858157] **2487**

FACTS ON FILE. WORLD NEWS DIGEST WITH INDEX *CEASED.* (US) **4474**

FACTS ON FILE YEARBOOK (US/0196-2981) [01774753] **2616**

FACTS ON FILE YEARBOOK [MICROFORM] (US) [16514645] **2487, 2616**

FACTS ON THE FUNDS (US/0430-0009) [04484416] **898**

FACTS ON THE MAJOR KILLING AND CRIPPLING DISEASES IN THE UNITED STATES TODAY *See* KILLERS AND CRIPPLERS, THE **3602**

FACTS (OTTAWA) (CN/0705-856X) [04249955] **1669**

FACTS (SEATTLE, WASH. : 1962) (US/0427-8879) [09287142] **5760**

FACTS (WASHINGTON) *CEASED.* (US/0163-3899) [04351627] **4001**

FACTSHEET - BRITISH COLUMBIA. AQUACULTURE AND COMMERCIAL FISHERIES BRANCH (CN/0848-6743) [23455452] **2300, 83**

FACTSHEET FIVE (US/0890-6823) [14239080] **385**

FACTUM (SZ) **5060**

FACTUM : BOLETIN OFICIAL DEL COLEGIO DE ABOGADOS DE PUERTO RICO (PR) [09539763] **2968**

FACULDADE SALESIANA *See* REVISTA DA FACULDADE SALESIANA **2552**

FACULTIES, PUBLICATIONS, AND DOCTORAL THESES IN CHEMISTRY, AND CHEMICAL ENGINEERING AT UNITED STATES UNIVERSITIES *See* DIRECTORY OF GRADUATE RESEARCH **974**

FACULTY & ADMINISTRATIVE DIRECTORY - THE UNIVERSITY OF BRITISH COLUMBIA (CN/0706-6724) [04955113] **1864**

FACULTY AND ADMINISTRATIVE SALARIES (US) [06705851] **1864**

FACULTY CHARACTERISTICS, PUBLIC COLLEGES AND UNIVERSITIES IN WEST VIRGINIA (US/0146-2296) [02917069] **1823**

FACULTY DIALOGUE (US/8756-2146) [11503065] **4958**

● FACULTY GRANTS DIRECTORY (US/1064-8003) [26407357] **1746**

FACULTY OF ACTUARIES IN SCOTLAND *See* TRANSACTIONS OF THE FACULTY OF ACTUARIES **2894**

FACULTY OF BUILDING *See* REGISTER OF MEMBERS - FACULTY OF BUILDING **626**

FACULTY OUTPUT AND SALARY COSTS OF STATE-RELATED AND STATE OWNED COLLEGES AND UNIVERSITIES : STAFF REPORT OF THE JOINT STATE GOVERNMENT COMMISSION OF THE GENERAL ASSEMBLY OF THE COMMONWEALTH OF PENNSYLVANIA (US) [08455846] **1823**

FACULTY PAPER SERIES (US) [21191409] **83**

FACULTY PAPERS OF MIDWESTERN STATE UNIVERSITY (US/0273-2424) [04164222] **1864**

FACULTY PUBLICATION - TECHNION - ISRAEL INSTITUTE OF TECHNOLOGY, FACULTY OF CIVIL ENGINEERING (IS/0440-0917) [I0440091 7] **2023**

FACULTY SALARIES IN BACCALAUREATE AND GRADUATE PROGRAMS IN NURSING / INSTITUTE DATA SYSTEMS (US) [24536789] **3855**

FACULTY SALARY SURVEY (US) [05873706] 1746, **1669**

FACULTY STUDIES - CARSON-NEWMAN COLLEGE (US/0734-1539) [05320610] **4958**

FADUM REPORT, THE (US/0748-3236) [10931919] **4233**

FAELLESUDVALGET FOR STATENS MEJERI-OG HUSDYRBRUGSFORSG *See* BERETNING - FAELLESUDVALGET FOR STATENS MEJERI- OG HUSDYRBRUGSFORSG **207**

FAENGSELSVASENET (DK) [02403406] **3164**

FAENZA (IT/0014-679X) [01018405] **2589**

FAG RAG (US/0046-3167) [02547737] **2794**

FAG TIDSSKRIFTET SYKEPLEIEN (NO/0802-9768) [21901051] **3856**

FAGINFO (NO/0803-2173) [24341036] **83**

FAGOPYRUM (LJUBLJANA) (YU/0352-3020) [21146003] **83**

FAHRPLANE (AU) [03100689] **5382**

FAHRT FREI (MICROFORM) (US) [07098170] **5431**

FAI ABSTRACT SERVICE (II) [12139921] **171**

FAIG ARTS (SP/0214-4514) [21220523] **320**

FAILED BANK AND THRIFT LITIGATION REPORTER (US/0887-7807) [13368296] **3086**

FAILED LBO LITIGATION REPORTER (US/1055-9485) [22622081] **3086**

FAILSAFE LONDON (UK/0956-5590) [I09565590] **1296**

FAIM DEVELOPPEMENT MAGAZINE PARIS (FR/0760-6443) [I07606443] **4958**

FAIN KEMIKARU (JA) [09289132] **1024**

FAIPAR (HU/0014-6897) [08161090] **2379**

FAIR EMPLOYMENT COMPLIANCE (US/0885-7172) [05381066] **3148**

FAIR EMPLOYMENT PRACTICE CASES (US/0525-552X) [01328492] **3148**

FAIR EMPLOYMENT PRACTICE NEWSLETTER (US) **1669**

FAIR EMPLOYMENT PRACTICES GUIDELINES (US/1069-921X) [28201699] 2968, **940**

FAIR EMPLOYMENT REPORT (US/0014-6919) [03346895] 4508, **1669**

FAIR FACTS (GLOSTRUP, DENMARK) (DK) [20778935] **2905**

FAIR LABOR STANDARDS HANDBOOK FOR STATES, LOCAL GOVERNMENTS AND SCHOOLS / GILBERT J. GINSBURG, DANIEL B. ABRAHAMS (US) [12594098] **3148**

FAIR SCOPE (CN) **674**

FAIR TIMES (US/0889-0714) [09210667] **4860**

FAIRBANKS ARTS : A PUBLICATION OF THE FAIRBANKS ARTS ASSOCIATION (US/1058-7667) [24369755] **320**

FAIRBANKS DAILY NEWS-MINER (US/8750-5495) [01367792] **5629**

FAIRCHILD TROPICAL GARDEN BULLETIN (US/0014-6943) [01353369] **2414**

FAIRCHILD TROPICAL GARDEN, COCONUT GROVE, FLA *See* FAIRCHILD TROPICAL GARDEN BULLETIN **2414**

FAIRCHILDE INTERNATIONAL LIBRARY INSTITUTE : [NEWSLETTER] / FILI (US/1060-314X) [24929857] **3210**

FAIRCHILD'S ELECTRONICS INDUSTRY FINANCIAL DIRECTORY *CEASED.* (US) [24519685] **2054**

FAIRCHILD'S FINANCIAL MANUAL OF RETAIL STORES *See* FAIRCHILD'S RETAIL STORES FINANCIAL DIRECTORY **954**

● FAIRCHILD'S RETAIL STORES FINANCIAL DIRECTORY (US) [24864707] **954**

FAIRCHILD'S TEXTILE & APPAREL FINANCIAL DIRECTORY (US/1067-7062) [01588900] 1084, **5350**

● FAIRCHILD'S TRAVEL INDUSTRY PERSONNEL DIRECTORY (US) [29300418] **5469**

FAIRES & FESTIVALS *CEASED.* (US/1054-2167) [22517519] **4861**

FAIRFAX *CEASED.* (US/0885-1999) [12603360] **2533**

FAIRFAX (COLUMBIA, MD.) (US/1057-7459) [24111687] **3387**

FAIRFAX COUNTY GOVERNMENT ORGANIZATION MANUAL (US/0094-3967) [01793548] **4647**

FAIRFAX COUNTY (VA.). OFFICE OF COMPREHENSIVE PLANNING *See* ANNUAL PLAN REVIEW - OFFICE OF COMPREHENSIVE PLANNING (VIRGINIA) **2814**

FAIRFAX COUNTY (VA.). OFFICE OF COMPREHENSIVE PLANNING *See* ANNUAL PLAN REVIEW: AREA II **2814**

FAIRFAX COUNTY (VA.). OFFICE OF COMPREHENSIVE PLANNING *See* ANNUAL PLAN REVIEW: AREA I **2814**

FAIRFAX COUNTY (VA.). OFFICE OF COMPREHENSIVE PLANNING *See* ANNUAL PLAN REVIEW: AREA III **2814**

FAIRFAX COUNTY (VA.). OFFICE OF COMPREHENSIVE PLANNING *See* ANNUAL PLAN REVIEW: AREA IV **2814**

FAIRFAX COUNTY, VA. OFFICE OF COMPREHENSIVE PLANNING *See* COUNTYWIDE ANNUAL PLAN REVIEW / FAIRFAX COUNTY, VA. OFFICE OF COMPREHENSIVE PLANNING **2819**

● FAIRFAX DIRECTORY SERVICE (US) **4837**

FAIRFAX JOURNAL (SPRINGFIELD. 1980), THE (US/0273-6403) [06780189] **5758**

FAIRFAX STANDARD (US) [01568753] **5695**

FAIRFIELD COUNTY BUSINESS JOURNAL (US/0898-9818) [17963112] **674**

FAIRFIELD COUNTY EXECUTIVE *CEASED.* (US/0161-7419) [04023971] **674**

FAIRFIELD HERITAGE QUARTERLY (US) **2446**

FAIRFIELD LEDGER (1966) (US/1061-4508) [14218387] **5670**

FAIRFIELD TIMES, THE (US) [12068367] **5705**

FAIRFIELD TRACE (US) **2446**

FAIRMONT SENTINEL (US) [01568756] **5695**

FAIRMOUNT NEWS (FAIRMOUNT, N.D. : 1965) *See* RICHLAND COUNTY NEWS-MONITOR **5726**

FAIROUZ (AT) **2768**

FAIRPLAY (LONDON, ENGLAND : 1985) (UK) [12263414] **5449**

FAIRPLAY MARINE COMPUTING GUIDE (UK) [11582302] **4176**

FAIRPLAY WORLD PORTS DIRECTORY (UK/0261-2356) [07943254] **5449**

FAIRPLAY WORLD SHIPPING DIRECTORY (UK/0959-3101) [22409989] **5449**

FAIRPRESS *CEASED.* (US/0192-3110) [05054077] **5645**

FAIRS AND FESTIVALS IN THE NORTHEAST *See* FAIRS AND FESTIVALS, NORTHEAST AND SOUTHEAST **4850**

FAIRS AND FESTIVALS IN THE SOUTHEAST *See* FAIRS AND FESTIVALS, NORTHEAST AND SOUTHEAST **4850**

FAIRS AND FESTIVALS, NORTHEAST AND SOUTHEAST (US/1059-5929) [24640158] **4850**

FAIRSHARE (US/0273-3560) [07048911] **3120**

FAIRTEST EXAMINER, THE (US/0898-2511) [16859866] **1746**

FAIRUZ (LE) **1084**

FAIRVIEW REPUBLICAN (US) [18398933] **5732**

FAIT-FEIGHT-FATE (US/0093-6634) [01792172] **2446**

● FAIT FRANCAIS EN AMERIQUE DU NORD (CN/1183-4854) [25066339] **2733**

FAITH (US) **5016**

FAITH AND FELLOWSHIP (US) [01568759] **5060**

FAITH & FORM (US/0014-7001) [01568760] **298**

FAITH AND FREEDOM (UK) [02446834] **4958**

FAITH AND FREEDOM OXFORD (UK/0014-701X) [I0014701X] **4958**

FAITH AND MISSION (US/0740-0659) [09865377] **4958**

FAITH AND PHILOSOPHY : JOURNAL OF THE SOCIETY OF CHRISTIAN PHILOSOPHERS (US/0739-7046) [09801750] 4958, **4346**

FAITH & REASON (US/0098-5449) [02242103] **4958**

FAITH & RENEWAL *CEASED.* (US/1051-8762) [22142573] **4958**

FAITH-LIFE (US/0360-9065) [01568765] **5060**

FAITH (PORTSLADE BY SEA, E. SUSSEX) (UK) [03182894] **4958**

FAMILY

FAITH TODAY (TORONTO) (CN/0706-7003) [04879565] **4958**

FAITH TODAY (WILLOWDALE) (CN/0832-1191) [16052848] **4958**

FAITHFUL WORD, THE (US/0360-9057) [01775340] **4958**

FAITS & CHIFFRES (FR/0290-0378) [05232318] 1561, **1532**

FAITS DE LANGUES EVRY (FR/1244-5460) [I12445460] **3387**

FAITS ET CHIFFRES, LES MINES AU CANADA (CN/0228-9547) [07869960] **1606**

FAITS ET CHIFFRES REUNIONNAIS (RE) [11699117] **5327**

FAITS MARQUANTS (FR) [11735703] **2054**

FAITS STRATEGIQUES (FR) [19827820] **4474**

FAITS SUR LES ASSURANCES DE PERSONNES AU CANADA (CN/0836-3374) [17240700] **2880**

FAIZULISLAM (PK) [02239406] **5285**

FAJAR ISLAM (MUSLIM RELIGIOUS COUNCIL OF SINGAPORE) (SI) [20064963] **5042**

FAJR (JERUSALEM) (IS) [09704534] **2503**

FAKSIMILE-REIHE BACHSCHER WERKE UND SCHRIFTSTUCKE (GW/0430-0246) [04265655] **4117**

FAKTA EUROPA (SW/1100-049X) [20922638] **1561**

FAKTY (PL) [01787696] **2516**

FALCON DIGEST (US/8756-579X) [11617594] **19**

FALCON (EASTERN AIR LINES, INC.) (US/8756-5781) [11615563] **19**

FALCON FLYER (CN/0316-5639) [02247512] **5784**

FALCON (MANSFIELD), THE (US/0014-7079) [01804452] **3387**

FALFURRIAS FACTS (US) [13695658] **5749**

FALK SYMPOSIUM (US/0161-5580) [03972977] 4190, **3576**

FALKE, DER (GW) [05755656] **5583**

FALL COLLEGE ENROLLMENTS BY RACIAL/ETHNIC CATEGORY (US/0734-2659) [08691328] 2261, **1823**

FALL ENROLLMENT (US) [07374431] **1823**

FALL MEETING, TECHNICAL COMMITTEE REPORTS (US) [10717920] **2288**

FALL SURVEY OF STUDENTS IN TEXAS PUBLIC ELEMENTARY AND SECONDARY SCHOOL DISTRICTS (US) [07549772] **1746**

FALLEN LEAF MUSIC REFERENCE BOOKS (US/8755-268X) [11279044] **4117**

FALLEN LEAF PUBLICATIONS IN CONTEMPORARY MUSIC (US/8755-2698) [11277089] **4117**

FALLIMENTO E FISCO (IT) **4723**

FALLIMENTO E LE ALTRE PROCEDURE CONCORSUALI, IL (IT/0394-2740) [09221741] **2968**

FALLS CITY JOURNAL, THE (US) [13400397] **5706**

FALMOUTH OUTLOOK, THE (US/0891-8694) [13082553] **5680**

FALU, A (HU/0237-4323) [I02374323] **2822**

FAMA (TEANECK, N.J.) (US/1056-5760) [23742816] **2533**

FAMEPAR (ORGANIZATION) *See* BOLETIM DOS MUNICIPIOS **4633**

FAMIGLIA CRISTIANA (IT/0014-7095) **5029**

FAMILIA (SA/0014-7117) [01285004] **2447**

FAMILIA CRISTIANA (MX) **5029**

FAMILIA DE HOY, LA (US/1049-9717) [21359679] **2278**

FAMILIA DE LA CIUDAD, LA (US/1077-3215) [30768926] **2278**

FAMILIA LATINA (US/0741-7403) [10239612] **2278**

FAMILIAR (MCALLEN, TEX.), EL (US) [05395929] **5749**

FAMILIE UND RECHT : FUR (GW/0937-2180) [21995013] **3120**

FAMILIEN UND HAUSHALTE / HERAUSGEGEBEN VOM STATISTISCHEN LANDESAMT BADEN-WURTTEMBERG (GW) [08578401] **2279**

FAMILIENPLANUNG / WISSENSCHAFTLICHE TAGUNG DER OSTERREICHISCHEN GESELLSCHAFT FUER FAMILIENPLANUNG (AU) [10895145] **588**

FAMILIES (CN/0030-2945) [02009414] **2447**

FAMILIES AND DISABILITY NEWSLETTER (US/1044-8217) [19909452] **4388**

●FAMILIES IN CRISIS FUNDING REPORT (US/1075-3184) [30050765] 2279, **5285**

FAMILIES IN SOCIETY (US/1044-3894) [19766242] **5285**

FAMILIES OF WYOMING CO., WV (US/0890-0353) [14126820] **2447**

FAMILIES OF YANCEY COUNTY, NC (US/0890-0361) [14122948] **2447**

FAMILJA KANA (MM) **2279**

FAMILLE AVERTIE (CN/0315-954X) [02247175] **4775**

FAMILLE ET DEVELOPPEMENT (TG) [02244105] 1746, 2909, **4775**

FAMILLE MAGAZINE (FR) **2279**

FAMILLE QUEBEC (CN/0318-0581) [02248283] 5029, **2279**

FAMILY ADVOCATE (US/0163-710X) [04161321] **3120**

FAMILY AFFAIRS (US) [17826067] **2279**

FAMILY ALBUM, THE (US/0094-5862) [01789135] **3387**

FAMILY & COMMUNITY HEALTH (US/0160-6379) [03719463] 3737, **4775**

FAMILY AND CONCILIATION COURTS REVIEW (US/1047-5699) [20487112] **3120**

FAMILY AND SOCIAL AFFAIRS COUNCIL *See* OBJECTIFS DANS LE DOMAINE DES AFFAIRES SOCIALES ET DE LA FAMILLE, LES **5300**

FAMILY ASSOCIATION NEWSLETTER, DRODDY, DRODY, DRAWDY & VARIANTS, THE (US/0749-4505) [11109325] **2447**

FAMILY BACKTRACKING (US/0735-682X) [08252813] **2447**

FAMILY (BOCA RATON) (US/0272-992X) [04454068] **2279**

FAMILY (BOSTON, MASS.), THE (JS/0899-1529) [18032914] **5029**

FAMILY BUSINESS (US/1047-255X) [20646645] **674**

●FAMILY BUSINESS ADVISOR, THE (US/1060-3603) [24946320] **674**

FAMILY BUSINESS REVIEW (US/0894-4865) [16115306] **674**

FAMILY CAREGIVER APPLICATIONS SERIES (US) [24626164] **4775**

FAMILY-CENTERED COMMUNITY NURSING (US/0273-3544) [06544144] **3856**

FAMILY CHILD CARING (US) **2279**

FAMILY CIRCLE (US/0014-7206) [04178274] **2790**

FAMILY CIRCLE. BRITISH EDITION (UK) **5555**

FAMILY CIRCLE COOKBOOK (US/0890-1481) [14181694] **2790**

FAMILY CONNECTION (REGINA) (CN/0846-0353) [23302861] **2279**

FAMILY CONNECTIONS (CN/1195-9428) **2279**

FAMILY COURT REPORTER (UK/0952-8199) [17282055] **3120**

FAMILY CREATIVE WORKSHOP, THE (US/0360-0190) [02012787] **373**

FAMILY DYNAMICS OF ADDICTION QUARTERLY *CEASED*. (US/1054-8726) [23001893] 5285, **1344**

FAMILY ECONOMICS REVIEW (US/0425-676X) [01568778] **2790**

●FAMILY ENTERTAINMENT CENTER (US/1064-542X) [26326108] **4861**

FAMILY EXPENDITURE IN CANADA (1978) (CN/0838-3715) [19049343] **1490**

FAMILY FINDER (HEIDELBERG, GERMANY) (GW/1040-4821) [18427340] **2447**

FAMILY FINDINGS (US/0533-0939) **2447**

FAMILY FOOD EXPENDITURE IN CANADA (1982) (CN/0838-3898) [19914134] **1490**

FAMILY FOOTPRINTS (US/0277-6936) [07603859] **2447**

FAMILY FOOTSTEPS QUARTERLY (US/0894-0487) [15792970] 2478, **2447**

FAMILY GUIDANCE ASSOCIATION OF ETHIOPIA *See* ANNUAL REPORT - FAMILY GUIDANCE ASSOCIATION OF ETHIOPIA **588**

FAMILY GUIDE, THE (US/0747-024X) [10478296] **2279**

FAMILY GUIDE (TORONTO) (CN/1189-623X) [27391070] **1063**

FAMILY HANDYMAN, THE (US/0014-7230) [01105125] **2790**

FAMILY HEALTH BULLETIN (US/0014-7257) [01367820] **3576**

FAMILY HISTORIAN QUARTERLY, THE *CEASED*. (US/1057-946X) [15667515] **2447**

FAMILY HISTORY (UK/0014-7265) [04427136] **2447**

FAMILY HISTORY CAPERS (US/0742-1419) [08080546] **2447**

FAMILY HISTORY FOR BEGINNERS (AT/0815-3922) [I08153922] **2447**

FAMILY HISTORY NEWS AND DIGEST (UK/0309-8559) [05296929] **2447**

FAMILY IN AMERICA, THE (US/0892-2691) [15140229] **2279**

FAMILY-IN-TOUCH (US/0732-0213) [08291362] **2279**

FAMILY INCOME DATA FOR COUNTIES AND REGIONS (US) [06347925] **1490**

FAMILY INCOMES. CENSUS FAMILIES (CN/0703-7368) [01788126] 2279, **2287**

FAMILY INFORMATION SERVICES (US/1042-0878) [18937703] **2279**

●FAMILY JOURNAL (ALEXANDRIA, VA.), THE (US/1066-4807) [26949658] 4587, **2279**

FAMILY JOURNAL (PUTNEY, VT.) (US/0272-2089) [06801461] **2279**

●FAMILY JUSTICE BULLETIN (CN/1189-4245) [26498112] **3120**

FAMILY LAW. BENDER PAMPHLET EDITION (US/0099-1988) [02239691] **3120**

FAMILY LAW (CHICHESTER) (UK/0014-7281) [01568786] **3120**

FAMILY LAW QUARTERLY (US/0014-729X) [01568788] **3120**

FAMILY LAW REPORTER, THE (US/0148-7922) [02242550] **3120**

FAMILY LAW REPORTS (SYDNEY, N.S.W.) (AT) [19051882] **3120**

FAMILY LAW REVIEW (US/0149-1431) [03429691] **3120**

FAMILY LAW TRIAL SUMMARIES (US) [09517825] **3120**

FAMILY LIFE (CN/0014-7303) [02395633] **2279**

FAMILY LIFE *CEASED*. (UK) **2279**

FAMILY LIFE EDUCATOR (US/0732-9962) [08500495] **2279**

FAMILY LIFE MATTERS (US/1064-6167) [26342177] **2279**

●FAMILY LIFE (NEW YORK, N.Y.) (US/1072-0332) [28867531] **2279**

FAMILY LIFE TODAY *CEASED*. (US/0273-9054) [07016180] **2279**

FAMILY LIFE (TORONTO) (CN/0319-5961) [02442286] **2279**

●FAMILY MATTERS LONDON (UK/0967-7119) [I09677119] **2968**

FAMILY MATTERS (MELBOURNE, VIC.) (AT/1030-2646) [18006021] **2279**

FAMILY MEDICINE (US/0742-3225) [09241221] **3737**

FAMILY MEDICINE REVIEW, THE (US/0197-6974) [06080947] **3737**

FAMILY MINISTRIES (US/0277-4518) [07568453] **4958**

FAMILY MOTOR COACHING (US/0360-3024) [02243810] **5382**

●FAMILY PC (US/1076-7754) [30620046] **1184**

FAMILY PEDIGREES (US/1057-9451) [24123447] **2447**

FAMILY PERSPECTIVE (US/0014-7311) [01568795] **2279**

FAMILY PHARMACY NEWSLETTER, THE (US/0190-5406) [04657686] **4304**

FAMILY PHYSICIAN (KUALA LUMPUR, MALAYSIA) (MY) [23110707] **3737**

FAMILY PLANNING ASSOCIATION OF HONG KONG *See* ANNUAL REPORT OF THE FAMILY PLANNING ASSOCIATION OF HONG KONG **588**

FAMILY PLANNING ASSOCIATION OF INDIA *See* REPORT - FAMILY PLANNING ASSOCIATION OF INDIA **590**

FAMILY PLANNING ASSOCIATION OF KENYA *See* ANNUAL REPORT - FAMILY PLANNING ASSOCIATION OF KENYA **588**

FAMILY PLANNING DIGEST (US/0046-3213) [01295989] **588**

FAMILY PLANNING GRANTEES, DELEGATES & CLINICS (US/0742-1893) [10266617] **588**

FAMILY PLANNING IN FIVE CONTINENTS *CEASED*. (UK/0538-9089) [02932842] **588**

●FAMILY PLANNING MANAGER, THE (US/1060-9172) [25107747] **5285**

FAMILY PLANNING PERSPECTIVES (US/0014-7354) [00829761] 2279, **588**

FAMILY PLANNING RESEARCH AND EVALUATION MANUAL (US/0093-352X) [05452350] **588**

FAMILY PLANNING SERVICES. ANNUAL SUMMARY (US/0094-4424) [01794422] **589**

FAMILY — Alphabetical Title Index

FAMILY PLANNING TODAY (UK/0309-1112) [02936036] **589**

FAMILY PRACTICE (UK/0263-2136) [11330496] **3737**

FAMILY PRACTICE ALERT *CEASED.* (US/0899-9562) [18277324] **3737**

FAMILY PRACTICE (GLENDALE, CALIF.) (US/0271-1362) [01778666] **1894**, **3737**

FAMILY PRACTICE JOURNAL (US/0191-2461) [04794896] **3737**

●FAMILY PRACTICE MANAGEMENT (US/1069-5648) [28104832] **3737**

FAMILY PRACTICE NEWS (US/0300-7073) [00977061] **3737**

FAMILY PRACTICE NEWSLETTER, THE (US/1041-2271) [18706861] **3576**

FAMILY PRACTICE PEDIATRICS (US/1047-0638) [20590765] 3903, **3737**

FAMILY PRACTICE RECERTIFICATION (US/0163-6642) [04430816] **3737**

FAMILY PRACTICE RESEARCH JOURNAL, THE *CEASED.* (US/0270-2304) [06368524] **3737**

●FAMILY PRACTICE RESIDENT, THE *SUSPENDED.* (US/1063-8555) [26150096] **3737**

FAMILY PRACTITIONER SERVICES, THE (UK/0305-9669) [02145013] **3737**

FAMILY PROCESS (US/0014-7370) [01285012] **2279**

FAMILY RECORDS TODAY (US/0736-1858) [08863765] **2447**

FAMILY RELATIONS (US/0197-6664) [05885388] **2279**

FAMILY RESOURCE COALITION REPORT (US/1041-8660) [14221800] **2280**

FAMILY (ROCHESTER, N.Y.), THE *CEASED.* (US/0739-442X) [05460994] **2280**

FAMILY ROOTS : JOURNAL OF THE FAMILY ROOTS FAMILY HISTORY SOCIETY. EASTBOURNE AND DISTRICT (UK) **2447**

FAMILY SAFETY AND HEALTH (CANADIAN ED.) (US/0749-3118) [11124686] **4775**

FAMILY SAFETY AND HEALTH (U.S. ED.) (US/0749-310X) [11110139] **4775**

FAMILY SERVICE AMERICA *See* DIRECTORY OF MEMBER AGENCIES IN THE UNITED STATES AND CANADA **5283**

FAMILY SERVICES IN UTAH (US/0361-4158) [02246549] **5285**

FAMILY SNOOP (US) **2447**

FAMILY SPENDING / CENTRAL STATISTICAL OFFICE (UK/0965-1403) [25352402] **1490**

●FAMILY SYSTEMS (US/1070-0609) [28261390] **2280**

FAMILY SYSTEMS MEDICINE (US/0736-1718) [09091663] **3737**

FAMILY SYSTEMS MEDICINE NEWSLETTER (US) [24469953] 3576, **2597**

FAMILY TAX PLANNING (US) [01764321] **4723**

FAMILY THERAPY (US/0091-6544) [01731055] **3925**

FAMILY THERAPY NETWORKER, THE (US/0739-0882) [08760181] **2280**

FAMILY THERAPY NEWS (US/0277-6464) [07607198] 2280, **4587**

FAMILY TIES (HOLLAND GENEALOGICAL SOCIETY) (US/0736-9883) [07864807] **2447**

FAMILY TIMES (EAU CLAIRE, WIS.) (US/1056-9243) [23896836] **2280**

FAMILY TIMES (TORONTO) (CN/1184-6801) [24267053] **5285**

FAMILY TO FAMILY (CN/1187-5712) [25423449] **2280**

FAMILY TREE *See* HEART OF TEXAS RECORDS **2452**

FAMILY TREE (DAYTON, OHIO) (US/1047-0956) [11408520] **2447**

FAMILY TREE (HOWARD COUNTY, MD), THE (US/1064-1106) [09071885] **2447**

FAMILY TREE MAGAZINE (UK/0267-1131) [13756514] **2447**

FAMILY TREE QUARTERLY : A PUBLICATION OF THE COBB COUNTY, GEORGIA, GENEALOGICAL SOCIETY, INC (US/1059-0803) [24434706] **2447**

FAMILY TREE TALK (US/0747-9441) [10157017] **2447**

FAMILY VINES (US/0749-1530) [11063298] **2447**

FAMILY VIOLENCE & SEXUAL ASSAULT BULLETIN (US/1067-7283) [27089443] **5285**

FAMILY VOICE / CONCERNED WOMEN FOR AMERICA (US) [24616714] 5555, **4474**

FAMILYFUN (NEW YORK, N.Y.) (US/1056-6333) [23751017] **2280**

FAMILYSEARCH. INTERNATIONAL GENEALOGICAL INDEX. BRITISH ISLES (US/1063-4711) [26243028] **2447**

FAMILYSEARCH. INTERNATIONAL GENEALOGICAL INDEX. DENMARK (US/1063-4738) [26243318] **2448**

FAMILYSEARCH. INTERNATIONAL GENEALOGICAL INDEX. U.S. AND CANADA (US/1063-4703) [26242890] **2448**

FAMILYSEARCH. INTERNATIONAL GENEALOGICAL INDEX. WALES (US/1063-472X) [26243176] **2448**

FAMOUS ARTISTS ANNUAL (US/0071-3783) [01568805] **350**

FAMOUS FIRST FACTS; A RECORD OF FIRST HAPPENINGS, DISCOVERIES AND INVENTIONS IN THE UNITED STATES (US) [02700660] **2733**

FAMOUS MONSTERS (US/0278-4203) [07789514] **4068**

FAMOUS PULP CLASSICS (US/0363-0560) [02404259] 5074, **3387**

FAMUAN (TALLAHASSEE, FLA.), THE (US/1063-9942) [26187664] 5648, **5649**

FAN CLUB DIRECTORY, THE (US) [12126101] **5231**

FAN. FEMINIST ARTS NEWS *CEASED.* (UK/0264-7060) [16439081] **320**

FAN I TUNG HSUN (CC) [07186115] **3281**

FAN VA TURMUSH (UZ) [06232941] **5104**

FANATIC READER, THE *SUSPENDED.* (US/0889-7972) [14066424] **2533**

FANCIERS DIGEST, THE (CN/0849-3405) [23231312] **4286**

FANCY FOOD (US/1046-2880) [17159261] **2335**

FANCY FOOD & CANDY *See* FANCY FOOD **2335**

FANCY FOOD. BUYERS GUIDE (US) [16736270] **2335**

●F&S INDEX EUROPE ANNUAL (1993) (US/1076-6596) [29989122] **674**

●F&S INDEX INTERNATIONAL (US) [28933654] 675, **728**

●F&S INDEX INTERNATIONAL ANNUAL (US/1076-6588) [29999007] **1606**

F&S INDEX PLUS TEXT. INTERNATIONAL (US/1065-5956) [23967950] 675, **729**

F&S INDEX PLUS TEXT. UNITED STATES (US/1065-5964) [23967871] 675, **729**

●F&S INDEX UNITED STATES ANNUAL (US/1076-4941) [29994936] **675**

FANFARE (TENAFLY, N.J.) (US/0148-9364) [03386493] **4117**

FANFARES (CN/0046-3256) [02398993] **320**

FANG YEN (CC) [05143391] **3281**

FANGORIA (US/0164-2111) [04618144] **4068**

FANGZHI GONGCHENG XUEKAN (CC/0254-6469) [08518994] **5350**

FANGZHI KEXUE (CC/0251-0804) [04321778] **5350**

FANGZHI XUEBAO (CH/0253-9721) [09235478] **5350**

FANON CENTER JOURNAL *CEASED.* (US/0273-3366) [07040060] **5285**

FANON RESEARCH AND DEVELOPMENT CENTER *See* FANON CENTER JOURNAL **5285**

FANTASIAE *CEASED.* (US/0094-2375) [05093061] **5074**

FANTASTIC (US/0014-7508) [01220232] **3387**

FANTASTIC (FLUSHING. 1958) (US/0014-7508) [04878636] **3387**

FANTASTIC FOUR (US/0274-5291) [06387681] **4861**

FANTASY & SCIENCE FICTION (US/0024-984X) [18737979] **3387**

FANTASY AND SCIENCE FICTION CONVENTIONEER'S GUIDE, THE (US/0898-5979) [17860527] **3387**

FANTASY BASEBALL (US/1046-9125) [20585140] **4894**

FANTASY BOOK (US/0277-0717) [07494637] 5074, **3387**

FANTASY COMMENTATOR (US/1051-5011) [11112346] 3342, **3387**

FANTASY FOOTBALL (US/0898-9672) [17961934] **4894**

FANTASY FRONTIERS (US/1040-757X) [18515236] **373**

FANTASY VOICES (US/0271-7808) [06683938] 5074, **3387**

FAO AGRICULTURAL SERVICES BULLETIN (IT/1010-1365) [05849365] **83**

FAO ANIMAL PRODUCTION AND HEALTH PAPER (IT/0254-6019) [04109140] **226**

FAO ANIMAL PRODUCTION AND HEALTH SERIES (IT) [03966688] **211**

FAO COMMODITY POLICY STUDIES (IT) [01293734] **83**

FAO COMMODITY REVIEW AND OUTLOOK (IT/0071-7002) [01280027] **83**

FAO CONSERVATION GUIDE (IT) [03673063] **2193**

FAO-DOC CURRENT BIBLIOGRAPHY (MICROFORM) (IT) [06705736] 83, **2335**

FAO DOCUMENTATION. CURRENT BIBLIOGRAPHY / DOCUMENTATION DE LA FAO. BIBLIOGRAPHIE COURANTE / DOCUMENTACION DE LA FAO. BIBLIOGRAFIA CORRIENTE (IT) [01771437] 153, **83**

FAO ECONOMIC AND SOCIAL DEVELOPMENT PAPER (IT) [05469469] **83**

FAO ECONOMIC AND SOCIAL DEVELOPMENT SERIES (IT) [03863559] **83**

FAO ENVIRONMENT AND ENERGY PAPER (IT) [15069039] 2216, **83**

FAO FERTILIZER AND PLANT NUTRITION BULLETIN (IT/0824-3974] **171**

FAO FISHERIES (IT) **2300**

FAO FISHERIES BIOLOGY REPORT (IT/0427-8038) [01443428] **2300**

FAO FISHERIES CIRCULAR (IT/0429-9329) [01947720] **2300**

FAO FISHERIES REPORT (IT/0429-9337) [01569615] **2300**

FAO FISHERIES SERIES (IT) [05957253] **2300**

FAO FISHERIES STUDIES (IT/0071-7037) [01437483] **2300**

FAO FISHERIES SYNOPSIS (IT/0014-5602) [01487738] **2300**

FAO FISHERIES TECHNICAL PAPER (IT/0429-9345) [01443090] **2301**

FAO FOOD AND NUTRITION PAPER (IT/0254-4725) [04399951] **4190**

FAO FOOD AND NUTRITION SERIES (IT) [03986920] **4190**

FAO FORESTRY DEVELOPMENT PAPER (IT/0071-7029) [01338103] **2379**

FAO FORESTRY PAPER (IT/0258-6150) [04676902] **2379**

FAO FORESTRY SERIES (IT) [06359712] **2379**

FAO IN ... (IT) [09519712] **83**

FAO INVESTMENT CENTRE TECHNICAL PAPER (IT) [13500891] **2909**

FAO IRRIGATION AND DRAINAGE PAPER (IT/0254-5284) [05231695] **2089**

FAO LEGISLATIVE SERIES (IT/0071-7045) [02310800] **83**

FAO NUTRITION MEETINGS REPORT SERIES (IT/0071-707X) [01320507] **4191**

FAO NUTRITIONAL STUDIES (US/0071-7088) [I00717088] **83**

FAO PLANT PRODUCTION AND PROTECTION PAPER (IT/0259-2517) [I02592517] **509**

FAO PLANT PRODUCTION AND PROTECTION PAPERS (IT) [03282547] **2414**

FAO PLANT PRODUCTION AND PROTECTION SERIES (IT/0259-2525) [04162632] 2414, **171**

FAO PLANT PROTECTION BULLETIN (IT/0014-5637) [08413999] **2414**

FAO QUARTERLY BULLETIN OF STATISTICS (IT/1011-8780) [18590354] **153**

FAO RESEARCH AND TECHNOLOGY PAPER (IT) [16107290] **2335**

FAO SOILS BULLETIN (IT/0253-2050) [04293406] **171**

FAO STATISTICAL DEVELOPMENT SERIES (IT) [15118627] **84**

FAO TRAINING SERIES (IT) [07871541] **4871**

FAO YEARBOOK. FERTILIZER (IT) [19839086] **84**

FAO YEARBOOK. PRODUCTION (IT) [19298751] **84**

FAPRI STAFF REPORT / FOOD AND AGRICULTURAL POLICY RESEARCH INSTITUTE (US) [12630148] **84**

FAPUQ NOUVELLES BREVES (CN/0316-5159) [02247456] **1823**

FAR EAST AND AUSTRALASIA, THE (UK/0071-3791) [01345792] **1925**

●FAR EAST FOCUS (UK/1354-5299) 1297, **4775**

FAR EAST REPORTER *CEASED.* (US/0014-7575) [05725173] **2487**

FAR EAST, STUDIES BY SOVIET SCHOLARS SERIES, THE (RU/0235-6813) [21187537] **2503**

FAR EAST TRAVEL DIGEST (US) [08208727] **5469**

FAR EAST TRAVELLER (JA) **5469**

FARMERS

FAR EASTERN AFFAIRS (RU) [01799511] **1561**

FAR EASTERN AGRICULTURE (UK/0266-8025) [10035921] **84**

FAR EASTERN AND RUSSIAN RESEARCH SERIES (US) [01605049] **4521**

FAR EASTERN ECONOMIC REVIEW (US/0014-7591) [05146170] **1635**

FAR EASTERN ECONOMIC REVIEW (HK/0014-7591) [01568821] **1561**

FAR EASTERN LAW REVIEW (PH/0046-3272) [07928513] **2968**

FAR EASTERN QUARTERLY, THE (US/0363-6917) [01780178] **2651**

FAR EASTERN TECHNICAL REVIEW *See* ASIAN REVIEW OF BUSINESS AND TECHNOLOGY **640**

FAR EASTERN TECHNICAL REVIEW (UK/0144-8218) [01448218] 1975, **835**

FAR NORTHEAST CITIZEN-SENTINEL, THE (US) [14146923] **5736**

FAR-WESTERN FORUM *SUSPENDED.* (US/0094-0887) [01793834] **3387**

FAR-WESTERNER, THE (US/0430-0688) [02355656] **2733**

FARADAY DISCUSSIONS (UK) [26046758] **1052**

FARAVID (FI/0356-5629) [06022018] **2616**

FARBE (GW/0014-7680) [01327548] **1024**

FARBE + I.E. UND LACK ADRESSBUCH MIT BEZUGSQUELLENNACHWEIS (GW) [05758786] **4223**

FARBE + LACK (GW/0014-7699) [09915034] **4223**

FARBE UND GLAS *See* FARBE UND RAUM **614**

FARBE UND RAUM (SZ/0014-7702) [02999896] **614**

FARE ELETTRONICA (IT) 2773, **2054**

FARE MUSICA (IT) **4117**

FARE VELA (IT) **593**

FARG OCH LACK SCANDINAVIA (DK/0106-7559) [09296343] **4223**

FARHANG-I IRAN ZAMIN (IR/0014-7788) [01568839] **2651**

FARHANG-I MARDUM (AF) [11106215] **2319**

FARIBAULT COUNTY REGISTER (1989) (US/1045-7429) [20223716] **5695**

FARIBAULT DAILY NEWS (US/0889-8898) [09887364] **5695**

FARM AND COUNTRY (TORONTO) (CN/0046-3299) [02009488] **84**

FARM AND DAIRY (SALEM, OHIO : 1914) (US/0014-7826) [04075097] **5728**

FARM & FOOD / TEAGASC (IE) [24588557] **84**

FARM & POWER EQUIPMENT DEALER *See* NAEDA EQUIPMENT DEALER **160**

FARM & POWER EQUIPMENT DEALER (US/0892-6085) [15220518] **158**

FARM & RANCH LIVING (US/0276-170X) [04202912] **84**

FARM BROADCASTERS LETTER (US/0364-5444) [02563831] **84**

FARM BUILDING PROGRESS (UK/0309-4111) [06746508] **158**

FARM BUILDINGS AND ENGINEERING : JOURNAL OF THE FARM BUILDINGS INFORMATION CENTRE AND THE FARM BUILDINGS ASSOCIATION *CEASED.* (UK/0265-5373) [12348714] **614**

FARM BUILDINGS TOPICS (UK) [05338462] **158**

FARM BULLETIN (ST. PIERRE, MAN.) (CN/0826-2985) [11085120] **84**

FARM BUREAU JOURNAL (US) **84**

FARM BUREAU NEWS (KANSAS FARM BUREAU) (US) [14580752] **84**

FARM BUREAU NEWS (WASHINGTON) (US/0197-5617) [02229468] **84**

FARM BUREAU PERSPECTIVE (US/0744-4990) [08376590] **84**

FARM BUSINESS ANALYSIS ... DAIRY ENTERPRISE / SASKATCHEWAN AGRICULTURE, MARKETING AND ECONOMICS DIVISION (CN) [10890511] **194**

FARM CASH RECEIPTS (QUARTERLY ED.) (CN/0703-7945) [02442559] **84**

FARM CHEMICALS (1973) (US/0092-0053) [01608593] **84**

FARM CHEMICALS HANDBOOK (US/0430-0750) [01568864] **171**

FARM CHEMICALS INTERNATIONAL (US/1043-8858) [19595723] **84**

FARM COMPUTING (AT) 171, **1184**

FARM CREDIT CORPORATION *See* ANNUAL REPORT - FARM CREDIT CORPORATION **771**

FARM CREDIT STATISTICS (CN/0825-7019) [10206937] **729**

FARM DEVELOPMENT REVIEW (UK) **84**

FARM ECONOMICS : FACTS AND OPINIONS (US/0886-5906) [03184862] 1490, **84**

FARM ECONOMICS (UNIVERSITY PARK, PA.) (US/0555-9456) [08674840] 1490, **84**

FARM ECONOMY (BG) [06852435] 1490, **84**

FARM EQUIPMENT (US/0014-7958) [01585918] **159**

FARM EQUIPMENT INTERNATIONAL *See* AGRICULTURE & EQUIPMENT INTERNATIONAL **53**

FARM FAMILY WEST (CN/1185-2119) [24368424] **84**

FARM FINANCE REVIEW (US) [02071352] **84**

FARM FINANCIAL CONDITIONS REVIEW (US/0883-2188) [12074641] 1490, **84**

FARM FORESTRY NEWS (US/1061-5539) [16816294] **2379**

FARM GATE, THE (CN/0705-8748) [04433011] **84**

FARM IMPLEMENT NEWS *See* IMPLEMENT & TRACTOR **159**

FARM IMPLEMENTS AND TRACTORS *See* NORTHWEST FARM EQUIPMENT JOURNAL **160**

FARM INCOME SERIES / MINISTRY OF AGRICULTURE AND FISHERIES (UK) [08416451] **84**

FARM INDUSTRY NEWS (1984) (US/0892-8312) [14124639] **159**

FARM INDUSTRY NEWS SOUTH *See* FARM INDUSTRY NEWS SUNBELT **84**

FARM INDUSTRY NEWS SUNBELT (US/0744-7787) [08556135] **84**

FARM INPUT PRICE INDEX (CN/0383-4875) [03196587] **84**

FARM JOURNAL (PHILADELPHIA. 1956) (US/0014-8008) [05843575] **85**

FARM LABOR AND WAGE RATES / IOWA CROP AND LIVESTOCK REPORTING SERVICE (US) [06203784] 85, **1669**

FARM LABOR REPORT (CASPER) (US/0095-389X) [01796234] 85, **1669**

FARM LABOR (WASHINGTON) (JS/0363-8545) [02533105] **85**

FARM LIGHT & POWER (ALBERTA EDITION) (CN/0229-2106) [08078613] **85**

FARM LIGHT & POWER (MANITOBA EDITION) (CN/0229-2092) [08078602] **85**

FARM MACHINERY AND LAWN AND GARDEN EQUIPMENT (US/0278-9035) [07889470] **159**

FARM MACHINERY & TRACTOR FACTS *CEASED.* (US/0192-8317) [05065903] **159**

FARM MACHINERY COSTS AS A GUIDE TO CUSTOM RATES (CN/0709-6216) [07293910] **159**

FARM MACHINERY CUSTOM AND RENTAL RATES, DETAILED SUPPLEMENT (CN/0225-9346) [06174163] **159**

FARM MANAGEMENT (KENILWORTH) (UK/0014-8059) [02939173] 1606, **85**

FARM MANAGEMENT NEWS AND VIEWS (US) [08245087] **85**

FARM MANAGEMENT NOTES FOR ASIA AND THE FAR EAST (TH/0430-084X) [01568887] 171, **85**

FARM MARKET CHARTS *See* AG. MARKET CHARTS **45**

FARM NEWS AND VIEWS (US) [17554772] **85**

FARM NEWS OF ERIE AND WYOMING COUNTIES (US) [15637755] **85**

FARM PAPER (CN/0715-5042) [09336483] **85**

FARM POND HARVEST (US/0014-8083) [01568892] **2301**

FARM PRODUCT PRICE INDEX (CN/0835-0906) [15904864] 85, **153**

FARM PRODUCTION EXPENDITURE SURVEY (US) [03799495] **85**

FARM PRODUCTION EXPENDITURES / UNITED STATES DEPARTMENT OF AGRICULTURE, STATISTICAL REPORTING SERVICE, CROP REPORTING BOARD (US/0191-0531) [11210196] **85**

FARM, RANCH & COUNTRY VACATIONS (US/0195-8437) [05122989] **5469**

FARM, RANCH & SUBURBAN ACREAGE (US/0192-9437) [05135109] **85**

FARM REAL ESTATE TAXES (US/0071-4003) [00930369] **85**

FARM REVIEW (JOLIET, ILL.) (US) [09350643] **85**

FARM SHOW (US/0163-4518) [03676332] **159**

FARM STORE (US/1057-3542) [22190079] **85**

FARM STORE MERCHANDISING *See* FARM STORE **85**

FARM SURVEYS REPORT (AT/0818-027X) [13975876] **85**

FARM TAXATION (AT) **4723**

FARM WEEKLY *See* ELDERS WEEKLY **210**

FARMA 7 (IT) **4304**

FARMACEUTICO HOSPITALES, EL (SP/0214-4697) [26146381] **4304**

FARMACEUTISCH NIEUWS *CEASED.* (NE) **4304**

FARMACEUTISCH TIJDSCHRIFT VOOR BELGIE (BE/0369-9714) [01295276] **4304**

FARMACEUTISCH TIJDSCHRIFT VOOR BELGIE 1971 (BE/0771-2367) [I07712367] **4304**

FARMACEUTSKI GLASNIK (CI/0014-8202) [10242604] **4304**

FARMACEVTISK REVY (SW/0014-8210) [01586623] **4304**

FARMACEVTSKI VESTNIK (LJUBLJANA) (XV/0014-8229) [09562274] **4304**

FARMACEVTYCNYJ ZURNAL (KIIV. 1928) (UN/0367-3057) [04186099] **4304**

FARMACI (IT) **4304**

FARMACI E TERAPIA (IT/0393-9693) [I03939693] **4304**

FARMACIA; BOLLETTINO UFFICIALE DEL SINDACATO NAZIONALE FASCISTA DEI FARMACISTI, LA *CEASED.* (IT) [20316504] **4304**

FARMACIA (BUCURESTI) (RM/0014-8237) [10240754] **4304**

FARMACIA CLINICA (SP/0212-6583) [12745409] **4304**

FARMACIA HOSPITALARIA (SP/1130-6343) [I11306343] **4304**

FARMACIA PORTUGUESA (PO/0870-0230) [I08700230] **4304**

FARMACIJA (BU/0428-0296) [09288368] **4304**

FARMACIJA (RU/0367-3014) [03390150] **4304**

FARMACIJA (KIEV) (UN/0301-5394) [01336794] **4304**

FARMACJA POLSKA (PL/0014-8261) [09585584] **4304**

FARMACO (SOCIETA CHIMICA ITALIANA : 1989) (IT) [19853803] 975, **4305**

FARMACOTERAPIA MADRID (SP/0214-8935) [02148935] **4305**

FARMAKOLOGIIA I TOKSIKOLOGIIA (MOSCOW, R.S.F.S.R.) *See* EKSPERIMENTALNAIA I KLINICHESKAIA FARMAKOLOGIIA **4303**

FARMAKOLOGIJA I TOKSIKOLOGIJA (KIEV) (RU/0430-0939) [10769337] **4305**

FARMAKOTERAPEUTICKE ZPRAVY SPOFA. SUPPLEMENTUM (XR/0533-0300) [05533502] **4305**

FARMAKOTERAPI (NO/0014-8326) [07720280] **4305**

FARMATELEX (SP) **4305**

FARMER AND PARLIAMENT (II/0014-8369) [01568909] **85**

FARMER AND STOCK-BREEDER YEAR BOOK AND DESK DIARY (UK) [05826214] **85**

FARMER COOPERATIVE STATISTICS (US/0742-9495) [08362427] 1542, **1532**

FARMER COOPERATIVES (US/0364-0736) [02200788] 85, **1542**

FARMER (MINNESOTA ED.) (US/0896-5579) [10742562] **85**

FARMER-RANCHER (CN/1185-2178) [24368430] **85**

FARMER STOCKMAN OF THE MIDWEST (US/0739-9235) [09834361] 211, **85**

FARMERS' ADVANCE, THE (US/0745-211X) [08917082] **5692**

FARMERS & CONSUMERS MARKET BULLETIN (US/0889-5619) [04242900] **85**

FARMERS BRANCH TIMES (US/8750-9199) [11907357] **5749**

FARMERS' BULLETIN (US/0193-4392) [01696411] **85**

FARMERS BULLETIN (WEST CUMBERLAND) (UK/0430-0998) [08469780] **85**

FARMERS' CHOICE (CN/1182-1248) [22281288] **85**

FARMERS' CLUB JOURNAL (LONDON, ENGLAND) (UK) [14173103] **85**

FARMER'S DIGEST (US/0046-3337) [01568919] **85**

FARMERS EXCHANGE (US) **85**

FARMER'S — Alphabetical Title Index

FARMER'S EXCHANGE, THE (US) [01568922] **85**

FARMERS FASTLINE - ILLINOIS EDITION (US) **86**

FARMERS FASTLINE (INDIANA EDITION) (US) **86**

FARMERS FASTLINE - IOWA EDITION (US) **86**

FARMERS FASTLINE - KENTUCKY EDITION (US) **86**

FARMERS FEDERAL TAX ALERT (US/0731-4612) [08198428] **4723, 86**

FARMERS HOT LINE (US/0192-6322) [05069524] **86**

FARMER'S MARKET (GALESBURG, ILL.) (US/0748-6022) [09320486] **3387**

FARMERS' NEWSLETTER (AT/0014-844X) [01357494] **86**

FARMERS' NEWSLETTER, LARGE AREA (AT/0467-5282) [01357603] **86**

FARMER'S WEEKLY (UK/0014-8474) [05138965] **86**

FARMERSVILLE HERALD (FARMERSVILLE, CALIF.) (US/1072-1827) [28877306] **5635**

FARMFUTURES (US/0091-1305) [01624516] **86**

FARMING BUSINESS *See* ENTERPRISE FARMING **82**

FARMING FACTS (CN/0835-6246) [16862139] **86**

FARMING FOR THE FUTURE (CN/0821-2724) [09387144] **86**

FARMING FORUM **CEASED.** (AT) [03067968] **86**

FARMING IN SOUTH AFRICA AND WOMAN AND HER HOME (SA) [01771971] **86**

FARMING JAPAN (JA) [08595660] **86**

FARMING NEWS (UK) **86**

FARMING NEWS LONDON. 1982 (UK/0265-1645) [I02651645] **86**

FARMING REVIEW (NAIROBI, KENYA) (KE) [12063080] **86**

FARMING SYSTEMS ANALYSIS PAPER (NE/0925-6563) [I09256563] **86**

FARMING SYSTEMS AND RESOURCE ECONOMICS IN THE TROPICS (GW/0932-6154) [I09326154] **1490, 2414**

FARMING SYSTEMS RESEARCH PAPER SERIES (US/0893-424X) [11123749] **86**

FARMING SYSTEMS SUPPORT PROJECT NEWSLETTER (US) [10387162] **86**

FARMING TODAY (NAIROBI, KENYA) (KE) [18511019] **86**

FARMING TODAY (WELLINGTON-WATERLOO-PERTH ED.) (CN/0838-8512) [18367757] **86**

FARMINGTON NEWS, THE (US) [26018446] **5645**

FARMINGTON OBSERVER (US/0888-6199) [13678124] **5692**

FARMLAND NEWS (US/0093-5832) [02629914] **86**

FARMLIFE (US/1056-3210) [23661226] **194**

FARMLINE **CEASED.** (US/0270-5672) [06214820] **86**

FARMSAFE (CN/0382-781X) [02843006] **86**

FARMVILLE HERALD (US) **5758**

FARMWEEK (BLOOMINGTON) (US/0197-6680) [06073866] **86**

FARMWEEK (EASTERN ED.) (US/0164-8640) [04309264] **86**

FARO DEL POETA : REVISTA TRIMESTRAL DE POESIA (SP) **3463**

FARO DEL SILENCIO (SP) **4388**

FARO (NEW WILMINGTON, PA.), IL **CEASED.** (US/0747-0126) [08857013] **5200**

FAROL (AG) [01327223] **4256**

FARR FOOTNOTES (US/0897-778X) [15720153] **2448**

FARSKA FAKTA OCH SORTERADE SIFFRUR (SW) [16569454] **5327**

FARUMASHIA (JA/0014-8601) [10286837] **4305**

FARUMASHIA REBYU (JA) [10314835] **4305**

FASB ACTION ALERT (US) [10869783] **744**

FASB DISCUSSION MEMORANDUM (US) [01864609] **744**

FASB EMERGING ISSUES TASK FORCE *See* EITF ABSTRACTS **743**

FASB INTERPRETATION (US/0193-7855) [03048223] **744**

FASB TECHNICAL BULLETIN (US/0886-4535) [05918022] **744**

FASCICLES OF FLORA OF INDIA (II) [08622813] **509**

FASCICULI ARCHAEOLOGIAE HISTORICAE (PL/0860-0007) [15934641] **268**

FASCICULI MATHEMATICI (PL/0044-4413) [08759219] **3505**

FASEB JOURNAL, THE (US/0892-6638) [15231392] **455**

FASHION (IT) **1084**

FASHION ACCESSORIES (HK/0255-7290) [14771702] **1084**

FASHION & CRAFTS (PALM COAST, FLA.) (US/1051-6921) [22092724] **373**

FASHION CALENDER (US) **1084**

FASHION FORECAST (UK) [04788112] **1084**

FASHION FORECAST INTERNATIONAL (UK/0952-701X) [I0952701X] **1084**

FASHION GALLERIA, THE **CEASED.** (US/0274-5100) [06370260] **1084**

FASHION GUIDE DUSSELDORF (GW/0942-8151) [I09428151] **5555, 1084**

FASHION IMAGES (CN/0228-829X) [08036638] **404, 1084**

FASHION INTERNATIONAL (US) **2914, 5350, 1084**

FASHION JEWELRY PLUS (US/1056-2559) [23603639] **2914**

FASHION KNITTING (US/8750-8869) [11885302] **5184**

FASHION NEWSLETTER (US/0300-7111) [01335345] **1084**

FASHION TEXTILES MODE (CN/0318-8701) [02443296] **5350**

FASHIONEWS (BURLINGAME, CALIF.) (US/0892-5216) [15217516] **1084**

FASLNAMAH-I HUNAR (IR) [12014148] **320**

FAST AND HEALTHY MAGAZINE (US/1078-0203) [30954925] **2597**

FAST (COMMUNITY LEADERS' ED.) (CN/1183-0484) [23686642] **5179**

FAST FERRY INTERNATIONAL (UK/0954-3988) [19453611] **593**

FAST FOLK MUSICAL MAGAZINE (US/8755-9137) [11406779] **4117**

FAST FOOD RESTAURANTS WAGE SURVEY. BELL COUNTY, TX *See* OCCUPATIONAL COMPENSATION SURVEY--PAY ONLY. BELL COUNTY, TX--FAST FOOD RESTAURANTS / U.S. DEPARTMENT OF LABOR, BUREAU OF LABOR STATISTICS **1697**

FAST FOOD RESTAURANTS WAGE SURVEY. DUVAL COUNTY, FL *See* OCCUPATIONAL COMPENSATION SURVEY--PAY ONLY. DUVAL COUNTY, FL--FAST FOOD RESTAURANTS / U.S. DEPARTMENT OF LABOR, BUREAU OF LABOR STATISTICS **1697**

FAST FOOD RESTAURANTS WAGE SURVEY. ESCAMBIA COUNTY, FL *See* OCCUPATIONAL COMPENSATION SURVEY--PAY ONLY. ESCAMBIA COUNTY, FL--FAST FOOD RESTAURANTS / U.S. DEPARTMENT OF LABOR, BUREAU OF LABOR STATISTICS **1697**

FAST FOOD RESTAURANTS WAGE SURVEY. HARDIN COUNTY, KY *See* OCCUPATIONAL COMPENSATION SURVEY--PAY ONLY. HARDIN COUNTY, KY--FAST FOOD RESTAURANTS / U.S. DEPARTMENT OF LABOR, BUREAU OF LABOR STATISTICS **1697**

FAST FOOD RESTAURANTS WAGE SURVEY. HARRISON COUNTY, MS *See* OCCUPATIONAL COMPENSATION SURVEY--PAY ONLY. HARRISON COUNTY, MS--FAST FOOD RESTAURANTS / U.S. DEPARTMENT OF LABOR, BUREAU OF LABOR STATISTICS **1697**

FAST FOOD RESTAURANTS WAGE SURVEY. ISLAND COUNTY, WA *See* OCCUPATIONAL COMPENSATION SURVEY--PAY ONLY. ISLAND COUNTY, WA--FAST FOOD RESTAURANTS / U.S. DEPARTMENT OF LABOR, BUREAU OF LABOR STATISTICS **1698**

FAST FOOD RESTAURANTS WAGE SURVEY. LAKE COUNTY, IL *See* OCCUPATIONAL COMPENSATION SURVEY--PAY ONLY. LAKE COUNTY, IL--FAST FOOD RESTAURANTS / U.S. DEPARTMENT OF LABOR, BUREAU OF LABOR STATISTICS **1698**

FAST FOOD RESTAURANTS WAGE SURVEY. LAUDERDALE COUNTY, MS *See* OCCUPATIONAL COMPENSATION SURVEY--PAY ONLY. LAUDERDALE COUNTY, MS--FAST FOOD RESTAURANTS / U.S. DEPARTMENT OF LABOR, BUREAU OF LABOR STATISTICS **1698**

FAST FOOD RESTAURANTS WAGE SURVEY. LEAVENWORTH COUNTY, KS *See* OCCUPATIONAL COMPENSATION SURVEY--PAY ONLY. LEAVENWORTH, KS--FAST FOOD RESTAURANTS / U.S. DEPARTMENT OF LABOR, BUREAU OF LABOR STATISTICS **1698**

FAST FOOD RESTAURANTS WAGE SURVEY. MONTGOMERY COUNTY, MD *See* OCCUPATIONAL COMPENSATION SURVEY--PAY ONLY. MONTGOMERY COUNTY, MD--FAST FOOD RESTAURANTS / U.S. DEPARTMENT OF LABOR, BUREAU OF LABOR STATISTICS **1698**

FAST FOOD RESTAURANTS WAGE SURVEY. NORFOLK, VA *See* OCCUPATIONAL COMPENSATION SURVEY--PAY ONLY. NORFOLK, VA--FAST FOOD RESTAURANTS / U.S. DEPARTMENT OF LABOR, BUREAU OF LABOR STATISTICS **1698**

FAST FOOD RESTAURANTS WAGE SURVEY. WASHINGTON, DC *See* OCCUPATIONAL COMPENSATION SURVEY--PAY ONLY. WASHINGTON, DC--FAST FOOD RESTAURANTS / U.S. DEPARTMENT OF LABOR, BUREAU OF LABOR STATISTICS **1699**

FAST FOURS & ROTARIES (AT/1033-7369) [I10337369] **5414**

FAST LANE (UK/0266-5182) [12492953] **2487**

FASTBACK (US/8756-6494) [10050110] **1746**

FASTENER TECHNOLOGY INTERNATIONAL (US/0746-2441) [09882028] **2114**

●FASTEST STREET CARS IN AMERICA (US/1072-8422) [29212359] **5414**

FASTFACTS EUROPEAN HOTEL LOCATOR (US/0192-1347) [04952920] **2805**

FASTFACTS HOTEL MOTEL LOCATOR, UNITED STATES & CANADA (US/0742-0722) [10249401] **2805**

FASTFACTS U.S.A. HOTEL MOTEL LOCATOR *See* FASTFACTS HOTEL MOTEL LOCATOR, UNITED STATES & CANADA **2805**

FASTI ARCHAEOLOGICI (IT) [01568954] **268**

FASTIE REPORT, THE **CEASED.** (US/1047-6202) [20765474] **1184**

FASZINATION MUSIK / ZDF (GW) [19659021] **4117**

FAT-BERICHTE (SZ/1018-502X) [I1018502X] **86**

FAT FENDERED STREET RODS **CEASED.** (US/1057-0330) [23914466] **5414**

FAT FREDDY'S COMICS & STORIES (US) [16519542] **4861**

FAT-SCHRIFTENREIHE (GW/0933-050X) [16167364] **5414**

FAT TUESDAY (US/0276-2072) [07322320] **5268**

FATABUREN (SW/0348-971X) [01568956] **236**

FATAL ACCIDENT REPORTING SYSTEM (US/0732-9792) [07211598] **5440**

FATAL ACCIDENT SUMMARY (VICTORIA) (CN/0226-0484) [06213484] **2862**

FATAL MOTOR VEHICLE ACCIDENT COMPARATIVE DATA REPORT (US/0737-6332) [09400907] **5440**

FATE (MARION) (US/0014-8776) [01780183] **4241**

FATEH (LE) [01568957] **5806**

FATH (KARACHI, PAKISTAN) (PK) [05725167] **2616**

FATHOM (NORFOLK) (US/0014-8822) [01568959] **4176**

FATIGUE & FRACTURE OF ENGINEERING MATERIALS & STRUCTURES (UK/8756-758X) [11658100] **2102**

FATIMA CRUSADER (CN/0713-0163) [08693653] **4958**

FATIPEC CONGRESS / ORGANISE PAR L'ASSOCIATION FRANCAISE DES TECHNICIENS DES PEINTURES ET VERNIS (A.F.T.P.V.) (GE/0430-2222) [08400330] **4224**

FATOS & I.I. FOTOS (BL) [06193291] **2551**

FATS AND OILS IN CANADA (CN/0014-8857) [02960476] **1606**

FATS AND OILS. PRODUCTION, CONSUMPTION, AND FACTORY AND WAREHOUSE STOCKS (ANNUAL) (US/0273-4397) [06935057] **1606**

FATTURATO, PRODOTTO LORDO, INVESTIMENTI DELLE IMPRESE INDUSTRIALI, DEL COMMERCIO, DEI TRASPORTI E COMUNICAZIONI E DI ALTRI TIPI DI SERVIZI (IT) [19892726] **5382**

FAULKNER & GRAY'S BANKRUPTCY LAW REVIEW **CEASED.** (US/1043-0547) [19288994] **2968**

●FAULKNER & GRAY'S ... EUROPEAN BUSINESS DIRECTORY (US/1055-2421) [23124549] **675**

FAULKNER & GRAY'S MEDICINE & HEALTH (US/1047-8892) [20752303] **3576**

FAULKNER APPLICATIONS SOFTWARE REPORTS (US) **1184**

FAULKNER CLIENT SERVER INFODISK (US) **1184**

FAULKNER COMMUNICATIONS INFODISK CD ROM (US) **1111**

FAULKNER COMPUTER AND COMMUNICATIONS LIBRARY (US) 1111, **1184**

FAULKNER DATAWORLD (US) **1184**

FAULKNER DATAWORLD INFODISC (US) **1184**

FAULKNER EDP LIBRARY (US) **1184**

FAULKNER ELECTRONIC OFFICE AUTOMATION (US) **1184**

FAULKNER ENTERPRISE NETWORKING (US) **1184**

FAULKNER FACTS AND FIDDLINGS (US/0430-1188) [02320687] **2733**

FAULKNER IMAGING SYSTEMS (US) **1184**

FAULKNER JOURNAL, THE (US/0884-2949) [11909870] **3387**

FAULKNER LOCAL AREA NETWORKING (US) **1184**

FAULKNER MANAGING DISTRIBUTED SYSTEMS (US) **1184**

FAULKNER MANAGING OPEN SYSTEMS (US) **1184**

FAULKNER MICROCOMPUTER AND SOFTWARE (US) **1184**

FAULKNER MICRODATA INFODISK (US) **1185**

FAULKNER MINICOMPUTER REPORTS (US) **1185**

FAULKNER NEWSLETTER AND YOKNAPATAWPHA REVIEW, THE (US/0733-6357) [07128528] 3342, **432**

FAULKNER SOFTWARE REPORTS (US) **1185**

FAULKNER STANDARD EDP REPORTS (US) **1185**

FAULKNER SYSTEMS SOFTWARE REPORTS (US) **1185**

FAULKNER TELECOMMUNICATIONS STRATEGIES (US) **1155**

FAULKNER TELECOMMUNICATIONS WORLD (US) **1155**

FAULT, THE (US/0146-5848) [02987281] **350**

FAUNA D'ITALIA (IT/0430-1226) [01421714] **5583**

FAUNA ENTOMOLOGICA SCANDINAVICA (DK/0106-8377) [01781879] **5608**

FAUNA NA BULGARIIA / BULGARSKA AKADEMIIA NA NAUKITE, INSTITUT PO ZOOLOGIIA (BU/0428-0636) [06133767] **5583**

FAUNA NORVEGICA. SER. A., NORWEGIAN FAUNA EXCEPT ENTOMOLOGY AND ORNITHOLOGY (NO/0332-768X) [07368776] **5583**

FAUNA NORVEGICA. SER. B (NO/0332-7698) [06161980] **5608**

FAUNA NORVEGICA. SER. C., CINCLUS (NO/0332-7701) [09934435] **5583**

FAUNA OCH FLORA (SW/0014-8903) [08652266] **509**

FAUNA OF NEW ZEALAND (NZ/0111-5383) [09926676] **5608**

FAUNA OF THE NATIONAL PARKS OF THE UNITED STATES : FAUNA SERIES (US) [01320385] **5583**

FAUNA (OSLO) (NO/0014-8881) [02278189] **5583**

FAUNA POLSKI (PL/0303-4909) [01449965] **5583**

FAUNA UKRAINY (UN) [01801695] **5583**

FAUNE DE L'EUROPE ET DU BASSIN MEDITERRANEEN (FR) [01568967] **5583**

FAUNE DE MADAGASCAR (FR/0428-0709) [02981081] **5583**

FAUNISTISCHE ABHANDLUNGEN (LEIPZIG) (GW/0375-2135) [04520676] **5608**

FAUQUIER TIMES-DEMOCRAT (US/1050-7655) [21588170] **5758**

FAUT LIRE, IL (CN/0709-6488) [05765450] **3210**

FAUX TITRE: ETUDES DE LANGUE ET LITTERATURE FRANCAISES PUBLIEES (NE/0167-9392) 3387, **3281**

FAVENTIA (SP) [07624297] 3281, **3387**

FAVONIUS SUPPLEMENTARY VOLUME (US/1047-0212) [18728861] **1076**

FAVORITE CROSSWORD PUZZLES (US/0195-0142) [05213119] **4861**

FAVORITE WESTERNS, SERIAL WORLD (US/0891-074X) [14562062] **4068**

FAWCETT'S FISHING JOURNAL (US/0362-6652) [02419479] **2301**

FAX & BUSINESS DIRECTORY (US/1052-2190) [22220947] **1111**

FAX BY TWIGG (CN/1184-7549) [24279934] **835**

FAX/NET, PUBLIC ACCESS FACSIMILE STATION DIRECTORY (US/0749-2715) [11085444] **1155**

●FAX-STAT ON DRUGS (US/1064-5055) [26319915] **4305**

FAXES OF THE WORLD (GW) 1155, **4211**

●FAXON BUSINESS INFORMATION CATALOG (US/1059-6844) [24679627] **675**

FAXON GUIDE TO CD-ROM (US/1053-6396) [22600974] **1185**

●FAXON GUIDE TO SERIALS (US/1059-6852) [24679647] **3210**

●FAXON HEALTH INFORMATION CATALOG (US/1059-6836) [24679597] **4775**

FAXON INTERNATIONAL NEWSLETTER (US/0740-347X) [09961061] **675**

FAXON ... LIBRARIANS' GUIDE TO CONTINUATIONS (US/0272-4537) [06840900] **3210**

FAXON ... LIBRARIANS' GUIDE TO SERIALS See FAXON GUIDE TO SERIALS **3210**

FAXON PLANNING REPORT, THE (US/1043-1187) [19318545] **3210**

FAXON REPORT, THE (US/1048-3403) [20921207] **3210**

FAYETTE ADVERTISER, THE (US/0746-9942) [10454566] **5703**

FAYETTE ANCESTORS SURNAME INDEX (US/0732-6661) [08371866] **2448**

FAYETTE CONNECTION, THE (US/0739-8093) [09779580] **2448**

FAYETTE COUNTY GENEALOGICAL SOCIETY (OHIO) See FAYETTE CONNECTION, THE **2448**

FAYETTE COUNTY NEWS, THE (US) [21964997] **5653**

FAYETTE COUNTY RECORD (LA GRANGE, TEX. : 1922) (US) [14209204] **5749**

FAYETTE FACTS (US/0737-1012) [05347942] **2448**

FAYETTE FALCON, THE (US) [19176500] **5745**

FAYETTE LEGAL JOURNAL (US/0196-4194) [01568974] **2968**

FAYETTE NEIGHBOR, THE (US/0192-0669) [04902058] **5653**

FAYETTE REVIEW, THE (US/1065-0083) [09771467] **5728**

FAYETTE TRIBUNE, THE (US) [12776047] **5763**

FAYETTEVILLE OBSERVER-TIMES, THE (US/1052-9829) [22441454] **5723**

FAZENDA DO ULTRAMAR (PO) [01788992] **4647**

●FBC (MADISON, ALA.) (US/1077-0291) [30681213] 1286, **1233**

FBI LAW ENFORCEMENT BULLETIN (US/0014-5688) [02557429] **3164**

FBI NEWS (US) [27637209] **4508**

FBIS REPORT. SOVIET UNION. BALTIC STATES AND REPUBLIC AFFAIRS (US) [24995895] **1132**

FBIS REPORT. SOVIET UNION. REPUBLIC AFFAIRS (US) [23987617] **1132**

FBM FERTIGUNGS-TECHNOLOGIE (GW/0934-7054) [20073405] **4001**

FBN (SPARTA, N.J.) (US/1059-2393) [24515876] **2335**

FBO See AIRPORT BUSINESS **637**

FBR AKTUELLT (SW/01791784) **3210**

FCC CALENDAR OF EVENTS FOR WEEK OF ... (US) [07298846] **1111**

FCC NEWS REPORT (US) **1111**

FCC RECORD (US/1057-5766) [14964165] **1155**

FCC RULES (US) **1155**

FCCAA STATISTICAL REPORTING SERVICE / MEN'S BASEBALL (US) 5327, **4894**

FCCSET COMMITTEE ON EDUCATION AND HUMAN RESOURCES See BY THE YEAR 2000: REPORT OF THE FCCSET COMMITTEE ON EDUCATION AND HUMAN RESOURCES **1729**

FCL NEWSLETTER (US/0532-7091) [05575262] 2968, **4647**

FCM FORUM (ENGLISH ED.) (CN/0381-1352) [23004050] **4647**

FCNL WASHINGTON NEWSLETTER (US) [02738969] **4647**

FCS SPECIAL REPORT (US) [02786323] 86, **1542**

FCTL. FOLIA CHIMICA THEORETICA LATINA (SP/0378-4843) [03740890] **1052**

FCX See FCX CAROLINA COOPERATOR **86**

FCX CAROLINA COOPERATOR (US/0195-3346) [05425649] 1542, **86**

FDA CONSUMER (US/0362-1332) [01685864] **4647**

FDA DRUG AND DEVICE PRODUCT APPROVALS / CENTER FOR DRUGS AND BIOLOGICS, CENTER FOR DEVICES AND RADIOLOGICAL HEALTH, CENTER FOR VETERINARY MEDICINE (US) [18329524] **4305**

FDA DRUG AND DEVICE PRODUCT APPROVALS LIST / (U.S.) FOOD AND DRUG ADMINISTRATION (US) [15812122] 3576, **4305**

FDA ENFORCEMENT REPORT (US/1057-9397) [03131334] 4775, **1344**

FDA FREEDOM OF INFORMATION LOG (US/0161-7044) [04010454] **4647**

FDA MEDICAL BULLETIN (US/1063-8067) [23209869] **4305**

●FDA NEWS (US/1069-5109) [28081545] 4305, **2335**

FDA QUARTERLY ACTIVITIES REPORT (US/0145-126X) [02663461] **4647**

FDA VETERINARIAN (US/1057-6223) [15040069] **5510**

FDC REPORTS. HEALTH NEWS DAILY (US/1042-2781) [18994932] **4775**

FDC REPORTS. PRESCRIPTION AND OTC PHARMACEUTICALS (US/0734-6514) [08673691] **4305**

FDC REPORTS. PRESCRIPTION AND OTC PHARMACEUTICALS. MID-WEEK REPORT CEASED. (US/0734-6506) [08673617] **4305**

FDC REPORTS. TOILETRIES, FRAGRANCES AND SKIN CARE (US/0279-1110) [07000555] **404**

FDDI NEWS (US/1051-1903) [21887558] **1111**

FDGB REVIEW CEASED. (GW/0323-7028) [05853876] **1669**

FDI NEWS See DENTAL WORLD / FDI **1322**

●FDI WORLD (UK) [30637967] **1323**

FDIC ENFORCEMENT DECISIONS (US) [18887234] **3086**

FDIC WATCH See AMERICAN BANKER'S WASHINGTON WATCH **769**

FDL (IT) [03547211] **320**

FDM, FURNITURE DESIGN & MANUFACTURING (US/0192-8058) [01570331] **634**

FE Y VIDA (US/0745-8215) [09492565] **5060**

FEASTS & SEASONS (US/0197-5137) [06061123] **3387**

FEAT MAGAZINE, THE (US/0732-8044) [08456112] **2230**

FEATHER FANCIER (CN/0380-352X) [02009509] **211**

FEATURE - CANADIAN UNIVERSITY PRESS (CN/0381-842X) [02604382] **1823**

FEATURE FILMS : A DIRECTORY OF FEATURE FILMS ON 16MM AND VIDEOTAPE AVAILABLE FOR RENTAL, SALE, AND LEASE CEASED. (US) [12047698] **4068**

FEATURE NEWS PUBLICITY OUTLETS (US/1054-4240) [20366484] **5736**

FEATURED FILL-IT-INS (US/0194-3170) [05430245] **4861**

FEATURES AND NEWS FROM BEHIND THE IRON CURTAIN (UK) [02079988] **2516**

FEBS LETTERS (NE/0014-5793) [01569056] **487**

FEBS SYMPOSIUM (GW) [03639537] **487**

FED IN PRINT: ECONOMICS AND BANKING TOPICS (US) [23291108] **729**

FED LETTER, THE (US/0363-9371) [02548452] **4702**

FEDDES REPERTORIUM (GW/0014-8962) [02251371] **509**

FEDERACION ARGENTINA DE COLEGIOS DE ABOGADOS See REVISTA - FEDERACION ARGENTINA DE COLEGIOS DE ABOGADOS **3042**

FEDERACION ARGENTINA DE PERIODISTAS See GACETA **2920**

FEDERAL ACQUISITION REPORT (US/8755-9285) [11464579] **4647**

FEDERAL ADP AND TELECOMMUNICATIONS STANDARDS INDEX (US/1057-5804) [23024611] 1155, **1185**

●FEDERAL ADVISORY DIRECTORY (US/1074-2727) [29647528] **4647**

FEDERAL AID IN SPORT FISH AND WILDLIFE RESTORATION PROGRAMS (US) [26118274] **2193**

FEDERAL AID IN SPORT FISH RESTORATION PROGRAM : PROJECT REPORTS (US) [30088188] **2193**

FEDERAL AID IN WILDLIFE RESTORATION PROGRAM : PROJECT REPORTS (US) [31001705] **2193**

FEDERAL

Alphabetical Title Index

FEDERAL AID PAID TO NEW YORK STATE SCHOOL DISTRICTS (US/0095-3709) [03149485] **1864**

FEDERAL AID PLANNER (US/0363-5899) [02251372] **1864**

FEDERAL AID TO ILLINOIS STATE AGENCIES (US) [05589817] **4723**

●FEDERAL AND ONTARIO INSOLVENCY LEGISLATION (CN/1195-3144) [29592999] **3100**

FEDERAL & STATE INSURANCE WEEK (US) [17012153] **2880**

FEDERAL AND STATE JUDICIAL CLERKSHIP DIRECTORY (US/0882-5041) [11858004] **2968**

FEDERAL AQUISITION REGULATIONS / DISKETTE (US) **4647**

FEDERAL ASSISTANCE MONITOR (US/1050-3242) [17285206] **1490**

FEDERAL AVIATION REGULATIONS *CEASED.* (US) [17832512] **19**

FEDERAL AVIATION REGULATIONS & AIRMAN'S INFORMATION MANUAL : BASIC REFERENCE BOOK (US/0092-3532) [01784471] **19**

FEDERAL AVIATION REGULATIONS. N.PART 39, P. AIRWORTHINESS DIRECTIVES (US/0276-1785) [04021147] **19**

FEDERAL AVIATION REGULATIONS. PART 1. DEFINITIONS AND ABBREVIATIONS (US) [02777745] **19**

FEDERAL AVIATION REGULATIONS. PART 11. GENERAL RULE-MAKING PROCEDURES (US) [02923217] **19**

FEDERAL AVIATION REGULATIONS. PART 13. ENFORCEMENT PROCEDURES (US) [02923146] **19**

FEDERAL AVIATION REGULATIONS. PART 21. CERTIFICATION PROCEDURES FOR PRODUCTS AND PARTS (US) [02786170] **19**

FEDERAL AVIATION REGULATIONS. PART 23. AIRWORTHINESS STANDARDS, NORMAL, UTILITY, AND ACROBATIC CATEGORY AIRPLANES (US) [02786013] **19**

FEDERAL AVIATION REGULATIONS. PART 25. AIRWORTHINESS STANDARDS, TRANSPORT CATEGORY AIRPLANES (US) [02786205] **19**

FEDERAL AVIATION REGULATIONS. PART 27. AIRWORTHINESS STANDARDS, NORMAL CATEGORY ROTORCRAFT (US) [02921959] **19**

FEDERAL AVIATION REGULATIONS. PART 29. AIRWORTHINESS STANDARDS, TRANSPORT CATEGORY ROTORCRAFT (US) [02923072] **19**

FEDERAL AVIATION REGULATIONS. PART 31. AIRWORTHINESS STANDARDS, MANNED FREE BALLOONS (US) [02922914] **19**

FEDERAL AVIATION REGULATIONS. PART 33. AIRWORTHINESS STANDARDS, AIRCRAFT ENGINES (US) [02786573] **19**

FEDERAL AVIATION REGULATIONS. PART 36. NOISE STANDARDS, AIRCRAFT TYPE AND AIRWORTHINESS CERTIFICATION (US) [02785934] **19**

FEDERAL AVIATION REGULATIONS. PART 37. TECHNICAL STANDARD ORDER AUTHORIZATION (US) [02785923] **19**

FEDERAL AVIATION REGULATIONS. PART 61. CERTIFICATION, PILOTS AND FLIGHT INSTRUCTORS (US) [03289113] **19**

FEDERAL AVIATION REGULATIONS. PART 63. CERTIFICATION, FLIGHT CREWMEMBERS OTHER THAN PILOTS (US) [02777779] **19**

FEDERAL AVIATION REGULATIONS. PART 67. MEDICAL STANDARDS AND CERTIFICATION (US) [02921835] **20**

FEDERAL AVIATION REGULATIONS. PART 91. GENERAL OPERATING AND FLIGHT RULES (US) [02785970] **20**

FEDERAL AVIATION REGULATIONS. PART 93. GENERAL AIR TRAFFIC RULES AND AIRPORT TRAFFIC PATTERNS (US) [02785955] **20**

FEDERAL AVIATION REGULATIONS. PART 107. AIRPORT SECURITY (US) [02921777] **20**

FEDERAL AVIATION REGULATIONS. PART 109. INDIRECT AIR CARRIER SECURITY (US) [06310589] **20**

FEDERAL AVIATION REGULATIONS. PART 121. CERTIFICATION AND OPERATIONS : DOMESTIC, FLAG, AND SUPPLEMENTAL AIR CARRIERS AND COMMERCIAL OPERATION UNITED STATES. FEDERAL AVIATION ADMINISTRATION (US) [04173238] **20**

FEDERAL AVIATION REGULATIONS. PART 123. CERTIFICATION AND OPERATIONS, AIR TRAVEL CLUBS USING LARGE AIRPLANES (US) [02786145] **20**

FEDERAL AVIATION REGULATIONS. PART 127. CERTIFICATION AND OPERATIONS OF SCHEDULED AIR CARRIERS AND HELICOPTERS (US) [03288889] **20**

FEDERAL AVIATION REGULATIONS. PART 129. OPERATIONS OF FOREIGN AIR CARRIERS (US) [02921708] **20**

FEDERAL AVIATION REGULATIONS. PART 133. ROTORCRAFT EXTERNAL-LOAD OPERATIONS (US) [02921657] **20**

FEDERAL AVIATION REGULATIONS. PART 135. AIR TAXI OPERATORS AND COMMERCIAL OPERATORS OF SMALL AIRCRAFT (US) [02921609] **20**

FEDERAL AVIATION REGULATIONS. PART 137. AGRICULTURAL AIRCRAFT OPERATIONS (US) [03802909] **20**

FEDERAL AVIATION REGULATIONS. PART 139. CERTIFICATION AND OPERATIONS, LAND AIRPORTS SERVING CAB-CERTIFICATED SCHEDULED AIR CARRIERS (US) [02786537] **20**

FEDERAL AVIATION REGULATIONS. PART 145. REPAIR STATIONS (US) [02921561] **20**

FEDERAL AVIATION REGULATIONS. PART 147. AVIATION MAINTENANCE TECHNICIAN SCHOOLS (US) [03137032] **20**

FEDERAL AVIATION REGULATIONS. PART 152. AIRPORT AID PROGRAM (US) [03285486] **20**

FEDERAL AVIATION REGULATIONS. PART 159. NATIONAL CAPITAL AIRPORTS (US) [03136976] **20**

FEDERAL AVIATION REGULATIONS. PART 183. REPRESENTATIVES OF THE ADMINISTRATOR (US) [02921478] **20**

FEDERAL AVIATION REGULATIONS. PART 191. WITHHOLDING SECURITY INFORMATION FROM DISCLOSURE UNDER THE AIR TRANSPORTATION SECURITY ACT OF 1974 (US) [03137142] **20**

FEDERAL BAR COUNCIL *See* SECOND CIRCUIT REDBOOK **3143**

FEDERAL BAR COUNCIL NEWS (US/1075-8534) [29948864] **2969**

FEDERAL BAR NEWS & JOURNAL (US/0279-4691) [07905080] **2969**

FEDERAL BENEFITS FOR VETERANS AND DEPENDENTS (US/0883-3370) [06433912] **4044**

FEDERAL BUDGET AND THE CITIES - UNITED STATES CONFERENCE OF MAYORS, THE (US) [06433458] 4723, **4647**

FEDERAL BUDGET; FOCUS AND PERSPECTIVES, THE (US/0363-5422) [02486549] **4723**

FEDERAL CAPITAL IMPROVEMENTS PROGRAM FOR THE NATIONAL CAPITAL REGION (US/0275-6404) [06419177] **898**

FEDERAL CARRIERS CASES (CHICAGO) *CEASED.* (US/0093-2108) [01564321] **2969**

FEDERAL CIRCUIT BAR JOURNAL, THE (US/1055-8195) [23351803] **2969**

FEDERAL CIRCUIT COURT RULES (US) **3140**

FEDERAL CIVIL RIGHTS ENFORCEMENT BUDGET, THE (US/0734-2454) [08695863] 4723, **4508**

FEDERAL CIVIL SERVICE, HISTORY, ORGANIZATION AND ACTIVITIES / OFFICE OF PERSONNEL MANAGEMENT, LIBRARY, THE (US) [06582629] **4647**

FEDERAL CIVILIAN WORK FORCE STATISTICS (US/0163-8270) [03812462] 1669, **1532**

●FEDERAL CLAIMS REPORTER (US/1067-4934) [27128486] **2969**

FEDERAL COAL MANAGEMENT REPORT (US/0192-3862) [04860198] **2139**

FEDERAL COMMUNICATIONS BAR ASSOCIATION *See* DIRECTORY - FEDERAL COMMUNICATIONS BAR ASSOCIATION **2961**

FEDERAL COMMUNICATIONS COMMISSION RULES AND REGULATIONS.--INDIVIDUAL PARTS (US) 1111, **2969**

FEDERAL COMMUNICATIONS LAW JOURNAL (US/0163-7606) [04099879] 1111, **2969**

FEDERAL COMPUTER MARKET REPORT (US/1042-721X) [12048849] 1264, 4647, **1237**

FEDERAL COMPUTER WEEK (US/0893-052X) [15336806] 4647, **1247**

FEDERAL CONTRACT COMPLIANCE MANUAL (US) [05918266] **1669**

FEDERAL CONTRACT DISPUTES (US/0747-9700) [10861199] **2969**

FEDERAL CONTRACTS REPORT (US/0014-9063) [02052285] **2969**

FEDERAL CORPORATE TAX RETURN, THE (CN/0713-7257) [09026026] **4723**

●FEDERAL COURT APPOINTMENTS REPORT (US/1059-6828) [24688354] **2969**

FEDERAL COURT CLERKS' NEWS, THE (US/0428-111X) [04263940] **2969**

FEDERAL COURT MANAGEMENT STATISTICS (US/0741-692X) [10077554] 2969, **3080**

FEDERAL COURT OF APPEAL DECISIONS (CN/0227-0390) [08996121] **2969**

FEDERAL COURT OF CANADA SERVICE (UK) **2969**

FEDERAL COURT PROCUREMENT DECISIONS (US/0734-9513) [08835576] **2969**

FEDERAL COURT REPORTER (AT/0728-6082) [107286082] 3093, **2969**

FEDERAL COURT REPORTS, THE (AT) [11921091] **2969**

FEDERAL DATA BASE FINDER, THE *SUSPENDED.* (US/0897-4810) [10995417] **1254**

FEDERAL DATA REPORT (US/1048-4051) [20943650] **4647**

FEDERAL DIRECTORY, THE (US/0360-3512) [02244106] **4648**

FEDERAL DISASTER ASSISTANCE PROGRAM, INSURANCE HANDBOOK FOR PUBLIC ASSISTANCE (US) [02927638] **2880**

FEDERAL DOCUMENT DEPOSITORIES AND RESOURCE INFORMATION FOR FLORIDA AND THE CARIBBEAN : A DIRECTORY (US) [24619915] **3210**

●FEDERAL EEO UPDATE (US/1065-9943) [26823713] **2969**

FEDERAL EMPLOYEE, THE (US/0014-9071) [01332315] **4702**

FEDERAL EMPLOYEES ALMANAC (US/0071-4127) [01303909] **4702**

FEDERAL EMPLOYEES NEWS DIGEST (US/1065-0970) [24609769] **4702**

FEDERAL ENVIRONMENTAL REGULATIONS (UK) **2193**

●FEDERAL EQUAL OPPORTUNITY ... DESK BOOK (US/1066-8764) [26707608] **4702**

FEDERAL EQUAL OPPORTUNITY RECRUITMENT PROGRAM (FEORP), REPORT TO CONGRESS (US) [27924980] **4702**

FEDERAL EQUAL OPPORTUNITY REPORTER (US/1043-7274) [19534722] **1669**

FEDERAL EQUAL OPPORTUNITY REPORTER (US) [15193984] **3148**

FEDERAL EXCISE TAX REPORTS (US/0414-0141) [01564324] **4723**

FEDERAL EXECUTIVE DIRECTORY (US/0270-563X) [06192813] **4648**

●FEDERAL EXECUTIVE DIRECTORY ANNUAL (US/1056-7275) [23826225] **4648**

FEDERAL EXPENDITURE BY STATE FOR FISCAL YEAR (US/0737-7444) [09270874] **1561**

FEDERAL FACILITIES ENVIRONMENTAL JOURNAL (US/1048-4078) [20943851] **3112**

FEDERAL FAST FINDER (US/0278-4580) [05578884] **4648**

FEDERAL FIFTH CIRCUIT CITATIONS (US) **2969**

FEDERAL FINANCIAL INSTITUTIONS EXAMINATION COUNCIL (U.S.) *See* ANNUAL REPORT / FEDERAL FINANCIAL INSTITUTIONS EXAMINATION COUNCIL (U.S.) **771**

FEDERAL FINANCIAL MANAGEMENT DIRECTORY (US/0092-0126) [01787395] **4723**

FEDERAL FINANCIAL REGULATORY DIGEST (US/0730-5028) [07995617] **2969**

FEDERAL FORECAST FOR ENGINEERS (US) [05153109] **1975**

FEDERAL FUNDS FOR RESEARCH AND DEVELOPMENT (US/0198-8700) [05802765] **5104**

FEDERAL GOVERNMENT FINANCE (CN/0575-8521) [01785284] **4723**

FEDERAL GOVERNMENT, THE (AT/0815-032X) [15175665] **2669**

FEDERAL GRANT-IN-AID ACTIVITY IN FLORIDA : A SUMMARY REPORT (US/0361-1582) [02240668] **4723**

FEDERAL GRANT-IN-AID PROGRAMS (PHOENIX) (US/0093-8300) [02243042] **4723**

FEDERAL GRANTS & CONTRACTS WEEKLY (US/0194-2247) [04510678] **1746**

FEDERAL GRANTS MANAGEMENT HANDBOOK (US/0195-2617) [05182859] **4723**

FEDERAL HEALTH MONITOR, THE (US) [18494086] **2969**

FEDERAL HOME LOAN BANK OF INDIANAPOLIS. ECONOMICS DEPT *See* BULLETIN - [ECONOMICS DEPARTMENT, FEDERAL HOME LOAN BANK OF INDIANAPOLIS] **781**

Alphabetical Title Index — FEDERAL

FEDERAL HOME LOAN MORTGAGE CORPORATION *See* REPORT OF THE FEDERAL HOME LOAN MORTGAGE CORPORATION **808**

FEDERAL HOSPITAL PHONE BOOK (US) 4702, **3914**

FEDERAL INCENTIVES TO INDUSTRY (CN) [06958196] **1606**

FEDERAL INCOME, GIFT, AND ESTATE TAXATION, BY JACOB RABKIN AND MARK H. JOHNSON (US) [04536931] **4723**

FEDERAL INCOME TAX (ENGLEWOOD CLIFFS), THE (US/0195-4768) [05434776] **4723**

FEDERAL INCOME TAX GUIDE (US/0196-1349) [04558838] **4723**

FEDERAL INCOME TAX PROCEDURES (US/0278-1875) [07669108] **4724**

FEDERAL INCOME TAX REGULATIONS (1986) (US/1043-7371) [19498710] **4724**

FEDERAL INCOME TAX (RESTON, VA.) (US/0191-2364) [04814118] **4724**

FEDERAL INCOME TAXATION (US/1071-0825) [22202869] **4724**

FEDERAL INCOME TAXATION OF CORPORATIONS AND SHAREHOLDERS; FORMS (US) [02313017] **4724**

FEDERAL INCOME TAXATION OF CORPORATIONS. SUPPLEMENT (US) [02844912] **4724**

FEDERAL INCOME TAXATION OF DEBT INSTRUMENTS (US) **4724**

FEDERAL INCOME TAXATION OF REAL ESTATE. SUPPLEMENTS (US) [04224131] **4837**

FEDERAL INDEX (1985) *CEASED.* (US/1046-3631) [14284170] **2969**

FEDERAL INDUSTRIAL LAWS SERVICE (UK) **2969**

FEDERAL INFORMATION DISCLOSURE (US) [06128143] **4648**

FEDERAL INFORMATION PROCESSING STANDARDS PUBLICATION (US/0083-1816) [01597446] **4648**

FEDERAL INFORMATION RESOURCES MANAGEMENT REGULATION AND BULLETINS THROUGH TRANSMITTAL CIRCULAR (US/1068-7386) [24516350] **4648**

FEDERAL JOBS DIGEST (US/0739-1684) [08279277] **4204**

FEDERAL JUDICIAL CENTER *See* ANNUAL REPORT / FEDERAL JUDICIAL CENTER **2934**

FEDERAL JUDICIAL CENTER *See* MANUAL FOR COMPLEX AND MULTIDISTRICT LITIGATION **3006**

FEDERAL JUDICIAL WORKLOAD STATISTICS (US/0192-625X) [04720999] 2969, **3080**

FEDERAL LABOR AND EMPLOYEE RELATIONS UPDATE (US) 940, **1669**

FEDERAL LABOR LAWS (US) [02785911] **3148**

FEDERAL LABOR-MANAGEMENT AND EMPLOYEE RELATIONS CONSULTANT, THE (US/0885-3061) [11061386] **1669**

●FEDERAL LABOR RELATIONS ... DESK BOOK (US/1065-8238) [26787173] **1669**

FEDERAL LABOR RELATIONS REPORTER (US/0199-4883) [05933973] **1669**

FEDERAL LABOR RELATIONS UPDATE (US/0898-2821) [17778710] 4648, **1669**

●FEDERAL LABORATORY CONSORTIUM HANDBOOK SERIES (US/1065-6375) [26659143] **5104**

FEDERAL LANDS (US/0731-7190) [07486824] **1944**

FEDERAL LAW ENFORCEMENT TRAINING CENTER *See* ANNUAL REPORT - FEDERAL ENFORCEMENT TRAINING CENTER **3157**

FEDERAL LAW JOURNAL (OVIEDO) (US/0273-3641) [05083468] **2969**

FEDERAL LAW REPORTS (AUSTRALIA), THE (AT) [01569001] **2969**

FEDERAL LAW REVIEW (AT/0067-205X) [01299291] **2969**

FEDERAL LITIGATOR (US/0886-621X) [12871324] **3089**

●FEDERAL LOBBYISTS, THE (CN/1193-2821) [26715043] **4474**

FEDERAL LOCAL COURT RULES (US/0745-2306) [06810649] **3089**

FEDERAL MANAGER'S EDGE, THE (US/1065-0032) [26492003] **868**

FEDERAL MANAGERS GUIDE TO DISCIPLINE (US) **868**

FEDERAL MANAGERS GUIDE TO PREVENTING SEXUAL HARASSMENT (US) **868**

FEDERAL MANAGERS GUIDE TO TQM (US) **868**

FEDERAL MANAGERS QUARTERLY (US/0893-8415) [14064311] **868**

FEDERAL MANAGERS SURVIVAL GUIDE (US) **868**

FEDERAL MARITIME COMMISSION DIGEST SERVICE (US) **3181**

FEDERAL MARKETING HANDBOOK AND YEARBOOK, THE (US/1044-4467) [19796760] **924**

FEDERAL MEDICAL CENTERS, HOSPITALS, AND MEDICAL CLINICS WITH REPORTED MORBIDITY DATA (US/0192-2211) [04960361] 4044, **3780**

FEDERAL MERIT SYSTEMS DESK BOOK (US) **2969**

FEDERAL MERIT SYSTEMS REPORTER (US/0746-035X) [12047606] **4702**

FEDERAL MILK ORDER MARKET STATISTICS (US/0501-4670) [02244484] 195, **153**

FEDERAL MOTOR VEHICLE FLEET REPORT FOR THE FISCAL YEAR ENDING ... (US/0093-0180) [05300833] 4648, **5382**

FEDERAL MOTOR VEHICLE SAFETY STANDARDS AND REGULATIONS (US/0364-6858) [01623763] 4775, **5382**

FEDERAL MOTOR VEHICLE SAFETY STANDARDS AND REGULATIONS (US/0364-6858) [01827637] 5414, **4648**

FEDERAL OCEAN PROGRAM : THE ANNUAL REPORT OF THE PRESIDENT TO THE CONGRESS ON THE NATION'S EFFORTS TO COMPREHEND, CONSERVE, AND USE THE SEA, THE (US) [01137219] **1449**

FEDERAL-ONTARIO AEROMAGNETIC SURVEY MAPS (CN) [01761280] **1375**

FEDERAL ORGANIZATION SERVICE (US/0741-5109) [09837594] **4648**

FEDERAL OUTLAYS IN TERRITORIES AND OTHER AREAS ADMINISTERED BY THE U.S (US) [01986747] **1490**

FEDERAL PARKS AND RECREATION (US) [09673433] **4706**

FEDERAL PARKS & RECREATION (US/0740-3690) [09953301] **4850**

FEDERAL PAY AND BENEFITS REPORTER (US/0888-269X) [13141833] 2969, **4702**

FEDERAL PERSONNEL GUIDE (US/0163-7665) [04922981] **4702**

FEDERAL PERSONNEL INDEX (US) **4702**

FEDERAL PERSONNEL MANUAL (US) [02784567] **4702**

FEDERAL PERSONNEL MANUAL SYSTEM. FPM SUPPLEMENT 271-1. DEVELOPMENT OF QUALIFICATION STANDARDS (US) [02782382] **4702**

FEDERAL PERSONNEL MANUAL SYSTEM. FPM SUPPLEMENT 271-2. TESTS AND OTHER APPLICANT APPRAISAL PROCEDURES (US) [02783003] **4702**

FEDERAL PERSONNEL MANUAL SYSTEM. FPM SUPPLEMENT 293-31. BASIC PERSONNEL RECORDS AND FILES SYSTEM (US) [02782974] **4702**

FEDERAL PERSONNEL MANUAL SYSTEM. FPM SUPPLEMENT 305-1. EMPLOYMENT UNDER THE EXECUTIVE ASSIGNMENT SYSTEM (US) [02782876] **4703**

FEDERAL PERSONNEL MANUAL SYSTEM. FPM SUPPLEMENT 330-1. EXAMINING PRACTICES (US) [02783019] **4703**

FEDERAL PERSONNEL MANUAL SYSTEM. FPM SUPPLEMENT 339-31. REVIEWING AND ACTING ON MEDICAL INFORMATION (US) [02782946] **4703**

FEDERAL PERSONNEL MANUAL SYSTEM. FPM SUPPLEMENT 512-1. JOB GRADING SYSTEM FOR TRADES AND LABOR OCCUPATIONS (US) [02783050] **4703**

FEDERAL PERSONNEL MANUAL SYSTEM. FPM SUPPLEMENT 532-1. FEDERAL WAGE SYSTEM (US) [02782960] **4703**

FEDERAL PERSONNEL MANUAL SYSTEM. FPM SUPPLEMENT 532-2. FEDERAL WAGE SYSTEM, NON-APPROPRIATED EMPLOYEES (US) [02783058] **4703**

FEDERAL PERSONNEL MANUAL SYSTEM. FPM SUPPLEMENT 711-1. LABOR-MANAGEMENT RELATIONS PROGRAMS PROVISIONS AND TECHNICAL GUIDE (US) [02783060] **4703**

FEDERAL PERSONNEL MANUAL SYSTEM. FPM SUPPLEMENT 711-2. LABOR-MANAGEMENT CASE FINDER (US) [02783031] **4703**

FEDERAL PERSONNEL MANUAL SYSTEM. FPM SUPPLEMENT 731-1. DETERMINING SUITABILITY FOR FEDERAL EMPLOYMENT (US) [02786990] **4703**

FEDERAL PERSONNEL MANUAL SYSTEM. FPM SUPPLEMENT 752-1. ADVERSE ACTIONS BY AGENCIES (US) [02782364] **4703**

FEDERAL PERSONNEL MANUAL SYSTEM. FPM SUPPLEMENT 792-1. OCCUPATIONAL HEALTH SERVICES FOR FEDERAL CIVILIAN EMPLOYEES (US) [02782402] 3576, **4703**

FEDERAL PERSONNEL MANUAL SYSTEM. FPM SUPPLEMENT 831-1. RETIREMENT (US) [02784316] **4703**

FEDERAL PERSONNEL MANUAL SYSTEM. FPM SUPPLEMENT 870-1. LIFE INSURANCE (US) [02782337] 2880, **4703**

FEDERAL PERSONNEL MANUAL SYSTEM. FPM SUPPLEMENT 890-1. FEDERAL EMPLOYEES HEALTH BENEFITS (US) [02782852] **4703**

FEDERAL PERSONNEL MANUAL SYSTEM. FPM SUPPLEMENT 910-1. NATIONAL EMERGENCY READINESS OF FEDERAL PERSONNEL MANAGEMENT (US) [02782923] **4703**

FEDERAL PERSONNEL MANUAL SYSTEM. FPM SUPPLEMENT 990-1. CIVIL SERVICE LAWS, EXECUTIVE ORDERS, RULES AND REGULATIONS (US) [02784392] **4703**

FEDERAL PERSONNEL MANUAL SYSTEM. FPM SUPPLEMENT 990-2. HOURS OF DUTY, PAY, AND LEAVE, ANNOTATED (US) [02782394] **4703**

FEDERAL PERSONNEL MANUAL SYSTEM. FPM SUPPLEMENT 990-3. NATIONAL EMERGENCY STANDBY REGULATIONS (PERSONNEL AND MANPOWER) (US) [02782888] **4703**

FEDERAL PHARMACIST (US/0428-1179) [01377492] **4305**

FEDERAL PLAN FOR METEOROLOGICAL SERVICES AND SUPPORTING RESEARCH / U.S. DEPARTMENT OF COMMERCE, NATIONAL OCEANIC AND ATMOSPHERIC ADMINISTRATION, THE (US/0565-9248) [01788588] **1425**

FEDERAL POET, THE (US/1041-4886) [18597303] **3463**

FEDERAL POWER COMMISSION NEWS RELEASE. MONTHLY FUEL COST AND QUALITY INFORMATION, FPC ISSUES REPORT ON FUEL COST (US) [03458279] **4256**

FEDERAL PRISONS JOURNAL (US) [21258082] **3164**

FEDERAL PROBATION (US/0014-9128) [02062391] **3164**

FEDERAL PROCUREMENT DATA SYSTEM. STANDARD REPORT / PREPARED BY FEDERAL PROCUREMENT DATA CENTER (US) [09866277] **4648**

FEDERAL PROCUREMENT REGULATIONS (US) [02786091] **4648**

FEDERAL PRODUCTIVITY MEASUREMENT (US/0278-0488) [07506906] **4648**

FEDERAL PROGRAM EXPENDITURES FOR MARYLAND PUBLIC SCHOOLS (US) [12741945] 4648, **1746**

FEDERAL PROPERTY MANAGEMENT REGULATIONS / DISKETTE (US) **4648**

FEDERAL-PROVINCIAL ENVIRONMENTAL ASSESSMENT REVIEW PANEL, HALIFAX-DARTMOUTH METROPOLITAN WASTEWATER MANAGEMENT SYSTEM (CANADA) *See* NEWS / FEDERAL-PROVINCIAL ENVIRONMENTAL ASSESSMENT REVIEW PANEL, HALIFAX-DARTMOUTH METROLITAN WASTEWATER MANAGEMENT SYSTEM **2237**

FEDERAL-PROVINCIAL PROGRAMS AND ACTIVITIES, A DESCRIPTIVE INVENTORY (CN/0848-5607) [23247973] **4648**

●FEDERAL QUALITY NEWS (US) [25937274] **4648**

FEDERAL RAILROAD ADMINISTRATION SPRING PREVIEW (US) [04792786] **5431**

FEDERAL REAL AND PERSONAL PROPERTY INVENTORY REPORT (CIVILIAN AND MILITARY) OF THE UNITED STATES GOVERNMENT COVERING ITS PROPERTIES LOCATED IN THE UNITED STATES, IN THE TERRITORIES, AND OVERSEAS (US/0498-9791) [01280884] **4648**

FEDERAL RECREATION FEE REPORT (US/0736-8364) [08576391] 4648, **4850**

FEDERAL RECREATION FEE REPORT TO CONGRESS : INCLUDING FEDERAL RECREATION VISITATION AND FEE DATA WITH STATE PARK INFORMATION SUPPLEMENT (US) [27478745] 2193, **4850**

FEDERAL REGIONAL EXECUTIVE DIRECTORY (US/0742-1729) [10270932] **4648**

●FEDERAL REGIONAL YELLOW BOOK (US/1061-3153) [25249756] 4648, **1925**

FEDERAL REGISTER (US/0097-6326) [01768512] 4648, **2969**

FEDERAL REGISTER (US/0364-1406) [02505035] **2970**

FEDERAL REGISTER DIGEST SERVICE (US/0734-7308) [08795058] **1746**

FEDERAL — Alphabetical Title Index

FEDERAL REGISTER HIGHLIGHTS NEWSLETTER (US) **2970**

FEDERAL REGISTER MONITOR, THE (US/1066-5862) [27002591] **2970**

FEDERAL REGISTER REPRINT FOR HAZARDOUS MATERIALS AND WASTE REGULATION (US) **2230**

FEDERAL REGISTER [MICROFORM] (US/0097-6326) [07940596] **2970**

FEDERAL REGULATION OF EMPLOYMENT NEWSLETTER (US/0746-5653) [09269645] **3148**

FEDERAL REGULATIONS AND THE EMPLOYMENT PRACTICES OF COLLEGES AND UNIVERSITIES (US) [02256563] 1823, **1669**

FEDERAL REGULATORY DIRECTORY (US/0195-749X) [05250786] **4648**

●FEDERAL REGULATORY PLAN (CN/0833-7322) [26497970] **4648**

FEDERAL REGULATORY PROCESS : AGENCY PRACTICES & PROCEDURES (US) [09663418] **2970**

FEDERAL RESEARCH REPORT (US/0148-4109) [03320918] **4724**

FEDERAL RESERVE ACT OF 1913, WITH AMENDMENTS AND LAWS RELATING TO BANKING, THE (US) [03181845] **3086**

FEDERAL RESERVE BANK OF ATLANTA See UPDATE - FEDERAL RESERVE BANK OF ATLANTA **815**

FEDERAL RESERVE BANK OF ATLANTA. RESEARCH DEPT See READINGS IN SOUTHERN FINANCE **806**

FEDERAL RESERVE BANK OF BOSTON See LANDMARK **796**

FEDERAL RESERVE BANK OF BOSTON See CONFERENCE SERIES - FEDERAL RESERVE BANK OF BOSTON **784**

FEDERAL RESERVE BANK OF CHICAGO. RESEARCH DEPT See RETAIL CREDIT SURVEY FOR SEVENTH FEDERAL RESERVE DISTRICT **809**

FEDERAL RESERVE BANK OF CLEVELAND See ECONOMIC COMMENTARY (CLEVELAND) **1482**

FEDERAL RESERVE BANK OF CLEVELAND See MEMBER BANK OPERATING RATIOS, FOURTH FEDERAL RESERVE DISTRICT **797**

FEDERAL RESERVE BANK OF CLEVELAND See ANNUAL REPORT - FEDERAL RESERVE BANK OF CLEVELAND **771**

FEDERAL RESERVE BANK OF DALLAS See MONTHLY BUSINESS REVIEW - FEDERAL RESERVE BANK OF DALLAS **1506**

FEDERAL RESERVE BANK OF KANSAS CITY See MEMBER BANK CONDITION, TENTH FEDERAL RESERVE DISTRICT **797**

FEDERAL RESERVE BANK OF MINNEAPOLIS See QUARTERLY REVIEW - FEDERAL RESERVE BANK OF MINNEAPOLIS **805**

FEDERAL RESERVE BANK OF NEW YORK See QUARTERLY REVIEW - FEDERAL RESERVE BANK OF NEW YORK **805**

FEDERAL RESERVE BANK OF NEW YORK See OPERATING RATIOS OF SECOND DISTRICT MEMBER BANKS **802**

FEDERAL RESERVE BANK OF SAN FRANCISCO. RESEARCH DEPT See FRB SF WEEKLY LETTER **1492**

FEDERAL RESERVE BANK OF ST. LOUIS See INTERNATIONAL ECONOMIC CONDITIONS **1496**

FEDERAL RESERVE BANK OF ST. LOUIS See RATES OF CHANGE IN ECONOMIC DATA FOR TEN INDUSTRIAL COUNTRIES **806**

FEDERAL RESERVE BANK OF ST. LOUIS See U.S. FINANCIAL DATA **1525**

FEDERAL RESERVE BANK OF ST. LOUIS See NATIONAL ECONOMIC TRENDS **1507**

FEDERAL RESERVE BANK OF ST. LOUIS See MONETARY TRENDS **1505**

FEDERAL RESERVE INDUSTRIAL PRODUCTION (US) [03183120] **1606**

FEDERAL RESERVE RELATIONS COMMITTEE See PROCEEDINGS OF THE MEETING. - FEDERAL RESERVE RELATIONS COMMITTEE **804**

FEDERAL RULES OF EVIDENCE NEWS (US/0364-3581) [02640692] **2970**

FEDERAL RULES SERVICE (US/0164-4564) [01357450] **3140**

FEDERAL SALES TAX *CEASED.* (CN/0832-0705) [15226819] **4724**

FEDERAL SAVINGS AND LOAN INSURANCE CORPORATION See LIST OF MEMBER INSTITUTIONS - FEDERAL SAVINGS AND LOAN INSURANCE CORPORATION **2887**

FEDERAL SCIENCE EXPENDITURES AND PERSONNEL (CN/0226-3726) [09074935] **4648**

FEDERAL SCIENTIFIC ACTIVITIES (CN/0824-0310) [11657532] 5104, **5174**

FEDERAL SCIENTIFIC AND TECHNICAL COMMUNICATION ACTIVITIES : PROGRESS REPORT (US/0145-2282) [02711032] **5105**

FEDERAL SECURITIES ACT: PRIMARY SOURCE MANUAL (US) [01589722] **2970**

FEDERAL SENTENCING REPORTER : FSR (US/1053-9867) [18294744] **3164**

FEDERAL SERVICE LABOR RELATIONS REVIEW *CEASED.* (US/0890-6947) [07568049] **1669**

FEDERAL SEVENTH CIRCUIT CITATIONS (US) **2970**

FEDERAL SOFTWARE EXCHANGE CATALOG *CEASED.* (US/0738-3266) [03454211] **1279**

FEDERAL STAFF DIRECTORY (US/0735-3324) [08152681] **4648**

FEDERAL STAFFING DIGEST (US/1053-4652) [20274008] **4703**

FEDERAL/STATE EXECUTIVE DIRECTORY See STATE EXECUTIVE DIRECTORY ANNUAL **4687**

FEDERAL/STATE EXECUTIVE DIRECTORY See FEDERAL EXECUTIVE DIRECTORY ANNUAL **4648**

FEDERAL-STATE-LOCAL GOVERNMENT DIRECTORY, THE (US/1041-6722) [17653150] **4648**

FEDERAL-STATE MARKET NEWS REPORTS (US/0363-2288) [02438419] **2335**

FEDERAL-STATE MARKET NEWS SERVICE See BOSTON, FRESH FRUIT AND VEGETABLE WHOLESALE MARKET PRICES **2329**

FEDERAL-STATE MARKET NEWS SERVICE See MARKETING FLORIDA AVOCADOS, LIMES, MANGOS **2349**

FEDERAL-STATE MARKET NEWS SERVICE See MARKETING CALIFORNIA ONIONS **2349**

FEDERAL-STATE MARKET NEWS SERVICE See MARKETING CALIFORNIA POTATOES **2349**

FEDERAL-STATE MARKET NEWS SERVICE See MARKETING CALIFORNIA TOMATOES **2349**

FEDERAL-STATE MARKET NEWS SERVICE See NEW ORLEANS, FRESH FRUIT AND VEGETABLE WHOLESALE MARKET PRICES **112**

FEDERAL-STATE MARKET NEWS SERVICE See MARKETING CALIFORNIA ARTICHOKES **2348**

FEDERAL-STATE MARKET NEWS SERVICE See MARKETING CALIFORNIA BROCCOLI **2349**

FEDERAL-STATE MARKET NEWS SERVICE See MARKETING MICHIGAN VEGETABLES **2349**

FEDERAL-STATE MARKET NEWS SERVICE See MARKETING CALIFORNIA PLUMS **2349**

FEDERAL-STATE MARKET NEWS SERVICE See MARKETING CALIFORNIA CARROTS **2349**

FEDERAL-STATE MARKET NEWS SERVICE See MARKETING LETTUCE FROM IMPERIAL VALLEY AND BLYTHE DISTRICTS **178**

FEDERAL-STATE MARKET NEWS SERVICE See MARKETING CALIFORNIA APRICOTS **2348**

FEDERAL-STATE MARKET NEWS SERVICE See MARKETING CALIFORNIA CELERY **2349**

FEDERAL-STATE MARKET NEWS SERVICE See MARKETING CALIFORNIA POTATOES FROM THE KERN DISTRICT AND STOCKTON DELTA DISTRICT **2349**

FEDERAL-STATE MARKET NEWS SERVICE See CALIFORNIA FRESH FRUIT AND VEGETABLE SHIPMENTS BY RAIL, TRUCK, AND AIR **2330**

FEDERAL-STATE MARKET NEWS SERVICE See MARKETING CALIFORNIA ASPARAGUS **2349**

FEDERAL-STATE MARKET NEWS SERVICE See MARKETING CALIFORNIA CHERRIES **2349**

FEDERAL-STATE PARTNERSHIP (US/0363-5902) [02511462] **320**

FEDERAL-STATE-PRIVATE COOPERATIVE SNOW SURVEYS. BASIC DATA SUMMARY OF SNOW SURVEY AND SOIL MOISTURE MEASUREMENTS FOR WESTERN UNITED STATES, INCLUDING COLUMBIA RIVER DRAINAGE IN CANADA (US) [04168040] **171**

FEDERAL STATISTICAL SOURCE : WHERE TO FIND AGENCY EXPERTS & PERSONNEL / BY WILLIAM R. EVINGER (US) [24813548] **4697**

FEDERAL STATISTICS USERS' CONFERENCE See NEWSLETTER - FEDERAL STATISTICS USERS' CONFERENCE **5334**

FEDERAL STUDENT FINANCIAL AID HANDBOOK (US/0730-8922) [08054682] **1823**

FEDERAL SUPERVISORS GUIDE TO DRUG TESTING (US) **1344**

FEDERAL SUPPLY CATALOG. SECTION IV, ALPHABETICAL INDEX OF EXPENDABLE ITEMS See FEDERAL SUPPLY CATALOG. SECTION VII, CLASSIFICATION OF PROPERTY WITH ALPHABETICAL INDEX OF EXPENDABLE ITEMS **4837**

FEDERAL SUPPLY CATALOG. SECTION VII, CLASSIFICATION OF PROPERTY See FEDERAL SUPPLY CATALOG. SECTION VII, CLASSIFICATION OF PROPERTY WITH ALPHABETICAL INDEX OF EXPENDABLE ITEMS **4837**

●FEDERAL SUPPLY CATALOG. SECTION VII, CLASSIFICATION OF PROPERTY WITH ALPHABETICAL INDEX OF EXPENDABLE ITEMS (US) [25897047] **4837**

●FEDERAL SUPPORT FOR NONPROFITS (US/1066-8896) [27082231] **4335**

FEDERAL SUPPORT TO UNIVERSITIES, COLLEGES AND SELECTED NONPROFIT INSTITUTIONS (US) [01249482] **1823**

FEDERAL TAX ARTICLES: INCOME, ESTATE, GIFT, EXCISE, EMPLOYMENT TAXES (US) [01564326] **4724**

FEDERAL TAX COMPLIANCE PLANNING (US/0735-9918) [09069616] **4724**

FEDERAL TAX COORDINATOR 2D (US/0738-8632) [08950448] **4724**

FEDERAL TAX COORDINATOR 2D. LISTING OF CURRENT TAX ARTICLES (US) [08068633] 4724, **2970**

FEDERAL TAX COORDINATOR 2D. WEEKLY ALERT (US/0163-996X) [04553182] **4724**

FEDERAL TAX COURSE (STUDENTS ED.) (US/0737-8718) [09457652] 4724, **2970**

FEDERAL TAX MANUAL (US/0888-0522) [12986721] 2970, **4724**

FEDERAL TAX VALUATION DIGEST (US/0194-1798) [05364741] **4724**

FEDERAL TAXATION (HOUSTON, TEX.) (US/0742-7816) [10438127] **4724**

FEDERAL TAXATION OF LIFE INSURANCE COMPANIES (US) [01771810] 4724, **2880**

FEDERAL TAXATION OF MUNICIPAL BONDS DESKBOOK (US) 898, **4724**

FEDERAL TAXATION OF OIL AND GAS TRANSACTIONS (US) [01569330] 4256, **4724**

FEDERAL TAXES (US) **4724**

FEDERAL TAXES (UK) **4724**

FEDERAL TAXES ADMINISTRATION REPORT (PK) [02405271] **4649**

FEDERAL TAXES CITATOR (US) **4724**

FEDERAL TECHNOLOGY TRANSFER *CEASED.* (US) [13685511] **5105**

FEDERAL TIMES (US/0014-9233) [01569042] **4703**

FEDERAL TRADE COMMISSION DECISIONS (US/0891-7515) [01768407] **3100**

FEDERAL TRAVEL DIRECTORY (WASHINGTON, D.C. : 1981) *CEASED.* (US/0278-0941) [07721664] **5469**

FEDERAL UPDATE (US/0898-4298) [17456201] **4649**

FEDERAL VETERINARIAN, THE (US/0164-6257) [01569045] **5510**

FEDERAL WAY NEWS (US) [14234851] **5760**

FEDERAL YELLOW BOOK (US/0145-6202) [02666012] 4649, **1926**

●FEDERALISM REPORT, THE (US) [25536110] **4474**

FEDERALIST (WASHINGTON, D.C. : 1980), THE (US/0736-8151) [09226043] 4649, **2733**

FEDERALISTA, IL (IT/0392-1042) [05055853] **4521**

FEDERALISTE; REVUE DE POLITIQUE, LE (IT/0014-925X) [01633958] **4474**

FEDERALLY EMPLOYED WOMEN (ASSOCIATION). ACCOUNTABILITY COMMITTEE See AGENCY ACCOUNTABILITY SURVEY **1642**

FEDERATIE NEDERLANDSE VAKBEWEGING See FNV JAARVERSLAG **1675**

FEDERATION AUTO-QUEBEC See RALLYE : REGLEMENTS **4914**

FEDERATION BULLETIN (FULTON) (US/0014-9306) [01569061] **3740**

FEDERATION CANADIENNE DES ARCHERS See LIVRET DES REGLEMENTS DE LA FEDERATION CANADIENNE DES ARCHERS (1974) **4903**

FEDERATION CULTURELLE DES CANADIENS-FRANCAIS See RESSOURCES CULTURELLES DES FRANCOPHONES HORS QUEBEC **2757**

Alphabetical Title Index — FELICITER

FEDERATION DE CROSSE DU QUEBEC See VOTRE BOTTIN DE CROSSE **4928**

FEDERATION DE L'AGRICULTURE DE L'ONTARIO See RECUEIL DES MEMBRES - LA FEDERATION DE L'AGRICULTURE DE L'ONTARIO **125**

FEDERATION DE MONTREAL DES CAISSES DESJARDINS See BULLETIN DE LA FEDERATION DE MONTREAL DES CAISSES DESJARDINS **825**

FEDERATION DES ASSOCIATIONS COOPERATIVES D'ECONOMIE FAMILIALE DU QUEBEC See MEMOIRE AUX GOUVERNEMENTS CANADIEN ET QUEBECOIS **2792**

FEDERATION DES ASSOCIATIONS DE PROFESSEURS DES UNIVERSITES DU QUEBEC See FAPUQ NOUVELLES BREVES **1823**

FEDERATION DES CENTRES LOCAUX DE SERVICES COMMUNAUTAIRES DU QUEBEC See INFORMATION - FEDERATION DES C. L. S. C. DU QUEBEC. SUPPLEMENT, L' **5290**

FEDERATION DES COMMISSIONS SCOLAIRES CATHOLIQUES DU QUEBEC See COMMISSAIRE D'ECOLES **1861**

FEDERATION DES ENSEIGNANTS DE L'ONTARIO See NOUS LES ENSEIGNANTS DE L'ONTARIO **1867**

FEDERATION DES ENTREPRISES DE BELGIQUE See BULLETIN **1600**

FEDERATION DES MEDECINS OMNIPRATICIENS DU QUEBEC See NOUVELLES DE LA F M O Q (ENGLISH EDITION) **3623**

FEDERATION DES SPORTS DU CANADA. CONGRES See CONGRESS ... PROCEEDINGS - FEDERATION DES SPORTS DU CANADA **4891**

FEDERATION DES TRAVAILLEURS DU NOUVEAU-BRUNSWICK See NEW BRUNSWICK FEDERATION OF LABOUR. ANNUAL SUBMISSION TO THE PREMIER AND MEMBERS OF THE CABINET OF THE GOVERNMENT OF NEW BRUNSWICK **1693**

FEDERATION HIGHLIGHTS (US/1048-3063) [18697560] **5533**

FEDERATION INTERNATIONALE DE FOOTBALL ASSOCIATION See FIFA NEWS **4894**

FEDERATION INTERNATIONALE DE GYMNASTIQUE See BULLETIN / FEDERATION INTERNATIONALE DE GYMNASTIQUE **4888**

FEDERATION INTERNATIONALE DES DROITS DE L'HOMME See LETTRE DE LA F.I.D.H. / FEDERATION INTERNATIONALE DES DROITS DE L'HOMME, LA **4510**

FEDERATION INTERNATIONALE DES SOCIETES D'AVIRON. CONGRESS See MINUTES OF THE REGULAR ANNUAL CONGRESS ... / FEDERATION INTERNATIONALE DES SOCIETES D'AVIRON **2519**

FEDERATION MONDIALE DES CONCOURS INTERNATIONAUX DE MUSIQUE : BROCHURE (SZ) [20290310] **4117**

FEDERATION MUSEUMS JOURNAL (MY/0126-561X) [01986851] **4087**

FEDERATION NATIONALE DES CHAMBRES DE COMMERCE, D'INDUSTRIE ET D'AGRICULTURE DE LA REPUBLIQUE DU ZAIRE See CIRCULAIRE D'INFORMATION **819**

FEDERATION NATIONALE DES INDUSTRIES ELECTRONIQUES See ELECTRONIQUE FRANCAISE, L' **2050**

FEDERATION NATIONALE DES TRAVAUX PUBLICS See REPERTOIRE ET CARACTERISTIQUES DES PRINCIPAUX MATERIELS DE GENIE CIVIL **626**

FEDERATION NATIONALE DU BATIMENT See MENSUALISATION DES OUVRIERS DU BATIMENT, LA **1690**

FEDERATION NEWS / FEDERATION OF NOVA SCOTIAN HERITAGE (CN/1197-5334) [29970237] **2733**

FEDERATION NEWS (LOS ANGELES, CALIF.), THE (US/0738-0550) [09534889] **1669**

FEDERATION NEWSLETTER (UNITARIAN UNIVERSALIST WOMEN'S FEDERATION) (US) [05870034] **5555**

FEDERATION OF AMERICAN SCIENTISTS See F.A.S. PUBLIC INTEREST REPORT **5104**

FEDERATION OF CANADIAN ARCHERS See RULES BOOK OF THE FEDERATION OF CANADIAN ARCHERS **4916**

FEDERATION OF CANADIAN MUNICIPALITIES. CONFERENCE See SUMMARY PROCEEDINGS OF THE ANNUAL CONFERENCE - FEDERATION OF CANADIAN MUNICIPALITIES **4689**

FEDERATION OF CHILDREN'S BOOK GROUPS (GREAT BRITAIN) See FEDERATION OF CHILDREN'S BOOK GROUPS YEARBOOK **4828**

FEDERATION OF CHILDREN'S BOOK GROUPS YEARBOOK (UK) [02244075] **4828**

FEDERATION OF EUROPEAN MICROBIOLOGICAL SOCIETIES See FEMS MICROBIOLOGY REVIEWS **563**

FEDERATION OF EUROPEAN MICROBIOLOGICAL SOCIETIES See FEMS MICROBIOLOGY LETTERS **562**

FEDERATION OF GENEALOGICAL SOCIETIES (U.S.) See FORUM **2449**

FEDERATION OF HONG KONG INDUSTRIES See MEMBERS' DIRECTORY / FEDERATION OF HONG KONG INDUSTRIES **1618**

FEDERATION OF INDIAN PUBLISHERS See DIRECTORY OF MEMBERS - FEDERATION OF INDIAN PUBLISHERS **4814**

FEDERATION OF INSURANCE & CORPORATE COUNSEL QUARTERLY (US/0887-0942) [12989894] 3100, **2880**

FEDERATION OF MILITARY AND UNITED SERVICES INSTITUTES OF CANADA See NATIONAL NEWS LETTER - FEDERATION OF MILITARY AND UNITED SERVICES INSTITUTES OF CANADA **4052**

FEDERATION OF SCHOOLS OF ACCOUNTANCY (U.S.) See NEWSLETTER / FEDERATION OF SCHOOLS OF ACCOUNTANCY **749**

FEDERATION OF STATE MEDICAL BOARDS OF THE UNITED STATES See FSMB HANDBOOK **4204**

FEDERATION OF STATE MEDICAL BOARDS OF THE UNITED STATES See FEDERATION BULLETIN (FULTON) **3740**

FEDERATION OF TAX ADMINISTRATORS See RESEARCH REPORT - FEDERATION OF TAX ADMINISTRATORS **4746**

FEDERATION OF UGANDA EMPLOYERS, COMMERCE & INDUSTRY See NEWSLETTER - FEDERATION OF UGANDA EMPLOYERS, COMMERCE & INDUSTRY **1619**

FEDERATION OF WOMEN TEACHERS' ASSOCIATIONS OF ONTARIO See FWTAO NEWSLETTER **1747**

FEDERATION OF WOMEN TEACHERS' ASSOCIATIONS OF ONTARIO See FWTAO GUIDEBOOK **1879**

FEDERATION OF WOMEN ZIONISTS OF GREAT BRITAIN AND IRELAND See FWZ REVIEW **5557**

FEDERATION PROFESSIONNELLE DES PRODUCTEURS ET DISTRIBUTEURS D'ELECTRICITE DE BELGIQUE See REPERTOIRE DES CENTRALES ELECTRIQUES **2006**

FEDERATION PROTESTANTE DE FRANCE See ANNUAIRE DE LA FRANCE PROTESTANTE **5055**

FEDERATION QUEBECOISE DE HOCKEY SUR GLACE See LIVRE DE REGLEMENTS ADMINISTRATIFS / FEDERATION QUEBECOISE DE HOCKEY SUR GLACE INC **4903**

FEDERATION QUEBECOISE DES SPORTS AERIENS. SECTEUR PARACHUTISME See BULLETIN DE NOUVELLES / FEDERATION QUEBECOISE DES SPORTS AERIENS, SECTEUR PARACHUTISME **4888**

FEDERATION QUEBECOISE DES SPORTS AERIENS. SECTEUR VOL LIBRE See BULLETIN DE NOUVELLES / FEDERATION QUEBECOISE DES SPORTS AERIENS, SECTEUR VOL LIBRE **4888**

FEDERATION QUEBECOISE DU LOISIR SCIENTIFIQUE See ANNUAIRE DES LOISIRS SCIENTIFIQUES **5083**

FEDGAZETTE (MINNEAPOLIS, MINN.) (US/1045-3334) [19967784] 1490, **675**

FEDLINK TECHNICAL NOTES (US/0737-4178) [09359460] **3210**

FEDNEWS, THE (US/0430-2761) [05438939] **1669**

FEDSTAT (ALEXANDRIA, VA.) (US/1063-0961) [25857465] **4553**

FEED ADDITIVE COMPENDIUM (1966) (US/0071-450X) [06290509] **86**

FEED & FARM SUPPLY DEALER *CEASED.* (CN/0046-3604) [01880290] **200**

FEED & FEEDING DIGEST (US/0886-5884) [08796983] **200**

FEED & GRAIN (US/1055-3223) [23150373] **200**

FEED & GRAIN FARM EQUIPMENT See FEED & GRAIN TIMES **200**

FEED & GRAIN TIMES (US/0163-4119) [04392780] **200**

FEED COMPOUNDER (UK/0950-771X) [10950771X] **200**

FEED GRAIN, WHEAT, UPLAND COTTON AND RICE PROGRAMS, DISASTER AND DEFICIENCY PROVISIONS (US/0193-984X) [03803214] **200**

FEED INDUSTRY RED BOOK (US) [02948253] **201**

FEED INGREDIENT ANALYSES FOR OFFICIAL SAMPLES (US) [02271055] **201**

FEED INTERNATIONAL (US/0274-5771) [06413497] **201**

FEED MAGAZINE (GW/0937-9134) [20346633] **201**

FEED MANAGEMENT (US/0014-956X) [04294319] **201**

FEED TRADER AND RETAILER, THE See FEED & FEEDING DIGEST **200**

FEEDBACK (CALGARY) (CN/0229-3110) [08443907] **2822**

FEEDBACK ELISE (FR) **1490**

FEEDBACK (MILLBRAE) (US/0198-6635) [05780354] **1894**

FEEDBACK PAPERS (GW) [07804139] **1240**

FEEDBACK (SYDNEY, N.S.W.) (AT/1030-8474) [19815863] **211**

FEEDBACK (WASHINGTON) (US/0147-4871) [03175448] **1132**

FEEDS & FEEDING *CEASED.* (UK/0961-978X) [0961978X] 211, **201**

FEEDSTUFFS (US/0014-9624) [01335250] **201**

FEEDSTUFFS INDEX, THE (US) [02664116] **201**

FEELING FINE (CN/0826-2594) [11847649] 2597, **4191**

FEELINGS & THEIR MEDICAL SIGNIFICANCE (US/0430-2869) [02261061] **3576**

FEESTELIJK ZAKENDOEN MAGAZINE (NE) **675**

FEGATO, IL *SUSPENDED.* (IT/0014-9659) [01778975] **3796**

● FEHB GUIDE FOR CSRS/FERS ANNUITANTS (US) [29204758] **2880**

● FEHB GUIDE. OPEN SEASON FOR FEDERAL CIVILIAN EMPLOYEES / FEDERAL EMPLOYEES HEALTH BENEFITS PROGRAM (US) [29233675] 4703, **2880**

● FEHB GUIDE. OPEN SEASON FOR FEDERAL CIVILIAN EMPLOYEES / FEDERAL EMPLOYEES HEALTH BENEFITS PROGRAM (LARGE PRINT EDITION) (US) [29353430] 4703, **2880**

● FEHB GUIDE. OPEN SEASON FOR FEDERAL CIVILIAN EMPLOYEES IN POSITIONS OUTSIDE THE CONTINENTAL UNITED STATES / FEDERAL EMPLOYEES HEALTH BENEFITS PROGRAM (US) [29242451] 4703, **2880**

● FEHB GUIDE. OPEN SEASON FOR INDIVIDUALS ELIGIBLE TO ENROLL FOR TEMPORARY CONTINUATION OF COVERAGE, COVERAGE UNDER THE SPOUSE EQUITY LAW OR SIMILAR STATUTES PROVIDING COVERAGE TO FORMER SPOUSES / FEDERAL EMPLOYEES HEALTH BENEFITS PROGRAM (US) [29233746] 4703, **2880**

● FEHB GUIDE. OPEN SEASON FOR INDIVIDUALS RECEIVING COMPENSATION FROM THE OFFICE OF WORKERS' COMPENSATION PROGRAMS (OWCP) (US) [29233865] 4703, **2880**

● FEHB GUIDE. OPEN SEASON FOR RETIREMENT SYSTEMS PARTICIPATING IN THE FEDERAL EMPLOYEES HEALTH BENEFITS PROGRAM (US) [29204722] 4703, **2880**

● FEHB GUIDE. OPEN SEASON FOR UNITED STATES POSTAL SERVICE EMPLOYEES / FEDERAL EMPLOYEES HEALTH BENEFITS PROGRAM (US) [29242538] 4703, **2880**

FEHERJE ES BIOTERMEK (HU/0866-482X) [10866482X] **86**

FEIJINSHUKUANG (CC/0253-2298) [08862811] **1439**

FEINWERKTECHNIK & MESSTECHNIK See F & M / ORGAN DER VDI/VDE-GESELLSCHAFT MIKRO- UND FEINWERKTECHNIK **5104**

FEITEN (BE) **4649**

FEJER MEGYEI KONYVTAROS (HU/0139-2115) [I01392115] **3210**

FEL ACTUALITES HEBDO : MARCHES EUROPEENS DES FRUITS ET LEGUMES (FR/1241-3682) [11487881] **171**

FEL ACTUALITES HEBDO : MARCHES EUROPEENS DES FRUITS ET LEGUMES (FR) [11820600] **86**

FEL ACTUALITES : MARCHES EUROPEENS DES FRUITS ET LEGUMES (FR) [11679579] **171**

FELA REPORTER AND RAILROAD LIABILITY MONITOR (US/1044-6648) [19455028] **2970**

FELD WALD WASSER. SCHWEIZERISCHE JAGDZEITUNG (SZ/0014-9756) [04023665] 4894, **4871**

FELDSER I AKUSERKA (RU/0014-9772) [10500186] **3760**

FELDWIRTSCHAFT (GW/0014-9799) [03754755] **86**

FELICITER (CN/0014-9802) [01569080] **3210**

FELINE HEALTH TOPICS (US) [13387448] **5510**

FELINE PRACTICE (1990) (US/1057-6614) [22177732] **5510**

FELIX (US) [26409523] 1132, **320**

FELIX RAVENNA (IT/0391-7517) [01569082] 250, **268**

FELLOWS LECTURE (CN/0384-7225) [03951106] **4088**

FELLOWSCRIP (US) **4958**

FELLOWSHIP IN PRAYER (US/0014-9837) [03372402] **4958**

FELLOWSHIP (NEW YORK) (US/0014-9810) [01569084] **4521**

FELLOWSHIP OF BELIEVERS See FELLOWSHIP OF BELIEVERS BULLETIN **4958**

FELLOWSHIP OF BELIEVERS BULLETIN (CN/0316-7909) [02569372] **4958**

FELLOWSHIP PROGRAM - INSURANCE INSTITUTE OF CANADA (CN/0225-2449) [06156676] **2880**

FELLOWSHIP YEARBOOK (CN/0317-266X) [02588520] **5060**

FELLOWSHIPS, SCHOLARSHIPS, AND RELATED OPPORTUNITIES IN INTERNATIONAL EDUCATION (US/0735-8830) [05575275] **1823**

●FELL'S GUIDE TO COLLEGE MONEY FOR THE ASKING IN FLORIDA (US/1040-9513) [18591358] **1824**

FELL'S INTERNATIONAL COIN BOOK (US/0430-2958) [04943597] **2781**

FELL'S UNITED STATES COIN BOOK (US/1041-6951) [02053377] **2781**

FELS MONOGRAPH SERIES (US/0428-2094) [01351340] **580**

FELSBAU (GW) [12071343] **1458**

FELSOOKTATASI SZEMLE : A MUVELODESUGYI MINISZTERIUM FOLYOIRATA (HU) [19226111] **1824**

FEM (MX/0185-4666) [04122068] **5555**

FEM. FACTORY EQUIPMENT & MATERIALS (SA/0014-6552) [I00146552] **2102**

FEM. FINANCIEEL-ECONOMISCH MAGAZINE (NE/0165-5655) [I01655655] **1490**

FEMALE BODYBUILDING AND WEIGHT TRAINING (US/0888-4102) [13566782] **5555**, **2597**

FEMALE LIVING See MPH LIVING **2792**

FEMALE PATIENT. PRACTICAL ADVICE FOR PRIMARY CARE, THE (US/0888-2398) [13535486] **3760**

FEMALE PATIENT. PRACTICAL OB/GYN MEDICINE, THE (US/0888-2401) [13535457] **3760**

FEMINA (MY) [04849155] **5555**

FEMINARIA (AG) [19702222] **5555**

FEMINIE (CN) **5555**

FEMININ PLURIEL (CN/0707-9036) [08465934] **5555**

FEMINISM & PSYCHOLOGY (UK/0959-3535) [23367452] 4587, **5555**

●FEMINISM AND THE SOCIAL SCIENCES (US/1070-549X) [28407077] 5556, **5200**

FEMINISME EN REVUE, LE (CN/0832-5340) [17846625] **5556**

FEMINISMS (COLUMBUS, OHIO) CEASED. (US/1041-1801) [18095403] **5556**

FEMINIST ACTION CEASED. (CN/0831-3377) [16516675] **5556**

FEMINIST ACTION (LONDON) (UK) [12191547] **5556**

FEMINIST BOOKSTORE NEWS (US/0741-6555) [10196440] **5556**

FEMINIST BOOKSTORE NEWSLETTER See FEMINIST BOOKSTORE NEWS **5556**

FEMINIST COLLECTIONS (MADISON, WIS.) (US/0742-7441) [06467769] **5556**

FEMINIST, DER (GW/0179-8367) [10969437] 2846, **5556**

●FEMINIST ECONOMICS (UK/1354-5701) 5556, **1490**

FEMINIST FORUM (UK/0732-6378) [08393814] **5556**

FEMINIST ISSUES (US/0270-6679) [06482659] **5556**

FEMINIST PARTY OF CANADA See NEWS - FEMINIST PARTY OF CANADA **5562**

FEMINIST PERIODICALS (MADISON, WIS.) (US/0742-7433) [07729295] **5556**

FEMINIST PRAXIS (UK) [25023592] **5556**

FEMINIST REVIEW (UK/0141-7789) [06191763] **5556**

FEMINIST STUDIES (US/0046-3663) [01632609] **5556**

FEMINIST TEACHER (US/0882-4843) [11660672] 5556, **1894**

FEMME (CN/0318-2452) [02441777] **5556**

FEMME ACTUELLE (FR/0764-0021) [I07640021] **5556**

FEMME ET LA LOI, LA (CN/0847-5261) [23263368] 5556, **2970**

●FEMME FATALE (US/1064-6302) [26345105] **4861**

●FEMME FATALES OF THE FILMS (US/1062-3906) [25609998] **320**

FEMME-LINES (US/0014-9918) [04157541] **1084**

FEMME PARIS, 1984 (FR/0764-4523) [I07644523] **5556**

FEMME PLUS (MONTREAL) (CN/0838-9446) [18310202] **5556**

FEMME PRATIQUE (FR/0014-9926) [I00149926] **5556**

FEMMES D'ACTION (CN/0226-9902) [07966287] **5556**

FEMMES DEMOCRATIQUES (CN/0828-6558) [12097942] **4474**

FEMMES D'ICI (CN/0705-3851) [03979966] **5556**

●FEMS IMMUNOLOGY AND MEDICAL MICROBIOLOGY (NE/0928-8244) [27447797] **3669**

FEMS MICROBIOLOGY (NE/0921-8254) **562**

FEMS MICROBIOLOGY, ECOLOGY (NE/0168-6496) [I01686496] 2216, **562**

FEMS MICROBIOLOGY IMMUNOLOGY (NE/0920-8534) [17515756] 3669, **562**

FEMS MICROBIOLOGY LETTERS (NE/0378-1097) [03217327] 2216, **562**

FEMS MICROBIOLOGY REVIEWS (NE) [11901735] **563**

FEMS SYMPOSIUM (UK/0163-9188) [03920673] **563**

FEN. FINITE ELEMENT NEWS (UK/0309-6688) [04123149] **5105**

FEN HSI SHIH YEN SHIH (CC) [14292058] **1015**

FENAISON (CN/0712-3566) [08890882] **3387**

FENCE POST, THE (US/0274-7308) [06539922] **5642**

FENCING CEASED. (UK) [19356671] **4894**

FENESTRATION ... BUYERS' GUIDE (US/1054-156X) [22770013] **1606**

FENESTRATION (RIVERTON, N.J.) (US/0895-450X) [16643907] **614**

FENG KUANG HUA PAO (HK) [04418360] **5469**

FENIX (NE) [24334638] **3210**

FENIX (US) [05543804] **3281**

FENIX (LIMA) (PE/0015-0002) [01983660] **3258**

FENNELL ORCHID COMPANY See FENNELL'S ORCHID NEWS **2414**

FENNELL ORCHID COMPANY See OFFERINGS FOR ... **2426**

FENNELL'S ORCHID NEWS (US) [12228438] **2414**

FENNIA (FI/0015-0010) [01569097] **2560**

FENNIMORE TIMES (US/8755-3694) [11283935] **5767**

FENNVILLE HERALD (US) **5692**

FENOLOGICKA ROCENKA SLOVENSKEJ SOCIALISTICKEJ REPUBLIKY / HYDROMETEOROLOGICKY USTAV BRATISLAVA (YU) [10089798] **510**

FENOMENOLOGIA E SOCIETA (IT) [12544250] **4346**

FENWAY COURT (US/0430-3091) [02261072] **350**

FENXI HUAXUE (CC/0253-3820) [01799836] **1015**

FENZI CUIHUA (CC/1001-3555) [I10013555] **455**

FENZI KEXUE YUEBAO (CC/0253-3677) [08725007] **1052**

FEP GUIDELINES (US/0093-7630) [01793071] **3148**

FER DE LANCE (FR/0557-5737) [10224949] **350**

FERC DATA ON CD-ROM (US) 898, 4256, **1944**

FERC PRACTICE AND PROCEDURE MANUAL (US/0745-6131) [09399415] **1944**

FERC REPORT, THE (US) [19090519] **3086**

FERDINAND NEWS, THE (US) [14223143] **5664**

FERGUS-ELORA PHOENIX (CN/0714-8135) [09084913] **5784**

FERGUSON FILES (US/1040-2276) [18354961] **2448**

FERGUSON FOUNDATION AGRICULTURAL ENGINEERING SERIES, THE (US/0430-3121) [01378621] **87**

FERGUSON'S SRI LANKA DIRECTORY (CE) [10141299] **2503**

FERMENT (LONDON) (UK/0957-7041) [18045356] **2367**

FERMILAB REPORT (US/0897-5566) [04310038] **4447**

FERN GAZETTE, THE (UK/0308-0838) [02242614] **510**

FERNALD CLUB YEARBOOK (US/0196-2140) [01359623] **5583**

FERNAND BRAUDEL CENTER FOR THE STUDY OF ECONOMIES, HISTORICAL SYSTEMS, AND CIVILIZATIONS See REVIEW - FERNAND BRAUDEL CENTER FOR THE STUDY OF ECONOMIES, HISTORICAL SYSTEMS, AND CIVILIZATIONS **1517**

FERNANDINA BEACH NEWS-LEADER (US) 5648, **5649**

FERNBANK QUARTERLY (US/0742-650X) [10450933] **5105**

FERNMELDE-INGENIEUR (GW/0015-010X) [I0015010X] **1111**

FERNSEH- UND KINOTECHNIK (GW/0015-0142) [05167600] **4068**

FERNSEHSPIEL IM ZDF / HERAUSGEGEBEN VOM ZWEITEN DEUTSCHEN FERNSEHEN, INFORMATION UND PRESSE/OFFENTLICHKEITSARBEIT, DAS (GW) [08912905] 1155, 4068, **1132**

FERNSTROM FOUNDATION SERIES (NE/0167-7004) [08498707] **3576**

FERNVERKEHR DEUTSCHER LASTKRAFTFAHRZEUGE ... IN SEINER BEWEGUNG NACH VERKEHRSGEBIETEN, GUTERHAUPTGRUPPEN UND WICHTIGEREN GUTERGRUPPEN : GEMEINSAMER BERICHT DER BUNDESANSTALT FUR DEN GUTERFERNVERKEHR UND DES KRAFTFAHRT-BUNDESAMTES (GW) [07936512] **5414**

FERNWAERME INTERNATIONAL (GW/0340-3572) [04179206] **2605**

FERRARA. CIVICO MUSEO DE STORIA NATURALE See PUBBLICAZIONI - FERRARA. CIVICO MUSEO DE STORIA NATURALE **4171**

FERRARA (ITALY). ASSESSORATO ALLE ISTITUZIONI CULTURALI See MUSEI FERRARESI **325**

FERRARA. UNIVERSITA See ANNALI DELL'UNIVERSITA DI FERRARA. SEZIONE 7 : SCIENZE MATEMATICHE **3494**

FERRARI WORLD (UK/0958-7462) [I09587462] **5415**

●FERRARI'S PLACES OF INTEREST (US/1078-0068) [27040674] **2794**

FERRIES, BRIDGES, CRUISES (CN/0708-3300) [08271717] **5382**

FERRIS STATE UNIVERSITY. COLLEGE OF ALLIED HEALTH SCIENCES See ALUMNI DIRECTORY / FERRIS STATE UNIVERSITY, COLLEGE OF ALLIED HEALTH SCIENCES **1098**

FERRO-ALLOY DIRECTORY (UK/0266-3198) [12011351] **4001**

FERRO-ALLOY DIRECTORY & DATABOOK (UK/0266-3198) [20099279] **4002**

FERRO ALLOYS MONTHLY (UK) **4002**

FERROALLOYS (US) [03028882] 4002, **4025**

FERROELECTRICS (US/0015-0193) [00840694] **4402**

FERROELECTRICS AND POLAR MATERIAL (UK/0883-8283) [12229490] **4402**

FERROELECTRICS AND RELATED PHENOMENA (UK/0275-9608) [07285895] **1032**

FERROELECTRICS. LETTERS SECTION (US/0731-5171) [08209340] **2054**

FERROSILICON See SILICON IN ... - U.S. DEPARTMENT OF THE INTERIOR, BUREAU OF MINES **4026**

FERROVIAS DO BRASIL (BL) [01335408] **5431**

FERTCON MONTHLY REPORT See WORLD FERTILIZER REVIEW **191**

FERTECON QUARTERLY SULPHUR REPORT See OUTLOOK SULPHUR **1037**

FERTIG LOS (IT) **1746**

FERTIGUNGSTECHNIK UND BETRIEB (GW/0015-024X) [02446887] **2114**

FERTILE JOURNAL (US) [01569119] **5695**

FERTILISER & ALLIED AGRICULTURAL STATISTICS, NORTHERN REGION (II) [07996447] 87, **153**

FERTILISER ASSOCIATION OF INDIA See PRODUCTION AND CONSUMPTION OF FERTILISERS; ANNUAL REVIEW **122**

FERTILISER ASSOCIATION OF INDIA See FERTILISER STATISTICS **153**

FERTILISER MARKETING NEWS (II) [01620859] **87**

FERTILISER NEWS (II/0015-0266) [03008299] **87**

FERTILISER STATISTICS (II/0430-327X) [01569120] **153**

FERTILITAT (GW/0179-1796) [13405111] **3760**

FERTILITY AND STERILITY (US/0015-0282) [01569122] **3576**

FERTILITY ASSISTANCE (US/0740-3178) [09921787] **3576**

FERTILITY OF AMERICAN WOMEN ... ADVANCE REPORT / U.S. DEPARTMENT OF COMMERCE, BUREAU OF THE CENSUS (US) [08731611] **3760**

FERTILIZANTES NITROGENADOS NACIONALES *See* DESARROLLO DEL MERCADO DE LOS FERTILIZANTES NITROGENADOS EN ESPANA **78**

FERTILIZER FOCUS (UK) [11219646] **171**

FERTILIZER INDICATORS / ECONOMICS COMMITTEE (FR) [12190472] **1606**

FERTILIZER INDUSTRY ROUND TABLE, WASHINGTON, D.C *See* PROCEEDINGS OF THE ANNUAL MEETING - FERTILIZER INDUSTRY ROUND TABLE **183**

FERTILIZER INTERNATIONAL (UK/0015-0304) [04023690] **87**

FERTILIZER MARKET BULLETIN (UK) [08437291] **87**

FERTILIZER MARKETS (US/1051-9130) [22148418] **87**

FERTILIZER RECOMMENDATIONS FOR VANCOUVER ISLAND, ZONE 1 *See* GUIDE TO THE USE OF FERTILIZERS FOR VANCOUVER ISLAND, ZONE 1 **91**

FERTILIZER RESEARCH (NE/0167-1731) [06777949] **171**

FERTILIZER SCIENCE AND TECHNOLOGY SERIES (US/0071-4623) [01569127] **87**

FERTILIZER SOCIETY OF SOUTH AFRICA JOURNAL (SA/0367-3073) [10522726] **87**

FERTILIZER SUMMARY DATA (US/0146-1850) [01286708] **87**

FERTILIZER TECHNOLOGY *CEASED.* (US/0378-0430) [02823483] **171**

FERTILIZER WEEK (UK/0951-7472) [19558255] **1606**

FESPP NEWSLETTER (DK) [09608998] **580**

FESTIN, LE (FR/1143-676X) [21469598] **320**

FESTIVAL D'ETE DE QUEBEC *See* REVUE DE PRESSE DU ... FESTIVAL D'ETE DE QUEBEC, LA **5269**

FESTIVAL DU VOYAGEUR (ST-BONIFACE, MAN.) *See* PROGRAMME SOUVENIR. FESTIVAL DU VOYAGEUR, ST. BONIFACE, MANITOBA **4853**

FESTIVAL INTERNATIONAL DU FILM DE LA CRITIQUE QUEBECOISE *See* FESTIVAL INTERNATIONAL DU FILM DE LA CRITIQUE QUEBECOISE **4069**

FESTIVAL INTERNATIONAL DU FILM DE LA CRITIQUE QUEBECOISE (CN/0703-9824) [04433196] **4069**

● FESTIVAL MANAGEMENT & EVENT TOURISM (US/1065-2701) [26562635] **5469**

FESTIVAL OF AMERICAN FOLKLIFE *See* FESTIVAL OF AMERICAN FOLKLIFE / SMITHSONIAN INSTITUTION AND NATIONAL PARK SERVICE **2319**

FESTIVAL OF AMERICAN FOLKLIFE / SMITHSONIAN INSTITUTION AND NATIONAL PARK SERVICE (US/1056-6805) [04147473] **2319**

FESTIVAL OF FRIENDS (CN/0822-4978) [10156723] **4117**

FESTIVAL QUARTERLY (US/8750-3530) [01780883] **4959**

FESTIVAL USA (US/0094-1263) [01793856] **2733**

● FESTIVALS & ATTRACTIONS (CN/1196-4790) [31095581] **4850**

FESTKORPERPROBLEME (GW/0430-3393) [01569130] **4402**

● FETAL AND MATERNAL MEDICINE REVIEW (UK/0965-5395) [27924174] **3760**

FETAL DIAGNOSIS AND THERAPY (SZ/1015-3837) [23338607] **3760**

FETAL MEDICINE REVIEW *See* FETAL AND MATERNAL MEDICINE REVIEW **3760**

FETES & FESTIVALS *See* FESTIVALS & ATTRACTIONS **4850**

FETES ET FESTIVALS (CN/0836-6926) [17743270] **4850**

FETES ET SAISONS (FR/0015-0371) [09849706] **4959**

FETT IN DER PARENTERALEN ERNAHRUNG (GW/0720-8731) [10466528] **4191**

FETT WISSENSCHAFT TECHNOLOGIE : ORGAN DER DEUTSCHEN GESELLSCHAFT FUER FETTWISSENSCHAFT E.V. / FAT SCIENCE TECHNOLOGY (GW/0931-5985) [15807859] **1024**

FETTFLECK (AU) [06830315] **3387**

FETUS (NASHVILLE, TENN.), THE (US/1057-137X) [23953934] **3761**

FEU ET LUMIERE SAINT-BROLADRE (FR/0760-5099) [07605099] **5029**

FEU NOUVEAU (BE) **4959**

FEUERVERZINKEN (GW) [05092894] **4002**

FEUILLES FAMILIALES *See* NOUVELLES FEUILLES FAMILIALES **2284**

FEUILLET BIBLIQUE, LE (CN/0225-2112) [06035261] **5016**

FEUILLET D'INFORMATION DE LA VILLE DE SAINT-LEONARD, LE (CN/0711-396X) [08690332] **4649**

FEUILLET SPIRITUEL DE L'OEUVRE DU PELERINAGE DES MALADES (CN/0824-1546) [12064636] **4959**

FEUILLETS DE BIOLOGIE (FR/0428-2779) [09362759] **455**

FEUILLETS DE RADIOLOGIE (FR/0181-9801) [04772293] **3941**

FEUX ET SIGNAUX DE BRUME (FR) [02927928] **4176**

FEVE NEWS (BE) **5778**

FEW-BODY SYSTEMS (AU/0177-7963) [13446320] **4447**

FEW-BODY SYSTEMS. SUPPLEMENTUM (AU/0177-8811) [15500798] **4447**

FF COMMUNICATIONS (FI/0014-5815) [01336752] **2319**

FFA NEW HORIZONS (US/1069-806X) [21316482] **87**

FFTC BOOK SERIES (CH/0253-9616) [09165337] **2414**

FGD NEWSLETTER (UNITED STATES. FEDERAL GEOGRAPHIC DATA COMMITTEE) *See* FGDC NEWSLETTER : A PUBLICATION OF THE FEDERAL GEOGRAPHIC DATA COMMITTEE **2581**

● FGDC NEWSLETTER : A PUBLICATION OF THE FEDERAL GEOGRAPHIC DATA COMMITTEE (US) [28103417] **2581**

FGL : BOLETIN DE LA FUNDACION FEDERICO GARCIA LORCA (SP/0214-3771) [18131184] **3387**

FHA HOMES. DATA FOR STATES AND SELECTED AREAS ON CHARACTERISTICS OF FHA OPERATIONS UNDER SECTION 245, GRADUATED PAYMENT MORTGAGE PROGRAM (US/0275-1267) [07036456] **2822**

FHA MONTHLY REPORT OF OPERATIONS. HOME MORTGAGE PROGRAMS (US/0145-5648) [03455399] **2822**

FHA MONTHLY REPORT OF OPERATIONS. PROJECT MORTGAGE INSURANCE PROGRAMS (US/0145-5656) [03454865] **2880**, **2822**

F+I-BAU (GW/0340-2967) [01792993] **615**

F+I-BAU BAUEN MIT SYSTEMEN (GW) **615**

FIA JOURNAL (AT/1322-4409) **2597**

FIA WEEKLY BULLETINS (US/0199-5669) [06008747] **1606**

FIABCI INTERNATIONAL DIRECTORY (FR) [05671741] **4837**

FIABCI PANORAMA (FR) [20980587] **4837**

FIABCI REPORTER (FR) [05142248] **4837**

FIAT (FIRM) *See* OPERATING YEAR ANNUAL REPORT **5422**

FIAT LUX (SA) [04709939] **2639**

FIAT LUX / UNIVERSITY OF CALIFORNIA, RIVERSIDE (US/1056-4276) [23660152] **1091**

FIBA BASKETBALL MONTHLY (UK/0959-888X) [22724875] **4894**

FIBER AND INTEGRATED OPTICS (US/0146-8030) [03040751] **4434**

FIBER OPTIC SENSORS AND SYSTEMS (US/1051-1946) [21887345] **4403**

FIBER OPTICS AND COMMUNICATIONS (US/0275-0457) [07075520] **1155**

FIBER OPTICS AND COMMUNICATIONS MONTHLY NEWS SERVICE (US) **1155**

FIBER OPTICS AND COMMUNICATIONS NEWSLETTER *See* FIBER OPTICS AND COMMUNICATIONS **1155**

FIBER OPTICS & COMMUNICATIONS WEEKLY NEWS SERVICE *See* FIBER OPTICS WEEKLY UPDATE **1155**

FIBER OPTICS BUSINESS NEWSLETTER (US/1057-5375) [24072067] **1155**

FIBER OPTICS CROSS-REFERENCE PATENT ABSTRACTS SERVICE (US/0270-3076) [06395208] **1304**

FIBER OPTICS DEVELOPMENTS (UK) **4434**

FIBER OPTICS DIRECTORY UPDATE SERVICE (US/0270-3068) [06395179] **1155**

FIBER OPTICS HANDBOOK & BUYERS GUIDE *See* FIBER OPTICS YELLOW PAGES **1155**

FIBER OPTICS MAGAZINE *CEASED.* (US/1045-6422) [20179230] **1155**

FIBER OPTICS NEWS (US/8756-2049) [11491985] **4434**

FIBER OPTICS PATENT ABSTRACTS SERVICE (US/0270-3084) [06395239] **1304**

FIBER OPTICS WEEKLY UPDATE (US/1051-189X) [21887575] **1155**

FIBER OPTICS YELLOW PAGES (US/1075-5268) [27695203] **1155**

FIBER ORGANON (US) [19533262] **5350**

FIBER SCIENCE SERIES (US/0071-4682) [01360823] **5105**

FIBER TO THE HOME (US/1051-192X) [21887488] **1155**

FIBER WORLD (US/0748-0733) [10882326] **5351**

FIBERARTS (US/0164-324X) [03301202] **5351**, **5184**

FIBEROPTIC APPLICATIONS ... (US/1057-9362) [24123222] **4434**

FIBEROPTIC PRODUCT NEWS (US/0890-653X) [14348357] **1155**

FIBERSCOPE (US/0198-8387) [06255256] **5184**, **5351**

FIBERWORKS QUARTERLY *CEASED.* (US/8756-7121) [11635894] **5351**

FIBONACCI QUARTERLY, THE (US/0015-0517) [15693137] **3505**

FIBRE BOX ASSOCIATION *See* HANDBOOK, CORRUGATED AND SOLID FIBREBOARD BOXES AND PRODUCTS **4219**

FIBRE BOX ASSOCIATION *See* FIBRE BOX HANDBOOK **4219**

FIBRE BOX HANDBOOK (US/0196-7215) [05870159] **4219**

FIBRE CHEMISTRY (US/0015-0541) [01382093] **1024**, **5351**

FIBRE MARKET NEWS (US/0046-3728) [04075120] **5351**

FIBRE OPTIC SENSORS (UK) **4434**

FIBRE REPORT (UK) [20649982] **5351**

FIBRINOLYSIS (UK/0268-9499) [15994268] **455**

FIBULA (NE/0015-5676) **268**, **2616**

FIBV STATISTICAL DATA (FR) [04274304] **898**, **729**

FIBV STATISTICS (FR) [08375640] **898**, **729**

FICHA DE CARACTERISTICAS (PO) [04039463] **2379**

FICHAS (UY) [01787947] **2733**

FICHE 'N REEL NEWS : MICROFORM COLLECTIONS AT THE NEW YORK STATE LIBRARY (US) [20066710] **3210**

FICHERO BIBLIOGRAFICO HISPANOAMERICANO (PR/0015-0592) [01569143] **416**

FICHES BIBLIOGRAPHIQUES *See* FICHES BIBLIOGRAPHIQUES (SYCOMORE) **416**

FICHES BIBLIOGRAPHIQUES (SYCOMORE) (FR) [14362213] **416**

FICHES D'IDENTIFICATION DU PLANCTON (DK/0109-2529) [15175387] **5583**

FICHES DU CINEMA (FR/0336-9331) [04821628] **4069**

FICHES PRATIQUES DE LA FORMATION CONTINUE MISE A JOUR, LES (FR/1166-0600) [11660600] **1746**

FICHIER BIOLOGIQUE (CN/0701-9033) [03991726] **455**

FICHIER CENTRAL DES AUTOMOBILES, PARC ET IMMATRICULATIONS / MINISTERE DES TRANSPORTS, DIRECTION DES AFFAIRES ECONOMIQUES, FINANCIERES ET ADMINISTRATIVES, DEPARTEMENT DES STATISTIQUES DES TRANSPORTS (FR) [11449769] **5415**

FICHIER PERMANENT DES CORPS ET GRADES ES ETS SANITAIRES ET SOCIAUX (FR) **4775**

FICHTE-SCHRIFTEN (GW) [06077930] **1746**

FICTA — Alphabetical Title Index

FICTA (AG) [03621150] **4117**

FICTION (US/0046-3736) [01785786] **3387**

FICTION CATALOG (US/0160-4880) [04207648] **416**

FICTION FOCUS (AT/0819-5358) [17944622] **3387**

FICTION INDEX (UK/0428-2957) [02098366] **416**

FICTION INTERNATIONAL (US/0092-1912) [01789240] **3387**

FICTION (NOVATO, CALIF.) (US/0883-7503) [10680317] **3387**

FICTION ON FICHE (UK/1350-4339) **3387**

FID/CR NEWSLETTER (II) [05852689] **3210**

FID/CR REPORT (II/0074-5804) [01587418] **3210**

FID DIRECTORY (NE/0379-3680) [19210147] **4649**

FIDDLE & A BOW *SUSPENDED.* (US/0160-0850) [03600711] **4117**

FIDDLEHEAD, THE (CN/0015-0630) [01306400] **3387**

FIDE, COYUNTURA Y DESARROLLO (AG/0325-5476) [05164036] **1561**

FIDE : THE ARGENTINE ECONOMIC REVIEW (AG) [10168491] **1490**

●FIDELIO (WASHINGTON, D.C.) (US/1059-9126) [24807859] **2533**

FIDELITY & SURETY NEWS : FSN (US/0747-6582) [10812251] 2880, **2970**

FIDELITY INSIGHT (US/1064-170X) [18894100] **898**

FIDELITY (MARSHFIELD, WIS.) (US/0730-0271) [07941555] **4959**

FIDES ET HISTORIA (US/0884-5379) [01780884] **4959**

FIDIA RESEARCH FOUNDATION SYMPOSIUM SERIES (US/1040-0451) [18300714] **3833**

FIDIA RESEARCH SERIES (IT) [12761847] **3576**

FIDUCIARY REPORTER (US) [02261078] **2970**

FIDUCIARY TAX RETURN GUIDE (US/0736-0975) [03782087] **4724**

FIELD & STREAM BASS FISHING ANNUAL (US/0163-5468) [04389612] **2301**

FIELD & STREAM DEER HUNTING ANNUAL (US/0163-5042) [04389148] **4871**

FIELD & STREAM (FAR WEST ED.) (US/8755-8572) [11405923] **4872**

FIELD & STREAM FISHING ANNUAL (US/0362-6385) [02314337] **2301**

FIELD & STREAM GUIDE TO CAMPING ON WHEELS (US) [01790995] 5382, **4872**

FIELD & STREAM HUNTING ANNUAL (US/0361-3011) [02246471] **4872**

FIELD & STREAM (MIDWEST ED.) (US/8755-8599) [11405833] **4872**

FIELD & STREAM (NORTHEAST ED.) (US/8755-8580) [11405735] **4872**

FIELD & STREAM (SOUTH ED.) (US/8755-8602) [11405810] **4872**

FIELD & STREAM SPORTSMAN (US/0091-0651) [01786415] **4872**

FIELD & STREAM (WEST ED.) (US/8755-8610) [11405900] **4872**

FIELD ARCHAEOLOGIST, THE (UK/0265-9921) [19792144] **268**

FIELD ARTILLERY (US/0899-2525) [16516511] **4044**

FIELD CONTEMPORARY POETRY AND POETICS (US) **3463**

FIELD CROP ABSTRACTS (UK/0015-069X) [01569151] 171, **153**

FIELD CROP REPORTING SERIES (CN/0575-8548) [02831095] **171**

FIELD CROPS PRODUCTION, DISPOSITION, VALUE (US/0147-457X) [02992484] **171**

FIELD CROPS : PRODUCTION, DISPOSITION, VALUE / IOWA CROP AND LIVESTOCK REPORTING SERVICE (US) [06347973] **171**

FIELD CROPS RESEARCH (NE/0378-4290) [03788311] **172**

FIELD DIRECTORIO GREMIAL DEL PERU *See* FIELD SERVICIO DE INFORMACIONES DEL PERU **835**

FIELD FOR INVESTMENT, A (RH) [07374510] **898**

FIELD FOUNDATION OF ILLINOIS *See* ANNUAL REPORT - FIELD FOUNDATION OF ILLINOIS **5239**

FIELD GUIDE - GEOLOGICAL SOCIETY OF AUSTRALIA (INC.), SPECIALIST GROUP IN TECTONICS AND STRUCTURAL GEOLOGY (AT/0810-588X) [I0810588X] **1375**

FIELD GUIDE - NEBRASKA GEOLOGICAL SURVEY (US) [05460743] **1375**

FIELD GUIDE TO THE PALEONTOLOGY OF ... / CANADIAN PALEONTOLOGY CONFERENCE, A (CN/1183-0298) [25589886] **4227**

FIELD GUIDES TO COLLECTING SHAKER ANTIQUES (US/1053-136X) [22460552] **250**

FIELD HOCKEY RULES. NATIONAL FEDERATION ED (US/0275-5394) [04185891] **4894**

FIELD (LONDON, ENGLAND : 1853) (UK) [10228365] **4872**

FIELD MUSEUM OF NATURAL HISTORY *See* FIELD MUSEUM OF NATURAL HISTORY ... BIENNIAL REPORT **4165**

FIELD MUSEUM OF NATURAL HISTORY ... BIENNIAL REPORT (US) [24817503] **4165**

FIELD NOTES - ARKANSAS ARCHEOLOGICAL SOCIETY (US/0015-0711) [01362193] **268**

FIELD (OBERLIN, OHIO) (US/0015-0657) [01569147] **3463**

FIELD OF VISION (PITTSBURGH) *CEASED.* (US/0193-9548) [05270063] **320**

●FIELD POLL, THE (US/0195-4520) [26234504] **5245**

FIELD PROCEDURES FOR MONITORING RELOCATION AND REAL PROPERTY ACQUISITION ACTIVITIES (US) [03114819] **2822**

FIELD REPORT EUROPE (IE) **2516**

FIELD SERVICIO DE INFORMACIONES DEL PERU (PE) [03714581] **835**

FIELD STUDIES (UK/0428-304X) [02324873] **4165**

FIELD, THE (UK) [01569146] **4871**

FIELD TRIP GUIDEBOOK (COLUMBIA) (US/0197-0976) [04326355] **1375**

FIELDIANA. ANTHROPOLOGY (US/0071-4739) [01226057] **236**

FIELDIANA. BOTANY (US/0015-0746) [01780190] **510**

FIELDIANA. GEOLOGY (US/0096-2651) [01569159] **1375**

FIELDIANA : ZOOLOGY (US/0015-0754) [01569158] **5583**

●FIELDING'S ALPINE EUROPE (US/1064-0932) [25355478] **5469**

●FIELDING'S AUSTRALIA (US/1061-4842) [24863259] **5469**

●FIELDING'S BENELUX (US/1064-0924) [25611407] **5470**

FIELDING'S BERMUDA AND THE BAHAMAS (US/0739-0769) [09688605] **5470**

●FIELDING'S BRITAIN (US/1064-0940) [24820911] **5470**

FIELDING'S CARIBBEAN (US/0736-2358) [07375267] **5470**

FIELDING'S ECONOMY CARIBBEAN (US/0739-0750) [09679146] **2560**

FIELDING'S EUROPE (US/0192-5326) [04605527] **5470**

FIELDING'S HAVENS AND HIDEAWAYS USA (US/0739-0807) [09688559] **2805**

FIELDING'S HAWAII (US/1061-3366) [22754111] **5470**

FIELDING'S ITALY (US) [23137485] **5470**

FIELDING'S MEXICO (US/0739-0793) [09679479] **5470**

●FIELDING'S SCANDINAVIA (US/1061-4834) [24760983] **5470**

FIELDING'S SELECTIVE SHOPPING GUIDE TO EUROPE (US/0071-478X) [05457402] **954**

FIELDING'S SELECTIVE SHOPPING GUIDE TO EUROPE *See* FIELDING'S SHOPPING EUROPE **954**

●FIELDING'S SHOPPING EUROPE (US/1068-641X) [26928550] **954**

●FIELDING'S SPAIN AND PORTUGAL (US/1064-0991) [25450853] **5470**

FIELDS WITHIN FIELDS WITHIN FIELDS (US/0015-0770) [01569161] **1185**

FIELDSTON COAL TRANSPORTATION MANUAL (US) [11697825] 2139, **1944**

FIEP BULLETIN (FR) [05301568] **1855**

FIESER AND FIESER'S REAGENTS FOR ORGANIC SYNTHESIS (US/0271-616X) [06674031] **1041**

FIET INFO / INTERNATIONAL FEDERATION OF COMMERCIAL, CLERICAL, PROFESSIONAL AND TECHNICAL EMPLOYEES (SZ) [18527179] **1669**

FIFA MAGAZINE : A PUBLICATION OF THE FEDERATION INTERNATIONALE DE FOOTBALL ASSOCIATION (SZ) [27990337] **4894**

FIFA NEWS (SZ) [02746828] **4894**

FIFTEENTH CENTURY STUDIES (GW/0164-0933) [04358047] **2616**

FIFTH COLUMN (CN/0229-7094) [09137695] **298**

FIFTH ESTATE (US/0015-0800) [01569163] **4541**

FIFTY BILLION DOLLAR DIRECTORY, THE (US/0741-8892) [10232654] **954**

FIFTY-FIVE PLUS (BATTERSEA) (CN/0840-4496) [19916349] **5179**

FIFTY SOMETHING (AT) **5179**

FIGA (US/0196-187X) [05753825] **4117**

FIGARO, LE (FR) [01569166] **5800**

FIGARO MAGAZINE, LE (FR) [04388119] **2516**

FIGHT BEAT (US/8756-2340) [11508397] **4894**

FIGHT DIRECTOR, THE (UK) [07193640] 4069, **5364**

FIGHT RACISM, FIGHT IMPERIALISM! : ANTI-IMPERIALIST BULLETIN OF THE REVOLUTIONARY COMMUNIST GROUP (UK/0143-5426) [22753334] **4474**

FIGHTING WOMAN NEWS (US/0146-8812) [03054837] 1855, **2597**

FIGURA (SW/0071-481X) [01327781] **350**

FIGURE (SALERNO, ITALY) (IT) [21022389] **320**

FIGURE SKATING COACHES OF CANADA *See* NEWSLETTER - FIGURE SKATING COACHES OF CANADA **4908**

FIGURES FOR THE YEAR ENDED MARCH 31 ... / THE OVERSEAS TELECOMMUNICATIONS COMMISSION (AUSTRALIA) (AT) [11560481] **1155**

FIGYELO (HU/0015-086X) [09305134] **675**

FIJI AGRICULTURAL JOURNAL (FJ/0015-0886) [02410738] **87**

FIJI AIRCRAFT STATISTICS (FJ) [18139014] **20**

FIJI. BOARD OF FIRE COMMISSIONERS *See* REPORT FOR THE YEAR ... / BOARD OF FIRE COMMISSIONERS **2292**

FIJI. BUREAU OF STATISTICS *See* SOCIAL INDICATORS FOR FIJI **5259**

FIJI. BUREAU OF STATISTICS *See* CURRENT ECONOMIC STATISTICS **1531**

FIJI. BUREAU OF STATISTICS *See* INSURANCE REPORT AND STATISTICS OF FIJI **2897**

FIJI. BUREAU OF STATISTICS *See* CENSUS OF BUILDING AND CONSTRUCTION (FIJI) **607**

FIJI. COCONUT BOARD *See* ANNUAL REPORT ... / COCONUT BOARD (FIJI) **1597**

FIJI. DEPT. OF POSTS AND TELECOMMUNICATIONS *See* REPORT - DEPT. OF POSTS AND TELECOMMUNICATIONS **1147**

FIJI LIBRARY ASSOCIATION *See* FIJI LIBRARY ASSOCIATION NEWSLETTER **3210**

FIJI LIBRARY ASSOCIATION NEWSLETTER (FJ) [05204417] **3210**

FIJI MINERAL RESOURCES DEPARTMENT HYDROGEOLOGICAL REPORT (FJ) **1355**

FIJI. MINERAL RESOURCES DEPT *See* REPORT FOR THE YEAR ... - MINERAL RESOURCES DEPARTMENT (FIJI) **1360**

FIJI. MINERALS RESOURCES DEPARTMENT *See* BULLETIN - MINERAL RESOURCES DIVISION (SUVA) **1370**

FIJI. MINISTRY OF FINANCE. E.D.P. BRANCH *See* REPORT OF E.D.P. BRANCH, MINISTRY OF FINANCE FOR THE YEAR ... **4745**

FIJI NATIONAL BIBLIOGRAPHY (FJ) [06509604] **416**

FIJI. NATIONAL TRAINING COUNCIL *See* REPORT - FIJI NATIONAL TRAINING COUNCIL **1706**

FIJI. PARLIAMENT. SENATE *See* PARLIAMENTARY DEBATES (HANSARD), THE SENATE **4672**

FIJI. POSTS AND TELEGRAPH DEPT. REPORT *See* REPORT - DEPT. OF POSTS AND TELECOMMUNICATIONS **1147**

FIJI REPUBLIC GAZETTE (FJ) **5800**

FIJI. SUGAR BOARD *See* ANNUAL REPORT FOR ... SEASON (FIJI. SUGAR BOARD) **60**

FIJI SUN (FJ) [19705755] **5800**

FIJI TIMES, THE (FJ) [19706068] **5800**

FIKIR VE SAN'ATTA HAREKET (TU/0300-2314) [01784707] **2503**

FIKIR (LE) [04130133] **2651**

FIKR O NAZAR (PK/0430-4055) [06157499] **5042**

FIL DE LIAISON (CN/1180-3444) [23658915] **5231**

Alphabetical Title Index — FILOSOFIIA

FIL DES PHIL- ANTHROPES, LE (CN/0710-5665) [08774046] **385**

FIL DIRECTEUR (FR) **1490**

●FIL MAGAZIN (AU) **4894**

FILASTIN (LE) [05860931] **4521**

FILASTIN AL-MUHTALLAH (LE) [04099573] **2651**

FILASTIN AL-THAWRAH (LE) [03324909] **2651**

FILATELIA CUBANA (CU) [04573490] **2785**

FILATELISTA : DWUTYGODNIK POLSKIEGO ZWIAZKU FILATELISTOW (PL) [09033341] **2785**

FILEMAKER REPORT, THE (US/0896-0313) [16891010] 1254, **1286**

FILET (MONTREAL, QUEBEC) (CN/0836-6918) [17743312] **4959**

FILIERA CARNE (IT) **2335**

FILIERE FARINE *See* FILIERE GOURMANDE **2335**

FILIERE GOURMANDE (FR) [I12439681] **2335**

FILIERES VIANDE ET PECHE *See* PRODUITS FRAIS LEVALLOIS-PERRET **2354**

FILIERES VIANDE ET PECHE LEVALLOIS-PERRET (FR/1143-7375) [I11437375] **2335**

●FILIGRANE (MONTREAL) (CN/1192-1412) [27018794] **3925**

FILING STATEMENT (VANCOUVER STOCK EXCHANGE) (CN) [10057312] **898**

FILIPINAS JOURNAL OF SCIENCE AND CULTURE, THE (PH) [08608868] **5105**

●FILIPINAS (SAN FRANCISCO, CALIF.) (US/1063-4630) [26041532] **2261**

FILIPINIANA UNION CATALOG (PH) [03854902] **416**

FILIPINKA WARSZAWA (PL/0426-1216) [I04261216] **1063**

FILIPINO-AMERICAN HERALD, THE (US) [03758757] **2261**

FILIPINO AMERICAN, THE (US/0745-905X) [08294897] **2261**

FILIPINO CATHOLIC (US/0273-7280) [06880776] **5029**

FILIPINO DIRECTORY OF CALIFORNIA, THE (US/0739-4802) [09729107] **2733**

FILIPINO METHODIST MAGAZINE, THE (PH/0430-4144) [06698091] **5060**

FILIPINO PHYSICIANS IN AMERICA (US/0739-8131) [09868471] **3576**

FILLERS FOR PUBLICATIONS (US/0739-0033) [09688507] **2919**

FILLES D'AUJOURD'HUI (CN/0227-0315) [08036483] **1063**

FILLING YOU IN -- (US) [24572195] **1323**

FILM (PL) [05249562] **4069**

FILM A DOBA (XR/0015-1068) [05249564] **5268**

FILM ACTORS GUIDE (US/1055-0836) [23076427] **4069**

FILM & FAKTEN : EIN MAGAZIN DER FSK (GW/0934-0378) [22475754] **4069**

FILM & HISTORY (NEWARK, N.J.) (US/0360-3695) [02578168] **4069**

FILM & KINO (NO/0015-1351) [09880649] **4069**

FILM AND PAMPHLET CATALOG (US) [12616799] **4810**

FILM AND TELEVISION HANDBOOK *See* BFI FILM AND TELEVISION HANDBOOK **4064**

FILM AND TELEVISION HANDBOOK / BRITISH FILM INSTITUTE (UK/0956-8409) [20944678] **4069**

FILM AND TELEVISION TECHNICIAN (UK) [05257961] **4069**

FILM AND VIDEO CATALOGUE / VIENNA INTERNATIONAL CENTRE LIBRARY (AU) [25816106] **1944**

FILM & VIDEO FINDER (US/0898-1582) [15047373] 1895, **4069**

FILM & VIDEO (LOS ANGELES, CALIF.) (US/1041-1933) [18676714] **4069**

FILM AND VIDEO MAKERS DIRECTORY, THE (US/0270-3289) [06364223] **4069**

FILM AND VIDEO (OTTAWA) (CN/1181-6708) [25066252] 4069, **4080**

●FILM ANNUAL (US/1061-4214) [25306071] **4069**

FILM AUSTRALIA EDUCATION CATALOGUE (AT) **4069**

FILM BULLETIN (US/0015-1165) [05089599] **4069**

FILM CATALOGUE ... / VIENNA INTERNATIONAL CENTRE LIBRARY (AU) [10978916] **4447**

FILM COMMENT (US/0015-119X) [02266507] **4069**

FILM COMPOSERS GUIDE (US/1055-081X) [23076375] 4117, **4069**

FILM CRITICISM (US/0163-5069) [04021815] **4069**

FILM CULTURE (US/0015-1211) [01569194] **4069**

FILM (DENVER, COLO.) **SUSPENDED.** (US/0740-1566) [09882831] **4069**

FILM DIRECTIONS (IE) [06885983] **4069**

FILM DOPE (UK/0305-1706) [06497960] 432, **4069**

FILM ECHANGE (FR/0181-4141) [11980388] **4069**

FILM EN TELEVISIE EN VIDEO (BE) 320, **4069**

FILM EXTRUSION MATERIALS AND MARKETS BULLETIN (UK) **4219**

FILM FILE ... , THE **SUSPENDED.** (US/0731-5716) [08205606] **4069**

... FILM FINANCIAL RECORD, THE (US/1056-6945) [23729808] **4069**

FILM FRANCAIS 1983, LE (FR/0759-0385) [I07590385] **4070**

FILM FRANCAIS, LE (FR) [04067599] **4069**

FILM/HISTORIA (BO) [05239151] **4070**

FILM IN FINLAND (HELSINKI, FINLAND) (FI) [10329289] **4070**

FILM INDEX (AT) [01787943] **4070**

FILM INDUSTRY GAZETTE (US/0742-6739) [10412001] **4070**

FILM INFORMATION (US/0015-1297) [01569201] **3210**

FILM JOURNAL (HOLLINS), THE **SUSPENDED.** (US/0046-3787) [01569202] **4070**

FILM JOURNAL (NEW YORK), THE (US/0199-7300) [06106518] **4070**

FILM LIBRARY CATALOGUE / NATIONAL HEALTH AND WELFARE (CN/0713-6099) [08871452] **3210**

FILM LITERATURE INDEX (US/0093-6758) [01792681] 385, 4070, **4080**

FILM (LONDON, ENGLAND : 1954) (UK/0015-1025) [06101893] **4070**

FILM NA SWIECIE 1974 (PL/0137-4877) [I01374877] **4070**

FILM NEWS (IO) [03994808] **4070**

FILM NEWS INTERNATIONAL (US/0067-7676) **4070**

FILM OG KINO / KOMMUNALE KINEMATOGRAFERS LANDSFORBUND (NO) [10708532] **4070**

FILM POLSKI *See* POLISH ANIMATED FILMS CATALOGUE **4076**

FILM PRODUCERS, STUDIOS, AGENTS, AND CASTING DIRECTORS GUIDE (US/1058-2630) [22261557] **4070**

FILM QUARTERLY (US/0015-1386) [01569205] **4070**

FILM REFERENCE GUIDE FOR MEDICINE AND ALLIED SCIENCES (US/0071-4909) [01295489] **3576**

FILM REVIEW (US) [01345159] **4070**

FILM REVIEW (UK) [05215241] **4070**

FILM REVIEW ANNUAL (US/0737-9080) [09101779] **4070**

FILM REVIEW DIGEST (MILLWOOD) (US/0098-0471) [02246439] **4070**

FILM REVIEW (ENGLAND) (UK) **4070**

FILM STUDIES (US/0524-1324) [03256824] **4070**

FILM STUDIES ASSOCIATION OF CANADA *See* NEWSLETTER - FILM STUDIES ASSOCIATION OF CANADA **4075**

FILM THREAT (US/0896-6389) [24890367] **4070**

FILM THREAT (US/0896-6389) [17247866] **4070**

FILM : TUTTI I FILM DELLA STAGIONE (IT) [26332798] **4070**

FILM UND FARBE (GW/0934-0378) [21664807] **4070**

FILM UND FERNSEHEN (GW/0323-3227) [07094962] **4070**

FILM- UND TV-KAMERAMANN (GW/0343-5571) [03435571] **4070**

FILM/VIDEO CANADIANA (CN/0836-1002) [18121299] 4369, **4070**

FILM WRITERS GUIDE (US/0894-864X) [16270180] **4070**

FILMCRITICA (IT) [05258452] **4070**

FILMECHO, FILMWOCHE, FILMBLAETTER (GW) **4070**

FILMFAUST (GW) [05594184] **4070**

FILMFAX (US/0895-0393) [14292774] **4070**

FILMFORDERUNG, STATISTIK *See* FILMFORDERUNG ... STATISTIK, FILMEINFUHR, STATISTIK / EIDGENOSSISCHES AMT FUER KULTURELLE ANGELEGENHEITEN, SEKTION FILM **4080**

FILMFORDERUNG ... STATISTIK, FILMEINFUHR, STATISTIK / EIDGENOSSISCHES AMT FUER KULTURELLE ANGELEGENHEITEN, SEKTION FILM (SZ) [08982283] 4070, **4080**

FILMHAFTET : TIDSKRIFT OM FILM OCH TV (SW/0345-3057) [I03453057] 385, **4070**

FILMIHULLU (FI) [07500515] **4071**

FILMKULTURA (HU/0015-1580) [08039636] **4071**

FILMKUNST (AU/0015-1599) [05258455] **4071**

FILMLOGBUCH (AU) **4071**

●FILMMAKER (LOS ANGELES, CALIF.) (US/1063-8954) [26168124] **4071**

FILMNEWS (AT/1036-8701) **4071**

FILMOTECA ULTRAMARINA PORTUGUESA *See* BOLETIM DA FILMOTECA ULTRAMARINA PORTUGUESA **2611**

FILMROW (US/0195-7546) [05623731] **4071**

FILMRUTAN (SW/0015-1661) [05248429] **4071**

FILMS / A CATALOG OF THE FILM COLLECTION (US) [02414460] **4071**

FILMS A L'ECRAN (CN/0046-3825) [02443064] **4071**

FILMS BY AND/OR ABOUT WOMEN **CEASED.** (US/0361-4581) [02026484] 5556, **4071**

FILMS IN REVIEW (US/0015-1688) [01569214] **4071**

FILMS ON OFFER ... / COMPILED BY NIGEL ALGAR AND STEPHEN JENKINS (UK) [08181052] **4071**

FILMS/VIDEO (US/0882-8490) [12026929] **1132**

FILMSPIEGEL (SZ) [04095337] **4071**

FILMSSONEN, DANSK FILMFORTEGNELSE / UDGIVIT AF BIBLIOTEKSCENTRALEN OG DET DANSKE FILMMUSEUM (DK/0107-1033) [07626287] **4071**

FILMVIDEO-JOURNAL (GW) [08869362] **4071**

FILMVILAG (HU) [21057723] **4071**

FILO METALLICO, IL (GW/0430-4578) [03096447] **4002**

FILOLOGIA (AG/0071-495X) [01569216] **1076**

FILOLOGIA ANGIELSKA - UNIWERSYTET IM. ADAMA MICKIEWICZA W POZNANIU (PL/0554-8144) [I05548144] **3281**

FILOLOGIA E CRITICA (SALERNO EDITRICE) (IT/0391-2493) [04294673] 3281, **3387**

FILOLOGIA MODERNA (IT) [04222566] **3281**

FILOLOGIA MODERNA **SUSPENDED.** (SP/0046-3841) [02261094] **3281**

FILOLOGIA NEOTESTAMENTARIA (SP) [20003371] 5016, **3281**

FILOLOGIA POLSKA (PL) [03536952] 3281, **3388**

FILOLOGIA VENETA (IT) [20404112] **3281**

FILOLOGIAI KOZLONY (HU/0015-1785) [01569218] 3342, **3281**

●FILOLOGICHESKIE NAUKI (RU) [27474399] **3281**

FILOLOGICHESKIE ZAPISKI (RU) [05883241] **3281**

FILOLOGIJA (CI/0449-363X) [01782906] **3281**

FILOLOGIKE PROTOHRONIA (GR/1105-1000) [04940177] 1077, **3281**

FILOLOGISKT ARKIV (SW/0083-6745) [01644926] **3281**

FILOLOHIIA (UN) [05637617] **3281**

FILOMATA (PL/0015-1815) [I00151815] **1077**

FILON (CN/0712-2861) [08878692] **1439**

FILOSOFIA (IT/0015-1823) [01635250] **4346**

FILOSOFIA (ATHENAI) (GR/1105-2120) [01792200] **4346**

FILOSOFIA E SOCIETA (IT) [16705789] **5200**

FILOSOFIA OGGI (IT) [04612110] **4346**

FILOSOFIA POLITICA (BL) [13154389] **4346**

FILOSOFIE EN PRAKTIJK (NE) **4346**

FILOSOFIIA I FIZIKA (RU) [01788104] **4403**

FILOSOFIIA — Alphabetical Title Index

FILOSOFIIA I SOVREMENNYI MIR / MINISTERSTVO NARODNOGO OBRAZOVANIIA BSSR [I] BELORUSSKII ORDENA TRUDOVOGO KRASNOGO ZNAMENI GOSUDARSTVENNYI UNIVERSITET IMENI V.I. LENINA (BW/0868-6718) [24040894] **4541**

FILOSOFIJA, SOCIOLOGIJA / LIETUVOS MOKSLU AKADEMIJA (LI/0235-7186) [23134007] 5245, **4346**

FILOSOFSKA MISUL (BU/0015-184X) [02362902] **4346**

●FILOSOFSKI ALTERNATIVI (BU/0861-7899) [27261164] **4346**

FILOSOFSKIE NAUKI (RU/0235-1188) [15625645] **4347**

FILOSOFSKIE NAUKI (ALMA-ATA) (KZ/0320-5452) [05637709] 4541, **4347**

FILOSOFSKIE OSNOVANIIA TEORII MEZHDUNARODNYKH OTNOSHENII (RU) [19247988] **4521**

FILOZOFIA (BRATISLAVA) (XO/0046-385X) [05667271] **4347**

FILOZOFICKY CASOPIS (USTAV PRO FILOZOFII A SOCIOLOGII CSAV) (XR/0015-1831) [08303633] **4347**

FILOZOFSKA ISTRAZIVANJA (CI/0351-4706) [16707314] **4347**

FILOZOFSKI VESTNIK / SLOVENSKA AKADEMIJA ZNANOSTI IN UMETNOSTI, ZNANSTVENORAZISKOVALNI CENTER SAZU, FILOZOFSKI INSTITUT (XV/0353-4510) [20863688] **4347**

FILS, TUBES, BANDES, PROFILES (FR/0249-6704) [02496704] **2114**

FILSON CLUB HISTORY QUARTERLY, THE (US/0015-1874) [06674913] **2733**

FILTER (BRANTFORD) (CN/0833-8493) [15134220] **3941**

FILTER PERTH **CEASED.** (AT/0310-6020) [103106020] 5105, **1895**

FILTRATION & SEPARATION (UK/0015-1882) [06894603] **2012**

FILUGELLO (IT) **3342**

FIN TECH. 1, TELECOM MARKETS (UK/0267-1484) [I02671484] **1155**

FINAL ACT / ORGANIZATION OF AMERICAN STATES, CIES (US) [08793937] **1669**

FINAL BUDGET / COUNTY OF LOS ANGELES (US) [17344595] **4724**

FINAL BUDGET PROPOSAL / ROYAL NORWEGIAN MINISTRY OF FINANCE (NO) [13842666] **4724**

FINAL BUDGET SUMMARY / STATE OF CALIFORNIA (US) [08035522] **4724**

FINAL COMPREHENSIVE ANNUAL SERVICES PLAN FOR NORTH CAROLINA PURSUANT TO TITLE XX OF THE FEDERAL SOCIAL SECURITY ACT *See* FINAL TITLE XX COMPREHENSIVE ANNUAL SERVICES PLAN FOR NORTH CAROLINA **5285**

FINAL COMPREHENSIVE ANNUAL SERVICES PROGRAM PLAN FOR TITLE XX - SOCIAL SECURITY ACT (US) [04964462] **5285**

FINAL COMPREHENSIVE ANNUAL SOCIAL SERVICE PROGRAM PLAN (US) [03645071] **5285**

FINAL CONTROL ELEMENTS; PROCEEDINGS (US/0091-7699) [01800066] **2114**

FINAL FRONTIER (US/0899-4161) [18097244] **20**

FINAL GRAPE CRUSH REPORT (US/0271-6127) [06643258] **87**

FINAL NEBRASKA COMPREHENSIVE ANNUAL SERVICES PLAN (US) [04020041] **5285**

FINAL REPORT / INTERGOVERNMENTAL COMMITTEE FOR PHYSICAL EDUCATION AND SPORT (FR) [08748052] **4894**

FINAL REPORT ON APPROPRIATIONS AND ESTIMATED REVENUES *See* LEGISLATIVE ASSEMBLY REPORT ON APPROPRIATIONS AND ESTIMATED REVENUES **4736**

FINAL REPORT - TEXAS LEGISLATIVE SERVICE (US/0093-1381) [01784509] **2970**

FINAL REPORTS OF INTERIM JOINT AND SPECIAL COMMITTEES (US) [06244140] **2970**

FINAL STATISTICAL REPORT - CALIFORNIA. PRUNE MARKETING COMMITTEE (US/0737-4852) [09367287] 835, **729**

FINAL TABLES AND INDEX TO LEGISLATIVE MEASURES (US) [02407356] **2970**

FINAL TITLE XX COMPREHENSIVE ANNUAL SERVICES PLAN FOR NORTH CAROLINA (US) [08080965] **5285**

FINANCAS E ORCAMENTO (BL) [02245096] **4724**

FINANCAS PUBLICAS MUNICIPAIS (BL) [02618879] **4724**

FINANCE (AT) [02173963] **4724**

FINANCE ACCOUNTS, GOVERNMENT OF ORISSA (II) [05218423] **4724**

FINANCE ACTS (UK) **4724**

FINANCE AND COMMERCE (US) [01757619] **3086**

FINANCE AND COMMERCE (REGULAR DAILY ED.) (US/8750-6149) [11163060] **2970**

FINANCE & DEVELOPMENT (US/0015-1947) [02246726] 2909, **1635**

FINANCE AND DEVELOPMENT (MY) [01797932] 4724, **1490**

FINANCE AND ECONOMICS DISCUSSION SERIES (US) [17432921] **1490**

FINANCE AND GENERAL STATISTICS (UK) [09178064] **4724**

●FINANCE & TREASURY (US/1070-9215) [27194128] **898**

FINANCE AUTHORITY OF MAINE *See* ANNUAL REPORT / FINANCE AUTHORITY OF MAINE **771**

FINANCE BILLS. COMMONS & LORDS (UK) **4724**

FINANCE BILLS. ORIGINALS & AMENDMENTS (UK) **4724**

●FINANCE (BOSTON, MASS.) (US/1070-9193) [27038410] **4204**

FINANCE DIRECTOR'S REVIEW (UK) **4724**

●FINANCE, INSURANCE & REAL ESTATE USA (US/1066-7350) [27039041] 4837, **2880**

FINANCE (PARIS) (FR/0752-6180) [11046002] **4725**

FINANCE QUARTERLY BULLETIN (US) [19829149] **4725**

FINANCE STANDING COMMITTEE DEBATES (UK) **4725**

FINANCES & DEVELOPPEMENT (US/0430-473X) [05187203] **2909**

FINANCES DES DEPARTEMENTS, LES (FR) [10488895] **4725**

FINANCES OF EMPLOYEE-RETIREMENT SYSTEMS OF STATE AND LOCAL GOVERNMENTS (US/0096-3224) [01798446] 4649, **1669**

FINANCIADORA DE ESTUDOS E PROJETOS (BRAZIL) *See* RELATORIO DE ATIVIDADES - FINANCIADORA DE ESTUDOS E PROJETOS **807**

FINANCIAL 1000 YELLOW BOOK *See* FINANCIAL YELLOW BOOK **1926**

FINANCIAL ACCOUNTABILITY & MANAGEMENT IN GOVERNMENTS, PUBLIC SERVICES, AND CHARITIES (UK/0267-4424) [12439748] 675, **4649**

FINANCIAL ACCOUNTING STANDARDS BOARD *See* EXPOSURE DRAFT (STAMFORD, CONN. 1974) **743**

FINANCIAL ACCOUNTING STANDARDS BOARD *See* FASB DISCUSSION MEMORANDUM **744**

FINANCIAL ACCOUNTING STANDARDS BOARD *See* FASB TECHNICAL BULLETIN **744**

FINANCIAL ACCOUNTING STANDARDS BOARD *See* FASB INTERPRETATION **744**

FINANCIAL ACCOUNTING STANDARDS BOARD *See* ANNUAL REPORT / FINANCIAL ACCOUNTING STANDARDS BOARD **738**

FINANCIAL ACCOUNTING STANDARDS BOARD *See* STATUS REPORT - FINANCIAL ACCOUNTING STANDARDS BOARD **751**

FINANCIAL ADVERTISING REVIEW (US/0748-1845) [10909152] **759**

FINANCIAL AID FOR FIRST DEGREE STUDY AT COMMONWEALTH UNIVERSITIES (UK/0260-0749) [07993041] **1824**

●FINANCIAL AID FOR RESEARCH AND CREATIVE ACTIVITIES ABROAD (US) [25895261] **1746**

FINANCIAL AID FOR RESEARCH, STUDY AND TRAVEL ABROAD *See* FINANCIAL AID FOR RESEARCH AND CREATIVE ACTIVITIES ABROAD **1746**

FINANCIAL AID FOR RESEARCH, STUDY AND TRAVEL ABROAD *See* FINANCIAL AID FOR STUDY AND TRAINING ABROAD **1746**

●FINANCIAL AID FOR STUDY AND TRAINING ABROAD (US) [25770932] **1746**

FINANCIAL AID FOR THE DISABLED AND THEIR FAMILIES (US/0898-9222) [17949275] **1824**

FINANCIAL AID FOR VETERANS, MILITARY PERSONNEL, AND THEIR DEPENDENTS (US/0896-7792) [17287247] 4044, **5285**

FINANCIAL AIDS FOR HIGHER EDUCATION (US/0364-8877) [02665307] **1824**

FINANCIAL ANALYSIS OF THE MOTOR CARRIER INDUSTRY **CEASED.** (US/0099-2445) [02241885] **5382**

FINANCIAL ANALYSTS FEDERATION *See* MEMBERSHIP DIRECTORY CLASSIFIED BY SPECIALTY **906**

FINANCIAL ANALYSTS FEDERATION *See* MEMBERSHIP DIRECTORY - THE FINANCIAL ANALYSTS FEDERATION **906**

FINANCIAL ANALYSTS JOURNAL, THE (US/0015-198X) [04889170] **898**

FINANCIAL & COMMON STOCK INFORMATION / WATER UTILITY INDUSTRY (US) **675**

FINANCIAL AND OPERATING STATISTICS CLASS I MOTOR CARRIERS OF PASSENGERS (US/0362-9317) [02465860] **5401**

FINANCIAL AND STATISTICAL REPORT - MICHIGAN. PUBLIC SCHOOL EMPLOYEES' RETIREMENT SYSTEM (US) [04915453] 1864, **1795**

FINANCIAL AND STATISTICAL REPORT: SPECIAL EDUCATION (ILLINOIS) (US) [01786996] 4388, **1879**

FINANCIAL ASSISTANCE BY GEOGRAPHIC AREA. REGION I, BOSTON, MASS (US/0196-9226) [04280707] **4725**

FINANCIAL ASSISTANCE BY GEOGRAPHIC AREA. REGION II, NEW YORK, N.Y (US/0192-4613) [05010577] **4725**

FINANCIAL ASSISTANCE BY GEOGRAPHIC AREA. REGION III, PHILADELPHIA, PENNA (US/0192-4982) [05015401] **4725**

FINANCIAL ASSISTANCE BY GEOGRAPHIC AREA. REGION IX, SAN FRANCISCO, CALIFORNIA (US/0192-6586) [05039224] **4725**

FINANCIAL ASSISTANCE BY GEOGRAPHIC AREA. REGION V, CHICAGO, ILLINOIS (US/0192-4966) [05015728] **4725**

FINANCIAL ASSISTANCE BY GEOGRAPHIC AREA. REGION VI, DALLAS, TEXAS (US/0192-5598) [05020320] **4725**

FINANCIAL ASSISTANCE BY GEOGRAPHIC AREA. REGION VII, KANSAS CITY, MISSOURI (US/0192-8074) [05032683] **4725**

FINANCIAL ASSISTANCE BY GEOGRAPHIC AREA. REGION VIII, DENVER, COLORADO (US/0192-6578) [05039277] **4725**

FINANCIAL ASSISTANCE BY GEOGRAPHIC AREA. REGION X, SEATTLE, WASHINGTON (US/0192-6608) [05039321] **4725**

FINANCIAL ASSISTANCE BY GEOGRAPHIC AREA (UNITED STATES. DEPT. OF EDUCATION. OFFICE OF FINANCIAL MANAGEMENT) (US/0277-3570) [07539793] **1824**

●FINANCIAL ASSISTANCE FOR LIBRARY AND INFORMATION STUDIES (US) [27079134] **3210**

FINANCIAL ASSISTANCE FOR LIBRARY EDUCATION (US/0569-6275) [02577404] **3210**

FINANCIAL ASSISTANCE SCHEMES FOR LOCAL GOVERNMENTS / PREPARED BY RESEARCH SECTION, DEPARTMENT OF LOCAL GOVERNMENT (AT) [16817691] **4649**

FINANCIAL COMPUTING (US/0743-0159) [10501665] **1185**

FINANCIAL CONDITION OF PENN CENTRAL TRANSPORTATION COMPANY, THE (US/0098-3128) [02240904] **5431**

FINANCIAL CONNECTION, THE (US) [24451660] **4725**

FINANCIAL COUNSELING AND PLANNING (US/1052-3073) [22258133] **898**

FINANCIAL DAILY CARD SERVICE, CUMULATIVE (US/0093-4070) [03149568] **898**

FINANCIAL DATA, COMMERCIAL AIR CARRIERS / RENSEIGNEMENTS FINANCIERS, TRANSPORTEURS AERIENS COMMERCIAUX / DATOS FINANCIEROS, TRANSPORTISTAS AEREOS COMERCIALES / FINANSOVYE DANNYE, KOMMERCHESKIE AVIAPEREVOZCHIKI (CN) [06719394] **20**

FINANCIAL DIRECTORY OF PENSION FUNDS. ALABAMA (US/0742-0072) [10236881] **1669**

FINANCIAL DIRECTORY OF PENSION FUNDS. ALASKA (US/0742-0099) [10237085] **1669**

FINANCIAL DIRECTORY OF PENSION FUNDS. ARIZONA (US/0742-0110) [10237212] **1669**

FINANCIAL DIRECTORY OF PENSION FUNDS. ARKANSAS (US/0742-0102) [10237135] **1669**

FINANCIAL DIRECTORY OF PENSION FUNDS. CALIFORNIA, NORTHERN, EXCLUDING SAN FRANCISCO. OAKLAND, SAN JOSE, FRESNO & OTHERS (US/0739-2737) [09693948] **1670**

FINANCIAL DIRECTORY OF PENSION FUNDS. CALIFORNIA, SOUTHERN, EXCLUDING LOS ANGELES AREA (SAN DIEGO, SANTA ANA, SAN BERNARDINO & OTHERS) (US/0739-3385) [09692590] **1670**

FINANCIAL DIRECTORY OF PENSION FUNDS. CALIFORNIA, SOUTHERN. LOS ANGELES CITY PROPER (US/0739-2591) [09690918] **1670**

FINANCIAL DIRECTORY OF PENSION FUNDS. CALIFORNIA, SOUTHERN, NO. SUBURBAN LOS ANGELES. VENTURA, PASADENA, ALHAMBRA & OTHERS (US/0739-2729) [09695259] **1670**

FINANCIAL DIRECTORY OF PENSION FUNDS. CALIFORNIA, SOUTHERN, SO. SUBURBAN LOS ANGELES. INGLEWOOD, WHITTIER, LONG BEACH & OTHERS (US/0739-2672) [09693789] **1670**

FINANCIAL DIRECTORY OF PENSION FUNDS. CALIFORNIA, UPPER NORTHERN (STOCKTON, SACRAMENTO & OTHERS) (US/0278-2405) [07720163] **1670**

FINANCIAL DIRECTORY OF PENSION FUNDS. COLORADO (US/0741-4714) [10142455] **1670**

FINANCIAL DIRECTORY OF PENSION FUNDS. CONNECTICUT, NORTHERN. HARTFORD, WILLIMANTIC, WATERBURY & OTHERS (US/0739-280X) [09693132] **1670**

FINANCIAL DIRECTORY OF PENSION FUNDS. CONNECTICUT, SOUTHERN. STAMFORD, NEW HAVEN, NEW LONDON & OTHERS (US/0739-2621) [09695080] **1670**

FINANCIAL DIRECTORY OF PENSION FUNDS. DELAWARE, THE (US/0882-2980) [11722406] **1670**

FINANCIAL DIRECTORY OF PENSION FUNDS. DISTRICT OF COLUMBIA (US/0742-0080) [10236972] **1670**

FINANCIAL DIRECTORY OF PENSION FUNDS. FLORIDA, CENTRAL (TAMPA, LAKELAND, ORLANDO & OTHERS) (US/0278-0348) [07680978] **1670**

FINANCIAL DIRECTORY OF PENSION FUNDS. FLORIDA, NORTHERN. JACKSONVILLE, TALLAHASSEE, GAINESVILLE & OTHERS (US/0739-2656) [09694745] **1670**

FINANCIAL DIRECTORY OF PENSION FUNDS. FLORIDA, SOUTHERN. WEST PALM BEACH, MIAMI, FT. MYER & OTHERS (US/0739-2664) [09694852] **1670**

FINANCIAL DIRECTORY OF PENSION FUNDS. GEORGIA, ATLANTA AREA (US/0739-3245) [09692643] **1670**

FINANCIAL DIRECTORY OF PENSION FUNDS. GEORGIA, EXCLUDING ATLANTA AREA (US/0731-7328) [08216693] **1670**

FINANCIAL DIRECTORY OF PENSION FUNDS. HAWAII, THE (US/0882-2956) [11718924] **1670**

FINANCIAL DIRECTORY OF PENSION FUNDS. IDAHO (US/0742-5139) [10237784] **1670**

FINANCIAL DIRECTORY OF PENSION FUNDS. ILLINOIS, CHICAGO CITY PROPER (US/0739-2834) [09691388] **1670**

FINANCIAL DIRECTORY OF PENSION FUNDS. ILLINOIS, NO. SUBURBAN CHICAGO (OAK PARK, SKOKIE, EVANSTON & OTHERS) (US/0731-3748) [08156857] **1670**

FINANCIAL DIRECTORY OF PENSION FUNDS. ILLINOIS, NORTHERN, EXCLUDING CHICAGO AREA. KANKAKEE, ROCKFORD, PEORIA & OTHERS (US/0739-2818) [09695633] **1671**

FINANCIAL DIRECTORY OF PENSION FUNDS. ILLINOIS, SO. SUBURBAN CHICAGO (EVERGREEN PARK, CHICAGO HEIGHTS, JOLIET & OTHERS) (US/0731-3756) [08157148] **1671**

FINANCIAL DIRECTORY OF PENSION FUNDS. ILLINOIS, SOUTHERN DOWNSTATE (CHAMPAIGN, SPRINGFIELD, EAST ST. LOUIS & OTHERS) (US/0732-7145) [08396153] **1671**

FINANCIAL DIRECTORY OF PENSION FUNDS. INDIANA, NORTHERN. SOUTH BEND, FT. WAYNE, MUNCIE & OTHERS (US/0739-2583) [09693001] **1671**

FINANCIAL DIRECTORY OF PENSION FUNDS. INDIANA, SOUTHERN (INDIANAPOLIS, TERRE HAUTE, EVANSVILLE & OTHERS) (US/0739-2869) [09691333] **1671**

FINANCIAL DIRECTORY OF PENSION FUNDS. IOWA (US/0742-0129) [10237690] **1671**

FINANCIAL DIRECTORY OF PENSION FUNDS. KANSAS, THE (US/0882-083X) [11718851] **1671**

FINANCIAL DIRECTORY OF PENSION FUNDS. KENTUCKY (US/0731-7395) [08216753] **1671**

FINANCIAL DIRECTORY OF PENSION FUNDS. LOUISIANA (US/0742-0137) [10237726] **1671**

FINANCIAL DIRECTORY OF PENSION FUNDS. MAINE (US/0741-8663) [10195868] **1671**

FINANCIAL DIRECTORY OF PENSION FUNDS. MARYLAND, EASTERN (BALTIMORE, ANNAPOLIS, EASTERN SHORE & OTHERS) (US/0278-0283) [07677337] **1671**

FINANCIAL DIRECTORY OF PENSION FUNDS. MARYLAND, WESTERN (FREDERICK, ROCKVILLE, WALDORF & OTHERS) (US/0278-2162) [07696969] **1671**

FINANCIAL DIRECTORY OF PENSION FUNDS. MASSACHUSETTS, BOSTON CITY PROPER (US/0278-2081) [07719938] **1671**

FINANCIAL DIRECTORY OF PENSION FUNDS. MASSACHUSETTS, EXCLUDING BOSTON & SUBURBS. WORCESTER, SPRINGFIELD, PITTSFIELD & OTHERS (US/0739-2648) [09695365] **1671**

FINANCIAL DIRECTORY OF PENSION FUNDS. MASSACHUSETTS, SUBURBAN BOSTON (LYNN, FRAMINGHAM & OTHERS) (US/0278-209X) [07719971] **1671**

FINANCIAL DIRECTORY OF PENSION FUNDS. MICHIGAN, DETROIT CITY PROPER (US/0731-7379) [08217466] **1671**

FINANCIAL DIRECTORY OF PENSION FUNDS. MICHIGAN, SOUTHERN, EXCLUDING DETROIT & SUBURBS (FLINT, GRAND RAPIDS, KALAMAZOO & OTHERS) (US/0731-7484) [08217269] **1671**

FINANCIAL DIRECTORY OF PENSION FUNDS. MICHIGAN, SUBURBAN DETROIT (PONTIAC, ANN ARBOR, MONROE & OTHERS) (US/0278-2170) [07696825] **1671**

FINANCIAL DIRECTORY OF PENSION FUNDS. MINNESOTA (EXCLUDING MINNEAPOLIS-ST. PAUL AREA) (US/0731-7301) [08217320] **1671**

FINANCIAL DIRECTORY OF PENSION FUNDS. MINNESOTA, MINNEAPOLIS-ST. PAUL AREA (US/0739-5787) [09752827] **1672**

FINANCIAL DIRECTORY OF PENSION FUNDS. MISSISSIPPI (US/0741-868X) [10195594] **1672**

FINANCIAL DIRECTORY OF PENSION FUNDS. MISSOURI, EASTERN. ST. LOUIS, JEFFERSON CITY & OTHERS (US/0739-2877) [09691582] **1672**

FINANCIAL DIRECTORY OF PENSION FUNDS. MISSOURI, WESTERN. KANSAS CITY, ST. JOSEPH, SPRINGFIELD & OTHERS (JS/0739-2826) [09691209] **1672**

FINANCIAL DIRECTORY OF PENSION FUNDS. MONTANA (US/0742-0153) [10237835] **1672**

FINANCIAL DIRECTORY OF PENSION FUNDS. NEBRASKA (US/0741-5117) [10141204] **1672**

FINANCIAL DIRECTORY OF PENSION FUNDS. NEVADA (US/0741-8671) [10196171] **1672**

FINANCIAL DIRECTORY OF PENSION FUNDS. NEW HAMPSHIRE (US/0741-4706) [10142061] **1672**

FINANCIAL DIRECTORY OF PENSION FUNDS. NEW JERSEY, NORTHERN, EXCLUDING NEWARK AND ENVIRONS (HACKENSACK, PATTERSON, SUMMIT & OTHERS) (US/0278-6001) [07790333] **1672**

FINANCIAL DIRECTORY OF PENSION FUNDS. NEW JERSEY, NORTHERN, NEWARK AND ENVIRONS (NEWARK, PASSAIC, JERSEY CITY & OTHERS) (US/0278-579X) [07790354] **1672**

FINANCIAL DIRECTORY OF PENSION FUNDS. NEW JERSEY, SOUTHERN. TRENTON, CAMDEN, ATLANTIC CITY & OTHERS (US/0739-2567) [09692439] **1672**

FINANCIAL DIRECTORY OF PENSION FUNDS. NEW MEXICO, THE (US/0882-2964) [11721481] **1672**

FINANCIAL DIRECTORY OF PENSION FUNDS. NEW YORK. BROOKLYN, S.I., BRONX, QUEENS (US/0739-2680) [09693848] **1672**

FINANCIAL DIRECTORY OF PENSION FUNDS. NEW YORK, EASTERN UPSTATE. POUGHKEEPSIE, ALBANY, GLENS FALLS & OTHERS (US/0739-2761) [09692787] **1672**

FINANCIAL DIRECTORY OF PENSION FUNDS. NEW YORK, MANHATTAN-DOWNTOWN. WALL ST. TO 40 ST (US/0739-2605) [09694607] **1672**

FINANCIAL DIRECTORY OF PENSION FUNDS. NEW YORK, MANHATTAN-MIDTOWN, 41 ST. TO 50 ST (US/0739-2745) [09694019] **1672**

FINANCIAL DIRECTORY OF PENSION FUNDS. NEW YORK, MANHATTAN-UPTOWN. 51 ST. TO HARLEM RIVER (US/0739-2842) [09691433] **1672**

FINANCIAL DIRECTORY OF PENSION FUNDS. NEW YORK (NASSAU & SUFFOLK COUNTIES ONLY) (US/0278-0305) [07677543] **1672**

FINANCIAL DIRECTORY OF PENSION FUNDS. NEW YORK, WEST CENTRAL UPSTATE (UTICA, SYRACUSE, BINGHAMTON & OTHERS) (US/0278-0291) [07677508] **1672**

FINANCIAL DIRECTORY OF PENSION FUNDS. NEW YORK, WESTCHESTER COUNTY AREA (YONKERS, WHITE PLAINS, MIDDLETOWN & OTHERS) (US/0278-0356) [07678141] **1672**

FINANCIAL DIRECTORY OF PENSION FUNDS. NEW YORK, WESTERN UPSTATE. ROCHESTER, BUFFALO, ELMIRA & OTHERS (US/0739-2850) [09691473] **1672**

FINANCIAL DIRECTORY OF PENSION FUNDS. NORTH CAROLINA, EASTERN. RALEIGH, FAYETTEVILLE, WILMINGTON & OTHERS (US/0739-2796) [09693238] **1673**

FINANCIAL DIRECTORY OF PENSION FUNDS. NORTH CAROLINA, WESTERN. WINSTON-SALEM, LEXINGTON, GREENSBORO, CHARLOTTE & OTHERS (US/0739-263X) [09693982] **1673**

FINANCIAL DIRECTORY OF PENSION FUNDS. NORTH DAKOTA (US/0741-479X) [10140968] **1673**

FINANCIAL DIRECTORY OF PENSION FUNDS. OHIO, MIDEASTERN (AKRON, YOUNGSTOWN, ZANESVILLE, CANTON & OTHERS) (US/0278-0321) [07678047] **1673**

FINANCIAL DIRECTORY OF PENSION FUNDS. OHIO, NORTHERN, CLEVELAND AREA (US/0731-7026) [08215857] **1673**

FINANCIAL DIRECTORY OF PENSION FUNDS. OHIO, NORTHWESTERN (TOLEDO, MANSFIELD, LIMA & OTHERS) (US/0278-0275) [07677414] **1673**

FINANCIAL DIRECTORY OF PENSION FUNDS. OHIO, SOUTHERN, CINCINNATI AREA (US/0731-700X) [08215918] **1673**

FINANCIAL DIRECTORY OF PENSION FUNDS. OHIO, SOUTHERN, EXCLUDING CINCINNATI AREA (COLUMBUS, DAYTON, ATHENS & OTHERS) (US/0731-7018) [08216011] **1673**

FINANCIAL DIRECTORY OF PENSION FUNDS. OREGON (US/0742-0161) [10237896] **1673**

FINANCIAL DIRECTORY OF PENSION FUNDS. PENNSYLVANIA, EASTERN, EXCLUDING PHILADELPHIA AREA. HARRISBURG, WILKESBARRE & OTHERS (US/0739-2575) [09692930] **1673**

FINANCIAL DIRECTORY OF PENSION FUNDS. PENNSYLVANIA, EASTERN, PHILADELPHIA CITY PROPER (US/0739-5779) [09752886] **1673**

FINANCIAL DIRECTORY OF PENSION FUNDS. PENNSYLVANIA, EASTERN, SUBURBAN PHILADELPHIA (UPPER DARBY, WEST CHESTER, KING OF PRUSSIA & OTHERS) (US/0278-0364) [07680837] **1673**

FINANCIAL DIRECTORY OF PENSION FUNDS. PENNSYLVANIA, WESTERN, EXCLUDING PITTSBURGH AREA. ERIE, NEW CASTLE, GREENSBURG & OTHERS (US/0739-2710) [09694824] **1673**

FINANCIAL DIRECTORY OF PENSION FUNDS. PENNSYLVANIA, WESTERN (PITTSBURGH AREA) (US/0741-5427) [10141328] **1673**

FINANCIAL DIRECTORY OF PENSION FUNDS. PUERTO RICO, THE (US/0882-2972) [11721792] **1673**

FINANCIAL DIRECTORY OF PENSION FUNDS. RHODE ISLAND (US/0741-871X) [10196074] **1673**

FINANCIAL DIRECTORY OF PENSION FUNDS. SOUTH CAROLINA, THE (US/0882-293X) [11721289] **1673**

FINANCIAL DIRECTORY OF PENSION FUNDS. SOUTH DAKOTA (US/0741-8701) [10196238] **1673**

FINANCIAL DIRECTORY OF PENSION FUNDS. TENNESSEE (US/0742-017X) [10237954] **1673**

FINANCIAL DIRECTORY OF PENSION FUNDS. TEXAS, NORTH CENTRAL & EASTERN (WACO, BRYAN, CONROE, LUFKIN, TYLER, LONGVIEW, TEXARKANA) (US/0278-2189) **1673**

FINANCIAL DIRECTORY OF PENSION FUNDS. TEXAS, NORTHERN (DALLAS, DENTON, SHERMAN) (US/0739-3237) **1673**

FINANCIAL DIRECTORY OF PENSION FUNDS. TEXAS, NORTHWESTERN (FORT WORTH, AMARILLO, LUBBOCK, MIDLAND, EL PASO) (US/0278-2103) **1674**

FINANCIAL DIRECTORY OF PENSION FUNDS. TEXAS, SOUTHERN (AUSTIN, SAN ANTONIO, VICTORIA, CORPUS CHRISTI) (US/0731-7484) **1674**

FINANCIAL DIRECTORY OF PENSION FUNDS. TEXAS, SOUTHERN, HOUSTON & EAST COAST (PASADENA & BEAUMONT) (US/0739-2788) **1674**

FINANCIAL DIRECTORY OF PENSION FUNDS. UTAH (US/0742-0188) [10238017] **1674**

FINANCIAL DIRECTORY OF PENSION FUNDS. VERMONT (US/0742-0196) [10238074] **1674**

FINANCIAL   Alphabetical Title Index

FINANCIAL DIRECTORY OF PENSION FUNDS. VIRGINIA, NORTHERN. (ARLINGTON, WINCHESTER, HARRISONBURG & OTHERS) (US/0739-2613) [09695000] **1674**

FINANCIAL DIRECTORY OF PENSION FUNDS. VIRGINIA, SOUTHERN (RICHMOND, NORFOLK, ROANOKE & OTHERS) (US/0278-212X) [07698705] **1674**

FINANCIAL DIRECTORY OF PENSION FUNDS. WASHINGTON, EASTERN (SPOKANE, YAKIMA, PASCO & OTHERS) (US/0278-0313) [07677591] **1674**

FINANCIAL DIRECTORY OF PENSION FUNDS. WASHINGTON, WESTERN, EXCLUDING SEATTLE AREA (TACOMA, OLYMPIA & OTHERS) (US/0278-2073) [07707380] **1674**

FINANCIAL DIRECTORY OF PENSION FUNDS. WASHINGTON, WESTERN (SEATTLE AREA ONLY) (US/0278-2111) [07707458] **1674**

FINANCIAL DIRECTORY OF PENSION FUNDS. WEST VIRGINIA, THE (US/0882-0821) [11717788] **1674**

FINANCIAL DIRECTORY OF PENSION FUNDS. WISCONSIN, MILWAUKEE CITY PROPER (US/0739-277X) [09693431] **1674**

FINANCIAL DIRECTORY OF PENSION FUNDS. WISCONSIN, MILWAUKEE (SHEBOYGAN, WAUWATOSA, RACINE & OTHERS) (US/0278-2154) [07696907] **1674**

FINANCIAL DIRECTORY OF PENSION FUNDS. WISCONSIN, NORTHERN (GREENBAY, WAUSAU, EAU CLAIRE & OTHERS) (US/0278-033X) [07678079] **1674**

FINANCIAL DIRECTORY OF PENSION FUNDS. WISCONSIN, SOUTHERN, EXCLUDING MILWAUKEE AREA. MADISON, LACROSSE, OSHKOSH & OTHERS) (US/0739-2753) [09693060] **1674**

FINANCIAL DIRECTORY OF PENSION FUNDS. WYOMING, THE (US/0882-2948) [11721625] **1674**

FINANCIAL ENGINEERING AND THE JAPANESE MARKETS (NE/1830-2011) **1975**

●FINANCIAL ESTIMATES OF COMMONWEALTH PUBLIC TRADING ENTERPRISES, AUSTRALIA (AT/1038-7609) [I10387609] **675, 729**

FINANCIAL EXECUTIVE (1987) (US/0895-4186) [16641710] **868, 675**

FINANCIAL EXECUTIVES INSTITUTE *See* MEMBER DIRECTORY - FINANCIAL EXECUTIVES INSTITUTE **693**

FINANCIAL EXPRESS (II) [01642779] **5803**

FINANCIAL FACTS ON WYOMING TAXING UNITS (US/0270-5605) [06438631] **4725**

FINANCIAL FREEDOM REPORT (US/0196-514X) [05836664] **4837, 898**

FINANCIAL FUTURES (US/0890-1309) [09696912] **1490**

FINANCIAL INDUSTRY NUMBER STANDARD DIRECTORY (US/0362-1405) [02303152] **898**

FINANCIAL INDUSTRY SALARY SURVEY (DENVER, COLO. : 1982) (US/0734-967X) [08820036] **1674**

FINANCIAL INFORMATION, COLORADO SCHOOL DISTRICTS (US/0360-9219) [02244632] **1864**

FINANCIAL MANAGEMENT MANUAL (UNITED STATES POSTAL SERVICE) *SUSPENDED.* (US) [04441340] **1145**

●FINANCIAL MANAGER'S REPORT ON COST CUTTING, THE (US/1070-2210) [28299300] **940**

FINANCIAL MANAGERS SOCIETY FOR SAVINGS INSTITUTIONS. SYSTEMS AUTOMATION DIVISION *See* AUTOMATION SURVEY **773**

FINANCIAL MANAGERS' STATEMENT *CEASED.* (US/0887-4808) [13260058] **868**

FINANCIAL MARKET TRENDS (FR/0378-651X) [03411611] **1491**

FINANCIAL MARKETING LETTER, THE (US/1044-3231) [19751715] **924**

FINANCIAL MARKETING UPDATE (UK/0962-1474) [I09621474] **1491**

●FINANCIAL OFFICER'S TAX & MANAGEMENT REPORT (US/1065-6456) [26288896] **4725, 868**

FINANCIAL OPERATIONS AND ACCOUNTING PROCEDURES FOR INSURED MULTIFAMILY PROJECTS (US) [02927480] **744, 2880, 2822**

FINANCIAL PLAN AND ... EXECUTIVE BUDGET / TRIBOROUGH BRIDGE AND TUNNEL AUTHORITY (US) [25014393] **4725**

FINANCIAL PLAN STATUS REPORT / OFFICE OF THE STATE DEPUTY COMPTROLLER FOR THE CITY OF NEW YORK (US) [24036666] **4725**

FINANCIAL PLANNING FOCUS [SOUND RECORDING] (US/0889-0552) [16006442] **2880**

FINANCIAL PLANNING GUIDE FOR MILITARY PERSONNEL (US/0146-7328) [03048557] **4725, 4044**

FINANCIAL PLANNING NEWS (US/0893-7060) [15625985] **898**

FINANCIAL PLANNING ON WALL STREET (US) **898**

FINANCIAL PLANNING SERIES. MONEYLINES MAGAZINE (US) **898, 675**

FINANCIAL POST, THE *See* DIRECTORY OF DIRECTORS. [EXECUTIVES OF CANADA] **728**

FINANCIAL POST, THE *See* FINANCIAL POST GOVERNMENT & MUNICIPAL SURVEY **4649**

FINANCIAL POST GOVERNMENT & MUNICIPAL SURVEY (CN/0701-4724) [03341231] **4649**

FINANCIAL POST OUTLOOK (CN) **675**

FINANCIAL POST, THE (CN/0015-2021) [05741613] **898**

FINANCIAL PREDICTIONS (US/1062-9033) [25799086] **675**

FINANCIAL PROCEDURES BULLETIN (CN/0709-4981) [06273621] **4649**

●FINANCIAL PROJECTIONS AND CAPITAL PLAN (US) [22036829] **4725**

FINANCIAL REPORT / ADJUTANT-GENERAL'S DEPARTMENT (TEXAS) (US) [06566644] **4044**

FINANCIAL REPORT AND AUDITED FINANCIAL STATEMENTS FOR THE YEAR ENDED 31 DECEMBER ... AND REPORT OF THE BOARD OF AUDITORS / UNITED NATIONS DEVELOPMENT PROGRAMME (US) [06895318] **1635**

FINANCIAL REPORT AND PROGRESS REPORT ON SPRUCE BUDWORM PROGRAMS (US/0272-9407) [06484436] **2379**

FINANCIAL REPORT - CARNEGIE ENDOWMENT FOR INTERNATIONAL PEACE (US/0094-3029) [01793508] **4521**

FINANCIAL REPORT - COMMISSION OF THE EUROPEAN COMMUNITIES (LU) [19540064] **4725**

FINANCIAL REPORT - DEPARTMENT OF HEALTH & SOCIAL SERVICES, DIVISION OF HEALTH (US/0362-7187) [03149580] **4775**

FINANCIAL REPORT - DIVISION OF FEDERAL PROGRAMS (US) [05250819] **1864**

FINANCIAL REPORT - ENERGY RESEARCH AND DEVELOPMENT ADMINISTRATION (US/0362-5192) [02289717] **1944**

FINANCIAL REPORT - MANITOBA DEPARTMENT OF FINANCE (CN/0710-8435) [08394510] **4725**

FINANCIAL REPORT / MARYLAND INDUSTRIAL DEVELOPMENT FINANCING AUTHORITY (US) [12218926] **1607**

FINANCIAL REPORT - NORTHERN STATE COLLEGE (US) [06057154] **1824**

FINANCIAL REPORT OF OHIO LOCAL HEALTH DEPARTMENTS *See* FINANCIAL REPORT, OHIO'S LOCAL HEALTH DEPARTMENT / PREPARED BY GRANTS MANAGEMENT UNIT, BUREAU OF ADMINISTRATIVE SERVICES, OHIO DEPARTMENT OF HEALTH **4775**

FINANCIAL REPORT OF THE COUNTY COLLEGES OF THE STATE OF NEW JERSEY FOR THE FISCAL YEAR ENDED JUNE 30 ... (US) [08336691] **1824**

FINANCIAL REPORT OF THE GENERAL SUPERINTENDENT - BOARD OF SCHOOL COMMISSIONERS OF THE CITY OF INDIANAPOLIS (US/0090-7375) [01785306] **1864**

FINANCIAL REPORT OF THE MISSOURI DEPARTMENT OF REVENUE (US) [17665103] **4725**

FINANCIAL REPORT, OHIO'S LOCAL HEALTH DEPARTMENT / PREPARED BY GRANTS MANAGEMENT UNIT, BUREAU OF ADMINISTRATIVE SERVICES, OHIO DEPARTMENT OF HEALTH (US) [07320608] **4775**

FINANCIAL REPORT / OLD DOMINION UNIVERSITY (US/0883-4636) [12086819] **1824**

FINANCIAL REPORT ON REGISTERED CHARITABLE ORGANIZATIONS (US/0147-8508) [03243245] **5285**

FINANCIAL REPORT - PURDUE UNIVERSITY (US) [05179259] **1824**

FINANCIAL REPORT - STATE INVESTMENT COUNCIL (US) [06110307] **898, 4725**

FINANCIAL REPORT - STATE OF NEVADA, DIVISION OF COLORADO RIVER RESOURCES (US/0149-6662) [03520736] **2089**

FINANCIAL REPORT / STATE OF NEW MEXICO, OFFICE OF STATE TREASURER (US) [08379501] **4725**

FINANCIAL REPORT TO MANAGEMENT (US) [06846608] **5440**

FINANCIAL REPORT - UNIVERSITY OF MASSACHUSETTS (US/0461-2981) [03276955] **1824**

FINANCIAL REPORT - UNIVERSITY OF VIRGINIA (US/0091-6110) [02173836] **1824**

FINANCIAL REPORT - VIRGINIA COMMUNITY COLLEGE SYSTEM (US) [06558799] **1824**

FINANCIAL REPORT - WEST TEXAS STATE UNIVERSITY (US) [01783471] **1824**

FINANCIAL REPORTING... A SURVEY OF UK PUBLISHED ACCOUNTS (UK) [09586782] **744**

FINANCIAL REPORTING DEVELOPMENTS (TORONTO, ONT.) (CN/0823-0196) [09819114] **744**

FINANCIAL REPORTING IN CANADA (CN/0071-5115) [02740225] **744**

FINANCIAL RESEARCH ASSOCIATES *See* FINANCIAL STUDIES OF THE SMALL BUSINESS **675**

FINANCIAL RESOURCES FOR INTERNATIONAL STUDY : A DEFINITIVE GUIDE TO ORGANIZATIONS OFFERING AWARDS FOR OVERSEAS STUDY (US) [20265060] **1824**

FINANCIAL RESULTS - GOVERNMENT OF CANADA (CN/0848-5194) [23248030] **4725**

FINANCIAL REVIEW OF ALIEN INSURERS (US/0270-5656) [06439454] **2880**

FINANCIAL SERVICES LAW LETTER (UK) **2970**

FINANCIAL SERVICES LAW REPORT (US/0883-2447) [12099604] **3086**

FINANCIAL SOURCEBOOKS' SOURCES (US/0892-7812) [15259510] **924**

FINANCIAL STATEMENT (US) [01589997] **4725**

FINANCIAL STATEMENT AFTER ALLOCATION (US/0145-2924) [02722245] **5382**

FINANCIAL STATEMENT - DEPARTMENT OF FINANCE (NORTHERN IRELAND) (IE) [02245971] **4725**

FINANCIAL STATEMENT FOR THE PERIOD COVERING FROM 1ST JANUARY TO 31ST DECEMBER ... / TANZANIA LIBRARY ASSOCIATION (TZ) [11139668] **3210**

FINANCIAL STATEMENTS & FINANCIAL STATISTICS / CAISSE DE DEPOT ET PLACEMENT DU QUEBEC (CN/0825-7043) [11762244] **4725, 4649**

FINANCIAL STATEMENTS AND SCHEDULES : (WITH ACCOUNTANTS' REPORT THEREON) / UNITED CHURCH BOARD FOR WORLD MINISTRIES (US) [11730726] **744, 4959**

FINANCIAL STATEMENTS AND SUPPLEMENTAL SCHEDULES FOR THE YEARS ENDED SEPTEMBER 30 ... AND INDEPENDENT AUDITOR'S REPORT (US) [23852013] **5415**

FINANCIAL STATEMENTS / BRITISH COLUMBIA LIQUOR DISTRIBUTION BRANCH (CN/0709-4531) [05590419] **2367**

FINANCIAL STATEMENTS - CITY TREASURER (SA) [03219140] **4725**

FINANCIAL STATEMENTS / CONSORZIO DI CREDITO PER LE OPERE PUBBLICHE (IT) [25720826] **4726**

FINANCIAL STATEMENTS - DEPARTMENT OF HOUSING AND URBAN DEVELOPMENT, OFFICE OF FINANCE AND ACCOUNTING (US/0145-1081) [02670362] **2822**

FINANCIAL STATEMENTS OF QUEBEC GOVERNMENT ENTERPRISES (CN) [02249908] **4726**

FINANCIAL STATEMENTS, STATE OF COLORADO, STATE CONTROLLER (US) [04127422] **4726**

FINANCIAL STATEMENTS WITH SUPPLEMENTAL SCHEDULES (US/0360-5469) [02350142] **1824**

FINANCIAL STATISTICS (FR) [02092973] **729**

FINANCIAL STATISTICS LONDON (UK/0015-203X) [I0015203X] **1532**

FINANCIAL STATISTICS MONTHLY. INTERNATIONAL MARKETS (FR) [13429086] **1491**

FINANCIAL STATISTICS MONTHLY. SECTION 2, DOMESTIC MARKETS, INTEREST RATES (FR) [10509342] **729**

FINANCIAL STATISTICS OF INSTITUTIONS OF HIGHER EDUCATION: CURRENT FUNDS, REVENUES AND EXPENDITURES SUMMARY DATA (US/0565-7458) [02740637] **1824, 1795**

FINANCIAL STATISTICS OF JAPAN (JA/0289-1522) [10647448] **4726, 4697**

Alphabetical Title Index — FINISHING

FINANCIAL STATISTICS OF MAJOR INVESTOR-OWNED ELECTRIC UTILITIES *See* FINANCIAL STATISTICS OF MAJOR U.S. INVESTOR-OWNED ELECTRIC UTILITIES **2004**

●FINANCIAL STATISTICS OF MAJOR U.S. INVESTOR-OWNED ELECTRIC UTILITIES (US) [29870347] 2055, **2004**

FINANCIAL STATISTICS OF PUBLIC UTILITIES (US/0430-4845) [01767864] 5533, **4761**

FINANCIAL STATISTICS OF SELECTED PUBLICLY OWNED ELECTRIC UTILITIES (US) [23183014] **4761**

FINANCIAL STATISTICS OF THE MAJOR PRIVATELY OWNED UTILITIES IN NEW YORK STATE (US/0363-2113) [02434691] 4761, **4697**

FINANCIAL STATISTICS, TAIWAN DISTRICT, THE REPUBLIC OF CHINA (CH) [07781899] **729**

FINANCIAL STATISTICS : VERMONT SCHOOL SYSTEMS (US/0363-3012) [02439001] 1746, **1795**

FINANCIAL STATUS OF MAJOR FEDERAL ACQUISITIONS (US/0193-2721) [05122349] **4649**

FINANCIAL STOCK GUIDE SERVICE. DIRECTORY OF ACTIVE STOCKS (US/0364-0752) [02579854] **898**

FINANCIAL STUDIES OF THE SMALL BUSINESS (US/0363-8987) [02551324] **675**

FINANCIAL SUMMARY AND BUDGETARY REVIEW (CN/0226-6458) [06512722] **4726**

FINANCIAL SUMMARY - DELAWARE. OFFICE OF THE GOVERNOR (US) [10210550] **4726**

FINANCIAL TECHNOLOGY INTERNATIONAL BULLETIN (UK/0265-1661) [I02651661] **5105**

●FINANCIAL TECHNOLOGY REVIEW (US/1071-3646) [28620299] **898**

FINANCIAL TIMES BUSINESS TRAVEL COSTS (UK) [09864138] **675**

FINANCIAL TIMES COAL STATISTICS (UK) 1439, **1362**

FINANCIAL TIMES (FRANKFURT ED.) (GW/0174-7363) [11962086] **675**

FINANCIAL TIMES INDUSTRIAL COMPANIES. CHEMICALS (UK/1065-2841) [23606397] **1024**

FINANCIAL TIMES INDUSTRIAL COMPANIES. VOLUME III, ENGINEERING (US) [19753335] **2098**

FINANCIAL TIMES INVESTOR'S 500 (CN) **898**

FINANCIAL TIMES LAW REPORTS (UK/0268-8433) [20044754] **2970**

FINANCIAL TIMES LIMITED *See* FINANCIAL TIMES WORLD HOTEL DIRECTORY, THE **2805**

FINANCIAL TIMES (LONDON ED.) (UK/0307-1766) [01383680] **5812**

FINANCIAL TIMES MARKETSHARE (CN) **898**

FINANCIAL TIMES MINING INTERNATIONAL YEAR BOOK (UK/0141-3244) [09962967] **2139**

FINANCIAL TIMES MONEY GUIDE (CN) **898**

FINANCIAL TIMES (NORTH AMERICAN EDITION) (US/0884-6782) [12412740] **675**

FINANCIAL TIMES NORTH SEA LETTER AND EUROPEAN OFFSHORE NEWS (UK/0950-1037) [10690783] **1944**

FINANCIAL TIMES OIL AND GAS INTERNATIONAL YEAR BOOK (UK/0141-3228) [10495320] **4256**

FINANCIAL TIMES TAX NEWSLETTER (UK) [01787381] **4726**

FINANCIAL TIMES WHO'S WHO IN WORLD OIL AND GAS (UK/0141-3236) [04625492] **1607**

FINANCIAL TIMES WORLD HOTEL DIRECTORY, THE (UK/0308-8464) [03548097] **2805**

FINANCIAL TIMES WORLD INSURANCE YEARBOOK, THE (UK) [03995499] **2897**

FINANCIAL TREND'S CORPORATE DIRECTORY SERVICE FOR TEXAS, OKLAHOMA, LOUISIANA, ARKANSAS, NEW MEXICO (US) [07496008] **675**

FINANCIAL WOMAN TODAY (US/1059-3950) [23368768] **5556**

FINANCIAL WORLD (US/0015-2064) [01569242] **898**

●FINANCIAL YELLOW BOOK (US/1058-2878) [24255527] **1926**

FINANCIAMIENTO DEL DESARROLLO (US/0250-6157) [04608655] **4726**

FINANCIEEL EKONOMISCHE TIJD, DE (BE/0772-0890) [I07720890] **1491**

FINANCIEEL MANAGEMENT (NE) **868**

FINANCIEEL OVERHEIDSMANAGEMENT (NE/0922-1026) **4649**

FINANCIELE GEGEVENS KERKGENOOTSCHAPPEN / CENTRAAL BUREAU VOOR DE STATISTIEK, HOOFDAFDELING FINANCIELE STATISTIEKEN (NE/0168-5481) [10339650] **4959**

FINANCIELE POSITIE VAN DE LANDBOUW, DE (NE) [04202078] 1491, **87**

FINANCIEN BERICHT-PERSBERICHT FINANCIEN (NE) **5806**

FINANCIERA NACIONAL DE CUBA *See* MEMORIA - FINANCIERA NACIONAL DE CUBA **798**

FINANCIERO; REVISTA INTERNACIONAL DE ECONOMIA, COMERCIO E INDUSTRIA **SUSPENDED.** (SP/0015-2102) [06579366] **1491**

FINANCING AGRICULTURE (II/0015-2110) [01774329] **87**

FINANCING AND EXTERNAL DEBT OF DEVELOPING COUNTRIES (FR) [14150361] **4726**

FINANCING LOCAL GOVERNMENT (US) [18269835] **4726**

FINANCING THE OREGON UNEMPLOYMENT INSURANCE PROGRAM (US/0149-0109) [03415775] 1674, 2880, **1532**

FINANICAL POST INVESTORS GUIDE *See* INVESTOR'S DIGEST **903**

FINANSIELE STATE VAN DIE OLIESADERAAD VIR DIE BOEKJAAR ... (SA) [12095923] **1607**

●FINANSY (RU) [25600706] **4726**

FINANSY I KREDIT *See* KHOZRASCHET, FINANSY I KREDIT **795**

FINANSY SSSR *See* FINANSY **4726**

FINANZ JOURNAL (AU/1017-5695) [04875277] **4726**

FINANZ-RUNDSCHAU (GW/0340-9007) [06070310] **4726**

FINANZ-RUNDSCHAU FUER EINKOMMENSTEUER UND KORPERSCHAFTSTEUER : FR (GW/0176-7771) [16152022] **3128**

FINANZA IMPRESE E MERCATI (IT/1120-9461) [I11209461] **835**

FINANZA ITALIANA (IT) **1491**

FINANZA, MARKETING E PRODUZIONE : RIVISTA DELL'UNIVERSITA L. BOCCONI (IT) [15130788] 868, **924**

FINANZARCHIV (GW/0015-2218) [01285011] **4726**

FINANZEN UND STEUEREN. REIHE 2 : STEUERHAUSHALT VON BUND, LANDERN UND GEMEINDEN (GW/0072-1883) [02042170] **4726**

FINANZEN UND STEUERN. REIHE 3.5, RECHNUNGSERGEBNISSE DER OFFENTLICHEN HAUSHALTE FUER SOZIALE SICHERUNG UND FUER GESUNDHEIT, SPORT, ERHOLUNG (GW) [19915322] **2516**

FINANZEN UND STEUERN. REIHE 5: SCHULDEN DER OFFENTLICHEN HAUSHALTE (GW/0418-7929) **4726**

FINANZEN UND STEUERN. REIHE 7.S.1, WIRTSCHAFTLICHE GLIEDERUNG DER EINKOMMEN- UND KORPERSCHAFTSTEUERPFLICHTIGEN (GW) [19028019] **4726**

FINANZIERE (IT/0015-2242) [I00152242] **4044**

FINANZPLAN DES BUNDES, DER (GW) [02381223] **4726**

●FINANZPLAN DES KANTONS BERN (SZ) [24189686] **4726**

FINANZPLANUNG DES LANDES BERLIN *See* FINANZPLANUNG VON BERLIN **4726**

FINANZPLANUNG VON BERLIN (GW) [02441306] **4726**

FINANZWIRTSCHAFT : ZEITSCHRIFT FUR DAS FINANZ-, PREIS- UND KREDITWESEN DER DDR (GW) [21412759] **4726**

FINANZWISSENSCHAFTLICHE FORSCHUNGSARBEITEN (GW/0430-4977) [02354711] **1491**

FINCASTLE HERALD, THE (US/8750-7323) [11048662] **5758**

FIND CATALOG (US/0091-7591) [01788194] 5316, **4117**

FINDBUCHER ZU BESTANDEN DES BUNDESARCHIV (GW) [02031138] **2481**

FINDER BINDER. ARIZONA'S UPDATED MEDIA DIRECTORY (US/0196-8548) [05913014] 1111, **2919**

FINDER BINDER. DALLAS/FORT WORTH METROPLEX AREA NEWS MEDIA (US/0276-2153) [07324482] **759**

FINDER BINDER. DETROIT AREA UPDATED MEDIA DIRECTORY (US/0276-2196) [07324355] **759**

FINDER BINDER, (NEW ORLEANS, LA.) (US/0739-8190) [08775950] **759**

FINDER BINDER. NORTHEAST OHIO/GREATER CLEVELAND (US/0196-8726) [05913988] **759**

FINDER BINDER. OKLAHOMA CITY METROPOLITAN UPDATED MEDIA DIRECTORY (US/0196-8734) [05913935] **759**

FINDER BINDER. THE SACRAMENTO, STOCKTON AND NORTHERN CALIFORNIA UPDATED NEWS MEDIA DIRECTORY (US/1057-0888) [23534561] **1111**

FINDER BINDER. WILLAMETTE VALLEY'S UPDATED MEDIA DIRECTORY (US/0196-8513) [05913477] **759**

FINDERBINDER (US/0196-853X) [05913693] **759**

FINDEX (US/0273-4125) [04812049] **924**

FINDING (US/0892-7367) [15249493] **3210**

FINDING A JOB IN THE NONPROFIT SECTOR (US/1050-3757) [21472041] **4204**

FINDING AIDS TO THE MICROFILMED MANUSCRIPT COLLECTION OF THE GENEALOGICAL SOCIETY OF UTAH (US) [04674838] **2448**

FINDING THE RIGHT SPEAKER (US) [07778070] **3388**

●FINE ART & ANTIQUES INTERNATIONAL (US/1071-1015) [28552067] **320**

FINE ART & AUCTION REVIEW (CN/0833-0891) [16073631] 250, **350**

●FINE ART INDEX (NORTH AMERICAN ED.), THE (US/1057-8269) [24124182] **350**

FINE ART PUBLICATIONS ... / NATIONAL GALLERY OF CANADA (CN/0848-726X) [23247580] **320**

FINE ARTS; A WEEKLY GUIDE (US) [02104154] **320**

FINE ARTS AND ARCHITECTURE [MICROFORM] / NEWSBANK, INC (US) [12009729] 298, **320**

FINE ARTS FEDERATION OF NEW YORK *See* CALENDAR OF REGULAR MEETINGS OF THE ART ORGANIZATIONS IN NEW YORK CITY ... **346**

FINE CRAFTS IN PENNSYLVANIA : A SIGHTSEERS AND SHOPPERS GUIDE (US) [07529513] **373**

FINE CUISINE D'HENRI BERNARD, LA (CN/0709-3225) [06017472] **2790**

FINE DINING (US/0747-2560) [10682422] **5071**

FINE (EDMONTON. 1974) (CN/0318-7489) [02011662] **1746**

FINE GARDENING (US/0896-6281) [17223836] **2414**

FINE HOMEBUILDING (US/0273-1398) [07011591] **615**

FINE LINE (AT/0818-3473) [I08183473] **3388**

FINE MADNESS (US/0737-4704) [09206999] **3388**

FINE PRINT (SAN FRANCISCO) (US/0361-3801) [02246344] **4565**

FINE TOOL JOURNAL, THE (US/0745-6824) [09396520] **250**

FINE WOODWORKING (US/0361-3453) [02246347] **634**

FINESCALE MODELER (US/0277-979X) [07674178] **2773**

FINEST HOUR (US/0882-3715) [11832978] **2688**

FINGER LAKES (US) [25010507] **2533**

FINGER LAKES LIBRARY SYSTEM *See* NEWSLETTER - FINGER LAKES LIBRARY SYSTEM **3235**

FINGER LAKES MAGAZINE (US) **2733**

FINGER LAKES TIMES (US) [10928789] **5716**

FINGER LAKES TRAVEL GUIDE, THE (US) [04961779] **2773**

FINGER PRINTS (US) 4088, **1063**

FINGERPRINT WHORLD (UK/0951-1288) [I09511288] **3164**

FINGERTIP FACTS & FIGURES (US/0470-0384) [08081488] **2379**

FINIGAN WINE LETTER, THE (US/0891-0774) [14638944] **2367**

FINISHED BROADWOVEN FABRIC PRODUCTION (US/0276-3389) [03246316] 5351, **3479**

FINISHED FABRICS. PRODUCTION, INVENTORIES, AND UNFILLED ORDERS (US/0272-5509) [06458916] 5351, **3479**

FINISHERS' MANAGEMENT (US/0015-2358) [04414085] 4002, **868**

FINISHING (UK/0264-2506) [08735046] **4224**

FINISHING INTERNATIONAL (US/0195-1076) [05284520] **1975**

FINISHING LINE QUARTERLY (US) **3479**

FINITE
Alphabetical Title Index

FINITE ELEMENTS IN ANALYSIS AND DESIGN (NE/0168-874X) [12178292] **1233**

FINITE ELEMENTS IN FLUIDS (UK/0196-6375) [04728268] **2089**

FINITE STRING *See* PROCEEDINGS OF THE CONFERENCE - ASSOCIATION FOR COMPUTATIONAL LINGUISTICS. MEETING **3312**

FINK AND BORNSTEIN WORKER'S COMPENSATION NEWSLETTER, THE (CN) **1674, 675**

FINLAND *See* REGERINGENS BERATTELSE TILL RIKSDAGEN OM UTVECKLINGSSAMARBETET **1516**

FINLAND *See* HALLITUKSEN KEHITYSYHTEISTYOKERTOMUS EDUSKUNNALLE VUODELTA **1565**

FINLAND AND ENERGY (FI) [19574227] **1944**

FINLAND. ASUNTOHALLITUS *See* ENERGIATALOUDELLISEEN KOBJAUSTOIMINTAAN VUONNA ... MYONNETTAVAT AVUSTUKSET **4646**

FINLAND. EDUSKUNTA. KIRJASTO *See* VALTION VIRALLISJULKAISUT **4693**

FINLAND HANDBOOK (FI/0355-5100) [04986415] **5470**

FINLAND. KANSANTALOUSOSASTO *See* NATIONAL BUDGET FOR FINLAND **4738**

FINLAND. KORKEIN HALLINTO-OIKEUS *See* TOIMINTAKERTOMUS / KORKEIN HALLINTO-OIKEUS **3143**

FINLAND. LAAKINTOHALLITUS *See* TERVEYDENHUOLTO **4804**

FINLAND. MAATALOUSHALLITUS. TILASTOTOIMISTO. MAATALOUSTILASTOLLINEN KUUKAUSIKATSAUS *See* MAATALOUSTILASTOLLINEN KUUKAUSIKATSAUAS. MONTHLY REVIEW OF AGRICULTURAL STATISTICS **154**

FINLAND. MAATILAHALLITUS. TILASTOTOIMISTO *See* MAATALOUSTILASTOLLINEN KUUKAUSIKATSAUAS. MONTHLY REVIEW OF AGRICULTURAL STATISTICS **154**

FINLAND. MERENKULKUHALLITUS *See* SUOMEN RANNIKON LOISTOT **4183**

FINLAND. METSAHALLITUS *See* METSAHALLITUKSEN VUOSIKERTOMUS **2388**

FINLAND. OPETUSMINISTERIO *See* KESKIASTEEN KOULUTUKSEN KEHITTAMISOHJELMA VUOSILLE **1760**

FINLAND. PANKKITARKASTUSVIRASTO *See* TOIMINTAKERTOMUS **814**

FINLAND SISAASIAINMINISTERIO KAAVOITUS- JA RAKENNUSOSASTO *See* KR-TIEDOTE / SISAASIAINMINISTERIO, KAAVOITUS- JA RAKENNUSOSASTO **2827**

FINLAND. SOSIAALIHALLITUS SUNNNITTELU- JA TILASTOTOIMISTO *See* KASVATUSNEUVOLATOIMINTA. VERKSAMHETEN VID RADGIVNINGSBYRAER FOR UPPFOSTRINGSFRAGOR **5294**

FINLAND. SOSIAALIHALLITUS SUNNNITTELU- JA TILASTOTOIMISTO *See* KODINHOITOAPU **5294**

FINLAND. SOSIAALIHALLITUS. SUUNNITTELU- JA TILASTOTOIMISTO *See* ELATUSTUKI **5284**

FINLAND. SOSIAALIHALLITUS. SUUNNITTELU- JA TILASTOTOIMISTO *See* HUOLTOAPU **5288**

FINLAND. TAITEEN KESKUSTOIMIKUNTA *See* TAITEEN KESKUSTOIMIKUNNAN TIEDOTUSLEHTI **331**

FINLAND. TILASTOKESKUN *See* PERUSKOULUT **1773**

FINLAND. TILASTOKESKUS *See* RAVITSEMIS- JA MAJOITUSLIIKKEIDEN TYONTEKIJOIDEN JA TOIMIHENKILOIDEN PALKAT. LONERNA FOR ARBETSTAGARE OCH FUNKTIONARER INOM FORPLAGNADS- OCH HARBARGERINGSRORELSER **1705**

FINLAND. TILASTOKESKUS *See* KORKEAKOULUISSA SUORITETUT TUTKINNOT **1833**

FINLAND. TILASTOKESKUS *See* KUORMA-AUTO LINJALIIKENNE **5418**

FINLAND. TILASTOKESKUS *See* KUNTIEN TALOUS: KUNNITTAISET TIEDOT. KOMMUNERNAS EKONOMI: UPPGIFTER ENLIGT KOMMUN **4735**

FINLAND. TILASTOKESKUS *See* TEKSTIILITEOLLISUUDEN KONEKANTA. TEXTILINDUSTRINS MASKINER **5356**

FINLAND. TILASTOKESKUS *See* KUNNALLISTEN VIRANHALTIJOIDEN JA KUUKAUSIPALKKAISTEN TYONTEKIJOIDEN JA TOIMIHENKILOIDEN PALKAT **4660**

FINLAND. TILASTOKESKUS *See* TYOLLISYYSKURSSIN SUORITTANEET **1715**

FINLAND. TILASTOKESKUS *See* KOULUTUSLUOKITUS **1899**

FINLAND. TILASTOKESKUS *See* AMMATILLISET OPPILAITOKSET. YRKESUTBILDNINGSANSTALTERNA **1910**

FINLAND. TILASTOKESKUS *See* ENNAKKOTIETOJA TUTKIMUS- JA KEHIITTAMISTOIMINNASTA SUOMESSA **1560**

FINLAND. TILASTOKESKUS *See* VALTIOLLISET VAALIT : KANSANEDUSTAJAIN VAALIT **4503**

FINLAND. TILASTOKESKUS *See* TIELIIKENNEONNETTOMUUDET **5445**

FINLAND. TILASTOKESKUS *See* KESKEYTTAMISET AMMATILLISISSA OPPILAITOKSISSA SEKA KANSANOPISTOISSA JA-KORKEAKOULUISSA **1760**

FINLAND. TILASTOKESKUS *See* PALKKATILASTO **1700**

FINLAND. TILASTOKESKUS *See* TUOMIOISTUINTEN TUTKIMAT RIKOKSET **3084**

FINLAND. TILASTOKESKUS *See* AMMATILLISIIN OPPILAITOKSIIN JA KANSANOPISTOIHIN PYRKINEET JA OTETUT **1724**

FINLAND. TILASTOKESKUS *See* KUNTAINLIITTOJEN TALOUS **4735**

FINLAND. TILASTOKESKUS *See* LIIKEVAIHTOVEROVELVOLLISET YRITYKSET **4736**

FINLAND. TILASTOKESKUS *See* AMMATILLISIIN OPPILAITOKSIIN SEKA KANSANOPISTOIHIN JA KANSANKORKEAKOULUTHIN PYUKINEET JAOTETUT **1910**

FINLAND. TILASTOKESKUS *See* KOTITALOUSESINEIDEN KORJAUS **2812**

FINLAND. TILASTOKESKUS *See* ENNAKKOTIETOJA ORKEAKOULUOPISKELIHAIM LUKUMAARASTA **1822**

FINLAND. TILASTOKESKUS *See* ENNAKKOTIEDOT SUORITETUISTA KORKEAKOULUTUTKINNOISTA JA HYVAKSYTYISTA VAITOSKIRJOISTA **1894**

FINLAND. TILASTOKESKUS *See* KAUPPAMERENKULUN SEKA HUOLINTA- JA AHTAUSTOIMINNAN TASETILASTO **5451**

FINLAND. TILASTOKESKUS *See* KORKEAKOULUOPETTAJIEN LUKUMAARA **1760**

FINLAND. TILASTOKESKUS *See* ENNAKKOTIEDOT KORKEAKOULUISSA SUORITETUISTA TUTKINNOISTA JA HYVAKSYTYISTA TOHTORINVAITOSKIRJOISTA **1822**

FINLAND. TILASTOKESKUS *See* VALTION VIRKAMIESTEN PALKAT MARRASKUUSSA **4693**

FINLAND. TILASTOKESKUS *See* AMMATILLISTEN OPPILAITOSTEN SEKA KANSANOPISTOJEN JA-KORKEAKOULUJEN OPPILASMAARA **1724**

FINLAND. TILASTOKESKUS *See* OPPILAITOSLUETTELO **1770**

FINLAND. TILASTOKESKUS *See* AMMATILLISTEN OPPILAITOSTEN OPPILASMAARA **1910**

FINLAND. TILASTOKESKUS *See* MOOTTORIAJONEUVO- JA KUMIKORJAAMOT **5419**

FINLAND. TILASTOKESKUS *See* POLIISIN JA TULLIN TIETON TULLEET RIKOKSET, PAIHTYNEENA SAILOON OTETUT JA PYSAKOINTIVIRHEET **3172**

FINLAND. TILASTOKESKUS *See* OPPIKOULUT **1770**

FINLAND. TILASTOKESKUS *See* REKISTERIIN MERKITYT UUDET MOOTTORIAJONEUVOT **5424**

FINLAND. TILASTOKESKUS *See* TUOMIOISTUIMISSA KASITELLYT RIKOS- , SIVIILI- JA HALLINTOOIKEUDELLISET ASIAT **3084**

FINLAND. TILASTOKESKUS *See* MAALAISKUNTIEN JA KUNTAINLIITTOJEN TUNTIPALKKAISTEN TYONTEKIJOIDEN PALKAT **4663**

FINLAND. TILASTOKESKUS *See* TYOVOIMA-ARVIO **1715**

FINLAND. TILASTOKESKUS *See* KANSANEDUSTAJAIN VAALIT **4659**

FINLAND. TILASTOKESKUS *See* VANKITILASTO **3178**

FINLAND. TILASTOKESKUS *See* ALIOIKEUKSISSA VIREILLEPANNUT JA LOPPUUNKASITELLTY KONKURSSIT **769**

FINLAND. TILASTOKESKUS *See* KORKOTILASTOA **796**

FINLAND. TILASTOKESKUS *See* ULKOMAANKAUPPA; KUUKAUSIJULKAISU. UTRIKESHANDEL MANADSPUBLIKATION **856**

FINLAND. TILASTOKESKUS *See* SUOMEN MAKSUTASE **813**

FINLAND. TILASTOKESKUS *See* TILASTOKATSAUKSIA **5345**

FINLAND. TILASTOKESKUS *See* MYONNETYT RAKENNUSLUVAT **621**

FINLAND. TILASTOKESKUS. PERHETILASTO *See* PERHEET **2285**

FINLAND. TILASTOTIEDOTUS. MAASSAMUUTTO KUNNITTAIN *See* MAASAAMUUTTO MUUTON SUUNNAN MUKAAN KUNNITTAIN ... **4554**

FINLAND. VALTIONTAKAUSLAITOS *See* STATSGARANTIANSTALTEN **813**

FINLAND. VALTIONTAKAUSLAITOS *See* VALTIONTAKAUSLAITOS **815**

FINLAND. VANKEINHOIDON KOULUTUSKESKUS *See* TAYDENNYSKOULUTUS VUONNA ... **3177**

FINLAND. VEROHALLITUS *See* VEROHALLINNON KASIKIRJA: MAATILATALOUDEN VEROTUS **4757**

FINLAND. VEROHALLITUS *See* VEROHALLITUKSEN YHTENAISTAMISOHJEET VUODELTA ... TOIMITETTAVAA VEROTUSIA VARTEN **4757**

FINMECCANICA AMBIENTE (IT) **2171**

FINNAM NEWSLETTER / FINNISH-AMERICAN HISTORICAL SOCIETY OF THE WEST (US) [02253861] **2261**

FINNEGANS WAKE CIRCULAR, A (UK/0267-9612) [15088963] **3388**

FINNIGAN SPECTRA (US/0161-2220) [02714911] **4434**

FINNISCH-UGRISCHE FORSCHUNGEN (FI/0355-1253) [01569289] **3281**

FINNISCH-UGRISCHE MITTEILUNGEN (GW/0341-7816) [04543797] **3281**

FINNISH AMERICAN ANNUAL (US/0362-2576) [02298318] **2733**

FINNISH AMERICANA (US/0162-5462) [03900863] **2733**

FINNISH BUSINESS REPORT (FI) [09876102] **675**

FINNISH ECONOMIC PAPERS (FI/0784-5197) [18822298] **1491**

FINNISH FISHERIES RESEARCH (FI/0301-908X) [01793157] **2301**

FINNISH FOUNDATION FOR ALCOHOL STUDIES (SERIES) (FI/0356-2654) [03062637] **5105**

FINNISH GAME RESEARCH (FI/0783-4365) [19414388] **2216**

FINNISH JOURNAL OF DAIRY SCIENCE *See* AGRICULTURAL SCIENCE IN FINLAND **52**

FINNISH MARINE RESEARCH (FI/0357-1076) [04969033] **1449**

FINNISH MUSIC QUARTERLY (FI/0782-1069) [13355483] **4117**

FINNISH TRADE REVIEW *CEASED.* (FI/0015-2463) [01569294] **835**

FINNLAND : ENERGIEWIRTSCHAFT (GW) [05063942] **1944**

FINNLAND, LAND-, FORST- UND HOLZWIRTSCHAFT / BUNDESSTELLE FUER AUSSENHANDELSINFORMATION (GW) [11564725] **2379, 87**

FINNLAND, LANDWIRTSCHAFT / BUNDESSTELLE FUER AUSSENHANDELSINFORMATION (GW) [10931687] **87**

FINNLAND : WIRTSCHAFT IN ZAHLEN UND WIRTSCHAFTSDOKUMENTATION (GW) [06234257] **1561**

FINNLAND: WIRTSCHAFTLICHE ENTWICKLUNG (GW) [03101055] **1561**

FINNO-UGRISTIKA / MINISTERSTVO VYSSHEGO I SREDNEGO SPETSIALNOGO OBRAZOVANIIA RSFSR, MORDOVSKII GOSUDARSTVENNYI UNIVERSITET IMENI N.P. OGAREVA (RU/0135-6569) [08683226] **3281**

FINNPAP WORLD (FI/0781-7789) [07817789] **4233**

FINOMMECHANIKA-MIKROTECHNIKA (HU/0231-2662) [01795442] **3479**

FINS AND FEATHERS (US) [14644950] **4872**

FINS AND FEATHERS (CONNECTICUT ED.) (US/0741-3866) [10216788] **5583**

FINS AND FEATHERS (KANSAS, ED.) (US/0741-3874) [10216947] **5583**

FINS AND FEATHERS (SOUTH DAKOTA ED.) (US/0741-4005) [10217786] **5583**

FINS AND FEATHERS (VIRGINIA, ED.) (US/0741-7101) [10196209] **5584**

FINSK PALSTIDSKRIFT (FI/0430-5817) [04305817] **3183**

FINSK TIDSKRIFT (FI) [18131448] **2516, 3343**

Alphabetical Title Index — FISCAL

FINSKA LAKARESALLSKAPET See FINSKA LAKARESALLSKAPETS HANDLINGAR **3576**

FINSKA LAKARESALLSKAPETS HANDLINGAR (FI/0015-2501) [01569298] **3576**

FINSKT MUSEUM (US) [06139269] **263**

FINTECH. 2, ELECTRONIC OFFICE (UK/0266-7797) [I02667797] **2055**

FINTECH. 3, PERSONAL COMPUTER MARKETS (UK/0267-8446) [I02678446] **1267**

FINTECH. 5, SOFTWARE MARKETS (UK/0267-9078) [I02679078] **1286**

FINTECH. ADVANCED MANUFACTURING (UK) **3479**

FINTECH. MOBILE COMMUNICATIONS (UK) **1155**

FIORINO (IT/0391-6405) [I03916405] **5804**

FIRA BULLETIN (UK/0014-5904) [01645759] **2905**

FIRA NAFM (US/0163-2930) [04336350] **2905**

FIRE ALARM SIGNALING SYSTEMS (US) **2288**

FIRE AND ARSON INVESTIGATOR, THE (US/1059-7298) [01795291] **3164, 2288**

FIRE AND CASUALTY, LIFE AND DISABILITY INSURANCE MANUAL (US/0738-8187) [09334880] **2880**

FIRE & EMERGENCY WORLD (US/0738-3940) [09582708] **2288**

FIRE & FLAMMABILITY BULLETIN (UK) [17315844] **2288**

FIRE AND MATERIALS (UK/0308-0501) [03356397] **2289, 615**

FIRE & MOVEMENT (US/0147-0051) [03061065] **4861**

FIRE AND POLICE PERSONNEL REPORTER (US/0164-6397) [04448971] **1674, 4775**

FIRE AND RESCUE (UK) **2289**

FIRE & SECURITY PROTECTION *CEASED*. (UK) [14882119] **2289, 5177**

FIRE APPARATUS JOURNAL (US/0885-8837) [12753894] **5382, 2289**

FIRE-BALL MAIL (NE) **4117**

FIRE CASUALTY & SURETY BULLETINS 301. STANDARD LINES SET (US/0163-8882) [04523100] **2880**

FIRE CASUALTY & SURETY BULLETINS 304. GUIDE TO POLICIES (US) **2880**

FIRE CASUALTY & SURETY BULLETINS 308. COMPANIES & COVERAGES (US) **2880**

FIRE CASUALTY & SURETY BULLETINS 325. COMPLETE SERVICE (US/0163-8874) [04523133] **2881**

FIRE CHIEF (US/0015-2552) [01385729] **2289**

FIRE CONTROL DIGEST (US/0889-5740) [06150658] **2289**

FIRE CONTROL NOTES (CALIFORNIA. DIVISION OF FORESTRY : 1975) See CALIFORNIA FIRE CONTROL NOTES (CALIFORNIA. DEPT. OF FORESTRY) **2288**

FIRE DEPARTMENT PERSONNEL REPORTER See FIRE AND POLICE PERSONNEL REPORTER **4775**

FIRE DIRECTORY, THE (UK/0264-4827) **2289**

FIRE/EMERGENCY SERVICES SOURCEBOOK See EMERGENCY SERVICES SOURCEBOOK **4774**

FIRE ENGINEERING (US/0015-2587) [01291160] **2289**

FIRE ENGINEERS JOURNAL (UK/0143-5337) [01786954] **2289**

FIRE FIGHTING IN CANADA (CN/0015-2595) [01988408] **2289**

FIRE INDEPENDENT, THE (US/0098-3276) [02241652] **2289**

FIRE INTERNATIONAL (UK/0015-2609) [02630295] **2289**

FIRE ISLAND NEWS (US) [11386187] **5716**

FIRE LOSSES IN BRITISH COLUMBIA IN ... (CN/0821-820X) [09610710] **2289**

FIRE MANAGEMENT NOTES *CEASED*. (US/0194-214X) [02538444] **2379, 2289**

FIRE NEWS (BOSTON) (US/0015-2625) [01569305] **2289**

FIRE NEWS (BOSTON) (US/0015-2625) [19037295] **2289**

FIRE PREVENTION (LONDON, 1971) (UK/0309-6866) [02446933] **2289**

FIRE PREVENTION NOTES (US/0734-0702) [06832422] **2289**

FIRE PROTECTION CONTRACTOR, THE (US/1043-2485) [09095156] **2289**

FIRE PROTECTION GUIDE TO HAZARDOUS MATERIALS (US/0362-0786) [02441083] **2289**

FIRE PROTECTION HANDBOOK (US/0734-5984) [07759949] **2289**

FIRE PROTECTION SYSTEMS (US) **2289**

FIRE PROTECTION VIDEO, FILM AND SLIDE CATALOGUE (CN/1185-2607) [24571407] **2289**

FIRE RESEARCH NEWS (UK/0261-1589) [I02611589] **2289**

●FIRE RESEARCH NEWS (CN/1188-4053) [26758248] **2289**

FIRE RESISTANCE DIRECTORY (US) [03010207] **2289**

FIRE RESISTANT MATERIALS AND PRODUCTS, PATENTS AND ABSTRACTS *CEASED*. (US/1043-464X) [19480943] **2290**

FIRE SAFETY ENGINEERING (UK) **2290**

FIRE SAFETY JOURNAL (SZ/0379-7112) [06118734] **2290**

FIRE SCIENCE AND TECHNOLOGY (JA/0285-9521) [08677747] **2290**

FIRE SERVICE EXTENSION SCHOOL, WEST VIRGINIA UNIVERSITY See PROCEEDINGS - FIRE SERVICE EXTENSION SCHOOL, WEST VIRGINIA UNIVERSITY **2029**

FIRE SERVICE INFORMATION (US/0015-2668) [04077467] **2290**

FIRE SERVICE LABOR MONTHLY (US/0890-8494) [14401854] **1674**

FIRE SERVICE STATISTICS ... ACTUALS (UK/0309-622X) [20437792] **2290**

FIRE SURVEYOR (UK/0262-7981) [01788822] **2290**

FIRE TECHNOLOGY (US/0015-2684) [01569307] **2290**

FIRE TECHNOLOGY ABSTRACTS (US/0148-6675) [03220341] **2290**

FIRE (TUNBRIDGE WELLS) (UK/0142-0510) [10032075] **2290**

FIREBIRD (HARMONDSWORTH, MIDDLESEX) (UK) [08755054] **3388**

FIREFIGHTER'S NEWS (USUS/1061-4818) [12256513] **2290**

FIREHEART (MAYNARD, MASS.) (US/1046-6029) [20462508] **4241, 4185**

FIREHOUSE (US/0145-4064) [02733088] **2290**

FIREHOUSE LAWYER MONTHLY NEWSLETTER (US/0896-8314) [17303619] **2970**

... FIREHOUSE MAGAZINE. BUYER'S GUIDE, THE (US/0276-4881) [07352300] **2290**

●FIRELINE (US/1065-0210) [26483968] **2290**

FIREMAN MELBOURNE, THE (AT/0812-0056) [I08120056] **2290**

FIRENZE (IT) [01788073] **2688**

FIRENZE IERI, OGGI, DOMANI (IT/1120-7248) [22365523] **2516**

FIRENZE SPETTACOLO (IT) **385**

FIREPOINT ROSEVILLE (AT/1035-2287) [110352287] **2290**

FIRESIDE CHATS (US/0015-2714) [09559616] **2785**

FIRESIDE SENTINEL : THE ALEXANDRIA LIBRARY, LLOYD HOUSE NEWSLETTER, THE (US/1042-2307) [17248964] **2733**

FIREWATCH / NAFED (US) [08372795] **2290**

FIREWEED (CN/0706-3857) [04677989] **5556**

FIREWEED : A FEMINIST QUARTERLY (CN/0383-7912) [03230487] **5557**

FIREWORKS BUSINESS (US/8755-4372) [11306862] **675**

FIRM FOUNDATION (US/8750-9377) [01293772] **5060**

FIRMA (PL/0137-9674) [09632174] **1607**

FIRMS IN THE 8(A) BUSINESS DEVELOPMENT PROGRAM (US/0195-5411) [05427390] **675, 2261**

FIRST AID BULLETIN See VIRGINIA LIFELINE **3650**

FIRST AIDER (US) [02252150] **1855, 3954**

FIRST AND READMISSIONS TO STATE AND COUNTY PSYCHIATRIC HOSPITALS BY COUNTY, MUNICIPALITY OF RESIDENCE, AND SERVICE AREA (US) [04042380] **3925, 3780**

FIRST BOSTON CORPORATION. PUBLIC FINANCE DEPT See SURVEY OF GENERATION AND TRANSMISSION COOPERATIVES **1543**

FIRST BOSTON WORKING PAPER SERIES (US/1047-9546) [15062542] **1491**

FIRST BREAK (UK/0263-5046) [09219764] **1405**

FIRST CATHOLIC SLOVAK UNION OF AMERICA See MINUTES OF THE ANNUAL MEETING OF THE FIRST CATHOLIC SLOVAK UNION OF THE UNITED STATES OF AMERICA AND CANADA **2747**

FIRST CATHOLIC SLOVAK UNION OF AMERICA. BOARD OF DIRECTORS See MINUTES OF THE SEMI-ANNUAL MEETING OF THE BOARD OF DIRECTORS OF THE FIRST CATHOLIC SLOVAK UNION OF THE UNITED STATES AND CANADA **5032**

FIRST CHICAGO GUIDE : MAJOR PUBLICLY HELD CORPORATIONS AND FINANCIAL INSTITUTIONS HEADQUARTERED IN NORTHERN ILLINOIS (US) [12621732] **1491**

FIRST CHOICE CANADA (CN/0820-8859) [11817730] **5382**

FIRST CLASS ALFELD (GW/0939-8414) [I09398414] **868, 5071, 2805**

FIRST DATA BANK BLUE BOOK (US) **4305**

FIRST DAYS (US/0428-4836) [03977942] **2785**

FIRST DAYS RECORD : A JOURNAL OF LIBERAL RELIGIOUS RESPONSES, THE (GW/1050-7507) [21583394] **4959**

FIRST DRAFT (US) **2919**

FIRST DROP / COASTER NEWS (UK) **4861**

FIRST FOR WOMEN (US/1040-9467) [18587622] **5557**

FIRST FREEDOM : A NEWSLETTER OF THE PUEBLA INSTITUTE, THE (US) [22590708] **4508**

FIRST HAND (US/0744-6349) [08460731] **2794**

FIRST INTERSTATE BANCORP See ANNUAL REPORT / FIRST INTERSTATE BANCORP **639**

FIRST LANGUAGE (UK/0142-7237) [07472982] **3281**

FIRST NATIONAL CITY BANK (NEW YORK, N.Y.) See INDONESIA STATISTICS **1534**

FIRST NATIONAL STORES, INC See ANNUAL REPORT - FIRST NATIONAL STORES INC **2327**

FIRST NATIONAL STORES, INC. PRESIDENT'S REPORT TO THE STOCKHOLDERS See ANNUAL REPORT - FIRST NATIONAL STORES INC **2327**

FIRST PAYMENTS, WEEKS COMPENSATED AND BENEFITS PAID TO WOMEN, BY INDUSTRIAL GROUP UNDER OHIO UNEMPLOYMENT COMPENSATION LAW / OHIO BUREAU OF EMPLOYMENT SERVICES (US) [07340999] **3148**

FIRST PEOPLE, THE (CN/0703-8437) [03948030] **2733**

FIRST PERSPECTIVE (CN) **2261**

●FIRST PLACE [COMPUTER FILE] (US) [25363991] **2335**

FIRST PRINCIPLES (US/0363-0447) [02417536] **4508**

FIRST-RATE CUSTOMER SERVICE (US) **675**

FIRST READING (CN/0824-197X) [11816174] **5245**

FIRST REPORT OF THE PUBLIC ACCOUNTS COMMITTEE TO THE NATIONAL ASSEMBLY, THE (MW) [06929117] **4726**

FIRST STEPS ON THE LADDER OF LEARNING (AT) **1804**

FIRST STRIKE (US/0896-4432) [17159008] **2781**

FIRST TEACHER (US/0744-7434) [08523814] **1895**

FIRST THINGS (NEW YORK, N.Y.) (US/1047-5141) [20708061] **4959**

FIRST THINGS (RUSH CITY, MINN.) (US/0890-7277) [14472144] **5060**

FIRST TUESDAY (US/0272-8230) [06930013] **4837**

FIRSTCLASS (IRVING, TEX.) (US/0192-2289) [05002348] **5470**

FIRSTS (LOS ANGELES, CALIF.) (US/1066-5471) [23035338] **4821**

FISCAL ACCOUNTABILITY ACT; SUMMARY REPORT TO THE GENERAL ASSEMBLY (US) [06190297] **4726**

FISCAL GUIDELINES FOR FEDERAL AND STATE AIDED GRANTS (US) [23905619] **4726, 1746**

FISCAL LETTER, THE (US/0197-288X) [04329311] **4726**

FISCAL NOTES (US) [03867893] **744**

FISCAL REPORT FOR THE FISCAL PERIOD ENDED JUNE 30 ... / COMMONWEALTH OF PENNSYLVANIA, OFFICE OF THE AUDITOR GENERAL (US) [11273911] **4726**

FISCAL STUDIES (UK/0143-5671) [07879424] **4726**

FISCAL SUMMARY OF ... / VERMONT DEPARTMENT OF FINANCE AND MANAGEMENT (US) [17197293] **4726**

FISCAL — Alphabetical Title Index

FISCAL SURVEY OF THE STATES (US/0198-6562) [04694448] **4726**

FISCAL YEAR ... ALABAMA TRANSIT DATA REPORT / MASS TRANSPORTATION DIVISION, BUREAU OF URBAN PLANNING, ALABAMA HIGHWAY DEPARTMENT (US) [08672457] **5415**

FISCAL YEAR BUDGET ESTIMATES - DEPT. OF TRANSPORTATION, OFFICE OF THE SECRETARY (US/0278-2987) [03079476] **5382**

FISCAL YEAR BUDGET ESTIMATES - FEDERAL AVIATION ADMINISTRATION (US) [03762111] 20, **4726**

● FISCAL YEAR ESTIMATED TAX ON UNRELATED BUSINESS TAXABLE INCOME FOR TAX-EXEMPT ORGANIZATIONS (WORKSHEET) (US) [26861393] 4335, **4726**

FISCAL YEAR HIGHER EDUCATION BUDGET RECOMMENDATIONS : CAPITAL IMPROVEMENTS (US/0095-7321) [01798514] **1824**

FISCAL YEAR HIGHER EDUCATION BUDGET RECOMMENDATIONS : OPERATIONS AND GRANTS (US/0097-7683) [01798575] **1824**

FISCAL YEAR ... PROGRAM REPORT, GRANT NO ... FOR U.S. DEPARTMENT OF THE INTERIOR, GEOLOGICAL SURVEY (US) [22459827] **1376**

FISCAL YEAR PROGRAM REPORT / WATER RESOURCES RESEARCH CENTER, PURDUE UNIVERSITY (US) [12959604] **5533**

FISCAL YEAR REPORT - STATE OF MONTANA. BOARD OF INVESTMENTS (US/0090-9122) [01785752] **899**

FISCAL YEAR SUMMARY REPORT OF POPULATION MOVEMENT (US/0362-7322) [03620579] **3164**

FISCALITE AFRICAINE: REVUE DU DROIT DES AFFAIRES AFRICAINES (FR) **3128**

FISCALITE AFRICAINES. REVUE DU DROIT DES AFFAIRES AFRICAINES (FR) **675**

FISCALITE AU CANADA, LA (CN/0319-2423) [01904453] **4726**

FISCALITE DE L'INNOVATION ET DU CAPITAL RISQUE DANS LA CEE, LA (FR) **1491**

FISCALITE EUROPEENNE (FR) [01569602] **4727**

FISCALITE IMMOBILIERE (FR/0750-8662) [I07508662] 2970, **4727**

FISCH-MAGAZIN (WALDSOLMS) (GW/0930-6544) [I09306544] **1746**

FISCH UND FANG (GW/0015-2838) [21551441] **4894**

FISCHER UND TEICHWIRT (GW/0342-5703) [I03425703] **4872**

FISCHERBLATT, DAS (GW/0015-2854) [I00152854] **2301**

FISCHEREI-FORSCHUNG (GW/0428-4984) [02778869] **2301**

FISCHERS TARIF-NACHRICHTEN FUER EISENBAHN UND KRAFTWAGEN (GW/0015-2862) [I00152862] **4727**

FISCHWAID (1982) (GW/0722-706X) [08419884] **2301**

FISCO, IL (IT) **744**

FISCOMAT (BL) [07406915] **4727**

FISH AND CHIPS AND FAST FOODS (UK) **2335**

FISH AND FISH EGG DISTRIBUTION REPORT OF THE NATIONAL FISH HATCHERY SYSTEM (US/1043-299X) [17979705] **2301**

● FISH & FISHERIES WORLDWIDE (US/1069-9309) [28202174] **2301**

FISH AND GAME CODE (US) [07536340] **4872**

FISH & GAME HIGHLIGHTS (US/1041-4762) [18778398] **4872**

FISH AND SHELLFISH IMMUNOLOGY (UK/1050-4648) [21501593] **5584**

● FISH AND WILDLIFE INFORMATION EXCHANGE NEWSLETTER (US/1071-3239) [27995592] 1185, **2193**

FISH AND WILDLIFE LEAFLET (US/0899-451X) [12438362] **2193**

FISH AND WILDLIFE NEWS (US) [02335613] **2193**

FISH AND WILDLIFE REFERENCE SERVICE NEWSLETTER (US/0160-4740) [01592797] **4872**

FISH AND WILDLIFE RESEARCH (US/1040-2411) [15311274] **2193**

FISH AND WILDLIFE TECHNICAL REPORT (US/0899-3505) [12211512] 2193, **2301**

FISH CATCH IN JAPANESE FISHERIES (JA) [02242212] **2301**

FISH CONSERVATION HIGHLIGHTS (US/0430-6015) [01569322] **2301**

FISH CULTURIST, THE (US/0015-2919) [01381029] **2301**

FISH DIRECTORY (US/0090-7081) [01784413] **5285**

FISH DISEASE LEAFLET (US/0071-5492) [02250361] **2301**

FISH FARM NEWS See PACIFIC COAST AQUACULTURE **2310**

FISH FARM NEWS, THE (CN/1180-5633) [23598537] **2301**

FISH FARMER (UK) [06428223] **2301**

FISH FARMER INTERNATIONAL FILE (UK/0262-9615) [24385427] **2301**

FISH FARMING INTERNATIONAL (UK/0262-0820) [01791751] **2301**

FISH INTERNATIONAL (GW/0930-6552) [15096972] **2301**

FISH KILLS CAUSED BY POLLUTION IN ... (1975) (US/0193-3558) [05157062] 2171, **2301**

FISH MARKETING REVIEW (PH) [09823896] **2301**

FISH MEAL AND OIL (US/0364-0140) [02494238] **2301**

FISH PHYSIOLOGY (US) [01781028] 2301, **580**

FISH PHYSIOLOGY AND BIOCHEMISTRY (NE/0920-1742) [13637540] **2301**

FISH SNIFFER (NORTHERN CALIFORNIA-NEVADA ED.), THE (US/0747-3397) [10755805] **5635**

FISH STICKS, PORTIONS, AND BREADED SHRIMP See PROCESSED FISHERY PRODUCTS, ANNUAL SUMMARY **2311**

FISH SUPPLIES INTERNATIONAL : PROCESSING & MARKETING NEWS (CN/0229-1924) [08260363] **2301**

FISH TRADER (UK) [02401000] **2301**

FISH TRADER YEARBOOK (UK/0953-8860) [I09538860] **2301**

FISH TRADES GAZETTE See FISH TRADER **2301**

FISHER REPORTER (US) **2487**

FISHERIES AND WILDLIFE RESEARCH AND DEVELOPMENT (US/0891-7523) [12163721] 2193, **2301**

FISHERIES, AUSTRALIA (AT) [08073225] **2302**

FISHERIES (BETHESDA) (US/0363-2415) [02146875] **2302**

FISHERIES BULLETIN (MW) [01785499] **2302**

FISHERIES BULLETIN (BATON ROUGE) (US/0460-1815) [01387177] **2302**

FISHERIES BULLETIN OF THE KENTUCKY DEPARTMENT OF FISH AND WILDLIFE RESOURCES (US) [05797907] **2302**

FISHERIES BULLETIN (PRETORIA) (SA/1015-6186) [01354128] 554, **2302**

FISHERIES (CANBERRA, A.C.T.) See FISHERIES, AUSTRALIA **2302**

FISHERIES COUNCIL OF CANADA See BULLETIN - FISHERIES COUNCIL OF CANADA **2297**

FISHERIES DATA REPORT (CN/0225-9818) [06270566] **2302**

FISHERIES DEVELOPMENT ACT, ANNUAL REPORT (CN) [09379703] 4649, **2302**

FISHERIES ECONOMICS NEWSLETTER (UK/0309-4294) [03862150] **2317**

FISHERIES LABORATORY, LOWESTOFT, ENG See REPORT OF THE DIRECTOR OF FISHERY RESEARCH **2311**

FISHERIES LABORATORY, LOWESTOFT, ENG. ANNUAL REPORT OF THE DIRECTOR OF FISHERY RESEARCH See REPORT OF THE DIRECTOR OF FISHERY RESEARCH **2311**

● FISHERIES MANAGEMENT AND ECOLOGY (UK/0969-997X) [30443288] **2302**

FISHERIES MANAGEMENT ANNUAL PROGRESS REPORT ON PROJECTS IN THE ... WORK SCHEDULE (US/0740-4387) [09926895] **2302**

FISHERIES MANAGEMENT REPORT (ALBERTA. FISH AND WILDLIFE DIVISION) (CN/0707-8498) [02442799] **2302**

FISHERIES MANUSCRIPT REPORT (CN/0706-9596) [04589467] **2302**

FISHERIES NEWS (CN/1183-3416) [25351927] **2302**

● FISHERIES OCEANOGRAPHY (US/1054-6006) [22922240] 2302, **1449**

FISHERIES OF JAPAN (JA) [03290966] **2302**

FISHERIES OF THE UNITED STATES (US) [01873631] **2302**

FISHERIES POLLUTION REPORT (LETHBRIDGE) (CN/0707-2783) [04801242] 2193, **2302**

FISHERIES PRODUCT NEWS (US/1047-2525) [20667720] **2302**

FISHERIES RESEARCH (NE/0165-7836) [08006898] **2302**

FISHERIES RESEARCH BOARD OF CANADA See FISHERIES RESEARCH BOARD OF CANADA REPORTS **2302**

FISHERIES RESEARCH BOARD OF CANADA REPORTS (CN/0384-3149) [02871567] **2302**

FISHERIES RESEARCH DATA REPORT (UK/0264-5130) [11639586] **2302**

FISHERIES RESEARCH JOURNAL OF THE PHILIPPINES (PH) [04969796] **2302**

FISHERIES RESEARCH REPORT (PERTH) (AT/1035-4549) [24272335] **2193**

FISHERIES REVIEW (FORT COLLINS, COLO.) (US/1042-6299) [13529972] 2302, **2317**

FISHERIES SCIENCE (JA) 554, **2302**

FISHERIES STATISTICS OF JAPAN (JA) [02240008] 2302, **2317**

FISHERIES TODAY (PH/0115-4443) [05791946] **2302**

FISHERMAN (FLORIDA ED.), THE (US/1059-5295) [24617195] 4872, **2302**

FISHERMAN (GRAND HAVEN, MICH.), THE (US/8755-4216) [07099821] **2302**

FISHERMAN (LONG ISLAND, METROPOLITAN NEW YORK ED.), THE (US/1040-0109) [09547094] **2302**

FISHERMAN (NEW ENGLAND ED.), THE (US/1040-0125) [18294925] **2302**

FISHERMAN (NEW JERSEY, DELAWARE BAY ED.), THE (US/1040-0117) [18294947] **4894**

FISHERMAN, THE (CN/0015-2986) [03341331] **2302**

FISHERMAN'S HANDBOOK, THE (US) [01293739] **2303**

FISHERMEN'S NEWS, THE (US/0015-2994) [04077481] **2303**

FISHER'S DESCRIPTIVE BIBLIOGRAPHY OF SCHOOL SOCIAL WORK (US) [22939064] **1747**

FISHERS SUN-HERALD (US) [13803540] **5664**

FISHERY BULLETIN (US/0090-0656) [01783998] **2303**

FISHERY MANAGEMENT REPORT (US) [22357724] **2303**

FISHERY MARKET NEWS (SEATTLE, WASH.) (US) [05525231] **2303**

FISHERY PUBLICATION (SPRINGFIELD) (US/0445-3034) [01331705] **2303**

FISHERY RESEARCH BULLETIN See ALASKA FISHERY RESEARCH BULLETIN **2293**

FISHERY RESEARCH REPORT (US) [02971827] **2303**

FISHERY STATISTICS OF THE UNITED STATES (US/0095-7682) [01798265] 2303, **2317**

FISHERY TECHNOLOGY (II/0015-3001) [01771430] **2303**

FISHES OF THE WESTERN NORTH ATLANTIC (US) [01296004] **2303**

FISHING & HUNTING JOURNAL (US/0886-3008) [12874312] **4872**

FISHING & HUNTING NEWS (WESTERN WASHINGTON ED.) (US/0015-301X) [04077498] **4872**

FISHING BOAT WORLD (HK/1033-1247) [10331247] **2303**

FISHING FACTS (NORTHERN ED.) (US/0899-9597) [18281099] **2303**

FISHING FACTS (SOUTHERN ED.) (US/0899-9589) [18281062] **2303**

FISHING GAZETTE (MARGATE, N.J.) (US/0747-2250) [10648990] **2303**

FISHING GUIDEBOOK (US) [01997894] 4872, **2303**

FISHING HOLES (US/1063-1577) [25506339] 2303, **4872**

FISHING IN MARYLAND (US/0164-0941) [04556335] 4872, **2303**

FISHING IN MARYLAND & VIRGINIA See FISHING IN MARYLAND **2303**

FISHING IN NEW JERSEY CEASED. (US) 4872, **2303**

FISHING IN NEW YORK (US/0192-9267) [05086497] **2303**

FISHING IN THE MID ATLANTIC CEASED. (US/0363-552X) [02483462] **2303**

FISHING INCOME TAX GUIDE (CN/0848-6913) [23454907] 2303, **4727**

FISHING (NEW YORK, N.Y.) (US/0742-0587) [08426442] **2303**

FISHING NEWS INTERNATIONAL (UK/0015-3044) [01569329] **2303**

FISHING SECRETS (US/0742-0595) [10248770] **2303**

FISHING TACKLE RETAILER (1984) (US/8750-1287) [11009167] **675**

FISHING TACKLE TRADE NEWS (US/0015-3060) [04351638] **2303**

●FISHING TRIP MAGAZINE (US/1060-5444) [25032560] **4872**

●FISHING VESSELS OF THE UNITED STATES (US/1065-5069) [26621612] 593, 5449, **2303**

FISHING WORLD (US/0015-3079) [02381756] **2303**

FISHING WORLD SYDNEY (AT/0158-572X) [I0158572X] 2303, **4872**

FISICA E TECNOLOGIA (IT/0391-9757) [05509834] **5105**

FISIOTERAPIA (SP/0211-5638) [02115638] **4380**

FISK(E) FAMILY ASSOCIATION : NEWSLETTER (US) [07891730] **2448**

FISKE GUIDE TO COLLEGES, THE (US/1042-7368) [18604341] **1824**

FISKE (STOCKHOLM) (SW/0301-6668) [01792990] **2303**

FISKEN OG HAVET (NO/0071-5638) [01569331] **2303**

FISKERI- OG FANGSTPRODUKTER KBT AF PRODUKTIONSANLG I GRNLAND / MINISTERIET FOR GRNLAND (DK) [10494247] **2304**

FISKERIDIREKTORATETS SKRIFTER. SERIE ERNAERING (NO/0332-5083) [03252404] **2304**

FISKERIDIREKTORATETS SKRIFTER. SERIE HAVUNDERSKELSER (NO/0015-3117) [01760746] 554, **2304**

FISKERISTATISTIKK (NO) [01589819] **2317**

FISKOLOOG (BE/0772-4837) [107724837] **1491**

FISSION ENERGY PROGRAM OF THE U.S. DEPARTMENT OF ENERGY (US) [06726592] **1944**

FIT : FORMATION INFORMATIQUE TECHNOLOGIE (FR/0980-322X) **3211**

FIT THIRD AGE (CN/0827-3103) [11847664] 2597, **3751**

FITCH INVESTORS SERVICE See FITCH RATINGS **899**

FITCH RATINGS (US) [23859933] **899**

FITCHBURG STAR (US) [11950730] **5767**

FITECH (UK/0307-2118) [01796388] **2290**

FITECH INTERNATIONAL (UK) [31061232] **2290**

FITNESS AND LIFESTYLE RESEARCH REVIEWS (CN/0227-7751) [06688400] 4587, **2597**

●FITNESS AND SPORTS REVIEW INTERNATIONAL (US/1068-5952) [26100109] 4895, **1855**

FITNESS BULLETIN, THE (CN/0820-6163) [08671267] **2597**

FITNESS CYCLING *CEASED*. (US/1046-1701) [20347246] 429, **2597**

FITNESS MANAGEMENT (SOLANA BEACH, CALIF.) (US/0882-0481) [11731020] **2597**

●FITNESS, PHYSICAL HEALTH AND RECREATION EDUCATION (EASTERN U.S. ED.) (CN/1189-329X) [25796427] **2597**

●FITNESS, PHYSICAL HEALTH AND RECREATION EDUCATION (WESTERN U.S. ED.) (CN/1189-3303) [25796429] 4850, **2597**

FITNESS PLUS (US/1054-674X) [22278938] **2597**

FITNESS REPORT, THE See ACTIVE LIVING (TORONTO) **2595**

FITNESS WORKS! (CN/1181-6988) [23598335] 2862, **2597**

FITOPATOLOGIA (PE/0430-6155) [01772629] **510**

FITOPATOLOGIA BRASILEIRA (BL/0100-4158) [02438360] 510, **172**

FITOPATOLOGIA COLOMBIANA (CK/0120-0143) [08428778] **510**

FITOPATOLOGIA VENEZOLANA (VE/0798-0035) [20536748] **510**

FITOTERAPIA (IT/0367-326X) [09262368] 3576, **510**

●FITZPATRICK'S JOURNAL OF CLINICAL DERMATOLOGY (US/1072-2521) [28895831] **3720**

FITZWILLIAM MUSEUM See ANNUAL REPORTS OF THE SYNDICATE AND OF THE FRIENDS OF THE FITZWILLIAM FOR THE YEAR ENDING ..., THE **4084**

FIVE FINGERS REVIEW (US/0898-0233) [10782817] **3388**

FIVE HUNDRED (US/1045-4209) [20618166] **2733**

FIVE LIBRARY REGIONS ..., PROVINCE OF NEW BRUNSWICK, THE (CN/0826-3671) [11139083] **3211**

FIVE OWLS, THE (US/0892-6735) [15178423] **1063**

FIVE STONES, THE (US/1064-136X) [13107766] 4959, **5060**

FIVE-YEAR BUDGET PROJECTIONS See REPORT TO THE SENATE AND HOUSE COMMITTEES ON THE BUDGET, A **1516**

FIVE-YEAR CAPITAL PLAN See FINANCIAL PROJECTIONS AND CAPITAL PLAN **4725**

FIVE-YEAR FORECAST OF BUSINESS CLIMATE TRENDS IN 85 COUNTRIES (US/0897-0653) [17390006] **1491**

FIVE YEAR FOREST AND RANGE RESOURCE PROGRAM (CN/0229-1886) [09175254] **2379**

FIVE-YEAR GOVERNMENTAL FUNDS PROJECTIONS See FINANCIAL PROJECTIONS AND CAPITAL PLAN **4725**

FIVE-YEAR INDEX TO ASTM TECHNICAL PAPERS AND REPORTS (US) [02257430] **2102**

FIVE YEAR MEDICAL FACILITY DEVELOPMENT PLAN (US) [15997101] **3780**

FIVE YEAR PLAN / CONNECTICUT DEPARTMENT OF CORRECTION (US) [18697224] **3164**

FIVE YEAR PROJECTIONS, KENTUCKY'S SCHOOL ENROLLMENT (US) [08371715] **1864**

FIW-SCHRIFTENREIHE (GW/0429-9485) [02003509] **1491**

FIX UND FOXI (GW) **378**

FIX YOUR VOLKSWAGEN (US/0071-5697) [05885161] **5415**

FIXED INCOME JOURNAL, THE (US/0739-4799) [09728422] **899**

FIZICESKIE SVOJSTVA METALLOV I SPLAVOV (RU/0136-3638) [10814043] **4002**

FIZICHESKAIA KHIMIIA (RU) [10292673] **1052**

FIZIKA AERODISPERSNYH SISTEM (KIEV) (UN/0367-1631) [01800081] 5105, **1425**

FIZIKA ATMOSFERY (RU/0135-1419) [I01351419] **1425**

FIZIKA ATOMNOGO IADRA / AKADEMIIA NAUK SSSR, LENINGRADSKII INSTITUT IADERNOI FIZIKI IM. B.P. KONSTANTINOVA (RU) [23686406] **4447**

●FIZIKA B : A JOURNAL OF EXPERIMENTAL AND THEORETICAL PHYSICS (CI/1330-0016) [27135066] 5105, **4403**

FIZIKA ELEMENTARNYKH CHASTITS / AKADEMIIA NAUK SSSR, LENINGRADSKII INSTITUT IADERNOI FIZIKI IM. B.P. KONSTANTINOVA (RU) [23686243] **4447**

FIZIKA ELEMENTARNYKH CHASTITS I ATOMNOGO IADRA (RU) [02351451] **4403**

FIZIKA GORENIIA I VZRYVA (RU/0430-6228) [09327848] **4403**

FIZIKA I HIMIJA STEKLA (RU/0132-6651) [02243252] **2589**

FIZIKA I KHIMIIA OBRABOTKI MATERIALOV (UK/0264-729X) [09959510] 975, **4403**

FIZIKA I KHIMIIA OBRABOTKI MATERIALOV (RU/0015-3214) [01374874] **2114**

FIZIKA I KHIMIIA STEKLOOBRAZUIUSHCHIKH SISTEM (LV/0134-7071) [02750633] 2589, **1015**

FIZIKA I MEKHANIKA GORNYKH POROD (GS) [02365638] **2023**

FIZIKA I TECHNIKA POLUPROVODNIKOV (RU/0015-3222) [01374928] **2055**

FIZIKA I TEHNIKA VYSOKIH DAVLENIJ (RU/0203-4654) [I02034654] **4403**

FIZIKA I TEKHNIKA VYSOKIH DAVLENII / AKADEMIIA NAUK UKRAINSOI SSR, DONETSKII FIZIKO-TEKHNICHESKII INSTITUT (RU) [08138255] **4427**

FIZIKA KRISTALLIZATSII (RU) [19001775] **1032**

FIZIKA MAGNITNYKH MATERIALOV (RU) [02412038] **4443**

FIZIKA METALLOV I METALLOVEDENIE (RU/0015-3230) [01569341] **4002**

FIZIKA MNOGOCHASTICHNYKH SISTEM (UN) [09339531] **4403**

FIZIKA MOLEKUL (KIEV) (UN/0131-176X) [02998901] **1052**

FIZIKA NIZKIH TEMPERATUR (KIEV) (UN/0132-6414) [02244414] **4430**

FIZIKA PLAZMY (MOSKVA. 1975) (RU/0134-5052) [02243251] **4403**

FIZIKA (SOFIA) (BU/0204-6946) [03601532] **4403**

FIZIKA TVERDOGO TELA (DONETSKII GOSUDARSTRENNYI UNIVERSITET) (UN/0202-2915) [09382085] **4427**

FIZIKA V SHKOLE : NAUCHNO-METODICHESKII ZHURNAL MINISTERSTVO PROSVESHCHENIIA SSSR (RU/0130-5522) [11047093] **4403**

FIZIKA VERKHNEI ATMOSFERY VYSOKIKH SHIROT (RU) [02671855] **1425**

FIZIKA VYSOKIKH ENERGII / AKADEMIIA NAUK SSSR, LENINGRADSKII INSTITUT IADERNOI FIZIKI IM. B.P. KONSTANTINOVA (RU) [23686329] **4447**

●FIZIKA ZEMLI / ROSSIISKAIA AKADEMIIA NAUK (RU) [26813360] **1405**

FIZIKA ZHIDKOGO SOSTOIANIIA (UN/0302-5470) [01796675] **4403**

FIZIKAI SZEMLE (HU/0015-3257) [02385776] **4403**

FIZIKO-HIMICESKA MEHANIKA (BU/0204-5958) [02244425] 4403, **1052**

FIZIKO-HIMICESKAJA MEHANIKA MATERIALOV (UN/0430-6252) [02351487] **1052**

FIZIKO-KHIMICHESKAIA MEKHANIKA I LIOFILNOST DISPERSNYKH SISTEM (UN/0367-2409) [05587826] **455**

FIZIKO-KHIMICHESKIE ISSLEDOVANIIA METALLURGICHESKIKH PROTSESSOV (RU) [03340087] **4002**

FIZIKO-MATEMATICHESKO SPISANIE (BU/0015-3265) [06002786] 3505, **4403**

FIZIKO-TEKHNICHESKIE PROBLEMY RAZRABOTKI POLEZNYKH ISKOPAEMYKH (RU/0015-3273) [06370254] **2139**

FIZIOLOGICESKIJ ZURNAL (UN/0201-8489) [04622355] **580**

FIZIOLOGICESKIJ ZURNAL SSSR IMENI I.M. SECENOVA (RU/0015-329X) [07660374] **580**

FIZIOLOGICHESKI AKTIVNYE VESHCHESTVA (UN/0533-1153) [06729217] **455**

FIZIOLOGIIA RASTENII (RU/0015-3303) [02989528] **510**

FIZIOLOGIIA RASTENII. ENGLISH. RUSSIAN PLANT PHYSIOLOGY See RUSSIAN JOURNAL OF PLANT PHYSIOLOGY : A COMPREHENSIVE RUSSIAN JOURNAL ON MODERN PHYTOPHYSIOLOGY **527**

FIZIOLOGIIA RASTENII. ENGLISH. SOVIET PLANT PHYSIOLOGY See RUSSIAN PLANT PHYSIOLOGY **527**

FIZIOLOGIJA CELOVEKA (RU/0131-1646) [02244548] **580**

FIZIOLOGIJA I BIOHIMIJA KULTURNYH RASTENIJ (UN/0256-1425) [02989551] **510**

FIZIOLOGIJA NA RASTENIJATA (BU/0324-0290) [02242407] **510**

FIZKULTURA I SPORT (RU) [08260495] **4895**

FIZKULTURA I ZDOROVE (RU) [19609227] **2597**

FIZYKA DIELEKTRYKOW I RADIOSPEKTROSKOPIA (PL/0137-8996) [01789179] **4443**

FIZYKO-TEKHNICHNYI INSTYTUT NYZKYKH TEMPERATUR (AKADEMIIA NAUK UKRAINSKOI RSR) See VOPROSY GIDRODINAMIKI I TEPLOOBMENA V KRIOGENNYH SISTEMAH **2096**

FIZYKOCHEMICZNE PROBLEMY MINERALURGII (PL/0137-1282) [11465411] **1439**

FJC DIRECTIONS (US/1055-5277) [23199933] **3140**

FKTU NEWS (KO) [05438885] **1674**

FLACS (US/0014-5920) [08205584] **975**

FLAG (US/0090-7308) [01785656] **4117**

FLAG BULLETIN, THE (US/0015-3370) [04077515] **2616**

FLAG : THE FOOTHILLS LIBRARY ASSOCIATION GAZETTE, THE (CN/0228-7137) [08045851] **3211**

FLAGLER NEWS, THE (US) [15476714] **5642**

FLAGS, DIAMONDS, AND STATUES (US/0271-7638) [06659963] **5431**

FLAGSCAN (CN/0833-1510) [16642024] **2448**

FLAGSHIP (CN/0705-1824) [03991746] **593**

FLAGSTAFF INSTITUTE See JOURNAL OF THE FLAGSTAFF INSTITUTE **1637**

FLAMBEE, LA (CN/0705-1751) [05840615] **4256**

FLAMBOROUGH NEWS *CEASED*. (CN/0710-5339) [08700943] **5784**

FLAME RETARDANCY NEWS (US/1058-0948) [24207591] **2290**

FLAME RETARDANCY OF POLYMERIC MATERIALS (US/0361-6320) [01377899] 2290, **5351**

FLAME (SEATTLE, WASH.) (US) [08375975] 4959, **5557**

FLAMING CARROT COMICS (US/0826-256X) [11564278] **4861**

FLAMING CRESCENT, THE (US) **4474**

FLAMING

FLAMING GORGE RESERVOIR FISHERIES INVESTIGATIONS (US/0738-2359) [09536023] **2304**

FLAMMABILITY INSTITUTE *See* NEWS BULLETIN (DETROIT) **2292**

FLAMMABLE AND COMBUSTIBLE LIQUIDS CODE (US) 2290, **2862**

FLAMMABLE AND COMBUSTIBLE LIQUIDS CODE HANDBOOK (US) 2290, **2862**

FLAMMES VIVES (FR/0015-3486) [06162254] **3343**

FLANDERS (BE) [20972013] **2516**

FLANDREAU SPIRIT, THE (US) [06169139] **1747**

FLANNERY O'CONNOR BULLETIN (US/0091-4924) [01786926] 3343, **432**

FLAP INTERNACIONAL (BL) [03217474] **20**

●FLARE ADVENTURES (US/1057-2910) [24004092] **378**

FLARE FIRST EDITION (US/1054-0997) [22745232] **378**

FLARE (TORONTO) (CN/0708-4927) [06019069] **5557**

FLASH (BE) **1674**

FLASH 10 (CN/0227-4604) [08010214] **1864**

FLASH ART (INTERNATIONAL EDITION) (IT/0394-1493) [09227733] **350**

FLASH (BANFF) (CN/1182-9265) [23242533] **4895**

FLASH (CAIRO, EGYPT) (UA) [09723104] **2503**

FLASH ESPACE TOULOUSE (FR/1154-2675) [l11542675] **395**

FLASH ETAT-UNIS (FR/0985-2662) 3576, **455**

FLASH INFORMATIONS - CHAMBRE DE COMMERCE FRANCO-SOVIETIQUE *See* CHAMBRE DE COMMERCE FRANCO-RUSSE **819**

FLASH INFORMATIONS - CHAMBRE DE COMMERCE FRANCO-SOVIETIQUE (FR/1157-8394) [11578394] **819**

FLASH JAPON (FR/0985-2654) 3576, **455**

FLASH. (LOS ANGELES/WEST ED.) (US/1055-3142) [23138013] **378**

FLASH ... SUR LA RECHERCHE SCIENTIFIQUE ET MEDICALE A L'UNIVERSITE PIERRE ET MARIE CURIE (FR/0769-1432) [20055120] 5105, **3576**

FLASHBACK (FAYETTEVILLE, ARK.) (US/0428-5573) [03600937] **2733**

FLASHES FROM THE TRADE UNIONS (XR) [05120747] **1674**

FLASHLIGHT (PASADENA, CALIF.) (US/0274-6522) [02250363] **4959**

FLASHMAPS INSTANT GUIDE TO BOSTON (US/0740-7653) [09991964] **5470**

FLASHMAPS INSTANT GUIDE TO DALLAS, FORT WORTH (US/0278-8942) [07901398] **2560**

FLASHY BUT CHEAP (US/1064-6027) [26338683] 1286, **1233**

FLAT EARTH NEWS (US/8756-0313) [11455295] **1405**

FLAT GLASS (US/0146-566X) [02715774] **2589**

FLATBUSH GUIDE, THE (US) **5470**

FLATHEAD COURIER, THE (US) [14082275] **5705**

FLATONIA ARGUS, THE (US) [14219098] **5749**

Alphabetical Title Index

FLAVOR AND FRAGRANCE MATERIALS (US/1051-0281) [08941613] **1024**

FLAVOUR AND FRAGRANCE JOURNAL (UK/0882-5734) [11893334] **2335**

FLAVOUR NEWS (BE) [05871912] **195**

FLEA MARKET TRADER (US/0364-023X) [02574481] **836**

FLEA NEWS (UK) [08850558] **5584**

FLEET EQUIPMENT (US/0747-2544) [10665854] **5382**

FLEET INTERNATIONAL *See* AUTOMOBILE INTERNATIONAL **5405**

FLEET MANAGEMENT (US) **5382**

FLEET MANAGEMENT NEWS (PORT READING, N.J.) (US/1042-1769) [18967081] **5382**

FLEET NEWS (UK) **5382**

FLEET RENTING AND LEASING (US) **5382**

●FLEET SAFETY & HEALTH (CN/1183-9856) [26497803] **2862**

FLEET STREET LETTER (UK/0300-4228) [01445252] **899**

FLEET STREET PATENT LAW REPORTS *See* FLEET STREET REPORTS OF INDUSTRIAL PROPERTY CASES FROM THE COMMONWEALTH AND EUROPE **2970**

FLEET STREET REPORTS (UK/0141-9455) [25800079] **1304**

FLEET STREET REPORTS OF INDUSTRIAL PROPERTY CASES FROM THE COMMONWEALTH AND EUROPE (UK) [06301718] **2970**

FLEET SUPERVISOR, THE *See* FLEET SAFETY & HEALTH **2862**

FLEETLINE (AT/0312-4681) [l03124681] **5382**

FLEET'S GUIDE (US/0899-9147) [18263973] **4837**

FLEETWOOD'S STANDARD FIRST DAY COVER CATALOG (US/0190-7433) [04762745] **2785**

FLEISCH (GW/0015-3575) [03754887] **2335**

FLEISCHEREI (GW/0015-3613) [04023718] **2335**

FLEISCHFORSCHUNG UND PRAXIS (GW/0430-6465) [01844506] **211**

FLEISCHWIRTSCHAFT, DIE (GW/0015-363X) [01771974] 5510, **211**

FLEMINGSBURG GAZETTE (FLEMINGSBURG, KY. : 1978) (US) [14351381] **5680**

FLEMISH AMERICAN HERITAGE (US) **2448**

FLESCHNER SERIES IN CRITICAL CARE NURSING, THE (US/0732-9644) [08425502] **3856**

FLESNEWS (US/1064-3540) [18182227] **1804**

FLETCHER (US/0161-8350) [04030762] **1102**

FLETCHER FORUM OF WORLD AFFAIRS, THE (US/1046-1868) [19187936] **4521**

FLETCHER-O'LEARY PERIODICAL, THE (CN/0715-4518) [09166918] **2448**

FLETCHER SCHOOL OF LAW AND DIPLOMACY *See* FLETCHER **1102**

FLEUR DESIGN (CN/0827-150X) [13844143] **2435**

FLEURISTE DU QUEBEC (CN/0380-3163) [02011976] **2435**

FLEURS, PLANTES ET JARDINS (CN/1180-159X) [22570020] **2414**

FLEX AND SPEX INFORMATION BULLETIN (US/1051-578X) [21170647] **3576**

●FLEXIBLE BENEFITS (US/1073-7111) [29513560] **2881**

FLEXLINES (US) **1185**

FLEXO (RONKONKOMA, N.Y.) (US/1051-7324) [10499536] **4565**

FLEXOGRAPHIC TECHNICAL ASSOCIATION *See* REPORT OF THE PROCEEDINGS : ANNUAL MEETING AND TECHNICAL FORUM **4569**

FLEXPACK MATERIALS & MARKETS BULLETIN (UK) **4219**

FLICC NEWSLETTER (US/0882-908X) [11664885] **3211**

FLICKERTALES (ERIE, N.D.) (US/0274-0001) [02250364] **5725**

FLIEGER-REVUE (GW) [03492656] **20**

FLIES OF THE NEARCTIC REGION (GW) [07494724] **5584**

FLIGHT GUIDE : EASTERN MANUAL (US) **5382**

FLIGHT GUIDE : WESTERN MANUAL (US) **5382**

FLIGHT INTERNATIONAL (UK/0015-3710) [06674288] **20**

FLIGHT INTERNATIONAL DIRECTORY. PART 1, UNITED KINGDOM (UK) [19701681] **21**

FLIGHT INTERNATIONAL DIRECTORY. PART II, MAINLAND EUROPE AND IRELAND (UK) [22607152] **21**

FLIGHT OPERATIONS (US/0361-5030) [02246052] **21**

FLIGHT REPORTS *CEASED.* (US/0194-9039) [05092290] 5470, **21**

FLIGHT SAFETY BULLETIN (US) [03457304] **21**

FLIGHT SAFETY BULLETIN (CN/0826-032X) [11085132] **21**

FLIGHT SAFETY DIGEST (1988) (US/1057-5588) [24059296] **21**

FLIGHT SAFETY FOUNDATION *See* INTERNATIONAL AIR SAFETY SEMINAR PROCEEDINGS **24**

FLIGHT SAFETY FOUNDATION NEWS (US/1057-557X) [24059157] **21**

FLIGHT SERVICES (US) [02786123] **21**

FLIGHT STANDARDS INFORMATION MANUAL (US/0565-4866) [01799415] **21**

FLIGHT TRAINING (US/1047-6415) [20738521] **21**

●FLIGHT TRAINING ACADEMIC ENHANCER. BOOK 2, INSTRUMENTS (US/1066-078X) [26844881] **21**

FLIGHTLOG (US/0164-8691) [04312116] **1674**

FLIGHTPATH (AT) **21**

FLINDERS JOURNAL OF HISTORY AND POLITICS (AT/0726-7215) [01989325] 2616, **4474**

FLINDERS UNIVERSITY OF SOUTH AUSTRALIA. INSTITUTE FOR ATOMIC STUDIES, FIAS-R (AT/0725-783X) [08334706] **2155**

FLINT JOURNAL (1935) (US) [09974225] **5692**

FLINT LABOR MARKET REVIEW *See* FLINT'S LABOR MARKET NEWS **1674**

●FLINT'S LABOR MARKET NEWS (US) [25953616] **1674**

FLIS NEWSLETTER (CN/0845-3020) [20008065] **3211**

FLLESRADET FOR DANSKE TJENESTEMANDS- OG FUNKTIONRORGANISATIONER *See* KILDESKATTELEKSIKON **4735**

FLOATING (US) [03260306] **4850**

FLOATING ISLAND (US/0147-1686) [03114849] **3463**

FLOCK BOOK OF DORSET HORN AND POLL DORSET SHEEP, THE (UK) [10517637] **211**

FLOCK BOOK OF DORSET HORN SHEEP *See* FLOCK BOOK OF DORSET HORN AND POLL DORSET SHEEP, THE **211**

FLOH KISTE (GW) **1063**

FLOODTIDE (US) [01586082] **4959**

FLOOR COVERING BUSINESS (US/1041-2506) [18694870] **2905**

FLOOR COVERING NEWS / U.S.A (US/1045-5116) [20128304] 615, **2905**

●FLOOR COVERING PLUS (CN/1193-8781) [28311870] 2905, **615**

FLOOR COVERING WEEKLY (US/0015-3761) [02446945] **2905**

●FLOOR FOCUS (US/1064-7627) [26391159] 2905, **615**

FLOORING (NEW YORK, N.Y.) (US/0162-881X) [01299356] **615**

FLOPPY ANBAR *See* ELECTRONIC ANBAR **671**

FLOPPY ANBAR (MCB UNIVERSITY PRESS) (UK/0962-3922) [I09623922] **1185**

FLOPPYLAND. COMPUTER DISK (US) **1267**

FLORA BUTTENSIS (US) [10573565] **510**

FLORA DA GUINE-BISSAU (PO) [07967221] **510**

FLORA DE VERACRUZ (MX) [05160822] **510**

FLORA ET VEGETATIO MUNDI *CEASED.* (SZ/0071-576X) [01371101] **510**

FLORA GRUZII (GS) [02970682] **510**

FLORA IRANICA : FLORA DES IRANISCHEN HOCHLANDES UND DER UMRAHMENDEN GEBIRGE (AU) [01588963] **510**

FLORA LEVY LECTURE IN THE HUMANITIES, THE (US/0897-1323) [17006047] **2846**

●FLORA-LINE, THE (US/1062-855X) [25771911] **2435**

FLORA (LONDON) (UK/0306-882X) [02329061] **2435**

FLORA MALESIANA. SERIES I, SPERMATOPHYTA (NE/0374-7778) [05179232] **510**

FLORA MALESIANA. SERIES II, PTERIDOPHYTA (NE/0071-5786) [05179735] **510**

FLORA MEDITERRANEA (IT/1120-4052) [24649213] **510**

FLORA. MORPHOLOGIE, GEOBOTANIK, OKOLOGIE (GW/0367-2530) [18733812] **2216**

FLORA NEOTROPICA (US/0071-5794) [01776032] **510**

FLORA OF BANGLADESH (BG) [08456047] **511**

FLORA OF BHUTAN (UK) **511**

FLORA OF CYPRUS (UK) **511**

FLORA OF ECUADOR (SW/0347-8742) [02789897] **511**

FLORA OF TEXAS (US) [01345556] **511**

FLORA OF THE GUIANAS. SERIES A : PHANEROGAMAE (GW) **511**

FLORA OF TROPICAL EAST AFRICA (UK/0451-7814) [01641158] **511**

FLORA OG FAUNA (DK/0015-3818) [03076448] 511, 2216, **5584**

FLORA ONLINE (US/0892-9106) [17217968] **511**

FLORA REPUBLICAE POPULARIS SINICAE (CC) **5105**

Alphabetical Title Index

FLORIDA

FLORACULTURE INTERNATIONAL (US/1051-9076) [22147783] **2414**

FLORAL & NURSERY TIMES (US/1042-2145) [18973488] **511**

FLORAL DIGEST *See* FLORAL & NURSERY TIMES **511**

FLORAL MARKETING DIRECTORY & BUYER'S GUIDE (US) [08143897] **2435 924**

FLORALA NEWS, THE (US) [12926701] **5626**

FLORE DE FRANCE (FR/0430-6651) [09637371] **511**

FLORE DE LA NOUVELLE CALEDONIE ET DEPENDANCES (FR) 455, **511**

FLORE DE MADAGASCAR ET DES COMORES (FR) **511**

FLORE DU CAMBODGE, DU LAOS ET DU VIETNAM (FR/0071-5867) [01569385] **511**

FLORE DU CAMEROUN (FR/0071-5875) [02995828] **511**

FLORE DU GABON (FR) [02995846] **511**

FLORENCE CITIZEN, THE (US) [21947987] **5642**

FLORENCE MINING NEWS, THE (US) [11978369] **5767**

FLORENCE MORNING NEWS (US) [27969756] **5742**

FLORENCE (PROVENCE). CAMERA DI COMMERCIO, INDUSTRIA E AGRICOLTURA *See* ARTI E MERCATURE **823**

FLORENTIA ILIBERRITANA (SP/1131-8848) [I11318848] **3388**

FLORESTA (BL/0015-3826) [03346018] **2379**

FLORESVILLE CHRONICLE-JOURNAL (US) [12717345] **5750**

FLORICULTURE (IT) **2435**

FLORICULTURE CROPS (US/0272-6793) [04168529] **2414**

FLORICULTURE DIRECTIONS ***CEASED***. (US/1043-9137) [08462206] **2414**

FLORIDA *See* FLORIDA ADMINISTRATIVE CODE; THE OFFICIAL COMPILATION OF RULES AND REGULATIONS OF REGULATORY STATE AGENCIES **4649**

FLORIDA *See* FLORIDA STATUTES **2971**

FLORIDA *See* LAWS OF FLORIDA **2997**

FLORIDA *See* FLORIDA STATUTES ANNOTATED **2971**

FLORIDA ACCIDENTAL DEATH STATISTICS (US) [04401493] **5327**

FLORIDA AD VALOREM VALUATIONS AND TAX DATA (US/0146-7034) [03013755] **4727**

FLORIDA ADMINISTRATIVE CODE SUPPLEMENT SERVICE (US) **4649**

FLORIDA ADMINISTRATIVE CODE; THE OFFICIAL COMPILATION OF RULES AND REGULATIONS OF REGULATORY STATE AGENCIES (US) [01569412] **4649**

FLORIDA ADMINISTRATIVE LAW REPORTS (US/0194-4800) [04636113] **3093**

FLORIDA ADMINISTRATIVE WEEKLY (US/0098-874X) [02241337] **4649, 2970**

FLORIDA ADVISORY COUNCIL ON INTERGOVERNMENTAL RELATIONS *See* ANNUAL REPORT - ADVISORY COUNCIL ON INTERGOVERNMENTAL RELATIONS **4709**

FLORIDA. AGRICULTURAL AND MECHANICAL UNIVERSITY, TALLAHASSEE *See* QUARTERLY JOURNAL - FLORIDA AGRICULTURAL AND MECHANICAL UNIVERSITY, TALLAHASSEE, THE **1843**

FLORIDA. AGRICULTURAL AND MECHANICAL UNIVERSITY, TALLAHASSEE *See* REPORT - FLORIDA AGRICULTURAL AND MECHANICAL UNIVERSITY **1844**

FLORIDA. AGRICULTURAL EXPERIMENT STATION, GAINESVILLE. LIBRARY *See* MISCELLANEOUS PUBLICATIONS - FLORIDA. AGRICULTURAL EXPERIMENT, GAINESVILLE. LIBRARY **109**

FLORIDA AGRICULTURAL STATISTICS (US) [01421628] **153**

FLORIDA AGRICULTURAL STATISTICS : CITRUS SUMMARY (US/0428-6413) [01794036] 87, **153**

FLORIDA AGRICULTURAL STATISTICS. COMMERCIAL CITRUS INVENTORY (US/0092-3656) [19684677] **87**

FLORIDA AGRICULTURAL STATISTICS. LIVESTOCK, DAIRY, AND POULTRY SUMMARY (US) [26770785] 211, **195**

FLORIDA AGRICULTURAL STATISTICS. LIVESTOCK SUMMARY (US) [01327304] **87**

FLORIDA AGRICULTURAL STATISTICS: VEGETABLE SUMMARY (US/0428-6456) [03082555] **87**

FLORIDA AGRICULTURE *See* FLORIDAGRICULTURE (GAINESVILLE, FLA.) **87**

FLORIDA ALMANAC (US/0361-9796) [01325795] **2533**

FLORIDA ANTHROPOLOGIST, THE (US/0015-3893) [01569447] **236**

FLORIDA ARCHAEOLOGY (US/0888-4277) [13567254] **268**

FLORIDA ARCHITECT (US/0015-3907) [06827129] **298**

FLORIDA ARCHITECTURE (1966) (US/1040-0893) [07708919] **298**

FLORIDA ARMCHAIR RESEARCHER, THE (US/0748-0113) [10692596] **2448**

FLORIDA. ARTHRITIS FOUNDATION *See* NEWSLETTER - FLORIDA ARTHRITIS FOUNDATION **3806**

FLORIDA. ATLANTIC UNIVERSITY, BOCA RATON *See* PRESIDENT'S REPORT - FLORIDA. ATLANTIC UNIVERSITY, BOCA RATON **1842**

FLORIDA. ATTORNEY-GENERAL. REPORT *See* REPORT OF ATTORNEY GENERAL TO THE GOVERNOR AND THE LEGISLATURE **3142**

FLORIDA ATTORNEYS-SECRETARYS HANDBOOK (US) 4211, **2970**

FLORIDA BAPTIST WITNESS / ORGAN OF THE FLORIDA BAPTIST STATE CONVENTION (US) [10673991] **5060**

FLORIDA BAR *See* FLORIDA BAR CASE SUMMARY SERVICE, THE **2970**

FLORIDA BAR *See* FLORIDA BAR NEWS **2970**

FLORIDA BAR CASE SUMMARY SERVICE, THE ***CEASED***. (US/0164-6427) [04448923] **2970**

FLORIDA BAR JOURNAL, THE (US/0015-3915) [02076103] **2970**

FLORIDA BAR NEWS (US/0360-0114) [02243343] **2970**

FLORIDA BLUE SHEET (US) [28299833] **4071**

FLORIDA. BOARD OF CONTROL *See* FLORIDA HIGHER EDUCATION **1824**

FLORIDA. BOARD OF REAL ESTATE. BOARD OF REAL ESTATE HANDBOOK *See* FLORIDA REAL ESTATE COMMISSION HANDBOOK / STATE OF FLORIDA **4838**

FLORIDA BOARD OF REAL ESTATE NEWS & REPORT *See* FLORIDA REAL ESTATE COMMISSION NEWS & REPORTS **4838**

FLORIDA. BOARD OF REGENTS *See* ENROLLMENT IN FLORIDA'S INSTITUTIONS OF HIGHER LEARNING **1822**

FLORIDA. BOARD OF REGENTS *See* CHARACTERISTICS OF COLLEGE STUDENTS, ENTERING FRESHMEN, AND TRANSFER UNDERGRADUATES : JUNIOR COLLEGE SURVEY **1815**

FLORIDA BUILDER (US) **615**

FLORIDA BUILDER & DEVELOPER *See* FLORIDA BUILDER **615**

FLORIDA. BUREAU OF EDUCATION FOR EXCEPTIONAL STUDENTS *See* FLORIDA STATE PLAN FOR THE EDUCATION OF EXCEPTIONAL STUDENTS **1879**

FLORIDA. BUREAU OF GEOLOGY *See* MAP SERIES (TALLAHASSEE, FLA.) **2582**

FLORIDA. BUREAU OF INTERGOVERNMENTAL RELATIONS *See* FEDERAL GRANT-IN-AID ACTIVITY IN FLORIDA : A SUMMARY REPORT **4723**

FLORIDA BUSINESS (CLEVELAND, OHIO) (US/1042-590X) [19089740] **675**

FLORIDA BUSINESS DIRECTORY (US/1048-7093) [21012917] **676**

FLORIDA BUSINESS GUIDE, THE (US/0733-964X) [07884103] **676**

FLORIDA BUSINESS LEADER (US/0428-707X) [01381426] **676**

FLORIDA BUSINESS LETTER. SPECIAL MAPS AND GRAPHS OF FLORIDA (US/0428-7088) [01396722] 2560, **676**

FLORIDA BUSINESS PUBLICATIONS INDEX (US/0191-183X) [03721043] **676**

FLORIDA BUSINESS SOUTHWEST (US/1047-6105) [20734268] **676**

FLORIDA CANCER NEWS ***CEASED***. (US) [01402001] **3817**

FLORIDA CANNERS ASSOCIATION *See* STATISTICAL SUMMARY - FLORIDA CANNERS ASSOCIATION **2362**

FLORIDA CASES REPORTED IN SOUTHERN REPORTER, SECOND SERIES (US/0744-981X) [08690646] **2970**

FLORIDA CATHOLIC, THE (US/0746-4584) [01381806] **5029**

FLORIDA CATTLEMAN AND DAIRY JOURNAL *See* FLORIDA CATTLEMAN AND LIVESTOCK JOURNAL, THE **211**

FLORIDA CATTLEMAN AND LIVESTOCK JOURNAL, THE (US/0015-3958) [09105128] **211**

FLORIDA CERTIFIED PUBLIC ACCOUNTANT, THE (US/0015-3966) [01381951] **744**

FLORIDA CHAMBERS ENVIRONMENTAL NETWORK ***CEASED***. (US) **2172**

FLORIDA CIRCLE, THE (US) [01382107] **2605**

FLORIDA CITRUS PROCESSORS ASSOCIATION *See* STATISTICAL SUMMARY - FLORIDA CITRUS PROCESSORS ASSOCIATION **2358**

FLORIDA CITRUS TREE INVENTORY (US) [01786903] **2414**

FLORIDA COACHING DIRECTORY (US/1044-9000) [19943872] **4895**

FLORIDA COLLEGE COMMUNIQUE (US/1057-9044) [24151456] **1091**

FLORIDA. COMMISSION ON HUMAN RELATIONS *See* SESQUIANNUAL REPORT - FLORIDA COMMISSION ON HUMAN RELATIONS **4513**

FLORIDA COMMUNICATION JOURNAL, THE (US/1050-3366) [18658764] **1111**

FLORIDA COMP (US/1078-2362) [29907680] **1675**

FLORIDA CONSTRUCTOR ***CEASED***. (US) [20032578] **615**

FLORIDA CONTRACTOR ***CEASED***. (US/0046-4112) [04902181] **2605**

FLORIDA CORRECTIONAL EDUCATION ASSOCIATION *See* PROCEEDINGS - FLORIDA CORRECTIONAL EDUCATION ASSOCIATION **3173**

FLORIDA. COUNCIL FOR THE BLIND *See* REPORT - FLORIDA COUNCIL FOR THE BLIND **4393**

FLORIDA COUNCIL OF TEACHERS OF ENGLISH *See* DIRECTORY OF MEMBERSHIP - FLORIDA COUNCIL OF TEACHERS OF ENGLISH **3277**

FLORIDA CPA TODAY : A PUBLICATION OF THE FLORIDA INSTITUTE OF CERTIFIED PUBLIC ACCOUNTANTS (US) [16074492] **744**

FLORIDA CREATIVE DIRECTORY *See* ... SOUTHEAST SOURCEBOOK, THE **766**

FLORIDA CRIME AND DELINQUENCY (US/0733-804X) [03961599] **3164**

FLORIDA CROP AND LIVESTOCK REPORTING SERVICE *See* FLORIDA AGRICULTURAL STATISTICS **153**

FLORIDA CROP AND LIVESTOCK REPORTING SERVICE *See* FLORIDA CITRUS TREE INVENTORY **2414**

FLORIDA CROP AND LIVESTOCK REPORTING SERVICE *See* FLORIDA AGRICULTURAL STATISTICS : CITRUS SUMMARY **153**

FLORIDA CUT FLOWER AND FERN REPORT (US/0744-3714) [08223837] **2435**

FLORIDA. DEPARTMENT OF HEALTH AND REHABILITATIVE SERVICES. DIVISION OF MENTAL HEALTH *See* REPORT - FLORIDA. DEPARTMENT OF HEALTH AND REHABILITATIVE SERVICES. DIVISION OF MENTAL HEALTH **4798**

FLORIDA. DEPARTMENT OF STATE *See* BIENNIAL REPORT - STATE OF FLORIDA DEPARTMENT OF STATE **4632**

FLORIDA. DEPT. OF ADMINISTRATION. DIVISION OF PERSONNEL *See* RECOMMENDED SALARIES AND BENEFITS FOR CAREER SERVICE EMPLOYEES **4678**

FLORIDA. DEPT. OF ADMINISTRATION. DIVISION OF PERSONNEL *See* CLASSIFICATION AND PAY PLAN - (TALLAHASSEE) DIVISION OF PERSONNEL **4638**

FLORIDA. DEPT. OF AGRICULTURE *See* INDUSTRIAL FLORIDA **1610**

FLORIDA. DEPT. OF AGRICULTURE AND CONSUMER SERVICES. DECISION OF MARKETING *See* FLORIDA STATE FARMERS' MARKETS ... ANNUAL SUMMARY **87**

FLORIDA. DEPT. OF BANKING AND FINANCE *See* STATE OF FLORIDA: LOCAL GOVERNMENT FINANCIAL REPORT **4749**

FLORIDA. DEPT. OF CRIMINAL LAW ENFORCEMENT. UNIFORM CRIME REPORTS, STATE OF FLORIDA *See* CRIME IN FLORIDA **3080**

FLORIDA. DEPT. OF EDUCATION *See* MONDAY REPORT (TALLAHASSEE, FLA.), THE **1866**

FLORIDA — Alphabetical Title Index

FLORIDA. DEPT. OF HEALTH AND REHABILITATIVE SERVICES *See* STATE OF FLORIDA PROPOSED COMPREHENSIVE ANNUAL SERVICES PROGRAM PLAN FOR SOCIAL SECURITY ACT TITLE XX **5311**

FLORIDA. DEPT. OF HEALTH AND REHABILITATIVE SERVICES *See* FLORIDA ACCIDENTAL DEATH STATISTICS **5327**

FLORIDA. DEPT. OF HEALTH AND REHABILITATIVE SERVICES. OFFICE OF THE ASSISTANT SECRETARY FOR PROGRAM PLANNING AND DEVELOPMENT *See* FINAL COMPREHENSIVE ANNUAL SERVICES PROGRAM PLAN FOR TITLE XX - SOCIAL SECURITY ACT **5285**

FLORIDA. DEPT. OF LEGAL AFFAIRS *See* DIGEST OF OFFICIAL OPINIONS - ATTORNEY GENERAL (TALLAHASSEE) **3140**

FLORIDA. DEPT. OF LEGAL AFFAIRS *See* REPORT OF ATTORNEY GENERAL TO THE GOVERNOR AND THE LEGISLATURE **3142**

FLORIDA. DEPT. OF PROFESSIONAL REGULATION *See* ANNUAL REPORT / DEPARTMENT OF PROFESSIONAL REGULATION (FLORIDA) **1649**

FLORIDA. DEPT. OF REVENUE *See* FLORIDA AD VALOREM VALUATIONS AND TAX DATA **4727**

FLORIDA. DEPT. OF TRANSPORTATION *See* OFFICIAL FINANCIAL STATEMENT **5388**

FLORIDA. DEPT. OF TRANSPORTATION *See* FINANCIAL STATEMENT AFTER ALLOCATION **5382**

FLORIDA. DEPT. OF TRANSPORTATION. DIVISION OF SAFETY *See* FLORIDA SUMMARY OF ACCIDENT DATA **5440**

FLORIDA. DEPT. OF VETERAN AND COMMUNITY AFFAIRS *See* FLORIDA HOUSING LAND ACQUISITION AND SITE DEVELOPMENT AND TRUST FUND... ANNUAL REPORT TO GOVERNOR ... **2823**

FLORIDA DIGEST (US) [02976046] **2971**

FLORIDA DIRECTORY : A GUIDE TO FLORIDA GOVERNMENT, THE (US) [24187050] **4649**

FLORIDA. DIVISION OF ARCHIVES, HISTORY, AND RECORDS MANAGEMENT *See* CATALOG OF THE FLORIDA STATE ARCHIVES **2481**

FLORIDA. DIVISION OF CORRECTIONS *See* CORRECTIONAL COMPASS; OFFICIAL NEWSLETTER **3161**

FLORIDA. DIVISION OF EMPLOYMENT SECURITY *See* ANNUAL PLANNING INFORMATION REPORT. ORLANDO SMSA AND ORANGE COUNTY, ORLANDO CITY, SEMINOLE COUNTY CETA PRIME SPONSOR AREAS **1529**

FLORIDA. DIVISION OF EMPLOYMENT SECURITY *See* ANNUAL PLANNING INFORMATION REPORT ... TALLAHASSEE SMSA AND LEON-GADSDEN CETA CONSORTIUM **1647**

FLORIDA. DIVISION OF EMPLOYMENT SECURITY *See* ANNUAL PLANNING INFORMATION REPORT ... MIAMI SMSA AND SOUTH FLORIDA CETA CONSORTIUM **1647**

FLORIDA. DIVISION OF EMPLOYMENT SECURITY *See* ANNUAL PLANNING INFORMATION, STATE OF FLORIDA **1648**

FLORIDA. DIVISION OF EMPLOYMENT SECURITY. OFFICE OF RESEARCH AND STATISTICS *See* ANNUAL PLANNING REPORT - STATE OF FLORIDA, DEPARTMENT OF COMMERCE, DIVISION OF EMPLOYMENT SECURITY **1648**

FLORIDA. DIVISION OF FAMILY SERVICES *See* ANNUAL STATISTICAL REPORT - DIVISION OF FAMILY SERVICES **5266**

FLORIDA. DIVISION OF HEALTH *See* SUMMARY OF RECEIPTS, DISBURSEMENTS, AND BALANCES **4804**

FLORIDA. DIVISION OF PLANT INDUSTRY *See* PLANT PATHOLOGY CIRCULAR **524**

FLORIDA. DIVISION OF PLANT INDUSTRY *See* NEMATOLOGY CIRCULAR **466**

FLORIDA. DIVISION OF RETIREMENT *See* FLORIDA RETIREMENT SYSTEM ANNUAL REPORT / PREPARED BY THE DIVISION OF RETIREMENT'S STATE RETIREMENT ACTUARY, RESEARCH, EDUCATION, & POLICY SECTION, BUREAU OF ACCOUNTING AND DIVISION AUDIT STAFF **1675**

FLORIDA. DIVISION OF VETERANS AFFAIRS *See* ANNUAL REPORT - DIVISION OF VETERAN'S AFFAIRS (FLORIDA) **4035**

FLORIDA EDUCATION (US/0015-4016) [01387153] **1747**

FLORIDA EDUCATION ASSOCIATION *See* LEGISLATIVE BULLETIN - FLORIDA **3001**

FLORIDA EDUCATIONAL RESEARCH AND DEVELOPMENT COUNCIL *See* RESEARCH BULLETIN - FLORIDA EDUCATIONAL RESEARCH AND DEVELOPMENT COUNCIL **1778**

FLORIDA EMPLOYMENT LAW DESK BOOK (US) **1675**

FLORIDA EMPLOYMENT LAW LETTER (US/1041-3537) [18731767] **3148**

FLORIDA ENGINEERING SOCIETY *See* JOURNAL / FLORIDA ENGINEERING SOCIETY **1981**

FLORIDA ENGLISH JOURNAL, THE (US) [01387431] **3281**

FLORIDA ENTOMOLOGIST, THE (US/0015-4040) [01569453] **5608**

●FLORIDA ENVIRONMENTAL COMPLIANCE UPDATE (US/1064-1874) [26224163] **3112**

FLORIDA ENVIRONMENTS (US/0894-9743) [16387192] **2172**

FLORIDA ESTIMATES OF POPULATION / PREPARED BY THE POPULATION PROGRAM, BUREAU OF ECONOMIC AND BUSINESS RESEARCH, COLLEGE OF BUSINESS ADMINISTRATION, UNIVERSITY OF FLORIDA (US/0145-4668) [18265683] **4553**

FLORIDA EXPORT GUIDE (US/0146-9703) [03093833] **836**

FLORIDA FACTS (DALLAS, TEX.) (US/0895-8084) [16809696] **2533**

FLORIDA FAMILY PHYSICIAN (US/0015-4067) [01347781] **3737**

FLORIDA FIELD NATURALIST (US/0738-999X) [03018654] **5584**

FLORIDA FIREMAN (US/0274-8797) [01388085] **2290**

FLORIDA FISHING NEWS (US/0164-5188) [04587019] **2304**

FLORIDA FLAMBEAU, THE (US) [01388554] 5648, **5649**

FLORIDA FOLIAGE (US) [09118999] **2414**

FLORIDA FOLIAGE (US/0741-1448) [09257421] **511**

FLORIDA FOLK ARTS DIRECTORY (US/0162-5616) [04167976] **320**

FLORIDA FOOD DEALER (US/0191-9857) [05090280] **2335**

FLORIDA FORUM (US/0191-4618) [04901876] **615**

FLORIDA FOSSIL HORSE NEWSLETTER *See* PONY EXPRESS (GAINESVILLE, FLA.) **4170**

FLORIDA FRIENDS OF BLUEGRASS SOCIETY *See* NEWSLETTER - FLORIDA FRIENDS OF BLUEGRASS SOCIETY **4141**

FLORIDA FUNDING (US/0887-3038) [13207559] 5285, **868**

FLORIDA FUNERAL DIRECTOR, THE (US/0273-9747) [01405263] **2407**

FLORIDA GAME & FISH (MARIETTA, GA.) (US/0889-3322) [13848985] **4872**

FLORIDA GARDENER, THE (US/0426-5750) [01405395] 2194, **2414**

FLORIDA GENEALOGICAL SOCIETY *See* NEWSLETTER - FLORIDA GENEALOGICAL SOCIETY **2463**

FLORIDA GENEALOGICAL SOCIETY, TAMPA, FLA *See* YEAR BOOK - FLORIDA GENEALOGICAL SOCIETY, TAMPA, FLA **2478**

FLORIDA GENEALOGIST, THE (US/0161-4932) [03957742] **2448**

FLORIDA. GENERAL EXTENSION DIVISION *See* UNIT PICTURE COLLECTIONS AND ART PRINTS **367**

FLORIDA GEOGRAPHER, THE (US/0739-0041) [09688538] **2560**

FLORIDA GOVERNMENT SERIES (US/0071-5972) [01406238] **4649**

FLORIDA GOVERNOR *See* HOUSING IN FLORIDA **2824**

FLORIDA GOVERNOR ... BIENNIAL BUDGET RECOMMENDATION. AMENDMENT (US) [10832702] **4727**

FLORIDA. GOVERNOR'S COMMISSION ON THE STATUS OF WOMEN *See* ANNUAL REPORT. THE STATUS OF WOMEN IN FLORIDA **5551**

FLORIDA GROCER (US/0191-586X) [01417152] **2335**

FLORIDA GROUP CHILD CARE ASSOCIATION *See* PROCEEDINGS OF THE ANNUAL MEETING - FLORIDA GROUP CHILD CARE ASSOCIATION **5301**

FLORIDA GROWER & RANCHER (US/0015-4091) [01406406] **87**

●FLORIDA GROWER'S ORNAMENTAL OUTLOOK (US/1064-6558) [26347263] 511, **87**

FLORIDA HANDBOOK, THE (US/0361-9788) [01306297] **2733**

FLORIDA. HEALTH CARE COST CONTAINMENT BOARD *See* ANNUAL REPORT TO THE GOVERNOR AND LEGISLATURE / STATE OF FLORIDA, HEALTH CARE COST CONTAINMENT BOARD **3776**

●FLORIDA HEALTH CARE IN PERSPECTIVE (US/1065-4119) [26604916] **4775**

FLORIDA HIGHER EDUCATION (US) [01417244] **1824**

FLORIDA HISTORICAL QUARTERLY, THE (US/0015-4113) [01569457] **2733**

FLORIDA HISTORY NEWSLETTER *CEASED.* (US) [01406452] **2733**

FLORIDA HOME & GARDEN (US/0898-9494) [17699910] **2900**

FLORIDA HORSE, THE (US/0090-967X) [01407026] **2799**

FLORIDA. HOSPITAL COST CONTAINMENT BOARD *See* PROGRAM STATUS REPORT ... TO THE GOVERNOR AND LEGISLATURE / STATE OF FLORIDA, HOSPITAL COST CONTAINMENT BOARD **3791**

FLORIDA. HOSPITAL COST CONTAINMENT BOARD *See* CURRENT CHARGES FOR SELECTED HOSPITAL SERVICES ... / STATE OF FLORIDA, HOSPITAL COST CONTAINMENT BOARD **3779**

FLORIDA HOTEL & MOTEL JOURNAL (US/8750-6807) [11671634] **2805**

FLORIDA HOUSING LAND ACQUISITION AND SITE DEVELOPMENT AND TRUST FUND... ANNUAL REPORT TO GOVERNOR ... (US) [08914785] **2823**

FLORIDA IN PERSPECTIVE (US/1065-5387) [25703648] **5327**

FLORIDA, IN REVIEW (US/0733-9658) [08030125] **1344**

FLORIDA INDIANS (US) [01407528] 2261, **2733**

FLORIDA INDUSTRIAL COMMISSION *See* EMPLOYMENT AND PAY ROLLS IN FLORIDA COVERED BY THE UNEMPLOYMENT COMPENSATION LAW **1666**

FLORIDA INDUSTRIES GUIDE, THE (US) [01313273] **1561**

FLORIDA INSIGHT (US/1068-4433) [27674180] **4649**

FLORIDA INSTITUTE OF CONSULTING ENGINEERS *See* DIRECTORY & GUIDE - FLORIDA INSTITUTE OF CONSULTING ENGINEERS **1970**

FLORIDA INTERCOM (US) [01408812] **3211**

FLORIDA J.O.H.P.E.R (US/0430-7739) [01409974] 4850, **4776**

FLORIDA JOB BANK, THE (US/1069-8981) [16826310] 676, **4204**

FLORIDA JOURNAL OF ANTHROPOLOGY, THE (US/0164-1662) [04583137] **236**

FLORIDA JOURNAL OF ENVIRONMENTAL HEALTH (US/0897-4624) [17539681] 4776, **2172**

FLORIDA JOURNAL OF PUBLIC HEALTH (US/1045-9758) [19917667] **4776**

FLORIDA JURY VERDICT REPORTER (US/1059-6275) [12529052] **2971**

FLORIDA JURY VERDICT REVIEW AND ANALYSIS (US/1058-8604) [24435206] **3089**

FLORIDA KEYS KEYNOTER (US/8756-6427) [11627669] 5648, **5649**

FLORIDA KEYS MAGAZINE (US/0271-6100) [06643182] **2733**

FLORIDA LABOR MARKET TRENDS (US) [20257191] **1675**

FLORIDA LAND OWNER (US/1053-3060) [22513813] **4837**

FLORIDA LAND OWNER MAGAZINE (US/1047-1413) [20620726] **4837**

FLORIDA LAW OF TRUSTS (US) **2971**

FLORIDA LAW REVIEW (US/1045-4241) [19905486] **2971**

FLORIDA LAW WEEKLY, THE (US/0274-8533) [06653512] **2971**

●FLORIDA LEADER (US/0898-4387) [24642270] **1824**

FLORIDA LEGAL DIRECTORY, THE (US/0145-7829) [02782059] **2971**

FLORIDA. LEGISLATURE. HOUSE OF REPRESENTATIVES. OFFICE OF THE CLERK *See* LOBBYING IN THE FLORIDA HOUSE OF REPRESENTATIVES **4662**

FLORIDA. LEGISLATURE. INTERIM EDUCATIONAL COMMITTEE *See* EXPANDING HORIZONS FOR THE FUTURE OF FLORIDA THROUGH EDUCATION, REPORT **1746**

FLORIDA. LEGISLATURE. JOINT INTERIM COMMITTEE ON MENTAL HEALTH *See* REPORT - FLORIDA. LEGISLATURE. JOINT INTERIM COMMITTEE ON MENTAL HEALTH **4680**

FLORIDA

FLORIDA. LEGISLATURE. JOINT LEGISLATIVE MANAGEMENT COMMITTEE See SUMMARY OF GENERAL LEGISLATION (TALLAHASSEE) **4689**

FLORIDA. LEGISLATURE. JOINT LEGISLATIVE MANAGEMENT COMMITTEE. STATUTORY REVISION DIVISION See DIGEST OF GENERAL LAWS ENACTED BY THE REGULAR SESSION AND SPECIAL SESSION OF THE FLORIDA LEGISLATURE **2961**

FLORIDA. LEGISLATURE. SENATE See FLORIDA SENATE, THE **4649**

FLORIDA. LEGISLATURE. SENATE See JOURNAL OF THE SENATE, STATE OF FLORIDA **2990**

FLORIDA. LEGISLATURE. SENATE. WAYS AND MEANS COMMITTEE See SUPPLEMENTAL GENERAL APPROPRIATIONS AND LEGISLATIVE INTENT FOR THE ... BIENNIUM **4751**

FLORIDA LIBRARY ASSOCIATION See MEMBERSHIP DIRECTORY - FLORIDA LIBRARY ASSOCIATION **3230**

FLORIDA LIBRARY DIRECTORY (US) [01569460] **3211**

FLORIDA LIVESTOCK ROUNDUP (US) [01420988] **211**

FLORIDA LIVING (US/0888-9600) [13804987] **2533**

FLORIDA MANUFACTURERS REGISTER (US/0882-9438) [12019911] **3479**

FLORIDA MARINE RESEARCH PUBLICATIONS (US/0095-0157) [01596830] **455**

FLORIDA MARKET UPDATE (US/0886-2729) [12877724] **1561**

FLORIDA MEDICAL ASSOCIATION See FLORIDA MEDICAL DIRECTORY **3576**

FLORIDA MEDICAL DIRECTORY (US) [01327587] **3576**

FLORIDA MONTHLY (US/0148-9143) [03740132] **2533**

FLORIDA MOTEL JOURNAL (US/0015-4156) [01421345] **2805**

FLORIDA MUNICIPAL PROFILES (US/1051-242X) [21896785] **1926**

FLORIDA NATURALIST, THE (US/0015-4172) [01569463] 2172, **226**

FLORIDA NEWS MEDIA DIRECTORY (US) [04937786] **1111**

FLORIDA NURSE, THE (US/0015-4199) [06674304] **3856**

FLORIDA NURSERYMAN (US) [01412897] **2414**

FLORIDA NURSING REVIEW (US/0887-5006) [13262038] **3856**

FLORIDA. OFFICE OF THE GOVERNOR See FLORIDA GOVERNOR ... BIENNIAL BUDGET RECOMMENDATION. AMENDMENT **4727**

FLORIDA. OFFICE OF THE GOVERNOR See STATE OF FLORIDA BUDGET RECOMMENDATIONS **4688**

FLORIDA ORCHIDIST, THE (US/0430-778X) [01314350] **2414**

FLORIDA OUTDOOR RECREATIONAL DEVELOPMENT COUNCIL See MINUTES OF THE FLORIDA OUTDOOR RECREATIONAL DEVELOPMENT COUNCIL, FLORIDA OUTDOOR RECREATIONAL PLANNING COMMITTEE **4874**

FLORIDA OUTLOOK, THE (US/0147-7986) [03230806] 1491, **1533**

FLORIDA PAINTBALL PRESS (US) 4861, **4895**

FLORIDA PARENT (US/0887-1310) [13107002] **2280**

FLORIDA PARISHES GENEALOGICAL NEWSLETTER (US/8756-2316) [11520045] **2448**

FLORIDA PATRIOT (US) [01421490] **2533**

FLORIDA PHARMACY TODAY (US/0897-4616) [17539147] **4305**

FLORIDA PLANNING (TALLAHASSEE, FLA. : 1981) (US/0279-0297) [07471835] **2823**

FLORIDA PLAYERS NEWSLETTER (US/0426-5912) [01411094] **1824**

FLORIDA PLUMBING AND HEATING CONTRACTOR See FLORIDA CONTRACTOR **2605**

FLORIDA POLICE ADVISOR (US) **3107**

FLORIDA POLICE INFORMANT (XXU) [03906707] **3107**

FLORIDA POLICE JOURNAL (US/0015-4229) [01411125] **3164**

●FLORIDA POPULATION STUDIES (US) [27923326] **4553**

FLORIDA POWER AND LIGHT COMPANY See FLORIDA POWER & LIGHT COMPANY TEN YEAR POWER PLANT SITE REPORT **2055**

FLORIDA POWER & LIGHT COMPANY TEN YEAR POWER PLANT SITE REPORT (US/0734-7723) [08462776] **2055**

FLORIDA PRESERVATION NEWS (US) [17646623] **2194**

FLORIDA PRESS, THE CEASED. (US/0426-5920) [01663110] **2919**

FLORIDA PSYCHOLOGIST, THE (US/0046-4171) [01413048] **4587**

FLORIDA PUBLIC EMPLOYEE REPORTER DIGEST (US) [08981314] **1675**

FLORIDA RAILROAD DIRECTORY (US/1053-959X) [22700917] **5431**

FLORIDA READING QUARTERLY, THE (US/0015-4261) [01413790] **1747**

FLORIDA REAL ESTATE CEASED. (US/0897-9383) [17671054] **4837**

FLORIDA REAL ESTATE & DEVELOPMENT UPDATE (US/0887-3208) [13211000] **4837**

FLORIDA REAL ESTATE BROKER & THE LAW, THE (US/0735-9071) [08997981] 2971, **4837**

FLORIDA REAL ESTATE COMMISSION See FLORIDA REAL ESTATE COMMISSION HANDBOOK / STATE OF FLORIDA **4838**

FLORIDA REAL ESTATE COMMISSION HANDBOOK / STATE OF FLORIDA (US) [10961305] **4838**

FLORIDA REAL ESTATE COMMISSION NEWS & REPORTS (US/0744-6152) [08440540] **4838**

FLORIDA REAL ESTATE JOURNAL (US/0892-0524) [15080207] **4838**

FLORIDA REALTOR (US/0199-5839) [06018956] **4838**

FLORIDA REALTY JOURNAL See FLORIDA REALTOR **4838**

FLORIDA RELATIVE VALUE STUDIES (US/0733-1223) [08507962] **3576**

FLORIDA RESTAURATEUR (US/0192-348X) [05062751] **5071**

FLORIDA RESTAURATEUR & PURVEYOR NEWS (US/0046-418X) [01415509] **5071**

FLORIDA RETIREMENT LIVING (US/0160-5739) [03714636] **5179**

FLORIDA RETIREMENT SYSTEM ANNUAL REPORT / PREPARED BY THE DIVISION OF RETIREMENT'S STATE RETIREMENT ACTUARY, RESEARCH, EDUCATION, & POLICY SECTION, BUREAU OF ACCOUNTING AND DIVISION AUDIT STAFF (US) [14702430] 5179, **1675**

FLORIDA REVIEW (ORLANDO, FLA.), THE (US/0742-2466) [10284641] 3388, **3463**

FLORIDA RULES OF COURT. STATE (US/1047-1782) [15272373] **3140**

FLORIDA RUNNING (US/1048-7891) [21020036] **2597**

FLORIDA SCHOOL SURVEY SERIES (US) [01357470] **1747**

FLORIDA SCIENCE NEWSLETTER (US) [01407230] **5105**

FLORIDA SCIENTIST (US/0098-4590) [02241060] **5105**

FLORIDA SCUBA NEWS (US/0897-2621) [17452041] **4895**

FLORIDA SDB DIRECTORY : A DIRECTORY OF MINORITY-OWNED MANUFACTURERS (US/1061-0995) [24095043] **676**

FLORIDA SECURITY & INVESTIGATORS JOURNAL (US/0747-3117) [10715887] **3164**

FLORIDA SENATE, THE (US/0093-4089) [01783741] **4649**

FLORIDA SHIPPER MAGAZINE See FLORIDA SHIPPER MAGAZINE, THE **5449**

FLORIDA SHIPPER MAGAZINE, THE (US/1067-1455) [27142627] **5449**

FLORIDA SHIPPER, THE (US/0884-8548) [12491979] **5449**

FLORIDA SOLAR COALITION NEWSLETTER (US/0276-9964) [07455613] **1944**

FLORIDA SOLAR ENERGY CENTER See ACTIVITIES / FLORIDA SOLAR ENERGY CENTER **1930**

FLORIDA SOUTHERN COLLEGE See ALUMNI DIRECTORY - FLORIDA SOUTHERN COLLEGE **1098**

FLORIDA SPORTSMAN (MIAMI) (US/0015-3885) [01408010] **4895**

FLORIDA STAR (JACKSONVILLE, FLA. : 1951), THE (US/0740-798X) [02261130] **2616**

FLORIDA. STATE BEEKEEPERS ASSOCIATION See PROCEEDINGS OF THE ANNUAL MEETING - FLORIDA STATE BEEKEEPERS ASSOCIATION **122**

FLORIDA. STATE BEVERAGE DEPT See WINE & LIQUOR SALES **2372**

FLORIDA. STATE BOARD OF ACCOUNTANCY See DIRECTORY - STATE BOARD OF ACCOUNTANCY, STATE OF FLORIDA **743**

FLORIDA STATE BOARD OF ARCHITECTURE See ROSTER - FLORIDA STATE BOARD OF ARCHITECTURE **308**

FLORIDA. STATE BOARD OF BEAUTY CULTURE See REPORT - FLORIDA. STATE BOARD OF BEAUTY CULTURE **405**

FLORIDA. STATE BOARD OF ENGINEER EXAMINERS See YEAR BOOK - FLORIDA STATE BOARD OF ENGINEER EXAMINERS **2001**

FLORIDA. STATE BOARD OF INDEPENDENT COLLEGES AND UNIVERSITIES See REPORT OF THE STATE BOARD OF INDEPENDENT COLLEGES AND UNIVERSITIES (TALLAHASSEE) **1915**

FLORIDA. STATE BOARD OF PROFESSIONAL ENGINEERS AND LAND SURVEYORS See SUPPLEMENTAL YEAR BOOK - STATE BOARD OF PROFESSIONAL ENGINEERS AND LAND SURVEYORS **1997**

FLORIDA STATE CHAMBER OF COMMERCE See DIRECTORY OF FLORIDA INDUSTRIES **666**

FLORIDA. STATE DEPT. OF EDUCATION See COMMUNITY EDUCATION **1891**

FLORIDA. STATE DEPT. OF EDUCATION. PROFESSIONAL PRACTICES COUNCIL See REPORT - FLORIDA. STATE DEPT. OF EDUCATION. PROFESSIONAL PRACTICES COUNCIL **1869**

FLORIDA STATE EMPLOYMENT SERVICE See ANNUAL PLANNING INFORMATION REPORT ... PENSACOLA SMSA AND OKALOOSA COUNTY **1529**

FLORIDA STATE FARMERS' MARKETS See FLORIDA STATE FARMERS' MARKETS ... ANNUAL SUMMARY **87**

FLORIDA STATE FARMERS' MARKETS ... ANNUAL SUMMARY (US) [11074084] **87**

FLORIDA STATE HORTICULTURAL SOCIETY. MEETING See PROCEEDINGS OF THE ANNUAL MEETING OF THE FLORIDA STATE HORTICULTURAL SOCIETY **2429**

FLORIDA STATE MANPOWER COUNCIL See FLORIDA STATE MANPOWER PLAN **1675**

FLORIDA STATE MANPOWER PLAN (US/0093-7126) [01792682] **1675**

FLORIDA. STATE MANPOWER PLANNING COUNCIL See STATE OF FLORIDA COMPREHENSIVE MANPOWER PLAN **1712**

FLORIDA. STATE PERSONNEL BOARD See REPORT - FLORIDA. STATE PERSONNEL BOARD **4705**

FLORIDA STATE PLAN FOR THE EDUCATION OF EXCEPTIONAL STUDENTS (US/0099-2135) [02242908] 4388, **1879**

FLORIDA STATE PLAN FOR VOCATIONAL EDUCATION UNDER TITLE II OF THE VOCATIONAL EDUCATION AMENDMENTS OF 1976 (P.L. 94-482). PART II, ANNUAL PROGRAM PLAN (US) [04410878] **1913**

FLORIDA. STATE ROAD DEPARTMENT. DIVISION OF TRAFFIC AND PLANNING See TABULATION SHOWING ANNUAL AVERAGE DAILY TRAFFIC VOLUME AT RECORDER LOCATIONS AND PERCENT OF CHANGE IN VOLUME OVER PREVIOUS YEARS **5445**

FLORIDA STATE UNIVERSITY. CENTER FOR YUGOSLAV-AMERICAN STUDIES, RESEARCH, AND EXCHANGES See PROCEEDINGS AND REPORTS - FLORIDA STATE UNIVERSITY, CENTER FOR YUGOSLAV-AMERICAN STUDIES, RESEARCH AND EXCHANGES **2703**

FLORIDA STATE UNIVERSITY. COLLEGE OF LAW See FLORIDA STATE UNIVERSITY LAW REVIEW **2971**

FLORIDA STATE UNIVERSITY LAW REVIEW (US/0096-3070) [01774925] **2971**

FLORIDA STATE UNIVERSITY NOTES IN ANTHROPOLOGY (US) [06611372] **236**

FLORIDA STATE UNIVERSITY RESEARCH IN REVIEW (US/1043-4275) [18089888] **1824**

FLORIDA. STATE UNIVERSITY, TALLAHASSEE. OCEANOGRAPHIC INSTITUTE See REPORT - FLORIDA. STATE UNIVERSITY, TALLAHASSEE. OCEANOGRAPHIC INSTITUTE **1456**

FLORIDA. STATE UNIVERSITY TALLAHASSEE. OCEANOGRAPHIC INSTITUTE See PAPERS - FLORIDA STATE UNIVERSITY, TALLAHASSEE. OCEANOGRAPHIC INSTITUTE **1455**

FLORIDA. STATE UNIVERSITY, TALLAHASSEE. OFFICE OF INSTITUTIONAL RESEARCH AND SERVICE See ANALYSIS OF FACTORS RELATED TO THE OPERATION OF THE COLLEGES AND THE SCHOOLS AND THE INSTRUCTIONAL DEPARTMENTS OF THE FLORIDA STATE UNIVERSITY, AN **1808**

FLORIDA — Alphabetical Title Index

FLORIDA. STATE UNIVERSITY, TALLAHASSEE. SCHOOL OF EDUCATION See TEACHING OF ENGLISH **3327**

FLORIDA. STATE UNIVERSITY, TALLAHASSEE. SEDIMENTOLOGY RESEARCH LABORATORY See SEDIMENTOLOGY RESEARCH LABORATORY CONTRIBUTION **1396**

FLORIDA STATISTICAL ABSTRACT (US/0071-6022) [01333015] **5327**

FLORIDA STATUTES (US) [01569414] **2971**

FLORIDA STATUTES ANNOTATED (US) [01569415] **2971**

FLORIDA SUMMARY OF ACCIDENT DATA (US/0092-007X) [01788296] 4776, **5440**

FLORIDA SUNLINK NEWS : SCHOOL LIBRARY MEDIA NETWORK / UNIVERSITY OF CENTRAL FLORIDA, COLLEGE OF EDUCATION (US/1059-034X) [24462505] **3211**

FLORIDA. SUPREME COURT See FLORIDA RULES OF COURT. STATE **3140**

●FLORIDA TAX REVIEW (US/1066-3487) [26822112] **4727**

FLORIDA TAX REVIEW (US) 744, **2971**

FLORIDA TEACHING PROFESSION See FTP-NEA ADVOCATE **1747**

FLORIDA TECHNOLOGY IN EDUCATION QUARTERLY : A PUBLICATION OF FLORIDA A&M UNIVERSITY IN CONJUNCTION WITH THE STATE OF FLORIDA, DEPARTMENT OF EDUCATION (US) [23677410] 1747, **1223**

FLORIDA THOROUGHBRED TIMES (US/1049-9032) [21347645] **2799**

FLORIDA TIMES-UNION (JACKSONVILLE, FLA. : 1910) (US/0740-2325) [08334948] **5649**

FLORIDA TODAY (US/1051-8304) [14366320] **5649**

FLORIDA TOUR BOOK (US/0516-9674) [01793898] **5470**

FLORIDA TOURISM HOTLINE (US/0743-0744) [10560289] **5470**

FLORIDA TOURISM INDUSTRY REPORT *SUSPENDED.* (US/0889-0099) [13787186] **5470**

FLORIDA TRAFFIC CRASH FACTS See TRAFFIC CRASH DATA / FLORIDA DEPARTMENT OF HIGHWAY SAFETY AND MOTOR VEHICLES **5446**

FLORIDA TREND (US/0015-4326) [01327598] **1561**

FLORIDA TRUCK NEWS (US/0015-4334) [01379916] **5382**

FLORIDA TURF GROWER (US/0430-7887) [01383411] **87**

FLORIDA UNDERWRITER (US/0743-3441) [10553750] **2881**

FLORIDA UNITED METHODIST (US) [01383658] **5060**

FLORIDA. UNIVERSITY. COOPERATIVE EXTENSION SERVICE See ANNUAL REPORT - FLORIDA COOPERATIVE EXTENSION SERVICE **60**

FLORIDA. UNIVERSITY. DEPT. OF AGRONOMY See AGRONOMY RESEARCH REPORT AG **56**

FLORIDA. UNIVERSITY, GAINESVILLE. AGRICULTURAL EXTENSION SERVICE See ECONOMICS SERIES- FLORIDA. UNIVERSITY, GAINESVILLE. AGRICULTURAL EXTENSION SERVICE **81**

FLORIDA. UNIVERSITY, GAINESVILLE. AGRICULTURAL EXTENSION SERVICE See REPORT TO FARMERS ... ANNUAL SWINE FIELD DAY **5596**

FLORIDA. UNIVERSITY, GAINESVILLE. BUREAU OF ECONOMIC AND BUSINESS RESEARCH See ECONOMIC LEAFLETS. - FLORIDA. UNIVERSITY, GAINESVILLE. BUREAU OF ECONOMIC AND BUSINESS RESEARCH **1557**

FLORIDA. UNIVERSITY, GAINESVILLE. BUREAU OF EDUCATIONAL RESEARCH See BULLETIN - FLORIDA. UNIVERSITY, GAINESVILLE. BUREAU OF EDUCATIONAL RESEARCH **1729**

FLORIDA. UNIVERSITY, GAINESVILLE. CANCER RESEARCH LABORATORY See REPORT - FLORIDA. UNIVERSITY, GAINESVILLE. CANCER RESEARCH LABORATORY **3823**

FLORIDA. UNIVERSITY, GAINESVILLE. COLLEGE OF ARTS AND SCIENCES See PUBLICATION INDEX - COLLEGE OF ARTS & SCIENCES, UNIVERSITY OF FLORIDA **1843**

FLORIDA. UNIVERSITY, GAINESVILLE. COLLEGE OF MEDICINE. DEPARTMENT OF PHYSIOLOGY See COLLECTED PAPERS - FLORIDA. UNIVERSITY, GAINESVILLE. COLLEGE OF MEDICINE. DEPARTMENT OF PHYSIOLOGY **579**

FLORIDA. UNIVERSITY, GAINESVILLE. DEPT. OF CHEMICAL ENGINEERING See PAPERS PRESENTED AT THE SHORT COURSE IN PAINT TECHNOLOGY **2015**

FLORIDA. UNIVERSITY, GAINESVILLE. ENGINEERING AND INDUSTRIAL EXPERIMENT STATION See POWER REACTOR CONFERENCE PROCEEDINGS **2158**

FLORIDA. UNIVERSITY, GAINESVILLE. GRADUATE SCHOOL See ADMISSIONS DECISIONS STUDY - FLORIDA. UNIVERSITY, GAINESVILLE. GRADUATE SCHOOL **1792**

FLORIDA. UNIVERSITY, GAINESVILLE. PANHELLENIC ASSOCIATION See PANHELLENICALLY SPEAKING ... THE RUSHEE'S HANDBOOK **5235**

FLORIDA. UNIVERSITY, GAINESVILLE. STATE MUSEUM See CONTRIBUTIONS. ANTHROPOLOGY AND HISTORY **234**

FLORIDA VEGETABLES. CABBAGE REPORT (US) [09319448] **2335**

FLORIDA VENTURE CAPITAL DIRECTORY (US) [11012745] **1491**

FLORIDA VIEW. CAREERS (US) [26175798] 1913, **4204**

FLORIDA VISITOR STUDY (US) [07685690] **836**

FLORIDA VITAL STATISTICS. HRS DISTRICT SUPPLEMENT (US) [09567636] **4776**

FLORIDA VOCATIONAL JOURNAL *CEASED.* (US/0145-9376) [02807973] **1913**

FLORIDA VOTER, THE (US/0426-6072) [01350506] **4474**

FLORIDA WATER RESOURCES JOURNAL (US/0896-1794) [16942871] **5533**

FLORIDA WATERMELON REPORT (US/0744-5997) [08423440] **172**

FLORIDA WEATHER AND CROP NEWS (US) [01442734] **172**

FLORIDA WILDLIFE (US/0015-4369) [01332620] 4872, **2194**

FLORIDA WORKERS COMPENSATION INSTITUTE REPORTER (US) 1675, **2881**

FLORIDA ZIP+4 STATE DIRECTORY (US) [11636860] **1145**

FLORIDAGRICULTURE (GAINESVILLE, FLA.) (US/0015-3869) [07473435] **87**

FLORIDA'S FISCAL ANALYSIS (US) [24810460] **4727**

FLORIDA'S FISCAL ANALYSIS. EXECUTIVE SUMMARY (US) [24811926] **4727**

FLORIDA'S WOOD-USING INDUSTRY *CEASED.* (US) [05274215] **2400**

FLORIDA'S WOOD USING INDUSTRY, A DIRECTORY (US) [04075785] **2400**

FLORIJN, DE See BEELDENAAR, DE **2780**

FLORILEGIUM (CN/0709-5201) [05528289] 4347, **2616**

FLORISSANT VALLEY QUARTERLY (US/0887-5235) [10377933] **2733**

FLORISSANT VALLEY REPORTER, THE (US) [20615168] **5703**

FLORIST (GUNZBURG, GERMANY) (GW/0015-4393) [11127847] **2435**

FLORIST (SOUTHFIELD, MICH.) (US/0015-4385) [01714065] **2435**

FLORIST TRADE MAGAZINE (UK/0015-4415) [10834476] **2435**

FLORISTS' REVIEW (US/0015-4423) [05577640] **2435**

FLORTECNICA (IT) [08276459] **2414**

FLOTATION SLEEP INDUSTRY (US/0164-5749) [04558476] **2905**

FLOTATION SLEEP INDUSTRY. BUYERS GUIDE (US/0734-1571) [08659874] **2905**

FLOUR MILLING AND BAKING RESEARCH ASSOCIATION See ABSTRACTS - FLOUR MILLING AND BAKING RESEARCH ASSOCIATION **2325**

FLOUR MILLING PRODUCTS (US) [02564281] **201**

FLOW, ITS MEASUREMENT AND CONTROL IN SCIENCE AND INDUSTRY (US/0098-5384) [02239684] **2089**

FLOW MEASUREMENT AND INSTRUMENTATION (UK/0955-5986) [21109462] **2089**

FLOW OF FUNDS ACCOUNTS. FINANCIAL ASSETS AND LIABILITIES YEAR-END See FLOW OF FUNDS ACCOUNTS, FLOWS AND OUTSTANDINGS **4727**

●FLOW OF FUNDS ACCOUNTS, FLOWS AND OUTSTANDINGS (US) [27052276] **4727**

FLOW OF FUNDS ACCOUNTS. SEASONALLY ADJUSTED FLOWS See FLOW OF FUNDS ACCOUNTS, FLOWS AND OUTSTANDINGS **4727**

FLOW OF FUNDS SUMMARY STATISTICS / BOARD OF GOVERNORS OF THE FEDERAL RESERVE SYSTEM (US) [10177607] 4727, **4698**

FLOW OF RESOURCES FROM NEW ZEALAND TO DEVELOPING COUNTRIES, THE (NZ/0110-0424) [02244032] **2909**

FLOW SYSTEMS NEWSLETTERS (US/0278-5145) [07788102] **536**

FLOWER AND GARDEN (KANSAS CITY, MO. : 1982) (US/0891-9534) [09660184] **2414**

FLOWER AND NURSERY REPORT FOR COMMERCIAL GROWERS (US/0886-5833) [03018476] **2414**

FLOWER ARRANGER (UK/0046-421X) **2435**

FLOWER ESSENCE JOURNAL, THE (US/0732-8389) [08445020] **4776**

FLOWER LINK (AT/0815-4112) [08154112] **2448**

FLOWER NEWS : THE FLORAL INDUSTRY'S NATIONAL WEEKLY (US/0015-4490) [02250866] **2414**

FLOWER OF THE FOREST BLACK GENEALOGICAL JOURNAL (US/0738-159X) [09511302] **2448**

FLOWER SHOP *CEASED.* (CN/0836-3749) [18033049] **2435**

FLOWER TRADES JOURNAL (UK) [06061569] **2435**

FLOWER VETERINARY LIBRARY See NEWSLETTER / CORNELL UNIVERSITY LIBRARIES, FLOWER VETERINARY LIBRARY **3235**

FLOWERING PLANT INDEX (US/1061-9011) [23122667] **2415**

FLOWERING PLANTS OF AFRICA, THE (SA/0015-4504) [06678860] **2415**

FLOWERS& (US/0199-4751) [05907158] **2435**

FLOYD COUNTY HESPERIAN, THE (US) [14106399] **5750**

FLOYD COUNTY TIMES (US) [15377623] **5680**

FLRA REPORT OF CASE DECISIONS AND FSIP RELEASES (US/0732-0345) [07320345] **4649**

FLUCTUACIONES MONETARIAS; METODO GENERAL DE ACTUALIZACION (AG) [01794771] **1561**

FLUE (US/0731-2636) [08150495] **320**

FLUE CURED TOBACCO FARMER, THE (US/0015-4512) [04170575] **5373**

FLUG REVUE (GW/0015-4547) [08969782] **21**

FLUGHAFEN ZURICH See JAHRESBERICHT / FLUGHAFEN ZURICH **25**

FLUGTECHNISCHE REIHE (SZ/0428-7703) [01383603] **21**

FLUID (GW/0015-461X) [I0015461X] 2114, **2089**

FLUID ABSTRACTS. CIVIL ENGINEERING (UK/0962-7170) [24188209] 1975, **2004**

FLUID ABSTRACTS. PROCESS ENGINEERING (UK/0962-7162) [24307874] 2089, **2004**

FLUID AIP (IT) **5105**

FLUID APPARECCHIATURE IDRAULICHE E PNEUMATICHE (IT/0374-3225) [I03743225] **2089**

FLUID DYNAMICS (US/0015-4628) [01569487] **2023**

FLUID DYNAMICS RESEARCH (NE/0169-5983) [13680443] **5105**

FLUID INCLUSION RESEARCH (US) [01569488] **1376**

FLUID INCLUSION RESEARCH (US/0375-6327) [07760497] **1439**

FLUID MECHANICS AND ITS APPLICATIONS (NE/0926-5112) [I09265112] **2089**

FLUID MECHANICS OF ASTROPHYSICS AND GEOPHYSICS, THE (US/0260-4353) [07219320] **1405**

FLUID MECHANICS PAPERS (US/0069-6099) [03227387] **2089**

●FLUID MECHANICS RESEARCH (US/1064-2277) [26276310] **2114**

FLUID MECHANICS : SOVIET RESEARCH (US/0096-0764) [01437883] **2089**

FLUID / PARTICLE SEPARATION JOURNAL (US/1043-2558) [19239467] **1024**

FLUID PHASE EQUILIBRIA (NE/0378-3812) [03417536] **1052**

FLUID POWER ABSTRACTS (UK/0015-4644) [01795482] **2089**

FLUID POWER AND CONTROL (US) [10501799] **1975**

FLUID POWER HANDBOOK & DIRECTORY (US/0428-7738) [07386499] **2089**

FLUID POWER INDUSTRY OUTLOOK SURVEY (US/0193-5518) [05203682] **3479**

FOCUS

Alphabetical Title Index

FLUID POWER INTERNATIONAL (UK/0015-4652) [01383645] **2089**

FLUID POWER SERVICE CENTER (US/1062-6018) [25680890] **2089**

FLUID SEALING ABSTRACTS (UK/0015-4660) [01795407] **2089**

FLUIDEX [ONLINE DATABASE] (UK) 2090, **2004**

FLUIDOS (SP/0211-1136) [I02111136] **2090**

FLUORESCENT LAMP BALLASTS (US/0145-5184) [02545293] **2055**

FLUORESCENT LAMP BALLASTS (US) **2055**

FLUORESCENT LAMP BALLASTS (US) [07042100] **1607**

FLUORIDATED DRINKING WATER, PROFICIENCY TESTING (US) [08623656] **5533**

FLUORIDE (US/0015-4725) [03546935] **487**

FLUSHING OBSERVER, THE (US/0747-1718) [10620892] **5692**

FLUSHING TIMES (US) [11414693] **5716**

FLUSSIGES OBST (GW/0015-4539) [04024508] 2367, **2335**

FLUTE, LA (CN/0703-4725) [06638617] **3164**

FLUTE LIBRARY, THE (NE) [12194811] **4118**

FLUTE TALK (US/0744-6918) [08292905] **4118**

FLUTE WORKER, THE (US/0737-8459) [09449859] **4118**

FLUTIST QUARTERLY, THE (US/8756-8667) [10873979] 385, **4118**

FLUVANNA COUNTY HISTORICAL SOCIETY BULLETIN (US) **2733**

●FLY! (BALDWIN, N.Y.) (US/1065-4631) [26613523] **4118**

FLY FISHERMAN (US/0015-4741) [01785913] **2304**

FLY FISHING DIRECTORY, THE (US/1051-046X) [21798491] **4872**

FLY ROD & REEL (US/1045-0149) [19976806] **2304**

FLY-TACKLE DEALER (US) **2304**

FLYER (EDMONTON, ALTA.) (CN/0833-3424) [15535552] **21**

FLYER (EVANSTON, ILL.) (US) [08372984] 4959, **5557**

FLYFAIRE VACATIONS (US/0895-6154) [16704343] **5470**

FLYFISHER, THE (US/0147-8834) [02642732] **2304**

FLYFISHING (US/0744-7191) [08507865] **2304**

FLYFISHING THE WEST See FLYFISHING **2304**

FLYING BUYERS' GUIDE (US/0738-3800) [08339724] **21**

FLYING DISC MAGAZINE (US/0275-4703) [07148750] **21**

FLYING (LOS ANGELES, CALIF.) (US/0015-4806) [01569490] **21**

FLYING MODELS (US/0015-4849) [04077576] 5382, **2773**

FLYING NEEDLE, THE (US/0270-2959) [03821169] **5184**

FLYING REVIEW (US/0274-5798) [06413430] **21**

FLYING SAFETY (1981) (US/0279-9308) [07149726] **21**

FLYING SAUCER REVIEW (UK/0015-4881) [02254407] **21**

FLYING SAUCERS (US/0015-489X) [01383668] **21**

FLYPAPER (CALGARY) (CN/0317-2481) [02248013] **4895**

FLYPAST (UK/0262-6950) [09779461] **21**

FM ATLAS / BY BRUCE F. ELVING (US) [23915840] **1132**

FM RADIO LOG (US/1061-8325) [25473980] **1111**

FM STATION ADDRESS BOOK (US/0899-5303) [18131392] **1132**

●FM TECHNOLOGY REPORT (US/1067-6244) [27345097] **1185**

FMG NEWSLETTER / CIVIC RESEARCH CENTER (US/0885-7032) [12719307] **3576**

FMG, THE (US/0744-589X) [08412312] **3576**

FMI ISSUES BULLETIN (US/0275-8059) [07228396] 2335, **924**

FMR (ED. ITALIANA) (IT/0393-0033) [08956598] **350**

FMR (ENGLISH ED.) (US/0747-6388) [10764669] **350**

FNP NEWSLETTER. FOOD INDUSTRY REPORT (US/0888-1332) [10489349] **2335**

FNP NEWSLETTER : FOOD, NUTRITION AND HEALTH (US/0160-8053) [03299481] 2335, **4191**

FNP NEWSLETTER, FOOD PACKAGING AND LABELING (US/0194-2980) [03281052] 2335, **4219**

FNP NEWSLETTER : PRICE TRENDS OF FOOD INGREDIENTS *CEASED.* (US/0194-2972) [03281076] **2335**

FNV JAARVERSLAG (NE) [05233190] **1675**

FNV : LE MAGAZINE DE LA FONDATION NOR-VAL (CN/1183-6326) [24690432] **5285**

FOAL REGISTRATIONS, ILLINOIS CONCEIVED & FOALED STANDARDBREDS (US/0884-1322) [12175807] **2799**

FOAL REGISTRATIONS OF ILLINOIS CONCEIVED AND FOALED, AND ILLINOIS FOALED THOROUGHBREDS (US/0884-0105) [10733747] **2799**

FOARD COUNTY NEWS AND CROWELL INDEX (US) [13695555] **5750**

●FOCAL POINT (CN/1189-5012) [26776203] **4071**

FOCAL POINT (ENGLEWOOD, COLO.) (US/0279-8840) [07332016] **5060**

FOCAL POINTS (US/0891-8260) [12492849] **3874**

FOCUS (CE) [05123088] **5200**

FOCUS (SI) [04868185] **1824**

FOCUS (US) [22163112] **5695**

FOCUS (US) [16577717] **4587**

FOCUS (US) [22163105] **5695**

FOCUS (US) [01768526] **2597**

FOCUS AFRICA (CN/1193-7351) [27203154] **2639**

FOCUS (AMERSFOORT) (NE/0015-4997) [02993825] **5105**

FOCUS & OPINION : INTERNAL MEDICINE (US) **3796**

●FOCUS & OPINION, INTERNAL MEDICINE (US/1072-0863) [28856297] **3796**

FOCUS AND OPINION: PEDIATRICS (US) [30800200] **3903**

FOCUS (AUSTIN, TEX. 1985) (US/0883-8194) [12227962] **1247**

FOCUS (AUSTIN, TEX. 1989) (US/1041-2549) [18695280] **1185**

FOCUS AUSTRALIA (AT/0815-4902) [I08154902] **2669**

FOCUS (BANGKOK, THAILAND) (TH) [11000157] **2526**

FOCUS : BIOLOGY (US/0098-8251) [02242505] **455**

FOCUS : BLACK AMERICAN BIBLIOGRAPHY SERIES. SUPPLEMENT (US/0090-9513) [02255326] **2276**

FOCUS (BOSTON, MASS.) (US) [06336503] **3576**

FOCUS (BURBANK, CALIF.) (US/1054-4208) [22881906] **4241**

FOCUS - CANADIAN STANDARDS ASSOCIATION (CN/0831-4888) [15271320] **4030**

FOCUS : CHICAGO (US/0362-0905) [02190964] **4071**

FOCUS (CHICAGO. 1977) (US/0148-026X) [03258820] **2971**

FOCUS (CHICAGO, ILL. : 1982) See DA UPDATE **1319**

FOCUS, FIBRE OPTIC COMMUNICATION & USER SYSTEMS (UK/0959-0188) [I09590188] **1155**

FOCUS HAWAII See COMTEC CABLE TELEVISION VIEWERS GUIDE **1130**

FOCUS, ISRAEL (US/1056-8557) [23882243] **2651**

FOCUS. JAPAN (JA/0388-0311) [01798314] 1635, **676**

FOCUS JAPAN. NOW IN JAPAN (JA/0388-032X) [04715841] 1607, **836**

FOCUS - JOINT CENTER FOR POLITICAL STUDIES (US/0740-0195) [01786901] 5245, **2261**

FOCUS, LIBRARY SERVICE TO OLDER ADULTS, PEOPLE WITH DISABILITIES (US/0740-4956) [09965722] 5179, 4388, **3211**

FOCUS : MACROECONOMICS (US/0362-3297) [03154975] **1592**

FOCUS (MADISON, WIS.) (US/0195-5705) [04396567] 5285, **1491**

FOCUS MAGAZINE (US) [10672526] **4071**

FOCUS (MATHEMATICAL ASSOCIATION OF AMERICA) (US/0731-2040) [08094602] **3505**

FOCUS (MENLO PARK, CALIF.) (US/0733-5555) [08616145] **1824**

FOCUS MHL See FOCUS MUL : ZEITSCHRIFT FUER WISSENSCHAFT, FORSCHUNG UND LEHRE AN DER MEDIZINISCHEN UNIVERSITAT ZU LUBECK **3576**

FOCUS MUL : ZEITSCHRIFT FUER WISSENSCHAFT, FORSCHUNG UND LEHRE AN DER MEDIZINISCHEN UNIVERSITAT ZU LUBECK (GW/0940-9998) [30108477] **3576**

FOCUS (NEW BRUNSWICK TEACHERS' ASSOCIATION. SOCIAL STUDIES COUNCIL) (CN/0710-7692) [08720487] **5200**

FOCUS (NEW YORK, N.Y. 1950) (US/0015-5004) [01334365] 1491, **2561**

FOCUS ON AFRICA : BBC MAGAZINE (UK/0959-9576) [22498362] **2499**

FOCUS ON AFRICAN INDUSTRY (ET) [18095388] **899**

FOCUS ON AGING (CN/0822-3637) [11240712] **5200**

FOCUS ON ASIAN STUDIES *CEASED.* (US/0046-4295) [01036290] **2651**

FOCUS ON AUTISTIC BEHAVIOR (US/0887-1566) [13113682] **3577**

FOCUS ON BEHAVIORAL HEALTH (US) [05695669] **4587**

FOCUS ON CANADIAN EMPLOYMENT AND EQUALITY RIGHTS (CN/0831-4535) [14709174] **1675**

●FOCUS ON CATALYSTS (UK/1351-4180) **975**

FOCUS ON CHEMICALS (UK) **2012**

FOCUS ON CHRISTIAN-MUSLIM RELATIONS *CEASED.* (UK/0950-9720) [18042884] **4959**

FOCUS ON COMMERICAL AVIATION SAFETY (UK) **21**

FOCUS ON CRITICAL CARE *CEASED.* (US/0736-3605) [09103998] **3856**

FOCUS ON CULTURE (CN/0843-7548) [21095111] **4553**

FOCUS ON DENTAL COMPUTERS *CEASED.* (US/0748-1810) [10905478] **1323**

●FOCUS ON DIAGNOSTICS (UK/0969-6229) **975**

FOCUS ON EARLY CHILDHOOD : FOR THE MEMBERS OF THE DIVISION FOR EARLY CHILDHOOD / ACEI (US) [20744907] 1804, **1895**

FOCUS ON EDUCATION (TORONTO) (CN/1183-4757) [25423815] **4369**

●FOCUS ON ELECTRONICS CHEMICALS (UK/0969-6202) 2055, **975**

FOCUS ON EQUALITY (CN/0838-6595) [18241755] **4508**

FOCUS ON EXCEPTIONAL CHILDREN (US/0015-511X) [00809741] **1879**

FOCUS ON FARMING (US/0745-8355) [06456482] **88**

FOCUS ON FOOD SERVICE (CN/0229-1770) [07966356] **2335**

FOCUS ON FOUR (US) [10318788] **4176**

●FOCUS ON GENDER (0968-2864) [I09682864] **5557**

FOCUS ON GERIATRIC CARE & REHABILITATION (US/0892-7103) [15239812] **3751**

FOCUS ON GLOBAL CHANGE *CEASED.* (US/1062-3086) [22297427] **2172**

FOCUS ON HEALTH (NEW YORK, N.Y.) (US/0271-3152) [06600180] **4776**

FOCUS ON HONDURAS (US) [25420028] **4508**

FOCUS ON INDIANA LIBRARIES (US/0015-5152) [01569502] **3211**

FOCUS ON INDONESIA *CEASED.* (US/0430-8301) [02116026] **2651**

FOCUS ON INFANCY : FOR THE MEMBERS OF THE DIVISION FOR INFANCY / ACEI (US) [20745025] 1804, **1895**

●FOCUS ON INTERMEDIATES AND CONTRACT CHEMICALS (UK/1352-3538) **975**

FOCUS ON INTERNATIONAL & COMPARATIVE LIBRARIANSHIP (UK/0305-8468) [05792174] **3211**

FOCUS ON ISSUES / UNITED STATES COUNCIL FOR INTERNATIONAL BUSINESS (US) [09690798] **676**

FOCUS ON JAMAICA (UK/0015-5160) [01357982] **5470**

FOCUS ON KEY ECONOMIC ISSUES (SA) [04688145] **1561**

FOCUS ON LATER CHILDHOOD/EARLY ADOLESCENCE : FOR MEMBERS OF THE DIVISION FOR LATER CHILDHOOD/EARLY ADOLESCENCE / ACEI (US) [20745161] **1895**

FOCUS ON LAW STUDIES : TEACHING ABOUT LAW IN THE LIBERAL ARTS (US) [12925184] 320, **2971**

FOCUS ON LEARNING PROBLEMS IN MATHEMATICS (US/0272-8893) [06970505] 3505, **1879**

FOCUS ON MALAYSIA (MY) [11610215] **836**

FOCUS ON MISSIONS; OCCASIONAL NEWS SUPPLEMENT FOR MISSIONARIES (US) [01776995] **4959**

FOCUS
Alphabetical Title Index

FOCUS ON NIGERIA (CN/0827-3022) [11847727] **2639**

FOCUS ON OHIO DENTISTRY (US/1042-2528) [18978207] **1323**

FOCUS ON PAKISTAN (PK/0046-4325) [01334463] **5470**

●FOCUS ON PAPER CHEMICALS (UK/1351-4199) **1024**

FOCUS ON PHYTOCHEMICAL PESTICIDES (US/0899-7837) [18216788] **511**

●FOCUS ON PIGMENTS (UK/0969-6210) **975**

FOCUS ON RENEWABLE NATURAL RESOURCES (US/0273-009X) [02709993] **2194**

FOCUS ON RESEARCH (SA) [07011999] **5105**

FOCUS ON RURAL HEALTH (US) **3577**

FOCUS ON SABAH (MY) [07302806] **899**

●FOCUS ON SECURITY (US/1071-9997) [28823715] **3211**

●FOCUS ON SOLVENTS (UK/1351-4202) **975**

FOCUS ON SPECIAL EDUCATION LEGAL PRACTICES (US/0747-959X) [07725918] **1879**, **2971**

FOCUS ON. SPORTS, SCIENCE AND MEDICINE (US/1069-7004) [28197392] **3954**, **4895**

●FOCUS ON SURFACTANTS (UK/1351-4210) **1024**

FOCUS ON SURGICAL EDUCATION (US/0742-9819) [10462787] **3965**

FOCUS ON THE BAKING INDUSTRY See BAKERS JOURNAL **2328**

FOCUS ON THE CENTER FOR RESEARCH LIBRARIES (US/0275-4924) [07142604] **3211**

FOCUS ON THE FAMILY (ARCADIA, CALIF. 1982) (US/0894-3346) [15998712] **4959**, **2280**

FOCUS ON THE FAMILY CLUBHOUSE (US/0895-1136) [16678218] **2280**, **1063**

FOCUS ON THE NEWS (US/0890-2682) [14203936] **5660**

FOCUS ON TIN (UK/0967-9618) [I09679618] **4002**

●FOCUS ON VETERINARY SCIENCE & MEDICINE (US/1067-8964) [27365864] **5510**

FOCUS ON YOUTH FOR CHRIST CALGARY (CN/0319-3837) [10595729] **4959**

FOCUS - ONTARIO VETERINARY MEDICAL ASSOCIATION (CN/1182-8781) [23598575] **5510**

FOCUS (RED DEER) (CN/0712-2691) [08808186] **2823**

FOCUS (ROCKVILLE) (US/0533-1242) [01450501] **455**

FOCUS (ROSSYLN, VA.) See NEW FOCUS **1767**

FOCUS (SAN FRANCISCO, CALIF.) (US/1047-0719) [15924051] **3713**, **3669**

FOCUS / SOCIETY FOR MANITOBANS WITH DISABILITIES (CN/1182-1353) [23598923] **4388**

●FOCUS SOUTH (CN/1188-3375) [25796424] **1635**

FOCUS SYSTEMS JOURNAL ENCYCLOPEDIA (US/1074-4037) [27865079] **1279**

FOCUS: TEACHING ENGLISH LANGUAGE ARTS (US/0163-5425) [04397303] **1895**, **3281**

FOCUS (WASHINGTON, D.C. 1990) (US/1056-3199) [23661516] **5557**, **1824**

FOCUS (WASHINGTON, D.C. 1991) (US/1062-7472) [25725938] **2172**

FOCUS WOMEN (CN/0713-8547) [09050400] **5557**

FOCUSES (BOONE, N.C.) (US/1040-3205) [18377342] **3388**, **2919**

FOCUSING FOLIO, THE (US/0890-3379) [14227711] **4347**

FODERBALANCER : RESSOURCER (LU) [03990993] **201**

FODOR'S ... ACAPULCO (US) [18841804] **5470**

●FODOR'S ACAPULCO, IXTAPA, ZIHUATANEJO (US/1070-8642) [26513979] **5470**

●FODOR'S ... AFFORDABLE FRANCE (US/1068-3593) [25471852] **5470**

FODOR'S ALASKA (US/0271-2776) [06575173] **5470**

FODOR'S AMSTERDAM (US/0883-6043) [11189968] **5470**

FODOR'S ARIZONA (US) [12813878] **5470**

FODOR'S ... AUSTRALIA (US) [22831007] **5470**

●FODOR'S ... AUSTRALIA & NEW ZEALAND (US) [26791244] **5470**

FODOR'S AUSTRALIA, NEW ZEALAND AND THE SOUTH PACIFIC (US/0191-2321) [03832723] **5470**

FODOR'S AUSTRIA (US/0071-6340) [01996649] **5470**

FODOR'S BAHAMAS (US) [12579605] **5470**

FODOR'S BAJA & THE PACIFIC COAST RESORTS (US/1050-737X) [20939232] **5470**

FODOR'S ... BARBADOS (US/1050-9771) [20569658] **5470**

FODOR'S BEIJING, GUANGZHOU, SHANGHAI (US) [19501212] **5470**

FODOR'S BELGIUM AND LUXEMBOURG (US) [02109105] **5470**

●FODOR'S ... BERLIN (US/1065-4593) [25488335] **5470**

FODOR'S BERMUDA (US/0192-3765) [04988389] **5471**

FODOR'S BOSTON (US/0882-0074) [10844924] **5471**

FODOR'S BRAZIL (US/0163-0628) [04270622] **5471**

●FODOR'S BUDAPEST (US/1065-4607) [25662075] **5471**

FODOR'S BUDGET EUROPE (US/0197-4998) [05872618] **5471**

FODOR'S CALIFORNIA (US/0192-9925) [05094074] **5471**

FODOR'S CANADA (US/0160-3906) [03548165] **5471**

FODOR'S ... CANADA'S ATLANTIC PROVINCES See FODOR'S NOVA SCOTIA, PRINCE EDWARD ISLAND, AND NEW BRUNSWICK **5472**

FODOR'S ... CANCUN, COZUMEL, YUCATAN PENINSULA (US/1051-6336) [20738025] **5471**

FODOR'S CAPE COD, MARTHA'S VINEYARD, NANTUCKET (US/1047-6768) [13441658] **5471**

FODOR'S CARIBBEAN (US) [12570462] **5471**

FODOR'S CARIBBEAN, BAHAMAS AND BERMUDA See FODOR'S BERMUDA **5471**

FODOR'S CENTRAL AMERICA (US/0270-8183) [06465612] **5471**

FODOR'S CHICAGO (US/0743-9326) [10584529] **5471**

FODOR'S CHINA (US/1070-6895) [22871093] **5471**

FODOR'S CIVIL WAR SITES (US/0195-7317) [05577861] **5471**

FODOR'S COLORADO (US/0276-9018) [07298764] **5471**

FODOR'S CRUISES AND PORTS OF CALL (US/1070-4477) [22632236] **5471**

FODOR'S DALLAS AND FORT WORTH (US) [10133478] **5471**

FODOR'S ... DISNEY WORLD & THE ORLANDO AREA (US/1070-6402) [18764040] **5471**

FODOR'S ... EASTERN EUROPE (US/0734-8010) [06228961] **5471**

FODOR'S EGYPT (US/0147-8176) [03231116] **5471**

FODOR'S EUROPE (US/0362-0204) [01299593] **5471**

FODOR'S ... EUROPE'S GREAT CITIES (US/1074-1216) [21283012] **5471**

FODOR'S FAR WEST (US/0192-3730) [04123214] **5471**

FODOR'S FLORIDA (US/0193-9556) [05255402] **5471**

FODOR'S FRANCE (US/0532-5692) [01988637] **5471**

FODOR'S FUN IN PUERTO RICO. / J.P. MACBEAN (US) [11912143] **5471**

FODOR'S FUN IN RIO DE JANEIRO (US) **5471**

FODOR'S ... GERMANY (US) [19372988] **5471**

FODOR'S GREAT BRITAIN (US/0071-6405) [01996715] **5471**

FODOR'S GREAT TRAVEL VALUES See FODOR'S ITALY **5472**

FODOR'S GREECE (US/0071-6413) [01988810] **5471**

FODOR'S GUIDE TO EUROPE See FODOR'S EUROPE **5471**

FODOR'S HAWAII (US/0071-6421) [02016764] **5471**

FODOR'S HEALTHY ESCAPES (US/1057-8048) [23472280] **2597**, **5471**

FODOR'S HOLLAND (US/0071-643X) [01988729] **5471**

FODOR'S ... HONG KONG (US/1070-6887) [19601465] **5471**

FODOR'S HUNGARY (US/0361-9761) [02002848] **5471**

FODOR'S I-75 MICHIGAN TO FLORIDA (US/1045-2745) [16141439] **5471**

FODOR'S INDIA, INCLUDING NEPAL (US) [17966657] **5472**

FODOR'S IRAN (US/0147-7919) [03231000] **5472**

FODOR'S IRELAND (UK/0071-6464) [01334847] **5472**

FODOR'S IRELAND (US/0090-0648) [01784736] **5472**

FODOR'S ISRAEL (US/0071-6588) [02016019] **5472**

FODOR'S ITALY (US/0361-977X) [02006499] **5472**

FODOR'S ... JAMAICA (US) [20374145] **5472**

FODOR'S JAPAN (US/0736-9956) [08978799] **5472**

FODOR'S JORDAN AND THE HOLY LAND *CEASED*. (US/0193-9114) [05070032] **5472**

FODOR'S KENYA & TANZANIA (US) [12061158] **5472**

FODOR'S KOREA (US) [09710219] **5472**

FODOR'S ... LAS VEGAS See FODOR'S ... LAS VEGAS, RENO, TAHOE **5472**

●FODOR'S ... LAS VEGAS, RENO, TAHOE (US/1070-6909) [25236621] **5472**

FODOR'S LISBON (US) [10746811] **5472**

FODOR'S LOIRE VALLEY (US) [15566328] **5472**

FODOR'S LONDON (US/0149-631X) [03506233] **5472**

FODOR'S LOS ANGELES (US) [19587013] **5472**

FODOR'S LOS ANGELES AND NEARBY ATTRACTIONS (US/0743-3336) [09151100] **5472**

FODOR'S MADRID (US/0884-0393) [09468926] **5472**

FODOR'S MAUI (US) [18607436] **5472**

FODOR'S MEXICO (US/0196-5999) [01639224] **5472**

FODOR'S MEXICO CITY AND ACAPULCO (US/1045-277X) [08841916] **5472**

FODOR'S ... MIAMI & THE KEYS (US/1070-6399) [22855049] **5472**

FODOR'S MID-ATLANTIC (US/0192-4540) [04998476] **5472**

FODOR'S ... MONTREAL & QUEBEC CITY (US) [21282981] **5472**

FODOR'S MOROCCO (US) [23931927] **5472**

●FODOR'S MOSCOW, ST. PETERBURG, KIEV (US) [29785158] **5472**

FODOR'S MUNICH (US) [10677802] **5472**

FODOR'S NEW ENGLAND (US/0192-3412) [04123166] **5472**

FODOR'S NEW MEXICO (US) [11911851] **5472**

FODOR'S NEW ORLEANS (US/0743-9385) [10414507] **5472**

FODOR'S NEW YORK CITY (US) [17247219] **5472**

FODOR'S NEW YORK STATE See FODOR'S VACATIONS IN NEW YORK STATE **5474**

FODOR'S NEW ZEALAND (US) [13434951] **5472**

●FODOR'S NOVA SCOTIA, PRINCE EDWARD ISLAND, AND NEW BRUNSWICK (US/1064-7643) [26391239] **5472**

FODOR'S PACIFIC NORTH COAST (US/1072-0391) [10881214] **5472**

FODOR'S PARIS (US/0149-1288) [03259446] **5472**

FODOR'S PEOPLE'S REPUBLIC OF CHINA See FODOR'S CHINA **5471**

FODOR'S PHILADELPHIA (US) [12147869] **5472**

FODOR'S ... POCKET GUIDE TO LONDON (US) [18841627] **5472**

FODOR'S ... POCKET GUIDE TO NEW YORK CITY (US/1056-7712) [19247366] **5472**

FODOR'S ... POCKET GUIDE TO PARIS (US) [19247093] **5473**

FODOR'S ... POCKET GUIDE TO SAN FRANCISCO (US/1046-8978) [19100507] **5473**

FODOR'S ... POCKET GUIDE TO THE BAHAMAS (US/1041-9373) [18658268] **5473**

FODOR'S PORTUGAL (US/0071-6510) [02650074] **5473**

FODOR'S ROME (US/0276-2560) [06775252] **5473**

●FODOR'S RUSSIA & THE BALTIC COUNTRIES (US) [27193395] **5473**

FODOR'S RUSSIA, THE REPUBLICS AND THE BALTICS (US/1062-6816) [25053878] **5473**

FODOR'S ... SAINT MARTIN, SINT MAARTEN (US) [18842234] **5473**

FODOR'S SAN DIEGO (US/1053-5950) [13441668] **5473**

FODOR'S ... SAN FRANCISCO (US) [19595856] **5473**

FODOR'S SCANDINAVIA (US/0071-6529) [01569508] **5473**

FODOR'S SCANDINAVIAN CITIES (US) **5473**

FODOR'S SCOTLAND (US/0743-0973) [09617607] **5473**

FODOR'S SELECTED RESORTS AND HOTELS OF THE U.S (US) [17513303] **5473, 2805**

FODOR'S SHOPPING IN EUROPE (US/1047-5680) [19587665] **5473**

FODOR'S SINGAPORE (US) [14039541] **5473**

FODOR'S SKIING IN NORTH AMERICA (US/1050-5180) [20543191] **5473**

FODOR'S SOUTH (US/0147-8680) [04819724] **5473**

FODOR'S SOUTH AMERICA (US/0362-0220) [02014892] **5473**

FODOR'S SOUTH-EAST ASIA (US/0160-8991) [02349357] **5473**

FODOR'S SOUTH PACIFIC (US) [13435061] **5473**

FODOR'S SOVIET UNION *See* FODOR'S ... RUSSIA, THE REPUBLICS AND THE BALTICS **5473**

FODOR'S SPAIN (US/0361-9648) [02000486] **5473**

FODOR'S SUNBELT LEISURE GUIDE (US/0196-1055) [05635529] **5473**

FODOR'S SWEDEN (US) [13461426] **5473**

FODOR'S SWITZERLAND (US/0071-6553) [02697337] **5473**

FODOR'S SYDNEY (US) [12254647] **5473**

FODOR'S TEXAS (US/0743-3328) [09617573] **5473**

FODOR'S THE CAROLINAS AND THE GEORGIA COAST (US) [16903648] **5473**

FODOR'S THE HIMALAYAN COUNTRIES (US/1073-6573) [21543019] **5473**

●FODOR'S THE NETHERLANDS, BELGIUM, LUXEMBOURG (US/1070-4590) [27670805] **5473**

FODOR'S THE ROCKIES (US) [17163392] **5473**

FODOR'S ... THE U.S. & BRITISH VIRGIN ISLANDS (US/1070-6380) [27021044] **5473**

FODOR'S THE UPPER GREAT LAKES REGION (US/1070-4485) [23378824] **5473**

FODOR'S TOKYO (US) [11936919] **5473**

FODOR'S ... TORONTO (US/1044-6133) [19294762] **5473**

FODOR'S TUNISIA (US/0090-2349) [01784811] **5474**

FODOR'S TURKEY (US/0071-6618) [01335206] **5474**

FODOR'S ... USA (US) [20437305] **5474**

FODOR'S VACATIONS IN NEW YORK STATE (US) [23157787] **5474**

FODOR'S VIENNA (US) [11808950] **5474**

FODOR'S ... VIRGIN ISLANDS (US/1048-1060) [20832710] **5474**

FODOR'S VIRGINIA & MARYLAND (US/1075-0711) [23365589] **5474**

FODOR'S WAIKIKI (US/1044-923X) [18763774] **5474**

FODOR'S WASHINGTON, D.C (US/0743-9741) [10584450] **5474**

FODOR'S WILLIAMSBURG, JAMESTOWN & YORKTOWN (US/1045-2737) [15704348] **5474**

FODOR'S YUGOSLAVIA (US/0071-657X) [02043822] **5474**

FOELDRAJZI ERTESITO (HU/0015-5403) [01569509] **2561**

FOERDERN UND HEBEN (GW/0373-6482) [02447002] **2114**

FOGLI ANNUNZI LEGALI (IT) **4649**

FOGLI DI COLLEGAMENTO DELLA L O C (IT) **4521**

FOGLIO ANNUNCI LEGALI. MILANO (IT) **1491**

FOGLIO ANNUNCI LEGALI ROMA (IT) **2971**

FOGLIO ANNUNZI LEGALI : IMPERIA (IT) **2971**

FOGLIO ANNUNZI LEGALI PROVINCIA DI BERGAMO (IT) **2971**

FOGLIO ANNUNZI LEGALI : SAVONA (IT) **2971**

FOGLIO TORINO, IL (IT/0393-7380) [I03937380] **4365**

FOGORVOSI SZEMLE (HU/0015-5314) [02261162] **3577**

FOGRA-LITERATURDIENST (GW/0015-5322) [I00155322] **3388**

FOGTDALS MAGASIN OM DANMARK (DK) [07855485] **2688**

FOHN (AU) [07694950] **2280**

FOI AUJOURD HUI (FR/0152-139X) **5029**

FOI ET LA VIE, LA (FR/0015-5357) [01774931] **4959**

FOI ET LE TEMPS (BE/0430-8522) [05657202] **4959**

FOIA UPDATE (US/1056-9413) [05900477] **2919**

FOKUROA (JA) [04070068] **236**

FOKUS PA FAMILIEN (NO/0332-5415) [I03325415] **2280**

FOLCLORICA (GOIANIA) (GW/0302-752X) [01793372] **2319**

FOLDING CARTON INDUSTRY (UK/0306-168X) [02685962] **4219**

FOLDING KAYAKER (US/1056-2273) [23591506] **4872, 4895**

FOLDRAJZI KOZLEMENYEK (HU/0015-5411) [02261163] **2561**

FOLDTANI KOZLONY (HU/0015-542X) [01569510] **1376**

FOLGER DOCUMENTS OF TUDOR AND STUART CIVILIZATION (US/0428-8203) [01443159] **2688**

FOLGER FACSIMILES, THE (US) [01421527] **3211**

FOLGER MONOGRAPHS ON TUDOR AND STUART CIVILIZATION (US) [01421391] **2688**

FOLHA MEDICA (BL/0015-5454) [09598782] **3577**

FOLHAS PEDAGOGICAS *See* REVISTA DA FACULDADE SALESIANA **2552**

FOLIA (IT) [24570716] **2415**

FOLIA ARCHAEOLOGICA BUDAPEST (HU/0133-2023) [I01332023] **268**

FOLIA BIOLOGICA (XR/0015-5500) [01569525] **455**

FOLIA BIOLOGICA (WARSZAWA) (PL/0015-5497) [01569526] **5584**

FOLIA BIOTECHNOLOGICA (HU/0237-0743) [I02370743] **3692**

FOLIA ENTOMOLOGICA HUNGARICA (HU/0373-9465) [09348528] **5609**

FOLIA ENTOMOLOGICA MEXICANA (MX/0430-8603) [03084287] **5609**

FOLIA FACULTATIS MEDICAE UNIVERSITATIS COMENIANAE BRATISLAVIENSIS (XO/0430-8611) [04756615] **3577**

FOLIA FACULTATIS SCIENTIARUM NATURALIUM UNIVERSITATIS PURKYNIANAE BRUNENSIS. GEOLOGIA (XR/0323-0139) [03029691] **5105**

FOLIA FACULTATIS SCIENTIARUM NATURALIUM UNIVERSITATIS PURKYNIANAE BRUNENSIS. PHYSICA (XR/0323-0287) [06415652] **4403**

FOLIA FORESTALIA (FI/0015-5543) [01569533] **2379**

FOLIA FORESTALIA POLONICA. SERIA A. LESNICTWO (PL/0071-6677) [01317539] **2379**

FOLIA GEOBOTANICA & PHYTOTAXONOMICA (XR/0015-5551) [07014595] **511**

FOLIA GEOGRAPHICA DANICA (DK/0071-6693) [01383700] **2561**

FOLIA HEREDITARIA ET PATHOLOGICA (IT/0015-5578) [01623936] **545**

FOLIA HISTOCHEMICA ET CYTOBIOLOGICA (PL/0239-8508) [11059238] **536**

FOLIA HISTORIAE ARTIUM (PL/0071-6723) [01996143] **350**

FOLIA HISTORICA (HU/0133-6622) [02339205] **2688**

FOLIA HORTICULTURAE (PL/0867-1761) [I08671761] **2415**

FOLIA HUMANISTICA (SP/0015-5594) [01299618] **2846**

FOLIA LINGUISTICA (NE/0165-4004) [01569541] **3282**

FOLIA LINGUISTICA HISTORICA (NE/0168-647X) [07906041] **3282**

FOLIA LITERARIA (AG) [05653958] **3388**

FOLIA MEDICA CRACOVIENSIA (PL/0015-5616) [01778982] **3577**

FOLIA MEDICA FACULTATIS MEDICINAE UNIVERSITATIS SARAEVIENSIS (BN/0350-0705) [01359280] **3577**

FOLIA MICROBIOLOGICA (XR/0015-5632) [01569543] **563**

FOLIA MORPHOLOGICA (PL/0015-5659) [06201707] **455, 5584**

FOLIA MUSEI HISTORICO-NATURALIS BAKONYIENSIS (HU/0231-035X) [10240133] **4165**

●FOLIA NEUROPATHOLOGICA / ASSOCIATION OF POLISH NEUROPATHOLOGISTS AND MEDICAL RESEARCH CENTRE, POLISH ACADEMY OF SCIENCES (PL) [31021491] **3833**

FOLIA NEUROPSIQUIATRICA GRANADA (SP/0211-2558) [I02112558] **3833**

FOLIA NUMISMATICA (XR/0862-1195) [19092995] **2781**

FOLIA ONCOLOGICA (IT/0392-047X) [05845431] **3817**

FOLIA OPHTHALMOLOGICA (GW/0323-4932) [02512843] **3874**

FOLIA OPHTHALMOLOGICAL *See* AKTUELLE AUGENHEILKUNDE **3871**

FOLIA ORIENTALIA (PL/0015-5675) [01569548] **2651**

FOLIA PARASITOLOGICA / CZECHOSLOVAK ACADEMY OF SCIENCE (XR/0015-5683) [07047492] **5584**

FOLIA PHARMACEUTICA (PRAHA) (XR/0139-939X) [08341672] **4305**

FOLIA PHONIATRICA (SZ/0015-5705) [01335356] **3888**

●FOLIA PHONIATRICA ET LOGOPAEDICA : OFFICIAL ORGAN OF THE INTERNATIONAL ASSOCIATION OF LOGOPEDICS AND PHONIATRICS (IALP) (SZ/1021-7762) [29750095] **3888**

FOLIA PRIMATOLOGICA (SZ/0015-5713) [01299595] **5584**

FOLIA QUATERNARIA (PL/0015-573X) [04637956] **1376**

FOLIA VETERINARIA (XO/0015-5748) [03302977] **5510**

FOLIA VETERINARIA LATINA (IT/0301-0724) [02111551] **5510**

FOLIA ZOOLOGICA (BRNO) (XR/0139-7893) [03143060] **5584**

FOLIAGE DIGEST *See* FLORIDA FOLIAGE **511**

FOLIO (BROCKPORT, N.Y.) *CEASED*. (US/0882-3030) [03918686] **3282, 3388**

FOLIO-DEX VOCAL, PIANO AND ORGAN FINDING LIST (US) [02252976] **4118**

FOLIO (LOUISVILLE, KY.) (US/0741-1537) [09706721] **5060**

FOLIO (NORTH HOLLYWOOD) (US/0274-4856) [06347135] **1132**

FOLIO. PUBLIC RELATIONS, THE (US/0198-7143) [06202271] **615, 2971**

FOLIO (SAINT LOUIS, MO.) (US/0896-3096) [16998012] **2733**

FOLIO (SASKATOON) (CN/0381-9469) [02585336] **350**

FOLIO SERIES - LOUISIANA GEOLOGICAL SURVEY (US/0458-3329) [03968572] **1376**

FOLIO, THE (UK/0015-5772) [03260746] **4828**

FOLIO : THE MAGAZINE FOR MAGAZINE MANAGEMENT (US/0046-4333) [01335416] **4815**

FOLIO'S MEDICAL DIRECTORY OF CONNECTICUT AND RHODE ISLAND (US/1042-4644) [19057454] **3914**

FOLIO'S MEDICAL DIRECTORY OF MASSACHUSETTS (US/0741-241X) [06853545] **3914**

FOLIO'S PUBLISHING NEWS *CEASED*. (US/1053-4563) [22600935] **4815**

FOLK AND KINFOLK OF HARRIS COUNTY (US/0190-8189) [04744439] **2448**

FOLK ART FINDER (US/0738-8357) [08067457] **350**

FOLK ART MESSENGER (US/1043-5026) [18397508] **2319, 350**

FOLK ART SAMPLER (US/0271-3098) [06586107] **373**

FOLK DANCE DIRECTORY (US/0163-528X) [04399240] **1313**

FOLK DANCE SCENE (US) [01787698] **1313**

FOLK DIRECTORY, THE (UK/0430-876X) [04866380] **1313, 4118, 5231**

FOLK HARP JOURNAL (US/0094-8934) [01794972] **4118**

FOLK (KBENHAVN) (DK/0085-0756) [01569562] **236**

FOLK LETTER, THE (US/0145-3734) [02729202] **4118**

FOLK LIFE (UK/0430-8778) [01998728] **2319**

FOLK LITERATURE OF THE SEPHARDIC JEWS (US) [01421431] **3388**

FOLK MICHEL (GW/0934-6449) [20920745] **4118**

●FOLK MUSIC CATALOGUE (CN/1186-7523) [24368441] **4118**

FOLK MUSIC JOURNAL (UK/0531-9684) [01569568] **2319, 4118**

FOLK MUSIC MAGAZINE (US/0190-6577) [04733001] **4118**

FOLK MUSIC MINISTRY (US/0276-6655) [07399121] **4118**

FOLK NEWS (UK) [01789498] **4118**

FOLK NEWS (WASHINGTON, D.C.) (US) [13678875] **4118**

FOLK OG FORSKNING / UDG. AF UNIVERSTETSFORENINGEN FOR DET SYDLIGE OG VESTLIGE JYLLAND (DK/0105-712X) [10932747] 5200, **2846**

FOLK OG KULTUR (DK/0105-1024) [01998813] **2319**

FOLK REVIEW (UK) [06283984] **4118**

FOLK ROOTS (UK/0951-1326) [12960391] 2319, **4118**

FOLK, VELT UN MEDINE (IS) [02245694] **2651**

FOLKEHJSKOLER OG LANDBRUGSSKOLER SAMT HUSHOLDNINGGKOLER (DK) [19889206] **88**

FOLKETINGSTIDENDE. ARBOG OG REGISTRE (DK/0903-6946) [18243758] **4474**

FOLKETS HISTORIA (SW/0349-6279) [12337694] 5200, **2616**

FOLKLIFE CENTER NEWS (US/0149-6840) [03543980] **2319**

FOLKLOR ARCHIVUM (HU) [04279280] 2261, **2319**

FOLKLOR (MOSCOW, R.S.F.S.R.) (RU) [08883888] **2319**

FOLKLOR NARODOV RSFSR (RU) [04350908] **2319**

FOLKLORE (BG) [03930057] **2319**

FOLKLORE AMERICANO (PE/0071-6774) [01775372] **2319**

FOLKLORE AND FOLKLIFE IN VIRGINIA (US/0272-5711) [05468583] **2320**

FOLKLORE AND MYTHOLOGY STUDIES (LOS ANGELES, CALIF. : 1977) (US/0162-6280) [04179185] **2320**

FOLKLORE AND MYTHOLOGY STUDIES (LOS ANGELES, CALIF. : 1980) (US/0731-1524) [06930238] **2320**

FOLKLORE BIBLIOGRAPHY (US/0272-8494) [06346982] **2325**

FOLKLORE BRABANCON (BE/0015-590X) [01569578] 2688, **2320**

FOLKLORE (CALCUTTA) (II/0015-5896) [01336470] **2320**

FOLKLORE DE CHAMPAGNE (FR) [04574454] **2320**

FOLKLORE DE FRANCE (FR/0015-5918) [06441059] **2320**

FOLKLORE FELLOWS *See* FF COMMUNICATIONS **2319**

FOLKLORE FORUM (US/0015-5926) [01647186] **2320**

FOLKLORE HISTORIAN (MIDDLETOWN, DAUPHIN COUNTY, PA.), THE (US/1041-8644) [16727333] **2320**

FOLKLORE (LONDON) (UK/0015-587X) [01569566] **2320**

FOLKLORE (MOOSE JAW) (CN/0824-3085) [10195284] 2733, **2320**

FOLKLORE OF AMERICAN HOLIDAYS, THE (US) 5268, **2320**

FOLKLORE (OTTAWA) (CN/0705-1158) [03963472] **2320**

FOLKLORE PAPERS OF THE UNIVERSITY FOLKLORE ASSOCIATION (US/0730-3181) [07252428] **2320**

FOLKLORE SOCIETY OF GREATER WASHINGTON *See* FOLKLORE SOCIETY OF GREATER WASHINGTON NEWSLETTER **2320**

FOLKLORE SOCIETY OF GREATER WASHINGTON *See* NEWSLETTER **4140**

FOLKLORE SOCIETY OF GREATER WASHINGTON NEWSLETTER (US) [01295992] **2320**

FOLKLORE STUDIES ASSOCIATION OF CANADA *See* BULLETIN OF THE FOLKLORE STUDIES ASSOCIATION OF CANADA **2318**

FOLKLORE SUISSE (SZ/0015-5969) [02336842] **2320**

FOLKLORE VERZEICHNIS FUER EUROPA (GW) [09509317] **2320**

FOLKLORE WOMEN'S COMMUNICATION (US/0160-9831) [03795482] 5557, **2320**

FOLKMANGD (SW) [01783811] **4562**

FOLKMANGDEN INOM ADMINISTRATIVA OMRADEN *See* FOLKMANGD **4562**

FOLKNIK, THE (US/0146-9169) [03059475] **4118**

FOLKOR VE ETNOGRAFYA ARASTRMALARI (TU) [11377529] **2320**

FOLKS-SHTIME *CEASED.* (PL) [10124699] **5808**

FOLLETOS MUNDO CRISTIANO (SP) 1747, **2280**

FOLLIA DI NEW YORK (US/0015-6000) [01569587] **2846**

FOLLIES *CEASED.* (US/0162-721X) [04221942] **3343**

FOLLOWING CHAIN AND COMPASS : NEWSLETTER OF THE ARCHIVAL AND HISTORY COMMITTEE OF SMITH TOWNSHIP (CN/0847-382X) [24266682] **2733**

FOLLOWUP FILE (US/0888-3955) [13562998] **2919**

FOLQ UN MEDINAH (IS/0302-8186) [01790778] **2651**

FOMENTO DE LA PRODUCCION (SP/0015-6035) [15726104] **676**

FOMENTO DEL TRABAJO (SP) [29717197] **1561**

FOMRHI QUARTERLY (UK) [05158452] **4118**

FONAIAP DIVULGA / FONDO NACIONAL DE INVESTIGACIONES AGROPECUARAIAS (VE) [09233321] **88**

FONAMENTS (SP/0210-2366) [07937949] **2688**

FOND DU LAC CLARION, THE (US/0747-4415) [10865830] **5767**

FONDAMENTI (IT) [13509254] **2846**

FONDATION LOUIS DE BROGLIE *See* ANNALES DE LA FONDATION LOUIS DE BROGLIE **4396**

FONDAZIONE GIANGIACOMO FELTRINELLI *See* ANNALI - FONDAZIONE GIANGIACOMO FELTRINELLI **4539**

FONDAZIONE GIORGIO CINI, VENICE. CENTRO DI CULTURA E CIVILTA. ISTITUTO DI STORIA DELL'ARTE *See* CATALOGHI DI MOSTRE **347**

FONDAZIONE GIORGIO CINI, VENICE. CENTRO DI CULTURA E CIVILTA. ISTITUTO DI STORIA DELLA SOCIETA E DELLO STATO. BOLLETTINO (IT) [05791281] **2688**

FONDAZIONE LUIGI EINAUDI *See* ANNALI DELLA FONDAZIONE LUIGI EINAUDI **5190**

FONDERIA (IT/0015-6078) [02446984] **4002**

FONDERIA ITALIANA *See* FONDERIA **4002**

FONDERIE, FONDEUR D'AUJOURD'HUI (FR/0249-3136) [07476583] **4002**

FONDO DE CULTURA ECONOMICA, MEXICO *See* CATALOGO GENERAL - FONDO DE CULTURA ECONOMICA, MEXICO **1531**

FONDS DE DEVELOPPEMENT ECONOMIQUE ET SOCIAL. CONSEIL DE DIRECTION *See* RAPPORT - CONSEIL DE DIRECTION DU FONDS DE DEVELOPPEMENT ECONOMIQUE ET SOCIAL **4744**

FONDS DER CHEMISCHEN INDUSTRIE (GERMANY) *See* STATISTISCHE UBERSICHTEN : CHEMIE AN DER HOCHSCHULEN DER BUNDESREPUBLIK DEUTSCHLAND **1012**

FONDS DER CHEMISCHEN INDUSTRIE ZUR FORDERUNG VON FORSCHUNG, WISSENSCHAFT UND LEHRE *See* STATISTISCHE UUBERSICHTEN : BESTAND UND BEDARF AN CHEMIKERN IN DER CHEMISCHEN INDUSTRIE DER BUNDESREPUBLIK DEUTSCHLAND **1012**

FONDS FCAR (QUEBEC) *See* RAPPORT ANNUEL / FONDS FCAR, FONDS POUR LA FORMATION DE CHERCHEURS ET L'AIDE A LA RECHERCHE **5144**

FONDS NATIONAL DE LA RECHERCHE SCIENTIFIQUE (BELGIUM) *See* LISTE DES BENEFICIAIRES D'UNE SUBVENTION DU FONDS NATIONAL DE LA RECHERCHE SCIENTIFIQUE OU D'UN DES TROIS FONDS ASSOCIES AVEC INDICATION DES RECHERCHES POURSUIVIES ET DE L'INSTITUTION D'ACCUEIL **5126**

FONO FORUM (GW/0015-6140) [03331875] **4118**

FONOWEEK 40 (NE) [02246450] **5316**

FONTANE BLATTER (GW/0015-6175) [02029297] **3388**

FONTANELLE OBSERVER (FONTANELLE, IOWA : 1904) (US) [12935821] **5670**

FONTANUS FROM THE COLLECTIONS OF MCGILL UNIVERSITY (CN/0838-2026) [18573529] **3211**

FONTES ARCHAEOLOGICI POSNANIENSES (PL/0071-6863) [01998902] **268**

FONTES ARTIS MUSICAE (SZ/0015-6191) [01569603] **4118**

FONTES DE FINANCIAMENTO PARA O SETOR PUBLICO ESTADUAL (BL) [06463026] **4727**

FONTES RERUM AUSTRIACARUM. OSTERREICHISCHE GESCHICHTS-QUELLEN. 1. ABTEILUNG. SCRIPTORES (AU/0071-6871) [01569605] **2688**

FONTES RERUM MEXICANARUM (AN) [03161919] **3388**

FONTI E DOCUMENTI / CENTRO STUDI PER LA STORIA DEL MODERNISMO (IT) [02544923] **2616**

FONTI MUSICALI IN ITALIA, LE (IT/1120-8260) [I11208260] **4118**

FONTI ORALI-STUDI E RICERCHE (IT) [09600645] **2688**

FONTI PER LA STORIA D'ITALIA (IT) [01569609] **2688**

FONTILLES (SP/0367-2743) [03620871] **3720**

FOOD ADDITIVES ANALYTICAL MANUAL (US) [19612977] **2335**

FOOD ADDITIVES AND CONTAMINANTS (UK/0265-203X) [11154369] **2335**

FOOD ADDITIVES INFORMATION FILE (UK) [02195464] **2335**

FOOD AID CONVENTION (UK) [17847905] 2335, **5285**

FOOD AID IN FIGURES (IT/0259-4064) [11705088] **2909**

FOOD AID MONITOR / WORLD FOOD PROGRAMME, THE (IT) [21540696] **2335**

FOOD ANALYST. CD-ROM (US) **4191**

FOOD ANALYST PLUS. CD-ROM (US) **4191**

FOOD AND AGRICULTURAL IMMUNOLOGY (UK/0954-0105) [20028489] 88, **563**

FOOD AND AGRICULTURAL LEGISLATION (IT/0015-6221) [01569611] 88, 2971, **2336**

FOOD AND AGRICULTURE : BIBLIOGRAPHY OF GAO DOCUMENTS (US) [21184078] **88**

FOOD AND AGRICULTURE IN AFRICA / UNITED NATIONS ECONOMIC COMMISSION FOR AFRICA, FOOD AND AGRICULTURE ORGANIZATION OF THE UNITED NATIONS (ET) [25122636] 88, 2336, **2909**

FOOD AND AGRICULTURE ORGANIZATION OF THE UNITED NATIONS *See* WORLD FOOD SURVEY **147**

FOOD AND AGRICULTURE ORGANIZATION OF THE UNITED NATIONS *See* FAO FISHERIES STUDIES **2300**

FOOD AND AGRICULTURE ORGANIZATION OF THE UNITED NATIONS *See* COMMODITY BULLETIN SERIES **1602**

FOOD AND AGRICULTURE ORGANIZATION OF THE UNITED NATIONS *See* FAO-DOC CURRENT BIBLIOGRAPHY (MICROFORM) **2335**

FOOD AND AGRICULTURE ORGANIZATION OF THE UNITED NATIONS *See* FAO ANIMAL PRODUCTION AND HEALTH PAPER **226**

FOOD AND AGRICULTURE ORGANIZATION OF THE UNITED NATIONS *See* FAO LEGISLATIVE SERIES **83**

FOOD AND AGRICULTURE ORGANIZATION OF THE UNITED NATIONS *See* ESTUDIOS AGROPECUARIOS DE LA FAO **82**

FOOD AND AGRICULTURE ORGANIZATION OF THE UNITED NATIONS *See* NATIONAL GRAIN POLICIES **203**

FOOD AND AGRICULTURE ORGANIZATION OF THE UNITED NATIONS *See* FAO NUTRITION MEETINGS REPORT SERIES **4191**

FOOD AND AGRICULTURE ORGANIZATION OF THE UNITED NATIONS *See* FAO ANIMAL PRODUCTION AND HEALTH SERIES **211**

FOOD AND AGRICULTURE ORGANIZATION OF THE UNITED NATIONS *See* FAO IN ... **83**

FOOD AND AGRICULTURE ORGANIZATION OF THE UNITED NATIONS *See* FAO COMMODITY POLICY STUDIES **83**

FOOD AND AGRICULTURE ORGANIZATION OF THE UNITED NATIONS *See* REVIEW OF THE REGULAR PROGRAMME **128**

FOOD AND AGRICULTURE ORGANIZATION OF THE UNITED NATIONS. COMMISSION FOR CONTROLLING THE DESERT LOCUST IN NORTHWEST AFRICA *See* REPORT OF THE ... SESSION OF THE COMMISSION FOR CONTROLLING THE DESERT LOCUST IN NORTHWEST AFRICA **184**

FOOD AND AGRICULTURE ORGANIZATION OF THE UNITED NATIONS. COMMODITIES AND TRADE DIVISION *See* FAO COMMODITY REVIEW AND OUTLOOK **83**

Alphabetical Title Index — FOOD

FOOD AND AGRICULTURE ORGANIZATION OF THE UNITED NATIONS. CONFERENCE See REPORT OF THE CONFERENCE OF FAO **2355**

FOOD AND AGRICULTURE ORGANIZATION OF THE UNITED NATIONS. CONSULTATIVE SUB-COMMITTEE ON THE ECONOMIC ASPECTS OF RICE See REPORT OF THE ... SESSION OF THE CONSULTATIVE SUB-COMMITTEE ON THE ECONOMIC ASPECTS OF RICE TO THE COMMITTEE ON COMMODITY PROBLEMS **1516**

FOOD AND AGRICULTURE ORGANIZATION OF THE UNITED NATIONS. COUNCIL See REPORT OF THE COUNCIL OF FAO (ENGLISH EDITION) **126**

FOOD AND AGRICULTURE ORGANIZATION OF THE UNITED NATIONS. DOCUMENTATION CENTER See FORESTRY **2381**

FOOD & BEVERAGE MARKETING (US/0731-3799) [08174116] 2367, **2336**

FOOD AND BIOPRODUCTS PROCESSING : TRANSACTIONS OF THE INSTITUTION OF CHEMICAL ENGINEERS, PART C (UK/0960-3085) [24327073] 1975, **2336**

FOOD AND CHEMICAL TOXICOLOGY (UK/0278-6915) [07864235] **3980**

FOOD & COOKERY REVIEW (UK) [04023757] **2336**

FOOD & DRINK DAILY (US) [23469314] **2336**

FOOD AND DRUG ADMINISTRATION PUBLIC ADVISORY COMMITTEES : AUTHORITY, STRUCTURE, FUNCTIONS, MEMBERS (US) [03062757] **4649**

●FOOD AND DRUG LAW JOURNAL (US/1064-590X) [26135015] **2971**

FOOD AND DRUG LAW REPORTS (US/1053-9034) [21308653] 2336, **2971**

FOOD & DRUG LETTER, THE (US/0362-6466) [02290086] 4305, **2336**

FOOD AND DRUG PACKAGING (US/0015-6272) [02446991] **4219**

FOOD & DRUG PACKAGING See NEW FOOD & DRUG PACKAGING, THE **4220**

●FOOD AND DRUG REPORT (US/1071-8869) [28691569] 2336, **2971**

FOOD & DRUGS INDUSTRY BULLETIN (UK/0266-9366) [I02669366] **2336**

FOOD & FIBER LETTER, THE (US/0739-6791) [09792382] **2336**

FOOD & FOODWAYS (SZ/0740-9710) [10063778] 2336, **5245**

FOOD AND HOME NOTES (US/0090-9688) [01642628] **88**

FOOD AND JUSTICE (US/0885-0704) [12561452] 2336, **172**

FOOD AND NUTRITION BULLETIN (JA/0379-5721) [05348644] 2909, **4191**

FOOD AND NUTRITION IN AFRICA (GH) [04795992] 4191, **2336**

FOOD & NUTRITION NEWS (US/0015-6310) [03581217] **4191**

FOOD & NUTRITION PROGRAMS (US/0360-4594) [02243716] **2909**

FOOD AND NUTRITION QUARTERLY INDEX CEASED. (US/0887-0535) [13072297] **4191**

FOOD AND NUTRITION UPDATE (UK) **2336**

FOOD AND NUTRITION (WASHINGTON, 1971) (US/0046-4394) [01533512] 2336, **4191**

FOOD & SERVICE / TEXAS RESTAURANT ASSOCIATION (US/0891-0154) [14525621] 5071, **2336**

FOOD & WINE (NEW YORK, N.Y.) (US/0741-9015) [09801741] **2790**

FOOD ARTS (US/1042-9123) [19252166] **2336**

FOOD AUSTRALIA : OFFICIAL JOURNAL OF CAFTA AND AIFST (AT/1032-5298) [19015915] **2336**

FOOD BIOTECHNOLOGY (US/0890-5436) [14261865] 2336, **3692**

FOOD BIOTECHNOLOGY (LONDON) (UK/0952-357X) [15680557] 2336, **3692**

FOOD BROKER QUARTERLY (US/0884-7185) [12425899] 924, **2336**

FOOD BUSINESS ANNUAL (US/1057-6959) [23676744] **2336**

FOOD BUSINESS (CHICAGO, ILL.) (US/1049-5568) [20881779] **2336**

FOOD BUSINESS MERGERS & ACQUISITIONS (US/8756-8772) [08636278] **2336**

FOOD BUSINESS OPPORTUNITIES (US/1057-6940) [24100687] **676**

FOOD CHANNEL, THE (US/1062-8665) [25772487] **2336**

FOOD CHEMICAL NEWS (US/0015-6337) [02256520] **1024**

FOOD CHEMICAL NEWS GUIDE (US) **2336**

FOOD CHEMISTRY (UK/0308-8146) [02728297] 4191, 2336, **1024**

FOOD COMPOSITION AND NUTRITION TABLES / DIE ZUSAMMENSETZUNG DER LEBENSMITTEL, NAEHRWERT-TABELLEN (GW/0721-6912) [09734894] **4191**

FOOD CONSUMPTION, PRICES, AND EXPENDITURES / UNITED STATES DEPARTMENT OF AGRICULTURE, ECONOMIC RESEARCH SERVICE (US) [11607596] **2336**

FOOD CONSUMPTION STATISTICS (FR) [01381462] **2362**

FOOD CONTROL (UK) [22155024] **2336**

FOOD, COSMETICS AND DRUG PACKAGING 1986 (UK/0951-4554) [I09514554] **4219**

FOOD DISTRIBUTION MAGAZINE : FDM (US/1048-8197) [20957713] **2337**

FOOD DISTRIBUTION RESEARCH SOCIETY See QUARTERLY NEWSLETTER / FOOD DISTRIBUTION RESEARCH SOCIETY, INC **2355**

FOOD, DRUG, COSMETIC, AND MEDICAL DEVICE LAW DIGEST (US/1057-2759) [23964914] **2971**

FOOD, DRUG, COSMETIC LAW JOURNAL See FOOD AND DRUG LAW JOURNAL **2971**

FOOD DRUG COSMETIC LAW REPORTS (RX EDITION) (US/0162-1122) [04116300] **3100**

FOOD ENGINEERING'S ... DIRECTORY OF U.S. FOOD & BEVERAGE PLANTS (US/0730-1413) [07936047] **2337**

FOOD EUROPE ENGLISH ED CEASED. (UK/0956-6783) [I09566783] **2337**

FOOD FILE (UK/0967-5302) [I09675302] **2337**

FOOD FIRST DEVELOPMENT REPORT (US/0895-3090) [16567233] **5285**

FOOD FIRST NEWS See FOOD FIRST NEWS & VIEWS **2337**

●FOOD FIRST NEWS & VIEWS (US) [28608569] **2337**

FOOD FOR PEACE PROGRAM ANNUAL REPORT (US) [02868959] **2909**

FOOD FOR THOUGHT (VANCOUVER) (CN/0712-2934) [08781479] **88**

FOOD FREEZING AND PROCESSING EQUIPMENT (US/0199-5286) [05965909] **2337**

FOOD HISTORY NEWS (US/1067-1951) [25261105] **2337**

FOOD HYDROCOLLOIDS (UK/0268-005X) [14942784] 2337, **1041**

FOOD + I.E. UND NONFOOD (GW) [06834294] **2337**

FOOD IN CANADA BUYERS' DIRECTORY & SERVICES INDEX (CN/0317-3364) [02248188] **2337**

FOOD INDUSTRIES OF SOUTH AFRICA (SA/0015-6450) [09400297] **2337**

FOOD INDUSTRIES OF SOUTH AFRICA (SA/0015-6450) [21133572] **2337**

FOOD INDUSTRIES (OTTAWA) (CN/0835-0000) [17365270] **2337**

FOOD INDUSTRY BULLETIN (UK/0965-4682) [I09654682] **2337**

FOOD INDUSTRY DIRECTORY, THE (US/0145-3610) [02724769] **2337**

FOOD INDUSTRY FUTURES (US/0046-4414) [03415806] **2337**

FOOD INDUSTRY NEWS AUCKLAND (NZ/0113-8901) [I01138901] **2337**

FOOD INDUSTRY NEWSLETTER (FAIRFAX, VA.), THE (US/0890-720X) [03415841] **2337**

FOOD INDUSTRY REPORT (US/1040-9076) [18575781] **2337**

FOOD INDUSTRY TOPICS (US) **2337**

●FOOD INGREDIENTS AND ANALYSIS INTERNATIONAL (US/0968-574X) [28598886] **2337**

FOOD INGREDIENTS & PROCESSING INTERNATIONAL (UK) **2337**

FOOD INGREDIENTS & PROCESSING INTERNATIONAL (UK/0968-574X) [24425675] **2337**

FOOD INNOVATION INTERNATIONAL (UK) **2337**

FOOD INSIGHT (US/1065-1497) [22992863] **2337**

FOOD INSTITUTE REPORT, THE (US/0745-4503) [09184975] **2337**

FOOD INSTITUTE'S REPORT ON FOOD MARKETS See FOOD INSTITUTE REPORT, THE **2337**

FOOD INSTITUTE'S WASHINGTON FOOD REPORT See FOOD INSTITUTE REPORT, THE **2337**

FOOD INSTITUTE'S WEEKLY DIGEST See FOOD INSTITUTE REPORT, THE **2337**

FOOD INVESTMENT REPORT CEASED. (US/1067-9871) [27407870] **2337**

FOOD IRELAND (IE/0790-0430) [I07900430] **2337**

FOOD IRRADIATION NEWSLETTER (AU/1011-2588) [13485573] **2337**

●FOOD IRRADIATION UPDATE (US/1065-142X) [26514293] **2338**

FOOD IRRADIATION [COMPUTER FILE] (US) [25321122] **2338**

●FOOD LABELING NEWS (US/1064-6329) [26345529] **2338**

FOOD LABORATORY NEWS SUSPENDED. (SW/1100-3227) [21474925] **2338**

FOOD LAUNCH AWARENESS BULLETIN (UK/0965-4690) [I09654690] **2338**

FOOD LAW MONTHLY (UK) 2338, **2971**

FOOD MAGAZINE LONDON. 1988 (UK/0953-5047) [I09535047] **2338**

FOOD MANAGEMENT (US/0091-018X) [01780205] **2338**

FOOD MANAGEMENT AMERSFOORT (NE/0168-325X) [I0168325X] **2338**

FOOD MANAGEMENT NEWS (AT) **2338**

FOOD MANUFACTURE (UK/0015-6477) [01569649] **2338**

FOOD MANUFACTURE INGREDIENT & MACHINERY SURVEY (UK) [03785708] **2338**

FOOD MANUFACTURE INTERNATIONAL (UK/0267-1506) [15478767] **2338**

FOOD MANUFACTURING NEWS (AT/0816-3634) [I08163634] **2338**

FOOD MANUFACTURING NEWS See FOOD MANAGEMENT NEWS **2338**

FOOD MARKET ABSTRACTS (UK/0268-0408) [I02680408] **2338**

FOOD MARKET COMMENTARY (CN/0709-5864) [06026354] **2338**

FOOD MARKETING & TECHNOLOGY (GW/0932-2744) [25783240] **2338**

FOOD MARKETING BRIEFS (US/0896-4203) [17154270] 924, **2338**

FOOD MARKETING INDUSTRY SPEAKS : DETAILED TABULATIONS, THE (US/0190-504X) [04696785] **2338**

FOOD MARKETING INDUSTRY SPEAKS, THE (US/0190-3349) [03451913] **2338**

FOOD MARKETING INSTITUTE See ANNUAL FINANCIAL REVIEW - FOOD MARKETING INSTITUTE **2327**

FOOD MARKETING INSTITUTE. FACTS ABOUT NEW SUPER MARKETS OPENED See FACTS ABOUT STORE DEVELOPMENT **2334**

FOOD MARKETING INSTITUTE. INFORMATION SERVICE See CUMULATIVE INDEX - FOOD MARKETING INSTITUTE, INFORMATION SERVICE **2332**

FOOD MARKETING POLICY CENTER RESEARCH REPORT (US) [20607040] **2338**

FOOD MARKETS IN REVIEW (US) [12928984] **2338**

FOOD MERCHANDISING FOR NON-FOOD RETAILERS (US/0279-3105) [07749332] **2338**

FOOD MERCHANTS ADVOCATE (US/0015-6493) [04077586] **2338**

FOOD MICROBIOLOGY (UK/0740-0020) [09848338] 2338, **563**

FOOD NEWS FOR CONSUMERS / UNITED STATES DEPT. OF AGRICULTURE, FOOD SAFETY AND QUALITY SERVICE CEASED. (US/1057-7785) [06310154] 1297, **2338**

FOOD, NUTRITION AND AGRICULTURE (IT) [25680983] 4191, **88**

FOOD OUTLOOK (ROME, ITALY) (IT) [04861822] **2338**

FOOD OUTLOOK. STATISTICAL SUPPLEMENT (IT) [09249381] 2338, **2362**

FOOD PACKER INTERNATIONAL (UK/0957-5189) [I09575189] 2338, **4219**

FOOD PAPER (LOS ANGELES, CALIF.), THE (US/1062-0192) [25505637] **2338**

FOOD PEOPLE AND THEIR COMPANIES (US/0279-9839) [07411297] **2338**

FOOD PERSONALITY (NE/0925-8051) [I09258051] **2339**

FOOD PLANT EQUIPMENT (US/0887-3895) [13206439] 1024, **2339**

●FOOD PLANT STRATEGIES (US/1072-298X) [28903102] **2339**

FOOD POLICY (UK/0306-9192) [02441275] **2339**

FOOD POLICY INTERNATIONAL (BE/0778-7065) [I07787065] 2339, **88**

FOOD PRICE SPREADS IN CALIFORNIA (US) [06972198] **2339**

FOOD PROCESSING (US/0015-6523) [04568525] **2339**

FOOD
Alphabetical Title Index

FOOD PROCESSING (BROMLEY, LONDON, ENGLAND) (UK/0264-9462) [09423548] **2339**

FOOD PROCESSING EQUIPMENT AND TESTING (UK) **2339**

FOOD PROCESSING MACHINERY AND SUPPLIES ASSOCIATION *See* BLUE BOOK : MEMBERSHIP DIRECTORY & BUYER'S GUIDE **2329**

FOOD PROCESSOR (AT) **2339**

FOOD PRODUCT DESIGN (US/1065-772X) [26732720] **2339**

FOOD PRODUCTION MANAGEMENT (US/0191-6181) [01569654] **2339**

FOOD PRODUCTS & EQUIPMENT (US/1056-5078) [23726220] **2339**

FOOD PROFESSIONAL'S GUIDE, THE (US/1046-2414) [20367394] **2339**

FOOD PROTECTION REPORT (US/0884-0806) [12303699] **2339**

FOOD PURITY PERSPECTIVES (US/0091-7605) [01788145] **2339**

FOOD QUALITY AND PREFERENCE (UK/0950-3293) [20189521] **2339**

FOOD R.A. ABSTRACTS FROM CURRENT SCIENTIFIC AND TECHNICAL LITERATURE (UK) [04024308] **2339**

FOOD RESEARCH INSTITUTE STUDIES (1975) *CEASED.* (US/0193-9025) [02256695] 1491, **88**

● FOOD RESEARCH INTERNATIONAL (CN/0963-9969) [25848747] **2339**

FOOD REVIEW (SA/0257-8867) [12131337] **2339**

FOOD REVIEWS INTERNATIONAL (US/8755-9129) [11427078] **2339**

● FOOD SAFETY & SECURITY (UK/0964-4164) [I09644164] **2340**

FOOD SAFETY CONCERNS BULLETIN, THE (UK/0968-1647) [I09681647] **2340**

FOOD SAFETY NOTEBOOK (US/1050-1843) [21420216] **2340**

● FOOD SAFETY SERIES (UK) [28358456] **2340**

FOOD SCIENCE AND TECHNOLOGY: A SERIES OF MONOGRAPHS (US/0532-0984) [02256086] **2340**

FOOD SCIENCE AND TECHNOLOGY ABSTRACTS (UK/0015-6574) [01569660] 2340, **2362**

FOOD SCIENCE AND TECHNOLOGY (NEW YORK, N.Y. 1984) (US/0891-8961) [11535135] **2340**

FOOD SCIENCE AND TECHNOLOGY SERIES (JA) [03829948] **2340**

FOOD SCIENCE & TECHNOLOGY TODAY (UK/0950-9623) [17256560] **2340**

FOOD SCIENCES AND NUTRITION *See* INTERNATIONAL JOURNAL OF FOOD SCIENCES AND NUTRITION **4192**

FOOD-SERVICE EAST (US/0885-6877) [12699453] **2340**

FOOD SERVICE RECIPE NEWSLETTER; MAKE IT TASTY SPICE BLENDS (US) **2340**

FOOD SERVICE RESEARCH ABSTRACTS (US/0532-0992) [03979828] **2340**

● FOOD SITUATION REPORT FOR THE MONTH OF ... [MICROFORM] (BG) [26776543] 2340, **5286**

FOOD STAMP PROGRAM : STATISTICAL SUMMARY OF OPERATIONS (US/0276-0320) [02807436] 5286, **5266**

FOOD STRUCTURE (US/1046-705X) [20496653] **2340**

FOOD SURVEILLANCE PAPER (UK/0141-8521) [10278157] **2340**

FOOD TALK (US) **2340**

FOOD TECHNOLOGY ABSTRACTS (II/0253-4924) [I02534924] **2362**

FOOD TECHNOLOGY (CHICAGO) (US/0015-6639) [01569663] **2340**

FOOD TECHNOLOGY IN NEW ZEALAND (NZ/0015-6655) [01569665] **2340**

FOOD TODAY *See* HOTEL MANAGEMENT TODAY **2806**

FOOD (TORONTO) (CN/0829-643X) [12706421] **2340**

FOOD TRADE NEWS (US/0015-6663) [04977121] **2340**

FOOD TRADE REVIEW (UK/0015-6671) [10522698] **2340**

FOOD TRENDS NEWSLETTER (US) **2340**

FOOD WORLD (HK) **2340**

FOOD WORLD (COLUMBIA) (US/0191-619X) [04912508] **2340**

FOOD WORLD NEWS (UK/0260-1974) [11980629] **2340**

FOODAY *See* FOODDAY UPDATE **5733**

FOODBORNE DISEASE SURVEILLANCE. ANNUAL SUMMARY (US/0270-4072) [06257440] **4776**

FOODCORP (II) [01236413] **2340**

FOODDAY UPDATE (US/0746-6404) [10195776] **5733**

FOODLETTER (US/8756-1514) [11520161] **2341**

FOODLINES (US/0736-0010) [09068287] **5286**

FOODNEWS (UK/0951-130X) [I0951130X] **2341**

FOODPRESS (NE/0015-6701) [I00156701] **2341**

FOODREVIEW (WASHINGTON, D.C.) (US/1056-327X) [23472649] **2341**

FOODS ADLIBRA (1975) (US/0146-9304) [02256521] 2341, **2362**

● FOODS INTELLIGENCE ON COMPACT DISC (US/1063-4169) [26019758] 4191, 2341, **2362**

FOODSERVICE & HOSPITALITY (CN/0007-8972) [01901941] 2805, **5071**

FOODSERVICE DIRECTOR (US/0897-7208) [17605123] **2341**

FOODSERVICE DIRECTORY (US/0883-1912) [12069573] **2341**

FOODSERVICE DISTRIBUTION NEWS (US/0199-9400) [06313402] **2341**

FOODSERVICE DISTRIBUTOR, THE (US/0896-4505) [17155171] **2341**

FOODSERVICE EQUIPMENT & SUPPLIES SPECIALIST (US/0888-8515) [13738167] **2341**

FOODSERVICE EQUIPMENT DEALER. BUYERS GUIDE AND PRODUCT DIRECTORY (US/0363-1303) [02429528] **2341**

FOODSERVICE EQUIPMENT SPECIALIST. BUYERS GUIDE AND PRODUCT DIRECTORY (US) [06846449] **2341**

FOODSERVICE OPERATORS GUIDE (US/1040-4546) [18422448] 5071, **2341**

FOODSERVICE PRODUCT NEWS (US/0199-7696) [06138948] **2341**

● FOODSERVICE YEARBOOK INTERNATIONAL (US/1062-7324) [25732103] **2341**

FOODSTORE MAGAZINE (CN/0834-3365) [16440471] **2341**

FOODTALK (SAN FRANCISCO, CALIF.) (US/1065-0067) [08341574] **4191**

FOODWEEK (AT) **2341**

FOODWEEK NEWSLETTER (US) **2341**

FOOKIEN TIMES PHILIPPINES YEARBOOK, THE (PH) [04789120] **2651**

FOOM (US/0192-8090) [05065888] **3388**

FOOT & ANKLE (US/0198-0211) [06182855] **3881**

FOOT & ANKLE *See* FOOT & ANKLE INTERNATIONAL **3918**

● FOOT & ANKLE INTERNATIONAL (US/1071-1007) [28552032] **3918**

● FOOT AND ANKLE QUARTERLY (US/1068-3100) [27644559] **3918**

FOOT AND MOUTH DISEASE BULLETIN (UK/0950-1878) [09180773] **5510**

FOOT MAGAZINE (BE/0770-321X) [I0770321X] **4850**

FOOT NOTES - BEEF AND SHEEP BRANCH (EDMONTON) (CN/0225-0888) [06170166] 211, **836**

FOOT PRINTS PAST AND PRESENT (US) [10204800] **2448**

FOOT, THE (UK/0958-2592) [23739283] **3881**

FOOT WORSHIP NEWS (US) **5268**

FOOTBALL ASSOCIATION INTERNATIONAL FEDERATION *See* LAWS OF THE GAME AND UNIVERSAL GUIDE FOR REFEREES **2997**

FOOTBALL ASSOCIATION INTERNATIONAL FEDERATION *See* DIRECTORY OF ADDRESSES - FEDERATION INTERNATIONALE DE FOOTBALL ASSOCIATION **4892**

FOOTBALL, BASKETBALL & HOCKEY COLLECTOR *CEASED.* (US/1051-1997) [21893552] 4895, **2773**

FOOTBALL CASE BOOK (US/0163-6200) [04396923] **4895**

FOOTBALL DIGEST (US/0015-6760) [02789827] **4895**

FOOTBALL HANDBOOK (US) [18204325] **4895**

FOOTBALL HANDBOOK (US) [05273388] **4895**

FOOTBALL JOURNAL (CN/0317-2163) [02247940] **4895**

FOOTBALL KICK (UK) **4895**

FOOTBALL MONTHLY (1980) (UK/0266-481X) [I0266481X] **4895**

FOOTBALL NEWS (DETROIT) (US/0161-9020) [04052792] **4895**

FOOTBALL OFFICIALS MANUAL (US/0163-6219) [04396913] **4895**

FOOTHILLS SENTINEL (US/8750-3026) [11253570] **5630**

FOOTHILLS TRADER (US/0191-7463) [04947888] **5645**

FOOTLOOSE LIBRARIAN, THE *CEASED.* (US/0733-3196) [08575130] 3211, **5474**

FOOTNOTE, THE (US) [01569673] **744**

FOOTNOTE (WASHINGTON) (US/0533-1250) [01569674] **4649**

FOOTNOTES (US) [01381535] **1313**

FOOTNOTES* (US) [04799423] **385**

FOOTNOTES (RESTON, VA.) (US/8755-9048) [11445962] **4895**

FOOTNOTES / STATE LIBRARY COMMISSION OF IOWA (US) [03188399] **3211**

FOOTNOTES (WASHINGTON, D.C.) (US/0749-6931) [04810374] **5245**

FOOTPRINTS (UK) **2448**

FOOTPRINTS (FORT WORTH) (US/0426-8261) [02763879] **2448**

FOOTPRINTS IN MARION COUNTY (US/8755-6928) [10271835] **2448**

FOOTPRINTS (MARIETTA, GA.) *CEASED.* (US/1051-4597) [21967134] **2487**

FOOTWEAR FORUM (CN/0706-7534) [05018184] **1084**

FOOTWEAR INDUSTRY REVITALIZATION PROGRAM / UNITED STATES DEPARTMENT OF COMMERCE (US) [04744093] **1084**

FOOTWEAR MANUAL (US/0095-1048) [01796182] **1084**

FOOTWEAR NEWS (US/0162-914X) [04255291] **1084**

FOOTWEAR NEWS AUSTRALIA (AT/0725-3362) [I07253362] **1084**

FOOTWEAR NEWS FACT BOOK (US/0429-0208) [01799374] **1084**

FOOTWEAR NEWS MAGAZINE (US/0888-2053) [06780064] **1084**

FOOTWEAR PLUS (US/1054-898X) [23010173] **1084**

FOOTWEAR STATISTICS (CN/0380-707X) [02443812] 1084, **1088**

FOOTWORK (US/0743-2259) [10535826] **2846**

FOR (US) [02510606] **2379**

FOR A CHANGE (CN) **2533**

FOR FORMULATION CHEMISTS ONLY (US/0887-736X) [23895071] **975**

FOR HIM (UK) **3995**

FOR PARENTS *CEASED.* (US/0277-612X) [07612107] **2280**

FOR QUATTRO (US/0895-5603) [16689240] **1286**

FOR REFERENCE FROM METRO (US) [21370379] **3211**

● FOR THE BRIDE BY DEMETRIOS (UNITED KINGDOM ED.) (US/1064-7996) [26393916] 5557, **2280**

FOR THE CORPORATE EXECUTIVE (US) [16810893] **676**

FOR THE DEFENSE (AUSTIN) (US/0091-1011) [01786471] **3107**

FOR THE DEFENSE (MILWAUKEE, WIS.) (US/0015-6884) [01569686] **3089**

FOR THE LEARNING OF MATHEMATICS : AN INTERNATIONAL JOURNAL OF MATHEMATICS EDUCATION (CN/0228-0671) [07805838] 1895, **3505**

FOR THE LOVE OF CROSS STITCH (US/1040-3965) [18396349] **5184**

FOR THE RECORD (US/0896-1913) [16947094] **3140**

FOR THE RECORD (US/0891-2653) [04742110] **2481**

FOR THE RECORD (PORTLAND, OR.) (US) [18031407] **2971**

FOR THE WORKING ARTIST (US) **320**

FOR YOU FROM CZECHOSLOVAKIA (XR/0015-6892) [02351407] **819**

FOR YOUNGER READERS (US/0093-2825) [01569687] 1063, **4388**

FOR YOUR CAREER INFORMATION (CN/0316-4764) [02603520] **1824**

FOR YOUR INFORMATION (NEW YORK, N. Y.) (US/0890-2992) [11843243] **320**

FOR YOUR INFORMATION (SAN DIEGO, CALIF.) (US/1064-1351) [09417150] 2971, **3211**

FORAGE NOTES (CN/0045-4168) [02950518] **88**

FORAGE RESEARCH (II/0379-0444) [01916853] **88**

FORAGE SEED UPDATE (CN/1186-7175) [24402046] **88**

FORAGES (FR/0046-4481) [I00464481] **2139**

Alphabetical Title Index — FOREIGN

FORAS TALUNTAIS See ECONOMICS AND RURAL WELFARE RESEARCH REPORT **81**

FORBES (US/0015-6914) [06465733] **676**

●FORBES MEDIACRITIC (US/1067-4926) [27247584] **2919**

●FORBES MEDIAGUIDE 500 (US/1067-4918) [27247545] **2919**

FORBUNDET MOD IMPERIALISMEN. AFRIKAKOMITEEN See AFRIKA BULLETIN **2637**

FORCA SINDICAL (BL) [26970783] **1675**

FORCE (ALBANY, N.Y.) (US) [09929817] **1675**

FORCE DE VENTE INFOS (FR) **676**

FORCE OUVRIERE HEBDO (FR/0399-4708) [10052226] **1675**

FORCE (ROME, ITALY) (IT/0394-5243) [19796783] **3164**

FORCES ARMEES RWANDAISES, LES (RW) [11202662] **4044**

FORCES FOLK (GW) [01791472] **4118**

FORCES (MONTREAL) (CN/0015-6957) [01081651] **2734**

FORCES SOUS-MARINES (FR) [11109094] **4176**

FORD FERGIE FARMER (US/0272-5290) [06874046] **88**

FORD FOUNDATION See CURRENT INTERESTS OF THE FORD FOUNDATION **5281**

FORD FOUNDATION See FORD FOUNDATION ANNUAL REPORT **4335**

FORD FOUNDATION ANNUAL REPORT (US/0071-7274) [01143142] **4335**

FORD FOUNDATION. LETTER - FORD FOUNDATION See FORD FOUNDATION REPORT, THE **1824**

●FORD FOUNDATION REPORT, THE (US/1063-7281) [25842541] **1824**

FORDERUNG DER BERUFLICHEN WEITERBILDUNG (GW) [22769394] **1913**

FORDERUNGSDIENST, DER (AU/0015-525X) [03101436] **88**

FORDHAM ENTERTAINMENT, MEDIA & INTELLECTUAL PROPERTY LAW FORUM (US/1056-4128) [22995466] **385, 1304, 2971**

●FORDHAM INTELLECTUAL PROPERTY, MEDIA & ENTERTAINMENT LAW JOURNAL (US) [29688269] **385, 1304, 2971**

FORDHAM INTERNATIONAL LAW JOURNAL (US/0747-9395) [07355022] **3128**

FORDHAM LAW REVIEW (US/0015-704X) [01569695] **2971**

FORDHAM URBAN LAW JOURNAL, THE (US/0199-4646) [01112939] **2971**

FORD'S DECK PLAN GUIDE (US/0096-1353) [01790841] **5449, 5474**

FORD'S FREIGHTER TRAVEL GUIDE ... AND WATERWAYS OF THE WORLD (US) [11694611] **5474**

FORD'S INTERNATIONAL CRUISE GUIDE (US/0015-7066) [01847053] **5449**

FORD'S TRAVEL GUIDES See FORD'S DECK PLAN GUIDE **5474**

FORDYCE LETTER, THE (US/0733-0324) [08510861] **1675**

FORDYCE NEWS-ADVOCATE (US/8750-4995) [11499966] **5631**

FORE (NORTH HOLLYWOOD, CALIF.) (US/0300-8509) [01390291] **4895**

FORECAST (US) **676**

FORECAST FM See FORECAST (SILVER SPRING) **1425**

FORECAST (LONDON, ONT.) (CN/0713-4150) [09099697] **1425**

FORECAST (LOS ANGELES) (US/0071-7282) [03574217] **1561**

FORECAST OF CONTRACTING OPPORTUNITIES / PREPARED BY OFFICE OF SMALL AND DISADVANTAGED BUSINESS UTILIZATION (US) [25030513] **676**

FORECAST OF HOUSING ACTIVITY (US/1056-5159) [23734319] **2823**

FORECAST (SILVER SPRING) (US/0270-3386) [06769157] **1425**

FORECASTER (US/0095-294X) [01456555] **1491**

FORECLOSURE LAW BULLETIN *CEASED.* (US/0889-9274) [12893653] **3086**

FORECOURT RETAILING (UK) [20053877] **4256**

FOREDRAG VID PYROTEKNIKDAGEN (SW/0348-6613) [02242764] **975**

FOREFRONT (BERKELEY) (US/0146-6232) [01351927] **1975**

FOREFRONT CO **4959**

FOREFRONT (COLUMBUS, OHIO) (US/1040-8495) [18550216] **4215**

FOREFRONT (NEW YORK) (US/0162-7260) [04182983] **3817**

FOREIGN ACTIVITY REPORT (US) **4649**

FOREIGN AFFAIRS (NEW YORK, N.Y.) (US/0015-7120) [01569702] **4521**

FOREIGN AFFAIRS RECORD (II/0536-9258) [01604654] **4522**

FOREIGN AFFAIRS REPORTS (II/0015-7155) [01774330] **4522**

FOREIGN AFFAIRS RESEARCH DOCUMENTATION CENTER See FOREIGN AFFAIRS RESEARCH SPECIAL PAPERS AVAILABLE, UNION OF SOVIET SOCIALIST REPUBLICS **416**

FOREIGN AFFAIRS RESEARCH SPECIAL PAPERS AVAILABLE, UNION OF SOVIET SOCIALIST REPUBLICS (US/0271-0226) [04452415] **416**

FOREIGN-AFFILIATED ENTERPRISES IN JAPAN--FULL TEXT OF ENTERPRISE BUREAU OF M.I.T.I. REPORT-- (JA) [01791295] **1635**

FOREIGN AGRICULTURAL ECONOMIC REPORT (US) [04687924] **88**

FOREIGN AGRICULTURAL TRADE OF THE UNITED AND STATES FISCAL YEAR ... SUPPLEMENT (US) [12542675] **836, 88**

FOREIGN AGRICULTURAL TRADE OF THE UNITED STATES (US/0046-4546) [04175706] **1635, 88**

FOREIGN AND COMPARATIVE STUDIES. SOUTH ASIAN SERIES (US) [06140861] **2651**

FOREIGN ANIMAL DISEASE REPORT (US/0091-8199) [01639625] **5510**

FOREIGN ASSISTANCE PROGRAM (US/0362-4153) [02338071] **2909**

FOREIGN BANK FOCUS See INTERNATIONAL BANKING FOCUS **792**

FOREIGN CAPITAL AFFILIATED ENTERPRISES IN JAPAN (JA) [02586337] **676**

FOREIGN CAR PRICES NEW & USED See PACE BUYER'S GUIDES. FOREIGN AND JAPANESE CAR PRICES, NEW & USED **5422**

FOREIGN COMMERCE HANDBOOK (US/8755-0679) [01299401] **836**

FOREIGN COMMERCE STATISTICAL REPORT : PORT OF BALTIMORE AND OTHER MARYLAND PORTS (US/0191-0434) [04769897] **836, 729**

FOREIGN COMMISSION RANKING REPORT (US) **899**

FOREIGN CONSULAR OFFICES IN THE UNITED STATES (US/0071-7320) [01241455] **4522**

FOREIGN CREDITS BY THE UNITED STATES GOVERNMENT See STATUS OF ACTIVE FOREIGN CREDITS OF THE U.S. GOVT.: FOREIGN CREDITS BY U.S. GOVT. AGENCIES **4750**

FOREIGN DIRECT INVESTMENT (FR) **899**

FOREIGN DIRECT INVESTMENT IN THE UNITED STATES ... TRANSACTIONS (US/0732-0418) [08276605] **899**

FOREIGN ECONOMIC TRENDS AND THEIR IMPLICATIONS FOR THE UNITED STATES *CEASED.* (US/0090-9467) [01786363] **1561**

FOREIGN EXCHANGE LETTER (US) **899**

FOREIGN EXCHANGE LONG-TERM OUTLOOK (US/0883-3575) [12031302] **1635**

FOREIGN FORUM YEARBOOK INTERNATIONAL (US/0732-1384) [08303360] **836**

FOREIGN GOVERNMENT AWARDS See FOREIGN GOVERNMENT AWARDS PROGRAM **4649**

●FOREIGN GOVERNMENT AWARDS PROGRAM (CN/1191-3282) [26290295] **4649**

FOREIGN INTELLIGENCE LITERARY SCENE (US/0749-9132) [09440378] **4522**

FOREIGN INVESTMENT ADVISORY SERVICE OCCASIONAL PAPER (US/1018-4902) [24336007] **899**

FOREIGN INVESTMENT IN CENTRAL AND EASTERN EUROPE (NE) **1635**

FOREIGN INVESTMENT IN THE UNITED STATES (US) [06113023] **899**

FOREIGN INVESTMENT IN THE US (UK/0958-3076) **899**

FOREIGN INVESTMENT REVIEW (CN/0702-6005) [03944303] **899**

FOREIGN INVESTORS' HANDBOOK : MAKING SUCCESSFUL US INVESTMENTS, THE (US) **899**

FOREIGN LABOR TRENDS. EASTERN CARIBBEAN (US) [17757045] **1675**

FOREIGN LANGUAGE ANNALS (US/0015-718X) [01334424] **1895, 3282**

FOREIGN LANGUAGE BOOKS (US/0748-4615) [10947201] **4828, 4388**

FOREIGN LODGING LIST (US) [08229227] **2805**

FOREIGN MEAT INSPECTION (US/0164-1824) [03336515] **211**

●FOREIGN MILITARY MARKETS, ASIA & PACIFIC RIM (US) **4522, 4044**

●FOREIGN MILITARY MARKETS, LATIN AMERICA & CARIBBEAN BASIN (US) **4522, 4044**

FOREIGN MILITARY MARKETS, MIDDLE EAST & AFRICA (US) **4522, 4044**

FOREIGN MILITARY MARKETS, NATO & EUROPE (US) **4522, 4044**

FOREIGN MILITARY SALES, FOREIGN MILITARY CONSTRUCTION SALES AND MILITARY ASSISTANCE FACTS AS OF ... (US/8756-5536) [08428710] **4044**

FOREIGN POLICY (US/0015-7228) [01785489] **4522**

FOREIGN POLICY ASSOCIATION See GREAT DECISIONS **4523**

FOREIGN POLICY BULLETIN (WASHINGTON, D.C.) (US/1052-7036) [21814773] **4522**

FOREIGN PROSPECTS (US) **836**

FOREIGN-RELATED TAX LAWS AND REGULATIONS OF THE PEOPLE'S REPUBLIC OF CHINA (NE) **4727**

FOREIGN RELATIONS JOURNAL (PH) [13844035] **4522**

FOREIGN RELATIONS OF THE UNITED STATES (US/0071-7355) [07809779] **4522**

FOREIGN REPORT (UK/0532-1328) [01569729] **4474**

FOREIGN SCOUTING SERVICE. LATIN AMERICA (SZ/0253-0279) [09454294] **4256**

FOREIGN SERVICE INSTITUTE (U.S.) See COMMUNICATIONS AND CLERICAL SKILLS PROGRAM; SCHEDULE OF COURSES **1912**

FOREIGN SERVICE JOURNAL (US/0146-3543) [01569733] **4522**

FOREIGN TAX LAW BI-WEEKLY BULLETIN (US/0095-7291) [01795055] **3128**

FOREIGN TECHNOLOGY / NTIS See NTIS ALERT. FOREIGN TECHNOLOGY **5135**

FOREIGN TOURIST ARRIVALS BY SELECTED STATES- AND PORTS-OF-ENTRY (US/0270-7985) [06007682] **5474**

FOREIGN TRADE ACCORDING TO THE STANDARD INTERNATIONAL TRADE CLASSIFICATION (SITC)--SPECIAL TRADE / FEDERAL STATISTICAL OFFICE, WIESBADEN (GW) [09554461] **836**

FOREIGN TRADE ANNUAL REPORT; VIRGINIA PORTS (US/0095-3903) [01796736] **836**

FOREIGN TRADE, AUSTRALIA, EXPORTS See FOREIGN TRADE, AUSTRALIA, MERCHANDISE EXPORTS, DETAILED COMMODITY TABLES **729**

FOREIGN TRADE AUSTRALIA, INTERNATIONAL CARGO (AT) [I10379088] **5382, 5401**

FOREIGN TRADE, AUSTRALIA. MERCHANDISE EXPORTS / AUSTRALIAN BUREAU OF STATISTICS (AT/1036-9449) [25119936] **836, 729**

FOREIGN TRADE, AUSTRALIA, MERCHANDISE EXPORTS, DETAILED COMMODITY TABLES (AT/1037-888X) [I1037888X] **836, 729**

FOREIGN TRADE, AUSTRALIA. MERCHANDISE IMPORTS / AUSTRALIAN BUREAU OF STATISTICS (AT/1036-904X) [25111318] **836, 729**

FOREIGN TRADE, AUSTRALIA. MERCHANDISE IMPORTS. DETAILED COMMODITY TABLES (AT/0819-9868) [25473248] **836, 729**

FOREIGN TRADE BULLETIN (II/0015-7317) [06126607] **836**

FOREIGN TRADE BY COMMODITIES / OECD DEPARTMENT OF ECONOMICS AND STATISTICS (FR) [10059444] **836**

FOREIGN TRADE FAIRS NEW PRODUCTS NEWSLETTER (US/0883-4687) [12157727] **836**

FOREIGN TRADE (MCLEAN, VA.) (US/1055-1468) [23093391] **836**

FOREIGN TRADE OF THE COMMUNITY (LU) [19614584] **836**

FOREIGN TRADE OF THE DEMOCRATIC PEOPLE'S REPUBLIC OF KOREA (KN) [02349368] **836**

FOREIGN TRADE OF THE PEOPLE'S REPUBLIC OF CHINA. LE COMMERCE EXTERIEUR DE LA REPUBLIQUE POPULAIRE DE CHINE (LU) [06219965] **836**

FOREIGN TRADE REVIEW (II/0015-7325) [01774331] **836**

FOREIGN TRADE STATISTICAL DIGEST (SJ/0522-246X) [02242032] **836, 729**

FOREIGN — Alphabetical Title Index

FOREIGN TRADE STATISTICS FOR AFRICA. SERIES A: DIRECTION OF TRADE. STATISTIQUES AFRICAINES DU COMMERCE EXTERIEUR. SERIE. ECHANGES PAR PAYS (US) [05796004] 836, **729**

FOREIGN TRADE STATISTICS FOR AFRICA. SERIES B. TRADE BY COMMODITY. STATISTIQUES AFRICAINES DU COMMERCE EXTERIEUR. SERIE ECHANGES PAR PRODUITS (US) [05792136] 836, **729**

FOREIGN TRADE STATISTICS OF ASIA AND THE PACIFIC (US/1011-4858) [18095453] **836**

FOREIGN TRADE STATISTICS OF THE PHILIPPINES (PH) [02920769] 836, **729**

FOREIGN TRADE STATISTICS QUARTERLY (ISRAEL. LISHKAH HA-MERKAZIT LI-STATISTIKAH : 1980) (IS) [07312454] 836, **729**

FOREIGN TRADE : THE PORT OF NEW YORK AND NEW JERSEY (US/0163-9382) [04525348] **836**

FOREIGN TRAVEL & IMMUNIZATION GUIDE (US) [07044684] 4776, **5474**

FOREMOST FILM OF ... (US/0145-3556) [04279039] **4071**

FORENINGER REGISTRERET I (DK) [19549640] **2734**

FORENSIA See FORENSIA JAHRBUCH **3833**

FORENSIA JAHRBUCH (GW) **3833**

FORENSIC ACCOUNTING REVIEW (US/8756-8888) [11679694] 3164, **3100**

FORENSIC BULLETIN (US/0277-982X) [07674117] **3164**

FORENSIC DRUG ABUSE ADVISOR, THE (US/1048-8731) [21056567] 3980, **1344**

FORENSIC LINGUISTICS: THE INTERNATIONAL JOURNAL OF LANGUAGE AND THE LAW (UK/1350-1771) 2972, **3282**

FORENSIC OF PI KAPPA DELTA, THE (US/0015-735X) [05669707] **1111**

FORENSIC PHOTOGRAPHY (UK) [01778985] **4369**

FORENSIC PSYCHIATRIC SERVICES COMMISSION OF BRITISH COLUMBIA See ANNUAL REPORT / FORENSIC PSYCHIATRIC SERVICES COMMISSION OF BRITISH COLUMBIA **3920**

FORENSIC QUARTERLY, THE (US/0196-304X) [02447011] **1111**

FORENSIC REPORTS **CEASED.** (US/0888-692X) [13692275] **3740**

FORENSIC SCIENCE INTERNATIONAL (SZ/0379-0738) [04590488] **3740**

FORENSIC SCIENCE PROGRESS (GW/0930-1461) [13196063] **3740**

FORENSIC SCIENCE REVIEW (US/1042-7201) [19114973] **3740**

FORENSIC SERVICES DIRECTORY (US/0192-3145) [05015248] **2972**

FORESIGHT (EDMONTON) (CN/0711-3927) [08507343] **5179**

FORESIGHT (LONDON, ENGLAND) (UK) [19714763] **868**

FORESIGHT (MONTREAL) (CN/0384-5958) [03279098] **2881**

FORESIGHT (RESTON, VA.) (US/1063-8407) [26152607] **676**

FORESIGHT (SACKVILLE) (CN/0228-2429) [06859925] **1824**

FORESIGHT (TORONTO) (CN/0710-0663) [08693674] 5415, **4776**

FORESIGHT (WESTLAKE VILLAGE, CALIF.) (US/1040-0753) [18311795] **868**

FORESKRIFTER OM STATLIG TJANSTEPENSIONERING / STATENS ARBETSGIVARVERK (SW/0348-1115) [10210671] **1675**

FOREST (US/0965-2051) **5373**

FOREST AND BIRD (NZ) [05873430] **4165**

FOREST & CONSERVATION HISTORY (US/1046-7009) [20496086] 2194, **2379**

FOREST AND TIMBER **SUSPENDED.** (AT/0015-7392) [01569748] **2400**

FOREST CITY SUMMIT (FOREST CITY, IOWA : 1947) (US) [16151448] **5670**

FOREST ECOLOGY AND MANAGEMENT (NE/0378-1127) [03131594] **2379**

FOREST ENGINEERING RESEARCH INSTITUTE OF CANADA See WORK PROGRAM / FERIC **2398**

FOREST FARMER (US/0015-7406) [01569750] **2379**

FOREST FIRE NEWS (US/0886-5841) [02771582] 2290, **2379**

FOREST GENETIC RESOURCES INFORMATION (IT/0259-2894) [07389661] **2380**

●FOREST GENETICS (XO/1335-048X) 545, **2380**

FOREST-GRAM SOUTH (US) [02771957] **2380**

FOREST H. BELT'S YEARBOOK OF CONSUMER ELECTRONICS (US/0093-3155) [01791226] **2055**

FOREST HILL VILLAGER (CN/0715-464X) [09166873] **5784**

FOREST HISTORY SOCIETY See MEMBERSHIP DIRECTORY - FOREST HISTORY SOCIETY **2388**

FOREST INDUSTRIES DIRECTORY, BUYERS' AND SELLERS' GUIDE **CEASED.** (AT) [09543730] **2380**

FOREST INDUSTRIES (PORTLAND, OR.) See WOOD TECHNOLOGY **2406**

FOREST INDUSTRIES (SAN FRANCISCO, CALIF.) (US/0015-7430) [01569754] **2400**

FOREST INDUSTRY LECTURE SERIES (CN) [05513996] **2380**

FOREST INSECT AND DISEASE CONDITIONS : CARIBOO FOREST REGION (CN/0226-3793) [06758488] **2380**

FOREST INSECT AND DISEASE CONDITIONS IN THE NORTHERN REGION (US/0195-8410) [05904197] **2380**

FOREST INSECT AND DISEASE CONDITIONS IN THE PACIFIC NORTHWEST (US/0198-8018) [05835568] **2380**

FOREST INSECT AND DISEASE CONDITIONS IN THE UNITED STATES (US/0160-5143) [02096739] **2380**

FOREST INSECT AND DISEASE CONDITIONS. INTERMOUNTAIN REGION (US/0272-8737) [06935055] **2380**

FOREST INSECT AND DISEASE CONDITIONS : KAMLOOPS FOREST REGION (CN/0226-3777) [06758434] **2380**

FOREST INSECT AND DISEASE CONDITIONS: NELSON FOREST REGION (CN/0226-3785) [06758449] **2380**

FOREST INSECT AND DISEASE CONDITIONS : PRINCE GEORGE FOREST REGION (CN/0226-3769) [06758442] **2380**

FOREST INSECT AND DISEASE CONDITIONS: PRINCE RUPERT FOREST REGION (CN/0226-3750) [06758421] **2380**

FOREST INSECT AND DISEASE CONDITIONS: VANCOUVER FOREST REGION (CN/0226-3742) [06758482] **2380**

FOREST INSECT AND DISEASE CONDITIONS : YUKON TERRITORY (CN/0226-4188) [06758474] **2380**

FOREST LOG (SALEM) (US/0015-7449) [01569758] **2380**

FOREST MANAGEMENT UPDATE (US) **2380**

FOREST NOTES (US/0015-7457) [01569762] **2380**

FOREST PARK NEWS (US/8750-7455) [11723683] **5660**

●FOREST PEOPLE (WILLOWDALE) (CN/1195-0560) [29790323] **2380**

FOREST PEST CONDITIONS IN THE NORTHEAST (US/0160-6492) [03145258] **2380**

FOREST PESTS AND DISEASES / FORESTRY COMMISSION, TASMANIA (AT) [10462539] **2380**

FOREST PLANNING-CANADA (CN/0832-1655) [15561697] **2380**

FOREST PRESS (TIONESTA, PA. : 1953) (US) [12396468] **5736**

FOREST PRODUCTS (UK/0951-581X) [20314306] **2380**

FOREST PRODUCTS (IT) [19979292] **2380**

FOREST PRODUCTS ABSTRACTS (UK/0140-4784) [03821089] 2380, **2399**

FOREST PRODUCTS AND PAPER MONTHLY See PAPER AND FOREST PRODUCTS / SALOMON BROTHERS **2390**

FOREST PRODUCTS DIRECTORY FOR THE STATE OF WASHINGTON (US) [06070242] **2380**

FOREST PRODUCTS JOURNAL (US/0015-7473) [01569763] **2380**

FOREST PRODUCTS NEWS (US) [05167670] **2381**

FOREST PRODUCTS RESEARCH LABORATORY, PRINCES RISBOROUGH See BULLETIN - FOREST PRODUCTS RESEARCH. DEPARTMENT OF THE ENVIRONMENT **2376**

FOREST PRODUCTS RESEARCH SOCIETY See MEMBER NEWSLETTER - FOREST PRODUCTS RESEARCH SOCIETY **2388**

FOREST REPUBLICAN, THE (US) [13139060] **5767**

FOREST RESEARCH BULLETIN (TH) [05314101] **2381**

FOREST RESEARCH COUNCIL OF BRITISH COLUMBIA See ANNUAL REPORT - FOREST RESEARCH COUNCIL OF BRITISH COLUMBIA **2374**

FOREST RESEARCH IN THE SOUTHEAST (US/0748-1586) [02902330] **2381**

FOREST RESEARCH INFORMATION PAPER (CN/0319-9118) [03820973] **2381**

FOREST RESEARCH NOTE (CN/0381-2650) [02444222] **2381**

FOREST RESEARCH NOTE (US) [01482809] **2381**

FOREST RESEARCH NOTE / SOLOMON ISLANDS, FORESTRY DIVISION (BP) [10235381] **2381**

FOREST RESEARCH REPORT (MY) [04225230] **2381**

FOREST RESEARCH REPORT (CN) [03588659] **2381**

FOREST RESEARCH SERIES / DEPARTMENT OF FORESTRY (US) [05592878] **2381**

FOREST RESEARCH (TORONTO) (CN/0704-2809) [10433928] **2381**

FOREST RESOURCE REPORT - UNITED STATES. FOREST SERVICE (US/0071-755X) [01127102] **2381**

FOREST SCENE, THE (CN/0046-4589) [02012104] **2381**

FOREST SCIENCE (US/0015-749X) [01569773] **2381**

FOREST SCIENCE. MONOGRAPH **CEASED.** (US/0071-7568) [01426122] **2381**

FOREST SERVICE ORGANIZATIONAL DIRECTORY (US/0160-9904) [01978365] **2381**

FOREST SERVICE RESEARCH ACCOMPLISHMENTS See FOREST SERVICE RESEARCH ACCOMPLISHMENTS **2381**

FOREST SERVICE RESEARCH ACCOMPLISHMENTS (US/0090-239X) [01784885] **2381**

FOREST SERVICE RESEARCH PAPER ITF (PR/0565-6338) [02671049] **2381**

FOREST SERVICE RESOURCE BULLETIN SE (US) [04511466] **2381**

FOREST STATISTICS FOR IOWA (US/0146-4159) [02943357] 2381, **2399**

FOREST TIMES (CN/0706-7747) [05018375] **2381**

FOREST WATCH (US/1057-2724) [13515018] **2381**

FORESTA: ROMANIAN WOOD AND FURNITURE REVIEW (RM) [09544230] 2905, **2400**

FORESTERIE ATOUT (CN/0711-5660) [08482327] **2381**

FORESTERIE SANS DETOUR, LA (CN/0844-6334) [19869684] **2381**

FORESTRY (IT) [08658886] **2381**

FORESTRY ABSTRACTS (UK/0015-7538) [01282465] 2381, **2399**

FORESTRY AND BRITISH TIMBER (UK) [03188434] **2400**

FORESTRY, ANNUAL REPORT (AT) [14286530] **2381**

FORESTRY ASSOCIATION OF NIGERIA See PROCEEDINGS OF THE ANNUAL CONFERENCE OF THE FORESTRY ASSOCIATION OF NIGERIA **2391**

FORESTRY BULLETIN (CLEMSON, S.C.) (US/0093-0083) [04387116] **2381**

FORESTRY CHRONICLE, THE (CN/0015-7546) [01306287] **2381**

FORESTRY COMMISSION BULLETIN (UK) [13857586] **2382**

FORESTRY COMMISSION FIELD BOOK (UK) [16943670] **2382**

FORESTRY, GAS AND OIL REVIEW See CANADIAN RESOUCRES REVIEW **2377**

FORESTRY-GEOLOGICAL REVIEW (US) [01287362] 1376, **2382**

FORESTRY INFORMATION PAMPHLET / SOLOMON ISLANDS, FORESTRY DIVISION (BP) [10235400] **2382**

FORESTRY LOG (AT) [01780561] **2382**

FORESTRY (LONDON) (UK/0015-752X) [01310944] **2382**

FORESTRY NEWSLETTER (AVONDALE ESTATES) (US/0164-4661) [04748223] **2382**

FORESTRY NEWSLETTER (SAULT STE. MARIE) (CN/0825-1770) [11076563] **2382**

●FORESTRY, OIL & GAS REVIEW (CN/1196-278X) [29205941] **2382**

FORESTRY ON THE HILL **CEASED.** (CN/1185-9598) [25882742] **2382**

FORESTRY REPORT (OTTAWA) (CN/0824-3824) [10392495] **2382**

FORESTRY REPORT R8-FR (US/1057-2139) [10500945] **2382**

FORESTRY RESEARCH INSTITUTE OF NIGERIA See ANNUAL REPORT OF THE FORESTRY RESEARCH INSTITUTE OF NIGERIA FOR THE PERIOD ... **2375**

Alphabetical Title Index   **FORSCHUNGSBERICHT**

FORESTRY RESEARCH NOTE (CAMAS) *CEASED.* (US/0094-4181) [01780581] **2382**

FORESTRY RESEARCH REPORT (US/0091-1313) [01952262] **2382**

FORESTRY RESEARCH WEST (US/0195-5861) [05140649] **2382**

FORESTRY SCIENCES (NE/0924-5480) [09188752] **2382**

FORESTRY SUPPLIERS, INC *See* CATALOG - FORESTRY SUPPLIERS, INC **2377**

FORESTRY TECHNICAL REPORT (CN/0381-1786) [02573077] **2382**

FORESTRY WAGE SURVEY. ARKANSAS *See* OCCUPATIONAL COMPENSATION SURVEY--PAY ONLY. ARKANSAS--FORESTRY / U.S. DEPARTMENT OF LABOR, BUREAU OF LABOR STATISTICS **1697**

FORESTRY WAGE SURVEY. MISSISSIPPI *See* OCCUPATIONAL COMPENSATION SURVEY--PAY ONLY. MISSISSIPPI--FORESTRY / U.S. DEPARTMENT OF LABOR, BUREAU OF LABOR STATISTICS **1698**

FORESTS AND PEOPLE (US/0015-7589) [01371302] **2382**

FORET CONSERVATION (CN/0380-321X) [01569789] 2194, **2382**

FORET DE CHEZ-NOUS (1990) (CN/1180-4270) [23237060] **2382**

FORET ET PAPIER (CN/0319-762X) [02442927] **4233**

FORET, LA (SZ) [09545144] **2382**

FORET MEDITERRANEENNE (FR/0245-484X) [06545560] **2382**

FORET PRIVEE (1977), LA (FR/0153-0216) [03307753] **2382**

FORET WALLONE (BE) **2382**

FORETS DE FRANCE ET ACTION FORESTIERE (FR) [09545218] **2382**

FORFATTNINGAR OM UPPBORD M.M (SW) [02336102] **4727**

FORGE (JONESVILLE, MICH.) (US/0735-6218) [08253623] **2448**

FORGE (MONTREAL) (CN/0703-4520) [03453041] **4541**

FORGE (MONTREAL. EDITION FRANCAISE) (CN/0703-4539) [03439517] **4541**

FORGET ME NOT (ANCHORAGE) (US/0145-3009) [02722206] **2320**

FORGING (CLEVELAND, OHIO) (US/1054-1756) [22775255] **4565**

FORHANDLINGER - DET KONGELIGE NORSKE VIDENSKABERS SELSKAB (NO/0368-6302) [01760493] **5105**

FORIEGN LAW. CURRENT SOURCES OF CODES AND BASIC LEGISLATION IN JURISDICTIONS OF THE WORLD (US) **3128**

FORKS FORUM-PENINSULA HERALD (US) [16999379] **5761**

FORKTAIL (UK/0950-1746) [I09501746] **5617**

FORM (SW/0015-766X) [01569795] 298, **2900**

FORM (ALEXANDRIA) (US/0532-1700) [05141290] 924, **4565**

FORM & FUNCTION (US/0015-7686) [06333083] **615**

FORM (CAMBRIDGE, ENGLAND) (UK/0532-1697) [01569792] **350**

FORM FUNCTION FINLAND (FI/0358-8904) [07782355] **2098**

FORM (SEEHEIM-JUGENHEIM, WEST GERMANY) (GW/0015-7678) [01569793] **2098**

FORMA Y COLOR COLOMBIA (CK) [25839627] **350**

FORMA Y FUNCION (CK/0120-338X) [09021647] **3282**

FORMACION POLITICA PARA LA DEMOCRACIA (AG) [10428001] **4649**

FORMAL ASPECTS OF COMPUTING (UK/0934-5043) [19718812] **1247**

FORMAL ETHICS OPINION *See* FORMAL ETHICS OPINION / BOARD OF PROFESSIONAL RESPONSIBILITY OF THE SUPREME COURT OF TENNESSEE **2250**

FORMAL ETHICS OPINION / BOARD OF PROFESSIONAL RESPONSIBILITY OF THE SUPREME COURT OF TENNESSEE (US) [09038344] **2250**

FORMAL METHODS IN SYSTEM DESIGN (US/0925-9856) **1247**

FORMAL OPINIONS - COMMITTEE ON PROFESSIONAL ETHICS, NEW YORK STATE BAR ASSOCIATION (US) [04866821] 2250, **2972**

FORMAT (ANN ARBOR, MICH.) (US/1053-1742) [19372910] 1185, **1209**

FORMAT CINEMA (CN/0711-3315) [08649527] **4071**

FORMAT (MINNETONKA, MINN.) (US/0279-6058) [07114410] **759**

FORMAT (ST. CHARLES) (US/0190-678X) [06767747] **350**

FORMATION EMPLOI (FR) [10560739] **1675**

FORMATION FRANCE (FR/0395-9740) [I03959740] **1747**

FORMATION FRANCE *See* FORMATION LE MENSUEL **1747**

FORMATION GENERALE DES JEUNES, L'EDUCATION PRESCOLAIRE, L'ENSEIGNEMENT PRIMAIRE ET L'ENSEIGNEMENT SECONDAIRE, INSTRUCTION, LA (CN/1187-4813) [25352056] **1747**

FORMATION LE MENSUEL (FR) **1747**

FORMATION PROFESSIONNELLE CONTINUE, RAPPORT D'ACTIVITE (FR) [10755558] **1675**

FORMATION PROFESSIONNELLE DES JEUNES ET DES ADULTES DANS LES COMMISSIONS SCOLAIRES, INSTRUCTION, LA (CN/1182-476X) [25589770] **1747**

FORMATIONS DE RECHERCHE, LES (FR) [02353197] **5105**

FORMATO 16 (PN) [12207722] **4071**

FORMAZIONE 80 (IT) **1800**

FORMAZIONE DOMANI (IT) **1879**

FORMAZIONE E LAVORO (IT) **1879**

FORMAZIONE E SOCIETA (IT) [11648063] **1747**

FORMAZIONE INDICATIVA DEL COSTA DI PRODUZIONE DEI GETTI DI GHISA (IT) **4002**

FORMAZIONE PSICHIATRICA : PERIODICO TRIMESTRALE A CURA DELLA CLINICA PSICHIATRICA DELL'UNIVERSITA DI CATANIA (IT) [09848872] **3925**

FORME E LA STORIA, LE (IT) [16714089] 5200, **3388**

FORMER U.S.S.R. MONITOR *CEASED.* (US/1062-614X) [25331762] **2688**

FORMES ET STRUCTURES : ARCHITECTURE, GENIE CIVIL, ENVIRONNEMENT (FR) [25540325] 2023, **298**

FORMING AND FABRICATING (US) **2098**

FORMIROVANIE I KONTROL KACESTVA POVERHNOSTNYH VOD (RU/0130-5824) [03690526] 5533, **455**

FORMIROVANIE ISTORICHESKOGO MYSHLENIIA SHKOLNIKOV / MINISTERSTVO PROSVESHCHENIIA RSFSR, CHELIABINSKII GOSUDARSTVENNYI PEDAGOGICHESKII INSTITUT [I] CHELIABINSKII INSTITUT USOVERSHENSTVOVANIIA UCHITELEI (RU) [07792700] **1747**

FORMS AND DIRECT MAIL MANUFACTURERS MARKET PLACE (US) **676**

FORMS OF BUSINESS AGREEMENTS *See* FORMS OF BUSINESS AGREEMENTS & RESOLUTIONS **676**

FORMS OF BUSINESS AGREEMENTS & RESOLUTIONS (US/0730-2665) [09434571] **676**

FORMSMFG (US/1042-3028) [17915683] **676**

FORMULA (IT) **4474**

FORMULA 80 (IT) **4474**

FORMULARIO 4 CODICI TRIBUTARI *See* FORMULARIO TRIBUTARIO ADEMPIMENTI E RICORSI **1491**

FORMULARIO TRIBUTARIO ADEMPIMENTI E RICORSI (IT) **2972**

FORMULARIO TRIBUTARIO ADEMPIMENTI E RICORSI (IT) **1491**

FORMULARY OF PAINTS AND OTHER COATINGS (US) [04367178] **4224**

FORNERI, IL (CN/0713-0627) [08655586] **3282**

FORNEY MESSENGER (US) [14249787] **5750**

FORNVANNEN (SW/0015-7813) [02003175] **2688**

FORO AMMINISTRATIVO (ANNUAL) (IT) [10461643] **3093**

FORO AMMINISTRATIVO E DELLE ACQUE PUBBLICHE (ANNUAL) *See* FORO AMMINISTRATIVO (ANNUAL) **3093**

FORO ARCHIVISTICO : REVISTA TECNICA DEL SISTEMA NACIONAL DE ARCHIVOS (MX/0199-669X) [25564910] **2481**

FORO DEL JURISTA (CK/0121-0335) [I01210335] **2972**

FORO INTERNACIONAL (MX/0185-013X) [01569808] **4474**

FORO INTERNACIONAL (IN STRUGGLE (ORGANIZATION)) (CN/0229-172X) [08436285] **4542**

FORO ITALIANO, IL (IT/0015-783X) [01569809] **2972**

FORO ITALIANO. MASSIMARIO, IL (IT) [04379160] **2972**

FORO MONDIALE DELLA SANITA (IT) **4776**

FORPRIDECOM TECHNICAL NOTE (PH) [09065269] **2382**

FORRILIUM CATALOGUS. I: ANIMALIA (NE) [02113597] **4227**

FORRUM (MONTREAL) (CN/1188-2344) [25796400] **4305**

FORSAKRINGSTIDNINGEN (STOCKHOLM, SWEDEN) (SW/0015-7880) [09462767] **2881**

FORSCHENDE KOMPLEMENTARMEDIZIN (SZ) **3577**

FORSCHUNG AN DER TECHNISCHEN UNIVERSITAT BERLIN (GW) [03337967] **5105**

FORSCHUNG (BOPPARD) (GW/0172-1518) [08614692] **5105**

FORSCHUNG IM INGENIEURWESEN (GW/0015-7899) [01569812] **1975**

FORSCHUNG UND DOKUMENTATION IN OSTERREICH (AU) [03720240] **1562**

FORSCHUNG UND ERGEBNISSE DES BEREICHES MEDIZIN (GW/0440-1298) [10982850] **3577**

FORSCHUNG UND FORTBILDUNG IN DER CHIRURGIE DES BEWEGUNGSAPPARATES (GW) [11176351] **3965**

FORSCHUNG UND VEROFFENTLICHUNGEN DES INTERNATIONALEN INSTITUTS FUR UMWELT UND GESELLSCHAFT (GW) [10221143] **2172**

FORSCHUNG ZUR BIBEL (GW) [06052335] **4959**

FORSCHUNGEN UND BERICHTE - STAATLICHE MUSEEN BERLIN (GW/0067-6004) [01519594] **4088**

FORSCHUNGEN ZU PAUL VALERY (GW/0934-5337) [20780654] **3388**

FORSCHUNGEN ZUE ANTIKEN SKLAVEREI (GW/0071-7665) [01604712] **4508**

FORSCHUNGEN ZUM ROMISCHEN RECHT (GW) [01569818] **1077**

FORSCHUNGEN ZUR ETHNOLOGIE UND SOZIALPSYCHOLOGIE (GW/0429-1530) [01372865] **236**

FORSCHUNGEN ZUR GESCHICHTE DER ALTEREN DEUTSCHEN LITERATUR (GW/0177-9370) [09201820] **3388**

FORSCHUNGEN ZUR GESCHICHTE DER STAEDTE UND MAERKTE OESTERREICHS (AU/05261217) **2688**

FORSCHUNGEN ZUR GESCHICHTE OBEROSTERREICHS (AU/0429-1565) [01372902] **2688**

FORSCHUNGEN ZUR KIRCHEN- UND DOGMENGESCHICHTE (GW/0532-2154) [01373986] **4959**

FORSCHUNGEN ZUR KUNSTGESCHICHTE UND CHRISTLICHEN ARCHAOLOGIE (GW) [01569828] **350**

FORSCHUNGEN ZUR KUNSTGESCHICHTE UND CHRISTLICHEN ARCHAOLOGIE (GW/0532-2189) [01374060] 268, **350**

FORSCHUNGEN ZUR MITTELALTERLICHEN GESCHICHTE (GW/0071-7673) [01374078] **2688**

FORSCHUNGEN ZUR OBERRHEINISCHEN LANDESGESCHICHTE (GW/0532-2197) [02001637] **2688**

FORSCHUNGEN ZUR OSTEUROPAISCHEN GESCHICHTE (GW/0067-5903) [01077848] **2688**

FORSCHUNGEN ZUR RAUMENTWICKLUNG (GW/0341-244X) [03866766] **2823**

FORSCHUNGEN ZUR RELIGION UND LITERATUR DES ALTEN UND NEUEN TESTAMENTS (GW) [01569832] **5016**

FORSCHUNGEN ZUR SYSTEMATISCHEN UND OEKUMENISCHEN THEOLOGIE (GW/0429-162X) [05967998] **4959**

FORSCHUNGEN ZUR VOLKS- UND LANDESKUNDE (RM/0015-7902) [02261242] **2261**

FORSCHUNGEN ZUR VOR- UND FURGESCHICHTE (LEIPZIG, 1955-) (GE/0532-2243) [01997678] **2616**

FORSCHUNGS- UND SITZUNGSBERICHTE (GW/0515-9083) [01728454] **2823**

FORSCHUNGSBEITRAGE ZUR MUSIKWISSENSCHAFT (GW/0532-226X) [01374544] **4118**

FORSCHUNGSBERICHT AGRARTECHNIK DES ARBEITSKREISES FORSCHUNG UND LEHRE DER MAX-EYTH-GESELLSCHAFT (MEG) (GW) [12043312] 1976, **88**

FORSCHUNGSBERICHT — Alphabetical Title Index

FORSCHUNGSBERICHT AGRARTECHNIK DES ARBEITSKREISES FORSCHUNG UND LEHRE DER MEG *See* FORSCHUNGSBERICHT AGRARTECHNIK DES ARBEITSKREISES FORSCHUNG UND LEHRE DER MAX-EYTH-GESELLSCHAFT (MEG) **88**

FORSCHUNGSBERICHT / ARBEITSGEMEINSCHAFT GESAMTKONZEPT NEUSIEDLER SEE (AU) [19506486] **4165**

FORSCHUNGSBERICHT - BUNDESMINISTERIUM FUER FORSCHUNG UND TECHNOLOGIE. T, TECHNOLOGISCHE FORSCHUNG UND ENTWICKLUNG (GW/0340-7608) [03407608] **5105**

FORSCHUNGSBERICHT DER FREIEN UNIVERSITAT BERLIN (GW) [02515805] **1824**

FORSCHUNGSBERICHT DER UNIVERSITAT AUGSBURG (GW) [24262281] **455**

FORSCHUNGSBERICHT / DEUTSCHE FORSCHUNGSANSTALT FUER LUFT- UND RAUMFAHRT (GW/0939-2963) [24091480] **21**

FORSCHUNGSBERICHT / DEUTSCHE SPORTHOCHSCHULE KOLN (GW) [19762867] **4872**

FORSCHUNGSBERICHT / INSTITUT FUER PLASMAFORSCHUNG DER UNIVERSITAT STUTTGART (GW) [08753045] 4403, **3771**

FORSCHUNGSBERICHT. MATERIALBAND / UNIVERSITAT HAMBURG (GW/0344-1008) [11311304] **1824**

FORSCHUNGSBERICHT - UNIVERSITAT ULM (GW) [02828105] **5105**

FORSCHUNGSBERICHTE AUS TECHNIK UND NATURWISSENSCHAFTEN (GW/0343-5520) [12245195] **5105**

FORSCHUNGSBERICHTE DER BUNDESANSTALT FUER LANDTECHNIK, WIESELBURG (AU) [12223225] **88**

FORSCHUNGSBERICHTE DES INSTITUTS FUR VERKEHRSWISSENSCHAFT AN DER UNIVERSITAT ZU KOLN (GW/0588-3377) [04126106] **1824**

FORSCHUNGSBERICHTE DES LANDES NORDRHEIN-WESTFALEN (GW/0367-2492) [04643148] **5105**

FORSCHUNGSBERICHTE / INSTITUT FUER PHONETIK UND SPRACHLICHE KOMMUNIKATION DER UNIVERSITAT MUNCHEN (GW/0342-782X) [08600051] **3282**

FORSCHUNGSDOKUMENTATION RAUMORDNUNG, STADEBAU, WOHNUNGSWESEN *CEASED*. (GW) [05937446] **2823**

FORSCHUNGSFORDERUNGEN UND FORSCHUNGSAUFTRAGE (AU) [04375028] **5106**

FORSCHUNGSFORDERUNGSFONDS FUR DIE GEWERBLICHE WIRTSCHAFT *See* BERICHT - FORSCHUNGSFORDERUNGSFONDS FUR DIE GEWERBLICHE WIRTSCHAFT **5087**

FORSCHUNGSGESELLSCHAFT FUR STRASSEN- UND VERKEHRSWESEN (GERMANY) (GW) [10969306] **5440**

FORSCHUNGSINSTITUT FUR PHYSIK DER STRAHLANTRIEBE (STUTTGART, GERMANY) *See* MITTEILUNGEN **28**

FORSCHUNGSINSTITUT FUR WIRTSCHAFTSVERFASSUNG UND WETTBEWERB, COLOGNE *See* FIW-SCHRIFTENREIHE **1491**

FORSCHUNGSINSTITUT FUR WIRTSCHAFTSVERFASSUNG UND WETTBEWERB (COLOGNE, GERMANY) *See* SCHWERPUNKTE DES KARTELLRECHTS **3103**

FORSCHUNGSPOLITISCHE DOKUMENTATION (AU) [01788788] **5200**

FORSCHUNGSPOLITISCHE ZIELVORSTELLUNGEN (SZ) [09910506] **5106**

FORSCHUNGSPROGRAMM - BUNDESANSTALT FUR STRASSENWESEN, BEREICH UNFALLFORSCHUNG (GW/0170-5431) [04456152] 4776, **5440**

FORSCHUNGSPROJEKTE SOZIALISATION UND SOZIALPAEDAGOGIK (GW) [05714570] 5245, **1879**

FORSCHUNGSREPORT, ERNAHRUNG, LANDWIRTSCHAFT, FORSTEN (GW/0931-2277) [14282104] 2382, **88**

FORSCHUNGSVORHABEN / ZENTRALSTELLE FUER AGRARDOKUMENTATION UND -INFORMATION (GW/0939-7701) [26186933] 5510, 2382, **88**

FORSCHUNGSZENTRUM JULICH *See* JAHRESBERICHT **4448**

FORSIKRINGSSELSKAPER (NO/0801-0056) [01760747] **2881**

FORSIM REVIEW (US/0190-1257) [04621617] **2400**

FORSKINIGSSTIFTELSEN SKOGSARBETEN (STOCKHOLM, SWEDEN) *See* NYTT - FORSKNINGSSTIFTELSEN SKOGSARBETEN **2390**

FORSKNING, UTVECKLING OCH DEMONSTRATION INOM ENERGIOMRADET--EN GLOBAL OVERSIKT (SW) [06558384] **1944**

FORSKNINGSBIBLIOTEKSRADET (SWEDEN) *See* FBR AKTUELLT **3210**

FORSKNINGSRAPPORT (STOCKHOLMS UNIVERSITET. SOCIOLOGISKA INSTITUTIONEN) (SW/0284-351X) [21016036] **5245**

FORSKNINGSSTATISTIK, RESSOURCEFORBRUGET VED FORSKNING OG UDVIKLINGSARBEJDE I DEN OFFENTLIGE SEKTOR (DK) [20291857] **4649**

FORST UND HOLZ (HANNOVER, GERMANY : 1988) (GW/0932-9315) [17850639] **2383**

FORSTARCHIV (GW/0300-4112) [02407584] **2383**

FORSTLICHE FORSCHUNGSBERICHTE MUNCHEN (GW/0174-1810) [07967373] **2383**

FORSTLICHE UMSCHAU *CEASED*. (GW/0015-7988) [01375703] **2383**

FORSTTECHNISCHE INFORMATIONEN (GW/0427-0029) [04024449] **2383**

FORSTWISSENSCHAFTLICHE BEITRAEGE / ETH ZURICH, FACHBEREICH FORSTOKONOMIE UND FORSTPOLITIK (SZ) [16816446] **2383**

FORSTWISSENSCHAFTLICHES CENTRALBLATT (GW/0015-8003) [01377053] **2383**

FORSYNINGSBALANCER (LU) [03991017] **1607**

FORSYTH COUNTY GENEALOGICAL SOCIETY *See* FORSYTH COUNTY GENEALOGICAL SOCIETY JOURNAL, THE **2448**

FORSYTH COUNTY GENEALOGICAL SOCIETY JOURNAL, THE (US/0741-8159) [09810877] **2448**

FORSYTH COUNTY NEWS, THE (US/0747-2242) [10639106] **5653**

FORT (UK/0261-586X) [10916601] **4044**

FORT BRAGG ADVOCATE-NEWS (US/0886-8840) [13026220] **5635**

FORT BRANCH TIMES *See* SOUTH GIBSON STAR-TIMES **5667**

FORT BURGWIN RESEARCH CENTER *See* PUBLICATION - FORT BURGWIN RESEARCH CENTER **5143**

FORT COLLINS COLORADOAN (US) [15651945] **5642**

FORT COLLINS REVIEW (US/0744-3870) [08247057] **5642**

FORT COLLINS REVIEW (FORT COLLINS, COLO. : 1981) *See* FORT COLLINS TRIANGLE REVIEW **5643**

FORT COLLINS TRIANGLE REVIEW (US/1076-4631) [30608814] **5643**

FORT CONCHO AND THE SOUTH PLAINS JOURNAL *CEASED*. (US/1049-3239) [21204309] **2734**

FORT COVINGTON SUN *See* SUN (1993) **5721**

FORT FRANCES TIMES (CN) [03188480] **5784**

FORT HARE PAPERS (SA/0015-8054) [01317528] 1491, 2846, **5106**

FORT HENRIETTA NEWSLETTER (US/0899-658X) [14270241] **2734**

FORT INDUSTRY REFLECTIONS (US/0749-8381) [11165793] **2448**

FORT LAUDERDALE NEWS (US/0744-8147) [08582178] **5649**

FORT LUPTON PRESS (1981) (US/1056-2419) [19527934] **5643**

FORT MADISON DAILY DEMOCRAT (US/0746-4266) [10036563] **5670**

FORT MCMURRAY EXPRESS (CN/0715-4925) [09506538] **5784**

FORT MCMURRAY TODAY (CN/0316-7542) [02247842] **5784**

FORT MILL TIMES (US) [13622336] **5742**

FORT MORGAN TIMES, THE (US) [21479746] **5643**

FORT MYERS BEACH OBSERVER (US/0199-2945) [05759511] **5649**

FORT MYERS NEWS-PRESS (US) [01379240] **5649**

● FORT NORFOLK COURIER (US/1065-5263) [26625750] **2734**

FORT RILEY POST, THE (US) [11321544] **5675**

FORT SCOTT TRIBUNE, THE (US/8755-3171) [09694054] **5675**

FORT SMITH HISTORICAL SOCIETY *See* JOURNAL / FORT SMITH HISTORICAL SOCIETY, THE **2740**

FORT STOCKTON PIONEER, THE (US) [08564879] **5750**

FORT WORTH (US/0015-8089) [04010292] **2533**

FORT WORTH COMMERCIAL RECORDER (US/0015-8097) [06905905] **2972**

FORT WORTH STAR-TELEGRAM (US/0889-0013) [11420948] **5750**

FORTE (MILWAUKEE, WIS.) (US/0893-2220) [15466971] **4118**

FORTECKNING OVER ADVOKATER OCH ADVOKATBYRAER AR JAMIE STADGAR FOR SVERIGES ADVOKATSAMFUND (SW/0300-2055) [01784743] **2972**

FORTEGNELSE OVER NYERHVERVELSER / RADET FOR DE EUROPAEISKE FAELLESSKABER, BIBLIOTEKER-DOKUMENTATION *CEASED*. (BE) [10113389] **416**

FORTH DIMENSIONS (US/0884-0822) [05526288] **1286**

FORTHCOMING BOOKS (US/0015-8119) [01569855] **416**

FORTHCOMING BOOKS FOR CHILDREN *CEASED*. (US/0000-0965) [14277525] **3388**

FORTHCOMING BOOKS - NATIONAL LIBRARY OF CANADA (CN/1187-6301) [26066817] 3343, **3211**

FORTHCOMING INTERNATIONAL SCIENTIFIC AND TECHNICAL CONFERENCES (UK/0046-4686) [06831061] **5106**

FORTID OG NUTID (DK/0106-4797) [01569856] **2616**

FORTIN MAPOCHO DIARIO (CL) [20547397] **5798**

FORTITUDINE (US/0362-9910) [02397858] **4176**

FORTNIGHT (BELFAST) (IE/0046-4694) [01688014] 320, **3343**

● FORTNIGHTLY : THE NORTH AMERICAN UTILITIES BUSINESS MAGAZINE (US/1074-6099) [28880059] **4761**

FORTRAN FORUM (US/1061-7264) [11685858] **1279**

FORTRAN JOURNAL (US/1060-0221) [24849217] 1279, **1185**

FORTRESS *CEASED*. (UK) [20386407] **615**

FORTSCHRITT-BERICHTE DER VDI-ZEITSCHRIFTEN. REIHE 4, BAUINGENIEURWESEN (GW/0532-2669) [09022274] **2023**

FORTSCHRITT-BERICHTE DER VDI ZEITSCHRIFTEN. REIHE 8, MESS-, STEUERUNGS- UND REGELUNGSTECHNIK (GW/0341-1672) [11546199] **2055**

FORTSCHRITT-BERICHTE DER VDI ZEITSCHRIFTEN. REIHE 11, SCHWINGUNGS TECHNIK, LARMBEKAMPFUNG (GW/0506-3159) [09434606] **2230**

FORTSCHRITT BERICHTE DER VDI ZEITSCHRIFTEN. SERIES 1 : KONSTRUKTIONSTECHNIK (GW) **1976**

FORTSCHRITT BERICHTE DER VDI ZEITSCHRIFTEN. SERIES 16 : TECHNIK UND WIRTSCHAFT (GW) **1976**

FORTSCHRITT-BERICHTE VDI. REIHE 17, BIOTECHNIK (GW/0178-9600) [12365394] **456**

FORTSCHRITT-BERICHTE VDI-ZEITSCHRIFT. REIHE 4: BAUINGENIEURWESEN *See* FORTSCHRITT-BERICHTE DER VDI-ZEITSCHRIFTEN. REIHE 4, BAUINGENIEURWESEN **2023**

FORTSCHRITT UND FORTBILDUNG IN DER MEDIZIN (GW/0170-3331) [11876166] **3577**

FORTSCHRITTE AUF DEM GEBIETE DER RONTGENSTRAHLEN UND DER NUKLEARMEDIZIN. ERGANZUNGSBAND (GW/0178-4609) [01644093] **3941**

FORTSCHRITTE DER CHEMIE ORGANISCHER NATURSTOFFE (AU/0071-7886) [01278222] **1041**

FORTSCHRITTE DER DIAGNOSTIK (GW/0938-9407) [22457210] **3577**

FORTSCHRITTE DER FERTILITATSFORSCHUNG (GW/0344-6204) [04106910] **3761**

FORTSCHRITTE DER KIEFER- UND GESICHTS-CHIRURGIE (GW/0071-7916) [01569872] **1323**

FORTSCHRITTE DER KIEFERORTHOPAEDIE (GW/0015-816X) [01569873] **1323**

FORTSCHRITTE DER MEDIZIN (GW/0015-8178) [01569875] **3577**

FORTSCHRITTE DER MEDIZIN. SUPPLEMENT : DIE KONGRESSINFORMATION FUER DIE PRAXIS (GW/0932-5611) [19843905] **3577**

FORTSCHRITTE DER NEUROLOGIE, PSYCHIATRIE (GW/0720-4299) [07417093] 3925, **3833**

FORTSCHRITTE DER NEUROLOGIE - PSYCHIATRIE EDICION ESPANOLA (SP/0212-100X) [I0212100X] **3925**

FORTSCHRITTE DER OPERATIVEN DERMATOLOGIE (GW/0932-3848) [12960732] **3720**

FORTSCHRITTE DER OPHTHALMOLOGIE *See* GERMAN JOURNAL OF OPHTHALMOLOGY **3875**

FORTSCHRITTE DER OPHTHALMOLOGIE *See* OPHTHALMOLOGE : ZEITSCHRIFT DER DEUTSCHEN OPHTHALMOLOGISCHEN GESELLSCHAFT, DER **3877**

FORTSCHRITTE DER PFLANZENZUCHTUNG (GW/0301-2727) [01771975] **172**

FORTSCHRITTE DER PHYSIK (BERLIN : 1953) (GW/0015-8208) [02334398] **4403**

FORTSCHRITTE DER PHYSIKALISCHEN CHEMIE (GW/0071-7924) [01569883] **1052**

FORTSCHRITTE DER SICHERHEITSTECHNIK : BERICHTE AUS DER DECHEMA-FACHAUSSCHUSSE (GW) [19452168] **2862**

FORTSCHRITTE DER VERHALTENSFORSCHUNG (GW) [01145548] **4587**, **5510**

FORTSCHRITTE DER VETERINARMEDIZIN (GW/0301-2794) [01158427] **5510**

FORTSCHRITTE DER WASSERCHEMIE UND IHRER GRENZGEBIETE (GW/0071-7983) [01310938] **5533**

FORTSCHRITTE DER ZOOLOGIE (STUTTGART) (GW/0071-7991) [01569890] **5584**

FORTSCHRITTE IM ACKER- UND PFLANZENBAU *CEASED.* (GW/0301-2735) [01453308] **88**

FORTSCHRITTE IN DER ATOMSPEKTROMETRISCHEN SPURENANALYTIK (GW/0176-7984) [12396820] **4434**

FORTSCHRITTE IN DER GEOLOGIE VON RHEINLAND UND WESTFALEN (GW/0071-8009) [01569891] **1355**

FORTSCHRITTLICHE BETRIEBSEHRUNG UND INDUSTRIAL ENGINEERING (GW/0340-8302) [02241942] **2098**

FORTSCHRITTLICHE LANDWIRT, DER (AU) **88**

FORTSCHRITTSBERICHTE FUER ERNAHRUNG UND HANDWIRTSCHAFT (GW) [26266504] **88**

FORTUNE (US/0015-8259) [01569892] **676**

FORTUNE DIGEST (US/1048-8065) [21064130] **677**

FORTUNE FRANCE (FR/0989-2869) [20841589] **677**

FORTUNE INTERNATIONAL (US/0738-5587) [09590555] **677**

FORTUNE NEWS (US/0015-8275) [02326773] **3164**

FORUM (US) [18042915] **4959**

FORUM (GW) [19006391] **3282**

FORUM (US/1042-6817) [19105722] **4838**

FORUM (US) [06429177] **589**

FORUM (SZ) [20426874] **836**

FORUM (CI/0015-8445) [02081767] **3388**

FORUM (US/0894-3265) [20231308] **2449**

FORUM (AL-ANON), THE (US/0194-8121) [05033054] **1344**

FORUM (AMSTERDAM, NETHERLANDS : 1984) (NE) [11462305] **299**

FORUM / ASSOCIATION OF CANADIAN MEDICAL COLLEGES (CN/0836-3463) [18028059] **1824**, **3577**

FORUM BARCELONA (SP/0212-9965) [I02129965] **3577**

FORUM (BONNER, MONT.) (US/0883-4970) [12140990] **5016**

FORUM - CANADIAN COUNCIL ON 4-H CLUBS (CN/0715-5301) [09502411] **5231**

FORUM / CANADIAN SOCIETY FOR INDUSTRIAL SECURITY (CN/0823-0382) [09816163] **5177**

FORUM - CANADIAN TELEMATICS FORUM (CN/1181-8654) [23237401] **1111**

FORUM - CANADIAN URBAN TRANSIT ASSOCIATION (CN/1183-2282) [24266271] **5382**

FORUM - CANADIAN URBAN TRANSIT ASSOCIATION (CN/1183-2282) [24266264] **5382**

FORUM (CHICAGO), THE (US) [09567778] **2881**, **2972**

FORUM / CONFERENCE OF DEFENCE ASSOCIATIONS (CN/0848-8886) [21540562] **4044**

FORUM - COUNCIL OF EUROPE (FR/0252-0958) [04258237] **2516**

FORUM DER LETTEREN (NE/0015-8496) [01569900] 3282, **3388**

FORUM DER PSYCHOANALYSE (GW/0178-7667) [12960736] **4587**

FORUM DES AUDIOPHILES PARIS (FR/0760-7245) [I07607245] **4118**

FORUM (DEVON) (US/0149-967X) [03585799] 4388, **1747**

FORUM (DON MILLS) (CN/0380-3147) [02012153] **2881**

FORUM DU COMMERCE INTERNATIONAL (SZ) **836**

FORUM EKONOMI (IO) [08908654] **1491**

FORUM (FARGO, N.D.), THE (US/0895-1292) [09563116] **5725**

FORUM (FEDERATION CANADIENNE DES MUNICIPALITES) (CN/0704-7177) [23004057] **4649**

FORUM FOR ADVANCING BASIC EDUCATION AND LITERACY, THE (US) [25533477] **1747**

FORUM FOR APPLIED RESEARCH AND PUBLIC POLICY (US/0887-8218) [13419464] **1944**

FORUM FOR COMMERCE AND INDUSTRY (UK) [02438890] **836**

●FORUM FOR DEVELOPMENT STUDIES (NO) [27552716] **2909**

FORUM FOR EKONOMI OCH TEKNIK (FI/0533-070X) [09574097] **5106**

FORUM FOR MODERN LANGUAGE STUDIES (UK/0015-8518) [01335911] 3388, **3282**

FORUM FOR PROMOTING 3-19 COMPREHENSIVE EDUCATION (UK/0963-8253) [24765773] **1747**

FORUM FOR READING (US/0738-9523) [09712408] **1824**

FORUM FOR SOCIAL ECONOMICS, THE (US/0736-0932) [09038620] **1491**

FORUM FOR THE PROBLEMS OF ZIONISM, WORLD JEWRY AND THE STATE OF ISRAEL (IS) [08485771] **5047**

FORUM FOR UTVIKLINGSSTUDIER *See* FORUM FOR DEVELOPMENT STUDIES **2909**

FORUM - FORUM FOR YOUNG CANADIANS (CN/0826-1458) [10926462] **4474**

FORUM GAZETA MERCANTIL (BL) [10895720] **1562**

FORUM HACENDARIO (MX) [01792305] **4727**

FORUM HOMOSEXUALITAT UND LITERATURE (GW/0931-4091) [18203119] 2794, **3388**

FORUM INDEX, THE (US/0738-8411) [09674340] **5814**

FORUM INFORMATION BULLETIN : A SERVICE OF THE NATIONAL IMMIGRATION, REFUGEE & CITIZENSHIP FORUM (US) [19746715] **1918**

FORUM INSIDER, THE (US/1051-5666) [21990590] **2449**

FORUM INTERNATIONAL (MONTREAL. 1991) (CN/1183-1359) [25314066] **4522**

FORUM ITALICUM (US/0014-5858) [01568702] **3388**

FORUM IULII (IT/0393-0041) [05050096] 4088, **268**

FORUM - KIELER WISSENSCHAFTSVERLAG VAUK (GW/0721-474X) [11059478] **88**

FORUM KRITISCHE PSYCHOLOGIE (GW/0720-0447) [05217977] **4587**

FORUM LETTER (US/0046-4732) [01624256] **5060**

FORUM LINGUISTICUM (US/0163-0768) [03092663] **3282**

FORUM LITERARIO (US) [05325053] **3343**

FORUM MATHEMATICUM (GW/0933-7741) [19409050] **3506**

FORUM MODERNES THEATER (GW/0930-5874) [14878861] **5364**

FORUM MONDIAL DE LA SANTE (SZ/0251-8716) [I02518716] **4776**

FORUM MUSIKBIBLIOTHEK (GW/0173-5187) [08374792] 4118, **3211**

FORUM (NORTH HOLLYWOOD) (US/0164-6931) [04417140] **3107**

FORUM OF EDUCATION, THE *SUSPENDED.* (AT/0015-8542) [04578580] **1824**

FORUM OF PHI SIGMA IOTA, THE (US/0883-5640) [12173533] **3282**

●FORUM OF THE AMERICAN TARANTULA SOCIETY (US/1062-9718) [25826677] **5609**

FORUM - OHIO COALITION FOR THE EDUCATION OF HANDICAPPED CHILDREN (US/1073-225X) [29355539] **1879**

FORUM ON CORRECTIONS RESEARCH (CN/0847-0464) [20879223] **3164**

FORUM ON INFECTION (US/0148-4710) [03291233] **3577**

FORUM (ONTARIO CONFEDERATION OF UNIVERSITY FACULTY ASSOCIATIONS) (CN/0225-6096) [06958646] **1825**

FORUM PASCASARJANA (IO) [17276064] **88**

FORUM PENDIDIKAN SCIENCE DAN MATEMATIKA (IO) [01795847] **5106**

FORUM (REGINA, SASK.) (CN/0831-3016) [15996863] **3211**

FORUM / RISK MANAGEMENT FOUNDATION (US) [19963449] **3780**

FORUM (ROSSLYN, VA.) *See* NCBE FORUM **1766**

FORUM (ROSSLYN, VA.) (US/0884-7568) [04303066] **1747**

FORUM (SCRANTON, PA.) (US/0015-8399) [01569897] **2516**

FORUM (SEMARANG) (IO/0376-5687) [02393555] **5200**

FORUM, STADTE, HYGIENE (GW/0342-202X) [03645980] **2194**

FORUM STATISTICUM / VERBAND SCHWEIZERISCHER STATISTISCHER AMTER (SZ) [11109496] **5327**

FORUM / THE ASSOCIATION OF CANADIAN FACULTIES OF DENTISTRY (CN/0820-5949) [16856721] **1323**

FORUM (TORONTO. 1975) (CN/0381-1018) [03244997] **1825**

FORUM - UNITED STATES INFORMATION AGENCY (1982) (US/8755-0393) [09974250] **1895**

FORUM (VICTORIA) (CN/0709-2180) [05377979] **3140**

FORUM (VIENNA, AUSTRIA : 1946) (AU) [13152384] **1747**

FORUM (VIENNA, AUSTRIA : 1980) (AU) [06347998] **2516**

FORUM WARE (GW/0340-7705) [I03407705] **2194**

FORUM WARE (GW/0340-7705) [07492125] 1491, **677**

FORUM (WASHINGTON, D.C.) *See* NATIONAL SECURITY AFFAIRS FORUM, THE **4052**

FORUM (WASHINGTON, D.C.), THE (US/0015-8305) [04077680] **2972**

FORWARD (COLOMBO, SRI LANKA) (CE) [09390818] **2503**

FORWARD (MADISON, WIS.) (US/0745-3086) [08677200] **5557**

FORWARD (NEW YORK, N.Y.) (US/1051-340X) [21929953] **5716**

FORWARD PLAN FOR THE HEALTH SERVICES ADMINISTRATION (US/0196-4909) [03988509] **4776**

FORZA 7 *SUSPENDED.* (IT) **593**

FORZA MILAN (IT) **2487**

FOSSIL CNIDARIA (US) [08333122] **1376**

FOSSIL ENERGY PROGRAM REPORT (US/0146-1931) [04342207] **1944**

FOSSIL ENERGY RESEARCH AND DEVELOPMENT PROGRAM OF THE U.S. DEPARTMENT OF ENERGY (US/0190-1141) [04168289] **1944**

FOSSILIUM CATALOGUS. II: PLANTAE (NE) [02116601] **4227**

FOSSILS AND STRATA (NO/0300-9491) [00972371] **1376**

FOSTER ASSOCIATES (WASHINGTON, D.C.) *See* FOSTER NATURAL GAS REPORT FROM WASHINGTON **4256**

FOSTER ASSOCIATES (WASHINGTON, D.C.). REPORT FROM WASHINGTON TO PRODUCERS OF NATURAL GAS *See* FOSTER NATURAL GAS REPORT FROM WASHINGTON **4256**

FOSTER BULLETIN ON DEREGULATED GAS *CEASED.* (US/0749-7377) [11160796] **4256**

FOSTER ELECTRIC REPORT (US) **2055**

FOSTER NATURAL GAS REPORT FROM WASHINGTON (US/0095-1587) [01795865] **4256**

FOSTER PARENT (CN/0046-4767) [03219800] 5286, **2280**

FOSTERLETTER (CN/0701-3418) [03042260] **2280**

FOSTER'S BOTANICAL & HERB REVIEWS (US/1047-000X) [20581774] **2415**

FOSTER'S DAILY DEMOCRAT (US/0892-6026) [10728920] **5708**

FOTO (NE/0015-8682) [07988584] **4369**

FOTO & DOKA (NE/0165-5531) [I01655531] **4369**

FOTO CREATIV *CEASED.*
(GW/0721-7730) [I07217730] **4369**

FOTO FINDER (US/0272-1252)
[06744755] **4369**

FOTO GALAXIS (SP) [03697094] **4369**

FOTO MAGAZIN (GW/0340-6660)
[01569917] **4369**

FOTO PROFESIONAL *See* REVISTA
FOTO SL **4376**

FOTO PROFESIONAL (SP/0211-9552)
[I02119552] **4369**

FOTO SHOE 15 (IT) **3183**

FOTO (STOCKHOLM, SWEDEN : 1983)
(SW/0345-3626) [09380099] **4369**

FOTO (WARSAW, POLAND)
(PL/0324-8453) [08224381] **4369**

FOTOGESCHICHTE (GW/0720-5260)
[07505157] **4369**

FOTOGRAFARE (IT) [08847394] **4369**

FOTOGRAFIA (WARSAW, POLAND)
(PL/0015-8801) [04088002] **4369**

FOTOGRAFIE *CEASED.*
(SZ/0015-8836) [04088095] **4369**

FOTOGRAFIE (XR/0009-0549)
[23379133] **4369**

FOTOGRAFISKA MUSEET / STATENS
KONSTMUSEER (SW) [11322399] **4369**

FOTOGRAMETRIA,
FOTOINTERPRETACION Y GEODESIA
(MX) [01795652] 1976, **4369**

FOTOGUIDE, LE (IT) **4369**

FOTOHANDEL (NE) **4369**

FOTOINTERPRETACJA W GEOGRAFII
(PL/0071-8076) [07720427] **2561**

FOTOLOGIA (IT) [14510961] **4369**

FOTOMAGAZIN (GW/0340-6660)
[00818152] **4369**

FOTOMUVESZET (HU/0532-3010)
[08766954] **4369**

FOTON FAKUTORI NYUSU
(JA/0288-691X) [10416488] **1944**

FOTOTECNICA (CU) [02960735] **4369**

FOTOWIRTSCHAFT, DIE
(GW/0340-6644) [I03406644] **4369**

FOUILLES DE DELPHES (FR)
[01567345] **268**

FOULING PREVENTION RESEARCH
DIGEST (UK/0143-3598) [10347631]
1976

FOUNDATION (US/0306-4964)
[04973611] **5106, 3388**

FOUNDATION 500 (US/0145-6067)
[02766186] **5286**

●FOUNDATION 1000, THE
(US/1067-7828) [26814050] **4336**

●FOUNDATION & CORPORATE
GRANTS ALERT (US/1062-4686)
[25635596] **4336**

FOUNDATION BULLETIN (NEW YORK)
(US/0196-5034) [05827761] **2785**

FOUNDATION (DAGENHAM)
(UK/0306-4964) [02299047] **3388**

●FOUNDATION DIRECTORY. PART 2, A
GUIDE TO GRANT PROGRAMS,
$25,000-$100,000, THE (US/1058-6210)
[22995180] **4336**

FOUNDATION DIRECTORY, THE
(US/0071-8092) [00918159] **4336**

FOUNDATION DRILLING
(US/0274-5186) [06386865] **615**

FOUNDATION FACTS (US/0015-8933)
[01385693] **2023**

FOUNDATION FOR BIOTECHNICAL
AND INDUSTRIAL FERMENTATION
RESEARCH (FI/0780-6655) [14696124]
2367

FOUNDATION FOR BUSINESS
RESPONSIBILITIES *See* SEMINAR
PAPERS (LONDON, 1972-) **710**

FOUNDATION FOR ORTHODONTIC
RESEARCH *See* PROCEEDINGS OF
THE FOUNDATION FOR
ORTHODONTIC RESEARCH **1333**

FOUNDATION GIVING (US/1066-0445)
[24492002] **4336**

FOUNDATION GIVING WATCH
(US/0741-7004) [07750112] **4336**

FOUNDATION GRANTS INDEX
QUARTERLY, THE (US) [21421578]
4336

FOUNDATION GRANTS INDEX, THE
(US/0090-1601) [01128405] **4336**

FOUNDATION GRANTS TO
INDIVIDUALS / COMPILED BY THE
FOUNDATION CENTER (US)
[03775240] **4336**

FOUNDATION NEWS (US/0015-8976)
[01569923] **4336**

●FOUNDATION NEWS & COMMENTARY
(US/1076-3961) [29961212] **4336**

FOUNDATION OF THANATOLOGY *See*
ARCHIVES OF THE FOUNDATION OF
THANATOLOGY (1976) **4341**

FOUNDATION ONE (US/0272-5622)
[06804801] **4776**

FOUNDATION REPORTER (1990)
(US/1055-4998) [22571643] **5286**

●FOUNDATION REPORTER (1990)
(US/1055-4998) [24643337] **4727**

FOUNDATION: THE REVIEW OF
SCIENCE FICTION (UK) **3388**

FOUNDATIONAL STUDIES
(US/0145-4331) [02735451] **1747**

FOUNDATIONS IN LIBRARY AND
INFORMATION SCIENCE (US)
[03979701] **3211**

FOUNDATIONS IN WISCONSIN
(US/0360-8042) [02243825] **4336**

FOUNDATIONS OF COMPUTING AND
DECISION SCIENCE (PL) **1185**

FOUNDATIONS OF CONTROL
ENGINEERING (PL/0324-8747)
[05508302] **1976**

FOUNDATIONS OF LINGUISTICS (US)
[01385844] **3282**

FOUNDATIONS OF NEUROLOGY (US)
[23045734] **3833**

FOUNDATIONS OF PHYSICS
(US/0015-9018) [01569928] **4403**

FOUNDATIONS OF PHYSICS LETTERS
(US/0894-9875) [16389088] **4403**

FOUNDATIONS OF SEMIOTICS
(NE/0168-2555) [12377889] 1111, **3282**

FOUNDATIONS (ST. ALBANS, HERTS)
(UK) [09879300] **5060**

FOUNDRY CATALOG FILE *CEASED.*
(US/0533-005X) [02963169] **4002**

FOUNDRY MANAGEMENT &
TECHNOLOGY (US/0360-8999)
[02240682] **4002**

FOUNDRY OPERATIONS PLANBOOK
(US/0147-8796) [03238163] **4002**

FOUNDRY TRADE JOURNAL, THE
(UK/0015-9042) [01921701] **4002**

FOUNDRY YEAR BOOK (UK/0264-5319)
[03247015] **4002**

FOUNDRYMAN, THE (UK/0007-0718)
[17184963] **4002**

FOUNTAIN COUNTY NEIGHBOR
(US/1060-5495) [25034549] **5664**

FOUR BY FOUR (MONTREAL,
QUEBEC) (CN/0714-9093) [09658154]
3463

FOUR CORNERS ADVISOR, THE
CEASED. (US/0162-6647) [04290874]
1491

●FOUR DIRECTIONS (TELLICO PLAINS,
TENN.), THE (US/1070-7549)
[28367853] **3388**

FOUR DRAGONS GUIDEBOOK : A
COMPREHENSIVE GUIDE TO HONG
KONG, THAILAND, SINGAPORE,
TAIWAN, THE (US/1055-8853)
[23363715] **5474**

FOUR HUNDRED (NEW YORK, N.Y.),
THE (US/1049-7757) [21308623] **1267**

FOUR QUARTERS (US/0015-9107)
[01585683] **3388**

FOUR SEASONS, THE (US/0532-3215)
[03030493] **511**

FOUR-TOWN JOURNAL
(CN/0712-6387) [09502121] **5784**

FOUR WHEELER (US/0015-9123)
[04077760] **5382**

FOUR WHEELER (AT) **5383**

FOUR ZOAS JOURNAL (US/0198-9928)
[06287816] **3388**

FOURNEE, LA (CN/0015-9158)
[02014233] **2341**

FOURRAGES (FR) [09546037] **201**

FOURRAGES ACTUALITES
(FR/0395-8515) [01671512] **88**

FOURRURES MAGAZINE, L'OFFICIAL
DE LA FOURRURE *See* OFFICIEL DE
LA FOURRURE 1960, L' **3185**

FOURSQUARE WORLD ADVANCE
(US/0015-9182) [04077783] **4959**

FOURTH CIRCUIT AND DISTRICT OF
COLUMBIA BANKRUPTCY COURT
REPORTER, THE (US/1048-2768)
[20906767] **2972**

FOURTH CIRCUIT REVIEW
(LOUISVILLE, KY.) (US/0889-3578)
[12812323] **2972**

FOURTH INTERNATIONAL (LONDON,
ENGLAND) (US/0015-9204) [02261275]
4542, 4474

FOURTH QUARTER AND ANNUAL
REPORT ON THE TEXAS BOVINE
BRUCELLOSIS PROGRAM / TEXAS
ANIMAL HEALTH COMMISSION,
AUSTIN TEXAS (US/0748-7754)
[10148456] **211**

FOURTH R, THE (US) **4959**

FOURTH SEASON (US/1056-3423)
[23665789] **5179**

FOURTH WORLD JOURNAL
(US/0882-3723) [11835111] **1491**

FOURTHOUGHT NEWSLETTER
(CN/0711-3897) [08499746] **4347**

FOWLERVILLE REVIEW, THE
(US/0191-6920) [04926824] **5692**

FOX FAMILY FACTS (US/1044-9809)
[19472061] **2449**

FOX (NEW YORK, N.Y. 1984)
(US/1041-9470) [18891210] **3995**

FOX POINT-BAYSIDE-RIVER HILLS
HERALD (US) [11958651] **5767**

FOX VALLEY LIVING *CEASED.*
(US/1047-3963) [20689972] **2487**

FOXFIRE (US/0015-9220) [01569938]
3388

FOXPRO ADVISOR (US/1066-7261)
[27033845] **1286**

FOXTALK (FEDERAL WAY, WASH.)
(US/1042-6302) [19096675] **1279**

FP: FUSION PLANNING *CEASED.* (JA)
4403

FPRDI JOURNAL : A PUBLICATION OF
THE FOREST PRODUCTS RESEARCH
AND DEVELOPMENT INSTITUT,
NATIONAL SCIENCE AND
TECHNOLOGY AUTHORITY
(PH/0115-0456) [11238229] **2400**

FPS (US/0362-9066) [02092566] **1063**

FQSE EN ACTION, LA (CN/0846-4618)
[20778312] **4895**

FR. MCBRIDE HOMILY SERVICE *See*
SCRIPTURE COMES ALIVE **5019**

FRA BORNHOLMS MUSEUM
(DK/0107-4849) [11862042] **4088**

FRA FYSIKKENS VERDEN
(NO/0015-9247) [09390793] **4403**

FRACASTORO, IL (IT/0015-9271)
[01778989] **3577**

●FRACTALS (SI/0218-348X) [28056668]
3506

FRACTURE MECHANICS OF
CERAMICS (US/0197-2766) [04298543]
2055, **2589**

●FRAGMENT (XO) [25614662] **3389**

FRAGMENT K *See* FRAGMENT **3389**

FRAGMENTA BALCANICA - MUSEI
MACEDONICI SCIENTARIUM
NATURALIUM (XN/0015-9298)
[03042979] **456**

FRAGMENTA ENTOMOLOGICA
(IT/0429-288X) [01569945] **5584**

FRAGMENTA FAUNISTICA
(PL/0015-9301) [01439815] **5584**

FRAGMENTA FLORISTICA ET
GEOBOTANICA (PL/0015-931X)
[01569947] **511**

FRAGMENTOS DE BARRO (US)
[06824142] **3389**

FRAGMENTS (US/0015-9344)
[03262661] **1825**

FRAGMENTS (SCARBOROUGH, ONT.)
(CN/0711-2211) [08858325] **4959**

FRAGUA; REVISTA DE
INVESTIGACION Y DOCUMENTACION
BIBLIOGRAFICA (SP) **416**

FRAM (BANGOR, ME.) (US/0739-8158)
[09816631] **5474**

FRAME BY FRAME (TORONTO, ONT.)
(CN/0821-6681) [09747725] **1132**

FRAME NEWS (UK/0268-4306)
[18631233] **226**

FRAME/WORK (LOS ANGELES, CALIF.)
(US/0895-6030) [16503884] 4071, **4369**

FRAMEFOCUS (US) **1286**

FRAMENTA HERBOLOGICA
JUGOSLAVICA (CI/0350-3615)
[09471589] **88**

FRAMERS FORUM (US) **1185**

FRAMER'S FORUM MAGAZINE : THE
MAGAZINE FOR DOCUMENT
PUBLISHERS (US) **1263**

FRAMES PORTE & FINESTRE (IT) **615**

FRAMEWORK *SUSPENDED.*
(UK/0306-7661) [05257024] **4071**

FRAMEWORK FOR ... BUDGET (IE)
[16167652] **4727**

FRAN RIKSDAG & I.E. OCH
DEPARTEMENT (SW) [06297037] **4727**

FRANC-NORD (CN/0822-7284)
[10926566] **2194**

FRANC-VERT (CN) **2194**

FRANCAIS AU NIGERIA
(NR/0015-9387) [09449033] **3282**

FRANCAIS AUJOURD'HUI: REVUE DE
L'ASSOCIATION FRANCAISE DES
ENSEIGNANTS DE FRANCAIS, LE
(FR/0184-7732) [03465156] **3282**

FRANCAIS DANS LE MONDE, LE
(FR/0015-9395) [01569951] **3282**

FRANCAIS MODERNE, LE
(FR/0015-9409) [01569952] **3282**

FRANCE *See* CODE DES LOYERS ET
DE LA COPROPRIETE **2818**

FRANCE *See* JOURNAL OFFICIEL DE
LA REPUBLIQUE FRANCAISE.
EDITION DES LOIS ET DECRETS :
NUMERO COMPLEMENTAIRE **2990**

FRANCE *See* JOURNAL OFFICIEL.
LOIS ET DECRETS **2990**

FRANCE *See* CODE PENAL **3105**

FRANCE *See* PRESENTATION
FONCTIONNELLE DU BUDGET DE
L'ETAT **4741**

Alphabetical Title Index — FRANCE

FRANCE (US) [03265990] **2516**

FRANCE See NOUVEAU CODE DE PROCEDURE CIVILE ET CODE DE PROCEDURE CIVILE **3090**

FRANCE See TEXTES D'INTERET GENERAL **3064**

FRANCE See JOURNAL OFFICIEL DE LA REPUBLIQUE FRANCAISE. AVIS ET RAPPORTS DU CONSEIL ECONOMIQUE ET SOCIAL **1501**

FRANCE See BULLETIN OFFICIEL DES DECORATIONS, MEDAILLES ET RECOMPENSES / REPUBLIQUE FRANCAISE **4038**

FRANCE See CODES DE LA SANTE PUBLIQUE DE LA FAMILLE ET DE L'AIDE SOCIALE **5279**

FRANCE See CODE ADMINISTRATIF **3092**

FRANCE See CODE GENERAL DES IMPOTS ET ANNEXES AVEC ANNOTATIONS ET RENVOIS **827**

FRANCE See CODE DE L'URBANISME **2818**

FRANCE See CODE RURAL; CODE FORESTIER - (FRANCE) **2952**

FRANCE See BULLETIN DES ANNONCES LEGALES OBLIGATOIRES **780**

FRANCE See CODE CIVIL **3089**

FRANCE See CODES DE LA SECURITE SOCIALE ET DE LA MUTUALITE, MUTUALITE SOCIALE AGRICOLE **5279**

FRANCE See BULLETIN OFFICIEL DES ANNONCES CIVILES ET COMMERCIALES **2945**

FRANCE 30,000 (FR) [18202879] **677**

FRANCE AFRIQUE (FR) [17617274] **2516**

FRANCE. AGENCE NATIONALE POUR L'AMELIORATION DES CONDITIONS DE TRAVAIL See LETTRE D'INFORMATION - ANACT **1687**

FRANCE AGRICOLE, LA (FR) [04024481] **89**

FRANCE. AMBASSADE (U.S.). SERVICE DE PRESSE ET D'INFORMATION See EUROPEAN AFFAIRS **2516**

FRANCE AMERIQUE (NEW YORK, N.Y.) (US/0747-2757) [01570052] **2261, 5716**

FRANCE. BIBLIOTHEQUE NATIONALE See CATALOGUES ET PUBLICATIONS EN VENTE **413**

FRANCE. BIBLIOTHEQUE NATIONALE. DEPARTEMENT DES LIVRES IMPRIMES. SALLE DES CATALOGUES ET DES BIBLIOGRAPHIES See NOUVEUX OUVRAGES DE REFERENCE, LISTE ANNUELLE / BIBLIOTHEQUE NATIONALE, DEPARTMENT DES LIVRES IMPRIMES, SALLE DES CATALOGUES ET DES BIBLIOGRAPHIES **421**

FRANCE. BIBLIOTHEQUE NATIONALE. DEPARTEMENT DES LIVRES IMPRIMES. SALLE DES CATALOGUES ET DES BIBLIOGRAPHIES See PUBLICATIONS EN SERIES RECUES REGULIEREMENT PAR LA SALLE DES CATALOGUES / SALLE DES CATALOGUES ET DES BIBLIOGRAPHIES **423**

FRANCE. BUREAU CENTRAL D'ETUDE POUR LES EQUIPEMENTS D'OUTRE-MER See INFORMATIONS ET DOCUMENTS - BCEOM **5113**

FRANCE. BUREAU DE RECHERCHES GEOLOGIQUES ET MINIERES See ANNUAL REPORT - BUREAU DE RECHERCHES GEOLOGIQUES ET MINIERES **1365**

FRANCE. BUREAU DE RECHERCHES GEOLOGIQUES ET MINI-ERES See DOCUMENTS - B.R.G.M **1439**

FRANCE. BUREAU DES LONGITUDES. CONNAISSANCE DES TEMPS OU DES MOUVEMENTS CELESTES A L'USAGE DES ASTRONOMES ET DES NAVIGATEURS See CONNAISSANCE DES TEMPS **4175**

FRANCE. BUREAU DES SYSTEMES D'INFORMATION SUR LA CONSTRUCTION ET L'URBANISATION See STATISTIQUES DE LA CONSTRUCTION **633**

FRANCE. BUREAU NATIONAL DE METROLOGIE See RAPPORT D'ACTIVITE / BUREAU NATIONAL DE METROLOGIE (FRANCE) **4032**

FRANCE CATHOLIQUE-ECCLESIA (US) [06341922] **5029**

FRANCE. CENTRE NATIONAL DE LA RECHERCHE SCIENTIFIQUE See BULLETIN SIGNALETIQUE 320: BIOCHEMIE. BIOPHYSIQUE. CHEMIE ANALYTIQUE BIOLOGIQUE. BIOPHYSIQUE. GENIE BIOLOGIQUE ET MEDICAL **450**

FRANCE. CENTRE NATIONAL DE LA RECHERCHE SCIENTIFIQUE See BULLETIN SIGNALETIQUE. [SECTION] 761. MICROSCOPIE ELECTRONIQUE, DIFFRACTION ELECTRONIQUE **572**

FRANCE. CENTRE NATIONAL DE LA RECHERCHE SCIENTIFIQUE See BULLETIN SIGNALETIQUE. [SECTION] 140. ELECTROTECHNIQUE **2037**

FRANCE. CENTRE NATIONAL DE LA RECHERCHE SCIENTIFIQUE. COMITE NATIONAL DE LA RECHERCHE SCIENTIFIQUE See RAPPORT NATIONAL DE CONJONCTURE SCIENTIFIQUE: INFORMATIQUE ET MOYENS DE CALCUL POLYVALENTS **1201**

FRANCE. CENTRE NATIONAL DE LA RECHERCHE SCIENTIFIQUE. COMITE NATIONAL DE LA RECHERCHE SCIENTIFIQUE See RAPPORT NATIONAL DE CONJONCTURE SCIENTIFIQUE: SCIENCES DE LA VIE **471**

FRANCE. CENTRE NATIONAL DE LA RECHERCHE SCIENTIFIQUE. COMITE NATIONAL DE LA RECHERCHE SCIENTIFIQUE See RAPPORT NATIONAL DE CONJONCTURE SCIENTIFIQUE : CHIMIE **990**

FRANCE. CENTRE NATIONAL DE LA RECHERCHE SCIENTIFIQUE. COMITE NATIONAL DE LA RECHERCHE SCIENTIFIQUE See RAPPORT NATIONAL DE CONJONCTURE SCIENTIFIQUE : MATHEMATIQUES PURES ET METHODOLOGIE MATHEMATIQUE **3530**

FRANCE. CENTRE NATIONAL DE LA RECHERCHE SCIENTIFIQUE. COMITE NATIONAL DE LA RECHERCHE SCIENTIFIQUE See RAPPORT NATIONAL DE CONJONCTURE SCIENTIFIQUE : SCIENCES DE L'HOMME **5254**

FRANCE. CENTRE NATIONAL DE LA RECHERCHE SCIENTIFIQUE. COMITE NATIONAL DE LA RECHERCHE SCIENTIFIQUE See RAPPORT NATIONAL DE CONJONCTURE SCIENTIFIQUE : RAPPORT DE SYNTHESE **5145**

FRANCE. CENTRE NATIONAL DE LA RECHERCHE SCIENTIFIQUE. COMITE NATIONAL DE LA RECHERCHE SCIENTIFIQUE See RAPPORT NATIONAL DE CONJONCTURE SCIENTIFIQUE : PHYSIQUE **4419**

FRANCE. CENTRE NATIONAL DE LA RECHERCHE SCIENTIFIQUE. COMITE NATIONAL DE LA RECHERCHE SCIENTIFIQUE See RAPPORT NATIONAL DE LA CONJONCTURE SCIENTIFIQUE : SCIENCES DE LA TERRE ET DE L'ESPACE **1359**

FRANCE. COMITE MONETAIRE DE LA ZONE FRANC. SECRETARIAT See ZONE FRANC, LA **817**

FRANCE. COMMISSARIAT A L'ENERGIE ATOMIQUE See ACTIVITES SCIENTIFIQUES ET TECHNIQUES - COMMISSARIAT A L'ENERGIE ATOMIQUE **2153**

FRANCE. COMMISSARIAT A L'ENERGIE ATOMIQUE See LISTE DES PUBLICATIONS DU COMMISSARIAT A L'ENERGIE ATOMIQUE / CENTRE D'ETUDES NUCLEAIRES DE SACLAY, SERVICE DE DOCUMENTATION **1949**

FRANCE. COMMISSION BANCAIRE See RAPPORT - COMMISSION BANCAIRE **806**

FRANCE. COMMISSION DE LA SECURITE DES CONSOMMATEURS See RAPPORT ANNUEL AU PRESIDENT DE LA REPUBLIQUE ET AU PARLEMENT / COMMISSION DE LA SECURITE DES CONSOMMATEURS **849**

FRANCE. COMMISSION DES COMPTES DE LA SECURITE SOCIALE See PROCES-VERBAL DE LA REUNION DU ... / MINISTERE DE LA SANTE ET DE LA SECURITE SOCIALE, COMMISSION DES COMPTES DE LA SECURITE SOCIALE **5302**

FRANCE. COMMISSION DES OPERATIONS DE BOURSE See RAPPORT AU PRESIDENT DE LA REPUBLIQUE **806**

FRANCE. COMMISSION D'HISTOIRE ECONOMIQUE ET SOCIALE DE LA REVOLUTION FRANCAISE See MEMOIRES ET DOCUMENTS - COMMISSION D'HISTOIRE ECONOMIQUE ET SOCIALE DE LA REVOLUTION FRANCAISE **1505**

FRANCE COMPOSITES (FR/0985-0503) [20022562] **2102**

FRANCE. CONSEIL DES IMPOTS See RAPPORT AU PRESIDENT DE LA REPUBLIQUE **4744**

FRANCE. CONSEIL D'ETAT See ETUDES ET DOCUMENTS - CONSEIL D'ETAT **3093**

FRANCE. CONSEIL D'ETAT See RECUEIL DES DECISIONS DU CONSEIL D'ETAT, STATUANT AU CONTENTIEUX ET DU TRIBUNAL DES CONFLITS ET DES JUGEMENTS DES TRIBUNAUX ADMINISTRATIFS **4679**

FRANCE. COUR DE CASSATION See ANNUAIRE DE LA COUR DE CASSATION **3138**

FRANCE. DELEGATION A L'AMENAGEMENT DU TERRITOIRE ET A L'ACTION REGIONALE See RAPPORT ANNUEL DE LA DATAR, LE **4678**

FRANCE. DEPARTEMENT DES STATISTIQUES DES TRANSPORTS See TRANSPORTS ROUTIERS DE MARCHANDISES **5397**

FRANCE. DEPARTEMENT DES STATISTIQUES DES TRANSPORTS See AUXILIAIRES DES TRANSPORTS TERRESTRES **5377**

FRANCE DES COMMERCES, LA (FR) [07227950] **837**

FRANCE. DIRECTION DE LA DOCUMENTATION See POLITIQUE ETRANGERE DE LA FRANCE, LA **4491**

FRANCE. DIRECTION DE LA DOCUMENTATION See BULLETIN QUOTIDIEN (TEXTES DU JOUR ET PRESSE ETRANGERE) **2612**

FRANCE. DIRECTION DE L'AIDE AU DEVELOPPEMENT. SECTEUR INFORMATION ECONOMIQUE ET CONJONCTURE See NIGER **1575**

FRANCE. DIRECTION DE L'AIDE AU DEVELOPPEMENT. SECTEUR INFORMATION ECONOMIQUE ET CONJONCTURE See MALI **1573**

FRANCE. DIRECTION DE L'AIDE AU DEVELOPPEMENT. SECTOUR INFORMATION ECONOMIQUE ET CONJONCTURE See COTE D'IVOIRE **1552**

FRANCE. DIRECTION DU BATIMENT ET DES TRAVAUX PUBLICS ET DE LA CONJONCTURE See TABLEAU DE BORD CONJONCTUREL DU LOGEMENT **2836**

FRANCE. DIRECTION DU GAZ, DE L'ELECTRICITE ET DU CHARBON See STATISTIQUES DE L'INDUSTRIE GAZIERE EN FRANCE **4284**

FRANCE. DIRECTION DU GAZ ET DE L'ELECTRICITE. STATISTIQUES OFFICIELLES DE L'INDUSTRIE GAZIERE EN FRANCE See STATISTIQUES DE L'INDUSTRIE GAZIERE EN FRANCE **4284**

FRANCE. DIRECTION GENERALE DE L'AVIATION CIVILE See BULLETIN OFFICIEL. SECTION II : AVIATION CIVILE ET METEOROLOGIE **15**

FRANCE. DIRECTION GENERALE DE L'AVIATION CIVILE. BULLETIN STATISTIQUE DE LA DIRECTION GENERALE A L'AVIATION CIVILE See BULLETIN STATISTIQUE DE LA DGAC / MINISTERE DES TRANSPORTS, AVIATION CIVILE **41**

FRANCE. DIRECTION GENERALE DES DOUANES ET DROITS INDIRECTS See TARIF DES DOUANES **853**

FRANCE. DIRECTION GENERALE DES POSTES. SERVICE DU PERSONNEL. FORMATION PROFESSIONNELLE CONTINUE DU PERSONNEL See FORMATION PROFESSIONNELLE CONTINUE, RAPPORT D'ACTIVITE **1675**

FRANCE. DIRECTION GENERALE DES TELECOMMUNICATIONS See RAPPORT D'ACTIVITE **1162**

FRANCE. DIRECTION GENERALE DES TELECOMMUNICATIONS See RESULTATS FINANCIERS **1163**

FRANCE. DIRECTOR GENERALE DE LA PROTECTION DE LA NATURE See TRAUVUX SCIENTIFIQUES DU PARC NATIONAL DE LA VANOISE **4173**

FRANCE-ECO-PECHE (FR/0986-5748) [23706241] **2304**

FRANCE ECOPECHE (FR) **2216**

FRANCE-EURAFRIQUE (FR) [01839191] **1918**

FRANCE FOOTBALL (FR) [06478013] **4895**

FRANCE FORUM (FR/0046-4910) [10135267] **2516**

FRANCE FRUITS ET LEGUMES (FR/0152-6790) [08120358] **172**

FRANCE GRAPHIQUE, LA (FR/0015-9565) [09036734] **4565**

FRANCE. GROUPE INTERMINISTERIEL D'EVALUATION DE L'ENVIRONNEMENT See RAPPORT ANNUEL - GROUPE INTERMINISTERIEL D'EVALUATION DE L'ENVIRONNEMENT **2241**

FRANCE. HAUT COMITE D'ETUDE ET D'INFORMATION SUR L'ALCOOLISME. BULLETIN D'INFORMATIONS See BULLETIN D'INFORMATION SUR L'ALCOOLISME **1342**

FRANCE HORLOGERE, LA (FR/0015-9573) [00159573] **2916**

FRANCE. INSPECTION GENERALE DE L'ADMINISTRATION DE L'EDUCATION NATIONALE See RAPPORT GENERAL / MINISTERE DE L'EDUCATION NATIONALE **1869**

FRANCE. INSTITUT DE RECHERCHE ET D'HISTOIRE DES TEXTES See DOCUMENTS, ETUDES ET REPERTOIRES **267**

FRANCE. INSTITUT NATIONAL DE LA STATISTIQUE ET DES ETUDES ECONOMIQUES. SERVICE DE LA CONJONCTURE See SITUATION ET PERSPECTIVES DANS LE COMMERCE D'APRES LES CHEFS D'ENTREPRISE **1584**

FRANCE ITALIE (FR/1146-0024) [11460024] **1491, 4474**

FRANCE — Alphabetical Title Index

FRANCE ITALIE (IT) **2487**

FRANCE LATINE, LA (FR/0222-0334) [I02220334] **3389, 3282**

FRANCE MAGAZINE (US/0886-2478) [12601735] **2517**

FRANCE. MINISTERE DE LA JEUNESSE, DES SPORTS ET DES LOISIRS *See* STATISTIQUES DU TOURISME **5501**

FRANCE. MINISTERE DE LA JEUNESSE, DES SPORTS ET DES LOISIRS. DIVISION DES ETUDES ET DE LA STATISTIQUE. ANNUAIRE *See* STATISTIQUES TEMPS LIBRE, JEUNESSE ET SPORTS **4924**

FRANCE. MINISTERE DE LA JUSTICE *See* BULLETIN OFFICIEL DU MINISTERE DE LA JUSTICE (FRANCE) **2945**

FRANCE. MINISTERE DE LA JUSTICE *See* COMPTE GENERAL DE L'ADMINISTRATION DE LA JUSTICE PENALE / MINISTERE DE LA JUSTICE **3079**

FRANCE. MINISTERE DE LA QUALITE DE LA VIE *See* BULLETIN DE DOCUMENTATION - MINISTERE DE LA QUALITE DE LA VIE **2225**

FRANCE. MINISTERE DE L'AGRICULTURE *See* BULLETIN D'INFORMATION DU MINISTERE DE L'AGRICULTURE (FRANCE) **69**

FRANCE. MINISTERE DE L'AGRICULTURE ET DU DEVELOPPEMENT RURAL. BULLETIN D'INFORMATION *See* BULLETIN D'INFORMATION DU MINISTERE DE L'AGRICULTURE (FRANCE) **69**

FRANCE. MINISTERE DE L'AMENAGEMENT DU TERRITOIRE, DE L'EQUIPEMENT, DU LOGEMENT ET DU TOURISME *See* BULLETIN OFFICIEL **4635**

FRANCE. MINISTERE DE L'ECONOMIE *See* BULLETIN ADMINISTRATIF DES ASSURANCES **2944**

FRANCE. MINISTERE DE L'ECONOMIE *See* BULLETIN OFFICIEL DES ASSURANCES / REPUBLIQUE FRANCAISE, MINISTERE DE L'ECONOMIE **2945**

FRANCE. MINISTERE DE L'ECONOMIE. BULLETIN ADMINISTRATIF DES ASSURANCES *See* BULLETIN OFFICIEL DES ASSURANCES / REPUBLIQUE FRANCAISE, MINISTERE DE L'ECONOMIE **2945**

FRANCE. MINISTERE DE L'ECONOMIE ET DES FINANCES *See* ANNUAIRE GENERAL - FRANCE. MINISTERE DE L'ECONOMIE ET DES FINANCES **1462**

FRANCE. MINISTERE DE L'EDUCATION NATIONALE. DEPARTEMENT DE LA DOCUMENTATION ET DE LA DIFFUSION DE L'INFORMATION STATISTIQUE *See* REPERTOIRE THEMATIQUE DES DOCUMENTS STATISTIQUES DU SERVICE DE L'INFORMATIQUE DE GESTION ET DES STATISTIQUES, CENTRALISES PAR LE DEPARTEMENT DE LA DOCUMENTATION ET DE LA DIFFUSION DE L'INFORMATION STATISTIQUE / MINISTERE DE L'EDUCATION NATIONALE **1796**

FRANCE. MINISTERE DE L'EDUCATION. SERVICE CENTRAL DES STATISTIQUES ET SONDAGES *See* LISTE DES DIPLOMES INSTITUES SUR LE PLAN NATIONAL ET SANCTIONNANT UNE FORMATION PROFESSIONNELLE **1834**

FRANCE. MINISTERE DE L'ENVIRONNEMENT ET DU CADRE DE VIE *See* BULLETIN OFFICIEL DU MINISTERE DE L'ENVIRONNEMENT ET DU CADRE DE VIE ET DU MINISTERE DES TRANSPORTS **3110**

FRANCE. MINISTERE DE L'EQUIPEMENT *See* RAPPORT D'ACTIVITE - MINISTERE DE L'EQUIPEMENT **5254**

FRANCE. MINISTERE DE L'EQUIPEMENT ET DE L'AMENAGEMENT DU TERRITOIRE *See* BULLETIN OFFICIEL DU MINISTERE DE L'EQUIPEMENT ET DE L'AMENAGEMENT DU TERRITOIRE **2816**

FRANCE. MINISTERE DE L'INTERIEUR *See* REPERTOIRE MENSUEL DU MINISTERE DE L'INTERIEUR **4680**

FRANCE. MINISTERE DELEGUE CHARGE DE LA MER *See* BULLETIN OFFICIEL DU MINISTERE DELEGUE CHARGE DE LA MER **3180**

FRANCE. MINISTERE DES AFFAIRES ETRANGERES *See* BULLETIN PERIODIQUE DE LA PRESSE TCHCOSLOVAQUE ... **2681**

FRANCE. MINISTERE DES P.T.T.. DIRECTION DU PERSONNEL ET DES AFFAIRES SOCIALES *See* STATISTIQUES DE PERSONNEL / MINISTERE DES PTT, DIRECTION DU PERSONNEL ET DES AFFAIRES SOCIALES **1125**

FRANCE. MINISTERE DES TRANSPORTS *See* BULLETIN OFFICIEL DU MINISTERE DES TRANSPORTS MARINE MARCHANDE (FRANCE) **3180**

FRANCE. MINISTERES CHARGES DE L'EMPLOI ET DU TRAVAIL *See* BULLETIN OFFICIEL DES MINISTERES CHARGES DE L'EMPLOI ET DU TRAVAIL **1657**

FRANCE. MINISTETE DE L'AGRICULTURE. DIRECTION DE LA QUALITE *See* RAPPORT GENERAL D'ACTIVITE / MINISTERE DE L'AGRICULTURE, DIRECTION DE LA QUALITE **4678**

FRANCE MODERNE (FR) [01789192] **4650**

FRANCE (NEW YORK, N.Y. 1983) (US/0883-2617) [09373051] **5474**

FRANCE. OFFICE NATIONAL DES FORETS *See* RAPPORT ANNUEL / OFFICE NATIONAL DES FORETS **2391**

FRANCE. PARLEMENT (1946-). ASSEMBLEE NATIONALE *See* JOURNAL OFFICIEL DE LA REPUBLIQUE FRANCAISE. DEBATS PARLEMENTAIRES, ASSEMBLEE NATIONALE. QUESTIONS ECRITES ET REPONSES DES MINISTRES **4659**

FRANCE. PARLEMENT (1946-). ASSEMBLEE NATIONALE *See* BULLETIN - FRANCE. PARLEMENT (1946-). ASSEMBLEE NATIONALE **4634**

FRANCE. PARLEMENT (1946-). ASSEMBLEE NATIONALE *See* IMPRESSIONS **2980**

FRANCE. PARLEMENT (1946-). ASSEMBLEE NATIONALE *See* JOURNAL OFFICIEL DE LA REPUBLIQUE FRANCAISE. DEBATS PARLEMENTAIRES, ASSEMBLEE NATIONALE (CUMULATIF) **4479**

FRANCE. PARLEMENT (1946-). ASSEMBLEE NATIONALE *See* PROGRAMMES ET ENGAGEMENTS ELECTORAUX **4492**

FRANCE. PARLEMENT (1946-). ASSEMBLEE NATIONALE *See* JOURNAL OFFICIEL DE LA REPUBLIQUE FRANCAISE. DEBATS PARLEMENTAIRES, ASSEMBLEE NATIONALE. COMPTE RENDU INTEGRAL **4659**

FRANCE. PARLEMENT (1946-). SENTA. SERVICE DES ARCHIVES *See* TABLE DES DEBATS DU SENAT. TABLE NOMINATIVE / ETABLIE PAR LE SERVICE DES ARCHIVES DU SENAT **4689**

FRANCE. PARLEMENT (1946-). SENTA. SERVICE DES ARCHIVES *See* TABLE DES DEBATS DU SENAT. TABLE DES MATIERES / ETABLIE PAR LE SERVICE DES ARCHIVES DU SENAT **4689**

FRANCE PAYS ARABES (FR/0533-0866) [04927112] **2651**

FRANCE PECHE *See* FRANCE ECOPECHE **2216**

FRANCE. PREMIER MINISTRE *See* BULLETIN OFFICIEL DES SERVICES DU PREMIER MINISTRE **4702**

FRANCE. SECRETARIAT D'ETAT AUX DEPARTEMENTS ET TERRITOIRES D'OUTRE-MER *See* BULLETIN OFFICIEL DU SECRETARIAT D'ETAT AUX DEPARTEMENTS ET TERRITOIRES D'OUTRE-MER (FRANCE) **2945**

FRANCE. SECRETARIAT GENERAL A L'AVIATION CIVILE *See* BULLETIN STATISTIQUE DU SECRETARIAT GENERAL A L'AVIATION CIVILE **41**

FRANCE. SERVICE CENTRAL DE L'ACTION SOCIALE DES ARMEES *See* PROJET DE BUDGET DE PROGRAMMES **4054**

FRANCE. SERVICE CENTRAL DE L'ACTION SOCIALE DES ARMEES *See* BUDGET DE PROGRAMMES / SECRETARIAT GENERAL POUR L'ADMINISTRATION, ACTION SOCIALE DES ARMEES **4038**

FRANCE. SERVICE CENTRAL DES ENQUETES ET ETUDES STATISTIQUES *See* COMPTES DE L'AGRICULTURE, LES **76**

FRANCE. SERVICE CENTRAL DES ENQUETES ET ETUDES STATISTIQUES *See* COLLECTIONS DE STATISTIQUE AGRICOLE. ETUDE **75**

FRANCE. SERVICE CENTRAL DES ENQUETES ET ETUDES STATISTIQUES *See* PRODUITS D'EXPLOITATION FORESTIERE ET DE SCIERIE, ET PRINCIPAUX PRODUITS DERIVES **2404**

FRANCE. SERVICE CENTRAL DES ENQUETES ET ETUDES STATISTIQUES *See* RESULTATS DE L'ENQUETE ANNUELLE SUR LA COOPERATION AGRICOLE **128**

FRANCE. SERVICE CENTRAL DES ENQUETES ET ETUDES STATISTIQUES *See* BILANS ALIMENTAIRES ET AUTRES BILANS **151**

FRANCE. SERVICE CENTRAL DES ENQUETES ET ETUDES STATISTIQUES *See* RESULTATS DEFINITIFS DE L'ENQETE SUR LE CHEPTEL BOVIN **220**

FRANCE. SERVICE CENTRAL DES ENQUETES ET ETUDES STATISTIQUES *See* CAHIERS DE STATISTIQUES AGRICOLES **71**

FRANCE. SERVICE CENTRAL DES ENQUETES ET ETUDES STATISTIQUES. REGION DE PROGRAMME BOURGOGNE *See* ANNUAIRE REGIONAL - SERVICE CENTRAL DES ENQUETES ET ETUDES STATISTIQUES, REGION DE PROGRAMME BOURGOGNE **151**

FRANCE. SERVICE CENTRAL D'ORGANISATION ET METHODES *See* REVUE DU SCOM **4683**

FRANCE. SERVICE DES TOPOGRAPHICS SOUTERRAINES *See* ETUDES DES GITES MINERAUX DE LA FRANCE **2138**

FRANCE. SERVICE DU TRAITEMENT DE L'INFORMATION ET DES STATISTIQUES INDUSTRIELLES *See* RESULTATS : SOCIETES D'ETUDES ET DE CONSEILS, INGENIEURS-CONSEILS **1994**

FRANCE. SERVICE HYDROGRAPHIQUE *See* FEUX ET SIGNAUX DE BRUME **4176**

FRANCE. SERVICE HYDROGRAPHIQUE ET OCEANOGRAPHIQUE DE LA MARINE *See* RAPPORT ANNUEL DU SERVICE HYDROGRAPHIQUE ET OCEANOGRAPHIQUE DE LA MARINE **1455**

FRANCE. SERVICE HYDROGRAPHIQUE ET OCEANOGRAPHIQUE DE LA MARINE *See* ANNALES HYDROGRAPHIQUES **1412**

FRANCE. SERVICE HYDROGRAPHIQUE ET OCEANOGRAPHIQUE DE LA MARINE *See* GUIDE DU NAVIGATEUR **4176**

FRANCE. SERVICE REGIONAL DE STATISTIQUE AGRICOLE DE LA REGION DE CHAMPAGNE-ARDENNE *See* CHAMPAGNE-ARDENNE, STATISTIQUE AGRICOLE **73**

FRANCE-SOIR (FR) [02261310] **5800**

FRANCE... SPECIALIZED CATALOGUE OF ARTIST PROOFS, DE LUXE SHEETS, IMPERFORATES, COLOR ESSAYS, FIRST DAY COVERS, COLLECTIVE PROOFS, PRINTERS INSPECTION PROOFS, ILLUSTRATIONS (US/0197-7202) [06109689] **2785**

FRANCE TABAC (FR) [12700232] **5373**

FRANCE TELECOM ED. NATIONALE *CEASED*. (FR/0984-8916) [I09848916] **1156**

FRANCE TELECOM NEWS (US/0898-1027) [17735034] **1156**

FRANCE TELECOM QUARTERLY (FR) **1156**

FRANCE TENNIS DE TABLE MAGAZINE (FR/0984-421X) [I0984421X] **4895**

FRANCE TODAY (SAN FRANCISCO, CALIF. 1987) (US/0895-3651) [16573447] **2688**

FRANCESVILLE TRIBUNE (US/0747-1793) [10617059] **5664**

FRANCEXPORT (FR/0244-710X) [10847140] **837**

FRANCHE-COMTE EN QUELQUES CHIFFRES, LA (FR/01798404) **5327**

FRANCHISE ANNUAL HANDBOOK AND DIRECTORY (US) **954**

FRANCHISE ANNUAL (LEWISTON), THE (CN/0318-8752) [02760899] **899, 677**

FRANCHISE HANDBOOK, THE (US/0882-5505) [11881278] **1297**

FRANCHISE LAW JOURNAL (US/8756-7962) [11332359] **3100**

FRANCHISE LEGAL DIGEST (US/0739-8239) [09654422] **3100**

FRANCHISE MAGAZINE (UK/0268-8395) **677**

FRANCHISE OPPORTUNITIES HANDBOOK (US) [02430498] **677**

FRANCHISING (AT/1321-408X) **677**

FRANCHISING BUSINESS AND LAW ALERT (US) 2972, **1747**

FRANCHISING IN THE ECONOMY (US/0193-9017) [06035362] **954**

FRANCHISING (NEW YORK, N.Y.) (US) [17701864] 3100, **954**

FRANCHISING (PITTSBURGH, PA.) (US/0895-7274) [09572678] **677**

FRANCHISING WORLD (US/1041-7311) [06713809] **677**

FRANCIA 1 MITTELALTER (GW/0937-7735) [I09377735] **2616**

FRANCIA 2 FRUHE NEUZEIT (GW/0937-7743) [I09377743] **2616**

FRANCIA 3 19./20. JAHRHUNDERT (GW/0937-7751) [I09377751] **2616**

FRANCIS. 617, ECODOC / RESEAU D'INFORMATION EN ECONOMIE GENERALE *CEASED*. (FR/1157-383X) [24346254] **1491**

FRANCIS BIBLIOGRAPHIE GEOGRAPHIQUE INTERNATIONALE. 531 (FR/1157-3805) [24898885] **2561**

FRANCIS BULLETIN SIGNALETIQUE. 519, PHILOSOPHIE (FR/1157-3694) [24237389] **4347**

FRANCIS BULLETIN SIGNALETIQUE. 520, SCIENCES DE L'EDUCATION (FR/1157-3708) [24363948] **1747**

FRANCIS BULLETIN SIGNALETIQUE. 521, SOCIOLOGIE (FR/1157-3716) [24237483] **5245**

FRANCIS BULLETIN SIGNALETIQUE. 522, HISTOIRE DES SCIENCES ET DES TECHNIQUES (FR/1157-3724) [24237088] **5106**

FRANCIS BULLETIN SIGNALETIQUE. 523, HISTOIRE ET SCIENCES DE LA LITTERATURE (FR/1157-3732) [24229075] **3389**

FRANCIS BULLETIN SIGNALETIQUE. 524, SCIENCES DU LANGAGE (FR/1157-3740) [24236911] **3282**

FRANCIS BULLETIN SIGNALETIQUE. 525, PREHISTOIRE ET PROTOHISTOIRE (FR/1157-3759) [24251065] **236**

FRANCIS BULLETIN SIGNALETIQUE. 526, ART ET ARCHEOLOGIE (FR/1157-3767) [24237203] 350, **268**

FRANCIS BULLETIN SIGNALETIQUE. 527, HISTOIRE ET SCIENCES DES RELIGIONS (FR/1157-3775) [24236988] **4959**

FRANCIS BULLETIN SIGNALETIQUE. 528, BIBLIOGRAPHIE INTERNATIONALE DE SCIENCE ADMINISTRATIVE (FR/1157-3783) [24237556] **4650**, **868**

FRANCIS BULLETIN SIGNALETIQUE. 529, ETHNOLOGIE (FR/1157-3791) [24325809] **236**

FRANCIS : HISTOIRE DES SCIENCES ET DES RELIGIONS. 527 (FR) **2616**

FRANCISATION EN MARCHE (CN/0226-5400) [08574647] **4650**

FRANCISCAN ESSAYS (UK) [01343667] **4959**

FRANCISCAN MISSIONARY (CN/0319-6739) [02578291] **5029**

FRANCISCAN STUDIES (US/0080-5459) [01570060] **5029**

FRANCISCAN, THE (UK) [06008850] **5029**

FRANCISCAN, THE (UK/0532-579X) [08973526] **4959**

FRANCISCANA (BE/0015-9840) [02353580] **5029**

FRANCISCANUM (CK/0120-1468) [01369489] **4959**, **4347**

FRANCO-BRITISH STUDIES : JOURNAL OF THE BRITISH INSTITUTE IN PARIS (UK/0952-8571) [17447948] **3282**

FRANCOFONIA (IT) [09674299] **3389**

FRANCOIS AUJOURD'HUI (CN/0821-3488) [09586167] **4959**

FRANCOIS MAURIAC (FR) [02307096] **3389**

FRANCOPHONIE RUGBY (UK/0957-1744) [09571744] **3282**

FRANCOPHONIES D'AMERIQUE (CN/1183-2487) [24623655] **2261**

FRANCUZSKIJ EZEGODNIK (RU/0532-6060) [01375305] **2688**

FRANK (FR/0738-9299) [09689986] 350, **3343**

FRANK GERSTEIN LECTURES, THE (CN/0532-582X) [01369519] **211**

FRANK LLOYD WRIGHT QUARTERLY (US) [21867241] **299**

FRANK NORRIS STUDIES (US) **3389**

FRANK SCHAFFER'S SCHOOLDAYS (US/0746-2018) [09848148] **1895**

FRANK W. PIERCE MEMORIAL LECTURES, THE (US/0532-5838) [01369544] **1675**

FRANKFORT AREA NEWS (US/1056-8174) [23859257] **2533**

FRANKFORT-MOKENA STAR See STAR (FRANKFORT, ILL.), THE **5662**

FRANKFURT AM MAIN. DEUTSCHES INSTITUT FUR INTERNATIONALE PADGOGISCHE FORSCHUNG. JAHRESBERICHT See BERICHT - DEUTSCHES INSTITUT FUR INTERNATIONALE PADAGOGISCHE FORSCHUNG **1889**

FRANKFURT AM MAIN. INSTITUT FUR ANGEWANDTE GEODASIE See NACHRICHTEN AUS DEM KARTEN- UND VERMESSUNGSWESEN. REIHE I **2569**

FRANKFURT AM MAIN. UNIVERSITAT. INSTITUT FUR METEOROLOGIE UND GEOPHYSIK See BERICHTE DES INSTITUTES FUER METEOROLOGIE UND GEOPHYSIK DER UNIVERSITAT FRANKFUERT/MAIN **1420**

FRANKFURTER ALLGEMEINE (GW/0174-4909) [07321360] **5801**

FRANKFURTER BEITRAEGE ZUR GERMANISTIK (GW/0071-9226) [01412059] **3282**

FRANKFURTER FORSCHUNGEN ZUR ARCHITEKTURGESCHICHTE (GW/0429-5714) [01412071] **299**

FRANKFURTER FORSCHUNGEN ZUR KUNST (GW) [05633001] **350**

FRANKFURTER GEOGRAPHISCHE HEFTE (GW/0071-9234) [02319786] **2561**

FRANKFURTER HEFTE See INFORMATION LETTER - FRANKFURTER HEFTE **2517**

FRANKFURTER HISTORISCHE ABHANDLUNGEN (GW) [02017972] **2688**

FRANKFURTER RUNDSCHAU (GW) [06560516] **5801**

FRANKFURTER WIRTSCHAFTS- UND SOZIALWISSENSCHAFTLICHE STUDIEN (GW/0532-6028) [01372973] **5200**

FRANKFURTER WISSENSCHAFTLICHE BEITRAGE. RECHTS- UND WIRTSCHAFTSWISSENSCHAFTLICHE REIHE (GW) [02334589] 1491, **2972**

FRANKIE CROCKER'S MUSIC TRACK (US/0883-0223) [12033836] **4118**

FRANKLIN ADVOCATE, THE (US) [15500630] **5700**

FRANKLIN AND MARSHALL COLLEGE. LANCASTER, PENNSYLVANIA See FRANKLIN AND MARSHALL COLLEGE STUDIES **1825**

FRANKLIN AND MARSHALL COLLEGE STUDIES (US) [01373261] **1825**

FRANKLIN CHALLENGER (US/8750-7390) [11722761] **5664**

FRANKLIN COUNTY CITIZEN (US) [19679814] **5653**

FRANKLIN COUNTY ENTERPRISE (US) [17157850] **5761**

FRANKLIN COUNTY GRAPHIC (US) [17157856] **5761**

FRANKLIN COUNTY HISTORICAL REVIEW, THE (US/0046-4651) [02029344] **2734**

FRANKLIN COUNTY LEGAL JOURNAL (US/0164-2820) [04343735] **2972**

FRANKLIN COUNTY TIMES (US) [09140200] **5626**

FRANKLIN COUNTY TRIBUNE (US) [21665755] **5703**

FRANKLIN FAVORITE, THE (US) [14173515] **5680**

FRANKLIN FOUNDATION See INDIVIDUAL AND THE FUTURE OF ORGANIZATIONS, THE **5203**

FRANKLIN-HALES CORNERS HUB (US) [12043029] **5767**

FRANKLIN HISTORICAL REVIEW (US/0888-6342) [05854728] **2734**

FRANKLIN INSTITUTE (PHILADELPHIA, PA.). SCIENCE INFORMATION SERVICE See BIBLIOGRAPHIC SERIES - FRANKLIN INSTITUTE, PHILADELPHIA, PA **409**

FRANKLIN JOURNAL AND FARMINGTON CHRONICLE, THE (US) [09249237] **5685**

FRANKLIN LECTURES IN THE SCIENCES AND HUMANITIES, THE (US/0533-0130) [01413801] 2846, **5200**

FRANKLIN MCLEAN MEMORIAL RESEARCH INSTITUTE See ANNUAL REPORT - THE FRANKLIN MCLEAN MEMORIAL RESEARCH INSTITUTE **3809**

FRANKLIN MINT See SCULPTORS **2783**

FRANKLIN OFFSET CATALOG (US/0738-6427) [09654565] **4565**

● FRANKLIN PIERCE TIMES (US/1060-5312) [25036055] **2304**

FRANKLIN SUN (WINNSBORO, LA.) (US) [09909889] **5684**

FRANKLIN TIMES, THE (US) [11560974] **5723**

FRANKLINTONIAN (COLUMBUS, OHIO), THE (US/1059-4051) [08341535] **2449**

FRANKREICH : ENERGIEWIRTSCHAFT (GW) [04263351] **1944**

FRANKREICH, FORSCHUNGSPOLITIK UND FORSCHUNGSPRAXIS / BUNDESSTELLE FUR AUSSENHANDELSINFORMATION (GW) [09363567] **5106**

FRANKREICH : WIRTSCHAFT IN ZAHLEN UND WIRTSCHAFTSDOKUMENTATION (GW) [06229940] **1562**

FRANKSTON CITIZEN, THE (US) [14218834] **5750**

FRANSE NEDERLANDEN: JAARBOEK. LES PAYS-BAS FRANCAIS: ANNALES, DE (BE) [04512696] **2688**

FRANZISKANISCHE STUDIEN (GW/0016-0067) [01282481] 4347, **5029**

FRANZOSISCH HEUTE (GW/0342-2895) [06182254] **1895**

FRAPPE (CN/0823-8006) [11054347] **1675**

FRASER BROS. LTD See ENCAN - FRASER BROS. LTD **349**

FRASER FORUM (CN/0827-7893) [14878428] 677, **1491**

FRASER OPINION LETTER, THE (US/0740-0276) [09856121] **1492**

FRASER'S CANADIAN TRADE DIRECTORY (CN/0071-9277) [02441808] 837, **729**

FRASER'S POTATO NEWSLETTER (CN/0384-7322) [03264639] **172**

FRAT UNIVERSITESI DERGISI. SOSYAL BILIMLER (TU) [20521753] **5200**

FRATERNA (CENTRAL POINT, OR.) (US/1055-4564) [23185300] **2415**

FRATERNAL HERALD (US/0006-9256) [03486459] **5231**

FRATERNAL MONITOR, THE (US/0016-0105) [04077824] **2881**

FRATERNALLY YOURS (CN/0823-6577) [10763739] **2261**

FRATERNITE MATIN (MICROFICHE) (IV) [02400701] **5805**

FRATERNITE (PARTI SOCIAL CHRETIENE D'HAITI) (HT) [07386600] **4542**

FRATERNITY NEWS - FRATERNITY FOR CANADIAN ASTROLOGERS (CN/0710-510X) [08649760] **390**

FRATERNITY-SORORITY DIRECTORY... LELAND'S ANNUAL (US) [01570097] **5231**

FRAUD BUREAU NEWSLETTER (US) [23809361] **2881**

FRAUEN UND FILM (GW) [04421946] 5557, **4071**

FRAUENARZT (GW) **3761**

FRAUENARZT HERNE, DER (GW/0016-0237) [00160237] **1747**

FRAUENFRAGE IN DEUTSCHLAND, BIBLIOGRAPHIE / DEUTSCHER AKADEMIKERINNENBUND, DIE (GW/0344-1415) [10470511] **416**

FRAUENHANDBUCH / BROT UND ROSEN (GW) [04627121] **589**

FRAUNHOFER-GESELLSCHAFT ZUR FORDERUNG DER ANGEWANDTEN FORSCHUNG. INSTITUT FUR FESTKORPERMECHANIK See INSTITUTSVEROFFENTLICHUNGEN - INSTITUT FUR FESTKORPERMECHANIK DER FRAUNHOFER-GESELLSCHAFT **1979**

FRAUNHOFER-INSTITUT FUR TREIB- UND EXPLOSIVSTOFFE. INTERNATIONALE JAHRESTAGUNG See INTERNATIONALE JAHRESTAGUNG / FRAUNHOFER-INSTITUT FUER TREIB-UND EXPLOSIVSTOFFE **2013**

FRAZEE FORUM (US) [01570100] **5696**

FRB SF WEEKLY LETTER (US/0890-927X) [03698734] **1492**

FRD OCCASIONAL PAPER (NP) [29838934] **2383**

FRDA REPORT (CN/0835-0752) [17696932] **2383**

FRED ... ANNUAL REPORT TO THE ALASKA STATE LEGISLATURE (US) [15295296] **2304**

FRED : FOOD REGULATIONS EUROPEAN DIRECTORY (FR) **2341**

FRED TROST'S OUTDOORS DIGEST (US/0884-9137) [12033585] **4872**

● FRED TROST'S PRACTICAL SPORTSMAN (US/1067-5914) [27305280] **4895**

FREDDO (IT/0016-0296) [09534388] **2605**

FREDERIC W. H. MYERS MEMORIAL LECTURES (UK) [01570107] **3389**

FREDERICK FINDINGS (US/0899-4188) [18098069] **2449**

FREDERICK LEADER, THE (US) [13676408] **5732**

FREDERICK POST, THE (US) [09977690] **5686**

FREDERICKSBURG STANDARD RADIO POST (US/8755-9331) [11450337] **5750**

● FREDERICTON, NEW BRUNSWICK, ATLANTIC CANADA TOUR PLANNING MANUAL (CN/1184-7530) [24279935] **5474**

FREDERICTON TOUR PLANNING MANUAL See FREDERICTON, NEW BRUNSWICK, ATLANTIC CANADA TOUR PLANNING MANUAL **5474**

FREDERIKSBERG GENNEM TIDERNE (DK/0108-8777) [01752155] **2688**

FREDERIKSHAVN KUNSTMUSEUM See INTER-EXLIBRIS **3217**

FREE (IT) **2487**

FREE ASSOCIATIONS (UK/0267-0887) [12660458] **3925**

FREE CASH FLOW (US/0740-5170) [09972957] **1492**

FREE Alphabetical Title Index

FREE CHINA JOURNAL, THE (CH) [10332516] **5798**

FREE CHINA REVIEW (CH/0016-030X) [01378099] **2651**

FREE CHINA TODAY (CH/0304-1204) [01796629] **2503**

FREE CHURCH CHRONICLE (UK/0016-0326) [05349731] **4960**

FREE CHURCH OF SCOTLAND See MONTHLY RECORD OF THE FREE CHURCH OF SCOTLAND, THE **5065**

FREE-FALL (BANFF, ALTA.) (CN/0714-4172) [09071168] **3389**

FREE FLIGHT (OTTAWA ONT.) (CN/0827-2557) [11734434] 21, **4895**

●FREE FOOD FOR THOUGHT (US) [26662813] **350**

FREE INQUIRY (BUFFALO) (US/0272-0701) [06753572] 4960, **4347**

FREE INQUIRY IN CREATIVE SOCIOLOGY (US/0736-9182) [05274230] **5246**

FREE LABOUR WORLD (BE/0770-1470) [01343828] **1675**

FREE LANCE (US) [27945699] **5635**

FREE LANCE STAR, THE (US) **5758**

FREE LANCE, THE (US/0016-0369) [01308644] **3389**

FREE-LANCE WRITING & PHOTOGRAPHY (UK) 3389, **4369**

FREE LOAN FILMS (US/0093-0881) [01791648] **4071**

FREE LUNCH (US/1041-0945) [18631459] **3463**

FREE MATERIALS FOR SCHOOLS AND LIBRARIES (US/0836-0073) [17514257] **1895**

FREE METHODIST HERALD (CN/0823-4590) [10365075] **5060**

FREE MUSIC MAGAZINE (CN/0826-5984) [11355484] **4118**

FREE PHILOSOPHER QUARTERLY, THE (US/0742-3748) [10305141] **4347**

FREE PRESS (US) [15579049] **5696**

●FREE PRESS (COLUMBUS, OHIO), THE (US/1063-1267) [25882195] **2920**

FREE PRESS-COURIER (GALETON ED.) (US) [13287047] **5736**

FREE PRESS (DIBOLL, TEX.) (US) [16727102] **5750**

FREE PRESS (SPARWOOD) (CN/0715-5131) [09318351] **5784**

FREE PRESS STANDARD, THE (US) [09753132] **5728**

FREE PRESS, THE (US) [22960616] **5723**

FREE PRESS TRIBUNE-TRESS (US) [21719387] **5696**

FREE QUERIES CEASED. (US/1050-3668) [17938826] **2449**

FREE RADICAL BIOLOGY & MEDICINE (US/0891-5849) [14917670] **487**

●FREE RADICAL RESEARCH (US/1071-5762) [28679237] **1052**

FREE RADICAL RESEARCH COMMUNICATIONS (SZ/8755-0199) [11241977] **1052**

FREE ROMANIAN : ORGAN OF THE WORLD UNION OF FREE ROMANIANS, THE (UK) [17673678] **2261**

FREE SPACE (CN/0821-5294) [09606647] **5557**

FREE SPEECH MONITOR (CN/1182-008X) [22366845] **4508**

FREE SPEECH YEARBOOK (US/0899-7225) [01830689] **3093**

●FREE SPIRIT (MIAMI, FLA.) (US/1062-8134) [25751375] **4388**

FREE SPIRIT (MINNEAPOLIS, MINN.) CEASED. (US/0895-2256) [16517697] 1895, **1063**

FREE STOCK PHOTOGRAPHY DIRECTORY, THE (US/0190-1567) [04644358] **4369**

FREE STUFF FOR KIDS (DEEPHAVEN, MINN.) (US/1056-9693) [16910475] **1063**

FREE TIME (US/1064-2757) [26243553] **2533**

FREE TO BE (AT/0815-9564) [I08159564] **1804**

FREE TRADE ADVISORY : THE BIWEEKLY ADVISORY ON HOW THE NORTH AMERICAN FREE TRADE TALKS WILL AFFECT YOUR BUSINESS AND INVESTMENTS IN MEXICO (US/1058-5745) [24333477] **837**

FREE TRADE LAW REPORTER (CN) [20615320] 837, **2972**

FREE-TRADE WINDS See NAFTA DIGEST / NORTH AMERICAN FREE TRADE AGREEMENT INFORMATION CENTER, THE GRADUATE SCHOOL OF INTERNATIONAL TRADE & BUSINESS ADMINISTRATION, LAREDO STATE UNIVERSITY **847**

FREE-TRADE WINDS / OFFICE FOR THE STUDY OF A U.S.-MEXICO FREE-TRADE AGREEMENT, LAREDO STATE UNIVERSITY (US) [23950207] **837**

FREE VENICE BEACHHEAD (US/0884-9641) [12536923] **5635**

FREE WEEKLY, THE CEASED. (US) [23108144] **5643**

FREEBIES (SANTA MONICA) (US/0148-2092) [05109367] **1297**

FREEBORN COUNTY TRACER (US) **2449**

FREEDOM : A DOCUMENTARY HISTORY OF EMANCIPATION 1861-1867 (UK) **2688**

FREEDOM DAILY / THE FUTURE OF FREEDOM FOUNDATION (US) [25680783] **4508**

FREEDOM DIGEST (KO) [10249032] **4522**

FREEDOM IN EDUCATION (US/0740-5936) [06411691] **1747**

FREEDOM IN THE WORLD (US/0732-6610) [05796565] **4508**

FREEDOM MAGAZINE (US) [06698981] **2533**

FREEDOM MONITOR CEASED. (US/0898-9265) [17799885] **4522**

FREEDOM OF INFORMATION AND PROTECTION OF INDIVIDUAL PRIVACY. DIRECTORY OF GENERAL RECORDS (CN/0835-9733) [18060151] **4650**

FREEDOM OF INFORMATION REVIEW (AT/0817-3532) [I08173532] **3179**

FREEDOM OF INFORMATION SERVICE (CN) 4508, **2972**

FREEDOM REVIEW (US/1054-3090) [22841714] **4508**

FREEDOM SOCIALIST, THE (US/0272-4367) [06859494] 5557, **4542**

FREEDOM SPEECH (US/1057-3682) [24032384] **5635**

FREEDOM TO READ FOUNDATION NEWS (US/0046-5038) [01792767] **3211**

FREEDOM TO READ FOUNDATION (U.S.) See FREEDOM TO READ FOUNDATION NEWS **3211**

FREEDOM WRITER (GREAT BARRINGTON, MASS.) (US/1059-6372) [15208738] **4960**

FREELANCE DIRECTORY (US) [08841961] 3577, **2920**

FREELANCE EDITORS' ASSOCIATION OF CANADA See DIRECTORY OF MEMBERS - FREELANCE EDITORS' ASSOCIATION OF CANADA **4814**

FREELANCE GRAPHICS REPORT, THE CEASED. (US/1059-6119) [24647481] **378**

FREELANCE (REGINA) (CN/0705-1379) [03991657] **3389**

FREELANCE UPDATE See TRAVELWRITER MARKETLETTER **2925**

FREELANCE (VANCOUVER) (CN/0711-2335) [08489228] **677**

●FREELANCE WRITER'S NEWSLETTER (KNOXVILLE, TENN.) (US/1064-9050) [26459369] **2920**

FREELANCE WRITER'S REPORT (US/0731-549X) [08215246] **2920**

FREELANCER (MAYERTHORPE) (CN/0706-7224) [04955078] **5784**

FREEMAN (IRVINGTON-ON-HUDSON, N.Y.), THE (US/0016-0652) [01570149] **1592**

FREEMAN REPORTS. MASS STORAGE OUTLOOK (US/1058-8299) [24350945] **1237**

●FREEMAN (WAUKESHA, WIS.), THE (US/1062-9041) [25587081] **5767**

FREEMAN'S INTERNATIONAL CATALOGUE (UK) **416**

FREEPORT FACTS See BRAZOSPORT FACTS, THE **5747**

FREEPORT JOURNAL-STANDARD (US) [11087856] **5660**

FREER GALLERY OF ART See OCCASIONAL PAPERS - FREER GALLERY OF ART **360**

FREER PRESS, THE (US) [16752306] **5750**

FREESAIL (AT/0727-615X) [I0727615X] **4895**

FREESTONE FRONTIERS (US/0735-3278) [08895303] **2449**

FREESTYLE BMX MAGAZINE See INVERT MAGAZINE **429**

FREETHINKER, THE (UK/0016-0687) [05249570] **4347**

●FREETHOUGHT HISTORY (US/1071-7269) [25681110] **4347**

FREETHOUGHT TODAY (US/0882-8512) [10121502] **4960**

FREEWAY EVOLUTION, THE (US) [06258218] **5440**

FREEWAY/L.A (US/0740-3003) [09910800] **5440**

FREEWHEELIN' (CN/0228-6831) [07857889] **4081**

FREEZE (UK/0306-5782) [01830109] **2341**

FREIBERGER FORSCHUNGSHEFTE. REIHE A (GW/0071-9390) [01570156] **2139**

FREIBERGER FORSCHUNGSHEFTE. REIHE B (GW/0071-9420) [04203866] **4002**

FREIBERGER FORSCHUNGSHEFTE. REIHE C (GW/0071-9404) [01570157] **1376**

FREIBERGER FORSCHUNGSHEFTE. REIHE D (GW/0071-9412) [02397736] **2139**

FREIBEUTER (GW/0171-9289) [06703208] **2517**

FREIBORD (AU) [04954266] **3389**

FREIBURG I.B. ARNOLD-NERGSTRAESER-INSTITUT FUR KULTURWISSENSCHAFTLICHE FORSCHUNG See ORDO POLITICUS **4486**

FREIBURGER DIOEZESAN-ARCHIV (GW) [01788849] **5029**

FREIBURGER ISLAMSTUDIEN (GW) [01380582] **5042**

FREIBURGER RECHTS- UND STAATSWISSENSCHAFTLICHE ABHANDLUNGEN (GW/0429-6524) [01570160] **4474**

FREIBURGER RUNDBRIEF (GW/0344-1385) [06240282] **4960**

FREIBURGER THEOLOGISCHE STUDIEN (GW) [02038691] **4960**

FREIBURGER ZEITSCHRIFT FUER PHILOSOPHIE UND THEOLOGIE (SZ/0016-0725) [01682285] 4960, **4347**

FREIE ARGUMENTE (AU) [07886039] **4650**

FREIE UNIVERSITAT BERLIN See RECHENSCHAFTSBERICHT DES PRASIDENTEN / FU BERLIN **1843**

FREIE UNIVERSITAT BERLIN. JAHRESBERICHT See RECHENSCHAFTSBERICHT DES PRASIDENTEN / FU BERLIN **1843**

FREIE UNIVERSITAT BERLIN. STANDIGE KOMMISSION FUR FORSCHUNG UND WISSENSCHAFTLICHEN NACHWUCHS See FORSCHUNGSBERICHT DER FREIEN UNIVERSITAT BERLIN **1824**

FREIE ZAHNARZT, THE (GW/0340-1766) [01372862] **1323**

FREIEN DEUTSCHES HOCHSTIFT (FRANKFURT AM MAIN, GERMANY) See JAHRBUCH DES FREIEN DEUTSCHEN HOCHSTIFTS **3398**

FREIER DEUTSCHER GEWERKSCHAFTSBUND See FDGB REVIEW **1669**

FREIES DEUTSCHES HOCHSTIFT (FRANKFURT AM MAIN, GERMANY) See REIHE DER SCHRIFTEN - FREIES DEUTSCHES HOCHSTIFT **3428**

FREIGHT COMMODITY STATISTICS. MOTOR CARRIERS OF PROPERTY (US/0194-0562) [04084462] **5401**

FREIGHT FORWARDING See WORLD FREIGHT SHIPPER **5458**

FREIGHT MANAGEMENT (UK/0016-0873) [I00160873] **5383**

FREIGHT MANAGEMENT INTERNATIONAL (UK/0965-4704) [I09654704] **5383**

FREIGHT NEWS (1983) (UK) [09649686] **5383**

FREIGHT NEWS (1983) See FREIGHT NEWS EXPRESS **5383**

FREIGHT NEWS EXPRESS CEASED. (UK) [12281791] **5383**

FREIGHT SERVICE DIRECTORY. CHICAGO EDITION (US/0278-5404) [07815854] **5383**

FREIGHT TRAFFIC FORECAST (SZ) [16988482] **21**

FREIGHTER, THE (CN/0820-5280) [16723081] **5784**

FREIGHTER TRAVEL NEWS (US/0016-089X) [04689053] **837**

FREIHEIT (BERLIN, GERMANY) (GW) [12620609] **5801**

FREITAG (GW) [24314289] **2517**

FREIZEIT REVUE (GW) **2773**

FREIZEITPADAGOGIK (GW/0721-1244) [07211244] **1747**

FREMANTLE ARTS REVIEW (AT/0816-6919) [I08166919] **320**

FREMDENVERKEHR See FREMDENVERKEHR + I.E. UND DAS REISEBURO, DER **5474**

FREMDENVERKEHR + I.E. UND DAS REISEBURO, DER (GW) [04677426] **5474**

FREMDENVERKEHR IM LANDE SALZBURG IM ..., DER (AU) [10764847] **837**

Alphabetical Title Index — FRIGIDAIRE

FREMDENVERKEHRSBILANZ DER SCHWEIZ / LA BALANCE TOURISTIQUE DE LA SUISSE, DIE (SZ) [08356706] **5474**

FREMDSPRACHE DEUTSCH (GW) **1895**

FREMDSPRACHEN *CEASED.* (GW/0016-0970) [01381053] **3282**

FREMDSPRACHEN LEHREN UND LERNEN (GW/0932-6936) [18008622] **3282**

FREMDSPRACHENUNTERRICHT (GW/0016-0989) [01570165] **1879**

FREMDSPRACHLICHE UNTERRICHT, DER (GW/0340-2207) [01785417] 1895, **3282**

FREMONT COUNTY HERALD-CHRONICLE (US) [18436129] **5656**

FREMONT COUNTY NOSTALGIA NEWS *CEASED.* (US/8756-8446) [11633133] **2449**

FREMONT GAZETTE (US) [15863237] **5670**

FREMONT-MILLS BEACON-ENTERPRISE (TABOR, IOWA : 1981) (US) [16126942] **5670**

FREMONT TRIBUNE (US/1049-8338) [10579597] **5706**

FREMONTIA (SACRAMENTO, CALIF.) (US/0092-1793) [01789066] **511**

FREMY, DOMINIQUE *See* QUID? **1928**

FRENCH 17 (US/0191-9199) [04633102] **3458**

FRENCH AMERICAN REVIEW (US/1052-3952) [22283139] **2688**

FRENCH ANCESTORS : HERITAGE OF THE FRENCH SETTLERS IN WESTERN OHIO (US/1064-3591) [26271090] **2734**

FRENCH COLONIAL HISTORICAL SOCIETY. MEETING *See* PROCEEDINGS OF THE ... MEETING OF THE FRENCH COLONIAL HISTORICAL SOCIETY **2703**

FRENCH COMPANY HANDBOOK (FR) [07217047] **677**

FRENCH CULTURAL STUDIES (UK/0957-1558) [21550146] **2846**

FRENCH-ENGLISH TRANSLATORS EXCHANGE (US/0275-4436) [07147692] **3282**

FRENCH EQUATORIAL AFRICA. GRAND CONSEIL *See* SESSION BUDGETAIRE / GRAND CONSEIL DE L'AFRIQUE EQUATORIALE FRANCAISE **4747**

FRENCH FOREIGN POLICY (US/0532-6729) [01383476] **4522**

FRENCH FORUM (US/0098-9355) [02246903] **3343**

FRENCH FORUM MONOGRAPHS (US) [06136516] 3283, **3389**

FRENCH HISTORICAL STUDIES (US/0016-1071) [01570174] **2688**

FRENCH HISTORY (UK/0269-1191) [15209899] **2689**

FRENCH ICE (US/0892-7960) [15262481] **373**

FRENCH JOURNAL OF ORTHOPAEDIC SURGERY *See* JOURNAL OF ORTHOPAEDIC SURGERY, THE **3882**

FRENCH LITERATURE SERIES (US/0271-6607) [02025530] 3389, **3343**

FRENCH MONOGRAPHS (AT) [02300285] 3389, **3283**

FRENCH PERIODICAL INDEX (US/0362-5044) [02294165] **416**

FRENCH POLITICS AND SOCIETY (US/0882-1267) [11681085] 5246, **4474**

FRENCH RAILWAY REVIEW (UK/0264-5769) [10384219] **5431**

FRENCH REVIEW, THE (US/0016-111X) [01238339] 1895, **3283**

FRENCH RIVIERA. COTE D'AZUR (UK) [02227687] **5415**

FRENCH, SAMUEL, FIRM, PUBLISHERS *See* GUIDE TO SELECTING PLAYS, THE **3392**

FRENCH SCIENCE NEWS (FR/0532-6826) [02165897] **5106**

FRENCH SETTLEMENT HISTORICAL REGISTER, THE (US/0160-0907) [03600650] **2734**

FRENCH STUDIES (UK/0016-1128) [01242098] **3343**

FRENCH STUDIES BULLETIN (UK/0262-2750) [08224183] 3283, **3389**

FRENCH STUDIES IN SOUTHERN AFRICA (SA/0259-0247) [02245018] **3389**

FRENCH XX BIBLIOGRAPHY (US/0085-0888) [02014769] 3389, **3458**

FRENESIE (FR/0767-3744) [15863854] **3925**

FRENTE DE TORMENTA (AG/0327-4071) [25239131] **2734**

FREQUENCY CONTROL SYMPOSIUM. PROCEEDINGS OF THE ... ANNUAL FREQUENCY CONTROL SYMPOSIUM *See* PROCEEDINGS OF THE ... IEEE FREQUENCY CONTROL SYMPOSIUM **4418**

FREQUENT FLYER (US/1046-0330) [20286528] **5474**

FREQUENT UPDATE *See* INSIDE FLYER **5384**

FREQUENZ ZEITSCHRIFT FUER SCHWINGUNGS-UND SCHWACHSTROMTECHNIK (GW/0016-1136) [01570184] **2055**

●FRESENIUS ENVIRONMENTAL BULLETIN (SZ/1018-4619) [26350423] **2172**

FRESENIUS' JOURNAL OF ANALYTICAL CHEMISTRY (GW/0937-0633) [21067721] **1015**

FRESH! (US/0886-9596) [13079672] **4118**

FRESH FRUIT AND VEGETABLE ARRIVAL TOTALS FOR 23 CITIES / UNITED STATES DEPARTMENT OF AGRICULTURE, AGRICULTURAL MARKETING SERVICE, FRUIT AND VEGETABLE DIVISION (US/0749-5390) [10167202] **837**

FRESH FRUIT AND VEGETABLE ARRIVALS IN EASTERN CITIES BY COMMODITIES, STATES, AND MONTHS (US/0738-1786) [09528262] 837, **1607**

FRESH FRUIT AND VEGETABLE ARRIVALS IN WESTERN CITIES BY COMMODITIES, STATES, AND MONTHS (US/0738-2243) [09528209] **1607**

FRESH FRUIT AND VEGETABLE PRICES (US/0740-4735) [09048052] **89**

FRESH FRUIT AND VEGETABLE SHIPMENTS BY STATES, COMMODITIES, COUNTIES, STATIONS (US/0565-2065) [02245925] **837**

FRESH FRUIT AND VEGETABLE UNLOADS IN MIDWESTERN CITIES BY COMMODITIES, STATES AND MONTHS (US/0501-462X) [02275919] **837**

FRESH FRUIT AND VEGETABLE UNLOADS IN SOUTHERN CITIES BY COMMODITIES, STATES AND MONTHS (US/0501-4603) [02276287] **837**

FRESH FRUIT AND VEGETABLES, ORNAMENTAL CROPS. WEEKLY SUMMARY--SHIPMENTS AND UNLOADS (US) [07559317] **89**

FRESH MEN (US/1060-5266) [25023189] **2533**

FRESH PRODUCE JOURNAL (UK/0016-2256) **172**

FRESH START, THE (US/0888-2525) [13545864] **1607**

FRESH TRACKS (US/1058-8191) [24386406] **385**

FRESH TRENDS (US/1062-2705) [25515135] **2341**

FRESHMAN ENGLISH NEWS *See* COMPOSITION STUDIES : FRESHMAN ENGLISH NEWS **3274**

FRESHMAN YEAR EXPERIENCE NEWSLETTER, THE (US/1053-2048) [18036063] **1825**

FRESHWATER (CN/0834-4302) [13714952] **4176**

FRESHWATER AND AQUACULTURE CONTENTS TABLES. ACTUALITES DES EAUX DOUCES ET DE L'AQUACULTURE (IT) [04371859] 2304, **2317**

FRESHWATER AND MARINE AQUARIUM (US/0160-4317) [03673498] **2304**

FRESHWATER BIOLOGICAL ASSOCIATION *See* SCIENTIFIC PUBLICATION - FRESHWATER BIOLOGICAL ASSOCIATION **472**

FRESHWATER BIOLOGICAL ASSOCIATION *See* LIST OF MEMBERS / FRESHWATER BIOLOGICAL ASSOCIATION **463**

FRESHWATER BIOLOGY (UK/0046-5070) [01793027] 2216, **456**

FRESHWATER CATCH *CEASED.* (NZ/0111-3232) [I01113232] **2304**

FRESHWATER FISHERIES LABORATORY (PITLOCHRY, SCOTLAND) *See* ANNUAL REVIEW / FRESHWATER FISHERIES LABORATORY, PITLOCHRY **2295**

FRESHWATER FISHING AUSTRALIA (AT/1032-125X) [I1032125X] **2304**

FRESHWATER FORUM (UK/0961-4664) [23723046] **456**

FRESNO BEE, THE (US/0889-6070) [08822010] **5635**

FRESNO BUSINESS AND INDUSTRY NEWS : SERVING THE GREATER FRESNO/CLOVIS METROPOLITAN AREA (US/1059-0986) [24479640] **677**

FRESNO PAST AND PRESENT (US/0429-7164) [02353712] **2734**

FRETTED INSTRUMENT GUILD OF AMERICA *See* FIGA **4117**

FRETZLETTER (US/0730-2495) [07958412] **2449**

FREUNDIN MUNCHEN (GW/0016-1187) [I00161187] **2790**

FRI BULLETIN / FOREST RESEARCH INSTITUTE, NEW ZEALAND FOREST SERVICE (NZ/0111-8129) [10068496] **2383**

FRIA TIDER (SW/0283-7560) [I02837560] **4850**

FRIC OCCASIONAL PAPER (NP) [25307737] **2383**

FRIDAY CITIZEN, THE (CN/0711-4451) [08534451] **5784**

FRIDAY REPORT (US) [20021651] **759**

FRIDAY TIMES (CN/0707-543X) [04875716] **5785**

FRIDAY (TORONTO) (CN/0229-2319) [07865667] **4850**

FRIDAY WEEKLY (SI) **1063**

FRIEDENSWARTE, DIE (SZ/0340-0255) [01570199] 4522, **3128**

FRIEDRICH GOTTLIEB KLOPSTOCK WERKE UND BRIEFE (GW) **3389**

FRIELING THEATER-JAHRBUCH (GW) [25898073] **5364**

FRIEND (LONDON), THE (UK/0016-1268) [01417494] **5060**

FRIEND OF AUSTRALIA AND NEW ZEALAND *See* AUSTRALIAN FRIEND (SYDNEY, N.S.W.) **4937**

FRIEND OF THE FAMILY FARM, THE (US/0890-8176) [12634399] **89**

FRIEND O'WILDLIFE (US/0016-1284) [04080429] **2194**

FRIEND (SALT LAKE CITY), THE (US/0009-4102) [04080412] **4960**

FRIENDLY EXCHANGE (US/0279-6856) [07198421] **5474**

FRIENDLY FAIRWAYS OF MICHIGAN (US/0193-0443) [05108188] **4895**

FRIENDLY LETTER, A *CEASED.* (US/0739-5418) [07789443] **5060**

FRIENDLY WOMAN, THE (US/0740-5618) [09286253] 5060, **5557**

FRIENDLY WORD, THE (IE/0790-3642) [I07903642] **5060**

FRIENDS COMMITTEE ON LEGISLATION OF CALIFORNIA *See* FCL NEWSLETTER **4647**

FRIENDS COMMITTEE ON NATIONAL LEGISLATION, WASHINGTON, D.C *See* FCNL WASHINGTON NEWSLETTER **4647**

FRIENDS (HALIFAX) (CN/0821-638X) [09808992] **5286**

FRIENDS' HISTORICAL SOCIETY *See* JOURNAL OF THE FRIENDS' HISTORICAL SOCIETY, THE **5062**

FRIENDS JOURNAL (US/0016-1322) [01570228] **4960**

FRIENDS OF FINANCIAL HISTORY (US/0278-8861) [07889259] **899**

FRIENDS OF FLORIDA FOLK (US/0892-2500) [15154815] 4118, **2320**

FRIENDS OF KEBYAR (US/0890-9717) [11420127] **299**

FRIENDS OF MICRONESIA (ASSOCIATION) *See* NEWSLETTER - FRIENDS OF MICRONESIA **2670**

FRIENDS OF THE COURT / LITTLE ROCK (US) [29687294] **3140**

FRIENDS OF THE COURT : NEWSLETTER OF THE ARKANSAS JUDICIAL DEPARTMENT (US) [08198379] **3140**

FRIENDS OF THE EARTH (US/1054-1829) [22753366] 2194, **2216**

FRIENDS OF THE LILLY LIBRARY NEWSLETTER, THE (US/0749-4092) [10480986] **3211**

FRIENDS OF WINE, THE (US/0364-9474) [02693448] **2367**

FRIENDS' QUARTERLY (US) 2616, **4088**

FRIENDS' QUARTERLY, THE (UK/0016-1357) [02509191] **4960**

FRIENDS (WARREN, MICH.) *CEASED.* (US/0884-9889) [01624397] 5474, **5415**

FRIENDS WORLD NEWS : NEWS BULLETIN OF THE FRIENDS WORLD COMMITTEE FOR CONSULTATION (UK/0016-1365) [01696749] **4960**

FRIENDSCRIPT (US/0192-5539) [05081463] **3211**

FRIENDSHIP FORUM (CN/0709-6259) [05694741] **5286**

FRIENDSHIP REPORTER (US) [15113636] **5767**

FRIESIAN BULLS WITH IMPROVED CONTEMPORARY COMPARISION. 2D SERIES (UK) [04186767] **211**

FRIESLAND POST (NE/0165-313X) [I0165313X] 5474, **4850**

FRIGHTEN THE HORSES (US/1072-5644) [26533508] **5187**

FRIGIDAIRE (IT) [23077095] **2487**

FRIIDRETT Alphabetical Title Index

FRIIDRETT (NO/0332-9666) [I03329666] **1091**

FRIM TECHNICAL INFORMATION (MY/0127-9793) [I01279793] **2383**

FRINGE BENEFITS FOR ADMINISTRATORS IN PUBLIC SCHOOLS (US/0742-1664) [08232048] **1864**

FRINGE BENEFITS FOR SUPERINTENDENTS IN PUBLIC SCHOOLS (US/0743-7390) [08232067] **1864**

FRINGE BENEFITS FOR TEACHERS IN PUBLIC SCHOOLS (US/0742-082X) [08232023] **1864**

●FRINGE WARE REVIEW (US/1069-5656) [28104824] 3389, **1237**

FRIO, CALOR, AIRE ACONDICIONADO (SP/0210-0665) [I02100665] **2605**

FRIONA STAR (US) [14114995] **5750**

FRIPOUNET PARIS (FR/0016-1446) [I00161446] **4850**

FRISKO (US) **2533**

FRM WEEKLY (US) **677**

FRODSKAPARRIT (FA/0367-1704) [09370543] **3283**

FROEIGN TRADE, AUSTRALIA. IMPORTS See FOREIGN TRADE, AUSTRALIA. MERCHANDISE IMPORTS. DETAILED COMMODITY TABLES **729**

FROHE BOTSCHAFT GOTTINGEN (GW/0340-6091) [I03406091] **4960**

FROHLINGER'S MARKETING REPORT (US/1057-5316) [24060825] **924**

●FROM INFORMATION TO EDUCATION (US/1064-9034) [26459492] **1747**

FROM NINE TO FIVE (US/0016-1616) [02251641] **677**

FROM SEA TO SEA (CN/1181-9014) [23237466] **2449**

FROM THE BROTHERS GRIMM (US/1070-8898) [21939346] **2320**

FROM THE DRAGON'S DEN (US/0732-5517) [08408031] **2785**

FROM THE GROUND UP (CN/0317-056X) [02247635] **22**

FROM THE GYM TO THE JURY (US/1054-1950) [20719616] 4895, **2972**

FROM THE HORSE'S MOUTH (PITTSBURGH) (US/0270-6865) [05853963] **1675**

FROM THE LAWYERS COLLECTIVE (II) [20023732] **2972**

●FROM THE OLDE BOOKSHELF (US/1066-2979) [26915910] **4828**

FROM THE PAGES OF EXPERIMENTAL MUSICAL INSTRUMENTS (US) **4118**

FROM THE ROOFTOPS (CN/0702-696X) [03412305] **1542**

FROM THE SOURDOUGH CROCK (US/0532-7334) [01789076] **2320**

FROM THE STATE CAPITALS. ALCOHOLIC BEVERAGE CONTROL (US/0734-0842) [08522814] **3164**

FROM THE STATE CAPITALS. CIVIL RIGHTS (US/0741-353X) [10175625] **4508**

FROM THE STATE CAPITALS. CONSTRUCTION POLICIES (US/0749-2766) [11135100] **615**

FROM THE STATE CAPITALS. ECONOMIC DEVELOPMENT (US/1061-9712) [21997684] **1492**

FROM THE STATE CAPITALS. EMPLOYEE POLICY FOR THE PRIVATE & PUBLIC SECTORS (US/1061-9674) [25259819] **4703**

FROM THE STATE CAPITALS. ENVIRONMENTAL REGULATION (US/1061-9682) [25042920] **2230**

FROM THE STATE CAPITALS. FAMILY RELATIONS (US/0741-3505) [10175389] **2280**

FROM THE STATE CAPITALS. FEDERAL ACTION AFFECTING THE STATES (NEW HAVEN, CONN.) (US/0734-1202) [08719321] **4650**

FROM THE STATE CAPITALS. FISH AND GAME REGULATION See FROM THE STATE CAPITALS. PARKS AND RECREATION TRENDS, (NEW HAVEN, CONN.) **4706**

FROM THE STATE CAPITALS. HIGHWAY FINANCING AND CONSTRUCTION (US/0016-1705) [05018474] 615, **5440**

FROM THE STATE CAPITALS. INSURANCE REGULATION (US/0016-1748) [02447070] **2881**

FROM THE STATE CAPITALS. JUSTICE POLICIES (US/0749-2790) [11130957] **3165**

FROM THE STATE CAPITALS. LABOR RELATIONS (US/0734-1105) [08601113] **3148**

FROM THE STATE CAPITALS. MOTOR VEHICLE REGULATION (US/0016-1810) [08699515] 4776, **5415**

FROM THE STATE CAPITALS. PARKS AND RECREATION See FROM THE STATE CAPITALS. PARKS AND RECREATION TRENDS, (NEW HAVEN, CONN.) **4706**

FROM THE STATE CAPITALS. PARKS AND RECREATION TRENDS, (NEW HAVEN, CONN.) (US/0749-2804) [08698956] 2194, **4706**

FROM THE STATE CAPITALS. PUBLIC ASSISTANCE & WELFARE TRENDS (NEW HAVEN, CONN.) (US/0734-1601) [08698719] **5286**

FROM THE STATE CAPITALS. PUBLIC EMPLOYEE POLICY (US/0741-3521) [10175665] **940**

FROM THE STATE CAPITALS. PUBLIC HEALTH (1982) (US/0734-1156) [08600262] 2972, **4776**

FROM THE STATE CAPITALS. PUBLIC SAFETY & JUSTICE POLICIES (US/1061-9704) [24632823] 4776, **3165**

FROM THE STATE CAPITALS. PUBLIC UTILITIES (US/0016-1888) [02254194] **4650**

FROM THE STATE CAPITALS. TAXATION AND REVENUE POLICIES (US/0749-2820) [11130549] **4727**

FROM THE STATE CAPITALS. TAXES-PROPERTY (NEW HAVEN, CONN.) (US/0734-1121) [08602902] **4727**

FROM THE STATE CAPITALS. THE OUTLOOK FROM THE STATE CAPITALS (US/1061-9690) [24785603] 4650, **2972**

FROM THE STATE CAPITALS. TOURIST BUSINESS PROMOTION (NEW HAVEN, CONN.) (US/0734-1199) [08697735] **5474**

FROM THE STATE CAPITALS. TRANSPORTATION POLICIES (US/0749-2774) [11134999] **5383**

FROM THE STATE CAPITALS. URBAN DEVELOPMENT (US/0741-3483) [10169137] **2823**

FROM THE STATE CAPITALS. WORKERS' COMPENSATION (US/0734-0931) [08606210] 4650, **1675**

FROM THE UNICEF WATERFRONT (US) [10587370] **2230**

FROMMER'S ALASKA (US) **5474**

FROMMER'S AMSTERDAM AND HOLLAND (US/0899-3181) [18065394] **5474**

●FROMMER'S ARIZONA (US/1053-2471) [22485344] **5474**

FROMMER'S ATHENS See FROMMER'S COMPREHENSIVE TRAVEL GUIDE. ATHENS **5475**

FROMMER'S ATLANTIC CITY & CAPE MAY See FROMMER'S COMPREHENSIVE TRAVEL GUIDE. ATLANTIC CITY & CAPE MAY **5475**

FROMMER'S AUSTRALIA See FROMMER'S COMPREHENSIVE TRAVEL GUIDE. AUSTRALIA **5475**

FROMMER'S AUSTRALIA ON $ ... A DAY See FROMMER'S BUDGET TRAVEL GUIDE. AUSTRALIA ... ON $ ... A DAY **5474**

FROMMER'S BARCELONA, PLUS MAJORCA, IBIZA, AND MINORCA See FROMMER'S COMPREHENSIVE TRAVEL GUIDE. BARCELONA **5475**

FROMMER'S BELGIUM, HOLLAND & LUXEMBOURG (US/1044-2413) [19716657] **5474**

●FROMMER'S BERLIN ON ... $ A DAY (US/1055-5366) [23200827] **5474**

FROMMER'S BERMUDA AND THE BAHAMAS, PLUS TURKS AND CAICOS See FROMMER'S COMPREHENSIVE TRAVEL GUIDE. BERMUDA & THE BAHAMAS **5475**

FROMMER'S BOSTON (US/0899-322X) [18065234] **5474**

●FROMMER'S BUDGET TRAVEL GUIDE. AUSTRALIA ... ON $ ... A DAY (US) [22472993] **5474**

●FROMMER'S BUDGET TRAVEL GUIDE. EASTERN EUROPE ... ON $ ... A DAY (US) [23830718] **5474**

FROMMER'S BUDGET TRAVEL GUIDE. HAWAII ... ON $ ... A DAY (US/1059-7603) [22653707] **5475**

●FROMMER'S BUDGET TRAVEL GUIDE. LONDON ... ON $ ... A DAY (US/1055-5331) [23200779] **5475**

●FROMMER'S BUDGET TRAVEL GUIDE. MADRID ... ON $ ... A DAY (US/1055-5323) [23200762] **5475**

FROMMER'S BUDGET TRAVEL GUIDE. MEXICO ... ON $ ... A DAY (US/1058-2541) [22653712] **5475**

●FROMMER'S BUDGET TRAVEL GUIDE. SPAIN ... ON $ ... A DAY (US/1053-2439) [22485542] **5475**

●FROMMER'S BUDGET TRAVEL GUIDE. WASHINGTON, D.C. ... ON $ ... A DAY (US/1065-4585) [25268876] **5475**

FROMMER'S CALIFORNIA WITH KIDS (US/1040-9386) [18587724] **5475**

FROMMER'S CANADA See FROMMER'S COMPREHENSIVE TRAVEL GUIDE. CANADA **5475**

FROMMER'S CHICAGO (US/1040-936X) [18587658] **5475**

●FROMMER'S COLORADO (US/1053-2463) [22485372] **5475**

FROMMER'S COMPREHENSINVE TRAVEL GUIDE (US) [22881060] **5475**

●FROMMER'S COMPREHENSIVE TRAVEL GUIDE. ACAPULCO, IXTAPA & TAXCO (US/1066-4939) [26963643] **5475**

●FROMMER'S COMPREHENSIVE TRAVEL GUIDE. ATHENS (US/1064-3060) [22932991] **5475**

●FROMMER'S COMPREHENSIVE TRAVEL GUIDE. ATLANTA (US/1047-7888) [22932980] **5475**

●FROMMER'S COMPREHENSIVE TRAVEL GUIDE. ATLANTIC CITY & CAPE MAY (US/1064-525X) [22932966] **5475**

●FROMMER'S COMPREHENSIVE TRAVEL GUIDE. AUSTRALIA (US/1064-3036) [25860735] **5475**

FROMMER'S COMPREHENSIVE TRAVEL GUIDE. AUSTRIA & HUNGARY (US/1057-4018) [22535349] **5475**

●FROMMER'S COMPREHENSIVE TRAVEL GUIDE. BANGKOK (US/1055-5374) [23200856] **5475**

●FROMMER'S COMPREHENSIVE TRAVEL GUIDE. BARCELONA (US/1064-3427) [24527167] **5475**

FROMMER'S COMPREHENSIVE TRAVEL GUIDE. BED & BREAKFAST, NORTH AMERICA (US/1064-3435) [23881397] **2805**

●FROMMER'S COMPREHENSIVE TRAVEL GUIDE. BELGIUM, HOLLAND & LUXEMBOURG (US/1040-9378) [18587687] **5475**

●FROMMER'S COMPREHENSIVE TRAVEL GUIDE. BERLIN (US/1048-2660) [23353158] **5475**

●FROMMER'S COMPREHENSIVE TRAVEL GUIDE. BERMUDA & THE BAHAMAS (US/1044-2383) [24507157] **5475**

FROMMER'S COMPREHENSIVE TRAVEL GUIDE. CALIFORNIA (US/1064-3044) [25310980] **5475**

FROMMER'S COMPREHENSIVE TRAVEL GUIDE. CALIFORNIA & LAS VEGAS See FROMMER'S COMPREHENSIVE TRAVEL GUIDE. CALIFORNIA **5475**

●FROMMER'S COMPREHENSIVE TRAVEL GUIDE. CANADA (US/1064-3443) [25720411] **5475**

FROMMER'S COMPREHENSIVE TRAVEL GUIDE. CARIBBEAN (US/1058-2304) [22471444] **5475**

FROMMER'S COMPREHENSIVE TRAVEL GUIDE. CRUISES (US/1057-6266) [22610929] 5449, **5475**

●FROMMER'S COMPREHENSIVE TRAVEL GUIDE. DELAWARE, MARYLAND, PENNSYLVANIA & THE NEW JERSEY SHORE (US/1055-5382) [23201055] **5475**

FROMMER'S COMPREHENSIVE TRAVEL GUIDE. ENGLAND & SCOTLAND See FROMMER'S SCOTLAND **5477**

FROMMER'S COMPREHENSIVE TRAVEL GUIDE. ENGLAND & SCOTLAND See FROMMER'S ENGLAND **5477**

FROMMER'S COMPREHENSIVE TRAVEL GUIDE. FLORIDA (US/1057-2791) [22471673] **5475**

FROMMER'S COMPREHENSIVE TRAVEL GUIDE. FRANCE (US/1059-2830) [22835756] **5475**

FROMMER'S COMPREHENSIVE TRAVEL GUIDE. HAWAII See FROMMER'S COMPREHENSIVE TRAVEL GUIDE. HONOLULU & OAHU **5476**

●FROMMER'S COMPREHENSIVE TRAVEL GUIDE. HONOLULU & OAHU (US/1064-1238) [26210420] **5476**

FROMMER'S COMPREHENSIVE TRAVEL GUIDE. ITALY (US) [23248936] **5476**

●FROMMER'S COMPREHENSIVE TRAVEL GUIDE. JAPAN (US/1064-5233) [25725715] **5476**

●FROMMER'S COMPREHENSIVE TRAVEL GUIDE. LAS VEGAS (US/1064-5195) [22973385] **5476**

●FROMMER'S COMPREHENSIVE TRAVEL GUIDE. LISBON, MADRID & THE COSTA DEL SOL (US/1064-5225) [22973330] **5476**

●FROMMER'S COMPREHENSIVE TRAVEL GUIDE. LOS ANGELES (US) [22881268] **5476**

FROMMER'S COMPREHENSIVE TRAVEL GUIDE. MEXICO CITY & ACAPULCO See FROMMER'S COMPREHENSIVE TRAVEL GUIDE. ACAPULCO, IXTAPA & TAXCO **5475**

●FROMMER'S COMPREHENSIVE TRAVEL GUIDE. MIAMI (US/1047-790X) [23187968] **5476**

●FROMMER'S COMPREHENSIVE TRAVEL GUIDE. MINNEAPOLIS & ST. PAUL (US/1051-6980) [22093715] **5476**

Alphabetical Title Index — FRONTIERS

- FROMMER'S COMPREHENSIVE TRAVEL GUIDE. MONTREAL & QUEBEC CITY (US/1064-5284) [23304377] **5476**
- FROMMER'S COMPREHENSIVE TRAVEL GUIDE. NEPAL (US/1055-5439) [23201264] **5476**

FROMMER'S COMPREHENSIVE TRAVEL GUIDE. NEW ENGLAND (US/1056-5787) [22905249] **5476**

- FROMMER'S COMPREHENSIVE TRAVEL GUIDE. NEW MEXICO (US/1053-2455) [22485402] **5476**

FROMMER'S COMPREHENSIVE TRAVEL GUIDE. NEW ORLEANS (US/1057-7645) [22773311] **5476**

FROMMER'S COMPREHENSIVE TRAVEL GUIDE. NEW YORK STATE (US/1064-5276) [25180878] **5476**

FROMMER'S COMPREHENSIVE TRAVEL GUIDE. NORTHWEST (US) [23903517] **5476**

- FROMMER'S COMPREHENSIVE TRAVEL GUIDE. PARIS (US) [22485601] **5476**
- FROMMER'S COMPREHENSIVE TRAVEL GUIDE. PORTUGAL (US/1064-5268) [25931597] **5476**
- FROMMER'S COMPREHENSIVE TRAVEL GUIDE, PUERTO RICO (US/1062-4775) [25636270] **5476**
- FROMMER'S COMPREHENSIVE TRAVEL GUIDE. PUERTO VALLARTA, MANZANILLO & GUADALAJARA (US/1060-3727) [24947899] **5476**
- FROMMER'S COMPREHENSIVE TRAVEL GUIDE. RIO (US/1064-5241) [23018277] **5476**

FROMMER'S COMPREHENSIVE TRAVEL GUIDE. ROME (US/1056-5795) [22653710] **5476**

FROMMER'S COMPREHENSIVE TRAVEL GUIDE SALT LAKE CITY (US) [23089622] **5476**

- FROMMER'S COMPREHENSIVE TRAVEL GUIDE, SAN DIEGO (US/1047-787X) [20793018] **5476**

FROMMER'S COMPREHENSIVE TRAVEL GUIDE. SAN FRANCISCO (US) [22881467] **5476**

- FROMMER'S COMPREHENSIVE TRAVEL GUIDE. SANTA FE, TAOS & ALBUQUERQUE (US/1064-5209) [24014281] **5476**
- FROMMER'S COMPREHENSIVE TRAVEL GUIDE. SEATTLE & PORTLAND (US/1064-5187) [25618040] **5476**
- FROMMER'S COMPREHENSIVE TRAVEL GUIDE. SOUTH PACIFIC (US) [25512189] **5476**
- FROMMER'S COMPREHENSIVE TRAVEL GUIDE. ST. LOUIS & KANSAS CITY (US/1051-6840) [22051673] **5476**
- FROMMER'S COMPREHENSIVE TRAVEL GUIDE. SWITZERLAND & LIECHTENSTEIN (US) [24863326] **5476**
- FROMMER'S COMPREHENSIVE TRAVEL GUIDE. TAMPA & ST. PETERSBURG (US/1047-7896) [20793163] **5477**
- FROMMER'S COMPREHENSIVE TRAVEL GUIDE. THE CAROLINAS & GEORGIA (US/1058-4943) [24775765] **5477**
- FROMMER'S COMPREHENSIVE TRAVEL GUIDE. THE VIRGIN ISLANDS (US/1055-5447) [23201283] **5477**
- FROMMER'S COMPREHENSIVE TRAVEL GUIDE. TORONTO (US/1047-7853) [20792930] **5477**
- FROMMER'S COMPREHENSIVE TRAVEL GUIDE, U.S.A (US) [23658826] **5477**
- FROMMER'S COMPREHENSIVE TRAVEL GUIDE. VIRGINIA (US/1058-4943) [24314751] **5477**

- FROMMER'S COMPREHENSIVE TRAVEL GUIDE, YUCATAN (US/1064-1416) [26216417] **5477**
- FROMMER'S COPENHAGEN ON ... $ A DAY (US/1055-5358) [23200813] **5477**

FROMMER'S COSTA RICA, GUATEMALA & BELIZE ON $ ... A DAY (US/1051-6859) [22050152] **5477**

FROMMER'S DOLLARWISE NORTHWEST, INCLUDING OREGON, WASHINGTON, VANCOUVER/VICTORIA, SUN VALLEY, & CRUISES TO ALASKA See FROMMER'S NORTHWEST **5477**

FROMMER'S DOLLARWISE SKIING EUROPE PLUS SUMMER SKIING IN ARGENTINA (US/0899-3327) [18066237] **5477**

FROMMER'S DOLLARWISE SOUTHEAST ASIA (US/1040-9394) [18588089] **5477**

FROMMER'S DOLLARWISE SOUTHWEST (US/0899-3335) [18066192] **5477**

FROMMER'S DOLLARWISE USA See FROMMER'S COMPREHENSIVE TRAVEL GUIDE, U.S.A **5477**

FROMMER'S EASTERN EUROPE & YUGOSLAVIA ON $ ... A DAY See FROMMER'S BUDGET TRAVEL GUIDE. EASTERN EUROPE ... ON $ ... A DAY **5474**

FROMMER'S EGYPT (US/1044-226X) [19719088] **5477**

- FROMMER'S ENGLAND (US/1055-5404) [23201196] **5477**
- FROMMER'S FAMILY TRAVEL GUIDE. LOS ANGELES WITH KIDS (US/1058-496X) [24335119] **5477**
- FROMMER'S FAMILY TRAVEL GUIDE. NEW YORK CITY WITH KIDS (US/1060-3719) [24948016] **5477**
- FROMMER'S FAMILY TRAVEL GUIDE. SAN FRANCISCO WITH KIDS (US/1058-4951) [24335150] **5477**
- FROMMER'S FAMILY TRAVEL GUIDE. WASHINGTON, D.C., WITH KIDS (US/1058-4978) [24335178] **5477**

FROMMER'S ... GUIDE TO PHILADELPHIA & ATLANTIC CITY (US/0739-7143) [07125910] **5477**

FROMMER'S HAWAII ON $ ... A DAY (US/8755-9250) [07347503] **5477**

FROMMER'S HOW TO LIVE IN FLORIDA ON $10,000 A YEAR (US/0276-9034) [07151096] **1492**

FROMMER'S INDIA ON $ ... A DAY (US/1051-6816) [18046351] **5477**

FROMMER'S ISRAEL ON $ ... & $ ... A DAY (US/8755-8440) [08188774] **5477**

- FROMMER'S JAMAICA, BARBARDOS (US/1061-9429) [25489342] **5477**

FROMMER'S JAPAN & HONG KONG See FROMMER'S COMPREHENSIVE TRAVEL GUIDE. JAPAN **5476**

FROMMER'S LAS VEGAS See FROMMER'S COMPREHENSIVE TRAVEL GUIDE. LAS VEGAS **5476**

FROMMER'S LISBON, MADRID & THE COSTA DEL SOL See FROMMER'S COMPREHENSIVE TRAVEL GUIDE. LISBON, MADRID & THE COSTA DEL SOL **5476**

FROMMER'S LOS ANGELES See FROMMER'S COMPREHENSIVE TRAVEL GUIDE. LOS ANGELES **5476**

FROMMER'S MID-ATLANTIC STATES See FROMMER'S COMPREHENSIVE TRAVEL GUIDE. DELAWARE, MARYLAND, PENNSYLVANIA & THE NEW JERSEY SHORE **5475**

FROMMER'S MONTREAL & QUEBEC CITY See FROMMER'S COMPREHENSIVE TRAVEL GUIDE. MONTREAL & QUEBEC CITY **5476**

FROMMER'S NEW ORLEANS (US/0899-2908) [18065320] **5477**

FROMMER'S NEW YORK (US/0899-7675) [18248660] **5477**

FROMMER'S NEW YORK ON $ ... A DAY (US/8755-5433) [08262582] **5477**

FROMMER'S NEW YORK STATE See FROMMER'S COMPREHENSIVE TRAVEL GUIDE. NEW YORK STATE **5476**

- FROMMER'S NORTHWEST (US/1051-6808) [22045297] **5477**

FROMMER'S PARIS See FROMMER'S COMPREHENSIVE TRAVEL GUIDE. PARIS **5476**

- FROMMER'S PARIS ON ... $ A DAY (US/1055-5315) [23200742] **5477**

FROMMER'S PHILADELPHIA (US/0899-3211) [18065286] **5477**

FROMMER'S PORTUGAL, MADEIRA, AND THE AZORES See FROMMER'S COMPREHENSIVE TRAVEL GUIDE. PORTUGAL **5476**

FROMMER'S RIO See FROMMER'S COMPREHENSIVE TRAVEL GUIDE. RIO **5476**

- FROMMER'S SALT LAKE CITY (US/1047-7861) [20792989] **5477**

FROMMER'S SANTA FE, TAOS AND ALBUQUERQUE See FROMMER'S COMPREHENSIVE TRAVEL GUIDE. SANTA FE, TAOS & ALBUQUERQUE **5476**

FROMMER'S SCANDINAVIA ON $ ... A DAY (US/0278-1069) [07349633] **5477**

- FROMMER'S SCOTLAND (US/1055-5390) [23201162] **5477**

FROMMER'S SEATTLE & PORTLAND See FROMMER'S COMPREHENSIVE TRAVEL GUIDE. SEATTLE & PORTLAND **5476**

FROMMER'S SOUTH AMERICA ON $ ... A DAY (US/0277-7827) [07631357] **5478**

FROMMER'S SOUTH PACIFIC See FROMMER'S COMPREHENSIVE TRAVEL GUIDE. SOUTH PACIFIC **5476**

FROMMER'S SOUTHERN ATLANTIC STATES See FROMMER'S COMPREHENSIVE TRAVEL GUIDE. THE CAROLINAS & GEORGIA **5477**

FROMMER'S SOUTHERN ATLANTIC STATES See FROMMER'S COMPREHENSIVE TRAVEL GUIDE. VIRGINIA **5477**

FROMMER'S SPAIN AND MOROCCO PLUS THE CANARY ISLANDS ON $ ... A DAY See FROMMER'S BUDGET TRAVEL GUIDE. SPAIN ... ON $ ... A DAY **5475**

- FROMMER'S STOCKHOLM ON ... $ A DAY (US/1055-534X) [23200791] **5478**

FROMMER'S SWITZERLAND AND LIECHTENSTEIN See FROMMER'S COMPREHENSIVE TRAVEL GUIDE. SWITZERLAND & LIECHTENSTEIN **5476**

FROMMER'S SYDNEY (US/0899-2770) [18057457] **5478**

- FROMMER'S THAILAND (US/1055-5412) [23201221] **5478**

FROMMER'S TOURING GUIDE TO BRAZIL (US/0899-2800) [18059057] **5478**

FROMMER'S TOURING GUIDE TO LENINGRAD/MOSCOW (US/1044-078X) [19681600] **5478**

FROMMER'S WASHINGTON, D.C. AND HISTORIC VIRGINIA ON $ ... A DAY See FROMMER'S BUDGET TRAVEL GUIDE. WASHINGTON, D.C. ... ON $ ... A DAY **5475**

FRONIMO; RIVISTA TRIMESTRALE DI CHITARRA E LIUTO, IL (IT) [01788283] **4118**

FRONT AND FINISH (US) [04908565] **4286**

FRONT COMMUN SECTEUR PUBLIC See BULLETIN DE LIAISON - SECTEUR PUBLIC **1656**

FRONT (KINGSTON. 1978) (CN/0709-2830) [10356321] **3389**

FRONT-LINE SERVICE (US/1053-1726) [22469566] **941**

FRONT LINE SUPERVISOR'S BULLETIN (US) **941**

FRONT PAGE DETECTIVE (US/0016-2043) [04080474] **5074**

FRONT PAGE NEWS PLUS BUSINESS (US/1059-5937) [24640120] **2920**

FRONT ROW (US/0885-0747) [12492474] **385**

FRONTAL (MARBURG) (GW/0340-0921) [01798802] **1825**

FRONTENAC HISTORIC FOUNDATION See NEWSLETTER - FRONTENAC HISTORIC FOUNDATION **304**

FRONTERA NORTE (MX/0187-7372) [21488877] **5200**

- FRONTERAS (ARLINGTON, TEX.) (US/1062-8444) [25770483] **2581**

FRONTIER (UK/0951-7677) [16506996] **4960, 4542**

FRONTIER : A VIEW FROM TOKYO, THE (JA) **2503**

FRONTIER CHRONICLES (US/1050-3560) [21473277] **2616**

- FRONTIER-FREE EUROPE / COMMISSION OF THE EUROPEAN COMMUNITIES, DIRECTORATE-GENERAL FOR AUDIOVISUAL MEDIA, INFORMATION, COMMUNICATION AND CULTURE (BE/1021-2353) [27689709] 3128, **1562**

FRONTIER MILITARY SERIES (US/0071-9641) [01388401] 2616, **4044**

FRONTIER NURSING SERVICE QUARTERLY BULLETIN (US/0016-2116) [01328559] **3856**

FRONTIER PERSPECTIVES (US/1062-4767) [25636275] **5106**

FRONTIERES (MONTREAL) (CN/1180-3479) [24368326] **5200**

FRONTIERS (BOULDER) (US/0160-9009) [02586280] **5557**

FRONTIERS IN AGING SERIES (US/0271-955X) [06369328] **3751**

FRONTIERS IN APPLIED MATHEMATICS (US) [19841284] **3506**

FRONTIERS IN APPLIED MICROBIOLOGY (II) [14402565] **563**

- FRONTIERS IN CARBOHYDRATE RESEARCH (US) [26571672] **976**

FRONTIERS IN DIABETES (SZ/0251-5342) [07921954] **3730**

FRONTIERS IN FUEL CELLS (US/0532-744X) [01388593] **2055**

FRONTIERS IN HEADACHE RESEARCH (US/1066-8322) [25545601] **3577**

FRONTIERS IN IMMUNOASSAY AND BIOTECHNOLOGY **CEASED.** (US/0893-6129) [13076197] **3692**

FRONTIERS IN LASERS/MASERS (US) [01287426] **2055**

FRONTIERS IN PHYSICS (US/0429-7725) [06733368] **4403**

FRONTIERS OF CLINICAL NEUROSCIENCE (US/0887-3658) [08994938] **3833**

FRONTIERS OF ECONOMICS (US/0362-6911) [02316188] **1492**

FRONTIERS OF ENTREPRENEURSHIP RESEARCH : PROCEEDINGS OF THE ... ANNUAL BABSON COLLEGE ENTREPRENEURSHIP RESEARCH CONFERENCE (US) [14208509] **677**

FRONTIERS
Alphabetical Title Index

FRONTIERS OF GASTROINTESTINAL RESEARCH (SZ/0302-0665) [01618037] **3744**

FRONTIERS OF HEALTH SERVICES MANAGEMENT (US/0748-8157) [11010909] **5286**

FRONTIERS OF HORMONE RESEARCH (SZ/0301-3073) [01388634] **487**

FRONTIERS OF MEDICAL AND BIOLOGICAL ENGINEERING (NE/0921-3775) [19582038] **3692**

FRONTIERS OF ORAL PHYSIOLOGY (SZ/0301-536X) [00974805] **1323**

FRONTIERS OF PLANT SCIENCE (US/0016-2167) [01293799] **172**

FRONTIERS OF RADIATION THERAPY AND ONCOLOGY (US/0071-9676) [01570270] 3941, **3817**

FRONTIERS (PHILADELPHIA) (US/0016-2159) [05978880] **4165**

FRONTIERS (POINTE-CLAIRE) (CN/1180-5668) [23237289] **3692**

FRONTLINE DUNEDIN (NZ/0113-1990) [I01131990] **3724**

FRONTLINE (MADRAS, INDIA) (II) [12086614] **2651**

FROSTPROOF NEWS, THE (US) [01388691] **5649**

FROTH FLOTATION (US) [05504384] **2139**

FROZEN & CHILLED FOODS (UK/0265-6485) [10953232] **2341**

FROZEN & CHILLED FOODS YEAR BOOK (UK) [12763111] **2341**

FROZEN FISHERY PRODUCTS (US/0364-0604) [02496764] **2304**

FROZEN FOOD AGE (US/0016-2191) [01792329] **2341**

FROZEN FOOD DIGEST (US/0889-5902) [13980854] **2341**

FROZEN FOOD EXECUTIVE, THE (US/0279-1498) [07593531] **2341**

FROZEN FOOD MANAGEMENT (UK) **2341**

FROZEN FOOD PACK STATISTICS (US/0469-7405) [05918389] 2342, **2362**

FROZEN FOOD REPORT (US/0192-0367) [05002298] **2342**

FRP REPORT (BG/0253-5475) [05633024] 589, **3761**

FRUCHTHANDEL DUSSELDORF (GW/0429-7830) [I04297830] 924, 950, **172**

FRUCTIDOR INTERNATIONAL (FR) [01785555] 89, **837**

FRUGTAVLEREN (DK/0106-004X) [03076476] **2342**

FRUHMITTELALTERLICHE STUDIEN (GW/0071-9706) [01570276] **2689**

FRUIT AND TROPICAL PRODUCTS *CEASED*. (UK/0142-1883) [06030268] **172**

FRUIT & VEGETABLE MARKETS (UK/0961-0464) **89**

FRUIT AND VEGETABLE NATIONAL SHIPPING POINT TRENDS (US) 2342, **837**

FRUIT AND VEGETABLE PRESERVATION *See* PACK OF APPLES AND APPLE PRODUCTS **2352**

FRUIT AND VEGETABLE PRESERVATION (CN/0380-5042) [02443641] **2342**

FRUIT AND VEGETABLE PRODUCTION (CN/0383-008X) [03290431] **172**

FRUIT AND VEGETABLE TRUCK RATE REPORT / UNITED STATES DEPARTMENT OF AGRICULTURE, AGRICULTURAL MARKETING SERVICE, FRUIT AND VEGETABLE MARKET NEWS SERVICE (US) [06308002] **837**

FRUIT BELGE, LE (BE/0016-2248) [02833415] **2415**

FRUIT COUNTRY (US) **89**

FRUIT CROPS FACT SHEET (US/1054-8319) [01388740] **172**

FRUIT GARDENER, THE (US/1049-4545) [16369992] **2415**

FRUIT GROWER MAIDSTONE (UK/0953-2188) [I09532188] **172**

FRUIT NOTES (US/0427-6906) [08774434] **89**

FRUIT PRODUCTION, TASMANIA *See* FRUIT, TASMANIA **1607**

FRUIT SCIENCE REPORTS (PL/0137-1479) [01945011] **172**

FRUIT SOUTH *CEASED*. (US/0192-0847) [03757175] **172**

FRUIT, TASMANIA (AT) [05764362] **1607**

FRUIT TRADES JOURNAL *See* FRESH PRODUCE JOURNAL **172**

FRUIT TREE AND GRAPEVINE SURVEY *See* PENNSYLVANIA ORCHARD AND VINEYARD SURVEY **2427**

FRUIT VARIETIES JOURNAL (US/0091-3642) [01785961] **2415**

FRUITBOWL *See* ONE TO ONE **1135**

FRUITS (FR/0760-7237) [11151137] **3389**

FRUITS (FR/0016-2299) [10171003] **2415**

FRUITS & LEGUMES (FR/0754-0698) [I07540698] **2342**

FRUITS (QUEBEC) (CN/0481-2417) [06522089] **1607**

FRUITTEELT, DE (NE/0016-2302) [04024567] **172**

FRUSTULA ENTOMOLOGICA (IT/0532-7679) [03138216] **5584**

FRUT (SP/0214-0578) [I02140578] **172**

FS (US) [04073661] **89**

FSF ACCIDENT PREVENTION BULLETIN *See* ACCIDENT PREVENTION (ARLINGTON, VA.) **3**

FSF AIRPORT OPERATIONS SAFETY BULLETIN *See* AIRPORT OPERATIONS **10**

FSF CABIN CREW SAFETY BULLETIN (US/0898-5758) [17855849] 4776, **22**

FSF HUMAN FACTORS BULLETIN & AVIATION MEDICINE (US/0898-5723) [17852967] 4776, **22**

FSIS FOOD SAFETY REVIEW (US/1072-0758) [24564481] 4776, **2342**

FSMB HANDBOOK (US/0888-5656) [13657640] **4204**

FSMBNEWSLINE (FORT WORTH, TEX.) (US/1062-5380) [25651467] **3577**

FT. GARRY PIONEER (CN/0700-9410) [03402931] **5785**

FT GUIDE TO NORTH SEA OPERATORS (UK) **4256**

FT SYSTEMS (US/0740-4980) [09966381] 1274, **1254**

FTC FREEDOM OF INFORMATION LOG (US/0161-7036) [04010422] **837**

FTC NEWS NOTES / FEDERAL TRADE COMMISSION, OFFICE OF PUBLIC AFFAIRS (US) [09249209] **837**

FTC : WATCH (US/0196-0016) [05184963] 837, **2972**

●FTCA NEWS (US/1063-9209) [26183258] **2972**

FTD FAMILY (US/0745-4201) [09141860] **2435**

FTMS MULTICULTURAL EDUCATION REVIEW (US/1059-1508) [24486709] **1895**

FTP-NEA ADVOCATE (US/0738-8470) [04391918] **1747**

FTS FRENCH TECHNOLOGY SURVEY *CEASED*. (FR/0985-2220) [25667807] **5106**

FU-CHIEN CHIAO YU (CC) [11319969] **1747**

FU-CHIEN CHING NIEN (CH) [09004691] **2503**

FU-CHIEN NUNG YEH KO CHI (CC/0253-2301) [19904682] **89**

FU-CHIEN WEN HSUEH (CH) [09004663] **3389**

FU-CHUN-CHIANG HUA PAO : FCJ (CC) [10061694] **4861**

FU-INFO *See* FU-NACHRICHTEN **1825**

FU INFO / [HERAUSGEGEBEN VON DER PRESSE- UND INFORMATIONSSTELLE DER FREIEN UNIVERSITAT BERLIN (FU)] (GW) [08663829] **1825**

FU JEN STUDIES : LITERATURE & LINGUISTICS (CH/1015-0021) [02572988] 3389, **3283**

FU JEN STUDIES : NATURAL SCIENCES (CH/1016-1538) [02246970] **5106**

FU JEN STUDIES. SCIENCE AND ENGINEERING (CH) [30034208] 1976, **5106**

FU-MITTEILUNGEN *See* MITTEILUNGEN FU BERLIN : AMTSBLATT DER FREIEN UNIVERSITAT BERLIN **1093**

FU-NACHRICHTEN (GW) [I09440585] **1825**

FU NU SHENG HUO (CC) [11419072] **5557**

FU NU SHENG HUO (CHENG-CHOU SHIH, CHINA) (CC) [11576670] **5246**

FU TAN HSUEH PAO. TZU JAN KO HSUEH PAN (CC/0427-7104) [10756326] **5106**

FUDOSAN KANKEI HOREI SHU (JA) [02870482] **4838**

FUDOSAN ROPPO (JA) [03179977] **2972**

FUDOSAN SHINROPPO (JA) [03512136] **4838**

FUEL AND ENERGY ABSTRACTS (UK/0140-6701) [03731607] **1944**

FUEL CELLS (US) [01301264] **2055**

FUEL CONSUMPTION GUIDE (CN/0225-9214) [06167220] 5383, **5415**

FUEL ECONOMY NEWS : THE NEWSLETTER OF THE VOLUNTARY TRUCK AND BUS FUEL ECONOMY PROGRAM (US) [05157448] **4256**

FUEL (GUILFORD) (UK/0016-2361) [06259052] **4256**

FUEL INJECTION & ELECTRONIC ENGINE CONTROLS. AUDI, BMW, JAGUAR, MERCEDES-BENZ, PEUGEOT, SAAB, STERLING, VOLKSWAGEN, VOLVO (US/1050-1150) [21395684] **2055**

FUEL LINE / DEFENSE FUEL SUPPLY CENTER (US) [12354246] **4256**

FUEL LINE [MICROFORM] / DEFENSE FUEL SUPPLY CENTER (US) [21884511] **4256**

FUEL OIL IN WORLD MARKETS (US) **4256**

FUEL OIL NEWS (US/0016-2396) [02447089] **4256**

FUEL PROCESSING TECHNOLOGY (NE/0378-3820) [03459859] **1025**

FUEL REFORMULATION (US/1062-3744) [25601015] **4257**

FUEL SCIENCE AND TECHNOLOGY (II/0254-3567) [09228150] **4257**

FUEL SCIENCE & TECHNOLOGY INTERNATIONAL (US/0884-3759) [12365605] **2139**

FUELOIL & OIL HEAT WITH AIR CONDITIONING (US/1060-9725) [25139347] **4257**

FUELSAVER (CN/0822-2142) [25652487] **5383**

FUENTES E INVESTIGACIONES PARA LA HISTORIA DEL PERU. SERIE : TEXTOS CRITICOS (PE/0532-7865) [01391629] **2734**

FUENTES HISTORICAS (VE/0506-6220) [01496560] 237, **2616**

FUENTES HISTORICAS ARAGONESAS (SP) [01284989] **2689**

FUENTES PARA LA HISTORIA SOCIAL Y ECONOMICA DEL RIO DE LA PLATA (UY/0581-1856) [01391922] **2734**

FUER DIE MEDIZINISCHE PRAXIS (GW/0863-2693) [20050254] **3577**

FUER SIE HAMBURG (GW/0016-2450) [I00162450] **2517**

FUERZA AEREA DE CHILE *See* FUERZA AEREA (SANTIAGO, CHILE) **4044**

FUERZA AEREA (SANTIAGO, CHILE) (CL) [08253088] 22, **4044**

FUERZAS ARMADAS (CK/0016-2485) [01390152] **4044**

FUERZAS ARMADAS DE VENEZUELA (VENEZUELA. MINISTERIO DE LA DEFENSA : 1971) (VE) [01390201] **4044**

FUGATE FAMILY NEWSLETTER, THE (US/0749-3541) [11101414] **2449**

FUGUE (CN/0702-8393) [03520243] 5316, **4118**

FUHE CAILIAO XUEBAO (CC/1000-3851) [21980594] **2102**

FUJI ELECTRIC REVIEW (JA/0429-8284) [10755991] **2055**

FUJI FIRUMU KENKYU HOKOKU (JA/0915-1478) [23346984] **4369**

FUJI JIHO (JA/0367-3332) [10467554] **2055**

FUJIAN NONGYE KEJI (CC/0253-2301) [08862983] **89**

FUJIAN SHIFAN DAXUE XUEBAO (ZIRAN KEXUE BAN) (CC/1000-5277) [18996969] **5106**

FUJIN KORON (JA) [05840496] **5557**

FUJIN KYOIKU JOHO (JA/0388-1709) [06712721] 5557, **1747**

FUJIN RODO NO JITSUJO (JA) [01797251] 5557, **1675**

FUJITA GAKUEN IGAKKAISHI (JA) [10314924] **3577**

FUJITSU (JA/0016-2515) **1976**

FUJITSU SCIENTIFIC & TECHNICAL JOURNAL (JA/0016-2523) [01939196] **2055**

FUKUI DAIGAKU KOGAKUBU KENKYU HOKOKU (JA/0429-8373) [09443685] **1976**

FUKUI DAIGAKU KOGAKUBU SENI KINOSEI ZAIRYO KENKYU SHISETSU HOKOKU (JA) [11188714] **5106**

FUKUI-KEN KOGYO SHIKENJO *See* NEMPO **5132**

FUKUI-KEN NOGYO SHIKENJO HOKOKU (JA/0388-7790) [10266719] **89**

FUKUOKA ACTA MEDICA (JA) [01641747] **3577**

FUKUOKA DAIGAKU JINBUN RONSO (JA) [02243523] **2846**

Alphabetical Title Index **FUNDAMENTALS**

FUKUOKA DAIGAKU. KENKYUJO *See* FUKUOKA DAIGAKU KENKYUJO HO **2503**

FUKUOKA DAIGAKU. KENKYUJO *See* FUKUOKA DAIGAKU KENKYUSHO HO : SHIZEN KAGAKU HEN **5106**

FUKUOKA DAIGAKU. KENKYUJO *See* FUKUOKA DAIGAKU KOGAKU SHUHO **5106**

FUKUOKA DAIGAKU. KENKYUJO *See* FUKUOKA DAIGAKU JINBUN RONSO **2846**

FUKUOKA DAIGAKU. KENKYUJO *See* FUKUOKA DAIGAKU KENKYUSHO HO : JINBUN KAGAKU HEN **1825**

FUKUOKA DAIGAKU. KENKYUJO *See* FUKUOKA DAIGAKU RIGAKU SHUHO **5106**

FUKUOKA DAIGAKU. KENKYUJO *See* FUKUOKA DAIGAKU TAIIKUGAKU KENKYU **1855**

FUKUOKA DAIGAKU KENKYUJO HO (JA) [03896102] **2503**

FUKUOKA DAIGAKU KENKYUSHO HO : JINBUN KAGAKU HEN (JA) [04793620] **1825**

FUKUOKA DAIGAKU KENKYUSHO HO : SHIZEN KAGAKU HEN (JA) [04967453] **5106**

FUKUOKA DAIGAKU KOGAKU SHUHO (JA) [04020394] **5106**

FUKUOKA DAIGAKU RIGAKU SHUHO (JA/0386-118X) [04687826] **5106**

FUKUOKA DAIGAKU TAIIKUGAKU KENKYU (JA) [03791194] **1855**

FUKUOKA IGAKU ZASSHI (JA/0016-254X) [07586353] **3577**

FUKUOKA JOSHI DAIGAKU KASEI GAKUBU KIYO (JA/0288-3953) [09914986] 976, **456**

FUKUOKA KANKU KISHODAI *See* BAIU TO TAIFU NO YOSO **1420**

FUKUOKA KOGYO DAIGAKU EREKUTORONIKUSU KENKYUJO SHOHO (JA/0911-050X) [27475331] **2055**

FUKUOKA KOKUZEIKYOKU TOKEISHO (JA) [01799693] **4727**

FUKUOKA KYOIKU DAIGAKU KIYO. DAI 3-BUNSATSU, SUGAKU, RIKA, GIJUTSUKA HEN (JA) [12182652] **5106**

FUKUOKA-SHI EISEI SHIKENJO HO (JA/0388-6166) [10315517] 4776, **2230**

FUKUOKA SHIKA DAIGAKU GAKKAI ZASSHI (JA/0385-0064) [09567556] **1324**

FUKUSHIMA IGAKU ZASSHI (JA/0016-2582) [09344187] **3577**

FUKUSHIMA JOURNAL OF MEDICAL SCIENCE (JA/0016-2590) [01570303] **3577**

FUKUSHIMA-KEN NOGYO SHIKENJO KENKYU HOKOKU (JA/0388-7723) [l03887723] **89**

FUKUSHIMA-KEN NOGYO SHIKENJO TOKUBETSU KENKYU HOKOKU (JA/0387-3714) [l03873714] **89**

FUKUSHIMA-KEN TANKA SENSHU (JA) [09868258] **3463**

FUKUZAWA YUKICHI NENKAN (JA) [02441134] **1747**

FUL-, ORR-, GEGEGYOGYASZAT (HU/0016-237X) [06284615] **3888**

FULBRIGHT AND OTHER GRANTS FOR GRADUATE STUDY ABROAD (US) [19291496] **1825**

FULBRIGHT NEWSLETTER (ll/0046-5259) [01695184] **1747**

FULCRUM REPORT *See* PUBLIC SAFETY ON-LINE **1162**

FULD & COMPANY LETTER, THE (US/1054-9986) [23043799] **1635**

FULDAER GESCHICHTSBLATTER (GW/0016-2612) [l00162612] **2689**

FULDAER HOCHSCHULSCHRIFTEN / HERAUSGEGEBEN VON DER THEOLOGISCHEN FAKULTAT FULDA (GW) [16978232] **4960**

FULFILL *See* WHAT'S WORKING **719**

FULL BLAST (US/0191-1953) [04791863] **4119**

FULL-COURT PRESS, THE (US/0892-5364) [15212558] **5696**

FULL CRY (SEDALIA) (US/0016-2620) [04080496] **4872**

FULL GOSPEL BUSINESS MEN'S VOICE (US/0042-8264) [01775237] **4960**

FULL PAGES IMAGES (US) **1286**

FULL SPECTRUM. CD-ROM (US) 1263, **1233**

FULL-TIME DADS (US/1055-2367) [23123806] 3995, **2280**

●FULLERENE SCIENCE AND TECHNOLOGY (US/1064-122X) [26210286] **5106**

FULLTEXT SOURCES ONLINE (US/1040-8258) [18544257] **3211**

FULTON COUNTY DAILY REPORT (ATLANTA) (US) **2972**

FULTON COUNTY FOLK FINDER (US/0896-1980) [16989618] **2449**

FULTON COUNTY HISTORICAL AND GENEALOGICAL SOCIETY NEWSLETTER (US) [04375246] 2449, **2734**

FULTON COUNTY IMAGES (US) [28563846] **2734**

FULTON COUNTY IMAGES (US/1070-7735) [25863846] **2616**

FULTON COUNTY NEWS (MCCONNELLSBURG, PA.) (US) [14408945] **5736**

FULTON-HICKMAN GENEALOGICAL JOURNAL (US/1065-0164) [15674092] **2449**

FULTON LEADER (US) [21506629] **5680**

FULTON PATRIOT (FULTON, N.Y. : 1892) (US) [18230060] **5716**

FULTON SUN, THE (US/8750-6696) [11680504] **5703**

FUN E LAFFS (US/1059-3209) [24562801] **4861**

FUN LETSTN HURBN : TSAYTSHRIFT FAR GESHIKHTE FUN YIDISHN LEBN BEYSN NATSI-REZSHIM (GW) [20485863] **2616**

FUN RUNNER (AT/0157-5295) [l01575295] **4895**

FUN ZONE, THE *CEASED.* (US/1059-6135) [24647414] **4861**

FUNCTION (AT/0313-6825) [l03136825] **3506**

FUNCTIONAL ANALYSIS AND ITS APPLICATIONS (US/0016-2663) [01570309] **3506**

FUNCTIONAL AND DEVELOPMENTAL MORPHOLOGY (XR/0862-8416) [25007385] **456**

FUNCTIONAL ECOLOGY (UK/0269-8463) [15596280] **2216**

FUNCTIONAL NEUROLOGY (IT/0393-5264) [16358631] **3833**

FUNCTIONAL ORTHODONTIST, THE (US/8756-3150) [10969269] **1324**

FUNCTIONES ET APPROXIMATIO COMMENTARII MATHEMATICI (PL/0208-6573) [03823874] **3506**

FUNCTIONS (CN/0821-2708) [09528041] **3506**

FUNCTIONS OF LANGUAGE (NE/0929-9998) 3389, **3283**

FUND ACTION (US/1054-5956) [22239104] **899**

FUND AND GIFT SUPPLEMENT TO THE FINANCIAL REPORT FOR THE FISCAL YEAR (US) [08270082] **1825**

FUND FOR THE CITY OF NEW YORK *See* THREE-YEAR REPORT / FUND FOR THE CITY OF NEW YORK **5312**

FUND OG FORSKNING I DET KONGELIGE BIBLIOTEKS SAMLINGER (DK/0069-9896) [01565066] **3211**

FUND RAISER'S GUIDE TO HUMAN SERVICE FUNDING (US/1045-1951) [19380380] **4336**

FUND RAISER'S GUIDE TO PRIVATE FORTUNES *See* GUIDE TO PRIVATE FORTUNES **678**

FUND RAISER'S GUIDE TO RELIGIOUS PHILANTHROPY (US/1042-0053) [18861196] **4336**

FUND RAISING EVENT REPORT (CN/0228-3891) [08099511] **5286**

FUND RAISING INSTITUTE *See* F R I MONTHLY PORTFOLIO **4335**

FUND RAISING MANAGEMENT (US/0016-268X) [01780894] **868**

FUND WATCH (US/1057-6703) [24092844] **899**

●FUND YOUR WAY THROUGH COLLEGE (US/1071-040X) [28535954] **1825**

FUNDACAO CALOUSTE GULBENKIAN. SERVICOS DE BIBLIOTECAS *See* BOLETIM INFORMATIVO - FUNDACAO CALOUSTE GULBENKIAN, SERVICOS DE BIBLIOTECAS **3196**

FUNDACAO CENTRO REGIONAL DE PRODUTIVIDADE DO PIAUI *See* CARTA CEPRO **1550**

FUNDACAO EDUCACIONAL PADRE LANDELL DE MOURA *See* RELATORIO DE ATIVIDADES - FUNDACAO EDUCACIONAL PADRE LANDELL DE MOURA **1777**

FUNDACAO ESTUDOS DO MAR. ASSOCIACAO DOS DIPLOMADOS *See* REVISTA DA ADISMAR **4182**

FUNDACAO GETULIO VARGAS *See* MONOGRAFIA - FUNDACAO GETULIO VARGAS **5233**

FUNDACAO INSTITUTO BRASILEIRO DE GEOGRAFIA E ESTATISTICA. DEPARTAMENTO DE ESTATISTICAS INDUSTRIAIS, COMERCIAIS E DE SERVICOS *See* INQUERITO NACIONAL DE PRECOS : GENEROS ALIMENTICIOS E ARTIGOS DO VESTUARIO, COMERCIO ATACADISTA E VAREJISTA NAS UNIDADES DA FEDERACAO **1085**

FUNDACAO INSTITUTO BRASILEIRO DE GEOGRAFIA E ESTATISTICA. DEPARTAMENTO DE ESTATISTICAS INDUSTRIAIS, COMERCIAIS E DE SERVICOS *See* INDUSTRIA DA CONSTRUCAO : PRECOS DE MATERIAL DE CONSTRUCAO NO COMERCIO ATACADISTA - SALARIOS NA INDUSTRIA DA CONSTRUCAO **1610**

FUNDACAO INSTITUTO BRASILEIRO DE GEOGRAFIA E ESTATISTICA. SUPERINTENDENCIA DE CARTOGRAFIA *See* TRABALHOS TECNICOS - FUNDACAO INSTITUTO BRASILEIRO DE GEOGRAFIA E ESTATISTICA, SUPERINTENDENCIA DE CARTOGRAFIA **2577**

FUNDACAO INSTITUTO DE PESQUISAS ECONOMICAS *See* ANALISE CONJUNTURAL DO EMPREGO **1643**

FUNDACAO JONES DOS SANTOS NEVES *See* REVISTA DA FUNDACAO JONES DOS SANTOS NEVES **2834**

FUNDACAO JORGE DUPRAT FIGUEIREDO DE SEGURANCA E MEDICINA DO TRABALHO *See* BOLETIM ESTATISTICO **2859**

FUNDACAO NACIONAL DO INDIO *See* INFORMATIVO FUNAI - FUNDACAO NACIONAL DO INDIO **2739**

FUNDACAO PARA O LIVRO DO CEGO NO BRASIL *See* RELATORIO DE ATIVIDADES - FUNDACAO PARA O LIVRO DO CEGO NO BRASIL **5304**

FUNDACAO SERVICOS DE SAUDE PUBLICA *See* REVISTA DA FUNDACAO SESP **4799**

FUNDACAO ZOOBOTANICA DO RIO GRANDE DO SUL *See* RELATORIO - FUNDACAO ZOOBOTANICA DO RIO GRANDE DO SUL **4171**

FUNDACION CIENTIFICA DE LA ASOCIACION ESPANOLA CONTRA EL CANCER INFORMA (SP) [08799160] **3817**

FUNDACION DE INVESTIGACIONES ECONOMICAS LATINOAMERICANAS (BUENOS AIRES, ARGENTINA) *See* ENCUESTAS DE COYUNTURA. SERIE 2 : LA SITUACION FINANCIERA DE LA INDUSTRIA MANUFACTURERA **1605**

FUNDACION DE INVESTIGACIONES ECONOMICAS LATINOAMERICANAS (BUENOS AIRES, ARGENTINA) *See* ENCUESTAS DE COYUNTURA. SERIE 1 : EVOLUCION DE LA ACTIVIDAD INDUSTRIAL **1560**

FUNDACION JUAN MARCH *See* ANALES DE LA FUNDACION JUAN MARCH **4334**

FUNDACION MIGUEL LILLO *See* MISCELANEA - FUNDACION MIGUEL LILLO **4167**

FUNDACION PARA LA EDUCACION SUPERIOR Y EL DESARROLLO *See* COYUNTURA ANDINA **1554**

FUNDACION VITORIA Y SUAREZ *See* PUBLICACIONES - FUNDACION VITORIA Y SUAREZ **5235**

●FUNDAMENTA INFORMATICAE (NE/0169-2968) [25956265] **1185**

FUNDAMENTA MATHEMATICAE (PL/0016-2736) [01570315] **3506**

FUNDAMENTA PSYCHIATRICA (GW/0931-0428) [17816655] **3925**

●FUNDAMENTAL AND APPLIED NEMATOLOGY (FR/1164-5571) [25269281] **456**

FUNDAMENTAL AND APPLIED TOXICOLOGY (US/0272-0590) [06753527] **3980**

FUNDAMENTAL AND CLINICAL CARDIOLOGY (US/1067-5264) [24914385] **3704**

FUNDAMENTAL & CLINICAL PHARMACOLOGY (FR/0767-3981) [16462006] **4305**

FUNDAMENTAL CONCEPTS OF ESTATE ADMINISTRATION (US/0164-1255) [04289944] **3118**

FUNDAMENTAL CONCEPTS OF ESTATE PLANNING (US/0733-0057) [05249068] **3118**

FUNDAMENTAL RESEARCH IN HOMOGENEOUS CATALYSIS (US/0271-1842) [11672499] **1052**

FUNDAMENTAL STUDIES IN COMPUTER SCIENCE (US) [01421031] **1185**

FUNDAMENTAL STUDIES IN ENGINEERING (NE) [07163446] **1976**

FUNDAMENTAL THEORIES OF PHYSICS (NE/0168-1222) [l01681222] **4403**

FUNDAMENTALS OF AEROSPACE INSTRUMENTATION (US/0094-3975) [06744967] **22**

FUNDAMENTALS OF BANKRUPTCY LAW : ALI-ABA COURSE OF STUDY, MATERIALS (US) [08414597] **3086**

FUNDAMENTALS OF CANCER MANAGEMENT (US/0739-7364) [08988014] **3817**

FUNDAMENTALS — Alphabetical Title Index

FUNDAMENTALS OF COSMIC PHYSICS (US/0094-5846) [01793904] 4403, **395**

FUNDAMENTALS OF MEDICAL CELL BIOLOGY (US) **456**

FUNDAMENTALS OF PURE AND APPLIED ECONOMICS (SZ/0191-1708) [12095384] **1592**

FUNDAMENTALS OF SECURED TRANSACTIONS (US/0732-4561) [08336563] **2972**

FUNDAMENTY (PL) [01785188] **1562**

FUNDBERICHTE AUS BADEN-WURTTEMBERG (GW) [02541020] **268**

FUNDBERICHTE AUS HESSEN (GW/0071-9889) [02356044] **268**

FUNDBERICHTE AUS OSTERREICH (AU) [09302249] **268**

FUNDE UND AUSGRABUNGEN IM BEZIRK TRIER (GW/0723-8630) [08966929] **268**

FUNDEVOGEL (GW/0176-2753) [I01762753] **3389**

FUNDHEFT FUER STEUERRECHT (GW) [02255694] **2972**

FUNDHEFT FUR OFFENTLICHES RECHT (GW/0071-9919) [01607217] **2972**

● FUNDHOLDING MANAGEMENT HANDBOOK (UK) **868**

● FUNDING DECISION MAKERS (US/1058-1235) [24223138] **5286**

FUNDING OF EDUCATION IN ALBERTA, A SCHOOL FINANCE BROCHURE, THE (CN/1189-4296) [26758247] 4727, **1747**

FUNDING REPORT - CONNECTICUT JUSTICE COMMISSION (US/0148-9291) [03392948] **3165**

FUNDMUNZEN DER ROMISCHEN ZEIT IN OSTERREICH. ABTEILUNG I, BURGENLAND, DIE (AU) [20404134] **2781**

FUNDS, AGENTS, CUSTODIANS, SUPPLIERS (US/0887-8161) [13388402] **899**

FUNDSTELLEN- UND INHALTSNACHWEIS ARBEITS- UND SOZIALRECHT (GW) [03252370] **2972**

FUNE NO KAGAKU (JA/0387-0863) [10755712] **1976**

FUNERAL DIRECTORS (CN/0575-8629) [01792777] **2407**

FUNERAL SERVICE JOURNAL ENGLAND (UK) **2407**

FUNGAL GENETICS NEWSLETTER (US/0895-1942) [13926143] **563**

FUNGI CANADENSES (CN/0823-0552) [02248667] **575**

FUNGICIDE AND NEMATICIDE TESTS (US/0148-9038) [03398911] **172**

FUNK-TECHNIK. AUSGABE ZV (MUNCHEN) (GW/0342-0426) [01303844] **1156**

FUNKCIALAJ EKVACIOJ (JA/0532-8721) [01570322] **3506**

FUNKCIONALNYJ ANALIZ I EGO PRILOZENIA (RU/0374-1990) [01393284] **3506**

FUNKSCHAU (GW/0016-2841) [01793555] 1132, **2055**

FUNKSCHAU. SONDERHEFT (GW/0172-2778) [09268494] **2055**

FUNKTIONELLE BIOLOGIE & MEDIZIN (GW/0722-3684) [09148622] 3577, **456**

FUNKTIONSANALYSE BIOLOGISCHER SYSTEME (GW/0340-0840) [01615578] 580, **456**

FUNKTIONSKRANKHEITEN DES BEWEGUNGSAPPARATES (GW/0258-2015) [15900235] **3804**

FUNKTSIONAL'NYI ANALIZ. SPEKTRAL'NAIA TEORIIA (RU) [24019319] **3506**

FUNLINE (PK) [24335218] **4861**

FUNNEL EXPERIMENTAL FILM THEATRE See CATALOGUE - FUNNEL **4065**

FUNNYWORLD (US/0071-9943) [03067704] **4861**

FUNPARKS DIRECTORY (US/0147-5606) [03194063] **4861**

FUNRUNNER See NEW FUN RUNNER **4907**

FUNTAI KOGAKKAISHI (JA/0386-6157) [09586196] **5106**

FUNTAI OYOBI FUMMATSU YAKIN (JA/0532-8799) [09354304] **4002**

FUNUN (UA) [07243559] **320**

FUNUN ARABIYAH (UK) [09559725] **350**

FUNUN (CAIRO, EGYPT : 1979) (UA) [08013379] **320**

FUNWORLD (US/0892-3752) [15172046] **4861**

FUQUA SCHOOL OF BUSINESS (DUKE UNIVERSITY) See ALUMNI DIRECTORY / DUKE, THE FUQUA SCHOOL OF BUSINESS **1098**

FUR AGE WEEKLY (US/0016-2884) [04080502] **3184**

FUR-BEARERS, THE (CN/0715-5891) [10334939] **226**

FUR BULLETIN (GW/0016-2914) **3184**

FUR CHIC (CN/0225-6452) [06136544] **3184**

FUR-FISH-GAME (US/0016-2922) [01570325] **4872**

FUR PRODUCTION See LIVESTOCK STATISTICS / STATISTICS CANADA, AGRICULTURE DIVISION, LIVESTOCK AND ANIMAL PRODUCTS SECTION **154**

FUR RANCHER (US/0744-7701) [03583331] **3184**

FUR SEAL INVESTIGATIONS (US) [06756478] **3184**

FUR TAKER, THE (US/0016-2965) [05134169] **3184**

FUR TRADE JOURNAL OF CANADA (1987) (CN/0845-6798) [20243313] **3184**

FURANI'S DIGEST OF THE OFFICIAL GAZETTE AL KUWAIT AL YOUM (KU) [09572414] **2972**

FURANSUGO FURANSU BUNGAKU KENKYU (JA/0425-4929) [12138013] **3283**

FURASUCHIKKU GAIDO; GENTAIRYE FUKUZAIRYO HEN (JA) [04472524] **4455**

FUREGURANSU JANARU : FJ / FRAGRANCE JOURNAL (JA) [10316223] **1025**

FURI JANARISUTO NENKAN (JA) [02959227] **2920**

● FURIOUS FICTIONS (US/1065-7983) [26739091] **3389**

● FURKINDRED (SEATTLE, WASH.) (US/1059-082X) [24487501] **378**

FURMAN ALUMNI ASSOCIATION See FURMAN UNIVERSITY ALUMNI DIRECTORY **1102**

FURMAN HUMANITIES REVIEW (US/1064-0037) [26187914] **2846**

FURMAN STUDIES (US/0190-4701) [01663373] **2846**

FURMAN UNIVERSITY ALUMNI DIRECTORY (US/0148-2580) [03284167] **1102**

FURNISHING FLOORS. DOMESTIC AND CONTRACT (AT/0816-5947) [I08165947] **2905**

FURNITURE & CABINET MANUFACTURING (US/0894-8348) [16265714] 3479, **2905**

FURNITURE AND FIXTURE INDUSTRIES (CN/0828-9891) [13786835] **2905**

FURNITURE HISTORY (UK/0016-3058) [01570335] 250, **2905**

FURNITURE INDUSTRY RESEARCH ASSOCIATION See FURNITURE LITERATURE. SUPPLEMENT **2905**

FURNITURE LITERATURE : A SELECT BIBLIOGRAPHY ON FURNITURE AND ALLIED SUBJECTS (UK) [01974314] **2905**

FURNITURE LITERATURE. SUPPLEMENT (UK) [08000179] **2905**

FURNITURE MAGAZINE SUSPENDED. (CN/0849-6692) [21486700] **2905**

FURNITURE MANUFACTURER (UK/0306-0519) [I03060519] 2905, **3479**

FURNITURE RETAILER (GREENSBORO, N.C.) See HOME FURNISHINGS EXECUTIVE (GREENSBORO, N.C.) **2906**

FURNITURE RETAILER (GREENSBORO, N.C.) (US/1047-4676) [20214290] 954, **2905**

FURNITURE/TODAY (US/0194-360X) [05423145] **2905**

FURNITURE WORKERS PRESS (US/0016-3090) [01393956] **1675**

FURNITURE WORLD (NEW YORK, N.Y.) (US/0738-890X) [09640118] **2906**

FUROR (SZ/0250-8044) [09734978] **2517**

FURQAN (CASABLANCA, MOROCCO) (MR) [11926560] **5042**

FURROW (MOLINE, ILL. : SOUTHEAST EDITION) (US) [12199682] **89**

FURROW, THE (IE/0016-3120) [01570339] **5029**

FURTHER ASPECTS OF PIAGET'S WORK CEASED. (UK) [01299451] **4587**

FURUKAWA REVIEW (JA/0429-9159) [09567509] **2055**

FUSE MAGAZINE (CN/0838-603X) [18241642] **320**

FUSHOKU BOSHOKU BUMON IINKAI KENKYU SHUKAI SHIRYO (JA) [10316344] **2102**

FUSHOKU BOSHOKU BUMON IINKAI SHIRYO (JA) [10316403] **2102**

FUSILIER (LA PUENTE) (US/0092-5322) [01789910] **4044**

FUSION ASIA (II/0970-0080) [11172088] **2504**

FUSION BRIEFINGS See NEW ENERGY NEWS **1951**

FUSION ENERGY UPDATE CEASED. (US/0163-3856) [03806867] **2155**

FUSION ENGINEERING AND DESIGN (NE/0920-3796) [15906736] **2155**

FUSION FACTS (SALT LAKE CITY, UTAH) (US/1051-8738) [22143365] **1945**

FUSION MAGAZINE (CN/0832-9656) [16390663] **2589**

FUSION POWER ASSOCIATES EXECUTIVE NEWSLETTER (US) **1945**

FUSION POWER PROGRAM QUARTERLY PROGRESS REPORT (US) [05305420] **1945**

FUSION POWER REPORT (US/0276-2919) [07330424] 2155, **1945**

FUSION TECHNOLOGY (US/0748-1896) [10904749] **2155**

FUSION WILMINGTON, DEL (US/0016-3155) [I00163155] **2589**

FUSSBALL MAGAZIN (GW) **4895**

FUSSBALL TRAINER (GW/0016-3228) **4895**

FUT / BREWERS ASSOCIATION OF CANADA / L'ASSOCIATION DES BRASSEURS DU CANADA, EN (CN/0832-2589) [16220970] **2367**

FUTRAL, FUTRELL, FUTRELLE AND RELATED FAMILIES, WATKINS, CLIFFORD, WOOD (US/0734-080X) [06246396] **2449**

FUTUR ANTERIEUR (FR) [22838632] **4474**

FUTURA (IE/0016-3252) **1084**

● FUTURA : ERGEBNISSE DER FORSCHUNGSPOLITISCHEN FRUEHERKENNUNG (FER) DES SCHWEIZERISCHEN WISSENSCHAFTSRATES RESULTATS DE LA DETECTION AVANCEE EN POLITIQUE DE LA RECHERCHE DU CONSEIL SUISSE DE LA SCIENCE FINDINGS OF THE EARLY WARNING SYSTEM IN SCIENCE POLICY OF THE SWISS SCIENCE COUNCIL (SZ) [29919787] **5106**

FUTURA FER See FUTURA : ERGEBNISSE DER FORSCHUNGSPOLITISCHEN FRUEHERKENNUNG (FER) DES SCHWEIZERISCHEN WISSENSCHAFTSRATES RESULTATS DE LA DETECTION AVANCEE EN POLITIQUE DE LA RECHERCHE DU CONSEIL SUISSE DE LA SCIENCE FINDINGS OF THE EARLY WARNING SYSTEM IN SCIENCE POLICY OF THE SWISS SCIENCE COUNCIL **5106**

FUTURA FER : ERGEBNISSE DER FORSCHUNGSPOLITISCHEN FRUEHERKENNUNG (FER) DES SCHWEIZERISCHEN WISSENSCHAFTSRATES / RESULTATS DE LA DETECTION AVANCEE EN POLITIQUE DE LA RECHERCHE DU CONSEIL SUISSE DE LA SCIENCE / FINDINGS OF THE EARLY WARNING SYSTEM IN SCIENCE POLICY OF THE SWISS SCIENCE COUNCIL (SZ) [19524806] **5106**

FUTURAIL : REVUE BIMESTRIELLE DE L'OCTRA - OFFICE DU CHEMIN DE FER TRANSGABONAIS (FR) [08148334] **5431**

FUTURE (UK) **1304**

● FUTURE AT WORK, THE (US/1069-4951) [28132191] **868**

FUTURE CHOICES CEASED. (US/1047-191X) [20376222] **5286**

● FUTURE CONSUMER NEWSLETTER (CN/1197-4699) [29874017] **1592**

FUTURE ENERGY CONFERENCES AND SYMPOSIA (US/0897-9138) [17661158] **1945**

FUTURE EUROPEAN AGRICULTURE (UK) **89**

FUTURE FOCUS (US) **1855**

FUTURE FOR OUR PAST / COUNCIL OF EUROPE, A (FR/0252-0842) [12144169] **299**

FUTURE GENERATIONS COMPUTER SYSTEMS : FGCS (NE/0167-739X) [11619996] 1279, **1247**

FUTURE HEALTH (CN/0225-395X) [06296077] **3577**

FUTURE HOME TECHNOLOGY NEWS (US/1051-9971) [22164397] **1111**

FUTURE IS TODAY, THE (CN/0712-8320) [09586284] **4960**

FUTURE (NEW DELHI, INDIA) (II/0252-1873) [08855855] 5246, **2280**

FUTURE OF CHILDREN / CENTER FOR THE FUTURE OF CHILDREN, THE DAVID AND LUCILE PACKARD FOUNDATION, THE (US/1054-8289) [22979213] **5286**

FUTURE PLANNER (CN/0821-4808) [09964682] **5200**

FUTURE REFLECTIONS (US/0883-3419) [10610252] 1879, **4388**

Alphabetical Title Index — GAKUEN

FUTURE RESOURCES (US/0895-979X) [16878927] **1607**

FUTURE SURVEY (US/0190-3241) [04693322] 1635, **1533**

FUTURE SURVEY ANNUAL (US/0273-0138) [06716993] **5107**

FUTUREBUS+ DESIGN (US/1059-0846) [24452814] **1241**

●FUTURECAST (LA CANADA, CALIF.) (US/1062-3280) [25588272] **1492**

FUTURES AND OPTIONS WORLD (UK/0953-6620) [16503586] **924**

FUTURES CANADA (1984) (CN/0834-3241) [16410134] **5200**

FUTURES (CEDAR FALLS, IOWA) (US/0746-2468) [09881835] **899**

FUTURES CHART SERVICE. AGRICULTURAL (US) [22252969] 837, **89**

FUTURES CHARTS (US/1065-9722) [24031275] **837**

FUTURES (EAST LANSING, MICH.) (US/0748-1578) [08378003] **89**

FUTURES INDUSTRY ASSOCIATION *See* FIA WEEKLY BULLETINS **1606**

FUTURES INDUSTRY (WASHINGTON, D.C.) (US/1065-6855) [26678966] **1492**

FUTURES INDUSTRY'S MANAGED ACCOUNT REPORTS (US/0197-5382) [06057528] **899**

●FUTURES INTERNATIONAL LAW LETTER (US) [25598726] 837, **2973**

FUTURES (LONDON) (UK/0016-3287) [01287420] **1492**

FUTURES MARKET SERVICE (US) [05182453] **899**

FUTURES RESEARCH QUARTERLY (US/8755-3317) [11276457] **5107**

FUTURESCAN (US) 1492, **677**

FUTURETECH'S STRATEGIC MARKETS (US) **5107**

FUTUREVIEWS *CEASED.* (US/0739-0823) [09716006] **1185**

FUTURIBLERNE (DK) [06683375] **5107**

FUTURIBLES (PARIS) (FR/0337-307X) [07294682] 1492, **5246**

FUTURICS (US/0164-1220) [05018534] **5107**

FUTURIFIC (US/0738-9264) [09689917] **2487**

FUTURISMO-OGGI (IT) [09874557] **320**

FUTURIST, THE (US/0016-3317) [02244782] **5107**

FUTURIST. [MICROFILM], THE (US/0016-3317) [07440118] **5107**

FUTURO SOSTENIBILE (IT) [23284841] **2216**

FUTUTETECH (US) **5107**

FUZZY SETS AND SYSTEMS (NE/0165-0114) [03767356] **3506**

FV. FOTO-VIDEO ACTUALIDAD (SP/0214-2244) [I02142244] **4369**

FVUS (US/0090-3078) [01784833] **89**

FW FINANCIAL WORLD (US) **899**

FWP JOURNAL (SA/0015-9026) [10522595] **4027**

FWP : MATERIALS ENGINEERING JOURNAL *CEASED.* (SA) [26940386] **1976**

FWS (US) [04843363] 2194, **2383**

FWTAO GUIDEBOOK (CN/0842-8425) [19276452] **1879**

FWTAO NEWSLETTER (CN/0381-9183) [02603499] **1747**

FWZ REVIEW (UK) [05703023] 2261, 5047, **5557**

FX WEEK (US/1050-0782) [21385065] **677**

FY ... ACCOUNTABILITY REPORT FOR VOCATIONAL EDUCATION (WYOMING) (US) [11848503] **1913**

FY ... ANNUAL REPORT / ALABAMA DEPARTMENT OF CONSERVATION AND NATURAL RESOURCES (US) [11668721] **2194**

FY ANNUAL REPORT ON IN-HOUSE ENERGY MANAGEMENT (US/0730-6954) [08040031] **1945**

FY ... UNIT COST REPORT FOR THE PUBLIC COMMUNITY COLLEGES OF ILLINOIS (US) [10035652] **1825**

●FYI EVERYWOMAN'S RESOURCE GUIDE TO L.I (US/1062-7367) [25723339] 5478, **5557**

FYI/FMHA : FOR YOUR INFORMATION / INFORMATION STAFF, FARMERS HOME ADMINISTRATION, U.S. DEPARTMENT OF AGRICULTURE (US) [06315495] **89**

FYI : NOTES FOR BUSINESS AND INDUSTRY (US) **677**

FYLKESTINGSVALGET. COUNTY COUNCIL ELECTIONS (NO) [02469644] **4698**

FYNS KOMMUNALE TELEFONSELSKAB *See* BERETNING OG REGNSKAB FOR ARET ... **1150**

FYNS KOMMUNALE TELEFONSELSKAB. AARSBERETNING *See* BERETNING OG REGNSKAB FOR ARET ... **1150**

FYNSKE MINDER (DK/0427-7945) [I04277945] 268, **2689**

FYSIATRICKY A REUMATOLOGICKY VESTNIK (XR/0072-0038) [06341483] **3577**

FYSIK-KEMI (DK) [03136552] 976, **4403**

FYSISK TIDSSKRIFT (DK/0016-3392) [01570358] **4403**

G.A.S. LITES (US/0882-8377) [11961370] **2449**

●G & B : GIORNALE DI CLINIA MEDICA & BASI RAZIONALI DELLA TERAPIA (IT/1120-8392) [28171006] **3578**

G.C.B. BULLETIN (US/0095-196X) [01795311] **3165**

G. CULUKIZIS SAXELOBIS SAMTO MEKANIKIS INSTITUTI *See* FIZIKA I MEKHANIKA GORNYKH POROD **2023**

G. GESCHICHTE MIT PFIFF (GW/0173-539X) [I0173539X] **2616**

G.H.S. FOOT-NOTES (US/0090-4368) [01785169] **2734**

G.I. JOE *CEASED.* (US/0746-7397) [10248397] **4861**

G-I-T (GW/0016-3538) [06053327] **2589**

G.R.I. NEWS 'N' NOTES (US) [10023794] **2449**

G.S.M.C. RECORD (US) [10129693] **2449**

G. V. OLSEN ASSOCIATES *See* OLSEN'S AGRIBUSINESS REPORT **117**

G. W. REVIEW, THE (US/8756-8640) [09384676] **3389**

GA DOCUMENT (JA/0389-0066) [07099622] **299**

GA. GAS + ARCHITEKTUR (GW/0016-3406) [I00163406] **2605**

GA HOUSES (JA) [03880888] **299**

GA PLAINSONG NOTES (CN/0821-509X) [09606634] **4119**

GAAP (US/0883-4245) [11705259] **744**

GAAS NEWS (US) **1025**

GABBITAS, TRUMAN & THRING GUIDE TO BOARDING SCHOOLS AND COLLEGES, THE (UK/0951-872X) [I0951872X] **1747**

GABBITAS TRUMAN & THRING GUIDE TO ENGLISH LANGUAGE SCHOOLS AND SUMMER COURSES *See* LANGUAGES IN EUROPE **1761**

GABLERS MAGAZIN (GW/0932-3961) [I09323961] **868**

GABON. DIRECTION DE LA STATISTIQUE ET DES ETUDES ECONOMIQUES *See* SITUATION ECONOMIQUE, FINANCIERE ET SOCIALE DE LA REPUBLIQUE GABONAISE **4748**

GABON. DIRECTION DE LA STATISTIQUE ET DES ETUDES ECONOMIQUES *See* BULLETIN MENSUEL DE STATISTIQUE - DIRECTION DE LA STATISTIQUE ET DES ETUDES ECONOMIQUES (GABON) **1530**

GABON SELECTION PARIS (FR/0247-8315) [I02478315] **837**

GABONAIPAR (HU/0133-0918) [02244272] **201**

GABRIELI (GW) **4119**

GABRIOLA SOUNDER, THE (CN/1187-0702) [24570882] **5785**

GABUN : ENERGIEWIRTSCHAFT (GW) [05121614] **1607**

GABUN : WIRTSCHAFTLICHE ENTWICKLUNG (GW) [02244005] **5327**

GABUN, WIRTSCHAFTSDATEN UND WIRTSCHAFTSDOKUMENTATION / BUNDESSTELLE FUER AUSSENHANDELSINFORMATION (GW) [12045716] **1562**

GABUNGAN IMPORTIR NASIONAL SELURUH INDONESIA *See* HIMPUNAN PERATURAN IMPOR **839**

GABUNGAN IMPORTIR NASIONAL SELURUH INDONESIA *See* BUSINESS GUIDE : JAKARTA **648**

GABUNGAN PERUSAHAAN EKSPOR INDONESIA *See* IER, INDONESIAN EXPORT REVIEW **839**

GACETA (AG) [01785264] **2920**

GACETA ARQUEOLOGICA ANDINA (PE/0254-8240) [09124770] **268**

GACETA DE CUBA (CU/0138-8770) [15715443] **320**

GACETA DE INVENCIONES Y MARCAS (MX) [05916564] **1304**

GACETA DE LAS ARTES (AG) [01445446] **350**

GACETA DE LOS NEGOCIOS, LA (SP) **5810**

GACETA FISCAL : REVISTA MENSUAL DE ORIENTACION JURIDICO-TRIBUTARIA (SP/0212-6591) [20600966] **4727**

GACETA INFORMATIVA DE LEGISLACION NACIONAL (MX/0185-4356) [12936185] **2973**

GACETA JUDICIAL (CK) [01445847] **2973**

GACETA JURIDICA DE LA CEE (SP) **2973**

GACETA LITERARIA (SP) [01793044] 3389, **3283**

GACETA MATEMATICA (SP/0016-3805) [04268853] **3506**

GACETA MEDICA DE BILBAO (SP/0304-4858) [01361867] **3578**

GACETA MEDICA DE CARACAS (VE/0367-4762) [01715448] **3578**

GACETA MEDICA DE MEXICO (MX/0016-3813) [01570372] **3578**

GACETA (MEXICO CITY, MEXICO : 1954) (MX/0185-3716) [01569599] **5231**

GACETA (MEXICO CITY, MEXICO), LA (MX) [07390473] **1492**

GACETA NUMISMATICA (SP/0210-2137) [I02102137] **2781**

GACETA OFICIAL - PROCURADURIA GENERAL DE JUSTICIA DEL DISTRITO FEDERAL (MX) [05986839] **3140**

GACETA OFICIAL - REPUBLICA DOMINICANA (DR) [02808900] **2973**

GACETA POETICA : REVISTA TRIMESTRAL DE POESIA (SP) **3463**

GACETA SANITARIA (SP/0213-9111) [19079114] **4776**

GACETA SINDICAL : ORGANO DE LA CONFEDERACION DE CC.OO (SP) [07525606] **1675**

GACETA (TAMPA, FLA.), LA (US/0016-3724) [01445676] **5649**

GADES (SP) [05858674] 4347, **1825**

GADGETS FOR DIVERS (US/1059-3853) [24579973] **4895**

GADSDEN COUNTY TIMES (US) [01445941] **5649**

GADSDEN TIMES (GADSDEN, ALA. : 1925) (US) [13433271] **5626**

GAELIC GLEANINGS *SUSPENDED.* (US/0882-2166) [11687934] **2449**

GAELIC SOCIETY OF INVERNESS *See* TRANSACTIONS OF THE GAELIC SOCIETY OF INVERNESS **3329**

GAELIC SPORT (IE) [14515143] **4895**

GAFFNEY LEDGER, THE (US/0748-934X) [11036230] **5742**

GAGARINSKIE NAUCHNYE CHTENIIA PO KOSMONAVTIKE I AVIATSII / AKADEMIIA NAUK SSSR, INSTITUT PROBLEM MEKHANIKI (RU) [11425951] **22**

GAHPERD JOURNAL (US) [17214329] **1855**

GAI SABER (TOLOZA) (FR/0047-4916) [02219636] **3389**

GAIAN SCIENCE FOR GEOPHYSIOLOGY RESEARCHERS & TEACHERS *CEASED.* (US/1051-6689) [22043892] 1376, **1405**

GAIKO TO BUNKA (JA/0285-0206) [10841659] **2651**

GAIKOKU BOEKI GAIKYO. THE SUMMARY REPORT, TRADE OF JAPAN (JA) [04205057] **837**

GAIKOKU BUNGAKU (JA) [02779132] **3389**

GAIKOKU GENSHIRYOKU KIKAN KANKO SHIRYO GEPPO. / MONTHLY LIST OF SELECTED ATOMIC ENERGY PUBLICATIONS (JA) [03209654] **4447**

GAIKOKU GIJUTSU DONYU NENJI HOKOKU (JA) [01797170] **899**

GAIKOKUGO GAIKOKU BUNGAKU KENKYU (JA) [02246989] **3283**

GAINES COUNTY NEWS (US) [14292342] **5750**

GAINESVILLE SUN (US/0163-4925) [01446379] **5649**

GAIRM (UK/0016-3929) [12488010] 320, **3343**

GAIS DE L'OUTAOUAIS *See* GO INFO **5231**

GAISHI REBYU (JA) [02245383] **2055**

●GAIT & POSTURE (UK/0966-6362) [28387280] **3578**

GAITHERSBURG GAZETTE, THE (US/0195-2447) [05424149] **5686**

GAIU HANDBOOK OF WAGES, HOURS, AND FRINGE BENEFITS (US/0094-4211) [01794083] 378, **1675**

GAIYO - HOKKAIDO KAIHATSUKYOKU DOBOKU SHIKENJO (JA) [02711567] **2023**

GAKKAI SENTA NEWS (JA) [05665513] **5107**

GAKKO ICHIRAN (JA) [03180281] **1748**

GAKUEN RONSHU (JA/0385-7271) [11520297] **1825**

GAKUJUTSU — Alphabetical Title Index

GAKUJUTSU KENKYU : GAIKOKUGO GAIKOKU BUNGAKU HEN (JA) [03401504] **3283**

GAKUJUTSU KENKYU: KYOIKU, SHAKAI KYOIKU, KYOIKU SHINRI, TAIIKU HEN (JA) [03400999] **1748**

GAKUJUTSU KENKYU NEMPO / DOSHISHA JOSHI DAIGAKU (JA/0418-0038) [07981673] **5231**

GAKUJUTSU KENKYU : SEIBUTSU CHIGAKU HEN (JA) [03610181] **1355**

GAKUJUTSU KIYO / KOCHI KOGYO KOTO SENMON GAKKO (JA) [10420471] 1091, **5107**

GAKUJUTSU ZASSHI SOGO MOKUROKU. OBUN HEN. HOIBAN (JA) [10843032] **5175**

GAKUSHIKAI *See* GAKUSHIKAI KAIHO **1825**

GAKUSHIKAI KAIHO (JA) [04735144] **1825**

GAKUSHUIN MINZOKU (JA) [09372437] **2320**

GAKUSO - KYOTO KOKURITSU HAKUBUTSUKAN (JA) [06657249] **4088**

GALA REALIST (US) [22407767] **2794**

GALACTIC CENTRAL BIBLIOGRAPHIES FOR THE AVID READER (US/1049-6386) [21268480] **416**

GALACTIC CENTRAL PUBLISHER CHECKLISTS (US/1049-6394) [21268498] **4815**

GALAKSIJA (YU/0350-123X) [01794957] **5107**

GALAKTIKA (HU/0133-2430) [101332430] **5107**

GALANG / LEMBAGA STUDI PEMBANGUNAN (IO) [10523934] **4727**

GALASSIA (IT) [23685357] **2487**

GALAXIA 71 [I.E. SETENTA Y UNO] (VE) [03501447] **320**

GALAXY MAGAZINE (US/0435-0464) [02113667] **3389**

GALE COMPOSITE BIOGRAPHICAL DICTIONARY SERIES (US) [02949253] **432**

●GALE DIRECTORY OF DATABASES (US/1066-8934) [27083744] **1237**

GALE DIRECTORY OF PUBLICATIONS AND BROADCAST MEDIA (US/1048-7972) [20820864] **1132**

●GALE ENVIRONMENTAL SOURCEBOOK (US/1059-0919) [24478627] **2172**

GALE GLOBAL ACCESS. ASSOCIATIONS *See* ENCYCLOPEDIA OF ASSOCIATIONS CD-ROM **1925**

GALE GLOBAL ACCESS. ASSOCIATIONS (US/1065-5050) [26621486] **5231**

GALE RESEARCH COMPANY *See* TWENTIETH-CENTURY LITERARY CRITICISM **3355**

GALED (IS/0334-4258) [01798530] **2261**

●GALENA GENEALOGY (US/1062-7448) [25724656] **2449**

GALERIA ANTIQUARIA (SP/1130-2747) [23710842] **350**

GALERIE DES MONNAIES OF GENEVA, LTD *See* RARE COINS & MEDALS **2783**

GALERIE JOLLIET *See* GALERIE JOLLIET **350**

GALERIE JOLLIET (CN/0228-3778) [08023763] **350**

GALERIE PAUL VALLOTTON *See* ENSEMBLE D'AQUARELLES ET DE DESSINS DE MAITRES SUISSES ET FRANCAIS DU XIXE ET DU XXE SIECLE, UN **349**

GALERIES MAGAZINE (INTERNATIONAL EDITION) (FR) [16928769] **350**

GALE'S AUTO SOURCEBOOK *CEASED.* (US/1056-4330) [23711328] **5415**

●GALE'S LITERARY INDEX (US/1066-7709) [27046032] **3389**

GALESVILLE REPUBLICAN (US) [07435257] **5767**

GALIBO : REVISTA DE LITERATURA (SP) [22137423] **3389**

GALICIA, CATALOGO DE EXPORTADORES/COMERCIO EXTERIOR (SP) [19409590] **837**

GALICIA CLINICA (SP/0304-4866) [103044866] **3578**

GALLATIN COUNTY NEWS, THE (US) [13151540] **5680**

GALLATIN TRAILS (US/0883-1920) [12089246] **2449**

GALLAUDET TODAY (US/0016-4089) [02336415] 4388, **1879**

GALLERIA (IT/0016-4097) [01633207] **3389**

GALLERIE E GRANDI OPERE SOTTERRANEE (IT/0393-1641) [103931641] **2023**

GALLERIE (NORTH VANCOUVER, B.C.) (CN/0838-1658) [18935907] **321**

GALLERIES (UK/0265-7511) [102657511] **4088**

GALLERIES (WASHINGTON, D.C.) (US/0739-0475) [07934428] **4088**

GALLERY (LETHBRIDGE) (CN/0826-1121) [10832003] **351**

GALLERY (NEW YORK, N.Y.) (US/0195-072X) [05256904] **3995**

GALLERY OF FINE HOME PLANS (US/0899-4404) [18096842] **299**

GALLERY WORKS (US/0730-5206) [08042906] **3463**

GALLEY (HARRISONBURG, VA.), THE (US/0743-9040) [10674653] **2449**

GALLEY SAIL REVIEW, THE (US/0016-4100) [03270300] **3343**

GALLIA (FR/0016-4119) [02365297] **2689**

GALLIA INFORMATIONS ARCHEOLOGIQUES (FR) **269**

GALLIA INFORMATIONS : PREHISTORIE ET HISTORIE (FR/0994-8899) [19701381] **2689**

GALLIA PREHISTOIRE. SUPPLEMENT (FR/0072-0100) [02040149] **269**

GALLIA, SUPPLEMENT (FR/0072-0119) [09349058] **2689**

GALLIMAUFRY (US/0161-2549) [03270321] **3389**

GALLIPOLIS DAILY TRIBUNE, THE (US) [15028266] **5728**

GALLIUM IN ... (US) [09372227] 4002, 2139, **4025**

GALLO SILVESTRE, IL (IT) **3463**

GALLUP MONTHLY REPORT ON EATING OUT, THE *CEASED.* (US/0739-9502) [09837615] **5071**

GALLUP ORGANIZATION *See* NATIONAL GARDENING SURVEY **2425**

GALLUP POLITICAL & ECONOMIC INDEX (UK) [23028033] **4474**

GALLUP POLL MONTHLY, THE (US/1051-2616) [21351921] **5327**

GALLUP POLL, THE (US/0195-962X) [05216944] **5246**

●GALLUP POLL (TORONTO. 1993) (CN/1197-4303) [29873917] **5246**

GALLUP REPORT INTERNATIONAL (US/0736-9514) [09262738] **5327**

GALLUP REPORT, THE (US/0754-0770) **5246**

GALLUP REPORT (TORONTO. 1990) (CN/1184-891X) [24368406] **5246**

GALLUP REPORT (TORONTO, ONT. : 1990) *See* GALLUP POLL (TORONTO. 1993) **5246**

GALPAGUCCHA (II) [10510167] **3283**

GALPIN SOCIETY *See* MEMBERSHIP LIST - THE GALPIN SOCIETY **4130**

GALPIN SOCIETY *See* JOURNAL - GALPIN SOCIETY **4125**

GALT HERALD, THE (US) [26728201] **5635**

GALVA NEWS, THE (US/0747-282X) [08807677] **5660**

GALVANO-ORGANO (FR/0302-6477) [22221021] **4002**

GALVANOTECHNIK (GW/0016-4232) [10989098] **2055**

GALVANOTECNICA & NUOVE FINITURE (IT/1120-6454) [I11206454] **487**

GALVANOTECNICA & PROCESSI AL PLASMA (IT) [11953132] **487**

GALVES AUTO PRICE LIST (AMERICAN USED CARS ED.) (US/0890-149X) [09079327] **5415**

GALVESTON DAILY NEWS (HOUSTON, TEX.: 1865) (US/0738-8047) [09690957] **5750**

GALVESTON (GALVESTON CHAMBER OF COMMERCE) (US/8750-4421) [11423614] **819**

GAM ON LAKE SAILING *See* GAM ON YACHTING **593**

GAM ON YACHTING (CN/0016-4259) [02014608] **593**

GAMA NEWS JOURNAL (US/1058-0808) [24189555] **2881**

GAMBIA WEEKLY, THE (GM/0046-5380) [21667079] **5801**

GAMBIT MAGAZINE : A JOURNAL OF THE OHIO VALLEY (US) [15123210] **3343**

GAMBIT (NEW ORLEANS, LA.) (US/0279-6589) [07149056] **5684**

GAMBLERS WORLD (US/0092-069X) [01789052] **4861**

GAMBLING / INFORMATION AIDS (US) [14196392] **3165**

GAMC NEWS (US/0743-7307) [10661302] **868**

GAMC NEWS JOURNAL (US/1052-424X) [22288252] **868**

GAME BIRD BREEDERS, AVICULTURISTS, ZOOLOGISTS AND CONSERVATIONISTS GAZETTE (US/0164-3711) [02642749] **211**

GAME BIRD BULLETIN (US) [04683586] 5617, **2149**

GAME CONSERVANCY (GREAT BRITAIN) *See* ANNUAL REVIEW FOR ... / THE GAME CONSERVANCY **2187**

GAME COUNTRY *See* GAME JOURNAL : THE BEST OF HUNTING AND FISHING **4872**

GAME DEVELOPER (US/1073-922X) [29558874] **1185**

GAME JOURNAL : THE BEST OF HUNTING AND FISHING (US) **4872**

GAME NEWS (US/8755-0989) [11401655] **4861**

GAME PLAYERS *See* PC GAMER **4864**

GAME PLAYER'S MS-DOS STRATEGY GUIDE (US/1041-5424) [18797987] **1185**

GAME PLAYER'S NINTENDO BUYER'S GUIDE (US/1041-0376) [18614535] **4861**

GAME PLAYERS NINTENDO GUIDE (US/1059-2172) [24508372] **4861**

GAME PLAYERS NINTENDO-SEGA (US/1068-1809) [27464100] **4861**

GAME PLAYERS PC ENTERTAINMENT (US/1059-2180) [24508479] 1185, **4861**

GAME PLAYER'S PC STRATEGY GUIDE *See* GAME PLAYERS PC ENTERTAINMENT **4861**

GAME PLAYER'S SEGA GENESIS STRATEGY GUIDE *See* GAME PLAYERS SEGA GUIDE **4861**

GAME PLAYERS SEGA GUIDE (US/1065-3376) [26576462] **4861**

●GAME PLAYERS SEGA NINTENDO (US/1074-2425) [29630393] **4861**

GAME PLAYERS STRATEGY GUIDE TO GAME BOY GAMES (US/1050-5601) [21534301] **1230**

GAME RESEARCH PROJECT *See* WILDLIFE RESEARCH **2209**

GAMECOCK, THE (US/0016-4313) [04080575] **211**

GAMEDAY (US/8755-1470) [11197169] **4896**

GAMEPLAN COLLEGE FOOTBALL ... ANNUAL PREVIEW (US/1055-9256) [20033975] **4896**

GAMEPRO (BELMONT, CALIF.) (US/1042-8658) [19231826] **4861**

GAMEROOM MAGAZINE *See* GAMEROOM (NEW ALBANY, IND.) **4861**

GAMEROOM (NEW ALBANY, IND.) (US/1049-3948) [21214106] **4861**

●GAMER'S CONNECTION, THE (US/1061-611X) [25380516] **4861**

GAMES AND ECONOMIC BEHAVIOR (US/0899-8256) [18232121] 1492, **3506**

GAMES (BASIC ED.) (US/0199-9788) [04578677] **4861**

GAMES (DELUXE ED.) *See* GAMES (BASIC ED.) **4861**

GAMES INTERNATIONAL (UK/0955-4424) [109554424] **4861**

GAMES JUNIOR *CEASED.* (US/0897-196X) [17429730] **4861**

GAMES (SPECIAL ED.) *See* GAMES (BASIC ED.) **4861**

GAMING CONFERENCE *See* ANNUAL GAMING CONFERENCE **3156**

GAMING REVENUE REPORT QUARTERLY (US) 4861, **4727**

GAMMA FIELD SYMPOSIA (JA/0435-1096) [01570403] 545, **511**

GAMMA (KBENHAVN) (DK/0108-0954) [08902028] **4434**

GAMMALT FRA STANGE OG ROMEDAL (NO) [03026005] **2689**

GAMMIE & DE SOUZA LAND TAXATION UPDATES (UK) **4727**

GAMUT (CLEVELAND, OHIO), THE *CEASED.* (US/0275-0589) [07078307] **2533**

GAMUT (GEORGIA ASSOCIATION OF MUSIC THEORISTS) (US) [16461691] **4119**

GAMUT (TORONTO) (CN/0713-3545) [09025964] **321**

GAN NO RINSHO (JA/0021-4949) [05214853] **3817**

GAN TO KAGAKU RYOHO (JA/0385-0684) [04684987] **3817**

GANADERIA (CK) [05304703] **211**

GANDAIA (BL) [04231780] **3463**

GANDHI MARG (ENGLISH ED.) (II/0016-4437) [06522861] **4522**

GANDHI MEMORIAL LECTURE (UK/0533-7224) [01432433] **2651**

Alphabetical Title Index GAS

GANDHI PEACE FOUNDATION LECTURE (II) [08751971] **2651**

GANDHIAN PERSPECTIVES (II) [05634384] **2651**

●GANG JOURNAL, THE (US/1061-5326) [25343998] 5246, **3165**

GANGAN BUCH (AU) [19250636] **3463**

GANGANATHA JHA KENDRIYA SANSKRIT VIDYAPEETHA *See* JOURNAL OF THE GANGANATHA JHA KENDRIYA SANSKRIT VIDYAPEETHA **3292**

GANGTIE (CC/0449-749X) [09235636] **4002**

GANGUANG KEXUE YU GUANGHUAXUE (CC/1000-3231) [21663588] 976, **4370**

GANIT (BG) [09221440] **3506**

GANITA (II/0046-5402) [01570407] **3506**

GANITA BHARATI (II/0970-0307) [08101734] **3506**

GANITA SANDESH (II/0970-9169) [I09709169] **3506**

GANKI (JA) [30939140] **3875**

GANKO : GANSEKI KOBUTSU KOSHO GAKKAI SHI (JA/0914-9783) [19403466] **1355**

GANN MONOGRAPH ON CANCER RESEARCH (JA) [05165544] **3817**

GANNETTEER (US/0433-163X) [01440527] 4815, **2920**

GANTAVYA (II/0377-9653) [01790402] **2504**

GANZE WOCHE, DIE (AU) **2517**

GAO JOURNAL (US) **744**

GAO WORK INVOLVING TITLE V OF THE ENERGY POLICY AND CONSERVATION ACT OF 1975 (US) [05277772] 1945, **2973**

GAODENG XUEXIAO HUAXUE XUEBAO (CC/0251-0790) [07441442] **976**

GAODENG XUEXIAO JISUAN SHUXUE XUEBAO (CC/1000-081X) [09296918] **3506**

GAOFENZI CAILIAO KEXUE YU GONGCHENG (CC/1000-7555) [I10007555] **976**

GAONENG WULI YU HE WULI (CC/0254-3052) [04372563] **4447**

GAO'S ... BIENNIAL REPORT ON THE TRANSFER OF EXCESS AND SURPLUS FEDERAL PERSONAL PROPERTY TO NONFEDERAL ORGANIZATIONS (US) [25739211] 4838, **4650**

GAP CONFERENCE REPORT / RESEARCH PROGRAM, CYSTIC FIBROSIS FOUNDATION (US/0740-7025) [08775529] **3578**

GARAGE NEWS (UK) **5415**

GARBAGE (BROOKLYN, NEW YORK, N.Y.) *CEASED.* (US/1044-3061) [19744968] 2230, **2194**

GARBAGE COALITION (CN/0382-6015) [02788449] **2230**

GARBAGE COALITION BULLETIN (CN/0382-6023) [02627653] **2230**

GARBO (SP) [11539245] **2517**

GARCIA DE ORTA : SERIE DE ANTROPOBIOLOGIA : REVISTA DA JUNTA DE INVESTIGACOES CIENTIFICAS DO ULTRAMAR (PO) [11459110] **237**

GARCIA DE ORTA : SERIE DE BOTANICA (PO/0379-9506) [01795489] **511**

GARCIA DE ORTA : SERIE DE ESTUDOS AGRONOMICOS (PO/0378-8032) [02555650] **89**

GARCIA DE ORTA : SERIE DE GEOGRAFIA (PO) [02239952] **2561**

GARCIA DE ORTA : SERIE DE GEOLOGIA (PO/0378-1240) [01795545] **1376**

GARCIA DE ORTA : SERIE DE ZOOLOGIA (PO/0253-0597) [01795546] **5584**

GARCILLA (SP/0212-923X) [14930251] 5617, **4165**

GARDAR (SW/0280-6487) [01776237] **3389**

GARDAVUE (LONGUEUIL) (CN/0842-1986) [19568699] **5286**

GARDEN ANSWERS (UK) [11143872] **2415**

GARDEN BOOK / WHITE FLOWER FARM, THE (US) [08468647] **2415**

GARDEN CENTER BULLETIN *See* BULLETIN **2411**

GARDEN CENTER BULLETIN, THE (US/0892-564X) [15059357] **2415**

GARDEN CITY OBSERVER (US) **5692**

GARDEN CITY TELEGRAM (GARDEN CITY, KAN. : 1953) (US) [11167137] **5675**

GARDEN CLIPPINGS *CEASED.* (CN/0318-7705) [02014708] **2415**

GARDEN CLUB OF AMERICA NEWSLETTER, THE (US/0896-8373) [16969652] **2415**

GARDEN CONSERVANCY *See* NEWSLETTER OF THE GARDEN CONSERVANCY, THE **2425**

GARDEN DESIGN (US/0733-4923) [08610163] **2415**

GARDEN HISTORY (UK/0307-1243) [01795341] **2415**

GARDEN HISTORY SOCIETY (GREAT BRITAIN) *See* NEWSLETTER - GARDEN HISTORY SOCIETY (1981) **2425**

GARDEN IDEAS & OUTDOOR LIVING (US/0733-0340) [08497447] 4872, **2415**

GARDEN ISLAND, THE (US/0744-4028) [08244899] **5655**

●GARDEN LITERATURE (US/1061-3722) [25277381] **2434**

GARDEN (LONDON 1975) (UK/0308-5457) [02255696] **2415**

●GARDEN NEWS / FAIRCHILD TROPICAL GARDEN (US) [27825025] 511, **2415**

GARDEN PATH, THE (US/0016-4607) [04080583] **2415**

GARDEN RAILWAYS (US/0747-0622) [10515249] 2023, **5431**

GARDEN STATE HOME & GARDEN (US/1044-3576) [19757703] **2900**

GARDEN STATE REPORT (US/8756-6605) [11617350] **4650**

GARDEN TALK (US/0897-280X) [16349660] **2415**

●GARDEN TOURIST, THE (JS/1062-6093) [25612490] **2415**

GARDEN WRITERS NEWSLETTER (US) **2415**

GARDENER (US/0016-464X) [01780219] **2415**

GARDENERS' CHRONICLE NEWSPAPER, THE (UK) [19098927] **5812**

GARDENERS DIGEST (CN/0821-5855) [09670579] **2415**

GARDENER'S EYE, THE (US/1041-2875) [18710016] **2415**

GARDENIA (IT/0393-585X) [I0393585X] **2415**

GARDENING AUSTRALIA (AT) **2415**

●GARDENING IN ALBERTA (CN/1188-2972) [25882966] **2416**

GARDENING NEWS (AT) **2416**

GARDENING NEWSLETTER (US/0164-7482) [04410796] **2416**

GARDENING WHICH (UK) [11226417] **2416**

GARDENS & COUNTRYSIDES (US/1049-9431) [21357884] **5478**

GARDENS AND MORE *See* NEIL SPERRY'S GARDENS **2425**

GARDENS' BULLETIN, SINGAPORE, THE (SI/0374-7859) [10510586] **89**

GARDENS OF ENGLAND AND WALES 1988 (UK/0953-8550) [I09538550] **2416**

GARDENS WEST (CN/0836-4974) [17237115] **2416**

GARDNER NEWS (1983), THE (US/0740-0837) [09863969] **5688**

GARFIELD COUNTY NEWS (TROPIC, UTAH) (US/1064-7309) [12625892] **5756**

GARFIELD MAGAZINE *CEASED.* (US/1049-0191) [21109486] **2533**

GARFIELD-MAPLE HEIGHTS SUN (US/0746-2611) [09898418] **5728**

GARGANOSTUDI : RIVISTA DEL CENTRO STUDI GARGANICI (IT/0393-005X) [19690632] **2616**

GARGOUILLE MAGAZINE *CEASED.* (CN/0831-2591) [14556569] **4861**

GARGOYLE (MADISON), THE (US/0148-9623) [03403249] **2973**

GARIMA (NP) [08849465] **3389**

GARLAND LIBRARY OF MEDIEVAL LITERATURE (US) [08341104] 2689, **3389**

GARLAND MEDIEVAL TEXTS (US) [07597981] 2689, **3389**

GARLAND NEWS (1989), THE (US/1045-3997) [20104998] **5750**

GARLAND REFERENCE LIBRARY OF THE HUMANITIES (US/1059-3454) [12435807] **2846**

GARLAND'S BANKRUPTCY BULLETIN *CEASED.* (US/0891-611X) [14926580] **3086**

GARMENT MANUFACTURERS INDEX (US/1065-1330) [03437620] **1084**

GARMONIIA (RU/0869-8902) [24614523] 5533, **4776**

GARNER LEADER AND SIGNAL AND GARNER HERALD, THE (US) [16145757] **5670**

GARNER'S CONTROL OF POLLUTION *See* GARNER'S ENVIRONMENTAL LAW **3112**

GARNER'S ENVIRONMENTAL LAW (UK) **3112**

GARNET AND WHITE, THE (US/0746-7079) [06678868] **5231**

GARNETT REVIEW, THE (US) [09365405] **5675**

GARRETT CLIPPER (GARRETT, IND. : 1919) (US) [15698173] **5664**

GARTEN ORGANISCH (GW) [21397911] **2416**

GARTEN UND KLEINTIERZUCHT. B : RASSEGEFLUGELZUCHTER (SZ/0433-1818) [04024600] **211**

GARTEN UND KLEINTIERZUCHT. D : KLEINTIERZUCHTER (SZ/0433-1834) [04024615] **211**

GARTEN UND LANDSCHAFT (GW/0016-4720) [01570441] **2416**

GARTENAMT, DAS (GW/0016-4739) [I00164739] **2416**

GARTENBAU *See* GARTENBAU MAGAZIN **2407**

●GARTENBAU MAGAZIN (GW/0942-0118) [26992270] **2407**

GARTENBAU- UND FELDGEMUSE-ANBAUERHEBUNG / BEARBEITET IM OSTERREICHISCHEN STATISTISCHEN ZENTRALAMT (AU) [11463486] 2416, **2434**

GARTENBAU UND WEINWIRTSCHAFT. III. WEINWIRTSCHAFT (GW) [01227708] **2416**

GARTENBAULICHE VERSUCHSBERICHTE (GW) [04851366] **2416**

GARTENBAUTECHNISCHE INFORMATIONEN (GW) [04990698] **2416**

GARTENBAUWISSENSCHAFT (GW/0016-478X) [01570442] **2416**

GARTENKUNST, DIE (GW/0935-0519) [21309833] **2416**

GARTENMOBEL INTERNATIONAL (US/8756-2871) [11699964] **837**

GARTENPRAXIS (GW/0341-2105) [01930715] **2416**

GARTH ANALYSIS, THE (US/0745-6468) [09328808] **5246**

GARTNER-TIDENDE : ORGAN FOR ALMINDELIG DANSK GARTNERFORENING (DK/0106-8393) [09790058] **2416**

●GARTNERBORSE (GW/0945-9111) [29900192] **2416**

GARTNERBORSE, GARTENWELT (GW/0936-3734) [I09363734] **2416**

GARTNERBORSE UND GARTENWELT *See* GARTNERBORSE **2416**

GARTNERMEISTER (SZ) [04919983] **2416**

GARTNERYRKET (NO/0046-5437) [03104525] **89**

GARUDA (II) [02239620] **2651**

GARVIN'S LARGE PRINT READER (US/1045-2907) [20074475] **3389**

GARY AMERICAN, THE (US) [13231213] **5664**

GARY CRUSADER (US) [02400666] **5664**

GARY NORTH'S RARE COIN INVESTMENT REVIEW (US/1052-8741) [22400688] **2781**

GARYOUNIS SCIENTIFIC BULLETIN (LY/0253-634X) [06401512] **5107**

GAS (NE/0016-4828) [02447123] **4257**

GAS (US) [01441615] **4257**

GAS ABSTRACTS (US/0016-4844) [01570447] 4257, **4283**

GAS AKTUELL (GW/0340-6067) [18712204] **4257**

GAS & CHEMICAL REPORTER (JA/0913-283X) [I0913283X] 1025, **4257**

●GAS & LIQUID CHROMATOGRAPHY LITERATURE, ABSTRACTS & INDEX (US/1059-3160) [24565281] 1015, **1011**

GAS AND OIL EQUIPMENT DIRECTORY (US) [03800743] **4257**

GAS (BARCELONA, SPAIN) (SP) [10587218] **4257**

GAS BUYERS GUIDE (US/0897-8778) [13919268] **4257**

GAS CHROMATOGRAPHY LITERATURE, ABSTRACTS AND INDEX (US/0016-4895) [02270484] **1015**

GAS CHROMATOGRAPHY LITERATURE, ABSTRACTS & INDEX *See* GAS & LIQUID CHROMATOGRAPHY LITERATURE, ABSTRACTS & INDEX **1011**

GAS CHROMATOGRAPHY-MASS SPECTROMETRY ABSTRACTS (UK/0046-5461) [04024661] **1015**

GAS COUNCIL RESEARCH COMMUNICATION (UK/0433-1931) [I04331931] **4257**

GAS DAILY (US/0885-5935) [12043252] **4257**

GAS DAILY NATURAL GAS MARKETING. INDUSTRY DIRECTORY (US/1061-5024) [23462336] **4257**

●GAS DAILY'S GAS MARKETS WEEK (US/1065-867X) [26782863] **4257**

GAS DAILY'S GAS STORAGE REPORT (US/1057-2279) [23980511] **4257**

●GAS DAILY'S NG (US/1068-1299) [27448090] **4257**

GAS DATA BOOK; BRIEF EXCERPTS FROM GAS FACTS (US/0433-194X) [01203693] **4257**

GAS DIGEST (US/0161-4851) [03937900] **4257**

GAS DIRECTORY AND WHO'S WHO (UK/0307-3084) [02176442] **4257**

GAS DISTRIBUTION INDUSTRY AND PERFORMANCE INDICATORS (AT/1039-8112) **4257**

GAS ENERGY REVIEW (US/8756-5471) [05133260] **4257**

GAS ENGINE MAGAZINE (US/0435-1304) [01570451] 159, **250**

GAS ENGINEERING AND MANAGEMENT (UK/0306-6444) [02240512] **4257**

GAS FACTS (US/0361-4298) [01189798] **4283**

GAS INDUSTRIES (1978) (US/0194-2468) [05347900] 1945, **4257**

GAS INDUSTRY DIRECTORY (UK/0954-853X) [I0954853X] **4257**

GAS MATTERS (UK/0964-8496) [I09648496] **4257**

GAS (MUNCHEN) (GW/0343-2092) [04715302] **4257**

●GAS PROCESSING AND PIPELINING (US/1067-1021) [27134262] **4257**

GAS PROCESSORS ASSOCIATION *See* PROCEEDINGS, ANNUAL CONVENTION - GAS PROCESSORS ASSOCIATION **4275**

GAS PROCESSORS REPORT (US/0740-5278) [09979221] **4258**

GAS PRODUCTION LEDGER (US) **4258**

GAS REVIEW NIPPON (JA/0913-2090) [I09132090] **4258**

GAS (SAN CARLOS, CALIF.) *SUSPENDED.* (US/1058-532X) [24324696] **3463**

GAS SEPARATION & PURIFICATION (UK/0950-4214) [17457421] 1025, **4258**

●GAS SHALES TECHNOLOGY REVIEW (US/1065-786X) [25742421] **4258**

GAS STATS (US/1049-4103) [18097672] **4258**

GAS SUPPLIES OF INTERSTATE NATURAL GAS PIPELINE COMPANIES / FEDERAL POWER COMMISSION, BUREAU OF NATURAL GAS, THE (US/0565-0127) [05368814] **4258**

GAS TRANSACTIONS REPORT (US/1072-5113) **4258**

●GAS TRANSPORTATION REPORT (US/1065-8661) [26782723] 5383, **4258**

GAS TURBINE FORECAST (US) **2114**

GAS TURBINE WORLD (1984) (US/0747-7988) [10787234] **2114**

GAS TURBINE WORLD HANDBOOK (US/0883-458X) [10984743] **2114**

GAS- UND WASSERFACH. GAS, ERDGAS : GWF, DAS (GW/0016-4909) [02394198] **4258**

GAS- UND WASSERFACH. WASSER, ABWASSER : GWF, DAS (GW/0016-3651) [02393508] **5533**

GAS UTILITIES (CN/0380-2329) [02443805] **4258**

GAS UTILITIES. TRANSPORT AND DISTRIBUTION SYSTEMS (CN/0527-5318) [01786180] **4258**

GAS UTILITY INDUSTRY IN JAPAN (JA) [02370819] **4258**

●GAS UTILITY REPORT (US) [29689912] **4761**

GAS WARME INTERNATIONAL (GW/0020-9384) [09534200] **4258**

GAS, WASSER, WARME (AU/0016-5018) [06857486] **4258**

GAS WORLD INTERNATIONAL (UK/0960-1635) [I09601635] **4258**

GAS WORLD (LONDON, ENGLAND : 1974) (UK/0308-7654) [06691925] **4258**

GASAVERS NEWS (US/0271-082X) [06545931] **4258**

GASCOYNE, REGIONAL PROFILE (AT) [20206158] **2669**

GASES AND WELDING DISTRIBUTOR, THE (US) 924, **4027**

GASETA MUNICIPAL (SP) [12211153] **4650**

GASEUNDERSGELSER I JAMESON LAND / GRNLANDS FISKERI- OG MILJUNDERSGELSER (DK) [11946590] **5617**

GASKELL SOCIETY JOURNAL, THE (UK/0951-7200) [20481363] **3389**

GASKIYA TA FI KWABO (NR) [02261412] **5807**

●GASLIGHT (CLEVELAND, MINN.) (US/1062-015X) [25505424] 5074, **3389**

GASLINI GENOVA (IT/0390-5845) [I03905845] **3903**

GASNYTT (SW/0039-6834) [I00396834] **4258**

GASOHOL TAX EXEMPTIONS (US) [07586925] **4727**

GASOLINE CONSUMPTION IN FLORIDA DURING THE FISCAL YEAR ... (US) [09139374] **1607**

GASOLINE RAINBOW (CN/0706-5280) [04590139] **3390**

GASPESIE (GASPE. 1979) (CN/0227-1370) [06688501] **2734**

GASSTATISTIK FUR DIE BUNDESREPUBLIK DEUTSCHLAND (GW) [03262604] 4258, **4283**

GASTECH : PREPRINTS OF CONFERENCE PAPERS / THE ... INTERNATIONAL LNG/LPG CONFERENCE & EXHIBITION ; ORGANISED BY GASTECH LTD (UK) [25617748] **4258**

GASTRIC SECRETION (UK/0142-8098) [01428098] **3744**

GASTROENTEROLOGIA CLINICA (IT/1120-3757) [11203757] **3745**

GASTROENTEROLOGIA JAPONICA (JA/0435-1339) [01778998] **3745**

GASTROENTEROLOGIA Y HEPATOLOGIA (SP/0210-5705) [11136068] **3745**

GASTROENTEROLOGIE CLINIQUE ET BIOLOGIQUE (FR/0399-8320) [03122984] **3745**

GASTROENTEROLOGISCHE FORTBILDUNGSKURSE FUER DIE PRAXIS *CEASED.* (SZ/0302-9255) [10101643] **3745**

●GASTROENTEROLOGIST (BOSTON, MASS.), THE (US/1065-2477) [26537843] **3745**

GASTROENTEROLOGIST'S CLINICAL UPDATE (US/1042-5713) [19085882] **3745**

GASTROENTEROLOGY (NE) [02242907] **3745**

GASTROENTEROLOGY & ENDOSCOPY NEWS (US/0883-8348) [11979411] **3745**

GASTROENTEROLOGY & RHEUMATOLOGY IN PRACTICE (UK/0959-3314) [22238799] **3745**

GASTROENTEROLOGY CLINICS OF NORTH AMERICA (US/0889-8553) [14091836] **3745**

GASTROENTEROLOGY (GLENDALE, CALIF.) (US/0892-9386) [15552570] **3745**

GASTROENTEROLOGY IN PRACTICE (UK/0264-7478) [15351711] **3745**

GASTROENTEROLOGY INTERNATIONAL (IT/0950-5911) [19743448] **3745**

GASTROENTEROLOGY JOURNAL CLUB (US) **3745**

●GASTROENTEROLOGY MEDICINE TODAY (US/1063-1291) [25895204] **3745**

GASTROENTEROLOGY (NEW YORK, N.Y. 1943) (US/0016-5085) [01570457] **3745**

GASTROENTEROLOGY (NEW YORK, N.Y. : 1983) (US/0892-1601) [10549042] **3745**

GASTROENTEROLOGY NURSING (US/1042-895X) [19243364] 3745, **3856**

GASTROINTESTINAL CARCINOGENESIS (US) [03457871] 3745, **3817**

●GASTROINTESTINAL DISEASES TODAY (US/1061-6004) [25377381] **3745**

GASTROINTESTINAL ENDOSCOPY (US/0016-5107) [01570459] **3746**

GASTROINTESTINAL ENDOSCOPY CLINICS OF NORTH AMERICA (US/1052-5157) [22298969] **3746**

GASTROINTESTINAL HORMONES (UK/0142-8101) [01428101] **3746**

GASTROINTESTINAL RADIOLOGY (US/0364-2356) [02512906] 3746, **3941**

GASTRONOME (NEW YORK, N.Y.) (US/0895-3910) [09696919] **5071**

GASTRONOMIE (GW/0323-4762) [09743457] **3746**

GASTROPODIA (US/0435-1363) [01941180] **5584**

GASTRUM (SP/0211-058X) [I0211058X] **3746**

GASVERWENDUNG (GW/0016-5182) [02900807] **4259**

GATE ESCHBORN (GW/0723-2225) [I07232225] **5107**

GATEKEEPER SERIES (UK/1018-7235) [21283171] **89**

GATELODGE : THE PRISON OFFICERS' MAGAZINE (UK) [13448675] **3165**

GATER RACING PHOTO NEWS (US/0161-7834) [04025795] **4896**

GATES GAZETTE (US/0897-7798) [17470235] **2449**

GATESVILLE MESSENGER AND STAR-FORUM (US/0894-4954) [14201739] **5750**

GATEWAY (US) 5060, **1102**

GATEWAY ENGINEER (US/0747-1270) [10560559] **1976**

GATEWAY HERITAGE (US/0198-9375) [06268045] **2734**

GATEWAY: THE JOURNAL OF THE BELL COUNTY HISTORICAL SOCIETY (US) [09363890] 2449, **2734**

GATEWAYS OF EASTERN AFRICA (KE/0302-8089) [01792540] **5449**

GATFWORLD (PITTSBURGH, PA.) (US/1048-0293) [19571360] **378**

GATHERING (CN/0823-1869) [11046547] **4960**

GATHERING GIBSONS (US/0893-3162) [15477997] **2449**

GATHERING OF THE TRIBES, A (US/1058-9112) [24426129] 351, **3390**

GATHERINGS FROM THE ADIRONDACK FOOTHILLS (US/0882-0856) [11701264] **2734**

GATHERINGS (PENTICTON) (CN/1180-0666) [24257009] **3390**

GATO NEGRO, EL (AG) [23660335] **3390**

GATO TUERTO, EL (US/8755-3651) [11276269] **3390**

GATOR BAIT (US/0744-0995) [08028578] **4896**

GATOR GREEK, THE (US/0433-2091) [01424089] **5231**

GATORRIG DAIHAG UIHAG-BU RONMUN-JIB (KO/0377-9483) [02080097] 456, **3578**

GATOS TIMES-OBSERVER (GENERAL NEWS ED.), LOS (US/8750-4766) [11460378] **5635**

GATT ACTIVITIES IN ... / GENERAL AGREEMENT ON TARIFFS AND TRADE (SZ) [01564994] **837**

GATT BIBLIOGRAPHY, 1947-1953; THE TEXT OF THE GATT, SELECTED GATT PUBLICATIONS, A CHRONOLOGICAL LIST OF REFERENCES TO THE GATT. SUPPLEMENT (SZ/0589-5634) [01564999] **729**

GATT FOCUS (ENGLISH ED.) (SZ/0256-0119) [08730650] 4727, **837**

GATT STUDIES IN INTERNATIONAL TRADE (SZ) [06453816] 1635, **837**

GAUCHE, LA (CN/1183-2053) [24266045] **4542**

GAUCHE SOCIALISTE (CN/0823-9177) [11847666] **4542**

GAUER DISTINGUISHED LECTURE IN LAW AND PUBLIC POLICY, THE (US/1054-4674) [22901323] **2973**

GAUGE RAIL-ROADING, O (US/1062-1482) [25532893] **2773**

GAUHATI LAW REPORTS (II) [09491765] **2973**

GAUNTLET (US/1047-4463) [20696450] **5246**

GAVEA-BROWN (US/0276-7910) [07413787] **3390**

GAVEL (BISMARCK) (US/0093-1845) [01789574] **2973**

GAVEL (SACRAMENTO), THE (US/0363-5783) [02498240] **2973**

GAVIN REPORT (US) **4119**

●GAY AIRLINE & TRAVEL CLUB NEWSLETTER, THE (US) 5478, **2794**

GAY CHRISTIAN WITNESS (CN/0226-0441) [08027915] 4960, **2794**

GAY COMMUNITY NEWS (BOSTON, MASS.) *CEASED.* (US/0147-0728) [03079323] **2794**

GAY/LESBIAN MEDIA DIRECTORY WORLDWIDE (US/0730-3297) [07958371] **2794**

GAY LUTHERAN, THE (US/0360-571X) [01780900] 5060, **2794**

GAY MONTREAL (CN/0381-6931) [02802190] **2794**

GAY NEWS (UK) [05130155] **2794**

GAY PEOPLES UNION *See* GPU NEWS **2794**

GAY RISING (CN/0700-3536) [03348870] **2794**

GAY TIMES (UK) [15783043] **2794**

GAY TIMES LONDON. 1984 (UK/0950-6101) [I09506101] **2794**

GAYANA : BOTANICA (CL/0016-5301) [01441761] **511**

GAYANA : ZOOLOGIA (CL/0016-531X) [01424321] **5584**

Alphabetical Title Index — GEGEVENS

GAYELLOW PAGES. NORTHEAST ED (US) [05915277] **2794**

GAYLORD HUB, THE (US/0742-1591) [01570466] **5696**

GAYOSO STREET REVIEW, THE (US/0270-0085) [06310094] **3390**

GAYS, LESBIANS, AND BISEXUALS OF AMES *See* GLBAMES NEWSLETTER **2794**

GAYS OF OTTAWA *See* GO INFO **2794**

GAZ ACTUALITES (FR) [02482077] **4259**

GAZ D'AUJOURD'HUI (FR/0016-5328) [06385182] **4259**

GAZ DE FRANCE. DEPARTEMENT DES RELATIONS PUBLIQUES. INFORMATION *See* INFORMATION / GAZ DE FRANCE **4260**

GAZ, WODA I TECHNIKA SANITARNA (PL/0016-5352) [09390828] **2230**

GAZANKULU (SOUTH AFRICA). PUBLIC SERVICE COMMISSION *See* ANNUAL REPORT OF THE GAZANKULU PUBLIC SERVICE COMMISSION, GAZANKULU GOVERNMENT **4701**

GAZATIM-BAOVAO - MINISTERAN'NY FAMPANDROSOANA NY AMBANIVOHITRA SY NY FANAVAOZANA NY FIZAKAN-TANY (MG) [04815537] **89**

GAZDASAG (HU/0016-5360) [01424429] **1492**

GAZETA AGRI'COLA DE ANGOLA (AO) [09791254] **89**

GAZETA CUKROWNICZA (PL/0016-5395) [04024685] **172**

GAZETA DE MATEMATICA (PO/0373-2681) [01570467] **3506**

GAZETA DE MONTEVIDEO (UY) [01425526] **2734**

GAZETA KRAKOWSKA 1980 (PL/0208-7693) [02087693] **5808**

GAZETA LUBUSKA 1975 (PL/0137-9518) [01379518] **5808**

GAZETA MATEMATICA (BUCHAREST, ROMANIA : 1974) *CEASED.* (RM/1010-9943) [02759725] **3506**

GAZETA MERCANTIL (BL) [05715629] **1562**

GAZETA MERCANTIL : ADMINISTRACAO E SERVICOS (BL) [05977574] **868**

GAZETA MERCANTIL (NEW YORK WEEKLY EDITION) (US) [11115103] **1562**

GAZETA OBSERWATORA (PL) [01788377] 1413, **1425**

GAZETA OLSZTYNSKA (PL/0137-9127) [01379127] **5808**

GAZETA POLICYJNA (PL/0867-0390) [08670390] **3165**

GAZETA POZNANSKA 1981 (PL/0208-8746) [02088746] **5808**

GAZETA ROBOTNICZA (PL/0137-9143) [01379143] **5808**

GAZETA WSPOCZESNA (PL/0137-9488) [01379488] **5808**

GAZETA WYBORCZA (PL/0860-908X) [19986122] **5808**

GAZETTE (NE/0016-5492) [01570469] **1111**

GAZETTE (US) [21549475] **5696**

GAZETTE - AUSTRALIAN MATHEMATICAL SOCIETY (AT/0311-0729) [05138937] **3506**

GAZETTE - CANADIAN FORCES BASE GAGETOWN (1981) (CN/0713-391X) [09000533] **4044**

GAZETTE (CEDAR RAPIDS, IOWA), THE (US/1066-0291) [12380738] **5670**

GAZETTE DE LA BUTTE, LA (CN/0711-3528) [08770648] **5286**

GAZETTE DE L'HOTEL DROUOT, LA (FR) [09022282] **321**

GAZETTE DE L'UNIVERSITE DE MONCTON (CN/0380-6774) [02578912] **1091**

GAZETTE DE MALARTIC, LA (CN/0703-7198) [03439463] **5785**

GAZETTE DE METZ ET DE LORRAINE (FR) [21009797] **5800**

GAZETTE DE QUEBEC (CN/0710-1686) [08415757] **4650**

GAZETTE-DEMOCRAT, THE TALK AND COBDEN REVIEW, THE (US) [27648372] **5660**

GAZETTE DES ARCHIVES, LA (FR/0016-5522) [01570478] **2481**

GAZETTE DES BEAUX-ARTS (FR/0016-5530) [01570479] **351**

GAZETTE DES FEMMES, LA (CN/0704-4550) [06295646] **5557**

GAZETTE DES TRIBUNAUX IVOIRIENS (IV) [09400378] **2973**

GAZETTE DU C. L. S. C, LA (CN/0227-1206) [06562842] **5785**

GAZETTE DU CEFI *CEASED.* (FR) **1976**

GAZETTE DU GRANIT, LA (CN/1180-2677) [24571061] **2734**

GAZETTE DU LIVRE MEDIEVAL (FR/0753-5015) [10635017] **4828**

GAZETTE DU PALAIS (FR) [01570485] **2973**

GAZETTE, GOOCHLAND, THE (US/0739-0106) [09710493] **5758**

GAZETTE (GRAND FALLS) (CN/0228-9164) [08003171] **5785**

GAZETTE (HAVERHILL, MASS.) (US/0740-2090) [09889717] **5688**

GAZETTE (HURT, VA.), THE (US/8750-5738) [11544503] **5758**

GAZETTE; INTERNATIONAL JOURNAL OF SCIENCE OF THE PRESS (NE) [01425569] **2920**

GAZETTE - KADUNA STATE OF NIGERIA (NR) [05088786] **2973**

GAZETTE - LAURENTIAN UNIVERSITY (CN/0226-7934) [06689146] **1825**

GAZETTE - LAW SOCIETY OF THE AUSTRALIAN CAPITAL TERRITORY (AT/1038-1872) [10381872] **2973**

GAZETTE LEADER (US) [13727652] **5710**

GAZETTE / MALAWI *See* MALAWI GOVERNMENT GAZETTE, THE **4664**

GAZETTE MEDICALE (FR/0760-758X) [11822611] **3578**

GAZETTE (MIAMI, FLA.), THE (US/8755-0776) [08455181] **321**

GAZETTE (MONTREAL) (CN/0384-1294) [05901687] **5785**

GAZETTE (NEOLA, IOWA) (US) [16838656] **5670**

GAZETTE (NEW YORK. 1979), THE (US/0193-533X) [05225287] **3390**

GAZETTE - NIGER STATE OF NIGERIA (NR) [07238576] **2973**

GAZETTE OF LAW AND JOURNALISM (AT/0818-0148) [08180148] **2973**

GAZETTE OF THE AMERICAN FRIENDS OF LAFAYETTE (US) [01479894] **2689**

GAZETTE OF THE EGYPTIAN PAEDIATRIC ASSOCIATION (UA/0304-484X) [03048083] **3903**

GAZETTE OFFICIELLE DU QUEBEC. PARTIE 1. AVIS JURIDIQUE (CN/0703-5756) [02249971] **2533**

GAZETTE OFFICIELLE DU QUEBEC, PARTIE 2; LOIS ET REGLEMENTS (CN/0703-5721) [02602836] **2973**

GAZETTE, POWHATAN, THE (US/0745-8614) [09512031] **5758**

GAZETTE, THE (US) [25513151] **5728**

GAZETTE - THE LAW SOCIETY OF UPPER CANADA (CN/0023-9364) [02244791] **2973**

GAZETTE / THE UNIVERSITY OF SYDNEY, THE (AT) [13925131] **1091**

GAZETTE YEARBOOK (UK) [04048440] **2973**

GAZETTEER OF INDIA; INDIAN UNION, THE (II/0072-0348) [01774943] **2504**

GAZETTEER - UNITED STATES BOARD ON GEOGRAPHIC NAMES (US/0498-6415) [01156610] **2561**

GAZI UNIVERSITESI, ECZACILIK FAKULTESI DERGISI (TU/1015-9592) [10159592] **4305**

GAZOVAIA PROMYSHLENNOST (RU/0016-5581) [02430543] **4259**

GAZOVAIA PROMYSHLENNOST. SERIIA EKONOMIKA, ORGANIZATSIIA I UPRAVLENIE V GAZOVOI PROMYSHLENNOSTI / MINISTERSTVO GAZOVOI PROMYSHLENNOSTI (RU) [07148643] **4259**

GAZZETTA ANTIQUARIA (IT/0016-559X) [I0016559X] **250**

GAZZETTA CHIMICA ITALIANA (IT/0016-5603) [01780898] **976**

GAZZETTA DEL MEZZOGIORNO (IT) **5804**

GAZZETTA DEL SUD (IT) **5804**

GAZZETTA DELLA PICCOLA INDUSTRIA *CEASED.* (IT/0391-6138) [I03916138] **1492**

GAZZETTA DELLE ARTI (IT) **351**

GAZZETTA DELLO SPORT, LA (IT/1120-5067) [11205067] **5804**

GAZZETTA DI AREZZO, LA (IT) **5804**

GAZZETTA DI FIRENZE *SUSPENDED.* (IT) [01570501] **5804**

GAZZETTA DI PARMA (IT) **5804**

GAZZETTA DI REGGIO : 6 DAYS A WEEK (IT) **5804**

GAZZETTA MEDICA ITALIANA, ARCHIVIO PER LE SCIENZE MEDICHE (IT/0393-3660) [11088708] **3578**

GAZZETTA UFFICIALE DELLA REPUBBLICA ITALIANA (IT) [03590084] **2973**

GAZZETTA UFFICIALE DELLA REPUBBLICA ITALIANA. SUPPLEMENTO ORDINARIO (IT) [04419160] **5804**

GAZZETTA UFFICIALE : INDICE REPERTORIO ANNUALE CRONOLOGICO PER MATERIE (IT) **2973**

GAZZETTA UFFICIALE REGIONE SICILIANA. SERIE SPECIALE CONCORSI (IT) **4650**

GAZZETTINO DELLA PESCA (IT) **2304**

GAZZETTINO LIBRARIO (IT) **3212**

GB PROGETTI (IT/0394-1132) [25936467] **299**

GBC RADIO AND TV TIMES *SUSPENDED.* (GH) [02578132] **1132**

GBF MONOGRAPHS / GESELLSCHAFT FUER BIOTECHNOLOGISCHE FORSCHUNG (GW/0930-4320) [18045839] **3692**

GB+GW; GARTNERBORSE UND GARTENWELT (GW/0342-4731) [03423758] **2416**

'GBH (BOSTON, MASS.) (US/1066-8586) [27078222] **1132**

GC. GRUNER MARKT, GARTENCENTER + (GW/0721-4499) [07214499] **2416**

GC/MS UPDATE. PART A ENVIRONMENTAL (UK/0962-9327) [09629327] **2172**

GC/MS UPDATE PART B BIOMEDICAL, CLINICAL, DRUGS (UK/0962-9335) [09629335] **4305**

GDANSK. AKADEMIA MEDYCZNA *See* ANNALES ACADEMIAE MEDICAE GEDANENSIS **3549**

GDG REPORT, THE (US/0883-3087) [12118793] **3165**

GDI IMPULS (SZ) [11643231] **5200**

GDR BULLETIN: NEWSLETTER FOR LITERATURE AND CULTURE IN THE GERMAN DEMOCRATIC REPUBLIC (US) [05267780] 3390, **3283**

GDR : FACTS AND FIGURES (GW) [02382763] **2689**

GDR MARKET (GW) [22152286] **1492**

GDS INFO PARIS (FR/1157-4569) [11574569] **211**

GE NEWS (US/0272-3212) [05862535] **2055**

GE RI CO NEWS : BOLLETINO DI INFORMAZIONE E INNOVAZIONE RICERCA TECNOLOGICA (IT) **5107**

GEA (IT/0394-8382) [20655372] **2230**

GEAR TECHNOLOGY (US/0743-6858) [10639427] 3479, **2114**

GEARTEST (UK/0308-6437) [03714266] **4176**

GEBBIE PRESS *See* GEBBIE PRESS ALL-IN-ONE DIRECTORY **1111**

GEBBIE PRESS ALL-IN-ONE DIRECTORY (US/0097-8175) [01783747] **1111**

GEBURTSHILFE UND FRAUENHEILKUNDE (GW/0016-5751) [01570506] **3761**

GEC JOURNAL OF RESEARCH (UK/0264-9187) [10092073] 2055, **1976**

GEC REVIEW (UK/0267-9337) [13544546] **2055**

GECAMINES *See* RAPPORT ANNUEL - GENERALE DES CARRIERES ET DES MINES **1623**

GEDRAG & GEZONDHEID (NE/0921-5360) [14053162] 3578, **4587**

GEDRAG EN ORGANISATIE (NE/0921-5077) [09215077] **4587**

GEDRAGSTHERAPIE (NE) **4776**

GEFAEHRLICHE LADUNG (GW/0016-5808) [03284613] **5383**

GEFAHRGUT-BEAUFTRAGTE, DER (GW) **4776**

GEFAHRGUT - DANGEROUS GOODS CD-ROM (GW) **2862**

GEFAHRLICHE ARBEITSSTOFFE (GW/0932-4712) **4776**

GEFIEDERTE WELT, DIE (GW/0016-5816) [03143149] **5584**

GEGENBAURS MORPHOLOGISCHES JAHRBUCH *CEASED.* (GW/0016-5840) [09106755] **5584**

GEGENSCHEIN (US) [03092678] **3463**

GEGENWART (SZ/0016-5867) [02261430] 4347, **4960**

GEGENWARTSFRAGEN DER OST-WIRTSCHAFT (GW/0072-0534) [01448955] **1562**

GEGENWARTSKUNDE (GW/0016-5875) [01633270] 1895, **5200**

GEGEVENS BETREFFENDE HET NAUTISCH ONDERWIJS (NE) [02636260] **4176**

GEHALTS — Alphabetical Title Index

GEHALTS- UND LOHNSTRUKTURERHEBUNG / HERAUSGEGEBEN VOM STATISTISCHEN LANDESAMT BADEN-WURTTEMBERG (GW) [10261569] **1675**

GEIBI CHIHOSHI KENKYU / GEIBI CHIHOSHI KENKYUKAI (JA) [10441704] **2651**

GEIJUTSU-GAKU (JA) [03245633] **321**

GEIJUTSU NENKAN (OSAKA, JAPAN) (JA/0385-5694) [09651014] **321**

GEIJUTSU SHINCHO (JA) [01570515] **351**

GEIRIADUR PRIFYSGOL CYMRU (UK) [02936123] **1926**

GEIRIADUR, Y (UK) **3283**

GEISHA GIRL PORCELAIN (US/8756-9213) [11669901] **2589**

GEIST GAZETTE (US) [18371007] **5664**

GEIST UND LEBEN (WURZBURG) (GW/0016-5921) [05306742] 4960, **3390**

GEIST (VANCOUVER) (CN/1181-6554) [25127714] 385, **3390**

GEITEHOUDER, DE (NE) [09791661] 5510, **211**

GEKA CHIRYO (JA/0433-2644) [01380674] **3965**

GEKA SHINRYO (JA) [10268822] **3965**

GEKA TO TAISHA, EIYO (JA/0389-5564) [10316681] 4191, **3965**

GEKKAN ASAGUMO (JA) [04821836] **4044**

GEKKAN BOEKI SEISAKU (JA) [01797366] **837**

GEKKAN BOEKI TO SANGYO / HENSHU, TSUSHO SEISAKU KENKYUKAI (JA) [07982144] 4650, **1607**

GEKKAN HAIKIBUTSU (JA/0285-6220) [09582834] **2230**

GEKKAN KOMPYUTA DAIJESUTO (JA) [08482912] **1185**

GEKKAN MIKKYO KOZA. THE MIKKYO KOZA (JA) [04320933] **5021**

GEKKAN NIRA *See* NIRA NEWS **5211**

GEKKAN RAMU (JA) [10377668] 1267, **1274**

GEKKAN SHAKAITO (JA) [01797192] **4542**

GEKKAN YAKUJI (JA) [10436964] **4305**

GELBE SEITEN. 99, ORTSNETZ MUNCHEN (GW) [20176696] **1112**

GELBEN HEFTE, DIE (GW/0016-6006) [03333551] **3578**

GELBVIEH EYEOPENER (CN/0703-8356) [03439621] **211**

GELIOTEHNIKA (TASKENT) (UZ/0130-0997) [10768937] **1945**

●GELLIS & KAGAN'S CURRENT PEDIATRIC THERAPY (US/1069-2460) [27964908] **3903**

GELORA PEMBANGUNAN INDONESIA (IO) [09163935] **1562**

GELUID ALPHEN AAN DEN RIJN (NE/0925-9406) [l09259406] **5316**

●GEM & LAPIDARY QUARTERLY (US/1044-3622) [19759180] **2914**

GEM CRAFT *See* MODEL BOATS **594**

GEM (FINDLAY, OHIO), THE (US/0745-3019) [09055470] **4960**

GEMA D.P.R.D. TINGKAT I JAWA TENGAH (IO) [02481083] **4650**

GEMATOLOGIYA I TRANSFUZIOLOGIYA (RU) [09475010] **3771**

GEMEENSCHAPPELIJK ADMINISTRATIEKANTOOR (NETHERLANDS) *See* VERSLAG OVER HET BOEKJAAR ... / GAK **1631**

GEMEENTE (BE) **4650**

GEMEENTESTEM, DE (NE) [21282493] **2823**

GEMEENTEWERKEN *See* STADSWERK **2031**

GEMEETEWERKEN (NE/0046-5577) [09335585] **2023**

GEMEINDE (VIENNA, AUSTRIA) (GW) [11492352] **4650**

GEMEINDEDATEN (GW) [02714546] **5327**

GEMEINDEERGEBNISSE DER FINANZSTATISTIK ... AUSGEWAHLTE EINNAHME UND AUSGABEARTEN, STEUERKRAFTZAHLEN, HEBESATZE, SCHULDENSTAND UND PERSONALSTAND (GW) [20237244] **4727**

GEMEINDEERGEBNISSE DER FINANZSTATISTIK ... STEUERKRAFT, HEBESATZE, STEUEREINNAHMEN, ALLGEMEINE FINANZZUWEISUNGEN, KREISUMLAGEAUSGABE, SCHULDENSTAND UND PERSONALSTAND *See* GEMEINDEERGEBNISSE DER FINANZSTATISTIK ... AUSGEWAHLTE EINNAHME UND AUSGABEARTEN, STEUERKRAFTZAHLEN, HEBESATZE, SCHULDENSTAND UND PERSONALSTAND **4727**

GEMEINDEN NORDRHEIN-WESTFALEN, DIE (GW) [03610402] **5327**

GEMEINDERVERZEICHNIS DER SCHWEIZ / BUNDESAMT FUR STATISTIK (SZ) [08735075] **5478**

GEMEINDEUBERSICHT (AU) [03135092] **4553**

GEMEINDEVERZEICHNIS FUER NIEDERSACHSEN (GW) [01792115] **2823**

GEMEINDEWACHSTUM (GW/0177-2082) [I01772082] **4553**

GEMEINSAME WEG, DER (GW) [03676452] **321**

GEMEINSAMES AMTSBLATT DES KULTUSMINISTERIUMS UND DES MINISTERIUMS FUR WISSENSCHAFT UND FORSCHUNG DES LANDES NORDRHEIN-WESTFALEN (GW) [03564626] **1748**

GEMEINSCHAFTSKATALOG (GW) [01783988] **4119**

GEMEINWIRTSCHAFT *See* ZEITSCHRIFT FUER GEMEINWIRTSCHAFT **1589**

GEMINI (ELMIRA, N.Y.) (US/0898-8331) [17927483] **2449**

GEMINI (HERSTMONCEUX, EAST SUSSEX) (UK/0960-670X) [10602460] **390**

GEMINI (HERSTMONCEUX, ENGLAND) *See* SPECTRUM : NEWSLETTER OF THE ROYAL OBSERVATORIES **390**

GEMINI PROJECT *See* GEMINI PROJECT NEWSLETTER **395**

●GEMINI PROJECT NEWSLETTER (US) [25469292] **395**

GEMMA : REVISTA INTERNACIONAL DE LITERATURA (SP) **3390**

GEMS & GEMOLOGY (GEMOLOGICAL INSTITUTE OF AMERICA : 1967) (US/0016-626X) [07921950] **1439**

GEMS OF POETRY AND PROSE (CN/0834-1737) [16219864] **3390**

GEMS WODEN (AT/1032-2302) [I10322302] 5107, **3506**

GEMSHORN (US/0270-7101) [05255407] **4119**

GEMSTONE PRICE REPORT (BE) **2914**

GEMSTONE REGISTRY BULLETIN, THE (US/0882-6269) [11910598] **2914**

GEMUSE (MUNCHEN) (GW/0016-6286) [04025636] **172**

GEMUTLICHKEIT (HAYWARD, CALIF.) (US/1043-1756) [19334273] **2561**

GEN, GASTROENTEROLOGIA, ENDOCRINOLOGIA I NUTRICION (VE/0016-3503) [01778269] **3746**

GEN GUIDE TO BIOTECHNOLOGY COMPANIES (US/1063-0341) [19771269] **3692**

GENAVA (FR/0072-0585) [06687147] **351**

GENDAI (JA) [06561297] **2504**

GENDAI HAIKU NENKAN (JA) [11994633] **3463**

GENDAI KAGAKU. CHEMISTRY TODAY (JA) [03898824] **976**

GENDAI KORIA (JA) [11566486] **2651**

GENDAI NI IKIRU JOSEI JITEN (JA) [08710592] **5557**

GENDAI NOGYO (JA) [09791893] **89**

GENDAI TANKA (JA) [02322767] **3390**

GENDAI TO SHISO (JA) [01797097] **5200**

GENDAI TOYO IGAKU (JA/0388-6719) [08021482] **3578**

GENDAI YOGO NO KISO CHISHIKI (JA/0431-1213) [02434678] **3283**

GENDAISHI KENKYU (JA) [15187086] **4474**

GENDER AND EDUCATION (UK/0954-0253) [19946680] 1748, **5187**

GENDER & HISTORY (UK/0953-5233) [19587394] 3995, **5557**

GENDER & SOCIETY (US/0891-2432) [14687475] **5200**

GENDER DYSPHORIA (UK) [24914370] **3925**

●GENDER, PLACE AND CULTURE: A JOURNAL OF FEMINIST GEOGRAPHY (UK/0966-369X) 5557, **5268**

GENDER, WORK AND ORGANISATION (UK/0968-6673) [30016412] 677, **5246**

GENDERS (AUSTIN, TEX.) (US/0894-9832) [16388863] **2846**

GENE (NE/0378-1119) [03424642] **545**

GENE AMPLIFICATION AND ANALYSIS (US/0275-2778) [07113249] **545**

GENE EXPRESSION (US/1052-2166) [22222277] **545**

GENE EXPRESSION (UK/0957-3526) 487, **545**

GENE GEOGRAPHY : A COMPUTERIZED BULLETIN ON HUMAN GENE FREQUENCIES (IT/0394-249X) [22814752] **545**

●GENE THERAPY (UK/0969-7128) [29814485] **545**

GENE THERAPY (UK/1356-1308) 487, **3578**

GENE THERAPY WEEKLY (US/1078-2842) **545**

GENEAGRAM (US/8756-7989) [11592086] **2449**

GENEALOGICAL AIDS BULLETIN (1978) (US/0738-5226) [09603722] **2449**

GENEALOGICAL AND HISTORICAL MAGAZINE OF THE SOUTH, THE (US/0743-5843) [10613982] 2734, **2449**

GENEALOGICAL & LOCAL HISTORY BOOKS IN PRINT (US/0146-616X) [02998564] 2449, **4828**

GENEALOGICAL CLEARINGHOUSE QUARTERLY, THE (US/0882-0422) [11788142] **2449**

GENEALOGICAL COMPUTER PIONEER (US/0735-0287) [08851609] 1185, **2449**

GENEALOGICAL COMPUTING (US/0277-5913) [07605404] 1185, **2450**

GENEALOGICAL FORUM OF OREGON *See* BIENNIAL MEMBERSHIP BOOK / GENEALOGICAL FORUM OF PORTLAND, OREGON **2439**

GENEALOGICAL GEMS (US/0882-1623) [11714899] **2450**

GENEALOGICAL GOLDMINE (US/0738-3770) [07023476] **2450**

GENEALOGICAL HELPER *See* EVERTON'S GENEALOGICAL HELPER **2446**

GENEALOGICAL JOURNAL (LEXINGTON, N.C.), THE (US/0731-9606) [08155106] **2450**

GENEALOGICAL JOURNAL OF JEFFERSON COUNTY, NEW YORK (US/1045-8166) [20256062] **2450**

GENEALOGICAL JOURNAL (SALT LAKE CITY, UTAH) (US/0146-2229) [02250993] **2450**

GENEALOGICAL MAGAZINE OF NEW JERSEY, THE (US/0016-6367) [01570536] **2450**

GENEALOGICAL PERIODICAL ANNUAL INDEX (US/0072-0593) [04205809] 2450, **2478**

GENEALOGICAL RECORD (HOUSTON, TEX.), THE (US/0433-3209) [07323731] **2450**

GENEALOGICAL RECORD OF STRAFFORD COUNTY, THE (US/0739-1447) [04234693] **2450**

GENEALOGICAL REFERENCE BUILDERS NEWSLETTER (US/0533-7275) [02242484] **2450**

GENEALOGICAL RESEARCH DIRECTORY (SYDNEY, N.S.W. : 1989) (AT) [22357785] **2450**

GENEALOGICAL SOCIETY OF CHICKASAW COUNTY, THE (US/1055-2693) [23109054] **2450**

GENEALOGICAL SOCIETY OF EAST MIDLANDS *See* NOTTINGHAMSHIRE FAMILY HISTORY SOCIETY : JOURNAL **2465**

GENEALOGICAL SOCIETY OF IREDELL COUNTY, N.C *See* IREDELL COUNTY TRACKS / GENEALOGICAL SOCIETY OF IREDELL COUNTY, N.C **4554**

GENEALOGICAL SOCIETY OF IREDELL COUNTY, N.C *See* GENEALOGICAL SOCIETY OF IREDELL COUNTY, N.C, THE **2450**

GENEALOGICAL SOCIETY OF IREDELL COUNTY, N.C *See* IREDELL COUNTY TRACKS / GENEALOGICAL SOCIETY OF IREDELL COUNTY, N.C **4554**

GENEALOGICAL SOCIETY OF IREDELL COUNTY, N.C, THE (US/0740-5006) [09948138] **2450**

GENEALOGICAL SOCIETY OF NEW JERSEY *See* NEWSLETTER - GENEALOGICAL SOCIETY OF NEW JERSEY **2463**

GENEALOGICAL SOCIETY OF OLD TRYON COUNTY *See* BULLETIN - GENEALOGICAL SOCIETY OF OLD TRYON COUNTY **2440**

GENEALOGICAL SOCIETY OF RIVERSIDE. LIFE-LINE *See* LIFELINER **2458**

GENEALOGICAL SOCIETY OF THE CHURCH OF JESUS CHRIST OF LATTER-DAY SAINTS. RESEARCH PAPER: SERIES C *See* RESEARCH PAPERS : SERIES C - THE GENEALOGICAL DEPARTMENT OF THE CHURCH OF JESUS CHRIST OF LATTER-DAY SAINTS **2470**

Alphabetical Title Index — GENERAL

GENEALOGICAL SOCIETY OF WASHTENAW COUNTY, MICHIGAN *See* HISTORY OF WASHTENAW COUNTY, MICHIGAN **2453**

GENEALOGICAL TIPS (US/0433-3233) [07980768] **2450**

GENEALOGIE (GW/0016-6383) [07511231] **2450**

GENEALOGIE UND LANDESGESCHICHTE (GW) [02432731] **2450**

GENEALOGIES BOURBONNAISES ET DU CENTRE / CERCLE GENEALOGIQUE ET HERALDIQUE DU BOURBONNAIS (FR/0223-7237) [09801961] 432, **2450**

GENEALOGISCHES HANDBUCH DES ADELS (GW) [01570546] **2450**

GENEALOGIST (MANCHESTER, N.H.), THE (US/0196-4259) [04311048] **2450**

GENEALOGIST MELBOURNE (AT) [I03111776] **2450**

GENEALOGIST (NEW YORK), THE (US/0197-1468) [05969918] **2450**

GENEALOGISTS IN THE UNITED STATES AND CANADA (US/0742-4094) [10209597] **2450**

GENEALOGISTS' MAGAZINE : OFFICIAL ORGAN OF THE SOCIETY OF GENEALOGISTS, THE (UK/0016-6391) [01635751] **2450**

GENEALOGY AND LOCAL HISTORY TITLES ON MICROFICHE (US/0736-5292) [09157055] 2734, **2450**

GENEALOGY CLUB OF THE ALBUQUERQUE PUBLIC LIBRARY NEWSLETTER (US) [24478578] **2450**

GENEALOGY GLEANINGS (US/0882-5106) [11714796] **2450**

GENEES- EN VERBANDMIDDELENINDUSTRIE / CENTRAAL BUREAU VOOR DE STATISTIEK, HOOFDAFDELING STATISTIEKEN VAN INDUSTRIE EN BOUWNIJVERHEID (NE/0168-437X) [12046404] **3578**

GENEES- EN VERBANDMIDDELENINDUSTRIE PRODUKTIESTATISTIEKEN *See* GENEES- EN VERBANDMIDDELENINDUSTRIE / CENTRAAL BUREAU VOOR DE STATISTIEK, HOOFDAFDELING STATISTIEKEN VAN INDUSTRIE EN BOUWNIJVERHEID **3578**

GENEESKUNDE EN SPORT (NE/0016-6448) [06599295] **3954**

GENEESKUNDIG ADRESBOEK VOOR NEDERLAND (NE) [12045542] **3914**

GENEESKUNDIGE GIDS (1969-) (NE/0016-6464) [01779005] **3578**

GENEESMIDDELENBULLETIN (NE/0304-4629) [I03044629] 3578, **4305**

GENEL YAYIN - TURKEY. TOPRASKU GENEL MUDURLUGU (TU) [04165192] 2090, **172**

GENERAL ACCOUNTING OFFICE POLICY AND PROCEDURES MANUAL FOR GUIDANCE OF FEDERAL AGENCIES (US) [02784856] **4650**

GENERAL AGREEMENT ON TARIFFS AND TRADE (ORGANIZATION) *See* INTERNATIONAL TRADING ENVIRONMENT : REPORT BY THE DIRECTOR-GENERAL, THE **842**

GENERAL AGREEMENT ON TARIFFS AND TRADE (ORGANIZATION) *See* GATT ACTIVITIES IN ... / GENERAL AGREEMENT ON TARIFFS AND TRADE **837**

GENERAL AGREEMENT ON TARIFFS AND TRADE (ORGANIZATION) *See* BASIC INSTRUMENTS AND SELECTED DOCUMENTS. SUPPLEMENT / GENERAL AGREEMENTS ON TARIFFS AND TRADE **1633**

GENERAL AIRCRAFT FIXED- AND ROTARY-WINGED PRICE GUIDE *See* AIRCRAFT BLUEBOOK-PRICE DIGEST **9**

GENERAL AND APPLIED ENTOMOLOGY (AT/0158-0760) [04318415] **5609**

GENERAL AND COMPARATIVE ENDOCRINOLOGY (US/0016-6480) [01427438] **3730**

GENERAL AND SPECIAL LAWS OF THE STATE OF TEXAS (US) [06770789] **2973**

GENERAL AND SYNTHETIC METHODS *CEASED*. (UK/0141-2140) [04534841] **1041**

GENERAL ANNOUNCEMENT - MCGILL UNIVERSITY, MONTREAL (CN) [02554183] **1825**

GENERAL ASSEMBLY OF GEORGIA, THE (US/0098-6534) [02239353] **4650**

GENERAL ASSSEMBLY - INTER AMERICAN PRESS ASSOCIATION. ASAMBLEA GENERAL - SOCIEDAD INTERNAMERICANA DE PRENSA (US) [06125881] **2920**

GENERAL AVIATION *See* GENERAL AVIATION NEWS **22**

GENERAL AVIATION ACCIDENT REPORT (US/0887-7823) [13368552] 22, **2973**

GENERAL AVIATION ACTIVITY AND AVIONICS SURVEY (US/0272-4502) [06804427] **22**

GENERAL AVIATION NEWS (US/0191-927X) [03989556] **22**

GENERAL AVIATION NEWS AND FLYER (US/1052-9136) [22408481] **22**

GENERAL AVIATION STATISTICAL DATABOOK (US) [08309970] **41**

GENERAL BUSINESSFILE [COMPUTER FILE] (US) 677, **730**

GENERAL CATALOG OF INFORMATION SERVICES / NATIONAL TECHNICAL INFORMATION SERVICE (US) [09375519] **5107**

GENERAL CATALOGUE OF PRINTED BOOKS / BRITISH MUSEUM (UK) [01537333] **4088**

GENERAL COMPETITION RULES (DENVER) (US/0196-7630) [05880009] **5415**

GENERAL CONSTRUCTION COSTBOOK (US/1059-6046) [24614559] **615**

GENERAL CONSTRUCTION ESTIMATING STANDARDS: THE RICHARDSON RAPID SYSTEM (US) [03954474] **615**

GENERAL CONVENTION OF THE NEW JERUSALEM IN THE UNITED STATES OF AMERICA *See* JOURNAL OF THE GENERAL CONVENTION OF THE NEW JERUSALEM **5062**

GENERAL DENTISTRY (US/0363-6771) [02328603] **1324**

GENERAL ELECTION. REPORT *See* REPORT OF THE DIRECTOR OF ELECTIONS **4493**

GENERAL ELECTRIC COMPANY *See* GE NEWS **2055**

GENERAL ELECTRIC COMPANY. RESEARCH AND DEVELOPMENT CENTER *See* HEAT TRANSFER AND FLUID FLOW DATA BOOK **4431**

GENERAL ELECTRIC COMPANY. RESEARCH LABORATORY *See* BULLETIN - GENERAL ELECTRIC COMPANY. RESEARCH LABORATORY **2037**

GENERAL ELECTRIC COMPANY. TUBE DEPT *See* RECEIVING TUBE MANUAL **2078**

GENERAL FISHERIES COUNCIL FOR THE MEDITERRANEAN *See* STUDIES AND REVIEWS - GENERAL FISHERIES COUNCIL FOR THE MEDITERRANEAN **2314**

GENERAL FISHERIES COUNCIL FOR THE MEDITERRANEAN (FOOD AND AGRICULTURE ORGANIZATION OF THE UNITED NATIONS) *See* REPORT OF THE ... SESSION / GENERAL FISHERIES COUNCIL FOR THE MEDITERRANEAN **2311**

GENERAL FOODS CORPORATION *See* GF NEWS **2342**

GENERAL HETEROCYCLIC CHEMISTRY SERIES (US/0363-8626) [02540072] **976**

GENERAL HISTORY OF AFRICA, THE (FR) [05175841] **2639**

GENERAL HOSPITAL PSYCHIATRY (US/0163-8343) [04508188] **3925**

GENERAL HOUSEHOLD SURVEY LABOUR FORCE CHARACTERISTICS: QUARTERLY REPORT (HK) [18028836] **1675**

GENERAL INDEX TO PUBLISHED REPORTS, MINERAL RESOURCES GROUP (CN/0824-9210) [10609077] **2139**

●GENERAL INFORMATION AND GUIDELINES FOR THE SUMMER INDIVIDUAL EXCHANGE PROGRAM (CN/1193-249X) [26714884] **1748**

GENERAL INFORMATION CONCERNING PATENTS (US/0160-9491) [03362926] **1304**

GENERAL INFORMATION HANDBOOK (ZA) [02243685] **1825**

GENERAL INFORMATION PROGRAMME. UNISIST NEWSLETTER (FR/0379-2218) [05533194] **5107**

GENERAL INFORMATION PROGRAMME, UNISIST NEWSLETTER. SUPPLEMENT ON BIBLIOGRAPHICAL SERVICES THROUGHOUT THE WORLD IN ... (FR/0252-5380) [06677949] **416**

GENERAL INFORMATION: THE VIRGIN ISLANDS OF THE UNITED STATES (US/0083-2952) [01149015] **2533**

GENERAL INSURANCE REGISTER (CN/0380-223X) [02443368] **2881**

GENERAL LAWS OF RHODE ISLAND (US) [01764284] **2973**

GENERAL LEGAL PUBLICATIONS UNION LIST / COMPILED AND EDITED BY THE UNION LIST COMMITTEE; FRANCES G. DURAKO - CHAIRPERSON, SIMA DABIRASHTIANI, ELMO F. DATTALO, ROBERT E. DICKEY, AND BETH E. SMITH (US) [25466493] 3212, **2973**

GENERAL LINGUISTICS (US/0016-6553) [01774945] **3283**

GENERAL MINUTES OF THE ANNUAL CONFERENCES OF THE UNITED METHODIST CHURCH (US/0503-3551) [01796302] **5060**

GENERAL MOTORS COLLISION ESTIMATING GUIDE (US) **5415**

GENERAL MOTORS CORPORATION. PONTIAC MOTOR DIVISION *See* PONTIAC; CHASSIS SHOP MANUAL **5423**

GENERAL MOTORS CORPORATION. PONTIAC MOTOR DIVISION *See* NEW MODEL PRODUCT INFORMATION MANUAL, PONTIAC **5421**

GENERAL MOTORS OF CANADA *See* PONTIAC SHOP MANUAL SUPPLEMENT **5423**

GENERAL MUSIC JOURNAL *CEASED*. (US/8755-5905) [11387689] 1895, **4119**

GENERAL MUSIC TODAY (US/1048-3713) [18845554] 1895, **4119**

GENERAL OPHTHALMOLOGY (US/0891-2084) [07525489] **3875**

GENERAL PERIODICALS INDEX [COMPUTER FILE] (US) 2487, **2496**

GENERAL PERIODICALS ONDISC (RESEARCH 1 ED.) (US/1064-8380) [26429024] 2487, **2496**

GENERAL PHARMACOLOGY (UK/0306-3623) [01342601] **4306**

GENERAL PHYSICS ADVANCE ABSTRACTS (US/0749-4823) [11129514] **4403**

GENERAL PHYSIOLOGY AND BIOPHYSICS (XO/0231-5882) [09921346] 495, **580**

GENERAL PRACTICE SECTION DIRECTORY AND OPERATING MANUAL (US/1061-7108) [18140550] **2973**

GENERAL PRACTITIONER (UK/0046-5607) [09186749] **3737**

●GENERAL PUBLICATIONS CATALOG - INTERNATIONAL IRRIGATION MANAGEMENT INSTITUTE (CE/1018-4899) [I10184899] **172**

GENERAL REGISTER OF MEDICAL PRACTITIONERS. PART 1, FULLY REGISTERED MEDICAL PRACTITIONERS AS AT ... / THE MEDICAL COUNCIL (IE/0790-567X) [11580045] **3914**

GENERAL RELATIVITY AND GRAVITATION (US/0001-7701) [01794406] **4403**

GENERAL REPORT / COMMITTEE ON WORK ON PLANTATIONS (US/0535-1219) [20384057] **1675**

GENERAL REPORT OF THE LEGISLATIVE COUNCIL TO THE LEGISLATURE (US/0362-9686) [02386816] **4650**

GENERAL REPORT ON THE ACTIVITIES OF THE COMMUNITIES (BE/0069-6749) [01406976] **1492**

GENERAL REPORT / THE PARLIAMENT OF THE COMMONWEALTH OF AUSTRALIA, PARLIAMENTARY STANDING COMMITTEE ON PUBLIC WORKS (AT) [21006147] **4761**

GENERAL REVIEW OF THE MINERAL INDUSTRIES. MINES, QUARRIES AND OIL WELLS (CN/0575-8645) [02301704] 1440, **1362**

GENERAL RULES AND REGULATIONS UNDER THE INVESTMENT COMPANY ACT OF 1940 (US) [03228236] **899**

GENERAL RULES AND RULES OF PRACTICE (US) **4259**

GENERAL SCIENCE INDEX (US/0162-1963) [06057436] 5107, **5175**

GENERAL SCIENCE INDEX. CD-ROM (US/0162-1963) **5107**

●GENERAL SCIENCE SOURCE (US/1073-1954) [29354642] 5107, **5175**

GENERAL SEMANTICS BULLETIN (US/0072-0771) [01570577] **3283**

GENERAL SERIES - CENTER FOR REAL ESTATE AND URBAN ECONOMIC STUDIES, SCHOOL OF BUSINESS ADMINISTRATION, UNIVERSITY OF CONNECTICUT (US/0069-9047) [02250817] 2823, **4838**

GENERAL SERIES REPRINT (US) [04753631] 1492, **5200**

GENERAL SERIES - UTAH WATER RESEARCH LABORATORY (US/0888-5168) [07451979] **5533**

GENERAL SOCIETY OF COLONIAL WARS (U.S.) *See* YEARBOOK / GENERAL SOCIETY OF COLONIAL WARS **2766**

GENERAL STAFF JOURNAL, THE (CN/0828-4733) [11873829] **4861**

GENERAL STATUTES OF CONNECTICUT (US) [03704136] **2973**

GENERAL STUDIES REVIEW *CEASED*. (UK/0960-7609) [I09607609] **2487**

GENERAL — Alphabetical Title Index

GENERAL SURGERY AND LAPARASCOPY NEWS (US) **3965**

GENERAL SURGERY & LAPARASCOPY NEWS (US/1065-7088) [26698691] **3965**

GENERAL SURGERY (GLENDALE, CALIF.) (US/1047-6954) [20745445] **3965**

GENERAL SURGERY NEWS See GENERAL SURGERY AND LAPARASCOPY NEWS **3965**

GENERAL SURGERY REPORT (US/1040-7898) [18530446] **3965**

GENERAL SYSTEMS (US/0072-0798) [01429672] 1251, **5200**

GENERAL TECHNICAL REPORT FPL (US/0196-321X) [05781907] **2401**

GENERAL TECHNICAL REPORT FPL-IMP-GTR (US) [25680103] **5107**

GENERAL TECHNICAL REPORT INT (US/0748-1209) [08241479] **2383**

GENERAL TECHNICAL REPORT NC (US) [08852667] **2383**

GENERAL TECHNICAL REPORT NE (US/0748-1314) [08655077] **2383**

GENERAL TECHNICAL REPORT PNW (US/0887-4840) [06785246] **2383**

GENERAL TECHNICAL REPORT PSW (US/0196-2094) [05756879] **2383**

GENERAL TECHNICAL REPORT RM (US/0277-5786) [04926185] **2383**

GENERAL TECHNICAL REPORT SE (1981) (US/0887-4859) [10683395] **2383**

GENERAL TECHNICAL REPORT SO (US/0887-4875) [08278223] **2383**

GENERAL TECHNICAL REPORT WO (US/0197-6109) [03997168] **2383**

GENERAL TEEN SYNDICATED STUDY (US/0741-9120) [10213497] 924, **1492**

GENERAL THEOLOGICAL CENTER OF MAINE See BULLETIN OF THE GENERAL THEOLOGICAL CENTER OF MAINE **4941**

GENERAL UROLOGY (US/0892-1245) [09654315] **3990**

GENERAL WAGE DETERMINATIONS ISSUED UNDER THE DAVIS-BACON AND RELATED ACTS. VOLUME 1, ESA REGIONS 1-4 (US) [15226797] **1675**

GENERALIST PAPERS, THE (US/1048-0870) [20850452] **3390**

GENERALISTE PARIS, LE (FR/0183-4568) [l01834568] **3578**

GENERATION : A JOURNAL OF AUSTRALIAN JEWISH LIFE, THOUGHT AND COMMUNITY (AT) [25006486] **2261**

GENERATION : THE MAGAZINE OF YOUNG BUSINESSMEN (US) [01429790] **677**

GENERATIONAL JOURNAL, THE **SUSPENDED.** (US/0898-5928) [17857412] **5246**

GENERATIONS (BALTIMORE) (US/0191-6939) [04909023] **5047**

GENERATIONS (FREDERICTON) (CN/0821-5359) [10296785] **2450**

GENERATIONS (SAN FRANCISCO, CALIF.) (US/0738-7806) [08433296] **5179**

GENERATIONS (WINNIPEG) (CN/0226-6105) [07097853] **2451**

GENERATOR (US) **2451**

GENERICS MAGAZINE **CEASED.** (US/0742-308X) [10315590] **4306**

GENES & DEVELOPMENT (US/0890-9369) [14470918] **545**

GENES, CHROMOSOMES & CANCER (US/1045-2257) [20043281] 3817, **545**

GENESES (FR/1155-3219) [23994411] 2616, **5200**

GENESIS 2 **CEASED.** (US/0016-6669) [05717227] **5047**

GENESIS (MITCHELLVILLE, MD.) **CEASED.** (US/0893-6617) [15609855] **4960**

GENESIS (NEW ORLEANS, LA.) (US) [07437841] **3165**

GENESIS OF BEHAVIOR (US/0195-5594) [04683569] **4587**

GENESIS REPORT/DX, THE (US/1061-2289) [25218341] **3578**

GENESIS REPORT/RX, THE (US/1061-2270) [25218297] 677, **4306**

GENESIS (WASHINGTON, D.C.) (US/0744-0596) [08002024] **3761**

GENETIC ANALYSIS, TECHNIQUES AND APPLICATIONS (US/1050-3862) [21144189] 3692, **545**

GENETIC AND CELLULAR TECHNOLOGY (US/0732-8079) [08277544] 536, **545**

GENETIC COUNSELING (US) [02253358] **545**

GENETIC COUNSELING (GENEVA, SWITZERLAND) (SZ/1015-8146) [22424924] **545**

GENETIC ENGINEER & BIOTECHNOLOGIST, THE (UK/0959-020X) [21832452] **3692**

GENETIC ENGINEERING (US/0196-3716) [05271667] 3692, **545**

GENETIC ENGINEERING AND BIOTECHNOLOGY MONITOR / UNITED NATIONS INDUSTRIAL DEVELOPMENT ORGANIZATION (AU) [12763747] 3692, **545**

GENETIC ENGINEERING AND BIOTECHNOLOGY RELATED FIRMS WORLDWIDE DIRECTORY (US/0890-0906) [13144948] **3692**

GENETIC ENGINEERING AND BIOTECHNOLOGY YEARBOOK (NE/0921-2604) [10164138] 545, **3692**

GENETIC ENGINEERING LETTER (US/0276-1882) [07332306] **545**

GENETIC ENGINEERING NEWS (US/0270-6377) [06463337] **545**

GENETIC EPIDEMIOLOGY (US/0741-0395) [10075991] 546, **3735**

GENETIC EPIDEMIOLOGY. SUPPLEMENT (US) [15915649] **3735**

GENETIC EPISTEMOLOGIST, THE (GW/0740-9583) [04394115] 4587, **546**

GENETIC MANIPULATION IN PLANTS (CH) **511**

GENETIC MAPS (US/0738-5269) [07294590] **546**

●GENETIC RESOURCES AND CROP EVOLUTION (NE/0925-9864) [25449777] 173, **511**

GENETIC RESOURCES COMMUNICATION (AT/0159-6071) [09547420] **173**

GENETIC, SOCIAL, AND GENERAL PSYCHOLOGY MONOGRAPHS (US/8756-7547) [11659641] **4587**

GENETIC STUDIES OF GENIUS (US) [01429864] 546, **4587**

GENETIC TECHNOLOGY NEWS (US/0272-9032) [06961419] **5107**

GENETICA (NE/0016-6707) [01570586] **546**

GENETICA POLONICA (PL/0016-6715) [01570588] 546, **2416**

GENETICAL RESEARCH (UK/0016-6723) [02113809] **546**

GENETICS ABSTRACTS (US/0016-674X) [01570591] 546, **478**

GENETICS (AUSTIN) (US/0016-6731) [01570590] **546**

GENETICS, SELECTION, EVOLUTION (FR) [19993483] 211, **546**

GENETICS SOCIETY OF CANADA See BULLETIN - GENETICS SOCIETY OF CANADA **543**

GENETIK (GW/0435-284X) [01430065] **546**

GENETIKA (YU/0534-0012) [02254552] **546**

GENETIKA (RU/0016-6758) [03066093] **546**

GENETIKA A SLECHTENI (XR) [25523536] 546, **173**

GENETIKA I SELEKTSIIA V AZERBAIDZHANE (AJ/0320-0035) [04062572] **546**

GENETIKA I SELEKTSIYA (BU/0016-6766) [03104472] 546, **2416**

GENEVA CHRONICLE (BERKELEY, CALIF.) (US/1054-9226) [23021544] **2262**

GENEVA. GRADUATE INSTITUTE OF INTERNATIONAL STUDIES See PUBLICATIONS DE L'INSTITUT UNIVERSITAIRE DE HAUTES ETUDES INTERNATIONALES **1843**

GENEVA. GRADUATE INSTITUTE OF INTERNATIONAL STUDIES See ETUDES ET TRAVAUX **1823**

GENEVA PAPERS ON RISK AND INSURANCE : ISSUES AND PRACTICE (SZ) [23124325] **2881**

GENEVA PAPERS ON RISK AND INSURANCE THEORY (US/0926-4957) [23124337] **2881**

GENEVA. UNIVERSITE. DEPARTEMENT D'HISTOIRE ECONOMIQUE See BULLETIN - UNIVERSITE DE GENEVE, DEPARTEMENT D'HISTOIRE ECONOMIQUE **1550**

GENEVA. UNIVERSITE. LABORATOIRE DE PALEONTOLOGIE See NOTES DU LABORATOIRE DE PALEONTOLOGIE DE L'UNIVERSITE DE GENEVA **4228**

GENEVE-AFRIQUE **CEASED.** (SZ/0016-6774) [01570600] 4474, **5246**

GENEWATCH (US/0740-9737) [10063547] 546, **3692**

GENGO BUNKA KENKYU (JA) [03284571] **3283**

GENGO BUNKA KENKYU (MATSUYAMA-SHI, JAPAN) (JA/0286-2093) [10509698] 3390, **3283**

GENGO BUNKA RONSHU (JA) [06881889] **3283**

GENGO BUNKABU KIYO (JA/0286-3855) [09652813] **3283**

GENGO KENKYU (JA) [01570601] **3283**

GENGO NO KAGAKU (JA) [03579673] **3283**

GENIE BUG (US/0739-6090) [09754713] **2451**

GENIE CHIMIQUE INDUSTRIES CHIMIQUE ET PARACHIMIQUE. F23 (FR) **976**

GENIE CIVIL (FR/0016-6812) [09877234] **1976**

GENIE CIVIL, LE (FR/0016-6812) [01570603] **2023**

GENIE EN FORMATION (CN/1183-7349) [25066715] **1976**

GENIE LOGICIEL & SYSTEMES EXPERTS (FR/1166-4738) [25177482] 1279, **1286**

GENIE RURAL **CEASED.** (FR/0395-8663) [03102087] **89**

GENIE, THE (US/0534-0020) [04153657] **2451**

GENII (US/0016-6855) [04080593] **4862**

GENIO RURALE (IT/0016-6863) [09792874] **89**

GENITOURINARY MEDICINE (UK/0266-4348) [11844378] **4776**

GENIUS OF ARCHITECTURE (UK) [12730962] **299**

GENJI MONOGATARI NO TANKYU (JA) [04552325] **3283**

GENKEN KENKYU SEIKA SHOROK SHU (JA) [04065294] **2155**

GENOA. UNIVERSITA. ISTITUTO DI FILOSOFIA DEL DIRITTO See MATERIALI PER UNA STORIA DELLA CULTURA GIURIDICA **3007**

GENOA. UNIVERSITA. ISTITUTO DI PROGETTAZIONE ARCHITETTONICA See QUADERNO **307**

GENOME (CN/0831-2796) [15354799] **546**

GENOME ANALYSIS (US/1050-8430) [21653952] **546**

●GENOME PRIORITY REPORTS (SZ/1021-6278) [29692747] **546**

●GENOME SCIENCE & TECHNOLOGY (US/1070-2830) [28317228] **546**

GENOMICS (SAN DIEGO, CALIF.) (US/0888-7543) [13716294] **546**

GENOS (FI/0016-6898) [06536471] **2451**

GENOS (WINNIPEG, MAN.) (CN/0712-3221) [08828177] **2794**

●GENOTYPE-BY-ENVIRONMENT, INTERACTION, AND PLANT BREEDING SYMPOSIUM (US/1051-662X) [22105063] **511**

GENRE (US) [24835116] **2794**

GENRE HUMAIN, LE (FR/0293-0277) [08609664] **237**

GENRE (NORMAN, OKLA.) (US/0016-6928) [01570607] **3343**

GENS D'AFFAIRES (CN/0823-6100) [09819010] **1607**

GENS D'AFFAIRES (RIMOUSKI, QUEBEC) See BUSINEST **1600**

GENS NOSTRA (NE/0016-6936) [I00166936] **2451**

GENSHIRYOKU ANZEN IINKAI GEPPO (JA) [06706173] **2155**

GENSHIRYOKU KISEI KANKEI HOREISHU / KAGAKU GIJUTSUCHO GENSHIRYOKU ANZENKYOKU KANSHU (JA) [08874072] 1945, **2155**

GENSHIRYOKU KOGYO (JA/0433-4035) [09444024] **2155**

GENTE (MX) [06039409] **2488**

GENTE (IT) [09096327] **2517**

GENTE (BUENOS AIRES, ARGENTINA) (AG) [10243179] **2551**

GENTE DE AZTLAN, LA (US) [18999673] **2262**

GENTE MOTORI (IT) **2115**

GENTE VIAGGI (IT/0393-7895) [I03937895] **5478**

GENTE Y LA ACTUALIDAD See GENTE (BUENOS AIRES, ARGENTINA) **2551**

GENTEMONEY (IT) [17303123] **899**

GENTES HERBARUM **SUSPENDED.** (US/0072-0879) [01570608] **512**

GENTILE OPERE (IT) **3343**

GENTRY FAMILY GAZETTE AND GENEALOGY See GENTRY FAMILY GAZETTE AND GENEALOGY EXCHANGE **2451**

GENTRY FAMILY GAZETTE AND GENEALOGY EXCHANGE (US/0742-0994) [10282172] **2451**

GENTSE BIJDRAGEN TOT DE KUNSTGESCHIEDENIS EN OUDHEIDKUNDE (BE) [23031591] **351**

GENUINE CORVETTE BLACK BOOK, THE (US) [15042523] **5415**

GENUS (IT/0016-6987) [02024069] **4553**

GEO (FR) **1355**

GEO (GW/0342-8311) [04472812] **4165**

Alphabetical Title Index

GEOGRAPHIC

GEO-ARCHEOLOGIA (IT/0390-2196) [02481826] **269**

GEO (DEE WHY WEST, A.C.T.) (AT/0157-1338) [07618351] **2561**

GEO-ECO-TROP (BE/0379-0452) [04656981] 2561, **2216**

GEO ED. FRANCAISE (FR/0220-8245) [I02208245] **2517**

GEO (ED. FRANCAISE) (FR/0220-8245) [29542205] **2488**

GEO, GEOGRAPHIE, ECOLOGIE, ENVIRONNEMENT, ORGANISATION DE L'ESPACE (BE) [04869917] **2561**

GEO INFO (CN/0843-5030) [20316064] **4650**

GEO INFO SYSTEMS (US/1051-9858) [22162232] **2561**

GEO-KATALOG (GW) [02126657] **5478**

GEO MAGAZINE (UK) **2561**

GEO-MARINE LETTERS (US/0276-0460) [07318326] 1405, **554**

● GEO PLEIN-AIR (CN/1194-5303) [28558060] **4896**

GEO STORM SERVICE MANUAL (US) [20790694] **5415**

GEO2 (US/0735-0511) [03163347] **1376**

GEOACTIVE (UK/0956-0629) **2561**

GEOARCHAEOLOGY (US/0883-6353) [12181174] **269**

GEOARCHIVE HANDBOOK (UK) **1376**

● GEOARCHIVE ON CD-ROM (US/1070-6046) [28427826] **1376**

GEOBASE (UK) 1355, **2561**

GEOBIOS (JODHPUR) (II/0251-1223) [01188606] **456**

GEOBIOS (LYON, FRANCE) (FR/0293-843X) [04067637] **4227**

GEOBIOS (LYON, FRANCE) (FR/0016-6995) [02336429] 1376, **4227**

GEOBIOS NEW REPORTS (II) [09168344] **456**

GEOBOTANICA SELECTA (GW) [09792974] **512**

GEOBOTANISCHE KOLLOQUIEN (GW/0940-6581) **2216**

GEOBOTANISCHE KOLLOQUIEN (GW/0940-6581) [28627651] **2216**

GEOBULLETIN / THE GEOLOGICAL SOCIETY OF SOUTH AFRICA, DIE GEOLOGIESE VERENIGING VAN SUID-AFRIKA (SA) [11195207] **1376**

GEOBYTE *CEASED.* (US/0885-6362) [12690404] **2139**

GEOCARTO INTERNATIONAL (HK/1010-6049) [13633929] 1976, **2561**

GEOCHEMICAL JOURNAL (JA/0016-7002) [01570623] **1376**

● GEOCHEMISTRY AND COSMOCHEMISTRY (US/1056-7518) [23835314] **976**

GEOCHEMISTRY AND THE ENVIRONMENT (US) [04743627] 4776, **2172**

GEOCHEMISTRY INTERNATIONAL (US/0016-7029) [01570625] **1376**

GEOCHILE (CL/0431-1930) [02607622] **2561**

GEOCHIMICA *CEASED.* (US/0096-3089) [01798770] 976, **1376**

GEOCHIMICA BRASILIENSIS (BL/0102-9800) [I01029800] 976, **1376**

GEOCHIMICA ET COSMOCHIMICA ACTA (US/0016-7037) [01570626] **1376**

GEOCHRONIQUE (FR/0292-8477) [08324396] **1376**

● GEOCRYOLOGY (MOSCOW, R.S.F.S.R.) (RU/1061-7574) [25442280] **1355**

GEODATE (AT) 2172, **2561**

GEODERMA (NE/0016-7061) [01158192] **173**

GEODESIA (NE) [06409452] **2561**

GEODETICAL INFO MAGAZINE (NE/0924-2023) [22689975] **1405**

GEODETICKY A KARTOGRAFICKY OBZOR (XR/0016-7096) [05060260] **2561**

GEODEX INTERNATIONAL *See* GEODEX SYSTEM/S **3212**

GEODEX STRUCTURAL INFORMATION SERVICE *See* GEODEX SYSTEM/S **3212**

GEODEX SYSTEM-A (US/0161-1569) [03774387] **299**

GEODEX SYSTEM/S (US/0161-1550) [03918916] **3212**

GEODEZIA ES KARTOGRAFIA (HU/0016-7118) [03267232] **2581**

GEODEZIIA I KARTOGRAFIJA (RU/0016-7126) [02414731] **2581**

GEODEZJA I KARTOGRAFIA (PL/0016-7134) [03901367] **2581**

GEODINAMICA ACTA (FR/0985-3111) [16265923] **2561**

GEODRILLING (UK/0268-0165) [07243789] **1405**

● GEODRILLING INTERNATIONAL (UK/0969-3769) [28190238] **1405**

GEODYNAMICS PROJECT : U.S. PROGRESS REPORT (US/0363-0455) [02407280] **1376**

GEODYNAMICS SERIES (US/0277-6669) [07243674] **1376**

GEODYNAMIQUE (FR/0766-5105) [13820294] 1405, **1377**

GEOECOLOGICAL RESEARCH (GW/0170-3250) [I01703250] **2216**

● GEOEKOLOGIIA, INZHENERNAIA GEOLOGIIA, GIDROGEOLOGIIA, GEOKRIOLOGIIA / ROSSIISKAIA AKADEMIIA NAUK (RU/0869-7809) [29240230] 1976, **1377**

GEOEXPLORATION *See* JOURNAL OF APPLIED GEOPHYSICS **1407**

GEOEXPLORATION MONOGRAPHS (GW) [01570631] **1405**

GEOFILE (UK/0267-7563) [I02677563] **2517**

GEOFISICA INTERNACIONAL : REVISTA DE LA UNION GEOFISICA MEXICANA AUSPICIADA POR EL INSTITUTO DE GEOFISICA DE LA UNIVERSIDAD NACIONAL AUTONOMA DE MEXICO (MX/0016-7169) [01453687] 1377, **4404**

GEOFIZICHESKII SBORNIK (RU) [02414058] **1405**

GEOFIZICHESKII ZHURNAL (UN/0203-3100) [05859242] **1405**

GEOFIZIKA ZAGREB (CI/0352-3659) [I03523659] **1405**

GEOFORUM (UK/0016-7185) [01570632] **1355**

● GEOGRAFFITY (BLACKSBURG, VA.) (US/1063-9837) [26185070] **2517**

GEOGRAFIA (BL) [04294366] **2561**

GEOGRAFIA (IT) **2562**

GEOGRAFIA FISICA E DINAMICA QUATERNARIA (IT/0391-9838) [06433899] **1377**

GEOGRAFIA NELLE SCUOLE, LA (IT) [23020185] **2562**

GEOGRAFIA W SZKOLE (PL/0137-7566) [I01377566] **2562**

GEOGRAFICHESKOE OBSHCHESTVO SSSR *See* IZVESTIIA VSESOIUZNOGO GEOGRAFICHESKOGO OBSHCHESTVA **2566**

GEOGRAFICHESKOE OBSHCHESTVO SSSR. ZABAIKALSKII FILIAL. OTDELENIE GEOLOGII *See* TRUDY **1400**

GEOGRAFICKY CASOPIS. GEOGRAFICHESKII ZHURNAL. GEOGRAPHICAL REVIEW. GEOGRAPHISCHE ZEITSCHRIFT. REVUE DE GEOGRAPHIE (XO/0016-7193) [01570637] **2562**

GEOGRAFICKY USTAV V BRNE *See* ZPRAVY GEOGRAFICKENO USTAVU CSAV **2580**

● GEOGRAFIE (NE/0926-3837) [26732094] **2562**

GEOGRAFIIA V SHKOLE / UPRAVLENIE NACHALNOI I SREDNEI SHKOLY NARKOMPROSA RSFSR (RU/0016-7207) [01570638] **2562**

GEOGRAFISCH TIJDSCHRIFT *See* GEOGRAFIE **2562**

GEOGRAFISK TIDSKRIFT DET KNOGELIGE DANSKI GEOGRAFISKE SELSKAB (DK) **2562**

GEOGRAFISK TIDSSKRIFT (DK/0016-7223) [01570640] **2562**

GEOGRAFISKA ANNALER. SERIES A, PHYSICAL GEOGRAPHY (SW/0435-3676) [01570642] **2562**

GEOGRAFISKA ANNALER. SERIES B, HUMAN GEOGRAPHY (NO/0435-3684) [01570643] 4553, **2823**

GEOGRAFSKI ZBORNIK. ACTA GEOGRAPHICA (XV/0373-4498) [01570645] **2562**

GEOGRAPHER, THE (II/0072-0909) [01570647] **2562**

GEOGRAPHERS : BIOBIBLIOGRAPHICAL STUDIES (US) [03509074] 432, **2562**

GEOGRAPHIA (PL) [07384327] **2562**

● GEOGRAPHIA ANTIQUA (IT/1121-8940) [28520740] **2562**

GEOGRAPHIA MEDICA (BUDAPEST) (HU/0300-807X) [02365404] **3735**

GEOGRAPHIA MEDICA. SUPPLEMENT / GEOGRAPHIA MEDICA. SONDERBAND (HU/0866-4323) [18474030] **3735**

GEOGRAPHIA POLONICA (PL/0016-7282) [01570648] **2562**

● GEOGRAPHIC AND GLOBAL ISSUES QUARTERLY / UNITED STATES DEPARTMENT OF STATE, BUREAU OF INTELLIGENCE AND RESEARCH (US/0083-016X) [28564483] **2562**

GEOGRAPHIC BULLETIN *CEASED.* (US/0083-0100) [06121629] **2562**

GEOGRAPHIC COST OF LIVING DIFFERENTIALS : LARGE CITIES (US/0271-3381) [09138023] **1492**

GEOGRAPHIC DISTRIBUTION OF FEDERAL FUNDS IN ALABAMA (US/0192-3218) [03922291] **1562**

GEOGRAPHIC DISTRIBUTION OF FEDERAL FUNDS IN ALASKA (US/0162-0576) [03922503] **1562**

GEOGRAPHIC DISTRIBUTION OF FEDERAL FUNDS IN ARIZONA (US/0161-9799) [03922413] **1562**

GEOGRAPHIC DISTRIBUTION OF FEDERAL FUNDS IN ARKANSAS (US/0162-0398) [03920303] **1562**

GEOGRAPHIC DISTRIBUTION OF FEDERAL FUNDS IN CALIFORNIA (US/0162-0479) [03910242] **1562**

GEOGRAPHIC DISTRIBUTION OF FEDERAL FUNDS IN COLORADO (US/0161-8997) [03909775] **1562**

GEOGRAPHIC DISTRIBUTION OF FEDERAL FUNDS IN CONNECTICUT (US/0190-1230) [03909811] **1562**

GEOGRAPHIC DISTRIBUTION OF FEDERAL FUNDS IN DELAWARE (US/0162-0711) [03910359] **1562**

GEOGRAPHIC DISTRIBUTION OF FEDERAL FUNDS IN DISTRICT OF COLUMBIA (US/0192-3722) [03910536] **1562**

GEOGRAPHIC DISTRIBUTION OF FEDERAL FUNDS IN FLORIDA (US/0162-0495) [03910638] **1562**

GEOGRAPHIC DISTRIBUTION OF FEDERAL FUNDS IN GEORGIA (US/0162-0754) [03919921] **1562**

GEOGRAPHIC DISTRIBUTION OF FEDERAL FUNDS IN HAWAII (US/0161-9012) [03919153] **1562**

GEOGRAPHIC DISTRIBUTION OF FEDERAL FUNDS IN IDAHO (US/0192-3803) [03919989] **1562**

GEOGRAPHIC DISTRIBUTION OF FEDERAL FUNDS IN ILLINOIS (US/0161-9969) [03920092] **1562**

GEOGRAPHIC DISTRIBUTION OF FEDERAL FUNDS IN INDIANA (US/0161-8989) [03815467] **1562**

GEOGRAPHIC DISTRIBUTION OF FEDERAL FUNDS IN IOWA (US/0161-8199) [03919094] **1562**

GEOGRAPHIC DISTRIBUTION OF FEDERAL FUNDS IN KANSAS (US/0162-0487) [03916113] **1562**

GEOGRAPHIC DISTRIBUTION OF FEDERAL FUNDS IN KENTUCKY (US/0192-5024) [03909504] **1563**

GEOGRAPHIC DISTRIBUTION OF FEDERAL FUNDS IN LOUISIANA (US/0161-8547) [03916155] **1563**

GEOGRAPHIC DISTRIBUTION OF FEDERAL FUNDS IN MAINE (US/0162-0355) [03916188] **1563**

GEOGRAPHIC DISTRIBUTION OF FEDERAL FUNDS IN MARYLAND (US/0162-1688) [03916224] **1563**

GEOGRAPHIC DISTRIBUTION OF FEDERAL FUNDS IN MASSACHUSETTS (US/0162-0622) [03916268] **1563**

GEOGRAPHIC DISTRIBUTION OF FEDERAL FUNDS IN MICHIGAN (US/0162-0347) [03920211] **1563**

GEOGRAPHIC DISTRIBUTION OF FEDERAL FUNDS IN MINNESOTA (US/0161-8539) [03920150] **1563**

GEOGRAPHIC DISTRIBUTION OF FEDERAL FUNDS IN MISSISSIPPI (US/0162-1874) [03917063] **1563**

GEOGRAPHIC DISTRIBUTION OF FEDERAL FUNDS IN MISSOURI (US/0161-9985) [03917017] **1563**

GEOGRAPHIC DISTRIBUTION OF FEDERAL FUNDS IN MONTANA (US/0162-0460) [03919732] **1563**

GEOGRAPHIC DISTRIBUTION OF FEDERAL FUNDS IN NEBRASKA (US/0161-9128) [03916345] **1563**

GEOGRAPHIC DISTRIBUTION OF FEDERAL FUNDS IN NEVADA (US/0162-0991) [03916390] **1563**

GEOGRAPHIC DISTRIBUTION OF FEDERAL FUNDS IN NEW HAMPSHIRE (US/0161-8911) [03916420] **1563**

GEOGRAPHIC DISTRIBUTION OF FEDERAL FUNDS IN NEW JERSEY (US/0162-1769) [03916457] **1563**

GEOGRAPHIC DISTRIBUTION OF FEDERAL FUNDS IN NEW MEXICO (US/0162-0509) [03916880] **1563**

GEOGRAPHIC DISTRIBUTION OF FEDERAL FUNDS IN NEW YORK (US/0162-9492) [03916905] **1563**

GEOGRAPHIC DISTRIBUTION OF FEDERAL FUNDS IN NORTH CAROLINA (US/0161-9802) [03916929] **1563**

GEOGRAPHIC DISTRIBUTION OF FEDERAL FUNDS IN NORTH DAKOTA (US/0162-0452) [03916967] **1563**

GEOGRAPHIC DISTRIBUTION OF FEDERAL FUNDS IN OHIO (US/0161-8962) [03918217] **1563**

GEOGRAPHIC — Alphabetical Title Index

GEOGRAPHIC DISTRIBUTION OF FEDERAL FUNDS IN OKLAHOMA (US/0162-1882) [03918267] **1563**

GEOGRAPHIC DISTRIBUTION OF FEDERAL FUNDS IN OREGON (US/0161-8512) [03918389] **1563**

GEOGRAPHIC DISTRIBUTION OF FEDERAL FUNDS IN PENNSYLVANIA (US/0161-8873) [03918445] **1563**

GEOGRAPHIC DISTRIBUTION OF FEDERAL FUNDS IN RHODE ISLAND (US/0161-8849) [03918833] **1563**

GEOGRAPHIC DISTRIBUTION OF FEDERAL FUNDS IN SOUTH CAROLINA (US/0161-8970) [03919351] **1563**

GEOGRAPHIC DISTRIBUTION OF FEDERAL FUNDS IN SOUTH DAKOTA (US/0161-9101) [03919302] **1563**

GEOGRAPHIC DISTRIBUTION OF FEDERAL FUNDS IN TENNESSEE (US/0162-1548) [03919205] **1564**

GEOGRAPHIC DISTRIBUTION OF FEDERAL FUNDS IN TERRITORIES & OTHER AREAS ADMINISTERED BY THE U.S (US/0162-3419) [03922688] **1564**

GEOGRAPHIC DISTRIBUTION OF FEDERAL FUNDS IN TEXAS (US/0161-8881) [03918505] **1564**

GEOGRAPHIC DISTRIBUTION OF FEDERAL FUNDS IN UTAH (US/0161-9195) [03918590] **1564**

GEOGRAPHIC DISTRIBUTION OF FEDERAL FUNDS IN VERMONT (US/0163-335X) [03765027] **1564**

GEOGRAPHIC DISTRIBUTION OF FEDERAL FUNDS IN VIRGINIA (US/0161-892X) [03918644] **1564**

GEOGRAPHIC DISTRIBUTION OF FEDERAL FUNDS IN WASHINGTON (US/0161-8520) [03919781] **1564**

GEOGRAPHIC DISTRIBUTION OF FEDERAL FUNDS IN WEST VIRGINIA (US/0161-8636) [03919431] **1564**

GEOGRAPHIC DISTRIBUTION OF FEDERAL FUNDS IN WISCONSIN (US/0161-9187) [03918926] **1564**

GEOGRAPHIC DISTRIBUTION OF FEDERAL FUNDS IN WYOMING (US/0161-889X) [03918963] **1564**

GEOGRAPHIC DISTRIBUTION OF VA EXPENDITURES (US/0741-0611) [10052995] **4044**

GEOGRAPHIC INFORMATION : THE YEARBOOK OF THE ASSOCIATION FOR GEOGRAPHIC INFORMATION (UK) [24187179] **2562**

GEOGRAPHIC NOTES *See* GEOGRAPHIC AND GLOBAL ISSUES QUARTERLY / UNITED STATES DEPARTMENT OF STATE, BUREAU OF INTELLIGENCE AND RESEARCH **2562**

GEOGRAPHIC NOTES / DEPARTMENT OF STATE, BUREAU OF INTELLIGENCE AND RESEARCH, THE GEOGRAPHER (US/0083-016X) [13551738] **2562**

GEOGRAPHIC PROFILE OF EMPLOYMENT AND UNEMPLOYMENT (US/0145-7330) [02806807] **1675**

GEOGRAPHIC REFERENCE (NEWPORT BEACH, CALIF.) *See* GEOGRAPHIC REFERENCE REPORT **1492**

●GEOGRAPHIC REFERENCE REPORT (US/1061-7469) [24948232] **1492**

GEOGRAPHIC SALARY DIFFERENTIALS (US/0161-3146) [03888125] **1675**

GEOGRAPHIC THESAURUS (US/0894-9190) [16318775] **2562**

GEOGRAPHICA (FI) [04756147] **2562**

GEOGRAPHICA HELVETICA (SZ/0016-7312) [01570649] **2562**

GEOGRAPHICA IUGOSLAVICA : BILTEN SAVEZA GEOGRAFSKIH DRUSTAVA JUGOSLAVIJE (YU/0351-3238) [12278554] **2562**

GEOGRAPHICA (KUALA LUMPUR) (MY/0126-6101) [02124109] **2562**

GEOGRAPHICAL ABSTRACTS. HUMAN GEOGRAPHY (UK/0953-9611) [19272596] 2562, **2580**

GEOGRAPHICAL ABSTRACTS : PHYSICAL GEOGRAPHY (UK/0954-0504) [19092921] 1355, 2562, **2580**

GEOGRAPHICAL ANALYSIS (US/0016-7363) [00842896] **2562**

GEOGRAPHICAL ASSOCIATION OF TANZANIA *See* JOURNAL OF THE GEOGRAPHICAL ASSOCIATION OF TANZANIA **2567**

GEOGRAPHICAL BULLETIN (YPSILANTI, MICH.), THE (US/0731-3292) [01570657] **2563**

GEOGRAPHICAL DIGEST (LONDON, ENGLAND: 1986) *See* PHILIP'S GEOGRAPHICAL DIGEST **2572**

GEOGRAPHICAL DISTRIBUTION OF FINANCIAL FLOWS TO DEVELOPING COUNTRIES (FR) [07414431] **2909**

GEOGRAPHICAL DISTRIBUTION OF FINANCIAL FLOWS TO LESS DEVELOPED COUNTRIES (COMMITMENTS) (US) [02243058] **2909**

GEOGRAPHICAL EDUCATION (AT/0085-0969) [05544457] 1895, **2563**

GEOGRAPHICAL INDEX SUPPLEMENT (US/0739-9499) [09839666] **2563**

GEOGRAPHICAL JOURNAL, THE (UK/0016-7398) [01570660] **2563**

GEOGRAPHICAL LOCATION CODES (WASHINGTON. 1976) (US/0148-7000) [03197801] **2563**

GEOGRAPHICAL MOBILITY (US) [08638162] **4553**

GEOGRAPHICAL MONOGRAPHS (CN/0829-7622) [02023119] **2563**

GEOGRAPHICAL OBSERVER, THE (II/0072-0925) [01570663] **2563**

GEOGRAPHICAL PAPERS (CI) [05537962] **2563**

GEOGRAPHICAL PAPERS. DEPARTMENT OF GEOGRAPHY, UNIVERSITY OF READING (UK/0305-5914) [02215187] **2563**

GEOGRAPHICAL PERSPECTIVE (II) [20612575] **2563**

GEOGRAPHICAL PERSPECTIVES *CEASED*. (US/0199-994X) [01188791] **2563**

GEOGRAPHICAL REPORTS OF TOKYO METROPOLITAN UNIVERSITY (JA/0386-8710) [01453860] **1377**

GEOGRAPHICAL RESEARCH STUDIES SERIES (UK/0277-2388) [07532287] **2563**

GEOGRAPHICAL REVIEW (US/0016-7428) [01570664] **2563**

GEOGRAPHICAL REVIEW OF INDIA (II) [01570665] **2563**

GEOGRAPHICAL REVIEW OF JAPAN. SERIES B (JA/0289-6001) [11857245] **2563**

●GEOGRAPHICAL SYSTEMS (US/1069-2665) [27965915] **2563**

GEOGRAPHICAL : THE MONTHLY MAGAZINE OF THE ROYAL GEOGRAPHICAL SOCIETY (UK) [19761293] **2563**

GEOGRAPHIE AKTUELL (GW/0178-7810) [I01787810] **2563**

GEOGRAPHIE HEUTE (GW/0721-8400) [12252574] **2563**

GEOGRAPHIE IM UNTERRICHT *See* GEOGRAPHIE HEUTE **2563**

GEOGRAPHIE PHYSIQUE ET QUATERNAIRE (CN/0705-7199) [03580173] 1355, **2563**

GEOGRAPHIE UND IHRE DIDAKTIK (GW/0343-7256) [I03437256] **2564**

GEOGRAPHIE UND SCHULE (GW/0171-8649) [I01718649] **2564**

GEOGRAPHIES FOR ADVANCED STUDIES (US/0275-2514) [07155407] **2564**

GEOGRAPHIKA CHRONIKA (GR) [01795970] **2564**

GEOGRAPHISCHE GESELLSCHAFT IN MUNCHEN *See* MITTEILUNGEN DER GEOGRAPHISCHEN GESELLSCHAFT IN MUNCHEN **2569**

GEOGRAPHISCHE RUNDSCHAU (GW/0016-7460) [01570674] **2564**

GEOGRAPHISCHE ZEITSCHRIFT (GW/0016-7479) [01570675] **2564**

GEOGRAPHISCHER JAHRESBERICHT AUS OSTERREICH (AU/0376-1738) [02227946] **2564**

GEOGRAPHISCHES JAHRBUCH *CEASED*. (GW) [01780902] **2564**

GEOGRAPHISCHES JAHRBUCH BURGENLAND (AU) [03595307] **2564**

GEOGRAPHISCHES TASCHEMBUCH UND JAHRWEISER FUER LANDESKUNGE *See* GEOGRAPHISCHES TASCHENBUCH **2564**

GEOGRAPHISCHES TASCHENBUCH (GW/0072-0968) [26187732] **2564**

GEOGRAPHY (UK/0016-7487) [02447169] **2564**

GEOGRAPHY BULLETIN (AT) 1895, **2564**

GEOGRAPHY (GUILFORD, CONN.) (US) [13047055] **2564**

GEOGRAPHY RESEARCH FORUM (US/0333-5275) [11672617] **2564**

GEOGRAPHY REVIEW (UK) [17959384] **2564**

GEOGRAPHY TEACHER (II) [01774338] **2564**

GEOHIMIA I RUDOOBRAZOVANIE (UN/0130-1128) [09793103] 1440, **1355**

GEOHIMIJA (RU/0016-7525) [02397661] **1377**

GEOJOURNAL (GE/0343-2521) [03693750] 1355, **2564**

GEOKHIMIYA, MINERALOGIYA I PETROLOGIYA (BU/0324-1718) [02145129] 1458, **1440**

GEOKOMPENDIER (DK/0105-8258) [10819521] **2564**

GEOLINGUISTICS (US/0190-4671) [02381164] **3283**

GEOLIT (GW) [05958038] **2564**

GEOLOG (GEOLOGICAL ASSOCIATION OF CANADA) (CN/0227-3713) [06858419] **1377**

GEOLOGEN-KALENDER *CEASED*. (GR) [09564059] **1377**

GEOLOGI INDONESIA (IO/0126-1061) [02515245] **1377**

GEOLOGIA (PL/0138-0974) [02703423] **1377**

GEOLOGIA APPLICATA E IDROGEOLOGIA (IT/0435-3870) [03873750] **1377**

GEOLOGIA E METALURGIA (BL/0100-4921) [06213897] **4002**

GEOLOGIA SUDETICA (PL/0072-100X) [02251538] **1377**

GEOLOGIAI ES GEOFIZIKAI SZAKIROLDALMI TAJEKOZTATO (HU/0230-7065) [I02307065] 1405, **1377**

GEOLOGIC INDEX OF THE PUBLICATIONS OF THE UNITED STATES GEOLOGICAL SURVEY, AND HAYDEN, KING, POWELL, AND WHEELER SURVEYS (US) [01479042] **1377**

GEOLOGIC INVESTIGATIONS OF RADIOACTIVE DEPOSITS, SEMIANNUAL PROGRESS REPORT (US) [01343419] **1377**

GEOLOGIC MAP - MONTANA BUREAU OF MINES AND GEOLOGY (US/0735-0600) [06749747] **1377**

GEOLOGIC MAP SERIES (US) [01566079] **1377**

GEOLOGICA BALCANICA (BU/0324-0894) [02828180] **1377**

GEOLOGICA BAVARICA (GW/0016-755X) [01435766] **1377**

GEOLOGICA ET PALAEONTOLOGICA (GW/0072-1018) [04101275] 4227, **1377**

GEOLOGICA HUNGARICA. SERIES GEOLOGICA (HU/0367-4150) [09182489] **1377**

GEOLOGICA HUNGARICA. SERIES PALAEONTOLOGICA (HU/0374-1893) [01443582] **4227**

GEOLOGICA ROMANA (IT/0435-3927) [01570679] **1377**

GEOLOGICAL ABSTRACTS (UK/0954-0512) [19642244] 1377, **1362**

GEOLOGICAL ASSOCIATION OF CANADA SPECIAL PAPER, THE (CN) [08327165] **1377**

GEOLOGICAL CIRCULAR (US/0082-3309) [04625184] **1377**

GEOLOGICAL CONTRIBUTIONS / ABILENE GEOLOGICAL SOCIETY (US) [08408581] **1377**

GEOLOGICAL CURATOR / GCG, THE (UK/0144-5294) [07528382] 1377, **4088**

GEOLOGICAL EXCURSION HANDBOOK (AT/0158-720X) [I0158720X] **1377**

GEOLOGICAL JOURNAL (CHICHESTER, ENGLAND) (UK/0072-1050) [00843976] **1378**

GEOLOGICAL MAGAZINE (UK/0016-7568) [02139602] **1378**

GEOLOGICAL MILESTONES (US/0196-3090) [02471128] **1378**

GEOLOGICAL, MINING AND METALLURGICAL SOCIETY OF INDIA *See* BULLETIN OF THE GEOLOGICAL, MINING AND METALLURGICAL SOCIETY OF INDIA **1370**

GEOLOGICAL NEWSLETTER (PORTLAND) (US/0270-5451) [06464069] **1378**

GEOLOGICAL NOTE (COLUMBUS, OHIO) (US/0163-9757) [02490686] **1378**

GEOLOGICAL REPORT (TORONTO) (CN/0472-9889) [01265165] **1378**

GEOLOGICAL SOCIETY OF AMERICA *See* MEMBERSHIP DIRECTORY / GEOLOGICAL SOCIETY OF AMERICA **1387**

GEOLOGICAL SOCIETY OF AMERICA *See* GEOLOGICAL SOCIETY OF AMERICA BULLETIN **1378**

GEOLOGICAL SOCIETY OF AMERICA *See* MEMORIALS - GEOLOGICAL SOCIETY OF AMERICA **1387**

GEOLOGICAL SOCIETY OF AMERICA *See* ABSTRACTS WITH PROGRAMS - GEOLOGICAL SOCIETY OF AMERICA **1364**

GEOLOGICAL SOCIETY OF AMERICA BULLETIN (US/0016-7606) [09407678] **1378**

GEOLOGICAL SOCIETY OF AMERICA BULLETIN (US/0016-7606) [01570691] **1378**

GEOLOGICAL SOCIETY OF AMERICA DATA REPOSITORY. MICROFORM *CEASED*. (US/1049-5886) [13535209] **1378**

GEOLOGICAL SOCIETY OF ASSAM *See* JOURNAL **1384**

GEOLOGICAL SOCIETY OF AUSTRALIA *See* SPECIAL PUBLICATION - GEOLOGICAL SOCIETY OF AUSTRALIA **1397**

GEOLOGICAL SOCIETY OF INDIA *See* JOURNAL OF THE GEOLOGICAL SOCIETY OF INDIA **1385**

GEOLOGICAL SOCIETY OF IRAQ *See* JOURNAL OF THE GEOLOGICAL SOCIETY OF IRAQ **1385**

GEOLOGICAL SOCIETY OF JAMAICA *See* JOURNAL - GEOLOGICAL SOCIETY OF JAMAICA **1384**

GEOLOGICAL SOCIETY OF JAPAN *See* JOURNAL - GEOLOGICAL SOCIETY OF JAPAN **1384**

GEOLOGICAL SOCIETY OF LONDON *See* JOURNAL OF THE GEOLOGICAL SOCIETY **1385**

GEOLOGICAL SOCIETY OF LONDON. SPECIAL PUBLICATION OF THE GEOLOGICAL SOCIETY OF LONDON *See* GEOLOGICAL SOCIETY SPECIAL PUBLICATION **1378**

GEOLOGICAL SOCIETY OF SOUTH AFRICA *See* SPECIAL PUBLICATION - GEOLOGICAL SOCIETY OF SOUTH AFRICA **1398**

GEOLOGICAL SOCIETY OF SOUTH AFRICA *See* GEOBULLETIN / THE GEOLOGICAL SOCIETY OF SOUTH AFRICA, DIE GEOLOGIESE VERENIGING VAN SUID-AFRIKA **1376**

GEOLOGICAL SOCIETY SPECIAL PUBLICATION (UK/0305-8719) [13256989] **1378**

GEOLOGICAL SURVEY BULLETIN (BLOOMINGTON, IND.) (US/0160-3051) [01667345] **1378**

GEOLOGICAL SURVEY BULLETIN (HOBART) (AT/0082-2043) [01345652] **1378**

GEOLOGICAL SURVEY CIRCULAR (BLOOMINGTON) (US/0445-8370) [01585859] **1378**

GEOLOGICAL SURVEY GUIDEBOOK (US/0160-0826) [02668756] **1378**

GEOLOGICAL SURVEY MINERAL ECONOMICS SERIES (US/0537-2925) [01752999] **1378**

GEOLOGICAL SURVEY OCCASIONAL PAPER (US/0149-2470) [03466208] **1378**

GEOLOGICAL SURVEY OF ALABAMA *See* MONOGRAPH - GEOLOGICAL SURVEY OF ALABAMA **1388**

GEOLOGICAL SURVEY OF ALABAMA *See* ATLAS SERIES - GEOLOGICAL SURVEY OF ALABAMA **1366**

GEOLOGICAL SURVEY OF ALABAMA *See* CIRCULAR / GEOLOGICAL SURVEY OF ALABAMA **1372**

GEOLOGICAL SURVEY OF ALABAMA *See* REPRINT SERIES - GEOLOGICAL SURVEY OF ALABAMA **1395**

GEOLOGICAL SURVEY OF ALABAMA. DIVISION OF ENERGY RESOURCES RESEARCH *See* SPECIAL MAP / GEOLOGICAL SURVEY OF ALABAMA, ENERGY RESOURCES DIVISION **1397**

GEOLOGICAL SURVEY OF ALABAMA INFORMATION SERIES (US/0568-7888) [01147802] **1378**

GEOLOGICAL SURVEY OF CANADA *See* MEMOIR - GEOLOGICAL SURVEY OF CANADA **1387**

GEOLOGICAL SURVEY OF CANADA *See* GEOLOGICAL SURVEY PAPER **1378**

GEOLOGICAL SURVEY OF CANADA *See* CURRENT RESEARCH - GEOLOGICAL SURVEY OF CANADA **1372**

GEOLOGICAL SURVEY OF INDIA *See* BULLETINS OF THE GEOLOGICAL SURVEY OF INDIA **1412**

GEOLOGICAL SURVEY OF INDIA *See* GEOLOGICAL SURVEY OF INDIA MISCELLANEOUS PUBLICATION **1378**

GEOLOGICAL SURVEY OF INDIA *See* BULLETINS OF THE GEOLOGICAL SURVEY OF INDIA. SERIES A : ECONOMIC GEOLOGY **1371**

GEOLOGICAL SURVEY OF INDIA MISCELLANEOUS PUBLICATION (II/0579-4706) [05084023] **1378**

GEOLOGICAL SURVEY OF IRELAND *See* BULLETIN - GEOLOGICAL SURVEY OF IRELAND **1369**

GEOLOGICAL SURVEY OF NEW SOUTH WALES *See* RECORDS OF THE GEOLOGICAL SURVEY OF NEW SOUTH WALES **1393**

GEOLOGICAL SURVEY OF NEW SOUTH WALES *See* 1:250,000 GEOLOGICAL SERIES. EXPLANATORY NOTES **1364**

GEOLOGICAL SURVEY OF NEW SOUTH WALES *See* BULLETIN - GEOLOGICAL SURVEY OF NEW SOUTH WALES **1369**

GEOLOGICAL SURVEY OF NEW SOUTH WALES *See* QUARTERLY NOTES / GEOLOGICAL SURVEY OF NEW SOUTH WALES **1392**

GEOLOGICAL SURVEY OF NEW SOUTH WALES *See* BULLETIN - GEOLOGICAL SURVEY OF NEW SOUTH WALES **1369**

GEOLOGICAL SURVEY OF NEW SOUTH WALES, MINERAL INDUSTRY OF NEW SOUTH WALES (AT/0369-6715) [02353953] **2139**

GEOLOGICAL SURVEY OF PAKISTAN *See* RECORDS OF THE GEOLOGICAL SURVEY OF PAKISTAN **1393**

GEOLOGICAL SURVEY OF SOUTH AFRICA *See* SEISMOLOGIC SERIES **1410**

GEOLOGICAL SURVEY OF SOUTH AUSTRALIA *See* QUARTERLY GEOLOGICAL NOTES - GEOLOGICAL SURVEY OF SOUTH AUSTRALIA **1392**

GEOLOGICAL SURVEY OF SOUTH AUSTRALIA *See* BULLETIN / GEOLOGICAL SURVEY OF SOUTH AUSTRALIA **1352**

GEOLOGICAL SURVEY OF SOUTH AUSTRALIA *See* REPORT OF INVESTIGATIONS - GEOLOGICAL SURVEY OF SOUTH AUSTRALIA **1394**

GEOLOGICAL SURVEY OF VICTORIA *See* MEMOIR - GEOLOGICAL SURVEY OF VICTORIA **1387**

GEOLOGICAL SURVEY OF WESTERN AUSTRALIA *See* BULLETIN - GEOLOGICAL SURVEY OF WESTERN AUSTRALIA **1369**

GEOLOGICAL SURVEY OF WESTERN AUSTRALIA *See* MINERAL RESOURCES BULLETIN - GEOLOGICAL SURVEY OF WESTERN AUSTRALIA **1388**

GEOLOGICAL SURVEY OF WYOMING *See* MEMOIR - GEOLOGICAL SURVEY OF WYOMING **1387**

GEOLOGICAL SURVEY OF WYOMING *See* PUBLIC INFORMATION CIRCULAR - GEOLOGICAL SURVEY OF WYOMING **1392**

GEOLOGICAL SURVEY OF WYOMING, EDUCATIONAL SERIES (US) **1355**

GEOLOGICAL SURVEY PAPER (AT/0313-1688) [08803383] **1378**

GEOLOGICAL SURVEY PAPER (CN) [02009879] **1378**

GEOLOGICAL SURVEY REPORT OF PROGRESS (US/0885-9876) [08621430] **1378**

GEOLOGICAL SURVEY REPORT. TASMANIA (AT/0371-7240) [I03717240] **2139**

GEOLOGICAL SURVEY RESEARCH (US/0083-1115) [04962906] **1378**

GEOLOGICAL SURVEY (SOUTH AFRICA) *See* MEMOIR - GEOLOGICAL SURVEY. SOUTH AFRICA **1387**

GEOLOGICAL SURVEY (SOUTH AFRICA) *See* ANNUAL TECHNICAL REPORT OF THE GEOLOGICAL SURVEY OF SOUTH AFRICA **1365**

GEOLOGICAL SURVEY SPECIAL REPORT (US/0537-2933) [01265699] **1379**

GEOLOGICAL SURVEY (U.S.) *See* WATER-RESOURCES ACTIVITIES OF THE U.S. GEOLOGICAL SURVEY IN ILLINOIS **5544**

GEOLOGICAL SURVEY (U.S.) *See* SUMMARY OF HYDROLOGIC DATA COLLECTED IN DADE COUNTY, FLORIDA **1418**

GEOLOGICAL SURVEY (U.S.) *See* GUIDE TO OBTAINING INFORMATION FROM THE USGS, A **1381**

GEOLOGICAL SURVEY (U.S.) *See* WATER-RESOURCES ACTIVITIES OF THE U.S. GEOLOGICAL SURVEY IN NEW MEXICO **5544**

GEOLOGICAL SURVEY (U.S.) *See* U.S. GEOLOGICAL SURVEY IN ALASKA ..., PROGRAMS, THE **1400**

GEOLOGICAL SURVEY (U.S.). CENTRAL REGION *See* TELEPHONE DIRECTORY / UNITED STATES DEPARTMENT OF THE INTERIOR, GEOLOGICAL SURVEY, CENTRAL REGION **1399**

GEOLOGICAL SURVEY (U.S.). WATER RESOURCES DIVISION *See* WRD INFORMATION GUIDE **1419**

GEOLOGICAL SURVEY (U.S.). WATER RESOURCES DIVISION *See* WATER RESOURCES DIVISION TRAINING BULLETIN **5546**

GEOLOGICAL SURVEY (U.S.). WATER RESOURCES DIVISION *See* INVESTIGATION OF FLOODS IN HAWAII **1415**

GEOLOGICAL SURVEY (U.S.). WATER RESOURCES DIVISION. NEW MEXICO DISTRICT *See* WATER-RESOURCES INVESTIGATIONS OF THE U.S. GEOLOGICAL SURVEY NEW MEXICO DISTRICT **5547**

GEOLOGICAL SURVEY (U.S.). WATER RESOURCES DIVISION. TEXAS DISTRICT *See* WATER-RESOURCES INVESTIGATIONS IN TEXAS **5547**

GEOLOGICARTOGRAPHY (AT/0810-6185) [04683173] **2582**

GEOLOGICESKIJ ZURNAL (KIEV. 1968) (UN/0367-4290) [06073109] **1379**

GEOLOGICESKOE STROENIE I POLEZNYE ISKOPAEMYE NIZNEGO POVOLZJA (RU/0132-7003) [02999092] **1379**

GEOLOGICKY PRUZKUM (XR/0016-772X) [05031415] **1379**

GEOLOGICKY PRUZKUM *See* UHLI- RUDY- GEOLOGICKY PRUZKUM **1400**

GEOLOGICKY PRUZKUM, N. P., OSTRAVA *See* SBORNIK GPO **1396**

GEOLOGICKY ZBORNIK / GEOLOGICA CARPATHICA (XO/0016-7738) [02367462] **2139**, **1379**

GEOLOGIE AFRICAINE (FR) [08584947] **1362**

GEOLOGIE ALPINE (FR/0367-3685) [06253404] **1379**

GEOLOGIE DE LA FRANCE (FR/0246-0874) [10684739] **1379**

GEOLOGIE EN MIJNBOUW (NE/0016-7746) [00997482] **2139**, **1379**

GEOLOGIE MEDITARRANEENNE (FR/0397-2844) [02381192] **1379**

GEOLOGIIA I GEOFIZIKA. ENGLISH. SOVIET GEOLOGY AND GEOPHYSICS *See* RUSSIAN GEOLOGY AND GEOPHYSICS **1396**

GEOLOGIIA I GEOFIZIKA (NOVOSIBIRSK) (RU/0016-7886) [06660728] **1405**, **1379**

GEOLOGIIA I GEOKHIMIIA GORIUCHIKH ISKOPAEMYKH (KIEV, UKRAINE : 1974) (UN/0135-2164) [20280585] **2139**

GEOLOGIJA I NEFTEGAZONOSNOST TURKMENISTANA (RU/0135-1605) [06718791] **4259**

GEOLOGIJA NEFTI I GAZA (RU/0016-7894) [10331110] **1379**

GEOLOGIJA RUDNYH MESTOROZDENIJ (RU/0016-7770) [02430398] **1379**, **2139**

GEOLOGIJA SIBIRI I DALNEGO VOSTOKA (RU/0130-1098) [02808803] **1379**

GEOLOGIKAI ANAGNORISEIS (GR) [06731888] **1379**

GEOLOGISCHE ABHANDLUNGEN HESSEN (GW/0341-4043) [04510981] **1379**

GEOLOGISCHE BUNDESANSTALT (AUSTRIA) *See* ABHANDLUNGEN DER GEOLOGISCHEN BUNDESANSTALT **1364**

GEOLOGISCHE RUNDSCHAU (GW/0016-7835) [02167347] **1379**

GEOLOGISCHES JAHRBUCH *See* GEOLOGISCHES JAHRBUCH, REIHE C : HYDROGEOLOGIE, INGENIEURGEOLOGIE **1413**

GEOLOGISCHES JAHRBUCH HESSEN (GW/0341-4027) [03856350] **1379**

GEOLOGISCHES JAHRBUCH, REIHE A : ALLGEMEINE UND REGIONALE GEOLOGIE BR DEUTSCHLAND UND NACHBARGEBIETE, TEKTONIK, STRATIGRAPHIE, PALAONTOLOGIE (GW/0341-6399) [01792106] **1379**

GEOLOGISCHES JAHRBUCH, REIHE B : REGIONALE GEOLOGIE, AUSLAND (GW/0341-6402) [01792105] **1379**

GEOLOGISCHES JAHRBUCH, REIHE C : HYDROGEOLOGIE, INGENIEURGEOLOGIE (GW/0341-6410) [01792104] **1413**

GEOLOGISCHES JAHRBUCH, REIHE D : MINERALOGIE, PETROGRAPHIE, GEOCHEMIE, LAGERSTATTENKUNDE (GW/0341-6429) [01794411] **1379**

GEOLOGISCHES JAHRBUCH, REIHE E : GEOPHYSIK (GW/0341-6437) [01795493] **1405**

GEOLOGISCHES JAHRBUCH, REIHE F : BODENKUNDE (GW/0341-6445) [02242498] **1379**

GEOLOGISKA FORENINGENS I STOCKHOLM FORHANDLINGAR (SW/0016-786X) [10612377] **1380**

GEOLOGISKA FORENINGENS I STOCKHOLM FORHANDLINGAR (1978) *See* GFF **1381**

GEOLOGISTS' ASSOCIATION *See* PROCEEDINGS OF THE GEOLOGISTS' ASSOCIATION **1391**

GEOLOGIST'S DIRECTORY (UK) [08295790] **1380**

GEOLOGOS (US/0732-4286) [08323990] **2564**, **1380**

GEOLOGUES (FR/0016-7916) [03973143] **1380**

GEOLOGY (BOULDER) (US/0091-7613) [01788177] **1380**

GEOLOGY OF IRAQ: A BIBLIOGRAPHY (IQ) **1380**

GEOLOGY Alphabetical Title Index

● GEOLOGY OF ORE DEPOSITS (RU/1075-7015) [30415968] **1440**

GEOLOGY OF PETROLEUM (NEW YORK, N.Y.) (US/0275-3960) [07125417] 1380, **4259**

GEOLOGY SERIES (LAWRENCE, KAN.) (US/0735-9810) [04182291] **1380**

GEOLOGY STUDIES (US/0068-1016) [05514310] **1380**

GEOLOGY STUDIES. SPECIAL PUBLICATIONS (US/0525-5201) [02250669] **1380**

GEOLOGY TODAY (UK/0266-6979) [11894556] **1380**

GEOLOSKI VJESNIK (YU/0016-7924) [06254365] **1380**

GEOMAGNETIC DATA (US/0163-4402) [04370513] **4443**

GEOMAGNETIC INDICES BULLETIN (US) [20433842] **1405**

GEOMAGNETISM AND AERONOMY (US/0016-7932) [01570719] 4443, **22**

GEOMAGNETIZM I AERONOMIJA (RU/0016-7940) [02397693] **4443**

● GEOMATICA (CN/1195-1036) [28323777] **2582**

● GEOMBINATORICS : [A MINI-JOURNAL OF OPEN PROBLEMS OF COMBINATORIAL AND DISCRETE GEOMETRY AND RELATED AREAS] / UNIVERSITY OF COLORADO AT COLORADO SPRINGS AND CENTER FOR EXCELLENCE IN MATHEMATICAL EDUCATION (US/1065-7371) [26726988] **3506**

GEOMECHANICS COMPUTING PROGRAMME (AT) [01846963] **1380**

GEOMETHODICA; VEROFFENTLICHUNGEN DES BASLER GEOMETHODISCHEN COLLOQUIUMS (SZ) [06274978] **2564**

GEOMETRA DELLA PROVINCIA GRANDA (IT) **2023**

GEOMETRE (FR/0016-7967) [03287675] **2023**

GEOMETRIAE DEDICATA (NE/0046-5755) [01785115] **3507**

GEOMETRIC AND FUNCTIONAL ANALYSIS : GAFA (SZ/1016-443X) [23352252] **3507**

GEOMETRICHESKII SBORNIK (RU/0134-8817) [02778849] **3507**

GEOMETRY (GW/0720-2598) [09449724] **3507**

GEOMICROBIOLOGY JOURNAL (US/0149-0451) [04205644] **563**

GEOMIMET (MX/0185-1314) [01771452] **2139**

GEOMORFOLOGIJA (MOSKVA) (RU/0435-4281) [02407884] **2564**

GEOMORPHOLOGY (NE/0169-555X) [16581898] **1380**

GEOMORPHOLOGY TEXTS (UK) [01409713] **1380**

GEOMUNDO (PN/0256-7253) [03591006] 237, **2564**

GEOOKODYNAMIK (GW/0720-454X) [0720454X] **1355**

GEOPHYSICA (FI/0367-4231) [01570720] **1405**

GEOPHYSICAL ABSTRACTS IN PRESS (US/1055-2383) [23124771] **1405**

GEOPHYSICAL AND ASTROPHYSICAL FLUID DYNAMICS (US/0309-1929) [02764582] 395, **1405**

GEOPHYSICAL DIRECTORY, THE (US) [01269813] **1405**

GEOPHYSICAL JOURNAL (US/0275-9128) [07250566] **1405**

GEOPHYSICAL JOURNAL INTERNATIONAL (UK/0956-540X) [20060716] **1405**

GEOPHYSICAL MAGAZINE, THE (JA/0016-8017) [01443345] **1406**

GEOPHYSICAL MONOGRAPH (US/0065-8448) [01775740] **1406**

GEOPHYSICAL PROSPECTING (NE/0016-8025) [01570723] **1406**

GEOPHYSICAL RESEARCH LETTERS (US/0094-8276) [01795290] **1406**

GEOPHYSICS (US/0016-8033) [01570724] **1406**

GEOPHYSICS ABSTRACTS **SUSPENDED.** (UK) **1406**

GEOPHYSICS AND ASTROPHYSICS MONOGRAPHS (NE/0165-1307) [01443370] 395, **1406**

GEOPHYSICS REPRINT SERIES (US/0734-5631) [05303152] **1406**

GEOPHYSICS, THE LEADING EDGE OF EXPLORATION (US/0732-989X) [08504812] **1406**

GEOPHYSIK UND GEOLOGIE (BERLIN, DDR) (GW/0138-2357) [04756345] 1380, **1406**

GEOPHYTOLOGY (II/0376-5156) [01790520] **512**

GEOPOLITICA (INSTITUTO DE ESTUDIOS GEOPOLITICOS (BUENOS AIRES, ARGENTINA)) (AG/0325-2035) [02623844] **2616**

GEOPOLITICA (INSTITUTO URUGUAYO DE ESTUDIOS GEOPOLITICOS) (UY) [03265661] **4474**

GEOPOLITICS OF ENERGY (CN/0273-1371) [07028267] **1945**

GEOPOLITIQUE (FR/0752-1693) [10330997] **4522**

GEOPUB REVIEW OF GEOGRAPHICAL LITERATURE (US/0360-8492) [02244783] **2564**

GEOREF (CD-ROM) (US/0197-7482) [25005560] 1380, **1363**

GEOREF NEWSLETTER, THE (US/0730-8116) [08081434] **1380**

GEOREF SERIALS LIST (US) [08405270] **416**

GEORG BRANDES ARBOG (DK) [03247264] **3390**

GEORG BUECHNER JAHRBUCH (GW) [09430292] **3390**

GEORGE B. PEGRAM LECTURES (US/0435-4389) [01433219] **1825**

GEORGE COUNTY TIMES, THE (US) [15647838] **5700**

GEORGE D. HALL COMPANY See GEORGE D. HALL'S NEW YORK MANUFACTURERS DIRECTORY **3479**

GEORGE D. HALL'S CONNECTICUT SERVICE DIRECTORY (US/0743-4502) [09327803] **1607**

GEORGE D. HALL'S DIRECTORY OF CENTRAL ATLANTIC STATES MANUFACTURERS (US/0889-0390) [11795987] **3479**

GEORGE D. HALL'S DIRECTORY OF CONNECTICUT MANUFACTURERS (US/0196-8270) [05900340] **3479**

GEORGE D. HALL'S DIRECTORY OF MASSACHUSETTS MANUFACTURERS (US/0149-6913) [01468952] **3479**

● GEORGE D. HALL'S DIRECTORY OF NEW ENGLAND MANUFACTURERS (US) [27763087] **3479**

● GEORGE D. HALL'S DIRECTORY OF NEW JERSEY MANUFACTURERS (US/1069-5176) [27652729] **3479**

● GEORGE D. HALL'S DIRECTORY OF NEW YORK MANUFACTURES (US) [27321850] **3479**

GEORGE D. HALL'S DIRECTORY OF NORTH CAROLINA MANUFACTURERS (US/0892-8282) [15287834] **3479**

GEORGE D. HALL'S MASSACHUSETTS SERVICE DIRECTORY (US/0196-7185) [05203141] **1607**

GEORGE D. HALL'S NEW JERSEY MANUFACTURERS DIRECTORY (US/0278-9124) [07494300] **3479**

GEORGE D. HALL'S NEW YORK MANUFACTURERS DIRECTORY (US/0272-1074) [06586753] **3479**

GEORGE D. HALL'S THE NEW ENGLAND INDUSTRIAL SERVICE DIRECTORY (US/0147-2356) [02590002] **1607**

GEORGE EASTMAN HOUSE See MONOGRAPH **5234**

GEORGE ELIOT FELLOWSHIP REVIEW See GEORGE ELIOT REVIEW : JOURNAL OF THE GEORGE ELIOT FELLOWSHIP, THE **3390**

GEORGE ELIOT, GEORGE HENRY LEWES NEWSLETTER, THE (US/0953-0754) [10361769] **3390**

● GEORGE ELIOT REVIEW : JOURNAL OF THE GEORGE ELIOT FELLOWSHIP, THE (UK) [26603984] **3390**

GEORGE HERBERT JOURNAL (US/0161-7435) [04010387] **3390**

GEORGE MACAULAY TREVELYN LECTURES (US/0433-5082) [01433241] **2689**

● GEORGE MASON INDEPENDENT LAW REVIEW (US/1068-3801) [27667362] **2973**

GEORGE MASON UNIVERSITY CIVIL RIGHTS LAW JOURNAL (US/1049-4766) [21085585] 4508, **3090**

GEORGE MASON UNIVERSITY LAW REVIEW (US/0741-8736) [07821833] **2973**

● GEORGE MASON UNIVERSITY LAW REVIEW (US) [30482842] **2973**

GEORGE ODIORNE LETTER, THE **CEASED.** (US/0890-0914) [06177156] **868**

GEORGE PHILIPP TELEMANN MUSIKALISCHE WERKE (GW) **4119**

GEORGE SAND STUDIES (US/0897-0483) [16149728] **3343**

GEORGE WASHINGTON JOURNAL OF INTERNATIONAL LAW AND ECONOMICS, THE (US/0748-4305) [08419381] 1635, 4522, **3128**

GEORGE WASHINGTON JOURNAL OF INTERNATIONAL LAW AND ECONOMICS, THE (US) [09247088] **3128**

GEORGE WASHINGTON LAW REVIEW, THE (US/0016-8076) [01570730] **2973**

GEORGE WASHINGTON UNIVERSITY See GW TIMES **1827**

GEORGE WASHINGTON UNIVERSITY. SOCIAL RESEARCH GROUP See TOWARD INTERAGENCY COORDINATION: FEDERAL RESEARCH AND DEVELOPMENT ON ADOLESCENCE **2286**

GEORGE WRIGHT FORUM, THE (US/0732-4715) [08325239] 4706, **2194**

GEORGETOWN CURRENT (US) **5647**

GEORGETOWN GAZETTE & TOWN CRIER See EL DORADO GAZETTE, GEORGETOWN GAZETTE & TOWN CRIER **5634**

GEORGETOWN GRAPHIC (US/0886-5965) [12832593] **5680**

GEORGETOWN IMMIGRATION LAW JOURNAL (US/0891-4370) [13563154] 1918, **2974**

GEORGETOWN INDEPENDENT (CN/0834-6518) [16310321] **5785**

GEORGETOWN INTERNATIONAL ENVIRONMENTAL LAW REVIEW (US/1042-1858) [17997905] **3112**

GEORGETOWN INTERNATIONAL REVIEW (US/0360-6082) [02244377] **3128**

GEORGETOWN JOURNAL OF LANGUAGES & LINGUISTICS, THE **CEASED.** (US/1048-4205) [20951708] **3283**

GEORGETOWN JOURNAL OF LEGAL ETHICS, THE (US/1041-5548) [15649826] 2250, **2974**

GEORGETOWN JOURNAL ON FIGHTING POVERTY (UK) **5286**

GEORGETOWN LAW JOURNAL, THE (US/0016-8092) [01570732] **2974**

GEORGETOWN MAGAZINE (1993) (US/1074-8784) [29869667] **1825**

GEORGETOWN MEDICAL BULLETIN (US/0016-8106) [01570733] **3780**

GEORGETOWN NEWS & TIMES, THE (US) [13112922] **5680**

● GEORGETOWN REVIEW (GEORGETOWN, KY.) (US/1066-1506) [26877055] **3390**

GEORGETOWN SHIPYARD INC. (P.E.I.) See ANNUAL REPORT - GEORGETOWN SHIPYARD INC **4174**

GEORGETOWN TIMES, THE (US/0746-5734) [10134297] **5742**

GEORGETOWN UNIVERSITY. CENTER FOR STRATEGIC AND INTERNATIONAL STUDIES See CENTER FOR STRATEGIC AND INTERNATIONAL STUDIES, GEORGETOWN UNIVERSITY, THE **4517**

GEORGETOWN UNIVERSITY ROUND TABLE ON LANGUAGES AND LINGUISTICS (US/0196-7207) [03876236] **3283**

GEORGETOWN UNIVERSITY, WASHINGTON, D.C. GRADUATE SCHOOL. ACADEMY IN THE PUBLIC SERVICE See APS REVIEW, THE **4464**

GEORGETOWN (WASHINGTON, D.C. : 1987) See GEORGETOWN MAGAZINE (1993) **1825**

GEORGETOWN (WASHINGTON, D.C. : 1987) (US/0895-1624) [16511646] **1091**

GEORGETOWNER, THE (US/0730-9082) [08079438] **2534**

GEORGIA. ADMINISTRATIVE OFFICE OF THE COURTS See ANNUAL REPORT ON THE WORK OF THE GEORGIA COURTS **2935**

GEORGIA ADVANCE SHEETS (US/8750-0515) [10932291] **2974**

GEORGIA ALERT; A LOOK AT EDUCATION'S ROLE TODAY **CEASED.** (US) [01786765] **1748**

GEORGIA ALUMNI RECORD (US/0016-8130) [04080599] **1102**

GEORGIA ANCHORAGE (US/0016-8149) [01446231] **5449**

GEORGIA ARMCHAIR RESEARCHER, THE (US/0882-9209) [10658911] **2451**

GEORGIA BULLETIN (US) **5030**

GEORGIA BUSINESS AND ECONOMIC CONDITIONS (US/0279-3857) [07767938] 1492, **677**

GEORGIA BUSINESS DIRECTORY (US/1048-7220) [17977799] **677**

GEORGIA BYWAYS (US/1055-1921) [23102332] **2734**

GEORGIA CATTLEMAN (US/0744-4451) [01657858] **211**

GEORGIA CONGRESS OF PARENTS AND TEACHERS See GEORGIA PTA TODAY **1748**

GEORGIA. COOPERATIVE EXTENSION SERVICE See BULLETIN - COOPERATIVE EXTENSION SERVICE (ATHENS) **1541**

GEORGIA COUNTY GOVERNMENT (US/1066-0119) [I10660119] **4650**

GEORGIA COUNTY GUIDE, THE (US/1044-0976) [08586712] **5327**

Alphabetical Title Index — GEOS

GEORGIA. COURT OF APPEALS *See* GEORGIA ADVANCE SHEETS **2974**

GEORGIA COURT RULES AND PROCEDURE. FEDERAL (US/1055-7245) [16955150] **3140**

GEORGIA COURTS DIRECTORY (US) [02721015] **3140**

GEORGIA COURTS JOURNAL (US/0147-7161) [03221380] **3141**

GEORGIA CRIMINAL TRIAL PRACTICE / BY WILLIAM W. DANIEL (US/0884-1632) [11619875] **3107**

GEORGIA. DEPT. OF ARCHIVES AND HISTORY *See* GENERAL ASSEMBLY OF GEORGIA, THE **4650**

GEORGIA. DEPT. OF AUDITS AND ACCOUNTS *See* AUDIT REPORT : SECRETARY OF STATE - GEORGIA. DEPT. OF AUDITS AND ACCOUNTS **4631**

GEORGIA. DEPT. OF EDUCATION *See* BULLETIN - GEORGIA. DEPT. OF EDUCATION **1890**

GEORGIA. DEPT. OF HUMAN RESOURCES *See* GEORGIA VITAL AND MORBIDITY STATISTICS **5328**

GEORGIA. DEPT. OF TRANSPORTATION *See* ANNUAL REPORT / GEORGIA DEPARTMENT OF TRANSPORTATION **5376**

GEORGIA. DEPT. OF TRANSPORTATION *See* CONTINUOUS COUNT TRAFFIC DATA **5439**

GEORGIA DOCLIST : STATE DOCUMENTS ADDED DURING ... / UNIVERSITY OF GEORGIA LIBRARIES, GOVERNMENT DOCUMENTS DEPARTMENT (US) [23305885] **4650**

GEORGIA ECONOMIC OUTLOOK (US/0884-1179) [10988893] **1492**

GEORGIA. EMPLOYEES' RETIREMENT SYSTEM *See* ANNUAL REPORT - EMPLOYEES' RETIREMENT SYSTEM **1649**

GEORGIA EMPLOYMENT LAW LETTER (US/1040-4813) [18425832] **3148**

GEORGIA ENVIRONMENTAL LAW LETTER (US/1044-2324) [19732347] **3112**

GEORGIA. ENVIRONMENTAL PROTECTION DIVISION *See* WATER QUALITY MONITORING DATA FOR GEORGIA STREAMS **5543**

GEORGIA FACTS (US/1044-9086) [19946190] **2734**

GEORGIA FARM BUREAU NEWS (US/0735-696X) [08621412] **90**

GEORGIA FARMER (BALTIMORE, MD.) (US/0741-1251) [10092703] **90**

GEORGIA FIREFIGHTER (US/0739-4349) [09752954] **2290**

GEORGIA FOREST RESEARCH PAPER (US/0435-5377) [06795855] **2383**

GEORGIA FORESTRY / [GEORGIA FORESTRY COMMISSION] (US) [01589086] **2383**

GEORGIA FUTURE FARMER, THE (US) [09793160] **90**

GEORGIA GAZETTE (SAVANNAH, GA.: 1978), THE (US/0730-1138) [07949651] **5653**

GEORGIA GENEALOGICAL MAGAZINE (US/0435-5393) [01446578] **2451**

GEORGIA GENEALOGICAL SOCIETY QUARTERLY, THE (US/0435-5393) [10709426] **2451**

GEORGIA. GENERAL ASSEMBLY. HOUSE OF REPRESENTATIVES. STATE PLANNING AND COMMUNITY AFFAIRS COMMITTEE *See* SESSION REPORT / STATE PLANNING AND COMMUNITY AFFAIRS COMMITTEE **4685**

GEORGIA. GOVERNOR'S OFFICE OF ENERGY RESOURCES *See* GOVERNOR'S OFFICE OF ENERGY RESOURCES ANNUAL REPORT **1945**

●GEORGIA HEALTH CARE IN PERSPECTIVE (US/1065-4127) [26604947] **4776**

GEORGIA HERPETOLOGICAL SOCIETY *See* BULLETIN OF THE GEORGIA HERPETOLOGICAL SOCIETY **5579**

GEORGIA HISTORICAL QUARTERLY, THE (US/0016-8297) [01751094] **2734**

GEORGIA HISTORICAL SOCIETY *See* G.H.S. FOOT-NOTES **2734**

GEORGIA HISTORICAL SOCIETY *See* COLLECTIONS / GEORGIA HISTORICAL SOCIETY **2728**

GEORGIA IN PERSPECTIVE (US/1065-5395) [26628435] **5327**

GEORGIA. INSTITUTE OF TECHNOLOGY, ATLANTA. LIBRARY *See* SERIALS HOLDINGS LIST **424**

GEORGIA JOURNAL (ATHENS, GA.) (US/0746-5963) [07019570] **2534**

GEORGIA JOURNAL OF HOSPITAL PHARMACY (US) [21133785] **4306**

GEORGIA JOURNAL OF INTERNATIONAL AND COMPARATIVE LAW, THE (US/0046-578X) [01589909] **3128**

GEORGIA JOURNAL OF READING (US/0890-698X) [09534932] **1748**

GEORGIA JOURNAL OF SCIENCE (US/0147-9369) [03224690] **5107**

GEORGIA JOURNAL OF SOUTHERN LEGAL HISTORY, THE (US/1047-9228) [20812399] **2974**

GEORGIA. LABOR INFORMATION SYSTEMS *See* GEORGIA LABOR MARKET TRENDS **1675**

GEORGIA LABOR MARKET TRENDS (US/0147-9865) [03262857] **1675**

GEORGIA LANDINGS, ANNUAL SUMMARY (US/0148-5245) [03260032] **2304**

GEORGIA LAW LETTER (US/0884-1217) [12308165] **2974**

GEORGIA LAW REVIEW (ATHENS, GA.: 1966) (US/0016-8300) [01751097] **2974**

GEORGIA LEGAL DIRECTORY, THE (US/0145-2991) [02720960] **3141**

GEORGIA LEGISLATIVE REVIEW (US/0362-5931) [02303080] **2974**

GEORGIA LIBRARIAN, THE (US/0016-8319) [01447071] **3212**

GEORGIA LICENSED NURSERIES (US) [12221436] 4245, **2416**

GEORGIA LIVING (US/1049-6432) [21269980] **2488**

GEORGIA MANAGED CARE (US) **3578**

GEORGIA MANUFACTURERS REGISTER (US/0896-4009) [17064744] **3479**

GEORGIA MANUFACTURING DIRECTORY (US/0435-5482) [02493910] **3479**

GEORGIA MORTALITY VITAL STATISTICS REPORT (US) [21267549] **5327**

GEORGIA MUNICIPAL YEARBOOK, THE (US/0146-5295) [02970619] **2823**

GEORGIA MUSEUM OF ART *See* BULLETIN - GEORGIA MUSEUM OF ART, THE UNIVERSITY OF GEORGIA **4085**

GEORGIA MUSIC NEWS (US/0046-5798) [01439691] **4119**

GEORGIA NEWS MEDIA DIRECTORY (US) [09438338] **1112**

GEORGIA NURSING (US/0016-8335) [01437709] **3856**

GEORGIA. OFFICE OF PLANNING AND BUDGET *See* CAPITAL BUDGET (GEORGIA) **4716**

GEORGIA. OFFICE OF PLANNING AND BUDGET *See* STATE INVESTMENT PLAN **2836**

GEORGIA. OFFICE OF PLANNING AND BUDGET *See* BUDGET IN BRIEF / STATE OF GEORGIA **4714**

GEORGIA OFFICIAL AND STATISTICAL REGISTER (US/1070-7816) [05092556] **4650**

GEORGIA OPERATOR, THE (US/0433-6054) [10781792] **1492**

GEORGIA. ORGANIZED CRIME PREVENTION COUNCIL *See* ANNUAL REPORT - GEORGIA ORGANIZED CRIME PREVENTION COUNCIL **3157**

GEORGIA OUTDOOR NEWS (US/0895-3295) [16570106] **4872**

GEORGIA PHARMACEUTICAL JOURNAL (US/0194-4290) [04647912] **4306**

GEORGIA PTA TODAY (US/1064-6159) [04856104] **1748**

GEORGIA REAL ESTATE LAW LETTER (US/1040-4805) [17944099] 4838, **2974**

GEORGIA REVIEW, THE (US/0016-8386) [01751100] **3390**

GEORGIA SCHOOL LAW REPORTER (US) 1748, **2974**

GEORGIA. SECRETARY OF STATE *See* MANUAL OF THE GENERAL ASSEMBLY OF THE STATE OF GEORGIA **4664**

GEORGIA SOCIAL SCIENCE JOURNAL *CEASED.* (US/0016-8408) [05904554] **5200**

GEORGIA SPORTSMAN (US/0199-6517) [03659525] **4872**

GEORGIA STATE BAR JOURNAL (US/0016-8416) [02276231] **2974**

GEORGIA STATE BAR NEWS (US) [02417936] **2974**

GEORGIA. STATE BOARD OF REGISTRATION FOR FORESTERS *See* ROSTER OF CURRENT LICENSES - GEORGIA. STATE BOARD OF REGISTRATION FOR FORESTERS **2394**

GEORGIA. STATE DATA CENTER *See* CITY POPULATION ESTIMATES - GEORGIA. STATE DATA CENTER **4551**

GEORGIA. STATE DATA CENTER *See* ANNUAL ESTIMATE OF POPULATION FOR THE STATE OF GEORGIA **4549**

GEORGIA. STATE HIGHWAY DATA. CONTINUOUS COUNT TRAFFIC DATA *See* CONTINUOUS COUNT TRAFFIC DATA **5439**

GEORGIA STATE LITERARY STUDIES (US/0884-8696) [12487102] **3390**

GEORGIA STATE UNIVERSITY. COLLEGE OF BUSINESS ADMINISTRATION *See* REPORT OF PUBLICATION AND RESEARCH - GEORGIA STATE UNIVERSITY. COLLEGE OF BUSINESS ADMINISTRATION **707**

GEORGIA STATE UNIVERSITY FACT BOOK (US/0098-3071) [02240783] **1825**

GEORGIA STATE UNIVERSITY LAW REVIEW (US/8755-6847) [11383007] **2974**

GEORGIA STATE UNIVERSITY. OFFICE OF AFFIRMATIVE ACTION *See* AFFIRMATIVE ACTION PLAN FOR EQUAL EMPLOYMENT OPPORTUNITY **1807**

GEORGIA STATE UNIVERSITY. OFFICE OF AFFIRMATIVE ACTION *See* GEORGIA STATE UNIVERSITY'S APPROACH TO AFFIRMATIVE ACTION **1825**

GEORGIA STATE UNIVERSITY. SCHOOL OF BUSINESS ADMINISTRATION *See* RESEARCH MONOGRAPH **707**

GEORGIA STATE UNIVERSITY'S APPROACH TO AFFIRMATIVE ACTION (US/0098-5163) [02240041] **1825**

GEORGIA STATISTICAL ABSTRACT (US/0085-1043) [01440913] **5328**

GEORGIA TREND (US/0882-5971) [11907414] **1492**

GEORGIA. UNIVERSITY. COLLEGE OF AGRICULTURE. COOPERATIVE EXTENSION SERVICE *See* CIRCULAR - UNIVERSITY OF GEORGIA. COLLEGE OF AGRICULTURE **75**

GEORGIA. UNIVERSITY. COLLEGE OF AGRICULTURE. EXTENSION SERVICE *See* BULLETIN - GEORGIA. UNIVERSITY. COLLEGE OF AGRICULTURE. EXTENSION SERVICE **69**

GEORGIA VETERINARIAN, THE (US/0886-5760) [01448413] **5510**

GEORGIA VITAL AND MORBIDITY STATISTICS (US) [01785595] **5328**

GEORGIA VOTER (US/0739-9251) [05886816] **4474**

GEORGIA WILDLIFE (US/0164-8608) [04308828] **2194**

GEORGIAN ANNUAL (US) **4241**

●GEORGIAN BAY ISLANDS NATIONAL PARK, MANAGEMENT PLANNING (CN/1191-4734) [26758067] **4706**

GEORGIAN BAY REGIONAL LIBRARY SYSTEM *See* DIRECTORY, NON-OPERATING LIBRARY BOARDS / GEORGIAN BAY REGIONAL LIBRARY SYSTEMS **3206**

GEORGIAN BAY REGIONAL LIBRARY SYSTEM *See* BULLETIN - GEORGIAN BAY REGIONAL LIBRARY SYSTEM **3198**

GEORGIAN BAY REGIONAL LIBRARY SYSTEM *See* DIRECTORY OF OPERATING LIBRARIES / GEORGIAN BAY REGIONAL LIBRARY SYSTEM **3207**

GEORGIAN BAY REGIONAL LIBRARY SYSTEM *See* LARGE PRINT BOOKS / GEORGIAN BAY REGIONAL LIBRARY SYSTEM **4829**

GEORGIAN BAY REGIONAL LIBRARY SYSTEM *See* DIRECTORY, MEMBER LIBRARIES, GEORGIAN BAY REGIONAL LIBRARY SYSTEM **3206**

GEORGIAN GROUP JOURNAL, THE (UK/0963-1070) [24163091] **299**

GEORGIAN GROUP (LONDON, ENGLAND). REPORT AND JOURNAL *See* GEORGIAN GROUP JOURNAL, THE **299**

●GEORGIAN MATHEMATICAL JOURNAL (US/1072-947X) [29242284] **3507**

GEORGIAN (STEPHENVILLE) (CN/0381-9566) [02861831] **5785**

GEORGIAN SUN (CN/1182-5804) [23226672] **5785**

GEORGIAN SUN (CN/1182-5804) [23598385] **5785**

GEORGIA'S CITIES (US) [21151279] **4650**

GEORGICON FOR AGRICULTURE (HU/0239-1260) [24584650] **90**

GEORGIKE EREUNA - HYPERESIA GEORGIKON EREUNON, GREECE (GR) [06901354] **90**

GEORGIST JOURNAL, THE (US/0887-6290) [13313663] **677**

GEORGOFILI; ATTI DELLA ACCADEMIA DEI GEORGOFILI, I (IT/0367-4134) [03474526] **90**

GEOS (CN/0374-3268) [01791372] 2139, **2194**

GEOS
Alphabetical Title Index

GEOS - UNION GEOFISICA MEXICANA (MX/0186-1891) [08822240] **1406**

GEOSAURUS (UK) [05063650] **1380**

GEOSCIENCE AND MAN (US/0072-1395) [02254730] 237, **2564**

GEOSCIENCE CANADA (CN/0315-0941) [01794385] **1380**

GEOSCIENCE CANADA REPRINT SERIES (CN/0821-381X) [06021629] **1355**

GEOSCIENCE CONTENTS *CEASED.* (US/0883-895X) [12253378] **1380**

GEOSCIENCE DOCUMENTATION (UK/0016-8483) [02046872] 1355, **1363**

GEOSCIENCE INFORMATION SOCIETY *See* PROCEEDINGS - GEOSCIENCE INFORMATION SOCIETY **1359**

GEOSCIENCE RESEARCH GRANT PROGRAM, SUMMARY OF RESEARCH (CN/0225-5316) [08830161] **1380**

GEOSCIENCE SOFTWARE DIRECTORY FOR THE IBM PC & COMPATIBLES (NE) [12390493] 1356, **1286**

GEOSCIENCE TEXTS (US/0278-7091) [07867470] **1356**

GEOSCIENCE WISCONSIN (US/0164-2049) [03505351] **1380**

GEOSCIENCES IN CANADA (1976) (CN/0707-2422) [04632224] **1356**

GEOSCIENTIST (UK/0961-5628) [23372286] **1380**

GEOSCITECH CITATION INDEX (US/0732-0558) [08297273] **1356**

GEOSCOPE (MONTREAL) (CN/0317-6029) [02015658] **2564**

GEOSCOPE (OTTAWA) (CN/0046-581X) [02015355] **2564**

GEOSTANDARDS NEWSLETTER (FR/0150-5505) [03645955] **1380**

GEOSUR / [ASOCIACION SUDAMERICANA DE ESTUDIOS GEOPOLITICOS E INTERNACIONALES] (UY) [08427052] **4522**

GEOSYSTEMS NEWS (UK/0142-6516) [09035568] **1380**

GEOTECHNICAL ABSTRACTS *CEASED.* (US/0016-8491) [01587538] 1381, **1363**

●GEOTECHNICAL AND GEOLOGICAL ENGINEERING (UK/0960-3182) 1381, **2139**

GEOTECHNICAL ENGINEERING (TH/0046-5828) [01432515] **2023**

GEOTECHNICAL FABRICS REPORT (US/0882-4983) [09922845] **5351**

GEOTECHNICAL NEWS (CN/0823-650X) [09951539] **1381**

GEOTECHNICAL SPECIAL PUBLICATION (US/0895-0563) [13687783] **2023**

GEOTECHNIK (GW/0172-6145) [06697417] 1381, **2023**

GEOTECHNIQUE (UK/0016-8505) [01751108] **2023**

GEOTECHNIQUE [MICROFORM] (UK/0016-8505) [04422544] 1381, **1976**

GEOTECHNOLOGY (US/0732-7110) [08405518] **1356**

GEOTECNIA (BL/0379-9522) [07935500] **2024**

GEOTECNICA; GEOLOGIA TECNICA, FONDAZIONI, COSTRUZIONI DI TERRA (IT) [06739771] **1381**

GEOTECTONICS (US/0016-8521) [01751109] **1381**

GEOTECTURE *CEASED.* (AT/0812-2253) [I08122253] **1381**

GEOTEKTONIKA (RU/0016-853X) [02456910] **1381**

GEOTEKTONIKA, TEKTONOFIZIKA I GEODINAMIKA (BU/0324-1661) [02244352] **1381**

GEOTEKTONISCHE FORSCHUNGEN (GW/0016-8548) [01448942] **1381**

GEOTEXTILES AND GEOMEMBRANES (UK/0266-1144) [11850170] **495**

GEOTHERMAL ENERGY (OAK RIDGE, TENN.) (US/0896-6257) [17236024] **1945**

GEOTHERMAL HOT LINE (US/0735-0503) [07233661] **1945**

GEOTHERMAL REPORT (US/0733-9100) [08672473] **1945**

GEOTHERMAL REPORT. MINERAL RESOURCES DIVISION, FIJI (FJ/0250-7277) [08655782] **1945**

GEOTHERMAL RESOURCES COUNCIL *See* TRANSACTIONS - GEOTHERMAL RESOURCES COUNCIL **1959**

GEOTHERMAL SCIENCE AND TECHNOLOGY (UK/0890-5363) [14262559] **1406**

GEOTHERMAL TECHNOLOGY PUBLICATIONS AND RELATED REPORTS, A BIBLIOGRAPHY (US/0741-5656) [09941833] **1962**

GEOTHERMICS (UK/0375-6505) [01751110] **1413**

GEOTHERMIE ACTUALITES *See* RESEAUX ET CHALEUR (ORLEANS) **1955**

GEOTIMES (US/0016-8556) [01643792] **1381**

GEOTITLES (UK/0952-2700) [16146158] 1356, **1363**

GEOVIEWS (SECUNDERABAD) (II/0253-679X) [03393321] **1356**

GEOWISSENSCHAFTEN (BOPPARD) (GW/0343-9712) [06211943] **1381**

GEOWISSENSCHAFTEN (WEINHEIM AN DER BERGSTRASSE, GERMANY) (GW/0933-0704) [17606653] **1356**

GEPESZETI SZAKIRODALMI TAJEKOZTATO (HU/0231-0686) [I02310686] **2115**

GEPGYARTASTECHNOLOGIAI ES SZERSZAMGEPIPARI SZAKIRODALMI TAJEKOZTATO (HU/0231-0694) [I02310694] **2115**

GEPROGRAMMEERDE INSTRUCTIE *See* ONDERWIJS IN MEDIA **1902**

GERALDTON-LONGLAC TIMES STAR (CN/0834-6275) [23004469] **5785**

GERANIUMS AROUND THE WORLD (US/0016-8599) [03087547] **2416**

GERARD HENDERSON'S MEDIA WATCH (AT/1031-1211) [I10311211] **1112**

GERATRIE FUER DIE TAEGLICHE PRAXIS (SZ/1011-2901) [26012111] **3751**

●GERBINO INVESTMENT LETTER, THE (US/1077-0119) [30677446] **899**

GEREFORMEERD THEOLOGISCH TIJDSCHRIFT (NE/0016-8610) [04441201] **4960**

GEREFORMEERDE GEMEENTEN IN NEDERLAND EN NOORD-AMERIKA *See* KERKELIJK JAARBOEKJE DER GEREFORMEERDE GEMEENTEN **4972**

GERFAUT, LE (BE/0251-1193) [01644358] **5617**

GERIACTION (AT/1032-4410) [I10324410] **3751**

GERIATRIC CARDIOVASCULAR MEDICINE (UK/0951-5216) [18770407] **3751**

GERIATRIC CARE (US) [02251654] **3751**

GERIATRIC CARE NEWS (US/1048-7514) [21022601] **3751**

GERIATRIC CONSULTANT *CEASED.* (US/0745-1202) [08828857] **3751**

GERIATRIC GUIDE TO PERTINENT PUBLICATIONS *See* DIRECTORY OF GERIATRIC PUBLICATIONS, THE **3750**

GERIATRIC LENGTH OF STAY BY DIAGNOSIS AND OPERATION, UNITED STATES (US/0891-2173) [09426449] **3751**

GERIATRIC MEDICINE ANNUAL *CEASED.* (US/0882-4614) [12757715] **3751**

GERIATRIC MEDICINE CURRENTS (US/0890-7811) [07479721] **3751**

GERIATRIC MEDICINE (HORTON KIRBY. 1985) (UK/0268-201X) [12706938] **3751**

GERIATRIC NEPHROLOGY AND UROLOGY (NE/0924-8455) [24540060] 3751, **3990**

GERIATRIC NURSING (NEW YORK) (US/0197-4572) [06035515] 3751, **3856**

GERIATRIC (SZ/1011-4831) [20293916] **3751**

GERIATRICS (US/0016-867X) [01751111] **3751**

GERIATRICS ED. ITALIANA (IT/0392-9663) [I03929663] **3751**

GERIATRIE & REHABILITATION / IM AUFTRAG DER DEUTSCHEN GESELLSCHAFT FUER GERIATRIE UND IN ZUSAMMENARBEIT MIT DER DEUTSCHEN GESELLSCHAFT FUER MEDIZINISCHE PSYCHOLOGIE UND PSYCHOPATHOMETRIE (GW) [19345715] **3751**

GERIATRIKA (SP/0212-9744) [15697890] **3751**

GERION / DEPARTAMENTO DE HISTORIA ANTIGUA (SP) [13453178] **2689**

GERMAN AMERICAN TRADE (CN/1182-803X) [22754245] **837**

GERMAN ANCESTRY *See* HIGHWAYMAN (WILLOW STREET, PA.), THE **2453**

GERMAN ANCESTRY (US/1061-0529) [25173943] **2451**

GERMAN AND CENTRAL EUROPEAN EMIGRATION (US/0195-735X) [05623407] 2451, **1918**

GERMAN BLUES CIRCLE *See* INFO / GERMAN BLUES CIRCLE **4122**

GERMAN BLUES GUIDE (GW) [07889261] **4119**

GERMAN BRIEF (GW) 677, **1492**

GERMAN CANADIAN STUDIES (ASSOCIATION) *See* SYMPOSIUM / DEUTSCHKANADISCHE STUDIEN **3443**

GERMAN-CANADIAN YEARBOOK (CN/0316-8603) [02593314] **2734**

GERMAN COMMENTS (GW) [10721485] **4522**

GERMAN CONNECTION, THE (US/8755-1756) [11215173] **2451**

GERMAN ENGRAVINGS ETCHINGS AND WOODCUTS (NE) **351**

GERMAN FASHION GUIDE *See* FASHION GUIDE DUSSELDORF **1084**

GERMAN GENEALOGICAL DIGEST (US) [12335732] **2451**

GERMAN HISTORY : THE JOURNAL OF THE GERMAN HISTORY SOCIETY (UK/0266-3554) [13379520] **2689**

GERMAN INTERNATIONAL *SUSPENDED.* (GW/0016-8769) [01449331] **2488**

●GERMAN JOURNAL OF OPHTHALMOLOGY (GW/0941-2921) [25786145] **3875**

GERMAN JOURNAL OF PSYCHOLOGY, THE (GW/0705-5870) [03864112] **4587**

GERMAN LANGUAGE AND LITERATURE MONOGRAPHS *CEASED.* (NE/0378-4150) [04734149] 3283, **3390**

GERMAN LIFE AND CIVILIZATION (US/0899-9899) [18283385] **2689**

GERMAN OPINION ON PROBLEMS OF TODAY (GW/0072-1468) [01451043] **2517**

GERMAN PATENTS GAZETTE : PARTS I-III COMPLETE (UK) [02474019] **1304**

GERMAN PATENTS GAZETTE: SECTION II, ELECTRICAL (UK/0533-7534) [01792776] **2056**

GERMAN PATENTS GAZETTE : SECTION III, MECHANICAL & GENERAL (UK/0533-7542) [01792768] **1304**

GERMAN PHOTOGRAPHIC ANNUAL, THE (US/0435-5806) [01751122] **4370**

●GERMAN POLITICS (UK/0964-4008) [26101668] **4474**

GERMAN POLITICS AND SOCIETY (US/1045-0300) [14816520] **5200**

GERMAN PRESS (TORONTO. 1991) (CN/1187-3388) [25589907] **5785**

GERMAN QUARTERLY, THE (US/0016-8831) [01258410] **3390**

GERMAN RESEARCH : REPORTS OF THE DFG (GW/0172-1526) [07849640] **5107**

GERMAN STUDIES IN INDIA (II) [07140525] **3283**

GERMAN STUDIES REVIEW (US/0149-7952) [03556144] 3390, **2689**

GERMAN TEACHING (UK/0953-4822) [I09534822] **3283**

GERMAN TRIBUNE, THE *CEASED.* (GW/0016-8858) [01642971] **2517**

GERMAN TRIBUNE. THIRD WORLD REVIEW, THE (GW) [07213250] **2910**

GERMAN WINE REVIEW : THE GERMAN WINE & BEVERAGE MAGAZINE *CEASED.* (GW) [29437182] **2367**

GERMAN YEARBOOK OF INTERNATIONAL LAW (GW/0344-3094) [04255021] **3128**

GERMAN YEARBOOK ON BUSINESS HISTORY (GW/0722-2416) [08208010] **1564**

GERMANIA (BERLIN) (GW/0016-8874) [02032669] **269**

GERMANIA SACRA (GW) [01751128] **5030**

GERMANIA SLAVICA (GW) [07264269] **2689**

GERMANIC NOTES *See* GERMANIC NOTES AND REVIEWS **2846**

●GERMANIC NOTES AND REVIEWS (US) [25357082] 2689, **2846**

GERMANIC REVIEW, THE (US/0016-8890) [01242828] **3343**

GERMANIC STUDIES IN AMERICA (SZ/0721-3727) [06392708] **3390**

GERMANICA (FR/0072-1484) [01936623] **3391**

GERMANICA OLOMUCENSIA (XR) [08150381] **3391**

GERMANISCH-ROMANISCHE MONATSSCHRIFT (GW/0016-8904) [01751131] **3283**

GERMANISCHE DENKMALER DER VOLKERWANDERUNGSZEIT. SERIES B. DIE FRANKISCHEN ALTERTUMER DES RHEINLANDES (GW/0418-9779) [01566505] **269**

GERMANISCHES NATIONALMUSEUM NURNBERG *See* ANZEIGER DES GERMANISCHEN NATIONALMUSEUMS **337**

Alphabetical Title Index — GERMANY

GERMANISCHES NATIONALMUSEUM NURNBERG See ERWERBUNGEN, GESCHENKE UND LEIHGABEN **4087**

GERMANISTIK (BERLIN) (GW/0524-8414) [02737339] 3391, **3284**

GERMANISTIK (TUEBINGEN) (GW/0016-8912) [01696129] 3284, **3336**

GERMANISTISCHE ABHANDLUNGEN (STUTTGART) (GW/0435-5903) [01587706] **3284**

GERMANISTISCHE ARBEITSHEFTE (GW) [01451699] **3284**

GERMANISTISCHE LINGUISTIK (GW/0072-1492) [01780905] **3284**

GERMANISTISCHE MITTEILUNGEN (BE/0771-3703) [06125606] 3391, **3284**

GERMANISTISCHE SCHRIFTENREIHE DER NORWEGISCHEN UNIVERSITATEN UND HOCHSCHULEN (SW/0435-5911) [01451949] 3391, **3284**

GERMANISTISCHE TEXTE UND STUDIEN (GW/0175-9388) [09807890] 3391, **3284**

GERMANO-SLAVICA (CN/0317-4956) [01432630] **3391**

GERMANSKOE RABOCHEE I DEMOKRATICHESKOE DVIZHENIE V NOVEISHEE VREMIA (RU) [05626993] **1676**

GERMANTOWN COURIER (US) [12347513] **5736**

GERMANTOWN CRIER (US/0742-6631) [14184400] **2734**

GERMANTOWN PAPER, THE (US) [12323252] **5736**

GERMANTOWNE CRIER See GERMANTOWN CRIER **2734**

GERMANY. AUSWARTIGES AMT See AKTEN ZUR DEUTSCHEN AUSWARTIGEN POLITIK, 1918-1945. SER. E : 1941-1945 **2609**

GERMANY (DEMOCRATIC REPUBLIC, 1949-) See GESETZBLATT DER DEUTSCHEN DEMOKRATISCHEN REPUBLIK. TEIL 2 **4475**

GERMANY (DEMOCRATIC REPUBLIC, 1949-). METEOROLOGISCHER DIENST See ABHANDLUNGEN DES METEOROLOGISCHEN DIENSTES DER DEUTSCHEN DEMOKRATISCHEN REPUBLIK **1419**

GERMANY (DEMOCRATIC REPUBLIC, 1949-). OBERSTES GERICHT See ENTSCHEIDUNGEN IN ARBEITSRECHTSSACHEN **2966**

GERMANY (DEMOCRATIC REPUBLIC, 1949-). PRESSEAMT BEIM VORSITZENDEN DES MINISTERRATES See PRESSE-INFORMATIONEN **2703**

GERMANY (DEMOCRATIC REPUBLIC, 1949-). STAATLICHE ZENTRALVERWALTUNG FUR STATISTIK See KONTENRAHMEN FUR VOLKSEIGENE BETRIEBE UND KOMBINATE MIT VEREINFACHTEN ANFORDERUNGEN AN RECHNUNGSFUHRUNG UND STATISTIK **747**

GERMANY (DEMOCRATIC REPUBLIC, 1949-). ZENTRALINSTITUT FUER INFORMATION UND DOKUMENTATION See INFORMATION UND DOKUMENTATION : ANNOTIERTE TITELLISTE **3217**

GERMANY (EAST) See GESETZBLATT DER DEUTSCHEN DEMOKRATISCHEN REPUBLIK. SONDERDRUCK **2974**

GERMANY (EAST). AMT FUR STANDARDISIERUNG, MESSWESEN UND WARENPRUFUNG See MITTEILUNGEN DES AMTES FUR STANDARDISIERUNG, MESSWESEN UND WARENPRUFUNG **5129**

GERMANY (EAST) MINISTERIUM FUR VOLKSBILDUNG See VERFUGUNGEN UND MITTEILUNGEN DES MINISTERIUMS FUR VOLKSBILDUNG **1789**

GERMANY (EAST). MUSIKRAT See BULLETIN / MUSIKRAT DER DEUTSCHEN DEMOKRATISCHEN REPUBLIK, SEKTION DDR DES INTERNATIONALEN MUSIKRATES **4106**

GERMANY (FEDERAL REPUBLIC, 1949-) See VERMOEGENSTEUER-HAUPTVERANLAGUNG, DIE **3071**

GERMANY (FEDERAL REPUBLIC, 1949-). BEVOLLMACHTIGTER DER BUNDESREGIERUNG IN BERLIN. WIRTSCHAFT See JAHRESBERICHT - DER BEVOLLMACHTIGTE DER BUNDESREGIERUNG IN BERLIN, WIRTSCHAFT **1568**

GERMANY (FEDERAL REPUBLIC, 1949-). BUNDESARBEITSGERICHT See ENTSCHEIDUNGEN DES BUNDESARBEITSGERICHTS **3147**

GERMANY (FEDERAL REPUBLIC, 1949-) BUNDESARCHIV See FINDBUCHER ZU BESTANDEN DES BUNDESARCHIV **2481**

GERMANY (FEDERAL REPUBLIC, 1949-). BUNDESMINISTERIUM FUR ERNAHRUNG, LANDWIRTSCHAFT UND FORSTEN. ABTEILUNG 2, PLANUNGSKOORDINATION UND WIRTSCHAFTSBEOBACHTUNG. REFERAT 221 See ABSCHLUSSBERICHT UBER DIE BESONDERE ERNTEERMITTLUNG BEI GETREIDE UND KARTOFFELN / C.BUNDESMINISTERIUM FUR ERNAHRUNG, LANDWIRTSCHAFT UND FORSTEN, ABTEILUNG VI, WIRTSCHAFTSBEOBACHTUNG, VERBRAUCHERANGELEGENHEITEN, REFERAT VI A 2 **42**

GERMANY (FEDERAL REPUBLIC, 1949-). BUNDESMINISTERIUM FUR INNERDEUTSCHE BEZIEHUNGEN See ZAHLENSPIEGEL **5347**

GERMANY (FEDERAL REPUBLIC, 1949-). BUNDESMINISTERIUM FUR WIRTSCHAFT UND FINANZEN VERTRETUNG BERLIN See JAHRESBERICHT - BUNDESMINISTERIUM FUR WIRTSCHAFT UND FINANZEN. VERTRETUNG BERLIN **1568**

GERMANY (FEDERAL REPUBLIC, 1949-). BUNDESMINISTERIUM FUR WIRTSCHAFTLICHE ZUSAMMENARBEIT See ENTWICKLUNGSPOLITIK; JAHRESBERICHT **1560**

GERMANY (FEDERAL REPUBLIC, 1949-). BUNDESMINISTERIUM FUR WIRTSCHAFTLICHE ZUSAMMENARBEIT See WISSENSCHAFTLICHE SCHRIFTENREIHE **1527**

GERMANY (FEDERAL REPUBLIC, 1949-). BUNDESSTELLE FUR AUSSENHANDELSINFORMATION See URUGUAY: ENERGIEWIRTSCHAFT **1960**

GERMANY (FEDERAL REPUBLIC, 1949-). BUNDESSTELLE FUR AUSSENHANDELSINFORMATION See SAUDI-ARABIEN: ENERGIEWIRTSCHAFT **1956**

GERMANY (FEDERAL REPUBLIC, 1949-). BUNDESSTELLE FUR AUSSENHANDELSINFORMATION See LAND- UND FORSTWIRTSCHAFT, FISCHEREI. REIHE 4.3.1 : SCHLACHTTIER- UND FLEISCHBESCHAU **3482**

GERMANY (FEDERAL REPUBLIC, 1949-). BUNDESSTELLE FUR AUSSENHANDELSINFORMATION See ITALIEN : ENERGIEWIRTSCHAFT **1948**

GERMANY (FEDERAL REPUBLIC, 1949-). BUNDESSTELLE FUR AUSSENHANDELSINFORMATION See KOLUMBIEN : ENERGIEWIRTSCHAFT **1949**

GERMANY (FEDERAL REPUBLIC, 1949-). BUNDESSTELLE FUR AUSSENHANDELSINFORMATION See FINNLAND : ENERGIEWIRTSCHAFT **1944**

GERMANY (FEDERAL REPUBLIC, 1949-). BUNDESSTELLE FUR AUSSENHANDELSINFORMATION See USA : WIRTSCHAFTLICHE ENTWICKLUNG DER SUDOSTSTAATEN **1588**

GERMANY (FEDERAL REPUBLIC, 1949-). BUNDESSTELLE FUR AUSSENHANDELSINFORMATION See KENIA : ENERGIEWIRTSCHAFT **1949**

GERMANY (FEDERAL REPUBLIC, 1949-). BUNDESSTELLE FUR AUSSENHANDELSINFORMATION See PHILIPPINEN : ENERGIEWIRTSCHAFT **1953**

GERMANY (FEDERAL REPUBLIC, 1949-). BUNDESSTELLE FUR AUSSENHANDELSINFORMATION See MEXIKO : WIRTSCHAFTLICHE ENTWICKLUNG **1574**

GERMANY (FEDERAL REPUBLIC, 1949-). BUNDESSTELLE FUR AUSSENHANDELSINFORMATION See MOSAMBIK : ENERGIEWIRTSCHAFT **1950**

GERMANY (FEDERAL REPUBLIC, 1949-). BUNDESSTELLE FUR AUSSENHANDELSINFORMATION See MADAGASKAR : ENERGIEWIRTSCHAFT **1950**

GERMANY (FEDERAL REPUBLIC, 1949-). BUNDESSTELLE FUR AUSSENHANDELSINFORMATION See MALAWI : ENERGIEWIRTSCHAFT **1950**

GERMANY (FEDERAL REPUBLIC, 1949-). BUNDESSTELLE FUR AUSSENHANDELSINFORMATION See KAMERUN : ENERGIEWIRTSCHAFT **1949**

GERMANY (FEDERAL REPUBLIC, 1949-). BUNDESSTELLE FUR AUSSENHANDELSINFORMATION See LUXEMBURG : ENERGIEWIRTSCHAFT **1949**

GERMANY (FEDERAL REPUBLIC, 1949-). BUNDESSTELLE FUR AUSSENHANDELSINFORMATION See UGANDA : ENERGIEWIRTSCHAFT **1959**

GERMANY (FEDERAL REPUBLIC, 1949-). BUNDESSTELLE FUR AUSSENHANDELSINFORMATION See JAPAN. WIRTSCHAFTLICHE ENTWICKLUNG **1498**

GERMANY (FEDERAL REPUBLIC, 1949-). BUNDESSTELLE FUR AUSSENHANDELSINFORMATION See GROSSBRITANNIEN : ENERGIEWIRTSCHAFT **1945**

GERMANY (FEDERAL REPUBLIC, 1949-). BUNDESSTELLE FUR AUSSENHANDELSINFORMATION See SENEGAL : ENERGIEWIRTSCHAFT **1956**

GERMANY (FEDERAL REPUBLIC, 1949-). BUNDESSTELLE FUR AUSSENHANDELSINFORMATION See JORDANIEN : ENERGIEWIRTSCHAFT **1948**

GERMANY (FEDERAL REPUBLIC, 1949-). BUNDESSTELLE FUR AUSSENHANDELSINFORMATION See IRAK : ENERGIEWIRTSCHAFT **1948**

GERMANY (FEDERAL REPUBLIC, 1949-). BUNDESSTELLE FUR AUSSENHANDELSINFORMATION See NORWEGEN : ENERGIEWIRTSCHAFT **1951**

GERMANY (FEDERAL REPUBLIC, 1949-). BUNDESSTELLE FUR AUSSENHANDELSINFORMATION See IRAN : ENERGIEWIRTSCHAFT **1948**

GERMANY (FEDERAL REPUBLIC, 1949-). BUNDESSTELLE FUR AUSSENHANDELSINFORMATION See GRIECHENLAND : ENERGIEWIRTSCHAFT **1945**

GERMANY (FEDERAL REPUBLIC, 1949-). BUNDESSTELLE FUR AUSSENHANDELSINFORMATION See GUATEMALA : ENERGIEWIRTSCHAFT **1945**

GERMANY (FEDERAL REPUBLIC, 1949-). BUNDESSTELLE FUR AUSSENHANDELSINFORMATION See PARAGUAY : ENERGIEWIRTSCHAFT **1952**

GERMANY (FEDERAL REPUBLIC, 1949-). BUNDESSTELLE FUR AUSSENHANDELSINFORMATION See INDIEN : ENERGIEWIRTSCHAFT **1946**

GERMANY (FEDERAL REPUBLIC, 1949-). BUNDESSTELLE FUR AUSSENHANDELSINFORMATION See ELFENBEINKUSTE : ENERGIEWIRTSCHAFT **1937**

GERMANY (FEDERAL REPUBLIC, 1949-). BUNDESSTELLE FUR AUSSENHANDELSINFORMATION (GERMANY) See LIBYEN : WIRTSCHAFTLICHE ENTWICKLUNG **1572**

GERMANY (FEDERAL REPUBLIC, 1949-). BUNDESSTELLE FUR AUSSENHANDELSINFORMATION (GERMANY) See KATAR : WIRTSCHAFTLICHE ENTWICKLUNG **1570**

GERMANY (FEDERAL REPUBLIC, 1949-). BUNDESSTELLE FUR AUSSENHANDELSINFORMATION (GERMANY) See REPUBLIK KOREA : WIRTSCHAFTLICHE ENTWICKLUNG **1581**

GERMANY (FEDERAL REPUBLIC, 1949-). BUNDESSTELLE FUR AUSSENHANDELSINFORMATION (GERMANY) See NEUSEELAND : WIRTSCHAFTLICHE ENTWICKLUNG **1575**

GERMANY (FEDERAL REPUBLIC, 1949-). BUNDESSTELLE FUR AUSSENHANDELSINFORMATION (GERMANY) See KANADA : WIRTSCHAFTLICHE ENTWICKLUNG **1501**

GERMANY (FEDERAL REPUBLIC, 1949-). BUNDESVERSICHERUNGSAMT See TATIGKEITSBERICHT DES BUNDESVERSICHERUNGSAMTES **1713**

GERMANY (FEDERAL REPUBLIC, 1949-). BUNDESVERWALTUNGSGERICHT See ENTSCHEIDUNGEN DES BUNDESVERWALTUNGSGERICHT **2966**

GERMANY (FEDERAL REPUBLIC, 1949-). PATENTAMT See JAHRESBERICHT - DEUTSCHES PATENTAMT **1305**

GERMANY (FEDERAL REPUBLIC, 1949-) SEEWETTERAMT See WITTERUNG IN UBERSEE, DIE **1437**

GERMANY (FEDERAL REPUBLIC, 1949-). STATISTISCHES BUNDESAMT See AUSSENHANDEL. REIHE 8 : AUSSENHANDEL NACH DEM INTERNATIONALEN WARENVERZEICHNIS FUR DEN AUSSENHANDEL, SITC-REV. II, UND LANDERN, SPEZIALHANDEL **824**

GERMANY (FEDERAL REPUBLIC, 1949). STATISTISCHES BUNDESAMT See LANDERKURZBERICHTE : HONG KONG **5332**

GERMANY (FEDERAL REPUBLIC, 1949-). STATISTISCHES BUNDESAMT See LANDERBERICHT : GABUN **5331**

GERMANY (FEDERAL REPUBLIC) STATISTISCHES BUNDESAMT See GARTENBAU UND WEINWIRTSCHAFT. III. WEINWIRTSCHAFT **2416**

GERMANY (FEDERAL REPUBLIC). STATISTISCHES BUNDESAMT See DUNGEMITTELVERSORGUNG **170**

GERMANY (FEDERAL REPUBLIC). STATISTISCHES BUNDESAMT See WARENVERZEICHNIS FUER DIE AUSSENHANDELSSTATISTIK **1929**

GERMANY — Alphabetical Title Index

GERMANY. REICHSMINISTERIUM DES INNERN *See* REICHSMINISTERIALBLATT : ZENTRALBLATT FUER DAS DEUTSCHE REICH / HERAUSGEGEBEN IM REICHSMINISTERIUM DES INNERN **2705**

GERMANY REPORTS (GW) [01468630] **2689**

GERMANY. STATISTISCHES BUNDESAMT *See* VERZEICHNIS DER VEROFFENTLICHUNGEN / STATISTISCHES BUNDESAMT **4820**

GERMANY (SYRACUSE, N.Y.) (US/1056-4721) [23717079] **4475, 1564**

GERMANY (WEST) *See* BUNDESANZEIGER **4635**

GERMANY (WEST) *See* BUNDESGESETZBLATT **2945**

GERMANY (WEST). AUSWARTIGES AMT *See* LISTE DER DIPLOMATISCHEN MISSIONEN UND ANDEREN VERTRETUNGEN IN BONN **4662**

GERMANY (WEST). AUSWARTIGES AMT *See* KONSULARISCHE VERTRETUNGEN UND ANDERE VERTRETUNGEN IN DER BUNDESREPUBLIK DEUTSCHLAND UND BERLIN (WEST) **3132**

GERMANY (WEST). BUDNESSTELLE FUR AUSSENHANDELSINFORMATION *See* SRI LANKA (CEYLON) : WIRTSCHAFTLICHE ENTWICKLUNG **1585**

GERMANY (WEST). BUNDESAUFSICHTSAMT FUER DAS VERSICHERUNGS- UND BAUSPARWESEN. VEROFFENTLICHUNGEN *See* VEROFFENTLICHUNGEN **3071**

GERMANY (WEST). BUNDESAUFSICHTSAMT FUER DAS VERSICHERUNGSWESEN *See* VEROFFENTLICHUNGEN **3071**

GERMANY (WEST) BUNDESGERICHTSHOF *See* ENTSCHEIDUNGEN DES BUNDESGERICHTSHOFES IN ZIVILSACHEN **2966**

GERMANY (WEST). BUNDESGESUNDHEITSAMT. INSTITUT FUR WASSER-, BODEN- UND LUFTHYGIENE, FORSCHUNGSSTATTE FUR ALLGEMEINE HYGIENE UND GESUNDHEITSTECHNIK *See* VERZEICHNIS DER WISSENSCHAFTLICHEN VEROFFENTLICHUNGEN **4811**

GERMANY (WEST). BUNDESMINISTERIUM DER FINANZE *See* FINANZPLAN DES BUNDES, DER **4726**

GERMANY (WEST). BUNDESMINISTERIUM DER FINANZEN *See* CHRONIK DER FINANZ- UND WAHRUNGSPOLITIK **4717**

GERMANY (WEST). BUNDESMINISTERIUM DES INNERN. REFERAT OFFENTLICHKEITSARVEIT. VERFASSUNGSSCHUTZ *See* VERFASSUNGSSCHUTZBERICHT **1309**

GERMANY (WEST). BUNDESMINISTERIUM FUER BILDUNG UND WISSENSCHAFT *See* BERUFLICHE AUS- UND FORTBILDUNG **1911**

GERMANY (WEST). BUNDESMINISTERIUM FUER JUGEND, FAMILIE UND GESUNDHEIT *See* DATEN DES GESUNDHEITSWESENS **4809**

GERMANY (WEST). BUNDESMINISTERIUM FUER WIRTSCHAFT *See* ECONOMIC SITUATION IN THE FEDERAL REPUBLIC OF GERMANY, THE **1485**

GERMANY (WEST). BUNDESMINISTERIUM FUR ARBEIT UND SOZIALORDNUNG *See* ARBEITS- UND SOZIALSTATISTIKEN **1529**

GERMANY (WEST). BUNDESMINISTERIUM FUR FORSCHUNG UND TECHNOLOGIE *See* BMFT FORDERUNGSKATALOG **5089**

GERMANY (WEST). BUNDESMINISTERIUM FUR RAUMORDNUNG, BAUWESEN UND STADTEBAU *See* STADTEBAUBERICHT **2836**

GERMANY (WEST). BUNDESRAT *See* DRUCKSACHE - BUNDESRAT **4472**

GERMANY (WEST). BUNDESSTELLE FUR AUSSENHANDELSINFORMATION *See* HONDURAS, WIRTSCHAFTLICHE ENTWICKLUNG **1565**

GERMANY (WEST). BUNDESSTELLE FUR AUSSENHANDELSINFORMATION *See* PAKISTAN, WIRTSCHAFTLICHE ENTWICKLUNG **1577**

GERMANY (WEST). BUNDESSTELLE FUR AUSSENHANDELSINFORMATION *See* USA, WIRTSCHAFTSPOLITIK UND -ENTWICKLUNG **1588**

GERMANY (WEST). BUNDESSTELLE FUR AUSSENHANDELSINFORMATION *See* BOLIVIEN, WIRTSCHAFTLICHE ENTWICKLUNG **1549**

GERMANY (WEST). BUNDESSTELLE FUR AUSSENHANDELSINFORMATION *See* PORTUGAL, WIRTSCHAFTLICHE ENTWICKLUNG **1578**

GERMANY (WEST). BUNDESSTELLE FUR AUSSENHANDELSINFORMATION *See* TANSANIA: WIRTSCHAFTLICHE ENTWICKLUNG **1586**

GERMANY (WEST). BUNDESTAG *See* PROTOKOLL - DEUTSCHER BUNDESTAG **4492**

GERMANY (WEST). BUNDESVARFASSUNGSGERICHT *See* ENTSCHEIDUNGEN DES BUNDESVERFASSUNGSGERICHTS **2966**

GERMANY (WEST). FERNMELDETECHNISCHES ZENTRALAMT *See* AMTLICHES VERZEICHNIS DER TEILNEHMER DES OFFENTLICHEN BILDUBERTRAGUNGSNETZES **1148**

GERMANY (WEST). PRESSE- UND INFORMATIONSAMT *See* GERMANY REPORTS **2689**

GERMANY (WEST). PRESSE- UND INFORMATIONSAMT *See* AMTLICHE SCHRIFTTUM DER BUNDESREPUBLIK, DAS **407**

GERMANY (WEST). STATISTISCHES BUNDESAMT *See* LANDERKURZBERICHTE: KUBA **5332**

GERMANY (WEST). STATISTISCHES BUNDESAMT *See* BEVOLKERUNG UND ERWERBSTATIGKEIT. REIHE 4.1.1: STAND UND ENTWICKLUNG DER ERWERBSTATIGKEIT **1655**

GERMANY (WEST). STATISTISCHES BUNDESAMT *See* BAUTATIGKEIT UND WOHNUNGEN. REIHE 3: BESTAND AN WOHNUNGEN, FORTGESCHRIEBENE ERGEBNISSE **2815**

GERMANY (WEST). STATISTISCHES BUNDESAMT *See* HANDEL, GASTGEWERBE, REISEVERKEHR. REIHE 3.1: BESCHAFTIGTE UND UMSATZ IM EINZELHANDEL, MESSZAHLEN **955**

GERMANY (WEST). STATISTISCHES BUNDESAMT *See* FINANZEN UND STEUERN. REIHE 5: SCHULDEN DER OFFENTLICHEN HAUSHALTE **4726**

GERMANY (WEST). STATISTISCHES BUNDESAMT *See* LANDERKURZBERICHTE : BOLIVIEN **5331**

GERMANY (WEST). STATISTISCHES BUNDESAMT *See* LANDERKURZBERICHTE : VENEZUELA **5332**

GERMANY (WEST). STATISTISCHES BUNDESAMT *See* SOZIALLEISTUNGEN. REIHE 1: VERSICHERTE IN DER KRANKEN- UND RENTENVERSICHERUNG **5310**

GERMANY (WEST). STATISTISCHES BUNDESAMT *See* PREISE. REISE 6 : INDEX DER GROSSHANDELSVERKAUFSPREISE **1594**

GERMANY (WEST). STATISTISCHES BUNDESAMT *See* PRODUZIERENDES GEWERBE. REIHE 6.3: KOSTENSTRUKTUR DER UNTERNEHMEN IN DER ENERGIE- UND WASSERVERSORGUNG **2126**

GERMANY (WEST). STATISTISCHES BUNDESAMT *See* LANDERKURZBERICHTE : NEPAL **5332**

GERMANY (WEST). STATISTISCHES BUNDESAMT *See* PRODUZIERENDES GEWERBE. REIHE 4.1.1: BESCHAFTIGUNG, UMSATZ UND ENERGIEVERSORGUNG DER UNTERNEHMEN UND BETRIEBE IM BERGBAU UND IM VERARBEITENDEN GEWERBE **1703**

GERMANY (WEST). STATISTISCHES BUNDESAMT *See* LANDERKURZBERICHTE : PANAMA **5332**

GERMANY (WEST). STATISTISCHES BUNDESAMT *See* AUSSENHANDEL. REIHE 4.1 : EIN- UND AUSFUHR VON MINERALOL, GENERALHANDEL **4251**

GERMANY (WEST). STATISTISCHES BUNDESAMT *See* UNTERNEHMEN UND ARBEITSSTATTEN. REIHE 1 : DIE KOSTENSTRUKTUR IN DER WIRTSCHAFT. V. GROSSHANDEL, HANDELVERTRETER UND HANDELSMAKLER, VERLAGSWESEN **856**

GERMANY (WEST). STATISTISCHES BUNDESAMT *See* AUSSENHANDEL. REIHE 4: GENERALHANDEL. EIN- UND AUSFUHR VON MINERALOEL **4251**

GERMANY (WEST). STATISTISCHES BUNDESAMT *See* LANDERKURZBERICHT : NAMIBIA (SUDWESTAFRIKA) **5331**

GERMANY (WEST). STATISTISCHES BUNDESAMT *See* LOHNE UND GEHALTER. REIHE 2. 1 : ARBEITERVERDIENSTE IN DER INDUSTRIE **1688**

GERMANY (WEST). STATISTISCHES BUNDESAMT *See* LANDERKURZBERICHTE : PERU **5332**

GERMANY (WEST). STATISTISCHES BUNDESAMT *See* HANDEL, GASTGEWERBE, REISEVERKEHR. REIHE 6 WARENVERKEHR MIT DER DEUTSCHEN DEMOKRATISCHEN REPUBLIK UND BERLIN, OST **838**

GERMANY (WEST). STATISTISCHES BUNDESAMT *See* AUSSENHANDEL. REIHE 1: ZUSAMMENFASSENDE UBERSICHTEN FUER DEN AUSSENHANDEL **824**

GERMANY (WEST). STATISTISCHES BUNDESAMT *See* LANDERKURZBERICHTE : FRANZ. -GUAYANA **5331**

GERMANY (WEST). STATISTISCHES BUNDESAMT *See* AUSGEWAHLTE ZAHLEN FUER DIE BAUWIRTSCHAFT **599**

GERMANY (WEST). STATISTISCHES BUNDESAMT *See* LAND- UND FORSTWIRTSCHAFT, FISCHEREI. REIHE 3 : VIEHWIRTSCHAFT **2307**

GERMANY (WEST). STATISTISCHES BUNDESAMT *See* LANDERBERICHT : UNGARN **5331**

GERMANY (WEST). STATISTISCHES BUNDESAMT *See* GESUNDHEITSWESEN. REIHE 3: SCHWANGERSCHAFTSABBRUECHE **589**

GERMANY (WEST). STATISTISCHES BUNDESAMT *See* LANDERKURZBERICHTE : BAHRAIN, KATAR **5331**

GERMANY (WEST). STATISTISCHES BUNDESAMT *See* LANDERBERICHTE. CHILE **2552**

GERMANY (WEST). STATISTISCHES BUNDESAMT *See* GROSS- UND EINZELHANDEL, GASTGEWERBE, REISEVERKEHR. REIHE 8 : REISEVERKEHR. IV. GRENZUBERSCHREITENDER REISEVERKEHR **5478**

GERMANY (WEST). STATISTISCHES BUNDESAMT *See* LANDERKURZBERICHT : BELIZE **1572**

GERMANY (WEST). STATISTISCHES BUNDESAMT *See* AUSSENHANDEL. REIHE 3: AUSSENHANDEL NACH LAENDERN UND WARENGRUPPEN, SPEZIALHANDEL **824**

GERMANY (WEST). STATISTISCHES BUNDESAMT *See* LAND- UND FORSTWIRTSCHAFT, FISCHEREI. REIHE 2.1.1 : BETRIEBSGROSSENSTRUKTUR **103**

GERMANY (WEST). STATISTISCHES BUNDESAMT *See* LANDERKURZBERICHTE : JORDANIEN **5332**

GERMANY (WEST). STATISTISCHES BUNDESAMT *See* PREISE. REIHE 8 : PREISE UND PREISINDIZES FUER DIE EIN UND AUSFUHR **1594**

GERMANY (WEST). STATISTISCHES BUNDESAMT *See* LANDERKURZBERICHT : VIETNAM **1572**

GERMANY (WEST). STATISTISCHES BUNDESAMT *See* LANDERKURZBERICHTE : BAHAMAS **5331**

GERMANY (WEST). STATISTISCHES BUNDESAMT *See* VERKEHR. REIHE 6 : LUFTVERKEHR **39**

GERMANY (WEST). STATISTISCHES BUNDESAMT *See* LANDERKURZBERICHTE : REPUBLIK KOREA **5332**

GERMANY (WEST). STATISTISCHES BUNDESAMT *See* FINANZEN UND STEUERN. REIHE 2 : STEUERHAUSHALT VON BUND, LANDERN UND GEMEINDEN **4726**

GERMANY (WEST). STATISTISCHES BUNDESAMT *See* LANDERKURZBERICHTE : ZYPERN **5332**

GERMANY (WEST). STATISTISCHES BUNDESAMT *See* STATISTISCHER WOCHENDIENST **5343**

GERMANY (WEST). STATISTISCHES BUNDESAMT *See* LANDERKURZBERICHTE : KONGO **5332**

GERMANY (WEST). STATISTISCHES BUNDESAMT *See* VEROFFENTLICHUNGSVERZEICHNIS / STATISTISCHES BUNDESAMT **427**

GERMANY (WEST). STATISTISCHES BUNDESAMT. LANDERBERICHTE: KOLUMBIEN *See* STATISTIK DES AUSLANDES. LANDERBERICHT. KOLOMBIEN / HERAUSGEBER STATISTISCHES BUNDESAMT **5342**

GERMANY (WEST). STATISTISCHES BUNDESAMT. VEROFFENTLICHUNGSVERZEICHNIS *See* VERZEICHNIS DER VEROFFENTLICHUNGEN / STATISTISCHES BUNDESAMT **4820**

GERMANY (WEST). STATISTISCHES BUNDESAMT. VERZEICHNIS DER VEROFFENTLICHUNGEN DES STATISTISCHEN BUNDESAMTES *See* VEROFFENTLICHUNGSVERZEICHNIS / STATISTISCHES BUNDESAMT **427**

GERMANY'S TOP 300 : A HANDBOOK OF GERMANY'S LARGEST CORPORATIONS (GW) [24931681] **677**

GERMINATION (CN/0704-6286) [03790815] **3463**

GERMINATOR (LETHBRIDGE) (CN/1186-0049) [24265795] **173**

GERODONTOLOGY *SUSPENDED*. (US/0734-0664) [08731707] **3751**

GERONTOLOGICAL ABSTRACTS *CEASED*. (US/0736-4342) [03916304] **3751, 3659**

GERONTOLOGIE (FR) [06785299] **3751**

GERONTOLOGIE ET SOCIETE (PARIS) (FR/0151-0193) [20362217] **3751**

GERONTOLOGIST, THE (US/0016-9013) [01642377] **3751**

GERONTOLOGY & GERIATRICS EDUCATION (US/0270-1960) [06352193] **3752**

GERONTOLOGY (BASEL) (SZ/0304-324X) [01911556] **3752**

GERONTOLOGY SPECIAL INTEREST SECTION NEWSLETTER (US/0279-4101) [07841591] **3752**

GERONTOPHILE (SAINTE-FOY) (CN/0225-4271) [08063672] **5179**

GERSHON'S ... SPECIALIZED CATALOGUE OF ISRAEL AND THE HOLY LAND (US/0275-4967) [04836301] **2785**

GERTSENOVSKIE CHTENIIA: INOSTRANNYE IAZYKI (RU) [04990054] **3284**

GERTSENOVSKIE CHTENIIA; KHIMIIA (RU) [05699460] **976**

GESAMMELTE AUFSATZE ZUR KULTURGESCHICHTE SPANIENS (GW) [06723561] **2689**

GESAMMELTE WERKE GEORG WILHELM FRIEDRICH HEGEL (GW) **4347**

GESAMMELTE WERKE IN EINZELAUSGABEN *CEASED*. (GW) **3391**

GESAMTAUSGABE NICOLAUS COPERNICUS (GW) **5108**

GESAMTKATALOG DER DUSSELDORFER KULTURINSTITUTE (GDK) [MICROFORM] / BIBLIOTHEKSSTELLE DER DUSSELDORFER KULTURINSTITUTE (GW/0178-9775) [17460161] **4088, 351**

GESAMTSCHUL-INFORMATIONEN (GW/0340-7268) [04308082] **1748**

GESAR (US/0738-2294) [03923031] **5021**

GESCHAEFTSPARTNER UNGARN *CEASED*. (HU/0237-5478) [I02375478] **838**

GESCHAFTSBERICHT (AU) [19019002] **4650**

GESCHAFTSBERICHT (AU) [20640822] **1145**

GESCHAFTSBERICHT - ALLGEMEINE ORTSKRANKENKASSE BERLIN (GW) [01793873] **1676**

GESCHAFTSBERICHT DER BUNDESBAHN-VERSICHERUNGSANSTALT (GW) [03176007] **1676**

GESCHAFTSBERICHT DER INDUSTRIEGEWERKSCHAFT BAU, STEINE, ERDEN FUER DIE BUNDESREPUBLIK DEUTSCHLAND (GW/0340-6636) [01794174] **1607**

GESCHAFTSBERICHT / DEUTSCHE LUFTHANSA AKTIENGESELLSCHAFT (GW) [07086189] **22**

GESCHAFTSBERICHT / GEORG-AUGUST-UNIVERSITAT GOTTINGEN (GW) [20179065] **1800**

GESCHAFTSBERICHT (SCHWEIZERISCHE REEDEREI UND NEPTUN AG) (SZ) [02563916] **5449**

GESCHAFTSBERICHT UBER DIE TATIGKEIT DER GESELLSCHAFT (SZ) [04838297] **924**

GESCHAFTSBERICHT UND RECHNUNGSABSCHLUSS - STEIERMARKISCHE LANDESBAHNEN (AU) [03043763] **5431**

GESCHICHTE (SZ) [03146572] **2616**

GESCHICHTE DER DEUTSCHEN LITERATUR VON DEN ANFAENGEN BIS ZUR GEGENWART (GW) **3391**

GESCHICHTE DER PHARMAZIE (GW/0939-334X) **4306**

GESCHICHTE DES HOSPITALS (GW) [04814500] **3780**

GESCHICHTE IM WESTEN (GW/0930-3286) [16949012] **2689**

GESCHICHTE IN KOLN (GW/0720-3659) [09251490] **2689**

GESCHICHTE IN WISSENSCHAFT UND UNTERRICHT (GW/0016-9056) [01751172] **2616**

GESCHICHTE UND GESELLSCHAFT (GOTTINGEN) (GW/0340-613X) [02244423] **5201**

GESCHICHTLICHE ARBEITEN ZUR WESTFAELISCHEN LANDESFORSCHUNG (GW/0433-8413) [01452326] **2689**

GESCHICHTLICHE LANDESKUNDE (GW/0072-4203) [04366156] **2689**

GESCHICHTSBLATTER / ARBEITSKREIS WINDEGG IM SCHWERTBERGER KULTURRING (AU) [19224499] **2689**

GESCHIED- EN OUDHEIDKUNDIGE KRING VOOR LEUVEN EN OMGEVING *See* MEDEDELINGEN VAN DE GESCHIED- EN OUDHEIDKUNDIGE KRING VOOR LEUVEN EN OMGEVING **2697**

GESCHMACKSMUSTERBLATT (GW/0934-7062) [I09347062] **2974**

GESELLSCHAFT DER ORGELFREUNDE *See* VEROFFENTLICHUNG - GESELLSCHAFT DER ORGELFREUNDE **4158**

GESELLSCHAFT FUER BIOLOGISCHE CHEMIE *See* COLLOQUIUM DER GESELLSCHAFT FUER BIOLOGISCHE CHEMIE **485**

GESELLSCHAFT FUER KANADA-STUDIEN : MITTEILUNGEN (GW/0936-4595) [19730468] **2734**

GESELLSCHAFT FUER REAKTORSICHERHEIT *See* UBERSETZUNGEN, KERNTECHNISCHE REGELN **2159**

GESELLSCHAFT FUER SOZIALEN FORTSCHRITT *See* SCHRIFTEN - GESELLSCHAFT FUER SOZIALEN FORTSCHRITT **5257**

GESELLSCHAFT FUR BIOLOGISCHE CHEMIE *See* COLLOQUIUM - GESELLSCHAFT FUR BIOLOGISCHE CHEMIE **973**

GESELLSCHAFT FUR DIE GESCHICHTE UND BIBLIOGRAPHIE DES BRAUWESENS (BERLIN, GERMANY) *See* JAHRBUCH / GESELLSCHAFT FUR DIE GESCHICHTE UND BIBLIOGRAPHIE DES BRAUWESENS E.V **2368**

GESELLSCHAFT FUR INFORMATIK *See* JAHRESTAGUNG - GESELLSCHAFT FUER INFORMATIK E.V **1260**

GESELLSCHAFT FUR INFORMATIK *See* FACHTAGUNG UBER PROGRAMMIERSPRACHEN **1279**

GESELLSCHAFT FUR INFORMATION UND DOKUMENTATION *See* JAHRESBERICHT / GESELLSCHAFT FUR INFORMATION UND DOKUMENTATION **3219**

GESELLSCHAFT FUR NIEDERSACHSISCHE KIRCHENGESCHICHTE *See* JAHRBUCH DER GESELLSCHAFT FUER NIEDERSACHSISCHE KIRCHENGESCHICHTE **4967**

GESELLSCHAFT FUR OKOLOGIE (GERMANY) *See* VERHANDLUNGEN / GESELLSCHAFT FUER OKOLOGIE **2222**

GESELLSCHAFT FUR SCHLESWIG-HOLSTEINISCHE GESCHICHTE *See* MITGLIEDERVERZEICHNIS DER GESELLSCHAFT FUER SCHLESWIG-HOLSTEINISCHE GESCHICHTE **1574**

GESELLSCHAFT NATURFORSCHENDER FREUNDE (BERLIN, GERMANY) *See* SITZUNGS-BERICHTE DER GESELLSCHAFT NATURFORSCHENDER FREUNDE ZU BERLIN **4172**

GESELLSCHAFT UND POLITIK (AU/0016-9099) [01874627] **5201**

GESETZBLATT DER DEUTSCHEN DEMOKRATISCHEN REPUBLIC. SONDERDRUCK *CEASED*. (GE/0232-4849) [10470539] **2974**

GESETZBLATT DER DEUTSCHEN DEMOKRATISCHEN REPUBLIK. TEIL 2 (GW) [01587409] **4475**

GESETZE UND KOMMENTARE (AU) [21016224] **1676**

GESETZLICHE RENTENVERSICHERUNG, DIE (GW) [10962205] **5286**

GESHER (NEW YORK, N.Y.) (US) [03484451] **5047**

GESHER (WORLD JEWISH CONGRESS. ISRAEL EXECUTIVE) (IS/0435-8406) [02381264] **5047**

GESNERIAD JOURNAL (US) [21942932] **2416**

GESNERIAD SAINTPAULIA NEWS *See* SAINTPAULIA INTERNATIONAL NEWS **2430**

GESNERUS (SZ/0016-9161) [01751188] **3578**

GEST-GUEST QUARTERLY (US/1058-8736) [10740660] **2451**

GESTA (FORT TRYON PARK, N.Y.) (US/0016-920X) [01606201] **2689, 351**

GESTALT: ABHANDLUNGEN ZU EINER ALLGEMEINEN MORPHOLOGIE, DIE (GW) [01454860] **4347**

GESTALT JOURNAL, THE (US/0190-0412) [04519364] **3926, 4588**

GESTALT THEORY (GW/0170-057X) [06569258] **4588**

GESTION 2000 (BE/0773-0543) [12428053] **868**

GESTION ACTUALITE *SUSPENDED*. (FR) **868**

GESTION & SOCIETE (MR) [05623326] **868**

GESTION DE L'ENSEIGNEMENT SUPERIEUR (INT/1013-8501) [I10138501] **868, 1825**

GESTION HOSPITALARIA (SP/0214-8919) [I02148919] **3856**

GESTION (LAVAL) (CN/0701-0028) [03403197] **868**

GESTION SOCIALE (FR) **5201**

GESTIONESCUOLA (IT/0393-5523) [19037869] **869**

GESTIONS HOSPITALIERES (FR/0016-9218) [I00169218] **3780**

GESTOS (IRVINE, CALIF.) (US/1040-483X) [13684075] **5364**

GESTUS (US/0749-7644) [11193419] **3391**

GESUIDO KYOKAI SHI (JA/0021-4639) [08659610] **2230**

GESUNDE PFLANZEN (GW/0367-4223) [03084388] **2230**

GESUNDHEITSPOLITISCHE UMSCHAU (GW/0016-9307) [03974137] **3578, 4306**

GESUNDHEITSREPORT INTERN (GW) **3578**

●GESUNDHEITSWESEN, DAS (GW/0941-3790) [25545527] **4776**

GESUNDHEITSWESEN DER BUNDESREPUBLIK DEUTSCHLAND, DAS (GW) [02041064] **4776**

GESUNDHEITSWESEN IN NORDRHEIN-WESTFALEN, DAS (GW) [02474576] **4810**

GESUNDHEITSWESEN. REIHE 2, MELDEPFLICHTIGE KRANKHEITEN / HERAUSGEBER STATISTISCHES BUNDESAMT (GW) [11775764] **3713**

GESUNDHEITSWESEN. REIHE 2.3, SONSTIGE MELDEPFLICHTIGE KRANKHEITEN (STUTTGART. KOHLHAMMER. 1977) (GW/0173-3869) [04622733] **3713**

GESUNDHEITSWESEN. REIHE 3: SCHWANGERSCHAFTSABBRUECHE (GW) [04200430] **589**

●GET A CLUE: GUIDE TO CORNELL & ITHACA, NY (US/1063-1127) [25866576] **1091**

GET FIT (US/8750-8079) [11799936] **2597**

GET READY SHEET, THE (US/0148-7566) [03429733] **3212**

GET RICH NEWS *CEASED*. (US) **677**

GETAWAY (SA) **4872**

GETEROGENNYJ KATALIZ (BU/0254-4946) [10518308] **1015**

GETETZBLATT DER VERWALTUNG DES VEREINIGTEN WIRTSCHAFTGEBIETES *See* BUNDESGESETZBLATT **2945**

GETRANKETECHNIK (GW) [13528627] **2367**

GETREIDE, MEHL UND BROT (1972) (GW/0367-4177) [01771999] **201**

GETTING ABOUT BRITAIN (UK/0954-0369) [I09540369] **5478**

GETTING AHEAD IN DP *CEASED*. (US/0271-8669) [06697440] **1259**

GETTING INJURED WORKERS BACK TO WORK (US) **3086**

GETTING MARRIED (US/0891-1657) [14687394] **2280**

GETTING READY (US/1064-0827) [26221638] **1063**

●GETTING THE LOW-DOWN ON EMPLOYERS AND A LEG-UP ON THE JOB MARKET (US/1062-9238) [25809361] **4204**

●GETTING THE MOST FOR YOUR MEDICAL DOLLAR (US/1066-2367) [I10662367] **3578, 1297**

GETTING THERE (BURLINGTON, ONT.) (CN/0822-8450) [10809708] **1072**

GETTING THERE BY TRAIN, TRANSIT, BOAT & BUS (US/0731-5473) [07432138] **5383**

GETTING TOGETHER (AT/0155-1019) [I01551019] **1063**

GETTYSBURG REVIEW (1988) (US/0898-4557) [17598861] **3391**

GEURIN GAZETTE (US/0736-2838) [09086417] **2451**

GEUZENPENNING *See* BEELDENAAR, DE **2780**

GEVAARLIJKE STOFFEN (NE) **5383**

GEVANGENISSTATISTIEK (NE) [06401300] **3165**

GEWASBESCHERMING (NE/0166-6495) [04025685] **512**

GEWASSERKUNDLICHER Alphabetical Title Index

GEWASSERKUNDLICHER JAHRESBERICHT DES LANDES BERLIN (GW/0525-4787) [10356084] **1413**

GEWASSERKUNDLICHER JAHRESBERICHT FUER BERLIN UND UMLAND (GW) [27992934] **1413**

GEWASSERSCHUTZ, WASSER, ABWASSER (GW/0342-6068) [11287539] **5533**

GEWERBLICHER RECHTSSCHUTZ UND URHEBERRECHT (GW) [07375860] **1304**

GEWERBLICHER RECHTSSCHUTZ UND URHEBERRECHT. INTERNATIONALER TEIL (GW/0435-8600) [05921626] **2974**

GEWERKSCHAFTER, DER (GW/0433-9118) [05252098] **1676**

GEWERKSCHAFTLICHE MONATSHEFTE (GW/0016-9447) [03427718] **1676**

GEWERKSCHAFTLICHE RUNDSCHAU (SZ) [01798874] **1676**

GEWERKSCHAFTLICHE RUNDSCHAU FUER DIE SCHWEIZ *See* GEWERKSCHAFTLICHE RUNDSCHAU **1676**

GEWERKSCHAFTS JAHRBUCH (GW) [12337364] **1676**

● GEWINA (NE) [26111629] 3507, 3578, **5108**

GEWUSST WO? IN OFFENBACH (GW) [06616138] **2689**

GEYER'S OFFICE DEALER *CEASED.* (US/0746-8997) [10378634] **4211**

GEZELLIANA (BE/0776-4111) [24488459] 3391, **3284**

GEZIN LISSE *CEASED.* (NE/0921-9684) [I09219684] **2280**

GEZINSBELEID IN VLAANDEREN (BE) **2280**

GF NEWS (US/0271-7328) [05853828] **2342**

● GFF (SW/1103-5897) [30338230] **1381**

GFG REPORT (IO/0852-0070) [I08520070] **2383**

GFOA NEWSLETTER (US/1051-6964) [21478687] **4727**

GFWC CLUBWOMAN (US/0745-2209) [08924574] **5557**

GGD-NIEWS (GRAVENHAGE) (NE/0921-8343) [I09218343] 3780, **4776**

GH MAGAZINE *See* HQ MAGAZINE **2510**

GHAA'S NATIONAL DIRECTORY OF HMOS (US/0897-3059) [13179121] **4776**

GHANA BROADCASTING CORPORATION *See* GBC RADIO AND TV TIMES **1132**

GHANA ECONOMIC REVIEW (GH) [01787505] **1564**

GHANA: ENERGIEWIRTSCHAFT (GW) [05063941] **1945**

GHANA ENTERPRISE (GH) [02711036] **838**

GHANA FARMER, THE (GH/0046-5917) [09793638] **90**

GHANA GEOGRAPHICAL ASSOCIATION *See* BULLETIN OF THE GHANA GEOGRAPHICAL ASSOCIATION **2557**

GHANA JOURNAL OF CHEMISTRY (GH/0855-0484) [I08550484] **976**

GHANA JOURNAL OF EDUCATION (GH/0534-0349) [05883075] **1748**

GHANA JOURNAL OF SCIENCE (GH/0016-9544) [01751201] **5108**

GHANA JOURNAL OF SOCIOLOGY (GH/0435-9380) [01455493] **5246**

GHANA MEDICAL JOURNAL (GH/0016-9560) [03101522] **3578**

GHANA NATIONAL BIBLIOGRAPHY (GH/0072-4378) [01751202] **416**

GHANA NATIONAL BIBLIOGRAPHY BI MONTHLY (GH) [17743634] **416**

GHANA RADIO & TELEVISION TIMES *See* GBC RADIO AND TV TIMES **1132**

GHANA REVIEW (GH) [02246693] **2499**

GHANA SOCIAL SCIENCE JOURNAL (GH/0046-5925) [01457564] **5201**

GHANA : WIRTSCHAFTLICHE ENTWICKLUNG (GW) [05143404] **1564**

GHANA : WIRTSCHAFTSDATEN UND WIRTSCHAFTSDOKUMENTATION (GW) [06218209] **1564**

GHENT. RIJKSUNIVERSITEIT. HOGERE SCHOOL VOOR HANDELS- EN ECONOMISCHE WETENSCHAPPEN *See* WERKEN - GHENT. RIJKSUNIVERSITEIT. HOGERE SCHOOL VOOR HANDELS- EN ECONOMISCHE WETENSCHAPPEN **1853**

GHOST DANCE (US/0016-9633) [01457729] **3391**

● GHOST RIDER & BLAZE : SPIRITS OF VENGEANCE (US/1065-8785) [26782428] **4862**

GHOST TOWN QUARTERLY *CEASED.* (US) **2534**

● GI CANCER (US/1064-9700) [26478212] **3817**

GI. GESUNDHEITS-INGENIEUR (1985) (GW/0932-6200) [12164483] **2230**

GI JOE (US) **4862**

GIA NET NEWS *See* LOUPE (SANTA MONICA, CALIF.) **2915**

GIA QUARTERLY (US/1070-7794) [28131154] **4119**

GIAIDS. GIORNALE ITALIANO DELL' AIDS (IT/1120-7892) [I11207892] 4776, **3669**

GIALLO MONDADORI (IT) **3463**

GIANNINI FOUNDATION RESEARCH REPORT (1987) (US/0899-3068) [16991865] 1492, **90**

GIANTS NEWSWEEKLY, THE (US/0279-0238) [07444995] **4896**

GIAPPONE, IL (IT) [01798089] **2651**

GIARDINI (IT/0394-0853) [I03940853] **2417**

GIARDINO FIORITO, IL (IT) [04025722] **2417**

GIATROS DERMATOLOGIE (GW/0932-8661) [I09328661] **3720**

GIATROS HNO (GW/0930-8318) [I09308318] **3888**

GIATROSERTHOPAEDIE (GW/0930-8326) [I09308326] **3881**

GIATROSGYNAKOLOGIE (GW/0177-9109) [I01779109] **3761**

GIATROSPAEDIATRIE (GW/0177-9095) [I01779095] **3903**

GIATROSUROLOGIE (GW/0178-7527) [I01787527] **3990**

GIBBONS STAMP MONTHLY (UK) [03611511] **2785**

GIBIER, FAUNE SAUVAGE (FR/0761-9243) [19039753] 456, **2216**

GIBRIDNYE VYCHISLITELNYE MASHINY I KOMPLEKSY (UN/0207-0111) [06700438] **1251**

GIBSON COUNTY LINES *See* COUNTY LINES (PRINCETON, IND.) **2444**

GIBSON COUNTY LINES (US/1053-4946) [19033710] **2451**

GICOCAM : GUIDE INDUSTRIEL & COMMERCIAL DU CAMEROUN (CM) [07486592] **1564**

GIDDINGS TIMES AND NEWS (US) [15925130] **5750**

GIDEON, THE (US) [01776434] **5016**

GIDROBIOLOGICESKIJ ZURNAL (UN/0375-8990) [03128549] **495**

GIDROKHIMICHESKIE MATERIALY (RU/0367-4665) [01640337] 5533, **976**

GIDROLIZNAIA I LESOKHIMICHESKAIA PROMYSHLENNOST. ENGLISH. HYDROLYSIS AND WOOD CHEMISTRY USSR *See* HYDROLYSIS AND WOOD CHEMISTRY **4234**

GIDROLIZNAIA I LESOKHIMICHESKAILA PROMYSHLENNOST (RU/0016-9706) [04025760] **2401**

GIDROLIZNAIA I LESOKHIMISCHESKAIA PROMYSHLENNOST (US/0730-8124) [05877806] **4233**

GIDROTEHNICESKOE STROITELSTVO (MOSKVA) (RU/0016-9714) [01645524] **5533**

GIDS (NE/0016-9730) [01751214] **3343**

GIDS (AMSTERDAM, NETHERLANDS) (NE) [09601393] 3391, **4475**

GIDS OP MAATSCHAPPELIJK GEBIED (BE/0378-4657) [103784657] **5286**

GIDS VOOR HET AANVRAGEN VAN Z. W.O.-STEUN / NEDERLANDSE ORGANISATIE VOOR ZURIVER-WETENSCHAPPELIJK ONDERZOEK (NE) [11609664] **5108**

GIDS VOOR PERSONEELSMANAGEMENT (NE/0165-0289) [16733002] **941**

GIESSEN. UNIVERSITAT BIBLIOTHEK *See* KURZBERICHTE AUS DEN PAPYRUSSAMMLUNGEN / BIBLIOTHEK DER JUSTUS LIEBIG-HOCHSCHULE **1078**

GIESSENER BEITRAEGE ZUR ENTWICKLUNGSFORSCHUNG. REIHE 2 : MONOGRAPHIEN (GW/0435-9763) [09925163] **90**

GIESSENER BEITRAEGE ZUR KUNSTGESCHICHTE (GW/0342-104X) [02489527] **351**

GIESSENER GEOGRAPHISCHE SCHRIFTEN (GW/0435-978X) [04025835] **2565**

GIESSENER STUDIENREIHE HEIL - UND SONDERPADAGOGIK (GW/0174-481X) [05671347] **1879**

GIESSEREI (GW/0016-9765) [09871876] **4003**

GIESSEREI RUNDSCHAU (AU/0016-979X) [11009406] **4003**

GIESSEREIFORSCHUNG (GW/0046-5933) [01936641] **4003**

GIETERIJEN / CENTRAAL BUREAU VOOR DE STATISTIEK, HOOFDAFDELING STATISTIEKEN VAN INDUSTRIE EN BOUWNIJVERHEID (NE/0168-5961) [10283220] **1607**

GIFAP BULLETIN (BE/0770-920X) [11449615] **1025**

GIFAP DIRECTORY (BE) [10066956] **1607**

GIFFORD PINCHOT NATIONAL FOREST (US/0091-7680) [01787533] **2383**

GIFT AND ART BUYERS DIRECTORY *See* GIFT AND DECORATIVE ACCESSORY BUYERS DIRECTORY, THE **2584**

GIFT AND DECORATIVE ACCESSORY BUYERS DIRECTORY, THE (US/0072-4505) [01793738] **2584**

GIFT & STATIONERY BUSINESS (US/0896-4092) [16905637] **2584**

GIFT BASKET IDEA NEWSLETTER (US) 2584, **2584**

GIFT BASKET REVIEW (US/1050-0316) [21378129] 1607, **2584**

GIFT BUYER INTERNATIONAL (UK) **2584**

GIFT REPORTER (US/0894-4113) [16086737] **2584**

GIFTED CHILD QUARTERLY, THE (US/0016-9862) [03337727] **1879**

GIFTED CHILD TODAY *See* GIFTED CHILD TODAY MAGAZINE **1879**

● GIFTED CHILD TODAY MAGAZINE (US/1076-2175) [29578458] **1879**

GIFTED CHILD TODAY, THE (US/0892-9580) [14217612] 1879, **1063**

GIFTED CHILDREN MONTHLY *SUSPENDED.* (US/8750-684X) [11672084] **1879**

GIFTED EDUCATION INTERNATIONAL (UK/0261-4294) [09614729] **1879**

GIFTED EDUCATION PRESS QUARTERLY (US/1064-0053) [26188724] **1879**

GIFTED EDUCATION REVIEW (US/1060-3166) [24929956] **1879**

GIFTS & DECORATIVE ACCESSORIES (US/0016-9889) [01751222] **2584**

GIFTS & HOME PRODUCTS (HK) [28616037] 2584, **2906**

GIFTS AND HOUSEWARES ACCESSORIES (CH) 2584, **2811**

GIFTS & TABLEWARES (CN/0700-9380) [03348698] **2584**

GIFTS AND TABLEWARES TRADE DIRECTORY (CN) **2584**

GIFTS TODAY (UK) **2584**

GIFTS YOU CAN MAKE FOR CHRISTMAS (US/0092-3850) [01789783] 373, **2584**

GIFTWARE NEWS (US/0193-2551) [05165541] **2584**

GIFU DAIGAKU GAKUGEI GAKUBU KENKYU HOKOKU. SHIZEN KAGAKU *See* KYOIKUGAKUBU KENKYU HOKOKU. SHIZEN KAGAKU (GIFU) **5124**

GIFU DAIGAKU IGAKUBU KIYO (JA/0072-4521) [06297106] **3578**

GIFU DAIGAKU. KYOIKUGAKUBU FUZOKU SHOGAKKO *See* KENKYU HOKOKU - GIFU DAIGAKU KYOIKUGAKUBU FUZOKU SHOGAKKO **1899**

GIFU DAIGAKU. NOGAKUBU *See* GIFU DAIGAKU NOGAKUBU KENKYU HOKOKU **90**

GIFU DAIGAKU NOGAKUBU KENKYU HOKOKU (JA/0072-4513) [09476475] **90**

GIFU, JAPAN. UNIVERSITY. FACULTY OF EDUCATION *See* SCIENCE REPORT OF THE FACULTY OF EDUCATION, GIFU UNIVERSITY (NATURAL SCIENCE) **5153**

GIFU-KEN EISEI KENKYUJOHO (JA/0385-1575) [10266795] **4776**

GIFU-KEN (JAPAN). KANKYOBU *See* KANKYO HAKUSHO **2234**

GIFU-KEN SEISHIN EISEI SENTA *See* GIFU-KEN SEISHIN EISEI SENTA SHOHO **4777**

GIFU-KEN SEISHIN EISEI SENTA SHOHO (JA) [01790264] **4777**

GIFU SHIKA GAKKAI ZASSHI (JA/0385-0072) [08025218] **1324**

GIFU UNIVERSITY. FACULTY OF AGRICULTURE *See* RESEARCH BULLETIN OF THE FACULTY OF AGRICULTURE, GIFU UNIVERSITY **127**

GIFU YAKKA DAIGAKU *See* GIFU YAKKA DAIGAKU KIYO **4306**

GIFU YAKKA DAIGAKU KIYO (JA/0434-0094) [09390859] **4306**

GIGIENA I SANITARIIA (1943) (RU/0016-9900) [09418930] **2597**

GIGIENA NASELENIH MISC (UN/0301-2468) [05175731] **4777**

Alphabetical Title Index — GIS

GIGIENA TRUDA I PROFESSIONALNYE ZABOLEVANIJA (RU/0016-9919) [05755476] **2862**

GIGIENICESKIE ASPEKTY OHRANY OKRUZAJUSCEJ SREDY (RU/0131-1697) [02972879] **2172**

GIGUERERIE (EDITION FRANCAISE) (CN/0713-3162) [08794532] **2451**

GIHO (BOEICHO GIJUTSU KENKYU HONGU (JAPAN)) See GIJUTSU KENKYU HONBU GIHO **5108**

GIJUTSU JOHO (JA) [03407617] **5108**

GIJUTSU KENKYU HONBU GIHO (JA) [09553532] **5108**

GIJUTSU RENKAN CHOSA KENKYU HOKOKUSHO (JA) [03127386] **4003**

GIJUTSU TO NINGEN (JA) [03352286] **5108**

GIKAI SHIRYO (JA) [02498037] **4650**

GIKEN GEPPO (JA) [09262339] **1132**

GILA BEND SUN NEWSPAPER (US) **5630**

GILA HERITAGE (US/0893-7753) [13421771] **2451**

GILBERT & SULLIVAN NEWS (UK/0263-7995) [I02637995] **385**

GILBERT CRIMINAL LAW AND PROCEDURE OF NEW YORK (US) [06109819] **3107**

GILBERT LAW SUMMARIES. CONFLICT OF LAWS (US/0270-2908) [06333681] **2974**

GILBERT LAW SUMMARIES CONTRACTS (US) [05626958] **2974**

GILBERT LAW SUMMARIES. CRIMINAL LAW (US/0193-7200) [05232500] **3107**

GILBERT LAW SUMMARIES: CRIMINAL PROCEDURE (US/0193-8010) [05232137] **3107**

GILCHRIST COUNTY JOURNAL (US) [01458649] **2534**

●GILCREASE JOURNAL (US/1070-7808) [28136012] **351**

GILCREASE MAGAZINE OF AMERICAN HISTORY AND ART See GILCREASE JOURNAL **351**

GILCREASE MAGAZINE OF AMERICAN HISTORY AND ART, THE (US/0730-5036) [05111161] 2734, **4088**

GILDEA REVIEW (US/0892-1776) [15144803] **2194**

GILES COUNTY HISTORICAL SOCIETY BULLETIN, THE (US) [25264801] **2451**

GILGAMESH (IQ) [15139508] **321**

GILMER MIRROR, THE (US/8750-0884) [10961415] **5750**

GILMORE SUGAR MANUAL, THE (US/0748-6782) [08741586] **173**

●GIM. GEODETICAL INFO MAGAZINE (NE/0928-1436) [I09281436] **1406**

GIMTOJI KALBA (LI) [23361618] **1112**

GINE-DIPS (SP/0211-6901) [08061173] **3761**

GINECOLOGIA CLINICA (IT/0392-2944) [13104284] **3761**

GINECOLOGIA DELL'INFANZIA E DELL'ADOLESCENZA **CEASED.** (IT/0393-5337) [I03953537] **3761**

GINECOLOGIA Y OBSTETRICIA DE MEXICO (MX/0300-9041) [01751227] **3761**

GINECOLOGIA Y OBSTETRICIA : TEMAS ACTUALES (SP) **3761**

GINEKOLOGIA POLSKA. SUPLEMENT (PL) [05878903] **3761**

GINKA (JA) **2774**

GINKO TORIHIKI SHOROPPO / HAYASHI RYOHEI ... HOKA HENSHU (JA) [08879620] **3086**

GINNASTA (IT) **4896**

GINNASTICA MEDICA, LA (IT/0431-8722) [I04318722] **3954**

GIOIA (IT/0017-0062) [I00170062] **5557**

GIORGIO LEVI DELLA VIDA CONFERENCES (US/0340-6369) [05230528] 2651, **2639**

GIORNALE BOTANICO ITALIANO (FLORENCE, ITALY : 1962) (IT/0017-0070) [03133191] **512**

GIORNALE CRITICO DELLA FILOSOFIA ITALIANA (IT/0017-0089) [01715115] **1077**

GIORNALE DEGLI ECONOMISTI E ANNALI DI ECONOMIA (IT/0017-0097) [06706022] **1492**

GIORNALE DEGLI IGIENISTI INDUSTRIALI (IT) **2862**

GIORNALE DEI CONGRESSI MEDICI : GCM : L'AGGIORNAMENTO IN DIRETTA DAI CONGRESSI, IL (IT/0391-8866) [26319999] **3578**

GIORNALE DEI GENITORI, IL **SUSPENDED.** (IT) [01787299] **1804**

GIORNALE DEL FARMACISTA, IL (IT/0393-8476) [I03938476] **4306**

GIORNALE DEL GENIO CIVILE (IT/0017-016X) [06012737] **2024**

GIORNALE DEL MEDICO, IL (IT/0393-8492) [I03938492] **3578**

GIORNALE DELL EDILIZIA E DEL RIVENDITORE EDILE, IL (IT) **615**

GIORNALE DELL ICE (IT) **2056**

GIORNALE DELL' INSTALLATORE ELETTRICO, IL (IT/0392-3630) [I03923630] **2056**

GIORNALE DELL' OFFICINA (IT/0017-0240) [I00170240] **2115**

GIORNALE DELLA LIBRERIA (IT) [06842326] **4815**

GIORNALE DELLA MUSICA, IL (IT/1120-6195) [23234686] **4119**

GIORNALE DELLA NATURA (IT) **2216**

GIORNALE DELLA SUBFORNITURA, IL (IT/0392-3622) [I03923622] **1607**

GIORNALE DELLA VELA, IL (IT) **593**

GIORNALE DELL'ARTE (TURIN, ITALY) (IT/0394-0543) [09739371] **321**

GIORNALE DELL'ARTERIOSCLEROSI (IT/0017-0224) [01641586] **3704**

GIORNALE DELLE ASSICURAZIONI (IT) **2881**

GIORNALE DELLE PROVE NON DISTRUTTIVE (IT) **5108**

GIORNALE DELL'INGEGNERE, IL (IT) **1976**

GIORNALE DELL'INSTALLATORE TELEFONICO, IL (IT/1120-219X) [I1120219X] 1156, **1976**

GIORNALE DELLO SPETTACOLO (IT/0017-0232) [I00170232] **385**

GIORNALE DI AGRICOLTURA **SUSPENDED.** (IT/0304-064X) [I0304064X] **90**

GIORNALE DI AGRICOLTURA See ITALIA AGRICOLA, L' **98**

GIORNALE DI ANESTESIA STOMATOLOGICA (IT/0391-5670) [13554435] **1324**

GIORNALE DI BRESCIA (IT) **5804**

GIORNALE DI CHIRURGIA, IL (IT/0391-9005) [22238710] **3965**

GIORNALE DI CLINICA MEDICA See G & B : GIORNALE DI CLINIA MEDICA & BASI RAZIONALI DELLA TERAPIA **3578**

GIORNALE DI EMODINAMICA **CEASED.** (IT/0392-7679) [10904610] **3704**

GIORNALE DI GEOLOGIA (IT/0017-0291) [01787413] 1449, **1381**

GIORNALE DI GERONTOLOGIA (IT/0017-0305) [01586563] **3752**

GIORNALE DI MALATTIE INFETTIVE E PARASSITARIE (IT/0017-0321) [07482034] **4777**

GIORNALE DI MARKETING (IT/0391-6413) [I03916413] **924**

GIORNALE DI MEDICINA MILITARE (IT/0017-0364) [01590009] **3578**

GIORNALE DI METAFISICA (IT) [05809006] **4347**

GIORNALE DI MONCALIERI (IT) **5804**

GIORNALE DI NAPOLI (IT) **5804**

GIORNALE DI NEUROPSICHIATRIA DELL'ETA EVOLUTIVA : ORGANO UFFICIALE DELLA SOCIETA ITALIANA DI NEUROPSICHIATRIA INFANTILE (IT/0392-4483) [13405921] 4588, **3833**

GIORNALE DI NEUROPSICOFARMACOLOGIN (IT/0391-9048) [I03919048] **4306**

GIORNALE DI RIABILITAZIONE CARDIOLOGICA ANGIOLOGICA RESPIRATORIA (IT) **3704**

GIORNALE DI SCIENZE AMBIENTALI **SUSPENDED.** (IT) **5108**

GIORNALE DI TECNICHE NEFROLOGICHE & DIALITICHE (IT/0394-9362) [I03949362] **3990**

GIORNALE DI VICENZA (IT) **5804**

GIORNALE D'ITALIA (IT) **5804**

GIORNALE INTERNAZIONALE DI DERMATOLOGIA PEDIATRICA (IT/1120-0499) [I11200499] 3903, **3720**

GIORNALE ITALIANO DELLE MALATTIE DEL TORACE **CEASED.** (IT/0017-0437) [06341874] **3949**

GIORNALE ITALIANO DI ALLERGOLOGIA E IMMUNOLOGIA CLINICA (IT/1120-6373) [I11206373] **3670**

GIORNALE ITALIANO DI ANGIOLOGIA (IT/0392-1387) [12700359] **3705**

GIORNALE ITALIANO DI CARDIOLOGIA (IT/0046-5968) [01590248] **3705**

GIORNALE ITALIANO DI CHEMIOTERAPIA **CEASED.** (IT/0017-0445) [01779016] **3578**

GIORNALE ITALIANO DI CHIMICA CLINICA (IT/0392-2227) [07788158] **976**

GIORNALE ITALIANO DI CHIRURGIA (IT/0017-0453) [01779017] **3965**

GIORNALE ITALIANO DI DERMATOLOGIA E VENEREOLOGIA (IT/0392-0488) [06764756] **3720**

GIORNALE ITALIANO DI DIABETOLOGIA (IT/0391-7525) [11247186] **3730**

GIORNALE ITALIANO DI ENDOSCOPIA DIGESTIVA : ORGANO UFFICIALE DELLA SOCIETA ITALIANA DI ENDOSCOPIA DIGESTIVA (IT) [19022364] **3796**

GIORNALE ITALIANO DI ENTOMOLOGIA (IT/0392-7296) [09553832] **5609**

GIORNALE ITALIANO DI FARMACIA CLINICA (IT/1120-3749) [I11203749] **4306**

GIORNALE ITALIANO DI FILOLOGIA (IT/0017-0461) [01458904] 3343, **3284**

GIORNALE ITALIANO DI MEDICINA DEL LAVORO (IT/0391-9889) [06026118] **3578**

GIORNALE ITALIANO DI NEFROLOGIA (IT/0393-5590) [I03935590] **3990**

GIORNALE ITALIANO DI ONCOLOGIA (IT/0392-128X) [12700567] 3965, **3817**

GIORNALE ITALIANO DI ORTOPEDIA E TRAUMATOLOGIA (IT/0390-0134) [04578691] **3881**

GIORNALE ITALIANO DI OSTETRICIA E GINECOLOGIA (IT/0391-9013) [13644393] **3761**

GIORNALE ITALIANO DI PSICOLOGIA (IT/0390-5349) [02246238] **4588**

GIORNALE ITALIANO DI RICERCHE CLINICHE E TERAPEUTICHE (IT/0393-5957) [I03935957] **3578**

GIORNALE ITALIANO PROVE NON DISTRUTTIVE See GIORNALE DELLE PROVE NON DISTRUTTIVE **5108**

GIORNALE STORICO DELLA LETTERATURA ITALIANA (IT/0017-0496) [01200595] **3391**

GIORNALE STORICO DELLA LUNIGIANA (IT/0017-050X) [02408160] 2689, **269**

GIORNALE STORICO DI PSICOLOGIA DINAMICA (IT/0391-2515) [05259484] **4588**

GIORNALINO (IT) **2488**

GIORNALINO (NEW YORK, N.Y.), IL **CEASED.** (US/0434-0299) [09292214] **1748**

GIORNI CANTATI (ROME, ITALY) (IT) [16678289] **351**

GIORNO, IL (IT) **5804**

GIPOTEZY, PROGNOZY (RU) [20860787] **5108**

GIPPSLAND WRITER (AT/0817-4148) [I08174148] **3463**

GIRARD GAZETTE, THE (US) [08807663] **5660**

GIRARD HOME NEWS (US) [12328867] **5736**

GIRARD PRESS, THE (US) [10828889] **5675**

GIRL GROUPS GAZETTE, THE (US) **4119**

GIRL GUIDES OF CANADA See POLICY, ORGANIZATION AND RULES - GIRL GUIDES OF CANADA **5235**

GIRL SCOUT LEADER (US/0017-0577) [01751247] **5231**

GIRL SCOUTS AROUND NEW YORK (US/0747-508X) [10733311] **5231**

GIRLS & BOYS TOGETHER (US/0361-9729) [02441353] **3458**

GIRLS' AND WOMEN'S TAEKWONDO NEWSLETTER, THE (US/0882-5920) [11893603] **4896**

GIRLS BASKETBALL RULES BOOK. NATIONAL FEDERATION EDITION (US/0361-5839) [02246908] **4896**

GIRLS CLUBS OF AMERICA, INC See ANNUAL REPORT / GIRLS CLUBS OF AMERICA **1060**

GIRLS GYMNASTICS JUDGING MANUAL. NATIONAL FEDERATION EDITION (US/0197-162X) [04185802] **4896**

GIRONALE DEI GIOCATTOLI (IT) **2584**

GIROZENTRALE UND BANK DER OSTERREICHISCHEN SPARKASSEN See BORSE (WIEN) **892**

GIS APPLICATION NOTE (US/1054-0563) [22438039] 1247, **2384**

GIS FORUM, THE **CEASED.** (US/1041-2697) [18702150] **3212**

GIS. GEO-INFORMATIONS-SYSTEME (GW/0935-1523) [I09351523] **1356**

... GIS GUIDE TO FOUR-YEAR COLLEGES, THE **CEASED.** (US/0897-8956) [17658949] **1825**

●GIS LAW (US/1065-2027) [26528855] **2974**

GIS NEWSLETTER (US/1062-791X) [02640226] **1381**

GIS SOURCEBOOK See INTERNATIONAL GIS SOURCEBOOK **2566**

GIS WORLD (US/0897-5507) [17541993] **2565**

GISSING JOURNAL, THE (UK) [23200276] **3391**

GIST (CAMPO, CALIF.) (US/0732-7781) [08433412] **4347**

GISTER EN VANDAG (SA) 2617, **1895**

GIT SPEZIAL. CHROMATOGRAPHIE (GW/0940-032X) [27052236] **1015**

GITARRE + LAUTE (GW/0172-9683) [05976344] **4119**

GITE (ST-JOSEPH) (CN/0705-7520) [04256105] 5071, **2805**

GITES DU PASSANT AU QUEBEC (CN/1187-421X) [25796299] **2805**

GITES DU PASSANT AU QUEBEC (CN/1187-421X) [25796296] **2805**

GIUNTE E COMMISSIONI PARLAMENTARI (IT) [07288553] **4475**

GIURISPRUDENZA AGRARIA ITALIANA (IT) **2974**

GIURISPRUDENZA ANNOTATA DI DIRITTO INDUSTRIALE (IT) [01792183] **2974**

GIURISPRUDENZA : BANCA DATI LAVORO SU CD-ROM (IT) **2974**

GIURISPRUDENZA COMMERCIALE (IT) [02244556] **3100**

GIURISPRUDENZA COSTITUZIONALE (IT/0436-0222) [01641229] **3093**

GIURISPRUDENZA DELLE IMPOSTE : RASSEGNA DELLE DECISIONI DI MASSIMA DELLA CORTE DI CASSAZIONE E DELLA COMMISSIONE CENTRALE DELLE IMPOSTE ... / ASSOCIAZIONE FRA LE SOCIETA ITALIANE PER AZIONI (IT) [11730844] 4727, **2974**

GIURISPRUDENZA DI MERITO (IT) [01639473] **2974**

GIURISPRUDENZA ITALIANA (IT) [29176899] **2974**

GIURISPRUDENZA PIEMONTESE (IT) **2974**

GIURISPRUDENZA PREVIDENZIALE : BANCA DATI LAVORO SU CD-ROM (IT) **2974**

GIUS - RASSEGNA DI GIURISPRUDENZA (IT) **2974**

GIUSTIZIA AMMINISTRATIVA IN EMILIA ROMAGNA (IT) **4650**

GIUSTIZIA CIVILE (IT/0017-0631) [09473121] **3090**

GIUSTIZIA CIVILE. MASSIMARIO ANNOTATO DELLA CASSAZIONE / A CURA DELLA DIREZIONE E REDEZIONE DELLA RIVISTA DI GIURISPRUDENZA (IT) [17278381] **2974**

GIUSTIZIA E COSTITUZIONE : RIVISTA TRIMESTRALE DELL'ASSOCIAZIONE DI STUDI GIURIDICI E COSTITUZIONALI (IT) [26391616] **2975**

GIUSTIZIA OGGI (IT) **4650**

GIUSTIZIA PENALE (IT/0017-0658) [I00170658] **2975**

GIUSTIZIA TRIBUTARIA E IMPOSTE DIRETTE (IT) **2975**

GIVE BUT GIVE WISELY / PHILANTHROPIC ADVISORY SERVICE, COUNCIL OF BETTER BUSINESS BUREAUS (US) [11700258] **4336**

GIVEAWAY, THE (US) [12090313] **5664**

GIVING USA (US/0436-0257) [03500843] **4336**

GIVING USA UPDATE (US/0899-3793) [17757084] **4336**

GJUTERIET (SW/0017-0682) [02447229] **4003**

GKSS JAHRESBERICHT (GW/0174-4933) [10056041] **4176**

GLABC DIRECTORY (CN/0821-5693) [09666922] **3212**

GLACIER REPORTER, THE (US) [11718964] **5705**

GLACIOLOGICAL DATA (US/0149-1776) [03427101] **1413**

GLAD DIRECTORY OF RESOURCES AVAILABLE TO DEAF & HARD-OF-HEARING PERSONS IN THE SOUTHERN CALIFORNIA AREA (US/0146-8340) [03038884] **5286**

GLAD NEWS, THE (US/0739-7453) [09804309] **4388**

GLAD RAG : JOURNAL OF THE TRANSVESTITE/TRANSSEXUAL SOCIAL GROUP (UK), THE (UK/0265-8143) [14261221] **5187**

GLADES COUNTY DEMOCRAT (US/0745-4120) [01461464] **5649**

GLADIATOR SPORTS MAGAZINE (US) **4896**

GLADIO GRAMS *CEASED.* (US/0431-9168) [01461478] **2417**

GLADIOLUS ANNUAL : BEING THE YEARBOOK OF THE BRITISH GLADIOLUS SOCIETY, THE (UK/0072-4580) [03066673] **2417**

GLADIUS (SP/0436-029X) [03236970] **4044**

GLADWIN COUNTY RECORD AND BEAVERTON CLARION, THE (US/1071-0019) [28528869] **5692**

GLADYS PORTER ZOO *See* GLADYS PORTER ZOO NEWS **5584**

GLADYS PORTER ZOO NEWS (US) [04794888] **5584**

GLAMOUR (US/0017-0747) [05259082] 404, 1084, **5557**

●GLAMOUR MILANO (IT) [I11215348] **5557**

GLAMOUR PARIS (FR/0990-6479) [I09906479] 404, 1084, **5557**

GLANEUSE (SZ) **4388**

GLAS (RU) [25335332] **3391**

GLAS (RU/0869-3102) [24896834] **3391**

GLAS-EMAIL-KERAMO-TECHNIK *See* SILIKAT JOURNAL **2594**

GLAS ISTRE (CI/0017-0771) [I00170771] **5799**

GLAS K O H T-A (CN/0700-8139) [03399870] **3578**

GLAS KANADSKIH SRBA (US) [06476922] **3284**

GLAS OCH PORSLIN (SW/0017-078X) [I0017078X] **2589**

GLAS. ODELJENJE MEDICINSKIH NAUKA (YU/0081-3966) [10215674] **3579**

GLAS OSTERREICHISCHE GLASER ZEITUNG (AU) **2589**

GLAS SLAVONIJE (CI/0350-3968) [I03503968] **5799**

GLAS - SRPSKA ADADEMIJA NAUKA I UMETNOSTI. ODELJENJE TEHNICKIH NAUKA (YU/0081-3974) [I00813974] **5108**

GLAS - SRPSKA AKADEMIJA NAUKA I UMETNOSTI, ODELJENJE PRIRODNO-MATEMATICKIKH NAUKA (YU) [02970501] **2589**

GLAS UND RAHMEN (GW/0036-3065) [06365364] **2589**

GLASCO SUN (GLASCO, KAN. : 1937) (US) [14575086] **5675**

GLASFORD GAZETTE (US) [08807442] **5660**

GLASFORUM (GW/0017-0852) [05150860] **2589**

GLASGOW ARCHAEOLOGICAL JOURNAL (UK) [02396325] **269**

GLASGOW COURIER, THE (US) [12317058] **5705**

GLASGOW DAILY TIMES, THE (US) [14192213] **5680**

GLASGOW. FIRE SERVICE *See* REPORT OF THE FIREMASTER OF THE CITY OF GLASGOW **2292**

GLASGOW MATHEMATICAL JOURNAL (UK/0017-0895) [02447236] **3507**

GLASGOW NATURALIST (UK/0373-241X) [01751257] **4165**

GLASGOW REPUBLICAN, THE (US) [14178420] **5680**

GLASGOW (STRATHCLYDE) *See* DIARY OF THE CORPORATION OF THE CITY OF GLASGOW & C **4642**

GLASGOW. TRADING STANDARDS DEPARTMENT *See* REPORT BY THE CHIEF INSPECTOR - GLASGOW. TRADING STANDARDS DEPARTMENT **850**

GLASNIK CETINJSKIH MUZEJA. BULLETIN DES MUSEES DE CETIGNE (YU/0350-8714) [05234671] **237**

GLASNIK ETNOGRAFSKOG INSTITUTA (YU/0350-0861) [09988879] **237**

GLASNIK - INSTITUT ZA NACIONALNA ISTORIJA SKOPJE (YU/0583-4961) [I05834961] **2689**

GLASNIK MATEMATICKI. SERIJA III (CI/0017-095X) [00853358] **3507**

GLASNIK (NORTH BURNABY) (CN/0836-7124) [17631659] 2262, **2689**

GLASNIK PRIRODNJACKOG MUZEJA U BEOGRADU. SERIJA C. SUMARSTVO I LOV (YU) [03246927] **2384**

GLASNIK SLOVENSKEGA ETNOLOSKEGA DRUSTVA (XV/0351-2908) [04821865] **237**

GLASNIK ZA SUMSKE POKUSE (CI/0352-3861) [I03523861] **2384**

GLASNIK ZEMALJSKOG MUZEJA BOSNE I HERCEGOVINE U SARAJEVU. ARHEOLOGIJA (BN) [01788923] **269**

GLASNOST (RU) [22991606] **5809**

GLASRA (IE/0332-0235) [05283260] **512**

GLASS AGE (UK/0017-0992) [02447240] **2589**

GLASS AND CERAMICS (US/0361-7610) [02117066] **2589**

GLASS & GLAZING (UK) 615, 2589, **299**

GLASS & PORSELEN (NO/0802-5428) [I08025428] **2589**

GLASS ART (BROOMFIELD, COLO.) (US/1068-2147) [27469735] **2589**

GLASS ART MAGAZINE (BROOMFIELD, COLO.) *See* GLASS ART (BROOMFIELD, COLO.) **2589**

GLASS ART MAGAZINE (BROOMFIELD, COLO.) (US/0886-8131) [12996099] **2589**

GLASS ART SOCIETY PHOTOGRAPHIC DIRECTORY (US/0740-8889) [10036980] **2589**

GLASS AUDIO (US/1045-5027) [20181421] **4404**

GLASS CANADA (CN/0843-7041) [20287047] **2589**

GLASS CAR GUIDE (UK) **5415**

GLASS CIRCLE, THE (UK) [01783641] **2589**

GLASS CLUB BULLETIN (US) **2589**

GLASS COLLECTOR'S DIGEST (US/0893-8660) [15679841] **2589**

GLASS CONTAINERS (WASHINGTON) (US/0364-1872) [02548406] **2589**

GLASS DIGEST (US/0017-1018) [02447242] **2589**

GLASS FACTORY DIRECTORY (US) [04388801] **2590**

GLASS INDUSTRY DIRECTORY ISSUE, THE (US) [00892147] **2590**

GLASS INDUSTRY INTERNATIONAL DIRECTORY *See* GLASS INDUSTRY DIRECTORY ISSUE, THE **2590**

GLASS INDUSTRY, THE (US/0017-1026) [01751261] **2590**

GLASS INTERNATIONAL (UK/0143-7836) [08997983] **2590**

GLASS MAGAZINE (US/0747-4261) [10843561] **2590**

GLASS NEWS *CEASED.* (US/0890-3743) [13240789] **2590**

GLASS ON METAL. THE ENAMELISTS' NEWSLETTER (US) **2590**

●GLASS, PHYSICS & CHEMISTRY (US) 976, **4404**

GLASS (PORTLAND, OR.) (US/0147-8427) [03232351] **2590**

GLASS (PRINCETON) (US/0091-6625) [01786991] **2590**

GLASS PRODUCTION TECHNOLOGY INTERNATIONAL (UK/0959-0838) [I09590838] **2590**

GLASS (REDHILL) (UK/0017-0984) [02447239] **2590**

GLASS REVIEW (PRAGUE, CZECH REPUBLIC) *See* NEW GLASS REVIEW (PRAHA) **2592**

GLASS REVIEW (PRAGUE, CZECHOSLOVAKIA) (CS/0323-0635) [05771679] **2590**

GLASS TECHNOLOGY (UK/0017-1050) [01751262] **2590**

GLASS TOKYO. 1986, THE (JA/0916-0388) [I09160388] **2590**

GLASS UDYOG (II/0379-0460) [05162310] **2590**

GLASS UDYOG *See* KANCH. NEW DELHI **1984**

GLASS WORKERS NEWS (US/0017-1069) [02261549] **2590**

GLASSWORK *CEASED.* (JA) **2590**

GLASSWORKS (US/0145-6792) [02767577] **3463**

GLASTECHNISCHE BERICHTE (GW/0017-1085) [01433058] **2590**

GLASTEKNISK TIDSKRIFT (SW/0017-1093) [05150721] **2590**

GLASTONBURY CITIZEN, THE (US) [26347116] **5645**

GLASUL BISERICII (RM) [06629262] **5039**

GLASWELT (GW/0017-1107) [I00171107] **2590**

GLAUBE UND DENKEN : JAHRBUCH DER KARL-HEIM-GESELLSCHAFT (GW/0934-0785) [20999799] **4960**

GLAUBE UND HEIMAT (SZ/0323-8202) [08188704] **5060**

GLAUBE UND LERNEN (GW/0179-3551) [18344967] **4960**

GLAUCOMA ABSTRACTS INTERNATIONAL (FR) [23535636] **3875**

GLAUCOMA (MIAMI) (US/0164-4645) [04743666] **3875**

GLAVNYI BOTANICHESKII SAD (AKADEMIIA NAUK SSSR) *See* BIULLETEN GLAVNOGO BOTANICHESKOGO SADA **502**

GLAZED EXPRESSIONS (UK/0261-0329) [I02610329] **299**

GLAZIERS JOURNAL *See* GLASS DIGEST **2589**

GLAZING TODAY (UK) **2590**

GLBAMES NEWSLETTER (US/1059-065X) [24469523] **2794**

GLEANER (HENDERSON, KY.) (US) [14156704] **5680**

GLEANER INDEX / NATIONAL LIBRARY OF JAMAICA, THE (JM/0259-0336) [14701412] **5805**

GLEANER (KOKOMO, IND.) (US/0897-9723) [17692730] **4960**

GLEANER (PORTLAND, OR.) (US/0746-5874) [10153800] **4960**

GLEANINGS (BEAVER FALLS, PA.) (US/0883-2765) [12009123] **2451**

GLEANINGS (CAMBRIDGE) (US/0160-2373) [02403717] 3343, **4960**

GLEANINGS FROM THE HEART OF THE CORNBELT (US) **2451**

GLEANINGS ... FROM THE WEST FIELDS (US) [12758704] **2451**

GLEANINGS IN BEE CULTURE (US/0017-114X) [02587368] 2774, **5585**

GLEANINGS (KEOKUK) (US) **2451**

GLEBE REPORT (CN/0702-7796) [03412159] **5785**

GLEDITSCHIA (GW) [06055307] **512**

GLEN ECHO PARK (US) [07982745] **1800**

GLEN INNES AGRICULTURAL RESEARCH AND ADVISORY STATION *See* BIENNIAL REPORT / GLEN INNES AGRICULTURAL RESEARCH AND ADVISORY STATION **66**

GLEN RIDGE PAPER (US) [16893438] **5710**

GLEN ROSE REPORTER, THE (US) [17661636] **5750**

GLENBOW (EXHIBITIONS AND EVENTS) (CN/0710-3697) [08205682] **4088**

GLENBOW MUSEUM *See* GLENBOW (EXHIBITIONS AND EVENTS) **4088**

GLENCOE ENTERPRISE (US) [01715144] **5696**

GLENCOE NEWS/VOICE (US/0747-3311) [10742855] **5660**

GLENDALE-HIGHLINE GAZETTE *See* HIGHLINE TIMES **5761**

GLENDALE LAW REVIEW (US/0363-2423) [02438862] **2975**

GLENDALE NEWS-PRESS (1993) (US/1071-3476) [28620169] **5635**

GLENDALE REGISTER (US) [11386235] **5716**

GLENDIVE RANGER-REVIEW (US) [13555771] **5705**

GLENGARRY HISTORICAL SOCIETY *See* GLENGARRY HISTORICAL SOCIETY **2734**

GLENGARRY HISTORICAL SOCIETY (CN/0229-6705) [08099252] **2734**

GLENGARRY LIFE (CN/0703-1556) [03951171] **2734**

GLENVIEW NEWS/VOICE (US/0745-9815) [09650449] **5660**

GLENVILLE DEMOCRAT, THE (US/0746-5890) [10135501] **5763**

GLENVILLE PATHFINDER, THE (US/0746-5882) [10135524] **5763**

GLENVILLE STATE COLLEGE *See* ALUMNI DIRECTORY / GLENVILLE STATE COLLEGE **1098**

GLENWOOD HERALD, THE (US) [23589689] **5631**

GLENWOOD POST (US) [11164465] **5643**

GLI SCAMBI COMMERCIAL CON L'ESTERO *See* SCAMBI COMMERCIALI CON L'ESTERO, GLI **850**

GLIA (NEW YORK, N.Y.) (US/0894-1491) [15804228] **3833**

GLIDDEN ENTERPRISE, THE (US) [13549588] **5767**

GLIDDEN GRAPHIC, THE (US/0746-6196) [10164185] **5670**

GLIDER RIDER'S ULTRALIGHT FLYING (US/0883-7937) [12212379] **22**

GLIEDERUNG DES LANDTAGS RHEINLAND-PFALZ ... WAHLPERIODE (GW) [11910373] **4650**

GLIM NEWSLETTER, THE (UK) [10617860] **5328**

●GLIMMER TRAIN STORIES (US/1055-7520) [23298128] **3391**

GLIMPSE : INTERNATIONAL CENTRE FOR DIARRHOEAL DISEASE RESEARCH, BANGLADESH NEWSLETTER (BG) [12744433] **3579**

GLIMPSES IN PLANT RESEARCH (II) [07481828] **512**

GLIMTAR UR ALANDS FOLKKULTUR (FI/0782-0011) [18152788] **2320**

GLITCHES (BEND, ORE.) *CEASED.* (US/0732-667X) [08428721] **1233**

GLITTER (CN/0316-5965) [02247616] **2534**

GLIWICE, UPPER SILESIA (CITY). POLITECHNIKA SLASKA. INSTYTUT ELEKTROENERGETYKI I STEROWANIA UKADOW *See* PRACE INSTYTUTU ELEKTROENERGETYKI I STEROWANIA UKADOW POLITECHNIKI SLASKIEJ **2075**

●GLOBAL ACCESS TO STD DIAGNOSTICS (US/1063-8423) [26149738] 4777, **3713**

GLOBAL AFFAIRS *CEASED.* (US/0886-6198) [12954805] **4522**

●GLOBAL AFRICA (US/1048-6216) [20990495] **2499**

GLOBAL AFRICA (WASHINGTON, D.C.) (US/1055-7636) [23295624] **2639**

GLOBAL AGENDA *CEASED.* (AT/1038-8451) **2172**

●GLOBAL AGENDA, A (US/1057-1213) [23958427] **4522**

●GLOBAL AIDSNEWS: THE NEWSLETTER OF THE WORLD HEALTH ORGANIZATION GLOBAL PROGRAMME ON AIDS (SZ/1020-007X) [24480521] **3713**

GLOBAL ALTERNATIVE SCENARIOS (US) [20375079] **1564**

GLOBAL AND PLANETARY CHANGE (NE/0921-8181) [18993035] **1356**

GLOBAL ASSESSMENT (US) [15139150] 1635, **4522**

GLOBAL ATMOSPHERIC BACKGROUND MONITORING FOR SELECTED ENVIRONMENTAL PARAMETERS BAPMON DATA FOR ... (US/0278-9132) [07867754] **2172**

GLOBAL AUTOMOTIVE REVIEW AND OUTLOOK (US/1070-9975) [28528223] **5415**

●GLOBAL BIODIVERSITY (CN/1195-3101) [28695309] **456**

GLOBAL BIOGEOCHEMICAL CYCLES (US/0886-6236) [12954754] **1041**

GLOBAL BUSINESS (UK) [19933636] **677**

GLOBAL BUSINESS WHITE PAPERS (US/1062-1261) [24033194] **677**

GLOBAL CERAMIC REVIEW (UK) **2590**

●GLOBAL CHANGE BIOLOGY (UK/1354-1013) **456**

GLOBAL CHANGE / IGBP (SW/0284-8015) [20033020] **1356**

GLOBAL CHURCH GROWTH (US/0731-1125) [08123835] **4960**

●GLOBAL CITY REVIEW (US/1068-0586) [27422346] 2794, 2172, **3343**

GLOBAL CLIMATE CHANGE DIGEST (US/0897-4268) [17494983] **1425**

GLOBAL COMMUNICATIONS (US/0195-2250) [05384825] **1112**

GLOBAL COMMUNIQUE/ THE EDP AUDITORS ASSOCIATION, INC (US/1055-3940) [23163074] **744**

●GLOBAL COMPANY NEWS DIGEST (US/1061-3714) [25277299] **678**

●GLOBAL CONNECTOR, THE (US/1055-3371) [23156498] **869**

GLOBAL CUSTODIAN (US/1047-8736) [20778911] **899**

GLOBAL DEVELOPMENT REPORT (US/0882-3251) [11809105] **2910**

GLOBAL DIALOGUE (US/0017-1190) [01865749] **4523**

GLOBAL DIRECTORY OF GAS COMPANIES (US/0094-6303) [01794869] **4259**

GLOBAL ECOLOGY AND BIOGEOGRAPHY LETTERS (UK/0960-7447) [23156550] **2216**

GLOBAL ECONOMIC OUTLOOK (TORONTO) (CN/0820-5167) [16728427] **1492**

GLOBAL ECONOMIC PROSPECTS AND THE DEVELOPING COUNTRIES (US/1014-8906) [23959250] **1492**

GLOBAL ENVIRONMENTAL CHANGE (UK/0959-3780) [23706833] **2172**

GLOBAL ENVIRONMENTAL CHANGE REPORT (US/1049-9083) [20777415] **2216**

GLOBAL FINANCE JOURNAL (US/1044-0283) [19650278] **789**

GLOBAL FINANCIAL REPORT ON TELECOMMUNICATIONS AND COMPUTER COMPANIES (US/1069-9899) [28211349] 1156, **789**

GLOBAL FOCUS (CN/1188-1917) [25882989] **869**

GLOBAL FUTURES DIGEST (CN/0226-9465) [09938434] **1592**

GLOBAL GAS TURBINE NEWS (US) **4259**

●GLOBAL GEORGIA (US/1063-9772) [26184428] **838**

GLOBAL GOVERNANCE (US/1075-2846) [29999410] **4475**

GLOBAL GUARANTY'S CREDIT ENHANCEMENT AND FINANCIAL GUARANTY DIRECTORY (US/1057-8714) [23066968] **2881**

GLOBAL INVESTMENT TECHNOLOGY (US/1058-3920) [24291393] **899**

GLOBAL INVESTOR (UK/0951-3604) [16503701] **899**

GLOBAL ISSUES (GUILFORD, CONN.) (US) [11792460] **5201**

●GLOBAL JOURNAL ON CRIME AND CRIMINAL LAW (NE/0928-9313) 3107, 3128, **3165**

GLOBAL JUSTICE (US/1060-0884) [24864649] 3128, **4523**

●GLOBAL M AND A (US) **789**

GLOBAL MEETING LINE, INC. [COMPUTER FILE] : MEETINGS DATA BASE MANAGEMENT (US/1056-6406) [23816659] **869**

GLOBAL MONEY MANAGEMENT (US) **789**

GLOBAL NETWORKS (US/1057-1620) [23961078] **1185**

GLOBAL NEWS (CN/0704-0202) [03791095] **5785**

GLOBAL NOMAD, THE (US/1062-466X) [25635967] **5231**

GLOBAL OIL REPORT (UK) **4259**

GLOBAL OIL STOCKS & BALANCES (US) 900, **4259**

GLOBAL OUTLOOK (CN/0226-8205) [06688335] **4475**

GLOBAL PAGES (US) [14915465] **1895**

GLOBAL PERSPECTIVES ON HEPATITIS : NEWSLETTER OF THE INTERNATIONAL TASK FORCE ON HEPATITIS B IMMUNIZATION (US/1049-2771) [21191658] **3797**

GLOBAL PLASTICS REPORT *CEASED.* (CN/0835-1791) [18027977] **4455**

GLOBAL POSITIONING & NAVIGATION NEWS (US/1072-3080) [28902355] 2565, **4176**

GLOBAL PRAYER DIGEST (US/1045-9731) [12123609] **237**

GLOBAL PROGRAMME ON AIDS (WORLD HEALTH ORGANIZATION) *See* PROGRESS REPORT / GLOBAL PROGRAMME ON AIDS **3676**

GLOBAL REPORT (VANCOUVER) (CN/0229-6543) [08730623] **869**

GLOBAL REPORTER, THE *SUSPENDED.* (US) [09457875] **237**

GLOBAL RISK ASSESSMENTS: ISSUES, CONCEPTS, AND APPLICATIONS (US/0739-4640) [09736713] **900**

GLOBAL STANDARDS & SPECIFICATIONS BULLETIN (US/1058-4285) [24296564] **1976**

●GLOBAL STOCK GUIDE (US/1060-8702) [25083975] **789**

GLOBAL STUDIES. JAPAN AND THE PACIFIC RIM (US/1059-5988) [24613310] **2651**

GLOBAL STUDIES PROGRAM NOTES (US/0890-4987) [14252117] **2488**

GLOBAL TAPESTRY (UK) [03277006] **3463**

GLOBAL TECTONICS AND METALLOGENY (GW/0163-3171) [04349619] **1356**

●GLOBAL TELECOM *SUSPENDED.* (US/1065-8424) [26776739] **1156**

GLOBAL TELECOM REPORT (US/1059-4485) [24595124] **1156**

GLOBAL TELECOMMS BUSINESS (UK) **1156**

●GLOBAL TELEPHONY (US/1067-6317) [27316932] **1156**

GLOBAL TELEVISION REPORT *See* GLOBOSPORTS **1132**

●GLOBAL TOURISM FORECASTS TO THE YEAR 2000 AND BEYOND : AFRICA (SP) **5478**

●GLOBAL TOURISM FORECASTS TO THE YEAR 2000 AND BEYOND : MIDDLE EAST (SP) **5478**

GLOBAL TRADE (US/1060-0906) [18370973] **838**

●GLOBAL TRADE & TRANSPORTATION *CEASED.* (US/1069-2843) [27393650] **838**

GLOBAL TRADE TALK (US/1056-3857) [23195704] **838**

GLOBAL TRADE WHITE PAGES *CEASED.* (US/1054-8742) [23004347] **838**

GLOBAL VISIONS (US/1060-3891) [24956832] **4523**

GLOBALITA (IT) **3343**

GLOBE (FR) **5201**

GLOBE AND LAUREL (UK/0017-1204) [I00171204] **4044**

GLOBE AND MAIL (CN/0319-0714) [18680540] **5785**

GLOBE AND MAIL, THE (CN/0319-0714) [06155622] **5785**

GLOBE AND TRAVELLER (LONDON, ENGLAND : 1907) (UK) [19094542] **5812**

GLOBE, LE (SZ) [01751276] **2565**

GLOBE (MELBOURNE) (AT/0311-3930) [02459103] **2565**

GLOBEFISH — Alphabetical Title Index

GLOBEFISH EUROPEAN FISH PRICE REPORT (IT) [19406804] **2304**

GLOBEFISH HIGHLIGHTS (IT/1014-9201) [19992187] **2304**

GLOBEHOPPER (CN/0711-7108) [08659502] **5478**

GLOBOSPORTS (US) **4896, 1132**

GLOBULE ROUGE (CN/0712-337X) [08890925] **1091**

GLOOM, BOOM AND DOOM REPORT, THE (HK/1017-1371) [I10171371] **1492**

GLORY OF INDIA (II) [04596250] **2504**

GLORY SONGS (US/0731-0781) [08120376] **4119**

GLOSSA / LES CAHIERS DE L'UNADRIO (FR) **3284**

GLOSSARIA INTERPRETUM (US/0072-4750) [01462324] **3284**

GLOT *CEASED.* (NE/0166-5790) [10025750] **3284**

GLOTTA (CK/0120-6516) [14913504] **3284**

GLOTTA (GOTTINGEN) (GW/0017-1298) [01714662] **3284**

GLOTTODIDACTICA (PL/0072-4769) [01751281] **3284**

GLOTTOMETRIKA (GW/0932-7991) [05121705] **3507, 3284**

GLOUCESTER COUNTY TIMES (US) [11218944] **5710**

GLOUCESTER GUIDE (CN/0704-7371) [03991628] **385**

GLOUCESTERSHIRE FAMILY HISTORY SOCIETY JOURNAL (UK/0143-0513) [12381211] **2451**

GLOUCESTERSHIRE RECORD SERIES (UK) [20844022] **2689**

GLOVES AND MITTENS (US/0272-958X) [03057436] **3479**

GLOXINIAN, THE (US/0017-1352) [01589351] **512**

GLP *See* REVISTA DO GAS **4277**

● GLQ (NEW YORK, N.Y.) (US/1064-2684) [26239715] **2794**

GLUCKAUF (ESSEN) (GW) [02702800] **2139**

GLUCKAUF-FORSCHUNGSHEFTE (GW/0017-1387) [01590452] **2139**

GLUCKAUF MINING REPORTER (GW) [09507390] **2139**

GLUCKAUF. WITH ENGLISH TRANSLATION (ESSEN) (GW/0174-1799) [08308678] **2140**

GLUT (CN/0824-7706) [11825346] **2735**

GLYCOBIOLOGY (OXFORD) (UK/0959-6658) [23364007] **487**

GLYCOBIOLOGY RESEARCH (UK/1356-1316) **487, 3579**

GLYCOCONJUGATE JOURNAL (UK/0282-0080) [13341010] **1025**

GLYCOCONJUGATES, THE (US/0164-081X) [04554114] **487**

GLYCOSYLATION AND DISEASE (UK/0969-3653) **3579**

GLYPH (US/0364-1708) [02618711] **3391**

GMAT REVIEW (US) **1825**

● GMB DIRECT (UK) [25808132] **1676, 838**

GMB JOURNAL *See* GMB DIRECT **838**

GMBH-RUNDSCHAU (GW/0016-3570) [13783447] **678**

GMDA BULLETIN (US/0884-6898) [09105647] **1324**

GMELIN HANDBOOK OF INORGANIC AND ORGANOMETALLIC CHEMISTRY (GW) **1036**

GMELIN HANDBUCH DER ANORGANISCHEN CHEMIE *See* GMELIN HANDBOOK OF INORGANIC AND ORGANOMETALLIC CHEMISTRY **1036**

GMP AWARENESS REPORT (US/0734-9505) [08835496] **4306**

GMP HORIZONS (US/1065-1640) [18348179] **1676**

GMP LETTER, THE (US/0196-626X) [05865907] **3479**

GMP TRENDS (US/1047-6555) [07072898] **1015, 4306, 3480**

GMRMLN FAX DIRECTORY (US) [17849704] **1156**

GMRMLN UPDATE (US/0743-9008) [10701228] **5108, 3212**

GMT CALENDAR OF COURSES (US) [04165748] **1676**

GNOMON (MUNCHEN) (GW/0017-1417) [01160828] **3284**

GNOSIS ANTHOLOGY (US/0748-884X) [11025460] **4347**

GNOSIS (MONTREAL) (CN/0316-618X) [02247644] **4347**

GNOSIS (SAN FRANCISCO, CALIF.) (US/0894-6159) [13719816] **4960**

GNOSTICA (US/0145-885X) [02255335] **4241**

GNOSTICA NEWS AND VIEWS (US) [06606338] **4241**

GNOZIS (US/0017-1425) [03277055] **4347**

GNSI NEWSLETTER (US/0199-5464) [05978832] **5108**

GO (US/0893-0643) [04654626] **5478**

GO! *CEASED.* (US/1047-3858) [20704702] **5478**

GO (EDMONTON) (CN/0046-6042) [02441938] **4850**

GO FOR SPORTS (CN/0704-0385) [03791143] **4896**

GO-GIOVANE ODONTOIATRIA (IT) **3579**

GO INFO (CN/0315-0151) [02014175] **5231**

GO INFO (CN/0315-0151) [02014761] **2794**

GO SYSTEM TIMETABLE (CN/0225-9842) [06180399] **5383**

GO (TORRANCE, CALIF.) *CEASED.* (US/1048-8758) [20921823] **429**

GOA, DAMAN, AND DIU (INDIA) *See* STATEMENT SHOWING THE SUPPLEMENTARY GRANTS **4750**

GOAL ATTAINMENT REVIEW (US/0147-7811) [03227620] **4777**

GOAL FLASH (IT) **4896**

GOAL (NEW YORK, N.Y.) *CEASED.* (US/0273-5601) [07079154] **4896**

GOAL, THE (US) [07389529] **1676**

GOALGETTER (CN/0708-5427) [05258104] **4896**

GOALS & GUIDELINES (US) [08442604] **678**

GOAT VETERINARY SOCIETY JOURNAL (UK) [09150037] **5510**

GOBBLES (US/0017-1506) [01751285] **211**

GOBIERNOS DEPARTAMENTALES : EJECUCION PRESUPUESTAL (CK) [01783838] **4650, 4727**

GODEBERT M REISS (FIRM) *See* AUKTION (GODEBERT M REISS) **408**

GODFREY MEMORIAL LIBRARY *See* AMERICAN GENEALOGICAL-BIOGRAPHICAL INDEX **2478**

GODISEN ZBORNIK - FILOZOFSKI FAKULTET NA UNIVERZITETOT, SKOPJE (XN/0350-1892) [I03501892] **4347**

GODISEN ZBORNIK NA MEDICINSKIOT FAKULTET VO SKOPJE (XN/0065-1214) [04727492] **3579**

GODISEN ZBORNIK NA ZEMJODELSKIOT FAKULTET NA UNIVERZITETOT VO SKOPJE (XN/0351-9112) [05869862] **90**

GODISHNIK NA IKONOMICHESKI UNIVERSITET GR. VARNA (BU) [26084550] **1492**

GODISHNIK NA MINNO-GEOLOZHKIIA UNIVERSITET, SOFIIA / ANNUAL OF THE MINE AND GEOLOGY UNIVERSITY, SOFIA (BU) [26638889] **2140, 1381**

GODISHNIK NA SOFIISKIIA UNIVERSITET "KLIMENT OKHRIDSKI," BIOLOGICHESKI FAKULTET *See* GODISHNIK NA SOFIISKIIA UNIVERSITET "SV. KLIMENT OKHRIDSKI," BIOLOGICHESKI FAKULTET / ANNUAIRE DE L'UNIVERSITE DE SOFIA "ST. KLIMENT OHRIDSKI," FACULTE DE BIOLOGIE **456**

GODISHNIK NA SOFIISKIIA UNIVERSITET "KLIMENT OKHRIDSKI", FIZICHESKI FAKULTET *See* GODISHNIK NA SOFIISKIIA UNIVERSITET "SV. KLIMENT OKHRIDSKI", FIZICHESKI FAKULTET **4404**

GODISHNIK NA SOFIISKIIA UNIVERSITET "KLIMENT OKHRIDSKI." FIZIKA I TEKHNIKA NA POLUPROVODNITSITE *See* GODISHNIK NA SOFIISKIIA UNIVERSITET "SV. KLIMENT OKHRIDSKI." INSTITUT PO FIZIKA I TEKHNIKA NA POLUPROVODNITSITE / ANNUAIRE DE L'UNIVERSITE DE SOFIA "ST. KLIMENT OHRIDSKI." INSTITUTE DE PHYSIQUE ET TECHNOLOGIE DES SEMI-CONDUCTEURS **2056**

GODISHNIK NA SOFIISKIIA UNIVERSITET "KLIMENT OKHRIDSKI," KHIMICHESKI FAKULTET *See* GODISHNIK NA SOFIISKIIA UNIVERSITET "SV. KLIMENT OKHRIDSKI," KHIMICHESKI FAKULTET / ANNUAIRE DE L'UNIVERSITE DE SOFIA "ST. KLIMENT OHRIDSKI," FACULTE DE CHIMIE **976**

GODISHNIK NA SOFIISKIIA UNIVERSITET "SV. KLIMENT OKHRIDSKI," BIOLOGICHESKI FAKULTET / ANNUAIRE DE L'UNIVERSITE DE SOFIA "ST. KLIMENT OHRIDSKI," FACULTE DE BIOLOGIE (BU) [28228533] **456**

GODISHNIK NA SOFIISKIIA UNIVERSITET "SV. KLIMENT OKHRIDSKI", FIZICHESKI FAKULTET (BU) [28209591] **4404**

GODISHNIK NA SOFIISKIIA UNIVERSITET "SV. KLIMENT OKHRIDSKI." INSTITUT PO FIZIKA I TEKHNIKA NA POLUPROVODNITSITE / ANNUAIRE DE L'UNIVERSITE DE SOFIA "ST. KLIMENT OHRIDSKI." INSTITUTE DE PHYSIQUE ET TECHNOLOGIE DES SEMI-CONDUCTEURS (BU) [28226912] **2056**

● GODISHNIK NA SOFIISKIIA UNIVERSITET "SV. KLIMENT OKHRIDSKI," KHIMICHESKI FAKULTET / ANNUAIRE DE L'UNIVERSITE DE SOFIA "ST. KLIMENT OHRIDSKI," FACULTE DE CHIMIE (BU) [28614008] **976**

GODISHNIK NA VISSHIIA MINNO-GEOLOZHKI INSTITUT, SOFIIA *See* GODISHNIK NA MINNO-GEOLOZHKIIA UNIVERSITET, SOFIIA / ANNUAL OF THE MINE AND GEOLOGY UNIVERSITY, SOFIA **1381**

GODISHNIK NA VISSIJA HIMIKO-TEHNOLOGICESKI INSTITUT--SOFIJA (BU/0489-6211) [01796098] **2012**

GODISNIK NA VISSIJA INSTITUT PO ARHITEKTURA I STROITELSTVO. SVITK II HISROTEHNIKA (BU/0205-0439) [08162066] **615, 1976**

GODISNJAK - AKADEMIJA NAUKA I UMJETNOSTI BOSNE I HERCEGOVINE. CENTAR ZA BALKANOLOSKA ISPITIVANJA (BN/0350-0020) [02257099] **2847**

GODISNJAK DRUSTVA ISTORICARA BOSNE I HERCEGOVINE (BN/0350-1981) [05730779] **2689**

GODISNJAK GRADA BEOGRADA (YU/0436-1105) [02396352] **4088**

GODISNJAK JUGOSLOVENSKIH POZORISTA (YU/0351-9120) [11771697] **5364**

GODISNJAK - NARODNA BIBLIOTEKA SRBIJE (YU) [06311131] **3212**

GODISNJAK / UNIVERZITET U SARAJEVU (BN/0352-2695) [09850535] **1825**

GODISNJAK VOJNOMEDICINSKE AKADEMIJE (CI/0352-664X) [13753764] **4044, 3579**

GODISNJAK ZA ... / VOJVOANSKA AKADEMIJA NAUKA I UMETNOSTI (YU) [11255832] **5231**

GODISNJAK ZASTITE SPOMENIKA KULTURE HRVATSKE / REPUBLICKI ZAVOD ZA ZASTITU SPOMENIKA KULTURE ZAGREB (CI/0350-2589) [06594418] **351**

GODO GODO (IV/1011-016X) [03703407] **2639**

GODS REVIVALIST AND BIBLE ADVOCATE (US/0745-0788) [04295369] **5016**

GOD'S SPECIAL PEOPLE (US/0896-2413) [16976352] **4960**

GOD'S WORD TODAY (US/0199-3429) [05802813] **5016**

GOD'S WORLD TODAY (US/1054-1837) [22777675] **4960, 1063**

GOELAND (MONTREAL) (CN/0820-7518) [09448574] **4388, 5286**

GOETHE DIE SCHRIFTEN ZUR NATURWISSENSCHAFT (GW) **3391**

GOETHE-GESELLSCHAFT (WEIMAR, GERMANY) *See* SCHRIFTEN DER GOETHE-GESELLSCHAFT **3434**

GOETHE-JAHRBUCH (JA) [05507712] **3391**

GOETHE-JAHRBUCH (WEIMAR) (GW/0323-4207) [01796254] **3391**

GOETHE WORTEBUCH (UK) **3391**

GOETHE YEARBOOK (US/0734-3329) [08756336] **3343, 432**

GOFFS/GOUGHS, THEIR ANCESTORS & DESCENDANTS (US/0882-7559) [11791453] **2451**

GOHAN TOKEI (JA) [08157435] **2401, 2399**

GOIAS, BRAZIL (STATE). ASSESSORIA DE RELACOES PUBLICAS *See* RELACAO DE AUTORIDADES - ASSESSORIA DE RELACOES PUBLICAS **4679**

GOIAS, BRAZIL (STATE). SECRETARIA DA INDUSTRIA E COMERCIO *See* SIC INFORMATIVO **4679**

GOING DOWN SWINGING (AT/0157-3950) [I01573950] **3391**

GOING INTERNATIONAL, INTERNATIONAL TRADE FOR THE NONSPECIALIST : ALI-ABA COURSE OF STUDY, MATERIALS (US) [07684359] **3100**

GOING PUBLIC (US/0882-9489) [11963461] **789**

GOING PUBLIC, THE IPO REPORTER (US/0278-0038) [06244882] **789**

GOINGSNAKE MESSENGER, THE (US) [10865291] **2451, 2735**

GOIRNALE DI DIRITTO DEL LAVORO E DI RELAZIONI INDUSTRIALI (IT) [07336969] **3148**

GOITIBERA (SP) **1356**

GOKANEN KEIZAI YOSOKU (JA) [02441452] **1564**

GOLD (UK) [04434002] **2140**

GOLD & BLACK ILLUSTRATED (US) **1564**

GOLD & SILVER SURVEY *SUSPENDED.* (US/0196-3546) [05794861] **4003**

GOLD BOOK. CONTEMPORARY VEHICLES, THE (US/1057-0535) [23272492] **5415**

GOLD BOOK (EL PASO, TEX.), THE (US) [04735819] **5415**

GOLD BOOK OF LIFE INSURANCE SELLING AND MARKETING *See* INSURANCE MAGAZINE'S GOLD BOOK OF INSURANCE MARKETING **2883**

GOLD BOOK OF MULTI-HOUSING (SOUTH EDITION), THE *SUSPENDED.* (US) [07054475] **615**

GOLD BOOK OF NAVAL AVIATION, THE (US/0884-1128) [11885965] **22**

GOLD BOOK OF PHOTOGRAPHY PRICES (US/0894-6663) [11989671] **4370**

GOLD BOOK. OLDER VEHICLES, THE (US/1057-0136) [23269529] **5415**

GOLD BUG, THE (US/0195-0398) [05231753] **789**

GOLD BULLETIN & GOLD PATENT DIGEST (SZ/0017-1557) [18188476] **789**

GOLD / BUREAU OF MINES, U.S. DEPARTMENT OF THE INTERIOR (US) [09637815] **2140**

● GOLD COAST (US/1071-4251) [28681516] **2534**

GOLD COAST GAZETTE (SEA CLIFF, N.Y.) (US/1065-1748) [24568603] **5716**

GOLD COAST LIFE MAGAZINE *See* GOLD COAST **2534**

GOLD GAZETTE (AT/0816-455X) [I0816455X] **4003**

GOLD NEWS (WASHINGTON, D.C.) (US/1058-6164) [24329774] **2140**, **1440**

GOLD POST (CN/0229-0723) [08072159] **4838**

GOLD PROSPECTOR (US/0745-6344) [09316852] **2140**

GOLD REVIEW AND OUTLOOK (US/0884-1292) [12179626] **1607**

GOLD + SILBER, UHREN + SCHMUCK (GW/0017-1573) [02447246] **2914**

GOLD STAR FAMILY ALBUM *See* FAMILY ALBUM, THE **3387**

GOLD STAR MOTHER (WASHINGTON, D.C. : 1985) (US) [14582371] **5231**

GOLD STATISTICS AND ANALYSIS (US/0736-1777) [07638900] **789**, **730**

GOLDBELT GAZETTE (CN/0849-8288) [21486644] **5785**

GOLDEN BALL GRAPEVINE, THE (US/0887-5898) [09773033] **2735**

GOLDEN BOUGH, THE (UK) [09565517] **512**

GOLDEN EAGLE FILM AWARDS (US/0436-1377) [05234541] **4071**

GOLDEN GATE AQUARIST (US) **554**

GOLDEN GATE BAPTIST THEOLOGICAL SEMINARY *See* ALUMNI DIRECTORY / GOLDEN GATE BAPTIST THEOLOGICAL SEMINARY **1098**

GOLDEN GATE UNIVERSITY LAW REVIEW (US/0363-0307) [02147023] **2975**

GOLDEN GATE UNIVERSITY. SCHOOL OF LAW *See* GOLDEN GATE UNIVERSITY LAW REVIEW **2975**

GOLDEN NUGGETS (US) [07834228] **2735**

GOLDEN PRAIRIE NEWS (US) [22779047] **5660**

GOLDEN ROOTS OF THE MOTHER LODE. NEWSLETTER (US/8755-5697) [11358598] **2451**

GOLDEN ROOTS OF THE MOTHER LODE, THE (US/8755-3023) [09572506] **2451**

GOLDEN TRANSCRIPT, THE (US/0746-6382) [10199885] **5643**

GOLDEN VALLEY NEWS (US) [01642217] **5725**

GOLDEN YEARS MAGAZINE (US) **5179**

GOLDENDALE SENTINEL, THE (US) [17311643] **5761**

GOLDENE KEYT, DI (IS) [01149076] **3391**

GOLDEN'S DIAGNOSTIC RADIOLOGY (US/0161-2824) [03887034] **3941**

GOLDENSEAL (US/0099-0159) [02242808] **2320**

GOLDFINCH, THE (US/0278-0208) [07695131] **2735**, **1063**

GOLDMAN SACHS EUROMONEY FOREIGN EXCHANGE DIRECTORY (UK) [22187834] **1493**

GOLDMINE (1985) (US/1055-2685) [13070910] **4119**, **2774**

GOLDSMITHS REVIEW (UK/0953-0355) [I09530355] **2914**

GOLDSTREAM GAZETTE (CN/0383-1213) [03202302] **5785**

GOLEM NEWSLETTER *CEASED.* (IT) **5108**

GOLEMBE REPORTS (US) [03935622] **789**

GOLF & CLUB ANNUAL *See* GOLFGUIDE ANNUAL **4897**

GOLF & CLUB YEARBOOK (US/0092-6914) [01791251] **4896**

GOLF & SPORTSTURF *See* SPORTSTURF (1992) **2431**

GOLF & SPORTSTURF (US/1049-0000) [21104445] **2417**

GOLF AUSTRALIA (AT/0818-5077) [I08185077] **4896**

GOLF BUSINESS (1976) (US/0148-3706) [03081275] **4896**

GOLF COURSE MANAGEMENT (US/0192-3048) [04596906] **869**, **4896**

GOLF COURSE SUPERINTENDENTS ASSOCIATION OF AMERICA *See* WHO'S WHO IN GOLF COURSE MANAGEMENT : DIRECTORY & SOURCE BOOK **4929**

GOLF DIGEST (US/0017-176X) [01751307] **4896**

GOLF DIGEST ALMANAC, THE (US/0742-4485) [10340444] **4896**

GOLF DIRECTORY (US/0275-5734) [07137685] **4896**

GOLF FOR WOMEN : GFW (US/0898-4719) [17823374] **5557**, **4896**

GOLF GUIDE, ANNUAL GOLF COURSE DIRECTORY, BRITISH COLUMBIA, ALBERTA, SASKATCHEWAN (CN/1184-6291) [24266579] **4896**

GOLF GUIDE (SANTA MONICA) (US/0099-1783) [02243561] **4896**

GOLF ILLUSTRATED (COVINA, CALIF.) *CEASED.* (US/0160-6808) [12858218] **4896**

GOLF INDUSTRY *CEASED.* (US/0160-6824) [03725073] **4896**

● GOLF INTERNATIONAL (CN/1189-4830) [26714778] **4896**

GOLF JOURNAL (US/0017-1794) [06287268] **4896**

GOLF-MAGAZIN HAMBURG. 1987 (GW/0933-7415) [I09337415] **4896**

GOLF MAGAZINE (1991) (US/1056-5493) [23740392] **4896**

GOLF MONTHLY (UK/0017-1816) [I00171816] **4896**

GOLF NEWS MAGAZINE (US) **4896**

GOLF PRO (US/1072-1274) [28871677] **4897**

GOLF PRO MERCHANDISER *See* GOLF PRO **4897**

GOLF PROPERTY (US) **4838**

GOLF REPORTER, THE (US/0745-7502) [09424454] **4897**

GOLF TIPS (US/1051-7758) [22121715] **4897**

GOLF TRAVELER, THE (US/0191-717X) [04942777] **4897**

● GOLF VACATIONS (BURLINGTON) (CN/1189-4849) [26714729] **5478**, **4897**

GOLF WORLD (UK/0017-1883) [06491142] **4897**

GOLF WORLD (US/0017-1891) [01466107] **4897**

GOLFGUIDE AND GOLF & CLUB *See* GOLF GUIDE (SANTA MONICA) **4896**

GOLFGUIDE ANNUAL (US/0360-0858) [02243775] **4897**

GOLFKARTON- EN KARTONNAGE-INDUSTRIE PRODUKTIESTATISTIEKEN (NE) [05589176] **4233**

GOLFSHOP OPERATIONS (US/0017-1824) [04298926] **4897**, **924**

GOLFWEEK (US/0890-3514) [14206141] **4897**

GOLIARD (WOOSTER, OHIO) (US/1056-1498) [23474457] **3391**

GOLOB'S OIL POLLUTION BULLETIN (US/1051-6255) [21998164] **4259**, **2230**

GOLOS ARMENII : ORGAN TSENTRALNOGO KOMITETA KOMMUNISTICHESKOI PARTII ARMENII (AI) [22522583] **5777**

GOLOS INSTYTUTU (CN/0318-0042) [01779738] **2320**, **2262**

GOLOS RODINY (RU) [13521840] **5809**

GOLTDAMMER'S ARCHIV FUER STRAFRECHT (GW/0017-1956) [01751309] **2975**

GOMER'S BUDGET TRAVEL DIRECTORY (US/0163-6227) [04396980] **5478**

GOMU HAGHOI JI (KO/0253-3138) [07930437] **5075**

GONDWANA GEOLOGICAL MAGAZINE (II) [19026421] **1381**

GONG FU (HK/0376-6535) [01799805] **4897**

GONGCHENG REWULI XUEBAO (CC/0253-231X) [08862716] **4430**

GONGYE WEISHENG YU ZHIYEBING (CC/1000-7164) [17725203] **2862**

GONGYE WEISHENGWU (CC/1001-6678) [14251349] **563**

GONJUN BOGEN JABJI (KO/0023-401X) [05257195] **4777**

GONZAGA LAW REVIEW (US/0046-6115) [01644234] **2975**

GONZAGA SPECIAL REPORT (US/0885-9868) [06347704] **2975**

GOOD APPLE NEWSPAPER, THE (US/0884-688X) [08680555] **1895**

GOOD BEGINNINGS NEWSLETTER (CN/0712-5038) [09156980] **1748**

GOOD BOOK GUIDE (UK) **4828**

GOOD BUILDING GUIDES (UK) **615**

● GOOD COUNTRY PEOPLE (US/1047-7225) [20749416] **2534**, **2320**

GOOD DEEDER *See* CLUBHOUSE (BERRIEN SPRINGS, MICH.) **4948**

GOOD FOOD + FITNESS A WINNING LIFESTYLE (US/1040-3140) [18374563] **2342**

GOOD FOOD MAGAZINE *CEASED.* (US/0885-0690) [12561359] **2342**

GOOD FRUIT & VEGETABLES (AT) **2417**

GOOD HEALTH (DON MILLS) (CN/0229-5903) [07966397] **4191**, **1297**

GOOD HEALTH WARBURTON *CEASED.* (AT/0819-5668) [I08195668] **2597**

GOOD HOPE NEWS *See* AFRICAN HERALD, THE **5746**

GOOD HOUSEKEEPING (BRITISH EDITION) (UK/0017-2081) [06396418] **2790**

GOOD HOUSEKEEPING NEEDLECRAFT (US/0436-1539) [01777156] **5184**

GOOD HOUSEKEEPING (U.S. ED.) (US/0017-209X) [02497043] **5557**, **2790**

● GOOD HOUSEKEEPING'S LIVING WELL : IN COOPERATION WITH THE AMERICAN MEDICAL ASSOCIATION (US) [26585873] **2597**

GOOD HOUSEKEEPING'S MOMS WHO WORK (US/0733-4478) [08570548] **2280**

GOOD NEWS (US) [10623426] **5767**

GOOD NEWS EXETER (UK/0954-562X) [I0954562X] **4960**

GOOD NEWS FROM NARAMATA CENTRE (CN/0229-091X) [08436313] **4961**

GOOD-NEWS-LETTER (CN/0713-3677) [09929617] **4961**

GOOD NEWS LETTER (WASHINGTON, D.C.), THE (US/0738-6419) [09654520] **5030**

GOOD NEWS (NEW BERLIN, WIS.) (US/1047-2320) [20643759] **4961**

GOOD NEWS OF TOMORROW'S WORLD (US/0093-5026) [02135955] **4961**

GOOD NEWS (WILMORE) (US/0436-1563) [01588016] **5060**

GOOD OLD DAYS (US/0046-6158) [05423956] **3391**

GOOD OLD DAYS. SPECIAL ISSUES (US/0160-7510) [01794395] **2735**

GOOD OLD DAYS. SPECIAL ISSUES (1991) (US/1056-1871) [24238641] **3391**

GOOD PACKAGING MAGAZINE (US/1049-3158) [14219108] **4219**

GOOD READING (CHICAGO, ILL.) *SUSPENDED.* (US) [04872691] **2496**

GOOD TIMES (US/0164-4033) [04708924] **2534**

GOOD TIMES (GREENVILLE, NY.) (US/0191-4995) [04936172] **2534**

GOOD TIMES (TORONTO) (CN/0847-1126) [22104208] **5179**

GOODALE'S DIRECTORY OF CLASSIFIED ADVERTISING (US/1058-2355) [24242442] **759**

GOODE'S WORLD ATLAS (US) **1926**

GOODFELLOW REVIEW OF CRAFTS, THE (US/0162-2765) [04148877] **373**

GOODFRUIT GROWER, THE (US/0046-6174) [04080634] **2417**

GOODING COUNTY LEADER (US) [20546338] **5656**

GOODLAND DAILY NEWS, THE (US/0893-0562) [12621744] **5676**

GOODLET FAMILY NEWSLETTER, THE (US/0738-8268) [09672888] **2451**

GOODLIFE (TORONTO) (CN/0823-9398) [11449436] **2534**

GOODS & SERVICES BULLETIN, THE (US/8750-8524) [11170840] **1297**

GOODS AND SERVICES TAX LEGISLATION (NZ/0112-9392) [I01129392] **4727**

GOODWIN NEWS, THE (US/0892-1423) [14093371] **2451**

GOODYEAR CHEMICAL REVIEW (US/0432-0905) [01466723] **5075**

GOOSE CREEK GAZETTE (US) [29485755] **5742**

● GOOSE (WILLOW STREET, PA.), THE (US/1062-7219) [25704989] **2452**

GOPHER MUSIC NOTES (US/0017-2235) [01716442] **4119**

GOPPINGER ARBEITEN ZUR GERMANISTIK (GW/0179-1834) [01751286] **3284**

GORDIAN (1948) (GW/0017-2243) [04025883] **2342**

GORDON JOURNAL (US) **5706**

GORDON QUARTERLY, THE (US/0746-5483) [10124958] **4286**

GORDON'S PRINT PRICE ANNUAL (US/0160-6298) [03719502] **378**

GORE-BROWNE ON COMPANIES (UK) **2975**

GOREN BRIDGE LETTER (US/8756-3908) [11556530] **4862**

GOREZONE (NEW YORK, N.Y.) *CEASED.* (US/0896-8802) [17313713] **385**

● GORGE GUIDE (US/1063-7656) [26134563] **4850**

GORGET ET SASH : JOURNAL OF THE EARLY MODERN WARFARE SOCIETY (US/0892-466X) [08436489] **4044**

GORIUCHIE SLANTSY *CEASED.* (ER/0208-189X) [12267997] **1381**

GORKHA (II) [08748818] **2651**

GORLITZ. NATURKUNDEMUSEUM *See* ABHANDLUNGEN UND BERICHTE DES NATURKUNDEMUSEUMS GORLITZ **4161**

GORMAN PROGRESS, THE (US) [14249614] **5750**

GORMAN'S NEW PRODUCT NEWS (US/1048-020X) [16678617] **678**

GORNICTWO (PL/0138-0990) [04388355] **2140**

GORNYI ZHURNAL (RU/0017-2278) [19654609] **1440**

GORRES GESELLSCHAFT ZUR PFLEGE DER WISSENSCHAFT IM KATHOLISCHEN DEUTSCHLAND *See* PORTUGIESISCHE FORSCHUNGEN **5254**

GORTANIA (IT/0391-5859) [103915859] **4165**

GORTERIA (NE/0017-2294) [02447674] **512**

GOS NAUCZYCIELSKI (PL/0017-1263) [I00171263] **1748**

GOS POMORZA (PL/0137-9526) [I01379526] **5808**

GOS PORANNY (PL/0867-4590) [I08674590] **5808**

GOS SZCZECINSKI (PL/0137-9178) [I01379178] **5808**

GOS WIELKOPOLSKI (PL/0137-9186) [I01379186] **5808**

GOS WYBRZEZA (PL/0137-9194) [I01379194] **5808**

GOSC NIEDZIELNY (PL/0137-7604) [I01377604] **4961**

GOSEI GOMU (JA) [10269015] **5075**

GOSEI JUSHI (JA/0387-0936) [16318335] **2102**

GOSEI SENZAI KENKYUKAISHI (JA/0911-1166) [27463367] **976**

GOSHEN COLLEGE BULLETIN (US/0017-2308) [04080640] **1825**

GOSHEN COLLEGE RECORD, THE (US/0740-865X) [09698345] **1825**

GOSHEN NEWS, THE (US/8750-3867) [11408565] **5664**

GOSHEN UNLIMITED NEWS (US) [23887322] **5716**

GOSIP (UK) **4650**

GOSPEL ADVOCATE (NASHVILLE) (US/0195-1297) [02447253] **4961**

GOSPEL EVANGEL, THE (US/0744-2203) [08117227] **4961**

GOSPEL HERALD AND THE SUNDAY SCHOOL TIMES (US/0746-0880) [09607312] **4961**

GOSPEL HERALD BEAMSVILLE (CN/0829-4666) [I08294666] **4961**

GOSPEL HERALD (JELLICO), THE (US/0273-7167) [04070964] **4961**

GOSPEL MESSAGE, THE (US/0744-5814) [01776437] **4961**

GOSPEL MISSION OF SOUTH AMERICA (US/0199-2953) [01606012] **4961**

GOSPEL MUSIC ASSOCIATION *See* GOSPEL MUSIC ASSOCIATION ANNUAL DIRECTORY & YEARBOOK **4119**

GOSPEL MUSIC ASSOCIATION ANNUAL DIRECTORY & YEARBOOK (US/0362-7330) [02312747] **4119**

GOSPEL MUSIC DIRECTORY & YEARBOOK *See* GOSPEL MUSIC ASSOCIATION ANNUAL DIRECTORY & YEARBOOK **4119**

GOSPEL MUSIC OFFICIAL DIRECTORY *CEASED.* (US/0739-604X) [09677129] **4119**

GOSPEL STANDARD (UK/0017-2367) [I00172367] **4961**

GOSPEL STANDARD, OR, FEEBLE CHRISTIAN'S SUPPORT, THE (UK) [10761440] **4961**

GOSPEL TIDINGS (AUSTIN, TEX.) (US/0017-2375) [04080654] **4961**

GOSPEL TIDINGS (OMAHA, NEB.) (US/0745-7618) [09428423] **5060**

GOSPEL VOICE (US) **4119**

GOSPEL WITNESS (TORONTO. 196?) (CN/0828-1769) [07566054] **4961**

GOSPEL WORLD (US/0278-3436) [07777708] **4119**

GOSPODARKA, ADMINISTRACJA PANSTWOWA (PL/0860-3081) [15141463] **4650**

GOSPODARKA MIESNA (PL/0367-4916) [04025897] **211**

GOSPODARKA MORSKA / INSTYTUT MORSKI (PL) [10606879] **5449**

GOSPODARKA NARODOWA (WARSAW, POLAND : 1990) (PL/0867-0005) [21768009] **1564**

GOSPODARKA RYBNA (PL) [01972640] **2304**

GOSPODARKA WODNA (PL/0017-2448) [02510182] **5533**

GOSPODARSKI CHOW ZWIERZAT (PL) [02175062] **90**

GOSPODYNI WARSZAWA (PL/0137-4249) [I01374249] **5558**

GOSSE BIRD CLUB (JAMAICA) *See* BROADSHEET / GOSSE BIRD CLUB **5616**

GOSUDARSTVENNII OOKENOGRAFICHESKII INSTITUT *See* TRUDY GOSUDARSTVENNOGO OKEANOGRAFICESKOGO INSTITUTA **1457**

GOSUDARSTVENNYE STANDARTY SSSR : UKAZATEL / GOSUDARSTVENNYI KOMITET STANDARTOV SOVETA MINISTROV SSSR (RU/0134-8752) [10643488] **4030**

GOSUDARSTVENNYI BIUDZHET SSSR (RU) [19992843] **4727**

GOSUDARSTVENNYI BIUDZHET SSSR / MINISTERSTVO FINANSOV SSSR, BIUDZHETNOE UPRAVLENIE (RU) [19687010] **1493**

GOSUDARSTVENNYI ERMITAZH (SOVIET UNION) *See* SOOBSHCHENIIA **1121**

GOSUDARSTVENNYI MUZEI ISKUSSTVA NARODOV VOSTOKA. SOOBSHCHENIIA *See* NAUCHNYE SOOBSHCHENIIA (MOSCOW, R.S.R.S.R.) **359**

GOSUDARSTVENNYI NAUCH NOISSLEDOVATELSKII I PROEKTNYI INSTITUT NEFTIANOI PROMYSHLENNOSTI *See* TRUDY - GOSUDARSTVENNYJ NAUCNO-ISSLEDOVATELSKIJ I PROEKTNYJ INSTITUT NEFTJANOJ PROMYSLENNOSTI **4280**

GOSUDARSTVENNYI NAUCHNO-ISSLEDOVATELSKII I PROEKTNYI INSTITUT REDKOMETALLICHESKOI PROMYSHLENNOSTI *See* NAUCHNYE TRUDY **4013**

● GOSUDARSTVO I PRAVO / INSTITUT GOSUDARSTVA I PRAVA, ROSSIISKAIA AKADEMIIA NAUK (RU) [25897483] **2975**

GOTEBORG STUDIES IN CONSERVATION (SW/0284-6578) [I02846578] **2194**

GOTEBORGER GERMANISTISCHE FORSCHUNGEN (SW/0072-4793) [01434495] **3284**

GOTEBORGS-EMIGRANTEN (SW) [19496173] **1918**

GOTEBORGS ETHOGRAFISKA MUSEUM *See* ARSTRYCK - GOTEBORGS ETNOGRAFISKA MUSEUM **231**

GOTEBORGS ETNOGRAFISKA MUSEUM *See* ETNOLOGISKA STUDIER **236**

GOTEBORGS UNIVERSITET *See* INFORMATION OM ORGANISATION, STYRELSEORGAN, FAKULTETER, INSTITUTIONER OCH ANSTALLDA **1830**

GOTHENBURG STUDIES IN ART & ARCHITECTURE (SW/0348-4114) [06970780] 299, **351**

GOTHENBURG, SWEDEN. STADSKONTORET *See* STATISTISKA MEDDELANDEN **5344**

GOTTESDIENST (GW/0343-8732) [I03438732] **4961**

GOTTESDIENST UND KIRCHENMUSIK (GW/0017-2499) [06622607] **4961**, **4119**

GOTTINGER ABHANDLUNGEN ZUR SOZIOLOGIE (GW/0072-4874) [01437703] **5246**

GOTTINGER ARBEITEN ZUR GEOLOGIE UND PALAONTOLOGIE (GW/0534-0403) [05511869] 4227, **1381**

GOTTINGER ARBEITSKREIS *See* EASTERN GERMANY; A HANDBOOK **2686**

GOTTINGER GEOGRAPHISCHE ABHANDLUNGEN (GW/0341-3780) [02042425] **2565**

GOTTINGER HANDWERKSWIRTSCHAFTLICHE STUDIEN (GW/0434-1473) [01588214] **1607**

GOTTINGER MISZELLEN (GW) [02410175] **2847**

GOTTINGER PREDIGTMEDITATIONEN (GW/0340-6083) [I03406083] **4961**

GOTTINGER RECHTSWISSENSCHAFTLICHE STUDIEN (GW) [01751294] **2975**

GOTTINGER THEOLOGISCHE ARBEITEN (GW) [06511807] **4961**

GOTTINGER UNIVERSITATSREDEN (GW) [02395185] **1825**

GOTTINGER WIRTSCHAFTS- UND SOZIALWISSENSCHAFTLICHE STUDIEN *See* GOTTINGER WIRTSCHAFTSWISSENSCHAFTLICHE STUDIEN **1493**

GOTTINGER WIRTSCHAFTSWISSENSCHAFTLICHE STUDIEN (GW) **1493**

GOTTINGISCHE GELEHRTE ANZEIGEN (GW/0017-1549) [06342904] **2847**

GOTUJS' (TORONTO) (CN/0046-8061) [02417259] **1064**

GOUCHER (US/0739-5795) [09754629] **1091**

GOUE VAG (SA) [09798621] **211**

GOULBOURN MIRROR (CN/0316-6635) [02247729] **5785**

GOULCAE JOURNAL OF EDUCATION (AT/0157-8944) [I01578944] **1748**

GOULD LEAGUER, THE *SUSPENDED.* (AT) [03297597] **2172**

GOULD'S CRIMINAL LAW HANDBOOK OF NEW YORK (US/1045-1625) [19917434] **3107**

GOULD'S PRIVATE SECURITY REPORTER : SERVING THE HOSPITALITY AND REAL ESTATE INDUSTRIES (US/1059-6607) [24661244] 5478, **4838**

GOURD, THE (US/0888-5672) [03271384] **90**

GOURGUES REPORT, THE (US/0743-5185) [10598443] 789, **900**

GOURMAN REPORT. A RATING OF GRADUATE AND PROFESSIONAL PROGRAMS IN AMERICAN AND INTERNATIONAL UNIVERSITIES, THE (US/1049-717X) [13568806] **1825**

GOURMAN REPORT. A RATING OF UNDERGRADUATE PROGRAMS IN AMERICAN AND INTERNATIONAL UNIVERSITIES, THE (US/1049-7188) [01410699] **1825**

GOURMET (US/0017-2553) [01751350] **2790**

GOURMET BOUTIQUE (CN/0711-7973) [08977470] **2811**

GOURMET FOOD & WINE FESTIVALS OF NORTH AMERICA (US/0886-0793) [12813368] **5268**

GOURMET NEWS (YARMOUTH, ME.) (US/1052-4630) [22293713] **2342**

GOURMET RETAILER, THE (US/0199-0357) [05529642] **2342**

GOURMET'S NOTEBOOK, A *CEASED.* (US/0279-8247) [07324605] **2342**

GOUSHA TRUCKER'S ROAD ATLAS (US/1054-4127) [22865536] **5440**

GOUT DE VIVRE, LE (CN/0383-6738) [03284817] **5246**

GOUVERNEMENT DU QUEBEC : PUBLIC ACCOUNTS (CN) [06071967] **4728**

GOVBANK TECHNICAL PAPERS (PR/0436-2233) [01438952] **789**

GOVERNANCE DIRECTORY (US/0735-0201) [08830816] **1825**

GOVERNANCE (OXFORD) (UK/0952-1895) [18473705] **4651**

GOVERNING BOARD MONTHLY MINUTES (US) **4651**

GOVERNING FLORIDA (US/1057-0675) [22869252] **4728**

GOVERNING NORTH DAKOTA (US/0271-3497) [06341970] **4651**

GOVERNING (WASHINGTON, D.C.) (US/0894-3842) [16067967] **4651, 4475**

GOVERNMENT ACCOUNTANTS JOURNAL, THE (US/0883-1483) [02287198] **4728, 744**

GOVERNMENT ACCOUNTING AND AUDITING UPDATE (US/1048-1389) [20859598] **744**

GOVERNMENT AFFAIRS REPORT (US/0146-8405) [03041272] **4651**

GOVERNMENT AFFAIRS UPDATE (US/1055-4920) [23191122] **2590**

GOVERNMENT AND INDUSTRY (UK) 1607, **4651**

GOVERNMENT AND MUNICIPAL BUYERS GUIDE (UK/0967-3873) **4651**

GOVERNMENT AND OPPOSITION (LONDON) (UK/0017-257X) [00843083] **4475**

GOVERNMENT & POLITICS ALERT *CEASED.* (US/1054-5859) [22547480] **4651**

GOVERNMENT ASSISTANCE ALMANAC (US/0883-8690) [12247571] **4651**

GOVERNMENT (BOCA RATON, FLA.) (US/1058-1774) [24233558] **4651**

GOVERNMENT BOND RECORD (CN/0833-9430) [15310622] **789**

GOVERNMENT BUSINESS OPPORTUNITIES (CN/0840-870X) [19916821] **4651, 950**

GOVERNMENT BUSINESS WORLD REPORT (US/0017-2588) 1635, **678**

GOVERNMENT BUYER *CEASED.* (US/0199-7394) [06118330] **950**

GOVERNMENT CHEMICAL LABORATORIES (WESTERN AUSTRALIA) *See* REPORT OF THE GOVERNMENT CHEMICAL LABORATORIES **1018**

GOVERNMENT COMPUTER NEWS (US/0738-4300) [09369246] 1238, **4651**

GOVERNMENT COMPUTER PROCUREMENT *See* FEDERAL COMPUTER MARKET REPORT **1237**

GOVERNMENT COMPUTING (UK/0951-7537) [I09517537] **1238**

GOVERNMENT COMPUTING (UK) **1185**

GOVERNMENT CONTRACT, COSTS, PRICING & ACCOUNTING REPORT (US/1052-5777) [22332089] **744**

GOVERNMENT CONTRACTOR, THE (US/0017-2596) [01716863] **4651**

●GOVERNMENT CONTRACTS & SUBCONTRACT LEADS DIRECTORY (US/1064-6795) [25986571] **4651**

GOVERNMENT CONTRACTS CITATOR (US/0434-2593) [01696676] **3100**

GOVERNMENT CONTRACTS DIRECTORY (US/0072-5137) [04897890] **1607**

GOVERNMENT CONTRACTS REPORTS (US/0162-1076) [01564329] **4651**

GOVERNMENT CONTRACTS SECTION NEWSLETTER (US/0742-8901) [10514295] **2975**

GOVERNMENT CONTRACTS SERVICE (US/0145-6598) [02771188] 4651, **2975**

GOVERNMENT DEVELOPMENT BANK FOR PUERTO RICO *See* SPECIAL REPORT ON PUERTO RICO INDUSTRIAL DEVELOPMENT COMPANY (PRIDCO), A **1585**

GOVERNMENT DEVELOPMENT BANK FOR PUERTO RICO *See* SPECIAL REPORT ON SAN JUAN, CAPITAL OF PUERTO RICO **1585**

GOVERNMENT DEVELOPMENT BANK FOR PUERTO RICO *See* SPECIAL REPORT ON PUERTO RICO HIGHWAY AUTHORITY, A **5444**

GOVERNMENT DEVELOPMENT BANK FOR PUERTO RICO *See* GOVBANK TECHNICAL PAPERS **789**

GOVERNMENT DIRECTORY FOR BRITISH COLUMBIA WITH SELECTED FEDERAL CONTACTS (CN/0822-8620) [10643457] **4651**

●GOVERNMENT DIRECTORY OF ADDRESSES AND TELEPHONE NUMBERS, THE (US/1062-1466) [26702426] **4651**

GOVERNMENT DISC. 1, US FEDERAL GOVERNMENT [COMPUTER FILE], THE (US/1053-282X) [22501055] **4651**

GOVERNMENT DOCUMENTS CATALOG SUBSCRIPTION SERVICE [COMPUTER FILE] (US) [22287018] **4651**

GOVERNMENT EMPLOYEE RELATIONS REPORT (US/0017-260X) [01751355] **4703**

GOVERNMENT ESTIMATES (CN/0842-4810) [15203546] **4728**

GOVERNMENT EXECUTIVE (US/0017-2626) [01624137] **4651**

GOVERNMENT FINANCE REVIEW (US/0883-7856) [11976429] **4728**

GOVERNMENT FINANCE STATISTICS, AUSTRALIA (AT/1031-7104) [I10317104] 4728, **4698**

GOVERNMENT FINANCE STATISTICS / NATIONAL STATISTICAL OFFICE (PP) [18738190] **4728**

GOVERNMENT FINANCE STATISTICS YEARBOOK (US/0250-7374) [03579749] 4728, **4698**

GOVERNMENT FINANCES IN ... (US) [17415194] **4728**

GOVERNMENT FINANCES IN DENMARK (DK) [10048620] **4728**

GOVERNMENT FINANCIAL ESTIMATES: AUSTRALIA (AT) [07044141] **4728**

GOVERNMENT FINANCIAL MANAGEMENT TOPICS (US/0199-1744) [05689721] **4728**

GOVERNMENT FUNDING REPORT (US) **4651**

GOVERNMENT GAZETTE (PP) [01783033] 4651, **4475**

GOVERNMENT GAZETTE OF MAURITIUS, THE (MF) [04262711] **4651**

GOVERNMENT GAZETTE OF THE COLONY OF MAURITIUS *See* GOVERNMENT GAZETTE OF MAURITIUS, THE **4651**

GOVERNMENT GAZETTE OF THE STATE OF NEW SOUTH WALES (AT) [02551103] **4651**

●GOVERNMENT IMAGING (US) **4651**

GOVERNMENT INFORMATION INSIDER (US) [22379360] 4475, **4651**

GOVERNMENT INFORMATION QUARTERLY (US/0740-624X) [10024704] **3212**

GOVERNMENT INVENTIONS FOR LICENSING / NTIS *See* NTIS ALERT. GOVERNMENT INVENTIONS FOR LICENSING **1306**

GOVERNMENT LIBRARIES ASSOCIATION OF BRITISH COLUMBIA *See* GLABC DIRECTORY **3212**

GOVERNMENT MANAGER, THE *CEASED.* (US/0148-7949) [02385133] 941, **4704**

GOVERNMENT MICRO USER'S GUIDE, THE (US/1040-1636) [17435682] **1267**

GOVERNMENT MICROCOMPUTER LETTER (US/0882-6587) [11991881] 4651, **1267**

GOVERNMENT NATIONAL MORTGAGE ASSOCIATION EXAMINATION OF FINANCIAL STATEMENTS (US/0360-6279) [02243449] **789**

GOVERNMENT OF CANADA PUBLICATIONS. QUARTERLY CATALOGUE (CN/0709-0412) [05297744] **4698**

GOVERNMENT OF CANADA. TELEPHONE DIRECTORY. CENTRAL REGION (CN/0848-5909) [23247469] **1156**

GOVERNMENT OF CANADA. TELEPHONE DIRECTORY. NATIONAL CAPITAL REGION (CN/0382-1846) [02814334] **1156**

GOVERNMENT OF MADHYA PRADESH: REPORT OF THE COMPTROLLER AND AUDITOR GENERAL *See* REPORT OF THE COMPTROLLER AND AUDITOR-GENERAL OF INDIA (REVENUE RECEIPTS) **4745**

GOVERNMENT OF NEW SOUTH WALES DIRECTORY OF ADMINISTRATION AND SERVICES, THE *CEASED.* (AT) [05578163] **4651**

GOVERNMENT OF ONTARIO TELEPHONE DIRECTORY (CN/0701-9599) [02249596] 4651, **1156**

GOVERNMENT PAPER SPECIFICATION STANDARDS *CEASED.* (US/0364-1260) [02476060] **4651**

GOVERNMENT PRIME CONTRACTS MONTHLY (US/0887-4085) [08462214] **4651**

GOVERNMENT PRINTING & BINDING REGULATIONS (US/0161-5181) [01370624] **4565**

●GOVERNMENT PROCUREMENT (US) **950**

GOVERNMENT PRODUCT NEWS (US/0017-2642) [01236269] **950**

GOVERNMENT PRODUCTION PRIME CONTRACTORS DIRECTORY (US/0887-4107) [04687010] **4652**

GOVERNMENT PRODUCTIVITY NEWS (US/0896-0674) [16899532] **4652**

●GOVERNMENT PROGRAMS (US/1055-825X) [23352173] **4652**

GOVERNMENT PROGRAMS AND PROJECTS DIRECTORY (US/0737-5255) [09405005] **4652**

GOVERNMENT PROPERTY CONTRACTS BULLETIN (UK/0969-4110) **4652**

GOVERNMENT PUBLICATIONS CHECKLIST / MAINE STATE LIBRARY (US) [08042088] **416**

GOVERNMENT PUBLICATIONS GUIDE (US/0091-7915) [02239677] **416**

GOVERNMENT PUBLICATIONS REVIEW (1982) (US/0277-9390) [07674859] 4652, **3212**

GOVERNMENT PUBLICATIONS REVIEW (NEW YORK, N.Y. : 1982) *See* JOURNAL OF GOVERNMENT INFORMATION **4658**

GOVERNMENT PURCHASING GUIDE (TORONTO) (CN/0046-6220) [01856245] **950**

GOVERNMENT R & D REPORT (US/0161-1127) [01409656] 4652, **5108**

GOVERNMENT REFERENCE BOOKS (US/0072-5188) [01028303] 1926, **4652**

GOVERNMENT RELATIONS (CN/0715-1608) [09387059] **1826**

GOVERNMENT RELATIONS NOTE (US) [04651878] 4652, **3579**

GOVERNMENT RELATIONS STATUS REPORT (US/0199-9990) [06290068] **3087**

GOVERNMENT REPORT FOR NONPROFITS. ONTARIO (CN/0709-9142) [06960345] **5286**

GOVERNMENT REPORTS ANNOUNCEMENTS & INDEX (US/0097-9007) [02242215] **5175**

GOVERNMENT REPORTS ANNUAL INDEX (US/0145-532X) [01781413] **5108**

GOVERNMENT RESEARCH DIRECTORY (US/0882-3766) [11826223] **5108**

GOVERNMENT SALES STRATEGIST (US/0733-5156) [08605915] **4652**

GOVERNMENT SECURITIES MANUAL (US) **4475**

GOVERNMENT TENDER REPORT (US/0738-3096) [09587827] **4652**

GOVERNMENT UNION CRITIQUE, THE (US/0738-3312) [08611728] **1676**

GOVERNMENT UNION REVIEW (US/0270-2487) [06263365] **3148**

GOVERNMENTAL ACCOUNTING STANDARDS BOARD (SUBSCRIPTION SERVICE) (US) [11554819] **744**

GOVERNMENTAL AFFAIRS NEWSLETTER *See* GOVERNMENTAL SERVICES NEWSLETTER (ASHLAND, MO.) **4652**

GOVERNMENTAL AFFAIRS REVIEW *CEASED.* (US/0731-0730) [07806297] **4388**

GOVERNMENTAL FINANCE (US) [02723902] **4728**

GOVERNMENTAL FINANCES AND EMPLOYMENT AT A GLANCE (US/0097-868X) [01799259] 4704, **4728**

GOVERNMENTAL FLEET MANAGEMENT (US/0193-4775) [05198663] **4652**

GOVERNMENTAL GUIDE. TENNESSEE EDITION (US) [03742778] **4652**

GOVERNMENTAL RESEARCH ASSOCIATION *See* DIRECTORY OF ORGANIZATIONS AND INDIVIDUALS PROFESSIONALLY ENGAGED IN GOVERNMENTAL RESEARCH AND RELATED ACTIVITIES **4472**

GOVERNMENTAL RESEARCH INSTITUTE, CLEVELAND *See* ELECTION RESULTS DATABOOK FOR CUYAHOGA COUNTY **4645**

GOVERNMENTAL RISK MANAGEMENT REPORTS (US/1056-8123) [05143821] **2881**

●GOVERNMENTAL SERVICES NEWSLETTER (ASHLAND, MO.) (US/1074-9845) [28124362] **4652**

GOVERNMENT'S EXPENDITURE PLANS / PRESENTED TO PARLIAMENT BY THE CHANCELLOR OF THE EXCHEQUER BY COMMAND OF HER MAJESTY, THE (UK) [08490065] **4728**

GOVERNMENTS OF ALABAMA (US/0883-3753) [12148062] **4728**

GOVERNMENTS OF ARKANSAS (US/0883-3761) [12148141] **4728**

GOVERNMENTS OF AUSTRALIA (AT) **4652**

GOVERNMENTS OF CALIFORNIA (US/0883-377X) [12148204] **4728**

GOVERNMENTS OF COLORADO (US/0883-3788) [12148257] **4728**

GOVERNMENTS OF CONNECTICUT (US/0883-3796) [12148288] **4728**

GOVERNMENTS OF FLORIDA (US/0883-380X) [12148330] **4728**

GOVERNMENTS OF GEORGIA (US/0883-3818) [12148362] **4728**

GOVERNMENTS OF ILLINOIS (US/0883-3826) [12148396] **4728**

GOVERNMENTS OF INDIANA (US/0883-3834) [12148425] **4728**

GOVERNMENTS OF IOWA (US/0883-3842) [12148461] **4728**

GOVERNMENTS — Alphabetical Title Index

GOVERNMENTS OF KANSAS (US/0883-3850) [12148504] **4728**

GOVERNMENTS OF KENTUCKY (US/0883-3869) [12148627] **4728**

GOVERNMENTS OF LOUISIANA (US/0883-3877) [12148670] **4728**

GOVERNMENTS OF MAINE (US/0883-3885) [12148734] **4728**

GOVERNMENTS OF MASSACHUSETTS (US/0883-3893) [12148776] **4728**

GOVERNMENTS OF MICHIGAN (US/0883-3907) [12148822] **4728**

GOVERNMENTS OF MINNESOTA (US/0883-3915) [12148848] **4728**

GOVERNMENTS OF MISSISSIPPI (US/0883-3923) [12148874] **4728**

GOVERNMENTS OF MISSOURI (US/0883-3931) [11870744] **4728**

GOVERNMENTS OF NEBRASKA (US/0883-394X) [12148976] **1493**

GOVERNMENTS OF NEW JERSEY (US/0883-3958) [12149205] **4729**

GOVERNMENTS OF NEW YORK (US/0883-3966) [12149237] **4729**

GOVERNMENTS OF NORTH DAKOTA (US/0883-3974) [12149260] **4729**

GOVERNMENTS OF OHIO (US/0883-3982) [12149307] **4729**

GOVERNMENTS OF OKLAHOMA (US/0883-3990) [12149330] **4729**

GOVERNMENTS OF PENNSYLVANIA (US/0883-4008) [12149358] **4729**

GOVERNMENTS OF SOUTH DAKOTA (US/0883-4016) [12149380] **4729**

GOVERNMENTS OF TENNESSEE (US/0883-4024) [12149401] **4729**

GOVERNMENTS OF TEXAS (US/0883-4032) [12149424] **4729**

GOVERNMENTS OF THE CAROLINAS (US/0883-4091) [12150948] **4729**

GOVERNMENTS OF THE NORTHEAST (US/0883-4121) [12151046] **4729**

GOVERNMENTS OF THE NORTHWEST (US/0883-4105) [12150984] **4729**

GOVERNMENTS OF THE WEST (US/0883-4113) [12151017] **4729**

GOVERNMENTS OF VERMONT (US/0883-4040) [12149455] **4729**

GOVERNMENTS OF VIRGINIA (US/0883-4059) [12149473] **4729**

GOVERNMENTS OF WASHINGTON (US/0883-4067) [12149503] **4729**

GOVERNMENTS OF WEST VIRGINIA (US/0883-4075) [12149527] **4729**

GOVERNMENTS OF WISCONSIN (US/0883-4083) [12159729] **4729**

GOVERNMENTS QUARTERLY REPORT. GR, FINANCES OF SELECTED PUBLIC EMPLOYEE RETIREMENT SYSTEMS (US) [03455233] **1676**

GOVERNMENTS QUARTERLY REPORT. GT, PRELIMINARY QUARTERLY SUMMARY OF STATE TAX REVENUE (US) [03904040] **4729**

GOVERNMENTS QUARTERLY REPORTS. GR, HOLDINGS OF SELECTED PUBLIC EMPLOYEE RETIREMENT SYSTEMS *See* GOVERNMENTS QUARTERLY REPORT. GR, FINANCES OF SELECTED PUBLIC EMPLOYEE RETIREMENT SYSTEMS **1676**

GOVERNO *CEASED.* (IT) **4475**

GOVERNOR'S BIENNIAL REPORT (MONTANA) (US) [06632566] **4652**

GOVERNOR'S BUDGET (US) [19681839] **4729**

GOVERNOR'S BUDGET - CALIFORNIA (US) [03761184] **4729**

GOVERNOR'S ... BUDGET IN-BRIEF (US) [11422286] **4729**

●GOVERNOR'S BUDGET REPORT, PREPARED BY THE DIVISION OF THE BUDGET, THE (US) [23295399] **4729**

GOVERNOR'S BUDGET REPORT - SOUTH DAKOTA (US) [05996836] **4729**

GOVERNOR'S BUDGET SUMMARY *See* FINANCIAL SUMMARY - DELAWARE. OFFICE OF THE GOVERNOR **4726**

GOVERNOR'S COORDINATION AND APECIAL SERVICES PLAN FOR THE PERIOD OF ... / [PREPARED BY] ILLINOIS DEPARTMENT OF COMMERCE AND COMMUNITY AFFAIRS (US) [09781845] **4652**

GOVERNOR'S COORDINATON AND SPECIAL SERVICES PLAN FOR JTPA AND RELATED PROGRAMS IN NEW YORK STATE... *See* NEW YORK STATE PLAN FOR COORDINATION OF TRAINING, EMPLOYMENT AND RELATED PROGRAMS **5298**

GOVERNOR'S LEGISLATIVE MESSAGE AND BUDGET REPORT, THE (US) [03289223] 4729, **4652**

GOVERNOR'S MANPOWER PLAN (JUNEAU) (US/0091-9535) [01788635] **1676**

GOVERNOR'S OFFICE OF ENERGY RESOURCES ANNUAL REPORT (US/0883-363X) [12057640] **1945**

●GOVERNOR'S PROPOSED ... OPERATING BUDGET SUPPORTING DATA, STATEWIDE SUMMARY TABLES (US) [27360231] **4729**

GOVERNOR'S PROPOSED SUPPORTING DATA AND ... OPERATING BUDGET (US) [23153489] **4729**

GOVERNOR'S REPORT FOR THE PERIOD ... / TEXAS COSMETOLOGY COMMISSION (US) [05858441] **404**

GOVERNOR'S REPORT ON ENVIRONMENTAL QUALITY, THE (US) [05957744] **2172**

GOVERNOR'S STATE OF THE STATE MESSAGE AND BUDGET SUMMARY (US) [03259366] **4729**

GOVERNOR'S YOUTH CONFERENCE (US) [07684692] **5286**

GOVORIT I POKAZYVAET MOSKVA (RU) [06460240] **1156**

GOWER FEDERAL SERVICE: MINING (US) [01715852] 2140, **2975**

GOWER FEDERAL SERVICE - MISCELLANEOUS LANDS DECISIONS SERVICE (US) [02536260] **2975**

GOWER FEDERAL SERVICE ROYALTY VALUATION AND MANAGEMENT (US) 4652, **1440**

GOWER FEDERAL SERVICES PLAN (US) 4652, **4838**

GOWRIE NEWS, THE (US) [14398231] **5670**

GOYA (SP/0017-2715) [01605491] **351**

GOZDARSKI VESTNIK (XV) [03761937] **5108**

GOZDARSKI VESTNIK (YU/0017-2723) [I00172723] **2384**

●GP (ATLANTA, GA.) *CEASED.* (US/1063-3324) [25980042] **1324**

GP GENERAL PRACTITIONER *CEASED.* (NZ/1039-7469) 3914, **3738**

●GP WEEKLY (NZ/1171-347X) [I1171347X] **3738**

GPA BULLETIN, THE (US/8750-6181) [11594598] **2920**

GPA IRISH ARTS REVIEW YEARBOOK *See* IRISH ARTS REVIEW YEARBOOK **353**

GPA IRISH ARTS REVIEW YEARBOOK, THE (UK/0791-038X) [19988829] **351**

GPLLA NEWSLETTER (US/1061-3072) [03416040] 2975, **3212**

GPMC NEWSLETTER (CN/0824-6181) [10852411] **2342**

GPN NEWSLETTER (US/0738-7555) [05091726] **1132**

GPO MONTHLY CATALOG [COMPUTER FILE] (US) [24006780] **4698**

GPO NEW SALES PUBLICATIONS (1991) (US/1058-0891) [24203515] **4652**

GPO SALES PUBLICATIONS REFERENCE FILE (US/1058-0824) [06343237] **4652**

GPS REPORT (US/1056-7127) [23819497] **1156**

GPS WORLD (US/1048-5104) [20961257] 4176, **2565**

GPU NEWS (US/0145-5400) [02745084] **2794**

GQ (US/0016-6979) [10858788] 1084, **3995**

GQ (UK EDITION) (UK/0954-8750) [29591690] **3995**

GR. GROCERS REPORT (US/0160-8894) [03940923] **2342**

GRA REPORTER (US/0016-3619) [02261596] **4652**

GRAA ZA PROUCAVANJE SPOMENIKA KULTURE VOJVODINE (YU/0434-300X) [06473823] **351**

GRAAFINEN TEOLLISUUS (FI/0785-0522) [19489183] **4565**

GRABBE-JAHRBUCH (GW) [09604536] **3391**

GRACE SEMINARY SPIRE (US) [01588058] **5016**

GRACE THEOLOGICAL JOURNAL *CEASED.* (US/0198-666X) [06203551] **4961**

GRACE THEOLOGICAL SEMINARY, WINONA LAKE, INDIANA *See* GRACE SEMINARY SPIRE **5016**

GRADBENI VESTNIK (YU/0017-2774) [I00172774] **615**

GRADHIVA (FR/0764-8928) [17398464] **237**

GRADIVA (US/0363-8057) [02529558] **3343**

GRADUATE AND UNDERGRADUATE PROGRAMS AND COURSES IN MIDDLE EAST STUDIES IN THE UNITED STATES, CANADA, AND ABROAD (1982) (US/0731-9320) [01244766] **1826**

●GRADUATE ASSISTANTSHIP DIRECTORY IN COMPUTING / ASSOCIATION FOR COMPUTING MACHINERY (US) [28368046] **1185**

GRADUATE ASSISTANTSHIP DIRECTORY IN THE COMPUTER SCIENCES (US/0072-5234) [02061746] **1185**

GRADUATE ASSISTANTSHIP DIRECTORY IN THE COMPUTER SCIENCES *See* GRADUATE ASSISTANTSHIP DIRECTORY IN COMPUTING / ASSOCIATION FOR COMPUTING MACHINERY **1185**

GRADUATE COMMUNICATION STUDIES (US/0161-2077) [03854243] **1112**

GRADUATE COMPUTERWORLD (CN/1186-1460) [24367974] **1238**

GRADUATE COURSE (MANCHESTER BUSINESS SCHOOL) UNIVERSITY OF MANCHESTER *See* MBA COURSE, THE DPBA COURSE, THE **1835**

●GRADUATE CURRICULA IN EDUCATIONAL COMMUNICATIONS AND TECHNOLOGY (US) [26434900] **1826**

GRADUATE EDUCATION BULLETIN (US) [12163811] 1826, **3579**

●GRADUATE FACULTY AND PROGRAMS IN POLITICAL SCIENCE (US/1065-6049) [26134253] **4475**

GRADUATE FACULTY PHILOSOPHY JOURNAL (US/0093-4240) [02546864] **4347**

GRADUATE FORUM (MINDANAO STATE UNIVERSITY. UNIVERSITY RESEARCH CENTER) (PH) [20113385] **2504**

GRADUATE LIBRARY EDUCATION PROGRAMS (US) [08995026] 1826, **3212**

GRADUATE MANAGEMENT ADMISSION TEST (US) [09180178] **678**

●GRADUATE MEDICAL EDUCATION DIRECTORY (US) [28038384] 3579, **1926**

GRADUATE MEDICAL EDUCATION IN THE EUROPEAN REGION. SUPPLEMENTARY REPORT (DK/0254-2609) [05065697] 1826, **3579**

GRADUATE OPPORTUNITIES (LONDON, ENGLAND : 1987) (UK) [16997148] 1826, **4204**

GRADUATE OUTLOOK (AT/0314-0679) [I03140679] 4204, **1826**

GRADUATE PROGRAMS IN PHYSICS, ASTRONOMY AND RELATED FIELDS (US/0147-1821) [04139865] 395, **4404**

GRADUATE RESEARCH IN URBAN EDUCATION AND RELATED DISCIPLINES (US/0888-1014) [04217665] **1826**

GRADUATE SCHOOL RESEARCH JOURNAL : A PUBLICATION OF GRADUATE SCHOOL OF BUSINESS ADMINISTRATION AND GRADUATE SCHOOL OF EDUCATION (PH/0030-7858) [11299091] **1826**

GRADUATE SCIENCE EDUCATION STUDENT SUPPORT AND POSTDOCTORALS (US/0094-7881) [01398706] **5108**

●GRADUATE STUDIES IN MATHEMATICS (US/1065-7339) [26710093] **3507**

GRADUATE STUDIES JOURNAL (US/0742-7522) [10428067] **1800**

GRADUATE STUDIES (LONDON, ENGLAND) (UK/0072-5269) [01774952] **1826**

●GRADUATE STUDY IN PSYCHOLOGY (US) [25904262] **4588**

GRADUATE STUDY IN PSYCHOLOGY AND ASSOCIATED FIELDS *See* GRADUATE STUDY IN PSYCHOLOGY **4588**

GRADUATE TEXTS IN MATHEMATICS (US/0072-5285) [02252251] **3507**

GRADUATE, THE (US/0098-3284) [02241443] **1091**

GRADUATES' GAZETTE, THE (CN/0702-8814) [03439558] **1826**

GRADUATING ENGINEER (US/0193-2276) [05160967] **1976**

GRADY COUNTY GENEALOGICAL SOCIETY QUARTERLY (US) **2452**

GRAECO-ARABICA / HETAIREIA HELLENOARAVIKON SPOUDON (GR) [10455586] **2651**

GRAEFE'S ARCHIVE FOR CLINICAL AND EXPERIMENTAL OPHTHALMOLOGY (GW/0721-832X) [08163108] **3875**

GRAELLSIA *CEASED.* (SP/0367-5041) [01411812] **5585**

GRAF ITI (OTTAWA) (CN/0381-9590) [02624854] **378**

GRAFICA (SALERNO, ITALY) (IT) [19071118] **378**

GRAFICAS (SP/0017-2901) [02652423] **4565**

GRAFICAS TECNICAS DE VALORES (MX) [21253505] **900**

Alphabetical Title Index — GRANT$

GRAFICUS (NE/0017-2936) [I00172936] **4565**

GRAFICUS MAGAZINE (NE) **4565**

GRAFIEK (BE) [16705791] **4565**

GRAFISCH NIEUWS (BE/0773-591X) [I0773591X] 378, **4815**

GRAFISKE FAG, DE (DK) [05654158] **4815, 4565**

GRAFISKT FORUM (SW) [05985186] **378**

GRAHAM HOUSE REVIEW (US/0145-7780) [02781731] **3463**

GRAHAM LEADER (GRAHAM, TEX. : 1975) (US) [14237911] **5750**

GRAIL (WATERLOO) (CN/0828-4083) [18595786] **4961**

GRAIN (CN/0315-7423) [01791701] **3391**

GRAIN AGE (US/0017-3029) [02251404] **201**

GRAIN & FEED JOURNALS (1978) (US/0164-3681) [04618742] **201**

GRAIN AND FEED MARKET NEWS / UNITED STATES DEPARTMENT OF AGRICULTURE, AGRICULTURAL MARKETING SERVICE, LIVESTOCK DIVISION (US) [08208017] **201**

GRAIN & FEED MARKETING (US/1047-4978) [14644252] **201**

GRAIN & FEED MERCHANT, THE (US/0199-2287) [05723488] **201**

GRAIN & FEED REVIEW (DES MOINES, IOWA) (US/0191-5959) [04622445] **201**

GRAIN AND OILSEEDS (UK) 2342, **90**

GRAIN DE SOLEIL PARIS (FR/0993-0787) [I09930787] **5030**

GRAIN DUST ABSTRACTS / COMPILED BY FANG S. LAI (US) [07792846] 159, **201**

GRAIN ELEVATORS IN CANADA (CN/0410-7470) [02443473] **201**

GRAIN GUIDE (US/1049-4073) [14235998] **201**

GRAIN JOURNAL (DECATUR, ILL.) (US/0274-7138) [06533908] **201**

GRAIN (LONDON, ENGLAND) (UK/0951-5798) [18941233] **838**

GRAIN MARKET NEWS (BELL, CALIF.) (US/0744-1533) [08072925] **90**

GRAIN MARKET REPORT (UK) [23938225] **90**

GRAIN MATTERS (CN/0383-4417) [03196453] **201**

GRAIN POOL OF WESTERN AUSTRALIA See ANNUAL REPORT / THE GRAIN POOL OF W. A **200**

GRAIN POOL OF WESTERN AUSTRALIA. GRAIN POOL OF WESTERN AUSTRALIA ANNUAL REPORT See ANNUAL REPORT / THE GRAIN POOL OF W. A **200**

GRAIN SORGHUM RESEARCH AND UTILIZATION CONFERENCE (US) [03744523] **201**

GRAIN STATISTICS WEEKLY (CN/0381-3010) [02754857] 201, **153**

GRAIN STOCKS (US/0193-5585) [02153663] **201**

GRAIN STORAGE & HANDLING (US/0199-4336) [05865308] **202**

GRAIN STORAGE, PROCESSING AND MARKETING. RESEARCH REPORT (US) [03297438] **202**

GRAIN TRADE OF CANADA (CN/0072-5358) [01791246] **202**

GRAIN TRANSPORTATION (US) [22913551] **202**

●GRAIN, WORLD MARKETS AND TRADE (US/1076-3929) [29829435] **202**

GRAINEWS (CN/0229-8090) [07285158] **173**

GRAINGER JOURNAL See GRAINGER SOCIETY JOURNAL, THE **4119**

GRAINGER SOCIETY JOURNAL, THE (UK/0141-5085) [12211872] 5231, **4119**

GRAINS JOURNAL (PH/0115-222X) [02510053] **202**

GRAMBLING STATE UNIVERSITY See ALUMNI DIRECTORY / GRAMBLING STATE UNIVERSITY **1098**

GRAMERCY REVIEW, THE (US/0194-4029) [04237087] **3391**

GRAMMA / TTT (NE) **3284**

GRAMMATEION (TORONTO) (CN/0836-0421) [18367567] **321**

GRAMMATICA (TOULOUSE, FRANCE) (FR) [01791725] **3284**

GRAMMATICA UNIVERSALIS (GW/0436-2829) [01452995] **3284**

GRAMODYOGA (II) [02239376] **1607**

GRAMOPHONE (UK/0017-310X) [22393171] **4119**

●GRAMOPHONE CLASSICAL CATALOGUE, THE (UK) [29763572] **5316**

GRAMOPHONE INCLUDING COMPACT DISC NEWS AND REVIEWS (UK/0017-310X) [12317734] **5316**

GRAMOPHONE NEWS (US/0147-8494) [03243276] 4119, **5317**

GRAMOPHONE. SPOKEN WORD AND MISCELLANEOUS CATALOGUE *SUSPENDED*. (UK) [02530223] **5317**

GRAMOPHONE, WIRELESS & TALKING MACHINE NEWS (UK) [04690897] 4119, **5317**

GRAMPIAN BUSINESS DIRECTORY (UK) **3480**

GRAMPIAN DIRECTORY (UK/0261-572X) [I0261572X] **1926**

GRAN BAZAAR (IT) **1084**

GRANA (SW/0017-3134) [00830748] **512**

GRANBURY TABLET, THE (US/0746-2131) [09864443] **5750**

GRAND ANGLE SUR L'EMPLOI ISSY-LES-MOULINEAUX (FR/0992-7662) [I09927662] **1676**

●GRAND BABILLARD, LE (CN/1196-0612) [28558021] **4652**

GRAND BATON, LE (US/0434-3336) [06509168] **4119**

GRAND BEND SUN (CN/0227-3470) [06702765] **5785**

GRAND BLANC NEWS, THE (US/0747-1742) [10620984] **5692**

GRAND FALLS ADVERTISER (CN/0833-1014) [20254363] **5785**

GRAND FORKS GAZETTE (CN) **5785**

GRAND FORKS HERALD (US/0745-9661) [01751382] **5725**

GRAND GOURMET (IT) **2488**

GRAND HOTEL (IT) **2488**

GRAND ISLAND DAILY INDEPENDENT (MAIL ED.) See GRAND ISLAND INDEPENDENT **5706**

GRAND ISLAND DAILY INDEPENDENT (REGULAR ED.) See GRAND ISLAND INDEPENDENT **5706**

GRAND ISLAND INDEPENDENT (US/1049-3018) [21212650] **5706**

GRAND LEDGE INDEPENDENT (US/1043-593X) [12115835] **5692**

GRAND MAGHREB : REVUE MENSUELLE DU CENTRE D'INFORMATION SUR LE GRAND MAGHREB (CIGMA) *CEASED*. (FR/0249-6879) [12954304] **2499**

GRAND MANAN HISTORIAN, THE (CN/0316-2702) [02248221] **2735**

GRAND MARAIS PILOT & PICTURED ROCKS REVIEW, THE (US/0746-617X) [10164354] **5692**

GRAND NEWS (CN/0316-7739) [02247917] **2785**

GRAND PORTAGE RESERVATION BUSINESS COMMITTEE See MOCCASIN TELEGRAPH **695**

GRAND PRAIRIE NEWS (GRAND PRAIRIE, TEX.) (US/1044-0097) [19682127] **5750**

GRAND PRIX DU CANADA See GRAND PRIX LABATT DU CANADA. REGLEMENTS **5415**

GRAND PRIX LABATT DU CANADA. REGLEMENTS (CN/0822-5222) [10061725] 4897, **5415**

GRAND RAPIDS BUSINESS JOURNAL (US/1045-4055) [12223622] **678**

GRAND RAPIDS HERALD-REVIEW (US/0744-544X) [01589644] **5696**

●GRAND RAPIDS' LABOR MARKET NEWS (US) [25953833] **1676**

GRAND RAPIDS LABOR MARKET REVIEW See GRAND RAPIDS' LABOR MARKET NEWS **1676**

GRAND RAPIDS LEGAL NEWS (US) **2975**

GRAND RAPIDS PRESS, THE (US) [09975013] **5692**

GRAND RIVER VALLEY REVIEW, THE (US/0739-084X) [06644697] **2735**

GRAND ROUNDS IN INFECTIOUS DISEASES (CN/1186-2947) [24368296] **3713**

GRAND ROUNDS PRESS, THE (US/1053-6620) [22603127] **3579**

GRAND SALINE SUN, THE (US) [14249855] **5750**

GRAND SLAM (OTTAWA) (CN/0701-0745) [03402736] **4897**

GRAND STREET (US/0734-5496) [08412070] **3391**

●GRAND TIMES (US/1068-1345) [27449767] **5179**

GRAND TRUNK POPLAR PRESS, THE (CN/0226-6415) [06515354] **5785**

GRAND VALLEY STAR AND VIDETTE (CN/0834-616X) [25589854] **5785**

GRANDE DIZIONARIO DELLA LINGUA ITALIANA. REDAZIONE, DIRETTORE: GIORGIO BARBERI SQUAROTTI (IT) [07458201] **3284**

GRANDE PRAIRIE, ALBERTA, CITY DIRECTORY See GRANDE PRAIRIE CITY DIRECTORY **4652**

●GRANDE PRAIRIE CITY DIRECTORY (CN/1193-4077) [27019164] **4652**

GRANDE PROMESSA (IT) **5246**

GRANDES COMPANHIAS, AS (BL) [01792482] **678**

GRANDES TEMAS ARGENTINOS, LOS (AG) [05770762] **2735**

GRANDS DOCUMENTS. LES EDITIONS DE MINUIT (US/0436-306X) [01457560] **2847**

GRANDS REPORTAGES (LOUVECIENNES, FRANCE) (FR) [07510412] **2517**

GRANDVIEW HERALD (US) [17410348] **5761**

GRANGE NEWS, THE (US/0043-0587) [09798729] **90**

GRANGER'S INDEX TO POETRY (US) [04815866] **3463**

GRANI (GW/0017-3185) [01590827] 2847, **2517**

GRANITE & MARBLE DIRECTORY ... / AMERICAN MONUMENT ASSOCIATION (US/0731-4094) [08160910] **2140**

GRANITE CUTTERS' JOURNAL, THE (US/0017-3207) [02261603] **1676**

GRANITE STATE LIBRARIES (US) [01586245] **3212**

GRANITSA; LENINGRADSKIE PISATELI O POGRANICHNIKAKH (RU) [01783428] **3392**

GRANMA (DAILY EDITION, SPANISH) (CU/0017-3223) [08676843] **5799**

GRANMA INTERNACIONAL (CU/0864-4616) [23959853] **5799**

GRANMA INTERNATIONAL (CU/0864-4624) [23828189] **5799**

GRANT/ACCESS (US/1054-769X) [22969318] **4652**

GRANT ADVISOR, THE (US/0740-5383) [09983273] **1826**

GRANT ALERT FOR THE GUIDE TO FEDERAL FUNDING FOR ANTI-DRUG PROGRAMS See ANTI-DRUG FUNDING ALERT **4630**

GRANT APPLICATION FOR CONTINUATION OF FULL DESIGNATION (US) [06236568] **4777**

GRANT AWARDS - U.S. DEPARTMENT OF TRANSPORTATION (US/0090-6492) [01785036] **5383**

GRANT AWARDS - UNITED STATES CIVIL SERVICE COMMISSION, BUREAU OF INTERGOVERNMENTAL PERSONNEL PROGRAMS (US/0095-6171) [01798447] **4704**

GRANT COUNTY BEACON / GRANT COUNTY GENEALOGY CLUB (US) [16410623] **2452**

GRANT COUNTY GENEALOGY CLUB See GRANT COUNTY BEACON / GRANT COUNTY GENEALOGY CLUB **2452**

GRANT COUNTY HERALD INDEPENDENT (US) [14403243] **5767**

GRANT COUNTY JOURNAL (US) [18591629] **5761**

GRANT COUNTY NEWS, THE (US) [01751390] **5725**

GRANT COUNTY NEWS (WILLIAMSTOWN, KY.) (US) [13151760] **5680**

GRANT COUNTY PRESS (US) [12789219] **5763**

GRANT COUNTY REVIEW (MILBANK, S.D.) (US) [12814338] **5743**

●GRANT$ FOR ALCOHOL AND DRUG ABUSE (US) [25074035] 1344, **4336**

GRANT$ FOR ARTS, CULTURE & THE HUMANITIES (US) [22615895] 321, **4336**

GRANT$ FOR CRIME, LAW ENFORCEMENT, & ABUSE PREVENTION (US) [22637397] 3165, **4336**

GRANT$ FOR ENVIRONMENTAL PROTECTION AND ANIMAL WELFARE (US) [22576372] 2172, **4336**

●GRANT$ FOR HEALTH PROGRAMS FOR CHILDREN AND YOUTH (US) [25199697] **5286**

GRANT$ FOR HIGHER EDUCATION (US/1045-2761) [10004160] 1826, **4336**

GRANT$ FOR HOSPITALS, MEDICAL CARE, & RESEARCH (US) [22637556] 3780, **4337**

GRANT$ FOR HUMAN SERVICES, MULTIPURPOSE AGENCIES See GRANT$ FOR SOCIAL SERVICES **4337**

GRANT$ FOR LIBRARIES AND INFORMATION SERVICES (US) [16260928] 3212, **4337**

●GRANT$ FOR MENTAL HEALTH, ADDICTIONS & CRISIS SERVICES (US) [25074259] 5286, **4337**

GRANT$ — Alphabetical Title Index

GRANT$ FOR MUSEUMS, ZOOS, & BOTANICAL GARDENS (US) [22602010] **4337**

GRANT$ FOR PUBLIC HEALTH AND DISEASES (US) [22607333] 4777, **4337**

GRANT$ FOR PUBLIC POLICY AND PUBLIC AFFAIRS (US) [22611943] 4652, **4337**

GRANT$ FOR RECREATION, SPORTS, & ATHLETICS (US) [22601054] 4850, **4337**

GRANT$ FOR RELIGION, RELIGIOUS WELFARE, & RELIGIOUS EDUCATION (US) [22601158] 4961, **4337**

●GRANT$ FOR SCHOLARSHIPS, STUDENT AID & LOANS (US) [25101673] 1826, **4337**

GRANT$ FOR SOCIAL AND POLITICAL SCIENCE PROGRAMS (US) [22577559] 5201, **4337**

●GRANT$ FOR SOCIAL SERVICES (US) [25199687] 5286, **4337**

GRANT$ FOR THE AGED / THE FOUNDATION CENTER (US) [12442219] 5286, **4337**

●GRANT$ FOR THE HOMELESS (US) [25074139] 5286, **4337**

GRANT LIST / DIVISION OF SOCIAL AND ECONOMIC SCIENCE (US) [08416393] **5201**

GRANT PROPOSAL NEWS (US/0893-9128) [15713503] **4729**

GRANT UPDATE! FOR GUIDE TO FEDERAL FUNDING FOR GOVERNMENTS & NONPROFITS (US/1055-596X) [23295284] **4729**

GRANTA (UK/0017-3231) [06619122] **3343**

GRANTECHS See GOVERNMENT FUNDING REPORT **4651**

GRANTEE REPORTS - FULBRIGHT EDUCATIONAL DEVELOPMENT PROGRAM (AT/0155-2996) [I01552996] **1748**

GRANTEE REPORTS - FULBRIGHT UNIVERSITY ADMINISTRATOR PROGRAM (AT/0155-8986) [I01558986] **1748**

GRANTHAGARA PARIKRAMA (BG) [26648820] **3212**

●GRANTHANA. INDIAN JOURNAL OF LIBRARY STUDIES (II) [24116509] **3212**

GRANTS ADMINISTRATION (US) [02778317] **4652**

GRANTS ADMINISTRATION MANUAL (US) [02788277] **4652**

GRANTS ADMINISTRATION NEWS (US/0889-8871) [14155880] **4652**

GRANTS AND AWARDS AVAILABLE TO AMERICAN WRITERS (US/0092-5268) [01790019] **3392**

GRANTS AND AWARDS AVAILABLE TO FOREIGN WRITERS (US/0093-3163) [01791695] **3392**

GRANTS AND AWARDS GUIDE - MEDICAL RESEARCH COUNCIL (CN/0703-2595) [02248430] **3579**

GRANTS / ARKANSAS MUSEUM SERVICES (US) [09500299] **4088**

GRANTS FOR ELEMENTARY AND SECONDARY EDUCATION / THE FOUNDATION CENTER (US) [11204524] 1748, **4337**

GRANTS FOR FILM, MEDIA & COMMUNICATIONS / THE FOUNDATION CENTER (US) [12493668] 1112, **4337**

GRANTS FOR FOREIGN AND INTERNATIONAL PROGRAMS (US/1056-649X) [22611954] 2910, **4337**

●GRANTS FOR LITERACY, READING & ADULT EDUCATION (US) [25074343] **1800**

GRANTS FOR MEDICAL AND PROFESSIONAL HEALTH EDUCATION (US) [14173354] 1826, **4337**

GRANTS FOR MINORITIES / FOUNDATION CENTER (US) [10004305] 2262, **4337**

GRANTS FOR PHYSICALLY AND MENTALLY DISABLED (US) [14173722] 4388, **4337**

GRANTS FOR RESEARCH ON DESEGREGATION (US/0278-1611) [07714741] **1748**

GRANTS FOR RESEARCH ON EDUCATION AND WORK (US/0148-3129) [03133864] **1913**

GRANTS FOR RESEARCH ON LAW AND GOVERNMENT IN EDUCATION (US/0196-4593) [04756563] 2975, 4653, **1748**

GRANTS FOR SCIENCE AND TECHNOLOGY PROGRAMS (US) [18422702] 5108, **4337**

GRANTS FOR WOMEN AND GIRLS (US/1064-4377) [10003929] 5558, **4337**

●GRANTS-IN-AID APPLICATION AND REFERENCE MATERIALS (US) [24607819] **4653**

GRANT'S INTEREST RATE OBSERVER (US/0748-8424) [11013046] **1493**

GRANTS PASS DAILY COURIER (US) **5733**

GRANTS REGISTER, THE (US/0072-5471) [01411991] **1826**

GRANTS - U.S. DEPARTMENT OF HEALTH, EDUCATION, AND WELFARE. OFFICE OF HUMAN DEVELOPMENT. OFFICE OF YOUTH DEVELOPMENT (US/0094-1387) [01793172] **5286**

GRANTSEEKER, THE (US/1076-1500) [30414853] **4653**

GRANTSLINE (US) **1826**

GRANTSMANSHIP NEWS **CEASED.** (US/0741-2487) [01751394] **4337**

GRANTSVILLE GAZETTE (US/8750-7684) [11743099] **5756**

GRANVILLE SENTINEL (GRANVILLE, N.Y. : 1885) (US) [18045905] **5716**

GRAPE ACREAGE (US) [18395591] **173**

GRAPE BELT (1959) (US) [11205336] **5716**

GRAPE GROWER (FRESNO, CALIF.) (US/1049-670X) [21275984] **173**

GRAPE RESEARCH NEWS (US) [22759914] **2342**

GRAPE VINE NEWSLETTER, THE (US/0890-5819) [14289854] **2617**

GRAPELAND MESSENGER, THE (US) [14153372] **5750**

GRAPEVINE (DOWNERS GROVE, ILL.), THE (US/0892-6611) [15266744] **2488**

GRAPEVINE GAZETTE (US/8750-7412) [11722565] **2534**

GRAPEVINE (SARATOGA) (US/0092-0592) [01788254] **4119**

GRAPEVINES FINGER LAKES MAGAZINE See FINGER LAKES MAGAZINE **2733**

GRAPH-AGRI : ANNUAIRE DE GRAPHIQUES AGRICOLES (FR/0242-2085) [07592832] **90**

GRAPH AGRI REGIONS (FR/0755-1908) [17165110] **90**

GRAPH THEORY NEWSLETTER **CEASED.** (US/0161-3324) [03623217] **3507**

GRAPHIC ARTISTS GUILD'S DIRECTORY OF ILLUSTRATION (US) [19040272] **378**

GRAPHIC ARTS ABSTRACTS (US) [19771637] **378**

GRAPHIC ARTS BLUE BOOK (US/1044-7970) [19913345] **4565**

GRAPHIC ARTS BLUE BOOK (METROPOLITAN NEW YORK-NEW JERSEY ED.) (US/1044-8527) [19576092] **4565**

GRAPHIC ARTS BLUE BOOK (MIDWESTERN ED.) (US/1044-8535) [19926348] **378**

GRAPHIC ARTS BLUE BOOK (NORTHEASTERN ED.) (US/1044-646X) [18575715] **378**

GRAPHIC ARTS BLUE BOOK (SOUTHEASTERN ED.) (US/1044-7989) [19913435] 4565, **378**

GRAPHIC ARTS BLUE BOOK (WEST COAST ED.) (US/1046-8005) [20535167] 4565, **378**

●GRAPHIC ARTS BULLETIN OF THE INSTITUTE OF PAPER SCIENCE AND TECHNOLOGY (US/1064-9638) [25310390] 379, **334**

GRAPHIC ARTS IN FINLAND (FI/0359-2464) [07588572] **379**

GRAPHIC ARTS INTERNATIONAL UNION. CONTRACT & RESEARCH DEPT See GAIU HANDBOOK OF WAGES, HOURS, AND FRINGE BENEFITS **1675**

GRAPHIC ARTS LITERATURE ABSTRACTS See GRAPHIC ARTS BULLETIN OF THE INSTITUTE OF PAPER SCIENCE AND TECHNOLOGY **334**

GRAPHIC ARTS MARKET IN CANADA (1978) (CN/0705-7571) [04233384] **379**

GRAPHIC ARTS MONTHLY (1987) (US/1047-9325) [17406060] 4565, **379**

GRAPHIC ARTS PRODUCT NEWS (CHICAGO) **CEASED.** (US/0274-5976) [06434053] **379**

GRAPHIC ARTS PURCHASE PREFERENCE STUDY (CN/0380-917X) [03400146] **379**

GRAPHIC ARTS TECHNICAL FOUNDATION : GATF (US) [10729181] **379**

GRAPHIC ARTS TRADE DIRECTORY & REGISTER (US/0072-5498) [01786315] 4565, **379**

GRAPHIC COMMUNICATIONS WORLD (US/0884-6901) [07879731] **4565**

GRAPHIC DESIGN BRITAIN (UK) [01412044] **379**

GRAPHIC DESIGN IN JAPAN / JAPAN GRAPHIC DESIGNERS ASSOCIATION (JA) [08643149] **379**

GRAPHIC DESIGN, USA (US) [12653724] **379**

GRAPHIC DESIGN USA (NEW YORK, N.Y. : 1986) (US) [14712875] **379**

GRAPHIC DESIGNERS' INDEX (SZ) **379**

GRAPHIC MONTHLY, THE (CN/0227-2806) [08063632] **4565**

GRAPHIC NOTICES AND SUPPLEMENTAL DATA See INTERNATIONAL FLIGHT INFORMATION MANUAL **24**

GRAPHIC (RICHMOND, IND.) (US) [13085393] **5664**

●GRAPHICAL MODELS AND IMAGE PROCESSING (US) **1233**

GRAPHICOMMUNICATOR (US/0746-3626) [09978715] **1112**

GRAPHICS DESIGN JOURNAL, THE (US/1047-7004) [20750985] **379**

GRAPHICS EXCHANGE (CN/0821-5588) [09670475] **379**

●GRAPHICS INTERNATIONAL (UK/1350-0937) [28838852] **379**

GRAPHICS WORLD (UK/0142-8853) [I01428853] **379**

GRAPHICUS (IT/0017-3436) [I00173436] **2488**

GRAPHIS (SZ/0017-3452) [01751402] **379**

GRAPHIS ANNUAL REPORTS (SZ) [18671168] **379**

GRAPHIS DESIGN (SZ) [18968333] **379**

GRAPHIS DIAGRAM (SZ) [18765582] **379**

GRAPHIS LETTERHEAD (SZ) [24441610] **379**

GRAPHIS LOGO (SZ) [25472658] 4565, **379**

GRAPHIS PACKAGING (SZ) [19610824] **379**

GRAPHIS PHOTO (SZ) [18500689] **4370**

GRAPHIS POSTERS (SZ) [01786992] **379**

GRAPHISCHE KUNST (GW) [02493891] **379**

GRAPHIX PRAHRAN (AT/0314-6685) [I03146685] **379**

GRAPHOSCOPE, THE (CN/0046-631X) [02016805] **900**

GRAPHS AND COMBINATORICS (JA/0911-0119) [12116743] **3507**

GRAPHS OF NEUTRON INTENSITIES (JA) [07033068] **4404**

GRAPPA **SUSPENDED.** (US/0742-7700) [10466649] **2367**

GRASAS Y ACEITES (SEVILLA) (SP/0017-3495) [01775751] 2342, **488**

GRASDUINEN (NE/0167-2932) [I01672932] 2384, **512**

GRASS AND FORAGE SCIENCE (UK/0142-5242) [05013604] **90**

GRASS FARMER **CEASED.** (UK) [07958288] **90**

GRASS ROOTS CAMPAIGNING (US) [08872964] **4475**

GRASS ROOTS FORUM **SUSPENDED.** (US/0017-3517) [01606788] **4475**

GRASS ROOTS INTERNATIONAL FOLK RESOURCE DIRECTORY (US/8755-6855) [11383426] **5268**

GRASS ROOTS PERSPECTIVES ON AMERICAN HISTORY (US/0148-771X) [03531643] **2735**

GRASS ROOTS SHEPPARTON (AT/0310-2890) [I03102890] **90**

●GRASSLANDS AND FORAGE ABSTRACTS (UK/1350-9837) [30096784] 90, **153**

GRASSROOTS CATALOG (US) **2452**

GRASSROOTS DEVELOPMENT (US/0733-6608) [08636417] **2910**

GRASSROOTS ECONOMIC ORGANIZING NEWSLETTER (US/1071-0590) [26868238] **1592**

GRASSROOTS EDITOR (US/0017-3541) [01751405] **2920**

GRASSROOTS FOR HIGH RISQUE LIBRARIANS (US/0889-5198) [10245488] **3212**

GRASSROOTS FUNDRAISING JOURNAL (US/0740-4832) [09723993] **4337**

GRASSROOTS (MADISON) **CEASED.** (US/0361-1515) [02241247] **1344**

GRASSROOTS / VIRGINIA DEPARTMENT OF CONSERVATION AND RECREATION, DIVISION OF SOIL AND WATER CONSERVATION (US) [25778582] **2194**

GRATIA (GW/0343-1258) [05758217] **3392**

GRATIS (SCARBOROUGH, ONT.) (CN/0225-381X) [08659477] **4862**

GRAUE LITERATUR AUS OSTASIEN (GW) [06368760] **2651**

Alphabetical Title Index — GREAT

GRAVE MATTERS : NEWSLETTER FOR CIVIL WAR NECROLITHOLOGISTS (US) [24460871] **2735**

GRAVELBOURG GAZETTE (CN/0715-4488) [09223223] **5785**

GRAVENHURST LEADER, THE (CN/0710-1082) [08295026] **5785**

GRAVES FAMILY NEWSLETTER, THE (US/0146-0269) [02846358] **2452**

GRAVETTE NEWS-HERALD, THE (US) [18391022] **5631**

GRAVURE (NEW YORK, N.Y. 1987) (US/0894-4946) [16116464] **4565**

GRAVURE RESEARCH INSTITUTE See GRI NEWSLETTER **4565**

●GRAY AREAS (US/1062-5712) [25669057] **2534**

GRAY BOOK (II) [01790416] **321**

GRAY PANTHER NETWORK (US/0739-2001) [04736337] **5286**

●GRAYS HARBOR BEACON (US/1064-4806) [26294868] **5761**

●GRAY'S SPECIALTY CAR VALUE GUIDE (US/1064-2404) [26238120] **5415**

GRAY'S SPORTING JOURNAL (US/0273-6691) [02177591] **4873**

GRAYSON COUNTY (KY.). FISCAL COURT See REPORT OF THE AUDITOR OF PUBLIC ACCOUNTS. AUDIT EXAMINATION OF THE GRAYSON COUNTY FISCAL COURT **4745**

GRAYSON COUNTY NEWS-GAZETTE (US) [13958182] **5680**

GRAYSON JOURNAL-ENQUIRER (US) [14407520] **5680**

GRAYWOLF ANNUAL, THE (US/0743-7471) [10666837] **3392**

GRAZ. JOANNEUM. ABTEILUNG FUR GEOLOGIE, PALAONTOLOGIE UND BERGBAU See MITTEILUNGEN DER ABTEILUNG FUER GEOLOGIE, PALAONTOLOGIE UND BERGBAU AM LANDESMUSEUM JOANNEUM. SH **1388**

GRAZ. JOANNEUM. ABTEILUNG FUR GEOLOGIE, PALAONTOLOGIE UND BERGBAU See MITTEILUNGEN DER ABTEILUNG FUER GEOLOGIE, PALAONTOLOGIE UND BERGBAU AM LANDESMUSEUM JOANNEUM **1388**

GRAZER BEITRAEGE (AU/0376-5253) [01794820] **3284**

GRAZER BEITRAEGE. SUPPLEMENTBAND (AU) [07500220] **269**

GRAZER LINGUISTISCHE STUDIEN (AU/1015-0498) [05392660] **3284**

GRAZER MUSIKWISSENSCHAFTLICHE ARBEITEN (AU) [20330128] **4119**

GRAZER PHILOSOPHISCHE STUDIEN (NE/0165-9227) [02697494] **4347**

GRAZIA (IT) **5558**

GRAZIER (CORVALLIS, OR.), THE (US/1057-2430) [13529122] **90**

GRAZIERS' REVIEW See QUEENSLAND COUNTRY LIFE **124**

GREAT ACTIVITIES (US/0886-764X) [12983197] **1855**

●GREAT AMERICAN BASEBALL STAT BOOK (US/1056-5116) [23728311] **4897**

GREAT AMERICAN COW TRADER, THE (US/0744-5008) [08376489] **211**

●GREAT AMERICAN STORIES (US/1046-008X) [20306698] **2488**

GREAT BARRIER REEF MARINE PARK AUTHORITY See ANNUAL REPORT / THE GREAT BARRIER REEF MARINE PARK AUTHORITY **2187**

GREAT BARRINGTON HISTORICAL SOCIETY NEWSLETTER (US/0895-7851) [11656823] **2617**

GREAT BASIN NATURALIST MEMOIRS (US/0160-239X) [02862690] **4166**

GREAT BASIN NATURALIST, THE (US/0017-3614) [01715991] **4165**

●GREAT BATTLES (US/1071-670X) [28683955] **4044, 2617**

GREAT BEND TRIBUNE (1972) (US/0891-7078) [14289378] **5676**

GREAT BIBLIOGRAPHERS SERIES (US) [06082655] **416**

GREAT BLAFIGRIA IS, THE (US) [03283938] **90**

GREAT BRITAIN See LONDON GAZETTE, THE **5812**

GREAT BRITAIN See SCOTS MERCANTILE LAW STATUTES **3103**

GREAT BRITAIN See INDEX TO GOVERNMENT ORDERS IN FORCE 31ST DECEMBER ... **2981**

GREAT BRITAIN See STATUTORY INSTRUMENTS **4689**

GREAT BRITAIN See HALSBURY'S STATUTORY INSTRUMENTS : BEING A COMPANION WORK TO HALSBURY'S STATUTES OF ENGLAND **2976**

GREAT BRITAIN See PUBLIC GENERAL ACTS AND GENERAL SYNOD MEASURES, THE **4676**

GREAT BRITAIN. ADVISORY COMMITTEE ON PESTICIDES See ANNUAL REPORT / ADVISORY COMMITTEE ON PESTICIDES **4244**

GREAT BRITAIN AGRICULTURAL DEVELOPMENT AND ADVISORY SERVICE See HORTICULTURAL ENTERPRISES **2419**

GREAT BRITAIN. AGRICULTURAL DEVELOPMENT AND ADVISORY SERVICE. POULTRY SECTION See QUARTERLY JOURNAL - AGRICULTURAL DEVELOPMENT AND ADVISORY SERVICE, POULTRY SECTION. ABSTRACTS SECTION **220**

GREAT BRITAIN. ARMY. ROYAL ARMY MEDICAL CORPS See JOURNAL OF THE ROYAL ARMY MEDICAL CORPS **3599**

GREAT BRITAIN. BOARD OF INLAND REVENUE See REPORT OF THE COMMISSIONERS OF HIS MAJESTY'S INLAND REVENUE **4745**

GREAT BRITAIN. BOARD OF TRADE See BOILER EXPLOSIONS ACTS, 1882 AND 1890, REPORT OF PRELIMINARY INQUIRY **3476**

GREAT BRITAIN. BREEDING AND PRODUCTION ORGANISATION See BULLS (OTHER THAN FRIESIAN) WITH IMPROVED CONTEMPORARY COMPARISONS **208**

GREAT BRITAIN. CABINET OFFICE See ANNUAL REVIEW OF GOVERNMENT FUNDED R&D / CABINET OFFICE **4630**

GREAT BRITAIN. CENTRAL STATISTICAL OFFICE See PRICE INDEX NUMBERS FOR CURRENT COST ACCOUNTING **1594**

GREAT BRITAIN. CENTRAL STATISTICAL OFFICE See GUIDE TO OFFICIAL STATISTICS **5328**

GREAT BRITAIN. CENTRAL STATISTICAL OFFICE See UNITED KINGDOM BALANCE OF PAYMENTS **5345**

GREAT BRITAIN. CENTRAL STATISTICAL OFFICE See MONTHLY DIGEST OF STATISTICS **5333**

GREAT BRITAIN. CENTRAL STATISTICAL OFFICE See ANNUAL ABSTRACT OF STATISTICS **5321**

GREAT BRITAIN. CIVIL SERVICE DEPT See PUBLISHED BY CSD **4705**

GREAT BRITAIN. COLONIAL OFFICE See ANNUAL REPORT ON ST. LUCIA, B.W.I **5461**

GREAT BRITAIN. COMMITTEE ON MEDICAL ASPECTS OF FOOD POLICY. SUBCOMMITTEE ON NUTRITIONAL SURVEILLANCE See REPORT BY THE SUB-COMMITTEE ON NUTRITIONAL SURVEILLANCE (LONDON) **4198**

GREAT BRITAIN. COMMITTEE ON SAFETY OF DRUGS See REPORT - GREAT BRITAIN. COMMITTEE ON SAFETY OF DRUGS **4798**

GREAT BRITAIN. COMMONWEALTH INSTITUTE See ANNUAL REPORT OF THE DIRECTOR TO THE BOARD OF GOVERNORS **4628**

GREAT BRITAIN. COUNCIL ON TRIBUNALS See ANNUAL REPORT OF THE COUNCIL ON TRIBUNALS FOR THE PERIOD, THE **4628**

GREAT BRITAIN. COURT OF APPEAL See CRIMINAL APPEAL REPORTS (SENTENCING), THE **3105**

GREAT BRITAIN. COURT OF APPEAL See CRIMINAL APPEAL REPORTS, THE **3105**

GREAT BRITAIN. COURT OF CRIMINAL APPEALS. CRIMINAL APPEAL REPORTS See CRIMINAL APPEAL REPORTS, THE **3105**

GREAT BRITAIN. COURTS See KNIGHT'S LOCAL GOVERNMENT AND MAGISTERIAL REPORTS, WITH STATUTES, STATUTORY INSTRUMENTS, & C **4660**

GREAT BRITAIN. DEPARTMENT OF EMPLOYMENT See NEW EARNINGS SURVEY (LONDON, 1970-) **1693**

GREAT BRITAIN. DEPT. OF EDUCATION AND SCIENCE See STATISTICS OF EDUCATION; SPECIAL SERIES - GREAT BRITAIN **1798**

GREAT BRITAIN. DEPT. OF EDUCATION AND SCIENCE See EDUCATION STATISTICS FOR THE UNITED KINGDOM **1794**

GREAT BRITAIN DEPT. OF EMPLOYMENT See EMPLOYMENT GAZETTE **1666**

GREAT BRITAIN. DEPT. OF EMPLOYMENT See ANNUAL REPORT ON TRAINING RESEARCH / EMPLOYMENT DEPARTMENT **938**

GREAT BRITAIN. DEPT. OF EMPLOYMENT See RESEARCH **1707**

GREAT BRITAIN. DEPT. OF ENERGY See DEVELOPMENT OF THE OIL AND GAS RESOURCES OF THE UNITED KINGDOM **4254**

GREAT BRITAIN. DEPT. OF ENERGY See DIGEST OF UNITED KINGDOM ENERGY STATISTICS **1961**

GREAT BRITAIN. DEPT. OF HEALTH AND SOCIAL SECURITY See HEALTH AND PERSONAL SOCIAL SERVICES STATISTICS FOR ENGLAND WITH SUMMARY TABLES FOR GREAT BRITAIN **5266**

GREAT BRITAIN. DEPT. OF HEALTH AND SOCIAL SECURITY See ON THE STATE OF THE PUBLIC HEALTH (1963) **4795**

GREAT BRITAIN. DEPT. OF HEALTH AND SOCIAL SECURITY See SOCIAL SECURITY STATISTICS **5267**

GREAT BRITAIN. DEPT. OF HEALTH AND SOCIAL SECURITY See REPORTED DECISIONS OF THE SOCIAL SECURITY COMMISSIONER. SOCIAL SECURITY, CHILD BENEFIT, FAMILY INCOME SUPPLEMENTS, AND SUPPLEMENTARY BENEFIT ACTS / DEPARTMENT OF HEALTH AND SOCIAL SECURITY **5305**

GREAT BRITAIN. DEPT. OF SCIENTIFIC AND INDUSTRIAL RESEARCH. ROAD RESEARCH BOARD See BULLETIN - GREAT BRITAIN DEPARTMENT OF SCIENTIFIC AND INDUSTRIAL RESEARCH. ROAD RESEARCH BOARD **5439**

GREAT BRITAIN. DEPT. OF THE ENVIRONMENT. LIBRARY See LIBRARY BULLETIN **3224**

GREAT BRITAIN. DEPT. OF THE ENVIRONMENT. LIBRARY SERVICES See ANNUAL LIST OF PUBLICATIONS - DEPARTMENT OF THE ENVIRONMENT. DEPARTMENT OF TRANSPORT. LIBRARY SERVICES **2160**

GREAT BRITAIN. DEPT. OF THE ENVIRONMENT. WATER DATA UNIT See WATER DATA - GREAT BRITAIN. DEPT. OF THE ENVIRONMENT. WATER DATA UNIT **5542**

GREAT BRITAIN. DEPT. OF TRADE AND INDUSTRY See INSURANCE BUSINESS: ANNUAL REPORT **2883**

GREAT BRITAIN. DEPT. OF TRANSPORT See ROAD ACCIDENTS GREAT BRITAIN **5443**

GREAT BRITAIN. DIPLOMATIC SERVICE ADMINISTRATION OFFICE See DIPLOMATIC SERVICE LIST (GREAT BRITAIN), THE **4471**

GREAT BRITAIN. DIRECTORATE OF CONSTRUCTIONAL DESIGN See TIMBER ECONOMY **2405**

GREAT BRITAIN. DIRECTORATE OF MILITARY SURVEY. MAP LIBRARY. SELECTED ACCESSIONS (UK) [08005579] **2565**

GREAT BRITAIN. EQUAL OPPORTUNITIES COMMISSION See ANNUAL REPORT / EQUAL OPPORTUNITIES COMMISSION **4504**

GREAT BRITAIN. EQUAL OPPORTUNITIES COMMISSION. ANNUAL REPORT OF THE EQUAL OPPORTUNITIES COMMISSION See ANNUAL REPORT / EQUAL OPPORTUNITIES COMMISSION **4504**

GREAT BRITAIN. FORESTRY COMMISSION See FORESTRY COMMISSION FIELD BOOK **2382**

GREAT BRITAIN. FORESTRY COMMISSION See ANNUAL REPORT AND ACCOUNTS OF THE FORESTRY COMMISSION **2374**

GREAT BRITAIN. FORESTRY COMMISSION See REPORT ON FOREST RESEARCH **2392**

GREAT BRITAIN. HEALTH AND SAFETY EXECUTIVE See CERAMICS, HEALTH AND SAFETY **2860**

GREAT BRITAIN. HEALTH AND SAFETY EXECUTIVE See COAL MINES - (GREAT BRITAIN) **2137**

GREAT BRITAIN. HEALTH AND SAFETY EXECUTIVE. RESEARCH AND LABORATORY SERVICES DIVISION See HEALTH AND SAFETY RESEARCH AND TECHNOLOGICAL SERVICES **2862**

GREAT BRITAIN. HER MAJESTY'S STATIONERY OFFICE See HMSO MONTHLY CATALOGUE **4654**

GREAT BRITAIN. HER MAJESTY'S STATIONERY OFFICE See HMSO AGENCY CATALOGUE **4654**

GREAT BRITAIN. HOME DEPT See HOME OFFICE RESEARCH STUDIES **5479**

GREAT BRITAIN. HOME OFFICE. PROBATION AND AFTER-CARE STATISTICS, ENGLAND AND WALES See PROBATION STATISTICS, ENGLAND AND WALES / HOME OFFICE **3082**

GREAT BRITAIN. HOME OFFICE. RESEARCH UNIT See SUMMARY OF RESEARCH WITHIN THE UNIT AND OF RESEARCH SUPPORTED BY GRANT **3177**

GREAT BRITAIN HOUSE OF COMMONS PARLIAMENTARY PAPERS. MICROFORM (UK) [08858587] **4653**

GREAT BRITAIN. HYDROGRAPHIC DEPT *See* ARCTIC PILOT **4174**

GREAT BRITAIN. LAND AUTHORITY FOR WALES *See* ANNUAL REPORT / LAND AUTHORITY FOR WALES **4627**

GREAT BRITAIN LAW COMMISSION. WORKING PAPERS (UK) **2975**

GREAT BRITAIN. MILK MARKETING BOARD *See* ANNUAL RREPORT AND ACCOUNTS / MILK MARKETING BOARD **192**

GREAT BRITAIN. MILK MARKETING BOARD *See* NATIONAL MILK RECORDS. ANNUAL REPORT, ENGLAND & WALES **197**

GREAT BRITAIN. MILK MARKETING BOARD *See* REPORT AND ACCOUNTS ... : INCORPORATING THE REPORT AND ACCOUNTS OF DAIRY CREST LIMITED / MILK MARKETING BOARD **198**

GREAT BRITAIN. MILK MARKETING BOARD. ANNUAL REPORT AND ACCOUNTS *See* REPORT AND ACCOUNTS ... : INCORPORATING THE REPORT AND ACCOUNTS OF DAIRY CREST LIMITED / MILK MARKETING BOARD **198**

GREAT BRITAIN. MINES AND QUARRIES INSPECTORATE *See* REPORTS OF H. M. INSPECTORS OF MINES AND QUARRIES UNDER THE MINES AND QUARRIES ACT 1954 : THE NORTH OF ENGLAND DISTRICT **2150**

GREAT BRITAIN. MINES AND QUARRIES INSPECTORATE *See* REPORTS OF H.M. INSPECTORS OF MINES AND QUARRIES UNDER THE MINES AND QUARRIES ACT 1954 : SOUTH WALES DISTRICT **2150**

GREAT BRITAIN. MINISTRY OF AGRICULTURE, FISHERIES AND FOOD *See* AGRICULTURE, FISHERIES, FOOD **53**

GREAT BRITAIN. MINISTRY OF AGRICULTURE, FISHERIES AND FOOD *See* TECHNICAL BULLETIN - MINISTRY OF AGRICULTURE, FISHERIES AND FOOD **139**

GREAT BRITAIN. MINISTRY OF AGRICULTURE, FISHERIES AND FOOD. ECONOMICS DIVISION II *See* RETAIL PRICES IN THE EEC **1625**

GREAT BRITAIN. MINISTRY OF DEFENCE *See* NAVY LIST, THE **4180**

GREAT BRITAIN. MINISTRY OF OVERSEAS DEVELOPMENT *See* BRITISH AID STATISTICS **5323**

GREAT BRITAIN. MUSEUMS AND GALLERIES COMMISSION. CONSERVATION UNIT *See* CONSERVATION UPDATE : NEWSLETTER OF THE CONSERVATION UNIT, MUSEUMS & GALLERIES COMMISSION **348**

GREAT BRITAIN. NATIONAL GALLERY *See* NATIONAL GALLERY TECHNICAL BULLETIN **359**

GREAT BRITAIN. NATIONAL WATER COUNCIL *See* ANNUAL REPORT AND ACCOUNTS - NATIONAL WATER COUNCIL **5529**

GREAT BRITAIN. NATURAL ENVIRONMENT RESEARCH COUNCIL *See* REPORT OF THE COUNCIL / NATURAL ENVIRONMENT RESEARCH COUNCIL **2181**

GREAT BRITAIN. OFFICE OF FAIR TRADING *See* ANNUAL REPORT OF THE DIRECTOR GENERAL OF FAIR TRADING TO THE SECRETARY OF STATE FOR PRICES AND CONSUMER PROTECTION (GREAT BRITAIN) **823**

GREAT BRITAIN. OFFICE OF POPULATION CENSUSES & SURVEYS *See* OPCS MONITOR. INFANT AND PERINATAL MORTALITY **4555**

GREAT BRITAIN. OFFICE OF POPULATION CENSUSES & SURVEYS *See* OPCS MONITOR. CONGENITAL MALFORMATIONS **4555**

GREAT BRITAIN. OFFICE OF POPULATION CENSUSES & SURVEYS *See* OPCS MONITOR. INFECTIOUS DISEASES **4555**

GREAT BRITAIN. OFFICE OF POPULATION CENSUSES & SURVEYS *See* OPCS MONITOR. REGISTRAR GENERAL'S WEEKLY RETURN FOR ENGLAND AND WALES **4555**

GREAT BRITAIN. OFFICE OF POPULATION CENSUSES & SURVEYS *See* OPCS MONITOR. MID-YEAR ESTIMATES OF THE POPULATION OF NEW COMMONWEALTH AND PAKISTANI ETHNIC ORIGIN **4555**

GREAT BRITAIN. OFFICE OF POPULATION CENSUSES AND SURVEYS *See* POPULATION TRENDS **4562**

GREAT BRITAIN. OFFICE OF POPULATION CENSUSES & SURVEYS *See* OPCS MONITOR. DEATHS FROM ACCIDENTS **4555**

GREAT BRITAIN. OFFICE OF POPULATION CENSUSES & SURVEYS *See* OPCS MONITOR. DEATHS BY CAUSE **4555**

GREAT BRITAIN. OFFICE OF POPULATION CENSUSES & SURVEYS *See* OPCS MONITOR. BIRTHS BY BIRTH PLACE OF PARENT **4555**

GREAT BRITAIN. OFFICE OF POPULATION CENSUSES & SURVEYS *See* OPCS MONITOR. ADOPTIONS **4555**

GREAT BRITAIN. OFFICE OF POPULATION CENSUSES & SURVEYS *See* OPCS MONITOR. POPULATION PROJECTIONS **4555**

GREAT BRITAIN. OFFICE OF POPULATION CENSUSES & SURVEYS *See* OPCS MONITOR. BIRTHS AND DEATHS **4555**

GREAT BRITAIN. OFFICE OF POPULATION CENSUSES & SURVEYS *See* OPCS MONITOR. LEGAL ABORTIONS / OFFICE OF POPULATION CENSUS & SURVEYS **4555**

GREAT BRITAIN. PARLIAMENT. HOUSE OF COMMONS *See* WEEKLY INFORMATION BULLETIN - HOUSE OF COMMONS **4694**

GREAT BRITAIN. PARLIAMENT. HOUSE OF COMMONS *See* GREAT BRITAIN HOUSE OF COMMONS PARLIAMENTARY PAPERS. MICROFORM **4653**

GREAT BRITAIN. PARLIAMENT. HOUSE OF COMMONS *See* PARLIAMENTARY DEBATES (HANSARD). HOUSE OF COMMONS OFFICIAL REPORT **4672**

GREAT BRITAIN. PARLIAMENT. HOUSE OF COMMONS *See* STANDING ORDERS OF THE HOUSE OF COMMONS **3136**

GREAT BRITAIN. PARLIAMENT. HOUSE OF COMMONS. COMMITTEE OF PUBLIC ACCOUNTS *See* REPORT FROM THE COMMITTEE OF PUBLIC ACCOUNTS TOGETHER WITH THE PROCEEDINGS OF THE COMMITTEE AND THE MINUTES OF EVIDENCE TAKEN BY THE COMMITTEE OF PUBLIC ACCOUNTS ON **4680**

GREAT BRITAIN. PARLIAMENT. HOUSE OF COMMONS. PARLIAMENTARY COMMISSIONER *See* ANNUAL REPORT - PARLIAMENTARY COMMISSIONER FOR ADMINISTRATION **4629**

GREAT BRITAIN. PARLIAMENT. HOUSE OF COMMONS. SELECT COMMITTEE ON SCIENCE AND TECHNOLOGY. SUB-COMMITTEE D *See* MINUTES OF EVIDENCE **1145**

GREAT BRITAIN. PARLIAMENT. HOUSE OF LORDS *See* PARLIAMENTARY DEBATES (HANSARD). HOUSE OF LORDS OFFICIAL REPORT, THE **4672**

GREAT BRITAIN. PATENT OFFICE *See* OFFICIAL JOURNAL (PATENTS) **1307**

GREAT BRITAIN. REGISTRY OF FRIENDLY SOCIETIES *See* REPORT OF THE CHIEF REGISTRAR / REGISTRY OF FRIENDLY SOCIETIES **2892**

GREAT BRITAIN. ROYAL AIR FORCE *See* ROYAL AIR FORCE RETIRED LIST, THE **4056**

GREAT BRITAIN. SCOTTISH DEVELOPMENT DEPT *See* REPORT - GREAT BRITAIN. SCOTTISH DEVELOPMENT DEPT **2833**

GREAT BRITAIN. SCOTTISH EDUCATION DEPT *See* EDUCATIONAL RESEARCH - GREAT BRITAIN. SCOTTISH EDUCATION DEPT **1893**

GREAT BRITAIN. SCOTTISH EDUCATION DEPT *See* SCOTTISH TEACHERS' SALARIES MEMORANDUM **1710**

GREAT BRITAIN. SEA FISH INDUSTRY AUTHORITY *See* ANNUAL REPORT / SEA FISH INDUSTRY AUTHORITY **2295**

GREAT BRITAIN. STATIONERY OFFICE *See* CONSOLIDATED INDEX TO GOVERNMENT PUBLICATIONS **4640**

GREAT BRITAIN. STATUE LAW COMMITTEE *See* TABLE OF GOVERNMENT ORDERS **4689**

GREAT BRITAIN. SUPREME COURT OF JUDICATURE *See* SUPREME COURT PRACTICE, THE **3143**

GREAT BRITAIN. TRAINING COMMISSION *See* ANNUAL REPORT / EMPLOYMENT DEPARTMENT GROUP, TRAINING COMMISSION **1649**

GREAT BRITAIN. TREASURY *See* GOVERNMENT'S EXPENDITURE PLANS / PRESENTED TO PARLIAMENT BY THE CHANCELLOR OF THE EXCHEQUER BY COMMAND OF HER MAJESTY, THE **4728**

GREAT BRITAIN. TREASURY. INFORMATION DIVISION *See* ECONOMIC PROGRESS REPORT **1557**

GREAT BRITAIN. WELSH OFFICE *See* STAFF OF SOCIAL SERVICES DEPARTMENTS ... / WELSH OFFICE **5311**

GREAT BRITAIN. WELSH OFFICE *See* HEALTH AND PERSONAL SOCIAL SERVICES STATISTICS FOR WALES **5266**

GREAT BRITAIN. WORKING PARTY OF PESTICIDE RESIDUES *See* REPORT OF THE WORKING PARTY ON PESTICIDE RESIDUES **4248**

GREAT CANADIAN HOMESTEADER, THE (CN/0705-7210) [04249870] **90**

GREAT CIRCLE (AT/0156-8698) [10502009] **4176**

GREAT CONTEMPORARY ISSUES. GROUP 1, UPDATE, THE (US/0275-2182) [07118734] **2617**

GREAT DECISIONS (US/0072-727X) [01334810] **4523**

GREAT EXPECTATIONS (CN/0823-9266) [I08239266] **3579**

GREAT EXPEDITIONS (US/0706-7682) [05018423] **5478**

GREAT FALLS TRIBUNE (GREAT FALLS, MONT. : 1921) (US) [09374534] **5705**

GREAT FOODS MAGAZINE (US/8756-2553) [11494157] **2342**

GREAT IDEAS FOR LONG TERM CARE (US/1041-2352) [18691719] **3579**

GREAT IDEAS TODAY, THE (US/0072-7288) [01751544] **1926**

GREAT ISSUES *CEASED.* (US/0364-1465) [01936948] **1748**

GREAT ISSUES OF THE DAY (US/0270-7497) [06501138] **2488**

GREAT LAKER, THE (CN/0317-1078) [02247902] **4233**

GREAT LAKES CAMPBOOK (US/0734-8517) [06469292] **4873**

GREAT LAKES ENTOMOLOGIST, THE (US/0090-0222) [01787278] **5609**

GREAT LAKES ENVIRONMENTAL RESEARCH LABORATORY *See* DETAILED TECHNICAL PLAN FOR THE GREAT LAKES ENVIRONMENTAL RESEARCH LABORATORY **2163**

GREAT LAKES FISHERMAN (CN/0847-0685) [07730397] **2304**

GREAT LAKES FISHERMAN (COLUMBUS, OHIO) *SUSPENDED.* (US/0194-5564) [04824375] **2304**

GREAT LAKES FISHERY COMMISSION *See* ANNUAL REPORT - GREAT LAKES FISHERY COMMISSION **2294**

GREAT LAKES GEOGRAPHER (CN) **2565**

GREAT LAKES JOURNAL *See* FISHERMAN (GRAND HAVEN, MICH.), THE **2302**

● GREAT LAKES LOG (US/1067-4144) [27206307] **5449**

GREAT LAKES MONITOR (US/1054-1071) [22748150] **1132**

GREAT LAKES NAVIGATION (CN/0824-8583) [02441801] **5449**

GREAT LAKES REPORTER, THE *CEASED.* (US/0748-9544) [11039775] **1635, 2172**

GREAT LAKES RESEARCH CHECKLIST (US/0072-7326) [02261633] **5533, 5549**

GREAT LAKES RESEARCH VESSELS SUPPLEMENT; PRELIMINARY SCHEDULES (US) [06618647] **5533**

GREAT LAKES SAILING SCANNER (US/0194-4622) [04676709] **593**

GREAT LAKES SAILOR (AKRON, OHIO) *SUSPENDED.* (US/0892-5410) [15212544] **593**

GREAT LAKES SCIENCE ADVISORY BOARD *See* REPORT / GREAT LAKES SCIENCE ADVISORY BOARD **5538**

GREAT LAKES STATES *See* GREAT LAKES TOUR BOOK **5478**

GREAT LAKES TOUR BOOK (US) [02742058] **5478**

GREAT LAKES TRAVEL & LIVING (US/0887-6223) [13302604] **5478**

GREAT LAKES TROLLING ANNUAL *CEASED.* (US/0749-0526) [11039159] **2304**

GREAT LAKES UNITED, THE (US) [14282635] **5533, 2172**

GREAT LAKES VEGETABLE GROWERS NEWS, THE (US/1049-8494) [10148562] **173**

GREAT LAKES WASTE & POLLUTION REVIEW MAGAZINE (US/0742-1230) [10292234] **2230**

GREAT LAKES WATER LEVELS (US/0090-2187) [01784835] **1413**

GREAT LAKES WATER QUALITY BOARD *See* REPORT ON GREAT LAKES WATER QUALITY : REPORT TO THE INTERNATIONAL JOINT COMMISSION / GREAT LAKES WATER QUALITY BOARD **5538**

GREAT LAKES WETLANDS (US/1062-5356) [21263864] **2216**

GREAT LIBRARY PROMOTION IDEAS (US/1050-9372) [14228183] **924**

Alphabetical Title Index — GREEN

GREAT LIVES OBSERVED (US) [04280413] **432**

GREAT MASTERS OF THE PAST (US/0434-5797) [01489694] **5231**

GREAT METROPOLIS, OR NEW-YORK ALMANAC, THE (US) [01770819] **2534**

GREAT MODEL RAILROADS *CEASED.* (US/1048-8685) [21063906] **5431**

GREAT OUTDOORS (UK/0140-7570) [I01407570] **4873**

GREAT OUTDOORS (SA) **2194**

GREAT PLAINS AGRICULTURAL COUNCIL *See* PROCEEDINGS OF THE GREAT PLAINS AGRICULTURAL COUNCIL **122**

GREAT PLAINS GAME & FISH (US/1055-6532) [23249605] **4873**

GREAT PLAINS JOURNAL (US/0017-3673) [01751559] **2735**

GREAT PLAINS QUARTERLY (US/0275-7664) [07235796] **2735**

GREAT PLAINS RESEARCH (US/1052-5165) [22298828] **5201, 4166**

GREAT PLAINS-ROCKY MOUNTAIN GEOGRAPHICAL JOURNAL *CEASED.* (US/0095-1315) [01793794] **2565**

GREAT PLAINS SOCIOLOGIST, THE (US/0896-0054) [16885650] **5246**

GREAT RECIPES OF THE WORLD (US/0272-796X) [06931377] **2342**

GREAT RIVER REVIEW (US/0160-2144) [03492233] **3392**

GREAT RIVERS (US/0747-7686) [10791338] **2565**

GREAT SOUTHERN MANUFACTURERS DIRECTORY (AT) [08422781] **3480**

GREAT STREAM REVIEW *CEASED.* (US/1042-8208) [19225712] **3392**

GREAT TASTE (US/0886-3504) [12873609] **2342**

GREAT WEST AND INDIAN SERIES (US/0072-7342) [02052167] **2735**

GREAT WESTERN SERIES, THE (US/0533-2052) [01492420] **2488**

GREATER ANCHORAGE AREA BOROUGH. INFORMATION OFFICE *See* BLUE BOOK, THE **4633**

GREATER AVOYELLES JOURNAL, THE (US) [18422148] **5684**

GREATER BATON ROUGE BUSINESS REPORT, THE (US/0747-4652) [09356044] **678**

GREATER BOSTON MEDIA DIRECTORY (US/0275-8369) [07095122] **1112**

GREATER CAROLINAS REGIONAL INDUSTRIAL BUYING GUIDE (US/1042-2935) [19002447] **1607**

GREATER CHICAGO JOB BANK *See* CHICAGO JOB BANK, THE **4203**

GREATER CHICAGO JOB BANK, THE (US/1070-9142) [15238784] **4204**

GREATER CINCINNATI BUSINESS RECORD *See* BUSINESS RECORD, THE **652**

GREATER CINCINNATI BUSINESS RECORD, THE (US/1044-9264) [18531884] **678**

GREATER EUROPE REPORT *See* EUROPE REPORT, THE **2516**

GREATER GREENWOOD BUSINESS JOURNAL, THE (US) **678**

●GREATER KINGSTON, ONTARIO CANADA, VISITOR'S GUIDE (CN/1189-3311) [25796432] **5478**

GREATER LANSING BUSINESS MONTHLY (US) **678**

GREATER LLANO ESTACADO SOUTHEAST HERITAGE, THE *CEASED.* (US/0145-8825) [02800230] **2735**

GREATER LONDON COUNCIL *See* PROGRAMME BUDGET **4742**

GREATER LONDON COUNCIL *See* REVENUE ESTIMATES - GREATER LONDON COUNCIL **4746**

GREATER LONDON COUNCIL *See* GREATER LONDON COUNCIL, INNER LONDON EDUCATION AUTHORITY REPORT ON ACCOUNTS **4729**

GREATER LONDON COUNCIL *See* BUDGET - GREATER LONDON COUNCIL **4714**

GREATER LONDON COUNCIL. DEPT. OF PUBLIC HEALTH ENGINEERING *See* ANNUAL REPORT - GREATER LONDON COUNCIL. DEPT. OF PUBLIC HEALTH ENGINEERING **4765**

GREATER LONDON COUNCIL, INNER LONDON EDUCATION AUTHORITY REPORT ON ACCOUNTS (UK) [06510239] **4729**

GREATER LONDON COUNCIL. INTELLIGENCE UNIT *See* LONDON BOROUGH COUNCIL ELECTIONS **4481**

GREATER LONDON INTELLIGENCE JOURNAL (UK/0264-6315) [04028756] **2823**

GREATER LONDON LOCAL HISTORY DIRECTORY AND BIBLIOGRAPHY (UK) **2689**

GREATER LONDON RECORD OFFICE *See* REPORT - GREATER LONDON RECORD OFFICE AND LIBRARY **2483**

GREATER LOS ANGELES 3-D MAP (US/1045-4918) [20137579] **2582**

GREATER LOS ANGELES COUNCIL ON DEAFNESS *See* GLAD DIRECTORY OF RESOURCES AVAILABLE TO DEAF & HARD-OF-HEARING PERSONS IN THE SOUTHERN CALIFORNIA AREA **5286**

GREATER LOS ANGELES PUBLIC SERVICE GUIDE (US) [06674886] **4653**

GREATER MADISON (US) [04153623] **2534**

GREATER NEW YORK DIRECTORY, THE (US/0743-6904) [10636532] **2881**

GREATER PHILADELPHIA ECONOMIST, THE (US/0744-4532) [08275798] **1493**

GREATER PHILADELPHIA LAW LIBRARY ASSOCIATION *See* GPLLA NEWSLETTER **3212**

GREATER PHOENIX JEWISH NEWS (US/0747-444X) [10863768] **5047**

GREATER QUEBEC AREA TOUR OPERATOR MANUAL (CN/0847-3846) [22378659] **5478**

GREATER SAN DIEGO CHAMBER OF COMMERCE ECONOMIC BULLETIN (US) [30307276] **1493**

GREATER SEATTLE (US) [25518835] **2534**

GREATER SEATTLE BUSINESS ASSOCIATION *See* GSBA GUIDE/DIRECTORY **2794**

●GREATER SILICON VALLEY TECHNOLOGY RESOURCE GUIDE (US/1060-1600) [24881432] **5108**

GREATER TORONTO PROFESSIONAL AND SERVICE DIRECTORY (CN/1191-0879) [25652407] **615**

GREATER VANCOUVER (B.C.) *See* GVRD NEWS **4653**

GREATER WASHINGTON BOARD OF TRADE NEWS, THE (US/0274-5496) [06398256] **1564**

GREATER WINNIPEG BUSINESS (CN/0830-8535) [13490254] **678**

GRECA *CEASED.* (SP) [02121654] **351**

GREECE *See* PHOROLOGIKE ENEMEROSIS **4741**

GREECE & ROME (UK/0017-3835) [01751570] **1077**

GREECE AND YUGOSLAVIA ON $15 & $20 A DAY (US/0270-4358) [06402046] **5478**

GREECE. ETHNIKE STATISTIKE HYPERESIA *See* DELTION STATISTIKE DEMASION OIKONOMIKON **4697**

GREECE. GENIKE GRAMMATEIA KOINONIKON ASPHALISEON. D/NSE EPITHEORESES *See* KOINONIKOS PROYPOLOGISMOS ETOUS ... / HYPOURGEIO HYGEIAS, PRONOIAS, KAI KOINONIKON ASPHALISEON, GENIKE GRAMMATEIA KOINONIKON ASPHALISEON, D/NSE EPITHEORESES **5294**

GREECE. HYPERESIA GEORGIKON EREUNON *See* GEORGIKE EREUNA - HYPERESIA GEORGIKON EREUNON, GREECE **90**

GREECE. HYPERESIA POLITIKES AEROPORIAS *See* HODEGOS HYPERESIAS POLITIKES AEROPORIAS **23**

GREECE. HYPERESIA POLITIKES AEROPORIAS *See* ETESIA EKTHESIS PEPRAGMENON - HYPERESIA POLITIKES AEROPORIAS **18**

GREECE. HYPERESIA POLITIKES AEROPORIAS *See* PROGRAMMA DRASEOS HYPERESIAS POLITIKES AEROPORIAS **32**

GREECE. HYPOURGEION TON OIKONOMIKON *See* EISEGETIKE EKTHESE OIKONOMIKOU ETOUS ... HYPOURGOI OIKONOMIKON **4721**

GREECE POST, THE (US) [08065518] **5716**

GREECE. STRATOS. GEOGRAPHIKE HYPERESIA *See* DELTION **4042**

GREECE'S WEEKLY FOR BUSINESS & FINANCE (GR) [10290698] **789**

GREECE'S WEEKLY FOR BUSINESS & FINANCE YEARBOOK (GR) [10522532] **1564**

GREECE'S WEEKLY : GREECE'S INTERNATIONAL NEWS MAGAZINE (GR) [26569302] **789**

GREEK ACCENT *CEASED.* (US/0279-1234) [07565677] **2689**

GREEK-AMERICAN REVIEW (US/1056-215X) [23591801] **2262**

GREEK BUSINESS MONITOR (GR) **678**

GREEK ECONOMIC REVIEW (GR/1010-9994) [06481431] **1493**

GREEK FORUM (KAVALA, GREECE) (GR) [20339166] **1564**

GREEK HERALD (AT) **5777**

GREEK ORTHODOX THEOLOGICAL REVIEW, THE (US/0017-3894) [01751574] **4961**

GREEK REPORT : MONTHLY INTELLIGENCE NEWSLETTER (GR) **2517**

GREEK REVIEW OF SOCIAL RESEARCH (GR) [06436477] **5201**

GREEK, ROMAN AND BYZANTINE MONOGRAPHS (US/0072-7474) [01507926] **1077**

GREEK, ROMAN AND BYZANTINE STUDIES (US/0017-3916) [06415521] **1077**

GREEK, ROMAN AND BYZANTINE STUDIES. SCHOLARLY AIDS (US/0072-7482) [01507967] **1077**

GREEK SHIPPING DIRECTORY (GR) [08961711] **5449**

GREEKAMERICAN, THE (US/0890-0035) [14126119] **2262**

GREELEY COUNTY REPUBLICAN AND THE GREELEY COUNTY NEWS (US) [11312907] **5676**

GREELEY STYLE MAGAZINE (US) **2488**

GREELEY TRIBUNE (US) [15699710] **5643**

GREEN (CN/0823-6380) [09860040] **4897**

GREEN ALTERNATIVES FOR HEALTH AND THE ENVIRONMENT *CEASED.* (US/1064-8852) [26448478] **2172**

GREEN AMERICA (US/0090-8088) [01780593] **2384**

GREEN BAY CATHOLIC COMPASS, THE (US/8755-9323) [11031850] **5030**

GREEN BAY NEWS-CHRONICLE, THE (US) [15158705] **5767**

GREEN BAY PRESS-GAZETTE (US) [10787057] **5767**

GREEN BOOK BATH (UK/0265-0088) [I02650088] **321**

GREEN BOOK BATH *See* CONTEMPORARY ART **317**

GREEN BOOK BUYERS' GUIDE FOR GARDEN MERCHANDISE (US/0147-3891) [02246957] **2417**

GREEN BOOK (LONDON) (UK/0017-3932) [03099568] **159**

GREEN BOOK (LONDON, ENGLAND) *See* MEMBERS' HANDBOOK & BUYERS' GUIDE : THE GREEN BOOK / THE INSTITUTION OF AGRICULTURAL ENGINEERS **160**

GREEN BOOK (MEMPHIS, TENN.) (US/0882-4568) [11801771] **2401, 1607**

●GREEN BOOK. NEW YORK/NEW JERSEY, THE (US/1062-9211) [25809526] **2172**

GREEN BOOK : OFFICIAL DIRECTORY OF THE CITY OF NEW YORK, THE (US) [10867448] **2565**

●GREEN BOOK REPORT, THE (US/1062-4589) [25625181] **2172**

●GREEN BOOK (WOBURN, MASS.), THE (US/1055-6893) [23271316] **2172**

GREEN BOOK'S HARDWOOD LUMBER MARKETING DIRECTORY (US/0884-7894) [12423624] **2401**

●GREEN BUSINESS LETTER, THE (US/1056-490X) [23725292] **2172**

GREEN CAR JOURNAL (US/1059-6143) [24647374] **2230, 5415**

GREEN CONSUMER LETTER, THE *CEASED.* (US/1049-2747) [21191431] **1297, 2172**

GREEN COUNTRY QUARTERLY, THE (US/0743-2828) [10509748] **2452**

●GREEN COUNTRY SCIENCE & ENGINEERING JOURNAL (US/1057-2953) [24004126] **1976**

GREEN COUNTY REVIEW (US/1042-4725) [06749550] **2452**

GREEN EGG (US/1066-7385) [23864810] **4241**

GREEN ENERGY MATTERS *CEASED.* (UK/0964-8755) [I09648755] **4259**

GREEN ENERGY UPDATE (CN/1183-417X) [24257012] **1945**

GREEN ENGINEERING *CEASED.* (UK/0960-8796) [I09608796] **1976, 2173**

GREEN EUROPE (BRUSSELS, BELGIUM) (UK/0250-5886) [07475629] **90**

GREEN FOREST TRIBUNE, THE (US) [20118937] **5631**

GREEN GUIDE FOR ELECTRIC LIFT TRUCKS (US/0731-9819) [08290733] **5383**

GREEN GUIDE FOR LIFT TRUCKS (US/0731-9827) [08286609] **5383**

GREEN GUIDE FOR OFF-HIGHWAY TRUCKS & TRAILERS (US/0731-9835) [08290776] **5383**

GREEN — Alphabetical Title Index

GREEN HORSE FOR POETRY, THE (US) [03285818] **3463**

● GREEN INDEX (US/1055-9396) [23369174] **2173**

GREEN-KEEPING (ANNANDALE-ON-HUDSON, N.Y.) *CEASED.* (US/1058-594X) [24336011] **2194**

GREEN LAKE COUNTY REPORTER (GREEN LAKE, WIS. : 1983) (US/8755-3988) [11292053] **5767**

GREEN LANDS (US/0888-3408) [06987131] **2173**

GREEN LEAVES. BRITISH COLUMBIA EDITION (CN/0380-8572) [02585082] **2384**

GREEN LEAVES. WESTERN CANADA ED, THE (CN/0705-1697) [04079770] **2384**

GREEN LEFT WEEKLY (AT/1036-126X) [24633962] **4542**

GREEN LIBRARY JOURNAL *See* GREEN LIBRARY JOURNAL (BERKELEY, CALIF. 1992) **2173**

GREEN LIBRARY JOURNAL (BERKELEY, CALIF. : 1992) *See* ELECTRONIC GREEN JOURNAL **2165**

GREEN LIBRARY JOURNAL (BERKELEY, CALIF. 1992) (US/1059-0838) [24563935] **2173**

GREEN LIVING (CN/1185-0957) [23686598] **2194**

GREEN MAGAZINE (US/0883-5462) [12143414] **2173**

GREEN MAN, THE (US/1069-3211) [27994971] 4185, **4241**

GREEN MARKETALERT *CEASED.* (US/1052-1755) [22202746] **2173**

GREEN MARKETING HANDBOOK (CN) **925**

GREEN MARKETING REPORT (US/1051-7316) [22101456] **925**

GREEN MARKETS (US/0149-5569) [03523154] **90**

GREEN MARKETS DEALER REPORT (US/0895-772X) [16797264] **2417**

GREEN MARKETS FERTILIZER PRICE HANDBOOK (US/0193-9106) [05267737] 173, **1607**

GREEN MOUNTAIN GAZETTE *See* HARDWICK GAZETTE, THE **5757**

GREEN MOUNTAIN'S LITERATURE NEWSLETTER *See* TEACHING AND LEARNING LITERATURE WITH CHILDREN AND YOUNG ADULTS **1906**

GREEN MOUNTAINS REVIEW (US/0895-9307) [16506765] **3392**

GREEN PAGES REHAB SOURCEBOOK, THE (US/0196-9870) [04597191] 4388, **5286**

GREEN PRINTS (US/1064-0118) [26190920] **2417**

GREEN REVOLUTION (YORK, PA.) (US/0017-3983) [01751579] **4542**

GREEN RIVER NEWS *See* SEBREE BANNER, THE **5682**

GREEN RIVER REPUBLICAN (US) [13905322] **5680**

GREEN SCENE, THE (US/0190-9789) [01188073] **2417**

GREEN SHEET (US/0533-2508) [01508155] **4071**

GREEN SHEET (MURRAY, UTAH), THE (US/1043-2949) [19406456] **1826**

GREEN SHEET - UNITED STATES. DEPT. OF HEALTH AND HUMAN SERVICES, THE (US/0732-9385) [08500670] **4777**

GREEN TEACHER (BRITISH EDITION) (UK/0953-3028) [I09533028] 1895, **2173**

GREEN TEACHER (TORONTO) (CN/1192-1285) [27193690] **2173**

GREEN THUMB NEWS (US/0749-2138) [10278143] 512, **2417**

GREEN THUMB (OAKLAND) (US/0160-3965) [03674686] **2417**

GREEN VALLEY NEWS (US) **5707**

GREEN2000 (WEST CHESTER, PA.) (US/1053-6418) [22600910] **2173**

GREENBELT NEWS REVIEW (US) [19952343] **5686**

GREENBOOK (NEW YORK, N.Y.) (US/8756-534X) [04644595] **925**

GREENBORO (CN/0703-7821) [07298480] **2735**

GREENBORO HUNT CLUB PARK NEWS [MICROFORM] (CN/1186-4303) [25313933] **5785**

GREENBURGH ENQUIRER, THE (US/0883-1637) [12062225] **5716**

GREENBUSH AREA NEWS (US) [17197132] **5716**

GREENDALE VILLAGE LIFE, THE (US) [13390853] **5767**

GREENE COUNTY DEMOCRAT (EUTAW, ALA.), THE (US/0889-518X) [09238773] **5626**

GREENE COUNTY HERALD (US) [15581873] **5700**

GREENE COUNTY HISTORICAL JOURNAL (US/0894-8135) [08566725] **2735**

GREENE COUNTY INDEPENDENT (US) [15580838] **5626**

GREENE COUNTY MAGAZINE (US) [05519293] **2735**

GREENE COUNTY NEWS (US) [10721772] **5716**

GREENE GENES (US/0898-9974) [17965178] **2452**

GREENE RECORDER, THE (US) [16107214] **5670**

GREENER MANAGEMENT INTERNATIONAL (UK) [I09669671] **2173**

GREENFIELD OBSERVER (1984) (US/1050-1185) [13390777] **5767**

GREENFIELD PARK JOURNAL (CN/0821-3038) [09515259] **5785**

GREENFIELD QUARTERLY (US/0883-170X) [12191518] **2452**

GREENFIELDS : THE TOTAL AGRICULTURAL MAGAZINE (PH) [14685807] **90**

GREENHILL JOURNAL OF ADMINISTRATION (GH/0379-8658) [02056511] **4653**

GREENHOUSE CANADA (CN/0712-4996) [09106592] **2417**

GREENHOUSE EFFECT REPORT (US/1042-5039) [19086077] **2230**

GREENHOUSE GASES BULLETIN *CEASED.* (UK/0964-9107) [26632108] **2140**

GREENHOUSE GROWER (US/0745-7324) [09421564] **2417**

GREENHOUSE INDUSTRY (CN/0527-5369) [02443614] **2417**

GREENHOUSE IPM UPDATE (US) [26629029] 90, **2417**

GREENHOUSE MANAGER (US/0744-8988) [08648282] **2417**

GREENHOUSE PRODUCT NEWS (US/1053-7104) [22612535] **2417**

GREENHOUSE REVIEW (US/0162-0304) [03285928] **3343**

GREENHOUSE VEGETABLE PRODUCTION GUIDE (EDMONTON) (CN/0848-6751) [23264911] **173**

GREENLINE GUIDE TO RESIDENTIAL ARCHITECTS (US/1047-6997) [20747006] **299**

GREENMASTER (CN/0380-3333) [02017029] **4897**

● GREENPACKAGING 2000 (US/1068-4271) [27671778] 2173, **4219**

GREENPEACE BUSINESS (UK/0962-9467) [I09629467] **2173**

GREENPEACE (CANADA ED.) (US/0836-5040) [17241091] **2194**

GREENPEACE NEWS (IT/0111-4506) **2216**

GREENPEACE (WASHINGTON, D.C.) (US/0899-0190) [16718179] **2173**

GREENPOINT GAZETTE (US) **5717**

GREEN'S BUSINESS LAW BULLETIN (UK) **3100**

● GREEN'S COURT PRACTICE BULLETIN (UK) **2975**

GREEN'S CRIMINAL LAW BULLETIN (UK) **3107**

● GREEN'S EMPLOYMENT LAW BULLETIN (UK) **3148**

● GREEN'S ENVIRONMENTAL LAW BULLETIN (UK) **3112**

● GREEN'S FAMILY LAW BULLETIN (UK) **3120**

GREENS GEORGIA LAW OF EVIDENCE (US) **2975**

GREEN'S MAGAZINE (CN/0824-2992) [03285966] **3392**

● GREEN'S PROPERTY LAW BULLETIN (UK) **2975**

● GREEN'S REPARATION LAW BULLETIN (UK) **2975**

GREENS WEEKLY DIGEST, CURRENT SCOTTISH CASE LAW (UK) [17680496] **2975**

GREENSBORO NEWS AND RECORD *See* NEWS & RECORD (GREENSBORO, N.C.) **5724**

GREENSBORO NEWS & RECORD (US/0747-1858) [10623286] **5723**

GREENSBORO REVIEW, THE (US/0017-4084) [01523797] **3392**

GREENSBORO WATCHMAN (US) [12380826] **5626**

GREENSBURG DAILY NEWS (US) [11981334] **5664**

GREENSBURG RECORD-HERALD (1941) (US) [17220658] **5680**

GREENSBURG TIMES, THE (US) [11983532] **5664**

GREENSBURG TRIBUNE-REVIEW (US) **5736**

GREENSCAPE (CN/0712-1822) [08720689] 4873, **2417**

GREENSWARD (UK/0017-4092) [03276879] **90**

GREENVILLE ADVOCATE (US) [11027303] **5626**

GREENVILLE ADVOCATE (GREENVILLE, ILL.) (US) [11326136] **5660**

GREENVILLE NEWS, THE (US) [12959349] **5742**

GREENVILLE PIEDMONT, THE (US) [26217539] **5742**

GREENWATCH : LETTERA CONFIDENZIALE IN DIFESA DI AGRICOLTURA E INDUSTRIA (IT) **2230**

GREENWEEK (AT/1034-5876) [10345876] 2230, **2194**

GREENWICH (GREENWICH, CONN.) (US/1072-2432) [28893252] **2488**

GREENWICH MAGAZINE (US/1051-0745) [21795021] **2488**

GREENWICH NEWS (US/0746-8539) [10339838] **5645**

GREENWICH REGISTER: THE DIRECTORY OF PERSONNEL MANAGERS, HUMAN RESOURCE EXECUTIVES AND CORPORATE RECRUITERS, THE (US/1060-9873) [25147806] **941**

GREENWICH RESEARCH ASSOCIATES *See* INTERNATIONAL CORPORATE BANKING REPORT TO PARTICIPANTS **792**

GREENWICH RESEARCH ASSOCIATES *See* MIDDLE MARKET FINANCIAL MANAGEMENT; REPORT TO PARTICIPANTS **879**

GREENWICH RESEARCH ASSOCIATES *See* LARGE CORPORATE BANKING **796**

GREENWOOD AND SOUTHSIDE CHALLENGER, THE (US/1068-6673) [18438236] **5664**

GREENWOOD COMMONWEALTH (GREENWOOD, MISS. : 1976) (US) [15193645] **5700**

GREENWOOD ENCYCLOPEDIA OF AMERICAN INSTITUTIONS, THE (US/0271-9509) [06753807] **1926**

GREENWOOD ENCYCLOPEDIA OF BLACK MUSIC, THE (US/0272-0264) [06740293] **4119**

GREENWOOD GAZETTE, THE (US) [14582970] **5664**

GREENWOOD LAKE AND WEST MILFORD NEWS (US/1065-1144) [24147864] **5717**

GREENWOOD'S GUIDE TO GREAT LAKES SHIPPING (US/0072-7490) [01197806] **5449**

GREER CITIZEN, THE (US) [24328907] **5742**

GREETING CARD MAGAZINE *See* GREETINGS MAGAZINE **2584**

● GREETINGS AND GIFT STATIONER (UK) **2584**

GREETINGS AND GIFTS (AT/1036-5915) [10365915] 373, **2584**

GREETINGS MAGAZINE (US/1064-2048) [26229395] **2584**

GREGG-GRANITEVILLE LIBRARY *See* REPORT OF THE DIRECTOR **3245**

GREGORIANUM (IT/0017-4114) [01715549] **4961**

GREGORIOS O PALAMAS (GR/1011-3010) [01791538] **4961**

GREGORIUS NYSSENUS OPERA (NE) **4119**

GREGORIUSBLAD *CEASED.* (NE) [06616935] **4119**

GREGORY'S A-SERIES TECHNICAL JOURNAL (US/0892-4856) [15307547] 1279, **1238**

GRENADA CONSOLIDATED INDEX OF STATUTES AND SUBSIDIARY LEGISLATION TO ... (US) [13717865] **3081**

GRENADA. MINISTRY OF FINANCE *See* BUDGET SPEECH DELIVERED BY THE MINISTER FOR FINANCE ... IN THE HOUSE OF REPRESENTATIVES ON **4715**

GRENADA, WIRTSCHAFTSDATEN / BUNDESSTELLE FUER AUSSENHANDELSINFORMATION (GW) [11453881] **1564**

GRENVILLE SENTINEL (CN/0715-3783) [09145936] **2735**

GRENZGEBIETE DER WISSENSCHAFT (GW) [09349408] **5108**

GRESHAM OUTLOOK (US) **5733**

GREY/CLARK TRADE NEWS (CN/0711-2947) [08465784] **838**

GREY MATTER. RETAIL EDITION (US/0432-658X) [01510209] **759**

GREYFRIAR (LOUDONVILLE N.Y.) *SUSPENDED.* (US/0533-2869) [04925150] **3392**

GREYHOUND BREEDER'S JOURNAL (US/0191-7633) [04913118] **4286**

GRHA VIBHAGANUM ANDAJAPATRA. BUDGET ESTIMATES OF HOME DEPARTMENT (II) [04286698] **4729**

GRI NEWSLETTER (US/0534-0489) [05040067] **4565**

GRIAL (SP/0017-4181) [02253073] **5268, 321**

GRID (US) [05515894] **4259**

GRID NEWS (LANSING, MICH.) (US/1054-9315) [23032575] **1277**

GRIDIRON COACH (US/1071-1902) [28566134] **4897**

GRIDLEY HERALD, THE (US) [27053477] **5635**

GRIECHENLAND : ENERGIEWIRTSCHAFT (GW) [05063419] **1945**

GRIECHENLAND : WIRTSCHAFTSDATEN UND WIRTSCHAFTSDOKUMENTATION (GW) [06234221] **1564**

GRIEVANCE AND ADJUDICATION SECTION REPORTS / PUBLIC SERVICE ALLIANCE OF CANADA (CN/0822-7810) [11355493] **2975**

GRIFFIN DAILY NEWS (US/0746-3324) [09925680] **5653**

GRIFFIN (HALIFAX) (CN/0383-7335) [03258586] **299**

GRIFFIN REPORT OF FOOD MARKETING, THE (US/0192-4400) [05047714] **2342**

GRIFFIN REPORT, THE (US) [02684772] **2342**

GRIFFITH OBSERVER (US/0195-3982) [01751590] **395**

GRIFFITHIANA (IT/0393-3857) [12125035] **4071**

GRIFFON (FR/0299-7827) [02997827] **1748**

GRIFFON (DRUMMONDVILLE) (CN/0710-5649) [08774067] **5785**

GRIGSBY CACTUS GARDENS *See* WISH LETTER / GRIGSBY CACTUS GARDENS **2433**

GRILLED FLOWERS (US) [02589998] **3463**

GRIMM & GRIPS (GW) [17822917] **1064, 5364**

GRIMSBY INDEPENDENT (CN/0834-6623) [16310160] **5785**

GRINNELL REVIEW, THE (US/0737-8912) [09461541] **1826**

GRINZ YEARBOOK (NZ/0113-2431) [01132431] **2452**

GRIO' (BLACK HISTORY ED.) (US/0886-1668) [12897145] **2735**

GRIOT (HOUSTON, TEX.), THE (US/0737-0873) [09298185] **2735**

GRIOT, THE (GD) [20252896] **5802**

●GRIPE/ GROUP FOR RESEARCH IN PATHOLOGY EDUCATION (US) **3894**

GRIST INTERNATIONAL (UK) **2342**

GRIST (WASHINGTON, D.C.) (US) [01780594] **4706**

GRIT AND STEEL (US/0017-4297) [04080937] **4873**

GRIT (CAYUGA, IND.) (US/0883-6876) [12193424] **5286**

GRIT (NATIONAL ED.) (US/0017-4289) [04080668] **5676**

GRN VIDEN. HAVEBRUG / STATENS PLANTEAVLSFORSG (DK/0903-0719) [19832353] **2417**

GRN VIDEN. LANDBRUG / STATENS PLANTEAVLSFORSG (DK/0903-0727) [19832343] **173**

GRNLAND (1953) (DK/0017-4556) [01751597] **4553**

GRNLANDS GEOLOGISKE UNDERGSELSE *See* RAPPORT - GRONLANDS GEOLOGISKE UNDERSOGELSE **1393**

GRNLANDS GEOLOGISKE UNDERGSELSE *See* ARSBERETNING - GRONLANDS GEOLOGISKE UNDERSOGELSE **860**

GRNLANDS TEKNISKE ORGANISATION *See* BILAG TIL GTO RAPPORT **2019**

GRO NEWSLETTER / NASA GODDARD SPACE FLIGHT CENTER (US/1061-8252) [24121580] **395**

●GROCER FOOD & DRINK DIRECTORY, THE (UK/0967-5892) [I09675892] **2342**

GROCER JOURNAL OF CALIFORNIA *See* CALIFORNIA GROCER **2330**

GROCER. MONTHLY SUPPLEMENT, THE (UK) [09798882] **2342**

GROCER TODAY (CN/1196-0817) [28558069] **838**

GROCERS JOURNAL OF CALIFORNIA (US/0745-4104) [09135519] **2342**

GROCERS' REVIEW (NZ/0113-1850) [I01131850] **2342**

GROCERY DISTRIBUTION (US/0361-4034) [02246534] **2342**

GROCERY DISTRIBUTION ANALYSIS AND GUIDE (1983) (US/0749-551X) [10128725] **2342**

●GROCERY EQUIPMENT PRODUCT NEWS (US) **2342**

GROCERY INDUSTRY ANNUAL REPORT, THE (US) [05685974] **2342**

GROCERY MARKETING (US/0888-0360) [13448004] **2343**

GROEI EN BLOEI (NE) [04025991] **2417, 512**

GROEN (NE/0166-3534) [06848568] **2417**

GROENE AMSTERDAMMER; ONAFHANKELIJK WEEKBLAD VOOR NEDERLAND. (MICROFICHE), DE (US) [04693246] **4523**

GROENTEN EN FRUIT : G & F (NE/0017-4491) [09798988] **2417**

GROENTEN + FRUIT. ALGEMEEN (NE/0925-9708) [I09259708] **2417**

GROENTEN + FRUIT. FRUIT (NE/0925-9694) [I09259694] **2417**

GROENTEN + FRUIT. GLASGROENTEN (NE/0925-9686) [I09259686] **2417**

GROENTEN + FRUIT. PADDESTOELEN (NE/0925-9716) [I09259716] **2417**

GROENTEN + FRUIT. VOLLEGRONDSGROENTEN (NE/0925-9678) [I09259678] **2417**

GROESBECK JOURNAL (US) [14249969] **5750**

GROFSMEDERIJEN, STAMP- EN PERSBEDRIJVEN / CENTRAAL BUREAU VOOR DE STATISTIEK, HOOFDAFDELING STATISTIEKEN VAN INDUSTRIE EN BOUWNIJVERHEID (NE/0168-3128) [10287362] **1608**

GROLIER CLUB *See* OFFICERS, COMMITTEES, CONSTITUTION AND BY-LAWS, MEMBERS / GROLIER CLUB **5234**

GROLIER CLUB *See* OFFICERS, COMMITTEES, CONSTITUTION AND BY-LAWS, MEMBERS, REPORTS OF OFFICERS AND COMMITTEES **5234**

GROLIER POETRY PRIZE (US/0743-7242) [10656776] **3463**

GROLIER'S LEARNING TREE (US/0898-6932) [17826636] **1748**

GROMADA ROLNIK POLSKI (PL/0137-9208) [04026005] **91**

GRONDBOOR EN HAMER (NE/0017-4505) [06347737] **1381**

GRONDVERZET & BOUWTRANSPORT (NE/0920-8380) [I09208380] **615**

GRONIGEN COLLOQUIA ON THE NOVEL (NE) [19117850] **3392**

GRONINGER ARBEITEN ZUR GERMANISTISCHEN LINGUISTIK (NE/0924-655X) [I0924655X] **3284**

GRONK (CN/0017-453X) [03286108] **3343**

GROOM & BOARD (US/0199-8366) [06207908] **4286**

●GROOM'S GUIDE, THE (US/1056-4551) [23719042] **2280, 3995**

GROOTCONSUMENT AMSTERDAM (NE/0926-6976) [I09266976] **2790**

GROOTHANDEL IN VOEDINGS- EN GENOTMIDDELEN / CENTRAAL BUREAU VOOR DE STATISTIEK, HOOFDAFDELING STATISTIEKEN VAN BINNENLANDSE HANDEL EN DIENSTVERLENING (NE/0168-4647) [12003780] **838**

GROSS-BERLINER ARZTEBLATT, ARZTLICHES MITTEILUNGSBLATT FUR BERLIN *See* BERLINER ARZTEBLATT **3555**

GROSS DOMESTIC PRODUCT AND EXPENDITURE (PP) **5328**

GROSS DOMESTIC PRODUCT BY INDUSTRY (MONTHLY EDITION) (CN/0711-852X) [08342252] **1533**

GROSS NATIONAL PRODUCT GROWTH RATES AND TREND DATA BY REGION AND COUNTRY (US/0097-8698) [01795904] **1564**

GROSS- UND EINZELHANDEL, GASTGEWERBE, REISEVERKEHR. REIHE 8 : REISEVERKEHR. IV. GRENZUBERSCHREITENDER REISEVERKEHR (GW) [03472618] **5478**

GROSS- UND EINZELHANDELSSTATISTIK (AU) [03393688] **838**

GROSSBRITANNIEN : ENERGIEWIRTSCHAFT (GW) [05063945] **1945**

GROSSE NATURFORSCHER (GW/0072-7741) [01511377] **4166**

GROSSE POINTER, THE (US/0017-4629) [04080958] **593, 5478**

GROSSEN 500, DIE (GW) [01781967] **678**

GROSSEN DARSTELLUNGEN DER MUSIKGESCHICHTE IN BAROCK UND AUFKLARUNG, DIE (AU/0533-3067) [01511628] **4119**

GROSSWETTERLAGEN EUROPAS, DIE (GW/0017-4645) [01511897] **4030**

GROTE SECRETARESSE HANDBOEK (NE) **4211**

GROTIANA (1980) (NE) [07103206] **3128**

GROTTA DELLA VIPERA, LA (IT) [07334965] **321**

GROTTAFERRATA, ITALY (BASILIAN MONASTERY) *See* BOLLETTINO DELLA BADIA GRECA DI GROTTAFERRATA **5024**

GROUND DEFENCE INTERNATIONAL *See* STRATEGY & DEFENCE **4058**

GROUND ENGINEERING (UK/0017-4653) [01751599] **2024**

GROUND ENGINEERING YEARBOOK (UK/0959-9959) [22853463] **2024**

GROUND FLOOR (US) **678**

●GROUND IMPROVEMENT (UK) **2024**

GROUND WATER (US/0017-467X) [01751600] **1413**

GROUND WATER AGE (US/0046-645X) [02512237] **5533**

GROUND-WATER DATA FOR MICHIGAN (US/0098-3691) [03157280] **5533**

GROUND-WATER LEVELS IN ARKANSAS (US) [13613630] **5533**

GROUND-WATER LEVELS IN NEW MEXICO. BASIC DATA REPORT (US/0548-6165) [01152446] **5533**

GROUND-WATER LEVELS IN THE UNITED STATES. NORTH-CENTRAL STATES (US/0499-5198) [03145570] **1381, 5534**

GROUND-WATER LEVELS IN THE UNITED STATES : NORTHEASTERN STATES (US/0502-1456) [02701497] **2090**

GROUND-WATER LEVELS IN THE UNITED STATES. NORTHWESTERN STATES (US) [03634231] **1413**

GROUND-WATER LEVELS IN THE UNITED STATES. SOUTH-CENTRAL STATES (US/0502-1464) [03145780] **1381, 5534**

GROUND-WATER LEVELS IN THE UNITED STATES. SOUTHEASTERN STATES (US) [03634310] **1413**

GROUND-WATER LEVELS IN THE UNITED STATES. SOUTHWESTERN STATES (US) [03145341] **5534**

GROUND WATER MODELING NEWSLETTER (US/0741-8507) [09959415] **1413, 5534**

●GROUND WATER MONITORING & REMEDIATION (US/1069-3629) [27344498] **1413**

GROUND WATER MONITORING REVIEW (US/0277-1926) [07472800] **1413**

GROUND WATER NEWSLETTER / WATER INFORMATION CENTER, WIC, THE (US/0090-5070) [01514812] **5534**

GROUND-WATER SERIES (LAWRENCE, KAN.) (US/0193-0761) [03990003] **1414**

GROUNDNUT NEWS (II) [26509667] **2343**

GROUNDS MAINTENANCE (US/0017-4688) [01344099] **2417**

GROUNDS MANAGEMENT FORUM (US/0742-5511) [07352897] **2418**

GROUNDSMAN (UK/0017-4696) [I00174696] **4897, 2418**

GROUNDSWELL *CEASED.* (US/0162-7899) [04254444] **2155**

GROUNDWATER INVESTIGATION PROGRAM (AT) [10031845] **1414**

GROUNDWATER MONITOR (US/0882-6188) [11863017] **1414**

GROUNDWATER NEWS *See* WATER POLLUTION CONTROL NEWS **2247**

GROUNDWATER POLLUTION NEWS (US/0899-3521) [18075626] **2230**

GROUNDWATER QUALITY MONITORING PROGRAM (US/0738-1204) [09505014] **5534**

GROUNDWATER RESEARCH / CSIRO, [DIVISION OF GROUNDWATER RESEARCH] (AT/0810-8404) [09773958] **5534**

GROUP ANALYSIS (UK/0533-3164) [01447188] **3926**

●GROUP & ORGANIZATION MANAGEMENT (US/1059-6011) [24640799] **869**

GROUP & ORGANIZATION STUDIES *See* GROUP & ORGANIZATION MANAGEMENT **869**

●GROUP DECISION AND NEGOTIATION (US/0926-2644) [26821095] **5201**

GROUP — Alphabetical Title Index

GROUP FOR THE STUDY OF ATOMS AND MOLECULES FROM RADIO-ELECTRIC RESEARCH *See* BULLETIN DU GROUPEMENT D'INFORMATIONS MUTUELLES AMPERE **4399**

GROUP HEALTH INSTITUTE *See* PROCEEDINGS ... ANNUAL GROUP HEALTH INSTITUTE / GROUP HEALTH ASSOCIATION OF AMERICA **4796**

GROUP HQ DIRECTORY (US/0277-108X) [07511305] **5231**

GROUP INSURANCE PLANS. HEALTH, DENTAL, PRESCRIPTION, OPTICAL (US/0730-2460) [04535040] **2881**

GROUP INSURANCE SURVEY (CN/0821-1493) [10195218] **2881**

GROUP (LOVELAND, COLO.) (US/0163-8971) [04523050] **4961**, **1064**

GROUP (NEW YORK. 1977) (US/0362-4021) [03076013] **4588**

GROUP OF THIRTY *See* ANNUAL REPORT / GROUP OF THIRTY **771**

GROUP PRACTICE FACILITIES (US) [03787764] **2823**

GROUP PRACTICE JOURNAL (US/0199-5103) [05934640] **3780**

GROUP PRACTICE (NEWSLETTER) (US/0190-440X) [04704164] **3780**

GROUP PROCESS (UK/0046-6468) [02240407] **4588**

GROUP RESEARCH, INC. (ATLANTA, GA.) *See* GROUP RESEARCH REPORT **4475**

GROUP RESEARCH REPORT (US/0017-4742) [01774959] **4475**

GROUP STUDIES JOURNAL (US/0363-714X) [02529335] **3926**

GROUP TRAVEL ORGANISER (UK/0962-8266) [I09628266] **5478**

GROUPE D'ETUDE D'ALGEBRE *See* GROUPE D'ETUDE D'ALGEBRE. EXPOSES **3507**

GROUPE D'ETUDE D'ALGEBRE. EXPOSES (FR) [05107907] **3507**

GROUPE D'ETUDE D'ANALYSE ULTRAMETRIQUE. EXPOSES *CEASED*. (FR) [02441455] **3507**

GROUPE D'ETUDE D'ANALYSE ULTRAMETRIQUE (PARIS, FRANCE) *See* GROUPE D'ETUDE D'ANALYSE ULTRAMETRIQUE. EXPOSES **3507**

GROUPE D'ETUDE DE THEORIES STABLES *See* GROUPE D'ETUDE DE THEORIES STABLES. [EXPOSES] **3507**

GROUPE D'ETUDE DE THEORIES STABLES. [EXPOSES] (FR) [07228823] **3507**

GROUPE D'ETUDE DES MONUMENTS ET OEUVRES D'ART DU BEAUVAISIS (FR/0224-0475) [I02240475] **351**

GROUPE FAMILIAL, LE (FR/0180-9857) [I01809857] **1748**, **2280**

GROUPEMENT TECHNIQUES VETERINAIRES *See* BULLETIN DES G.T.V **5506**

GROUP'S JR. HIGH MINISTRY (US/0884-0504) [12298242] **1064**

GROUPS WITH HISTORICALLY HIGH INCIDENCES OF UNEMPLOYMENT *See* MINIMUM WAGE AND MAXIMUM HOURS STANDARDS UNDER THE FAIR LABOR STANDARDS ACT **1690**

GROUPWORK LONDON (UK/0951-824X) [I0951824X] **4588**, **5286**

GROVE CITY COLLEGE *See* ALUMNI DIRECTORY / GROVE CITY COLLEGE **1098**

GROVE CITY SOUTHWEST MESSENGER (US/0891-2270) [14703049] **5728**

GROVE: CONTEMPORARY POETRY AND TRANSLATION (US) [02169148] **3463**

GROVE EXAMINER, THE (CN/0318-1650) [02441709] **5785**

GROVE MESSENGER *See* GROVE SUN, THE **5732**

GROVE SUN, THE (US) [20556575] **5732**

GROW ELECTRIC HANDBOOK (UK) [04616856] **2418**

GROWER (UK/0017-4785) [03147150] **2418**

GROWER ADVISOR (US/0737-9935) [09086561] **2418**

GROWER (SHAWNEE MISSION, KAN.), THE (US/0745-1784) [08899890] **173**

GROWER (STORRS, CONN.) (US/1059-2563) [17574157] **173**

GROWER TALKS (US/0276-9433) [01680753] **2418**

GROWER (TORONTO) (CN/0017-4777) [01751604] **2418**

GROWING CHILD RESEARCH REVIEW (US/0737-0318) [09292868] **1748**

GROWING CHURCHES (US/1045-8948) [20282725] **5060**

GROWING EDGE (CORVALLIS, OR.), THE (US/1043-2906) [19403207] **2418**

GROWING EDGE (LOS ANGELES, CALIF.), THE (US/0741-4498) [10197292] **1748**

GROWING NATIVE PLANTS *CEASED*. (AT) [03147211] **2418**

GROWING OLDER (US) [06185661] **5179**

GROWING POINT *CEASED*. (UK/0046-6506) [01779713] **3392**, **1064**

GROWING POINTS, CENTRAL COAST COUNTRIES (US) [03903750] **2418**

GROWING TOGETHER (US) **5286**

GROWING WITHOUT SCHOOLING (US/0745-5305) [06151851] **1895**

GROWTH AND CHANGE (US/0017-4815) [01715590] **1493**, **2823**

GROWTH AND MATURATION FACTORS (US/0743-0779) [09811572] **580**

GROWTH, DEVELOPMENT, AND AGING (US/1041-1232) [18299765] **456**

GROWTH FACTORS & CYTOKINES (UK/0964-7554) **3730**, **581**

GROWTH FACTORS (CHUR, SWITZERLAND) (SZ/0897-7194) [17605004] **456**

GROWTH FUND GUIDE (US/0017-4831) [04539894] **900**

GROWTH FUND RESEARCH, INC *See* GROWTH FUND GUIDE **900**

GROWTH GENETICS & HORMONES (US/0898-6630) [12028906] **3903**

GROWTH INDEX, THE (US/0744-7205) [08507691] **820**

GROWTH INDUSTRY NEWS *See* INDUSTRIES IN TRANSITION **682**

GROWTH (MELBOURNE, VIC.) (AT/0085-1280) [02410166] **1564**

GROWTH OF CRYSTALS (US) [01713569] **1032**

GROWTH (PRETORIA, SOUTH AFRICA) (SA) [11577839] **1564**

GROWTH REGULATION (UK/0956-523X) [23835727] **547**

GROWTH REPORT (US) [11220752] **4961**

GROWTH STOCK OUTLOOK (US) [03190870] **900**

GRUB STREET (US/0149-4228) [03491422] **3392**

GRUDNAIA I SERDECHNO-SOSUDISTAIA KHIRURGIIA (RU/0236-2791) [21291205] **3705**

GRUMMAN AEROSPACE HORIZONS *See* HORIZONS **23**

GRUMMAN PLANE NEWS (US) [09036797] **22**

GRUNDFOERBAETTRING (SW/0017-4904) [01443147] **91**

GRUNDGESETZ KOMMENTAR (GW) **2975**

GRUNDLAGEN DER GERMANISTIK (GW/0533-3350) [01437470] **3284**

GRUNDLAGEN DER LANDTECHNIK (GW/0017-4920) [01751609] **91**

GRUNDLAGEN UND PRAXIS DES WIRTSCHAFTSRECHTS (GW) [01751610] **3100**

GRUNDLAGEN ZUR PFLANZENQUARANTAENE (GW/0420-0136) [04885978] **173**

GRUNDLAGENSTUDIEN AUS KYBERNETIK UND GEISTESWISSENSCHAFT (GW/0017-4939) [01866252] **1251**

GRUNDLEHREN DER MATHEMATISCHEN WISSENSCHAFTEN (GW) [05819764] **3507**

GRUNDRISS DER SLAVISCHEN PHILOLOGIE UND KULTURGESCHICHTE (JA) [01751611] **3284**

GRUNDRISSE ZUM NEUEN TESTAMENT (GW) **5016**

GRUNDSCHULZEITSCHRIFT, DIE (GW/0932-3910) [I09323910] **1895**

GRUNDTVIG STUDIER (DK/0107-4164) [09297702] **4961**

GRUNDWISSEN MATHEMATIK (GW) [13588637] **3507**

GRUNE, DIE (SZ) [03104571] **91**

GRUPO ANDINO *CEASED*. (PE/0252-9041) [02230404] **2735**

GRUPO ANDINO : LEGISLACION ECONOMICA Y SOCIAL DE LOS PAISES MIEMBROS (PE) [01786682] **2975**

GRUPPE & SPIEL (GW/0724-3332) [10261615] **1895**

GRUPPENDYNAMIK (GW/0046-6514) [08462233] **4588**

GRUPPENPRAXIS, DIE (GW/0341-7344) [02829755] **3579**

GRUPPO E FUNZIONE ANALITICA *See* KOINOS - GRUPPO E FUNZIONE ANALITICA **4602**

GRUVER STATESMAN (US) [14156984] **5750**

GRUYTER STUDIES IN ORGANIZATION, DE (GW) [11250832] **869**

GRYGLA EAGLE, THE (US) [21379028] **5696**

GS NEWS TECHNICAL REPORT (JA/0385-7204) [10467868] **5108**

GSA SUPPLY CATALOG (UNITED STATES. GENERAL SERVICES ADMINISTRATION : 1983) (US) [09431017] **4653**

GSA TODAY (US/1052-5173) [22298497] **1381**

GSBA DIRECTORY *See* GSBA GUIDE/DIRECTORY **2794**

● GSBA GUIDE/DIRECTORY (US) [24136964] **678**, **2794**

GSD NEWS (1983) (US/0746-3677) [09977318] **299**

GSF-BERICHT (GW/0721-1694) [14037388] **2173**

GSF-BERICHT. P (GW/0172-9446) [11417763] **2517**

GSI-REPORT (GW/0171-4546) [I01714546] **976**

GSI REPORT ON REAL ESTATE AND FACILITY MANAGEMENT AUTOMATION (US/1056-5604) [23739548] **4838**

GT. BRIT. DEPT. OF SCIENTIFIC AND INDUSTRIAL RESEARCH. FOREST PRODUCTS RESEARCH DEPT. BULLETIN *See* BULLETIN - FOREST PRODUCTS RESEARCH. DEPARTMENT OF THE ENVIRONMENT **2376**

GT GUIDE TO WORLD EQUITY MARKETS *See* GUIDE TO WORLD EQUITY MARKETS, THE **900**

GT. II GIORNALE DEL TERMOIDRAULICO (IT/1120-5377) [I11205377] **2090**

GTE JOURNAL OF RESEARCH AND DEVELOPMENT (US/0097-7721) [02173908] **2056**

GTE LENKURT *See* GTE LENKURT DEMODULATOR **2056**

GTE LENKURT DEMODULATOR (US/0163-982X) [04550311] **2056**

GTE NETWORK SYSTEMS WORLD-WIDE COMMUNICATIONS JOURNAL (US/0742-6151) [09859059] **1112**

GTE SYLVANIA NEWS (US/0271-731X) [05853931] **2056**

GTEC NEWS (CN/0833-0611) [16629269] **1879**

GTM, GENERALTULLSTYRELSENS MEDDELANDEN (SW) [03142548] **4729**

GTRI TECHNICAL JOURNAL (US/1060-7153) [25053589] **1976**

GTV L'ANTENNA (IT) [11893875] **2056**

GU, THE JOURNAL OF GENITOURINARY MEDICINE (US/0164-4912) [04757712] **3990**

GUA PAPERS OF GEOLOGY. SERIES 1 *CEASED*. (NE/0165-1358) [03990318] **1381**

GUADALIMAR (SP) [I02101254] **321**, **4455**

GUADALUPE COUNTY COMMUNICATOR (US/0746-1399) [09796399] **5712**

GUAJANA (PR/0017-498x) [01468969] **3463**

GUAM & MICRONESIA GLIMPSES *CEASED*. (GU/0889-2938) [13849463] **2669**

GUAM BUSINESS NEWS (GU/1045-053X) [11326592] **678**

GUAM DAILY NEWS *See* PACIFIC DAILY NEWS **5802**

GUAM. DEPARTMENT OF COMMERCE *See* BUSINESS DIRECTORY (AGANA) **647**

GUAM REPORTS : CONTAINING OPINIONS OF THE DISTRICT, SUPERIOR AND SUPREME COURTS *CEASED*. (US) [08008667] **2975**

GUANABARA: INDICADORES ECONOMICOS *See* ESTADO DO RIO DE JANEIRO : INDICADORES ECONOMICOS **1560**

GUANGARA LIBERTARIA (US/0890-0280) [10907880] **5201**, **2617**

GUANGDONG YIXUE (CC/1001-9448) [21728275] **3579**

GUANGHUA (ZHONG-YINGWEN BAN) (US/0256-9043) [20549278] **2262**

GUANGXI NONGXUEYUAN XUEBAO (CC/1000-2553) [I10002553] **91**

GUANGXUE XUEBAO (CC/0253-2239) [09005697] **4434**

GUARD THE NORTH (CN/0700-9917) [03291557] **3392**

GUIDANCE

GUARDIA CIVIL. REVISTA OFICIAL Y PROFESIONAL DEL CUERPO (SP) **4044**

GUARDIA COSTIERA (IT) **4044**

GUARDIAN (GW) **5801**

GUARDIAN (CN) **5785**

GUARDIAN CAPITAL'S VIEWPOINT (CN/0824-6696) [11254718] **1493**

GUARDIAN (LEXINGTON, KY.), THE (US/1059-6224) [24655626] **4653, 2250**

GUARDIAN (LONDON) (UK/0261-3077) [08082962] **5812**

GUARDIAN (NEW YORK, N.Y.), THE (US/0017-5021) [02243323] **2920**

GUARDIAN OF TRUTH (US/0273-5504) [07076662] **4961**

GUARDIAN (WINDSOR) (CN/0700-7167) [02829651] **5785**

GUARDIAN - WRIGHT STATE'S STUDENT NEWSPAPER (US) **5728**

GUARDIANS OF THE GALAXY (US/1052-102X) [22159579] **4862**

GUARDIANSHIP NEWS (US/0276-6272) [07389370] **3121**

GUARDMOUNT *SUSPENDED.* (US/0883-0843) [12041799] **3182**

GUARDS MAGAZINE, THE (UK) [08567748] **4044**

GUATEMALA *See* DIARIO DE CENTRO AMERICA **2960**

●GUATEMALA BULLETIN (US/1068-0187) [27402880] **4508**

GUATEMALA (CITY). BIBLIOTECA NACIONAL *See* BOLETIN - GUATEMALA (CITY) BIBLIOTECA NACIONAL **3196**

GUATEMALA : ENERGIEWIRTSCHAFT (GW) [05064394] **1945**

GUATEMALA INDIGENA (GT/0017-5056) [01588413] **237**

GUATEMALA. INSTITUTO GEOGRAFICO NACIONAL *See* CALIDAD DEL AGUA - GUATEMALA. INSTITUTO GEOGRAFICO NACIONAL **2226**

GUATEMALA-NACHRICHTEN / HRSG. SOLIDARITATSBEWEGUNG MIT DEM VOLK VON GUATEMALA (GW) [11180900] **2735**

GUATEMALA NEWS WATCH (GT) [25044196] **1565**

GUATEMALA : REVISTA CULTURAL DEL EJERCITO (GT) [11643920] **4044**

GUATEMALA UPDATE (US) [21115275] **2512**

GUATEMALA, WIRTSCHAFTLICHE ENTWICKLUNG / BUNDESSTELLE FUR AUSSENHANDELSINFORMATION (GW) [09402630] **1565**

GUATEMALA, WIRTSCHAFTSDATEN / BUNDESSTELLE FUER AUSSENHANDELSINFORMATION (GW) [11508785] **1565**

GUATEMALA WIRTSCHAFTSDATEN UND WIRTSCHAFTSDOKUMENTATION / BUNDESSTELLE FUR AUSSENHANDELSINFORMATION (GW) [07336942] **1565**

GUATEMALAN-AMERICAN CHAMBER OF COMMERCE *See* MEMBERSHIP DIRECTORY **845**

GUATEMALAN CHURCH IN EXILE : [NEWSLETTER] (NQ) [21507619] **4508**

GUATEMALTECO *See* DIARIO DE CENTRO AMERICA **2960**

GUAYULERO, EL (US/0890-7242) [12765442] **3480**

GUBENER HEIMATKALENDER (GW) [01792430] **2690**

GUDOK (RU) [05294766] **5809**

●GUDOK (RU) 5431, **5809**

GUELPH EXAMINER, THE (CN/0229-6799) [08023767] **5785**

GUELPH HISTORICAL SOCIETY NEWSLETTER (CN/0712-2179) [08737679] **2735**

GUELPH MAGAZINE (CN/0710-3425) [08091660] **5478**

GUELPH THIS WEEK (CN/0226-6326) [06511157] **5785**

GUERNSEY BREEDERS' JOURNAL (US/0017-5110) [01751619] **211**

GUERNSEY BREEDERS' JOURNAL (UK) [09802370] **211**

GUERNSEY EVENING PRESS AND STAR (UK) **5812**

GUERNSEY GAZETTE, THE (US/1061-1789) [22417469] **5772**

GUERNSEY IRON GAZETTE *See* GUERNSEY GAZETTE, THE **5772**

GUERRA CIVIL ESPANOLA (SP) **4475**

GUERRES ET CONFLITS D'AUJOURD'HUI (FR) [11965690] **4523, 4044**

GUERRES MONDIALES ET CONFLITS CONTEMPORAINS (FR) [15702247] **2617, 4045**

GUEST AUTHOR (US/0160-6565) [03725044] **3392**

GUEST SECURITY BULLETIN (US) **2805**

GUETERVERKEHR, DER (GW/0017-5137) [l00175137] **5383**

GUFFEY'S JOURNAL (US/0895-5360) [16687358] **4838**

GUGONG XUESHU JIKAN (CH/1011-9094) [l10119094] **351**

GUIA - ADMINISTRACAO-GERAL DO PORTO DE LISBOA (PO) [05088037] **5449**

GUIA ANUAL ISRAELITA (AG) [02862192] 2262, **5048**

GUIA-ANUARIO DE CENTROS DE ENSENANZA MEDIA DE LA IGLESIA (BL) [01792508] **1748**

GUIA-ANUARIO DOS EXPORTADORES E IMPORTADORES DE ANGOLA (AO) [02242725] **838**

GUIA BANCARIO DO BRASIL (BL) [02300676] **789**

GUIA BIBLIOGRAFICA DEL SERVICIO INTERNACIONAL DE INFORMACION SOBRE SUBNORMALES *See* GUIA BIBLIOGRAFICA (SERVICIO INTERNACIONAL DE INFORMACION SOBRE SUBNORMALES) **5266**

GUIA BIBLIOGRAFICA (SERVICIO INTERNACIONAL DE INFORMACION SOBRE SUBNORMALES) (SP) [08652259] **5266**

GUIA BRASILEIRO DE INSTITUCOES DE PESQUISA EM AGRICULTURA / MINISTERIO DA AGRICULTURA, BINAGRI (BL/0101-4684) [09860415] **91**

GUIA CATALOGO PLASTICOS ESPANOLES (SP) [02245160] **4455**

GUIA CHIP (SP/0211-8688) [l02118688] **678**

GUIA COLOMBIANA DEL TRANSPORTE (CK) [03277357] **5383**

GUIA COMERCIAL Y TELEFONICA DEL DEPARTAMENTO DE SORIANO (UY) [05045450] **1112**

GUIA COMPLETA DE LA CIUDAD DE MEXICO, DISTRITO FEDERAL Y SUS ALREDEDORES (MX) [09634901] **5478**

GUIA DAS EDITORAS BRASILEIRAS (BL) [05217321] **4815**

GUIA DAS INSTITUICOES EM FISICA NO BRASIL / CENTRO BRASILEIRO DE PESQUISAS FISICAS, COORDENACAO DE DOCUMENTACAO E INFORMACAO CIENTIFICA, DIVISAO DE INFORMACAO CIENTIFICA (BL) [10732436] **4404**

GUIA DAS LIVRARIAS E PONTOS DE VENDA DE LIVROS NO BRASIL (BL) [02673167] **4828**

GUIA DE ABONADOS : PARANA, VICTORIA, GUALEGUAY (AG) [05639275] **1112**

GUIA DE ARTE (BARCELONA, SPAIN) (SP) [10150435] **351**

GUIA DE COMUNICACAO A DISTANCIA (BL) [01798868] **838**

GUIA DE CONCURSOS : REVISTA DE INFORMACION CULTURAL Y LITERARIA (SP) **3392**

GUIA DE CULTURA *See* NUESTRA CIUDAD **326**

GUIA DE ENDERECOS DO RIO DE JANEIRO (BL) [24362676] **5440**

GUIA DE ENTIDADES E INSTALACIONES DEPORTIVAS (SP) [01798060] **2597**

GUIA DE EXPORTADORES E IMPORTADORES ARGENTINOS (AG) [14955809] **838**

GUIA DE HOTELES : ESPANA (SP) [01785946] **2806**

GUIA DE LA INDUSTRIA ALIMENTARIA (MX) [01226502] **2343**

GUIA DE LA INDUSTRIA QUIMICA : PRODUCTOS QUIMICOS (MX) [06272452] **2012**

GUIA DE LA INDUSTRIA REPUBLICA DEL PARAGUAY (PY) [10137068] **838**

GUIA DE LA UNIVERSIDAD NACIONAL DE EDUCACION A DISTANCIA (SP) [09868629] **1826**

GUIA DE LOS MEDIOS, LA (SP) [21388052] **1112**

GUIA DE MEDICAMENTOS (UY) [05243920] **3579**

GUIA DE PROFESIONALES URUGUAYOS (UY) [06419307] **1676**

GUIA DE PROFESIONALES Y TECNICOS DE LA INDUSTRIA Y DE LA CONSTRUCCION (UY) [11208145] **1676**

GUIA DE REUNIONES CIENTIFICAS Y TECNICAS EN ARGENTINA (AG/0301-7567) [01793013] **5108**

GUIA DE TELEVISION Y ENTRETENIMEINTO (PR/1055-6141) [23245831] **1132**

GUIA DE TRIBUNALES NACIONALES Y DE LA PROVINCIA DE BUENOS AIRES (AG) [04403140] **3141**

GUIA DE TURISMO : REPUBLICA ARGENTINA (AG) [04273192] **5478**

GUIA DEL COMERCIO Y DE LA INDUSTRIA (SP) [04740448] **820**

GUIA DEL ESTUDIANTE (AG) [05049798] **1826**

GUIA DEL SECTOR FINANCIERO ECUATORIANO (EC) [25880713] **789**

GUIA DEL TERCER MUNDO (AG) [03008893] **4653**

GUIA DIRIGENTES (BL) [01785761] **1565**

GUIA DOS EXPORTADORES DO RIO GRANDE DO SUL (BL) [10937534] **838**

GUIA ECLESIASTICA LATINOAMERICANA (CK) [03511612] **5030**

GUIA, EL (SP) **321**

GUIA FINANCIERA (UY) [09407491] **900**

GUIA FINANCIERA MAGUI *See* GUIA FINANCIERA **900**

GUIA INDUSTRIAL ABRIL (BL) [01787001] **5108**

GUIA INDUSTRIAL Y COMERCIAL DE PUERTO RICO (PR) [01799198] 1608, **838**

GUIA INTERNACIONAL DAS ARTES (BL) [09906308] **351**

GUIA NACIONAL DE BANCOS, COMPANIAS DE SEGUROS, ENTIDADES DE AHORRO Y PRESTAMO, SOCIEDADES FINANCIERAS *See* GUIBANCA **3087**

GUIA NACIONAL DO TRANSPORTE RODOVIARIO DE CARGA (BL) [02242717] **5383**

GUIA-NOMENCLATOR DE LA BANCA EN ESPANA (SP) [01788899] **789**

GUIA, O (BL) [02246508] **2565**

GUIA PRACTICA DEL EXPORTADOR E IMPORTADOR *See* GUIA PRACTICA DEL EXPORTADOR E IMPORTADOR Y PARA TODO HOMBRE DE NEGOCIOS **838**

GUIA PRACTICA DEL EXPORTADOR E IMPORTADOR. SUPLEMENTO. FASCICULO DE RESOLUCIONES DE CLASIFICACION (AG) [08518431] **2975**

GUIA PRACTICA DEL EXPORTADOR E IMPORTADOR Y PARA TODO HOMBRE DE NEGOCIOS (AG/0432-8884) [06855760] **838**

GUIA PRACTICA DEL EXPORTADOR E IMPORTADOR Y PARA TODO HOMBRE DE NEGOCIOS. SUPLEMENTO (AG) [06855860] 4729, **838**

GUIA PRACTICA DEL EXPORTADOR E IMPORTADOR Y PARA TODO HOMBRE DE NEGOCIOS. SUPLEMENTO DE LA SECCION INFORMATIVA (AG) [06855924] 838, **2975**

GUIA PROFESIONAL Y JUDICIAL (SP) [04292878] **3141**

GUIA RELACIONES INSTITUCIONALES DEL ESTADO ARGENTINO (AG) [09233672] **4653**

GUIA ROJI (GUIA ROJA) : INFORMACION Y GUIA DE LA CIUDAD DE MEXICO *See* GUIA COMPLETA DE LA CIUDAD DE MEXICO, DISTRITO FEDERAL Y SUS ALREDEDORES **5478**

GUIA SOCIAL DEL TRABAJADOR (CN/0826-8673) [11919053] **3148**

GUIA TELEFONICA : SAN SALVADOR DE JUJUY (AG) [06974920] **1156**

GUIA TURISTICA Y DE CALLES DE LA CIUDAD DE MAR DEL PLATA (AG) [02242337] **5478**

GUIA TURISTICA Y HOTELES DE VENEZUELA (VE) [01787794] **2806**

GUIA TURISTICO INFORMATIVO DE CURITIBA E DO PARANA (BL) [02243924] **2735**

GUIA VERDE INDUSTRIAL Y COMERCIAL (PE) [04233574] **1565**

GUIBANCA (VE) [03851514] **3087**

●GUIDA AGLI ACQUISTI PER GLI ENTI PUBBLICI (IT) [26081356] **678**

GUIDA CUCINA (IT) **5558**

GUIDA DEL CAVALIERE (IT) [01794713] **2799**

GUIDA DELLA PELLICCERIA (IT) **3184**

GUIDA DI VETERINARIA E ZOOTECNIA (IT) [27797296] **5510**

GUIDA MENSILE (CN/1185-3131) [24368120] **2735**

GUIDA SOCIAL DO TRABALHADOR (CN/0826-8681) [11919050] **3148**

GUIDA SOCIALE DEL LAVORATORE (CN/0826-869X) [12030778] **3148**

GUIDANCE & COUNSELLING (CN/0831-5493) [12933388] 4588, **1748**

GUIDANCE

GUIDANCE AND COUNSELLING ASSOCIATION (SASK.) *See* NEWSLETTER - GUIDANCE AND COUNSELLING ASSOCIATION **1882**

GUIDANCE EXCHANGE (US/0017-520X) [01507508] **1879**

GUIDANCE ON DESIGN CONSTRUCTION OF OFFSHORE INSTALLATIONS AMENDMENT SERVICE (UK) **2090**

GUIDARGUS DE LA PEINTURE DU XIXE SIECLE A NOS JOURS, LE (FR) [10827800] **351**

GUIDAZZURRA ALL'AMMINISTRAZIONE PUBBLICA (IT) [25648679] **4653**

GUIDE (JA) [01786503] **2090**

GUIDE, AGENCIES, BOARDS & COMMISSIONS, GOVERNMENT OF ONTARIO, A (CN/1183-7705) [24401828] **4653**

GUIDE BOOK FOR FIRST YEAR STUDENTS IN THE SCHOOL OF NATURAL SCIENCES (ZA) [02742574] **5108**

GUIDE BOOK OF UNITED STATES COINS, A (US/0072-8829) [02115595] **2781**

GUIDE BOOK / OKLAHOMA GEOLOGICAL SURVEY (US/0078-4400) [01681066] **1381**

GUIDE BOUNTY DE LA GROSSESSE, LE (CN/1183-0689) [25127691] **3579**

GUIDE BOUNTY DES SOINS AU NOURRISSON (CN/1183-0662) [24623489] **2280**

GUIDE BUDGETAIRE COMMUNAL, DEPARTEMENTAL ET REGIONAL (FR) [16836552] **4730**

GUIDE CASTELRIAND (CN/0708-983X) [05257125] **2735**

GUIDE CUISINE PARIS (FR/0767-8177) [07678177] **2790**

GUIDE D'ACHAT DE LA VOITURE USAGEE (CN/0820-8964) [09551518] **5415**

GUIDE DE L' AUTO (MONTREAL) (CN/0315-9205) [01795126] **5415**

GUIDE DE LA BIBLIOTHEQUE DU CENTRE AUDIO-VISUEL - COLLEGE JEAN-DE-BREBEUF (CN/0712-8533) [08777653] **3212**

GUIDE DE LA CHIMIE *See* GUIDE DE LA CHIMIE INTERNATIONAL **976**

GUIDE DE LA CHIMIE INTERNATIONAL (FR) [09872445] **976**

GUIDE DE LA CONCURRENCE ET DE LA CONSOMMATION (FR) [11556661] **838**

GUIDE DE LA DECLARATION D'EFFECTIF SCOLAIRE (DCS) (CN/1187-2977) [25590193] **1748**

GUIDE DE LA MOTO (MONTREAL, 1984) (CN/0823-8499) [11431415] **4081**

GUIDE DE LA MUSIQUE, LE (BE) **4119**

GUIDE DE LA ROUTE, FLORIDE (CN/0838-0015) [17759084] **5478**

GUIDE DE LA ROUTE, PROVINCES DE L'ATLANTIQUE ET DU QUEBEC (CN/0225-2600) [06184798] **5478**

GUIDE DE L'ACHETEUR ANNUEL - EXPOSITION COMMERCIALE DE L'HORTICULTURE ORNEMENTALE (CN/1187-2268) [25314203] **2418**

GUIDE DE L'AUDIOVISUEL EUROPEEN, LE (FR) [24596850] **4071**

GUIDE DE L'AUTOMOBILE AMERICAINE, LE (CN/0228-9776) [07869951] **5415**

GUIDE DE L'AVIATION GENERALE (FR) [05699490] **22**

GUIDE DE L'AVIATION GENERALE EN FRANCE *See* GUIDE DE L'AVIATION GENERALE **22**

GUIDE DE L'EAU (FR) [04950148] **5534**

GUIDE DE L'ENVIRONNEMENT (CN/1183-4803) [24623458] **2173**

GUIDE DE L'EQUIPEMENT ET DE L'OUTILLAG (FR) **5415**

GUIDE DE L'INDUSTRIE SENEGALAISE (SG/0376-5245) [01793602] **1608**

GUIDE DE L'INVESTISSEUR INDUSTRIEL AU SENEGAL (SG) [01788420] **1565**

GUIDE DE LOCATION (MONTREAL) (CN/0384-0077) [03230245] **2115**

GUIDE DE L'USAGER / UNIVERSITE DU QUEBEC A TROIS-RIVIERES, SERVICE DE LA BIBLIOTHEQUE, LE (CN/0823-5686) [11422259] **3212**

GUIDE DE ROUTE (CN/0318-9414) [02443124] **5478**

GUIDE DELLE REGIONI D'ITALIA (IT) [04538236] **5479**

GUIDE DES AUTOS USAGEES, LE (CN/1186-9321) [24690584] **5415**

GUIDE DES CONVENTIONS INTERNATIONALES DE SECURITE SOCIALE (FR/0767-1830) [I07671830] **2811**

GUIDE DES COSMETIQUES *CEASED.* (CN/0316-9898) [02247559] **404**

GUIDE DES GUIDES, LE (FR) [10599893] **4698**

●GUIDE DES MEMBRES DE LA STQ (CN/1187-922X) [26497860] **3284**

●GUIDE DES MEMBRES DE LA STQ (FRENCH EDITION) (CN/1187-922X) [26497862] **3284**

GUIDE DES ORGANISMES, CONSEILS ET COMMISSIONS DU GOUVERNEMENT DE L'ONTARIO (CN/1183-7713) [24401830] **4653**

GUIDE DES RATIOS DES COMMUNES DE PLUS DE 10 000 HABITANTS / MINISTERE DE L'INTERIEUR, DIRECTION GENERALE DES COLLECTIVITES LOCALES, MISSION D'ETUDES ET DE STATISTIQUES (FR) [04837725] **4730**

GUIDE DES RATIOS DES REGIONS / MINISTERE DE L'INTERIEUR, LE SECRETAIRE D'ETAT AUPRES DU MINISTRE DE L'INTERIEUR CHARGE DES COLLECTIVITES TERRITORIALES, DIRECTION GENERALE DES COLLECTIVITES LOCALES, MISSION D'ETUDES ET DE STATISTIQUES (FR/0762-0195) [20327418] **5328**

GUIDE DES RELATIONS PRESSE, LE (FR) [11846375] **4347**

GUIDE DES RESSOURCES PROFESSIONNELLES EN URBANISME (CN) [23238244] **2823**

GUIDE DES USAGERS / UNIVERSITE DE SHERBROOKE-BIBLIOTHEQUE GENERALE (CN/0824-8095) [09313027] **3212**

GUIDE DES VILLES DU MONDE, LE (FR) [18933872] **2565**

GUIDE D'IMPOT SUR LE REVENU DES AGRICULTEURS (CN/0710-8915) [08828264] **91, 4730**

GUIDE DU BANQUIER, LE (FR) [18338198] **789**

GUIDE DU CADEAU ET DES ARTS DE LA TABLE (FR/0997-2676) [I09972676] **351**

GUIDE DU CONTRIBUABLE CANADIEN, LE (CN/0432-9368) [02247821] **678**

GUIDE DU DEPOSANT (GW) **2976**

GUIDE DU NAVIGATEUR (FR) [06077979] **4176**

GUIDE DU PASSAGE A LA RETRAITE (CN/0846-0671) [23658911] **5179**

GUIDE DU PORT DE MONTREAL & REPERTOIRE DU TRANSPORT (CN/0844-1871) [19759148] **5383**

GUIDE DU PRODUCTEUR DE DISQUES, LE (BE) **4119, 5317**

GUIDE DU TRANSPORT PAR CAMION INC (CN/0706-9995) [04677967] **5415, 5383**

GUIDE DU TRAVAIL (FR) **1676**

GUIDE DU TRAVAIL DES METAUX (FR/0301-8539) [01792633] **4003**

GUIDE DU VIN, LE (CN/0823-6682) [10052306] **2367**

GUIDE ECONOMIQUE DE LA TUNISIE (TI) [02694417] **1565**

GUIDE EUROPEEN DES PROGICIELS. EDITION COMPLEMENTAIRE / CXP (FR/0294-0701) [11292575] **1286**

●GUIDE EXPRESS DES VINS (CN/1191-1522) [25883056] **2367**

GUIDE FOR ACCREDITED VETERINARIANS, A (US) [02197652] **5510**

GUIDE FOR APPLICANTS FOR UNDERGRADUATE COURSES (UK) [02366327] **1826**

GUIDE FOR THE CARE AND USE OF LABORATORY ANIMALS / PREPARED BY THE COMMITTEE ON CARE AND USE OF LABORATORY ANIMALS OF THE INSTITUTE OF LABORATORY ANIMAL RESOURCES, COMMISSION OF LIFE SCIENCES, NATIONAL RESEARCH COUNCIL (US) [04923005] **5510**

GUIDE FOR THE PREPARATION OF PROPOSALS FOR FACULTY DEVELOPMENT PROJECTS IN ENERGY EDUCATION (US) [05246890] **1945**

GUIDE FOR THE SELECTION OF TANKERS (US/0882-2913) [10474567] **4176**

GUIDE FRANCE ... / GAULT ET MILLAU (FR) [08702356] **5071**

GUIDE GENERAL DES COMITES - ASTED (CN/0824-8613) [10595682] **3212**

GUIDE GRIMALDI DE MONTREAL, LE (CN/0825-6764) [09581973] **5479**

GUIDE HACHETTE DES VINS DE FRANCE (FR) [20395013] **2367**

GUIDE (HAWKESBURY) (CN/0227-5368) [08003276] **5785**

GUIDE INTERNATIONAL DE L'ENERGIE NUCLEAIRE (FR) [03997802] **2155**

GUIDE LINES (ROUND ROCK, TEX.) *CEASED.* (US/1057-6193) [24082886] **865**

GUIDE MARKETING MIX, LE (FR) [17195454] **789**

GUIDE MEDIA - CONCORDES (CN/0820-0645) [09459962] **4897**

GUIDE MEDICAL ET PHARMACEUTIQUE ROSENWALD *See* GUIDE ROSENWALD **3914**

GUIDE MOTOR CLUB *See* GUIDE MOTOR CLUB'S ANNUAL EMERGENCY ROAD SERVICE GUIDE **5415**

GUIDE MOTOR CLUB'S ANNUAL EMERGENCY ROAD SERVICE GUIDE (US/0160-1318) [03610220] **5415**

GUIDE NERET DES CARIERES : ECOLES, DIPLOMES ET DEBOUCHS POUR JEUNES GENS ET JEUNES FILLES A PARTIR DE LA CLASSE DE TROISIEME (FR) [02637371] **1913**

GUIDE OF CHINESE TRADING (US/1042-7198) [19114878] **838**

GUIDE OFFICIEL DU BATIMENT / PUBLIE SOUS LE PATRONAGE OU AVEC LA COLLABORATION DE LA FEDERATION NATIONAL BELGE DU BATIMENT ET DES TRAVAUX PUBLICS ... [ET AL.] (BE) [20498036] **615**

GUIDE ORGANIZZATIVA / CONFINDUSTRIA, DIREZIONE CENTRALE RAPPORTI INTERNI (IT) [19806224] **1608**

GUIDE PLEIN AIR DU QUEBEC (CN/0847-4834) [22135330] **4873**

GUIDE PRATIQUE DE L'ORGANISATEUR DE CONGRES, RIMOUSKI LA PREFERENCE (CN/1186-1886) [24368167] **5479**

GUIDE PRATIQUE DES ETUDES COLLEGIALES (CN/0714-5780) [09340503] **1826**

GUIDE PRATIQUE DU SALARIE (FR) **1676**

GUIDE. PUBLIC SERVICES, ORGANISATION OF PUBLIC AND PRIVATE LAW, BANKS, DIPLOMATIC CORPS, AIR COMPANIES, CONCISE GUIDE TO THESSALONIKI (GR) [05332263] **4653**

GUIDE RESSOURCES (1991) (CN/1187-502X) [25652306] **2597, 4588**

GUIDE ROSENWALD (FR) [05530014] **3914**

GUIDE ROUTIER ET TOURISTIQUE: MADAGASCAR, REUNION, MAURICE, COMORES ET SEYCHELLES (MG) [01797951] **5479**

GUIDE SANTE (SILLERY) (CN/1191-1123) [25796559] **2597**

GUIDE SERIES - GEOLOGICAL SURVEY OF IRELAND (IE/0790-0260) [03953175] **1381**

GUIDE SPECIFICATIONS FOR BRIDGE CONSTRUCTION (AT) [17020690] **615, 2024**

GUIDE STATISTIQUE DE LA FISCALITE DIRECTE LOCALE / MINISTERE DE L'INTERIEUR ET DE LA DECENTRALISATION, DIRECTION GENERALE LOCALES, MISSION D'ETUDES ET DESTATISTIQUES (FR) [11767611] **4730, 4698**

GUIDE TO A WORLD OF LEARNING (CN/1185-8923) [25590213] **1748**

GUIDE TO ACCOUNTING CONTROLS. SUPPLEMENT *SUSPENDED.* (US/0734-8525) [07829103] **744**

GUIDE TO ACCREDITATION OF CANADIAN MENTAL HEALTH SERVICES (CN/0383-2457) [03209897] **5287**

GUIDE TO ACCREDITED CAMPS (US/1046-5774) [19051363] **4873, 1064**

GUIDE TO AGRICULTURAL PRODUCTION IN MALAWI (MW/0542-3007) [01785459] **91**

GUIDE TO AMERICAN DIRECTORIES (US/0533-5248) [06009110] **1926**

GUIDE TO AMERICAN DIRECTORIES FOR COMPILING MAILING LISTS *See* GUIDE TO AMERICAN DIRECTORIES **1926**

GUIDE TO AMERICAN EDUCATIONAL DIRECTORIES (US/0072-8225) [01325382] **1748**

GUIDE TO AMUSEMENT RIDES (US/0145-8159) [02792351] **4862**

●GUIDE TO ARCHITECTURE SCHOOLS (US) [29991596] **299**

GUIDE TO ARCHITECTURE SCHOOLS IN NORTH AMERICA *See* GUIDE TO ARCHITECTURE SCHOOLS **299**

●GUIDE TO ARTS ADMINISTRATION TRAINING. / CENTER FOR ARTS ADMINISTRATION, GRADUATE SCHOOL OF BUSINESS, UNIVERSITY OF WISCONSIN - MADISON, AND ASSOCIATION OF ARTS ADMINISTRATION EDUCATORS (US) [28860443] **321**

GUIDE TO AUDITS OF EMPLOYEE BENEFIT PLANS (US/1060-2933) [24916788] **744**

GUIDE TO AUSTRALIAN GOVERNMENTS *See* AUSTRALIAN RESOURCES GUIDE **4631**

Alphabetical Title Index — GUIDE

GUIDE TO BACKGROUND INVESTIGATIONS, THE (US/0897-3156) [17454333] **1676**

GUIDE TO BIBLES IN PRINT (US/0072-8241) [01624321] **5012**

GUIDE TO BIOMEDICAL STANDARDS, THE (US/0085-1353) [01908072] **3579**

GUIDE TO BUSINESS AND FINANCIAL NEWS MEDIA (US) [17630162] **1493, 2920**

GUIDE TO BUSINESS & INVESTMENT BOOKS *See* SIE GUIDE TO BUSINESS & INVESTMENT BOOKS **914**

GUIDE TO BUSINESS VALUATIONS (US/1058-4897) [24333580] **678**

GUIDE TO CALIFORNIA COLLEGES & UNIVERSITIES... (US) [10197287] **1826**

GUIDE TO CALIFORNIA FOUNDATIONS (US/0163-4623) [04372419] **5287**

GUIDE TO CALIFORNIA GOVERNMENT, A (US) [06731726] **4653**

GUIDE TO CANADIAN HEALTH CARE FACILITIES (CN) **3780**

GUIDE TO CANADIAN MANUFACTURERS (CN/0227-2059) [06563033] **3480**

GUIDE TO COAL CONTRACTS (US) [16268932] **1945**

GUIDE TO COLLECTIONS OF MANUSCRIPTS RELATING TO AUSTRALIA (AT/0072-8578) [02950811] **416**

GUIDE TO COLLEGE COURSES IN FILM AND TELEVISION (US) [02559572] **1826**

GUIDE TO COLLEGE MANAGEMENT (UK) **869**

●GUIDE TO COLLEGE PROGRAMS IN HOSPITALITY AND TOURISM : A DIRECTORY OF CHRIE MEMBER COLLEGES AND UNIVERSITIES, A (US) [23479601] **5479**

GUIDE TO CONSTRUCTION ACTIVITY IN MANHATTAN (US) [14438787] **4838**

GUIDE TO COOKING SCHOOLS, THE (US/1040-2616) [18361011] **2343**

GUIDE TO DIRECT SOURCES OF INDIANA AGRICULTURAL PRODUCTS (US) [19372548] **91**

GUIDE TO ELECTRONICS INDUSTRY IN INDIA (II/0376-5229) [02245620] **2056**

GUIDE TO ENVIRONMENTAL LEGISLATION IN ONTARIO (CN) **3112**

GUIDE TO ETHNIC MEDIA IN VICTORIA / VICTORIAN ETHNIC AFFAIRS COMMISSION (AT/0811-6636) [12432573] 1112, **2262**

GUIDE TO EXTERNAL & CONTINUING EDUCATION *See* CHRONICLE GUIDE TO EXTERNAL & CONTINUING EDUCATION **1800**

GUIDE TO FEDERAL ASSISTANCE FOR EDUCATION *See* GUIDE TO FEDERAL ASSISTANCE. NEWSLETTER, THE **4730**

GUIDE TO FEDERAL ASSISTANCE. NEWSLETTER, THE (US/0278-5064) [07819328] **4730**

●GUIDE TO FEDERAL FUNDING FOR ANTI-CRIME PROGRAMS (US) 3165, **4653**

GUIDE TO FEDERAL FUNDING FOR ANTI-DRUG PROGRAMS (US/1056-9340) [23865720] 3165, **1344**

GUIDE TO FEDERAL FUNDING FOR EDUCATION (US/0275-8393) [07238591] 4653, **1748**

GUIDE TO FEDERAL FUNDING FOR GOVERNMENTS AND NONPROFITS (US/1055-596X) [23113913] **4653**

GUIDE TO FEDERAL GOVERNMENT LABOUR STATISTICS (CN) [01785406] 1676, **1533**

GUIDE TO FEDERAL PROCUREMENT (US/0276-9891) [07467046] 950, **4653**

GUIDE TO FEDERAL PROGRAMS AND SERVICES (CN/0848-4597) [21832522] **4653**

GUIDE TO FLORIDA GOVERNMENT (US) [03957358] **4653**

GUIDE TO FLORIDA RETIREMENT LIVING (US/0889-051X) [13818448] 2823, **5179**

GUIDE TO FLORIDA STATE PROGRAMS, A (US/1070-7832) [17672319] **4338**

GUIDE TO FOREIGN TRADE STATISTICS (US/0565-0933) [01792725] 838, **730**

GUIDE TO FREE COMPUTER MATERIALS (US/0748-6235) [09914291] 1185, **1895**

GUIDE TO GEORGIA (US/0434-8877) [13754439] **5479**

GUIDE TO GIFTS AND BEQUESTS, CALIFORNIA, THE (US/0163-383X) [04354667] **4338**

GUIDE TO GIFTS AND BEQUESTS. NEW YORK/FLORIDA, THE (US) [17853937] **5201**

GUIDE TO GLOBAL INSTITUTIONAL INVESTORS (US) **900**

GUIDE TO GOVERNMENT IN HAWAII (US/0072-8454) [01590453] **4653**

GUIDE TO GOVERNMENT-LOAN FILMS (US/0072-8462) [05289796] **4071**

GUIDE TO GRADUATE DEGREE PROGRAMS IN ARCHITECTURAL HISTORY (US/0740-8102) [08704324] **299**

GUIDE TO GRADUATE DEPARTMENTS OF SOCIOLOGY (US/0091-7052) [01511015] **5246**

GUIDE TO GRADUATE EDUCATION IN SPEECH-LANGUAGE PATHOLOGY AND AUDIOLOGY (US/0884-7347) [06879158] 4388, **1826**

GUIDE TO GRADUATE PROGRAMS IN CRIMINAL JUSTICE AND CRIMINOLOGY (US/1055-4688) [22102117] **3165**

GUIDE TO GRADUATE STUDY IN BOTANY FOR THE UNITED STATES AND CANADA (US/0072-8500) [02512880] 1826, **512**

GUIDE TO GRADUATE STUDY IN POLITICAL SCIENCE *See* GRADUATE FACULTY AND PROGRAMS IN POLITICAL SCIENCE **4475**

GUIDE TO GRANTS & FELLOWSHIPS IN LINGUISTICS (US/1041-5459) [13202189] **3284**

GUIDE TO HEALTH SERVICES OF THE WORLD (UK) **4777**

GUIDE TO HONG KONG SCHOOLS, A (HK) [01790390] **1748**

GUIDE TO HOSPITALITY AND TOURISM EDUCATION *See* GUIDE TO COLLEGE PROGRAMS IN HOSPITALITY AND TOURISM : A DIRECTORY OF CHRIE MEMBER COLLEGES AND UNIVERSITIES, A **5479**

GUIDE TO HOSPITALITY AND TOURISM EDUCATION, THE (US/1050-933X) [20375424] **1826**

GUIDE TO INCOME TAX PREPARATION (US) [17315006] **4730**

GUIDE TO INDIAN PERIODICAL LITERATURE (II/0017-5285) [01751626] **416**

GUIDE TO INDUSTRIAL INVESTMENT, A (KE) [01783356] **900**

GUIDE TO INDUSTRIAL PARKS AND AREA DEVELOPMENT (US/0072-8535) [01169399] **1565**

GUIDE TO INFORMATION TECHNOLOGY (UK) **5108**

GUIDE TO INTERNATIONAL EDUCATION IN THE UNITED STATES (US/1052-9586) [22423873] **1748**

GUIDE TO INTERNATIONAL SUBSCRIPTION AGENCIES (US) **1926**

GUIDE TO JAPANESE TAXES (JA/0072-8551) [01641645] **4730**

GUIDE TO JAPAN'S AUTO INDUSTRY, FACTS & INFO (JA) [14339781] **5415**

GUIDE TO JEWISH CANADA & USA (US) [21652833] **5048**

GUIDE TO JEWISH CHICAGO, AND YEARBOOK (US/0272-1066) [06739761] **2262**

GUIDE TO JEWISH EUROPE (US) **5479**

GUIDE TO JEWISH ITALY *CEASED*. (US) **5479**

GUIDE TO JEWISH USA (US) [16799828] **4961**

GUIDE TO KEY BRITISH ENTERPRISES *See* KEY BRITISH ENTERPRISES : KBE / COMPILED AND PUBLISHED BY PUBLICATIONS DIVISION, DUN & BRADSTREET LIMITED **688**

GUIDE TO LEGISLATION ON RESTRICTIVE BUSINESS PRACTICES *CEASED*. (FR) [01761447] **2976**

GUIDE TO LIBRARIES AND INFORMATION UNITS IN GOVERNMENT DEPARTMENTS AND OTHER ORGANISATIONS (UK) [22599217] **3212**

●GUIDE TO LITERARY AGENTS & ART/PHOTO REPS (US/1055-6087) [23239176] **321**

GUIDE TO LITERARY PRIZES, GRANTS AND AWARDS *CEASED*. (UK) [18129673] **3392**

GUIDE TO LOCATION INFORMATION (US/0148-8538) [03388310] **4071**

GUIDE TO MANAGEMENT IMPROVEMENT PROJECTS IN LOCAL GOVERNMENT, THE (US) [02833812] **4653**

GUIDE TO MANUFACTURED HOMES (US/0160-7340) [03786523] **615**

GUIDE TO MARINES IN REUNION (US/1063-1364) [25898552] **4176**

GUIDE TO MARTIN COUNTY (US/1056-862X) [23881485] **5479**

GUIDE TO MEDICAL AND SCIENCE NEWS MEDIA (US) [16170755] 3579, **2920**

GUIDE TO MICROFORMS IN PRINT. AUTHOR, TITLE (GW/0164-0747) [03898516] **416**

GUIDE TO MICROFORMS IN PRINT. SUBJECT (GW/0163-8386) [03898468] **3212**

GUIDE TO MICROFORMS IN PRINT. SUPPLEMENT (US/0164-0739) [04572280] **416**

GUIDE TO MICROGRAPHIC EQUIPMENT (US/0360-8654) [02244682] **4370**

GUIDE TO MIDDLE STATES SCHOOLS IN DELAWARE, DISTRICT OF COLUMBIA, MARYLAND, PUERTO RICO, CANAL ZONE, VIRGIN ISLANDS, OVERSEAS (US/0192-2572) [04973557] **1749**

GUIDE TO MIDDLE STATES SCHOOLS IN NEW JERSEY (US/0192-2580) [04973492] **1749**

GUIDE TO MIDDLE STATES SCHOOLS IN NEW YORK (US/0192-2564) [04973579] **1749**

GUIDE TO MIDDLE STATES SCHOOLS IN PENNSYLVANIA (US/0192-2599) [04973530] **1749**

GUIDE TO MILITARY INSTALLATIONS IN THE U.S (US) [17834262] **4045**

GUIDE TO MINORITY BUSINESS DIRECTORIES (US/0362-3459) [02059436] **678**

GUIDE TO MUSCLE CARS *CEASED*. (US/0895-6782) [14117332] **5415**

GUIDE TO NEBRASKA STATE AGENCIES (US/0091-0716) [01786367] **4653**

GUIDE TO NEW AUSTRALIAN BOOKS (AT/1035-5391) [I10355391] **3392**

GUIDE TO NEW INDUSTRIAL POLICY OF GOVERNMENT OF INDIA (II) [10953208] **1608**

GUIDE TO NEW ZEALAND'S FOREIGN RELATIONS, A (NZ) [13041664] **4523**

GUIDE TO NORTH SUMATRA, INDONESIA (IO/0377-7200) [01790712] **5479**

GUIDE TO OBTAINING INFORMATION FROM THE USGS, A (US) [08091892] **1381**

GUIDE TO OBTAINING MINORITY BUSINESS DIRECTORIES (US/1045-0319) [03713643] **678**

GUIDE TO OFFICIAL STATISTICS (UK) [03092019] **5328**

GUIDE TO ORANGE COUNTY FREELANCE MARKETS (US/1055-1174) [23077526] **678**

GUIDE TO OVER 100 PROPERTIES / NATIONAL TRUST FOR SCOTLAND (UK) [14081176] 299, **2690**

GUIDE TO PARENTERAL ADMIXTURES (US) [02255341] **2280**

GUIDE TO PERIODICALS AND NEWSPAPERS (TORONTO) (CN/0315-7288) [02443191] **416**

GUIDE TO PERSONAL FINANCIAL PLANNING (US) [25121552] **789**

GUIDE TO PETROLEUM STATISTICAL INFORMATION (US/0742-8464) [09306423] 4259, **4283**

GUIDE TO PHOTOGRAPHY WORKSHOPS & SCHOOLS (US/1054-8904) [22943396] **4370**

GUIDE TO PORT ENTRY (UK) [07661586] **5449**

GUIDE TO POSTGRADUATE DEGREES, DIPLOMAS AND COURSES IN MEDICINE (UK/0265-2730) [11689276] 1826, **3579**

GUIDE TO POSTGRADUATE STUDY (UK) [13411067] **1827**

GUIDE TO PRACTICE AND PROCEDURE, U.S. DEPARTMENT OF ENERGY, BOARD OF CONTRACT APPEALS, CONTRACT ADJUSTMENT BOARD, FINANCIAL ASSISTANCE APPEALS BOARD, INVENTION LICENSING APPEALS BOARD (US/0270-000X) [05924967] **1945**

GUIDE TO PREPARING FINANCIAL STATEMENTS (CN/0848-7855) [23238184] **789**

●GUIDE TO PRIVATE FORTUNES (US/1070-7964) [27198739] **678**

GUIDE TO PROFESSIONAL BODIES IN MALAWI (MW) [07365507] **5231**

GUIDE TO PROGRAMS & SERVICES / THE MASSACHUSETTS COUNCIL ON THE ARTS AND HUMANITIES (US) [06046517] **321**

GUIDE TO PROGRAMS - NATIONAL ENDOWMENT FOR THE ARTS (US/0360-3407) [02441072] **321**

GUIDE TO PROGRAMS / NATIONAL SCIENCE FOUNDATION (US) [01142423] 4730, **5108**

GUIDE TO PSI PERIODICALS *See* INTERNATIONAL GUIDE TO PSI PERIODICALS AND ORGANIZATIONS **4243**

GUIDE TO PUBLISHERS AND RELATED INDUSTRIES IN JAPAN *See* DIRECTORY OF JAPANESE PUBLISHING INDUSTRY **4814**

GUIDE — Alphabetical Title Index

GUIDE TO QUALITY CONSTRUCTION PRODUCTS (US/0197-6214) [03598694] **616**

GUIDE TO REAL ESTATE AND MORTGAGE BANKING SOFTWARE (US) **1286**

GUIDE TO RECORD RETENTION REQUIREMENTS (US/0271-6461) [02481622] **2976**

GUIDE TO RESTAURANTS AND BARS (US/1059-583X) [24640880] **5071**

●GUIDE TO RETAIL SHOPS (US/1061-2106) [25255623] **954**

GUIDE TO SAFETY *See* ACCIDENT PREVENTION MAGAZINE **2858**

●GUIDE TO SELECTED DOMESTIC BOND MARKETS, THE (UK) [25236659] **900**

GUIDE TO SELECTING PLAYS, THE (UK) [01570169] 5364, **3392**

GUIDE TO SERIAL PUBLICATIONS - MANAGEMENT STUDIES LIBRARY, UNIVERSITY OF TORONTO (CN/0709-8065) [07805771] **730**

GUIDE TO SERVICES (US/0148-7841) [03367840] **4653**

GUIDE TO SIMULATIONS/GAMES FOR EDUCATION AND TRAINING, THE (US) [06875294] 4862, **1749**

GUIDE TO SOCIAL SCIENCE AND RELIGION (US/1054-0946) [19989872] 5201, 5266, **5012**

GUIDE TO SOCIAL SECURITY AND MEDICARE *See* MERCER GUIDE TO SOCIAL SECURITY AND MEDICARE **2888**

GUIDE TO SOFTWARE PRODUCTIVITY AIDS (US/0740-8374) [10028622] 1286, **1238**

GUIDE TO SOURCES OF INTERNATIONAL POPULATION ASSISTANCE (US) [05037923] **4553**

GUIDE TO SOURCES OF INTERNATIONAL POPULATION ASSISTANCE. SUPPLEMENT (US) [05039447] **2910**

GUIDE TO SPECIFICATIONS FOR INTERIOR LANDSCAPING, A (US/0271-3373) [06593795] **2418**

GUIDE TO SPRINGFIELD (US) **2534**

GUIDE TO STABILISATION IN ROADWORKS / NATIONAL ASSOCIATION OF AUSTRALIAN STATE ROAD AUTHORITIES (AT) [16704204] 2024, **5440**

GUIDE TO STATE AND FEDERAL RESOURCES FOR ECONOMIC DEVELOPMENT, THE (US/0894-4202) [16074650] **1493**

GUIDE TO STATIONARY PHASES FOR GAS CHROMATOGRAPHY (US/0533-9855) [09860359] **4259**

GUIDE TO SUMMER CAMPS AND SUMMER SCHOOLS, THE (US/0072-8705) [02432902] 1749, **4850**

GUIDE TO TANKER PORTS (UK) **5449**

GUIDE TO TAXATION, PUBLIC FINANCE AND RELATED LITERATURE (US) [01452138] **4730**

●GUIDE TO TEXAS FRANCHISE TAX (US/1064-7732) [26392953] 4730, **2976**

GUIDE TO THE ADMISSIONS TESTING PROGRAM (US/0196-7576) [05332277] **1827**

GUIDE TO THE AMERICAN LEFT (KANSAS CITY, MO. 1984) (US/0894-4547) [11857054] 4542, **4502**

GUIDE TO THE AMERICAN RIGHT (KANSAS CITY, MO. 1984) (US/8756-0216) [11859906] **4502**

GUIDE TO THE ANTIQUE SHOPS OF BRITAIN (UK) [02550531] **250**

●GUIDE TO THE ATLANTA UNIVERSITY CENTER AND ATLANTA, THE (US/1064-5306) [26279737] **1827**

GUIDE TO THE AUSTRALIAN FEDERAL PARLIAMENT (AT) [05630247] **4475**

GUIDE TO THE CANADIAN FINANCIAL SERVICES INDUSTRY (CN/0827-0864) [13828675] **789**

GUIDE TO THE COALFIELDS (UK/0072-8713) [02255710] **2140**

GUIDE TO THE CRAFT WORLD (US/0097-7012) [01799217] **373**

GUIDE TO THE DEPARTMENT, UNIVERSITY FARMS AND EXPERIMENTAL STATIONS WITH A SUMMARY OF RESEARCH (UK) [03676278] **91**

GUIDE TO THE ECONOMY / NEDBANK GROUP (SA/0258-6754) [15649405] **1493**

GUIDE TO THE ENERGY INDUSTRIES (US/0732-7366) [08422935] **1945**

●GUIDE TO THE EUROPEAN VAT DIRECTIVES: COMMENTARY ON THE VALUE ADDED TAX OF THE EUROPEAN COMMUNITY (NE) **4730**

GUIDE TO THE EVALUATION OF EDUCATIONAL EXPERIENCES IN THE ARMED SERVICES (US/0732-3034) [04442280] 4045, **1827**

GUIDE TO THE FEDERAL BUDGET, THE (US/0730-9511) [08098349] **4730**

GUIDE TO THE HANDLING AND DISPOSAL OF HAZARDOUS SUBSTANCES IN THE SCHOOLS, A (CN/1187-2195) [25352194] 1749, **2230**

GUIDE TO THE HIGH TECHNOLOGY INDUSTRIES (US/0738-2324) [09545620] **5108**

GUIDE TO THE HOTELS IN SOUTH AFRICA (SA/0376-5210) [01796728] **2806**

GUIDE TO THE HOUSE OF COMMONS (UK) [02304296] **4475**

GUIDE TO THE JEWISH WEST (US) 5048, **5479**

GUIDE TO THE MOTOR INDUSTRY OF JAPAN (JA) [04088806] **5415**

GUIDE TO THE NATIONAL ENDOWMENT FOR THE ARTS (US) [13694500] **321**

GUIDE TO THE NATION'S BEST OUTLETS / OUTLET BOUND (US) [22619477] **1297**

... GUIDE TO THE NATION'S HOSPICES, THE (US/1045-0548) [11420637] **3579**

GUIDE TO THE PORT OF NEW YORK-NEW JERSEY (US) [19073663] **5449**

GUIDE TO THE TORONTO REGION'S TOP EMPLOYERS (CN/1183-7373) [25066338] **1608**

GUIDE TO THE UNITED STATES TREATIES IN FORCE, A (US/0736-5713) [09157644] **3128**

GUIDE TO THE USE OF FERTILIZERS FOR VANCOUVER ISLAND, ZONE 1 (CN) [03780308] **91**

GUIDE TO THE USE OF THE GRADUATE RECORD EXAMINATIONS (US/0196-5263) [03417662] **1827**

GUIDE TO TRAINING OPPORTUNITIES FOR INDUSTRIAL DEVELOPMENT (AU) [05087141] **2910**

GUIDE TO TRAVEL AND RESIDENCE EXPENSES FOR THE MULTINATIONAL EXECUTIVE (US/0193-9130) [05144263] **5479**

GUIDE TO U.S. CITIES (CN/0705-3711) [03956540] **5479**

GUIDE TO U.S. FOOD LABELING LAW (US) **2343**

●GUIDE TO U.S. FOUNDATIONS, THEIR TRUSTEES, OFFICERS, AND DONORS (US/1071-202X) [27942862] **4338**

GUIDE TO U.S. TAXES FOR CITIZENS ABROAD (US/0278-3576) [04256847] **4730**

GUIDE TO VINTAGE WINE PRICES (US/0191-7838) [04965369] **2367**

GUIDE TO WHO'S WHO IN CANADIAN PLACEMENT *See* CONTACTS AND COURSES, WHO'S WHO IN CANADIAN PLACEMENT **1818**

●GUIDE TO WORLD EQUITY MARKETS, THE (UK) [26155125] **900**

GUIDE TO WORLDWIDE BUNKERING SERVICES (UK) [24536440] **5449**

GUIDE TO WRITERS CONFERENCES, THE (US/0897-4195) [17494704] **3392**

GUIDE TO YOUTH HOSTELS AROUND THE WORLD, A (UK) [13188967] **5287**

GUIDE (TORONTO) (CN/0533-5051) [02017060] **1676**

GUIDE TOURISTIQUE, CHAUDIERE-APPALACHES (CN/0849-1992) [23237438] **5479**

GUIDE TOURISTIQUE EUROPEEN POUR ISRAELITES (BE) [01791901] **5479**

GUIDE TOURISTIQUE, LANAUDIERE (CN/1180-0305) [23242610] **5479**

●GUIDE UNIVERSITAIRE DE LA MEDECINE (CN/1188-1380) [25883039] **3579**

GUIDE (WASHINGTON) (US/0017-5226) [04080976] 1064, **5060**

GUIDEBOOK (AMERICAN ASSOCIATION OF PETROLEUM GEOLOGISTS (US) [03818776] **1381**

GUIDEBOOK FOR THE ... ANNUAL FIELD CONFERENCE OF PENNSYLVANIA GEOLOGISTS (US/0375-5630) [03786481] **1381**

GUIDEBOOK - ILLINOIS STATE GEOLOGICAL SURVEY DIVISION (US) [15350355] **1382**

GUIDEBOOK - NEW MEXICO GEOLOGICAL SOCIETY (US/0077-8567) [02196216] **1382**

GUIDEBOOK OF U.S. & CANADIAN POSTDOCTORAL DENTAL PROGRAMS (US/0361-9273) [02382792] **1324**

GUIDEBOOK SERIES-MINNESOTA GEOLOGICAL SURVEY (US/0192-6268) [05069974] **1382**

GUIDEBOOK - STATE OF OHIO, DEPARTMENT OF NATURAL RESOURCES, DIVISION OF GEOLOGICAL SURVEY (US/0097-9473) [01799414] **1382**

GUIDEBOOK TO FAIR EMPLOYMENT PRACTICES (US/0196-7975) [02899451] **3148**

GUIDEBOOK TO FLORIDA TAXES (US/0093-8637) [01792765] **4730**

GUIDEBOOK TO LABOR RELATIONS (US/0072-8853) [01452697] **3148**

GUIDEBOOK TO NEW JERSEY TAXES (US/0072-8888) [05867383] **4730**

GUIDEBOOK TO NEW YORK TAXES (US/0072-8896) [02476799] **4730**

GUIDEBOOK TO OHIO TAXES (US/0091-4010) [01787192] **4730**

GUIDEBOOK TO PENNSYLVANIA TAXES (US/0072-890X) [05867356] **4730**

GUIDEBOOK TO WISCONSIN TAXES (US/0093-8645) [01792912] **4730**

GUIDEBOOK (UNIVERSITY OF TEXAS AT AUSTIN. BUREAU OF ECONOMIC GEOLOGY) (US/0363-4132) [01586365] **1382**

GUIDEBOOK - WEST TEXAS GEOLOGICAL SOCIETY (US/0510-1387) [01769644] **1382**

GUIDEBOOK - WYOMING GEOLOGICAL ASSOCIATION (US/0160-2829) [01736926] **1382**

GUIDELINE FOR THE PREPARATION OF A HAZARD COMMUNICATION RIGHT-TO-KNOW PROGRAM / PREPARED BY HAZARDOUS COMMUNICATION AND RIGHT-TO-KNOW TASK FORCE, AMERICAN BOILER MANUFACTURERS ASSOCIATION (US/1061-043X) [25105590] **2230**

GUIDELINES (AT/0156-6717) [01566717] 3212, **3258**

GUIDELINES (SI/0129-7767) [07797569] **3284**

GUIDELINES FOR INDUSTRIES (NEW DELHI) (II/0302-7538) [01640758] **1608**

GUIDELINES FOR PASTORAL LITURGY (CN/0317-7203) [05586096] **5030**

GUIDELINES FOR PREPARATION OF GRANT APPLICATIONS. RESEARCH AND DEVELOPMENT PROJECTS IN AGING, TITLE IV-B OF THE OLDER AMERICANS ACT (US) [05036647] **3752**

●GUIDELINES FOR THE ROLLING PLAN (NR) [26295126] **4730**

GUIDELINES FOR TODAY (US/0891-1452) [14628581] **4961**

GUIDELINES IN MEDICINE (US/0270-0646) [05778876] **3579**

GUIDELINES LETTER (US) [04083472] 1976, **299**

GUIDELINES (SASKATOON) (CN/0048-9190) [02017089] **1749**

GUIDELINES TO METABOLIC THERAPY (US/0364-2577) [02577402] **488**

GUIDEPOST (WASHINGTON, D.C.) (US/0017-5323) [01776439] **4588**

GUIDEPOSTS (CARMEL) (US/0017-5331) [01681063] **4961**

GUIDES AND HANDBOOKS (UK/0080-4398) [01764589] **2617**

GUIDES FOR FAMILY BUDGETING (CN/0823-6860) [10057363] **2790**

GUIDES OF UNDERWRITERS' LABORATORIES OF CANADA (CN/0710-4588) [08465755] **2881**

GUIDES TO CONTEMPORARY ISSUES (US) [08513372] **2488**

GUIDES TO EUROPEAN TAXATION *CEASED.* (NE/0072-8926) [01645961] **4730**

GUIDES TO EVALUATION OF PERMANENT IMPAIRMENT (US) **3579**

GUIDES TO FOREST AND CONSERVATION HISTORY OF NORTH AMERICA (US/0196-5395) [03747288] **2194**

●GUIDES TO MAJOR SOCIAL SCIENCE DATA BASES (US/1058-4862) [24332630] **5201**

GUIDES TO MULTINATIONAL BUSINESS, INC *See* AMERICAN EXECUTIVE TRAVEL COMPANION **5461**

GUIDES TO OFFICIAL PUBLICATIONS (UK) [05672391] **4653**

GUIDES TO THE HARVARD LIBRARIES (US) [01639614] **3212**

GUIDING IN AUSTRALIA (AT/0159-0340) [01590340] **1064**

GUIDING LIGHT, THE (CN/0318-7365) [02017228] **2534**

GUILD GAZETTE (CN/0823-7875) [10785418] **4119**

GUILD (NEW YORK, N.Y.) (US/0885-3975) [12629218] **373**

GUILD NEWS (TORONTO. 1979) (CN/0834-1656) [16220576] **4120**

GUILD NOTES (US/0148-0588) [01779715] 2976, **4508**

GUILD OF BOOK WORKERS *See* GUILD OF BOOK WORKERS JOURNAL **4828**

GUILD OF BOOK WORKERS *See* MEMBERSHIP DIRECTORY / GUILD OF BOOK WORKERS **4830**

GUILD OF BOOK WORKERS JOURNAL (US/0434-9245) [01642298] **4828**

GUILD OF CARILLONNEURS IN NORTH AMERICA *See* BULLETIN OF THE GUILD OF CARILLONNEURS IN NORTH AMERICA **4106**

GUILD OF NATURAL SCIENCE ILLUSTRATORS (U.S.) *See* GNSI NEWSLETTER **5108**

GUILD PRACTITIONER *See* NATIONAL LAWYER'S GUILD PRACTITIONER **3013**

GUILD REPORTER, THE (US/0017-5404) [01454482] 2920, **1676**

GUILDS' ENGINEER *See* SPANNER **365**

GUILFORD GENEALOGIST, THE (US/0731-3179) [08058583] **2452**

GUILFOYLE REPORT, THE (US/0889-8235) [14092499] **925**

GUILLEMOT, LE (CN/0714-8283) [09084902] **5585**

GUILT & GARDENIAS / THE ARTS COUNCIL (US/1055-8985) [23366475] **3392**

GUINEA, WIRTSCHAFTSDATEN (KURZFASSUNG), WIRTSCHAFTSDOKUMENTATION UND PROJEKTE / BUNDESSTELLE FUER AUSSENHANDELSINFORMATION (GW) [12070781] **1565**

GUINEA WIRTSCHAFTSDATEN UND WIRTSCHAFTSDOKUMENTATION / BUNDESSTELLE FUR AUSSENHANDELSINFORMATION (GW) [07344821] **1565**

GUINNESS BOOK OF RECORDS (NEW YORK, N.Y.) (US/1057-4557) [22474859] **1926**

GUINNESS BOOK OF SPORTS RECORDS, THE (US/1054-4178) [22879799] **4897**

GUINNESS DISC OF RECORDS [COMPUTER FILE], THE *CEASED.* (US) [24239524] **1926**

GUION (CK) [04289084] **2488**

GUION LITERARIO (ES/0017-5447) [01454678] **3392**

GUIPREX, GUIA DE PRODUCTORES Y EXPORTADORES LATINOAMERICANOS (AG) [02294736] **838**

GUISUANYAN TONGBAO (CC/1001-1625) [12955663] **1036**

GUITAR & LUTE (US/0199-9117) [05747606] **4120**

GUITAR & MANDOLIN *SUSPENDED.* (US/0270-9325) [06510434] **4120**

GUITAR CANADA *CEASED.* (CN/0830-8721) [15226782] **4120**

●GUITAR CLASSICS, THE (US/1061-4400) [25307543] **4120**

GUITAR FOR THE PRACTICING MUSICIAN (US) [12894674] **4120**

GUITAR INTERNATIONAL (UK) [12489847] **4120**

GUITAR MAGAZINE (UK/0962-2640) [09622640] **4120**

GUITAR NEWS (UK/0434-9342) [01454765] **4120**

GUITAR PLAYER LEGENDS OF GUITAR (US/0884-7517) [12415198] **4120**

GUITAR REVIEW, THE (US/0017-5471) [01751643] **4120**

GUITAR SCHOOL (US/1058-0220) [24182867] **4120**

GUITAR WORLD (US/1045-6295) [07982091] **4120**

GUITARE ET CLAVIERS (FR) **4120**

GUITARRA MAGAZINE *CEASED.* (US/0434-9350) [07617392] **4120**

GUITARS & MUSICAL INSTRUMENTS (US/1046-3879) [19539586] **4120**

GUJARAT *See* AGRICULTURAL CENSUS **150**

GUJARAT AGRICULTURAL UNIVERSITY *See* GUJARAT AGRICULTURAL UNIVERSITY RESEARCH JOURNAL **91**

GUJARAT AGRICULTURAL UNIVERSITY RESEARCH JOURNAL (II/0250-5193) [03064026] **91**

GUJARAT (INDIA) *See* ANNUAL FINANCIAL STATEMENT (BUDGET) OF THE GOVERNMENT OF GUJARAT FOR THE YEAR ... **4709**

GUJARAT (INDIA). AGRICULTURE, FORESTS, AND CO-OPERATION DEPARTMENT *See* PERFORMANCE BUDGET OF AGRICULTURE, FORESTS, AND CO-OPERATION DEPARTMENT. CO-OPERATION **1543**

GUJARAT (INDIA). AGRICULTURE, FORESTS, AND CO-OPERATION DEPARTMENT *See* PERFORMANCE BUDGET OF AGRICULTURE, FORESTS, AND CO-OPERATION DEPARTMENT. FOREST **119**

GUJARAT (INDIA). AGRICULTURE, FORESTS, AND COOPERATION DEPT *See* PERFORMANCE BUDGET OF AGRICULTURE, FORESTS, AND CO-OPERATION DEPARTMENT. AGRICULTURE **119**

GUJARAT (INDIA). HEALTH AND FAMILY WELFARE DEPT *See* PERFORMANCE BUDGET OF HEALTH AND FAMILY WELFARE DEPARTMENT **4795**

GUJARAT (INDIA). HOME DEPT *See* GRHA VIBHAGANUM ANDAJAPATRA. BUDGET ESTIMATES OF HOME DEPARTMENT **4729**

GUJARAT (INDIA). PORTS AND FISHERIES DEPT *See* PERFORMANCE BUDGET OF PORTS AND FISHERIES DEPARTMENT (FISHERIES) **4740**

GUJARAT, INDIA (STATE) *See* ANNUAL ADMINISTRATION REPORT ON SCHEDULED AREAS IN GUJARAT STATE **2814**

GUJARAT, INDIA (STATE). BUREAU OF ECONOMICS AND STATISTICS *See* SOCIO-ECONOMIC REVIEW: GUJARAT STATE **1584**

GUJARAT, INDIA (STATE) REVENUE DEPT *See* PERFORMANCE BUDGET OF REVENUE DEPARTMENT - GUJARAT, INDIA (STATE) **4740**

GUJARAT RESEARCH SOCIETY *See* GUJARATA SAMSODHANA MANDALANUM TRAIMASIKA **2504**

GUJARAT SMALL INDUSTRIES CORPORATION *See* ANNUAL REPORT AND ACCOUNTS - GUJARAT SMALL INDUSTRIES CORPORATION **1597**

GUJARAT STATISTICAL REVIEW (II/0379-3419) [03246100] 3507, **3542**

GUJARAT UNIVERSITY, AHMEDABAD *See* THESES PUBLICATION SERIES **1850**

GUJARATA SAMSODHANA MANDALANUM TRAIMASIKA (II) [01454892] **2504**

GUJIZHUI DONGWU XUEBAO (CC/1000-3118) [12841753] **4227**

GUL-I KHANDAN (PK) [02239398] **4962**

GULA INDONESIA (IO) [22541484] 2343, **173**

GULDEN PASSER, DE (BE) [01640478] **4570**

GULF AND CARIBBEAN FISHERIES INSTITUTE *See* PROCEEDINGS OF THE ANNUAL GULF AND CARIBBEAN FISHERIES INSTITUTE AND THE ANNUAL INTERNATIONAL GAME FISH RESEARCH CONFERENCE **2310**

GULF COAST (US/0896-2251) [16970549] **3392**

GULF COAST ASSOCIATION OF GEOLOGICAL SOCIETIES *See* TRANSACTIONS / GULF COAST ASSOCIATION OF GEOLOGICAL SOCIETIES **1400**

GULF COAST ASSOCIATION OF GEOLOGICAL SOCIETIES *See* SPECIAL PUBLICATIONS : GULF COAST ASSOCIATION OF GEOLOGICAL SOCIETIES **1398**

GULF COAST CATTLEMAN (US/0017-5552) [06230020] **211**

GULF COAST HISTORICAL REVIEW (US/0892-9025) [12619134] **2735**

GULF COAST LUMBERMAN AND BUILDING MATERIAL DISTRIBUTOR (HOUSTON, TEX. : 1982) (US/0745-6603) [09342425] **2401**

GULF COAST OIL AND GAS WORLD (US/1070-4914) [28385006] **4259**

GULF COAST OIL DIRECTORY (US/0739-3547) [08572048] **4259**

GULF COAST OIL WORLD (US/0884-7967) [12438811] **4259**

GULF COAST RECORD, THE (US) [14366519] **5750**

GULF COAST TRIBUNE (US) [16902427] **5750**

GULF COMMS GUIDE (UK) **5108**

GULF COUNTY BREEZE (US) [01456402] **5649**

GULF DAILY NEWS (BA) **5778**

GULF DEALER (CN/0704-5980) [03790886] **4259**

GULF ISLANDS GUARDIAN, THE (CN/1191-1670) [25883019] **5479**

GULF NEWS (CN/0833-1065) [l08331065] **5785**

GULF OF MEXICO DRILLING REPORT (US/1058-5850) [24335637] **1608**

GULF OF MEXICO NEWSLETTER (US/1058-5885) [24338696] **1608**

GULF OF MEXICO REPORT. NEWSLETTER EDITION (US/0885-355X) [12621017] **4259**

GULF OF MEXICO UPDATE : OUTER CONTINENTAL SHELF OIL & GAS ACTIVITIES (US) [20974647] **2090**

GULF RESEARCH REPORTS (US/0072-9027) [01278029] **554**

GULF STATES MARINE FISHERIES COMMISSION *See* TECHNICAL SUMMARY - GULF STATES MARINE FISHERIES COMMISSION **2314**

GULF STATES MARINE FISHERIES COMMISSION *See* RESEARCH PROSPECTUS - GULF STATES MARINE FISHERIES COMMISSION **2311**

GULF STATES MARINE FISHERIES COMMISSION *See* INFORMATIONAL SERIES - GULF STATES MARINE FISHERIES COMMISSION **2305**

GULF STATES NEWSLETTER (UK/0953-5411) [l09535411] 4475, **1493**

GULF STATES OIL AND GAS DIRECTORY (US/0191-9849) [04935417] **4259**

GULF STATES / PERMIAN BASIN PETROLEUM DIRECTORY (US) **4259**

GULF STATES PETROLEUM DIRECTORY *See* GULF STATES / PERMIAN BASIN PETROLEUM DIRECTORY **4259**

●GULF WAR CLAIMS REPORTER (US/1061-7345) [25425981] **3128**

GULFSHORE LIFE (US/0745-0079) [04949981] **2534**

GULLET (UK/0952-0643) [23269379] **3579**

GULLIVER (BARI, ITALY) (IT) [10436901] **1112**

GULLIVERIANA (US) [01458280] **3392**

GULLIVORE PARIS (FR/0987-237X) [l0987237X] **1749**

GUMMA KENRITSU HAKUBUTSUKAN *See* GUMMA KENRITSU HAKUBUTSUKAN HO **4088**

GUMMA KENRITSU HAKUBUTSUKAN HO (JA) [03040071] **4088**

GUMMA KENRITSU REKISHI HAKUBUTSUKAN NEMPO (JA) [08482883] **2651**

GUMMI BEREIFUNG (GW) [06678223] **5075**

GUMMI, FASERN, KUNSTSTOFFE (GW/0176-1625) [10988667] 4455, **5076**

GUMSOG PYOMYEN CERI (KO/0253-3081) [08191542] **4003**

GUN (US) **4897**

GUN DOG (US/0279-5086) [07929835] **4873**

GUN LIST (US/0894-8119) [16261172] **4873**

GUN REPORT (US/0017-5617) [04081005] **250**

GUN SHOW CALENDAR (US/0896-6001) [17211197] 4873, **4850**

GUN TALK (CN/0017-5625) [02017720] **2774**

GUN TESTS (US/1042-6450) [19098776] **4045**

GUN TRADER'S GUIDE, THE (US/0883-4431) [11995468] **2774**

GUN WORLD (US/0017-5641) [02251406] **4897**

GUN WORLD ANNUAL (US/0362-2495) [02441494] **4897**

GUN WORLD HUNTING GUIDE (US/0362-4749) [02309517] 4873, **4897**

GUNAKESARI (NP) [01790427] **3392**

GUNDERSEN MEDICAL JOURNAL, THE (US) [25225978] **3579**

GUNMA DAIGAKU. KYOIKU GAKUBU *See* GUNMA DAIGAKU KYOIKU GAKUBU KIYO : SHIZEN KAGAKU HEN **5108**

GUNMA DAIGAKU KYOIKU GAKUBU KIYO. JINBUN SHAKAI KAGAKU HEN (JA/0386-4294) [08899608] **1864**

GUNMA DAIGAKU KYOIKU GAKUBU KIYO : SHIZEN KAGAKU HEN (JA/0017-5668) [06829546] **5108**

GUNMA DAIGAKU KYOYOBU KIYO (JA/0367-4061) [09913554] **2847**

GUNMA KENRITSU REKISHI HAKUBUTSUKAN *See* GUMMA KENRITSU REKISHI HAKUBUTSUKAN NEMPO **2651**

GUNMA KOSEN REBYU (JA) [10574032] **1827**

GUNMA NOGYO KENKYU. A, SOGO (JA/0289-4610) [l02894610] **91**

GUNMA SYMPOSIA ON ENDOCRINOLOGY (JA/0533-6724) [01779026] **3730**

GUNN SALUTE, THE (US/0738-4866) [09176020] **2452**

GUNNER (UK) **4045**

GUNNISON COUNTRY TIMES, THE (US/0892-1113) [11217462] **5643**

GUNNISON VALLEY NEWS, THE (US) [12893411] **5756**

GUNRUNNER (CN) **4897**

GUNS & AMMO (US/0017-5684) [02652620] **4897**

GUNS & AMMO ACTION SERIES (US/0883-9468) [12212593] **4897**

GUNS & AMMO ... HANDGUN ANNUAL (US/1059-1672) [12675976] **2811**

GUNS & WEAPONS FOR LAW ENFORCEMENT (US/1058-2975) [24258751] **3165**

GUNS AUSTRALIA (AT/0157-1729) [I01571729] **4897**

GUNS CONTROL (US) [15621580] **3165**

GUNS MAGAZINE (US/1044-6257) [19719227] **4873, 4897**

GUNS REVIEW (UK) [01789252] **4897**

GUNZO (JA) [02478509] **3392**

GUOFANG KE-JI DAXUE XUEBAO (CC/1001-2486) [I10012486] **4045**

GUOJI DIZHEN DONGTAI (CC/0253-4975) [08047628] **1406**

GUOJI RIBAO (US/0741-126X) [10102287] **5635**

GUOLI TAIWAN DAXUE YIXUEYUAN YANJIU BAOGAO (CH/0028-0275) [I00280275] **3579**

GUOLI ZHONGGUO YIYAO YANJIUSUO YANJIU BAOGAO (CH/0253-3197) [08694171] **3579**

GUOWAI ZAOZHI (CC/1001-3911) [I10013911] **4234**

GURAFU DE MIRU RODO JIJO / RODOSHO HEN (JA) [10842329] **1676**

GURAFU KANAGAWA (JA) [02864323] **2651**

GURAFU TOKYO (JA) [02245142] **2651**

GURNEE PRESS (US/0745-810X) [09477101] **5660**

GURU (MY) [06782714] **1749**

GURU NANAK JOURNAL OF SOCIOLOGY (II/0970-0242) [08021529] **5246**

GUSHENG WUXUE BAO (CC/0001-6616) [02444332] **4227**

GUSTAVIAN WEEKLY (US) [01751654] **5696**

GUSTO (BRONX) (US/0190-2253) [04675918] **3463**

GUT (UK/0017-5749) [01641120] **3746**

GUT (TORONTO) (CN/0710-5843) [08716785] **2534**

GUTENBERG-JAHRBUCH (GW/0072-9094) [01715243] **379, 4565**

GUTHRIE CENTER TIMES (GUTHRIE CENTER, IOWA : 1952) (US) [12745771] **5670**

GUTHRIE DAILY LEADER, THE (US) [13748544] **5732**

GUTHRIE JOURNAL OF THE DONALD GUTHRIE FOUNDATION FOR MEDICAL RESEARCH, THE (US/0882-696X) [11924771] **3579**

GUTHRIE NEW THEATER (US/0145-3750) [02728320] **5364**

GUTI RUNHUA (CC/1000-4084) [21663711] **2115**

GUTMANN PUMA/EXPLORER KNIFE ANNUAL (US/0731-1885) [08119511] **4897, 4873**

GUYANA. AUDITOR GENERAL *See* REPORT OF THE AUDITOR GENERAL ON THE PUBLIC ACCOUNTS OF THE GOVERNMENT OF GUYANA FOR THE FINANCIAL YEAR ENDED 31ST DECEMBER ... / GUYANA **4745**

GUYANA CONSOLIDATED INDEX TO STATUTES AND SUBSIDIARY LEGISLATION TO 1ST JAN. ... (US) [15160821] **3081**

GUYANA. GEOLOGICAL SURVEY *See* BULLETIN - GEOLOGICAL SURVEY OF GUYANA **1369**

GUYANA JOURNAL (GY/0046-6654) [01462228] **4475**

GUYANA JOURNAL OF SOCIOLOGY : OFFICIAL JOURNAL OF THE GUYANA SOCIOLOGICAL SOCIETY (GY) [10439395] **5246**

GUYANA LAW JOURNAL (GY) [05095040] **2976**

GUYANA LIBRARY ASSOCIATION BULLETIN (GY) [04862834] **3212**

GUYANA NATIONAL CO-OPERATIVE BANK *See* ANNUAL REPORT & ACCOUNTS - GUYANA NATIONAL CO-OPERATIVE BANK **770**

GUYANA SUGAR CORPORATION *See* REPORT AND ACCOUNTS - GUYANA SUGAR CORPORATION **2355**

GUYANA : WIRTSCHAFTLICHE ENTWICKLUNG (GW) [04196650] **1565**

GUYANA YEAR BOOK (SA/0533-6961) [01462379] **2499**

GUY'S GAZETTE (UK) [22294608] **3579**

GUY'S HOSPITAL GAZETTE (UK/0017-5870) [01751660] **3780**

GV-PRAXIS (GW/0342-376X) [I0342376X] **2343**

GV SWISS (GW/0935-1574) [I09351574] **2343**

GVRD NEWS (CN/0833-4641) [16073615] **4653**

GW TIMES (US/0279-2435) [04551564] **1827**

GW WASHINGTON STUDIES (US/0276-4091) [05063386] **1827**

GWIAZDA POLARNA (US/0740-5944) [09357644] **5767**

GWINNETT HOME WEEKLY *See* GWINNETT POST-TRIBUNE **5653**

●GWINNETT POST-TRIBUNE (US/1076-4852) [29527438] **5653**

GYERHAIG MIC HOHUBGI JIROHAN (KO/0378-0066) [01410632] **3949**

GYERMEKGYOGYASZAT (HU/0017-5900) [06380161] **3903**

GYMNASIUM (HEIDELBERG) (GW/0342-5231) [04384444] **1077**

GYMNASTE (FR) **4897**

GYMNASTIKK OG TURN (NO) [01463031] **4897**

●GYNAECOLOGICAL ENDOSCOPY (UK/0962-1091) [26146976] **3761**

GYNAIKA (GR) [05915166] **5558**

GYNAKOLOGE (BERLIN) (GW/0017-5994) [06978404] **3761**

GYNAKOLOGISCH-GEBURTSHILFLICHE RUNDSCHAU (SZ/1018-8843) [26207371] **3761**

GYNAKOLOGISCHE PRAXIS (GW/0341-0481) [03996064] **3761**

GYNAKOLOGISCHE RUNDSCHAU *See* GYNAKOLOGISCH-GEBURTSHILFLICHE RUNDSCHAU **3761**

GYNECOLOGIC AND OBSTETRIC INVESTIGATION (SZ/0378-7346) [04521112] **3761**

GYNECOLOGIC ONCOLOGY (US/0090-8258) [01785628] **3761, 3817**

GYNECOLOGICAL ENDOCRINOLOGY (UK/0951-3590) [18175592] **3761, 3730**

GYNECOLOGIE (FR/0301-2204) [05215117] **3761**

GYNECOLOGIE, OBSTETRIQUE, ANDROLOGIE. E82 (FR) **3761**

GYNECOLOGIE OBSTETRIQUE PRATIQUE (FR/0988-6990) [I09886990] **3761**

●GYNECOLOGIE : REVUE DU GYNECOLOGUE (FR) [30039768] **3761**

GYNLIT (GW) **3762**

GYOBYO KENKYU (JA/0388-788X) [06928160] **2304**

GYOGYO HAKUSHO (JA) [02245365] **2304**

GYOGYO YOSHOKUGYO SEISAN TOKEI NEMPO (JA) [01790167] **2304**

GYOGYSZERESZET (HU/0017-6036) [10970237] **4306**

GYOJI SAMBYAKU-ROKUJUGONICHI (JA) [01797070] **5268**

GYOKAI JITTAI CHOSA HOKOKUSHO (JA) [03252285] **678**

GYOMU BENRAN (JA) [05142160] **789**

GYOMU GAIYO (JA) [01797123] **1145**

GYOMU HOKOKU (JA/0389-0724) [09181569] **211**

GYOMU HOKOKU - NORINSHO SATOKIBIGEN GENSHU NOJO (JA) [02245307] **173**

GYOMU HOKOKUSHO (JA) [02849533] **678**

GYOMU HOKOKUSHO - NIHON KAIHATSU GINKO (JA) [02959068] **790**

GYOMU HOKOKUSHO - NIHON YUSHUTSUNYU GINKO (JA) [03512172] **790**

GYOMU NEMPO - HACHIROGATA SHINNOSON KENSETSU JIGYODAN (JA) [03024604] **91**

GYOMU NEMPO - OSAKA FURITSU KOGYO GIJUTSU KENKYUJO (JA) [05272954] **5108**

GYOMU NENPO (JA) [08794571] **2304**

GYOMU TOKEI NEMPO - NORIN GYOGYO KINYU KOKO (JA) [02881233] **790**

GYORUIGAKU ZASSHI (JA/0021-5090) [01751667] **2304**

GYOSEI KANKEI HANREI KAISETSU / GOSEI HANREI KENKYUKAI HEN (JA) [11745021] **3093**

GYOSEI KANRI KENKYU (JA) [02579959] **4653**

GYOSEI KANRICHO NO ARAMASHI (JA) [06030304] **4653**

GYOTEI HOKOKU - NIHON SEMBAI KOSHA UTSUNOMIYA TABAKO SHIKENJO (JA) [01797368] **5373**

GYPSUM PRODUCTS (CN/0380-7223) [02585676] **616, 632**

GYPSY (UK) [13819055] **2321, 237**

●GYPSY BLOOD REVIEW (US/1071-5126) [28012588] **3392**

GYPSY LORE SOCIETY. NORTH AMERICAN CHAPTER *See* MEMBERSHIP DIRECTORY - GYPSY LORE SOCIETY, NORTH AMERICAN CHAPTER **2322**

GYPSY LOU SERIES (US/0533-7127) [01463114] **2488**

GYUMOLCSTERMESZTES (HU) [02173869] **2418**

GZ : GOLDSCHMIEDE UND UHRMACHER ZEITUNG (GW) [16700388] **2914**

●H.A.C. JOURNAL (AT) [28121204] **1092**

H.A.N.D.S. ON GUIDE (US/0897-5345) [17533973] **2774, 373**

H & E COMPUTRONICS INC (US/0734-3159) [08713957] **1185**

H & R BLOCK ... INCOME TAX GUIDE (US/1054-9846) [20668835] **4730**

H & V ENGINEER (UK/0268-4225) [11638287] **2605**

H. G. WELLS NEWSLETTER, THE (UK/0306-5480) [09491237] **3392**

H + G ZEITSCHRIFT FUER HAUTKRANKHEITEN (GW/0301-0481) [01777670] **3720**

H.K.I.M.S. HONG KONG INDEX OF MEDICAL SPECIALTIES (SI/0300-4090) [10101777] **3579**

H.M. QUEEN ELIZABETH THE QUEEN MOTHER FELLOWSHIP (UK/0952-2433) [11136820] **3580**

H.P.O. NOTES *See* TRANSIT POSTMARK COLLECTOR **1147**

H.W. WILSON COMPANY *See* SENIOR HIGH SCHOOL LIBRARY CATALOG **3249**

H. W. WILSON COMPANY *See* JUNIOR HIGH SCHOOL LIBRARY CATALOG **418**

H. ZINDER & ASSOCIATES *See* SUMMARY OF RATE SCHEDULES OF NATURAL GAS PIPELINE COMPANIES AS FILED WITH THE FEDERAL ENERGY REGULATORY COMMISSION AND THE NATIONAL ENERGY BOARD OF CANADA **4284**

H2O (NE/0166-8439) [I01668439] **5534**

H2O TIJDSCHRIFT VOOR DRINKWATERVOORZIENING EN AFVALWATERBEHANDELING (NE) **5534**

HA-MAYAN (IS/0465-420X) [05256286] **2976**

HA-SHILTH-SA (CN/0715-4143) [10446112] **5785**

HA UY DI THI BAO (US) [23247092] **5655**

HAAGSE MONITOR (NE/0925-4218) **678**

HAANDBOG FOR DRIFTSPLANLGNING (DK) [02239454] **91**

HA'ARETZ (IS) [06619543] **5804**

HABARI - AFRICAN BIBLIOGRAPHIC CENTER (US/0360-9480) [02243983] **2639**

HABELTS DISSERTATIONSDRUCKE. REIHE KLASSISCHE ARCHAOLOGIE (GW) [06673166] **269**

HAB'GUK SONBAK YON'GUSO *See* LECTURE SERIES - HAN'GUK SONBAK YON'GUSO **875**

HABILITATIVE MENTAL HEALTHCARE NEWSLETTER, THE (US/1057-3291) [21277851] **3926**

HABILITES LOISIRS (CN/0821-7815) [09981842] **4388**

HABIS (SP) [02063121] **269, 1077**

HABITABEC (CN/0700-5040) [03403205] **2823**

HABITABEC QUEBEC (CN/0844-2487) [20244324] **616**

HABITAT (FALMOUTH, ME.) (US/0739-2052) [09848860] **4166, 2194**

HABITAT INTERNATIONAL (UK/0197-3975) [03762402] **2823**

HABITAT (LONDON) (UK/0028-9043) [05657079] **2194**

HABITAT (MELBOURNE) (AT/0310-2939) [01787795] **2194**

HABITAT NEWS (KE/0251-7205) [05381053] **2823**

HABITAT PAKISTAN : A JOURNAL OF ARCHITECTURE, PLANNING, ENVIRONMENT, AND THE ARTS IN ASIA (PK) [16516673] **351, 299**

●HABITAT : SUPPLEMENT ... AUX CAHIERS DE L'IAURIF (FR) [26407873] **2823**

HABITAT UFFICIO (IT/1120-236X) [I1120236X] **2900**

HABITATION *SUSPENDED.* (SZ) [02261708] **2823**

HABITATION SPACE (IT) [04601018] **299**

HABLAN LOS COMUNISTAS (DR) [13646403] **4542**

HABLEMOS DE CINE *SUSPENDED.* (PE/0046-6700) [05239149] **4071**

HABS. HOUSING ABSTRACTS (UK/0952-8156) [I09528156] **2823**

HAC. THE HEATING AND AIR CONDITIONING JOURNAL (UK/0307-7950) [02728255] **2605**

HACETTEPE BULLETIN OF NATURAL SCIENCES AND ENGINEERING (TU/0379-5918) [11349521] 1976, **1356**

HACETTEPE MEDICAL JOURNAL (TU/0259-2282) [11136946] **3580**

HACETTEPE SOSYAL VE BESERI BILIMLER DERGISI (TU/0304-2790) [07884360] **1749**

HACETTEPE UNIVERSITY BULLETIN ADMINISTRATIVE SCIENCES (TU) **678**

HACETTEPE UNIVERSITY BULLETIN OF HUMANITITES (TU) **2847**

HACHETTE GUIDE TO GREAT BRITAIN, THE (US/0895-3767) [16577324] **5479**

HACHIJUKAI TEN (JA) [03094886] **351**

HACHIROGATA SHINNOSON KENSETSU JIGYODAN See GYOMU NEMPO - HACHIROGATA SHINNOSON KENSETSU JIGYODAN **91**

HACHU RYOSEIRUIGAKU ZASSHI (JA/0285-3191) [03299946] **5585**

HACIENDA, LA (US/0017-6486) [01751678] **91**

HACIENDA PUBLICA ESPANOLA (SP) [05266796] **4730**

HACK'D (WOODBRIDGE, VA.) (US/1055-033X) [23063198] **4081**

HACTION (CN/0714-7066) [09562826] **5287**

HADASHOT ARKHEOLOGIYOT / AGAF HA-ATIKOT, MISRAD HA-HINUKH VEHA-TARBUT (IS/0047-1569) [02428194] **269**

HADASSAH MAGAZINE (US/0017-6516) [01696040] **5048**

HADITH (KE) [02261710] **2639**

HADRONIC JOURNAL (US/0162-5519) [04150480] **4447**

HADRONIC JOURNAL SUPPLEMENT (US/0882-5394) [11881973] **4404**

HADRONIC PRESS MONOGRAPHS IN THEORETICAL PHYSICS (US) [18595942] **4404**

HADSHOT HA-NEFT VEHA-ENERGYAH (IS) [02562443] **4259**

HADTORTENELMI KOZLEMENYEK (HU/0017-6540) [02430456] **2690**

HAEGI (KO) [11334647] **4176**

HAELSA OCH SJUKVAARDSKONSUMTION (SW) [04059109] **4777**

HAEMATOLOGIA (HU/0017-6559) [01751680] **3797**

HAEMATOLOGIA (BUDAPEST. 1976. SOROZAT) (HU/0133-4883) [03152591] **3772**

HAEMATOLOGICA (ROMA) (IT/0390-6078) [01118753] **3772**

HAEMATOLOGY AND BLOOD TRANSFUSION (GW/0171-7111) [03507622] **3772**

● HAEMOPHILIA (UK/1351-8216) **3580**

HAEMOSTASEOLOGIE (GW/0720-9355) [07936527] **3580**

HAEMOSTASIS (SZ/0301-0147) [01778124] **3580**

HAEOE CHONGSE (KO) [09100239] **4475**

HAEOE HANIN UIRYO CHONGNAM (US) [18649378] **3580**

HAEOE HANMIN (US) [07522059] **2651**

HAEOE KYONGGONGOP CHONGBO41 See CHUNGSO KIOP. HAEOE KYONGGONGOP **657**

HAEOE KYONGJE CHONGBO (KO) [01797431] **1565**

HAEOE MUNYE (KO) [06574920] **321**

HAEOE SASANGGYE (US) [06998099] **2651**

HAEOE SIJANG (KO) [08925000] **838**

HAEOE TONGPO (KO) [09084898] **2651**

HA'ERBIN KEXUE JISHU DAXUE XUEBAO (CC/1000-5897) [I10005897] **5108**

HAESA YONGAM (KO) [09753658] **5449**

HAEUN HANGMAN (KO) [04740090] **5450**

HAEUN YONBO (KO) [11837823] **5450**

HAEUSER (GW/0724-6528) [I07246528] **299**

HAEYANG YONGU (KO) [13390677] **1449**

HAFENBAUTECHNISCHE GESELLSCHAFT (GERMANY) See JAHRBUCH DER HAFENBAUTECHNISCHEN GESELLSCHAFT **2091**

HAFNIA CEASED. (DK/0085-1361) [06749824] **351**

HAFTEN FOR KRITISKA STUDIER (SW/0345-4789) [05187987] **4475**

HAGALO USTED MISMO - BRACE RESEARCH INSTITUTE (CN/0824-7773) [11579910] **4404**

HAGUE. LANDBOUW-ECONOMISCH INSTITUUT See TUINBOUWCIJFERS **2434**

HAGUE. LANDBOUW-ECONOMISCH INSTITUUT. AFDELING BEDRIJFSECONOMISCH ONDERZOEK LANDBOUW See MELKKOEIEN **196**

HAGUE. LANDBOUW-ECONOMISCH INSTITUUT. AFDELING LANDBOUW See BEDRIJFSUITKOMSTEN IN DE LANDBOUW **65**

HAGUE. LANDBOUW-ECONOMISCH INSTITUUT. AFDELING LANDBOUW See FINANCIELE POSITIE VAN DE LANDBOUW, DE **87**

HAGUE. LANDBOUW-ECONOMISCH INSTITUUT. AFDELING VISSERIJ EN BOSBOUW See BEDRIJFSRESULTATEN VAN DE KLEINE ZEEVISSERIJ **2297**

HAGUE YEARBOOK OF INTERNATIONAL LAW / ANNUAIRE DE LA HAYE DE DROIT INTERNATIONAL (NE) [18953858] **3128**

HAGUE-ZAGREB-GHENT : ESSAYS ON THE LAW OF INTERNATIONAL TRADE (NE) 838, **3128**

HAGWON (KO) [05929900] **2504**

HAHN-MEITNER-INSTITUT BERLIN See BERICHT / HAHN-MEITNER-INSTITUT BERLIN GMBH **962**

HAI CHIAO SHIH YEN CHIU (CH) [08855880] **5450**

HAI HSIA (CH) [10669063] **3392**

HAI KUAN TUNG CHI (CC) [11394157] **4730**

HAI WAI HSUEH JEN (CH) [01751695] **1749**

HAI WAI SHU LIN (CN/0714-9298) [09318440] **2735**

HAI YANG KO HSUEH (CC) [08738445] **1449**

HAI YANG WEN I (HK) [01797567] **3392**

HAI YANG YU HU CHAO (CC/0029-814X) [05958970] **1449**

HAIDE-ANZEIGER. SONDERAUSGABE, DER (GW) [21015924] **3463**

HAIGAN (JA/0386-9628) [I03869628] **3817**

HAIKIBUTSU GAKKAISHI (JA/0917-0855) [I09170855] **2230**

HAIKU BUNGAKUKAN KIYO (JA/0389-4274) [09310213] **3392**

HAIKU REVIEW (US) [08137980] **3463**

HAIR & BEAUTY NEWS (US/0897-3903) [17486608] **404**

HAIR CUT AND STYLE (US/1058-2983) [24258898] **404**

HAIR DESIGN (US) **404**

HAIR INTERNATIONAL NEWS (US/0887-803X) [13351596] **404**

HAIR (LONDON) (UK/0143-7968) [25022932] **404**

HAIR (NEW YORK, N.Y.) CEASED. (US/0888-6938) [13692636] **5268**

HAIRDO IDEAS (US/1058-0980) [24208125] **404**

HAIRDRESSERS JOURNAL INTERNATIONAL (UK/0143-6910) [I01436910] **404**

HAITI. ADMINISTRATION GENERALE DES CONTRIBUTIONS See BULLETIN ANNUEL - ADMINISTRATION GENERALE DES CONTRIBUTIONS (HAITI (REPUBLIC)) **4715**

HAITI-CULTURE (HT/0304-1220) [01796296] **2534**

HAITI INFORMATION LIBRE (FR/0296-807X) [I0296807X] **4475**

HAITI (REPUBLIC). BUREAU DE NUTRITION See RAPPORT DES ACTIVITES DU BUREAU DE NUTRITION **4198**

HAIYANG DIZHI YU DISIJI DIZHI (CC/0256-1492) [09591336] **1382**

HAIYANG KEXUE JIKAN (CC/0438-380X) [01548468] **554**

HAIYANG WENJI (CC/0253-245X) [08286488] **1449**

HAIYANG XUEBAO (ENGLISH ED.) (CC/0253-505X) [08656508] **1449**

HAIYANG XUEBAO (ZHONGGUOHUA) (CC/0253-4193) [06682326] **1449**

HAIYANG YUYE (CC/1004-2490) [I10042490] **2305**

HAJDU-BIHAR MEGYEI KONYVTARI TEKA (HU/0238-2512) [I02382512] **3213**

HAJDUBOESZOERMENY, HUNGARY. HAJDUSAGI MUZEUM See HAJDUSAGI MUZEUM EVKOENYVE, A **2690**

HAJDUSAGI MUZEUM EVKOENYVE, A (HU) [04546588] **2690**

HAJJ RESEARCH CENTRE STUDIES (UK) [08916806] **5042**

HAJOZASI SZAKIRODALMI TAJEKOZTATO (HU/0231-1941) [I02311941] **5450**

HAKKO KOGAKKAI SHI See SEIBUTSU KOGAKKAI SHI / SEIBUTSU-KOGAKU KAISHI **3696**

HAKKOKOGAKU KAISHI (JA/0385-6151) [03776302] **3693**

HAKLAUT BE-YISRAEL (IS) [02241523] **91**

HAKLUYT SOCIETY See ANNUAL REPORT / THE HAKLUYT SOCIETY **5461**

HAKLUYT SOCIETY See WORKS ISSUED BY THE HAKLUYT SOCIETY. EXTRA SERIES **5237**

HAKLUYT SOCIETY See LIST OF MEMBERS / THE HAKLUYT SOCIETY **2568**

HAKLUYT SOCIETY. PROSPECTUS AND LIST OF MEMBERS See LIST OF MEMBERS / THE HAKLUYT SOCIETY **2568**

HAKODATE EIRINKYOKU TOSHO MOKUROKU (JA) [02441396] **2399**

HAKODATE KOGYO KOTO SEMMON GAKKO See HAKODATE KOGYO KOTO SEMMON GAKKO KIYO **5108**

HAKODATE KOGYO KOTO SEMMON GAKKO KIYO (JA) [01790119] **5108**

HAKSAENG (KO) [04950242] **1749**

HAKSUL CHAPCHI MOKCHA SOKPO. KYONGYONG, KYONGJE PYON (KO) [08903031] 1493, **869**

HAKSUL CHAPCHI MOKCHA SOKPO. KYOYUKHAK, SIMNIHAK, SAHOEHAK PYON (KO) [08903617] **1795**

HAKSURWON NONMUNJIP. CHAYON KWAHAK PYON (KO/0440-1123) [02106825] **5109**

HAKTUNG (KO) [10582869] **2504**

HAKUBUTSUKAN KENKYU (JA) [01797369] **4088**

HAKUBUTSUKAN NYUSU (JA) [01797246] **4088**

HAKUSHI GAKUI ROMBUN NO GAIYO OYOBI SHINSA NO YOSHI (JA) [03351441] **5109**

HALASZAT (HU) [09802648] **2305**

HALBASIEN (GW/0939-3781) [24608688] **3392**

HALCYON (RENO) (US/0198-6449) [06176922] **2847**

HALES REPORT, INSURANCE BROKERAGE, THE (US/0889-4183) [13943626] **2881**

HALF MOON BAY REVIEW AND PESCADERO PEBBLE (US) [27927005] **5635**

HALF TONES TO JUBILEE (US/1074-0228) [12713300] **3463**

HALF-YEARLY BULLETIN OF ELECTRIC ENERGY STATISTICS FOR EUROPE. BULLETIN SEMESTRIEL DE STATISTIQUES DE L'ENERGIE ELECTRIQUE POUR L'EUROPE. POLUGODOVOI BIULLETEN EVROPEISKOI STATISTIKI ELECTROENERGII (US/0503-3772) [05719729] 1945, **1962**

HALF-YEARLY ECONOMIC REPORT (HK) [05375762] **1493**

HALF-YEARLY REPORT - INDIAN COUNCIL OF HISTORICAL RESEARCH (II) [01784280] **2652**

HALGAN : ORGAN OF THE SOMALI REVOLUTIONARY SOCIALIST PARTY (SO) [08183783] **4542**

HALI (UK/0142-0798) [05083241] **5351**

HALIBURTON FISHING GUIDE (CN/0846-3654) [25589815] 4873, **2305**

HALIEIA (GR) [01795849] **2305**

HALIFAX AND DARTMOUTH CLUBS AND ORGANIZATIONS (1983) (CN/0826-0095) [10935336] **5231**

HALIFAX ANTIQUARIAN SOCIETY, HALIFAX, ENG See TRANSACTIONS **2713**

HALIFAX CITY REGIONAL LIBRARY See MAGAZINES / HALIFAX CITY REGIONAL LIBRARY **419**

HALIFAX DISTRICT SCHOOL BOARD. LIBRARY DEPT See NEWSLETTER - HALIFAX DISTRICT SCHOOL BOARD. LIBRARY DEPT. (1989) **3235**

HALIFAX FIELD NATURALISTS NEWSLETTER (CN/0715-3627) [09128328] **4166**

HALIFAX HARBOUR CLEANUP INC. (N.S.) See CLEAN CURRENTS / HALIFAX HARBOUR CLEANUP INC **2226**

HALIFAX METRO PROFILE (CN/0849-2387) [23231258] **1493**

HALIFAX METROPOLITAN AREA BUSINESS DIRECTORY (CN/0834-0676) [15731950] **678**

HALIFAX SHOPPING GUIDE See PENNYSAVER SHOPPING GUIDE **1298**

HALIKSAI — Alphabetical Title Index

HALIKSAI : U.N.M. CONTRIBUTIONS TO ANTHROPOLOGY **CEASED.** (US) [08938108] 269, **237**

HALIOTIS (FR/0397-765X) [05656990] **5585**

HALL, GEORGE D., COMPANY *See* GEORGE D. HALL'S MASSACHUSETTS SERVICE DIRECTORY **1607**

HALL, GEORGE D., COMPANY, BOSTON *See* GEORGE D. HALL'S DIRECTORY OF CONNECTICUT MANUFACTURERS **3479**

HALL OF THE STATES MANDATE MONITOR (US/1057-7025) [24098374] **4653**

HALLE CONCERTS SOCIETY *See* HALLE YEARBOOK **4120**

HALLE SUD **CEASED.** (SZ/1013-5065) [I10135065] **5479**

HALLE YEARBOOK (UK) [11216440] **4120**

HALLEL CAPPOQUIN (IE/0791-1513) [I07911513] **5030**

HALLESCHE STUDIEN ZUR GESCHICHTE DER SOZIALDEMOKRATIE (GW/0138-1091) [06363504] **4542**

HALLITUKSEN KEHITYSYHTEISTYOKERTOMUS EDUSKUNNALLE VUODELTA (FI/0782-7873) [18993588] **1565**

HALLS GRAPHIC, THE (US/1060-1171) [19052260] **5745**

HALSBURY'S LAWS OF ENGLAND ANNUAL ABRIDGEMENT (UK/0308-4388) [02244170] **2976**

HALSBURY'S LAWS OF ENGLAND : CUMULATIVE SUPPLEMENT (UK) [06038642] **2976**

HALSBURY'S LAWS OF ENGLAND MONTHLY REVIEW (UK) [05979053] **2976**

HALSBURY'S STATUTES OF ENGLAND AND WALES (UK) **2976**

HALSBURY'S STATUTORY INSTRUMENTS : BEING A COMPANION WORK TO HALSBURY'S STATUTES OF ENGLAND (UK) [01644466] **2976**

HALSOUPPLYSNING (SW) [06462882] **4777**

HALSTAD VALLEY JOURNAL **CEASED.** (US) [01751711] **5696**

HALSTEAD INDEPENDENT (HALSTEAD, KAN. : 1892) *See* HARVEY COUNTY INDEPENDENT, THE **5676**

HALTE JEUNESSE ET FOI (1982) (CN/0823-261X) [10036607] **4962**

HALTON BUSINESS JOURNAL (1986) (CN/0833-384X) [15731172] **678**

HALTON CONSUMER (CN/0707-3941) [04747002] **1297**

HALTON FARM NEWS (CN/0704-9226) [04040525] **91**

HALTON-PEEL BRANCH NEWSLETTER (CN/1187-6360) [25883116] **2452**

● HALTON-PEEL FARM NEWS (CN/1192-0785) [27193897] **91**

HALVE MAEN, DE (US/0017-6834) [01799191] **2452**

HAM JOURNAL TOKYO (JA/0388-2306) [I03882306] **1112**

HAM RADIO TODAY (UK/0269-8269) [I02698269] **1156**

HAMBLEN CONNECTOR (US) **2452**

HAMBONE (STANFORD, CALIF.) (US/0733-6616) [06374282] **3392**

HAMBRO COMPANY GUIDE, THE (UK/0144-2015) [14347154] **678**

HAMBROOK HERALD, THE (CN/0821-5472) [09951407] **2452**

HAMBURG. AMT. FUR INGINEURWESEN 3. HAUPTABTEILUNG STADTENTWASSER *See* JAHRESBERICHT DER HAUPTABTEILUNG STADTENTWASSERUNG **2233**

HAMBURG. AMT FUR SCHULE *See* MITTEILUNGSBLATT DES AMTES FUR SCHULE **1764**

HAMBURG, GER. SCHULBEHORDE. MITTEILUNGSBLATT *See* MITTEILUNGSBLATT DES AMTES FUR SCHULE **1764**

HAMBURG HANDBUCH (GW/0302-9247) [05718468] **4475**

HAMBURG. INSTITUT FUR ALLGEMEINE BOTANIK *See* MITTEILUNGEN AUS DEM INSTITUT FUER ALLGEMEINE BOTANIK HAMBURG **518**

HAMBURG. MUSEUM FUR VOLKERKUNDE UND VORGESCHICHTE *See* MITTEILUNGEN AUS DEM MUSEUM FUER VOLKERKUNDE HAMBURG **241**

HAMBURG. MUSEUM FUR VOLKERKUNDE UND VORGESCHICHTE *See* MONOGRAPHIEN ZUR VOLKERKUNDE **241**

HAMBURG. MUSEUM FUR VOLKERKUNDE UND VORGESCHICHTE *See* BEITRAEGE ZUR MITTELAMERIKANISCHEN VOLKERKUNDE **2723**

HAMBURG. STATISTISCHES LANDESAMT *See* STATISTISCHES TASCHENBUCH **5343**

HAMBURG. UNIVERSITAT. INSTITUT FUR INTERNATIONALE ANGELEGENHEITEN *See* DOKUMENTE - INSTITUT FUER INTERNATIONALE ANGELEGENHEITEN DER UNIVERSITAT HAMBURG **3127**

HAMBURG. ZOOLOGISCHES MUSEUM UND INSTITUT *See* MITTEILUNGEN AUS DEM HAMBURGISCHEN ZOOLOGISCHEN MUSEUM UND INSTITUT **5591**

HAMBURGER BEITRAEGE ZUR FRIEDENSFORSCHUNG UND SICHERHEITSPOLITIK (GW/0936-0018) [I09360018] **4523**

HAMBURGER BEITRAEGE ZUR NUMISMATIK (GW/0072-9523) [03230938] **2781**

HAMBURGER GEOGRAPHISCHE STUDIEN (GW/0440-1697) [02057654] **2565**

HAMBURGER JAHRBUCH FUER MUSIKWISSENSCHAFT (GW) [05791166] **4120**

HAMBURGER JAHRBUCH FUER THEATER UND MUSIK (GW) [11390778] **4120, 5364**

HAMBURGER JAHRBUCH FUER WIRTSCHAFTS- UND GESELLSCHAFTSPOLITIK (GW/0072-9566) [02062958] **1493**

HAMBURGER KREBSDOKUMENTATION (GW/0170-3064) [11198958] **3817**

HAMBURGER PHILOLOGISCHE STUDIEN (GW/0072-9582) [02057218] **3392, 3285**

HAMBURGER ROMANISTISCHE DISSERTATIONEN (GW/0440-1727) [09661672] 1827, **3285**

HAMBURGER WIRTSCHAFT : ZEITSCHRIFT DER HANDELSKAMMER HAMBURG (GW) [20150062] **838**

HAMBURGER ZUSTANDE : JAHRBUCH ZUR GESCHICHTE DER REGION HAMBURG / HERAUSGEGEBEN VON "VEREIN HAMBURG-JAHRBUCH" E.V (GW) [19046706] **2517**

HAMBURGISCHE GESCHICHTS- UND HEIMATBLATTER (GW/0931-0185) [02461856] **2690**

HAMDARD ISLAMICUS (PK/0250-7196) [04333497] **5042**

HAMERSKY & ALLIED FAMILIES NEWSLETTER (US/0882-4150) [11838039] **2452**

HAMILTON COUNTY NEWS, THE (US) [10871178] **5717**

HAMILTON CUE MAGAZINE (CN/0822-9724) [11050400] **2534**

HAMILTON EXPRESS, LE (CN/0705-081X) [03960173] **5786**

HAMILTON GUIDEBOOK (CN/0227-6267) [07822602] **5479**

● HAMILTON LAWYER (CN/1188-4827) [11884827] **2976**

HAMILTON NEWS (HAMILTON, IND.) (US) [15494126] **5664**

HAMILTON PROGRESS, THE (US) [14265297] **5626**

HAMILTON REPORT (CN/0834-0536) [15624334] **678**

HAMILTON SPECTATOR (DAILY : 1984) (CN/0839-0185) [18925972] **5786**

HAMILTON THIS MONTH (CN/0829-1373) [19759344] **678**

HAMILTON TIGER-CAT FOOTBALL CLUB *See* TIGER-CAT FACT BOOK / TIGER-CATS FOOTBALL **4926**

HAMILTON'S COIN AND MEDAL DESPATCH **CEASED.** (UK) [06494440] **2781**

HAMLET STUDIES (II/0256-2480) [06822158] **5364, 3392**

HAMLIN HERALD (HAMLIN, TEX. : 1906) (US) [14265287] **5750**

HAMLINE JOURNAL OF PUBLIC LAW AND POLICY (US) [13593560] **2976**

HAMLINE LAW REVIEW (US/0198-7364) [04150047] **2976**

HAMLYN LECTURES, THE (UK) [01589007] 4475, **2976**

HAMMABURG : VOR- U. FRUHGESCHICHTLICHE FORSCHUNGEN AUS DEM NIEDERELBISCHEN RAUM (GW/0172-0886) [08569774] 269, **2690**

HAMMARSKJOLD FORUMS (US) [01695842] **4347**

HAMMASLAAKARIT (FI/0780-1807) [11093458] **1324**

HAMMER & DOLLY (US/1064-4822) [21139198] **5416**

HAMMOND CITATION WORLD ATLAS **CEASED.** (US) 2565, **2582**

HAMMOND ROAD ATLAS AMERICA (US) 5440, **2582**

HAMMOND ROAD ATLAS & VACATION GUIDE (US) 5479, **2582**

HAMMOND VINDICATOR, THE (US) [08811010] **5684**

HAMPDEN-SYDNEY POETRY REVIEW, THE (US/0190-6135) [02430214] **3463**

HAMPSHIRE HERDSMAN (US) [19289778] **212**

HAMPSHIRE HERDSMAN (US) [01772890] **5510**

HAMPSHIRE REVIEW AND THE SOUTH BRANCH INTELLIGENCER, THE (US/0736-5497) [09805487] **5763**

HAMPSHIRE WORLD (CUBA, ILL. : 1989) *See* BANNER (CUBA, ILL.), THE **207**

HAMPSTEAD JOURNAL (CN/0714-8844) [09088978] **5786**

HAMPTON COUNTY GUARDIAN (US) [13622346] **5742**

HAMPTON REVIEW : HR, THE (US) [19249068] **2262**

HAMPTON ROADS SHIPPING NEWS, THE **CEASED.** (US/0744-1061) [08203989] **5450**

HAMPTON UNION, THE (US) [22135658] **5708**

HAMPTONS : THE MAGAZINE OF THE WORLD'S MOST SOPHISTICATED RESORT, THE (US) [08458372] 2806, **5479**

HAMSTER INFORMATION SERVICE (US/0739-4276) [09522328] **5510**

HAN-GUK SUSAN HAKHOIJI (KO/0374-8111) [05055912] **2305**

HAN HSUEH YEN CHIU (CH/0254-4466) [10838867] **2652**

HAN HSUEH YEN CHIU TUNG HSUN (CH) [08912544] **2504**

HAN KAREM (KO) [04970076] **2504**

HAN SHENG (TAIPEI, TAIWAN) (CH) [04277382] **2652**

HANAZONO DAIGAKU. BUNGAKUBU *See* HANAZONO DAIGAKU KENKYU KIYO **1827**

HANAZONO DAIGAKU KENKYU KIYO (JA) [05458710] **1827**

HANCEVILLE HERALD, THE (US) [13067630] **5626**

HANCOCK CLARION, THE (US) [13918506] **5680**

HANCOCK COUNTY COURIER (NEW CUMBERLAND, W. VA. : 1943) (US) [12818418] **5764**

HANCOCK HERALD, THE (US) [12299933] **5717**

HANCOCK NEWS, THE (US) [17613400] **5686**

HAND CLINICS (US/0749-0712) [11078527] **3881**

HAND-MADE (CN/0703-7864) [03439612] **373**

HAND PAPERMAKING (US/0887-1418) [13109938] **4234**

HAND TO HAND (US) 1064, **4088**

HANDAI HOGAKU (JA/0438-4997) [19087596] **2976**

HANDBALL (FR) **4897**

HANDBALL-MAGAZIN (GW/0178-2983) [I01782983] **4897**

HANDBALL (SKOKIE, ILL.) (US/0046-6778) [02254411] **4897**

HANDBELLS FOR DIRECTORS AND RINGERS (US/8756-7407) [11637678] **4120**

HANDBOEK ADMINISTRATIE (NE) **744**

HANDBOEK ARBEIDS - EN MILIEUVEILIGHEID (NE) **2862**

HANDBOEK MACINTOSH & NIEUWSBRIEF (NE) 1267, **1263**

HANDBOEK VAN DE NEDERLANDSE PERS EN PUBLICITEIT (NE) [16260189] **5806**

HANDBOEK VOOR BEDRIJFSVEILIGHEID *See* HANDBOEK ARBEIDS - EN MILIEUVEILIGHEID **2862**

HANDBOG - DANSK MASKINHANDLERFORENING (DK/0302-5349) [01792696] **159**

HANDBOG I DANSK POLITIK (DK/0106-0392) [05258359] **1565**

HANDBOOK (US) [18313177] **1749**

HANDBOOK : A PUBLICATION OF THE COLORADO COUNCIL ON HIGH SCHOOL-COLLEGE RELATIONS (US/0898-4018) [17804285] **1749**

HANDBOOK - ALABAMA LAW INSTITUTE (US/0149-0842) [03427039] **2976**

HANDBOOK - ALBERTA BADMINTON ASSOCIATION (CN/0849-097X) [22154913] **4898**

HANDBOOK AND ANNUAL REVIEW (ZA) [08311183] **5109**

Alphabetical Title Index — HANDBOOK

HANDBOOK AND CALENDAR - MURDOCH UNIVERSITY 1986 (AT/0815-9068) [I08159068] **1827**

HANDBOOK AND COURSES DIRECTORY - DIVISION OF TECHNICAL AND FURTHER EDUCATION, EDUCATION DEPARTMENT HOBART (AT/1037-566X) [I1037566X] **1749**

HANDBOOK AND DIRECTORY - ASSOCIATION FOR EDUCATIONAL DATA SYSTEMS (US/0092-6280) [01791066] **1749**

HANDBOOK AND DIRECTORY - CANADIAN FIELD HOCKEY ASSOCIATION (CN/0225-0314) [06018202] **4898**

HANDBOOK AND DIRECTORY - CANADIAN WOMEN'S FIELD HOCKEY ASSOCIATION (CN/0225-0306) [06018216] **4898**

HANDBOOK AND DIRECTORY - CLASSIC CAR CLUB OF AMERICA (US/0163-1055) [04293824] **5416**

HANDBOOK AND ... LIST OF MEMBERS - INSTITUTE OF METALS (UK) [14908900] **4003**

HANDBOOK AND REPORT TO THE COMMISSIONERS - BUFFALO MUNICIPAL HOUSING AUTHORITY (US) [04019239] **2823**

HANDBOOK, ANNUAL CONFERENCE - ASSOCIATED CHURCHES OF CHRIST IN NEW ZEALAND (NZ/0304-1603) [01794408] **4962**

● HANDBOOK / ASSOCIATION OF AMERICAN LAW SCHOOLS (US/1063-8253) [25716819] **2976**

HANDBOOK - AUSTRALIAN ACADEMY OF TECHNOLOGICAL SCIENCES AND ENGINEERING (AT/1031-6892) [I10316892] **5109**

HANDBOOK - BRITISH COLUMBIA PROVINCIAL MUSEUM (CN/0068-1628) [02249294] **4088**

HANDBOOK / CANADIAN ASSOCIATION FOR UNIVERSITY CONTINUING EDUCATION (CN/0713-5858) [10935282] **1827**

HANDBOOK - CANADIAN BADMINTON ASSOCIATION (CN/0229-5806) [08360295] **4898**

HANDBOOK - COMMONWEALTH BROADCASTING ASSOCIATION (UK) [06611942] **1132**

HANDBOOK : CONSTITUTION, DIRECTORY, BYLAWS, POLICIES, BUDGET, LEGISLATION / ONTARIO PUBLIC SCHOOL FEDERATION (CN/0822-9104) [10809719] **1864**

HANDBOOK, CORRUGATED AND SOLID FIBREBOARD BOXES AND PRODUCTS (US) [01313245] **4219**

HANDBOOK - FACULTY OF MEDICINE, UNIVERSITY OF NEW SOUTH WALES (AT/0312-6137) [05705216] **3580**

HANDBOOK FOR CLASSROOM STUDENTS *See* HANDBOOK FOR CLASSROOM STUDENTS/ ALBERTA DISTANCE LEARNING CENTRE **1749**

● HANDBOOK FOR CLASSROOM STUDENTS/ ALBERTA DISTANCE LEARNING CENTRE (CN/0846-2658) [25351958] **1749**

HANDBOOK FOR FINANCIAL AID ADMINISTRATORS (US/0094-2227) [01794025] **1827**

HANDBOOK FOR GEORGIA LEGISLATORS (US/0438-5047) [01590743] **4654**

HANDBOOK FOR INDIANS IN OTTAWA-HULL, A (CN/0707-574X) [04784060] **2262**

HANDBOOK FOR MEMBERS OF THE NORTHWEST TERRITORIES TEACHERS' ASSOCIATION, A (CN/0825-0014) [10763874] **1895**

HANDBOOK FOR NO-LOAD FUND INVESTORS, THE (US/0736-6264) [07717375] **900**

HANDBOOK FOR NON-CLASSROOM STUDENTS *See* HANDBOOK FOR NON-CLASSROOM STUDENTS / ALBERTA DISTANCE LEARNING CENTRE **1749**

● HANDBOOK FOR NON-CLASSROOM STUDENTS / ALBERTA DISTANCE LEARNING CENTRE (CN/0846-264X) [25351961] **1749**

HANDBOOK FOR STAFF PHYSICIANS / CLINICAL CENTER, NATIONAL INSTITUTES OF HEALTH (US) [10169850] **3780**

HANDBOOK FOR STUDENTS TAKING COURSES IN GEOGRAPHY / UNIVERSITY OF ZAMBIA, SCHOOL OF EDUCATION, DEPARTMENT OF GEOGRAPHY (ZA) [08312542] **2565**

HANDBOOK FOR SUMMER SCHOOL PROGRAMS (US) [23886718] **1749**

HANDBOOK FOR THE FACULTY OF ARTS AND FACULTY OF SOCIAL SCIENCES (UG/0376-9526) [01786454] **1827**

HANDBOOK (GEOLOGICAL SURVEY OF SOUTH AFRICA) (SA/0560-9208) [01379467] **1382**

HANDBOOK / INSTITUTE OF EDUCATION (TZ) [08426679] **1749**

HANDBOOK - INSTITUTE OF PURCHASING AND SUPPLY *CEASED*. (UK) [06180559] **950**

HANDBOOK - INTERNATIONAL CHAMBER OF COMMERCE (FR/0378-049X) [01796197] **820**

HANDBOOK LONDON. ROYAL COLLEGE OF SURGEONS OF ENGLAND (UK) [05620619] **3965**

HANDBOOK - MAKERERE UNIVERSITY. SCIENCE FACULTY (UG) [01786349] **5109**

HANDBOOK / NATIONAL ASSOCIATION OF SCHOOLS OF ART AND DESIGN (US/0272-7552) [06912639] 1749, **351**

HANDBOOK / NATIONAL ASSOCIATION OF SCHOOLS OF DANCE (US/0735-9608) [09040582] 1749, **1313**

HANDBOOK - NATIONAL ASSOCIATION OF SCHOOLS OF MUSIC (US/0164-2847) [02807398] 1749, **4120**

HANDBOOK - NATIONAL ASSOCIATION OF SCHOOLS OF THEATRE (U.S.) (US/0739-9839) [09840315] **5364**

HANDBOOK - NEW YORK STATE PUBLIC HIGH SCHOOL ATHLETIC ASSOCIATION (US) [04866301] **4898**

HANDBOOK OF ADVERTISING & MARKETING SERVICES (US/0749-2243) [10815053] 925, **759**

HANDBOOK OF ANTIMICROBIAL THERAPY (US/0190-3454) [04622824] **4306**

HANDBOOK OF ASTRONOMY, ASTROPHYSICS, AND GEOPHYSICS (US/0141-0326) [04335961] **395**

HANDBOOK OF BASIC STATISTICS OF MAHARASHTRA STATE (II) [02434022] **5328**

HANDBOOK OF BEHAVIORAL ECONOMICS (US) 760, **925**

HANDBOOK OF BEHAVIORAL NEUROBIOLOGY (US/0194-0880) [05192346] **3833**

HANDBOOK OF BENDEL STATE OF NIGERIA (NR) [06795267] **4654**

HANDBOOK OF BRITISH ANAESTHESIA (UK/0260-2873) [06507862] **3683**

HANDBOOK OF BRITISH REFRIGERATION MATERIAL AND REFRIGERATION CATALOGUE, BUYERS' REFERENCE GUIDE (UK) [20292305] **2605**

HANDBOOK OF BUSINESS FINANCE AND CAPITAL SOURCES (US/0163-4615) [04387382] **790**

HANDBOOK OF BUSINESS LETTERS (US) [10610711] **679**

HANDBOOK OF CANADIAN CONSUMER MARKETS *CEASED*. (CN/0225-4190) [06136473] **1297**

HANDBOOK OF CANCER IMMUNOLOGY, THE (US/0736-8674) [07388172] **3817**

HANDBOOK OF CERTIFICATION/LICENSURE REQUIREMENTS FOR SCHOOL PSYCHOLOGISTS, THE (US) [06670821] **4588**

HANDBOOK OF CHEMICAL NEUROANATOMY (NE) [10385335] **1052**

HANDBOOK OF CIVIL PROCEDURE (US) **3090**

HANDBOOK OF CLINICAL NEUROLOGY (NE) [01777687] **3833**

HANDBOOK OF COLLECTIONS (US/0445-3387) [01741154] **4088**

HANDBOOK OF COMMERCE AND INDUSTRY IN NIGERIA (NR/0549-1940) [01189634] **838**

HANDBOOK OF COMMERCIAL ROOFING SYSTEMS (US) [17807818] **616**

HANDBOOK OF COMMUNICATIONS SYSTEMS MANAGEMENT. YEARBOOK (US/1051-7839) [20347205] **1156**

HANDBOOK OF COMPARATIVE ECONOMIC POLICIES (US/1054-7681) [22969272] **1493**

HANDBOOK OF CONTRACT FLOOR COVERING (US/0197-8209) [06119912] **616**

HANDBOOK OF CYCLICAL INDICATORS (US/0196-9366) [03585269] **4404**

HANDBOOK OF DEGREE AND ADVANCED COURSES IN INSTITUTES/COLLEGES OF HIGHER EDUCATION, UNIVERSITY DEPARTMENT OF EDUCATION, ENGLAND AND WALES *See* NATFHE HANDBOOK, THE **1836**

HANDBOOK OF ECONOMIC STATISTICS *See* HANDBOOK OF INTERNATIONAL ECONOMIC STATISTICS / DIRECTORATE OF INTELLIGENCE, CENTRAL INTELLIGENCE AGENCY **1493**

HANDBOOK OF ECONOMIC STATISTICS (WASHINGTON) (US/0195-9018) [04654549] 1565, **1533**

HANDBOOK OF ELECTRICITY SUPPLY STATISTICS *CEASED*. (UK/0440-1905) [01786391] **2004**

HANDBOOK OF ELECTROENCEPHALOGRAPHY AND CLINICAL NEUROPHYSIOLOGY (NE) [02255344] **3580**

HANDBOOK OF EMPLOYMENT SECURITY PROGRAM STATISTICS (US/0361-2902) [02246395] 1676, 2881, **1533**

HANDBOOK OF EXPERIMENTAL PHARMACOLOGY (GW/0171-2004) [04737381] **4306**

HANDBOOK OF FLORIDA SECURITIES (US) [01800059] **900**

HANDBOOK OF GEOPHYSICAL EXPLORATION SECTION 1 SEISMIC EXPLORATION (UK/0950-1401) [I09501401] **1406**

● HANDBOOK OF GYNECOLOGY & OBSTETRICS (US/1062-5704) [25669095] **3762**

HANDBOOK OF HYPERLIPIDAEMIA (UK) [21226800] **3705**

HANDBOOK OF HYPERTENSION (NE) [10478605] **3705**

HANDBOOK OF IBM TERMINOLOGY, THE (UK) **1247**

HANDBOOK OF ILLINOIS GOVERNMENT (US/0095-2842) [01783477] 4654, **4475**

HANDBOOK OF ILLINOIS POSTSECONDARY INSTITUTIONS (US) [04820223] **1827**

HANDBOOK OF INDUSTRIAL STATISTICS (NEW DELHI, INDIA) (II) [18596083] 1608, **1533**

HANDBOOK OF INFLAMMATION (NE/0167-5567) [06937495] **3580**

HANDBOOK OF INSURANCE (UK) **2881**

HANDBOOK OF INTERNATIONAL DOCUMENTATION AND INFORMATION (US) [09031231] **1926**

● HANDBOOK OF INTERNATIONAL ECONOMIC STATISTICS / DIRECTORATE OF INTELLIGENCE, CENTRAL INTELLIGENCE AGENCY (US) [27990932] **1493**

HANDBOOK OF INTERNATIONAL TRADE AND DEVELOPMENT STATISTICS (US) [01577385] **1533**

HANDBOOK OF IS MANAGEMENT (US) [26271365] **869**

HANDBOOK OF LABOR STATISTICS / U.S. DEPARTMENT OF LABOR, BUREAU OF LABOR STATISTICS (US/0082-9056) [01768204] **1533**

HANDBOOK OF LASER SCIENCE AND TECHNOLOGY (SZ/0899-2711) [18056078] **4434**

HANDBOOK OF LATIN AMERICAN STUDIES (US/0072-9833) [01751732] **2735**

HANDBOOK OF LEARNING AND COGNITIVE PROCESSES (US) [04044900] **1749**

HANDBOOK OF LIPID RESEARCH (US/0163-9102) [03974131] **1041**

HANDBOOK OF MASSACHUSETTS FAMILY LAW (US) **3121**

HANDBOOK OF MEDICAL EDUCATION (II/0253-7621) [04208221] 1749, **3580**

HANDBOOK OF MEDICAL TREATMENT (US/0072-9841) [04748438] **3580**

HANDBOOK OF MOTOR INSURANCE (UK) **2881**

HANDBOOK OF NEUROCHEMISTRY (US) [02254836] **3833**

HANDBOOK OF NEW ZEALAND AGRICULTURE *See* CONTACTS IN AGRICULTURE **76**

HANDBOOK OF NON-PRESCRIPTION DRUGS (US/0889-7816) [01751734] **4306**

HANDBOOK OF OBSTETRICS & GYNECOLOGY *See* HANDBOOK OF GYNECOLOGY & OBSTETRICS **3762**

HANDBOOK OF OCCUPATIONAL HYGIENE (UK) [15313145] **2862**

HANDBOOK OF OPTICAL MEMORY SYSTEMS & UPDATES (US) **1185**

HANDBOOK OF PENSIONS (UK) **2881**

HANDBOOK OF PHYSICAL PROPERTIES OF ROCKS (US) [08408506] **1458**

HANDBOOK OF POLYTECHNIC COURSES (UK/0305-6376) [01785456] **1913**

HANDBOOK OF POWDER TECHNOLOGY (NE/0167-3785) [07310271] **5109**

HANDBOOK ... OF PRIVATE ACCREDITED TRADE AND TECHNICAL SCHOOLS (US) [17829557] **1913**

HANDBOOK Alphabetical Title Index

HANDBOOK OF PRIVATE SCHOOLS, THE (US/0072-9884) [05689553] **1749**

HANDBOOK OF RAILROAD RETIREMENT AND UNEMPLOYMENT INSURANCE SYSTEMS See RAILROAD RETIREMENT AND UNEMPLOYMENT INSURANCE SYSTEMS HANDBOOK **2891**

HANDBOOK OF RENT REVIEW (UK) **2976**

HANDBOOK OF RISK MANAGEMENT (UK) **679**

HANDBOOK OF RUPEE COMPANIES (CE) [01751735] **900**

HANDBOOK OF SEC ACCOUNTING AND DISCLOSURE (US/1046-3534) [20372850] **744**

HANDBOOK OF SECURITY (UK) **1226**

HANDBOOK OF SECURITY (UK) **5177**

HANDBOOK OF STATE LEGISLATIVE LEADERS See INSIDE THE LEGISLATURE **4477**

HANDBOOK OF STATE LEGISLATIVE LEADERS, THE (US/0743-0728) [10497490] **4475**

HANDBOOK OF STATE PROGRAMS FOR LOCAL GOVERNMENTS (US) [04052882] **4654**

HANDBOOK OF STATISTICS (NE/0169-7161) [08234629] **5328**

HANDBOOK OF STATISTICS ON COTTON TEXTILE INDUSTRY (II) [09873879] **5360**

HANDBOOK OF SYSTEMS MANAGEMENT, DEVELOPMENT AND SUPPORT. YEARBOOK (US/1056-0998) [23281636] **1286**

HANDBOOK OF TABLES FOR MATHEMATICS (US/0362-8191) [02159208] **3507**

HANDBOOK OF THE BRITISH ASTRONOMICAL ASSOCIATION, THE (UK/0068-130X) [02672203] **395**

HANDBOOK OF THE GENERAL ASSEMBLY OF THE STATE OF GEORGIA See MANUAL OF THE GENERAL ASSEMBLY OF THE STATE OF GEORGIA **4664**

HANDBOOK OF THE HOSPITAL CORPS, UNITED STATES NAVY (US) [05191234] **4177**

HANDBOOK OF THE LABOUR MARKET OUTCOMES OF THE ... GRADUATES FROM UNIVERSITY OF PRINCE EDWARD ISLAND, HOLLAND COLLEGE POST SECONDARY COURSES, CANADA EMPLOYMENT AND IMMIGRATION COMMISSION SPONSORED COURSES (CN) [10983087] **1676**

HANDBOOK OF THE NATIONS (US/0194-3790) [05383780] **4475**

HANDBOOK OF THE NEVADA LEGISLATURE (US) [01246295] **4654**

HANDBOOK OF THE UNITED FREE CHURCH OF SCOTLAND, THE (UK/0082-7908) [07285355] **5061**

HANDBOOK OF TIDE TABLES, PARTICULARS OF DOCKS, &C (UK) [06598859] **4177**

HANDBOOK OF VEGETATION SCIENCE (NE/0302-3141) [17748193] **512**

HANDBOOK OF WAGES AND BENEFITS FOR CONSTRUCTION UNIONS (US/8755-979X) [06209099] **1676**

... HANDBOOK OF WORLD STOCK AND COMMODITY EXCHANGES, THE (UK) [24341132] **900**

HANDBOOK - OKLAHOMA BAR ASSOCIATION (US/0271-2571) [04343586] **2976**

HANDBOOK ON ERISA LITIGATION (US) **3148**

HANDBOOK ON LOUISIANA FAMILY LAW (US/1061-6489) [23950186] **3121**

HANDBOOK ON THE 1989 DOUBLE TAXATION CONVENTION BETWEEN THE FEDERAL REPUBLIC OF GERMANY AND THE UNITED STATES OF AMERICA (NE) 744, **4730**

HANDBOOK ON THE LATE EFFECTS OF POLIOMYELITIS FOR PHYSICIANS AND SURVIVORS (US) [19034094] **3580**

HANDBOOK - RUGBY FOOTBALL UNION (UK/0306-8218) [01795547] **4898**

HANDBOOK - SECURITIES EXCHANGE OF THAILAND (TH) [02634987] **900**

HANDBOOK SERIES / ZOOLOGICAL SURVEY OF INDIA (II) [07881285] **5585**

HANDBOOK (SOUTH AUSTRALIA. DEPT. OF MINES AND ENERGY) (AT/0726-1519) [11321533] **2140**

HANDBOOK / THE DEPARTMENT OF TECHNICAL AND FURTHER EDUCATION OF SOUTH AUSTRALIA (AT/0814-9283) [17463722] **1749**

HANDBOOK / THE UNIVERSITY OF ZAMBIA, SCHOOL OF EDUCATION, DEPARTMENT OF LITERATURE & LANGUAGES (ZA) [08462566] 3392, **3285**

HANDBOOK TO GRADUATE PROGRAMMES IN HISTORY IN CANADA (CN/1180-3673) [23242477] **2617**

HANDBOOK TO THE SEASON / CINCINNATI SYMPHONY ORCHESTRA (US/0732-2321) [08309823] **4120**

HANDBOOK - UNIVERSITI PERTANIAN MALAYSIA (MY/0377-7227) [02240563] **1827**

HANDBOOK / UNIVERSITY OF ZAMBIA, SCHOOL OF EDUCATION, DEPARTMENT OF EDUCATION (ZA) [11591666] **1827**

HANDBOOK - WORLD CONFEDERATION OF ORGANIZATIONS OF THE TEACHING PROFESSION (SZ) [21111212] **1895**

HANDBOOKS FOR THE IDENTIFICATION OF BRITISH INSECTS (UK) [02469881] **5609**

HANDBOOKS IN OPERATIONS RESEARCH AND MANAGEMENT SCIENCE (NE) [23944830] **5109**

HANDBUCH DER ALTERTUMSWISSENSCHAFT (GW) [05207618] **269**

HANDBUCH DER ARCHAEOLOGIE (GW) **269**

HANDBUCH DER AUSLANDSZOELLE (GW) **1635**

HANDBUCH DER DATENBANKEN FUER NATURWISSENSCHAFT, TECHNIK, PATENTE (GW/0936-1375) [09361375] **1185**

HANDBUCH DER DEUTSCHEN LITERATURGESCHICHTE (SZ) [01775761] **3392**

HANDBUCH DER DOGMENGESCHICHTE (GW) **4962**

HANDBUCH DER EXPERIMENTELLEN PHARMAKOLOGIE (GW/0073-0033) [01587877] **4306**

HANDBUCH DER GEFAHRLICHEN GUTER (GW/0172-9578) [05983081] **2230**

HANDBUCH DER GROSSFORSCHUNG / ARBEITSGEMEINSCHAFT DER GROSSFORSCHUNGSEINRICHTUNGEN (AGR) (GW/0174-5026) [12201125] **5109**

HANDBUCH DER GROSSUNTERNEHMEN (GW/0073-0068) [01453457] **1493**

HANDBUCH DER HAUT- UND GESCHLECHTSKRANKHEITEN. ERGANZUNGSWERK (GW) [09800589] **3580**

HANDBUCH DER HISTOCHEMIE (GW) [01777690] **536**

HANDBUCH DER INTERNATIONALEN DOKUMENTATION UND INFORMATION See HANDBOOK OF INTERNATIONAL DOCUMENTATION AND INFORMATION **1926**

HANDBUCH DER OFFENTLICHEN BIBLIOTHEKEN (GW/0301-9225) [01793168] **3213**

HANDBUCH DER ORIENTALISTIK, 1. ABT. DER NAHE UND DER MITTLERE OSTEN (NE/0169-9423) [01773142] **2768**

HANDBUCH DER OSTERREICHISCHEN SOZIALVERSICHERUNG FUER DAS JAHR (AU) [07442936] **5287**

HANDBUCH DER PALAOHERPETOLOGIE (GW) [06391924] **5585**

HANDBUCH DER PFLANZENANATOMIE (GW) [01777766] **512**

HANDBUCH DER WIRTSCHAFTSDATENBANKEN (GW/0931-2234) [17976268] **679**

HANDBUCH DER ZOOLOGIE (GW) [01588989] **5585**

HANDBUCH FUER PERSONAL- UND LOHNBUROS (AU) [21024823] **3148**

HANDBUCH PERSONLICHE SCHUTZAUSRUSTUNGEN (GW) **2862**

HANDBUCH SCHLESWIG-HOLSTEIN (GW) [08354992] **2690**

HANDBUCH ZUM NEUEN TESTAMENT (GW/0932-9706) [01775762] **5016**

HANDBUCHER ZUR SPRACH- UND KOMMUNIKATIONSWISSENSCHAFT (GW) [12745281] **3285**

HANDCHIRURGIE, MIKROCHIRURGIE, PLASTISCHE CHIRURGIE (GW/0722-1819) [09624128] **3965**

HANDCHIRURGISCHE TASCHENBUCHER (GW/0171-9734) [04795096] **3965**

HANDCRAFT & HOME (AT) **373**

● HANDEL, DER (GW) [26002508] **838**

HANDEL, GASTGEWERBE, REISEVERKEHR. REIHE 1.1, BESCHAFTIGTE UND UMSATZ IM GROSSHANDEL (MESSZAHLEN) (GW) [20083280] **838**

HANDEL, GASTGEWERBE, REISEVERKEHR. REIHE 3.1: BESCHAFTIGTE UND UMSATZ IM EINZELHANDEL, MESSZAHLEN (GW) [03400750] **955**

HANDEL, GASTGEWERBE, REISEVERKEHR. REIHE 6 WARENVERKEHR MIT DER DEUTSCHEN DEMOKRATISCHEN REPUBLIK UND BERLIN, OST (GW) [04424992] **838**

HANDEL JAHRBUCH (GW) **4120**

HANDEL WEWNETRZNY (PL/0438-5403) [02702249] **839**

HANDEL ZAGRANICZNY (PL/0017-7245) [02701543] **839**

HANDELINGEN DER MAATSCHAPPIJ VOOR GESCHIEDENIS EN OUDHEIDKUNDE TE GENT (BE/0774-286X) [05810158] 269, **2617**

HANDELINGEN / KONINKLIJKE ZUIDNEDERLANDSE MAATSCHAPPIJ VOOR TAAL- EN LETTERKUNDE EN GESCHIEDENIS (BE/0774-3254) [02226040] **3285**

HANDELINGEN VAN DE KONINKLIJKE KRING VOOR OUDHEIDKUNDE, LETTEREN EN KUNST VAN MECHELEN (BE/0776-2976) [07762976] **321**

HANDELINGEN VAN DEN GESCHIED- EN OUDHEIDKUNDIGE KRING VAN KORTRIJK (BE/0776-5533) [07765533] **321**

HANDELINGEN VAN HET GENOOTSCHAP VOOR GESCHIEDENIS (BE/0770-0822) [07700822] **2690**

HANDEL'S NATIONAL DIRECTORY FOR THE PERFORMING ARTS (US/0898-7955) [17554317] **385**

HANDELS- OG SFARTSMUSEET PA KRONBORG See ARBOG - HANDELS- OG SFARTSMUSEET PA KRONBORG **823**

HANDELSBLATT (GW/0017-7296) [10198531] **839**

HANDELSHOGSKOLAN I STOCKHOLM See KATALOG OVER PERSONAL, INSTITUTIONER OCH SEKTIONER **843**

HANDES AMSORYA (AU) [05377086] **3285**

HANDGUNNER (UK/0260-8693) [02608693] 4045, **4898**

● HANDGUNNING (US/1060-068X) [24859676] 4873, **4898**

HANDGUNS FOR SPORT & DEFENSE (US/1054-4135) [22878962] 4045, **4898**

HANDGUNS (LOS ANGELES, CALIF.) (US/1068-2635) [27520809] **4898**

HANDHAAF CEASED. (SA) [01789845] **2639**

HANDHAVING (NE) **2173**

HANDI-COMMUNICATIONS (CN/0255-030X) [11108216] **1186**

HANDICAP MAGAZINE (NE) **4388**

HANDICAP NEWS See CARING CONNECTION **4385**

HANDICAPPED FUNDING DIRECTORY See DIRECTORY OF GRANTS FOR ORGANIZATIONS SERVING PEOPLE WITH DISABILITIES **4387**

HANDICAPPED LIVING See CARING : FOR THE DISABLED CARERS AND THE ELDERLY **4385**

HANDICAPPED REQUIREMENTS HANDBOOK. SUPPLEMENT (US/0194-7818) [05015357] **4388**

HANDICAPS ET INADAPTATIONS PARIS (FR/0180-9040) [01809040] **4388**

HANDICRAFTS AND HANDLOOMS EXPORTS CORPORATION OF INDIA See VARSHIKA RIPORTA - HAINDIKRAPHTSA ENNDA HAINDALUMSA EKSAPORTASA KARPORESANA APHA INDIYA **376**

HANDLING & SHIPPING. PRESIDENTIAL ISSUE (US) [01784895] **869**

HANDLING CORPORATE EMPLOYMENT PROBLEMS (US/1059-0277) [24031310] **1676**

HANDLING EQUIPMENT DIRECTORY (UK) **2115**

HANDLINGAR OCH TIDSKRIFT (SW) [01782518] **4045**

HANDLOADER (US/0017-7393) [04081099] **4898**

HANDLOADER BULLETIN MAKING ANNUAL CEASED. (US) **4898**

HANDLOADER'S DIGEST (US/0073-0211) [04522536] **3480**

HANDMADE (AT) **373**

HANDMADE (ASHEVILLE, N.C.) (US/0275-9640) [07264972] **5184**

HANDS ON! (DAYTON, OHIO) (US/0197-6559) [06071818] **634**

HANDS-ON ENGLISH (US/1056-2680) [23613842] **3285**

HANDS ON (RABUN GAP, GA.) (US) [08191326] 2920, **1749**

HANDWERK IM LANDE NORDRHEIN-WESTFALEN, DAS (GW/0300-1059) [01784704] **679**

HANDWOVEN (US/0198-8212) [06758062] 5184, **5351**

HANDY APPRAISAL CHART (US/0891-2254) [04710285] **616**

HANDY POCKET DIRECTORY OF TELEVISION STATIONS IN OPERATION (US) [11451717] **1132**

HANDY-WHITMAN INDEX OF PUBLIC UTILITY CONSTRUCTION COSTS. BULLETIN, THE (US) [06327009] **4654**

HANFORD SENTINEL, THE (US) [27696061] **5635**

HANG-CHOU TA HSUEH HSUEH PAO. CHE HSUEH SHE HUI KO HSUEH PAN (CC) [06212489] **1827**

HANG GLIDING (US/0895-433X) [08024110] 4851, **4898**

HANG HAI (CC) [09425681] **4177**

HANG KUNG CHIH SHIH (CC/1000-0119) [08375948] **22**

HANG KUNG HSUEH PAO (CC) [10513440] **22**

HANGGONG SANOP KWA KUKPANG KYONGJE YONGU (KO) [08916424] **22**

HANGING LOOSE (US/0440-2316) [01877219] 3392, **3463**

HANGKONG DONGLI XUEBAO (CC/1000-8055) [I10008055] **22**

HANGKONG XUEBAO (CC/1000-6893) [I10006893] **22**

HANGTIAN YIXUE YU YIXUE GONGCHENG (CC/1002-0837) [I10020837] **3580**

HANGUG BUSIG HAGHOI JI (KO/0253-312X) [07862243] **1976**

HANGUG GYNNHAGHOI JI (KO/0253-651X) [05079477] **575**

HANGUG JAMSA HAGNOI JI (KO/0440-2332) [07986878] **5585**

HANGUG NUIHAG DOSEGWAN (KO/0250-9083) [05732368] **3580**

HANGUG NYENNYAN SIGRYAN HAGHOI JI (KO/0253-3154) [07930858] 2343, **4191**

HANGUG NYUJEN HAGHOI JI (KO/0254-5934) [08224063] **547**

HANGUG RAGNON HAGHOI JI (KO/0253-2980) [07930666] **195**

HANGUG SAINHWAR GWAHAG NYENGUNWEN RONCON (KO/0253-6501) [05537940] **456**

HANGUG SEMNYU GONHAGHOIJI (KO/0253-6420) [04725526] **5351**

HANGUK CHAEGYE INSAROK (KO) [08525626] **679**

HAN'GUK CHANGMUL HAKHOE See HANGUK CHANGMUL HAKHOE CHI **173**

HANGUK CHANGMUL HAKHOE CHI (KO) [03970115] **173**

HANGUK CHOJI YONGUHOE PO (KO) [12892298] **91**

HANGUK CHOLLYOK KONGSA See ELECTRIC POWER IN KOREA / KOREA ELECTRIC POWER CORPORATION **2043**

HANGUK CHONGSONYON SONDO KYOYUK YONGAM (KO) [25396657] **4388**

HANGUK CHONGWON HAKHOE CHI (KO) [10187875] **2418**

HAN'GUK CHONJA KONGOP TONGGYE YON'GAM (KO) [05711719] **2056**

HANGUK CHONJA YONGAM (KO) [11901001] **2056**

HANGUK CHONMUN HAKHOE See CEN MUN HAGHOI JI **394**

HAN'GUK CHUKSAN HAKHOE See HAN'GUK CHUKSAN HAKHOE CHI **5510**

HAN'GUK CHUKSAN HAKHOE CHI (KO/0367-5807) [04617341] **5510**

HANGUK CHUKSAN KWAHAK YONGU POGO (KO) [08605057] **5511**

● HANGUK DIJAIN CHONGNAM (KO) [26461002] **299**

HANGUK ENOJI YONGUSO HWIBO (KO) [08956847] **2155**

HANGUK HWAPYE KAGYOK TOROK / KIM IN-SIK CHO (KO) [07718785] **2781**

HANGUK ILBO (CHICAGO, ILL.) (US/0274-5801) [05540347] **5660**

HANGUK ILBO, HAWAI (US/0884-3139) [12334953] **5655**

HANGUK ILBO (HOUSTON, TEX.) (US/0744-5520) [08349296] **5750**

HAN'GUK ILBO NEW YORK PAN (US/0273-8031) [11219774] **5717**

HANGUK ILBO, ROSUENJELSU (US/0746-4312) [10037273] **5635**

HANGUK ILBO, SAEN PURANSISUKO (US/0747-8356) [10811857] **5635**

HANGUK ILBO, SOBUNGMI (US/0888-2290) [13506604] **5761**

HANGUK ILBO, TENBO (US/0884-3120) [12333712] **5643**

HANGUK IMHAKHOE See HANGUK IMHAKHOE CHI **2384**

HANGUK IMHAKHOE CHI (KO) [04901417] **2384**

HANGUK JAKMUL HAKHOE CHI (KO/0252-9777) [13565987] **173**

HAN'GUK KAEBAL YON'GU (KO) [05461430] **5195**

HANGUK KIDIKKYO CHANGNOHOE HOEBO (KO) [10474528] **5061**

HANGUK KIDOKKYO KYOHOE CHUSOROK (KO) [15870164] **5061**

HANGUK KIGYE KONGGU (KO) [11201368] **2115**

HANGUK KIGYE YONGUSO SOBO (KO) [09651970] **2115**

HANGUK KIOP CHONGNAM (KO) [17160654] **679**

HANGUK KIOP UI KYONGYONG CHIPYO (KO) [08838417] **790**

HANGUK KISUL (KO) [09265655] **5109**

HANGUK KISUL YONGUSO CHONGNAM (KO) [12094420] **5109**

HANGUK KOJON SIMPOJIUM (KO) [11171895] **2652**

HANGUK KOMI YONGUSO YONGU POGOSO (KO/1011-2014) [13077090] **5585**

HAN'GUK KOMU KONGHAKHOE See KOMU KONGHAKHOE CHI **5076**

HANGUK KONCHUNG HAKHOE CHI (KO/1011-9493) [02552980] **5609**

HAN'GUK KONCHUNG HAKKOE See HANGUK KONCHUNG HAKHOE CHI **5609**

HANGUK KUMHYONG KONGOP CHONGNAM (KO) [10509956] **4003**

HANGUK KWA KUKCHE CHONGCHI (KO) [12073099] **4523**

HANGUK KYOHOE CHUSOROK (KO) [28081793] **5061**

HAN'GUK KYONGJE SINMUN (KO/0897-697X) [17610477] **2920**

HANGUK KYOYUK (KO) [04388242] **1749**

HANGUK KYOYUK YONGU (KO) [07346148] **1749**

HANGUK KYUNHAKHOE See HANGUG GYNNHAGHOI JI **575**

HAN'GUK MISUL YON'GAM (KO) [04866581] **351**

HANGUK MULLIA HAKHOE See JOURNAL OF THE KOREAN PHYSICAL SOCIETY **4410**

HANGUK MUNHAK (KO) [01797427] **3392**

HANGUK MUNHAK PIPYONG SONJIP / HANGUK MUNHAK PYONGNONGA HYOPHOE (KO) [09093937] **3392**

HAN'GUK MUNHWA YESUL CHINHUNGWON See KOREAN CULTURE & ARTS FOUNDATION, THE **323**

HANGUK MUYOK HYOPHOE See CHANGSO MONGNOK **1551**

HAN'GUK NONGGONG HAKHOE See HAN'GUK NONGGONG HAKHOE CHI **91**

HAN'GUK NONGGONG HAKHOE CHI (KO/0253-3146) [05055546] **91**

HANGUK NONGHWA HAKHOE CHI (KO/0368-2897) [06105458] 976, **91**

HANGUK OR HAKHOE CHI (KO) [08752443] **5109**

HANGUK SA YONGU (KO) [07352621] **2652**

HAN'GUK SA YON'GU HWIBO (KO) [05135598] **2652**

HANGUK SAENGHWAHAKOE See HAN'GUK SAENGHWAHAKOE CHI **488**

HAN'GUK SAENGHWAHAKOE CHI (KO/0368-4881) [04608778] **488**

HANGUK SAHOE YONGU (KO) [10903627] **5246**

HANGUK SANGPUM CHONGNAM (KO) [07980023] **1565**

HAN'GUK SANOP UNHAENG See SANOP KISUL **5149**

HAN'GUK SIKPUM KWAHAKHOE See HAN'GUK SIKPUM KWAHAKHOE CHI **2343**

HAN'GUK SIKPUM KWAHAKHOE CHI (KO/0367-6293) [05587976] **2343**

HANGUK SIKPUM SANOP PYOLLAM (KO) [09671499] **2343**

HANGUK SINGMUL HAKHOE See SINGMUL HAKHOE CHI **528**

HANGUK SINHAK YONGUSO See ACTIVITY REPORT - KOREA THEOLOGICAL STUDY INSTITUTE **4932**

HANGUK SINMUN PANGSONG YONGAM (KO) [06836381] **2920**

HAN'GUK SOMYU KONGHAKHOE See HANGUG SEMNYU GONHAGHOIJI **5351**

HANGUK SONBAK YONGUSO See SOBO **4183**

HAN'GUK SUSAN HOKHOE See HAN-GUK SUSAN HAKHOIJI **2305**

HANGUK SUUI KONGJUNG POGON HAKHOE CHI (KO) [07959884] **5511**

HANGUK TOYANG PIRYO HAKHOE See HAN'GUK TOYANG PIRYO HAKHOE CHI **173**

HAN'GUK TOYANG PIRYO HAKHOE CHI (KO/0367-6315) [04860081] **173**

HANGUK UI CHUNGSO KIOP (KO) [07789666] **679**

HANGUK UI MUNHAK (KO) [09104155] **3393**

HANGUK UIKWAHAK : THE OFFICIAL JOURNAL OF RESEARCH INSTITUTE OF MEDICAL SCIENCE OF KOREA (KO/0379-1521) [06466193] **3580**

HAN'GUK UIRYU HAKHOE See HAN'GUK UIRYU HAKHOE CHI **1084**

HAN'GUK UIRYU HAKHOE CHI (KO) [04923776] 5351, **1084**

HANGUK UMHYANG HAKHOE CHI (KO) [08948519] 4452, **1977**

HANGUK UNGYONG KONCHUNG HAKHOE CHI (KO) [19739058] **5609**

HANGUK UNHAENG. CHOSABU See ECONOMIC STATISTICS YEARBOOK **728**

HANGUK WONYE HAKHOE See HANGUK WONYE HAKHOE CHI **2418**

HANGUK WONYE HAKHOE CHI (KO/0253-6498) [04911571] **2418**

HAN'GUK YAKCHE HAKHOE See YAKCHE HAKHOE CHI. JOURNAL OF KOREAN PHARMACEUTICAL SCIENCES **4333**

HANGUK YOK HAKHOE CHI (KO) [08672006] **3735**

HANGUK YONCHO HAKHOE CHI (KO) [07939711] **5373**

HAN'GUK YONGHWA YON'GAM (KO) [05758558] **4071**

HANGUK YONYE (KO) [07885759] **385**

HAN'GUK YOOP HAKHOE See YOOP HAKHOE CHI. JOURNAL OF THE KOREAN CERAMIC SOCIETY **2595**

HANGUK YWCA (KO) [11336197] **5558**

HANGUKHAK NONJIP (SEOUL, KOREA) (KO) [11998744] **2652**

HANGZHOU DAXUE XUEBAO. ZIRAN KEXUE BAN (CC/0253-3618) [08694220] **5109**

HANIL UNHAENG (1960-) See HANIL WOLBO **1565**

HANIL WOLBO (KO) [06570558] **1565**

HANJIE XUEBAO (CC/0253-360X) [08691063] **4027**

HANJUNG (KO) [09754756] **1608**

HANK STRAM'S PRO FOOTBALL SCOUTING REPORT (US) [24864077] **4898**

HANKINSON NEWS See RICHLAND COUNTY NEWS-MONITOR **5726**

HANNAH INSTITUTE FOR THE HISTORY OF MEDICINE See PUBLICATION OF THE HANNAH INSTITUTE FOR THE HISTORY OF MEDICINE **3631**

HANNAH RESEARCH INSTITUTE See REPORT / HANNAH RESEARCH INSTITUTE **198**

HANNOVERSCHE GEOGRAPHISCHE ARBEITEN (GW) [25357267] **2565**

HANNOVERSCHE STUDIEN UBER DEN MITTLEREN OSTEN (GW/0179-2784) [13854528] **2504**

HANNYAN NUI-DAI HAGSUR JI (KO/0254-5942) [08676513] **3580**

HANOVER. NIEDERSACHSISCHE LANDESBIBLIOTHEK.LEIBNIZ-ARCHIV See VEROFFENTLICHUNGEN DES LEIBNIZ-ARCHIVS **3540**

HANOVER POST POSTSCRIPTS, THE (CN/0847-8988) [20660689] **5786**

● HANOVER REPORT, THE (US/1065-8335) [26756901] **1608**

HANREI JIHO (JA) [12591524] **2976**

HANREI MINJI ROPPO ZENSHO / HENSHU, DAIICHI HOKI SHUPPAN KABUSHIKI KAISHA HENSHUBU (JA) [09986981] **2976**

HANREI TAIMUZU (JA) [17636407] **2976**

HANREITSUKI ROPPO ZENSHO (JA) [01784055] **2976**

HANS PFITZNER-GESELLSCHAFT See MITTEILUNGEN DER HANS PFITZNER-GESELLSCHAFT **4131**

HANSA (GW/0017-7504) [07894171] **4177**

HANSARD OFFICIAL REPORT (CJ) [07114684] **4654**

HANSARD
Alphabetical Title Index

HANSARD : OFFICIAL REPORT / LEGISLATIVE ASSEMBLY OF THE NORTHWEST TERRITORIES (CN/0713-0082) [08595080] **4654**

HANSARD OFFICIAL REPORT OF DEBATES (CN/0833-0476) [19503051] **4654**

HANSARD OFFICIAL REPORT OF DEBATES / LEGISLATIVE ASSEMBLY OF ONTARIO, STANDING COMMITTEE ON RESOURCES DEVELOPMENT (CN/0822-2193) [10465682] **4654**

HANSARD, OFFICIAL REPORT OF DEBATES / LEGISLATIVE ASSEMBLY OF ONTARIO, STANDING COMMITTEE ON SOCIAL DEVELOPMENT (CN/0822-126X) [10466845] **5246, 4654**

HANSEN REPORT ON AUTOMOTIVE ELECTRONICS, THE (US/1040-1105) [18326843] **2056**

HANSENIASE: RESUMOS E NOTICIAS. HANSENIASIS: ABSTRACTS AND NEWS (BL/0017-7512) [05720832] **4777**

HANSENOLOGIA INTERNATIONALIS (BL/0100-3283) [03148459] **3580**

HANSFORD & TILLEYS ALABAMA EQUITY (US) **2976**

HANSFORD PLAINSMAN, THE (US) [14156921] **5750**

HANSHIN KOSOKU DORO KODAN *See* HANSHIN KOSOKU DORO KODAN NEMPO **5440**

HANSHIN KOSOKU DORO KODAN NEMPO (JA) [03014191] **5440**

HANSISCHE GESCHICHTSBLATTER (GW/0073-0327) [01623679] **2690**

HANSKA HERALD, THE (US) [01587845] **5696**

HANSON REPORTER *CEASED.* (US/0747-4040) [10808176] **5688**

HANSON'S GUIDELINES (US/0739-3431) [09726422] **4212**

HANSON'S MANUAL OF EXAMINATION AND INSURANCE LAW HANDBOOK (US) [04818895] **2881, 2976**

HANVERK & INDUSTRI : ORGAN FOR NORSKE HANDVERKER OG INDUSTRIBEDRIFTERS FORBUND (NO) [20302629] **2098**

HANZAI-SHINRIGAKU KENKYU (JA/0017-7547) [I00177547] **4588**

HANZAI-SHINRIGAKU KENKYU (JA) [01790078] **3165**

HANZAIGAKU ZASSHI (JA/0302-0029) [01327021] **3740**

HAP. HEART OF AMERICA PURCHASER (US/0193-2004) [05166326] **950**

HAPPENINGS (CN/0844-5753) [20121199] **3213**

HAPPENINGS IN KAMLOOPS (CN/0225-7009) [06272652] **4851**

●HAPPENINGS IN SAN DIEGO COUNTY (US/1064-3397) [26198621] **2534**

HAPPINESS HOLDING TANK (US/0046-6832) [03289662] **3463**

HAPPY HANDS NEEDLECRAFT NEWS (US/0747-0940) [10542210] **5184**

HAPPY TIMES (US) **5016**

HAPPY WANDERER, THE (US/0195-2080) [05366727] **5479**

HAQQ (ST-LEONARD) (CN/0821-3186) [09586279] **5246**

HARALSON GATEWAY-BEACON, THE (US/0746-4169) [10029273] **5653**

HARAMATA (UK) [21470592] **91**

HARAMBEE (US) **2262**

HARARE (ZIMBABWE). DEPT. OF WORKS *See* ANNUAL REPORT OF THE DIRECTOR OF WORKS FOR THE YEAR **4628**

HARAS AL-WATANI (RIYADH, SAUDI ARABIA) (SU) [08119812] **2504**

HARAUI (PE/0440-2987) [02149751] **3463**

HARBOR SOUND, THE (US) [21432329] **5653**

HARBOUR & SHIPPING (CN/0017-7636) [02017816] **5450**

HARBOUR & SHIPPING. ANNUAL PORT ISSUE (CN) [02442991] **5450**

HARBOUR & SHIPPING. ANNUAL SHIPBUILDING EDITION (CN) [02443037] **5450**

HARBOUR & SHIPPING. ANNUAL SHIPPING DIRECTORY (CN) [02443038] **5450**

HARBOUR, HARBOR, HARBER, AND WITT, WHITT, WHIT FAMILY ASSOCIATION BULLETIN (US/0731-6968) [08209430] **2452**

HARBOUR MAGAZINE ON ART AND EVERYDAY LIFE (CN/1181-943X) [24256729] **351**

HARBUS NEWS, THE (US/0749-4882) [10270087] **869**

HARCERSTWO WARSZAWA (PL/0438-6019) [I04386019] **1064**

HARD ACT TO FOLLOW *CEASED.* (CN/0849-262X) [23598604] 1749, **2976**

HARD AND SOFT *CEASED.* (FR/0178-7586) [13832442] 2056, **1186**

HARD CHEESE (UK) [01788180] **1749**

HARD COPY OBSERVER, THE (US/1058-2444) [24242960] **1608**

HARD CRABS (US/0198-1099) [06181837] **3343**

HARD EN SOFTWARETUNING VOOR IBM PCS EN COMPATIBLES (NE) **1286**

HARD MONEY DIGEST *CEASED.* (US/8756-2413) [11500818] **790**

HARD REPORT (US) **1132**

HARD SCUFFLE. FOLIO *See* HIGH ROADS FOLIO **2534**

HARD TIMES (MERIDEN, CONN.) (US/0897-5035) [17526810] **2452**

HARDIN COUNTY HISTORICAL QUARTERLY (US/8755-6073) [10174439] **2735**

HARDIN COUNTY TIMES, THE (US) [12935746] **5670**

HARDIN FAMILY COURIER (US/0748-1888) [10897454] **2452**

HARDIN HERALD *See* BIG HORN COUNTY NEW **5705**

HARDWARE & GARDEN REVIEW (UK/0266-0539) [02660539] **2418**

HARDWARE & HOME CENTRE MAGAZINE (CN/0847-9968) [21101678] **2811**

HARDWARE MERCHANDISER (CHICAGO) *CEASED.* (US/0017-7709) [05090285] **2811**

HARDWARE MERCHANDISING (1993) (CN/1199-2786) [30714831] **2811**

HARDWARE MERCHANDISING, BUILDING SUPPLY DEALER (CN/0831-0807) [13816714] **2811**

HARDWARE, TOOL AND CUTLERY MANUFACTURERS (PRELIMINARY ED.) *CEASED.* (CN/0384-3394) [03251291] **2811**

HARDWICK GAZETTE, THE (US/0744-5512) [08349356] **5757**

HARDWOOD FLOORS (US/0897-022X) [17372041] 2900, **2401**

HARDWOOD MARKET REPORT (MEMPHIS, TENN.) (US/0888-9104) [01751766] **2401**

HARDWOOD PURCHASING HANDBOOK (US) [13588327] **2401**

HARDWOOD REVIEW EXPORT (US/1063-9322) [26187477] **2401**

HAREFUAH (IS/0017-7768) [02945149] **3580**

HARFORD HISTORICAL BULLETIN (US/0741-7802) [10118329] **2452**

HARGROVE NEWSLETTER, THE (US/0737-4798) [09359687] **2452**

HARLAN DAILY ENTERPRISE, THE (US/1041-7109) [15153136] **5680**

HARLAN FOOTPRINTS (US/0894-8925) [14056159] **2452**

HARLAN NEWS-ADVERTISER (US) [17109654] **5670**

HARLAN TRIBUNE, THE (US) [17109655] **5670**

HARLEM NEWS (HARLEM, MONT. : 1908) (US) [13811753] **5705**

HARLEM VALLEY TIMES (US) [17456971] **5717**

HARLEQUIN WORLD'S BEST ROMANCES (US/1183-5044) [23819696] **5074**

HARLEY WOMEN (US/0893-6447) [15626427] **4851**

HARLINGEN STATE CHEST HOSPITAL *See* AUDIT REPORT, HARLINGEN STATE CHEST HOSPITAL **3777**

HARLO'S ANTHOLOGY OF MODERN-DAY POETS AND AUTHORS *See* POETS AND AUTHORS **3424**

HARLOW REPORT, GEOGRAPHIC INFORMATION SYSTEMS, THE (US/1043-6146) [19301277] **869**

HARLOW'S WOODEN MAN (US/0887-5448) [10243931] **2617**

HARMON MEMORIAL LECTURES IN MILITARY HISTORY, THE (US/0073-0394) [01803956] **4045**

HARMONICA HAPPENINGS (US/0270-0832) [06323817] **4120**

HARMONICA HORIZONS (US) [22933361] **4120**

HARMONICA HOSPITAL NEWSLETTER (US) [21378234] **4120**

HARMONIE-QUEBEC : BULLETIN OFFICIEL, FEDERATION DES HARMONIES DU QUEBEC (CN/0713-8059) [08996232] **4120**

HARMONIE SYNDICALE, L' (CN/0319-4132) [02442847] **1676**

HARMONIKA INTERNATIONAL (GW) [20511769] **4120**

HARMONISATIERAAD WELZIJNSBELEID (NETHERLANDS) *See* JAARVERSLAG - HARMONISATIERAAD WELZIJNSBELEID **5291**

HARMONIZED TARIFF SCHEDULE OF THE UNITED STATES (US/1066-0925) [17427157] 2976, **4730**

HARMONIZER (KENOSHA, WIS.), THE (US/0017-7849) [04081198] **4120**

HARMONY (OTTAWA) (CN/1183-0077) [24256452] **2173**

HARNESS HANDBOOK, THE (US/1045-2648) [20074287] **2799**

HARNESS HORSEMEN INTERNATIONAL (US/0164-3703) [04635758] **2799**

HARNESS WORLD (CN/0381-7695) [03219718] **2799**

HARNETT COUNTY NEWS (US/8750-023X) [10916277] **5723**

HARO CHOSA HOKOKUSHO (JA) [10632440] **1449**

HAROLD L. LYON ARBORETUM *See* HAROLD L. LYON ARBORETUM LECTURE **456**

HAROLD L. LYON ARBORETUM LECTURE (US/0091-7079) [03299970] **456**

HARPA (SZ/1017-1142) [25002599] **4120**

HARPER HERALD (HARPER, TEX. 1917), THE (US/1040-6514) [14265203] **5750**

HARPERS & QUEEN (UK) [11825442] **5558**

HARPER'S BAZAAR (US/0017-7873) [01639362] **1085**

HARPERS BAZAAR COLLEZIONI (IT) **2488**

HARPER'S BAZAAR EN ESPANOL (US/0890-9598) [14473211] **1085**

HARPER'S BAZAAR ITALIA (IT/1121-7375) [I11217375] 5558, **1085**

HARPER'S BIOCHEMISTRY (US/1043-9811) [16965251] **488**

HARPERS DIRECTORY (UK) [05057800] **2367**

HARPERS DIRECTORY AND MANUAL *See* HARPERS DIRECTORY **2367**

HARPER'S (NEW YORK, N.Y.) (US/0017-789X) [04532730] **3343**

HARPERS WINE AND SPIRIT GAZETTE (UK/0017-7903) [01620099] **2367**

HARPETH GLEANINGS (US/0732-0396) [08269526] **2735**

●HARPIES & QUINES (UK/0966-2995) [I09662995] **5558**

HARPOON (BUFFALO, N.Y.) *See* AMERICAN HARPOON, THE **2527**

HARPOON (BUFFALO, N.Y.) (US/1060-6688) [25053317] **4862**

HARPSICHORD AND FORTEPIANO MAGAZINE, THE (UK) [17157579] **4120**

HARRIMAN INSTITUTE FORUM, THE (US/0896-114X) [16914734] **2690**

HARRINGTON JOURNAL, THE (US/0747-0975) [10545890] **5647**

HARRIS AUCTION GALLERIES *See* COLLECTORS' AUCTION (BALTIMORE) **4087**

HARRIS BANK ... ANNUAL RETAIL STUDY (US) [24594458] **955**

HARRIS COUNTY REAL ESTATE REPORT (US) **4838**

HARRIS FAMILY NEWSLETTER, THE (US/0737-478X) [09359634] **2452**

●HARRIS GEORGIA MANUFACTURERS DIRECTORY (US/1065-4755) [26612664] **3480**

HARRIS ILLINOIS INDUSTRIAL DIRECTORY (US/0734-3256) [10513663] **1608**

HARRIS INDIANA INDUSTRIAL DIRECTORY (US/0888-8175) [10035224] **1608**

HARRIS KENTUCKY INDUSTRIAL DIRECTORY (US/0887-4255) [13221354] **1608**

●HARRIS MANUFACTURERS DIRECTORY (NATIONAL ED.) (US/1061-2076) [25215171] **3480**

●HARRIS MANUFACTURERS DIRECTORY (NORTHEAST ED.) (US/1061-2041) [25215358] **3480**

●HARRIS MANUFACTURERS DIRECTORY (SOUTHEAST ED.) (US/1061-2033) [25215326] **3480**

●HARRIS MANUFACTURERS DIRECTORY (SOUTHWEST ED.), THE (US/1061-2068) [25215403] **3480**

●HARRIS MANUFACTURERS DIRECTORY (WEST & SOUTHWEST ED.) (US/1061-205X) [25215380] **3480**

HARRIS MARYLAND INDUSTRIAL DIRECTORY *CEASED.* (US/1055-5617) [23235914] **1608**

●HARRIS MARYLAND MANUFACTURERS DIRECTORY (US/1065-7231) [26708785] **3480**

HARRIS MICHIGAN INDUSTRIAL DIRECTORY (TWINSBURG, OHIO: 1984) (US/0888-8167) [10509171] **1608**

HARVARD

●HARRIS NORTH CAROLINA MANUFACTURERS DIRECTORY (US/1065-4720) [26612567] **3480**

HARRIS OHIO INDUSTRIAL DIRECTORY (US/0888-8140) [10292927] **1608**

HARRIS OHIO SERVICES DIRECTORY *CEASED.* (US/0894-296X) [15985478] **1608**

HARRIS PENNSYLVANIA INDUSTRIAL DIRECTORY (US/0734-8541) [08741578] **1608**

HARRIS POLL, THE (US/0895-7983) [16809487] **5246**

●HARRIS SOUTH CAROLINA MANUFACTURERS DIRECTORY (US/1065-4747) [26612628] **3480**

HARRIS SURVEY YEARBOOK OF PUBLIC OPINION, THE (US/0085-1442) [01751783] **5246**

HARRIS WEST VIRGINIA MANUFACTURING DIRECTORY (US/0887-4247) [13221546] **3480**

HARRISON DAILY TIMES (US) [18545584] **5631**

HARRISON HERITAGE (US/0740-9001) [10012430] **2452**

HARRISON INDEPENDENT (US/0892-4163) [09579690] **5717**

HARRISON NEWS-HERALD (US/1043-4992) [17460364] **5728**

HARRISON POST, THE (US) [11421451] **5664**

HARRISONBURG DAILY NEWS RECORD (US) **5758**

HARRISONBURG-ROCKINGHAM HISTORICAL SOCIETY NEWSLETTER (US/1064-6043) [21222589] **2736**

HARRISONS INLAND REVENUE (UK) **4730**

HARRISON'S INLAND REVENUE. INDEX TO TAX CASES (UK) **4730**

HARRISTON REVIEW, THE (CN/0381-0283) [02417281] **5786**

HARRODSBURG HERALD, THE (US) [13800327] **5680**

HARROWSMITH (CANADIAN ED.) (CN/0381-6885) [02979214] **2534**

HARROWSMITH COUNTRY LIFE (US/1049-4618) [21244654] **2534**

HARRY BROWNE'S SPECIAL REPORTS (US) [08547031] **900**

●HARSH MISTRESS (US/1070-6569) [28444494] **3393**

HART BEAT, THE (US/0892-239X) [15127383] **5750**

HART BULLETIN (NE/0301-8202) [06342544] **3705**

HART COUNTY NEWS-HERALD (US/1075-4628) [20314136] **5680**

HARTFORD ADVOCATE (US/0192-8503) [05119845] **5645**

HARTFORD AGENT. A JOURNAL OF FIRE INSURANCE, THE (US/0017-7962) [01805486] **2881**

HARTFORD "AREA" NEWS, THE (US/8750-7714) [11747796] **5743**

HARTFORD CITY NEWS-TIMES (US) [13454462] **5664**

HARTFORD COURANT, THE (US/1047-4153) [08807834] **5645**

HARTFORD MONTHLY (US/0897-7534) [17617018] **2534**

HARTFORD NEWS-HERALD, THE (US) [11828156] **5626**

HARTLEPOOL MAIL (UK) **5812**

HARTLEY SENTINEL, THE (US) [16719876] **5670**

HARTMANS TIJDSCHRIFT TER BEOEFENING VAN HET ADMINISTRATIEF RECHT *See* HARTMANS TIJDSCHRIFT VOOR STUDERENDEN OPENBAAR BESTUUR **3093**

HARTMANS TIJDSCHRIFT VOOR STUDERENDEN OPENBAAR BESTUUR (NE) [07419003] **3093**

HART'S PETROLEUM PROFESSIONALS (ROCKY MOUNTAIN ED.) *CEASED.* (US/0884-3007) [12303606] **4259**

HARTSELLE ENQUIRER, THE (US) [09191210] **5626**

HARTSVILLE MESSENGER, THE (US/8750-3972) [11377921] **5742**

HARTSVILLE VIDETTE, THE (US/0891-169X) [14709089] **5745**

HARTUNG & KARL *See* AUKTION **377**

HARTVILLE NEWS, THE (US/0746-8016) [10307077] **5728**

HARVARD ADVOCATE (CAMBRIDGE, MASS.), THE (US/0017-8004) [08158155] **3393**

HARVARD AIDS INSTITUTE SERIES ON GENE REGULATION OF HUMAN RETROVIRUSES (US/1063-0627) [24726518] 3713, **3670**

HARVARD ALUMNI ASSOCIATION *See* DIRECTORY OF CLUB OFFICERS **1101**

HARVARD ALUMNI DIRECTORY (US/0895-1683) [06574718] **1102**

HARVARD ARCHITECTURE REVIEW, THE *CEASED.* (US/0194-3650) [05384482] **299**

HARVARD ARMENIAN TEXTS AND STUDIES (US/0073-0459) [01607732] **2652**

HARVARD BELGIUM REVIEW (BE) **2517**

HARVARD BLACKLETTER JOURNAL, THE (US/0897-2761) [12934319] 2262, **4508**

HARVARD BOOKS IN BIOLOGY (US/0073-0467) [01807275] **456**

HARVARD BOOKS IN BIOPHYSICS (US/0073-0475) [01807327] **495**

HARVARD BUSINESS REVIEW (US/0017-8012) [01751795] 1565, **679**

HARVARD BUSINESS REVIEW (NE/0168-9444) [13854376] **1565**

HARVARD BUSINESS REVIEW (US/0017-8012) [03527639] 1565, **679**

HARVARD BUSINESS REVIEW CATALOG (US) [17791653] 1565, **679**

HARVARD BUSINESS SCHOOL BULLETIN (US/0017-8020) [03790464] **679**

HARVARD BUSINESS SCHOOL CAREER GUIDE (US) **679**

HARVARD BUSINESS SCHOOL CATALOG OF TEACHING MATERIALS (US/1042-654X) [18386089] **679**

HARVARD BUSINESS SCHOOL CORE COLLECTION (US/1044-2111) [19722094] **416**

HARVARD CASE HISTORIES IN EXPERIMENTAL SCIENCE (US) [01751796] **5109**

HARVARD CITY PLANNING STUDIES (US) [01751797] **2823**

HARVARD CIVIL RIGHTS-CIVIL LIBERTIES LAW REVIEW (US/0017-8039) [01751798] **4508**

HARVARD CLASS OF 1970 ANNIVERSARY REPORT (US/0361-7416) [02246703] **1827**

HARVARD COLLEGE ECONOMIST (US/0197-7636) [04562971] **1493**

HARVARD CRIMSON, THE (US) [06324327] **5688**

HARVARD DENTAL BULLETIN (US/1062-029X) [23465257] **1324**

HARVARD - DEUSTO BUSINESS REVIEW (SP/0210-900X) [I0210900X] **679**

HARVARD DIVINITY BULLETIN (US/0017-8047) [01774962] **4962**

HARVARD DIVINITY SCHOOL *See* HARVARD DIVINITY BULLETIN **4962**

HARVARD DIVINITY SCHOOL *See* ALUMNI/AE DIRECTORY / HARVARD DIVINITY SCHOOL **1097**

HARVARD EAST ASIAN MONOGRAPHS (US/0073-0483) [01751799] **2652**

HARVARD EAST ASIAN SERIES (US/0073-0491) [01936607] **2652**

HARVARD EDUCATION LETTER, THE (US/8755-3716) [11274478] **1749**

HARVARD EDUCATIONAL REVIEW (US/0017-8055) [07514547] **1749**

HARVARD EDUCATIONAL REVIEW (US/0017-8055) [01587741] **1749**

HARVARD EDUCATIONAL REVIEW. REPRINT SERIES (US/0362-8027) [01695215] **1750**

HARVARD ENGLISH STUDIES (US/0073-0513) [01809244] **3393**

HARVARD HEALTH LETTER (US/1052-1577) [22200621] **3580**

HARVARD HEART LETTER (US/1051-5313) [21985672] **3705**

HARVARD HERALD, THE (US) [08813886] **5660**

HARVARD HISTORICAL MONOGRAPHS (US/0073-0521) [01751803] **2617**

HARVARD HISTORICAL STUDIES (US/0073-053X) [01751804] **2617**

HARVARD HUMAN RIGHTS JOURNAL (US/1057-5057) [21743088] **4508**

HARVARD INDEPENDENT, THE (US) [09369698] **1092**

HARVARD INSTITUTE OF ECONOMIC RESEARCH DISCUSSION PAPERS (US) **1493**

HARVARD INTERNATIONAL LAW JOURNAL (US/0017-8063) [01796621] 4523, **3128**

HARVARD INTERNATIONAL REVIEW (US/0739-1854) [07942267] 1635, **4523**

HARVARD IRANIAN SERIES (US) [01810717] **1827**

HARVARD JOURNAL OF ASIATIC STUDIES (US/0073-0548) [01607880] 3393, **2652**

HARVARD JOURNAL OF HISPANIC POLICY (US/1074-1917) [29355926] **2262**

HARVARD JOURNAL OF LAW & PUBLIC POLICY (US/0193-4872) [04301245] **2976**

HARVARD JOURNAL OF LAW & TECHNOLOGY (US/0897-3393) [17465343] 5109, **2976**

●HARVARD JOURNAL OF WORLD AFFAIRS : AN INTERNATIONAL POLICY FORUM OF THE JOHN F. KENNEDY SCHOOL OF GOVERNMENT (US) [26348041] **4523**

HARVARD JOURNAL ON LEGISLATION (US/0017-808X) [01624014] **2977**

HARVARD JUDAIC MONOGRAPHS (US) [06404450] **5048**

HARVARD LAMPOON, THE (US) [01751806] **1092**

HARVARD LAW RECORD (US/0017-8101) [09093740] **2977**

HARVARD LAW REVIEW (US/0017-811X) [01751808] **2977**

HARVARD LAW SCHOOL *See* PAPERS USED AT THE ANNUAL EXAMINATIONS IN LAW HELD AT HARVARD UNIVERSITY **3024**

HARVARD LAW SCHOOL. EAST ASIAN LEGAL STUDIES PROGRAM *See* EALS NEWSLETTER : THE NEWSLETTER OF THE EAST ASIAN LEGAL STUDIES PROGRAM AT HARVARD LAW SCHOOL **2965**

HARVARD, L'EXPANSION (FR/0397-5495) [I03975495] **869**

HARVARD L'EXPANSION / LA REVUE DES RESPONSABLES *See* EXPANSION MANAGEMENT REVIEW, L' **867**

HARVARD LIBRARIAN, THE (US/0073-0564) [02242395] **3213**

HARVARD LIBRARY BULLETIN (US/0017-8136) [01751811] **3213**

HARVARD MAGAZINE (US/0095-2427) [01788529] **1092**

HARVARD MANAGER (GW) **869**

HARVARD MEDICAL ALUMNI BULLETIN (US/0191-7757) [03527383] 3580, **1102**

HARVARD MENTAL HEALTH LETTER, THE (US/1057-5022) [22636797] 4588, **3926**

HARVARD MIDDLE EASTERN STUDIES (US) [01642411] **2768**

HARVARD MONOGRAPHS IN THE HISTORY OF SCIENCE (US) [01815773] **5109**

HARVARD PAPERS IN BOTANY (US/1043-4534) [19475908] **512**

HARVARD POLITICAL REVIEW (US/0090-1032) [01784689] **4475**

HARVARD PUBLICATIONS IN MUSIC (US/0073-0629) [01816073] **4120**

HARVARD RADCLIFFE SCIENCE REVIEW *See* HARVARD SCIENCE REVIEW (1992) **5109**

HARVARD REVIEW (US) **3393**

HARVARD REVIEW OF PHILOSOPHY, THE (US/1062-6239) [25557273] **4347**

●HARVARD REVIEW OF PSYCHIATRY (US/1067-3229) [27190882] **3926**

●HARVARD SCIENCE REVIEW (1992) (US/1062-7022) [25376755] **5109**

HARVARD SEMITIC MONOGRAPHS (US/0073-0637) [01589503] **5016**

HARVARD SEMITIC STUDIES (US/0147-9342) [03254747] **5048**

HARVARD STUDENT AGENCIES *See* LET'S GO: THE BUDGET GUIDE TO BRITAIN AND IRELAND **5482**

HARVARD STUDENT AGENCIES *See* LET'S GO: THE BUDGET GUIDE TO FRANCE **5482**

HARVARD STUDIES IN BUSINESS HISTORY (US/0073-067X) [01751818] **679**

HARVARD STUDIES IN CLASSICAL PHILOLOGY (US/0073-0688) [01696996] 3285, **1077**

HARVARD STUDIES IN COMPARATIVE LITERATURE (US/0073-0696) [01751819] **3393**

HARVARD STUDIES IN ROMANCE LANGUAGES (US/0073-0718) [01680761] **3393**

HARVARD STUDIES IN TECHNOLOGY AND SOCIETY (US) [01819880] **5109**

HARVARD STUDIES IN URBAN HISTORY (US) [01820007] **2823**

HARVARD TEACHERS' NETWORK *See* TEACHERS' NETWORK NEWSLETTER **1906**

HARVARD THEOLOGICAL REVIEW, THE (US/0017-8160) [01535398] **4962**

HARVARD THEOLOGICAL STUDIES (US/0073-0726) [01589376] **4962**

HARVARD

Alphabetical Title Index

HARVARD TODAY (US/0017-8179) [02244596] **1827**

HARVARD UKRAINIAN STUDIES (US/0363-5570) [03011268] 3285, **2690**

HARVARD UNIVERSITY *See* FUND AND GIFT SUPPLEMENT TO THE FINANCIAL REPORT FOR THE FISCAL YEAR **1825**

HARVARD UNIVERSITY *See* DIRECTORY OF STUDENTS - HARVARD UNIVERSITY **1821**

HARVARD UNIVERSITY. ART MUSEUMS *See* HARVARD UNIVERSITY ART MUSEUMS REVIEW **4088**

●HARVARD UNIVERSITY ART MUSEUMS BULLETIN (US/1065-6448) [26662122] **351**

●HARVARD UNIVERSITY ART MUSEUMS REVIEW (US/1065-819X) [25721996] 352, **4088**

HARVARD UNIVERSITY. BLACK ROCK FOREST. CORNWALL, NEW YORK *See* BULLETIN - HARVARD UNIVERSITY. BLACK ROCK FOREST. CORNWALL, NEW YORK **1813**

HARVARD UNIVERSITY. CENTER FOR THE STUDY OF WORLD RELIGIONS *See* BULLETIN - CENTER FOR THE STUDY OF WORLD RELIGIONS, HARVARD UNIVERSITY **4940**

HARVARD UNIVERSITY. CLASS OF 1936 *See* REPORT - HARVARD UNIVERSITY. CLASS OF 1936 **1844**

HARVARD UNIVERSITY. CLASS OF 1959 *See* REPORT - HARVARD COLLEGE, CLASS OF 1959 **1844**

HARVARD UNIVERSITY. CLASS OF 1970 *See* HARVARD CLASS OF 1970 ANNIVERSARY REPORT **1827**

HARVARD UNIVERSITY. CLASS OF 1971 *See* ANNIVERSARY REPORT - HARVARD COLLEGE, CLASS OF 1971 **1808**

HARVARD UNIVERSITY. EAST ASIAN RESEARCH CENTER *See* PEOPLE'S REPUBLIC OF CHINA BIOGRAPHICAL APPEARANCES **4673**

HARVARD UNIVERSITY. FACULTY OF ARTS AND SCIENCES *See* PAPERS PRINTED FOR MID-YEAR EXAMINATIONS. SECTION 2. MATHEMATICS, SCIENCES **3526**

HARVARD UNIVERSITY GAZETTE (US/0364-7692) [02204435] **1092**

HARVARD UNIVERSITY. JACOB WERTHEIM RESEARCH FELLOWSHIP *See* PUBLICATIONS IN INDUSTRIAL RELATIONS **1704**

HARVARD UNIVERSITY. LIBRARY *See* HARVARD LIBRARY BULLETIN **3213**

HARVARD UNIVERSITY. MUSEUM OF COMPARATIVE ZOOLOGY *See* ANNUAL REPORT - HARVARD UNIVERSITY. MUSEUM OF COMPARATIVE ZOOLOGY **5576**

HARVARD UNIVERSITY. MUSEUM OF COMPARATIVE ZOOLOGY. DEPT. OF MOLLUSKS *See* OCCASIONAL PAPERS ON MOLLUSKS **5593**

HARVARD UNIVERSITY. UNIVERSITY LABORATORY OF PHYSICAL CHEMISTRY RELATED TO MEDICINE AND PUBLIC HEALTH *See* MEMOIRS - HARVARD UNIVERSITY / UNIVERSITY LABORATORY OF PHYSICAL CHEMISTRY **1055**

●HARVARD WOMEN'S HEALTH WATCH (US/1070-910X) [28490541] 5558, **3762**

HARVARD WOMEN'S LAW JOURNAL (US/0270-1456) [03967304] 5558, **2977**

HARVEST (DACCA, BANGLADESH) (BG) [07995825] **3285**

HARVEST (EDMONTON) (CN/0226-1499) [06273118] **3165**

HARVEST (FARMINGTON) (US/0362-7888) [01840359] **3393**

HARVEST FIELD MINISTRIES : NEWSLETTER (CN/0848-9386) [21664707] **4962**

HARVEST (PORT MORESBY) (PP/0378-8865) [04922816] **91**

HARVEST QUARTERLY (US/0146-5414) [02957474] **5246**

HARVEST STATES JOURNAL (US/8756-8845) [09766819] **202**

HARVEST, THE (US) [02250701] **5061**

HARVEST TODAY (US) [08550454] **91**

HARVESTER *See* AWARE **4937**

HARVESTER, THE (UK/0017-8217) [01781017] **5017**

●HARVEY COUNTY INDEPENDENT, THE (US/1065-3740) [26595849] **5676**

HARVEY INDUSTRIAL RELATIONS EMPLOYMENT LAW SERVICE (UK) **3148**

HARVEY INDUSTRIAL RELATIONS EMPLOYMENT LAW SERVICE (UK) 2977, **1676**

HARVEY LECTURES, THE (US/0073-0874) [01751852] **3580**

HARVEY STAR-TRIBUNE *See* STAR (HARVEY-MARKHAM AREA ED.), THE **5662**

HARYANA *See* NEW EXPENDITURE **4738**

HARYANA AGRICULTURAL UNIVERSITY *See* HARYANA AGRICULTURAL UNIVERSITY JOURNAL OF RESEARCH **91**

HARYANA AGRICULTURAL UNIVERSITY JOURNAL OF RESEARCH (II/0367-5610) [03251857] 5511, **91**

HARYANA BUDGET AT A GLANCE (II) [05174801] **4730**

HARYANA. ECONOMIC AND STATISTICAL ORGANISATION *See* ECONOMIC SURVEY OF HARYANA **1558**

HARYANA. ECONOMIC AND STATISTICAL ORGANISATION *See* STATISTICAL ABSTRACT OF PUBLIC FINANCE OF HARYANA STATE **4699**

HARYANA. FINANCE DEPT *See* HARYANA BUDGET AT A GLANCE **4730**

HARYANA JOURNAL OF AGRONOMY (II) [14160534] **91**

HARYANA JOURNAL OF HORTICULTURAL SCIENCES (II) [01730851] **2418**

HARYANA REVIEW (II/0440-4106) [01696467] **5479**

HARYANA VETERINARIAN, THE (II) [01716977] **5511**

HASAD (IS) [06832083] **2504**

HASAD AL-SHAHR (US/0749-6540) [11146383] **2488**

HASIL-HASIL RAPAT KERDJA KESEHATAN NASIONAL (IO/0216-9053) [07371605] **4777**

HASIL HASIL RAPAT LENGKAP BADAN KERJA SAMA PERGURUAN TINGGI NEGERI INDONESIA BAGIAN TIMUR (IO) [04518661] **1827**

HASIL PENELITIAN USAHA PETERNAKAN DI D.K.I. JAKARTA (IO) [04985604] **1608**

HASIL PENENELITIAN I.E. PENELITIAN KESEJAHTERAAN SOSIAL ANAK / KANTOR STATISTIK PROPINSI DKI JAKARTA (IO) [09755006] **5287**

HASIL RAPAT KERJA DEPARTEMEN PERINDUSTRIAN (IO) [03498203] **1565**

HASIL RAPAT-KERJA DIREKTORAT JENDERAL PERINDUSTRIAN PENERBANGAN (IO) [01797877] **22**

HASIL SURVEY PERGURUAN TINGGI DKI JAKARTA (IO) [04739954] **1827**

HASKELL COUNTY MONITOR-CHIEF, THE (US) [11634027] **5676**

HASKELL FREE PRESS, THE (US) [14156759] **5750**

HASKINS SOCIETY JOURNAL, THE (UK) [21984031] **2690**

HASLO OGRODNICZE (PL) [02111808] **2418**

HASSADEH (IS/0017-8314) [04026092] **91**

HASSADEH QUARTERLY : ISRAELI REVIEW OF AGRICULTURE (IS) [25396646] **91**

HASSELBLAD FORUM (SW/0282-5449) [13087840] **4370**

HASTINGS CENTER *See* RECENT ACTIVITIES - HASTINGS CENTER **2253**

HASTINGS CENTER *See* HASTINGS CENTER REPORT, THE **3580**

HASTINGS CENTER REPORT, THE (US/0093-0334) [02241292] 2250, **3580**

HASTINGS COMMUNICATIONS AND ENTERTAINMENT LAW JOURNAL (COMM/ENT) (US/1061-6578) [23676569] **2977**

HASTINGS CONSTITUTIONAL LAW QUARTERLY (US/0094-5617) [01606931] **3093**

HASTINGS DAILY TRIBUNE (US) [22718029] **5706**

HASTINGS HERALD (SPOKANE, WASH.) (US/0898-543X) [13233137] **2452**

HASTINGS INTERNATIONAL AND COMPARATIVE LAW REVIEW (US/0149-9246) [03424187] **3129**

HASTINGS LAW JOURNAL (US/0017-8322) [01586521] **2977**

HASTINGS STAR GAZETTE (US) [21400591] **5696**

HASTINGS WOMEN'S LAW JOURNAL (US/1061-0901) [19650978] **2977**

HATABAKO KENKYU (JA) [03022422] **5373**

HATARAKU HIROBA (JA) [05671732] **4388**

HATCHER REVIEW, THE (UK/0309-5118) [05087663] **2690**

HATCHERY PRODUCTION. SUMMARY (US/8755-2973) [11119006] **212**

HATCHERY REVIEW / REVUE SUR LES COUVOIRS (CN) [09455146] **212**

HATCHET (US/0017-8357) [04094479] **1102**

HATTATSU SHOGAI KENKYUJO *See* HATTATSU SHOGAI KENKYUJO NEMPO **547**

HATTATSU SHOGAI KENKYUJO NEMPO (JA/0303-0377) [01797142] **547**

HATTEN TOJO KOKU NO TOKEI SHIRYO MOKUROKU (JA/0301-9837) [01784058] **416**

HATTEN TOJOKOKU KEIZAI TOKEI YORAN (JA) [01790101] **1565**

HATTIESBURG AMERICAN (US) [10363305] **5700**

HATTON FREE PRESS (US) [01607923] **5725**

HATTORI SHOKUBUTSU KENKYUJO HOKOKU (JA/0073-0912) [02949410] **512**

HATTORI SHOKUBUTSU KENKYUSHO *See* HATTORI SHOKUBUTSU KENKYUJO HOKOKU **512**

HAUBENMACHER, DIE (GW) [03802998] **2452**

HAUPPAGE NEWS (US/8750-1023) [10988669] **5717**

HAUPTVERBAND DER OSTERREICHISCHEN SPARKASSEN *See* JAHRESBERICHT - HAUPTVERBAND DER OSTERREICHISCHEN SPARKASSEN **793**

HAUS, DAS (GW) [24232085] **2900**

HAUS TECH (SZ) [20403346] **616**

HAUSFRAU, MONATSSCHRIFT FUR DIE FRAUENWELT AMERIKAS, DIE (US/0017-842X) [03058772] **2517**

HAUSTECHNISCHE RUNDSCHAU (GW/0017-8438) [10258163] **616**

HAUSTEX (GW/0343-6853) **5351**

HAUSWIRTSCHAFT UND WISSENSCHAFT (GW/0017-8454) [01751864] **2790**

HAUT PARLEUR / JOURNAL DE VULGARISATION (FR) **3285**

HAUTARZT (GW/0017-8470) [01751865] **3720**

HAUTE-FIDELITE *See* HI-FI **5317**

HAUTES ETUDES ISLAMIQUES ET ORIENTALES D'HISTOIRE COMPAREE (SZ/0073-0947) [02086749] **2652**

HAUTES ETUDES MEDIEVALES ET MODERNES (SZ/0073-0955) [01848281] **2690**

HAUTES ETUDES ORIENTALES (SZ/0073-0971) [02086522] **2652**

HAVANA. BIBLIOTECA NACIONAL "JOSE MARTI." *See* REVISTA DE LA BIBLIOTECA NACIONAL JOSE MARTI **3246**

HAVANA HERALD (US) **5649**

HAVE YOU HEARD? (US) **4553**

HAVELOCK CITIZEN (CN/0382-0017) [02624981] **5786**

HAVELOCK PROGRESS, THE (US/0747-1149) [10552119] **5723**

HAVERSACK (TICONDEROGA, N.Y. 1991), THE (US/1062-340X) [25589688] **2736**

HAVING A BABY (US/1049-2402) [21183176] **2280**

HAVRE (CHANDLER) (CN/0226-6407) [06562497] **5786**

HAWAII *See* WORKERS' COMPENSATION LAW OF THE STATE OF HAWAII **3155**

HAWAII AGRICULTURAL STATISTICS SERVICE *See* HAWAII CHICKENS & EGGS **212**

HAWAII ANNUAL ECONOMIC REPORT (US/1043-6685) [12026420] **1565**

HAWAII AQUACULTURE (US) [26628419] 457, **2305**

HAWAII ARCHITECT (US/0191-8311) [04965737] **299**

HAWAII ARTS MONTHLY : A PUBLICATION OF HAWAII PUBLIC RADIO (US/1059-678X) [24676278] **321**

HAWAII BAR JOURNAL (1992) (US/1063-1585) [25909222] **2977**

HAWAII BAR JOURNAL MICROFORM (US) [07892648] **2977**

HAWAII BAR NEWS (HAWAII STATE BAR ASSOCIATION) *See* HAWAII BAR JOURNAL (1992) **2977**

HAWAII BEVERAGE GUIDE (US/0017-8543) [09764865] **2367**

HAWAII BUSINESS (US/0440-5056) [04844792] **679**

HAWAII BUSINESS DIRECTORY (US) [03111126] **679**

HAWAII CHICKENS & EGGS (US) [25480520] **212**

HAWAII COASTAL ZONE MANAGEMENT PROGRAM *See* ANNUAL REPORT / HAWAII COASTAL ZONE MANAGEMENT PROGRAM **2814**

HAWAII. COMMISSION ON AGING See REPORT OF ACHIEVEMENTS OF PROGRAMS FOR THE AGING **5305**

HAWAII. COMMISSION ON JUDICIAL DISCIPLINE See ANNUAL REPORT OF THE COMMISSION ON JUDICIAL DISCIPLINE, STATE OF HAWAII (FOR PERIOD JUNE 1, ... TO JUNE 30, ...) **3139**

HAWAII COMMUNITY DEVELOPMENT AUTHORITY See ANNUAL REPORT **2814**

HAWAII CRIMINAL JUSTICE STATISTICAL ANALYSIS CENTER. UNIFORM CRIME REPORTING DIVISION See CRIME IN HAWAII **3080**

HAWAII DENTAL JOURNAL (US/0891-9933) [10977703] **1324**

HAWAII. DEPARTMENT OF LABOR AND INDUSTRIAL RELATIONS See ANNUAL REPORT OF THE DEPARTMENT OF LABOR AND INDUSTRIAL RELATIONS, STATE OF HAWAII **1649**

HAWAII. DEPT. OF AGRICULTURE See ANNUAL REPORT / DEPARTMENT OF AGRICULTURE **60**

HAWAII. DEPT. OF EDUCATION See ANNUAL PROGRAM PLAN AMENDMENT FOR PART B OF THE EDUCATION OF THE HANDICAPPED ACT AS AMENDED BY PUBLIC LAW 94-142 **1875**

HAWAII. DEPT. OF EDUCATION See EDUCATIONAL DIRECTORY. STATE & DISTRICT OFFICES (HONOLULU) **1741**

HAWAII. DEPT. OF EDUCATION. DIRECTORY - STATE OF HAWAII, DEPARTMENT OF EDUCATION See EDUCATIONAL DIRECTORY. STATE & DISTRICT OFFICES (HONOLULU) **1741**

HAWAII. DEPT. OF HEALTH See POPULATION MOBILITY IN HAWAII **4557**

HAWAII. DEPT. OF LABOR AND INDUSTRIAL RELATIONS. RESEARCH AND STATISTICS OFFICE See LABOR FORCE STATISTICS (HONOLULU) **1535**

HAWAII. DEPT. OF PLANNING AND ECONOMIC DEVELOPMENT See STATE OF HAWAII DATA BOOK **5339**

HAWAII. DEPT. OF PLANNING AND ECONOMIC DEVELOPMENT See MILITARY PERSONNEL AND DEPENDENTS IN HAWAII **4062**

HAWAII. DEPT. OF SOCIAL SERVICES AND HOUSING See PROPOSED COMPREHENSIVE ANNUAL SERVICE PROGRAM PLAN FOR THE STATE OF HAWAII **5302**

HAWAII. DIVISION OF WATER AND LAND DEVELOPMENT See CIRCULAR - STATE OF HAWAII, DEPARTMENT OF LAND AND NATURAL RESOURCES, DIVISION OF WATER AND LAND DEVELOPMENT **1413**

HAWAII FACTS AND FIGURES **CEASED.** (US) [09317730] **5328**

HAWAII. FEDERAL-STATE MARKET NEWS SERVICE See HONOLULU PRICES, WHOLESALE FRESH FRUITS AND VEGETABLES **2343**

HAWAII FILIPINO NEWS HONOLULU, HAWAII : 1985) **CEASED.** (US) [13712111] **5655**

HAWAII FISHING NEWS (US/0194-651X) [04912885] **2305**

HAWAII FOOD PROCESSOR / COOPERATIVE EXTENSION SERVICE, UNIVERSITY OF HAWAII, U.S. DEPARTMENT OF AGRICULTURE, COOPERATING (US) [09804795] **2343**

●HAWAII HEALTH CARE IN PERSPECTIVE (US/1065-4135) [26604966] **4777**

HAWAII HERALD (1969) (US/8750-913X) [06671356] **2262**

HAWAII IN PERSPECTIVE (US/1065-5409) [26628519] **5328**

HAWAII INSTITUTE OF GEOPHYSICS See PUBLICATIONS - HAWAII INSTITUTE OF GEOPHYSICS **1409**

HAWAII INSTITUTE OF GEOPHYSICS See HAWAII INSTITUTE OF GEOPHYSICS : REPORT **1406**

HAWAII INSTITUTE OF GEOPHYSICS : REPORT (US) [20559635] **1406**

HAWAII INVESTOR (US/0745-7073) [09394904] **900, 4838**

HAWAII ISLAND GUIDE (US/0744-5792) [08412447] **5479**

HAWAII LEGAL REPORTER (US/0147-1392) [03131385] **2977**

HAWAII MAGAZINE (US) [27971891] **5479**

HAWAII MARINE (US) [11620857] **5656**

HAWAII. MARKET NEWS SERVICE BRANCH See HONOLULU WHOLESALE PRICES EGGS, POULTRY, PORK, BEEF AND RICE **93**

HAWAII. MARKET NEWS SERVICE BRANCH See OUTER-ISLAND PRICES OF WHOLESALE FRESH FRUITS AND VEGETABLES **180**

HAWAII MEDICAL JOURNAL (1962) (US/0017-8594) [01751888] **3581**

HAWAII. MENTAL HEALTH DIVISION. RESEARCH & RECORDS SERVICES See PSYCHIATRIC OUTPATIENT PROGRAM **3933**

HAWAII NAVY NEWS (US) [12306683] **5656**

HAWAII NEWS (US) [11775758] **5656**

HAWAII NURSE, THE (US/1047-4749) [20351318] **3856**

HAWAII OBSERVER (US/0091-9845) [01787130] **2534**

HAWAII. OFFICE OF INSTRUCTIONAL SERVICES. COMMUNITY SERVICES SECTION See ANNUAL SUMMARY OF CLASSES AND ENROLLMENT IN COMMUNITY SCHOOLS FOR ADULTS **1799**

HAWAII. OFFICE OF INSTRUCTIONAL SERVICES. COMPENSATORY EDUCATION SECTION See COMPENDIUM OF COMPENSATORY ACTIVITIES **1733**

HAWAII. OFFICE OF MANPOWER PLANNING See REPORT ON THE STATE PROGRAM FOR THE UNEMPLOYED / [PREPARED BY OFFICE OF MANPOWER PLANNING] **1707**

HAWAII. OFFICE OF THE LIEUTENANT GOVERNOR See DISTRICT AND PRECINCT BOUNDARIES, STATE OF HAWAII **4472**

HAWAII. OFFICE OF THE OMBUDSMAN See REPORT OF THE OMBUDSMAN **4681**

HAWAII ON TEN AND FIFTEEN DOLLARS A DAY (US) [02653338] **5479**

HAWAII PACIFIC ARCHITECT (US) **299**

HAWAII. PLANNING DIVISION See STATUS REPORT: CAPITAL IMPROVEMENT PROGRAM, BOND FUND SUMMARY **4750**

HAWAII. PLANNING DIVISION See STATUS REPORT : CAPITAL IMPROVEMENTS PROGRAM, CONSTRUCTION SUMMARY **1627**

HAWAII. PLANNING DIVISION See CAPITAL IMPROVEMENTS PROGRAM STATUS REPORT, FINANCIAL SUMMARY **894**

HAWAII PROSECUTOR-PUBLIC DEFENDER NEWSLETTER (US/0363-0463) [02433134] **3107**

HAWAII. PUBLIC EMPLOYMENT RELATIONS BOARD See DECISIONS OF THE HAWAII PUBLIC EMPLOYMENT RELATIONS BOARD **1662**

HAWAII REVIEW (US/0093-9625) [01787393] **3393**

HAWAII (SAN JUAN CAPISTRANO, CALIF.) (US/0892-0990) [15103977] **5479**

HAWAII (SAN JUAN CAPISTRANO, CALIF.) See HAWAII MAGAZINE **5479**

HAWAII SERIES (US/0073-1145) [02070938] **417**

HAWAII STATE BAR ASSOCIATION See ANNUAL DIRECTORY / HAWAII STATE BAR ASSOCIATION **2934**

HAWAII. STATE BOARD OF REGISTRATION OF PROFESSIONAL ENGINEERS, ARCHITECTS AND LAND SURVEYORS See ROSTER - STATE BOARD OF REGISTRATION OF PROFESSIONAL ENGINEERS, ARCHITECTS AND LAND SURVEYORS **1995**

HAWAII. STATE ETHICS COMMISSION See DIGEST OF ADVISORY OPINIONS **2249**

HAWAII. STATE KOHALA TASK FORCE See REPORT OF THE KOHALA TASK FORCE **1624**

HAWAII. STATE LAW ENFORCEMENT PLANNING AGENCY See COMPREHENSIVE LAW ENFORCEMENT AND CRIMINAL JUSTICE PLAN AND ACTION GRANT APPLICATION **3160**

HAWAII (TER.) DEPARTMENT OF LABOR AND INDUSTRIAL RELATIONS. ANNUAL REPORT - DEPARTMENT OF LABOR AND INDUSTRIAL RELATIONS, TERRITORY OF HAWAII See ANNUAL REPORT OF THE DEPARTMENT OF LABOR AND INDUSTRIAL RELATIONS, STATE OF HAWAII **1649**

HAWAII, THE BIG ISLAND (US/1042-8062) [19226872] **5479**

HAWAII, THE BIG ISLAND UPDATE (US/1042-8046) [19226742] **5479**

HAWAII TV DIGEST (US/0745-6565) [09332678] **1132**

HAWAII, WASHINGTON, ALASKA, OREGON COACHING DIRECTORY : AN OFFICIAL PUBLICATION OF THE NATIONAL INTERSCHOLASTIC ATHLETIC ADMINISTRATORS ASSOCIATION, THE ALASKA INTERSCHOLASTIC ATHLETIC ADMINISTRATORS ASSOCIATION, AND THE WASHINGTON SECONDARY SCHOOL ATHLETIC ADMINISTRATORS ASSOCIATION (US/1045-0017) [19968531] **4898**

HAWAIIAN ARCHAEOLOGY (US/0890-1678) [11805274] **269**

HAWAIIAN ENTOMOLOGICAL SOCIETY See PROCEEDINGS OF THE HAWAIIAN ENTOMOLOGICAL SOCIETY **5613**

HAWAIIAN FALCON (US) [12155320] **5656**

HAWAIIAN ISLAND HOME (US/1051-3787) [21941938] **299**

HAWAIIAN JOURNAL OF HISTORY, THE (US/0440-5145) [02071455] **2669**

HAWAIIAN SHELL NEWS (US/0017-8624) [01941145] **1449**

HAWAIIAN SUGAR MANUAL (US/1048-9428) [10991181] **91**

HAWAIIAN SUGAR TECHNOLOGISTS. CONFERENCE See PROCEEDINGS OF ... ANNUAL CONFERENCE / HAWAIIAN SUGAR TECHNOLOGISTS **183**

HAWAII'S FOREIGN TRADE (US) [06991969] **839**

●HAWAII'S VOICES (US/1061-4109) [25301775] **321, 5558**

HAWG (MT. MORRIS, N.Y.) (US/1060-8672) [25080217] **4898**

HAWK (US) **3995**

HAWK EYE, THE (US) [12948159] **5670**

HAWK MIGRATION ASSOCIATION OF NORTH AMERICA See NEWSLETTER OF THE HAWK MIGRATION ASSOCIATION OF NORTH AMERICA, THE **5592**

HAWK MOUNTAIN NEWS (US) [05873963] **2195**

HAWK : THE INDEPENDENT JOURNAL OF THE ROYAL AIR STAFF COLLEGE (UK) **22**

HAWKEN SCHOOL (LYNDHURST, OHIO) See ALUMNI DIRECTORY / HAWKEN SCHOOL **1098**

HAWKESBURY AGRICULTURAL COLLEGE JOURNAL See JOURNAL / HACOBU **99**

HAWKESBURY EXPRESS (CN/0226-6318) [06511135] **5786**

HAWKEYE HERITAGE (US/0440-5234) [03865834] **2452**

HAWKEYE OSTEOPATHIC JOURNAL (US) [18322769] **3581**

HAWKINSVILLE DISPATCH AND NEWS, THE (US) [15916452] **5653**

HAWLEY HERALD, THE (US) [01751900] **5696**

HAWLIYAT AL-JAMIAH AL-TUNISIYAH (TI) [02534168] **2652**

HAWLIYAT FAR AL-ADAB AL-ARABIYAH (LE/0250-9970) [09812138] **3285**

HAWLIYAT KULLIYAT AL-INSANIYAT WA-AL-ULUM AL-IJTIMAIYAH (UA) [09124909] **2847**

HAWLIYAT SIYASIYAH (FR) [09548328] **4475**

HAWORTH SERIES IN DRUG THERAPY FOR ADDICTION PROBLEMS (US/1051-4236) [21957335] **1344**

HAWORTH SERIES IN INTERNATIONAL LIBRARY ACQUISITIONS (US/1050-253X) [21431285] **3213**

HAWORTH SERIES ON WOMEN (US/1040-7359) [18506150] **5558**

HAWTHORNE WAVE (US) [10537051] **5635**

●HAWVER'S CAPITOL REPORT (US/1071-5401) [28589074] **4654**

HAXTUN HERALD, THE (US) [21259602] **5643**

HAY & FORAGE GROWER (US/0891-5946) [14923353] **202**

HAY ASSOCIATES. RESEARCH FOR MANAGEMENT See BASE REPORT: BUDGETING, ACCOUNTABILITY, AND STAFFING EVALUATION, PERSONNEL **938**

HAY DRAMAGITAKAN HANDES (US/0884-0180) [10255847] **2781**

HAY MARKET NEWS (BELL, CALIF.) (US/0744-1517) [08071687] **202, 925**

HAYAMA HANDBOOK See HAYAMA MISSIONARY SEMINAR ANNUAL REPORT **4962**

HAYAMA MISSIONARY SEMINAR ANNUAL REPORT (JA) **4962**

HAYATUNA (KU) [05318974] **2504**

HAYDEN VALLEY PRESS, THE (US) [21096385] **5643**

HAYDEN'S FERRY REVIEW (US/0887-5170) [13295749] **3344**

HAYDN-STUDIEN (GW/0440-5323) [02340867] **4120**

HAYDN YEARBOOK, THE **CEASED.** (UK/0073-1390) [01606131] **4121**

HAYES DRUGGIST DIRECTORY (US) [04767814] **4306**

HAYES' DRUGGISTS' DIRECTORY See HAYES DRUGGIST DIRECTORY **4306**

HAYES — Alphabetical Title Index

HAYES HISTORICAL JOURNAL: A JOURNAL OF THE GILDED AGE **CEASED.** (US/0364-5924) [02665217] **2736**

HAYES OF AMERICA HERALD **CEASED.** (US/0736-9468) [09184735] **2452**

HAYKAKAN ELLOPEYJ : KALIFORNIAHAY ENDARDZAK HERATSUTSAK (US/1054-2671) [22806898] **2262**

HAYKAKAN SSH GITUTYUNNERI AKADEMIA **See** IZVESTIJA AKADEMII NAUK ARMJANSKOJ SSR. MEHANIKA **2117**

HAYNES EAGLE (US/0438-8399) [02569171] **2452**

HAYS COUNTY FREE PRESS (US/1058-4471) [23982014] **5750**

HAYS DAILY NEWS, THE (US) [11144819] **5676**

HAZ-MAT TECHNOLOGY (US/0888-6849) [13694919] **4777**

HAZ PACKS **CEASED.** (US/1042-6574) [19100145] **2230**

HAZARD ASSESSMENT OF CHEMICALS (US/0730-5427) [08036600] **2173**

HAZARD HERALD-VOICE (US) [11699239] **5681**

HAZARD MONTHLY (US/0742-6410) [06714469] **2230**

HAZARD PREVENTION (US/0743-8826) [04877745] **2862**

HAZARD TIMES, THE (US/0883-752X) [12206017] **5681**

HAZARDOUS AND INDUSTRIAL WASTE (US/1044-0631) [19677150] **2230**

HAZARDOUS & SOLID WASTE MINIMIZATION & RECYCLING REPORT (US/0890-5509) [14261904] **2231**

HAZARDOUS AND TOXIC SUBSTANCES (US/0163-9099) [04536854] **3981**, **2231**

HAZARDOUS CARGO BULLETIN (UK/0143-6864) [08943563] **5450**

HAZARDOUS EMERGENCY RESPONSE (US/1062-8096) [25750120] **5287**

HAZARDOUS INFORMATION AND PACKAGING (UK) **2862**

HAZARDOUS LOCATION EQUIPMENT DIRECTORY (US) [04204328] **2231**

HAZARDOUS MATERIALS CONTROL (US/0895-3260) [16571414] **2231**

HAZARDOUS MATERIALS CONTROL BUYER'S GUIDE AND SOURCE BOOK (SILVER SPRING, MD. 1991) (US/1061-706X) [25347527] **2231**

HAZARDOUS MATERIALS INTELLIGENCE REPORT (US/0272-9628) [06984722] **2231**

HAZARDOUS MATERIALS MANAGEMENT (CN/1193-2074) [I11932074] **2231**

HAZARDOUS MATERIALS NEWSLETTER (BARRE, VT.) (US/0889-3454) [06956873] **2231**

HAZARDOUS MATERIALS RESPONSE HANDBOOK (US) **2290**, **2862**

HAZARDOUS MATERIALS TRANSPORTATION (BOSTON) (US/0197-3177) [06003813] **2231**

HAZARDOUS SUBSTANCES & PUBLIC HEALTH (US/1076-8920) [23110031] **2173**

HAZARDOUS SUBSTANCES (SUDBURY) (UK/0964-962X) [I0964962X] **2231**

HAZARDOUS WASTE & HAZARDOUS MATERIALS (US/0882-5696) [11880521] **2231**

HAZARDOUS WASTE & HAZARDOUS MATERIALS TRANSPORT DIRECTORY **See** HAZARDOUS WASTE & MATERIALS MANAGEMENT DIRECTORY, THE **2231**

HAZARDOUS WASTE & HAZARDOUS MATERIALS TRANSPORT DIRECTORY, THE (US/1057-0012) [23906350] **2231**

HAZARDOUS WASTE & MATERIALS MANAGEMENT DIRECTORY, THE (US) [28190069] **2231**

HAZARDOUS WASTE AND TOXIC TORTS (US/0884-3775) [12259050] **3112**

HAZARDOUS WASTE BUSINESS (US/0897-2699) [17450712] **2231**

HAZARDOUS WASTE CASE LAW UPDATE (US/1055-5099) [23194197] **2231**

HAZARDOUS WASTE CONSULTANT, THE (US/0738-0232) [09507325] **2231**

HAZARDOUS WASTE DRIVER SAFETY MANUAL, THE (US/1044-5080) [19817792] **2231**

HAZARDOUS WASTE LITIGATION (US/1048-9398) [20926876] **2977**

HAZARDOUS WASTE LITIGATION REPORTER (US/0275-0244) [07077881] **2231**, **3112**

HAZARDOUS WASTE MANAGEMENT & BUSINESS OPPORTUNITIES NEWSLETTER / CAE CONSULTANTS INC (US/1055-3495) [23158526] **2231**

HAZARDOUS WASTE MANAGEMENT HANDBOOK (CN/0711-7140) [08693670] **2231**

HAZARDOUS WASTE MANAGEMENT IN MASSACHUSETTS (US/0743-7331) [10644198] **2231**

HAZARDOUS WASTE NEWS (US/0275-374X) [07725439] **2231**

HAZARDOUS WASTE STRATEGIES UPDATE (US/1059-468X) [21468310] **3112**

●HAZARDOUS WASTE UPDATE SERVICE, THE (US/1074-1291) [29603692] **2231**

HAZARDS (UK/0267-7296) [I02677296] **2862**

HAZARDS AUSTRALIA (AT) **2862**

●HAZARDS IN THE OFFICE (UK/0966-906X) **2862**

HAZARD'S PAVILION (US/0892-6913) [15241548] **4121**

HAZARDS, POLLUTION AND LEGISLATION IN THE COATINGS FIELD **See** CORE. COATINGS, REGULATIONS AND THE ENVIRONMENT **4226**

HAZCHEM ALERT (US/0891-3072) [12888379] **4777**

HAZELL'S GUIDE AND THE BAR LIST (UK/0266-3597) **2977**

HAZELL'S GUIDE TO THE JUDICIARY AND THE COURTS (UK/0266-3597) [12737379] **3141**

HAZELNUT PRODUCTION / U.S. DEPT. OF AGRICULTURE, NATIONAL AGRICULTURAL STATISTICS SERVICE, AGRICULTURAL STATISTICS BOARD, (US) [25360236] **92**

HAZMAT NEWS (US/1054-7142) [22943957] **2231**

HAZMAT TRANSPORT NEWS (US) **2232**

HAZMAT TRANSPORTATION MANAGEMENT (US/1062-6026) [25681246] **869**, **5383**

HAZMAT WORLD (US/0898-5685) [17851442] **2232**

HAZTECH NEWS (US/1051-3221) [18462670] **2232**

HB. HOOSIER BANKER (US/0018-473X) [04094567] **790**

HBG-MITTEILUNGEN (GW) [02519318] **3480**

●HBJ MILLER ACCOUNTANTS' LEGAL LIABILILTY (US/1064-7155) [26379670] **2977**, **744**

HBJ MILLER ACCOUNTANTS' LEGAL LIABILILTY GUIDE **See** HBJ MILLER ACCOUNTANTS' LEGAL LIABILILTY **744**

●HBJ MILLER COMPREHENSIVE GOVERNMENTAL GAAP GUIDE (US) [25596488] **744**, **4730**

●HBJ MILLER COMPREHENSIVE LOCAL AUDIT GUIDE (US/1064-7163) [26379703] **744**

HBO'S GUIDE TO MOVIES ON VIDEOCASSETTE AND CABLE TV (US/1050-8996) [20697463] **4071**, **4370**

HCIMA QUARTERLY BIBLIOGRAPHY OF HOTEL AND CATERING MANAGEMENT (UK) [06668917] **2810**

HCL CATALOGING BULLETIN (US/0732-894X) [08458579] **3213**

HCSP ACTUALITE **See** ACTUALITE ET DOSSIER EN SANTE PUBLIQUE **4763**

HD : GIORNALE DI PSICOLOGIA E PEDAGOGIA DELL HANDICAPPATO E DELLE DISABILITA DI APPRENDIMENTO (IT) **4588**

HDTV NEWSLETTER (US/0892-5771) [15233781] **1156**, **1132**

HDTV REPORT (US/1055-9280) [23368990] **1132**

HE HUAXUE YU FANGSHE HUAXUE (CC/0253-9950) [09236722] **4447**, **976**

HE JUBIAN YU DENGLIZITI WULI (CC/0254-6086) [10346739] **4447**

HE LEXE (GR) [10858179] **321**, **3393**

HE RAMA (II) [04372237] **3393**

HE ZI KE XUE (CH/0029-5647) [04444471] **4447**

HEAD & NECK (US/1043-3074) [19016256] **3965**

HEAD INJURY UPDATE (US/0887-1779) [13194121] **3965**

HEAD-MEDIA TECHNOLOGY NEWSLETTER (US) **5109**

HEAD OFFICE AT HOME (CN/1183-6709) [25313853] **679**

HEAD START NEWSLETTER (US/0017-8721) [01751905] **5287**

HEAD TEACHERS REVIEW (UK/0017-873X) [I0017873X] **1895**

HEADACHE (US/0017-8748) [01037358] **3833**

HEADACHE QUARTERLY (US/1059-7565) [22154092] **3833**

HEADLAMP (ARMDALE) (CN/0229-6667) [10420708] **5416**

HEADLAND OBSERVER, THE (US) [11658328] **5626**

HEADLIGHT HERALD (US) **5733**

HEADLIGHTS (NEW YORK) (US/0091-8059) [01785592] **5431**

HEADLINE NEWS CURRENT AWARENESS SERVICE. BATTERIES/NEW DEVELOPMENTS (UK) **1132**

HEADLINE SERIES (US/0017-8780) [01607117] **4523**

HEADLINES (UK/0957-8714) **1864**

HEADQUARTERS HELIOGRAM (COUNCIL ON AMERICA'S MILITARY PAST) (US) [09310491] **4045**

HEADQUARTERS TELEPHONE DIRECTORY (US/0364-2488) [02512158] **22**

HEADS LEGAL GUIDE (UK) **2977**

HEAD'S LETTER, THE (US/1044-6389) [19855902] **1750**

HEADS OF SCIENCE (UK/0967-6813) [I09676813] **5109**

HEADWAY (NEW YORK, N.Y.) **See** WOMEN'S SPORTS EXPERIENCE, THE **4930**

HEALDSBURG TRIBUNE-ENTERPRISE AND SCIMITAR (US/0017-8810) [04094524] **5635**

HEALING HAND, THE (UK) [03768121] **3581**, **4962**

HEALING HEALTHCARE NETWORK NEWSLETTER (US/1055-0054) [23055336] **3581**

●HEALING (SACRAMENTO, CALIF.) (US/1064-4237) [26283302] **4777**

●HEALING WOMAN, THE (US/1065-8289) [26755924] **5287**

HEALTH ADVOCATE (MADISON, WIS.) (US/0897-3598) [11795895] **2977**, **3581**

HEALTH AFFAIRS (MILLWOOD, VA.) (US/0278-2715) [07760874] **4777**

HEALTH ALERT (PASADENA, CALIF.) **SUSPENDED.** (US/8755-4763) [11324569] **4777**

●HEALTH ALLIANCE ALERT (US/1075-024X) [29690084] **3581**, **2881**

HEALTH & ENVIRONMENT DIGEST (US/0893-6242) [15604856] **4777**

HEALTH AND FITNESS MAGAZINE (UK) **2597**

HEALTH & FITNESS MAGAZINE FOR HEALTHY, SOUND LIVING : HF (US/1048-8405) [21052229] **2598**, **4777**

●HEALTH & FITNESS TRIAD (US/1064-6728) [26368611] **2598**

HEALTH AND HEALTH INSURANCE : THE PUBLIC'S VIEW (US) [05420131] **4777**, **2882**

HEALTH AND HYGIENE (LONDON) (UK/0140-2986) [04008466] **4777**

HEALTH & LIBERATION : ANTI-APARTHEID MOVEMENT HEALTH COMMITTEE NEWSLETTER (UK/0267-2170) [13273407] **3581**

HEALTH & MEDICAL CARE DIRECTORY (US/1046-8900) [14994164] **3780**

HEALTH AND MEDICAL CARE DIRECTORY **See** MEDI PAGES **3607**

HEALTH & MEDICAL CARE DIRECTORY ON CD-ROM **CEASED.** (US) **3780**

HEALTH & MEDICAL HORIZONS **See** HEALTH & MEDICAL YEAR BOOK **3581**

●HEALTH & MEDICAL YEAR BOOK (US/1066-1786) [26694214] **3581**

●HEALTH AND MEDICINE (US/1061-6446) [25384889] **4777**

HEALTH & NUTRITION UPDATE (CN/0831-8530) [15202012] **4777**, **4191**

HEALTH AND PERSONAL SOCIAL SERVICES STATISTICS FOR ENGLAND WITH SUMMARY TABLES FOR GREAT BRITAIN (UK/0307-0824) [02240665] **5287**, **5266**

HEALTH AND PERSONAL SOCIAL SERVICES STATISTICS FOR WALES (UK/0307-0840) [01799028] **5287**, **5266**

HEALTH & PHYSICAL EDUCATION NEWSLETTER (CN/0824-4863) [12740238] **1855**

HEALTH AND POPULATION. PERSPECTIVES AND ISSUES **CEASED.** (SZ/0253-6803) [05732415] **589**, **4777**

HEALTH & SAFETY AT WORK (UK/0269-8188) [09148678] **2862**

HEALTH & SAFETY AT WORK (CROYDON) (UK/0141-8246) [05666806] **2862**

HEALTH

HEALTH AND SAFETY AT WORK DIRECTORY, THE (UK) [29706020] **2862**

HEALTH AND SAFETY BULLETIN *See* HEALTH, SAFETY AND ENVIRONMENT BULLETIN **4781**

HEALTH AND SAFETY BULLETIN (AT/0727-3304) [I07273304] **2862**

HEALTH & SAFETY CASE LAW INDEX (NE) 4777, **2977**

HEALTH AND SAFETY COMMISSION NEWSLETTER (UK) [13863211] **4777**

HEALTH AND SAFETY DIRECTORY *See* HEALTH AND SAFETY AT WORK DIRECTORY, THE **2862**

HEALTH AND SAFETY EXECUTIVE GUIDANCE NOTES. CHEMICAL SAFETY (UK) 976, **4778**

HEALTH AND SAFETY EXECUTIVE GUIDANCE NOTES. ENVIRONMENTAL HYGIENE (UK) **4778**

HEALTH AND SAFETY EXECUTIVE GUIDANCE NOTES. GENERAL SERIES (UK) **4778**

HEALTH AND SAFETY EXECUTIVE GUIDANCE NOTES. MEDICAL SERIES (UK) **4778**

HEALTH AND SAFETY EXECUTIVE GUIDANCE NOTES. PLANT AND MACHINERY (UK) 2115, **4778**

HEALTH AND SAFETY EXECUTIVE GUIDANCE NOTES. WORKPLACE AIR & BIOLOGICAL MONITORING DATABASE (UK) **4778**

HEALTH AND SAFETY FACTBOOK (UK) **4778**

HEALTH AND SAFETY GUIDE (SZ/0259-7268) [19376789] **2232**

HEALTH AND SAFETY IN INDUSTRY AND COMMERCE (UK) [06408939] **2862**

●HEALTH AND SAFETY MANAGER (UK/1352-5611) [I13525611] **4778**

HEALTH & SAFETY. MICROFILE (UK) **4778**

HEALTH & SAFETY MONITOR (UK/0140-8534) [06652294] **2862**

HEALTH AND SAFETY RESEARCH AND TECHNOLOGICAL SERVICES *CEASED.* (UK) [12860433] **2862**

HEALTH AND SAFETY SCIENCE ABSTRACTS (US/0892-9351) [15296645] 4778, **4810**

HEALTH & SAFETY SPECIFIER (UK) **4778**

HEALTH AND SEXUALITY (US/1054-2957) [22770495] **4778**

●HEALTH & SOCIAL CARE IN THE COMMUNITY (UK/0966-0410) [27415487] **5287**

HEALTH & SOCIAL WORK (US/0360-7283) [02198019] **5287**

HEALTH & WEALTH GUARDIAN (US) **3581**

HEALTH AND WELFARE ESTABLISHMENTS / QUEENSLAND (AT) [19523341] 4778, **4810**

... HEALTH & WELL-BEING RESOURCES DIRECTORY, THE (CN/0849-830X) [21530457] **3581**

HEALTH & YOU (CINNAMINSON, N.J.) (US/0898-3569) [17588526] **2598**

HEALTH AT WORK NEWSLETTER *SUSPENDED.* (AT/1033-1425) [I10331425] **2863**

HEALTH BENEFITS LETTER *CEASED.* (US/1055-3517) [23158414] **4778**

HEALTH BUILDING LIBRARY BULLETIN (UK) **4778**

HEALTH BULLETIN (EDINBURGH) (UK/0374-8014) [02824552] **4778**

HEALTH BULLETIN (MELBOURNE) (AT/0311-9254) [01003340] **4778**

HEALTH BULLETIN (RALEIGH), THE (US/0017-8934) [01533255] **4778**

HEALTH BUSINESS (US/1062-6107) [24055739] 3581, **925**

HEALTH BUSINESS NEWSLETTER (US) **4778**

HEALTH (CANBERRA) *CEASED.* (AT/0046-7006) [09566936] **4778**

HEALTH CARE (US) **3581**

HEALTH CARE 500 *See* HEALTH CARE 1000, THE **4778**

HEALTH CARE 500, THE (US/1050-9976) [21742680] **4778**

●HEALTH CARE 1000, THE (US/1070-9150) [28478164] **4778**

●HEALTH CARE ANALYSIS (UK/1065-3058) [26570043] 4778, **3581**

HEALTH CARE ARTICLES *See* HERE'S HELP (RENO, NEV.) **5287**

●HEALTH CARE BILLER, THE (US/1063-5335) [26057952] **4778**

HEALTH CARE BUYERS GUIDE (UK/0967-3881) [29706032] **950**

HEALTH CARE COMPENSATION & BENEFITS ADVISOR *CEASED.* (US/0889-5465) [13919273] **4778**

HEALTH CARE COMPETITION WEEK (US/0886-2095) [12813303] **4778**

HEALTH CARE COSTS (US/0739-8034) [09806310] **4778**

HEALTH CARE DIGEST (CN/0316-2141) [02247507] **3581**

HEALTH CARE EDUCATION (US/0160-7006) [03692990] **4778**

●HEALTH CARE ETHICS USA (US/1072-5490) [29015517] 2250, **3581**

HEALTH CARE EXPENDITURES IN KANSAS (US/0883-3699) [05374894] **4810**

HEALTH CARE FACILITIES : HILL-BURTON STATE PLAN DATA. EXISTING AND NEEDED (US) [08710193] **3781**

HEALTH CARE FEDERAL REGISTER ALERT *CEASED.* (US/1060-2909) [24915874] **4778**

HEALTH CARE FINANCING ADMINISTRATION RULINGS ON MEDICARE, MEDICAID, PROFESSIONAL STANDARDS REVIEW, AND RELATED MATTERS (US/0197-4246) [04625811] 3581, **2882**

HEALTH CARE FINANCING REVIEW (US/0195-8631) [05527522] **2897**

HEALTH CARE FOR WOMEN INTERNATIONAL (US/0739-9332) [09837689] 5558, **3762**

HEALTH CARE LABOR MANUAL (US/0095-3792) [05717466] **1676**

HEALTH CARE LAW NEWSLETTER (US/0893-6099) [14116197] 3781, **2977**

HEALTH CARE MANAGEMENT (UK/0269-2104) [15606493] **3781**

●HEALTH CARE MANAGEMENT (US/1069-6571) [28132135] **3781**

HEALTH CARE MANAGEMENT REVIEW (US/0361-6274) [02247030] **3781**

HEALTH CARE MARKETER (US) [15183918] **3581**

●HEALTH-CARE MEDIA SOURCE (US/1071-460X) [28642663] 3781, **760**

HEALTH CARE PARLIAMENTARY MONITOR (UK) **3581**

HEALTH CARE PR GRAPHICS (US) **760**

HEALTH CARE PRODUCTS AND CAPABILITIES IN ALBERTA (CN/1186-8201) [24571427] **3581**

●HEALTH CARE REFORM WEEK (US/1067-2214) [26994378] 2977, **3581**

HEALTH CARE REGISTRAR *See* HEALTH CARE REGISTRATION **4778**

●HEALTH CARE REGISTRATION (US) **4778**

HEALTH CARE RESOURCES IN PENNSYLVANIA, LONG TERM CARE FACILITIES (US/0883-900X) [12169314] **3581**

HEALTH CARE RISK REPORT (UK) **2863**

HEALTH CARE (SPRINGFIELD, VA.) *See* NTIS ALERT. HEALTH CARE / PREPARED BY THE NATIONAL TECHNICAL INFORMATION SERVICE, U.S. DEPARTMENT OF COMMERCE, TECHNOLOGY ADMINISTRATION **4794**

HEALTH CARE STANDARDS (US/1044-4076) [19770409] **4778**

●HEALTH CARE STATE RANKINGS (US/1065-1403) [26514227] **4778**

HEALTH CARE STRATEGIC MANAGEMENT (US/0742-1478) [10266690] **3781**

HEALTH CARE SUPERVISOR, THE (US/0731-3381) [08162085] **3781**

HEALTH CARE SYSTEMS (NEW YORK, N.Y.) (US/0745-1717) [08883312] **3581**

HEALTH CARE UK (UK/0267-3223) [13707965] **3581**

HEALTH CAREER PATHS (CN/0833-9457) [15367609] 4204, **3914**

HEALTH CAREERS (US/0362-8337) [02349235] **3581**

HEALTH CAREERS NEWS (CN/0701-1210) [03412003] 3581, **4204**

HEALTH CITY SUN (US) [10796022] **5712**

HEALTH COMMUNICATION (US/1041-0236) [18611352] **4779**

HEALTH CONFIDENTIAL (US/0894-4172) [16101265] **4779**

HEALTH CONSCIOUSNESS (OVIEDO, FLA.) (US/0895-9986) [16880834] **4779**

HEALTH CONSEQUENCES OF SMOKING, THE (US/0098-311X) [02241027] **4779**

HEALTH COST MANAGEMENT *CEASED.* (US/0740-2406) [09903945] **3581**

HEALTH DATA INVENTORY (US/0735-0848) [08851508] **4779**

HEALTH DATA MANAGEMENT (US) **745**

HEALTH DATA SUMMARIES FOR CALIFORNIA COUNTIES (US/8755-240X) [08381245] **4779**

HEALTH DEVELOPMENT IN AFRICA (US) [11014354] **4779**

HEALTH DEVICES (US/0046-7022) [02242189] **3581**

HEALTH DEVICES ALERTS (US/0163-0458) [03693951] 3581, **3659**

HEALTH DEVICES INSPECTION AND PREVENTIVE MAINTENANCE SYSTEM (US/8756-8713) [11688889] **4779**

HEALTH DEVICES SOURCEBOOK (US/0278-3452) [05384492] **3581**

●HEALTH DIET & NUTRITION (US/1055-8241) [23352143] 2598, **4191**

●HEALTH ECONOMICS (US/1057-9230) [24221931] 1493, **4779**

HEALTH EDUCATION (UK/0965-4283) [I09654283] **1855**

HEALTH EDUCATION BULLETIN (US/0270-0603) [06299021] **4779**

HEALTH EDUCATION INDEX AND GUIDE TO VOLUNTARY SOCIAL WELFARE ORGANISATIONS (UK) [02245894] **2598**

HEALTH EDUCATION JOURNAL, THE (UK/0017-8969) [01751913] **2598**

HEALTH EDUCATION QUARTERLY (US/0195-8402) [05660142] **4779**

HEALTH EDUCATION REPORT (OJAI) (US/0193-7138) [02928340] **4779**

HEALTH EDUCATION REPORTS (US/0193-5232) [05189140] **4779**

HEALTH EDUCATION RESEARCH (UK/0268-1153) [12824066] **4779**

HEALTH EDUCATION SUBSCRIPTION SERVICE (UK) 4779, **1750**

●HEALTH EDUCATOR : JOURNAL OF ETA SIGMA GAMMA (US) [29290320] **4779**

HEALTH EFFECTS ASSESSMENT SUMMARY TABLES (US) [23865750] **4779**

HEALTH EMPLOYMENT LAW UPDATE (US/0890-9245) [14472187] **3148**

HEALTH EQUIPMENT INFORMATION (UK/0261-0736) [I02610736] **3781**

HEALTH EQUIPMENT NOTE (UK/0141-1403) [03067893] **3581**

HEALTH ESTATE JOURNAL : JOURNAL OF THE INSTITUTE OF HOSPITAL ENGINEERING (UK/0957-7742) [21304377] **3781**

HEALTH FACILITIES COURT DIGEST, THE (US/0148-5385) [03321458] **2977**

HEALTH FACILITIES DIRECTORY (SACRAMENTO) (US/0361-2929) [02246059] **3781**

HEALTH FACILITIES ENERGY REPORT (US/0272-8443) [06959931] 3781, **1946**

HEALTH FACILITIES MANAGEMENT (US/0899-6210) [18161006] **4779**

●HEALTH FACILITIES REPORT (US/1062-4562) [25624701] **3781**

HEALTH FACT NEWS *CEASED.* (US/0279-5639) [07096974] **2598**

HEALTH FACTS (US/0738-811X) [06283406] 1297, **4779**

HEALTH (FAMILY MEDIA, INC.) *See* HEALTH (SAN FRANCISCO, CALIF.) **4781**

HEALTH FOODS BUSINESS (US/0149-9602) [03581773] **2343**

HEALTH FOODS COMMUNICATOR, THE (US/0194-5343) [04796937] **2343**

HEALTH FOODS RETAILING MERCHANDISING HANDBOOK (US/0163-304X) [04328965] **2343**

HEALTH FOR ALL SERIES (SZ/0254-9263) [08271547] **5287**

HEALTH FOR THE MILLIONS (II/0970-8685) [I09708685] **4779**

HEALTH FORUM (AT/1030-6072) [I10306072] **4779**

HEALTH FREEDOM NEWS (MONROVIA, CALIF.) (US/0749-4742) [09499675] **4779**

HEALTH FUNDS DEVELOPMENT LETTER (US/0193-7928) [05256404] 4654, **3581**

HEALTH GAZETTE (US) **2598**

HEALTH GRANTS & CONTRACTS WEEKLY (US/0194-2352) [05370999] **4780**

HEALTH GROUPS IN WASHINGTON : A DIRECTORY (US/0278-5323) [07322359] **4780**

HEALTH (GUILFORD, CONN.) (US/0278-4653) [07474200] **4780**

HEALTH HAZARD EVALUATION SUMMARIES (US/0277-8521) [07612915] **2863**

HEALTH IN NEW ZEALAND (NZ) [08160656] **4780**

HEALTH IN THE UNITED STATES (US/0148-7450) [03366885] **4780**

HEALTH IN WISCONSIN (US/0146-2768) [02884644] **4780**

HEALTH

HEALTH INDEX [COMPUTER FILE] (US) 4780, 2598, **2602**

HEALTH INDUSTRY BUYERS GUIDE : HIBG (US/0892-7731) [10181094] **3581**

HEALTH INDUSTRY TODAY (US/0745-4678) [09198985] **3581**

● HEALTH INFORMATICS (UK) **3582**

HEALTH INFORMATION AND LIBRARIES (HU/0864-991X) [22538042] **3213**

HEALTH INFORMATION BULLETIN / HEALTH INFORMATION SYSTEM, MINISTRY OF HEALTH, GOVERNMENT OF KENYA (KE) [11216988] **4780**

HEALTH INFORMATION FOR INTERNATIONAL TRAVEL (US/0095-3539) [02905736] **3713**

HEALTH INFORMATION RESOURCES IN THE FEDERAL GOVERNMENT / PREPARED BY ODPHP NATIONAL HEALTH INFORMATION CENTER (US) [24007325] 4654, **4780**

HEALTH INSURANCE SURVEY, AUSTRALIA (AT/0727-1611) [I07271611] 2882, **2897**

HEALTH INSURANCE UNDERWRITER, THE (US/0017-9019) [01791960] 4780, **2882**

HEALTH IS WEALTH (US/0884-0717) [12298001] **4780**

HEALTH ISSUES ON CAPITOL HILL (US/0145-336X) [02675292] **4780**

HEALTH, LABOR & SAFETY REPORT (CN/0824-5681) [10785494] **2863**

HEALTH LABOR RELATION REPORTS (US/0148-4761) [03301820] **1677**

HEALTH LAW BULLETIN (US/0549-804X) [07011222] 4780, **2977**

HEALTH LAW DIGEST / NATIONAL HEALTH LAWYERS ASSOCIATION (US) [06096814] 3582, **2977**

HEALTH LAW IN CANADA (CN/0226-8841) [06559623] 3582, **2977**

HEALTH LAW JOURNAL OF OHIO (US/1043-6081) [19496555] **2977**

● HEALTH LAW LITIGATION REPORTER (US/1075-0606) [29887241] 3762, **3740**

HEALTH LAW PROJECT LIBRARY BULLETIN (US/0163-3996) [04130448] 3582, **2978**

HEALTH LAW VIGIL *CEASED.* (US/0270-3343) [06370810] 3781, **2978**

● HEALTH LAW WEEK (US/1063-4061) [26018415] 4780, **2978**

HEALTH LAWYER, THE (US/0736-3443) [08644501] 3582, **2978**

HEALTH LAWYERS NEWS REPORT (US/0145-4129) [02732616] 4780, **2978**

HEALTH LEGISLATION AND REGULATION (US/0899-8965) [14211528] 2882, **2978**

HEALTH LETTER / AMERICAN HEALTH FOUNDATION (US) [18495433] **4780**

HEALTH LETTER ON THE CDC (US/1078-2907) **4780**

HEALTH LETTER (SAN ANTONIO, TEX.), THE *CEASED.* (US/0739-4217) [02255716] **4780**

HEALTH LETTER (WASHINGTON, D.C.) (US/0882-598X) [11906218] 1297, **3582**

HEALTH LIBRARIES ASSOCIATION OF B.C *See* HLABC FORUM **3213**

HEALTH LIBRARIES REVIEW (UK/0265-6647) [11723043] 3582, **3213**

HEALTH LITERATURE REVIEW (US/0740-7262) [09988191] **4780**

HEALTH MANAGEMENT QUARTERLY (US/0891-3250) [12031022] **3781**

● HEALTH MANAGEMENT TECHNOLOGY (US/1074-4770) [29649286] **3582**

HEALTH MANAGER'S UPDATE (US/0894-4679) [16104291] **4780**

HEALTH MANPOWER DIRECTORY (NP/0258-3178) [09103884] **3914**

HEALTH MANPOWER MANAGEMENT (UK/0955-2065) [18812336] **3582**

HEALTH MANPOWER PILOT PROJECTS PROGRAM. ANNUAL REPORT TO THE LEGISLATURE AND THE HEALING ARTS LICENSING BOARDS (US/0192-6101) [05032463] **3914**

HEALTH MANPOWER RESOURCES (UK) [04518056] **3914**

HEALTH MANPOWER STATISTICS (US/0740-1701) [09351548] 4045, **4062**

HEALTH MARKETING QUARTERLY (US/0735-9683) [09039468] 4780, **3582**

HEALTH MATRIX (US/0748-383X) [24360166] **3740**

HEALTH (NEW ZEALAND) (NZ) [09566948] **4780**

HEALTH NEWS & BREAKTHROUGHS (US/1068-770X) [27797634] **2598**

HEALTH NEWS & REVIEW (US/1056-1900) [16350973] 4201, **4191**

HEALTH NEWS DIGEST (MARLBOROUGH, MASS.) *CEASED.* (US/1065-1810) [26520320] **4780**

HEALTH NEWS (TORONTO) (CN/0821-3925) [09808988] **3582**

HEALTH OF AMERICA'S CHILDREN, THE (US/0899-4137) [18089404] **4780**

HEALTH OF ANIMALS (CN/0846-4782) [20779509] **5511**

HEALTH OF KANSANS CHART BOOK, THE (US/0276-606X) [05823267] **4780**

HEALTH OF THE PEOPLE, THE (NZ/0301-0384) [10101862] **4780**

HEALTH ONE MEDICAL JOURNAL (US/1060-605X) [25043974] **3582**

HEALTH/PAC *See* HEALTH/PAC BULLETIN **4780**

HEALTH/PAC BULLETIN (US/0017-9051) [02483417] **4780**

HEALTH PATHWAYS (US/0164-7598) [04359419] **4780**

HEALTH PERIODICALS DATABASE [ONLINE DATABASE] (US) 4780, 2598, **2602**

HEALTH PERSONNEL IN CANADA (CN/0837-7251) [18120990] **4780**

HEALTH PHYSICS (1958) (US/0017-9078) [01639509] **4404**

HEALTH PHYSICS/RADIATION PROTECTION ENROLLMENTS AND DEGREES (US/0748-3333) [10917181] **3941**

● HEALTH PLANNING AND ADMINISTRATION (US/1065-0679) [26496761] 3781, **3659**

HEALTH PLANNING AND ADMINISTRATION DATABASE (HEALTH) (US) **3781**

HEALTH POLICY (AMSTERDAM) (NE/0168-8510) [10960514] **3582**

HEALTH POLICY AND PLANNING (UK/0268-1080) [13579422] **4780**

HEALTH POLICY ANNUAL (US/1056-2389) [23593579] **4780**

HEALTH POLICY COUNCIL (VT.) *See* ANNUAL IMPLEMENTATION PLAN / HEALTH POLICY COUNCIL **4765**

HEALTH POLICY (NEW YORK, N.Y.) (US/0733-9143) [07523437] **4780**

HEALTH POLICY WEEK (US/0732-7439) [08416533] **4780**

HEALTH POLICY WEEK *See* HEALTH CARE REFORM WEEK **3581**

HEALTH PROFESSIONS REPORT (US/0888-9465) [10728396] **3582**

HEALTH PROFESSIONS SCHOOLS. SELECTED ENROLLMENT DATA (US) [04698188] 1827, **3582**

HEALTH PROGRESS (SAINT LOUIS, MO.) (US/0882-1577) [11228094] **3781**

● HEALTH PROMOTION IN CANADA (CN/1195-6747) [29333826] **4781**

HEALTH PROMOTION INTERNATIONAL (UK/0957-4824) [21315959] **4781**

HEALTH PROMOTION JOURNAL OF AUSTRALIA (AT/1036-1073) **3582**

HEALTH PROMOTION NEWSLETTER (US/0882-0252) [11778206] **4781**

HEALTH PROMOTION (OTTAWA) (CN/0833-7594) [13958108] **4781**

HEALTH PROMOTION (OTTAWA, ONT.) *See* HEALTH PROMOTION IN CANADA **4781**

● HEALTH PROMOTION PRACTITIONER (US/1060-5517) [25034768] **4781**

HEALTH PSYCHOLOGY (US/0278-6133) [07856766] 3582, **4588**

HEALTH QUEST (CN/1188-6250) [25883014] **4781**

HEALTH REFERENCE CENTER [COMPUTER FILE] (US) [28189997] 3582, **3659**

HEALTH REPORTS / RAPPORT SUR LA SANTE / STATISTIQUE CANADA, DIVISION DE LA SANTE. STATISTICS CANADA, HEALTH DIVISION (CN/0840-6529) [20544288] **4781**

HEALTH REPORTS. SUPPLEMENT. BIRTHS (CN/1180-3088) [22773481] **3762**

HEALTH REPORTS. SUPPLEMENT. CANCER IN CANADA (CN/1180-3053) [23004750] **3817**

HEALTH REPORTS. SUPPLEMENT. CANCER IN CANADA *See* CANCER IN CANADA (1989) **3811**

HEALTH REPORTS. SUPPLEMENT. CAUSES OF DEATH (CN/1180-2421) [21516189] **4553**

HEALTH REPORTS. SUPPLEMENT. DEATHS (CN/1180-3096) [25314226] 4781, **4810**

HEALTH REPORTS. SUPPLEMENT. DIVORCES (CN/1180-3126) [22774305] 2280, **2287**

HEALTH REPORTS. SUPPLEMENT. HOSPITAL STATISTICS, PRELIMINARY ANNUAL REPORT (CN/1180-2456) [21493861] **3781**

HEALTH REPORTS. SUPPLEMENT. LIFE TABLES, CANADA AND PROVINCES (CN/1180-307X) [24986800] 4553, **4562**

HEALTH REPORTS. SUPPLEMENT. LIST OF CANADIAN HOSPITALS (CN/1180-2391) [21516202] **3781**

HEALTH REPORTS. SUPPLEMENT. LIST OF RESIDENTIAL CARE FACILITIES IN CANADA (CN/1180-3045) [23235962] **5287**

HEALTH REPORTS. SUPPLEMENT. MENTAL HEALTH STATISTICS (CN/1180-3037) [22773049] **4588**

HEALTH REPORTS. SUPPLEMENT. NO. 7, LIST OF RESIDENTIAL CARE FACILITIES IN CANADA *See* LIST OF RESIDENTIAL CARE FACILITIES / STATISTICS CANADA, CANADIAN CENTRE FOR HEALTH INFORMATION **5295**

HEALTH REPORTS. SUPPLEMENT. RESIDENTIAL CARE FACILITIES (CN/1181-8832) [23166739] **5287**

HEALTH REPORTS. SUPPLEMENT. SURGICAL PROCEDURES AND TREATMENTS (CN/1180-243X) [21516145] **3965**

HEALTH REPORTS. SUPPLEMENTS. RESIDENTIAL CARE FACILITIES *See* RESIDENTIAL CARE FACILITIES, MENTAL / STATISTICS CANADA, CANADIAN CENTRE FOR HEALTH INFORMATION **5306**

HEALTH RESOURCES AND SERVICES ADMINISTRATION MEDICAL SUPPLY CATALOG *See* MEDICAL SUPPLY CATALOG / U.S. PUBLIC HEALTH SERVICE **3611**

HEALTH RESOURCES MEDICAL MANPOWER (AT) [10812627] **3914**

HEALTH, SAFETY & EDUCATION (US/0161-6765) [03971516] **4781**

HEALTH, SAFETY AND ENVIRONMENT BULLETIN (UK) 2173, **4781**

● HEALTH (SAN FRANCISCO, CALIF.) (US/1059-938X) [24813732] **4781**

HEALTH SCIENCE (1985) (US/0883-8216) [12241306] 4191, **4781**

HEALTH SCIENCE REVIEW (NEW YORK, N.Y.) (US/0731-5694) [08215535] **3582**

HEALTH SCIENCES AUDIOVISUALS *CEASED.* (US/0278-7318) [09933442] **4781**

HEALTH SCIENCES INFORMATION IN CANADA. LIBRARIES *CEASED.* (CN/0708-9465) [05585741] 3582, **3213**

HEALTH SCIENCES SERIALS (US/0162-0843) [04094060] 3582, **3213**

HEALTH SCIENCES VIDEOLOG, THE (US/0731-5945) [07384113] **4781**

HEALTH SENTRY (US/1042-699X) [19111444] **2598**

HEALTH SERVICE ABSTRACTS (UK/0268-0459) [17578169] 3582, **3659**

HEALTH SERVICE BUYERS GUIDE *See* HEALTH CARE BUYERS GUIDE **950**

HEALTH SERVICE JOURNAL, THE (UK/0952-2271) [13409134] **4781**

HEALTH SERVICE REPORT (UK) **2863**

HEALTH SERVICES ADMINISTRATION EDUCATION (US/0160-4961) [03693268] **4781**

HEALTH SERVICES DIRECTORY (US/0731-6607) [07382900] 5287, **3781**

HEALTH SERVICES IN CZECHOSLOVAKIA (XR) [09796250] **4781**

HEALTH SERVICES INTERNATIONAL (UK/1011-5153) [I10115153] **4781**

HEALTH SERVICES MANAGEMENT *CEASED.* (UK/0953-8534) [18149474] **3781**

HEALTH SERVICES MANAGEMENT RESEARCH : AN OFFICIAL JOURNAL OF THE ASSOCIATION OF UNIVERSITY PROGRAMS IN HEALTH ADMINISTRATION (UK/0951-4848) [18713778] **3781**

HEALTH SERVICES RESEARCH (US/0017-9124) [01589868] **3582**

HEALTH SHORTS (US) **2598**

HEALTH, SOCIETY, AND CULTURE (US/0891-7795) [14999544] **5246**

● HEALTH SOURCE (PEABODY, MASS.) (US/1063-9810) [26185100] 4781, 2598, **2602**

HEALTH SPECTRUM (US/0737-7568) [09455603] 4191, **4781**

HEALTH STATISTICS (DUBLIN, IRELAND) (IE) [15799134] **4810**

HEALTH STATISTICS IN THE NORDIC COUNTRIES / HELSESTATISTIKK I DE NORDISKE LAND / NOMESKO (DK/0900-7962) [10203665] **4810**

HEALTH STATISTICS PLAN (US/0147-0949) [03110375] **4810**

Alphabetical Title Index — HEAT

HEALTH SYSTEMS AGENCIES, STATE HEALTH PLANNING AND DEVELOPMENT AGENCIES, AND STATEWIDE HEALTH COORDINATING COUNCILS (US) [08293064] **4781**

HEALTH SYSTEMS AGENCY OF NORTHEASTERN NEW YORK *See* HSA/NENY NEWS **5288**

HEALTH SYSTEMS PLAN (HOUSTON, TEX.) (US/0892-7677) [07399137] **4781, 2978**

HEALTH SYSTEMS REPORT ALMANAC ON FEDERAL HEALTH ISSUES, PROPOSALS, ADMINISTRATIVE ACTIONS, LEGISLATION, PUBLIC LAWS (US/0194-3049) [04556113] **3582, 2978**

HEALTH SYSTEMS REVIEW (US/1055-7466) [23100330] **3782**

HEALTH TECHNICAL MEMORANDUM / DEPARTMENT OF HEALTH AND SOCIAL SECURITY ; WELSH OFFICE (UK) [12444451] **3782**

HEALTH TECHNOLOGY CASE STUDY (US/0892-0036) [10904793] **3582**

HEALTH TECHNOLOGY MANAGEMENT (US) **3582**

HEALTH TECHNOLOGY TRENDS (US/1041-6072) [18809841] **3583**

HEALTH TIPS (US) **4781**

●HEALTH TRANSITION REVIEW : THE CULTURAL, SOCIAL, AND BEHAVIOURAL DETERMINANTS OF HEALTH (AT/1036-4005) [24732380] **4781**

HEALTH TRENDS (UK/0017-9132) [01794804] **4781**

HEALTH, UNITED STATES (US/0361-4468) [03151554] **4781**

HEALTH VALUES (US/0147-0353) [03085059] **4782**

●HEALTH VISION (CN/1189-475X) [26621402] **4782**

HEALTH VISITOR : THE JOURNAL OF THE HEALTH VISITORS' ASSOCIATION (UK/0017-9140) [09604659] **4782, 3856**

HEALTH WATCH (LOUISVILLE, KY.) (US/1051-9726) [22160130] **4782**

HEALTH WATCH (TORONTO) (CN/0845-8251) [20244432] **4782**

HEALTH WORLD (US/0888-7330) [13712443] **4782**

HEALTH YOURSELF (AT) **2598**

HEALTHACTION MANAGERS *CEASED.* (US/0895-108X) [16462964] **4782**

HEALTHCARE ADVERTISING REVIEW (US/8756-4513) [11561145] **4782, 760**

●HEALTHCARE ADVOCATE (EDMONTON) (CN/1197-4710) [29970276] **3782**

HEALTHCARE BOTTOM LINE (US/1062-032X) [16896797] **3782**

HEALTHCARE CAI DIRECTORY (US) [24914402] 1223, **1324**

HEALTHCARE CAREER DIRECTORY *See* HEALTHCARE CAREER DIRECTORY. NURSES AND PHYSICIANS **3914**

●HEALTHCARE CAREER DIRECTORY. NURSES AND PHYSICIANS (US) [28446265] **3914**

●HEALTHCARE CD-ROM/CD-I DIRECTORY (US) [30677908] 1277, **3583**

HEALTHCARE CD-ROM DIRECTORY (US/1074-6064) [24706564] **3583**

HEALTHCARE COMMUNITY RELATIONS & MARKETING LETTER (US/0894-9980) [16396781] 925, **3583**

HEALTHCARE COMPUTING & COMMUNICATIONS CANADA (CN/0842-5353) [19730299] 1186, **3782**

HEALTHCARE ENVIRONMENTAL MANAGEMENT SYSTEM (US/1055-5250) [23199456] **4782**

HEALTHCARE EXECUTIVE (US/0883-5381) [12148474] **3782**

HEALTHCARE FINANCIAL MANAGEMENT (US/0735-0732) [08504366] 869, **3782**

HEALTHCARE FORUM JOURNAL, THE (US/0899-9287) [17276109] 3782, **3583**

HEALTHCARE FUND RAISING NEWSLETTER (US) **3782**

HEALTHCARE FUNDRAISING NEWSLETTER (US/0193-9939) **3782**

HEALTHCARE HAZARDOUS MATERIALS MANAGEMENT (US/1050-575X) [21540678] 2863, **4782**

●HEALTHCARE HUMAN RESOURCES (US/1060-9253) [25111425] **3914**

HEALTHCARE INFORMATICS (US/1050-9135) [21140357] **3782**

HEALTHCARE INFORMATION AND MANAGEMENT SYSTEMS SOCIETY *See* CATALOG OF HEALTHCARE INFORMATION AND MANAGEMENT SYSTEMS PUBLICATIONS / AHA **3778**

HEALTHCARE INFORMATION MANAGEMENT (US) [17416323] **3782**

HEALTHCARE ISSUES & TRENDS (US/1058-028X) [24183803] **4782**

HEALTHCARE MANAGEMENT FORUM (CN/0840-4704) [17694891] **3782**

HEALTHCARE MANAGEMENT TEAM LETTER (US/0891-9267) [15042315] **3583**

HEALTHCARE MARKET RESEARCH, REPORTS, STUDIES, & SURVEYS (US/8755-9153) [11401954] **4782**

HEALTHCARE MARKETING ABSTRACTS (US/0891-5016) [14872182] 4782, **925**

HEALTHCARE MARKETING REPORT (US/0741-9368) [10269196] 925, **3782**

HEALTHCARE MICROCOMPUTING NETWORK (US/0737-6219) [09425456] 3782, **1267**

HEALTHCARE PACKAGING *CEASED.* (US/1068-0802) [27457085] 3583, **4219**

HEALTHCARE PLANNING AND MARKETING. SOCIETY FOR HEALTHCARE PLANNING AND MARKETING OF THE AMERICAN HOSPITAL ASSOCIATION (US) [17692793] **2863**

●HEALTHCARE PR & MARKETING NEWS (US) [28935424] 760, **3782**

HEALTHCARE PR NEWS (US/1068-0403) [27408316] 760, **3782**

HEALTHCARE PRODUCT COMPARISON SYSTEM - IMAGING AND RADIOLOGY (US) **3583**

HEALTHCARE PRODUCT COMPARISON SYSTEM - SURGICAL (US) **3583**

HEALTHCARE RECRUITMENT RESOURCE GUIDE (US/1046-4603) [21309213] **3583**

●HEALTHCARE RECRUITMENT RESOURCE GUIDE (US/1046-4603) [24479873] **3583**

HEALTHCARE RECRUITMENT RESOURCE GUIDE (CLEARWATER, FLA.) *See* HEALTHCARE RECRUITMENT RESOURCE GUIDE **3583**

HEALTHCARE STAFFING MANAGEMENT *CEASED.* (US/1055-9183) [23378940] **3782**

HEALTHCARE SYSTEM REFORM ALERT (US/1068-0853) [25198297] **5201**

HEALTHCARE SYSTEMS STRATEGY REPORT (US) **4782**

HEALTHCARE TECHNOLOGY BUSINESS OPPORTUNITIES (US/1049-4499) 679, **3583**

HEALTHCARE TRENDS & TRANSITION (US/1047-7276) [20770851] **3583**

HEALTHCARE TRENDS REPORT (US/0894-7961) [16244597] **3782**

HEALTHCARE VIDEODISC DIRECTORY (US) [24706701] 3583, **4370**

HEALTHCOVER SYDNEY (AT/1036-1901) [I10361901] **2598**

HEALTHIER YOUTH (CN/1181-6139) [23347165] **2598**

HEALTHLINE (SAN MATEO, CALIF.) (US/0736-7929) [09208705] **2598**

HEALTHLINES (ANN ARBOR, MICH.) (US/8756-453X) [11561255] **4782**

HEALTHLINES (WACO, TEX.) (US/1048-5562) [20973129] **4782**

HEALTHMARKETING (US/0745-4538) [09181433] **4782**

HEALTHPLAN / NATIONAL LIBRARY OF MEDICINE / [COMPUTER FILE] (US) [22498510] **3583**

●HEALTHSERVICE LEADER, THE (US/1070-0978) [28277732] **4782**

HEALTHSHARING *CEASED.* (CN/0226-1510) [06295890] 5558, **4782**

HEALTHSPAN (US/0883-0452) [11829624] **3740**

HEALTHTALK (MERRICK, N.Y.) (US/0898-8560) [17932452] **2598**

HEALTHTEXAS (AUSTIN, TEX.) (US/1048-4167) [19071009] **3782**

HEALTHTRAC (US) **3583**

HEALTHWAYS (US/0897-9251) [17669927] **4191**

HEALTHWEEK *CEASED.* (US/0890-2259) [14175224] **4782**

HEALTHWISE (US/0740-1086) [09868282] **2598**

HEALTHY CITIES (UK/0955-5358) [I09555358] **4782**

HEALTHY COMPANIES *CEASED.* (US/0897-7615) [17616912] **679**

HEALTHY EATING (CN/0846-0663) [23658904] **4191**

HEALTHY EXCHANGE (OTTAWA) (CN/1183-4331) [24690704] **2598**

HEALTHY EXCHANGE (OTTAWA) (CN/1183-4331) [24690699] **4782**

HEALTHY HORIZONS (CN/0823-7352) [10386428] 4191, **2343**

HEALTHY INTERCHANGE (CN/1191-0054) [25607911] **4782**

HEALTHY KIDS. 4-10 YEARS (US/1062-4236) [25623279] 2280, **2598**

●HEALTHY KIDS. BIRTH-3 (US/1063-0945) [25856232] 2280, **2598**

HEALTHY LIVING LONDON *SUSPENDED.* (UK/0017-9167) [I00179167] **2598**

HEALTHY OFFICE REPORT, THE (US/1057-199X) [23979087] **2863**

HEALTHY PEOPLE (US/0884-2094) [12323313] **4782**

●HEALTHY WEIGHT JOURNAL (US/1075-0169) [29917355] 4782, **4191**

HEARD HERITAGE (US/0149-5046) [03503023] **2736**

HEARING & SPEECH ACTION (US/0162-5667) [03916598] **4388**

HEARING BOARD DECISIONS AND SUMMARIES . [MICROFORM] (US) [21199939] **1493**

HEARING CALENDAR (US) **4654**

HEARING HEALTH (US/0888-2517) **1297**

HEARING INSTRUMENTS (US/0092-4466) [01789026] **3888**

HEARING JOURNAL, THE (US/0745-7472) [09267554] **3888**

HEARING REHABILITATION QUARTERLY (US/0360-9278) [02245706] **4388**

HEARING RESEARCH (NE/0378-5955) [04410062] **3888**

HEARINGS AND REPORTS OF COMMITTEES OF THE CALIFORNIA LEGISLATURE : A LISTING (US/0362-9929) [02255606] **2978**

HEARINGS IN PUBLIC ASSISTANCE (US/0161-2417) [03819447] **5287**

HEARNE DEMOCRAT, THE (US) [14265209] **5750**

HEARSAY (US) [13923913] **4388**

HEARSAY : LEGAL AID PRACTICE NOTES AND INFORMATION BULLETIN OF THE LEGAL AID COMMISSION OF WESTERN AUSTRALIA (AT) [08077039] **3179**

HEART & LUNG (US/0147-9563) [01590400] **3856**

HEART AND VESSELS (JA/0910-8327) [12260817] **3705**

HEART AND VESSELS. SUPPLEMENT (JA/0935-736X) [12940545] **3705**

HEART DISEASE AND STROKE *CEASED.* (US/1058-2819) [24251790] **3705**

HEART FAILURE (US/8755-7673) [11403103] **3705**

HEART HEALTH DIGEST *CEASED.* (US/0897-5949) [17560031] **4782**

HEART LONDON. 1987 (UK/0953-0495) [I09530495] **3705**

HEART OF TEXAS RECORDS (US/0093-9854) [01792868] **2452**

HEARTBEAT (US/1047-1014) [20607784] **4962**

HEARTBEAT (LOS ANGELES) (US/0194-8032) [05031854] **589**

HEARTBEAT (VANCOUVER) (CN/0849-3111) [23238137] **3583**

HEARTBOUND (US) **3995**

HEARTCARE *CEASED.* (US) **3705**

HEARTH AND HOME (GILFORD, N.H. : 1989) (US/0273-5695) [19465387] 2906, **1946**

HEARTHEALTH (CN/1183-1340) [24256736] **2598**

●HEARTHSIDE READER, THE (US/1061-4567) [25312441] **3393**

HEARTLAND BOATING (US/1042-1009) [18941297] **593**

HEARTLAND JOURNAL *CEASED.* (US/0887-2597) [11179064] 352, **3393**

HEARTLAND OF SOUTHERN ONTARIO DIRECTORY (CN/0225-5677) [06131659] **893**

HEARTS AFLAME (US/0893-536X) [15565199] 1064, **5030**

HEARTWOOD *CEASED.* (CN/0825-5318) [11802926] **4588**

HEAT AND MASS TRANSFER (GW) **4430**

HEAT AND TECHNOLOGY (IT/0392-8764) [11644337] **4430**

HEAT ENGINEERING (LIVINGSTON) (US/0017-9329) [01751930] 1977, **1946**

HEAT EXCHANGER DESIGN HANDBOOK : HEDH *CEASED.* (US/0741-2533) [10111337] **4430**

HEAT PIPE TECHNOLOGY (US/0046-7146) [04022471] **2605**

HEAT RECOVERY SYSTEMS & CHP (UK/0890-4332) [14225988] **4430**

HEAT

HEAT SHOCK PROTEINS (UK/0950-0510) [I09500510] **488**

HEAT TECHNOLOGY (US/0017-9337) [02007940] **4431**

HEAT TRANSFER AND FLUID FLOW DATA BOOK (US) [04964726] **4431**

HEAT TRANSFER AND FLUID MECHANICS INSTITUTE *See* PROCEEDINGS OF THE HEAT TRANSFER AND FLUID MECHANICS INSTITUTE **2125**

HEAT TRANSFER ENGINEERING (US/0145-7632) [03818353] **2012**

HEAT TRANSFER. JAPANESE RESEARCH (US/0096-0802) [01289442] **4431**

● HEAT TRANSFER RECENT CONTENTS (US/1063-1313) [25895276] **2115**

● HEAT TRANSFER RESEARCH (US/1064-2285) [26275498] **2056**

HEAT TRANSFER: SOVIET RESEARCH *See* HEAT TRANSFER RESEARCH **2056**

HEAT TREATING (US/0017-9345) [04935561] **4003**

HEAT TREATMENT OF METALS (UK/0305-4829) [04551739] **4003**

HEATHCLIFF *CEASED.* (US/0888-0751) [13118289] **4862**

HEATHER SOCIETY BULLETIN, THE (UK) [07295575] **5231**

HEATING, AIR CONDITIONING & PLUMBING PRODUCTS *CEASED.* (US/8750-4774) [11484440] **2605**

HEATING & VENTILATING REVIEW (UK/0017-9396) [02246297] **2605**

HEATING, PIPING, AND AIR CONDITIONING (US/0017-940X) [01751932] **2605**

HEATING-PLUMBING, AIR CONDITIONING (CN/0017-9418) [02021786] **2605**

HEATING, PLUMBING, AIR CONDITIONING. BUYER'S GUIDE (CN/0382-6996) [02851823] **2605**

HEATING, VENTILATING, REFRIGERATION AND AIR CONDITIONING YEAR BOOK AND DAILY BUYERS GUIDE *See* SPECIFIER'S GUIDE TO HEATING, VENTILATING, AIR CONDITIONING AND REFRIGERATION **2608**

HEAVEN BONE (US/1042-5381) [17606046] **3393**

HEAVEN EARTH (US/1055-9884) [23441292] **2652**

HEAVENER LEDGER (US) [13663946] **5732**

HEAVY CONSTRUCTION NEWS (CN/0017-9426) [02470737] **616**

HEAVY DUTY TRUCKING (US/0017-9434) [02244755] **5383**

HEAVY EQUIPMENT & FARM MACHINERY MAGAZINE (US/1060-6718) [25053774] **159**

HEAVY HORSE WORLD (UK/0951-2640) [I09512640] **2799**

HEAVY-ION REACTIONS *CEASED.* (US/8756-1964) [11492185] **4404**

HEAVY METAL (US/0885-7822) [04963999] **3393**

HEAVY METAL TIMES (US/0739-4306) [09722712] **4121**

HEAVY OILER *SUSPENDED.* (US/1015-0714) [19612094] **4259**

HEAVY TRUCK COLLISION ESTIMATING GUIDE: CHEVROLET, DIAMOND REO, DODGE, FORD, FREIGHTLINER, GMC, INTERNATIONAL, KENWORTH, MACK, PETERBILT, WHITE (US/0272-8591) [06932383] **5383**

HEBAMME, DIE (GW/0932-8122) [23835117] **3762**

HEBBEL JAHRBUCH (GW/0073-1560) [01751935] **3393**

HEBDO A H P Q (CN/0707-204X) [04635083] **3783**

HEBDO CARRIERES (MONTREAL) (CN/0823-518X) [10381556] **1677**

HEBDO COLLEGE (CN/0710-2089) [08418974] **1827**

HEBDO-COOP (CN/0713-4231) [08898906] **1542**

HEBDO-COOP. ENGLISH EDITION (CN/0713-424X) [08898911] **1542**

HEBDO DE BELLECHASSE (DORCHESTER), L' (CN/0714-4784) [09071200] **5786**

HEBDO DE LA ROUGE, L' (CN/0711-8074) [08503277] **5786**

HEBDO DE L'ACTUALITE SOCIALE, L' (FR) [29805390] **2617**

HEBDO DE LAVAL, L' (CN/0822-7535) [10436298] **5786**

HEBDO JOURNAL (CN/0229-9887) [08300750] **5786**

HEBDO PENINSULE (CN/1184-2814) [23598428] **5786**

HEBDO POLICE (CN/0229-6470) [08489368] **3165**

HEBDO, PUBLI-MAISON (CN/1183-2290) [24690513] **2534**

HEBDO SCIENCE (CN/0711-3463) [08605199] **5109**

HEBDO-TEX, L' (FR/0989-4985) [I09894985] 1025, **5351**

HEBDOCUIR (FR/0399-5461) [I03995461] **3184**

HEBEI DAXUE XUEBAO ZIRAN KEXUE BAN (CC/1000-1565) [I10001565] **5201**

HEBEI DIZHI XUEYUAN XUEBAO (CC/1001-9707) [18892875] **1382**

HEBEI GONGXUEYUAN XUEBAO (CC/1000-5358) [I10005358] **5109**

HEBEI SHENG KEXUEYUAN XUEBAO (CC/1001-9383) [21708251] **5109**

HEBEI SHIFAN DAXUE XUEBAO ZIRAN KEXUE BAN (CC/1000-5854) [I10005854] **5109**

HEBEI YIXUEYUAN XUEBAO (CC/1000-1581) [21722307] **3583**

HEBERT'S CATALOGUE OF USED PLATE NUMBER SINGLES (US/0098-2326) [01798739] **2785**

HEBEZEUGE UND FORDERMITTEL (GW/0017-9442) [I00179442] **2115**

HEBRAICA, A (BL) [07189792] **2262**

HEBRAICA EM REVISTA *See* HEBRAICA, A **2262**

HEBREW ANNUAL REVIEW *SUSPENDED.* (US/0193-7162) [03898672] **5017**

HEBREW STUDIES (US/0146-4094) [02942269] 5017, **5048**

HEBREW UNION COLLEGE *See* MONOGRAPHS OF THE HEBREW UNION COLLEGE **5051**

HEBREW UNION COLLEGE *See* HEBREW UNION COLLEGE ANNUAL **5048**

HEBREW UNION COLLEGE ANNUAL (US/0360-9049) [01589746] **5048**

HEBREW UNION COLLEGE ANNUAL. SUPPLEMENTS (US/0275-9993) [03638278] **5048**

HEBREW UNIVERSITY STUDIES IN LITERATURE AND THE ARTS *CEASED.* (IS/0792-0393) [10419453] 321, **3393**

HEC FORUM (NE/0956-2737) [19771189] 2250, **3783**

HECATE (AT/0311-4198) [02530248] **5558**

HECB ADVISORY COMMITTEES, STATUS REPORT / PREPARED BY THE STAFF OF THE MINNESOTA HIGHER EDUCATION COORDINATING BOARD (US) [10033192] **1827**

HECLA INDEPENDENT (US) [12813985] **5743**

HEDONGLI GONGCHENG (CC/0258-0926) [I02580926] **2155**

HEENSCHUT (NE/0017-9515) [I00179515] **299**

HEER MELSUNGEN (GW/0941-2808) [I09412808] **4045**

HEFTE DES ARCHAOLOGISCHEN SEMINARS DER UNIVERSITAT BERN (SZ) [03611164] **2690**

HEFTE ZUR UNFALLHEILKUNDE (GW/0085-1469) [01354454] **2863**

HEGEL-STUDIEN (GW/0073-1587) [01751937] **4347**

HEGEL-STUDIEN. BEIHEFT, (GW/0440-5927) [02578465] **4348**

HEGIS IX REQUIREMENTS AND SPECIFICATIONS FOR THE SURVEY OF SALARIES AND TENURE OF FULL-TIME INSTRUCTIONAL FACULTY (US) [04011884] **1827**

HEI-LUNG-CHIANG FA HSIAO / HEI-LUNG-CHIANG SHENG FA HSIAO KUNG YEH KO CHI CHING PAO CHAN (CC) [08634719] **1025**

HEIAN HAKUBUTSUKAN *See* HEIAN HAKUBUTSUKAN KENKYU KIYO **4088**

HEIAN HAKUBUTSUKAN KENKYU KIYO (JA) [02246042] **4088**

HEIDEGGER STUDIES (GW/0885-4580) [12641227] **4348**

HEIDELBERG BULLETIN, THE (US/1044-3851) [19768462] **1092**

HEIDELBERG SCIENCE LIBRARY (US/0073-1595) [02762889] **5109**

HEIDELBERGER AKADEMIE DER WISSENSCHAFTEN *See* SITZUNGSBERICHTE DER HEIDELBERGER AKADEMIE DER WISSENSCHAFTEN, MATHEMATISCH-NATURWISSENSCHAFTLICHE KLASSE **5158**

HEIDELBERGER AKADEMIE DER WISSENSCHAFTEN *See* JAHRBUCH DER HEIDELBERGER AKADEMIE DER WISSENSCHAFTEN **5117**

HEIDELBERGER AKADEMIE DER WISSENSCHAFTEN. PHILOSOPHISCH-HISTORISCHE KLASSE *See* ABHANDLUNGEN DER HEIDELBERGER AKADEMIE DER WISSENSCHAFTEN, PHILOSOPHISCH-HISTORISCHE KLASSE **4339**

HEIDELBERGER ALTHISTORISCHE BEITRAEGE UND EPIGRAPHISCHE STUDIEN (GW/0930-1208) [I09301208] **1077**

HEIDELBERGER BEITRAEGE ZUR ROMANISTIK (GW/0170-8821) [02078302] 3393, **3285**

HEIDELBERGER FORSCHUNGEN (GW/0440-6044) [02078361] 3393, **3285**

HEIDELBERGER GEOGRAPHISCHE ARBEITEN (GW/0375-6572) [02069903] **2565**

HEIDELBERGER JAHRBUCHER (GW/0073-1641) [01751946] **5109**

HEIDELBERGER TASCHENBUCHER (GW/0073-1684) [02843213] **4828**

HEIFER INTERNATIONAL EXCHANGE, THE (US) [23460443] **212**

HEIGHTS HERALD (US/0887-476X) [13260957] **5664**

HEILBERUFE, DIE (GW/0017-9604) [04660929] **3583**

HEILIGER DIENST (AU/0017-9620) [I00179620] **4962**

HEILPADAGOGISCHE BLATTER *See* ZEITSCHRIFT FUER HEILPAEDAGOGIK **1859**

HEILPADAGOGISCHE FORSCHUNG (GW) [05826705] **1750**

HEIMATBUCH DER DEUTSCHEN AUS RUSSLAND (GW) [01751949] **1918**

HEIMATKALENDER (HANNOVER, GERMANY) (GW) [20926018] **2690**

HEIMATKUNDLICHE HEFTE DES ARCHIVS DER STADT REMSCHEID (GW) [18095439] **2517**

HEIMATLEBEN. COSTUMES ET COUTUMES (SZ) [04980006] **5268**

HEIMEN (NO/0017-9841) [01751952] **2690**

HEIMTEX (GW/0017-9876) [I00179876] **2900**

HEIMTEX AKTUELL, HAUSTEX *See* HAUSTEX **5351**

HEINE-JAHRBUCH (GW/0073-1692) [00923884] **3393**

HEIN'S U.S. TREATY INDEX ON CD-ROM [COMPUTER FILE] (US) [24768091] **4523**

HEIR-LINES (LAKE ORION, MICH.) (US/0739-6082) [07802690] **2452**

HEIR LINES (LEBANON, OHIO) (US/0742-4779) [10336374] **2452**

HEIRS (US/0017-9884) [01955845] **3393**

HEISEY NEWS (US/0731-8014) [08236899] **2590**

HEIZUNG UND LUFTUNG (SZ) [25895166] **2605**

HEJIRA (MONTREAL, QUEBEC) (CN/0826-0133) [11426737] **3463**

HEJISHU (CH/0253-3219) [08724793] **2155**

HEJNA (US/0748-7568) [10978606] **2262**

HEKIMA (KE) [08471569] **1827**

HEL ACHAU. MICROFORM. : JOURNAL OF THE CLWYD FAMILY HISTORY SOCIETY (UK/0260-1753) [19725313] **2453**

HELDIA (GW/0176-2621) [12896793] **5585**

HELEN FORESMAN SPENCER MUSEUM OF ART *See* REGISTER OF THE SPENCER MUSEUM OF ART, THE **4095**

HELEN K. MUSSALLEM LIBRARY *See* PERIODICAL HOLDINGS / HELEN K. MUSSALLEM LIBRARY, CANADIAN NURSES ASSOCIATION **3866**

HELENA-WEST HELENA WORLD *See* DAILY WORLD (HELENA, ARK.), THE **5631**

HELGOLAENDER MEERESUNTERSUCHUNGEN (GW/0174-3597) [07043681] **554**

HELIA (NOVI SAD) (YU/1018-1806) [25088170] **2418**

HELICOBACTER (UK/1351-5284) 488, **3583**

HELICOM FROM MIRABEL (CN/0828-5683) [11919066] **1608**

HELICON (II) [01784173] **3463**

HELICON; REVUE INTERNATIONALE DES PROBLEMES GENERAUX DE LA LITTERATURE (NE) [02261856] **3393**

HELICOPTER (UK/0143-1005) [01431005] **22**

HELICOPTER ANNUAL (US/0739-5728) [09430702] **22**

HELICOPTER EQUIPMENT LISTS & PRICES. RECIPROCATING ENGINE HELICOPTERS (US/1056-7747) [23848625] **22**

Alphabetical Title Index — HERALD

HELICOPTER EQUIPMENT LISTS & PRICES. TURBINE ENGINE HELICOPTERS : H.E.L.P (US/1045-9464) [20292495] **22**

HELICOPTER NEWS (US/0363-8227) [02521083] **23**

HELICOPTER SAFETY (ARLINGTON, VA.) (US/1042-2048) [18923844] **23**

HELICOPTER WORLD (LONDON. 1982) (UK/0262-0448) [09262424] **23**

HELICOPTERS (CN/0227-3160) [11108180] **23**

HELICTITE (AT/0017-9973) [02447359] **5109**

HELIKON (HU/0017-999X) [09716408] **3393**

HELIKON (ROMA) (IT/0017-9981) [02261857] 1077, **3285**

HELINIUM (BE/0018-0009) [01890322] **2690**

HELIOGRAPHIC MAPS OF THE PHOTOSPHERE (SZ) [06971948] **395**

HELIOS (DR) [01794770] **2736**

HELIOS (LUBBOCK) (US/0160-0923) [02464767] **1077**

HELIUM RESOURCES OF THE UNITED STATES (US) [09735669] **2140**

HELLAS (IT) [10708765] **3393**

HELLAS (US/1044-5331) [19829713] **3393**

HELLENEWS (GR) **2517**

HELLENIC CHRONICLE, THE (US) [10462892] **2262**

HELLENIC TIMES (US/1059-2121) [10462933] **5717**

HELLENIKA STOMATOLOGIKA CHRONIKA (GR/1011-4181) [06466395] **1324**

HELLENIKA VIVLIA. GREEK BOOKS (GR) [04340026] **2847**

HELLENIKE LAIKE TECHNE (GR) [01793031] **352**

HELLENIKE THEOLOGIKE VIVLIOGRAPHIA (GR) [10630730] **4962**

HELLENIKO PERIODIKO GIA STOMATIKE & GNATHOPROSOPIKE CHEIROURGIKE / EPISEMO ORGANO TES HETAIREIAS STOMATOGNATHOPROSOPIKES CHEIROURGIKES, TO (GR) [20999657] 1324, **3965**

HELLENOKANADIKI HEBDOMADA (CN/0705-1336) [03963375] **5786**

HELLER AND HUNT LAW PRACTICE MANAGEMENT REPORT (US) [18345908] **2978**

HELLER REPORT ON EDUCATIONAL TECHNOLOGY AND TELECOMMUNICATIONS MARKETS, THE (US/1047-5230) [20732337] **5109**

HELLIS NEWSLETTER (II/0254-2595) [08857567] **3213**

HELLO (UK) **2517**

HELMANTICA (SP/0018-0114) [01936080] **1077**

HELMINTHOLOGIA (XO/0440-6605) [05428628] **5585**

HELMINTHOLOGICAL ABSTRACTS (UK/0957-6789) [21107637] 5585, **5604**

HELMINTOLOGIJA (SOFIJA) (BU/0324-1947) [02618769] **5585**

HELO (II) [03217457] **3393**

HELP FOR LIVING (US/1056-1986) [23535973] **5061**

HELP (WASHINGTON) (US/0363-9185) [02569224] **1297**

HELPER (AMERICAN SOCIAL HEALTH ASSOCIATION) (US) [08986334] 5287, **4782**

●HELPING CHILDREN LEARN (US/1065-6405) [26661527] 2280, **1750**

HELPING HAND (JANESVILLE, WIS.), THE (US/0745-029X) [06435220] **4962**

HELPING OUT IN THE OUTDOORS (US/8756-310X) [09524955] 4204, **4706**

HELPING PERSON IN THE GROUP (US/0073-1706) [01640935] **5287**

HELPING THE EXOFFENDER (US/0364-3441) [02625475] **3165**

HELPS FOR STUDENTS OF HISTORY (UK/0073-1714) [01751966] **2617**

HELR. THE HARVARD ENVIRONMENTAL LAW REVIEW (US/0147-8257) [03231039] **3113**

HELSINGIN SANOMAT (FI/0355-2047) [01751971] **5800**

HELSINGIN VAESTO (FI/0357-3370) [10314689] **5328**

HELSINGIN YLIOPISTON YMPARISTONSUOJELUN LAITOKSEN JULKAISUJA (FI/0782-2790) [07822790] **2195**

HELSINKI (FINLAND). TELASTOKESKUS See TILK : NELJANNESVUOSIKATSAUS **5345**

HELTIDSLANDBRUGETS KONOMI / JORDBRUGSKONOMISK INSTITUT (DK/0108-6561) [09711543] **92**

HELVETICA CHIMICA ACTA (SZ/0018-019X) [01751975] **976**

HELVETICA CHIRURGICA ACTA CEASED. (SZ/0018-0181) [01624504] **3903**

HELVETICA PAEDIATRICA ACTA (SZ/0018-022X) [01751980] **3903**

HELVETICA PAEDIATRICA ACTA. SUPPLEMENTUM (SZ/0073-1811) [01751981] **3904**

HELVETICA PHYSICA ACTA (SZ/0018-0238) [01751982] **4404**

HEM O FRITID (SW) [08611736] **2517**

●HEM/ONC ANNALS (US/1067-2370) [27166182] 3818, **3772**

HEMATOLOGIC PATHOLOGY (US/0886-0238) [12788658] **3894**

HEMATOLOGICAL ONCOLOGY (UK/0278-0232) [07684096] 3818, **3772**

HEMATOLOGIE. E80 (FR) **488**

HEMATOLOGY CASE STUDIES (US/0091-2336) [01784528] **3772**

HEMATOLOGY (NEW YORK, N.Y.) (US/0891-9763) [11258918] **3772**

HEMATOLOGY/ONCOLOGY CLINICS OF NORTH AMERICA (US/0889-8588) [14091884] 3818, **3772**

HEMATOLOGY REVIEWS AND COMMUNICATIONS (SZ/0882-8083) [11984944] **3772**

●HEMATOPOIETIC THERAPY (US/1061-5318) [25343942] **3797**

HEMEL HEMPSTEAD & DISTRICT BUSINESS DIRECTORY (UK/0957-1043) [09571043] **679**

HEMET NEWS, THE (US) [13042317] **5635**

HEMIJSKI PREGLED (YU/0440-6826) [11101457] **976**

HEMINGWAY REVIEW, THE (US/0276-3362) [07342953] **3344**

HEMISFILE: PERSPECTIVES ON POLITICAL AND ECONOMIC TRENDS IN THE AMERICAS (US) [21572643] 1493, **4475**

HEMISPHERE (MIAMI, FLA.) (US/0898-3038) [17784270] **4475**

HEMISPHERES / [POLISH ACADEMY OF SCIENCES, INSTITUTE OF HISTORY, CENTER FOR STUDIES ON NON-EUROPEAN COUNTRIES] (PL/0239-8818) [13960077] **2617**

HEMLOCK QUARTERLY See TIMELINES (EUGENE, OR) **2253**

HEMMINGS MOTOR NEWS (US) [01781701] **5416**

HEMOGLOBIN (US/0363-0269) [02720226] **3797**

HEMOPHILIA ONTARIO (CN/0822-5974) [10199282] **3772**

HEMOPHILIA TODAY (CN/0046-7251) [10365081] **3705**

HEMOPHILIE DE NOS JOURS, L' (CN/0226-6644) [06515203] **3583**

HEMOSTASIS AND THROMBOSIS (US/0360-7607) [01924593] **3772**

HEMPSTEAD TRAILS (US) **2453**

HEMSON PLANNING & DEVELOPMENT REPORT (CN/0848-8622) [21343897] **2824**

HEMSON TORONTO LAND USE REPORT (CN/0848-8541) [21343880] 4838, **4654**

HENA (GR) [12714192] **5328**

HENCEFORTH (US/0895-7622) [02250382] **4962**

HENCKEL GENEALOGICAL BULLETIN SUSPENDED. (US/0739-6341) [05398492] **2453**

HENDERSON DAILY NEWS (US) [14265341] **5750**

HENDERSON ELECTRONIC MARKET FORECAST (US) **2056**

HENDERSON HOME NEWS (US) [10686708] **5707**

HENDERSONVILLE STAR NEWS (US/0193-5143) [05229146] **5745**

HENDRICKS PIONEER, THE (US) [01751989] **5696**

HENINGER/NOELL WEEKLY M&A "GREEN SHEET", THE (US/1041-1860) [18686295] **790**

HENKEL-REFERATE : EXCERPTS OF HENKEL RESEARCH PAPERS (GW/0720-9428) [08598580] **976**

HENLEIN-HEINLEIN CHANTICLEER : NEWSLETTER OF THE HENLEIN-HEINLEIN FAMILY ASSOCIATION, THE (US/1057-008X) [23071971] **2453**

HENNEPIN COUNTY LIBRARY. CATALOGING SECTION. CATALOGING BULLETIN See HCL CATALOGING BULLETIN **3213**

HENNEPIN COUNTY LIBRARY. TECHNICAL SERVICES DIVISION See HCL CATALOGING BULLETIN **3213**

HENNEPIN HISTORY (US) [24054161] **2736**

HENNEPIN LAWYER, THE (US) [01752000] **2978**

HENNESSEY CLIPPER (US) [13756250] **5732**

HENRIETTA POST, THE (US) [08065537] **5717**

HENRY AND CLAYTON SUN See CLAYTON SUN **5652**

HENRY B. ZIMMER'S INCOME TAX PROBLEMS WITH DETAILED SOLUTIONS (CN/0824-667X) [11634767] **4730**

HENRY B. ZIMMER'S PROBLEMS & QUESTIONS IN CANADIAN TAXATION (CN/0824-6378) [10840863] 4731, **2978**

HENRY BRADSHAW SOCIETY (SERIES) (UK/0144-0241) [18096291] **4962**

HENRY COUNTY NEWS REPUBLICAN, THE (US) [13730837] **5664**

HENRY E. HUNTINGTON LIBRARY AND ART GALLERY See ANNUAL REPORT - HUNTINGTON LIBRARY, ART GALLERY, BOTANICAL GARDENS **3190**

HENRY E. HUNTINGTON LIBRARY AND ART GALLERY See HUNTINGTON LIBRARY PUBLICATIONS **3213**

HENRY E. HUNTINGTON LIBRARY AND ART GALLERY, SAN MARINO, CALIFORNIA See HUNTINGTON LIBRARY QUARTERLY, THE **352**

HENRY E. SIGERIST SUPPLEMENTS TO THE BULLETIN OF THE HISTORY OF MEDICINE, THE (US/0194-1100) [04337944] **3583**

HENRY GEORGE NEWS (US/0018-0424) [01606144] **1827**

HENRY HERALD, THE (US/1045-6678) [19646987] **5653**

HENRY JAMES REVIEW, THE (US/0273-0340) [06060016] **3344**

HENRY L. DOHERTY SERIES (US/0149-6409) [01713919] **4259**

HENRY LUCE FOUNDATION See HIGHLIGHTS - HENRY LUCE FOUNDATION **1750**

HENRY NEIGHBOR, THE (US/0192-0677) [04972855] **5653**

HENS REVISTA TECHNICO-GANADERA (SP) [09567229] **212**

HENSTON VETERINARY BOVINE VADE MECUM (UK) **5511**

HENSTON VETERINARY EQUINE VADE MECUM (UK/0969-2681) [09692681] **5511**

HENSTON VETERINARY VADE MECUM. LARGE ANIMALS See HENSTON VETERINARY BOVINE VADE MECUM **5511**

HENSTON VETERINARY VADE MECUM. LARGE ANIMALS See HENSTON VETERINARY EQUINE VADE MECUM **5511**

HENSTON VETERINARY VADE MECUM. LARGE ANIMALS, THE (UK/0268-4276) [13487976] **5511**

HENSTON VETERINARY VADE MECUM. SMALL ANIMALS, THE (UK/0268-4268) [12993660] **5511**

HENTY SOCIETY LITERARY SUPPLEMENT (UK) [18723010] **3344**

HEP ... COLLEGES AND UNIVERSITY COMPUTER DIRECTORY, THE (US/0898-2279) [15972196] **1827**

HEP HIGHER EDUCATION DIRECTORY, THE (US/0736-0797) [09068387] **1827**

HEPATITIS B COALITION NEWS (US) **3670**

HEPATO-GASTROENTEROLOGY (GW/0172-6390) [06298177] **3746**

HEPATOLOGY (US) **3583**

HEPATOLOGY (GW/0171-6123) [06635338] **3797**

HEPATOLOGY (BALTIMORE, MD.) (US/0270-9139) [06848614] 3746, **3797**

HEPATOLOGY LETTERS (NE) **3583**

HEPCATS (US/1045-201X) [20061086] **5074**

HEPHAISTOS (BAD BRAMSTEDT) (GW/0174-2086) [07445742] **269**

HER MAJESTY'S CONSULS' LIST (UK) [02397665] **4654**

HER MAJESTY'S INSPECTORATE OF CONSTABULARY ANNUAL REPORT (UK) **4654**

HER WORLD ANNUAL (SI) [03448266] **5558**

HERACLES (FR) [09787939] **4045**

HERALD AND TRIBUNE (JONESBORO, TENN. : 1869) (US) [11961030] **5745**

HERALD (BROWN DEER, GLENDALE, WIS. ED.) (US) [15513855] **5768**

HERALD-CHRONICLE

Alphabetical Title Index

HERALD-CHRONICLE (WINCHESTER, TENN.), THE (US/0893-3707) [15512017] **5745**

HERALD-CITIZEN (COOKEVILLE, TENN.) (US/8750-5541) [11501842] **5745**

HERALD-COASTER, THE (US) [14407668] **5750**

HERALD (CONROE, TEX.), THE (US/0730-6520) [07901651] **2453**

HERALD-DEMOCRAT (BEAVER, OKLA.) (US) [13663868] **5732**

HERALD-DISPATCH (HUNTINGTON, W. VA.) (US) [12897734] **5764**

HERALD-DISPATCH (LOS ANGELES, CALIF. : 1981) (US/8750-2038) [10568995] **5635**

HERALD (EVERETT, WASH.), THE (US) [09331946] **5761**

HERALD (FLORIDA SCHOOL FOR THE DEAF AND BLIND) (US) [17886009] **4388**, **1092**

HERALD (GARY, IND. : EAST GARY ED.) *See* LAKE STATION HERALD **5665**

HERALD (HAYWARD, CALIF.), THE (US/1046-865X) [20551707] **5635**

HERALD (HIGH SPRINGS, FLA.) *See* HIGH SPRINGS HERALD **5649**

HERALD (JASPER, IND.) (US) [14227360] **5664**

HERALD-JOURNAL, THE (US) [12546157] **5756**

HERALD-LEADER (SILOAM SPRINGS, ARK.) (US/1061-9542) [24980543] **5631**

HERALD-LEADER, THE (US) [19965752] **5653**

HERALD LEDGER (US) [14145738] **5681**

HERALD (MACKENZIE) (CN/0318-1863) [02441815] **5786**

HERALD (MILBANK, S.D.) *See* MILBANK HERALD ADVANCE **5744**

HERALD (MONTEREY, CALIF.), THE (US/0889-3101) [13461387] **5635**

HERALD-NEWS (EDMONTON, KY.), THE (US/0889-9711) [14126508] **5681**

HERALD-NEWS (PASSAIC, N.J.) (US) [10336463] **5710**

HERALD-NEWS (WOLF POINT, MONT.) (US) [13984691] **5705**

HERALD OF CHRISTIAN SCIENCE (AUDIO CASSETTE ED.) *See* CHRISTIAN SCIENCE SENTINEL (RADIO ED.) **2530**

HERALD OF CHRISTIAN SCIENCE (AUDIO CASSETTE ED. : 1988) *See* HERALD OF CHRISTIAN SCIENCE (AUDIO CASSETTE ED.), THE **4962**

HERALD OF CHRISTIAN SCIENCE (AUDIO CASSETTE ED.), THE (US/1061-6659) [25394258] **4962**

HERALD OF CHRISTIAN SCIENCE, THE (US/0146-7174) [03006632] **4962**

HERALD OF FREEDOM (MANVILLE), THE (US/0018-0483) [04331741] **2534**

HERALD OF HIS COMING (US) [01775768] **4962**

HERALD OF HOLINESS (US/0018-0513) [01431126] **5061**

HERALD OF LIBRARY SCIENCE (II/0018-0521) [01752007] **3213**

HERALD OF REPRESSION IN UKRAINE (US/0749-8616) [11182872] **4508**

●HERALD OF THE RUSSIAN ACADEMY OF SCIENCES (RU/1019-3316) [25704277] **5109**

HERALD-PRESS (HUNTINGTON, IND.) (US) [14508002] **5664**

HERALD RECORD (WEST UNION, W. VA.) (US) [12768460] **5764**

HERALD-REPUBLICAN (ANGOLA, IND.) (US) [12149728] **5664**

HERALD REVIEW (BANGALORE, INDIA) (II) [11660338] **2504**

HERALD (RINCON, GA.), THE (US/0899-627X) [18171726] **5654**

HERALD (ROCKPORT, TEX. 1990), THE (US/1055-5005) [23192632] **5750**

HERALD (SHARON, PA.), THE (US/0744-7302) [02261871] **5736**

HERALD (SHARPSBURG, PA. : 1953) (US) [02261872] **5736**

HERALD-STANDARD (UNIONTOWN, PA. : 1980) (US) [15238984] **5736**

HERALD-STAR, THE (US/0890-8656) [14510835] **5728**

HERALD STATESMAN (US/1060-460X) [10088884] **5717**

HERALD-SUN (DURHAM, N.C.), THE (US/1055-4467) [22992790] **5723**

HERALD, THE (PK) [01589238] **2504**

HERALD, THE (US) [10610642] **5712**

HERALD, THE (US) [08782955] **5645**

HERALD, THE (US) [28436872] **5742**

HERALD, THE (US) [25084644] **5660**

HERALD, THE (US) [23308737] **5660**

HERALD-TIMES (BLOOMINGTON, IND.), THE (US/1044-4246) [19784589] **5664**

HERALD TRIBUNE CROSSWORD PUZZLES ONLY (US/1054-8149) [22978964] **4862**

HERALD TRIBUNE CROSSWORDS & OTHER WORD GAMES (US/1054-8165) [22979164] **4862**

HERALD-TRIBUNE, THE (US) [20411789] **5654**

HERALD-TRIBUNE, THE (US/0746-2042) [09856572] **5664**

HERALD-VOICE (BELLE CENTER, OHIO : 1928) (US) [17358946] **5728**

HERALD (WHITEFISH BAY, WIS. ED.) (US) [15499532] **5768**

HERALDIQUE ET GENEALOGIE VILLAINE-LA-JUHEL (FR/1142-4966) [11424966] **2453**

HERALDO DE LA CIENCIA CRISTIANA, EL (US/0439-0148) [03243659] **4962**

HERALDO DE SANTIDAD *See* DIRECCION (KANSAS CITY, MO.) **4953**

●HERALDO DE SANTIDAD (1992), EL (US/1060-2135) [24887686] **4962**

HERALDO DEL CINE (AG) [05377059] **4071**

HERALDO, EL (HO) [29040213] **5802**

HERALDRY IN CANADA (CN/0441-6619) [02021900] **2453**

HERALDRY SOCIETY OF SCOTLAND *See* JOURNAL OF THE HERALDRY SOCIETY OF SCOTLAND **2455**

HERALDRY, THE ARMIGER'S NEWS (US) [09444396] **2453**

HERANCA JUDAICA (BL) [09603401] **5048**

HERAUT DE LA SCIENCE CHRETIENNE, LE (US/0145-7470) [02777179] **4962**

HERAUT VAN DE CHRISTELIJKE WETENSCHAP, DE (US/0145-756X) [03243939] **4962**

HERB AND SPICE SAMPLER (US/1050-9941) [21741471] **2343**

HERB COMPANION, THE (US/1040-581X) [18474078] **2343**

HERB IRELAND'S SALES PROSPECTOR. CALIFORNIA, ARIZONA, NEVADA AND HAWAII (US/0270-8833) [06519074] **925**

HERB IRELAND'S SALES PROSPECTOR. CANADA (US/0270-8817) [06515888] **616**

HERB IRELAND'S SALES PROSPECTOR. COLORADO, IDAHO, MONTANA, OREGON, UTAH, WASHINGTON, WYOMING AND ALASKA (US/0270-8825) [06515959] **925**

HERB IRELAND'S SALES PROSPECTOR. GEORGIA, FLORIDA, ALABAMA AND NORTH AND SOUTH CAROLINA (US/0270-8752) [05917263] **925**

HERB IRELAND'S SALES PROSPECTOR. ILLINOIS AND INDIANA (US/0270-8736) [06513437] **925**

HERB IRELAND'S SALES PROSPECTOR. LOUISIANA, MISSISSIPPI, ARKANSAS, OKLAHOMA, KENTUCKY AND TENNESSEE (US/0270-8779) [06515792] **925**

HERB IRELAND'S SALES PROSPECTOR. MARYLAND, VIRGINIA, WEST VIRGINIA, NORTH AND SOUTH CAROLINA, AND DISTRICT OF COLUMBIA (US/0270-8760) [06515128] **925**

HERB IRELAND'S SALES PROSPECTOR. MISSOURI, KANSAS, IOWA AND NEBRASKA (US/0270-8795) [06515804] **925**

HERB IRELAND'S SALES PROSPECTOR. NEW ENGLAND (US/0270-8698) [06512806] **925**

HERB IRELAND'S SALES PROSPECTOR. NEW YORK, NEW JERSEY AND SOUTHERN CONNECTICUT (US/0270-8701) [06513049] **925**

HERB IRELAND'S SALES PROSPECTOR. OHIO AND MICHIGAN (US/0270-8728) [06513278] **925**

HERB IRELAND'S SALES PROSPECTOR. OHIO RIVER VALLEY (US/0270-8744) [06514998] **925**

HERB IRELAND'S SALES PROSPECTOR. PENNSYLVANIA, DELAWARE AND SOUTHERN NEW JERSEY (US/0270-871X) [06513233] **925**

HERB IRELAND'S SALES PROSPECTOR. TEXAS, OKLAHOMA AND NEW MEXICO (US/0270-8787) [06515443] **925**

HERB IRELAND'S SALES PROSPECTOR. WISCONSIN, MINNESOTA, IOWA, NORTH AND SOUTH DAKOTA (US/0270-8809) [06515837] **925**

HERB QUARTERLY, THE (US/0163-9900) [04550387] **2418**

HERB, SPICE, AND MEDICINAL PLANT DIGEST, THE (US/1048-3160) [13078341] **2418**

HERBA (NO/0800-5419) [I08005419] **2418**, **2343**

HERBA GALLICA CHEMILLE (FR/0998-4399) [I09984399] 92, **512**

HERBA POLONICA (PL/00l8-0599) [03577863] 3583, **512**

HERBAGE ABSTRACTS (UK/0018-0602) [01644974] 92, **154**

HERBAL ROSE REPORT, THE (US/1055-8578) [23363849] **2418**

HERBALGRAM (AUSTIN, TEX.) (US/0899-5648) [13799895] **512**

HERBARIST, THE (US/0740-5979) [02447371] **2418**

HERBARIUM NEWS (US/0731-7824) [07980872] **512**

HERBERGEN DER CHRISTENHEIT; JAHRBUCH FUER DEUTSCHE KIRCHENGESCHICHTE (GE/0437-3014) [02432613] 4962, **300**

HERBERTIA (1984) (US/8756-9418) [10988608] 512, **2418**

HERBES ROUGES *CEASED.* (CN/0441-6627) [02021929] **2534**

HERBS, SPICES & MEDICINAL PLANTS *See* JOURNAL OF HERBS, SPICES & MEDICINAL PLANTS **2421**

HERBS, SPICES, AND MEDICINAL PLANTS : RECENT ADVANCES IN BOTANY, HORTICULTURE, AND PHARMACOLOGY (US/0890-6653) [13195370] **173**

HERCEGOVINA (MOSTAR, BOSNIA AND HERCEGOVINA: 1981) (BN/0351-4552) [19129034] **2690**

HERCULES MIXER, THE (US/0191-1775) [04810313] **679**

HERCYNIA *CEASED.* (GW/0018-0637) [03485760] **5109**

HERD BOOK - BRITISH GOAT SOCIETY (UK) [03854307] 212, **195**

HERDER-KORRESPONDENZ (GW/0018-0645) [01606254] **5030**

●HERDER YEARBOOK: PUBLICATIONS OF THE INTERNATIONAL HERDER SOCIETY (US/1062-3582) [25596244] **212**

HERDSA NEWS (AT/0157-1826) [I01571826] **1828**

HERE IS YOUR INDIANA GOVERNMENT (US/0894-6434) [03436900] **4654**

HEREDITAS (SW/0018-0661) [01752016] **547**

HEREDITY (UK/0018-067X) [01752017] **547**

HEREFORD BRAND, THE (US) [13695046] **5750**

HEREFORD'S NORTH AMERICA (UK/0143-5906) [05636806] **23**

HERE'S HEALTH (WEST BYFLEET) (UK/0018-0696) [I00180696] **4782**

HERE'S HELP (RENO, NEV.) (US/1064-2080) [26231249] **5287**

HERE'S HOW (NEW YORK) (US/0092-5365) [01783677] **4370**

HERE'S HOW (RESTON, VA.) (US/0735-0031) [08843317] **1864**

HERESIES (US/0146-3411) [02917688] 352, **5558**

HERINGTON TIMES (HERINGTON, KAN. : 1973) (US) [11116848] **5676**

HERITAGE (SI) [04618428] **4088**

HERITAGE (AUSTIN, TEX.) (US/1047-5613) [16199992] **2736**

HERITAGE BOOK, THE (CN/0711-4737) [08534435] **4962**

HERITAGE (BURNHAM-ON-CROUCH, ENG.) (UK/0950-5245) [15472577] **2690**

HERITAGE (CARSON, CALIF.) (US/0895-0792) [16685585] 2652, **2262**

HERITAGE CONSERVATION AND RECREATION SERVICE *See* NOTIFICATIONS / HCRS INFORMATION EXCHANGE **2201**

HERITAGE (COOPERSTOWN, N.Y.) (US/8755-9064) [11285512] **2736**

HERITAGE COUNTRY (US/1055-9515) [23374969] **2736**

HERITAGE ECHOES (CN) **2453**

HERITAGE EDUCATION QUARTERLY (US/0897-6775) [17597436] 3213, **2481**

HERITAGE FOUNDATION, WASHINGTON, D.C *See* CRITICAL ISSUES (WASHINGTON DC) **5197**

HERITAGE HEARTH (CN/0841-923X) [19115473] **4088**

HERITAGE INSTITUTIONS (CN/0847-0146) [21094868] **4088**

HERITAGE INTERPRETATION (UK/0265-3664) [10357767] **2690**

HERITAGE LINK (CN/0820-2893) [16450476] **2690**

HERITAGE (LONDON) (UK) [09650735] **5048**

HERITAGE NEWS (CANBERRA, A.C.T.) (AT/0103-626X) [18992950] **2510**

HERITAGE NEWS / DALLAS COUNTY HISTORICAL SOCIETY (US) [13658109] **2617**

HERITAGE NEWSLETTER (US) **2453**

HERITAGE NOTES (LOUISBOURG) (CN/1183-5834) [25652404] **2736**

HERITAGE OF THE GREAT PLAINS (US/0739-4772) [07027594] **2617**

HERITAGE OF VERMILION COUNTY, THE (US/0018-0718) [04094552] **2617**

HERITAGE OF ZIMBABWE (RH) [16140660] **2639**

HERITAGE OUTLOOK *See* URBAN FOCUS LONDON **2714**

HERITAGE OUTLOOK (UK/0261-1988) [09297329] 2195, **300**

HERITAGE QUEST *See* HERITAGE QUEST MAGAZINE **2453**

HERITAGE QUEST (US/0886-0262) [12867827] **2453**

HERITAGE QUEST MAGAZINE (US/1074-5238) [27398939] **2453**

HERITAGE REVIEW (US/0162-8267) [02253521] **2690**

HERITAGE SCOTLAND : THE MAGAZINE OF THE NATIONAL TRUST FOR SCOTLAND (UK/0264-9144) [10378568] **2690**

HERITAGE SEEKERS (CN/0707-0780) [04631910] **2453**

HERITAGE TALES (US/0193-998X) [05277928] **2736**

HERITAGE. THE YORKER SCENE (US/0883-1513) [11372748] **2736**

HERITAGE (TROIS-RIVIERES) (CN/0709-3365) [09639281] **2453**

HERITAGE (VAN BUREN), THE (US/0439-027X) [02416971] **2736**

HERITAGE WEST (SACRAMENTO, CALIF.) (US/0738-8829) [09679122] **251**

HERITAGE WINDOWS (US) **2736**

HERIZONS (CN/0711-7485) [08559632] **5558**

HERMAEA (GW/0440-7164) [01967159] **3393**

HERMAN OTTO MUZEUM EVKONYVE, A (HU/0544-4225) [I05444225] 352, **4088**

HERMATHENA (IE/0018-0750) [01752025] 1077, **4348**

HERMENEIA (GW/0930-6897) [18059662] 4962, **352**

HERMENEIA; A CRITICAL AND HISTORICAL COMMENTARY ON THE BIBLE (US) [01779728] **5017**

HERMENEUTICS OF ART (US/0899-9856) [18283133] **352**

HERMES (1936) (GW) [02280693] **1077**

HERMES AMERICANUS (US/0741-1286) [09925607] **3285**

HERMES (LANSING, MICH.) (US/1061-494X) [25323554] **839**

HERMES (PARIS, FRANCE : 1988) (FR/0767-9513) [20615812] **4476**

HERMES (WIESBADEN) (GW/0018-0777) [01166984] **3393**

HERMETIKKINDUSTRIENS LABORATORIUM (STAVANGER, NORWAY). ARSBERETNING *See* HL-INFORMASJON **2343**

HERMETIKKINDUSTRIENS LABORATORIUM (STRAVANGER NORWAY) *See* HL-INFORMASJON **2343**

HERMINE (CN/0823-6348) [09981989] 2900, **2882**

HERMISTON HERALD AND BUYER'S BONUS, THE (US/8750-4782) [11484529] **5733**

HERMOSILLO, MEXICO. UNIVERSIDAD DE SONORA. ESCUELA DE DERECHO Y CIENCIAS SOCIALES *See* REVISTA DE LA ESCUELA DE DERECHO Y CIENCIAS SOCIALES **3041**

HERMSDORFER TECHNISCHE MITTEILUNGEN : HTM (GE/0439-0377) [11104951] **2590**

HERNANADO DEED REPORT (US) **4838**

HERNE, L' (FR/0440-7237) [02342009] 3285, 3393, **4348**

HERODOTE (FR/0338-487X) [05714903] **2565**

HEROLD DER CHRISTLICHEN WISSENSCHAFT, DER (US/0145-7578) [03244134] **4962**

HEROLD DER WAHRHEIT (US/0300-8851) [01385749] **4962**

HEROLD EXPORT-ADRESSBUCH VON OSTERREICH (AU) [19273690] **839**

HEROLD'S COMPARATIVE APPRAISAL REPORTS (US) [26508506] **4259**

●HEROLD'S OIL HEADLINER (US/1062-3485) [25590391] 1608, **4260**

HEROLD'S OIL SHARE MARKET PERFORMANCE (US/1060-9431) [25344385] **679**

HERON (NE/0046-7316) [02689935] **2024**

HERP (US/0440-7296) [03290487] **5585**

HERPETOFAUNA (AT) [07558207] **5585**

HERPETOFAUNA NEWS (UK/0269-8498) [I02698498] 2195, **5585**

HERPETOLOGICA (US/0018-0831) [01644484] **5585**

HERPETOLOGICAL ASSOCIATION OF AFRICA *See* JOURNAL OF THE HERPETOLOGICAL ASSOCIATION OF AFRICA **5589**

HERPETOLOGICAL CIRCULAR (US/0161-147X) [03902236] **5585**

HERPETOLOGICAL JOURNAL, THE (UK/0268-0130) [13719388] **5585**

HERPETOLOGICAL REVIEW (US/0018-084X) [00918558] **5585**

HERPETOLOGY (PASADENA) (US/0441-666X) [03282351] **5585**

HERPETON (US/0440-7326) [02651542] **5585**

HERPETON (GLENDORA, CALIF.) (US/0090-5410) [01785162] **5585**

HERRI-ARDURALARITZAZKO EUSKAL ALDIZKARIA (SP/0211-9560) [10742415] **3093**

HERS NEWSLETTER (US/0892-628X) [15249554] **3762**

HERTFORDSHIRE ARCHAEOLOGY (UK/0440-7342) [02428397] **269**

HERTFORDSHIRE PEOPLE (UK/0309-913X) [I0309913X] **2453**

HERTIS *See* HERTIS OCCASIONAL PAPER **3213**

HERTIS OCCASIONAL PAPER *CEASED.* (UK/0440-7334) [05392807] **3213**

HERTS AND ESSEX TRADES' DIRECTORY (UK) [19042543] **839**

HERVORMD UTRECHT (NE) **4962**

HERVORMDE TEOLOGIESE STUDIES (SA) [05870057] **4962**

HERVORMER, DIE (SA) [03384474] **4962**

HERZ (GW/0340-9937) [03955104] **3705**

HERZ + GEFASSE (GW/0720-0730) [10637360] **3583**

HERZ-KREISLAUF (GW/0046-7324) [04654697] **3705**

HERZOGIA (GW/0018-0971) [03392935] **512**

HERZSCHRITTMACHERTHERAPIE & ELEKTROPHYSIOLOGIE (GW/0938-7412) [I09387412] **2056**

HESPERIA (US/0018-098X) [01752035] **1077**

HESPERIDE, L' (FR/0018-0998) [01911054] **2690**

HESPERIS TAMUDA (MR/0018-1005) [08661236] **2639**

HESPERUS REVIEW (II) **3393**

HESSE (GERMANY). KULTUSMINISTERIUM *See* AMTSBLATT DES HESSISCHEN KULTUSMINISTERS **2841**

HESSE (GERMANY). MINISTERIUM FUR ERZIEHUNG UND VOLKSBILDUNG. AMTSBLATT *See* AMTSBLATT DES HESSISCHEN KULTUSMINISTERS **2841**

HESSE. STATISTISCHES LANDESAMT *See* VEROFFENTLICHUNGEN DES HESSISCHEN STATISTISCHEN LANDESAMTES **5345**

HESSISCHE AUSFUHR, DIE (GW) [05090264] 839, **730**

HESSISCHE FLORISTISCHE BRIEFE (GW/0439-0687) [04100284] **512**

HESSISCHE POSTGESCHICHTE (GW) [02242262] **2785**

HESSISCHES JAHRBUCH FUER LANDESGESCHICHTE (GW/0073-2001) [02083557] **2690**

HESSTON RECORD, THE (US) [11587067] **5676**

HESTIA (GW/0440-7563) [02083991] **4348**

HETAIREIA BYZANTINON SPOUDON *See* EPETERIS ETAIREIAS BUZANTINON SPOUDON **2686**

HETAIREIA MAKEDONIKON SPOUDON *See* ETHNIKE BIBLIOTHEKE **3209**

HETEROATOM CHEMISTRY (US/1042-7163) [19116292] **976**

HETEROCYCLES (JA/0385-5414) [01851247] **1041**

●HETEROCYCLIC COMMUNICATIONS (UK/0793-0283) **976**

●HETERODOXY (STUDIO CITY, LOS ANGELES, CALIF.) (US/1069-7268) [25911106] **4476**

HETEROFONIA (MX/0018-1137) [02489377] **4121**

●HETEROGENEOUS CHEMISTRY REVIEWS (UK/1068-6983) [27757302] **977**

HETI VILAGGAZDASAG : HVG (HU/0139-1682) [10705988] **1635**

HEURES CLAIRES DES FEMMES (FR) [06080272] **5558**

HEUREUX QUI COMMUNIQUE (CN/0843-4441) [19916218] **1112**

HEURISTICS (ROCKVILLE, MD.) (US/1040-6433) [18480992] **1229**

HEUTIGES DEUTSCH. REIHE 1: LINGUISTISCHE GRUNDLAGEN (US/0073-201X) [02071105] **3285**

HEVES MEGYEI HIRLAP (HU/0865-9109) [I08659109] **5802**

HEVRAH U-REVAHAH (IS) [06633907] **5287**

HEWLETT-PACKARD COMPANY *See* ANNUAL REPORT / HEWLETT-PACKARD COMPANY **639**

HEWLETT-PACKARD JOURNAL (US/0018-1153) [02447377] **1186**

HEYTHROP JOURNAL (UK/0018-1196) [01587186] 4348, **5030**

HFD (US/0746-7885) [10341073] **2906**

HFD/RETAILING HOME FURNISHINGS *See* HFD **2906**

HGS INTERNATIONAL'S REAS LETTER (US/0733-1304) [08522427] **4838**

HHS FELLOWS PROGRAM, THE (US) [07530705] **5287**

HI-DESERT STAR (US/0746-2301) [09869459] **5635**

HI-FASHION (JA) **1085**

HI-FI (FR) [02441245] **5317**

HI-FI ANSWERS (UK) [01788746] **5317**

HI-FI NEWS & RECORD REVIEW (UK/0142-6230) [07590767] **5317**

HI FI VIDEO TEST (NE) 1297, **5317**

HI-HAKAI KENSA (JA/0367-5866) [10270722] **5109**

HI-LITES OF NATIVE BUSINESS (US/0732-166X) [07799416] **679**

HI-PERFORMANCE CARS *See* CARS **5409**

HI-RISE (CN/0715-5948) [10330377] **2534**

HI TECH (IT) **5109**

HI-TECH AD PLACEMENT REPORT (US/0889-9606) [14108337] **760**

HI-TECH COACHING & TRAINING (US/1051-6905) [22092020] **1855**

HI-TEEN STUDENT *See* HI-TEEN STUDENT GUIDE **4962**

●HI-TEEN STUDENT GUIDE (US/1059-3365) [24568201] **4962**

HI-TEEN TEACHER *See* HI-TEEN TEACHER GUIDE **4962**

●HI-TEEN TEACHER GUIDE (US/1059-3357) [24568177] 1750, **4962**

HIARI / COMMUNITY DEVELOPMENT TRUST FUND (TZ) [13237317] **4654**

HIAS BULLETIN (US/0097-0263) [02245726] **1919**

HIAWATHA DAILY WORLD HIAWATHA, KAN. : 1908) (US) [09899517] **5676**

HIBAKUSHA (JA) [11796237] **5287**

HIBALLER FOREST MAGAZINE (CN/0708-2169) [05018648] **2384**

HIBARINO : TOYOHASHI GIJUTSU KAGAKU DAIGAKU JIMBUN KAGAKUKEI KIYO (JA) [07624566] **5231**

HIBBING TRIBUNE (US) [01586989] **5696**

HIBOU (ST-LAMBERT) (CN/0709-9177) [06472022] 1750, **1064**

HICALL *See* TEEN LIFE (SPRINGFIELD, MO.) **5002**

HICKMAN COUNTY GAZETTE, THE (US) [08789966] **5681**

HICKMAN COURIER, THE (US) [12495733] **5681**

HICKSON MONEY REPORT (US/0732-8354) [08440972] **790**

HICKSVILLE ILLUSTRATED NEWS (US/0895-5476) [16687469] **5717**

HIDA MANUFACTURERS DIRECTORY (US/1045-6058) [20073963] 3480, **4782**

HIDALGUIA (SP/0018-1285) [05212624] **2690**

●HIDDEN JOB MARKET (US/1064-1769) [26236132] **4204**

HIDDEN PICTURES MAGAZINE *See* FUN ZONE, THE **4861**

HIDDEN VALLEY JOURNAL (US/0741-4773) [10142374] **2453**

HIDROBIOLOGIA (RM/0073-2087) [01395836] **554**

HIDROLOGIAI KOZLONY (HU/0018-1323) [02510154] 2090, **1414**

HIDROTEHNICA — Alphabetical Title Index

HIDROTEHNICA (RM/0439-0962) [03665574] **2090**

HIDRYMA KOINONIKON ASPHALISEON. D/NSIS LOGISTERIOU *See* OIKONOMIKA APOTELESMATA ETOUS ... / VASILEION TES HELLADOS, HIDRYMA KOINONIKON ASPHALISEON, DIOIKESIS, OIKON. HYPERESIAI, D/NSIS LOGISTERIOU **1700**

HIDUP (IO/0377-9610) [01795487] **5030**

HIERZULAND NICHT NUR BADISCHES VON RHEIN, NECKAR UND MAIN : ORGAN DES ARBEITSKREISES HEIMATPFLEGE NORDABADEN / REGIERUNGSBEZIRK KARLSRUHE (GW/0930-4878) [18058487] **2517**

HIFI & TV (GW/0343-4206) [I03434206] **1132**

HIFI EXKLUSIV *See* STEREO **5319**

HIFI STEREO, VIDEO (FR/0337-1891) [15743655] **5317**, **4121**

HIFI VIDEO MAGAZINE (FR/0247-7769) [I02477769] **4071**

HIFU. SKIN RESEARCH (JA/0018-1390) [06478673] **3720**

HIG (SERIES) (US/0440-4866) [01779724] **1406**

HIGASHI AJIA NO KODAI BUNKA (JA) [02501644] **2652**

HIGASHI NIHON RYOKAKU TETSUDO KABUSHIKI KAISHA *See* FACT BOOK **5431**

HIGASHI NIHON RYOKAKU TETSUDO KABUSHIKI KAISHA *See* ANNUAL REPORT **5429**

HIGASHI NIHON SHIGAKU ZASSHI (JA/0910-9722) [15484293] **1324**

HIGDON FAMILY NEWSLETTER (US/0739-3199) [09697045] **2453**

HIGGINSON JOURNAL *CEASED.* (US/0164-145X) [04599511] **3464**

HIGH ADVENTURE (US/0190-3802) [04707513] **1064**

HIGH ALTITUDE POLLUTION PROGRAM (U.S.) *See* BIENNIAL REPORT PREPARED IN ACCORDANCE WITH THE OZONE PROTECTION PROVISION, SECTION 153 (G), OF THE CLEAN AIR ACT AMENDMENTS OF 1977 **2225**

HIGH AND LOW (CN/0315-2782) [02442045] **900**

HIGH BLOOD PRESSURE AND CARDIOVASCULAR PREVENTION (US/1120-9879) **3705**

HIGH BLOOD PRESSURE HIGHLIGHTS (US/0164-758X) [04359474] **3705**

HIGH COLOR *See* PC GRAPHICS & VIDEO **1234**

HIGH COLOR (US/1060-5282) [25019533] **1233**

HIGH COUNTRY INDEPENDENT PRESS (US/0746-3359) [09929995] **5705**

HIGH COUNTRY NEWS (US/0191-5657) [03032858] **2195**

HIGH COUNTRY, THE *CEASED.* (US/0018-1420) [03295346] **2736**

HIGH ENERGY CHEMISTRY (US/0018-1439) [01752049] **1052**

HIGH ENERGY PHYSICISTS & GRADUATE STUDENTS / PREPARED BY U.S. DEPARTMENT OF ENERGY, DIRECTORATE, OFFICE OF ENERGY RESEARCH, DIVISION OF HIGH ENERGY PHYSICS (US) [08995108] **1946**

HIGH ENERGY PHYSICS & NUCLEAR PHYSICS (US/0899-9996) [18286624] **4447**

HIGH ENERGY PHYSICS INDEX / HOCHENERGIEPHYSIK-INDEX (GW/0018-1447) [05789772] **4404**

HIGH FIDELITY (UK) **5317**

HIGH FIDELITY'S BUYING GUIDE TO SPEAKER SYSTEMS *See* SPEAKERS **5319**

HIGH FIDELITY'S BUYING GUIDE TO STEREO COMPONENTS (US/0198-7224) [06154876] **5317**

HIGH FIDELITY'S BUYING GUIDE TO TAPE SYSTEMS (US/0161-4371) [03920024] **5317**

HIGH FLIGHT *SUSPENDED.* (CN/0708-4331) [06516467] **23**

HIGH FRONTIER NEWSWATCH (US/0892-5674) [15233613] **4045**

HIGH INCOME TAX RETURNS (US/0148-2947) [03111183] **4731**

HIGH INTEGRITY SYSTEMS (UK/0967-2648) **1247**

HIGH LEVEL ECHO (CN) **5786**

HIGH LEVEL RADIOACTIVE WASTE NEWSLETTER / NATIONAL CONFERENCE OF STATE LEGISLATORS (US) [15732561] **2232**

HIGH-PERFORMANCE COMPUTING REVIEW *CEASED.* (US/1068-0365) [27156361] **1186**

HIGH PERFORMANCE LIQUID CHROMATOGRAPHY SHEFFIELD (UK/0261-4707) [I02614707] **1011**

HIGH PERFORMANCE (LOS ANGELES) (US/0160-9769) [03797950] **385**

HIGH PERFORMANCE OPTOMETRY (US/0894-5810) [16149607] **4215**

HIGH PERFORMANCE PLASTICS (UK/0264-7753) [10331413] **4455**

HIGH PERFORMANCE POLYMERS (UK/0954-0083) [20520705] **977**

HIGH-PERFORMANCE PONTIAC (US/0745-5941) [09313484] **5416**

HIGH PERFORMANCE REVIEW (US/0277-1357) [07506165] **5317**

HIGH PERFORMANCE TEXTILES (UK/0144-5871) [08875542] **5351**

HIGH PLAINS APPLIED ANTHROPOLOGIST (US/0882-4894) [11907822] **237**

HIGH PLAINS JOURNAL, THE (US/0018-1471) [04094557] **5676**

HIGH PLAINS LITERARY REVIEW (US/0888-4153) [13564017] **3344**

HIGH POINT ENTERPRISE, THE *CEASED.* (US/0747-1491) [10579072] **5723**

HIGH PRAIRIE REPORTER (CN/0316-7534) [02247918] **5786**

HIGH PRESSURE RESEARCH (US/0895-7959) [16798650] **4404**

HIGH PROFIT INVESTING (US/8756-8403) [11667770] **900**

HIGH-PURITY SUBSTANCES *CEASED.* (US/0897-4403) [17500166] **977**

HIGH QUALITY : HQ (GW) [17536758] **379**, **4565**

HIGH RELIABILITY ELECTRONIC COMPONENTS (US/0899-8531) [18247649] **2056**

HIGH ROADS FOLIO (US/0742-6240) [10341104] **2534**

HIGH ROLLER (US/0197-6044) [03287960] **3213**

HIGH SCHOOL BASEBALL RULES (US) [26891868] **4898**

●HIGH SCHOOL GIRLS GYMNASTICS RULES AND MANUAL (US/1069-6393) [24416712] **4898**

HIGH SCHOOL JOURNAL, THE (US/0018-1498) [01642826] **1750**

●HIGH SCHOOL MAGAZINE, THE (US/1070-9533) [28521404] **1864**

HIGH SCHOOL NEWS AND GRAPHICS (US/0746-2425) [09881458] **2920**

HIGH SCHOOL SOFTBALL RULES (US) [27995266] **4898**

●HIGH SCHOOL SOFTBALL UMPIRES MANUAL (US/1075-1920) [29780604] **4898**

HIGH SCHOOL SPORTS (US) [19107623] **4898**

HIGH SCHOOL SWIMMING, DIVING, AND WATER POLO RULES (US) [22288614] **4898**

HIGH SCHOOL WRESTLING RULES (US/1054-3600) [22688726] **4898**

HIGH SCHOOL WRITER OF THE MIDWEST *See* HIGH SCHOOL WRITER, THE **2920**

HIGH SCHOOL WRITER, THE (US/1048-3373) [20920965] **1092**, **2920**

HIGH/SCOPE EARLY CHILDHOOD POLICY PAPERS (US/0898-6495) [13777070] **5246**

HIGH/SCOPE EDUCATIONAL RESEARCH FOUNDATION *See* MONOGRAPHS OF THE HIGH/SCOPE EDUCATIONAL RESEARCH FOUNDATION **1765**

HIGH SCOPE RESOURCE (US/0887-2007) [13175410] **1750**

HIGH/SCOPE SURVEY OF EARLY CHILDHOOD SOFTWARE (US) [19637495] **1223**, **1804**

HIGH SOLIDS COATINGS *CEASED.* (US/0146-4752) [02941961] **977**

HIGH SPEED DIESELS & DRIVES (US/1041-5416) [18799758] **5416**

●HIGH SPEED TRANSPORT NEWS (US/1076-8408) [30620551] **4443**

HIGH SPRINGS HERALD (US/0746-1046) [09779087] **5649**

HIGH STANDARDS *See* QUALITY POSTINGS **706**

HIGH TECH CERAMICS NEWS (US/1045-2397) [20065025] **2590**

HIGH TECH DEUTSCHE AUSG (GW/0176-3474) [I01763474] **5109**

HIGH TECH DIGEST *CEASED.* (FR) **5110**

HIGH TECH GROWTH FORECASTER (US) **900**

HIGH TECH INVESTOR (US/0736-427X) [09125151] **900**

HIGH-TECH MATERIALS ALERT (US/0741-0808) [10081132] **1977**

HIGH TECH PROCUREMENT (US) **1186**

HIGH TECH SEPARATIONS NEWS (US/1046-039X) [20313362] **1015**

HIGH TECHNOLOGY AND OTHER GROWTH STOCKS (US) **900**

HIGH-TECHNOLOGY BUSINESSTRENDS (US/0893-5424) [15579077] **679**

HIGH TECHNOLOGY LAW JOURNAL (US/0885-2715) [12615792] **5110**, **2978**

HIGH TECHNOLOGY MARKET PLACE DIRECTORY *CEASED.* (US) [12688729] **5110**

HIGH TEMPERATURE (US/0018-151X) [01752056] **4431**

HIGH-TEMPERATURE GAS-COOLED REACTOR SAFETY STUDIES FOR THE DIVISION OF ACCIDENT EVALUATION QUARTERLY PROGRESS REPORT (US) [09697966] **2155**

HIGH TEMPERATURE MATERIALS AND PROCESSES (IS/0334-6455) [11713567] **4404**

HIGH TEMPERATURE REACTION RATE DATA (UK) [20649937] **1052**

HIGH TEMPERATURE SCIENCE (US/0018-1536) [01715228] **1025**, **1052**

HIGH TEMPERATURES - HIGH PRESSURES (UK/0018-1544) [01714957] **2102**, **4431**

HIGH TIDINGS (US/0737-5867) [09417701] **4166**, **4088**

HIGH TIMBER TIMES (US) [23097025] **5643**

HIGH TIMES (US/0362-630X) [02326986] **2488**

HIGH VOLUME PRINTING (US/0737-1020) [08767696] **4565**

●HIGH YIELD SECURITIES JOURNAL (US/1065-089X) [26498227] **900**

HIGHER EDUCATION (NE/0018-1560) [01586372] **1828**

HIGHER EDUCATION ABSTRACTS (US/0748-4364) [10941211] **1828**, **1795**

HIGHER EDUCATION & NATIONAL AFFAIRS (US/0018-1579) [01479725] **1828**

HIGHER EDUCATION AND SCHOOL REFORM : CREATING THE PARTNERSHIP (US) **1828**

HIGHER EDUCATION DAILY *See* EDUCATION DAILY **1739**

HIGHER EDUCATION DATA BOOK (US/0146-5902) [02990052] **1828**

HIGHER EDUCATION DESKBOOK, THE (US/0192-4338) [05043381] **1828**

HIGHER EDUCATION DIRECTORY (US/0740-9230) [03909143] **1828**

HIGHER EDUCATION GROUP ANNUAL (CN/1180-467X) [24256745] **1828**

HIGHER EDUCATION IN EUROPE (RM/0379-7724) [02590141] **1828**

HIGHER EDUCATION IN MONTANA DIRECTORY (US/0145-2207) [02711715] **1828**

HIGHER EDUCATION IN THE UNITED KINGDOM (UK) [05998464] **1828**

HIGHER EDUCATION LAW REPORT (US/0742-0803) [10248864] **1828**, **2978**

HIGHER EDUCATION MANAGEMENT (PARIS, FRANCE) (FR/1013-851X) [19744715] **1828**

HIGHER EDUCATION (NEW YORK, N.Y. : 1985) (US/0882-4126) [11830722] **1828**

HIGHER EDUCATION OPPORTUNITIES FOR MINORITIES AND WOMEN ANNOTATED SELECTIONS (US) [09513842] **5558**, **2250**, **1828**

HIGHER EDUCATION POLICY (UK/0952-8733) [18584491] **1828**

HIGHER EDUCATION POLICY SERIES (UK) [18937921] **1828**

... HIGHER EDUCATION PUBLIC ADMINISTRATION DIRECTORY, THE (US/0747-9743) [10828980] **1828**, **4654**

HIGHER EDUCATION QUARTERLY / SOCIETY FOR RESEARCH INTO HIGHER EDUCATION (UK/0951-5224) [15236888] **1828**

HIGHER EDUCATION RESEARCH AND DEVELOPMENT (AT/0729-4360) [I07294360] **1828**

HIGHER EDUCATION REVIEW (UK/0018-1609) [02447384] **1828**

HIGHER EDUCATION REVIEW (LAHORE, PAKISTAN) (II) [10854909] **1828**

HIGHER EDUCATION STATISTICAL ABSTRACT / SOUTH CAROLINA COMMISSION ON HIGHER EDUCATION (US) [08795127] **1828**, **1795**

HIGHER EDUCATION TUITION (US/1045-7968) [20235577] **1828**

HIGHER, THE (UK) [24259228] **1828**

HIGHER [MICROFORM], THE (US) [25575526] **1828**

HIGHLAND HERITAGE (CN/0707-2554) [05359764] **2453**

HIGHLAND NEWS LEADER (US/8750-0957) [10969770] **5660**

HIGHLAND PARK LIFE (US/0191-5460) [05011068] **5660**

HIGHLAND PARK NEWS (HIGHLAND PARK, ILL.) (US/1053-2846) [22501886] **5660**

HIGHLAND PARK NEWS/VOICE *See* HIGHLAND PARK NEWS (HIGHLAND PARK, ILL.) **5660**

HIGHLAND RECORDER *See* RECORDER (MONTEREY, VA.) **5759**

HIGHLAND VIDETTE (HIGHLAND, KAN.) (US) [11086722] **5676**

HIGHLANDER (BARRINGTON), THE (US/0161-5378) [03727367] **2262**

HIGHLANDER, THE (US) [27856860] **5649**

HIGHLANDER, THE (US) [17307949] **5750**

HIGHLANDS PRESS (US) **5650**

HIGHLANDS STAR, THE (US) [17446603] **5751**

HIGHLIGHT QUEBEC (CN/0825-4850) [11431458] **4963**

HIGHLIGHT (VICTORIA) (CN/0848-7804) [23264722] **4782**

HIGHLIGHTS (MW) [01785444] 2195, **92**

HIGHLIGHTS : BUDGET SPEECH AND ESTIMATES (CN) [02243627] 679, **1493**

HIGHLIGHTS (CALGARY. 1978) (CN/0712-5879) [09502371] **352**

HIGHLIGHTS FOR CHILDREN (US/0018-165X) [01589689] 1750, **1064**

HIGHLIGHTS FROM INFECTIONS IN SURGERY (US/0743-9202) [10703623] **3965**

HIGHLIGHTS FROM STUDENT DRUG USE IN AMERICA / THE INSTITUTE FOR SOCIAL RESEARCH, THE UNIVERSITY OF MICHIGAN (US) [08541332] **1345**

HIGHLIGHTS - HENRY LUCE FOUNDATION (US/0884-1748) [12290294] **1750**

HIGHLIGHTS (LONDON, ONT.) (CN/0712-5828) [09448345] **5328**

HIGHLIGHTS (MISSISSAUGA) (CN/0226-272X) [06860431] **385**

HIGHLIGHTS NEWSLETTER (CN/0384-1162) [03284820] **352**

HIGHLIGHTS OF AGRICULTURAL AND FOOD RESEARCH IN ONTARIO (CN/1183-5796) [22948586] **92**

HIGHLIGHTS OF AGRICULTURAL RESEARCH (US/0018-1668) [01478887] **92**

HIGHLIGHTS OF FEDERAL UNEMPLOYMENT COMPENSATION LAWS (US/0886-246X) [12887792] **3148**

HIGHLIGHTS OF OPHTHALMOLOGY LETTER (MINI-HIGHLIGHTS) / BENJAMIN F. BOYD (PN) [12057140] **3875**

HIGHLIGHTS OF STATE UNEMPLOYMENT COMPENSATION LAWS (US/0730-7624) [08069502] **3149**

HIGHLIGHTS OF THE COLLECTIONS / THE MONTREAL MUSEUM OF FINE ARTS (CN/0711-7078) [11050376] **4088**

HIGHLIGHTS OF THE YEAR ... (US/1055-6427) [22743211] **1356**

HIGHLIGHTS (SAIPAN) (NW/0196-2523) [05173663] **4654**

HIGHLIGHTS: WALLOWA-WHITMAN NATIONAL FOREST (US) [04165925] **2384**

HIGHLINE TIMES (US) [17212591] **5761**

HIGHLINES (US) [05044160] **1946**

HIGHWAY 12 WEEKENDER (CN/0821-4824) [09586338] **5786**

HIGHWAY 43 LEADER (CN/0704-0458) [03791102] **5786**

HIGHWAY ACCIDENT REPORTS. SUMMARY FORMAT (US/8755-9196) [08119270] **5440**

HIGHWAY & HEAVY CONSTRUCTION *See* HIGHWAY & HEAVY CONSTRUCTION PRODUCTS **5440**

HIGHWAY & HEAVY CONSTRUCTION PRODUCTS (US/1062-5194) [25647318] **5440**

HIGHWAY & URBAN MASS TRANSPORTATION (US/0364-3468) [01695944] **5383**

HIGHWAY & VEHICLE SAFETY REPORT (US/0161-0325) [03811306] 4782, **5440**

HIGHWAY BUILDER (US) [06957646] **2024**

HIGHWAY COMMISSION UPDATE (US) [19101198] **5440**

HIGHWAY IMPROVEMENT PROGRAM / INDIANA DEPARTMENT OF TRANSPORTATION (US) [22170495] **5440**

HIGHWAY LOSS DATA INSTITUTE *See* AUTOMOBILE INSURANCE LOSSES COLLISION COVERAGES VARIATIONS BY MAKE AND SERIES **2875**

HIGHWAY PATROLMEN'S FUND, STATEMENT TO EMPLOYEES (US) [01589975] **5287**

HIGHWAY RESEARCH ABSTRACTS (1990) (US/1050-0804) [21387752] 2024, **2004**

HIGHWAY, ROAD, STREET AND BRIDGE CONTRACTORS (CN/0835-1058) [15974887] **616**

HIGHWAY SAFETY LITERATURE (1973) (US/0738-5277) [09054602] 4782, **5440**

HIGHWAY SAFETY PERFORMANCE. FATAL AND INJURY ACCIDENT RATES ON PUBLIC ROADS IN THE UNITED STATES (US/8755-8688) [10686769] **5440**

HIGHWAY SAFETY PLAN / OTSC (US) [08754073] 4782, **5441**

HIGHWAY SAFETY PLAN - WASHINGTON (STATE). TRAFFIC SAFETY COMMISSION (US) [06284556] 4782, **5441**

HIGHWAY SAFETY STEWARDSHIP REPORT, THE (US/0277-2310) [07513904] **5441**

HIGHWAY STATISTICS (US/0095-344X) [01796740] **5441**

HIGHWAY STATISTICS AND RELATED INFORMATION *See* NEW MEXICO ... HIGHWAY STATISTICS AND RELATED INFORMATION **5401**

HIGHWAY SUFFICIENCY REPORT (US/0147-9539) [03248945] **5441**

HIGHWAY TAXES AND FEES (US/0732-8230) [08428042] **5441**

HIGHWAY TRAFFIC STATISTICS (US/0364-0825) [02567168] **5401**

HIGHWAY TRANSPORT BOARD BULLETIN (CN/0701-8568) [08311683] **5383**

HIGHWAY TRANSPORTATION RESEARCH AND DEVELOPMENT STUDIES (US/0092-3389) [01788587] **5441**

HIGHWAY USER REVENUES AND DISTRIBUTION FOR THE CALENDAR YEAR ENDING ... / ARKANSAS STATE HIGHWAY AND TRANSPORTATION DEPARTMENT, PLANNING DIVISION (JS) [09410648] **5416**

●HIGHWAYMAN (WILLOW STREET, PA.), THE (US/1062-7200) [25717207] **2453**

HIGHWAYS AND TRANSPORTATION (UK/0265-6868) [10104796] **5441**

HIGHWAYS AND TRANSPORTATION STATISTICS ... ESTIMATES (UK/0260-9894) [10661606] **5401**

HIGHWAYS (CROYDON, LONDON, ENGLAND) (UK) [12115031] **2024**

HIGHWAYS EXPENDITURE / SOCIETY OF COUNTY TREASURERS AND COUNTY SURVEYORS' SOCIETY (UK) [12940604] **5383**

HIGIENA I ZDRAVEOPAZVANE (BU/0018-8247) [09490080] **3583**

HIKAKU BUNGAKU (JA/0440-8047) [01588765] **3393**

HIKAKU BUNKA ZASSHI (JA) [10509088] **2617**

HIKAKU KAGAKU (JA/0018-1811) [I00181811] 977, **3184**

HIKAKU SEIRI SEIKAGAKU (JA/0916-3786) [I09163786] 581, **488**

HIKAKU TOSHISHI KENKYU (JA) [09128945] 1565, **2824**

HIKE CANADA (CN/1183-6288) [24623499] **4873**

HIKING AFRICA (SA) **4873**

HIKING (HIGHLAND PARK) (US/0094-0291) [01793182] 4898, **4873**

HIKKEI GAKKO SHOROPPO (JA) [10862808] **2978**

HIKMAH AL-YAMANIYAH *See* AL-HIKMAH **3358**

HIKOBIA / HIROSHIMA SHOKUBUTSUGAKU KENKYUKAI (JA/0046-7413) [03325265] **512**

HIKUIN (DK) [01799126] 269, **2690**

HILBORN FAMILY JOURNAL **CEASED.** (CN/0707-3836) [05071970] **2453**

HILEIA MEDICA (BL/0101-9597) [08126138] **3583**

HILEIA MEDICA. SUPLEMENTO (BL/0101-9600) [08538172] **3583**

HILGARDIA (US/0073-2230) [01644088] **92**

HILITES DATABASE [ONLINE DATABASE] (US) 1186, **1209**

HILL CITY TIMES, THE (US) [11377748] **5676**

HILL COUNTRY ALMANAC (US) [25613942] **1926**

HILL COUNTRY GENEALOGICAL SOCIETY QUARTERLY, THE (US) [09706031] **2453**

HILL COUNTRY NEWS (CEDAR PARK, TEX. : 1978) (US) [16826355] **5751**

HILLANDALE NEWS, THE (UK/0018-1846) [I00181846] **4121**

●HILLARY CLINTON QUARTERLY, THE (US/1067-0777) [27129929] **2534**

●HILLEL GUIDE TO JEWISH LIFE ON CAMPUS, THE (US) [23174692] 1829, **2262**

HILLIARD NORTHWEST NEWS (US) [25028466] **5728**

HILLS AND HARBORS (US/0193-8614) [05266890] **2534**

HILLSBORO ARGUS (HILLSBORO, OR.) (US/8750-5479) [11502176] **5733**

HILLSBORO BANNER (US) [01752077] **5725**

HILLSBORO SENTRY-ENTERPRISE (US/0749-7016) [11165666] **5768**

HILLSBOROUGH BEACON (US) [15649333] **5710**

HILLSDALE MAGAZINE (US) **1092**

HILLSDALE REVIEW (US/0735-2387) [08868348] **2534**

HILLSIDE JOURNAL OF CLINICAL PSYCHIATRY, THE **CEASED.** (US/0193-5216) [05190393] **3926**

HILLSIDE TIMES, THE (US) [15794589] **5710**

HILO TIMES, THE (US/1053-0045) [11397069] **5656**

HILO TRIBUNE HERALD (US) [13046272] **5656**

HIM MONTHLY *See* GAY TIMES **2794**

HIMA DIRECTORY (US/0741-8191) [10179564] **4783**

HIMACHAL PRADESH, INDIA. LEGISLATIVE ASSEMBLY. PUBLIC ACCOUNTS COMMITTEE *See* REPORT - PUBLIC ACCOUNTS COMMITTEE **4746**

HIMACHAL PRADESH, INDIA. STATE EMPLOYMENT MARKET INFORMATION UNIT *See* REPORT ON SHORTAGE OCCUPATIONS **4209**

HIMALANGUE (NP) [01797695] **3285**

HIMALAYA TODAY (II) [18958429] **2652**

HIMALAYAN CHEMICAL AND PHARMACEUTICAL BULLETIN : HCPB (II/0970-1281) [14179958] **1025**

HIMALAYAN CULTURE (NP) [05979879] **2652**

HIMALAYAN INSTITUTE QUARTERLY GUIDE TO PROGRAMS AND OTHER OFFERINGS (US/0891-6144) [14928132] 4588, **4348**

HIMALAYAN JOURNAL OF ENVIRONMENT AND ZOOLOGY (II/0970-2903) [26666661] 5585, **2216**

HIMALAYAN JOURNAL, THE (II) [01643102] **4873**

HIMALAYAN PLANT JOURNAL (II) [09182173] **2418**

HIMALAYAN RESEARCH BULLETIN (US/0891-4834) [09751251] **2652**

HIMALI SAUGATA (NP/0377-9661) [01790471] **3393**

HIMEJI KOGYO DAIGAKU KOGAKUBU KENKYU HOKOKU (JA) [24346561] 1977, **5110**

HIMICESKAJ PROMYSLENNOST (RU/0023-110X) [09467381] **977**

HIMICESKAJA FIZIKA (RU/0207-401X) [08535483] **1052**

HIMICESKAJA PROMYSLENNOST. SERIJA, FOSFORNAJA PROMYSLENNOST (RU/0204-3998) [11058862] 4260, **1025**

HIMICESKAJA TEHNOLOGIJA (KIEV. 1971) (UN/0368-556X) [04079416] **977**

HIMICESKAJA TEHNOLOGIJA VOLOKNISTYH MATERIALOV (RU/0320-023X) [02997178] **1025**

HIMICESKAJA TERMODINAMIKA I RAVNOVESIJA (RU/0302-9751) [05728311] **1052**

HIMICESKIE VOLOKNA (RU/0023-1118) [04079523] **4455**

HIMICESKOE I NEFTJANOE MASINOSTROENIE (RU/0023-1126) [06263371] **1025**

HIMICESKOE MASINOSTROENIE (KIEV) (UN/0451-8306) [10790956] 2115, **2012**

HIMIJA DREVESINY (LV/0201-7474) [02241929] **2401**

HIMIJA GETEROCIKLICESKIH SOEDINENIJ (LV/0132-6244) [04084303] **977**

HIMIJA I TEHNOLOGIJA CELLJULOZY (RU/0132-7046) [03027272] 4234, **1025**

HIMIJA I TEHNOLOGIJA TOPLIV I MASEL (RU/0023-1169) [09490295] **4260**

HIMIJA I TEHNOLOGIJA VODY (UN/0204-3556) [07042293] **5534**

HIMIJA I TERMODINAMIKA RASTVOROV (RU/0454-8833) [10872585] **977**

HIMIJA I ZIZN (RU/0130-5972) [04084315] **488**

HIMIJA TVERDOGO TELA (RU/0137-0340) [10814382] **977**

HIMIJA

Alphabetical Title Index

HIMIJA TVERDOVO TOPLIVA (RU/0023-1177) [02448127] **4260**

HIMIJA VYSOKIH ENERGIJ (RU/0023-1193) [04084341] **1052**

HIMIKO-FARMACEVTICESKIJ ZURNAL (RU/0023-1134) [01210417] **4306**

HIMIZACI A SELSKOGO HOZAJSTVA (RU/0235-2516) [18036772] **92**

HIMPUNAN NELAYAN SELURUH INDONESIA. DEWAN PIMPINAN PUSAT *See* LAPORAN KEGIATAN - DEWAN PIMPINAN PUSAT, HIMPUNAN NELAYAN SELURUH INDONESIA **1687**

HIMPUNAN PERATURAN IMPOR (IO) [05121921] **839**

HINCKLEY NEWS (US) [01588958] **5696**

HINDI EKSAPRESA (II) [08620014] **2652**

HINDI PRACARAKA PATRIKA (II) [02239585] **4828**

HINDI PRAYOGA VARSHIKI KOSA (II) [11176314] **3285**

HINDI SAHITYABDAKOSA (II) [02437233] **3393**

HINDSIGHT CAMBRIDGE (UK/0958-3637) [I09583637] **2617**

HINDU-CHRISTIAN STUDIES BULLETIN (CN/0844-4587) [20285844] **5041**

HINDU (MADRAS, INDIA : DAILY) (II) [01781415] **5803**

HINDU REGENERATION (II) [01790482] **5041**

HINDU TEXT INFORMATION (US/0277-1349) [07511160] **417**

HINDU VISVA (II) [03198241] **5041**

HINDUISM (UK/0018-1927) [02430263] **4963**

HINDUISM TODAY (US/0896-0801) [13910211] **4185, 5041**

HINDUSTAN ANTIBIOTICS BULLETIN (II/0018-1935) [01641662] **4306**

HINDUSTAN ANTIBIOTICS, PIMPRI, INDIA *See* HINDUSTAN ANTIBIOTICS BULLETIN **4306**

HINDUSTAN TIMES (II) [01781416] **5803**

HINDUSTAN YEAR-BOOK AND WHO'S WHO (II/0970-1168) [I09701168] **5012**

HINDUTVA (II) [01784229] **5041**

HINE'S DIRECTORY OF INSURANCE ADJUSTERS (US) [05256046] **2882**

HINE'S DIRECTORY OF INSURANCE COUNSEL, RAILROAD AND BANK COUNSEL, INSURANCE ADJUSTERS *See* HINE'S INSURANCE COUNSEL **2978**

HINE'S INSURANCE ADJUSTERS *See* HINE'S DIRECTORY OF INSURANCE ADJUSTERS **2882**

HINE'S INSURANCE COUNSEL (US) [08095936] **2882, 2978**

HINNAT JA KILPAILU (FI/0356-5092) [12056073] **1608**

HINSHITSU (JA) [09227993] **3480**

HINSHITSU KANRI (JA/0018-1951) [I00181951] **5110, 1977**

HINTERALIA (AT/1035-624X) [I1035624X] **3213**

HINTERLAND ENGLISH ED (BE/0773-1922) [I07731922] **5110**

HINTERLAND WHO'S WHO (CN/0703-7481) [02248610] **4166**

HINTON NEWS (US) [13241045] **5764**

HINTS TO POTATO GROWERS (US) [03269439] **173**

HINUK MERUGARIM BE-YISRAEL (IS/0303-1527) [01784360] **1800**

HINWEISE UND STUDIEN ZUM LEBENSWERK VON ALBERT STEFFEN (SZ/0258-235X) [18152662] **3393**

HINYOKIKA KIYO (JA/0018-1994) [02835176] **3990**

HIP INTERNATIONAL : THE JOURNAL OF CLINICAL AND EXPERIMENTAL RESEARCH ON HIP PATHOLOGY AND THERAPY (IT/1120-7000) [25047278] **3804**

HIP REPORT, THE (US/1065-1918) [26522820] **4388**

HIP; THE JAZZ RECORD DIGEST *See* JAZZ DIGEST **4124**

HIPERTENSION (SP/0212-8241) [I02128241] **3705**

HIPERTENSION Y ARTERIOESCLEROSIS *CEASED*. (SP/0214-6436) [23656668] **3705**

HIPPO MAGAZINE (US/1050-6802) [20506979] **3393**

HIPPOCAMPUS (NEW YORK, N.Y.) (US/1050-9631) [21725124] **3797**

HIRAGANA TAIMUZU (JA/0915-9975) [I09159975] **2504**

HIRAM (IT) **4241**

HIRAM POETRY REVIEW, THE (US/0018-2036) [02242807] **3464**

HIRATRA / SAMPANA TENY SY LAHABOLANA ARY RIBA MALAGASY (MG) [09781989] **3393**

HIROSAKI DAIGAKU HOKEN KANRI GAIYO (JA/0286-5890) [12151483] **2882**

HIROSAKI DAIGAKU. IRYO GIJUTSU TANKI DAIGAKUBU *See* KIYO - HIROSAKI DAIGAKU IRYO GIJUTSU TANKI DAIGAKUBU **5232**

HIROSAKI DAIGAKU. NOGAKUBU *See* HIROSAKI DAIGAKU NÃOGAKUBU GAKUJUTSU HOKOKU **92**

HIROSAKI DAIGAKU NÃOGAKUBU GAKUJUTSU HOKOKU (JA/0073-229X) [03324789] **92**

HIROSAKI IGAKU (JA/0018-2044) [01752087] **3583**

HIROSHIMA DAIGAKU *See* JOURNAL OF SCIENCE OF THE HIROSHIMA UNIVERSITY. SERIES A. PHYSICS AND CHEMISTRY (1971) **4410**

HIROSHIMA DAIGAKU *See* JOURNAL OF SCIENCE OF THE HIROSHIMA UNIVERSITY. SERIES B. DIVISION 1. ZOOLOGY **5588**

HIROSHIMA DAIGAKU *See* JOURNAL OF SCIENCE OF THE HIROSHIMA UNIVERSITY. SERIES B. DIVISION 2. BOTANY **516**

HIROSHIMA DAIGAKU. DAIGAKU KYOIKU KENKYU SENTA *See* KORIGU : HIROSHIMA DAIGAKU KYOIKU KENKYU SENTA TSUSHIN **1833**

HIROSHIMA DAIGAKU IGAKU ZASSHI (JA/0018-2087) [07618182] **3584**

HIROSHIMA DAIGAKU KOGAKUBU KENKYU HOKOKU (JA/0018-2060) [09937899] **1977**

HIROSHIMA DAIGAKU KYOIKUGAKUBU GAKUBU FUZOKU KYODO KENKYU TAISEI *See* KENKYU KIYO - HIROSHIMA DAIGAKU KYOIKUGAKUBU GAKUBU FUZOKU KYODO KENKYU TAISEI **1760**

HIROSHIMA DAIGAKU SEIBUTSU GAKKAI *See* HIROSHIMA DAIGAKU SEIBUTSU GAKKAI SHI **457**

HIROSHIMA DAIGAKU SEIBUTSU GAKKAI SHI (JA/0367-5912) [06922468] **457**

HIROSHIMA DAIGAKU SEIBUTSU SEISANGAKUBU KIYO (JA/0387-7647) [05755694] **457**

HIROSHIMA DAIGAKU SHIGAKU ZASSHI (JA/0046-7472) [10278386] **1324**

HIROSHIMA DAIGAKU SOGO KAGAKUBU KIYO. 3, JOHO KODO KAGAKU KENKYU (JA) [07996047] **5110**

HIROSHIMA FORUM FOR PSYCHOLOGY (JA/0386-3158) [02526871] **4588**

HIROSHIMA JOURNAL OF MEDICAL SCIENCES (JA/0018-2052) [01681363] **3584**

HIROSHIMA-KEN KANKYO SENTA KENKYU HOKOKU (JA/0389-0082) [07855505] **2232**

HIROSHIMA KENRITSU NOGYO SHIKENJO HOKOKU (JA/0439-1799) [10278349] **92**

HIROSHIMA KENRITSU SEIBU KOGYO GIJUTSU SENTA KENKYU HOKOKU (JA/0915-194X) [I0915194X] **5110**

HIROSHIMA KOKUZEIKYOKU TOKEISHO (JA) [01799677] **4731**

HIROSHIMA MATHEMATICAL JOURNAL (JA/0018-2079) [01714327] **3507**

HIROSHIMA NOGYO TANKI DAIGAKU, SAIJO, JAPAN *See* BULLETIN OF THE HIROSHIMA AGRICULTURAL COLLEGE **69**

HIROSHIMA SHOSEN KOTO SEMMON GAKKO *See* HIROSHIMA SHOSEN KOTO SEMMON GAKKO KIYO **4177**

HIROSHIMA SHOSEN KOTO SEMMON GAKKO KIYO (JA) [06567132] **4177**

HIRSCH, PHIL *See* HIRSCH REPORT, THE **1186**

HIRSCH REPORT, THE (US/0193-466X) [05211252] **1186**

HIRURGIJA (MOSKVA) (RU/0023-1207) [01755139] **3965**

HIRURGIJA (SOFIJA) (BU/0450-2167) [01902562] **3965**

HIS (GW) [01786540] **1750**

HIS DOMINION (REGINA) (CN/0229-7175) [04301882] **4963**

HISLA (PE) [10189349] **2736, 1565**

HISPALIS MEDICA (SP/0018-2125) [01777993] **3584**

HISPAMERICA (US/0363-048X) [02407319] **3394**

HISPAMERICA (COLLEGE PARK) (US/0363-0471) [00975223] **3394**

HISPANIA (US/0018-2133) [01200188] **1895, 3285**

HISPANIA (MADRID) (SP/0018-2141) [01752090] **2690**

HISPANIA SACRA (SP/0018-215X) [01774966] **5030**

HISPANIC AMERICAN ARTS (UY/0738-5625) [05004402] **321**

HISPANIC AMERICAN HISTORICAL REVIEW, THE (US/0018-2168) [01752092] **2262**

HISPANIC AMERICAN HISTORICAL REVIEW [MICROFORM], THE (US/0018-2168) [03518594] **2736**

HISPANIC AMERICAN PERIODICALS INDEX (LOS ANGELES, CALIF.) (US/0270-8558) [03864464] **2496**

HISPANIC AMERICANS (BOULDER, COLO.) (US/1056-7992) [23238025] **2262**

HISPANIC AMERICANS INFORMATION DIRECTORY (US/1046-3933) [20398621] **2262**

HISPANIC ARTICLES IN SCHOLARLY PERIODICALS : ANNUAL BIBLIOGRAPHY (UK) [24357243] **3394, 3285**

HISPANIC BOOKS BULLETIN (US/0894-2358) [15876010] **4828**

HISPANIC BUSINESS (US/0199-0349) [05525730] **2262, 679**

HISPANIC CLASSICS (UK) **1077**

HISPANIC ENGINEER (US) [13847847] **1977**

HISPANIC FOCUS (US/0737-7029) [08913512] **2276**

HISPANIC HOTLINE (US/1064-0916) [26224007] **4204**

HISPANIC ISSUES (US/0893-2395) [15467122] **3394**

HISPANIC JOURNAL (US/0271-0986) [06059630] **3285, 3394**

HISPANIC JOURNAL OF BEHAVIORAL SCIENCES (US/0739-9863) [05062173] **2262**

HISPANIC LINGUISTICS (US/0742-5287) [10361860] **3285**

HISPANIC LINK (US) [07311187] **1112, 2262**

HISPANIC LINK WEEKLY REPORT (US) [10295017] **2262**

● HISPANIC MEDIA & MARKET SOURCE (US/1071-4553) [28642396] **925**

HISPANIC MEDIA AND MARKETS *See* HISPANIC MEDIA & MARKET SOURCE **925**

HISPANIC NOTABLES IN THE UNITED STATES OF NORTH AMERICA (US/0191-6297) [04898558] **2262**

HISPANIC OUTLOOK IN HIGHER EDUCATION, THE (US/1054-2337) [22789380] **1829**

HISPANIC POPULATION IN THE UNITED STATES. ADVANCE REPORT, THE (US) [16783935] **5328**

HISPANIC RESOURCE DIRECTORY (US) [25174724] **2262**

HISPANIC REVIEW (US/0018-2176) [01752093] **3344, 3285**

HISPANIC TIMES *See* HISPANIC TIMES MAGAZINE **4204**

HISPANIC TIMES MAGAZINE (US/0892-1369) [15100479] **2262, 4204**

HISPANIC TODAY (US) [20252958] **2262**

HISPANIC (WASHINGTON, D.C.) (US/0898-3097) [17770329] **2262**

HISPANICA POSNANIENSIA / UNIWERSYTET IM. ADAMA MICKIEWICZA W POZNANIU (PL) [23721024] **3285**

HISPANISTISCHE STUDIEN (SZ/0170-8570) [09825393] **3285, 3394**

HISPANO AMERICANO; SEMINARIO DE LA VIDA Y LA VERDAD (MX) [04928187] **2534**

HISPANO NEWS, EL (US) [21741763] **2263**

HISPANO (SACRAMENTO, CALIF.) (US) [06039484] **2263, 5635**

HISPANOFILA (US/0018-2206) [01607299] **3394**

HISPO / ASSOCIATION D'HISTOIRE ET DE SCIENCE POLITIQUE (SZ) [10053491] **4476**

HISSU AMINOSAN KENKYU (JA/0387-4141) [I03874141] **4191**

HISTECHNICON (DELFT) *See* ERFGOED VAN INDUSTRIE EN TECHNIEK **2686**

HISTOCHEMICAL JOURNAL (UK/0018-2214) [01752094] **536**

HISTOCHEMISTRY (BERLIN) (GW/0301-5564) [01793014] **536**

HISTOIRE & GENEALOGIE PARIS (FR/0984-7677) [I09847677] **2453**

HISTOIRE & MESURE (FR/0982-1783) [15566803] **2617**

HISTOIRE COMPAREE DES LITTERATURES DE LANGUES EUROPEENNES (HU) [11023703] **3285, 3394**

HISTOIRE DE L'ART (PARIS, 1988) (FR/0992-2059) [18889261] **321**

HISTOIRE DE L'EDUCATION (FR/0221-6280) [07602855] **1750**

HISTOIRE DES ACCIDENTS DU TRAVAIL (FR/0181-9739) [08604643] **2863**

HISTOIRE DES SCIENCES MEDICALES (FR/0440-8888) [02432739] **3584**

HISTOIRE DU ROCK (CN) [02443315] **4121**

HISTOIRE, ECONOMIE ET SOCIETE (FR) [08924328] 5201, **1565**

HISTOIRE EN SAVOIE MAGAZINE, L' (FR) [25357269] **2690**

HISTOIRE EPISTEMOLOGIE LANGAGE : HEL (FR) [10292250] **3285**

HISTOIRE ET NATURE (FR/0396-9681) [01290450] **4166**

HISTOIRE ET SOCIOLOGIE DE LA CULTURE **CEASED.** (CN) [02076939] **5246**

HISTOIRE : H (FR) [05869813] **2690**

HISTOIRE, L' (FR/0182-2411) [06047757] **2617**

HISTOIRE LITTERAIRE DE LA FRANCE (FR) [01695908] **3394**

HISTOIRE RELIGIEUSE DU CANADA (CN/0440-8934) [02076998] **4963**

HISTOIRE SOCIALE (CN/0018-2257) [01586704] **5201**

HISTOIRES DE DEVELOPPEMENT LYON (FR/0990-915X) [I0990915X] **2910**

HISTOLOGIA MEDICA (SP/0213-2990) [20626691] **537**

HISTOLOGY AND HISTOPATHOLOGY (SP/0213-3911) [13918649] 3894, **537**

HISTONIUM EN SU NUEVA DIMENSION (AG) [01788325] **2551**

HISTOPATHOLOGY (UK/0309-0167) [03146859] **3894**

HISTORAMA (PARIS, FRANCE : 1984) **See** HISTORAMA SPECIAL **2617**

HISTORAMA (PARIS, FRANCE : 1984) (FR/0752-3408) [10636831] **2690**

HISTORAMA SPECIAL (FR/0995-709X) [28698773] **2617**

HISTORIA (PO) [05961116] **2617**

HISTORIA (PE) [03005913] **2736**

HISTORIA (IT) **2617**

HISTORIA 16 (SP/0210-6353) [03719984] **2691**

HISTORIA 16 I.E. DIECISEIS. EXTRA (SP) [06236393] **2691**

HISTORIA AGRICULTURAE (NE/0439-2027) [03289288] **92**

HISTORIA ANDINA (PE) [02077400] **2736**

HISTORIA (BUENOS AIRES, ARGENTINA : 1981) (AG/0326-1352) [08009319] **2736**

HISTORIA CRITICA (BOGOTA, COLOMBIA) (CK) [20311938] **2736**

HISTORIA DE LA EDUCACION (SP/0212-0267) [22692834] **1750**

HISTORIA DE LA REVOLUCION MEXICANA (MX) [05279481] **2736**

HISTORIA. EINZELSCHRIFTEN (GW/0440-8969) [05230783] **2691**

HISTORIA GRAFICA DE CATALUNYA DIA A DIA (SP) [06336302] **2691**

HISTORIA HOSPITALIUM (GW/0440-9043) [01397548] **3783**

HISTORIA INFANTIAE (HU/0236-929X) [14125061] **1804**

HISTORIA, INSTITUCIONES, DOCUMENTOS (SP/0210-7716) [04354191] **2691**

HISTORIA LATINOAMERICANA EN EUROPA (GW/1010-0466) [14258183] **2617**

HISTORIA MATHEMATICA (US/0315-0860) [02240703] **3507**

HISTORIA MEDICINAE VETERINARIAE (DK/0105-1423) [02627669] **5511**

HISTORIA MEXICANA (MX/0185-0172) [00833659] **2736**

HISTORIA NATURAL Y PRO NATURA (GT/0018-2346) [02653563] **4166**

HISTORIA OBRERA (MX) [02242924] **1677**

HISTORIA PARAGUAYA (PY/0440-9094) [01752103] **2736**

HISTORIA (PARIS) (FR/0018-2281) [01586868] **2617**

HISTORIA, QUESTOES & DEBATES (BL/0100-6932) [10357566] **2736**

HISTORIA RELIGIONUM (SW/0439-2132) [02095473] **4963**

HISTORIA (SANTIAGO) (CL/0073-2435) [02080066] **2736**

HISTORIA SCIENTIARUM (JA/0285-4821) [07066089] **5110**

HISTORIA SOCIAL (VALENCIA, SPAIN) (SP/0214-2570) [19738349] **5201**

HISTORIA (THREE RIVERS) (SA/0018-229X) [01928379] **2640**

HISTORIA / UNIVERSIDADE ESTADUAL PAULISTA (BL) [10567506] **2617**

HISTORIA (WIESBADEN) (GW/0018-2311) [01752100] **2617**

HISTORIA Y CULTURA (LIMA) (PE/0073-2486) [01585713] 237, **2617**

HISTORIA Y FUENTE ORAL (SP) [21062457] **2691**

HISTORIA Y SOCIEDAD (PR) [18927054] **2617**

HISTORIA Y VIDA (SP/0018-2354) [01787693] **2617**

HISTORIALLINEN AIKAKAUSKIRJA (FI/0018-2362) [02428424] **2617**

HISTORIALLINEN ARKISTO (FI/0073-2540) [02067743] **2691**

HISTORIAN (KINGSTON), THE (US/0018-2370) [01713899] **2618**

HISTORIAN, THE (AT) [05212974] **2669**

HISTORIANS OF EARLY MODERN EUROPE (US/0883-3559) [01605543] **2691**

HISTORIANS OF NETHERLANDISH ART NEWSLETTER (US/1067-4284) [27211468] 300, **352**

HISTORIAS (MX) [09605464] **2618**

HISTORIC BRASS SOCIETY JOURNAL (US/1045-4616) [20128252] **4121**

HISTORIC BRASS SOCIETY NEWSLETTER (US/1045-4594) [20127854] **4121**

HISTORIC CLAY TOBACCO PIPE STUDIES (US/0747-8801) [10618601] 237, **269**

HISTORIC DOCUMENTS (JS/0892-080X) [01783719] **4476**

HISTORIC ENVIRONMENT (AT/0726-6715) [07266715] **2669**

HISTORIC GUELPH (CN/0709-5562) [05694788] 432, **2736**

HISTORIC HOTELS OF AMERICA (US) [23069585] **2806**

HISTORIC HOUSE (UK) **300**

HISTORIC HOUSES, CASTLES, AND GARDENS IN GREAT BRITAIN AND IRELAND (UK/0073-2567) [01798121] **2691**

HISTORIC HUNTSVILLE QUARTERLY OF LOCAL ARCHITECTURE AND PRESERVATION, THE (US/1074-567X) [29746603] **300**

HISTORIC ILLINOIS (US/0164-5293) [03990610] **2737**

HISTORIC KINGSTON (CN/0440-9191) [02247176] **2737**

HISTORIC LANDMARKS OF BLACK AMERICANS (US) **2737**

HISTORIC MADISON, INC **See** JOURNAL OF HISTORIC MADISON, INC. OF WISCONSIN, THE **2741**

HISTORIC MAURY (US/1065-0016) [10603295] **2737**

HISTORIC NANTUCKET (US/0439-2248) [01752107] **2737**

HISTORIC NEIGHBORHOODS NEWSLETTER (US/1051-5852) [20576913] **2824**

HISTORIC PRESERVATION FORUM (US/1056-6309) [23348310] **2618**

HISTORIC PRESERVATION NEWS (US/1065-3562) [22046089] **2618**

HISTORIC PRESERVATION (WASHINGTON, D.C.) (US/0018-2419) [04604083] **2737**

HISTORIC SCHAEFFERSTOWN RECORD (US/0892-6336) [15244725] **2737**

HISTORIC SOCIETY OF LANCASHIRE AND CHESHIRE **See** OCCASIONAL SERIES - HISTORIC SOCIETY OF LANCASHIRE AND CHESHIRE **2701**

HISTORIC TRAVELER, THE (US/1074-4665) [23361874] 5479, **2618**

HISTORICA (MX) [02547543] **2737**

HISTORICA (CESKOSLOVENSKA AKADEMIE VED. SEKCE HISTORICKA) **CEASED.** (XR/0440-9205) [01752110] **2691**

HISTORICA (LIMA) (PE/0252-8894) [05094781] **2737**

HISTORICAL ABSTRACTS ON DISC [COMPUTER FILE] (US/1074-7869) [24892955] **2618**

HISTORICAL ABSTRACTS. PART A, MODERN HISTORY ABSTRACTS (US/0363-2717) [01000370] 2618, **2635**

HISTORICAL ABSTRACTS. PART B, TWENTIETH CENTURY ABSTRACTS (US/0363-2725) [01000359] 2618, **2635**

HISTORICAL AND CULTURAL DICTIONARIES OF ASIA (US) [02084948] **2652**

HISTORICAL ARCHAEOLOGY (US/0440-9213) [01752118] **269**

HISTORICAL ASSOCIATION, LONDON **See** ANNUAL BULLETIN OF HISTORICAL LITERATURE **2610**

HISTORICAL BIOLOGY (UK/0891-2963) [14709289] **457**

HISTORICAL BOOKLETS / THE CANADIAN HISTORICAL ASSOCIATION (CN/0068-886X) [02810086] **2737**

HISTORICAL BULLETIN (MADISON, WIS.) (US/0275-1968) [01755931] **2618**

HISTORICAL BULLETIN / PHILIPPINE HISTORICAL ASSOCIATION (PH/0116-3655) [08228713] **2652**

HISTORICAL COLLECTIONS OF THE DANVERS HISTORICAL SOCIETY (US/0362-000X) [01565935] **2737**

HISTORICAL COLLECTIONS OF THE ESSEX INSTITUTE **See** ESSEX INSTITUTE HISTORICAL COLLECTIONS **2732**

HISTORICAL ENERGY STATISTICS (US) [06856666] **1962**

HISTORICAL EVALUATION AND RESEARCH ORGANIZATION **See** COMBAT DATA SUBSCRIPTION SERVICE **4039**

HISTORICAL FIREARMS SOCIETY OF SOUTH AFRICA **See** JOURNAL - HISTORICAL FIREARMS SOCIETY OF SOUTH AFRICA **251**

HISTORICAL FOOTNOTES (ST. LOUIS, MO.) (US/0360-9030) [01776445] **2618**

HISTORICAL FOOTNOTES (STONINGTON, CONN.) (US/0886-5272) [02461845] 2453, **2737**

●HISTORICAL GARDENER, THE (US/1067-5973) [26106917] **2418**

HISTORICAL GENEALOGICAL MAGAZINE SPECIALIZING IN CLINTON AND BOONE COUNTIES (US/1064-041X) [23984081] **2453**

HISTORICAL GEOGRAPHY (US) [06085239] **2565**

HISTORICAL GUIDES TO THE WORLD'S PERIODICALS AND NEWSPAPERS (US/0742-5538) [10370868] **2920**

HISTORICAL INTELLIGENCER (US/0270-4919) [06461992] **5061**

HISTORICAL JOURNAL (CAMBRIDGE, CAMBRIDGESHIRE) (UK/0018-246X) [01752122] **2618**

HISTORICAL JOURNAL OF FILM, RADIO, AND TELEVISION (UK/0143-9685) [07522224] 1132, **4071**

HISTORICAL JOURNAL OF MASSACHUSETTS (US/0276-8313) [06420039] **2737**

HISTORICAL JOURNAL / OTAKI HISTORICAL SOCIETY (NZ/0110-5647) [09890356] **2669**

HISTORICAL LABOUR FORCE STATISTICS (CN/1181-957X) [24623909] 1677, **1533**

HISTORICAL METALLURGY (UK/0142-3304) [02250385] **4003**

HISTORICAL METHODS (US/0161-5440) [03977420] **5201**

HISTORICAL MICROFICHE SERIES (AT/1038-6424) [I10386424] **1926**

HISTORICAL MONOGRAPH / RANDWICK & DISTRICT HISTORICAL SOCIETY (AT) [16949184] **2669**

HISTORICAL NEW HAMPSHIRE (US/0018-2508) [01752126] **2737**

HISTORICAL NEWS (NZ/0439-2345) [02113164] **2618**

HISTORICAL NEWS LETTER (US/0199-9664) [01776101] **2737**

HISTORICAL NEWS. MIFFLIN COUNTY HISTORICAL SOCIETY (US) **2618**

HISTORICAL NEWSLETTER (O'NEILL, NEB.) (US/0895-3058) [16567174] **2618**

HISTORICAL ORGAN BROADSHEETS (UK) [19706166] **4121**

HISTORICAL ORGAN NOTES (UK) [19706028] **4121**

HISTORICAL PAPERS / CANADIAN SOCIETY OF CHURCH HISTORY (CN/0848-1563) [21103082] **4963**

HISTORICAL PERFORMANCE (US/0898-8587) [17932492] **4121**

HISTORICAL PORT HOPE (CN/0846-3190) [25066653] **2737**

HISTORICAL PRICING--PETROCHEMICALS (US) [28389587] 2012, **1025**

HISTORICAL PUBLICATIONS - CANADIAN WAR MUSEUM (CN) [03505160] **2737**

HISTORICAL RECORDS OF AUSTRALIAN SCIENCE (AT/0727-3061) [07511064] **5110**

HISTORICAL REFLECTIONS (CN/0315-7997) [02027177] **2618**

HISTORICAL REPORT OF THE SECRETARY OF STATE, ARKANSAS (US/0196-4720) [03401850] **4476**

HISTORICAL — Alphabetical Title Index

HISTORICAL RESEARCH FOR HIGHER DEGREES IN THE UNITED KINGDOM. PART I, THESES COMPLETED (UK/0268-6716) [13816588] **1829**

HISTORICAL RESEARCH FOR HIGHER DEGREES IN THE UNITED KINGDOM. PART II, THESES IN PROGRESS (UK/0268-6724) [13816619] **2618**

HISTORICAL RESEARCH : THE BULLETIN OF THE INSTITUTE OF HISTORICAL RESEARCH (UK/0950-3471) [15263309] **2618**

HISTORICAL REVIEW (NZ/0018-2516) [02082365] **2669**

HISTORICAL REVIEW OF BERKS COUNTY (US/0018-2524) [01589887] **2737**

HISTORICAL SERIES / ROLLS-ROYCE HERITAGE TRUST (UK) [17361655] 5416, **2618**

HISTORICAL SOCIAL RESEARCH (KOLN) (GW/0172-6404) [07920282] 4476, **5246**

HISTORICAL SOCIAL RESEARCH (QUANTUM (ASSOCIATION) : 1979) (GW/0172-6404) [18733716] **5201**

HISTORICAL SOCIETY MIRROR (US/0440-940X) [01752131] **2737**

HISTORICAL SOCIETY OF FAIRFAX COUNTY YEARBOOK (US) **2737**

HISTORICAL SOCIETY OF GHANA *See* TRANSACTIONS OF THE HISTORICAL SOCIETY OF GHANA **2667**

HISTORICAL SOCIETY OF HARFORD COUNTY *See* HARFORD HISTORICAL BULLETIN **2452**

HISTORICAL SOCIETY OF HOPKINS COUNTY (KENTUCKY) *See* YEAR BOOK - HISTORICAL SOCIETY OF HOPKINS COUNTY **2766**

HISTORICAL SOCIETY OF MONTGOMERY COUNTY (PENNSYLVANIA) *See* BULLETIN OF THE HISTORICAL SOCIETY OF MONTGOMERY COUNTY, PENNSYLVANIA **2725**

HISTORICAL SOCIETY OF SOUTH AUSTRALIA *See* JOURNAL OF THE HISTORICAL SOCIETY OF SOUTH AUSTRALIA **2669**

HISTORICAL SOCIETY OF SOUTHERN CALIFORNIA *See* SOUTHERN CALIFORNIAN, THE **2761**

HISTORICAL SOCIETY OF WASHINGTON COUNTY, VIRGINIA *See* PUBLICATION - HISTORICAL SOCIETY OF WASHINGTON COUNTY, VIRGINIA **2755**

HISTORICAL SOCIETY OF YORK COUNTY (PA.) *See* ANNUAL REPORT - HISTORICAL SOCIETY OF YORK COUNTY (PA.) **2720**

HISTORICAL STATISTICAL BULLETIN (SP) [09698279] 2305, **2317**

HISTORICAL STATISTICS OF FOREIGN TRADE / ORGANISATION FOR ECONOMIC CO-OPERATION AND DEVELOPMENT (FR) [09167500] **730**

HISTORICAL STREAMFLOW SUMMARY, ALBERTA (CN/0318-5877) [01785765] **1414**

HISTORICAL STREAMFLOW SUMMARY : ATLANTIC PROVINCES (CN) [01785770] **1414**

HISTORICAL STREAMFLOW SUMMARY: BRITISH COLUMBIA (CN) [01785767] **1414**

HISTORICAL STREAMFLOW SUMMARY: MANITOBA.(CN) [01785771] **1414**

HISTORICAL STREAMFLOW SUMMARY: SASKATCHEWAN (CN/0318-5923) [01785772] **1414**

HISTORICAL STREAMFLOW SUMMARY : YUKON TERRITORY AND NORTHWEST TERRITORIES (CN) [01785769] **1414**

HISTORICAL STUDIES IN EDUCATION (CN/0843-5057) [20601349] **1750**

HISTORICAL STUDIES IN THE PHYSICAL AND BIOLOGICAL SCIENCES (US/0890-9997) [13900123] 457, **4404**

HISTORICAL STUDIES OTTAWA. 1990 (CN/1193-1981) [I11931981] 4963, **2618**

HISTORICAL WHISPERINGS (US) [08630111] **2737**

HISTORICALLY SPEAKING (US/0275-8385) [04255331] **2737**

HISTORICAS : BOLETIN DE INFORMACION DEL INSTITUTO DE INVESTIGACIONES HISTORICAS UNAM (MX) [07618230] **2618**

HISTORICKE STUDIE (XO) **2618**

HISTORICKY CASOPIS (XO/0018-2575) [02261936] **2691**

HISTORIE A VOJENSTVI (XR/0018-2583) [07319152] **2691**

HISTORIE; JYSKE SAMLINGER (DK) [01752135] **2691**

HISTORIELARARNAS FORENINGS ARSSKRIFT (SW/0439-2434) [05872344] **2618**

HISTORIEN MUNICIPAL, L' (CN/0826-5283) [12093245] **2737**

HISTORIENS ET GEOGRAPHES (FR/0046-757X) [09518751] **2618**

HISTORIGRAM (CN/0821-1469) [09747521] **2737**

HISTORIJSKI ZBORNIK (CI/0351-2193) [01752136] **2691**

HISTORIOGRAPHER, THE (US) [06140222] **5061**

HISTORIOGRAPHIA LINGUISTICA (NE/0302-5160) [01784474] **3285**

HISTORISCH GEOGRAFISCH TIJDSCHRIFT (NE/0167-9775) [12018043] **2565**

HISTORISCH-POLITISCHE BUCH, DAS (GW/0018-2605) [01752139] 3344, **2618**

HISTORISCH POLITISCHE MILLEILUNGEN (GW/0943-691X) **4523**

HISTORISCHE ANTHROPOLOGIE (GW/0942-8704) **237**

HISTORISCHE FORSCHUNGEN (BERLIN) (GW) [02079585] **2619**

HISTORISCHE MITTEILUNGEN (GW/0936-5796) [20696528] **2619**

HISTORISCHE SOZIALFORSCHUNG (GW/0173-2145) [08593669] **5201**

HISTORISCHE SPRACHFORSCHUNG (GW/0935-3518) [18726557] **3285**

HISTORISCHE SPRACHFORSCHUNG. ERGANZUNGSHEFT (GW) [21994701] **3286**

HISTORISCHE VEREINIGUNG WYNENTAL *See* JAHRESSCHRIFT DER HISTORISCHEN VEREINIGUNG WYNENTAL **2694**

HISTORISCHE ZEITSCHRIFT (GW/0018-2613) [01752145] **2619**

HISTORISCHE ZEITSCHRIFT. BEIHEFT (GW) [02094580] **2619**

HISTORISCHE ZEITSCHRIFT. SONDERHEFT (GW/0440-971X) [02094440] **2619**

HISTORISCHER VEREIN DER PFALZ *See* MITTEILUNGEN DES HISTORISCHEN VEREINS DER PFALZ **2699**

HISTORISCHER VEREIN DILLINGEN AN DER DONAU *See* JAHRBUCH DES HISTORISCHEN VEREINS DILLINGEN AN DER DONAU **2693**

HISTORISCHER VEREIN FUER DAS FURSTENTUM LIECHTENSTEIN *See* JAHRBUCH DES HISTORISCHEN VEREINS FUER DAS FURSTENTUM LIECHTENSTEIN **2693**

HISTORISCHER VEREIN FUER NIEDERBAYERN *See* VERHANDLUNGEN DES HISTORISCHEN VEREINS FUER NIEDERBAYERN **2714**

HISTORISCHER VEREIN FUR SCHWABEN *See* ZEITSCHRIFT DES HISTORISCHEN VEREINS FUER SCHWABEN **2634**

HISTORISCHER VEREIN FUR STEIERMARK *See* ZEITSCHRIFT DES HISTORISCHEN VEREINES FUER STEIERMARK **2671**

HISTORISCHER VEREIN FUR STRAUBING UND UMGEBUNG *See* JAHRESBERICHT DES HISTORISCHEN VEREINS FUER STRAUBING UND UMGEBUNG **2694**

HISTORISCHES JAHRBUCH (GW/0018-2621) [01696568] **2619**

HISTORISCHES JAHRBUCH DER STADT LINZ (AU/0440-9736) [02084615] **2691**

HISTORISCHES MUSEUM BASEL *See* JAHRESBERICHTE / HISTORISCHES MUSEUM BASEL **4089**

HISTORISCHES MUSEUM SCHLOSS THUN *See* HISTORISCHES MUSEUM SCHLOSS THUN **2691**

HISTORISCHES MUSEUM SCHLOSS THUN (SZ) [12626341] 4088, **2691**

HISTORISK-FILOSOFISKE MEDDELELSER (DK/0106-0481) [06665593] 4348, **2619**

HISTORISK TIDSKRIFT FOR FINLAND (FI/0046-7596) [01697075] **2691**

HISTORISK TIDSKRIFT (STOCKHOLM) (SW/0345-469X) [01641165] **2691**

HISTORISK TIDSSKRIFT (NO/0018-263x) [01588341] **2691**

HISTORISK TIDSSKRIFT (DK) [01638964] **2691**

HISTORISK-TOPOGRAFISK SELSKAB FOR FREDERIKSBERG *See* FREDERIKSBERG GENNEM TIDERNE **2688**

HISTORISKA OCH LITTERATURHISTORISKA STUDIER (FI/0073-2702) [01696867] **3394**

HISTORISKE MEDDELELSER OM KBENHAVN. ARBOG (DK/0439-2620) [02256709] **2691**

HISTORY AND ANTHROPOLOGY (SZ/0275-7206) [07208057] **237**

HISTORY AND COMPUTING (UK) [16582278] **1259**

HISTORY & COMPUTING (UK/0957-0144) [22659624] 2619, **1186**

● HISTORY AND LANGUAGE (US/1062-2306) [25540797] **2619**

HISTORY AND MEMORY (US/0935-560X) [20506305] **2619**

HISTORY AND PHILOSOPHY OF LOGIC (UK) **4348**

HISTORY AND PHILOSOPHY OF THE LIFE SCIENCES (UK/0391-9714) [06256347] **457**

HISTORY AND TECHNOLOGY (SZ/0734-1512) [08682103] **5110**

HISTORY AND THEORY (US/0018-2656) [01752159] **2635**

HISTORY; ANNUAL SUPPLEMENT (US/0091-2271) [01786369] **4045**

HISTORY (BOCA RATON, FLA.) (US/1058-174X) [24233466] **2619**

HISTORY FORUM BRIDGEWATER (AT/1034-7577) [I10347577] 2619, **1896**

HISTORY HIGHLIGHTS : NEWSLETTER OF THE WASHINGTON STATE HISTORICAL SOCIETY (US) [09203293] **2619**

HISTORY IN AFRICA (US/0361-5413) [02246846] **2640**

HISTORY IN NEWSPAPER FRONT PAGES, A (US/0098-163X) [02243996] **2619**

HISTORY LIVES HERE (US/0883-8143) [12225657] **2737**

HISTORY (LONDON) (UK/0018-2648) [02164044] **2619**

HISTORY MICROCOMPUTER REVIEW (US/0887-1078) [13179768] **2619**

HISTORY NEWS DISPATCH (US) [13142922] **2737**

HISTORY NEWS (NASHVILLE, TENN.) (US/0363-7492) [01752160] **2737**

HISTORY NOTES / LAKE CHELAN HISTORICAL SOCIETY (US/1065-0024) [16112224] **2453**

HISTORY NOTES : THE NEWSLETTER OF THE VIRGINIA HISTORICAL SOCIETY (US) [23153086] **2737**

HISTORY OF AGRICULTURE (II/0378-7524) [09805569] **92**

HISTORY OF ANTHROPOLOGY NEWSLETTER (US/0362-9074) [01172585] **237**

HISTORY OF ECONOMIC THOUGHT NEWSLETTER (UK/0440-9884) [02243299] **1592**

HISTORY OF EDUCATION QUARTERLY (US/0018-2680) [01752162] **1750**

HISTORY OF EDUCATION REVIEW (AT/0819-8691) [09851277] **1750**

HISTORY OF EDUCATION SOCIETY BULLETIN (UK/0018-2699) [05138298] **1750**

HISTORY OF EDUCATION SOCIETY (GREAT BRITAIN) *See* HISTORY OF EDUCATION SOCIETY BULLETIN **1750**

HISTORY OF EDUCATION (TAVISTOCK) (UK/0046-760X) [01787160] **1750**

HISTORY OF EUROPEAN IDEAS (UK/0191-6599) [04964760] **2691**

HISTORY OF GEOGRAPHY JOURNAL (US) [21356892] **2565**

HISTORY OF GEOPHYSICS (US/8755-1217) [11241038] **1406**

HISTORY OF HIGHER EDUCATION ANNUAL (US/0737-2698) [08626232] **1829**

HISTORY OF LINCOLNSHIRE *CEASED.* (UK) **2691**

HISTORY OF LOGIC (IT) [10579114] 2619, **4348**

HISTORY OF MATHEMATICS (US/0899-2428) [18042917] **3507**

HISTORY OF NURSING BULLETIN (UK) [18713843] **3856**

HISTORY OF PHILOSOPHY QUARTERLY (US/0740-0675) [09886163] **4348**

HISTORY OF PHOTOGRAPHY (UK/0308-7298) [02691911] **4370**

HISTORY OF PHYSICAL EDUCATION AND SPORT: RESEARCH AND STUDIES *CEASED.* (JA) [04204606] 4898, **1855**

HISTORY OF POLITICAL ECONOMY (US/0018-2702) [01715102] **1565**

HISTORY OF POLITICAL THOUGHT (UK/0143-781X) [06574358] **4476**

HISTORY OF PSYCHIATRY (UK/0957-154X) [22167445] **3926**

HISTORY OF PSYCHOANALYSIS MONOGRAPH *CEASED.* (US/0734-9831) [08859672] 4588, **3926**

HISTORY OF PSYCHOLOGY IN AUTOBIOGRAPHY (US/0097-6091) [01782291] **4588**

HISTORY OF PSYCHOLOGY SERIES (US/0146-0331) [02830284] **4588**

HISTORY OF RELIGIONS (US/0018-2710) [01752164] **4963**

Alphabetical Title Index — HOCKEY

HISTORY OF SCIENCE (UK/0073-2753) [00971471] **5110**

● HISTORY OF SCIENCE AND TECHNOLOGY (US/1062-5445) [25660814] **5110**

HISTORY OF TECHNOLOGY (UK/0307-5451) [02841646] **5110**

HISTORY OF THE GENEVA BIBLE (UK) **5017**

HISTORY OF THE HUMAN SCIENCES (UK/0952-6951) [19287751] **5201**

HISTORY OF THE TARIFF SCHEDULES OF THE UNITED STATES ANNOTATED *CEASED.* (US) [08125339] **839**

HISTORY OF UNIVERSITIES (UK/0144-5138) [07703318] **1829**

HISTORY OF WASHTENAW COUNTY, MICHIGAN (US) [22959728] **2453**

HISTORY OF WOMEN RELIGIOUS NEWS AND NOTES (US/1054-545X) [20365962] **4963**

HISTORY REVIEW (US) **2619**

HISTORY SOURCE (US/1063-9799) [26185120] 2619, **2635**

HISTORY SOURCE CD-ROM *See* HUMANITIES SOURCE **2857**

HISTORY (SYDNEY, N.S.W.) (AT) [19453778] **2669**

HISTORY TEACHER BRISBANE (AT/0729-154X) [I0729154X] 2619, **1896**

HISTORY TEACHER (LONG BEACH, CALIF.), THE (US/0018-2745) [01794874] **1896**

HISTORY, TECHNOLOGY, AND ART MONOGRAPH (CN/0316-1269) [06693870] **5110**

HISTORY TODAY (UK/0018-2753) [01644842] **2619**

HISTORY TRAILS (US/0889-6186) [13997035] **2737**

HISTORY (WASHINGTON) (US/0361-2759) [01202184] **2619**

HISTORY WORKSHOP (UK/0309-2984) [02328483] **2619**

HISTORYKA (PL/0073-277X) [01713909] **2619**

HISTRIA ARCHAEOLOGICA (CI/0350-6320) [04202029] 2691, **269**

HISUTORIA (JA) [01639167] **2619**

HIT PARADER (US/0162-0266) [02250386] **2534**

HITACHI CABLE REVIEW (JA/0914-899X) [I0914899X] **2155**

HITACHI KINZOKU GIHO (JA/0916-0930) [I09160930] **4003**

HITACHI REVIEW (JA/0018-277X) [02510097] **5110**

HITACHI TECHNOLOGY (JA/0018-277X) [11223052] **5110**

HITACHI ZOSEN GIHO (JA/0018-2788) [10278166] **5110**

HITCH (DK) [02242521] **4072**

● HITCHCOCK ANNUAL (US/1062-5518) [25663236] **4072**

HITCHHIKER (US) [02251674] **3213**

HITEL (HU) [19745193] **2691**

HITHADSHUT (IS/0303-1519) [01784358] **2652**

HITKRANT (NE) **4121**

HITMAKERS (US) **1133**

HITMEN (US/0737-7959) [09449021] **4121**

HITO TO KOKUDO (JA) [02441254] **2824**

HITOTSUBASHI DAIGAKU KENKYU NENPO. SHAKAIGAKU KENKYU (JA/0559-7102) [22293970] **5201**

HITOTSUBASHI DAIGAKU, TOKYO. KEIZAI KENKYUJO *See* ECONOMIC RESEARCH SERIES **1484**

HITOTSUBASHI JOURNAL OF ARTS & SCIENCES (JA/0073-2788) [01752169] 5110, **321**

HITOTSUBASHI JOURNAL OF COMMERCE AND MANAGEMENT (JA/0018-2796) [01752170] **839**

HITOTSUBASHI JOURNAL OF ECONOMICS (JA/0018-280X) [01752171] **1493**

HITOTSUBASHI JOURNAL OF LAW & POLITICS (JA/0073-2796) [01696142] 2978, **4476**

HITOTSUBASHI JOURNAL OF SOCIAL STUDIES (JA/0073-280X) [01588535] **5201**

HITOTSUBASHI RONSO (JA/0018-2818) [02539072] **5201**

HITS (US) [15994494] **4121**

HIV/AIDS SURVEILLANCE (US/1048-759X) [19372125] **3670**

HIV/AIDS UPDATE / PENNSYLVANIA DEPARTMENT OF HEALTH, BUREAU OF HIV/AIDS (US) [23437342] 3670, 3713, **4783**

HIV HOTLINE (US) [25047383] **4783**

HIVELY'S CHOICE (US/0748-3325) [10916236] **1750**

HJARTA, KARL, LUNGOR (SW/0280-4638) [08498931] **3949**

HK, HOLZ- UND MOBELINDUSTRIE (GW/0721-2585) [18335927] **634**

HL-INFORMASJON (NO) [20008192] **2343**

HLA JOURNAL / HAWAII LIBRARY ASSOCIATION *SUSPENDED.* (US) [08141677] **3213**

HLABC FORUM (CN/0826-0125) [11100290] 3584, **3213**

HLAS L'UDU (XO/0018-2869) [I00182869] **5810**

HLAS PRAVOSLAVI : ORGAN PRAVOSLAVNE CIRKVE V CESKOSLOVENSKU (XR) [10040009] **4963**

HLASATEL (US) [08814906] **5660**

HLB NEWSLETTER, THE (US/0887-3712) [13228187] **3797**

HLH (GW/0017-9906) [02339871] **2605**

HLI REPORT (US/0899-2673) [14393787] **2280**

HM CUSTOM AND EXCISE TARIFF AMENDMENT (UK/0262-0421) [I02620421] **4731**

HM CUSTOMS AND EXCISE NEWS RELEASES (UK) **4731**

HM CUSTOMS & EXCISE.VAT GUIDE (UK) **4731**

HMC&M, HAZARDOUS MATERIAL CONTROL & MANAGEMENT [COMPUTER FILE] : HMIS, HAZARDOUS MATERIALS INFORMATION SYSTEM (US) [25621808] **2232**

HMC&M [COMPUTER FILE] : HAZARDOUS MATERIAL CONTROL & MANAGEMENT ; HMIS : HAZARDOUS MATERIAL INFORMATION SYSTEM / DEPT. OF DEFENSE (US) [25494925] **2232**

HMD. THEORIE UND PRAXIS DER WIRTSCHAFTSINFORMATIK (GW/0939-2602) [I09392602] **1186**

HML NEWS (CN/0228-9296) [07869923] **457**

HM/M (XR/0323-1283) [25857069] **4121**

HMO EXECUTIVE SALARY SURVEY (US/0278-1247) [07706334] 4783, **1677**

HMO MAGAZINE (US/1050-9038) [21719118] **2882**

HMO MANAGERS LETTER (US/1050-902X) [16502762] **3783**

● HMO PERFORMANCE DIGEST (US/1063-1704) [25908641] **5287**

HMO PPO DIRECTORY (US) **3584**

HMO PRACTICE (US/0891-6624) [14948058] **5287**

HMSO AGENCY CATALOGUE (UK) [19007951] **4654**

HMSO ANNUAL CATALOGUE (UK/0951-8584) [14523756] **417**

HMSO BOOKS IN PRINT. [MICROFICHE] (UK) **4828**

HMSO CHEMICAL SAFETY SERIES (UK) **977**

HMSO ENVIRONMENTAL HYGIENE SERIES (UK) **4783**

HMSO MEDICAL SERIES (UK) **3584**

HMSO MONTHLY CATALOGUE (UK/0263-7197) [14797261] **4654**

HMTC UPDATE (US/0882-1976) [11788442] **4783**

HN MAGAZINE (NE/0168-8693) [13260853] **4963**

HNO (GW/0017-6192) [01751671] **3888**

HNO PRAXIS HEUTE (GW/0173-9859) [06633603] **3888**

HO (US) [03836166] **2418**

HO EPHEMERIOS (GR) [10648974] **5039**

HO HAI KUNG CHENG (CH) [07025583] **2090**

HO KO HSUEH YU KUNG CHENG (CC) [10698013] **2155**

HO-NAN WEN SHIH TZU LIAO HSUAN CHI / CHUNG-KUO JEN MIN CHENG CHIH HSIEH SHANG HUI I HO-NAN SHENG WEI YUAN HUI, WEN SHIH TZU LIAO YEN CHIU WEI YUAN HUI PIEN (CC) [08716956] **2652**

HO NENG I CHI TSU NIEN TU KUNG TSO PAO KAO (CH) [10898610] **2155**

HO NENG YEN CHIU SO. HO NENG I CHI TSU *See* HO NENG I CHI TSU NIEN TU KUNG TSO PAO KAO **2155**

HO NUNG HSUEH PAO (CC/1000-8551) [19916390] **92**

HO-PEI HSUEH KAN (CC) [10681482] **5231**

HO-PEI HUA PAO (CC) [11654535] **2652**

HO-PEI KO MING HUI I LU (CH) [09538695] **2652**

HO-PEI MEI TAN (CC) [11281677] **2140**

HO-PEI SHIH FAN TA HSUEH HSUEH PAO. CHE HSUEH SHE HUI KO HSUEH PAN (CC) [09492669] **2652**

HO-PEI WEN SHIH TZU LIAO HSUAN CHI / CHUNG-KUO JEN MIN CHENG CHIH HSIEH SHANG HUI I HO-PEI SHENG WEI YUAN HUI, WEN SHIH TZU LIAO YEN CHIU WEI YUAN HUI PIEN (CH) [08882910] **2652**

HO TO CHITSUJO (JA) [02245301] **2978**

HOARD'S DAIRYMAN (US/0018-2885) [01713791] **195**

HOB. DIE HOLZBEARBEITUNG (GW/0018-3822) [I00183822] **5110**

HOBART AND WILLIAM SMITH COLLEGES *See* ALUMNI AND ALUMNAE DIRECTORY **1097**

HOBART COLLEGE *See* ALUMNI AND ALUMNAE DIRECTORY / HOBART AND WILLIAM SMITH COLLEGES **1097**

HOBART GAZETTE (HOBART, IND. : 1939) (US) [15117860] **5664**

HOBBES STUDIES (NE/0921-5891) [18634086] **4348**

HOBBS FLARE, THE (US) [16877658] **5712**

HOBBY ARTIST NEWS (US/0145-6016) [02757355] **2774**

HOBBY BULLETIN (NE) **2774**

HOBBY ELECTRONICS (UK/0142-6192) [06711450] 2774, **2056**

HOBBY GREENHOUSE (US/1040-6212) [13077414] **2418**

HOBBY HANDIG (NE) **2774**

HOBBY INDEX (US/1053-8011) [22606037] **2774**

HOBBY MERCHANDISER ANNUAL TRADE DIRECTORY (US) **2774**

HOBBY MERCHANDISER (NEW YORK, N.Y.) (US/0744-1738) [08085732] **2774**

HOBBYISTS' SOURCEBOOK (US/1045-0602) [19990468] **2774**

HOBIE HOT LINE (US/0745-1628) [08879705] **593**

HOBO JUNGLE : A QUARTERLY JOURNAL OF NEW WRITING (US/1045-2591) [20067510] **2488**

HOBUNSHU / KYOTO DAIGAKU GENSHIRO JIKKENJO GAKUJUTSU KOENKAI (JA/0917-1746) [23806339] 4447, **1053**

HOCHPARTERRE (SZ) [21022769] 300, **2098**

HOCHSCHUL-DIENST (GW/0439-2965) [02653593] **1750**

HOCHSCHUL-INFORMATIONS-SYSTEM GMBH *See* HIS **1750**

HOCHSCHULBERICHT (AU) [01786899] **1829**

HOCHSCHULBUCHER FUER MATHEMATIK (GW/0073-2842) [I00732842] **3507**

HOCHSCHULE FUR BAUWESEN LEIPZIG *See* WISSENSCHAFTLICHE ZEITSCHRIFT DER HOCHSCHULE FUER BAUWESEN LEIPZIG **311**

HOCHSCHULWESEN : WISSENSCHAFTSPOLITISCHE RUNDSCHAU, DAS (SZ/0018-2974) [02419278] **1750**

HOCHUDOKU (JA/0915-9606) [I09159606] **3740**

HOCKEY AMATEUR (CN/0826-5313) [11888297] **4898**

● HOCKEY, ART OF THE STATE (US/1064-6892) [28153190] **4898**

HOCKEY AUJOURD'HUI (CN/0841-6982) [18926577] **4898**

HOCKEY (BLOOMINGTON, MINN.) (US/1064-6892) [26375600] **4898**

HOCKEY CIRCLE (AT) **4898**

HOCKEY COACHING JOURNAL (CN/0835-8044) [18056637] **4899**

HOCKEY DIGEST (EVANSTON, ILL.) (US/0046-7693) [02790054] **4899**

HOCKEY DIGEST (HARROW) (UK/0950-9550) [I09509550] **4899**

HOCKEY FIELD (UK/0018-3008) [09072321] **4899**

HOCKEY (MONTREAL) (CN/0704-7983) [03797435] **4899**

HOCKEY NEWS, THE (CN/0018-3016) [01775795] **4899**

HOCKEY NEWS ... YEARBOOK, THE (CN/0845-2563) [09242520] **4899**

HOCKEY (NORWALK) (US/0361-5847) [02247016] **4899**

HOCKEY ONTARIO MAGAZINE (CN/0821-4700) [09590460] **4899**

HOCKEY PROFESSIONNEL (CN/0712-8428) [08898737] **4899**

HOCKEY SCOUTING REPORT *See* HOCKEY SCOUTING REPORT **4899**

● HOCKEY SCOUTING REPORT (CN/0836-5148) [25423667] **4899**

HOCKEY
Alphabetical Title Index

HOCKEY STARS OF ... (US/0073-2869) [02367696] **4899**

HOCKEY TODAY (NEW YORK, N.Y.) (US/1059-4795) [24639342] **4899**

HOCKEY'S HERITAGE *SUSPENDED.* (CN/0317-9257) [02248335] **4899**

HODA *See* AL-HUDA AL-JADIDAH **5713**

HODEGOS HYPERESIAS POLITIKES AEROPORIAS (GR) [01798154] **23**

HODEGOS PAIDIKOU KAI NEANIKOU VIVLIOU (GR) [19566277] **1072**

HODO SHASHIN (JA) [03713947] **4370**

HODOWCA DROBNEGO INWENTARZA (PL) [04026159] **92**

HODOWCA GOEBI POCZTOWYCH (PL) [02173966] **5585**

HODOWLA ROSLIN AKLIMTYZACJA I NASIENNICTWO (PL/0018-3040) [01771341] **173**

HOEBO (US) [04967927] **1750**

HOEGYE WA SEMU (KO) [05189885] **745**

HOER ZU (GW/0018-3113) [I00183113] **5479**

HOFMANNSTHAL BLATTER (GW/0441-6813) [02098255] **3394**

HOFMANNSTHAL-FORSCHUNGEN (SZ) [02083646] **3394**

● HOFMANNSTHAL : JAHRBUCH ZUR EUROPAISCHEN MODERNE (GW) [28922702] **3344**

HOFSTRA ENVIRONMENTAL LAW DIGEST (US/0882-6765) [11520073] **3113**

HOFSTRA LABOR LAW JOURNAL (US/1052-3332) [11898384] **3149**

HOFSTRA LAW REVIEW (US/0091-4029) [01787015] **2978**

HOFSTRA PROPERTY LAW JOURNAL *CEASED.* (US/1050-2076) [18433361] **2978**

HOFSTRA UNIVERSITY BUSINESS REVIEW (US) [12532877] **679**

HOFSTRA UNIVERSITY CULTURAL & INTERCULTURAL STUDIES (US/0195-802X) [05661694] **3394**

HOFSTRA UNIVERSITY YEARBOOK OF BUSINESS (US/0073-2907) [02113397] **680**

HOG DIGEST *SUSPENDED.* (US/0195-1947) [03416283] **212**

HOG FARM MANAGEMENT (US/0018-3180) [01771342] **212**

HOG MARKET PLACE QUARTERLY (CN/0380-3651) [02443069] **212**

HOGAKU *CEASED.* (US/0886-1862) [09659192] **4121**

HOGAKU (JA) [02465177] **4476**, **2978**

HOGAKU KYOKAI ZASSHI (JA/0022-6815) [09382778] **2978**

HOGAKU NO TOMO (JA) [01752182] **2978**

HOGAKU RONSO (KYOTO. 1919) (JA/0387-2866) [09938003] **2978**

HOGAKU SEMINA (JA) [19089084] **2978**

HOGAKU SHINPO (JA/0009-6296) [11641376] **2978**

HOGAKU ZASSHI (JA/0441-0351) [I04410351] **2978**

HOGG FOUNDATION NEWS (US) [06993637] **3926**

HOGS AND PIGS / IOWA CROP AND LIVESTOCK REPORTING SERVICE (US) [06204078] **212**

HOGS AND PIGS (WASHINGTON, D.C.) (US/0565-2189) [02572120] **212**

HOGTOWN HERALDRY (CN/1183-1766) [24265686] **2453**

HOGUK (KO) [11392780] **4045**

HOHENHEIMER ARBEITEN (GW/0340-9783) [02993812] **92**

HOHERE TECHNISCHE BUNDES-LEHR-UND VERSUCHSANSTALT WIEN I *See* BERICHT **5087**

HOHLE, DIE (AU/0018-3091) [08973118] **1356**

HOIKU HAKUSHO (JA) [03252572] **5287**

HOISINGTON DISPATCH, THE (US) [09580086] **5676**

HOITOTIEDE (FI/0786-5686) [23363165] **3856**

HOJA DE INFORMACION (INTERNATIONAL OLIVE OIL COUNCIL) (SP) [15026150] **2343**

HOJA DE INFORMACION SOBRE AYUDA FEDERAL PARA ESTUDIANTES, UNA (US) [25474097] **1750**

HOJAS DE CULTURA POPULAR COLOMBIANA (CK) [01590548] **2512**

HOJAS DIVULGADORAS - MINISTERIO DE AGRICULTURA, PESCA Y ALIMENTACION (SP/0213-2613) [I02132613] **92**

HOJAS DIVULGADORAS / MINISTERIO DE AGRICULTURA, SECCION DE PUBLICACIONES, PRENSA Y PROPAGANDA (SP) [03803758] **92**

HOJINZEIHO SOMATOME (JA) [01783591] **680**

HOJOKIN SORAN / [HENJA, ZAISEI CHOSAKAI] (JA) [10587087] **1565**

HOKEI RON SHU: KENKYU KIYO (JA) [01797128] **2978**

HOKEI RONSO (MORIOKA, 1980) (JA/0389-6498) [09485955] **1493**, **2978**

HOKEN BUTSURI (JA/0367-6110) [10278135] **3584**

HOKEN ROPPO / HOKEN SEIDO KENKYUKAI HEN (JA) [08867740] **2882**, **2978**

HOKEN TAIIKUGAKU KENKYU KIYO / OSAKA SHIRITSU DAIGAKU (JA/0474-795X) [10818384] **3954**, **1855**

HOKENGAKU ZASSHI (JA) [06613417] **2882**

HOKENJO UNEI HOKOKU (JA) [02245422] **4783**

HOKHMAH (SZ/0379-7465) [03286194] **5061**

HOKKAI GAKUEN DAIGAKU HOGAKKAI HOGAKU KENKYU (JA/0385-7255) [01797034] **2978**

HOKKAI GAKUEN DAIGAKU KAIHATSU KENKYUJO *See* KAIHATSU RONSHU **2826**

HOKKAI GAKUEN DAIGAKU. KOGAKUBU *See* HOKKAI GAKUEN DAIGAKU KOGAKUBU KENKYU HOKOKU **5110**

HOKKAI GAKUEN DAIGAKU KOGAKUBU KENKYU HOKOKU (JA) [02240174] **5110**

HOKKAIDO DAIGAKU BUNGAKUBU KIYO (JA/0437-6668) [06900244] **321**

HOKKAIDO DAIGAKU CHIKYU BUTSURIGAKU KENKYU HOKOKU (JA/0439-3503) [11343183] **1406**

HOKKAIDO DAIGAKU (JAPAN). SHAKAIGAKU KENKYUSHITSU *See* KENKYUSHITSU IHO **5250**

HOKKAIDO DAIGAKU. KOGAKUBU *See* HOKKAIDO DAIGAKU KOGAKUBU KENKYU HOKOKU. BULLETIN OF THE FACULTY OF ENGINEERING, HOKKAIDO UNIVERSITY **1977**

HOKKAIDO DAIGAKU. KOGAKUBU *See* MEMOIRS OF THE FACULTY OF ENGINEERING, HOKKAIDO UNIVERSITY **1987**

HOKKAIDO DAIGAKU KOGAKUBU KENKYU HOKOKU. BULLETIN OF THE FACULTY OF ENGINEERING, HOKKAIDO UNIVERSITY (JA/0385-602X) [09349356] **1977**

HOKKAIDO DAIGAKU KYOIKUGAKUBU KIYO (JA) [06484381] **1750**

HOKKAIDO DAIGAKU. NOGAKUBU *See* HOKKAIDO DAIGAKU. NOGAKUBU ENSHURIN KENKYU HOKOKU **2384**

HOKKAIDO DAIGAKU. NOGAKUBU *See* HOKKAIDO DAIGAKU NOGAKUBU HOBUN KIYO **92**

HOKKAIDO DAIGAKU NOGAKUBU ENSHURIN KENKYU HOKOKU (JA/0367-6129) [01765021] **2384**

HOKKAIDO DAIGAKU NOGAKUBU HOBUN KIYO (JA/0367-5726) [01643411] **92**

HOKKAIDO DAIGAKU NOGAKUBU NOJO KENKYU HOKOKU (JA/0385-6445) [10286053] **92**

HOKKAIDO DAIGAKU. OYO DENKI KENKYUJO *See* HOKKAIDO DAIGAKU OYO DENKI KENKYUJO YORAN **2056**

HOKKAIDO DAIGAKU OYO DENKI KENKYUJO YORAN (JA) [01797341] **2056**

HOKKAIDO DAIGAKU. RIGAKUBU *See* JOURNAL OF THE FACULTY OF SCIENCE, HOKKAIDO UNIVERSITY. SERIES VII. GEOPHYSICS **1408**

HOKKAIDO DAIGAKU, SAPPORO, JAPAN. KYOIKUGAKUBU *See* HOKKAIDO DAIGAKU KYOIKUGAKUBU KIYO **1750**

HOKKAIDO DAIGAKU, SAPPORO, JAPAN. NOGAKUBU. ENSHURIN *See* KENKYU HOKOKU. RESEARCH BULLETINS OF THE COLLEGE EXPERIMENT FORESTS, HOKKAIDO UNIVERSITY **2386**

HOKKAIDO DAIGAKU, SAPPORO, JAPAN. RIGAKUBU *See* JOURNAL OF THE FACULTY OF SCIENCE, HOKKAIDO UNIVERSITY. SERIES 4. GEOLOGY AND MINERALOGY **1357**

HOKKAIDO DAIGAKU, SAPPORO, JAPAN. RIGAKUBU. KAISO KENKYUJO, MURORAN *See* SCIENTIFIC PAPERS OF THE INSTITUTE OF ALGOLOGICAL RESEARCH, FACULTY OF SCIENCE, HOKKAIDO UNIVERSITY **527**

HOKKAIDO DAIGAKU, SAPPORO, JAPAN. SUISANGAKUBU, HAKODATE *See* MEMOIRS OF THE FACULTY OF FISHERIES, HOKKAIDO UNIVERSITY **2308**

HOKKAIDO DAIGAKU, SAPPORO, JAPAN. SURABU KENKYU SHISETSU *See* HOKKAIDO DAIGAKU SURABU KENKYU SHISETSU BENRAN **2691**

HOKKAIDO DAIGAKU SUISANGAKUBU, HAKODATE *See* HOKKAIDO DAIGAKU SUISANGAKUBU KENKYU IHO **2305**

HOKKAIDO DAIGAKU SUISANGAKUBU KENKYU IHO (JA/0018-3458) [01771470] **2305**

HOKKAIDO DAIGAKU SURABU KENKYU SHISETSU BENRAN (JA) [03698827] **2691**

HOKKAIDO EIRINKYOKU JIGYO TOKEISHO : CHOKKATSU (JA) [06671495] **2384**

HOKKAIDO IGAKU ZASSHI (JA/0367-6102) [09726140] **3584**

HOKKAIDO KAITAKU KINENKAN *See* HOKKAIDO KAITAKU KINENKAN DAYORI **2652**

HOKKAIDO KAITAKU KINENKAN *See* HOKKAIDO KAITAKU KINENKAN CHOSA HOKOKU **2652**

HOKKAIDO KAITAKU KINENKAN CHOSA HOKOKU (JA) [02246990] **4088**, **2652**

HOKKAIDO KAITAKU KINENKAN DAYORI (JA) [03634775] **2652**

HOKKAIDO KEIZAI CHOSA (JA) [09372357] **1565**

HOKKAIDO KOGAI BOSHI KENKYUJO *See* KOKKAIDO KOGAI BOSHI KENKYUJO HO **2235**

HOKKAIDO KOGYO DAIGAKU KENKYU KIYO (JA/0385-0862) [10278118] **5110**

HOKKAIDO KOGYO KAIHATSU SHIKENJO *See* HOKKAIDO KOGYO KAIHATSU SHIKENJO HOKOKU **5110**

HOKKAIDO KOGYO KAIHATSU SHIKENJO *See* YORAN - HOKKAIDO KOGYO KAIHATSU SHIKENJO **5172**

HOKKAIDO KOGYO KAIHATSU SHIKENJO *See* HOKKAIDO KOGYO KAIHATSU SHIKENJO NEMPO **5110**

HOKKAIDO KOGYO KAIHATSU SHIKENJO HOKOKU (JA/0441-0734) [01797146] **5110**

HOKKAIDO KOGYO KAIHATSU SHIKENJO NEMPO (JA) [01797145] **5110**

HOKKAIDO-KU SUISAN KENKYUJO KENKYU HOKOKU (JA) [22203318] **2305**

HOKKAIDO KYOIKU DAIGAKU *See* HOKKAIDO KYOIKU DAIGAKU KIYO. DAI 2-BU ; C KATEI-, TAIIKU-HEN **5110**

HOKKAIDO KYOIKU DAIGAKU *See* HOKKAIDO KYOIKU DAIGAKU KIYO. DAI L-BU C : KYOIKU KAGAKU HEN **1750**

HOKKAIDO KYOIKU DAIGAKU *See* HOKKAIDO KYOIKU DAIGAKU KIYO. A SUGAKU-, BUTSURIGAKU-, KAGAKU-, KOGAKU-HEN. DAI 2-BU **5110**

HOKKAIDO KYOIKU DAIGAKU *See* HOKKAIDO KYOIKU DAIGAKU KIYO. DAI 1-BU A : JIMBUN-KAGAKU HEN **1829**

HOKKAIDO KYOIKU DAIGAKU *See* HOKKAIDO KYOIKU DAIGAKU KIYO. DAI 2-BU **457**

HOKKAIDO KYOIKU DAIGAKU KIYO. A SUGAKU-, BUTSURIGAKU-, KAGAKU-, KOGAKU-HEN. DAI 2-BU (JA/0367-5939) [07060623] **5110**

HOKKAIDO KYOIKU DAIGAKU KIYO. DAI 1-BU A : JIMBUN-KAGAKU HEN (JA) [06911687] **1829**

HOKKAIDO KYOIKU DAIGAKU KIYO. DAI 2-BU (JA/0018-3393) [03993442] **457**

HOKKAIDO KYOIKU DAIGAKU KIYO. DAI 2-BU; C KATEI-, TAIIKU-HEN (JA) [07115386] **5110**

HOKKAIDO KYOIKU DAIGAKU KIYO. DAI L-BU C : KYOIKU KAGAKU HEN (JA) [06910219] **1750**

HOKKAIDO MATHEMATICAL JOURNAL (JA/0385-4035) [01788079] **3507**

HOKKAIDO NOGYO SHIKENJO (JA) [02808922] **92**

HOKKAIDO NOGYO SHIKENJO (JAPAN) *See* HOKKAIDO NOGYO SHIKENJO **92**

HOKKAIDO NOGYO SHIKENJO KENKYU HOKOKU (JA/0367-5955) [01608375] **92**

HOKKAIDO NOGYO SHIKENJO, SAPPORO, JAPAN *See* HOKKAIDO NOGYO SHIKENJO KENKYU HOKOKU **92**

HOKKAIDO NOGYO SHIKENJO SHUHO (JA/0441-0807) [07236296] **92**

HOKKAIDO OKIAI SOKOBIKIAMI GYOGYO-GYOJOBETSU GYOKAKU TOKEI NEMPO (JA) [02245330] **2305**

HOKKAIDO SAKE MASU FUKAJO *See* SCIENTIFIC REPORTS OF THE HOKKAIDO SALMON HATCHERY **2312**

HOKKAIDO SEIKEI SAIGAI GEKA ZASSHI (JA/0018-3377) [I00183377] **3965**, **3881**

HOKKAIDO. SUISAN SHIKENJO, YOICHI *See* HOKOKU **2305**

HOKKAIDORITSU HAKODATE SUISAN SHIKENJO JIGYO HOKOKUSHO (JA) [08788549] **2305**

HOKKAIDORITSU KINDAI BIJUTSUKAN *See* HOKKAIDORITSU KINDAI BIJUTSUKAN NENPO **352**

HOKKAIDORITSU KINDAI BIJUTSUKAN NENPO (JA) [10832620] **352**

HOKKAIDORITSU MIGISHI KOTARO BIJUTSUKAN *See* DORITSU MIGISHI KOTARO BIJUTSUKAN HO **349**

HOKKAIDORITSU NOGYO SHIKENJO *See* SHUHO. BULLETIN OF THE HOKKAIDO PREFECTURAL AGRICULTURAL EXPERIMENT STATIONS **134**

HOKKAIDORITSU NOGYO SHIKENJO *See* HOKKAIDORITSU NOGYO SHIKENJO HOKOKU **92**

HOKKAIDORITSU NOGYO SHIKENJO HOKOKU (JA/0367-6048) [03340843] **92**

HOKKAIDORITSU SEISHIN EISEI SENTA *See* HOKKAIDORITSU SEISHIN EISEI SENTA NEMPO **4783**

HOKKAIDORITSU SEISHIN EISEI SENTA NEMPO (JA) [08515142] **4783**

HOKKAIDÃO DAIGAKU. BUNGAKUBU *See* HOKKAIDO DAIGAKU BUNGAKUBU KIYO **321**

HOKKE BUNKA KENKYU (JA) [02490851] **5021**

HOKKEJ (MOSKVA) (RU/0302-7260) [01793239] **4899**

HOKKYOKUSEI HOIKAKU HYO (JA) [03283551] **4177**

HOKOKU (JA) [03362667] **2305**

HOKOKU. JOURNAL OF THE FACULTY OF AGRICULTURE, IWATE UNIVERSITY (JA/0579-2746) [03427858] **92**

HOKOKU (TOHOKU DAIGAKU. NOGAKU KENKYUJO). (JA/0040-8697) [10516484] **92**

HOKUBEI HOCHI (US/8756-6451) [11627889] **5761**

HOKURIKU KEIZAI TOKEI NEMPO (JA) [01797274] **1565**

HOKURIKU KOSHU EISEI GAKKAISHI (JA/0386-3530) [10270839] **4783**

HOKURIKU MASUIGAKU ZASSHI (JA/0367-5947) [06342281] **3683**

HOKURIKU NO DENKI TO KOGYO (JA) [01797292] **2056**

HOKURIKU NOGYO SHIKENJO HOKOKU (JA/0439-3600) [02616886] **93**

HOKURIKU YUSEIKYOKU TOKEI NEMPO (JA) [01797347] **1145**

HOKUSHINETSU CHIKU KOKURITSU DAIGAKU TOSHOKAN KYOGIKAI *See* HOKUSHINETSU CHIKU KOKURITSU DAIGAKU TOSHOKAN KYOGIKAI NEMPO **3213**

HOKUSHINETSU CHIKU KOKURITSU DAIGAKU TOSHOKAN KYOGIKAI NEMPO (JA) [04073023] **3213**

HOLA (SP) [08593123] **2517**

HOLARCTIC ECOLOGY *See* ECOGRAPHY **2213**

●HOLART REPORT (US/1062-6360) [25686886] **352**

HOLBROOK TRIBUNE-NEWS AND SNOWFLAKE HERALD (US/8750-5363) [11489277] **5630**

HOLDERLIN FRIEDRICH SAMTLICHE WERKE (GW) **4348**

HOLDERLIN-JAHRBUCH (GW/0340-6849) [01283738] 1077, **3394**

HOLDSWORTH LAW REVIEW / UNIVERSITY OF BIRMINGHAM (UK) [08204625] 3129, **2979**

HOLE (CN/1180-1670) [22254379] **3394**

HOLIDAY CRAFTS (US/0278-7490) [06845460] **373**

HOLIDAY CRAFTS & GRANNY SQUARES (US) [22426249] 373, **5184**

HOLIDAY HOMES INTERNATIONAL *See* HOMES INTERNATIONAL **2824**

HOLIDAY NIAGARA (CN/0318-9104) [02441913] **5479**

HOLIDAY TIME IN THAILAND *SUSPENDED.* (TH/0439-3678) [02098212] **5479**

HOLINESS DIGEST (US/1040-8584) [17205159] **4963**

HOLISTIC EDUCATION REVIEW (US/0898-0926) [17719244] **1751**

HOLISTIC MASSAGE (US/0748-6855) [11002814] **2598**

HOLISTIC MEDICINE *See* JOURNAL OF INTERPROFESSIONAL CARE **3775**

HOLISTIC MEDICINE (SEATTLE, WASH.) (US/0898-6029) [16743654] **3584**

HOLISTIC NURSING PRACTICE (US/0887-9311) [13448695] **3856**

HOLISTIC OPTOMETRIST, THE (US/0748-9307) [11036651] **4215**

HOLISTIC RESOURCE MANAGEMENT NEWSLETTER (US/1048-8472) [21056790] **93**

●HOLISTIC RESOURCE MANAGEMENT QUARTERLY (US/1069-2789) [27966938] **93**

HOLLABRUNNER ZEITUNG (AU) [20349367] **5778**

HOLLAND & KNIGHT'S FLORIDA ENVIRONMENTAL & LAND USE LETTER (US/1047-4641) [20697294] **3113**

HOLLAND & KNIGHT'S FLORIDA ENVIRONMENTAL & LAND USE NEWSLETTER *See* FLORIDA ENVIRONMENTAL COMPLIANCE UPDATE **3112**

HOLLAND EVENING SENTINEL (HOLLAND, MICH. : 1952) (US) [13440201] **5692**

HOLLAND HERALD (NE) [05131691] **2517**

HOLLAND REPORTER, THE (US/0300-8800) [01345283] **5635**

HOLLAND SENTINEL (1977), THE (US/1050-4044) [13799746] **5692**

HOLLANDE (FR) [06642490] **2691**

HOLLANDS MAANDBLAD *CEASED.* (NE) [17759071] **3394**

HOLLANDSE KRANT (CN/0837-1342) [I08371342] **2263**

HOLLINGER MINES LIMITED *See* ANNUAL REPORT - HOLLINGER MINES LIMITED **2133**

HOLLINS CRITIC, THE (US/0018-3644) [01752196] **3344**

HOLLIS EUROPE (UK/0962-3590) [I09623590] **760**

HOLLIS PRESS & PUBLIC RELATIONS ANNUAL (UK/0073-3059) [03753983] **760**

HOLLY HOBBIE'S HOME TIMES (US/0194-2522) [05365817] **2790**

HOLLY SOCIETY JOURNAL (US/0738-2421) [09547575] **5231**

HOLLYWOOD AGENTS DIRECTORY *See* HOLLYWOOD AGENTS/MANAGERS DIRECTORY **4072**

HOLLYWOOD AGENTS/MANAGERS DIRECTORY (US/1075-6531) [25882368] 321, **4072**

HOLLYWOOD MAGAZINE *CEASED.* (US/1045-361X) [20109993] **2488**

HOLLYWOOD REPORTER, THE (US/0018-3660) [01752197] **4072**

HOLLYWOOD REPORTER TV SPECIAL, THE (US/0195-7481) [05532505] **4072**

HOLLYWOOD STUDIO MAGAZINE *CEASED.* (US/0894-2188) [05314947] **4072**

HOLLYWOOD SUN *CEASED.* (US) [20739849] **2488**

HOLMES COMMUNITY COLLEGE *See* ALUMNI DIRECTORY / HOLMES COMMUNITY COLLEGE **1098**

HOLMES COUNTY ADVERTISER (US) **5650**

HOLMES COUNTY HERALD (US) [15612520] **5700**

HOLOCAUST AND GENOCIDE STUDIES (UK/8756-6583) [11613306] **2691**

HOLOCAUST STUDIES ANNUAL *CEASED.* (US/0738-0739) [09507952] **2691**

HOLOCENE (SEVENOAKS) (UK/0959-6836) [23749848] 269, **1382**

HOLODILNAJA TEHNIKA I TEHNOLOGIJA (UN/0453-8307) [10765636] **5110**

HOLOGRAPHICS INTERNATIONAL *SUSPENDED.* (UK/0951-3914) [19692139] 379, **4434**

HOLOGRAPHY NEWS (US/0895-9080) [16854944] **1608**

HOLOS SPASYTELIA (CN/0381-5129) [08369165] **4963**

HOLOSPHERE *SUSPENDED.* (US/0739-120X) [09718904] **4370**

HOLSTEIN-FRIESIAN HERD-BOOK (US) [01606476] **195**

HOLSTEIN FRIESIAN JOURNAL (RICKMANSWORTH) (UK/0954-6219) [19566985] **195**

HOLSTEIN JOURNAL (CN/0710-1309) [08091504] **195**

HOLSTEIN SIRE CATALOGUE (CN/0713-2050) [08850971] **195**

HOLSTEIN WORLD (US/0199-4239) [05856917] **195**

HOLSTON PASTFINDER (US/0887-3135) [13207111] **2453**

HOLT ADVISORY, THE (US/1047-9791) [15506683] **900**

HOLTON RECORDER (HOLTON, KAN. : 1908) (US) [11663353] **5676**

HOLY CROSS (US) [06126812] **4963**

HOLY LAND (US) [08712588] **4963**

HOLYOKE ENTERPRISE (HOLYOKE, COLO.) (US) [15490929] **5643**

HOLZ ALS ROH- UND WERKSTOFF (GW/0018-3768) [01752203] **2401**

HOLZ-BERFUSGENOSSENSCHAFT *See* HBG-MITTEILUNGEN **3480**

HOLZ IM HANDWERK (AU/0018-3776) [I00183776] **2906**

HOLZ-KUNSTSTOFF (GW) [02804767] **2401**

HOLZ KURIER (AU) [09695972] **2384**

HOLZ-ZENTRALBLATT (GW/0018-3792) [03755404] **2384**

HOLZFORSCHUNG (GW/0018-3830) [01752204] **2401**

HOLZFORSCHUNG UND HOLZVERWERTUNG (AU/0018-3849) [09451743] 4234, **2401**

HOLZZUCHT, DIE (GW/0437-7168) [05261739] **2384**

HOMBRE DE MUNDO *See* HOMBRE INTERNACIONAL **3995**

●HOMBRE INTERNACIONAL (US/1064-8976) [25533810] **3995**

HOME (IT) 2906, **5351**

HOME ACCENTS TODAY (US) **2900**

HOME & AWAY (US/8750-5649) [11522056] **5479**

HOME & AWAY (CHICAGO, ILL.) (US/0199-7521) [06129611] **4081**

HOME & AWAY. IOWA (US/0744-1576) [08073081] **5479**

HOME & AWAY (OMAHA, NEB.) (US/0199-7009) [06083311] **5479**

HOME AND CONDO (US) 2900, **2418**

HOME AND COUNTRY : THE MAGAZINE OF THE NATIONAL FEDERATION OF WOMEN'S INSTITUTES (UK) [09806938] 2790, **5558**

HOME & FREEZER DIGEST *See* HOME COOKING **2790**

HOME AND GARDEN BULLETIN (US/0073-3075) [01608035] **2790**

HOME AND GARDEN SUPPLY MERCHANDISER *See* GREEN BOOK BUYERS' GUIDE FOR GARDEN MERCHANDISE **2417**

HOME AND STUDIO RECORDING *See* RECORDING : THE MAGAZINE FOR THE RECORDING MUSICIAN **5318**

HOME & STUDIO RECORDING (US/0896-7172) [17285024] **5317**

HOME-BASED & SMALL BUSINESS NETWORK (US/1067-7739) [18048420] **680**

●HOME BASED HOMERUN (US/1061-4222) [25306036] **680**

HOME BUILDER MAGAZINE (CN/0840-4348) [19486600] **616**

HOME BUILDER'S JOURNAL, THE (US/0884-6774) [12410693] **616**

HOME BUILDING & REMODELING (US/0360-1382) [02244013] **616**

HOME BUSINESS ADVISOR *CEASED.* (US/0893-7621) [15640363] **680**

HOME BUSINESS ADVOCATE, THE (US/0832-8595) [15732016] **680**

HOME CARE ECONOMICS *CEASED.* (US/0891-9364) [15033835] **5287**

HOME CARE REPORT (US/1072-3617) [28919765] **3584**

●HOME CARE SALARY & BENEFITS REPORT (US/1058-7934) [24370771] **5287**

HOME CARE SERVICES IN NEW YORK STATE (US/0277-7401) [05060129] **4783**

HOME CARE TODAY *CEASED.* (CN/0847-2378) [22285006] 3856, **5288**

HOME CARE UPDATE *See* CONTINUING CARE CONNECTION : LINKING LONG-TERM, HOME AND COMMUNITY CARE SYSTEMS **5280**

●HOME CARING (US/1061-0227) [25157316] **5288**

HOME CENTER PRODUCTS REPORT (US/0883-0436) [12046098] **839**

HOME COMPUTER & SOFTWARE MERCHANDISING (US/8750-4928) [11451262] 1286, **1267**

HOME COOKING (US/1071-4782) [28643757] **2790**

●HOME COOKING (UK/0965-366X) [I0965366X] **2790**

HOME DEVELOPMENT MUTUAL FUND (PHILIPPINES) *See* ANNUAL REPORT / HOME DEVELOPMENT MUTUAL FUND (PHILIPPINES) **2814**

HOME EC NEWS (CN/0018-4004) [02297663] **2790**

HOME ECONOMICS (UK) [03314170] **2791**

HOME ECONOMICS ASSOCIATION OF AUSTRALIA JOURNAL *See* JOURNAL OF HOME ECONOMICS. INSTITUTE OF AUSTRALIA **2791**

HOME — Alphabetical Title Index

HOME ECONOMICS RESEARCH JOURNAL (US/0046-7774) [01642571] **2791**

HOME ECONOMIST, THE (UK) [10007994] **2791**

HOME EDUCATION MAGAZINE (US/0888-4633) [13615236] **1751**

HOME ENERGY (BERKELEY, CALIF.) (US/0896-9442) [17344484] 616, **1946**

HOME ENERGY DIGEST, WOOD BURNING QUARTERLY (US/0195-1874) [04247244] **1946**

HOME ENTERTAINMENT GUIDE (FM GUIDE ED.) (CN/0827-2484) [11734663] **4851**

HOME FASHIONS (US/1078-0289) [30958018] **2900**

HOME FASHIONS MAGAZINE (US/0896-7962) [17252938] **2900**

●HOME FURNISHINGS EXECUTIVE (GREENSBORO, N.C.) (US/1073-5585) [29462355] **2906**

HOME FURNISHINGS REPRESENTATIVES CONTACT (US/8750-4979) [11484361] **2906**

HOME FURNISHINGS TONBRIDGE (UK/0954-1071) [I09541071] **2906**

HOME GOODS RETAILING (CN/0848-8312) [21490452] 955, **2906**

HOME GROUND (US/1053-0762) [22448054] **2824**

HOME-GROWN CEREALS AUTHORITY BULLETIN & DIGEST (UK) **202**

HOME HEALTH CARE (CN/0841-1883) [19996802] **4783**

●HOME HEALTH CARE REIMBURSEMENT REPORT (US/1074-4541) [29713951] **4783**

HOME HEALTH CARE SERVICES QUARTERLY (US/0162-1424) [04111751] **5288**

●HOME HEALTH FOCUS (US/1075-2188) [29968709] **3856**

HOME HEALTH HANDBOOK (US) **2598**

HOME HEALTH JOURNAL **CEASED.** (US/0734-7588) [08799535] **3584**

HOME HEALTH LINE (US) [03416301] **4783**

●HOME HEALTH PRODUCTS (US/1070-2431) [28309019] **2598**

HOME HEALTHCARE NURSE (US/0884-741X) [10290548] **3856**

HOME HOW-TO NEWS (US/1053-7260) [22617933] **2811**

HOME IMPROVEMENT & REPAIR (US/0361-2813) [02246473] **616**

HOME IMPROVEMENT CENTER **CEASED.** (US/1045-9367) [20289951] 2906, **616**

HOME IMPROVEMENT IDEAS *See* IMPROVEMENT IDEAS **300**

HOME IMPROVEMENTS JOURNAL (UK/0142-0704) [I01420704] **616**

HOME LANDSCAPE PLANS (US/1048-8537) [21061847] **2418**

HOME LIFE (NASHVILLE) (US/0018-4071) [01776447] 2280, **5061**

HOME LIGHTING & ACCESSORIES (US/0162-9077) [04252700] **2906**

HOME MAGAZINE'S BEST IDEAS KITCHEN AND BATH (US/1050-494X) [21506774] **2900**

●HOME MAGAZINE'S BUILDING/REMODELING PLANNER (US/1061-6667) [25394749] **616**

HOME MECHANIX (US/8755-0423) [11246280] **634**

HOME MEDIA TECHNOLOGY (US) **1112**

HOME MEDIA TECHNOLOGY NEWS *See* MULTIMEDIA WEEK **1118**

HOME MISSIONS IMPACT / THE WESLEYAN CHURCH (US) [08578635] **4963**

HOME MISSIONS (TORONTO) (CN/0823-8464) [11431399] **4963**

HOME NEWS (BATH, PA.) (US) [17465490] **5736**

HOME OFFICE COMPUTING (US/0899-7373) [18201745] **1267**

HOME OFFICE RESEARCH STUDIES (UK/0072-6435) [05212702] **5479**

HOME OFFICE : THE OFFICIAL PUBLICATIN OF THE NATIONAL HOME BUSINESS INSTITUTE, INC (CN/1183-3564) [24267082] **869**

HOME OFFICE WORKER (US/1053-0444) [22441320] **680**

HOME (ORADELL, N.J.) (US/0278-2839) [07674501] **2900**

HOME OWNERS' (CN/0225-5871) [06183506] **2791**

●HOME PC (US/1073-1784) [29349092] **1267**

HOME PLAN IDEAS (US/0194-0627) [05296674] 300, **616**

HOME PLANET NEWS (US/0273-303X) [07046822] **3394**

HOME PLANNER (US/1040-547X) [18448386] 300, **616**

HOME PLANNING AND DECORATING (US/0363-8758) [02546514] **2900**

HOME PLANNING & DESIGN (US/0360-2079) [02243956] **300**

HOME PLANS & PROJECTS (US/0364-653X) [02667484] 2900, **300**

HOME PLANS GUIDE (US/0899-4374) [08008920] 616, **300**

HOME PLANS TO BUILD (US/0899-4366) [08462617] 616, **300**

HOME POWER (US/1050-2416) [21428817] **1946**

HOME PRESS, THE (US/0746-1666) [09819765] **5703**

HOME QUARTER (CN/0823-6410) [10763700] **212**

HOME RENOVATIONS (CN/0714-8151) [09106481] **2811**

HOME REPORTER (US) **5717**

HOME SALES (US/1063-0511) [16786239] **4838**

HOME SALES *See* REAL ESTATE OUTLOOK MARKET TRENDS AND INSIGHTS **4845**

HOME SALES REPORT (US) **4838**

HOME SALES YEARBOOK (US) [25162847] **4838**

HOME SATELLITE NEWSLETTER, THE (US/0892-5143) [15217021] **1156**

●HOME SCHOOL ADVANTAGE (US/1065-7754) [26733542] **1751**

HOME SCHOOL RESEARCHER (US/1054-8033) [22973352] **1751**

HOME SHOP MACHINIST, THE (US/0744-6640) [08482836] **2115**

HOME SOFTWARE NEWSLETTER *See* PC LETTER **1198**

●HOME STUDIO FORUM (US/1061-3765) [25277432] **4370**

HOME SUPPORT SERVICES IN METROPOLITAN TORONTO (CN/0822-9406) [10935312] **5288**

HOME-TECH REMODELING AND RENOVATION COST ESTIMATOR (US/1043-8831) [09654948] 300, **2900**

HOME TEXTILES TODAY (US/0195-3184) [05523644] **5351**

HOME VIDEO REPORT, THE (US/0161-9055) [04053467] **4370**

HOME WINE AND BEER MAKERS INFORMATION (US/0270-4668) [06467002] **2367**

HOME WINEMAKER, THE (US/0739-5434) [09788778] **2367**

HOME, YARD, AND GARDEN PEST NEWSLETTER (US) [05111799] **4245**

HOMEBUYER'S GUIDE. DALLAS/FT. WORTH (US/0894-0258) [15729686] **4838**

●HOMECARE DIRECTION (US/1069-4560) [28050764] **3584**

HOMECARE (LOS ANGELES, CALIF.) (US/0882-2700) [11845275] **5288**

... HOMECARE MARKET REPORT, THE (US/0882-9152) [11999763] **3584**

HOMEGROWN (ROHNERT PARK) (US/0095-6910) [01798295] **2321**

HOMEHEALTH MAGAZINE (US/0883-0835) [12057178] **4783**

HOMELESS *See* GRANT$ FOR THE HOMELESS **4337**

HOMEMAKER OF THE NATIONAL EXTENSION HOMEMAKERS COUNCIL, THE (US/0146-9487) [03058218] 5558, **2791**

HOMEMAKER'S MAGAZINE (CN/0318-7802) [02027634] **5558**

HOMEOPATHIE FRANCAISE, L' (FR) **3774**

HOMEOSTASIS IN HEALTH AND DISEASE : INTERNATIONAL JOURNAL DEVOTED TO INTEGRATIVE BRAIN FUNCTIONS AND HOMEOSTATIC SYSTEMS (XR/0960-7560) [24490174] **3833**

HOMEOTHERAPY (US/0363-2776) [01041698] **3774**

HOMEOWNER REPAIR AND RENOVATION EXPENDITURE IN CANADA (CN/0840-8106) [21472606] **634**

HOMEOWNER, THE **SUSPENDED.** (US/0747-3176) [09794026] **616**

HOMEOWNERS ANALYSIS (US) **2882**

HOMEOWNERS GUIDE (US) **2882**

HOMEOWNER'S GUIDE TO GLASS, THE (US/1041-3510) [18729837] **2591**

HOMEOWNERS PROGRAM GUIDE (US) **2882**

HOMEOWNERSHIP FOR LOWER-INCOME FAMILIES, SECTION 235 (I), BASIC INSTRUCTIONS (US) [03116532] **2824**

HOMER INDEX, THE (US/0891-1398) [12147206] **5692**

HOMER NEWS (US) **5629**

HOMES AND GARDENS INCORPORATING HOME (UK/0018-4233) [02251416] **2824**

HOMES AND HOMEBUILDING *See* REFERENCE GUIDE TO HOMEBUILDING ARTICLES **307**

HOMES FOR LEISURE LIVING (US/0364-6548) [02667473] 2900, **300**

HOMES FOR THE AGED (CN/0229-415X) [08071365] **3783**

HOMES INTERNATIONAL **SUSPENDED.** (US/0740-7211) [10025183] **2824**

HOMESCHOOLING TODAY (US) [29354140] **1751**

HOMESTEAD (KENTVILLE) (CN/0712-6476) [09467832] **5786**

HOMESTYLES HOME PLANS (US/0897-621X) [17570788] **300**

HOMETOWN PRESS (US/1064-1742) [26246170] **2534**

HOMEWORDS (WASHINGTON, D.C.) **CEASED.** (US/0896-355X) [17009655] **5288**

HOMEWORKS (US) **2824**

HOMEWORLD BUSINESS (US/1048-0641) [20845034] **1608**

HOMICIDE IN CALIFORNIA (US) [06617216] **3165**

HOMICIDE SURVEILLANCE (US/0749-2286) [11081580] **3165**

HOMILETIC (US/0738-0534) [02770866] **4963**

HOMILETIC & PASTORAL REVIEW (US/0018-4268) [05739991] **5030**

HOMILETICA (SP/0439-4208) [06034019] **5030**

HOMILETICS (NORTH CANTON, OHIO) (US/1040-6255) [18474246] **4963**

HOMILY HELPS *See* SUNDAY HOMILY HELPS **5037**

HOMILY HELPS *See* WEEKDAY HOMILY HELPS **5038**

HOMILY HINTS (CN/1184-2652) [24257170] **4963**

HOMILY SERVICE (US/0732-1872) [01585646] **4963**

HOMINES (PR/0252-8908) [07138537] **5201**

HOMINY NEWS-PROGRESS, THE (US) [27786967] **5732**

HOMME (FR/0439-4216) [01752231] **237**

HOMME ET LA SOCIETE, L' (FR/0018-4306) [01604122] **5247**

HOMME ET L'HUMANITE, L' (FR) [01795884] **5247**

HOMMES & MIGRATIONS (FR/1142-852X) [15360833] **1919**

HOMMES ET EGLISE; ANNUAIRE DU QUEBEC (FR) [07005019] **4963**

HOMMES ET FONCTIONS (FR/0755-8074) [I07558074] **4476**

HOMMES ET FONDERIE (FR/0018-4357) [09681407] **4428**

HOMMES ET LIBERTES (FR/0180-8524) [I01808524] **4508**

HOMMES ET TERRES DU NORD (FR/0018-439X) [01752232] **2565**

HOMMES, LA TERRE, L'EAU *See* HOMMES, TERRE & I.E. ET EAUX **93**

HOMMES, TERRE & I.E. ET EAUX (MR) [07032919] **93**

HOMMES VOLANTS PARIS, LES (FR/0018-4411) [I00184411] **4899**

HOMO (GW/0018-442X) [01949648] **237**

HOMO (TOULOUSE) (FR/0563-9743) [02242253] **5247**

HOMU SOGO KENKYUJO *See* BULLETIN OF THE CRIMINOLOGICAL RESEARCH DEPARTMENT **3159**

HOMU SOGO KENKYUJO (JAPAN) *See* HOMU SOGO KENKYUJO KENKYUBU KIYO **3165**

HOMU SOGO KENKYUJO KENKYUBU KIYO (JA/0386-0728) [01790162] **3165**

HON VIET (VM) [12852464] **2263**

HON VIET (GARDEN GROVE, CALIF.) (US/1066-6311) [26607895] **2263**

HONDO ANVIL HERALD, THE (US) [15149265] **5751**

HONDURAS ... : ORGANO DE LA SECRETARIA DE PRENSA DE LA JUNTA MILITAR DE GOBIERNO (HO) [06494372] **2738**

HONDURAS ROTARIA (HO) [03734409] **680**

HONDURAS UPDATE **SUSPENDED.** (US/0741-8167) [09519534] **2512**

HONDURAS, WIRTSCHAFTLICHE ENTWICKLUNG (GW) [01798762] **1565**

HONES MUTUAL MONTHLY (CN/0228-2399) [06860008] **2534**

Alphabetical Title Index — HOOSIER

HONEST ULSTERMAN, THE (UK/0018-4543) [03295693] **3394**

HONEY HOLE (US/0895-4046) [16630550] **4899**

HONEYMOON HIDEAWAYS (US/0736-6736) [09181307] 4851, **5480**

HONEYWELL COMPUTER JOURNAL, THE (US/0046-7847) [01798583] **1259**

HONG KONG See HONG KONG GOVERNMENT GAZETTE, THE **4654**

HONG KONG See CONSULAR POSTS, OFFICIALLY RECOGNIZED REPRESENTATIVES AND BODIES ESTABLISHED UNDER THE SINO-BRITISH JOINT DECLARATION / HONG KONG **3126**

HONG KONG See CLERICAL OFFICERS AND TYPISTS LISTS **4638**

HONG KONG See REGULATIONS OF HONG KONG / INCLUDING PROCLAMATIONS, ORDERS IN COUNCIL, ETC. FOR THE YEAR ..., THE **4679**

HONG KONG See HALF-YEARLY ECONOMIC REPORT **1493**

HONG KONG ANNUAL DIGEST OF STATISTICS (HK) [05324946] 4654, **4698**

HONG KONG. AUDIT DEPT See REPORT OF THE DIRECTOR OF AUDIT ON THE RESULTS OF VALUE FOR MONEY AUDITS **4681**

HONG KONG. BROADCASTING DEPT See ... REPORT OF THE BROADCASTING AUTHORITY ON THE PROGRESS OF TELEVISION BROADCASTING IN HONG KONG, THE **1138**

HONG KONG BUILDER DIRECTORY (HK) [02246380] **616**

HONG KONG BUSINESS (HK) **680**

HONG KONG. CENSUS AND STATISTICS DEPT See HONG KONG TRADE STATISTICS **730**

HONG KONG. CENSUS AND STATISTICS DEPT See HONG KONG MONTHLY DIGEST OF STATISTICS **4698**

HONG KONG. CENSUS AND STATISTICS DEPT See ESTIMATES OF GROSS DOMESTIC PRODUCT **1560**

HONG KONG. CENSUS AND STATISTICS DEPT See HONG KONG SOCIAL & ECONOMIC TRENDS **1533**

HONG KONG. CENSUS AND STATISTICS DEPT See ANNUAL SUPPLEMENT TO HONG KONG TRADE STATISTICS, COUNTRY BY COMMODITY IMPORTS **726**

HONG KONG CHENG FU YU NUNG CHU KAN WU (HK) [09581979] 5609, 2305, **93**

HONG KONG. CHINESE UNIVERSITY See HSIANG-KANG CHUNG WEN TA HSUEH HSUEH PAO **1829**

HONG KONG. COLONIAL SECRETARIAT. STAFF BIOGRAPHIES, HONG KONG GOVERNMENT See STAFF BIOGRAPHIES, HONG KONG GOVERNMENT / COMPILED IN THE GOVERNMENT SECRETARIAT / HSIANG-KANG CHENG FU KUNG WU YUAN CHIEN CHIEH / PU CHENG SSU SHU PIEN **4687**

HONG KONG COUNTDOWN (HK/0257-3636) [I02573636] **680**

HONG KONG. CUSTOMS AND EXCISE DEPT See REVIEW / CUSTOMS AND EXCISE DEPARTMENT **4747**

HONG KONG DEPARTMENTAL REPORT BY THE COMMISSIONER FOR TRANSPORT (HK) [01788124] **5383**

HONG KONG ECONOMIC PAPERS (HK/0018-4578) [02092788] **1493**

HONG KONG ECONOMIC TRENDS (HK) [17646715] **1565**

HONG KONG ELECTRONICS (HK) **2056**

HONG KONG ENERGY STATISTICS (HK) [10781536] **2056**

HONG KONG ENTERPRISE (HK/0018-4586) [02454863] **680**

HONG KONG EXTERNAL TRADE (HK) [01789294] 1635, **839**

HONG KONG. FINANCIAL SECRETARY See ... BUDGET, THE **4714**

HONG KONG GIFTS & PREMIUMS (HK) **2584**

HONG KONG GOVERNMENT GAZETTE, THE (HK) [02434916] **4654**

HONG KONG. GOVERNMENT SECRETARIAT See STAFF LIST, HONG KONG GOVERNMENT **4687**

HONG KONG. GOVERNMENT SECRETARIAT See STAFF BIOGRAPHIES, HONG KONG GOVERNMENT / COMPILED IN THE GOVERNMENT SECRETARIAT / HSIANG-KANG CHENG FU KUNG WU YUAN CHIEN CHIEH / PU CHENG SSU SHU PIEN **4687**

HONG KONG. INDEPENDENT COMMISSION AGAINST CORRUPTION See ANNUAL REPORT ON THE ACTIVITIES OF THE INDEPENDENT COMMISSION AGAINST CORRUPTION **4629**

HONG KONG JEWELLERY (HK) **2914**

HONG KONG JOURNAL OF BUSINESS MANAGEMENT (HK) [10773098] **869**

HONG KONG LANDS TRIBUNAL LAW REPORTS, THE (HK) [06984322] **2979**

HONG KONG LAW JOURNAL (HK/0378-0600) [01752245] **2979**

HONG KONG LAW REPORTS, THE (CH) [01752246] **2979**

HONG KONG. LAWS, STATUTES, ETC See ORDINANCES OF HONG KONG **4671**

HONG KONG. LEGISLATIVE COUNCIL. FINANCE COMMITTEE. PUBLIC WORKS SUBCOMMITTEE See REPORT OF THE PUBLIC WORKS SUBCOMMITTEE OF FINANCE COMMITTEE APPOINTED TO REVIEW THE PUBLIC WORKS PROGRAMME **4762**

HONG KONG LIBRARY ASSOCIATION See HONG KONG LIBRARY ASSOCIATION JOURNAL **3213**

HONG KONG LIBRARY ASSOCIATION JOURNAL (HK) [02468532] **3213**

HONG KONG MANAGER. K'O HSUEH KUAN LI (HK) [06577190] **869**

HONG KONG MONITOR (CN/0836-6667) [17526625] **1635**

HONG KONG MONTHLY DIGEST OF STATISTICS (HK/0300-418X) [01402244] 4654, **4698**

HONG KONG NURSING JOURNAL (HK) **3856**

HONG KONG. OFFICE OF THE COMMISSIONER OF BANKING See ANNUAL REPORT OF THE OFFICE OF THE COMMISSIONER OF BANKING **772**

HONG KONG PEAK (HK) [10691732] **5061**

HONG KONG. PRINTING DEPT See BUDGET : ECONOMIC BACKGROUND **1549**

HONG KONG PSYCHOLOGICAL SOCIETY BULLETIN (HK/0379-4490) [I03794490] **4588**

HONG KONG. QUARTERLY ECONOMIC REPORTS See HALF-YEARLY ECONOMIC REPORT **1493**

HONG KONG. RATING AND VALUATION DEPT See PROPERTY REVIEW **4843**

HONG KONG. RATING AND VALUATION DEPT See ANNUAL SUMMARY BY THE COMMISSIONER OF RATING AND VALUATION (HONGKONG) **4711**

HONG KONG REGISTER (US/1046-1655) [20338782] 900, **4838**

HONG KONG SHIPPING STATISTICS (HK) [15028413] **5450**

HONG KONG SOCIAL & ECONOMIC TRENDS (HK) [06984059] 1493, **1533**

HONG KONG. STANDING COMMISSION ON CIVIL SERVICE SALARIES AND CONDITIONS OF SERVICE See PROGRESS REPORT **4675**

HONG KONG. STANDING COMMISSION ON CIVIL SERVICE SALARIES AND CONDITIONS OF SERVICE See ... REPORT ON THE PAY LEVEL SURVEY, THE **4682**

HONG KONG TRADE DIRECTORY **SUSPENDED.** (UK) **839**

HONG KONG TRADE STATISTICS (HK) [02241142] 839, **730**

HONG KONG TRADE STATISTICS. SUPPLEMENT See ANNUAL SUPPLEMENT TO HONG KONG TRADE STATISTICS, COUNTRY BY COMMODITY IMPORTS **726**

HONG KONG. TRANSPORT DEPT See HONG KONG DEPARTMENTAL REPORT BY THE COMMISSIONER FOR TRANSPORT **5383**

HONG KONG. TREASURY See ACCOUNTS OF HONG KONG AND ANNUAL REPORT OF THE ACCOUNTANT GENERAL **4708**

HONG KONG. TREASURY. DEPARTMENTAL REPORT BY THE ACCOUNTANT GENERAL See ACCOUNTS OF HONG KONG AND ANNUAL REPORT OF THE ACCOUNTANT GENERAL **4708**

HONG KONG. URBAN COUNCIL See OFFICIAL RECORD OF PROCEEDINGS / HONG KONG URBAN COUNCIL **4671**

HONG KONG WATCHES & CLOCKS (HK) **2916**

HONGBO INMUL YONGAM (KO) [10009223] **432**

HONGKONG. LANDS TRIBUNAL See HONG KONG LANDS TRIBUNAL LAW REPORTS, THE **2979**

HONGKONG PAPERS IN LINGUISTICS AND LANGUAGE TEACHING (HK/1015-2059) [I10152059] **3286**

HONGKONG. PRISON DEPT See ANNUAL DEPARTMENTAL REPORT BY THE COMMISSIONER OF PRISONS **3156**

HONGKONG, WIRTSCHAFTSDATEN UND WIRTSCHAFTSDOKUMENTATION / BUNDESSTELLE FUER AUSSENHANDELSINFORMATION (GW) [10257211] **1565**

HONGKONGIANA (HK) [05629682] **2504**

HONOLULU (US/0441-2044) [01752250] **2534**

HONOLULU ACADEMY OF ARTS See JOURNAL - HONOLULU ACADEMY OF ARTS **323**

HONOLULU ADVERTISER, THE (US/1072-7191) [08807414] **5656**

HONOLULU ARRIVALS, FRESH FRUITS AND VEGETABLES (US) [11087263] **2343**

HONOLULU PRICES, WHOLESALE FRESH FRUITS AND VEGETABLES (US/0360-9626) [02245070] **2343**

HONOLULU STAR-BULLETIN (US) [08807359] **5656**

HONOLULU WEEKLY (US/1057-414X) [24032407] **5656**

HONOLULU WHOLESALE PRICES EGGS, POULTRY, PORK, BEEF AND RICE (US/0148-3358) [03297120] **93**

HONOR AWARDS PROGRAM / SEATTLE CHAPTER, AMERICAN INSTITUTE OF ARCHITECTS (US) [17869973] **300**

HONOURABLE SOCIETY OF CYMMRODORION (LONDON, ENGLAND) See TRAFODION ANRHYDEDDUS GYMDEITHAS Y CYMMRODORION **3447**

HONYAKU NO SEKAI (JA) [04165614] **3286**

HONYURUI KAGAKU (JA/0385-437X) [18555049] **5585**

HOO-DOO (US) [01928064] **3464**

HOOD COUNTY GENEALOGICAL SOCIETY (US/1071-1112) [28602832] **2453**

HOOD COUNTY NEWS (US) [17659294] **5751**

HOOD RIVER NEWS (US/0746-5823) [10133661] **5733**

HOODOOS HIGHLANDER, THE (CN/0229-768X) [08295192] **5786**

HOOF BEATS (COLUMBUS, OHIO) (US/0018-4683) [02251417] **2799**

HOOFBEATS (AT/0811-8698) [I08118698] **2799**

●HOOFCARE & LAMENESS (US) [26667108] **2799**

HOOFCARE AND LAMENESS QUARTERLY REPORT See HOOFCARE & LAMENESS **2799**

HOOFDBLAD DE INDUSTRIELE EIGENDOM (NE) **1608**

HOOFPRINTS (US) [21360284] **2799**

HOOFPRINTS FROM THE YELLOWSTONE CORRAL OF THE WESTERNERS (US/0742-7727) [03342019] **2738**

HOOFS AND HORNS (AT) [20581647] **2799**

HOOGSTEDER MERCURY, THE **CEASED.** (NE/0924-9419) [22253586] **352**

HOOK (BONITA, CALIF.), THE (US/0736-9220) [09269387] 23, **4177**

HOOK N' COOK (CN) [03963696] **4654**

HOOKED ON CROCHET! (US/0893-1879) [15377076] **5184**

HOOKER'S ICONES PLANTARUM **CEASED.** (UK) [03333414] **513**

HOOKUP (US) **2305**

HOOP/NBA TODAY (US/0749-5285) [11136090] **4899**

HOOSHARAR (US/0018-4721) [01588085] **2263**

HOOSIER BUSINESS WOMAN, THE (US/0194-5319) [04795940] 680, **5558**

HOOSIER CONSERVATION (US/0199-6894) [04251014] 2173, **2216**

HOOSIER EQUESTRIAN (US/0199-6266) [05589442] **2799**

HOOSIER FAMILY ARCHIVES (US/0149-1253) [03422411] **2454**

HOOSIER FARMER (US/0018-4748) [04094572] **93**

HOOSIER GENEALOGIST, THE (US/1054-2175) [01696561] **2454**

HOOSIER JOURNAL OF ANCESTRY, THE (US/0147-1228) [03110502] **2454**

HOOSIER OUTDOORS (US/0018-4780) [04094582] 2195, **4873**

HOOSIER SCENE (US) [04735602] **4899**

HOOSIER UNITED METHODIST NEWS (US/1056-4624) [23492790] **5061**

HOOVER — Alphabetical Title Index

HOOVER ESSAYS (US/0748-4380) [10935334] **4476**

HOOVER INSTITUTION ON WAR, REVOLUTION, AND PEACE **See** PUBLICATION **4532**

HOOVER PRESS BIBLIOGRAPHY (US) [18903529] **2619**

HOOVER'S HANDBOOK **See** HOOVER'S HANDBOOK OF WORLD BUSINESS **680**

HOOVER'S HANDBOOK **See** HOOVER'S HANDBOOK OF AMERICAN BUSINESS **1608**

●HOOVER'S HANDBOOK OF AMERICAN BUSINESS (US/1055-7202) [23274858] **1608**

●HOOVER'S HANDBOOK OF WORLD BUSINESS (US/1055-7199) [23274547] **680**

●HOOVER'S MASTERLIST OF MAJOR U.S. COMPANIES (US/1066-291X) [26912611] **680**

HOP STOCKS / CROP REPORTING BOARD, ECONOMICS, STATISTICS, & COOPERATIVES SERVICE, U.S. DEPARTMENT OF AGRICULTURE (US) [04072864] **173**

HOPE BOLETIN DE SALUD (US/1050-0111) [21370308] **4783**

HOPE HEALTH LETTER (US/0891-3374) [14714459] **4783**

HOPE NEWS (US) [03944808] **4783**

HOPFEN-RUNDSCHAU (GW) [04026389] **173**

HOPITAL A PARIS, L' **SUSPENDED.** (FR/0018-4861) [01955928] **3783**

HOPITAL GENERAL DE SAINT-BONIFACE **See** PERSPECTIVES - ST. BONIFACE GENERAL HOSPITAL **3790**

HOPKINS COUNTY ECHO, THE (US) [15045476] **5751**

HOPKINS QUARTERLY **SUSPENDED.** (CN/0094-9086) [01795643] **3344**

HOPPLANTER, DE (BE/0018-490X) [02393409] **173**

HOPPO BUNKA KENKYU (JA/0385-6046) [I03856046] **5268, 321**

HOPPO KAGAKU CHOSA HOKOKU (JA) [09455928] **2652**

HOPSCOTCH (SARATOGA SPRINGS, N.Y.) (US/1044-0488) [19674433] **1064**

HOR YEZH (FR/0769-0088) [14642938] **3286**

HORA DE POESIA (SP/0212-9442) [04941321] **3464**

HORA (NEW YORK, N.Y.) (US/0741-9384) [05318382] **2263, 1313**

HORACE (PROVIDENCE, R.I.) (US/1052-8938) [17931464] **1829**

HORAIRE PROVISOIRE DE RADIODIFFUSION A ONDES DECAMETRIQUES (GW) [03261351] **1156**

HORBUCHVERZEICHNIS (GW) [04306431] **5266**

HORECA (NE) **2343**

HORECA ENTRE (UK) **2806**

HORECO (SP) **2806, 5071**

HOREN : JUNGER LITERATURKREIS, DIE (GW/0018-4942) [02085433] **3394**

HORGESCHADIGTEN PADAGOGIK (GW/0342-4898) [02830040] **1880, 4388**

HORICON REPORTER (US) [15113401] **5768**

HORISON (IO/0441-2168) [02535622] **3394**

HORISONT (FI/0439-5530) [I04395530] **2847**

HORISONT (VASSA, FINLAND) (FI/0018-4950) [01696710] **3394**

HORITSU JIHO (JA) [11641569] **2979**

HORIZON (CHICAGO, ILL.) (US/1042-8461) [19226823] **4963**

HORIZON D'OR (CN/0701-1490) [03406428] **5288**

HORIZON JEUNESSE (CN/0822-8469) [10809696] **1072**

HORIZON (MONTREAL. 1979) (CN/0708-580X) [05528702] **2263**

HORIZON. OCEANOGRAPHIE HYDROBIOLOGIE (FR/1142-2505) [I11422505] **1363**

HORIZON. SCIENCES DE LA TERRE (FR/0998-4771) [I09984771] **1363**

HORIZON. SCIENCES DU MONDE VEGETAL ET ANIMAL (FR/1142-2521) [I11422521] **478**

HORIZON. SCIENCES ECONOMIQUES ET SOCIALES (FR/1142-2513) [I11422513] **5227, 1533**

HORIZON SEPHARDI (CN/0315-7946) [02441926] **2619**

HORIZONS (US/0196-3120) [05777810] **23**

HORIZONS 80 I.E. QUATRE-VINGT (CG) [02158538] **1565**

HORIZONS (ARMDALE) (CN/0318-5362) [02442088] **2565**

HORIZONS (CHICAGO. 1980) **CEASED.** (US/0197-5056) [06036505] **1324**

HORIZONS (GAMBRILLS, MD.) (US/1064-6434) [20229008] **4388**

HORIZONS IN BIBLICAL THEOLOGY (US/0195-9085) [05700913] **5017**

HORIZONS IN BIOCHEMISTRY AND BIOPHYSICS **CEASED.** (US/0096-2708) [02243969] **457**

HORIZONS LONDON. 1991 **CEASED.** (UK/0967-5698) [I09675698] **5480**

HORIZONS (OAKVILLE) (CN/0712-6077) [09340481] **4963**

●HORIZONS OF VIETNAMESE THOUGHT AND EXPERIENCE (US/1062-7006) [25699839] **5268**

HORIZONS P.T.A. DIRECTORY, THE (KE) [21214134] **839**

HORIZONS PHILOSOPHIQUES (CN/0709-4469) [23761549] **4348**

HORIZONS (SAINT JOHN. 1982) (CN/0823-2393) [10220830] **4088**

HORIZONS (SAN ANTONIO, TEX.) (US) [12414188] **2195**

HORIZONS SF (CN/0229-1215) [07865657] **3394**

HORIZONS (TORONTO. 1966) (CN/0381-3789) [02249378] **1829**

HORIZONS (VILLANOVA) (US/0360-9669) [01947569] **4963**

HORIZONS (WINNIPEG. 1990) (CN/1180-5455) [23236577] **321**

HORIZONT (BERLIN, GERMANY) **CEASED.** (GW) [17728850] **4476**

HORIZONTE EMPRESARIAL (SP/0212-0607) [09736835] **1566**

HORIZONTE EMPRESIARAL **See** FOMENTO DEL TRABAJO **1561**

HORIZONTES (PONCE, P.R.) (PR/0018-5027) [01697154] **2847**

HORIZONTN FUN KULTUR UN LEBN / WORKMEN'S CIRCLE (US/1055-2049) [23104573] **5247**

HORMONAL STEROIDS : PROCEEDINGS (NE/0534-9303) [02252929] **3584**

HORMONE AND METABOLIC RESEARCH (GW/0018-5043) [01588475] **3730**

HORMONE AND METABOLIC RESEARCH. SUPPLEMENT SERIES (GW/0170-5903) [01607904] **3730**

HORMONE RESEARCH (SZ/0301-0163) [01787438] **581, 3730**

HORMONES AND BEHAVIOR (US/0018-506X) [01696259] **3730**

HORMONES AND THEIR ACTIONS. PART I (NE) **3730**

HORMONES AND THEIR ACTIONS. PART II (NE) **3730**

HORN BOOK GUIDE TO CHILDREN'S AND YOUNG ADULT BOOKS, THE (US/1044-405X) [19770536] **3394, 1064**

HORN BOOK MAGAZINE (1945), THE (US/0018-5078) [06715359] **1064**

HORN CALL, THE (US/0046-7928) [04828279] **4121**

HORN OF AFRICA (US/0161-4703) [03936168] **2640**

HORN OF AFRICA BULLETIN (SW) [24520827] **4523, 2640**

HORN REVIEW, THE (US/1056-4659) [23716107] **2640**

HORNBILL (II) [03955468] **457**

HORNERO, EL (AG/0073-3407) [01586333] **5586**

HORNS OF PLENTY, MALCOLM COWLEY AND HIS GENERATION (US/0896-9965) [17361374] **3394**

HOROLOGICAL DIALOGUES (US/0273-3374) [07039976] **2916**

HOROLOGICAL JOURNAL (UK/0018-5108) [01640391] **2916**

HOROLOGICAL TIMES (US/0145-9546) [02843251] **2916**

HOROSCOPE (ANDRE MAURICE) (CN/1182-6304) [23296421] **4241**

HOROSCOPE GUIDE (US/8750-3042) [11252846] **390**

HOROSCOPE (NEW YORK) (US/0018-5116) [02253776] **390**

HOROSCOPE (VERONIQUE CHARPENTIER) (CN/1182-6312) [23296414] **390**

HORROR SHOW, THE (US/0748-2914) [10952309] **3394**

HORRY INDEPENDENT, THE (US) [13387326] **5742**

HORS CADRE (FR/0755-0863) [10654101] **4072**

HORS D'ORDRE (CN/0823-6119) [09818957] **5202**

HORS LIGNE (SZ) **680**

HORSE ACTION (WINFIELD) (CN/1183-3173) [24368294] **2799**

HORSE AND HORSEMAN (US/0094-3355) [04148819] **2799**

HORSE AND HOUND HUNTER CHASERS AND POINT-TO-POINTERS (UK) [03442425] **4899, 2799**

HORSE & PONY (UK/0262-5814) **2799**

HORSE & RIDER (US/0018-5159) [05718624] **2799**

HORSE & RIDER ALL-WESTERN YEARBOOK (US/0193-2950) [02588475] **2799**

HORSE AND RIDER (LONDON, ENGLAND) (UK) [07603699] **2799**

HORSE ILLUSTRATED (US/0145-9791) [02831286] **2799**

HORSE INDUSTRY DIRECTORY (US/0890-233X) [02465656] **2799**

HORSE INDUSTRY DIRECTORY OF CANADA (CN/0828-4679) [11830292] **2799**

HORSE MAGAZINE (AT/0817-7686) [I08177686] **2799**

HORSE PLAY (US/0092-6353) [04104703] **2799**

HORSE RACING MAGAZINE (CN/0380-2779) [02583547] **4899, 2799**

HORSE SHEETS (US) **2799**

HORSE SHOW MAGAZINE (US) [08620269] **2799**

HORSE TIMES (US/0744-4257) [08256067] **2799**

HORSE WORLD (US/0018-5191) [01642239] **2800**

HORSE WORLD : PONY EXPRESS (UK/0018-5183) [01369232] **2800**

HORSE WORLD USA (US/0897-4497) [17537293] **2800**

HORSECARE **CEASED.** (US/0162-8127) [04249367] **2800**

HORSELESS CARRIAGE CLUB GAZETTE **See** HORSELESS CARRIAGE GAZETTE **5416**

HORSELESS CARRIAGE GAZETTE (US/0018-5213) [01588923] **251, 5416**

HORSEMAN (HOUSTON, TEX.) (US/0018-5221) [01752274] **2800**

HORSEMAN'S CONNECTION OF OREGON (US/1045-6066) [20147947] **2800**

HORSEMEN'S JOURNAL, THE **CEASED.** (US/0018-5256) [04094594] **2800**

HORSEMEN'S YANKEE PEDLAR (US/0199-6436) [06070289] **2800**

HORSEPOWER (AURORA) (CN/0840-6715) [20286782] **2800**

HORSES ALL (CN/0225-4913) [06136557] **2800**

HORSES (CARLSBAD, CALIF.) (US/0046-7936) [04094605] **2800**

HORSESHOE PITCHER'S NEWS DIGEST, THE (US) [05464680] **4899**

HORSETRADER, THE (US/0742-7999) [10446596] **2800**

HORTI SUL (BL/0103-3700) [I01033700] **2418**

HORTICULTURA BRASILEIRA (BL) [11452220] **2419**

HORTICULTURAL ABSTRACTS (UK/0018-5280) [01752276] **2419, 2434**

HORTICULTURAL ECONOMIC NEWSLETTER (NE) **2419**

HORTICULTURAL ENTERPRISES (UK) [04175386] **2419**

HORTICULTURAL NEWS (NEW BRUNSWICK, N.J.) (US/0886-5779) [09438935] **2419**

HORTICULTURAL PRODUCTS REVIEW (US/0894-8429) [15249484] **2419**

HORTICULTURAL REVIEWS (US/0163-7851) [04476218] **2419**

HORTICULTURE (US/0018-5329) [01752281] **2419**

HORTICULTURE ADVANCE (II) [01752282] **2419**

HORTICULTURE AND HOME PEST NEWSLETTER (US) [15732760] **2419**

HORTICULTURE DIGEST (US/0046-6964) [09809248] **2419**

HORTICULTURE FRANCAISE (FR/0395-8531) [04026419] **2419**

HORTICULTURE IN NEW ZEALAND : JOURNAL OF THE ROYAL NEW ZEALAND INSTITUTE OF HORTICULTURE (NZ/1170-1803) [23364381] **2419**

HORTICULTURE NEWS (NZ) **2419**

HORTICULTURE RESEARCH INTERNATIONAL (GREAT BRITAIN) **See** ANNUAL REPORT / HORTICULTURE RESEARCH INTERNATIONAL **2409**

HORTICULTURE REVIEW (CN/0823-8472) [11449412] **2419**

HORTICULTURE WEEK (UK/0269-9478) [13173458] **2419**

HOSPITAL

●HORTICULTURIST/ INSTITUTE OF HORTICULTURE, THE (UK/0964-8992) [25322740] **2419**

HORTIDEAS (US/0742-8219) [10486765] **2419**

HORTON HEADLIGHT (HORTON, KAN. : 1933) (US) [09931238] **5676**

HORTSCIENCE (US/0018-5345) [01752284] **2419**

HORTTECHNOLOGY (ALEXANDRIA, VA.) (US/1063-0198) [25298367] **2419**

HORTUS (FARNHAM) (UK/0950-1657) [15720918] **2419**

HORTUS MUSICUS (GW) [02057451] **4121**

HORTUS NORTHWEST (US) [21884897] **2419**

HORTUS TUBIGENSIS INDEX SEMINUM (GW) [04913856] **2420**

HORUMON TO RINSHO (JA/0045-7167) [01360413] **3731**

HORUS (SILVER SPRINGS, MD.) (US/8756-3029) [11506552] **4963**

HOSANNA (PHOENIX, ARIZ.) (US) [10412700] **4963**

HOSANNA (PHOENIX, ARIZ.) (US/0276-3729) [05018828] **4963**

HOSE & NOZZLE (SHREVEPORT) (US/0191-6653) [04913419] 925, **4260**

HOSEI DAIGAKU ION BIMU KOGAKU KENKYUJO HOKOKU (JA) [11605092] **4447**

HOSEI SHIGAKU (JA/0386-8893) [03868893] 1829, **2620**

HOSEKI GAKKAI SHI (JA/0385-5090) [02841570] **2914**

HOSHANO CHOSA HOKOKUSHO (JA) [08405722] **1449**

HOSHASEN (JA/0285-3604) [09580479] **4434**

HOSHASEN IGAKU SOGO KENKYUJO (JAPAN) *See* HOSHASEN IGAKU SOGO KENKYUJO NENPO **3584**

HOSHASEN IGAKU SOGO KENKYUJO NENPO (JA) [03209283] **3584**

HOSHASEN SEIBUTSU KENKYU (JA/0441-747X) [01900113] **457**

HOSIERY AND UNDERWEAR *See* BODY FASHIONS/INTIMATE APPAREL **1082**

HOSIERY NEWS / NATIONAL ASSOCIATION OF HOSIERY MANUFACTURERS (US/0742-8065) [08604020] **5351**

HOSIERY STATISTICS / NAHM (US) [03982980] **5351**

HOSOGAKU KENKYU / [HENSHU, NIHON HOSO KYOKAI HOSO BUNKA KENKYUJO HOSOGAKU KENKYUSHITSU] (JA) [12782496] **1133**

HOSPICE FORUM (US/0891-3781) [14714174] **5288**

HOSPICE JOURNAL, THE (US/0742-969X) [10485224] 3584, **5288**

HOSPICE LETTER (US/0193-6816) [05250781] **3783**

●HOSPICE SALARY & BENEFITS REPORT (US/1065-3155) [26570709] **3783**

HOSPIMEDICA *CEASED.* (US/0898-7270) [17383195] **3584**

HOSPITAL 2000 *SUSPENDED.* (SP/0214-2422) [02142422] 1977, 3783, **300**

HOSPITAL ACCESS MANAGEMENT (US) **3783**

HOSPITAL ADMINISTRATION (NEW DELHI) (II/0018-5531) [01681259] **3783**

HOSPITAL ADMITTING MONTHLY (US/0745-1466) [08868081] **3783**

HOSPITAL & COMMUNITY PSYCHIATRY (US/0022-1597) [00871477] **3926**

HOSPITAL & COMMUNITY PSYCHIATRY. MICROFILM *CEASED.* (US/0022-1597) [05320360] **3926**

●HOSPITAL AND HEALTH ADMINISTRATION INDEX (US/1077-1719) [30714319] 3783, **3659**

HOSPITAL AND HEALTH ADMINISTRATION INDEX. ANNUAL CUMULATION (US) 3783, **3659**

HOSPITAL AND HEALTH CARE REPORT (US/0146-7360) [03027166] **3783**

HOSPITAL & HEALTH SERVICES ADMINISTRATION (US/8750-3735) [02473360] **3783**

HOSPITAL AND HEALTH SERVICES REVIEW, THE (UK/0308-0234) [02483542] **3783**

HOSPITAL & HEALTHCARE AUSTRALIA (AT/0813-7471) [11535141] **3783**

HOSPITAL AND NURSING YEAR BOOK OF SOUTH AFRICA *See* HOSPITAL AND NURSING YEAR BOOK OF SOUTHERN AFRICA (JOHANNESBURG (SOUTH AFRICA) : 1971)) **3783**

HOSPITAL AND NURSING YEAR BOOK OF SOUTHERN AFRICA (JOHANNESBURG (SOUTH AFRICA) : 1971)) (SA) [07444557] **3783**

HOSPITAL AND PRIMARY HEALTH CARE (UK) **3783**

HOSPITAL AND SELECTED MORBIDITY DATA (NZ/0548-9938) [02436854] **4810**

HOSPITAL ASSOCIATION OF NEW YORK STATE *See* NEWS - HOSPITAL ASSOCIATION OF NEW YORK STATE **3790**

HOSPITAL BED USE STATISTICS / WELSH OFFICE [AND] WELSH HEALTH COMMON SERVICES AUTHORITY (UK/0959-2512) [20578636] **3783**

HOSPITAL BLUE BOOK (OFFICIAL NATIONAL ED.) (US/1047-6903) [20496011] **3783**

HOSPITAL COMARCAL (SP/0211-4437) [02114437] **3584**

HOSPITAL/COMMUNITY RELATIONS PROFESSIONAL (US/0740-3674) [09953199] **3783**

HOSPITAL CONTRACTS MANUAL (US/0734-0028) [08672271] 3783, **2979**

HOSPITAL COST MANAGEMENT AND ACCOUNTING (US/1045-1765) [19729471] **3783**

HOSPITAL DEVELOPMENT (UK/0300-5720) [05069251] **3784**

HOSPITAL DOCTOR (UK/0262-3145) [02623145] **3584**

HOSPITAL EDITORS' IDEA EXCHANGE (US/1046-1647) [20338893] 925, **1112**

HOSPITAL, EL (US/0018-5485) [01470141] **3783**

HOSPITAL EMPLOYEE HEALTH (US/0744-6470) [08466867] **3784**

HOSPITAL ENGINEERING BULLETIN / AMERICAN SOCIETY FOR HOSPITAL ENGINEERING OF THE AMERICAN HOSPITAL ASSOCIATION (US) [12076657] **3784**

HOSPITAL ENGINEERING (CHICAGO) (US/0163-3465) [04338493] **1977**

HOSPITAL EQUIPMENT & SUPPLIES (UK/0018-5620) [00185620] **3784**

HOSPITAL ETHICS (US/8756-8519) [11671943] 3584, **2251**

HOSPITAL FINANCIAL MANAGEMENT ASSOCIATION ANNUAL REPORT (US/0271-406X) [06595928] **3784**

HOSPITAL FINANCIAL MANAGEMENT ASSOCIATION (U.S.) *See* HOSPITAL FINANCIAL MANAGEMENT ASSOCIATION ANNUAL REPORT **3784**

HOSPITAL FOOD & NUTRITION FOCUS (US/0747-7376) [10789034] **4192**

HOSPITAL FOOD SERVICE (US/0046-7979) [05845433] 2343, **3784**

HOSPITAL FOR SPECIAL SURGERY *See* JOURNAL OF THE HOSPITAL FOR SPECIAL SURGERY, THE **3968**

HOSPITAL FORMULARY (US/0098-6909) [01512185] **4306**

HOSPITAL FUND RAISING NEWSLETTER (US/0193-9939) [05283333] **3784**

HOSPITAL GIFT SHOP MANAGEMENT *CEASED.* (US/0738-7946) [09651479] 2584, **869**

HOSPITAL GRAPHICS (US/0739-3466) [09726480] 3784, **379**

HOSPITAL HOME HEALTH *CEASED.* (US/0884-8998) [12491192] **3584**

HOSPITAL INFECTION CONTROL (US/0098-180X) [01395733] **3584**

HOSPITAL LAW MANUAL. ADMINISTRATORS VOLUME (US) [07821283] 3784, **2979**

HOSPITAL LAW MANUAL. ATTORNEYS VOLUME (US/0018-5728) [07809536] 3784, **2979**

●HOSPITAL LAW MANUAL BULLETIN (US/1065-2817) [26563366] **3740**

HOSPITAL LAW MANUAL. NEWSLETTER AND QUARTERLY SUPPLEMENT (US) [01752295] 3784, **2979**

HOSPITAL LAW NEWSLETTER (US/0738-0984) [09511591] **3741**

HOSPITAL LITERATURE INDEX (US/0018-5736) [01752296] 3784, **3659**

HOSPITAL LITIGATION REPORTER (US/1048-5201) [20966869] 3784, **2979**

HOSPITAL MAGAZINE (UK) **3784**

●HOSPITAL MANAGED CARE & DIRECT CONTRACTING (US/1061-7620) [25453502] **3784**

HOSPITAL MANAGEMENT INTERNATIONAL / INTERNATIONAL HOSPITAL FEDERATION (UK/0953-9743) [19861562] **3784**

HOSPITAL MANAGEMENT REVIEW (US/0737-903X) [09476015] 3784, **3659**

HOSPITAL MANAGEMENT SERIES (US/0363-390X) [02386732] **3784**

HOSPITAL MANAGEMENT SMARTS *CEASED.* (CN/1195-0390) **5786**

HOSPITAL MANAGEMENT SYSTEMS SOCIETY. CONFERENCE *See* PROCEEDINGS OF THE ... ANNUAL CONFERENCE OF THE HOSPITAL MANAGEMENT SYSTEMS SOCIETY **3791**

HOSPITAL MARKETING MONITOR (US/8755-3392) [11283996] **869**

HOSPITAL MATERIALS MANAGEMENT (US/0888-3068) [13544881] **3784**

HOSPITAL MATERIALS MANAGEMENT NEWS (US/0749-6672) [11181666] **3784**

HOSPITAL MATERIEL MANAGEMENT QUARTERLY (US/0192-2262) [05002369] **3784**

HOSPITAL MEDICINE (NEW YORK, N.Y.) (US/0441-2745) [01715055] **3584**

HOSPITAL MORBIDITY - CANADIAN CENTRE FOR HEALTH INFORMATION (CN/1195-4000) [30999324] 3784, **3659**

HOSPITAL NEWS FOR HEALTHCARE PROVIDERS. (EASTERN MASS/BOSTON ED.) (US/1056-3040) [23657375] **3784**

HOSPITAL NEWS FOR HEALTHCARE PROVIDERS (NORTHERN NEW ENGLAND ED.) (US/1056-3032) [23657385] **3784**

HOSPITAL NEWS (PITTSBURGH, PA. 1986) (US/1071-0582) [28873967] **3784**

HOSPITAL NEWS. WISCONSIN (US/1062-9947) [25841292] **3784**

HOSPITAL PATIENT RELATIONS REPORT (US/1048-4477) [20949911] **3784**

HOSPITAL PAYMENT & INFORMATION MANAGEMENT *CEASED.* (US/1074-8334) [29858384] 2882, **3784**

HOSPITAL PEER REVIEW (US/0149-2632) [03451297] **3785**

HOSPITAL PHARMACIST REPORT (US/1052-3146) [22254998] **4306**

●HOSPITAL PHARMACIST, THE (UK/1352-7967) **4306**

HOSPITAL PHARMACY DIRECTOR'S MONTHLY MANAGEMENT SERIES (US/0739-957X) [09899216] **4306**

HOSPITAL PHARMACY (PHILADELPHIA) (US/0018-5787) [01587834] **4306**

HOSPITAL PHARMACY SERVICE "INSTANT UP-DATE" (US/0739-9561) [09899281] **4307**

HOSPITAL PHONE BOOK, THE (US/0278-5153) [06939188] **3785**

HOSPITAL PHYSICIAN (SURGERY/EMERGENCY/SPECIALTIES ED.) (US/0888-2428) [13532791] **3584**

HOSPITAL PRACTICE (ED. EN ESPANOL) *CEASED.* (SP/0213-4845) [02134845] **3584**

HOSPITAL PRACTICE (HOSPITAL ED.) (US/8755-4542) [11307940] **3785**

HOSPITAL PRACTICE (OFFICE EDITION) (US/8750-2836) [10716242] 457, **3584**

HOSPITAL PRODUCT COMPARISON SYSTEM (US) [15875915] **3785**

HOSPITAL PRODUCT LINE REPORT (US) [17588458] **3785**

HOSPITAL PRODUCTS AND TECHNOLOGY *CEASED.* (CN/0823-6798) [10061627] **3584**

HOSPITAL PSIQUIATRICO DE LA HABANA, MAZORRA, CUBA *See* REVISTA DEL HOSPITAL PSIQUIATRICO DE LA HABANA **3936**

HOSPITAL PUBLIC RELATIONS (US/0195-9824) [05639030] **760**

HOSPITAL PUBLIC RELATIONS ADVISOR (US/0892-709X) [15239779] **760**

HOSPITAL PURCHASING NEWS (US/0279-4799) [07904984] **3785**

HOSPITAL REHAB (US) **3585**

HOSPITAL REVENUE REPORT (US/1052-8733) [22400017] **3785**

HOSPITAL RISK CONTROL SYSTEM (US) **3585**

HOSPITAL RISK MANAGEMENT (US/0199-6312) [06065988] 3785, **869**

HOSPITAL SAFETY INFORMATION SERVICE (US/0276-2323) [07237040] 4783, **3785**

HOSPITAL SALARY SURVEY REPORT (US) [23303671] **3785**

HOSPITAL SALARY SURVEY REPORT (US/0277-2353) [23003671] **3785**

HOSPITAL SECURITY AND SAFETY MANAGEMENT (US/0745-1148) [08828501] **3785**

HOSPITAL STATISTICS. VOLUME 1. BEDS, SERVICES, PERSONNEL (CN/0383-574X) [03244911] 3785, **3660**

HOSPITAL STRATEGY REPORT (US/1040-6263) [18475695] **3785**

HOSPITAL — Alphabetical Title Index

HOSPITAL SUPERVISOR'S BULLETIN (US/0018-585X) [04094617] **3785, 941**

HOSPITAL TECHNOLOGY ALERTS (US/0887-672X) [12306051] **3785**

HOSPITAL TECHNOLOGY SERIES (US/0888-711X) [11826648] **3785**

HOSPITAL TOPICS (US/0018-5868) [01643911] **3785**

HOSPITAL TOPICS. [MICROFICHE] (US) **3785**

HOSPITAL TRUSTEE (CN/0704-0407) [03797300] **3785**

HOSPITAL UPDATE (UK/0305-4136) [03693035] **3585**

HOSPITAL UTILIZATION DATA, WISCONSIN (US) [03736919] **3785**

HOSPITAL WAGE, SALARY, AND BENEFITS SURVEY (US/0198-6384) [06175682] **3785**

HOSPITALITE, HOTELLERIE, RESTAURATION, L' (CN/0838-6854) [18242003] **2806**

HOSPITALITE (TORONTO) (CN/0704-6359) [03887260] **5071**

●HOSPITALITY (NZ) [28894536] **2343, 2806**

HOSPITALITY (UK) [06567177] **2343**

HOSPITALITY & CATERING (NZ) [28902227] **2343**

HOSPITALITY & TOURISM EDUCATOR (US) [19340108] **5480, 2806**

●HOSPITALITY DESIGN (US/1062-9254) [25810496] **2900**

HOSPITALITY DIRECTIONS (US) **5480, 5071**

HOSPITALITY FOODSERVICE (AT) [27579207] **2343**

HOSPITALITY INDEX, THE (US) [18650465] **5480, 869**

HOSPITALITY LAW (US/0889-5414) [13940986] **2979**

HOSPITALITY MANAGEMENT (US) [18490579] **869, 5071**

HOSPITALITY RESEARCH JOURNAL (US/1060-9350) [22334764] **2806**

HOSPITALITY SERIES (US/0363-1427) [02433227] **93, 2806**

●HOSPITALS & HEALTH NETWORKS (US/1068-8838) [27839964] **3785**

HOSPITALS & HEALTH NETWORKS (US) [28572910] **3785**

HOSPITALS & HEALTH SERVICES YEAR BOOK AND DIRECTORY OF HOSPITAL SUPPLIERS, THE (UK/0300-5968) [01793818] **3785**

HOSPITALS & HEALTH SERVICES YEARBOOK AUSTRALIA (AT) [04457989] **3786**

HOSPITALS (CHICAGO, ILL. : 1936) *See* HOSPITALS & HEALTH NETWORKS **3785**

HOSPITALS (CHICAGO, ILL. 1936) (US/0018-5973) [01752305] **3786**

HOSPITALS (CHICAGO, ILL. : 1936) *See* HOSPITALS & HEALTH NETWORKS **3785**

HOSPITAL'S MEDICARE POLICY & PAYMENT REPORT *See* HOSPITAL PAYMENT & INFORMATION MANAGEMENT **3784**

HOSPITAL'S MEDICARE POLICY & PAYMENT REPORT, THE (US/1060-7838) [25060461] **2882, 3786**

HOSPITALS, NURSING HOMES AND RELATED HEALTH FACILITIES (US/0094-9833) [01076657] **3786**

HOSPITALTA (1991) *See* HEALTHCARE ADVOCATE (EDMONTON) **3782**

HOSPODAR (US/0018-599X) [01752308] **2263**

HOSPODARSKE DEJINY (XR) [08096979] **1566**

HOST/PATHOGEN NEWS (US/0747-6116) [10763679] **3585**

HOSTA JOURNAL : A PUBLICATION OF THE AMERICAN HOSTA SOCIETY, THE (US/1041-553X) [13422147] **513**

HOSTELER (MINNEAPOLIS, MINN.) (US) [01606932] **2806**

HOSTELLING INTERNATIONAL, BUDGET ACCOMMODATION (UK) [27960656] **2806**

HOSTELLING NORTH AMERICA : A GUIDE TO HOSTELS IN CANADA AND THE UNITED STATES (US) [23614211] **5480**

HOSTETLER MEMO FOR BROKERS ONLY, THE (US/1052-7575) [22366736] **790**

HOT BIKE (US/8750-3212) [11252739] **4081**

HOT BOAT (US/0892-8320) [15267105] **593**

HOT BUTTERED SOUL (UK/0302-0762) [01792429] **4121**

HOT CLUB DE FRANCE *See* BULLETIN - HOT CLUB DE FRANCE **4106**

HOT CLUB DE FRANCE *See* BULLETIN DU HOT-CLUB DE FRANCE **4106**

HOT CLUB DE FRANCE. BULLETIN *See* BULLETIN DU HOT-CLUB DE FRANCE **4106**

HOT COCO (US/0740-3186) [09935395] **1267**

HOT FLASH: A NEWSLETTER FOR MIDLIFE AND OLDER WOMEN (US) [08488628] **5558**

HOT GRAPHICS INTERNATIONAL *See* GRAPHICS INTERNATIONAL **379**

HOT HOUSE (US) **4121**

HOT LINE CONSTRUCTION EQUIPMENT MONTHLY UPDATE (US/1047-4382) [20694952] **616**

HOT LINE FARM EQUIPMENT GUIDE'S QUICK REFERENCE GUIDE FOR FARM TRACTORS AND COMBINES (US/0743-7730) [09981133] **159**

HOT METAL (AT/1033-7423) [I10337423] **4027**

HOT OFF THE COMPUTER (US/0737-8076) [09460924] **1267, 3213**

HOT PRESS (IE) [I03320847] **2517**

HOT ROD (US/0018-6031) [04084734] **4899, 5416**

HOT ROD ... ANNUAL (US/0735-083X) [08842341] **5416**

HOT ROD BIKES (US) **4899**

HOT ROD MAGAZINE CHEVROLET (US/0271-0919) [06534374] **5416**

HOT ROD MAGAZINE CORVETTE (US/0273-0383) [06984283] **5416**

HOT ROD MAGAZINE ENGINES (US/0730-4811) [07992235] **5416**

HOT ROD MAGAZINE KIT CAR (US/0731-3314) [08142310] **5416**

HOT ROD MAGAZINE PICKUPS & MINI-TRUCKS (US/0730-5044) [08001744] **5416**

HOT ROD PERFORMANCE AND CUSTOM DIRECTORY (US/0196-7010) [05859968] **5416**

●HOT ROD SWIMSUIT SPECIAL (US/1066-4181) [26945442] **3995**

HOT SHEET (FAIRFIELD, WASH.) (US/1064-1831) [26224282] **2290**

HOT SHOE INTERNATIONAL (UK/0959-6933) [I09596933] **4370**

HOT STOVE BASEBALL (US/1057-0179) [23912120] **4899**

HOT TOPICS (US/0273-4990) [11336808] **2535**

HOT WACKS (CN/0714-864X) [09375283] **4121**

HOT WIRE *CEASED.* (US/0747-8887) [10828405] **322, 5558**

HOTADS INTERNATIONAL *See* ADS INTERNATIONAL **754**

HOTEL & CATERING REVIEW (BLACKROCK, DUBLIN) (US/0332-4400) [09856333] **5071, 2806**

HOTEL AND CATERING TECHNOLOGY (UK) **2806**

HOTEL & MOTEL MANAGEMENT (US/0018-6082) [01681167] **869, 2806**

HOTEL & RESORT INDUSTRY (US/0149-3639) [03504256] **2806**

HOTEL AND RESTAURANT EMPLOYEES AND BARTENDERS INTERNATIONAL UNION *See* OFFICERS' REPORT & DAILY CONVENTION PROCEEDINGS - HOTEL AND RESTAURANT EMPLOYEES AND BARTENDERS INTERNATIONAL UNION **5072**

HOTEL AND RESTAURANT GUIDE INDIA (II) [09446375] **5071, 2806**

HOTEL & TRAVEL INDEX (US/0162-9972) [02903155] **5480, 2806**

HOTEL & TRAVEL INDEX (ABC INTERNATIONAL ED.) (US/1056-4713) [23666428] **2806, 5480, 23**

HOTEL BUSINESS (US) **2806**

HOTEL CATERING AND INSTITUTIONAL MANAGEMENT ASSOCIATION *See* HCIMA QUARTERLY BIBLIOGRAPHY OF HOTEL AND CATERING MANAGEMENT **2810**

HOTEL DES ENCANS DE MONTREAL *See* VENTES AUX ENCHERES PUBLIQUES **367**

HOTEL- EN RESTAURANTGIDS NEDERLAND (NE) [11175366] **5071, 2806**

HOTEL EXECUTIVE, THE (AT/1032-0954) [I10320954] **2806**

HOTEL MANAGEMENT TODAY (UK) **869, 2806**

HOTEL/MOTEL SECURITY AND SAFETY MANAGEMENT (US/8750-5126) [10149585] **2806**

HOTEL RESTAURANT (GW) **2806, 5071**

HOTEL- UND GASTGEWERBE RUNDSCHAU (SZ) [08556367] **5071, 2806**

HOTEL UPDATE NEWSLETTER (US) **2806**

●HOTELBUSINESS (HAUPPAUGE, N.Y.) (US/1065-8432) [26776049] **2806**

HOTELDOMANI (IT) **2806**

HOTELIER & CATERER (NAIROBI) (SA) **2806**

HOTELIER & CATERER : OFFICIAL MAGAZINE OF FEDHASA (SA) [22942687] **2343, 2806**

HOTELIER SINGAPORE (SI/0217-9695) [I02179695] **2806**

HOTELL & PENSIONAT (SW/0283-748X) [16799404] **2806**

HOTELL & PENSIONAT I SVERIGE *See* HOTELL & PENSIONAT **2806**

HOTELLI- JA RAVINTOLALEHTI *See* VITRIINI **2810**

HOTELLILUOKITTELUTYORYHMA : MUISTIO (FI) [19689277] **2806**

HOTELS, CAFES, RESTAURANTS EN ... (FR) [20347513] **5071, 2806**

HOTELS DE FRANCE, LES (FR) [04991658] **2806**

HOTELS (NEWTON, MASS.) (US/1047-2975) [20461276] **2807**

HOTHEAD PAISAN (US/1069-5281) [27865696] **2794**

HOTLINE (KE) [02306676] **5480**

HOTLINE (US/0730-2274) [07979663] **3213**

HOTLINE *CEASED.* (US) **4476, 680**

HOTLINE - CHILDREN'S RIGHTS OF NEW YORK (ORGANIZATION) (US/0895-3171) [16570296] **5288**

HOTLINE - NEWSLETTER ASSOCIATION OF AMERICA (US/0749-1255) [11093695] **4815, 2920**

HOTLINE ON OBJECT-ORIENTED TECHNOLOGY *CEASED.* (US/1044-4319) [19784719] **1186**

HOTLINE (SPRINGFIELD, ILL.) (US/0273-5946) [07479399] **5288**

HOTLINE, THE (US) **4476**

HOTLINE THE OFFICIAL NEWSLETTER OF AMERICA'S MOST WANTED (US) [25001157] **3165**

HOTLINE (VANCOUVER) (CN/0710-2232) [08205718] **1677**

HOTLINE (WILLISTON, N.D.) *SUSPENDED.* (US/0747-1173) [10554549] **4260**

HOTTEST NEW BUSINESS IDEAS, THE (US/0273-0618) [04671906] **680**

HOTUBA YA WAZIRI WA MAMBO YA NJE (TZ) [19502907] **3129**

HOUALLET (CN/0714-8275) [09088985] **2454**

HOUGHTON POULTRY RESEARCH STATION *See* REPORT OF THE HOUGHTON POULTRY RESEARCH STATION **220**

HOUGHTON STAR, THE (US) [08815110] **2535**

HOUILLE BLANCHE, LA (FR/0018-6368) [01752315] **2090**

HOUMA DAILY COURIER (US) [17500164] **5684**

HOUNDS AND HUNTING (US/0018-6384) [04094620] **4286**

HOUR BOOK (MICROFORM), THE (US) [06435582] **2535**

●HOUR (MONTREAL) (CN/1192-6708) [28311966] **2535**

HOUR, THE (US) [27905790] **5645**

HOURLY EARNINGS INDEX, THE (US/0362-692X) [02316103] **1677**

HOURLY PRECIPITATION DATA. HAWAII AND PACIFIC (US) [05934132] **1425**

HOURLY PRECIPITATION DATA, ILLINOIS (US) [02563760] **1425**

HOURLY PRECIPITATION DATA. INDIANA (US/0364-6165) [02621542] **1425**

HOURLY PRECIPITATION DATA. KENTUCKY (US/0364-5401) [02630333] **1425**

HOURLY PRECIPITATION DATA, MICHIGAN (US) [02564868] **1425**

HOURLY PRECIPITATION DATA, MINNESOTA (US) [02564888] **1425**

HOURLY PRECIPITATION DATA, MISSOURI (US) [02564925] **1425**

HOURLY PRECIPITATION DATA, PENNSYLVANIA (US/0364-619X) [02262003] **1425**

HOURLY PRECIPITATION DATA. PUERTO RICO AND VIRGIN ISLANDS (US) [06598133] **1425**

HOURLY PRECIPITATION DATA, SOUTH CAROLINA (US) [02565750] **1425**

HOURLY PRECIPITATION DATA. TENNESSEE (US/0364-6386) [02621359] **1426**

HOURLY PRECIPITATION DATA, TEXAS (US) [02565822] **1426**

Alphabetical Title Index — HOW

HOURLY PRECIPITATION DATA, WEST VIRGINIA (US) [02566031] **1426**

HOUSE & GARDEN (BRITISH EDITION, 1948) (UK/0043-5759) [01752317] 2420 **2901**

HOUSE & GARDEN (NEW YORK) *CEASED.* (US/0018-6406) [01752319] 300, **2901**

HOUSE & GARDEN PLANS GUIDE (1979) (US/0271-2881) [06113229] **2420**

HOUSE & HOME WOODWORKER (AT/1037-1354) [I10371354] **634**

HOUSE AND SENATE REPORTS ON PUBLIC BILLS (NUMBERED, UNBOUND) (US) [05795487] **2979**

HOUSE BEAUTIFUL (US/0018-6422) [01752321] 2901, **300**

HOUSE BEAUTIFUL'S COLONIAL HOMES *See* COLONIAL HOMES **295**

HOUSE BEAUTIFUL'S HOME BUILDING (US) [21095221] 2901, **616**

HOUSE BEAUTIFUL'S HOME REMODELING AND DECORATING (US) [15805971] **2901**

HOUSE BEAUTIFUL'S HOUSES AND PLANS (US) [06899838] **300**

HOUSE BEAUTIFUL'S KITCHENS, BATHS (US) [22369840] **2901**

HOUSE BILL SUMMARIES (US/0148-3005) [03283140] **4654**

HOUSE BUILDER (UK) [09406402] **2824**

HOUSE EAR INSTITUTE. REVIEW (US) **3888**

HOUSE IN THE HAMPTONS (US) [08458371] **2535**

HOUSE JOURNAL OF THE ... LEGISLATURE OF THE STATE OF MONTANA (US) [08183665] **4476**

HOUSE MAGAZINE (UK/0309-0426) [I03090426] **4476**

HOUSE OF COMMONS BOUND DEBATES (UK) **4476**

HOUSE OF COMMONS DEBATES (OTTAWA. DAILY ED.) (CN/0704-5603) [02587761] **4654**

HOUSE OF COMMONS DEBATES (OTTAWA. RETROSPECTIVE COMPILATION) (CN/0229-1398) [02885876] **4654**

HOUSE OF DELEGATES REPORTS (1966) (US/0195-5713) [05390877] **3856**

HOUSE PLAN FAVORITES (US) [07600649] **300**

HOUSE PRICE TRENDS (US/1200-2062) [31235268] **4838**

HOUSE PRICE TRENDS AND RESIDENTIAL CONSTRUCTION COSTS IN THE TORONTO REAL ESTATE BOARD MARKET AREA AND IN CANADA (CN/0705-9515) [04233342] **4838**

HOUSE PRICES (UK/0263-3639) [I02633639] **4838**

HOUSE (WESTHAMPTON BEACH, N.Y.) (US/1074-4274) [29699231] **2901**

●HOUSEBOAT MAGAZINE (US) **593**

HOUSEHOLD AND FAMILY CHARACTERISTICS (US) [08620642] **2280**

HOUSEHOLD & PERSONAL PRODUCTS INDUSTRY : HAPPI (US/0090-8878) [02027593] 404, **977**

HOUSEHOLD BRIGADE MAGAZINE *See* GUARDS MAGAZINE, THE **4044**

HOUSEHOLD ENERGY CONSUMPTION AND EXPENDITURES. PART I, NATIONAL DATA (US) [21024334] **1946**

HOUSEHOLD ENERGY CONSUMPTION AND EXPENDITURES. SUPPLEMENT: REGIONAL (US) [28658441] **1946**

HOUSEHOLD FACILITIES AND EQUIPMENT (CN/0318-5273) [01798152] **2811**

HOUSEHOLD FACILITIES BY INCOME AND OTHER CHARACTERISTICS (CN/0226-4560) [02438757] 2811, **1493**

HOUSEHOLD FACILITIES BY INCOME AND OTHER CHARACTERISTICS, REVISED ESTIMATES (CN/0848-502X) [22938771] 2811, **2812**

HOUSEHOLD FISH CONSUMPTION IN GREAT BRITAIN (UK/0262-3269) [I02623269] **2305**

HOUSEHOLD SUBSISTANCE LEVEL IN THE MAJOR URBAN CENTRES OF THE REPUBLIC OF SOUTH AFRICA, THE (SA) [08690929] **1494**

HOUSEHOLD VEHICLES ENERGY CONSUMPTION (US/1057-5006) [21570869] 5416, **1946**

HOUSEMENDING NOTEBOOK (US/1054-6421) [20717779] **616**

●HOUSEPLANT MAGAZINE (US/1061-4079) [25301882] **2420**

HOUSER HUNTERS NEWSLETTER (US/0748-2736) [10218748] **2454**

HOUSEWARES CANADA *CEASED.* (CN/0829-9889) [13784666] **2811**

HOUSEWARES EUROPE (UK) **2812**

HOUSEWARES MERCHANDISING (US/0747-3885) [10786892] **2812**

HOUSEWARES TONBRIDGE (UK/0264-8563) [I02648563] **2812**

HOUSING AFFAIRS LETTER (US/0018-6554) [02432102] **2824**

HOUSING AND BUILDING RESEARCH INSTITUTE, DACCA *See* ANNUAL REPORT / HOUSING AND BUILDING RESEARCH INSTITUTE, DACCA **598**

HOUSING AND CONSTRUCTION QUARTERLY (AT) [02246386] 616, **2824**

HOUSING AND CONSTRUCTION STATISTICS (ANNUAL) (UK/0308-9819) [09458008] **632**

HOUSING & DEVELOPMENT REPORTER (US/0091-5939) [01787686] 4654, **2824**

HOUSING & PLANNING REVIEW (UK/0018-6589) [06498426] **2824**

HOUSING & PROPERTY DIGEST (MY) [10471303] **2824**

HOUSING AND SOCIETY (US/0888-2746) [04551227] **2824**

HOUSING AND URBAN AFFAIRS ... : A BIBLIOGRAPHIC GUIDE TO THE MICROFORM COLLECTION (US) [07582711] **2840**

HOUSING AND URBAN DEVELOPMENT ASSOCIATION OF CANADA. ECONOMIC RESEARCH COMMITTEE *See* NEWSLETTER **2829**

HOUSING AND URBAN DEVELOPMENT ASSOCIATION OF CANADA. SALES AND MARKETING COUNCIL *See* SMC NATIONAL REPORT **2835**

HOUSING ASSISTANCE PAYMENTS PROGRAM. SUBSTANTIAL REHABILITATION PROCESSING HANDBOOK (US) [04171537] **2824**

HOUSING CHARACTERISTICS FOR SELECTED METROPOLITAN AREAS (US) [02540310] **2824**

HOUSING CHEAP OR ON A BUDGET NEWSLETTER (US) **2824**

HOUSING COUNSELING HANDBOOK (US) [02927705] **2824**

HOUSING ECONOMICS (US/1056-5140) [16640623] **2824**

HOUSING FINANCE AND DEVELOPMENT AGENCIES PROCESSING HANDBOOK (US) [02924458] **2824**

HOUSING FINANCE FOR OWNER OCCUPATION, AUSTRALIA (AT/1031-0320) [I10310320] 2824, **2840**

HOUSING IN FLORIDA (US) [05422451] **2824**

HOUSING IN SOUTHERN AFRICA (SA) **2824**

HOUSING LAW BULLETIN (US/0277-8491) [07641378] 2824, **2979**

HOUSING LAW REPORTS (UK) [10915355] 2824, **2979**

HOUSING (LONDON. 1978) (UK/0261-0280) [04071598] **2824**

HOUSING MARKET REPORT (US/0363-4744) [02429300] **2824**

HOUSING MARKET STATISTICS (US/1056-5132) [23042472] **2824**

HOUSING NEW JERSEY (US/1071-2585) [25425192] **2824**

HOUSING NEW JERSEY (US) **2824**

HOUSING NEWSLETTER (OTTAWA) (CN/0710-7323) [08720434] **2825**

HOUSING PERFORMANCE INDICATORS (US/0145-1359) [02670373] **2825**

HOUSING POLICY DEBATE (US/1051-1482) [21880928] **2825**

HOUSING PRODUCTION (BALTIMORE, MD.) (US/0742-6178) [05211003] 616, **2825**

HOUSING QUEENSLAND (AT/0813-7978) [I08137978] **2825**

HOUSING REPORT FOR KENTUCKY (US/0732-9342) [08460495] **2825**

HOUSING REVIEW (LONDON) (UK/0018-6651) [11806912] **2825**

HOUSING STUDIES (UK/0267-3037) [14362544] **2825**

HOUSING THE ELDERLY REPORT (US/1050-3234) [12893412] 5288, **5179**

HOUSMAN SOCIETY *See* HOUSMAN SOCIETY JOURNAL **3394**

HOUSMAN SOCIETY JOURNAL (UK/0305-926X) [02244011] 432, **3394**

HOUSTON AREA APARTMENT OWNERSHIP GUIDE (US) **4838**

HOUSTON ARTS MAGAZINE (US) [09460544] **322**

HOUSTON BAR BULLETIN (US/0279-3997) [05509475] **2979**

HOUSTON BUSINESS JOURNAL (US/0277-4976) [05438977] **680**

HOUSTON CHRONICLE (1912) (US/1074-7109) [01607806] **5751**

HOUSTON CITY MAGAZINE *CEASED.* (US/0884-0628) [04716730] **2738**

HOUSTON CORPORATE DIRECTORY (US/0278-4963) [04156584] **680**

HOUSTON FORWARD TIMES (US) [03968075] **5751**

HOUSTON-GALVESTON AREA COUNCIL. HEALTH SYSTEMS AGENCY *See* HEALTH SYSTEMS PLAN (HOUSTON, TEX.) **2978**

HOUSTON GEOLOGICAL SOCIETY *See* BULLETIN OF THE HOUSTON GEOLOGICAL SOCIETY, THE **1370**

HOUSTON HOME JOURNAL (US) [19673986] **5654**

HOUSTON HOME JOURNAL (PERRY, GA. : 1924) *See* HOUSTON TIMES-JOURNAL **5654**

HOUSTON INFORMER AND TEXAS FREEMAN, THE (US) [10536597] **5751**

HOUSTON INTERNATIONAL BUSINESS DIRECTORY (US/0197-3630) [04025975] **680**

HOUSTON JOURNAL OF INTERNATIONAL LAW (US/0194-1879) [04092705] **3129**

HOUSTON JOURNAL OF MATHEMATICS (US/0362-1588) [02009613] **3507**

HOUSTON LAW REVIEW (US/0018-6694) [01752338] **2979**

HOUSTON LAWYER (US/0439-660X) [02255037] **2979**

HOUSTON MONTHLY (US/0272-8060) [06956871] **2535**

HOUSTON MONTHLY (US/0272-6602) [06886070] **5071**

HOUSTON OIL DIRECTORY (US/0739-3555) [03953219] **4260**

HOUSTON POST (1932) (US/1060-3484) [05871627] **5751**

HOUSTON POST INDEX, THE (US/0893-2476) [15475281] **5692**

●HOUSTON REAL ESTATE FINANCE SOURCEBOOK (US/1065-853X) [26778068] **4838**

HOUSTON REAL ESTATE TRENDS (US/1045-8638) [20274743] **4838**

HOUSTON REVIEW, THE (US/0272-4030) [05298290] **2738**

HOUSTON SUN, THE (US/1071-2941) [27155880] **5751**

●HOUSTON TIMES-JOURNAL (US/1075-1874) [29960392] **5654**

HOUSTONIAN (HUNTSVILLE, TEX.) (US) [15021861] **5751**

HOUSTONIAN MAGAZINE (US/0888-4013) [13577351] **2535**

HOUSTON'S PUBLIC COMPANIES (US/0099-0426) [02243111] **790**

HOUT- EN MEUBELINDUSTRIE, EXCL. METALEN MEUBELEN / CENTRAAL BUREAU VOOR DE STATISTIEK, HOOFDAFDELING STATOSTOELEM VAN INDUSTRIE EN BOUWNIJVERHEID (NE/0168-4663) [11879783] **2906**

HOUTWERELD (NE) **634**

HOVEDSTADSOMRADETS TRAFIKSELSKAB (HOVEDSTADSRADET) *See* ARSBERETNING **5377**

HOVORYT I POKOZUIE UKRAINA (UN) [01788546] **1133**

HOW (II) [07015016] **5247**

HOW (BETHESDA, MD.) (US/0886-0483) [12818188] **380**

HOW FEDERAL AGENCIES HAVE SERVED THE HANDICAPPED (US/0091-4584) [01784594] 5288, **4388**

HOW NORTH CAROLINA RANKS EDUCATIONALLY AMONG FIFTY STATES (US) [04251744] 1751, **1795**

●HOW ON EARTH! (US/1062-7723) [25736563] **4192**

HOW OTTAWA SPENDS (CN/0822-6482) [10441054] **4655**

●HOW PRODUCTS ARE MADE (US/1072-5091) [28989437] **680**

●HOW TO ADOPT YOUR BABY PRIVATELY (US/1063-9071) [26177382] **5288**

HOW TO AVOID RIPPING YOUR HAIR OUT WHEN PURCHASING NEW OR USED FOREIGN OR DOMESTIC TAX FREE CARS DIRECT STATESIDE, OVERSEAS OR CANADA (US/1042-6434) [19098440] **5416**

●HOW TO BE A PERFECT COOK (US/1063-1747) [25909703] **2791**

HOW TO BUY A NEW OR USED POWER BOAT WITHOUT GETTING BURNED (US/1054-3856) [22874584] **593**

HOW TO DEFEND AND UPHOLD YOUR RIGHTS VS. THE POLICE (US/1061-8627) [25482166] **3165**

HOW TO DOUBLE YOUR INCOME (US/0277-0334) [07510361] **404**

HOW TO FIND BUSINESS INTELLIGENCE IN WASHINGTON (US/1044-7784) [13778506] 4655, **680**

HOW TO FIND COMPANY INTELLIGENCE IN STATE DOCUMENTS *CEASED.* (US/1041-8024) [17316567] **680**

HOW TO FIND INFORMATION ABOUT COMPANIES (US/0278-372X) [07787464] **680**

HOW TO GET A JOB IN ATLANTA : THE INSIDER'S GUIDE (US) [20824688] **1677**

HOW TO GET A JOB IN CHICAGO : THE INSIDER'S GUIDE (US) [18521551] **680**

HOW TO GET A JOB IN DALLAS/FORT WORTH : THE INSIDER'S GUIDE (US) [20824681] **1677**

HOW TO GET A JOB IN HOUSTON : THE INSIDER'S GUIDE (US) [20824664] **1677**

HOW TO GET A JOB IN LOS ANGELES/SAN DIEGO : THE INSIDER'S GUIDE (US) [18256916] **680**

HOW TO GET A JOB IN NEW YORK : THE INSIDER'S GUIDE (US) [19670225] **680**

HOW TO GET A JOB IN SAN FRANCISCO : THE INSIDER'S GUIDE (US) [18742451] **680**

HOW TO GET A JOB IN SEATTLE/PORTLAND (US) [21196769] **680**

HOW TO GET A JOB IN WASHINGTON, DC : THE INSIDER'S GUIDE (US) [20824673] **1677**

HOW TO GET RICHES FROM GOD SCRIPTURALLY (US/1057-0861) [23934755] **5017**

"HOW TO GROW" SERIES (ZA) [04276954] **93**

HOW TO (INDIANAPOLIS) (US/0095-4705) [01796528] 2420, **616**

HOW TO MANAGE YOUR LAW OFFICE (US) [09484816] **2979**

HOW TO PREPARE AN INITIAL PUBLIC OFFERING (US/1076-3376) [14202266] **3100**

HOW TO RECOVER FOR LOSS OR DAMAGE TO GOODS IN TRANSIT (US) [04344077] **5383**

HOW, WHEN, & WHERE IN TENNESSEE (US/0278-8926) [07901438] **2535**

HOW YOU CAN STOP SMOKING (US/1055-6052) [23237396] **2598**

HOWARD COUNTY TIMES (COLUMBIA, MD.) (US/0748-5298) [10963177] **5686**

HOWARD COURANT-CITIZEN, THE (US) [11208265] **5676**

HOWARD FLOREY INSTITUTE OF EXPERIMENTAL PHYSIOLOGY AND MEDICINE *See* ANNUAL REPORT AND ACCOUNTS - HOWARD FLOREY INSTITUTE OF EXPERIMENTAL PHYSIOLOGY AND MEDICINE **3726**

HOWARD JOURNAL OF COMMUNICATIONS, THE (US/1064-6175) [18321455] **1112**

HOWARD JOURNAL OF CRIMINAL JUSTICE, THE (UK/0265-5527) [10482022] **3165**

HOWARD LAKE HERALD (US) [01752346] **5696**

HOWARD LAW JOURNAL (US/0018-6813) [01641246] **2979**

HOWARD UNIVERSITY. COLLEGE OF MEDICINE *See* ANNUAL REPORT / HOWARD UNIVERSITY COLLEGE OF MEDICINE **1809**

HOWARD UNIVERSITY JOURNAL OF SCIENCE, THE (US) [05332169] **5110**

HOWARD UNIVERSITY REVIEWS OF SCIENCE, THE (US/0093-6057) [01787209] **5110**

HOWARD UNIVERSITY, WASHINGTON, DC. PHYSICS DEPARTMENT *See* HOWARD UNIVERSITY REVIEWS OF SCIENCE, THE **5110**

HOWARD UNIVERSITY, WASHINGTON, DC. PHYSICS DEPARTMENT *See* HOWARD UNIVERSITY JOURNAL OF SCIENCE, THE **5110**

HOWARD W. SAMS AND CO *See* SAMS AUTO RADIO SERVICE DATA **2080**

HOWARD W. SAMS & CO *See* TUBE SUBSTITUTION HANDBOOK **2085**

HOWARD W. SAMS & CO *See* TRANSISTOR SUBSTITUTION HANDBOOK **2085**

HOWARD W. SAMS & CO *See* SAMS TRANSISTOR RADIO **5149**

HOWARD W. SAMS & CO *See* SAMS TAPE RECORDER SERVICE DATA **5318**

HOWARD WAY LETTER, THE (US/0891-8244) [15026272] **869**

HOWE ENTERPRISE, THE (US) [17359487] **5751**

HOWLING DOG (US/0888-3521) [13562896] 3464, **3394**

HOWNIKAN (US) **2263**

HOXIE SENTINEL (HOXIE, KAN. : 1931) (US/1041-2921) [12590806] **5676**

HOY (CL/0716-3460) [04181058] **3344**

HOY DIA *CEASED.* (US/0018-6856) [04094625] 1896, **3286**

HOY ES HISTORIA (UY) [11299354] **2738**

HOYT'S ISSUE (US/0749-6176) [11139191] **2454**

HOZON KAGAKU (JA) [03494475] **352**

HP CHRONICLE. EUROPE, THE *CEASED.* (US/0895-0342) [16414219] **1186**

HP CHRONICLE, THE (US/0892-2829) [15145105] **1186**

HP-DE TIJD (NE) **4476**

HP DESIGN & AUTOMATION *See* WORKSTATION (AUSTIN, TEX.) **1207**

HP ENERGIA TRASPORTI (IT/0391-2019) [03912019] **5383**

HP PALMTOP PAPER, THE (US/1065-6189) [26656920] **1186**

HP PROFESSIONAL (US/0896-145X) [16925953] **1186**

HP WORLD : THE INDEPENDENT EUROPEAN MAGAZINE FOR HEWLETT PACKARD COMPUTER USERS (UK/0953-4091) **1186**

HPB SURGERY (SZ/0894-8569) [16270260] **3965**

HPI MARKET DATA (US) [06074611] **1025**

HPI MARKET DATA (US) [27165581] **4260**

HPI OUTLOOK *See* HPI MARKET DATA **4260**

HPI OUTLOOK, THE (US) [23452140] **4260**

HPV NEWS (INDIANAPOLIS, IND.) (US/0898-6894) [17885830] 5383, **1977**

HQ MAGAZINE (AT/1321-9820) [13219820] **2510**

● HR COMPUTING (US/1060-5916) [25039933] **1186**

HR FOCUS (US/1059-6038) [24642533] **941**

HR HORIZONS *CEASED.* (US/1053-3656) [22518517] **941**

HR MANAGERS LEGAL REPORTER (US/1053-0363) [22439132] **3149**

HR MANAGER'S SOURCEBOOK & BUYER'S GUIDE (CN/1193-2449) [11932449] **941**

HR/PC (US/0884-9129) [12533642] **941**

HR POWER: THE NEWSLETTER FOR INFLUENTIAL HUMAN RESOURCE PROFESSIONALS (US) **680**

HR REPORTER (US/0741-6997) [10203787] 1677, **941**

HRA, HSA, CDC, OASH, & ADAMHA PUBLIC ADVISORY COMMITTEES *See* ADAMHA PUBLIC ADVISORY COMMITTEES **1338**

HRAF NEWSLETTER (US/0195-3869) [03426227] **5202**

HRANA I ISHRANA (YU/0018-6872) [02999971] 4192, **2343**

HRANITELNOPROMISHLENA NAUKA (BU/0205-177X) [13506919] **2343**

HRD DIGEST AND ABSTRACTS *CEASED.* (US/1055-1182) [23077561] **2847**

HRD TREND REPORT (CN/0847-5407) [23237435] **941**

HRF, OSTERREICHISCHES HANDELSREGISTER (AU) [05937577] **680**

● HRM DOWNSIZING STRATEGIES (US) [25496981] **941**

HRMAGAZINE (ALEXANDRIA, VA.) (US/1047-3149) [20665218] **941**

HRNEWS (ALEXANDRIA, VA.) (US/1047-3157) [20665052] **941**

HRONIKA AISTHETIKES (GR/1105-0462) [11050462] **322**

HRONIKO (ATHENAI) (GR/0302-136X) [01792527] **322**

HRPLANNING NEWSLETTER, THE (US/0733-0332) [07761114] **941**

HRVATSKA KRSCANSKA BIBLIOGRAFIJA (CI) [08613089] 4963, **5012**

HRVATSKI GODNISNJAK ZA GODINU (CN/0841-2200) [20113559] **1926**

HRVATSKI KATOLICKI GLASNIK (US/0018-6910) [01586125] **4963**

HRVATSKO PRAVO : VJESTNIK HOB-A I PRAVASKOG HOP-A ZA DOMOVINU I INOZEMSTVO (SP) [11000521] **2692**

HSA/NENY NEWS (US/8755-1241) [10263159] **5288**

HSB INTERNATIONAL (NE/0923-666X) [20793801] **5450**

HSE LANGUAGE SERVICES BULLETIN (US) **4783**

HSI-AN CHIAO TUNG TA HSUEH *See* HSI-AN CHIAO TUNG TA HSUEH **1977**

HSI-AN CHIAO TUNG TA HSUEH (CC/0253-987X) [07075016] **1977**

HSI CHU : CHUNG YANG HSI CHU HSUEH YUAN HSUEH PAO (CC) [15996004] **5365**

HSI CHU HSUEH HSI / CHUNG YANG HSI CHU HSUEH YUAN PIEN (CH) [11012566] 5365, **3394**

HSI CHU I SHU (CC) [05387749] **5365**

HSI CHU LUN TSUNG (CC) [05142777] **5365**

HSI NAN MIN TSU YEN CHIU / CHUNG-KUO HSI NAN MIN TSU YEN CHIU HUI PIEN (CC) [11571634] **2652**

HSI PEI SHIH TA HSUEH PAO. SHE HUI KO HSUEH PAN (CC) [21732118] **5202**

HSI PEI TA HSUEH PAO (CH) [09330533] **1829**

HSI PEI YU (US) [03453859] **2652**

HSI-TSANG YEN CHIU (CC) [11406715] **2652**

HSI TUNG KO HSUEH YU SHU HSUEH (CC/1000-0577) [08273119] **3508**

HSIA CHAO LUN TAN (CH) [11459558] **2652**

HSIA-MEN TA HSUEH HSUEH PAO. CHE HSUEH SHE HUI KO HSUEH PAN (CC) [06656752] 5202, **4348**

HSIA-MEN TA HSUEH HSUEH PAO. TZU JAN KO HSUEH PAN (CC/0438-0479) [10288069] **5110**

HSIANG-KANG CH'IN HUI HSUEH YUAN HSUEH PAO (HK/0367-5920) [03675920] 5061, **1092**

HSIANG-KANG CHUNG WEN TA HSUEH CHIAO YU HSUEH PAO (HK) [06013538] **1751**

HSIANG-KANG CHUNG WEN TA HSUEH HSUEH PAO (HK) [01797492] **1829**

HSIANG-KANG CHUNG WIEN TA HSHUEH CHUNG-KUO WIEN HUA YEN CHIU SO HSHUEH PAO (HK) [02535645] **1829**

HSIANG-KANG FO CHIAO (HK/0073-3253) [02510245] **5021**

HSIANG-KANG KUNG YEH CHIH PIN NIEN CHIEN (HK) [01797659] **1608**

HSIAO HSI LIU (CH) [09005343] **1064**

HSIAO HSI TSUNG KAN (CC) [08663948] **3394**

HSIAO HSING WEI HSING CHI SUAN CHI HSI TUNG (CC) [11322694] **1186**

HSIAO PENG YU *CEASED.* (CC) [12789136] 1064, **3394**

HSIAO SHUO LIN (HARBIN, CHINA) (CH) [10518446] **3394**

HSIAO SHUO YUEH PAO (CC) [06660395] **3394**

HSIEN TAI AO-MEN (MH) [01799800] **5480**

HSIEN TAI CHUN SHIH (HK) [21020050] **4045**

HSIEN TAI HUA / CHUNG-KUO KO HSUEH CHI SHU HSIEH HUI (CH) [09004598] **1566**

HSIEN TAI TUNG HSIN (CC) [08664168] **1156**

HSIEN TAI WEN I LUN TSUNG / HSIEN TAI WEN I LUN TSUNG PIEN WEI HUI CHU PIEN (CC) [11853390] **322**

HSIEN TAI WU LI CHIH SHIH / MODERN PHYSICS (CC/1001-0610) [20640655] **4404**

HSIN-CHIA-PO CHING CHI NIEN CHIEN (CC) [03673882] **1494**

HSIN CHIA PO WEN I (SI) [09467471] **322**

HSIN-CHIANG CHIAO YU (CH) [08933834] **1751**

HSIN-CHIANG HUA PAO (CC) [11446271] **2652**

HSIN-CHIANG I SHU (CC) [11379195] **322**

HSIN-CHIANG MIN CHIEN WEN HSUEH (CC) [09300982] 2321, **3395**

HSIN-CHIANG NUNG YEH KO HSUEH / HSIN-CHIANG NUNG YEH KO HSUEH YUAN, HSIN-CHIANG PA I NUNG HSUEH YUAN (CH) [08779995] **93**

HSIN-CHIANG WEN HSUEH (CH) [08998088] **3395**

HSIN CHIAO YU (HK) [03283512] **1751**

HSIN HAI (CH) [09425438] **3395**

HSIN HSIN WEN CHOU KAN (CH) [19586936] **5799**

HSIN HUA WEN CHAI (CC) [08016011] **2504**

HSIN KANG (CC) [06660406] **3395**

HSIN KUAN CHA (HK) [01790393] **2504**

HSIN LI KO HSUEH (CC/1000-6648) [23954760] **4588**

HSIN SHIH HSUEH (CH) [23453249] **2620**

HSIN SHIH / LIEN-HO-KUO CHIAO KO WEN TSU CHIH (CH/0250-8869) [08832630] **4655**

HSIN SHU YUEH KAN (CH) [11446181] **4815**

HSIN TSUN (CH) [09005305] **3395**

HSIN WEN HSUEH SHIH LIAO (CC) [06520034] **3395**

HSIN WEN TA HSUEH (CH) [08882937] **2920**

HSIN WEN YEN CHIU TZU LIAO (CC) [06202373] **2920**

HSIN YA HSUEH SHU CHI KAN. NEW ASIA ACADEMIC BULLETIN (HK) [06064993] **2847**

HSIN YUEH HUA PAO (VM) [12889531] **5813**

HSING CHENG YUAN KUO CHIA KO HSUEH WEI YUAN HUI NIEN PAO (CH) [07870211] **5111**

HSING CHENG YUAN SO SHU KO CHI KUAN ... YEN CHIU FA CHAN CHENG KUO NIEN PAO / HSING CHENG YUAN YEN CHIU FA CHAN KAO HO WEI YUAN HUI PIEN (CH) [08372024] **4655**

HSING HO (HK) [02245554] **2504**

HSING HUO LIAO YUAN (CC) [10653286] **2652**

HSING HUO LIAO YUAN (SELECTIONS) (CC) [11123145] **2653**

HSING TA KUNG CHENG HSUEH PAO (CH/1017-4397) [24438454] **1977**

HSING-TAO LU YU (HK) [02280468] **5480**

HSIU TZU HSUEH HSI (CC) [09424267] **3286**

HSMAI MARKETING REVIEW (US/0746-9985) [10461496] **2807**

HSU CHAN YEN CHIU. JOURNAL OF THE TAIWAN LIVESTOCK RESEARCH (CH) [02638591] **212**

HSU-CHOU SHIH FAN HSUEH YUAN HSUEH PAO. CHE HSUEH SHE HUI KO HSUEH PAN XUZHOU SHIFAN XUEYUAN XUEBAO (CC) [10048756] **5231**

HSU MU SHOU I HSUEH PAO / CHUNG-KUO HSU MU SHOU I HSUEH HUI (CC/0529-5127) [03133788] **212, 5511**

HSU SHIH SHIH TSUNG KAN (CH) [10591874] **3464**

HSUEH HSI TSA CHIH (CH) [10669127] **4476**

HSUEH LI LUN (CC) [11418906] **5202**

HSUEH PAO. CHE HSUEH SHE HUI KO HSUEH PAN (CC) [11295333] **5202**

HSUEH PAO (SHAN-HSI TSAI CHING HSUEH YUAN) (CH) [08964721] **1592**

HSUEH PAO (SHAN-HSI TSAI CHING HSUEH YUAN, TAI-YUAN SHIH, CHINA) (CC) [11337393] **1592**

HSUEH PAO (SHAN-TUNG CHUNG I HSUEH YUAN) (CH) [08752083] **3585**

HSUEH PAO. SHE HUI KO HSUEH PAN (CC) [11294432] **1829**

HSUEH PAO (SSU-CHUAN TA HSUEH) (CC) [07427746] **5202**

HSUEH PAO. TZU JAN KO HSUEH PAN (CC) [19380162] **1977, 5111**

HSUEH PAO (WU-HAN KUNG HSUEH YUAN) (CC) [08924774] **5111**

HSUEH SHU CHI KAN (CC) [14089145] **5202**

HSUEH SHU YEN CHIU (CC) [06660459] **1751**

HSUEH SHU YEN TAO HUI PAO KAO (CH) [09611171] **93**

HSUS NEWS (US/1059-1621) [20079591] **226**

HTFS DIGEST (1987) (UK/0952-2654) [15601520] 2012, 4431, **2004**

HTM. HARTEREI-TECHNISCHE MITTEILUNGEN (GW/0341-101X) [I0341101X] **5111**

HU-NAN KAO KU CHI KAN / HU-NAN SHENG PO WU KUAN PIEN (CC) [10252446] **269**

HU-NAN LI SHIH TZU LIAO / HU-NAN LI SHIH TZU LIAN PIEN CHI SHIH (CC) [08693996] **2653**

HU-PEI CHIAO YU (CH) [08912583] **1751**

HU-PEI CHING NIEN (CH) [09844050] **2504**

HU-PEI WEN I *See* CHANG-CHIANG WEN I **317**

HU WAI SHENG HUO (CH) [08488867] **4873**

HUA CHENG (CC) [07130149] **3395**

HUA FAN FO HSUEH NIEN KAN (CH) [10066136] **5021**

HUA-HSI I KO TA HSUEH HSUEH PAO (CC/0257-7712) [14189591] **3585**

HUA HSIEH HUEI T'UNG HSIN (CN/0824-5851) [10785411] **2535**

HUA HSUEH. CHEMISTRY (CH/0441-3768) [01644102] **977**

HUA HSUEH HSUEH PAO (CC/0567-7351) [07038450] **977**

HUA HSUEH SHIH CHIEH (CC/0367-6358) [21237442] **977**

HUA HSUEH TUNG PAO / CHUNG-KUO HUA HSUEH HUI (CC/0441-3776) [02530271] **977**

HUA JEN YUEH KAN (HK) [11906315] **2504**

HUA-KANG LI KO HSUEH PAO (CH) [09842413] **5111**

HUA-KANG NUNG KO HSUEH PAO / CHUNG-KUO WEN HUA HSUEH YUAN NUNG HSUEH PU (CH) [09729132] **93**

HUA-KANG SHE HUI KO HSUEH PAO (CH) [10305983] **5202**

HUA PEI NUNG HSUEH PAO (CC/1000-7091) [24451440] **93**

HUA WEN ZA ZHI (US/1056-3873) [23740700] **2263**

HUADONG HUAGONG XUEYUAN XUEBAO (CC/0253-9683) [09270760] **1025**

HUAFU YOUBAO (US/0739-831X) [09813355] **5686**

HUAGONG JINZHAN (CC/1000-6613) [14037328] **2012**

HUAGONG JIXIE (CC/0254-6094) [10319327] **2013**

HUAGONG YEJIN (CH/1001-2052) [I10012052] 4003, **2013**

HUAGONG ZIDONGHUA JI YIBIAO (CC/1000-3932) [21767832] **2013**

HUAMAN RESOURCES AND PRACTICE AND IDEAS (US/1075-8321) [30053806] **869**

HUAN CHING KO HSUEH TSA CHIH (CH) [11492104] **2232**

HUANAN LIGONG DAXUE XUEBAO ZIRAN KEXUE BAN (CC/1000-565X) [I1000565X] **5111**

HUANG KUAN (CH) [01713589] **3395**

HUANG PO HAI HAI YANG (CC) [14277612] **1449**

HUANJING BAOHU (BEIJING) (CC/0253-9705) [09250726] 2173, **2232**

HUANJING HUAXUE (CC/0254-6108) [10331686] **2173**

HUANJING KEXUE (CC/0250-3301) [04392373] **2173**

HUANJING KEXUE XUEBAO (CC/0253-2468) [08873773] 2173, **1977**

HUANJING WURAN YU FANGZHI (CC/1001-3865) [21722336] **2232**

HUAXUE FANYING GONGCHENG YU GONGYI (CC/1001-7631) [21708131] **2013**

HUAXUE SHIJI (CH/0258-3283) [10377616] **5365**

HUAXUE YU ZHANHE (CC/1001-0017) [I10010017] **2013**

HUAYU KUAIBAO (US/0891-561X) [14970578] **5717**

HUB (HAY RIVER) (CN/0714-5810) [16766760] **2535**

HUBEI YIXUEYUAN XUEBAO (CC/1000-243X) [I1000243X] **3585**

HUD COMPUTERIZED PERSONNEL SYSTEMS USERS MANUAL *See* CRC SUBSYSTEM HANDBOOK **1661**

HUD INTERNATIONAL INFORMATION SERIES (US) [01559273] **2825**

HUD SALES CONNECTION, THE (US) [23448176] **2825**

HUDEBNI ROZHLEDY (XR/0018-6996) [02494315] **4121**

HUDEBNI VEDA (XR/0018-7003) [02407897] **4121**

HUDOBNY ARCHIV (XO) [03078406] **4121**

HUDOZESTVENNOE NASLEDIE (RU/0205-5295) [I02055295] **322**

HUDOZNIK (RU/0131-7555) [I01317555] **322**

HUDSON BAY POST REVIEW (CN) **5786**

HUDSON BAY ROUTE ASSOCIATION *See* ANNUAL CONVENTION OF THE HUDSON BAY ROUTE ASSOCIATION **5447**

HUDSON FAMILY ASSOCIATION (SOUTH) *See* BULLETIN - HUDSON FAMILY ASSOCIATION, SOUTH **2440**

HUDSON INSTITUTE *See* HUDSON INSTITUTE REPORT TO THE MEMBERS, THE **5111**

HUDSON INSTITUTE REPORT TO THE MEMBERS, THE (US/0073-3776) [02246885] **5111**

HUDSON REGISTER STAR (US) **5717**

HUDSON REVIEW, THE (US/0018-702X) [01639704] 3344, **322**

HUDSON STAR-OBSERVER (US/0749-7008) [01775800] **5768**

HUDSON VALLEY (US/0191-9288) [04826145] **2535**

HUDSON VALLEY BUSINESS JOURNAL (ORANGE COUNTY ED.) (US/1050-1096) [21397045] **680**

HUDSON VALLEY GREEN TIMES (US/0888-661X) [13707517] 1946, **2173**

HUDSON VALLEY REGIONAL REVIEW, THE (US/0742-2075) [10285928] **2847**

HUDSONIANA BULLETIN *See* BULLETIN - HUDSON FAMILY ASSOCIATION, SOUTH **2440**

HUDSON'S NEWSLETTER DIRECTORY *See* HUDSON'S SUBSCRIPTION NEWSLETTER DIRECTORY **4815**

HUDSON'S STATE CAPITALS DIRECTORY (US) **2565**

HUDSON'S STATE CAPITALS NEWS MEDIA CONTACTS DIRECTORY (US/0885-1328) [12173643] **1133**

HUDSON'S SUBSCRIPTION NEWSLETTER DIRECTORY (US/1046-8110) [20071925] **2488**

HUDSON'S SUBSCRIPTION NEWSLETTER DIRECTORY (US) **4815**

HUDSON'S WASHINGTON NEWS MEDIA CONTACTS DIRECTORY (US/0441-389X) [02166135] **2920**

HUDSPETH COUNTY HERALD AND DELL VALLEY RREVIEW (US) [14175453] **5751**

HUDSPETH REPORT, THE (US/0896-7296) [17283690] **5480**

HUELLAS : REVISTA DE LA UNIVERSIDAD DEL NORTE (CK/0120-2537) [27415078] **1092**

HUENEFELD REPORT (US) **4815**

HUERFANO (US) [03295971] **5288**

HUESO HUMERO (PE) [04273357] 3464, **322**

HUFACT QUARTERLY *SUSPENDED.* (US/0893-3529) [15493872] 300, **1977**

HUFVUDSTADSBLADET (FI/0356-0724) [03560724] **5800**

HUGH LE CAINE PROJECT NEWSLETTER, THE (CN/0229-6659) [08071024] **4121**

HUGHES ESTATE, SUMMARY OF PROBATE PROCEEDINGS (US/0145-6083) [02766464] **2979**

HUGHES FAMILY LETTER (US/0747-5675) [10738063] **2454**

HUGHSTON HEALTH ALERT (US/1070-7778) [21440148] **3954**

HUGIN, LOKALHISTORISK TIDSSKRIFT FOR EGEBJERG KOMMUNE (DK) [03634865] **2692**

HUGO DAILY NEWS, THE (US) [13676420] **5732**

HUGUENOT HISTORIAN, THE (US/0199-9583) [06283472] **2738**

HUGUENOT SOCIETY OF GREAT BRITAIN AND IRELAND *See* PROCEEDINGS OF THE HUGUENOT SOCIETY OF GREAT BRITAIN AND IRELAND **5066**

HUGUENOT SOCIETY OF SOUTH CAROLINA *See* TRANSACTIONS OF THE HUGUENOT SOCIETY OF SOUTH CAROLINA **5237**

HUGUENOT TRAILS (CN/0441-6910) [02029199] **2454**

HUI YUAN MING LU (SI) [05341468] **820**

HUIBAO - TAIWAN UMU SHOUYI XUEHUI (CH/0253-9128) [01799780] **5511**

HUISARTS & PRAKTIJK (NE/0165-7054) [03720007] **3738**

HUISARTS EN WETENSCHAP (NE/0018-7070) [I00187070] **3585**

HUISARTS NU : MAANDBLAD VAN DE WETENSCHAPPELIJKE VERENIGING DER VLAAMSE HUISARTSEN : HANU (BE/0775-0501) [13104254] **3738**

HUISGENOOT, DIE (SA) [08804223] **5810**

HUKUM (IO) [02651110] **2979**

HUKUM DAN PEMBANGUNAN (IO) [03826964] **2979**

HUKUM NASIONAL (IO) [02801912] **2979**

HULBERT FINANCIAL DIGEST, THE (US/1042-4261) [17010148] **900**

HULL CLAIMS ANALYSIS (UK/0265-5934) [14764676] **2882**

HULL MONOGRAPHS ON SOUTH-EAST ASIA (UK) [06748934] **2653**

HUMA (TEHRAN, IRAN) (IR) [12087453] **2504**

HUMAN AFFAIRS (CN/0714-4873) [09313105] **5202**

HUMAN & EXPERIMENTAL TOXICOLOGY (UK/0960-3271) [21307548] **3981**

HUMAN — Alphabetical Title Index

HUMAN ANTIBODIES AND HYBRIDOMAS (US/0956-960X) [22143642] **457**

HUMAN BEHAVIOR AND ENVIRONMENT (US/0148-8686) [02954472] 4588, **5247**

HUMAN BIOLOGY (US/0018-7143) [01752384] 237, **457**

●HUMAN BRAIN MAPPING (US/1065-9471) [26813384] **3833**

HUMAN CAPITAL *SUSPENDED.* (US/1043-8998) [19596927] **869**

HUMAN CELL : OFFICIAL JOURNAL OF HUMAN CELL RESEARCH SOCIETY (JA/0914-7470) [20055105] **537**

HUMAN COMMUNICATION AND ITS DISORDERS (NORWOOD, N.J.) (US/1046-7599) [17009620] 3286, **1112**

HUMAN COMMUNICATION RESEARCH (US/0360-3989) [01875171] **1112**

HUMAN-COMPUTER INTERACTION (US/0737-0024) [09287660] 4588, **1186**

HUMAN DEVELOPMENT (SZ/0018-716X) [01641127] 237, **4588**

HUMAN DEVELOPMENT (GUILFORD, CT.) (US/0278-4661) [06697884] **4589**

HUMAN DEVELOPMENT (NEW YORK) (US/0197-3096) [06006051] 4963, **4589**

HUMAN ECOLOGIST, THE (US/8755-7878) [11423149] **5202**

HUMAN ECOLOGY & ENERGY BALANCING SCIENTIST, THE (US/1045-2729) [20073625] 5111, **4783**

HUMAN ECOLOGY FORUM (US/0018-7178) [01607768] **2216**

HUMAN ETHOLOGY NEWSLETTER (US/0739-2036) [09718528] 457, 4589, **237**

HUMAN EVENTS (WASHINGTON) (US/0018-7194) [02228324] **4476**

HUMAN EVOLUTION (IT/0393-9375) [13882564] 457, **237**

HUMAN FACTORS (US/0018-7208) [01329271] **1251**

HUMAN FACTORS AND ERGONOMICS SOCIETY. MEETING *See* PROCEEDINGS OF THE HUMAN FACTORS AND ERGONOMICS SOCIETY ... ANNUAL MEETING **2125**

HUMAN FACTORS BULLETIN *See* FSF HUMAN FACTORS BULLETIN & AVIATION MEDICINE **22**

HUMAN FACTORS SOCIETY *See* BULLETIN - HUMAN FACTORS SOCIETY **1250**

HUMAN FACTORS SOCIETY *See* DIRECTORY AND YEARBOOK - HUMAN FACTORS SOCIETY **1970**

HUMAN FACTORS SOCIETY *See* PROCEEDINGS OF THE HUMAN FACTORS SOCIETY ANNUAL MEETING **2125**

HUMAN FACTORS SOCIETY. BULLETIN - HUMAN FACTORS SOCIETY *See* BULLETIN / HUMAN FACTORS AND ERGONOMICS SOCIETY **1250**

HUMAN FACTORS SOCIETY. PROCEEDINGS OF THE HUMAN FACTORS SOCIETY ANNUAL MEETING *See* PROCEEDINGS OF THE HUMAN FACTORS AND ERGONOMICS SOCIETY ... ANNUAL MEETING **2125**

HUMAN GENE THERAPY (US/1043-0342) [19283546] **547**

HUMAN GENETICS (GW/0340-6717) [02699217] **547**

HUMAN GENETICS. SUPPLEMENT (ROCKVILLE) (US/0197-8160) [06114485] **547**

HUMAN GENOME ABSTRACTS (US/1045-4470) [20113728] 547, **478**

HUMAN GENOME NEWS (US/1050-6101) [21569225] **547**

HUMAN HEREDITY (SZ/0001-5652) [01752389] **547**

HUMAN IMMUNOLOGY (US/0198-8859) [06272568] **3670**

HUMAN LIFE REVIEW, THE (US/0097-9783) [01799422] **589**

HUMAN LYMPHOCYTE DIFFERENTIATION (UK/0144-3909) [06374467] **537**

●HUMAN MOLECULAR GENETICS (UK/0964-6906) [25594670] 488, **547**

HUMAN MOSAIC (US/0018-7240) [02246041] 237, **5247**

HUMAN MOVEMENT SCIENCE (NE/0167-9457) [08857527] **5202**

●HUMAN MUTATION (US/1059-7794) [24767962] **547**

HUMAN NATURE (HAWTHORNE, N.Y.) (US/1045-6767) [20187035] **2847**

HUMAN ORGANIZATION (US/0018-7259) [04970693] **237**

HUMAN PATHOLOGY (US/0046-8177) [01752392] **3895**

HUMAN PERFORMANCE (US/0895-9285) [16854846] **4589**

HUMAN PERFORMANCE REPORTS (1960) (UK/0461-5905) [18525013] **4589**

HUMAN PHYSIOLOGY (US/0362-1197) [02302497] **581**

HUMAN POWER (US/0898-6908) [17884008] **1977**

HUMAN PSYCHOPHARMACOLOGY (UK/0885-6222) [12681804] 4589, **4307**

HUMAN QUEST (US/0897-8786) [20851560] **4963**

HUMAN RELATIONS AREA FILES, INC *See* HRAF NEWSLETTER **5202**

HUMAN RELATIONS (NEW YORK) (US/0018-7267) [01752393] **5202**

HUMAN REPRODUCTION (OXFORD) (UK/0268-1161) [13829792] **541**

HUMAN REPRODUCTION UPDATE (UK/1355-4786) **581**

HUMAN REPRODUCTIVE MEDICINE (NE/0165-7100) [03999808] **3762**

HUMAN RESEARCH REPORT (US/0885-0615) [12561295] 2251, **3585**

HUMAN RESOURCE ADVISOR *See* HUMAN RESOURCE BRIEFINGS **869**

HUMAN RESOURCE BRIEFINGS (US) **869**

HUMAN RESOURCE DEVELOPMENT JOURNAL *SUSPENDED.* (PH) [03574184] **1677**

HUMAN RESOURCE DEVELOPMENT QUARTERLY (US/1044-8004) [19906481] **941**

HUMAN RESOURCE EXECUTIVE (US/1040-0443) [16069021] **941**

HUMAN RESOURCE LINE, THE (US/1058-5001) [24316516] **1677**

HUMAN RESOURCE MANAGEMENT (SA/1010-8092) [I10108092] **941**

HUMAN RESOURCE MANAGEMENT (US/0090-4848) [01201641] **941**

HUMAN RESOURCE MANAGEMENT JOURNAL (UK/0954-5395) [23131787] **942**

HUMAN RESOURCE MANAGEMENT NEWS (US) [10864685] **942**

HUMAN RESOURCE MANAGEMENT REVIEW (US/1053-4822) [22538329] **942**

HUMAN RESOURCE MANAGEMENT YEARBOOK, THE (UK) [19715584] **942**

HUMAN RESOURCE PLANNING (US/0199-8986) [06281631] **942**

HUMAN RESOURCE REPORT (AT) **942**

HUMAN RESOURCES (US) [18661596] **1677**

HUMAN RESOURCES ABSTRACTS (US/0099-2453) [02241815] 1677, 5288, **1533**

HUMAN RESOURCES AND SERVICES, DIRECTORY (US) [03276911] **5288**

HUMAN RESOURCES BRIEFING (US/1051-3760) [21322504] 1677, **942**

●HUMAN RESOURCES FORECAST (US/1066-2758) [26912080] **942**

HUMAN RESOURCES INTERNATIONAL (IE/0791-847X) **942**

HUMAN RESOURCES; MANAGEMENT AND STRATEGY (UK) **942**

HUMAN RESOURCES MANAGEMENT INTERNATIONAL DIGEST (UK) [I09670734] **942**

HUMAN RESOURCES MANAGEMENT. PERSONNEL PRACTICES/COMMUNICATIONS (US/0745-0621) [08794681] **942**

HUMAN RESOURCES NEWS (AT) **942**

HUMAN RESOURCES NEWSLETTER *CEASED.* (US/0883-0851) [12041526] **942**

HUMAN RESOURCES PROFESSIONAL (CN/0847-9453) [20787188] **942**

HUMAN RESOURCES PROFESSIONAL (NEW YORK, N.Y.), THE (US/1040-5232) [18436346] **942**

HUMAN RESOURCES YEARBOOK (US/0887-5316) [13294833] **942**

HUMAN RIGHTS (US/0273-2521) [06941597] **4508**

HUMAN RIGHTS BULLETIN (US) [24614067] **4508**

HUMAN RIGHTS BULLETIN (BERKELEY, CALIF.) (US/1041-5866) [17976572] **4508**

HUMAN RIGHTS CANBERRA (AT/0729-2716) [I07292716] **4508**

HUMAN RIGHTS CASE DIGEST (UK) [24620909] **4508**

HUMAN RIGHTS (CHICAGO, ILL.) (US/0046-8185) [01752394] 4508, **2979**

HUMAN RIGHTS COMMISSION OF BRITISH COLUMBIA *See* NEWSLETTER - HUMAN RIGHTS COMMISSION OF BRITISH COLUMBIA **4511**

HUMAN RIGHTS DIRECTORY WESTERN EUROPE (US/0732-0906) [08301639] **4508**

HUMAN RIGHTS IN SWEDEN (US/1044-193X) [16411665] **4509**

HUMAN RIGHTS, INFORMATION SHEET (FR) [09268537] **4509**

HUMAN RIGHTS INTERNET REPORTER (US/0275-049X) [06938307] 4476, 4509, **4502**

HUMAN RIGHTS LAW JOURNAL : HRLJ (GW/0174-4704) [07343144] 4509, **3129**

HUMAN RIGHTS (MONTREAL) (CN/0711-2122) [08730720] **4509**

HUMAN RIGHTS (MONTREAL) (CN/0711-2122) [16850998] **4509**

HUMAN RIGHTS ORGANIZATIONS & PERIODICALS DIRECTORY *CEASED.* (US/0098-0579) [01790837] **4509**

HUMAN RIGHTS QUARTERLY (US/0275-0392) [07070148] **4509**

HUMAN RIGHTS TEACHING / UNESCO (FR) [08570585] **4509**

HUMAN RIGHTS TRIBUNE *See* CHINA RIGHTS FORUM **4505**

●HUMAN RIGHTS TRIBUNE (OTTAWA) (CN/1188-6226) [25527562] **4509**

HUMAN RIGHTS UPDATE (CHICAGO, ILL.) (US/0792-7797) [22711958] **4509**

HUMAN RIGHTS UPDATE / JAMAICA COUNCIL FOR HUMAN RIGHTS (JM) [15114698] **4509**

HUMAN RIGHTS UPDATES & ALERTS (US) **4509**

●HUMAN RIGHTS WATCH/AMERICAS (US/1077-6710) [30486545] **4509**

HUMAN RIGHTS WATCH QUARTERLY NEWSLETTER (US) [27836152] **4509**

HUMAN RIGHTS WATCH WORLD REPORT (US/1054-948X) [23031425] **4509**

HUMAN RIGHTS WORKING PAPER (CK) [25265268] **4509**

HUMAN SCIENCES RESEARCH COUNCIL. INSTITUTE FOR INFORMATION AND SPECIAL SERVICES *See* EDUCATION OF WHITES IN THE REPUBLIC OF SOUTH AFRICA, THE **1740**

HUMAN SERVICE BUSINESS JOURNAL *See* HUMAN SERVICE MONEY SOURCE **5288**

HUMAN SERVICE EDUCATION (US/0890-5428) [14263475] **1751**

HUMAN SERVICE MONEY SOURCE (US) **5288**

HUMAN SERVICE YELLOW PAGES OF MASSACHUSETTS (US/1051-5844) [19037401] **5288**

HUMAN SERVICE YELLOW PAGES OF MASSACHUSETTS & RHODE ISLAND (US) **5288**

●HUMAN SERVICE YELLOW PAGES OF MASSACHUSETTS & RHODE ISLAND (US) [29395549] **5288**

HUMAN SERVICE YELLOW PAGES OF RHODE ISLAND *See* HUMAN SERVICE YELLOW PAGES OF MASSACHUSETTS & RHODE ISLAND **5288**

HUMAN SERVICES IN THE RURAL ENVIRONMENT (US/0193-9009) [04126243] **5288**

HUMAN SERVICES MONOGRAPH SERIES (PROJECT SHARE) (US) [03342471] **5288**

HUMAN SERVICES NEWS (US) [05387725] **5288**

HUMAN SERVICES (WOODHAVEN, N.Y.) (US/0745-2616) [09009565] **5288**

HUMAN SEXUALITY (US) [06536555] **5187**

HUMAN SEXUALITY (UK/0142-811X) [I0142811X] 457, **3585**

HUMAN SIDE OF SUPERVISION (US) **870**

HUMAN STRESS (US/0885-1174) [12565637] 581, **4589**

HUMAN STUDIES (NE/0163-8548) [03946108] **4348**

HUMAN SYSTEMS MANAGEMENT (NE/0167-2533) [06176184] **5111**

HUMAN/TECHNOLOGY INTERACTION IN COMPLEX SYSTEMS (US) 870, **5111**

HUMAN, THE (CN/0711-7388) [08559660] **589**

HUMANA CIVILITAS (US/0742-115X) [06415823] **2847**

●HUMANE INNOVATIONS AND ALTERNATIVES (US/1062-4805) [25637372] **226**

HUMANE MEDICINE (CN/0828-7090) [12670449] **3585**

HUMANE TRAPPING PROGRAM *See* HUMANE TRAPPING PROGRAM ANNUAL REPORT **226**

HUMANE TRAPPING PROGRAM ANNUAL REPORT (CN/1184-1524) [23259446] **226**

HUMANIDADES (BRASILIA, BRAZIL) (BL/0102-9479) [10259362] **5231**

HUMANIORA (COPENHAGEN, DENMARK : 1988) (DK/0903-2401) [18733735] **2847**

HUMANISME (FR) [06802347] **5288**

HUMANISMUS UND TECHNIK (GW/0439-884X) [08693923] 2847, **2620**

HUMANIST ALMANAC AND DATEBOOK, A (US/1052-5203) [22295926] **4348**

HUMANIST (BUFFALO, N.Y.), THE (US/0018-7399) [01587384] **4348**

HUMANIST IN CANADA (CN) [02029218] **4348**

HUMANIST OUTLOOK (II/0018-7429) [02255718] **4348**

HUMANISTIC JUDAISM (US/0441-4195) [07779394] 4348, **5048**

●HUMANISTIC MATHEMATICS NETWORK JOURNAL (US/1065-8297) [26059308] **3508**

HUMANISTIC PSYCHOLOGIST, THE (US/0887-3267) [13210734] **4589**

HUMANISTICA LOVANIENSIA (BE/0774-2908) [01781417] **3286**

HUMANISTISCHE BIBLIOTHEK. REIHE III: SKRIPTEN (GW) [02123477] **2847**

HUMANISTISCHE GYMNASIUM *See* GYMNASIUM (HEIDELBERG) **1077**

HUMANITAS BERLIN, DDR *CEASED.* (GW/0018-7445) [00187445] **2847**

HUMANITAS (BRESCIA, ITALY) (IT) [01988912] 5030, **4348**

HUMANITAS (COIMBRA) (PO) [02098491] **3286**

HUMANITE (MONTREAL) (CN/0712-2780) [08808153] **5288**

HUMANITE PARIS, L' (FR/0242-6870) [02426870] **2847**

HUMANITIES ASSOCIATION OF CANADA NEWSLETTER (CN/0229-4699) [08311751] **2847**

HUMANITIES EDUCATION (US/0882-5475) [11891002] **2847**

HUMANITIES IN THE SOUTH (US/0018-7577) [02130615] **2847**

HUMANITIES INDEX (US/0095-5981) [02244583] 2847, **2857**

HUMANITIES INDEX. CD-ROM (US/0095-5981) **2847**

HUMANITIES INDEX (CD-ROM ED.) (US/1063-3294) [22294297] **2857**

●HUMANITIES SOURCE (US/1073-1962) [29354668] 2847, **2857**

HUMANITIES (WASHINGTON) (US/0018-7526) [05918184] **2847**

HUMANITY & SOCIETY (US/0160-5976) [03695809] **5247**

HUMANIZACJA PRACY (PL/0137-3013) [03409668] **1608**

HUMANOMICS (UK/0828-8666) [18931437] **1608**

HUMBER COLLEGE OF APPLIED ARTS AND TECHNOLOGY *See* MULTI-YEAR PLAN - HUMBER COLLEGE OF APPLIED ARTS AND TECHNOLOGY **1836**

HUMBER COLLEGE OF APPLIED ARTS AND TECHNOLOGY. CENTRE FOR WOMEN *See* NEWSMAGAZINE - CENTRE FOR WOMEN. HUMBER COLLEGE OF APPLIED ARTS AND TECHNOLOGY. CENTRE FOR CONTINUOUS LEARNING **1838**

HUMBER HIGHLIGHTS (CN/0821-2465) [09506607] **3786**

HUMBER MAGAZINE WORLD (CN/0711-3269) [08605162] **4815**

HUMBLE ECHO, THE (US) [17473767] **5751**

HUMBOLDT BEACON AND FORTUNA ADVANCE, THE (US/0746-777X) [10261698] **5635**

HUMBOLDT JOURNAL OF SOCIAL RELATIONS (US/0160-4341) [01082933] **5202**

HUMBOLDT (PORTUGIESISCHE AUSGABE) (GW/0018-7623) [01795763] **2517**

HUMBOLDT SPANISCHE AUSGABE (GW/0018-7615) [00187615] **2847**

HUMBOLDT SUN (US) [13775980] **5707**

HUME PAPERS ON PUBLIC POLICY (UK) **4655**

HUME STUDIES (US/0319-7336) [02442960] **4348**

HUMMER, THE (US/0199-2708) [05744986] **4851**

HUMOR (IO/0852-8225) [23093900] **3395**

HUMOR AND CARTOON MARKETS *CEASED.* (US/1043-240X) [19359190] **380**

HUMOR (BERLIN, GERMANY) (GW/0933-1719) [18129584] **4589**

HUMOR GRAPHIC (IT) [11377866] **4862**

HUMOR INTERIOR (AG) [11802405] **2488**

HUMORESQUES (FR/0996-9942) [22913972] **3344**

HUMPTY DUMPTY'S MAGAZINE (US/0273-7590) [06903786] **1064**

HUMUS (BL) [01791085] **1751**

HUN NING TU CHI CHIA CHIN HUN NING TU (CC) [11631975] **2024**

HUNAN DAXUE XUEBAO (CC/1001-943X) [21708239] **1092**

HUNAN SHIFAN DAXUE XUEBAO (ZIRAN KEXUE BAN) (CC/1000-2537) [18994427] **5111**

HUNAN YIKE DAXUE XUEBAO (CC/1000-5625) [21979240] **3585**

HUNAR VA MIMARI. ART AND ARCHITECTURE (IR) [06629148] 352, **300**

HUNG CHI (US) [05430628] **4476**

HUNGARIAN AGRICULTURAL ENGINEERING (HU/0864-7410) [08647410] **93**

●HUNGARIAN AGRICULTURAL RESEARCH / MINISTRY OF AGRICULTURE, HUNGARY (HU/1216-4526) [27920442] **93**

HUNGARIAN BUSINESS BRIEF (UK) **680**

HUNGARIAN BUSINESS HERALD : HBH : QUARTERLY REVIEW OF THE HUNGARIAN CHAMBER OF COMMERCE (HU) [12361819] **820**

HUNGARIAN CINEMA (HU) [21289998] **4072**

HUNGARIAN ECONOMIC REVIEW : HER (HU/1215-2439) [24401518] 1494, **839**

HUNGARIAN ECONOMY (BUDAPEST. 1972), THE (HU/0133-0365) [02255039] **1566**

HUNGARIAN FOREIGN TRADE (FR/0018-7747) [01939859] **1635**

HUNGARIAN HERITAGE REVIEW (US/0889-2695) [13240456] **2263**

HUNGARIAN INSTITUTE OF INTERNATIONAL AFFAIRS *See* POLICY PAPERS **4532**

HUNGARIAN JOURNAL OF INDUSTRIAL CHEMISTRY (HU/0133-0276) [05691602] **977**

HUNGARIAN LAW REVIEW (HU) [01696508] **2979**

HUNGARIAN LIBRARY AND INFORMATION SCIENCE ABSTRACTS (HU/0046-8304) [01423321] 3213, **3258**

HUNGARIAN MARKET REPORT (HU/0865-8579) [25638019] **1494**

HUNGARIAN MUSIC QUARTERLY *CEASED.* (HU/0238-9401) [19841040] **4121**

HUNGARIAN OBSERVER, THE (HU/0238-9932) [19621862] **2488**

●HUNGARIAN QUARTERLY, THE (HU) [28135576] **3395**

HUNGARIAN STATISTICAL YEARBOOK / HUNGARIAN CENTRAL STATISTICAL OFFICE (HU) [25403587] **5328**

HUNGARIAN STUDIES : HS (HU/0236-6568) [12616916] **2692**

HUNGARIAN STUDIES IN ENGLISH : HSE (HU) [28763021] **3395**

HUNGARIAN STUDIES NEWSLETTER (US/0194-164X) [01680865] **2692**

HUNGARIAN STUDIES REVIEW (CN/0713-8083) [09639231] **2692**

HUNGARIKA IRODALMI SZEMLE (HU) [03719474] **2692**

HUNGARY. KOHO- ES GEPIPARI MINISZTERIUM. TERVEZO IRODAI *See* K.G.M.T.I. KOZLEMENYEI **1984**

HUNGARY. KOZLEKEDES- ES POSTAUGYI MINISZTERIUM. VASUTI FOOSZTALY *See* NEMZETKOZI VASUTI OESSZEKOETTETESEK KIVONATOS MENETRENDJE **5433**

HUNGARY. KOZPONTI STATISZTIKAI HIVATAL *See* STATISZTIKAI HAVI KOZLEMENYEK **5344**

HUNGARY. KOZPONTI STATISZTIKAI HIVATAL *See* STATISZTIKAI SZEMLE **1540**

HUNGARY. KOZPONTI STATISZTIKAI HIVATAL. ARES MODSZERTANI OSZTALY *See* KISKERESKEDELMI ARALAKULAS **1593**

HUNGARY. KOZPONTI STATISZTIKAI HIVATAL. BERUHAZASI ES EPITOIPARI STATISZTIKAI FOOSZTALY *See* EPITOIPARI ARAK ALAKULASA, AZ **614**

HUNGARY. KOZPONTI STATISZTIKAI HIVATAL. BERUHAZASIES EPITOIPARI STATISZTIKAI FOOSZTALY *See* BERUHAZASI, EPITOIPARI, LAKASEPITESI ZSEBKONYV **600**

HUNGARY. KOZPONTI STATISZTIKAI HIVATAL. IPARGAZDASAGI OSZTALY *See* IPARI TERMELES SZERKEZETENEK ALAKULASA, AZ **1568**

HUNGARY. KOZPONTI STATISZTIKAI HIVATAL. KOHO- ES GEPIPARI OSZTALY *See* ANYAMOZGATAS GEPESITESE A GEPIPARBAN, AZ **1598**

HUNGARY. KOZPONTI STATISZTIKAI HIVATAL KOMMUNALIS ES IGAZGATASI SZOLGALTATASOK STATISZTIKAI OSZTALAYA *See* KORNYEZETSTATISZTIKAI ADATGYUJTEMENY **2176**

HUNGARY. KPZPONTI STATISZTIKAI HIVATAL. IDEGENFORGALMI OSZTALY *See* IDEGENFORGALMI **5480**

HUNGARY, STATISTICAL DATA / CENTRAL STATISTICAL OFFICE OF HUNGARY (HU/0230-5755) [07632889] **5328**

HUNGARY. TERMELOSZOVETKEZETEK ORSZAGOS TANACSA *See* MEZOGAZDASAGI SZOVETKEZETEK GAZDALKODASA A SZAMOK TUKREBEN **108**

HUNGARY UNDER SOVIET RULE (US) [01679222] **2692**

HUNGATE (US/0147-2364) [03132200] **2454**

HUNGER NOTES (US) [07062923] **5288**

HUNGER NOTES (US/0740-1116) [06849972] **2910**

HUNGER PROJECT PAPERS, THE (US/0743-6416) [10630907] **5288**

HUNGRY HORSE NEWS (US) [11227489] **5705**

HUNGRY MIND REVIEW (US/0887-5499) [13291726] **4829**

●HUNGRY POET, THE (US/1065-6421) [26661595] **3464**

HUNT (US) **4873**

HUNT INSTITUTE FOR BOTANICAL DOCUMENTATION *See* BULLETIN OF THE HUNT INSTITUTE FOR BOTANICAL DOCUMENTATION **505**

HUNT PETRO INFORMATION *See* GULF OF MEXICO DRILLING REPORT **1608**

●HUNT-SCANLON'S EXECUTIVE RECRUITERS OF NORTH AMERICA (US/1063-1143) [25866563] **4204**

HUNTER & SPORT HORSE (US/1057-8501) [24130100] **2800**

HUNTER CASUALTY REPORT / ARKANSAS GAME AND FISH COMMISSION (US) [07667079] 4873, **4856**

HUNTER EDUCATION NEWS (PETERBOROUGH) (CN/0846-104X) [24256945] **4873**

HUNTER SAFETY INSTRUCTOR (US/0737-6227) [09450411] **4899**

HUNTERDON COUNTY DEMOCRAT (US/0018-7844) [04094634] **5710**

HUNTERDON REVIEW AND THE HIGH BRIDGE GAZETTE (US/0746-3863) [10012916] **5710**

HUNTERDON REVIEW (LEBANON, N.J.) (US/1059-8715) [24798697] **5710**

HUNTERS FRONTIER TIMES (US) **4873**

HUNTER'S HORN, THE (US/0018-7860) [04094638] **4899**

HUNTIA (US/0073-4071) [02447473] **513**

●HUNTING HORIZONS (US/1059-3837) [24601491] **4873**

HUNTING (NEW YORK, N.Y.) (US/0276-8895) [07426924] **4899**

HUNTING REGULATIONS (US) [03316974] **4873**

HUNTING RETRIEVER (US/8750-6629) [11641551] **4873**

●HUNTING TRIP MAGAZINE (US/1060-5452) [25032678] **4873**

HUNTINGTON BEACH INDEPENDENT (US/0194-6021) [04872611] **5635**

HUNTINGTON LIBRARY PUBLICATIONS (US) [02079534] **3213**

HUNTINGTON LIBRARY QUARTERLY, THE (US/0018-7895) [01752421] 3395, **352**

HUNTSMAN MARINE LABORATORY *See* HML NEWS **457**

HUNTSMAN MARINE SCIENCE NEWS (CN/0843-5340) [19752357] **1449**

HUNTSVILLE ASSOCIATION OF FOLK MUSICIANS *See* NEWSLETTER - HUNTSVILLE ASSOCIATION OF FOLK MUSICIANS **4141**

HUNTSVILLE HISTORICAL REVIEW, THE (US/1048-3152) [07993191] **2738**

HUNTSVILLE ITEM, THE (US/0888-4145) [10263733] **5751**

HUNTSVILLE LETTER, THE *CEASED.* (US/0887-3747) [13227232] **1494**

HUNTSVILLE NEWS (US) [11832200] **5627**

HUNTSVILLE TIMES, THE (US) [02665831] **5627**

HUOLTOAPU (FI/0355-4759) [03880753] **5288**

HUONEKALU- JA MUU TEOLLISUUS (FI/0786-003X) [19862472] **2906**

HUQUQUK (MR) [12119189] **2979**

HURDY GURDY (US/0191-6785) [04936843] **4121**

HURON DAILY PLAINSMAN (US) [12862498] **5743**

HURON HISTORICAL NOTES (CN/0822-9503) [02247387] **2738**

HURON REVIEW (US) [03296043] **3344**

HURON SOIL AND CROP NEWS (1964) (CN/0319-6038) [02442999] **173**

●HURONIA YEARLY VACATION PLANNER (CN/1189-3001) [25882700] **5480**

HURRICANE ALICE (US/0882-7907) [10741971] **5558**

HURRICANE BREEZE (US) [13196253] **5764**

HURRICANE RESEARCH DIVISION FISCAL YEAR ... PROGRAMS, FISCAL YEAR ... PROJECTIONS (US) [11134824] **1426**

HURRIYAH (BEIRUT, LEBANON : 1981) (LE) [08213736] **2653**

HURRIYAH (NICOSIA, CYPRUS) (CY) [11790863] **2653**

HURRIYET INSANLAR, OLAYLAR, SAYLARYLA ... YLLG (TU) [17959472] **1926**

HUSDJUR : SVENSK HUSDJURSSKOTSEL, LADUGARDEN (SW/0046-8339) [09809314] **212**

HUSKY FEVER (CN/0715-495X) [09543090] **4899**

HUSMODERN (SW/0018-8026) [01587512] **5558**

HUSSERL STUDIES (NE/0167-9848) [10331466] **4348**

HUSSERLIANA DEN HAAG (NE/0923-4128) [l09234128] **4349**

HUSTLER (COLUMBUS) (US/0149-4635) [03487803] **3995**

HUSTLER HUMOR (US/0199-5405) [05978460] **3995**

HUSTLER, THE (US/1074-0236) [29579502] **760**

HUTCHINSON LEADER (US) [01645827] **5696**

HUTCHINSON NEWS (HUTCHINSON, KAN. : 1957) (US) [08814408] **5676**

HUTCHINSON RECORD, THE (US) [12362585] **5676**

HUTHE PAPERS ON PUBLIC POLICY (UK/1350-7516) **4655**

HUTNICKE LISTY (XR/0018-8069) [02447474] **4003**

HUTNIK (KATOWICE) (PL/0018-8077) [02447476] **4003**

HUTNIK (WARSZAWA) See HUTNIK, WIADOMOSCI HUTNICZE **4003**

HUTNIK, WIADOMOSCI HUTNICZE (PL/1230-3534) [l12303534] **4003**

HUTOIPAR (HU/0018-8085) [04026449] 2605, **2343**

HUTTON CONSTRUCTION CATALOG : MECHANICAL PRODUCTS (US/0737-6316) [09159815] **2115**

HUWA WA-HIYA (CY/0250-6343) [05912610] 1297, **1064**

HUWELIKE EN EGSKEIDINGS / REPUBLIEK VAN SUID-AFRIKA, SENTRALE STATISTIEKDIENS / MARRIAGES AND DIVORCES / REPUBLIC OF SOUTH AFRICA, CENTRAL STATISTICAL SERVICE (SA) [30686078] 2281, **4553**

HUXFORD GENEALOGICAL SOCIETY See MAGAZINE / HUXFORD GENEALOGICAL SOCIETY, INC **2459**

HVAC DUCT CONSTRUCTION STANDARDS. (METAL & FLEXIBLE) (US) **4003**

HVAC PRODUCT NEWS (US/0887-445X) [13229814] **2605**

HVAC PROFITMAKER (US/0899-9791) [18302381] 790, **2605**

HVEDEKORN (DK/0018-8093) [01752433] 352, **3464**

HVEM ER HVEM? (NO) [01752434] **432**

HWAHAE (GW) [11203143] **4964**

HWAHAK KWA HWAHAK KONGOP (KO) [06517682] **2013**

HWAHAK KWA KONGOP UI CHINBO See HWAHAK SEGYE: CHEMWORLD **977**

HWAHAK KYOYUK. CHEMICAL EDUCATION (KO/0304-5277) [04507555] **977**

●HWAHAK SEGYE: CHEMWORLD (KO) [25838360] **977**

HWAHWE HYOPHOE PO (KO) [10265825] **2435**

HWANGTO / HWANGTO SI TONGIN (KO) [11172640] **3464**

HWANGYONG KWA KONGHAE (KO) [09328970] **2232**

HWANGYONG POJON (KO) [10009842] **2232**

HWANGYONG YONGU (KO) [09205388] **2232**

HWASUL (KO) [10048434] **3286**

HYBRID CIRCUIT TECHNOLOGY (US/0747-1599) [10621104] **5111**

HYBRID CIRCUITS See MICROELECTRONICS INTERNATIONAL **2072**

HYBRID CIRCUITS : JOURNAL OF THE INTERNATIONAL SOCIETY FOR HYBRID MICROELECTRONICS-UK / INTERNATIONAL SOCIETY FOR HYBRID ELECTRONICS, UNITED KINGDOM (UK/0265-3028) [11280822] **2056**

HYBRID GRAIN SORGHUM YIELD RESULTS (AT/0815-7383) [19576645] **173**

HYBRIDOMA (US/0272-457X) [06842358] 537, **3670**

HYBRIDOMA PROFILES (US/0732-1368) [08256500] **547**

HYBRIDS (JA/0914-2568) [l09142568] 547, **513**

HYDATA NEWS AND VIEWS (US) [16519609] **5534**

HYDE PARK TRIBUNE, THE MATTAPAN TRIBUNE (US/0745-9262) [09612824] **5689**

HYDINARSTVO (XO/0139-8822) [03785602] **212**

HYDRAULIC RESEARCH IN THE UNITED STATES AND CANADA (US/0094-1832) [01793242] **2090**

HYDRAULICS AND HYDROLOGY SERIES (US/0730-9678) [07428408] 1414, **2090**

HYDRAULICS & PNEUMATICS (US/0018-814X) [01752437] **2090**

HYDRAULICS PAPERS (US/0069-6102) [02192472] **2090**

HYDRO-ABSTRACTS (US/0731-6445) [06525090] **5534**

HYDRO-INDEX (US/0735-0309) [07214171] **1414**

HYDRO PLUS (FR) **2090**

HYDRO-QUEBEC See PROPOSITION TARIFAIRE **1513**

HYDRO-QUEBEC See PROPOSITION TARIFAIRE **1513**

HYDRO-QUEBEC. BIBLIOTHEQUE See AU-COURANT (HYDRO-QUEBEC. BIBLIOTHEQUE) **408**

HYDRO REVIEW (US/0884-0385) [10642585] **2090**

HYDROBIOLOGIA (NE/0018-8158) [01644557] **457**

HYDROBIOLOGICAL BULLETIN (NE/0165-1404) [02240667] 2217, **457**

HYDROBIOLOGICAL JOURNAL (US/0018-8166) [01696562] **457**

HYDROBIOLOGICAL STUDIES (XR/0577-3644) [01752438] **1414**

HYDROCARBON CONTAMINATED SOILS AND GROUNDWATER (US) [25607995] **174**

HYDROCARBON PROCESSING (INTERNATIONAL ED.) (US/0018-8190) [01752439] **4260**

HYDROCARBON PROCESSING (U.S. ED.) (US/0887-0284) [11016827] **4260**

HYDRODATA [COMPUTER FILE] (US) [22299028] **1414**

HYDROELECTRIC POWER RESOURCES OF THE UNITED STATES, DEVELOPED AND UNDEVELOPED (US/0073-4209) [02230512] **2115**

HYDROGEN ENERGY COORDINATING COMMITTEE ANNUAL REPORT-SUMMARY OF DOE HYDROGEN PROGRAMS (US/8755-3058) [10153667] **1946**

HYDROGEN ENERGY QUARTERLY LITERATURE REVIEW / ASSEMBLED AND DISSEMINATED BY THE TECHNOLOGY TRANSFER OFFICE OF GLOBAL RESOURCES AND ASSOCIATES (US) [09548148] **1946**

HYDROGEN LETTER, THE (US/1057-0713) [17861939] **977**

HYDROGEN PROGRESS CEASED. (US/0162-8402) [04244668] **2090**

HYDROGEOLOGIE (ORLEANS) (FR/0246-1641) [13042715] **1414**

HYDROGRAM See UNDERWATER LETTER, THE **1458**

HYDROGRAPHIC JOURNAL (UK/0309-7846) [03353377] 1449, **1414**

HYDROLOGIC AND CLIMATOLOGIC DATA, SOUTHEASTERN UINTA BASIN, UTAH AND COLORADO (US) [06070209] 1426, **1414**

HYDROLOGIC DATA (US) [23985146] 5534, **1414**

HYDROLOGIC DATA - CALIFORNIA. DEPT. OF WATER RESOURCES. SAN JOAQUIN DISTRICT (US/0737-7681) [09433141] **1414**

HYDROLOGIC DATA FOR EXPERIMENTAL AGRICULTURAL WATERSHEDS IN THE UNITED STATES (US/0503-5139) [05368663] 93, **1414**

HYDROLOGIC DATA REDUCTION AND ANALYSIS SERIES (US/0163-7592) [04452426] **1414**

HYDROLOGIC REPORT (LOS ANGELES) (US/0147-3697) [03148427] 2090, **5534**

HYDROLOGIC REPORT (NEW MEXICO. BUREAU OF MINES AND MINERAL RESOURCES) (US/0090-709X) [01785244] **1414**

HYDROLOGICAL ANNUAL (CE/0304-0925) [01798600] **1414**

HYDROLOGICAL EVENTS (CN/0382-2656) [02755168] **1414**

HYDROLOGICAL PROCESSES (UK/0885-6087) [12681914] **1414**

HYDROLOGICAL SCIENCE AND TECHNOLOGY (US/0887-686X) [13317544] **1415**

HYDROLOGICAL SCIENCES JOURNAL (UK/0262-6667) [08293191] **1415**

HYDROLOGIE CONTINENTALE (FR/0246-1528) [12867159] **1415**

HYDROLOGY AND WATER RESOURCES IN ARIZONA AND THE SOUTHWEST (US/0272-6106) [03910313] 5534, **1415**

HYDROLYSIS AND WOOD CHEMISTRY (US/1068-3658) [27658594] **4234**

HYDROMETALLURGY (NE/0304-386X) [02147037] **4003**

HYDROMETEOROLOGICAL REPORT (WASHINGTON) (US/0093-5859) [01260008] 1415, **1426**

HYDROTECHNICAL CONSTRUCTION (US/0018-8220) [01752442] **2090**

HYDROTITLES DIDCOT (UK/0953-7589) [l09537589] 1356, **1363**

HYDROWIRE (US/0886-697X) [11768088] **2056**

HYGIE (FR/0751-7149) [08832140] 1896, **4783**

HYGIENE + MEDIZIN (GW/0172-3790) [09726493] **3585**

HYMN SOCIETY OF GREAT BRITAIN AND IRELAND See BULLETIN - HYMN SOCIETY OF GREAT BRITAIN AND IRELAND **4106**

HYMN, THE (US/0018-8271) [01605454] 4964, **4121**

HYMNOLOGISKE MEDDELELSER (DK/0106-4940) [10141674] 4964, **4121**

HYMNOLOGY ANNUAL, THE (US/1054-7495) [22964252] **4122**

HYMY (FI/0355-4317) [l03554317] **2774**

HYOGO-KEN KOGAI KENKYUJO KENKYU HOKOKU (JA/0385-9290) [01397007] 2173, 2195, **2232**

HYOGO KENRITSU SUISAN SHIKENJO See HYOGO KENRITSU SUISAN SHIKENJO KENKYU HOKOKU **2305**

HYOGO KENRITSU SUISAN SHIKENJO KENKYU HOKOKU (JA) [07038585] **2305**

HYOGO KENRITSU TOSHOKAN See HYOGO KENRITSU TOSHOKAN ZOSHO MOKUROKU **3214**

HYOGO KENRITSU TOSHOKAN See NENPO **3233**

HYOGO KENRITSU TOSHOKAN ZOSHO MOKUROKU (JA) [02441458] **3214**

HYOMEN (JA/0367-648X) [10265370] **1025**

HYOMEN GIJUTSU (JA/0915-1869) [24768136] **1025**

HYOMEN KAGAKU (JA/0388-5321) [28109041] **1025**

HYONDAE HAEYANG (KO) [09752184] **2305**

HYONDAE MISUL CHODAEJON (KO) [11835253] **352**

HYONDAE MOKHOE (KO) [11356825] **4964**

HYONDAE MUNHAK (KO) [05045921] **3395**

HYONDAE PYONGNON (KO) [10244310] **2504**

HYONDAE SAENGHWAL (KO) [10707700] **2504**

HYONDAE SAHOE (KO) [12090069] **1566**

HYONDAE YESUL (KO) [04584701] **322**

HYONDAESA (KO) [07528423] **2620**

HYPATIA (EDWARDSVILLE, ILL.) (US/0887-5367) [13312118] **5558**

HYPE (US/0097-6539) [01799349] **4122**

HYPER G.A.P (FR/0756-368X) [l0756368X] **680**

HYPERACTIVITY NEWSLETTER See ADHD NEWSLETTER **4571**

Alphabetical Title Index — IATUL

HYPERFINE INTERACTIONS (NE/0304-3843) [02428078] **4443**

HYPERION (BERKELEY) *SUSPENDED.* (US/0018-8328) [02110721] **3395**

HYPERION PC (CN/0825-5784) [11734531] **1186**

HYPERLINK MAGAZINE (US/1045-4624) [17776600] **1186**

HYPERMEDIA (UK/0955-8543) [20363137] **1223**

HYPERNEXUS (US) [29395072] 1751, **1186**

HYPERTENSIE IN DE HUISARTSENPRAKTIJK (BE/0770-1276) [07856470] **3705**

HYPERTENSION ANNUAL (UK/0956-2311) [I09562311] **3705**

HYPERTENSION (DALLAS, TEX. 1979) (US/0194-911X) [04798824] **3705**

●HYPERTENSION IN PREGNANCY (US/1064-1955) [26226712] 5558, 3705, **3762**

HYPERTENSION INDEX & REVIEWS (US/1044-8071) [19904731] **3705**

HYPERTENSION (NEW YORK) (US/0362-4323) [02289529] **3705**

●HYPERTENSION RESEARCH, CLINICAL AND EXPERIMENTAL (JA/0916-9636) [I09169636] **3706**

HYPERTENSION SHEFFIELD (UK/0143-117X) [I0143117X] 488, **3585**

HYPHEN MAGAZINE (US/1058-3297) [24265313] **3395**

HYPNOSIS REPORTS *CEASED.* (US/0882-6072) [11900523] **2858**

HYPNOTHERAPY TODAY (US/0882-8652) [12010264] **2858**

HYPOTENUSE (US) [17867721] **3508**

HYPOTHETICAL ADVISORY OPINIONS (US/0146-7808) [03038768] **2251**

HYPOTHETICAL U.S. TAX TABLES FOR U.S. CITIZENS ABROAD (US) [08272295] **4731**

HYSTERIA (KITCHENER) (CN/0229-5385) [08036553] 322, **5558**

HYSTRIO (IT) [19224088] **385**

HYST'RY MYST'RY MAGAZINE (US/0735-4576) [08936865] **2620**

HYUNDAI NEWSLETTER (US) **681**

I (US/8755-4771) [11320034] **2504**

I.A.A.F. DIRECTORY *See* DIRECTORY & CALENDAR / IAAF **4892**

I.A.A.F. DIRECTORY / I.A.A.F (UK) [10421487] **4899**

I.A.M.R. REPORT (II/0418-5633) [01566106] **1677**

I A S M H F NEWSLETTER (US) **4089**

I AIN'T LYING (US/0885-7970) [09718116] **2318**

I & I.E. Y A (NQ) [03417275] 616, **2024**

I & L / INSTITUTE FOR THE STUDY OF IDEOLOGIES AND LITERATURE (US) [11888926] **3395**

I & P (FR) [07969975] **4523**

●I & T MAGAZINE (BE) [29778227] **1148**

I.B.I. GUIDE (US/1053-7198) [06549535] **2115**

I.B.N.S. JOURNAL (UK) [04304886] **790**

I.C.A.R. TECHNICAL BULLETIN (AGRIC) (II/0537-1309) [01608128] **93**

I.C.E.U.M (SP) [01798287] **1896**

I.C.I.D. BULLETIN (II/0300-2810) [01640944] **2090**

I.C. NACHRICHTEN (AU) [04508764] **269**

I C O M NEWS (FR/0018-8999) [01753487] **4089**

I CARE (IT/0394-817X) [I0394817X] **3585**

I CHUAN HSUEH PAO (CC) [01797639] **547**

I CONTRATTI : PRINCIPI FORMULE PROCEDURE (IT) **1677**

●I.D (US/0894-5373) [25225852] **2098**

I.D.A.A. COMMUNIQUE (US/0360-7224) [01920031] **1324**

I.D.B.I. GUIDE, INTERNATIONAL DRIVE BELT INTERCHANGE (US/0748-5824) [10951842] **2115**

I.D. CHECKING GUIDE (US/1041-5793) [12026395] **4655**

I.D.E.A.S. INTERIORS, DESIGN, ENVIRONMENT, ARTS, STRUCTURES (US/0161-1895) [03863958] 300, **2901**

I.D.E.E (BRIGHAM) (CN/1192-7755) [28166417] **5289**

I-D MAGAZINE (UK) **1064**

I D R C REPORTS (CN/0315-9981) [02825154] **2910**

●I/E (CHANDLER, ARIZ.) (US/1064-9859) [26495297] **4122**

I.E. (CHICAGO) (US/0422-4108) [01716996] **4964**

I E E E PUBLICATIONS BULLETIN (US) [01752466] **2042**

I.E.E.-I.E.R.E. PROCEEDINGS INDIA (UK/0018-9146) [03758578] **2056**

I F O-INSTITUT FUR WIRTSCHAFTSFORSCHUNG, MUNICH *See* I F O-STUDIEN ZUR ENTWICKLUNGSFORSCHUNG **1635**

I F O-STUDIEN ZUR ENTWICKLUNGSFORSCHUNG (GW) [06034010] **1635**

I.F. PUBLICATIONS (BG) [10526791] **5042**

I F TRASPORTI E COMUNICAZIONE (IT) **5383**

I GOVERNI LOCALI (IT) **4655**

I GRANDI LIBRI (IT) [15157803] **4829**

●I.H.I. GUIDE HOSES (US/1056-6155) [23747816] **3480**

I HAI TSA CHIH (CH) [04742237] **322**

I LOVE CATS (US/0899-9570) [19277361] **4286**

I LOVE ENGLISH (FR) **1751**

●I LOVE NY GROUP TRAVEL GUIDE FOR NEW YORK STATE (US) [26758834] **5480**

I N I S REFERENCE SERIES (US) [01540886] **4447**

I.N. REVUE DES TECHNIQUES NOUVELLES EN SERRURERIE MENUISERIE MIROITERIE (FR/0750-0181) [I07500181] 2906, **634**

I NAIFS E L'ARTE POPOLARE (IT) [02244214] **352**

I/O NEWS *CEASED.* (US/0274-9998) [06834292] **1267**

I.O.S. CRUISE REPORT (UK/0960-6009) [I09606009] **1449**

I P H INFORMATION (GW/0250-8338) [08483586] **4234**

I P L O NEWS (CN/0319-4442) [02604372] **3214**

I.P.R.E. REVIEW, THE (UK) [06896362] **2056**

I P R NEWS, A *See* CONSCIOUSNESS **4241**

I. P. REPORTS FROM SOCIALIST COUNTRIES (UK) [07308005] **1304**

I POVERI, STRENNA POETICA VERONESE (IT) [19966024] **3464**

I.R.C.A. FOREIGN LOG (US/0093-1926) [01791863] **1133**

I S A BULLETIN (1975) (CN/0383-8501) [03304074] **5247**

I.S.A.M. MONOGRAPHS (US) [06444227] **4122**

I/S ANALYZER (US/0896-3231) [16670566] **4212**

I.S.C.A. QUARTERLY, THE (US/0741-2940) [10101624] **380**

I. S. E. R. SECTOR REPORTS (US) **1494**

I.S.I. GUIDE, INTERNATIONAL SEAL INTERCHANGE (US/0748-7665) [10951804] **2115**

I T L G (UK/0954-917X) [I0954917X] **5161**

I.T. MAGAZINE (TORONTO) (CN/1196-4715) [27699066] **1259**

I.V.R.I. CAMPUS, BANGALORE *See* ANNUAL SCIENTIFIC REPORT OF THE I.V.R.I. CAMPUS, BANGALORE, FOR THE YEAR ... **5504**

I.V.U.N. NEWS (US/1066-534X) [25680185] **3949**

I YUAN TO YING (CC) [05578476] **322**

I2-PROCESTECHNOLOGIE (NE/0169-4200) [25997929] **1977**

IA. INGEGNERIA AMBIENTALE (IT/0394-5871) [I03945871] **2232**

IA, THE JOURNAL OF THE SOCIETY FOR INDUSTRIAL ARCHEOLOGY (US/0160-1040) [03617256] **269**

IAAH NEWSLETTER (AT/0819-9558) [I08199558] **4783**

IAALD NEWS (UK) [10665384] **3214**

IAAO UPDATE *See* ASSESSMENT JOURNAL **4711**

IAB (MC/0256-3517) [I02563517] **352**

IABSE REPORTS (SZ) [09837315] **2024**

IACD QUARTERLY (US/8756-2189) [11487168] **4589**

IACE/AEDS NEWSLETTER (US) [15718586] **1913**

IACEE NEWSLETTER (FI/0786-9916) [I07869916] **1977**

IACFA NEWSLETTER (US) **3585**

IACM BULLETIN OF THE INTERNATIONAL ASSOCIATION FOR COMPUTATIONAL MECHANICS (UK/1046-6606) [13866724] **2115**

IACP LAW ENFORCEMENT LEGISLATION AND LITIGATION REPORT (US/0047-0554) [01785518] **3107**

IAEA NEWSBRIEFS : INTERNATIONAL ATOMIC ENERGY AGENCY (AU) [15188037] 4447, **1946**

IAEA SAFETY SERIES (AU/0074-1892) [01695579] **4783**

IAEA YEARBOOK (AU) [20639106] **4447**

IAEI NEWS (US/0020-5974) [04062521] 2056, **2290**

IAFC COMMITTEE LIST (US/0743-0248) [10480182] **616**

IAFC ON SCENE (US/0893-3936) [15506940] **2291**

IAFP FINANCIAL PLANNING UPDATE (US/0733-5687) [08612129] **4731**

IAHPER JOURNAL, THE (US) [05772915] **1855**

IAHR BULLETIN (NE) [11869489] **2090**

IAHS-AISH PUBLICATION (UK/0144-7815) [08359644] **1415**

IAIABC JOURNAL (US/0145-1561) [02703150] **2863**

IAJRC JOURNAL (US/0098-9487) [02161808] 2774, **4122**

IAL PLASTICS YEARBOOK, THE (UK) **4455**

IALL JOURNAL OF LANGUAGE LEARNING TECHNOLOGIES, THE (US/1050-0049) [21363417] **3286**

IAM (NEW YORK) (US/0146-9274) [03059772] **2738**

IANUA (AT/0729-6010) [I07296010] **1804**

IAO INSPECTOR (CN/0226-2460) [10789988] **2232**

IAPA NEWS (US/0018-8409) [04540385] **2920**

IAPONIIA (RU) [02808672] **2653**

IAPQR TRANSACTIONS (II/0970-0102) [11743854] **5328**

IAR HOTLINE (US/0273-9518) [07042678] **5317**

IAR NEWSLETTER OF AGRICULTURAL RESEARCH (ET/1015-9762) [25087942] **93**

IARC INTERNAL TECHNICAL REPORT (FR/0254-9719) [06716805] **3818**

IARC MONOGRAPHS ON THE EVALUATION OF CARCINOGENIC RISKS TO HUMANS (FR/1017-1606) [19175507] 2863, **3818**

IARC MONOGRAPHS ON THE EVALUATION OF CARCINOGENIC RISKS TO HUMANS. SUPPLEMENT (FR/1014-711X) [19175543] **3818**

IARCA *See* MEMBERSHIP DIRECTORY / INTERNATIONAL ASSOCIATION OF RESIDENTIAL AND COMMUNITY ALTERNATIVES **5296**

IARCA JOURNAL (US) [21096630] **5289**

IAS NEWSLETTER (INTERNATIONAL ASSOCIATION OF SEDIMENTOLOGISTS) (DK) [16378923] **1382**

●IASA JOURNAL / INTERNATIONAL ASSOCIATION OF SOUND ARCHIVES (HU/1021-562X) [28643426] **5317**

IASB : INTERNATIONAL ACCOUNTANCY SOFTWARE BULLETIN (UK) 1286, **745**

IASB SCHOOL BOARD NEWSBULLETIN (US) [15089161] **1864**

IASC BULLETIN (CN/0227-1338) [07869954] **3214**

IASCP BULLETIN : [A PUBLICATION OF IASCP], THE (US) [08147976] **1112**

IASLIC BULLETIN (II/0018-8441) [02105575] **3214**

IASLIC SPECIAL PUBLICATION (II/0073-6279) [01752834] **3214**

IASP NEWSLETTER (INTERNATIONAL ASSOCIATION OF SCHOLARLY PUBLISHERS) (NO/0333-3620) [11584890] **4815**

IASSI QUARTERLY (II/0970-9061) [23449526] **5202**

IASSIST QUARTERLY (US/0739-1137) [09693936] 5202, 3214, **3258**

IASSW DIRECTORY (US/0098-8278) [02163697] **5289**

IATA LOCATION IDENTIFIERS HANDBOOK (CN) [06930949] **23**

IATA PASSENGER AGENCY CONFERENCE RESOLUTIONS MANUAL (SZ) **23**

IATREIA MEDELLIN (CK/0121-0793) [I01210793] **3585**

IATROGENICS : SAFETY IN HEALTH CARE (DK) **4783**

IATROGENICS : THE OFFICIAL JOURNAL OF THE INTERNATIONAL SOCIETY FOR THE PREVENTION OF IATROGENIC COMPLICATIONS (ISPIC) (DK/0905-717X) [24538311] **3585**

IATSS RESEARCH (JA/0386-1112) [04400034] 4783, **5441**

IATUL NEWS (DK/1102-6103) [11026103] **3214**

IATUL — Alphabetical Title Index

IATUL QUARTERLY See IATUL NEWS **3214**

IAU BULLETIN : THE BIMONTHLY NEWSLETTER OF THE INTERNATIONAL ASSOCIATION OF UNIVERSITIES (FR) [21506022] **1829**

IAWA BULLETIN (NE/0254-3915) [04671507] **2401**

IAWA BULLETIN. NEW SERIES (NE) [07394818] **2401**

● IAWA JOURNAL / INTERNATIONAL ASSOCIATION OF WOOD ANATOMISTS (NE/0928-1541) [28238907] **2401**

IAWCM BULLETIN (US/0744-9941) [08701690] **3480**

IAZYK I OBSHCHESTVO (RU) [05435308] **3286**

IAZYKI I TOPONIMIIA (RU) [03512087] **3286**

IB MAGAZINE See IB SUISSE **681**

IB SUISSE (SZ) 4212, **681**

IBA REPORTS (US) 1609, **3693**

IBA REVIEW (JM) [04658168] **4003**

IBAC MITTEILUNGEN (GW) [02411597] **616**

IBADAN, NIGERIA. UNIVERSITY See STUDENT HANDBOOK OF INFORMATION ON UNIVERSITY POLICIES AND PRACTICES **1848**

IBAO NEWS (CN/0712-5887) [09336573] **2882**

IBAR (IE/0332-1118) [14521984] **681**

IBARAKI DAIGAKU. IZURA BIJUTSU BUNKA KENKYUJO See IBARAKI DAIGAKU IZURA BIJUTSU BUNKA KENKYUJO HO **5232**

IBARAKI DAIGAKU IZURA BIJUTSU BUNKA KENKYUJO HO (JA) [01790297] **5232**

IBARAKI DAIGAKU KOGAKUBU KENKYU SHUHO (JA/0367-7389) [10442245] **1977**

IBARAKI DAIGAKU. KYOIKUGAKUBU See IBARAKI DAIGAKU KYOIKUGAKUBU KIYO : JIMBUN SHAKAI KAGAKU **1829**

IBARAKI DAIGAKU. KYOIKUGAKUBU See IBARAKI DAIGAKU KYOIKUGAKUBU KIYO : SHIZEN KAGAKU **5111**

IBARAKI DAIGAKU KYOIKUGAKUBU KIYO : JIMBUN SHAKAI KAGAKU (JA) [06361806] **1829**

IBARAKI DAIGAKU KYOIKUGAKUBU KIYO. JIMBUN, SHAKAI KAGAKU, GEIJUTSU (JA/0386-765X) [08000493] **2504**

IBARAKI DAIGAKU KYOIKUGAKUBU KIYO : SHIZEN KAGAKU (JA) [04758449] **5111**

IBARAKI DAIGAKU. NOGAKUBU See IBARAKI DAIGAKU NOGAKUBU GAKUJUTSU HOKOKU **93**

IBARAKI DAIGAKU NOGAKUBU GAKUJUTSU HOKOKU (JA/0445-1694) [01208719] **93**

IBARAKI DAIGAKU. RIGAKUBU. SUGAKU KYOSHITSU See BULLETIN OF THE FACULTY OF SCIENCE, IBARAKI UNIVERSITY. SERIES A : MATHEMATICS **3498**

IBARAKI-KEN EISEI KENKYUJO See IBARAKI-KEN EISEI KENKYUJO NEMPO **4783**

IBARAKI-KEN EISEI KENKYUJO NEMPO (JA) [06706376] 5111, **4783**

IBARAKI-KEN KOGAI GIJUTSU SENTA See IBARAKI-KEN KOGAI GIJUTSU SENTA NEMPO **2232**

IBARAKI-KEN KOGAI GIJUTSU SENTA NEMPO (JA) [02245360] **2232**

IBARAKI-KEN NI OKERU HOSHANO CHOSA (JA) [03457446] **2232**

IBARNKI-KEN KOGAI GIJUTSU SENTA See IBARAKI-KEN NI OKERU HOSHANO CHOSA **2232**

IBAS ANNUAL / INDONESIAN BUSINESS ASSOCIATION OF SINGAPORE (SI) [07815748] **900**

IBBD/CDU INFORMATIVO (BL) [03158447] **417**

IBC/DONOGHUE'S MONEY FUND DIRECTORY (US/1060-8516) [23687018] **900**

● IBC/DONOGHUE'S MONEY FUND REPORT (US) [20917413] **790**

IBC/DONOGHUE'S MUTUAL FUNDS ALMANAC (US/1060-8524) [23687064] **900**

IBCAM (UK/0306-2910) [01794007] 3480, **5416**

IBCD (US/0738-3398) [09581897] **1566**

IBC'S MONEY MARKET INSIGHT (US/1043-285X) [19371551] **900**

IBC'S QUARTERLY REPORT ON MONEY FUNDS PERFORMANCE (US) **790**

IBD NETWORK PROFILE (US/0894-6574) [16162489] **681**

IBD WATCH (US) **3797**

IBDA (UA) [09520499] **322**

IBE DOCUMENTATION CENTRE See DOCUMENTATION CENTRE CATALOGUE **1737**

IBERIAN STUDIES (UK/0307-3262) [01587067] **2517**

IBERICA (US/1056-5000) [23725628] **3395**

IBERICA (FR) [05262655] **2620**

IBERICA. ACTUALIDAD CIENTIFICA (SP/0211-0776) [02377469] **5111**

IBERO-AMERICANA (SW/0046-8444) [01098014] **5202**

IBERO-AMERICANA PRAGENSIA (XR/0536-2520) [02262098] **2738**

IBERO-AMERIKANISCHES ARCHIV (GW/0340-3068) [01490884] **2738**

IBEROAMERICANA (GW/0342-1864) [05115735] **2738**

IBEROROMANIA (SP/0019-0993) [01752497] **3286**

IBEW JOURNAL (US/0897-2826) [17452097] **1677**

IBEX BULLETIN (UK) **1186**

IBFAN NEWS (US/0889-4000) [13900826] **5289**

IBI BULLETIN (NE) [19574046] **300**

IBI DIENST (GW/0946-4441) **2920**

IBIS, DE (NE) [03525722] **2640**

IBIS LINKS (AT/0811-5559) [I08115559] **2454**

IBIS (LONDON, ENGLAND) (UK/0019-1019) [01377260] **5617**

IBIS REVIEW (US) [19573820] **2882**

IBJ INDUSTRY RESEARCH (JA) [24423781] **1609**

IBLA (TI/0018-862X) [02098293] **3286**

IBM DIRECTIONS (US/0897-0289) [16899451] **1186**

IBM FUTURES (UK/0958-4579) [I09584579] **1186**

IBM FUTURES See COMPUTER FINANCE **1236**

● IBM INTERNET JOURNAL (US/1068-1396) [27450306] **1186**

IBM JOURNAL OF RESEARCH AND DEVELOPMENT (US/0018-8646) [01716542] 1259, **2056**

IBM NACHRICHTEN (GW/0018-8662) [07079875] **1186**

IBM PC INDEX, THE (US/0741-2355) [10108243] **1186**

IBM SYSTEM USER (UK/0950-303X) [I0950303X] **1186**

IBM SYSTEMS JOURNAL (US/0018-8670) [01445487] **1259**

IBM TECHNICAL DISCLOSURE BULLETIN (US/0018-8689) [01752459] **1187**

IBON FACTS AND FIGURES (PH/0115-8007) [06273174] **1494**

IBPGR NEWSLETTER FOR ASIA AND THE PACIFIC / INTERNATIONAL BOARD FOR PLANT GENETIC RESOURCES (II) [23741849] 547, **513**

IBPGR TRAINING COURSES. LECTURE SERIES (IT) [18033221] 547, **513**

IBRM (UK) 4851, **2807**

IBRO HANDBOOK SERIES (UK/0742-504X) [09656236] **3833**

IBRO NEWS (US/0361-0713) [02001973] 581, **3834**

IBS SEMINAR (BG) [12762872] **2653**

IBSEN NEWS AND COMMENT : NEWSLETTER OF THE IBSEN SOCIETY OF AMERICA (US) [10237932] **3344**

● IBSNAT VIEWS (US/1076-3112) [30449572] **93**

IBT-RAPPORT / [NORGES LANDBRUKSHGSKOLE, INSTITUTT FOR BYGNINGSTEKNIKK] (NO) [12685275] 1977, **93**

● IC CARD SYSTEMS & DESIGN (US/1074-6269) [29694458] **1187**

IC. INFORMATION CONSTRUCTION (CN/0713-6919) [08985146] **616**

IC MASTER (US/0894-6809) [03037953] **2057**

ICA INFORMA (CK/0046-9920) [04674051] **93**

ICA INFORMATION (IS/0334-6056) [I03346056] 1259, **4655**

ICA INFORMATION : BULLETIN DE L'INSTITUT CULTUREL AFRICAIN (SG) [05231318] **2640**

ICA. INTERNATIONAL COLOUR AUTHORITY (UK/0952-0708) [I09520708] **5351**

ICA-KURIREN (SW/0345-5068) [I03455068] **2517**

ICA NEWS / INTERNATIONAL CO-OPERATIVE ALLIANCE (SZ) [16318438] **1542**

ICAA NEWS (SZ/1012-8360) [I10128360] **1345**

ICAE NEWS (CN/0834-9789) [16888306] **1800**

ICAEW TAXATION SERVICE (UK) **4731**

ICAM NEWS (NE/0844-1901) [19598177] **300**

ICAME JOURNAL / INTERNATIONAL COMPUTER ARCHIVE OF MODERN ENGLISH (NO/0801-5775) [16637656] 1187, **3286**

ICAO JOURNAL (CN/0018-8778) [21967611] **23**

ICARA REPORT / INTERNATIONAL CONFERENCE ON ASSISTANCE TO REFUGEES IN AFRICA (SZ) [08751200] **2910**

ICARBS SUSPENDED. (US/0360-8409) [01794308] **3214**

ICARDA (SY) [19639584] **93**

ICARDA ANNUAL REPORT / INTERNATIONAL CENTER FOR AGRICULTURAL RESEARCH IN THE DRY AREAS (SY) [09523840] **93**

ICARE (FR/0445-1767) [05159591] **23**

ICARUS (IE/0019-1027) [03296329] **3395**

ICARUS SUSPENDED. (US/0163-0954) [03296309] **3464**

ICARUS (NEW YORK, N.Y. 1962) (US/0019-1035) [01752499] **395**

ICARUS (NEW YORK, N.Y. : 1991) CEASED. (US/1054-1381) [22762024] **3395**

ICASALS NEWSLETTER (US/0018-8808) [03418217] **174**

ICASALS PUBLICATION (US/0538-5318) [02146457] 93, **2565**

ICB (UK/0953-5632) [17979902] **790**

ICB CARPET DIRECTORY (UK/0269-1450) [18544138] **5351**

ICB DIRECTORY See ICB CARPET DIRECTORY **5351**

ICB. INTERNATIONAL CARPET BULLETIN (UK/0268-2966) [I02682966] **5351**

ICB MAGAZINE (UK/0968-6118) [27077508] **900**

ICBA. INDEPENDENT CANADIAN BUSINESS ASSOCIATION OF BRITISH COLUMBIA (CN/0822-7187) [10513286] **1609**

ICBP TECHNICAL PUBLICATION (US/0277-1330) [07511116] **2195**

ICC (CN) [04405604] **352**

ICC BUSINESS WORLD : MAGAZINE OF THE INTERNATIONAL CHAMBER OF COMMERCE (FR) [09743892] **820**

ICC COMMERCIAL CRIME INTERNATIONAL (UK/1012-2710) [22161352] 3165, **1609**

ICC INTERNATIONAL COURT OF ARBITRATION BULLETIN, THE (FR/1017-284X) [24102276] **3129**

ICC NEWS (US) [03564144] **839**

ICC REGISTER (US/0749-0534) [10527894] 839, **2979**

ICC STANDARDS METHODS (AU) 202, **2343**

ICCA JOURNAL (CN/0920-234X) [I0920234X] **1230**

ICCM BULLETIN See AICCM BULLETIN **2841**

ICCSASW SOLIDARITY BULLETIN (CN/0823-7468) [10398325] **1609**

ICE (UK/0019-1043) [01752500] **1415**

ICE CREAM AND FROZEN CONFECTIONERY (UK) [12609868] **2343**

ICE CREAM REPORTER (US/0897-3261) [17461055] **2343**

ICE, INSIDE CODE ENFORCEMENT (US/0161-3367) [03897845] **2979**

ICE RIVER (US/1043-7010) [19538298] **3395**

ICE SUMMARY AND ANALYSIS: EASTERN CANADIAN SEABOARD (CN/0068-7766) [01814089] **1415**

ICE THICKNESS DATA FOR CANADIAN SELECTED STATIONS. FREEZE-UP, BREAK-UP (CN/0225-1094) [02442486] **1415**

ICEA. INSTITUT CANADIEN D'EDUCATION DES ADULTES (CN/0318-8205) [02041752] **1800**

ICEC QUARTERLY (US) [06963746] **1880**

ICELAND (IC) [01606090] **2517**

ICELAND REVIEW (REYKJAVIK, ICELAND : 1984) (IC/0019-1094) [10821383] **2692**

ICELANDIC CANADIAN (CN/0046-8452) [01681256] 2738, **2263**

ICES JOURNAL CEASED. (US/0882-2115) [06825785] **2024**

ICES JOURNAL OF MARINE SCIENCE (UK/1054-3139) [22841287] **1449**

ICES MARINE SCIENCE SYMPOSIA (DK/0906-060X) [24456993] 2305, **1449**

ICES OCEANOGRAPHIC DATA LISTS AND INVENTORIES (DK) [03792511] **1450**

ICHI *CEASED.* (JA) [02246930] **2504**

ICHIOKUNIN NO SHOWA SHI (JA) [02243666] **2653**

ICHNEUTES (GR) **5202**

ICHNOS (CHUR, SWITZERLAND) (SZ/1042-0940) [18940319] **269**

ICHNUSA (IT) [09336825] **2692**

ICHOR (CN/0229-1495) [07821222] **3395**

ICHPER JOURNAL *See* ICHPER-SD JOURNAL : THE OFFICIAL MAGAZINE OF THE INTERNATIONAL COUNCIL FOR HEALTH, PHYSICAL EDUCATION, RECREATION, SPORT AND DANCE **1856**

ICHPER JOURNAL : THE OFFICIAL MAGAZINE OF THE INTERNATIONAL COUNCIL FOR HEALTH, PHYSICAL EDUCATION, AND RECREATION (US) [26666664] **1855**

● ICHPER-SD JOURNAL : THE OFFICIAL MAGAZINE OF THE INTERNATIONAL COUNCIL FOR HEALTH, PHYSICAL EDUCATION, RECREATION, SPORT AND DANCE (US) [29986547] **1856**

ICHR NEWSLETTER (II/0376-9682) [02172530] **2653**

ICHTHYOLITH ISSUES (AT/1032-1314) [I10321314] **5586**

ICHTHYOLOGIA (YU/0579-7152) [05463617] **5586**

ICHTHYOLOGICAL BULLETIN OF THE J.L.B. SMITH INSTITUTE OF ICHTHYOLOGY (SA/0251-1258) [05437311] **5586**

ICHTHYOLOGICAL EXPLORATION OF FRESHWATERS (GW/0936-9902) [21190899] **2305**

ICHTHYOS LJUBLJANA (XV/0352-3837) [I03523837] **1356**

ICHTYOPHYSIOLOGICA ACTA (FR/0245-8608) [I02458608] **457**

● ICI BOUCHERVILLE (CN/1187-872X) [26497507] **4655**

ICI QUEBEC (REPENTIGNY) (CN/0704-0334) [03827617] **417**

ICI...ROSEMONT (CN/0318-2622) [02441931] **1829**

ICI TRENDS IN MUTUAL FUND ACTIVITY (US/0273-0898) [04621371] **900**

ICIASF RECORD (US/0730-2010) [07030923] **23**

ICID TECHNICAL MEMOIRS (II) [01011683] **2090**

ICIDH AND ENVIRONMENTAL FACTORS INTERNATIONAL NETWORK (CN/1198-3795) 4389, **5289**

ICIDH INTERNATIONAL NETWORK (CN/1182-5049) [23296515] 4389, **5289**

ICIE INNOVAZIONE *SUSPENDED.* (IT) **2825**

ICIMOD OCCASIONAL PAPER (NP) [20181926] 5534, **1494**

ICIT, INDEX, COMMERCIAL, INDUSTRIEL, TOURISTIQUE (HT) [06182605] **1609**

ICJ NEWSLETTER (SZ) [06176554] **4509**

ICL TECHNICAL JOURNAL (UK/0142-1557) [05397587] **1187**

ICLA BOLETIN (PE) [06494439] **5030**

ICLARM BIBLIOGRAPHIES (PH/0115-5997) [16843918] **2317**

ICLARM CONFERENCE PROCEEDINGS (PH/0115-4435) [I01154435] **2305**

ICLARM REPORT (PH/0115-4494) [09539094] **2305**

ICLARM STUDIES AND REVIEWS (PH/0115-4389) [08253285] **2305**

ICLARM TECHNICAL REPORTS (PH/0115-5547) [09292203] **2305**

ICLAS BULLETIN *See* ICLAS NEWS **5511**

ICLAS NEWS (FI/1018-4635) [24177623] **5111**

ICLAS NEWS (FI/1018-4635) **5511**

ICMA NEWSLETTER (US/0047-0651) [02262107] **4655**

ICMA REPORTS ON PERSONNEL (US) **942**

ICMC NEWSLETTER (SZ) [04308311] **5202**

ICMC TODAY / INTERNATIONAL CATHOLIC MIGRATION COMMISSION *CEASED.* (SZ) [25184055] **4964**

ICMM NEWS (US/0883-1343) [12119617] **4089**

ICMR ANNALS : ANNUAL REPORTS OF THE INTERNATIONAL CENTER FOR MEDICAL RESEARCH (JA) [08516326] **3585**

ICNAF HANDBOOK (CN) [02248059] **2305**

ICO (SW/0106-1348) [07695683] **352**

ICO. INTELLIGENCE ARTIFICIELLE ET SCIENCES COGNITIVES AU QUEBEC (CN/1189-6078) [I11896078] **5111**

ICOC : ISTANBUL CHAMBER OF COMMERCE (TU) [16744532] **820**

ICOM EDUCATION (FR) [05906977] **4089**

ICOMOS BULLETIN (FR) [06401620] **2692**

ICOMOS/INFORMATION (IT) [13028852] 352, **300**

ICOMOS INFORMATION (IT/0394-218X) [I0394218X] **300**

ICON (TORONTO) *CEASED.* (CN/1183-6962) [25313615] **322**

ICONES / LE JOURNAL DU MACINTOSH (FR) **1187**

ICOT JOURNAL (JA) [13720700] **1187**

ICP (IT/0390-2358) [I03902358] **4260**

ICP ADMINISTRATIVE & ACCOUNTING SOFTWARE (US/0747-2102) [10633255] 1286, **681**

ICP INFORMATION NEWSLETTER (US/0161-6951) [02434546] **1015**

ICP REFERENCE SERIES SOFTWARE DIRECTORY (US) [02252254] **1286**

ICP SOFTWARE DIRECTORY. MICROCOMPUTER SERIES (US) [14270025] 1267, **1279**

ICP SOFTWARE GUIDE : BANKING (US/0094-8020) [01795283] **790**

ICP SOFTWARE JOURNAL (US/0734-466X) [08738842] 1238, **1286**

ICPM. SERIES 1 (US/0196-4925) [05758322] **3918**

ICPS NEWLETTER / INSTITUTE FOR CULTURAL POLICY STUDIES (AT) **5268**

ICPSR BULLETIN (US/0198-6848) [06213628] **5202**

ICRAF WORKING PAPER (KE) [15431703] **2384**

ICRP PUBLICATION (UK/0074-2740) [02022120] **3941**

ICRU REPORT (US/0579-5435) [09767564] **3941**

ICSC MEMBERSHIP DIRECTORY (US/8756-9337) [17832246] **681**

ICSC RESEARCH BULLETIN (US) [25124001] **955**

ICSID REVIEW (US/0258-3690) [13275772] **3129**

ICSSR JOURNAL OF ABSTRACTS AND REVIEWS : ECONOMICS (II) [06676921] 4523, **1533**

ICSSR JOURNAL OF ABSTRACTS AND REVIEWS: GEOGRAPHY (II) [04221276] **2565**

ICSSR JOURNAL OF ABSTRACTS AND REVIEWS : POLITICAL SCIENCE (II/0250-9660) [05504479] **4476**

ICSSR JOURNAL OF ABSTRACTS AND REVIEWS. SOCIOLOGY AND SOCIAL ANTHROPOLOGY / INDIAN COUNCIL OF SOCIAL SCIENCE RESEARCH (II) [05816662] **5202**

ICSSR NEWSLETTER (II/0018-9049) [02106019] **5202**

ICSSR RESEARCH ABSTRACTS QUARTERLY (II) [01752851] **5202**

ICSU SHORT REPORTS (UK/0952-1097) [12084998] **488**

ICTA ROSTER (US/0094-3517) [01794315] **5480**

ICTP SERIES IN THEORETICAL PHYSICS, THE (SI) [15500284] **4405**

ICU FORUM (US/8756-7857) [11654199] **3585**

ICUC (US/0899-5451) [18132675] **2488**

ICUIS BIBLIOGRAPHY SERIES (US/0161-5483) [03966557] **5012**

ICUIS METRO-MINISTRY NEWS : THE INTERDENOMINATIONAL NEWSLETTER OF THE INSTITUTE ON THE CHURCH IN URBAN INDUSTRIAL SOCIETY (US) [12863327] **4964**

ID HANDBOOK OF FOODSERVICE DISTRIBUTION (US/0731-518X) [08209467] **2343**

ID MAGAZINE (US/0897-5027) [17526241] **5202**

ID (NEW YORK, N.Y. : 1984) (US/0894-5373) [12139124] **2098**

ID SYSTEM BUYER'S GUIDE (US/1043-8319) [19571195] **1494**

ID SYSTEMS (US/0892-676X) [15212786] **5111**

IDA COUNTY COURIER, THE (US) [16688828] **5670**

IDA COUNTY PIONEER RECORD (US) [16688777] **5670**

IDACA NEWS: THE INSTITUTE FOR THE DEVELOPMENT OF AGRICULTURAL COOPERATION IN ASIA (JA) 1542, **93**

IDAHI VELFAIYAR JARNAL (US/1058-0514) [24202821] **5289**

IDAHO ACADEMY OF SCIENCE *See* JOURNAL OF THE IDAHO ACADEMY OF SCIENCE **5120**

IDAHO. AGRICULTURAL EXPERIMENT STATION *See* PROGRESS REPORT - IDAHO. AGRICULTURAL EXPERIMENT STATION **123**

IDAHO AGRICULTURAL STATISTICS (US/0094-1271) [01792542] 93, **154**

IDAHO ARCHAEOLOGIST (US/0893-2271) [07807041] **270**

IDAHO ARGONAUT *See* ARGONAUT (MOSCOW, IDAHO) **5656**

IDAHO BEVERAGE ANALYST (US/0191-5290) [04902577] **2367**

IDAHO BLUE BOOK (US) [01253347] **4655**

IDAHO BROADCASTING GUIDE (US/0748-0237) [10837356] **1133**

IDAHO BUSINESS REVIEW, THE (US/8750-4022) [11406176] **681**

IDAHO CASE NAMES CITATOR (US) **2979**

IDAHO CITIES (US) [05523334] **4655**

IDAHO COUNTY FREE PRESS (US) [13137622] **5656**

IDAHO CROP AND LIVESTOCK REPORTING SERVICE *See* IDAHO AGRICULTURAL STATISTICS **154**

IDAHO. DEPARTMENT OF HEALTH AND WELFARE *See* IDAHO DEPARTMENT OF HEALTH & WELFARE ANNUAL REPORT **4783**

IDAHO DEPARTMENT OF HEALTH & WELFARE ANNUAL REPORT (US/0272-5916) [06835381] **4783**

IDAHO. DEPT. OF HEALTH AND WELFARE *See* ANNUAL REPORT - DEPARTMENT OF HEALTH & WELFARE **5272**

IDAHO. DEPT. OF HEALTH AND WELFARE *See* ANNUAL REPORT AND GUIDE TO PROGRAMS / IDAHO DEPARTMENT OF HEALTH AND WELFARE **4765**

IDAHO. DEPT. OF HEALTH AND WELFARE. ANNUAL REPORT - DEPARTMENT OF HEALTH AND WELFARE *See* ANNUAL REPORT AND GUIDE TO PROGRAMS / IDAHO DEPARTMENT OF HEALTH AND WELFARE **4765**

IDAHO. DEPT. OF LABOR AND INDUSTRIAL SERVICES *See* ANNUAL REPORT OF THE IDAHO DEPARTMENT OF LABOR AND INDUSTRIAL SERVICES **1649**

IDAHO. DEPT. OF PARKS AND RECREATION *See* IDAHO STATE PARKS AND RECREATION **4706**

IDAHO. DEPT. OF WATER RESOURCES *See* ANNUAL REPORT OF THE IDAHO DEPARTMENT OF WATER RESOURCES **5529**

IDAHO ECONOMIC FORECAST, THE (US/8756-1840) [06617653] **1566**

IDAHO EMPLOYMENT / STATE OF IDAHO, DEPARTMENT OF EMPLOYMENT, BUREAU OF RESEARCH AND ANALYSIS (US) [04079868] **1566**

IDAHO ENTERPRISE, THE (US) [13170040] **5656**

IDAHO FARMER-STOCKMAN (US/1041-1682) [01224625] **212**

IDAHO FISCAL YEAR ANNUAL PROGRAM PLAN UNDER PART B OF THE EDUCATION OF THE HANDICAPPED ACT AS AMENDED BY PUBLIC LAW 94-142 (US) [06272144] **1880**

IDAHO. FISH AND GAME DEPARTMENT *See* ANNUAL UPLAND GAME BIRD REPORT (BOISE) **5576**

IDAHO. FISH AND GAME DEPT *See* BIENNIAL REPORT OF THE FISH AND GAME DEPARTMENT OF THE STATE OF IDAHO **2297**

IDAHO FRUIT TREE CENSUS / U.S. DEPARTMENT OF AGRICULTURE, ECONOMICS AND STATISTICS SERVICE AND IDAHO DEPARTMENT OF AGRICULTURE (US) [08249896] **2420**

IDAHO GENEALOGICAL SOCIETY QUARTERLY (US/0445-2127) [06591620] **2454**

● IDAHO HEALTH CARE IN PERSPECTIVE (US/1065-4143) [26605008] **4783**

IDAHO IN PERSPECTIVE (US/1065-5417) [26628894] **5328**

IDAHO LAW REVIEW (US/0019-1205) [01752531] **2979**

IDAHO LEGISLATIVE FISCAL REPORT TO THE JOINT SENATE FINANCE-HOUSE APPROPRIATIONS COMMITTEE : A PUBLICATION OF THE LEGISLATIVE BUDGET OFFICE (US) [10540799] **4655**

IDAHO — Alphabetical Title Index

IDAHO. LEGISLATURE. LEGISLATIVE BUDGET OFFICE See LEGISLATIVE BUDGET BOOK : A PUBLICATION OF THE LEGISLATIVE BUDGET OFFICE / JOINT SENATE FINANCE-HOUSE APPROPRIATIONS COMMITTEE **4661**

IDAHO. LEGISLATURE. LEGISLATIVE BUDGET OFFICE See IDAHO LEGISLATIVE FISCAL REPORT TO THE JOINT SENATE FINANCE-HOUSE APPROPRIATIONS COMMITTEE : A PUBLICATION OF THE LEGISLATIVE BUDGET OFFICE **4655**

IDAHO LIBRARIAN, THE (US/0019-1213) [01752532] **3214**

IDAHO MANUFACTURING DIRECTORY (US/1057-347X) [21142589] **3480**

IDAHO MOUNTAIN EXPRESS (US/0279-8964) [07341817] **5656**

IDAHO. OFFICE OF THE GOVERNOR See EXECUTIVE BUDGET FOR FISCAL YEAR ... / STATE OF IDAHO **4722**

IDAHO PHARMACIST, THE (US/0019-1221) [04979484] **4307**

IDAHO POTATO COMMISSION See REPORT TO THE GOVERNOR OF IDAHO AND THE LEGISLATURE FROM THE IDAHO POTATO COMMISSION **184**

IDAHO POTATO COMMISSION See REPORT - IDAHO POTATO COMMISSION **184**

IDAHO PRESS-TRIBUNE (US) [18630835] **5657**

IDAHO. PUBLIC EMPLOYEE RETIREMENT BOARD See ANNUAL REPORT OF THE PUBLIC EMPLOYEE RETIREMENT SYSTEM OF IDAHO **4629**

IDAHO. PUBLIC EMPLOYEE RETIREMENT BOARD See PERSI COMPONENT UNIT FINANCIAL REPORT FOR THE FISCAL YEAR ENDED ... **4704**

IDAHO PUBLIC UTILITIES COMMISSION See REPORT / IDAHO. PUBLIC UTILITIES COMMISSION **4680**

IDAHO. STATE BOARD FOR VOCATIONAL EDUCATION See ANNUAL DESCRIPTIVE REPORT OF PROGRAM ACTIVITIES FOR VOCATIONAL EDUCATION **1910**

IDAHO. STATE BOARD FOR VOCATIONAL EDUCATION See ANNUAL PLAN FOR VOCATIONAL EDUCATION AND ... ACCOUNTABILITY REPORT (IDAHO) **1910**

IDAHO. STATE BOARD OF EDUCATION See OFFICIAL MINUTES: MEETING OF THE STATE BOARD OF EDUCATION **1868**

IDAHO. STATE DEPT. OF EDUCATION See IDAHO STATE TESTING PROGRAM : TABLES OF STANDARD SCORES WITH CORRESPONDING PERCENTILE NORMS FOR THE IOWA TESTS OF EDUCATIONAL DEVELOPMENT **1751**

IDAHO. STATE DEPT. OF EDUCATION See IDAHO FISCAL YEAR ANNUAL PROGRAM PLAN UNDER PART B OF THE EDUCATION OF THE HANDICAPPED ACT AS AMENDED BY PUBLIC LAW 94-142 **1880**

IDAHO. STATE DEPT. OF EDUCATION See AUDIT REPORT, IDAHO DEPARTMENT OF EDUCATION FOR THE FISCAL YEARS ENDED JUNE 30 ... **1726**

IDAHO STATE DIVISION OF VOCATIONAL EDUCATION. ANNUAL PERFORMANCE REPORT (US) **1913**

IDAHO STATE JOURNAL (US) [08801227] **5657**

IDAHO STATE PARKS AND RECREATION (US/0149-662X) [03520669] **4706**

IDAHO STATE TAX INSTITUTE See PAPERS AND PROCEEDINGS, IDAHO STATE TAX INSTITUTE **4740**

IDAHO STATE TESTING PROGRAM : TABLES OF STANDARD SCORES WITH CORRESPONDING PERCENTILE NORMS FOR THE IOWA TESTS OF EDUCATIONAL DEVELOPMENT (US/0095-7992) [01798509] **1751**

IDAHO STATESMAN, THE (US) [09543462] **5657**

IDAHO. TRAFFIC SAFETY COMMISSION See STATE OF IDAHO ANNUAL WORK PROGRAM **5444**

IDAHO. UNIVERSITY. FOREST, WILDLIFE, AND RANGE EXPERIMENT STATION, MOSCOW See BULLETIN - FOREST, WILDLIFE AND RANGE EXPERIMENT STATION **2189**

IDAHO WHEAT (US) [08207012] **174**

IDAHO WILDLIFE (US/8755-2469) [04647497] **4899**, **4873**

IDAHO WOOL GROWER'S BULLETIN (US) [08429030] **212**

IDAHO YESTERDAYS (US/0019-1264) [01752534] **2738**

IDAHONIAN (US/8755-9080) [11449867] **5657**

IDB : MONTHLY NEWS FROM THE INTER-AMERICAN DEVELOPMENT BANK, THE (US) [16621334] **790**

IDB NEWSLETTER (US/0018-9073) [07302450] **790**

●IDB PROJECTS (US/1076-8424) [30620870] 681, **1635**

IDC : INFORMATION, DOCUMENTS, COMMENTARIES (BU) [10900634] **2692**

IDC JAPAN REPORT (US) [20686622] **1609**

IDEA (JA/0019-1299) [01846290] **380**

IDEA (GW) **5061**

IDEA (CONCORD, N.H.) (US/0019-1272) [01607064] **1304**

IDEA FACTORY, THE (US/0891-3978) [11503017] **3286**

IDEA INK (US/8755-6871) [11383852] **5030**

IDEA LETTER FOR HEALTH CARE MANAGERS, THE (US/1068-5286) [27695185] **3786**

IDEA (ROME) (IT/0019-1280) [02106120] **2620**

IDEA SPEKTRUM (GW) **4964**

IDEA TODAY (US/1040-8126) [18543076] 2598, **1313**

IDEAL HOME (UK/0019-1361) [20240583] **616**

IDEAL HOME PLANS (US/1049-2968) [20620142] **300**

●IDEAL TRAVELER (US/1055-8314) [23352440] **5480**

IDEALISTIC STUDIES (US/0046-8541) [01786353] **4349**

IDEALS (US/0019-137X) [01752535] **5558**

IDEAS '92: A PUBLICATION OF THE 1992 INSTITUTE (US) [17730383] **2620**

IDEAS AND DEBATES : A JOURNAL OF ART WRITING (CN) **352**

IDEAS & INFORMATION ABOUT DEVELOPMENT EDUCATION (US/1040-6352) [18477036] **1751**

IDEAS CONCRETAS (VE) [01785263] **5232**

IDEAS EN ARTE Y TECNOLOGIA / UNIVERSIDAD DE BELGRANO CEASED. (AG/0326-3878) [11598709] **300**

IDEAS EN CIENCIAS SOCIALES / UNIVERSIDAD DE BELGRANO (AG/0326-386X) [11451559] **5202**

IDEAS FORUM (SZ/0252-5119) [I02525119] **5811**

IDEAS (HYDERABAD) (II/0301-9101) [01797675] **2738**

IDEAS. IDEES (CN) [03353706] **2263**

IDEAS PLUS (US/1042-5330) [11794429] 3286, **1896**

IDEAS (RESTON, VA.) (US/0896-1441) [16928548] **925**

IDEAS UNLIMITED (WASHINGTON, D.C.) (US/1054-4747) [12660505] **2791**

IDEAS (YOUTH SPECIALTIES (ORGANIZATIONS)) (US/0738-2715) [03499219] **1064**

IDECO BULLETIN (CN/0834-0889) [15726917] **1751**

IDEELE (PE) [25325362] **4509**

IDEES (GR) [01791566] **5203**

IDEES DE MA MAISON, LES (CN/0822-4269) [10335077] **2901**

IDEES ET PRATIQUES ALTERNATIVES CEASED. (CN/0823-5724) [10615637] **2217**

IDEGENFORGALMI (HU) [01791118] **5480**

IDEGENFORGALMI EVKONYV / OSSZEALLITOTTA A KSH KERESKEDELMI ES KOZLEKEDESI STATISZTIKAI FOOSZTALY, IDEGENFORGALMI OSZTALY (HU/0230-4414) [09518369] **5480**

IDEGENFORGALMI KOZLEMENYEK (HU) [04533784] **5480**

IDEMITSU BIJUTSUKAN KANPO (JA/0389-0902) [09167450] **352**

IDEN (JA/0387-0022) [I03870022] **547**

IDENGAKU ZASSHI See JAPANESE JOURNAL OF GENETICS **548**

IDENTIDAD (AG) [25302962] **2738**

IDENTIDEX. CD-ROM (US) **3981**

IDENTIFICATION CANADA (CN/0826-8142) [19032679] **5289**

IDENTIFICATION JOURNAL CEASED. (US/0747-962X) [10846593] **870**

IDENTIFIED SOURCES OF SUPPLY, THE CEASED. (US) [13198135] **950**

●IDENTITIES (YVERDON, SWITZERLAND) (SZ/1070-289X) [28315522] **2263**

IDENTITY (CINCINNATI, OHIO) (US/0899-3483) [18068425] **380**

IDEOLOGIA I POLITYKA (PL) [01787428] **4542**

IDES ... ET AUTRES (BE/0772-3784) [I07723784] **3395**

IDESIA (CL/0073-4675) [03333331] **2195**

IDF BULLETIN (US/0306-4980) [01130932] **3731**

IDH, THE HANDBOOK See INTERIOR DECORATORS' HANDBOOK : IDH **2901**

IDIA, INFORMATIVO DE INVESTIGACIONES AGRICOLAS (AG/0018-9081) [01713540] **93**

IDIOM (AT) 3286, **1896**

IDIOM 23 (AT/1032-1640) [I10321640] 3464, **3395**

IDIOMATICA (GW) [02100843] **3286**

IDIS (US/0891-8511) [11194622] **4307**

IDIS-LITERATURLISTE. ARBEITSMEDIZIN / IDIS (GW/0932-2876) [30039920] **3797**

IDIS-LITERATURLISTE. SOZIALMEDIZIN / IDIS (GW/0932-5034) [27124824] **4783**

IDIS-LITERATURLISTE. SUCHTINFORMATION / IDIS (GW/0932-4240) [27124991] **1345**

IDIS SYSTEM / CD-ROM (US) 4307, **4334**

IDISHE FOLK. THE JEWISH PEOPLE, DOS CEASED. (UK) [06685560] **2653**

IDISHE GAS, DI (RU) 352, **3395**

IDISHE VORT, DOS (US/0513-5419) [05966787] **5048**

IDISHER KEMFER (US/1050-5296) [10590960] **2504**

IDLER (TORONTO) CEASED. (CN/0828-1289) [12847221] **2535**

IDO KANSOKUJO JIGYO HOKOKU (JA) [02441205] **395**

IDO KANSOKUJO (MIZUSAWA-SHI, JAPAN) See IDO KANSOKUJO JIGYO HOKOKU **395**

IDO KANSOKUJO (MIZUSAWA-SHI, JAPAN) See IDO KANSUKOJO GAIYO **395**

IDO KANSOKUJO (MIZUSAWA-SHI, JAPAN) See IDO KANSUKOJO YORAN **1406**

IDO KANSOKUJO YORAN (JA) [03443671] **1406**

IDO KANSUKOJO GAIYO (JA) [03296241] **395**

IDOC INTERNAZIONALE (IT) [12962197] 5203, **4964**

IDOC MIDDLE EAST QUARTERLY (US/0887-9044) [01641873] **2768**

IDOJARAS (BUDAPEST 1897) (HU/0367-7443) [05015241] 93, **1426**

IDP REPORT (US/0197-0178) [05947398] 4815, **1254**

IDR. INDUSTRIAL DIAMOND REVIEW (UK/0019-8145) [01645049] **2115**

IDRA (IT) **3395**

IDRC ACQUIRES (CN/1180-0410) [23248175] **417**

IDRC MONOGRAPHS See IDRC (SERIES) **1829**

IDRC (SERIES) (CN) [11939390] **1829**

IDROTECNICA. L'ACQUA NELL'AGRICOLTURA NELL'IGIENE NELL'INDUSTRIA (IT/0390-6655) [02659415] **2090**

IDS BRIEF (UK/0308-9312) [06722620] **1677**

IDS BULLETIN (UNIVERSITY OF SUSSEX. INSTITUTE OF DEVELOPMENT STUDIES : 1985) (UK) [12879804] **1494**

IDS COMMUNICATION (UK) [03182223] **1112**

IDS EMPLOYMENT LAW CASES (UK) **3149**

IDS EUROPEAN REPORT (UK/0959-2199) [19548859] **1677**

IDS FOCUS (UK/0144-0209) [I01440209] **1609**

IDS PAY DIRECTORY (UK/0265-6019) [I02656019] 942, **1677**

IDS PENSIONS SERVICE BULLETIN (UK/1353-1573) 2882, **3149**

IDS STUDY (UK/0308-9339) [06140524] **1677**

IDSA JOURNAL SUSPENDED. (II) [05380043] **4045**

IDSA NEWS REVIEW ON AFRICA (II) [17205070] **4523**

IDSA NEWS REVIEW ON EAST ASIA (II) [17645290] **2526**

IDSA NEWS REVIEW ON NORTH AMERICA, EUROPE (II) [12742477] **4045**

IDSA NEWS REVIEW ON SOUTH ASIA/INDIAN OCEAN (II) [12397373] **4045**

IDSA NEWS REVIEW ON SOUTHEAST ASIA (II) [22201767] **2504**

IDSA PAPERS (US/0277-173X) [07515099] **2098**

Alphabetical Title Index   IEEE

IDYLLWILD TOWN CRIER (US) [27263446] **5635**

IE, INVESTMENT EXECUTIVE (CN/0840-9137) [19652507] **900**

IEA COAL RESEARCH *See* ANNUAL REPORT / IEA COAL RESEARCH **2133**

IEA LECTURE (UK) [02380265] **1494**

IEA/NEA ADVOCATE / ILLINOIS EDUCATION ASSOCIATION/NEA (US) [08963209] **1751**

IEC BULLETIN (SW/0018-9138) [03348260] **2057**

IED STAFF REPORT (US) [07560573] **1635**

IEE BRIEF (US/1059-2776) [24562017] **1751**

IEE CONFERENCE PUBLICATION (UK/0537-9989) [02139514] **2057**

IEE CONTROL ENGINEERING SERIES (UK/0262-1797) [03723015] **2057**

IEE DIGITAL ELECTRONICS AND COMPUTING SERIES (UK) [12003992] **2057**

IEE ELECTRICAL MEASUREMENT SERIES (UK) [10329474] **2057**

IEE ELECTROMAGNETIC WAVES SERIES (UK) [13588632] **2057**

IEE HISTORY OF TECHNOLOGY SERIES (UK/0266-1721) [10311045] **2057**

IEE MANAGEMENT OF TECHNOLOGY SERIES (UK/0268-6171) [I02686171] **5111**

IEE MANAGEMENT OF TECHNOLOGY SERIES (UK) [20240761] **2057**

IEE MATERIALS & DEVICES SERIES (UK/0953-5985) [17165748] **2057**

IEE NEWS (UK/0308-0684) [02447490] **2057**

IEE PROCEEDINGS. A, SCIENCE, MEASUREMENT AND TECHNOLOGY (UK/0960-7641) [23045170] **2057**

IEE PROCEEDINGS. C, GENERATION, TRANSMISSION, AND DISTRIBUTION (UK/0143-7046) [05973062] **2057**

●IEE PROCEEDINGS. CIRCUITS, DEVICES AND SYSTEMS (UK/1350-2409) [29965674] **2057**

●IEE PROCEEDINGS. COMMUNICATIONS (UK/1350-2425) [29855603] **1156**

●IEE PROCEEDINGS. COMPUTERS AND DIGITAL TECHNIQUES (UK/1350-2387) [29965679] **1229**

●IEE PROCEEDINGS. CONTROL THEORY AND APPLICATIONS (UK/1350-2379) [29973264] **2057**

IEE PROCEEDINGS. D, CONTROL THEORY AND APPLICATIONS (UK/0143-7054) [05987124] **2057**

●IEE PROCEEDINGS. ELECTRIC POWER APPLICATIONS (UK/1350-2352) [29965686] **2058**

IEE PROCEEDINGS. F, RADAR AND SIGNAL PROCESSING (UK/0956-375X) [19110246] **1156**

IEE PROCEEDINGS. G, CIRCUITS, DEVICES, AND SYSTEMS (UK/0956-3768) [19250529] **2058**

●IEE PROCEEDINGS. GENERATION, TRANSMISSION, AND DISTRIBUTION (UK/1350-2360) [29923918] **2058**

IEE PROCEEDINGS. I, COMMUNICATIONS, SPEECH, AND VISION (UK/0956-3776) [19239750] **1156**

IEE PROCEEDINGS INDEX *CEASED*. (UK) **2058**

●IEE PROCEEDINGS. MICROWAVES, ANTENNAS AND PROPAGATION (UK/1350-2417) [29965297] **2058**

●IEE PROCEEDINGS. OPTOELECTRONICS (UK/1350-2433) [29965305] **2058**

IEE PROCEEDINGS. PART B. ELECTRIC POWER APPLICATIONS (UK/0143-7038) [05958499] **2058**

IEE PROCEEDINGS. PART E. COMPUTERS AND DIGITAL TECHNIQUES (UK/0143-7062) [05987851] **1229**

IEE PROCEEDINGS. PART F, RADAR AND SIGNAL PROCESSING *See* IEE PROCEEDINGS. RADAR, SONAR, AND NAVIGATION **1156**

IEE PROCEEDINGS. PART H, MICROWAVES, ANTENNAS, AND PROPAGATION (UK/0950-107X) [12070418] **2058**

IEE PROCEEDINGS. PART I. SOLID-STATE AND ELECTRON DEVICES (UK/0143-7100) [06895493] **2058**

IEE PROCEEDINGS. PART J, OPTOELECTRONICS (UK/0267-3932) [11811682] **2058**

●IEE PROCEEDINGS. RADAR, SONAR, AND NAVIGATION (UK/1350-2395) [29903951] **1156**

●IEE PROCEEDINGS. SCIENCE, MEASUREMENT AND TECHNOLOGY (UK/1350-2344) [29965317] **2058**

IEE PROCEEDINGS: VISION, IMAGE AND SIGNAL PROCESSING (UK/1350-245X) **1156**

IEE PRODUCTRONIC (GW) [08752033] 3480, **2058**

IEE REVIEW (UK/0953-5683) [17349294] **2058**

IEE TELECOMMUNICATIONS SERIES (UK/0263-5852) [05133509] **1156**

IEE TOPICS IN CONTROL SERIES (UK/0265-2986) [10056197] **2058**

IEE 802.3 REPORT (US/0897-6813) [17595031] **2058**

●IEEE/ACM TRANSACTIONS ON NETWORKING (US/1063-6692) [26108948] 1112, **1241**

IEEE AEROSPACE AND ELECTRONIC SYSTEMS MAGAZINE (US/0885-8985) [12760485] 2058, **23**

●IEEE ANNALS OF THE HISTORY OF COMPUTING (US/1058-6180) [24344740] **1187**

IEEE ANTENNAS & PROPAGATION MAGAZINE (US/1045-9243) [20287815] **2058**

IEEE BULLETIN (US/0162-3842) [04162450] **2059**

IEEE/CHMT INTERNATIONAL ELECTRONIC MANUFACTURING TECHNOLOGY SYMPOSIUM : [PROCEEDINGS] (US) [21347560] **2059**

IEEE CIRCUITS AND DEVICES MAGAZINE (US/8755-3996) [11292098] **2059**

IEEE COMMUNICATIONS MAGAZINE (US/0163-6804) [04447692] **1157**

IEEE COMMUNICATIONS SOCIETY *See* IEEE COMMUNICATIONS MAGAZINE **1157**

IEEE COMMUNICATIONS SOCIETY *See* IEEE TRANSACTIONS ON COMMUNICATIONS **1157**

●IEEE COMPUTATIONAL SCIENCE AND ENGINEERING (US/1070-9924) [28525313] **1187**

IEEE COMPUTER APPLICATIONS IN POWER (US/0895-0156) [16402053] **2059**

IEEE COMPUTER GRAPHICS AND APPLICATIONS (US/0272-1716) [06794952] **1233**

IEEE CONFERENCE RECORD-ABSTRACTS (US/0730-9244) [08010879] **2024**

IEEE CONFERENCE RECORD OF ... ANNUAL CONFERENCE OF ELECTRICAL ENGINEERING PROBLEMS IN THE RUBBER AND PLASTICS INDUSTRIES (US/0272-4685) [02535636] 4455, **2059**

IEEE CONFERENCE RECORD OF ANNUAL PETROLEUM AND CHEMICAL INDUSTRY TECHNICAL CONFERENCE *See* RECORD OF CONFERENCE PAPERS - PETROLEUM AND CHEMICAL INDUSTRY CONFERENCE **2016**

IEEE CONFERENCE RECORD OF ... POWER MODULATOR SYMPOSIUM (US/0736-590X) [08864069] **2059**

IEEE CONTROL SYSTEMS (US/1066-033X) [26522522] **2059**

IEEE DESIGN & TEST OF COMPUTERS (US/0740-7475) [10024072] **1229**

IEEE ELECTRICAL INSULATION MAGAZINE (US/0883-7554) [12221132] **2059**

IEEE ELECTRO TECHNOLOGY REVIEW (US/0748-9196) [12143227] **2059**

IEEE ELECTRON DEVICE LETTERS (US/0741-3106) [07797465] **2059**

IEEE ENGINEERING IN MEDICINE AND BIOLOGY MAGAZINE (US/0739-5175) [08878354] **3693**

IEEE ENGINEERING IN MEDICINE AND BIOLOGY SOCIETY. CONFERENCE *See* PROCEEDINGS OF THE ANNUAL INTERNATIONAL CONFERENCE OF THE IEEE ENGINEERING IN MEDICINE AND BIOLOGY SOCIETY **3696**

IEEE ENGINEERING MANAGEMENT REVIEW (US/0360-8581) [01961379] **2059**

IEEE ENGINEERING MANAGEMENT SOCIETY *See* IEEE ENGINEERING MANAGEMENT REVIEW **2059**

IEEE EXPERT (US/0885-9000) [12760395] **1229**

IEEE GRID (US/0018-9189) [04062633] **2059**

IEEE IECI PROCEEDINGS (US/0271-8308) [06696060] **2059**

IEEE IMPACT (US/0274-8207) [06619834] **2059**

IEEE INDUSTRY APPLICATIONS MAGAZINE (US) **3480**

IEEE INSTRUMENTATION AND MEASUREMENT SOCIETY *See* IEEE INSTRUMENTATION AND MEASUREMENT SOCIETY NEWSLETTER **2059**

IEEE INSTRUMENTATION AND MEASUREMENT SOCIETY NEWSLETTER (US/0161-1038) [03834723] **2059**

IEEE INTERNATIONAL SYMPOSIUM ON CIRCUITS AND SYSTEMS : [SELECTED PAPERS] (US) [25014786] **2059**

IEEE JOURNAL OF OCEANIC ENGINEERING (US/0364-9059) [02460306] **2090**

IEEE JOURNAL OF QUANTUM ELECTRONICS (US/0018-9197) [04760477] **2060**

IEEE JOURNAL OF SOLID-STATE CIRCUITS (US/0018-9200) [01589745] **2060**

IEEE JOURNAL ON SELECTED AREAS IN COMMUNICATIONS (US/0733-8716) [08649040] **1157**

IEEE JOURNAL ON SELECTED TOPICS IN QUANTUM ELECTRONICS (US) **2060**

IEEE LTS : THE MAGAZINE OF LIGHTWAVE TELECOMMUNICATIONS SYSTEMS *CEASED*. (US/1055-6877) [23269746] **4434**

IEEE MEMBERSHIP DIRECTORY (US/0073-9146) [03225575] **2060**

IEEE MICRO (US/0272-1732) [06795047] **1267**

IEEE MICROWAVE AND GUIDED WAVE LETTERS (US/1051-8207) [22134434] **2060**

IEEE ... MICROWAVE AND MILLIMETER-WAVE MONOLITHIC CIRCUITS SYMPOSIUM DIGEST OF PAPERS (US) [10985617] **2060**

IEEE MTT-S INTERNATIONAL MICROWAVE SYMPOSIUM DIGEST (US/0149-645X) [03490335] **2060**

●IEEE MULTIMEDIA (US/1070-986X) [28524907] **1187**

IEEE NETWORK (US/0890-8044) [14393593] **1241**

●IEEE/NPSS SYMPOSIUM FUSION ENGINEERING : PROCEEDINGS (US) [30842885] **1977**

IEEE NUCLEAR AND PLASMA SCIENCES SOCIETY *See* IEEE TRANSACTIONS ON PLASMA SCIENCE **3693**

IEEE OCEANIC ENGINEERING SOCIETY. NEWSLETTER (US/0746-7834) [10267724] **2060**

●IEEE PARALLEL AND DISTRIBUTED TECHNOLOGY (US) [26104210] **2060**

●IEEE PARALLEL & DISTRIBUTED TECHNOLOGY : SYSTEMS & APPLICATIONS (US/1063-6552) [27749578] **1187**

●IEEE PERSONAL COMMUNICATIONS MAGAZINE (US) [28525286] **1112**

IEEE PHOTONICS TECHNOLOGY LETTERS (US/1041-1135) [18633549] **4435**

IEEE POTENTIALS (US/0278-6648) [07856947] **2060**

IEEE POWER ENGINEERING REVIEW (US/0272-1724) [06795095] **2060**

IEEE POWER ENGINEERING SOCIETY *See* IEEE POWER ENGINEERING SOCIETY DISCUSSIONS AND CLOSURES OF ABSTRACTED PAPERS FROM THE SUMMER MEETING **2060**

IEEE POWER ENGINEERING SOCIETY *See* TEXT OF "A" PAPERS FROM THE WINTER MEETING - IEEE POWER ENGINEERING SOCIETY **2084**

IEEE POWER ENGINEERING SOCIETY *See* DISCUSSIONS AND CLOSURES OF ABSTRACTED PAPERS FROM THE WINTER MEETING **2042**

IEEE POWER ENGINEERING SOCIETY DISCUSSIONS AND CLOSURES OF ABSTRACTED PAPERS FROM THE SUMMER MEETING (US/0160-0141) [03594822] **2060**

IEEE PROFESSIONAL COMMUNICATION SOCIETY. IEEE PROFESSIONAL COMMUNICATION SOCIETY NEWSLETTER *See* NEWSLETTER / IEEE PROFESSIONAL COMMUNICATION SOCIETY **2073**

IEEE PUBLICATIONS BULLETIN (US/0046-8371) [03930493] **2060**

●IEEE ROBOTICS AND AUTOMATION MAGAZINE (US/1070-9932) [28528271] **1219**

●IEEE SIGNAL PROCESSING LETTERS (US/1070-9908) [28525247] **1977**

IEEE SIGNAL PROCESSING MAGAZINE (US/1053-5888) [22582650] **2060**

IEEE SOFTWARE (US/0740-7459) [10024196] **1286**

IEEE SPECTRUM (US/0018-9235) [01752538] **2060**

IEEE STUDENT PAPERS (US/0362-4536) [02287379] **2061**

IEEE STUDENT PRIZE PAPERS, THE (US/0360-8956) [03157198] **2061**

IEEE TECHNICAL ACTIVITIES GUIDE (US/0278-520X) [07501739] **2061**

IEEE Alphabetical Title Index

IEEE TECHNOLOGY & SOCIETY MAGAZINE (US/0278-0097) [07677068] **5111**

IEEE TRANSACTIONS ON AEROSPACE AND ELECTRONIC SYSTEMS (US/0018-9251) [04935918] 23, **2061**

IEEE TRANSACTIONS ON ANTENNAS AND PROPAGATION (US/0018-926X) [01752540] **2061**

IEEE TRANSACTIONS ON APPLIED SUPERCONDUCTIVITY (US/1051-8223) [22134485] **2061**

IEEE TRANSACTIONS ON AUTOMATIC CONTROL (US/0018-9286) [01752543] **1219**

IEEE TRANSACTIONS ON BROADCASTING (US/0018-9316) [01642875] **1133**

IEEE TRANSACTIONS ON CIRCUITS AND SYSTEMS *See* IEEE TRANSACTIONS ON CIRCUITS & SYSTEMS. PART 1, FUNDAMENTAL THEORY AND APPLICATIONS **2061**

IEEE TRANSACTIONS ON CIRCUITS AND SYSTEMS *See* IEEE TRANSACTIONS ON CIRCUITS AND SYSTEMS. PART 2, ANALOG AND DIGITAL SIGNAL PROCESSING **2061**

IEEE TRANSACTIONS ON CIRCUITS AND SYSTEMS FOR VIDEO TECHNOLOGY (US/1051-8215) [22134460] **1133**

●IEEE TRANSACTIONS ON CIRCUITS & SYSTEMS. PART 1, FUNDAMENTAL THEORY AND APPLICATIONS (US/1057-7122) [24103431] **2061**

●IEEE TRANSACTIONS ON CIRCUITS AND SYSTEMS. PART 2, ANALOG AND DIGITAL SIGNAL PROCESSING (US/1057-7130) [24103498] **2061**

IEEE TRANSACTIONS ON COMMUNICATIONS (US/0090-6778) [01785858] **1157**

IEEE TRANSACTIONS ON COMPONENTS, HYBRIDS AND MANUFACTURING TECHNOLOGY (US/0148-6411) [03523341] **2061**

●IEEE TRANSACTIONS ON COMPONENTS, PACKAGING, AND MANUFACTURING TECHNOLOGY. PART A (US/1070-9886) [28525047] **3480**

IEEE TRANSACTIONS ON COMPUTER-AIDED DESIGN OF INTEGRATED CIRCUITS AND SYSTEMS (US/0278-0070) [07677291] 1233, **2061**

IEEE TRANSACTIONS ON COMPUTERS (US/0018-9340) [01799331] 1977, **2247**

IEEE TRANSACTIONS ON CONSUMER ELECTRONICS (US/0098-3063) [02241216] **2061**

●IEEE TRANSACTIONS ON CONTROL SYSTEMS TECHNOLOGY (US/1063-6536) [26104129] **1977**

●IEEE TRANSACTIONS ON DIELECTRICS AND ELECTRICAL INSULATION (US/1070-9878) [28524935] **2061**

IEEE TRANSACTIONS ON EDUCATION (US/0018-9359) [01752549] **2062**

IEEE TRANSACTIONS ON ELECTRICAL INSULATION (US/0018-9367) [01352217] **2062**

IEEE TRANSACTIONS ON ELECTROMAGNETIC COMPATIBILITY (US/0018-9375) [01645452] **2062**

IEEE TRANSACTIONS ON ELECTRON DEVICES (US/0018-9383) [00935837] **2062**

IEEE TRANSACTIONS ON ENERGY CONVERSION (US/0885-8969) [12761083] **2062**

IEEE TRANSACTIONS ON ENGINEERING MANAGEMENT (US/0018-9391) [01752550] **2062**

●IEEE TRANSACTIONS ON FUZZY SYSTEMS (US/1063-6706) [26109022] **1187**

IEEE TRANSACTIONS ON GEOSCIENCE AND REMOTE SENSING (US/0196-2892) [05792014] **1406**

●IEEE TRANSACTIONS ON IMAGE PROCESSING (US/1057-7149) [24103523] **2062**

IEEE TRANSACTIONS ON INDUSTRIAL ELECTRONICS (1982) (US/0278-0046) [07677112] **2062**

IEEE TRANSACTIONS ON INDUSTRY APPLICATIONS (US) [05244837] **2062**

IEEE TRANSACTIONS ON INDUSTRY APPLICATIONS (US/0093-9994) [01695800] **2062**

IEEE TRANSACTIONS ON INFORMATION THEORY (US/0018-9448) [01752552] **2062**

IEEE TRANSACTIONS ON INSTRUMENTATION AND MEASUREMENT (US/0018-9456) [00936505] **2063**

IEEE TRANSACTIONS ON KNOWLEDGE AND DATA ENGINEERING (US/1041-4347) [18766852] **2063**

IEEE TRANSACTIONS ON MAGNETICS (US/0018-9464) [03938336] **4443**

IEEE TRANSACTIONS ON MEDICAL IMAGING (US/0278-0062) [07677152] 2063, **3941**

IEEE TRANSACTIONS ON MICROWAVE THEORY AND TECHNIQUES (US/0018-9480) [01752555] **2063**

IEEE TRANSACTIONS ON NEURAL NETWORKS (US/1045-9227) [20284540] **1229**

IEEE TRANSACTIONS ON NUCLEAR SCIENCE (US/0018-9499) [01605747] **2155**

IEEE TRANSACTIONS ON PARALLEL AND DISTRIBUTED SYSTEMS (US/1045-9219) [20284447] **1259**

IEEE TRANSACTIONS ON PATTERN ANALYSIS AND MACHINE INTELLIGENCE (US/0162-8828) [04253074] 1212, **1229**

IEEE TRANSACTIONS ON PLASMA SCIENCE (US/0093-3813) [01787960] **3693**

IEEE TRANSACTIONS ON POWER APPARATUS AND SYSTEMS (US) [06366867] **2063**

IEEE TRANSACTIONS ON POWER DELIVERY (US/0885-8977) [12761155] **2063**

IEEE TRANSACTIONS ON POWER ELECTRONICS (US/0885-8993) [12760678] **2063**

IEEE TRANSACTIONS ON POWER SYSTEMS (US/0885-8950) [12760783] **2063**

IEEE TRANSACTIONS ON PROFESSIONAL COMMUNICATION (US/0361-1434) [01752470] 1112, **2063**

●IEEE TRANSACTIONS ON REHABILITATION ENGINEERING (US/1063-6528) [26104092] **3693**

IEEE TRANSACTIONS ON RELIABILITY (US/0018-9529) [01752560] **2063**

IEEE TRANSACTIONS ON ROBOTICS AND AUTOMATION (US/1042-296X) [19003543] 1219, **1212**

IEEE TRANSACTIONS ON ROBOTICS AND AUTOMATION (US/1042-296X) [19580071] **1213**

IEEE TRANSACTIONS ON SEMICONDUCTOR MANUFACTURING (US/0894-6507) [16152423] **2063**

IEEE TRANSACTIONS ON SIGNAL PROCESSING (US/1053-587X) [22582682] **2064**

IEEE TRANSACTIONS ON SOFTWARE ENGINEERING (US/0098-5589) [01465815] **1286**

IEEE TRANSACTIONS ON SOFTWARE ENGINEERING (US/0098-5589) [01434336] 1279, **1286**

●IEEE TRANSACTIONS ON SPEECH AND AUDIO PROCESSING (US/1063-6676) [26108901] **5317**

IEEE TRANSACTIONS ON SYSTEMS, MAN, AND CYBERNETICS (US/0018-9472) [01752562] **1251**

IEEE TRANSACTIONS ON ULTRASONICS, FERROELECTRICS, AND FREQUENCY CONTROL (US/0885-3010) [12615923] **4452**

IEEE TRANSACTIONS ON VEHICULAR TECHNOLOGY (US/0018-9545) [01644964] **2064**

●IEEE TRANSACTIONS ON VERY LARGE SCALE INTEGRATION (VLSI) SYSTEMS (US/1063-8210) [26142392] **1187**

IEEE TRANSLATION JOURNAL ON MAGNETICS IN JAPAN *CEASED*. (US/0882-4959) [11874165] 2064, **4444**

IEEE VISUALIZATION AND COMPUTER GRAPHICS (US) **1233**

IEEMA JOURNAL (II/0970-2946) [24925416] **3480**

IEG DIRECTORY OF SPONSORSHIP MARKETING (US/1058-613X) [23437921] **926**

IEICE TRANSACTIONS ON COMMUNICATIONS (JA/0916-8516) [25533083] 2064, **1112**

IEICE TRANSACTIONS ON COMMUNICATIONS, ELECTRONICS, INFORMATION, AND SYSTEMS *See* IEICE TRANSACTIONS ON INFORMATION AND SYSTEMS **5111**

IEICE TRANSACTIONS ON COMMUNICATIONS, ELECTRONICS, INFORMATION, AND SYSTEMS *See* IEICE TRANSACTIONS ON ELECTRONICS **2064**

IEICE TRANSACTIONS ON COMMUNICATIONS, ELECTRONICS, INFORMATION, AND SYSTEMS *See* IEICE TRANSACTIONS ON FUNDAMENTALS OF ELECTRONICS, COMMUNICATIONS AND COMPUTER SCIENCES **1157**

●IEICE TRANSACTIONS ON ELECTRONICS (JA/0916-8524) [25533087] **2064**

●IEICE TRANSACTIONS ON FUNDAMENTALS OF ELECTRONICS, COMMUNICATIONS AND COMPUTER SCIENCES (JA/0916-8508) [25533095] 2064, **1157**

●IEICE TRANSACTIONS ON INFORMATION AND SYSTEMS (JA/0916-8532) [25533102] **5111**

IEMA JOURNAL *See* IEEMA JOURNAL **3480**

IEN. INDUSTRIAL EQUIPMENT NEWS (SUTTON) (UK/0019-8277) [I00198277] 2115, **1609**

IEPS JOURNAL *See* INTERNATIONAL JOURNAL OF MICROCIRCUITS AND ELECTRONIC PACKAGING, THE **4219**

IER, INDONESIAN EXPORT REVIEW (IO) [03216937] **839**

IES LIGHTING HANDBOOK. APPLICATION VOLUME *See* LIGHTING HANDBOOK. REFERENCE & APPLICATION **2071**

IES LIGHTING HANDBOOK. REFERENCE VOLUME *See* LIGHTING HANDBOOK. REFERENCE & APPLICATION **2071**

IEVANHELSKYI RANOK (US/1051-5143) [03566898] **5061**

IF. INDUSTRIALIZATION FORUM (CN/0380-0857) [03916218] **616**

IF REPORT SERIES (US/0492-8539) [01441745] **2305**

IFA CONGRESS SEMINAR SERIES (INT/1016-7560) [I10167560] **1494**

IFAC NEWSLETTER (AU) **681**

IFAC NEWSLETTER (UK) [05540006] **4655**

IFAC PROCEEDINGS SERIES (UK/0742-5953) [10088596] **1219**

IFAC SYMPOSIA SERIES *CEASED*. (UK/0962-9505) [21927007] **1219**

IFAD ANNUAL REPORT (IT) [23451906] **93**

IFAD STUDIES IN RURAL POVERTY (US) [25126422] **5289**

IFAD UPDATE (IT) **93**

IFAR REPORTS (US/8756-7172) [11635845] **352**

●IFBWW EDUCATION NEWS (SZ) [26686351] **1677**

IFC GENERAL POLICIES (US/0160-9238) [02748426] **790**

IFCC NEWS (UK/0142-0143) [05533943] **977**

IFCD REPORT (SPANISH EDITION) (US/0149-5852) [03522230] **93**

●IFCI FIRE CODE JOURNAL (US/1061-5334) [25344233] **2291**

IFCO NEWS (US/1065-1675) [09516222] **4964**

IFC'S FINANCIAL NEWS REVIEW (US/0741-3785) [10137950] **790**

IFDA DOSSIER / INTERNATIONAL FOUNDATION FOR DEVELOPMENT ALTERNATIVES *SUSPENDED*. (SZ) [05590685] **4523**

IFDC REPORT (US/0149-3434) [03473202] **94**

IFDC REPORT (FRENCH ED.) (US/1044-4521) [19789192] **174**

IFES REVIEW (UK/1010-8734) [I10108734] **4964**

IFF BULLETIN (GW/0340-0743) [01786505] **4428**

IFF REPORT *See* REPORT - INSTITUTE FOR THE FUTURE **5215**

IFI : MEMORIA (CK) [20288434] **1609**

IFI RESEARCH CENTER *See* TECHNICAL BULLETIN - IFI RESEARCH CENTER **5356**

IFI RESEARCH CENTER *See* FABRICS-FASHIONS **5350**

IFIP CONGRESS SERIES (NE/0924-5812) [I09245812] **1187**

IFIP TRANSACTIONS B: COMPUTER APPLICATIONS IN TECHNOLOGY (NE/0926-5481) 1223, **1229**

IFIP TRANSACTIONS C: SYSTEMS COMMUNICATIONS (NE) [28894768] 1254, **1241**

●IFIP TRANSACTIONS. COMPUTER SCIENCE AND TECHNOLOGY (NE/0926-5473) [I09265473] 1229, 1279, **1247**

IFLA ANNUAL (GW) [03961857] **3214**

IFLA DIRECTORY (NE/0074-6002) [04607184] **3214**

IFLA JOURNAL (GW/0340-0352) [01286525] **3214**

IFLA PROFESSIONAL REPORTS / INTERNATIONAL FEDERATION OF LIBRARY ASSOCIATIONS AND INSTITUTIONS (NE) [17570706] **3214**

IFMA ENCYCLOPEDIA OF THE FOODSERVICE INDUSTRY, THE (US/8755-0334) [09100048] **2344**

IFMA JOURNAL *See* FACILITY MANAGEMENT JOURNAL : A PUBLICATION OF THE INTERNATIONAL FACILITY MANAGEMENT ASSOCIATION **867**

IFO-DIGEST (GW) [06955113] **1566**

IFO-INSTITUT FUER WIRTSCHAFTSFORSCHUNG *See* SCHRIFTENREIHE DES IFO-INSTITUT FUER WIRTSCHAFTSFORSCHUNG **1396**

IFO-INSTITUT FUER WIRTSCHAFTSFORSCHUNG. ABTEILUNG BAU- UND WOHNUNGSWIRTSCHAFT *See* BAUVORAUSSCHAETZUNG **600**

IFO-INSTITUT FUR WIRTSCHAFTSFORSCHUNG *See* SONDERSCHRIFT DES IFO-INSTITUTS FUR WIRTSCHAFTSFORSCHUNG **1521**

IFO-INSTITUT FUR WIRTSCHAFTSFORSCHUNG *See* IFO SPIEGEL DER WIRTSCHAFT **1533**

IFO-INSTITUT FUR WIRTSCHAFTSFORSCHUNG, MUNICH *See* IFO-DIGEST **1566**

IFO SCHNELLDIENST (GW/0018-974X) [07887835] **1494, 681**

IFO SPIEGEL DER WIRTSCHAFT (GW/0170-3617) [02887055] **1635, 1533**

IFO-STUDIEN (GW/0018-9731) [02084278] **1494**

●IFO WIRTSCHAFTSKONJUNKTUR : MONATSBERICHTE DES IFO INSTITUTS FUER WIRTSCHAFTSFORSCHUNG (GW) [24775714] **1494**

IFOAM BULLETIN (US/0195-0304) [05226360] **94**

IFOR REPORT (NE/0167-174X) [I0167174X] **4509**

IFPA COMMUNICATOR (US/0099-1090) [02239934] **4072**

IFPAAW NEWS *See* INFO / FITPAS **1679**

IFPRA BULLETIN (UK/1012-7720) [I10127720] **4706**

IFPRI REPORT (US/0272-3700) [06364106] **1494, 94**

IFR (US/0894-6620) [16160430] **23**

IFR AIRCRAFT HANDLED (US/0092-3567) [06832474] **23**

IFR GLOBAL FINANCING DIRECTORY, THE (UK) [17530721] **790**

IFR NEWS (UK) **2344**

IFR OFF-AIRWAY ROUTES, NON PART 95 (US) [04455985] **23**

IFR REFRESHER (US/0896-9868) [17360244] **23**

IFR-- SUPPLEMENT, UNITED STATES (US) [04508668] **4045**

IFT BASIC SYMPOSIUM SERIES (US/0730-9198) [08122550] **4192**

IFT SHORT COURSE MANUALS (US) **2344**

IFW. INTERNATIONAL FREIGHTING WEEKLY (UK/0032-5007) [08546917] **681, 5383**

IFYGL BULLETIN (US/0149-4023) [02291650] **839**

IGA GROCERGRAM (US/0018-9766) [02447493] **2344**

IGAKU KENSA (JA/0915-8669) [I09158669] **3585**

IGAKU NO AYUMI (JA/0039-2359) [09947154] **3585**

IGAKU TO SEIBUTSUGAKU (JA/0019-1604) [I00191604] 458, **3585**

IGAKU TO YAKUGAKU (JA/0389-3898) [I03893898] **3585**

IGCAR (II/0970-2210) [15618534] **2156**

IGD, INITIATION GENERALE AU DROIT (FR) [06844994] **2980**

IGIENE DEL LAVORO (IT) **2863**

IGIENE E SANITA PUBBLICA (IT/0019-1639) [03048186] **4783**

IGIENE MODERNA (IT/0019-1655) [01752564] **4783**

IGLESIA EVANGELICA ESPANOLA *See* PRESUPUESTO - IGLESIA EVANGELICA ESPANOLA **4987**

IGLESIA Y SOCIEDAD EN AMERICA LATINA *See* FICHAS **2733**

IGLOOS *See* REVUE QUART MONDE **4512**

IGLU. INSTITUTO DE GESTION Y LIDERAZGO UNIVERSITARIO (CN/1183-5052) [24623394] **1829**

IGLU. INSTITUTO DE GESTION Y LIDERAZGO UNIVERSITARIO (CN/1183-5052) [24623387] **1829**

IGNACE COURIER (CN/0715-5352) [09499055] **5786**

IGOTI NAUKI I TEKHNIKI. SERIIA KRISTALLOKHIMIIA (RU/0202-7984) [21440523] **1032**

IGT GASCOPE (US/0270-1022) [05534467] **4260**

IGU BULLETIN (UK/0018-9804) [03006300] **2565**

IGU NEWSLETTER (CN/0251-0464) [07817238] 4553, **2565**

IGW-REPORT UBER WISSENSCHAFT UND TECHNOLOGIE (GW) [20160563] **5111**

IGY OCEANOGRAPHY REPORT (US/0536-1699) [01167526] **1450**

IGY WORLD DATA CENTER A: OCEANOGRAPHY *See* IGY OCEANOGRAPHY REPORT **1450**

IH REVIEW *See* COMMUNITY MOVES **4385**

IHAK NONJIP (KO) [22271218] **5111**

IHD, THE HANDBOOK (US/1055-5013) [22099757] **2901**

IHERINGIA. BOTANICA *See* IHERINGIA. SERIE BOTANICA **513**

IHERINGIA. SERIE BOTANICA (BL/0073-4705) [02447495] **513**

IHERINGIA. SERIE ZOOLOGIA (BL/0073-4721) [02447496] **5586**

IHI ENGINEERING REVIEW (JA/0018-9820) [10265864] **1977**

IHN NEWS (US/1042-4334) [19056814] **1113**

IHO *See* HOKOKU (TOHOKU DAIGAKU. NOGAKU KENKYUJO) **92**

IHPS REPORT (US/0892-1318) [08160363] **4784**

IHRC ETHNIC BIBLIOGRAPHY (US) [06101890] 3149, **2276**

IHSA AL-TALIM BI-AL-MADARIS WA-AL-MAAHID WA-MARAKIZ AL-TADRIB AL-GHAYR KHADIAH L.-WIZARAT AL-TALIM WA-AL-BAHTH AL-ILMI WA-AL-AZHAR / AL-JIHAZ A.-MARKAZI LIL-TABIAH AL-AMMAH WA-AL-IHSA (UA) [08819640] **1751**

IHSA AL-TASHYID WA-AL-BINA. SHARIKAT AL-QITA AL-AMM. AL-JIHAZ AL-MARKAZI LIL-TABIAH AL-AMMAH WA-AL-IHSA (UA) [09351256] **617**

IHSAAT AL-IQTISADIYAH WA-AL-MALIYAH LIL-BUNUK WA-AL-TA-MIN / AL-JIHAZ AL-MARKAZI LIL-TABIAH AL-AMMAH WA-AL-IHSA (UA) [08815203] 790, **730**

IHSAAT AL-TALIM FI AL-MAMLAKAH AL-ARABIYAH AL-SAUDIYAH / AL-MAMLAKAH AL-ARABIYAH AL-SAUDIYAH, WIZARAT AL-MAARIF, QISM AL-IHSA (SU) [04635294] 1751, **1795**

IHWA UMAK (KO) [07345348] **4122**

IHWA YOJA TAEHAKKYO, SEOUL, KOREA. TAEHAGWON *See* YON'GU NONJIP - IHWA YOJA TAEHAKKYO, TAEHAGWON **5237**

II COMPUTING (US/0889-9134) [14104975] **1187**

IIASA COLLABORATIVE PROCEEDINGS SERIES (AU/1012-909X) [09500579] **1187**

IIASA PUBLICATIONS (AU) [04231341] **1187**

IIC DOCUMENT SERVICE (US/0738-7938) [08963317] **1113**

IIC; INTERNATIONAL REVIEW OF INDUSTRIAL AND COPYRIGHT LAW (GW/0018-9855) [01714535] **1304**

IIC NEWS (UK/0536-1737) [01171302] **2195**

IICCG BULLETIN (CN/0843-6657) [23295780] 2620, **322**

IIE TRANSACTIONS (US/0740-817X) [08390286] **2098**

III-VS REVIEW (UK/0961-1290) [24495367] **2064**

IIMC NEWSLETTER *See* NEWS DIGEST - INTERNATIONAL INSTITUTE OF MUNICIPAL CLERKS **4669**

IIMI CASE STUDY (CE) [19596761] **2091**

IIMI COUNTRY PAPER, NEPAL (CE) [24385679] **174**

IIMI COUNTRY PAPER, SRI LANKA (CE) [22657594] **174**

IIMS, INDONESIA INDEX OF MEDICAL SPECIALITIES (SI/0300-4147) [04351503] **4307**

IINFANCIA : BOLETIN DEL INSTITUTO INTERAMERICANO DEL NINO-OEA (UY) [25991688] **5289**

IIPA NEWSLETTER (II/0536-1761) [01588977] **4655**

IIPS NEWSLETTER (II) [06963097] **4553**

IIR REVIEW, THE (US/1062-2799) [25580016] **2863**

IISH CIMINAL LW JURNAL (IE/0791-539X) [25416669] **3107**

IISRP (ORGANIZATION) *See* ANNUAL MEETING PROCEEDINGS - INTERNATIONAL INSTITUTE OF SYNTHETIC RUBBER PRODUCERS, INC **5075**

IISRP (ORGANIZATION) *See* PROCEEDINGS ... ANNUAL GENERAL MEETING **5077**

IISRP (ORGANIZATION). ANNUAL MEETING PROCEEDINGS - INTERNATIONAL INSTITUTE OF SYNTHETIC RUBBER PRODUCERS, INC *See* PROCEEDINGS ... ANNUAL GENERAL MEETING **5077**

IITA RESEARCH (NR/1115-3067) [23236821] **94**

IJA REPORT (US/0018-991X) [01795173] **3090**

IJA REVIEW / THE INSTITUTE OF JUDICIAL ADMINISTRATION (US) [08524110] **4655**

IJCAI (UNITED STATES) (US/1045-0823) [08018488] **1213**

IJDL. INTERNATIONAL JOURNAL OF DRAVIDIAN LINGUISTICS (II/0378-2484) [01753568] **3286**

IJS JAZZ REGISTER (US/0889-8723) [05626914] **4122**

IJU KENKYU (JA) [02262147] **1919**

IK. ZEITSCHRIFT FUER INDUSTRIEKAUFLEUTE (GW/0939-9909) [I09399909] **1609**

IKA KIKAIGAKU (JA/0385-440X) [05845436] **3585**

IKATAN PEMINAT DAN AHLI DEMOGRAFI INDONESIA *See* KONGRES IPADI **1593**

IKATAN PUSTAKAWAN INDONESIA *See* MAJALAH IPI **3229**

IKEDA KYODO KENKYU (JA) [03927746] **2653**

IKEN TO ISHIKI NO HYAKKA JITEN (JA) [03197970] **5247**

IKON (IT/0019-1744) [11501702] **1113**

IKONOMI (SA) [08968271] **1566**

IKONOMIKA I UPRAVLENIE NA SELSKOTO STOPANSTVO (BU/0205-3845) [21068716] **94**

IKONOMISUTU (SEOUL, KOREA) (KO) [10727857] **1566**

IKONOTHEKA : PRACE INSTYTUTU HISTORII SZTUKI UNIWERSYTETU WARSZAWSKIEGO (PL/0860-5769) [26287402] **322**

IKUSHUGAKU SAIKIN NO SHINPO (JA/0388-8177) [10326494] **548**

IKUSHUGAKU ZASSHI (JA/0536-3683) [01640786] **94**

IL, L' (FR/0183-3014) [01761030] **352**

IL-MERILL (MM) [04126857] **5586**

ILA AL-AMAM, MIN AJLI TAHRIR AL-ARD WA-AL-INSAN (LE) [04152554] **2653**

ILA BULLETIN (II/0970-4728) [26905188] **3214**

ILAM GUIDE TO GOOD PRACTICE IN LEISURE MANAGEMENT (UK) **870**

ILAR NEWS (US/0018-9960) [01639311] 5511, **3585**

ILBON CHUNCHU (KO) [04403367] **2653**

ILBON WANGNAE (KO) [04648738] **2653**

ILCA ... ANNUAL REPORT AND PROGRAMME HIGHLIGHTS (ET/1014-9015) [25226450] **212**

ILCA BULLETIN (ET/0255-0008) [I02550008] **212**

ILCA RESEARCH REPORT / INTERNATIONAL LIVESTOCK CENTRE FOR AFRICA (ET) [09796635] **212**

ILE CAMERA (US) **5692**

ILE-DE-FRANCE, NOTE DE CONJONCTURE REGIONALE (FR/0181-0162) [07906114] **1566**

ILE : INDUSTRIAS LACTEAS ESPANOLAS (SP) **2367**

ILE LETTREE, L' (CN/0226-7233) [06511425] **5786**

ILEIA NEWSLETTER (NE/0920-8771) [18689594] 2232, **174**

ILERDA CIENCIES: ANUARI DE L'INSTITUT D'ESTUDIS ILERDENCS (SP) [24013809] **5111**

ILF CALENDAR NEWSLETTER (US/1061-9232) [25492439] **3395**

ILGA PINK BOOK (NE) [19369408] **2794**

ILHA DO DESTERRO / DEPTO. DE LINGUA E LITERATURA ANGLO-AMERICANAS, UNIVERSIDADE FEDERAL DE SANTA CATARINA (BL) [08160272] **3395**

ILIAD (UK) **1077**

ILIFF REVIEW, THE *CEASED.* (US/0019-1795) [01776452] **4964**

ILIRIA (AA) [02661500] **2692**

ILKE (TU) [02240893] **4655**

ILL. IA. MO. SEARCHER, THE *CEASED.* (US/0737-5239) [09372515] **2454**

●ILLAHEE (SEATTLE, WASH.) (US/1073-0478) [29297046] **2173**

ILLIANA GENEALOGIST (US/0019-1809) [06217462] **2454**

ILLIMANI (BO/1013-9796) [02262148] **2738**

ILLINI REVIEW (US) [13505660] **4476**

ILLINOIAN-STAR DAILY (US) [24616382] **5660**

ILLINOIS
Alphabetical Title Index

ILLINOIS See BOILER AND PRESSURE VESSEL SAFETY ACT AND RULES AND REGULATIONS **2942**

ILLINOIS See ILLINOIS CRIMINAL LAW AND PROCEDURE **3107**

ILLINOIS AGRI-NEWS (US/0194-7443) [04984505] **94**

ILLINOIS AGRICULTURAL STATISTICS (US/0442-2562) [03348216] **94, 154**

ILLINOIS AIRPORT DIRECTORY (US) [02806891] **23**

ILLINOIS. ALCOHOLISM DIVISION See ANNUAL REPORT, STATE OF ILLINOIS ALCOHOLISM PLANS AND PROGRAMS **1341**

ILLINOIS. APPELLATE COURT See ILLINOIS APPELLATE REPORTS **2980**

ILLINOIS APPELLATE REPORTS (US/0884-0482) [06442781] **2980**

ILLINOIS APPLICATIONS, INSTRUCTIONS, AND FEES, INTERNATIONAL REGISTRATION PLAN (US) [18096153] **5384**

ILLINOIS ARCHITECTURE REFERENCE DIRECTORY, THE (US/0747-6345) [10761167] **300**

ILLINOIS AUDUBON (US/1061-9801) [12083856] 5617, **4166**

ILLINOIS AVIATION (SPRINGFIELD, ILL. : 1979) (US/0276-640X) [05781560] **23**

ILLINOIS BANKER (US/0019-185X) [04062927] **790**

ILLINOIS BAPTIST (US/0019-1868) [01781889] **5061**

ILLINOIS BAR JOURNAL (US/0019-1876) [06777213] **2980**

ILLINOIS BENEDICTINE MAGAZINE, THE (US/0744-5806) [08416568] **1092**

ILLINOIS BEVERAGE JOURNAL (US/0019-1892) [04074061] **2367**

ILLINOIS BIOLOGICAL MONOGRAPHS (US/0073-4748) [01402561] **458**

ILLINOIS. BOARD OF HIGHER EDUCATION See STATEWIDE SPACE SURVEY **1848**

ILLINOIS. BOARD OF HIGHER EDUCATION See FISCAL YEAR HIGHER EDUCATION BUDGET RECOMMENDATIONS : OPERATIONS AND GRANTS **1824**

ILLINOIS. BOARD OF HIGHER EDUCATION See FISCAL YEAR HIGHER EDUCATION BUDGET RECOMMENDATIONS : CAPITAL IMPROVEMENTS **1824**

ILLINOIS BOND WATCHER, THE (US) [08143184] **901**

ILLINOIS. BUREAU OF EMPLOYMENT SECURITY. RESEARCH AND ANALYSIS DIVISION See ANNUAL PLANNING REPORT, FISCAL YEAR ... CHAMPAIGN SMSA **1529**

ILLINOIS. BUREAU OF EMPLOYMENT SECURITY. RESEARCH AND STATISTICS SECTION See ESTIMATES OF EMPLOYMENT, HOURS, AND EARNINGS IN NONAGRICULTURAL ESTABLISHMENTS: DECATUR STANDARD METROPOLITAN STATISTICAL AREA **1668**

ILLINOIS. BUREAU OF EMPLOYMENT SECURITY. RESEARCH AND STATISTICS SECTION See ESTIMATES OF EMPLOYMENT, HOURS, AND EARNINGS IN NONAGRICULTURAL ESTABLISHMENTS. SPRINGFIELD STANDARD METROPOLITAN STATISTICAL AREA **1668**

ILLINOIS BUSINESS REVIEW (US/0019-1922) [01608178] **681**

ILLINOIS CAREER EDUCATION JOURNAL See ILLINOIS VOCATIONAL EDUCATION JOURNAL **1913**

ILLINOIS. CITIES AND VILLAGES MUNICIPAL PROBLEMS COMMISSION See ILLINOIS MUNICIPAL PROBLEMS; REPORT OF THE CITIES AND VILLAGES MUNICIPAL PROBLEMS COMMISSION TO THE GENERAL ASSEMBLY OF ILLINOIS **4655**

ILLINOIS CLASSICAL STUDIES (US/0363-1923) [02460661] **1077**

ILLINOIS CODE OF CIVIL PROCEDURE AND COURT RULES (US/8756-8969) [09672170] **3090**

ILLINOIS COLLEGE HANDBOOK See HANDBOOK OF ILLINOIS POSTSECONDARY INSTITUTIONS **1827**

ILLINOIS COMMISSION ON ATOMIC ENERGY See BIENNIAL REPORT - ILLINOIS COMMISSION ON ATOMIC ENERGY **4632**

ILLINOIS COMMISSION ON ATOMIC ENERGY. REPORT TO THE ... GOVERNOR OF THE STATE OF ILLINOIS, THE PRESIDENT OF THE SENATE ... OF THE ... GENERAL ASSEMBLY FROM THE ILLINOIS COMMISSION ON ATOMIC ENERGY See BIENNIAL REPORT - ILLINOIS COMMISSION ON ATOMIC ENERGY **4632**

ILLINOIS. COMMISSION ON LABOR LAWS See REPORT AND RECOMMENDATIONS TO THE GOVERNOR AND THE GENERAL ASSEMBLY **3153**

ILLINOIS. COMMISSION ON THE STATUS OF WOMEN See REPORT AND RECOMMENDATIONS TO THE GOVERNOR AND THE GENERAL ASSEMBLY - ILLINOIS. COMMISSION ON THE STATUS OF WOMEN **5565**

ILLINOIS COMMUNITY COLLEGE BOARD See STATE FUNDING CLAIMS PROCESSED AND PAID BY THE ILLINOIS COMMUNITY COLLEGE BOARD **1848**

ILLINOIS COMMUNITY COLLEGE BOARD See OPERATING FINANCE REPORT FOR ILLINOIS PUBLIC COMMUNITY COLLEGES **1839**

ILLINOIS COMMUNITY COLLEGE BOARD See RESEARCH REPORT - ILLINOIS COMMUNITY COLLEGE BOARD **1845**

ILLINOIS COMMUNITY COLLEGE BOARD See ILLINOIS COMMUNITY COLLEGE BOARD CURRICULUM ENROLLMENT SUMMARY IN THE PUBLIC COMMUNITY COLLEGES OF ILLINOIS **1829**

ILLINOIS COMMUNITY COLLEGE BOARD See STUDENT ENROLLMENT IN THE PUBLIC COMMUNITY COLLEGES OF ILLINOIS **1848**

ILLINOIS COMMUNITY COLLEGE BOARD CURRICULUM ENROLLMENT SUMMARY IN THE PUBLIC COMMUNITY COLLEGES OF ILLINOIS (US) [06582990] **1829**

ILLINOIS COMMUNITY COLLEGE BOARD DISADVANTAGED STUDENT GRANT PROGRAM FOR ILLINOIS PUBLIC COMMUNITY COLLEGES See DISADVANTAGED STUDENT GRANT ANNUAL REPORT FOR FY ... **1821**

ILLINOIS. COMPTROLLER'S OFFICE See STATEWIDE SUMMARY OF FIRE PROTECTION DISTRICT FINANCE IN ILLINOIS **2292**

ILLINOIS CONFERENCE ON MEDICAL INFORMATION SYSTEMS (US/0147-0191) [03054591] **3585**

ILLINOIS CONSTRUCTION LAW (US/8755-691X) [11358106] 617, **2980**

ILLINOIS COUNTY AND TOWNSHIP OFFICIAL (US/0019-1949) [04074218] **4655**

ILLINOIS. CREDIT UNION DIVISION See CONSOLIDATED ANNUAL REPORT OF ILLINOIS STATE CHARTERED CREDIT UNIONS **784**

ILLINOIS CREDIT UNION LEAGUE See YEARBOOK - ILLINOIS CREDIT UNION LEAGUE (1988) **817**

ILLINOIS CRIMINAL LAW AND PROCEDURE (US) [04735874] **3107**

ILLINOIS. DANGEROUS DRUGS COMMISSION See ANNUAL REPORT TO THE GENERAL ASSEMBLY ON THE ABUSE OF DANGEROUS DRUGS IN ILLINOIS **1341**

ILLINOIS DENTAL JOURNAL (US/0019-1973) [01752643] **1324**

ILLINOIS. DEPT. OF ADULT, VOCATIONAL, AND TECHNICAL EDUCATION See ANNUAL REPORT, FISCAL YEAR ... VOCATIONAL EDUCATION IN ILLINOIS **1910**

ILLINOIS. DEPT. OF ALCOHOLISM & SUBSTANCE ABUSE See COMPREHENSIVE STATE PLAN AND HUMAN SERVICES PLAN FOR THE PREVENTION/INTERVENTION/TREATMENT OF ALCOHOLISM AND OTHER DRUG DEPENDENCY FOR FISCAL YEARS, A **1342**

ILLINOIS. DEPT. OF BUSINESS AND ECONOMIC DEVELOPMENT See ANNUAL REPORT - ILLINOIS DEPARTMENT OF BUSINESS AND ECONOMIC DEVELOPMENT **1546**

ILLINOIS. DEPT. OF COMMERCE AND COMMUNITY AFFAIRS See ANNUAL CETA REPORT FOR ... - ILLINOIS. DEPT. OF COMMERCE AND COMMUNITY AFFAIRS **1644**

ILLINOIS. DEPT. OF CONSERVATION See LAND AND WATER REPORT **2197**

ILLINOIS. DEPT. OF CORRECTIONS. DIVISION OF RESEARCH AND LONG RANGE PLANNING See POPULATION ANALYSIS OF THE ILLINOIS ADULT PRISON SYSTEM **3172**

ILLINOIS. DEPT. OF HUMAN RIGHTS See ANNUAL REPORTS / STATE OF ILLINOIS, DEPARTMENT OF HUMAN RIGHTS [AND] HUMAN RIGHTS COMMISSION **4504**

ILLINOIS. DEPT. OF INSURANCE See REPORT OF EXAMINATION, PUBLIC EMPLOYEES' PENSION FUNDS **4680**

ILLINOIS. DEPT. OF INSURANCE See ANNUAL REPORT AND SUMMARY OF ANNUAL STATEMENTS BY THE DIRECTOR OF INSURANCE TO ... GOVERNOR, FOR YEAR ENDING DECEMBER 31 ... INCLUDING FISCAL REPORT FOR YEAR ENDING JUNE 30 ... **2873**

ILLINOIS DEPT. OF MENTAL HEALTH AND DEVELOPMENTAL DISABILITIES See AFFIRMATIVE ACTION PROGRAM - ILLINOIS DEPT. OF MENTAL HEALTH AND DEVELOPMENTAL DISABILITIES **4763**

ILLINOIS. DEPT. OF MENTAL HEALTH AND DEVELOPMENTAL DISABILITIES See ANNUAL PLAN ... OF THE ILLINOIS DEPARTMENT OF MENTAL HEALTH AND DEVELOPMENTAL DISABILITIES **4765**

ILLINOIS. DEPT. OF PUBLIC AID See MEDICAL ASSISTANCE PROGRAM **5295**

ILLINOIS. DEPT. OF REGISTRATION AND EDUCATION See LICENSEES, DENTAL PRACTICE ACT **1329**

ILLINOIS. DEPT. OF REHABILITATION SERVICES See PLAN FOR ILLINOIS DEPARTMENT OF REHABILITATION SERVICES **4673**

ILLINOIS. DEPT. OF REVENUE See REVENUE **4746**

ILLINOIS. DEPT. OF TRANSPORTATION. OFFICE OF PLANNING, PROGRAMMING, AND ENVIRONMENTAL SCIENCE See UNIFIED WORK PROGRAM **5398**

ILLINOIS. DEPT. ON AGING See COMMUNITY CARE **5279**

ILLINOIS. DIVISION OF AIR POLLUTION CONTROL See SEMIANNUAL REPORT - DIVISION OF AIR POLLUTION CONTROL **2243**

ILLINOIS. DIVISION OF ALCOHOLISM See STATE OF ILLINOIS PLAN FOR THE TREATMENT AND PREVENTION OF ALCOHOL ABUSE AND ALCOHOLISM **1349**

ILLINOIS. DIVISION OF CREDIT UNIONS See ANNUAL REPORT OF ILLINOIS STATE CHARTERED CREDIT UNIONS **771**

ILLINOIS DOCUMENTS LIST (US/0190-6887) [02623812] **417**

ILLINOIS ECONOMIC OUTLOOK (US) [08225937] **1494**

ILLINOIS ECONOMIC REPORT (US/0744-6683) [08489557] **1494**

ILLINOIS. EDUCATIONAL TELEVISION COMMISSION See ANNUAL REPORT - STATE OF ILLINOIS, EDUCATIONAL TELEVISION COMMISSION **1809**

ILLINOIS EMPLOYMENT LAW LETTER (US/1049-9385) [21356998] **3149**

ILLINOIS ENERGY CONSUMPTION (US/0730-7209) [08012429] **1946**

ILLINOIS ENGINEER (US/0019-2015) [01587804] **1977**

ILLINOIS ENGLISH BULLETIN : OFFICIAL PUBLICATION OF THE ILLINOIS ASSOCIATION OF TEACHERS OF ENGLISH (US) [06957629] **3395**

ILLINOIS ENVIRONMENTAL FACILITIES FINANCING AUTHORITY See ANNUAL REPORT / ILLINOIS ENVIRONMENTAL FACILITIES FINANCING AUTHORITY **2160**

● ILLINOIS ENVIRONMENTAL LAW LETTER (US/1059-5074) [24609848] 2173, **2980**

ILLINOIS. ENVIRONMENTAL PROTECTION AGENCY See WATER POLLUTION CONTROL PLAN (SPRINGFIELD) **5543**

ILLINOIS ENVIRONMENTAL PROTECTION AGENCY See NEWSROOM DIRECTORY & GUIDE TO THE ILLINOIS ENVIRONMENTAL PROTECTION AGENCY **4669**

ILLINOIS. ENVIRONMENTAL PROTECTION AGENCY See LAKE MICHIGAN WATER QUALITY REPORT **5535**

ILLINOIS ENVIRONMENTAL PROTECTION AGENCY See REPORT OF PROGRESS BY THE ILLINOIS ENVIRONMENTAL PROTECTION AGENCY **2181**

ILLINOIS FACTS (US/1041-2778) [18229367] **1926**

ILLINOIS FAIR EMPLOYMENT PRACTICE REPORTS (US) [04185025] **3149**

ILLINOIS. FAIR EMPLOYMENT PRACTICES COMMISSION See ILLINOIS FAIR EMPLOYMENT PRACTICE REPORTS **3149**

ILLINOIS FOODSERVICE NEWS (US/0279-9618) [07386501] **5071**

ILLINOIS. GENERAL ASSEMBLY See LEGISLATIVE SYNOPSIS AND DIGEST ... GENERAL ASSEMBLY, STATE OF ILLINOIS **4661**

ILLINOIS. GENERAL ASSEMBLY. LEGISLATIVE ADVISORY COMMITTEE TO THE REGIONAL TRANSPORTATION AUTHORITY See BIENNIAL REPORT / LEGISLATIVE ADVISORY COMMITTEE TO THE REGIONAL TRANSPORTATION AUTHORITY **5377**

ILLINOIS. GENERAL ASSEMBLY. LEGISLATIVE INVESTIGATING COMMISSION See ANNUAL REPORT - ILLINOIS. GENERAL ASSEMBLY. LEGISLATIVE INVESTIGATING COMMITTEE **4627**

Alphabetical Title Index — ILLINOIS

ILLINOIS. GENERAL ASSEMBLY. LEGISLATIVE INVESTIGATING COMMISSION *See* ANNUAL REPORT OF ... / BY THE ILLINOIS LEGISLATIVE INVESTIGATING COMMISSION **4628**

ILLINOIS. GENERAL ASSEMBLY. LEGISLATIVE INVESTIGATION COMMISSION. ANNUAL REPORT *See* ANNUAL REPORT OF ... / BY THE ILLINOIS LEGISLATIVE INVESTIGATING COMMISSION **4628**

ILLINOIS GEOGRAPHICAL SOCIETY *See* BULLETIN - ILLINOIS GEOGRAPHICAL SOCIETY **2557**

ILLINOIS. GOVERNOR *See* ILLINOIS STATE BUDGET DETAIL **4731**

ILLINOIS. GOVERNOR *See* GOVERNOR'S COORDINATION AND APECIAL SERVICES PLAN FOR THE PERIOD OF ... / [PREPARED BY] ILLINOIS DEPARTMENT OF COMMERCE AND COMMUNITY AFFAIRS **4652**

ILLINOIS GOVERNOR'S ADVISORY COUNCIL ON MANPOWER *See* EMPLOYMENT AND TRAINING REPORT TO THE GOVERNOR - ILLINOIS GOVERNOR'S ADVISORY COUNCIL ON MANPOWER **1666**

ILLINOIS GRAIN & LIVESTOCK MARKET NEWS (US/0745-8525) [06413879] 212, **202**

ILLINOIS GUARDIANSHIP AND ADVOCACY COMMISSION *See* ANNUAL REPORT / ILLINOIS GUARDIANSHIP AND ADVOCACY COMMISSION **2934**

ILLINOIS GUIDANCE AND PERSONNEL ASSOCIATION QUARTERLY *See* IACD QUARTERLY **4589**

ILLINOIS HANDCRAFTS DIRECTORY (US/0095-5337) [01798146] **373**

●ILLINOIS HEALTH CARE IN PERSPECTIVE (US/1065-4151) [26605035] **4784**

ILLINOIS HEALTH FACILITIES AUTHORITY *See* ANNUAL REPORT - ILLINOIS HEALTH FACILITIES AUTHORITY **3776**

ILLINOIS HEALTH FINANCE AUTHORITY *See* ANNUAL REPORT / ILLINOIS HEALTH FINANCE AUTHORITY **3776**

ILLINOIS HERITAGE ASSOCIATION NEWSLETTER (US/0890-3719) [10640501] **2454**

ILLINOIS HISTORICAL JOURNAL (US/0748-8149) [11010786] **2738**

ILLINOIS HISTORY (US/0019-2058) [01752650] **2738**

ILLINOIS HOME ENERGY ASSISTANCE PROGRAM FY ... ANNUAL REPORT (US) [10037512] **5289**

ILLINOIS IN PERSPECTIVE (US/1065-5425) [26628931] **5328**

ILLINOIS INFORMER, THE (US) [06038504] **2535**

ILLINOIS INSIGHTS (US/0275-4096) [04748578] **5289**

ILLINOIS INSTITUTE FOR ENVIRONMENTAL QUALITY *See* ANNUAL REPORT - ILLINOIS INSTITUTE FOR ENVIRONMENTAL QUALITY **2160**

ILLINOIS INSURANCE (US/0094-7660) [01795506] **2882**

ILLINOIS INTERSCHOLASTIC, THE *CEASED.* (US/0892-9130) [08562085] **4899**

ILLINOIS INVENTORY OF EDUCATIONAL PROGRESS. MATHEMATICS ITEM RESULTS (US) [08164474] 1751, **3508**

ILLINOIS INVENTORY OF EDUCATIONAL PROGRESS. READING ITEM RESULTS (US) [08164498] **1896**

ILLINOIS IRRIGATION NEWSLETTER *CEASED.* (US) [06178944] **174**

ILLINOIS ISSUES (US/0738-9663) [03859340] **4476**

ILLINOIS JOURNAL OF HEALTH, PHYSICAL EDUCATION, RECREATION, AND DANCE (US/1062-2764) [22362330] **1751**

ILLINOIS JOURNAL OF MATHEMATICS (US/0019-2082) [01752652] **3508**

ILLINOIS. JUNIOR COLLEGE BOARD *See* OPERATING FINANCIAL DATA FOR ILLINOIS PUBLIC JUNIOR COLLEGES **1839**

ILLINOIS LABOR MARKET REVIEW (US/0883-3338) [05509253] **1677**

ILLINOIS LAW ENFORCEMENT OFFICERS LAW BULLETIN (US/0445-4111) [08561262] **3165**

ILLINOIS LAW OF CRIMINAL INVESTIGATION, THE (US) [14048102] **3165**

ILLINOIS. LEGISLATIVE COUNCIL *See* OVERVIEW OF LEGISLATION IN THE SESSION OF THE ILLINOIS GENERAL ASSEMBLY, AN **3024**

ILLINOIS. LEGISLATIVE COUNCIL *See* ILLINOIS LEGISLATIVE DIRECTORY **4655**

ILLINOIS LEGISLATIVE DIRECTORY (US) [01752595] **4655**

ILLINOIS LIBRARIES (US/0019-2104) [01752654] **3214**

ILLINOIS LOCAL GOVERNMENTAL LAW ENFORCEMENT OFFICERS TRAINING BOARD *See* BIENNIAL REPORT **3158**

ILLINOIS LOCAL GOVERNMENTAL LAW ENFORCEMENT OFFICERS TRAINING BOARD *See* STATEWIDE SYSTEM OF IN-SERVICE TRAINING : ANNUAL REPORT, A **3177**

ILLINOIS MAGAZINE **SUSPENDED.** (US/0747-9794) [10827910] **2738**

ILLINOIS MANUFACTURERS DIRECTORY (US/0160-3302) [02704397] **3480**

ILLINOIS MAPNOTES (US) [08004926] **2582**

ILLINOIS MASTER PLUMBER (US/0019-2112) [02447500] **2606**

ILLINOIS MATHEMATICS TEACHER, THE (US) [08863404] **3508**

ILLINOIS MEDICINE (US/1044-6400) [19095702] **3585**

ILLINOIS. MERIT COMMISSION *See* ANNUAL REPORT - SECRETARY OF STATE, MERIT COMMISSION **4701**

ILLINOIS MINERALS / DEPARTMENT OF ENERGY AND NATURAL RESOURCES, ILLINOIS STATE GEOLOGICAL SURVEY (US) [22970977] **1440**

ILLINOIS MOSQUITO AND VECTOR CONTROL ASSOCIATION. MEETING *See* PROCEEDINGS OF THE ILLINOIS MOSQUITO AND VECTOR CONTROL ASSOCIATION **5613**

ILLINOIS MUNICIPAL PROBLEMS; REPORT OF THE CITIES AND VILLAGES MUNICIPAL PROBLEMS COMMISSION TO THE GENERAL ASSEMBLY OF ILLINOIS (US/0442-0713) [01697106] **4655**

ILLINOIS MUNICIPAL REVIEW (US/0019-2139) [01752658] **4655**

ILLINOIS MUNICIPAL REVIEW, TO IMPROVE THE QUALITY AND DECREASE THE COST OF MUNICIPAL SERVICE *See* ILLINOIS MUNICIPAL REVIEW **4655**

ILLINOIS MUSIC COUNTRY MAGAZINE (US/0098-3535) [02241414] **4122**

ILLINOIS MUSIC EDUCATOR, THE (US/0019-2147) [01645450] **4122**

ILLINOIS. NATURAL HISTORY SURVEY DIVISION *See* CIRCULAR - ILLINOIS NATURAL HISTORY SURVEY **4164**

ILLINOIS NATURAL HISTORY SURVEY REPORTS, THE (US/0536-4132) [02447503] **4166**

ILLINOIS NATURAL HISTORY SURVEY SPECIAL PUBLICATION (US/0888-9546) [10016018] **4166**

ILLINOIS NATURE PRESERVES COMMISSION *See* REPORT - ILLINOIS NATURE PRESERVES COMMISSION **2203**

ILLINOIS NURSERY NOTES FOR THE PLANT INDUSTRIES (US) [04420888] **2420**

ILLINOIS OFFICE OF EDUCATION *See* ILLINOIS PUBLIC SCHOOL DISTRICTS **1864**

ILLINOIS. OFFICE OF EDUCATION. DEPT. OF PLANNING, RESEARCH, AND EVALUATION *See* ILLINOIS TEACHER SUPPLY AND DEMAND **1751**

ILLINOIS. OFFICE OF EDUCATION. PROGRAM EVALUATION AND ASSESSMENT SECTION *See* ANNUAL REPORT ON TITLE I, PUBLIC LAW 89-313 **1860**

ILLINOIS. OFFICE OF PLANNING AND ANALYSIS *See* STATE OF ILLINOIS STATISTICAL REPORT **5339**

ILLINOIS. OFFICE OF SECRETARY OF STATE *See* HANDBOOK OF ILLINOIS GOVERNMENT **4475**

ILLINOIS. OFFICE OF SECRETARY OF STATE *See* PUBLICATIONS OF THE STATE OF ILLINOIS **4677**

ILLINOIS. OFFICE OF SECRETARY OF STATE *See* REPORT OF THE SECURITIES DIVISION **912**

ILLINOIS. OFFICE OF SECRETARY OF STATE. COMMERCIAL AND FARM TRUCK DIVISION *See* APPLICATION AND INSTRUCTIONS FOR VEHICLE PRORATION **5377**

ILLINOIS. OFFICE OF THE GOVERNOR *See* ILLINOIS STATE BUDGET IN BRIEF **4731**

ILLINOIS. OFFICE OF THE SUPERINTENDENT OF PUBLIC INSTRUCTION. HANDICAPPED CHILDREN SECTION *See* STATE OF ILLINOIS REPORT ON TITLE I, PUBLIC LAW 89-313 **1885**

ILLINOIS. OFFICE OF THE SUPERINTENDENT OF PUBLIC INSTRUCTION. HANDICAPPED CHILDREN SECTION *See* FINANCIAL AND STATISTICAL REPORT: SPECIAL EDUCATION (ILLINOIS) **1879**

ILLINOIS. OFFICE OF THE SUPERINTENDENT OF PUBLIC INSTRUCTION. PUBLICATIONS AND LIBRARY RESOURCES SECTION *See* PUBLICATIONS RESOURCE MANUAL (SPRINGFIELD) **3243**

ILLINOIS. OFFICE OF THE SUPERINTENDENT OF PUBLIC INSTRUCTION. RESEARCH SECTION *See* ILLINOIS TEACHER SALARY SCHEDULE AND POLICY STUDY **1864**

ILLINOIS PARKS & RECREATION (US/0019-2155) [02385435] **4706**

ILLINOIS PETROLEUM (US/0073-5108) [01261013] **4260**

ILLINOIS PHARMACIST (1979) (US/0195-2099) [05367054] **4307**

ILLINOIS POLICE & LAW ENFORCEMENT DIRECTORY (US) [05583629] **3165**

ILLINOIS POLICE ASSOCIATION *See* OFFICIAL JOURNAL - ILLINOIS POLICE ASSOCIATION **3171**

ILLINOIS POPULATION TRENDS FROM ... TO ... (US) [09085409] **4553**

ILLINOIS PREP TOP TIMES. CROSS COUNTRY EDITION (US) **4899**

ILLINOIS PREP TOP TIMES. TRACK FIELD EDITION (US) **4899**

ILLINOIS PRINCIPAL *CEASED.* (US/0019-218X) [04074329] **1864**

ILLINOIS PSYCHOLOGICAL ASSOCIATION NEWSLETTER *See* ILLINOIS PSYCHOLOGIST : NEWSLETTER OF THE ILLINOIS PSYCHOLOGICAL ASSOCIATION **4589**

ILLINOIS PSYCHOLOGIST : NEWSLETTER OF THE ILLINOIS PSYCHOLOGICAL ASSOCIATION (US/0019-2198) [09693771] **4589**

ILLINOIS PUBLIC EMPLOYEE RELATIONS REPORT / INSTITUTE OF LABOR AND INDUSTRIAL RELATIONS, UNIVERSITY OF ILLINOIS AT URBANA-CHAMPAIGN, THE (US) [11059315] **4655**

ILLINOIS PUBLIC EMPLOYEE REPORTER (US) [11717566] **3149**

ILLINOIS PUBLIC PENSIONS (US/0891-7256) [15011470] **901**

ILLINOIS PUBLIC SCHOOL DISTRICTS (US) [03722161] **1864**

ILLINOIS RAIL PLAN ... UPDATE (US) [06756066] **5431**

ILLINOIS REASONABLE FURTHER PROGRESS REPORT FOR ... OZONE AND CARBON MONOXIDE (US) [17369652] **977**

ILLINOIS REGIONAL PLANNING AGENCY DIRECTORY (US/0361-6932) [02441414] **2825**

ILLINOIS REGISTER (US) [03763989] **2980**

ILLINOIS REGISTER OF EXPERT WITNESSES, THE (US/1058-5435) [24329527] **2980**

ILLINOIS REGISTER [MICROFICHE] (US) [09191326] **2980**

ILLINOIS REPORTS (US/0160-1199) [03600451] **2980**

●ILLINOIS REVIEW, THE (US/1067-4128) [27206041] **3344**

ILLINOIS RUNNER (US/0747-4911) [10729084] **4899**

ILLINOIS SCHOOL BOARD JOURNAL (US/0019-221X) [04073427] 870, **1864**

ILLINOIS SCHOOL RESEARCH AND DEVELOPMENT (US/0163-822X) [03358563] **1751**

ILLINOIS SCHOOLS JOURNAL (US/0019-2236) [01586450] **1896**

ILLINOIS SERVICES DIRECTORY (US/0092-3818) [01789583] **1609**

ILLINOIS SMALL PRESS DIRECTORY *CEASED.* (US/0743-2925) [10546285] **4815**

ILLINOIS SPEECH & THEATRE ASSOCIATION *See* JOURNAL OF THE ILLINOIS SPEECH & THEATRE ASSOCIATION **5365**

ILLINOIS STATE ACADEMY OF SCIENCE *See* TRANSACTIONS OF THE ILLINOIS STATE ACADEMY OF SCIENCE **5166**

ILLINOIS STATE AFL-CIO *See* WEEKLY NEWS LETTER - ILLINOIS STATE AFL-CIO **1717**

ILLINOIS STATE AFL-CIO LABORLETTER (US) [20581526] **1677**

ILLINOIS STATE BAR ASSOCIATION *See* BLUE BOOK / ILLINOIS STATE BAR ASSOCIATION **2942**

ILLINOIS STATE BAR ASSOCIATION. SECTION ON INDIVIDUAL RIGHTS AND RESPONSIBILITIES *See* NEWSLETTER - ILLINOIS STATE BAR ASSOCIATION **3017**

ILLINOIS STATE BAR ASSOCIATION. SECTION ON PUBLIC UTILITIES AND TRANSPORTATION *See* PUBLIC UTILITIES AND TRANSPORTATION NEWSLETTER **4677**

ILLINOIS STATE BOARD OF EDUCATION (1973-) *See* ANNUAL PROGRAM PLAN FOR VOCATIONAL EDUCATION IN ILLINOIS **1910**

ILLINOIS — Alphabetical Title Index

ILLINOIS STATE BOARD OF EDUCATION (1973-) *See* PROPOSED BUDGET / ADOPTED BY THE STATE BOARD OF EDUCATION **1869**

ILLINOIS. STATE BOARD OF ELECTIONS *See* MACHINE MANUAL OF INSTRUCTIONS FOR JUDGES OF ELECTION. PRIMARY ELECTION **4663**

ILLINOIS. STATE BOARD OF ELECTIONS *See* DEMOCRATIC PARTY. YEAR BOOK **4471**

● ILLINOIS STATE BUDGET DETAIL (US) [23201437] **4731**

ILLINOIS STATE BUDGET IN BRIEF (US/0360-9340) [02245043] **4731**

ILLINOIS STATE EMPLOYEE, THE (US) [06059571] **1677**

ILLINOIS. STATE EMPLOYMENT SERVICE. LABOR MARKET UNIT *See* ANNUAL MANPOWER PLANNING REPORT. CHICAGO STANDARD METROPOLITAN STATISTICAL AREA **1645**

ILLINOIS STATE FEDERATION OF LABOR *See* PROCEEDINGS ... ANNUAL CONVENTION ... / ILLINOIS STATE FEDERATION OF LABOR **1702**

ILLINOIS STATE GENEALOGICAL SOCIETY QUARTERLY (US/0046-8622) [01585725] **2454**

ILLINOIS STATE LIBRARY *See* LIBRARY STATISTICS OF ILLINOIS COLLEGES AND UNIVERSITIES **3259**

ILLINOIS STATE MUSEUM *See* HANDBOOK OF COLLECTIONS **4088**

ILLINOIS STATE WATER SURVEY *See* BULLETIN - ILLINOIS STATE WATER SURVEY **5531**

ILLINOIS STATEWIDE WAGE AND SALARY SURVEY OF SELECTED OCCUPATION *See* ILLINOIS WAGE SURVEY / ILLINOIS DEPARTMENT OF LABOR, BUREAU OF EMPLOYMENT SECURITY, RESEARCH AND ANALYSIS **1677**

● ILLINOIS STEWARD, THE (US/1058-9309) [24439479] **2195**

ILLINOIS STUDIES IN ANTHROPOLOGY (US/0073-5167) [01586016] **238**

ILLINOIS STUDIES IN LANGUAGE AND LITERATURE / UNIVERSITY OF ILLINOIS *CEASED.* (US/0073-5175) [07563734] **3286**

ILLINOIS. SUPREME COURT *See* ILLINOIS REPORTS **2980**

ILLINOIS. SUPREME COURT *See* REPORT / SUPREME COURT, STATE OF ILLINOIS **3143**

ILLINOIS TAX CLIMATE, THE (US/8755-7770) [05145861] **4731**

ILLINOIS TAX RATE AND LEVY MANUAL / OFFICE OF COMMUNITY SERVICES DEPARTMENT OF LOCAL GOVERNMENT AFFAIRS (US) [04254359] **4731**

ILLINOIS TEACHER SALARY SCHEDULE AND POLICY STUDY (US/0146-0668) [02871753] **1864**

ILLINOIS TEACHER SUPPLY AND DEMAND (US) [06240246] **1751**

● ILLINOIS TECHNOLOGY RESOURCE GUIDE (US/1065-7770) [26740375] **5112**

ILLINOIS TIMES (US/0199-7823) [06150732] **5660**

ILLINOIS TRAFFIC ACCIDENT FACTS AND STATISTICS (US) [20795327] 4784, **5441**

ILLINOIS TRUCK NEWS (US/0019-2309) [04943393] **5384**

ILLINOIS UNIFORM CRIME REPORTS USER'S GUIDE UPDATE (US/0732-9849) [08482927] 3165, **3081**

ILLINOIS. UNIVERSITY AT URBANA-CHAMPAIGN. COLLEGE OF FINE AND APPLIED ARTS *See* CONTEMPORARY AMERICAN PAINTING AND SCULPTURE **348**

ILLINOIS. UNIVERSITY AT URBANA-CHAMPAIGN. SMALL HOMES COUNCIL-BUILDING RESEARCH COUNCIL *See* COUNCIL NOTES **2819**

ILLINOIS. UNIVERSITY AT URBANA-CHAMPAIGN. WATER RESOURCES CENTER *See* WRC RESEARCH REPORT **5549**

ILLINOIS VOCATIONAL EDUCATION JOURNAL (US/0279-0491) [07479394] **1913**

ILLINOIS WAGE SURVEY / ILLINOIS DEPARTMENT OF LABOR, BUREAU OF EMPLOYMENT SECURITY, RESEARCH AND ANALYSIS (US) [09543258] **1677**

ILLINOIS WEATHER & CROPS (US/0273-8635) [06996866] **174**

ILLINOIS WILDLIFE (US/0019-2317) [01752674] **2195**

ILLINOIS WORKERS' COMP LAW BULLETIN (US) **3087**

● ILLINOIS WORKERS' COMPENSATION LAW BULLETIN (US/1067-2338) [27166027] 2882, **2980**

ILLINOIS WRITERS REVIEW *CEASED.* (US/0733-9526) [07939382] **3344**

ILLISIBLE (CN/0821-543X) [09635133] **5786**

ILLNESS CRISIS & LOSS (US/1054-1373) [22762044] 3752, **2251**

ILLUMINATING ENGINEERING SOCIETY *See* JOURNAL OF THE ILLUMINATING ENGINEERING SOCIETY **2069**

ILLUMINATIONS (VANCOUVER) (CN/1180-9558) [22425474] **373**

ILLUMINITECNICA (IT) **2064**

ILLUSIONS (NZ/0112-9341) [16349844] 322, **4072**

● ILLUSTRATED CASE REPORTS IN GASTROENTEROLOGY (UK/1352-8513) **3746**

ILLUSTRATED CATALOG OF FREE CATALOGS AND SOURCES FOR EVERYTHING IMAGINABLE (CN/0823-7956) [10840877] **2488**

ILLUSTRATED DIGEST OF BASEBALL (US/0091-3901) [01784421] **4899**

ILLUSTRATED DIRECTORY OF HANDICAPPED PRODUCTS, THE (US/1053-6035) [20967917] **4389**

ILLUSTRATED ENCYCLOPAEDIA YEARBOOK, THE (US/0145-1790) [02917413] **1926**

ILLUSTRATED GARDEN BOOK / KRIDER'S (US) [12408792] **2420**

ILLUSTRATED HOUSE PLANS (US/0197-7806) [06098466] **300**

ILLUSTRATED LIGHT (US/1059-2660) [24357293] **4370**

ILLUSTRATED LONDON NEWS, THE (UK/0019-2422) [01752679] **2517**

ILLUSTRATED RANCH HOMES *See* SINGLE FAMILY HOME PLANS **308**

ILLUSTRATED WEEKLY OF INDIA ANNUAL, THE (II/0302-8623) [01790600] **2504**

ILLUSTRATED WEEKLY OF INDIA, THE *CEASED.* (II) [06772824] **2504**

ILLUSTRATED WEEKLY OF INDIA, THE (II/0019-2430) [01752682] **5803**

ILLUSTRATION 63. I.E. DREIUNDSECHZIG (GW/0019-2457) [02673241] **380**

ILLUSTRATION IN JAPAN (TOKYO, JAPAN) (JA) [08071057] **380**

ILLUSTRATION INDEX (US) [01775121] **380**

ILLUSTRATOR, THE (US/0019-2465) [07352095] **380**

ILLUSTRATORS (US/0073-5477) [01752685] **373**

ILLUSTRAZIONE ITALIANA (MILAN, ITALY : 1974) (IT) [12820424] **4089**

ILLUSTRE COLEGIO PROVINCIAL DE ABOGADOS DE LERIDA *See* LISTA DE SENORES COLEGIADOS, GUIA JUDICIAL Y ADMINISTRATIVA **3003**

ILLUSTRIERTE NEUE WELT (AU) [01788903] **2517**

ILMATIETEEN LAITOS *See* KUUKAUSIKATSAUS SUOMEN ILMASTOON **1427**

ILMOITUS TARTTUVISTA ELAINTAUDEISTA / SUOMI (FI) [09810415] **5511**

ILMU ALAM (MY/0126-7000) [02239416] **2653**

ILMU MASYARAKAT : TERBITAN PERSATUAN SAINS SOSIAL MALAYSIA (MY) [10238449] **5203**

ILO CATALOGUE OF PUBLICATIONS IN PRINT (US/0376-9690) [02174198] **1533**

ILO INFORMATION. U.S. EDITION (US/0379-1734) [01172527] **1677**

ILOCOS REVIEW, THE (PH/0019-2538) [02105801] **2653**

ILP MAGAZINE *SUSPENDED.* (UK/0951-2187) [15874117] **1677**

ILR JOURNAL, THE (US/1058-6962) [24358557] **3464**

ILR PAPERBACK (US/0070-0177) [01781316] **1677**

ILRAD REPORTS (KE/0255-4585) [10318249] **5511**

ILRU INSIGHTS (US/0732-1953) [08357900] **4389**

ILSI NEWSLETTER (US) **4192**

ILUSTRADORES DO BRASIL (BL) [10675208] **352**

ILUSTRE COLEGIO DE ABOGADOS DE OVIEDO *See* LISTA DE SENORES COLEGIADOS **3003**

ILUSTRE COLEGIO PROVINCIAL DE ABOGADOS (SALAMANCA, SPAIN (PROVINCE)) *See* GUIA PROFESIONAL Y JUDICIAL **3141**

ILUZJON WARSZAWA (PL/0209-3537) [02093537] **4072**

ILVS REVIEW (US/1043-3023) [19379224] **4089**

IM; INFORMATICA EN MEDICINA Y BIOLOGIA (SP) 458, **3586**

IM. INZYNIERIA MATERIALOVA (PL/0208-6247) [09707837] **1977**

IMA BULLETIN : THE NEWSLETTER OF THE INTERNATIONAL MIDI ASSOCIATION, THE (US) [16388031] 4122, **1247**

IMA JOURNAL OF APPLIED MATHEMATICS (UK/0272-4960) [06855428] **3508**

IMA JOURNAL OF MATHEMATICAL CONTROL AND INFORMATION (UK/0265-0754) [11580583] **3508**

IMA JOURNAL OF MATHEMATICS APPLIED IN BUSINESS AND INDUSTRY (UK/0953-0061) [21984716] 681, **3508**

IMA JOURNAL OF MATHEMATICS APPLIED IN MEDICINE AND BIOLOGY (UK/0265-0746) [11580554] 3586, **3508**

IMA JOURNAL OF NUMERICAL ANALYSIS (UK/0272-4979) [06855501] **3508**

IMA MONOGRAPH SERIES (UK) [13468064] **3508**

IMA VOLUMES IN MATHEMATICS AND ITS APPLICATIONS, THE (US) [14207589] **3508**

IMAC, INTERNATIONAL MARINE AND AIR CATERING (UK) [06765393] **2344**

IMACS ANNALS ON COMPUTING AND APPLIED MATHEMATICS *CEASED.* (SZ/1012-2435) [I10122435] **1187**

IMAGE (SI/0129-704X) [09064682] 352, **4964**

IMAGE AND VISION COMPUTING (UK/0262-8856) [09320255] **1233**

IMAGE BUILDER (US/1055-9973) [23441761] **870**

IMAGE DE LA MAURICIE (CN/0704-7428) [03797390] **5480**

IMAGE DE LA RIVE SUD, L' (CN/0227-5430) [08027933] **5786**

IMAGE ET SON *See* REVUE DU CINEMA (PARIS. 1969) **4077**

IMAGE FILE (US/1046-6614) [20484314] **4089**

IMAGE LACHINE (CN/0705-923X) [04130156] **2535**

IMAGE PROCESSING (UK) [25791307] **1187**

IMAGE PROCESSING TECHNOLOGY (US/0886-8042) [13131524] **5112**

IMAGE (ROCHESTER) (US/0536-5465) [01752688] **4370**

IMAGE SCH. RELEASE (US/1056-3814) [23703914] **1829**

IMAGE (ST. LOUIS, MO.) (US/0748-1780) [10906063] **3395**

IMAGE TECHNOLOGY (LONDON) (UK/0950-2114) [14257070] **4072**

IMAGE--THE JOURNAL OF NURSING SCHOLARSHIP (US/0743-5150) [09629646] **3857**

IMAGE UNDERSTANDING (US/0748-0059) [10858195] **1219**

IMAGE (VANCOUVER) *CEASED.* (CN/0383-9710) [03222191] 4389, **3586**

IMAGE WORLD (US/8756-6664) [11640032] **1092**

IMAGEM DO BRASIL E DA AMERICA LATINA (BL) [02239717] **2738**

IMAGEN (PE) [01795414] **4370**

IMAGEN : ARTES, LETRAS, ESPECTACULOS (VE) [05332436] **3395**

IMAGEN (SAN JUAN, P.R.) (PR/0890-6548) [14348520] **2488**

IMAGENES *CEASED.* (PR) [14137774] **4072**

IMAGENES DE LA FE (SP/0211-5441) [I02115441] **5030**

IMAGES (DAYTON, OHIO) *CEASED.* (US/0884-819X) [03299709] **3464**

IMAGES DE LA CHIMIE (FR) [05791421] **977**

IMAGES DOC PARIS (FR/0995-1121) [I09951121] **4370**

IMAGES D'OUTREMONT (CN/1180-5579) [24279922] **2738**

IMAGES ECONOMIQUES DES ENTERPRISES. ENERGIE, TRANSPORTS ET TELECOMMUNICATIONS AU (FR) [20185312] **1609**

IMAGES ECONOMIQUES DES ENTERPRISES. SERVICES AU (FR) [20315709] **1494**

IMAGES ECONOMIQUES DES ENTREPRISES. INDUSTRIES AGRICOLES ET ALIMENTAIRES AU ... (FR) [20315379] 94, 2344, **154**

IMAGES (MONTREAL. 1991) (CN/1187-7162) [25652174] **2535**

IMAGES (MONTREAL. 1991) (CN/1187-7162) [25652170] **2535**

IMAGES (NELSON) *CEASED.* (CN/0384-5990) [05785061] **5558**

Alphabetical Title Index

●IMAGES OF A CHANGING PLANET COMPUTER FILE (US) [25608530] **2173**

IMAGES OF EXCELLENCE (US/0899-1138) [17993281] **2738**

IMAGES (RESTON, VA.) (US/1055-1476) [23093473] 3857, **3941**

IMAGINARY TALES (CN/0846-1015) [24256961] **3395**

IMAGINATION, COGNITION AND PERSONALITY (US/0276-2366) [07340895] **4589**

●IMAGINE (BALTIMORE, MD.) (US/1071-605X) [28689601] **1751**

IMAGINE (BOSTON, MASS.) (US/0747-489X) [10729012] **3464**

IMAGINE (MONTREAL) (CN/0709-8855) [06021301] **3395**

IMAGINE (WATERBURY, CONN.) (US/0162-6450) [04201928] **4122**

IMAGING ABSTRACTS (US/0896-100X) [16909598] 4370, **4378**

●IMAGING : AN INTERNATIONAL JOURNAL OF CLINICO-RADIOLOGICAL PRACTICE (UK/0965-6812) [25723553] **3942**

IMAGING AND CLINICAL ANATOMY (SZ) **3679**

IMAGING AND SURGICAL ANATOMY (SZ) **3586**

IMAGING BUSINESS REPORT *See* DOCUMENT IMAGING REPORT **1183**

IMAGING BUSINESS REPORT, THE (US/1050-7019) [21576318] 1609, **2064**

●IMAGING DECISIONS (US/1073-9718) [29571891] **3942**

●IMAGING (NEW YORK, N.Y.) (US/1063-4320) [25558037] **1187**

IMAGING NEWS (ALEXANDRIA, VA.) (US/1058-7705) [24383215] **1113**

IMAGING RETAIL NEWS (US/1048-2296) [20874730] **1113**

IMAGING SERVICE BUREAU NEWS (US/1055-8098) [23347903] **1609**

IMAGING SOLUTIONS INFODISK (US) **1187**

IMAGING TECHNOLOGY NEWS : THE NEWSLETTER FOR IMAGING END USERS (US/1059-4043) [24603306] **4435**

IMAGING TECHNOLOGY REPORT (US/1041-4320) [18005885] 1187, 1238, **1277**

IMAGING UPDATE *CEASED.* (US/0889-9142) [14109363] **4565**

●IMAGINGWORLD (CAMDEN, ME.) (US/1060-894X) [25101065] **4212**

IMAGO MUNDI (LYMPNE) (UK/0308-5694) [02227740] **2582**

IMANUEL (IS/0302-8127) [01784359] **5048**

IMBALLAGGIO : ORGANO UFFICIALE DELL'ISTITUTO ITALIANO IMBALLAGGIO (IT/0019-2708) [04088129] **5112**

IMBOTTIGLIAMENTO (IT/0392-792X) [I0392792X] **2367**

IMC JOURNAL (US/0019-0012) [02252706] 1187, 4370, **4212**

IMENOVANJE DIREKTORA RADNIH ORGANIZACIJA (YU) [01798777] **681**

IMERA (PE) [01787217] **2064**

IMF NEWS (SZ) [05533956] **4003**

IMF SURVEY (US/0047-083X) [02323476] **790**

IMF WORKING PAPER (US) [18708242] **790**

IMFAMA (SA/0019-2724) [I00192724] **4389**

IMHE. INFORMACION DE MAQUINAS-HERRAMIENTAS, EQUIPOS Y ACCESORIOS (SP/0210-1777) [I02101777] **2115**

IMI DESCRIPTIONS OF FUNGI AND BACTERIA / C.A.B. INTERNATIONAL (UK/0009-9716) [24150783] **458**

IMI. INTERACTIVE MEDIA INTERNATIONAL (UK/0953-7856) [I09537856] **1113**

IMLS GAZETTE (UK/0267-2928) [15551923] **3586**

IMM ABSTRACTS (UK/0019-0020) [06371234] 2140, **4003**

IMMAGINE (IT) [17303832] **4072**

IMMAGINE RIFLESSA, L' (IT) [04536366] 5247, **3395**

IMMATRICULATIONS DES VEHICULES UTILITAIRES *See* FICHIER CENTRAL DES AUTOMOBILES, PARC ET IMMATRICULATIONS / MINISTERE DES TRANSPORTS, DIRECTION DES AFFAIRES ECONOMIQUES, FINANCIERES ET ADMINISTRATIVES, DEPARTEMENT DES STATISTIQUES DES TRANSPORTS **5415**

IMME BOLETIN TECNICO (VE/0376-723X) [03917591] **2024**

IMMEDIATE IMPACT (US) **1113**

IMMERGRUNE BLATTER (GW/0170-8414) [02569630] **2420**

IMMERSION REGISTRY (CN/1187-0850) [25066826] **3286**

IMMI : THE INDEX OF MEDIEVAL MEDICAL IMAGES IN NORTH AMERICA (US) [19489681] **3586**

IMMIGRANT COMMUNITIES & ETHNIC MINORITIES IN THE UNITED STATES & CANADA (US/0749-5951) [11171159] **2263**

IMMIGRANTS & MINORITIES (UK/0261-9288) [09309620] **1919**

IMMIGRANTS IN AUSTRALIA (AT) [02095428] **1919**

IMMIGRATION AND NATIONALITY LAW AND PRACTICE *See* TOLLEY'S IMMIGRATION AND NATIONALITY LAW AND PRACTICE **1921**

IMMIGRATION AND NATURALIZATION INSTITUTE *See* ANNUAL IMMIGRATION AND NATURALIZATION INSTITUTE. PROCEEDINGS **2934**

IMMIGRATION AND NATURALIZATION INSTITUTE *See* ANNUAL IMMIGRATION AND NATURALIZATION INSTITUTE **2934**

IMMIGRATION APPEAL TRIBUNAL (GREAT BRITAIN) *See* IMMIGRATION APPEALS : SELECTED DETERMINATIONS OF THE IMMIGRATION APPEAL TRIBUNAL **1919**

IMMIGRATION APPEALS : SELECTED DETERMINATIONS OF THE IMMIGRATION APPEAL TRIBUNAL (UK) [02334960] **1919**

IMMIGRATION BRIEFINGS (US/0897-6708) [17568320] 1919, **2980**

IMMIGRATION DIGEST (US/0899-5400) [17217719] **2454**

IMMIGRATION HISTORY NEWSLETTER, THE (US/0579-4374) [02247048] **1919**

IMMIGRATION ISSUES : A COMPARISON OF ALIEN ADMISSIONS BEFORE AND AFTER IRCA / U.S. DEPARTMENT OF JUSTICE, IMMIGRATION AND NATURALIZATION SERVICE, STATISTICS DIVISION, OFFICE OF PLANS AND ANALYSIS (US) [23378749] **1919**

IMMIGRATION LAW & BUSINESS NEWS (US) [17718414] 1919, **2980**

IMMIGRATION LAW AND PROCEDURE (US) [01607655] 1919, **2980**

IMMIGRATION LAW BULLETIN (US) [07341669] 1919, **2980**

IMMIGRATION LAW REPORT (US/0731-5767) [07586705] 1919, **2980**

IMMIGRATION LAW REPORTER (DON MILLS) (CN/0835-3808) [13999683] 1919, **2980**

IMMIGRATION NEWSLETTER (US/0145-3416) [02727956] **1919**

IMMIGRATION POLICY & LAW (US/0892-547X) [15214430] 1919, **2980**

IMMIGRATION PROCEDURES HANDBOOK (US/0887-1205) [12230081] **1919**

IMMIGRATION UPDATE (AT/1034-5051) [I10345051] **1919**

IMMINENCE! (ARLINGTON, VA.) *CEASED.* (US/1056-0467) [23449919] **2263**

IMMOBILIEN-BERATER (GW/0934-5693) **4839**

IMMR (INSTITUTE FOR MINING AND MINERALS RESEARCH, UNIVERSITY OF KENTUCKY) (US/0192-4680) [05043265] **2140**

IMMUNE INTERVENTION (UK/0887-7750) [12015750] **3670**

IMMUNITAT UND INFEKTION (GW/0340-1162) [01357834] **3670**

●IMMUNITY (CAMBRIDGE, MASS.) (US/1074-7613) [29819797] **3670**

IMMUNIZATION ALERT, THE (US/1054-8866) [23010720] **4784**

IMMUNO ANALYSE & BIOLOGIE SPECIALISEE (FR/0923-2532) [I09232532] **458**

IMMUNOASSAY KIT DIRECTORY. SERIES A, CLINICAL CHEMISTRY, THE (NE/0926-2067) [25366597] **3586**

IMMUNOASSAY. SUPPLEMENT (UK/0262-8740) [09179976] **3670**

IMMUNOASSAY TECHNOLOGY *CEASED.* (GW/0930-9160) [13388507] **3670**

IMMUNOBIOLOGY (1979) (GW/0171-2985) [06192325] **3670**

IMMUNOCLONES (FR/0994-9895) [24317901] **458**

IMMUNODEFICIENCY (CHUR, SWITZERLAND) (UK/1067-795X) [27351341] **3670**

IMMUNODEFICIENCY REVIEWS (UK/0893-5300) [15559491] **3670**

IMMUNOFACTS (US) **4307**

IMMUNOGENETICS (NEW YORK) (US/0093-7711) [01793392] **3670**

IMMUNOHEMATOLOGY (US/0894-203X) [15924480] **3772**

IMMUNOHISTOCHEMISTRY (UK/0142-8136) [I01428136] **537**

IMMUNOLOGIA CLINICA *CEASED.* (IT) [18838040] **3670**

IMMUNOLOGIA POLSKA (PL/0324-8534) [03459191] **3670**

IMMUNOLOGIC RESEARCH (SZ/0257-277X) [13999087] **3670**

IMMUNOLOGICAL DISORDERS UPDATE (US/1056-4896) [23723013] **3671**

IMMUNOLOGICAL INVESTIGATIONS (US/0882-0139) [11718387] **3671**

IMMUNOLOGICAL REVIEWS (DK/0105-2896) [02885127] **3671**

IMMUNOLOGIE MEDICALE (FR/0755-0871) [17382818] **3671**

IMMUNOLOGIJA I ALLERGIJA (UKU/0130-2019) [02550696] **3671**

IMMUNOLOGIJA (MOSKVA) (RU/0206-4952) [07100987] **3671**

●IMMUNOLOGIST (TORONTO) (US/1192-5612) [29186464] **3671**

IMMUNOLOGY (UK/0019-2805) [01752695] **3671**

IMMUNOLOGY ABSTRACTS (US/0307-112X) [02082330] 3671, **3660**

IMMUNOLOGY AND ALLERGY CLINICS OF NORTH AMERICA (US/0889-8561) [14091852] 3786, **3671**

IMMUNOLOGY & ALLERGY PRACTICE *CEASED.* (US/0194-7508) [04986792] **3671**

IMMUNOLOGY AND CELL BIOLOGY (AT/0818-9641) [15718354] **3671**

IMMUNOLOGY AND INFECTIOUS DISEASES (UK/0959-4957) [23364328] **3671**

IMMUNOLOGY LETTERS (NE/0165-2478) [05434613] **3671**

IMMUNOLOGY SERIES (US/0092-6019) [01349256] **3671**

IMMUNOLOGY. SUPPLEMENT (UK) [18179672] **3671**

IMMUNOLOGY TODAY (AMSTERDAM. REGULAR ED.) (UK/0167-5699) [06828159] **3671**

IMMUNOLOGY TRIBUNE *CEASED.* (US/0271-3284) [06569580] **3672**

●IMMUNOMETHODS (SAN DIEGO, CALIF.) (US/1058-6687) [24351991] **3672**

IMMUNOPATHOLOGY IMMUNOTHERAPY FORUM (US) [20763697] **3672**

IMMUNOPHARMACOLOGY (US/0162-3109) [04148651] **3672**

IMMUNOPHARMACOLOGY AND IMMUNOTOXICOLOGY (US/0892-3973) [15178708] 3981, **3672**

IMMUNOPHARMACOLOGY REVIEWS (US) [21461197] 4307, **3672**

IMMUNOTECHNOLOGY (NE/1380-2933) **3672**

IMMUNOTHERAPY AND CLINICAL CANCER IMMUNOLOGY (US) [03457731] **3672**

IMO NEWS (UK) [08824087] **5450**

IMO STATE (NIGERIA). MILITARY ADMINISTRATOR *See* BUDGET SPEECH - MILITARY ADMINISTRATOR, IMO STATE OF NIGERIA **4715**

IMONO (JA/0021-4396) [09174446] 4027, **977**

IMOP KWA IMHAK *See* HANGUK IMHAKHOE CHI **2384**

IMOP YONGUQON YONGU POGO (KO) [18807014] **2384**

IMP, INDUSTRIAL MODELS & PATTERNS (US/0146-0161) [02829803] **3481**

IMPAC REPORTS (US/0198-8042) [06038908] 2384, **870**

IMPACT (CN/0703-6922) [03564276] **4655**

IMPACT (AT) [06589032] **5203**

IMPACT 80 (CN/0227-2644) [08651759] **1609**

IMPACT / ACADEMY OF GENERAL DENTISTRY (US) [24150424] **1324**

IMPACT AGBIOBUSINESS (UK/0961-4745) [25745578] **681**

IMPACT AGBIOINDUSTRY *CEASED.* (UK/0964-069X) 94, **3693**

IMPACT ASSESSMENT BULLETIN (US/0734-9165) [08816000] **2173**

IMPACT BEVERAGE TRENDS IN AMERICA REVIEW AND FORECAST, THE (US/0882-6277) [11905266] **2367**

IMPACT (CLAREMONT) (US/0194-0422) [05292975] **4964**

IMPACT COMPRESSORS (US/0884-2264) [12317354] **2115**

IMPACT (CONSERVATIVE BAPTIST FOREIGN MISSION SOCIETY) (US/0019-2821) [01779748] **5061**

IMPACT — Alphabetical Title Index

IMPACT (ENGLEWOOD CLIFFS, N.J.) **CEASED.** (US) [08947633] **942**

IMPACT (GAINESVILLE, FLA.) (US/0748-2353) [10908183] **94**

IMPACT (GREAT FALLS, MONT.) (US/0740-3445) [09910439] **4045**

IMPACT INTERNAT (FR) **3586**

IMPACT INTERNATIONAL (UK/0046-8703) [04600278] **4523**

IMPACT INTERNATIONAL DIRECTORY *See* IMPACT WORLD DIRECTORY : LEADING SPIRITS, WINE & BEER COMPANIES : WHO'S WHO OF INDUSTRY EXECUTIVES **2367**

IMPACT INTERNATIONAL (NEW YORK, N.Y.) (US/0268-8212) [16411652] **2367**

IMPACT JOURNAL (US/0162-1300) [04103769] **4655**

IMPACT, LABOUR LAW & MANAGEMENT PRACTICES (CN/0843-7114) [20279212] **3149**

IMPACT (MANILA) (PH/0300-4155) [01424350] **5203**

IMPACT MEDECIN (NOUV. FORMULE) (FR) [20857359] **3586**

IMPACT MEDECIN QUOTIDIEN (FR) **3586**

IMPACT (MONTREAL. ENGLISH EDITION) **CEASED.** (CN/0700-4869) [03956689] **839**

IMPACT (NEW YORK. 1970) (US/0363-9444) [02546924] **2367**

IMPACT OF COMPUTING IN SCIENCE AND ENGINEERING **CEASED.** (US/0899-8248) [18234643] 1187, **3508**

IMPACT OF SCIENCE ON SOCIETY **CEASED.** (UK/0019-2872) [01590753] **5112**

IMPACT OF SCIENCE ON SOCIETY (KO) [11789398] **5112**

IMPACT OF SCIENCE ON SOCIETY (UA) [09288994] **5112**

IMPACT OF TAX CHANGES ON INCOME DISTRIBUTION, THE (UK/0308-1958) [03792857] **4731**

IMPACT OF TRAVEL ON STATE ECONOMIES, THE (US/0730-9813) [06435676] **5480**

IMPACT (PHILADELPHIA) (US/0090-3930) [01785116] **2263**

IMPACT - PROFESSIONAL ASSOCIATION OF CANADIAN THEATRES (CN/0848-1482) [21190689] **5365**

IMPACT PUMP NEWS (US/0887-5081) [13277022] 1304, **2115**

IMPACT PUMP NEWS & PATENTS (US/1056-1536) [23476141] 1304, **2115**

IMPACT PUMPS (US/0899-031X) [17974915] **2115**

IMPACT (SAVE THE CHILDREN (U.S.)) (US) [20742544] **5289**

IMPACT, SCIENCE ET SOCIETE **CEASED.** (FR/0304-2944) [04187752] **5112**

IMPACT SINGAPORE (SI/0129-2862) [01292862] **4964**

IMPACT SYDNEY, 1986 (AT/1030-3847) [10303847] **3113**

IMPACT (SYRACUSE) (US/0163-8262) [04376357] **5187**

IMPACT - UNIVERSITE DU QUEBEC (CN/1181-8034) [23242547] **1829**

IMPACT (VAL-BELAIR (QUEBEC)) (CN/0824-4286) [10420468] **2535**

IMPACT VALVE NEWS & PATENTS (US/1056-1544) [23476036] 1304, **2115**

IMPACT VALVES (US/0883-7619) [12207053] **2115**

IMPACT (WASHINGTON) (US/0162-4989) [04090347] 5416, **2980**

●IMPACT WORLD DIRECTORY : LEADING SPIRITS, WINE & BEER COMPANIES : WHO'S WHO OF INDUSTRY EXECUTIVES (US) [25730648] **2367**

IMPACT YEARBOOK (US/0749-7946) [11193897] **2367**

IMPACTO (US/0273-530X) [07058720] **2551**

IMPACTO (MEXICO) (MX/0019-2880) [01792826] **2535**

IMPAKUTO (JA) [07100776] **2504**

IMPARCIAL [MICROFORM], EL (GT/0536-5708) [02411450] **5802**

IMPART (AT/0813-6939) [I08136939] **3214**

IMPARTIAL CITIZEN (SYRACUSE, N.Y. : 1980), THE (US/0738-9116) [09668392] **2263**

IMPARTIAL DE LA MEURTHE ET DES VOSGES, L' (FR) [21075171] **5800**

IMPEGNO OSPEDALIERO (IT/0393-0394) [08897675] 3786, **1677**

IMPERIAL COUNTY FARM BUREAU MONTHLY (US/8750-5355) [11489179] **94**

IMPERIAL MYCOLOGICAL INSTITUTE. DISTRIBUTION MAPS OF PLANT DISEASES *See* DISTRIBUTION MAPS OF PLANT DISEASES **508**

IMPERIAL OIL REVIEW (1989) (CN/0848-8843) [21253189] **4260**

IMPERIAL QUARTERLY *See* IMPERIAL QUARTERLY MAGAZINE **2517**

IMPERIAL QUARTERLY MAGAZINE **CEASED.** (CN/1188-0066) [26245294] **2517**

IMPERIAL VALLEY PRESS (US) [27084787] **5635**

IMPERMEABILIZZARE (IT) **2825**

IMPIANTI (IT/0390-6132) [11826904] **1609**

IMPIANTI ATTREZZATURE SPORTIVE E RICREATIVE (IT) **4899**

IMPIANTISTICA ITALIANA (IT/0394-1582) [I03941582] **617**

IMPIANTO ELETTRICO, L' (IT/0394-5634) [I03945634] **2064**

●IMPLANT DENTISTRY (US/1056-6163) [23747904] **1324**

IMPLANT SOCIETY, THE (US/1059-3489) [24172677] **3586**

IMPLANTATION D'UNE ENTREPRISE AU CANADA, L' (CN/0225-7238) [06316254] **1609**

IMPLANTATION ETRANGERE DANS L'INDUSTRIE AU IER JANVIER, L' (FR/0244-7118) [05080283] **901**

IMPLEMENT & TRACTOR (US/0019-2953) [08820078] **159**

IMPLEMENT & TRACTOR TRADE JOURNAL (KANSAS CITY, MO. :1929) *See* IMPLEMENT & TRACTOR **159**

IMPLEMENTATION DIVISION ACTIVITIES *See* IMPLEMENTATION DIVISION ACTIVITIES REPORT / FEDERAL HIGHWAY ADMINISTRATION, OFFICES OF RESEARCH AND DEVELOPMENT **5384**

IMPLEMENTATION DIVISION ACTIVITIES REPORT / FEDERAL HIGHWAY ADMINISTRATION, OFFICES OF RESEARCH AND DEVELOPMENT (US) [09135416] **5384**

IMPLEMENTATION OF LITTLE BLUE RIVER BASIN WATER QUALITY MANAGEMENT PLAN (US) [06175831] **2232**

IMPOR MENURUT JENIS BARANG DAN NEGERI ASAL (IO) [02900665] **839**

IMPORT AUTOMOTIVE PARTS & ACCESSORIES (US/0199-4468) [05872595] **5416**

IMPORT BANKSTOWN (AT/1034-7313) [I10347313] **839**

IMPORT BULLETIN (US) [01644248] **839**

IMPORT CAR AND TRUCK TRANSMISSION MANUAL (US) **5416**

IMPORT COLLISION ESTIMATING GUIDE (US) **5416**

IMPORT EXPORT BULLETIN (CN/0228-0043) [08730645] **839**

IMPORT EXPORT OPPORTUNITIES *See* WORLD TRADE LINK **858**

IMPORT/EXPORT WOOD PURCHASING NEWS (US/0194-1186) [05363790] **2401**

IMPORT FILE (1982) (CN/0822-6687) [10339519] **839**

IMPORT LICENSING SCHEDULE (NZ) [02474597] **839**

IMPORT SERVICE (US/0896-5722) [17211177] **5416**

IMPORTANT ADVANCES IN ONCOLOGY (US/0883-5896) [11616140] **3818**

●IMPORTCAR (1993) (US/1069-4714) [28056942] **5416**

IMPORTCAR & TRUCK (US/1040-5267) [18438394] **5416**

IMPORTED CAR REPAIR MANUAL PARTS / LABOR ESTIMATING MANUAL (US) **5416**

IMPORTED CARS & TRUCKS, ELECTRICAL SERVICE & REPAIR (US) [08128007] **5416**

IMPORTED CARS & TRUCKS, TRANSMISSION SERVICE & REPAIR (US/0741-0158) [06178798] **5416**

IMPORTED CARS, LIGHT TRUCKS, AND VANS SERVICE AND REPAIR MANUAL. ANNUAL DATA ENGINE PERFORMANCE / ELECTRICAL / MECHANICAL (US) **5416**

IMPORTED CARS, LIGHT TRUCKS, AND VANS SERVICE AND REPAIR MANUAL. ELECTRICAL (US) **5416**

IMPORTED CARS, LIGHT TRUCKS, AND VANS SERVICE AND REPAIR MANUAL ENGINE PERFORMANCE (US) **5417**

IMPORTED CARS, LIGHT TRUCKS, AND VANS SERVICE AND REPAIR MANUAL. HEATING AND AIR CONDITIONING (US) **5417**

IMPORTED WINE MARKET IN AMERICA, THE (US/0730-8728) [08077469] **2367**

IMPORTED WOOD PURCHASING GUIDE (US) [08295617] **2401**

IMPORTED WOOD PURCHASING NEWS *See* IMPORT/EXPORT WOOD PURCHASING NEWS **2401**

●IMPORTERS MANUAL USA (US/1065-5158) [26621426] **839**

IMPORTS AND EXPORTS STATISTICS (CY/0253-858X) [19060514] **5328**

IMPORTS BY COUNTRY, H.S. BASED (CN/0844-837X) [20189496] **839**

IMPORTS, MERCHANDISE TRADE, H.S. BASED (CN/0844-8353) [20189279] **839**

IMPORTWEEK (CN/0702-8385) [03960129] **839**

IMPOSTE LAVORO PREVIDENZA (IT) 2980, **1677**

IMPOSTO DE RENDA APLICADO, PESSOA JURIDICA (BL) [03765783] **4731**

IMPOSTO DE RENDA. JURISPRUDENCIA / CAMARA SUPERIOR DE RECURSOS FISCAIS (BL) [10657416] **2980**

IMPOSTO DE RENDA NA FONTE : TABELAS PRATICAS (BL) [06246791] **2980**

IMPOSTO DE RENDA PESSOA JURIDICA (BL) [05322592] **4731**

IMPOSTO FISCAL (BL) [09987413] **4731**

IMPOSTURE (MONTREAL) (CN/0838-2239) [18595871] **352**

IMPOTS EN FRANCE, LES (FR) [20276229] **4731**

IMPRENDITORIALITA (IT) **870**

IMPRESA (IT/0035-6816) [06574341] **1609**

IMPRESA AMBIENTE, L' (IT) [28052847] **2173**

IMPRESA & STATO (IT) [20499366] **1566**

IMPRESA E SOCIETA **CEASED.** (IT/0390-9212) [I03909212] **901**

IMPRESA : PER IL CONSULENTE DELLE IMPRESE INDUSTRIALI E COMMERCIALI (IT) **870**

IMPRESA PUBBLICA *See* IMPRESA PUBBLICA MUNICIPALIZZAZIONE : RIVISTA BIMESTRALE DELLA CISPEL, CONFEDERAZIONE ITALIANA DEI SERVIZI PUBBLICI DEGLI ENTI LOCALI, L' **4655**

IMPRESA PUBBLICA : CIVILTA POSTINDUSTRIALE **CEASED.** (IT) **4731**

IMPRESA PUBBLICA. CIVILTA POSTINDUSTRIALE, L' **SUSPENDED.** (IT) **1494**

IMPRESA PUBBLICA MUNICIPALIZZAZIONE : RIVISTA BIMESTRALE DELLA CISPEL, CONFEDERAZIONE ITALIANA DEI SERVIZI PUBBLICI DEGLI ENTI LOCALI, L' (IT) [26387911] **4655**

IMPRESSION (MONTREAL) (CN/0704-7150) [03791122] **380**

IMPRESSION (VALLEYFIELD) (CN/0228-9830) [08601786] **5786**

IMPRESSIONS (FR) [04122197] **2980**

IMPRESSIONS (DALLAS, TEX.) (US/1043-6839) [11180628] 4899, **1085**

IMPRESSIONS/EXPRESSIONS (WINNIPEG) (CN/1184-6178) [24266561] **3286**

IMPRESSIONS MONOGRAPH (CN) [02248336] **4370**

IMPREVUE (MONTPELLIER) (FR/0242-5149) [07669092] **3395**

IMPRIMATUR (MUNCHEN) (GW/0073-5620) [01641030] **4829**

IMPRIMIS (US/0277-8432) [03890282] **1494**

IMPRINT (II/0019-3046) [02630245] **2504**

IMPRINT (HILLSDALE, N.J.) (US/0279-0408) [07471801] **4589**

IMPRINT (NEW YORK, N.Y. : 1976) (US/0277-7061) [06212941] **380**

IMPRINT (NEW YORK, NEW YORK) (US/0019-3062) [01305590] **3857**

IMPRINT (SYRACUSE, N.Y.), THE (US/0046-8746) [04899274] **3214**

IMPRINT (WATERLOO) (CN/0706-7380) [04955207] **1829**

●IMPRINTING BUSINESS (US/1066-7083) [27032887] **1085**

IMPRINTS : QUARTERLY PUBLICATION OF THE GENEALOGICAL SOCIETY OF BROWARD COUNTY, INC (US) [12824878] **2454**

●IMPROVED RECOVERY WEEK (US/1061-3692) [25277504] **1609**

IMPROVEMENT IDEAS **CEASED.** (US/0092-6140) [01789415] **300**

IMPROVING UNIVERSITY TEACHING : JOURNAL OF THE UNIVERSITY OF MALAWI TEACHING METHODS COMMITTEE (MW) **1829**

INCIDENTS

IMPROVISOR (US/0892-1911) [15124289] **4122**

IMPUESTO A LA RENTA; REGIMEN LEGAL TRIBUTARIO (CK/0120-0550) [01800080] **4731**

IMPUESTOS : BOLETIN INFORMATIVO MENSUAL AL SERVICIO DE LOS CONTRIBUYENTES (AG) [03738916] **4731**

IMPUESTOS SUCESORIALES; REGIMEN LEGAL TRIBUTARIO (CK) [04393967] **2980**

IMPULS MODA IN PELLE (GW) **1085**

IMPULS VOOR EEN OPEN SCHOOLGEMEENSCHAP (BE) **1751**

IMPULSE (AUGSBURG, GERMANY) (GW) [17759837] **2263**

●IMPULSE (CHAMPAIGN, ILL.) (US/1063-8520) [26150233] 3586, **1313**

IMPULSE (WIEN) (AU/0304-1239) [01798321] **3395**

IMQ NOTIZIE (IT) **681**

IMRO RULE BOOK (UK) **901**

IMS AMERICA LTD *See* NATIONAL PRESCRIPTION AUDIT: THERAPEUTIC CATEGORY REPORT **4317**

IMS LIST, SANITATION COMPLIANCE AND ENFORCEMENT RATINGS OF INTERSTATE MILK SHIPPERS (US/0898-9877) [16570714] **195**

IMSA JOURNAL (US/1064-2560) [07529443] **5441**

IMSIL MUNHWA (KO) [09530244] **322**

IMSS NEWSLETTER (CN/0823-8812) [11431463] **4964**

IMT; ILUSTROWANY MAGAZYN TURYSTYCZNY (PL) [01786579] **5480**

IMVS NEWSLETTER / PREPARED BY THE STAFF OF THE INSTITUTE OF MEDICAL AND VETERINARY SCIENCE (AT/0813-1643) [16635187] **5511**

IMYONG MUNHWA (KO) [05691034] **2653**

IN (GW) [01792944] **1829**

IN BETWEEN YEARS, THE (US/1050-7949) [21613814] **2281**

IN BRIEF (SYDNEY, N.S.W.) *See* MEAT & LIVESTOCK REVIEW / PRODUCED BY THE AUSTRALIAN MEAT AND LIVESTOCK CORPORATION, MARKETING INTELLIGENCE UNIT **2349**

IN BRITAIN (UK/0019-3143) [05025648] **5480**

IN BUSINESS (US/0190-2458) [04676753] 790, **2232**

IN BUSINESS WINDSOR (CN/0848-1008) [20984613] **681**

IN CHRISTO : A QUARTERLY FOR RELIGIOUS (II) [09746553] **5030**

IN COMPETITION (UK/0965-3597) [l09653597] **2980**

IN CONFIDENCE (US) **3586**

IN CONTEXT (CROWNSVILLE, MD.) (US/1059-5511) [24624360] **2738**

IN CONTEXT (SEQUIM, WASH.) (US/0741-6180) [10188761] **4349**

IN CONTROL (HOUSTON, TEX.) (US/1045-7046) [20212503] **1609**

IN DANCE *CEASED.* (US/0883-9956) [12277127] **1313**

IN DE WAAGSCHAAL (NE) [08257353] 4476, **4964**

IN DEFENSE OF THE ALIEN (US/0275-634X) [07219679] **1919**

IN DEPTH (WASHINGTON, D.C.) (US/1055-9809) [23436560] **4476**

IN DIE SKRIFLIG (SA/1018-6441) [I10186441] **4964**

IN FACT (MILWAUKEE, WIS.) (US) [13076011] **2980**

IN FASHION (US/0883-6183) [24271084] **1085**

●IN/FIRE ETHICS (US/1062-9564) [25814717] **2251**

IN-FISHERMAN ANGLING ADVENTURES TRAVEL GUIDE (US/1048-4892) [20955607] **4873**

IN-FISHERMAN, THE (US/0276-9905) [06228644] 4873, **2305**

IN-FISHERMAN WALLEYE IN-SIDER *See* WALLEYE IN-SIDER **2315**

IN FORMA DI PAROLE *CEASED.* (IT) [07753171] **3395**

IN-FORMAZIONE (IT) **5289**

IN FORMAZIONE (IT) [13864952] **4542**

IN GEARDAGUM : ESSAYS ON OLD ENGLISH LANGUAGE AND LITERATURE (US) [11172567] **3286**

IN GOD'S IMAGE (KO) **4964**

IN GOOD TILTH (US/1065-1527) [22807104] **94**

IN HEALTH (US/1047-0549) [20588917] **3586**

IN-HOUSE (UK/0308-8154) [l03088154] **300**

IN HOUSE GRAPHICS (US/0883-6973) [12570859] **380**

IN (IOWA CITY) (US/0091-6994) [01788069] 3165, **322**

IN IURE PRAESENTIA (IT) [03603772] **2980**

IN JOPLIN METROPOLITAN (US/0743-1503) [10535698] 2535, **5480**

IN KULTUR : DAS MAGAZIN DER HAMBURGER VOLKSBUHNE (GW) [25518581] **5365**

IN MOTION FILM & VIDEO PRODUCTION MAGAZINE (US/0889-6208) [13997219] 4072, **4370**

IN-NAZZJON TAGHNA HAMRUN (MM/1017-2106) [I10172106] **5806**

IN OTHER WORDS (US/0279-3172) [04123106] **5017**

IN OTHER WORDS NUNAWADING (AT/1036-1421) [I10361421] **3286**

IN OUR OPINION (US) [12098745] **745**

IN PERSPECTIVE OF THE BLACK AMERICAN VETERAN (US/1053-7864) [22646566] 2263, **4045**

●IN-PLANT PRINTER (1993) (US/1071-832X) [28738388] **4565**

IN-PLANT PRINTER & ELECTRONIC PUBLISHER (US/0891-8996) [15132062] **4565**

IN-PLANT REPRODUCTIONS (1988) (US/1043-1942) [19340328] 1263, **4566**

IN-PLANT REPRODUCTIONS & ELECTRONIC PUBLISHING (US/0886-3121) [14913748] **4815**

IN POLITICS (US/0275-8954) [07243337] **4476**

IN PRACTICE (LONDON 1979) (UK/0263-841X) [04752211] **5511**

IN PRINT (TRENTON, N.J.) (US/1067-5132) [21268284] **4815**

IN PROCESS (NEW YORK, N.Y.) (US/1060-6734) [25054003] **322**

IN PROCESS (OTTAWA) (CN/0711-2971) [08486328] **4655**

IN RE, EAGLE-PICHER INDUSTRIES, INC., ET AL (US/1061-3536) [25259371] **790**

IN REVIEW / INTER-AMERICAN FOUNDATION (US) [25763647] **2910**

IN REVIEW (TORONTO) (CN/0019-3259) [02593663] **1064**

IN REVIEW (TORONTO. 1975) (CN/0700-3854) [03399941] **5247**

IN SEASON (US) **4964**

IN-SERVICE REVIEWS IN CLINICAL LABORATORY SCIENCE (US/1042-7430) [19121576] **3586**

IN SERVICE REVIEWS IN DIAGNOSTIC MEDICAL SONOGRAPHY (US/1041-0104) [18610470] **3586**

IN SERVICE REVIEWS IN NUCLEAR MEDICINE (US/1041-0090) [18610565] **3848**

IN SERVICE REVIEWS IN RADIOLOGIC TECHNOLOGY (US/1041-0082) [18610642] **3942**

IN SERVICE REVIEWS IN RESPIRATORY THERAPY (US/1041-0058) [18609971] **3949**

IN SERVICE REVIEWS IN RESPIRATORY THERAPY *See* CLINICAL ADVANCES IN CARDIO-RESPIRATORY CARE **3949**

IN-SITE (VERNON HILLS, ILL.) *SUSPENDED.* (US/1042-7562) [19133434] **2420**

IN SITU (US/0146-2520) [03132001] 2140, **1440**

IN SITU (LUSAKA) (ZA/1015-0862) [08971731] **300**

IN-STAT ELECTRONICS REPORT (US/0888-9406) [10386762] **2064**

IN-STORE BAKERY PRODUCTION AND MARKETING *CEASED.* (US/0733-4796) [08581448] **2344**

IN SUMMARY (CN/0228-2518) [06860187] **5203**

IN THE COMPANY OF POETS (US/1055-0038) [23044412] **3464**

IN THE CREASE *CEASED.* (US/0744-5172) [08333091] **4899**

IN THE DRIVER'S SEAT (CN/0702-5785) [04678064] **5417**

IN THE FIELD (CHICAGO, ILL.) (US/1051-4546) [21962192] 4166, **4089**

IN THE GROVE (US/0737-5972) [09425177] **3214**

IN THE MAINSTREAM (WASHINGTON, D.C.) (US/0888-9724) [05983859] **4389**

IN THE MARKETPLACE (US/1064-0649) [26207591] **4964**

IN THE MIDDLE (CN/0823-695X) [10082644] **1751**

IN THE PUBLIC INTEREST (AMHERST, N.Y.) (US/0897-1331) [06365424] **2980**

IN THE PUBLIC INTEREST / OFFICE OF THE ATTORNEY GENERAL (NEW MEXICO) (US) [11404707] **3165**

IN THE WIND (ANGOURA HILLS, CALIF.) (US/1059-759X) [24726603] **4081**

IN THE WORKS (LITTLE ROCK, ARK.) (US/8756-2162) [09338854] 1801, **1913**

IN THEORY ONLY *SUSPENDED.* (US/0360-4365) [02244773] **4122**

IN THESE TIMES (US/0160-5992) [03690551] **5203**

IN TOUCH (CN/1180-9205) [22185827] **1804**

IN TOUCH (OTTAWA) *CEASED.* (CN/0826-0648) [10884135] **5112**

IN TOUCH WITH FLOWERS (UK) **2420**

IN TRANSIT (WASHINGTON) (US/0019-3291) [04074428] **5384**

IN TRUST (UK/0141-0415) [I01410415] **301**

IN TUNE (EDMONTON) (CN/1186-6055) [24368273] **4122**

IN UNITY (AT/0442-3844) [06122680] **4964**

IN VERKEHR GESETZTE NEUE MOTORFAHRZEUGE (LH) [03219828] **5417**

IN VIEW (US/1047-3777) [20707618] 5559, **1829**

IN VITRO CELLULAR & DEVELOPMENTAL BIOLOGY. ANIMAL (US/1071-2690) [23906300] **537**

IN VITRO CELLULAR & DEVELOPMENTAL BIOLOGY. PLANT (US/1054-5476) [22918530] **513**

IN-VITRO-DIAGNOSTICA-NACHRICHTEN (GW/0938-0922) [I09380922] **3797**

IN VITRO. MONOGRAPH (US/0363-521X) [02370877] 3586, **458**

IN VITRO TOXICOLOGY (US/0888-319X) [13535703] **3981**

IN VIVO (ATHENS) (GR/0258-851X) [18319328] **458**

IN VIVO (NEW YORK, N.Y.) (US/0733-1398) [08536463] 3586, **681**

IN YOUR EAR *See* QRM (WASHINGTON, D.C.) **4148**

IN YOUR FACE (US/1059-1230) [24478991] 3395, **2263**

IN YOUR INTEREST (CN/0847-2785) [21344656] **790**

INA NEWSLETTER (UK/0255-013X) [I0255013X] **4227**

INA NEWSLETTER (INSTITUTE OF NAUTICAL ARCHAEOLOGY (U.S.)) *See* INA QUARTERLY, THE **270**

INA NEWSLETTER / INTERNATIONAL NANNOPLANKTON ASSOCIATION (NE) [06760702] **4231**

INA PROFESSIONAL LIABILITY BULLETIN, ATTORNEYS (US/0736-8399) [09224138] 2882, **2980**

INA PROFESSIONAL LIABILITY BULLETIN, SCHOOLS (US/0736-8380) [09224717] **2980**

●INA QUARTERLY, THE (US) [26536606] **270**

INACTIVE OIL AND GAS FIELDS (US/0360-6236) [02244257] **4260**

INAUGURAL LECTURE SERIES / UNIVERSITY COLLEGE CORK *CEASED.* (IE) [14580615] **4655**

INAZUCAR (DR/1013-980X) [03431717] **2344**

INBOARD BOAT TRADE-IN GUIDE, BLUE BOOK (US) [11526327] **593**

INBOUND LOGISTICS (US) [21894848] 839, **5450**

INBOUND/OUTBOUND (US/1042-6116) [18679765] 1157, **926**

INC. (BOSTON, MASS.) (US/0162-8968) [04251282] **681**

INC HEBDO CONSOMMATEURS ACTUALITES (FR/1145-0673) [I11450673] **1297**

INCAST (DALLAS, TEX.) (US/1045-5779) [20156713] **4003**

INCENTIVE MARKETING AND SALES PROMOTION: ANNUAL REVIEW AND BUYERS' GUIDE (UK) [06937207] 955, **760**

INCENTIVE (NEW YORK) (US/0019-3348) [03565688] **955**

INCENTIVE (NEW YORK, N.Y. 1988) (US/1042-5195) [17990331] **760**

INCENTIVE TAXATION (US/0896-4556) [09530963] **4731**

INCENTIVE TRAVEL AND BUSINESS MEETINGS (US/0090-8533) [01785686] 5480, **1677**

INCHIESTA (IT) [05937336] **5247**

INCHON SANGUI (KO) [10378067] **820**

INCIDENTS OF SUSPECTED CHILD ABUSE IN MARYLAND (US/0092-0169) [01788795] **5289**

INCIDENTS — Alphabetical Title Index

INCIDENTS OF THE WAR (US) [13393126] 2620, **4370**

INCIPIT (AG/0326-0941) [11018228] **3395**

INCITE INFORMATION (US/1056-3504) [23669405] **5247**

INCITE INFORMATION (US/1056-3504) [24103587] **4815**

INCITE (SYDNEY) (AT/0158-0876) [06804709] **3214**

INCITE (TORONTO) **CEASED.** (CN/0829-9013) [10191584] **352**

INCL JOURNAL (US/0270-2061) [06324027] 2882, **2980**

INCLUSIVE DIRECTORY OF INDEPENDENT OPERATING TELEPHONES (US/0361-3437) [02246285] **1157**

INCOGNITA (LEIDEN, NETHERLANDS) **CEASED.** (NE/0923-7135) [23057804] **2848**

INCOME AFTER TAX, DISTRIBUTIONS BY SIZE IN CANADA (CN/0319-0374) [02240934] **1566**

INCOME & SAFETY *See* INCOME FUND OUTLOOK **901**

INCOME ASSISTANCE, SOCIAL SERVICES, AND MEDICAL ASSISTANCE / WASHINGTON STATE, DEPARTMENT OF SOCIAL & HEALTH SERVICES (US) [24139656] **5289**

INCOME DISTRIBUTIONS BY SIZE IN CANADA (CN/0575-8750) [01787153] 1494, **1533**

INCOME ESTIMATES FOR SUBPROVINCIAL AREAS (CN/0825-124X) [09631103] **1494**

INCOME/EXPENSE ANALYSIS : FEDERALLY-ASSISTED APARTMENTS (US) [15099266] **2825**

INCOME/EXPENSE ANALYSIS. OFFICE BUILDINGS, DOWNTOWN AND SUBURBAN (US) [09006625] **4839**

INCOME FUND OUTLOOK (US) **901**

INCOME MAINTENANCE BULLETIN / COMMONWEALTH OF PENNSYLVANIA, DEPARTMENT OF PUBLIC WELFARE (US) [08054218] **5289**

INCOME OPPORTUNITIES (NEW YORK, N.Y.) (US/0019-3429) [01775571] **681**

INCOME PER SHARE BEFORE SECURITIES GAINS OR LOSSES (US/0749-8543) [09892946] **790**

INCOME PLU$ (US/1046-1736) [20344369] **681**

INCOME SECURITY PROGRAMS (CN/0707-3283) [10128707] **5289**

INCOME STOCKS HANDBOOK (US/0741-1812) [10090599] **901**

INCOME TAX ACT (CN/0317-9060) [02248267] **4731**

INCOME TAX ACT AND REGULATIONS, DEPARTMENT OF FINANCE TECHNICAL NOTES (CN/1187-7502) [25652195] **4731**

INCOME TAX ACT ... ANNOTATED (CN/0527-7884) [02247190] 4731, **2981**

INCOME TAX AND FAMILY LAW HANDBOOK (CN) 4731, **3121**

INCOME TAX BULLETINS, CIRCULARS, RULINGS (CN/1193-3879) [27019134] **4731**

INCOME TAX GUIDE FOR MILITARY PERSONNEL (US/0098-1729) [01799535] 4045, **745**

INCOME TAX PROCEDURE (US/0091-2816) [01783409] **4731**

INCOME TAX REPORTS, THE (II/0019-3453) [01586688] **4731**

INCOME TAX RULING (CN/0704-2930) [03980417] **4731**

INCOME TAX TECHNIQUES **CEASED.** (US) [05630217] **4731**

INCOMES DATA PANORAMA (UK/0579-3149) [05506972] **1677**

INCOMES DATA REPORT (UK/0019-3451) [05506988] **4731**

INCOMES DATA SERVICES *See* IDS STUDY **1677**

INCOMINDIOS (SZ) [05814645] **2738**

INCOMPATEX (FR) **681**

INCONNU PARIS, L' (FR/0338-8190) [I03388190] **5074**

INCONTRI CEF (IT/0394-3690) [I03943690] **942**

INCONTRI DE ANESTESIA, RIANIMAZIONE E SCIENZE AFFINI (IT/0391-8629) [07355725] **3965**

INCONTRI LINGUISTICI (IT/0390-2412) [02105889] **3286**

INCORPORATED ASSOCIATION OF ARCHITECTS AND SURVEYORS *See* REFERENCE BOOK & LIST OF MEMBERS / THE INCORPORATED ASSOCIATION OF ARCHITECTS & SURVEYORS **307**

INCORPORATED MUNICIPALITIES, MUNICIPAL OFFICIALS AND STATE STREET AID ALLOCATIONS (US/0098-6933) [02242367] **4655**

INCORPORATED SOCIETY OF MUSICIANS (GREAT BRITAIN) *See* YEARBOOK & REGISTER OF MEMBERS / INCORPORATED SOCIETY OF MUSICIANS **4159**

INCORPORATION AND INCOME TAX IN CANADA (CN/0319-5953) [02443073] **4731**

INCREASE (US/0274-5569) [06401440] **4964**

INCREASING UNDERSTANDING OF PUBLIC PROBLEMS AND POLICIES (US/0430-0785) [02239243] **94**

INCREDIBLE HULK, THE (US/0274-5275) [06387665] **4862**

INCREMENTAL MOTION CONTROL SYSTEMS AND DEVICES NEWSLETTER (US/0362-3858) [02222565] **2064**

INCUNABULA GRAECA (IT/0073-5752) [01752714] **1077**

INDA JOURNAL OF NONWOVENS RESEARCH (US) **5351**

INDAGATIONES MATHEMATICAE (NE/0019-3577) [01779751] **3508**

INDAGINE SPECIALE SULLE VACANZE DEGLI ITALIANI (IT) [04397720] 1677, **1533**

INDAGINI E QUADERNI (IT) **3344**

INDEBTEDNESS / BUREAU OF LOCAL FINANCIAL ASSISTANCE (US) [03820968] **790**

INDEC COMMUNICATOR, THE (CN/0705-1166) [03991650] **1751**

INDECOSA (FR) **870**

INDEFUND LIMITED *See* ANNUAL REPORT AND ACCOUNTS / INDEFUND LIMITED **770**

INDEKS BERITA DAN ARTIKEL SURAT KABAR BIDANG ILMU-ILMU SOSIAL DAN KEMANUSIAAN (IO) [06776734] **5803**

INDEKS HARGA PERDAGANGAN BESAR BAHAN BANGUNAN/KONSTRUKSI DI INDONESIA (IO) [04864432] 617, **1609**

INDEKS MAJALAH ILMIAH INDONESIA / INDEX OF INDONESIAN LEARNED PERIODICALS (IO/0216-6216) [10355089] **417**

INDEKS; MESECNI PREGLED PRIVREDNE STATISTIKE FNRJ (YU/0513-0689) [05530739] **5328**

INDEKS PEMILU (IO) [08635017] **4655**

INDEPENDANT PROFESSIONAL AND FLORIDA BUSINESS JOURNAL, THE (US/0746-4754) [10063039] **681**

INDEPENDENCE (AT) 1864, **1751**

INDEPENDENCE DAILY REPORTER (INDEPENDENCE, KAN. : 1927) (US) [12228688] **5676**

INDEPENDENCE NEWS (CN/0821-0756) [10330226] **901**

INDEPENDENCE NEWS (INDEPENDENCE, KAN.) (US) [12228818] **5676**

INDEPENDENICA (PO) [12233075] **2692**

INDEPENDENT (US) [10674822] **5712**

INDEPENDENT ADJUSTER, THE (US) [04412249] **2882**

INDEPENDENT AGENT (US/0002-7197) [02245002] **2882**

INDEPENDENT ASSOCIATION OF QUESTIONED DOCUMENT EXAMINERS, INC. : [JOURNAL] *See* JOURNAL OF QUESTIONED DOCUMENT EXAMINATION **3167**

INDEPENDENT AUDIT REPORT ON REVENUES BY SOURCE FOR TEXAS PUBLIC ELEMENTARY AND SECONDARY SCHOOL DISTRICTS (US) [08099491] **1864**

INDEPENDENT BANKER (US/0019-3674) [01644026] **790**

INDEPENDENT BAPTIST VOICE, THE (US/8756-1816) [11479813] **5061**

INDEPENDENT BROADCASTING AUTHORITY *See* ANNUAL REPORT / INDEPENDENT BROADCASTING AUTHORITY **1126**

INDEPENDENT BROADCASTING AUTHORITY. ANNUAL REPORT AND ACCOUNTS *See* ANNUAL REPORT / INDEPENDENT BROADCASTING AUTHORITY **1126**

INDEPENDENT BUSINESS FORUM (CN/0710-0531) [08078883] **681**

INDEPENDENT BUSINESS : IB (US/1047-2347) [20643697] 1229, **681**

INDEPENDENT CANADIAN BUSINESS ASSOCIATION OF BRITISH COLUMBIA *See* ICBA. INDEPENDENT CANADIAN BUSINESS ASSOCIATION OF BRITISH COLUMBIA **1609**

INDEPENDENT CANADIAN BUSINESSMEN ASSOCIATION OF BRITISH COLUMBIA *See* DIRECTORY - INDEPENDENT CANADIAN BUSINESSMEN ASSOCIATION OF BRITISH COLUMBIA **666**

INDEPENDENT DE SOTO PRESS (US) [09410942] **5703**

INDEPENDENT (DEERFIELD, WIS.) (US) [11858918] **5768**

INDEPENDENT DEMOCRAT (WAVERLY) (US) **5670**

INDEPENDENT EDUCATION (AT/0310-7175) [I03107175] **1751**

INDEPENDENT (ELMIRA) (CN/0833-8019) [15216618] **5786**

INDEPENDENT (ELMIRA, ONT. : LOCAL ED.) *See* ELMIRA INDEPENDENT **5784**

INDEPENDENT ENERGY (US/1043-7320) [19533716] **1946**

INDEPENDENT (FENTON, MICH.) **SUSPENDED.** (US/8750-8230) [11822534] **5692**

INDEPENDENT FLORIDA ALLIGATOR, THE (US/0889-2423) [13827512] **1092**

INDEPENDENT HERALD (ONEIDA, TENN.) (US/0744-1711) [08085926] **5745**

INDEPENDENT-HERALD (PINEVILLE, W.VA.) (US) [13416136] **5764**

INDEPENDENT INVESTOR (MIAMI BEACH, FLA.) (US/1046-3291) [20379361] **901**

INDEPENDENT LIVING (AT/0815-2276) [I08152276] **4389**

INDEPENDENT LIVING (1989) (US/1048-3772) [20832152] **4389**

INDEPENDENT (LONDON, ENGLAND) (UK) [15051443] **5812**

INDEPENDENT-MESSENGER (US/0746-794X) [10282128] **5758**

INDEPENDENT METHODIST BULLETIN, THE (US/0744-4087) [08246378] **5061**

INDEPENDENT MONTHLY, THE (AT/1033-9957) [I10339957] 681, **4476**

INDEPENDENT (NEW YORK, N.Y. : 1978) (US/0731-5198) [08228619] **4072**

INDEPENDENT NEWSPAPER FROM RUSSIA (US/1064-4431) [23886902] **5759**

INDEPENDENT-OBSERVER (CONRAD, MONT.) (US) [11834281] **5705**

INDEPENDENT-OBSERVER (SCOTTDALE, PA.) (US) [13739216] **5736**

INDEPENDENT ON SUNDAY, THE (UK) [22223654] **5812**

INDEPENDENT (PORT HOPE) (CN/0712-4953) [09137683] **5786**

● INDEPENDENT POWER MARKETS QUARTERLY (US/1065-870X) [26784333] **4761**

INDEPENDENT POWER REPORT (US/1049-0744) [18832228] **2064**

INDEPENDENT POWER REPORT'S AVOIDED-COST QUARTERLY *See* INDEPENDENT POWER MARKETS QUARTERLY **4761**

INDEPENDENT PRESS (BLOOMFIELD, N.J.) (US/0747-4075) [10810658] **5710**

INDEPENDENT PRESS-TELEGRAPH *See* PRESS-TELEGRAM **5638**

INDEPENDENT-PROSPECTOR *See* NORTH JERSEY PROSPECTOR, THE **5711**

INDEPENDENT-RECORD (HELENA, MONT.) (US) [11978496] **5705**

INDEPENDENT-REGISTER, THE (US) [13728147] **5768**

INDEPENDENT REPORTER JOLIMONT (AT/1037-0242) [I10370242] 1896, **1751**

INDEPENDENT REPUBLIC QUARTERLY, THE (US/0046-8843) [01897333] **2738**

INDEPENDENT REPUBLICAN (US/8750-2364) [11148294] **4476**

INDEPENDENT REPUBLICAN, 1812 (US) [23885781] **2488**

INDEPENDENT (ROBERTSDALE, ALA.) (US) [12393483] **5627**

INDEPENDENT (RURAL HALL) (US) **5723**

INDEPENDENT SCHOLAR, THE (US/1066-5633) [15925430] **1829**

INDEPENDENT SCHOOL (BOSTON, MASS.) (US/0145-9635) [02568937] **1751**

INDEPENDENT SCHOOLS ASSOCIATION *See* YEARBOOK - INDEPENDENT SCHOOLS ASSOCIATION **1792**

INDEPENDENT SCHOOLS (PRINCETON, N.J.) (US/0736-0177) [07757297] **1752**

● INDEPENDENT SCHOOLS YEARBOOK (UK) [27697733] **1830**

INDEPENDENT SCHOOLS YEARBOOK. BOYS' SCHOOLS, CO-EDUCATIONAL SCHOOLS & PREPARATORY SCHOOLS *See* INDEPENDENT SCHOOLS YEARBOOK **1830**

Alphabetical Title Index INDEX

INDEPENDENT SCHOOLS YEARBOOK. GIRLS' SCHOOLS See INDEPENDENT SCHOOLS YEARBOOK **1830**

INDEPENDENT SCHOOLS YEARBOOK. GIRLS' SCHOOLS : THE OFFICIAL BOOK OF REFERENCE OF THE GIRLS' SCHOOLS ASSOCIATION (UK) [14104606] 5559, **1752**

INDEPENDENT SECTOR (US/0743-1236) [10497289] **4655**

INDEPENDENT SECTOR (FIRM) See INDEPENDENT SECTOR **4655**

INDEPENDENT SENIOR, THE (CN/0847-5288) [22185888] **5179**

INDEPENDENT SHAVIAN, THE (US/0019-3763) [01894528] 5365, **3396**

INDEPENDENT STUDY (US/0191-3042) [04822234] **1752**

INDEPENDENT STUDY CATALOG (PRINCETON, N.J.), THE (US/0733-6020) [08618029] **1830**

INDEPENDENT STUDY LINK (CN/1183-4951) [24368009] **1830**

INDEPENDENT TEACHER FORTITUDE VALLEY (AT/1033-2464) [I10332464] **1896**

INDEPENDENT TELCO NEWS See TELEPHONE WEEK **1167**

INDEPENDENT TELEVISION (US/1064-6833) [26373194] **1133**

INDEPENDENT TRUCKER CEASED. (CN/0840-3945) [19573621] **5384**

INDEPENDENT WOMAN See WIDENING HORIZONS **5568**

INDEPENDENT WOMEN'S SPECIALTY STORES & BOUTIQUES (US) [12698711] **1085**

INDEPENDIENTE (SP) **3344**

INDESIGN (IT) [23067448] **2098**

INDEX AND ABSTRACT DIRECTORY, THE (US/1041-1321) [18650387] **3258**

INDEX AND CUMULATIVE LIST OF PAPERS ON RADIATION CHEMISTRY (US/0096-1345) [01798199] **978**

INDEX AURELIENSIS (GW) [01643253] **4566**

INDEX : CANADA TREATY SERIES (CN) [02248392] **3129**

INDEX CHEMICUS (1987) (US/0891-6055) [14923744] 978, **1011**

INDEX CHRONOLOGIQUE / INDEX CHRONOLOGIQUE - CONSEIL DU PATRONAT DU QUEBEC (CN/0820-7933) [10008089] **1678**

INDEX COMMERCIAL DE MONTREAL (CN/0821-7254) [09977341] **839**

INDEX COMMERCIAL, JUDICIAIRE, FINANCIER, L' (CN/0317-6150) [02441734] **2981**

INDEX DE LA LEGISLATION OUVRIERE (CN/0712-340X) [08871393] **3149**

INDEX DE L'ACTUALITE, L' (CN/0838-0449) [19038797] **5786**

INDEX DES AFFAIRES, L' (CN/0838-0457) [18603705] **870**

INDEX-DIGEST OF PRECEDENT DECISIONS (US) [01552446] **2882**

INDEX-DIGEST - UNITED STATES DEPARTMENT OF THE INTERIOR, OFFICE OF HEARINGS AND APPEALS (US/0192-2602) [02536296] **3081**

INDEX - ENGINEERING SCIENCES DATA UNIT (UK) [04557792] **1977**

INDEX ESTADISTICO. ANALISIS DE COYUNTURA (AG) [22477188] **1566**

INDEX, FEDERAL EMPLOYEE APPEALS DECISIONS / MERIT SYSTEMS PROTECTION BOARD CEASED. (US) [09614900] **4655**

INDEX FOR FISCAL YEAR APPROPRIATIONS (US) [06132876] **4731**

INDEX HOLMIENSIS (SW) [20381973] **513**

INDEX INDIA (II/0019-3844) [01774363] **417**

INDEX INDO-ASIATICUS (II/0019-3852) [01774364] **2653**

INDEX INTERNATIONALIS INDICUS (II) [06724853] **5021**

INDEX ISLAMICUS (UK) [09664134] 5042, **5012**

INDEX-JOURNAL, THE (US/0747-0231) [10470620] **5742**

INDEX KOMMUNALWISSENSCHAFTLICHER LITERATUR: BUCHER (AU) [01784564] **4656**

●INDEX LOS ANGELES TIMES-ORANGE COUNTY SECTIONS (US/1065-8203) [26750667] **1286**

INDEX MEDICUS (1960) (US/0019-3879) [01752728] 3586, **3660**

INDEX MEDICUS FOR WHO SOUTH-EAST ASIA REGION (II/1013-5499) [10125076] **3586**

INDEX MEDICUS LATINO-AMERICANO SUSPENDED. (BL/0100-4743) [08411637] **3586**

INDEX MEDICUS / NATIONAL LIBRARY OF MEDICINE. [MICROFICHE] (US) 3586, **3660**

INDEX NEW ZEALAND [MICROFORM] : INNZ (NZ/0113-6526) [20379636] **417**

INDEX / NIGER BASIN AUTHORITY, DOCUMENTATION CENTRE (NG) [08835574] **1415**

INDEX NOMINUM / ELBORE PAR LE CENTRE SCIENTIFIQUE DE LA SOCIETE SUISSE DE PHARMACIE (SZ) [03465188] **4307**

INDEX NUMBERS OF STOCK EXCHANGE SECURITIES (PK/0081-4466) [01978152] **901**

INDEX OF ACTIVE REGISTERED INVESTMENT COMPANIES UNDER THE INVESTMENT COMPANY ACT OF 1940 AND RELATED INVESTMENT ADVISERS, PRINCIPAL UNDERWRITERS, SPONSORS (I.E. DEPOSITORS) AND UNDERLYING COMPANIES (US/0147-9504) [03249110] **901**

INDEX OF AFRICAN SOCIAL SCIENCE PERIODICAL ARTICLES / COUNCIL FOR THE DEVELOPMENT OF ECONOMIC AND SOCIAL RESEARCH IN AFRICA (SG) [20409546] **5203**

INDEX OF AIR FORCE-NAVY AERONAUTICAL (AN), AIR FORCE-NAVY AERONAUTICAL DESIGN (AND) AND MILITARY (MS) STANDARDS (US) [06076342] 23, **4045**

INDEX OF AMERICAN PERIODICAL VERSE (US/0090-9130) [01784376] 3396, **3458**

INDEX OF ART IN THE PACIFIC NORTHWEST (US/0085-1760) [06404474] **352**

INDEX OF ARTICLES See INDEX OF AVIATION ARTICLES **23**

INDEX OF AUSTRALIAN IMPORTERS CEASED. (AT) [06985511] **840**

INDEX OF AVIATION ARTICLES (UK) **23**

INDEX OF BLANK FORMS - UNITED STATES. DEPT. OF THE ARMY (US) [06342242] **4045**

INDEX OF COMPANIES REGISTERED IN NEW ZEALAND (NZ) [01789606] **1609**

INDEX OF CONFERENCE PROCEEDINGS. ANNUAL CUMULATION (UK/0959-4906) [19499867] **3214**

INDEX OF CONFERENCE PROCEEDINGS RECEIVED (UK) [06456980] **3214**

INDEX OF CONFERENCE PROCEEDINGS / THE BRITISH LIBRARY, DOCUMENT SUPPLY CENTRE (UK/0144-7556) [19370401] **3214**

INDEX OF CURRENT B.C. REGULATIONS (CN/0701-760X) [04632280] **2981**

INDEX OF CURRENT GOVERNMENT AND GOVERNMENTAL-SUPPORTED RESEARCH IN ENVIRONMENTAL POLLUTION IN GREAT BRITAIN (UK) [02459611] **2232**

INDEX OF CURRENT REGULATIONS OF THE MARITIME ADMINISTRATION, MARITIME SUBSIDY BOARD, NATIONAL SHIPPING AUTHORITY (US/0735-8679) [02974646] **3181**

INDEX OF CURRENT RESEARCH GRANTS AND CONTRACTS ADMINISTERED BY THE NATIONAL INSTITUTE ON AGING (US) [06351810] **3752**

INDEX OF CURRENT RESEARCH ON PIGS / AGRICULTURAL RESEARCH COUNCIL (UK/0568-2800) [01478564] **94**

INDEX OF DCAA MEMORANDUMS FOR REGIONAL DIRECTORS (MRDS) (US) [22342629] **4045**

INDEX OF DCAA NUMBERED PUBLICATIONS AND MEMORANDUMS (US) [12071628] **745**

INDEX OF ECONOMIC ARTICLES IN JOURNALS AND COLLECTIVE VOLUMES (US/0536-647X) [01752732] 1494, **1533**

INDEX OF EIA & JEDEC STANDARDS & ENGINEERING PUBLICATIONS (US) [04920481] **2064**

INDEX OF EMPLOYMENT OPPORTUNITIES. PROFESSIONAL CAREERS EDITION (US/0091-648X) [01787810] **4205**

INDEX OF ENGLISH LITERARY MANUSCRIPTS (UK) **3396**

INDEX OF ENTOMOPHAGOUS INSECTS (FR) [01752733] **5586**

INDEX OF FAA NATIONAL AND WA ORDERS (US) [06972242] **23**

INDEX OF FDA REGULATORY LETTERS (US/0161-7028) [04010354] **4656**

INDEX OF FEDERAL SPECIFICATIONS, STANDARDS AND COMMERCIAL ITEM DESCRIPTIONS (US/0198-9138) [05730039] **4656**

INDEX OF FEDERALLY SUPPORTED PROGRAMS IN HEART, BLOOD VESSEL, LUNG, AND BLOOD DISORDERS (US/0192-5385) [04859393] **3706**

INDEX OF FUNGI / COMMONWEALTH MYCOLOGICAL INSTITUTE (UK/0019-3895) [06168547] **513**

INDEX OF INSTITUTIONS OF HIGHER EDUCATION BY STATE AND CONGRESSIONAL DISTRICT See INSTITUTIONS OF HIGHER EDUCATION INDEX, BY STATE AND CONGRESSIONAL DISTRICT **1830**

INDEX OF ISLAMIC LITERATURE (UK) [16639145] 3396, 5042, **3458**

INDEX OF LABOUR LEGISLATION (CN/0712-3418) [08871388] **3149**

INDEX OF LEGISLATION (US/0160-0656) [03597047] **2981**

INDEX OF LOCAL LAWS OF THE COUNTIES CITIES TOWNS AND VILLAGES BY SUBJECT AND BY MUNICIPALITY FILED DURING THE YEAR (US) [08658050] **2981**

INDEX OF MAJORS See INDEX OF MAJORS AND GRADUATE DEGREES **1830**

●INDEX OF MAJORS AND GRADUATE DEGREES (US/1065-2787) [26385615] **1830**

INDEX OF NATIONAL AEROSPACE STANDARDS (US) [05688062] **23**

INDEX OF NEW PRODUCTS (UK/0019-3925) [01714707] 4307, **4334**

INDEX OF PROCEEDINGS / CANADA. PARLIAMENT. STANDING JOINT COMMITTEE ON REGULATIONS AND OTHER STATUTORY INSTRUMENTS (CN) [20870101] **2981**

INDEX OF PSYCHOANALYTIC WRITINGS (WITH PREFACE BY ERNEST JONES), THE (US) [06432332] **4589**

INDEX OF PUBLICATIONS / TECHNICAL AIDS BRANCH, OFFICE OF INDUSTRIAL RESOURCES, INTERNATIONAL COOPERATION ADMINISTRATION (US) [15371255] **5112**

INDEX OF PUBLICATIONS - WORLD BANK (US/0259-7357) [14399171] **1533**

INDEX OF SELECTED PUBLICATIONS See CENTER FOR NAVAL ANALYSES PUBLICATIONS CLEARED FOR PUBLIC RELEASE **4175**

INDEX OF SOVIET AND CHINESE MILITARY AFFAIRS IN ANNUAL US DEFENSE DEPARTMENT REPORTS (US/0739-5892) [09768994] **4045**

INDEX OF SPECIFICATIONS AND STANDARDS (US/0363-8464) [02459477] **4045**

INDEX OF STATISTICS PUBLISHED BY THE DEPARTMENT OF HEALTH / NATIONAL HEALTH STATISTICS CENTRE, DEPARTMENT OF HEALTH (NEW ZEALAND) (NZ) [07761767] **4810**

INDEX OF STORAGE AND OUTLOADING DRAWINGS FOR AMMUNITION COMMODITIES (US) [05918668] **4046**

INDEX OF TRADE OPPORTUNITIES : A LISTING OF EXPORT LEADS (US) [09671908] **840**

INDEX OF TRADEMARKS ISSUED FROM THE UNITED STATES PATENT AND TRADEMARK OFFICE (US/0099-0809) [02243146] **1304**

INDEX OF VETERINARY SPECIALITIES (UK/0019-3941) [03949610] **5511**

INDEX OF WELLS SHOT FOR VELOCITY (US/0560-6225) [03881536] **4260**

INDEX ON CENSORSHIP (UK/0306-4220) [01785255] 4509, **3344**

INDEX/ PARK PRACTICE PROGRAM (US) [22204591] **4706**

INDEX : QUADERNI CAMERTI DI STUDI ROMANISTICI (IT/0392-2391) [02133810] **2981**

INDEX RADIOLOGIAE (GW/0343-3331) [04564214] **3942**

INDEX SEMINUM (HU) [04928238] **513**

INDEX SEMINUM (NO) [05325097] **2420**

INDEX SEMINUM. JARDIM-MUSEU AGRICOLA TROPICAL (PO) **2420**

INDEX SEMINUM / UNIVERSITY BOTANIC GARDENS (NE) [25635659] **174**

INDEX TO 35MM EDUCATIONAL FILMSTRIPS (US/0735-021X) [02253409] **1896**

INDEX TO ACCOUNTING AND AUDITING TECHNICAL PRONOUNCEMENTS (US/0163-7150) [04426772] **745**

INDEX TO AMERICAN REFERENCE BOOKS ANNUAL (US/0192-6969) [05109415] **1926**

INDEX TO ARCHITECTURE SERIES--BIBLIOGRAPHY (US/0194-1356) [05267979] **301**

INDEX   Alphabetical Title Index

INDEX TO ART EXHIBITION CATALOGUES ON MICROFICHE (UK) [03743641] **352**

INDEX TO ART PERIODICALS. SUPPLEMENT (US/0099-0965) [03157090] **352**

INDEX TO ARTICLES ON JEWISH STUDIES (IS/0073-5817) [10166775] **2263**

INDEX TO AUDIO EQUIPMENT REVIEWS *CEASED*. (US/0277-8424) [07644808] **5317**

INDEX TO AV PRODUCERS & DISTRIBUTORS (US/1044-3967) [19640654] **1896**

INDEX TO BANK LETTERS, BULLETINS, AND REVIEWS : SOURCES (US) [04792264] **790**

INDEX TO BILLS INTRODUCED IN UTAH LEGISLATIVE SESSION (US/0149-1601) [03429846] **2981**

INDEX TO BLACK PERIODICALS (US/0899-6253) [18171277] **2263, 2276**

INDEX TO BOOK REVIEWS IN RELIGION (US/0887-1574) [13114508] **4964, 5012**

INDEX TO BRITISH LITERARY BIBLIOGRAPHY (UK) [01931793] **3458**

INDEX TO BUSINESS REPORTS (UK) [09825587] **681, 730**

INDEX TO CANADIAN LEGAL LITERATURE (CN) [22098382] **2981**

INDEX TO CANADIAN LEGAL LITERATURE (LIBRARY ED.) (CN/0832-9257) [16220550] **3081**

INDEX TO CANADIAN LEGAL PERIODICAL LITERATURE (CN/0316-8891) [02247419] **2981, 3081**

INDEX TO CANADIAN POETRY IN ENGLISH (CN) 3464, **3458**

INDEX TO CHINA DAILY (AT/1035-3380) [23957415] **417**

INDEX TO CHINESE PERIODICAL LITERATURE / CHUNG-HUA MIN KUO CHI KAN LUN WEN SO YIN (CH) [01535446] **3396**

INDEX TO CHIROPRACTIC LITERATURE (US/0882-8318) [09275363] **3804**

INDEX TO COLORADO STATE PUBLICATIONS (US/0891-3129) [09121621] **4656**

INDEX TO COMMONWEALTH LITTLE MAGAZINES *CEASED*. (US/0362-8183) [01589999] **2488**

INDEX TO COMPUTER-PRODUCED STANDARD INTEREST PROFILES IN CHEMISTRY, APPLIED CHEMISTRY, CHEMICAL ENGINEERING, AND METALLURGY *See* INDEX TO STANDARD INTEREST PROFILES IN SCIENCE AND TECHNOLOGY, AN **5112**

INDEX TO COURSE HANDBOOKS (US/0731-440X) [07341707] **2981**

INDEX TO CPL EXCHANGE BIBLIOGRAPHIES (US) [03251864] **2825**

INDEX TO CURRENT URBAN DOCUMENTS (US/0046-8908) [01785237] **4656**

INDEX TO DECISIONS OF THE OCCUPATIONAL SAFETY AND HEALTH REVIEW COMMISSION (US/0270-4242) [05000756] **2863**

INDEX TO DENTAL LITERATURE (US/0019-3992) [04839041] 1324, **1338**

INDEX TO DEVELOPMENT LITERATURE (UK) [19419169] **3396**

INDEX TO DOCTORAL DISSERTATIONS IN BUSINESS EDUCATION, 1900-1975 (US) [01887759] **1752**

INDEX TO ELECTRIC UTILITY WEEK (US/0743-3492) [10553434] **4761**

●INDEX TO ... ETHICS ADVISORY OPINIONS (US) [27653779] **2251**

INDEX TO FEDERAL TAX ARTICLES. SUPPLEMENT (US/0149-6166) [03170320] **4731**

INDEX TO FOREIGN LEGAL PERIODICALS (UK/0019-400X) [01752740] **3081**

INDEX TO FREE PERIODICALS (US/0147-5630) [02867177] 2488, **2496**

INDEX TO GOVERNMENT ORDERS IN FORCE 31ST DECEMBER ... (UK) [01715321] **2981**

INDEX TO GOVERNMENT REGULATION (US/0195-9492) [05732624] **2981**

INDEX TO HOW TO DO IT INFORMATION (US/0073-5930) [03620639] 2774, **2779**

INDEX TO ICAO PUBLICATIONS (CN/0074-249X) [01715386] **23**

INDEX TO IEEE PUBLICATIONS (US/0099-1368) [01115344] 2064, **2004**

INDEX TO INDIAN ECONOMIC JOURNALS (II/0019-4026) [01590204] **1494**

INDEX TO INDIAN LEGAL PERIODICALS (II/0019-4034) [01752937] **2981**

INDEX TO INFORMATION (WASHINGTON, D.C.) (US/0882-2204) [08748696] **942**

INDEX TO INTERNATIONAL PUBLIC OPINION (US/0193-905X) [05267822] **5247**

INDEX TO INTERNATIONAL STATISTICS (US/0737-4461) [09179279] **5328**

INDEX TO JEWISH PERIODICALS (US/0019-4050) [01048671] 5048, **5013**

INDEX TO LAWS OF FLORIDA. SPECIAL AND LOCAL LAWS (US) [08260473] **2981**

INDEX TO LEGAL PERIODICALS (US/0019-4077) [01585611] 2981, **3081**

INDEX TO LEGAL PERIODICALS. CD-ROM (US/0019-4077) **3081**

●INDEX TO MARQUIS WHO'S WHO PUBLICATIONS (US) [30135055] 1926, **433**

INDEX TO MEED. MIDDLE EAST ECONOMIC DIGEST (UK/0963-5572) [I09635572] **1566**

INDEX TO MUSEOLOGICAL LITERATURE (CN/0846-6327) [21095500] **4089**

INDEX TO NEW ENGLAND PERIODICALS *SUSPENDED*. (US/0163-0466) [03700294] **417**

INDEX TO NEW JERSEY LEGAL DECISIONS (US/8756-2383) [11486409] **2981**

INDEX TO PERIODICAL ARTICLES RELATED TO LAW (US/0019-4093) [00988168] 2981, **3081**

INDEX TO PHILIPPINE PERIODICALS (PH/0073-599X) [01606272] 2504, **2496**

INDEX TO PRAVDA (US/0099-0876) [02241991] **2920**

INDEX TO PROCEEDINGS OF THE ECONOMIC AND SOCIAL COUNCIL (US/0082-8084) [01248189] **4523**

INDEX TO PROCEEDINGS OF THE GENERAL ASSEMBLY (US) [01768033] **4523**

INDEX TO PROCEEDINGS OF THE IEEE (US/0897-151X) [17417128] **2064**

INDEX TO PROCEEDINGS OF THE SECURITY COUNCIL / DAG HAMMARSKJOLD LIBRARY (US/0082-8408) [01768034] **4523**

INDEX TO PUBLIC ADMINISTRATION SERIES--BIBLIOGRAPHY (US) [05205871] **4656**

INDEX TO RECENT NEW HAMPSHIRE CASES (US/0199-5626) [05987272] **2981**

INDEX TO REPRODUCTIONS IN ART PERIODICALS : IRAP (US/0893-0139) [15313739] **352**

INDEX TO RESEARCH FRONTS IN ISI/GEOSCITECH (US/0734-0273) [08672707] **1382**

INDEX TO RESOLUTIONS OF THE GENERAL ASSEMBLY (US) [01799328] **3129**

INDEX TO SCIENCE FICTION ORIGINAL ANTHOLOGIES (US/0882-5947) [11893262] **3396**

INDEX TO SCIENTIFIC & TECHNICAL PROCEEDINGS (US/0149-8088) [03562096] **5112**

INDEX TO SCIENTIFIC BOOK CONTENTS (US/0884-8440) [12488141] **5112**

INDEX TO SCIENTIFIC REVIEWS (US/0360-0661) [02240320] 5112, **5175**

INDEX TO SOCIAL SCIENCES & HUMANITIES PROCEEDINGS (US/0191-0574) [04785721] 2848, **5203**

INDEX TO SOUTH AFRICAN PERIODICALS (SA) [01752748] **3214**

INDEX TO ST. LOUIS NEWSPAPERS (US/0098-6062) [02854804] **5703**

INDEX TO STANDARD INTEREST PROFILES IN SCIENCE AND TECHNOLOGY, AN (US) [05038959] **5112**

INDEX TO STATISTICS CANADA SURVEYS AND QUESTIONNAIRES (CN/0843-6142) [20740049] **4698**

INDEX TO THE ABSTRACTS ON CRIME AND JUVENILE DELINQUENCY, AN (US) [13370697] 3166, **3081**

INDEX TO THE CATALOGING SERVICE BULLETIN (US/0887-4158) [05432293] **3215**

INDEX TO THE CODE OF FEDERAL REGULATIONS (US/0198-9014) [06260698] **2981**

INDEX TO THE GRAND FORKS HERALD (US/0272-779X) [06855394] **2535**

INDEX TO THE HISTORICAL MICROFICHE SERIES (AT/1038-6300) [I10386300] **1926**

INDEX TO THE JOURNALS OF THE NORTH DAKOTA HISTORICAL SOCIETY (US) [03820259] **2738**

INDEX TO THE LONG ISLANDER, THE (US/0730-9783) [03909162] **5717**

INDEX TO THE PUBLIC SCHOOLS (ALBANY) (US/0091-3251) [01786749] **1752**

INDEX TO THE SCIENCE FICTION MAGAZINES (1979) (US/0732-0655) [08274521] **3396**

INDEX TO THE SEMI-PROFESSIONAL FANTASY MAGAZINES (US/0743-4103) [10528452] **3396**

INDEX TO THE SPORTING NEWS (US/1041-2859) [18708903] **4899**

INDEX TO THE TIMES OF INDIA (II/0304-162X) [02241177] **5803**

INDEX TO THE U.S. PATENT CLASSIFICATION (US/0161-9470) [04010459] **1304**

INDEX TO THESES WITH ABSTRACTS ACCEPTED FOR HIGHER DEGREES BY THE UNIVERSITIES OF GREAT BRITAIN AND IRELAND AND THE COUNCIL FOR NATIONAL ACADEMIC AWARDS (UK/0073-6066) [15499176] **1830**

INDEX TO TITLE 40 OF THE CODE OF FEDERAL REGULATIONS : PROTECTION OF ENVIRONMENT (US/0192-3773) [04521330] **3113**

INDEX TO UNITED NATIONS DOCUMENTS AND PUBLICATIONS [COMPUTER FILE] (US) [23370507] **417**

INDEX TRANSLATIONUM (FR/0073-6074) [02433763] **3286**

INDEX (TULSA, OKLA.), THE (US/0278-5900) [07845200] **4900**

INDEX VETERINARIUS (UK/0019-4123) [01589903] 5511, **5528**

INDEXER (UK/0019-4131) [01716604] **3215**

INDEXES OF PRICES RECEIVED AND PAID BY FARMERS (AT) [24905266] **94**

INDEXES TO ONTARIO MUNICIPAL BOARD APPLICATIONS DISPOSED OF... AND TO LAND COMPENSATION BOARD APPLICATIONS DISPOSED OF ... (CN/0703-2501) [04232967] **2981**

INDEXING : THE STATE OF OUR KNOWLEDGE AND THE STATE OF OUR IGNORANCE (US) **3215**

INDEXPORT (II) [01784186] **840**

INDIA, A REFERENCE ANNUAL (II/0073-6090) [01752763] **2653**

INDIA ABROAD (US/0046-8932) [01781854] 2653, **2263**

INDIA BRIEFING (US/0894-5136) [16119131] **2653**

●INDIA BUSINESS & INDUSTRY NEWSLETTER (US/1064-1408) [26211131] 1609, **681**

INDIA CALLING (II) [06039572] **1133**

INDIA. CARDAMON BOARD *See* CARDAMOM STATISTICS (INDIA) **2362**

INDIA. CENTRAL ADVISORY BOARD OF EDUCATION *See* ADDRESSES AND RESOLUTIONS / CENTRAL ADVISORY BOARD OF EDUCATION **1722**

INDIA. CENTRAL BOARD OF IRRIGATION AND POWER. RESEARCH AND DEVELOPMENT SESSION *See* PROCEEDINGS / RESEARCH AND DEVELOPMENT SESSION (INDIA) **2095**

INDIA. CENTRAL ELECTRICITY AUTHORITY *See* POWER SUPPLY POSITION IN THE COUNTRY **2075**

INDIA. CENTRAL STATISTICAL ORGANISATION *See* MASIKA ANKARA SARA. MONTHLY ABSTRACT OF STATISTICS **5332**

INDIA. CENTRAL TEA BOARD. ANNUAL ADMINISTRATION REPORT *See* ANNUAL ADMINISTRATION REPORT FOR THE YEAR ... / TEA BOARD (INDIA) **4626**

INDIA. COMPTROLLER AND AUDITOR-GENERAL *See* REPORT OF THE COMPTROLLER AND AUDITOR GENERAL OF INDIA, GOVERNMENT OF TAMIL NADU : REVENUE RECEIPTS **4745**

INDIA. COMPTROLLER AND AUDITOR-GENERAL *See* REPORT OF THE COMPTROLLER AND AUDITOR GENERAL OF INDIA FOR THE YEAR ..., (REVENUE RECEIPTS) GOVERNMENT OF RAJASTHAN **4745**

INDIA. COMPTROLLER AND AUDITOR-GENERAL *See* REPORT OF THE COMPTROLLER AND AUDITOR GENERAL OF INDIA GOVERNMENT OF TAMIL NADU : CIVIL **4745**

INDIA. COMPTROLLER AND AUDITOR-GENERAL *See* APPROPRIATION ACCOUNTS, GOVERNMENT OF ORISSA **4711**

INDIA. COMPTROLLER AND AUDITOR-GENERAL *See* VINIYOJANA LEKHE, UTTARA PRADESA SARAKARA **4758**

INDIA. COMPTROLLER AND AUDITOR-GENERAL *See* REPORT, GOVERNMENT OF TAMIL NADU **4744**

INDIA. COMPTROLLER AND AUDITOR-GENERAL *See* REPORT OF THE COMPTROLLER AND AUDITOR-GENERAL OF INDIA (REVENUE RECEIPTS) **4745**

INDIA CURRENTS (US/0896-095X) [16911656] **2488**

Alphabetical Title Index — INDIA

INDIA. DEPT. OF AGRICULTURAL RESEARCH AND EDUCATION See ANNUAL REPORT 60

INDIA. DEPT. OF CHEMICALS & PETROCHEMICALS See ANNUAL REPORT / GOVERNMENT OF INDIA, MINISTRY OF PETROLEUM AND CHEMICALS, DEPARTMENT OF CHEMICALS & PETROCHEMICALS 4250

INDIA. DEPT. OF COMMUNITY DEVELOPMENT See REPORT ON COMMUNITY DEVELOPMENT WEEK 5255

INDIA. DEPT. OF FOREIGN TRADE See REPORT - DEPARTMENT OF FOREIGN TRADE 850

INDIA. DEPT. OF NON-CONVENTIONAL ENERGY SOURCES See ANNUAL REPORT / GOVERNMENT OF INDIA, DEPARTMENT OF NON-CONVENTIONAL ENERGY SOURCES, MINISTRY OF ENERGY 1932

INDIA. DEPT. OF OCEAN DEVELOPMENT See ANNUAL REPORT 1446

INDIA. DEPT. OF RURAL DEVELOPMENT See ANNUAL REPORT. INDIA. DEPT. OF RURAL DEVELOPMENT 1546

INDIA. DEPT. OF SCIENCE AND TECHNOLOGY See ANUDANOM KI MANGEM (INDIA. DEPT. OF SCIENCE AND TECHNOLOGY) 5084

INDIA. DEPT. OF SOCIAL WELFARE See NEWS LETTER - INDIA (REPUBLIC). DEPT. OF SOCIAL WELFARE, THE 5298

INDIA. DEPT. OF SPACE See ANTARIKSHA VIBHAGA KI ANUDANOM KI MANGEM 12

INDIA DIRECTORATE GENERAL OF TECHNICAL DEVELOPMENT See STATISTICS RELATING TO DGTD UNITS 1539

INDIA INTERNATIONAL CENTRE See INDIA INTERNATIONAL CENTRE QUARTERLY 2653

INDIA INTERNATIONAL CENTRE QUARTERLY (II/0376-9771) [02245565] 2653

INDIA JOURNAL, THE (US/1059-4973) [24606744] 2653

INDIA LEATHER & LEATHER PRODUCTS DIRECTORY (II/0376-978X) [02245606] 3184

INDIA MAGAZINE OF HER PEOPLE AND CULTURE, THE (II) [07224432] 2504, 2263

INDIA. MINISTRY OF COMMERCE See EXPORT TRADE CONTROL HAND-BOOK OF POLICY AND PROCEDURE 834

INDIA. MINISTRY OF COMMUNICATIONS See SANCARA MANTRALAYA KI ANUDANOM KI MANGEM 1121

INDIA. MINISTRY OF DEFENCE See ARMED FORCES PERSONNEL AND CIVILIANS IN DEFENCE ESTABLISHMENT BOOK ON SERVICE CONDITIONS 4036

INDIA. MINISTRY OF EDUCATION AND CULTURE (DEPT. OF EDUCATION). PLANNING, MONITORING, AND STATISTICS DIVISION See ANALYSIS OF BUDGETED EXPENDITURE ON EDUCATION 1860

INDIA. MINISTRY OF EDUCATION AND SOCIAL WELFARE See PAY SCALES OF SCHOOL TEACHERS IN INDIA 1868

INDIA. MINISTRY OF EDUCATION AND SOCIAL WELFARE See SELECTED EDUCATIONAL STATISTICS 1797

INDIA. MINISTRY OF EDUCATION AND SOCIAL WELFARE. EXPENDITURE ON EDUCATION AS SHOWN IN CENTRAL AND STATE ANNUAL BUDGETS See ANALYSIS OF BUDGETED EXPENDITURE ON EDUCATION 1860

INDIA. MINISTRY OF EDUCATION AND YOUTH SERVICES See EDUCATIONAL STATISTICS : DISTRICT-WISE 1794

INDIA. MINISTRY OF EXTERNAL AFFAIRS See VIDESA MANTRALAYA KI ANUDANOM KI MANGEM 4693

INDIA. MINISTRY OF HEALTH AND FAMILY WELFARE See ANNUAL REPORT 5272

INDIA. MINISTRY OF HEALTH AND FAMILY WELFARE. REPORT See ANNUAL REPORT 5272

INDIA. MINISTRY OF INDUSTRY AND CIVIL SUPPLIES See REPORT - GOVERNMENT OF INDIA, MINISTRY OF INDUSTRY AND CIVIL SUPPLIES 4680

INDIA. MINISTRY OF SHIPPING AND TRANSPORT See ANUDANOM KI MANGEM, NAUVAHANA AURA PARIVAHANA MANTRALAYA 5447

INDIA. MINISTRY OF SOCIAL WELFARE See ANUDANOM KIMANGEM, SAMAJA KAJANA MANTRALAYA 5273

INDIA. MINISTRY OF URBAN DEVELOPMENT See ANUDANOM KI MANGEM, NAGARA VIKASA MANTRALAYA 2815

INDIA. MINISTRY OF WORKS AND HOUSING. ANUDANOM KI MANGEM See ANUDANOM KI MANGEM, NAGARA VIKASA MANTRALAYA 2815

INDIA. NATIONAL POLICE COMMISSION See REPORT OF THE NATIONAL POLICE COMMISSION (INDIA) 3174

INDIA. NATIONAL REMOTE SENSING AGENCY See ANNUAL REPORT - INDIA. NATIONAL REMOTE SENSING AGENCY 2554

INDIA. PARLIAMENT. HOUSE OF THE PEOPLE See LOK SABHA. PARLIAMENTARY COMMITTEES. SUMMARY OF WORK 4663

INDIA PERSPECTIVES (II) [18824431] 4523

INDIA. PLANNING COMMISSION See REPORT / INDIA. PLANNING COMMISSION 4680

INDIA. PROCEEDINGS OF THE ANNUAL RESEARCH SESSION See PROCEEDINGS / RESEARCH AND DEVELOPMENT SESSION (INDIA) 2095

INDIA. PROTOCOL DIVISION See DIPLOMATIC LIST (INDIA) 4643

INDIA QUARTERLY (II/0251-3048) [01752770] 4523

INDIA. RAJASTHAN HIGH COURT See RAJASTHAN LAW WEEKLY, THE 3034

INDIA (REPUBLIC) See ACTS OF PARLIAMENT 4624

INDIA (REPUBLIC). ARCHAEOLOGICAL SURVEY See ANNUAL REPORT ON INDIAN EPIGRAPHY FOR... / DEPARTMENT OF ARCHAEOLOGY 255

INDIA (REPUBLIC) ARCHAEOLOGICAL SURVEY See INDIAN ARCHAEOLOGY 270

INDIA (REPUBLIC). CENTRAL BUREAU OF HEALTH INTELLIGENCE See POCKET BOOK OF HEALTH STATISTICS 4810

INDIA (REPUBLIC). CENTRAL STATISTICAL ORGANISATION See MONTHLY PRODUCTION OF SELECTED INDUSTRIES OF INDIA 1536

INDIA (REPUBLIC). CENTRAL STATISTICAL ORGANISATION See STATISTICAL ABSTRACT, INDIA 5339

INDIA (REPUBLIC) COFFEE BOARD See REPORT - INDIA (REPUBLIC) COFFEE BOARD 184

INDIA (REPUBLIC). COFFEE BOARD See COFFEE STATISTICS 152

INDIA (REPUBLIC). COMPTROLLER AND AUDITOR-GENERAL See REPORT, GOVERNMENT OF NAGALAND 4744

INDIA (REPUBLIC). COMPTROLLER AND AUDITOR-GENERAL See AUDIT REPORT, GOVERNMENT OF ORISSA 4712

INDIA (REPUBLIC). COMPTROLLER AND AUDITOR-GENERAL See REPORT, GOVERNMENT OF THE UNION TERRITORY OF PONDICHERRY 4744

INDIA (REPUBLIC). COMPTROLLER AND AUDITOR-GENERAL See REPORT, GOVERNMENT OF THE UNION TERRITORY OF GOA, DAMAN, AND DIU 4744

INDIA (REPUBLIC). COMPTROLLER AND AUDITOR-GENERAL See REPORT : UNION GOVERNMENT (POSTS AND TELEGRAPHS) 1147

INDIA (REPUBLIC). COMPTROLLER AND AUDITOR-GENERAL See FINANCE ACCOUNTS, GOVERNMENT OF ORISSA 4724

INDIA (REPUBLIC). COMPTROLLER AND AUDITOR-GENERAL See REPORT OF THE COMPTROLLER AND AUDITOR GENERAL OF INDIA, UNION GOVERNMENT (RAILWAYS) 5436

INDIA (REPUBLIC). COMPTROLLER AND AUDITOR-GENERAL See REPORT OF THE COMPTROLLER AND AUDITOR GENERAL OF INDIA, GOVERNMENT OF KERALA, CIVIL 4745

INDIA (REPUBLIC). COMPTROLLER AND AUDITOR-GENERAL See REPORT OF THE COMPTROLLER AND AUDITOR-GENERAL OF INDIA. GOVERNMENT OF GUJARAT 4745

INDIA (REPUBLIC). DEPT. OF COMPANY AFFAIRS See ANUDANOM KI MANGEM (INDIA. DEPT. OF COMPANY AFFAIRS) 4630

INDIA (REPUBLIC). DEPT. OF CULTURE See ANUDANOM KI MANGEM 313

INDIA (REPUBLIC). DEPT. OF ECONOMIC AFFAIRS. BUDGET DIVISION See KEY TO THE BUDGET DOCUMENTS 4735

INDIA (REPUBLIC). DEPT. OF EDUCATION See PERFORMANCE BUDGET - DEPARTMENT OF EDUCATION 1773

INDIA (REPUBLIC). DEPT. OF ELECTRONICS See ANNUAL REPORT 2035

INDIA (REPUBLIC). DEPT. OF ELECTRONICS See ANUDANOM KI MANGEM (INDIA. DEPT. OF ELECTRONICS) 2035

INDIA (REPUBLIC). DEPT. OF PERSONNEL AND ADMINISTRATIVE REFORMS (ADMINISTRATIVE REFORMS) See REPORT - DEPARTMENT OF PERSONNEL AND ADMINISTRATIVE REFORMS (ADMINISTRATIVE REFORMS) 4680

INDIA (REPUBLIC). DEPT. OF POWER See REPORT - GOVERNMENT OF INDIA, DEPARTMENT OF POWER 2079

INDIA (REPUBLIC). DEPT. OF SPACE See ANNUAL REPORT - DEPARTMENT OF SPACE. GOVERNMENT OF INDIA 11

INDIA (REPUBLIC). DIRECTORATE-GENERAL OF MINES SAFETY See STATISTICS OF MINES IN INDIA: COAL 2151

INDIA (REPUBLIC). DIRECTORATE-GENERAL OF MINES SAFETY See STATISTICS OF MINES IN INDIA: NON-COAL 2151

INDIA (REPUBLIC). DIRECTORATE OF ECONOMICS AND STATISTICS See BULLETIN OF AGRICULTURAL PRICES (INDIA) 69

INDIA (REPUBLIC). DIRECTORATE OF INSPECTION (RESEARCH, STATISTICS AND PUBLICATION) See DIRECT TAXES BULLETIN 4720

INDIA (REPUBLIC). DIRECTORATE OF PLANT PROTECTION, QUARANTINE AND STORAGE See PLANT PROTECTION BULLETIN 524

INDIA (REPUBLIC). MINISTRY OF EDUCATION AND SOCIAL WELFARE See REPORT ON EDUCATIONAL DEVELOPMENTS IN INDIA 1778

INDIA (REPUBLIC). MINISTRY OF EXTERNAL AFFAIRS See FOREIGN AFFAIRS RECORD 4522

INDIA (REPUBLIC). MINISTRY OF EXTERNAL AFFAIRS. DEMANDS FOR GRANTS See VIDESA MANTRALAYA KI ANUDANOM KI MANGEM 4693

INDIA (REPUBLIC). MINISTRY OF FINANCE See BUDGET / GOVERNMENT OF INDIA, MINISTRY OF FINANCE 4714

INDIA (REPUBLIC). MINISTRY OF FOREIGN TRADE See VIDESA VYAPARA MANTRALAYA KI ANUDANOM KI MANGEM 857

INDIA (REPUBLIC). MINISTRY OF HEAVY INDUSTRIES See BHARI UDYOGA MANTRALAYA KI ANUDANOM KI MANGEM 1599

INDIA (REPUBLIC). MINISTRY OF LAW AND JUSTICE See ANUDANOM KI MANGEM (INDIA. MINISTRY OF LAW AND JUSTICE) 2935

INDIA (REPUBLIC). MINISTRY OF LAW. ANUANOM KI MANGEM See ANUDANOM KI MANGEM (INDIA. MINISTRY OF LAW AND JUSTICE) 2935

INDIA (REPUBLIC). MINISTRY OF WORKS AND HOUSING See ANUDANOM KI MANGEM (INDIA. MINISTRY OF WORKS AND HOUSING) 2815

INDIA (REPUBLIC). OIL AND NATURAL GAS COMMISSION See BULLETIN OF THE OIL AND NATURAL GAS COMMISSION 4252

INDIA (REPUBLIC). PARLIAMENT. JOINT COMMITTEE ON OFFICES OF PROFIT See REPORT - JOINT COMMITTEE ON OFFICES OF PROFIT 4680

INDIA (REPUBLIC). RUBBER BOARD See RUBBER BOARD BULLETIN 5077

INDIA (REPUBLIC). SUPREME COURT See SUPREME COURT CASES, THE 3061

INDIA (REPUBLIC). ZOOLOGICAL SURVEY See RECORDS OF THE ZOOLOGICAL SURVEY OF INDIA 5596

INDIA. STAFF SELECTION COMMISSION See REPORT - STAFF SELECTION COMMISSION 4705

INDIA STAR See CANADIAN INDIA STAR, THE 2648

INDIA. SUPREME COURT See SUPREME COURT REPORTS 3061

INDIA. SUPREME COURT See CURRENT TAX REPORTER 4719

INDIA. SUPREME COURT See UNREPORTED JUDGEMENTS, THE 3069

INDIA. TEA BOARD See ANNUAL ADMINISTRATION REPORT FOR THE YEAR ... / TEA BOARD (INDIA) 4626

INDIA TIMES (LOS GATOS, CALIF.) (US/1040-628X) [18474217] 5203

INDIA TODAY (II) [02675526] 2504

● INDIA TODAY (CN/0254-8399) [27003242] 2653

INDIA TODAY (INTERNATIONAL ED) (II) [08800679] 2488

INDIA — Alphabetical Title Index

INDIA TODAY (INTERNATIONAL ED.) See INDIA TODAY **2653**

INDIA TODAY. NORTH AMERICAN EDITION (CN/0709-6178) [04750736] **2535**

INDIA. UNIVERSITY GRANTS COMMISSION See BULLETIN OF HIGHER EDUCATION **1813**

INDIA. UNIVERSITY GRANTS COMMISSION See UNIVERSITY DEVELOPMENT IN INDIA; BASIC FACTS AND FIGURES **1852**

INDIA-WEST (US/0883-721X) [05218030] **5636**

INDIA-WEST GUIDE AND BUSINESS DIRECTORY (US/0740-2589) [09885969] **1609**

INDIA WHO'S WHO (II/0073-6244) [01714937] **433**

INDIA WORLDWIDE (US/0895-4283) [16643235] **2653**

INDIAN ACADEMY OF APPLIED PSYCHOLOGY See JOURNAL OF THE INDIAN ACADEMY OF APPLIED PSYCHOLOGY **4602**

INDIAN ACADEMY OF FORENSIC SCIENCES See JOURNAL OF THE INDIAN ACADEMY OF FORENSIC SCIENCES **3741**

INDIAN ACADEMY OF GEOSCIENCE See JOURNAL - INDIAN ACADEMY OF GEOSCIENCE **1384**

INDIAN ACADEMY OF MATHEMATICS See JOURNAL OF THE INDIAN ACADEMY OF MATHEMATICS, THE **3515**

INDIAN ACADEMY OF PHILOSOPHY See JOURNAL OF THE INDIAN ACADEMY OF PHILOSOPHY, THE **4351**

INDIAN ACADEMY OF WOOD SCIENCE See JOURNAL OF THE INDIAN ACADEMY OF WOOD SCIENCE **2402**

INDIAN ADVOCATE (II/0019-4301) [01752822] **2981**

INDIAN AFFAIRS (NEW YORK) (US/0046-8967) [01681425] **2263**

INDIAN AGRICULTURE IN BRIEF (II/0536-8510) [03357220] **94**

INDIAN AGRICULTURIST (II/0019-4336) [01587611] **94**

INDIAN-AMERICAN (NEW YORK, N.Y.), THE (US/1054-1640) [22772625] **2263**

INDIAN AND ESKIMO AFFAIRS PROGRAM (CANADA) See JOINT VENTURES (OTTAWA) **1498**

INDIAN ANTHROPOLOGIST (II) [01752831] **238**

INDIAN ARCHAEOLOGY (II/0536-7832) [02592284] **270**

INDIAN ARCHITECT & BUILDER (II) [18676989] **301**

INDIAN ARCHITECT, THE (II/0019-4409) [01752833] **301**

INDIAN ARCHIVES (II/0367-7435) [01774628] **2481**

INDIAN-ARTIFACT MAGAZINE (US/0736-265X) [09064525] 2738, **270**

INDIAN ARTS & CRAFTS ASSOCIATION (U.S.) See DIRECTORY OF MEMBERS AND BUYERS GUIDE / INDIAN ARTS & CRAFTS ASSOCIATION **372**

INDIAN ASSOCIATION FOR THE STUDY OF CONSERVATION OF CULTURAL PROPERTY See CONSERVATION OF CULTURAL PROPERTY IN INDIA **2190**

INDIAN ASSOCIATION FOR WATER POLLUTION CONTROL NEWSLETTER - IAWPC (II) [11590037] **2232**

INDIAN ASSOCIATION OF SPECIAL LIBRARIES AND INFORMATION CENTRES See IASLIC BULLETIN **3214**

INDIAN ASSOCIATION OF SPECIAL LIBRARIES AND INFORMATION CENTRES See IASLIC SPECIAL PUBLICATION **3214**

INDIAN ASTRONOMICAL EPHEMERIS, THE (II) [06725644] **395**

INDIAN AWARENESS CENTER NEWS LETTER (US/0896-1972) [16989767] **2263**

INDIAN BAR REVIEW (II) [11208566] **2981**

INDIAN BEE JOURNAL (II/0019-4425) [01714093] **94**

INDIAN BEHAVIOURAL SCIENCES ABSTRACTS **SUSPENDED.** (II/0018-8727) [01639973] **5203**

INDIAN BIOLOGIST (II/0302-7554) [01797676] **458**

INDIAN BOOK INDUSTRY (II/0019-4433) [01774630] **4829**

INDIAN BOOK REVIEW (II) [07718606] **4829**

INDIAN BOTANICAL CONTACTOR : IBC (II) [14124788] **5112**

INDIAN BOTANICAL CONTRACTOR (II/0970-1389) [09701389] **513**

INDIAN BOTANICAL REPORTER (II/0254-4091) [09770667] **513**

INDIAN BOTANICAL SOCIETY See JOURNAL OF THE INDIAN BOTANICAL SOCIETY, THE **516**

INDIAN BROADCAST MEDIA YEAR BOOK (II) [10827410] **1133**

INDIAN BUYER (II) [01604139] **950**

INDIAN CASHEW JOURNAL (II/0019-4484) [03342557] **2344**

INDIAN CERAMIC SOCIETY See TRANSACTIONS OF THE INDIAN CERAMIC SOCIETY **2594**

INDIAN CERAMICS (II/0019-4492) [02385150] **2591**

INDIAN CHAMBER OF COMMERCE (CALCUTTA, INDIA). WORLD TRADE DEPT See SURVEY OF INDIA'S IMPORTS **852**

INDIAN CHEMICAL ABSTRACTS (II/0253-6838) [09270465] **978**

INDIAN CHEMICAL ENGINEER (II/0019-4506) [01696113] **2013**

INDIAN CHURCH HISTORY REVIEW (II/0019-4530) [01713588] **4964**

INDIAN COCOA, ARECANUT & SPICES JOURNAL (II/0970-1184) [07855673] **174**

INDIAN COCONUT JOURNAL (COCHIN) (II/0367-7281) [04752970] **174**

INDIAN COFFEE (II/0019-4549) [01752842] **174**

INDIAN CONCRETE JOURNAL, THE (II/0019-4565) [01752843] 2024, **617**

INDIAN CONSTRUCTION : JOURNAL OF THE BUILDERS' ASSOCIATION OF INDIA (II) [09534385] **617**

INDIAN CONSUMER COOPERATOR (II/0376-981X) [01797797] **1542**

INDIAN COOPERATIVE REVIEW (II/0019-4581) [01774633] **1542**

INDIAN COTTON MILLS' FEDERATION See JOURNAL - INDIAN COTTON MILLS' FEDERATION **5353**

INDIAN COUNCIL FOR AFRICA. LIBRARY. DOCUMENTATION LIST : AFRICA See AFRICA : A DOCUMENTATION LIST **407**

INDIAN COUNCIL FOR CULTURAL RELATIONS. AFRICA SECTION See AFRICA : A DOCUMENTATION LIST **407**

INDIAN COUNCIL OF AGRICULTURAL RESEARCH See I.C.A.R. TECHNICAL BULLETIN (AGRIC) **93**

INDIAN COUNCIL OF HISTORICAL RESEARCH See HALF-YEARLY REPORT - INDIAN COUNCIL OF HISTORICAL RESEARCH **2652**

INDIAN COUNCIL OF HISTORICAL RESEARCH See ICHR NEWSLETTER **2653**

INDIAN COUNCIL OF SOCIAL SCIENCE RESEARCH See ICSSR RESEARCH ABSTRACTS QUARTERLY **5202**

INDIAN COUNCIL OF SOCIAL SCIENCE RESEARCH See ICSSR JOURNAL OF ABSTRACTS AND REVIEWS : POLITICAL SCIENCE **4476**

INDIAN COUNCIL OF SOCIAL SCIENCE RESEARCH See ICSSR JOURNAL OF ABSTRACTS AND REVIEWS : ECONOMICS **1533**

INDIAN COUNCIL OF SOCIAL SCIENCE RESEARCH See ICSSR JOURNAL OF ABSTRACTS AND REVIEWS: GEOGRAPHY **2565**

INDIAN COUNCIL OF SOCIAL SCIENCE RESEARCH See ICSSR NEWSLETTER **5202**

● INDIAN COUNTRY TODAY (US/1066-5501) [26771949] **5743**

INDIAN DAIRYMAN (II/0019-4603) [01752852] **195**

INDIAN DENTAL ASSOCIATION See JOURNAL OF THE INDIAN DENTAL ASSOCIATION **1328**

INDIAN DISSERTATION ABSTRACTS (II) [01779763] **5203**

INDIAN DRUGS (II/0019-462X) [01752855] **4307**

INDIAN ECONOMIC AND SOCIAL HISTORY REVIEW, THE (II/0019-4646) [01752856] **1566**

INDIAN ECONOMIC DIARY (II/0019-4654) [01752857] **1566**

INDIAN ECONOMIC EMPLOYMENT ASSISTANCE PROGRAM, PROGRESS REPORT (US) [04103001] 2263, **5289**

INDIAN ECONOMIC JOURNAL, THE (II/0019-4662) [01752858] **1566**

INDIAN ECONOMIC REVIEW (II/0019-4670) [01774641] **1494**

INDIAN ECONOMY (II) [20516091] **1494**

INDIAN EDUCATION (US) [06188755] 2263, **1752**

INDIAN EDUCATION ABSTRACTS (II/0019-4697) [01752859] **1752**

INDIAN EDUCATION ACT OF 1972; REPORT OF PROGRESS, THE (US/0361-1590) [02246078] 2263, **1752**

INDIAN EDUCATIONAL REVIEW (II/0019-4700) [01752860] 2263, **1752**

INDIAN ELECTRONICS DIRECTORY (II/0377-7340) [01797742] **2064**

INDIAN ENERGY AND POWER UPDATE (II) **1946**

INDIAN ENGINEER (II) [01752862] **1978**

INDIAN EXPORT TRADE JOURNAL, THE (II/0019-4735) [09570607] 840, **4523**

INDIAN EXPORT YEAR-BOOK (II) [07112254] **840**

INDIAN EXPRESS (II) [09693826] **5803**

INDIAN FACTORIES JOURNAL, THE (II/0019-476X) [01585754] **3481**

INDIAN FARMERS' DIGEST (II) [01643835] **94**

INDIAN FARMING (II/0019-4786) [01585649] **94**

INDIAN FERN JOURNAL (II/0970-2741) [14171581] **513**

INDIAN FILM CULTURE (IT) [10048679] **4072**

INDIAN FILMS (POONA) (II/0377-7359) [01790604] **4072**

INDIAN FINANCE (II/0019-4794) [01588828] **790**

INDIAN FISHERIES BULLETIN (II/0537-1643) [02385154] **2305**

INDIAN FOOD INDUSTRY (II/0253-5025) [09103870] **2344**

INDIAN FOOD PACKER (II/0019-4808) [01752865] **2344**

INDIAN FORESTER, THE (II/0019-4816) [01752876] **2384**

INDIAN FOUNDRY JOURNAL (II/0379-5446) [11071297] **4003**

INDIAN GEOGRAPHICAL JOURNAL, THE (II/0019-4824) [08226473] **2566**

INDIAN GEOGRAPHICAL STUDIES: RESEARCH BULLETIN (II) [02643228] **2566**

INDIAN GEOLOGICAL INDEX (II/0379-511X) [02477721] **1382**

INDIAN GEOLOGISTS' ASSOCIATION See BULLETIN - INDIAN GEOLOGISTS' ASSOCIATION **1369**

INDIAN GEOPHYSICAL UNION See JOURNAL OF THE INDIAN GEOPHYSICAL UNION **1408**

INDIAN GEOSCIENCE ABSTRACTS (II) [08026607] 1356, **1363**

INDIAN GEOSCIENCE ASSOCIATION. JOURNAL See JOURNAL - INDIAN ACADEMY OF GEOSCIENCE **1384**

INDIAN GEOTECHNICAL JOURNAL (II/0046-8983) [02689727] **2024**

INDIAN HEALTH PROGRAM OF THE U.S. PUBLIC HEALTH SERVICE, THE (US) [01784593] **4784**

INDIAN HEART JOURNAL (II/0019-4832) [01752880] **3706**

INDIAN HIGHWAYS (II/0376-7256) [01790571] **5441**

INDIAN HIGHWAYS (TEMPE, ARIZ.) (US/0892-6654) [10238323] 5061, **2263**

INDIAN HISTORICAL REVIEW, THE (II/0376-9836) [01797780] **2653**

INDIAN HISTORY AND GENEALOGY (US) **2454**

INDIAN HORIZONS (II/0378-2964) [01784195] **2848**

INDIAN HORTICULTURE (II/0019-4875) [01607417] **2420**

INDIAN HOTELKEEPER AND TRAVELLER (II) [01752883] **2807**

INDIAN IMPORT EXPORT DIRECTORY (II) [25696856] **840**

INDIAN INDUSTRIES (II/0442-6851) [02689591] **681**

INDIAN INDUSTRIES (MADRAS) (II/0019-4891) [01716411] **3481**

INDIAN INSTITUTE OF BANKERS See JOURNAL OF THE INDIAN INSTITUTE OF BANKERS **795**

INDIAN INSTITUTE OF FOREIGN TRADE See ANNUAL REPORT - INDIAN INSTITUTE OF FOREIGN TRADE **823**

INDIAN INSTITUTE OF MANAGEMENT. CENTRE FOR MANAGEMENT IN AGRICULTURE See MONOGRAPH - CENTRE FOR MANAGEMENT IN AGRICULTURE, INDIAN INSTITUTE OF MANAGEMENT **109**

INDIAN INSTITUTE OF METALS See TRANSACTIONS OF THE INDIAN INSTITUTE OF METALS **4022**

INDIAN INSTITUTE OF PUBLIC ADMINISTRATION See IIPA NEWSLETTER **4655**

INDIAN INSTITUTE OF PUBLIC OPINION See MONTHLY PUBLIC OPINION SURVEYS **2526**

INDIAN INSTITUTE OF SCIENCE, BANGALORE See JOURNAL OF THE INDIAN INSTITUTE OF SCIENCE. SECTION C: BIOLOGICAL SCIENCES **5121**

Alphabetical Title Index

INDIAN

INDIAN INSTITUTE OF SCIENCE, BANGALORE *See* JOURNAL OF THE INDIAN INSTITUTE OF SCIENCE. SECTION A: ENGINEERING AND TECHNOLOGY **5120**

INDIAN INSTITUTE OF SCIENCE, BANGALORE *See* JOURNAL OF THE INDIAN INSTITUTE OF SCIENCE **5120**

INDIAN INSTITUTE OF SCIENCE, BANGALORE *See* JOURNAL OF THE INDIAN INSTITUTE OF SCIENCE. SECTION B: PHYSICAL AND CHEMICAL SCIENCES **5121**

INDIAN INSTITUTE OF TECHNOLOGY, BOMBAY *See* RESEARCH BULLETIN - INDIAN INSTITUTE OF TECHNOLOGY, BOMBAY **5146**

INDIAN INVESTMENT CENTRE *See* MONTHLY NEWSLETTER - INDIAN INVESTMENT CENTRE **907**

INDIAN JOURNAL OF ADMINISTRATIVE SCIENCE (II) [24606876] **4656**

INDIAN JOURNAL OF ADULT EDUCATION (US/0019-5006) [03173499] **1801**

INDIAN JOURNAL OF AGRICULTURAL BIOCHEMISTRY (II/0970-6399) [l09706399] 488, **94**

INDIAN JOURNAL OF AGRICULTURAL CHEMISTRY (II/0367-8229) [01085050] 978, **94**

INDIAN JOURNAL OF AGRICULTURAL ECONOMICS, THE (II/0019-5014) [01752888] 1494, **94**

●INDIAN JOURNAL OF AGRICULTURAL ENGINEERING, THE (II/0971-2356) [27905998] 1978, **95**

INDIAN JOURNAL OF AGRICULTURAL RESEARCH (II/0367-8245) [01771509] **95**

INDIAN JOURNAL OF AGRICULTURAL SCIENCES, THE (II/0019-5022) [01771510] **95**

INDIAN JOURNAL OF AGRONOMY (II/0537-197X) [01752889] **95**

INDIAN JOURNAL OF AMERICAN STUDIES (II/0019-5030) [01714923] **2738**

INDIAN JOURNAL OF ANAESTHESIA (II/0019-5049) [01752890] **3683**

INDIAN JOURNAL OF ANIMAL HEALTH (II/0019-5057) [01752891] **5511**

INDIAN JOURNAL OF ANIMAL NUTRITION (II/0970-3209) [12771156] 5511, **212**

INDIAN JOURNAL OF ANIMAL PRODUCTION AND MANAGEMENT (II) [13500638] **212**

INDIAN JOURNAL OF ANIMAL REPRODUCTION : JOURNAL OF THE INDIAN SOCIETY FOR THE STUDY OF ANIMAL REPRODUCTION, THE (II) [12030736] **5511**

INDIAN JOURNAL OF ANIMAL RESEARCH (II/0367-6722) [01644436] 5511, **212**

INDIAN JOURNAL OF ANIMAL SCIENCES, THE (II/0367-8318) [06267258] **5511**

INDIAN JOURNAL OF APPLIED AND PURE BIOLOGY (II/0970-2091) [15102119] **458**

INDIAN JOURNAL OF APPLIED CHEMISTRY (II/0019-5065) [01752893] **2013**

INDIAN JOURNAL OF APPLIED LINGUISTICS (II/0379-0037) [03497484] **3286**

INDIAN JOURNAL OF APPLIED PSYCHOLOGY (II/0019-5073) [01680850] **4589**

INDIAN JOURNAL OF ASIAN STUDIES (II) [05696923] **2653**

INDIAN JOURNAL OF BEHAVIOUR (II/0970-0897) [04533461] **4589**

INDIAN JOURNAL OF BIOCHEMISTRY & BIOPHYSICS (II/0301-1208) [01696706] 495, **488**

INDIAN JOURNAL OF BOTANY (II/0250-829X) [05362771] **513**

INDIAN JOURNAL OF BUDDHIST STUDIES BAUDDHA ADHYAYANA KI BHARATIYA PATRIKA, THE (II) [21264541] **5021**

INDIAN JOURNAL OF CANCER (II/0019-509X) [01752894] **3818**

INDIAN JOURNAL OF CANCER CHEMOTHERAPHY (II/0970-2563) [15617149] **3818**

●INDIAN JOURNAL OF CHEMICAL TECHNOLOGY (II/0971-457X) [30678983] **1025**

INDIAN JOURNAL OF CHEMISTRY. SECTION A, INORGANIC, BIO-INORGANIC, PHYSICAL, THEORETICAL & ANALYTICAL CHEMISTRY (II/0376-4710) [24334417] 1036, 1053, **1015**

INDIAN JOURNAL OF CHEMISTRY. SECTION B : ORGANIC INCLUDING MEDICINAL (II/0376-4699) [02720948] **1042**

INDIAN JOURNAL OF CHEST DISEASES & ALLIED SCIENCES, THE (II/0377-9343) [02594075] 3949, **3706**

INDIAN JOURNAL OF CLINICAL BIOCHEMISTRY (II/0970-1915) [14124343] **488**

INDIAN JOURNAL OF CLINICAL PSYCHOLOGY (II/0303-2582) [01797763] **4589**

INDIAN JOURNAL OF COMMERCE, THE (II/0019-512x) [01586033] **840**

INDIAN JOURNAL OF COMMUNICATION ARTS (II) [03498891] **385**

INDIAN JOURNAL OF COMMUNITY GUIDANCE SERVICE (II/0970-1346) [12170059] **4784**

INDIAN JOURNAL OF COMPARATIVE ANIMAL PHYSIOLOGY (II/0255-7150) [10387964] **5586**

INDIAN JOURNAL OF COMPARATIVE LAW (II) [10480214] **3129**

INDIAN JOURNAL OF COMPARATIVE MICROBIOLOGY, IMMUNOLOGY, AND INFECTIOUS DISEASES (II) [10413003] **5511**

INDIAN JOURNAL OF COMPARATIVE SOCIOLOGY (II) [02441181] **5247**

INDIAN JOURNAL OF CRIMINOLOGY (II/0376-9844) [01790595] **3166**

INDIAN JOURNAL OF CRIMINOLOGY & CRIMINALISTICS, THE (II/0970-4345) [08226471] **3166**

INDIAN JOURNAL OF CRYOGENICS (II/0379-0479) [08227897] **4405**

INDIAN JOURNAL OF CURRENT PSYCHOLOGICAL RESEARCH (II) [25636778] **4589**

INDIAN JOURNAL OF DAIRY SCIENCE (II/0019-5146) [01752897] **195**

INDIAN JOURNAL OF DERMATOLOGY (II/0019-5154) [01715007] **3720**

INDIAN JOURNAL OF DERMATOLOGY, VENEREOLOGY AND LEPROLOGY (II/0378-6323) [02884822] 4784, **3720**

INDIAN JOURNAL OF DRYLAND AGRICULTURAL RESEARCH AND DEVELOPMENT (II) [26726630] **95**

INDIAN JOURNAL OF ECOLOGY (II/0304-5250) [02245626] **2217**

INDIAN JOURNAL OF ECONOMICS (II/0019-5170) [01774651] **1494**

●INDIAN JOURNAL OF ENGINEERING & MATERIALS SCIENCES (II/0971-457X) **1978**

INDIAN JOURNAL OF ENGLISH STUDIES (II/0537-6554) [01752899] **3396**

INDIAN JOURNAL OF ENTOMOLOGY, THE (II/0367-8288) [01608123] **5609**

INDIAN JOURNAL OF ENVIRONMENTAL HEALTH (II/0367-827X) [01771498] **2174**

INDIAN JOURNAL OF ENVIRONMENTAL PROTECTION (II/0253-7141) [09179128] **2174**

INDIAN JOURNAL OF EXPERIMENTAL BIOLOGY (II/0019-5189) [01752900] **458**

INDIAN JOURNAL OF EXTENSION EDUCATION (II/0537-1996) [01774652] 95, **1752**

INDIAN JOURNAL OF FIBRE & TEXTILE RESEARCH (II/0971-0426) [22102377] **5351**

INDIAN JOURNAL OF FINANCE AND RESEARCH (II/0971-0566) [25097032] **870**

INDIAN JOURNAL OF FISHERIES (II/0537-2003) [01752901] **2305**

INDIAN JOURNAL OF FORENSIC SCIENCES : THE OFFICIAL PUBLICATION OF THE FORENSIC SCIENCE SOCIETY OF INDIA (II/0970-1982) [19376624] **3741**

INDIAN JOURNAL OF FORESTRY (II/0250-524X) [04327218] **2384**

INDIAN JOURNAL OF GASTROENTEROLOGY (II/0254-8860) [11257416] **3746**

INDIAN JOURNAL OF GENDER STUDIES (US/0971-52155) **5203**

INDIAN JOURNAL OF GENETICS & PLANT BREEDING, THE (II/0019-5200) [01715141] 513, **548**

INDIAN JOURNAL OF GEOGRAPHY, THE (II/0537-2011) [01752902] **2566**

INDIAN JOURNAL OF GEOLOGY (II/0970-1354) [16929827] **1382**

INDIAN JOURNAL OF GERONTOLOGY (II/0019-5219) [03389955] **3752**

INDIAN JOURNAL OF HELMINTHOLOGY / HELMINTHOLOGICAL SOCIETY OF INDIA (II/0019-5227) [01589715] **5586**

INDIAN JOURNAL OF HEREDITY (II/0374-826X) [02887857] **548**

INDIAN JOURNAL OF HETEROCYCLIC CHEMISTRY / PUBLISHED IN ASSOCIATION WITH NATIONAL ACADEMY OF CHEMISTRY AND BIOLOGY (INDIA) (II/0971-1627) [25614604] **978**

INDIAN JOURNAL OF HILL FARMING (II/0970-6429) [l09706429] **2420**

INDIAN JOURNAL OF HISTORY OF MEDICINE (II/0019-5677) [01624493] **3586**

INDIAN JOURNAL OF HISTORY OF SCIENCE (II/0019-5235) [01752903] **5112**

INDIAN JOURNAL OF HORTICULTURE, THE (II/0019-5251) [01641719] **2420**

INDIAN JOURNAL OF HOSPITAL PHARMACY (II/0019-526X) [01714995] **4307**

INDIAN JOURNAL OF INDUSTRIAL MEDICINE (II/0019-5278) [01695666] **2863**

INDIAN JOURNAL OF INDUSTRIAL RELATIONS (II/0019-5286) [01752904] **681**

INDIAN JOURNAL OF INTERNATIONAL LAW, THE (II/0019-5294) [01752905] **3129**

INDIAN JOURNAL OF LABOUR ECONOMICS (II/0019-5308) [01604587] 1678, **1566**

INDIAN JOURNAL OF LEPROSY (II/0254-9395) [11206847] **4784**

INDIAN JOURNAL OF LIBRARY SCIENCE (II/0970-4302) [06670192] **3215**

INDIAN JOURNAL OF MALARIOLOGY (II/0367-8326) [01644179] **3797**

INDIAN JOURNAL OF MARINE SCIENCES (II/0379-5136) [01771499] **1450**

INDIAN JOURNAL OF MARKETING (II) [08641401] **926**

INDIAN JOURNAL OF MARKETING GEOGRAPHY, THE (II/0970-1095) [13536046] 926, **2566**

INDIAN JOURNAL OF MATHEMATICS (II/0019-5324) [01752906] **3508**

INDIAN JOURNAL OF MECHANICS AND MATHEMATICS (II/0537-2038) [06748958] **3508**

INDIAN JOURNAL OF MEDICAL EDUCATION (II/0019-5332) [01752907] 1752, **3586**

INDIAN JOURNAL OF MEDICAL MICROBIOLOGY (II/0255-0857) [15085386] **563**

INDIAN JOURNAL OF MEDICAL RESEARCH. SECTION A, INFECTIOUS DISEASES (II/0970-955X) [21248308] **3586**

INDIAN JOURNAL OF MEDICAL RESEARCH. SECTION B, BIOMEDICAL RESEARCH OTHER THAN INFECTIOUS DISEASES (II/0970-9568) [21248314] **3586**

INDIAN JOURNAL OF MEDICAL SCIENCES (II/0019-5359) [01752908] **3586**

INDIAN JOURNAL OF MENTAL RETARDATION (II/0019-5375) [08637668] **1880**

INDIAN JOURNAL OF MICROBIOLOGY (II/0046-8991) [01586408] **563**

INDIAN JOURNAL OF MUSHROOMS (II) [09104562] **575**

INDIAN JOURNAL OF MYCOLOGY AND PLANT PATHOLOGY (II/0303-4097) [01772595] **575**

INDIAN JOURNAL OF NATURAL PRODUCTS (II/0970-129X) [14707476] **4307**

INDIAN JOURNAL OF NATURAL RUBBER RESEARCH (II/0970-2431) [20344618] **5076**

INDIAN JOURNAL OF NEMATOLOGY : OFFICIAL PUBLICATION OF THE NEMATOLOGICAL SOCIETY OF INDIA (II/0303-6960) [01604973] **5586**

INDIAN JOURNAL OF NUTRITION AND DIETETICS, THE (II/0022-3174) [01771511] **4192**

INDIAN JOURNAL OF OCCUPATIONAL HEALTH (II/0019-5391) [01752911] **2863**

INDIAN JOURNAL OF OPHTHALMOLOGY (II/0301-4738) [01590475] **3875**

INDIAN JOURNAL OF ORTHOPAEDICS (II/0019-5413) [01752912] **3881**

INDIAN JOURNAL OF OTOLARYNGOLOGY (II/0019-5421) [01752913] **3888**

●INDIAN JOURNAL OF OTOLARYNGOLOGY, AND HEAD, AND NECK : OFFICIAL PUBLICATION OF THE ASSOCIATION OF OTOLARYNGOLOGISTS OF INDIA (II) [28382811] **3888**

INDIAN JOURNAL OF PARASITOLOGY (II/0253-7168) [04660964] **563**

INDIAN JOURNAL OF PATHOLOGY & MICROBIOLOGY (II/0377-4929) [02134140] **3895**

INDIAN JOURNAL OF PEDIATRICS (II/0019-5456) [01752915] **3904**

INDIAN JOURNAL OF PETROLEUM GEOLOGY (II/0971-2542) [l09712542] 1382, **4260**

INDIAN JOURNAL OF PHARMACEUTICAL EDUCATION (II/0019-5464) [01587097] **4307**

INDIAN — Alphabetical Title Index

INDIAN JOURNAL OF PHARMACEUTICAL SCIENCES (II/0250-474X) [04237329] **4307**

INDIAN JOURNAL OF PHARMACOLOGY (II/0253-7613) [04896540] **4307**

INDIAN JOURNAL OF PHYSICAL & NATURAL SCIENCES. SECTION A (II/0970-0811) [15609604] **5112**

INDIAN JOURNAL OF PHYSICAL ANTHROPOLOGY AND HUMAN GENETICS (II/0378-8156) [03131357] **238**, **548**

INDIAN JOURNAL OF PHYSICS A AND PROCEEDINGS OF THE INDIAN ASSOCIATION FOR THE CULTIVATION OF SCIENCE A (II/0252-9262) [03689333] **4405**

INDIAN JOURNAL OF PHYSICS AND PROCEEDINGS OF THE INDIAN ASSOCIATION FOR THE CULTIVATION OF SCIENCE (II/0019-5480) [01752916] **4405**, **5112**

INDIAN JOURNAL OF PHYSICS B AND PROCEEDINGS OF THE INDIAN ASSOCIATION FOR THE CULTIVATION OF SCIENCE B (II/0252-9254) [03689359] **4405**

INDIAN JOURNAL OF PHYSIOLOGY AND ALLIED SCIENCES (II/0367-8350) [01752917] **581**

INDIAN JOURNAL OF PHYSIOLOGY AND PHARMACOLOGY (II/0019-5499) [01352235] **4307**, **581**

INDIAN JOURNAL OF PLANT PATHOLOGY (II/0970-342X) [19026739] **513**

INDIAN JOURNAL OF PLANT PHYSIOLOGY (II/0019-5502) [01752918] **513**

INDIAN JOURNAL OF PLANT PROTECTION (II/0253-4355) [05659888] **513**

INDIAN JOURNAL OF PLANT SCIENCES (II/0970-0404) [11640460] **513**

INDIAN JOURNAL OF PLASTIC SURGERY (II/0970-0358) [09817283] **3966**

INDIAN JOURNAL OF POLITICAL SCIENCE, THE (II/0019-5510) [01752919] **4476**

INDIAN JOURNAL OF POLITICAL STUDIES, THE (II/0251-303X) [03719593] **4524**, **4476**

INDIAN JOURNAL OF POLITICS (II/0303-9951) [01680822] **4476**

INDIAN JOURNAL OF POULTRY SCIENCE (II/0019-5529) [01752920] **212**

INDIAN JOURNAL OF POWER AND RIVER VALLEY DEVELOPMENT (II/0019-5537) [01752921] **5534**

INDIAN JOURNAL OF PREVENTIVE AND SOCIAL MEDICINE (II/0301-1216) [10101994] **3586**

INDIAN JOURNAL OF PSYCHIATRIC SOCIAL WORK (II/0302-1610) [01797684] **5289**

INDIAN JOURNAL OF PSYCHIATRY (II/0019-5545) [01589371] **3926**

INDIAN JOURNAL OF PSYCHOLOGICAL MEDICINE (II/0253-7176) [05828881] **3926**

INDIAN JOURNAL OF PSYCHOLOGY (II/0019-5553) [01752922] **4589**

INDIAN JOURNAL OF PSYCHOMETRY AND EDUCATION (II/0378-1003) [06096835] **1752**

INDIAN JOURNAL OF PSYCHOPHYSIOLOGY (II) **4589**

INDIAN JOURNAL OF PUBLIC ADMINISTRATION, THE (II/0019-5561) [01752923] **4656**

INDIAN JOURNAL OF PUBLIC HEALTH (II/0019-557X) [01752924] **4784**

INDIAN JOURNAL OF PULSES RESEARCH (II/0970-6380) [I09706380] **513**

INDIAN JOURNAL OF PURE AND APPLIED MATHEMATICS (II/0019-5588) [01639468] **3508**

INDIAN JOURNAL OF PURE & APPLIED PHYSICS (II/0019-5596) [00843065] **4405**

INDIAN JOURNAL OF QUANTITATIVE ECONOMICS (II/0970-1532) [14135650] **1494**

INDIAN JOURNAL OF RADIO & SPACE PHYSICS (II/0367-8393) [01640515] **4405**

INDIAN JOURNAL OF RADIOLOGY & IMAGING, THE (II/0970-2016) [11428897] **3942**

INDIAN JOURNAL OF REGIONAL SCIENCE (II/0046-9017) [01204580] **2825**

INDIAN JOURNAL OF SERICULTURE (II/0445-7722) [02887998] **5586**

INDIAN JOURNAL OF SEXUALLY TRANSMITTED DISEASES (II/0253-7184) [07857217] **3762**, **4784**

INDIAN JOURNAL OF SOCIAL RESEARCH (II/0019-5626) [01752927] **5203**

INDIAN JOURNAL OF SOCIAL SCIENCES (II/0376-9879) [01797759] **5203**

INDIAN JOURNAL OF SOCIAL WORK, THE (II/0019-5634) [01607790] **5289**

INDIAN JOURNAL OF SOIL CONSERVATION (II/0970-3349) [07407667] **174**

INDIAN JOURNAL OF SURGERY (II/0019-5650) [01752929] **3966**

INDIAN JOURNAL OF TECHNICAL EDUCATION, THE (II) [01790429] **1913**

INDIAN JOURNAL OF TECHNOLOGY (II/0019-5669) [01752930] **5112**

INDIAN JOURNAL OF THEOLOGY, THE *CEASED.* (II/0019-5685) [01752931] **4964**

INDIAN JOURNAL OF THEORETICAL PHYSICS (II/0019-5693) [01752932] **3509**, **4405**

INDIAN JOURNAL OF TRAINING & DEVELOPMENT (II) [06428132] **1752**, **870**

INDIAN JOURNAL OF TUBERCULOSIS (II/0019-5707) [01752933] **3949**

●INDIAN JOURNAL OF UNANI MEDICINE : DEVOTED TO INTERDISCIPLINARY RESEARCH IN UNANI MEDICINE AND ALLIED SCIENCES (II) [25698413] **3586**

INDIAN JOURNAL OF UROLOGY (II/0970-1591) [12862061] **3990**

INDIAN JOURNAL OF VETERINARY ANATOMY (II/0971-1937) [I09711937] **5512**

INDIAN JOURNAL OF VETERINARY MEDICINE (II/0970-051X) [10016171] **5512**

INDIAN JOURNAL OF VETERINARY PATHOLOGY (II/0250-4758) [04406006] **5512**

INDIAN JOURNAL OF VETERINARY SURGERY (II/0254-4105) [09248836] **5512**

INDIAN JOURNAL OF VIROLOGY (II/0970-2822) [14275750] **458**

INDIAN JOURNAL OF WEED SCIENCE (II/0253-8040) [03392957] **95**

INDIAN JOURNAL OF ZOOLOGICAL SPECTRUM (II/0971-104X) [I0971104X] **5586**

INDIAN JOURNAL OF ZOOLOGY (II/0302-7562) [01790578] **5586**

INDIAN JUDGMENT REPORTER : IJR (II) [09891075] **2981**

INDIAN JUTE MILLS ASSOCIATION. STATISTICS DEPT *See* MONTHLY SUMMARY OF JUTE AND GUNNY STATISTICS **155**

INDIAN LABOUR JOURNAL (II/0019-5723) [01774653] **1678**

INDIAN LAW REPORTER (US/0097-1154) [01796534] **2981**

INDIAN LAW REPORTS *See* INDIAN LAW REPORTS, THE **2981**

INDIAN LAW REPORTS; DELHI SERIES (II) [01752943] **2981**

INDIAN LAW REPORTS, THE (II) [02381635] **2981**

INDIAN LEADER, THE (US/0364-8028) [01752948] **2264**, **1752**

INDIAN LEATHER (II/0019-574X) [I0019574X] **3184**

INDIAN LIBERTARIAN, THE (II/0019-5766) [01643786] **1592**

INDIAN LIBRARY SCIENCE ABSTRACTS (II/0019-5790) [02666124] **3215**, **3258**

INDIAN LIFE MAGAZINE (CN/0226-9317) [06169243] **2264**

INDIAN LINGUISTICS (II/0378-0759) [01713804] **3286**

INDIAN LISTENER *See* AKASHVANI (NEW DELHI) **1126**

INDIAN LITERARY REVIEW, THE (II) [10411562] **3396**

INDIAN LITERATURE (NEW DELHI) (II/0019-5804) [01716981] **3396**

INDIAN MANAGEMENT (II/0019-5812) [01774655] **870**

INDIAN MANAGEMENT ABSTRACTS (II) [09108059] **870**

INDIAN MARINE DIRECTORY (II) [10265649] **5450**

INDIAN MARKET (US/0892-6409) [15304903] **352**, **2264**

INDIAN MEDICAL GAZETTE (II/0019-5863) [01169166] **3587**

INDIAN MEDICAL JOURNAL (II/0019-5871) [01778021] **3587**

INDIAN MERCHANTS' CHAMBER *See* JOURNAL OF THE INDIAN MERCHANTS' CHAMBER **843**

INDIAN MILLER (II/0376-9887) [02246224] **202**

●INDIAN MINERAL RESOURCE HORIZONS / BIA DIVISION OF ENERGY AND MINERAL RESOURCES (US) [26273150] **2140**

INDIAN MINERALOGIST, THE (II/0019-5928) [01752956] **1440**

INDIAN MINERALS (II/0019-5936) [01716773] **2140**

INDIAN MINERALS YEARBOOK (II/0445-7897) [09204099] **2140**

INDIAN MINING & ENGINEERING JOURNAL, THE (II/0019-5944) [07995512] **2140**

INDIAN MISSIOLOGICAL REVIEW : IMR / SACRED HEART THEOLOGICAL COLLEGE (II) [09538103] **4964**

INDIAN MOTION PICTURE ALMANAC (II) [02441515] **4072**

INDIAN MOUNTAINEER (II) [05997553] **4873**

INDIAN MUSEUM, CALCUTTA *See* BULLETIN - INDIAN MUSEUM **4085**

INDIAN MUSIC JOURNAL (II/0019-5995) [01752959] **4122**

INDIAN MUSICOLOGICAL SOCIETY *See* JOURNAL OF THE INDIAN MUSICOLOGICAL SOCIETY **4127**

INDIAN NATION, THE (II) [12594401] **5803**

INDIAN NATIONAL BIBLIOGRAPHY (II/0019-6002) [01645018] **417**

INDIAN NATIONAL CONGRESS *See* CONGRESS BULLETIN - INDIAN NATIONAL CONGRESS **2649**

INDIAN NATIONAL SCIENCE ACADEMY *See* PROCEEDINGS OF THE INDIAN NATIONAL SCIENCE ACADEMY. PART B, BIOLOGICAL SCIENCES **469**

INDIAN NATIONAL SCIENCE ACADEMY *See* PROCEEDINGS OF THE INDIAN NATIONAL SCIENCE ACADEMY. PART A, PHYSICAL SCIENCES **5140**

INDIAN NATIONAL SCIENCE ACADEMY *See* BIOGRAPHICAL MEMOIRS OF FELLOWS OF THE INDIAN NATIONAL SCIENCE ACADEMY **430**

INDIAN NATIONAL SCIENCE ACADEMY *See* YEAR BOOK OF THE INDIAN NATIONAL SCIENCE ACADEMY, THE **5171**

INDIAN NATIONAL SCIENTIFIC DOCUMENTATION CENTRE *See* ANNUAL REPORT - INDIAN NATIONAL SCIENTIFIC DOCUMENTATION CENTRE **3190**

INDIAN NEWS OF THE AMERICAS / INTER-AMERICAN INDIAN INSTITUTE (MX/0185-6278) [12812864] **2264**

INDIAN NEWSPAPER SOCIETY PRESS HANDBOOK (II) [20611811] **1113**, **5803**

INDIAN OCEAN NEWS & VIEWS / SOCIETY FOR INDIAN OCEAN STUDIES, THE (II) [25536537] **1450**

INDIAN OCEAN NEWSLETTER / LA LETTRE DE L'OCEAN INDIEN, THE (FR/0294-6475) [10179748] **4476**, **1494**

INDIAN OCEAN POLICY PAPERS (AT/1030-1976) [I10301976] **1566**

INDIAN OCEAN REVIEW, THE (AT/1031-2331) [18542412] **2510**

INDIAN ODONATOLOGY (II) [23606129] **5609**

INDIAN OUTLOOK (II) [03318261] **2653**

INDIAN PEDIATRICS (II/0019-6061) [01752963] **3904**

INDIAN PERFUMER (II/0019-607X) [09742526] **404**

INDIAN PHARMACEUTICAL GUIDE (II/0073-6635) [01639646] **4307**

INDIAN PHILOSOPHICAL QUARTERLY (II/0376-415X) [01780934] **4349**

●INDIAN PHYCOLOGICAL REVIEW (II) [27905572] **513**

INDIAN PHYTOPATHOLOGY (II/0367-973X) [01752966] **513**

INDIAN POLICE JOURNAL, THE (II/0537-2429) [01752967] **3166**

INDIAN POULTRY INDUSTRY YEARBOOK (II) [01588040] **212**

INDIAN POULTRY REVIEW (II/0019-6150) [01688492] **213**

INDIAN PRACTITIONER (II/0019-6169) [01588018] **3587**

INDIAN PRESS INDEX (II/0019-6177) [01752970] **5803**

INDIAN PRINT AND PAPER (II) [09067048] **4234**

INDIAN PROGRESS (US/0019-6193) [05303311] **2264**

INDIAN PSYCHOLOGICAL ABSTRACTS (II) [01784202] **4589**

INDIAN PSYCHOLOGICAL ABSTRACTS AND REVIEWS (US/0971-524X) **4589**

INDIAN PSYCHOLOGICAL REVIEW (II/0019-6215) [01644511] **4589**

INDIAN PSYCHOLOGIST (II/0970-2520) [09772033] **4589**

INDIAN PUBLISHER AND BOOKSELLER, THE (II/0019-6223) [01752972] **4829**, **4815**

INDIAN RAILWAY TECHNICAL BULLETIN (II/0019-6266) [I00196266] **5432**

INDIAN RAILWAYS (II/0019-6274) [02666278] **5432**

INDIAN REVIEW (CHICAGO), THE *SUSPENDED.* (US/0194-3391) [05175627] **2653**

INDIAN REVIEW (MADRAS) (II/0019-6304) [01606107] **2505**

INDIAN REVIEW OF AFRICAN AFFAIRS : IRAA (II) [13494800] 4477, **1494**

INDIAN REVIEW OF LIFE SCIENCES (II/0253-4436) [08255747] **458**

INDIAN REVIEW OF PUBLIC AND CO-OPERATIVE ECONOMY (II) [01784163] **1495**

INDIAN SAFETY ENGINEER, THE (II/0368-0029) [I03680029] **1978**

INDIAN SCHOLAR (II) [07641192] **3344**

INDIAN SCHOOL JOURNAL (US/0364-7056) [02371409] 2264, **1752**

INDIAN SCIENCE ABSTRACTS (II/0019-6339) [01642963] 5112, **5175**

INDIAN SCIENCE INDEX (II) [03216869] **5112**

INDIAN SCIENTIFIC TRANSLATORS ASSOCIATION *See* JISTA **3289**

INDIAN SHIPPING (II/0970-4299) [06578569] **5450**

INDIAN SILK (II/0019-6355) [03342579] **5351**

INDIAN SOCIETY FOR AFRO-ASIAN STUDIES *See* ISAAS NEWSLETTER / INDIAN SOCIETY FOR AFRO-ASIAN STUDIES **4526**

INDIAN SOCIETY OF AGRICULTURAL STATISTICS *See* JOURNAL OF THE INDIAN SOCIETY OF AGRICULTURAL STATISTICS **154**

INDIAN SOCIETY OF ORIENTAL ART *See* JOURNAL OF THE INDIAN SOCIETY OF ORIENTAL ART **354**

INDIAN SOCIETY OF SOIL SCIENCE *See* JOURNAL OF THE INDIAN SOCIETY OF SOIL SCIENCE **177**

INDIAN SOCIETY OF SOIL SCIENCE *See* BULLETIN - INDIAN SOCIETY OF SOIL SCIENCE **165**

INDIAN SOCIO-LEGAL JOURNAL (II/0970-7972) [04555087] 5247, **2981**

INDIAN SPICES (II/0019-6401) [01641073] 2344, **840**

INDIAN STATISTICAL ASSOCIATION *See* JOURNAL OF THE INDIAN STATISTICAL ASSOCIATION **5330**

INDIAN SUB-CONTINENT SERVICE (UK) **4260**

INDIAN SUGAR (II/0019-6428) [03755462] **2344**

INDIAN SUGAR CROPS JOURNAL, THE (II) [03519474] **174**

INDIAN SUGAR YEAR BOOK (II/0537-2631) [01771515] **2344**

INDIAN TEXTILE BULLETIN (II/0537-0078) [02394007] **5351**

INDIAN TEXTILE JOURNAL, THE (II/0019-6436) [02128554] **5351**

INDIAN THEOLOGICAL STUDIES (II/0253-620X) [03681971] **4964**

INDIAN THOUGHT AND CULTURE *See* INDIAN THOUGHT LEIDEN **2653**

● INDIAN THOUGHT LEIDEN (NE/0924-8986) [I09248986] **2653**

INDIAN TIME (ROOSEVELTOWN, N.Y.) (US/0893-3820) [12958901] **5717**

INDIAN TIMES (US/0278-7202) [02385166] **5643**

INDIAN TOBACCO (II/0445-7951) [02245613] **5373**

INDIAN TOBACCO (GUNTUR, INDIA) (II) [08938314] **5373**

INDIAN TRADE JOURNAL (II/0019-6444) [02163794] **840**

INDIAN TRADER, THE (US/0046-9076) [04112458] 2264, **2738**

INDIAN TRUST FUNDS INVESTMENT OPERATIONS (US) [07338549] **901**

INDIAN VERSE (II) [01790504] **3464**

INDIAN VETERINARY JOURNAL, THE (II/0019-6479) [01752985] **5512**

INDIAN VETERINARY MEDICAL JOURNAL (II/0250-5266) [03784325] **5512**

INDIAN VOICE (SANTA CLARA) (US/0091-102X) [01786483] 2264, **2738**

INDIAN WELDING JOURNAL (II/0046-9092) [02716876] **4027**

INDIAN WORKER, THE (II/0537-2682) [05621454] **1678**

INDIAN YEAR BOOK OF INTERNATIONAL AFFAIRS, THE (II/0537-2704) [01752988] **4524**

INDIAN ZOOLOGIST (II/0368-0983) [I03680983] **5586**

INDIANA *See* INDIANA ENVIRONMENTAL STATUTES **3113**

INDIANA *See* LABOR LAWS OF INDIANA **3150**

INDIANA *See* INDIANA CODE. SUPPLEMENT **2981**

INDIANA *See* INDIANA EMPLOYMENT SECURITY ACT **1678**

INDIANA ACADEMY OF SCIENCE *See* PROCEEDINGS OF THE INDIANA ACADEMY OF SCIENCE **5140**

INDIANA ACADEMY OF SCIENCE *See* MONOGRAPH - INDIANA ACADEMY OF SCIENCE **5129**

INDIANA ACADEMY OF THE SOCIAL SCIENCES *See* PROCEEDINGS / INDIANA ACADEMY OF THE SOCIAL SCIENCES **5213**

INDIANA AGRI-NEWS (US/0745-7103) [09394952] **95**

INDIANA AGRICULTURAL STATISTICS (US) [17244799] **95**

INDIANA ALWAYS (US/0739-9391) [09586162] **2738**

INDIANA APOSTOLIC TRUMPET (US/8750-8176) [11796508] **5061**

INDIANA ARCHITECT (US/0445-8605) [02673134] **301**

INDIANA ARTS COMMISSION *See* ANNUAL REPORT - INDIANA ARTS COMMISSION **312**

INDIANA. AUDITOR OF STATE'S OFFICE *See* INDIANA COMPREHENSIVE ANNUAL FINANCIAL REPORT FOR THE FISCAL YEAR ENDED ... **4731**

INDIANA AUDUBON QUARTERLY (US/0019-6525) [01753029] **5617**

INDIANA BAPTIST (US) **4964**

● INDIANA BASKETBALL HISTORY : A PUBLICATION OF THE INDIANA BASKETBALL HALL OF FAME (US) [27690980] **4900**

INDIANA BEER BOOK (US) **2367**

INDIANA (BERLIN, GERMANY) (GW) [02452883] **2738**

INDIANA BEVERAGE JOURNAL (US/0274-547X) [06398346] **2367**

INDIANA BUSINESS DIRECTORY (US/1048-7255) [15327861] **682**

INDIANA BUSINESS MAGAZINE (US/1060-4154) [23001621] **682**

INDIANA BUSINESS MODERNIZATION AND TECHNOLOGY CORPORATION *See* BMT NEWS / INDIANA BUSINESS MODERNIZATION AND TECHNOLOGY CORPORATION **1599**

INDIANA BUSINESS REVIEW (US/0019-6541) [01753032] **1495**

INDIANA CASES REPORTED IN NORTH EASTERN REPORTER, SECOND SERIES (US/0744-9046) [04904049] **2981**

INDIANA CHAMBER OF COMMERCE *See* BUSINESS DIRECTORY & RESOURCE GUIDE **647**

INDIANA. CIVIL RIGHTS COMMISSION *See* TRIENNIAL REPORT / INDIANA CIVIL RIGHTS COMMISSION **4513**

INDIANA CODE. SUPPLEMENT (US) [04097989] **2981**

INDIANA COMPREHENSIVE ANNUAL FINANCIAL REPORT FOR THE FISCAL YEAR ENDED ... (US) [21011131] **4731**

INDIANA COMPREHENSIVE ASSESSMENT AND PROGRAM PLANNING SYSTEM ANNUAL REPORT ... READING, COMPOSITION, SPELLING (US) [08755348] **1896**

INDIANA COUNTY HERITAGE (US) [02262249] **2454**

INDIANA CRIMINAL LAW REVIEW (US) [04784134] **3107**

INDIANA DAILY STUDENT, THE (US/0740-9664) [07980535] **1092**

INDIANA DECISIONS AND LAW REPORTER (US/0445-8664) [04162557] **2981**

INDIANA DENTAL ASSOCIATION *See* YEARBOOK / INDIANA DENTAL ASSOCIATION **1337**

INDIANA. DEPT. OF MENTAL HEALTH *See* ANNUAL REPORT OF THE INDIANA DEPARTMENT OF MENTAL HEALTH, THE **4766**

INDIANA. DEPT. OF NATURAL RESOURCES *See* ANNUAL STATE HISTORIC PRESERVATION PLAN (INDIANA) **2721**

INDIANA. DEPT. OF TRANSPORTATION. DIVISION OF PROGRAM DEVELOPMENT *See* HIGHWAY IMPROVEMENT PROGRAM / INDIANA DEPARTMENT OF TRANSPORTATION **5440**

INDIANA. DIVISION OF ADULT AND COMMUNITY EDUCATION *See* ADULT EDUCATION **1799**

INDIANA. DIVISION OF FISH AND GAME *See* ANNUAL REPORT OF THE DIVISION OF FISH AND GAME, INDIANA DEPARTMENT OF CONSERVATION **2186**

INDIANA. DIVISION OF MUSEUMS AND MEMORIALS *See* ANNUAL PRESERVATION PROGRAM, THE **2186**

INDIANA. EMERGENCY MEDICAL SERVICES COMMISSION *See* COMPREHENSIVE PLAN FOR EMERGENCY MEDICAL SERVICES **3723**

INDIANA EMPLOYMENT LAW LETTER (US/1053-6191) [22589688] **3149**

INDIANA EMPLOYMENT SECURITY ACT (US) [05741920] **1678**

INDIANA. EMPLOYMENT SECURITY DIVISION *See* COUNTY EMPLOYMENT PATTERNS **1661**

INDIANA. EMPLOYMENT SECURITY DIVISION *See* LABOR FORCE STATUS OF INDIANA RESIDENTS **1683**

INDIANA. EMPLOYMENT SECURITY DIVISION *See* OCCUPATIONAL OUTLOOK AND DEVELOPMENT **4207**

INDIANA. EMPLOYMENT SECURITY DIVISION *See* INDIANA RURAL MANPOWER REPORT **1678**

INDIANA. EMPLOYMENT SECURITY DIVISION. RESEARCH AND STATISTICS SECTION *See* NEED FOR WORKERS IN SELECTED OCCUPATIONS RELATED TO VOCATIONAL & TECHNICAL EDUCATION PROGRAMS. REGION 9 **1693**

INDIANA. EMPLOYMENT SECURITY DIVISION. RESEARCH AND STATISTICS SECTION *See* NEED FOR WORKERS IN SELECTED OCCUPATIONS RELATED TO VOCATIONAL & TECHNICAL EDUCATION PROGRAMS. REGION 8 **1693**

INDIANA. EMPLOYMENT SECURITY DIVISION. RESEARCH AND STATISTICS SECTION *See* NEED FOR WORKERS IN SELECTED OCCUPATIONS RELATED TO VOCATIONAL & TECHNICAL EDUCATION PROGRAMS. REGION 6 **1693**

INDIANA. EMPLOYMENT SECURITY DIVISION. RESEARCH AND STATISTICS SECTION *See* NEED FOR WORKERS IN SELECTED OCCUPATIONS RELATED TO VOCATIONAL & TECHNICAL EDUCATION PROGRAMS. REGION 12 **1693**

INDIANA. EMPLOYMENT SECURITY DIVISION. RESEARCH AND STATISTICS SECTION *See* NEED FOR WORKERS IN SELECTED OCCUPATIONS RELATED TO VOCATIONAL & TECHNICAL EDUCATION PROGRAMS. REGION 10 **1693**

INDIANA. EMPLOYMENT SECURITY DIVISION. RESEARCH AND STATISTICS SECTION *See* NEED FOR WORKERS IN SELECTED OCCUPATIONS RELATED TO VOCATIONAL & TECHNICAL EDUCATION PROGRAMS. REGION 1 **1693**

INDIANA. EMPLOYMENT SECURITY DIVISION. RESEARCH AND STATISTICS SECTION *See* NEED FOR WORKERS IN SELECTED OCCUPATIONS RELATED TO VOCATIONAL & TECHNICAL EDUCATION PROGRAMS. REGION 4 **1693**

INDIANA. EMPLOYMENT SECURITY DIVISION. RESEARCH AND STATISTICS SECTION *See* NEED FOR WORKERS IN SELECTED OCCUPATIONS RELATED TO VOCATIONAL & TECHNICAL EDUCATION PROGRAMS. REGION 7 **1693**

INDIANA. EMPLOYMENT SECURITY DIVISION. RESEARCH AND STATISTICS SECTION *See* NEED FOR WORKERS IN SELECTED OCCUPATIONS RELATED TO VOCATIONAL & TECHNICAL EDUCATION PROGRAMS. REGION 3 **1693**

INDIANA. EMPLOYMENT SECURITY DIVISION. RESEARCH AND STATISTICS SECTION *See* NEED FOR WORKERS IN SELECTED OCCUPATIONS RELATED TO VOCATIONAL & TECHNICAL EDUCATION PROGRAMS. REGION 11 **3916**

INDIANA. EMPLOYMENT SECURITY DIVISION. RESEARCH AND STATISTICS SECTION *See* NEED FOR WORKERS IN SELECTED OCCUPATIONS RELATED TO VOCATIONAL & TECHNICAL EDUCATION PROGRAMS. REGION 5 **1693**

INDIANA. EMPLOYMENT SECURITY DIVISION. RESEARCH AND STATISTICS SECTION *See* NEED FOR WORKERS IN SELECTED OCCUPATIONS RELATED TO VOCATIONAL & TECHNICAL EDUCATION PROGRAMS. REGION 13 **1693**

INDIANA. EMPLOYMENT SECURITY DIVISION. RESEARCH AND STATISTICS SECTION *See* NEED FOR WORKERS IN SELECTED OCCUPATIONS RELATED TO VOCATIONAL & TECHNICAL EDUCATION PROGRAMS. REGION 14 **1693**

INDIANA — Alphabetical Title Index

INDIANA. EMPLOYMENT SECURITY DIVISION. RESEARCH AND STATISTICS SECTION *See* NEED FOR WORKERS IN SELECTED OCCUPATIONS RELATED TO VOCATIONAL & TECHNICAL EDUCATION PROGRAMS. REGION 2 **1693**

INDIANA ENGLISH (US/1070-9371) [03867942] **3286**

INDIANA ENVIRONMENTAL LAW LETTER (US/1053-6183) [22589628] 2174, **2981**

INDIANA ENVIRONMENTAL RULES (US/1061-916X) [24839470] **3113**

INDIANA ENVIRONMENTAL STATUTES (US/1061-7957) [24839299] **3113**

INDIANA FACTBOOK (BLOOMINGTON, IND.) (US/0886-330X) [12873936] 5328, **2535**

INDIANA FACTS (US/0893-2298) [15464926] **2535**

INDIANA FAMILY HEALTH COUNCIL *See* COUNCIL NOTES - INDIANA FAMILY HEALTH COUNCIL, INC **3569**

INDIANA FARM LABOR REPORT *See* INDIANA RURAL MANPOWER REPORT **1678**

INDIANA FREEMASON, THE (US/0019-6622) [04079580] **5232**

INDIANA GAME & FISH (US/0897-8980) [17657539] **4873**

INDIANA GAZETTE (INDIANA, PA.) (US) [15096706] **5736**

INDIANA. GENERAL ASSEMBLY *See* INDIANA GENERAL ASSEMBLY LEGISLATIVE DIRECTORY **4656**

INDIANA GENERAL ASSEMBLY LEGISLATIVE DIRECTORY (US) [08401642] **4656**

INDIANA. GEOLOGICAL SURVEY *See* GEOLOGICAL SURVEY CIRCULAR (BLOOMINGTON) **1378**

INDIANA GEOLOGICAL SURVEY *See* GEOLOGICAL SURVEY GUIDEBOOK **1378**

INDIANA. GEOLOGICAL SURVEY *See* DEPARTMENT OF NATURAL RESOURCES GEOLOGICAL SURVEY GUIDEBOOK **2191**

INDIANA. GEOLOGICAL SURVEY *See* GEOLOGICAL SURVEY BULLETIN (BLOOMINGTON, IND.) **1378**

INDIANA GRAPPLER (US) **4900**

INDIANA HAND CENTER NEWSLETTER (US) [28916638] 3882, **3587**

● INDIANA HEALTH CARE IN PERSPECTIVE (US/1065-416X) [26605063] **4784**

INDIANA HISTORICAL SOCIETY PUBLICATIONS (US/0073-6902) [01680927] **2738**

INDIANA HISTORY BULLETIN (US/0019-6649) [01641806] **2739**

INDIANA IN PERSPECTIVE (US/1065-5433) [25224361] **5328**

INDIANA INDUSTRIAL DIRECTORY, THE (US) [02214928] **3481**

INDIANA INTERNATIONAL & COMPARATIVE LAW REVIEW (US/1061-4982) [23673041] **3129**

INDIANA JOURNAL FOR HEALTH, PHYSICAL EDUCATION, RECREATION, DANCE, THE (US) [19864239] **1856**

● INDIANA JOURNAL OF HISPANIC LITERATURES (US/1065-0350) [26489877] **3396**

INDIANA JOURNAL OF POLITICAL SCIENCE *SUSPENDED.* (US/0737-7355) [08840488] **4477**

INDIANA LABOR MARKET. PROFILE OF ECONOMIC REGION 1 *See* PROFILE OF ECONOMIC REGION 1 **1703**

INDIANA LABOR MARKET. PROFILE OF ECONOMIC REGION 2 *See* PROFILE OF ECONOMIC REGION 2 **1703**

INDIANA LABOR MARKET. PROFILE OF ECONOMIC REGION 3 *See* PROFILE OF ECONOMIC REGION 3 **1703**

INDIANA LABOR MARKET. PROFILE OF ECONOMIC REGION 4 *See* PROFILE OF ECONOMIC REGION 4 **1703**

INDIANA LABOR MARKET. PROFILE OF ECONOMIC REGION 5 *See* PROFILE OF ECONOMIC REGION 5 **1703**

INDIANA LABOR MARKET. PROFILE OF ECONOMIC REGION 6 *See* PROFILE OF ECONOMIC REGION 6 / PREPARED BY OCCUPATIONAL INFORMATION UNIT **1704**

INDIANA LABOR MARKET. PROFILE OF ECONOMIC REGION 7 *See* PROFILE OF ECONOMIC REGION 7 **1704**

INDIANA LABOR MARKET. PROFILE OF ECONOMIC REGION 8 *See* PROFILE OF ECONOMIC REGION 8 **1704**

INDIANA LABOR MARKET. PROFILE OF ECONOMIC REGION 9 *See* PROFILE OF ECONOMIC REGION 9 **1704**

INDIANA LABOR MARKET. PROFILE OF ECONOMIC REGION 10 *See* PROFILE OF ECONOMIC REGION 10 **1704**

INDIANA LABOR MARKET. PROFILE OF ECONOMIC REGION 11 *See* PROFILE OF ECONOMIC REGION 11 **1704**

INDIANA LABOR MARKET. PROFILE OF ECONOMIC REGION 12 *See* PROFILE OF ECONOMIC REGION 12 **1704**

INDIANA LABOR MARKET. PROFILE OF ECONOMIC REGION 13 *See* PROFILE OF ECONOMIC REGION 13 **1704**

INDIANA LABOR MARKET. PROFILE OF ECONOMIC REGION 14 *See* PROFILE OF ECONOMIC REGION 14 **1704**

INDIANA LABOR MARKET TRENDS (US) [06578914] **1678**

INDIANA LAW JOURNAL (BLOOMINGTON) (US/0019-6665) [02322874] **2982**

INDIANA LAW REVIEW (US/0090-4198) [01774980] **2982**

● INDIANA LEGISLATIVE SOURCEBOOK (US) [23149003] 4656, **4477**

INDIANA LIBRARIES (US/0275-777X) [07219192] **3215**

INDIANA LIBRARY FEDERATION *See* MEMBERSHIP DIRECTORY AND HANDBOOK / INDIANA LIBRARY DERATION **3230**

INDIANA MAGAZINE OF HISTORY (US/0019-6673) [02371402] **2739**

INDIANA MANUFACTURERS DIRECTORY (US/0735-2417) [08418056] **3481**

INDIANA MATHEMATICS TEACHER (US/0889-6941) [13998563] 1896, **3509**

INDIANA MEDIA JOURNAL (US/0164-7660) [04370836] **3215**

INDIANA MEDICINE (US/0746-8288) [10307039] **3587**

INDIANA MUSICATOR (US/0273-9933) [06752255] **4122**

INDIANA NEWSPAPER DIRECTORY AND RATE BOOK (US) [06259096] **5664**

INDIANA. OFFICE OF SOCIAL SERVICES *See* STATE OF INDIANA FINAL COMPREHENSIVE ANNUAL SERVICES PLAN **5311**

INDIANA OFFICE OF SOCIAL SERVICES *See* PROPOSED COMPREHENSIVE ANNUAL SERVICES PLAN (INDIANAPOLIS) **5302**

INDIANA PHARMACIST (US) [01753041] **4307**

INDIANA PRAIRIE FARMER (US/0162-7104) [04212490] **95**

INDIANA PRESERVATIONIST, THE (US/0737-8602) [09350921] 2739, **5480**

INDIANA PUBLIC EMPLOYEE REPORTER (US) **1678**

INDIANA PUBLIC MANAGEMENT (US/0099-1023) [02243157] **4656**

INDIANA PUBLISHER, THE (US/0019-6711) [04079618] **4815**

INDIANA QUERIES (US/1044-694X) [17928104] **2454**

INDIANA RAIL PLAN UPDATE (US) [17959211] **5432**

INDIANA READING QUARTERLY (US/0019-672X) [08000796] **1896**

INDIANA REGISTER (US/0193-1520) [04859868] **2982**

INDIANA REVIEW (US/0738-386X) [09399570] **3344**

INDIANA ROOTS *CEASED.* (US/8755-2612) [11248033] **2454**

INDIANA RURAL MANPOWER REPORT (US/0092-3222) [01789270] 95, **1678**

INDIANA STATE ADVISORY COUNCIL ON VOCATIONAL EDUCATION *See* ANNUAL REPORT / INDIANA STATE ADVISORY COUNCIL ON VOCATIONAL EDUCATION **1910**

INDIANA STATE BAR ASSOCIATION (1916-) *See* DIRECTORY OF THE OFFICERS, BOARD OF MANAGERS, COMMITTEES AND SECTIONS AFFILIATED AND COOPERATING ORGANIZATIONS **2962**

INDIANA STATE BOARD OF HEALTH BULLETIN, THE (US/0019-6754) [02447563] **4784**

INDIANA. STATE BOARD OF VOCATIONAL AND TECHNICAL EDUCATION *See* INDIANA STATE PLAN FOR VOCATIONAL EDUCATION **1913**

INDIANA. STATE BUDGET AGENCY *See* LIST OF APPROPRIATIONS : MADE BY THE REGULAR SESSION OF THE ... GENERAL ASSEMBLY AND THE ... SPECIAL SESSION THEREOF FOR THE BIENNIUM **4736**

INDIANA. STATE HIGHWAY COMMISSION (1961-1981). DIVISION OF ACCOUNTING AND CONTROL *See* ANNUAL REPORTS - INDIANA STATE HIGHWAY COMMISSION, DIVISION OF ACCOUNTING & CONTROL **5438**

INDIANA STATE PLAN FOR VOCATIONAL EDUCATION (US) [01799420] **1913**

INDIANA STATE UNIVERSITY. DEPT. OF GEOGRAPHY AND GEOLOGY *See* PROFESSIONAL PAPER - INDIANA STATE UNIVERSITY. DEPT. OF GEOGRAPHY AND GEOLOGY **2573**

INDIANA THEORY REVIEW (US/0271-8022) [04216235] **4122**

INDIANA UNDERWRITER, THE *CEASED.* (US/0195-7805) [05664551] **2882**

INDIANA UNIVERSITY *See* PUBLICATIONS. AFRICAN SERIES **2642**

INDIANA UNIVERSITY *See* ARBUTUS **1810**

INDIANA UNIVERSITY *See* PUBLICATIONS. GEOGRAPHIC MONOGRAPH SERIES **2574**

INDIANA UNIVERSITY ART MUSEUM BULLETIN (US/0161-1003) [03834902] 352, **4089**

INDIANA UNIVERSITY, BLOOMINGTON. ART MUSEUM *See* INDIANA UNIVERSITY ART MUSEUM BULLETIN **4089**

INDIANA. UNIVERSITY. GRADUATE LIBRARY SCHOOL *See* NORTH AMERICAN LIBRARY EDUCATION DIRECTORY AND STATISTICS **3259**

INDIANA UNIVERSITY MATHEMATICS JOURNAL (US/0022-2518) [01753019] **3509**

INDIANA UNIVERSITY STUDIES ON HUNGARY (HU) **4524**

INDIANA UNIVERSITY URALIC AND ALTAIC SERIES (US/0893-2913) [15483144] **3287**

INDIANA WATERSHED PROGRESS (US/0092-2366) [01787335] **2091**

INDIANA WEEKLY WEATHER AND CROP REPORT *See* INDIANA WEEKLY WEATHER CROP REPORT **174**

INDIANA WEEKLY WEATHER CROP REPORT (US/0442-817X) [08566879] **174**

INDIANA ZIP+4 STATE DIRECTORY (US) [11585612] **1145**

INDIANAPOLIS 500 YEARBOOK, THE (US/1055-3355) [04918509] 4900, **5417**

INDIANAPOLIS. BOARD OF SCHOOL COMMISSIONERS *See* FINANCIAL REPORT OF THE GENERAL SUPERINTENDENT - BOARD OF SCHOOL COMMISSIONERS OF THE CITY OF INDIANAPOLIS **1864**

INDIANAPOLIS BUSINESS JOURNAL (US/0274-4929) [06363753] **682**

INDIANAPOLIS MONTHLY (US/0899-0328) [08348365] **2535**

INDIANAPOLIS MUSEUM OF ART PREVIEWS MAGAZINE (US) **353**

INDIANAPOLIS NEWS (INDIANAPOLIS, IND. : 1876) (US) [08808048] **5664**

INDIANAPOLIS RECORDER, THE (US) [08797400] **5664**

INDIANAPOLIS STAR, THE (US) [07980466] **5665**

INDIANAPOLIS SYMPHONY ORCHESTRA *See* INDIANAPOLIS SYMPHONY ORCHESTRA : [PROGRAMS] **4122**

INDIANAPOLIS SYMPHONY ORCHESTRA : [PROGRAMS] (US) [06963882] **4122**

INDICA (II/0019-686X) [01774666] 270, **2653**

INDICADOR DO SETOR ENERGETICO NACIONAL (BL) [02242724] **2064**

INDICADORES DA CONJUNTURA SERGIPANA (BL) [05164149] **1566**

INDICADORES DE COMERCIO EXTERIOR (CL/0716-2405) [06974805] **840**

INDICADORES DE COYUNTURA (AG/0537-3468) [06020307] 1566, **1534**

INDICADORES DE COYUNTURA (CK/0120-9299) [17283881] **1566**

INDICADORES DEL SECTOR EXTERNO (MX) [08720848] 1495, **840**

INDICADORES ECONOMICOS (CK) [02659652] **790**

INDICADORES ECONOMICOS (BANCOO DE MEXICO (1925-). SUBDIRECCION DE INVESTIGACION ECONOMICA) (MX) [08922405] 1495, **1534**

INDICADORES ECONOMICOS PORTUGAL / PORTUGAL ECONOMIC INDICATORS / BANCO DE PORTUGAL (PO) [09391597] **1566**

INDICADORES IBGE. ESTATISTICA DA PRODUCAO AGRICOLA ANUAL (BL) [26937040] **1566**

INDICADORES IBGE. INDICADORES CONJUNTURAIS DA INDUSTRIA, PRODUCAO FISICA. BRASIL (BL) [26937127] **1566**

INDICADORES IBGE. INDICADORES CONJUNTURAIS DA INDUSTRIA, PRODUCAO FISICA. REGIONAL (BL) [26937303] **1566**

INDICADORES IBGE. INDICES DE PRECOS AO CONSUMIDOR, INPC, IPCA (BL) [26985605] **1566**

INDICADORES IBGE. PRODUTO INTERNO BRUTO (BL) [26937419] **1567**

INDICADORES IBGE / SECRETARIA DE PLANEJAMENTO DA PRESIDENCIA DA REPUBLICA, FUNDACAO INSTITUTO BRASILEIRO DE GEOGRAFIA E ESTATISTICA, IBGE (BL) [09640165] **1567**

INDICADORES SOCIAIS DE SERGIPE / GOVERNO DO ESTADO DE SERGIPE, SECRETARIA DO PLANEJAMENTO, COORDENACAO DE PLANEJAMENTO E ESTATISTICA, CPE (BL) [08041700] **5203**

INDICATEUR FISCAL (BE) **1495**

INDICATEUR HORAIRES VILLE A VILLE (FR/1243-4671) [I12434671] **2982**

INDICATEUR OFFICIEL DES POSTES DE BELGIQUE (BE) [05842264] **1145**

INDICATEUR OFFICIEL VILLE A VILLE See INDICATEUR HORAIRES VILLE A VILLE **2982**

INDICATEUR OFFICIEL VILLE A VILLE (FR/1164-7701) [I11647701] **2982**

INDICATEUR (OTTAWA) CEASED. (CN/0828-7201) [19032496] **1978**

INDICATEUR PUBLICITAIRE MEDIA (BE) **1113**

INDICATEUR STATISTIQUE (CAISSE NATIONALE DE L'ASSURANCE MALADIE DES TRAVAILLEURS SALARIES (FRANCE)) (FR) [09982074] 2882, **1678**

INDICATEUR SUISSE (SZ) [10742465] **2916**

INDICATEURS DE L'ECONOMIE TOGOLAISE (TG/0302-4423) [01793213] **1567**

INDICATEURS RAPIDES. SPECIAL D ISSUE (LU) **1495**

INDICATION (BE) **1064**

INDICATIONS INDEX See PDR GUIDE TO DRUG INTERACTIONS, SIDE EFFECTS, INDICATIONS **4319**

INDICATOR (NANAIMO) (CN/0381-0917) [03680940] **4848**

INDICATOR (SAINT PAUL, MINN. 1985) (US/0898-5308) [12483408] 3481, **2140**

INDICATOR, THE (US/0019-6924) [04079712] 458, **978**

INDICATORE CARTARIO : RASSEGNA BIBLIOGRAFICA MENSILE (IT/0392-9108) [08203385] **4234**

INDICATORI MENSILI / ISTAT, ISTITUTO CENTRALE DI STATISTICA (IT/0390-6620) [01786747] **5328**

INDICATORS OF EDUCATIONAL QUALITY, SUMMARY (US/0148-4591) [03312701] **1752**

INDICATORS OF INDUSTRIAL ACTIVITY (FR/0250-4278) [05065391] **1609**

INDICATORS OF SCIENCE AND TECHNOLOGY (OTTAWA) (CN/0843-753X) [20653396] **5112**

INDICATORS OF SOCIO-ECONOMIC DEVELOPMENT OF GOA, DAMAN & DIU SINCE LIBERATION (II/0376-9925) [01790536] **1567**

INDICE, ARTICULOS SOBRE EDUCACION EN PUBLICACIONES PERIODICAS NACIONALES / MINISTERIO DE EDUCACION, INIDE, CENTRO NACIONAL DE DOCUMENTACION E INFORMACION EDUCACIONAL (PE) [10624949] **1752**

INDICE BIBLIOGRAFICO - ARMO (MX) [04269596] **417**

INDICE BIBLIOGRAFICO - CENTRO DE INFORMACION TECNICA Y DOCUMENTACION See INDICE BIBLIOGRAFICO - ARMO **417**

INDICE BOLIVIANO DE CIENCIAS DE LA SALUD (BO/0253-5521) [06680247] **4784**

INDICE COLOMBIANO DE ECONOMIA Y NEGOCIOS (CK/0121-2613) [I01212613] 1495, **682**

INDICE DE LA LITERATURA DENTAL PERIODICA EN CASTELLANO (AG/0325-0679) [10707179] **1324**

INDICE DE PRECIOS AL CONSUMIDOR (CK) [06912131] **1495**

INDICE DE PRECIOS AL CONSUMIDOR. AREA URBANA (EC) [09368206] **1592**

INDICE DE PRECIOS AL POR MAYOR (CL) [04112234] 682, **730**

INDICE DE PRECOS AO CONSUMIDOR (FUNDACAO INSTITUTO DE PLANEJAMENTO DO CEARA. COORDENADORIA DE ESTATISTICA E INFORMATICA) See INDICE DE PRECOS AO CONSUMIDOR (FUNDACAO INSTITUTO DE PLANEJAMENTO DO CEARA. COORDENADORIA DE PLANEJAMENTO GLOBAL) **1495**

INDICE DE PRECOS AO CONSUMIDOR (FUNDACAO INSTITUTO DE PLANEJAMENTO DO CEARA. COORDENADORIA DE PLANEJAMENTO GLOBAL) (BL) [09347952] **1495**

INDICE DE PROFESIONALES DEL URUGUAY (UY) [10287257] **4205**

INDICE DE RESUMENES ANALITICOS SOBRE EDUCACION EN AMERICA LATINA Y EL CARIBE (CL) [22456832] **1752**

INDICE DE TECNICOS PAPELEROS ESPANOLES (SP/0376-9933) [02240602] **4234**

INDICE DE VENTAS NOMINALES DE COMERCIO INTERIOR (CL) [03098832] 840, **730**

INDICE DEI LIBRI DEL MESE, L' (IT) [12575799] **4829**

INDICE DU COUT DE LA VIE (MR) [07984884] 1495, **955**

INDICE ESPANOL DE CIENCIA Y TECNOLOGIA (SP/0210-9409) [09823263] **5112**

INDICE ESPANOL DE CIENCIAS SOCIALES. SERIE A, PSICOLOGIA Y CIENCIAS DE LA EDUCACION (SP/0213-019X) [11981761] 1752, 4590, **5203**

INDICE ESPANOL DE CIENCIAS SOCIALES. SERIE C, DERECHO (SP) [17816794] **3081**

INDICE GENERAL DE PUBLICACIONES PERIODICAS CUBANAS (CU) [01786982] **5203**

INDICE HISPANOAMERICANO DE CIENCIAS SOCIALES (CK/0120-6478) [13385786] **5203**

INDICE HISTORICO ESPANOL (SP/0537-3522) [01753053] 2692, **2635**

INDICE INDUSTRIAL (UY/0376-9941) [01798453] **1609**

INDICE MEDICO ESPANOL (SP) [07567443] 3587, **3660**

INDICE MENSUEL DES PRIX DE DETAIL A LA CONSOMMATION / POLYNESIE FRANCAISE (FP) [22257846] **1297**

INDICE-O BANCO DE DADOS See BRAZILIAN INDEX **780**

INDICE PENALE, L' (IT/0019-7084) [01753054] **3107**

INDICES AGROPECUARIOS / FUNDACAO GETULIO VARGAS, INSTITUTO BRASILEIRO DE ECONOMIA, DIVISAO DE ESTATISTICA E ECONOMETRIA, CENTRO DE ESTUDOS AGRICOLAS CEASED. (BL) [06912956] **95**

INDICES CE DE PRECIOS AGRICOLAS. GLOSSARIUM (LU) [19059104] **95**

INDICES DE PRECIOS (MX) [08920689] 1495, **1534**

INDICES - MONOGRAPHS IN PHILOSOPHICAL LOGIC & FORMAL LINGUISTICS (US) 4349, **3287**

INDICES OF EXTERNAL TRADE (JM) [02262868] **840**

INDICI COSTO LAVORO INDUSTRIA (IT) **1678**

INDICI E SUSSIDI BIBLIOGRAFICI (IT/0567-6746) [06340503] **417**

INDICI MENSILI PIROLA (IT) **1495**

INDICITALIA COMUNICAZIONI (IT) **760**

INDICIZZAZIONE, L' (IT/0394-0810) [I03940810] **3215**

INDIEN : ENERGIEWIRTSCHAFT (GW) [05055926] **1946**

INDIEN, FORSCHUNGSPOLITIK UND FORSCHUNGSPRAXIS / BUNDESSTELLE FUER AUSSENHANDELSINFORMATION (GW) [11407449] **2653**

INDIGENA (US) [02694648] **2264**

INDIGENISMO : BOLETIN DEL SEMINARIO ESPANOL DE ESTUDIOS INDIGENISTAS, INSTITUTO DE COOPERACION IBEROAMERICANA (SP) [19604391] **2264**

INDIGENOUS AFFAIRS (DK) **238**

INDIGENOUS WOMAN (US/1070-1400) [26228788] **2264**

INDIGENOUS WORLD (US) [15475559] **2264**

●INDIGENOUS WORLD / INTERNATIONAL WORK GROUP FOR INDIGENOUS AFFAIRS (DK) [30981676] **2982**

INDIKATOR EKONOMI (IO) [01795453] **1567**

INDIKATOR EKONOMI BALI (IO) [09186206] **1567**

INDIKATOR EKONOMI DKI JAKARTA (IO) [08913055] **1495**

INDIKATOR EKONOMI KALIMANTAN SELATAN (IO) [05734548] **1567**

INDIKATOR EKONOMI PROPINSI SULAWESI SELATAN See INDIKATOR EKONOMI ... SULAWESI SELATAN **1567**

INDIKATOR EKONOMI ... SULAWESI SELATAN (IO) [09250685] **1567**

INDIKATOR KESEJAHTERAAN RAKYAT / WELFARE INDICATORS (IO) [08001535] **5289**

INDIKATOR PEMBANGUNAN INDUSTRI PERTANIAN (IO) [11482472] 1567, **95**

INDILEX (UY) [02242929] **2982**

INDIRECTIONS (CN/0227-2547) [06702720] **3287**

INDIVIDUAL AND THE FUTURE OF ORGANIZATIONS, THE (US/0161-4177) [03916009] **5203**

INDIVIDUAL EMPLOYMENT RIGHTS (US) [14239399] **3149**

INDIVIDUAL INVESTOR (NEW YORK, N.Y.) (US/1049-4596) [21220037] **790**

INDIVIDUAL INVESTOR'S GUIDE TO INVESTMENT PUBLICATIONS, THE (US) [18962334] **901**

INDIVIDUAL INVESTOR'S GUIDE TO NO-LOAD MUTUAL FUNDS, THE CEASED. (US) [11629292] **901**

INDIVIDUAL ONSITE WASTEWATER SYSTEMS (US/0160-6662) [03735234] **2232**

INDIVIDUAL PSYCHOLOGY (US/0277-7010) [07625417] **4590**

INDIVIDUAL PSYCHOLOGY REPORTER CEASED. (US/0888-4595) [13592890] **4590**

INDIVIDUAL RETIREMENT PLANS GUIDE : IRA, SEP, KEOGH (US/0744-6268) [08290988] 901, **790**

INDIVIDUAL STUDIES BY PARTICIPANTS TO THE INTERNATIONAL INSTITUTE OF SEISMOLOGY AND EARTHQUAKE ENGINEERING (JA) [06608545] **1407**

INDIVIDUAL TAXATION (US/0742-7832) [10438202] **4732**

INDIVIDUAL WITH DISABILITIES EDUCATION LAW REPORT (US/1055-520X) [23196419] 4389, **2982**

INDIVIDUALIST, THE (UK) [04863128] **1567**

INDIVIDUALLY GUIDED EDUCATION (US) [01795436] **1896**

INDIVIDUALS' FILLED-IN TAX RETURN FORMS (US) [02094880] **4732**

INDO ASIA (GW/0019-719X) [01715691] **2653**

INDO-BRITISH REVIEW (II/0019-7211) [01589524] **2692**

INDO-BURMA PETROLEUM COMPANY See INDO-BURMA PETROLEUM COMPANY LIMITED ANNUAL REPORT **4260**

INDO-BURMA PETROLEUM COMPANY LIMITED ANNUAL REPORT (II/0376-9968) [01790638] **4260**

INDO-CANADIAN NATIONAL NEWS (CN/0843-8145) [20493964] **2739**

INDO-CANADIAN TIMES (CN/0708-949X) [05257153] **5786**

INDO-IRANIAN JOURNAL (NE/0019-7246) [01929743] 3287, **4349**

INDO-IRANICA (II) [01642208] 3396, **2505**

INDO-KOREAN FRIENDSHIP (II) [01790434] **5247**

INDO-PACIFIC FISHERY COMMISSION See PROCEEDINGS / INDO-PACIFIC FISHERY COMMISSION **2310**

INDO-PACIFIC FISHES (US/0736-0460) [09068886] 2305, **5586**

INDO-PACIFIC PREHISTORIC ASSOCIATION BULLETIN (AT/0156-1316) [07434237] **270**

INDO-PACIFIC PREHISTORY ASSOCIATION See INDO-PACIFIC PREHISTORIC ASSOCIATION BULLETIN **270**

INDOCHINA CHRONOLOGY (US/0897-4519) [11553676] 4477, **2653**

INDOCHINA JOURNAL (US/0742-907X) [10443008] **2653**

INDOCHINA NEWSLETTER (US) [14254358] **4509**

INDOCHINA REPORT SUSPENDED. (SI/0217-8451) [12714078] **4524**

INDOGAKU BUKKYOGAKU KENKYU (JA/0019-4344) [01753061] **2653**

INDOGERMANISCHE FORSCHUNGEN (GW/0341-1850) [01588506] **3287**

INDOLOGIA BEROLINENSIS (GW) [02123660] **3287**

INDOLOGICA TAURINENSIA (IT) [02666251] **3287**

INDONESHIA Alphabetical Title Index

INDONESHIA NO GUN-SEI SHIDOSHA ICHIRAN (JA) [02245309] **4656**

INDONESIA. BADAN KOORDINASI KELUARGA BERENCANA NASIONAL. BIRO PELAPORAN DAN DOKUMENTASI *See* AREA REPORT SERIES **588**

INDONESIA. BADAN URUSAN LOGISTIK *See* PEDOMAN PELAKSANAAN PENGADAAN DALAM NEGERI **203**

INDONESIA. BIRO KLASIFIKASI *See* LAPORAN PERUSAHAAN - BIRO KLASIFIKASI INDONESIA **5451**

INDONESIA. BIRO PUSAT STATISTIC *See* PRODUKSI TANAMAN BAHAN MAKANAN DI INDONESIA **183**

INDONESIA. BIRO PUSAT STATISTIK *See* SURVEY PERTANIAN **138**

INDONESIA. BIRO PUSAT STATISTIK *See* STATISTIK KENDARAAN BERMOTOR DAN PANJANG JALAN **5402**

INDONESIA BIRO PUSAT STATISTIK *See* PRODUKSI PERIKANAN LAUT YANG DIJUAL DI PELELANGAN/TEMPAT PENDARATAN IKAN DI JAWA-MADURA **2311**

INDONESIA. BIRO PUSAT STATISTIK *See* INDEKS HARGA PERDAGANGAN BESAR BAHAN BANGUNAN/KONSTRUKSI DI INDONESIA **1609**

INDONESIA. BIRO PUSAT STATISTIK *See* KOMPILASI DATA OUTPUT & [I.E. DAN] INPUT USAHA TANI PADI INTENSIFIKASI PER KABUPATEN DI JAWA-MADURA **177**

INDONESIA. BIRO PUSAT STATISTIK *See* PENDUDUK CINA JAWA-MADURA : HASIL REGISTRASI PENDUDUK **4556**

INDONESIA. BIRO PUSAT STATISTIK *See* DAFTAR PENERBITAN PENERBITAN BIRO PUSAT STATISTIK **5326**

INDONESIA. BIRO PUSAT STATISTIK *See* PERKEMBANGAN BULANAN HARGA ECERAN BAHAN MAKANAN POKOK & BAHAN PENTING LIANNYA DI IBUKOTA PROPINSI INDONESIA **1594**

INDONESIA. BIRO PUSAT STATISTIK *See* IMPOR MENURUT JENIS BARANG DAN NEGERI ASAL **839**

INDONESIA. BIRO PUSAT STATISTIK *See* PETERNAKAN DAN UNGGAS **217**

INDONESIA. BIRO PUSAT STATISTIK *See* LUAS & INTENSITAS SERANGAN HAMA & PENYAKIT DI INDONESIA **2424**

INDONESIA. BIRO PUSAT STATISTIK *See* STATISTIK BONGKAR MUAT BARANG DI PELABUHAN INDONESIA **5457**

INDONESIA. BIRO PUSAT STATISTIK *See* KEPADATAN PERUSAHAAN INDUSTRI DAN TENAGA KERJA DI SEKTOR INDUSTRI TERHADAP JUMLAH PENDUDUK DI TIAP-TIAP PROPINSI, KABUPATEN, KOTAMADYA **1682**

INDONESIA. BIRO PUSAT STATISTIK *See* INDIKATOR EKONOMI **1567**

INDONESIA. BIRO PUSAT STATISTIK *See* KEADAAN ANGKATEN KERJA DI INDONESIA : ANGKA SEMENTARA **1682**

INDONESIA. BIRO PUSAT STATISTIK *See* LUAS TANAMAN, PRODUKSI, DAN PERSEDIAAN TANAMAN PERKEBUNAN YANG TERPENTING **178**

INDONESIA BUYER'S GUIDE & WHO'S WHO (IO) [10177253] **433**

INDONESIA (CHASE MANHATTAN BANK, N.A.) (IO) [09179614] **901**

INDONESIA CIRCLE : [JOURNAL] (UK/0306-2848) [02668673] **2505**

INDONESIA. DEPARTEMEN PEKERJAAN UMUM DAN TENAGA LISTRIK. BIRO TUJUH: UMUM *See* LAPORAN TAHUNAN - DEPARTEMEN PEKERJAAN UMUM DAN TENAGA LISTRIK, BIRO VII : UMUM **1615**

INDONESIA. DEPARTEMEN PENDIDIKAN DAN KEBUDAYAAN. KANTOR WILAYAH DKI JAKARTA *See* PROGRAM KEGIATAN - KANTOR WILAYAH DEPARTEMEN P DAN K DKI JAKARTA **1775**

INDONESIA. DEPARTEMEN PENERANGAN *See* SIARAN UMUM - DEPARTEMEN PENERANGAN R.I **4686**

INDONESIA. DEPARTEMEN PERDAGANGAN. KANTOR WILAYAH PROPINSI JAWA TIMUR *See* LAPORAN - KANTOR WILAYAH DEPARTEMEN PERDAGANGAN PROPINSI JAWA TIMUR **844**

INDONESIA. DEPARTEMEN PERDAGANGAN. PERWAKILAN PROPINSI JAWA TIMUR *See* LAPORAN TRIWULAN - PERWAKILAN DEPARTEMEN PERDAGANGAN PROPINSI DJAWA-TIMUR **844**

INDONESIA. DEPARTEMEN PERIDUSTRIAN. KANTOR WILAYAH PROPINSI BALI. LAPORAN - KANTOR WILAYAH DEPARTEMEN PERINDUSTRIAN PROPINSI BALI *See* LAPORAN TAHUNAN - KANTOR WILAYAH DEPARTEMEN PERINDUSTRIAN PROPINSI BALI **1572**

INDONESIA. DEPARTEMEN PERINDUSTRIAN *See* HASIL RAPAT KERJA DEPARTEMEN PERINDUSTRIAN **1565**

INDONESIA. DEPARTEMEN PERINDUSTRIAN. KANTOR WILAYAH DAERAH ISTIMEWA YOGYAKARTA *See* LAPORAN - KANTOR WILAYAH DEPARTEMEN PERINDUSTRIAN DAERAH ISTIMEWA YOGYAKARTA **1572**

INDONESIA. DEPARTEMEN PERINDUSTRIAN. KANTOR WILAYAH PROPINSI BALI *See* LAPORAN TAHUNAN - KANTOR WILAYAH DEPARTEMEN PERINDUSTRIAN PROPINSI BALI **1572**

INDONESIA. DEPARTEMEN PERINDUSTRIAN. KANTOR WILAYAH PROPINSI RIAU *See* LAPORAN TAHUNAN **1572**

INDONESIA. DEPARTEMEN PERINDUSTRIAN. KANTOR WILAYAH PROPINSI SULAWESI TENGAH *See* LAPORAN TAHUNAN - KANTOR WILAYAH DEPARTEMEN PERINDUSTRIAN PROPINSI SULAWESI TENGAH **1535**

INDONESIA. DEPARTEMEN SOSIAL *See* LAPORAN KEGIATAN DEPARTEMEN SOSIAL **5251**

INDONESIA. DEPARTEMEN SOSIAL *See* BULLETIN STATISTIK DEPARTEMEN SOSIAL (INDONESIA) **5276**

INDONESIA. DEPARTEMEN SOSIAL. KANTOR WILAYAH PROPINSI LAMPUNG *See* LAPORAN KEGIATAN KANTOR WILAYAH DEP. SOSIAL & DINAS SOSIAL PROPINSI DAERAH TINGKAT I LAMPUNG **5294**

INDONESIA. DEPARTEMEN SOSIAL. PERWAKILAN DAERAH TINGKAT I SUMATERA SELATAN *See* LAPORAN KERJA - PERWAKILAN DEPARTEMEN SOSIAL DAERAH TINGKAT I SUMATERA SELATAN **5294**

INDONESIA. DEPARTEMEN TENAGA KERJA, TRANSMIGRASI DAN KOPERASI *See* LAPORAN TENTANG PELAKSANAAN PROYEK-PROYEK PEMBANGUNAN YANG DIPERTANGGUNG JAWABKAN PADA DEPARTEMEN TENAGA KERJA, TRANSMIGRASI DAN KOPERASI R.I **1687**

INDONESIA. DEPARTEMEN TENAGA KERJA, TRANSMIGRASI DAN KOPERASI *See* LAPORAN DEPARTEMEN TENAGA KERJA, TRANSMIGRASI DAN KOPERASI **1687**

INDONESIA. DEPARTEMEN TENAGA KERJA, TRANSMIGRASI DAN KOPERASI. TEAM POLICY RESEARCH *See* KUMPULAN KERTAS KARYA - DEPARTEMEN TENAGA KERJA, TRANSMIGRASI DAN KOPERASI, TEAM POLICY RESEARCH **1683**

INDONESIA. DEPARTEMENT PEKERJAAN UMUM DAN TENAGA LISTRIK *See* JAWABAN UNTUK D.P.R.-R.I **1613**

INDONESIA. DEPARTMEN TENAGA KERJA, TRANSMIGRASI DAN KOPERASI. BIRO PERENCANAAN. BAGIAN PENGUMPULAN DAN PENGOLAHAN DATA *See* LAPORAN STATISTIK BULANAN - BAGIAN PENGUMPULAN DAN PENGOLAHAN DATA, BIRO PERENCANAAN, DEPARTEMEN TENAGA KERJA, TRANSMIGRASI DAN KOPERASI **1535**

INDONESIA. DEPARTMENT PERDAGANGAN. PERWAKILAN PROPINSI SUMATERA UTARA *See* DAFTAR PERUSAHAAN DAGANG/JASA YANG IZINNYA DITERBITKAN **664**

INDONESIA DEVELOPMENT NEWS *See* INDONESIA DEVELOPMENT NEWS QUARTERLY **1495**

INDONESIA DEVELOPMENT NEWS *See* INDONESIA DEVELOPMENT NEWS MONTHLY STATISTICAL BULLETIN **1495**

INDONESIA DEVELOPMENT NEWS MONTHLY STATISTICAL BULLETIN (US) [26862577] **1495**

● INDONESIA DEVELOPMENT NEWS QUARTERLY (US) [27213901] **1495**

INDONESIA. DIREKTORAT BINA SARANA USAHA KEHUTANAN *See* STATISTIK EKSPOR HASIL HUTAN BUKAN KAYU **2399**

INDONESIA. DIREKTORAT BINAWISATA *See* PENUNTUN WISATA **2662**

INDONESIA. DIREKTORAT FILM *See* FILM NEWS **4070**

INDONESIA. DIREKTORAT JENDERAL BANTUAN SOSIAL *See* LAPORAN PELAKSANAAN TUGAS-TUGAS & I.E. DAN PEDOMAN PELAKSANAAN TUGAS-TUGAS **5294**

INDONESIA. DIREKTORAT JENDERAL BIMAS KATOLIK *See* MAJALAH BIMAS KATOLIK **5032**

INDONESIA. DIREKTORAT JENDERAL BIMAS KATOLIK. MADJALAH *See* MAJALAH BIMAS KATOLIK **5032**

INDONESIA. DIREKTORAT JENDERAL BINA KARYA *See* PROJECT STATEMENT DAN PEDOMAN PELAKSANAAN D.I.K. & D.I.P **5302**

INDONESIA. DIREKTORAT JENDERAL BINA KARYA *See* KEBIJAKSANAAN OPERASIONIL DAN RENCANA KERJA ROUTINE & PEMBANGUNAN **1682**

INDONESIA. DIREKTORAT JENDERAL HUBUNGAN EKONOMI LUAR NEGERI *See* LAPORAN TAHUNAN - DIREKTORAT JENDERAL HUBUNGAN EKONOMI LUAR NEGERI **844**

INDONESIA. DIREKTORAT JENDERAL MINYAK DAN GAS BUMI *See* BERITA MIGAS **4252**

INDONESIA. DIREKTORAT JENDERAL PAJAK *See* LAPORAN TRIWULAN - DIREKTORAT JENDERAL PAJAK **4735**

INDONESIA. DIREKTORAT JENDERAL PEMBANGUNAN MASYARAKAT DESA *See* KEGIATAN L.S.D. SELURUH INDONESIA **5207**

INDONESIA. DIREKTORAT JENDERAL PENCEGAHAN, PEMBRANTASAN/PEMBASNIAN PENYAKIT MENULAR *See* BERITA EPIDEMIOLOGI **3712**

INDONESIA. DIREKTORAT JENDERAL PERHUBUNGAN LAUT. KANTOR WILAYAH II. PELABUHAN DUMAI *See* LAPORAN TAHUNAN / DIREKTORAT JENDERAL PERHUBUNGAN LAUT, KANTOR WILAYAH II, PELABUHAN DUMAI **1615**

INDONESIA. DIREKTORAT JENDERAL PERINDUSTRIAN KIMIA *See* CATALOGUE P.N.P2S, PERUM. P2S, P.T.P2S INDUSTRI KIMIA **1601**

INDONESIA. DIREKTORAT JENDERAL PERINDUSTRIAN PENERBANGAN *See* HASIL RAPAT-KERJA DIREKTORAT JENDERAL PERINDUSTRIAN PENERBANGAN **22**

INDONESIA. DIREKTORAT JENDERAL TRANSMIGRASI *See* LAPORAN TAHUN ANGGARAN DIREKTORAT JENDERAL TRANSMIGRASI **1502**

INDONESIA. DIREKTORAT NAVIGASI *See* LAPORAN TAHUNAN DIREKTORAT NAVIGASI **5451**

INDONESIA. DIREKTORAT PEMBANGUNAN MASYARAKAT SUKU-SUKU TERASING *See* SERI PMST **4685**

INDONESIA. DIREKTORAT PERLINDUNGAN DAN PEDGAWETAN ALAM *See* LAPORAN TAHUNAN DIREKTORAT PERLINDUNGAN DAN PENGAWETAN ALAM **4167**

INDONESIA. DIREKTORAT PERTAMBANGAN *See* LAPORAN TAHUNAN KEGIATAN USAHA PERTAMBANGAN SWASTA NASIONAL DAN PERUSAHAAN PERTAMBANGAN DAERAH **1615**

INDONESIA: ECONOMIC STATISTICS *See* INDONESIA STATISTICS **1534**

INDONESIA ECONOMIC TRENDS REPORT (IO) [02365167] **1567**

INDONESIA, FOREIGN AFFAIRS (IO) [09698195] **2653**

INDONESIA HOTEL DIRECTORY (IO) [03349320] **2807**

INDONESIA (INDONESIA. DIREKTORAT JENDERAL PARIWISATA) (IO) [08446224] **5480**

INDONESIA. INSPEKTORAT PERKEBUNAN BESAR DAERAH IV RIAU *See* LAPORAN TAHUNAN - INSPEKTORAT PERKEBUNAN BESAR DAERAH IV RIAU **104**

INDONESIA ISSUES (US/0889-9355) [14116027] **2654**

INDONESIA (ITHACA) (US/0019-7289) [01606205] **2654**

INDONESIA. KANTOR SENSUS DAN STATISTIK DKI JAKARTA *See* HASIL PENELITIAN USAHA PETERNAKAN DI D.K.I. JAKARTA **1608**

INDONESIA. KANTOR SENSUS DAN STATISTIK PROPINSI SUMATERA UTARA *See* PENDUDUK SUMATERA UTARA **5335**

INDONESIA. KANTOR WILAYAH PERDAGANGAN PROPINSI JAWA TIMUR *See* LAPORAN TAHUNAN / DEPARTEMEN PERDAGANGAN DAN KOPERASI, KANTOR WILAYAH PERDAGANGAN PROPINSI JAWA TIMUR **844**

INDONESIA LETTER, THE (HK/0019-7297) [02663421] **682**, **1495**

● INDONESIA, MALAYSIA & SINGAPORE HANDBOOK (US/1061-9852) [25499389] **5480**

INDONESIA MIRROR (US/0889-9347) [14116032] **2654**

INDONESIA NEWS SERVICE (US/1044-3665) [18270505] **2505**

INDONESIA. PERHUTANI, DJAWA TENGAH. DIREKSI *See* LAPORAN TAHUNAN **2386**

INDONESIA REPORTS (US/0749-5315) [11135917] **2654**

INDUSTRIAL

INDONESIA. SIREKTORAT JENDERAL INDUSTRI KIMIA *See* LAPORAN DIREKTORAT JENDERAL INDUSTRI KIMIA **984**

INDONESIA STATISTICS (IO/0376-9984) [01794336] **1534**

INDONESIAN ACQUISITIONS LIST (AT/0310-6659) [03380891] **3215**

INDONESIAN AGRICULTURAL RESEARCH & DEVELOPMENT JOURNAL (IO) [05875979] **95**

INDONESIAN CAPITAL MARKET DIRECTORY (IO) [23194779] **791**

INDONESIAN COMMERCIAL NEWSLETTERS (IO/0377-0001) [02245652] **1495**

INDONESIAN ECONOMIC BULLETIN (NE) [12226728] **1495**

INDONESIAN ECONOMY BULLETIN (IO) **1495**

INDONESIAN ECONOMY, THE (IO/0215-1561) [17829424] **1495**

INDONESIAN IMPORTERS (IO) [08158436] **840**

INDONESIAN JOURNAL OF CROP SCIENCE (IO/0216-8170) [13922608] **174**

INDONESIAN MONTHLY ACTIVITIES REPORT (SI) **4260**

INDONESIAN NEWS SELECTIONS : BULLETIN OF THE INDONESIA ACTION GROUP (AT) [04671243] **4509**

INDONESIAN OBSERVER (IO) [02770713] **5803**

INDONESIAN PETROLEUM ASSOCIATION *See* PROCEEDINGS OF THE ANNUAL CONVENTION - INDONESIAN PETROLEUM ASSOCIATION **4275**

INDONESIAN PRODUCT REFERENCE (IO) [10381713] **1609**

INDONESIAN QUARTERLY, THE (IO) [01789266] **2654**

INDONESIAN STUDIES (AT/0813-4820) [16220522] **5203**

INDONESIAN TRADE, INDUSTRY, AND TOURISM REVIEW (SI) [08101817] **1567**

INDONESIEN : WIRTSCHAFTLICHE ENTWICKLUNG (GW) [02515939] **1567**

INDONESIEN : WIRTSCHAFTSDATEN UND WIRTSCHAFTSDOKUMENTATION (GW) [06234309] **1567**

INDOOR AIR (DK/0905-6947) [26899889] **2232**

INDOOR AIR BULLETIN (US/1055-5242) [23199425] **2174**

INDOOR AIR QUALITY UPDATE (US/1040-5313) [18441118] **2606**

INDOOR AIR REVIEW (US/1055-1050) [23072669] **1609**

INDOOR COMFORT NEWS (US/0446-0138) [07329768] **2901**

●INDOOR ENVIRONMENT : THE JOURNAL OF INDOOR AIR INTERNATIONAL (SZ/1016-4901) [24527286] **2174**

INDOOR GARDEN, THE (US/8750-4081) [11143983] **2420**

INDOOR POLLUTION LAW REPORT (US/0894-0533) [15743187] **3113**

INDOOR POLLUTION NEWS (US/0896-8594) [17306959] **2232**

INDOPOP NONCHONG (KO) [05120460] **3166**

INDORAIR (CN/0712-2063) [08924012] **4784**

INDORE, INDIA (CITY). UNIVERSITY *See* RESEARCH JOURNAL : HUMANITIES & SOCIAL SCIENCE **2853**

INDRAMA (II) [07121304] **2505**

INDUS (PK) [01642001] **2505**

INDUSTRIA (BL) [05720860] **1567**

INDUSTRIA (GT) [06122674] **1609**

INDUSTRIA ALIMENTICIA *SUSPENDED.* (CU) [06698584] **2344**

INDUSTRIA & FORMAZIONE (IT) **1678**

INDUSTRIA AVICOLA (US/0019-7467) [03339249] **213**

INDUSTRIA AZUCARERA, LA (AG/0325-0326) [09813463] **95**

INDUSTRIA CARBOQUIMICA CATARINENSE. DIRETORIA *See* RELATORIO DA DIRETORIA **1624**

INDUSTRIA CARNICA LATINOAMERICANA, LA (AG/0325-3414) [09148731] **213**

INDUSTRIA CONSERVE (IT/0019-7483) [02385304] **2344**

INDUSTRIA CONSERVERA (VIGO) *SUSPENDED.* (SP) [02379595] **1609**

INDUSTRIA COTONIERA (IT/0019-7491) [06822078] 1609, **5352**

INDUSTRIA DA CONSTRUCAO *See* INDUSTRIA DA CONSTRUCAO : PRECOS DE MATERIAL DE CONSTRUCAO NO COMERCIO ATACADISTA - SALARIOS NA INDUSTRIA DA CONSTRUCAO **1610**

INDUSTRIA DA CONSTRUCAO : PRECOS DE MATERIAL DE CONSTRUCAO NO COMERCIO ATACADISTA - SALARIOS NA INDUSTRIA DA CONSTRUCAO (BL) [02241993] **1610**

INDUSTRIA DE SAO PAULO: ORGAOS DIRIGENTES (BL) [02943102] **1567**

INDUSTRIA DEI FARMACI (IT/0446-0243) [04460243] **4307**

INDUSTRIA DEI LATERIZI, L' (IT) [22426552] **617**

INDUSTRIA DEL LATTE (IT) **195**

INDUSTRIA DEL LEGNO & DEL MOBILE, L' (IT) [01132373] **634**

INDUSTRIA DEL LEGNO & DEL MOBILE, L' (IT/0392-9086) [03929086] **634**

INDUSTRIA DEL MOBILE, L' (IT) [06569416] **634**

INDUSTRIA DELLA CARTA (IT/0019-7548) [06678057] **4234**

INDUSTRIA DELLA GOMMA, L' (IT/0019-7556) [06457244] **5076**

INDUSTRIA DELLE CARNI (IT) **2344**

INDUSTRIA DELLE CONSTRUZIONI (IT) **617**

INDUSTRIA DELLE COSTRUZIONI (IT) **617**

INDUSTRIA FARMACEUTICA (SP/0213-5574) [02135574] **4307**

INDUSTRIA GRAFICA & ARTES GRAFICAS (US/1054-2434) [22831522] **1610**

INDUSTRIA HOTELERA EN ESPANA (SP) [19548802] **2807**

INDUSTRIA INTERNACIONAL (SP) **1610**

INDUSTRIA ITALIANA DEL CEMENTO, L' (IT/0019-7637) [11070676] **1978**

INDUSTRIA ITALIANA DELLA MACCHINA UTENSILE NEL ..., L' (IT) [20225731] **1567**

INDUSTRIA LECHERA : ORGANO DEL CENTRO NACIONAL DE LA INDUSTRIA LECHERA, LA (AG/0046-9181) [09813489] **195**

INDUSTRIA LEMNULUI (BUCHAREST, ROMANIA : 1986) (RM) [14958363] **2384**

INDUSTRIA MECCANICA, L' (IT/0393-1331) [03931331] **2115**

INDUSTRIA MERCATO (IT) **840**

INDUSTRIA MINERA (SP/0210-2307) [12123561] **2140**

INDUSTRIA MINERARIA (ROMA. 1957) (IT/0391-1586) [06785077] 4003, **1382**

INDUSTRIA PORCINA (US/0279-7771) [07252331] **213**

INDUSTRIA, RIVISTA DI ECONOMIA E POLITICA INDUSTRIALE, L' (IT/0390-041X) [08150188] **1610**

INDUSTRIA SACCARIFERA ITALIANA (IT/0019-7734) [03388736] **2344**

INDUSTRIA SIDERURGICA EN ... / UNION DE EMPRESAS SIDERURGICAS, LA (SP) [09286040] **1610**

INDUSTRIA TESSILE (IT) **5352**

INDUSTRIA TURISTICA (MIAMI) (US/0019-7777) [05065910] **5480**

INDUSTRIA USOARA (RM) [07548648] **5352**

INDUSTRIA USOARA (1974) (RM/1017-2270) [11070345] **3184**

INDUSTRIA Y QUIMICA (AG) [06665690] **978**

INDUSTRIAL ACCOUNTANT (PK/0019-7793) [04672213] **745**

INDUSTRIAL AND BUSINESS DIRECTORY OF TENNESSEE, ARKANSAS AND MISSISSIPPI (US/0362-1286) [02441507] **1610**

INDUSTRIAL AND COMMERCIAL TRAINING (UK/0019-7858) [06588320] **942**

●INDUSTRIAL AND CORPORATE CHANGE (UK/0960-6491) [25855432] **1610**

INDUSTRIAL & ENGINEERING CHEMISTRY RESEARCH (US/0888-5885) [13659424] 2098, **2013**

●INDUSTRIAL & ENVIRONMENTAL CRISIS QUARTERLY (US) [27258806] 1610, **2174**

INDUSTRIAL & MARINE GAS TURBINE ENGINES (US/8756-2375) [11486148] **2115**

INDUSTRIAL & PRODUCTION ENGINEERING *See* EUROPEAN PRODUCTION ENGINEERING : EPE **1975**

INDUSTRIAL AND SCIENTIFIC INSTRUMENTS (UK) **3481**

INDUSTRIAL AND SOCIAL RELATIONS (SA) [29984732] **1610**

INDUSTRIAL AND TRADE DIRECTORY (MW) [20688138] 1610, **840**

INDUSTRIAL AND TRADE DIRECTORY (KE) [10032953] **840**

INDUSTRIAL AND TRADE DIRECTORY OF MALAWI (MW/0377-0028) [02243421] **840**

INDUSTRIAL AND TRADE WORLD (II) [02256124] **1567**

INDUSTRIAL ARBITRATION REPORTS, NEW SOUTH WALES, THE (AT/0155-2589) [01759971] **3149**

INDUSTRIAL ARBITRATION SERVICE INDUSTRIAL REPORTS *See* INDUSTRIAL REPORTS **3149**

INDUSTRIAL ARCHAEOLOGY REVIEW (UK/0309-0728) [03423583] **270**

INDUSTRIAL ARCHAEOLOGY (TAVISTOCK) (UK/0019-7971) [06115534] **270**

INDUSTRIAL ARTS INITIATIVE *See* INITIATIVE (ST. JOHN) **5114**

INDUSTRIAL ASSISTANCE PROGRAMS IN CANADA (CN/0826-5828) [11245775] **1610**

INDUSTRIAL BANK OF KOREA *See* ANNUAL REPORT / INDUSTRIAL BANK OF KOREA **771**

INDUSTRIAL BIOPROCESSING (US/1056-7194) [23823201] **1946**

INDUSTRIAL BULLETIN *See* INDUSTRIAL PRODUCT BULLETIN **3481**

INDUSTRIAL CASES REPORTS (UK/0306-2163) [02481058] **3149**

INDUSTRIAL CERAMICS (IT) [16149903] 1025, **2591**

INDUSTRIAL CHEMICALS AND SYNTHETIC RESINS (CN/0712-8592) [13474520] **1025**

INDUSTRIAL COMMISSION OF NEW SOUTH WALES *See* INDUSTRIAL ARBITRATION REPORTS, NEW SOUTH WALES, THE **3149**

INDUSTRIAL COMMISSION OF OHIO *See* ANNUAL REPORT / OHIO INDUSTRIAL COMMISSION [AND] OHIO BUREAU OF WORKERS' COMPENSATION **1649**

INDUSTRIAL COMMUNICATIONS (US/0737-0415) [09293288] **1113**

INDUSTRIAL COMPUTING PLUS PROGRAMMABLE CONTROLS (US/1045-0203) [20180916] **1238**

●INDUSTRIAL CONTROLS INTELLIGENCE & THE PLC INSIDER'S NEWSLETTER (US/1074-0511) [29609044] **1188**

INDUSTRIAL CORPORATIONS, FINANCIAL STATISTICS, PRELIMINARY DATA (CN/0225-9168) [02585931] **1610**

INDUSTRIAL CORROSION (UK/0265-0584) [I02650584] **2102**

INDUSTRIAL CORROSION ABSTRACTS (UK/0955-7040) [19966946] **2013**

INDUSTRIAL CRISIS QUARTERLY (NE/0921-8106) [15355954] **682**

●INDUSTRIAL CROPS AND PRODUCTS (NE/0926-6690) [26558437] **174**

INDUSTRIAL CROPS RESEARCH JOURNAL (IO/0215-8981) [21735325] **95**

INDUSTRIAL DESIGN IN AMERICA (US/0446-0375) [01541943] **2098**

INDUSTRIAL DESIGN: JOURNAL OF JAPAN INDUSTRIAL DESIGNERS ASSOCIATION *CEASED.* (JA) **2098**

INDUSTRIAL DESIGNERS SOCIETY OF AMERICA *See* DIRECTORY OF INDUSTRIAL DESIGNERS **2098**

INDUSTRIAL DEVELOPERS ASSOCIATION OF CANADA *See* MEMBERSHIP DIRECTORY - INDUSTRIAL DEVELOPERS ASSOCIATION OF CANADA **1618**

INDUSTRIAL DEVELOPERS ASSOCIATION OF CANADA. DIRECTORY *See* DIRECTORY / ECONOMIC DEVELOPERS ASSOCIATION OF CANADA **1479**

INDUSTRIAL DEVELOPMENT ABSTRACTS (US/0378-2654) [04236664] **1610**

INDUSTRIAL DEVELOPMENT AND THE SOCIAL FABRIC (US) [07237420] **1610**

INDUSTRIAL DEVELOPMENT BANK LIMITED *See* ANNUAL REPORT AND ACCOUNTS - INDUSTRIAL DEVELOPMENT BANK LIMITED **770**

INDUSTRIAL DIAMOND INFORMATION BUREAU, LONDON *See* DIAMOND RESEARCH **2138**

INDUSTRIAL DIGEST (BE) **1610**

INDUSTRIAL DIRECTORY (NR) [01787436] **1610**

INDUSTRIAL DIRECTORY FOR THE RESTIGOUCHE REGION (CN/0710-0507) [08078915] **1610**

INDUSTRIAL DIRECTORY -- NIAGARA FALLS AREA (US) [06663747] **1610**

INDUSTRIAL DIRECTORY OF SOUTH CAROLINA *See* SOUTH CAROLINA INDUSTRIAL DIRECTORY **1627**

INDUSTRIAL — Alphabetical Title Index

INDUSTRIAL DIRECTORY OF WALES (UK) [02441196] **1610**

INDUSTRIAL DIRECTORY / THE CHAMBER OF COMMERCE (US) [13997453] 820, **1610**

INDUSTRIAL DISPUTES DUBLIN (IE/0791-329X) [I0791329X] 1678, **1495**

INDUSTRIAL DISTRIBUTION (US/0019-8153) [04636591] 950, **926**

INDUSTRIAL EDUCATION *SUSPENDED.* (US/0091-8601) [01753082] **1913**

INDUSTRIAL EMPLOYMENT, EARNINGS AND HOURS WORKED, DETAILS FOR SUPPLEMENTARY NACE SUB-SECTORS (IE/0791-2927) [I07912927] 1678, **1610**

INDUSTRIAL ENERGY (US/0094-1646) [01791581] 1946, **4260**

INDUSTRIAL ENERGY BULLETIN (US/0894-5764) [16144567] **1610**

INDUSTRIAL ENERGY EFFICIENCY IMPROVEMENT PROGRAM, THE (US/0732-9776) [08480380] **1946**

INDUSTRIAL ENERGY EFFICIENCY IMPROVEMENT PROGRAM (U.S.) *See* INDUSTRIAL ENERGY EFFICIENCY IMPROVEMENT PROGRAM, THE **1946**

INDUSTRIAL ENERGY TECHNOLOGY (US/1057-4247) [24036827] **1946**

INDUSTRIAL ENGINEERING (US) [10181938] **2098**

INDUSTRIAL ENGINEERING NEWS. (EUROPEAN EDITION) (BE) **2098**

INDUSTRIAL ENGINEERING (NORCROSS, GA.) (US/0019-8234) [08262407] **2098**

●INDUSTRIAL EQUIPMENT NEWS (NEW YORK) (US/0019-8285) [01753086] **2098**

INDUSTRIAL FABRIC PRODUCTS REVIEW (US/0019-8307) [01753087] **5352**

INDUSTRIAL FABRIC PRODUCTS REVIEW BUYERS GUIDE (US) **5352**

INDUSTRIAL FINISHING. BUYERS' GUIDE (US) [11952131] **4224**

INDUSTRIAL FINISHING (WHEATON) (US/0019-8323) [01753088] **4224**

INDUSTRIAL FIRE JOURNAL (UK/0964-9719) [I09649719] **2291**

INDUSTRIAL FIRE SAFETY *CEASED.* (US) 2863, **2291**

INDUSTRIAL FIRE WORLD (US/0749-890X) [11241066] **2291**

INDUSTRIAL FISHERY PRODUCTS, ANNUAL SUMMARY *See* PROCESSED FISHERY PRODUCTS, ANNUAL SUMMARY **2311**

INDUSTRIAL FLORIDA (US) [01321476] **1610**

INDUSTRIAL GROUPINGS IN JAPAN (JA) [08392794] **682**

INDUSTRIAL HANDLING REVUE (SZ) [03533138] **1219**

INDUSTRIAL HEALTH (JA/0019-8366) [02262281] **2863**

INDUSTRIAL HEALTH & HAZARDS UPDATE (US/0890-3018) [14222020] **2863**

INDUSTRIAL HEALTH AND SAFETY (UK) **2863**

INDUSTRIAL HEATING (US/0019-8374) [02138806] **4431**

INDUSTRIAL HERALD (II) [19230746] **5113**

INDUSTRIAL HYGIENE DIGEST (US/0019-8382) [01639807] 2863, **2872**

INDUSTRIAL HYGIENE FIELD OPERATIONS MANUAL (US) [06582673] **2863**

INDUSTRIAL HYGIENE FOUNDATION OF AMERICA *See* TRANSACTIONS BULLETIN - INDUSTRIAL HYGIENE FOUNDATION OF AMERICA **2871**

INDUSTRIAL HYGIENE FOUNDATION OF AMERICA *See* MEDICAL SERIES, BULLETIN **3611**

INDUSTRIAL HYGIENE NEWS (PITTSBURGH) (US/0147-5401) [03504386] **2863**

INDUSTRIAL INDIA : OFFICIAL ORGAN OF THE ALL-INDIA MANUFACTURERS' ORGANIZATION (II/0970-5155) [01589648] **1610**

INDUSTRIAL INSIGHT (UK) **1610**

INDUSTRIAL LABORATORY (US/0019-8447) [01753092] **1015**

INDUSTRIAL LASER ANNUAL HANDBOOK, THE *See* INDUSTRIAL LASER HANDBOOK, THE **4435**

INDUSTRIAL LASER BUYERS' GUIDE (US) **1610**

●INDUSTRIAL LASER HANDBOOK, THE (US/0941-4185) [25907699] **4435**

INDUSTRIAL LASER REVIEW (US/0888-935X) [13751975] **4435**

INDUSTRIAL LAUNDERER (US/0046-9211) [03863495] **5352**

INDUSTRIAL LAW JOURNAL, INCLUDING THE INDUSTRIAL LAW REPORTS (SA) [06548464] **2982**

INDUSTRIAL LAW JOURNAL (LONDON) (UK/0305-9332) [01753093] **3149**

INDUSTRIAL LAW REPORTS (KUALA LUMPUR, MALAYSIA) (MY/0127-3051) [10238508] **3149**

INDUSTRIAL LAWS OF SOUTH AFRICA (SA) [01766034] **3149**

INDUSTRIAL LUBRICATION AND TRIBOLOGY (UK/0036-8792) [06529627] **3481**

INDUSTRIAL MACHINERY (US) **1610**

INDUSTRIAL MANAGEMENT (AT) [02246730] **1610**

INDUSTRIAL MANAGEMENT & DATA SYSTEMS (UK/0263-5577) [07087002] 682, **1259**

INDUSTRIAL MANAGEMENT (DES PLAINES) (US/0019-8471) [02225952] **1610**

INDUSTRIAL MARKET PLACE (US) **1610**

INDUSTRIAL MARKETING MANAGEMENT (US/0019-8501) [01904848] 870, **926**

INDUSTRIAL MATHEMATICS (US/0019-8528) [01716544] **3509**

INDUSTRIAL METROLOGY (NE/0921-5956) [21730519] **4030**

INDUSTRIAL MINERALS (UK/0019-8544) [01715245] **1440**

INDUSTRIAL NATION (US/1062-449X) [25623835] **2535**

INDUSTRIAL NEWS AND RESEARCH (SI) [01791304] **5113**

INDUSTRIAL NEWS (IAEGER, W.VA.) (US) [13223043] **5764**

INDUSTRIAL ORGANIZATIONAL PSYCHOLOGIST, THE (US/0739-1110) [08228905] **4590**

●INDUSTRIAL PAINT & POWDER (US/1073-4651) [29180638] **4224**

INDUSTRIAL PARKS AND AREAS IN HAWAII (US) [06158046] **1567**

INDUSTRIAL PERFORMANCE ANALYSIS (UK) [20857603] **682**

INDUSTRIAL PHOTOGRAPHY (US/0019-8595) [01639191] **4370**

INDUSTRIAL POLICY IN OECD COUNTRIES : ANNUAL REVIEW / ORGANISATION FOR ECONOMIC CO-OPERATION AND DEVELOPMENT, INDUSTRY COMMITTEE (FR) [20737445] **1610**

INDUSTRIAL POLICY NEWS (US/0888-871X) [13745690] **1611**

INDUSTRIAL PROCESS RESEARCH AND DEVELOPMENT DIVISIONAL ANNUAL REPORT / INDUSTRIAL PROCESSING DIVISION, DEPARTMENT OF SCIENTIFIC AND INDUSTRIAL RESEARCH, NEW ZEALAND (NZ) [10553478] **2099**

INDUSTRIAL PRODUCT BULLETIN (US/0199-2074) [05714171] **3481**

INDUSTRIAL PRODUCT IDEAS! (CN/0820-6759) [09403338] 4003, **3481**

INDUSTRIAL PRODUCTION AND CAPACITY UTILIZATION (US) [22190332] **1611**

INDUSTRIAL PRODUCTION. PRODUCTION INDUSTRIELLE (FR) [02253012] **1567**

INDUSTRIAL PROJECT SEARCH. ALBERTA & N.W.T (CN/1184-633X) [24266523] **617**

INDUSTRIAL PROJECT SEARCH. MANITOBA, SASKATCHEWAN, NORTHWEST ONTARIO (CN/1184-6356) [24266536] **617**

INDUSTRIAL PROPERTY (SZ/0019-8625) [01753097] **1304**

INDUSTRIAL PSYCHOLOGY (SA/0258-5200) [15799856] **4590**

INDUSTRIAL PURCHASING AGENT (US/0019-8641) [08546886] **950**

INDUSTRIAL R&D MANAGEMENT (US) [12299947] **1978**

INDUSTRIAL REHABILITATION QUARTERLY *CEASED.* (US) **1611**

INDUSTRIAL RELATIONS & MANAGEMENT LETTER (AT) **1678**

INDUSTRIAL RELATIONS (BERKELEY) (US/0019-8676) [01697206] 942, **1678**

INDUSTRIAL RELATIONS BULLETIN (VANCOUVER) (CN/0710-5940) [08858212] **1678**

INDUSTRIAL RELATIONS EUROPE (BE) [04975690] **1678**

INDUSTRIAL RELATIONS JOURNAL (KARACHI, PAKISTAN) (PK) [12714128] 942, **1678**

INDUSTRIAL RELATIONS JOURNAL (LONDON, ENGLAND) (UK/0019-8692) [01941434] **1678**

INDUSTRIAL RELATIONS JOURNAL OF SOUTH AFRICA *See* INDUSTRIAL AND SOCIAL RELATIONS **1610**

INDUSTRIAL RELATIONS LAW (UK) **3149**

INDUSTRIAL RELATIONS LAW BULLETIN (UK/0969-3637) [I09693637] **3149**

INDUSTRIAL RELATIONS LAW JOURNAL (US/0145-188X) [02341172] **3149**

INDUSTRIAL RELATIONS LAW REPORTS (UK) [06220618] **3149**

INDUSTRIAL RELATIONS LEGAL INFORMATION BULLETIN (UK) [06584288] **3149**

INDUSTRIAL RELATIONS LEGISLATION IN CANADA (CN/1192-7283) [28195039] **3149**

INDUSTRIAL RELATIONS REPORT (US) [06572694] **1678**

INDUSTRIAL RELATIONS RESEARCH ASSOCIATION *See* INDUSTRIAL RELATIONS RESEARCH ASSOCIATION SERIES NEWSLETTER **1678**

INDUSTRIAL RELATIONS RESEARCH ASSOCIATION *See* PUBLICATIONS - INDUSTRIAL RELATIONS RESEARCH ASSOCIATION **1704**

INDUSTRIAL RELATIONS RESEARCH ASSOCIATION *See* PROCEEDINGS OF THE ANNUAL MEETING - INDUSTRIAL RELATIONS RESEARCH ASSOCIATION (1978) **1703**

INDUSTRIAL RELATIONS RESEARCH ASSOCIATION SERIES NEWSLETTER (US/0749-2162) [10259886] 942, **1678**

INDUSTRIAL RELATIONS RESEARCH ASSOCIATION. SPRING MEETING *See* PROCEEDINGS OF THE ... SPRING MEETING (INDUSTRIAL RELATIONS RESEARCH ASSOCIATION : 1979) **1703**

INDUSTRIAL RELATIONS REVIEW AND REPORT (UK/0309-7269) [06129183] **1678**

INDUSTRIAL REPORTS (AT) [26702748] **3149**

INDUSTRIAL RESEARCH AND DEVELOPMENT STATISTICS ... WITH ... FORECASTS (CN/0824-8133) [11539895] 5113, **5175**

INDUSTRIAL RESEARCH IN THE UNITED KINGDOM (UK/0265-3214) [07113856] **5113**

INDUSTRIAL RESEARCH NEWS / CSIRO (AT) [08505185] **5113**

INDUSTRIAL RESEARCHER (II) [06599843] 926, **901**

INDUSTRIAL REVIEW (NAIROBI, KENYA) (KE) [12063017] 1567, **1611**

INDUSTRIAL REVIEW OF GREAT BRITAIN, THE (UK) [01791908] **1611**

INDUSTRIAL ROBOT, THE (UK/0143-991X) [03935626] 1213, **1219**

INDUSTRIAL SAFETY AND APPLIED HEALTH PHYSICS ANNUAL REPORT FOR ... (US/0734-0346) [05952007] **2863**

INDUSTRIAL SAFETY & HEALTH BULLETIN *CEASED.* (II/0019-8765) [01753106] **2863**

INDUSTRIAL SAFETY CHRONICLE (II/0301-4746) [01784268] **2863**

INDUSTRIAL SAFETY DATA FILE (UK/0262-3226) [I02623226] **2863**

INDUSTRIAL SITUATION IN INDIA (II) [01790428] **1611**

INDUSTRIAL SPECIALTIES NEWS (CN/0835-5134) [18116104] **4455**

INDUSTRIAL STATISTICS (FI) **5328**

INDUSTRIAL STATISTICS (VALLETTA, MALTA) (MM) [22835152] 1611, **1534**

INDUSTRIAL STATISTICS YEARBOOK (US) [12067944] 1611, **1534**

INDUSTRIAL STRUCTURE STATISTICS / STATISTIQUES DES STRUCTURES INDUSTRIELLES (FR) [10810904] 1495, **1534**

INDUSTRIAL TECHNOLOGY APPLICATION PROGRAM (EGYPT) *See* ANNUAL REPORT / INDUSTRIAL TECHNOLOGY APPLICATION PROGRAM **2096**

INDUSTRIAL TRAINING COMMISSION OF VICTORIA *See* ANNUAL REPORT - INDUSTRIAL TRAINING COMMISSION OF VICTORIA **370**

INDUSTRIAL VEGETATION MANAGEMENT (1982) (US/0749-145X) [09336499] **95**

INDUSTRIAL VISTA (II/0377-7383) [01790582] **1611**

INDUSTRIAL WASTE CONFERENCE, PURDUE UNIVERSITY, LAFAYETTE, IND *See* PROCEEDINGS - INDUSTRIAL WASTE CONFERENCE **1028**

INDUSTRIAL WASTE MANAGEMENT (UK/0961-4710) [I09614710] **2232**

INDUSTRIAL WASTES *CEASED.* (US/0046-9262) [02038241] **2233**

●INDUSTRIAL WASTEWATER (US/1067-5337) [27261315] 2233, **5534**

INDUSTRIAL WATER ENGINEERING See INDUSTRIAL WATER TREATMENT **5534**

INDUSTRIAL WATER TREATMENT (US/1058-3645) [24278406] **5534**

INDUSTRIAL WELDER (II/0377-7391) [01797705] **4027**

INDUSTRIAL WEST (EL MONTE, CALIF.) (US/0743-3271) [10550993] **1611**

INDUSTRIALIZACION, COMERCIO Y DESARROLLO (MX) [12438056] 1611, **840**

INDUSTRIAS (CHILE. SERVICIO NACIONAL DE ESTADISTICA Y CENSOS) See INDUSTRIAS MANUFACTURERAS **3481**

INDUSTRIAS MANUFACTURERAS (CL/0577-7976) [02349624] **3481**

INDUSTRIAS PESQUERAS (SP) [02401156] **2305**

INDUSTRIE (BE) **1611**

INDUSTRIE (GW) [02776445] **1611**

INDUSTRIE ADRESBOEK VAN NOORD-HOLLAND (NE) [01798828] **1567**

INDUSTRIE ALIMENTARI (PINEROLO) (IT/0019-901X) [10283460] **2344**

INDUSTRIE-ALMANACH UNGARN (HU/1215-007X) [25453368] **1611**

INDUSTRIE-ANZEIGER (GW/0019-9036) [03939140] **617**

INDUSTRIE CERAMIQUE, L' (FR/0019-9044) [02447612] **2591**

INDUSTRIE CFE See CFE INDUSTRIE **2038**

INDUSTRIE DE LA CHAUSSURE ET DES CUIRS ET PEAUX BRUTS ET TANNES DANS LES PAYS DE L'OCDE; STATISTIQUES. THE FOOTWEAR, RAW HIDES AND SKINS AND LEATHER INDUSTRY IN OECD COUNTRIES; STATISTICS, L' (FR) [02413833] **3184**

INDUSTRIE DE L'HABITATION MANUFACTUREE, L' (CN/0709-6836) [05761779] **2825**

INDUSTRIE DE L'INFORMATION (FR/0754-1996) [I07541996] **3215**

INDUSTRIE DELLE BEVANDE (IT/0390-0541) [06463822] **2367**

INDUSTRIE DES PATES ET PAPIERS (FR) [01131643] **4234**

INDUSTRIE, DIE (AU) [05690468] **1611**

INDUSTRIE DU CUIR (PARIS, FRANCE : 1987) (FR/0980-1367) [15814024] **3184**

INDUSTRIE ELEKTRIK + ELEKTRONIK (GW/0019-9079) [25058042] **2064**

INDUSTRIE EN ... ENERGIE, EAU, CHAUFFAGE URBAIN, MINERAIS ET MATERIAUX DIVERS, METALLURGIE (FR) [18809273] **1611**

INDUSTRIE EN ... TEXTILES, HABILLEMENT, CUIR, PAPIER, BOIS, INDUSTRIES DIVERSES / MINISTERE DE L'INDUSTRIE DES P ET T ET DU TOURISME, SESSI, DIRECTION GENERALE DE L'INDUSTRIE, SERVICE DES STATISTIQUES INDUSTRIELLES, CENTRE D'ENQUETES STATISTIQUES DE CAEN, L' (FR) [27773955] 1611, **1534**

INDUSTRIE ET ARTISANAT (FR/0073-7739) [02714368] **1611**

INDUSTRIE IN NORDRHEIN-WESTFALEN, DIE (GW) [03422537] **5328**

INDUSTRIE LACKIER BETRIEB (GW/0019-9109) [11308746] **4224**

INDUSTRIE LAITIERE See REVUE LAITIERE FRANCAISE **220**

INDUSTRIE MEISTER (GW) [24245193] **870**

INDUSTRIE SENEGALAISE, L' (SG) [06280880] **1611**

INDUSTRIE SERVICE (GW) [08832087] **3481**

INDUSTRIE SIDERURGIQUE. IRON AND STEEL INDUSTRY, L' (FR) [05203458] 1611, **4004**

INDUSTRIE SIDERURGIQUE. THE IRON AND STEEL INDUSTRY, L' (FR) [04661187] 4004, **1611**

INDUSTRIE TEXTILE (PARIS) (FR/0019-9176) [03582097] **5352**

INDUSTRIE- UND GEWERBESTATISTIK / BEARBEITET IM OSTERREICHISCHEN STATISTISCHEN ZENTRALAMT (AU) [11108474] 1611, **1534**

INDUSTRIE UND HANDELSREVUE AKTUELLE OSTHANDELS INFORMATIONEN (GW) **682**

INDUSTRIE, ZWANGSARBEIT UND KONZENTRATIONSLAGER IN OSTERREICH WIEN (AU) [18579006] **2692**

INDUSTRIEABWASSER (GW/0073-7755) [02689712] **2233**

INDUSTRIEBAU HANNOVER (GW/0935-2023) [I09352023] **617**

INDUSTRIEFEUERUNG (GW/0367-7788) [11135054] **2606**

INDUSTRIEGEWERKSCHAFT BAU, STEINE, ERDEN See GESCHAFTSBERICHT DER INDUSTRIEGEWERKSCHAFT BAU, STEINE, ERDEN FUER DIE BUNDESREPUBLIK DEUTSCHLAND **1607**

INDUSTRIEKONJUNKTUR / INDUSTRIAL TRENDS / [EUROSTAT] (LU/0258-1922) [13622681] **1611**

INDUSTRIEL DE VAUCLUSE, L' (FR) [20335533] **5800**

INDUSTRIEL SUR BOIS (SZ) **2401**

INDUSTRIELE ARCHEOLOGIE See ERFGOED VAN INDUSTRIE EN TECHNIEK **2686**

INDUSTRIELL DATATEKNIK (SW) **1611**

INDUSTRIELLE OBST- UND GEMUESEVERWERTUNG, DIE (GW/0367-939X) [03582523] **2344**

INDUSTRIELLE WELT (GW/0537-5762) [02123337] **5203**

INDUSTRIELLER PFLANZENBAU (AU) [01523877] **2420**

INDUSTRIENS UTREDNINGSINSTITUT (SWEDEN) See CURRENT RESEARCH PROJECTS **5197**

INDUSTRIES AGRO-ALIMENTAIRES (FR/0245-985X) [10193233] **2344**

INDUSTRIES ALIMENTAIRES ET AGRICOLES (FR/0019-9311) [03755507] **95**

INDUSTRIES DES CEREALES (FR/0245-4505) [08294629] **202**

INDUSTRIES ELECTRIQUES ET ELECTRONIQUES (PARIS, 1973) (FR/0302-2609) [01786061] **2064**

INDUSTRIES ET TECHNIQUES (FR/0150-6617) [11954728] **1611**

INDUSTRIES GRAPHIQUES PARIS (FR/1164-0863) [I11640863] **4566**

INDUSTRIES IN TRANSITION (US) [21590943] **682**

INDUSTRIES PARIS (FR/1167-7287) [I11677287] **1611**

INDUSTRIESTATISTIK (AU) [01785849] 1611, **1534**

INDUSTRIJA (YU) [01789039] **1611**

INDUSTRIJSKA PREDUZECA (YU) [01795719] **5328**

INDUSTRIJSKE ORGANIZACIJE (YU) [02244640] **1611**

INDUSTRIJSKI PROIZVODI (YU) [01789034] 840, **730**

INDUSTRISCOPE (RICHMOND) (US/0094-1352) [01793954] **901**

INDUSTRISTATISTIK CEASED. (DK/0070-3532) [03694117] 1611, **1534**

INDUSTRISTATISTIKK. HEFTE 1, NRINGSTALL (NO/0078-1886) [12930438] **5328**

INDUSTRISTATISTIKK. HEFTE 2, VARETALL (NO/0800-5818) [12933561] 1611, **1534**

INDUSTRITEHEMEN; PR-MAGAZIN FUER DIE INVESTITIONSGUESTERINDUSTRIE (GW) **901**

INDUSTRIVERKETS HOSTRAPPORT / STATENS INDUSTRIVERK (SW/0346-5748) [10497163] **1495**

INDUSTRY AGENTS' HANDBOOK / AIRLINES REPORTING CORPORATION (US) [11559670] **5480**

INDUSTRY & COMMERCIAL OF ZIMBABWE RHODESIA See ZIMBABWE INDUSTRY AND COMMERCE **858**

INDUSTRY AND DEVELOPMENT. GLOBAL REPORT / UNITED NATIONS INDUSTRIAL DEVELOPMENT ORGANIZATION (US) [12727935] **1611**

INDUSTRY AND DEVELOPMENT (NEW YORK. ENGLISH EDITION) (US/0197-7253) [04340054] **1611**

INDUSTRY AND ENVIRONMENT (ENGLISH EDITION) (FR/0378-9993) [07077622] **2863**

INDUSTRY AND FINANCE SERIES (US/0256-2235) [11422655] **791**

INDUSTRY AND HEALTH CARE (CAMBRIDGE, MASS.) CEASED. (US/0887-1086) [09897628] **2863**

INDUSTRY & HIGHER EDUCATION (UK/0950-4222) [17457356] 1830, **1611**

INDUSTRY & RESOURCES (CN) [05635453] **1611**

INDUSTRY CLASSIFICATION GUIDE BOOKLET FOR CONTRACTORS-EXECUTIVE SUPERVISORS (US) **1612**

INDUSTRY DIGEST (PH/0115-4419) **1612**

●INDUSTRY ENGINEER (US/1064-5683) [26330166] **1978**

INDUSTRY FACT SHEET (US/0884-8238) [02406660] **4234**

INDUSTRY INTERNATIONAL (US/0276-7317) [07411801] **682**

INDUSTRY NEWS (US) **1612**

INDUSTRY NEWS (RICHMOND, VA.) (US/8750-5525) [11505241] **5071**

INDUSTRY NORMS AND KEY BUSINESS RATIOS (US/8755-2396) [08969832] **745**

INDUSTRY NORMS & RATIOS, ONE YEAR. FINANCE, REAL ESTATE, SERVICES (US) [23131169] **791**

INDUSTRY OF FREE CHINA (CH/0019-946X) [02100887] **791**

INDUSTRY OUTLOOK UPDATE ... (CN/0712-7626) [08659387] **159**

INDUSTRY PERFORMANCE IN ... AND PROSPECTS FOR ... (PH) [12014935] **682**

INDUSTRY PLANNING SERVICE (US/0749-5870) [10292135] **1567**

INDUSTRY PRICE INDEXES (CN/0700-2033) [03421642] 1612, **1534**

INDUSTRY REFERENCE GUIDE (US) [02210488] **2420**

INDUSTRY REPORT ON SUPERVISORY MANAGEMENT COMPENSATION (US/1041-908X) [18802988] 1679, **942**

●INDUSTRY REPORT ON TECHNICIAN AND SKILLED TRADES PERSONNEL COMPENSATION (US/1063-0058) [25692964] 942, **1679**

●INDUSTRY RESOURCES / THEATER CRAFTS (US) [26088465] **5365**

INDUSTRY REVIEW (US) [04696966] 5352, **5360**

INDUSTRY REVIEW DEAKIN CEASED. (AT/1035-4107) [I10354107] **1612**

INDUSTRY STANDARD (US) [01483648] **4370**

INDUSTRY STANDARDS AND ENGINEERING DATA (US) [20960112] **4030**

INDUSTRY STANDARDS SERVICE (US/8756-9825) [11071185] **1978**

INDUSTRY WAGE AND PRACTICES SURVEY, SOUTH CAROLINA / PREPARED BY STATE BOARD FOR TECHNICAL & COMPREHENSIVE EDUCATION (US) [06638219] **1679**

INDUSTRY WAGE SURVEY. APPLIANCE REPAIR (US) [11388215] **1679**

INDUSTRY WAGE SURVEY. APPLIANCE REPAIR SHOPS See INDUSTRY WAGE SURVEY. APPLIANCE REPAIR **1679**

INDUSTRY WAGE SURVEY. BASIC IRON AND STEEL (US) [13449969] **1679**

INDUSTRY WAGE SURVEY. BITUMINOUS COAL (US/8755-559X) [08818191] **1679**

INDUSTRY WAGE SURVEY. BITUMINOUS COAL MINING See INDUSTRY WAGE SURVEY. BITUMINOUS COAL **1679**

INDUSTRY WAGE SURVEY. CANDY AND OTHER CONFECTIONERY PRODUCTS (US) [08818158] **1679**

INDUSTRY WAGE SURVEY. CIGARETTE MANUFACTURING / U.S. DEPARTMENT OF LABOR, BUREAU OF LABOR STATISTICS (US) [10680607] 3481, **1679**

INDUSTRY WAGE SURVEY. CORRUGATED AND SOLID FIBER BOXES (US/0148-9208) [03389808] 4219, **1679**

INDUSTRY WAGE SURVEY. DEPARTMENT STORES (US/0360-2060) [02244008] **1679**

INDUSTRY WAGE SURVEY. INDUSTRIAL CHEMICALS (US/0091-8156) [01786836] **1679**

INDUSTRY WAGE SURVEY, MEAT PRODUCTS (US) [03363859] **1679**

INDUSTRY WAGE SURVEY. MEAT PRODUCTS, MEATPACKING, PREPARED MEAT PRODUCTS See INDUSTRY WAGE SURVEY, MEAT PRODUCTS **1679**

INDUSTRY WAGE SURVEY : METAL MINING (US/0360-0718) [02243970] **1679**

INDUSTRY WAGE SURVEY : NONFERROUS FOUNDRIES (US/0148-9194) [03389759] **1679**

INDUSTRY WAGE SURVEY. NURSING AND PERSONAL CARE FACILITIES (US/0749-5102) [09597374] 3857, **1679**

INDUSTRY WAGE SURVEY. PETROLEUM REFINING (US) [08887862] **1679**

INDUSTRY WAGE SURVEY. SHIPBUILDING AND REPAIRING (US/0148-9747) [03397934] **1679**

INDUSTRY WEEK (US/0039-0895) [01753122] 1612, **4004**

INDUSTRYGUIDE (US) [12258351] **1612**

INDY CAR RACING See INDY CAR RACING MAGAZINE **4900**

INDY CAR RACING MAGAZINE (US/1071-1759) [28054813] **4900**

INDY REVIEW (US/1059-3179) [24563004] **4900**

INEDITOS (BL) [03031415] **322**

INF INN : INFORMAZIONE INNOVATIVA (IT) **5113**

INF-O-RAL (VERDUN) (CN/1185-7331) [25313884] **1324**

INF TELECOM & TELEMATIQUE *See* QUOTIDIEN DES TELECOMS, LE **1162**

INF TELECOM ET TELEMATIQUE PARIS (FR/0241-0362) [I02410362] **1157**

INFA ... PRESS AND ADVERTISERS YEAR BOOK *See* PRESS AND ADVERTISERS YEAR BOOK **764**

INFANCIA Y APRENDIZAJE (SP/0210-3702) [05901709] **4590**

INFANCIA Y SOCIEDAD (SP) [26114178] 1752, 5289, **4784**

INFANT BEHAVIOR & DEVELOPMENT (US/0163-6383) [03834915] **4590**

INFANT MENTAL HEALTH JOURNAL (US/0163-9641) [04540648] 3904, **4590**

INFANT SCREENING (US/0886-1315) [12832412] **3904**

INFANT-TODDLER INTERVENTION (US/1053-5586) [22576561] **3904**

INFANTRY (US/0019-9532) [04741952] **4046**

INFANTS AND YOUNG CHILDREN (US/0896-3746) [17016150] **3904**

INFANZIA (IT/0390-2420) [I03902420] **4590**

INFECTIOLOGIE (FR) [20857336] **3713**

INFECTIOLOGIE IMMUNOLOGIE (FR) **3713**

INFECTION (GW/0300-8126) [03388280] **3714**

INFECTION AND IMMUNITY (US/0019-9567) [01753126] 3672, **563**

INFECTION CONTROL AND HOSPITAL EPIDEMIOLOGY (US/0899-823X) [17410391] **3735**

INFECTION CONTROL & UROLOGICAL CARE *CEASED.* (US/0740-3615) [05024351] **3990**

INFECTION CONTROL BULLETIN (US) **4784**

INFECTION CONTROL DIGEST *CEASED.* (US/0275-0236) [07078040] **3587**

INFECTION CONTROL IN LONG-TERM CARE FACILITIES NEWSLETTER (US/1071-6580) [28697471] **4784**

●INFECTION CONTROL WEEKLY (US/1074-2905) **3714**

INFECTION REPORTER, THE (US) [14164240] **3587**

INFECTIONS IN MEDICINE (US/0749-6524) [11166619] **3735**

INFECTIONS IN UROLOGY (US/0896-9647) [17349054] **3990**

●INFECTIOUS AGENTS AND DISEASE (US/1056-2044) [23542941] **3714**

INFECTIOUS AND MEDICAL DISEASE LETTERS FOR OBSTETRICS AND GYNECOLOGY, THE (US) [14076497] **3762**

INFECTIOUS DISEASE (US) **3714**

INFECTIOUS DISEASE ALERT (US/0739-7348) [08436403] 3714, **3672**

INFECTIOUS DISEASE AND THERAPY (US/1043-2981) [19346238] **3714**

INFECTIOUS DISEASE CLINICS OF NORTH AMERICA (US/0891-5520) [14781687] **3714**

INFECTIOUS DISEASE NEWS (US/1056-9251) [19523564] **3714**

INFECTIOUS DISEASE PRACTICE (US/0162-6493) [04200093] **3587**

INFECTIOUS DISEASE REPORT (US/1040-791X) [18530558] **4784**

INFECTIOUS DISEASE WEEKLY (US/1078-2850) **3672**

INFECTIOUS DISEASES AND ANTIMICROBIAL AGENTS (US/0734-4627) [07523527] **3714**

INFECTIOUS DISEASES CAPSULE & COMMENT (US/0741-7462) [08470646] **4784**

INFECTIOUS DISEASES IN CHILDREN (US/1044-9779) [19743870] **3714**

●INFECTIOUS DISEASES IN OBSTETRICS AND GYNECOLOGY (US/1064-7449) [26387724] **3762**

INFECTIOUS DISEASES NEWSLETTER (NEW YORK, N.Y.) (US/0278-2316) [08253287] **3714**

INFECTIOUS DISEASES NEWSLETTER (NEW YORK, N.Y.) *See* ANTIMICROBICS AND INFECTIOUS DISEASES NEWSLETTER **559**

INFECTIOUS WASTES NEWS (US) **2233**

INFECTOLOGIA (MX/0185-0628) [26050066] **3714**

INFECTOLOGIKA (SP/0212-3800) [12169319] 3714, **3672**

INFEKTIONEN UND KLINIKHYGIENE *CEASED.* (GW/0178-9090) [I01789090] **3587**

INFEKTOLOGIA (BU/0861-8259) [I08618259] **3714**

INFERMIERE : NOTIZIARIO AGGIORNAMENTI PROFESSIONALI, L' (IT) **174**

INFERMIERISTICA NEUROCHIRURGICA *See* NEU **3839**

INFERTILITY *CEASED.* (US/0160-7626) [03763807] 3731, **3762**

INFERTILITY AND REPRODUCTIVE MEDICINE CLINICS OF NORTH AMERICA (US/1047-9422) [20818551] **3762**

INFFO FLASH (FR/0397-3301) [I03973301] **1752**

INFINI, L' (FR/0754-023X) [09377608] **2517**

INFINITY LIMITED (US/1050-7280) [21582076] **3396**

●INFIRMIERE DU QUEBEC (CN/1195-2695) [30013231] **3857**

INFIRMIERE ENSEIGNANTE *See* SOINS. FORMATION, PEDAGOGIE, ENCADREMENT : AVEC LA PARTICIPATION DU CEEIEC **3869**

INFIRMIERE MAGAZINE, L' (FR/0981-0560) [17801033] **3857**

INFLAMMATION (GW/0360-3997) [02245180] **3587**

INFLAMMATION RESEARCH (SZ/1023-3830) **3587**

INFLAMMATORY DISEASE AND THERAPY (US/1047-5028) [20567216] **3587**

INFLAMMOPHARMACOLOGY (NE/0925-4692) [24539380] **3587**

INFLATION IMPACT STATMENTS (US) [03116631] **1495**

INFLATION IN CANADA *CEASED.* (CN/0229-3234) [08143719] **791**

INFLATION MEASURES FOR SCHOOLS & COLLEGES (US/1057-7394) [24111353] **1830**

INFLUENZA SURVEILLANCE (1973) (US/0362-3351) [02209302] **3587**

INFLUX (MONTREAL, QUEBEC) (CN/0712-6069) [09332456] **3464**

INFO (US) [06513945] **2195**

INFO (CN) **3215**

INFO 9 (CN/0228-2453) [08071174] **5289**

INFO-AEF : FEUILLET D'INFORMATION DU RESEAU D'ACTION-EDUCATION-FEMMES (CN/0843-798X) [20495800] **5559**

INFO BASKET (CN/0710-1414) [08371771] **4900**

INFO (BERLIN, GERMANY) *See* FU INFO / [HERAUSGEGEBEN VON DER PRESSE- UND INFORMATIONSSTELLE DER FREIEN UNIVERSITAT BERLIN (FU)] **1825**

INFO-BOURG (CN/0715-7592) [10611194] **4656**

INFO CANADA (DOWNSVIEW) (CN/1187-7081) [26244844] **1188**

INFO CDAME (CN/0831-540X) [14091181] 1896, **1223**

INFO CLUB (CN/0846-2917) [25066305] **1542**

INFO CLUB (OTTAWA ED.) (CN/0846-2917) [25066309] **1495**

INFO COMMERCE (CN/0823-5414) [10420449] **840**

INFO-COMPTOIR MUSICAL (CN/0822-8167) [10517677] **4122**

INFO-COOP (CN/0826-8045) [18620029] **1495**

INFO-CREPUQ (CN/0835-1732) [17500417] **1830**

INFO DAF. INFORMATIONEN DEUTSCH ALS FREMDSPRACHE (GW/0724-9616) [I07249616] 3287, **1830**

INFO DE L'A U C C (CN/0703-8917) [03589210] **1830**

INFO-DETAIL (1991 ENGLISH ED.) (CN/1187-5321) [25882792] **840**

INFO-DETAIL / LE CONSEIL QUEBECOIS DU COMMERCE DE DETAIL (CN/1187-5313) [25882789] **840**

INFO DGA (FR) **682**

INFO-DIABETE : BULLETIN D'INFORMATION DE LA SECTION PROFESSIONNELLE DE L'ASSOCIATION DU DIABETE DU QUEBEC *CEASED.* (CN/0832-9958) [16309639] **3731**

INFO DOCUMENTATION (DRUMMONDVILLE) (CN/1183-5540) [24368699] **3215**

INFO / EUROPEAN TRADE UNION INSTITUTE (BE) [27301995] **840**

INFO-FAC (CN/1188-1356) [25423692] **5289**

●INFO / FITPAS (SZ) [26408294] 95, **1679**

INFO FRANCHISE NEWSLETTER, THE (US/0147-5924) [03200688] 926, 955, **840**

INFO (GARY, IND.) (US) [15504502] **5665**

INFO-GENEALOGIE (SAINTE-FOY) (CN/1183-0840) [24368091] **2454**

INFO / GERMAN BLUES CIRCLE (GW) [07465479] **4122**

INFO-INFOGETTABLE (GW) **1064**

INFO / ISM LIBRARY INFORMATION SERVICES (CN) **3215**

INFO IVANHOE *See* IVANOUVELLES (MONTREAL) **872**

INFO IVANHOE *See* IVANOUVELLES (MONTREAL) **872**

INFO J4B *See* ICI BOUCHERVILLE **4655**

INFO JEUNES PC (CN/0826-2616) [11240709] **4477**

INFO JOURNAL / INTERNATIONAL FORTEAN ORGANIZATION (US/0019-0144) [07095910] **4241**

INFO-LINE (WASHINGTON, D.C.) (US/8755-9269) [11464706] **1679**

INFO-LOG MAGAZINE *CEASED.* (CN/0847-4915) [22154888] **1245**

INFO LONGUEUIL (CN/0383-1272) [03202223] **4656**

INFO-MATHS (CN/0710-0027) [08192544] **3509**

INFO MEMO (US) [03458521] **3706**

INFO MEP (CN/0822-0409) [10386294] **1752**

INFO-NATURE : ILE DE LA REUNION (RE) [02686872] **4166**

INFO / NORTH YORK (CN/0821-2368) [09506628] **4656**

INFO - NURSES ASSOCIATION OF NEW BRUNSWICK (CN/0842-3210) [19486453] **3857**

INFO OCEANS (HALIFAX) *CEASED.* (CN/1180-1816) [24368234] **554**

●INFO-PARENTS (CN/1193-1833) [26758177] **2281**

INFO PC (NEUILLY-SUR-SEINE) (FR/0981-6402) [I09816402] **1268**

INFO-POINTELIERE (CN/0712-3949) [08898892] **4656**

INFO PRESSE COMMUNICATIONS (CN/0827-4711) **1113**

INFO PRESSE PARIS (FR/0991-8248) [I09918248] **1495**

INFO PREVENTION (CN/0822-6776) [10676891] **5384**

INFO-QUEBEC (CN/0226-6598) [07294922] **1259**

INFO-R.A.A.Q (CN/0820-7429) [09631067] **5289**

INFO RENOVATION. SECTEUR EST DE MTL (CN/1187-0303) [25066584] **617**

INFO RENOVATION. SECTEUR RIVE-SUD (CN/1187-029X) [25066579] **617**

INFO-RESEAU - MINISTERE DE L'EDUCATION (CN/0820-9200) [10832212] **1752**

INFO-RURAL (CN/0822-7314) [11046657] **95**

INFO-SAINT-BRUNO (CN/0714-3885) [09029873] **4656**

INFO-SARDEC (CN/0822-5591) [10105695] **1679**

INFO SECURITY NEWS (US/1066-7822) [27047208] **1226**

INFO (SHERBROOKE) (CN/0382-7755) [02801952] **1752**

INFO SID TELIDON II (CN/0822-9236) [10668957] **1133**

INFO SOURCE (ED. FRANCAISE) (CN/1184-8111) [24401723] **4656**

INFO SOURCE (ENGLISH ED.) (CN/1184-8103) [24401724] **4656**

INFO SOURCE. GUIDE TO SOURCES OF FEDERAL GOVERNMENT INFORMATION (CN/1188-7907) [27018996] **4656**

●INFO-SOUTH ABSTRACTS (US/1059-5910) [24640034] 1567, 4477, **1534**

INFO TECH *See* MAGAZINE INFO TECH **5126**

INFO TRENDS *See* TRENDS IN HEALTH CARE, LAW & ETHICS **2253**

INFO-VISU: BULLETIN D'INFORMATION ET DE LIAISON DU CLUB VISUALISATION (FR) **1113**

INFO-VOLLEY (CN/0823-6305) [09938394] **4900**

INFO WORLD DIRECT *CEASED.* (US/1067-1595) [27153241] **1188**

INFO ZAIRE (BE) [09299356] **2499**

INFOAAU (US/0279-9863) [07417700] 4900, **2598**

Alphabetical Title Index — INFORMATION

INFOBANK (IO) [07137770] 791, **730**

INFOBRAZIL / CENTER OF BRAZILIAN STUDIES (US/0736-8666) [06912857] 4477, **1567**

INFOBRIEF RESEARCH AND TECHNOLOGY (GW/0170-4664) [I01704664] **5113**

INFOBUS REPORT *See* EMBEDDED COMPUTER TRENDS **1184**

INFOCONNECTION / NEVADA STATE LIBRARY AND ARCHIVES (US) [23820804] **3215**

INFOCUS (CN/0834-3187) [16440075] **4072**

INFOCUS (EDMONTON) (CN/0839-8631) [18460001] **1752**

INFOCUS NEWS MAGAZINE (AT/0815-6905) [I08156905] **2264**

INFOCUS (PHILADELPHIA, PA.) (US/0889-6836) [14079003] **1188**

INFOCUS (PORTLAND, OR.) (US/1040-2179) [18353251] 3215, **870**

INFODB (US/0891-6004) [14942438] **1254**

INFODEX, INDEX DE LA PRESSE *SUSPENDED.* (CN/0831-2052) [15997070] **2488**

INFOFISH INTERNATIONAL (MY/0127-2012) [16841004] **2305**

INFOLETTER - INTERNATIONAL PLANT PROTECTION CENTER (US/0145-6288) [02765275] 4245, **174**

INFOLINE (BETHESDA, MD.) (US) [18718682] 3772, **5289**

INFOLIOS (CK) [05285693] **2982**

INFOMANE (CN/0229-2068) [08072109] **5786**

INFOMARKT (GW) **682**

INFOMAT (ENGLISH ED.) (CN/0380-0547) [01586374] **4698**

INFOMAT INTERNATIONAL BUSINESS [ONLINE DATABASE] (US) 682, **730**

INFOMATICS *CEASED.* (UK/0260-7247) [I02607247] **1259**

INFOMEDIARY (NE/0169-2763) [12991645] **3215**

INFONET (AT/1031-953X) **5113**

INFONETICS ANALYST, THE *CEASED.* (US/0895-8726) [16836242] **1188**

INFOOD (EDMONTON) (CN/1184-9762) [24690786] **2344**

INFOPERSPECTIVES (US/0733-9305) [08674931] **1238**

INFOPERSPECTIVES INTERNATIONAL (UK/1044-8764) [19933670] **1238**

INFOPRENEUR (US/0742-633X) [10407897] **1157**

INFOR. INFORMATION SYSTEMS AND OPERATIONAL RESEARCH (CN/0315-5986) [01752484] **1259**

INFOR MARECHALERIE (BE/0774-4323) [I07744323] **3396**

INFOR-MER. MINES (CN/0713-1445) [08874906] **2004**

INFORM - A P I Q, L' (CN/0227-1842) [07314019] **3914**

INFORM ACTION - ACTION LIBAN (CN/0712-8045) [08861983] **2654**

INFORM-ACTION - EDUCATEURS FRANCO-MANITOBAINS (CN/0822-5109) [10087981] **1752**

INFORM LETTER (WICHITA, KAN.), THE (US/0889-308X) [13866096] **5676**

INFORM REPORTS (US/0275-522X) [07164532] **2195**

INFORM (RICHMOND, VA.) (US/1047-8353) [20790475] **301**

INFORM (SILVER SPRING, MD.) (US/0892-3876) [15132949] 1188, **4370**

INFORM (WINNIPEG) (CN/0848-757X) [23659127] **1188**

INFORMA *CEASED.* (SA) [05045894] **1113**

INFORMAA QUARTERLY (AT/0816-200X) [I0816200X] **3215**

INFORMACAO BIBLIOGRAFICA (PO) [09242194] **95**

INFORMACCUEIL, L' (CN/0229-4338) [08401622] **5289**

INFORMACIO ARQUEOLOGICA : BULLETI INFORMATIU DE L'INSTITUT DE PREHISTORIA I ARQUEOLOGIA DE LA DIPUTACIO PROVINCIAL DE BARCELONA (SP) [11864802] **270**

INFORMACIO - CASA NOSTRA DE GINEBRA (SZ) [03813665] **2692**

INFORMACIO ESTADISTICA DEL DEPARTAMENT DE TREBALL (SP/1130-4553) [23893455] **1679**

INFORMACION AL DIA: ALERTA DASONOMOS *CEASED.* (CR) [04479536] **2384**

INFORMACION CIENTIFICA Y TECNOLOGICA (MX/0185-0261) [05773563] **5113**

INFORMACION COMERCIAL ESPANOLA (SP/0019-977X) [05746392] **1612**

● INFORMACION ESTADISTICA MENSUAL / BANCO CENTRAL DEL ECUADOR (EC) [26968584] **791**

INFORMACION ESTADISTICA QUINCENAL *See* INFORMACION ESTADISTICA MENSUAL / BANCO CENTRAL DEL ECUADOR **791**

INFORMACION FINANCIERA (SANTIAGO, CHILE) (CL) [04928337] **791**

INFORMACION IBERO AMERICANA (SP) [21426353] **4656**

INFORMACION LABORAL (HAVANA, CUBA) (CU/0864-0122) [17459071] **5289**

INFORMACION (MEXICO. SECRETARIA DE COMUNICACIONES Y TRANSPORTES) (MX) [05976843] **1113**

INFORMACION SISTEMATICA *CEASED.* (MX/0185-2973) [04756623] **5806**

INFORMACION SOBRE GRASAS Y ACEITES (AG/0368-0088) [03046612] **4192**

INFORMACION TECNOLOGICA DE PATENTES *See* BOLETIN DE RESUMENES DE PATENTES **1301**

INFORMACION TERAPEUTICA DEL SISTEMA NACIONAL DE SALUD (SP) [25785300] **4307**

INFORMACIONES : A.L.A.L.C., GRUPO ANDINO, S.E.L.A. Y MERCADO COMUN CENTROAMERICANO (AG) [05339274] **1567**

INFORMACIONES ARGENTINAS SOBRE GRASAS Y ACEITES *See* INFORMACION SOBRE GRASAS Y ACEITES **4192**

INFORMACIONES ESTADISTICAS (CR/0379-7015) [04579360] **3786**

INFORMACIONES GEOGRAFICAS (CL/0537-6041) [01589628] **2566**

INFORMACIONES PSIQUIATRICAS (SP/0210-7279) [03257913] **3926**

INFORMACIONES (UNIVERSIDAD NACIONAL DE LA PLATA. BIBLIOTECA PUBLICA) (AG/0326-2642) [12920284] **3215**

INFORMACIONES Y MEMORIAS DE LA SOCIEDAD DE INGENIEROS DEL PERU (PE) [03742769] **1978**

INFORMACNI BULLETIN O UCEBNICH POMUCKACH (XR) [01791735] **1896**

INFORMACNI PRIRUCKA / CESKOSLOVENSKA AKADEMIE VED (XR/0231-5386) [06855842] 2848, **5232**

INFORMACOES ECONOMICAS - INSTITUTO DE ECONOMIA AGRICOLA (BL/0100-4409) [01788049] 95, **1495**

INFORMACOES SOBRE A INDUSTRIA CINEMATOGRAFICA BRASILEIRA (BL) [03285499] **4072**

INFORMADOR APICOLA, EL (MX) [02322576] **5586**

INFORMADOR, EL (CR) [15321477] **4509**

INFORMADOR UNIVERSITARIO (VE) [06164525] **1830**

INFORMAFRICA (PO) [19797222] **2499**

INFORMAG (CN/0225-5510) [06141337] **2535**

INFORMAL LOGIC (WINDSOR, ONT.) (CN/0824-2577) [10921157] **4349**

INFORMAL MANUSCRIPT - U.S. NAVAL OCEANOGRAPHIC OFFICE (US/0565-856X) [01688740] **1450**

● INFORMAL : ORGANO INDEPENDIENTE DE LA PEQUENA, MICROEMPRESA Y DEL SECTOR INFORMAL, EL (PE) [26794385] 1495, **682**

INFORMASI (IO) [04664126] **2505**

INFORMASI POTENSI INDUSTRI (IO) [08143689] **1567**

INFORMAT (SA) [12207591] **3215**

INFORMATEUR CATHOLIQUE (1985) (CN/0833-9228) [15465607] **4964**

INFORMATEUR, L' (CG) [01787866] **1830**

INFORMATEUR (LONGUEUIL) (CN/0226-9961) [08292986] **682**

INFORMATIC USERS (BE) **1188**

INFORMATICA 70 [I.E. SETTANTA] (IT) [01795826] 2064, **1259**

INFORMATICA DEL FARMACO E DEL PARAFARMACO (IT) **4307**

INFORMATICA E DIRITTO (IT/0390-0975) [02441206] **2982**

INFORMATICA E DIRITTO: BIBLIOGRAFIA INTERNAZIONALE *See* INFORMATION TECHNOLOGY AND THE LAW: AN INTERNATIONAL BIBLIOGRAPHY **3129**

INFORMATICA I. KWADRAAT ELEKTROTECHNIEK (NE) **2064**

INFORMATICA I. KWADRAAT INGENIEURS INFORMATIE (NE) **1978**

INFORMATICA I. KWADRAAT WERKTUIGBOUW (NE) **2115**

INFORMATICA MUSEOLOGICA (XN/0350-2325) [I03502325] **4089**

INFORMATICA OGGI (IT/0392-8888) [I03928888] **1188**

INFORMATICA OGGI *See* INFORMATICA OGGI E UNIX **1188**

INFORMATICA OGGI E UNIX (IT) **1188**

INFORMATICA OGGI MENSILE (IT) **1188**

INFORMATICA OGGI SETTIMANALE (IT) **1188**

INFORMATICS ABSTRACTS (RU/0203-3054) [04224149] **3215**

INFORMATIE (NE/0019-9907) [11134777] **1297**

INFORMATIE VOOR DE BUITENDIENST (NE/0165-0041) [I01650041] **942**

INFORMATIE VOOR DE VERKOOPBINNENDIENST (NE/0167-398X) **682**

INFORMATIEBULLETIN - RAAD VOOR DE KUNST *See* RAADSADVIEZEN / RAAD VOOR DE KUNST **328**

INFORMATIEF NVR (NE/0922-4122) [I09224122] 5076, **4455**

INFORMATIERECHT (NE) [14074129] **2982**

INFORMATIERECHT AMI (NE) **2982**

INFORMATIK *SUSPENDED.* (SZ/0019-9915) [05808861] **5113**

INFORMATIK, BIOMETRIE UND EPIDEMIOLOGIE IN MEDIZIN UND BIOLOGIE (GW) [29334813] 458, **3587**

INFORMATIK - FORSCHUNG UND ENTWICKLUNG (GW/0178-3564) [26012007] **1188**

INFORMATIK IN DER LAND-, FORST- UND ERNAHRUNGSWIRTSCHAFT (GW/0939-9534) [I09399534] **95**

INFORMATIK-SPEKTRUM (GW/0170-6012) [05797269] **1259**

INFORMATION - A R C A D (CN/0702-875X) [03436747] **3166**

INFORMATION ABOUT THE OIL INDUSTRY, FOR THE OIL INDUSTRY *CEASED.* (UK) [09892963] **4260**

INFORMATION ADVISOR, THE (US/1050-1576) [18882237] **682**

INFORMATION AGE (UK/0261-4103) [08157497] **1226**

INFORMATION AGRICOLE, L' (FR/0019-994X) [03389976] **95**

INFORMATION AMERICA (US/0738-1522) [09529545] **3215**

● INFORMATION AND APPLICATION GUIDE / CANADIAN STUDIES AND SPECIAL PROJECTS DIRECTORATE (CN/1187-8401) [26290290] **2739**

INFORMATION AND BEHAVIOR (US/0740-5502) [09965070] **1113**

INFORMATION AND COMPUTATION (US/0890-5401) [14262272] **1219**

INFORMATION AND DECISION TECHNOLOGIES (AMSTERDAM) *CEASED.* (NE/0923-0408) [18811394] **2116**

INFORMATION & I.E. E DOCUMENTAZIONE (IT/0390-2439) [02401099] **1260**

INFORMATION & INSTRUCTION TECHNOLOGIES (US) 3215, **3258**

INFORMATION & INTERACTIVE SERVICES REPORT (US/1059-731X) [23996196] **1157**

INFORMATION AND LIAISON BULLETIN / INSTITUT KURDE DE PARIS (FR/0761-1285) [17169263] **2768**

INFORMATION AND LIBRARY MANAGER (UK/0260-6879) [08037226] **3215**

INFORMATION & MANAGEMENT (NE/0378-7206) [03726682] 1260, **1254**

INFORMATION AND PRIVACY COMMISSIONER/ONTARIO *See* IRC PERSPECTIVES **4658**

INFORMATION AND REFERRAL (US/0278-2383) [07347248] **5289**

INFORMATION AND SOCIETY (AT/1033-6273) 1113, **5247**

INFORMATION AND SOFTWARE TECHNOLOGY (UK/0950-5849) [15431174] 1286, **1260**

INFORMATION & TECHNOLOGY (IT) **5113**

INFORMATION AND TECHNOLOGY (IT) **5113**

INFORMATION BELLECOMBE (CN/0823-6879) [10032102] **2535**

INFORMATION BROKER (HOUSTON, TEX.) (US/0895-9927) [15433415] **3215**

INFORMATION BULLETIN - AMERICAN BAR ASSOCIATION. STANDING COMMITTEE ON SPECIALIZATION (US/0736-2765) [09086404] **2982**

INFORMATION BULLETIN - AMERICAN INDONESIAN CHAMBER OF COMMERCE, INC (US/0517-2292) [01666897] **820**

INFORMATION

INFORMATION BULLETIN - ASH (UK/0261-0590) [I02610590] **4784**

INFORMATION BULLETIN / BRI (AT) [25366662] **4192**

INFORMATION BULLETIN / CALIFORNIA AUCTIONEER COMMISSION (US) [25493049] **682**

INFORMATION BULLETIN (CENTRE DE DONNEES STELLAIRES) *See* BULLETIN D'INFORMATION - CENTRE DE DONNEES STELLAIRES **394**

INFORMATION BULLETIN - CHILDREN'S COURT OF NEW SOUTH WALES (AT/1031-6590) [I10316590] **2982**

INFORMATION BULLETIN - CHRISTIAN SOCIAL ASSOCIATION *CEASED.* (PL) [04892208] **4965**

INFORMATION BULLETIN / COMISION DE DERECHOS HUMANOS DE GUATEMALA, USA (US) [11818814] **4509**

INFORMATION BULLETIN / CORNELL FELINE HEALTH CENTER (US) [10182685] **5512**

INFORMATION BULLETIN - CORPORATIONS TAX BRANCH (CN/0709-860X) [05843439] **4732**

INFORMATION: BULLETIN DE L'A.U.A (GH) [03882409] **1830**

INFORMATION BULLETIN / ERIC CLEARINGHOUSE FOR SCIENCE, MATHEMATICS AND ENVIRONMENTAL EDUCATION (US/0888-1723) [09568168] **5113**

INFORMATION BULLETIN (GUATEMALA HUMAN RIGHTS COMMISSION/USA) *See* GUATEMALA BULLETIN **4508**

INFORMATION BULLETIN / INTERNATIONAL ASSOCIATION FOR THE STUDY OF THE CULTURES OF CENTRAL ASIA (RU/1012-6570) [08739122] **2654**

INFORMATION BULLETIN / INTERNATIONAL ASSOCIATION OF SOUND ARCHIVES (NE) [21322171] **2481**

INFORMATION BULLETIN / INTERNATIONAL ASSOCIATION ON THE POLITICAL USE OF PSYCHIATRY (IAPUP) (UK/0922-7857) [22376856] **3926**

INFORMATION BULLETIN / INTERNATIONAL ASTRONOMICAL UNION (NE/0538-4753) [02766223] **395**

INFORMATION BULLETIN - INTERNATIONAL UNION OF RADIO SCIENCE. / BULLETIN D'INFORMATION - UNION RADIO-SCIENTIFIQUE INTERNATIONALE (BE) [05299661] **1407**

INFORMATION BULLETIN - MISSISSIPPI. AGRICULTURAL AND FORESTRY EXPERIMENT STATION, MISSISSIPPI STATE (US) [06070615] 2384, **96**

INFORMATION BULLETIN, MUNICIPAL AND REGIONAL MATTERS (FR) [03522512] **2825**

INFORMATION BULLETIN - NATIONAL CENTER FOR ATMOSPHERIC RESEARCH (US/0161-6625) [03967175] **1426**

INFORMATION BULLETIN OF THE CENTRAL BUREAU FOR SATELLITE GEODESY (US/0161-2921) [02996836] **1407**

INFORMATION BULLETIN ON LEGAL ACTIVITIES WITHIN THE COUNCIL OF EUROPE AND IN MEMBER STATES (FR/0252-0877) [04586196] **3129**

INFORMATION BULLETIN ON VARIABLE STARS / COMMISSION 27 OF THE I.A.U (HU/0538-4761) [02723592] **395**

INFORMATION BULLETIN. P & R (AT/0725-6558) [I07256558] **2174**

INFORMATION BULLETIN - PACIFIC SCIENCE ASSOCIATION (US/0030-8889) [02726012] **5113**

INFORMATION BULLETIN (ROMANIAN-AMERICAN HERITAGE CENTER (U.S.) (US/0748-6502) [10989688] 2264, **2739**

INFORMATION BULLETIN : SPOD (UK) 5187, **4389**

INFORMATION BULLETIN - THE NATURE CONSERVANCY (US/0470-3847) [01348242] **2195**

INFORMATION BULLETIN / WESTERN ASSOCIATION OF MAP LIBRARIES (US/0049-7282) [06663431] 2566, **3215**

INFORMATION C B (CN/0705-307X) [03827610] **1133**

INFORMATION - CANADIAN ASSOCIATION OF SOCIAL WORKERS (CN/0315-3150) [01850770] **5289**

INFORMATION CARDIOLOGIQUE, L' (FR/0220-2476) [07791951] **3706**

INFORMATION CATALOG, THE (US/1045-3652) [09487210] **682**

INFORMATION CENTER QUARTERLY *See* INFORMATION CENTER QUARTERLY REPORTS **870**

INFORMATION CENTER QUARTERLY REPORTS *CEASED.* (US/1062-6824) [25703061] **870**

INFORMATION CHICAGO (US/0196-3643) [05795007] **2535**

INFORMATION CIRCULAR - ALASKA. DIVISION OF GEOLOGICAL AND GEOPHYSICAL SURVEYS (US/0065-5759) [03994511] **1356**

INFORMATION CIRCULAR / ALBERTA TREASURY, CORPORATE TAX ADMINISTRATION (CN/0711-5431) [08444237] **4656**

INFORMATION CIRCULAR - ARKANSAS GEOLOGICAL COMMISSION (US/0732-9075) [04913506] **1382**

INFORMATION CIRCULAR - EXPORT DEVELOPMENT CORPORATION (CN/0226-3165) [06477210] **840**

INFORMATION CIRCULAR - GEOLOGICAL SURVEY OF CANADA (1990) (CN/1184-6941) [24280218] **1382**

INFORMATION CIRCULAR / IDAHO GEOLOGICAL SURVEY (US) [13292650] **1382**

INFORMATION CIRCULAR / KENTUCKY GEOLOGICAL SURVEY (US/0451-6915) [07583485] **1382**

INFORMATION CIRCULAR (MARYLAND GEOLOGICAL SURVEY) (US/0076-4795) [01639462] **1382**

INFORMATION CIRCULAR - MINNESOTA GEOLOGICAL SURVEY (US/0544-3105) [01639064] **1382**

INFORMATION CIRCULAR - MISSOURI. DIVISION OF GEOLOGICAL SURVEY AND WATER RESOURCES (US/0884-8246) [01284002] 5534, **1382**

INFORMATION CIRCULAR - OCCUPATIONAL SUPERANNUATION GROUP (AT/1031-5543) [I10315543] **1679**

INFORMATION CIRCULAR - PENNSYLVANIA. BUREAU OF TOPOGRAPHIC AND GEOLOGIC SURVEY (US/0553-5719) [02253573] **1382**

INFORMATION CIRCULAR / SOUTH PACIFIC COMMISSION (NL/1013-9915) [05244074] **96**

INFORMATION CIRCULAR - STATE OF OHIO, DEPARTMENT OF NATURAL RESOURCES, DIVISION OF GEOLOGICAL SURVEY (US/0097-5605) [01371745] **1383**

INFORMATION CIRCULAR - STATE OF OHIO, DEPARTMENT OF NATURAL RESOURCES, DIVISION OF WATER (US/0471-265x) [01117319] **5534**

INFORMATION CIRCULAR - STATE OF TENNESSEE, DEPARTMENT OF CONSERVATION, DIVISION OF GEOLOGY (US/0492-7079) [01306588] **1383**

INFORMATION CIRCULAR - STATE OF WASHINGTON, DEPARTMENT OF NATURAL RESOURCES, DIVISION OF GEOLOGY AND EARTH RESOURCES (US/0147-1783) [01795556] **1383**

INFORMATION CIRCULAR - UNITED STATES. BUREAU OF MINES (US/1066-5544) [27023052] **2140**

INFORMATION CIRCULAR - UNIVERSITY OF THE WITWATERSRAND, ECONOMIC GEOLOGY RESEARCH UNIT (SA/0375-8087) [06184807] **1383**

INFORMATION CIRCULAR (WISCONSIN GEOLOGICAL AND NATURAL HISTORY SURVEY) (US/0512-0640) [01282288] **1383**

INFORMATION COMMUNICATION (CN) **3287**

INFORMATION, COMPUTER, COMMUNICATIONS POLICY (FR/0924-3461) [05255499] 1113, **1188**

INFORMATION COULEUR (MONTREAL) (CN/0822-8493) [11360448] **4435**

INFORMATION DENTAIRE, L' (FR/0020-0018) [09374122] **1325**

INFORMATION DESIGN JOURNAL (UK/0142-5471) [07115409] **3215**

INFORMATION DEVELOPMENT (UK/0266-6669) [12151554] **3215**

INFORMATION DIETETIQUE COLOMBES, L' (FR/0020-0034) [I00200034] **4192**

INFORMATION DIGEST (SOUTH AFRICA FOUNDATION) *See* SOUTH AFRICA / SOUTH AFRICA FOUNDATION **2643**

INFORMATION DIGEST (U.S. NUCLEAR REGULATORY COMMISSION : POCKET REFERENCE ED.) (US) [20074061] 1946, **4656**

INFORMATION DISPLAY (1975) (US/0362-0972) [12183552] **2064**

INFORMATION DOCUMENT (SOUTH PACIFIC COMMISSION) (ML/0081-2838) [09086743] **2620**

INFORMATION DU VEHICULE, L' (FR/0397-6440) [I03976440] **5384**

INFORMATION EAUX (FR/0012-9003) [03368020] 2233, **5534**

INFORMATION ECONOMICS AND POLICY (NE/0167-6245) [10007698] 1495, **1157**

INFORMATION ECONOMIQUE AFRICAINE (TI/0020-0050) [I00200050] **1495**

INFORMATION ET DOCUMENTATION - ASSOCIATION NATIONALE DE LA RECHERCHE TECHNIQUE (FR) [03658691] **3215**

INFORMATION EXPRESS / NATIONAL STANDARDS ASSOCIATION, INC (US) [10351897] **4815**

INFORMATION, FAMILY PLANNING PROGRAM (IO) [23820429] **589**

INFORMATION - FEDERATION DES C. L. S. C. DU QUEBEC. SUPPLEMENT, L' (CN/0705-8101) [04249970] **5290**

INFORMATION - FEDERATION QUEBECOISE DES DIRECTEURS D'ECOLE *SUSPENDED.* (CN/0227-5899) [07865720] **1864**

INFORMATION FILM PRODUCERS OF AMERICA *See* IFPA COMMUNICATOR **4072**

INFORMATION FINANCIERE ET LES FLUCTUATIONS DES PRIX, L' (CN/0713-3804) [09586260] **745**

INFORMATION FOR COLLECTORS (CN/0712-3620) [08831434] **1383**

INFORMATION FOR DECISION-MAKING, ANNUAL PROGRAM FOR LIBRARY DEVELOPMENT IN ARKANSAS (US) [10258865] **3215**

INFORMATION FOR MEMBERS / NOVA SCOTIA LIBRARY ASSOCIATION (CN/0826-1946) [11426768] **3215**

●INFORMATION FOR NETWORK USERS (US/1065-0660) [26496664] **1241**

INFORMATION FOR PERSONS WITH HANDICAPS OR DISABILITIES : FOR USE IN PREPARING ... RETURNS (US) [27742711] 4732, **4389**

INFORMATION FOR SENIORS (CN/0228-3123) [06960284] **5290**

INFORMATION FROM THE VOLUNTEER CENTRE MEDIA PROJECT : THE ... YEAR REPORT OF THE MEDIA PROJECT (UK) [08082639] **1113**

●INFORMATION FUTURES (US/1062-1059) [25526228] **1113**

INFORMATION / GAZ DE FRANCE (FR) [06638145] **4260**

INFORMATION GEOGRAPHIQUE, L' (FR/0020-0093) [02255727] **2566**

INFORMATION GERONTOLOGIQUE INTERNATIONALE BULLETIN (SZ) **3752**

INFORMATION GRAMMATICALE (PARIS), L' (FR/0222-9838) [08919780] **3287**

INFORMATION GROUP INC *See* RESEARCH AND DEVELOPMENT PROGRAMS GUIDE **4055**

INFORMATION GUIDE - ARIZONA DEPARTMENT OF HEALTH SERVICES (US) [06830115] **4784**

INFORMATION GUIDE FOR DOING BUSINESS IN ECUADOR *See* DOING BUSINESS IN ECUADOR **667**

INFORMATION GUIDE FOR DOING BUSINESS IN NIGERIA *See* DOING BUSINESS IN NIGERIA **668**

INFORMATION HANDLING SERVICES. LIBRARY AND EDUCATION DIVISION *See* UNITED STATES SUPREME COURT RECORDS AND BRIEFS INDEX **3068**

INFORMATION HIGHWAYS (CN/1195-3616) **1188**

INFORMATION HIPPIQUE (FR) [16286368] **2800**

INFORMATION HISTORIQUE, L' (FR/0046-9351) [02098245] **2692**

INFORMATION HOTLINE (US/0360-5817) [01910448] **3216**

INFORMATION; I C C MEMBERS' BULLETIN (FR) [02253074] **820**

INFORMATION INDUSTRY ASSOCIATION *See* INFORMATION SOURCES **3216**

INFORMATION INDUSTRY BULLETIN (US/0885-7660) [12746232] **3216**

INFORMATION INDUSTRY DIRECTORY (US/1051-6239) [21996923] **3216**

INFORMATION INDUSTRY FACTBOOK : THE INFORMATION INDUSTRY'S ANNUAL REPORT *CEASED.* (US) [17283275] **4815**

INFORMATION INDUSTRY SCAN (US/1053-0428) [22441047] **1188**

INFORMATION INFRASTRUCTURE POLICY (NE) **1188**

INFORMATION INTELLIGENCE, INC *See* INFORMATION INTELLIGENCE ONLINE NEWSLETTER **1274**

INFORMATION INTELLIGENCE, ONLINE LIBRARIES, AND MICROCOMPUTERS (US/0737-7770) [09462024] 1268, 1274, **3216**

INFORMATION

INFORMATION INTELLIGENCE ONLINE NEWSLETTER (US/0194-0694) [05312746] 1277, **1274**

INFORMATION INTERCHANGE (ATLANTA, GA.) (US/0197-2847) [05427249] **3216**

INFORMATION - L'ASSOCIATION QUEBECOISE DU TRANSPORT ET DES ROUTES (CN/0319-1818) [02442229] **5384**

INFORMATION LEGISLATIVE SERVICE (1969) (US/0020-0115) [02399374] 1752, **2982**

INFORMATION LETTER - FRANKFURTER HEFTE (GW) [01304525] **2517**

INFORMATION LETTER (LUTHERAN WORLD FEDERATION. DEPT. OF STUDIES) (SZ) [03705468] **5203**

INFORMATION LETTER / UNITED NATIONS, DIVISION OF NARCOTIC DRUGS (AU/0378-2220) [02214905] **4307**

INFORMATION LISTING / REGIONAL CLERK'S DEPT (CN/0826-0613) [10805542] **4656**

INFORMATION LITTERAIRE, L' (FR/0020-0123) [01639904] **3396**

INFORMATION - LUTHERAN WORLD FEDERATION NEWS SERVICE (SZ) [01779507] **5061**

INFORMATION MALAYSIA See INFORMATION MALAYSIA ... YEARBOOK **2654**

INFORMATION MALAYSIA ... YEARBOOK (MY) [27376303] **2654**

INFORMATION MANAGEMENT & COMPUTER SECURITY (UK/0968-5227) [28873934] **1188**

●INFORMATION MANAGEMENT & TECHNOLOGY (UK) [25289535] 1209, 5113, **3258**

INFORMATION MANAGEMENT & TECHNOLOGY / ANBAR ABSTRACTS (UK/0959-2350) [22877241] **5175**

INFORMATION MANAGEMENT BULLETIN (US/1046-9303) [20242098] **1188**

●INFORMATION MANAGEMENT IN HEALTH CARE / FULL SERVICE (UK/1353-8853) **870**

●INFORMATION MANAGEMENT IN HEALTH CARE / HOSPITAL SYSTEMS SERVICE (UK/1353-8888) **3786**

●INFORMATION MANAGEMENT IN HEALTH CARE / IM & T SERVICE (UK/1353-8861) 3786, **3587**

●INFORMATION MANAGEMENT IN HEALTH CARE / PRIMARY CARE SERVICE (UK/1353-887X) 3738, **3587**

INFORMATION MANAGEMENT (MUNCHEN) (GW/0930-5181) [I09305181] **682**

INFORMATION MANAGEMENT POLICIES AND SERVICES (US) **3216**

INFORMATION MANAGEMENT REPORT (UK/0961-7612) [23591518] **1157**

INFORMATION MANAGEMENT SOURCEBOOK (US/0897-3199) [15511977] 1188, **3216**

INFORMATION MARKETING HANDBOOK, THE (US) [20714444] **926**

●INFORMATION MARKETPLACE DIRECTORY (US/1065-0393) [26491340] **682**

INFORMATION MEDIA & TECHNOLOGY See INFORMATION MANAGEMENT & TECHNOLOGY **3258**

INFORMATION MONT-ROLLAND (CN/0710-586X) [08777524] **4656**

INFORMATION MOSCOW (RU) [06190312] **5480**

●INFORMATION NETWORKS (US/1073-8126) [29534462] **1113**

INFORMATION NORTH (CN/0315-2561) [01690883] **2535**

INFORMATION OM ORGANISATION, STYRELSEORGAN, FAKULTETER, INSTITUTIONER OCH ANSTALLDA (SW) [02979033] **1830**

INFORMATION PAMPHLET - CALIFORNIA. DEPT. OF JUSTICE (US) [01784769] **3107**

INFORMATION PAMPHLET - DEPARTMENT OF EMPLOYMENT AND SOCIAL SERVICES (BALTIMORE) (US/0092-9476) [01787265] **5290**

INFORMATION PAMPHLET - SOUTH DAKOTA GEOLOGICAL SURVEY (US/0091-9012) [03791657] **1383**

INFORMATION PAPER - AUSTRALIAN BUREAU OF STATISTICS (AT/0817-9344) [I08179344] **1926**

INFORMATION PAPER - COMMITTEE FOR ECONOMIC DEVELOPMENT OF AUSTRALIA (AT) [03725585] **1495**

INFORMATION PHARMACEUTIQUES (FR) [01188450] **4307**

INFORMATION PHILOSOPHIE (SZ) [19750291] **4349**

INFORMATION PLEASE ALMANAC, ATLAS AND YEARBOOK (US/0073-7860) [01389167] **1926**

●INFORMATION PLEASE ENVIRONMENTAL ALMANAC, THE (US/1057-8293) [24124264] **2174**

... INFORMATION PLEASE SPORTS ALMANAC, THE (US/1046-4980) [20429949] **4900**

INFORMATION PRACTICES IN WYOMING STATE GOVERNMENT (US/0364-9334) [02709081] **4656**

INFORMATION PROCESSING & MANAGEMENT (UK/0306-4573) [02243314] **3216**

●INFORMATION PROCESSING COMPENSATION SURVEY (CN/1188-1305) [26497864] **1679**

INFORMATION PROCHE-ORIENT (CN/0711-2157) [08767146] **2654**

INFORMATION PSYCHIATRIQUE (FR/0020-0204) [20848799] **3926**

INFORMATION PUBLISHING (US/1058-4730) [24303953] 4815, **2920**

INFORMATION PUMPEN UND VERDICHTER (GW) [10639210] **2116**

INFORMATION REPORT (CN) [25360057] **2384**

INFORMATION REPORT BC-X/ FORESTRY CANADA, PACIFIC AND YUKON REGION, PACIFIC FORESTRY CENTRE (CN) [21491330] **2384**

INFORMATION REPORT - DEPARTMENT OF CONSUMER AFFAIRS AND ENVIRONMENT, RESEARCH AND ASSESSMENT BRANCH (CN/0713-1682) [08963956] **1297**

INFORMATION REPORT DPC-X (CN/0705-324X) [I0705324X] **2384**

INFORMATION REPORT / FORESTRY CANADA (CN) [21967908] **2384**

INFORMATION REPORT - GREAT LAKES FORESTRY CENTRE (CN/0832-7122) [20034507] **2384**

INFORMATION REPORT - NEWFOUNDLAND FORESTRY CENTRE (CN/0831-8255) [16685510] **2385**

INFORMATION REPORT - NORTHERN FORESTRY CENTRE (CN/0831-8247) [14368739] **2385**

INFORMATION REPORT / PETAWAWA NATIONAL FORESTRY INSTITUTE (CN/0706-1854) [09166965] **2385**

INFORMATION REPORT (WASHINGTON, D.C.), THE (US/0733-8961) [03905842] **682**

INFORMATION REPORTS AND BIBLIOGRAPHIES (US/0360-0971) [02243762] **3216**

INFORMATION REPORTS (OREGON. DEPARTMENT OF FISH AND WILDLIFE. FISH DIVISION) (US) [10057444] **2305**

INFORMATION RESEARCH AND RESOURCE REPORTS (US) [09358894] **5113**

INFORMATION RESEARCH NEWS (UK/0959-8928) **3216**

INFORMATION RESOURCES MANAGEMENT JOURNAL (US/1040-1628) [18337047] **3216**

INFORMATION RETRIEVAL & LIBRARY AUTOMATION (US/0020-0220) [02463301] **1275**

INFORMATION SAINT-CONSTANT (CN/0714-508X) [09054291] **4656**

INFORMATION (SAINTE-JULIE) (CN/0700-9062) [03248530] **5786**

INFORMATION SCIENCE ABSTRACTS (US/0020-0239) [02244657] 3216, **3258**

INFORMATION SCIENCES (US/0020-0255) [01753138] **3216**

●INFORMATION SCIENCES, APPLICATIONS (US/1069-0115) [27880854] **3216**

INFORMATION SCIENTIFIQUE DU BIOLOGISTE, L' *CEASED.* (FR/0337-2723) [17287895] **458**

INFORMATION SEARCHER (US/1055-3916) [23161427] **1752**

INFORMATION SECURITY SERVICE (UK) **1226**

INFORMATION SERIES - ASPHALT INSTITUTE (US/0097-4560) [01334739] **2024**

INFORMATION SERIES / COLORADO GEOLOGICAL SURVEY (US/0271-0285) [02129065] **1383**

INFORMATION SERIES - COLORADO WATER RESOURCES RESEARCH INSTITUTE (US/0198-8735) [03957225] 5534, **2195**

INFORMATION SERIES. GROUP 2: DESIGN AND CONSTRUCTION OF TRANSPORTATION FACILITIES (US/0148-8473) [03389536] **5384**

INFORMATION SERIES / INTERNATIONAL GRAIN LEGUME INFORMATION CENTRE *CEASED.* (NR) [08933023] **174**

INFORMATION SERIES (MISSISSIPPI. BUREAU OF GEOLOGY) (US) [08745494] 1383, **1356**

INFORMATION SERIES - NATIONAL TRUST FOR HISTORIC PRESERVATION IN THE UNITED STATES (US/1054-6855) [21457203] **2739**

INFORMATION SERIES - QUEENSLAND DEPARTMENT OF PRIMARY INDUSTRIES (AT/0727-6273) [23735709] **458**

INFORMATION SERIES - TENNESSEE STATE BOARD OF VOCATIONAL EDUCATION (US/0093-9889) [01792968] **1913**

INFORMATION SERIES - VIRGINIA POLYTECHNIC INSTITUTE AND STATE UNIVERSITY. COLLEGE OF AGRICULTURE AND LIFE SCIENCES (US/0742-7425) [10437112] **96**

INFORMATION SERVICE (IT) [03574014] **4965**

INFORMATION SERVICE / AMERICAN GAS ASSOCIATION (US) [08311509] **4260**

INFORMATION SERVICE FOR THE DISABLED (UK) **4389**

INFORMATION SERVICE NEWS AND ABSTRACTS / ADVISORY, CONCILIATION AND ARBITRATION SERVICE, WORK RESEARCH UNIT (UK/0951-0524) [14096664] **942**

INFORMATION SERVICES & USE (NE/0167-5265) [07904883] **3216**

INFORMATION SERVICES UPDATE (US/1052-1658) [22200767] **3216**

INFORMATION SHARING INDEX (US) [08680168] **5290**

INFORMATION SHEET - MISSISSIPPI STATE UNIVERSITY. AGRICULTURAL AND FORESTRY EXPERIMENT STATION (US/0090-256X) [03755604] **96**

INFORMATION SHEET - MISSISSIPPI STATE UNIVERSITY. COOPERATIVE EXTENSION SERVICE (US/0886-5787) [09772620] **1542**

INFORMATION SHEETS (UK) **2344**

INFORMATION SOCIETY, THE (US/0197-2243) [05986609] **3216**

INFORMATION SOLUTIONS/ INFORMATION PLUS (CN/0824-3514) [10446048] 870, **926**

INFORMATION SOURCES (US/0734-9637) [08565041] **3216**

INFORMATION STANDARDS QUARTERLY (US/1041-0031) [18606259] **3217**

INFORMATION STATEMENT FOR APPLICANTS AND GRANTEES MODEL PROJECTS ON AGING (US) [04271070] **5179**

INFORMATION STRATEGY (US/0743-8613) [10686488] **870**

INFORMATION SUR LES TEXTILES SYNTHETIQUES ET CELLULOSIQUES (FR) [02803757] **5352**

●INFORMATION SYSTEMS IN GROUP PRACTICE SURVEY (US/1065-8009) [26739193] **3587**

●INFORMATION SYSTEMS JOURNAL (US/0887-5561) [13306511] **3217**

●INFORMATION SYSTEMS JOURNAL (UK) [29858565] **1247**

INFORMATION SYSTEMS MANAGEMENT (US/1058-0530) [24100837] 1247, **870**

INFORMATION SYSTEMS (OXFORD) (UK/0306-4379) [02241895] **1254**

INFORMATION SYSTEMS RESEARCH (US/1047-7047) [20750174] **1188**

●INFORMATION SYSTEMS SECURITY (US/1065-898X) [26331817] **1226**

INFORMATION SYSTEMS SECURITY PRODUCTS AND SERVICES CATALOGUE / PREPARED BY THE NATIONAL SECURITY AGENCY (US) [19674136] **3693**

INFORMATION SYSTEMS SPENDING: AN ANALYSIS OF TRENDS AND STRATEGIES (US) **1188**

INFORMATION TECHNOLOGIES (FR) **5113**

INFORMATION TECHNOLOGY & LEARNING (UK/0952-7923) [24565851] 1264, **1286**

INFORMATION TECHNOLOGY AND LIBRARIES (US/0730-9295) [08144340] **3217**

INFORMATION TECHNOLOGY AND PEOPLE *CEASED.* (UK/0261-1732) [09812799] 1188, **3217**

●INFORMATION TECHNOLOGY & PEOPLE (WEST LINN, OR.) (US/0959-3845) [26406505] **870**

INFORMATION TECHNOLOGY & PUBLIC POLICY (UK/0266-8513) [I02668513] **1188**

INFORMATION TECHNOLOGY AND THE LAW: AN INTERNATIONAL BIBLIOGRAPHY (NE/0925-9872) **3129**

●INFORMATION TECHNOLOGY DIGEST/ INFORMATION TECHNOLOGY DIVISION, UNIVERSITY OF MICHIGAN (US) [25521960] 1241, 1279, **1268**

INFORMATION — Alphabetical Title Index

INFORMATION TECHNOLOGY IN EDUCATION. NETWORK USER (UK) 1752, **1242**

INFORMATION TECHNOLOGY IN HEALTH CARE (UK) **4784**

INFORMATION TECHNOLOGY INDEX (AT/1036-0352) [I10360352] **1188**

INFORMATION TECHNOLOGY MANAGEMENT (AT/1322-3526) 870, **5113**

INFORMATION TECHNOLOGY NEWSLETTER (HARRISBURG, PA.) (US/1057-7939) [23241975] **3217**

● INFORMATION TECHNOLOGY OUTLOOK: LES PERSPECTIVES DES TECHNOLOGIES DE L'INFORMATION (FR) [25686590] **5113**

● INFORMATION TECHNOLOGY SERVICES MEMBER DIRECTORY (US/1060-3344) [24933145] **5113**

INFORMATION TEXT SERIES / HAWAII INSTITUTE OF TROPICAL AGRICULTURE AND HUMAN RESOURCES (US/0271-9908) [06740223] **96**

INFORMATION TIMES (1983) ***CEASED.*** (US/8756-0941) [10953215] **3258**

INFORMATION TODAY (US/8755-6286) [10142299] 1268, 1274, **3217**

INFORMATION U.M.R.C (CN/0821-1094) [09747539] **4656**

INFORMATION UND DOKUMENTATION : ANNOTIERTE TITELLISTE (GW) [04121687] **3217**

INFORMATION UPDATE - CANADIAN STANDARDS ASSOCIATION (CN/1182-0187) [22366872] **1978**

INFORMATION UPDATE/ DATABASE TECHNOLOGY (UK/0951-9327) [16163057] **1188**

INFORMATION UPDATE - HUB, INFORMATION SERVICES (CN/0713-8474) [09084920] **4389**

INFORMATION UPDATE / LEAGUE OF OREGON CITIES (US/0731-1443) [06657933] **2535**

INFORMATION - VMS (SZ/1016-2690) [I10162690] **4089**

INFORMATION WORLD EN ESPANOL (UK/0965-3821) [I09653821] **3217**

INFORMATION WORLD REVIEW (UK/0950-9879) [05881600] 1242, 1275, **1277**

INFORMATIONAL BULLETIN - MARINE BIOLOGICAL LABORATORY ***CEASED.*** (US/0192-2300) [04964680] **554**

INFORMATIONAL LETTER - NEW YORK (STATE). DEPT. OF SOCIAL SERVICES (US) [05110661] **5290**

INFORMATIONAL SERIES - GULF STATES MARINE FISHERIES COMMISSION (US/0434-9474) [01331722] **2305**

INFORMATIONEN (GW) [01787183] **213**

INFORMATIONEN AUS ORTHODONTIE UND KIEFERORTHOPADIE (GW/0020-0336) [I00200336] **1325**

INFORMATIONEN FRESENIUS FUR KRANKENSCHWESTERN UND KRANKENPFLEGER (GW/0932-4313) [10719067] **3857**

INFORMATIONEN FUER DIE FISCHWIRTSCHAFT (GW/0020-0344) [02407618] **2305**

INFORMATIONEN FUER DIE MUSEEN DER DDR (GW) [01786073] **4089**

INFORMATIONEN FUR DIE BERATUNGS- UND VERMITTLUNGSDIENSTE (GW) [01789594] **1679**

INFORMATIONEN UND MATERIALIEN ZUR GEOGRAPHIE DER EUREGIO RHEIN-MAAS (GW/0343-494X) [07578105] **2566**

INFORMATIONEN - UNIVERSITAT BIELEFELD (GW) [05367213] **5113**

INFORMATIONEN ZUM STEUERRECHT (GW) **2982**

INFORMATIONEN ZUR DEUTSCHDIDAKTIK (AU) [05845350] **3287**

INFORMATIONEN ZUR MODERNEN STADTGESCHICHTE : IMS (GW/0340-1774) [02141729] **2825**

INFORMATIONEN ZUR ORTS-, REGIONAL- UND LANDESPLANUNG (SZ/0300-3981) [01423693] **96**

INFORMATIONEN ZUR POLITISCHEN BILDUNG (GW) [08015533] **4477**

INFORMATIONEN ZUR RAUMENTWICKLUNG (GW/0303-2493) [01793263] **2825**

INFORMATIONES SACRA CONGREGATIO PRO RELIGIOSIS ET INSTITUTIS SAECULARIBUS (IT) **5030**

INFORMATIONS - AEC, DEPARTEMENT ALIMENTATION ANIMALE (FR) [03962599] **5512**

INFORMATIONS CANADIENNES 1969 (FR/0768-9098) [I07689098] **820**

INFORMATIONS CHIMIE (EDITION FRANCAISE) (FR/0020-045X) [03582615] **978**

INFORMATIONS CHIMIE HEBDO (FR/0339-6045) [11416441] **978**

INFORMATIONS CNC (FR/0397-8435) [02710578] **4072**

INFORMATIONS DU COMMERCE EXTERIEUR (BE) [08661460] **840**

INFORMATIONS ECONOMIQUES (SHARIKAH AL-TUNISIYAH LIL-BANK) (TI) [08364619] **1567**

INFORMATIONS ET DOCUMENTS - BCEOM (FR) [03055808] **5113**

INFORMATIONS HOSPITALIERES (FR/0763-0387) [I07630387] **3786**

INFORMATIONS INTERNATIONALES (FR) **1635**

INFORMATIONS MONDIALES - UNDA (BE/0258-9494) [I02589494] **1133**

INFORMATIONS SOCIALES (FR/0046-9459) [02262318] **5247**

INFORMATIONS STATISTIQUES - MINISTERE DE L'EDUCATION NATIONALE, SERVICE DES STATISTIQUES (LU) [06462942] **1752**

INFORMATIONS STATISTIQUES RAPIDES (INSTITUT NATIONAL DE LA STATISTIQUE ET DES ETUDES ECONOMIQUES (FRANCE)) (RE/0336-3791) [09358024] **5329**

INFORMATIONS TECHNIQUES - CEMAGREF (FR/0755-2181) [I07552181] **96**

INFORMATIONS TECHNIQUES DE SERVICES VETERINAIRES (FR) [06236859] **5512**

INFORMATIONSBLATT FUR DEUTSCHE WISSENSCHAFTLER IM AUSLAND (GW) [01794113] **5113**

INFORMATIONSBRIEF AUSLANDERRECHT (GW/0174-2108) [10278852] **2982**

INFORMATIONSDIENST BIBLIOTHEKSWESEN ***CEASED.*** (GW/0044-1457) [I00441457] **3217**

INFORMATIONSDIENST SUDLICHES AFRIKA (GW/0721-5088) [I07215088] 1567, **4477**

INFORMATIONSDIENST VDI : INSTANDHALTUNG (GW/0724-1976) **1978**

INFORMATIONSDIENST - VEREIN DEUTSCHER INGENIEURE. BLECHBEARBEITUNG (GW/0170-9526) [I01709526] **4004**

INFORMATIONSDIENST - VEREIN DEUTSCHER INGENIEURE. ELEKTRISCH ABTRAGENDE FERTIGUNGSVERFAHREN (GW/0170-9569) [I01709569] **2064**

INFORMATIONSDIENST - VEREIN DEUTSCHER INGENIEURE. KALTMASSIVUMFORMUNG (GW/0170-9550) [I01709550] **1978**

INFORMATIONSDIENST - VEREIN DEUTSCHER INGENIEURE. MECHANISCHE VERBINDUNGSTECHNIK (GW/0720-9886) [I07209886] **1978**

INFORMATIONSDIENST - VEREIN DEUTSCHER INGENIEURE. NEUE FERTIGUNGSVERFAHREN (GW/0720-9878) [I07209878] **1978**

INFORMATIONSDIENST - VEREIN DEUTSCHER INGENIEURE. SCHMIEDEN UND PRESSEN (GW/0171-3647) [I01713647] **1978**

INFORMATIONSDIENST - VEREIN DEUTSCHER INGENIEURE. STRANGPRESSEN VON METALLEN (GW/0721-7242) [I07217242] **1978**

INFORMATIONSTAG FUR SPRENGTECHNIK INTERNATIONAL : PROCEEDINGS / MEDIENENHABER UND HERSTELLER, WIRTSCHAFTSFORDERUNGSTNSTIT UT DER KAMMER DER GEWERPLICHEN WIRTSCHAFT FUR GEROSTEREICH (AU) [11570411] **5113**

INFORMATIONSTECHNIK (GW/0179-9738) [13882483] **1188**

● INFORMATIONSTECHNIK UND TECHNISCHE INFORMATIK : IT + TI / ORGAN DER FACHBEREICHE 3 "TECHNISCHE INFORMATIK UND ARCHITEKTUR VON RECHENSYSTEMEN" UND 4 "INFORMATIONSTECHNIK UND TECHNISCHE NUTZUNG DER INFORMATIK" DER GI E.V (GW/0944-2774) [28981191] **1188**

INFORMATIONSZENTRUM DRITTE WELT *See* BLATTER DES IZ3W **1548**

INFORMATIONWEEK (MANHASSET, N.Y.) (US/8750-6874) [11636008] **1260**

INFORMATIQUE DANS LES ADMINISTRATIONS FRANCAISES, L' (FR) [03754251] **4656**

INFORMATIQUE DANS LES ENTREPRISES PUBLIQUES ET SON EVOLUTION AU COURS DES TROIS PROCHAINES ANNEES *See* INFORMATIQUE DANS LES ENTREPRISES PUBLIQUES, L' **4656**

INFORMATIQUE DANS LES ENTREPRISES PUBLIQUES, L' (FR) [03497239] **4656**

INFORMATIQUE DOCUMENTAIRE PARIS, L' (FR/0249-3381) [I02493381] **1189**

INFORMATIQUE. E33 (FR) **1189**

INFORMATIQUE ET BUREAUTIQUE : L'HEBDO ROMAND DE L'INFORMATIQUE (SZ) **1229**

INFORMATIQUE ET SCIENCES JURIDIQUES (FR) [06368015] **1226**

INFORMATIQUE ET STRATEGIE D'ENTREPRISE (FR) **5113**

INFORMATIQUE PROFESSIONNELLE, L' (FR/0750-1080) [09530670] **1260**

INFORMATIQUE QUEBEC (CN/0706-1773) [06141453] 1292, **1260**

INFORMATIQUE U.S. EN DIRECT, L' (FR/0243-4695) [I02434695] **5113**

INFORMATIQUE US EN DIRECT *See* INFORMATION TECHNOLOGIES **5113**

INFORMATIVE BULLETIN - CAPITAL MARKETS DEVELOPMENT PROGRAM (US) [02243532] **901**

INFORMATIVE BULLETIN (SAVEZNI ZAVOD ZA MEUNARODNU NAUCNU, PROSVJETNO-KULTURNU I TEHNICKU SARADNJU (YUGOSLAVIA)) (YU) [08260735] **5247**

INFORMATIVE CIRCULAR - OHIO BIOLOGICAL SURVEY (US/0270-5443) [01781442] **458**

INFORMATIVO (BL) [01792326] **3166**

INFORMATIVO (BL/0524-2932) [02813082] **5203**

INFORMATIVO ANUAL DA INDUSTRIA CARBONIFERA / MINISTERIO DAS MINAS E ENERGIA, DEPARTAMENTO NACIONAL DA PRODUCAO MINERAL, DNPM (BL) [09265630] **1612**

INFORMATIVO - ASSOCIACAO CATARINENSE DO MINISTERIO PUBLICO (BL) [03007635] **2982**

INFORMATIVO - CENTRO INTERAMERICANO DE ADMINISTRADORES TRIBUTARIOS (PN) [04361103] **4732**

INFORMATIVO CLAT (VE) [02942879] **1679**

INFORMATIVO DEL MINISTERIO / MINISTERIO DE AGRICULTURA, CHILE (CL) [23980368] **96**

INFORMATIVO DO INT (BL/0019-0233) [05076912] **5113**

INFORMATIVO ESTADISTICO (CL/0577-8514) [03115885] **5329**

INFORMATIVO ESTATISTICO DE MERCADO AGRICOLA DE GOIAS (BL) [01796207] **96**

INFORMATIVO FUNAI - FUNDACAO NACIONAL DO INDIO (BL) [02207953] **2739**

INFORMATIVO JURIDICO (WASHINGTON D.C.) (US/0747-6574) [10307123] **3129**

INFORMATIVO LEGAL AGRARIO : UNA PUBLICACION MENSUAL DEL CEPES / CENTRO PERUANO DE ESTUDIOS SOCIALES (PE) [19700450] **96**

INFORMATIVO LEGAL RODRIGO (PE) [06322862] **2982**

INFORMATIVO MAI DE ENSINO DO ESTADO DE MINAS GERAIS (BL) [02240000] 1752, **2982**

INFORMATIVO MENSUAL (AG) [05637761] **840**

INFORMATIVO - SNI (CK/0302-4830) [01793366] **5113**

INFORMATIZATION AND THE PUBLIC SECTOR (NE/0925-5052) [24487358] **1189**

INFORMATIZATION WHITE PAPER (JA) [17360970] **1189**

INFORMATOR I SKAD OSOBOWY NA ROK AKADEMICKI ... / POLITECHNIKA POZNANSKA (PL) [11462824] **1978**

INFORMATOR (MONTREAL) (CN/0381-131X) [08003210] **2982**

INFORMATOR ROBOTNICZY (PL) [01786575] **1679**

INFORMATORE AGRARIO, L' (IT) [03582633] **96**

INFORMATORE BOTANICO ITALIANO (IT/0020-0697) [03755674] **514**

INFORMATORE DEL RECUPERO, L' (IT/0393-0793) [I03930793] **2217**

INFORMATORE FARMACEUTICO : ANNUARIO ITALIANO DEI MEDICAMENTI E DEI LABORATORI, L' (IT/0392-3010) [03532953] **4308**

INFORMATORE FITOPATOLOGICO (IT/0020-0735) [01753143] **514**

INFORMATORE GIURIDICO DELLE ATTIVITA SPORTIVE, L' (IT/0394-9885) [I03949885] **2982**

INFORMATORE INAZ (IT) **1495**

INFORMATORE LEGISLATIVO (ITALY), L' ***CEASED.*** (IT) [04787860] **2982**

INFORMATORE MARITTIMO (IT) **5450**

INFORMATORE PIROLA (IT) **2982**

INFORMATORE. POLITICO ECONOMICO CULTURALE, L' (IT) **1635**

INFORMATORE SCOLASTICO (IT) **1092**

INFORMATORE ZOOTECNICO (IT/0020-0778) [03339276] **213**

INFORMATSIINYI BIULETEN - UKRAINSKA BIBLIOTEKA IMENY S. PETLIURY V PARYZHI (FR) [02457468] **3217**

INFORMATSIONEN BIULETIN. KHRANITELNA PROMISHLENOST (BU/0453-8315) [01791108] **2344**

INFORMATSIONNYE MATERIALY / AKADEMIIA NAUK SSSR, FILOSOFSKOE OBSHCHESTVO SSSR (RU/0207-6861) [15371845] **4349**

INFORMATSIONNYE MATERIALY INSTITUTA EKOLOGII RASTENII I ZHIVOTNYKH (RU) [02243255] **2217**

INFORMATSIONNYE MATERIALY ; KIBERNETIKA (RU) [01795481] **1251**

INFORMATSIONNYI MATERIAL / AKADEMIIA NAUK SSSR, NAUCHNYI TSENTR BIOLOGICHESKIKH ISSLEDOVANII ... ET AL (RU) [23600559] **174**

INFORMATSIONNYI UKAZATEL BIBLIOGRAFICHESKIKH RABOT, VYPOLNENNYKH BIBLIOTEKAMI I NAUCHNYMI UCHREZHDENIIAMI SISTEMY AN USSR V ... GODU / AKADEMIIA NAUK UKRAINSKOI SSR, TSENTRALNAIA BIBLIOTEKA (UN) [08899165] **5113**

INFORMATYKA / POLITECHNIKA SLASKA (PL/0208-7286) [08942059] **3217**

INFORMAZIONE (IT) **760**

INFORMAZIONE BIBLIOGRAFICA, L' (IT) [02725649] **4829**

INFORMAZIONE CARDIOLOGICA (IT) **3706**

INFORMAZIONE ELETTRONICA *CEASED.* (IT/0390-2455) [I03902455] **2064**

INFORMAZIONE FILOSOFICA (IT) **4349**

INFORMAZIONE INDUSTRIALE, L' (US) [04506721] **1612**

INFORMAZIONI ACRI (IT) **791**

INFORMAZIONI AZIENDALI E PROFESSIONALI (IT/0390-2447) [I03902447] **870**

INFORMAZIONI DOC (IT/0021-3128) [I00213128] **5432**

INFORMAZIONI E STUDI VIVALDIANI (IT/0393-2915) [07337079] **4122**

INFORMAZIONI PER IL COMMERCIO ESTERO *See* GIORNALE DELL ICE **2056**

INFORMAZIONI RIABILITAZIONE *SUSPENDED.* (IT) **3805**

INFORMAZIONI SANITAIRE EUROPEE (IT) **2174**

INFORMAZIONI SANITARIE (IT) **2174**

INFORMAZIONI SOCIALI (IT) **5290**

INFORMAZIONI SUI FARMACI (IT/1121-1644) [I11211644] **4308**

INFORME (CL/0529-2263) [03105733] **617**

INFORME - ACERIAS PAZ DEL RIO, S.A (CK) [05213969] **1612**

INFORME AGROPECUARIO (BL/0100-3364) [07386705] **96**

INFORME AGROPECUARIO (BELO HORIZONTE) (BL/0100-3364) [02243916] **96**

INFORME ANUAL (SP) [24385722] **791**

INFORME ANUAL / BANCO CENTRAL DE NICARAGUA (NQ/0067-3226) [01239891] **791**

INFORME ANUAL - BANCO DE ESPANA (SP/0067-3315) [02477262] **1567**

INFORME ANUAL - BANCO INTERAMERICANO DE DESARROLLO, INSTITUTO PARA LA INTEGRACION DE AMERICA LATINA (AG) [02758434] **791**

INFORME ANUAL - CENTRO INTERNATIONAL DE AGRICULTURA TROPICAL (CK) [05773452] **96**

INFORME ANUAL - COMISION EJECUTIVA HIDROELECTRICA DEL RIO LEMPA (ES) [02243001] **1612**

INFORME ANUAL DE ACTIVIDADES - SERVICIO ESPECIAL DE SALUD PUBLICA (PE/0253-8326) [05332555] **4784**

INFORME ANUAL DEL DIRECTOR ADMINISTRATIVO DE LOS TRIBUNALES (PR) [01713926] **2982**

INFORME ANUAL DEL DIRECTORIO EJECUTIVO - FONDO MONETARIO INTERNACIONAL *CEASED.* (US/0250-751X) [04702890] **1495**

INFORME ANUAL DEL TESORERO DE PUERTO RICO (PR) [06542353] **4732**

INFORME ANUAL - ESTADO LIBRE ASOCIADO DE PUERTO RICO, COMISION DE SERVICIO PUBLICO (PR/0478-8583) [01190650] **4656**

INFORME ANUAL - ESTADO LIBRE ASOCIADO DE PUERTO RICO, POLICIA DE PUERTO RICO (PR/0095-0483) [01795419] **3166**

INFORME ANUAL / INSTITUTO DE ESTUDIOS LATINOAMERICANOS. UNIVERSIDAD DE ESTOCOLMO (SW) [25739382] **2739**

INFORME ANUAL - INSTITUTO PANAMERICANO DE GEOGRAFIA E HISTORIA, SECCION NACIONAL (VE) [02852401] **2566**

INFORME ANUAL; SERVICIOS ODONTOLOGICOS (PR/0147-0221) [03054666] **1325**

INFORME ANUAL / UNIVERSIDAD CENTRAL DE VENEZUELA, FACULTAD DE AGRONOMIA, INSTITUTO DE PRODUCCION ANIMAL (VE) [09653974] **96**

INFORME BIENAL - BANCO DEL LIBRO (VE) [01792604] **3217**

INFORME CIENCIA E ARTE : BOLETIM (BL/0100-0365) [01793601] **2848**

INFORME COLOMBIANO (US/0882-3901) [11828336] **2739**

INFORME - COMISION DE INTEGRACION ELECTRICA REGIONAL. SUBCOMITE DE DISTRIBUCION ENERGIA ELECTRICA (PE) [01797972] **2064**

INFORME DA PESQUISA (BL/0100-9508) [I01009508] **2385**

INFORME DA PESQUISA - INSTITUTO AGRONOMICO DO PARANA (BL/0100-9508) [26091384] **96**

INFORME DE ACTIVIDADES / CORPORACION DE INVESTIGACIONES ECONOMICAS PARA LATINOAMERICA (CL) [06452272] **1495**

INFORME DE INVESTIGACION - CENTRO DE INVESTIGACIONES TECHNOGICAS (UY/0378-8601) [10407786] **5113**

INFORME DE INVESTIGACION - DIVISION DE CIENCIAS AGROPECUARIAS Y MARITIMAS, INSTITUTO TECNOLOGICO DE MONTEREY (MX) [05987342] **96**

INFORME DE LABORES (MX) [22781208] **4260**

INFORME DE LABORES - CENTRO DOMINICANO DE PROMOCION DE EXPORTACIONES (DR) [02242164] **840**

INFORME DE LABORES DE LA SECRETARIA EJECTIVA DEL CONVENIO ANDRES BELLO (CK) [03484207] **5203**

INFORME DE LABORES ... Y APERTURA DEL ANO JUDICIAL / CORTE SUPERIOR DEL DISTRITO JUDICIAL DE CHUQUISACA (BO) [11404250] **2982**

INFORME DE LAS LABORES *See* INFORME ANUAL - COMISION EJECUTIVA HIDROELECTRICA DEL RIO LEMPA **1612**

INFORME ... DEL PROGRAMA NACIONAL DE FISIOLOGIA VEGETAL (CK) [03947141] **2420**

INFORME - DISTRITO FEDERAL (VENEZUELA). CONTRALORIA MUNICIPAL (VE/0506-631X) [01773202] **4732**

INFORME ECONOMICO (VE/0067-3250) [01161877] **1495**

INFORME ECONOMICO. RESUMEN (AG) [02241536] **1567**

INFORME ESPECIAL - LATIN AMERICAN NEWSLETTERS (UK/0266-2914) [I02662914] 791, **1495**

INFORME ESTADISTICO ANUAL. PUERTO DE ACAJUTLA (ES) [19033985] **5450**

INFORME ESTADISTICO (INSTITUTO NACIONAL DE SEGUROS (SAN JOSE, COSTA RICA)) (CR) [08567096] 2882, **2897**

INFORME ESTATISTICO ANUAL, SETOR METALURGICO (BL) [08581886] 4004, **4025**

INFORME ESTATISTICO, PRODUTOS METALURGICOS (ANNUAL) *See* INFORME ESTATISTICO ANUAL, SETOR METALURGICO **4025**

INFORME ESTATISTICO, PRODUTOS METALURGICOS (MONTHLY) *See* INFORME ESTATISTICO, SETOR METALURGICO **1612**

INFORME ESTATISTICO, SETOR METALURGICO (BL) [08652204] 4004, **1612**

INFORME FINANCIERO Y ESTADISTICO, INSTITUTO NACIONAL DE ELECTRIFICACION, Y ESTADISTICAS DEL SECTOR ELECTRICO NACIONAL (GT) [08777004] 791, **730**

INFORME - INSTITUTO DEL MAR DEL PERU (PE/0458-7774) [01395159] **554**

INFORME INTERCONTINENTAL SOBRE GERENCIA AVANZADA (US/0739-4748) [09741675] **870**

INFORME LATNOAMERICANO (UK/0263-5372) [09306397] **2489**

INFORME PETROLERAS (BO) [05142608] **4260**

INFORME / PUBLICACION COORDINADA POR LA DIRECCION GENERAL DE ESTUDIOS ADMINISTRATIVOS (MX) [07807012] **1830**

INFORME R (BO) [11652342] **2174**

INFORME SOBRE CHILE (CK) [07901666] **5329**

INFORME SOBRE EL DESARROLLO MUNDIAL (US/0271-1737) [06562018] **791**

INFORME SOBRE ESTADO JURIDICO DE LAS SOLICITUDES VIGENTES DE LICENCIAS, PERMISOS, APORTES, ANTIGUOS PERMISOS DE ESMERALDAS Y RECONOCIMIENTO DE PROPIEDAD PRIVADA, PRESENTADAS ANTE EL MINISTERIO Y LAS GOBERNACIONES (CK) [19700471] **4839**

INFORME TECNICO DE BANANO (EC) [03300974] **2420**

INFORME TECNICO - DEPARTAMENTO DE ASSUNTOS UNIVERSITARIOS (BL) [04725501] **1830**

INFORME TECNICO - ESTACION EXPERIMENTAL REGIONAL AGROPECUARIA PERGAMINO (AG/0325-1799) [02920537] **96**

INFORME TECNICO (INSTITUTO FORESTAL (SANTIAGO, CHILE)) (CL/0581-6378) [01765003] **2385**

INFORME TECNICO - INSTITUTO NACIONAL DE INVESTIGACIONES AGROPECUARIAS (EC) [03571193] **96**

INFORME TRIBUTARIO (PE) [25880792] **4732**

INFORME - UNIVERSIDAD CENTRAL DE VENEZUELA, FACULTAD DE INGENIERIA, ESCUELA DE GEOLOGIA Y MINAS, LABORATORIO DE PETROGRAFIA Y GEOQUIMICA (VE/0378-1836) [03005241] **5113**

INFORME UNIVERSITARIO (BL) [03028498] **1830**

INFORMED. BLUE BANNER EDITION *CEASED.* (US/0730-6628) [08045547] **4308**

●INFORMED LIBRARIAN, THE (US/1061-3609) [25265763] **3217**

INFORMER (IT) **2517**

INFORMER (CALGARY) (CN/0227-5406) [08605150] **4965**

INFORMER (RALEIGH), THE (US/0195-4318) [05010157] **3217**

INFORMER, THE (CN/0227-7999) [06688768] **5786**

INFORMES ANTROPOLOGICOS / INSTITUTO COLOMBIANO DE ANTROPOLOGIA (CK/0121-2079) [17310801] **238**

INFORMES DE LA CONSTRUCCION (SP/0020-0883) [02673306] **617**

INFORMES TECNICOS / INSTITUTO ESPANOL DE OCEANOGRAFIA (SP/0212-1565) [11300836] **1450**

INFOROM (US) **1287**

INFORPRESS CENTROAMERICANA (SERIES) (GT/0252-8754) [05148542] **1567**

INFORUM (AT/0812-9304) [18319131] **3857**

INFORUM: ENVIRONMENTAL REPORT DATA SYSTEM (US/0360-4985) [02244689] **2174**

INFOS / CENTRE TECHNIQUE INTERPROFESSIONNEL DES FRUITS ET LEGUMES (FR) [12223372] **2420**

INFOS DE L'ISE (BE) **1679**

INFOS JUNIOR PARIS (FR/1240-4454) [I12404454] **4851**

INFOS PARIS (FR/0758-5373) [I07585373] 2344, **96**

INFOSEVEC (CN/0715-6065) [09670436] **1752**

INFOTECTURE (FR/0241-2640) [15648288] **1275**

INFOTECTURE (EUROPEAN ED.) (FR/0294-7544) [15648131] **1275**

INFOTERM NEWSLETTER (AU) [15689771] **3287**

INFOTEXT (IRVINE, CALIF.) (US/1043-3694) [19413869] **1113**

INFOWORLD (US/0199-6649) [06510141] 1274, **1268**

INFRACTIONS DE LA COMPETENCE DU TRIBUNAL D'INSTANCE STATUANT EN MATIERE PENALE (FR) [20378078] **3166**

INFRARED PHYSICS (UK/0020-0891) [01606379] **4405**

INFRARED PHYSICS AND ENGINEERING (UK) 1978, **4405**

●INFRARED PHYSICS & TECHNOLOGY (UK/1350-4495) [30056065] **4405**

●INFRASTRUCTURE FINANCE (US/1063-0260) [25844402] **791**

INFUSION (ANDOVER) *SUSPENDED.* (US/0160-757X) [03759246] **3587**

INFUSIONSTHERAPIE (BASEL, SWITZERLAND) *See* INFUSIONSTHERAPIE UND TRANSFUSIONSMEDIZIN **3772**

INFUSIONSTHERAPIE

●INFUSIONSTHERAPIE UND TRANSFUSIONSMEDIZIN (SZ/1019-8466) [26105365] **3772**

INGAA RATE AND POLICY ANALYSIS DEPARTMENTS REPORTS (US) **4260**

INGAN KAEBAL (KO) [10107438] **682**

IN'GAN KWAHAK (KO) [05055761] **3587**

INGEGNERI E COSTRUTTORI (IT) **2024**

INGEGNERIA (IT/0035-6263) [07003544] **1978**

INGEGNERIA ALIMENTARE. LE CONSERVE ANIMALI (IT/0394-588X) [I0394588X] **2344**

INGEGNERIA AMBIENTALE INQUINAMENTO E DEPURAZIONE (IT/0302-7775) [03219112] **4784**

INGEGNERIA ELETTRONICA (IT) **2065**

INGEGNERIA FERROVIARIA (IT/0020-0956) [11130111] **1978**

INGEGNERIA SANITARIA (IT) **1978**

INGEGNERIA SISMICA (IT/0393-1420) [I03931420] **2024**

INGENIERIA (MX) [06319150] **1978**

INGENIERIA AERONAUTICA Y ASTRONAUTICA (SP) [06368087] **24**

INGENIERIA CIVIL (LA HABANA) (CU/0020-1022) [02447629] **2024**

INGENIERIA CIVIL MADRID (SP/0213-8468) [I02138468] **2024**

INGENIERIA DE SISTEMAS (CL/0716-1174) [I07161174] **1978**

INGENIERIA ELECTRONICA, AUTOMATICA Y COMUNICACIONES (CU) [08247779] **2065**

INGENIERIA ENERGETICA (CU/0253-5645) [08331991] **1947**

INGENIERIA ESTRUCTURAL Y VIAL (CU) [21696626] **2024**

INGENIERIA HIDRAULICA (LA HABANA) (CU/0253-0678) [07664216] **2091**

INGENIERIA NAVAL (MADRID) (SP/0020-1073) [11129212] **4177**

INGENIERIA PETROLERA (MX/0185-3899) [06805145] **2013**

INGENIERIA QUIMICA (MADRID) (SP/0210-2064) [12123490] **2013**

INGENIERIA Y ARQUITECTURA *See* I & I.E. Y A **2024**

INGENIERIA Y CIENCIA QUIMICA (CR/0250-8303) [11353973] **2013**

INGENIEUR ARCHIV *See* ARCHIVES OF APPLIED MECHANICS **2110**

INGENIEUR CONSEIL DE FRANCE, L' (FR) [04237765] **1978**

INGENIEUR (DEN HAAG) (NE/0020-1146) [01753148] **1978**

INGENIEUR DER DEUTSCHEN BUNDESPOST, DER *See* INGENIEUR FUER POST UND TELEKOMMUNIKATION, DER **1978**

●INGENIEUR FUER POST UND TELEKOMMUNIKATION, DER (GW/0942-3915) [I09423915] **1978**

INGENIEURS-CONSEILS CANADA (1981) (CN/0821-4166) [09586362] **1978**

INGENIEURS DE L'AUTOMOBILE (PARIS) (FR/0020-1200) [11128110] **5417**

INGENIEURS D'ENTRETIEN (FR/0396-3586) [03298348] **870**

INGENIEURSBLAD (BE/0020-1235) [11178530] **1978**

INGENIEURWERKSTOFFE (GW) [I09355715] **1978**

INGENIEURWISSEN (GW) [20333690] **1978**

INGENIEURWISSENSCHAFTLICHE BIBLIOTHEK (GW/0173-0274) [05983457] **1978**

INGENIREN (KBENHAVN. 1975) (DK/0105-3205) [02244176] **1978**

●INGENUITY (UK/1354-9952) [30852932] **1189**

INGHAM COUNTY NEWS (US/1062-4260) [12221496] **5692**

INGLESIDE INDEX, THE (US) [14366706] **5751**

INGLEWOOD WAVE (US) [10537018] **5636**

INGRAM'S (KANSAS CITY, MO.) (US/1046-9958) [20576666] **870**

INGU MUNJE NONJIP (KO/0537-6998) [02813598] **4553**

INGXELO YO- MLAWULI NO-MPICOTHI-ZINCWADI JIKELELE ZEEAKHAWUNTI ZIKAGUNYAZIWE WAMAZWANA ASECIKEI KUNYE NOO- GUNYAZIEW ABANGEZANTSI KUMMANDLA WAKHE *See* INGXELO YOMLAWULI NOMPHICOTHI-ZINCWADI JIKELELE KWIIAKHAWUNTI ZORHULUMENTE WASECISKEI KUNYE NOOGUNYAZIWE ABANGEZANTSI KULOO MMANDLA **4732**

INGXELO YOMLAWULI NOMPHICOTHI-ZINCWADI JIKELELE KWIIAKHAWUNTI ZORHULUMENTE WASECISKEI KUNYE NOOGUNYAZIWE ABANGEZANTSI KULOO MMANDLA (SA) [02243307] **4732**

INHALATION TOXICOLOGY (UK/0895-8378) [16820956] **3981**

INHALATION TOXICOLOGY RESEARCH INSTITUTE *See* ANNUAL REPORT OF THE INHALATION TOXICOLOGY RESEARCH INSTITUTE **3979**

INHALO-SCOPE **SUSPENDED.** (CN/0824-8281) [11046522] **4308**

INHARMONIQUES (FR/0987-6960) [17417675] **4122**

INIQUITY (SAN DIEGO, CALIF.) (US/1056-1064) [23466818] **2535**

INIS ATOMINDEX (AU/0004-7139) [01779746] 4447, **4426**

INIS ATOMINDEX [MICROFORM] (AU) [18923053] 4447, **4426**

INIS. AUTHORITY LIST FOR CORPORATE ENTRIES AND REPORT NUMBER PREFIXES (AU/1014-1561) [04293340] 4447, **4426**

INIS : AUTHORITY LIST FOR JOURNAL TITLES (AU) [03331630] 4447, **4426**

INIS, CHARACTER SET REPRESENTATION AND CODING RULES (AU) [09904954] **1189**

INIS, DESCRIPTIVE CATALOGUING SAMPLES (AU) [04557429] 4447, **4426**

INIS GUIDELINES FOR STANDARDIZED ENTRY OF CORPORATE BODIES (AU) 1947, **1963**

INIS MANUAL FOR ONLINE RETRIEVAL (AU) **4447**

INIS SPECIFICATIONS FOR MACHINE READABLE DATA EXCHANGE (AU) **4447**

INIS : THESAURUS (AU) [04626658] 4447, **4426**

INITIAL CLOSING COMMITMENT FOR PROJECT MORTGAGE INSURANCE (US) [03116475] **2882**

INITIAL PUBLIC OFFERINGS ANNUAL **CEASED.** (US/1053-7163) [22615987] **1612**

INITIALES (HALIFAX) (CN/0710-4278) [08499705] **3396**

INITIATIONS ET ETUDES AFRICAINES (SG/0070-2625) [02123427] **2640**

INITIATIVE **SUSPENDED.** (CN/0827-4789) [12874524] **5290**

INITIATIVE (CN/0384-0719) [03284885] **1567**

INITIATIVE (AUSTIN, TEX.), THE (US/1060-0922) [24865889] **1189**

INITIATIVE EUROPE MONITOR (UK/0955-1697) [I09551697] **682**

●INITIATIVE (ST. JOHN) (CN/1197-4532) [29970307] **5114**

INITIATIVES IN POPULATION (PH/0115-2181) [02044868] 589, **4553**

INITIATIVES MICROFORM : [JOURNAL OF NAWDAC] (US/1042-413X) [21318658] **1830**

INITIATIVES (TORONTO) (CN/0836-866X) [16886077] 4965, **1896**

INITIATIVES (WASHINGTON, D.C.) (US/1042-413X) [18509875] 5559, **1864**

INJURED ATHLETE, THE (CN/0705-369X) [03900463] **3587**

INJURIES IN OIL AND GAS DRILLING AND SERVICES (US/8756-2405) [11488999] **2863**

INJURIES, WOUNDS, AND MULTIPLE BODY DAMAGES (US/1056-473X) [23719366] **3587**

INJURY (UK/0020-1383) [01715915] **3587**

INJURY AWARENESS AND PREVENTION CENTRE NEWS *See* INJURY PREVENTION NEWS **2598**

INJURY EXPERIENCE IN COAL MINING (US/0095-0432) [01096905] **2863**

INJURY EXPERIENCE IN METALLIC MINERAL MINING (US/0270-0042) [06191043] **2864**

INJURY EXPERIENCE IN SAND AND GRAVEL MINING (US/0270-2053) [06307129] **2864**

INJURY EXPERIENCE IN STONE MINING / U.S. DEPARTMENT OF LABOR, MINE SAFETY AND HEALTH ADMINISTRATION (US) [06162386] **2864**

●INJURY PREVENTION (UK) **4784**

INJURY PREVENTION NETWORK NEWSLETTER (US) [23110696] **4784**

●INJURY PREVENTION NEWS (CN/1197-4362) [29970239] **2598**

INK & GALL (US/0894-0479) [15793247] **353**

INK & PRINT (UK/0263-497X) [08721359] **4566**

INK & PRINT INTERNATIONAL (UK/0263-497X) [27330352] **4566**

INKLINGS (US/0190-0234) [04627023] **3396**

INKLINGS (GW/0176-3733) [12441341] **3396**

●INKS (COLUMBUS, OHIO) (US/1071-9156) [28763232] **380**

INKSHED (UK/0951-0427) [18206652] **3464**

INKSTONE (CN/0714-2870) [09379131] **3464**

INLAND ARCHITECT (US/0020-1472) [01753153] 617, **301**

INLAND EMPIRE *See* INLAND EMPIRE MAGAZINE **682**

INLAND EMPIRE MAGAZINE (US/0199-5073) [05953081] 1297, **682**

INLAND LUMBER PRICE INDEX (US) [11606651] **2401**

INLAND REVENUE OF OFFICIAL TAX GUIDES (UK) **4732**

INLAND REVENUE PRACTICES & CONCESSIONS (UK) 2982, **4732**

INLAND REVENUE STATISTICS (UK) [09490419] 4732, **4698**

INLAND REVENUE TAX CASE LEAFLETS (UK) **4732**

INLAND RIVER GUIDE (US/0198-859X) [04585411] **5450**

INLAND SEA COMBINED WITH RUDDER (US) [04372918] **593**

INLAND SEAS (US/0020-1537) [01588435] **2739**

INLAND SEAS INDEX (US) **5534**

INLAND WATERWAY GUIDE. GREAT LAKES EDITION *See* WATERWAY GUIDE (GREAT LAKES EDITION) **596**

INLAND WATERWAY GUIDE. NORTHERN EDITION *See* WATERWAY GUIDE. NORTHERN EDITION **597**

INLAND WATERWAY GUIDE. (SOUTHERN EDITION) *See* WATERWAY GUIDE. SOUTHERN EDITION **5458**

INLIGHTINSBULLETIN - NAVORSINGSINSTITUUT VIR SITRUS EN SUBTROPIESE VRUGTE (SA) [02789620] **174**

INLOGOV INFORMS (UK/0958-4021) [I09584021] **4657**

INMAN REVIEW AND BUHLER NEWS, THE (US) [11897831] **5676**

●INMATE POPULATION FORECAST UPDATE, STATE OF WASHINGTON (US) [18001222] **3166**

INMUN KWAHAK (KO) [12391981] **2848**

INMUN KWAHAK NONCHONG (KO) [08312664] **2654**

INMUNOLOGIA (1987) (SP/0213-9626) [19079036] **3672**

INN BUSINESS (ESSEX, ONT.) (CN/0821-7610) [09454631] **2807**

INN GUIDE, THE (US/0895-2965) [16567237] **2807**

INN MAGAZINE (CN/0710-6386) [08144148] **2807**

INNER HORIZONS **CEASED.** (US/0897-229X) [17446747] **5030**

INNER LONDON EDUCATION AUTHORITY *See* CAPITAL AND REVENUE ESTIMATES - INNER LONDON EDUCATION AUTHORITY **1861**

INNER LONDON EDUCATION STATISTICS (UK) [02351256] 1752, **1795**

INNER SOUND OF LIFE, THE (US/1056-1420) [23600477] **3464**

INNER WOMAN (US/1049-9709) [21261604] 4965, **5559**

INNERE MEDIZIN (GW/0303-4305) [01038362] **3797**

INNES REVIEW, THE (UK/0020-157X) [01624084] **5030**

INNFOCUS (NORTH VANCOUVER) (CN/1193-1922) [26883872] **2807**

INNISFIL SCOPE, THE (CN/0225-1604) [05842277] **5786**

INNKEEPER (CN/0847-9356) [20787321] 870, **2807**

INNKEEPING WORLD (US/0746-6498) [10200823] **2807**

INNOTECH JOURNAL (PH) [06350465] **1752**

INNOTECH NEWSLETTER (PH) [04979939] **1752**

INNOVATING (RENSSELAERVILLE, N.Y.) (US/1053-2587) [22495659] **870**

INNOVATION **CEASED.** (IS/0334-3847) [07371827] **5114**

INNOVATION ABSTRACTS (US/0199-106X) [05591865] **1896**

INNOVATION AND EMPLOYMENT (FR) **1679**

INNOVATION & MANAGEMENT (GW/0863-2790) [22405697] **1304**

INNOVATION AND MANAGEMENT (UK/0260-3748) [14928443] **870**

Alphabetical Title Index — INSIDE

INNOVATION AND TECHNOLOGY TRANSFER/ DG XIII (LU/0255-0806) [18678913] **5114**

INNOVATION ET TECHNOLOGIE EN BIOLOGIE ET MEDECINE (FR/0243-7228) [08359513] **3693**

INNOVATION IN AUSTRALIAN TECHNOLOGY / AUSTRALIAN ACADEMY OF TECHNOLOGICAL SCIENCES *CEASED.* (AT/0156-0069) [18066602] **5114**

INNOVATION IN MICROBIOLOGY SERIES (UK/0952-1127) [11374645] **563**

INNOVATION IN SOCIAL SCIENCE RESEARCH (UK/1012-8050) [27901187] **5203**

INNOVATION INFORMATION AND ANALYSIS PROJECT *See* CUMULATIVE DOCUMENT ACCESSION LIST **414**

INNOVATION (MCLEAN, VA.) (US/0731-2334) [08143097] **2099**

INNOVATION ST. ANDREWS (UK/0264-9861) [I02649861] 5114, **1979**

INNOVATIONS (CN/0836-0650) [18371780] **2791**

INNOVATIONS (US) [25479715] **96**

●INNOVATIONS & IDEAS (US/1059-2091) [24499108] **5114**

INNOVATIONS & RESEARCH IN CLINICAL SERVICES, COMMUNITY SUPPORT, AND REHABILITATION (US/1062-7553) [25732911] **3926**

INNOVATIONS IN CLINICAL PRACTICE : A SOURCE BOOK (US/0737-125X) [08516300] **4590**

●INNOVATIONS IN EDUCATION AND TRAINING TECHNOLOGY INTERNATIONAL (UK) **1753**

INNOVATIONS IN INTERNATIONAL COMPENSATION (US) **942**

INNOVATIONS IN POLYMER/ENGINEERING PLASTICS (US/1045-1889) [20030901] 4455, **2102**

INNOVATIONS IN SURGERY AT THE LAHEY CLINIC MEDICAL CENTER (US/0883-4954) [12153594] **3966**

INNOVATIONS IN UROLOGY (US/0883-4962) [12153670] **3990**

INNOVATIONS IN UROLOGY NURSING (US/1058-0166) [24179344] 3990, **3857**

INNOVATIONS (PALO ALTO) (US/0095-4519) [01159225] **5290**

INNOVATIVE GRADUATE PROGRAMS DIRECTORY (US/0363-2601) [02451941] **1830**

INNOVATIVE HIGHER EDUCATION (US/0742-5627) [10366072] **1830**

●INNOVATIVE IDEAS (US/1064-0576) [26208976] **1612**

INNOVATIVE PACKAGING PARIS (FR/0998-6249) [I09886249] **4219**

INNOVATIVE PROGRAMS FOR CHILD CARE : EVALUATION REPORT (US/0362-7063) [02330132] **1804**

INNOVATOR'S DIGEST (US/0890-300X) [13197548] **5114**

INNOVAZIONE : IMPIANTI E PRODUZIONE *CEASED.* (IT) **5114**

INNSBRUCK. UNIVERSITAT. THEOLOGISCHE FAKULTAT *See* STUDIEN UND ARBEITEN DER THEOLOGISCHEN FAKULTAT **5000**

INNSBRUCKER BEITRAEGE ZUR KULTURWISSENSCHAFT (AU/0537-7250) [02204384] **5247**

INNSBRUCKER HISTORISCHE STUDIEN (AU/0253-0899) [05430471] **2620**

INNSBRUCKER NACHRICHTEN (AU) [20077306] **5778**

INNSIDE ISSUES (US) [22173469] 682, **4839**

INNSIDE NEWS (CN/0710-992X) [08349000] **2807**

INNUIT GALLERY OF ESKIMO ART *See* NEWSLETTER - THE INNUIT GALLERY OF ESKIMO ART **360**

INOCHI ARU CHIKYU (JA) [02240150] **2195**

●INOCULUM (ITHACA, N.Y.) (US/1067-909X) [27143602] **5114**

INONIJA *CEASED.* (IT) [19946695] **3464**

INORGANIC BIOCHEMISTRY *CEASED.* (UK/0142-9698) [06135965] 1036, **488**

INORGANIC CHEMICALS AND GASES (US) **1036**

INORGANIC CHEMISTRY (US/0020-1669) [01753164] **1036**

INORGANIC CHEMISTRY CONCEPTS (GW/0172-7966) [05327122] **1036**

INORGANIC MATERIALS (US/0020-1685) [01911353] 4004, **1036**

INORGANIC PERSPECTIVES IN BIOLOGY AND MEDICINE (NE/0378-3790) [03266631] 3587, **458**

INORGANIC REACTIONS & METHODS (GW) **2013**

INORGANIC SYNTHESES (US) [04840878] **1036**

INORGANICA CHIMICA ACTA : BIOINORGANIC CHEMISTRY ARTICLES AND LETTERS (SZ/0020-1693) [06220680] **1036**

INOSTRANNYE IAZYKI V VUZAKH UZBEKISTANA (UZ) [02808878] **3287**

INOSTRANNYE IAZYKI V SKOLE (RU/0130-6073) [01753168] 3396, **3287**

INOZEMNA FILOLOGIJA (UN/0320-2372) [01753169] **3287**

INPHARMA WEEKLY (NZ/0156-2703) [21114249] **4308**

INPRINT (PETERBOROUGH) (CN/0705-6907) [04249847] **353**

INPSIDER (ATLANTA, GA.), THE *CEASED.* (US/1068-5340) [27697875] **4241**

INPUT *CEASED.* (CN/0706-151X) [05584962] **3217**

INPUT-OUTPUT BIBLIOGRAPHY (US) [04099809] **1534**

INPUT-OUTPUT STRUCTURE OF THE CANADIAN ECONOMY (CN/0226-2304) [05018712] **1612**

INPUT-OUTPUT TABELLER OG ANALYSER (DK/0902-7726) [19407294] **1496**

INQUERITO AO TRANSPORTE RODOVIARIO DE MERCADORIAS. FOLHA SINTESE (PO) [20311214] **5384**

INQUERITO NACIONAL DE PRECOS : GENEROS ALIMENTICIOS E ARTIGOS DO VESTUARIO, COMERCIO ATACADISTA E VAREJISTA NAS UNIDADES DA FEDERACAO (BL) [01798050] **1085**

INQUINAMENTO (IT/0001-4982) [03955107] **2233**

INQUIRER AND MIRROR (US/0891-8686) [02262335] **5689**

INQUIRER, THE (UK/0020-1723) [03425398] **4965**

INQUIRY & ANALYSIS (US/1069-0190) [27878602] **2982**

INQUIRY (CHICAGO) (US/0046-9580) [02057017] **3587**

INQUIRY (KINGSTON) (CN/0714-7198) [09250183] **682**

INQUIRY (OSLO) (NO/0020-174X) [01591883] **5149**

INQUIRY : SCIENCE AND TECHNOLOGY AT THE AMES LABORATORY (US) [23196049] **5114**

INRA MENSUEL LES DOSSIERS (FR/1156-1653) [I11561653] **2385**

INRA SCIENCES SOCIALES (FR/0988-3266) [I09883266] **5203**

INRIATHEQUE (FR) **2848**

INRS NOUVELLES (CN/0836-3218) [17884063] **5114**

INS AND OUTS (NE/0167-3696) [07083295] **3396**

INSAAT MUHENDISLERI ODAS *See* TEKNIK BULTEN **2095**

INSAM YONGU NONMUNJIP (KO) [09030686] **174**

INSATSU-KYOKU KENKYUJO HOKOKU (JA/0367-8547) [08182845] **4566**

INSATSU ZASSHI (JA) [09733716] **4566**

INSCAPE LONDON (UK/0264-7141) [I02647141] **353**

INSCAPE (PASADENA) (US/0094-2715) [05736561] **3396**

INSCHRIFTEN GRIECHISCHER STADTE AUS KLEINASIEN (GW) [02132331] **1077**

INSCOM JOURNAL (US/0270-8906) [06295560] **4046**

INSCRIPTIONS (STEVENS POINT, WIS.) (US/0882-2883) [11806033] 2407, **2454**

INSECT AND DISEASE CONTROL IN THE HOME GARDEN (CN/0713-1313) [08874960] **4245**

INSECT BIOCHEMISTRY *See* INSECT BIOCHEMISTRY AND MOLECULAR BIOLOGY **5609**

●INSECT BIOCHEMISTRY AND MOLECULAR BIOLOGY (UK/0965-1748) [25469033] **5609**

INSECT CONTROL GUIDE (US) [22968638] **4245**

INSECT LIBERATIONS IN CANADA (CN/0590-7748) [02442525] **5609**

●INSECT MOLECULAR BIOLOGY (UK) [26659497] **5609**

INSECT PEST SURVEY / TASMANIAN DEPARTMENT OF AGRICULTURE (AT) [09818360] **4245**

INSECT SCIENCE AND ITS APPLICATION (KE/0191-9040) [04964979] **5609**

INSECT WORLD (LANSING, MICH.) (US/1043-6057) [19494166] 5609, **1064**

INSECTA HELVETICA. CATALOGUS (SZ) [01753179] **5609**

INSECTA MATSUMURANA (JA/0020-1804) [01753180] **5609**

INSECTA MUNDI (US/0749-6737) [11166350] **5609**

INSECTES SOCIAUX (FR/0020-1812) [01753181] **5609**

INSECTICIDE & ACARACIDE TEST *See* ARTHROPOD MANAGEMENT TESTS **4244**

INSECTICIDE & ACARICIDE TESTS (US/0276-3656) [09227665] **4245**

INSECTICIDE, HERBICIDE, FUNGICIDE QUICK GUIDE, THE (US) [04240120] **4245**

INSECTS OF VIRGINIA, THE (US/0098-1222) [02240638] **5610**

INSEE CADRAGE. DEMOGRAPHIE-SOCIETE (FR/0998-4860) [I09984860] **4553**

INSEE CADRAGE. ECONOMIE GENERALE (FR/0998-4828) [I09984828] **1496**

INSEE. CADRAGE ET INSEE RESULTATS CONSOMMATIONS ET MODES DE VIE (FR/0998-4852) **1534**

INSEE. CADRAGE ET INSEE RESULTATS EMPLOIS REVENUS (FR/0998-4844) **5329**

INSEE. CADRAGE ET INSEE RESULTATS SYSTEME PRODUCTIF (FR/0998-4836) **5329**

INSEE ETUDES (FR/1140-5252) [I11405252] **1496**

INSEE METHODES (FR/1142-3080) [I11423080] **1496**

INSEE PREMIERE (FR/0997-3192) [21979091] **1496**

INSEE RESULTATS. EMPLOI-REVENUS (FR/0998-4747) [I09984747] **1680**

INSEE RESULTATS. SYSTEME PRODUCTIF (FR/0998-4895) [I09984895] **1496**

INSEGNANTE SPECIALIZZARO (IT) **1896**

INSEGNARE ALL' HANDICAPPATO (IT/0393-8859) [I03938859] 4389, **1880**

INSEGNARE RELIGIONE (IT/1121-1555) [I11211555] **4965**

INSEH INFORMA (MX/0188-5340) [I01885340] 1496, **5247**

INSELFUHRER (GW) [02648837] **2692**

INSEMINATION ARTIFICIELLE EN FRANCE, L' (FR) [02960306] **3762**

INSEMINATOR (PL) [02153691] **3587**

INSEPARABLES (CN/0711-2130) [08777680] **2281**

INSERM SYMPOSIUM (NE/0378-0546) [02826198] **3588**

INSERVICE QUARTERLY (CN/1183-4749) [24265874] **5290**

INSERVICE (SYRACUSE, N.Y.) (US/0732-3808) [07842607] **1864**

INSIDE 1-2-3 RELEASE 3 *CEASED.* (US/1052-2662) [22246185] **1287**

INSIDE ALABAMA POLITICS (US/0884-030X) [12374481] **4477**

INSIDE (ALBANY, N.Y.) (US/0736-0150) [09024864] **3100**

●INSIDE AMBULATORY CARE (US/1073-6506) [29501582] **3724**

INSIDE ARTS (US/1069-2029) [23944948] **385**

INSIDE ASTROPHYSICS : THE ASTROPHYSICS DIVISION NEWSLETTER (US) [24140099] **24**

●INSIDE AUTOCAD (US/1071-0728) [28540042] **1247**

INSIDE BLUEGRASS (US/0891-0537) [14507837] **4122**

INSIDE BRITISH TELECOM *See* INSIDE BT **1157**

●INSIDE BT (US/1061-2629) [25224834] 5114, **1157**

INSIDE CANADA (CN/0382-8174) [02130533] **2233**

●INSIDE CASE MANAGEMENT (US/1073-6514) [29501773] **870**

INSIDE CHICAGO (US) [15803084] **5480**

INSIDE CHINA MAINLAND (CH) [04918146] **4477**

INSIDE COLLECTOR, THE (US/1052-861X) [22400186] **251**

●INSIDE COMICS (GLASSBORO, N.J.) (US/1062-7405) [25723504] **4862**

INSIDE CONGRESS (US/0275-6714) [07208837] **617**

INSIDE CONTACTS U.S.A. MARKETING INFORMATION DIRECTORY. METRO PHOENIX MARKETING DIRECTORY (US) [24178955] **926**

●INSIDE CONTACTS U.S.A. METRO TUCSON MARKETING DIRECTORY (US/1059-3683) [24124735] **682**

INSIDE — Alphabetical Title Index

INSIDE CONTRACTING *See* INTERIOR CONSTRUCTION **617**

● INSIDE DBASE (US/1061-3293) [25252501] **1279**

INSIDE DEFENSE ELECTRONICS WEEKLY REPORT (US) [22612108] **4046**

INSIDE DETECTIVE *CEASED*. (US/0020-1847) [04079802] **5074**

INSIDE DINING (AT/0814-5806) [I08145806] **5071**

INSIDE DIRECT MARKETING (US/0882-7001) [11929911] **926**

INSIDE DOS (US/1049-5320) [21248014] **1247, 1268**

INSIDE DOT & TRANSPORTATION WEEK (US/1050-818X) [21709378] **5384**

INSIDE DPMA (US/0898-171X) [17737248] **1254, 683**

INSIDE E.P.A. WEEKLY REPORT (US/0270-8965) [06154087] **2174**

INSIDE EDGE (AT) **3995**

INSIDE EDGE (CN/0711-1126) [08713591] **4900**

● INSIDE EDGE FOR MEN (US/1064-7597) [26391628] **3995**

INSIDE ENERGY (UK) **1947**

INSIDE ENERGY/WITH FEDERAL LANDS (US) [08803338] **1947**

INSIDE ENTERPRISE BARGAINING (AT) **683**

INSIDE ENTERTAINMENT (CN/1186-7477) [24368628] **385**

INSIDE EPA'S CLEAN AIR REPORT (US) [21557366] **3113**

INSIDE EPA'S ENVIRONMENTAL POLICY ALERT (US/0894-6655) [11146791] **3113**

INSIDE EPA'S SUPERFUND REPORT (US/1049-6149) [15469999] **3113**

INSIDE F.E.R.C (US/0163-948X) [04543975] **4260, 1947**

INSIDE F.E.R.C.'S GAS MARKET REPORT (US/8756-3711) [11543098] **4260**

INSIDE FINANCIAL SERVICES MARKETING (US) **901, 791**

INSIDE FLORIDA POLITICS *CEASED*. (US/1059-2148) [24514468] **4477**

● INSIDE FLYER (US/1061-4494) [25317403] **4900**

INSIDE FREELANCE *CEASED*. (US/1058-6938) [24358287] **1287**

● INSIDE GTE (US/1061-2637) [25224855] **1113**

INSIDE HOCKEY (DON MILLS, ONT.) *CEASED*. (CN/0835-9806) [17361120] **4900**

INSIDE HOLLYWOOD *CEASED*. (US/1054-2825) [22831055] **385**

INSIDE HOUSING (US/1049-9725) [21359161] **617**

INSIDE HYPERCARD (US/1052-9470) [22416498] **1287**

INSIDE IMMIGRATION : THE PRACTICE ADVISORY (US/1054-7967) [22973299] **1919**

INSIDE INDIANA (US/1061-480X) [25321740] **4851**

INSIDE INDONESIA (AT/0814-1185) [11092900] **2505**

INSIDE INFORMATION WHITCHURCH (UK/0958-1790) [I09581790] **1189**

INSIDE INTERIOR (US/0364-6688) [02401131] **4657**

INSIDE IRELAND (IE/0332-2483) [21633786] **2518**

INSIDE ISHM MAGAZINE (US) **2065**

INSIDE IT (UK/0953-2625) [I09532625] **1189**

INSIDE IVHS (US/1054-2647) [22806585] **5384**

INSIDE JAPAN : HARVARD'S UNDERGRADUATE JAPAN JOURNAL (US/1054-8025) [22973233] **2654**

INSIDE JAPANESE SUPPORT *CEASED*. (US/1058-8671) [24413343] **5290**

INSIDE KARATE (US) **4900**

INSIDE KUNG-FU (US/0199-8501) [06211445] **4900, 2598**

INSIDE LINE *See* CAREER RESOURCE GUIDE **1658**

INSIDE LITIGATION (US/0890-7315) [14368089] **3090**

INSIDE LOBBYING (US/1056-6341) [23751069] **4657**

INSIDE MARKET DATA (US/1047-2908) [20653559] **926**

INSIDE MCI (US/1055-0283) [23060241] **1157**

INSIDE MEDIA (STAMFORD, CONN.) (US/1046-5316) [20437606] **760**

● INSIDE MICROSOFT ACCESS (US/1067-8204) [27361525] **1287**

INSIDE MICROSOFT BASIC *CEASED*. (US/1047-6067) [20730791] **1238, 1268**

INSIDE MICROSOFT C (US/1047-6075) [20730912] **1287**

INSIDE MICROSOFT WINDOWS (US/1051-9734) [22160185] **1287**

INSIDE MICROSOFT WORKS (US/1046-9648) [20580282] **1238, 1268**

INSIDE MORTGAGE CAPITAL MARKETS (US) **791**

INSIDE MORTGAGE FINANCE (US/8756-0003) [11456710] **791**

INSIDE MORTGAGE FINANCE'S CRA/HMDA UPDATE (US/1059-1400) [24487608] **791**

● INSIDE MOTOCROSS MAGAZINE (US/1066-419X) [26945485] **4081**

● INSIDE MOTOROLA (US/1065-6898) [26678179] **1157**

INSIDE MS (US/0739-9774) [09839654] **3834**

INSIDE N.R.C (US/0194-0252) [05294415] **1947**

INSIDE (NELSON) (CN/0380-2957) [02585097] **3396**

● INSIDE NETWARE (US/1061-7647) [25454283] **1287**

INSIDE NEW YORK TAXES (US) [18899048] **4732**

INSIDE NUTRITION (US/0742-3799) [10330487] **4192**

INSIDE OBJECTVISION *CEASED*. (US/1065-8475) [26777506] **1189**

INSIDE OLA (CN/0832-9605) [16074423] **3217**

INSIDE OLA SUPPLEMENT, OPINION SURVEY, AN (CN/1185-3816) [25066695] **1680**

INSIDE OPERATIONS (US/1071-2968) [28641145] **1189**

● INSIDE OS/2 (US/1063-3146) [25971473] **1287**

INSIDE OUT (NEW YORK) (US/0148-3714) [03301949] **3166**

INSIDE/OUT (NEW YORK, N.Y. : 1980) *CEASED*. (US/0275-021X) [07077803] **3396**

INSIDE OUTSIDE (II/0970-1761) [04469629] **2901**

INSIDE OUTSIDE MAGAZINE *CEASED*. (US) **3762**

INSIDE OXFAM (CN/0319-0323) [02442063] **4338**

● INSIDE PARADOX FOR WINDOWS (US/1069-0956) [27923465] **1287**

INSIDE PC TOOLS *CEASED*. (US/1061-5865) [25375790] **1287**

INSIDE (PHILADELPHIA, PA.) (US/0199-7602) [06757985] **2264**

INSIDE PHOENIX (US/0446-3013) [05123239] **1567**

INSIDE PR (US/1053-8828) [21930638] **760**

INSIDE QUATTRO PRO (US/1053-1467) [22464699] **1287**

INSIDE QUEBEC (QUEBEC, QUEBEC) (CN/0713-343X) [08867635] **2739**

INSIDE QUICKBASIC (US/1055-0577) [23065495] **1189**

INSIDE R & D : THE WEEKLY REPORT ON TECHNICAL INNOVATION (US/0300-757X) [01355805] **1025**

INSIDE RADIO (US/0731-9312) [08272420] **1133**

INSIDE REPORT ON NEW MEDIA (US) **1189**

INSIDE RETAILING (AT) **1496**

INSIDE RETAILING (US) [05949470] **955**

INSIDE RETAILING (AT/0310-5660) [I03105660] **955**

INSIDE ROUTES (CN/1180-4602) [22442987] **5384**

INSIDE SEMC (US/0195-833X) [04610634] **4089**

INSIDE SPORT CAMMERAY (AT/1037-1648) [I10371648] **4900**

INSIDE SPORTS (US/0195-3478) [05395512] **4900**

INSIDE SPRINT *See* INSIDE SPRINT CORP **1157**

● INSIDE SPRINT CORP (US/1065-8505) [26777839] **1157**

INSIDE STORY *CEASED*. (NE) [02111379] **1496**

● INSIDE TAE KWON DO (US/1065-4682) [26612204] **4900**

INSIDE TEXAS RUNNING (US/1042-3664) [19028480] **4900**

INSIDE TEXTILES (US/0733-8244) [08673319] **5352**

INSIDE THE ARMY (US) **4046**

INSIDE THE AUBURN TIGERS (AUBURN, ALA.) (US/0279-2273) [07645052] **4900**

INSIDE THE BLUE CHIPS : EXCLUSIVE NATIONAL COLLEGIATE RECRUITERS' REPORT (US) [07927826] **4900**

INSIDE THE LEADING MAIL ORDER HOUSES (US/0743-2895) [10546248] **760**

INSIDE THE LEGISLATURE (US/1075-6752) [27972508] **4477**

● INSIDE THE NEW COMPUTER INDUSTRY (US/1079-4573) [31408233] **1189**

INSIDE THE PENTAGON (US) [13302463] **4046**

INSIDE THE PENTAGON'S INSIDE THE AIR FORCE (US) **24**

INSIDE THE PENTAGON'S INSIDE THE NAVY (US) [19226979] **4046**

INSIDE THE WHITE HOUSE (US) [17867048] **4657**

● INSIDE TRAC, THE (US/1059-387X) [24579859] **1189, 926**

INSIDE TRACK (HAMMONTON, N.J.) (US/1052-1607) [22200186] **4851**

INSIDE TRACK (MIAMI, FLA.) (US/0885-6885) [12708630] **870**

INSIDE TUCSON BUSINESS (US/1069-5184) [24335519] **683**

INSIDE TURBO C *CEASED*. (US/1045-6791) [20186877] **1287**

INSIDE TURBO C++ (US/1052-9489) [22416615] **1287**

INSIDE TURBO PASCAL *CEASED*. (US/1045-6775) [20186586] **1238, 1268**

INSIDE U.S.A. VOLLEYBALL (US/1059-8227) [24289391] **4851, 4900**

INSIDE U.S. TRADE (US/0897-1676) [10004204] **840**

INSIDE UVA (US/0745-9432) [04885162] **1864**

● INSIDE VIEW (IRVING, TEX.) (US/1065-7320) [26714336] **3834**

INSIDE VISUAL BASIC (US/1059-1788) [24496621] **1287**

● INSIDE VISUAL BASIC FOR WINDOWS (US/1066-7555) [27043440] **1287**

INSIDE WASHINGTON (US) **4657**

INSIDE WELFARE BULLETIN (AT/0313-8496) [I03138496] **1496**

INSIDE WOMEN'S TENNIS (US/0738-7040) [09648665] **4900**

INSIDE WORCESTER (US) **2535**

INSIDE WORD FOR WINDOWS (US/1049-0795) [21122323] **1287**

INSIDE WORD (MACINTOSH ED.) (US/0893-9349) [15693681] **1287**

INSIDE WORD (PC ED.) *CEASED*. (US/1052-7605) [22367502] **1287**

INSIDE WORDPERFECT (US/1046-9656) [20580227] **1287**

● INSIDE WORDPERFECT WINDOWS (US/1063-2727) [25955798] **1287**

● INSIDE WORKERS' COMPENSATION (US/1065-2736) [26562569] **2882, 1680**

● INSIDE WORKS FOR WINDOWS (US/1061-5873) [25375752] **1287**

INSIDE WRESTLING (US/1047-9562) [20836342] **4900**

INSIDER FORECLOSURE GUIDE (US/1065-2310) [26530897] **4839**

INSIDER GUN NEWS, THE (US/0892-1180) [15186312] **4873**

● INSIDER REAL ESTATE GUIDE, THE (US/1068-1264) [27447323] **4839**

INSIDER REPORTING AND LIABILITY UNDER SECTION 16 OF THE SECURITIES EXCHANGE ACT OF 1934 (US/1061-3390) [18838416] **2982**

INSIDER / SOUTH AFRICA (SA) **2499**

INSIDER, THE (BU/0861-3117) [24031634] **2518**

INSIDER TRADING REGULATION (US/0897-490X) [17514419] **901**

INSIDER TRAVEL SECRETS (US/1057-9184) [24163798] **5480**

INSIDER'S BANKING & CREDIT ALMANAC, THE (US/0195-3311) [05383849] **791**

INSIDERS BASEBALL FACT-BOOK (US/0731-8162) [08252741] **4900**

INSIDERS BASEBALL FACT-BOOK EXTRA (US/0731-8146) [08252632] **4900**

INSIDERS' CHRONICLE *See* CDA/INVESTNET INSIDERS' CHRONICLE **894**

INSIDERS' CHRONICLE, THE (US/0162-5152) [03613653] **791**

INSIDER'S GUIDE TO BOOK EDITORS AND PUBLISHERS, THE (US/1052-0120) [21274564] **4815**

INSIDER'S GUIDE TO GRADUATE PROGRAMS IN CLINICAL PSYCHOLOGY (US/1061-7132) [25418998] 1830, 4590

INSIDER'S GUIDE TO PERSONAL WELLNESS (US/1064-6841) [26373037] 2598

INSIDER'S GUIDE TO PREP SCHOOLS, THE (US/0271-535X) [05223315] 1753

INSIDERS' GUIDE TO THE COLLEGES, THE (US/0093-5220) [01784519] 1830

INSIDERS OPTIONS (US) 901

INSIDERS REPORT (SCOTTSDALE, ARIZ.) (US/8756-6435) [11535268] 901

INSIDERS, THE (US/0730-2908) [07992263] 901

INSIEME (IT/0020-1871) [I00201871] 683

INSIEME (IT) 1753

INSIGHT (AKRON, OHIO) (US) [15158826] 3217

INSIGHT & HINDSIGHT (US/0737-7215) [09425321] 4590

●INSIGHT : AUSTRALIAN FOREIGN AFFAIRS AND TRADE ISSUES (AT/1038-6726) [26585289] 840, 4524

INSIGHT (BOSTON, MASS.) (US/0742-5244) [10382157] 3396

INSIGHT (CHICAGO, ILL.) (US/1053-8542) [22683254] 745

INSIGHT (HONG KONG) (CH) [07522765] 840

INSIGHT IBM (UK) 1238

INSIGHT INTO AMERICAN LIFE & OPINIONS REVEALED BY POLLS & SURVEYS (US/1057-0845) [23935330] 2739

INSIGHT INTO COURTS (US/1043-8467) [19579783] 3588, 2982

INSIGHT LAGOS. 1987 (NR/0794-7968) [I07947968] 4349, 4965

●INSIGHT (NORTHAMPTON) (UK/1354-2575) [30577044] 2102

INSIGHT ON COLLECTABLES (1987) (CN/0836-5873) [17463169] 251

INSIGHT ON SITE See ON SITE (WASHINGTON, D.C.) 623

INSIGHT ON THE NEWS (WASHINGTON, D.C.) (US/1051-4880) [20032347] 4477

INSIGHT (SAN FRANCISCO, CALIF.) (US/1060-135X) [23592777] 3875, 3857

INSIGHT (SINGAPORE) (SI/0129-6078) [09493785] 4784

INSIGHT (WASHINGTON) (US/0020-1944) [04086516] 5061

INSIGHTS (US/0898-1795) [17345712] 3217

INSIGHTS : A JOURNAL OF THE FACULTY OF AUSTIN SEMINARY (US/1056-0548) [22603695] 4965

●INSIGHTS & STRATEGIES (US/1065-6413) [26661574] 791

INSIGHTS (CLIFTON, N.J.) (US/0894-3524) [16050132] 3100

INSIGHTS FOR LIFE (US/1056-1978) [23535812] 4965

INSIGHTS FOR SUCCESS CEASED. (US/0891-4729) [14866609] 871

INSIGHTS INTO CHRISTIAN EDUCATION CEASED. (US/8756-3347) [11557051] 1753, 4965

INSIGHTS INTO OPEN EDUCATION/ UNIVERSITY OF NORTH DAKOTA (US/0740-5596) [02252341] 1896

INSIGHTS (MANHATTAN BEACH, CALIF.) (US/0894-3478) [16002151] 760

INSIGHTS OF MEMBERS OF THE JOHN DEWEY SOCIETY FOR THE STUDY OF EDUCATION AND CULTURE (US) [01753188] 1753

INSIGHTS (SPRINGFIELD, OHIO) (US/0164-7709) [01641206] 4965

INSIGHTS (WASHINGTON, D.C.) (US/0747-007X) [10462224] 4873, 4900

INSITA (XO/0046-9661) [02781910] 353

INSITE (CN/0020-2029) [02041384] 1753

INSOL INTERNATIONAL INSOLVENCY REVIEW See INTERNATIONAL INSOLVENCY REVIEW : JOURNAL OF THE INTERNATIONAL ASSOCIATION OF INSOLVENCY PRACTITIONERS 2984

INSOLVENCY BULLETIN (CN/0821-0012) [09812130] 3087

INSOLVENCY INTELLIGENCE (UK/0950-2645) [I09502645] 2983

INSOLVENCY LAW & PRACTICE (UK/0267-0771) [13303445] 3087

INSOLVENCY LAWYER CEASED. (UK) 2983

INSOLVENCY LAWYERS' ASSOCIATION (GREAT BRITAIN) See INSOLVENCY LAWYERS DIRECTORY / INSOLVENCY LAWYERS' ASSOCIATION 2983

●INSOLVENCY LAWYERS DIRECTORY / INSOLVENCY LAWYERS' ASSOCIATION (UK) [26136542] 2983

INSOURCE CUSTOM SERVICE (CD-ROM) (US) 2882

INSPEC MATTERS (UK) [06672882] 2065

INSPEC ONDISC (US/1063-7060) [25987734] 2065

INSPEC TOPICS. 390. POWER SYSTEM PROTECTION (UK) 2065

INSPEC TOPICS. T0740. SEMICONDUCTOR LASERS (UK) 2065

INSPEC [ONLINE DATABASE] (UK) 2065, 2004

INSPECTEUR DE GTA (1975) (CN/0226-2452) [10446039] 2233

INSPECTION & WEIGHING UPDATE / FEDERAL GRAIN INSPECTION SERVICE, U.S. DEPARTMENT OF AGRICULTURE (US) [05786552] 202

INSPEL (GW/0019-0217) [02146777] 3217

INSPIRATION (SZ/0020-2061) [02568681] 926

INSPIRATION (PITTSBURGH, PA.) CEASED. (US/1065-8092) [26749170] 4965

INSPIRATIONAL WRITER'S MARKET (US/0897-9804) [17682245] 3396

INSPIRED (US) [17868363] 301

INSTA-MATCH DIRECTORY OF MINORITY OWNED BUSINESSES IN TEXAS (US/0730-3521) [07988485] 683

INSTALACIONES DEPORTIVAS XXI (SP/0212-8519) [I02128519] 617

INSTALACIONES Y TECNICAS DEL CONFORT (SP/0214-4034) [I02144034] 2606

INSTALADOR, EL (SP) 2065

INSTALLATEUR EN CHAUFFAGE PLOMBERIE COUVERTURE GENIE CLIMATIQUE ELECTRICITE (FR/0399-9874) 2606

INSTALLATIE JOURNAAL (NE) 2065

INSTALLATION & CLEANING SPECIALIST (US/0192-1657) [05120403] 2906, 2901

INSTALLATION DES SYSTEMES DE GICLEURS, L' (CN/0708-2215) [05018628] 2291, 1979

INSTALLATION, DKZ (GW/0723-4775) [I07234775] 2065

INSTALLATION NEWS (US/0887-2287) [13147464] 1612

INSTALLATION OF SPRINKLER SYSTEMS (US) 2291

INSTALLATION SPECIALIST See INSTALLATION & CLEANING SPECIALIST 2901

INSTALLATORE ITALIANO (IT/0020-2118) [I00202118] 2606

INSTALLATORE TECNICO (IT) 5114

INSTALLMENT CREDIT REPORT (US/1041-6390) [18568036] 791

INSTAND SCHRIFTENREIHE / INSTITUT FUR STANDARDISIERUNG UND DOKUMENTATION IM MEDIZINISCHEN LABORATORIUM E.V. (INSTAND) (GW/0932-4682) [12138411] 3588

INSTANT AND SMALL COMMERCIAL PRINTER (US/1044-3746) [12639975] 4566

INSTANT ART (US) 3217

INSTANT BACKGROUND (US) [22168747] 1133

INSTANT HITS (US/1057-1604) [23959742] 4072

INSTANT (THEATRE DU GANOUE) (CN/0711-4648) [08555900] 3464

INSTANT (TORONTO) (CN/0316-9138) [02247392] 2781

INSTANTANES MATHEMATIQUES (CN/0226-2061) [06468561] 3509

INSTANTANES MEDICAUX, LES (FR/0020-2142) [10870837] 3588

INSTAURATION (US/0277-2302) [06406234] 4477

INSTELLINGEN (NE) 5179, 4784

INSTITUTI PENYELIDEKAN PERHUTANAN See RESEARCH PAMPHLET - FOREST RESEARCH INSTITUTE 2393

INSTITOUTON GEOLOGIAS KAI EREUNON HYPEDAPHOUS (GREECE) See EIDIKAI MELETAI EPI TES GEOLOGIAS TES ELLADOS (ATHENAI) 1355

INSTITOUTON GEORGIKON EREUNON (CYPRUS) See REVIEW FOR ... / AGRICULTURAL RESEARCH INSTITUTE, REPUBLIC OF CYPRUS 128

INSTITUT AFRICAIN POUR LE DEVELOPPEMENT ECONOMIQUE ET SOCIAL - FORMATION See RAPPORT D'ACTIVITE - INSTITUT AFRICAIN POUR LE DEVELOPPEMENT ECONOMIQUE ET SOCIAL - FORMATION 1776

INSTITUT ARCHEOLOGIQUE DU LUXEMBURG, ARLON, BELGIUM See BULLETIN TRIMESTRIEL DI L'INSTITUT ARCHEOLOGIQUE DU LUXEMBOURG 265

INSTITUT ARKHEOLOGII I ISKUSSTVOZNANIIA (ROSSIISKAIA ASSOTSIATSIIA NAUCHNO-ISSLEDOVATELSKIKH INSTITUTOV OBSHCHESTVENNYKH NAUK) See TRUDY SEKTSII ARKHEOLOGII 285

INSTITUT BELGE DE NORMALISATION See LISTE DES MEMBRES - INSTITUT BELGE DE NORMALISATION 4031

INSTITUT BELGE DES SCIENCES ADMINISTRATIVES See ADMINISTRATION PUBLIQUE 3091

INSTITUT BELGE DU PETROLE See STATUTS, LISTE DES MEMBRES - INSTITUT BELGE DU PETROLE 4279

INSTITUT BELGE DU PETROLE See ANNALES DE L'INSTITUT BELGE DU PETROLE 4249

INSTITUT BIOLOGII VNUTRENNIKH VOD (AKADEMIIA NAUK SSSR) See TRUDY - AKADEMIIA NAUK SSSR, INSTITUT BIOLOGII VNUTRENNIH VOD 475

INSTITUT CANADIEN D'EDUCATION DES ADULTES See ICEA. INSTITUT CANADIEN D'EDUCATION DES ADULTES 1800

INSTITUT CATALA DEL SOL (SPAIN) See ACTUACIONS INDUSTRIALS / INSTITUT CATALA DEL SOL, GENERALITAT DE CATALUNYA, DEPARTMENT DE POLITICA TERRITORIAL I OBRES PUBLIQUES 1596

INSTITUT CATALA DEL SOL (SPAIN) See ACTUACIONS RESIDENCIALS / INSTITUT CATALA DEL SOL, GENERALITAT DE CATALUNYA, DEPARTAMENT DE POLITICA TERRITORIAL I OBRES PUBLIQUES 2813

INSTITUT CATHOLIQUE DE PARIS See RECHERCHES ACTUELLES - INSTITUT CATHOLIQUE DE PARIS 5035

INSTITUT CULTUREL AFRICAIN See ICA INFORMATION : BULLETIN DE L'INSTITUT CULTUREL AFRICAIN 2640

INSTITUT D'AMENAGEMENT ET D'URBANISME DE LA REGION D'ILE-DE-FRANCE See CAHIERS DE L'INSTITUT D'AMENAGEMENT ET D'URBANISME DE LA REGION D'ILE-DE-FRANCE 2816

INSTITUT D'ASSURANCE DU CANADA See PROGRAMME D'ASSOCIE / INSTITUT D'ASSURANCE DU CANADA 2891

INSTITUT D'ASTRONOMIE ET DE GEOPHYSIQUE GEORGES LEMAITRE See CONTRIBUTION - INSTITUT D'ASTRONOMIE ET DE GEOPHYSIQUE GEORGES LEMAITRE. MEDEDELINGEN VAN HET ASTRONOMISCH INSTITUUT VAN DE KATHOLIEKE UNIVERSITEIT LEUVEN 394

INSTITUT DE PHONETIQUE D'AIX-EN-PROVENCE See TRAVAUX DE L'INSTITUT DE PHONETIQUE D'AIX 3329

INSTITUT DE POLICE DU QUEBEC See RAPPORT ANNUEL / INSTITUT DE POLICE DU QUEBEC 3174

INSTITUT DE RADIOTELEVISION POUR ENFANTS (CN/0824-6998) [11400803] 1133

INSTITUT DE RECHERCHE DES TRANSPORTS See PROGRAMME DE RECHERCHE - INSTITUT DE RECHERCHE DES TRANSPORTS 5390

INSTITUT DE RECHERCHE DES TRANSPORTS (FRANCE) See ACTIVITES DE L'INSTITUT DE RECHERCHE DES TRANSPORTS 5375

INSTITUT DE RECHERCHE EN CONSTRUCTION (CANADA) See CATALOGUE DE PUBLICATIONS EUROPEENNES 606

INSTITUT DE RECHERCHE EN CONSTRUCTION (CANADA) See PUBLICATIONS CATALOGUE - INSTITUTE FOR RESEARCH IN CONSTRUCTION (OTTAWA) 633

INSTITUT DE RECHERCHES DU COTTON ET DES TEXTILES EXOTIQUES. SECTION D'EXPERIMENTATION DE BOBO-DIOULASSO See RAPPORT - SECTION D'EXPERIMENTATION DE BOBO-DIOULASSO, INSTITUT DE RECHERCHES DU COTON ET DES TEXTILES EXOTIQUES 2429

INSTITUT DE RECHERCHES TECHNOLOGIQUES (LIBREVILLE, GABON) See RAPPORT D'ACTIVITE - INSTITUT DE RECHERCHES TECHNOLOGIQUES 5144

INSTITUT DE STATISTIQUE DES UNIVERSITES DE PARIS See PUBLICATIONS DE L'INSTITUT DE STATISTIQUE DE L'UNIVERSITE DE PARIS 5336

INSTITUT D'EMISSION DES DEPARTMENTS D'OUTRE-MER (FRANCE) See RAPPORT D'ACTIVITE - INSTITUT D'EMISSION DES DEPARTEMENTS D'OUTRE-MER 1580

INSTITUT — Alphabetical Title Index

INSTITUT DES BANQUIERS CANADIENS *See* REGLEMENTS RELATIFS AUX PROGRAMMES - INSTITUT DES BANQUIERS CANADIENS 807

INSTITUT DES HAUTES ETUDES SCIENTIFIQUES (PARIS, FRANCE) *See* PUBLICATIONS MATHEMATIQUES. INSTITUT DES HAUTES ETUDES SCIENTIFIQUES 3529

INSTITUT DES SCIENCES HUMAINES, YAOUNDE, CAMEROON. UNITE DE RECHERCHE LINGUISTIQUE ET PHONETIQUE *See* BULLETIN DE L'ALCAM 3270

INSTITUT D'ESTUDIS ILERDENCS *See* INSTITUT D'ESTUDIS ILERDENCS 2692

INSTITUT D'ESTUDIS ILERDENCS (SP) [18343030] 2692

INSTITUT D'ESTUDIS OCCITANS (FRANCE) *See* ANNALES DE L'INSTITUT D'ETUDES OCCITANES 3264

INSTITUT D'ETUDES SLAVES *See* TEXTES PUBLIES PAR L'INSTITUT D'ETUDES SLAVES 3328

INSTITUT D'HYGIENE ET D'EPIDEMIOLOGIE (BELGIUM) *See* RAPPORT D'ACTIVITE - INSTITUT D'HYGIENE ET D'EPIDEMIOLOGIE 4798

INSTITUT DOMINICAIN D'ETUDES ORIENTALES DU CAIRE *See* MELANGES - INSTITUT DOMINICAIN D'ETUDES ORIENTALES DU CAIRE 3302

INSTITUT EKOLOGII RASTENII I ZHIVOTHYKH (AKADEMIIA NAUK SSSR) *See* INFORMATSIONNYE MATERIALY INSTITUTA EKOLOGII RASTENII I ZHIVOTNYKH 2217

INSTITUT ETNOGRAFII IMENI N.N. MIKLUKHO-MAKLAIA *See* POLEVYE ISSLEDOVANIIA INSTITUTA ETNOGRAFII 243

INSTITUT FONDAMENTAL D'AFRIQUE NOIRE *See* MEMOIRES DE L'INSTITUT FONDAMENTAL D'AFRIQUE NOIRE 2499

INSTITUT FONDAMENTAL D'AFRIQUE NOIRE *See* RAPPORT ANNUEL - INSTITUT FONDAMENTAL D'AFRIQUE NOIRE 2642

INSTITUT FRANCAIS D'ARCHEOLOGIE ORIENTALE DU CAIRE *See* BULLETIN DE L'INSTITUT FRANCAIS D'ARCHEOLOGIE ORIENTALE 263

INSTITUT FRANCAIS D'ETUDES ANDINES *See* BULLETIN DE L'INSTITUT FRANCAIS D'ETUDES ANDINES 2724

INSTITUT FRANCAIS D'OCEANIE. CENTRE D'OCEANOGRAPHIE *See* RAPPORT SCIENTIFIQUE - INSTITUT FRANCAIS D'OCEANIE, CENTRE D'OCEANOGRAPHIE 1455

INSTITUT FRANCAIS D'OCEANIE. SECTION OCEANOGRAPHIE *See* RAPPORT SCIENTIFIQUE - INSTITUT FRANCAIS D'OCEANIE, SECTION OCEANOGRAPHIE 1455

INSTITUT FUER EUROPAISCHE GESCHICHTE (MAINZ, GERMANY) *See* VORTRAGE 2715

INSTITUT FUER EUROPAISCHE GESCHICHTE (MAINZ, GERMANY) *See* VEROFFENTLICHUNGEN 5007

INSTITUT FUER OESTERREICHISCHE GESCHICHTSFORSCHUNG (1947-) *See* MITTEILUNGEN DES INSTITUTS FUER OESTERREICHISCHE GESCHICHTSFORSCHUNG. ERGAENZUNGSBAND 2699

INSTITUT FUER REAKTORSICHERHEIT DER TECHNISCHEN UBERWACHUNGS-VEREINE. UBERSETZUNGEN, KERNTECHNISCHE REGELN *See* UBERSETZUNGEN, KERNTECHNISCHE REGELN 2159

INSTITUT FUR ARBEITSMARKT- UND BERUFSFORSCHUNG *See* ARBEITSMARKTSTATISTISCHE ZAHLEN IN ZEITREIHENFORM 1651

INSTITUT FUR INTERNATIONALE POLITIK UND WIRTSCHAFT *See* IPW BERICHTE 1636

INSTITUT FUR LANDES- UND STADTENTWICKLUNGSFORSCHUNG DES LANDES NORDRHEIN-WESTFALEN *See* TATIGKEITSBERICHT DES ILS 2836

INSTITUT FUR MITTELSTANDSFORSCHUNG *See* ARBEITSBERICHT DES INSTITUTS FUR MITTELSTANDSFORSCHUNG 639

INSTITUT FUR REAKTORSICHERHEIT DER TECHNISCHEN UBERWACHUNGS-VEREIN *See* IRS-SCHRIFTTUM 2156

INSTITUT FUR REAKTORSICHERHEIT DER TECHNISCHEN UBERWACHUNGS-VEREINE *See* TATIGKEITSBERICHT - INSTITUT FUR REAKTORSICHERHEIT DER TECHNISCHEN UBERWACHUNGS-VEREINE 2159

INSTITUT FUR SEEFISCHEREI *See* MITTEILUNGEN AUS DEM INSTITUT FUER SEEFISCHEREI DER BUNDESFORSCHUNGSANSTALT FUER FISCHEREI 2308

INSTITUT FUR SERVERKEHRSWIRTSCHAFT BERMEN *See* SHIPPING STATISTICS 5402

INSTITUT FUR ZEITGESCHICHTE, MUNICH. BIBLIOTHEK *See* ALPHABETISCHER KATALOG. NACHTRAGSBAND 2609

INSTITUT GEOLOGII I GEOKHIMII IM. ADAD. A.N. ZAVARITSKOGO *See* EZHEGODNIK / AKADEMIIA NAUK SSSR, URALSKII NAUCHNYI TSENTR, INSTITUT GEOLOGII I GEOKHIMII IM. AKAD. A. N. ZAVARITSKOGO 1375

INSTITUT HISTORIQUE BELGE DE ROME *See* BULLETIN DE L'INSTITUT HISTORIQUE BELGE DE ROME 2481

INSTITUT / INSTITUT DE FRANCE (FR/0768-2050) [18029879] 4089

INSTITUT INTERUNIVERSITAIRE DES SCIENCES NUCLEAIRES *See* MONOGRAPHIE - INSTITUT INTERUNIVERSITAIRE DES SCIENCES NUCLEAIRES 4448

INSTITUT KEGURUAN DAN ILMU PENDIDIKAN, MANADO, INDONESIA. FAKULTAS KEGURUAN SASTRA SENI *See* BERITA PENDIDIKAN SASTRA DAN SENI 3366

INSTITUT KEGURUAN DAN ILMU PENDIDIKAN, YOGYAKARTA, INDONESIA. DEPARTEMEN PENDIDIKAN EKONOMI *See* BULLETIN DEPARTEMEN PENDIDIKAN EKONOMI 1590

INSTITUT KEGURUAN DAN ILMU PENDIDIKAN, YOGYAKARTA, INDONESIA. DEPARTEMEN STUDIUM GENERALE *See* BULETIN DEPARTEMEN STUDIUM GENERALE IKIP YOGYAKARTA 1890

INSTITUT KEGURUAN DAN ILMU PENDIDIKAN, YOGYAKARTA, INDONESIA. PUSAT PENELITIAN PENDIDIKAN *See* BULLETIN P 3 - INSTITUT KEGURUAN DAN ILMU PENDIDIKAN, YOGYAKARTA, INDONESIA. PUSAT PENELITIAN PENDIDIKAN 1729

INSTITUT KOSMOFIZICHESKIKH ISSLEDOVANII I AERONOMII (AKADEMIIA NAUK SSSR) *See* FIZIKA VERKHNEI ATMOSFERY VYSOKIKH SHIROT 1425

INSTITUT MONETAIRE LUXEMBOURGEOIS *See* RAPPORT ANNUEL DE L'INSTITUTE MONETAIRE LUXEMBOURGEOIS POUR L'ANNEE ... / ANNUAL REPORT OF THE IML FOR THE YEAR ... INSTITUT MONETAIRE LUXEMBOURGEOIS 806

INSTITUT NATIONAL AGRONOMIQUE. (ALGERIA) *See* ANNALES DE L'INSTITUT NATIONAL AGRONOMIQUE 59

INSTITUT NATIONAL DE LA RECHERCHE AGRONOMIQUE *See* JOURNEES DE LA RECHERCHE PORCINE EN FRANCE 5515

INSTITUT NATIONAL DE LA RECHERCHE AGRONOMIQUE DE TUNISIE *See* ANNALES 59

INSTITUT NATIONAL DE LA RECHERCHE AGRONOMIQUE (FRANCE) *See* BIBLIOGRAPHIE - INSTITUT NATIONAL DE LA RECHERCHE AGRONOMIQUE, DEPARTEMENT D'ECONOMIE ET DE LA SOCIOLOGIE RURALES 151

INSTITUT NATIONAL DE LA SANTE ET DE LA RECHERCHE MEDICALE (FRANCE) *See* INSERM SYMPOSIUM 3588

INSTITUT NATIONAL DE LA STATISTIQUE ET DES ETUDES ECONOMIQUES (FRANCE) *See* POINT ECONOMIQUE DE L'AUVERGNE, LE 5253

INSTITUT NATIONAL DE LA STATISTIQUE ET DES -ETUDES -ECONOMIQUES (FRANCE) *See* DONNEES SOCIALES 5244

INSTITUT NATIONAL DE LA STATISTIQUE ET DES ETUDES ECONOMIQUES (FRANCE) *See* PERSPECTIVES ECONOMIQUES DE LA PROFESSION DU BATIMENT DANS LA REGION NORD (NORD-PAS-DE-CALAIS) 623

INSTITUT NATIONAL DE LA STATISTIQUE ET DES ETUDES ECONOMIQUES (FRANCE) *See* RAPPORT SUR LES COMPTES DE LA NATION 1580

INSTITUT NATIONAL DE LA STATISTIQUE ET DES ETUDES ECONOMIQUES (FRANCE) *See* STATISTIQUES ET INDICATEURS DES REGIONS FRANCAISES 1539

INSTITUT NATIONAL DE LA STATISTIQUE ET DES ETUDES ECONOMIQUES (FRANCE) *See* SUD; INFORMATION ECONOMIQUE : PROVENCE ALPES COTE D'AZUR 1585

INSTITUT NATIONAL DE LA STATISTIQUE ET DES ETUDES ECONOMIQUES (FRANCE) *See* PUBLICATIONS STATISTIQUES DES ADMINISTRATIONS 5336

INSTITUT NATIONAL DE LA STATISTIQUE ET DES ETUDES ECONOMIQUES (FRANCE) *See* BULLETIN MENSUEL DE STATISTIQUE 5324

INSTITUT NATIONAL DE LA STATISTIQUE ET DES ETUDES ECONOMIQUES. OBSERVATOIRE ECONOMIQUE DE L'EST *See* PETIT GUIDE STATISTIQUE DE LA LORRAINE 5336

INSTITUT NATIONAL DE PREPARATION PROFESSIONNELLE *See* CAHIER - INSTITUT NATIONAL DE PREPARATION PROFESSIONNELLE 1657

INSTITUT NATIONAL DE RECHERCHE ET DE SECURITE *See* TRAVAIL & SECURITE 2871

INSTITUT NATIONAL DE RECHERCHE SCIENTIFIQUE *See* RAPPORT ANNUEL / INSTITUT NATIONAL DE RECHERCHE SCIENTIFIQUE (I.N.R.S.) 5144

INSTITUT NATIONAL DE STATISTIQUE (BELGIUM) *See* STATISTIQUES DEMOGRAPHIQUES 4563

INSTITUT NATIONAL DE STATISTIQUE (BELGIUM) *See* BEVOLKINGSSTATISTIEKEN - NATIONAAL INSTITUUT VOOR DE STATISTIEK 4561

INSTITUT NATIONAL DE STATISTIQUE (BELGIUM) *See* VEHICULES A MOTEUR NEUFS MIS EN CIRCULATION 5427

INSTITUT NATIONAL DE STATISTIQUE (BELGIUM) *See* ENQUETE SOCIO-ECONOMIQUE 4562

INSTITUT NATIONAL DE STATISTIQUE (BELGIUM) *See* STATISTIQUE DU TRAFIC INTERNATIONAL DES PORTS 5457

INSTITUT NATIONAL DE STATISTIQUE (BELGIUM) *See* ANNUAIRE STATISTIQUE DE POCHE - INSTITUT NATIONAL DE STATISTIQUE 5321

INSTITUT NATIONAL DE STATISTIQUE (BELGIUM) *See* LANDBOUWSTATISTIEKEN 154

INSTITUT NATIONAL DE STATISTIQUE (BELGIUM) *See* STATISTIQUES INDUSTRIELLES 1539

INSTITUT NATIONAL DE STATISTIQUE (BELGIUM) *See* JAARSTATISTIEK OVER DE INTERNATIONALE TRAFIEK DER HAVENS 5401

INSTITUT NATIONAL DE STATISTIQUE (BELGIUM). STATISTIQUE ANNUELLE DE TRAFIC INTERNATIONAL DES PORTS; CHIFFRES DEFINITIFS *See* JAARSTATISTIEK OVER DE INTERNATIONALE TRAFIEK DER HAVENS 5401

INSTITUT NATIONAL DES INDUSTRIES EXTRACTIVES *See* RAPPORT 2149

INSTITUT NATIONAL DES LANGUES ET CIVILISATIONS ORIENTALES *See* LIVRET DE LA RECHERCHE / INSTITUT NATIONAL DES LANGUES ET CIVILISATIONS ORIENTALES 2658

INSTITUT NATIONAL DES SCIENCES DE L'UNIVERS (FRANCE) *See* RAPPORT D'ACTIVITE / INSTITUT NATIONAL DES SCIENCES DE L'UNIVERS 399

INSTITUT NATIONAL GENEVOIS *See* RAPPORT ADMINISTRATIF - INSTITUT NATIONAL GENEVOIS 2521

INSTITUT NATIONAL POUR L'ETUDE ET LA RECHERCHE AGRONOMIQUE *See* RAPPORT ANNUEL - INSTITUT NATIONAL POUR L'ETUDE ET LA RECHERCHE AGRONOMIQUE 124

INSTITUT OCEANOGRAPHIQUE *See* BULLETIN DE L'INSTITUT OCEANOGRAPHIQUE (MONACO) 1447

INSTITUT PASTEUR D'ALGERIE *See* ARCHIVES DE L'INSTITUT PASTEUR D'ALGERIE 3552

INSTITUT PASTEUR (PARIS, FRANCE) *See* BULLETIN DE L'INSTITUT PASTEUR 3667

INSTITUT RAZI *See* ARCHIVES DE L'INSTITUTE RAZI 5504

INSTITUT ROYAL DES SCIENCES NATURELLES DE BELGIQUE *See* BULLETIN - INSTITUT ROYAL DES SCIENCES NATURELLES DE BELGIQUE. BIOLOGIE 449

INSTITUT ROYAL DES SCIENCES NATURELLES DE BELGIQUE *See* BULLETIN - INSTITUT ROYAL DES SCIENCES NATURELLES DE BELGIQUE. ENTOMOLOGIE 5579

INSTITUT ROYAL DES SCIENCES NATURELLES DE BELGIQUE *See* BULLETIN - INSTITUT ROYAL DES SCIENCES NATURELLES DE BELGIQUE. SCIENCES DE LA TERRE 1352

INSTITUT ROYAL METEOROLOGIQUE DE BELGIQUE *See* ANNUAIRE; RAYONNEMENT SOLAIRE. JAARBOEK: ZONNESTRALING 1419

INSTITUT ROYAL METEOROLOGIQUE DE BELGIQUE *See* BULLETIN MENSUEL : OBSERVATIONS IONOSPHERIQUES ET DU RAYONNEMENT COSMIQUE 1421

Alphabetical Title Index — INSTITUTE

INSTITUT TEKNOLOGI BANDUNG *See* PROCEEDINGS - INSTITUT TEKNOLOGI BANDUNG **5140**

INSTITUT TEKNOLOGI BANDUNG *See* BERKALA ITB **5088**

INSTITUT UNIVERSITAIRE D'ETUDES DU DEVELOPPEMENT *See* RAPPORT D'ACTIVITE / INSTITUT UNIVERSITAIRE D'ETUDES DU DEVELOPPEMENT **1623**

INSTITUT VSEOBSHCHEI ISTORII (AKADEMIIA NAUK SSSR) *See* SREDNIE VEKA **2630**

INSTITUT VSEOBSHCHEI ISTORII (AKADEMIIA NAUK SSSR) *See* SREDNIE VEKA **2710**

INSTITUT ZA ZASTITU BILJA (BELGRADE, SERBIA) *See* POSEBNA IZDANJA INSTITUTA ZA ZASTITU BILJA **525**

INSTITUTA ET MONUMENTA. SERIE 2: INSTITUTA (IT/0073-8611) [01642426] **4122**

INSTITUTE FOR ANTIQUITY AND CHRISTIANITY (CLAREMONT, CALIF.) *See* BULLETIN / INSTITUTE FOR ANTIQUITY AND CHRISTIANITY **4941**

INSTITUTE FOR BRIQUETTING AND AGGLOMERATION. BIENNIAL CONFERENCE *See* PROCEEDINGS / THE INSTITUTE FOR BRIQUETTING AND AGGLOMERATION **2016**

INSTITUTE FOR BUSINESS PLANNING, INC *See* CORPORATE PLANNING IDEAS **661**

INSTITUTE FOR BUSINESS PLANNING, INC *See* ESTATE PLANNING (ENGLEWOOD CLIFFS, N.J.) **3118**

INSTITUTE FOR BUSINESS PLANNING, INC *See* TAX PRACTICE AND PROCEDURE **4754**

INSTITUTE FOR BUSINESS PLANNING, INC *See* LIFE INSURANCE IDEAS **2887**

INSTITUTE FOR BUSINESS PLANNING, INC *See* LIFE INSURANCE PLANNING **2887**

INSTITUTE FOR CHRISTIAN ECONOMICS (US) **4965, 1496**

INSTITUTE FOR CORPORATE COUNSEL *See* ANNUAL INSTITUTE FOR CORPORATE COUNSEL **3095**

INSTITUTE FOR DEVELOPMENT OF EDUCATIONAL ACTIVITIES *See* SERIES ON EDUCATIONAL CHANGE **1783**

INSTITUTE FOR ENERGY ANALYSIS NEWS (US) [04850161] **1947**

INSTITUTE FOR MATH MANIA PRESENTS WONDERFUL IDEAS, THE (US/1058-0573) [20962928] **1896, 3509**

INSTITUTE FOR NONPROFIT ORGANIZATIONS *See* NEWS FROM THE CENTRE - INSTITUTE FOR NONPROFIT ORGANIZATIONS **5298**

INSTITUTE FOR PERCEPTION RESEARCH *See* IPO ANNUAL PROGRESS REPORT **514**

INSTITUTE FOR RAPID TRANSIT (U.S.) *See* IRT DIGEST **5384**

INSTITUTE FOR RESEARCH IN CONSTRUCTION (CANADA) *See* EUROPEAN PUBLICATIONS CATALOGUE **614**

INSTITUTE FOR RESEARCH IN CONSTRUCTION (CANADA) *See* PUBLICATIONS CATALOGUE / INSTITUTE FOR RESEARCH IN CONSTRUCTION **625**

INSTITUTE FOR RESEARCH INTO MENTAL AND MULTIPLE HANDICAP *See* REVIEWS OF RESEARCH AND PRACTICE OF THE INSTITUTE FOR RESEARCH INTO MENTAL AND MULTIPLE HANDICAP **3935**

INSTITUTE FOR REWRITING INDIAN HISTORY *See* MEETING INVITATION, ANNUAL REPORT, HISTORICAL NOTES / INSTITUTE FOR REWRITING INDIAN HISTORY **2769**

INSTITUTE FOR SCIENTIFIC INFORMATION *See* ISI ALERT **5116**

INSTITUTE FOR STUDIES IN PSYCHOLOGICAL TESTING *See* ISPT JOURNAL OF RESEARCH **4592**

INSTITUTE FOR TELECOMMUNICATION SCIENCES *See* ITS ... TECHNICAL PROGRESS REPORT FOR THE PERIOD ... **1158**

INSTITUTE FOR TELECOMMUNICATION SCIENCES *See* ITS ANNUAL TECHNICAL PROGRESS REPORT **1158**

INSTITUTE FOR TELECOMMUNICATION SCIENCES *See* ITS ... TECHNICAL PROGRESS REPORT FOR THE PERIOD ... **1158**

INSTITUTE FOR THE CERTIFICATION OF COMPUTER PROFESSIONALS *See* ANNUAL REPORT - THE INSTITUTE FOR CERTIFICATION OF COMPUTER PROFESSIONALS **1255**

INSTITUTE FOR THE STUDY OF WOMEN *See* COMMUNIQUE / THE INSTITUTE FOR THE STUDY OF WOMEN **5553**

INSTITUTE FOR WORKERS' CONTROL PAMPHLET (UK/0579-5125) [06344738] **943**

INSTITUTE IN TECHNICAL AND INDUSTRIAL COMMUNICATIONS, COLORADO STATE UNIVERSITY *See* PROCEEDINGS OF THE INSTITUTE IN TECHNICAL AND INDUSTRIAL COMMUNICATIONS **1119**

INSTITUTE (NEW YORK, N.Y.), THE (US/1050-1797) [04853634] **2065**

INSTITUTE OF ACTUARIES (GREAT BRITAIN) *See* INSTITUTE OF ACTUARIES (GREAT BRITAIN) **2882**

INSTITUTE OF ACTUARIES (GREAT BRITAIN) (UK) [24193377] **2882**

INSTITUTE OF ACTUARIES YEAR BOOK, THE *CEASED.* (UK) [04761997] **2882**

INSTITUTE OF ANIMAL PHYSIOLOGY (GREAT BRITAIN) *See* REPORT / AGRICULTURAL RESEARCH COUNCIL, INSTITUTE OF ANIMAL PHYSIOLOGY **5520**

INSTITUTE OF ARABLE CROPS RESEARCH (GREAT BRITAIN) *See* REPORT FOR ... - INSTITUTE OF ARABLE CROPS RESEARCH **184**

INSTITUTE OF BIOLOGICAL RESOURCES (AUSTRALIA) *See* ANNUAL REPORT / INSTITUTE OF BIOLOGICAL RESOURCES **2186**

INSTITUTE OF BRITISH CARRIAGE AND AUTOMOBILE MANUFACTURERS *See* IBCAM **5416**

INSTITUTE OF BRITISH GEOGRAPHERS *See* SPECIAL PUBLICATION--INSTITUTE OF BRITISH GEOGRAPHIES **2576**

INSTITUTE OF BRITISH GEOGRAPHERS *See* TRANSACTIONS - INSTITUTE OF BRITISH GEOGRAPHERS (1965) **2577**

INSTITUTE OF BUILDING *See* YEAR BOOK AND DIRECTORY OF MEMBERS - INSTITUTE OF BUILDING **631**

INSTITUTE OF CANADIAN BANKERS *See* PROGRAMS REGULATIONS - INSTITUTE OF CANADIAN BANKERS **804**

INSTITUTE OF CERTIFIED TRAVEL AGENTS *See* ICTA ROSTER **5480**

INSTITUTE OF CHARTERED ACCOUNTANTS IN AUSTRALIA MEMBERS HANDBOOK (AT) **745**

INSTITUTE OF CHARTERED ACCOUNTANTS IN ENGLAND AND WALES *See* AUDITING AND REPORTING **739**

INSTITUTE OF CHARTERED ACCOUNTANTS IN ENGLAND AND WALES *See* LIST OF MEMBERS AND FIRMS **747**

INSTITUTE OF CHARTERED ACCOUNTANTS IN ENGLAND AND WALES. LIST OF MEMBERS *See* LIST OF MEMBERS AND FIRMS **747**

INSTITUTE OF CHARTERED ACCOUNTANTS IN ENGLAND AND WALES. LONDON. LIBRARY *See* CURRENT ACCOUNTING LITERATURE **742**

INSTITUTE OF CHARTERED ACCOUNTANTS OF ALBERTA *See* MONTHLY STATEMENT - INSTITUTE OF CHARTERED ACCOUNTANTS OF ALBERTA, A **748**

INSTITUTE OF CHARTERED FINANCIAL ANALYSTS *See* C.F.A. DIGEST, THE **781**

INSTITUTE OF CHARTERED FINANCIAL ANALYSTS *See* MEMBERSHIP DIRECTORY **906**

INSTITUTE OF CHILD HEALTH *See* ANNALS - INSTITUTE OF CHILD HEALTH **3900**

INSTITUTE OF CONTINUING LEGAL EDUCATION, ANN ARBOR, MICH *See* ANNUAL SECURITIES SEMINAR COURSE HANDBOOK **2935**

INSTITUTE OF CRIMINOLOGY & FORENSIC SCIENCES BULLETIN (US/0739-8514) [09889104] **3166**

INSTITUTE OF EARLY AMERICAN HISTORY AND CULTURE, WILLIAMSBURG, VA *See* NEWS LETTER FROM THE INSTITUTE OF EARLY AMERICAN HISTORY & CULTURE, A **2749**

INSTITUTE OF ECOLOGY *See* TIE REPORT **1714**

INSTITUTE OF ECONOMIC AFFAIRS (GREAT BRITAIN) *See* IEA LECTURE **1494**

INSTITUTE OF ECONOMIC GEOGRAPHY, INDIA *See* JOURNAL - INSTITUTE OF ECONOMIC GEOGRAPHY, INDIA **1569**

INSTITUTE OF ECONOMIC RESEARCH, DHARWAR *See* JOURNAL OF INSTITUTE OF ECONOMIC RESEARCH **1570**

INSTITUTE OF EDUCATION (DAR ES SALAAM, TANZANIA) *See* HANDBOOK / INSTITUTE OF EDUCATION **1749**

INSTITUTE OF ELECTRICAL AND ELECTRONIC ENGINEERS. REGION 6 CONFERENCE *See* PROCEEDINGS, REGION 6 CONFERENCE **2077**

INSTITUTE OF ELECTRICAL AND ELECTRONICS ENGINEERS *See* IEEE TRANSACTIONS ON COMPUTERS **1247**

INSTITUTE OF ELECTRICAL AND ELECTRONICS ENGINEERS *See* IEEE GRID **2059**

INSTITUTE OF ELECTRICAL AND ELECTRONICS ENGINEERS *See* IEEE MEMBERSHIP DIRECTORY **2060**

INSTITUTE OF ELECTRICAL AND ELECTRONICS ENGINEERS *See* IEEE STUDENT PAPERS **2061**

INSTITUTE OF ELECTRICAL AND ELECTRONICS ENGINEERS *See* IEEE PUBLICATIONS BULLETIN **2060**

INSTITUTE OF ELECTRICAL AND ELECTRONICS ENGINEERS *See* CONFERENCE PAPER [PREPRINTS] **2039**

INSTITUTE OF ELECTRICAL AND ELECTRONICS ENGINEERS *See* INDEX TO IEEE PUBLICATIONS **2004**

INSTITUTE OF ELECTRICAL AND ELECTRONICS ENGINEERS *See* IEEE IMPACT **2059**

INSTITUTE OF ELECTRICAL AND ELECTRONICS ENGINEERS *See* PROCEEDINGS OF THE IEEE **2076**

INSTITUTE OF ELECTRICAL AND ELECTRONICS ENGINEERS *See* IEEE IECI PROCEEDINGS **2059**

INSTITUTE OF ELECTRICAL AND ELECTRONICS ENGINEERS. LOS ANGELES COUNCIL *See* IEEE BULLETIN **2059**

INSTITUTE OF ELECTRICAL AND ELECTRONICS ENGINEERS. PHILADELPHIA SECTION *See* ALMANACK - INSTITUTE OF ELECTRICAL AND ELECTRONICS ENGINEERS, INC. PHILADELPHIA SECTION **2034**

INSTITUTE OF ENERGY AND EARTH RESOURCES (AUSTRALIA). DIVISION OF ENERGY CHEMISTRY *See* BIENNIAL RESEARCH REPORT / DIVISION OF ENERGY CHEMISTRY, CSIRO **1933**

INSTITUTE OF ENERGY AND EARTH RESOURCES (AUSTRALIA). DIVISION OF GEOMECHANICS *See* ABSTRACTS OF PUBLISHED PAPERS / CSIRO, INSTITUTE OF ENERGY AND EARTH RESOURCES, DIVISION OF GEOMECHANICS **1351**

INSTITUTE OF ENERGY AND EARTH RESOURCES (AUSTRALIA). DIVISION OF GEOMECHANICS *See* BIENNIAL REPORT / CSIRO DIVISION OF GEOMECHANICS **1367**

INSTITUTE OF ENERGY (GREAT BRITAIN) *See* JOURNAL OF THE INSTITUTE OF ENERGY **1949**

INSTITUTE OF ENVIRONMENTAL SCIENCES *See* PROCEEDINGS / INSTITUTE OF ENVIRONMENTAL SCIENCES **1991**

INSTITUTE OF ENVIRONMENTAL SCIENCES *See* PROCEEDINGS, ANNUAL TECHNICAL MEETING - INSTITUTE OF ENVIRONMENTAL SCIENCES **5140**

INSTITUTE OF FINANCE MANAGEMENT *See* PROSPECTUS - THE INSTITUTE OF FINANCE MANAGEMENT **883**

INSTITUTE OF FOOD SCIENCE AND TECHNOLOGY *See* PROCEEDINGS - INSTITUTE OF FOOD SCIENCE AND TECHNOLOGY (U.K.) **2353**

INSTITUTE OF GEOLOGICAL AND NUCLEAR SCIENCES MONOGRAPHS (NZ) **1383**

INSTITUTE OF HOUSING YEAR BOOK, THE (UK/0260-7239) [08059149] **2825**

INSTITUTE OF INDUSTRIAL TECHNOLOGIES (COMMONWEALTH SCIENTIFIC AND INDUSTRIAL RESEARCH ORGANIZATION (AUSTRALIA)). DIVISION OF MATERIALS SCIENCE AND TECHNOLOGY *See* ANNUAL REPORT / DIVISION OF MATERIALS SCIENCE AND TECHNOLOGY, CSIRO AUSTRALIA **2100**

INSTITUTE OF INTERNAL AUDITORS *See* RESEARCH REPORT - INSTITUTE OF INTERNAL AUDITORS **750**

INSTITUTE OF INTERNATIONAL EDUCATION (NEW YORK, N.Y.) *See* OPEN DOORS (NEW YORK) **1796**

INSTITUTE OF INTERNATIONAL LAW *See* ANNUAIRE DE L'INSTITUT DE DROIT INTERNATIONAL **3123**

INSTITUTE OF JUDICIAL ADMINISTRATION *See* IJA REPORT **3090**

INSTITUTE OF JUDICIAL ADMINISTRATION *See* INSTITUTE OF JUDICIAL ADMINISTRATION REPORT **2983**

INSTITUTE OF JUDICIAL ADMINISTRATION. LIBRARY *See* SELECTED LIST OF ACQUISITIONS CATALOGED **3047**

INSTITUTE OF JUDICIAL ADMINISTRATION REPORT (US/0146-7816) [03037918] **2983**

INSTITUTE — Alphabetical Title Index

INSTITUTE OF LABORATORY ANIMAL RESOURCES (U.S.) *See* ILAR NEWS **3585**

INSTITUTE OF MANAGEMENT CONSULTANTS (LONDON, ENGLAND) *See* YEARBOOK / INSTITUTE OF MANAGEMENT CONSULTANTS **889**

INSTITUTE OF MANAGEMENT CONSULTANTS (NEW YORK, N.Y.) *See* DIRECTORY OF MEMBERS - INSTITUTE OF MANAGEMENT CONSULTANTS **865**

INSTITUTE OF MANAGEMENT SCIENCES *See* PROCEEDINGS OF THE ... INTERNATIONAL MEETING OF THE INSTITUTE OF MANAGEMENT SCIENCES **883**

INSTITUTE OF MANAGEMENT SCIENCES *See* TIMS/ORSA BULLETIN **1629**

INSTITUTE OF MANPOWER STUDIES (GREAT BRITAIN) *See* ANNUAL REPORT / INSTITUTE OF MANPOWER STUDIES **1649**

INSTITUTE OF MATHEMATICAL STATISTICS *See* BULLETIN - INSTITUTE OF MATHEMATICAL STATISTICS **5324**

INSTITUTE OF MATHEMATICS AND ITS APPLICATIONS *See* BULLETIN - INSTITUTE OF MATHEMATICS AND ITS APPLICATIONS **3498**

INSTITUTE OF MEASUREMENT AND CONTROL *See* TRANSACTIONS OF THE INSTITUTE OF MEASUREMENT AND CONTROL **2131**

INSTITUTE OF MEAT *See* BULLETIN - THE INSTITUTE OF MEAT **2329**

INSTITUTE OF MEDICINE (U.S.) *See* NEWSLETTER - INSTITUTE OF MEDICINE **3621**

INSTITUTE OF METAL FINISHING *See* TRANSACTIONS OF THE INSTITUTE OF METAL FINISHING **4022**

INSTITUTE OF METALS *See* HANDBOOK AND ... LIST OF MEMBERS - INSTITUTE OF METALS **4003**

INSTITUTE OF METALS MONOGRAPH AND REPORT SERIES (UK/0073-9464) [01753244] **4004**

INSTITUTE OF MUNICIPAL ASSESSORS OF ONTARIO *See* TECHNICAL BULLETIN - INSTITUTE OF MUNICIPAL ASSESSORS OF ONTARIO **4690**

INSTITUTE OF NAVIGATION. NATIONAL TECHNICAL MEETING *See* PROCEEDINGS OF THE NATIONAL TECHNICAL MEETING / THE INSTITUTE OF NAVIGATION **4182**

INSTITUTE OF NUCLEAR MATERIALS MANAGEMENT *See* PROCEEDINGS, ANNUAL MEETING, INSTITUTE OF NUCLEAR MATERIALS MANAGEMENT **2158**

INSTITUTE OF OCEANOGRAPHIC AND FISHERIES RESEARCH *See* SPECIAL PUBLICATION - INSTITUTE OF OCEANOGRAPHIC AND FISHERIES RESEARCH **1457**

INSTITUTE OF OCEANOGRAPHIC SCIENCES DEACON LABORATORY (GREAT BRITAIN) *See* REPORT OF THE INSTITUTE OF OCEANOGRAPHIC SCIENCES DEACON LABORATORY FOR THE PERIOD 1ST APRIL ... TO 31ST MARCH ... **1456**

INSTITUTE OF PAPER CHEMISTRY (APPLETON, WIS.) *See* ABSTRACT BULLETIN OF THE INSTITUTE OF PAPER CHEMISTRY **4240**

INSTITUTE OF PAPER CHEMISTRY (APPLETON, WIS.) *See* ABSTRACT BULLETIN OF THE INSTITUTE OF PAPER CHEMISTRY. KEYWORD INDEX **4232**

INSTITUTE OF PAPER CONSERVATION *See* MEMBERSHIP DIRECTORY - INSTITUTE OF PAPER CONSERVATION **4235**

INSTITUTE OF PAPER SCIENCE AND TECHNOLOGY. EXECUTIVES' CONFERENCE *See* PROCEEDINGS / EXECUTIVES' CONFERENCE, INSTITUTE OF PAPER SCIENCE AND TECHNOLOGY **4237**

INSTITUTE OF PETROLEUM. STATISTICS SERVICE (UK) **4283**

INSTITUTE OF PHYSICS CONFERENCE SERIES (UK/0951-3248) [13258644] **4405**

INSTITUTE OF PRIMATE RESEARCH (KENYA) *See* IPR ... REPORT / INSTITUTE OF PRIMATE RESEARCH **5512**

INSTITUTE OF PRIMATE RESEARCH (KENYA). IPR ANNUAL REPORT *See* IPR ... REPORT / INSTITUTE OF PRIMATE RESEARCH **5512**

INSTITUTE OF PROFESSIONAL LIBRARIANS OF ONTARIO *See* I P L O NEWS **3214**

INSTITUTE OF PUBLIC POLICY STUDIES DISCUSSION PAPER (US) [21253336] **1496**

INSTITUTE OF PUBLIC RELATIONS JOURNAL, THE (UK) [28996027] **760**

INSTITUTE OF PUBLIC SERVICE STATE AND LOCAL GOVENMENT NEWSLETTER (US) [21274764] **4657**

INSTITUTE OF PURCHASING AND SUPPLY *See* HANDBOOK - INSTITUTE OF PURCHASING AND SUPPLY **950**

INSTITUTE OF ROAD TRANSPORT ENGINEERS *See* ANNUAL REPORT OF THE COUNCIL AND INSTITUTE ACCOUNTS **2018**

INSTITUTE OF SCRAP IRON AND STEEL *See* FACTS (WASHINGTON) **4001**

INSTITUTE OF SCRAP IRON & STEEL YEARBOOK *See* FACTS (WASHINGTON) **4001**

INSTITUTE OF SOCIAL STUDIES (NETHERLANDS) *See* PUBLICATIONS OF THE INSTITUTE OF SOCIAL STUDIES. PAPERBACK SERIES **5214**

INSTITUTE OF STATISTICS AND APPLIED ECONOMICS (UGANDA) *See* BROCHURE FOR ... / INSTITUTE OF STATISTICS AND APPLIED ECONOMICS **1530**

INSTITUTE OF TRADITIONAL CULTURES *See* BULLETIN OF THE INSTITUTE OF TRADITIONAL CULTURES **5194**

INSTITUTE OF TRANSPORTATION ENGINEERS *See* ITE JOURNAL **5384**

INSTITUTE OF TRANSPORTATION ENGINEERS. DISTRICT 7, CANADA *See* ANNUAL CONFERENCE PROCEEDINGS - INSTITUTE OF TRANSPORTATION ENGINEERS, CANADA **5376**

INSTITUTE OF TRANSPORTATION ENGINEERS. MEETING *See* COMPENDIUM OF TECHNICAL PAPERS : INSTITUTE OF TRANSPORTATION ENGINEERS ... ANNUAL MEETING **5439**

INSTITUTE OF TROPICAL FORESTRY (RIO PIEDRAS, P.R.) *See* FOREST SERVICE RESEARCH PAPER ITF **2381**

INSTITUTE OF TROPICAL FORESTRY (RIO PIEDRAS, SAN JUAN, P.R.) *See* ANNUAL LETTER **2374**

INSTITUTE OF TROPICAL FORESTRY (RIO PIEDRAS, SAN JUAN, P.R.). LETTER PRESENTING SOME OF THE HIGHLIGHTS OF ACTIVITIES AND PROGRESS AT INSTITUTE OF TROPICAL FORESTRY *See* ANNUAL LETTER **2374**

INSTITUTE OF URBAN STUDIES PUBLICATION (CN/0712-788X) [08569829] **2825**

INSTITUTE OF WOOD SCIENCE *See* JOURNAL OF THE INSTITUTE OF WOOD SCIENCE **2402**

INSTITUTE ON AGING NEWSLETTER (US/1059-2431) [24527141] **5179**

INSTITUTE ON FEDERAL TAXATION (US) [10064910] **4732**

INSTITUTE ON SECURITIES LAWS AND REGULATIONS *See* PROCEEDINGS OF THE ANNUAL INSTITUTE ON SECURITIES LAWS AND REGULATIONS **3031**

INSTITUTE ON SECURITIES REGULATION *See* ANNUAL INSTITUTE ON SECURITIES REGULATION **2934**

INSTITUTE ON THE CHURCH IN URBAN-INDUSTRIAL SOCIETY *See* ICUIS BIBLIOGRAPHY SERIES **5012**

INSTITUTE REPORT (KALAMAZOO, MICH.), THE (US/0738-4858) [08774254] **1680**

INSTITUTE TODAY (US/0897-4527) [17502179] **791**

INSTITUTES OF CHARTERED ACCOUNTANTS IN CANADA *See* APPROACHES TO ANSWERING THE UNIFORM FINAL EXAMINATIONS, PLUS EXAMINERS' COMMENTS **738**

INSTITUTES OF CHARTERED ACCOUNTANTS IN CANADA *See* INSTITUTS DE COMPTABLES AGREES DU CANADA. EXAMENS FINAL **745**

INSTITUTES OF CHARTERED ACCOUNTANTS IN CANADA AND BERMUDA *See* UNIFORM FINAL EXAMINATION REPORT / THE INSTITUTES OF CHARTERED ACCOUNTANTS IN CANADA AND BERMUDA **752**

INSTITUTION OF AGRICULTURAL ENGINEERS *See* MEMBERS' HANDBOOK & BUYERS' GUIDE : THE GREEN BOOK / THE INSTITUTION OF AGRICULTURAL ENGINEERS **160**

INSTITUTION OF CHEMICAL ENGINEERS *See* INSTITUTION OF CHEMICAL ENGINEERS SYMPOSIUM SERIES, THE **2013**

INSTITUTION OF CHEMICAL ENGINEERS SYMPOSIUM SERIES, THE (UK/0307-0492) [01641886] **2013**

INSTITUTION OF CIVIL ENGINEERS (GREAT BRITAIN) *See* PROCEEDINGS **2029**

INSTITUTION OF CIVIL ENGINEERS (GREAT BRITAIN) *See* PROCEEDINGS OF THE INSTITUTION OF CIVIL ENGINEERS. MUNICIPAL ENGINEER **2029**

INSTITUTION OF CIVIL ENGINEERS (GREAT BRITAIN) *See* PROCEEDINGS OF THE INSTITUTION OF CIVIL ENGINEERS. MUNICIPAL ENGINEER **2029**

INSTITUTION OF CIVIL ENGINEERS (GREAT BRITAIN) *See* PROCEEDINGS OF THE INSTITUTION OF CIVIL ENGINEERS. WATER, MARITIME AND ENERGY **2094**

INSTITUTION OF CIVIL ENGINEERS (GREAT BRITAIN) *See* PROCEEDINGS OF THE INSTITUTION OF CIVIL ENGINEERS. WATER, MARITIME AND ENERGY **2094**

INSTITUTION OF CIVIL ENGINEERS (GREAT BRITAIN) *See* YEARBOOK - INSTITUTION OF CIVIL ENGINEERS **2034**

INSTITUTION OF CIVIL ENGINEERS (GREAT BRITAIN). LIST OF MEMBERS *See* YEARBOOK - INSTITUTION OF CIVIL ENGINEERS **2034**

INSTITUTION OF CIVIL ENGINEERS (GREAT BRITAIN). PROCEEDINGS - INSTITUTION OF CIVIL ENGINEERS. PART 1, DESIGN AND CONSTRUCTION *See* PROCEEDINGS OF THE INSTITUTION OF CIVIL ENGINEERS. STRUCTURES AND BUILDINGS **2029**

INSTITUTION OF CIVIL ENGINEERS (GREAT BRITAIN). PROCEEDINGS - INSTITUTION OF CIVIL ENGINEERS. PART 2, RESEARCH AND THEORY *See* PROCEEDINGS OF THE INSTITUTION OF CIVIL ENGINEERS. STRUCTURES AND BUILDINGS **2029**

INSTITUTION OF CIVIL ENGINEERS (GREAT BRITAIN). RESEARCH COMMITTEE *See* REPORT OF THE RESEARCH COMMITTEE **1994**

INSTITUTION OF ELECTRICAL ENGINEERS *See* IEE CONFERENCE PUBLICATION **2057**

INSTITUTION OF ELECTRICAL ENGINEERS *See* IEE PROCEEDINGS. PART I. SOLID-STATE AND ELECTRON DEVICES **2058**

INSTITUTION OF ELECTRICAL ENGINEERS *See* I.E.E.-I.E.R.E. PROCEEDINGS INDIA **2056**

INSTITUTION OF ELECTRICAL ENGINEERS *See* IEE CONTROL ENGINEERING SERIES **2057**

INSTITUTION OF ELECTRICAL ENGINEERS *See* IEE TELECOMMUNICATIONS SERIES **1156**

INSTITUTION OF ELECTRICAL ENGINEERS *See* IEE NEWS **2057**

INSTITUTION OF ELECTRICAL ENGINEERS, LONDON *See* PROCEEDINGS OF THE INSTITUTION OF ELECTRICAL ENGINEERS **2077**

INSTITUTION OF ELECTRONICS AND TELECOMMUNICATION ENGINEERS (INDIA) *See* ANNUAL REPORT / IETE **2035**

INSTITUTION OF ELECTRONICS AND TELECOMMUNICATION ENGINEERS (INDIA) *See* JOURNAL OF THE INSTITUTION OF ELECTRONICS AND TELECOMMUNICATION ENGINEERS **1159**

INSTITUTION OF ENGINEERS AND SHIPBUILDERS IN SCOTLAND *See* TRANSACTIONS / INSTITUTION OF ENGINEERS AND SHIPBUILDERS IN SCOTLAND **1999**

INSTITUTION OF ENGINEERS, AUSTRALIA *See* NATIONAL CONFERENCE PUBLICATION - INSTITUTION OF ENGINEERS, AUSTRALIA **1988**

INSTITUTION OF ENGINEERS (INDIA) *See* BULLETIN OF THE INSTITUTION OF ENGINEERS (INDIA) **2037**

INSTITUTION OF ENGINEERS (INDIA) *See* JOURNAL OF THE INSTITUTION OF ENGINEERS (INDIA). CIVIL ENGINEERING DIVISION **2026**

INSTITUTION OF ENGINEERS (INDIA) *See* JOURNAL OF THE INSTITUTION OF ENGINEERS (INDIA). ELECTRONICS & TELECOMMUNICATION ENGINEERING DIVISION **2070**

INSTITUTION OF ENGINEERS (INDIA). ELECTRICAL ENGINEERING DIVISION *See* JOURNAL OF THE INSTITUTION OF ENGINEERS (INDIA) **2070**

INSTITUTION OF ENGINEERS (INDIA). ENVIRONMENTAL ENGINEERING DIVISION *See* JOURNAL OF THE INSTITUTION OF ENGINEERS (INDIA). PART EN CALCUTTA, ENVIRONMENTAL ENGINEERING DIVISION, THE **2176**

INSTITUTION OF ENGINEERS (INDIA). MECHANICAL ENGINEERING DIVISION *See* JOURNAL OF THE INSTITUTION OF ENGINEERS (INDIA). MECHANICAL ENGINEERING DIVISION **2118**

INSTITUTION OF ENGINEERS OF IRELAND *See* TRANSACTIONS - INSTITUTION OF ENGINEERS OF IRELAND **1999**

INSTITUTION OF ENGINEERS, SINGAPORE *See* JOURNAL - THE INSTITUTION OF ENGINEERS, SINGAPORE **1984**

Alphabetical Title Index

INSTITUTO

INSTITUTION OF ENVIRONMENTAL HEALTH OFFICERS (LONDON, ENGLAND) *See* MEMBERS DIRECTORY / THE INSTITUTION OF ENVIRONMENTAL HEALTH OFFICERS **4790**

INSTITUTION OF MECHANICAL ENGINEERS (GREAT BRITAIN) *See* PROCEEDINGS OF THE INSTITUTION OF MECHANICAL ENGINEERS **2125**

INSTITUTION OF MINING AND METALLURGY (GREAT BRITAIN) *See* IMM ABSTRACTS **4003**

INSTITUTION OF MINING AND METALLURGY. TRANSACTIONS. SECTION B : APPLIED EARTH SCIENCES (UK/0371-7453) [02401166] **2140**

INSTITUTION OF MINING AND METALLURGY. TRANSACTIONS. SECTION C : MINERAL PROCESSING AND EXTRACTIVE METALLURGY (UK/0371-9553) [02401167] **4004**

INSTITUTION OF PROFESSIONAL ENGINEERS NEW ZEALAND. CIVIL ENGINEERING SECTION *See* TRANSACTIONS OF THE INSTITUTION OF PROFESSIONAL ENGINEERS NEW ZEALAND, CIVIL ENGINEERING SECTION **2033**

INSTITUTION OF PROFESSIONAL ENGINEERS NEW ZEALAND. ELECTRICAL, MECHANICAL, CHEMICAL, ENGINEERING SECTION *See* TRANSACTIONS OF THE INSTITUTION OF PROFESSIONAL ENGINEERS NEW ZEALAND, ELECTRICAL/MECHANICAL/CHEMICAL ENGINEERING SECTION **1999**

INSTITUTION OF STRUCTURAL ENGINEERS (GREAT BRITAIN) *See* SESSIONAL YEARBOOK ... AND DIRECTORY OF MEMBERS **2030**

INSTITUTION OF WATER OFFICERS JOURNAL (UK/0962-0311) [I09620311] **5534**

INSTITUTIONAL CHARACTERISTICS OF COLLEGES AND UNIVERSITIES (US/0095-5272) [03165539] **1830**

INSTITUTIONAL DIRECTORY. POSTSECONDARY EDUCATION IN NEW YORK STATE *See* INTERIM INSTITUTIONAL DIRECTORY ... HIGHER EDUCATION IN NEW YORK STATE / THE UNIVERSITY OF THE STATE OF NEW YORK, THE STATE EDUCATION DEPARTMENT, BUREAU OF POSTSECONDARY PLANNING **1831**

INSTITUTIONAL DISTRIBUTION (US/0020-3572) [02447690] **2344**

INSTITUTIONAL EQUITY SERVICES (US/0741-0239) [08420312] **901**

INSTITUTIONAL FOOD SERVICE AND NUTRITIONAL CARE (US) **3857**

INSTITUTIONAL INVESTOR (INTERNATIONAL ED.) (US/0192-5660) [05031892] **901**

INSTITUTIONAL INVESTOR (U.S. ED.) (US/0020-3580) [01017201] **901**

INSTITUTIONAL MEAT PURCHASE SPECIFICATIONS (US) [02636988] **213**

INSTITUTIONAL REAL ESTATE LETTER, THE (US/1044-1662) [19699048] **4839**

INSTITUTIONAL REAL ESTATE MONITOR. FLORIDA ED *See* INSIDER FORECLOSURE GUIDE **4839**

INSTITUTIONS OF ENGINEERS (INDIA) *See* JOURNAL OF THE INSTITUTION OF ENGINEERS. INDIA. PART CH: CHEMICAL ENGINEERING DIVISION **2014**

INSTITUTIONS OF HIGHER EDUCATION INDEX, BY STATE AND CONGRESSIONAL DISTRICT (US/0145-7721) [02781608] **1830**

INSTITUTO AGRARIO NACIONAL (VENEZUELA) *See* BOLETIN - VENEZUELA. INSTITUTO AGRARIO NACIONAL **68**

INSTITUTO AGRONOMICA DO PARANA *See* CIRCULAR - FUNDACAO INSTITUTO AGRONOMICO DO PARANA **74**

INSTITUTO AGRONOMICO DO PARANA *See* BOLETIN TECNICO - IAPAR **68**

INSTITUTO AMERICANO DE ESTUDIOS VASCOS *See* BOLETIN DEL INSTITUTO AMERICANO DE ESTUDIOS VASCOS **3269**

INSTITUTO ANT ARTICO ARGENTINO *See* PUBLICACION - INSTITUTO ANTARTICO ARGENTINO **2574**

INSTITUTO ANTARTICO ARGENTINO *See* CONTRIBUCIONES CIENTIFICAS DEL INSTITUTO ANTARTICO ARGENTINO **5097**

INSTITUTO ARGENTINO DE OCEANOGRAFIA *See* CONTRIBUCIONES CIENTIFICAS DEL INSTITUTO ARGENTINO DE OCEANOGRAFIA **1448**

INSTITUTO ARGENTINO DE OCEANOGRAFIA *See* MEMORIA ANUAL - INSTITUTO ARGENTINO DE OCEANOGRAFIA **1452**

INSTITUTO ARGENTINO DE RACIONALIZACION DE MATERIALES. IRAM, TECNOLOGIA Y GESTION *See* TECNOLOGIA Y GESTION **5165**

INSTITUTO ARGENTINO DEL ENVASE (AG/0326-8365) [I03268365] **4219**

INSTITUTO AUTONOMO ADMINISTRACION DE FERROCARRILES DEL ESTADO (VENEZUELA). DIVISION DE PRESUPUESTO *See* PRESUPUESTO PRO PROGRAMA - INSTITUTO AUTONOMO ADMINISTRACION DE FERROCARRILES DEL ESTADO, DIVISION DE PRESUPUESTO **5434**

INSTITUTO BAHIANO DO FUMO *See* BOLETIM INFORMATIVO : COMERCIO EXTERIOR - EXPORTACAO DE FUMO EM FOLHAS **5372**

INSTITUTO BRASILEIRO DE BIBLIOGRAFIA E DOCUMENTACAO *See* IBBD/CDU INFORMATIVO **417**

INSTITUTO BRASILEIRO DE ECONOMIA. CENTRO DE ESTUDOS AGRICOLAS *See* PRECOS RECEBIDOS PELOS AGRICULTORES **121**

INSTITUTO BRASILEIRO DE GEOGRAFIA E ESTATISTICA *See* CENSO AGROPECUARIO; VIII RECENSEAMENTO GERAL **152**

INSTITUTO BRASILEIRO DE PETROLEO *See* RELATORIO DAS ATIVIDADES DE ... E PROGRAMACAO PARA ... **4276**

INSTITUTO BRASILEIRO DE PETROLEO. RELATORIO DAS ATIVIDADES EM . *See* RELATORIO DAS ATIVIDADES DE ... E PROGRAMACAO PARA ... **4276**

INSTITUTO BRASILEIRO DO CAFE *See* CAFE: RESULTADOS OBTIDOS **2365**

INSTITUTO BRASILEIRO DO CAFE ESCRITORIO DE NEW YORK *See* MERCADO DE CAFE NOS ESTADOS UNIDOS E NO CANADA. THE COFFEE MARKET IN THE UNITED STATES AND CANADA, O **2369**

INSTITUTO BRASILEIRO DO COURO, CALCADOS E AFINS *See* SISTEMA DE INFORMACAO ESTATISTICA PARA A INDUSTRIA NACIONAL DE COUROS : BOLETIM DE INFORMACOES **3186**

INSTITUTO BRASILEIRO DO COURO, CALCADOS E AFINS *See* SISTEMA DE INFORMACAO ESTATISTICA PARA A INDUSTRIA NACIONAL DE CALCADOS **1087**

INSTITUTO CALASANZ DE CIENCIAS DE LA EDUCACION *See* BOLETIN BIBLIOGRAFICO ICCE **1793**

INSTITUTO COLOMBIANO AGROPECUARIO. PROGRAMA NACIONAL DE FISIOLOGIA VEGETAL *See* INFORME ... DEL PROGRAMA NACIONAL DE FISIOLOGIA VEGETAL **2420**

INSTITUTO COORDINADOR DEL COMERCIO INTERNACIONAL *See* ARANCEL ADUANERO DE CHILE **823**

INSTITUTO DE ARQUEOLOGIA BRASILEIRA *See* BOLETIM DO INSTITUTO DE ARQUEOLOGIA BRASILEIRA **262**

INSTITUTO DE ARQUEOLOGIA BRASILEIRA *See* BOLETIM DO INSTITUTO DE ARQUEOLOGIA BRASILEIRA : SERIE ESPECIAL **2723**

INSTITUTO DE CREDITO OFICIAL (SPAIN) *See* INFORME ANUAL **791**

INSTITUTO DE CULTURA PUERTORRIQUENA *See* REVISTA DEL INSTITUTO DE CULTURA PUERTORRIQUENA **2758**

INSTITUTO DE DESENVOLVIMENTO ECONOMICO E GERENCIAL *See* ESTADO DO RIO DE JANEIRO : INDICADORES ECONOMICOS **1560**

INSTITUTO DE DESENVOLVIMENTO ECON,,OMICO SOCIAL DO PAR,A *See* INSTITUTO DO DESENCOLVIMENTO ECONOMICO-SOCIAL DO PARA: PEDQUISA EMPREGO E DESEMPREGO NA REGIAO METROPOLITANA DE BELEM **1680**

INSTITUTO DE DESENVOLVIMENTO INDUSTRIAL DE MINAS GERAIS *See* RELATORIO ANUAL / INDI **1624**

INSTITUTO DE DIREITO SOCIAL (SAO PAULO, BRAZIL) *See* ARQUIVOS DO INSTITUTO DE DIREITO SOCIAL **2937**

INSTITUTO DE DOCUMENTACION E INFORMACION CIENTIFICA Y TECNICA (ACADEMIA DE CIENCIAS DE CUBA) *See* ACTUALIDADES DE LA INFORMACION CIENTIFICA Y TECNICA **3187**

INSTITUTO DE DOCUMENTACION E INFORMACION CIENTIFICA Y TECNICA (ACADEMIA DE CIENCIAS DE CUBA) *See* PROBLEMAS DE ORGANIZACION DE LA CIENCIA **5139**

INSTITUTO DE DOCUMENTACION E INFORMACION CIENTIFICA Y TECNICA (ACADEMIA DE CIENCIAS DE CUBA). ACTUALIDADES DE LA INFORMACION CIENTIFICA Y TECNICA *See* CIENCIAS DE LA INFORMACION **3202**

INSTITUTO DE ENGENHARIA DE S‰AO PAULO *See* ANUARIO DO INSTITUTO DE ENGENHARIA **1965**

INSTITUTO DE ENGENHARIA NUCLEAR *See* RELATORIO TECNICO ANUAL DE ... / COMISSAO NACIONAL DE ENERGIA NUCLEAR, INSTITUTO DE ENGENHARIA NUCLEAR **2158**

INSTITUTO DE ESTUDIOS ASTURIANOS (OVIEDO, SPAIN) *See* BOLETIN DEL INSTITUTO DE ESTUDIOS ASTURIANOS **2679**

INSTITUTO DE ESTUDIOS GERUNDENSES *See* ANALES DEL INSTITUTO DE ESTUDIOS GERUNDENSES **2673**

INSTITUTO DE ESTUDIOS MADRILENOS (CONSEJO SUPERIOR DE INVESTIGACIONES CIENTIFICAS) *See* ANALES DEL INSTITUTO DE ESTUDIOS MADRILENOS **2673**

INSTITUTO DE ESTUDIOS POLITICOS (SPAIN). INSTITUTO DE LA JUVENTUD *See* REVISTA DEL INSTITUTO DE LA JUVENTUD **1068**

INSTITUTO DE FISIOGRAFIA Y GEOLOGIA "DR ALFREDO CASTELLANOS." *See* PUBLICACIONES - INSTITUTO DE FISIOGRAFIA Y GEOLOGIA **1392**

INSTITUTO DE FOMENTO INDUSTRIAL (BOGOTA, COLOMBIA) *See* IFI : MEMORIA **1609**

INSTITUTO DE GEOLOGIA REVISTA (MX/0185-0962) [04433271] **1383**

INSTITUTO DE HISTORIA DEL DERECHO RICARDO LEVENE *See* REVISTA DEL INSTITUTO DE HISTORIA DEL DERECHO RICARDO LEVENE **3041**

INSTITUTO DE INVESTIGACAO CIENTIFICA DE ANGOLA *See* RELATORIOS E COMUNICOES - INSTITUTO DE INVESTIGACAO CIENTIFICA DE ANGOLA **5145**

INSTITUTO DE INVESTIGACIONES BIOQUIMICAS, ANUARIO (AG) [03497007] **581**

INSTITUTO DE INVESTIGACIONES MARINAS DE PUNTA DE BETIN *See* ANALES DEL INSTITUTO DE INVESTIGACIONES MARINAS DE PUNTA DE BETIN **552**

INSTITUTO DE INVESTIGACIONES VETERINARIAS *See* ANALES DEL INSTITUTO DE INVESTIGACIONES VETERINARIAS **5502**

INSTITUTO DE MEDICINA TROPICAL DE SAO PAULO *See* REVISTA DO INSTITUTO DE MEDICINA TROPICAL DE SAO PAULO **3986**

INSTITUTO DE PESCA *See* BOLETIM DO INSTITUTO DE PESCA **2297**

INSTITUTO DE PESQUISAS DA MARINHA *See* PUBLICACAO DO INSTITUTO DE PESQUISAS DA MARINHA **470**

INSTITUTO DE PESQUISAS TECHNOLOGICAS *See* ATIVIDADES DESENVOLVIDAS **5086**

INSTITUTO DE RESSEGUROS DO BRASIL *See* RELATORIO ANUAL / IRB **2891**

INSTITUTO DE RESSEGUROS DO BRASIL. REVISTA *See* REVISTA DO IRB / INSTITUTO DE RESSEGUROS DO BRASIL **2892**

INSTITUTO DE TECNOLOGIA DE ALIMENTOS (S‰AO PAULO, BRAZIL) *See* COLETANEA DO INSTITUTO DE TECNOLOGIA DE ALIMENTOS **2331**

INSTITUTO DEL MAR DEL PERU *See* INFORME - INSTITUTO DEL MAR DEL PERU **554**

INSTITUTO DO ACUCAR E DO ALCOOL (BRAZIL) *See* COLETANEA DE RESOLUCOES DO CONSELHO DELIBERATIVO. COLETANEA DE ATOS DA PRESIDENCIA **2952**

INSTITUTO DO AZEITE E PRODUTOS OLEAGINOSO *See* BOLETIM - INSTITUTO DO AZEITE E PRODUTOS OLEAGINOSOS **5089**

INSTITUTO DO DESENCOLVIMENTO ECONOMICO-SOCIAL DO PARA: PEDQUISA EMPREGO E DESEMPREGO NA REGIAO METROPOLITANA DE BELEM (BL) [05056939] **1680**

INSTITUTO DOS ADVOGADOS BRASILEIROS *See* REVISTA DO INSTITUTO DOS ADVOGADOS BRASILEIROS **3042**

INSTITUTO DOS ADVOGADOS DO RIO GRANDE DO SUL. DIRETORIA *See* RELATORIO DA GESTAO DA DIRETORIA DO INSTITUTO DOS ADVOGADOS DO RIO GRANDE DO SUL **3037**

INSTITUTO ECUATORIANO DE CIENCIAS NATURALES *See* CONTRIBUCION - INSTITUTO ECUATORIANO DE CIENCIAS NATURALES **5097**

INSTITUTO EDUARDO TORROJA DE LA CONSTRUCCION Y DEL CEMENTO *See* MONOGRAFIAS DEL INSTITUTO EDUARDO TORROJA DE LA CONSTRUCCION Y DEL CEMENTO **621**

INSTITUTO ESPANOL DE MUSICOLOGIA *See* ANUARIO MUSICAL **4100**

INSTITUTO — Alphabetical Title Index

INSTITUTO FORESTAL LATINO-AMERICANO DE INVESTIGACION Y CAPACITACION *See* BIBLIOGRAPHICAL BULLETIN - LATIN AMERICAN FORESTRY INSTITUTE **2399**

INSTITUTO GENEALOGICO BRASILEIRO *See* REVISTA DO INSTITUTO GENEALOGICO BRASILEIRO **2470**

INSTITUTO GEOGRAFICO NACIONAL (GUATEMALA) *See* BOLETIN GEOLOGICO - INSTITUTO GEOGRAFICO NACIONAL **1367**

INSTITUTO GEOLOGICAL MINERO DE ESPANA *See* MEMORIA GENERAL - INSTITUTO GEOLOGICO Y MINERO DE ESPANA **1387**

INSTITUTO HISTORICO E GEOGRAFICO DE SAO PAULO *See* REVISTA DO INSTITUTO HISTORICO E GEOGRAFICO DE SAO PAULO **2758**

INSTITUTO INTERAMERICANO DE ETNOMUSICOLOGIA Y FOLKLORE *See* REVISTA INIDEF **4150**

INSTITUTO LATINOAMERICANO DEL FIERRO Y EL ACERO. SIDERURGIA EN AMERICA LATINA *See* SIDERURGIA LATINOAMERICANA EN ... Y SUS PERSPECTIVAS, LA **4019**

INSTITUTO "LUIS DE CAMOES." *See* BOLETIM DO INSTITUTO "LUIS DE CAMOES." **3368**

INSTITUTO MEXICANO DE PLANEACION Y OPERACIONE DE SISTEMAS *See* BOLETIN - INSTITUTO MEXICANO DE PLANEACION Y OPERACION DE SISTEMAS **1599**

INSTITUTO MEXICANO DEL PETROLEO *See* REVISTA DEL INSTITUTO MEXICANO DEL PETROLEO **4277**

INSTITUTO MIGUEL DE CERVANTES *See* BOLETIN INFORMATIVO **3269**

INSTITUTO NACIONAL DA PROPRIEDADE INDUSTRIAL *See* RELATORIO **5145**

INSTITUTO NACIONAL DE ASTROFISICA, OPTICA Y ELECTRONICA (MEXICO) *See* BOLETIN DEL INSTITUTO DE TONANTZINTLA **393**

INSTITUTO NACIONAL DE ELECTRIFICACION. UNIDAD ECONOMICA Y FINANCIERA *See* INFORME FINANCIERO Y ESTADISTICO, INSTITUTO NACIONAL DE ELECTRIFICACION, Y ESTADISTICAS DEL SECTOR ELECTRICO NACIONAL **730**

INSTITUTO NACIONAL DE ESTADISTICA (BOLIVIA) *See* ESTADISTICAS INDUSTRIALES **1532**

INSTITUTO NACIONAL DE ESTADISTICA (ECUADOR) *See* ANUARIO DE ESTADISTICA **5322**

INSTITUTO NACIONAL DE ESTADISTICA (SPAIN) *See* BOLETIN MENSUAL DE ESTADISTICA **5323**

INSTITUTO NACIONAL DE ESTADISTICA Y CENSOS (ARGENTINA) *See* BOLETIN ESTADISTICO TRIMESTRAL - INSTITUTO NACIONAL DE ESTADISTICA Y CENSOS **5323**

INSTITUTO NACIONAL DE ESTATISTICA (PORTUGAL). SERVICOS CENTRAIS *See* STATISTIQUES DES SOCIETES. ESTATISTICAS DAS SOCIEDADES **5343**

INSTITUTO NACIONAL DE ESTATISTICA (PORTUGAL). SERVICOS CENTRAIS *See* STATISTIQUES DES TRANSPORTS ET COMMUNICATIONS : CONTINENT, AZORES ET MADERE **5402**

INSTITUTO NACIONAL DE ESTATISTICA (PORTUGAL). SERVICOS CENTRAIS. STATISTIQUES DES SOCIETES *See* STATISTIQUES DES SOCIETES **713**

INSTITUTO NACIONAL DE HIDROCARBUROS (SPAIN) *See* ANNUAL REPORT / INH **4250**

INSTITUTO NACIONAL DE HIDROCARBUROS (SPAIN) *See* PREVIEW OF THE INSTITUTO NACIONAL DE HIDROCARBUROS ANNUAL REPORT FOR ... **4674**

INSTITUTO NACIONAL DE INVESTIGACAO DAS PESCAS *See* BOLETIM DO INSTITUTO NACIONAL DE INVESTIGACAO DAS PESCAS **553**

INSTITUTO NACIONAL DE INVESTIGACIONES AGROPECUARIAS *See* INFORME TECNICO DE BANANO **2420**

INSTITUTO NACIONAL DE INVESTIGACIONES AGROPECUARIAS *See* INFORME TECNICO - INSTITUTO NACIONAL DE INVESTIGACIONES AGROPECUARIAS **96**

INSTITUTO NACIONAL DE MEDICINA LEGAL DE COLOMBIA *See* REVISTA DEL INSTITUTO NACIONAL DE MEDICINA LEGAL DE COLOMBIA **3742**

INSTITUTO NACIONAL DE METEOROLOGIA E GEOFISICA *See* BOLETIM GEOMAGNETICO PRELIMINAR **4443**

INSTITUTO NACIONAL DE NUTRICION (VENEZUELA) *See* MEMORIA Y CUENTA **4194**

INSTITUTO NACIONAL DE PREVIDENCIA SOCIAL. PROCURADORIA-GERA *See* REVISTA - INSTITUTO NACIONAL DE PREVIDENCIA SOCIAL. PROCURADORIA-GERAL **5306**

INSTITUTO NACIONAL DE RACIONALIZACION Y NORMALIZACION *See* BOLETIN DE LA NORMALIZACION ESPANOLA UNE **1966**

INSTITUTO NACIONAL DE RACIONALIZACION Y NORMALIZACION. COMISION TECNICA DE TRABAJO NO. 53 INDUSTRIAS DE PLASTICOS Y CAUCHO *See* MEMORIA - INSTITUTO NACIONAL DE RACIONALIZACION Y NORMALIZACION. COMISION TECNICA DE TRABAJO NO. 53 INDUSTRIAS DE PLASTICS **4456**

INSTITUTO NACIONAL DE TECNOLOGIA AGROPECUARIA (ARGENTINA) *See* CAMPO Y TECNOLOGIA **5092**

INSTITUTO NACIONAL DEL CAFE (EL SALVADOR) *See* MEMORIA ANUAL / INSTITUTO NACIONAL DEL CAFE, INCAFE **178**

INSTITUTO NACIONAL DO CINEMA. SETOR DO INGRESSO PADRONIZADO *See* BOLETIM INFORMATIVO SIP **4064**

INSTITUTO RIVA AGUERO *See* BOLETIN DEL INSTITUTO RIVA-AGUERO **1074**

INSTITUTO TORCUATO DI TELLA. CENTRO DE INVESTIGACIONES SOCIALES *See* DOCUMENTO DE TRABAJO / INSTITUTO TORCUATO DI TELLA, CENTRO DE INVESTIGACIONES SOCIALES **1663**

INSTITUTO URUGUAYO DE DERECHO DE ARRENDAMIENTOS URBANOS *See* IUDAU **2985**

INSTITUTS DE COMPTABLES AGREES DU CANADA. EXAMENS FINAL (CN/0384-8639) [03304016] **745**

INSTITUTSVEROFFENTLICHUNGEN - INSTITUT FUR FESTKORPERMECHANIK DER FRAUNHOFER-GESELLSCHAFT (GW) [02242558] **1979**

INSTITUTUL AGRONOMIC "DR. PETRU GROZA." *See* BULETINUL INSTITULUI AGRONOMIC CLUJ-NAPOCA. SERIA AGRICULTURA **68**

INSTITUTUL AGRONOMIC DR. PETRU GROZA *See* BULETINUL INSTITULUI AGRONOMIC CLUJ-NAPOCA. SERIA ZOOTEHNIE SI MEDICINA VETERINARA **208**

INSTITUTUL AGRONOMIC N. BALCESCU *See* LUCRARI STIINTIFICE. ZOOTEHNIE **5590**

INSTITUTUL DE ARHEOLOGIE (ACADEMIA DE STIINTE SOCIALE SI POLITICE A REPUBLICII SOCIALISTE ROMANIA) *See* STUDII SI CERCETARI DE NUMISMATICA **2783**

INSTITUTUL DE CERCETARI PENTRU CEREALE SI PLANTE TEHNICE FUNDULEA *See* ANALELE INSTITUTULUI DE CERCETARI PENTRU CEREALE SI PLANTE TEHNICE, FUNDULEA **58**

INSTITUTUL DE CERCETARI PENTRU PEDOLOGIE SI AGROCHIMIE (ROMANIA) *See* ANALELE INSTITUTULUI DE CERCETARI PENTRU PEDOLOGIE SI AGROCHIMIE **162**

INSTITUTUL DE CERCETARI PENTRU VALORIFICAREA LEGUMELOR SI FRUCTELOR *See* LUCRARI STIINTIFICE - INSTITUTUL DE CERCETARI PENTRU VALORIFICAREA LEGUMELOR SI FRUCTELOR **178**

INSTITUTUL DE CONSTRUCTII (BUCHAREST, ROMANIA) *See* BULETINUL STIINTIFIC / INSTITUTUL DE CONSTRUCTII BUCURESTI **2019**

INSTITUTUL DE GEOLOGIE SI GEOFIZICA *See* DARI DE SEAMA ALE SEDINTELOR - INSTITUTUL DE GEOLOGIE SI GEOFIZICA. 4, STRATIGRAFIE **1373**

INSTITUTUL DE GEOLOGIE SI GEOFIZICA *See* ANUARUL INSTITUTULUI DE GEOLOGIE SI GEOFIZICA **1365**

INSTITUTUL DE GEOLOGIE SI GEOFIZICA *See* DARI DE SEAMA ALE SEDINTELOR - INSTITUTUL DE GEOLOGIE SI GEOFIZICA. 5. TECTONICA SI GEOLOGIE REGIONALA **1373**

INSTITUTUL DE ISTORIE (ACADEMIA REPUBLICII POPULARE ROMINE) STUDII SI MATERIALE DE ISTORIE MEDIE *See* STUDII SI MATERIALE DE ISTORIE MEDIE **2712**

INSTITUTUL DE ISTORIE "N. IORGA." *See* STUDII SI MATERIALE DE ISTORIE CONTEMPORANA **2711**

INSTITUTUL DE ISTORIE "N. IORGA." *See* STUDII SI MATERIALE DE ISTORIE MEDIE **2712**

INSTITUTUL DE LINGVISTICA DIN BUCURESTI *See* STUDII DE GRAMATICA **3326**

INSTITUTUL DE SPEOLOGIE "EMIL RACOVITA." *See* TRAVAUX DE L'INSTITUT DE SPEOLOGIE EMILE RACOVITZA **4173**

INSTITUTUL DE STUDII, CERCETARI SI PROIECTARI PENTRU GOSPODARIREA APELOR *See* STUDII DE ECONOMIA APELOR **5540**

INSTITUTUL DE STUDII, CERCETARI SI PROIECTARI PENTRU GOSPODARIREA APELOR *See* STUDII - INSTITUTUL DE CERCETARI SI PROIECTARI PENTRU GOSPODARIREA APELOR. EPURAREA APELOR **2244**

INSTITUTUL DE STUDII, CERCETARI SI PROIECTARI PENTRU GOSPODARIREA APELOR *See* STUDI ALIMENTARI CU APA **5540**

INSTITUUT VOOR BEWARING EN VERWERKING VAN LANDBOUWPRODUKTEN *See* PUBLIKATIE - INSTITUUT VOOR BEWARING EN VERWERKING VAN LANDBOUWPRODUKTEN **2355**

INSTITUUT VOOR CULTUURTECHNIEK EN WATERHUISHOUDING *See* MEDEDELING - INSTITUUT VOOR CULTUURTECHNIEK EN WATERHUISHOUDING **178**

INSTITUUT VOOR CULTUURTECHNIEK EN WATERHUISHOUDING *See* TECHNICAL BULLETIN - INSTITUTE FOR LAND AND WATER MANAGEMENT RESEARCH **189**

INSTITUUT VOOR MECHANISATIE, ARBEID EN GEBOUWEN (WAGENNGEN, NETHERLANDS) *See* PUBLIKATIE - INSTITUUT VOOR MECHANISATIE, ARBEID EN GEBOUWEN **123**

INSTITUUT VOOR PLANTENZIEKTENKUNDIG ONDERZOEK (WEGENINGEN, NETHERLANDS) *See* JAARVERSLAG - INSTITUUT VOOR PLANTENZEIKTENKUNDIG ONDERZOEK **2421**

INSTREAM FLOW INFORMATION PAPER (US/0198-1447) [03387794] **1415**

INSTRUCTION AND CODE TABLE BOOKLET / VA HEALTH PROFESSIONAL SCHOLARSHIP PROGRAM (US) [10361840] **4046**

INSTRUCTION DELIVERY SYSTEMS (US/0892-4872) [15307463] **1189**

INSTRUCTION IN MARYLAND (US) [04248071] **1753**

INSTRUCTIONAL CASSETTE RECORDINGS CATALOG (US/0145-2525) [04445748] **4389**, **4122**

INSTRUCTIONAL COURSE LECTURES (US/0065-6895) [01479261] **3882**, **3966**

INSTRUCTIONAL DEVELOPMENT AT WATERLOO (CN/0228-2313) [06965861] **1896**

INSTRUCTIONAL DISC RECORDINGS CATALOG (US/0145-2517) [06606404] **4389**, **4122**

INSTRUCTIONAL EQUIPMENT GRANTS : TITLE VI-A HIGHER EDUCATION ACT OF 1975 (US/0363-6429) [02531736] **1830**

INSTRUCTIONAL LEADER (US) **1753**

INSTRUCTIONAL MATERIALS ADOPTION DATA FILE (US/0191-9148) [04934931] **1896**

INSTRUCTIONAL SCIENCE (NE/0020-4277) [01779781] **1896**

INSTRUCTIONAL STRATEGIES (US/1072-1517) [28873790] **1753**, **683**

INSTRUCTIONS FOR FORM W-2, WAGE AND TAX STATEMENT (US) [25598315] **4732**

INSTRUCTIONS FOR MAILERS (US) [02784717] **1145**

INSTRUCTIONS RESPECTING VOCATIONAL TRAINING IN THE YOUTH AND ADULT SECTORS OF SCHOOL BOARDS (CN/1182-0802) [22281393] **1913**

INSTRUCTOR (1990) (US/1049-5851) [20868525] **1896**

● INSTRUMENT BUSINESS OUTLOOK (US/1061-2203) [25217755] **1612**

INSTRUMENT FLYING (US) [03456923] **24**

INSTRUMENT MAINTENANCE MANAGEMENT (US/0538-2351) [03728627] **2065**

INSTRUMENT REPORT (US) **5114**

INSTRUMENT SOCIETY OF AMERICA *See* ISA TRANSACTIONS **5116**

INSTRUMENT SOCIETY OF AMERICA *See* TENTATIVE RECOMMENDED PRACTICE (INSTRUMENT SOCIETY OF AMERICA) **3488**

INSTRUMENT UND FORSCHUNG (GW/0340-8655) [03571800] **5114**

Alphabetical Title Index — INSURANCE

INSTRUMENTA BIBLICA (BE) **5017**

INSTRUMENTA LEXICOLOGICA LATINA. SERIES A, ENUMERATIO FORMARUM, CONCORDANTIA FORMARUM, INDEX FORMARUM A TERGO ORDINATARUM (BE) [08924014] **4965**

INSTRUMENTA LEXICOLOGICA LATINA. SERIES B, ENUMERATIO LEMATUM, CONCORDANTIA LEMMATUM ET FORMARUM, INDEX FORMARUM ET LEMMATUM, INDEX LEMMATUM A TERGO ORDINATORUM, TABULA FREQUENTIARUM (BE) [09421953] **4965, 1077**

INSTRUMENTA PATRISTICA (NE/0534-4255) [06179004] **4965**

INSTRUMENTALIST, THE (US/0020-4331) [01753312] **4122**

INSTRUMENTALNYE I PODSHIPNIKOVYE STALI (RU) [01795949] **4004**

INSTRUMENTATION (US/0020-4366) [01753313] **2065**

●INSTRUMENTATION & AUTOMATION NEWS : IAN (US) [28884704] **1979**

INSTRUMENTATION & CONTROL ENGINEERING *CEASED.* (UK/0959-8286) **2065**

●INSTRUMENTATION & CONTROL SYSTEMS: I&CS (US) [25639549] **1979**

INSTRUMENTATION AND CONTROLS DIVISION ANNUAL PROGRESS REPORT (US) [04093416] **1947**

INSTRUMENTATION FOR ENVIRONMENTAL MONITORING (US) [02050599] **2174**

INSTRUMENTATION IN THE AEROSPACE INDUSTRY (US/0096-7238) [06745295] **24**

INSTRUMENTATION IN THE CHEMICAL AND PETROLEUM INDUSTRIES (US/0074-0551) [01753315] **4260**

INSTRUMENTATION IN THE FOOD AND BEVERAGE INDUSTRY (US/0095-0777) [01783675] **2345**

INSTRUMENTATION IN THE MINING AND METALLURGY INDUSTRIES (US/0361-3070) [02050536] **2140**

INSTRUMENTATION IN THE POWER INDUSTRY (US/0074-056X) [02733819] **2065**

INSTRUMENTATION IN THE PULP AND PAPER INDUSTRY (US/0361-4719) [01525027] **4234**

INSTRUMENTATION-RESEARCH (US/0883-7201) [11865197] **978**

●INSTRUMENTATION SCIENCE AND TECHNOLOGY (US/1073-9149) [29554273] **3588**

INSTRUMENTENBAU ZEITSCHRIFT, MUSIK INTERNATIONAL : IZ (GW/0934-3962) [23955120] **4122**

INSTRUMENTENBAUREPORT (GW/0936-014X) [I0936014X] **4123**

INSTRUMENTS AND EXPERIMENTAL TECHNIQUES (NEW YORK) (US/0020-4412) [01883598] **4405**

INSTRUMENTS INDIA (II/0047-0376) [03440210] **3481**

INSTUMENT REPORT (US) **5114**

INSTUTUT NATIONAL DE LA STATISTIQUE ET DES ETUDES ECONOMIQUES (FRANCE) *See* EQUIPEMENT DES MENAGES, L' **1489**

●INSTYLE (NEW YORK, N.Y.) (US/1076-0830) [30385219] **2535**

INSTYTUT BADANIA PRAWA SADOWEGO *See* ZESZYTY NAUKOWE INSTYTUTU BADANIA PRAWA SADOWEGO **3078**

INSTYTUT FIZYKI I TECHNIKI JADROWEJ AGH *See* RAPORT - INSTYTUT FIZYKI I TECHNIKI JADROWEJ AGH **4450**

INSTYTUT GEOFIZYKI (POLSKA AKADEMIA NAUK) *See* RESULTS OF GEOMAGNETIC OBSERVATIONS, BELSK **4445**

INSTYTUT HODOWLI I AKLIMATYZACJI ROSLIN *See* BIULETYN **66**

INSTYTUT METALURGII ZELAZA (GLIWICE, POLAND) *See* PRACE INSTYTUTU METALURGII ZELAZA IM, ST. STASZICA **4015**

INSTYTUT METEOROLOGII I GOSPODARKI WODNEJ *See* PRACE INSTYTUTU METEOROLOGII I GOSPODARKI WODNEJ **1433**

INSTYTUT OCHRONY ROSLIN *See* PRACE NAUKOWE INSTYTUT OCHRONY ROSLIN **4247**

INSTYTUT PODSTAW BUDOWY MASZYN (AKADEMIA GORNICZO-HUTNICZA IM. S. STASZICA W KRAKOWIE) MASZYN *See* PRACE - KRAKOW. AKADEMIA GORNICZO-HUTNICZA. INSTYTUT PODSTAW BUDOWY MASZY **2148**

INSTYTUT PODSTAWOWYCH PROBLEMOW TECHNIKI (POLSKA AKADEMIA NAUK) *See* SCIENTIFIC ACTIVITIES OF THE POLISH ACADEMY OF SCIENCES, INSTITUTE OF FUNDAMENTAL TECHNOLOGICAL RESEARCH **5155**

INSTYTUT TECHNOLOGII DREWNA (POZNAN, POLAND) *See* PRACE INSTYTUT TECHNOLOGII DREWNA **2403**

INSTYTUT ZIEMNIAKA BONIN *See* ZIEMNIAK **191**

INSTYTUT ZIEMNIAKA BONIN *See* BIULETYN INSTYTUTU ZIEMNIAKA **2329**

INSTYTUT ZOOTECHNIKI. (POLAND). ZAKAD INFORMACJI ZOOTECHNICZNEJ *See* BIULETYN INFORMACYJNY - INSTYTUT ZOOTECHNIKI **207**

INSTYTYT ZOOLOGII *See* KATALOG FAUNY POLSKI **5589**

INSULA (MADRID) (SP/0020-4536) [01589710] **417**

INSULATED WIRE AND CABLE (US/0278-9337) [03057588] **4004, 1612**

INSULATION GUIDE (US/0737-2817) [09342567] **1947**

INSULATION HANDBOOK, THE (UK) [05881956] **617**

INSULATION JOURNAL (RICKMARSWORTH) (UK/0950-1940) [10813442] **617**

INSULATOR'S GUIDE *See* CONTRACTORS GUIDE (LOMBARD, ILL.) **611**

INSULIN AND GLUCAGON (UK/0142-8144) [I01428144] **3731**

INSURANCE ACCOUNTING AND STATISTICAL ASSOCIATION *See* YEAR BOOK - INSURANCE ACCOUNTING AND STATISTICAL ASSOCIATION **2896**

INSURANCE ACT OF 1960 : ANNUAL REPORT FOR THE YEAR ENDED ON THE 30TH OF JUNE ..., THE (AT) [20999314] **2882**

INSURANCE ADVOCATE (US/0020-4587) [05325585] **2882**

INSURANCE AGE (UK/0142-6265) [I01426265] **2882**

INSURANCE AGENT *See* SOUTHERN INSURANCE **2894**

INSURANCE AGENT & BROKER IN CANADA *See* CANADIAN INSURANCE **2877**

INSURANCE ALMANAC (ENGLEWOOD. 1933), THE (US/0074-0675) [01753319] **2882**

INSURANCE & BANKING RECORD, THE (AT/0311-0192) [01795424] **2883, 791**

INSURANCE AND EMPLOYEE BENEFITS LITERATURE (US/0735-3944) [07807918] **2883**

INSURANCE AND FINANCIAL REVIEW, THE (US/0736-0126) [09068611] **791, 2883**

INSURANCE & LIABILITY REPORTER (US/1055-4556) [23185225] **2883**

INSURANCE & REINSURANCE SOLVENCY REPORT (UK/0950-5377) [I09505377] **2883**

INSURANCE AND RISK MANAGEMENT--FOR BUSINESS AND GOVERNMENT (US/0892-5887) [15217821] **2883**

INSURANCE & TAX NEWS *CEASED.* (US) **4732**

INSURANCE & TECHNOLOGY (US/1054-0733) [22753514] **1189, 2883**

INSURANCE ANTITRUST & TORT REFORM REPORT (US/0898-5170) [17845669] **2883, 3100**

INSURANCE BENEFITS SURVEY. TWIN CITY AREA (US/0736-5969) [09147916] **2883**

INSURANCE BROKERS' MONTHLY AND INSURANCE ADVISER (UK/0260-2385) [I02602385] **2883**

INSURANCE BUSINESS: ANNUAL REPORT (UK) [01786268] **2883**

INSURANCE COMPANY MARKET RANK (US) **2883**

INSURANCE COMPANY RATINGS REPORTER (US/0749-2847) [11105671] **2883**

INSURANCE COMPUTING NEWSLETTER (US/8755-6162) [11387518] **2883**

INSURANCE CONFERENCE PLANNER (US/0193-0516) [02600008] **2883**

INSURANCE CONTRACT LAW (UK) **2883**

INSURANCE CORPORATION OF BARBADOS *See* REPORT AND ACCOUNTS AT ... / INSURANCE CORPORATION OF BARBADOS **2891**

INSURANCE CORPORATION OF BRITISH COLUMBIA *See* ANNUAL REPORT - INSURANCE CORPORATION OF BRITISH COLUMBIA **2873**

INSURANCE DEPARTMENT SERVICE / ALL STATE SERVICE (US) **2883**

INSURANCE DIRECTORY (US) [06740323] **2883**

INSURANCE DIRECTORY AND YEAR BOOK : POST MAGAZINE ALMANACK, THE (UK) [10387396] **2883**

INSURANCE ECONOMICS SURVEYS (US/0020-4668) [01605776] **1496, 2883**

INSURANCE FIELD, THE *See* INSURANCE INDUSTRY NEWSLETTER **2883**

INSURANCE FORUM, THE (US/0095-2923) [01453444] **2883**

INSURANCE IN FINLAND (FI/0356-9993) [I03569993] **2883**

INSURANCE INDUSTRY IN COLORADO, STATISTICAL REPORT *See* COLORADO INSURANCE INDUSTRY STATISTICAL REPORT **2897**

INSURANCE INDUSTRY INTERNATIONAL (IE/0791-7201) **2883**

INSURANCE INDUSTRY LITIGATION REPORTER : THE NATIONAL JOURNAL OF RECORD OF INSURANCE LITIGATION (US/0887-7858) [13166843] **2883, 2983**

INSURANCE INDUSTRY NEWSLETTER (US) [06745412] **2883**

INSURANCE INSTITUTE FOR HIGHWAY SAFETY *See* YEAR'S WORK - INSURANCE INSTITUTE FOR HIGHWAY SAFETY, THE **5446**

INSURANCE INSTITUTE FOR HIGHWAY SAFETY *See* STATUS REPORT - INSURANCE INSTITUTE FOR HIGHWAY SAFETY **5444**

INSURANCE INSTITUTE OF CANADA *See* PROGRAMME F.I.A.C **2891**

INSURANCE INSTITUTE OF CANADA *See* FELLOWSHIP PROGRAM - INSURANCE INSTITUTE OF CANADA **2880**

INSURANCE JOURNAL (US/0020-4714) [05120362] **2883**

INSURANCE LAW (US/0148-2688) [03279903] **2883, 2983**

INSURANCE LAW & PRACTICE (UK) **2983, 2883**

INSURANCE LAW ANTHOLOGY (US/0892-4422) [15192622] **2883, 2983**

INSURANCE LAW JOURNAL (SYDNEY, N.S.W.) (AT/1030-2379) [18077712] **2983, 2883**

INSURANCE LAW MONTHLY (UK) **2883**

INSURANCE LAW REPORTS (HARLOW, ESSEX) (UK) [10013810] **2883, 2983**

INSURANCE LITIGATION REPORTER (US/0744-1045) [07863258] **2883, 2983**

INSURANCE MAGAZINE'S GOLD BOOK OF INSURANCE MARKETING (US/0097-6245) [01799195] **926, 2883**

INSURANCE MARKET PLACE, THE (US/0538-2629) [02665030] **2883**

INSURANCE MARKETER, THE (CN/0317-1272) [01787900] **2884**

INSURANCE MARKETING INSIDER (US/1040-6867) [18509448] **2884**

INSURANCE MATHEMATICS & ECONOMICS (NE/0167-6687) [08636479] **2884**

INSURANCE PERIODICALS INDEX (US/0074-073X) [01714698] **2884, 2897**

INSURANCE PHONE BOOK & DIRECTORY (US/1055-5749) [12545929] **2884**

INSURANCE RECORD (DALLAS, TEX.), THE (US/0020-4803) [04083698] **2884**

INSURANCE RECORD OF AUSTRALIA & NEW ZEALAND, THE (AT) [03460417] **2884**

INSURANCE REPORT AND STATISTICS OF FIJI (FJ) [06271489] **2884, 2897**

INSURANCE SAFETY DIRECTORY *See* WEISS RESEARCH'S INSURANCE SAFETY DIRECTORY **2896**

INSURANCE. SEIMEI HOKEN TOKEI-GO (JA/0910-5719) [I09105719] **2884, 2897**

INSURANCE SERVICE. COMMERCIAL INSURANCE MARKET STUDY / DATA RESOURCES, INC (US/0749-1840) [11074815] **2884**

INSURANCE SERVICE ECONOMIC INDICATORS / DRI, DATA RESOURCES, INC (US) [08484901] **1567, 2884**

INSURANCE SERVICE QUARTERLY REVIEW (US/0276-6361) [07367621] **2884**

INSURANCE SERVICE: REGIONAL REVIEW (US/0271-2628) [06570843] **2884**

INSURANCE SOFTWARE REVIEW (US/0892-8533) [15271944] **2884**

INSURANCE. SONGAI HOKEN TOKUBETSU TOKEI-GO (JA/0910-5727) [I09105727] **2884, 2897**

INSURANCE SOUTH MAGAZINE (US/1057-0349) [23914025] **2884**

INSURANCE

INSURANCE STATISTICS (NEW ZEALAND) (NZ) [09818461] **2897**

INSURANCE SYSTEMS BULLETIN (UK/0268-1935) [I02681935] **2884**

INSURANCE SYSTEMS INTERNATIONAL (UK/0954-5514) [I09545514] **2884**

INSURANCE T.R.A.C. REPORT, CANADA (CN/0714-8402) [09387108] **2884**

INSURANCE TAX REVIEW, THE (US/0890-9164) [14583110] **2884**

INSURANCE THEFT LOSSES. VANS, PICKUPS AND UTILITY VEHICLES, ... MODELS (US/0276-6280) [07399496] 5417, **2884**

INSURANCE TIMES (NEWTON, MASS.) (US/1042-7333) [19117483] **2884**

INSURANCE TRENDS (US) **2884**

INSURANCEWEEK (US/0020-4846) [04083723] **2884**

INSURED PROJECT SERVICING HANDBOOK (US) [03118066] **2884**

INSURED WORKERS IN WEST VIRGINIA / PREPARED BY WEST VIRGINIA DEPARTMENT OF EMPLOYMENT SECURITY, LABOR AND ECONOMIC RESEARCH SECTION (US) [10079268] 1680, **1534**

INSURING FOREIGN RISKS (UK) **2884**

INSWAEGYE (KO) [05154556] **4566**

INTEC (CL) [01793747] **5114**

INTECH (US/0192-303X) [04742665] **2065**

INTECOL NEWSLETTER (US/1012-6880) [I10126880] **2217**

INTEGER PROGRAMMING AND RELATED AREAS (GW/0722-7906) [04938763] **3509**

INTEGRACION EN CIFRAS (GT) [04367640] **1496**

INTEGRACION LATINOAMERICANA (AG) [02648975] **1635**

INTEGRAL (US) **4123**

INTEGRAL EQUATIONS AND OPERATOR THEORY (SZ/0378-620X) [04026585] **3509**

●INTEGRAL TRANSFORMS AND SPECIAL FUNCTIONS (US/1065-2469) [26537827] **5114**

INTEGRAL YOGA (US/0161-1380) [03856467] **4965**

INTEGRALNYE SKHEMY V DISKRETNOI TEKHNIKE (LV) [02239722] **2065**

INTEGRATED BAR OF THE PHILIPPINES *See* JOURNAL - INTEGRATED BAR OF THE PHILIPPINES **2986**

INTEGRATED CIRCUIT DISCONTINUED DEVICES (US/0730-2290) [06760722] **2065**

INTEGRATED CIRCUIT ENGINEERING CORPORATION *See* STATUS (SCOTTSDALE) **2082**

INTEGRATED CIRCUITS. CIRCUITS INTEGRES. INTEGRIERTE SCHALTUNGEN (BE) [03527424] **2065**

INTEGRATED CIRCUITS. DIGITAL (US/1057-4530) [23966807] **2065**

INTEGRATED CIRCUITS. INTERFACE (US/1057-4522) [23365724] **2065**

INTEGRATED CIRCUITS INTERNATIONAL (UK/0263-6522) [08752480] 1189, **2065**

INTEGRATED CIRCUITS. LINEAR (US/1059-3128) [24562586] **2065**

INTEGRATED CIRCUITS. MICROPROCESSORS (US/1049-2445) [20689010] **2065**

INTEGRATED CIRCUITS. SURFACE-MOUNTED ICS (US/1051-7707) [22106073] **2066**

●INTEGRATED COMPUTER AIDED ENGINEERING (US/1069-2509) [27965046] **1229**

INTEGRATED ENVIRONMENTAL MANAGEMENT (UK/0962-1113) [I09621113] **2174**

●INTEGRATED FERROELECTRICS (US/1058-4587) [24298433] **2066**

INTEGRATED IMAGE (US/1046-932X) [20569375] 683, **1189**

INTEGRATED MANUFACTURING (ROCKFORD, ILL.) (US/1055-3274) [23155502] **3481**

INTEGRATED MANUFACTURING SYSTEMS (UK/0957-6061) [21057095] **2116**

INTEGRATED MESSAGING NEWS (US/1056-1412) [23599779] **1157**

●INTEGRATED PEST MANAGEMENT REVIEWS (UK/1353-5226) **4245**

●INTEGRATED SAMPLE SURVEY FOR ESTIMATION OF ANIMAL PRODUCTS [MICROFORM] : MILK, WOOL, EGGS, AND MEAT / HIMACHAL PRADESH GOVERNMENT, ANIMAL HUSBANDRY DEPARTMENT (II) [26778208] 195, **213**

INTEGRATED TECHNOLOGY PLAN FOR THE CIVIL SPACE PROGRAM (US) [25612002] **24**

INTEGRATED WASTE MANAGEMENT (US/1049-1562) [21062179] **2233**

INTEGRATION (UK) **1189**

INTEGRATION AFRICAINE : REVUE TRIMESTRIELLE DE LA C.E.A.O (UV) [07558044] **1636**

INTEGRATION (AMSTERDAM) (NE/0167-9260) [10088850] **2066**

INTEGRATION / JOICFP (JA) [18437426] 4554, **589**

INTEGRATIVE PHYSIOLOGICAL AND BEHAVIORAL SCIENCE (US/0093-2213) [22684607] 581, **4590**

INTEGRATIVE PSYCHIATRY (US/0735-3847) [08917223] **3926**

INTEGREE, L' (FR/0397-1392) [I03971392] **4566**

INTEGRITY (CN/0848-1660) [21190716] **2251**

INTEGRITY FORUM (US/0095-2184) [05438995] **5204**

INTEL 16 BIT ASSEMBLER HANDBOEK (NE) **1279**

INTELCOL NEWSLETTER (UK) **2195**

INTELEC (US/0275-0473) [06237190] **1157**

INTELLECTICA / REVUE DE L'ARC (FR) **2848**

INTELLECTUAL ACTIVIST, THE (US/0730-2355) [07982719] 1496, **4477**

INTELLECTUAL PROPERTY FRAUD REPORTER (UK) [21885083] **1304**

INTELLECTUAL PROPERTY IN BUSINESS BRIEFING *CEASED.* (UK/0955-2197) [22258491] **1304**

INTELLECTUAL PROPERTY IN BUSINESS REVIEW *CEASED.* (UK) **1304**

INTELLECTUAL PROPERTY JOURNAL (CN/0824-7064) [11055037] **1305**

INTELLECTUAL PROPERTY LAW (CHUR, SWITZERLAND) (UK/0892-2365) [15127407] **1305**

INTELLECTUAL PROPERTY LAW REVIEW (US/0193-4864) [04584359] **1305**

INTELLECTUAL PROPERTY NEWSLETTER (UK) [06499443] **1305**

INTELLECTUAL PROPERTY REPORTS (AT/0812-2024) [15555897] **1305**

INTELLECTUAL PROPERTY STRATEGIST (US) **1305**

INTELLECTUELE EIGENDOM & RECLAMERECHT (NE/0169-1074) [21279817] **1305**

INTELLIGENCE AND NATIONAL SECURITY (UK/0268-4527) [13134789] **4524**

INTELLIGENCE DIGEST (UK/0020-4900) [04096114] 4477, **1496**

INTELLIGENCE (NEW YORK, N.Y. 1984) (US/1042-4296) [19056676] **1189**

INTELLIGENCE NEWSLETTER (FR) [27536208] **4046**

INTELLIGENCE (NORWOOD) (US/0160-2896) [03334510] **4590**

INTELLIGENCE REPORTS IN CARDIOVASCULAR DISEASE (US/0271-1141) [06550699] **3706**

INTELLIGENCER (US) [18728032] **5737**

INTELLIGENCER JOURNAL (US/0889-4140) [02262429] **5737**

INTELLIGENCER (WHEELING, W.VA.) (US) [13502342] **5764**

INTELLIGENT HIGHWAY, THE (US/0959-6631) [26065556] 5417, **5441**

INTELLIGENT INSTRUMENTS & COMPUTERS (US/0889-8308) [11900896] 1247, 1260, **1220**

INTELLIGENT NETWORK NEWS (US/1042-6930) [19109310] **1113**

INTELLIGENT SOFTWARE STRATEGIES (US/1052-7214) [22362025] **1287**

INTELLIGENT SYSTEMS ENGINEERING *CEASED.* (UK/0963-9640) [I09639640] 1247, **1979**

INTELLIGENT SYSTEMS REPORT (US/1054-8696) [22853454] **1213**

INTELLIGENT SYSTEMS : THE NEWSLETTER OF THE FOUNDATION FOR INTELLIGENT SYSTEMS IN THE SOCIAL SCIENCES, ARTS & HUMANITIES (US/1055-0542) [23065439] 2848, **5204**

INTELLIGENT TUTORING MEDIA *CEASED.* (UK/0957-9133) [I09579133] **1213**

INTELLIMOTION (RICHMOND, CALIF.) (US/1061-4311) [24617439] **5384**

●INTELPROP NEWS (UK/0967-3466) [I09673466] **1305**

INTENATIONALES GEWERBEARCHIV (GW/0020-9481) [I00209481] **683**

INTENSIV (GW) **3588**

INTENSIV UND NOTFALLBEHANDLUNG (GW) **3588**

INTENSIVBEHANDLUNG (GW/0341-3063) [04564251] **3588**

INTENSIVE AGRICULTURE (II/0020-4919) [09818513] **96**

INTENSIVE & CRITICAL CARE DIGEST (UK/0265-5241) [13039225] **3588**

●INTENSIVE & CRITICAL CARE NURSING : THE OFFICIAL JOURNAL OF THE BRITISH ASSOCIATION OF CRITICAL CARE NURSES (UK/0964-3397) [25560349] **3857**

INTENSIVE CARE MEDICINE (GW/0342-4642) [03176818] **3588**

INTENSIVE CARE MEDICINE SUPPLEMENT (GW/0935-1701) [I09351701] **3588**

INTENSIVE CARE NURSING *See* INTENSIVE & CRITICAL CARE NURSING : THE OFFICIAL JOURNAL OF THE BRITISH ASSOCIATION OF CRITICAL CARE NURSES **3857**

INTENSIVE CARE REVIEW (NE) **3588**

INTENSIVE CARE WORLD (BALDOCK) (UK/0266-7037) [13039230] **3588**

INTENSIVE MANAGEMENT PRACTICES ASSESSMENT CENTER *See* IMPAC REPORTS **870**

INTENSIVE THERAPY AND CLINICAL MONITORING *CEASED.* (UK) [15688931] **3588**

INTENSIVMEDIZIN + NOTFALLMEDIZIN (GW/0175-3851) [11319834] **3588**

INTENSIVMEDIZINISCHE PRAXIS (GW/0173-2315) [06312537] **3683**

INTENTION MISSIONNAIRE (CN/0849-133X) [22186050] **4965**

INTER-ACAO (BL) [04220697] **5232**

INTER-ACTIF, L' (CN/1191-1042) [25796533] **1830**

INTER-AFRICAN AND REGIONAL CONFERENCES. EDUCATION *See* REPORTS : E **1516**

INTER ALIA (US/0534-4638) [02255046] **2983**

INTER ALIA ADELAIDE (AT/1031-3575) [I10313575] **1864**

INTER ALIA (RENO) (US/0092-6086) [01786597] **2983**

INTER-AMERICAN ARBITRATION (CN/0715-4771) [09502108] **2983**

INTER-AMERICAN CENTER OF TAX ADMINISTRATORS *See* INFORMATIVO - CENTRO INTERAMERICANO DE ADMINISTRADORES TRIBUTARIOS **4732**

INTER-AMERICAN COMMISSION OF WOMEN *See* INTER-AMERICAN COMMISSION OF WOMEN : NEWSLETTER **5559**

INTER-AMERICAN COMMISSION OF WOMEN : NEWSLETTER (US) [08543862] **5559**

INTER-AMERICAN COMMISSION ON HUMAN RIGHTS *See* ANNUAL REPORT : INTER-AMERICAN COMMISSION ON HUMAN RIGHTS **4504**

INTER-AMERICAN COMMISSION ON HUMAN RIGHTS *See* ANNUAL REPORT OF THE INTER-AMERICAN COMMISSION ON HUMAN RIGHTS / ORGANIZATION OF AMERICAN STATES **4504**

INTER-AMERICAN CONFERENCE OF MINISTERS OF LABOR ON THE ALLIANCE FOR PROGRESS. FINAL ACT *See* FINAL ACT / ORGANIZATION OF AMERICAN STATES, CIES **1669**

INTER-AMERICAN DEVELOPMENT BANK *See* ANNUAL REPORT / INTER-AMERICAN DEVELOPMENT BANK **1462**

INTER-AMERICAN DEVELOPMENT BANK *See* IDB NEWSLETTER **790**

INTER-AMERICAN DEVELOPMENT BANK *See* ECONOMIC AND SOCIAL PROGRESS IN LATIN AMERICA **1556**

INTER-AMERICAN DEVELOPMENT BANK. INSTITUTE FOR LATIN AMERICAN INTEGRATION *See* INFORME ANUAL - BANCO INTERAMERICANO DE DESARROLLO, INSTITUTO PARA LA INTEGRACION DE AMERICA LATINA **791**

INTER-AMERICAN ECONOMIC AND SOCIAL COUNCIL *See* ALLIANCE FOR PROGRESS : REPORT ON THE PROGRESS OF ECONOMIC AND SOCIAL DEVELOPMENT IN LATIN AMERICA AND PROSPECTS FOR THE FUTURE, THE **1545**

INTER-AMERICAN FOUNDATION *See* IN REVIEW / INTER-AMERICAN FOUNDATION **2910**

INTER-AMERICAN INSTITUTE OF AGRICULTURAL SCIENCES *See* BOLETIN TECNICO / INTER-AMERICAN INSTITUTE OF AGRICULTURAL SCIENCES **68**

INTER-AMERICAN INSTITUTE SERIES (US) [01331379] **2739**

Alphabetical Title Index — INTERCOM

INTER-AMERICAN LEGAL MATERIALS / AMERICAN BAR ASSOCIATION, SECTION OF INTERNATIONAL LAW AND PRACTICE, INTER-AMERICAN LAW COMMITTEE (US/0886-7747) [09264568] **2983**

INTER-AMERICAN MUSIC REVIEW (US/0195-6655) [05055249] **4123**

INTER-AMERICAN ORGANIZATION FOR HIGHER EDUCATION *See* INTERAMERICA (ENGLISH ED.) **1831**

INTER-AMERICAN ORGANIZATION FOR HIGHER EDUCATION *See* INTERAMERICAN (ED. PORTUGUESA) **1831**

INTER-AMERICAN ORGANIZATION FOR HIGHER EDUCATION *See* INTERAMERICA (ED. ESPANOLA) **1830**

INTER-AMERICAN PRESS ASSOCIATION *See* IAPA NEWS **2920**

INTER-AMERICAN PRESS ASSOCIATION *See* GENERAL ASSSEMBLY - INTER AMERICAN PRESS ASSOCIATION. ASAMBLEA GENERAL - SOCIEDAD INTERNAMERICANA DE PRENSA **2920**

●INTER-AMERICAN TRADE AND INVESTMENT LAW (US/1078-2028) [29876130] **3129, 840**

INTER-AMERICAN TROPICAL TUNA COMMISSION *See* BULLETIN - INTER-AMERICAN TROPICAL TUNA COMMISSION **449**

INTER-AMERICAN TROPICAL TUNA COMMISSION *See* QUARTERLY REPORT OF THE INTER-AMERICAN TROPICAL TUNA COMMISSION, THE **2311**

INTER-AMERICAN TROPICAL TUNA COMMISSION *See* ANNUAL REPORT OF THE INTER-AMERICAN TROPICAL TUNA COMMISSION **2295**

INTER-ARTS *See* PRESENTING AND COMMISSIONING **328**

●INTER-ARTS. GRANTS TO PRESENTING ORGANIZATIONS, SERVICES TO PRESENTING ORGANIZATIONS, SPECIAL TOURING INITIATIVES: APPLICATION GUIDELINES (US) [23894260] **4732, 322**

INTER-ARTS. PRESENTING ORGANIZATIONS, ARTIST COLONIES, SERVICES TO THE ARTS *See* INTER-ARTS. GRANTS TO PRESENTING ORGANIZATIONS, SERVICES TO PRESENTING ORGANIZATIONS, SPECIAL TOURING INITIATIVES: APPLICATION GUIDELINES **322**

INTER BLOC (FR/0242-3960) [08425558] **3966**

INTER CDI ETAMPES (FR/0242-2999) [02422999] **683**

INTER-CITY EXPRESS (OAKLAND, CALIF.) (US/0274-7464) [06549847] **5636**

INTER-CITY WAGE & SALARY DIFFERENTIALS (US/0196-3457) [05780116] **1680**

INTER COOP (CN/1185-0744) [23599112] **1542**

INTER-CORPORATE OWNERSHIP (CN/0575-8823) [02241023] **1612**

INTER-COUNTY LEADER (FREDERIC, WIS.) (US/8750-9091) [11946885] **5768**

INTER DEPENDENT, THE (US/0094-5072) [01794070] **4524**

INTER DITS (FR) [11975454] **2692**

INTER ECONOMICS (GW/0020-5346) [01753365] **1636**

INTER ELECTRONIQUE *CEASED.* (FR) [06870144] **2066**

INTER-EXLIBRIS (DK) [06767580] **3217**

INTER FOLIA (MX) [06186961] **3217**

INTER (HAUTE-VILLE, QUEBEC) (CN/0825-8708) [19099132] **385**

INTER-INDUSTRY STUDY OF THE NEW ZEALAND ECONOMY (NZ/0110-7321) [02246856] **1496, 1534**

INTER-LEX (BL) [01790033] **5290**

INTER-MECANIQUE DU BATIMENT (CN/0831-411X) [14937980] **617**

INTER-MENNONITE CONFERENCE (ONTARIO) *See* YEARBOOK **5069**

INTER-MISSION (QUEBEC) (CN/0837-7111) [17863988] **4657**

INTER-MOUNTAIN (ELKINS, W.VA. : DAILY) (US) [13201772] **5764**

INTER-NOISE (US/0105-175X) [01037036] **2174**

INTER-NORD (FR/0074-1035) [02382427] **2620**

INTER NOS (US) [04538730] **4123**

INTER-PARLIAMENTARY BULLETIN (SZ/0020-5079) [06298052] **4524**

INTER-PARLIAMENTARY UNION *See* CONSTITUTIONAL AND PARLIAMENTARY INFORMATION **3092**

INTER-PARLIAMENTARY UNION *See* SERIES "REPORTS AND DOCUMENTS" / INTER-PARLIAMENTARY UNION **4685**

INTER REGIONS (FR/0240-9925) [26387320] **2825**

INTER-SOCIETY COLOR COUNCIL *See* NEWSLETTER - INTER-SOCIETY COLOR COUNCIL **5133**

INTER-SOCIETY COLOR COUNCIL NEWS (US/0731-2911) [08134800] **5114**

INTER-UNIVERSITY CONSORTIUM FOR POLITICAL AND SOCIAL RESEARCH *See* ICPSR BULLETIN **5202**

INTER URBA (CN/0710-7307) [08192602] **4657**

INTER-VIEWS (PHILADELPHIA, PA.) (US/1059-2768) [24530008] **5247**

INTER-VIH (CN/1187-5674) [25423773] **3672**

INTERACT (LOS ALTOS, CALIF.) (US/0279-2664) [07707641] **1260**

INTERACTA (AT/0159-9135) [I01599135] 353, **1896**

INTERACTING WITH COMPUTERS (UK/0953-5438) [20745502] **1189**

INTERACTION - CANADIAN CHILD DAY CARE FEDERATION (CN/0835-5819) [18909999] **5290**

INTERACTION (CANBERRA, A.C.T.) (AT/0818-6286) [18046522] **1880**

INTERACTION (COARSEGOLD, CALIF.) (US/1061-7183) [25418364] **4862**

INTERACTION/INSIGHT *See* BUREAU OF BUSINESS PRACTICE MANAGEMENT LETTER, THE **862**

INTERACTION (INTERGOVERNMENTAL COMMITTEE ON URBAN AND REGIONAL RESEARCH) (CN/0226-2878) [02586073] **4657**

INTERACTION MELBOURNE (AT/0310-7949) [I03107949] 2566, **1897**

INTERACTION : MONTHLY NEWSLETTER OF THE HENRY MARTYN INSTITUTE (II) [11425905] 5039, **5042**

INTERACTION (WASHINGTON. 1977) (US/0161-6749) [03953610] **3926**

INTERACTION (WASHINGTON, D.C. : 1981) (US/8756-6281) [10213335] **2195**

●INTERACTIONS BIBLIOGRAPHY, THE (US/1062-7278) [25717462] **417**

●INTERACTIONS / DELTA SOCIETY (US) [26559056] **4286**

●INTERACTIONS (NEW YORK, N.Y.) (US/1072-5520) [29010407] **1189**

INTERACTIONS OF MAN & ANIMALS *See* INTERACTIONS BIBLIOGRAPHY, THE **417**

INTERACTIONS (TILLSONBURG) (CN/1188-3146) [26066752] **2174**

INTERACTIVE AGE (US) **1113**

INTERACTIVE HEALTHCARE NEWSLETTER (US/1048-0501) [20791205] 1287, **4784**

INTERACTIVE LEARNING ENVIRONMENTS (US/1049-4820) [21236137] **1753**

INTERACTIVE LEARNING INTERNATIONAL *CEASED.* (UK/0748-5743) [10967200] 1897, **1223**

INTERACTIVE MEDIA BUSINESS (US/1065-629X) [26569352] 683, **1113**

INTERACTIVE MULTIMEDIA ASSOCIATION *See* COMPLETE MEMBERSHIP DIRECTORY OF THE INTERACTIVE MULTIMEDIA ASSOCIATION, THE **1222**

INTERACTIVE MULTIMEDIA ASSOCIATION COMPATIBILITY PROJECT *See* PROCEEDINGS **1248**

INTERACTIVE UPDATE (UK/0953-8771) [I09538771] **1189**

INTERACTIVE VIDEO (US/0743-4537) [10600097] **1133**

INTERACTIVE VIDEO INDUSTRY ASSOCIATION. INTERACTIVE VIDEO INDUSTRY DIRECTORY *See* COMPLETE MEMBERSHIP DIRECTORY OF THE INTERACTIVE MULTIMEDIA ASSOCIATION, THE **1222**

INTERACTIVE WORLD *CEASED.* (US/1062-2098) [25538958] **1113**

INTERAFRICAIN PHYTOSANITARY BULLETIN (NR) [01792235] 4245, **2420**

INTERAGENCY GRIZZLY BEAR STUDY TEAM *See* YELLOWSTONE GRIZZLY BEAR INVESTIGATIONS **5600**

INTERAGENCY TRAINING CALENDAR OF COURSES (US/0145-1049) [05514373] **943**

INTERAGENCY TRAINING CATALOG OF COURSES (US/0360-5019) [04789946] **4704**

INTERAGENCY TRAINING PROGRAMS CATALOG (US) [02239233] **4704**

INTERAMERICA (ED. ESPANOLA) (CN/0255-0334) [11197156] **1830**

INTERAMERICA (ED. FRANCAISE) (CN/0255-0350) [11197153] **1830**

INTERAMERICA (ENGLISH ED.) (CN/0255-0342) [11197152] **1831**

INTERAMERICAN CHILDREN'S INSTITUTE *See* REPORT OF THE GENERAL DIRECTOR - INTERAMERICAN CHILDREN'S INSTITUTE **5305**

INTERAMERICAN (ED. PORTUGUESA) (CN/0255-0369) [11197151] **1831**

INTERAMERICAN OPPORTUNITIES BRIEFING (US/1055-9299) [23369080] **683**

INTERAMERICAN PSYCHOLOGIST (US/0146-034X) [02830208] **4590**

INTERAMERICAN SOCIETY FOR TROPICAL HORTICULTURE *See* PROCEEDINGS OF THE INTERAMERICAN SOCIETY FOR TROPICAL HORTICULTURE **2429**

INTERAMERICAN SOCIETY OF PSYCHOLOGY *See* DIRECTORIO DE MIEMBROS - SOCIEDAD INTERAMERICANA DE PSICOLOGIA **4585**

INTERAMERICANA (RIO PIEDRAS, P.R.) (PR/8750-5428) [10731676] **5808**

INTERARMA (IT) **4046**

INTERAVIA, AEROSPACE WORLD *See* INTERAVIA : BUSINESS & TECHNOLOGY **24**

INTERAVIA, AEROSPACE WORLD : BUSINESS & TECHNOLOGY (SZ) [27045401] **24**

INTERAVIA AIR LETTER : WORLD AVIATION, SPACE AND ELECTRONICS (SZ) [08902602] **24**

●INTERAVIA : BUSINESS & TECHNOLOGY (SZ) [29868237] **24**

INTERAVIA (ENGLISH ED.) (UK/0020-5168) [01716195] **24**

INTERAVIA (ENGLISH EDITION) *See* INTERAVIA, AEROSPACE WORLD : BUSINESS & TECHNOLOGY **24**

INTERAVIA SPACE DIRECTORY *See* JANE'S SPACE DIRECTORY **25**

INTERBEHAVIORIST, THE (US/8755-612X) [11218975] **4590**

INTERBLOCS (CN/0705-0828) [03956650] **3786**

INTERCAMBIO (MX) [06966773] **840**

INTERCAMBIO ACADEMICO (MX) [20414046] **1831**

INTERCAMBIOS (LOS ANGELES, CALIF.) (US) [20495074] **5559**

INTERCERAM (GW/0020-5214) [02447722] **2591**

●INTERCESSION BIBLE STUDY LESSON (US) [25065779] **5017**

INTERCHAMBER (ET) [11387299] **841**

INTERCHANGE (US) [03113758] **2791**

INTERCHANGE (ALLIANCE FOR ARTS EDUCATION (U.S.)) (US/0890-8338) [05304745] 1753, **322**

●INTERCHANGE (CARRBORO, N.C.) (US/1065-6669) [26668193] **5290**

INTERCHANGE - CITIZENSHIP DEVELOPMENT BRANCH (TORONTO) (CN/0835-5681) [23005068] **5290**

INTERCHANGE - ERIC PROCESSING AND REFERENCE FACILITY (US/0738-7784) [02879238] **3217**

INTERCHANGE, IMPORTED CARS & TRUCKS (US) [12093553] **5417**

INTERCHANGE (PHILADELPHIA) (US/0195-9549) [05592292] **4784**

INTERCHANGE (SACRAMENTO) (US/0196-5743) [05842859] **4389**

INTERCHANGE - SCHOOL OF BUSINESS AND ECONOMICS. WILFRID LAURIER UNIVERSITY *SUSPENDED.* (CN/0823-9851) [11873816] 1831, **683**

INTERCHANGE SYDNEY (AT/0814-4834) [I08144834] **1801**

INTERCHANGE (SYDNEY, AUSTRALIA) (AT) [09380594] **5017**

INTERCHANGE (TORONTO. 1984) (CN/0826-4805) [11830186] **1753**

INTERCHANGE (TORONTO. 1984) (US/0826-4805) [12775917] **1753**

INTERCIENCIA (VE/0378-1844) [02513645] **5114**

... INTERCOLLEGIATE DEBATES (US) [02336721] **1113**

INTERCOLLEGIATE PRESS BULLETINS (US/0193-6824) [01753360] **1831**

INTERCOLLEGIATE REVIEW, THE (US/0020-5249) [01716938] **1831**

INTERCOM (IE) **1753**

INTERCOM (US/0164-6206) [04483731] **1113**

INTERCOM (US) [15181572] **2385**

INTERCOM / CO-OPERATIVE COLLEGE OF CANADA (CN/0821-6398) [09743341] **1542**

INTERCOM — Alphabetical Title Index

INTERCOM (DISTRICT OF COLUMBIA LIBRARY ASSOCIATION) (US/0047-0414) [02230143] **3217**

INTERCOM (LETCHWORTH DEVELOPMENTAL SERVICES) (US) [09102936] **1753**

INTERCOM (LIVINGSTON, N.J.) *CEASED.* (US/0887-963X) [13441652] **1157**

INTERCOM (MONTREAL. ENGLISH EDITION) (CN/0700-9429) [03291344] **3287**

INTERCOM (ONTARIO UNIVERSITY REGISTRARS' ASSOCIATION) (CN/0228-1074) [06959101] **1831**

INTERCOM (SASKATOON) (CN/0315-9892) [02062879] **1753**

INTERCOM (WASHINGTON. EDICION ESPANOL) (US/0163-7223) [04456619] **4554**

INTERCOM (WILLOWDALE) (CN/0383-6061) [02469793] **5061**

INTERCOM : WOMEN IN COMMUNICATIONS (US) **5559, 1113**

INTERCOMM - INTERPRETATION CANADA. ONTARIO SECTION (CN/0831-9103) [15271278] **4851, 4706**

INTERCONNECTION JOURNAL, THE (US/0746-9292) [10393479] **5559**

INTERCONNECTION TECHNOLOGY (US/1065-0415) [26491980] **1189**

INTERCONNECTIONS & CABLES (IT) **1979**

INTERCONTINENTAL ADVANCED MANAGEMENT REPORT, THE (US/0739-313X) [09370647] **871**

INTERCORP *CEASED.* (US/8750-2550) [11189311] **683**

INTERCULTURAL COMMUNICATION STUDIES (US/1057-7769) [24115200] **5247**

INTERCULTURAL HORIZONS *CEASED.* (CN/0827-1550) [13541633] **5247**

INTERCULTURAL STUDIES (US/1055-2804) [23132461] **5204**

INTERCULTURAL STUDIES (MONTREAL, QUEBEC) (CN/0715-5166) [09502358] **1753**

INTERCULTURE (CN/0828-797X) [15732479] **4965**

INTERCULTURE (MONTREAL. ED. FRANCAISE) (CN/0712-1571) [15732553] **5247, 4965**

INTERDATA FINANCIAL HANDBOOK (AT/0816-1224) [I08161224] **791**

INTERDATA LEISURE & TOURISM HANDBOOK, THE *SUSPENDED.* (AT/1034-148X) [I1034148X] **5480**

INTERDENOMINATIONAL THEOLOGICAL CENTER, ATLANTA *See* JOURNAL OF THE INTERDENOMINATIONAL THEOLOGICAL CENTER, THE **4971**

INTERDEPENDENCE (US/0362-4668) [02158361] **4965**

INTERDISCIPLINA (US) [02466479] **2535**

INTERDISCIPLINAIR TIJDSCHRIFT VOOR TAAL EN TEKSTWETENSCHAP *See* GRAMMA / TTT **3284**

INTERDISCIPLINARIA (AG/0325-8203) [12715624] **4590**

INTERDISCIPLINARY APPLIED MATHEMATICS (US) **3509**

● INTERDISCIPLINARY HUMANITIES (US/1056-6139) [23747713] **2848**

INTERDISCIPLINARY MATHEMATICS (US) [05586105] **3509**

INTERDISCIPLINARY SCIENCE REVIEWS : ISR (UK/0308-0188) [02320266] **5114**

INTERDISCIPLINARY TOPICS IN GERONTOLOGY (SZ/0074-1132) [01590457] **3752**

INTERDISZIPLINARE GERONTOLOGIE (GW/0723-8800) [08413223] **3752**

INTERDISZIPLINARES FORUM DER BUNDESARZTEKAMMER *See* FORTSCHRITT UND FORTBILDUNG IN DER MEDIZIN **3577**

INTERDIT (CN/0712-8339) [08862010] **5187**

INTEREST RATE SERVICE (US/0308-9002) [03248735] **791**

INTEREST RATES ON SELECTED CONSUMER INSTALLMENT LOANS AT REPORTING COMMERCIAL BANKS (US) [03458435] **791**

INTERFACCIA (IT) **1189**

INTERFACE (JA) **1189**

INTERFACE (US/0163-6626) [04430477] **1223**

INTERFACE *CEASED.* (US/0891-2912) [14701477] **1157**

INTERFACE (US) [05693925] **5030**

INTERFACE (AMSTERDAM) (NE/0303-3902) [01798812] **4123**

INTERFACE (ATLANTA) (US/0094-5838) [01794066] **5232**

INTERFACE (BETHESDA) (US/0020-5419) [02568440] **4784, 1189**

INTERFACE (CHICAGO) (US/0270-6717) [04851225] **3217**

INTERFACE DISCONTINUED DEVICES *CEASED.* (US) [16721792] **1238, 2066**

INTERFACE. INSURANCE INDUSTRY (US/0192-9046) [02378771] **2884**

INTERFACE: JOURNAL OF NEW MUSIC RESEARCH *See* JOURNAL OF NEW MUSIC RESEARCH **4126**

INTERFACE (MONTREAL. 1984) (CN/0826-4864) [11377303] **5114**

INTERFACE OPPREBOIS (BE/0770-4720) [I07704720] **5778**

INTERFACE OTTAWA-CARLETON (CN) [18641642] **1242**

INTERFACE QUARTERLY NEWSLETTER (AT) **1947**

INTERFACE (SANTA MONICA, CALIF.) (US/1071-295X) [28641047] **1189**

INTERFACE SCIENCE (US/0927-7056) **4428**

INTERFACE (SOCIETY FOR ENVIRONMENTAL GEOCHEMISTRY AND HEALTH) (US/0161-0120) [03805305] **4784, 2233**

INTERFACES IN PSYCHOLOGY (US/0743-2135) [10580067] **4590**

INTERFACES (PROVIDENCE) (US/0092-2102) [01795029] **871**

INTERFAITH ACTION FOR ECONOMIC JUSTICE (US/8755-9404) [11446252] **4477**

INTERFAITH WOMEN'S NEWS & NETWORK (US/0892-6719) [15236700] **5559**

INTERFAX (OTTAWA) (CN/1184-0552) [23247441] **4657**

INTERFEM (US/0742-9436) [10480050] **5559**

INTERFERENCE TECHNOLOGY ENGINEER'S MASTER (US/0190-0943) [04624920] **2066**

INTERFERENZEN (GW/0940-0117) [I09400117] **1979**

INTERFILM *See* INTERFILM REPORTS **4072**

INTERFILM REPORTS (NE) [04161019] **4072**

INTERFLO (US/0748-4631) [10938294] **841**

● INTERFOLIO LEVALLOIS-PERRET (FR/1251-9812) [I12519812] **301**

● INTERGENERATIONAL ISSUES IN SPEECH, HEARING, AND LANGUAGE (US/1058-9902) [24455646] **3287**

INTERGEO BULLETIN *CEASED.* (FR/0396-5880) [04296312] **2582**

INTERGOVERNMENTAL AFFAIRS FELLOWSHIP PROGRAM (US/0097-7780) [01798719] **4657**

INTERGOVERNMENTAL AIDS REPORTS (US/1051-0087) [20125867] **4784**

INTERGOVERNMENTAL COMMITTEE FOR PHYSICAL EDUCATION AND SPORT *See* FINAL REPORT / INTERGOVERNMENTAL COMMITTEE FOR PHYSICAL EDUCATION AND SPORT **4894**

INTERGOVERNMENTAL COUNCIL OF COPPER EXPORTING COUNTRIES. DOCUMENTATION CENTRE *See* STATISTICAL BULLETIN - CIPEC DOCUMENTATION CENTRE **1627**

INTERGOVERNMENTAL COUNCIL OF COPPER PRODUCING COUNTRIES *See* QUARTERLY REVIEW - CIPEC **1623**

INTERGOVERNMENTAL PERSPECTIVE (US/0362-8507) [02292830] **4657**

INTERIEUR (DK) [19346641] **2901**

INTERIGHTS BULLETIN (UK/0268-3709) [I02683709] **4509**

INTERIM CASE CITATIONS TO THE RESTATEMENTS OF THE LAW (US/0895-2523) [12269609] **2983**

INTERIM COLLECTION OF THE NATIONAL ELECTRICAL SAFETY CODE INTERPRETATIONS / NATIONAL ELECTRICAL SAFETY CODE COMMITTEE, ANSI C2 (US) [22611902] **2066**

INTERIM GUIDE FOR ENVIRONMENTAL ASSESSMENT (US) [04430399] **2825**

● INTERIM INSTITUTIONAL DIRECTORY ... HIGHER EDUCATION IN NEW YORK STATE / THE UNIVERSITY OF THE STATE OF NEW YORK, THE STATE EDUCATION DEPARTMENT, BUREAU OF POSTSECONDARY PLANNING (US) [25720968] **1831**

INTERIM (LAS VEGAS, NEV.) (US/0888-2452) [13534204] **3464**

INTERIM REPORT - B. C. HYDRO (CN/0226-3351) [06467860] **4657**

INTERIM REPORT / JOS PLATEAU ENVIRONMENTAL RESOURCES DEVELOPMENT PROGRAMME (UK) [27801324] **2217**

INTERIM REPORT OF THE ASSESSMENT COORDINATION DIVISION (US) [02309550] **4732**

INTERIM REPORT OF THE ELECTORAL BOUNDARIES COMMISSION OF THE PROVINCE OF ALBERTA (CN) [11806254] **4477**

INTERIM REPORT TO THE ... LEGISLATURE (US) [03188890] **2983**

INTERIM (TORONTO) (CN/0824-5401) [10669136] **3762**

INTERINDUSTRY REVIEW (US/0734-6557) [08774869] **1567**

INTERIOR (BL) [02246431] **1567**

INTERIOR BUDGET IN BRIEF, THE (US/0743-2844) [10524108] **4657**

INTERIOR CONSTRUCTION (US/0888-0387) [13448257] **617**

INTERIOR DECORATORS' HANDBOOK (US/0733-8511) [02253079] **2901**

● INTERIOR DECORATORS' HANDBOOK : IDH (US) [27425369] **2901**

INTERIOR DESIGN (NEW YORK, N.Y.) (US/0020-5508) [05965672] **2901**

INTERIOR JOURNAL (1984) (US/8750-7609) [11737767] **5681**

● INTERIOR LANDSCAPE (US/1063-1607) [25908196] **2420**

INTERIOR LANDSCAPE INDUSTRY (US/0742-1648) [10292000] **2420**

INTERIOR LONDON (UK/0954-1438) [I09541438] **5352**

INTERIOR MOTIVES (CN/1188-0635) [25423732] **2901**

INTERIOR VOICE (CN/0715-4011) [09157022] **3396**

INTERIORS & SOURCES (US/1059-5287) [21895519] **2901**

INTERIORS (NEW YORK, N.Y. : 1978) (US/0164-8470 #y 0148-012x) [04374237] **2901**

INTERIORS QUARTERLY (UK) **2901**

INTERIORSCAPE (US/0744-8635) [08338503] **2420**

INTERLAKE LEADER (CN/1184-7786) [24256982] **5786**

INTERLAKEN REVIEW, THE (US) [12889461] **5717**

INTERLAKE'S REGIONAL NEWS, THE (CN/0824-149X) [11807825] **5786**

INTERLENDING & DOCUMENT SUPPLY (UK/0264-1615) [09286784] **3217**

INTERLOCHEN CENTER FOR THE ARTS *See* ALUMNI DIRECTORY / INTERLOCHEN CENTER FOR THE ARTS **1098**

INTERLOCUTEUR (CN/0711-2009) [08690321] **1865**

INTERMEDIA (LONDON) (UK/0309-118X) [03049412] **1133, 1157**

INTERMEDIA (LOS ANGELES) (US/0147-5754) [02725788] **322**

INTERMEDIAIR (NE) **5114**

INTERMEDIAIR BELGIE (BE) **1567**

INTERMEDIAIRE DES CASANOVISTES, L' (IT) [13740274] **3396**

INTERMEDIAIRE DES CHERCHEURS ET CURIEUX, L' (FR/0020-5613) [01753367] **1926**

INTERMEDIAIRE DES GENEALOGISTES (BE/0020-5621) [I00205621] **2454**

INTERMEDIATE MINIMUM PROPERTY STANDARDS FOR SOLAR HEATING AND DOMESTIC HOT WATER SYSTEMS (US) [03454433] **2606**

INTERMEDIATE TEACHERS ASSOCIATION *See* NEWS - INTERMEDIATE TEACHERS ASSOCIATION **1867**

INTERMET *See* COMMUNIQUE - INTERMET **5242**

● INTERMETALLICS (UK/0966-9795) [28207563] **4004**

INTERMODAL ASIA (HK) **5450**

INTERMODAL REPORTER (US/0882-8059) [11985180] **5384**

INTERMOUNTAIN CATHOLIC (US/0273-6187) [06751940] **5030, 4965**

INTERMOUNTAIN CATHOLIC REGISTER *See* INTERMOUNTAIN CATHOLIC **4965**

INTERMOUNTAIN CONTRACTOR (US/0020-5656) [04083829] **617**

INTERMOUNTAIN JEWISH NEWS (US/0047-0511) [04083846] **5643**

INTERMOUNTAIN LOGGING NEWS *CEASED.* (US/0300-7405) [01355733] **2401**

INTERMOUNTAIN REGION ANNUAL QUALITY PLAN (US) [25145025] **2385**

INTERMOUNTAIN RESEARCH STATION (OGDEN, UTAH) See INTERCOM **2385**

INTERMUSE (US/0277-8017) [07623788] **322**

INTERNAL AUDITING *CEASED.* (IT) **1496**

INTERNAL AUDITING ALERT (US/0744-2947) [08037549] **745**

INTERNAL AUDITING (BOSTON, MASS.) (US/0897-0378) [12854478] **745**

INTERNAL AUDITOR, THE (US/0020-5745) [01585937] **745**

INTERNAL COMBUSTION ENGINES (US/0278-9302) [03093578] **2116**

INTERNAL CONTROL REPORT TO THE STATE LEGISLATURE (US) [05921766] **4732**

INTERNAL MEDICINE (US/0897-6309) [17575785] **3797**

●INTERNAL MEDICINE (JA) [25545226] **3797**

INTERNAL MEDICINE ALERT (US/0195-315X) [05523368] **3797**

INTERNAL MEDICINE BULLETIN *CEASED.* (US/1065-9498) [26813421] **3797**

INTERNAL MEDICINE (GLENDALE, CALIF.) (US/0271-1303) [03438123] **3797**

INTERNAL MEDICINE NEWS & CARDIOLOGY NEWS (US/0274-5542) [06400032] **3706, 3746**

INTERNAL MEDICINE (PLAINSBORO, N.J.) (US/1056-9286) [23273983] **3797**

●INTERNAL MEDICINE RESIDENT (US/1058-1685) [24235919] **3797**

INTERNAL MEDICINE WEEKLY (US/1078-2869) **3797**

INTERNAL REVENUE BULLETIN (US/0020-5761) [02447728] **4732**

INTERNAL REVENUE CODE (US/0163-7177) [01208088] **4732**

INTERNAL REVENUE CUMULATIVE BULLETIN (US/0364-0620) [02779188] **4732**

INTERNAL REVENUE MANUAL; AUDIT (US) [06349615] **4732**

INTERNAMERICA (NEEDHAM, MASS.) (US/1061-7337) [25422599] **1680**

INTERNASJONAL POLITIKK (OSLO, NORWAY) (NO/0020-577X) [01681224] **4524**

INTERNATIONAAL MARXISTISCH TIJDSCHRIFT (BE) [06399621] **4542**

INTERNATIONAL A. A. DIRECTORY (US/0361-7459) [02386602] **1345**

INTERNATIONAL ABC AEROSPACE DIRECTORY (UK/0074-1116) [22283395] **24**

INTERNATIONAL ABSTRACTS IN DERMATOLOGY (CN/0829-9935) [13924560] **3720**

INTERNATIONAL ABSTRACTS IN HYPERTENSION (CN/0836-7884) [17743247] **3706**

INTERNATIONAL ABSTRACTS IN OPERATIONS RESEARCH (UK/0020-580X) [01753369] **5114, 5175**

INTERNATIONAL ABSTRACTS, PEDIATRIC UROLOGY (CN/1185-5479) [24860883] **3904, 3990**

●INTERNATIONAL ACADEMY FOR BIOMEDICAL AND DRUG RESEARCH (SZ) [26320068] **978, 4308**

INTERNATIONAL ACADEMY FOR THE STUDY OF TOURISM See NEWSLETTER OF THE INTERNATIONAL ACADEMY FOR THE STUDY OF TOURISM **5486**

INTERNATIONAL ACADEMY OF PATHOLOGY See MONOGRAPHS IN PATHOLOGY **3896**

INTERNATIONAL ACCOUNTANT, THE (UK/0020-5826) [04456233] **745**

INTERNATIONAL ACCOUNTING BULLETIN (UK/0265-0223) [10320661] **745**

INTERNATIONAL ACCOUNTING SUMMARIES (US/1056-2583) [23603916] **745**

INTERNATIONAL ACTIVITIES (US/0197-1948) [05366214] **1979**

INTERNATIONAL ADVENTURE TRAVELGUIDE (US/0148-2300) [03594727] **5480**

INTERNATIONAL ADVERTISER (NEW YORK, N.Y. 1985) (US/0885-3363) [12609072] **760**

INTERNATIONAL AEROBIOLOGY NEWSLETTER (FI) [02046763] **458**

INTERNATIONAL AEROSPACE ABSTRACTS (US/0020-5842) [01696171] **24, 41**

INTERNATIONAL AEROSPACE DIRECTORY (US/0882-6730) [11909683] **24**

INTERNATIONAL AFFAIRS AND DEFENSE (US/0737-3767) [09354809] **4524**

INTERNATIONAL AFFAIRS BULLETIN (SA/0258-7270) [04060336] **4524**

INTERNATIONAL AFFAIRS (LONDON) (UK/0020-5850) [08698894] **4524**

INTERNATIONAL AFFAIRS (MOSCOW) (RU/0130-9641) [01697121] **4524**

INTERNATIONAL AFFAIRS REPORTS FROM QUAKER WORKERS (US/0534-6541) [02723613] **4524**

INTERNATIONAL AFFAIRS STUDIES (PL/0867-4493) [24460261] **4524**

INTERNATIONAL AFRICAN BIBLIOGRAPHY (UK/0020-5877) [01588491] **417**

INTERNATIONAL AG-SIEVE (US/1048-2962) [20915912] **96**

INTERNATIONAL AGRICULTURAL DEVELOPMENT (CROWBOROUGH, EAST SUSSEX) (UK/0261-4413) [08256295] **96**

INTERNATIONAL AIR FORCES & MILITARY AIRCRAFT DIRECTORY. MONTHLY NEWSLETTER SUPPLEMENT See AAS MILAVNEWS **4033**

INTERNATIONAL AIR REVIEW *CEASED.* (US/1056-5701) [23740263] **24**

INTERNATIONAL AIR SAFETY SEMINAR PROCEEDINGS (US/0270-5176) [06380782] **24**

INTERNATIONAL AIR TRANSPORT ASSOCIATION See PASSENGER SERVICES CONFERENCE RESOLUTIONS MANUAL / IATA **31**

INTERNATIONAL AIR TRANSPORT ASSOCIATION See IATA LOCATION IDENTIFIERS HANDBOOK **23**

INTERNATIONAL AIR TRANSPORT ASSOCIATION See TICKETING HANDBOOK **37**

INTERNATIONAL AIR TRANSPORT ASSOCIATION See AIRPORT HANDLING MANUAL **10**

INTERNATIONAL AIR TRANSPORT ASSOCIATION See DANGEROUS GOODS REGULATIONS **4773**

INTERNATIONAL AIR TRANSPORT ASSOCIATION See LIVE ANIMALS REGULATIONS / IATA **5386**

INTERNATIONAL AIR TRANSPORT ASSOCIATION See MANUAL OF TARIFF COORDINATING CONFERENCES RESOLUTIONS--PASSENGER; TC23/TC123 RESOLUTIONS, EUROPE/MIDDLE EAST-JAPAN/KOREA **845**

INTERNATIONAL AIR TRANSPORT ASSOCIATION. GENERAL MEETING See MINUTES **28**

INTERNATIONAL ALLIANCE OF THEATRICAL STAGE EMPLOYEES AND MOVING PICTURE MACHINE OPERATORS OF THE UNITED STATES AND CANADA See OFFICIAL BULLETIN OF THE THEATRICAL STAGE EMPLOYEES AND MOVING PICTURE MACHINE OPERATORS OF THE UNITED STATES AND CANADA **5367**

INTERNATIONAL AMATEUR ATHLETIC FEDERATION See I.A.A.F. DIRECTORY / I.A.A.F **4899**

INTERNATIONAL AMATEUR ATHLETIC FEDERATION See OFFICIAL HANDBOOK / INTERNATIONAL AMATEUR ATHLETIC FEDERATION **4909**

INTERNATIONAL AMATEUR ATHLETIC FEDERATION See DIRECTORY & CALENDAR / IAAF **4892**

INTERNATIONAL AMATEUR BASKETBALL FEDERATION See F.I.B.A. RULES CASEBOOK **4894**

INTERNATIONAL AMATEUR BASKETBALL FEDERATION See FIBA BASKETBALL MONTHLY **4894**

INTERNATIONAL AMATEUR BASKETBALL FEDERATION See OFFICIAL BASKETBALL RULES FOR MEN AND WOMEN **4909**

INTERNATIONAL AND COMPARATIVE LAW QUARTERLY, THE (UK/0020-5893) [01753375] **3129**

INTERNATIONAL AND INTERCULTURAL COMMUNICATION ANNUAL (US/0270-6075) [03496951] **1113**

INTERNATIONAL AND NON-U.S. NATIONAL STANDARDS NUMERIC INDEX TO ... (US) [20647583] **4030**

INTERNATIONAL ANESTHESIOLOGY CLINICS (US/0020-5907) [01753376] **3683**

INTERNATIONAL ANGIOLOGY (IT/0392-9590) [10637543] **3966**

INTERNATIONAL ANIMAL ACTION (UK) [20270570] **226**

INTERNATIONAL ANNALS OF ADOLESCENT PSYCHIATRY (US/1071-0752) [19408635] **3926**

INTERNATIONAL ANNUAL JOURNAL OF ARTS, SCIENCES, ENGINEERING, AGRICULTURE, AND TECHNOLOGY (US/0749-0682) [11078301] **5114**

INTERNATIONAL ANNUAL OF ORAL HISTORY See INTERNATIONAL YEARBOOK OF ORAL HISTORY AND LIFE STORIES **2620**

INTERNATIONAL ANTIVIRAL NEWS (UK) [29431220] **564**

●INTERNATIONAL APPLIED MECHANICS (US/1063-7095) [26117585] **2116**

INTERNATIONAL ARACHIS NEWSLETTER (II/1010-5824) [16471613] **174**

INTERNATIONAL ARBITRATION REPORT (US/0886-0114) [12792366] **3129**

INTERNATIONAL ARCHIVES OF ALLERGY AND APPLIED IMMUNOLOGY See INTERNATIONAL ARCHIVES OF ALLERGY AND IMMUNOLOGY **3672**

●INTERNATIONAL ARCHIVES OF ALLERGY AND IMMUNOLOGY (SZ/1018-2438) [25800185] **3672**

INTERNATIONAL ARCHIVES OF OCCUPATIONAL AND ENVIRONMENTAL HEALTH (GW/0340-0131) [01718978] **2864**

INTERNATIONAL ARCHIVES OF PHOTOGRAMMETRY See INTERNATIONAL ARCHIVES OF PHOTOGRAMMETRY AND REMOTE SENSING **1979**

INTERNATIONAL ARCHIVES OF PHOTOGRAMMETRY AND REMOTE SENSING (UK/0256-1840) [18183918] **4370, 1979**

INTERNATIONAL ARMAMENTS MONTHLY (US/0090-4813) [01785118] **4046**

INTERNATIONAL ARRIVALS AND DEPARTURES / PAPUA NEW GUINEA, NATIONAL STATISTICAL OFFICE (PP) [08119276] **1919**

INTERNATIONAL ART MATERIAL DIRECTORY AND BUYERS' GUIDE (US/0742-7387) [10407120] **353**

INTERNATIONAL ARTHURIAN SOCIETY See BULLETIN BIBLIOGRAPHIQUE DE LA SOCIETE INTERNATIONALE ARTHURIENNE **3457**

INTERNATIONAL ASSOCIATION FOR BRIDGE AND STRUCTURAL ENGINEERING See RAPPORTS DES COMMISSIONS DE TRAVAIL **1993**

INTERNATIONAL ASSOCIATION FOR BRIDGE AND STRUCTURAL ENGINEERING. CONGRESS See CONGRESS REPORT / CONGRESS **2021**

INTERNATIONAL ASSOCIATION FOR CEREAL CHEMISTRY. CONGRESS. BERICHTE DER INTERNATIONALEN GESELLSCHAFT FUR GETREIDECHEMIE See INTERNATIONALE GESELLSCHAFT FUER GETREIDEWISSENSCHAFT UND -TECHNOLOGIE **97**

INTERNATIONAL ASSOCIATION FOR CEREAL SCIENCE AND TECHNOLOGY. CONGRESS See INTERNATIONALE GESELLSCHAFT FUER GETREIDEWISSENSCHAFT UND -TECHNOLOGIE **97**

INTERNATIONAL ASSOCIATION FOR COMPUTING IN EDUCATION See IACE/AEDS NEWSLETTER **1913**

INTERNATIONAL ASSOCIATION FOR FRANCOPHONE SOLIDARITY See A.S.F. DOCUMENTATION **2671**

INTERNATIONAL ASSOCIATION FOR HYDRAULIC RESEARCH See PROCEEDINGS **2094**

INTERNATIONAL ASSOCIATION FOR MOBILIZATION OF CREATIVITY See BULLETIN - INTERNATIONAL ASSOCIATION FOR MOBILIZATION OF CREATIVITY **3560**

INTERNATIONAL ASSOCIATION FOR SHELL AND SPATIAL STRUCTURES See BULLETIN OF THE INTERNATIONAL ASSOCIATION FOR SHELL AND SPATIAL STRUCTURES **605**

INTERNATIONAL ASSOCIATION OF AGRICULTURAL LIBRARIANS AND DOCUMENTALISTS See IAALD NEWS **3214**

INTERNATIONAL ASSOCIATION OF AQUATIC AND MARINE SCIENCE LIBRARIES AND INFORMATION CENTERS See MEMBERSHIP DIRECTORY / INTERNATIONAL ASSOCIATION OF AQUATIC AND MARINE SCIENCE LIBRARIES AND INFORMATION CENTERS **1452**

INTERNATIONAL ASSOCIATION OF ASSESSING OFFICERS See MEMBERSHIP DIRECTORY - INTERNATIONAL ASSOCIATION OF ASSESSING OFFICERS (1977) **4737**

INTERNATIONAL ASSOCIATION OF ASSESSING OFFICERS. PERSONAL PROPERTY SECTION See MEMBERSHIP DIRECTORY - INTERNATIONAL ASSOCIATION OF ASSESSING OFFICERS. PERSONAL PROPERTY SECTION **4737**

INTERNATIONAL ASSOCIATION OF BIOLOGICAL STANDARDIZATION See BULLETIN D'INFORMATION - ASSOCIATION INTERNATIONALE DE STANDARDISATION BIOLOGIQUE. NEWSLETTER - INTERNATIONAL ASSOCIATION OF BIOLOGICAL STANDARDIZATION **4295**

INTERNATIONAL — Alphabetical Title Index

INTERNATIONAL ASSOCIATION OF BUDDHIST STUDIES *See* JOURNAL OF THE INTERNATIONAL ASSOCIATION OF BUDDHIST STUDIES, THE **5021**

INTERNATIONAL ASSOCIATION OF CHIEFS OF POLICE. LEGISLATIVE RESEARCH UNIT *See* IACP LAW ENFORCEMENT LEGISLATION AND LITIGATION REPORT **3107**

INTERNATIONAL ASSOCIATION OF ENGINEERING GEOLOGY *See* BULLETIN OF THE INTERNATIONAL ASSOCIATION OF ENGINEERING GEOLOGY **2019**

INTERNATIONAL ASSOCIATION OF FIRE CHIEFS *See* IAFC COMMITTEE LIST **616**

INTERNATIONAL ASSOCIATION OF FISH AND WILDLIFE AGENCIES *See* PROCEEDINGS OF THE CONVENTION - INTERNATIONAL ASSOCIATION OF FISH AND WILDLIFE AGENCIES **2202**

INTERNATIONAL ASSOCIATION OF INDUSTRIAL ACCIDENT BOARDS AND COMMISSIONS *See* IAIABC JOURNAL **2863**

INTERNATIONAL ASSOCIATION OF JAZZ RECORD COLLECTORS *See* IAJRC JOURNAL **4122**

INTERNATIONAL ASSOCIATION OF LAW LIBRARIES *See* DIRECTORY - INTERNATIONAL ASSOCIATION OF LAW LIBRARIES **2961**

INTERNATIONAL ASSOCIATION OF LIGHTHOUSE AUTHORITIES *See* LISTE DES MEMBRES / ASSOCIATION INTERNATIONALE DE SIGNALISATION MARITIME **4178**

INTERNATIONAL ASSOCIATION OF MACHINISTS AND AEROSPACE WORKERS *See* REPORT FROM HEADQUARTERS **1706**

INTERNATIONAL ASSOCIATION OF MARINE SCIENCE LIBRARIES AND INFORMATION CENTERS *See* MEMBERSHIP DIRECTORY / INTERNATIONAL ASSOCIATION OF MARINE SCIENCE LIBRARIES AND INFORMATION CENTERS **3230**

INTERNATIONAL ASSOCIATION OF MARINE SCIENCE LIBRARIES AND INFORMATION CENTERS *See* NEWSLETTER - IAMSLIC **1453**

INTERNATIONAL ASSOCIATION OF MARINE SCIENCE LIBRARIES AND INFORMATION CENTERS. CONFERENCE *See* INTERNATIONAL ASSOCIATION OF MARINE SCIENCE LIBRARIES AND INFORMATION CENTERS CONFERENCE SERIES **3218**

INTERNATIONAL ASSOCIATION OF MARINE SCIENCE LIBRARIES AND INFORMATION CENTERS CONFERENCE SERIES (US/8755-6332) [11361820] **3218**

INTERNATIONAL ASSOCIATION OF MARINE SCIENCE LIBRARIES AND INFORMATION CENTERS. MEMBERSHIP DIRECTORY *See* MEMBERSHIP DIRECTORY / INTERNATIONAL ASSOCIATION OF AQUATIC AND MARINE SCIENCE LIBRARIES AND INFORMATION CENTERS **1452**

INTERNATIONAL ASSOCIATION OF MILK FOOD AND ENVIRONMENTAL SANITARIANS 3A SANITARY STANDARDS (US) 2195, **2345**

INTERNATIONAL ASSOCIATION OF ORIENTALIST LIBRARIANS *See* BULLETIN - INTERNATIONAL ASSOCIATION OF ORIENTALIST LIBRARIANS **3198**

INTERNATIONAL ASSOCIATION OF PANORAMIC PHOTOGRAPHERS : (US/1063-7478) [19582572] **4370**

INTERNATIONAL ASSOCIATION OF PLUMBING AND MECHANICAL OFFICIALS *See* UNIFORM PLUMBING CODE **2608**

INTERNATIONAL ASSOCIATION OF PUPIL PERSONNEL WORKERS *See* JOURNAL OF THE INTERNATIONAL ASSOCIATION OF PUPIL PERSONNEL WORKERS, THE **1759**

INTERNATIONAL ASSOCIATION OF PUPIL PERSONNEL WORKERS. JOURNAL *See* JOURNAL FOR TRUANCY AND DROPOUT PREVENTION, THE **1756**

INTERNATIONAL ASSOCIATION OF SCHOOLS OF SOCIAL WORK *See* IASSW DIRECTORY **5289**

INTERNATIONAL ASSOCIATION OF SEDIMENTOLOGISTS *See* SPECIAL PUBLICATION ... OF THE INTERNATIONAL ASSOCIATION OF SEDIMENTOLOGISTS **1398**

INTERNATIONAL ASSOCIATION OF SOUND ARCHIVES *See* INFORMATION BULLETIN / INTERNATIONAL ASSOCIATION OF SOUND ARCHIVES **2481**

INTERNATIONAL ASSOCIATION OF SURVEY STATISTICIANS *See* DIRECTORY OF MEMBERS - INTERNATIONAL ASSOCIATION OF SURVEY STATISTICIANS **5326**

INTERNATIONAL ASSOCIATION OF THEORETICAL AND APPLIED LIMNOLOGY *See* MITTEILUNGEN - INTERNATIONALEN VEREINIGUNG FUER THEORETISCHE UND ANGEWANDTE LIMNOLOGIE **1416**

INTERNATIONAL ASSOCIATION OF THEORETICAL AND APPLIED LIMNOLOGY *See* VERHANDLUNGEN - INTERNATIONALE VEREINIGUNG FUER THEORETISCHE UND ANGEWANDTE LIMNOLOGIE **1418**

INTERNATIONAL ASSOCIATION OF WOOD ANATOMISTS *See* IAWA BULLETIN **2401**

INTERNATIONAL ASSOCIATION OF WOOD ANATOMISTS. IAWA BULLETIN *See* IAWA JOURNAL / INTERNATIONAL ASSOCIATION OF WOOD ANATOMISTS **2401**

INTERNATIONAL ASTROLOGICAL REGISTER (US/0095-0378) [01796168] **390**

INTERNATIONAL ASTRONAUTICAL FEDERATION *See* ASTRONAUTICAL RESEARCH **12**

INTERNATIONAL ASTRONOMICAL UNION *See* SYMPOSIUM - INTERNATIONAL ASTRONOMICAL UNION **401**

INTERNATIONAL ASTRONOMICAL UNION *See* INFORMATION BULLETIN / INTERNATIONAL ASTRONOMICAL UNION **395**

INTERNATIONAL ASTRONOMICAL UNION *See* TRANSACTIONS OF THE INTERNATIONAL ASTRONOMICAL UNION **401**

INTERNATIONAL ASTRONOMICAL UNION. CENTRAL BUREAU FOR ASTRONOMICAL TELEGRAMS *See* CIRCULAR - CENTRAL BUREAU FOR ASTRONOMICAL TELEGRAMS, INTERNATIONAL ASTRONOMICAL UNION **394**

INTERNATIONAL ATLAS. [EDITORS: RUSSEL L. VOISIN AND OTHERS] (US) [01642454] **1926**

INTERNATIONAL ATOMIC ENERGY AGENCY *See* LEGAL SERIES **1949**

INTERNATIONAL ATOMIC ENERGY AGENCY *See* OPERATING EXPERIENCE WITH NUCLEAR POWER STATIONS IN MEMBER STATES **2158**

INTERNATIONAL ATOMIC ENERGY AGENCY *See* INIS. AUTHORITY LIST FOR CORPORATE ENTRIES AND REPORT NUMBER PREFIXES **4426**

INTERNATIONAL ATOMIC ENERGY AGENCY *See* PANEL PROCEEDINGS SERIES - INTERNATIONAL ATOMIC ENERGY AGENCY **1952**

INTERNATIONAL ATOMIC ENERGY AGENCY *See* INIS, DESCRIPTIVE CATALOGUING SAMPLES **4426**

INTERNATIONAL ATOMIC ENERGY AGENCY *See* INTERNATIONAL ATOMIC ENERGY AGENCY PUBLICATIONS. CATALOGUE **1947**

INTERNATIONAL ATOMIC ENERGY AGENCY BULLETIN (AU/0020-6067) [20284215] **1947**

INTERNATIONAL ATOMIC ENERGY AGENCY PUBLICATIONS. CATALOGUE (AU) [02889876] **1947**

INTERNATIONAL AUCTION RECORDS (US/0074-1922) [01442496] **353**

INTERNATIONAL AUTHORS' AND WRITERS' WHO'S WHO *See* INTERNATIONAL WHO'S WHO IN POETRY AND POETS' ENCYCLOPAEDIA **3464**

INTERNATIONAL AUTHORS AND WRITERS WHO'S WHO, THE (UK/0143-8263) [02341010] **433**

INTERNATIONAL AUTO INDUSTRY NEWSLETTER (UK/0262-317X) [I0262317X] **5417**

INTERNATIONAL AUTOMOTIVE REVIEW *CEASED.* (UK/0261-2267) [10041235] **5417**

INTERNATIONAL AVIATION MECHANICS JOURNAL (US/0045-1193) [04083858] **24**

INTERNATIONAL AWARDS FOR BIOMEDICAL RESEARCH AND RESEARCH TRAINING *See* NATIONAL INSTITUTES OF HEALTH INTERNATIONAL AWARDS FOR BIOMEDICAL RESEARCH AND RESEARCH TRAINING **5130**

INTERNATIONAL BACK PAIN NEWS (UK) **3797**

INTERNATIONAL BAHAMA LIFE (BF) [01789434] **5480**

INTERNATIONAL BANK ACCOUNTING (UK) [16928970] **792**

INTERNATIONAL BANK CREDIT ANALYST, THE (CN/0020-6113) [14250330] **901**

INTERNATIONAL BANK DIRECTORY *CEASED.* (US/1046-266X) [13105732] **792**

INTERNATIONAL BANK FOR RECONSTRUCTION AND DEVELOPMENT *See* MONTHLY OPERATIONAL SUMMARY **1506**

INTERNATIONAL BANK FOR RECONSTRUCTION AND DEVELOPMENT *See* PUBLICATIONS UPDATE / THE WORLD BANK **804**

INTERNATIONAL BANK FOR RECONSTRUCTION AND DEVELOPMENT *See* WORLD BANK GROUP DIRECTORY, THE **1169**

INTERNATIONAL BANK FOR RECONSTRUCTION AND DEVELOPMENT *See* REPORT - WORLD BANK **808**

INTERNATIONAL BANK FOR RECONSTRUCTION AND DEVELOPMENT *See* WORLD BANK POLICY RESEARCH BULLETIN **816**

INTERNATIONAL BANK FOR RECONSTRUCTION AND DEVELOPMENT *See* WORLD BANK CATALOG. ACCESSION LIST **816**

INTERNATIONAL BANK FOR RECONSTRUCTION AND DEVELOPMENT *See* INDEX OF PUBLICATIONS - WORLD BANK **1533**

INTERNATIONAL BANK FOR RECONSTRUCTION AND DEVELOPMENT *See* ANNUAL REPORT - WORLD BANK **2907**

INTERNATIONAL BANK FOR RECONSTRUCTION AND DEVELOPMENT *See* WORLD BANK CATALOG OF PUBLICATIONS, THE **1540**

INTERNATIONAL BANK NOTE SOCIETY *See* I.B.N.S. JOURNAL **790**

INTERNATIONAL BANKING AND FINANCIAL LAW (UK) [24130492] **3087**

INTERNATIONAL BANKING AND FINANCIAL LAW BULLETIN (UK) 792, **2983**

INTERNATIONAL BANKING FOCUS (US/1042-3370) [18868869] **792**

INTERNATIONAL BAR ASSOCIATION. SECTION ON BUSINESS LAW *See* DIRECTORY OF MEMBERS - INTERNATIONAL BAR ASSOCIATION, SECTION ON BUSINESS LAW **3099**

INTERNATIONAL BAR NEWS (LONDON, ENGLAND) (UK/0143-7453) [06732881] **3129**

INTERNATIONAL BARBED WIRE GAZETTE, THE (US/0047-0597) [04083870] **159**

INTERNATIONAL BAROMETER (US/0882-7966) [11982203] **5204**

INTERNATIONAL BASKETBALL (HU/0139-4932) [I01394932] **4900**

INTERNATIONAL BEHAVIOURAL SCIENTIST (II/0020-613X) [02142392] **5204**

INTERNATIONAL BENEFITS INFORMATION SERVICE (US/0018-8611) [05924699] **2884**

INTERNATIONAL BEVERAGE NEWS *See* INTERNATIONAL BOTTLER AND PACKER, THE **4219**

INTERNATIONAL BIBLIOGRAPHIC BULLETIN OF WILDLAND FIRE (US/1064-184X) [26224351] **2291**

INTERNATIONAL BIBLIOGRAPHY OF ECONOMICS (US/0085-204X) [01753414] **1496**

INTERNATIONAL BIBLIOGRAPHY OF HISTORICAL SCIENCES (FR/0074-2015) [01753415] 2620, **2635**

INTERNATIONAL BIBLIOGRAPHY OF SOCIAL SCIENCES: ANTHROPOLOGY (US) **248**

INTERNATIONAL BIBLIOGRAPHY OF SOCIAL SCIENCES: ECONOMICS (US) **1534**

INTERNATIONAL BIBLIOGRAPHY OF SOCIAL SCIENCES: POLITICAL SCIENCE (US) **4477**

INTERNATIONAL BIBLIOGRAPHY OF SOCIAL SCIENCES: SOCIOLOGY (US) **5266**

INTERNATIONAL BIBLIOGRAPHY OF SOCIOLOGY (UK/0085-2066) [01753417] 5247, **5266**

INTERNATIONAL BIBLIOGRAPHY OF STUDIES ON ALCOHOL (US) [01604217] 1345, **1350**

INTERNATIONAL BIBLIOGRAPHY OF THE FORENSIC SCIENCES, THE *SUSPENDED.* (US/0098-2393) [01397787] **3660**

INTERNATIONAL BIBLIOGRAPHY OF THEATRE (US/0882-9446) [12019321] 5365, **5372**

● INTERNATIONAL BIBLIOGRAPHY OF WILDLAND FIRE (US/1051-4201) [21957206] 2195, **2291**

INTERNATIONAL BIBLIOGRAPHY ON BURNS (US/0090-0575) [02255013] **3660**

INTERNATIONAL BIBLIOGRAPHY ON BURNS. SUPPLEMENT (US/0360-1196) [02243676] **3660**

INTERNATIONAL BIBLIOGRAPHY ON OPERATIONS RESEARCH, CONTROL THEORY, SYSTEM SCIENCE (GW) [05085885] **5114**

INTERNATIONAL BIODETERIORATION *See* INTERNATIONAL BIODETERIORATION & BIODEGRADATION **1356**

●INTERNATIONAL BIODETERIORATION & BIODEGREDATION (UK/0964-8305) [25645577] **1356**

INTERNATIONAL BIOLOGICAL PROGRAMME. JAPANESE NATIONAL COMMITTEE *See* JIBP SYNTHESIS **460**

INTERNATIONAL BIOSCIENCE MONOGRAPH (II/0253-7206) [06835410] **458**

INTERNATIONAL BIOSCIENCE SERIES (II/0971-1716) [I09711716] **458**

INTERNATIONAL BIOTECHNOLOGY LABORATORY (US/0888-7225) [13703562] **3693**

INTERNATIONAL BLOOD/PLASMA NEWS (US/0742-7719) [10466487] **3772**

INTERNATIONAL BOAT INDUSTRY (UK/0020-6172) [01787700] **593**

INTERNATIONAL BOND AND MONEY MARKET PERFORMANCE (US/0895-299X) [15566928] **792**

INTERNATIONAL BOND EQUITIES LETTER : WEEKLY REVIEW OF THE INTERNATIONAL BOND & EQUITIES MARKET (UK) **901**

●INTERNATIONAL BOND INVESTOR (UK/1352-0431) [28598695] **901**

INTERNATIONAL BONSAI (US/0198-9561) [06108033] **2420**

INTERNATIONAL BOOK COLLECTORS ALMANAC/NEWSLETTER (US/0741-9953) [10240288] **4829**

INTERNATIONAL BOOK TRADE DIRECTORY : EUROPE, AUSTRALIA, OCEANIA, LATIN AMERICA, AFRICA AND ASIA / INTERNATIONALES BUCHHANDELSADRESSBUCH : EUROPA, AUSTRALIAN, OZEANIEN, LATEINAMERIKA, AFRIKA UND ASIEN (GW) [20232537] **4829**

INTERNATIONAL BOOKBINDER / OFFICIAL JOURNAL OF THE INTERNATIONAL BROTHERHOOD OF BOOKBINDERS OF NORTH AMERICA, THE (US/0020-6180) [01753420] **4829**

INTERNATIONAL BOOKS IN PRINT (GW/0170-9348) [04952175] **4821**

INTERNATIONAL BOTTLER AND PACKER, THE (UK/0020-6199) [04010245] **4219**

INTERNATIONAL BRAIN DOMINANCE REVIEW *CEASED*. (US/1046-5448) [20438432] **4590**

●INTERNATIONAL BRANDS AND THEIR COMPANIES (US/1050-8376) [21633427] **683**

INTERNATIONAL BREWER & DISTILLER *See* BREWERS' GUARDIAN **2365**

INTERNATIONAL BRIDGE, TUNNEL, AND TURNPIKE ASSOCIATION. MEETING *See* PRESENTATIONS **1991**

INTERNATIONAL BROADCAST ENGINEER : IBE (UK/0020-6229) [02447744] **1133**

INTERNATIONAL BROADCASTING (UK/0957-4425) [08752085] **1133**

INTERNATIONAL BROADCASTING OF ALL NATIONS; REPORT (US) [05253397] **1133**

INTERNATIONAL BROKER, THE (UK/0966-7733) [I09667733] **2884**

INTERNATIONAL BROTHERHOOD OF PAINTERS AND ALLIED TRADES. PAINTERS DISTRICT COUNCIL 9 OF NEW YORK CITY *See* PAINTERS & ALLIED TRADES DISTRICT COUNCIL 9 SPOTLITE NEWS **1700**

INTERNATIONAL BUILDING SC ENCE AND CONSTRUCTION ABSTRACTS *See* INTERNATIONAL BUILDING SCIENCE & STRUCTURAL ABSTRACTS **617**

INTERNATIONAL BUILDING SCIENCE & CONSTRUCTION ABSTRACTS (IE/0790-5769) [13956656] **2024**

INTERNATIONAL BUILDING SCIENCE & STRUCTURAL ABSTRACTS (IE/0791-492X) **617**

INTERNATIONAL BUILDING SERVICES ABSTRACTS (UK/0140-4237) [03925917] **2606**, **617**

INTERNATIONAL BULK JOURNAL : IBJ (UK/0260-1087) [08249068] **5384**

INTERNATIONAL BULLETIN (DK) [03415644] **4524**

INTERNATIONAL BULLETIN FOR THE RECONSTRUCTION & DEVELOPMENT OF ARMENIA (US/1047-4803) [20707046] **2910**

INTERNATIONAL BULLETIN OF BIBLIOGRAPHY ON EDUCATION (QUARTERLY) (SP/0211-8335) [08564682] **1795**

INTERNATIONAL BULLETIN OF LAW & MENTAL HEALTH (CN/0843-4964) [20367662] **2983**

INTERNATIONAL BULLETIN OF MISSIONARY RESEARCH (US/0272-6122) [06882616] **4965**

INTERNATIONAL BULLETIN OF MORITA THERAPY (CN/0847-415X) [23598817] **4590**

INTERNATIONAL BULLETIN OF SPORTS INFORMATION (NE/0378-4037) [05349778] 1856, **4900**

INTERNATIONAL BULLETIN OF WILDLAND FIRE (US/1063-049X) [25703829] **2291**

INTERNATIONAL BUREAU OF FISCAL DOCUMENTATION *See* TAX NEWS SERVICE **3062**

INTERNATIONAL BUREAU OF FISCAL DOCUMENTATION *See* ANNUAL REPORT. INTERNATIONAL BUREAU OF FISCAL DOCUMENTATION **4710**

INTERNATIONAL BUREAU OF FISCAL DOCUMENTATION *See* PUBLICATIONS OF THE INTERNATIONAL BUREAU OF FISCAL DOCUMENTATION **750**

INTERNATIONAL BUREAU OF FISCAL DOCUMENTATION *See* TAXATION IN LATIN AMERICA **4755**

INTERNATIONAL BUREAU OF FISCAL DOCUMENTATION *See* TAXATION IN LATIN AMERICA. SUPPLEMENT **4755**

INTERNATIONAL BUREAU OF FISCAL DOCUMENTATION, AMSTERDAM *See* TAXATION OF PATENT ROYALTIES, DIVIDENDS, INTEREST IN EUROPE **4755**

INTERNATIONAL BUSINESS (HK) **683**

INTERNATIONAL BUSINESS (US) [24327291] **683**

INTERNATIONAL BUSINESS CHRONICLE : THE REPORT ON INTERNATIONAL BUSINESS IN FLORIDA AND THE SOUTHEAST (US) [21922294] **683**

INTERNATIONAL BUSINESS CLIMATE, THE (US/1047-8698) [20803429] **683**

INTERNATIONAL BUSINESS LAWYER (UK/0309-7676) [01787580] **3129**

INTERNATIONAL BUSINESS MONTHLY (HK) **683**

INTERNATIONAL BUSINESS NEWS MAGAZINE (CN/0317-5340) [02248168] **841**

INTERNATIONAL BUSINESS OPPORTUNITIES SERVICE (US) [12732386] **683**

INTERNATIONAL BUSINESS OPPORTUNITIES SERVICES : IBOS (US) **683**

INTERNATIONAL BUSINESS REPORT (SA) [07533454] **792**

INTERNATIONAL BUSINESS REPORT (NEW YORK, N.Y.) (US/0278-5439) [07816807] **841**

INTERNATIONAL BUSINESS REVIEW (UK/0969-5931) [28933688] **683**

INTERNATIONAL BUSINESS TRAVEL AND RELOCATION DIRECTORY *See* CRAIGHEAD'S INTERNATIONAL BUSINESS, TRAVEL, AND RELOCATION GUIDE TO 71 COUNTRIES **5467**

INTERNATIONAL BUSINESS WEEK (US/0739-8409) [10014345] **683**

INTERNATIONAL BUSINESSMAN (US/8756-0623) [11711426] **792**

INTERNATIONAL BUSINESSMAN'S GUIDE TO OFFICIAL WASHINGTON, THE (US/0147-7293) [03220278] **683**

INTERNATIONAL BUYER'S GUIDE (US) [11732817] 5317, **4123**

INTERNATIONAL CABLE (US/1069-5494) [28101424] **1133**

●INTERNATIONAL CALIFORNIA MINING JOURNAL (US) [29572534] **2140**

INTERNATIONAL CAMELLIA JOURNAL (US/0159-656X) [02447745] **2420**

INTERNATIONAL CAMELLIA SOCIETY JOURNAL, THE (UK/0534-7750) [02028425] **2420**

INTERNATIONAL CANCER RESEARCH DATA BANK *See* DETECTION, DIAGNOSIS, AND THERAPY, AND PRE-CLINICAL BIOLOGY OF BREAST CANCER, THE **3815**

INTERNATIONAL CANCER RESEARCH DATA BANK *See* MAJOR HISTOCOMPATIBILITY COMPLEX, THE **538**

INTERNATIONAL CANCER RESEARCH DATA BANK *See* MACROMOLECULAR ALTERATION AND REPAIR IN CARCINOGENESIS **3820**

INTERNATIONAL CANCER RESEARCH DATA BANK *See* NUCLEAR MEDICINE IN CANCER DIAGNOSIS AND MANAGEMENT **3848**

INTERNATIONAL CANCER RESEARCH DATA BANK *See* DIAGNOSIS AND TREATMENT OF HODGKIN'S DISEASE **3816**

INTERNATIONAL CANCER RESEARCH DATA BANK *See* IMMUNOTHERAPY AND CLINICAL CANCER IMMUNOLOGY **3672**

INTERNATIONAL CANCER RESEARCH DATA BANK *See* DIAGNOSIS AND TREATMENT OF SARCOMAS AND RELATED TUMORS **3816**

INTERNATIONAL CANCER RESEARCH DATA BANK *See* DETECTION, DIAGNOSIS, AND THERAPY OF LUNG CANCER, THE **3815**

INTERNATIONAL CANCER RESEARCH DATA BANK *See* GASTROINTESTINAL CARCINOGENESIS **3817**

INTERNATIONAL CANCER RESEARCH DATE BANK *See* ACTIVATION AND METABOLISM OF CARCINOGENS **3808**

INTERNATIONAL CAR PARK DESIGN & CONSTRUCTION TRENDS (UK/0966-4955) [I09664955] **5441**

INTERNATIONAL CARDIOLOGICAL REPORTER (US/0147-3042) [03518515] **3706**

INTERNATIONAL CARGO HANDLING CO-ORDINATION ASSOCIATION *See* BIENNIAL REPORT - INTERNATIONAL CARGO HANDLING CO-ORDINATION ASSOCIATION **5447**

INTERNATIONAL CATALOGUING AND BIBLIOGRAPHIC CONTROL : QUARTERLY BULLETIN OF THE IFLA UBCIM PROGRAMME (UK/1011-8829) [17899703] **417**

INTERNATIONAL CATHOLIC MIGRATION COMMISSION *See* ICMC NEWSLETTER **5202**

INTERNATIONAL CATHOLIC ORGANIZATION FOR CINEMA AND AUDIOVISUAL. GENERAL ASSEMBLY *See* MINUTES / OCIC **4074**

INTERNATIONAL CD-ROM REPORT, THE *CEASED*. (CN/0847-0456) [24368175] **1189**

INTERNATIONAL CEMENT REVIEW (UK/0959-6038) [I09596038] 2024, **617**

INTERNATIONAL CENTER FOR AGRICULTURAL RESEARCH IN THE DRY AREAS *See* ICARDA ANNUAL REPORT / INTERNATIONAL CENTER FOR AGRICULTURAL RESEARCH IN THE DRY AREAS **93**

INTERNATIONAL CENTER FOR ARID AND SEMI-ARID LAND STUDIES *See* ICASALS NEWSLETTER **174**

INTERNATIONAL CENTER FOR ARID AND SEMI-ARID LAND STUDIES *See* ICASALS PUBLICATION **2565**

INTERNATIONAL CENTER FOR LIVING AQUATIC RESOURCES MANAGEMENT *See* ICLARM REPORT **2305**

INTERNATIONAL CENTER FOR THE DISABLED *See* ANNUAL REPORT / INTERNATIONAL CENTER FOR THE DISABLED **4383**

INTERNATIONAL CENTER OF PHOTOGRAPHY *See* ANNUAL REPORT / INTERNATIONAL CENTER OF PHOTOGRAPHY **4366**

INTERNATIONAL CENTRE FOR AFRICAN ECONOMIC AND SOCIAL DOCUMENTATION *See* BULLETIN OF INFORMATION ON CURRENT RESEARCH ON HUMAN SCIENCES CONCERNING AFRICA. BULLETIN D'INFORMATION SUR LES RECHERCHES DANS LES SCIENCES HUMAINES CONCERNANT L'AFRIQUE **5194**

INTERNATIONAL CENTRE FOR DIARRHOEAL DISEASE RESEARCH, BANGLADESH *See* ANNUAL REPORT - INTERNATIONAL CENTRE FOR DIARRHOEAL DISEASE RESEARCH **3743**

INTERNATIONAL CENTRE FOR RESEARCH IN AGROFORESTRY *See* ANNUAL REPORT / INTERNATIONAL CENTRE FOR RESEARCH IN AGROFORESTRY **2375**

INTERNATIONAL CENTRE FOR THE REGISTRATION OF SERIAL PUBLICATIONS *See* REGISTRE DE L'ISDS (ED. SUR MICROFICHE) **4819**

INTERNATIONAL CENTRE FOR THEORETICAL PHYSICS *See* ANNUAL REPORT - INTERNATIONAL CENTRE FOR THEORETICAL PHYSICS **4397**

INTERNATIONAL CENTRE NEWS (WINNIPEG) (CN/0838-8164) [18310293] **1919**

INTERNATIONAL CHALLENGES / FROM THE FRIDTJOF NANSEN INSTITUTE (NO/0801-4914) [16621007] **1450**

INTERNATIONAL CHAMBER OF COMMERCE *See* HANDBOOK - INTERNATIONAL CHAMBER OF COMMERCE **820**

INTERNATIONAL CHAMBER OF COMMERCE. CONGRESS *See* STATEMENTS AND RESOLUTIONS - INTERNATIONAL CHAMBER OF COMMERCE. CONGRESS **821**

INTERNATIONAL CHEMICAL ENGINEERING (US/0020-6318) [01753436] **2013**

INTERNATIONAL CHICKPEA NEWSLETTER (II) [06262182] **174**

INTERNATIONAL CHILD HEALTH (FR/1016-8699) [22134288] **4785**

INTERNATIONAL CHILDREN'S RIGHTS MONITOR (SZ/0259-3696) [18131063] 1065, 4509, **4477**

INTERNATIONAL CHIPS SNACKS MANAGEMENT *See* SNACKS MAGAZINE, THE **2358**

INTERNATIONAL CHORAL BULLETIN (US/0896-0968) [13806758] **4123**

INTERNATIONAL — Alphabetical Title Index

INTERNATIONAL CHRISTIAN DIGEST : ICD *CEASED.* (US/0890-4081) [14221546] **4965**

INTERNATIONAL CITY MANAGEMENT ASSOCIATION *See* ICMA NEWSLETTER **4655**

INTERNATIONAL CITY MANAGEMENT ASSOCIATION *See* WHO'S WHO IN LOCAL GOVERNMENT MANAGEMENT **889**

INTERNATIONAL CIVIL AVIATION ORGANIZATION *See* AIR NAVIGATION PLAN : MIDDLE EAST AND SOUTH EAST ASIA REGIONS / PLAN DE NAVIGATION AERIENNE : REGIONS MOYEN-ORIENT ET ASIE DU SUD-EST / PLAN DE NAVEGACION AEREA : REGIONES DEL ORIENTE MEDIO Y DEL ASIA SUDORIENTAL **7**

INTERNATIONAL CIVIL AVIATION ORGANIZATION *See* AIRCRAFT NOISE; INTERNATIONAL STANDARDS AND RECOMMENDED PRACTICES. ANNEX 16 TO THE CONVENTION ON INTERNATIONAL CIVIL AVIATION **9**

INTERNATIONAL CIVIL AVIATION ORGANIZATION *See* AERODROMES; INTERNATIONAL STANDARDS AND RECOMMENDED PRACTICES. ANNEX 14 TO THE CONVENTION ON INTERNATIONAL CIVIL AVIATION **4**

INTERNATIONAL CIVIL AVIATION ORGANIZATION *See* AIR NAVIGATION PLAN, CARRIBBEAN AND SOUTH AMERICAN REGIONS / PLAN DE NAVIGATION AERIENNE, REGIONS CARAIBES ET AMERIQUE DU SUD. PLAN DE NAVEGACION AEREA, REGIONES DEL CARIBE Y DE SUDAMERICA **7**

INTERNATIONAL CIVIL AVIATION ORGANIZATION *See* SEARCH AND RESCUE; INTERNATIONAL STANDARDS AND RECOMMENDED PRACTICES. ANNEX 12 TO THE CONVENTION ON INTERNATIONAL CIVIL AVIATION **35**

INTERNATIONAL CIVIL AVIATION ORGANIZATION *See* AIR NAVIGATION PLAN, EUROPEAN REGION **7**

INTERNATIONAL CIVIL AVIATION ORGANIZATION *See* AERONAUTICAL INFORMATION SERVICES; INTERNATIONAL STANDARDS AND RECOMMENDED PRACTICES. ANNEX 15 TO THE CONVENTION ON INTERNATIONAL CIVIL AVIATION **4**

INTERNATIONAL CIVIL AVIATION ORGANIZATION *See* ON-FLIGHT ORIGIN AND DESTINATION / ORIGINE ET DESTINATION PAR VOL **31**

INTERNATIONAL CIVIL AVIATION ORGANIZATION *See* REPERTOIRE DE TARIFS D'AEROPORTS ET DE TARIFS D'INSTALLATIONS ET DE SERVICES DE NAVIGATION AERIENNE **33**

INTERNATIONAL CIVIL AVIATION ORGANIZATION *See* AERONAUTICAL TELECOMMUNICATIONS, INTERNATIONAL STANDARDS AND RECOMMENDED PRACTICES. ANNEX 10 TO THE CONVENTION ON INTERNATIONAL CIVIL AVIATION **4**

INTERNATIONAL CIVIL AVIATION ORGANIZATION *See* RULES OF THE AIR; INTERNATIONAL STANDARDS. ANNEX 2 TO THE CONVENTION ON INTERNATIONAL CIVIL AVIATION **34**

INTERNATIONAL CIVIL AVIATION ORGANIZATION *See* DESIGNATORS FOR AIRCRAFT OPERATING AGENCIES, AERONAUTICAL AUTHORITIES AND SERVICES / INDICATIFS DES EXPLOITANTS D'AERONEF ET DES ADMINISTRATIONS ET SERVICES AERONAUTIQUES / DESIGNADORES DE EMPRESAS EXPLOTADORAS DE AERONAVES, DE ENTIDADES OFICIALES Y DE SERVICIOS AERONAUTICOS **17**

INTERNATIONAL CIVIL AVIATION ORGANIZATION *See* AERONAUTICAL CHARTS; INTERNATIONAL STANDARDS AND RECOMMENDED PRACTICES. ANNEX 4 TO THE CONVENTION ON INTERNATIONAL CIVIL AVIATION **4**

INTERNATIONAL CIVIL AVIATION ORGANIZATION *See* AIRCRAFT NATIONALITY AND REGISTRATION MARKS; INTERNATIONAL STANDARDS. ANNEX 7 TO THE CONVENTION ON INTERNATIONAL CIVIL AVIATION **9**

INTERNATIONAL CIVIL AVIATION ORGANIZATION *See* AIRCRAFT ACCIDENT INQUIRY; INTERNATIONAL STANDARDS AND PRACTICES. ANNEX 13 TO THE CONVENTION ON INTERNATIONAL CIVIL AVIATION **8**

INTERNATIONAL CIVIL AVIATION ORGANIZATION *See* AIRWORTHINESS OF AIRCRAFT; INTERNATIONAL STANDARDS. ANNEX 8 TO THE CONVENTION ON INTERNATIONAL CIVIL AVIATION **11**

INTERNATIONAL CIVIL AVIATION ORGANIZATION *See* FACILITATION; INTERNATIONAL STANDARDS AND RECOMMENDED PRACTICES. ANNEX 9 TO THE CONVENTION ON INTERNATIONAL CIVIL AVIATION **19**

INTERNATIONAL CIVIL AVIATION ORGANIZATION *See* AIR TRAFFIC SERVICES, AIR TRAFFIC CONTROL SERVICE, FLIGHT INFORMATION SERVICE, ALERTING SERVICE; INTERNATIONAL STANDARDS AND RECOMMENDED PRACTICES. ANNEX 11 TO THE CONVENTION OF INTERNATIONAL CIVIL AVIATION **8**

INTERNATIONAL CIVIL AVIATION ORGANIZATION *See* METEOROLOGY; INTERNATIONAL STANDARDS AND RECOMMENDED PRACTICES. ANNEX 3 TO THE CONVENTION ON INTERNATIONAL CIVIL AVIATION **28**

INTERNATIONAL CIVIL AVIATION ORGANIZATION *See* PERSONNEL LICENSING; INTERNATIONAL STANDARDS AND RECOMMENDED PRACTICES. ANNEX TO THE CONVENTION ON INTERNATIONAL CIVIL AVIATION **31**

INTERNATIONAL CIVIL AVIATION ORGANIZATION *See* INDEX TO ICAO PUBLICATIONS **23**

INTERNATIONAL CIVIL AVIATION ORGANIZATION *See* AERONAUTICAL INFORMATION SERVICES PROVIDED BY STATES / SERVICES D'INFORMATION AERONAUTIQUE ASSURES PAR LES ETATS / SERVICIOS DE INFORMACION AERONAUTICA SUMINISTRADOS POR LOS ESTADOS **4**

INTERNATIONAL CIVIL AVIATION ORGANIZATION *See* LOCATION INDICATORS. INDICATEURS D'EMPLACEMENT. INDICADORES DE LUGAR **27**

INTERNATIONAL CIVIL AVIATION ORGANIZATION *See* TRAFFIC BY FLIGHT STAGE / TRAFIC PAR ETAPES **37**

INTERNATIONAL CIVIL AVIATION ORGANIZATION *See* AIRCRAFT ACCIDENT DIGEST **8**

INTERNATIONAL CIVIL AVIATION ORGANIZATION *See* AERONAUTICAL CHART CATALOGUE / CATALOGUE DES CARTES AERONAUTIQUES / CATALOGO DE CARTAS AERONAUTICAS / KATALOG AERONAVIGATSIONNIKH KART **4**

INTERNATIONAL CIVIL AVIATION ORGANIZATION *See* CATALOGUE OF ICAO PUBLICATIONS AND AUDIO VISUAL TRAINING AIDS **41**

INTERNATIONAL CIVIL AVIATION ORGANIZATION. CATALOGUE OF ICAO AUDIO VISUAL AIDS *See* CATALOGUE OF ICAO PUBLICATIONS AND AUDIO VISUAL TRAINING AIDS **41**

INTERNATIONAL CIVIL AVIATION ORGANIZATION. CATALOGUE OF ICAO PUBLICATIONS *See* CATALOGUE OF ICAO PUBLICATIONS AND AUDIO VISUAL TRAINING AIDS **41**

INTERNATIONAL CIVIL AVIATION ORGANIZATION. ECONOMIC COMMISSION *See* REPORT AND MINUTES - ECONOMIC COMMISSION. INTERNATIONAL CIVIL AVIATION ORGANIZATION **33**

INTERNATIONAL CIVIL AVIATION ORGANIZATION. SECRETARIAT *See* TRAFFIC FLOW **37**

INTERNATIONAL CIVIL AVIATION ORGANIZATION. SECRETARIAT. DIGEST OF STATISTICS *See* DIGEST OF STATISTICS (INTERNATIONAL CIVIL AVIATION ORGANIZATION) **41**

INTERNATIONAL CIVIL ENGINEERING ABSTRACTS (IE/0332-4095) [08460571] 2024, **2005**

INTERNATIONAL CLASSIFICATION (GW/0340-0050) [01432243] **3218**

INTERNATIONAL CLINICAL NUTRITION REVIEW (AT/0813-9008) [12115699] **4192**

INTERNATIONAL CLINICAL PSYCHOPHARMACOLOGY (UK/0268-1315) [14076534] 4590, **4308**

INTERNATIONAL COAL (US/0146-3845) [02937418] **1636**

INTERNATIONAL COAL LETTER (BE) 1947, **2140**

INTERNATIONAL COAL PREPARATION CONGRESS (US/0534-8145) [06507631] **2140**

INTERNATIONAL COAL REPORT (UK/0260-4299) [08527035] **1947**

INTERNATIONAL COAL REPORT'S COAL YEAR / FINANCIAL TIMES (UK) [13718992] **1947**

INTERNATIONAL CODEN DIRECTORY (US/0364-3670) [03963458] **5114**

INTERNATIONAL COMET QUARTERLY, THE (US/0736-6922) [05953147] **395**

INTERNATIONAL COMMISSION FOR THE CONSERVATION OF ATLANTIC TUNAS *See* REPORT - INTERNATIONAL COMMISSION FOR THE CONSERVATION OF ATLANTIC TUNAS. ENGLISH VERSION **2311**

INTERNATIONAL COMMISSION FOR THE CONSERVATION OF ATLANTIC TUNAS *See* COLLECTIVE VOLUME OF SCIENTIFIC PAPERS. RECUEIL DE DOCUMENTS SCIENTIFIQUES. COLECCION DE DOCUMENTOS CIENTIFICOS **2299**

INTERNATIONAL COMMISSION FOR THE CONSERVATION OF ATLANTIC TUNAS *See* DATA RECORD. RECUEIL DE DONNEES STATISTIQUES. COLECCION DE DATOS ESTADISTICOS **2299**

INTERNATIONAL COMMISSION FOR THE CONSERVATION OF THE ATLANTIC TUNAS STATISTICAL BULLETIN (SP) **2306**

INTERNATIONAL COMMISSION FOR THE NORTHWEST ATLANTIC FISHERIES *See* ICNAF HANDBOOK **2305**

INTERNATIONAL COMMISSION FOR THE SCIENTIFIC EXPLORATION OF THE MEDITERRANEAN SEA *See* RAPPORTS ET PROCES-VERBAUX DES REUNIONS COMMISSION INTERNATIONALE POUR L'EXPLORATION SCIENTIFIQUE DE LA MER MEDITERRANEE **1455**

INTERNATIONAL COMMISSION FOR THE SOUTHEAST ATLANTIC FISHERIES *See* PROCEEDINGS AND REPORTS OF MEETINGS **2310**

INTERNATIONAL COMMISSION OF JURISTS (1952-) *See* ICJ NEWSLETTER **4509**

INTERNATIONAL COMMISSION ON IRRIGATION AND DRAINAGE *See* ICID TECHNICAL MEMOIRS **2090**

INTERNATIONAL COMMISSION ON RADIATION UNITS AND MEASUREMENTS. REPORT *See* ICRU REPORT **3941**

INTERNATIONAL COMMISSION ON ZOOLOGICAL NOMENCLATURE *See* BULLETIN OF ZOOLOGICAL NOMENCLATURE, THE **5580**

INTERNATIONAL COMMITTEE FOR AESTHETIC STUDIES *See* INTERNATIONAL REVIEW OF THE AESTHETICS AND SOCIOLOGY OF MUSIC **4123**

INTERNATIONAL COMMITTEE FOR MOSAICS CONSERVATION *See* NEWSLETTER **4094**

INTERNATIONAL COMMITTEE FOR SOCIOLOGY OF SPORT *See* BULLETIN - I C S S **4888**

INTERNATIONAL COMMITTEE OF HISTORICAL SCIENCES *See* BULLETIN D'INFORMATION - COMITE INTERNATIONAL DES SCIENCES HISTORIQUES **5091**

INTERNATIONAL COMMITTEE OF HISTORICAL SCIENCES. COMMISSION INTERNATIONALE D'HISTOIRE ECCLESIASTIQUE COMPAREE *See* BIBLIOGRAPHIE DE LA REFORME, 1450-1648; OOUVRAGES PARUS DE 1940 A 1955 **2634**

INTERNATIONAL COMMITTEE OF THE RED CROSS *See* ANNUAL REPORT - INTERNATIONAL COMMITTEE OF THE RED CROSS **5272**

INTERNATIONAL COMMITTEE ON URGENT ANTHROPOLOGICAL AND ETHNOLOGICAL RESEARCH *See* BULLETIN OF THE INTERNATIONAL COMMITTEE ON URGENT ANTHROPOLOGICAL AND ETHNOLOGICAL RESEARCH **233**

INTERNATIONAL COMMUNICATIONS IN HEAT AND MASS TRANSFER (US/0735-1933) [08892057] **4431**

INTERNATIONAL COMMUNICATIONS REPORT (UK) **1157**

● INTERNATIONAL COMPANIES AND THEIR BRANDS (US/1050-8384) [21633484] **683**

INTERNATIONAL COMPANY AND COMMERCIAL LAW REVIEW (UK/0958-5214) [I09585214] **3100**

INTERNATIONAL COMPARISON OF AVERAGE NET HOURLY EARNINGS BASED ON WORK TIME REQUIRED FOR THE PURCHASE OF VARIOUS CONSUMER ITEMS (SZ) [09251279] **1680**

INTERNATIONAL COMPUTER LAW ADVISER (US/0893-2859) [14996716] **1189**

● INTERNATIONAL COMPUTER LAWYER, THE (US/1067-6171) [27215234] 1189, **2983**

INTERNATIONAL COMPUTER MUSIC CONFERENCE PROCEEDINGS (US) **1240**

INTERNATIONAL COMPUTER PROGRAMS, INC *See* ICP SOFTWARE GUIDE : BANKING **790**

INTERNATIONAL COMPUTER PROGRAMS, INC *See* ICP REFERENCE SERIES SOFTWARE DIRECTORY **1286**

INTERNATIONAL COMPUTER UPDATE *CEASED.* (US/0897-411X) [17497305] **1189**

INTERNATIONAL COMPUTERS, LTD *See* ICL TECHNICAL JOURNAL **1187**

INTERNATIONAL COMPUTERS, LTD. ICL TECHNICAL JOURNAL *See* INGENUITY **1189**

INTERNATIONAL CONFEDERATION OF FREE TRADE UNIONS *See* BOLETIN ECONOMICO Y SOCIAL **1656**

INTERNATIONAL CONFEDERATION OF FREE TRADE UNIONS See REPORT OF THE ... WORLD CONGRESS / INTERNATIONAL CONFEDERATION OF FREE TRADE UNIONS **4533**

INTERNATIONAL CONFERENCE OF BUILDING OFFICIALS See UNIFORM FIRE CODE STANDARDS **2293**

INTERNATIONAL CONFERENCE OF BUILDING OFFICIALS See DWELLING CONSTRUCTION UNDER THE UNIFORM BUILDING CODE **2965**

INTERNATIONAL CONFERENCE OF BUILDING OFFICIALS See UNIFORM HOUSING CODE **631**

INTERNATIONAL CONFERENCE OF BUILDING OFFICIALS See DWELLING CONSTRUCTION UNDER THE UNIFORM MECHANICAL CODE **613**

INTERNATIONAL CONFERENCE OF BUILDING OFFICIALS See ANALYSIS OF REVISIONS OF THE UNIFORM BUILDING CODE, U.B.C. STANDARDS ... **2933**

INTERNATIONAL CONFERENCE OF BUILDING OFFICIALS See UNIFORM FIRE CODE **2293**

INTERNATIONAL CONFERENCE OF BUILDING OFFICIALS See UNIFORM BUILDING CODE **630**

INTERNATIONAL CONFERENCE OF BUILDING OFFICIALS See UNIFORM MECHANICAL CODE **631**

INTERNATIONAL CONFERENCE OF BUILDING OFFICIALS See MEMBERSHIP ROSTER - INTERNATIONAL CONFERENCE OF BUILDING OFFICIALS **621**

INTERNATIONAL CONFERENCE OF BUILDING OFFICIALS See UNIFORM BUILDING CODE STANDARDS **630**

INTERNATIONAL CONFERENCE OF BUILDING OFFICIALS See UNIFORM SIGN CODE **631**

INTERNATIONAL CONFERENCE OF BUILDING OFFICIALS. UNIFORM BUILDING CODE See UNIFORM SIGN CODE **631**

INTERNATIONAL CONFERENCE OF BUILDING OFFICIALS. UNIFORM BUILDING CODE See UNIFORM BUILDING CODE STANDARDS **630**

INTERNATIONAL CONFERENCE ON ENVIRONMENTAL PROBLEMS OF THE EXTRACTIVE INDUSTRIES (US/0270-2584) [06397401] **2174**

INTERNATIONAL CONFERENCE ON PATTERN RECOGNITION. INTERNATIONAL CONFERENCE ON PATTERN RECOGNITION [PROCEEDINGS] See PROCEEDINGS / IAPR INTERNATIONAL CONFERENCE ON PATTERN RECOGNITION **4440**

INTERNATIONAL CONFERENCE ON PUBLIC EDUCATION See INTERNATIONAL CONFERENCE ON PUBLIC EDUCATION. PROCEEDINGS AND RECOMMENDATIONS **1753**

INTERNATIONAL CONFERENCE ON PUBLIC EDUCATION. PROCEEDINGS AND RECOMMENDATIONS (SZ) [02234811] **1753**

INTERNATIONAL CONFERENCE ON THE PHYSICS OF SEMICONDUCTORS : PROCEEDINGS (SI) [19675727] **4405**

INTERNATIONAL CONFERENCES IN BRITAIN (UK) **5480**

INTERNATIONAL CONGRESS AND SYMPOSIUM SERIES / ROYAL SOCIETY OF MEDICINE (UK/0142-2367) [04365670] **3588**

INTERNATIONAL CONGRESS CALENDAR (GW/0538-6349) [10762268] **4657**

INTERNATIONAL CONGRESS OF NEURO-PSYCHOPHARMACOLOGY See PROCEEDINGS - INTERNATIONAL CONGRESS OF NEURO-PSYCHOPHARMACOLOGY **3844**

INTERNATIONAL CONGRESS OF PUBLIC TRANSPORT. PROCEEDINGS See INTERNATIONAL CONGRESS PROCEEDINGS **5384**

INTERNATIONAL CONGRESS OF THE INTERNATIONAL COUNCIL ON HEALTH, PHYSICAL EDUCATION, AND RECREATION (US/0074-4417) [01459319] **1856**

INTERNATIONAL CONGRESS ON PHYSICAL EDUCATION AND SPORTS FOR GIRLS AND WOMEN See REPORT - INTERNATIONAL CONGRESS ON PHYSICAL EDUCATION AND SPORTS FOR GIRLS AND WOMEN **4915**

INTERNATIONAL CONGRESS ON RHEOLOGY See PROCEEDINGS OF THE ... INTERNATIONAL CONGRESS ON RHEOLOGY **4418**

INTERNATIONAL CONGRESS PROCEEDINGS *CEASED.* (BE) [05796869] **5384**

INTERNATIONAL CONGRESS SERIES (NE/0531-5131) [01568571] **3588**

INTERNATIONAL CONSTRUCTION (UK/0020-6415) [02447751] **2024**

INTERNATIONAL CONSTRUCTION ANALYSTS See GENERAL CONSTRUCTION ESTIMATING STANDARDS: THE RICHARDSON RAPID SYSTEM **615**

INTERNATIONAL CONSTRUCTION ANALYSTS See PROCESS PLANT CONSTRUCTION ESTIMATING STANDARDS: THE RICHARDSON RAPID SYSTEM **624**

●INTERNATIONAL CONSTRUCTION DIRECTORY. INTERNATIONAL SECTION (US/1063-1135) [25866585] **617**

●INTERNATIONAL CONSTRUCTION DIRECTORY. USA SECTION (US/1063-1453) [25901665] **618**

INTERNATIONAL CONSTRUCTION LAW REVIEW, THE (UK/0265-1416) [15072227] 618, **3129**

INTERNATIONAL CONSTRUCTION WEEK (US/0149-5585) [03522808] **618**

INTERNATIONAL CONSUMER DIRECTORY (UK) [21462319] **1297**

INTERNATIONAL CONTACT LENS CLINIC (1987) (US/0892-8967) [15288718] 3875, **4216**

INTERNATIONAL CONTAINER DIRECTORY See PAPERBOARD PACKAGING'S INTERNATIONAL CONTAINER DIRECTORY **4221**

INTERNATIONAL CONTRACT ADVISER (US/0899-7799) [18216723] **3130**

INTERNATIONAL CONTRACT (DOWNSVIEW) (CN/1183-9708) [25882747] **2901**

INTERNATIONAL CONTRACT (DOWNSVIEW, ONT.) See ARCHITECTURE AND DESIGN INSITE **2898**

INTERNATIONAL CONTRACTORS (US) 4046, 2066, **24**

INTERNATIONAL CONTRIBUTIONS TO LABOUR STUDIES (UK/1052-9187) [22410049] **1680**

INTERNATIONAL CONVOCATION ON IMMUNOLOGY. [PROCEEDINGS] *CEASED.* (SZ/0074-4220) [04140643] **3672**

INTERNATIONAL COPPER INFORMATION BULLETIN *CEASED.* (UK/0309-2216) [05360476] 4004, **4025**

INTERNATIONAL CORPORATE 1000 YELLOW BOOK See INTERNATIONAL CORPORATE YELLOW BOOK **871**

INTERNATIONAL CORPORATE BANKING REPORT TO PARTICIPANTS (US/0198-8026) [06213248] **792**

INTERNATIONAL CORPORATE LAW (UK/0961-5326) [l09615326] **3100**

INTERNATIONAL CORPORATE YELLOW BOOK *CEASED.* (US/1058-2894) [24255577] **871**

INTERNATIONAL CORRESPONDANCE (MONTREAL) (CN/0228-9962) [08601766] **4542**

INTERNATIONAL CORRESPONDENCE BANKER NEWSLETTER (UK) **792**

INTERNATIONAL CORRESPONDENCE SOCIETY OF OBSTETRICIANS AND GYNECOLOGISTS See COLLECTED LETTERS OF THE INTERNATIONAL CORRESPONDENCE SOCIETY OF OBSTETRICIANS, GYNECOLOGISTS **3759**

INTERNATIONAL COTTON ADVISORY COMMITTEE See COTTON: MONTHLY REVIEW OF THE WORLD SITUATION **5349**

INTERNATIONAL COTTON INDUSTRY STATISTICS (SZ/0538-6829) [04823758] 5352, **5360**

INTERNATIONAL COUNCIL FOR BIRD PRESERVATION See BULLETIN OF THE INTERNATIONAL COUNCIL FOR BIRD PRESERVATION **2189**

INTERNATIONAL COUNCIL FOR RESEARCH IN AGROFORESTRY See ANNUAL REPORT OF THE INTERNATIONAL COUNCIL FOR RESEARCH IN AGROFORESTRY **2375**

INTERNATIONAL COUNCIL FOR RESEARCH IN AGROFORESTRY See REPORT / INTERNATIONAL COUNCIL FOR RESEARCH IN AGROFORESTRY **2392**

INTERNATIONAL COUNCIL FOR RESEARCH IN AGROFORESTRY. ANNUAL REPORT OF THE INTERNATIONAL COUNCIL FOR RESEARCH IN AGROFORESTRY See ANNUAL REPORT / INTERNATIONAL CENTRE FOR RESEARCH IN AGROFORESTRY **2375**

INTERNATIONAL COUNCIL FOR THE EXPLORATION OF THE SEA See ICES OCEANOGRAPHIC DATA LISTS AND INVENTORIES **1450**

INTERNATIONAL COUNCIL FOR THE EXPLORATION OF THE SEA See COOPERATIVE RESEARCH REPORT - INTERNATIONAL COUNCIL FOR THE EXPLORATION OF THE SEA (1972) **1448**

INTERNATIONAL COUNCIL FOR TRADITIONAL MUSIC See BULLETIN OF THE INTERNATIONAL COUNCIL FOR TRADITIONAL MUSIC **4106**

INTERNATIONAL COUNCIL OF MONUMENTS AND SITES See ICOMOS BULLETIN **2692**

INTERNATIONAL COUNCIL OF MUSEUMS See I C O M NEWS **4089**

INTERNATIONAL COUNCIL OF SCIENTIFIC UNIONS. SCIENTIFIC COMMITTEE ON PROBLEMS OF THE ENVIRONMENT See SCOPE MISCELLANEOUS PUBLICATION **2181**

INTERNATIONAL COUNCIL OF SHOPPING CENTERS See ICSC MEMBERSHIP DIRECTORY **681**

INTERNATIONAL COUNCIL ON HEALTH, PHYSICAL EDUCATION, AND RECREATION See INTERNATIONAL CONGRESS OF THE INTERNATIONAL COUNCIL ON HEALTH, PHYSICAL EDUCATION, AND RECREATION **1856**

INTERNATIONAL COUNCIL ON THE FUTURE OF THE UNIVERSITY See NEWSLETTER - THE INTERNATIONAL COUNCIL ON THE FUTURE OF THE UNIVERSITY **1837**

INTERNATIONAL COUNTERMEASURES HANDBOOK, THE (US/0145-2584) [02730757] 2066, **4046**

INTERNATIONAL COUNTERTERRORISM & SECURITY See COUNTERTERRORISM & SECURITY REPORT **4519**

INTERNATIONAL COUNTRY MUSIC NEWS (UK) **4123**

International COUNTRY RISK GUIDE (US/0278-6680) [07855175] **901**

INTERNATIONAL COURT OF JUSTICE See YEARBOOK / INTERNATIONAL COURT OF JUSTICE **3138**

INTERNATIONAL COURT OF JUSTICE See RECUEIL DES ARRETS, AVIS CONSULTATIFS ET ORDONNANCES / COUR INTERNATIONALE DE JUSTICE **3134**

INTERNATIONAL COURT OF JUSTICE (US) [01768077] **3130**

INTERNATIONAL CREATIVITY NETWORK NEWSLETTER : ICN (US/1055-4904) [23192728] **1753**

INTERNATIONAL CRIMINAL JUSTICE REVIEW (US/1057-5677) [24059483] **2983**

INTERNATIONAL CRIMINAL POLICE ORGANIZATION See STATISTIQUES CRIMINELLES INTERNATIONALES **3083**

INTERNATIONAL CRIMINAL POLICE REVIEW (FR/0367-729X) [04328458] **3166**

INTERNATIONAL CROPS RESEARCH INSTITUTE FOR THE SEMI-ARID TROPICS. ECONOMICS PROGRAM See OCCASIONAL PAPER - ECONOMICS PROGRAM **1509**

INTERNATIONAL CRUDE OIL AND PRODUCT PRICES (CY/1010-1179) [I10101179] **4261**

INTERNATIONAL CRUISE AND FERRY REVIEW (UK) **5450**

INTERNATIONAL CRYOGENICS ENGINEERING CONFERENCE (UK) **2116**

INTERNATIONAL CURRENCY REPORT (US/0738-8888) [09679285] **1636**

INTERNATIONAL CURRENCY REVIEW (UK/0020-6490) [01909533] **792**

INTERNATIONAL DAIRY FEDERATION See DOCUMENTS - INTERNATIONAL DAIRY FEDERATION **194**

INTERNATIONAL DAIRY FEDERATION See INTERNATIONAL STANDARD FIL-IDF **841**

INTERNATIONAL DAIRY FEDERATION See ANNUAL MEMENTO / INTERNATIONAL DAIRY FEDERATION **191**

INTERNATIONAL DAIRY FEDERATION See OFFICIAL NEWS AND INFORMATION - INTERNATIONAL DAIRY FEDERATION **197**

INTERNATIONAL DAIRY JOURNAL (UK/0958-6946) [24603186] **195**

INTERNATIONAL DANCE-EXERCISE ASSOCIATION See MEMBERSHIP DIRECTORY **2599**

INTERNATIONAL DECADE OF OCEAN EXPLORATION (US/0092-0002) [04587254] **1450**

INTERNATIONAL DEFENCE EQUIPMENT CATALOG : IDEC (GW) **4046**

INTERNATIONAL DEFENCE ET TECHNOLOGY (FR) **5114**

INTERNATIONAL DEFENSE BUSINESS: DEFENSE SURVEY (US/0161-0813) [03795219] **4046**

INTERNATIONAL DEFENSE BUSINESS : REPORT (US/0161-0805) [03795292] **4046**

INTERNATIONAL DEFENSE DIRECTORY (UK/0256-7822) [12373002] **4046**

INTERNATIONAL DEFENSE DMS INTELLIGENCE See INTERNATIONAL DEFENSE INTELLIGENCE **4046**

INTERNATIONAL DEFENSE INTELLIGENCE (US/1041-746X) [11809428] **4046**

INTERNATIONAL
Alphabetical Title Index

INTERNATIONAL DEFENSE REVIEW (SZ/0020-6512) [01893800] **4046**

INTERNATIONAL DEFENSE REVIEW. SPECIAL SERIES (SZ) [06596519] **4046**

INTERNATIONAL DEMOCRATIC TRUST. INTERNATIONAL NEWSLETTER ASSOCIATION *See* MAYFLOWER DIGEST **2490**

INTERNATIONAL DENDROLOGY SOCIETY *See* INTERNATIONAL DENDROLOGY SOCIETY YEARBOOK **514**

INTERNATIONAL DENDROLOGY SOCIETY YEARBOOK (UK/0307-322X) [01792144] **514**

INTERNATIONAL DENTAL JOURNAL (UK/0020-6539) [01753498] **1325**

INTERNATIONAL DESIGN *See* I.D **2098**

INTERNATIONAL DESIGN YEARBOOK, THE (US/0883-7155) [12226030] 2812, **2906**

INTERNATIONAL DEVELOPMENT ABSTRACTS (UK/0262-0855) [09041428] 2910, **2913**

INTERNATIONAL DEVELOPMENT RESEARCH CENTRE *See* IDRC (SERIES) **1829**

INTERNATIONAL DEVELOPMENT RESEARCH CENTRE (CANADA) *See* IDRC ACQUIRES **417**

INTERNATIONAL DEVELOPMENT RESEARCH CENTRE (CANADA). LIBRARY *See* EX LIBRIS (OTTAWA) **3210**

INTERNATIONAL DEVELOPMENT RESOURCE BOOKS (US/0738-1425) [09529718] **2910**

INTERNATIONAL DIATOMIST DIRECTORY (US/0882-2093) [11512700] **514**

INTERNATIONAL DICTIONARY OF ARCHITECTS AND ARCHITECTURE (US) **301**

INTERNATIONAL DICTIONARY OF ART AND ARTISTS (UK) [21228779] **353**

INTERNATIONAL DICTIONARY OF ART AND ARTISTS (US) **353**

INTERNATIONAL DICTIONARY OF BALLET (US) **385**

INTERNATIONAL DICTIONARY OF FILMS AND FILMMAKERS, THE (US) [19134883] **4072**

INTERNATIONAL DICTIONARY OF THEATRE (US) **385**

INTERNATIONAL DIGEST OF HEALTH LEGISLATION (SZ/0020-6563) [01642165] 4785, **2983**

INTERNATIONAL DIRECTORY (ALEXANDRIA, VA.) (US/0730-5354) [04923558] **5290**

INTERNATIONAL DIRECTORY OF ACCESS GUIDES, THE (US/0735-0112) [05455370] 5480, **4389**

INTERNATIONAL DIRECTORY OF APPROVED MUSIC EDUCATION DOCTORAL DISSERTATIONS IN PROGRESS (US) [19416785] **4123**

●INTERNATIONAL DIRECTORY OF AQUARIST ORGANIZATIONS (CN) **2306**

INTERNATIONAL DIRECTORY OF ASTROLOGERS & PSYCHICS, THE (US/0273-3749) [07034110] 4241, **390**

INTERNATIONAL DIRECTORY OF BEHAVIOR AND DESIGN RESEARCH (US/0094-4084) [01790846] **5204**

INTERNATIONAL DIRECTORY OF BOOK COLLECTORS (UK) [03572009] **4829**

INTERNATIONAL DIRECTORY OF BUSINESS INFORMATION AGENCIES AND SERVICES, THE (US) [16271951] **683**

INTERNATIONAL DIRECTORY OF CANCER INSTITUTES AND ORGANIZATIONS (SZ) [22548184] **3818**

INTERNATIONAL DIRECTORY OF CENTERS FOR ASIAN STUDIES *SUSPENDED.* (HK) [02591493] **5204**

INTERNATIONAL DIRECTORY OF CIVIL ENGINEERING/CONSTRUCTION SOFTWARE (IE/0791-4326) [I07914326] 618, 2024, **1287**

INTERNATIONAL DIRECTORY OF COMPANY HISTORIES (US) **683**

INTERNATIONAL DIRECTORY OF COMPUTER ANIMATION PRODUCERS (CN/0840-5905) [21665689] **1234**

INTERNATIONAL DIRECTORY OF CONSULTANTS AND CONTRACTORS ACTIVE IN EASTERN EUROPE, AN (US/1053-2501) [22486890] **618**

INTERNATIONAL DIRECTORY OF CONSULTANTS AND CONTRACTORS ACTIVE IN THE MIDDLE EAST *See* INTERNATIONAL DIRECTORY OF CONSULTANTS AND CONTRACTORS ACTIVE IN THE MIDDLE EAST AND AFRICA, AN **683**

●INTERNATIONAL DIRECTORY OF CONSULTANTS AND CONTRACTORS ACTIVE IN THE MIDDLE EAST AND AFRICA, AN (US/1058-580X) [24334101] **683**

●INTERNATIONAL DIRECTORY OF CONSULTANTS AND CONTRACTORS ACTIVE IN THE UNITED STATES AND CANADA, AN (US/1058-5796) [24334034] **1979**

INTERNATIONAL DIRECTORY OF CONSULTANTS AND CONTRACTORS ACTIVE IN WESTERN EUROPE, AN (US/1056-1099) [23466975] 2024, **618**

INTERNATIONAL DIRECTORY OF CONSULTING ENVIRONMENTAL AND CIVIL ENGINEERS (US/0191-9636) [04935303] **2025**

●INTERNATIONAL DIRECTORY OF CONTEMPORARY MUSIC. COMPOSERS (US/1054-6669) [22933624] **4123**

●INTERNATIONAL DIRECTORY OF CONTEMPORARY MUSIC. INSTRUMENTATION (US/1054-6677) [22933700] **4123**

INTERNATIONAL DIRECTORY OF DISCONTINUED ICS AND DISCRETE SEMICONDUCTORS (US/0887-008X) [13051589] **2066**

INTERNATIONAL DIRECTORY OF EIGHTEENTH-CENTURY STUDIES (UK) [12636699] **2692**

●INTERNATIONAL DIRECTORY OF ENGINEERING SOCIETIES AND RELATED ORGANIZATIONS (US/1067-9014) [26883662] **1979**

INTERNATIONAL DIRECTORY OF FILMS AND FILMMAKERS (US) **4072**

INTERNATIONAL DIRECTORY OF GOVERNMENT, THE (UK) [19672160] **4657**

INTERNATIONAL DIRECTORY OF IMPORTERS. AFRICA, THE (US/1050-5520) [12786949] 1636, **841**

INTERNATIONAL DIRECTORY OF IMPORTERS. EUROPE, THE (US/1050-5555) [10602923] **841**

INTERNATIONAL DIRECTORY OF IMPORTERS. MIDDLE EAST, THE (US/1050-5563) [07720976] 1636, **841**

INTERNATIONAL DIRECTORY OF IMPORTERS. NORTH AMERICA, THE (US/1050-5466) [07546522] 1636, **841**

INTERNATIONAL DIRECTORY OF IMPORTERS. SOUTH/CENTRAL AMERICA, THE (US/1050-5547) [12786929] 1636, **841**

INTERNATIONAL DIRECTORY OF LITTLE MAGAZINES & SMALL PRESSES (US/0092-3974) [01788072] **1926**

INTERNATIONAL DIRECTORY OF MARKETING RESEARCH HOUSES AND SERVICE; GREEN BOOK (US/0074-459X) [01753501] **926**

INTERNATIONAL DIRECTORY OF MEMBERS (US/0149-2039) [03441519] **4839**

INTERNATIONAL DIRECTORY OF MODEL & TALENT AGENCIES & SCHOOLS (US) [13239817] **760**

INTERNATIONAL DIRECTORY OF NON-OFFICIAL STATISTICAL SOURCES, THE (UK) [22454494] **730**

INTERNATIONAL DIRECTORY OF NUCLEAR CONTRACT SERVICE FIRMS (US/1045-2613) [20067844] **4657**

INTERNATIONAL DIRECTORY OF NUCLEAR UTILITIES (US/0742-5821) [09937755] 1947, **2156**

INTERNATIONAL DIRECTORY OF NURSES WITH DOCTORAL DEGREES (US/0091-9462) [01784438] **3857**

●INTERNATIONAL DIRECTORY OF OPERA (US) **4123**

INTERNATIONAL DIRECTORY OF PHILOSOPHY AND PHILOSOPHERS (US/0074-4603) [02587356] **4349**

●INTERNATIONAL DIRECTORY OF POWER GENERATION (UK) [I13542400] **1947**

●INTERNATIONAL DIRECTORY OF PRIMATOLOGY (US/1064-3826) [26083784] **5586**

INTERNATIONAL DIRECTORY OF RESOURCES FOR ARTISANS, THE (US/0898-1094) [17719767] **373**

INTERNATIONAL DIRECTORY OF SCHOLARLY PUBLISHERS (FR) [03923374] **4815**

INTERNATIONAL DIRECTORY OF SOCIAL SCIENCE ORGANIZATIONS / COMPILED AND EDITED BY INTERNATIONAL FEDERATION OF SOCIAL SCIENCE ORGANIZATIONS, IFSSO (SW) [07690438] **5204**

INTERNATIONAL DIRECTORY OF SOFTWARE (UK/0260-3438) [06453038] 1279, **1287**

INTERNATIONAL DIRECTORY OF SYSTEMS HOUSES AND COMPUTER OEM'S (US/0887-4921) [13256735] **1238**

INTERNATIONAL DIRECTORY OF TELECOMMUNICATIONS (UK) [16900523] 1133, **1158**

INTERNATIONAL DIRECTORY OF VOLUNTARY WORK (UK/0143-3474) [I01433474] **4338**

INTERNATIONAL DIRECTORY - ROYAL BANK OF CANADA (CN/0823-1362) [09964658] **792**

INTERNATIONAL DIRECTORY TO CANADIAN STUDIES *See* INTERNATIONAL DIRECTORY TO CANADIAN STUDIES **2739**

INTERNATIONAL DIRECTORY TO CANADIAN STUDIES *See* INTERNATIONAL DIRECTORY TO CANADIAN STUDIES **2739**

●INTERNATIONAL DIRECTORY TO CANADIAN STUDIES (CN/0846-5495) [26757931] **2739**

●INTERNATIONAL DIRECTORY TO CANADIAN STUDIES (CN/0846-5495) [26757925] **2739**

INTERNATIONAL DISABILITY STUDIES *See* DISABILITY AND REHABILITATION **4387**

INTERNATIONAL DISCUSSION BULLETIN *See* INTERNATIONAL SOCIALISM. SERIES 2 **4477**

INTERNATIONAL DIVER INDEX. WORLD INDIVEX EDITION (US/0091-6986) [01788138] 4873, **4900**

INTERNATIONAL DOCUMENTARY (US/0742-5333) [10378920] **4072**

INTERNATIONAL DOCUMENTARY ASSOCIATION *See* MEMBERSHIP DIRECTORY AND SURVIVAL GUIDE / INTERNATIONAL DOCUMENTARY ASSOCIATION **1134**

INTERNATIONAL DOCUMENTS ON PALESTINE (LE) [02349569] **4524**

INTERNATIONAL DOCUMENTS REVIEW (US/1054-4933) [22903084] **4524**

INTERNATIONAL DOLL WORLD (US/1050-3994) [21477974] 2584, **2774**

INTERNATIONAL DOMOTIQUE NEWS PARIS (FR/1148-3555) [I11483555] **5115**

INTERNATIONAL DREDGING REVIEW (US/0737-8181) [07942545] 4177, **1979**

INTERNATIONAL DRUG & DEVICE REGULATORY MONITOR (US/0888-6393) [11535161] **4308**

INTERNATIONAL DRUG PREVENTION QUARTERLY OF THE NAE PROJECT, THE (US/1060-815X) [25080309] **2910**

INTERNATIONAL DRUG REPORT (US/0148-4648) [03316014] **3166**

INTERNATIONAL DRUG REVIEW (US/0734-9084) [08840029] **4308**

INTERNATIONAL DRUG THERAPY NEWSLETTER (US/0020-6571) [01753503] 3926, **4308**

INTERNATIONAL DYER (UK) [24486505] **5352**

INTERNATIONAL ECONOMIC & ENERGY STATISTICAL REVIEW (US) [06911681] **1568**

INTERNATIONAL ECONOMIC ASSOCIATION *See* INTERNATIONAL ECONOMIC ASSOCIATION SERIES **1496**

INTERNATIONAL ECONOMIC ASSOCIATION SERIES (US) [06401123] **1496**

INTERNATIONAL ECONOMIC CONDITIONS (US/0190-7085) [03880026] **1496**

INTERNATIONAL ECONOMIC DATA SERVICE (US/0142-0771 y 0307-0379) [05397894] **1636**

INTERNATIONAL ECONOMIC INDICATORS (US) **1496**

INTERNATIONAL ECONOMIC INSIGHTS *CEASED.* (US/1050-8481) [21654144] **1636**

INTERNATIONAL ECONOMIC JOURNAL (KO) [17413482] **1496**

INTERNATIONAL ECONOMIC OUTLOOK / CENTRE FOR ECONOMIC FORECASTING, LONDON BUSINESS SCHOOL (UK/0960-8869) [24302404] **1636**

INTERNATIONAL ECONOMIC REPORT OF THE PRESIDENT (US/0091-2492) [01786559] **1636**

INTERNATIONAL ECONOMIC REVIEW (PHILADELPHIA) (US/0020-6598) [01753505] **1496**

INTERNATIONAL ECONOMIC SCOREBOARD (US/0270-045X) [05140402] **1636**

●INTERNATIONAL ECONOMIC SCOREBOARD (US/0270-045X) [28103364] **1636**

INTERNATIONAL ECONOMICS SERIES (NE) [02156200] **1636**

INTERNATIONAL ECONOMY, THE (US/0898-4336) [16912422] 4524, **1636**

INTERNATIONAL EDUCATION (US/0160-5429) [01753506] **1753**

INTERNATIONAL EDUCATION FORUM (PULLMAN, WASHINGTON) (US/1053-1750) [22201198] **1831**

INTERNATIONAL EDUCATION JOURNAL (US/0736-5276) [09156913] **1753**

INTERNATIONAL EDUCATOR (WASHINGTON, D.C.) (US/1059-4221) [24585343] **1753**

INTERNATIONAL EDUCATOR (WEST BRIDGEWATER, MASS.), THE (US/1044-3509) [19757999] **1897**

INTERNATIONAL

INTERNATIONAL EGG COMMISSION *See* INTERNATIONAL EGG MARKET REVIEW; SITUATION AND OUTLOOK REPORT **2345**

INTERNATIONAL EGG MARKET REVIEW; SITUATION AND OUTLOOK REPORT (UK) [03411306] **2345**

INTERNATIONAL ELECTROCHEMICAL PROGRESS *CEASED.* (US/0741-1413) [04471806] **978**

INTERNATIONAL ELECTRON DEVICES MEETING *See* TECHNICAL DIGEST / INTERNATIONAL ELECTRON DEVICES MEETING **2083**

INTERNATIONAL ELECTROTECHNICAL COMMISSION *See* IEC BULLETIN **2057**

INTERNATIONAL ELECTROTECHNICAL COMMISSION *See* ANNUAIRE - INTERNATIONAL ELECTROTECHNICAL COMMISSION **2035**

INTERNATIONAL ELECTROTECHNICAL COMMISSION *See* REPERTOIRE / COMMISSION ELECTROTECHNIQUE INTERNATIONALE **2079**

INTERNATIONAL ELECTROTECHNICAL COMMISSION *See* CATALOGUE OF IEC PUBLICATIONS COMPLETE TO ... / INTERNATIONAL ELECTROTECHNICAL COMMISSION **2038**

INTERNATIONAL ELECTROTECHNICAL COMMISSION *See* RAPPORT ANNUEL / CEI **2078**

INTERNATIONAL ELECTROTECHNICAL COMMITTEE. CENTRAL OFFICE. REPORT ON ACTIVITIES *See* RAPPORT ANNUEL / CEI **2078**

INTERNATIONAL EMPLOYMENT GAZETTE (US/1058-0506) [23988556] **4205**

INTERNATIONAL EMPLOYMENT HOTLINE (US/0748-8890) [09633782] **4205**

INTERNATIONAL ENCYCLOPAEDIA OF LAWS (NE) 1926, **2983**

INTERNATIONAL ENCYCLOPEDIA FOR LABOUR LAW AND INDUSTRIAL RELATIONS (NE) 1680, **2983**

INTERNATIONAL ENCYCLOPEDIA OF COMPOSITES *CEASED.* (GW) **1979**

INTERNATIONAL ENCYCLOPED A OF PHARMACOLOGY AND THERAPEUTICS (UK) [01771042] **4308**

INTERNATIONAL ENDODONTIC JOURNAL (UK/0143-2885) [06178313] **1325**

INTERNATIONAL ENERGY AGENCY *See* RAPPORT ANNUEL SUR L'ENERGIE: RECHERCHE, DEVELOPPEMENT ET DEMONSTRATION **1954**

INTERNATIONAL ENERGY AGENCY *See* ENERGY BALANCES OF OECD COUNTRIES. BILANS ENERGETIQUES DES PAYS DE L'OCDE **1939**

INTERNATIONAL ENERGY ANNUAL (US/0731-5341) [07138645] **1947**

INTERNATIONAL ENERGY OUTLOOK (US/1051-6360) [13696840] **1947**

INTERNATIONAL ENERGY STATISTICAL REVIEW *SUSPENDED.* (US/0163-3724) [04081957] 1947, **1963**

INTERNATIONAL ENERGY STATISTICS SOURCEBOOK (US/1058-2487) [24244049] 1947, **1963**

INTERNATIONAL ENGINEERING DIRECTORY (US/0074-5774) [01589959] **1979**

INTERNATIONAL ENVIRONMENT & SAFETY (UK/0141-4836) [06409319] **2174**

INTERNATIONAL ENVIRONMENT REPORTER. CURRENT REPORT (US/0149-8738) [03993028] **3113**

INTERNATIONAL ENVIRONMENTAL AFFAIRS (US/1041-4665) [18774412] 2217, **2195**

INTERNATIONAL ENVIRONMENTAL LAW. MULTILATERAL TREATIES (GW) [01254039] **3113**

INTERNATIONAL ENVIRONMENTAL TECHNOLOGY (UK/0963-7362) [I09637362] **2174**

INTERNATIONAL ENVIRONMENTAL UPDATE (AT/1035-8544) [I10358544] **2174**

INTERNATIONAL EQUIPMENT NEWS *See* INDUSTRIAL ENGINEERING NEWS. (EUROPEAN EDITION) **2098**

INTERNATIONAL ESSAYS FOR BUSINESS DECISION MAKERS, THE (US/0272-6289) [05695478] **683**

INTERNATIONAL ESTIMATING SERVICES. MANUAL OF COMMERCIAL AND INDUSTRIAL CONSTRUCTION ESTIMATING AND ENGINEERING STANDARDS *See* PROCESS PLANT CONSTRUCTION ESTIMATING STANDARDS: THE RICHARDSON RAPID SYSTEM **624**

INTERNATIONAL EXAMINER (SEATTLE, WASH. 1973) (US/1065-1500) [18330384] **2654**

INTERNATIONAL EXCHANGE OF INFORMATION ON CURRENT CRIMINOLOGICAL RESEARCH PROJECTS IN MEMBER STATES OF THE COUNCIL OF EUROPE / DIRECTORATE OF LEGAL AFFAIRS, COUNCIL OF EUROPE, DIVISION OF CRIME PROBLEMS, COUNCIL OF EUROPE (FR/0252-063X) [08505870] **3166**

INTERNATIONAL EXECUTIVE (US/0020-6652) [01753510] **4502**

INTERNATIONAL EXPLORATION NEWSLETTER (US/1064-9042) [26459441] 1383, **4261**

INTERNATIONAL FABRICARE INSTITUTE *See* TEXTILE CLEANING TECHNOLOGY **5357**

INTERNATIONAL FAIRS GUIDE (ROME, ITALY) (IT) [06396847] **683**

INTERNATIONAL FAMILY PLANNING PERSPECTIVES (US/0190-3187) [04692802] 589, **2281**

INTERNATIONAL FASHION TRENDS (GW/0940-7278) [I09407278] **1085**

INTERNATIONAL FEDERATION FOR DOCUMENTATION. COMMITTEE ON CLASSIFICATION RESEARCH *See* FID/CR REPORT **3210**

INTERNATIONAL FEDERATION FOR DOCUMENTATION. COMMITTEE ON CLASSIFICATION RESEARCH *See* FID/CR NEWSLETTER **3210**

INTERNATIONAL FEDERATION FOR HOUSING AND PLANNING *See* LIST OF MEMBERS - INTERNATIONAL FEDERATION FOR HOUSING AND PLANNING **2827**

INTERNATIONAL FEDERATION FOR INFORMATION AND DOCUMENTATION *See* FID DIRECTORY **4649**

INTERNATIONAL FEDERATION OF AUTOMATIC CONTROL *See* IFAC NEWSLETTER **4655**

INTERNATIONAL FEDERATION OF AUTOMATIC CONTROL *See* PROCEEDINGS OF THE IFAC WORLD CONGRESS **2125**

INTERNATIONAL FEDERATION OF AUTOMATIC CONTROL. AUTOMATIC AND REMOTE CONTROL; PROCEEDINGS OF THE CONGRESS *See* PROCEEDINGS OF THE IFAC WORLD CONGRESS **2125**

INTERNATIONAL FEDERATION OF FILM ARCHIVES *See* BIBLIOGRAPHY : F I A F MEMBERS PUBLICATIONS **4080**

INTERNATIONAL FEDERATION OF LIBRARY ASSOCIATIONS *See* PROGRESS REPORT - F.I.A.B **3242**

INTERNATIONAL FEDERATION OF LIBRARY ASSOCIATIONS AND INSTITUTIONS *See* IFLA DIRECTORY **3214**

INTERNATIONAL FEDERATION OF LIBRARY ASSOCIATIONS AND INSTITUTIONS *See* IFLA ANNUAL **3214**

INTERNATIONAL FEDERATION OF LIBRARY ASSOCIATIONS AND INSTITUTIONS. SECTION OF BIOLOGICAL AND MEDICAL SCIENCES LIBRARIES *See* NEWSLETTER - IFLA. SECTION OF BIOLOGICAL AND MEDICAL SCIENCES LIBRARIES **3235**

INTERNATIONAL FEDERATION OF LIBRARY ASSOCIATIONS AND INSTITUTIONS. UNIVERSAL DATAFLOW AND TELECOMMUNICATIONS CORE PROGRAM *See* UDT NEWSLETTER **3254**

INTERNATIONAL FEDERATION OF ORGANIC AGRICULTURE MOVEMENTS *See* IFOAM BULLETIN **94**

INTERNATIONAL FEDERATION OF PHYSICAL EDUCATION *See* FIEP BULLETIN **1855**

INTERNATIONAL FEDERATION OF STOCK EXCHANGES *See* FIBV STATISTICAL DATA **729**

INTERNATIONAL FELLOWSHIP NEWSLETTER, THE (US) **4965**

INTERNATIONAL FERTILIZER DEVELOPMENT CENTER *See* IFCD REPORT (SPANISH EDITION) **93**

INTERNATIONAL FERTILIZER DEVELOPMENT CENTER *See* ANNUAL REPORT / INTERNATIONAL FERTILIZER DEVELOPMENT CENTER **163**

INTERNATIONAL FERTILIZER DEVELOPMENT CENTER *See* IFDC REPORT **94**

INTERNATIONAL FIBER JOURNAL (US/1049-801X) [21320388] **5352**

INTERNATIONAL FIBER SCIENCE AND TECHNOLOGY SERIES (US) [11278703] **5352**

INTERNATIONAL FICTION REVIEW (CN/0315-4149) [01779793] **3396**

●INTERNATIONAL FIGURE SKATING (US/1070-9568) [28521371] **4900**

INTERNATIONAL FILE OF MICROGRAPHICS EQUIPMENT & ACCESSORIES (US/0148-5121) [03318127] **4370**

INTERNATIONAL FILM BUFF (US/0361-4131) [02246537] **4072**

INTERNATIONAL FILMARCHIVE CD-ROM. / FIAF (UK) [30093925] **4072**

INTERNATIONAL FINANCE CORPORATION *See* IFC GENERAL POLICIES **790**

INTERNATIONAL FINANCE SECTION PUBLICATIONS (US) **1496**

INTERNATIONAL FINANCIAL LAW PRACTICE FILES. REGULATION REPORTS (UK) 792, **2983**

INTERNATIONAL FINANCIAL LAW REVIEW (UK/0262-6969) [08442665] **3100**

INTERNATIONAL FINANCIAL PRODUCTS (UK) **792**

INTERNATIONAL FINANCIAL STATISTICS (US/0020-6725) [01753522] **730**

INTERNATIONAL FINANCIAL STATISTICS ANUARIO *CEASED.* (US/0250-7471) [05338823] 792, **730**

INTERNATIONAL FINANCIAL STATISTICS COMPUTER FILE / INTERNATIONAL MONETARY FUND (US) [25612688] **792**

INTERNATIONAL FINANCIAL STATISTICS YEARBOOK - INTERNATIONAL MONETARY FUND (US/0250-7463) [05374371] 792, **730**

INTERNATIONAL FINANCING REVIEW (UK/0953-0223) [11502677] **792**

INTERNATIONAL FINE ART COLLECTOR (US/1057-2023) [23979362] **353**

INTERNATIONAL FIRE AND SECURITY PRODUCT NEWS (UK/0961-3730) [I09613730] **2291**

INTERNATIONAL FIRE FIGHTER (US/0020-6733) [01753523] **2291**

INTERNATIONAL FIRE PHOTOGRAPHERS ASSOCIATION : NEWSLETTER : IFPA (US) [09523500] **4371**

INTERNATIONAL FISCAL ASSOCIATION *See* YEARBOOK - IFA **4759**

INTERNATIONAL FITNESS SCIENTIST *See* FITNESS AND SPORTS REVIEW INTERNATIONAL **1855**

INTERNATIONAL FLIGHT INFORMATION MANUAL (US/0364-0418) [05192872] **24**

INTERNATIONAL FLORICULTURE QUARTERLY REPORT (UK) [20570116] **2435**

INTERNATIONAL FLOW OF PRIVATE CAPITAL, THE (US) [01476907] **901**

INTERNATIONAL FLYING FARMER (US/0020-675X) [08741891] 24, **96**

INTERNATIONAL FOAMED PLASTIC MARKETS & DIRECTORY *See* U.S. FOAMED PLASTICS MARKETS & DIRECTORY **4460**

INTERNATIONAL FOLK MUSIC COUNCIL *See* MEMBERS - INTERNATIONAL FOLK MUSIC COUNCIL **4130**

INTERNATIONAL FOLKLORE BIBLIOGRAPHY (GW) **2325**

INTERNATIONAL FOOD INGREDIENT (NE/0924-5863) [I09245863] **2345**

INTERNATIONAL FOOD INGREDIENTS DIRECTORY (UK/27334596) **2345**

INTERNATIONAL FOOD POLICY RESEARCH INSTITUTE *See* IFPRI REPORT **94**

●INTERNATIONAL FOOD SAFETY NEWS (UK/0960-9784) [I09609784] 4785, **2345**

INTERNATIONAL FORUM : BULLETIN OF THE JEANNE SAUVE YOUTH FOUNDATION (CN/1183-1359) [25314062] **5290**

INTERNATIONAL FORUM (EN LUTTE (ORGANISATION)) (CN/0227-633X) [08436300] **4542**

INTERNATIONAL FORUM FOR LOGOTHERAPY, THE (US/0191-3379) [04865213] 1753, **4349**

INTERNATIONAL FORUM FOR PSYCHOANALYSIS (US/0738-8217) [09672307] **4590**

●INTERNATIONAL FORUM OF PSYCHOANALYSIS (NO/0803-706X) [27195919] **4590**

INTERNATIONAL FORUM ON INFORMATION AND DOCUMENTATION (NE/0304-9701) [02281313] **3218**

INTERNATIONAL FOUNDATION DIRECTORY, THE (US) [09176678] **4338**

INTERNATIONAL FOUNDATIONS OF EDUCATION QUARTERLY, THE (US/0095-506X) [01790865] **1753**

INTERNATIONAL FRANCHISING & DISTRIBUTION LAW (UK) **2983**

INTERNATIONAL FREE TRADE ZONE (UK) [20120345] **5384**

INTERNATIONAL　　　Alphabetical Title Index

INTERNATIONAL FREEDOM FOUNDATION (SA/0897-5086) 3130, 4524, **1636**

INTERNATIONAL FREQUENCY REGISTRATION BOARD *See* HORAIRE PROVISOIRE DE RADIODIFFUSION A ONDES DECAMETRIQUES **1156**

INTERNATIONAL FRIENDSHIP MAGAZINE (US/1055-3657) [23159971] **2791**

INTERNATIONAL FRUIT WORLD (SZ/0250-944X) [02406901] **2345**

INTERNATIONAL FUND FOR AGRICULTURAL DEVELOPMENT *See* IFAD ANNUAL REPORT **93**

INTERNATIONAL FUR FASHION REVIEW *CEASED.* (CN/0823-6976) [10105636] 1085, **3184**

INTERNATIONAL FUTURES DATABOOK (UK) **792**

INTERNATIONAL GAME WARDEN, THE (US/0890-0698) [13802039] **2195**

INTERNATIONAL GAMING & WAGERING BUSINESS (US/1066-145X) [23237755] **4657**

INTERNATIONAL GAS REPORT (UK) [21573731] **4261**

INTERNATIONAL GAS TECHNOLOGY HIGHLIGHTS (US/0276-4040) [05044208] **4261**

INTERNATIONAL GAY HOTEL & RESORT GUIDE (NE) **5480**

INTERNATIONAL GENEVA YEARBOOK (NE) [18078060] **3130**

INTERNATIONAL GEOGRAPHICAL UNION *See* IGU BULLETIN **2565**

INTERNATIONAL GEOGRAPHICAL UNION. COMMISSION OF POPULATION GEOGRAPHY *See* REPORT ON THE ACTIVITIES OF THE IGU COMMISSION ON POPULATION GEOGRAPHY **4559**

INTERNATIONAL GEOLOGY REVIEW (US/0020-6814) [01715633] **1383**

INTERNATIONAL GEOPHYSICS SERIES (US/0074-6142) [01753531] **1407**

●INTERNATIONAL GIS SOURCEBOOK (US/1057-3348) [24013918] **2566**

INTERNATIONAL GLASS/METAL CATALOG (US/0147-300X) [03133584] 4004, **2591**

INTERNATIONAL GOAT ASSOCIATION NEWSLETTER (US) [11522948] **213**

INTERNATIONAL GOLF DIRECTORY, THE (US/0272-1775) [06755261] **4900**

INTERNATIONAL GRAVIMETRIC BUREAU *See* BULLETIN D'INFORMATION - BUREAU GRAVIMETRIQUE INTERNATIONAL **4399**

INTERNATIONAL GROUP OF NATIONAL ASSOCIATIONS OF AGROCHEMICAL MANUFACTURERS *See* GIFAP DIRECTORY **1607**

INTERNATIONAL GROUP OF SCIENTIFIC, TECHNICAL, AND MEDICAL PUBLISHERS *See* STM INFORMATION BOOKLET **4820**

INTERNATIONAL GUIDE, EDMONTON (CN/1182-3062) [22569412] **5481**

●INTERNATIONAL GUIDE TO AFROCENTRIC EVENTS (US/1059-9452) [24822105] **2264**

●INTERNATIONAL GUIDE TO AFROCENTRIC MERCHANDISE (US/1059-7808) [24766228] **2264**

●INTERNATIONAL GUIDE TO AFROCENTRIC TALENT (US/1059-9460) [24822140] **2264**

INTERNATIONAL GUIDE TO MERGERS AND ACQUISITIONS (NE) **4732**

INTERNATIONAL GUIDE TO PARTNERSHIPS, THE (NE) **4732**

INTERNATIONAL GUIDE TO PERIODICALS & REFERENCE WORKS (US/0742-3985) [10339429] **5115**

INTERNATIONAL GUIDE TO PSI PERIODICALS AND ORGANIZATIONS (US/0277-9870) [07661591] **4243**

INTERNATIONAL GUILD GUIDE, THE (US/0361-4220) [02246280] 2807, **5071**

INTERNATIONAL GYMNAST (1986) (US/0891-6616) [14944601] **4900**

INTERNATIONAL HAIR ROUTE (CN/0820-6880) [09428041] 3731, **3720**

INTERNATIONAL HALLEY WATCH : IHW (US/0893-3618) [10264584] **396**

INTERNATIONAL HANDBOOK OF PARTICIPATION IN ORGANIZATIONS (UK) [21402138] **871**

●INTERNATIONAL HANDBOOK OF UNIVERSITIES (FR) [29432755] **1831**

INTERNATIONAL HANDBOOK OF UNIVERSITIES AND OTHER INSTITUTIONS OF HIGHER EDUCATION *See* INTERNATIONAL HANDBOOK OF UNIVERSITIES **1831**

INTERNATIONAL HANDBOOK OF UNIVERSITIES AND OTHER INSTITUTIONS OF HIGHER EDUCATION *See* WORLD LIST OF UNIVERSITIES, OTHER INSTITUTIONS OF HIGHER EDUCATION AND UNIVERSITY ORGANISATIONS. LISTE MONDIALE DES UNIVERSITES, AUTRES ETABLISSEMENTS D'ENSEIGNEMENT SUPERIEUR ET ORGANISATIONS UNIVERSITAIRES **1930**

INTERNATIONAL HANDBOOK ON COMMERCIAL ARBITRATION (NE) **2983**

INTERNATIONAL H&E / HEALTH & EFFICIENCY (UK) **4785**

INTERNATIONAL HARRY SCHULTZ LETTER, THE (SZ) [08821099] **902**

INTERNATIONAL HATCHERY PRACTICE (UK) [19287473] **213**

INTERNATIONAL HEALTH NEWS *CEASED.* (US/0731-7220) [08234884] **4785**

INTERNATIONAL HEALTH PLANNING SERIES (US/0731-6615) [05735133] **4785**

●INTERNATIONAL HEPATOLOGY COMMUNICATIONS (NE/0928-4346) [28551837] **3797**

INTERNATIONAL HERALD TRIBUNE (FR/0294-8052) [06906145] **5800**

INTERNATIONAL HIGH TECHNOLOGY REPORT *CEASED.* (US/0882-3553) [11823584] **5115**

INTERNATIONAL HISTORY REVIEW, THE (CN/0707-5332) [05133715] **2620**

INTERNATIONAL HOPKINS ASSOCIATION NEWSLETTER, THE (CN/0227-5414) [06537428] **3464**

INTERNATIONAL HORSE DIGEST *See* INTERNATIONAL SADDLERY AND APPAREL JOURNAL **2800**

INTERNATIONAL HOSPITAL EQUIPMENT : IHE (BE) [09053516] **3588**

INTERNATIONAL HOTEL GUIDE (FR) [04260391] **2807**

INTERNATIONAL HOTEL TELEX (GW/0340-0948) [01826956] **2807**

●INTERNATIONAL HOTEL TRENDS (US) [30344861] **2807**

INTERNATIONAL HUMANIST (NE) [07972624] 2251, **4349**

INTERNATIONAL HYDROGRAPHIC BULLETIN. BULLETIN HYDROGRAPHIQUE INTERNATIONAL (MC/0020-6938) [01585561] **5534**

INTERNATIONAL HYDROGRAPHIC BUREAU *See* REPORT ON THE WORK OF THE BUREAU SINCE THE PREVIOUS CONFERENCE **4182**

INTERNATIONAL HYDROGRAPHIC REVIEW, THE (MC/0020-6946) [02401183] 1450, **1415**

●INTERNATIONAL IMAGING SOURCE BOOK (US/1053-8291) [22651527] **1190**

INTERNATIONAL IMMUNOLOGY (UK/0953-8178) [20567176] **3672**

INTERNATIONAL IMPORT INDEX *See* INTERNATIONAL INTERTRADE INDEX **841**

INTERNATIONAL INDEX TO FILM PERIODICALS (US/0000-0388) [01783618] 4073, **4080**

INTERNATIONAL INDEX TO TELEVISION PERIODICALS (UK/0143-5663) [09721641] **1133**

INTERNATIONAL INDIRECT LAW REPORT (UK) **2983**

INTERNATIONAL INDUSTRIAL ENGINEERING CONFERENCE PROCEEDINGS (US/1055-7288) [23292187] **2099**

INTERNATIONAL INDUSTRIAL ENGINEERING CONFERENCE PROCEEDINGS (US) [18267527] **2099**

INTERNATIONAL INDUSTRIAL SENSOR DIRECTORY (US) [21423460] **1612**

INTERNATIONAL INDUSTRY DOSSIER (US/0748-206X) [10062078] **1612**

●INTERNATIONAL INFORMATION & LIBRARY REVIEW, THE (UK/1057-2317) [23983766] **3218**

INTERNATIONAL INFORMATION, COMMUNICATION & EDUCATION (II/0970-1850) [09477245] **3218**

INTERNATIONAL INFORMATION FLOWS / UNITED STATES COUNCIL FOR INTERNATIONAL BUSINESS (US) [09607508] **683**

INTERNATIONAL INFORMATION REPORT (US) **4524**

INTERNATIONAL INFORMATION SYSTEMS *CEASED.* (US/1056-0009) [23443198] **871**

INTERNATIONAL INSIDER (UK/0953-2714) [I09532714] **1496**

INTERNATIONAL INSIGHTS (CN/0829-321X) [15190829] **4524**

INTERNATIONAL INSOLVENCY REVIEW : JOURNAL OF THE INTERNATIONAL ASSOCIATION OF INSOLVENCY PRACTITIONERS (UK) [29019357] 683, **2984**

INTERNATIONAL INSTITUTE FOR AERIAL SURVEY AND EARTH SCIENCES *See* ITC JOURNAL, THE **1356**

INTERNATIONAL INSTITUTE FOR APPLIED SYSTEMS ANALYSIS *See* IIASA PUBLICATIONS **1187**

INTERNATIONAL INSTITUTE FOR CONSERVATION OF HISTORIC AND ARTISTIC WORKS. NORDISK KONSERVATORFORBUND *See* MEDDELELSER OM KONSERVERING **358**

INTERNATIONAL INSTITUTE FOR LAND RECLAMATION AND IMPROVEMENT *See* BULLETIN - INTERNATIONAL INSTITUTE FOR LAND RECLAMATION AND IMPROVEMENT **2189**

INTERNATIONAL INSTITUTE FOR LAND RECLAMATION AND IMPROVEMENT *See* ANNUAL REPORT - INTERNATIONAL INSTITUTE FOR LAND RECLAMATION AND IMPROVEMENT **4627**

INTERNATIONAL INSTITUTE FOR LAND RECLAMATION AND IMPROVEMENT *See* BIBLIOGRAPHY - INTERNATIONAL INSTITUTE FOR LAND RECLAMATION AND IMPROVEMENT **151**

INTERNATIONAL INSTITUTE FOR POPULATION STUDIES *See* IIPS NEWSLETTER **4553**

INTERNATIONAL INSTITUTE FOR SOCIAL HISTORY *See* ALPHABETICAL CATALOG OF THE BOOKS AND PAMPHLETS OF THE INTERNATIONAL INSTITUTE OF SOCIAL HISTORY, AMSTERDAM. SUPPLEMENT **407**

INTERNATIONAL INSTITUTE FOR STRATEGIC STUDIES *See* LIST OF MEMBERS - INTERNATIONAL INSTITUTE FOR STRATEGIC STUDIES **4049**

INTERNATIONAL INSTITUTE OF HUMANITARIAN LAW *See* SECRETARY GENERAL'S REPORT FOR THE YEAR ... / INTERNATIONAL INSTITUTE OF HUMANITARIAN LAW, THE **4512**

INTERNATIONAL INSTITUTE OF MANAGEMENT DATABASES PLUS (UK/0967-652X) **871**

INTERNATIONAL INSTITUTE OF MUNICIPAL CLERKS *See* NEWS DIGEST - INTERNATIONAL INSTITUTE OF MUNICIPAL CLERKS **4669**

INTERNATIONAL INSTITUTE OF PUBLIC FINANCE *See* PROCEEDINGS OF THE CONGRESS OF THE INTERNATIONAL INSTITUTE OF PUBLIC FINANCE **4742**

INTERNATIONAL INSTITUTE OF SEISMOLOGY AND EARTHQUAKE ENGINEERING *See* PROGRESS REPORT - INTERNATIONAL INSTITUTE OF SEISMOLOGY AND EARTHQUAKE ENGINEERING **1409**

INTERNATIONAL INSTITUTE OF SEISMOLOGY AND EARTHQUAKE ENGINEERING *See* BULLETIN OF THE INTERNATIONAL INSTITUTE OF SEISMOLOGY AND EARTHQUAKE ENGINEERING **1403**

INTERNATIONAL INSTITUTE OF TROPICAL AGRICULTURE *See* RECORD OF PUBLICATIONS / INTERNATIONAL INSTITUTE OF TROPICAL AGRICULTURE **156**

●INTERNATIONAL INSURANCE LAW REVIEW (UK/0968-2090) [I09682090] 2884, **2984**

INTERNATIONAL INSURANCE MONITOR (US/0020-6997) [03592548] **2884**

INTERNATIONAL INSURANCE REPORT (UK) [18861820] **2885**

INTERNATIONAL INTERACTIONS (UK/0305-0629) [02240874] **4524**

INTERNATIONAL INTERTRADE INDEX (US/0020-7004) [09764600] **841**

INTERNATIONAL INVENTION REGISTER (US/8755-9609) [11482758] **1305**

INTERNATIONAL INVENTORY OF MUSICAL SOURCES (GW/0538-8007) [02680040] **4123**

INTERNATIONAL INVESTMENT & BANKING REPORT *CEASED.* (UK) [24835893] **792**

INTERNATIONAL INVESTMENT LETTER *CEASED.* (US/0734-0656) [08678356] **902**

INTERNATIONAL INVESTMENT POSITION, AUSTRALIA (AT/1037-8782) [26344454] 902, **730**

INTERNATIONAL INVESTOR'S DIRECTORY (US/1040-6921) [18501120] **902**

INTERNATIONAL IRON & STEEL INSTITUTE *See* WORLD STEEL EXPORTS : QUANTITY **1631**

INTERNATIONAL IRON AND STEEL INSTITUTE. MEETINGS AND CONFERENCE *See* REPORT OF PROCEEDINGS / IISI ... ANNUAL MEETINGS AND CONFERENCE **1624**

INTERNATIONAL ISBN AGENCY *See* ISBN REVIEW **3218**

INTERNATIONAL ISDN YELLOW PAGES (US/1075-5276) [30065224] **1190**

INTERNATIONAL JEWELLERY & GIFTS (UK) [13518499] **2914**

INTERNATIONAL JOINT COMMISSION See BIENNIAL REPORT UNDER THE GREAT LAKES WATER QUALITY AGREEMENT OF 1978 **5531**

INTERNATIONAL JOURNAL (CN/0020-7020) [01640693] **2692**

INTERNATIONAL JOURNAL, ADVANCED MANUFACTURING TECHNOLOGY, THE (UK/0268-3768) [13500923] **3481**

INTERNATIONAL JOURNAL FOR DEVELOPMENT TECHNOLOGY **SUSPENDED.** (UK) [09481602] **5115**

INTERNATIONAL JOURNAL FOR HOUSING SCIENCE AND ITS APPLICATIONS (US/0146-6518) [03349199] **2825**

INTERNATIONAL JOURNAL FOR HYBRID MICROELECTRONICS See INTERNATIONAL JOURNAL OF MICROCIRCUITS AND ELECTRONIC PACKAGING, THE **4219**

INTERNATIONAL JOURNAL FOR NUMERICAL AND ANALYTICAL METHODS IN GEOMECHANICS (UK/0363-9061) [03057459] 174, **2025**

INTERNATIONAL JOURNAL FOR NUMERICAL METHODS IN ENGINEERING (UK/0029-5981) [01740575] 3509, **1979**

INTERNATIONAL JOURNAL FOR NUMERICAL METHODS IN FLUIDS (UK/0271-2091) [06569528] **2091**

INTERNATIONAL JOURNAL FOR PHILOSOPHY OF RELIGION (NE/0020-7047) [01753552] 4349, **4965**

●INTERNATIONAL JOURNAL FOR QUALITY IN HEALTH CARE : JOURNAL OF THE INTERNATIONAL SOCIETY FOR QUALITY IN HEALTH CARE (UK/1353-4505) [30575014] **3588**

INTERNATIONAL JOURNAL FOR THE ADVANCEMENT OF COUNSELLING (NE/0165-0653) [03975707] **4591**

INTERNATIONAL JOURNAL FOR THE JOINING OF MATERIALS, THE (DK/0905-6866) [I09056866] **1979**

INTERNATIONAL JOURNAL FOR THE SEMIOTICS OF LAW (UK/0952-8059) [18104166] **2984**

INTERNATIONAL JOURNAL FOR VETERINARY HOMOEOPATHY (NE) [14929406] **5512**

INTERNATIONAL JOURNAL FOR VITAMIN AND NUTRITION RESEARCH (SZ/0300-9831) [01785670] **4192**

INTERNATIONAL JOURNAL FOR VITAMIN AND NUTRITION RESEARCH (SUPPLEMENT) **CEASED.** (SZ/0300-9831) [08736378] **4192**

INTERNATIONAL JOURNAL IN COMPUTER SIMULATION (US/1055-8470) [23359071] **1282**

INTERNATIONAL JOURNAL OF ACAROLOGY (US/0164-7954) [03357196] 96, **5586**

INTERNATIONAL JOURNAL OF ACCOUNTING, THE (UK) [20927316] **745**

INTERNATIONAL JOURNAL OF ADAPTIVE CONTROL AND SIGNAL PROCESSING (UK/0890-6327) [14291657] **1979**

INTERNATIONAL JOURNAL OF ADHESION AND ADHESIVES (UK/0143-7496) [07021467] **1053**

INTERNATIONAL JOURNAL OF ADOLESCENCE AND YOUTH (UK/0267-3843) [17651275] 5290, **2281**

INTERNATIONAL JOURNAL OF ADULT ORTHODONTICS AND ORTHOGNATHIC SURGERY, THE (US/0742-1931) [10293302] **1325**

INTERNATIONAL JOURNAL OF ADVERTISING (UK/0265-0487) [09604797] **760**

INTERNATIONAL JOURNAL OF AESTHETIC SURGERY / INTERNATIONAL SOCIETY OF AESTHETIC SURGERY (JA/0285-6506) [11140587] **3966**

●INTERNATIONAL JOURNAL OF AFRICAN DANCE (US/1045-8042) [20243132] 2264, **1313**

INTERNATIONAL JOURNAL OF AFRICAN HISTORICAL STUDIES, THE (US/0361-7882) [01213103] **2640**

INTERNATIONAL JOURNAL OF AGING & HUMAN DEVELOPMENT, THE (US/0091-4150) [01788134] **5247**

INTERNATIONAL JOURNAL OF ALGEBRA AND COMPUTATION (SI/0218-1967) [23982144] **3509**

INTERNATIONAL JOURNAL OF AMBIENT ENERGY (UK/0143-0750) [07342020] **1947**

INTERNATIONAL JOURNAL OF AMERICAN LINGUISTICS (US/0020-7071) [01753556] **3287**

INTERNATIONAL JOURNAL OF ANALYTICAL AND EXPERIMENTAL MODAL ANALYSIS See MODAL ANALYSIS **2122**

INTERNATIONAL JOURNAL OF ANALYTICAL AND EXPERIMENTAL MODAL ANALYSIS, THE (US/0886-9367) [13041544] **2116**

INTERNATIONAL JOURNAL OF ANDROLOGY (UK/0105-6263) [03676831] **3588**

INTERNATIONAL JOURNAL OF ANDROLOGY. SUPPLEMENT (DK/0106-1607) [04991928] **3588**

●INTERNATIONAL JOURNAL OF ANGIOLOGY, THE (US/1061-1711) [25198667] **3706**

INTERNATIONAL JOURNAL OF ANIMAL SCIENCES (II/0970-2857) [18030998] **213**

INTERNATIONAL JOURNAL OF ANTHROPOLOGY (IT/0393-9383) [15161412] **238**

INTERNATIONAL JOURNAL OF ANTIMICROBIAL AGENTS (NE/0924-8579) [24466890] **3588**

INTERNATIONAL JOURNAL OF APPLIED ELECTROMAGNETICS IN MATERIALS (NE/0925-2096) [23726268] **4444**

INTERNATIONAL JOURNAL OF APPLIED ENGINEERING EDUCATION See INTERNATIONAL JOURNAL OF ENGINEERING EDUCATION, THE **1980**

INTERNATIONAL JOURNAL OF APPLIED EXPERT SYSTEMS (UK) **1213**

INTERNATIONAL JOURNAL OF APPLIED LINGUISTICS (NO/0802-6106) [23888158] **3287**

INTERNATIONAL JOURNAL OF APPLIED PHILOSOPHY, THE (US/0739-098X) [09693598] **2251**

INTERNATIONAL JOURNAL OF APPROXIMATE REASONING (US/0888-613X) [13681636] **1213**

INTERNATIONAL JOURNAL OF AROMATHERAPY (UK) [19576194] **404**

INTERNATIONAL JOURNAL OF ARTIFICIAL ORGANS, THE (IT/0391-3988) [03676874] **3798**

INTERNATIONAL JOURNAL OF ARTS MEDICINE (US/1057-4263) [24033837] 322, **3588**

INTERNATIONAL JOURNAL OF AVIATION PSYCHOLOGY, THE (US/1050-8414) [21653673] **4591**

INTERNATIONAL JOURNAL OF BANK MARKETING (UK/0265-2323) [11908302] 926, **792**

INTERNATIONAL JOURNAL OF BEHAVIORAL DEVELOPMENT (NE/0165-0254) [04131153] **4591**

INTERNATIONAL JOURNAL OF BEHAVIORAL GERIATRICS (US/0730-6695) [08030603] **3752**

●INTERNATIONAL JOURNAL OF BEHAVIORAL MEDICINE (US/1070-5503) [28407276] 3589, **4591**

INTERNATIONAL JOURNAL OF BIFURCATION AND CHAOS IN APPLIED SCIENCES AND ENGINEERING (SI/0218-1274) [23477115] **1979**

INTERNATIONAL JOURNAL OF BIOCHEMISTRY AND CELL BIOLOGY (UK) **488**

INTERNATIONAL JOURNAL OF BIOCHEMISTRY, THE (UK/0020-711X) [01338269] **488**

INTERNATIONAL JOURNAL OF BIOLOGICAL MACROMOLECULES (UK/0141-8130) [05059673] **581**

INTERNATIONAL JOURNAL OF BIOLOGICAL MARKERS, THE (IT/0393-6155) [17250991] **3818**

INTERNATIONAL JOURNAL OF BIOMEDICAL COMPUTING (UK/0020-7101) [01753560] **3589**

INTERNATIONAL JOURNAL OF BIOMETEOROLOGY (NE/0020-7128) [06745198] **1426**

INTERNATIONAL JOURNAL OF BIOSOCIAL AND MEDICAL RESEARCH (US/1044-811X) [19906283] 458, **5248**

INTERNATIONAL JOURNAL OF CANADIAN STUDIES (CN/1180-3991) [23238088] **2739**

INTERNATIONAL JOURNAL OF CANCER (US/0020-7136) [01753562] **3818**

INTERNATIONAL JOURNAL OF CANCER. SUPPLEMENT (US/0898-6924) [16689456] **3818**

INTERNATIONAL JOURNAL OF CARDIAC IMAGING (US/0167-9899) [12855040] **3706**

INTERNATIONAL JOURNAL OF CARDIOLOGY (NE/0167-5273) [07833068] **3706**

INTERNATIONAL JOURNAL OF CAREER MANAGEMENT, THE (HK/0955-6214) [20832237] **4205**

INTERNATIONAL JOURNAL OF CELL CLONING (US/0737-1454) [09328410] **537**

INTERNATIONAL JOURNAL OF CHEMICAL KINETICS (US/0538-8066) [01222779] **1053**

INTERNATIONAL JOURNAL OF CHILDBIRTH EDUCATION, THE (US/0887-8625) [13386204] **3762**

INTERNATIONAL JOURNAL OF CHILDREN'S RIGHTS, THE (NE/0927-5568) **3121**

INTERNATIONAL JOURNAL OF CIRCUIT THEORY AND APPLICATIONS (UK/0098-9886) [01776304] **2066**

INTERNATIONAL JOURNAL OF CLIMATOLOGY : A JOURNAL OF THE ROYAL METEOROLOGICAL SOCIETY (UK/0899-8418) [18236579] **1426**

INTERNATIONAL JOURNAL OF CLINICAL ACUPUNCTURE (US/1047-1979) [20621031] **3589**

INTERNATIONAL JOURNAL OF CLINICAL AND EXPERIMENTAL HYPNOSIS, THE (US/0020-7144) [01753563] **2858**

INTERNATIONAL JOURNAL OF CLINICAL AND LABORATORY RESEARCH (GW/0940-5437) [25786067] 3589, **458**

INTERNATIONAL JOURNAL OF CLINICAL MONITORING AND COMPUTING (NE/0167-9945) [12855001] **1190**

INTERNATIONAL JOURNAL OF CLINICAL NEUROPSYCHOLOGY, THE **CEASED.** (US/0749-8470) [10570784] **4591**

●INTERNATIONAL JOURNAL OF CLINICAL PHARMACOLOGY AND THERAPEUTICS (GW/0946-1965) [29934177] **4308**

INTERNATIONAL JOURNAL OF CLINICAL PHARMACOLOGY RESEARCH (SZ/0251-1649) [08069969] **4308**

INTERNATIONAL JOURNAL OF CLINICAL PHARMACOLOGY, THERAPY AND TOXICOLOGY (1980) (GW/0174-4879) [06004733] 3981, **4308**

INTERNATIONAL JOURNAL OF CLINICAL PHARMACOLOGY, THERAPY, AND TOXICOLOGY (INTERNATIONAL SYMPOSIA ON CLINICAL PHARMACOLOGY : 1980) See INTERNATIONAL JOURNAL OF CLINICAL PHARMACOLOGY AND THERAPEUTICS **4308**

INTERNATIONAL JOURNAL OF CLOTHING SCIENCE AND TECHNOLOGY (UK/0955-6222) [21352925] 5352, **1085**

INTERNATIONAL JOURNAL OF COAL GEOLOGY (NE/0166-5162) [06923547] **1383**

INTERNATIONAL JOURNAL OF COGNITIVE EDUCATION & MEDIATED LEARNING (UK/0957-4964) [27729865] **1753**

INTERNATIONAL JOURNAL OF COLORECTAL DISEASE (GW/0179-1958) [13162949] **3589**

INTERNATIONAL JOURNAL OF COMMERCE AND MANAGEMENT (US/1056-9219) [23897119] 871, **841**

●INTERNATIONAL JOURNAL OF COMMUNICATION SYSTEMS (UK/1074-5351) [29741428] **1158**

●INTERNATIONAL JOURNAL OF COMMUNICATIVE PSYCHOANALYSIS AND PSYCHOTHERAPY, THE (US/1062-3051) [25575073] **3927**

INTERNATIONAL JOURNAL OF COMPARATIVE AND APPLIED CRIMINAL JUSTICE (US/0192-4036) [03824725] **3166**

INTERNATIONAL JOURNAL OF COMPARATIVE LABOUR LAW AND INDUSTRIAL RELATIONS, THE (UK/0952-617X) [19582974] **3149**

INTERNATIONAL JOURNAL OF COMPARATIVE PSYCHOLOGY (US/0889-3667) [13855256] **4591**

INTERNATIONAL JOURNAL OF COMPARATIVE SOCIOLOGY (NE/0020-7152) [01654008] **5248**

●INTERNATIONAL JOURNAL OF COMPUTATIONAL FLUID DYNAMICS (UK/1061-8562) [25480245] **2116**

INTERNATIONAL JOURNAL OF COMPUTATIONAL GEOMETRY & APPLICATIONS (SI/0218-1959) [23812439] **3509**

INTERNATIONAL JOURNAL OF COMPUTER AIDED VLSI DESIGN **CEASED.** (US/1042-7988) [19219799] 1234, **2066**

INTERNATIONAL JOURNAL OF COMPUTER APPLICATIONS IN TECHNOLOGY (SZ/0952-8091) [19891151] **1190**

INTERNATIONAL JOURNAL OF COMPUTER INTEGRATED MANUFACTURING (UK/0951-192X) [18009321] **3481**

INTERNATIONAL JOURNAL OF COMPUTER MATHEMATICS (UK/0020-7160) [01753566] 1190, **3509**

●INTERNATIONAL JOURNAL OF COMPUTER RESEARCH (US) **1190**

INTERNATIONAL JOURNAL OF COMPUTER SYSTEMS SCIENCE & ENGINEERING (UK) [28855929] **1190**

INTERNATIONAL JOURNAL OF COMPUTER VISION (US/0920-5691) [15364035] **1190**

INTERNATIONAL Alphabetical Title Index

INTERNATIONAL JOURNAL OF COMPUTERS IN ADULT EDUCATION AND TRAINING **CEASED.** (UK/0952-6315) [18785226] **1190**

INTERNATIONAL JOURNAL OF CONFLICT MANAGEMENT, THE (US/1044-4068) [19770443] 1612, **871**

INTERNATIONAL JOURNAL OF CONSTRUCTION & REPAIR *See* CONSTRUCTION REPAIR **610**

INTERNATIONAL JOURNAL OF CONSTRUCTION MAINTENANCE & REPAIR, THE (UK/0959-5090) [21554357] **618**

INTERNATIONAL JOURNAL OF CONSTRUCTION MANAGEMENT & TECHNOLOGY (UK/0268-3938) [17486967] **618**

INTERNATIONAL JOURNAL OF CONTEMPORARY HOSPITALITY MANAGEMENT (HK/0959-6119) [21833162] 871, **2807**

INTERNATIONAL JOURNAL OF CONTEMPORARY SOCIOLOGY (FI/0019-6398) [02262574] **5248**

INTERNATIONAL JOURNAL OF CONTINUING ENGINEERING EDUCATION (SZ/0957-4344) [24672828] **1979**

INTERNATIONAL JOURNAL OF CONTROL (UK/0020-7179) [01607464] **5115**

INTERNATIONAL JOURNAL OF COSMETIC SCIENCE (UK/0142-5463) [04744124] 1015, **404**

●INTERNATIONAL JOURNAL OF CULTURAL PROPERTY (GW/0940-7391) [25724320] **1305**

●INTERNATIONAL JOURNAL OF DAMAGE MECHANICS (US/1056-7895) [23853169] **1979**

INTERNATIONAL JOURNAL OF DERMATOLOGY (US/0011-9059) [01753567] 3986, **3721**

INTERNATIONAL JOURNAL OF DEVELOPMENT BANKING : IJDB (II) [10166807] **792**

INTERNATIONAL JOURNAL OF DEVELOPMENT PLANNING LITERATURE (II) [16703527] **2910**

INTERNATIONAL JOURNAL OF DEVELOPMENTAL BIOLOGY, THE (SP/0214-6282) [20626707] **541**

INTERNATIONAL JOURNAL OF DEVELOPMENTAL NEUROSCIENCE (UK/0736-5748) [09161012] **3834**

INTERNATIONAL JOURNAL OF DIGITAL AND ANALOG COMMUNICATION SYSTEMS (UK/1047-9627) [20832096] **1158**

INTERNATIONAL JOURNAL OF DYNAMIC ASSESSMENT AND INSTRUCTION **CEASED.** (CN/0847-3269) [21349076] **1753**

INTERNATIONAL JOURNAL OF EARLY CHILDHOOD (CN/0020-7187) [02219661] **1753**

INTERNATIONAL JOURNAL OF EATING DISORDERS, THE (US/0276-3478) [07343037] **3798**

INTERNATIONAL JOURNAL OF ECO FORESTRY (CN) **2385**

INTERNATIONAL JOURNAL OF ECOLOGY AND ENVIRONMENTAL SCIENCES (II/0377-015X) [02245595] **2217**

INTERNATIONAL JOURNAL OF EDUCATIONAL DEVELOPMENT (UK/0738-0593) [08660698] **1754**

INTERNATIONAL JOURNAL OF EDUCATIONAL MANAGEMENT (UK) 1865, **871**

●INTERNATIONAL JOURNAL OF EDUCATIONAL REFORM (US/1056-7879) [23853144] **1754**

INTERNATIONAL JOURNAL OF EDUCATIONAL RESEARCH (UK/0883-0355) [12055045] **1897**

INTERNATIONAL JOURNAL OF EDUCOLOGY (AT/0818-0563) [22099123] **1754**

INTERNATIONAL JOURNAL OF ELECTRICAL ENGINEERING EDUCATION (UK/0020-7209) [01642734] 1897, **2066**

INTERNATIONAL JOURNAL OF ELECTRICAL POWER & ENERGY SYSTEMS (UK/0142-0615) [05212915] **2066**

INTERNATIONAL JOURNAL OF ELECTRONICS THEORETICAL & EXPERIMENTAL (UK/0020-7217) [06874213] **2066**

INTERNATIONAL JOURNAL OF ENERGY, ENVIRONMENT, ECONOMICS (US/1054-853X) [22994621] 2174, **1947**

INTERNATIONAL JOURNAL OF ENERGY RESEARCH (UK/0363-907X) [03024072] **1947**

INTERNATIONAL JOURNAL OF ENERGY SYSTEMS *See* INTERNATIONAL JOURNAL OF POWER & ENERGY SYSTEMS **1948**

INTERNATIONAL JOURNAL OF ENERGY SYSTEMS (US/0226-1472) [07309236] **1947**

●INTERNATIONAL JOURNAL OF ENGINEERING EDUCATION, THE (GW) [26272139] **1980**

INTERNATIONAL JOURNAL OF ENGINEERING FLUID MECHANICS **CEASED.** (US/0893-3960) [15506879] **2091**

INTERNATIONAL JOURNAL OF ENGINEERING SCIENCE (UK/0020-7225) [01753570] **1980**

●INTERNATIONAL JOURNAL OF ENTREPRENEURIAL BEHAVIOUR & RESEARCH (UK/1355-2554) **683**

INTERNATIONAL JOURNAL OF ENVIRONMENT AND POLLUTION (SZ/0957-4352) [25209892] **2174**

INTERNATIONAL JOURNAL OF ENVIRONMENTAL ANALYTICAL CHEMISTRY (US/0306-7319) [01796569] **1015**

INTERNATIONAL JOURNAL OF ENVIRONMENTAL HEALTH RESEARCH (UK/0960-3123) [23835805] **2174**

INTERNATIONAL JOURNAL OF ENVIRONMENTAL STUDIES. SECTION A, ENVIRONMENTAL STUDIES, THE (US/0020-7233) [12627355] 2217, **2195**

INTERNATIONAL JOURNAL OF ENVIRONMENTAL STUDIES. SECTION B, ENVIRONMENTAL SCIENCE AND TECHNOLOGY, THE (US/0020-7233) [12923068] **2175**

INTERNATIONAL JOURNAL OF ENVIRONMENTAL STUDIES, THE (US/0020-7233) [01642253] 5115, **2174**

●INTERNATIONAL JOURNAL OF ENVIRONMENTALLY CONSCIOUS MANUFACTURING (US/1062-6832) [25696042] 2175, **3481**

INTERNATIONAL JOURNAL OF EPIDEMIOLOGY (UK/0300-5771) [01784923] **3735**

INTERNATIONAL JOURNAL OF ESTUARINE AND COASTAL LAW (UK/0268-0106) [14442936] **3181**

INTERNATIONAL JOURNAL OF EXPERIMENTAL AND CLINICAL CHEMOTHERAPY (GW/0933-0453) [19743757] **3818**

INTERNATIONAL JOURNAL OF EXPERIMENTAL PATHOLOGY (UK/0959-9673) [22299064] **3895**

INTERNATIONAL JOURNAL OF EXPERT SYSTEMS (US/0894-9077) [16307915] **1213**

INTERNATIONAL JOURNAL OF FATIGUE (UK/0142-1123) [04815819] **2102**

INTERNATIONAL JOURNAL OF FERTILITY (US/0020-725X) [01645538] **581**

●INTERNATIONAL JOURNAL OF FERTILITY AND MENOPAUSAL STUDIES (US/1069-3130) [27702532] **3762**

INTERNATIONAL JOURNAL OF FETO-MATERNAL MEDICINE (GW/0933-0445) [19523312] **3762**

INTERNATIONAL JOURNAL OF FINANCE, THE (US/1041-2743) [18705076] **4732**

●INTERNATIONAL JOURNAL OF FLEXIBLE AUTOMATION AND INTEGRATED MANUFACTURING (US/1064-6345) [26345570] **3481**

INTERNATIONAL JOURNAL OF FLEXIBLE MANUFACTURING SYSTEMS (US/0920-6299) [17365737] **3481**

INTERNATIONAL JOURNAL OF FOOD MICROBIOLOGY (NE/0168-1605) [10835421] 564, **2345**

INTERNATIONAL JOURNAL OF FOOD SCIENCE AND TECHNOLOGY (UK/0950-5423) [15324897] **2345**

●INTERNATIONAL JOURNAL OF FOOD SCIENCES AND NUTRITION (UK/0963-7486) [26387565] **4192**

INTERNATIONAL JOURNAL OF FORECASTING (NE/0169-2070) [12658569] **684**

INTERNATIONAL JOURNAL OF FORENSIC DENTISTRY (UK/0306-9419) [01405999] **1325**

INTERNATIONAL JOURNAL OF FOUNDATIONS OF COMPUTER SCIENCE (SI/0129-0541) [20783011] **1190**

INTERNATIONAL JOURNAL OF FRACTURE (NE/0376-9429) [01771045] **2102**

INTERNATIONAL JOURNAL OF FRONTIER MISSIONS (US/0743-2429) [10566109] **4965**

INTERNATIONAL JOURNAL OF FUSION ENERGY **CEASED.** (US/0146-4981) [02945402] **495**

INTERNATIONAL JOURNAL OF GAME THEORY (GW/0020-7276) [01775294] **3509**

INTERNATIONAL JOURNAL OF GENERAL SYSTEMS (US/0308-1079) [02246672] **1247**

INTERNATIONAL JOURNAL OF GENOME RESEARCH **CEASED.** (SI/0218-1932) [26585548] **548**

INTERNATIONAL JOURNAL OF GEOGRAPHICAL INFORMATION SYSTEMS (UK/0269-3798) [15605763] **2566**

INTERNATIONAL JOURNAL OF GERIATRIC PSYCHIATRY (UK/0885-6230) [12681849] 3927, **3752**

INTERNATIONAL JOURNAL OF GLOBAL ENERGY ISSUES (SZ/0954-7118) [20837987] **1948**

INTERNATIONAL JOURNAL OF GOVERNMENT AUDITING (CN/0047-0724) [01794231] **4732**

INTERNATIONAL JOURNAL OF GROUP PSYCHOTHERAPY, THE (US/0020-7284) [01753571] **3927**

INTERNATIONAL JOURNAL OF GROUP TENSIONS (US/0047-0732) [01753572] 4591, **5248**

INTERNATIONAL JOURNAL OF GYNAECOLOGY AND OBSTETRICS (IE/0020-7292) [01753573] **3762**

INTERNATIONAL JOURNAL OF GYNECOLOGICAL CANCER (US/1048-891X) [21074512] 3763, **3818**

INTERNATIONAL JOURNAL OF GYNECOLOGICAL PATHOLOGY (US/0277-1691) [07520439] 3763, **3895**

INTERNATIONAL JOURNAL OF HEALTH CARE QUALITY ASSURANCE (UK/0952-6862) [21076985] **4785**

INTERNATIONAL JOURNAL OF HEALTH INFORMATICS (UK/0965-8335) [I09658335] **3857**

INTERNATIONAL JOURNAL OF HEALTH PLANNING & MANAGEMENT, THE (UK/0749-6753) [11166101] **4785**

INTERNATIONAL JOURNAL OF HEALTH SCIENCES (NE/0924-2287) [22178150] **4785**

INTERNATIONAL JOURNAL OF HEALTH SERVICES (US/0020-7314) [01115313] **4785**

INTERNATIONAL JOURNAL OF HEAT AND FLUID FLOW, THE (US/0142-727X) [05017673] **2116**

INTERNATIONAL JOURNAL OF HEAT AND MASS TRANSFER (UK/0017-9310) [01753576] **4431**

INTERNATIONAL JOURNAL OF HEMATOLOGY (NE/0925-5710) [24372334] **3772**

INTERNATIONAL JOURNAL OF HIGH SPEED COMPUTING (SI/0129-0533) [20747695] 1264, **1260**

INTERNATIONAL JOURNAL OF HIGH SPEED ELECTRONICS (SI/0129-1564) [22213026] **2066**

INTERNATIONAL JOURNAL OF HOSPITALITY MANAGEMENT (UK/0278-4319) [07827955] 871, **2807**

INTERNATIONAL JOURNAL OF HUMAN-COMPUTER INTERACTION (US/1044-7318) [19876683] **1220**

●INTERNATIONAL JOURNAL OF HUMAN-COMPUTER STUDIES (UK/1071-5819) [28682659] **1190**

INTERNATIONAL JOURNAL OF HUMAN FACTORS IN MANUFACTURING, THE (US/1045-2699) [20060415] 3481, **1220**

INTERNATIONAL JOURNAL OF HUMAN RELATIONS, THE (US/0148-1169) [03270737] **5248**

INTERNATIONAL JOURNAL OF HUMAN RESOURCE MANAGEMENT, THE (UK/0958-5192) [22462199] **943**

INTERNATIONAL JOURNAL OF HUMANITIES AND PEACE, THE (US/1042-4032) [19034394] 2857, **2848**

INTERNATIONAL JOURNAL OF HYDROGEN ENERGY (UK/0360-3199) [02335748] **1948**

INTERNATIONAL JOURNAL OF HYPERTHERMIA (UK/0265-6736) [12260804] **3589**

INTERNATIONAL JOURNAL OF IMAGING SYSTEMS AND TECHNOLOGY (US/0899-9457) [18271575] **5115**

INTERNATIONAL JOURNAL OF IMMUNOPATHOLOGY AND PHARMACOLOGY (IT/0394-6320) [20102895] **3672**

INTERNATIONAL JOURNAL OF IMMUNOPHARMACOLOGY (UK/0192-0561) [04985177] **4308**

INTERNATIONAL JOURNAL OF IMMUNOTHERAPY (SZ/0255-9625) [13406131] **3672**

INTERNATIONAL JOURNAL OF IMPACT ENGINEERING (UK/0734-743X) [08795319] **2103**

INTERNATIONAL JOURNAL OF IMPOTENCE RESEARCH (UK/0955-9930) [21592203] **3589**

●INTERNATIONAL JOURNAL OF INDUSTRIAL ENGINEERING (US/1072-4761) [28959523] **2099**

INTERNATIONAL JOURNAL OF INDUSTRIAL ERGONOMICS (NE/0169-8141) [14938548] **2099**

INTERNATIONAL JOURNAL OF INDUSTRIAL ORGANIZATION (NE/0167-7187) [09651742] **871**

INTERNATIONAL JOURNAL OF INFORMATION AND LIBRARY RESEARCH (UK/0953-556X) [20782489] **3218**

INTERNATIONAL JOURNAL OF INFORMATION MANAGEMENT (UK/0268-4012) [13894473] 5204, **3218**

INTERNATIONAL JOURNAL OF INFORMATION RESOURCE MANAGEMENT *See* INFORMATION MANAGEMENT & COMPUTER SECURITY **1188**

INTERNATIONAL JOURNAL OF INFRARED AND MILLIMETER WAVES (US/0195-9271) [05702014] **4435**

INTERNATIONAL JOURNAL OF INNOVATIVE HIGHER EDUCATION : THE OFFICIAL JOURNAL OF THE UNIVERSITY WITHOUT WALLS INTERNATIONAL COUNCIL (CN/0267-4386) [12922131] **1831**

INTERNATIONAL JOURNAL OF INSECT MORPHOLOGY & EMBRYOLOGY (UK/0020-7322) [01753577] **5610**

INTERNATIONAL JOURNAL OF INSTRUCTIONAL MEDIA (US/0092-1815) [01789161] **1897**

INTERNATIONAL JOURNAL OF INTELLIGENCE AND COUNTER INTELLIGENCE (US/0885-0607) [12566055] **4046**

●INTERNATIONAL JOURNAL OF INTELLIGENT & COOPERATIVE INFORMATION SYSTEMS : IJICIS (SI/0218-2157) [26519263] 1254, **1213**

INTERNATIONAL JOURNAL OF INTELLIGENT SYSTEMS (US/0884-8173) [12437702] **1213**

●INTERNATIONAL JOURNAL OF INTELLIGENT SYSTEMS IN ACCOUNTING, FINANCE & MANAGEMENT (UK/1055-615X) [23239085] 871, **745**

INTERNATIONAL JOURNAL OF INTERCULTURAL RELATIONS (US/0147-1767) [03111503] **5248**

INTERNATIONAL JOURNAL OF ISLAMIC AND ARABIC STUDIES (US/0740-5375) [09965942] **2768**

INTERNATIONAL JOURNAL OF KOREAN STUDIES (KO/0303-3007) [01793041] **2654**

●INTERNATIONAL JOURNAL OF KURDISH STUDIES, THE (US/1073-6697) [29450724] **2768**

INTERNATIONAL JOURNAL OF LAW AND INFORMATION TECHNOLOGY (UK/0967-0769) **2984**

INTERNATIONAL JOURNAL OF LAW AND PSYCHIATRY (US/0160-2527) [03655497] 3927, **2984**

INTERNATIONAL JOURNAL OF LAW AND THE FAMILY (UK/0950-4109) [14700373] **3121**

INTERNATIONAL JOURNAL OF LEGAL INFORMATION (US/0731-1265) [08127531] 2984, **3218**

INTERNATIONAL JOURNAL OF LEGAL MEDICINE (GW/0937-9827) [23022400] **3741**

●INTERNATIONAL JOURNAL OF LEISURE (UK/1352-2809) **4851**

INTERNATIONAL JOURNAL OF LEPROSY AND OTHER MYCOBACTERIAL DISEASES (US/0148-916X) [03398651] **4785**

INTERNATIONAL JOURNAL OF LEXICOGRAPHY (UK/0950-3846) [18409655] **3287**

INTERNATIONAL JOURNAL OF LIFELONG EDUCATION (UK/0260-1370) [08793697] **1801**

INTERNATIONAL JOURNAL OF LOGISTICS MANAGEMENT, THE (US) [21883064] **684**

INTERNATIONAL JOURNAL OF MACHINE TOOLS & MANUFACTURE (US/0890-6955) [14352846] **2116**

INTERNATIONAL JOURNAL OF MAN-MACHINE STUDIES (UK/0020-7373) [01753578] 2116, **1251**

INTERNATIONAL JOURNAL OF MANAGEMENT (UK/0813-0183) [11060406] **871**

INTERNATIONAL JOURNAL OF MANAGEMENT AND SYSTEMS (II/0970-7328) [I09707328] **871**

INTERNATIONAL JOURNAL OF MANPOWER (UK/0143-7720) [06822142] 943, **1680**

INTERNATIONAL JOURNAL OF MANUFACTURING SYSTEMS AND DESIGN (SI/0218-3382) **3481**

INTERNATIONAL JOURNAL OF MARINE AND COASTAL LAW, THE (NE/0927-3522) **3130**

INTERNATIONAL JOURNAL OF MARITIME HISTORY (CN/0843-8714) [21102214] **4177**

INTERNATIONAL JOURNAL OF MASS EMERGENCIES AND DISASTERS (SW/0280-7270) [10704767] **1073**

INTERNATIONAL JOURNAL OF MASS SPECTROMETRY AND ION PROCESSES (NE/0168-1176) [10180940] **4405**

INTERNATIONAL JOURNAL OF MATERIALS & PRODUCT TECHNOLOGY (SZ/0268-1900) [15202098] **1980**

INTERNATIONAL JOURNAL OF MATERIALS IN ENGINEERING APPLICATIONS (UK/0141-5530) [04448477] **2103**

●INTERNATIONAL JOURNAL OF MATHEMATICAL AND STATISTICAL SCIENCES (US/1055-7490) [23297958] 3509, **5115**

INTERNATIONAL JOURNAL OF MATHEMATICAL EDUCATION IN SCIENCE AND TECHNOLOGY (UK/0020-739X) [01605999] 3509, **1754**

INTERNATIONAL JOURNAL OF MATHEMATICS (SI/0129-167X) [21682643] **3509**

INTERNATIONAL JOURNAL OF MATHEMATICS AND MATHEMATICAL SCIENCES (US/0161-1712) [03873348] **3509**

INTERNATIONAL JOURNAL OF MECHANICAL ENGINEERING EDUCATION, THE (UK/0306-4190) [01792132] **2116**

INTERNATIONAL JOURNAL OF MECHANICAL SCIENCES (UK/0020-7403) [01740655] **2116**

INTERNATIONAL JOURNAL OF MEDICAL AND BIOLOGICAL FRONTIERS (US) 459, **3589**

INTERNATIONAL JOURNAL OF MEDICAL MICROBIOLOGY AND HYGIENE ABSTRACTS OF MICROBIOLOGY, VIROLOGY, PARASITOLOGY, PREVENTIVE MEDICINE AND ENVIRONMENTAL HYGIENE *CEASED*. (GW/0937-1591) [20182106] 3714, **564**

INTERNATIONAL JOURNAL OF MEDICINE AND LAW (UK/0334-3049) [06646874] **3741**

INTERNATIONAL JOURNAL OF MENTAL HEALTH (US/0020-7411) [01641095] **3927**

INTERNATIONAL JOURNAL OF METHODS IN PSYCHIATRIC RESEARCH (UK/1049-8931) [21343999] **3927**

INTERNATIONAL JOURNAL OF MICROBIOLOGY (II) [10701586] **564**

●INTERNATIONAL JOURNAL OF MICROCIRCUITS AND ELECTRONIC PACKAGING, THE (US/1063-1674) [25909306] 2066, **4219**

INTERNATIONAL JOURNAL OF MICROCIRCULATION: CLINICAL AND EXPERIMENTAL (NE/0167-6865) [08773168] **3798**

INTERNATIONAL JOURNAL OF MICROGRAPHICS & OPTICAL TECHNOLOGY (UK/0958-9961) [19998158] **1277**

INTERNATIONAL JOURNAL OF MICROWAVE AND MILLIMETER-WAVE COMPUTER-AIDED ENGINEERING (US/1050-1827) [21420115] **2066**

INTERNATIONAL JOURNAL OF MIDDLE EAST STUDIES (UK/0020-7438) [01226911] **2768**

INTERNATIONAL JOURNAL OF MINE WATER (AT) [13245302] **1415**

INTERNATIONAL JOURNAL OF MINERAL PROCESSING (NE/0301-7516) [01792778] **2140**

INTERNATIONAL JOURNAL OF MINI & MICROCOMPUTERS (US/0702-0481) [05937753] 1268, **1274**

INTERNATIONAL JOURNAL OF MINING AND GEOLOGICAL ENGINEERING (UK/0269-0136) [13507603] **2141**

INTERNATIONAL JOURNAL OF MINING & GEOLOGICAL ENGINEERING *See* GEOTECHNICAL AND GEOLOGICAL ENGINEERING **2139**

INTERNATIONAL JOURNAL OF MODELLING & SIMULATION (US/0228-6203) [08584340] 3509, **1282**

INTERNATIONAL JOURNAL OF MODERN PHYSICS A (SI/0217-751X) [13191064] **4405**

INTERNATIONAL JOURNAL OF MODERN PHYSICS B (SI/0217-9792) [18217515] **4406**

INTERNATIONAL JOURNAL OF MODERN PHYSICS. C (SI/0129-1831) [22160159] **4406**

●INTERNATIONAL JOURNAL OF MODERN PHYSICS. D, GRAVITATION, ASTROPHYSICS, COSMOLOGY (SI/0218-2718) [26920209] **4406**

●INTERNATIONAL JOURNAL OF MODERN PHYSICS. E, NUCLEAR PHYSICS (SI/0218-3013) [26920318] **4447**

INTERNATIONAL JOURNAL OF MORAL AND SOCIAL STUDIES *CEASED*. (UK/0267-9655) [13959309] 5204, **2251**

INTERNATIONAL JOURNAL OF MULTIPHASE FLOW (UK/0301-9322) [01793010] **2067**

INTERNATIONAL JOURNAL OF MUSIC EDUCATION / INTERNATIONAL SOCIETY FOR MUSIC EDUCATION (UK) [10163776] 1754, **4123**

INTERNATIONAL JOURNAL OF MYCOLOGY AND LICHENOLOGY *CEASED*. (GW/0723-3353) [09802692] **575**

INTERNATIONAL JOURNAL OF NAUTICAL ARCHAEOLOGY, THE (UK/1057-2414) [23987845] 4177, **270**

INTERNATIONAL JOURNAL OF NEONATAL AND LATER SCREENING (NE) **3904**

INTERNATIONAL JOURNAL OF NETWORK MANAGEMENT (UK/1055-7148) [23275085] **1113**

INTERNATIONAL JOURNAL OF NEURAL NETWORKS *CEASED*. (UK/0954-9889) [20929964] **1213**

INTERNATIONAL JOURNAL OF NEURAL SYSTEMS (SI/0129-0657) [21018895] **1190**

INTERNATIONAL JOURNAL OF NEUROLOGY (UY/0020-7446) [01585589] **3834**

INTERNATIONAL JOURNAL OF NEUROSCIENCE (US/0020-7454) [01643113] **3834**

INTERNATIONAL JOURNAL OF NON-LINEAR MECHANICS (US/0020-7462) [01589173] **4428**

●INTERNATIONAL JOURNAL OF NONLINEAR OPTICAL PHYSICS (SI/0218-1991) [25481741] **4435**

INTERNATIONAL JOURNAL OF NUMERICAL METHODS FOR HEAT & FLUID FLOW (UK/0961-5539) [25426026] **1980**

INTERNATIONAL JOURNAL OF NUMERICAL MODELLING (UK/0894-3370) [16014843] **2067**

INTERNATIONAL JOURNAL OF NURSING PRACTICE (AT/1322-7114) **3857**

INTERNATIONAL JOURNAL OF NURSING STUDIES (UK/0020-7489) [01713694] **3857**

INTERNATIONAL JOURNAL OF OBESITY *See* INTERNATIONAL JOURNAL OF OBESITY AND RELATED METABOLIC DISORDERS : JOURNAL OF THE INTERNATIONAL ASSOCIATION FOR THE STUDY OF OBESITY **3589**

●INTERNATIONAL JOURNAL OF OBESITY AND RELATED METABOLIC DISORDERS : JOURNAL OF THE INTERNATIONAL ASSOCIATION FOR THE STUDY OF OBESITY (UK) [26074170] **3589**

INTERNATIONAL JOURNAL OF OBSTETRIC ANESTHESIA (UK/0959-289X) [25047318] **3763**

●INTERNATIONAL JOURNAL OF OCCUPATIONAL AND ENVIRONMENT HEALTH (US/1077-3525) 2864, **2175**

INTERNATIONAL JOURNAL OF OCCUPATIONAL HEALTH AND TOXICOLOGY (US/1053-9557) [22699765] 3981, **2864**

INTERNATIONAL JOURNAL OF OFFENDER THERAPY AND COMPARATIVE CRIMINOLOGY (US/0306-624X) [01250617] **3166**

INTERNATIONAL JOURNAL OF OFFSHORE AND POLAR ENGINEERING (US/1053-5381) [22569468] **1980**

INTERNATIONAL JOURNAL OF ONCOLOGY (GR/1019-6439) [26667223] **3818**

INTERNATIONAL JOURNAL OF OPERATIONS & PRODUCTION MANAGEMENT (UK/0144-3577) [06807191] **871**

INTERNATIONAL JOURNAL OF OPTICAL COMPUTING *CEASED*. (UK/1047-8507) [20794002] **1190**

INTERNATIONAL JOURNAL OF OPTOELECTRONICS (UK/0952-5432) [18031879] **4435**

INTERNATIONAL JOURNAL OF ORAL AND MAXILLOFACIAL IMPLANTS, THE (US/0882-2786) [11800171] **1325**

INTERNATIONAL JOURNAL OF ORAL AND MAXILLOFACIAL SURGERY (DK/0901-5027) [13320581] 1325, **3966**

INTERNATIONAL JOURNAL OF ORAL IMPLANTOLOGY *See* IMPLANT DENTISTRY **1324**

●INTERNATIONAL JOURNAL OF ORGANIZATIONAL ANALYSIS (US/1055-3185) [23138726] **684**

INTERNATIONAL JOURNAL OF ORIENTAL MEDICINE (US/1044-0003) [19644047] **4308**

INTERNATIONAL JOURNAL OF OROFACIAL MYOLOGY, THE (US/0735-0120) [06911062] **1325**

INTERNATIONAL JOURNAL OF ORTHODONTICS *CEASED*. (US/0020-7500) [02028370] **1325**

INTERNATIONAL JOURNAL OF ORTHOPAEDIC TRAUMA (UK/0960-2941) [23665872] **3882**

INTERNATIONAL JOURNAL OF OSTEOARCHAEOLOGY (UK/1047-482X) [20698668] **270**

INTERNATIONAL — Alphabetical Title Index

INTERNATIONAL JOURNAL OF PAEDIATRIC DENTISTRY / THE BRITISH PAEDONDONTIC SOCIETY [AND] THE INTERNATIONAL ASSOCIATION OF DENTISTRY FOR CHILDREN (UK/0960-7439) [23737000] 3904, **1325**

INTERNATIONAL JOURNAL OF PALLIATIVE NURSING (UK) **3857**

INTERNATIONAL JOURNAL OF PANCREATOLOGY (NE/0169-4197) [13757728] **3798**

INTERNATIONAL JOURNAL OF PARALLEL PROGRAMMING (US/0885-7458) [12712733] **1279**

INTERNATIONAL JOURNAL OF PARTIAL HOSPITALIZATION *CEASED.* (US/0272-4308) [06842219] **3786**

INTERNATIONAL JOURNAL OF PATTERN RECOGNITION AND ARTIFICIAL INTELLIGENCE (SI/0218-0014) [17376720] **1213**

INTERNATIONAL JOURNAL OF PEDIATRIC OTORHINOLARYNGOLOGY (NE/0165-5876) [05702726] 3888, **3904**

INTERNATIONAL JOURNAL OF PEPTIDE AND PROTEIN RESEARCH (DK/0367-8377) [01607810] **1042**

INTERNATIONAL JOURNAL OF PERIODONTICS & RESTORATIVE DENTISTRY, THE (US/0198-7569) [06232619] **1325**

INTERNATIONAL JOURNAL OF PERSONAL CONSTRUCT PSYCHOLOGY (UK/0893-603X) [15600253] **4591**

●INTERNATIONAL JOURNAL OF PEST MANAGEMENT (UK/0967-0874) [28540875] **96**

INTERNATIONAL JOURNAL OF PHARMACEUTICAL TECHNOLOGY & PRODUCT MANUFACTURE *CEASED.* (UK/0260-6267) [07643054] **4308**

INTERNATIONAL JOURNAL OF PHARMACEUTICS (NE/0378-5173) [03687036] **4308**

INTERNATIONAL JOURNAL OF PHARMACOGNOSY (NE/0925-1618) [23372924] **4308**

INTERNATIONAL JOURNAL OF PHARMACY PRACTICE (UK/0961-7671) [25385253] **4309**

INTERNATIONAL JOURNAL OF PHILOSOPHICAL STUDIES, THE (UK/0967-2559) **4349**

●INTERNATIONAL JOURNAL OF PHILOSOPHY, PSYCHOLOGY, AND SPIRITUALITY (US/1061-530X) [25343864] 4591, **4349**

INTERNATIONAL JOURNAL OF PHYSICAL CHEMISTRY : BERICHTE DER BUNSEN-GESELLSCHAFT, AN (GW) [23587562] **1053**

INTERNATIONAL JOURNAL OF PHYSICAL DISTRIBUTION & LOGISTICS MANAGEMENT (UK/0960-0035) [21987179] **871**

INTERNATIONAL JOURNAL OF PHYSICAL EDUCATION (GW/0341-8685) [01782086] **1856**

INTERNATIONAL JOURNAL OF PIXE (SI/0129-0835) [22099078] **3942**

●INTERNATIONAL JOURNAL OF PLANT SCIENCES (US/1058-5893) [24335365] **514**

●INTERNATIONAL JOURNAL OF PLANT SCIENCES. MICROFORM (US/1058-5893) [25797422] **514**

INTERNATIONAL JOURNAL OF PLASTICITY (US/0749-6419) [11166895] **2103**

INTERNATIONAL JOURNAL OF POLITICAL ECONOMY (US/0891-1916) [14639715] **4477**

INTERNATIONAL JOURNAL OF POLITICS, CULTURE, AND SOCIETY (US/0891-4486) [14781350] 5204, 4477, **5248**

INTERNATIONAL JOURNAL OF POLYMERIC MATERIALS (US/0091-4037) [01786907] 4455, **978**

INTERNATIONAL JOURNAL OF POWDER METALLURGY (PRINCETON, N.J.) (US/0888-7462) [13320625] 2141, **4004**

●INTERNATIONAL JOURNAL OF POWER & ENERGY SYSTEMS (US/1078-3466) [30614808] **1948**

INTERNATIONAL JOURNAL OF PRESSURE VESSELS AND PIPING, THE (UK/0308-0161) [01791142] **2116**

INTERNATIONAL JOURNAL OF PRIMATOLOGY (US/0164-0291) [04556695] **5586**

INTERNATIONAL JOURNAL OF PRODUCTION ECONOMICS (NE/0925-5273) [24682470] **1612**

INTERNATIONAL JOURNAL OF PRODUCTION RESEARCH (UK/0020-7543) [01908523] **871**

INTERNATIONAL JOURNAL OF PROJECT MANAGEMENT (UK/0263-7863) [09500603] 618, **1980**

INTERNATIONAL JOURNAL OF PROSTHODONTICS, THE (US/0893-2174) [15434404] **1325**

INTERNATIONAL JOURNAL OF PSYCHIATRY IN MEDICINE, THE (US/0091-2174) [01778043] **3927**

INTERNATIONAL JOURNAL OF PSYCHO-ANALYSIS, THE (UK/0020-7578) [01640896] 3927, **4591**

INTERNATIONAL JOURNAL OF PSYCHOLINGUISTICS (JA/0165-4055) [01084609] 4591, **3287**

INTERNATIONAL JOURNAL OF PSYCHOLOGY (NE/0020-7594) [01753586] **4591**

●INTERNATIONAL JOURNAL OF PSYCHOLOGY RESEARCH (US) **4591**

INTERNATIONAL JOURNAL OF PSYCHOPHYSIOLOGY (NE/0167-8760) [10082177] **581**

INTERNATIONAL JOURNAL OF PSYCHOSOMATICS (US/0884-8297) [10985506] **3589**

INTERNATIONAL JOURNAL OF PUBLIC ADMINISTRATION (US/0190-0692) [04629549] **4657**

INTERNATIONAL JOURNAL OF PUBLIC OPINION RESEARCH (UK/0954-2892) [20779599] **5248**

INTERNATIONAL JOURNAL OF PUBLIC SECTOR MANAGEMENT, THE (UK/0951-3558) [18217545] **4657**

INTERNATIONAL JOURNAL OF PUNJAB STUDIES (US/0971-5223) **2768**

INTERNATIONAL JOURNAL OF PURCHASING AND MATERIALS MANAGEMENT (US/1055-6001) [23175993] **950**

INTERNATIONAL JOURNAL OF PURINE & PYRIMIDINE RESEARCH (SZ) **978**

INTERNATIONAL JOURNAL OF QUALITATIVE STUDIES IN EDUCATION : QSE (UK/0951-8398) [17887601] **1754**

INTERNATIONAL JOURNAL OF QUALITY & RELIABILITY MANAGEMENT, THE (UK/0265-671X) [11858289] **871**

INTERNATIONAL JOURNAL OF QUANTUM CHEMISTRY (US/0020-7608) [01753588] **978**

●INTERNATIONAL JOURNAL OF QUANTUM CHEMISTRY. QUANTUM BIOLOGY SYMPOSIUM : PROCEEDINGS OF THE INTERNATIONAL SYMPOSIUM ON THE APPLICATION OF FUNDAMENTAL THEORY TO PROBLEMS OF BIOLOGY AND PHARMACOLOGY (US) [29369218] **488**

INTERNATIONAL JOURNAL OF QUANTUM CHEMISTRY. QUANTUM CHEMISTRY SYMPOSIUM (US/0161-3642) [03757426] **1053**

INTERNATIONAL JOURNAL OF RADIATION APPLICATIONS AND INSTRUMENTATION. PART A, APPLIED RADIATION AND ISOTOPES (UK/0883-2889) [12101521] **4406**

INTERNATIONAL JOURNAL OF RADIATION APPLICATIONS AND INSTRUMENTATION. PART B, NUCLEAR MEDICINE AND BIOLOGY (UK/0883-2897) [12101408] **3848**

INTERNATIONAL JOURNAL OF RADIATION APPLICATIONS AND INSTRUMENTATION. PART C, RADIATION PHYSICS AND CHEMISTRY (UK) [13832377] **978**

INTERNATIONAL JOURNAL OF RADIATION APPLICATIONS AND INSTRUMENTATION. PART D, NUCLEAR TRACKS AND RADIATION MEASUREMENTS (UK) [13832408] 4435, **4447**

INTERNATIONAL JOURNAL OF RADIATION APPLICATIONS AND INSTRUMENTATION. PART E, NUCLEAR GEOPHYSICS *See* NUCLEAR GEOPHYSICS **1409**

INTERNATIONAL JOURNAL OF RADIATION APPLICATIONS AND INSTRUMENTATION. PART E, NUCLEAR GEOPHYSICS, THE (UK/0886-0130) [12789030] **1407**

INTERNATIONAL JOURNAL OF RADIATION BIOLOGY (UK/0955-3002) [18488886] 459, **3942**

INTERNATIONAL JOURNAL OF RADIATION ENGINEERING (IS) [06366081] **2156**

●INTERNATIONAL JOURNAL OF RADIATION HYGIENE (US/1066-7016) [27032841] **4435**

INTERNATIONAL JOURNAL OF RADIATION- ONCOLOGY, BIOLOGY, PHYSICS (US/0360-3016) [01865944] **3818**

INTERNATIONAL JOURNAL OF RADIOACTIVE MATERIALS TRANSPORT (UK/0957-476X) [22634728] **4435**

INTERNATIONAL JOURNAL OF RAPID SOLIDIFICATION (UK/0265-0916) [11620061] **4004**

INTERNATIONAL JOURNAL OF REFRACTORY METALS & HARD MATERIALS (UK/0263-4368) [21653614] **4004**

INTERNATIONAL JOURNAL OF REFRIGERATION (UK/0140-7007) [04554909] **2606**

INTERNATIONAL JOURNAL OF REFUGEE LAW (UK/0953-8186) [19349447] **3130**

●INTERNATIONAL JOURNAL OF REHABILITATION AND HEALTH (US) **3589**

INTERNATIONAL JOURNAL OF REHABILITATION RESEARCH (GW/0342-5282) [04554227] **4389**

INTERNATIONAL JOURNAL OF RELIABILITY, QUALITY & SAFETY ENGINEERING (SI/0218-5393) **1980**

INTERNATIONAL JOURNAL OF REMOTE SENSING (UK/0143-1161) [06498596] **1980**

INTERNATIONAL JOURNAL OF RESEARCH AND ENGINEERING (POSTAL APPLICATION) (US/1043-7134) [19537683] **1145**

INTERNATIONAL JOURNAL OF RESEARCH IN MARKETING (NE/0167-8116) [10731651] **926**

INTERNATIONAL JOURNAL OF RETAIL & DISTRIBUTION MANAGEMENT (UK/0959-0552) [21571249] **955**

INTERNATIONAL JOURNAL OF RISK & SAFETY IN MEDICINE, THE (NE/0924-6479) [22982503] **3589**

INTERNATIONAL JOURNAL OF ROBOTICS & AUTOMATION (US/0826-8185) [13569508] 1220, **1213**

INTERNATIONAL JOURNAL OF ROBOTICS RESEARCH, THE (US/0278-3649) [07793158] 1213, **1220**

INTERNATIONAL JOURNAL OF ROBUST AND NONLINEAR CONTROL (UK/1049-8923) [21344085] **1980**

INTERNATIONAL JOURNAL OF ROCK MECHANICS AND MINING SCIENCES & GEOMECHANICS ABSTRACTS (UK/0148-9062) [02139425] **2141**

INTERNATIONAL JOURNAL OF SALT LAKE RESEARCH (NE/1037-0544) 2175, **5115**

INTERNATIONAL JOURNAL OF SATELLITE COMMUNICATIONS (UK/0737-2884) [09329775] **1158**

INTERNATIONAL JOURNAL OF SCIENCE & ENGINEERING (II/0257-7828) [12031950] **1980**

INTERNATIONAL JOURNAL OF SCIENCE AND TECHNOLOGY (US/0891-5083) [14874437] **5115**

INTERNATIONAL JOURNAL OF SCIENCE EDUCATION (UK/0950-0693) [15531109] 1897, **5115**

INTERNATIONAL JOURNAL OF SEDIMENT RESEARCH (CC/1013-7866) [15582683] **1383**

●INTERNATIONAL JOURNAL OF SELECTION AND ASSESSMENT (UK/0965-075X) [28272363] **943**

●INTERNATIONAL JOURNAL OF SELF-PROPAGATING HIGH-TEMPERATURE SYSTEM (US/1061-3862) [25284273] **1980**

INTERNATIONAL JOURNAL OF SERVICE INDUSTRY MANAGEMENT (UK/0956-4223) [22212924] **872**

INTERNATIONAL JOURNAL OF SHORT-TERM PSYCHOTHERAPY (UK/0884-724X) [12437620] **4591**

INTERNATIONAL JOURNAL OF SIGN LINGUISTICS (UK/0959-6402) [23003161] 4389, **3287**

INTERNATIONAL JOURNAL OF SLAVIC LINGUISTICS AND POETICS (US/0538-8228) [01753591] 3464, **3287**

INTERNATIONAL JOURNAL OF SOCIAL ECONOMICS (UK/0306-8293) [01794620] 5204, **1496**

INTERNATIONAL JOURNAL OF SOCIAL EDUCATION, THE (US/0889-0293) [13778238] **5204**

INTERNATIONAL JOURNAL OF SOCIAL PSYCHIATRY, THE (UK/0020-7640) [01329560] **3927**

INTERNATIONAL JOURNAL OF SOCIOLOGY (US/0020-7659) [00820297] **5248**

INTERNATIONAL JOURNAL OF SOCIOLOGY & SOCIAL POLICY, THE (UK/0144-333X) [07680489] **5248**

INTERNATIONAL JOURNAL OF SOCIOLOGY OF THE FAMILY (II/0020-7667) [01789286] **2281**

INTERNATIONAL JOURNAL OF SOFTWARE ENGINEERING AND KNOWLEDGE ENGINEERING (SI/0218-1940) [24347302] 1287, **1229**

INTERNATIONAL JOURNAL OF SOLAR ENERGY (SZ/0142-5919) [04814017] **1948**

Alphabetical Title Index — INTERNATIONAL

INTERNATIONAL JOURNAL OF SOLIDS AND STRUCTURES (US/0020-7683) [01642851] 2103, 2116, **2025**

INTERNATIONAL JOURNAL OF SPACE STRUCTURES (UK) [18360616] **301**

INTERNATIONAL JOURNAL OF SPECIAL EDUCATION (CN/0827-3383) [14938024] **1880**

INTERNATIONAL JOURNAL OF SPEECH TECHNOLOGY (NE/1381-2416) **5115**

INTERNATIONAL JOURNAL OF SPELEOLOGY (IT/0020-7691) [02093416] **1407**

INTERNATIONAL JOURNAL OF SPORT BIOMECHANICS (US/0740-2082) [09901720] 4900, **495**

INTERNATIONAL JOURNAL OF SPORT MEDICINE (US/1049-9679) [21359413] **3954**

INTERNATIONAL JOURNAL OF SPORT NUTRITION (US/1050-1606) [21402212] 4900, **4192**

INTERNATIONAL JOURNAL OF SPORT PSYCHOLOGY (IT/0047-0767) [01753592] **4900**

INTERNATIONAL JOURNAL OF SPORTS MEDICINE (GW/0172-4622) [06828231] **3954**

INTERNATIONAL JOURNAL OF STD & AIDS (UK/0956-4624) [21176258] **3672**

●INTERNATIONAL JOURNAL OF STRESS MANAGEMENT (US/1072-5245) [28999556] **4591**

INTERNATIONAL JOURNAL OF STRUCTURES (II/0253-4754) [08913352] **2099**

INTERNATIONAL JOURNAL OF SUPERCOMPUTER APPLICATIONS *See* INTERNATIONAL JOURNAL OF SUPERCOMPUTER APPLICATIONS AND HIGH PERFORMANCE COMPUTING, THE **1287**

INTERNATIONAL JOURNAL OF SUPERCOMPUTER APPLICATIONS *See* INTERNATIONAL JOURNAL OF SUPERCOMPUTER APPLICATIONS AND HIGH-PERFORMANCE COMPUTING **1287**

●INTERNATIONAL JOURNAL OF SUPERCOMPUTER APPLICATIONS AND HIGH PERFORMANCE COMPUTING (US) **1287**

●INTERNATIONAL JOURNAL OF SUPERCOMPUTER APPLICATIONS AND HIGH PERFORMANCE COMPUTING, THE (US/1078-3482) [30855422] **1287**

INTERNATIONAL JOURNAL OF SUPERCOMPUTER APPLICATIONS, THE (US/0890-2720) [14191146] **1287**

●INTERNATIONAL JOURNAL OF SURGICAL PATHOLOGY (US/1066-8969) [27088858] 3966, **3895**

INTERNATIONAL JOURNAL OF SURGICAL SCIENCES (IT/1122-8687) **3966**

INTERNATIONAL JOURNAL OF SUSTAINABLE DEVELOPMENT AND WORLD ECOLOGY, THE (UK/1350-4509) **2217**

INTERNATIONAL JOURNAL OF SYSTEMATIC BACTERIOLOGY (US/0020-7713) [01643282] **564**

INTERNATIONAL JOURNAL OF SYSTEMS AUTOMATION, RESEARCH & APPLICATIONS *CEASED.* (US/1055-8462) [23359049] **1247**

INTERNATIONAL JOURNAL OF SYSTEMS SCIENCE (UK/0020-7721) [01695817] **2116**

INTERNATIONAL JOURNAL OF TECHNOLOGY & AGING *CEASED.* (US/0891-4478) [14780835] **3752**

INTERNATIONAL JOURNAL OF TECHNOLOGY AND DESIGN EDUCATION (NE/0957-7572) [09577572] **5115**

INTERNATIONAL JOURNAL OF TECHNOLOGY ASSESSMENT IN HEALTH CARE (UK/0266-4623) [12209782] **3589**

INTERNATIONAL JOURNAL OF TECHNOLOGY MANAGEMENT (SZ/0267-5730) [15080965] **5115**

INTERNATIONAL JOURNAL OF THE ADDICTIONS (US/0020-773X) [01753594] **1345**

●INTERNATIONAL JOURNAL OF THE CLASSICAL TRADITION (US/1073-0508) [29297230] **1077**

INTERNATIONAL JOURNAL OF THE HISTORY OF SPORT, THE (UK/0952-3367) [16314947] **4901**

INTERNATIONAL JOURNAL OF THE JAPAN SOCIETY FOR PRECISION ENGINEERING (JA) [24880431] **1980**

●INTERNATIONAL JOURNAL OF THE LEGAL PROFESSION (UK/0969-5958) **2984**

INTERNATIONAL JOURNAL OF THE SOCIOLOGY OF LANGUAGE (NE/0165-2516) [02024029] **3287**

INTERNATIONAL JOURNAL OF THE SOCIOLOGY OF LAW (UK/0194-6595) [04880624] 5248, **2984**

●INTERNATIONAL JOURNAL OF THE STRUCTURAL DESIGN OF TALL BUILDINGS, THE (UK/1062-8002) [25744751] **2025**

INTERNATIONAL JOURNAL OF THEOLOGY AND PHILOSOPHY IN AFRICA : TPA, THE (UK/0951-5429) [21314594] 4349, **4966**

INTERNATIONAL JOURNAL OF THEORETICAL PHYSICS (US/0020-7748) [00843108] **4406**

INTERNATIONAL JOURNAL OF THERAPEUTIC COMMUNITIES (UK/0196-1365) [05758753] **3589**

INTERNATIONAL JOURNAL OF THERMOPHYSICS (US/0195-928X) [05702905] **4406**

INTERNATIONAL JOURNAL OF TISSUE REACTIONS (SZ/0250-0868) [08994929] **537**

●INTERNATIONAL JOURNAL OF TOXICOLOGY, OCCUPATIONAL, AND ENVIRONMENTAL HEALTH (II) [25742960] **3981**

INTERNATIONAL JOURNAL OF TRANSLATION (II) [21104736] **3288**

●INTERNATIONAL JOURNAL OF TRANSPORTATION POLICY (US/1065-5174) [26622642] **5384**

●INTERNATIONAL JOURNAL OF TRAUMA NURSING (US/1075-4210) [30050879] **3857**

INTERNATIONAL JOURNAL OF TROPICAL AGRICULTURE (II/0254-8755) [10074955] **97**

INTERNATIONAL JOURNAL OF TROPICAL PLANT DISEASES (II/0254-0126) [10890669] **514**

INTERNATIONAL JOURNAL OF TURBO & JET-ENGINES (IS/0334-0082) [10617921] **24**

INTERNATIONAL JOURNAL OF TURKISH STUDIES (US/0272-7919) [06676065] **2692**

INTERNATIONAL JOURNAL OF UNCERTAINTY, FUZZINESS AND KNOWLEDGE BASED SYSTEMS (SI/0218-4885) [29644737] **1190**

INTERNATIONAL JOURNAL OF UNIVERSITY ADULT EDUCATION (CN/0074-3992) [04547295] **1801**

INTERNATIONAL JOURNAL OF URBAN AND REGIONAL RESEARCH (UK/0309-1317) [03776030] **2825**

INTERNATIONAL JOURNAL OF UROLOGY (JA/0919-8172) **3990**

INTERNATIONAL JOURNAL OF VALUE BASED MANAGEMENT (US/0895-8815) [16850850] **684**

INTERNATIONAL JOURNAL OF VALUE-BASED MANAGEMENT (NE/0895-8815) **1190**

INTERNATIONAL JOURNAL OF VEHICLE DESIGN (SZ/0143-3369) [05882271] 1980, **5417**

INTERNATIONAL JOURNAL OF VEHICLE DESIGN SERIES B : HEAVY VEHICLE DESIGN SYSTEMS (SZ/1351-7848) 1980, **5417**

INTERNATIONAL JOURNAL OF WATER RESOURCES DEVELOPMENT (UK/0790-0627) [09769587] **5534**

INTERNATIONAL JOURNAL OF WILDLAND FIRE, THE (US/1049-8001) [21311054] **2291**

INTERNATIONAL JOURNAL OF WINE MARKETING (HK/0954-7541) [21232495] 926, **2368**

●INTERNATIONAL JOURNAL OF WIRELESS INFORMATION NETWORKS (US/1068-9605) [27870247] 1158, **1242**

INTERNATIONAL JOURNAL OF WORLD STUDIES, THE (US/0742-4698) [10354549] **4524**

INTERNATIONAL JOURNAL OF ZOONOSES *CEASED.* (CH/0377-0168) [01350729] **3589**

●INTERNATIONAL JOURNAL ON ARTIFICIAL INTELLIGENCE TOOLS (SI/0218-2130) [02182130] **1213**

INTERNATIONAL JOURNAL ON DRUG POLICY, THE (UK/0955-3959) [22592772] **1345**

INTERNATIONAL JOURNAL ON GROUP RIGHTS (NE/0927-5908) **3130**

INTERNATIONAL JOURNAL ON POLICY AND INFORMATION (US/0251-1266) [07528105] **5204**

INTERNATIONAL JOURNAL ON THE UNITY OF THE SCIENCES *SUSPENDED.* (US/0896-2294) [16961732] 2848, **5115**

INTERNATIONAL JOURNAL ON WORLD PEACE (US/0742-3640) [10310754] **4524**

INTERNATIONAL LABMATE (UK/0143-5140) [23593924] **1015**

INTERNATIONAL LABOR AFFAIRS REPORT / UNITED STATES COUNCIL OF THE INTERNATIONAL CHAMBER OF COMMERCE INC (US) [08180516] **1680**

INTERNATIONAL LABOR AND WORKING CLASS HISTORY (US/0147-5479) [02270929] **1680**

INTERNATIONAL LABOR OFFICE. INTERNATIONAL OCCUPATIONAL SAFETY AND HEALTH INFORMATION CENTRE *See* LIST OF PERIODICALS ABSTRACTED **2865**

INTERNATIONAL LABORATORY ACCREDITATION CONFERENCE DIRECTORY (AT) **2117**

INTERNATIONAL LABORATORY. EUROPEAN ED (US/0010-2164) [00974796] **1016**

INTERNATIONAL LABOUR DOCUMENTATION (SZ/0020-7756) [09470121] 1680, **1534**

INTERNATIONAL LABOUR OFFICE *See* COST OF SOCIAL SECURITY. LE COUT DE LA SECURITE SOCIALE. EL COSTO DE LA SEGURIDAD SOCIAL, THE **5281**

INTERNATIONAL LABOUR OFFICE *See* OIT INFORMACIONES **1700**

INTERNATIONAL LABOUR OFFICE *See* ILO INFORMATION. U.S. EDITION **1677**

INTERNATIONAL LABOUR OFFICE *See* TECHNICAL GUIDE - INTERNATIONAL LABOUR OFFICE **1714**

INTERNATIONAL LABOUR OFFICE *See* OFFICIAL BULLETIN. SERIES B / INTERNATIONAL LABOUR OFFICE **1699**

INTERNATIONAL LABOUR OFFICE *See* OFFICIAL BULLETIN. SERIES A / INTERNATIONAL LABOUR OFFICE **3152**

INTERNATIONAL LABOUR OFFICE *See* ILO CATALOGUE OF PUBLICATIONS IN PRINT **1533**

INTERNATIONAL LABOUR OFFICE *See* SPECIAL REPORT OF THE DIRECTOR-GENERAL ON THE APPLICATION OF THE DECLARATION CONCERNING ACTION AGAINST APARTHEID IN SOUTH AFRICA / INTERNATIONAL LABOUR OFFICE **2643**

INTERNATIONAL LABOUR OFFICE. CENTRAL LIBRARY AND DOCUMENTATION BRANCH *See* INTERNATIONAL LABOUR DOCUMENTATION **1534**

INTERNATIONAL LABOUR OFFICE. GOVERNING BODY. SESSION *See* MINUTES OF THE ... SESSION OF THE GOVERNING BODY / INTERNATIONAL LABOUR OFFICE **1691**

INTERNATIONAL LABOUR OFFICE. ILO INFORMATION *See* WORLD OF WORK : THE MAGAZINE OF THE ILO **1720**

INTERNATIONAL LABOUR ORGANISATION *See* REPORT OF THE INTERNATIONAL LABOUR ORGANIZATION TO THE UNITED NATIONS **1706**

INTERNATIONAL LABOUR ORGANISATION. ADMINISTRATIVE TRIBUNAL *See* JUDGMENTS OF THE ADMINISTRATIVE TRIBUNAL OF THE INTERNATIONAL LABOUR ORGANISATION: ORDINARY SESSION **3150**

INTERNATIONAL LABOUR ORGANISATION. COMMITTEE ON WORK ON PLANTATIONS *See* GENERAL REPORT / COMMITTEE ON WORK ON PLANTATIONS **1675**

INTERNATIONAL LABOUR ORGANISATION. COMMITTEE ON WORK ON PLANTATIONS *See* NOTE ON THE PROCEEDINGS / COMMITTEE ON WORK ON PLANTATIONS **1695**

INTERNATIONAL LABOUR REVIEW (SZ/0020-7780) [01642893] **1680**

INTERNATIONAL LAND RIG DRILLING REPORT, THE (US/0732-9911) [08504955] **2141**

INTERNATIONAL LAW ASSOCIATION. CONFERENCE *See* REPORT OF THE ... CONFERENCE / THE INTERNATIONAL LAW ASSOCIATION **3134**

INTERNATIONAL LAW FIRM MANAGEMENT (US) **2984**

INTERNATIONAL LAW NEWS, THE (US/0047-0813) [01753619] **3130**

INTERNATIONAL LAW OF ARMS CONTROL (GW) 4525, **3130**

INTERNATIONAL LAW PRACTICUM (US/1041-3405) [18518566] **3130**

INTERNATIONAL LAW REPORTER, THE (II) [01784179] **3130**

INTERNATIONAL LAW REPORTS (UK/0309-0671) [06561091] **3130**

INTERNATIONAL LAWYER, THE (US/0020-7810) [01589271] **3130**

INTERNATIONAL LAWYERS' NEWSLETTER (US/0738-9728) [05996349] **3130**

INTERNATIONAL LAZARITE (CN) [02244241] **4966**

INTERNATIONAL LEAD AND ZINC STUDY GROUP *See* PRINCIPAL USES OF LEAD AND ZINC **4016**

INTERNATIONAL LEAD AND ZINC STUDY GROUP *See* WORLD DIRECTORY: SECONDARY LEAD PLANTS **4024**

INTERNATIONAL LEADS (US/0892-4546) [15194449] **3218**

INTERNATIONAL — Alphabetical Title Index

INTERNATIONAL LEAGUE FOR HUMAN RIGHTS *See* ANNUAL REVIEW - INTERNATIONAL LEAGUE FOR HUMAN RIGHTS **4504**

INTERNATIONAL LEATHER GUIDE (UK) [20553078] **3184**

INTERNATIONAL LEGAL BOOKS IN PRINT (UK) [21412885] **2984**

INTERNATIONAL LEGAL MATERIALS (US/0020-7829) [01753623] **3130**

INTERNATIONAL LEGAL PERSPECTIVES (US) [17892185] **3130**

INTERNATIONAL LEGAL PRACTITIONER (UK/0309-7684) [06740920] **3130**

INTERNATIONAL LEGAL STRATEGY : ILS (US/1072-7795) [29202546] **2984**

INTERNATIONAL LESSON ANNUAL, THE (US/0074-6770) [02369568] **4966**

INTERNATIONAL LIAISON GROUP ON GOLD MINERALIZATION NEWSLETTER (UK) 1440, **1383**

INTERNATIONAL LIBRARY MOVEMENT (II/0970-0048) [06988006] **3218**

INTERNATIONAL LIBRARY REVIEW *See* INTERNATIONAL INFORMATION & LIBRARY REVIEW, THE **3218**

INTERNATIONAL LICENSING DIRECTORY, THE (UK) [13001701] **1305**

INTERNATIONAL LICHENOLOGICAL NEWSLETTER (GW/0731-2830) [02447787] **514**

INTERNATIONAL LIGHTING REVIEW (NE/0020-7853) [01753626] **2067**

INTERNATIONAL LIMOUSIN JOURNAL (US/0744-3951) [05914534] **213**

INTERNATIONAL LITERARY MARKET PLACE (US/0074-6827) [01776268] **4821**

INTERNATIONAL LITIGATION : A GUIDE TO JURISDICTION PRACTICE & STRATEGY (US) **3130**

INTERNATIONAL LITIGATION PROCEDURE (UK/0958-9767) [21890101] **3130**

INTERNATIONAL LIVESTOCK CENTRE FOR AFRICA *See* ILCA ... ANNUAL REPORT AND PROGRAMME HIGHLIGHTS **212**

INTERNATIONAL LIVING (WASHINGTON, D.C.) (US/0277-2442) [07525256] **5481**

INTERNATIONAL LONGSHOREMEN'S AND WAREHOUSEMEN'S UNION *See* PROCEEDINGS OF THE ... BIENNIAL CONVENTION OF THE INTERNATIONAL LONGSHOREMEN'S AND WAREHOUSEMEN'S UNION **1703**

INTERNATIONAL LOSS CONTROL REVIEW (US) **2864**

INTERNATIONAL LOW VISION DIRECTORY (US/1040-9912) [18597764] **3875**

INTERNATIONAL MAIL MANUAL (US/1058-0875) [08269582] **1145**

INTERNATIONAL MAIZE AND WHEAT IMPROVEMENT CENTER *See* CIMMYT REVIEW **167**

INTERNATIONAL MANAGEMENT (UK) [08227925] 1612, **684**

INTERNATIONAL MANAGEMENT *CEASED*. (UK) [02250937] **872**

INTERNATIONAL MANAGEMENT (LAUSANNE, SWITZERLAND) *CEASED*. (SZ/0020-7888) [13348267] **872**

INTERNATIONAL MANAGER PROFILES (US) **872**

INTERNATIONAL MAPS AND ATLASES IN PRINT (UK) [01605264] **2582**

INTERNATIONAL MARINE BUSINESS (UK/0965-0644) [25180177] **684**

INTERNATIONAL MARINE BUSINESS JOURNAL (US) **593**

INTERNATIONAL MARINE SAFETY DIRECTORY (UK/0263-7618) [10841854] **4177**

INTERNATIONAL MARINE SCIENCE NEWSLETTER (IT/0020-7918) [01715775] **555**

INTERNATIONAL MARITIME COMMITTEE *See* DOCUMENTATION - INTERNATIONAL MARITIME COMMITTEE **4176**

INTERNATIONAL MARITIME COMMITTEE *See* YEARBOOK - INTERNATIONAL MARITIME COMMITTEE **4185**

●INTERNATIONAL MARITIME LAW (UK) **3181**

INTERNATIONAL MARITIME ORGANIZATION *See* PUBLICATIONS OF THE INTERNATIONAL MARITIME ORGANIZATION **4182**

INTERNATIONAL MARKET ALERT (US/1051-8061) [22123874] **841**

INTERNATIONAL MARKETING DATA AND STATISTICS (UK/0308-2938) [02636006] **730**

INTERNATIONAL MARKETING DATA AND STATISTICS (UK/0308-2938) [103082938] **926**

INTERNATIONAL MARKETING REPORT (US/0193-9661) [04411648] **926**

INTERNATIONAL MARKETING REVIEW (UK/0265-1335) [10860883] **926**

INTERNATIONAL MARKETS FOR MEAT, THE (SZ) [13768167] **213**

INTERNATIONAL MARXIST REVIEW : IMR / ORGAN OF THE REVOLUTIONARY MARXIST TENDENCY OF THE FOURTH INTERNATIONAL (UK) [05504478] **4477**

INTERNATIONAL MATERIALS REVIEWS (UK/0950-6608) [16107683] **4004**

INTERNATIONAL MATHEMATICS RESEARCH NOTICES (US) [23292047] **3509**

INTERNATIONAL MAURITIUS DIRECTORY (MF) [10012910] **2499**

INTERNATIONAL MEALS ON WHEELS DIRECTORY (US/0161-2522) [03862487] **5290**

INTERNATIONAL MEAT MARKET REVIEW (UK/0263-2217) [18777359] **213**

INTERNATIONAL MED-TECH DIRECTORY : THE INTERNATIONAL GUIDE TO PUBLIC HEALTH CARE COMPANIES (US) [24233706] **3589**

INTERNATIONAL MEDIA GUIDE. BUSINESS/PROFESSIONAL, ASIA/PACIFIC, MIDDLE EAST/AFICA (US/1073-8002) [24625106] **760**

INTERNATIONAL MEDIA GUIDE. BUSINESS/PROFESSIONAL, EUROPE (US/0730-5257) [17805123] **760**

INTERNATIONAL MEDIA GUIDE. BUSINESS/PROFESSIONAL THE AMERICAS (US/1069-4277) [20105447] **760**

INTERNATIONAL MEDIA GUIDE. CONSUMER MAGAZINES WORLDWIDE : IMG (US/0730-5257) [22724245] **761**

INTERNATIONAL MEDIA GUIDE. EDITION, BUSINESS/PROFESSIONAL PUBLICATIONS, EUROPE (US/0730-5273) [10008578] **761**

INTERNATIONAL MEDIA GUIDE. EDITION, BUSINESS/PROFESSIONAL PUBLICATIONS, MIDDLE EAST/AFRICA (US) [10060386] **761**

INTERNATIONAL MEDIA GUIDE. NEWSPAPERS WORLDWIDE : IMG (US) [17805279] **5814**

INTERNATIONAL MEDIA LAW (UK) [09203617] **3130**

INTERNATIONAL MEDICAL DEVICE REGULATORY MONITOR (US) **3589**

●INTERNATIONAL MEDICAL IMAGE REGISTRY (US) **3589**

INTERNATIONAL MEDICAL TRIBUNE SYNDICATE (US/1040-7588) [18515056] **3589**

INTERNATIONAL MEDICINE (LONDON) *SUSPENDED*. (UK/0143-4853) [06299577] **3589**

INTERNATIONAL MEDICINE. SUPPLEMENT (UK/0143-4853) [10603195] **3589**

INTERNATIONAL MEDIEVAL BIBLIOGRAPHY (UK/0020-7950) [01783429] 3396, **3458**

INTERNATIONAL MERGER LAW *CEASED*. (US/1053-4660) [22495734] **684**

INTERNATIONAL MERGER YEARBOOK *See* MERGER YEARBOOK, THE **693**

... INTERNATIONAL MERGER YEARBOOK, THE (US/1052-9942) [22188090] **684**

INTERNATIONAL METALLOGRAPHIC SOCIETY *See* MICROSTRUCTURAL SCIENCE **4012**

INTERNATIONAL METEOROLOGICAL INSTITUTE IN STOCKHOLM *See* ANNUAL REPORT - INTERNATIONAL METEOROLOGICAL INSTITUTE IN STOCKHOLM **1420**

INTERNATIONAL MICROFORM JOURNAL OF LEGAL MEDICINE AND FORENSIC SCIENCES *CEASED*. (US/8755-4933) [06958386] **3741**

INTERNATIONAL MICROGRAPHICS SOURCE BOOK *See* INTERNATIONAL IMAGING SOURCE BOOK **1190**

INTERNATIONAL MIGRATION (GENEVA, SWITZERLAND) (SZ/0020-7985) [01753637] **1919**

INTERNATIONAL MIGRATION REVIEW : IMR (US/0197-9183) [01753638] **1919**

INTERNATIONAL MILITARY REVIEW (US/1056-5728) [23740350] **4657**

INTERNATIONAL MILLING FLOUR & FEED (UK) [24653015] **202**

INTERNATIONAL MINDS : THE QUARTERLY JOURNAL OF PSYCHOLOGICAL INSIGHT INTO INTERNATIONAL AFFAIRS (UK/0957-1299) [22713443] **4525**

INTERNATIONAL MINERALS SCENE, THE (CN/0823-6488) [09859930] **1440**

INTERNATIONAL MINING (UK/0269-378X) [I0269378X] **2141**

INTERNATIONAL MINING REVIEW (UK) **2141**

INTERNATIONAL MOBILISATION (FI) [09847102] **4509**

INTERNATIONAL MONETARY FUND *See* JAHRESBERICHT DER EXECUTIVDIREKTOREN - INTERNATIONALER WAHRUNGSFONDS **1497**

INTERNATIONAL MONETARY FUND *See* ANNUAL REPORT OF THE EXECUTIVE BOARD - INTERNATIONAL MONETARY FUND **1632**

INTERNATIONAL MONETARY FUND *See* SELECTED DECISIONS OF THE INTERNATIONAL MONETARY FUND AND SELECTED DOCUMENTS **811**

INTERNATIONAL MONETARY FUND *See* REGLEMENTATION GENERALE, REGLES ET REGLEMENTS / FONDS MONETAIRE INTERNATIONAL **1516**

INTERNATIONAL MONETARY FUND *See* RAPPORT ANNUEL DU CONSEIL D'ADMINISTRATION - FONDS MONETAIRE INTERNATIONAL **1515**

INTERNATIONAL MONETARY FUND *See* IMF SURVEY **790**

INTERNATIONAL MONETARY FUND *See* SUMMARY PROCEEDINGS OF THE ANNUAL MEETING OF THE BOARD OF GOVERNORS. INTERNATIONAL MONETARY FUND **1523**

INTERNATIONAL MONETARY FUND *See* ESTATUTOS Y REGLAMENTO / FONDO MONETARIO INTERNACIONAL **1489**

INTERNATIONAL MONETARY FUND *See* INFORME ANUAL DEL DIRECTORIO EJECUTIVO - FONDO MONETARIO INTERNACIONAL **1495**

INTERNATIONAL MONETARY FUND *See* PAMPHLET SERIES - INTERNATIONAL MONETARY FUND **1511**

INTERNATIONAL MONETARY FUND *See* INTERNATIONAL FINANCIAL STATISTICS **730**

INTERNATIONAL MONETARY FUND *See* STAFF PAPERS - INTERNATIONAL MONETARY FUND **812**

INTERNATIONAL MONETARY FUND *See* BY-LAWS, RULES AND REGULATIONS. INTERNATIONAL MONETARY FUND **4635**

INTERNATIONAL MONETARY FUND *See* SELECTED DECISIONS AND SELECTED DOCUMENTS OF THE INTERNATIONAL MONETARY FUND **811**

INTERNATIONAL MONETARY FUND. SELECTED DECISIONS OF THE INTERNATIONAL MONETARY FUND AND SELECTED DOCUMENTS *See* SELECTED DECISIONS AND SELECTED DOCUMENTS OF THE INTERNATIONAL MONETARY FUND **811**

INTERNATIONAL MONEY MARKETING (UK/0958-3785) [I09583785] **902**

INTERNATIONAL MONEY MARKETS (TORONTO) (CN/0711-5644) [08700965] **792**

INTERNATIONAL MONOGRAPH SERIES ON EARLY CHILD CARE (UK/0140-668X) [07189666] 1804, **2281**

INTERNATIONAL MONOGRAPHS IN NUTRITION, METABOLISM, AND OBESITY (UK/0958-9414) [22449940] **4192**

INTERNATIONAL MONOGRAPHS ON OBESITY SERIES (UK/0957-0349) [14690882] **2598**

INTERNATIONAL MONOGRAPHS ON RISK (UK/0266-0512) [11634844] 4309, **3981**

INTERNATIONAL MOTION PICTURE ALMANAC (1956) (US/0074-7084) [04652879] **4073**

INTERNATIONAL MOTOR BUSINESS (UK/0267-8225) [12210855] **5417**

INTERNATIONAL MOTOR-CYCLE RACING BOOK (UK/0306-5898) [01795490] **4081**

INTERNATIONAL MUSIC CENTRE. IMZ BULLETIN INFORMATION *See* MUSIC IN THE MEDIA : IMZ BULLETIN **4133**

INTERNATIONAL MUSICIAN (US/0020-8051) [01753645] **4123**

INTERNATIONAL MUSICIAN AND RECORDING WORLD (UK) [02619432] **4123**

INTERNATIONAL NANNOPLANKTON ASSOCIATION *See* INA NEWSLETTER / INTERNATIONAL NANNOPLANKTON ASSOCIATION **4231**

INTERNATIONAL NARCOTIC ENFORCEMENT OFFICERS ASSOCIATION *See* OFFICIAL DIRECTORY **3171**

INTERNATIONAL NARCOTIC ENFORCEMENT OFFICERS ASSOCIATION *See* INTERNATIONAL DRUG REPORT **3166**

INTERNATIONAL

INTERNATIONAL NARCOTICS CONTROL BOARD *See* ESTIMATED WORLD REQUIREMENTS OF NARCOTIC DRUGS AND ESTIMATES OF WORLD PRODUCTION OF OPIUM **1344**

INTERNATIONAL NARCOTICS CONTROL BOARD *See* REPORT OF THE INTERNATIONAL NARCOTICS CONTROL BOARD **1348**

INTERNATIONAL NAUTICAL INDEX (US/0363-261X) [02457034] **4177**

INTERNATIONAL NEMATOLOGY NETWORK NEWSLETTER (US/1052-5408) [18932222] **5586**

INTERNATIONAL NETSUKE COLLECTORS SOCIETY *See* JOURNAL - THE INTERNATIONAL NETSUKE COLLECTORS SOCIETY **373**

INTERNATIONAL NETWORKS *CEASED.* (US/0739-9898) [09887149] 2067, **1158**

INTERNATIONAL NEW PRODUCT NEWSLETTER (US/1046-7211) [15813518] **5115**

INTERNATIONAL NEW PRODUCT REPORT (UK) 926, **684**

INTERNATIONAL NEW PRODUCT REPORT (UK) **2345**

INTERNATIONAL NEWS ON FATS, OILS AND RELATED MATERIALS (US/0897-8026) [17628586] **1025**

INTERNATIONAL NEWSLETTER *SUSPENDED.* (SW/0308-762X) [03819403] **2692**

INTERNATIONAL NEWSLETTER OF MARITIME HISTORY (CN/0843-8706) [19744682] **5450**

●INTERNATIONAL NEWSLETTER ON ROCK ART : I.N.O.R.A (FR) [25651555] 353, **270**

INTERNATIONAL NONPROPRIETARY NAMES (INN) FOR PHARMACEUTICAL SUBSTANCES / DENOMINATIONS COMMUNES INTERNATIONALES (DCI) POUR LES SUBSTANCES PHARMACEUTIQUES (SZ) [02862309] **4309**

INTERNATIONAL NONWOVENS DIRECTORY (US) [18239731] **5352**

INTERNATIONAL NOTICES TO AIRMEN (US/0364-6742) [02169082] **24**

INTERNATIONAL NUMISMATIC DIRECTORY (UK) [01788709] **2781**

INTERNATIONAL NURSING INDEX (US/0020-8124) [01753653] 3857, **3660**

INTERNATIONAL NURSING REVIEW (LONDON, ENGLAND) (SZ/0020-8132) [01753654] **3857**

INTERNATIONAL NUTRITION POLICY SERIES *CEASED.* (US/0190-8480) [04123377] **4192**

●INTERNATIONAL OBSERVER (WASHINGTON, D.C.) (US/1061-0324) [25162669] **2620**

INTERNATIONAL OFFICE OF EPIZOOTICS, PARIS *See* BULLETIN - OFFICE INTERNATIONAL DES EPIZOOTIES (PARIS) **5506**

●INTERNATIONAL OFFSHORE OIL COMPANY DIRECTORY (US/1059-7816) [24766284] **4261**

INTERNATIONAL OFFSHORE RIG OWNERS & PERSONNEL DIRECTORY (US/1058-6008) [24338755] **4261**

INTERNATIONAL OIL AND GAS DEVELOPMENT (US/0535-1634) [08003819] 4261, **4283**

INTERNATIONAL OIL AND GAS DEVELOPMENT YEARBOOK. PART 1: EXPLORATION (US/0535-1634) **4261**

INTERNATIONAL OIL AND GAS DEVELOPMENT YEARBOOK. PART 2: PRODUCTION (US) **4261**

INTERNATIONAL OIL NEWS (US/0043-8855) [09882496] **4261**

INTERNATIONAL OIL SCOUTS ASSOCIATION *See* ANNUAL MEETING - INTERNATIONAL OIL SCOUTS ASSOCIATION **4249**

INTERNATIONAL OIL SCOUTS ASSOCIATION *See* OIL SCOUTS DIRECTORY **4270**

INTERNATIONAL OLD LACERS *See* BULLETIN / INTERNATIONAL OLD LACERS **5348**

INTERNATIONAL OLD LACERS INC., BULLETIN (US/0740-6746) [09986457] **5352**

INTERNATIONAL OLYMPIC ACADEMY. SUMMER SESSION *See* REPORT OF THE ... SUMMER SESSION OF THE INTERNATIONAL OLYMPIC ACADEMY **1857**

INTERNATIONAL OLYMPIC LIFTER (US/0739-5396) [08692245] **4901**

INTERNATIONAL OMEGA ASSOCIATION. MEETING *See* PROCEEDINGS OF THE ... ANNUAL MEETING / INTERNATIONAL OMEGA ASSOCIATION **4181**

INTERNATIONAL ON-LINE INFORMATION MEETING : PAPERS (UK) [06348729] **3218**

INTERNATIONAL OOP DIRECTORY (US/1050-4354) [21489059] **1287**

INTERNATIONAL OPERATING ENGINEER, THE (US/0020-8159) [06360335] **1680**

INTERNATIONAL OPHTHALMOLOGICAL REPORTER (US/0145-370X) [02721197] **3875**

INTERNATIONAL OPHTHALMOLOGY (NE/0165-5701) [05095870] **3875**

INTERNATIONAL OPHTHALMOLOGY CLINICS (US/0020-8167) [01753661] **3875**

INTERNATIONAL ORGANISATIONS IN WORLD POLITICS YEARBOOK (US/0363-7123) [02522296] **4525**

INTERNATIONAL ORGANIZATION (US/0020-8183) [01753662] **4525**

INTERNATIONAL ORGANIZATION FOR BIOLOGICAL CONTROL OF NOXIOUS ANIMALS AND PLANTS. WEST PALAEARCTIC REGIONAL SECTION *See* BULLETIN SROP **450**

INTERNATIONAL ORGANIZATION FOR SEPTUAGINT AND COGNATE STUDIES *See* BULLETIN OF THE INTERNATIONAL ORGANIZATION FOR SEPTUAGINT AND COGNITE STUDIES **5046**

INTERNATIONAL ORGANIZATION FOR STANDARDIZATION *See* ISO CATALOGUE **4030**

INTERNATIONAL ORGANIZATION FOR STANDARDIZATION *See* ISO MEMENTO **4030**

INTERNATIONAL ORGANIZATION OF CITRUS VIROLOGISTS. CONFERENCE *See* PROCEEDINGS OF THE ... CONFERENCE OF THE INTERNATIONAL ORGANIZATION OF CITRUS VIROLOGISTS **183**

INTERNATIONAL ORGANIZATIONS REGULATORY GUIDEBOOK, THE (US) [07537476] 684, **3130**

INTERNATIONAL ORNITHOLOGICAL CONGRESS *See* PROCEEDINGS OF THE INTERNATIONAL ORNITHOLOGICAL CONGRESS **5595**

INTERNATIONAL ORTHOPAEDICS (GW/0341-2695) [03295014] **3882**

INTERNATIONAL OTORHINOLARYNGOLOGICAL REPORTER (US/0147-3026) [03511581] **3888**

INTERNATIONAL PACIFIC HALIBUT COMMISSION (CANADA AND UNITED STATES) *See* TECHNICAL REPORT - INTERNATIONAL PACIFIC HALIBUT COMMISSION **2314**

INTERNATIONAL PACIFIC HALIBUT COMMISSION (UNITED STATES AND CANADA) *See* ANNUAL REPORT - INTERNATIONAL PACIFIC HALIBUT COMMISSION **2294**

INTERNATIONAL PACKAGING ABSTRACTS (UK/0260-7409) [07429184] 4219, **4222**

INTERNATIONAL PAF USERS GROUP SOFTWARE (US) **1190**

INTERNATIONAL PAPER BOARD INDUSTRY (UK/0020-8191) [07754818] **4234**

INTERNATIONAL PAPERMAKER (CN) **4234**

INTERNATIONAL PARALLELS (US/1055-3649) [23159953] **841**

INTERNATIONAL PEACE AND DISARMAMENT SERIES (RU) [11256735] **4525**

INTERNATIONAL PEACE RESEARCH ASSOCIATION *See* PROCEEDINGS OF THE INTERNATIONAL PEACE RESEARCH ASSOCIATION **4532**

INTERNATIONAL PEACE RESEARCH ASSOCIATION *See* IPRA STUDIES IN PEACE RESEARCH **4526**

INTERNATIONAL PEACE RESEARCH NEWSLETTER (US) [19873731] **4525**

INTERNATIONAL PEACE STUDIES NEWSLETTER (US) [01588019] **4525**

INTERNATIONAL PEACEKEEPING (NE/1380-748X) **4525**

INTERNATIONAL PEACEKEEPING (UK/1353-3312) **4525**

INTERNATIONAL PEAT JOURNAL (FI/0782-7784) [15808125] **1948**

INTERNATIONAL PEAT SOCIETY *See* BULLETIN OF THE INTERNATIONAL PEAT SOCIETY **1934**

INTERNATIONAL PEDIATRIC ASSOCIATION *See* BULLETIN OF THE INTERNATIONAL PEDIATRIC ASSOCIATION **3901**

INTERNATIONAL PEDIATRICS (US/0885-6265) [12690449] **3904**

INTERNATIONAL PENTECOSTAL HOLINESS ADVOCATE, THE (US/0145-6970) [02776989] **5061**

INTERNATIONAL PERMACULTURE SOLUTIONS JOURNAL, THE (US/1046-8366) [20542028] **97**

INTERNATIONAL PERMACULTURE SPECIES YEARBOOK, THE (US/0896-5781) [16156634] **2217**

INTERNATIONAL PERSONNEL MANAGEMENT ASSOCIATION *See* WHO'S WHO IN THE INTERNATIONAL PERSONNEL MANAGEMENT ASSOCIATION **948**

INTERNATIONAL PERSONNEL MANAGEMENT ASSOCIATION. MEMBERSHIP DIRECTORY *See* WHO'S WHO IN THE INTERNATIONAL PERSONNEL MANAGEMENT ASSOCIATION **948**

INTERNATIONAL PERSPECTIVES IN PUBLIC HEALTH (US/8755-5328) [11358769] **4785**

●INTERNATIONAL PERSPECTIVES IN SOFTWARE ENGINEERING (US/1065-1349) [26513143] 1287, **1229**

INTERNATIONAL PERSPECTIVES IN UROLOGY (US/0276-2315) [07269467] **3990**

INTERNATIONAL PERSPECTIVES ON EDUCATION AND SOCIETY (US) [20551110] **1754**

INTERNATIONAL PEST CONTROL (UK/0020-8256) [08650660] **4245**

INTERNATIONAL PETROCHEMICAL DEVELOPMENT *CEASED.* (US/0270-1138) [06343690] **4261**

INTERNATIONAL PETROCHEMICAL REPORT, THE (US/0733-009X) [08504454] 4261, **978**

INTERNATIONAL PETROLEUM ABSTRACTS (UK/0309-4944) [01789050] 4261, **4283**

INTERNATIONAL PETROLEUM ABSTRACTS INCORPORATING OFFSHORE ABSTRACTS (UK/1052-9292) [22416307] **4261**

INTERNATIONAL PETROLEUM ANNUAL *See* INTERNATIONAL ENERGY ANNUAL **1947**

INTERNATIONAL PETROLEUM ENCYCLOPEDIA (US/0148-0375) [01203814] **4261**

INTERNATIONAL PETROLEUM FINANCE (US/0193-9270) [05294097] 792, **4261**

INTERNATIONAL PETROLEUM STATISTICS REPORT (US/1044-1816) [19688109] **4261**

INTERNATIONAL PHARMACEUTICAL ABSTRACTS (US/0020-8264) [01753672] 4309, **4334**

INTERNATIONAL PHARMACEUTICAL REGULATORY MONITOR (US) **4309**

INTERNATIONAL PHARMACEUTICAL TECHNOLOGY & PRODUCT MANUFACTURE ABSTRACTS *CEASED.* (UK/0264-2247) [10289843] **4309**

INTERNATIONAL PHARMACY JOURNAL (NE/1010-0423) [15258376] **4309**

INTERNATIONAL PHILOSOPHICAL QUARTERLY (US/0019-0365) [01876622] **4349**

INTERNATIONAL PHONETIC ASSOCIATION *See* JOURNAL OF THE INTERNATIONAL PHONETIC ASSOCIATION **3292**

INTERNATIONAL PHOTOGRAPHER (US/0020-8299) [04084087] **4371**

INTERNATIONAL PHYSICS SERIES (IT/0392-3967) [01624359] **4406**

INTERNATIONAL PIG TOPICS (UK/0963-5866) [l09635866] **213**

INTERNATIONAL PIGEONPEA NEWSLETTER (II) [08334046] **174**

INTERNATIONAL PIGLETTER (US) [10552932] **213**

INTERNATIONAL PIPE LINE & OFFSHORE CONTRACTORS ASSOCIATION *See* OFFICIAL IPLOCA DIRECTORY **4267**

INTERNATIONAL PIPER, THE (UK) [06515545] **4123**

INTERNATIONAL PLANNED PARENTHOOD DIRECTORY. WORLD LIST OF FAMILY PLANNING AGENCIES *See* WORLD LIST OF FAMILY PLANNING ADDRESSES / INTERNATIONAL PLANNED PARENTHOOD FEDERATION **591**

INTERNATIONAL PLANNED PARENTHOOD FEDERATION *See* PROGRAMME REVIEW AND FINANCIAL STATEMENTS **590**

INTERNATIONAL PLANNED PARENTHOOD FEDERATION *See* ANNUAL REPORT - INTERNATIONAL PLANNED PARENTHOOD FEDERATION **2276**

INTERNATIONAL PLANNED PARENTHOOD FEDERATION *See* ANNUAL REPORT / INTERNATIONAL PLANNED PARENTHOOD FEDERATION **4549**

INTERNATIONAL PLANNED PARENTHOOD *See* IPPF MEDICAL BULLETIN (ENGLISH EDITION) **589**

INTERNATIONAL PLANNED PARENTHOOD FEDERATION *See* IPPF CO-OPERATIVE INFORMATION SERVICE **589**

INTERNATIONAL PLANT BIOTECHNOLOGY NETWORK / TISSUE CULTURE FOR CROPS PROJECT, THE (US) [17858799] **514**

INTERNATIONAL

INTERNATIONAL PLANT PROPAGATORS' SOCIETY *See* COMBINED PROCEEDINGS / INTERNATIONAL PLANT PROPAGATORS' SOCIETY **2412**

INTERNATIONAL PLANT PROPAGATORS' SOCIETY *See* COMBINED PROCEEDINGS - INTERNATIONAL PLANT PROPAGATORS' SOCIETY **2412**

INTERNATIONAL PLANT PROTECTION CENTER *See* INFOLETTER - INTERNATIONAL PLANT PROTECTION CENTER **174**

●INTERNATIONAL PLAY JOURNAL (UK) [I09652531] **4851**

INTERNATIONAL PLAYERS CHESS NEWS, THE (US/0742-700X) [10411829] **4862**

INTERNATIONAL POETRY REVIEW (GREENSBORO) (US/0145-0786) [02707379] **3344**

INTERNATIONAL POETRY REVIEW (GREENSBORO, N.C.) (US/1063-9128) [26177399] **3464**

INTERNATIONAL POLICY CASE SERIES (US/1055-8209) [23351863] **684**

INTERNATIONAL POLICY REPORT (US/0738-6508) [03231802] **4525**

INTERNATIONAL POLITICAL ECONOMY YEARBOOK (US/8755-8335) [11412640] **1636**

INTERNATIONAL POLITICAL SCIENCE ABSTRACTS (FR/0020-8345) [01753679] 4477, **4502**

INTERNATIONAL POLITICAL SCIENCE ASSOCIATION *See* ABSTRACTS OF PAPERS PRESENTED AT THE ... WORLD CONGRESS OF THE INTERNATIONAL POLITICAL SCIENCE ASSOCIATION **4514**

INTERNATIONAL POLITICAL SCIENCE REVIEW (UK/0192-5121) [05035602] **4477**

INTERNATIONAL POLYMER PROCESSING (GW/0930-777X) [15923342] **4455**

INTERNATIONAL POLYMER SCIENCE AND TECHNOLOGY (UK/0307-174X) [01795358] 1042, **1011**

INTERNATIONAL POPULAR BRIDGE MONTHLY (UK/0951-1555) [I09511555] **4851**

INTERNATIONAL POPULAR CULTURE *CEASED.* (US/0734-4791) [06703592] **5204**

INTERNATIONAL POST-GRADUATE COURSE ON HYDROLOGICAL METHODS FOR DEVELOPING WATER RESOURCES MANAGEMENT (BUDAPEST, HUNGARY) *See* SERIES OF MANUALS **1418**

INTERNATIONAL POSTAL HANDBOOK (US) [03559650] **1145**

INTERNATIONAL POTASH INSTITUTE *See* PROCEEDINGS OF THE ... IPI-CONGRESS **1028**

INTERNATIONAL POTATO CENTER *See* CIP CIRCULAR (ENGLISH ED.) **167**

INTERNATIONAL POULTRY PRACTICE *See* VETMARK INTERNATIONAL POULTRY PRACTICE **223**

INTERNATIONAL POWER GENERATION (UK/0141-1918) [05114300] **2067**

INTERNATIONAL PRACTITIONER'S NOTEBOOK (US) [05664987] **3130**

INTERNATIONAL PRECIOUS METALS INSTITUTE. CONFERENCE *See* PRECIOUS METALS (TORONTO, ONT.) **4015**

INTERNATIONAL PRESERVATION NEWS (US/0890-4960) [14267649] **3218**

INTERNATIONAL PRESS JOURNAL (CN) [01791875] **2920**

INTERNATIONAL PRESS TELECOMMUNICATIONS COUNCIL *See* IPTC NEWS **1158**

INTERNATIONAL PRESS TELECOMMUNICATIONS COUNCIL. I.P.T.C. NEWSLETTER *See* IPTC NEWS **1158**

INTERNATIONAL PRINT BUYER'S DIRECTORY (UK) [11039091] **4566**

INTERNATIONAL PRISONERS AID ASSOCIATION *See* NEWSLETTER - INTERNATIONAL PRISONERS AID ASSOCIATION **3170**

●INTERNATIONAL PRIVATE POWER QUARTERLY (US/1070-2989) [27410966] **2067**

INTERNATIONAL PROBLEMS (IS/0020-840X) [02405714] **4525**

INTERNATIONAL PROBLEMS (BEOGRAD) (YU/0543-3665) [02153516] **5204**

INTERNATIONAL PRODUCT ALERT (US) **2345**

INTERNATIONAL PRODUCTIVITY JOURNAL (US/1053-9514) [22196459] **1612**

INTERNATIONAL PROGRAMS, GENERAL REPORT / CANADIAN TEACHERS' FEDERATION AND ITS MEMBERS (CN/0820-7305) [09519586] **1897**

INTERNATIONAL PROJECT BOOKLET (CN/0703-8976) [03790973] **2910**

INTERNATIONAL PROJECT MANAGEMENT YEARBOOK *CEASED.* (UK) [12090687] **5115**

INTERNATIONAL PROTECTION OF INDUSTRIAL PROPERTY (PL) [06391004] **3130**

INTERNATIONAL PSYCHOGERIATRICS / IPA (US/1041-6102) [18810324] 3927, **3752**

INTERNATIONAL PSYCHOLOGIST (US/0047-116X) [02833189] **4591**

INTERNATIONAL PUBLIC RELATIONS REVIEW (UK/0269-0357) [13745936] **761**

INTERNATIONAL PUBLIC WORKS REVIEW *CEASED.* (US/1053-783X) [22645968] **4657**

INTERNATIONAL PULP & PAPER DIRECTORY (US/0097-2509) [01798999] **4234**

INTERNATIONAL PULP & PAPER MARKETS (FI/0784-7289) [I07847289] **4234**

INTERNATIONAL QUARTERLY (CHESTERLAND, OHIO) (US/1041-3855) [18735868] 3130, **3100**

INTERNATIONAL QUARTERLY OF COMMUNITY HEALTH EDUCATION (US/0272-684X) [06728624] **4785**

INTERNATIONAL QUARTERLY OF ENTOMOLOGY (TU/0256-6672) [11898260] 4227, **5610**

INTERNATIONAL QUARTERLY (PRINCETON, N.J.) (US/0889-7417) [12397192] **1754**

●INTERNATIONAL QUARTERLY (TALLAHASS., FLA.) (US/1060-6084) [25044264] 353, **3396**

INTERNATIONAL RADIO CLUB OF AMERICA *See* I.R.C.A. FOREIGN LOG **1133**

INTERNATIONAL RADIO CONSULTATIVE COMMITTEE *See* DOC. - C.C.I.R **1153**

INTERNATIONAL RAILWAY JOURNAL AND RAPID TRANSIT REVIEW (UK/0744-5326) [06070542] **5432**

INTERNATIONAL RAILWAY TRAVELER, THE (US/0891-7655) [10622662] **5432**

INTERNATIONAL RARE BOOK PRICES (UK) [17432249] 301, 322, **4829**

INTERNATIONAL RARE BOOK PRICES. EARLY PRINTED BOOKS (UK) [17432117] **4829**

INTERNATIONAL RARE BOOK PRICES. MODERN FIRST EDITIONS (UK) [17432190] 3397, **4829**

INTERNATIONAL RARE BOOK PRICES. VOYAGES, TRAVEL & EXPLORATION (UK) [17431871] 5481, **4829**

INTERNATIONAL READING ASSOCIATION *See* SUMMARY OF INVESTIGATIONS RELATING TO READING **3327**

INTERNATIONAL READING ASSOCIATION. SPECIAL INTEREST GROUP ON LITERATURE FOR THE ADOLESCENT READER *See* SIGNAL **3436**

INTERNATIONAL REAL ESTATE FEDERATION *See* DIRECTORY - INTERNATIONAL REAL ESTATE FEDERATION **4836**

INTERNATIONAL REAL ESTATE FEDERATION *See* FIABCI INTERNATIONAL DIRECTORY **4837**

INTERNATIONAL REAL ESTATE FEDERATION *See* FIABCI REPORTER **4837**

INTERNATIONAL REAL ESTATE FEDERATION. FIABCI *See* FIABCI REPORTER **4837**

INTERNATIONAL REAL ESTATE JOURNAL (US/8755-6138) [09390309] **4839**

INTERNATIONAL RECORDING EQUIPMENT & STUDIO DIRECTORY (US/0889-4922) [11829197] **5317**

INTERNATIONAL RECORDS NEWS (IT) [09250123] **4525**

INTERNATIONAL REFERENCE (US/1059-3810) [24528204] **5329**

INTERNATIONAL REFERENCE GROUP ON GREAT LAKES POLLUTION FROM LAND USE ACTIVITIES *See* ANNUAL PROGRESS REPORT TO THE INTERNATIONAL JOINT COMMISSION FROM THE INTERNATIONAL REFERENCE GROUP ON GREAT LAKES POLLUTION FROM LAND USE ACTIVITIES (PLUARG) **2224**

INTERNATIONAL REGIONAL SCIENCE REVIEW (US/0160-0176) [01701088] 2566, **1497**

INTERNATIONAL REGISTER OF MARKETERS AND SUPPORTERS OF IBM PRODUCTS (US/0743-9695) [10701734] **1245**

INTERNATIONAL REGISTRY OF ORGANIZATION DEVELOPMENT PROFESSIONALS *See* INTERNATIONAL REGISTRY OF ORGANIZATION DEVELOPMENT PROFESSIONALS AND ORGANIZATION DEVELOPMENT HANDBOOK, THE **433**

INTERNATIONAL REGISTRY OF ORGANIZATION DEVELOPMENT PROFESSIONALS AND ORGANIZATION DEVELOPMENT HANDBOOK, THE (US/0749-2685) [10755538] 684, **433**

INTERNATIONAL REHABILITATION REVIEW (US/0020-8477) [01753685] 3927, **4389**

INTERNATIONAL RELATIONS (BULGARSKA AKADEMIIA NA NAUKITE. INSTITUT PO MEZHDUNARODNI OTNOSHENIIA I SOTSIALISTICHESKA) (BU) [07677663] **4525**

INTERNATIONAL RELATIONS (LONDON) (UK/0047-1178) [01607811] **4525**

INTERNATIONAL REPERTORY OF MUSIC LITERATURE (ORGANIZATION) *See* RILM ABSTRACTS **4160**

INTERNATIONAL REPERTORY OF MUSICAL ICONOGRAPHY (ORGANIZATION) *See* RIDIM/RCMI NEWSLETTER **363**

INTERNATIONAL REPORT (IRVINE, CALIF.) (US/0740-669X) [09746229] 1636, **4477**

INTERNATIONAL REPORT OF SALARY INCREASES (US) [23591820] **1680**

INTERNATIONAL REPORTS (US/0020-8507) [06818853] **792**

INTERNATIONAL RESCUER NEWSLETTER (US) [12170101] **4785**

INTERNATIONAL RESEARCH AND DEMONSTRATION PROJECTS. AN ANNOTATED LISTING (US) [03064829] **4785**

INTERNATIONAL RESEARCH AND EXCHANGES BOARD *See* IREX OCCASIONAL PAPERS **5204**

INTERNATIONAL RESEARCH CENTERS DIRECTORY (US/0278-2731) [07760703] **5115**

INTERNATIONAL RESEARCH DOCUMENT (US/0098-5643) [02242107] **5329**

INTERNATIONAL RESEARCH GROUP ON WOOD PRESERVATION *See* IRG AND ITS MEMBERS AND SPONSORS **2402**

INTERNATIONAL RESEARCH IN THE BUSINESS DISCIPLINES (US) **1636**

INTERNATIONAL REVIEW FOR THE SOCIOLOGY OF SPORT (GW/0074-7769) [11361860] **4901**

INTERNATIONAL REVIEW OF ADMINISTRATIVE SCIENCES (BE/0020-8523) [06515659] **4657**

INTERNATIONAL REVIEW OF AFRICAN AMERICAN ART, THE (US/1045-0920) [10955508] **353**

INTERNATIONAL REVIEW OF APPLIED ECONOMICS (UK/0269-2171) [15578967] **1497**

INTERNATIONAL REVIEW OF CHILDREN'S LITERATURE AND LIBRARIANSHIP (UK/0269-0500) [14402579] 1065, **3218**

INTERNATIONAL REVIEW OF COMPARATIVE PUBLIC POLICY (US/1051-4694) [21869676] **4657**

INTERNATIONAL REVIEW OF CONTEMPORARY LAW *SUSPENDED.* (BE) [09053578] **3130**

INTERNATIONAL REVIEW OF CRIMINAL POLICY (US/0074-7688) [03053641] **3166**

INTERNATIONAL REVIEW OF CRIMINAL POLICY (US) [01641031] **3166**

INTERNATIONAL REVIEW OF CYTOLOGY (US/0074-7696) [00928149] **537**

●INTERNATIONAL REVIEW OF ECONOMICS & FINANCE (US/1059-0560) [24467085] 792, **1497**

INTERNATIONAL REVIEW OF EDUCATION (NE/0020-8566) [01753693] **1754**

INTERNATIONAL REVIEW OF EXPERIMENTAL PATHOLOGY (US/0074-7718) [00988645] **3895**

●INTERNATIONAL REVIEW OF FINANCIAL ANALYSIS (US/1057-5219) [24047734] **792**

INTERNATIONAL REVIEW OF HISTORY AND POLITICAL SCIENCE *SUSPENDED.* (II/0020-8574) [01753696] **4525**

INTERNATIONAL REVIEW OF INDUSTRIAL AND ORGANIZATIONAL PSYCHOLOGY (UK/0886-1528) [12849430] **4591**

INTERNATIONAL REVIEW OF LAW AND ECONOMICS (US/0144-8188) [07617400] 3130, **1636**

INTERNATIONAL REVIEW OF MISSIONS (SZ/0020-8582) [01753698] **4966**

Alphabetical Title Index — INTERNATIONAL

INTERNATIONAL REVIEW OF MODERN SOCIOLOGY (II/0970-4841) [01775296] **5248**

INTERNATIONAL REVIEW OF NEUROBIOLOGY (US/0074-7742) [01753699] **3834, 459**

INTERNATIONAL REVIEW OF NUCLEAR PHYSICS (SI) [12178895] **4448**

INTERNATIONAL REVIEW OF PSYCHIATRY (US/1048-0021) [20837966] **3927**

INTERNATIONAL REVIEW OF PSYCHIATRY (ABINGDON, ENGLAND) (UK/0954-0261) [21969370] **3927**

●INTERNATIONAL REVIEW OF PSYCHIATRY (WASHINGTON, D.C.) (US/1066-3657) [26923212] **3927**

INTERNATIONAL REVIEW OF PSYCHO-ANALYSIS, THE (UK/0306-2643) [00999705] **4592**

INTERNATIONAL REVIEW OF RESEARCH IN MENTAL RETARDATION (US/0074-7750) [01585860] **3927**

INTERNATIONAL REVIEW OF RETAIL DISTRIBUTION CONSUMER RESEARCH (UK/0959-3969) [23263421] **955**

INTERNATIONAL REVIEW OF SOCIAL HISTORY (NE/0020-8590) [01607493] **5248**

INTERNATIONAL REVIEW OF SOCIOLOGY OF EDUCATION (AT/0726-4178) **5248**

INTERNATIONAL REVIEW OF STRATEGIC MANAGEMENT (UK/1047-7918) [20788805] **872**

INTERNATIONAL REVIEW OF STUDIES ON EMOTION (UK/1058-4994) [24314849] **4592**

INTERNATIONAL REVIEW OF THE AESTHETICS AND SOCIOLOGY OF MUSIC (CI/0351-5796) [01589350] **5248, 4123**

INTERNATIONAL REVIEW OF THE RED CROSS (SZ/0020-8604) [03527645] **5290**

INTERNATIONAL REVIEW OF VICTIMOLOGY (UK/0269-7580) [21574232] **3166**

INTERNATIONAL REVIEWS IN PHYSICAL CHEMISTRY (UK/0144-235X) [08203942] **1053**

INTERNATIONAL REVIEWS OF ERGONOMICS *CEASED.* (UK/0269-5839) [16412386] **2117**

INTERNATIONAL REVIEWS OF IMMUNOLOGY (SZ/0883-0185) [12033593] **3672**

INTERNATIONAL REVUE FUER SOZIALE SICHERHEIT (SW/0379-0282) [103790282] **1680**

INTERNATIONAL RICE RESEARCH INSTITUTE *See* INTERNATIONAL RICE RESEARCH NEWSLETTER **174**

INTERNATIONAL RICE RESEARCH INSTITUTE *See* IRRI REPORTER, THE **97**

INTERNATIONAL RICE RESEARCH INSTITUTE. INTERNATIONAL RICE RESEARCH NEWSLETTER *See* INTERNATIONAL RICE RESEARCH NOTES **175**

INTERNATIONAL RICE RESEARCH NEWSLETTER (PH/0115-0944) [03161237] **174**

●INTERNATIONAL RICE RESEARCH NOTES (PH) [28235864] **175**

INTERNATIONAL RISK CONTROL REVIEW (US/0739-389X) [09727529] **2864, 2872**

INTERNATIONAL RISK MANAGEMENT (UK) **792**

INTERNATIONAL ROAD FEDERATION *See* WORLD ROAD STATISTICS **5446**

INTERNATIONAL ROBOTICS YEARBOOK, THE (US/0739-1595) [09698468] **1213**

INTERNATIONAL ROUND TABLE *See* FOREIGN PROSPECTS **836**

INTERNATIONAL ROUND TABLE, THE (US) [08934222] **841**

INTERNATIONAL RUBBER DIGEST (UK) [05296668] **926, 5076**

INTERNATIONAL RUBBER STUDY GROUP *See* PROCEEDINGS OF THE ... MEETING OF THE INTERNATIONAL RUBBER STUDY GROUP **5077**

INTERNATIONAL RUBBER STUDY GROUP *See* PROCEEDINGS OF THE ... ASSEMBLY OF THE INTERNATIONAL RUBBER STUDY GROUP **5077**

INTERNATIONAL RUBBER STUDY GROUP *See* SUMMARY OF PROCEEDINGS OF THE ... ASSEMBLY / INTERNATIONAL RUBBER STUDY GROUP **5078**

INTERNATIONAL RUBBER STUDY GROUP. SUMMARY OF PROCEEDINGS OF THE MEETING *See* SUMMARY OF PROCEEDINGS OF THE ... ASSEMBLY / INTERNATIONAL RUBBER STUDY GROUP **5078**

INTERNATIONAL RURAL HOUSING JOURNAL, THE (VE) [07216912] **2825**

●INTERNATIONAL SADDLERY AND APPAREL JOURNAL (US/1062-7146) [25704582] **2800**

INTERNATIONAL SAMPE ELECTRONICS CONFERENCE (US/1051-1067) [21832462] **2117**

INTERNATIONAL SAMPE SYMPOSIUM AND EXHIBITION (US/0891-0138) [13842362] **2103**

INTERNATIONAL SAMPE TECHNICAL CONFERENCE SERIES (US/0892-2624) [15139423] **2103**

INTERNATIONAL SATELLITE DIRECTORY (US/1041-4541) [15080498] **1113**

INTERNATIONAL SAUDI-REPORT (UK/0265-5799) [10093801] **2505**

INTERNATIONAL SCHOOLS DIRECTORY / ECIS, THE (UK) [19287864] **1754**

INTERNATIONAL SCHOOLS JOURNAL, THE (UK) [09695915] **1754**

INTERNATIONAL SCIENCE AND TECHNOLOGY INSIGHT (US) [23670669] **5115**

INTERNATIONAL SCIENCE REVIEW SERIES (US/0074-7866) [05855263] **5115**

●INTERNATIONAL SEARCH AND RESCUE TRADE ASSOCIATION (INSARTA) (US/1065-2302) [26532178] **5290**

INTERNATIONAL SECURITIES IDENTIFICATION DIRECTORY (US/1049-6300) [21262177] **902**

INTERNATIONAL SECURITIES LENDING (UK/0964-9301) [25650709] **792**

INTERNATIONAL SECURITIES MARKET ASSOCIATION *See* MEMBERS' REGISTER **906**

INTERNATIONAL SECURITIES REGULATION (US/0149-1067) [03429327] **902**

INTERNATIONAL SECURITIES REGULATION REPORT (US/0896-3010) [16996584] **3130**

INTERNATIONAL SECURITY (US/0162-2889) [02682087] **4525**

INTERNATIONAL SECURITY DIRECTORY (UK/0074-7890) [02152922] **3166**

INTERNATIONAL SECURITY REVIEW (UK/0141-8017) [06063714] **1612, 872**

●INTERNATIONAL SEMINARS IN PAEDIATRIC GASTROENTEROLOGY AND NUTRITION (CN/1188-4525) [26714737] **3904, 3746**

INTERNATIONAL SEMIOTIC SPECTRUM (CN/0825-0456) [11108250] **5204, 4349, 2848**

INTERNATIONAL SERIES IN ANALYTICAL CHEMISTRY (US) [04031140] **1016**

INTERNATIONAL SERIES IN EXPERIMENTAL PSYCHOLOGY (UK/0364-0841) [01984475] **4592**

INTERNATIONAL SERIES IN EXPERIMENTAL SOCIAL PSYCHOLOGY (UK/0892-3175) [09106543] **4592**

INTERNATIONAL SERIES IN MODERN APPLIED MATHEMATICS AND COMPUTER SCIENCE (UK/0733-1932) [08531302] **1190, 3510**

INTERNATIONAL SERIES IN PURE AND APPLIED BIOLOGY. ZOOLOGY DIVISION (UK) [04074103] **5586**

INTERNATIONAL SERIES IN THE SCIENCE OF THE SOLID STATE (UK/0146-5589) [02987061] **5115**

INTERNATIONAL SERIES OF MONOGRAPHS ON COMPUTER SCIENCE, THE (UK) [17469197] **1190**

INTERNATIONAL SERIES OF MONOGRAPHS ON ELECTROMAGNETIC WAVES *CEASED.* (UK/0538-9992) [10512690] **2067**

INTERNATIONAL SERIES OF MONOGRAPHS ON METAL PHYSICS AND PHYSICAL METALLURGY (US/0074-8218) [01642388] **4004**

INTERNATIONAL SERIES OF MONOGRAPHS ON PHYSICS (UK) (UK/0950-5563) [10544390] **4406**

INTERNATIONAL SERIES OF MONOGRAPHS ON PURE AND APPLIED BIOLOGY. DIVISION: ZOOLOGY (US) [01644594] **459**

INTERNATIONAL SERIES ON APPLIED SYSTEMS ANALYSIS (UK/0271-7379) [06693811] **1190**

INTERNATIONAL SERIES ON SPORT SCIENCES *CEASED.* (US/0160-0559) [02254566] **3954**

INTERNATIONAL SERIES ON SYSTEMS AND CONTROL (UK/0733-1940) [08555754] **2067**

INTERNATIONAL SHIPBUILDING PROGRESS (NE/0020-868X) [01753719] **4177**

INTERNATIONAL SHIPPING REVIEW (UK/0967-1056) [l09671056] **5450**

INTERNATIONAL SKATING UNION *See* REGULATIONS / INTERNATIONAL SKATING UNION **4914**

INTERNATIONAL SKATING UNION *See* COMMUNICATION - INTERNATIONAL SKATING UNION **4891**

INTERNATIONAL SKI TRAILS (US/0092-1769) [01789248] **4873, 4901**

INTERNATIONAL SMALL BUSINESS JOURNAL (UK/0266-2426) [10680205] **684**

INTERNATIONAL SOCIAL MOVEMENT RESEARCH (US/1043-1365) [18844439] **5248**

INTERNATIONAL SOCIAL SCIENCE COUNCIL *See* INTERNATIONAL SOCIAL SCIENCE COUNCIL : [DIRECTORY] **5204**

INTERNATIONAL SOCIAL SCIENCE COUNCIL : [DIRECTORY] (FR) [11332210] **5204**

INTERNATIONAL SOCIAL SCIENCE JOURNAL (FR/0020-8701) [01645213] **5204**

INTERNATIONAL SOCIAL SCIENCE REVIEW (US/0278-2308) [07757493] **5204**

INTERNATIONAL SOCIAL SECURITY ASSOCIATION. COMMITTEE ON PROVIDENT FUNDS. MEETING *See* REPORTS AND SUMMARIES OF DISCUSSIONS / INTERNATIONAL SOCIAL SECURITY ASSOCIATION, COMMITTEE ON PROVIDENT FUNDS **2892**

INTERNATIONAL SOCIAL SECURITY ASSOCIATION. COMMITTEE ON PROVIDENT FUNDS. MEETING. REPORTS AND SUMMARY OF DISCUSSIONS *See* REPORTS AND SUMMARIES OF DISCUSSIONS / INTERNATIONAL SOCIAL SECURITY ASSOCIATION, COMMITTEE ON PROVIDENT FUNDS **2892**

INTERNATIONAL SOCIAL SECURITY ASSOCIATION. GENERAL SECRETARIAT *See* AFRICAN SOCIAL SECURITY DOCUMENTATION **5270**

INTERNATIONAL SOCIAL SECURITY ASSOCIATION. REGIONAL OFFICE FOR ASIA AND OCEANIA *See* SOCIAL SECURITY DOCUMENTATION. ASIAN SERIES **2893**

INTERNATIONAL SOCIAL SECURITY REVIEW (ENGLISH EDITION) (SZ/0020-871X) [01714005] **5290**

INTERNATIONAL SOCIAL WORK (UK/0020-8728) [01753722] **5290**

INTERNATIONAL SOCIALISM. SERIES 2 (UK/0020-8736) [02262631] **4477**

INTERNATIONAL SOCIETY FOR APPLIED CARDIOVASCULAR BIOLOGY *CEASED.* (SZ) [22741714] **3706**

INTERNATIONAL SOCIETY FOR HYBRID MICROELECTRONICS (US) **2067**

INTERNATIONAL SOCIETY FOR JAZZ RESEARCH *See* LIST OF MEMBERS - INTERNATIONAL SOCIETY FOR JAZZ RESEARCH. MITGLIEDERLISTE - INTERNATIONALE GESELLSCHAFT FUER JAZZFORSHCUNG. LISTE DE MEMBRES - SOCIETE INTERNATIONALE DE RECHERCHES SCIENTIFIQUE POUR LE JAZZ **4129**

INTERNATIONAL SOCIETY FOR MUSIC EDUCATION *See* INTERNATIONAL SOCIETY FOR MUSIC EDUCATION YEARBOOK **4123**

INTERNATIONAL SOCIETY FOR MUSIC EDUCATION YEARBOOK (UK/0172-0597) [01791873] **1754, 4123**

INTERNATIONAL SOCIETY FOR ROCK MECHANICS *See* NEWS / INTERNATIONAL SOCIETY FOR ROCK MECHANICS **1389**

INTERNATIONAL SOCIETY FOR THE HISTORY OF PHARMACY *See* VEROEFFENTLICHUNGEN DER INTERNATIONALEN GESELLSCHAFT FUER GESCHICHTE DER PHARMAZIE. NEUE FOLGE, DIE **4332**

INTERNATIONAL SOCIETY FOR THE STUDY OF XENOBIOTICS *See* ISSX PROCEEDINGS **4309**

INTERNATIONAL SOCIETY OF APPRAISERS *See* MEMBERSHIP DIRECTORY / INTERNATIONAL SOCIETY OF APPRAISERS **693**

INTERNATIONAL SOCIETY OF BASSISTS (US/0892-0532) [12568542] **4123**

INTERNATIONAL SOCIETY OF ORGANBUILDERS *See* ISO INFORMATION **4124**

INTERNATIONAL SOCIETY OF SOIL SCIENCE *See* BULLETIN OF THE INTERNATIONAL SOCIETY OF SOIL SCIENCE. BULLETIN DE L'ASSOCIATION INTERNATIONALE DE LA SCIENCE DU SOL. MITTEILUNGEN DER INTERNATIONALEN BODENKUNDLICHEN GESELLSCHAFT **165**

INTERNATIONAL SOCIETY OF SUGAR CANE TECHNOLOGISTS *See* PROCEEDINGS OF THE INTERNATIONAL SOCIETY OF SUGARCANE TECHNOLOGISTS **183**

INTERNATIONAL Alphabetical Title Index

INTERNATIONAL SOCIOLOGICAL ASSOCIATION See I S A BULLETIN (1975) **5247**

INTERNATIONAL SOCIOLOGY (UK/0268-5809) [13919989] **5248**

INTERNATIONAL SOLAR ENERGY INTELLIGENCE REPORT (US/1045-6325) [13136848] **1948**

INTERNATIONAL SOLAR ENERGY SOCIETY. UK SECTION. CONFERENCE See CONFERENCE - INTERNATIONAL SOLAR ENERGY SOCIETY UK SECTION **1936**

INTERNATIONAL SOLID FUEL BUYER'S GUIDE DIRECTORY (US/0277-870X) [06359906] **2606**

INTERNATIONAL SPECTATOR, THE (IT/0393-2729) [10571352] **4525**

INTERNATIONAL SPECTRUM (US/1050-9070) [21696052] **1190**

INTERNATIONAL SPORT SCIENCES (US/0190-9541) [04781670] **3954**

INTERNATIONAL SPORTS MAGAZINE (HU) **4901**

INTERNATIONAL STANDARD FIL-IDF (BE/0538-7094) [02252156] **841**

INTERNATIONAL STANDARDS INDEX (US) **4030**

INTERNATIONAL STATISTICAL INSTITUTE See LIST OF MEMBERS OF THE INTERNATIONAL STATISTICAL INSTITUTE **5332**

INTERNATIONAL STATISTICAL REVIEW (NE/0306-7734) [01533919] **5329**

INTERNATIONAL STEEL STATISTICS : SUMMARY TABLES (UK/0952-6803) [05337910] 4004, **4025**

INTERNATIONAL STEEL STATISTICS, UNITED KINGDOM (UK/0307-7608) [02242409] 4004, **4025**

INTERNATIONAL STEREOTYPERS AND ELECTROTYPERS UNION JOURNAL, THE (US) [09721307] **4566**

INTERNATIONAL STOCK EXCHANGE FACT SHEET (UK) [11743173] **902**

INTERNATIONAL STOCK EXCHANGE OFFICIAL YEARBOOK See STOCK EXCHANGE OFFICIAL YEARBOOK **916**

INTERNATIONAL STRUCTURAL ENGINEERING ABSTRACTS (IE/0790-5750) [13910749] **2025**

INTERNATIONAL STUDENT PARTICIPATION IN CANADIAN EDUCATION (CN/0840-7150) [19769805] **1754**

INTERNATIONAL STUDIES IN PHILOSOPHY (US/0270-5664) [02515233] **4349**

INTERNATIONAL STUDIES IN SOCIAL CHANGE (US/1055-7180) [23275039] **5249**

INTERNATIONAL STUDIES IN SOCIOLOGY AND SOCIAL ANTHROPOLOGY (NE/0074-8684) [02160215] 238, **5249**

INTERNATIONAL STUDIES IN SOCIOLOGY OF EDUCATION (UK/0962-0214) [25612969] 5249, **1754**

INTERNATIONAL STUDIES IN THE NORDIC COUNTRIES NEWSLETTER *CEASED.* (SW/0345-4975) [06657589] **4525**

INTERNATIONAL STUDIES IN THE PHILOSOPHY OF SCIENCE : I.S.P.S (UK/0269-8595) [16313452] 4349, **5116**

INTERNATIONAL STUDIES NEWSLETTER (US/0097-8965) [01799052] **4525**

INTERNATIONAL STUDIES NOTES (US/0094-7768) [01132943] **4525**

INTERNATIONAL STUDIES OF MANAGEMENT & ORGANIZATION (US/0020-8825) [01226965] **872**

INTERNATIONAL STUDIES QUARTERLY (US/0020-8833) [01941695] **4525**

INTERNATIONAL STUDIES (SAHIBABAD) (II/0020-8817) [01588728] **3131**

INTERNATIONAL SUBSCRIPTION AGENTS (US/0363-7549) [02179427] **3218**

INTERNATIONAL SUGAR JOURNAL (UK/0020-8841) [01753731] **2345**

INTERNATIONAL SUNFLOWER YEARBOOK (AT) [14254501] **2420**

INTERNATIONAL SURGERY (IT/0020-8868) [01753732] **3966**

INTERNATIONAL SWIMMING AND WATER POLO, DIVING & SYNCHRONIZED SWIMMING (HU) **4901**

INTERNATIONAL SYMPOSIUM ON FAULT-TOLERANT COMPUTING See DIGEST OF PAPERS - INTERNATIONAL SYMPOSIUM ON FAULT-TOLERANT COMPUTING (1979) **1182**

INTERNATIONAL SYMPOSIUM ON QUANTUM BIOLOGY AND QUANTUM PHARMACOLOGY. INTERNATIONAL JOURNAL OF QUANTUM CHEMISTRY. QUANTUM BIOLOGY SYMPOSIUM See INTERNATIONAL JOURNAL OF QUANTUM CHEMISTRY. QUANTUM BIOLOGY SYMPOSIUM : PROCEEDINGS OF THE INTERNATIONAL SYMPOSIUM ON THE APPLICATION OF FUNDAMENTAL THEORY TO PROBLEMS OF BIOLOGY AND PHARMACOLOGY **488**

INTERNATIONAL SYMPOSIUM ON THE PHARMACOLOGY OF THERMOREGULATION *CEASED.* (SZ/1013-9222) [I10139222] 488, 581, **4309**

INTERNATIONAL SYMPOSIUM ON THEORY AND PRACTICE IN TRANSPORT ECONOMICS : [PROCEEDINGS] / EUROPEAN CONFERENCE OF MINISTERS OF TRANSPORT (FR) [03789324] **1497**

INTERNATIONAL TAPE ASSOCIATION See NEWS DIGEST - ITA **5133**

●INTERNATIONAL TATTO ART (US/1065-643X) [26662093] **5268**

INTERNATIONAL TAX ADVISOR, THE *CEASED.* (NE/0920-315X) [14232755] **2984**

INTERNATIONAL TAX AGREEMENTS (US/0074-896X) [01642039] 3131, **4732**

INTERNATIONAL TAX AGREEMENTS / UNITED NATIONS, DEPARTMENT OF ECONOMIC AFFAIRS, FISCAL DIVISION (US) [09233278] **3131**

INTERNATIONAL TAX & BUSINESS LAWYER (US/0741-4269) [09926845] 4733, **3131**

INTERNATIONAL TAX AND PUBLIC FINANCE (NE/0927-5940) **4733**

INTERNATIONAL TAX FREE TRADER (UK) **1636**

INTERNATIONAL TAX-FREE TRADER & DUTY-FREE WORLD (UK/0306-6045) [18890807] 841, **4733**

INTERNATIONAL TAX-FREE TRADER. BUYERS GUIDE & DIRECTORY (UK/0263-5488) [I02635488] 841, **4733**

INTERNATIONAL TAX GLOSSARY (NE) [18766622] **4733**

INTERNATIONAL TAX HANDBOOK / HORWATH INTERNATIONAL (AT/1034-8506) [23747346] **4733**

INTERNATIONAL TAX REPORT, THE (UK/0300-1628) [01784691] 792, **902**

INTERNATIONAL TAX REVIEW (UK/0958-7594) [20743564] **4733**

INTERNATIONAL TAX SUMMARIES (US/8755-1551) [10345033] **4733**

INTERNATIONAL TAX SYSTEMS AND PLANNING TECHNIQUES (UK) **4733**

INTERNATIONAL TAX TREATIES SERVICE (IE) [05742468] **4733**

INTERNATIONAL TAX TREATIES SERVICE (UK) **4733**

INTERNATIONAL TEA COMMITTEE See ANNUAL BULLETIN OF STATISTICS **2362**

INTERNATIONAL TEA COMMITTEE MONTHLY STATISTICAL SUMMARY (UK/0309-0477) [07603830] 2368, **2362**

INTERNATIONAL TEA JOURNAL (NE) [14338163] **2368**

INTERNATIONAL TEAMSTER : OFFICIAL MAGAZINE, INTERNATIONAL BROTHERHOOD, TEAMSTERS, CHAUFFEURS, WAREHOUSEMEN & HELPERS OF AMERICA, THE (US/0020-8892) [02497284] **1680**

INTERNATIONAL TECHNICAL COMMUNICATIONS CONFERENCE. PROCEEDINGS See PROCEEDINGS / STC, SOCIETY FOR TECHNICAL COMMUNICATION ANNUAL CONFERENCE **5142**

INTERNATIONAL TECHNOLOGY & INNOVATION (UK) **2489**

INTERNATIONAL TECHNOLOGY DISCLOSURES (US/0742-4825) [10586915] **1305**

INTERNATIONAL TELECOMMUNICATION UNION See REPORT ON THE ACTIVITIES OF THE INTERNATIONAL TELECOMMUNICATION UNION **1163**

INTERNATIONAL TELECOMMUNICATION UNION See LIST OF PUBLICATIONS / INTERNATIONAL TELECOMMUNICATION UNION **1159**

INTERNATIONAL TELECOMMUNICATION UNION See REPORT BY THE INTERNATIONAL TELECOMMUNICATION UNION ON TELECOMMUNICATION AND THE PEACEFUL USES OF OUTER SPACE **1162**

INTERNATIONAL TELECOMMUNICATION UNION GENERAL SECRETARIAT See NOMENCLATURE DES VOIES DE TELECOMMUNICATION UTILISEES POUR LA TRANSMISSION DES TELEGRAMMES. LIST OF TELECOMMUNICATION CHANNELS USED FOR THE TRANSMISSION OF TELEGRAMS. NOMENCLATOR DE LA VIAS DE TELECOMUNICACION EMPLEADAS PARA LA TRANSMISION DEL TELEGRAMAS **1161**

INTERNATIONAL TELECOMMUNICATIONS SATELLITE ORGANIZATION See REPORT / INTELSAT **1162**

INTERNATIONAL TELEMETERING CONFERENCE See PROCEEDINGS - INTERNATIONAL TELEMETERING CONFERENCE **2076**

INTERNATIONAL TELEPHONE DIRECTORY OF THE DEAF (US/0160-7472) [03736072] 4389, **1158**

INTERNATIONAL TELEVISION & VIDEO ALMANAC (US/0895-2213) [15175861] 4371, **1133**

INTERNATIONAL TELEX (CN/0227-1176) [06634980] **1158**

INTERNATIONAL TELEX BOOK. AFRICAN-ASIAN-AUSTRALASIAN EDITION, THE (US/0099-2461) [02243411] **1158**

INTERNATIONAL TELEX BOOK. AMERICAS EDITION (US/0094-6923) [01794849] **1158**

INTERNATIONAL TELEX BOOK. EUROPEAN EDITION (US/0097-2525) [01798922] **1158**

INTERNATIONAL TELEX (DARMSTADT, GERMANY) (GW) [22643517] **1158**

INTERNATIONAL TELEX-DIRECTORY ITD (GW) [17616682] **1158**

INTERNATIONAL TELEX FAX DIRECTORY (BE) **1158**

INTERNATIONAL TENNIS (US/1063-0333) [24834441] **4901**

INTERNATIONAL TENNIS FEDERATION See RULES OF TENNIS **4916**

INTERNATIONAL TENNIS FEDERATION See RULES AND STANDING ORDERS OF THE INTERNATIONAL TENNIS FEDERATION **4915**

INTERNATIONAL TENNIS WEEKLY (US/0199-0853) [05581442] **4901**

INTERNATIONAL TEXTILE AND APPAREL ASSOCIATION See ITAA PROCEEDINGS. NATIONAL MEETING **5353**

INTERNATIONAL TEXTILE BULLETIN See INTERNATIONAL TEXTILE BULLETIN. YARN FORMING/NONWOVEN **5352**

INTERNATIONAL TEXTILE BULLETIN. DYING/PRINTING/FINISHING (SZ/1012-8417) [08547114] **5352**

INTERNATIONAL TEXTILE BULLETIN. DYING/FINISHING See INTERNATIONAL TEXTILE BULLETIN. DYING/PRINTING/FINISHING **5352**

INTERNATIONAL TEXTILE BULLETIN. FABRIC FORMING (SZ/1012-8425) [09678675] **5352**

INTERNATIONAL TEXTILE BULLETIN FABRIC FORMING AND YARN FORMING See INTERNATIONAL TEXTILE BULLETIN. YARN AND FABRIC FORMING **5352**

INTERNATIONAL TEXTILE BULLETIN. YARN AND FABRIC FORMING (SZ) **5352**

INTERNATIONAL TEXTILE BULLETIN. YARN FORMING/NONWOVEN (SZ) **5352**

INTERNATIONAL TEXTILE BULLETIN. YARN FORMING/NONWOVENS (SZ) [21000098] **5352**

INTERNATIONAL TEXTILE CALENDAR / TEXTILE INSTITUTE (UK/0263-5879) [12348624] **5352**

INTERNATIONAL TEXTILE MACHINERY SHIPMENT STATISTICS (SZ) [05253178] **5360**

INTERNATIONAL TEXTILE MANUFACTURERS FEDERATION See DIRECTORY - INTERNATIONAL TEXTILE MANUFACTURERS FEDERATION **5350**

INTERNATIONAL TEXTILE MANUFACTURING (SZ/1012-9545) [05016391] 1612, **5352**

INTERNATIONAL TEXTILES (NE/0020-8914) [01753740] **5352**

INTERNATIONAL TEXTILES INTERIOR (NE/0020-8922) [06818843] **5353**

INTERNATIONAL, THE (UK) [18298673] **792**

INTERNATIONAL THIRD WORLD STUDIES JOURNAL & REVIEW *CEASED.* (US/1041-3944) [18757653] **4526**

INTERNATIONAL THOROUGHBRED DIGEST (CN/0712-497X) [09156978] **2800**

INTERNATIONAL TIN COUNCIL See NOTES ON TIN **4014**

INTERNATIONAL TIN COUNCIL See ANNUAL REPORT - INTERNATIONAL TIN COUNCIL **3998**

INTERNATIONAL TIN STATISTICS (UK) **4004**

INTERNATIONAL TOURISM REPORTS (UK/0269-3747) [13517484] **5481**

INTERNATIONAL TRADE ALERT (BALTIMORE, MD.) (US/1055-5587) [23235890] **841**

INTERNATIONAL TRADE ALERT (NEW YORK, N.Y.) (US/0744-5660) [08372673] **841**

INTERNATIONAL TRADE AND DEVELOPMENT (II) [01753744] **841**

INTERNATIONAL TRADE & FINANCE REVIEW (US/0362-4307) [02289729] **841**

INTERNATIONAL TRADE AND SINGAPORE (SI/0377-0176) [01790742] **841**

INTERNATIONAL TRADE BUSINESS PLAN (CN/1199-1429) [30570952] **97**

INTERNATIONAL TRADE. EXPORTS (PP) [09807234] **841**

INTERNATIONAL TRADE FINANCE (UK/0968-4026) [I09684026] **684**

INTERNATIONAL TRADE FINANCE (UK) [15873253] **841**

INTERNATIONAL TRADE FORUM (SZ/0020-8957) [02447816] **841, 926**

INTERNATIONAL TRADE - GENERAL AGREEMENT ON TARIFFS AND TRADE (SZ/0589-5669) [01232931] **841**

INTERNATIONAL TRADE. IMPORTS (PP) [08677418] **841**

INTERNATIONAL TRADE, IMPORTS AND EXPORTS / STATISTICS OFFICE, MINISTRY OF FINANCE, REPUBLIC OF KIRIBATI (GB) [17223770] **841**

INTERNATIONAL TRADE IN SERVICES, AUSTRALIA (AT/1034-0505) [I10340505] **841, 730**

INTERNATIONAL TRADE JOURNAL, THE (US/0885-3908) [12629354] **841**

INTERNATIONAL TRADE NAMES DICTIONARY *See* INTERNATIONAL BRANDS AND THEIR COMPANIES **683**

INTERNATIONAL TRADE NAMES DICTIONARY. COMPANY INDEX *See* INTERNATIONAL COMPANIES AND THEIR BRANDS **683**

INTERNATIONAL TRADE REPORT (US/0890-5142) [12627764] **2401**

INTERNATIONAL TRADE REPORTER. CURRENT REPORTS (US/0748-0172) [10882565] **841**

INTERNATIONAL TRADE REPORTER. DECISIONS (1984) (US/0748-0709) [10881494] **842**

INTERNATIONAL TRADE REPORTER. EXPORT REFERENCE MANUAL (US/1043-5670) [19488497] **842**

INTERNATIONAL TRADE REPORTER. IMPORT REFERENCE MANUAL (US/1043-5662) [19488429] **842**

INTERNATIONAL TRADE REPORTER. REFERENCE FILE *See* INTERNATIONAL TRADE REPORTER. IMPORT REFERENCE MANUAL **842**

INTERNATIONAL TRADE REVIEW (II/0020-8981) [01779806] **842**

INTERNATIONAL TRADE STATISTICS YEARBOOK (US) [12857462] **842, 730**

INTERNATIONAL TRADE UNION NEWS (BE/0020-899X) [05238649] **1680**

INTERNATIONAL TRADING ENVIRONMENT : REPORT BY THE DIRECTOR-GENERAL, THE (SZ) [21615492] **842**

INTERNATIONAL TRAFFIC FORECAST. SCHEDULED AND CHARTER FREIGHT (SZ) [29394421] **24**

INTERNATIONAL TRAN SCRIPT (US/1059-1036) [24479713] **5249**

●INTERNATIONAL TRANSACTIONS IN OPERATIONAL RESEARCH : A JOURNAL OF THE INTERNATIONAL FEDERATION OF OPERATIONAL RESEARCH SOCIETIES (UK/0969-6016) [30340812] **1191**

INTERNATIONAL TRANSFER PRICING JOURNAL, THE (NE) **2984**

INTERNATIONAL TRANSPORT JOURNAL OVERSEAS DIGEST (SZ) **5384**

INTERNATIONAL TRANSPORT POLICY / UNITED STATES COUNCIL OF THE INTERNATIONAL CHAMBER OF COMMERCE INC (US) [08180495] **5384**

INTERNATIONAL TRANSPORT WORKERS FEDERATION *See* ITF JOURNAL **1681**

INTERNATIONAL TRAVEL, ADVANCE INFORMATION (CN/0705-5269) [02248898] **5481**

INTERNATIONAL TRAVEL AND HEALTH (SZ) [19321527] **4785**

INTERNATIONAL TRAVEL BRIEFINGS *See* PINKERTON EYE ON TRAVEL **5489**

INTERNATIONAL TRAVEL IMMUNIZATIONS (US/1065-1586) [26515372] **3590**

INTERNATIONAL TRAVEL NEWS (SACRAMENTO, CALIF.) (US/0191-8761) [04970648] **5481**

INTERNATIONAL TREASURY SERVICES (US/0883-4601) [12090780] **4733**

INTERNATIONAL TREE CROPS JOURNAL, THE (UK/0143-5698) [06939487] **2385**

INTERNATIONAL TRENDS IN THORACIC SURGERY **CEASED.** (US/0891-3382) [11093561] **3966**

INTERNATIONAL TROMBONE ASSOCIATION *See* INTERNATIONAL TROMBONE ASSOCIATION SERIES **4123**

INTERNATIONAL TROMBONE ASSOCIATION SERIES (US/0363-5708) [02469723] **4123**

INTERNATIONAL TROPICAL TIMBER COUNCIL *See* DECISION ADOPTED BY THE INTERNATIONAL TROPICAL TIMBER COUNCIL **2378**

INTERNATIONAL TRUMPET GUILD *See* ITG JOURNAL **4124**

INTERNATIONAL TRUMPET GUILD *See* MEMBERSHIP DIRECTORY / INTERNATIONAL TRUMPET GUILD **4130**

INTERNATIONAL TV & VIDEO GUIDE **SUSPENDED.** (UK) [09376481] **1133**

INTERNATIONAL TYPOGRAPHICAL UNION OF NORTH AMERICA *See* BULLETIN - INTERNATIONAL TYPOGRAPHICAL UNION, THE **4564**

INTERNATIONAL UFO REPORTER (US/0730-174X) [03527692] **24**

INTERNATIONAL ULTRAVIOLET EXPLORER (IUE) NASA NEWSLETTER (US/0738-2677) [05317595] **24**

INTERNATIONAL UNDERSTANDING AT SCHOOL **CEASED.** (FR) [05623219] **1897**

INTERNATIONAL UNDERSTANDING (LONDON, ENGLAND) (UK) [08122161] **1754**

INTERNATIONAL UNDERWATER SYSTEMS DESIGN (UK/0267-1085) [07000082] **1415, 2091**

INTERNATIONAL UNION FOR CONSERVATION OF NATURE AND NATURAL RESOURCES *See* IUCN OCCASIONAL PAPER **2196**

INTERNATIONAL UNION FOR CONSERVATION OF NATURE AND NATURAL RESOURCES *See* IUCN PUBLICATIONS NEW SERIES **2196**

INTERNATIONAL UNION FOR CONSERVATION OF NATURE AND NATURAL RESOURCES *See* IUCN BULLETIN **2196**

INTERNATIONAL UNION FOR CONSERVATION OF NATURE AND NATURAL RESOURCES *See* IUCN YEARBOOK **2196**

INTERNATIONAL UNION FOR CONSERVATION OF NATURE AND NATURAL RESOURCES *See* IUCN MONOGRAPH **2196**

INTERNATIONAL UNION FOR CONSERVATION OF NATURE AND NATURAL RESOURCES *See* IUCN PUBLICATIONS NEW SERIES. SUPPLEMENTARY PAPER **2196**

INTERNATIONAL UNION FOR THE SCIENTIFIC STUDY OF POPULATION *See* REPERTOIRE DES ACTIVITES SCIENTIFIQUES DES MEMBRES / UNION INTERNATIONALE POUR L'ETUDE SCIENTIFIQUE DE LA POPULATION **4559**

INTERNATIONAL UNION FOR THE SCIENTIFIC STUDY OF POPULATION *See* NEWSLETTER / INTERNATIONAL UNION FOR THE SCIENTIFIC STUDY OF POPULATION **4555**

INTERNATIONAL UNION OF BRICKLAYERS AND ALLIED CRAFTSMEN *See* JOURNAL - INTERNATIONAL UNION OF BRICKLAYERS AND ALLIED CRAFTSMEN **1681**

INTERNATIONAL UNION OF FOOD AND ALLIED WORKERS' ASSOCIATIONS *See* NEWS BULLETIN - INTERNATIONAL UNION OF FOOD & ALLIED WORKERS' ASSOCIATIONS **1694**

INTERNATIONAL UNION OF FOOD AND ALLIED WORKERS' ASSOCIATIONS. EXECUTIVE COMMITTEE *See* EXECUTIVE COMMITTEE MEETING - INTERNATIONAL UNION OF FOOD AND ALLIED WORKERS' ASSOCIATIONS. EXECUTIVE COMMITTEE **1668**

INTERNATIONAL UNION OF FORESTRY RESEARCH ORGANIZATIONS *See* IUFRO NEWS **2402**

INTERNATIONAL UNION OF GEODESY AND GEOPHYSICS *See* CHRONIQUE DE L'U.G.G.I **1404**

INTERNATIONAL UNION OF GEOLOGICAL SCIENCES *See* PUBLICATION - INTERNATIONAL UNION OF GEOLOGICAL SCIENCES **1392**

INTERNATIONAL UNION OF PHYSIOLOGICAL SCIENCES *See* WORLD DIRECTORY OF PHYSIOLOGISTS / INTERNATIONAL UNION OF PHYSIOLOGICAL SCIENCES **587**

INTERNATIONAL UNION OF PUBLIC TRANSPORT *See* INTERNATIONAL CONGRESS PROCEEDINGS **5384**

INTERNATIONAL UNION OF PURE AND APPLIED CHEMISTRY *See* COMPTES RENDUS DE LA CONFERENCE - UNION INTERNATIONALE DE CHIMIE PURE ET APPLIQUE **973**

INTERNATIONAL UNION OF RADIO SCIENCE *See* INFORMATION BULLETIN - INTERNATIONAL UNION OF RADIO SCIENCE. / BULLETIN D'INFORMATION - UNION RADIO-SCIENTIFIQUE INTERNATIONALE **1407**

INTERNATIONAL UNIVERSITY POETRY QUARTERLY, THE (US/0748-9676) [11055469] **3464**

INTERNATIONAL UNIVERSITY REPORT, THE (US) **1831**

INTERNATIONAL UROGYNECOLOGY JOURNAL (UK/0937-3462) [22304968] **3763**

INTERNATIONAL UROLOGY AND NEPHROLOGY (HU/0301-1623) [03431194] **3990**

INTERNATIONAL VAT MONITOR (NE/0925-0832) [21423200] **4733**

INTERNATIONAL VIDEO JOURNAL OF ENGINEERING RESEARCH **CEASED.** (UK/1052-9268) [22416816] **1980**

INTERNATIONAL VIDEOVUE (CN/0847-3994) [22470942] **4073**

INTERNATIONAL (VIENNA, AUSTRIA) (AU) [18540448] **4526**

INTERNATIONAL VIEWPOINT (FR/0294-2925) [12580188] **4477**

INTERNATIONAL VISITOR (US/1058-5575) [24329507] **5481**

INTERNATIONAL VOICE PROCESSING REVIEW *See* INTERNATIONAL VOICE SYSTEMS REVIEW **1158**

INTERNATIONAL VOICE SYSTEMS REVIEW (US) **1158**

INTERNATIONAL VOICEPOWER DIRECTORY & BUYERS GUIDE, THE (CN/1187-8193) [25882775] **1612**

INTERNATIONAL VOLLEY TECH (GW/0942-721X) [I0942721X] **4901**

INTERNATIONAL VOLLEYBALL REVIEW (US) [01606060] **4901**

●INTERNATIONAL WATER & IRRIGATION REVIEW (IS) [28278458] **5535, 175**

INTERNATIONAL WATER POWER & DAM CONSTRUCTION (UK/0306-400X) [02256540] **2091**

INTERNATIONAL WATER POWER & DAM CONSTRUCTION HANDBOOK (UK) [15540129] **2091**

INTERNATIONAL WATER REPORT (US/0893-8776) [04847275] **5535, 2233**

INTERNATIONAL WATER SUPPLY ASSOCIATION *See* IWSA YEAR BOOK : AN OFFICIAL PUBLICATION OF THE INTERNATIONAL WATER SUPPLY ASSOCIATION **5535**

INTERNATIONAL WATER SUPPLY ASSOCIATION. WORLD CONGRESS *See* PROCEEDINGS OF THE ... WORLD CONGRESS OF THE INTERNATIONAL WATER SUPPLY ASSOCIATION **5537**

INTERNATIONAL WEED SCIENCE SOCIETY *See* IWSS **2420**

INTERNATIONAL WHALING COMMISSION *See* REPORT OF THE INTERNATIONAL WHALING COMMISSION **5596**

INTERNATIONAL WHEAT COUNCIL *See* REVIEW OF THE WORLD WHEAT SITUATION **203**

INTERNATIONAL WHEAT COUNCIL *See* PRESS RELEASE - INTERNATIONAL WHEAT COUNCIL **203**

INTERNATIONAL WHEAT COUNCIL *See* SECRETARIAT PAPER - INTERNATIONAL WHEAT COUNCIL **203**

INTERNATIONAL WHEAT COUNCIL *See* WHEAT MARKET REPORT. PMR **204**

INTERNATIONAL WHEAT COUNCIL *See* REPORT FOR THE FISCAL YEAR **203**

INTERNATIONAL WHEAT COUNCIL. REPORT FOR THE CROP YEAR *See* REPORT FOR THE FISCAL YEAR **203**

INTERNATIONAL WHO'S WHO (US) **792, 684**

INTERNATIONAL WHO'S WHO IN ASIAN STUDIES (HK) [02482195] **2654, 433**

INTERNATIONAL WHO'S WHO IN COMMUNITY SERVICE (UK/0306-3488) [01014209] **4657, 433**

INTERNATIONAL WHO'S WHO IN MUSIC AND MUSICIANS' DIRECTORY (UK/0307-2894) [02247063] **4123, 433**

●INTERNATIONAL WHO'S WHO IN POETRY AND POETS' ENCYCLOPAEDIA (UK) [29482627] **3464**

INTERNATIONAL WHO'S WHO OF THE ARAB WORLD, THE (UK) [04362706] **433**

INTERNATIONAL Alphabetical Title Index

●INTERNATIONAL WHO'S WHO OF WOMEN, THE (UK/0965-3775) [27417944] **5559**

INTERNATIONAL WHO'S WHO, THE (UK/0074-9613) [01390904] **433**

INTERNATIONAL WILDLIFE (US/0020-9112) [01112911] **2195**

INTERNATIONAL WINE MARKET: IMPACT DATABANK REPORT, THE (US/1061-9305) [25494971] **2368**

INTERNATIONAL WOMEN'S NEWS JOURNAL OF THE INTERNATIONAL ALLIANCE OF WOMEN, INCORPORATING LE DROIT DES FEMMES (UK/0020-9120) [05705574] **5559**

INTERNATIONAL WORK GROUP FOR INDIGENOUS AFFAIRS *See* IWGIA DOCUMENTS **238**

INTERNATIONAL WORKCAMP DIRECTORY / VOLUNTEERS FOR PEACE (US/0896-565X) [12363530] **5290**

INTERNATIONAL WORKER (UK) **1680**

INTERNATIONAL WORKING PAPERS ON DANCE (UK) [29249699] **1313**

INTERNATIONAL WORKSHOP ON DIABETES AND CAMPING (US/0161-7524) [03995364] **3731**

INTERNATIONAL X-RAY EMISSION SPECTROMETRY (UK/0144-6789) [07361985] **1016**

INTERNATIONAL YEAR BOOK AND STATESMEN'S WHO'S WHO, THE (US/0074-9621) [01391134] **4478**, **433**

INTERNATIONAL YEAR BOOK COVERING THE YEAR... (US) [23366096] **1926**

INTERNATIONAL YEARBOOK (US) [01780691] **4177**

INTERNATIONAL YEARBOOK OF EDUCATION (FR) [01753766] **1754**

INTERNATIONAL YEARBOOK OF EDUCATIONAL AND TRAINING TECHNOLOGY (UK) [20156369] **1897**

INTERNATIONAL YEARBOOK OF FOREIGN POLICY ANALYSIS, THE (US/0095-1471) [01790818] **4526**

INTERNATIONAL YEARBOOK OF LAW, COMPUTERS AND TECHNOLOGY (UK/0965-528X) 1191, 2984, **5116**

●INTERNATIONAL YEARBOOK OF LAW, COMPUTERS, AND TECHNOLOGY (UK/0965-528X) [28883599] 1191, **2984**

INTERNATIONAL YEARBOOK OF NEPHROLOGY (US/0921-9862) [18476688] **3990**

●INTERNATIONAL YEARBOOK OF ORAL HISTORY AND LIFE STORIES (US) [27841381] **2620**

INTERNATIONAL YOGA GUIDE (US/0277-092X) [07495418] 4349, **2598**

INTERNATIONAL YOUTH HOSTELS HANDBOOK (UK) **5481**

INTERNATIONAL ZOO-NEWS (UK/0020-9155) [03527773] **5586**

INTERNATIONAL ZOO YEARBOOK (UK/0074-9664) [01420355] **5586**

INTERNATIONALE AGRAR-INDUSTRIE-ZEITSCHRIFT *CEASED.* (RU/0863-1840) [21487331] **97**

INTERNATIONALE BERG- UND SEILBAHN-RUNDSCHAU *See* ISR, INTERNATIONLE BERG- UND SEILBAHNRUNDSCHAU. INTERNATIONAL AERIAL TRAMWAY REVIEW **2117**

INTERNATIONALE BIBLIOGRAPHIE DER REPRINTS. INTERNATIONAL BIBLIOGRAPHY OF REPRINTS (US) [05631715] **417**

INTERNATIONALE BIBLIOGRAPHIE DER REZENSIONEN WISSENSCHAFTLICHER LITERATUR (GW/0020-918X) [12045575] 3344, **3357**

INTERNATIONALE BIBLIOGRAPHIE DER ZEITSCHRIFTENLITERATUR AUS ALLEN GEBIETEN DES WISSENS (GW) [11994937] 2848, 3344, **3357**

INTERNATIONALE BIBLIOTHEK FUER ALLGEMEINE LINGUISTIK (GW/0579-3998) [01753770] **3288**

INTERNATIONALE, DIE (GW) [03022556] **4542**

INTERNATIONALE FILMFESTSPIELE BERLIN *See* DOKUMENTATION. WETTBEWERB, PANORAMA, KINDERFILMFEST / INTERNATIONALE FILMFESTSPIELE BERLIN **4068**

INTERNATIONALE GESELLSCHAFT FUER GETREIDEWISSENSCHAFT UND -TECHNOLOGIE (AU) [19656426] **97**

INTERNATIONALE JAHRESBIBLIOGRAPHIE DER FESTSCHRIFTEN : IJBF (GW) [09299653] **417**

INTERNATIONALE JAHRESBIBLIOGRAPHIE DER KONGRESSBERICHTE (GW/0933-1905) [18028993] **417**

INTERNATIONALE JAHRESBIBLIOGRAPHIE SUDWESTASIEN (GW) [19117659] **417**

INTERNATIONALE JAHRESTAGUNG / FRAUNHOFER-INSTITUT FUER TREIB-UND EXPLOSIVSTOFFE (GW/0722-4087) [08479065] **2013**

INTERNATIONALE KATHOLISCHE ZEITSCHRIFT (GW/0341-8693) [01785469] **5030**

INTERNATIONALE KIRCHLICHE ZEITSCHRIFT (SZ/0020-9252) [01773897] **4966**

INTERNATIONALE MATHEMATISCHE NACHRICHTEN (AU) [01753774] **3510**

INTERNATIONALE REVUE DER GESAMTEN HYDROBIOLOGIE (GW/0020-9309) [01753778] **555**

INTERNATIONALE SAMENWERKING *See* ASPECTEN VAN INTERNATIONALE SAMENWERKING. MAANDBLAD VAN HET DIRECTORAAT-GENERAAL INTERNATIONALE SAMENWERKING VAN HET MINISTERIE VAN BUITENLANDSE ZAKEN **2907**

INTERNATIONALE SCHULBUCHFORSCHUNG (GW/0172-8237) [10552994] **1754**

INTERNATIONALE SPECTATOR (NE/0020-9317) [02146475] **4478**

INTERNATIONALE STIFTUNG MOZARTEUM SALZBURG *See* MITTEILUNGEN DER INTERNATIONALEN STIFTUNG MOZARTEUM **4131**

INTERNATIONALE TRANSPORT ZEITSCHRIFT (SZ/0020-9341) **5384**

INTERNATIONALE VOLKSKUNDLICHE BIBLIOGRAPHIE (GW) [08532141] **2325**

INTERNATIONALE ZEITSCHRIFT FUER PHILOSOPHIE (GW/0942-3028) [I09423028] **4349**

INTERNATIONALE ZEITSCHRIFTENSCHAU FUER BIBELWISSENSCHAFT UND GRENZGEBIETE (GW/0074-9745) [01753790] 5017, **5013**

INTERNATIONALER ELEKTRONIK-ARBEITSKREIS *See* MIKROELEKTRONIK **2072**

INTERNATIONALER HOLZMARKT (AU/0020-9422) [03755770] 4234, **2402**

INTERNATIONALES AFRIKA-FORUM (GW/0020-9430) [01799059] **4526**

INTERNATIONALES ARCHIV FUER SOZIALGESCHICHTE DER DEUTSCHEN LITERATUR (GW/0340-4528) [02592741] **3397**

INTERNATIONALES ASIEN FORUM (GW/0020-9449) [01140997] **5204**

INTERNATIONALES BODENSEE JAHRBUCH DER SPORTSCHIFFAHRT (GW) [03386290] **593**

INTERNATIONALES JAHRBUCH DER ERWACHSENENBILDUNG (GW/0074-9818) [I00749818] **1801**

INTERNATIONALES JAHRBUCH FUER GESCHICHTS- UND GEOGRAPHIE-UNTERRICH (GW/0074-9834) [01753796] **2620**

INTERNATIONALES KUNST-ADRESSBUCH (GW/0539-1849) [01639184] **334**

INTERNATIONALES RECHT UND DIPLOMATIE *CEASED.* (GW/0020-9503) [01605011] 3131, **4526**

INTERNATIONALES SAUNA-ARCHIV (GW/0178-7764) [11875976] **2599**

INTERNATIONALES VERKEHRSWESEN (GW/0020-9511) [10059472] **5384**

INTERNATIONALES VERZEICHNIS DER WIRTSCHAFTSVERBANDE (GW/0302-2196) [01793099] **842**

INTERNATIONALES WAFFEN-MAGAZIN (SZ/1017-5547) [10175547] 4901, **4046**

INTERNATIONALES WISSENSCHAFTLICHES KOLLOQUIUM (GW/0374-3365) [06369686] **5116**

INTERNATIONELLA STUDIER (SW/0020-952X) [02393934] **4526**

INTERNET BUSINESS JOURNAL, THE (CN/1192-8646) [28195339] **1242**

INTERNET BUSINESS REPORT (US) 684, **1191**

●INTERNET LETTER, THE (US/1070-9851) [28528669] **1242**

●INTERNET RESEARCH (US/1066-2243) [26904938] **1242**

●INTERNET WORLD (US) [26273275] **1242**

●INTERNET WORLD'S ON INTERNET (US/1066-9973) [27117990] **1242**

INTERNETWORKING (CHICHESTER, ENGLAND) (UK/1049-8915) [21344113] **1242**

INTERNI (IT/0020-9538) [08937074] **2901**

INTERNI ANNUAL (IT) [07806171] 2906, **1612**

INTERNIST (BERLIN), DER (GW/0020-9554) [01753799] **3798**

INTERNIST (SAN FRANCISCO, CALIF.), THE (US/0020-9546) [03527625] **3590**

INTERNISTISCHE PRAXIS (GW/0020-9570) [06380363] **3590**

INTERNISTISCHE WELT (GW/0344-4201) [04554253] **3798**

INTERNIST'S CLINICAL UPDATE *CEASED.* (US/0896-5021) [17187972] **3590**

INTERNSHIP OPPORTUNITIES AT THE SMITHSONIAN INSTITUTION (US) [21435800] **4205**

INTERNSHIPS (US/0272-5460) [06867434] **4205**

INTEROPERABILITY (US) [25105844] **1242**

INTERP CENTRAL CLEARINGHOUSE NEWSLETTER *CEASED.* (US/0890-1538) [08995571] **4205**

●INTERPERSONAL COMPUTING AND TECHNOLOGY (US/1064-4326) [26325657] **1191**

INTERPERSONAL DEVELOPMENT *SUSPENDED.* (SZ/0373-3793) [00997495] **3927**

●INTERPHARMACY FORUM (US/1065-9412) [26813065] **4309**

INTERPLAN (CN/0710-2291) [11422246] **1981**

INTERPLASTICS (MILANO) (IT/0392-3800) [08433570] **4455**

INTERPRES (IT) [06795966] **3397**

●INTERPRET YOUR DREAMS (US/1060-7978) [25064002] **4592**

INTERPRETACION ECONOMICA : ORGANO DE DIFUSION DE LA SOCIACION DE ECONOMISTAS ARGENTINOS (AG) [04914784] **1568**

INTERPRETATION BULLETIN / ALBERTA TREASURY, CORPORATE TAX ADMINISTRATION (CN/0826-9505) [10154090] **3100**

INTERPRETATION DE LA MUSIQUE FRANCAISE (SZ) **4123**

INTERPRETATION NEWSLETTER (UK/0964-6337) [I09646337] **2692**

INTERPRETATION REVENU QUEBEC (CN/0822-3726) [I08223726] **4733**

INTERPRETATION (RICHMOND) (US/0020-9643) [01715998] **4966**

INTERPRETATION (THE HAGUE) (US/0020-9635) [02381107] **4478**

INTERPRETE ALUMNOS, EL (US/0740-0071) [09873800] **1102**

INTERPRETE, L' (IT) [09002628] **3288**

INTERPRETE, L' (SZ/0047-1291) [03472807] **3288**

INTERPRETER (DURHAM, N.C.), THE (US/0020-9651) [07911025] **2885**

INTERPRETER (EVANSTON, ILL.), THE (US/0020-9678) [01776458] **5061**

INTERPRETER RELEASES (US) [05452978] 1919, **2984**

INTERPRETIVE PERSPECTIVES ON EDUCATION AND POLICY (US) **1754**

INTERPROVINCIAL COMPARISONS OF UNIVERSITY FINANCING (CN/0820-7763) [09603989] **1831**

INTERRACE (SCHENECTADY, N.Y.) (US/1047-5370) [20709204] 2281, **2264**

INTERRACIAL BOOKS FOR CHILDREN BULLETIN (US/0146-5562) [02972338] 2264, **1065**

INTERRACIAL DIGEST (US) [09770881] **2264**

INTERRELIGIOUS FOUNDATION FOR COMMUNITY ORGANIZATION (U.S.) *See* IFCO NEWS **4964**

INTERSCAMBIO (IT/0394-087X) [I0394087X] **1497**

INTERSCHOLASTIC ATHLETIC ADMINISTRATION (US/0097-871X) [03165587] **4901**

INTERSCIENCE MONOGRAPHS AND TEXTS IN PHYSICS AND ASTRONOMY (US/0074-9931) [02277438] 396, **4406**

INTERSCIENCE TRACTS ON PHYSICS AND ASTRONOMY *CEASED.* (US/0074-9958) [01695468] 396, **4406**

INTERSEARCH (US/0163-0997) [04698651] **4478**

INTERSECT (JA/0910-4607) [20479682] 5268, **4349**

INTERSECTIONS (US/0095-6945) [01798426] **5249**

INTERSERVICE JOURNAL OF MILITARY & POLICE SCIENCE AND THE INTELLIGENCE PROFESSION, THE (US/0734-3264) [08722263] **4046**

INTERSEZIONI (IT) [08984532] **2848**

INTERSPACE FLEET (UK/0269-3615) [I02693615] **1114**

INTERSTATE *CEASED.* (US/0363-9991) [05132105] 353, **3397**

INTERSTATE ACCOMODATION DIRECTORY (AT) [07000997] **2807**

Alphabetical Title Index — INVENTORY

INTERSTATE COMMERCE COMMISSION'S REPORT TO THE PRESIDENT AND THE CONGRESS. EFFECTIVENESS OF THE ACT. AMTRAK (US/0147-2178) [03117031] **5432**

INTERSTATE INFORMATION REPORT (US/0884-8394) [06262573] **5384**, **2984**

INTERSTATE OIL & GAS COMPACT & COMMITTEE BULLETIN, THE (US/1046-2333) [18110264] **4261**

INTERSTATE OIL AND GAS COMPACT COMMISSION See DIRECTORY, INTERSTATE OIL AND GAS COMPACT COMMISSION AND STATE OIL & GAS AGENCIES **4254**

INTERSTATE OIL COMPACT COMMISSION See DIRECTORY - INTERSTATE OIL COMPACT COMMISSION **4254**

INTERSTATE OIL COMPACT COMMISSION. DIRECTORY See DIRECTORY, INTERSTATE OIL AND GAS COMPACT COMMISSION AND STATE OIL & GAS AGENCIES **4254**

INTERSTATE OIL COMPACT COMMISSION. DIRECTORY OF THE INTERSTATE OIL COMPACT COMMISSION AND OIL AND GAS AGENCIES See DIRECTORY - INTERSTATE OIL COMPACT COMMISSION **4254**

INTERSTATE PIPELINE RATES ON CRUDE PETROLEUM OIL (US) **4261**

INTERSTATE PORT HANDBOOK (US/0074-9982) [01753813] **5450**

INTERSTATE RATES FOR GASOLINE AND PETROLEUM PRODUCTS (US) **4261**

INTERSTATE SECURITIES TELEPHONE AND ELECTRIC UTILITIES ATLAS, THE (US/1046-8544) [11145684] **4761**

INTERSTATE TAX REPORT (US/0731-5651) [08203317] **4733**

INTERSTUDY COMPETITIVE EDGE, THE (US/1058-1294) [24233742] **4785**

INTERSTUDY QUALITY EDGE, THE (US/1056-9618) [23903901] **3590**

INTERTAX (NE/0165-2826) [01681423] **4733**

● INTERTEC RECREATIONAL VEHICLE TRADE-IN GUIDE (US/1064-3079) [25163028] **5481**

INTERUNIVERSITAIR REACTOR INSTITUUT See JAARVERSLAG / UNIVERSITAIR REACTOR INSTITUUT **4448**

INTERUNIVERSITY CENTRE FOR EUROPEAN STUDIES See MISE A JOUR DE LA LISTE DES MEMBRES DU CIEE AU ... **2699**

INTERVAL (SAN DIEGO, CALIF.) SUSPENDED. (US/0276-3052) [04943383] **4123**

INTERVALLE (GW) [06457371] **4123**

INTERVENANT (CN/0823-213X) [10634835] **1345**

INTERVENCOES E DESINTERVENCOES DO ESTADO EM EMPRESAS / MINISTERIO DO TRABALHO (PO) [07643611] **3150**

INTERVENOR : NEWSLETTER OF THE CANADIAN ENVIRONMENTAL LAW ASSOCIATION (CN/0820-3458) [16641909] **3113**

INTERVENTION (CN/0047-1321) [02044282] **5290**

INTERVENTION IN SCHOOL AND CLINIC (US/1053-4512) [22424337] **1897**, **1880**

INTERVENTION (QUEBEC) (CN/0705-1972) [03991853] **2535**

● INTERVENTIONAL CARDIOLOGY NEWSLETTER (US/1063-4282) [26025147] **3706**

● INTERVENTIONAL CARDIOVASCULAR NEWSLETTER (US) **3706**

INTERVENTIONS ECONOMIQUES POUR UNE ALTERNATIVE SOCIALE (CN/0715-3570) [09344808] **1497**

INTERVENTIONS SONORES (CN/1181-7739) [24256971] **1880**, **4124**

INTERVIEW (AT/0159-625X) [I0159625X] **1754**

INTERVIEW (NEW YORK, N.Y. 1977) (US/0149-8932) [03596402] **2535**

INTERVIROLOGY (SZ/0300-5526) [01788734] **564**

INTERVISTA MEDICA (IT) **3590**

INTERWEAVE See HANDWOVEN **5351**

INTERZONE (UK/0264-3596) [11921760] **3397**

INTESTINAL FUNCTION (UK/0261-4995) [I02614995] **3746**

INTI (PROVIDENCE, R.I.) (US/0732-6750) [03863759] **3344**, **3397**

INTIMACY (US/0747-380X) [10769299] **5074**

INTIMATE APPAREL See BODY FASHIONS/INTIMATE APPAREL **1082**

INTIMATE FASHION NEWS (US/1061-5792) [09348067] **1085**

INTIMITA (IT) **5559**

INTIMO PIU MARE (IT) **1085**

INTISARI (IO/0535-4900) [01795121] **2505**

● INTOUCH (KNOXVILLE, TENN.) (US/1059-8081) [24773203] **1325**

INTOWNER, THE (US/0887-9400) [13435461] **5647**

INTRA-EUROPEAN COUNTRY-TO-COUNTRY TRAFFIC (BE) [11196654] **24**

● INTRACOASTAL WATERWAY FESTIVAL AND SERVICES DIRECTORY, THE (US) [25312487] **593**

INTRAMURALE GEZONDHEIDSZORG / CENTRAAL BUREAU VOOR DE STATISTIK, HOOFDAFDELING GEZINDHEIDSSTATISTIEKEN (NE/0168-4604) [10832724] **4785**

INTRAMUROS (FR/0769-3710) [I07693710] **301**

INTRASTATE PIPELINE RATES ON CRUDE PETROLEUM OIL (US) **4261**

INTRASTATE RATES FOR CRUDE PETROLEUM OIL (US) **4261**

INTRASTATE RATES FOR GASOLINE AND PETROLEUM PRODUCTS (US) **4261**

INTREPID (US/0020-9864) [01753815] **3397**

INTRINSIC (CN/0704-7290) [04040015] **3464**

NTRO TO COMPUTERIZED TAX PLANNING WITH AATAXCOM TO ACCOMPANY WEST'S FEDERAL TAXATION [COMPUTER FILE] (US) [17699991] **1191**, **4733**

INTRODUCING BUFFALO TO YOU (US/0091-3200) [01786580] **2535**

INTRODUCING COLUMBUS TO YOU (US/0091-3197) [01786581] **2535**

INTRODUCING COMPUTERS (US/1051-9246) [19651136] **1260**

INTRODUCING SYRACUSE TO YOU (US/0091-2980) [01786583] **2535**

INTRODUCTION TO AFRICAN CULTURE (FR) [08496286] **5268**

INTRODUCTION TO FEDERAL INCOME TAXATION IN CANADA (CN/0821-5340) [09688371] **4733**

● INTRODUCTION TO FEDERAL INCOME TAXES, AN (US/1070-8502) [28479209] **4733**

INTRODUCTION TO FEDERAL TAXATION (ENGLEWOOD CLIFFS, N.J.) (US/0731-7905) [07825112] **4733**

INTRODUCTION TO QUALIFIED PENSION AND PROFIT-SHARING PLANS (US/8756-9396) [07313638] **1680**

INTRODUCTION TO SYSTEMATIC GEOMORPHOLOGY, AN CEASED. (US/0074-9990) [06802851] **1356**

INTRODUCTORY MATHEMATICS FOR SCIENTISTS AND ENGINEERS (UK/0275-259X) [07116326] **3510**

INTRODUKTSIIA I AKKLIMATIZATSIIA RASTENII (KIEV, UKRAINE) (UN/0579-4005) [11584748] **2420**

INTRODUKTSIIA I EKOLOGIIA RASTENII (TK) [02741200] **514**

INTRODUKTSIIA TA AKLIMATYZATSIIA ROSLIN NA UKRAINI (UN/0579-4005) [03550217] **97**

INTV JOURNAL (US/0899-787X) [18216980] **1133**

INUIT (GL/0108-6898) [10768464] **2739**

INUIT ART ENTHUSIASTS NEWSLETTER, THE CEASED. (CN/0824-0639) [11825411] **353**

INUIT ART QUARTERLY (CN/0831-6708) [13712412] **353**

INUIT CULTURAL INSTITUTE See NEWSLETTER - INUIT CULTURAL INSTITUTE **2749**

INUKTITUT (ENGLISH AND INUIT EDITION) (CN/0020-9872) [04146119] **2264**

INUMMARIT (ESKIMO EDITION) (CN/0382-8085) [03193490] **2264**

INVANDRARNAS LEVNADSFORHALLANDEN (SW) [04187838] **1680**

INVANDRARTIDNINGEN PA LATT SVENSKA (SW/0345-4991) [I03454991] **1919**

INVASION & METASTASIS (SW/0251-1789) [08379001] **581**, **537**

INVATAMINTUL LICEAL SI TEHNIC PROFESIONAL (RM) [02244046] **5116**

INVENT! (WOODLAND HILLS, CALIF.) (US/1040-3485) [18390495] **1305**

INVENTAIRE AGRICOLE REGIONAL (FR) [01794909] **97**

INVENTAIRE DE LA RECHERCHE SUBVENTIONNEE ET COMMANDITEE (CN/0709-3896) [05695142] **1831**

INVENTAIRE DES INSECTES ET DES MALADIES DES ARBRES, AU QUEBEC (CN) [03645318] **2385**

INVENTAIRE DES MOYENS DE FORMATION DEPENDANT DES MINISTERES TECHNIQUES (IV) [05001248] **1913**

INVENTAIRE DES THESES DE DOCTORAT SOUTENUES DEVANT LES UNIVERSITES FRANCAISES. DROIT, SCIENCES ECONOMIQUES, SCIENCES DE GESTION, LETTRES, SCIENCES HUMAINES, THEOLOGIES / MINISTERE DE L'EDUCATION NATIONALE, DIRECTION GENERALE DES ENSEIGNEMENTS SUPERIEURS ET DE LA RECHERCHE (FR) [09657634] **417**

INVENTARE NICHTSTAATLICHER ARCHIVE (GW) [02199196] **2481**

INVENTARI DEI MANOSCRITTI DELLE BIBLIOTECHE D'ITALIA (IT/0075-0026) [01696610] **3218**

INVENTARIA ARCHAEOLOGICA. DENMARK (GW/0075-0050) [06715354] **270**

INVENTARIA ARCHAEOLOGICA. JUGOSLAVIJA (GW/0075-0115) [06723294] **270**

INVENTARISASI AKOMODASI PROPINSI MALUKU (IO) [03700138] **2807**, **5071**

INVENTARISATIE SPORTACCOMMODATIES (NE) [02980967] **4901**

INVENTING AND PATENTING SOURCEBOOK (US/1044-4742) [19795190] **1305**

INVENTING TOMORROW'S SCHOOLS (US/1070-6828) [28454239] **1754**

INVENTIONES MATHEMATICAE (GW/0020-9910) [01753817] **3510**

INVENTORS DIGEST (CN/0706-6902) [04955185] **1305**

INVENTORS' DIGEST (COLORADO SPRINGS, COLO.) (US/0883-9859) [12279456] **5116**

INVENTORS' VOICE (US/0748-7851) [11010391] **5116**

INVENTORY AND CRUISING NEWSLETTER / JOHN BELL & ASSOCIATES (US/0898-9737) [17968142] **2385**

INVENTORY OF ACADEMIC DEGREE PROGRAMS IN SOUTH CAROLINA, AN (US) [04728873] **1831**

INVENTORY OF AGRICULTURAL RESEARCH (US/0360-5841) [04791832] **97**

INVENTORY OF AMERICAN INTERMODAL EQUIPMENT (US/0097-9341) [01794033] **5450**

INVENTORY OF DEGREE PROGRAMS IN CONNECTICUT'S COLLEGES AND UNIVERSITIES, AN (US/0098-5287) [02241985] **1831**

INVENTORY OF DEGREE PROGRAMS/OPTIONS OFFERED BY N.J. INSTITUTIONS OF HIGHER LEARNING See INVENTORY OF PROGRAM OFFERINGS AT NEW JERSEY INSTITUTIONS OF HIGHER EDUCATION **1831**

INVENTORY OF HEALTH CARE FACILITY SURVEYORS, UNITED STATES (US/0190-3500) [04634736] **3590**

INVENTORY OF HOSPITAL FACILITIES (US) [06324441] **3786**

INVENTORY OF INTERSTATE CARRIER WATER SUPPLY SYSTEMS BY STATES AND ENVIRONMENTAL PROTECTION AGENCY REGIONS (US/0094-0569) [01793153] **5535**

INVENTORY OF MARRIAGE AND FAMILY LITERATURE (US/0094-7814) [02163984] **2281**

INVENTORY OF MUSIC ICONOGRAPHY (US/0889-6607) [13987957] **4124**

INVENTORY OF NONPURCHASED FOREIGN CURRENCIES (US/0093-1225) [02241091] **792**

INVENTORY OF PHYSICAL FACILITIES OF ONTARIO UNIVERSITIES / PREPARED BY THE RESEARCH DIVISION OF THE COUNCIL OF ONTARIO UNIVERSITIES (CN/0711-3250) [08465865] **1831**

INVENTORY OF POPULATION PROJECTS IN DEVELOPING COUNTRIES AROUND THE WORLD (US/0363-5155) [02475358] **589**, **4554**

INVENTORY OF POWER PLANTS IN THE UNITED STATES (US/0272-3743) [06732336] **2067**, **2005**

● INVENTORY OF PROGRAM OFFERINGS AT NEW JERSEY INSTITUTIONS OF HIGHER EDUCATION (US) [25002084] **1831**

INVENTORY OF REPORTS / OEA (US) [09014123] **842**

INVENTORY OF THE COLLECTIONS (US/0095-2893) [01457795] **4089**

INVENTORY OF WASTE WATER PRODUCTION AND WASTE WATER RECLAMATION PRACTICES IN CALIFORNIA (US/0092-9158) [01791475] **5535**, **2233**

INVENTORY — Alphabetical Title Index

INVENTORY REDUCTION REPORT (US/1049-9849) [21360101] **872**

INVENTORY SERIES - STATE OF NEVADA, DEPARTMENT OF CONSERVATION AND NATURAL RESOURCES (US/0548-3549) [01473458] **2195**

INVERELL TIMES, THE (AT) [11616840] **5777**

INVERMAY TECHNICAL REPORT (NZ/0113-051X) [I0113051X] **5116**

INVERSE PROBLEMS (UK/0266-5611) [11886741] **3510**

INVERSION Y DESARROLLO (BO) [25363840] **1497**

INVERT MAGAZINE (UK/0957-3828) **429**

INVERTEBRATE BIOLOGY (US) **459**

INVERTEBRATE NEUROBIOLOGY (UK/0261-4952) [I02614952] 488, **3590**

INVERTEBRATE REPRODUCTION & DEVELOPMENT (IS/0792-4259) [19737364] **5586**

INVERTEBRATE TAXONOMY (AT/0818-0164) [15160215] **5587**

INVEST CANADA (TORONTO, ONT. : 1984) (CN/0828-5721) [11919023] **902**

INVEST IN HUNGARY (HU/0239-1929) [I02391929] **902**

INVEST/NET INSIDE *See* CDA/INVESTNET INSIDERS' CHRONICLE **894**

INVEST YOURSELF (US/0148-6802) [03354467] **5290**

INVESTAMERICA (SAN FRANCISCO, CALIF.) (US/1040-2934) [18367298] **902**

INVESTECH MUTUAL FUND ADVISOR (US/0896-4165) [17160611] **902**

INVESTEXT (US) **684**

INVESTICIJE SR SRBIJE / SOCIJALISTICKA REPUBLIKA SRBIJA, REPUBLICKI ZAVOD ZA STATISTIKU (CI) [08286397] 1497, **1534**

INVESTIGACAO OPERACIONAL (PO) **1981**

INVESTIGACION AGRARIA. ECONOMIA (SP/0213-635X) [16254665] **97**

INVESTIGACION AGRARIA. PRODUCCION Y PROTECCION VEGETALES (SP/0213-5000) [15155183] **175**

INVESTIGACION AGRARIA. PRODUCCION Y SANIDAD ANIMALES (SP/0213-5205) [16929141] **213**

INVESTIGACION BIBLIOTECOLOGICA (MX/0187-358X) [19571923] **3218**

INVESTIGACION CLINICA (VE/0535-5133) [01587878] **3590**

INVESTIGACION E INFORMACION TEXTIL Y DE TENSIOACTIVOS *CEASED.* (SP/0302-5268) [04696351] **5353**

INVESTIGACION MEDICA INTERNACIONAL (MX/0377-0206) [01919982] **3590**

INVESTIGACION Y CIENCIA (SP/0210-136X) [I0210136X] **5116**

INVESTIGACION Y CLINICA LASER : ORGANO DEL GRUPO DE EXPERIMENTACION E INVESTIGACION CLINICA LASER (GRUPO LASER-ESPANA) (SP/0212-6605) [25865125] **3590**

INVESTIGACION Y DOCENCIA / UNIVERSIDAD NACIONAL DE ROSARIO, FACULTAD DE DERECHO, CONSEJO ASESOR DE INVESTIGACIONES, CENTRO DE INVESTIGACIONES DE FILOSOFIA JURIDICA Y FILOSOFIA SOCIAL (AG) [19462067] **2984**

INVESTIGACION Y EDUCACION EN ENFERMERIA : REVISTA DE LA FACULTAD DE ENFERMERIA, UNIVERSIDAD DE ANTIOQUIA (CK/0120-5307) [23968229] **3857**

INVESTIGACION Y TECNICA DEL PAPEL (SP/0368-0789) [11844329] **4234**

INVESTIGACIONES ECONOMICAS (SP/0210-1521) [04877920] **1568**

INVESTIGACIONES GEOGRAFICAS : BOLETIN DEL INSTITUTO DE GEOGRAFIA (MX/0188-4611) [24583255] **2566**

INVESTIGACIONES HISTORICAS (UNIVERSIDAD DE VALLADOLID. DEPARTAMENTO DO HISTORIA MODERNA) (SP) [06780501] **2692**

INVESTIGACIONES MARINAS (CL) [04937940] 1450, **2306**

INVESTIGACIONES MARINAS CICIMAR (MX/0186-5102) [15469841] **555**

INVESTIGACIONES OCEANOLOGICAS CHILENAS (CL) [03573112] **1450**

INVESTIGACIONES PSICOLOGICAS (MADRID, SPAIN) (SP) [19022297] **4592**

INVESTIGACIONES Y ENSAYOS (AG/0539-242X) [02158194] **2739**

INVESTIGATE NEWSLETTER (US/0276-7414) [07405914] **902**

INVESTIGATING (AT/0815-9602) [I08159602] **5116**

INVESTIGATION OF AIR POLLUTION; NATIONAL SURVEY, SMOKE AND SULPHUR DIOXIDE, THE (UK) [05351866] **2233**

INVESTIGATION OF FLOODS IN HAWAII (US/0094-9140) [05712338] **1415**

INVESTIGATION OF FLOODS IN HAWAII, WITH SELECTED DATA ON MAGNITUDE AND FREQUENCY *See* INVESTIGATION OF FLOODS IN HAWAII **1415**

INVESTIGATIONAL NEW DRUGS (US/0167-6997) [09862782] **3818**

INVESTIGATIONAL REPORT - DEPARTMENT OF NATURE CONSERVATION (SA/0528-0397) [01794676] **4166**

INVESTIGATIONAL REPORT - OCEANOGRAPHIC RESEARCH INSTITUTE (DURBAN) (SA/0078-320X) [01159425] 1450, **555**

INVESTIGATIONAL REPORT (SEA FISHERIES RESEARCH INSTITUTE (SOUTH AFRICA)) (SA) [10789071] **555**

INVESTIGATIONS IN SCIENCE EDUCATION *SUSPENDED.* (US) [04542231] 1754, **5116**

INVESTIGATIONS ON CETACEA (SZ/1010-3635) [07600064] **5587**

INVESTIGATIVE OPHTHALMOLOGY & VISUAL SCIENCE (US/0146-0404) [02834457] **3875**

INVESTIGATIVE RADIOLOGY (US/0020-9996) [01753822] **3942**

INVESTIGATIVE REPORTER, THE (US/0731-0978) [08118234] **2921**

INVESTIGATIVE REPORTERS AND EDITORS, INC *See* IRE JOURNAL, THE **2921**

INVESTIGATOR (AT/0021-0013) [01990576] **2669**

INVESTIGATOR (EL PASO, TEX.), THE (US/0730-2045) [07965484] **1297**

INVESTING & TRADING WITH SPANISH SPEAKING COUNTRIES (US/0735-9225) [09001493] 842, **902**

INVESTING COMMON CENTS (US/0733-351X) [08575302] **902**

INVESTING IN CRISIS (US/0740-3666) [09956006] **902**

INVESTING IN RADIO (US) [14875377] **1134**

INVESTING IN TELEVISION (US) [14875334] **1134**

INVESTING, LICENSING AND TRADING CONDITIONS ABROAD (US/0021-003X) [02256543] **684**

INVESTIR (PARIS) (FR/0759-7673) [26441767] **792**

INVESTIRE (IT) **902**

INVESTISSEMENTS PRIVES ET PUBLICS AU CANADA : PERSPECTIVES (CN) [01798477] **902**

INVESTMENT ADVISER DIRECTORY (US/0091-2328) [01786619] **902**

INVESTMENT ADVISERS GUIDE (US) **902**

●INVESTMENT ADVISOR (SHREWSBURY, N.J.) (US/1069-1731) [26784630] **902**

INVESTMENT & TAX SHELTER BLUE BOOK (US/1046-8803) [18453523] **4733**

INVESTMENT AND TAXATION IN THE PEOPLE'S REPUBLIC OF CHINA (NE) [12854375] **4733**

INVESTMENT BANKING (BOSTON, MASS.) *See* FINANCE (BOSTON, MASS.) **4204**

INVESTMENT BENCHMARKS (US/1051-7073) [22095231] **902**

INVESTMENT BULLETIN (US/0401-8680) [01671200] **902**

INVESTMENT BUSINESS COMPLIANCE MANUAL (UK) 902, **745**

INVESTMENT CANADA *See* ANNUAL REPORT / INVESTMENT CANADA **891**

INVESTMENT COMPANIES (ARTHUR WIESENBERGER & COMPANY) *See* INVESTMENT COMPANIES (CDA/WIESENBERGER (FIRM)) **902**

INVESTMENT COMPANIES (CDA/WIESENBERGER (FIRM)) *See* INVESTMENT COMPANIES YEARBOOK **902**

INVESTMENT COMPANIES (CDA/WIESENBERGER (FIRM)) (US/1070-2334) [26374373] **902**

INVESTMENT COMPANIES INTERNATIONAL YEARBOOK (US/0091-4533) [01783695] **902**

INVESTMENT COMPANIES (NEW YORK, N.Y. 1983) (US/0747-9484) [10351246] **3100**

INVESTMENT COMPANIES (PRACTISING LAW INSTITUTE) *See* INVESTMENT COMPANY REGULATION **3101**

INVESTMENT COMPANIES REREGULATION AND THE CHANGING ROLE OF OUTSIDE DIRECTORS (US/0731-8278) [08225188] **3101**

INVESTMENT COMPANIES, THE CHANGING ROLE OF OUTSIDE DIRECTORS *See* INVESTMENT COMPANIES REREGULATION AND THE CHANGING ROLE OF OUTSIDE DIRECTORS **3101**

●INVESTMENT COMPANIES YEARBOOK (US/1068-9958) [27875024] **902**

INVESTMENT COMPANY INSTITUTE (U.S.) RESEARCH DEPT *See* ICI TRENDS IN MUTUAL FUND ACTIVITY **900**

●INVESTMENT COMPANY REGULATION (US/1071-8265) [28740662] **3101**

INVESTMENT COMPANY SERVICE DIRECTORY, THE (US/1068-1159) [26977380] **902**

INVESTMENT DEALERS' ASSOCIATION OF CANADA *See* CONSTITUTION, BY-LAWS AND REGULATIONS - INVESTMENT DEALERS' ASSOCIATION OF CANADA **895**

INVESTMENT DEALERS' DIGEST, THE (US/0021-0080) [01753829] 902, **793**

INVESTMENT GUIDE (GREAT BARRINGTON, MASS.) (US/0739-9138) [06921397] **902**

INVESTMENT IN ASEAN (SI) [09238189] **1568**

INVESTMENT IN SINGAPORE (SI) [06687162] **902**

●INVESTMENT INFORMATION DIRECTORY (SEATTLE, WASH.) (US/1060-1481) [24881772] **902**

INVESTMENT INSIGHT (AT) [11276084] **903**

●INVESTMENT LAWYER, THE (US/1075-4512) [30060835] 903, **2984**

INVESTMENT LIMITED PARTNERSHIPS LAW REPORT (US/0893-1364) [15360519] **903**

INVESTMENT MANAGEMENT (UK/0267-3770) [26999285] **903**

INVESTMENT MANAGEMENT NEWSLETTER *See* AIMR NEWSLETTER **890**

INVESTMENT MANAGEMENT TECHNOLOGY (US/1057-5626) [24059236] **903**

INVESTMENT MANAGEMENT WEEKLY (US/0896-8500) [17254754] **903**

INVESTMENT MANAGEMENT WORLD (US/0887-2449) [13147640] **903**

INVESTMENT MANAGER PROFILES (US) **903**

INVESTMENT MONITOR (AT) **903**

INVESTMENT PORTFOLIO GUIDE (US/0883-1661) [12151045] **903**

INVESTMENT PRODUCT BUYER'S GUIDE *See* INVESTMENT INFORMATION DIRECTORY (SEATTLE, WASH.) **902**

INVESTMENT QUALITY TRENDS (US/0021-0110) [04990023] **903**

INVESTMENT REPORTER (CN/0700-5539) [I07005539] **903**

INVESTMENT REVIEW (AT/0094-8683) [01795701] **903**

INVESTMENT SPECIALTIES GUIDE (US/1059-7441) [12561272] **903**

INVESTMENT VISION (US/1055-2375) [22272186] **903**

INVESTMENTS LIMITED PARTNERSHIPS HANDBOOK (US/0893-3944) [15507040] **903**

INVESTOR ACTIVITY REPORT (US) **903**

INVESTOR LATIN AMERICA (UK) **903**

INVESTOR RELATIONS NEWSLETTER (US) **903**

INVESTOR, THE (II) [24041734] **903**

INVESTOR, U.S.A (US/0739-8026) [09810269] **903**

INVESTORS' BULLETIN (MILTON) (CN/0712-9904) [08890848] **4966**

INVESTOR'S BUSINESS DAILY (US/1061-2890) [24397457] **903**

INVESTORS CHRONICLE & FINANCIAL WORLD *See* INVESTORS CHRONICLE (LONDON, ENGLAND : 1983) **903**

INVESTORS CHRONICLE (LONDON, ENGLAND : 1983) (UK) [09962065] **903**

INVESTOR'S DAILY (US) [10755509] 793, **903**

INVESTOR'S DIGEST (CN) **903**

INVESTOR'S DIGEST (CN) **903**

INVESTOR'S DIGEST (FORT LAUDERDALE, FLA.) (US/1057-6711) [22882507] **903**

INVESTOR'S DIGEST OF CANADA (CN/0047-1356) [02036846] **903**

Alphabetical Title Index — IOWA

INVESTOR'S ENVIRONMENTAL REPORT / IRRC, ENVIRONMENTAL INFORMATION SERVICE (US/1055-2154) [23108902] **903**

INVESTOR'S GUIDE (SINGAPORE) (SI/0129-5276) [02649614] **903**

INVESTOR'S GUIDE TO SINGAPORE, THE (SI) [27758646] 1636, **903**

INVESTOR'S YEARBOOK (US/0741-9813) [10245373] **903**

INVIRONMENT (BUFFALO GROVE, ILL.) (US/1059-4078) [24600834] **2175**

INVISIBLE CITY (US/0147-4936) [02762908] **3464**

INVITATION A L'OPERA (CN/1188-0759) [25796505] 4124, **385**

INVITATION A L'OPERA (CN/1188-0759) [25796506] 4124, **385**

INVITATION. BIBLE STUDIES FOR AGES 3-4. TEACHER (US/0893-6331) [15620375] **4966**

INVITATION. BIBLE STUDIES FOR AGES 5-6 (LEAFLETS) (US/0893-6366) [15620457] **4966**

INVITATION. BIBLE STUDIES FOR AGES 5-6. TEACHER (US/0893-6382) [15620507] **4966**

INVITATION. BIBLE STUDIES FOR ELEMENTARY A (LEAFLETS) (US/0893-6390) [15620534] **4966**

INVITATION. BIBLE STUDIES FOR ELEMENTARY C (LEAFLETS) (US/0893-679X) [15620874] **4966**

INVIVO (CN/0836-3838) [16959292] **459**

INVOLVEMENT & PARTICIPATION See INVOLVEMENT : THE JOURNAL OF THE INVOLVEMENT & PARTICIPATION ASSOCIATION **872**

INVOLVEMENT & PARTICIPATION / IPA (UK) [23720641] **872**

●INVOLVEMENT : THE JOURNAL OF THE INVOLVEMENT & PARTICIPATION ASSOCIATION (UK) [30478888] **872**

INWARD LIGHT (US/0021-0250) [05525818] **4966**

INYO REGISTER (US) [27085036] **5636**

INZENERNO-FIZICESKIJ ZURNAL (BW/0021-0285) [02447830] 4406, **1981**

INZET (NE/0166-3658) [I01663658] **2885**

INZET AMSTERDAM (NE/0927-5770) [I09275770] **2910**

INZHENER (RU) [22621261] **1981**

INZHENERNAIA GEOLOGIIA See GEOEKOLOGIIA, INZHENERNAIA GEOLOGIIA, GIDROGEOLOGIIA, GEOKRIOLOGIIA / ROSSIISKAIA AKADEMIIA NAUK **1377**

INZHENERNAIA GEOLOGIIA / AKADEMIIA NAUK SSSR (RU/0203-0292) [05897039] 1981, **1383**

INZYNIERIA CHEMICZNA I PROCESOWA (PL/0208-6425) [07016145] **2013**

INZYNIERIA I APARATURA CHEMICZNA (PL/0368-0827) [11256421] **978**

INZYNIERIA MORSKA (PL/0138-0540) [I01380540] **1981**

IO (US/0021-0331) [02564883] 3397, **238**

IO, MANAGEMENT-ZEITSCHRIFT INDUSTRIELLE ORGANISATION (SZ/0019-9281) [05140945] **872**

IODINE (US) [03027765] 2141, **1440**

IOE LIBRARY BULLETIN See OFFSHORE ENGINEERING INFORMATION BULLETIN **3238**

IOF BULLETIN See ORIENTEERING WORLD **4911**

IOF REPORT See ORIENTEERING WORLD **4911**

IOH NEWS See HORTICULTURIST/ INSTITUTE OF HORTICULTURE, THE **2419**

IOJ NEWS LETTER / THE INTERNATIONAL ORGANIZATION OF JOURNALISTS (XR) [07492170] **2921**

IOLA HERALD, THE (US/0886-8360) [12100600] **5768**

IOLA REGISTER (IOLA, KAN. : 1939) (US) [09563684] **5676**

IOMAS GIC BIC YIELDS AND MARKET REPORT See DEFINED CONTRIBUTION PLAN INVESTING **896**

IOMA'S MONTHLY REPORT ON PROPERTY CASUALTY RATES AND RATINGS (US) **2984**

●IOMA'S REPORT ON COMPENSATION & BENEFITS FOR LAW OFFICES (US/1068-4239) [27671456] 3150, **1681**

●IOMA'S REPORT ON CONTROLLING BENEFITS COSTS FOR LAW, DESIGN, CPA, AND OTHER PROFESSIONAL SERVICE FIRMS (US/1062-7936) [25776668] **872**

●IOMA'S REPORT ON CONTROLLING LAW FIRM COSTS (US/1060-5924) [25038759] 872, **2984**

●IOMA'S REPORT ON MANAGING 401 (K) PLANS (US/1059-2741) [24529905] **903**

●IOMA'S REPORT ON MANAGING CREDIT, RECEIVABLES & COLLECTIONS (US/1074-8903) [29874562] **793**

●IOMA'S REPORT ON MANAGING LITIGATION COSTS (US/1074-3898) [29694365] **2984**

IOMA'S REPORT ON REDUCING BENEFITS COSTS (US/1056-7984) [23854517] **872**

●IOMA'S REPORT ON SALARY SURVEYS (US/1067-4551) [27242740] **684**

ION CHANNELS (US/1059-7514) [17733724] **488**

ION EXCHANGE AND MEMBRANES (US/0091-0619) [01798343] **1053**

ION EXCHANGE AND SOLVENT EXTRACTION (US/0092-0193) [01788139] **1053**

ION NEWSLETTER / THE INSTITUTE OF NAVIGATION, THE (US/1061-8244) [24154773] **4177**

IONIA SENTINEL-STANDARD See SENTINEL-STANDARD **5693**

IONNYE RASPLAVY (RU/0130-6359) [02652883] **1036**

IONNYE RASPLAVY I TVERDYE ELEKTROLITY (UN/0234-4483) [16547632] **4406**

IONNYI OBMEN I IONOMETRIIA / LENINGRADSKII GOSUDARSTVENNYI UNIVERSITET IMENI A.A. ZHDANOVA (RU) [09387058] **4406**

IONOSFERNYE ISSLEDOVANIIA. IONOSPHERIC RESEARCHES (RU) [03722794] **4406**

IONOSPHERIC PREDICTION SERVICE See ANNUAL REPORT - IONOSPHERE PREDICTION SERVICE (CANBERRA) **1420**

IONOSPHERIC STATION INFORMATION BULLETIN / IONOSPHERIC NETWORK ADVISORY GROUP (US) [10797506] **396**

IOP NEWSLETTER (US/1016-4928) [02553102] **514**

IOP SHORT MEETINGS SERIES (UK/0269-8986) [20590408] **4406**

IOTA (LASALLE) (CN/0229-7493) [07970412] **1831**

IOUDAIOS REVIEW (CN/1183-9937) [25652254] **5048**

IOWA See IOWA ELECTION HANDBOOK WITH ELECTION LAWS OF IOWA **2984**

IOWA ADMINISTRATIVE BULLETIN (US) [04072272] **2984**

IOWA ADVOCATE (US/0578-6533) [02255052] **2984**

IOWA AIR QUALITY REPORT UPDATE WITH ... AIR MONITORING DATA (US) [23478966] **2233**

IOWA AIRPORT SUFFICIENCY RATINGS (US) [03624107] **24**

IOWA ARCHEOLOGICAL SOCIETY See NEWSLETTER - IOWA ARCHEOLOGICAL SOCIETY **276**

IOWA ARCHEOLOGICAL SOCIETY See JOURNAL OF THE IOWA ARCHEOLOGICAL SOCIETY **272**

IOWA ARCHITECT (US/0021-0439) [02728419] **301**

IOWA BIRD LIFE (US/0021-0455) [01589829] **5617**

IOWA BUSINESS DIRECTORY (US/1048-7263) [11838531] **684**

IOWA CAPITOL COMPLEX TELEPHONE DIRECTORY / STATE OF IOWA, DEPARTMENT OF GENERAL SERVICES, DIVISION OF COMMUNICATIONS (US) [05979684] **4657**

IOWA CITY MAGAZINE (US) **2536**

IOWA CITY PRESS-CITIZEN (US) [02262691] **5670**

IOWA CIVIL RIGHTS COMMISSION See IOWA CIVIL RIGHTS COMMISSION, CASE REPORTS **4509**

IOWA CIVIL RIGHTS COMMISSION, CASE REPORTS (US) [03875576] 2984, **4509**

IOWA COMMERCE (US/8750-6645) [11560998] **842**

IOWA COMPREHENSIVE STATE PLAN FOR SUBSTANCE ABUSE (US) [16715473] **1345**

IOWA CONSERVATIONIST (US/0021-0471) [01696514] **2195**

IOWA. COOPERATIVE EXTENSION SERVICE See IOWA FARM OUTLOOK **97**

IOWA CRIMINAL LAW BULLETIN (US) [06363353] **3107**

IOWA CROP AND LIVESTOCK REPORTING SERVICE See PLANTING TO HARVEST; ANNUAL CROP WEATHER SUMMARY **182**

IOWA CROP REPORT (US/0745-0109) [08717536] 213, **175**

IOWA CROPS AND WEATHER / IOWA CROP AND LIVESTOCK REPORTING SERVICE (US/1041-9268) [06133880] **175**

IOWA DAIRY MARKETING NEWS (US/0744-608X) [08424806] **195**

IOWA DENTAL JOURNAL, THE (US/0021-0498) [01606415] **1325**

IOWA. DEPARTMENT OF PUBLIC INSTRUCTION See IOWA EDUCATIONAL DIRECTORY **1755**

IOWA. DEPT. FOR THE BLIND See ANNUAL REPORT - IOWA DEPARTMENT FOR THE BLIND **4383**

IOWA. DEPT. OF CORRECTIONS. BUREAU OF RESEARCH AND PLANNING See LOOKING TOWARD THE FUTURE: A FIVE YEAR PLAN FOR THE IOWA DEPARTMENT OF CORRECTIONS / PREPARED BY THE IOWA DEPARTMENT OF CORRECTIONS, BUREAU OF RESEARCH AND PLANNING **3169**

IOWA. DEPT. OF ELDER AFFAIRS See ANNUAL REPORT / IOWA DEPARTMENT OF ELDER AFFAIRS **3749**

IOWA. DEPT. OF PUBLIC INSTRUCTION See ANNUAL STATE PLAN FOR VOCATIONAL EDUCATION WITHIN CAREER EDUCATION. EXECUTIVE SUMMARY **1910**

IOWA. DEPT. OF PUBLIC INSTRUCTION See DATA ON IOWA'S AREA SCHOOLS AND PUBLIC JUNIOR COLLEGE **1819**

IOWA. DEPT. OF PUBLIC INSTRUCTION See BUDGET REQUEST - STATE DEPARTMENT OF PUBLIC INSTRUCTION **1812**

IOWA. DEPT. OF PUBLIC INSTRUCTION See OPPORTUNITIES IN IOWA'S AREA SCHOOLS **1839**

IOWA. DEPT. OF PUBLIC SAFETY See ANNUAL REPORT - IOWA DEPARTMENT OF PUBLIC SAFETY **4766**

IOWA. DEPT. OF PUBLIC SAFETY. RESEARCH AND STATISTICS SECTION See BICYCLE ACCIDENT STATISTICS **429**

IOWA. DEPT. OF REVENUE. RESEARCH & STATISTICS DIVISION See IOWA ELDERLY AND DISABLED PROPERTY TAX RELIEF REPORT **4733**

IOWA. DEPT. OF TRANSPORTATION See PLANNING AND RESEARCH PROGRAM **5389**

IOWA. DEPT. OF TRANSPORTATION See STATISTICAL PROFILE - IOWA DEPARTMENT OF TRANSPORTATION **5402**

IOWA. DEPT. OF TRANSPORTATION. PLANNING AND RESEARCH DIVISION See IOWA AIRPORT SUFFICIENCY RATINGS **24**

IOWA. DEPT. OF TREASURER OF STATE See REPORT OF THE TREASURER OF STATE - IOWA. DEPT. OF TREASURER OF STATE **4746**

IOWA. DEPT. OF WATER, AIR, AND WASTE MANAGEMENT See ANNUAL REPORT / IOWA DEPARTMENT OF WATER, AIR, AND WASTE MANAGEMENT **2224**

IOWA DEVELOPMENT COMMISSION See STATISTICAL PROFILE OF IOWA **1538**

IOWA. DIVISION OF SUBSTANCE ABUSE See IOWA COMPREHENSIVE STATE PLAN FOR SUBSTANCE ABUSE **1345**

IOWA DRUG INFORMATION SERVICE (US) [01771057] 4309, **4334**

IOWA EDUCATIONAL DIRECTORY (US) [01753846] **1755**

IOWA ELDERLY AND DISABLED PROPERTY TAX RELIEF REPORT (US/0148-8082) [03375262] **4733**

IOWA ELECTION HANDBOOK WITH ELECTION LAWS OF IOWA (US/0360-7526) [02240326] 4478, **2984**

IOWA EMPLOYMENT LAW LETTER (US/1075-962X) [30332442] **3150**

IOWA. EMPLOYMENT SECURITY COMMISSION. EMPLOYABILITY DEVELOPMENT SECTION See NEW SKILLS FOR PROGRESS : MDTA **1694**

IOWA ENERGY BULLETIN (US) [04442427] **1948**

IOWA ENGLISH BULLETIN (US/0444-4663) [03830322] 1897, **3288**

IOWA FACTS (DALLAS, TEX.) (US/0895-8092) [16809654] **2536**

IOWA FALLS CITIZEN (US) [12935738] **5670**

IOWA FARM BUREAU SPOKESMAN (US/0021-051X) [04084100] **97**

IOWA FARM OUTLOOK (US/0092-5209) [05531389] **97**

IOWA. FISHERIES SECTION See TECHNICAL SERIES - FISHERIES SECTION (DES MOINES) **2314**

IOWA FOOD DEALER, THE (US) [09820297] **2345**

IOWA GAME & FISH (US/0897-9197) [17664464] **4873**

IOWA — Alphabetical Title Index

IOWA GENEALOGICAL SOCIETY *See* IOWA GENEALOGICAL SOCIETY SURNAME INDEX **2454**

IOWA GENEALOGICAL SOCIETY SURNAME INDEX (US/0090-905X) [01786079] **2454**

IOWA. GENERAL ASSEMBLY HOUSE OF REPRESENTATIVES *See* JOURNAL OF THE HOUSE OF REPRESENTATIVES OF THE ... REGULAR SESSION OF THE GENERAL ASSEMBLY OF THE STATE OF IOWA **4659**

IOWA GEOLOGICAL SURVEY *See* PUBLIC INFORMATION CIRCULAR - IOWA GEOLOGICAL SURVEY **1392**

IOWA GEOLOGY (US/0193-4856) [05039787] **1383**

●IOWA HEALTH CARE IN PERSPECTIVE (US/1065-4178) [26605093] **4785**

IOWA. HIGHER EDUCATION FACILITIES COMMISSION *See* STATE OF IOWA SCHOLARSHIPS, TUITION GRANTS, MEDICAL TUITION LOANS : BIENNIUM REPORT **1785**

IOWA. HIGHWAY DIVISION *See* WEEKLY LETTING REPORT - IOWA. HIGHWAY DIVISION **2033**

IOWA IIA AUDIT UPDATE (US/0746-6579) [10199511] **745**

IOWA IN PERSPECTIVE (US/1065-5441) [26127733] **5329**

IOWA INDIVIDUAL INCOME TAX ANNUAL REPORT (US) [19260163] **4733**

IOWA. INSURANCE DIVISION *See* REPORT OF THE INSURANCE DIVISION OF IOWA **2892**

IOWA INTERLINK (US/1050-2270) [21258025] **4657**

IOWA JOURNAL OF COMMUNICATION (US) 3288, **1114**

IOWA JOURNAL OF RESEARCH IN MUSIC EDUCATION *CEASED.* (US/0270-7098) [05255736] 1755, **4124**

IOWA LAW REVIEW (US/0021-0552) [01753893] **2984**

IOWA LAWYER (US/1052-5327) [22298860] **2985**

IOWA LAWYERS DIARY AND MANUAL (US) [03787265] **2985**

IOWA. LEGISLATIVE SERVICE BUREAU *See* SUMMARY OF LEGISLATION APPROVED BY THE ... SESSION OF THE ... IOWA GENERAL ASSEMBLY MEETING IN THE YEAR ... **4689**

IOWA LOCAL GOVERNMENT SALARY AND BENEFIT SURVEY / IOWA MUNICIPAL SALARY SURVEY (US) [08901329] **1681**

IOWA MANUFACTURERS REGISTER (US/0737-7940) [09301128] **3481**

IOWA MEDICINE (US/0746-8709) [10351558] **3590**

IOWA. MERIT EMPLOYMENT DEPT *See* STATE OF IOWA CLASSIFIED SERVICE PAY PLAN **1712**

IOWA. MOTOR VEHICLE DIVISION. RESEARCH & STATISTICS SECTION *See* IOWA MOTOR VEHICLE TRAFFIC ACCIDENT FACTS **5441**

IOWA MOTOR VEHICLE TRAFFIC ACCIDENT FACTS (US) [04052039] **5441**

IOWA MUNICIPALITIES (US/0021-0595) [01753898] **4657**

IOWA. OFFICE FOR PLANNING AND PROGRAMMING *See* REPORT ON FEDERAL FUNDS RECEIVED IN IOWA **4746**

IOWA. OFFICE OF STATE ARCHAEOLOGIST *See* REPORT - OFFICE OF STATE ARCHAEOLOGIST **280**

IOWA PARK LEADER, THE (US) [16855513] **5751**

IOWA PHARMACIST (US/0889-7735) [04979392] **4309**

IOWA POLL, THE (US) [03761989] **2536**

IOWA PRESERVES BOARD *See* BIENNIAL REPORT / IOWA PRESERVES BOARD **4163**

IOWA PTA BULLETIN (US/0021-0617) [04084117] **1865**

IOWA PUBLIC LIBRARY STATISTICS / STATE LIBRARY COMMISSION OF IOWA (US) [06459142] 3218, **3258**

IOWA PUBLICATIONS IN PHILOSOPHY (US/0075-0395) [01753900] **4350**

IOWA QUERIES (US/1044-6931) [17928056] **2454**

IOWA REAL ESTATE COMMISSION *See* ROSTER OF REAL ESTATE LICENSEES (IOWA) **4847**

IOWA REVIEW QUARTERLY (US/0741-2924) [10101460] **4658**

IOWA REVIEW, THE (US/0021-065X) [01234380] **3397**

IOWA RULES OF COURT (US/0742-9967) [04008632] **3141**

IOWA RURAL COMMUNITY DEVELOPMENT PROGRAM *See* BIENNIAL REPORT / IRCD, IOWA RURAL COMMUNITY DEVELOPMENT PROGRAM **2816**

IOWA. SAVINGS AND LOAN DIVISION *See* REPORT ON THE CONDITION OF SAVINGS AND LOAN ASSOCIATIONS FOR THE YEAR ENDING ... **808**

IOWA SCHOOL BOARD DIALOGUE, THE (US/0021-0668) [04079747] **1865**

IOWA SCIENCE TEACHERS' JOURNAL (US/0021-0676) [04172750] 1897, **5116**

IOWA. STATE BOARD OF REGENTS *See* BUDGET REQUESTS - STATE BOARD OF REGENTS **1728**

IOWA. STATE BOARD OF REGENTS *See* SUMMARY OF BUDGET REQUESTS - STATE BOARD OF REGENTS **1872**

IOWA STATE DAILY (US) [11832768] **5670**

IOWA. STATE DEPT. OF HEALTH. DIVISION OF DISEASE PREVENTION *See* ANNUAL SUMMARY - IOWA. STATE DEPT. OF HEALTH. DIVISION OF DISEASE PREVENTION **3712**

IOWA STATE EDUCATION ASSOCIATION *See* ISEA COMMUNIQUE **1865**

IOWA. STATE EMPLOYMENT AND TRAINING COUNCIL *See* ... ANNUAL REPORT TO THE GOVERNOR ON EMPLOYMENT AND TRAINING, THE **1650**

IOWA. STATE MANPOWER SERVICES COUNCIL *See* STATE MANPOWER REPORT TO THE GOVERNOR - IOWA **1711**

IOWA STATE UNIVERSITY LIBRARY INSTRUCTION MANUAL (US) [06609041] **3218**

IOWA STATE UNIVERSITY VETERINARIAN (US/0099-5851) [06267055] **5512**

IOWA STATER, THE (US/0746-2204) [09864906] **1831**

IOWA STUDIES IN AFRICAN ART (US/0897-8573) [11027896] **353**

IOWA STYLE (US/0887-9788) [13433014] **404**

IOWA VOTER (US/0199-4212) [05857641] **4478**

IOWA WOMAN (US/0271-8227) [06685646] **5559**

IOWAN, THE (US/0021-0722) [01753910] **2536**

IP ASIA: INTELLECTUAL PROPERTY, MARKETING AND COMMUNICATIONS LAW (HK/1011-3649) [17643017] **1305**

IP MARK (SP) **684**

IP NUOVO DIRITTO (IT/0029-6368) [I00296368] **2985**

IPA INTERGOVERNMENTAL ASSIGNMENT PROGRAM : REPORT, THE (US/0360-6260) [02172521] **4658**

IPA REVIEW (1986) (AT/1030-4177) [15506576] **4733**

IPAC QUARTERLY (CN/0845-437X) [19900857] **4261**

IPADE ALAGBARA (US/0883-6620) [12195747] **5268**

IPARI FORMATERVEZESI SZAKIRODALMI TAJEKOZTATO (HU/0231-195X) [I0231195X] **2901**

IPARI TERMELES SZERKEZETENEK ALAKULASA, AZ (HU) [01789763] **1568**

IPC PAPERS: INSTITUTE OF PHILIPPINE CULTURE (PH) **2848**

IPECK PUKPANG KYONGJE (KO) [24593122] **1497**

IPEF, INSTITUTO DE PESQUISAS E ESTUDOS FLORESTAIS (BL/0100-4557) [01194377] **2385**

IPEK (GW/0075-0468) [01771746] **270**

IPH YEARBOOK (GW/1010-4054) [08783904] **4234**

IPI: ARRECADACAO SETORIAL (BL) [03598514] **4734**

IPI DATA SERVICE. EUROPE (US) [02457390] **4261**

IPI DATA SERVICE. EXPLORATION, PRODUCTION, TRANSPORTATION, REFINING & MARKETING (NORTH AMERICA) (US/0276-0061) [07329937] **4261**

IPI DATA SERVICE. EXPLORATION, PRODUCTION, TRANSPORTATION, REFINING & MARKETING (WORLD) (US/0276-0096) [07331532] **4261**

IPI DATA SERVICE. MIDDLE EAST (US) [02457402] **4261**

IPI DATA SERVICE. NORTH AMERICA. CONSOLIDATED TABLE OF CONTENTS (US) [10805528] **4262**

IPI DATA SERVICE. WORLD. CONSOLIDATED TABLE OF CONTENTS (US) [10805555] **4262**

IPI REPORT (SZ/0019-0314) [02447804] **2921**

●IPL NEWSLETTER : A PUBLICATION OF THE AMERICAN BAR ASSOCIATION SECTION OF INTELLECTUAL PROPERTY LAW (US) [29604251] **1305**

IPM, INTERPRESS MAGAZIN (HU) [04206481] **2518**

IPM JOURNAL *See* PEOPLE DYNAMICS **944**

IPM PRACTITIONER, THE (US/0738-968X) [07666007] **4245**

IPMA ASSESSMENT COUNCIL MONOGRAPH SERIES (US) **943**

IPMA MONOGRAPH SERIES (US) **943**

IPMA NEWS / INTERNATIONAL PERSONNEL MANAGEMENT ASSOCIATION (US) [02350391] **943**

IPMS BULLETIN (UK/0958-5222) [09585222] **5116**

IPMS-USA QUARTERLY *See* QUARTERLY - INTERNATIONAL PLASTIC MODELERS' SOCIETY. UNITED STATES BRANCH **4460**

IPN-BLATTER (GW/0179-5775) [I01795775] **1755**

IPN CINE / DIRECCION DE DIFUSION CULTURAL, DIRECCION DE PUBLICACIONES (NP) [09961789] **4073**

IPO ANNUAL PROGRESS REPORT (NE/0921-2566) [06172538] **514**

IPPA-NEWSLETTER (IO) [04282752] **589**

IPPAN KYOIKU GAKKAI *See* IPPAN KYOIKU GAKKAI SHI **1755**

IPPAN KYOIKU GAKKAI SHI (JA) [09279238] **1755**

IPPF CO-OPERATIVE INFORMATION SERVICE *CEASED.* (UK/0309-6904) [04610794] **589**

IPPF IN ACTION (UK) [08572453] **589**

IPPF MEDICAL BULLETIN (ENGLISH EDITION) (UK/0019-0357) [02254843] 2281, **589**

IPPF OPEN FILE (UK) [04766850] 5290, **589**

IPPOGRIFO (BOLOGNA, ITALY) (IT) [19093382] **3344**

IPPON : DEUTSCHER JUDO VERBAND (GW) **4901**

IPPTA (II/0379-5462) [11480496] **4234**

IPR ... REPORT / INSTITUTE OF PRIMATE RESEARCH (KE) [29263210] **5512**

IPRA STUDIES IN PEACE RESEARCH (NE/0074-7289) [02152775] **4526**

IPRAX : PRAXIS DES INTERNATIONALEN PRIVAT- UND VERFAHRENSRECHTS (GW) [08015594] **3131**

IPS PAPERS (LE) [06732411] **4526**

IPSCO INC. / MIDLAND WALWYN RESEARCH (CN/1186-8643) [24571261] **4734**

IPSWICH & SUFFOLK DIRECTORY OF INDUSTRY & COMMERCE, THE (UK/0269-2716) [17247998] **684**

IPTC NEWS (UK/1012-8719) [07409748] **1158**

IPU REVIEW (IE/0332-2130) [06288542] **4309**

IPW BERICHTE *CEASED.* (GW/0046-970X) [01578097] **1636**

IQBAL REVIEW (PK/0021-0773) [01607963] 5042, **3397**

IQTISADI (KHARTOUM, SUDAN) (SJ) [11137819] **1568**

IR & R NEWS REPORT / SECTION OF INDIVIDUAL RIGHTS AND RESPONSIBILITIES (US/1059-1729) [24222970] 4509, **2985**

IR. INVESTOR RELATIONS (UK/0958-6679) [22899132] **903**

IR VE-EZOR (IS) [01784369] **4658**

IRA BULLETIN (BRAINERD, MINN.) (US/1062-7499) [25724694] **904**

IRA REPORTER, THE (US/0739-2168) [09710463] **904**

IRAC JOURNAL (US/1050-1282) [21396727] **4658**

IRAK : ENERGIEWIRTSCHAFT (GW) [05023192] **1948**

IRAK, WIRTSCHAFTSDATEN UND WIRTSCHAFTSDOKUMENTATION / BUNDESSTELLE FUR AUSSENHANDELSINFORMATION (GW) [07756709] **1568**

IRAL, INTERNATIONAL REVIEW OF APPLIED LINGUISTICS IN LANGUAGE TEACHING (GW/0019-042X) [01641366] 1897, **3288**

●IRAM NEWSLETTER (FR) [25487157] **396**

IRAMANATAPURAM PANCANKAM (II) [08721275] **2505**

IRAN AGRICULTURAL RESEARCH (IR/1013-9885) [11951450] **97**

IRAN ECONOMIC NEWS (US/0161-0627) [02730965] **1497**

IRAN : ENERGIEWIRTSCHAFT (GW) [05023161] **1948**

IRAN FOCUS (UK/0935-1531) [20548142] **1497**

Alphabetical Title Index — IRISH

IRAN LIBERATION : BULLETIN D'INFORMATION DES MODJAHEDINES DU PEOPLE D'IRAN (FR) [15585978] **4510**

IRAN LIBERATION : NEWS BULLETIN OF THE PEOPLE'S MOJAHEDIN OF IRAN (US) [25330683] **4510**

IRAN (LONDON) (UK/0578-6967) [01589108] **2505**

IRAN MONITOR See BUSINESS MIDDLE EAST **650**

IRAN MONITOR / BUSINESS INTERNATIONAL (UK) [18460536] **684**

IRAN NAMEH. BUNYAD-I MUTALAAT-I IRAN (US/0892-4147) [10110175] **2654**

IRAN QUARTERLY (UK) 4478, **1568**

IRAN TIMES, THE (US) [03932325] **5647**

IRAN TODAY (US/0889-6291) [14086569] **4510**

IRAN-UNITED STATES CLAIMS TRIBUNAL See IRAN-UNITED STATES CLAIMS TRIBUNAL REPORTS **3131**

IRAN-UNITED STATES CLAIMS TRIBUNAL REPORTS (UK) [10253112] **3131**

IRAN VOICE (US) [05284622] **4526**

IRAN YEARBOOK (GW) [18240372] **2526**

IRAN YEARBOOK (IR) [03247329] **2768**

IRANIAN ASSETS LITIGATION REPORTER (US/0277-2922) [07530424] **3131**

IRANIAN JOURNAL OF AGRICULTURAL RESEARCH CEASED. (IR/0376-4524) [01771747] **97**

IRANIAN JOURNAL OF AGRICULTURAL SCIENCE (IR/1017-5652) [06203116] **97**

IRANIAN JOURNAL OF INTERNATIONAL AFFAIRS, THE (IR) [20678672] **4526**

IRANIAN JOURNAL OF MEDICAL SCIENCES (IR/0253-0716) [07785067] **3590**

IRANIAN JOURNAL OF PLANT PATHOLOGY (IR/0021-0838) [02262715] **514**

IRANIAN JOURNAL OF PUBLIC HEALTH (IR/0304-4556) [01357528] **4785**

IRANIAN STUDIES (US/0021-0862) [01753915] **2768**

IRANIAN STUDIES SEMINAR, ANNUAL PROCEEDINGS (US/0270-840X) [06505234] **2768**

IRANIAN STUDIES SEMINAR (UNIVERSITY OF PENNSYLVANIA) See IRANIAN STUDIES SEMINAR, ANNUAL PROCEEDINGS **2768**

IRANIAN WOMEN QUARTERLY (CN) **5559**

IRANICA ANTIQUA (NE/0021-0870) [01753916] **270**

IRANIYAN (TORONTO) (CN/0832-2007) [15731072] **5786**

IRANSHINASI (BETHESDA, MD.) (US/1051-5364) [20611385] **3397**

IRANSKOE IAZYKOZNANIE / AKADEMIIA NAUK SSSR, INSTITUT IAZYKOZNANIIA (RU) [08460211] **3288**

IRAQ (UK/0021-0889) [01714824] **2768**

IRAQ (BAGHDAD, IRAQ) (IQ) [07661270] **2768**

IRAQ OIL NEWS See IRAQ OIL NEWS BULLETIN / MINISTRY OF OIL **4262**

IRAQ OIL NEWS BULLETIN / MINISTRY OF OIL (IQ) [08165621] **4262**

IRAQ VIEWS & NEWS (US/0748-2639) [10899703] **2768**

IRAQI JOURNAL OF AGRICULTURAL SCIENCES ZANCO (IQ) [11752669] **97**

IRAQI JOURNAL OF SCIENCE (IQ/0067-2904) [03984106] **5116**

IRB (US/0193-7758) [05255051] 3590, **2251**

IRB-LITERATURAUSLESE (GW/0724-5548) [12122570] **3397**

IRC BULLETIN / UNITED STATES ENVIRONMENT PROTECTION AGENCY, NATIONAL TRAINING AND OPERATIONAL TECHNOLOGY CENTER CEASED. (US) [04635655] 2233, **5535**

IRC FIRE RESEARCH NEWS See FIRE RESEARCH NEWS **2289**

IRC NEWSLETTER (NE/0257-6333) [02576333] 4761, **4785**

●IRC PERSPECTIVES (CN/1188-2999) [26290920] **4658**

IRCIHE BULLETIN / INTERNATIONAL REFERRAL CENTRE FOR INFORMATION HANDLING EQUIPMENT (CI/0351-0123) [12369081] **3218**

IRCS MEDICAL SCIENCE. PSYCHOLOGY AND PSYCHIATRY (UK/0309-152X) [0309152X] 4592, **3927**

IRCWD NEWS (SZ/0253-4606) [02534606] **2233**

IRE EMPLOYMENT LAW : THE INTERNATIONAL NEWSLETTER ON ENGAGEMENTS AND DISMISSALS (BE) **3150**

IRE JOURNAL, THE (US/0164-7016) [04390579] **2921**

IREDELL COUNTY TRACKS / GENEALOGICAL SOCIETY OF IREDELL COUNTY, N.C (US) [15641473] **4554**

IRELAND See BUDGET IRELAND **4714**

IRELAND See FRAMEWORK FOR ... BUDGET **4727**

IRELAND : A PARLIAMENTARY DIRECTORY (IE) [02306952] **4658**

IRELAND AGENDA, THE (UK) [27954738] **1681**

IRELAND. CENTRAL STATISTICS OFFICE See TREND OF EMPLOYMENT AND UNEMPLOYMENT, THE **1715**

IRELAND. CENTRAL STATISTICS OFFICE. LIVE REGISTER STATEMENT (IE) 1681, **1497**

IRELAND. DEPT. OF AGRICULTURE AND FOOD See ANNUAL REPORT OF THE MINISTER FOR AGRICULTURE AND FOOD **61**

IRELAND. DEPT. OF FISHERIES AND FORESTRY See SEA AND INLAND FISHERIES REPORT FOR ... / AN ROINN IASCAIGH AGUS FORAOISEACHTA (DEPT. OF FISHERIES AND FORESTRY) **2313**

IRELAND. DEPT. OF FISHERIES. SEA AND INLAND FISHERIES REPORT See SEA AND INLAND FISHERIES REPORT FOR ... / AN ROINN IASCAIGH AGUS FORAOISEACHTA (DEPT. OF FISHERIES AND FORESTRY) **2313**

IRELAND. DEPT. OF INDUSTRY, COMMERCE, AND TOURISM See COMPANIES - IRELAND. DEPT. OF INDUSTRY, COMMERCE AND TOURISM **1602**

IRELAND (EIRE) See DEVELOPMENTS IN THE EUROPEAN COMMUNITIES (DUBLIN) **1555**

IRELAND (EIRE). CENTRAL FUND See ABSTRACT ACCOUNT - CENTRAL FUND (IRELAND) **4708**

IRELAND (EIRE). DEPT. OF HEALTH. PLANNING UNIT See STATISTICAL INFORMATION RELEVANT TO THE HEALTH SERVICES **3661**

IRELAND (EIRE). GEOLOGICAL SURVEY See GUIDE SERIES - GEOLOGICAL SURVEY OF IRELAND **1381**

IRELAND (EIRE). IRISH MANUSCRIPTS COMMISSION See FACSIMILES IN COLLOTYPE OF IRISH MANUSCRIPTS **4828**

IRELAND (EIRE). MERCHANDISE MARKS COMMISSION See REPORT - IRELAND (EIRE). MERCHANDISE MARKS COMMISSION **850**

IRELAND (EIRE). NATIONAL HEALTH COUNCIL See REPORT - NATIONAL HEALTH COUNCIL **4798**

IRELAND (EIRE). REGISTRY OF BUILDING SOCIETIES See REPORT OF THE REGISTRAR OF BUILDING SOCIETIES **808**

IRELAND (EIRE). RESTRICTIVE PRACTICES COMMISSION See ANNUAL REPORT - RESTRICTIVE PRACTICES COMMISSION. (IRELAND) **2935**

IRELAND (EIRE). SEA FISHERIES BOARD See ANNUAL REPORT - IRISH SEA FISHERIES BOARD **2294**

IRELAND. EMPLOYMENT APPEALS TRIBUNAL See ANNUAL REPORT FOR THE YEAR ENDED ... / EMPLOYMENT APPEALS TRIBUNAL **3144**

IRELAND. EMPLOYMENT APPEALS TRIBUNAL See REPORTS OF IMPORTANT DECISIONS BY THE EMPLOYMENT APPEALS TRIBUNAL UNDER THE UNFAIR DISMISSALS ACT, 1977 **3153**

IRELAND. EXCHEQUER AND AUDIT DEPT. APPROPRIATIONS ACCOUNTS See APPROPRIATION ACCOUNTS **4711**

IRELAND. GARDA SIOCHANA. COMPLAINTS BOARD See ANNUAL REPORT / GARDA SIOCHANA COMPLAINTS BOARD **4627**

●IRELAND / MICHELIN (UK) [25622807] **5481**

IRELAND OF THE WELCOMES (IE/0021-0943) [01753936] **2518**

IRELAND. OFFICE OF THE COMPTROLLER AND AUDITOR GENERAL See APPROPRIATION ACCOUNTS **4711**

IRELAND. OIREACHTAS. JOINT COMMITTEE ON THE SECONDARY LEGISLATION OF THE EUROPEAN COMMUNITIES See REPORT / JOINT COMMITTEE ON THE SECONDARY LEGISLATION OF THE EUROPEAN COMMUNITIES **2522**

IRELAND, PORTS & SHIPPING HANDBOOK (UK/0260-924X) [08073670] **5450**

IRELAND REPORT, WOMEN'S HEALTH MARKETING, THE (US/0896-8535) [17307890] 927, **2599**

IRELAND TODAY CEASED. (IE/0332-0103) [02243178] **5481**

IRELAND'S OWN (IE/0021-0951) [00210951] **5803**

IRENIKON (BE/0021-0978) [01776460] **4966**

IRES MATERIALI (IT) **1681**

IRETA'S SOUTH PACIFIC AGRICULTURAL NEWS (WS/1015-8502) [10158502] **97**

IREX OCCASIONAL PAPERS (US/0198-8875) [06239020] **5204**

IRG AND ITS MEMBERS AND SPONSORS (SW) [15874764] **2402**

IRHACE JOURNAL (NZ/0114-8257) [01148257] **2606**

IRIAN (IO/0304-2189) [02764859] 3288, **238**

IRIDE (LUCCA, ITALY) (IT) [20582705] **4350**

IRIS (US/0751-7033) [09425440] **4073**

IRIS AND RES NOVISSIMAE (AT/0310-9186) [03109186] **1077**

●IRIS (ATLANTA, GA.) (US/1068-9494) [27866796] **3344**

IRIS (CHARLOTTESVILLE, VA.) (US/0896-1301) [16919838] **5204**

IRIS (MONTPELLIER) (FR/0291-2066) [11011075] **3397**

IRIS YEAR BOOK / BRITISH IRIS SOCIETY, THE (UK/0075-0700) [03388713] **2420**

IRISH AMERICA (US/0884-4240) [12366619] **2739**

IRISH AMERICAN WHO'S WHO, THE (US/0742-6771) [10421486] **433**

IRISH ANCESTOR, THE (IE/0047-1437) [02158006] **2454**

IRISH ARCHITECT (IE/0790-8342) [07908342] **301**

IRISH ARCHIVES : JOURNAL OF THE IRISH SOCIETY FOR ARCHIVES (IE/0332-4303) [20655319] **2481**

●IRISH ARTS REVIEW YEARBOOK (IE) [25810423] **353**

IRISH ASTRONOMICAL JOURNAL, THE (UK/0021-1052) [01911485] **396**

IRISH BANKING REVIEW, THE (IE/0021-1060) [05523421] 1497, **793**

IRISH BAPTIST (IE) [01776461] **5061**

IRISH BAPTIST HISTORICAL SOCIETY See IRISH BAPTIST HISTORICAL SOCIETY JOURNAL **5061**

IRISH BAPTIST HISTORICAL SOCIETY JOURNAL (IE/0075-0727) [01776463] **5061**

IRISH BIBLICAL ASSOCIATION See PROCEEDINGS OF THE IRISH BIBLICAL ASSOCIATION **5019**

IRISH BIBLICAL STUDIES (IE/0268-6112) [04743101] **5017**

IRISH BIOTECH NEWS (IE/0790-1747) [07901747] **459**

IRISH BIRDS (IE/0332-0111) [04444951] **5617**

IRISH BOOKS IN PRINT & LEABHAIR GAEILGE I GCLO (IE) [11432937] **4829**

IRISH CATHOLIC DIRECTORY See IRISH CATHOLIC DIRECTORY & DIARY **5030**

●IRISH CATHOLIC DIRECTORY & DIARY (IE) [25215869] **5030**

IRISH CATHOLIC DIRECTORY, THE (IE/0075-0735) [02157987] **5030**

IRISH COLLEGES OF PHYSICIANS AND SURGEONS See JOURNAL OF THE IRISH COLLEGES OF PHYSICIANS AND SURGEONS **3598**

IRISH COUNCIL FOR CIVIL LIBERTIES See BULLETIN / IRISH COUNCIL FOR CIVIL LIBERTIES **4505**

IRISH ECHO (US/0192-1215) [04988765] **2264**

IRISH ECONOMIC AND SOCIAL HISTORY (IE/0332-4893) [03680172] **2692**

IRISH EDITION (US/1063-7532) [15585706] **2264**

IRISH EDUCATIONAL STUDIES (IE/0332-3315) [09909909] **1755**

IRISH FARMER'S JOURNAL (IE) [09821131] **97**

IRISH FORESTRY (IE/0021-1192) [01641262] **2385**

IRISH GENEALOGIST (UK/0306-8358) [01798086] **2454**

IRISH GENEALOGY DIGEST (US/8756-1484) [08973866] **2454**

IRISH GEOGRAPHY (IE/0075-0778) [03778634] **2566**

IRISH HERITAGE LINKS (UK/0957-0837) [10957083 7] **2454**

IRISH HISTORICAL STUDIES (IE/0021-1214) [01753943] **2692**

IRISH IN AMERICA, THE (US) 2264

IRISH INDEPENDENT (IE) [12066691] 5803

●IRISH JOURNAL OF AGRICULTURAL AND FOOD RESEARCH (IE/0791-6833) [26288783] 2345, 97

IRISH JOURNAL OF AGRICULTURAL ECONOMICS AND RURAL SOCIOLOGY See IRISH JOURNAL OF AGRICULTURAL AND FOOD RESEARCH 97

IRISH JOURNAL OF AGRICULTURAL RESEARCH (IE/0578-7483) [01753945] 97

IRISH JOURNAL OF EARTH SCIENCES (IE/0790-1763) [11295497] 1356

IRISH JOURNAL OF EDUCATION, THE (IE/0021-1257) [01624037] 1755

●IRISH JOURNAL OF EUROPEAN LAW (IE/0791-5403) [26346573] 2985

IRISH JOURNAL OF FOOD SCIENCE AND TECHNOLOGY See IRISH JOURNAL OF AGRICULTURAL AND FOOD RESEARCH 97

IRISH JOURNAL OF MEDICAL SCIENCE (IE/0021-1265) [01588106] 3590

IRISH JOURNAL OF PSYCHIATRY (IE/0790-1186) [11140651] 3927

IRISH JOURNAL OF PSYCHOLOGICAL MEDICINE (IE/0790-9667) [19485276] 3927

IRISH JOURNAL OF PSYCHOLOGY, THE (IE/0303-3910) [03306805] 4592

IRISH JURIST, THE (IE/0021-1273) [02262764] 2985

IRISH LAW TIMES AND SOLICITORS' JOURNAL, THE (IE/0021-1281) [01605399] 2985

IRISH LIBRARY BULLETIN (IE) [06368216] 3218

IRISH LITERARY STUDIES (US/0140-895X) [05157892] 3397

IRISH LITERARY SUPPLEMENT (US/0733-3390) [08574455] 3397

IRISH MARKETING REVIEW (IE/0790-7362) [I07907362] 927

IRISH MEDICAL JOURNAL (IE/0332-3102) [00999721] 3590

IRISH MUSICAL STUDIES (IE) [23155031] 4124

IRISH NATURALISTS' JOURNAL, THE (UK/0021-1311) [03402040] 4166

IRISH NEWS AND BELFAST MORNING NEWS, THE (IE) [10588281] 5803

IRISH OFFSHORE REVIEW (IE) [06257861] 1356

IRISH PEOPLE (NEW YORK, N.Y. : 1972) (US/0888-3556) [13545723] 2518

IRISH PHARMACY JOURNAL (IE/0332-0707) [02986576] 4309

IRISH PHILOSOPHICAL JOURNAL (UK/0266-9080) [13684700] 4350

IRISH PRESS, THE (IE) [14200392] 5803

IRISH QUERIES (US/1044-6923) [18490158] 2454

IRISH REPORTS (IE) [01753952] 2985

IRISH REVIEW (CORK, IRELAND) (IE/0790-7850) [16187371] 2518

IRISH RUNNER (IE/0332-2947) [I03322947] 4901

IRISH SKIPPER, THE (IE/0791-2137) [I07912137] 4177

IRISH SLAVONIC STUDIES (UK/0260-2067) [07689593] 2692

IRISH STAGE & SCREEN (IE/0791-105X) [21002885] 4073, 5365

IRISH STANDARDS CATALOGUE (IE) 417

IRISH STUDIES IN INTERNATIONAL AFFAIRS (IE/0332-1460) [07780646] 4526

IRISH STUDIES (NEW YORK, N.Y.) (US/1043-5743) [19489038] 2693

IRISH SWORD, THE (IE/0021-1389) [01587206] 2693

IRISH TATLER See IT MAGAZINE 2518

IRISH THEOLOGICAL QUARTERLY (IE/0021-1400) [01696940] 4966

IRISH TIMES ANNUAL REVIEW (IE) [06931787] 5803

IRISH TRAVEL TRADE NEWS (IE/0021-1419) [I00211419] 5481

IRISH UNIVERSITY REVIEW (IE/0021-1427) [01160264] 3344

IRISH VETERINARY JOURNAL (IE/0368-0762) [01624393] 5512

IRISH VETERINARY NEWS (IE) [12738272] 5512

IRISH VOICE (NEW YORK, N.Y.) (US/0895-4534) [16644967] 2264, 5717

IRKUTSKII MEDITSINSKII INSTITUT. KLINIKA NERVNYKH BOLEZNEI See SBORNIK NAUCNYH TRUDOV - KLINIKA NERVNYH BOLEZNEI IRKUTSKOGO MEDICINSKOGO INSTITUTA 3638

IRLAND : WIRTSCHAFT IN ZAHLEN UND WIRTSCHAFTSDOKUMENTATION (GW) [06234196] 1568

IRLAND : WIRTSCHAFTLICHE ENTWICKLUNGEN (GW) [02355945] 1568

IRMA JOURNAL (II/0250-5304) [10258166] 2591

IRODALOMTORTENET (BUDAPEST. 1912) (HU/0021-1478) [01713595] 3397

IRODALOMTORTENETI KOZLEMENYEK (HU/0021-1486) [01753957] 3458

IROHIN (US) [25762685] 2640

IRON (UK) [03308033] 3397

IRON AGE (NEW YORK, N.Y. 1987) (US/0897-4365) [17221237] 4004

IRON AGE (NEW YORK, N.Y. : 1987) See NEW STEEL 4013

IRON AND STEEL ANNUAL STATISTICS FOR THE UNITED KINGDOM See IRON AND STEEL INDUSTRY ANNUAL STATISTICS FOR THE UNITED KINGDOM 4025

IRON AND STEEL ENGINEER (US/0021-1559) [01753960] 4004

IRON AND STEEL FOUNDRIES AND STEEL INGOT PRODUCERS (US/0732-8621) [03092328] 1612, 4005

IRON AND STEEL INDUSTRY. ANNUAL STATISTICS FOR THE UNITED KINGDOM (UK/0572-709X) [01537380] 1612

IRON AND STEEL INDUSTRY ANNUAL STATISTICS FOR THE UNITED KINGDOM (UK/0952-5505) [I09525505] 4005, 4025

IRON & STEEL INTERNATIONAL (UK) 4005

IRON AND STEEL (LUXEMBOURG, LUXEMBOURG : 1986) (LU/0378-7559) [14772228] 4005

IRON AND STEEL. MONTHLY STATISTICS (LU) 4005

IRON & STEEL REVIEW (II/0578-7661) [01753968] 4005

IRON AND STEEL SCRAP (ANNUAL) See IRON AND STEEL SCRAP IN ... / U.S. DEPARTMENT OF THE INTERIOR, BUREAU OF MINES 1613

IRON AND STEEL SCRAP IN ... / U.S. DEPARTMENT OF THE INTERIOR, BUREAU OF MINES (US) [09310759] 4005, 1613

IRON AND STEEL WORKS OF THE WORLD (UK) [02363638] 4005

IRON & STEELMAKER (US/0275-8687) [06718366] 4005

IRON COUNTY MINER (US) [12094083] 5768

IRON GAME HISTORY (US/1069-7276) [21869675] 2599

IRON HORSE NEWS (US) 5432

IRON MAN (US/0047-1496) [02251706] 2599

IRON-MEN ALBUM MAGAZNE (US) [04295218] 2117

IRON METABOLISM (UK/0142-8152) [I01428152] 488, 3590

IRON MOUNTAIN (US/8756-3142) [11699277] 4966

IRON MOUNTAIN NEWS, THE (US) [09948265] 5692

IRON ORE (CLEVELAND, OHIO) (US/0075-0883) [01404221] 4005

IRON ORE MANUAL (JA) [04910002] 4005

IRONDEQUOIT PRESS (US) [08690449] 5717

IRONMAKING & STEELMAKING (UK/0301-9233) [01793328] 4005

IRONMAN (US) 4862

IRONTON TRIBUNE, THE (US/0279-5124) [07930249] 5728

IRONWOOD DAILY GLOBE (US) [10890811] 5692

IRONWORKER, THE (US/0021-163X) [02447845] 2025

IROQUOIA BRUCE TRAIL CLUB See IROQUOIAN, THE 4874

IROQUOIAN, THE (CN/0712-6336) [09340526] 4874

IROQUOIS STALKER, THE (US/0743-7579) [04153834] 2454

IRP REPORT (US/1074-3715) [29441802] 2067

IRPI. INTERNATIONAL REINFORCED PLASTICS INDUSTRY (UK/0261-5487) [I02615487] 4455

IRPTC BULLETIN (SZ/0250-4227) [08206999] 2233

IRRI REPORTER, THE (PH/0115-2467) [02341148] 97

IRRI RESEARCH PAPER SERIES CEASED. (PH/0115-3862) [02972633] 97

IRRICAB SUSPENDED. (IS/0376-5083) [02786015] 2091, 175

IRRIGATION AND DRAINAGE ABSTRACTS / COMMONWEALTH AGRICULTURAL BUREAUX (UK/0306-7327) [01581006] 175, 2091, 2005

IRRIGATION AND DRAINAGE SYSTEMS (NE/0168-6291) [12771113] 2091

IRRIGATION AND POWER (II/0367-9993) [01588221] 2091

IRRIGATION ASSOCIATION See TECHNICAL CONFERENCE PROCEEDINGS / IRRIGATION ASSOCIATION 2095

IRRIGATION ENGINEERING (US) 2091

IRRIGATION FARMER, THE CEASED. (AT) [08648156] 175

IRRIGATION JOURNAL (US/0047-1518) [01771751] 2091, 159

IRRIGATION MANAGEMENT INFORMATION NETWORK See SELECTED BIBLIOGRAPHY ON IRRIGATION MANAGEMENT, A 186

IRRIGATION MANAGEMENT NETWORK (OVERSEAS DEVELOPMENT INSTITUTE) See NEWSLETTER 179

IRRIGATION SCIENCE (GW/0342-7188) [04223147] 175

IRRIGAZIONE E DRENAGGIO (IT/0394-9338) [I03949338] 175

IRRIGAZIONE, L' (IT/0021-1680) [09821384] 97

IRRINEWS (IS/0304-3606) [04914440] 2091, 175

IRS LETTER RULING SERVICE (US) 4658, 745

IRS LETTER RULINGS (US/0148-1940) [03270137] 2985, 4734

IRS PRACTICE ALERT CEASED. (US/1053-1173) [18059672] 4734

IRS PRACTICE AND PROCEDURE MANUAL See IRS PROCEDURAL FORMS AND ANALYSIS 4734

IRS PRACTICE AND PROCEDURES (US/0194-8210) [05037299] 4734

●IRS PROCEDURAL FORMS AND ANALYSIS (US) [25080138] 4734

IRS-SCHRIFTTUM (GW) [02453593] 2156

IRS TAX PRACTICE INSIDER See TAX PRACTICE & CONTROVERSIES 752

IRS TAX PRACTICE INSIDER, THE (US/1063-4932) [24842334] 4734

IRS TECHNICAL ADVICE MEMORANDUMS AND IRS LETTER RULINGS (US/1066-6303) [15309179] 4734

IRSHAD (SANA, YEMEN) (YE) [07439968] 5042

IRSST / IRSST, INSTITUT DE RECHERCHE EN SANTE ET EN SECURITE DU TRAVAIL DU QUEBEC, L' (CN/0822-2754) [11147498] 2864

IRT DIGEST (US/0094-2707) [01793615] 5384

IRVINE WORLD NEWS, THE (US/0195-4822) [05519974] 5636

IRVING NEWS (US) 5751

IRVINGTON HERALD (US) [19844725] 5710

IRV'S BODYBUILDING DIGEST (US/1050-1363) [21398742] 2599

●IRWIN BUSINESS AND INVESTMENT ALMANAC, THE (US/1072-6136) [29049560] 684

IRYO (JA/0021-1699) [01778486] 3590

IRYO JOHOGAKU (JA/0289-8055) [02898055] 3590

●IS AUDIT & CONTROL JOURNAL (US/1076-4100) [30325500] 1260

●IS BUDGET (US/1076-2620) [30441757] 1260

IS CAPACITY MANAGEMENT HANDBOOK SERIES (US) 1191

IS : INDUSTRIAL SOCIETY MAGAZINE (UK) [16083511] 943

IS. INTER SERVICE (US/0273-7485) [06884995] 955

IS IT IN FORCE? ... : A GUIDE TO THE COMMENCEMENT OF STATUTES PASSED SINCE ... / PREPARED BY BUTTERWORTHS EDITORIAL STAFF (UK) [12789129] 2985

ISA DIRECTORY OF INSTRUMENTATION (TRADE EDITION) (US/0272-8141) [06922287] 3481

ISA INTERNATIONAL CONFERENCE AND EXHIBIT. ADVANCES IN INSTRUMENTATION AND CONTROL : PROCEEDINGS OF THE ISA ... INTERNATIONAL CONFERENCE AND EXHIBIT See ADVANCES IN INSTRUMENTATION AND CONTROL 5081

ISA TRANSACTIONS (US/0019-0578) [01752490] 5116

ISAAC ASIMOV'S SCIENCE FICTION MAGAZINE (1990) (US/1055-2146) [22928233] 3397

ISAAC ASIMOV'S SCIENCE FICTION MAGAZINE (NEW YORK, N.Y. : 1990) *See* ASIMOV'S SCIENCE FICTION **3364**

ISAAC PITBLADO LECTURES ... (CN/0827-441X) [15515311] **2985**

ISAAS NEWSLETTER / INDIAN SOCIETY FOR AFRO-ASIAN STUDIES (II) [11274063] **4526**

ISAKIMU (CN/0384-7349) [08581120] **2536**

ISANTI COUNTY NEWS (US/8750-2267) [11143748] **5696**

ISBA NEWS (US/1055-8705) [22965037] **2985**

ISBERETNING (DK) [01791528] **1415**

ISBN REVIEW (GW/0342-4634) [04669462] **3218**

ISDN (BROOKLINE, MASS.) (US/0735-1844) [08910616] **1191**

ISDN HANDBOOK & BUYERS GUIDE *See* INTERNATIONAL ISDN YELLOW PAGES **1190**

ISDN INFORMATION SOURCEBOOK (US) **1191**

ISDN NEWS (US/0899-9554) [18277269] **1114**

ISDN REPORT *See* BANDWIDTH REPORT **1150**

ISDN-REPORT (GW/0931-0827) [I09310827] **1191**

ISDN SMALL BUSINESS (US) **684, 1191**

ISDN USER MAGAZINE (US/1058-7470) [24364575] **1191**

ISDN USER NEWSLETTER (US/1078-1005) [30993416] **1191**

ISDOC BULLETIN (NP) [03961311] **1568**

ISDS REGISTER *See* ISSN REGISTER. TAPE EDITION **3219**

ISDS-SEA BULLETIN (TH/0125-4111) [07949625] **4815**

ISEA COMMUNIQUE (US/0019-0624) [02336753] **1865**

ISEGORIA : REVISTA DE FILOSOFIA MORAL Y POLITICA / INSTITUTO DE FILOSOFIA (SP/1130-2097) [22691733] **4350**

ISEGR REPORT (US) [01211245] **1568**

ISELYA (US) [04946027] **514**

ISFORHOLDENE I DE GRNLANDSKE FARVANDE (DK/0418-6591) [01566178] **1426**

ISHIDATAMI (JA) [02245398] **3218**

ISHIKAWA-KEN EISEI KOGAI KENKYUJO *See* ISHIKAWA-KEN EISEI KOGAI KENKYUJO NEMPO **4785**

ISHIKAWA-KEN EISEI KOGAI KENKYUJO NEMPO (JA) [08208671] **4785**

ISHIKAWA-KEN KOGYO SHIKENJO *See* ISHIKAWA-KEN KOGYO SHIKENJO SHIKENJO HOKOKU **5353**

ISHIKAWA-KEN KOGYO SHIKENJO SHIKENJO HOKOKU (JA/0285-869X) [01797144] **5353**

ISHIKAWA KENRITSU KYODO SHIRYOKAN *See* KYODO SHIRYOKAN DAYORI **2657**

ISHIKAWA NOGYO NO KENKYU (JA) [03116519] **98**

ISHIKAWAJIMA-HARIMA GIHO (JA/0578-7904) [10265715] **1981**

ISHOKU (JA) [02429194] **3798**

ISI ALERT (US) [06046195] **5116**

ISI ATLAS OF SCIENCE. BIOCHEMISTRY (US/0894-3753) [16059464] **488**

ISI ATLAS OF SCIENCE. IMMUNOLOGY (US/0894-3745) [16059615] **3672**

ISI ATLAS OF SCIENCE. SOCIAL SCIENCES (US/0899-7977) [18219465] **5204**

ISI LECTURE NOTES (II/0258-1736) [06478370] **5329**

ISI ONLINE NEWS (US/0892-094X) [15078268] **3219**

ISIE (US/0894-928X) [16387640] **5290**

ISIJ INTERNATIONAL / IRON AND STEEL INSTITUTE OF JAPAN (JA/0915-1559) [19284696] **4005, 1613**

ISILILI SAM SISE AFRIKA (SA) [06388309] **301**

ISIS *CEASED.* (IT) **4478**

ISIS (US/0021-1753) [01638942] **3590, 5116**

ISIS GUIDE TO THE HISTORY OF SCIENCE *CEASED.* (US) [07091443] **5116**

ISIS MAGAZINE : MAGAZINE OF THE INDEPENDENT SCHOOLS INFORMATION SERVICE, THE (UK) **1755**

ISIS NEWS (IT) [20664408] **3590**

ISKATEL (RU/0130-6634) [03281453] **3397**

ISKCON WORLD REVIEW, THE (US/0748-2280) [10906240] **4966**

ISKRA (GRAND FORKS) (CN/0021-1761) [02592285] **4966**

ISKUSSTVO *CEASED.* (RU/0021-177X) [02027398] **353**

ISKUSSTVO KINO (RU/0130-6405) [09170194] **4073**

ISKUSSTVO LEKTORA (RU) [02441089] **3397**

ISKUSSTVO UDMURTII : SBORNIK STATEI / UDMURTSKII NAUCHNO ISSLEDOVADTELSKII INSTITUT ISTORII, EKONOMIKI, LITERATURY I IAZYKA PRI SOVETE MINISTROV UDMURTSKOI ASSR (RU) [20272152] **373**

● ISLA (MANGILAO, GUAM) (GU/1054-9390) [23025071] **238**

ISLA (OAKLAND, CALIF.) (US/0741-1138) [06039511] **2739**

ISLAH (DUBAYY, UNITED ARAB EMIRATES) (TS) [09833217] **4526**

ISLAM (UK) [05141333] **5042**

ISLAM & CHRISTIAN MUSLIM RELATIONS (UK/0959-6410) [22222987] **5042**

ISLAM AND THE MODERN AGE (II/0021-1826) [01774507] **5042**

ISLAM AND THE MODERN WORLD (BG/0379-4032) [03603105] **5042**

ISLAM (BERLIN), DER (GW/0021-1818) [01753978] **5043**

ISLAM ET SOCIETES AU SUD DU SAHARA (FR/0984-7685) [17338628] **5043**

ISLAM INTERNATIONAL (DOVER, DEL.) *SUSPENDED.* (US/8755-8912) [11446440] **4478**

ISLAM, STORIS E CIVILTA (GW/0393-246X) [15586128] **5043**

ISLAM TETKIKLERI ENSTITUSU DERGISI (TU) [05289988] **5043**

ISLAMIC AFFAIRS (US/0748-0482) [10873008] **5043**

ISLAMIC AFFAIRS ANALYST (UK) [I09694234] **5043, 4478**

ISLAMIC AND COMPARATIVE LAW QUARTERLY *See* ISLAMIC AND COMPARATIVE LAW REVIEW **2985**

● ISLAMIC AND COMPARATIVE LAW REVIEW (II) [27301956] **2985**

ISLAMIC CULTURE (IS) [08175243] **2264**

ISLAMIC CULTURE (II/0021-1834) [01774508] **5043**

ISLAMIC DEFENCE REVIEW (UK/0952-116X) [07331494] **4046**

ISLAMIC DEVELOPMENT BANK *See* ANNUAL REPORT : ISLAMIC DEVELOPMENT BANK **771**

ISLAMIC DEVELOPMENT BANK *See* AL-TAQRIR AL-SANAWI **769**

ISLAMIC HERALD (MY/0126-852X) [03146424] **5043**

ISLAMIC HORIZONS (US/8756-2367) [02200584] **5043**

ISLAMIC LAW AND SOCIETY (NE/0928-9380) **5043**

ISLAMIC ORDER (PK) [05979900] **5043**

ISLAMIC PERSPECTIVE (II) [11121096] **5043**

ISLAMIC QUARTERLY, THE (UK/0021-1842) [01753982] **4966**

ISLAMIC REVOLUTION (US/0730-613X) [05360183] **5043**

ISLAMIC STUDIES (PK/0578-8072) [01753984] **5043**

ISLAMIC SURVEYS (UK/0075-093X) [01753985] **2768**

ISLAMIC THOUGHT AND SCIENTIFIC CREATIVITY : A QUARTERLY JOURNAL OF THE COMSTECH (PK) [23865454] **5116**

ISLAMOCHRISTIANA. ISLAMIYAT MASIHIYAT (IT) [03817880] **4966**

ISLAND (AT/1035-3127) [24524242] **322, 3397**

● ISLAND ARC, THE (AT/1038-4871) [27436636] **1383**

ISLAND DISPATCH (US/0892-2497) [15154663] **5717**

ISLAND: ENERGIEWIRTSCHAFT (GW) [05136395] **1948**

ISLAND ESCAPES (US/1056-392X) [23703513] **5481**

ISLAND FARMER (CN/0823-7735) [10638843] **98**

ISLAND FISH FINDER MAGAZINE (CN/1185-7145) [25313970] **4874**

ISLAND GROWER, THE (CN/0827-2824) [11762395] **2420**

ISLAND HOME (US/1064-6906) [26375840] **301**

ISLAND (LANTZVILLE) *SUSPENDED.* (CN/0227-0773) [08340636] **3464**

ISLAND MAGAZINE, THE (CN/0384-8175) [03564956] **2739**

ISLAND (OAKLAND, CALIF.) (US/0894-3494) [16046634] **2693**

ISLAND PACKET, THE (US/0746-4886) [10076001] **5742**

ISLAND PARENT MAGAZINE (CN/0838-5505) [19752325] **2281**

ISLAND PROPERTIES REPORT (US/0882-1879) [11769755] **4839**

ISLAND PROPERTIES REPORT. QUARTERLY REPORT (US/0882-1887) [11769685] **4839**

ISLAND. SANDY BAY (AT/1035-3127) [I10353127] **3397**

● ISLAND SCENE (US/1064-8674) [26433415] **2599**

ISLAND STAR (CN/0318-207X) [02441715] **5786**

ISLAND TIMES (HILTON HEAD ISLAND, S.C.) (US/1055-3215) [23138578] **5742**

ISLAND : WIRTSCHAFT IN ZAHLEN (GW) [06234182] **1568**

ISLANDER (GULF SHORES, ALA.), THE (US/1041-2662) [12291126] **5627**

ISLANDER, THE (US) [17937849] **5654**

ISLANDICA (US) [01771752] **3397**

ISLANDS *CEASED.* (NZ/0110-0858) [02240541] **3397**

ISLANDS/AUSTRALIA WORKING PAPERS (AT/0816-5165) [I08165165] **2910**

● ISLANDS OF ALOHA, THE (US/1062-3396) [25589538] **5481**

ISLANDS (SANTA BARBARA, CALIF.) (US/0745-7847) [08702233] **5481**

ISLANDSIDE MAGAZINE (CN/0849-6056) [21348532] **2739**

ISLANDWIDE RUNNER *CEASED.* (US/0740-6266) [08458386] **4901**

ISLAS (CU/0047-1542) [02186141] **2321**

ISLE / INTERDISCIPLINAREY STUDIES IN LITERATURE AND ENVIRONMENT (US) **3397, 2217**

ISLE OF MAN DIGEST OF ECONOMIC AND SOCIAL STATISTICS (UK) [02686205] **1497, 1534**

ISLE OF MAN NATURAL HISTORY AND ANTIQUARIAN SOCIETY *See* PROCEEDINGS - ISLE OF MAN NATURAL HISTORY AND ANTIQUARIAN SOCIETY **4170**

ISLE OF MAN OFFICIAL YEAR BOOK (UK) [09455789] **2693**

ISLE SONANTE, L' (US/0732-5886) [08423800] **3464**

ISLENHA (PO) [19106899] **5204**

ISLENSK SAMT,I : ALFRIARBOK VOKU-HELGAFELLS (IC) [25844223] **1927**

ISLETON JOURNAL *See* RIVER NEWS HERALD & ISLETON JOURNAL, THE **5639**

ISM. INFORMATION SECURITY MONITOR (UK/0950-7388) [I09507388] **1227**

ISMEC, MECHANICAL ENGINEERING ABSTRACTS (US/0896-7113) [17274450] **2117, 2005**

ISNAR SMALL-COUNTRIES STUDY PAPER (NE/0926-3225) [25023250] **98**

ISO 9000 REGISTERED COMPANY DIRECTORY, UNITED STATES / COMPILED BY QUALITY SYSTEMS UPDATE *CEASED.* (US/1064-5314) [26265782] **684**

ISO BULLETIN (SZ/0303-805X) [06049338] **4030**

ISO CATALOGUE (SZ/0303-3309) [02717941] **4030**

ISO INFORMATION (GW/0579-5613) [01753724] **4124**

ISO/IRAS NEWSLETTER (UK) [24155302] **396**

ISO MEMENTO (US/0536-2067) [04573003] **4030**

● ISO NEWS : THE QUARTERLY MAGAZINE OF THE INTERNATIONAL SOCIETY OF ORGANBUILDERS (BE/1017-7515) [24088967] **4124**

ISOCHRON/WEST (US/0099-6882) [01753990] **1383**

ISOCLARE CTA (IT) **618**

ISOKINETICS AND EXERCISE SCIENCE (US) [24025474] **2599**

ISOLATIE ENERGIEBESPARING *See* UIT EUROPOORTKRINGEN **5458**

● ISOLATION AND PURIFICATION (US/1065-6081) [26648523] **978**

ISOTECH JOURNAL OF THERMOMETRY (US) [22738724] **5116**

ISOTOPE AND RADIATION RESEARCH (UA/0021-1907) [09878217] **4435**

ISOTOPE GEOSCIENCE (SZ/0167-6695) [19969263] **1383**

ISOTOPE GEOSCIENCE (NE/0167-6695) [09428986] **1042**

ISOTOPENPRAXIS — Alphabetical Title Index

ISOTOPENPRAXIS (SW/0021-1915) [02447851] **4406**

ISOTOPES IN ORGANIC CHEMISTRY (NE) [03031728] **1042**

ISOZYME BULLETIN, THE (US/0197-887X) [03511471] **548**

ISOZYMES *CEASED.* (US/0160-3787) [03536758] 3590, **488**

ISPHS CIRCULAR LETTERS *See* PHONETICIAN, THE **3310**

ISPNEWS (FRAMINGHAM, MASS.) (US/1051-2500) [21368389] **1191**

ISPOLZOVANIE NEORGANICHESKIKH RESURSOV OKEANICHESKOI VODY (RU) [04431178] **2141**

ISPRS JOURNAL OF PHOTOGRAMMETRY AND REMOTE SENSING (NE/0924-2716) [20456482] **2067**

ISPT JOURNAL OF RESEARCH (II) [03339005] **4592**

ISR, INTERNATIONLE BERG- UND SEILBAHNRUNDSCHAU. INTERNATIONAL AERIAL TRAMWAY REVIEW (AU) [05758499] 5384, **2117**

ISR NEWSLETTER (US/0020-2622) [03673789] **5205**

ISRAEL AFFAIRS (UK) **2768**

ISRAEL AGRICULTURE (IS) [09821480] **98**

ISRAEL & PALESTINE *See* I & P **4523**

ISRAEL & PALESTINE POLITICAL REPORT : I & P (FR/0294-1341) [08816945] **4526**

ISRAEL BOOK TRADE DIRECTORY (IS) [02441375] **4829**

ISRAEL BUSINESS TODAY (US) [25612971] **1497**

ISRAEL ECONOMIC AND BUSINESS REVIEW, THE (IS) [14278207] 685, **1497**

ISRAEL ECONOMIST. ANNUAL, THE (IS) [06786452] **1497**

ISRAEL ENVIRONMENT BULLETIN (IS/0334-3804) [04840164] **2175**

ISRAEL EXPLORATION JOURNAL (IS/0021-2059) [01623888] **270**

ISRAEL EXPORT INSTITUTE. BOOK AND PRINTING CENTER *See* BOOKS FROM ISRAEL **4825**

ISRAEL FISHERIES IN FIGURES (IS) [03402059] **2306**

ISRAEL. HA-LISHKAH HA-MERKAZIT LI-STATISTIKAH *See* STATISTIKAH SHEL SEHAR HUTS **852**

ISRAEL HIGH TECH REPORT (US) **5116**

ISRAEL HORIZONS (US/0021-2083) [02262787] 4478, **5048**

ISRAEL JOURNAL OF BOTANY (IS/0021-213X) [03343908] **514**

ISRAEL JOURNAL OF CHEMISTRY (IS/0021-2148) [01605748] **978**

ISRAEL JOURNAL OF EARTH SCIENCES (IS/0021-2164) [01754005] **1383**

ISRAEL JOURNAL OF ENTOMOLOGY (IS/0075-1243) [01754006] **5610**

ISRAEL JOURNAL OF MATHEMATICS (IS/0021-2172) [01644326] **3510**

ISRAEL JOURNAL OF MEDICAL SCIENCES (IS/0021-2180) [01715159] **3590**

● ISRAEL JOURNAL OF PLANT SCIENCES (IS/0792-9978) [30600706] **514**

ISRAEL JOURNAL OF PSYCHIATRY AND RELATED SCIENCES, THE (IS/0333-7308) [07777482] **3927**

ISRAEL JOURNAL OF VETERINARY MEDICINE (IS/0334-9152) [24788532] **5512**

ISRAEL JOURNAL OF ZOOLOGY (IS/0021-2210) [03460725] **5587**

ISRAEL LAW REVIEW (IS/0021-2237) [01754008] 5048, **2985**

ISRAEL. LISHKAH HA-MERKAZIT LI-STATISTIKAH *See* YARHON HA-STATISTI LE-YISRAEL. MUSAF, HA- **5346**

ISRAEL. LISHKAH HA-MERKAZIT LI-STATISTIKAH *See* YARHON LI-STATISTIKAH SHEL MEHIRIM **1541**

ISRAEL. LISHKAH HA-MERKAZIT LI-STATISTIKAH *See* RIVON LI-STATISTIKAH SHEL TAHBURAH **5401**

ISRAEL. LISHKAH HA-MERKAZIT LI-STATISTIKAH *See* TOURISM AND HOTEL SERVICES STATISTICS QUARTERLY **5501**

ISRAEL. LISHKAH HA-MERKAZIT LI-STATISTITKAH *See* YARHON HA-STATISTI LE-YISRAEL, HA- **5346**

ISRAEL. LISHKAT HA-PATENTIM *See* YOMAN HA-PATENTIM VEHA-MIDGAMIN **1310**

ISRAEL MATHEMATICAL CONFERENCE PROCEEDINGS (IS) [25140346] **3510**

ISRAEL. MISRAD HA-PITUAH *See* SEKIRAH AL PEULOT MISRAD HA-PITUAH VE-HEVROT HA-PITUAH **1583**

ISRAEL MUSEUM JOURNAL, THE (IS/0333-7499) [08962984] **4089**

ISRAEL MY GLORY (US/8755-402X) [04619185] **4966**

ISRAEL NUMISMATIC JOURNAL (IS/0021-2288) [04735280] **2781**

ISRAEL NUMISMATIC SOCIETY OF TORONTO *See* INSTANT (TORONTO) **2781**

ISRAEL ON $ ... A DAY (US) [04313192] **5481**

ISRAEL PHARMACEUTICAL JOURNAL (IS/0334-2603) [11360824] **4309**

ISRAEL SCENE (AMERICAN EDITION) (US/0199-7424) [06124528] **5048**

ISRAEL SECURITIES REVIEW (1975) (US/0147-4316) [03162549] **904**

ISRAEL SOCIAL SCIENCE RESEARCH (IS) [10396910] **5205**

● ISRAEL STUDIES BULLETIN (US/1065-7711) [26732153] **2768**

ISRAEL STUDIES IN CRIMINOLOGY (IS/0075-1391) [01754013] **3166**

ISRAEL STUDIES IN MUSICOLOGY (IS) [04839521] **4124**

ISRAEL STUDIES : THE REVIEW OF THE JERUSALEM INSTITUTE FOR ISRAEL STUDIES (IS) [19117248] **2769**

ISRAEL YEARBOOK *See* ISRAEL YEARBOOK AND ALMANAC **1927**

● ISRAEL YEARBOOK AND ALMANAC (IS) [25910807] **1927**

ISRAEL YEARBOOK OF HUMAN RIGHTS (NE/0333-5925) [01754014] **4510**

ISRAELI DEMOCRACY *CEASED.* (IS) [17204071] 2768, **4478**

ISRAELI FOREIGN AFFAIRS (US/0883-9832) [12295430] **4526**

ISRAELI JOURNAL OF AQUACULTURE, BAMIDGEH (IS/0792-156X) [19056400] **2306**

ISS DIRECTORY OF OVERSEAS SCHOOLS (US/0732-7862) [07928576] **1755**

ISS MATCHBOOK (US/0738-3819) [09563047] **4212**

ISSA NEWSLETTER (SZ) [16503712] **793**

ISSAQUAH PRESS, THE (US) [17216061] **5761**

ISSLEDOVANIE EKOSISTEMY BALTIISKOGO MORIA / GOSUDARSTVENNYI KOMITET SSSR PO GIDROMETEOROLOGII I KONTROLIU PRIRODNOI SREDY; AGENSTVO PO ZASHCHITE OKRUZHAIUSHCHEI SREDY SHVETSII (RU) [17220874] **2175**

ISSLEDOVANIE, KONSTRUIROVANIE I RASCHET REZBOVYKH SOEDINENII (RU) [02245753] **2117**

ISSLEDOVANIE SOLNTSA I KRASNYKH ZVEZD (LV) [02242012] **396**

ISSLEDOVANIE ZEMLI IZ KOSMOSA (SZ/0275-911X) [07250726] **1981**

ISSLEDOVANIE ZEMLI IZ KOSMOSA (RU/0205-9614) [07036658] **2566**

ISSLEDOVANIIA PO ISTORII I TEORII RAZVITIIA AVIATSIONNOI I RAKETNO-KOSMICHESKOI NAUKI I TEKHNIKI / AKADEMIIA NAUK SSSR, INSTITUT ISTORII ESTESTVOZNANIIA I TEKHNIKI (RU) [10014636] **24**

ISSLEDOVANIIA PO ISTORII RUSSKO-GERMANSKIKH OTNOSHENII / MINISTERSTVO VYSSHEGO I SREDNEGO SPETSIALNOGO OBRAZOVANIIA SSSR, DNEPROPETROVSKII GOSUDARSTVENNYI UNIVERSITET IMENI 300-LETIIA VOSSOEDINENIIA UKRAINY S ROSSIEI (UN) [08155113] **4526**

ISSLEDOVANIIA PO NELINEINOI OPTIKE I SPEKTROSKOPII (RU) [02243249] **4435**

ISSLEDOVANIIA PO PODZEMNOI GIDROMEKHANIKE (RU) [05737654] 2091, **2141**

ISSLEDOVANIIA PO ROMANO-GERMANSKOMU IAZYKOZNANIIU (RU) [05045553] **3288**

ISSLEDOVANIIA PO RUSSKOMU IAZYKU I LITERATURE *See* SLAVICA TAMPERENSIA **3322**

ISSLEDOVANIIA PO UPRUGOSTI I PLASTICHNOSTI (RU/0578-9583) [06044423] **4428**

ISSLEDOVANIIA V OBLASTI KHIMII REDKOZEMELNYKH ELEMENTOV (RU) [05217455] **1036**

ISSLEDOVANIJA V OBLASTI HIMII I TEHNOLOGII PRODUKTOV PERERABOTKI GORJUCIH ISKOPAEMYH (RU/0132-7070) [03110953] **978**

● ISSN COMPACT (FR/1018-4783) [26079625] **3219**

ISSN REGISTER. TAPE EDITION (FR/1021-500X) **3219**

ISSO NEWSLETTER, THE (US/1064-4393) [26282057] **25**

ISSUE ALERT *See* ISSUE UPDATE / BONNEVILLE POWER ADMINISTRATION **2067**

ISSUE BRIEF : A MONTHLY PUBLICATION FROM THE PUBLIC POLICY INSTITUTE OF AARP (US) [25907552] **5290**

ISSUE BRIEFING PAPER / UNITED STATES DEPARTMENT OF AGRICULTURE (US/0886-635X) [05299249] **98**

ISSUE DESIGN MUSEUM (UK/0960-0892) [I09600892] **4089**

ISSUE (NEW YORK, N.Y. : 1984) *SUSPENDED.* (US) [12130264] **353**

ISSUE PAPER - OFFICE OF STATE PLANNING (US/0099-054X) [02242840] **1568**

ISSUE PAPER / U.S. COMMITTEE FOR REFUGEES (US/0882-9276) [12008689] **1919**

ISSUE PAPER / UNIVERSITY OF PENNSYLVANIA, NATIONAL HEALTH CARE MANAGEMENT CENTER (US/0195-5551) [05346722] **4785**

● ISSUE UPDATE / BONNEVILLE POWER ADMINISTRATION (US) [26296591] **2067**

ISSUE (VANCOUVER) (CN/0824-1368) [11807877] **353**

ISSUE (WALTHAM, MASS.) (US/0047-1607) [01241350] **2499**

ISSUE WATCH (US/0890-4642) [14281737] **4658**

ISSUES (US) **1755**

ISSUES (AIDS PROJECT LOS ANGELES) (US) [17645189] **3673**

ISSUES & INQUIRY IN COLLEGE LEARNING AND TEACHING *CEASED.* (US/1061-2017) [25215536] **1831**

ISSUES & OBSERVATIONS (US/1065-464X) [07448683] **872**

ISSUES AND REVIEWS IN TERATOLOGY (US/0740-8242) [09530222] 3981, **581**

ISSUES & STUDIES (CH/1013-2511) [02168831] **4526**

ISSUES & VIEWS (US/1041-3839) [16958586] **2264**

ISSUES BEFORE THE ... GENERAL ASSEMBLY OF THE UNITED NATIONS *See* GLOBAL AGENDA, A **4522**

ISSUES BRISBANE (AT/0814-303X) [I0814303X] **1755**

ISSUES (CHICAGO, ILL.) (US/0885-0046) [09308348] **3857**

ISSUES (DALLAS, TEX.) (US/0732-9806) [08497321] **2536**

ISSUES, EVENTS & IDEAS (CN/0704-6936) [04039447] **1804**

ISSUES - EXECUTIVE OFFICE OF THE PRESIDENT, OFFICE OF MANAGEMENT AND BUDGET (US/0146-8928) [03066365] **4734**

ISSUES IN ACCOUNTING EDUCATION (US/0739-3172) [09716801] **745**

● ISSUES IN AGRICULTURAL DATABASE MARKETING (US/1060-6017) [25043507] **927**

ISSUES IN APPLIED LINGUISTICS (US/1050-4273) [21486493] **3288**

ISSUES IN ARCHITECTURE (US/0361-4492) [02397831] **301**

ISSUES IN ARCHITECTURE ART AND DESIGN (UK/0960-8648) [26280953] 353, **301**

ISSUES IN BIOMEDICINE (SZ/1010-8408) [21015749] 3590, **459**

ISSUES IN CHILD ABUSE ACCUSATIONS (US/1043-8823) [19595831] **5291**

ISSUES IN COMPREHENSIVE PEDIATRIC NURSING (US/0146-0862) [02851873] 3904, **3857**

ISSUES IN CRIMINOLOGICAL AND LEGAL PSYCHOLOGY (UK/0266-6863) [I02666863] **4592**

ISSUES IN EDUCATION *CEASED.* (US/0747-6043) [10762583] **1755**

ISSUES IN EDUCATION (US) **1755**

ISSUES IN EGO PSYCHOLOGY (US/0097-6555) [01799079] **4592**

● ISSUES IN ENVIRONMENTAL SCIENCE AND TECHNOLOGY (UK/1350-7583) 2175, **5116**

ISSUES IN HR (US) [29826144] **943**

ISSUES IN INTEGRATIVE STUDIES (US) [14874164] **1755**

ISSUES IN INTERNATIONAL TAXATION (FR) [16350817] **4734**

ISSUES IN LAND INFORMATION MANAGEMENT (AT) [I1035235X] 4658, **1497**

ISSUES IN LAW & MEDICINE (US/8756-8160) [11695493] 3590, **2985**

Alphabetical Title Index IT

ISSUES IN MENTAL HEALTH NURSING (US/0161-2840) [03918233] 4592, **3858**

ISSUES IN PEDIATRIC MENTAL HEALTH (US) [19586336] **3904**

●ISSUES IN PSYCHOANALYTIC PSYCHOLOGY (US/1075-0754) [29768728] **4592**

ISSUES IN RACE AND EDUCATION (UK/0308-3233) [I03083233] **1755**

ISSUES IN REPRODUCTIVE AND GENETIC ENGINEERING : JOURNAL OF INTERNATIONAL FEMINIST ANALYSIS **CEASED.** (US/0958-6415) [21586549] 548, **3693**

ISSUES IN SCIENCE AND TECHNOLOGY (US/0748-5492) [10959486] **5116**

ISSUES IN SOCIAL WORK EDUCATION / ASSOCIATION OF TEACHERS IN SOCIAL WORK EDUCATION (UK/0261-4154) [09434758] **5291**

ISSUES IN THE CANADIAN ECONOMY (CN/0709-0501) [05362457] **1568**

ISSUES IN THE CANADIAN ECONOMY. TEACHER'S NOTES (CN/0714-7910) [09234467] 1755, **1497**

●ISSUES IN THE POSTMODERN THEORY OF EDUCATION (US/1058-1634) [24233827] **1755**

ISSUES IN WRITING (US/0897-0696) [17390251] **2921**

ISSUES OF THE AMERICAN COUNCIL FOR JUDAISM (US/0741-465X) [07001858] **5048**

ISSUES PAPER / INTERNATIONAL INSTITUTE FOR ENVIRONMENT AND DEVELOPMENT, DRYLAND NETWORKS PROGRAMME (UK) [23451776] **2175**

ISSUES (PENTICTON) (CN/1182-8757) [23237475] 3590, **4241**

ISSUES (SAINT LOUIS, MO.) (US/0888-9201) [13750893] **2251**

ISSUES (VANCOUVER. 1990) (CN/1181-6430) [22632356] **1497**

●ISSX PROCEEDINGS (US/1061-3439) [25257936] 3981, **4309**

ISTAHARA (II) [11334408] **3397**

ISTANBUL TIP FAKULTESI MECMUASI. MONOGRAFI SERISINDEN (TU/0379-1173) [03421983] **3590**

ISTANBUL TP FAKULTESI MECMUASI (TU/0301-7362) [02667632] **3590**

ISTANBUL. UNIVERSITE. EDEBIYAT FAKULTESI **See** TURK DILI VE EDEBIYAT DERGISI **3330**

ISTANBUL. UNIVERSITE. IKTISAT FAKULTESI **See** ISTANBUL UNIVERSITESI IKTISAT FAKULTESI MECMUAS **1592**

ISTANBUL. UNIVERSITE. ISLAM TETKIKLERI ENSTITUSU **See** ISLAM TETKIKLERI ENSTITUSU DERGISI **5043**

ISTANBUL UNIVERSITESI. COGRAFYA ENSTITUSU **See** REVIEW OF THE GEOGRAPHICAL INSTITUTE OF THE UNIVERSITY OF ISTANBUL **2574**

ISTANBUL UNIVERSITESI ECZACLK FAKULTESI MECMUAS (TU/0367-7524) [08520931] **4309**

ISTANBUL UNIVERSITESI IKTISAT FAKULTESI MECMUAS (TU) [06719971] **1592**

ISTANBUL UNIVERSITESI. ORMAN FAKULTESI **See** ISTANBUL UNIVERSITESI ORMAN FAKULTESI DERGISI. SERI A **2385**

ISTANBUL UNIVERSITESI ORMAN FAKULTESI DERGISI. SERI A (TU/0535-8418) [01605817] **2385**

ISTANBUL UNIVERSITESI. TARIH ENSTITUSU **See** TARIH ENSTITUSU DERGISI **2631**

ISTANBUL UNIVERSITESI. VETERINER FAKULTESI **See** ISTANBUL UNIVERSITESI VETERINER FAKULTESI DERGISI **5512**

ISTANBUL UNIVERSITESI VETERINER FAKULTESI DERGISI (TU/0378-2352) [03197995] **5512**

ISTANBULER MITTEILUNGEN (GW/0341-9142) [01566500] **270**

ISTC NEW BRUNSWICK/PRINCE EDWARD ISLAND (CN/1187-2950) [25590055] **1613**

ISTC NEW BRUNSWICK/PRINCE EDWARD ISLAND (CN/1187-2950) [25590057] **5117**

ISTERSCOPIA NELLA PRATICA CLINICA-S, L' (II) **3590**

ISTF NEWS (US/0276-2056) [07319919] **2385**

ISTF NOTICIAS (US/0743-5991) [10643900] **2385**

ISTF NOUVELLES (US/8755-5506) [11348349] **2385**

ISTINA (FR/0021-2423) [01754024] **4966**

ISTIQLAL (PK) [02239407] **4658**

ISTISAN-CONGRESSI (IT/0393-5620) [20293931] **3591**

ISTITUTO AGOSTINO GEMELLI PER LO STUDIO SPERIMENTALE DI PROBLEMI SOCIALI DELL'INFORMAZIONE VISIVA **See** ANNUARIO - ISTITUTO "AGOSTINO GEMELLI" PER LO STUDIO SPERIMENTALE DI PROBLEMI SOCIALI DELL'INFORMAZIONE VISIVA **1104**

ISTITUTO CENTRALE DI STATISTICA (ITALY) **See** NOTIZIARIO ISTAT. SERIE 3 : POPOLAZIONE. FOGLIO 31 : ANDAMENTO DEMOGRAFICO **5335**

ISTITUTO CENTRALE DI STATISTICA (ITALY) **See** INDICATORI MENSILI / ISTAT, ISTITUTO CENTRALE DI STATISTICA **5328**

ISTITUTO CENTRALE DI STATISTICA (ITALY) **See** STATISTICA ANNUALE DEL COMMERCIO CON L'ESTERO **733**

ISTITUTO CENTRALE DI STATISTICA (ITALY) **See** NOTIZIARIO ISTAT. SERIE 1 : ATTIVITA PRODUTTIVA. FOGLLIO 14 : STATISTICA DEL COMMERCIO CON L'ESTERO **5335**

ISTITUTO CENTRALE DI STATISTICA (ITALY) **See** INDAGINE SPECIALE SULLE VACANZE DEGLI ITALIANI **1533**

ISTITUTO DI CREDITO PER LE IMPRESE DI PUBBLICA UTILITA **See** REPORT AND ACCOUNTS - ISTITUTO DI CREDITO PER LE IMPRESE DI PUBBLICA UTILITA **807**

ISTITUTO DI DIRITTO ROMANO, ROME **See** BULLETTINO DELL'ISTITUTO DI DIRITTO ROMANO **2945**

ISTITUTO DI RICERCA SULLE ACQUE (ITALY) **See** QUADERNI - ISTITUTO DI RICERCA SULLE ACQUE **5538**

ISTITUTO DI RICERCA SULLE ACQUE (ITALY) **See** RAPPORTO DI ATTIVITA / ISTITUTO DI RICERCA SULLE ACQUE **5538**

STITUTO DI RICHERCHE FARMACOLOGICHE MARIO NEGRI **See** MONOGRAPHS OF THE MARIO NEGRI INSTITUTE FOR PHARMACOLOGICAL RESEARCH **4316**

ISTITUTO GIAPPONESE DI CULTURA **See** NOTIZIARIO - ISTITUTO GIAPPONESE DI CULTURA **2507**

ISTITUTO ITALIANO DI NAVIGAZIONE **See** ATTI DELL'ISTITUTO ITALIANO DI NAVIGAZIONE **4175**

ISTITUTO ITALIANO PER GLI STUDI STORICI **See** ANNALI DELL'ISTITUTO ITALIANO PER GLI STUDI STORICI **2610**

ISTITUTO NAZIONALE DELLE ASSICURAZIONI **See** RELAZIONI E BILANCIO / INA, ISTITUTO NAZIONALE DELLE ASSICURAZIONI **2891**

ISTITUTO NAZIONALE DELLE ASSICURAZIONI. CONSIGLIO DI AMMINISTRAZIONE. RELAZIONI E BILANCIO DEL CONSIGLIO DI AMMINISTRAZIONE E DEL COLLEGIO DEI SINDACI **See** RELAZIONI E BILANCIO / INA, ISTITUTO NAZIONALE DELLE ASSICURAZIONI **2891**

ISTITUTO NAZIONALE DELLE PREVIDENZA SOCIALE **See** ATTI UFFICIALI / ISTITUTO NAZIONALE DELLA PREVIDENZA SOCIALE **2874**

ISTITUTO NAZIONALE PER L'ASSICURAZIONE CONTRO GLI INFORTUNI SUL LAVORO. CENTRO DI INFORMAZIONE E DI DOCUMENTAZIONE INFORTUNISTICA **See** STATISTICHE PER LA PREVENZION **2870**

ISTITUTO ORIENTALE DI NAPOLI. SEZIONE ROMANZA **See** ANNALI - SEZIONE ROMANZA **3265**

ISTITUTO PER LA RICOSTRUZIONE INDUSTRIALE (ITALY) **See** YEARBOOK / GRUPPO IRI **1632**

ISTITUTO PER LA RICOSTRUZIONE INDUSTRIALE, ROME **See** ANNUARIO DEL GRUPPO IRI **1463**

ISTITUTO SPERIMENTALE AGRONOMICO **See** ANNALI DELL'ISTITUTO SPERIMENTALE AGRONOMICO **59**

ISTITUTO SPERIMENTALE PER IL TABACCO **See** ANNALI DELL'ISTITUTO SPERIMENTALE PER IL TABACCO **5372**

ISTITUTO SPERIMENTALE PER LA FLORICOLTURA **See** ANNALI DELL'ISTITUTO SPERIMENTALE PER LA FLORICOLTURA **2408**

ISTITUTO SPERIMENTALE PER LA FRUTTICOLTURA (ROME, ITALY) **See** ANNALI DELL'ISTITUTO SPERIMENTALE PER LA FRUTTICOLTURA **2326**

ISTITUTO SPERIMENTALE PER LA MECCANIZZAZIONE AGRICOLA **See** ANNALI DELL'ISTITUTO SPERIMENTALE PER LA MECCANIZZAZIONE AGRICOLA **59**

ISTITUTO SPERIMENTALE PER LA SELVICOLTURA **See** ANNALI DELL'ISTITUTO SPERIMENTALE PER LA SELVICOLTURA **2374**

ISTITUTO SPERIMENTALE PER LA VALORIZZAZIONE TECNOLOGICA DEI PRODOTTI AGRICOLI **See** ANNALI DELL'ISTITUTO SPERIMENTALE PER LA VALLORIZZAZIONE TECNOLOGICA DEI PRODOTTI AGRICOLI **2326**

ISTITUTO SPERIMENTALE PER LA ZOOTECNIA (ROME, ITALY) **See** ANNALI DELL'ISTITUTO SPERIMENTALE PER LA ZOOTECNIA **5575**

ISTITUTO SPERIMENTALE PER L'AGRUMICOLTURA **See** ANNALI DELL'ISTITUTO SPERIMENTALE PER L'AGRUMICOLTURA **59**

ISTITUTO STORICO ARTISTICO ORVIETANO **See** BOLLETTINO DELL'ISTITUTO STORICO ARTISTICO ORVIETANO **2612**

ISTITUTO STORICO E DI CULTURA DELL'ARMA DEL GENIO (ROME, ITALY) **See** BOLLETTINO DELL'ISTITUTO STORICO E DI CULTURA DELL'ARMA DEL GENIO **4038**

ISTITUTO STORICO ITALIANO PER IL MEDIO EVO **See** BULLETTINO DELL'ISTITUTO STORICO ITALIANO PER IL MEDIO EVO E ARCHIVIO MURATORIANO **2681**

ISTITUTO STORICO ITALO-GERMANICO **See** ANNALI DELL'ISTITUTO STORICO ITALO-GERMANICO IN TRENTO. JAHRBUCH DES ITALIENISCH-DEUTSCHEN HISTORISCHEN INSTITUTS IN TRIENT **2610**

ISTITUTO SUPERIORE AGRARIO. LABORATORIO DI ENTOMOLOGIA AGRARIA FILIPPO SILVESTRI **See** BOLLETTINO DEL LABORATORIO DI ENTOMOLOGIA AGRARIA FILIPPO SILVESTRI PORTICI **5578**

ISTITUTO VENETO DI SCIENZE, LETTERE ED ARTI. CLASSE DI SCIENZE MORALI, LETTERE ED ARTI **See** ATTI, ISTITUTO VENETO DI SCIENZE, LETTERE ED ARTI. CLASSE DI SCIENZE MORALI, LETTERE ED ARTI **3364**

ISTITUTO ZOOPROFILATTICO SPERIMENTALE DELLA LOMBARDIA E DELL'EMILIA **See** SELEZIONE VETERINARIA **5521**

ISTMO (MX/0021-261X) [02187345] **5249**

ISTO E SENHOR (BL) [18556574] **4966**

ISTOCNIKOVEDENIC OTECESTVENNOJ ISTORII (RU/0321-2858) [01791239] **2693**

●ISTOE (BL) [26209433] **2739**

ISTORICESKIE ZAPISKI (RU/0130-6685) [01754039] **2620**

ISTORICHESKI PREGLED (BU/0021-2636) [02262809] **2693**

ISTORIIA BIBLIOTECHNOGO DELA V SSSR (RU) [03384162] **3219**

ISTORIIA NARODNOHO HOSPODARSTVA TA EKONOMICHNOI DUMKY UKRAINSKOI RSR (UN/0320-4421) [08996558] **1497**

ISTORIIA SSSR **See** OTECHESTVENNAIA ISTORIIA **2466**

ISTORIJA 20. VEKA : CASOPIS INSTITUTA ZA SAVREMENU ISTORIJU (YU/0352-3160) [12028594] **2620**

ISTORIJA (SKOPJE) (XN/0579-0263) [01492842] **2693**

ISTORIJA SSSR (RU/0131-3150) [01754044] **2693**

ISTORIJSKI CASOPIS (YU/0350-0802) [11023546] **2620**

ISTORIJSKI GLASNIK (YU/0021-2644) [11024531] **2620**

ISTORIKA, TA (GR/1105-1663) [I11051663] **2620**

ISTORIKO-FILOSOFSKIE ISSLEDOVANIIA (BW) [25686407] 2620, **4350**

ISTORISKI GLASNIK **See** ISTORIJSKI GLASNIK **2620**

ISTORYCHNI DOSLIDZHENNIA. ISTORIIA ZARUBIZHNYKH KRAIN / AKADEMIIA NAUK UKRAINSKOI RSR, INSTYTUT ISTORII (UN/0135-2202) [04360036] 4542, **2620**

ISTORYCHNI DOSLIDZHENNIA : VITCHYZNIANA ISTORIIA (UN/0135-2210) [03093128] **2693**

ISTP SEARCH (US) **5117**

ISTRATIJYA (LE) [11001370] **4046**

ISTRUZIONE TECNICA E PROFESSIONALE 1959 (IT/0535-899X) [I0535899X] **1831**

ISURI : DO. HARISIMHA GAURA VISVAVIDYALAYA, SAGARA KE HINDI-VIBHAGA KE ANTARGATA KRIYASILA BUNDELI-PITHA KA AYOJANA (II) [11798376] 3397, **3288**

ISVESTIIA AKADEMII NAUK SSSR. SERIIA BIOLOGICHESKAIA **See** IZVESTIIA AKADEMII NAUK. SERIIA BIOLOGICHESKAIA / ROSSIISKAIA AKADEMIIA NAUK **459**

IT (UK/0019-073X) [01586681] **2518**

IT ASIA (HK/1012-8328) [I10128328] **2566**

IT BERGEN (NO/0801-5988) [I08015988] **943**

IT. IBEROAMERICANA DE TECHNOLOGIAS (GW/0937-3764) [I09373764] **5117**

● IT LAW TODAY (UK) [27702101] **2985**

IT LINK (UK/0954-2612) [I09542612] **3219**

IT MAGAZINE (IE) [10261555] **2518**

IT (MUNICH, GERMANY) See INFORMATIONSTECHNIK UND TECHNISCHE INFORMATIK : IT + TI / ORGAN DER FACHBEREICHE 3 "TECHNISCHE INFORMATIK UND ARCHITEKTUR VON RECHENSYSTEMEN" UND 4 "INFORMATIONSTECHNIK UND TECHNISCHE NUTZUNG DER INFORMATIK" DER GI E.V **1188**

IT SPECTRUM CEASED. (US) **5117**

IT STARTS IN THE CLASSROOM (US) [01754048] **1755**

IT TRAINING (UK/0954-7940) [I09547940] **1223**

ITA JOURNAL (US/0145-3513) [11974487] **4124**

ITAA PROCEEDINGS. NATIONAL MEETING (US/1067-2850) [25609104] **5353**

ITAL COMMERCE (CN/0225-1140) [06166689] **842**

ITALIA AGRICOLA, L' SUSPENDED. (IT/0021-275X) [03401910] **98**

ITALIA ARTISTICA (IT) **322**

ITALIA CHE SCRIVE, L' (IT/0021-2881) [01947795] **3397**

ITALIA CONTEMPORANEA (IT/0392-3568) [02246260] **2693**

ITALIA DIALETTALE, L' (IT) [02220865] **3288**

ITALIA FORESTALE E MONTANA (IT/0021-2776) [09720286] **1497**

ITALIA FRANCESCANA (IT/0391-7509) [I03917509] **3288**

ITALIA GRAFICA, L' (IT/0021-2784) [04756731] **4566**

ITALIA MEDIOEVALE E UMANISTICA (IT/0391-7495) [02262813] **3288**

ITALIA NELLA POLITICA INTERNAZIONALE, L' (IT/0303-4933) [01793666] **4526**

ITALIA NOSTRA (IT) [03137116] **2693**

ITALIA NOSTRA (ASSOCIATION) See ITALIA NOSTRA **2693**

ITALIA OGGI (IT) [20881081] **5804**

ITALIA, ORIENTE, MEDITERRANEO (IT) [15103184] **2518**

ITALIA SCACCHISTICA, L' (IT/0021-2849) [04137844] **5329**

ITALIAN-AMERICAN BUSINESS (IT) [03949418] 842, **1636**

ITALIAN-AMERICAN IDENTITY (US/0163-0423) [04270693] **2739**

ITALIAN AMERICANA (US/0096-8846) [01798891] **2264**

ITALIAN BOOKS AND PERIODICALS (IT/0021-2881) [01606514] 3397, **3458**

ITALIAN BUSINESS REVIEW (MC/1120-5997) **685**

ITALIAN CANADIANA (CN/0827-6129) [13563848] **3397**

ITALIAN CARS (UK/0960-3204) [I09603204] **5417**

ITALIAN CATHOLIC FEDERATION. CENTRAL COUNCIL See BOLLETTINO : OFFICIAL PUBLICATION OF THE ITALIAN CATHOLIC FEDERATION **5024**

ITALIAN CURRENT RADIOLOGY (IT/0394-1574) [I03941574] **3942**

ITALIAN ECONOMIC SURVEY (IT/0021-2911) [01643357] **1568**

ITALIAN GENEALOGIST (US/0884-9080) [12439564] **2455**

ITALIAN GENERAL REVIEW OF DERMATOLOGY (IT/0021-292X) [01644072] **3721**

ITALIAN GREYHOUND, THE (US/0735-8504) [09047901] **4286**

ITALIAN JOURNAL (US/0894-1793) [15969161] **2693**

ITALIAN JOURNAL OF ANATOMY & EMBRIOLOGY (IT) 541, **3679**

ITALIAN JOURNAL OF BIOCHEMISTRY (IT/0021-2938) [01754053] **488**

ITALIAN JOURNAL OF FOOD SCIENCE (IT/1120-1770) [21288524] **2345**

ITALIAN JOURNAL OF GASTROENTEROLOGY, THE (IT/0392-0623) [06096704] **3746**

ITALIAN JOURNAL OF MINERAL & ELECTROLYTE METABOLISM (IT/1121-1709) [I11211709] 495, **489**

ITALIAN JOURNAL OF NEUROLOGICAL SCIENCES (IT/0392-0461) [06596359] **3834**

ITALIAN JOURNAL OF ORTHOPAEDICS AND TRAUMATOLOGY CEASED. (IT/0390-5489) [01705976] **3882**

ITALIAN JOURNAL OF PSYCHOLOGY, THE (IT) [04770075] **4592**

ITALIAN JOURNAL OF SPORTS TRAUMATOLOGY (IT/0391-4089) [06459226] **3954**

ITALIAN JOURNAL OF SURGICAL SCIENCES, THE CEASED. (US/0392-3525) [08803148] **3966**

ITALIAN LIGHTING (IT) **2067**

ITALIAN LINK (CN/1184-1087) [23237407] **2264**

ITALIAN POLITICS, A REVIEW (IT) [17276276] **4478**

ITALIAN QUARTERLY (US/0021-2954) [01754054] **2693**

ITALIAN QUERIES (US/0897-7410) [17609733] **2455**

ITALIAN STUDIES (UK/0075-1634) [01604960] **3397**

● ITALIAN STUDIES IN LAW : A REVIEW OF LEGAL PROBLEMS / EDITED BY THE ITALIAN ASSOCIATION OF COMPARATIVE LAW (NE/0927-0523) [26028969] **2985**

ITALIAN TRADE TOPICS (US/0021-2997) [01714036] **842**

ITALIAN TRIBUNE NEWS (US) [12627845] 2264, **5710**

ITALIAN VOICE, THE (US) [16246716] **5710**

ITALIAN WINES & SPIRITS (IT) [06655906] **2368**

ITALIAN YEARBOOK OF CIVIL PROCEDURE (IT) [25481086] **3090**

ITALIAN YEARBOOK OF INTERNATIONAL LAW, THE (IT) [02735411] **3131**

ITALIAN YELLOW PAGES FOR THE U.S.A (IT) [16570181] **1158**

ITALIANA VITA (CN/0700-3234) [03436645] **2693**

ITALIANIST (UK/0261-4340) [09076300] 3288, **4397**

ITALIANISTICA (IT/0391-3368) [01786824] **3397**

ITALIANO & OLTRE (IT) [14108025] **3288**

ITALIANO (NEW YORK, N.Y.), L' (US/0883-086X) [12074893] **2693**

ITALICA (NEW YORK, N.Y.) (US/0021-3020) [06772822] **3288**

ITALICA ROMA (IT/0392-7601) [I03927601] **2848**

ITALIE (FR) [02657328] **5481**

ITALIEN : ENERGIEWIRTSCHAFT (GW) [05023175] **1948**

ITALIEN : WIRTSCHAFT IN ZAHLEN UND WIRTSCHAFTSDOKUMENTATION (GW) [06260066] **1568**

ITALIEN : WIRTSCHAFTLICHE ENTWICKLUNG (GW) [05136285] **1568**

ITALIENISCH (GW/0171-4996) [09899358] 1897, **3288**

ITALIENISCHE STUDIEN (AU) [08271268] **2693**

ITALIMUSE ITALIC NEWS (US/0021-3039) [04348587] **380**

ITALIQUES / UNIVERSITE DE LA SORBONNE NOUVELLE (PARIS III), U.E.R. D'ITALIEN ET ROUMAIN, CENTRE DE RECHERCHES SUR L'ITALIE MODERNE ET CONTEMPORAINE (FR/0751-2163) [13150978] **3397**

ITALY See GAZZETTA UFFICIALE DELLA REPUBBLICA ITALIANA **2973**

ITALY See GAZZETTA UFFICIALE DELLA REPUBBLICA ITALIANA. SUPPLEMENTO ORDINARIO **5804**

ITALY (IT/0021-3063) [05773975] **2518**

ITALY CANADA TRADE (CN/0021-3098) [01938692] **1636**

ITALY. CORET COSTITUZIONALE See SENTENZE DELLA CORTE COSTITUZIONALE NEL ..., LE **3048**

ITALY. CORTE COSTITUZIONALE See RACCOLTA UFFICIALE DELLE SENTENZE E ORDINANZE **3034**

ITALY. CORTE COSTITUZIONALE See REPERTORIO DELLE DECISIONI DELLA CORTE COSTITUZIONALE **4680**

ITALY. DIREZIONE GENERALE DEL CATASTO See RIVISTA DEL CATASTO E DEI SERVIZI TECNICI ERARIALI **2030**

ITALY. ISTITUTO CENTRALE DI STATISTICA See REGIONI IN CIFRE, LE **5337**

ITALY. ISTITUTO NAZIONALE PER IL COMMERCIO ESTERO. SERVIZIO ECONOMICO AGRARIO See PRODUZIONE E COMMERCIO : PRODOTTI AGRICOLO-ALIMENTARI E FLORICOLI **122**

ITALY ITALY (IT/0393-3725) [13477368] **5481**

ITALY JEWISH TRAVEL GUIDE (US) 5048, **5481**

ITALY. MINISTERIO DELL'INDUSTRIA, DEL COMMERCIO E DELL'ARTIGIANANTO See BOLLETTINO UFFICIALE - MINISTERO DELL'INDUSTRIA DEL COMMERCIO E DELL'ARTIGIANATO **825**

ITALY. MINISTERO DEL BILANCIO See RELAZIONE GENERALE SULLA SITUAZIONE ECONOMICA DEL PAESE **1516**

ITALY. MINISTERO DELL'INDUSTRIA E DEL COMMERCIO. BOLLETTINO See BOLLETTINO UFFICIALE - MINISTERO DELL'INDUSTRIA DEL COMMERCIO E DELL'ARTIGIANATO **825**

ITALY (NEW YORK, N.Y. 1984) (US/0883-2633) [09612922] **5481**

ITALY. PARLAMENTO. CAMERA DEI DEPUTATI See DISEGNI E PROPOSTE DI LEGGE, RELAZIONI **4472**

ITALY. PARLAMENTO. CAMERA DEI DEPUTATI. SEGRETARIATO GENERALE See BOLLETTINO DI INFORMAZIONI COSTITUZIONALI E PARLAMENTARI. NUOVA SERIE **3092**

ITALY. PARLAMENTO. SENATO See GIUNTE E COMMISSIONI PARLAMENTARI **4475**

ITALY. PARLAMENTO. SENATO See DISEGNO DI LEGGE **4645**

ITALY. PARLAMENTO. SENATO. 4. COMMISSIONE PERMANENTE DIFESA See ATTI PARLAMENTARI. RESOCONTI STENOGRAFICI DELLE SEDUTE **2938**

ITALY. SERVIZI DELLA INFORMAZIONI E DELLA PROPRIETA LETTERARIA, ARTISTICA E SCIENTIFICA See INFORMATORE LEGISLATIVO (ITALY), L' **2982**

ITALY. SERVIZIO GEOLOGICO See BOLLETTINO DEL SERVIZIO GEOLOGICO D'ITALIA **1368**

ITALY. UFFICIO CENTRALE DEI BREVETTI PER INVENZIONI, MODELLI E MARCHI See BOLLETTINO DEI BREVETTI PER INVENZIONI, MODELLI E MARCHI **1301**

ITALY. UFFICIO NAZIONALE MINERARIO PER GLI IDROCARBURI See BOLLETTINO UFFICIALE DEGLI IDROCARBURI E DELLA GEOTERMIA / MINISTERO DELL'INDUSTRIA, DEL COMMERCIO E DELL'ARTIGIANATO, DIREZIONE GENERALE DELLE MINIERE, UFFICIO NAZIONALE MINERARIO PER GLI IDROCARBURI E LA GEOTERMIA **4252**

ITALY. UFFICIO NAZIONALE MINERARIO PER GLI IDROCARBURI E LA GEOTERMIA See BOLLETTINO UFFICIALE DEGLI IDROCARBURI E DELLA GEOTERMIA / MINISTERO DELL'INDUSTRIA, DEL COMMERCIO E DELL'ARTIGIANATO, DIREZIONE GENERALE DELLE MINIERE, UFFICIO NAZIONALE MINERARIO PER GLI IDROCARBURI E LA GEOTERMIA **4252**

ITATE JOURNAL (AT/0812-1435) [I08121435] 1913, **1897**

ITAWAMBA COUNTY TIMES (US) [15153646] **5700**

ITAWAMBA SETTLERS (US/0737-7932) [07503557] **2455**

ITB See BERKALA ITB **5088**

ITC COMMUNICATOR (US/0885-8063) [12733696] **1114**

ITC JOURNAL, THE (NE/0303-2434) [01791718] 1981, 2566, **1356**

ITC NEWS - UNITED STATES. DEPT. OF AGRICULTURE. INFORMATION TECHNOLOGY CENTER (US/0893-7109) [10294660] 1191, **3219**

ITD. IZOTOPTECHNIKA, DIAGNOSZTIKA (HU/0865-0497) [08650497] **3591**

ITE JOURNAL (US/0162-8178) [04061418] **5384**

ITE RESEARCH PUBLICATION (UK/0957-7238) [I09577238] 1357, **2217**

ITE SYMPOSIUM (UK/0263-8614) [14772104] **2217**

ITEA. PRODUCCION VEGETAL (SP/1130-6017) [26618066] 2345, **175**

ITEM (SP/0214-0349) [17858810] **3219**

ITEM OF MILLBURN AND SHORT HILLS, THE (US) [12593151] **5710**

ITEM PROCESSING REPORT (US/1048-5120) [20961504] **793**

ITEM, THE (US) [29435081] **5742**

ITEMS See ITEMS VAK **301**

ITEMS (NE/0167-9082) [I01679082] 353, **301**

ITEMS - SOCIAL SCIENCE RESEARCH COUNCIL (U.S.) (US/0049-0903) [01604581] **5205**

ITEMS VAK (NE) 353, **301**

ITEST BULLETIN See BULLETIN / INSTITUTE FOR THEOLOGICAL ENCOUNTER WITH SCIENCE AND TECHNOLOGY **4941**

ITEXT (UK) **1191**

ITF JOURNAL (UK/0020-9007) [01963501] **1681**

ITF RAPPORT / NORGES LANDBRUKSHGSKOLE, INSTITUTT FOR TEKNISKE FAG (NO/0802-8532) [25162698] 1981, **98**

ITG JOURNAL (US/0363-2849) [02547459] **4124**

ITHACA COLLEGE *See* NATIONAL ALUMNI DIRECTORY - ITHACA COLLEGE **1102**

ITHACA JOURNAL (ITHACA, N.Y. : 1934) (US) [09802571] **5717**

ITHACA TIMES (US/0277-1187) [04351703] **5717**

ITHACAGUN HUNTING & SHOOTING ANNUAL (US/0361-4999) [02246996] **4874, 4901**

ITI INTERNATIONAL NEWS ROUND UP (AT) 5365, **385**

ITI. INTERNATIONAL TELECOMMUNICATIONS INTELLIGENCE (UK/0268-9960) [02689960] **1158**

ITINERA GEOBOTANICA (SP/0213-8530) [02138530] **514**

ITINERAIRE DE LA MONTEREGIE, L' (CN/0834-3950) [16656422] **5481**

ITINERARI DI RICERCA STORICA : PUBBLICAZIONE PERIODICA DEL DIPARTIMENTO DI STUDI STORICI DAL MEDIOEVO ALL'ETA CONTEMPORANEA / UNIVERSITA DEGLI STUDI DI LECCE (IT) [24868174] **2693**

ITINERARIO (NE/0165-1153) [04339970] **2693**

ITINERARIO (NAPLES, ITALY) (IT) [13494883] **2518**

ITINERARY (BAYONNE, N.J.), THE *CEASED.* (US/0743-5223) [10611395] **5481**

ITISAM (TEHRAN, IRAN) (IR) [10110609] **5043**

ITL. INSTITUUT VOOR TOEGEPASTE LINGUISTIK (BE/0019-0829) [01794915] 1897, **3288**

ITL : REVIEW OF APPLIED LINGUISTICS (BE) [11110102] **3288**

ITOGI NAUCHNYKH RABOT ZA ... GOD (RU) [01796804] **459**

ITOGI NAUKI I TECHNIKI. SERIIA GEOMAGNETIZM I VYSOKIE SLOI ATMOSFERY (RU/0202-7275) [17648488] **390**

ITOGI NAUKI I TEHNIKI - VSESOJUZNYI INSTITUT NAUCNOJ I TEHNICESKOJ INFORMACII. SERIJA TEORIJA VEROJATNOSTEJI, MATEMATICESKAJA STATISTIKA, TEORETICESKAJA KIBERNETIKA (RU/0202-7488) [03161013] 5329, **3510**

ITOGI NAUKI I TEHNIKI - VSESOJUZNYI INSTITUT NAUCNOJ I TEHNICESKOJINFORMACI SERIJA FIZIOLOGIJA CELOVEKA I ZIVOTNYH (RU/0134-2673) [03374697] **581**

ITOGI NAUKI I TEHNIKI - VSESOJUZNYJ INSTITUT NA UCNOJ I TEHNICESKOJ INFORMACII, SERIJA FIZIKA PLAZMY (RU/0202-7933) [07940486] **4406**

ITOGI NAUKI I TEHNIKI - VSESOJUZNYJ INSTITUT NAUCNOJ I TEHNICESKO J INFORMACII. SERIJA ALGEBRA, TOPOLOGIJA, GEOMETRIJA (RU/0202-7445) [01780969] **3510**

ITOGI NAUKI I TEHNIKI - VSESOJUZNYJ INSTITUT NAUCNOJ I TEHNICESKOJ INFORMACII. SERIJA PROBLEMY GEOMETRII (RU/0202-7461) [16751715] **3510**

ITOGI NAUKI I TEHNIKI - VSESOUZNYJ INSTITUT NAUCNOJ I TEHNICESKOJ INFORMACII. SERIA BIOTEHNOLOGIA (RU/0208-2330) [16150790] **3693**

ITOGI NAUKI I TEHNIKI - VSESOUZNYJ INSTITUT NAUCNOJ I TEHNICESKOJ INFORMACII. SERIA OHRANA PRIRODY I VOSPROIZVODSTVO PRIRODNYH RESURSOV (RU/0202-7321) [04388471] **2196**

ITOGI NAUKI I TEHNIKI - VSESOUZNYJ INSTITUT NAUCNOJ I TEHNICESKOJ INFORMACII. SERIA ZIVOTNOVODSTVO I VETERINARIJA (RU/0134-2681) [01296745] 213, **5512**

ITOGI NAUKI I TEHNIKI - VSESOUZNYJ INSTITUT NAUCNOJ I TEHNICESKOJ INFORMACII. SERIJA CITOLOGIJA (RU/0131-1751) [02549991] **537**

ITOGI NAUKI I TEKHNIKI: DIAGRAMMY SOSTOIANIIA NEMETALLICHESKIKH SISTEM. OKISNYE SISTEMY (RU) [04378579] **4005**

ITOGI NAUKI I TEKHNIKI: EKONOMIKA I ORGANIZATSIIA OTRASLEI TIAZHELOI PROMYSHLENNOSTI (RU) [03340960] **1613**

ITOGI NAUKI I TEKHNIKI: GORNOE I NEFTEPROMYSLOVOE MASHINOSTROENIE (RU) [03116370] **2141**

ITOGI NAUKI I TEKHNIKI : KHROMATOGRAFIA (RU) [05454466] **1016**

ITOGI NAUKI I TEKHNIKI: KORROZIIA I ZASHCHITA OT KORROZII (RU) [05792654] 2103, **2013**

ITOGI NAUKI I TEKHNIKI : KRISTALLOKHIMIIA (RU) [03075202] **1032**

ITOGI NAUKI I TEKHNIKI: MEDITSINSKAIA GEOGRAFIIA (RU) [03045388] 3591, **2566**

ITOGI NAUKI I TEKHNIKI : MEKHANIKA DEFORMIRUEMOGO TVERDOGO TELA (RU) [03575140] **4428**

ITOGI NAUKI I TEKHNIKI: MIROVAIA EKONOMIKA, EKONOMICHESKOE POLOZHENIE STRAN (RU) [03341017] **1568**

ITOGI NAUKI I TEKHNIKI: NEORGANICHESKAIA KHIMIIA (RU) [04196749] **1036**

ITOGI NAUKI I TEKHNIKI : OBSHCHAIA MEKHANIKA (RU) [03575256] **4428**

ITOGI NAUKI I TEKHNIKI. OBSHCHEOTRASLEVYE VOPROSY EKONOMIKI I ORGANIZATSII PROMYSHLENNOSTI (RU) [03954663] **1568**

ITOGI NAUKI I TEKHNIKI. OKEANOLOGIIA (RU/0202-7305) [03094719] **1450**

ITOGI NAUKI I TEKHNIKI. POCHVOVEDENIE I AGROKHIMIIA (RU/0202-7143) [04990654] **98**

ITOGI NAUKI I TEKHNIKI : RAZRABOTKA MESTOROZHDENII TVERDYKH POLEZNYKH ISKOPAEMYKH (RU) [05235038] **2141**

ITOGI NAUKI I TEKHNIKI. REZANIE METALLOV, STANKI I INSTRUMENTY (RU/0202-7623) [04222563] **2117**

ITOGI NAUKI I TEKHNIKI. SERIIA ATMOSFERA, OKEAN, KOSMOS PROGRAMMA RAZREZY (RU/0208-1245) [10803302] **1450**

ITOGI NAUKI I TEKHNIKI. SERIIA BIOLOGICHESKAIA KHIMIIA (RU/0202-795X) [09461147] **489**

ITOGI NAUKI I TEKHNIKI. SERIIA EKONOMIKA, ORGANIZATSIIA, TEKHNOLOGIIA I OBORUDOVANIE POLIGRAFICHESKOGO PROIZVODSTVA / VSESOJUZNYI INSTITUT NAUCHNOI I TEKHNICHESKOI INFORMATSII (RU/0202-8158) [09405362] **5117**

ITOGI NAUKI I TEKHNIKI. SERIIA ELEKTROKHIMIIA / GOSUDARSTVENNYI KOMITET SSSR PO NAUKE I TEKHNIKE, AKADEMIIA NAUK SSSR, VSESOIUZNYI INSTITUT NAUCHNOI I TEKHNICHESKOI INFORMATSII (RU/0202-8093) [09960598] **1034**

ITOGI NAUKI I TEKHNIKI. SERIIA FIZICHESKIE OSNOVY LAZERNOI I PUCHKOVOI TEKHNOLOGII (RU/0235-229X) [20181190] **2067**

ITOGI NAUKI I TEKHNIKI. SERIIA FIZIOLOGIIA RASTENII (RU/0202-7186) [20000927] **514**

ITOGI NAUKI I TEKHNIKI : SERIIA GEODEZIIA I AEROSEMKA (RU/0202-0726) [02513635] **396**

ITOGI NAUKI I TEKHNIKI: SERIIA GEOMORFOLOGIIA (RU) [02383520] **1383**

ITOGI NAUKI I TEKHNIKI. SERIIA KHIMIIA I TEKHNOLOGIIA VYSOKOMOLEKULIARNYKH SOEDINENII (RU) [03084240] **978**

ITOGI NAUKI I TEKHNIKI. SERIIA KINETIKA I KATALIZ / GOSUDARSTVENNYI KOMITET SSSR PO NAUKE I TEKHNIKE, AKADEMIIA NAUK SSSR, VSESOIUZNYI INSTITUT NAUCHNOI I TEKHNICHESKOI INFORMATSII (RU/0202-7968) [08592867] **978**

ITOGI NAUKI I TEKHNIKI. SERIIA MATEMATICHESKII ANALIZ / GOSUDARSTVENNYI KOMITET SSSR PO NAUKE I TEKHNIKE, AKADEMIIA NAUK SSSR, VSESOIUZNYI INSTITUT NAUCHNOI I TEKHNICHESKOI INFORMATSII (RU/0202-7453) [17845759] **3510**

ITOGI NAUKI I TEKHNIKI. SERIIA MIKROBIOLOGIIA (RU/0130-6758) [03014068] **564**

ITOGI NAUKI I TEKHNIKI. SERIIA NARKOLOGIIA (RU/0235-6007) [20191248] **1345**

ITOGI NAUKI I TEKHNIKI. SERIIA NEMETALLICHESKIE POLEZNYE ISKOPAEMYE (RU/0202-7364) [21708119] **1440**

ITOGI NAUKI I TEKHNIKI. SERIIA ORGANICHESKAIA KHIMIIA (RU/0137-0251) [16942119] **1042**

ITOGI NAUKI I TEKHNIKI. SERIIA ORGANIZATSIIA UPRAVLENIIA TRANSPORTOM (RU/0134-7799) [07563753] **5384**

ITOGI NAUKI I TEKHNIKI. SERIIA PATOLOGICHESKAIA ANATOMIIA (RU/0202-7135) [05672614] **3895**

ITOGI NAUKI I TEKHNIKI. SERIIA POZHARNAIA OKHRANA / GOSUDARSTVENNYI KOMITET SSSR PO NAUKE I TEKHNIKE, AKADEMIIA NAUK SSSR, VSESOIUZNYI INSTITUT NAUCHNOI I TEKHNICHESKOI INFORMATSII (RU/0137-0243) [08578794] **2291**

ITOGI NAUKI I TEKHNIKI. SERIIA PROTSESSY I APPARATY KHIMICHESKOI TEKHNOLOGII (RU) [19796709] **2013**

ITOGI NAUKI I TEKHNIKI. SERIIA RADIOTEKHNIKA (RU) [19862479] **1158**

ITOGI NAUKI I TEKHNIKI. SERIIA RASTENIEVODSTVO (RU/0202-716X) [19862422] **514**

ITOGI NAUKI I TEKHNIKI. SERIIA RASTVORY, RASPLAVY (RU) [16159654] **979**

ITOGI NAUKI I TEKHNIKI. SERIIA SOVREMENNYE PROBLEMY MATEMATIKI FUNDAMENTALNYE NAPRAVLENIIA (RU/0233-6723) [14198545] **3510**

ITOGI NAUKI I TEKHNIKI. SERIIA SOVREMENNYE PROBLEMY MATEMATIKI NOVEISHIE DOSTIZHENIIA (RU) [16954393] **3510**

ITOGI NAUKI I TEKHNIKI. SERIIA SVIAZ / GOSUDARSTVENNYI KOMITET SSSR PO NAUKE I TEKHNIKE, AKADEMIIA NAUK SSSR, VSESOIUZNYI INSTITUT NAUCHNOI I TEKHNICHESKOI INFORMATSII, 10 SVIAZ (RU/0235-2265) [19962035] **1158**

ITOGI NAUKI I TEKHNIKI. SERIIA TEKHNICHESKAIA KIBERNETIKA (RU/0130-6774) [20373494] **1251**

ITOGI NAUKI I TEKHNIKI. SERIIA TEKHNOLOGIIA ORGANICHESKIKH VESHCHESTV / GOSUDARSTVENNYI KOMITET SSSR PO NAUKE I TEKHNIKE, AKADEMIIA NAUK SSSR, VSESOIUZNYI INSTITUT NAUCHNOI I TEKHNICHESKOI INFORMATSII (RU/0202-8042) [10172056] **1042**

ITOGI NAUKI I TEKHNIKI. SERIIA TEKHNOLOGIIA SILIKATNYKH I TUGOPLAVKIKH NEMETALLICHESKIKH MATERIALOV (RU/0235-2273) [20659165] **1440**

ITOGI NAUKI I TEKHNIKI. SERIIA ZASHCHITA RASTENII / VSESOIUZNYI INSTITUT NAUCHNOI I TEKHNICHESKOI INFORMATSII (RU/0134-7780) [09707799] **4245**

ITOGI NAUKI I TEKHNIKI. SERIIA ZOOLOGIIA POZVONOCHNYKH (RU/0202-702X) [20026761] **5587**

ITOGI NAUKI I TEKHNIKI: TEKHNOLOGIIA I OBORUDOVANIE KUZNECHNO-SHTAMPOVOCHNOGO PROIZVODSTVA (RU/0202-7690) [07031799] **4005**

ITOGI NAUKI I TEKHNIKI: VOPROSY TEKHNICHESKOGO PROGRESSA I ORGANIZATSII PROIZVODSTVA V MASHINOSTROENII (RU) [06567332] **2117**

ITOGI NAUKI: MEDITSINSKAIA GEOGRAFIIA *See* ITOGI NAUKI I TEKHNIKI: MEDITSINSKAIA GEOGRAFIIA **2566**

ITOGI NAUKII TEKHNIKI SERIIA MEKHANIKA ZHIDKOSTEI I GAZA (RU/0202-781X) [18451677] **2117**

ITOGI, SUMMARIES OF SCIENTIFIC PROGRESS : DEVELOPMENT OF OIL AND GAS DEPOSITS (US/0360-036X) [01811563] 2141, **4262**

ITOGI, SUMMARIES OF SCIENTIFIC PROGRESS : HUMAN GENETICS (US/0360-0394) [01808380] **548**

ITOGI, SUMMARIES OF SCIENTIFIC PROGRESS : METEOROLOGY AND CLIMATOLOGY (US/0360-0408) [01808496] **1426**

ITOGI, SUMMARIES OF SCIENTIFIC PROGRESS : MICROBIOLOGY (US/0360-0416) [01877532] **564**

ITOGI, SUMMARIES OF SCIENTIFIC PROGRESS : OCEANOLOGY (US/0360-0424) [01811445] **1450**

ITOGI, SUMMARIES OF SCIENTIFIC PROGRESS: THEORETICAL PROBLEMS IN PHYSICAL AND ECONOMIC GEOGRAPHY (US/0360-0432) [01808240] **2566**

ITOGI, SUMMARIES OF SCIENTIFIC PROGRESS : VIROLOGY (US/0360-0440) [01811727] **564**

ITPI JOURNAL (II) [13201541] **2825**

ITRI PUBLICATION (UK/0144-3143) [01443143] **4005**

IT'S A FANZINE (US/1054-2620) [14581089] **4862**

ITS ANNUAL TECHNICAL PROGRESS REPORT (US/0196-4410) [05811624] **1158**

IT'S GOD'S WORLD (US/0278-9809) [07938197] **4966**

IT'S HAPPENING (US/0098-7549) [01592657] **1880**

IT'S ME (US/0279-6511) [07141688] **1085**

IT'S NEWS LONDON. 1983 (UK/0265-5551) [02655551] **1191**

IT'S
Alphabetical Title Index

IT'S SPORTS (US/0274-886X) [06668037] **4901**

ITS ... TECHNICAL PROGRESS REPORT FOR THE PERIOD ... (US) [25261922] **1158**

IT'S YOUR BUSINESS (ROCKVILLE CENTER) (US/0198-7232) [06191423] 4734, **2985**

ITTIHAD AL-SINAAT AL-IRAQI *See* AL-SINAI **1461**

ITTIHAD AL-SINAAT AL-MISRIYAH *See* YEAR BOOK **1528**

●ITU NEWSLETTER (SZ) [30125289] **1158**

ITV RESOURCES IN THE DEFINED MINIMUM PROGRAM (US) [20768217] **1158**

ITYB-INTELLECTUALLY TALENTED YOUTH BULLETIN (US) [04903504] **1880**

IUCN BULLETIN (SZ/0020-9058) [02396750] **2196**

IUCN MONOGRAPH (SZ) [01506924] **2196**

IUCN OCCASIONAL PAPER (SZ) [01506991] **2196**

IUCN PUBLICATIONS NEW SERIES (SZ/0074-9273) [01506903] **2196**

IUCN PUBLICATIONS NEW SERIES. SUPPLEMENTARY PAPER (SZ/0591-2741) [01506977] **2196**

IUCN RED LIST OF THREATENED ANIMALS (SZ) [17410157] **5512**

IUCN YEARBOOK (SZ) [01521642] **2196**

IUDAU (UY) [04292853] **2985**

IUE NEWS (US/0019-0861) [02262823] **1681**

IUFRO NEWS (AU/0256-5145) [05342285] **2402**

IUFRO WORLD SERIES (AU/1016-3263) [25565554] **2385**

IUG : IZDANIE NA DRUZHESTVOTO NA PISATELITE--KHASKOVO (RU) [08054758] **3398**

IUGOSLAVICA PHYSIOLOGICA ET PHARMOCOLOGICA ACTA (YU/0021-3225) [03410134] **581**

IUI YEARBOOK / INDUSTRIAL INSTITUTE FOR ECONOMIC AND SOCIAL RESEARCH (SW/0283-8974) [10362852] **1497**

IUNOSTJ (RU) **3398**

IUPAC CHEMICAL DATA SERIES (UK/0275-0910) [07080908] **979**

IUS CANONICUM (SP/0021-325X) [05741465] 4966, **2985**

IUS COMMUNE (GW) [01754079] **2985**

IUS COMMUNE. SONDERHEFTE. TEXTE UND MONOGRAPHIEN (GW) [01754080] **2985**

IUS ECCLESIAE : RIVISTA INTERNAZIONALE DI DIRITTO CANONICO (IT) [21320177] 4966, **2985**

IUSSP PAPERS (BE/0253-4010) [05538870] **4554**

IUSTITIA (BLOOMINGTON) (IT/0092-3524) [01587598] **2985**

IUVENIS (IT) **1755**

IV *See* INTERNATIONALES VERKEHRSWESEN **5384**

IVA (IT) **745**

IVANHOE (FIRM) *See* IVANOUVELLES (MONTREAL) **872**

IVANHOE (FIRME) *See* IVANOUVELLES (MONTREAL) **872**

●IVANOUVELLES (MONTREAL) (CN/1187-8606) [26497528] **872**

●IVANOUVELLES (MONTREAL) (CN/1187-8606) [26497531] **872**

IVF AND GIFT PREGNANCIES AUSTRALIA AND NEW ZEALAND / NATIONAL PERINATAL STATISTICS UNIT; FERTILITY SOCIETY OF AUSTRALIA (AT/1030-4711) [20999861] **3763**

IVF, INGENIEURS DES VILLES DE FRANCE (FR/0336-4410) [02676169] **1981**

●IVHS JOURNAL (SZ/1065-5123) [26621492] **5441**

IVHS REVIEW (US) **5441**

IVL. B (SW/0347-8696) [11490235] **2233**

IVME REPUBLIQUE, LA (FR) [20185448] **5800**

IVORY COAST. BUREAU DE DEVELOPPEMENT INDUSTRIEL *See* PROGRAMME D'ACTIVITE - B.D.I **1622**

IVORY COAST. BUREAU DE DEVELOPPEMENT INDUSTRIEL *See* COUTS DES FACTEURS EN COTE D'IVOIRE **1590**

IVORY COAST. BUREAU DE DEVELOPPEMENT INDUSTRIEL *See* RAPPORT D'ACTIVITES - REPUBLIQUE DE COTE D'IVOIRE, BUREAU DE DEVELOPPEMENT INDUSTRIEL **1623**

IVORY COAST. BUREAU DE DEVELOPPEMENT INDUSTRIEL *See* PROGRAMME TRIENNAL DES ACTIVITES DU BUREAU DE DEVELOPPEMENT INDUSTRIEL **1622**

IVORY COAST. DIRECTION DE LA COMPTABILITE PUBLIQUE ET DU TRESOR *See* CENTRALE DE BILANS **782**

IVORY COAST. DIRECTION DES MINES ET DE LA GEOLOGIE *See* RAPPORT PROVISOIRE SUR LES ACTIVITES DU SECTEUR **2149**

IVORY COAST. OFFICE NATIONALE DE FORMATION PROFESSIONELLE. DIRECTION ETUDES ET RECHERCHES *See* INVENTAIRE DES MOYENS DE FORMATION DEPENDANT DES MINISTERES TECHNIQUES **1913**

IVRA (IT/0021-3241) [02092801] **2985**

IVS ANNUAL CROWS NEST (AT/1033-2863) [110332863] **5512**

IVS. INDEX OF VETERINARY SPECIALITIES (SA/0019-0918) [I00190918] **5512**

IVY JOURNAL (US/0882-4142) [09568978] **514**

IVY LEAF (CHICAGO) (US/0021-3276) [04086637] **1102**

IWAA NEWS (US/0737-9447) [09265468] **353**

IWATE DAIGAKU, MORIOKA, JAPAN. NOGAKUBU *See* HOKOKU. JOURNAL OF THE FACULTY OF AGRICULTURE, IWATE UNIVERSITY **92**

IWATE-KEN EISEI KENKYUJO NENPO (JA) [10074684] **4785**

IWATE-KEN JOZO SHOKUHIN SHIKENJO *See* IWATE-KEN JOZO SHOKUHIN SHIKENJO HOKOKU **1026**

IWATE-KEN JOZO SHOKUHIN SHIKENJO HOKOKU (JA) [07855034] **1026**

IWATE SHIGAKU KENKYU (JA/0289-9582) [I02899582] **2620**

IWGIA DOCUMENTS (DK/0105-4503) [03704738] **238**

IWGIA NEWSLETTER (DK/0105-6387) [17560582] **5205**

IWGIA NEWSLETTER (DK) [24865701] **238**

IWK INTERNATIONALE WISSENSCHAFTLICHE KORRESPONDENZ ZUR GESCHICHTE DER DEUTSCHEN ARBEITERBEWEGUNG (GW/0046-8428) [01775298] **1681**

IWL-FORUM (GW/0537-796X) [16847236] **5535**

IWL UMWELTBRIEF (GW/0179-3462) 2175, **2196**

IWRB NEWS (INT/1016-1317) [I10161317] **2196**

IWSA YEAR BOOK : AN OFFICIAL PUBLICATION OF THE INTERNATIONAL WATER SUPPLY ASSOCIATION (UK) [10484845] **5535**

IWSS (US) [06261926] **2420**

IX-MAGAZINE PARIS (FR/0980-1529) [I09801529] **1229**

IX-MULTIUSER-MULTITASKING-MAGAZIN (GW/0935-9680) [I09359680] **1191**

IYAKUHIN KENKYU (JA/0287-0894) [10265799] **3591**

IYAKUHIN SOGO SAYO KENKYU (JA/0385-5015) [I03855015] **4309**

IYO DENSHI TO SEITAI KOGAKU (JA/0021-3292) [07619376] **3693**

IYUNIM BE-MUSIKAH (IS) [05092830] **4124**

IZ ISTORII ENERGETIKI, ELEKTRONIKI I SVIAZI (RU) [03593871] **2067**

IZ ISTORII SOTSIALISTICHESKOGO I KOMMUNISTICHESKOGO STROITELSTVA V SSSR (RU) [05811087] **4542**

IZARD COUNTY HISTORIAN, THE **SUSPENDED.** (US/0164-7539) [03773302] **2739**

IZBIRATELNYE SISTEMY S OBRATNOI SVIAZIU (RU) [02622025] **2067**

IZBORI NA DELEGACII I DELEGATI ZA SOBORITE NA SOBRANIJATA (XN) [02244639] **4608**

IZDATELSKOE DELO; BIBLIOGRAFICHESKAIA INFORMATSIIA (RU) [03281173] **4815**

IZDATELSTVO NAUKA *See* KATALOG KNIG IZDATELSTVA NAUKA **4816**

IZDATELSTVO NAUKA. GLAVNAIA REDAKTSIIA VOSTOCHNOI LITERATURY *See* KNIGI GLAVNOI REDAKTSII VOSTOCHNOI LITERATURY IZDATELSTVA NAUKA **4816**

IZKUSTVO (BU/0324-1238) [I03241238] **2921**

IZKUSTVOTO NA PREVODA (BU) [03854565] **3288**

IZMERITELNAJA TEHNIKA (RU/0368-1025) [09993918] **4030**

IZOBRAZITEL'NOE ISKUSSTVO; BIBLIOGRAFICHESKAIA INFORMATSIIA (RU) [05957901] **334**

IZOBRETENIIA I RATSIONALIZATORSKIE PREDLOZHENIIA V OBLASTI MEDITSINY (RU) [01799481] **3591**

IZOBRETENIIA : OFITSIALNYI PATENTNYI BIULLETEN (RU/0208-287X) [27056474] **1305**

IZRAZ (BN/0021-3381) [02262840] 353, **3398**

IZTAPALAPA (MX) [06826600] **5205**

IZVESTIA (RU) [01754085] **5809**

IZVESTIA AKADEMII NAUK SSSR. SERIA HIMICESKAA (RU/0002-3353) [09261446] **99**

IZVESTIA AKADEMII NAUK UZBEKSKIJ SSR. SERIA TEHNICESKIH NAUK (UZ/0516-2629) [09179577] 5117, **1981**

IZVESTIA NA ARHEOLOGICESKIA INSTITUT (BU/0323-9535) [I03239535] **270**

IZVESTIA NA NARODNATA BIBLIOTEKA KIRIL I METODIJ (BU/0204-6091) [I02046091] **3219**

IZVESTIA NA NARODNIA MUZEJ-VARNA (BU/0324-0533) [I03240533] **4089**

IZVESTIA VYSSIH UCEBNYH ZAVEDENIJ. PISEVAA TEHNOLOGIA (RU/0579-3009) [03755953] **2345**

IZVESTIIA (BU/0525-0811) [03020510] **5535**

IZVESTIIA (BU/0068-371X) [03020609] **5117**

IZVESTIIA AKADEMII NAUK ARMENII. FIZIKA (AI) [26885368] **4407**

IZVESTIIA AKADEMII NAUK ARMENII. MATEMATIKA HAYASTANI GITUTYUNNERI AKADEMIAYI TEGHEKAGIR. MATEMATIKA (AI) [25861762] **3510**

IZVESTIIA AKADEMII NAUK ARMENII. NAUKI O ZEMLE (AI) [24767844] **1357**

IZVESTIIA AKADEMII NAUK ARMENII. SERIIA TEKHNICHESKIKH NAUK (AI) [25861746] **1981**

IZVESTIIA AKADEMII NAUK BELARUSI. SERIIA FIZIKO-MATEMATISCHEKIKH NAUK (BW) [27407161] **3510**

●IZVESTIIA AKADEMII NAUK. ENERGETIKA (RU) [26700197] **1948**

●IZVESTIIA AKADEMII NAUK. FIZIKA ATMOSFERY I OKEANA / ROSSIISKAIA AKADEMIIA NAUK (RU) [26602560] **4407**

IZVESTIIA AKADEMII NAUK. FIZIKA ZEMLI *See* FIZIKA ZEMLI / ROSSIISKAIA AKADEMIIA NAUK **1405**

IZVESTIIA AKADEMII NAUK. FIZIKA ZEMLI / ROSSIISKAIA AKADEMIIA NAUK (RU) [26770609] **1407**

IZVESTIIA AKADEMII NAUK GRUZII. SERIIA BIOLOGICHESKAIA (GS/0321-1665) [27116592] **459**

IZVESTIIA AKADEMII NAUK GRUZINSKOI SSR : SERIIA KHIMICHESKAIA (GS/0132-6074) [02590797] **979**

IZVESTIIA AKADEMII NAUK KAZAKHSKOI SSR. SERIIA BIOLOGICHESKAIA (KZ/0002-3183) [09466847] **459**

IZVESTIIA AKADEMII NAUK KAZAKHSKOI SSR. SERIIA FIZIKO-MATEMATICHESKAIA (KZ/0002-3191) [25206398] **5117**

IZVESTIIA AKADEMII NAUK KAZAKHSKOI SSR. SERIIA KHIMICHESKAIA (KZ/0002-3205) [12000675] **979**

IZVESTIIA AKADEMII NAUK KAZAKHSKOI SSR. SERIIA KHIMICHESKAIA (1966) *See* IZVESTIIA AKADEMII NAUK RESPUBLIKI KAZAKHSTAN. SERIIA KHIMICHESKAIA **979**

IZVESTIIA AKADEMII NAUK KAZAKHSKOËI SSR. SERIIA GEOLOGICHESKAIA (1964) *See* IZVESTIIA AKADEMII NAUK RESPUBLIKI KAZAKHSTAN. SERIIA GEOLOGICHESKAIA **1384**

●IZVESTIIA AKADEMII NAUK. MEKHANIKA ZHIDKOSTI I GAZA / ROSSIISKAIA AKADEMIIA NAUK (RU) [26570625] **2117**

IZVESTIIA AKADEMII NAUK RESPUBLIKI KAZAKHSTAN. SERIIA FIZIKO-MATEMATICHESKAIA (KZ) [26441360] **5117**

IZVESTIIA AKADEMII NAUK RESPUBLIKI KAZAKHSTAN. SERIIA GEOLOGICHESKAIA (KZ) [26442560] **1384**

IZVESTIIA AKADEMII NAUK RESPUBLIKI KAZAKHSTAN. SERIIA KHIMICHESKAIA (KZ) [26386401] **979**

IZVESTIIA AKADEMII NAUK RESPUBLIKI KYRGYZSTAN. FIZIKO-TEKHNICHESKIE, MATEMATICHESKIE I GORNO-GEOLOGICHESKIE NAUKI (KG) [27242938] 3510, **1384**

●IZVESTIIA AKADEMII NAUK. SERIIA BIOLOGICHESKAIA / ROSSIISKAIA AKADEMIIA NAUK (RU) [26121656] **459**

Alphabetical Title Index — IZVESTIYA

● IZVESTIIA AKADEMII NAUK. SERIIA FIZICHESKAIA / ROSSIISKAIA AKADEMIIA NAUK (RU) [26628086] **4407**

● IZVESTIIA AKADEMII NAUK. SERIIA GEOGRAFICHESKAIA / ROSSIISKAIA AKADEMIIA NAUK (RU) [26770616] **2566**

● IZVESTIIA AKADEMII NAUK. SERIIA GEOLOGICHESKAIA / ROSSIISKAIA AKADEMIIA NAUK (RU) [26283331] **1384**

● IZVESTIIA AKADEMII NAUK. SERIIA KHIMICHESKAIA / ROSSIISKAIA AKADEMIIA NAUK (RU) [26022335] **979**

● IZVESTIIA AKADEMII NAUK. SERIIA LITERATURY I IAZYKA / ROSSIISKAIA AKADEMIIA NAUK (RU) [26340248] **3288**

IZVESTIIA AKADEMII NAUK. SERIIA MATEMATICHESKAIA / ROSSIISKAIA AKADEMIIA NAUK (RU) [26717063] **3510**

IZVESTIIA AKADEMII NAUK SSR MOLDOVA. BIOLOGICHESKIE I KHIMICHESKIE NAUKI (MV) [24887503] 979, **459**

IZVESTIIA AKADEMII NAUK SSSR. ENERGETIKA I TRANSPORT *See* IZVESTIIA AKADEMII NAUK. ENERGETIKA **1948**

IZVESTIIA AKADEMII NAUK SSSR. FIZIKA ATMOSFERY I OKEANA *See* IZVESTIIA AKADEMII NAUK. FIZIKA ATMOSFERY I OKEANA / ROSSIISKAIA AKADEMIIA NAUK **4407**

IZVESTIIA AKADEMII NAUK SSSR. FIZIKA ATMOSFERY I OKEANA. ENGLISH IZVESTIYA. ATMOSPHERIC AND OCEANIC PHYSICS *See* IZVESTIYA. ATMOSPHERIC AND OCEANIC PHYSICS **1407**

IZVESTIIA AKADEMII NAUK SSSR. FIZIKA ZEMLI (RU/0002-3337) [01839419] **4407**

IZVESTIIA AKADEMII NAUK SSSR. MEKHANIKA ZHIDKOSTI I GAZA *See* IZVESTIIA AKADEMII NAUK. MEKHANIKA ZHIDKOSTI I GAZA / ROSSIISKAIA AKADEMIIA NAUK **2117**

IZVESTIIA AKADEMII NAUK SSSR. SERIIA BIOLOGICHESKAIA (RU/0002-3329) [02444481] **459**

IZVESTIIA AKADEMII NAUK SSSR. SERIIA BIOLOGICHESKAIA (RU/0002-3329) [05227218] **459**

IZVESTIIA AKADEMII NAUK SSSR. SERIIA EKONOMICHESKAIA *See* OBSHCHESTVO I EKONOMIKA **1576**

IZVESTIIA AKADEMII NAUK SSSR. SERIIA GEOGRAFICHESKAIA (RU/0373-2444) [01644968] **2566**

IZVESTIIA AKADEMII NAUK SSSR. SERIIA GEOLOGICHESKAIA (RU/0321-1703) [06419365] **1384**

IZVESTIIA AKADEMII NAUK SSSR. SERIIA LITERATURY I IAZYKA *See* IZVESTIIA AKADEMII NAUK. SERIIA LITERATURY I IAZYKA / ROSSIISKAIA AKADEMIIA NAUK **3288**

IZVESTIIA AKADEMII NAUK SSSR. SERIIA MATEMATICHESKAIA *See* IZVESTIIA AKADEMII NAUK. SERIIA MATEMATICHESKAIA / ROSSIISKAIA AKADEMIIA NAUK **3510**

IZVESTIIA AKADEMII NAUK SSSR. TEKHNICHESKAIA KIBERNETIKA *See* IZVESTIIA AKADEMII NAUK. TEKHNICHESKAIA KIBERNETIKA / ROSSIISKAIA AKADEMIIA NAUK **5117**

IZVESTIIA AKADEMII NAUK SSSR. TEKHNICHESKAIA KIBERNETIKA. ENGLISH. SOVIET JOURNAL OF COMPUTER AND SYSTEMS SCIENCES *See* JOURNAL OF COMPUTER AND SYSTEMS SCIENCES INTERNATIONAL **1191**

● IZVESTIIA AKADEMII NAUK. TEKHNICHESKAIA KIBERNETIKA / ROSSIISKAIA AKADEMIIA NAUK (RU) [26570644] **5117**

IZVESTIIA AKADEMII NAUK TURKMENISTANA. SERIIA FIZIKO-MATEMATICHESKIKH, TEKHNICHESKIKH, KHIMICHESKIKH I GEOLOGICHESKIKH NAUK (TK) [26569215] 979, **4407**

IZVESTIIA AKADEMII NAUK TURKMENSKOI SSR. SERIIA BIOLOGICHESKIKH NAUK *See* TURKMENISTAN YLYMLAR AKADEMIIASYNYNG KHABARLARY. BIOLOGIK YLYMLARYNG SERIIASY **475**

IZVESTIIA AKADEMII NAUK TURKMENSKOI SSR. SERIIA FIZIKO-MATEMATICHESKIKH, TEKHNICHESKIKH, KHIMICHESKIKH I GEOLOGICHESKIKH NAUK (TK) [24223596] 979, **4407**

IZVESTIIA AKADEMII NAUK UZSSR. SERIIA FIZIKO-MATEMATICHESKIKH NAUK (UZ/0131-8012) [01968958] 3510, **4407**

IZVESTIIA AKADEMII NAUK UZSSR. TEKHNICHESKIE NAUKI (UZ) [26289807] 5117, **1981**

IZVESTIIA AKADEMIIA NAUK AZERBAIDZHANSKOI SSR. SERIIA BIOLOGICHESKIKH NAUK (AJ/0132-6112) [01478771] **459**

IZVESTIIA AKADEMIIA NAUK TURKMENSKOI SSR. SERIIA BIOLOGICHESKIKH NAUK (TK/0321-1746) [03499507] 98, **459**

IZVESTIIA GLAVNOI ASTRONOMICHESKOI OBSERVATORII V PULKOVE (RU/0367-7966) [09419119] **25**

IZVESTIIA : MEKHANIKA TVERDOGO TELA (RU/0572-3299) [01830967] **2117**

IZVESTIIA NA ARKHIVNIIA INSTITUT (BU) [05860607] **2481**

IZVESTIIA NA DURZHAVNITE ARKHIVI / MINISTERSTVO NA VUTRESHNITE RABOTI, OTDEL "DURZHAVEN ARKHIV" (BU/0323-9780) [03720459] **2481**

IZVESTIIA NA INSTITUTA ZA BULGARSKI EZIK (BU/0068-3787) [01537681] **3288**

IZVESTIIA NA INSTITUTA ZA ISTORIIA / BULGARSKA AKADEMIIA NA NAUKITE, OTDELENIE ZA ISTORICHESKI I PEDAGOGICHESKI NAUKI (BU) [09978714] **2693**

IZVESTIIA NA INSTITUTA ZA PRAVNI NAUKI (BU) [01537681] **2985**

IZVESTIIA NA NAUCHNIIA ARKHIV / BULGARSKA AKADEMIIA NA NAUKITE, TSENTRALNA BIBLIOTEKA SUS SLUZHBA ZA NAUCHNA INFORMATSIIA I NAUCHEN ARKHIV (BU/0525-0870) [03020534] **2481**

IZVESTIIA ORDENA TRUDOVOGO ASTROFIZICH ESKOI OBSERVATORII (US/0190-2717) [04697617] **396**

IZVESTIIA ORDENA TRUDOVOGO KRASNOGO ZNAMENI KRYMSKOI ASTROFIZICHESKOI OBSERVATORII (RU) [04388377] **396**

IZVESTIIA PO KHIMIIA *See* BULGARIAN CHEMICAL COMMUNICATIONS **963**

IZVESTIIA. SERIIA FIZICHESKAIA (RU) [01478799] **4407**

IZVESTIIA. SERIIA KHIMICHESKAIA *CEASED.* (RU/0002-3353) [01478802] **979**

IZVESTIIA SIBIRSKOGO OTDELENIIA AKADEMII NAUK SSSR. SERIIA BIOLOGICHESKIKH NAUK (RU/0568-6547) [03531522] **460**

IZVESTIIA SIBIRSKOGO OTDELENIIA AKADEMII NAUK SSSR. SERIIA REGION. EKONOMIDA I SOTSIOLOGIIA (RU/0868-5169) [23035975] **1568**

IZVESTIIA SIBIRSKOGO OTDELENIIA AN SSSR. SIBIRSKII FIZIKO-TEKHNICHESKII ZHURNAL (RU) [25223219] **5117**

IZVESTIIA SO AN SSSR. SIBIRSKII BIOLOGICHESKII ZHURNAL *See* IZVESTIIA SORAN. SIBIRSKII BIOLOGICHESKII ZHURNAL **460**

IZVESTIIA SO AN SSSR. SIBIRSKII FIZIKO-TEKHNICHESKII ZHURNAL *See* IZVESTIIA SORAN. SIBIRSKII FIZIKO-TEKHNICHESKII ZHURNAL **4407**

IZVESTIIA SO AN SSSR. SIBIRSKII KHIMICHESKII ZHURNAL *See* IZVESTIIA SORAN. SIBIRSKII KHIMICHESKII ZHURNAL **979**

● IZVESTIIA SORAN. SIBIRSKII BIOLOGICHESKII ZHURNAL (RU) [26717146] **460**

● IZVESTIIA SORAN. SIBIRSKII FIZIKO-TEKHNICHESKII ZHURNAL (RU) [26717158] **4407**

● IZVESTIIA SORAN. SIBIRSKII KHIMICHESKII ZHURNAL (RU) [26717190] **979**

IZVESTIIA TIMIRIAZEVSKOI SELSKOKHOZIAISTVENNOI AKADEMII (RU/0021-342X) [11120520] **98**

IZVESTIIA TSK TPSS *CEASED.* (RU/0235-7097) [19341922] **4658**

IZVESTIIA VNIIG IMENI B.E. VEDENEEVA / MINISTERSTVO ENERGETIKI I ELEKTRIFIKATSII SSSR GLAVNIPROEKT, VSESOIUZNYI ORDENA TRUDOVO KRASNOGO ZNAMENI NAUCHNO-ISSLEDOVATELSKII INSTITUT GIDROTEKHNIKI IMEMI B.E. VEDENEEVA (RU) [10715478] 2067, **1948**

IZVESTIIA VSESOIUZNOGO GEOGRAFICHESKOGO OBSHCHESTVA (RU/0373-353X) [01570636] **2566**

IZVESTIIA VYSSHIKH UCHEBMYKH ZAVEDENII. RADIOELEKTRONIKA (US/0735-2727) [03917350] **2067**

IZVESTIIA VYSSHIKH UCHEBNYKH ZAVEDENII. CHERNAIA METALLURGIIA (RU) [02447868] **4005**

IZVESTIIA VYSSHIKH UCHEBNYKH ZAVEDENII. ELEKTROMEKHANIKA (RU/0136-3360) [09467388] **2067**

IZVESTIIA VYSSHIKH UCHEBNYKH ZAVEDENII. FIZIKA / MINISTERSTVO VYSSHEGO OBRAZOVANIIA SSSR (RU/0021-3411) [19677705] **4407**

IZVESTIIA VYSSHIKH UCHEBNYKH ZAVEDENII. LESNOI ZHURNAL (RU/0536-1036) [01779818] **2385**

IZVESTIIA VYSSHIKH UCHEBNYKH ZAVEDENII. NEFT I GAZ / MINISTERSTVO VYSSHEGO I SREDNEGO SPETSIALNOGO OBRAZOVANIIA SSSR (AJ/0445-0108) [03359056] **4262**

IZVESTIIA VYSSHIKH UCHEBNYKH ZAVEDENII. PRAVOVEDENIE (RU/0131-8039) [03282943] **2985**

IZVESTIIA VYSSHIKH UCHEBNYKH ZAVEDENII. STROITELSTVO / GOSUDARSTVENNYI KOMITET SSSR PO NARODNOMU OBRAZOVANIIU (RU) [25910244] **301**

IZVESTIJA AKADEMII NAUK ARMJANSKOJ SSR. FIZIKA (AI/0002-3035) [04768491] **4407**

IZVESTIJA AKADEMII NAUK ARMJANSKOJ SSR. MEHANIKA (AI/0002-3051) [01478770] **2117**

IZVESTIJA AKADEMII NAUK AZERBAIDZANSKOI SSR. SERIJA NAUK O ZEMLE (AJ/0002-3124) [01478773] **1384**

IZVESTIJA AKADEMII NAUK AZERBAJDZANSKOJ SSR. SERIJA FIZIKO-TEHNICESKIH I MATEMATICESKIH NAUK (AJ/0002-3108) [09261581] 3510, **4407**

IZVESTIJA AKADEMII NAUK AZERBAJDZANSKOJ SSR. SERIJA NAUK O ZEMLE (AJ/0002-3124) [08164264] 2566, **1384**

IZVESTIJA AKADEMII NAUK SSSR. SERIJA FIZICESKAJA (RU/0367-6765) [09261407] **4407**

IZVESTIJA AKADEMII NAUK TADZIKSKOJ SSR. OTDELENIE BIOLOGICESKIH NAUK (TA/0002-3477) [04797072] **460**

IZVESTIJA. AKADEMIJA NAUK SSSR. NEORGANICESKIE MATERIALY (US/0002-337X) [01830942] **1036**

IZVESTIJA - DRZAVEN INSTITUT ZA KONTROL NA LEKARSTVENITE SREDSTVA (BU/0323-9438) [11248254] **3591**

IZVESTIJA NA INSTITUT PO TEHNICESKA MEHANIKA (BU/0068-3892) [03015091] **2117**

IZVESTIJA SEVERO-KAVKAZSKOGO NAUCNOGO CENTRA VYSSEJ SKOLY. ESTESTVENNYE NAUKI (RU/0321-3005) [10791463] **1384**

IZVESTIJA SEVERO-KAVKAZSKOGO NAUCNOGO CENTRA VYSSEJ SKOLY. TEHNICESKIE NAUKI (RU/0321-2653) [10792599] **5117**

IZVESTIJA VYSSIH UCEBNYH ZAVEDENIJ, ENERGETIKA (BW/0579-2983) [09419190] **1948**

IZVESTIJA VYSSIH UCEBNYH ZAVEDENIJ. GEODEZIJA I AEROFOTOSEMKI (RU/0536-101X) [03256447] **2566**

IZVESTIJA VYSSIH UCEBNYH ZAVEDENIJ. GORNYJ ZURNAL (RU/0536-1028) [01588657] **2141**

IZVESTIJA VYSSIH UCEBNYH ZAVEDENIJ. HIMIJA I HIMICESKAJA TEHNOLOGIJA (RU/0579-2991) [19227916] 2013, **979**

IZVESTIJA VYSSIH UCEBNYH ZAVEDENIJ. HIMIJA I HIMICESKAJA TEHNOLOGIJA (RU/0579-2991) [04058209] **979**

IZVESTIJA VYSSIH UCEBNYH ZAVEDENIJ. MASINOSTROENIE (RU/0536-1044) [09423864] **2117**

IZVESTIJA VYSSIH UCEBNYH ZAVEDENIJ. MATEMATIKA (RU/0021-3446) [01780970] **3510**

IZVESTIJA VYSSIH UCEBNYH ZAVEDENIJ. PRIBOROSTROENIE (RU/0021-3454) [09419607] **4124**

IZVESTIJA VYSSIH UCEBNYH ZAVEDENIJ. RADIOELEKTRONIKA (UN/0021-3470) [06935317] **2067**

IZVESTIJA VYSSIH UCEBNYH ZAVEDENIJ. RADIOFIZIKA (RU/0021-3462) [03324051] **1114**

IZVESTIJA VYSSIH UCEBNYH ZAVEDENIJ. TEHNOLOGIJA LEGKOJ PROMYSLENNOSTI *CEASED.* (UN/0021-3489) [09419598] **3482**

IZVESTIJA VYSSIH UCEBNYH ZAVEDENIJ. TEHNOLOGIJA TEKSTILNOJ PROMYSLENNOSTI *CEASED.* (RU/0021-3497) [04068380] **5353**

IZVESTIJA VYSSIH UCEBNYH ZAVEDNIJ. AVIACIONNAJA TEHNIKA (RU/0579-2975) [03461613] **25**

IZVESTIJA VYSSIKH UCEBNYH ZAVEDENIJ. CVETNAJA METALLURGIJA (RU/0021-3438) [02447869] **4005**

IZVESTIJA VYSSYHUCEBNYH ZAVEDENIJ. GEOLOGIJA I RAZVEDKA (RU/0016-7762) [03260058] **1384**

IZVESTIYA, ACADEMY OF SCIENCES, USSR. PHYSICS OF THE SOLID EARTH (US/0001-4354) [01478798] **1407**

● IZVESTIYA. ATMOSPHERIC AND OCEANIC PHYSICS (US/0001-4338) [28731658] **1407**

IZVESTIYA. ATMOSPHERIC AND OCEANIC PHYSICS (US/0001-4338) [01478792] **1407**

● IZVESTIYA. MATHEMATICS (US/1064-5632) [26329193] **3511**

J — Alphabetical Title Index

J & F RECORD SPECIAL (US/0363-8367) [02548586] **4124**

J.C.I. NEWS (US) **5232**

J. CROSS EXECUTIVE ALERT (US/0730-9368) [08036054] **685**

J.D.I (FR/0246-8298) [102468298] **1755**

J. IIC-CG : JOURNAL OF THE INTERNATIONAL INSTITUTE FOR CONSERVATION, CANADIAN GROUP (CN/0381-0402) [03963075] **353**

J.K. LASSER'S MONTHLY TAX LETTER (US/1056-3121) [23659417] **4734**

J.K. LASSER'S PERSONAL INVESTMENT ANNUAL (US/1041-2115) [18676871] **904**

J. L. NEWS (DK) [09229195] **4177**

J MAGAZINE (FR/0224-9928) [102249928] **1755**

J.O.P *See* N.Y. JOURNAL JAPAN **4529**

J P 4 (IT/0394-3437) [103943437] **25**

J.P. WEEKLY LAW DIGEST, THE (UK/0264-3723) [02652604] **2986**

J. PAUL GETTY MUSEUM *See* J. PAUL GETTY MUSEUM JOURNAL, THE **4089**

J. PAUL GETTY MUSEUM JOURNAL, THE (US/0362-1979) [02304305] 353, **4089**

J. PAUL GETTY TRUST *See* BULLETIN / THE J. PAUL GETTY TRUST **346**

J.T.R. INFORMATIONS (FR/0754-4618) [107544618] **5385**

J U C O REVIEW (US/0047-2956) [02253219] **4901**

J + W TELEFAX INTERNATIONAL (GW) **1158**

J + W TRAVEL INTERNATIONAL (GW) [24242901] **5481**

J3E L JOURNAL DE L EQUIPMENT ELECTRIQUE ET ELECTRONIQUE (FR/0758-3826) [107583826] **2067**

JA QUARTERLY (JA) **301**

JAARBERICHT / RIJKSWATERSTAAT (NE) [10528467] **2091**

JAARBERICHT VAN HET VOORAZIATISCH-EGYPTISCH GENOOTSCHAP EX ORIENTE LUX (NE) [01716288] 270, **2769**

JAARBOEK (NE) [01785855] **3288**

JAARBOEK (SA) [06784770] **1831**

JAARBOEK (AMSTERDAM (NETHERLANDS). BESTUURSINFORMATIE. AFDELING STATISTIEK) (NE) [07980210] **5329**

JAARBOEK - ARCA LOVANIENSIS ARTES ATQUE HISTORIAE RESERANS DOCUMENTA (BE/0774-2851) [107742851] 353, 2848, **322**

JAARBOEK (COMMISSION ROYALE BELGE DE FOLKLORE. SECTION FLAMANDE) *See* JAARBOEK MET VOLKSKUNDIGE BIBLIOGRAFIE / KONINKLIJKE BELGISCHE COMMISSIE VOOR VOLKSKUNDE, VLAAMSE AFDELING **2321**

JAARBOEK (FINANCIEELE DAGBLAD BV) (NE) [13494768] **1568**

JAARBOEK / KONINKLIJKE BELGISCHE COMMISSIE VOOR VOLKSKUNDE, VLAAMSE AFDELING (BE/0778-5607) [09528229] **2321**

JAARBOEK - MAATSCHAPPIJ DER NEDERLANDSE LETTERKUNDE TE LEIDEN (NE) [04598160] **5232**

JAARBOEK MET VOLKSKUNDIGE BIBLIOGRAFIE / KONINKLIJKE BELGISCHE COMMISSIE VOOR VOLKSKUNDE, VLAAMSE AFDELING (BE) [15683933] **2321**

JAARBOEK MONUMENTENZORG (NE/0925-7845) [25586551] 2693, **301**

JAARBOEK OPENBARE BIBLIOTHEKEN (NE) [04820367] **3219**

JAARBOEK / ORANJE-NASSAU MUSEUM (NE/0922-775X) [17343121] **4089**

JAARBOEK / STAD BRUGGE, STEDELIJKE MUSEA (BE/0771-839X) [14930219] 353, **4089**

JAARBOEK/VADEMECUM VOOR HET VERZEKERINGSWEZEN (NE) [01785808] **2885**

JAARBOEK VAN DE GESCHIED- EN OUDHEIDKUNDIGE KRING VOOR LEUVEN EN OMGEVING (BE/0774-5435) [107745435] **2693**

JAARBOEK VAN DE HAVEN VAN ANTWERPEN. ANNUAIRE DU PORT D'ANVERS. ANTWERP PORT ANNUAL (BE) [06286175] **5450**

JAARBOEK VAN HET CENTRAAL BUREAU VOOR GENEALOGIE EN VAN HET ICONOGRAFISCH BUREAU (NE/0922-6702) [09226702] 2482, **2455**

JAARBOEK VAN HET KATHOLIEK DOCUMENTATIE CENTRUM (NE) [01799492] **5030**

JAARBOEK VAN HET KONINKLIJK MUSEUM VOOR SCHONE KUNSTEN (BE) [03251773] **353**

JAARBOEK (VLAAMS INSTITUUT VOOR AMERIKAANSE KULTUREN) (BE) [10416751] **270**

JAARBOEK VOOR DE GESCHIEDENIS VAN BEDRIJF EN TECHNIEK (NE/0920-7724) [12690700] **5117**

JAARBOEK (WEST FLANDERS, BELGIUM) (BE) [18803114] **4658**

JAARLIKSE SEMINAAR OOR TEORETIESE FISIKA (SA/0254-1912) [10037634] **4428**

JAARLIKSE STRALINGSVERSLAG (SA/0377-0311) [01784863] **4435**

JAAROVERZICHT / GEMEENTEARCHIEF AMSTERDAM (NE) [19099219] 4658, **2482**

JAARSTATISTIEK OVER DE INTERNATIONALE TRAFIEK DER HAVENS (BE) [03218087] **5401**

JAARSTATISTIEK VAN DE BUITENLANDSE HANDEL PER LAND EN GOEDERENSOORT (NE) 842, **730**

JAARSTATISTIEK VAN DE IN-EN UITVOER PER LAND VAN DE NEDERLANDSE ANTILLEN (NE/0077-6645) [01248773] **842**

JAARSTATISTIEK VAN DE VEEVOEDERS (NE) [05818642] **213**

JAARSVERSLAG - INSTITUUT VOOR PLANTENZEIKTENKUNDIG ONDERZOEK (NE/0074-0446) [01623962] 4245, **2421**

JAARVERSLAG (NE) [17633405] 98, **4839**

JAARVERSLAG (SA) [25564268] 4205, **1681**

JAARVERSLAG / ADMINISTRASIE VIR KAVANGO'S (NE) [19224714] **1681**

JAARVERSLAG / ALGEMEEN WERKLOOSHEIDSFONDS (NE) [20949829] **2885**

JAARVERSLAG - ARBEIDSINSPECTIE (NE) [03884843] **1613**

JAARVERSLAG BETREFFENDE HET EXPERIMENT VERTROUWENSARTSEN INZAKE KINDERMISHANDELING (NE) [05817625] **3166**

JAARVERSLAG / COMMISSIE INDUSTRIEVESTIGING GRONINGEN (NE) [09071533] **1613**

JAARVERSLAG - DEPARTEMENT VAN KLEURLING-, REHOBOTH - EN NAMABETREKKINGE (SA) [03701639] **2640**

JAARVERSLAG / DEPARTEMENT VAN MANNEKRAG / ANNUAL REPORT / DEPARTMENT OF MANPOWER (SA) [25209145] 1681, **4658**

JAARVERSLAG / DIENST GRONDWATERVERKENNING TNO (NE) [09873601] **1415**

JAARVERSLAG FINANCIERING EN COORDINATIE (NE) [19523118] 1831, **793**

JAARVERSLAG / GEMEENTEARCHIEF AMSTERDAM (NE) [19572289] **2482**

JAARVERSLAG - HARMONISATIERAAD WELZIJNSBELEID (NE) [05250582] **5291**

JAARVERSLAG - KONINKLIJK NEDERLANDS VERBOND VAN DRUKKERIJEN (NE) [04202744] **4566**

JAARVERSLAG - KORINGRAAD (SA) [03314265] **1568**

JAARVERSLAG (NEDERLANDSCHE BANK (AMSTERDAM, NETHERLANDS)) (NE) [10993516] **793**

JAARVERSLAG - NEDERLANDSCHE SCHEEPVAART UNIE (NE) [01794013] **5385**

JAARVERSLAG - NEDERLANDSE FINANCIERINGS-MAATSCHAPPIJ VOOR ONTWIKKELINGSLANDEN (NE) [03592917] **4734**

JAARVERSLAG - NEDERLANDSE HOUTBOND EN AANGESLOTEN VERENIGINGEN (NE/0550-4554) [02239841] **1613**

JAARVERSLAG (NETHERLANDS. KONINKLIJKE LANDMACHT. SECTIE MILITAIRE GESCHIEDENIS) (NE) [09468668] **2693**

JAARVERSLAG (NETHERLANDS. RIJKSINKOOPBUREAU) (NE) [10896526] 950, **4658**

JAARVERSLAG - PRODUKTSCHAP VOOR LANDBOUWZAAIZADEN (NE) [04481601] **98**

JAARVERSLAG - PROVINCIALE WATERSTAAT IN LIMBURG (NE) [01793855] **2025**

JAARVERSLAG - RIJKSDIENST VOOR DE MONUMENTENZORG (NE) [02561361] **2693**

JAARVERSLAG / RIJKSINSTITUUT VOOR NATUURBEHEER (NE/0302-5276) [04093924] **4166**

JAARVERSLAG / RIJKSPROEFSTATION VOOR ZAADONDERZOEK (NE) [12027151] **175**

JAARVERSLAG / SOCIAAL-ECONOMISCHE RAAD (NE) [08039659] **1568**

JAARVERSLAG - SOCIALE VERZEKERINGSRAAAD (NE) [03762029] 2885, **5291**

JAARVERSLAG / SUID-AFRIKAANSE ONTWIKKELINGSTRUSTKORPORASIE BEPERK (STK) (SA) [16662772] **1568**

JAARVERSLAG - TECHNISCH PHYSISCHE DIENST TNO-TH (NE) [02403449] **4407**

JAARVERSLAG / UNIVERSITAIR REACTOR INSTITUUT (NE) [18269472] **4448**

JAARVERSLAG VAN DE NEDERLANDS-ZUIDAFRIKAANSE VERENIGING (NE) [08868274] **2693**

JAARVERSLAG VAN DE PERMANENTE COMMISSIE VOOR OVERHEIDSDOCUMENTATIE (NE) [05796019] **4658**

JAARVERSLAG VAN DIE OLIESADERAAD VIR DIE JAAR ... (SA) [12094387] **175**

JAARVERSLAG VAN DIE SUID-AFRIKAANSE REGSKOMMISSIE (SA) [02246332] **2986**

● JAB MAGAZINE (US) **2536**

JABALPUR LAW JOURNAL, THE (II) [01589192] **2986**

JABALPUR LEGAL QUARTERLY (II) [08022361] **2986**

JABBERWOCKY (UK/0305-8182) [02169986] **3398**

JABBERWOCKY (TORONTO) (CN/0316-6759) [02247899] **1065**

JABEGA : REVISTA DE LA DIPUTACION PROVINCIAL DE MALAGA (SP/0210-8496) [10330916] **2693**

JAC COURSES DIRECTORY (AT/1031-7805) [I10317805] **1755**

● JACA : JOURNAL OF THE ASSOCIATION FOR COMMUNICATION ADMINISTRATION (US/0360-0939) [28601760] 2921, **1114**

JACARANDA REVIEW, THE *CEASED.* (US/1042-7082) [18204316] **3398**

JACHT EN NATUURBEHEER (BE) [04473340] 2196, **4874**

JACHTFUNKDIENST MITTELMEER FUR NICHTAUSRUSTUNGSPFLICHTIGE SCHIFFE (GW) [03624977] **4177**

JACHTFUNKDIENST NORD- UND OSTSEE FUR NICHTAUSRUSTUNGSPFLICHTIGE SCHIFFE (GW) [04172967] **4177**

JACHTING WARSZAWA (PL/0867-4337) [I08674337] **593**

● JACK ANDERSON CONFIDENTIAL (1992) (US/1064-4458) [26285965] **4478**

JACK ANDERSON FIRST ALERT *See* JACK ANDERSON CONFIDENTIAL (1992) **4478**

JACK COUNTY HERALD, THE (US) [16707196] **5751**

JACK DARR'S SERVICE CLINIC (US/0360-2419) [02239221] **2067**

JACK O'DWYER'S NEWSLETTER (US/0047-1690) [06023456] **761**

JACK O'DWYER'S NEWSLETTER INDEX (US) **761**

JACK-PINE WARBLER (US) [23372950] **5617**

JACKPOT (CN/0703-1785) [03681052] **4862**

JACKPOT & RODEO NEWS (US/8750-8680) [11873960] **4901**

JACKSBORO GAZETTE *See* JACKSBORO GAZETTE-NEWS **5751**

JACKSBORO GAZETTE-NEWS (US) [14509618] **5751**

JACKSBORO NEWS *See* JACKSBORO GAZETTE-NEWS **5751**

JACKSON ADVOCATE (US/0047-1704) [04701538] **5700**

JACKSON CITIZEN PATRIOT, THE (US) [09939307] **5692**

JACKSON COUNTY BANNER (BROWNSTOWN, IND.) (US/1055-775X) [21962137] **5665**

JACKSON COUNTY CHRONICLES (US/1071-2348) [10293536] **2739**

JACKSON COUNTY FLORIDAN (US) [04280584] **5650**

JACKSON COUNTY HISTORY (US) **2739**

JACKSON COUNTY PILOT (US) [01604953] **5696**

JACKSON DAILY NEWS (JACKSON, MISS. : 1907) (US) [10935422] **5700**

JACKSON HERALD (US) [19638930] **5654**

JACKSON HERALD (RIPLEY, W.VA.) (US) [12889762] **5764**

JACKSON HOLE GUIDE, THE (US) [26281951] **5772**

JACKSON HOLE NEWS (US) [26281993] **5772**

JACKSON JOURNAL OF BUSINESS *See* METRO JACKSON BUSINESS NEWS **693**

JAHRBUCH

JACKSON LABOR MARKET REVIEW
See JACKSON'S LABOR MARKET
NEWS **1681**

JACKSON, LEWIS, SCHNITZLER AND
KRUPMAN See JLS & K PREVENTIVE
LABOR RELATIONS FOR EXECUTIVES
1681

JACKSON SUN (JACKSON, TENN. :
1895), THE (US/0890-9938) [12869760]
5745

JACKSONIAN (CIMARRON, KAN. :
1937) (US) [11457646] **5676**

JACKSONIANA (US/0738-6648)
[09627015] **2455**

● JACKSON'S LABOR MARKET NEWS
(US) [25954027] **1681**

JACKSONVILLE BUSINESS JOURNAL
(US/0885-453X) [12641996] **685**

JACKSONVILLE (JACKSONVILLE,
FLA.) (US/1070-5163) [28396149] **2536**

JACKSONVILLE JOURNAL *CEASED.*
(US/0743-0914) [08335069] **5650**

JACKSONVILLE MAGAZINE *CEASED.*
(US/0891-1428) [13054389] **2536**

JACKSONVILLE NEWS (US/0891-5601)
[14964158] **5631**

JACKSONVILLE NEWS
(JACKSONVILLE, ALA.) (US) [12717792]
5627

JACKSONVILLE PATRIOT
(US/1064-7260) [26381908] **5631**

JACKSONVILLE TODAY
(US/0885-4769) [12642148] **2536**

JACOBEAN DRAMA STUDIES (AU)
[01780971] 385, **5365**

JACOBEAN STUDIES (AU) **3398**

JACOBSEN'S FATS AND OILS
BULLETIN (US/0021-387X) [04013646]
2345

JACQUES (CN/0227-4450) [08063909]
4862

JACT REVIEW (UK/0268-0181)
[12541940] **1077**

JADAVPUR JOURNAL OF
COMPARATIVE LITERATURE
(II/0970-0692) [01587467] **3398**

JADERNA ENERGIE (XR/0448-116X)
[03877515] **1948**

JAEGER'S INTERTRAVEL (GW)
[03025461] **5481**

JAGUAR INTERNATIONAL MAGAZINE
(US) [13224784] **5417**

JAGUAR JOURNAL (US/0743-3913)
[10544531] **5417**

JAHAN-I ZANAN (IR) [10107577] **4478**

JAHRBUCH (SZ) [22770077] **5117**

JAHRBUCH (SZ) [02243665] **4124**

JAHRBUCH / AKADEMIE FORUM
MASONICUM (GW) [21016307] **5232**

JAHRBUCH - ALTONAER MUSEUM IN
HAMBURG (GW/0440-1417)
[01783236] **4089**

JAHRBUCH / BAYERISCHE AKADEMIE
DER SCHONEN KUNSTE
(GW/0932-0229) [18045582] **322**

JAHRBUCH BIOTECHNOLOGIE
(GW/0930-9152) [15259069] **3693**

JAHRBUCH / BORSENVEREIN DES
DEUTSCHEN BUCHHANDELS E.V
(GW/0937-261X) [21284573] **4829**

JAHRBUCH DER ABSATZ- UND
VERBRAUCHSFORSCHUNG
(GW/0021-3985) [06205508] **1568**

JAHRBUCH DER AKADEMIE DER
WISSENSCHAFTEN DER DDR
(GW/0304-2154) [01798897] **5232**

JAHRBUCH DER AKADEMIE DER
WISSENSCHAFTEN IN GOTTINGEN
(GW/0373-9767) [05859220] 2848, **322**

JAHRBUCH DER BAUTECHNIK, DAS
(GW) [11175451] **618**

JAHRBUCH DER BAYERISCHEN
STAATSOPER / ANLASSLICH DER
MUNCHNER OPERNFESTSPIELE ...
HERAUSGEGEBEN VON DER
GESELLSCHAFT ZUR FORDERUNG
DER MUNCHNER OPERNFESTSPIELE
ZUSAMMEN MIT DER INTENDANZ DER
BAYERISCHEN STAATSOPER (GW)
[09009181] **4124**

JAHRBUCH DER BERLINER MUSEEN
(GW/0075-2207) [01519595] **353**

JAHRBUCH DER BIBLIOTHEKEN,
ARCHIVE UND
INFORMATIONSSTELLEN DER
DEUTSCHEN DEMOKRATISCHEN
REPUBLIK *CEASED.* (GW/0075-2215)
[03873471] 2482, **3219**

JAHRBUCH DER
BUEROKOMMUNIKATION
(GW/0932-3635) [I09323635] **872**

JAHRBUCH DER COBURGER
LANDESSTIFTUNG (GW/0084-8808)
[03529429] **2693**

JAHRBUCH DER DEUTSCHEN
BIBLIOTHEKEN (GW/0075-2223)
[01696817] **3219**

JAHRBUCH DER DEUTSCHEN
BUNDESPOST (GW) [05189631] **1145**

JAHRBUCH DER DEUTSCHEN
MUSIKORGANISATION (GW)
[08655057] **4124**

JAHRBUCH DER DEUTSCHEN
SCHILLERGESELLSCHAFT
(GW/0070-4318) [01258453] **3398**

JAHRBUCH DER ESOTERIK (SZ)
[19870759] 390, **4241**

JAHRBUCH DER GEOLOGISCHEN
BUNDESANSTALT (AU) [12961101]
1384

JAHRBUCH DER GESELLSCHAFT
FUER NIEDERSACHSISCHE
KIRCHENGESCHICHTE
(GW/0072-4238) [02046111] 2693, **4967**

JAHRBUCH ... DER GEWERKSCHAFT
OFFENTLICHER DIENST (AU)
[07487010] **4704**

JAHRBUCH DER GRAPHISCHEN
UNTERNEHMUNGEN OSTERREICHS
(AU/0075-2266) [01782705] **4566**

JAHRBUCH DER
GRILLPARZER-GESELLSCHAFT (AU)
[01770820] **3398**

JAHRBUCH DER
HAFENBAUTECHNISCHEN
GESELLSCHAFT (GW/0340-4838)
[04412870] **2091**

JAHRBUCH DER HEIDELBERGER
AKADEMIE DER WISSENSCHAFTEN
(GW/0341-2865) [02084041] **5117**

JAHRBUCH DER HISTORISCHEN
FORSCHUNG IN DER
BUNDESREPUBLIK DEUTSCHLAND
(GW) [02170056] **2620**

JAHRBUCH DER
JEAN-PAUL-GESELLSCHAFT
(GW/0075-3580) [01754245] **3398**

JAHRBUCH DER KAMMER FUER
ARBEITER UND ANGESTELLTE FUER
NIEDEROSTERREICH (AU) [02241889]
1681

JAHRBUCH DER
KARL-MAY-GESELLSCHAFT
(GW/0300-1989) [01784875] **3398**

JAHRBUCH DER
KUNSTHISTORISCHEN
SAMMLUNGEN IN WIEN (AU)
[06543288] **322**

JAHRBUCH DER LUFT- UND
RAUMFAHRT (GW/0447-256X)
[03919074] **25**

JAHRBUCH DER MUSIKBIBLIOTHEK
PETERS (GW) [02223116] **4124**

JAHRBUCH DER
OSTERREICHISCHEN BYZANTINISTIK
(AU/0378-8660) [02173891] **1078**

JAHRBUCH DER PSYCHOANALYSE
(GW/0075-2363) [02262856] **3927**

JAHRBUCH DER
RAABE-GESELLSCHAFT
(GW/0075-2371) [01641940] **3398**

JAHRBUCH DER RHEINISCHEN
DENKMALPFLEGE (GW/0341-924X)
[05387024] **353**

JAHRBUCH DER SAMMLUNG
KIPPENBERG (GW/0448-133X)
[01782279] **3398**

JAHRBUCH DER
SCHIFFBAUTECHNISCHEN
GESELLSCHAFT (US/0374-1222)
[01916587] **4177**

JAHRBUCH DER SCHLESIER (GW)
[08787860] **2693**

JAHRBUCH DER SCHWEIZERISCHEN
GESELLSCHAFT FUER UR- UND
FRUHGESCHICHTE (SZ/0252-1881)
[04409374] 4227, **270**

JAHRBUCH DER SCHWEIZERISCHEN
GESELLSCHAFT FUER UR- UND
FRUHGESCHICHTE (SZ) [01925874]
270

JAHRBUCH DER
SOZIALDEMOKRATISCHEN PARTEI
DEUTSCHLANDS (GW) [01606942]
4658

JAHRBUCH DER STAATLICHEN
KUNSTSAMMLUNGEN DRESDEN
(GW/0419-733X) [07920882] **353**

JAHRBUCH DER STAATLICHEN
KUNSTSAMMLUNGEN IN
BADEN-WURTTEMBERG
(GW/0067-284X) [01607086] **354**

JAHRBUCH DER TURNKUNST (GW)
[06808973] 1856, **4901**

JAHRBUCH DER UHRENINDUSTRIE
UND IHRER VERWANDTEN ZWEIGE
(SZ) [01788470] **2916**

JAHRBUCH DER VILLA VIGONI
(GW/0938-863X) [I0938863X] **3398**

JAHRBUCH DER WEHRTECHNIK
(GW/0075-2428) [01783250] **4046**

JAHRBUCH DER WERBUNG IN
DEUTSCHLAND, OSTERREICH UND
DER SCHWEIZ (GW/0932-6251)
[18399402] **761**

JAHRBUCH DER WIENER
GESELLSCHAFT FUER
THEATERFORSCHUNG
(AU/0377-0354) [01795792] **5365**

JAHRBUCH DES ARBEITSKREISES
THURINGER MUNZ- UND
GELDGESCHICHTE (GW/0323-6919)
[17793967] **2781**

JAHRBUCH DES ARCHIVS DER
DEUTSCHEN JUGENDBEWEGUNG
(GW/0587-5277) [03357870] **5249**

JAHRBUCH DES DEUTSCHEN
ARCHAOLOGISCHEN INSTITUTS
(GW/0070-4415) [07906501] **270**

JAHRBUCH DES EISENBAHNWESENS
(GW/0075-2479) [01782551] **5432**

JAHRBUCH DES FREIEN DEUTSCHEN
HOCHSTIFTS (GW/0071-9463)
[01246792] **3398**

JAHRBUCH DES HISTORISCHEN
VEREINS DILLINGEN AN DER DONAU
(GW) [06746087] **2693**

JAHRBUCH DES HISTORISCHEN
VEREINS FUER DAS FURSTENTUM
LIECHTENSTEIN (LH) [02082723] **2693**

JAHRBUCH DES HISTORISCHEN
VEREINS FUER MITTELFRANKEN
(GW/0341-9339) [I03419339] **2693**

JAHRBUCH ... DES INSTITUTS FUER
DEUTSCHE SPRACHE (GW)
[09801998] **3288**

JAHRBUCH DES KREISES DUREN
(GW) [01785735] 685, **2566**

JAHRBUCH DES MUSEUVEREINES
WELS (AU) [06398211] **2693**

JAHRBUCH DES MUSEUMS FUER
KUNST UND GEWERBE HAMBURG
(GW/0723-7871) [09737207] **354**

JAHRBUCH DES
OBEROSTERREICHISCHEN
MUSEALVEREINES. ABHANDLUNGEN
(AU/0376-2556) [I03762556] **4089**

JAHRBUCH DES
OBEROSTERREICHISCHEN
MUSEALVEREINES. BERICHTE
(AU/0379-0819) [I03790819] **354**

JAHRBUCH DES OFFENTLICHEN
RECHTS DER GEGENWART
(GW/0075-2517) [01714123] **4478**

JAHRBUCH DES OO.
MUSEALVEREINES GESELLSCHAFT
FUER LANDESKUNDE (AU) [10221678]
2693

JAHRBUCH DES
RHEIN-SIEG-KREISES
(GW/0932-0377) [18095325] **2518**

JAHRBUCH DES
ROEMISCH-GERMANISCHES
ZENTRALMUSEUM MAINZ
(GW/0076-2741) [02263776] **2620**

JAHRBUCH DES SOZIALRECHTS DER
GEGENWART (GW) [08751870] **2986**

JAHRBUCH DES STAATLICHEN
INSTITUTS FUER MUSIKFORSCHUNG
PREUSSISCHER KULTURBESITZ
(GW/0572-6239) [01979029] **4124**

JAHRBUCH DES STIFTES
KLOSTERNEUBURG. NEUE FOLGE
(GW/0454-0158) [02273188] **5030**

JAHRBUCH DES VEREINS FUER
AUGSBURGER
BISTUMSGESCHICHTE E. V
(GW/0341-9916) [I03419916] **5031**

JAHRBUCH DES VEREINS FUER
GESCHICHTE DER STADT WIEN
(AU/1011-4726) [01714227] **2694**

JAHRBUCH DES VEREINS FUER
NIEDERDEUTSCHE
SPRACHFORSCHUNG (GW/0083-5617)
[01242847] 3398, **3288**

JAHRBUCH DES VEREINS ZUM
SCHUTZ DER BERGWELT
(GW/0171-4694) [04261606] **2196**

JAHRBUCH DES WIENER
GOETHE-VEREINS (AU) [01995213]
3398

JAHRBUCH DES ZENTRALINSTITUTS
FUER KUNSTGESCHICHTE *CEASED.*
(GW/0177-8978) [13138545] 301, **354**

JAHRBUCH DEUTSCH ALS
FREMDSPRACHE (GW/0342-6300)
[02808934] **3289**

JAHRBUCH - DEUTSCHE AKADEMIE
FUER SPRACHE UND DICHTUNG
(DARMSTADT) (GW/0070-3923)
[02260333] **3398**

JAHRBUCH. DEUTSCHE
GESELLSCHAFT FUER LUFT- UND
RAUMFAHRT (GW) [01789275] **25**

JAHRBUCH - DEUTSCHE
SHAKESPEARE-GESELLSCHAFT
WEST (GW/0070-4326) [01566449]
3398

JAHRBUCH - DEUTSCHES ROTES
KREUZ (GW) [03583292] 2910, **5291**

JAHRBUCH DRITTE WELT
(GW/0724-4762) [10768257] **2620**

JAHRBUCH (FREUNDESKREIS
LEBENDIGE GRAFSCHAFT) (GW)
[17257952] **2693**

JAHRBUCH FUER AFRIKANISCHES
RECHT (GW) [08771467] **2986**

JAHRBUCH FUER ANTIKE UND
CHRISTENTUM (GW/0075-2541)
[01754112] **4967**

JAHRBUCH FUER ANTIKE UND
CHRISTENTUM. ERGANZUNGSBAND
(GW/0448-1488) [02171455] **4967**

JAHRBUCH FUER BIBLISCHE
THEOLOGIE : JBTH (GW) [17866114]
4967

JAHRBUCH FUER DEN PRAKTIKER
(GW) [13677820] **979**

JAHRBUCH

JAHRBUCH FUER DIE
GEFLUEGELWIRTSCHAFT (GW)
[04524344] **213**

JAHRBUCH FUER DIE GESCHICHTE
DES PROTESTANTISMUS IN
OSTERREICH (AU/1013-6991)
[08158852] **5061**

JAHRBUCH FUER DIE GESCHICHTE
MITTEL- UND OSTDEUTSCHLANDS
CEASED. (GW/0075-2614) [04737243]
2694

JAHRBUCH FUER EUROPAISCHE
VERWALTUNGSGESCHICHTE : JEV
(GW) [20582484] **4658**

JAHRBUCH FUER
FINNISCH-DEUTSCHE
LITERATURBEZIEHUNGEN
(FI/0781-3619) [07985775] **3398**

JAHRBUCH FUER FRANKISCHE
LANDESFORSCHUNG
(GW/0446-3943) [01713612] **2694**

JAHRBUCH FUER
FREMDENVERKEHR (GW/0075-2649)
[l00752649] **5481**

JAHRBUCH FUER GEOLOGIE
CEASED. (GW/0448-1518) [03866075]
1384

JAHRBUCH FUER GESCHICHTE VON
STAAT, WIRTSCHAFT UND
GESELLSCHAFT LATEINAMERIKAS
(GW/0075-2673) [01783148] **2740**

JAHRBUCH FUER HAUSFORSCHUNG
(GW/0172-2727) [08933090] **301**

JAHRBUCH FUER INTERNATIONALE
GERMANISTIK (GW/0449-5233)
[01639003] **3289**

JAHRBUCH FUER INTERNATIONALES
RECHT (GW/0021-3993) [01754120]
3131

JAHRBUCH FUER KATHOLISCHE
ERZIEHUNG IN OSTERREICH (AU)
[19134769] **5031**

JAHRBUCH FUER LANDESKUNDE
VON NIEDEROSTERREICH
(AU/1016-2712) [02178885] **2518**

JAHRBUCH FUER LITURGIK UND
HYMNOLOGIE (GW/0075-2681)
[01782829] **4967, 4124**

JAHRBUCH FUER MUSIKALISCHE
VOLKS- UND VOLKERKUNDE
(GW/0075-2703) [01783108] **4124**

JAHRBUCH FUER NEUE POLITISCHE
OKONOMIE (GW/0722-5369)
[09015996] **1497**

JAHRBUCH FUER NUMISMATIK UND
GELDGESCHICHTE (GW/0075-2711)
[01782572] **2781**

JAHRBUCH FUER
OPERNFORSCHUNG (GW/0724-8156)
[13212718] **4124**

JAHRBUCH FUER OPTIK UND
FEINMECHANIK (GW/0075-272X)
[01783904] **4435**

JAHRBUCH FUER OSTDEUTSCHE
VOLKSKUNDE (GW/0075-2738)
[02208628] **2321**

JAHRBUCH FUER OSTRECHT
(GW/0075-2746) [10258133] **3131**

● JAHRBUCH FUER PADAGOGIK
(GW/0941-1461) [26280547] **1755**

JAHRBUCH FUER POLITIK (GW)
[25612979] **4478**

JAHRBUCH FUER
RECHTSSOZIOLOGIE &
RECHTSTHEORIE (GW) **2986**

JAHRBUCH FUER
REGIONALGESCHICHTE UND
LANDESKUNDE (GW) [26876459] **2694**

JAHRBUCH FUER
REGIONALWISSENSCHAFT /
HERAUSGEGEBEN VOM VORSTAND
DER GESELLSCHAFT FUER
REGIONALFORSCHUNG E. V.
(DEUTSCHSPRACHIGE GRUPPE DER
REGIONAL SCIENCE ASSOCIATION)
(GW/0173-7600) [08696561] **2694**

JAHRBUCH FUER
SOZIALWISSENSCHAFT
(GW/0075-2770) [01664352] **5205**

JAHRBUCH FUER VOLKSKUNDE
(GW/0171-9904) [06656152] **2321**

JAHRBUCH FUER
VOLKSLIEDFORSCHUNG
(GW/0075-2789) [01782287] **4124**

JAHRBUCH FUER WESTDEUTSCHE
LANDESGESCHICHTE (GW)
[02706960] **2694**

JAHRBUCH FUER
WIRTSCHAFTSGESCHICHTE
(GW/0075-2800) [01782983] **1568**

JAHRBUCH FUER ZEITGESCHICHTE
(AU/1012-6465) [06226272] **2694**

JAHRBUCH FUR ARCHITEKTUR *See*
ARCHITEKTUR JAHRBUCH **291**

JAHRBUCH FUR UMWELTSCHUTZ
(SZ) [02239771] **2175**

JAHRBUCH / GESELLSCHAFT FUER
DIE GESCHICHTE UND
BIBLIOGRAPHIE DES BRAUWESENS
E.V (GW/0072-422X) [03061544] **2368**

JAHRBUCH (GEWERKSCHAFT DER
OFFENTLICH BEDIENSTETEN) *See*
JAHRBUCH ... DER GEWERKSCHAFT
OFFENTLICHER DIENST **4704**

JAHRBUCH - JUNGE UNION
DEUTSCHLANDS (GW) [03637934]
2281

JAHRBUCH ... / MANNER VOM
MORGENSTERN, HEIMATBUND AN
ELB- UND WESERMUNDUNG
(GW/0931-8313) [12231953] **322**

JAHRBUCH MARKETING (GW)
[15814300] **927**

JAHRBUCH -
MAX-PLANCK-GESELLSCHAFT
(GW/0341-0218) [04385746] **5117**

JAHRBUCH OBERFLACHENTECHNIK
(GW/0075-2819) [01782417] **4005**

JAHRBUCH PHARMALABOR
(GW/0932-7770) [19960969] **4309**

JAHRBUCH PREUSSISCHER
KULTURBESITZ (GW/0342-0124)
[08211556] **4089**

JAHRBUCH - RUHR-UNIVERSITAT
BOCHUM (GW) [01791222] **1831**

JAHRBUCH - SACHSISCHE AKADEMIE
DER WISSENSCHAFTEN ZU LEIPZIG
(GW/0080-5262) [01764731] **1831**

JAHRBUCH SCHWEISSTECHNIK /
HERAUSGEBER, DEUTSCHER
VERBAND FUER SCHWEISSTECHNIK
E.V. (DVS) (GW) [16919424] **5117**

JAHRBUCH / SCHWEIZERISCHES
INSTITUT FUER
KUNSTWISSENSCHAFT
(GW/0258-9524) [08970181] **354**

JAHRBUCH STAHL / HERAUSGEBEN
VOM VEREIN DEUTSCHER
EISENHUTTENLEUTE (GW/0724-8482)
[12984856] **1613**

JAHRBUCH - STEIERMARKISCHE
GEBIETSKRANKENKASSE FUR
ARBEITER UND ANGESTELLTE
(AU/0379-2595) [02377399] **2885, 3591**

JAHRBUCH /
THOMAS-MORUS-GESELLSCHAFT
(GW/0723-0516) [10903517] **3398**

JAHRBUCH UBERBLICKE
MATHEMATIK (GW/0172-8512)
[l01728512] **3511**

JAHRBUCH ZUR GESCHICHTE VON
STADT UND LANDKREIS
KAISERSLAUTERN (GW/0448-1607)
[02182391] **2694**

JAHRBUCH ZUR LITERATUR IN DER
DDR / HERAUSGEGEBEN IM AUFTRAG
DES ARBEITSKREISES LITERATUR
UND GERMANISTIK IN DER DDR VON
PAUL GERHARD KLUSSMANN UND
HEINRICH MOHR (GW/0174-4720)
[07479243] **3398**

JAHRBUCH ZUR STAATS- UND
VERWALTUNGSWISSENSCHAFT (GW)
[16410975] **4478, 4658**

JAHRBUCHER DER
INTERNATIONALEN POLITIK (GW)
4526

JAHRBUCHER DER
ZENTRALANSTALT FUER
METEOROLOGIE UND GEODYNAMIK
(AU) [02160745] **1407, 1426**

JAHRBUCHER FUER GESCHICHTE
OSTEUROPAS (PL/0021-4019)
[01586336] **2694**

JAHRBUCHER FUER
NATIONALOKONOMIE UND STATISTIK
(GW/0021-4027) [01746790] **1497**

JAHRBUCHER FUR STATISTIK UND
LANDESKUNDE VON
BADEN-WURTTEMBERG
(GW/0408-1706) [03398457] **5329**

JAHRESBERICHT (GW) [21351956]
4734

JAHRESBERICHT (GE/0417-1489)
[04886051] **98**

JAHRESBERICHT (GW) [15180867]
5535

JAHRESBERICHT (GW) [22965434]
4448

JAHRESBERICHT (AU/0457-1231)
[02501021] **2885, 1681**

JAHRESBERICHT (AKADEMIE FUR
RAUMFORSCHUNG UND
LANDESPLANUNG (GERMANY))
(GW/0515-9091) [10114414] **2825**

JAHRESBERICHT / BAYERISCHE
STAATSGEMALDESAMMLUNGEN
(GW/0938-3611) [05366299] **2264, 238**

JAHRESBERICHT. BD. 2,
PROGRAMME UND PROJEKTE (GW)
[26711534] **5232**

JAHRESBERICHT - BERLINER
GASWERKE (GW) [02243807] **979**

JAHRESBERICHT - BIOLOGISCHE
BUNDESANSTALT FUER LAND- UND
FORSTWIRTSCHAFT IN BERLIN
UND BRAUNSCHWEIG
(GW/0521-2804) [l05212804] **460**

JAHRESBERICHT /
BUND-LANDER-KOMMISSION FUER
BILDUNGSPLANUNG UND
FORSCHUNGSFORDERUNG (GW)
[08518099] **1880**

JAHRESBERICHT -
BUNDESMINISTERIUM FUR
WIRTSCHAFT UND FINANZEN.
VERTRETUNG BERLIN (GW)
[01787879] **1568**

JAHRESBERICHT - BUNDESVERBAND
DER DEUTSCHEN GAS- UND
WASSERWIRTSCHAFT (GW)
[04220807] **2196**

JAHRESBERICHT - DER
BEVOLLMACHTIGTE DER
BUNDESREGIERUNG IN BERLIN,
WIRTSCHAFT (GW) [02242530] **1568**

JAHRESBERICHT DER
BUNDESANSTALT FUR
GEWASSERKUNDE / BFG
(GW/0170-5156) [11891495] **1415**

JAHRESBERICHT DER DEUTSCHEN
MATHEMATIKER-VEREINIGUNG
(GW/0012-0456) [01636417] **3511**

JAHRESBERICHT DER
EXECUTIVDIREKTOREN -
INTERNATIONALER
WAHRUNGSFONDS *CEASED.*
(US/0250-7528) [07679202] **1497**

JAHRESBERICHT DER
GEWERBEAUFSICHT (GW)
[02394940] **2864**

JAHRESBERICHT DER
HAUPTABTEILUNG
STADTENTWASSERUNG (GW)
[03953087] **2233**

JAHRESBERICHT DER TIROLER
GEBIETSKRANKENKASSE (AU)
[10520034] **2885**

JAHRESBERICHT ... DER
UNIVERSITAETSBIBLIOTHEK MAINZ
MIT VERZEICHNIS DER
UNIVERSITAETSBIBLIOTHEK
UEBERLASSENER SCHRIFTEN
MAINZER HOCHSCHULLEHRER (GW)
[20148234] **3219**

JAHRESBERICHT DER VIEH- UND
FLEISCHKOMMISSION BEIM
BUNDESMINISTERIUM FUER LAND-
UND FORSTWIRTSCHAFT (AU)
[05198563] **213, 2345**

JAHRESBERICHT DES
HISTORISCHEN VEREINS FUER
STRAUBING UND UMGEBUNG (GW)
[06720418] **2694**

JAHRESBERICHT DES
LANDESARBEITSAMTES TIROL (AU)
[06077750] **1681**

JAHRESBERICHT ... DES ZURCHER
LANDWIRTSCHAFTLICHER
KANTONALVEREINS UND DES
ZURCHER BAUERNSEKRETARIATES
(SZ) [05252582] **98**

JAHRESBERICHT - DEUTSCHE
GESELLSCHAFT FUER
AUSWAERTIGE POLITIK (GW)
[03584370] **4526**

JAHRESBERICHT - DEUTSCHES
PATENTAMT (GW) [05720156] **1305**

JAHRESBERICHT - DYNAMITRON-
TANDEM-LABORATORIUM, BOCHUM
(GW) [06702402] **4448**

JAHRESBERICHT / FLUGHAFEN
ZURICH (SZ) [11246562] **25**

JAHRESBERICHT (GERMANY (WEST).
BUNDESMINISTERIUM FUR
INNERDEUTSCHE BEZIEHUNGEN)
(GW) [08724661] **5205**

JAHRESBERICHT - GESELLSCHAFT
FUER STRAHLEN- UND
UMWELTFORSCHUNG MHB
MUNCHEN (GW/0721-930X) [07591929]
460

JAHRESBERICHT / GESELLSCHAFT
FUR INFORMATION UND
DOKUMENTATION (GW/0174-3287)
[07765536] **3219**

JAHRESBERICHT (HAMBURGER
SYNCHROTRONSTRAHLUNGSLABOR
HASYLAB) (GW) [19785055] **5117**

JAHRESBERICHT - HAUPTVERBAND
DER OSTERREICHISCHEN
SPARKASSEN (AU) [01794860] **793**

JAHRESBERICHT - INSTITUT FUER
MEERESKUNDE AN DER
UNIVERSITAT KIEL (GW) [06661259]
1450

JAHRESBERICHT (INSTITUT FUR
EMPIRISCHE SOZIOLOGIE
FORSCHUNG)) (GW) [08578256] **5249**

JAHRESBERICHT / INSTITUT FUR
FREIE BERUFE AN DER
FRIEDRICH-ALEXANDER-
UNIVERSITAT
ERLANGEN-NURNBERG (GW)
[08515688] **1831**

JAHRESBERICHT (JOHANNES
GUTENBERG-UNIVERSITAT. INSTITUT
FUR KERNPHYSIK) (GW) [14402325]
4448

JAHRESBERICHT /
KESTNER-MUSEUM (GW/0441-5590)
[13091863] **4089**

JAHRESBERICHT - LANDESMUSEUM
JOANNEUM GRAZ (AU/0378-6862)
[l03786862] **4089**

JAHRESBERICHT /
MAX-PLANCK-INSTITUT FUER
KERNPHYSIK (GW) [08927546] **4448**

JAHRESBERICHT /
MAX-PLANCK-INSTITUT FUER PHYSIK
UND ASTROPHYSIK,
WERNER-HEISENBERG-INSTITUT
FUR PHYSIK (GW) [11920241] **4407**

JAHRESBERICHT /
MAX-PLANCK-INSTITUT FUER
PHYSIK,
WERNER-HEISENBERG-INSTITUT
(GW) **4407**

JAHRESBERICHT / MAX-PLANCK-INSTITUT FUER QUANTENOPTIK (GW) [11460004] **4435**

JAHRESBERICHT / OSTERREICHISCHES FORSCHUNGSZENTRUM SEIBERSDORF (AU) [07742699] **4448**

JAHRESBERICHT (OSTERREICHISCHES PRODUKTIVITATS- UND WIRTSCHAFTLICHKEITS-ZENTRUM) (AU) [10052332] **1568**

JAHRESBERICHT - OSTEUROPA-INSTITUT (GW) [05724167] 1497, **5205**

JAHRESBERICHT - SCHWEIZERISCHE AKADEMIE DER MEDIZINISCHEN WISSENSCHAFTEN (1988) (SZ/1016-1562) [20567018] **3591**

JAHRESBERICHT - SCHWEIZERISCHES LANDESMUSEUM ZURICH (SZ/1015-3470) [02226062] **4089**

JAHRESBERICHT / SCHWEIZERISCHES ROTES KREUZ (SZ) [12026887] **5291**

JAHRESBERICHT - STEIERMARKISCHE GEBIETSKRANKENKASSE FUER ARBEITER UND ANGESTELLTE (AU/0561-9912) [01792378] **1681**

JAHRESBERICHT - STUDIENSTIFTUNG (GW) [02243844] **1831**

JAHRESBERICHT UBER DIE DEUTSCHE FISCHWIRTSCHAFT (GW/0075-2851) [02099255] **2306**

JAHRESBERICHT / VON DER HEYDT-MUSEUM KUNST- UND MUSEUMSVEREIN (GW/0176-9030) [17789110] **354**

JAHRESBERICHT - ZURCHER KUNSTGESELLSCHAFT (SZ/1013-6916) [I10136916] **354**

JAHRESBERICHTE FUER DEUTSCHE GESCHICHTE (GW/0075-286X) [01754151] **418**

JAHRESBERICHTE / HISTORISCHES MUSEUM BASEL (SZ/1013-6959) [04950032] 2620, **4089**

JAHRESBERICHTE UBER HOLZSCHUTA *CEASED.* (GW/0075-2878) [01780607] **2402**

JAHRESBERICHTE UND MITTEILUNGEN DES OBERRHEINISCHEN GEOLOGISCHEN VEREINES (GW/0078-2947) [05384335] 4227, **1384**

JAHRESBEZUGSNACHWEIS FUER DEN GESAMTEN METALLSEKTOR *CEASED.* (GW) [21049041] **4005**

JAHRESBIBLIOGRAPHIE / BIBLIOTHEK FUER ZEITGESCHICHTE, WELTKRIEGSBUCHEREI (GW) [10438351] **2620**

JAHRESFACHKATALOG: RECHT, WIRTSCHAFT, STEUERN (GW/0075-2886) [01782755] 4734, **2986**

JAHRESFORSCHUNGSBERICHT / UNIVERSITAT GOTTINGEN (GW) [10571258] **1832**

JAHRESGABE - KLAUS-GROTH-GESELLSCHAFT (GW/0453-9842) [06691945] **3398**

JAHRESHEFTE DES GEOLOGISCHEN LANDESAMTES IN BADEN-WURTTEMBERG (GW/0408-1560) [02327417] **1384**

JAHRESHEFTE DES OSTERREICHISCHEN ARCHAOLOGISCHEN INSTITUTES IN WIEN (AU/0078-3579) [01644741] **271**

JAHRESBERICHT - RHEINLAND PFALZ, MINISTERIUM FUER SOZIALES, GESUNDHEIT UND SPORT (GW) [02242672] **5205**

JAHRESKATALOG PSYCHOLOGIE UND VERWANDTE WISSENSCHAFTEN (GW/0075-2924) [02178911] **4592**

JAHRESSCHAU DER DEUTSCHEN INDUSTRIE. DIE ELEKTRO-INDUSTRIE, ELEKTRONIK UND IHRE HELFER (GW) [07218862] **2067**

JAHRESSCHRIFT DER HISTORISCHEN VEREINIGUNG WYNENTAL (SZ) [03662062] **2694**

JAHRESSCHRIFT FUER MITTELDEUTSCHE VORGESCHICHTE (GW/0075-2932) [02173764] **271**

JAHRESSCHRIFT / SALZBURGER MUSEUM CAROLINO AUGUSTEUM (AU/0558-3438) [09026362] 2620, **4089**

JAHRESSTATISTIK ... DER AMBULANTEN BERATUNGS- UND BEHANDLUNGSSTELLEN FUR SUCHTKRANKE IN DER BUNDESREPUBLIK DEUTSCHLAND / DEUTSCHER CARITASVERBAND E.V. ... ET AL (GW) [12182864] 1345, **1350**

JAHRESSTATISTIK DES AUSSENHANDELS DER SCHWEIZ. STATISTIQUE ANNUELLE DU COMMERCE EXTERIEUR DE LA SUISSE (SZ) [03106410] 842, **730**

JAHRESTAGUNG - GESELLSCHAFT FUER INFORMATIK E.V (GW/0343-3110) [01786615] **1260**

JAHRESTAGUNG KERNTECHNIK (GW/0720-9207) [08479380] **2156**

JAHRESVERZEICHNIS DER AUSLEGESCHRIFTEN UND ERTEILTEN PATENTE (GW) [06539519] **1305**

JAHRESVERZEICHNIS DER MUSIKALIEN UND MUSIKSCHRIFTEN (GW/0323-3693) [02830732] **4124**

JAIL & PRISONER LAW BULLETIN (US/0739-0998) [09819316] **3166**

JAIL COMMITMENTS AND CONFINEMENTS (US) [10713310] **3166**

J'AIME LIRE (SAINT-LAMBERT) (CN/0835-7714) [17759190] **1065**

JAIPUR, INDIA (RAJASTHAN). UNIVERSITY OF RAJASTHAN *See* RAJASTHAN UNIVERSITY STUDIES IN ENGLISH **3427**

JAKARTA BUSINESS DIRECTORY (IO) [02246803] **685**

JAKARTA BUYER'S GUIDE (IO) [04274484] **842**

JAKARTA JAKARTA (IO/0215-2770) [I02152770] **2510**

JAKARTA METROPOLITAN BUYERS' GUIDE (IO) [04619210] **842**

JAKARTA POST, THE (IO) [17635176] **5803**

JAKARTA PUSAT DALAM ANGKA STATISTIK (IO) [02412646] **5329**

JAKARTA PUSAT, INDONESIA. WALIKOTA *See* JAKARTA PUSAT DALAM ANGKA STATISTIK **5329**

JAKARTA PUSAT, INDONESIA. WALIKOTA *See* LAPORAN - WALIKOTA JAKARTA PUSAT **4661**

JAKARTA RAYA, INDONESIA *See* MEDIA JAYA **1574**

JAKARTA RAYA (INDONESIA). DINAS KESEHATAN *See* WARTA KESEHATAN **4807**

JAKARTA RAYA (INDONESIA). DINAS SOSIAL *See* PROGRESS REPORT PELITA P.K3A **5302**

JAKARTA RAYA, INDONESIA. KANTOR SENSUS DAN STATISTIK *See* PETUNJUK KELURAHAN WILAYAH JAKARTA PUSAT **5336**

JAKARTA RAYA, INDONESIA. KANTOR SENSUS DAN STATISTIK *See* PETUNJUK KELURAHAN WILAYAH JAKARTA UTARA **5336**

JAKARTA RAYA, INDONESIA. KANTOR SENSUS DAN STATISTIK. KANTOR PETUNJUK KELURAHAN WILAYAH JAKARTA TIMUR **5336**

JAKARTA RAYA, INDONESIA. KANTOR SENSUS DAN STATISTIK *See* PETUNJUK KELURAHAN WILAYAH JAKARTA BARAT **5336**

JAKARTA RAYA, INDONESIA. KANTOR SENSUS DAN STATISTIK *See* PETUNJUK KELURAHAN WILAYAH JAKARTA SELATAN **5336**

JAKARTA RAYA, INDONESIA. KANTOR SENSUS DAN STATISTIK *See* HASIL SURVEY PERGURUAN TINGGI DKI JAKARTA **1827**

JAKARTA RAYA (INDONESIA). KANTOR SENSUS DAN STATISTIK *See* LAPORAN KEPALA KANTOR SENSUS DAN STATISTIK DKI JAKARTA **5332**

JAKARTA TIMUR (INDONESIA). WALI KOTA *See* LAPORAN - WALIKOTA JAKARTA TIMUR **4661**

JAKATKURU (II) [08721326] **5041**

JAKUTO NYUSU / JACT NEWS. CHUZO GIJUTSU FUKKYU KYOKAI (JA) [10282599] **4005**

JALEO (US/0890-8672) [08836275] 1313, **4124**

JALONS (REPENTIGNY) (CN/0383-672X) [03284893] **5232**

JAMA EN ESPANOL (SP/0211-4445) [06435553] **3591**

JAMA FORUM, THE (JA/0286-5971) [08731195] **5417**

JAMA H (ED. FRANCAISE) (FR/1140-5031) [I11405031] **3591**

JAMA JOURNAL OF THE AMERICAN MEDICAL ASSOCIATION. EDITION FRANCAISE (FR/0221-7678) [06371173] **3591**

JAMA : THE JOURNAL OF THE AMERICAN MEDICAL ASSOCIATION (US/0098-7484) [01124917] **3591**

JAMAAT SAYYIDAT MISR *See* JAMAAT SAYYIDAT MISR : KITAB SANAWI **2281**

JAMAAT SAYYIDAT MISR : KITAB SANAWI (UA) [07338308] **2281**

JAMAHIRIYA REVIEW (UK/0260-0358) [09849124] **2640**

JAMAICA ARCHITECT *CEASED.* (JM/0448-214X) [03880911] **301**

JAMAICA. COCONUT INDUSTRY BOARD *See* ANNUAL REPORT AND ACCOUNTS FOR THE YEAR ENDED DECEMBER 31ST, ... / THE COCONUT INDUSTRY BOARD, JAMAICA, WEST INDIES **2327**

JAMAICA CONSOLIDATED INDEX OF STATUTES AND SUBSIDIARY LEGISLATION TO ... (BB) [13894746] **3131**

JAMAICA. DEPT. OF STATISTICS *See* NATIONAL INCOME AND PRODUCT **1536**

JAMAICA. DEPT. OF STATISTICS *See* STATISTICAL BULLETIN: PRODUCTION STATISTICS **1538**

JAMAICA. DEPT. OF STATISTICS *See* DEMOGRAPHIC STATISTICS **4561**

JAMAICA. ELECTORAL OFFICE *See* REPORT OF THE DIRECTOR OF ELECTIONS **4493**

JAMAICA. GEOLOGICAL SURVEY DIVISION *See* BIENNIAL REPORT / GEOLOGICAL SURVEY DIVISION, MINISTRY OF MINING, ENERGY AND TOURISM **1367**

JAMAICA HERALD (JM) [11760750] **5805**

JAMAICA JOURNAL (JM/0021-4124) [01797964] **2536**

JAMAICA. MINES AND GEOLOGY DIVISION *See* SPECIAL PUBLICATION - MINES & GEOLOGY DIVISION **2151**

JAMAICA. MINISTRY OF EXTERNAL AFFAIRS *See* DIPLOMATIC CORPS. MINISTRY OF EXTERNAL AFFAIRS (KINGSTON) **4520**

JAMAICA PLAIN CITIZEN *See* JAMAICA PLAIN CITIZEN ROXBURY CITIZEN **5689**

JAMAICA PLAIN CITIZEN ROXBURY CITIZEN (US/0745-9254) [09612896] **5689**

JAMAICA STOCK EXCHANGE YEARBOOK (JM) [15709456] **904**

JAMAICAN HISTORICAL REVIEW, THE (JM/1010-6367) [01782874] **2740**

JAMAICAN NATIONAL BIBLIOGRAPHY (JM) [04760593] **418**

JAMAICAN NURSE *SUSPENDED.* (JM/0021-4140) [03576533] **3858**

JAMAICAN VIEW (US/0276-0029) [07321161] **2536**

JAMAICAN WEEKLY GLEANER, THE (CN) [03597361] **5786**

JAMAIKA : WIRTSCHAFTLICHE ENTWICKLUNG (GW) [04177305] **1568**

JAMARC (JA) [07250510] **2306**

JAMBOREE COUNTRY MUSIC MAGAZINE (CN/0229-2203) [07821204] **4124**

JAMES BURNSIDE BULLETIN OF RESEARCH, THE *SUSPENDED.* (US/1046-2279) [19739265] **2740**

JAMES CAPEL EUROMONEY FUTURES & OPTIONS DIRECTORY (UK) **1497**

JAMES DICKEY NEWSLETTER (US/0749-0291) [11054993] **3464**

JAMES FENIMORE COOPER SOCIETY NEWSLETTER, THE (US) [22447518] **3398**

JAMES FORD BELL LECTURES, THE (US) [01590724] **842**

JAMES FORD BELL LIBRARY *See* LIST OF ADDITIONS, A **3259**

JAMES JOYCE BROADSHEET (UK/0143-6333) [07061384] **3398**

JAMES JOYCE LITERARY SUPPLEMENT (US/0899-3114) [17020504] **3345**

JAMES JOYCE QUARTERLY (US/0021-4183) [01754166] **3345**

JAMES MADISON JOURNAL, THE (US/0147-2046) [03110300] 1897, **745**

JAMES S. COLEMAN AFRICAN STUDIES CENTER NEWSLETTER (US) [20378395] **2264**

JAMES SPRUNT STUDIES IN HISTORY AND POLITICAL SCIENCE, THE (US/0361-6169) [02104766] 4478, **2620**

JAMES WHITE REVIEW, THE (US/0891-5393) [11104809] **3345**

JAMESTOWN SUN, THE (US) [01586324] **5725**

JAMIAH (DAMMAN, SAUDI ARABIC) *See* AL-JAMIAH / TUSDIRUHA JAMIAT AL-MALIK FAYSAL BI-AL-MINTAQAH AL-SHARQIYAH **5228**

JAMIAH-I NAVIN (IR) [10218046] **2654**

JAMIAT AL-KUWAYT. KULLIYAT AL-ULUM *See* JOURNAL OF THE UNIVERSITY OF KUWAIT, SCIENCE, THE **5121**

JAMIAT AL-MALIK ABD AL-AZIZ. MAHAD SHUUN AL-AQALLIYAT AL-MUSLIMAH *See* NASHRAT MAHAD SHUUN AL-AQALLIYAT AL-MUSLIMAH, JAMIAT AL-MALIK ABD AL-AZIZ BI-JIDDAH **5044**

JAMIAT AL-QARAWIYIN. KULLIYAT AL-SHARIAH *See* MAJALLAT KULLIYAT AL-SHARIAH **3005**

JAMI'AT ASYUT. KULLIYAT AL-ULUM *See* BULLETIN OF THE FACULTY OF SCIENCE, ASSIUT UNIVERSITY **5091**

JAMIAT — Alphabetical Title Index

JAMIAT HALAB. MAHAD AL-TURATH AL-ILMI AL-ARABI See RISALAT MAHAD AL-TURATH AL-ILMI AL-ARABI **5148**

JAMIAT MUHAMMAD AL-KHAMIS. MAHAD AL-ILMI See BULLETIN DE L'INSTITUT SCIENTIFIQUE (RABAT) **5090**

JAMIAT MUHAMMAD V. KULLIYAT AL-ADAB See MAJALLAT KULLIYAT AL-ADAB WA-AL-ULUM AL-INSANIYAH BI-AL-RABAT **5233**

JAMIATAL-RIYAD See UNIVERSITY BULLETIN / UNIVERSITY OF RIYADH, KINGDOM OF SAUDI ARABIA **1852**

JAMIYAH AL-KIMAWIYAH AL-IRAQIYAH See MAGALLAT AL-GAMIYYAT AL-KIMYAWIYAAT AL-IRAQIWAT **985**

JAMIYAH AL-MISRIYAH LI-ILM AL-HASHARAT See BULLETIN OF THE ENTOMOLOGICAL SOCIETY OF EGYPT. ECONOMIC SERIES **5579**

JAM'IYAH AL-MISRIYAH LIL-'ULUM AL-RIYADIYAH WA-AL-TABI'IYAH See PROCEEDINGS OF THE MATHEMATICAL AND PHYSICAL SOCIETY OF EGYPT **3528**

JAMIYAT MASARIF LUBNAN See BILANS DES BANQUES **779**

JAMMER'S HANDBOOK (US/0147-9652) [03251713] **4081**

JAMMU AND KASHMIR. FOOD SUPPLIES AND TRANSPORT DEPT See DETAILED DEMAND FOR GRANTS OF FOOD SUPPLIES AND TRANSPORT DEPARTMENT. GOVERNMENT OF JAMMU AND KASHMIR **4642**

JAMMU AND KASHMIR. HOUSING AND URBAN DEVELOPMENT DEPT See DETAILED DEMAND FOR GRANTS OF HOUSING AND URBAN DEVELOPMENT DEPARTMENT **2821**

JAMMU AND KASHMIR (INDIA) See BUDGET **4714**

JAMMU AND KASHMIR (INDIA). DEPT. OF INDUSTRIES & COMMERCE See DETAILED DEMAND FOR GRANTS OF INDUSTRIES & COMMERCE DEPARTMENT. GOVERNMENT OF JAMMU AND KASHMIR **831**

JAMMU AND KASHMIR (INDIA). EDUCATION DEPT See DETAILED DEMAND FOR GRANTS OF EDUCATION DEPARTMENT. GOVERNMENT OF JAMMU AND KASHMIR **1735**

JAMMU AND KASHMIR (INDIA). REVENUE DEPT See DETAILED DEMAND FOR GRANTS OF REVENUE DEPARTMENT FOR ... **4720**

JAMMU AND KASHMIR. LABOUR AND SOCIAL WELFARE DEPT See DETAILED DEMAND FOR GRANTS OF LABOUR AND SOCIAL WELFARE DEPARTMENT **1662**

JAMMU AND KASHMIR. LADAKH AFFAIR DEPT See DETAILED DEMAND FOR GRANTS OF LADAKH AFFAIR DEPARTMENT. GOVERNMENT OF JAMMU AND KASHMIR **1479**

JAMMU AND KASHMIR. LAW DEPT See DETAILED DEMAND FOR GRANTS OF LAW DEPARTMENT **2960**

JAMMU AND KASHMIR LEGISLATURE. LEGISLATIVE ASSEMBLY. COMMITTEE ON PUBLIC UNDERTAKINGS See REPORT - JAMMU AND KASHMIR. LEGISLATIVE ASSEMBLY. COMMITTEE ON PUBLIC UNDERTAKINGS **4680**

JAMMU AND KASHMIR. LEGISLATURE. LEGISLATIVE COUNCIL. COMMITTEE ON PRIVILEGES See REPORT - JAMMU AND KASHMIR LEGISLATIVE COUNCIL, COMMITTEE ON PRIVILEGES **4680**

JAMMU AND KASHMIR. PLANNING DEPT See DETAILED DEMAND FOR GRANTS OF PLANNING DEPARTMENT **1479**

JAMMU AND KASHMIR. PUBLIC WORKS DEPT See DETAILED DEMAND FOR GRANTS OF WORKS DEPARTMENT. GOVERNMENT OF JAMMU AND KASHMIR **4720**

JANARUCI (II) [02239612] **2526**

JANASAMKHYA (II) [10890687] **4554**

JANATA (II/0021-4221) [02225881] **4478**

JANE AUSTEN SOCIETY See REPORT FOR THE YEAR ... / JANE AUSTEN SOCIETY **3429**

JANE CORRIDOR, THE (CN/0701-1083) [03402645] **2536**

JANE'S A F V SYSTEMS (UK) **4046**

JANE'S AIR LAUNCHED WEAPONS (UK/0954-3848) [I09543848] **25, 4046**

JANE'S AIRPORT & ATC EQUIPMENT (UK) [24508791] **25**

JANE'S AIRPORT EQUIPMENT (UK) [08821507] **25**

JANE'S AIRPORT REVIEW (UK/0954-7649) [21283651] **25**

JANE'S ALL THE WORLD'S AIRCRAFT (LONDON, ENGLAND) (UK/0075-3017) [06494540] **25, 4046**

JANE'S ARMOUR AND ARTILLERY (UK/0143-9952) [05825057] **4046**

JANE'S ARMOURED FIGHTING VEHICLE RETROFIT SYSTEMS (UK) [22589082] **4046**

JANE'S AVIONICS (UK) [09001918] **25, 2068, 4047**

JANE'S BATTLEFIELD SURVEILLANCE SYSTEMS (UK) [20644252] **4047**

JANE'S C31 SYSTEMS (UK) **4047**

JANE'S CONTAINERISATION DIRECTORY (UK) [18806345] **5385**

JANE'S DEFENCE WEEKLY (UK/0265-3818) [10366120] **4047**

JANE'S DEFENSE SYSTEMS MODERNISATION (UK) **4047**

JANE'S FIGHTING SHIPS (UK/0075-3025) [05952041] **4047, 4177**

JANE'S HIGH-SPEED MARINE CRAFT (UK/0960-7994) [21991610] **4047**

JANE'S INFANTRY WEAPONS (UK) [01297291] **4047**

JANE'S INTELLIGENCE REVIEW (UK/1350-6226) [23933655] **4047**

JANE'S LAND-BASED AIR DEFENCE (UK) [20156974] **4047**

JANE'S MAJOR COMPANIES OF EUROPE (US/0075-3041) [06231341] **685**

JANE'S MERCHANT SHIPS *CEASED*. (UK) [08502488] **4177**

JANE'S MILITARY COMMUNICATIONS (UK/0144-0004) [05825020] **1158, 4047**

JANE'S MILITARY LOGISTICS See JANE'S MILITARY VEHICLES AND LOGISTICS **4047**

JANE'S MILITARY TRAINING SYSTEMS (UK) [19061151] **4047**

●JANE'S MILITARY VEHICLES AND LOGISTICS (UK) [23822124] **5385, 4047**

JANE'S NATO HANDBOOK *CEASED*. (UK/0958-126X) [19257528] **4047**

JANE'S NAVAL WEAPON SYSTEMS (UK) [20680519] **4047**

JANE'S NBC PROTECTION EQUIPMENT (UK) [19019641] **4047**

JANE'S RADAR AND ELECTRONIC WARFARE SYSTEMS (US) [20286586] **4047**

JANE'S SECURITY AND CO-IN EQUIPMENT (UK) [22807940] **4047**

●JANE'S SPACE DIRECTORY (UK) [29020435] **25**

JANE'S STRATEGIC WEAPON SYSTEMS (UK) **4047**

JANE'S UNDERWATER WARFARE SYSTEMS (UK) [20502000] **4047**

JANE'S URBAN TRANSPORT SYSTEMS (UK) [08491977] **5385**

JANE'S WORLD RAILWAYS (UK/0075-3084) [02220646] **5432**

JANESVILLE ARGUS (US) [01754179] **5696**

JANESVILLE GAZETTE (JANESVILLE, WIS. : 1969 : DAILY) (US) [15183737] **5768**

JANG (II) [01781424] **5803**

JANO. GUIA DE CONGRESOS MEDICOS (SP) **3591**

JANO. MEDICINA Y HUMANIDADES (SP/0210-220X) [I0210220X] **3591**

JANSSEN CHIMICA ACTA (BE/0771-4602) [I07714602] **979**

JANSSEN RESEARCH FOUNDATION SERIES (NE/0165-8352) [06433108] **4309**

JANSSEN RESEARCH NEWS (US) [07658039] **4309**

JANTAR (PL) [01783902] **2518**

JANUA LINGUARUM. SERIES MAIOR (NE/0075-3114) [01924058] **3289**

JANUB AL-WADI (UA) [07237031] **2640**

JANUS (SP) **5365**

JANUS (AMSTERDAM) *CEASED*. (NE/0021-4264) [01641906] **3591**

JANUS PANNONIUS MUZEUM EVKONYVE, A (HU/0553-4429) [I05534429] **4089**

JANYEN GWAHAG DAIHAG NONMUNJIB (KO/0253-6277) [08484024] **5117**

JAPAN See SAISHIN TOKI ROPPO / TODA SHUZO KANSHU **3091**

JAPAN See HANREITSUKI ROPPO ZENSHO **2976**

JAPAN See KASEN SHOROPPO **1416**

JAPAN See NOGYO ROPPO **3017**

JAPAN See AUDIT REPORT ON FINAL ACCOUNTS FOR FISCAL ..., THE **4712**

JAPAN See KAGAKU GIJUTSU ROPPO / HENSHU KAGAKU GIJUTSUCHO **5122**

JAPAN See BOSAI ROPPO **5275**

JAPAN See KINYU SHOROPPO **795**

JAPAN See ZAISEI SHOROPPO **4759**

JAPAN See FUDOSAN ROPPO **2972**

JAPAN See SUIDO JITSUMU ROPPO / KOSEISHO KANKYO EISEIKYOKU SUIDO KANKYOBU SUIDO SEIBIKA HENSHU **5540**

JAPAN See SHAKAI HOKEN ROMU ROPPO **3154**

JAPAN See SHOTOKUZEI HOREI SHU **4748**

JAPAN See SEMPAKU ROPPO **3182**

JAPAN See NINMEN KANKEI HOREISHU / HENSHU NIHON JINJI GYOSEI KENKYUJO **4704**

JAPAN See KYUKYU SHOROPPO / SHOBOCHO YOBO KYUKYUKA HEN **5294**

JAPAN See FUDOSAN KANKEI HOREI SHU **4838**

JAPAN See JIDO FUKUSHI ROPPO **5291**

JAPAN See SHOROPPO **3055**

JAPAN See MOHAN ROPPO **3011**

JAPAN See KOKKA OMUIN SAIGAI HOSHO KANKEI HOREI SHU **1682**

JAPAN See KENSETSUGYO ANZEN EISEI HOREI HYAKKA **618**

JAPAN See JITSUYO KAIJI ROPPO **3181**

JAPAN See JITSUMU ZEIHO ROPPO. HOREI / OKURASHO SHUZEIKYOKU SOMUKA KANSHU **4734**

JAPAN See SHAKAI FUKUSHI ROPPO / KOSEISHO SHAKAIKYOKU JIDO KATEIKYOKU ENGOKYOKU KANSHU **5307**

JAPAN See FUDOSAN SHINROPPO **4838**

JAPAN See SAISHIN CHUKAI SHOBO HOREI **2292**

JAPAN See KOTSU SHOROPPO **5385**

JAPAN See KAISETSU KYOIKU ROPPO **2992**

JAPAN See YUSEI GYOSEI ROPPO **1148**

JAPAN See KENSETSUSHO SETCHI HO KANKEI HOREISHU / KENSETSU DAIJIN KANBO BUNSHOKA KANSHU **2992**

JAPAN See KENSETSUGYO HOREI TSUTATSU ZENSHO **618**

JAPAN See HOKEN ROPPO / HOKEN SEIDO KENKYUKAI HEN **2978**

JAPAN See SENIN ROPPO **4183**

JAPAN See HIKKEI GAKKO SHOROPPO **2978**

JAPAN See CHUKAI JIDOSHA ROPPO **2950**

JAPAN See HANREI MINJI ROPPO ZENSHO / HENSHU, DAIICHI HOKI SHUPPAN KABUSHIKI KAISHA HENSHUBU **2976**

JAPAN See CHUKAI SHIN KYOIKU ROPPO **1732**

JAPAN See JUMIN KIHON DAICHO ROPPO / JICHISHO GYOSEIKYOKU KANSHU **2990**

●JAPAN 21ST (JA/0916-877X) [25335108] **1498, 685**

JAPAN AGRINFO NEWSLETTER : JAPAN'S FOOD AND AGRICULTURE-NEWS AND VIEWS (JA) [10652215] **98**

JAPAN ... AN INTERNATIONAL COMPARISON (JA/0389-3502) [08088969] **1569**

JAPAN AND THE WORLD ECONOMY (NE/0922-1425) [19224071] **1636**

JAPAN ANNUAL REVIEWS IN ELECTRONICS, COMPUTERS & TELECOMMUNICATIONS *CEASED*. (JA) [11057702] **1260, 2068**

JAPAN ARCHITECT See JA QUARTERLY **301**

JAPAN ASSOCIATION FOR PHILOSOPHY OF SCIENCE See ANNALS - JAPAN ASSOCIATION FOR PHILOSOPHY OF SCIENCE **5083**

JAPAN AUTO DIGEST (UK/1355-6118) **5417**

JAPAN AUTOMOBILE LETTER *CEASED*. (JA) **5417**

JAPAN AUTOMOTIVE NEWS (JA) **5417**

JAPAN AUTOTECH REPORT (JA) **5417**

JAPAN AVIATION DIRECTORY (JA/0286-0635) [07034550] **25**

JAPAN BANKING BRIEFS (JA/0448-8520) [05992848] **793**

JAPAN BIOINDUSTRY LETTERS (JA) **460**

JAPAN BIOTECH LETTER *CEASED*. (JA) **5117**

JAPAN CAMERA TRADE NEWS (JA) **4371**

JAPAN CHEMICAL ANNUAL (JA) [01789570] **1026**

JAPAN CHEMICAL DIRECTORY (JA/0075-3203) [01772504] **1026**

JAPAN CHEMICAL WEEK (JA/0047-1755) [03394184] **1026**

JAPAN. CHOKINKYOKU *See* YUBIN CHOKIN TO NI KANSURU SERON CHOSA KEKKA HOKOKUSHO **817**

JAPAN CHRISTIAN ACTIVITY NEWS **SUSPENDED.** (JA/0021-4353) [01639757] **4967**

JAPAN CHRISTIAN QUARTERLY *See* JAPAN CHRISTIAN REVIEW, THE **4967**

● JAPAN CHRISTIAN REVIEW, THE (JA/0918-516X) [27056742] **4967**

JAPAN. CHUGOKU SHIKOKU NOSEIKYOKU *See* CHUGOKU SHIKOKU NOGYO JOSEI HOKOKU **74**

JAPAN. CHUGOKU ZAIMUKYOKU *See* KANNAI KEIZAI JOSEI HOKOKU **1570**

JAPAN. CHUO RODO IINKAI *See* TAISHOKUKIN TEINENSEI OYOBI NENKIN JIJO CHOSA **5312**

JAPAN COMMERCE AND INDUSTRY **CEASED.** (JA/0447-5291) [11394416] **842, 1613**

JAPAN COMPANY HANDBOOK. FIRST SECTION FIRMS (JA) [16348250] **685**

JAPAN COMPANY HANDBOOK. SECOND SECTION (JA) [16291350] **685**

JAPAN COMPUTER QUARTERLY (JA/0910-6707) [12297801] **1260**

JAPAN COTTON STATISTICS AND RELATED DATA, THE (JA/0447-5321) [01783029] **98, 154**

JAPAN CULTURAL INSTITUTE IN ROME *See* ANNUARIO - INSTITUTO GIAPPONESE DI CULTURA IN ROMA **2645**

JAPAN. DAIICHI KOWAN KENSETSUKYOKU. NIIGATA CHOSA SEKKEI JIMUSHO *See* CHOSETSU KOHO NIIGATA **2088**

JAPAN DIRECTORY (JA) [01984073] **842**

JAPAN DIRECTORY OF PROFESSIONAL ASSOCIATIONS (JA/0287-9530) [10744748] **685**

JAPAN ECHO (JA/0388-0435) [02241573] **2654**

JAPAN ECONOMIC ALMANAC (JA/0910-8300) [12105697] **1569**

JAPAN ECONOMIC DAILY (US/0734-0575) [08691449] **1498**

JAPAN ECONOMIC REVIEW (JA) [01794884] **1569**

JAPAN ECONOMIC SURVEY (US/0888-5710) [06783627] **1636**

JAPAN ELECTRONIC PARTS GUIDE (JA) [10987209] **2068**

JAPAN ELECTRONICS ALMANAC (JA) [07729028] **2068**

JAPAN ELECTRONICS BUYERS' GUIDE (JA/0448-861X) [01783020] **2068**

JAPAN : ENERGIEWIRTSCHAFT (GW) [06605947] **1948**

JAPAN ENGLISH PUBLICATIONS IN PRINT (JA/0910-7908) [12441652] **4829**

JAPAN EXPORTS & IMPORTS (JA) [01782868] **842**

JAPAN FINANCE AND ECONOMIC REVIEW **CEASED.** (UK/0968-7122) **793**

JAPAN FINANCIAL REPORT **CEASED.** (JA) [14096784] **793**

JAPAN FORUM (JA/0024-127X) [03309012] **4526**

JAPAN FORUM (OXFORD, ENGLAND) (UK/0955-5803) [19966890] **2654**

JAPAN FOUNDATION NEWSLETTER, THE (JA/0385-2318) [04102509] **5249**

● JAPAN FOUNDATION PROGRAMS AVAILABLE IN CANADA, THE (CN/1183-885X) [25882936] **2654**

JAPAN FREIGHT RAILWAY COMPANY *See* BUSINESS REPORT **5430**

JAPAN. FUKUOKA KOKUZEIKYOKU *See* SOZEI TO ZAISEI NO ARAMASHI **4748**

JAPAN. FUKUOKA KOKUZEIKYOKU *See* FUKUOKA KOKUZEIKYOKU TOKEISHO **4727**

JAPAN. FUKUOKA TSUSHO SANGYOKYOKU *See* KYUSHU TSUSHO SANGYO NEMPO **1571**

JAPAN. GENSHIRYOKU ANZEN IINKAI *See* GENSHIRYOKU ANZEN IINKAI GEPPO **2155**

JAPAN GRAPHIC ARTS (JA) [19948705] **380, 4566**

JAPAN. GYOSEI KANRICHO *See* GYOSEI KANRICHO NO ARAMASHI **4653**

JAPAN. HAKODATE EIRINKYOKU. KEIRIKA. TOSHOSHITSU *See* HAKODATE EIRINKYOKU TOSHO MOKUROKU **2399**

JAPAN HARVEST (JA/0021-440X) [01776468] **4967**

JAPAN HIGH TECH REPORT (UK) **5117**

JAPAN. HIROSHIMA KOKUZEIKYOKU *See* HIROSHIMA KOKUZEIKYOKU TOKEISHO **4731**

JAPAN. HOKKAIDO EIRINKYOKU *See* HOKKAIDO EIRINKYOKU JIGYO TOKEISHO : CHOKKATSU **2384**

JAPAN. HOKKAIDO KAIHATSUKYOKU. DOBOKU SHIKENJO *See* GAIYO - HOKKAIDO KAIHATSUKYOKU DOBOKU SHIKENJO **2023**

JAPAN. HOKKAIDO ZAIMUKYOKU *See* YORAN - HOKKAIDO ZAIMUKYOKU **4759**

JAPAN. HOKURIKU YUSEIKYOKU *See* HOKURIKU YUSEIKYOKU TOKEI NEMPO **1145**

JAPAN. HOMUSHO. HOMU TOSHOKAN *See* SHUSHO NEMPO - HOMUSHO HOMU TOSHOKAN **3055**

JAPAN HOTEL AND RESORT INVESTMENT REPORT (US/1056-5043) [23747451] **2807**

JAPAN INSURANCE NEWS (JA/0910-4534) [I09104534] **2885**

JAPAN INTERPRETER (JA/0021-4450) [C1793685] **5205**

JAPAN INTRACTABLE DISEASES RESEARCH FOUNDATION PUBLICATION (JA) [17726654] **3591**

JAPAN (JAPAN. SORIFU. TOKEIKYOKU) (JA) [06637526] **5329**

JAPAN JOURNAL OF INDUSTRIAL AND APPLIED MATHEMATICS (JA/0916-7005) [23874993] **3511**

JAPAN. KAGAKU GIJUTSUCHO *See* SPACE IN JAPAN **36**

JAPAN. KAGAKU GIJUTSUCHO. SHINKOKYOKU *See* GAIKOKU GIJUTSU DONYU NENJI HOKOKU **899**

JAPAN. KAGAKU GIJUTSUCHO. SHINKOKYOKU *See* CHUMOKU HATSUMEI NO SENTEI **1303**

JAPAN. KAIJO HOANCHO *See* KAIJO HOAN TOKEI NEMPO **5450**

JAPAN. KAIJO HOANCHO. KEIBI KYUNANBU. KOKO ANZENKA. KAIJO KOSTU KIKAKUSHITSU *See* TSUKO SEMPAKU JITTAI CHOSA HOKOKUSHO **5458**

JAPAN. KAIJO HOANCHO. SUIROBU *See* DATA REPORT OF HYDROGRAPHIC OBSERVATIONS. SERIES OF OCEANOGRAPHY **1448**

JAPAN. KANAZAWA KOKUZEIKYOKU *See* KANAZAWA KOKUZEIKYOKU TOKEISHO **4735**

JAPAN. KANI HOKENKYOKU *See* KANI SEIMEI HOKEN NO SHIBORITSU SHOGAI HASSEIRITSU NI KANSURU CHOSA **2886**

JAPAN. KANTO SHIN-ETSU KOKUZEIKYOKU *See* KANTO SHIN-ETSU KOKUZEIKYOKU TOKEISHO **4735**

JAPAN. KANTO YUSEIKYOKU *See* KANTO YUSEIKYOKU TOKEI NEMPO **1145**

JAPAN. KANTO ZAIMUKYOKU *See* KANNAI KEIZAI JOSEI HOKOKU **1570**

JAPAN. KEIZAI KIKAKUCHO. BUKKAKYOKU *See* BUKKA REPOTO **1590**

JAPAN. KEIZAI KIKAKUCHO. CHOSAKYOKU *See* NIHON KEIZAI NO GENKYO **1575**

JAPAN. KENSETSUCHO. TOHOKU CHIHO KENSETSUKYOKU *See* JIGYO NO ARAMASHI - KENSETSUSHO TOHOKU CHIHO KENSETSUKYOKU **1613**

JAPAN. KENSETSUSHO *See* CURRENT CONDITIONS & PROBLEMS IN THE CONSTRUCTION INDUSTRY **612**

JAPAN. KENSETSUSHO *See* KANCHO EIZEN **618**

JAPAN. KENSETSUSHO. CHUBU CHIHO KENSETSUKYOKU *See* JIGYO NO ARAMASHI - KENSETSUSHO CHUBU CHIHO KENSETSUKYOKU **2025**

JAPAN. KENSETSUSHO. CHUGOKU CHIHO KENSETSUKYOKU *See* JIGYO GAIYO - KENSETSUSHO CHUGOKU CHIHO KENSETSUKYOKU **1613**

JAPAN. KENSETSUSHO HOKURIKU CHIHO KENSETSUKYOKU *See* JIGYO GAIYO - KENSETSUSHO HOKURIKU CHIHO KENSETSUKYOKU **1613**

JAPAN. KENSETSUSHO KEIKAKUKYOKU. CHOSA TOKEIKA *See* KENSETSU TOKEI GEPPO **618**

JAPAN. KENSETSUSHO KYUSHU CHIHO KENSETSUKYOKU *See* JIGYO GAIYO - KENSETSUSHO KYUSHU CHIHO KENSETSUKYOKU **1613**

JAPAN. KENSETSUSHO. SHIKOKU CHIHO KENSETSUKYOKU *See* JIGYO GAIYO - KENSETSUSHO SHIKOKU CHIHO KENSETSUKYOKU **1613**

JAPAN. KIOKU IGAKU JIKKENTAI *See* KOKU IGAKU JIKKENTAI KENKYU SEIKA GAIYO **3799**

JAPAN. KISHOCHO *See* KISHOCHO NENPO: ZENKOKU KISHOHYO. ANNUAL REPORT OF THE JAPAN METEOROLOGICAL AGENCY: METEOROLOGICAL OBSERVATIONS **1427**

JAPAN. KISHOCHO *See* KISHOCHO KAIYO KISHO BUI ROBOTTO KANSOKU SHIRYO. / DATA FROM OCEAN DATA BUOY STATIONS **1427**

JAPAN. KISHOCHO *See* KISHOCHO HARO KANSOKU SHIRYO. / THE RESULTS OF SEA WAVES OBSERVATIONS **1451**

JAPAN. KISHOCHO *See* OCEANOGRAPHICAL MAGAZINE **1454**

JAPAN. KISHOCHO *See* KISHOCHO GEPPO : ZENKOKU KISHOHYO **1427**

JAPAN. KITA KYUSHU ZAIMUKYOKU *See* KANNAI KEIZAI JOSEI HOKOKU **1570**

JAPAN. KOGYO GIJUTSUIN *See* KOGYO GIJUTSUIN SHOKAI **5124**

JAPAN. KOKU IGAKU JIKKENTAI *See* TOSHO MOKUROKU - KOKU IGAKU JIKKENTAI **3662**

JAPAN. KOKUSEICHO. SOMUKA *See* ZEIMU TOKEI KARA MITA MINKAN KYUYO NO JITTAI **1720**

JAPAN. KOKUZEICHO *See* SHOTOKUZEIHO SOCHIHO SANRIN SHOTOKU JOTO SHOTOKU KIHON TSUTATSU **4686**

JAPAN. KOSEISHO *See* YAKUJI KOGYO SEISAN DOTAI TOKEI NEMPO **4333**

JAPAN. KOSEISHO. DAIJIN KAMBO. TOKEI JOHOBU *See* EISEI GYOSEI GYOMU HOKOKU **4774**

JAPAN. KOSEISHO. TOKEI JOHOBU *See* HOKENJO UNEI HOKOKU **4783**

JAPAN. KUMAMOTO KOKUZEIKYOKU *See* KUMAMOTO KOKUZEIKYOKU TOKEISHO **4735**

JAPAN. KYUSHU NOSEIKYOKU *See* KYUSHU NOGYO JOSEI HOKOKU **103**

JAPAN. KYUSHU YUSEIKYOKU *See* KYUSHU YUSEIKYOKU TOKEI NEMPO **1145**

JAPAN LABOR BULLETIN (JA/0021-4469) [02187235] **1681**

JAPAN LASER REPORT (US/0887-9362) [13414610] **4435**

JAPAN LAW JOURNAL, THE (JA) [16811257] **2986**

JAPAN. LAWS, STATUTES, ETC *See* EHS LAW BULLETIN SERIES, JAPAN **2965**

JAPAN LETTER (US/0446-6241) [01794900] **2654**

JAPAN LETTER, THE (US) [02262876] **2505**

JAPAN LUMBER JOURNAL (JA) [09837506] **2402**

JAPAN LUMBER REPORTS (JA) [15193452] **2402**

JAPAN MANAGEMENT REVIEW (UK/0968-7130) **872**

JAPAN M&A REPORTER (US/1049-4383) [21218987] **793**

JAPAN M&A REPORTER *See* ASIAN M&A AND INVESTMENT DATABASE **891**

JAPAN MARKET, THE (US/0734-2853) [08471036] **842**

JAPAN MARKET TRENDS *See* JAPAN TOY & HOBBY MARKET REPORT **2584**

JAPAN ... MARKETING AND ADVERTISING YEARBOOK (JA/0918-4406) [24020129] **927, 761**

JAPAN MATERIALS NEWS (METALS PARK, OHIO) **CEASED.** (US/0894-1149) [15797898] **4005**

JAPAN MEDICAL JOURNAL. NIHON IJI SHIMPO (JA) **3591**

JAPAN METAL BULLETIN. AIR MAIL ED (JA/0021-4523) [I00214523] **4005**

JAPAN. MINAMI KYUSHU ZAIMUKYOKU *See* KANNAI KEIZAI JOSEI HOKOKU **1570**

JAPAN. MINAMI KYUSHU ZAIMUKYOKU *See* MINAMI KYUSHU ZAIMUKYOKU YORAN **4737**

JAPAN MISSION JOURNAL (JA) **4967**

JAPAN MISSIONARY BULLETIN *See* JAPAN MISSION JOURNAL **4967**

JAPAN MISSIONARY BULLETIN, THE (JA/0021-4531) [01773902] **4967**

JAPAN. MOMBUSHO *See* EDUCATIONAL STANDARDS IN JAPAN **1743**

JAPAN. MOMBUSHO. TOSHOKAN *See* MOMBUSHO TOSHOKAN YORAN **3232**

JAPAN NATIONAL CONGRESS FOR APPLIED MECHANICS *See* THEORETICAL AND APPLIED MECHANICS **2130**

JAPAN NEW MATERIALS LETTER (JA) **2068**

JAPAN — Alphabetical Title Index

JAPAN. NIHON GAKUJUTSU KAIGI. KOKUSAI CHIKYU KANSOKU TOKUBETSU IINKAI. TAIYO CHIKYUKAN BUTSURIGAKU BUNKAKAI *See* GRAPHS OF NEUTRON INTENSITIES **4404**

JAPAN. NOGYO SHIKENJO, KYUSHU *See* KYUSHU NOSHI NEMPO **103**

JAPAN. NORIN SUISANSHO. DAIJIN KAMBO. CHOSAKA *See* NOGYO KANSOKU **113**

JAPAN. NORIN SUISANSHO. KEIZAIKYOKU. TOKEI JOHOBU *See* NO-CHIKUSANGYOYO KOTEI SHISAN HYOKA HYOJUN **749**

JAPAN. NORIN SUISANSHO. KEIZAIKYOKU. TOKEI JOHOBU *See* NOKA KEIZAI CHOSA HOKOKU **113**

JAPAN. NORIN SUISANSHO. KEIZAIKYOKU. TOKEI JOHOBU *See* NORIN SUISANSHO TOKEIHYO **114**

JAPAN. NORIN SUISANSHO. KEIZAIKYOKU. TOKEI JOHOBU *See* NPGUO CHOSA HOKOKUSHO **115**

JAPAN. NORIN SUISANSHO. KEIZAIKYOKU. TOKEI JOHOBU *See* NORIN-SUISANGYO SEISAN SHISU **2389**

JAPAN. NORIN SUISANSHO. KEIZAIKYOKU. TOKEI JOHOBU *See* NOKA SHUGYO DOKO CHOSA HOKOKU **114**

JAPAN. NORIN SUISANSHO. KEIZAIKYOKU. TOKEI JOHOBU. KIKAKU CHOSAKA *See* NORIN-SUISANGYO NI KANSURU CHIIKI BUNSEKISHO SORAN **155**

JAPAN. NORINSHO *See* NORINSHO NEMPO **114**

JAPAN. NORINSHO *See* NOGYO HAKUSHO **113**

JAPAN. NORINSHO. NORIN KEIZAIKYOKU. TOKEI JOHOBU *See* SEISAN NOGYO SHOTOKU TOKEI **133**

JAPAN. NORINSHO. NORIN KEIZAIKYOKU. TOKEI JOHOBU *See* CHIKUSAMBUTSU SEISANHI CHOSA HOKOKU **209**

JAPAN. NORINSHO. NORIN KEIZAIKYOKU. TOKEI JOHOBU *See* RINGYO SEISAN TOKEI NEMPO **2394**

JAPAN. NORINSHO. NORIN KEIZAIKYOKU. TOKEI JOHOBU *See* SEIKABUTSU NISUGATA CHOSA KEKKA **1626**

JAPAN. NORINSHO. NORIN KEIZAIKYOKU. TOKEI JOHOBU *See* FISH CATCH IN JAPANESE FISHERIES **2301**

JAPAN. NORINSHO. NORIN KEIZAIKYOKU. TOKEI JOHOBU *See* OKINAWA-KEN TOKEISHO **116**

JAPAN. NORINSHO. NORIN KEIZAIKYOKU. TOKEI JOHOBU *See* KOGEI NOSAKUBUTSU TOKEI NEMPO **177**

JAPAN. NORINSHO. NORIN KEIZAIKYOKU. TOKEI JOHOBU *See* SEIKABUTSU SEISAN SHUKKA TOKEI **1520**

JAPAN. NORINSHO. NORIN KEIZAIKYOKU. TOKEI JOHOBU *See* NOKA SHIKIN DOTAI TOKEI **113**

JAPAN. NORINSHO. NORIN KEIZAIKYOKU. TOKEI JOHOBU *See* MOKUZAI RYUTSU KOZO HOKOKUSHO **2403**

JAPAN. NORINSHO. NORIN KEIZAIKYOKU. TOKEI JOHOBU *See* SHICHOSONBETSU KOCHI MENSEKI TOKEI **1520**

JAPAN. NORINSHO. NORIN KEIZAIKYOKU. TOKEI JOHOBU *See* CHA TOKEI NEMPO **73**

JAPAN NOTEBOOK *SUSPENDED.* (US/1053-4997) [22546464] **2654**

JAPAN. OKINAWA KAIHATSUCHO *See* OKINAWA NO SHINKO KAIHATSU **2830**

JAPAN. OKINAWA YUSEI KANRI JIMUSHO *See* OKINAWA YUSEI KANRI JIMUSHO TOKEI NEMPO **1146**

JAPAN. OKURASHO. KANZEIKYOKU *See* GAIKOKU BOEKI GAIKYO. THE SUMMARY REPORT, TRADE OF JAPAN **837**

JAPAN. OKURASHO. KOKUSAI KINYUKYOKU *See* OKURASHO KOKUSAI KINYUKYOKU NEMPO **910**

JAPAN. OKURASHO. SHUZEIKYOKU *See* OUTLINE OF JAPANESE TAXES, AN **4740**

JAPAN PATENTS & TRADEMARKS (JA) [03341585] **1305**

JAPAN PERIODICALS (JA) [10479283] **1534**

JAPAN PESTICIDE INFORMATION (JA/0368-265X) [01714407] **4245**

JAPAN PETROLEUM & ENERGY TRENDS (JA) [18723541] 1948, **4262**

JAPAN PETROLEUM & ENERGY TRENDS. MONTHLY STATISTICAL SUPPLEMENT (JA) [18723553] 1948, **4262**

JAPAN PETROLEUM & ENERGY YEARBOOK *SUSPENDED.* (JA) [04694674] **4262**

JAPAN PETROLEUM INDUSTRY YEARBOOK (JA) [11275970] **4262**

JAPAN PICTORIAL (NORTH AMERICAN EDITION) (JA/0388-6115) [09562568] **2536**

JAPAN PLASTICS AGE *CEASED.* (JA/0021-4582) [04795425] **4455**

JAPAN PLASTICS INDUSTRY ANNUAL (JA/0448-8679) [04042345] **4455**

JAPAN POLITICAL RESEARCH (US/1051-1776) [21388009] **4478**

JAPAN PUBLISHERS DIRECTORY (JA) [15026753] **4816**

JAPAN PULP AND PAPER (JA/0285-726X) [04125501] **4234**

JAPAN QUARTERLY (JA/0021-4590) [01754204] **2654**

JAPAN QUARTERLY (NEW DELHI) (II/0377-0370) [02246225] **2654**

JAPAN REPORT (CANADIAN EDITION) (CN/0226-5982) [09313036] **842**

JAPAN REPORT SERIES INFORMATION TECHNOLOGY (SP) **1191**

JAPAN REPORT SERIES MEDICAL TECHNOLOGY (SP) **3591**

JAPAN REPORT SERIES PRODUCT OPPORTUNITIES (SP) **1613**

JAPAN REPORT SERIES TELECOMMUNICATIONS (SP) **1158**

JAPAN REPORT : TELECOMMUNICATION *See* JAPANESE REPORT SERIES : TELECOMMUNICATIONS **1158**

JAPAN REVIEW OF INTERNATIONAL AFFAIRS (JA/0913-8773) [16968055] **4526**

JAPAN. RINYACHO *See* KOKUYU RINYA JIGYO TOKEISHO **2386**

JAPAN. RODOSHO. DAIJIN KAMBO. TOKEI JOHOBU. JOHO KAISEKIKA *See* RODOSHA FUKUSHI SOGO CHOSA HOKOKU **1708**

JAPAN. RODOSHO. DAIJIN KAMBO. TOKEI JOHOBU. KEIZAI TOKEI *See* RODO SEISANSEI TOKEI CHOSA HOKOKU **1582**

JAPAN. RODOSHO. ROSEIKYOKU *See* CHINGIN HIKIAGE TO NO JITTAI NI KANSURU CHOSA KEKKA HOKOKUSHO **1659**

JAPAN. RODOSHO. TOKEI JOHOBU *See* SHOKUBA NO ANZEN KANRI OYOBI EISEI KANRI NI KANSURU SOGO JITTAI CHOSA KEKKA HOKOKUSHO **2870**

JAPAN. RODOSHO. TOKEI JOHOBU *See* MAIGETSU KINRO TOKEI TOKUBETSU CHOSA HOKOKU **1689**

JAPAN. RODOSHO. TOKEI JOHOBU *See* KOYO KANRI CHOSA HOKOKU **943**

JAPAN. RODOSHO. TOKEI JOHOBU *See* OKUGAI RODOSHA SHOKUSHUBETSU CHINGIN CHOSA HOKOKU **1700**

JAPAN. RODOSHO. TOKEI JOHOBU *See* KOYO DOKO CHOSA KEKKA NO GAIYO **1682**

JAPAN. RODOSHO. TOKEI JOHOBU *See* KYUJIN TO JITTAI CHOSA HOKOKU **1683**

JAPAN. SAIKO SAIBANSHO *See* SERIES OF PROMINENT JUDGEMENTS OF THE SUPREME COURT UPON QUESTIONS OF CONSTITUTIONALITY **3048**

JAPAN. SAPPORO KOKUZEIKYOKU *See* SAPPORO KOKUZEIKYOKU TOKEISHO **4747**

JAPAN. SAPPORO TSUSHO SANGYOKYOKU *See* ME DE MIRU HOKKAIDO SANGYO **1574**

JAPAN. SENDAI TSUSHO SANGYOKYOKU *See* TOHOKU CHIHO KOGYO KAIHATSU YORAN **1629**

JAPAN. SETO NAIKAI RENGO KAIKU GYOGYO CHOSEI IINKAI *See* SETO NAIKAI RENGO KAIKU GYOGYO CHOSEI IINKAI GIJIROKU **2313**

JAPAN. SHIGEN ENERUGICHO. KOEKI JIGYOBU *See* DENGEN KAIHATSU NO GAIYO **2040**

JAPAN. SHIKOKU YUSEIKYOKU *See* SHIKOKU YUSEI TOKEI NEMPO **1147**

JAPAN. SHIKOKU ZAIMUKYOKU *See* KANNAI KEIZAI JOSEI HOKOKU **1570**

JAPAN SHIPBUILDING & MARINE ENGINEERING (JA/0021-4647) [05360558] 1981, **4177**

JAPAN SOCIETY (NEW YORK, N.Y.) *See* JAPAN SOCIETY NEWSLETTER **2654**

JAPAN SOCIETY NEWSLETTER (US/1070-9363) [28511176] **2654**

JAPAN. SORIFU. NAIKAKU SORI DAIJIN KAMBO *See* SERON CHOSA NENKAN. ZENKOKU SERON CHOSA NO GENKYO **5257**

JAPAN. SORIFU. TOKEIKYOKU *See* KOJIN KIGYO EIGYO CHOSA HOKOKU **1614**

JAPAN. SORIFU. TOKEIKYOKU *See* NEWS BULLETIN **4699**

JAPAN SOURCE CARD INNOVATION NEWSLETTER (JA) **685**

JAPAN STEEL JOURNAL *CEASED.* (JA) **4005**

JAPAN STOCK JOURNAL, THE (JA/0021-4736) [04042221] **904**

JAPAN SUGAR YEARBOOK (JA) [01787727] **175**

JAPAN. SUISANCHO *See* GYOGYO HAKUSHO **2304**

JAPAN. TAKAMATSU KOKUZEIKYOKU *See* TAKAMATSU KOKUZEIKYOKU TOKEISHO **4751**

JAPAN TECHNOLOGY MONITOR (US/1055-8004) [23243634] **5117**

JAPAN TELECOM REPORT (JA) **1158**

JAPAN TIMES (OVERSEAS ED.), THE (JA/0447-5763) [21225620] **5805**

JAPAN TIMES (TOKYO. 1956), THE (JA/0289-1956) [12002049] **5805**

JAPAN. TOHOKU ZAIMUKYOKU *See* KANNAI KEIZAI JOSEI HOKOKU **1570**

JAPAN. TOKYO TSUSHO SANGYOKYOKU *See* KANTO KO-SHIN-ETSU-SEI CHIIKI KEIZAI GAIKAN **1570**

JAPAN. TOKYO YUSEIKYOKU *See* TOKYO YUSEIKYOKU TOKEI NEMPO **1147**

JAPAN TOY & HOBBY MARKET REPORT (JA) **2584**

JAPAN TRADE DIRECTORY (NIHON BOEKI SHINKOKAI) (JA) [08794359] **842**

JAPAN TRAVEL BLUE BOOK (JA) **5481**

JAPAN. TSUSANSHO *See* TSUSANSHO KOHO **1587**

JAPAN. TSUSHO SANGYOSHO *See* WHITE PAPER ON INTERNATIONAL TRADE: JAPAN **735**

JAPAN. TSUSHO SANGYOSHO *See* NEWS FROM MITI **847**

JAPAN. TSUSHO SANGYOSHO. CHOSA TOKEIBU *See* ENERUGI TOKEI GEPPO **4255**

JAPAN. TSUSHO SANGYOSHO. CHOSA TOKEIBU *See* KOSAKU KIKAI SETSUBI TO TOKEI CHOSA HOKOKUSHO **1615**

JAPAN. TSUSHO SANGYOSHO. CHOSA TOKEIBU *See* SHIGEN TOKEI GEPPO **1445**

JAPAN. TSUSHO SANGYOSHO. CHOSA TOKEIBU *See* TOKUTEI SABISUGYO JITTAI TOKEI CHOSA HOKOKUSHO **1629**

JAPAN. TSUSHO SANGYOSHO DAIJIN KAMBO. CHOSA TOEKIBU *See* KIKAI KIGU RYUTSU NO DOKO: CHOSA NO YOSHI TO SONO KEKKA **1614**

JAPAN. TSUSHO SANGYOSHO DAIJIN KAMBO. CHOSA TOKEIBU *See* KOKOGYO SHISU NEMPO **1571**

JAPAN. TSUSHO SANGYOSHO. DAIJIN KAMBO. CHOSA TOKEIBU *See* WAGA KUNI NO KOKOGYO: KAMI PARUPU KOGYO HEN **4239**

JAPAN. TSUSHO SANGYOSHO. DAIJIN KAMBO. CHOSA TOKEIBU *See* WAGA KUNI NO KOKOGYO : KIKAI KOGYO HEN; CHU-TANZOGYO HEN **1631**

JAPAN. TSUSHO SANGYOSHO. DAIJIN KAMBO. CHOSA TOKEIBU *See* KAMI PARUPU KOGYO SETSUBI CHOSA HOKOKUSHO **4234**

JAPAN. TSUSHO SANGYOSHO. DAIJIN KAMBO. CHOSA TOKEIBU *See* WAGA KUNI NO KOKOGYO : SENI KOGYO HEN; SENI RYUTSU HEN **5359**

JAPAN. TSUSHO SANGYOSHO. DAIJIN KAMBO. CHOSA TOKEIBU *See* WAGA KUNI NO KOKOGYO : KAGAKU KOGYO HEN, GOMU SEIHIN HEN, PURASUCHIKKU SEIHIN HEN, YOGYO KENZAI HEN **1631**

JAPAN. TSUSHO SANGYOSHO. DAIJIN KAMBO. CHOSA TOKEIBU *See* WAGA KUNI NO KOGOGYO: TEKKO HEN **4023**

JAPAN. TSUSHO SANGYOSHO. KIGYOKYOKU *See* FOREIGN CAPITAL AFFILIATED ENTERPRISES IN JAPAN **676**

JAPAN. TSUSHO SANGYOSHO. KIGYOKYOKU *See* FOREIGN-AFFILIATED ENTERPRISES IN JAPAN--FULL TEXT OF ENTERPRISE BUREAU OF M.I.T.I. REPORT-- **1635**

JAPAN. TSUSHO SANGYOSHO. SANGYO SEISAKUKYOKU *See* SEKAI NO KIGYO NO KEIEI BUNSEKI: KOKUSAI KEIEI HIKAKU **811**

JAPAN. TSUSHO SANGYOSHO. SANGYO SEISAKUKYOKU *See* WAGA KUNI KIGYO NO KEIEI BUNSEKI. KIGYOBETSU TOKEI HEN **815**

JAPAN. TSUSHO SANGYOSHO. SANGYO SEISAKUKYOKU *See* WAGA KUNI KIGYO NO KAIGAI JIGYO KATSUDO, SONO GENJO TO MONDAITEN **919**

JAPAN. TSUSHO SANGYOSHO TOSHOKAN *See* TSUSHO SANGYOSHO TOSHOKAN TOSHO MOKUROKU **1596**

JAPAN. TSUSHO SANGYOSHO. TSUSHO SEISAKUKYOKU See BOEKI GYOTAI TOKEIHYO **825**

JAPAN. TSUSHO SANGYOSHO. TSUSHOKYOKU. BOEKI GYOTAI TOKEIHYO See BOEKI GYOTAI TOKEIHYO **825**

JAPAN-U.S. BUSINESS REPORT (US/0888-5702) [13113311] **685**

JAPAN-UNITED STATES FRIENDSHIP COMMISSION See ANNOUNCEMENT OF PROGRAMS / JAPAN-UNITED STATES FRIENDSHIP COMMISSION **4515**

JAPAN-UNITED STATES FRIENDSHIP COMMISSION See BIENNIAL REPORT / JAPAN-UNITED STATES FRIENDSHIP COMMISSION **4516**

JAPAN-UNITED STATES FRIENDSHIP COMMISSION See ANNUAL REPORT / THE JAPAN-UNITED STATES FRIENDSHIP COMMISSION **5239**

JAPAN. UNYUSHO See UNYUSHO KENKYU KIHON KEIKAKU **2000**

JAPAN. UNYUSHO. DAIJIN KAMBO. JOHO KANRIBU See KOKU YUSO TOKEI NENPO **27**

JAPAN. UNYUSHO. DAIJIN KAMBO. JOHO KANRIBU See SENIN RODO TOKEI **1710**

JAPAN. UNYUSHO. DAIJIN KAMBO. JOHO KANRIBU See SENIN TOKEI **1710**

JAPAN. UNYUSHO. DAIJIN KAMBO. JOHO KANRIBU See KAINAN TOKEI NENPO **4178**

JAPAN. UNYUSHO. DAIJIN KANBO. TOKEI CHOSABU. KAINAN TOKEI NENPO See KAINAN TOKEI NENPO **4178**

JAPAN UPDATE (JA/0912-3474) [24780673] **1569**

●JAPAN WATCH, USA (US/1062-3302) [25587658] **1498**

JAPAN. WIRTSCHAFTLICHE ENTWICKLUNG (GW) [03375813] **1498**

JAPAN, WIRTSCHAFTSDATEN / BUNDESSTELLE FUER AUSSENHANDELSINFORMATION (GW) [11778523] **1569**

JAPAN, WIRTSCHAFTSDATEN UND WIRTSCHAFTSDOKUMENTATION / BUNDESTELLE FUR AUSSENHANDELSINFORMATION (GW) [08948572] **1569**

JAPAN. ZEIKAN, KOBE See KOBE ZEIKAN. / KOBE CUSTOMS **5268**

JAPAN. ZEIKAN, OSAKA See OSAKA ZEIKAN **4740**

JAPAN. ZOHEIKYOKU See JIGYO ANNAI - ZOHEIKYOKU **793**

JAPANESE AEROSPACE DIRECTORY (JA/0304-1654) [02245981] **25**

JAPANESE AMERICAN VERNACULAR NEWSPAPERS, ABSTRACT-INDEX *SUSPENDED.* (US/0893-8598) [15474892] **3219**

JAPANESE ANAESTHESIA JOURNALS' REVIEW *CEASED.* (NE/0169-1066) [12397576] **3683**

JAPANESE ANNUAL OF INTERNATIONAL LAW, THE (JA/0448-8806) [01782891] **3131**

JAPANESE ASSOCIATION OF GROUNDWATER HYDROLOGY See JOURNAL - JAPANESE ASSOCIATION OF GROUNDWATER HYDROLOGY **1415**

JAPANESE BUSINESS JOURNAL (US/0047-181X) [01783581] **685**

JAPANESE CHILDREN'S BOOKS OF INTERNATIONAL INTEREST (JA) [08890738] **1065**

JAPANESE CIRCULATION JOURNAL (JA/0047-1828) [04610952] **3706**

JAPANESE ECONOMIC REVIEW (UK/1352-4739) **1498**

JAPANESE ECONOMIC STUDIES (US/0021-4841) [01784686] **1569**

JAPANESE FILMS (JA/0448-8830) [03694055] **4073**

JAPANESE FINANCE AND INDUSTRY : QUARTERLY SURVEY (JA/0385-2369) [02244411] **793**

●JAPANESE GOLF COURSE INVESTMENT REPORT (US/1054-3562) [22857938] **904**

JAPANESE INVESTMENT IN U.S. AND CANADIAN REAL ESTATE DIRECTORY (US/1047-7233) [20749793] **904**, **4839**

JAPANESE INVESTMENT IN U.S. REAL ESTATE REVIEW. WESTERN REGION *CEASED.* (US/0898-9761) [17969753] **904**, **4839**

JAPANESE JOURNAL OF ADVANCED AUTOMATION TECHNOLOGY (JA) **5117**

JAPANESE JOURNAL OF ADVANCED AUTOMATION TECHNOLOGY (JA) **2117**

JAPANESE JOURNAL OF AMERICAN STUDIES, THE (JA) [09104425] **2740**

JAPANESE JOURNAL OF ANTIBIOTICS, THE (JA/0368-2781) [01714965] **4309**

JAPANESE JOURNAL OF APPLIED PHYSICS. PART 1, REGULAR PAPERS & SHORT NOTES (JA) [08270740] **4407**

JAPANESE JOURNAL OF APPLIED PHYSICS. PART 2, LETTERS (JA) [08270811] **4408**

JAPANESE JOURNAL OF APPLIED PHYSICS. SUPPLEMENT (JA) [03999790] **4408**

JAPANESE JOURNAL OF BEHAVIOR THERAPY (JA) **4592**

JAPANESE JOURNAL OF BEHAVIORMETRICS (JA) **4592**

JAPANESE JOURNAL OF BREEDING See BREEDING SCIENCE **68**

JAPANESE JOURNAL OF CANCER RESEARCH : GANN (JA/0910-5050) [11876799] **3818**

JAPANESE JOURNAL OF CHILD AND ADOLESCENT PSYCHIATRY (JA) [07136415] **3904**, **3927**

JAPANESE JOURNAL OF CLINICAL ONCOLOGY (JA/0368-2811) [01771066] **3819**

JAPANESE JOURNAL OF ENDOUROLOGY AND ESWL (JA/0914-9635) [20102801] **3990**

JAPANESE JOURNAL OF ENTOMOLOGY TOKYO. 1989 (JA/0915-5805) [I09155805] **5610**

JAPANESE JOURNAL OF FUZZY THEORY AND SYSTEMS (US/1058-7349) [24364544] **3511**

JAPANESE JOURNAL OF GENETICS (JA) [27263135] **548**

●JAPANESE JOURNAL OF HUMAN GENETICS, THE (JA/0916-8478) [26253564] **548**

JAPANESE JOURNAL OF MATHEMATICS (JA/0075-3432) [02142996] **3511**

JAPANESE JOURNAL OF MEDICAL SCIENCE & BIOLOGY (JA/0021-5112) [01487384] **460**, **3591**

JAPANESE JOURNAL OF MEDICINE See INTERNAL MEDICINE **3797**

JAPANESE JOURNAL OF NEPHROLOGY, THE (JA/0385-2385) [10327768] **3990**

JAPANESE JOURNAL OF OPHTHALMOLOGY (JA/0021-5155) [01716924] **3875**

JAPANESE JOURNAL OF PHARMACOLOGY (JA/0021-5198) [01754223] **4309**

JAPANESE JOURNAL OF PHYSIOLOGY, THE (JA/0021-521X) [01754225] **581**

JAPANESE JOURNAL OF PSYCHIATRY AND NEUROLOGY, THE (JA/0912-2036) [13879119] **3834**, **3928**

JAPANESE JOURNAL OF RADIOLOGICAL TECHNOLOGY (JA) [09743376] **3942**

JAPANESE JOURNAL OF RELIGIOUS STUDIES (JA/0304-1042) [01796139] **4967**

JAPANESE JOURNAL OF RHEUMATOLOGY (NE/0169-1163) [15903676] **3805**

JAPANESE JOURNAL OF SPORTS SCIENCES (JA/0286-9322) [I02869322] **4901**

JAPANESE JOURNAL OF SURGERY (JA/0047-1909) [01644454] **3966**

JAPANESE JOURNAL OF SWINE HUSBANDRY RESEARCH (JA) [08658443] **213**

JAPANESE JOURNAL OF THORACIC SURGERY (JA) [01623621] **3949**

JAPANESE JOURNAL OF TRIBOLOGY (US/1045-7828) [20229930] **2117**

JAPANESE JOURNAL OF VETERINARY RESEARCH, THE (JA/0047-1917) [06190079] **5512**

JAPANESE LITERATURE TODAY (JA) [02715049] **3398**

JAPANESE MACHINE TOOL ... GUIDE (JA) [08938031] **2117**

JAPANESE MOTOR BUSINESS / EIU, THE ECONOMIST INTELLIGENCE UNIT (US) [11714477] **5417**

JAPANESE NEW MATERIALS IACA SERIES. ADVANCED ALLOYS & METALS (SP) **3482**

JAPANESE NEW MATERIALS IACA SERIES. ADVANCED PLASTICS (SP) **4455**

JAPANESE NEW MATERIALS IACA SERIES. ELECTRONIC MATERIALS (SP) **2068**

JAPANESE NEW MATERIALS IACA SERIES. HIGH-PERFORMANCE CERAMICS (SP) **2591**

JAPANESE OIL STATISTICS TODAY (JA) **4262**

JAPANESE PACKAGING REPORT (JA) **4219**

JAPANESE PATENTS ABSTRACTS (UK/0021-5333) [10388872] **1305**

JAPANESE PHARMACEUTICAL BUSINESS REPORT: JPB (JA) **4309**

JAPANESE PHILATELY (US/0146-0994) [02851813] **2785**

JAPANESE PRESS, THE (JA) [09229916] **5805**

JAPANESE PSYCHOLOGICAL RESEARCH (JA/0021-5368) [01353889] **4592**

JAPANESE PSYCHOLOGICAL REVIEW (JA) **4592**

JAPANESE RAILWAY ENGINEERING (JA/0448-8938) [04794138] **1981**, **5432**

JAPANESE RELIGIONS (JA/0448-8954) [06548536] **4967**

JAPANESE REPORT SERIES BIOTECHNOLOGY (SP) **3693**

JAPANESE REPORT SERIES : INFORMATION TECHNOLOGY (SP) **3219**

JAPANESE REPORT SERIES : MEDICAL TECHNOLOGY (SP) **3591**

JAPANESE REPORT SERIES : TELECOMMUNICATIONS (SP) **1158**

JAPANESE REVIEW (US/0735-6609) [08948025] **1498**

JAPANESE SENSOR NEWSLETTER (US) **2068**

JAPANESE SLAVIC AND EAST EUROPEAN STUDIES (JA/0389-1186) [08914439] **2694**

JAPANESE SOCIETY OF PHYCOLOGY See BULLETIN OF JAPANESE SOCIETY OF PHYCOLOGY, THE **4295**

JAPANESE TECHNOLOGY REVIEWS See JAPANESE TECHNOLOGY REVIEWS. SECTION B, COMPUTERS AND COMMUNICATION **1114**

JAPANESE TECHNOLOGY REVIEWS See JAPANESE TECHNOLOGY REVIEWS. SECTION E, BIOTECHNOLOGY **3693**

JAPANESE TECHNOLOGY REVIEWS See JAPANESE TECHNOLOGY REVIEWS. SECTION C, NEW MATERIALS **5117**

JAPANESE TECHNOLOGY REVIEWS See JAPANESE TECHNOLOGY REVIEWS. SECTION A, ELECTRONICS **2068**

JAPANESE TECHNOLOGY REVIEWS See JAPANESE TECHNOLOGY REVIEWS. SECTION D, MANUFACTURING ENGINEERING **1981**

●JAPANESE TECHNOLOGY REVIEWS. SECTION A, ELECTRONICS (US/1058-7292) [24364094] **2068**

●JAPANESE TECHNOLOGY REVIEWS. SECTION B, COMPUTERS AND COMMUNICATION (US/1058-7306) [24364145] **1191**, **1114**

●JAPANESE TECHNOLOGY REVIEWS. SECTION C, NEW MATERIALS (US/1058-7314) [24364191] **5117**

●JAPANESE TECHNOLOGY REVIEWS. SECTION D, MANUFACTURING ENGINEERING (US/1058-7322) [24364223] **1981**

●JAPANESE TECHNOLOGY REVIEWS. SECTION E, BIOTECHNOLOGY (US/1058-7330) [24364960] **3693**

JAPANESE TELECOMMUNICATIONS (US) **1159**

JAPANESE YEARBOOK ON BUSINESS HISTORY (JA/0910-2027) [13136335] **685**

JAPANINFO (GW/0931-3230) [I09313230] **685**

JAPANISCHE STUDIEN ZUR DEUTSCHEN SPRACHE UND LITERATUR (SZ/0721-3719) [I07213719] **3398**, **3289**

JAPAN'S CONSTRUCTION TODAY (JA) [06571281] **618**

JAPAN'S EXPANDING U.S. MANUFACTURING PRESENCE (US/1067-697X) [20399535] **904**

JAPAN'S IRON & STEEL INDUSTRY (JA/0075-3475) [01754236] **4005**, **1613**

JAPANSCAN. FOOD SCIENCE AND THE FOOD INDUSTRY (UK/0264-3812) [02643812] **2345**

JAPON ECONOMIE ET SOCIETE PARIS (FR/1140-4264) [I11404264] **1498**

JAPOS BULLETIN (US/0278-436X) [07806801] **2785**

JAQUE (SP) **4862**

JAR (UK) **25**

JARD. JOURNAL OF AGE RELATED DISORDERS (SA/1017-2572) [I10172572] **3752**

JARDIN BOTANIQUE DE MONTREAL See ANNUELLES ET LEGUMES. RESULTATS DES CULTURES D'ESSAI **2409**

JARDIN BOTANIQUE NATIONAL DE BELGIQUE See BULLETIN DU JARDIN BOTANIQUE NATIONAL DE BELGIQUE **504**

JARDIN DES MODES (FR/0021-5457) [01588916] **1085**

JARDINS — Alphabetical Title Index

JARDINS DE FRANCE PARIS (FR/0021-5481) [I00215481] **2421**

JARGON (HULL) (CN/0705-0569) [04954955] **1092**

JARIDAT AL-MISRIYIN (FR) [11183776] **2640**

JARMUVEK, MEZOGAZDASAGI GEPEK (HU/0021-5511) [01782978] **2117**

JARN : JAPAN AIR CONDITIONING, HEATING & REFRIGERATION NEWS (JA) **2606**

JARNIGOINE (CN/0228-3689) [07858014] **2321**

JARNVAGSHOBBY (SW) [03392615] **5432**

JARQ. JAPAN AGRICULTURAL RESEARCH QUARTERLY (JA/0021-3551) [01644908] **98**

JARROW LECTURES (UK) **4967**

JASA SHARE (US/0882-9411) [07639096] **5205**

JASENLUETTELO - SUOMEN TEOLLISUUSLIITTO (FI) [02414423] **1569**

JASHNVARAH (LOS ANGELES, CALIF.) (US/1059-6208) [24649469] **2265**

JASMU : JOURNAL POUR L'AVANCEMENT DES SOINS MEDICAUX D'URGENCE **CEASED.** (CN/0831-4411) [15226964] **3786**

JASNA NEWS (US/0892-8665) [15338663] **3398**

JASO : JOURNAL OF THE ANTHROPOLOGICAL SOCIETY OF OXFORD (UK/0044-8370) [13713080] **238**

JASON AND THE ARGONAUTS (US/1055-4815) [23189794] **380**

JASONVILLE LEADER, THE (US/0896-2790) [14204882] **5665**

JASPER COUNTY GLEANER, THE (US/0749-8314) [11170694] **2455**

JASPER COUNTY NEWS (BAY SPRINGS, MISS.), THE (US) [14508741] **5700**

JASPER JOURNAL, THE (US/0744-3110) [01754240] **5696**

JASPER JOURNAL, THE (US) [19255110] **5745**

JASPER NEWS-BOY, THE (US/0746-2824) [09926510] **5751**

JASSA (AT/0313-5934) [03135934] **793**

JASSY. INSTITUTUL AGRONOMIC PROFESOR ION IONESCU DE LA BRAD **See** LUCRARI STIINTIFICE - INSTITUTUL AGRONOMIC ION IONESCU DE LA BRAD. SERIA ZOOTEHNIE - MEDICINA VETERINARA **105**

JASSY. UNIVERSITATEA. DIN IASI **See** ANALELE STIINTIFICE ALE UNIVERSITATII "AL. I. CUZA" DIN IASI. SERIE NOUA. SECTIUNEA 1A, MATEMATICA **3492**

JATI COURIER (JA/0914-5230) [I09145230] **5417**

JATIKA USAS ADHYAPANA SABHAVARTAVAYI (CE) [03867851] **1832**

JATIKA USAS ADHYPANA SABHAVA **See** JATIKA USAS ADHYAPANA SABHAVARTAVAYI **1832**

JATIYA GRANTHAKENDRA BAMLADESA **See** QUARTERLY - NATIONAL BOOK CENTRE BANGLADESH **4831**

JATMA YEAR BOOK: JAPAN AUTOMOBILE TIRE MANUFACTURERS ASSOCIATION (JA) **5417**

JAUNA GAITA (CN/0448-9179) [01533570] **2848**

JAVANAN-I IMRUZ (IR) [11203358] **2505**

JAVELIER (LA POCATI'ERE) (CN/0841-9787) [19099604] **2740**

JAVIDAN (PK) [02239405] **2654**

JAVISKO (XO) [02826865] **5365**

JAVNI VODOVOD I KANALIZACIJA U NASELJIMA SR SRBIJE (YU) [01787465] 2233, **5535**

JAWA BARAT DALAM ANGKA (IO) [12687254] **5329**

JAWA BARAT, INDONESIA. KANTOR SENSUS DAN STATISTIK **See** PENDUDUK JAWA-BARAT, HASIL REGISTRASI PENDUDUK **5335**

JAWA TENGAH DALAM ANGKA (IO) [06801087] **5329**

JAWA TENGAH, INDONESIA. DEWAN PERWAKILAN RAKYAT DAERAH **See** GEMA D.P.R.D. TINGKAT I JAWA TENGAH **4650**

JAWABAN UNTUK D.P.R.-R.I (IO) [01790749] **1613**

JAWAHARLAL NEHRU. AGRICULTURAL UNIVERSITY **See** JNKVV RESEARCH JOURNAL **98**

JAWAHARLAL NEHRU UNIVERSITY. SCHOOL OF LANGUAGES **See** JSL, JOURNAL OF THE SCHOOL OF LANGUAGES **3293**

JAWETZ, MELNICK & ADELBERG'S MEDICAL MICROBIOLOGY (US/1054-2744) [22829980] **564**

JAWHAR AL-ISLAM (TI) [03340780] **5043**

JAX FAX **See** JAX FAX TRAVEL MARKETING MAGAZINE **5481**

JAX FAX TRAVEL MARKETING MAGAZINE (US/0279-7984) [07263610] 25, **5481**

JAY RECORD **See** GROVE SUN, THE **5732**

JAY SCHABACKER'S MUTUAL FUND INVESTING (US/8756-5161) [11576090] **904**

JAY SCHABACKER'S MUTUAL FUND YEARBOOK **See** JAY SCHABACKER'S YEARBOOK **904**

●JAY SCHABACKER'S YEARBOOK (US) [25677497] **904**

JAYA BAYA (IO) [03570397] **2505**

JAYANTI (II) [02404598] **3399**

JAYBEES **CEASED.** (US/0010-7646) [04070099] **2774**

JAYCEES MAGAZINE (GREENSBORO, N.C.) (US/0893-0031) [15313074] **5232**

JAYNE LECTURES (US) [02574869] **5117**

JAYSH AL-SHAB. JAYCH-ACH-CHAAB (AE) [03573941] **2499**

JAZYKOVEDNE AKTUALITY / VYDAVA JAZYKOVEDNE SDRUZENI PRI CSAV ... ET AL (XR) [05527501] **3289**

JAZYKOVEDNE STUDIE (XO/0448-9241) [01783099] **3289**

JAZYKOVEDNY CASOPIS (XO/0021-5597) [01782818] **3289**

JAZZ DIGEST (US/0092-0525) [01788874] **4124**

JAZZ EDUCATORS JOURNAL (US/0730-9791) [07074117] 1897, **4124**

JAZZ FESTIVALS INTERNATIONAL DIRECTORY (US/0882-0368) [11698949] **4124**

JAZZ FORUM **CEASED.** (US/0021-5635) [04061504] **4124**

JAZZ JOURNAL INTERNATIONAL (UK/0140-2285) [03290573] **4125**

JAZZ MAGAZINE (PARIS) (FR/0021-566X) [04798721] **4125**

JAZZ (MARSEILLE, FRANCE) (FR) [19835343] **4125**

JAZZ-PODIUM (GW/0021-5686) [05781142] **4125**

JAZZ RAG (US/0270-4048) [06392943] 5317, **4125**

JAZZ REPORT (TORONTO) (CN/0843-3151) [19647112] **4125**

JAZZ RESEARCH PAPERS (US) [11276465] **4125**

JAZZ REVIEW AND COLLECTOR'S DISCOGRAPHY, THE (US/1060-670X) [25060543] **4125**

JAZZ SCENE, LA (US) **4125**

JAZZ SPOTLITE NEWS (US) [09139186] **4125**

JAZZ TIMES (WASHINGTON) (US/0272-572X) [06498642] **4125**

JAZZ WORLD (NEW YORK, N.Y. 1984) (US/0749-4564) [10950649] **4125**

JAZZBAND (AG) [01788872] **4125**

JAZZFORSCHUNG (GRAZ) (AU/0075-3572) [02009633] **4125**

JAZZFREUND (MENDEN), DER (GW/0021-5724) [04801758] **4125**

JAZZIZ (GAINESVILLE, FLA.) (US/0741-5885) [10188255] **4125**

JAZZLETTER (US/0890-6440) [10697569] **4125**

JAZZNYTT (SW/0332-7248) [01792039] **4125**

JAZZOLOGIST, THE (US/0198-6805) [04801875] **4125**

JBI ABSTRACTS (JM) [10993430] 1440, **1363**

JBI JOURNAL, THE (JM) [08560537] **1613**

JBIS. JOURNAL OF THE BRITISH INTERPLANETARY SOCIETY (UK/0007-084X) [01537261] **25**

JBSP. JOURNAL OF THE BRITISH SOCIETY FOR PHENOMENOLOGY (UK/0007-1773) [01537369] **4350**

JCMCC : THE JOURNAL OF COMBINATORIAL MATHEMATICS AND COMBINATORIAL COMPUTING (CN/0835-3026) [16878153] 1191, **3511**

JCMT-UKIRT NEWSLETTER, THE (UK) [24155048] **396**

JCT, AN INTERDISCIPLINARY JOURNAL OF CURRICULUM STUDIES (US/1057-896X) [23193268] **1897**

JCT, JOURNAL OF COATINGS TECHNOLOGY (US/0361-8773) [01998749] **4224**

JCU : JOURNAL OF CLINICAL ULTRASOUND (US/0091-2751) [01786752] **3591**

JD/MBA QUARTERLY **CEASED.** (US/0747-9093) [10818706] **2986**

JD (WASHINGTON) (US/0272-0922) [05131868] 5061, **2986**

JDISK ORIENTERING (DK) [02241791] **2694**

●JDL NEWS & VIEWS : AN OFFICIAL PUBLICATION OF THE JEWISH DEFENSE LEAGUE (US) [26200051] **5048**

JDR 3RD FUND **See** JDR 3RD FUND REPORT, THE **323**

JDR 3RD FUND REPORT, THE (US/0273-012X) [06362108] **323**

JE BOUQUINE (FR/0756-564X) [I0756564X] **1065**

JE ME PETITDEBROUILLE **See** DEBROUILLARDS (MONTREAL) **1062**

JE ME PETITDERBROUILLE (CN/0714-4067) [09046706] **5117**

JE ME SOUVIENS (US/0195-7384) [05637917] **2455**

JE NE VEUX PAS MOURIR A L'ACADEMIE FRANCAISE (CN/0820-6333) [09981850] **3399**

JE TAI LIN YEH K'O CHI (CC) [17624728] **2385**

JE TAI TI LI (CC) [09492082] **2567**

JEALOUS MISTRESS, THE (US/0092-170X) [01787394] **2986**

JEAN-PAUL-GESELLSCHAFT **See** JAHRBUCH DER JEAN-PAUL-GESELLSCHAFT **3398**

JEAN RHYS REVIEW (US/0889-759X) [14051996] **3399**

JEANNETTE SPIRIT, THE (US/0746-5971) [10156922] **5737**

JEBAT (MY/0126-5644) [02245911] **2654**

JEC BATTERY NEWSLETTER (US) 2068, **979**

JEDNOTA (PL) [06203360] **5061**

JEDNOTA ALMANAC FURDEK **See** JEDNOTA ANNUAL FURDEK **2740**

JEDNOTA ANNUAL FURDEK (US/0449-4873) [01716958] **2740**

JEDNOTA BRATRSKA (CS) [06220077] **5061**

JEEPERS KREEPERS REFUND PEEPERS (US/0162-8380) [04235862] **2791**

JEEVADHARA (ENGLISH ED.) (II/0970-1125) [03944591] **4967**

JEFF DAVIS LEDGER (US) [19534173] **5654**

JEFFERSON (SW/0345-5653) [03875652] **4125**

JEFFERSON BEE, THE (US) [10936929] **5671**

JEFFERSON CITY POST-TRIBUNE (US) [10262804] **5814**

JEFFERSON COUNTY (ALA.). BOARD OF EDUCATION **See** SUMMARY OF ACTUAL RECEIPTS AND EXPENDITURES FOR ... AND ANNUAL SCHOOL BUDGET FOR ... / JEFFERSON COUNTY BOARD OF EDUCATION **1872**

JEFFERSON COUNTY CHRONICLE (US/0893-3693) [15492871] **5701**

JEFFERSON COUNTY HISTORICAL QUARTERLY (US) [04601325] **2620**

JEFFERSON COUNTY HISTORICAL SOCIETY (W. VA.) **See** MAGAZINE OF THE JEFFERSON COUNTY HISTORICAL SOCIETY **2745**

JEFFERSON COUNTY JOURNAL (US) [09695735] **5717**

JEFFERSON COUNTY LEGAL JOURNAL (US) **2986**

JEFFERSON COUNTY LINES (US) **2455**

JEFFERSON HERALD (JEFFERSON, IOWA) (US) [13115159] **5671**

JEFFERSON JIMPLECUTE (US/1060-3476) [14218513] **5751**

JEFFERSON JOURNAL OF PSYCHIATRY, THE (US) [10729131] **3928**

JEFFERSON PARISH TIMES & DEMOCRAT / KENNER CITY NEWS (US/0895-2132) [15114523] **5684**

JEFFERSON REPORTER, THE (US/8755-9501) [11429532] **5654**

JEFFERSONIAN-DEMOCRAT (BROOKVILLE, PA.) (US) [13379014] **5737**

JEFFERSONIAN REVIEW, THE (US/0094-1360) [01790850] **3399**

JEFFERSONIAN, THE (US) [18579888] **5686**

●JEFFERSONIANA (MARTINSVILLE, VA.) (US/1061-1878) [25218785] **4166**

JEFFREY HOARE AUCTIONS See JEFFREY HOARE NUMISMATIC AUCTION IN CONJUNCTION WITH TOREX **2781**

JEFFREY HOARE NUMISMATIC AUCTION IN CONJUNCTION WITH TOREX (CN/0848-9610) [21679973] **2781**

JEI. JOURNAL OF ECONOMIC ISSUES (US/0021-3624) [01754544] **1592**

JEI, JOURNAL OF THE ELECTRONICS INDUSTRY (JA/0385-4515) [02643149] **2068**

JEI REPORT (US/0744-6489) [07077306] **1498**

JEKYLL'S GOLDEN ISLANDER (US) [17561359] **5654**

JELENKOR (HU/0447-6425) [07470252] **3399**

JELENTES A MEZOGAZDASAG ... EVI FEJLODESEROL / KOZPONTI STATISZTIKAI HIVATAL (HU) [20286894] **1569**

JELLICO ADVANCE-SENTINEL See ADVANCE-SENTINEL, THE **5744**

JEMNA MECHANIKA A OPTIKA (XR/0447-6441) [01783021] 4435, **4428**

JEMS (US/0197-2510) [06001132] **3724**

JEN JEN TSA CHIH (HK) [01797541] **2505**

JEN KOU HSUEH KAN / KUO LI TAI-WAN TA HSUEH (CH) [09039712] **4554**

JEN MIN CHIAO YU (CH) [09840537] **1755**

JEN MIN JIH PAO (CC) [13056661] **5798**

JEN MIN JIH PAO SO YIN (CC) [01754250] **5798**

JEN MIN JIH PAO SO YIN HO TING PEN (MICROFORM) (CC) [08603139] **5798**

JEN MIN SHUI WU See TSAI CHENG **4757**

JEN MIN WEN HSUEH (CH) [01605226] **3399**

JEN SHOU PAO HSIEN YEH WU TUNG CHI NIEN PAO (CH) [03731439] **2885**

JEN WEN TSA CHIH RENWEN ZAZHI (CC) [07136181] **2505**

JEN YU SHE HUI (CH) [01790372] **2505**

JEN YU TI (CH) [11003150] **2196**

JENAER RUNDSCHAU. ENGLISH. JENA REVIEW See ZEISS INFORMATION WITH JENA REVIEW **4442**

JENGA : MAGAZINE OF THE NATIONAL DEVELOPMENT CORPORATION (TZ/0021-5872) [05994058] **1613**

JENGI HAGHOI RONMUN JI (KO/0254-4172) [09201475] **2068**

JENKS HEALTHCARE BUSINESS REPORT (US/1065-0881) [26498159] **3786**

JENS JURGEN'S ... CHARTER FLIGHT DIRECTORY AND GUIDE TO OTHER AIR TRAVEL BARGAINS (US) [17912797] **25**

JEOMORFOLOJI DERGISI (TU) [01796633] **2567**

JEOPARDY (BELLINGHAM, WASH.) (US/0021-5880) [03312921] **3399**

JEPPESEN SANDERSON AVIATION YEARBOOK (US/0364-331X) [02630824] **25**

JEPPESEN SANDERSON, INC See JEPPESEN SANDERSON AVIATION YEARBOOK **25**

JERAGEH (CN/0700-916X) [03304051] **2740**

JERICHO TRIBUNE, THE (US/8750-3476) [11269611] **5717**

JERNAL BAHAGIAN PERANCANG DAN PENYELIDIKAN PELAJARAN (MY/0126-5164) [01798284] **1755**

JERNAL FAKULTI KEJURUTERAAN, UNIVERSITI MALAYA (MY) [01794170] **1981**

JERNAL JIHAD (MY) [01790752] **5043**

JERNAL SEJARAH (MY/0126-5172) [01784303] **2654**

JERNAL UNDANG-UNDANG (MY/0126-6322) [02422809] **3131**

JERSEY See REPORT ON THE ESTABLISHMENT AND WORK OF THE STATES POLICE FORCE **3174**

JERSEY EVENING POST (UK) **5812**

JERSEY JOURNAL (US/0021-5953) [01754260] **213**

JERSEY JOURNAL AND JERSEY OBSERVER, THE (US) [10807106] **5710**

JERSEY JOURNEYS (US) **2740**

JERSEY PUBLISHER (US/0021-5961) [04070168] **4816**

JERSEY / THE JERSEY CATTLE SOCIETY OF THE UNITED KINGDOM, THE (UK) [09838153] **213**

JERSEY WILDLIFE PRESERVATION TRUST See WILDLIFE PRESERVATION TRUST ... ANNUAL REPORT **2209**

JERSEY WOMAN (US/0197-4610) [04940885] **5559**

JERUSALEM (TI) [25426300] **2265**

JERUSALEM. HEBREW UNIVERSITY. SOVIET AND EAST EUROPEAN RESEARCH CENTRE See RESEARCH PAPER - HEBREW UNIVERSITY OF JERUSALEM, SOVIET AND EAST EUROPEAN RESEARCH CENTRE **4534**

JERUSALEM JOURNAL OF INTERNATIONAL RELATIONS, THE CEASED. (US/0363-2865) [02256138] **4526**

JERUSALEM LETTER (IS) [06652549] 4526, **5048**

JERUSALEM POST, THE (IS) [15700704] **5804**

JERUSALEM POST [MICROFORM], THE (IS) [28659844] **5804**

JERUSALEM REPORT, THE (IS/0792-6049) [24088081] **2526**

JERUSALEM STUDIES IN ARABIC AND ISLAM (IS/0334-4118) [05506302] **2769**

JERUSALEM SYMPOSIA ON QUANTUM CHEMISTRY AND BIOCHEMISTRY, THE (IS/0075-3696) [07042026] 979, **489**

JESSAMINE JOURNAL (NICHOLASVILLE, KY.) (US) [12863594] **5681**

JESSE MEYER'S BEVERAGE DIGEST (US/0738-8853) [09705217] **2368**

JESUITS AND FRIENDS (UK) **5031**

JESUP CITIZEN HERALD (US) [15986823] **5671**

JESUS, MARIE ET NOTRE TEMPS (CN/0383-2635) [02455726] **4967**

JESUS PARIS. 1973 (FR/1154-7138) [11547138] **4967**

JET (US/0021-5996) [01781708] **2265**

JET (CALGARY) (CN/0710-5932) [08713563] **25**

JET CARGO NEWS (US/0021-6003) [05066202] 927, **5385**

JET CUTTING TECHNOLOGY (UK/0269-6533) [02696533] **2068**

JET FUEL INTELLIGENCE (US) **4262**

JET. JOURNAL OF EDUCATION FOR TEACHING (UK/0260-7476) [07154185] **1897**

JET PROGRAMS (UK) **25**

JET PROPULSION LABORATORY (U.S.) See JPL PUBLICATION **26**

JETI (JA) [10819348] **5117**

JETORO HAKUSHO. BOEKI-HEN (JA) [11737085] **1636**

JETP LETTERS (US/0021-3640) [01696920] **4408**

JETRO MARKETING SERIES (JA) [09004333] **927**

JEU (CN/0382-0335) [08710479] **5365**

JEUN. LIB (FR/0757-0171) [07570171] **1065**

JEUNE AFRIQUE ECONOMIE (PARIS, FRANCE : 1986) (FR) [15639410] **1498**

JEUNE AFRIQUE (PARIS, FRANCE : 1980) (FR/0021-6089) [06547270] **4526**

JEUNE CINEMA (FR) [03882336] **4073**

JEUNE ET JOLIE (FR) **1065**

JEUNES (IT) **1755**

JEUNES ANNEES See CROQUILOU **1062**

JEUNES ANNEES. AGES 3 TO 6 (FR) **1065**

JEUNESSE ET ORGUE CEASED. (FR/0021-6208) [02441492] **4125**

JEUNESSE ET SPORT (SZ) **4901**

JEUNESSE FRANCOIS D'ASSISE (CN/0822-5559) [10105660] **4967**

JEUNESSES MUSICALES DU CANADA See JMC BULLETIN **4125**

JEUX & JOUETS MAGAZINE (FR/0754-068X) [0754068X] **2584**

JEWELERS' CIRCULAR-KEYSTONE (1990) (US/1070-0242) [20844671] **2914**

JEWELL COUNTY RECORD (MANKATO, KAN.) (US) [11773590] **5676**

JEWELL COUNTY REPUBLICAN (US) [11794087] **5676**

JEWELLERY AUCTION / CHARLTON AUCTIONS (CN/0822-4897) [10007938] **2914**

JEWELLERY AUCTION - TOREX (CN/0822-4935) [10008010] **2914**

●JEWELLERY INTERNATIONAL (UK/0961-4559) [09614559] **2914**

JEWELLERY JOURNAL (CN/0710-4820) [08465846] **2914**

JEWELLERY NEWS ASIA (HK) **2914**

JEWELLERY REVIEW (HK) **2914**

JEWELLERY STUDIES (UK/0268-2087) [02682087] **2914**

JEWELLERY WORLD (CN/0383-9818) [02915558] **2914**

JEWELRY AD REVIEW (US/0883-7929) [12212752] **761**

JEWELRY DUPLEX (SP) **2915**

JEWELRY MARKETING REVIEW (US/1075-8143) [30209382] 2915, **927**

JEWISH ACTION (US/0447-7049) [05763983] **5048**

JEWISH ADVOCATE, THE (US) [16645134] **2265**

JEWISH AFFAIRS (SA) [01782433] **5048**

JEWISH AFFAIRS (NEW YORK, N.Y.) (US/0021-6305) [04070323] **2654**

JEWISH ART (JERUSALEM. 1986) (IS/0792-0660) [17285385] **354**

JEWISH BIBLE QUARTERLY, THE (IS/0792-3910) [21320204] **5017**

JEWISH BOOK ANNUAL (US/0075-3726) [02588712] **3399**

JEWISH BOOK NEWS (US/8755-299X) [11225731] **5048**

JEWISH BOOK NEWS & REVIEWS (UK/0269-4662) [13788217] **5048**

JEWISH CHRONICLE (LONDON, ENGLAND : 1845) (UK/0021-633X) [05955238] 2265, **5048**

JEWISH CHRONICLE, THE (US) [02262912] **2265**

JEWISH CURRENT EVENTS (ELMONT, N.Y.) (US/0021-6380) [04073226] 1897, **5048**

JEWISH CURRENTS (US/0021-6399) [05634669] **5048**

JEWISH DIALOGUE (CN/0315-2685) [01783899] **3399**

JEWISH EDUCATION (US/0021-6429) [01754277] 1755, **5049**

JEWISH EDUCATION DIRECTORY (US/0276-6310) [04813773] 1755, **5049**

JEWISH EDUCATION NEWS (US) 2265, **1755**

JEWISH EXPONENT, THE (US/0021-6437) [04073245] **5049**

JEWISH FOLKLORE AND ETHNOLOGY REVIEW (US/0890-9113) [14450866] 5049, **2321**

JEWISH FRONTIER (US/0021-6453) [01782361] **2265**

JEWISH HISTORICAL SOCIETY OF ENGLAND See BULLETIN OF THE JEWISH HISTORICAL SOCIETY OF ENGLAND **5046**

JEWISH HISTORICAL STUDIES : TRANSACTIONS OF THE JEWISH HISTORICAL SOCIETY OF ENGLAND (UK) [18398141] **5049**

JEWISH HISTORY (IS/0334-701X) [15433553] 2265, **5049**

JEWISH JOURNAL (BROOKLYN, N.Y.) (US/0745-0818) [07135171] **5717**

JEWISH JOURNAL OF GREATER LOS ANGELES, THE (US/0888-0468) [13450863] **5049**

JEWISH JOURNAL OF SOCIOLOGY, THE (UK/0021-6534) [01644644] 5049, **5249**

JEWISH JURISPRUDENCE (US/0276-1432) [07310521] **2986**

JEWISH LANGUAGE REVIEW (IS/0333-8347) [07785693] **3289**

JEWISH LAW ANNUAL, THE (NE/0169-8354) [04553741] **2986**

JEWISH LAW IN CONTEXT (SZ/1045-6015) [20155284] **5049**

JEWISH LEDGER (ROCHESTER NY) (US/0021-6550) [04073460] 5049, **5717**

JEWISH LIFE IN GREATER WASHINGTON (US/0732-4855) [08334490] **5049**

JEWISH LIFE ON CAMPUS See HILLEL GUIDE TO JEWISH LIFE ON CAMPUS, THE **2262**

JEWISH LIVING (US/0199-2929) [05757554] **2265**

JEWISH NEWS OF GREATER PHOENIX (US/1070-5848) [28402247] 2265, **5630**

JEWISH NEWS (RICHMOND, VA.), THE (US/0744-6632) [08463699] **5049**

JEWISH OBSERVER, THE (US/0021-6615) [04043008] **5049**

JEWISH POST & NEWS, THE (CN/0836-6063) [17365125] 2265, **5786**

JEWISH PRESS (BROOKLYN), THE (US/0021-6674) [04073546] **2265**

JEWISH QUARTERLY REVIEW (PHILADELPHIA, PA.) (US/0021-6682) [01754280] **5049**

JEWISH QUARTERLY, THE (UK/0449-010X) [03574617] **5049**

JEWISH SOCIAL STUDIES (US/0021-6704) [01714440] 5205, **5049**

JEWISH SOCIAL WORK FORUM, THE (US/0021-6712) [02262922] **5291**

JEWISH — Alphabetical Title Index

JEWISH SPECTATOR (US/0021-6720) [05576627] **5049**

JEWISH STANDARD (JERSEY CITY, N.J.) (US/0021-6747) [04117975] **2265**

JEWISH STANDARD (TORONTO) (CN/0021-6739) [02030716] **5049**

JEWISH STAR (CALGARY) (CN/0228-2283) [09086757] **5787**

JEWISH STAR (EDMONTON EDITION) (CN/0228-6017) [09086751] **5787**

JEWISH STORYTELLING NEWSLETTER (US/0896-8152) [17294755] **3399**

● JEWISH STUDIES QUARTERLY (GW/0944-5706) **5049**

JEWISH TELEGRAPHIC AGENCY See JTA WEEKLY NEWS DIGEST **2266**

JEWISH TELEVIMAGE REPORT (US/1056-3342) [23667013] 1134, **5049**

JEWISH TIMES (US) [15466286] **5737**

JEWISH TIMES (DOWNSVIEW) *CEASED.* (CN/0382-0254) [03032053] **5049**

JEWISH TRANSCRIPT, THE (US/0021-678X) [04123417] **2265**

JEWISH TRAVEL GUIDE, THE (UK/0075-3750) [02180302] **5481**

JEWISH VEGETARIAN (UK/0021-681X) [I0021681X] 2599, **2265**

JEWISH VEGETARIANS OF NORTH AMERICA : NEWSLETTER (US/0883-1904) [12089169] 5049, **4192**

JEWISH VETERAN, THE (US/0047-2018) [03350059] **2265**

JEWISH VOICE, THE (US/0021-6828) [04073692] **5049**

JEWISH WEEKLY NEWS (US/0021-6860) [04073891] 5049, **2265**

JEWISH WESTERN BULLETIN (CN/0021-6879) [03024046] **5787**

JEWISH WORLD (ALBANY), THE (US/0199-4441) [05867431] 5049, **2265**

JEWISH YEAR BOOK, THE (UK/0075-3769) [01696736] **5049**

JEZIK : CASOPIS ZA KULTURU HRVATSKOGA KNJIZEVNOG JEZIKA (CI/0021-6925) [02086172] **3399**

JEZIK IN SLOVSTVO (XV/0021-6933) [02086105] **3289**

JEZYK POLSKI (KRAKOW 1919) (PL/0021-6941) [01714789] **3289**

JEZYK ROSYJSKI (PL) [05821277] **3399**

JFCC REVIEW (JA/0916-4553) [I09164553] **2591**

JHP, JOURNAL OF HOMEOPATHIC PRACTICE (US/0190-1818) [04652112] **3591**

JIAJING HUABAO (CN/0711-6705) [08711066] **5787**

JIANGHAN KAOGU (CC/1001-0327) [I10010327] **271**

JIANGSU NONGYE KEXUE (CH/1002-1302) [I10021302] **98**

JIANGSU NONGYE XUEBAO (CH/1000-4440) [I10004440] **98**

JIANGSU YIYAO (CC/0253-3685) [08322494] **3591**

JIANGSU ZHONGYI ZAZHI (CC/0253-9799) [08421189] **3592**

JIANZHU XUEBAO (CC/0529-1399) [03603438] **301**

JIAOYU XINLIXUEBAO (CH/1011-5714) [03662610] 1755, **4592**

JIAOYU YU WENHUA (CH/0529-0554) [10347856] **1755**

JIAOYU ZILIAO YU TUSHUGUAN XUE (CH/1013-090X) [09126905] **3219**

JIB GEMS (CN/0839-105X) [18800395] **4089**

JIBI INKOKA RINSHO (JA/0032-6313) [09726172] **3888**

JIBI INKOKA TENBO (JA/0386-9687) [I03869687] **3888**

JIBI INKOKA, TOKEIBU GEKA 1988 (JA/0914-3491) [I09143491] **3888**

JIBI TO RINSHO (JA/0447-7227) [10281731] **3888**

JIBP SYNTHESIS (JA) [04008549] **460**

JICARILLA CHIEFTAIN (US/0021-695X) [04073951] **2265**

JICHI IKA DAIGAKU KIYO (JA/0387-0308) [I03870308] **3592**

JICHI NO UGOKI (JA) [01797323] **4658**

JIDO BUNGAKU ANYUARU (JA) [10801955] **3399**

JIDO BUNGAKU KENKYU (JA) [09257130] **3399**

JIDO FUKUSHI ROPPO (JA) [03189871] **5291**

JIDO NO GENGO SEITAI KENKYU (JA) [01790324] **1755**

JIDOKA GIJUTSU (JA/0287-8461) [I02878461] **1220**

JIDOKA GIJUTSU: MECHANICAL AUTOMATION (JA) **2117**

JIDOSHA CHOSA NENPO (JA) [02240166] **5385**

JIDOSHA GIJUTSUKAI RONBUNSHU / TRANSACTIONS OF THE SOCIETY OF AUTOMOTIVE ENGINEERS OF JAPAN, INC (JA) [10282341] **5417**

JIEFANG RIBAO (CC) **5798**

JIEFANGJUN HUABAO (CC/0009-3823) [I00093823] **2505**

JIEGOU HUAXUE (CC/0254-5861) [10346312] **979**

JIGYO ANNAI - ZOHEIKYOKU (JA) [03507190] **793**

JIGYO GAIYO See JIGYO NO ARAMASHI - KENSETSUSHO TOHOKU CHIHO KENSETSUKYOKU **1613**

JIGYO GAIYO - KENSETSUSHO CHUGOKU CHIHO KENSETSUKYOKU (JA) [02245141] **1613**

JIGYO GAIYO - KENSETSUSHO HOKURIKU CHIHO KENSETSUKYOKU (JA) [02482953] **1613**

JIGYO GAIYO - KENSETSUSHO KYUSHU CHIHO KENSETSUKYOKU (JA) [02244381] **1613**

JIGYO GAIYO - KENSETSUSHO SHIKOKU CHIHO KENSETSUKYOKU (JA) [03213990] **1613**

JIGYO NO ARAMASHI - KENSETSUSHO CHUBU CHIHO KENSETSUKYOKU (JA) [02246312] **2025**

JIGYO NO ARAMASHI - KENSETSUSHO TOHOKU CHIHO KENSETSUKYOKU (JA) [03189716] **1613**

JIGYO TOKEI (JA) [01790099] **1613**

JIGYO YORAN - KANI HOKEN YUBIN NENKIN FUKUSHI JIGYODAN (JA) [02242919] **1681**

JIGYO YORAN - KOKURITSU KOSHU EISEIIN (JA) [05194241] **4786**

JIGYOSHO MEIKAN. SONO 1, JIGYOSHO HEN / [HENSHU, SORIFU TOKEIKYOKU ; DENSAN SHORI, SHAKAI CHOSA KENKYUJO KONPYUTA JIGYOBU] (JA) [10662190] **1569**

JIGYOSHO MEIKAN. SONO 2, KAISHA KIGYO HEN / HENSHU, SORIFU TOKEIKYOKU (JA) [10599886] **1569**

JIH-PEN HSUEH KAN / JAPANESE STUDIES / CHUNG-HUA JIH-PEN HSUEH HUI, CHUNG-KUO SHE HUI KO HSUEH YUAN JIH-PEN YEN CHIU SO CHU PAN (CC) [25044544] **2654**

JIHAD (QOM, IRAN) (IR) [10023795] **2654**

JIHAD (TEHRAN, IRAN) (IR) [09754736] **2505**

JIHAD (TEHRAN, IRAN : MONTHLY) (IR) [09998561] **2769**

JIHOCESKY SBORNIK HISTORICKY (XR) [02897604] **2694**

JIJI EIGO KENKYU. THE STUDY OF CURRENT ENGLISH (JA) [05737829] **3289**

JIJNASA (II/0377-743X) [02256139] **2769**

JIJNASA (CALCUTTA, INDIA) (II) [10510436] **2654**

JIJNASA (KATHMANDU, NEPAL) (NP) [11985899] **5041**

JIKEIKAI MEDICAL JOURNAL (JA/0021-6968) [01605164] **3592**

JIKKEN DOBUTSU (JA/0007-5124) [04286779] **3592**

JIKKEN SHAKAI SHINRIGAKU KENKYU (JA/0387-7973) [10425941] **4592**

JILIN NONGYE DAXUE XUEBAO (CC/1000-5684) [13998853] **98**

JILINYIKE DAXUE XUEBAO (CC/0253-2719) [06906220] **3592**

● JIM CABELL'S WORLD TRAVEL COMMUNICATIONS PRESENTS THE '800' & FAX TRAVEL DIRECTORY (US) [26755514] **5481**

● JIM GILREATH'S EXECUTIVE JOB SEARCH GAZETTE (US/1064-7945) [26392830] **4205**

JIM HENSON'S MUPPET BABIES *CEASED.* (US/0888-532X) [12636977] **4862**

JIM HOGG COUNTY ENTERPRISE (US) [14265200] **5751**

JIM. JOURNAL INFORMATION MUNICIPALE (CN/0821-0810) [10330314] **4658**

JIM RENNIE'S SPORTS LETTER (CN/0712-2632) [08871318] **4901**

JIM TAYLOR'S CURRENTS (CN/0828-9662) [12643861] **4967**

JIMBUN CHIRI (JA) [01606620] **2567**

JIMBUN GAKUHO TOKYO. 1950 (JA/0386-8729) [I03868729] **2848**

JIMBUNGAKU RONSHU (JA) [06911904] **5205**

JIME REVIEW (UA) [23706988] **1948**

JINAN DAXUE XUEBAO ZIRAN KEXUE YU YIXUE BAN (CC/1000-9965) [I10009965] **3592**

JINBUN RONSHU / WASEDA DAIGAKU HOGAKKAI (JA/0441-4225) [09499935] **2986**

JINDAI ZHONGGUO SHI YANJIU TONGXUN (CH/1016-0566) [I10160566] **2694**

JING BAO JOURNAL (US) [10976586] **4047**

JINGJI-BU GUOLI TAIWAN DAXUE HEBANYUVE SHENGWU SHIYAN-SUO YANJIU BAOGAO *SUSPENDED.* (CH/0513-3483) [01797553] **2306**

JINJI KOSHINROKU (JA) [01754288] **433**

JINKO MONDAI KENKYU (JA/0387-2793) [01586136] **4554**

JINKO MONDAI KENKYUHO (JAPAN) See JINKO MONDAI KENKYUJO NENPO **4554**

JINKO MONDAI KENKYUJO (JAPAN) See JINKO MONDAI KENKYUJO YORAN **4554**

JINKO MONDAI KENKYUJO NENPO (JA/0449-0339) [18275857] **4554**

JINKO MONDAI KENKYUJO YORAN (JA) [03950783] **4554**

JINKO ZOKI (JA/0300-0818) [10102109] **3592**

JINKOGAKU KENKYU (JA/0386-8311) [07985854] **4554**

JINRUI IDENGAKU ZASSHI See JAPANESE JOURNAL OF HUMAN GENETICS, THE **548**

JINRUIGAKU ZASSHI See ANTHROPOLOGICAL SCIENCE : JOURNAL OF THE ANTHROPOLOGICAL SOCIETY OF NIPPON **229**

JINRUIGAKU ZASSHI. JOURNAL OF THE ANTHROPOLOGICAL SOCIETY OF NIPPON (JA/0003-5505) [02262929] **238**

JINRUIGAKU ZASSHI / THE JOURNAL OF THE ANTHROPOLOGICAL SOCIETY OF TOKYO (JA) [07512982] **238**

JINSHAN SHIBAO (US/0746-5432) [10125576] **5636**

JINSHU RECHULI (CC/0254-6051) [10346930] 2117, **4005**

JINSHU RECHULI XUEBAO (CC/0254-587X) [10346173] **4005**

J'INVESTRIE (CN/0714-3117) [09157008] **793**

JIS HANDOBUKKU : SEKIYU (JA) [02240165] **4262**

JISHIN GAKKAI (JAPAN) See JISIN **1407**

JISHIN YOCHI RENRAKUKAI. CHIIKI BUKAI See JISHIN YOCHI RENRAKUKAI CHIIKI BUKAI HOKOKU **1384**

JISHIN YOCHI RENRAKUKAI CHIIKI BUKAI HOKOKU (JA) [03401066] **1384**

JISHU, HE (CC/0253-3219) [I02533219] **1981**

JISHU YU XUNLIAN (CH/0253-5888) [10378747] **4006**

JISIN (JA/0037-1114) [03777715] **1407**

JISTA (II) [01784182] **3289**

JISUANJI XUEBAO (CH/0254-4164) [10476918] **1191**

JISUANJI YU YINGYONG HUAXUE (CC/1001-4160) [21741348] 979, **1191**

JITCHUKEN ZENRINSHO KENKYUHO (JA/0385-8502) [05078440] 5118, **4309**

JITENSHA GIJUTSU JOHO (JA/0387-7396) [10836817] **429**

JITSUGYO NO BURAJIRU. SELECOES ECONOMICAS (BL) [05759524] 904, **1569**

JITSUMU ZEIHO ROPPO. HOREI / OKURASHO SHUZEIKYOKU SOMUKA KANSHU (JA) [08909773] **4734**

JITSUYO KAIJI ROPPO (JA) [02561466] **3181**

JIVANA SAHITYA (II) [01784079] **3399**

JIVE (US/0277-8130) [07645525] **2536**

JIWAJU UNIVERSITY See JOURNAL : SCIENCE, TECHNOLOGY & MEDICINE **5122**

JJAP SERIES (JA) [I09149090] **4408**

JLAG REVIEW (US/0278-0178) [07684791] **323**

JLS & K PREVENTIVE LABOR RELATIONS FOR EXECUTIVES (US) [05579256] **1681**

JMA MANAGEMENT NEWS (JA) **872**

JMA NEWSLETTER./ JAPAN MANAGEMENT ASSOCIATION (JA) [08422803] **872**

JMC BULLETIN (CN/0317-0489) [02247648] **4125**

JMR ABSTRACTS See MRS BULLETIN **2107**

JMR ABSTRACTS (US/1066-2375) [I10662375] 2103, **2005**

JMR, JOURNAL OF MARKETING RESEARCH (US/0022-2437) [01783303] **927**

JMR. JOURNAL OF MOLECULAR RECOGNITION (UK/0952-3499) [18040299] **460**

● JN. JOURNAL OF NEPHROLOGY (IT/1121-8428) [I11218428] **3990**

JNANABHA (II) [06688330] **5118**

JNKVV RESEARCH JOURNAL (II/0023-3721) [04472830] **98**

JNMM : JOURNAL OF THE INSTITUTE OF NUCLEAR MATERIALS MANAGEMENT (US/0893-6188) [14633228] **2156**

JOB BANK GUIDE TO EMPLOYMENT SERVICES, THE (US) [15244666] **4205**

JOB CATALOG, THE (US/0278-5706) [07430497] **4205**

● JOB CHOICES ... IN BUSINESS (US) [28866007] **4205**

● JOB CHOICES ... IN HEALTHCARE (US) [28866094] **3592, 4205**

● JOB CHOICES ... IN SCIENCE & ENGINEERING (US) [28866194] **1981, 5118, 4205**

● JOB FINDER FOR HIGH TECH SILICON VALLEY (US/1065-4658) [26613708] **1681, 4205**

JOB FUTURES (CN/0833-7195) [17847105] **4205**

JOB GROWTH UPDATE See BLUE CHIP JOB GROWTH UPDATE **1465**

JOB HUNTER, THE (US/0889-9908) [16370791] **4205**

JOB HUNTER'S FINAL EXAM : WITH ALL THE ANSWERS!, THE (US) [20422855] **685**

JOB HUNTER'S SOURCEBOOK (US/1053-1874) [22469370] **4205**

JOB INFORMATION LETTER (US/8756-1670) [11509491] **4205**

JOB JARGON (US/1051-9017) [22147827] **4205**

JOB MARKET **CEASED.** (US) **685**

JOB MARKET PREVIEWS (US) **4205**

JOB OPENINGS FOR ECONOMISTS (US/0196-1551) [01133844] **4205**

JOB OPPORTUNITIES BULLETIN **CEASED.** (US/0731-3365) [08161772] **1681**

JOB PATTERNS FOR MINORITIES AND WOMEN IN STATE AND LOCAL GOVERNMENT / U.S. EQUAL EMPLOYMENT OPPORTUNITY COMMISSION (US) [22971116] **4704**

JOB PROSPECTS AUSTRALIA (AT/1031-0894) [I10310894] **4205**

JOB READY (US/1046-1353) [20334747] **1681**

JOB SAFETY & HEALTH; AN ADVISORY BULLETIN ON GOVERNMENT AND INDUSTRY SAFETY POLICIES, PROCEDURES AND PRACTICES (US/0149-7510) [07018590] **2864**

JOB SAFETY & HEALTH QUARTERLY (US/1057-5820) [21588730] **2864**

JOB SAFETY & HEALTH REPORT (US/0148-4079) [02447934] **2864**

JOB SAFETY & HEALTH (WASHINGTON. 1977) (US/0149-7510) [03547682] **2864**

JOB SAFETY CONSULTANT (US/1040-4198) [08971979] **2864**

JOB SEARCH. A GUIDE FOR UNIVERSITY OF VERMONT STUDENTS (US/0742-9223) [10470256] **4205**

● JOB SEEKER'S GUIDE TO PRIVATE AND PUBLIC COMPANIES (US/1061-3285) [25252127] **4205**

JOB SHOP TECHNOLOGY (MIDWEST EDITION) (US/0894-2005) [15876080] **1613**

JOB TRAINING AND PLACEMENT REPORT (US/1041-1488) [18660010] **872**

JOBBER NEWS ANNUAL MARKETING GUIDE (CN) **927**

JOBBER NEWS (TORONTO) (CN/0021-7050) [02030733] **685, 5417**

JOBBER RETAILER (US/0148-5792) [03337720] **5417**

JOBBER TOPICS (US/0021-7069) [03876438] **5417**

JOBFLO (US) [06011765] **1681**

JOBLESS NEWSLETTER (US/0738-0208) [09490701] **1681**

JOBS AVAILABLE (US/0738-7601) [09671983] **1681**

JOBS AVAILABLE - MIDWEST/EASTERN EDITION See PUBLIC SECTOR JOB BULLETIN **4209**

JOBS AVAILABLE (WESTERN ED.) (US/1065-6944) [26682196] **4205**

JOBS CANADA See JOBS FOR YOUR FUTURE **4205**

JOBS FOR YOUR FUTURE (CN/1195-5325) **4205**

● JOBS IN HIGHER EDUCATION (US/1074-5475) [29742954] **4205**

JOBS IN RECESSIONARY TIMES POSSIBILITY NEWSLETTER (US/1053-654X) [22603283] **1681**

JOBS MAGAZINE (US) **1681**

JOBSON'S BEER HANDBOOK (US) [29370939] **2368**

JOBSON'S BEVERAGE DYNAMICS (US/1046-1973) [20348857] **2368**

JOBSON'S CHEERS (US/1051-564X) [21990470] **2368**

JOBSON'S FINANCIAL SERVICES PTY See JOBSON'S WHO'S WHO IN AUSTRALIAN MINING & OIL **4262**

JOBSON'S HANDBOOK ADVANCE (US/1047-918X) [17831093] **2368**

● JOBSON'S LICENSED BEVERAGE MARKETING & MERCHANDISING FACT BOOK (US) [29865239] **2368**

JOBSON'S LIQUOR HANDBOOK (US/1046-8250) [12571688] **2368**

JOBSON'S MINING YEAR BOOK (AT/0075-3777) [01306699] **2141**

JOBSON'S PUBLICATIONS See JOBSON'S YEAR BOOK. PUBLIC COMPANIES OF AUSTRALIA & NEW ZEALAND **685**

JOBSON'S QUARTERLY (AT/0813-7455) [I08137455] **685**

JOBSON'S WHO'S WHO IN AUSTRALIAN MINING & OIL (AT) [08384472] **4262**

JOBSON'S WINE & SPIRITS INDUSTRY MARKETING (US) [19828905] **2368**

JOBSON'S WINE HANDBOOK (US) [28738258] **2368**

JOBSON'S WINE MARKETING HANDBOOK (US) [12848558] **2368**

JOBSON'S YEAR BOOK. PUBLIC COMPANIES OF AUSTRALIA & NEW ZEALAND (AT) [05175453] **685**

JOCHI DAIGAKU DOITSU BUNGAKU RONSHU (JA) [03321501] **3399**

JOCHI EIGO BUNGAKU KENKYU (JA/0388-6417) [I03886417] **3399, 3289**

JOCK (US/8756-1379) [11502947] **5187**

JOE (KE) [03806431] **2499**

● JOE FELLEGY'S MILLE LACS FISHING DIGEST (US/1062-5224) [25651431] **4874**

JOE FRANKLIN'S NOSTALGIA **CEASED.** (US/1047-0476) [20589240] **2489**

JOE WEIDER'S FLEX (US/8750-8915) [11891022] **2599**

JOE WEIDER'S MEN'S FITNESS (US/0893-4460) [15526786] **3995, 2599**

JOE WEIDER'S MUSCLE & FITNESS (US/0744-5105) [08374526] **2599**

JOE WEIDER'S MUSCLE AND FITNESS AUSTRALIAN ED (AT/1033-8292) [I10338292] **2599**

JOEL H. WELDON & ASSOCIATES See UNLIMITED TIMES, THE **717**

JOEL WHITBURN'S TOP POP SINGLES (US/0195-4040) [05463803] **4125, 4160**

JOERNAAL VIR EIETYDSE : GESKIEDENIS EN INTERNASIONALE VERHOUDINGE (SA) [04336616] **2620**

JOETSU KYOIKU DAIGAKU KENKYU KIYO (JA) [09844148] **1832**

JOGGING INTERNATIONAL (FR) **2774**

JOGTUDOMANYI KOZLONY (HU) [02262935] **2986**

JOGU (GW) [05218769] **1832**

JOHANNESBURG QUARTERLY GOLD STOCK REPORT (US/0276-9719) [07446205] **2141**

JOHANNESBURG (SOUTH AFRICA) See BUDGET **4714**

JOHANNESBURG STOCK EXCHANGE MONTHLY BULLETIN, THE (SA) [09502433] **904**

JOHANNESBURG. UNIVERSITY OF THE WITWATERSRAND. DEPT. OF GEOGRAPHY AND ENVIRONMENTAL STUDIES See OCCASIONAL PAPER - JOHANNESBURG. UNIVERSITY OF THE WITWATERSRAND. DEPT. OF GEOGRAPHY AND ENVIRONMENTAL STUDIES **2179**

JOHN A. PUGSLEY'S COMMON SENSE VIEWPOINT (US/0733-6152) [08609584] **904**

JOHN & MABLE RINGLING MUSEUM OF ART : NEWSLETTER (US) [14074674] **354**

JOHN & MARY'S JOURNAL (US/0364-6572) [02667438] **5232**

JOHN BERRYMAN STUDIES (US/0098-2199) [02241088] **3464**

JOHN BIRCH SOCIETY BULLETIN, THE (US/0449-0754) [13177453] **4542**

JOHN BURTON'S WORKERS' COMPENSATION MONITOR (US/1040-1008) [18320806] **2885**

JOHN COFFIN MEMORIAL LECTURE, THE (UK/0449-0789) [02186847] **2848**

JOHN COLET ARCHIVE OF AMERICAN LITERATURE, 1620-1920, THE **CEASED.** (US) [05987631] **3399**

JOHN CURTIN MEMORIAL LECTURE, THE (AT) [04851794] **1681**

JOHN D. AND CATHERINE T. MACARTHUR FOUNDATION See REPORT ON ACTIVITIES / JOHN D. AND CATHERINE T. MACARTHUR FOUNDATION **4339**

JOHN DONNE JOURNAL (US/0738-9655) [09528115] **433, 3345**

JOHN E. FOGARTY INTERNATIONAL CENTER FOR ADVANCED STUDY IN THE HEALTH SCIENCES See NATIONAL INSTITUTES OF HEALTH ANNUAL REPORT OF INTERNATIONAL ACTIVITIES **3619**

JOHN E FOGARTY INTERNATIONAL CENTER FOR ADVANCED STUDY IN THE HEALTH SCIENCES. INTERNATIONAL COOPERATION AND GEOGRAPHIC STUDIES BRANCH See STATISTICAL REFERENCE BOOK OF INTERNATIONAL ACTIVITIES **1930**

JOHN E. FOGARTY INTERNATIONAL CENTER FOR ADVANCED STUDY IN THE HEALTH SCIENCES. INTERNATIONAL COOPERATION AND GEOGRAPHIC STUDIES BRANCH See NATIONAL INSTITUTES OF HEALTH INTERNATIONAL AWARDS FOR BIOMEDICAL RESEARCH AND RESEARCH TRAINING **5130**

JOHN F. KENNEDY-INSTITUT FUR NORDAMERIKASTUDIEN. BIBLIOTHEK See VERZEICHNIS DER NEUERWERBUNGEN - JOHN F. KENNEDY-INSTITUT FUER NORDAMERIKASTUDIEN, FREIE UNIVERSITAT BERLIN BIBLIOTHEK **427**

JOHN F. KENNEDY SCHOOL OF GOVERNMENT See CATALOGUE / JOHN F. KENNEDY SCHOOL OF GOVERNMENT, HARVARD UNIVERSITY **1814**

JOHN HANCOCK COMPANIES ... ANNUAL REPORT (US/0739-7186) [09791250] **2885**

JOHN HANCOCK MUTUAL LIFE INSURANCE COMPANY See JOHN HANCOCK COMPANIES ... ANNUAL REPORT **2885**

JOHN HORAN'S SPORTS INK (US/0882-7877) [11991582] **4901**

JOHN HOWARD SOCIETY OF QUEBEC See QUARTERLY JOURNAL - JOHN HOWARD SOCIETY OF QUEBEC **3174**

JOHN KETTLE'S FUTURELETTER (CN/0712-8177) [09075026] **1498, 685**

JOHN LINER LETTER, THE (US/0021-7204) [03501880] **2885**

JOHN M. ECHOLS COLLECTION ON SOUTHEAST ASIA ACCESSIONS LIST, THE (US/0276-2676) [04943051] **2496**

JOHN MACMURRAY SOCIETY See NEWSLETTER - THE JOHN MACMURRAY SOCIETY **5234**

JOHN MACMURRAY STUDIES (US/1044-5757) [19834358] **4350**

● JOHN MARSHALL JOURNAL OF COMPUTER & INFORMATION LAW, THE (US) [30365829] **1191, 2986**

JOHN MARSHALL LAW JOURNAL (US/0147-3689) [03148473] **2986**

JOHN MARSHALL LAW REVIEW, THE (US/0270-854X) [06116366] **2986**

JOHN MILTON MAGAZINE (CN) [02251016] **4967**

JOHN NAISBITT'S TREND LETTER (US/0883-136X) [09962588] **1569**

JOHN PETER ZENGER AWARD FOR FREEDOM OF THE PRESS AND THE PEOPLE'S RIGHT TO KNOW, THE (US/0146-4957) [02254227] **2921**

JOHN SIMON GUGGENHEIM MEMORIAL FOUNDATION See REPORTS OF THE PRESIDENT AND THE TREASURER - JOHN SIMON GUGGENHEIM MEMORIAL FOUNDATION **5236**

JOHN T. REED'S REAL ESTATE INVESTOR'S MONTHLY (US/0887-1922) [13190965] **904, 4839**

JOHN TWIGG'S REPORT ON B.C (CN/0838-1542) [18047436] **685, 1498**

JOHN TYLER COMMUNITY COLLEGE See ANNUAL REPORT / JOHN TYLER COMMUNITY COLLEGE **1809**

JOHN WESLEY COLLEGE CRUSADER (US/0744-7213) [08509359] **1092**

JOHN WHITMER HISTORICAL ASSOCIATION JOURNAL, THE (US/0739-7852) [07865139] **5061**

JOHNS HOPKINS APL TECHNICAL DIGEST (US/0270-5214) [06283189] **1981**

JOHNS HOPKINS CENTER FOR ALTERNATIVES TO ANIMAL TESTING : NEWSLETTER, THE (US/1058-112X) [11810216] **2251, 3592**

JOHNS HOPKINS MAGAZINE (US/0021-7255) [01782714] **1102**

JOHNS HOPKINS MEDICAL LETTER HEALTH AFTER 50, THE (US/1042-1882) [18966179] **3592**

JOHNS HOPKINS OCEANOGRAPHIC STUDIES, THE (US/0075-3858) [01000260] **1450**

JOHNS HOPKINS SERIES IN THE MATHEMATICAL SCIENCES (US/0885-0062) [09722867] **3511**

JOHNS HOPKINS STUDIES IN HEALTH CARE FINANCE AND ADMINISTRATION (US/0888-7675) [11155938] **3786**

JOHNS HOPKINS STUDIES IN THE HISTORY OF TECHNOLOGY (US) [04412915] **5118**

JOHNS HOPKINS SYMPOSIA IN COMPARATIVE HISTORY, THE (US/0075-3874) [01779425] **2621**

JOHNS HOPKINS UNIVERSITY. APPLIED PHYSICS LABORATORY *See* JOHNS HOPKINS APL TECHNICAL DIGEST **1981**

JOHNS HOPKINS UNIVERSITY SCHOOL OF MEDICINE POSTGRADUATE COURSE IN INTERNAL MEDICINE, THE (US/0360-5914) [01877609] **3798**

JOHNS HOPKINS UNIVERSITY STUDIES IN GEOLOGY, THE (US/0075-3890) [01604393] **1384**

JOHNS HOPKINS UNIVERSITY STUDIES IN HISTORICAL AND POLITICAL SCIENCE, THE (US/0075-3904) [02194846] **4478**, **5205**

JOHNSON C. SMITH UNIVERSITY *See* ALUMNI DIRECTORY / JOHNSON C. SMITH UNIVERSITY **1098**

JOHNSON COUNTY GENEALOGIST, THE (US/0749-6850) [04852047] **2455**

JOHNSON COUNTY HISTORICAL SOCIETY JOURNAL (US/0747-6876) [03773346] **2740**

JOHNSON COUNTY SUN (US) [11956481] **5676**

JOHNSON JOURNAL (US/8755-1721) [11225270] **2455**

JOHNSON OUTBOARDS *See* JOHNSON OUTBOARDS BOATING **593**

JOHNSON OUTBOARDS BOATING (US/0271-2040) [06558571] **593**

JOHNSON REPORTER (LINCOLN, NEB.), THE (CN/0731-8979) [08264738] **2455**

JOHNSONBURG PRESS, THE (US) [15259035] **5737**

JOHNSONIA *CEASED.* (US/0075-3920) [01607451] **5587**

JOHNSONIAN NEWS LETTER (US/0021-728X) [01782595] **3399**

JOHNSON'S CHARTS (US) [10895235] **904**

JOHNSON'S INDEX TO CANADIAN ART AUCTIONS (CN/0823-5023) [11180189] **354**

JOHNSONVILLE LICENSING TRUST (N.Z.) *See* REPORT OF THE JOHNSONVILLE LICENSING TRUST FOR THE YEAR ENDED 31 MARCH ... **4681**

JOHNSTON COUNTY GENEALOGICAL SOCIETY *See* NEWSLETTER / JOHNSTON COUNTY GENEALOGICAL SOCIETY **2463**

JOHO KANRI (JA/0021-7298) [01083297] **3219**

JOHO NO KAGAKU TO GIJUTSU (JA) [16506767] **5118**

JOHO SANGYO KIJI SAKUINSHU. SHINBUNHEN (JA) [12190029] **1114**

JOHO SHORI GAKKAI RONBUN SHI / TRANSACTIONS OF INFORMATION PROCESSING SOCIETY OF JAPAN (JA/0387-5806) [12843825] **1234**, **1260**

JOHO SHORI KENKYU (JA/0388-5038) [02240168] **1242**, **1260**, **1213**

JOHOKA HAKUSHO / NIHON JOHO SHORI KAIHATSU KYOKAI HEN (JA) [17315782] **1191**

● JOICE. JOURNAL OF INTERNATIONAL AND COMPARATIVE ECONOMICS (GW/0840-4821) [I09408421] **1637**

JOICFP NEWS (JA/0911-0755) [I09110755] **589**

JOIDES JOURNAL (US/0734-5615) [02168626] **1450**

JOINING SCIENCES *CEASED.* (UK) **1981**

JOINT (CN/0380-4771) [02578343] **1832**

JOINT ACQUISITIONS LIST OF AFRICANA (US/0021-731X) [01754319] **418**

JOINT ASSOCIATION OF CLASSICAL TEACHERS *See* BULLETIN **1890**

JOINT AVIATION REQUIREMENTS AMENDMENT SERVICE (UK) **25**

JOINT BANK-FUND LIBRARY *See* LIST OF RECENT PERIODICAL ARTICLES **1503**

JOINT CAPITAL IMPROVEMENTS PROGRAM FOR CHICAGO *See* CAPITAL IMPROVEMENTS PROGRAM FOR CHICAGO **4716**

JOINT COAL BOARD (AUSTRALIA AND NEW SOUTH WALES) *See* REPORT - JOINT COAL BOARD **2149**

● JOINT COMMISSION JOURNAL ON QUALITY IMPROVEMENT, THE (US/1070-3241) [28321301] **3786**

JOINT COMMISSION ON ACCREDITATION OF HEALTHCARE ORGANIZATIONS *See* ACCREDITATION MANUAL FOR HOSPITALS / THE JOINT COMMISSION **3775**

JOINT COMMISSION ON ACCREDITATION OF HEALTHCARE ORGANIZATIONS *See* JOINT COMMISSION PERSPECTIVES **3786**

JOINT COMMISSION ON ACCREDITATION OF HEALTHCARE ORGANIZATIONS *See* AMH : ACCREDITATION MANUAL FOR HOSPITALS / THE JOINT MISSION **3776**

JOINT COMMISSION PERSPECTIVES (US/1044-4017) [17217187] **3786**

JOINT COUNCIL ON ECONOMIC EDUCATION *See* ECONOMIC EDUCATION EXPERIENCES OF ENTERPRISING TEACHERS **5199**

JOINT COUNCIL ON FOOD AND AGRICULTURAL SCIENCES (U.S.) *See* PRIORITIES FOR RESEARCH, EXTENSION, AND HIGHER EDUCATION : A REPORT TO THE SECRETARY OF AGRICULTURE **121**

JOINT ECE/CODEX ALIMENTARIUS GROUP OF EXPERTS ON STANDARDIZATION OF QUICK FROZEN FOODS *See* REPORT OF THE SESSION OF THE JOINT ECE/CODEX ALIMENTARIUS GROUP OF EXPERTS ON STANDARDIZATION OF QUICK FROZEN FOODS **3038**

JOINT ECONOMIC REPORT, THE (US/0162-5888) [03683609] **1498**

JOINT FAO/WHO CODEX ALIMENTARIUS COMMISSION. CODEX COMMITTEE ON COCOA PRODUCTS AND CHOCOLATE *See* REPORT OF THE CODEX COMMITTEE ON COCOA PRODUCTS AND CHOCOLATE **2355**

JOINT FAO/WHO CODEX ALIMENTARIUS COMMISSION. CODEX COMMITTEE ON FOODS FOR SPECIAL DIETARY USES *See* REPORT OF THE SESSION OF THE CODEX COMMITTEE ON FOODS FOR SPECIAL DIETARY USES **2355**

JOINT FEDERAL-STATE LAND USE PLANNING COMMISSION FOR ALASKA *See* ANNUAL REPORT - JOINT FEDERAL-STATE LAND USE PLANNING COMMISSION FOR ALASKA **4627**

JOINT FORCE QUARTERLY (US/1070-0692) [28261727] **4047**

JOINT FORUM FOR PHILIPPINE PROGRESS NEWS (US) **2910**

JOINT MEMBERSHIP DIRECTORY - AMERICAN SOCIETY OF HUMAN GENETICS (US/0883-4709) [11265377] **548**

JOINT MEMBERSHIP DIRECTORY / THE ASSOCIATION OF BIOMEDICAL COMMUNICATIONS DIRECTORS, THE ASSOCIATION OF MEDICAL ILLUSTRATORS, THE HEALTH SCIENCES COMMUNICATIONS ASSOCIATION (US) [13013779] **3592**, **1114**

JOINT NIOSH/OSHA CURRENT INTELLIGENCE BULLETIN (US) [04827875] **2864**

JOINT OCEANOGRAPHIC INSTITUTIONS FOR DEEP EARTH SAMPLING *See* JOIDES JOURNAL **1450**

JOINT PERSPECTIVES (US/0274-595X) [06434249] **4047**

JOINT TRAVEL REGULATIONS. VOLUME 1. MEMBERS OF UNIFORMED SERVICES: ARMY, NAVY, MARINE CORPS, AIR FORCE, COAST GUARD, NATIONAL OCEANIC AND ATMOSPHERIC ADMINISTRATION CORPS, PUBLIC HEALTH SERVICE (US) [02786756] **4048**

JOINT TRAVEL REGULATIONS. VOLUME 2, DEPARTMENT OF DEFENSE CIVILIAN PERSONNEL (US) [02786300] **943**

JOINT VENTURES (OTTAWA) (CN/0319-7239) [02443430] **1498**

JOINTURE (CN/0226-7667) [06562451] **1832**

JOJOBA HAPPENINGS (US/0746-3766) [02792798] **98**

JOKESMITH, THE (US/0749-4351) [11168088] **1114**

JOKULL (IC/0449-0576) [03919023] **1415**

JOLISO (SAINT-BASILE-LE-GRAND, QUEBEC) *See* GRAND BABILLARD, LE **4652**

JOM (1989) (US/1047-4838) [19289898] **4006**

JONATHAN (MONTREAL) *SUSPENDED.* (CN/0711-026X) [08584628] **5049**

JONCTION (ASTON JONCTION) (CN/0821-218X) [09428048] **4658**

JONES BEACH STATE PARKWAY AUTHORITY *See* CAUSEWAYS & THEATRE PROJECTS; ANNUAL REPORT **5439**

JONES JOURNEYS (US/0749-1522) [04831355] **2455**

JONESBORO SUN, THE (US) [22281703] **5631**

JONESREPORT (US/0889-485X) [14083403] **927**

JONG HOLLAND (NE/0168-9193) [13800332] **354**

JONGE KIND (NE) **1065**, **1755**

JONQUIERE (QUEBEC) *See* VILLE DE JONQUIERE, VILLE A CONGRES ET TOURISTIQUE **2765**

JONQUIERE (QUEBEC) *See* VIE MUNICIPALE A JONQUIERE, LA **4693**

JONQUIEROIS (JONQUIERE) (CN/1183-5699) [24368588] **4658**

JONQUIL (US/0744-3943) [08243765] **5232**

JONQUIL FOR ESA WOMEN *See* JONQUIL **5232**

JONXIS LECTURES, THE (NE/0166-2430) [05061463] **3592**

JOPERD (US/0730-3084) [23667439] **1313**, **1856**

JOPLIN GLOBE (US) [13433720] **5703**

JOPSOM. JOURNAL OF PREVENTIVE AND SOCIAL MEDICINE (BG/1012-8697) [10467356] **3592**

JOR QUARTERLY (US/1061-5032) [25174921] **4125**

● JORD OG VIDEN (DK/0906-7043) [25325359] **2385**, **2421**, **98**

JORDAN *See* AL-JARIDAH AL-RASMIYAH LIL-MAMLAKAH AL-URDUNIYAH AL-HASHIMIYAH **2929**

JORDAN (JO) [04292455] **2655**

JORDAN. DAIRAT AL-ATHAR AL-AMMAH *See* ANNUAL OF THE DEPARTMENT OF ANTIQUITIES **2645**

JORDAN INDEPENDENT (US) [01754335] **5696**

JORDAN. WIZARAT AL-SIYAHAH WA-AL-ATHAR *See* TRAVEL STATISTICS **5501**

JORDANIEN : ENERGIEWIRTSCHAFT (GW) [05064326] **1948**

JORDANIEN : WIRTSCHAFTSDATEN UND WIRTSCHAFTSDOKUMENTATION (GW) [06214213] **1569**

JORDANIEN, WIRTSCHAFTSSTRUKTUR / BUNDESSTELLE FUR AUSSENHANDELSINFORMATION (GW) [08933412] **1569**

JORDANS' JOURNEYS (US/8756-7970) [11580409] **2455**

JORDANS REGIONAL DIRECTORIES OF KEY BUSINESS PROSPECTS. VARIOUS AREAS IN UK (UK) **685**

JORDBRUGSKONOMISK INSTITUT *See* REGNSKABSRESULTATER FRA DANSKE LANDBRUG **125**

JORDBRUKETS ARBETSKRAFT (SW) [10252730] **98**, **1681**

JORDBRUKSEKONOMISKA MEDDELANDEN: JEM (SW/0021-7441) [09286662] **98**

JORDBRUKSSTATISTISK ARSBOK (SW) [02244062] **98**

JORDBRUKSTEKNISKA INSTITUTET (SWEDEN) *See* MEDDELANDE - JORDBRUKSTEKNISKA INSTITUTET **107**

JORDEMODERN (SW/0021-7468) [I00217468] **3763**

JORNADA (MEXICO CITY, MEXICO) (MX) [14208832] **5806**

JORNADAS (MX) [01697024] **5205**

JORNADAS DE TRABAJO SOBRE SUSTITUCIONES ARTICULARES (SP/0210-8240) [04083051] **3805**

JORNAL ARQUITECTOS (PO/0870-1504) [I08701504] **301**

JORNAL BRASILEIRO DE GINECOLOGIA (BL/0368-1416) [06382580] **3763**

JORNAL BRASILEIRO DE PSIQUIATRIA (BL/0047-2085) [01778514] **4592**, **3928**

JORNAL BRASILEIRO DE UROLOGIA (BL/0100-0519) [01562900] **3990**

JORNAL DA ABES (BL) [04573832] **4786**

JORNAL DA ARMAZENAGEM (BL) [06479555] **175**

JORNAL DA LIGA BRASILEIRA DE EPILEPSIA (BL) [20818199] **3834**

JORNAL DE ANGOLA, O (AO) **5777**

JORNAL DE EXERCITO (PO) [06203206] **4048**

Alphabetical Title Index — JOURNAL

JORNAL DE PEDIATRIA (BL/0021-7557) [I00217557] **3904**

JORNAL DE PNEUMOLOGIA : PUBLICACAO OFICIAL DA SOCIEDADE BRASILEIRA DE PNEUMOLOGIA E TISIOLOGIA (BL/0102-3586) [27065278] **3949**

JORNAL DE PSICOLOGIA (PO/0870-4783) [17257100] **4592**

●JORNAL DO BRASIL (BL) [26207675] **1026**

JORNAL DO BRASIL (BL) [01754340] **5779**

JORNAL DO COMERCIO (PO) **842**

JORNAL DOS REFLORESTADORES (BL) [10515549] **2385**

JORNAL DOS TRABALHADORES RURAIS SEM TERRA (BL) [22108100] **1681, 98**

JORNAL INDIGENA / UMA PUBLICACAO DA UNIAO DAS NACOES INDIGENAS, UNI (BL) [12061637] **2265**

JORNAL NOVO (PO) [03043751] **5808**

JORNAL PORTUGUES (SAN PABLO, CALIF.) (US/8756-2200) [05686672] **5636**

JORNAL SUL-AMERICANO DE BIOCIENCIAS (BL/0100-7319) [10908884] **5118**

JORNAL SUL-TROPICAL DE MEDICINA / SOUTH TROPICAL JOURNAL OF MEDICINE (BL/0103-054X) [19475867] **3986**

JOSA NYENGU BOGO - JANWEN GAIBAR NYENGUSO (KO/0253-3863) [04735586] **2141**

JOSE (BL) [02829878] **323**

JOSEI MONDAI TOSHO SOMOKUROKU (MICROFORM) (JA) [12248932] **5559**

JOSEMARIA ESCRIVA DE BALAGUER (EDITION FRANCAISE) (CN/0703-2757) [08767179] **4967**

JOSEMARIA ESCRIVA DE BALAGUER (ENGLISH EDITION) (CN/0703-9093) [03960064] **4967**

JOSEPH CONRAD TODAY (US/0162-413X) [03472846] **3345, 433**

JOSEPHITE HARVEST, THE (US/0021-7603) [01754341] **4967**

JOSHI EIYO DAIGAKU KIYO (JA/0286-0511) [10281766] **4192**

JOSLIN'S JAZZ JOURNAL (US/0735-1585) [08732994] **4125**

JOSSEY BASS HIGHER AND ADULT EDUCATION SERIES (US) **1832**

JOSSEY BASS MANAGEMENT SERIES (US) **872**

JOTS AND TITLES (US) [09279649] **4125**

JOTS FROM THE POINT (US/0277-4909) [04835710] **2455**

JOUETS ET JEUX (FR/0075-4056) [I00754056] **2584**

JOUETS (MONTREAL. 1976) (CN/0707-5081) [06264549] **2584**

JOUGWA (GP) [09582195] **2740**

JOUR (MONTREAL. 1977) (CN/0703-699X) [03519945] **5787**

JOURNAAL NV/BV (NE/0920-6280) [I09206280] **2986**

JOURNAAL / UITGAVE STICHTING VOOR CULTURELE SAMENWERKING (STICUSA) (NE) [09835056] **2694**

JOURNAL (US) [10649139] **2455**

JOURNAL (II) [01790467] **1384**

JOURNAL A (BE/0771-1107) [03919149] **1981**

JOURNAL ACTON REGIONAL (CN/0228-6289) [07802373] **5787**

JOURNAL - ADDICTION RESEARCH FOUNDATION, THE (CN/0044-6203) [02249760] **1345, 4786**

JOURNAL-ADVOCATE (US) [23131616] **5643**

JOURNAL / AGRI-MARK INC (US/1056-9537) [15244510] **195**

JOURNAL-AMERICAN (US/0744-947X) [08672432] **5761**

JOURNAL (AMERICAN ACADEMY OF GNATHOLOGIC ORTHOPEDICS) (US/0886-1064) [11265429] **1325**

JOURNAL - AMERICAN ASSOCIATION FOR MEDICAL TRANSCRIPTION (US/0745-2624) [09009482] **3592**

JOURNAL (AMERICAN CIVIL LIBERTIES UNION FOUNDATION. NATIONAL PRISON PROJECT) *See* NATIONAL PRISON PROJECT JOURNAL, THE **3170**

JOURNAL - AMERICAN CIVIL LIBERTIES UNION FOUNDATION. NATIONAL PRISON PROJECT (US/0748-2655) [10923014] **3167**

JOURNAL (AMERICAN PSYCHOLOGICAL ASSOCIATION. DIVISION OF CONSULTING PSYCHOLOGY) *See* CONSULTING PSYCHOLOGY JOURNAL **4582**

JOURNAL - AMERICAN PSYCHOLOGICAL ASSOCIATION. DIVISION OF CONSULTING PSYCHOLOGY (US/1061-4087) [25301859] **4592**

JOURNAL / AMERICAN RHODODENDRON SOCIETY (US/0745-7839) [08199975] **2421**

JOURNAL - AMERICAN SOCIETY OF SUGAR CANE TECHNOLOGISTS. FLORIDA DIVISIONS (US/1075-6302) [10786532] **2345, 175**

JOURNAL / AMERICAN WATER WORKS ASSOCIATION (US/0003-150X) [13118972] **5535**

JOURNAL - AMERICAN WINE SOCIETY (US/0364-698X) [02667545] **2368**

JOURNAL AND COURIER (LAFAYETTE, IND.) (US) [08807571] **5665**

JOURNAL AND GUIDE (NORFOLK, VA : 1977) (US) [06836057] **5759**

JOURNAL AND GUIDE, THE (US) [02262974] **5759**

JOURNAL AND PROCEEDINGS OF THE ROYAL SOCIETY OF NEW SOUTH WALES (AT/0035-9173) [01764619] **5118**

JOURNAL & REPORT - NATIONAL UNION OF THE FOOTWEAR, LEATHER & ALLIED TRADES *SUSPENDED.* (UK) [06352716] **3184**

JOURNAL AND REPORT OF PROCEEDINGS - PERMANENT WAY INSTITUTION (UK/0031-5524) [.00315524] 5432, **2025**

JOURNAL AND REPUBLICAN, THE (US) [09972200] **5717**

JOURNAL AND THE NOBLE COUNTY LEADER, THE (US) [17277844] **5729**

JOURNAL - ANDHRA PRADESH AKADEMI OF SCIENCES (II) [01790464] **5118**

JOURNAL - ANDHRA PRADESH, INDIA. LEGISLATURE. LEGISLATIVE COUNCIL (II) [01784191] **4478**

JCURNAL - ARCHIVES OF AMERICAN AFT (US/0003-9853) [09475849] **354**

JOURNAL / ARKLOW HISTORICAL SOCIETY (IE/0790-0090) [17642573] **2694**

●JOURNAL - ART GALLERY OF ONTARIO (CN/1191-9868) [27809711] **4090**

JOURNAL (ASHCROFT) (CN/0824-6394) [10862228] **5787**

JOURNAL ASIATIQUE (FR/0021-762X) [06837149] **3289**

JOURNAL - ASSOCIATION FOR HEALTHCARE PHILANTHROPY (U.S.) (US/1061-7655) [24523095] **3786**

JOURNAL - ASSOCIATION FOR HOSPITAL MEDICAL EDUCATION (US/0148-4869) [03259649] **3592**

JOURNAL - ASSOCIATION OF OFFICIAL ANALYTICAL CHEMISTS (US) [03758073] **979, 98**

JOURNAL / AUSTRALIAN JEWISH HISTORICAL SOCIETY (AT/0819-0615) [18425024] **2265**

JOURNAL - AVIATION HISTORICAL SOCIETY OF NEW ZEALAND (NZ/0110-5493) [I01105493] **25**

JOURNAL - BANGLADESH INSURANCE ACADEMY (BG) [02537013] **2885**

JOURNAL BARREAU, LE (CN/0833-921X) [15732369] **2986**

JOURNAL BELGE DE RADIOLOGIE (1924) (BE/0021-7646) [05436880] **3942**

JOURNAL BRASILEIRO DE NEUROCIRURGIA (BL) [23465223] **3834**

JOURNAL-BULLETIN RHODE ISLAND ALMANAC (US/0364-2909) [07620780] **2536**

JOURNAL / CALIFORNIA RARE FRUIT GROWERS (US/0894-8445) [14914260] **98**

JOURNAL / CALIFORNIA TRADITIONAL MUSIC SOCIETY (US/1053-3664) [17724778] **2321**

JOURNAL / CALIFORNIA TRIAL LAWYERS ASSOCIATION (US/0730-4919) [07992723] **2986**

JOURNAL - CAMBORNE SCHOOL OF MINES (UK/0308-3845) [06353215] **2141**

JOURNAL (CAMP VERDE, ARIZ.), THE (US/0744-3285) [08190106] **5630**

JOURNAL - CANADIAN DENTAL ASSOCIATION (CN/0709-8936) [05842178] **1325**

JOURNAL - CANADIAN DENTAL ASSOCIATION (FRENCH EDITION) (CN/0709-8936) [05842189] **1325**

JOURNAL - CANADIAN FEDERATION OF UNIVERSITY WOMEN (CN/0705-3843) [03979952] **5559**

JOURNAL (CANADIAN FOUNDATION FOR ILEITIS AND COLITIS) *See* JOURNAL / CROHN'S AND COLITIS FOUNDATION OF CANADA, THE **3746**

JOURNAL - CANADIAN FUSION FUELS TECHNOLOGY PROJECT (CN/0847-9437) [20782007] **4262**

JOURNAL - CANADIAN OLDTIMERS' HOCKEY ASSOCIATION (CN/0826-5887) [11453868] **4901**

JOURNAL - CANADIAN ORAL HISTORY ASSOCIATION (CN/0383-6894) [03258691] **2740**

JOURNAL - CANADIAN RED CROSS SOCIETY. BLOOD PROGRAMME (CN/0715-8602) [09819000] **3772, 5291**

JOURNAL - CANADIAN SOCIETY FOR EDUCATION THROUGH ART (CN/1196-4081) [22715623] **323**

JOURNAL CANNT, LE (CN) [22449926] **3990**

JOURNAL CHALEUR (CN/0318-2134) [02441718] **5787**

JOURNAL / CHARTERED INSURANCE INSTITUTE, THE (UK) [19416166] **2885**

JOURNAL - COLLEGE OF MEDICINE, THE OHIO STATE UNIVERSITY (US/0030-1132) [01449979] **3592**

JOURNAL - COLORADO DENTAL ASSOCIATION (US/0010-1559) [03974582] **1326**

JOURNAL / COLORADO EDUCATION ASSOCIATION (US/0279-3326) [07299399] **1755**

JOURNAL - CONNECTICUT STATE DENTAL ASSOCIATION, THE (US/0010-6232) [04062360] **1326**

JOURNAL - CONSEIL REGIONAL DE LA SANTE ET DES SERVICES SOCIAUX, REGION 01 (CN/0228-3425) [06960253] **5291**

JOURNAL CONSTRUCTO (CN/0047-2115) [02032481] **618**

JOURNAL CONTENTS IN QUANTITATIVE METHODS (UK/0142-5951) [12717202] **3511**

JOURNAL / CORNWALL FAMILY HISTORY SOCIETY (UK/0141-7614) [12796227] **2455**

JOURNAL COTE-DES-NEIGES (CN/0822-0794) [10003783] **5787**

JOURNAL / CROHN'S AND COLITIS FOUNDATION OF CANADA, THE (CN/1197-4982) [29970277] **3746**

JOURNAL (CROSBY, N.D.), THE (US/0886-6007) [01566810] **5725**

JOURNAL D ACOUTIQUE *See* ACTA ACUSTICA **4395**

JOURNAL D' ANALYSE MATHEMATIQUE (JERUSALEM) (IS/0021-7670) [01782744] **3511**

JOURNAL D'ACOUSTIQUE (FR/0988-4319) [19173429] **4452**

JOURNAL D'AGRICULTURE TRADITIONELLE ET DE BOTANIQUE APPLIQUEE *SUSPENDED.* (FR/0183-5173) [04204222] **514, 98**

JOURNAL DE BIOLOGIE BUCCALE *CEASED.* (FR/0301-3952) [03439807] **1326**

JOURNAL DE CHIMIE PHYSIQUE ET DE PHYSICO-CHIMIE BIOLOGIQUE (FR/0021-7689) [01782394] **1053**

JOURNAL DE CHIRURGIE (FR/0021-7697) [01754346] **3966**

JOURNAL DE CLAVIS, LE (CN/0702-5068) [03887330] **2536**

JOURNAL DE CORNWALL, LE (CN/0704-0660) [03889962] **5787**

JOURNAL DE DROIT FISCAL (BE) [02315168] **2986**

JOURNAL DE GENEVE (SZ) [13173419] **5811**

JOURNAL DE GENEVE ET GAZETTE DE LAUSANNE (SZ/1021-1721) [I10211721] **5811**

JOURNAL DE GYNECOLOGIE, OBSTETRIQUE ET BIOLOGIE DE LA REPRODUCTION (FR/0368-2315) [01771071] **3763**

JOURNAL DE JUGES DES PAIX, DE LEUR SUPPLANTS, DES OFFICIERS DU MINISTERE PUBLIC ET DES GREFFIERS *See* JOURNAL DES JUGES DE PAIX ET DE POLICE **2986**

JOURNAL DE LA COTE (CN/0227-2911) [06635230] **5787**

JOURNAL DE LA FORMATION CONTINUE & DE L'E.A.O, LE (FR/0761-9863) [I07619863] **1832**

JOURNAL DE L'A. I. H. P. Q, LE (CN/0705-0003) [03956590] **4786**

JOURNAL DE LA MAISON, LE (FR/0750-3288) [I07503288] **2906**

JOURNAL DE LA MARINE MARCHANDE ET DU TRANSPORT MULTIMODAL (FR/0983-0537) [19463385] **5450**

JOURNAL DE LA NAVIGATION FLUVIALE & I.E. ET MARITIME (MICROFICHE) (US) [04506642] **4177**

JOURNAL DE LA PAIX (FR/0021-7794) [I00217794] **4478**

JOURNAL DE LA PSYCHANALYSE DE L'ENFANT (FR) [27697736] **4592**

JOURNAL

Alphabetical Title Index

JOURNAL DE LA SOCIETE CHIMIQUE DE TUNISIE (TI/0253-1208) [10810318] **979**

JOURNAL DE LA SOCIETE DE STATISTIQUE DE PARIS (FR/0037-914X) [01330145] **5329**

JOURNAL DE LA SOCIETE DES AMERICANISTES (FR/0037-9174) [01765786] 238, **271**

JOURNAL DE LA SOCIETE DES OCEANISTES (FR/0300-953X) [01765793] **238**

JOURNAL DE LA SOCIETE DES OCEANISTES MICROFILM (FR/0300-953X) [25796967] 5205, **271**

JOURNAL DE L'AGE D'OR, LE (CN/0704-7029) [04039527] 5179, **5291**

JOURNAL DE L'ANNEE (FR/0449-4733) [01783389] **2621**

JOURNAL DE L'APUC (EDITION FRANCAISE) (CN/0709-2504) [05842558] 1681, **1832**

JOURNAL DE L'ASSOCIATION OUVRIERE CANADIENNE (CN/0225-3089) [06131593] **1681**

JOURNAL DE L'AUTO SPORT, LE *See* AUTO SPORT (MONTREAL. 1992) **4885**

JOURNAL DE L'IMMERSION, LE (CN/0833-1812) [16849859] 1897, **3289**

JOURNAL DE MATHEMATIQUES PURES ET APPLIQUEES (FR/0021-7824) [01782372] **3511**

JOURNAL DE MEDECINE DE LYON (FR/0021-7883) [01754360] **3592**

JOURNAL DE MEDECINE DE STRASBOURG (FR/0021-7905) [06382527] **3592**

JOURNAL DE MEDECINE LEGALE, DROIT MEDICAL (FR/0249-6208) [07715245] **3741**

JOURNAL DE MEDECINE NUCLEAIRE ET BIOPHYSIQUE *See* MEDECINE NUCLEAIRE **3848**

JOURNAL DE MEDECINE PRATIQUE *CEASED.* (FR/0987-2825) [19345465] **3592**

JOURNAL DE MICKEY 1952, LE (FR/0242-9225) [02429225] **1065**

JOURNAL DE MUSIQUE ANCIENNE (CN/0838-9349) [18314864] **4125**

JOURNAL DE MYCOLOGIE MEDICALE PARIS (FR/1156-5233) [I11565233] **575**

JOURNAL DE PARODONTOLOGIE *See* JOURNAL DE PARODONTOLOGIE & D'IMPLANTOLOGIE ORALE **1326**

●JOURNAL DE PARODONTOLOGIE & D'IMPLANTOLOGIE ORALE (FR) [30775420] **1326**

JOURNAL DE PATHOLOGIE DIGESTIVE (FR/1161-9147) [25007256] **3746**

JOURNAL DE PEDIATRIE ET DE PUERICULTURE (FR) [18660091] **3904**

JOURNAL DE PHARMACIE CLINIQUE (FR/0291-1981) [09832671] **4310**

JOURNAL DE PHARMACIE DE BELGIQUE (BE/0047-2166) [01754364] **4310**

JOURNAL DE PHARMACOLOGIE CLINIQUE (FR/0301-4762) [01866016] **4310**

JOURNAL DE PHYSIOLOGIE *See* JOURNAL OF PHYSIOLOGY, PARIS **583**

JOURNAL DE PHYSIQUE. I (LES ULIS) (FR/1155-4304) [22936696] **4408**

JOURNAL DE PHYSIQUE. II (LES ULIS) (FR/1155-4312) [22936713] **4408**

JOURNAL DE PHYSIQUE. III (LES ULIS) (FR/1155-4320) [22936721] **4408**

JOURNAL DE PHYSIQUE. IV (LES ULIS) (FR/1155-4339) [23449204] **4408**

JOURNAL DE PSYCHANALYSE DE L'ENFANT (FR) **3928**

JOURNAL DE RADIOLOGIE (FR/0221-0363) [04890024] 3848, **3942**

JOURNAL DE READAPTATION MEDICALE (FR) **3592**

JOURNAL DE READAPTATION MEDICALE (FR/0242-648X) [I0242648X] **3882**

JOURNAL DE RECHERCHE OCEANOGRAPHIQUE (FR/0397-5347) [03974246] **1450**

JOURNAL DE REFLEXION SUR L'INFORMATIQUE (BE) 5249, **1191**

JOURNAL DE ST-DOMINIQUE (CN/0822-6938) [10611145] **5787**

JOURNAL DE THERAPIE COMPORTEMENTALE ET COGNITIVE (FR) **4592**

JOURNAL DE TOXICOLOGIE CLINIQUE ET EXPERIMENTALE *CEASED.* (FR/0753-2830) [12618092] **3981**

JOURNAL DE TRAUMATOLOGIE (FR/0245-5811) [08326425] **3592**

JOURNAL DE TRAUMATOLOGIE DU SPORT (FR/0762-915X) [17193951] **3954**

JOURNAL DE VILLERAY, LE (CN/0821-5081) [09606612] **5787**

JOURNAL D'ECHOGRAPHIE ET DE MEDECINE ULTRASONORE : JEMU (FR/0245-5552) [08277855] **3592**

JOURNAL D'ECONOMIE MEDICALE (FR/0294-0736) [17250364] **3592**

JOURNAL DENTAIRE DU QUEBEC (CN) [02027054] **1326**

JOURNAL DENTAIRE DU QUEBEC (CN) [02049038] **1326**

JOURNAL D'ERGOTHERAPIE PARIS (FR/0249-6550) [I02496550] 4389, **4380**

JOURNAL DES AFRICANISTES (FR/0399-0346) [03672339] **238**

JOURNAL DES DEBATS : COMMISSIONS PARLEMENTAIRES (CN) [01786520] **4478**

JOURNAL DES DEBATS. INDEX (CN) [04531297] **2986**

JOURNAL DES DEBATS (QUEBEC) (CN/0709-3632) [04272169] **4478**

JOURNAL DES DEBATS - QUEBEC (PROVINCE). ASSEMBLEE NATIONALE. COMMISSION D'ETUDE DES QUESTIONS AFFERENTES A L'ACCESSION DU QUEBEC A LA SOUVERAINETE (CN/1189-0762) [25352197] **4658**

JOURNAL DES DEBATS - QUEBEC (PROVINCE). ASSEMBLEE NATIONALE. COMMISSION D'ETUDE SUR TOUTE OFFRE D'UN NOUVEAU PARTENARIAT DE NATURE CONSTITUTIONELLE (CN/1189-072X) [25352196] **4658**

JOURNAL DES DEBATS - QUEBEC (PROVINCE). ASSEMBLEE NATIONALE. COMMISSION PARLEMENTAIRE SUR L'AVENIR POLITIQUE ET CONSTITUTIONNEL DU QUEBEC (CN/0846-0361) [23455476] **4658**

JOURNAL DES ENFANTS ED. NATIONALE, LE (FR/0986-9050) [I09869050] 1065, **1755**

JOURNAL DES INGENIEURS (BRUSSELS, BELGIUM : 1984) (BE/0021-8065) [11097649] **1981**

JOURNAL DES INSTITUTEURS ET DES INSTITUTRICES (FR/0021-8073) [I00218073] **1865**

JOURNAL DES JEUNES (SAINT-BONIFACE) (CN/0849-5734) [21349028] **1065**

JOURNAL DES JUGES DE PAIX ET DE POLICE (BE) [19486948] **2986**

JOURNAL DES MALADIES VASCULAIRES (FR/0398-0499) [03570726] **3706**

JOURNAL DES PATES ET PAPIERS *CEASED.* (CN/0830-887X) [15483158] **4234**

JOURNAL DES PSYCHOLOGUES, LE (FR/0752-501X) [I0752501X] **4592**

JOURNAL DES SAVANTS (FR/0021-8103) [01713951] **4478**

JOURNAL DES TRAVAILLEURS D'HOPITAUX (CN/0707-7858) [04747134] **5787**

JOURNAL DES TRIBUNAUX DU TRAVAIL (BE) [17492940] **3150**

JOURNAL D'OUTREMONT, LE (CN/0824-1317) [11825458] **2536**

JOURNAL DU DROIT INTERNATIONAL (FR/0021-8170) [01754386] **3131**

JOURNAL DU JEUNE CINEMA QUEBECOIS, LE (CN/0705-5188) [04130094] **4073**

JOURNAL DU NORD-OUEST, LE (CN/0380-2051) [02583216] **5787**

JOURNAL DU PATISSIER: CONFISEUR GLACIER. CHOCOLATIER TRAITEUR, LE (FR) **2345**

JOURNAL DU R C M, LE (CN/0709-6003) [05765832] **4478**

JOURNAL DU SAMEDI, LE (CN/0229-981X) [08091440] **5787**

JOURNAL DU SIDA PARIS, LE (FR/1153-0863) [I11530863] **3592**

JOURNAL DU TEXTILE 1964 (FR/0021-8197) [I00218197] **5353**

JOURNAL DU TRAVAIL (QUEBEC. 1979) (CN/0708-4986) [05257960] **1681**

●JOURNAL DU VILLAGE D'EMILIE, LE (CN/1189-5071) [26758153] **5365**

JOURNAL D'UROLOGIE (FR/0248-0018) [06509815] **3990**

JOURNAL / ECONOMIC POLICY INSTITUTE (US/1061-8228) [23136924] **1498**

JOURNAL (ELLETTSVILLE, IND.) (US) [16700317] **5665**

JOURNAL-ENTERPRISE, THE (US) [14124366] **5681**

JOURNAL ETUDIANT - COLLEGE DE JONQUIERE (CN/0228-9059) [07817467] **1092**

JOURNAL EUROPEEN DE RADIOTHERAPIE *CEASED.* (FR/0243-1203) [11248572] **3942**

JOURNAL EUROPEEN DES URGENCIES : JEUR (FR) [19584821] **3725**

JOURNAL-EXPRESS (US) [17927743] **5671**

JOURNAL / FLINTSHIRE HISTORICAL SOCIETY (UK) [09537976] **2694**

JOURNAL / FLORIDA ENGINEERING SOCIETY (US/0015-4032) [01387321] **1981**

JOURNAL - FLORIDA GENEALOGICAL SOCIETY (1978) (US/0735-6420) [08937334] **2455**

JOURNAL FOR A JUST AND CARING EDUCATION (US) **1755**

JOURNAL FOR ANTHROPOSOPHY (US/0021-8235) [01795292] **4967**

JOURNAL FOR CHRISTIAN STUDIES, A (US/0889-5848) [12937308] **4967**

JOURNAL FOR COMPUTER USERS IN SPEECH AND HEARING *CEASED.* (US/8756-7342) [11638389] 1223, **4389**

JOURNAL FOR CONSTRUCTIVE CHANGE (US/0198-9383) [06284935] **873**

JOURNAL FOR CONTEMPORARY HISTORY / JOERNAAL VIR EIETYDSE GESKIEDENIS (SA) [07651254] 5205, **4526**

JOURNAL FOR CORPORATE GROWTH *CEASED.* (US/1048-1648) [19008973] **685**

JOURNAL FOR EDUCATION IN PHOTOJOURNALISM, THE (US/0273-9917) [07051163] **4371**

JOURNAL FOR FURTHER AND HIGHER EDUCATION IN SCOTLAND, A (UK) [08288279] **1832**

JOURNAL FOR GENERAL PHILOSOPHY OF SCIENCE (NE/0925-4560) [23013395] 5118, **4350**

JOURNAL FOR GERIATRIC CARE STAFF MEMBER (US/0093-7320) [00928283] **3752**

JOURNAL FOR GROWTH IN MARRIAGE, THE (US/0160-7804) [03765714] **2281**

JOURNAL FOR HAWAIIAN AND PACIFIC AGRICULTURE (US/1052-5394) [19038969] **99**

●JOURNAL FOR HEALTHCARE QUALITY (US/1062-2551) [25320984] **3858**

●JOURNAL FOR HEALTHCARE QUALITY: PROMOTING EXCELLENCE IN HEALTHCARE (US) [25465572] **4786**

JOURNAL FOR HIGHER EDUCATION MANAGEMENT (US) [13029495] **1832**

JOURNAL FOR PEACE & JUSTICE STUDIES (US) [19908928] **4526**

JOURNAL FOR POSTSECONDARY EDUCATION AND DISABILITY (US) **1880**

JOURNAL FOR PREACHERS (US/1057-266X) [06126432] **4967**

JOURNAL FOR QUALITY AND PARTICIPATION. PROFILES OF SERVICES AND PRODUCTS FOR EXCELLENCE, THE (US/1060-8494) [23226562] **1613**

JOURNAL FOR QUALITY AND PARTICIPATION, THE (US/1040-9602) [17497271] **1681**

JOURNAL FOR RESEARCH IN MATHEMATICS EDUCATION (US/0021-8251) [01790822] **3511**

JOURNAL FOR SEMITICS (SA/1013-8471) [21079909] **3289**

JOURNAL FOR SOCIAL JUSTICE STUDIES (AT/1035-4425) [I10354425] **5249**

JOURNAL FOR SPECIALISTS IN GROUP WORK, THE (US/0193-3922) [04183964] **4592**

JOURNAL FOR THE ANTHROPOLOGICAL STUDY OF HUMAN MOVEMENT AT NEW YORK UNIVERSITY (US/0891-7124) [08713137] 1313, **238**

JOURNAL FOR THE CALLIGRAPHIC ARTS (US) [13514600] **380**

JOURNAL FOR THE EDUCATION OF THE GIFTED (US/0162-3532) [04144776] **1880**

JOURNAL FOR THE HISTORY OF ARABIC SCIENCE (SY/0379-2927) [03697160] **5118**

JOURNAL FOR THE HISTORY OF ASTRONOMY (UK/0021-8286) [01784601] **396**

JOURNAL FOR THE OFFICE OF MENTAL RETARDATION & DEVELOPMENTAL DISABILITIES, THE (US/8750-3328) [11256707] **5291**

JOURNAL FOR THE SCIENTIFIC STUDY OF RELIGION (US/0021-8294) [01783125] **4967**

JOURNAL FOR THE STUDY OF JUDAISM IN THE PERSIAN, HELLENISTIC AND ROMAN PERIOD (NE/0047-2212) [01800061] **5050**

JOURNAL FOR THE STUDY OF RELIGION (SA/1011-7601) [18282563] **4967**

JOURNAL FOR THE STUDY OF THE NEW TESTAMENT (UK/0142-064X) [04536858] **5017**

JOURNAL FOR THE STUDY OF THE NEW TESTAMENT. SUPPLEMENT SERIES (UK/0143-5108) [08538123] **5017**

JOURNAL FOR THE STUDY OF THE OLD TESTAMENT (UK/0309-0892) [03295041] **5017**

JOURNAL FOR THE STUDY OF THE OLD TESTAMENT. SUPPLEMENT SERIES (UK/0309-0787) [04896638] **5017**

JOURNAL FOR THE STUDY OF THE PSEUDEPIGRAPHA (UK/0951-8207) [17504095] **4968**

JOURNAL FOR THE THEORY OF SOCIAL BEHAVIOUR (UK/0021-8308) [01695343] **4593**

●JOURNAL FOR TRUANCY AND DROPOUT PREVENTION, THE (US) [27606987] **1756**

JOURNAL FOR VOCATIONAL SPECIAL NEEDS EDUCATION, THE (US/0195-7597) [05049063] **1880**

JOURNAL FOR WEAVERS, SPINNERS & DYERS, THE (UK) [11611682] **5353**

JOURNAL - FORENSIC SCIENCE SOCIETY (UK/0015-7368) [11262669] **3741**

JOURNAL / FORT SMITH HISTORICAL SOCIETY, THE (US/0736-4261) [03463948] 2455, **2740**

JOURNAL FRANCAIS D'AMERIQUE (US/0195-2889) [05460001] **5636**

JOURNAL FRANCAIS D'HYDROLOGIE (FR/0335-9581) [11320169] **1415**

JOURNAL FRANCAIS D'OPHTALMOLOGIE (FR/0181-5512) [03942135] **3875**

JOURNAL FRANCAIS D'ORTHOPTIQUE (FR/0240-7914) [I02407914] **3875**

JOURNAL FRANCAIS D'OTO-RHINO-LARYNGOLOGIE (FR/0398-9771) [03443385] **3889**

JOURNAL-FREE PRESS, THE (US) [12193314] **5676**

JOURNAL FROM THE RADICAL REFORMATION, A (US/1058-3084) [24258371] **4968**

JOURNAL FROM THE ROYAL COLLEGE OF ART *See* ARK **226**

JOURNAL FUER BETRIEBSWIRTSCHAFT (AU/0344-9327) [I03449327] **685**

JOURNAL FUER BETRIEBSWIRTSCHAFT (AU) [04434567] **1613**

JOURNAL FUER DIE FRAU (GW/0178-7284) [I01787284] **5559**

JOURNAL FUER DIE REINE UND ANGEWANDTE MATHEMATIK (GW/0075-4102) [01782270] **3511**

JOURNAL FUER ENTWICKLUNGSPOLITIK : JEP (AU/0258-2384) [22197348] **1569**

JOURNAL FUER HIRNFORSCHUNG (GW/0021-8359) [01754401] **3834**

JOURNAL FUER ORNITHOLOGIE (GW/0021-8375) [01588080] **5618**

JOURNAL FUER PRAKTISCHE CHEMIE *See* JOURNAL FUER PRAKTISCHE CHEMIE, CHEMIKER-ZEITUNG **979**

●JOURNAL FUER PRAKTISCHE CHEMIE, CHEMIKER-ZEITUNG (GW/0941-1216) [25732865] **979**

JOURNAL FUER RECHTSPOLITIK (AU/0943-4011) **4478**

JOURNAL FUER SOZIALFORSCHUNG (AU/0253-3995) [08007447] **5249**

JOURNAL FUR SOZIALFORSCHUNG (VIENNA, AUSTRIA : 1987) (AU) [17545768] **5205**

JOURNAL - GALPIN SOCIETY (UK/0072-0127) [01439153] **4125**

JOURNAL (GARDEN CLUB OF VIRGINIA) (US/0431-0233) [08462224] **2421**

JOURNAL-GAZETTE (FORT WAYNE, IND.), THE (US/0734-3701) [07368210] **5665**

JOURNAL - GEOLOGICAL SOCIETY OF JAMAICA (JM) [01437073] **1384**

JOURNAL - GEOLOGICAL SOCIETY OF JAPAN (JA/0016-7630) [01456605] **1384**

JOURNAL / GERMAN-TEXAN HERITAGE SOCIETY, THE (US) [20364751] 2265, **2455**

JOURNAL / GLASS ART SOCIETY (US/0278-9426) [07921703] **2591**

JOURNAL / HACOBU (AT) [26296156] **99**

JOURNAL (HAWKESBURY AGRICULTURAL COLLEGE. OLD BOY'S UNION) *See* H.A.C. JOURNAL **1092**

JOURNAL-HERALD (JACKSON, OHIO) (US) [16823588] **5729**

JOURNAL-HERALD (WHITE HAVEN, PA.) (US) [15648013] **5737**

JOURNAL - HISTORICAL FIREARMS SOCIETY OF SOUTH AFRICA (SA) [01785088] **251**

JOURNAL HOLDINGS IN THE NATIONAL CAPITAL AREA (US/0893-5386) [15565417] **2921**

JOURNAL - HONOLULU ACADEMY OF ARTS (US/0360-4756) [02244542] **323**

JOURNAL / HOUSTON ARCHEOLOGICAL SOCIETY (US/8756-8071) [08495823] **271**

JOURNAL - ILLINOIS. OFFICE OF THE COMMISSIONER OF SAVINGS AND RESIDENTIAL FINANCE, THE (US/1057-283X) [24004227] **793**

JOURNAL INDEX TO THE ALBUQUERQUE JOURNAL (US/0190-7468) [04762688] **5712**

JOURNAL - INDIAN ACADEMY OF GEOSCIENCE (II/0379-5160) [01790414] **1384**

JOURNAL - INDIAN COTTON MILLS' FEDERATION (II) [01771504] **5353**

JOURNAL (INSTITUTE FOR SASKATCHEWAN STUDIES) (CN/0823-8715) [11734527] **1498**

JOURNAL - INSTITUTE OF ECONOMIC GEOGRAPHY, INDIA (II) [01784194] **1569**

JOURNAL / INSTITUTE OF MUSLIM MINORITY AFFAIRS (UK/0266-6952) [07070059] **2265**

JOURNAL / INSTITUTE OF STERILE SERVICES MANAGEMENT (UK/0951-2578) [20351426] **3592**

JOURNAL - INTEGRATED BAR OF THE PHILIPPINES (PH/0115-138X) [01791364] **2986**

JOURNAL - INTERNATIONAL CHINESE SNUFF BOTTLE SOCIETY (US/0734-5534) [06121215] **251**

JOURNAL INTERNATIONAL DE BIOETHIQUE (FR/1145-0762) [22926280] 2251, **460**

JOURNAL INTERNATIONAL DE MEDECINE, LE (FR/0241-0109) [08293480] **3592**

JCURNAL INTERNATIONAL DES SCIENCES DE LA VIGNE ET DU VIN (FR/1151-0285) [27137513] 99, **2368**

JOURNAL INTERNATIONAL DES SCIENCES DE LA VIGNE ET DU VIN (FR/1151-0985) 2368, **175**

JOURNAL INTERNATIONAL MEDICAL SCIENCES ACADEMY (II/0971-071X) [I0971071X] **3592**

JOURNAL - INTERNATIONAL UNION OF BRICKLAYERS AND ALLIED CRAFTSMEN (US/0362-3696) [02291774] **1681**

JOURNAL - IRISH GRASSLAND AND ANIMAL PRODUCTION (IE/0332-0588) [I03320588] **5512**

JOURNAL - JAPANESE ASSOCIATION CF GROUNDWATER HYDROLOGY (JA) [02474254] **1415**

JOURNAL JEUNESSE TIMOTHEE (CN/1186-6020) [24368301] **4968**

JOURNAL - KEMENTERIAN PELAJARAN MALAYSIA (MY/0126-7957) [02359487] **1756**

JOURNAL (KING GEORGE, VA.), THE (US/8750-2275) [11143497] **5759**

JOURNAL LA MITIS (CN/0228-2569) [06860215] **5787**

JOURNAL LA REPUBLIQUE (CN/0226-3580) [06515051] **5787**

JOURNAL (LACHUTE) (CN/0227-1249) [06562852] **5787**

JOURNAL L'ACTION (CN/0822-8116) [10615587] **1092**

JOURNAL L'ARISTOCRATE (CN/0849-3588) [23237136] **4593**

●JOURNAL LE MACAREUX (CN/1193-2562) [26758098] **4706**

●JOURNAL LE MACAREUX (FRENCH EDITION) (CN/1193-2562) [26758100] **4706**

JOURNAL LE NORD (CN/0228-278X) [06965975] **5787**

JOURNAL LE ST-FRANCOIS (CN/0227-1222) [06562863] **5787**

JOURNAL L'ECLAIREUR ABITIBIEN (CN/0384-6784) [04249516] **2921**

JOURNAL (LEWIS AND CLARK COLLEGE, PORTLAND, OR.) (US/0746-8873) [10416397] **1832**

JOURNAL - LEWIS COUNTY HISTORICAL SOCIETY (US/0895-500X) [05285498] **2740**

JOURNAL L'INFORMATION DU NORD (CN/0713-6420) [08890762] **5787**

JOURNAL : MACOMB COUNTY DENTAL SOCIETY (US/0744-9682) [08682307] **1326**

JOURNAL - MAINE WATER UTILITIES ASSOCIATION (US/0025-0805) [02263770] 5535, **4761**

JOURNAL / MANITOBA ELEMENTARY TEACHERS' ASSOCIATION (CN/0710-2712) [08268025] **1804**

JOURNAL MASKOUTAIN, LE (CN/0711-4745) [08700950] **5787**

JOURNAL MESSENGER, THE (US/0745-6859) [09396777] **5759**

JOURNAL - MICHIGAN ASSOCIATION OF TEACHER EDUCATORS, THE (US/1046-7254) [19706773] **1897**

JOURNAL MICHIGAN PHARMACIST (US/1045-6481) [20051203] **4310**

JOURNAL - MIDDLE STATES COUNCIL FOR THE SOCIAL STUDIES (U.S.) (US/0739-8069) [09809102] 2740, **5205**

JOURNAL - MINING AND METALLURGICAL INSTITUTE OF JAPAN (JA) [03005778] **4006**

JOURNAL - NATIONAL ASSOCIATION OF CAREERS AND GUIDANCE TEACHERS (UK/0954-3732) [I09543732] **1756**

JOURNAL / NATIONAL ASSOCIATION OF DESKTOP PUBLISHERS *See* NATIONAL ASSOCIATION OF DESKTOP PUBLISHERS JOURNAL **4817**

JOURNAL - NATIONAL PHARMACEUTICAL ASSOCIATION (US/0027-9897) [01759327] **4310**

JOURNAL / NATIONAL SOCIETY OF FUND RAISING EXECUTIVES, THE (US/1056-2443) [23599911] **761**

JOURNAL - NEW MEXICO HIGHLANDS UNIVERSITY (US/0270-0824) [06323838] **1832**

JOURNAL (NEW ULM, MINN.) (US/1059-1338) [01589813] **5696**

JOURNAL - NEW ZEALAND DIETETIC ASSOCIATION (NZ/0110-635X) [01947645] **4192**

JOURNAL / NORTH LA. HIST. ASSOC (US/0739-005X) [07767259] **2740**

JOURNAL - NORTHERN CERAMIC SOCIETY (UK) [04880037] **2591**

JOURNAL (ODON, IND.) (US) [14283555] **5665**

JOURNAL OF ABNORMAL CHILD PSYCHOLOGY (US/0091-0627) [01795095] 3928, **4593**

JOURNAL OF ABNORMAL PSYCHOLOGY (1965) (US/0021-843X) [01605720] **4593**

JOURNAL OF ABSTRACTS (AND ARTICLES) IN INTERNATIONAL EDUCATION (US/1064-0746) [26202430] 1756, **1795**

JOURNAL OF ACADEMIC LIBRARIANSHIP (US/0099-1333) [02243594] **3219**

JOURNAL OF ACADEMIC SKILLS (US/0730-1227) [07949575] **1832**

JOURNAL OF ACCESS STUDIES / FORUM FOR ACCESS STUDIES (UK/0269-2562) [18152621] **1801**

●JOURNAL OF ACCIDENT & EMERGENCY MEDICINE (UK/1351) [30325995] **3725**

JOURNAL OF ACCOUNTANCY (US/0021-8448) [01782226] **746**

JOURNAL OF ACCOUNTING & ECONOMICS (NE/0165-4101) [04968789] 1498, **746**

JOURNAL OF ACCOUNTING AND PUBLIC POLICY (US/0278-4254) [07828244] **746**

JOURNAL OF ACCOUNTING AUDITING & FINANCE (US/0148-558X) [03321499] **746**

●JOURNAL OF ACCOUNTING CASE RESEARCH, THE (CN/1192-2621) [27809696] **746**

JOURNAL OF ACCOUNTING EDUCATION (US/0748-5751) [09384181] 1756, **746**

JOURNAL OF ACCOUNTING, FINANCE AND BUSINESS HISTORY (UK) **685**

JOURNAL OF ACCOUNTING LITERATURE (US/0737-4607) [08625931] **746**

JOURNAL OF ACCOUNTING RESEARCH (US/0021-8456) [01754410] **746**

●JOURNAL OF ACCOUNTING, TAXATION AND FINANCE FOR BUSINESS, THE (US/1078-0726) [30983562] **746**

JOURNAL OF ACOUSTIC EMISSION (US/0730-0050) [07942395] **1981**

JOURNAL OF ACQUIRED IMMUNE DEFICIENCY SYNDROMES (US/0894-9255) [16314537] **3673**

JOURNAL OF ACQUIRED IMMUNE DEFICIENCY SYNDROMES AND RETROVIROLOGY (US) **3673**

●JOURNAL OF ACTUARIAL PRACTICE (US/1064-6647) [26368158] **2885**

JOURNAL OF ADDICTIONS & OFFENDER COUNSELING (US/1055-3835) [22696721] 3167, **4593**

JOURNAL OF ADDICTIVE DISEASES (US/1055-0887) [23070745] 3593, **1345**

JOURNAL OF ADHESION SCIENCE AND TECHNOLOGY (NE/0169-4243) [16908124] **1053**

JOURNAL — Alphabetical Title Index

JOURNAL OF ADHESION, THE (UK/0021-8464) [01790905] **1053**

JOURNAL OF ADOLESCENCE (LONDON, ENGLAND) (UK/0140-1971) [04041779] **4593, 3904**

JOURNAL OF ADOLESCENT CHEMICAL DEPENDENCY (US/0896-7768) [17287200] **1345**

JOURNAL OF ADOLESCENT HEALTH (US/1054-139X) [22762017] **3593**

JOURNAL OF ADOLESCENT RESEARCH (US/0743-5584) [10608553] **4593**

●JOURNAL OF ADULT DEVELOPMENT (US/1068-0667) [27422455] **4593**

JOURNAL OF ADULT EDUCATION (US/0090-4244) [01785080] **1801**

JOURNAL OF ADULT EDUCATION (UNIVERSITY OF ZAMBIA. CENTRE FOR CONTINUING EDUCATION.) (ZA) [09928375] **1801**

JOURNAL OF ADVANCED COMPOSITION (US/0731-6755) [08230989] **1897, 3289**

●JOURNAL OF ADVANCED MATERIALS (US/1070-9789) [28528320] **1981**

JOURNAL OF ADVANCED NURSING (UK/0309-2402) [02437500] **3858**

JOURNAL OF ADVANCED SCIENCE / SOCIETY OF ADVANCED SCIENCE (JA/0915-5651) [23054520] **5118**

JOURNAL OF ADVANCED TRANSPORTATION (US/0197-6729) [05121625] **5385**

JOURNAL OF ADVANCED ZOOLOGY (II/0253-7214) [08373712] **5587**

JOURNAL OF ADVANCEMENT IN MEDICINE (US/0894-5888) [16149659] **4192, 3593**

JOURNAL OF ADVANCES IN HEALTH AND NURSING CARE (UK/0960-9857) [I09609857] **3858**

JOURNAL OF ADVENTIST EDUCATION, THE (US/0021-8480) [04073976] **1897**

JOURNAL OF ADVENTURE EDUCATION AND OUTDOOR LEADERSHIP : THE JOURNAL OF THE NATIONAL ASSOCIATION FOR OUTDOOR EDUCATION, THE ASSOCIATION OF HEADS OF OUTDOOR EDUCATION CENTRES, [AND] THE OUTDOOR EDUCATION ASSOCIATION OF IRELAND, THE (UK) [25483617] **4874**

JOURNAL OF ADVERTISING (US/0091-3367) [01786755] **761**

JOURNAL OF ADVERTISING RESEARCH (US/0021-8499) [01783062] **927, 761**

JOURNAL OF AEROSOL MEDICINE (US/0894-2684) [15923625] **3949**

JOURNAL OF AEROSOL SCIENCE (UK/0021-8502) [01800058] **1053**

JOURNAL OF AEROSPACE ENGINEERING (US/0893-1321) [15357858] **25**

JOURNAL OF AESTHETIC EDUCATION, THE (US/0021-8510) [01754415] **2848**

JOURNAL OF AESTHETICS AND ART CRITICISM, THE (US/0021-8529) [01800235] **354**

JOURNAL OF AFFECTIVE DISORDERS (NE/0165-0327) [04939367] **3593**

●JOURNAL OF AFRICAN AMERICAN MALE STUDIES (US/1063-4460) [26035782] **2265**

JOURNAL OF AFRICAN CIVILIZATIONS (US/0270-2495) [05804573] **2640**

JOURNAL OF AFRICAN EARTH SCIENCES (AND THE MIDDLE EAST) (UK/0899-5362) [17526960] **1384**

●JOURNAL OF AFRICAN ECONOMIES (UK/0963-8024) [26862593] **1637**

JOURNAL OF AFRICAN HISTORY (UK/0021-8537) [01783006] **2640**

JOURNAL OF AFRICAN LANGUAGES AND LINGUISTICS (NE/0167-6164) [05107927] **3289**

JOURNAL OF AFRICAN LAW (UK/0021-8553) [01754418] **2986**

JOURNAL OF AFRICAN POLICY STUDIES (US/1058-5613) [24329692] **2640**

JOURNAL OF AFRICAN PSYCHOLOGY (SOUTH OF THE SAHARA, THE CARIBBEAN, AND AFRO-LATIN AMERICA) (NR/0795-3097) [20307925] **4593**

JOURNAL OF AFRICAN RELIGION AND PHILOSOPHY (UG/1018-8592) [24577196] **4350**

●JOURNAL OF AFRICAN RESEARCH (US/1047-9716) [20832677] **2640**

JOURNAL OF AFRICAN ZOOLOGY (BE/0776-7943) [22455295] **5587**

JOURNAL OF AFRO-LATIN AMERICAN STUDIES AND LITERATURES, THE (US/1051-1865) [21889783] **3399**

JOURNAL OF AGENT AND MANAGEMENT SELECTION AND DEVELOPMENT, THE *SUSPENDED*. (US/0278-5420) [07808628] **2885**

JOURNAL OF AGING AND HEALTH (US/0898-2643) [17766752] **3752**

●JOURNAL OF AGING AND PHYSICAL ACTIVITY (US/1063-8652) [26150256] **2599, 3752**

JOURNAL OF AGING & SOCIAL POLICY (US/0895-9420) [16859137] **5179**

JOURNAL OF AGING STUDIES (US/0890-4065) [14221706] **5180, 5249**

JOURNAL OF AGRIBUSINESS (US/0738-8950) [09487552] **99**

●JOURNAL OF AGRICULTURAL AND APPLIED ECONOMICS (US/1074-0708) [29394379] **99**

JOURNAL OF AGRICULTURAL & ENVIRONMENTAL ETHICS (CN/1187-7863) [24238888] **99, 2251**

JOURNAL OF AGRICULTURAL AND FOOD CHEMISTRY (US/0021-8561) [01800249] **979, 99**

●JOURNAL OF AGRICULTURAL & FOOD INFORMATION (US/1049-6505) [21269776] **2306, 99**

●JOURNAL OF AGRICULTURAL AND RESOURCE ECONOMICS (US/1068-5502) [26241509] **99**

JOURNAL OF AGRICULTURAL ECONOMICS (UK/0021-857X) [04217840] **1498, 99**

JOURNAL OF AGRICULTURAL ECONOMICS AND DEVELOPMENT (PH/0300-1717) [01771776] **1498, 99**

JOURNAL OF AGRICULTURAL ECONOMICS RESEARCH, THE *CEASED*. (US/1043-3309) [16263378] **1498, 99**

JOURNAL OF AGRICULTURAL EDUCATION (US/1042-0541) [18924760] **99**

JOURNAL OF AGRICULTURAL ENGINEERING RESEARCH (UK/0021-8634) [01782943] **99, 1981**

JOURNAL OF AGRICULTURAL ENTOMOLOGY (US/0735-939X) [09040746] **5610**

JOURNAL OF AGRICULTURAL LENDING / AMERICAN BANKERS ASSOCIATION (US) [15971239] **99, 793**

JOURNAL OF AGRICULTURAL RESEARCH (LAHORE) (PK/0368-1157) [01790657] **175**

JOURNAL OF AGRICULTURAL SCIENCE IN FINLAND *See* AGRICULTURAL SCIENCE IN FINLAND **52**

JOURNAL OF AGRICULTURAL SCIENCE, THE (UK/0021-8596) [01782362] **99**

JOURNAL OF AGRICULTURAL TAXATION & LAW *CEASED*. (US/0745-9181) [09591154] **99, 2986**

JOURNAL OF AGRICULTURE OF THE UNIVERSITY OF PUERTO RICO, THE (PR/0041-994X) [02449950] **99**

JOURNAL OF AGRICULTURE (SOUTH PERTH) (AT/0021-8618) [07051688] **100**

●JOURNAL OF AGROMEDICINE (US/1059-924X) [24814342] **100, 3593**

JOURNAL OF AGRONOMIC EDUCATION *See* JOURNAL OF NATURAL RESOURCES AND LIFE SCIENCES EDUCATION **100**

●JOURNAL OF AGSI (UK/0965-4380) [I09654380] **3219**

JOURNAL OF AHIMA (US/1060-5487) [24893687] **3786**

JOURNAL OF AIR LAW AND COMMERCE, THE (US/0021-8642) [01641887] **25, 2987**

JOURNAL OF AIR MEDICAL TRANSPORT *See* AIR MEDICAL JOURNAL **3547**

JOURNAL OF AIR TRAFFIC CONTROL, THE (US/0021-8650) [01783048] **25**

●JOURNAL OF AIR TRANSPORT MANAGEMENT (UK/0969-6997) **26**

JOURNAL OF AIRCRAFT (US/0021-8669) [01783071] **26**

JOURNAL OF ALABAMA ARCHAEOLOGY (US/0449-2153) [01783228] **271**

JOURNAL OF ALASKA NATIVE ARTS / INSTITUTE OF ALASKA NATIVE ARTS, INC (US) [11485103] **323**

JOURNAL OF ALCOHOL AND DRUG EDUCATION (US/0090-1482) [02227440] **1756, 1345**

JOURNAL OF ALGEBRA (US/0021-8693) [01754425] **3511**

JOURNAL OF ALGEBRAIC COMBINATORICS (US/0925-9899) **3511**

●JOURNAL OF ALGEBRAIC GEOMETRY (US/1056-3911) [23703491] **3511**

JOURNAL OF ALGORITHMS (US/0196-6774) [05874032] **1191, 3511**

JOURNAL OF ALLERGY AND CLINICAL IMMUNOLOGY (US/0091-6749) [01754426] **3673**

JOURNAL OF ALLIED HEALTH (US/0090-7421) [01785629] **3593**

JOURNAL OF ALLOYS AND COMPOUNDS (SZ/0925-8388) [24768995] **4006**

JOURNAL OF ALTERNATIVE AND COMPLEMENTARY MEDICINE (UK/0959-9886) [I09599886] **3660, 3593**

●JOURNAL OF ALTERNATIVE AND COMPLEMENTARY MEDICINE (NEW YORK, N.Y.), THE (US/1075-5535) [30084937] **3593**

JOURNAL OF AMBULATORY CARE MANAGEMENT, THE (US/0148-9917) [03527371] **3786**

JOURNAL OF AMBULATORY CARE MARKETING (US/0886-9723) [13048802] **3725**

JOURNAL OF AMBULATORY MONITORING (UK/0951-1830) [18489010] **3593**

JOURNAL OF AMERICAN AND CANADIAN STUDIES, THE (JA/0914-8035) [18900884] **2740**

JOURNAL OF AMERICAN COLLEGE HEALTH (US/0744-8481) [08598579] **3593**

JOURNAL OF AMERICAN CULTURE (US/0191-1813) [03904985] **2740**

JOURNAL OF AMERICAN DRAMA AND THEATRE, THE (US/1044-937X) [19816153] **5365**

●JOURNAL OF AMERICAN-EAST ASIAN RELATIONS, THE (US/1058-3947) [24291427] **4527**

JOURNAL OF AMERICAN ETHNIC HISTORY (US/0278-5927) [07845143] **2265**

JOURNAL OF AMERICAN FOLKLORE (US/0021-8715) [01782260] **2321**

JOURNAL OF AMERICAN HEALTH POLICY *See* JOURNAL OF THE AMERICAN HEALTH CARE, THE **5293**

JOURNAL OF AMERICAN HEALTH POLICY, THE (US/1055-324X) [23152872] **5291**

JOURNAL OF AMERICAN HISTORY, THE (US/0021-8723) [01754428] **2740**

JOURNAL OF AMERICAN INDIAN EDUCATION (US/0021-8731) [01604081] **1756**

JOURNAL OF AMERICAN INDIAN FAMILY RESEARCH, THE (US/0730-6148) [07805403] **2455**

JOURNAL OF AMERICAN INSURANCE *CEASED*. (US/0021-874X) [01754429] **2885**

JOURNAL OF AMERICAN ORGANBUILDING (US/1048-2482) [20879538] **4125**

JOURNAL OF AMERICAN ROMANIAN CHRISTIAN LITERARY STUDIES (US/0271-5139) [06605795] **2740**

JOURNAL OF AMERICAN STUDIES (UK/0021-8758) [01799967] **2740**

JOURNAL OF ANALYSIS AND PURIFICATION *SUSPENDED*. (US) [15639597] **1016**

●JOURNAL OF ANALYTIC SOCIAL WORK (US/1052-9950) [22440756] **4593, 5291**

JOURNAL OF ANALYTICAL AND APPLIED PYROLYSIS (NE/0165-2370) [05781401] **1016**

JOURNAL OF ANALYTICAL ATOMIC SPECTROMETRY (UK/0267-9477) [13213443] **1016**

JOURNAL OF ANALYTICAL CHEMISTRY (NEW YORK, N.Y.) (US/1061-9348) [25489675] **1016**

JOURNAL OF ANALYTICAL PSYCHOLOGY (UK/0021-8774) [01782845] **4593**

JOURNAL OF ANALYTICAL TOXICOLOGY (US/0146-4760) [02942106] **3981**

JOURNAL OF ANATOMY (UK/0021-8782) [02246129] **3679**

JOURNAL OF ANDROLOGY (US/0196-3635) [05794893] **581**

JOURNAL OF ANESTHESIA (GW) **3683**

JOURNAL OF ANESTHESIA (JA/0913-8668) [19460792] **3683**

JOURNAL OF ANIMAL BREEDING AND GENETICS (1986) (GW/0931-2668) [I09312668] **548**

JOURNAL OF ANIMAL ECOLOGY, THE (UK/0021-8790) [01800268] **2217, 5587**

JOURNAL OF ANIMAL MORPHOLOGY AND PHYSIOLOGY, THE (II/0021-8804) [01782965] **5513, 5587**

JOURNAL OF ANIMAL PHYSIOLOGY AND ANIMAL NUTRITION (1986) (GW/0931-2439) [I09312439] **5513**

JOURNAL OF ANIMAL PRODUCTION RESEARCH (NR/0189-0514) [12492934] **213**

JOURNAL OF ANIMAL SCIENCE (US/0021-8812) [01782370] **213, 5513**

JOURNAL OF ANKARA MEDICAL SCHOOL (TU) [21144269] **3593**

6506

JOURNAL OF ANTHROPOLOGICAL ARCHAEOLOGY (US/0278-4165) [07810050] 238, 271

JOURNAL OF ANTHROPOLOGICAL RESEARCH (US/0091-7710) [01787802] 238

JOURNAL OF ANTHROPOLOGY (DEKALB), THE (US/0163-0601) [04270660] 238

JOURNAL OF ANTHROPOSOPHIC MEDICINE (US/1067-4640) [27241582] 3593

JOURNAL OF ANTIBIOTICS (NIHON KOSEIBUSSHITSU GAKUJUTSU KYOGIKAI : 1968) (JA/0021-8820) [01642415] 4310

JOURNAL OF ANTIMICROBIAL CHEMOTHERAPY, THE (UK/0305-7453) [01343768] 564

JOURNAL OF ANXIETY DISORDERS (US/0887-6185) [13307332] 4593

●JOURNAL OF AOAC INTERNATIONAL (US/1060-3271) [24929715] 100, 1016

JOURNAL OF APHIDOLOGY (II/0970-3810) [I09703810] 4245, 5610

JOURNAL OF APICULTURAL RESEARCH (UK/0021-8839) [01754439] 5587

JOURNAL OF APPLIED ANIMAL RESEARCH (II/0971-2119) [I09712119] 5513

JOURNAL OF APPLIED AQUACULTURE (US/1045-4438) [20113535] 555, 2306

JOURNAL OF APPLIED BEHAVIOR ANALYSIS (US/0021-8855) [01783308] 4593

JOURNAL OF APPLIED BEHAVIORAL SCIENCE, THE (US/0021-8863) [01783135] 5205

JOURNAL OF APPLIED BIOMATERIALS (US/1045-4861) [20119099] 489, 3798

●JOURNAL OF APPLIED BIOMECHANICS (US/1065-8483) [26777588] 3694

JOURNAL OF APPLIED BUSINESS RESEARCH (US/0892-7626) [14227683] 685

JOURNAL OF APPLIED CHEMISTRY OF THE USSR (US/0021-888X) [01782492] 979

JOURNAL OF APPLIED COMMUNICATION RESEARCH : JACR (US/0090-9882) [08812632] 1114

JOURNAL OF APPLIED COSMETOLOGY (IT/0392-8543) [11265465] 3721

JOURNAL OF APPLIED CRYSTALLOGRAPHY (DK/0021-8898) [01783313] 1032

JOURNAL OF APPLIED DEVELOPMENTAL PSYCHOLOGY (US/0193-3973) [05214394] 4593

JOURNAL OF APPLIED ECOLOGY, THE (UK/0021-8901) [01783079] 2217

JOURNAL OF APPLIED ECONOMETRICS (CHICHESTER, ENGLAND) (UK/0883-7252) [12223426] 1592

JOURNAL OF APPLIED EDUCATIONAL STUDIES (UK) [01792473] 1756

JOURNAL OF APPLIED ELECTROCHEMISTRY (UK/0021-891X) [01799622] 1034

JOURNAL OF APPLIED ENTOMOLOGY 1986 (GW/0931-2048) [I09312048] 5610

JOURNAL OF APPLIED FIRE SCIENCE (US/1044-4300) [19784594] 2291

●JOURNAL OF APPLIED GEOPHYSICS (NE/0926-9851) [25388753] 1440, 1407

JOURNAL OF APPLIED GERONTOLOGY (US/0733-4648) [08586390] 3753

JOURNAL OF APPLIED ICHTHYOLOGY (GW/0175-8659) [12289901] 2306

JOURNAL OF APPLIED MANAGEMENT (US/0149-7901) [03549941] 873

JOURNAL OF APPLIED MANUFACTURING SYSTEMS, THE (US/0899-0956) [17989019] 3482, 1613

JOURNAL OF APPLIED MATHEMATICS AND MECHANICS (UK/0021-8928) [01754444] 4428

JOURNAL OF APPLIED MATHEMATICS AND STOCHASTIC ANALYSIS (US/1048-9533) [21134864] 3511, 1282

JOURNAL OF APPLIED MEASUREMENTS (US/0092-2447) [03164067] 5118

JOURNAL OF APPLIED MECHANICS (US/0021-8936) [06685991] 2117

JOURNAL OF APPLIED MECHANICS AND TECHNICAL PHYSICS (US/0021-8944) [01754446] 4408, 2117

JOURNAL OF APPLIED MEDICINE (II/0377-0400) [01903011] 3593

JOURNAL OF APPLIED METEOROLOGY (1988) (US/0894-8763) [16275214] 1426

JOURNAL OF APPLIED NON-CLASSICAL LOGICS (FR/1166-3081) [26536894] 3511

JOURNAL OF APPLIED NUTRITION, THE (US/0021-8960) [02052355] 4192

JOURNAL OF APPLIED PHILOSOPHY (UK/0264-3758) [10708539] 2251, 4350

JOURNAL OF APPLIED PHYCOLOGY (NE/0921-8971) [19905318] 514

JOURNAL OF APPLIED PHYSICS (US/0021-8979) [01754449] 4408

JOURNAL OF APPLIED PHYSICS. [MICROFICHE] (US) [22407195] 4408

JOURNAL OF APPLIED PHYSIOLOGY (1985) (US/8750-7587) [11603017] 581

JOURNAL OF APPLIED POLYMER SCIENCE (US/0021-8995) [01754451] 2013

JOURNAL OF APPLIED POLYMER SCIENCE. APPLIED POLYMER SYMPOSIUM (US/0271-9460) [06932074] 1042

●JOURNAL OF APPLIED POULTRY RESEARCH (US/1056-6171) [23747943] 213

JOURNAL OF APPLIED PROBABILITY (UK/0021-9002) [01800304] 3511

JOURNAL OF APPLIED PSYCHOLOGY (US/0021-9010) [01606821] 4593

JOURNAL OF APPLIED RABBIT RESEARCH See WORLD RABBIT SCIENCES 476

JOURNAL OF APPLIED RABBIT RESEARCH, THE (US/0738-9760) [07366061] 460

JOURNAL OF APPLIED RECREATION PESEARCH (CN/0843-9117) [22136364] 4851

JOURNAL OF APPLIED REHABILITATION COUNSELING (US/0047-2220) [01026850] 1880

JOURNAL OF APPLIED SEED PRODUCTION (US/8755-8750) [11452179] 175

JOURNAL OF APPLIED SOCIAL PSYCHOLOGY (US/0021-9029) [00855160] 4594

JOURNAL OF APPLIED SOCIAL SCIENCES, THE (US/0146-4310) [02942750] 5291

JOURNAL OF APPLIED SOCIOLOGY - SOCIETY FOR APPLIED SOCIOLOGY (U.S.) (US/0749-0232) [11054904] 5249

JOURNAL OF APPLIED SPECTROSCOPY (US/0021-9037) [01716341] 1016

JOURNAL OF APPLIED SPORT PSYCHOLOGY (US/1041-3200) [18717831] 4901, 4594

JOURNAL OF APPLIED SPORT SCIENCE RESEARCH See JOURNAL OF STRENGTH AND CONDITIONING RESEARCH 4902

JOURNAL OF APPLIED SPORT SCIENCE RESEARCH, THE (US) [19951864] 1856

●JOURNAL OF APPLIED STATISTICAL SCIENCE (US/1067-5817) [27300108] 3512, 5329

JOURNAL OF APPLIED STATISTICS (UK/0266-4763) [10566980] 5329

JOURNAL OF APPLIED TOXICOLOGY (UK/0260-437X) [07567999] 3981

JOURNAL OF APPROXIMATION THEORY (US/0021-9045) [01754453] 3512

JOURNAL OF AQUACULTURE IN THE TROPICS (II/0970-0846) [15088480] 2306

JOURNAL OF AQUARICULTURE & AQUATIC SCIENCES (US/0733-2076) [08529706] 460

JOURNAL OF AQUATIC ANIMAL HEALTH (US/0899-7659) [18212487] 2306

●JOURNAL OF AQUATIC ECOSYSTEM HEALTH (NE/0925-1014) [26206548] 555

JOURNAL OF AQUATIC ECOTOXICOLOGY See JOURNAL OF AQUATIC ECOSYSTEM HEALTH 555

●JOURNAL OF AQUATIC FOOD PRODUCTS TECHNOLOGY (US/1049-8850) [21342197] 2306

JOURNAL OF AQUATIC PLANT MANAGEMENT (US/0146-6623) [02988296] 515

JOURNAL OF ARAB AFFAIRS CEASED. (US/0275-3588) [07118804] 4527

JOURNAL OF ARABIC LITERATURE (NE/0085-2376) [01783632] 3399

JOURNAL OF ARACHNOLOGY, THE (US/0161-8202) [02215102] 5587

JOURNAL OF ARBORICULTURE (US/0278-5226) [01187180] 2421

●JOURNAL OF ARCHAEOLOGICAL METHOD AND THEORY (US/1072-5369) [29000783] 271

●JOURNAL OF ARCHAEOLOGICAL RESEARCH (US/1059-0161) [24458690] 271

JOURNAL OF ARCHAEOLOGICAL SCIENCE (UK/0305-4403) [01795941] 271

JOURNAL OF ARCHITECTURAL AND PLANNING RESEARCH (US/0738-0895) [09512258] 301

JOURNAL OF ARCHITECTURAL EDUCATION (WASHINGTON, D.C. : 1984) (US/1046-4883) [16633988] 301

●JOURNAL OF ARCHITECTURAL ENGINEERING (US/1076-0431) [30374299] 302, 2025

JOURNAL OF ARCHITECTURAL THEORY AND CRITICISM / UIA (UK/0953-220X) [18073298] 302

●JOURNAL OF AREA STUDIES (UK) [30857325] 5205

JOURNAL OF ARID ENVIRONMENTS (UK/0140-1963) [04041814] 1357

JOURNAL OF ARIZONA HISTORY, THE (US/0021-9053) [02397640] 2740

JOURNAL OF ARMAMENT STUDIES (II/0379-5470) [11484384] 5118, 4048

JOURNAL OF ART & DESIGN EDUCATION (UK/0260-9991) [08415688] 354

JOURNAL OF ART & ENTERTAINMENT LAW (US/1061-0553) [23831468] 2987

JOURNAL OF ARTHROPLASTY, THE (US/0883-5403) [12148812] 3966

JOURNAL OF ARTIFICIAL INTELLIGENCE IN EDUCATION (US/1043-1020) [19298482] 1897, 1213

●JOURNAL OF ARTIFICIAL NEURAL NETWORKS (US/1073-5828) [29484167] 1242

JOURNAL OF ARTS & IDEAS (II/0970-5309) [09221456] 3399, 323

JOURNAL OF ARTS MANAGEMENT AND LAW See JOURNAL OF ARTS MANAGEMENT, LAW, AND SOCIETY 323

JOURNAL OF ARTS MANAGEMENT AND LAW, THE (US/0733-5113) [08582293] 2987, 386

●JOURNAL OF ARTS MANAGEMENT, LAW, AND SOCIETY (US/1063-2921) [25961381] 323

●JOURNAL OF ASIA-PACIFIC BUSINESS (US/1059-9231) [24814213] 685

●JOURNAL OF ASIA PACIFIC ECONOMIES (UK/1354-7860) 2505, 1498

JOURNAL OF ASIAN AND AFRICAN AFFAIRS (US/1044-2979) [20277007] 4527

JOURNAL OF ASIAN AND AFRICAN STUDIES (LEIDEN) (NE/0021-9096) [01715841] 2769

●JOURNAL OF ASIAN BUSINESS (US/1068-0055) [27407995] 685

JOURNAL OF ASIAN CULTURE (US/0162-6795) [03583351] 2505

JOURNAL OF ASIAN ECONOMICS (US/1049-0078) [21104764] 1498

JOURNAL OF ASIAN HISTORY (GW/0021-910X) [01716294] 2655

●JOURNAL OF ASIAN MARTIAL ARTS (US/1057-8358) [24124424] 2599

JOURNAL OF ASIAN PACIFIC COMMUNICATION (UK/0957-6851) [22144161] 5249, 1114

JOURNAL OF ASIAN STUDIES, THE (US/0021-9118) [03409894] 2655

●JOURNAL OF ASSISTED REPRODUCTION AND GENETICS (US/1058-0468) [24202972] 548, 3763

JOURNAL OF ASSOCIATION OF EXPLORATION GEOPHYSICISTS (II/0257-1412) [07313031] 1407

JOURNAL OF ASTHMA, THE (US/0277-0903) [07414148] 3950

JOURNAL OF ASTROPHYSICS AND ASTRONOMY (II/0250-6335) [07118659] 396

●JOURNAL OF ATHLETIC TRAINING (US/1062-6050) [25538987] 1856

JOURNAL OF ATMOSPHERIC AND OCEANIC TECHNOLOGY (US/0739-0572) [09672043] 1450, 1426

JOURNAL OF ATMOSPHERIC AND TERRESTRIAL PHYSICS (UK/0021-9169) [01782553] 1407

JOURNAL OF ATMOSPHERIC CHEMISTRY (NE/0167-7764) [10444896] 980, 1426

JOURNAL OF ATMOSPHERIC ELECTRICITY (JA/0919-2050) [29838845] 1426

●JOURNAL OF AUDIOLOGICAL MEDICINE (UK/0963-7133) [26450634] 3889

JOURNAL OF AUDIOVISUAL MEDIA IN MEDICINE, THE (UK/0140-511X) [03879996] 3593

JOURNAL OF AUSTRALIAN POLITICAL ECONOMY, THE (AT/0156-5826) [06775140] 1498

JOURNAL OF AUSTRALIAN STUDIES (AT/0314-769X) [05192496] 2669

JOURNAL OF AUTISM AND DEVELOPMENTAL DISORDERS (US/0162-3257) [04147866] 1804, 3928

JOURNAL — Alphabetical Title Index

JOURNAL OF AUTOIMMUNITY (UK/0896-8411) [17305814] **3673**

JOURNAL OF AUTOMATED REASONING (NE/0168-7433) [11936798] 1214, **1220**

JOURNAL OF AUTOMATIC CHEMISTRY, THE (UK/0142-0453) [04770036] **1016**

JOURNAL OF AUTOMATIC WRITING, THE (CN/0315-5412) [01988581] **4241**

●JOURNAL OF AUTOMATION AND INFORMATION SCIENCES (US/1064-2315) [26271424] **1220**

JOURNAL OF AUTONOMIC PHARMACOLOGY (UK/0144-1795) [07517142] **4310**

●JOURNAL OF AVIAN BIOLOGY (DK/0908-8857) [30066747] **5618**

JOURNAL OF AVIATION/AEROSPACE EDUCATION & RESEARCH, THE (US/1065-1136) [23266509] **26**

JOURNAL OF AYURVEDA (JAIPUR, INDIA) (II) [11763216] **3593**

JOURNAL OF BACK AND MUSCULOSKELETAL REHABILITATION (US/1053-8127) [22647631] **3805**

JOURNAL OF BACTERIOLOGY (US/0021-9193) [01800435] **564**

JOURNAL OF BAHA'I STUDIES (CN/0838-0430) [18921520] **4968**

JOURNAL OF BALLISTICS (US/0146-4140) [09243128] **2014**

JOURNAL OF BALTIC STUDIES (US/0162-9778) [01784640] **2694**

JOURNAL OF BAND RESEARCH (US/0021-9207) [01754464] **4125**

JOURNAL OF BANGLADESH ACADEMY OF SCIENCES (BG/0378-8121) [04686979] **5118**

JOURNAL OF BANGLADESH COLLEGE OF PHYSICIANS & SURGEONS (BG/1015-0870) [17193795] **3593**

JOURNAL OF BANK ACCOUNTING & AUDITING, THE **CEASED.** (US/0895-853X) [16825906] **793**

JOURNAL OF BANK COST & MANAGEMENT ACCOUNTING, THE (US/1070-941X) [20520780] **746**

JOURNAL OF BANK TAXATION, THE (US/0895-4720) [16652451] **793**

JOURNAL OF BANKING & FINANCE (NE/0378-4266) [03401093] **793**

JOURNAL OF BANKING AND FINANCE LAW AND PRACTICE (AT/1034-3040) [I10343040] 2987, **793**

JOURNAL OF BANKING & FINANCE MICROFORM (SZ/0378-4266) [17154745] **793**

JOURNAL OF BANKRUPTCY, LAW, AND PRACTICE (US/1059-048X) [24464652] **793**

JOURNAL OF BASIC AND CLINICAL PHYSIOLOGY AND PHARMACOLOGY (UK/0792-6855) [22939438] 4310, **582**

JOURNAL OF BASIC MICROBIOLOGY (GW/0233-111X) [12062185] **564**

JOURNAL OF BASIC WRITING (US/0147-1635) [03117719] 1897, **3289**

JOURNAL OF BASQUE STUDIES (US/0747-6256) [09145122] **2694**

JOURNAL OF BECKETT STUDIES (US) [27607703] **3399**

JOURNAL OF BEHAVIOR THERAPY AND EXPERIMENTAL PSYCHIATRY (UK/0005-7916) [01800139] **3928**

JOURNAL OF BEHAVIORAL DECISION MAKING (UK/0894-3257) [16014697] **4594**

JOURNAL OF BEHAVIORAL EDUCATION (US/1053-0819) [22447968] 4594, **1880**

JOURNAL OF BEHAVIORAL MEDICINE (US/0160-7715) [03763102] 3593, **4594**

JOURNAL OF BEHAVIORAL OPTOMETRY (US/1045-8395) [20268909] **4216**

●JOURNAL OF BIBLICAL COUNSELING, THE (US/1063-2166) [25929605] **4968**

JOURNAL OF BIBLICAL ETHICS IN MEDICINE (US/1050-3404) [16501448] 4968, **2251**

JOURNAL OF BIBLICAL LITERATURE (US/0021-9231) [01782210] 4968, **5017**

JOURNAL OF BIBLICAL LITERATURE (US/0021-9231) [06207750] **5017**

JOURNAL OF BIBLICAL STORYTELLING (US/1075-0347) [28621224] **5017**

JOURNAL OF BIG BEND STUDIES (US/1058-4617) [19331154] **2740**

JOURNAL OF BIO-FEEDBACK, THE (US/0093-3597) [02242568] **4594**

JOURNAL OF BIOACTIVE AND COMPATIBLE POLYMERS (US/0883-9115) [12245885] **980**

JOURNAL OF BIOCHEMICAL AND BIOPHYSICAL METHODS (NE/0165-022X) [04936947] 495, **489**

●JOURNAL OF BIOCHEMICAL ORGANIZATION (US/1065-9668) [26820653] **489**

JOURNAL OF BIOCHEMICAL TOXICOLOGY (US/0887-2082) [12658406] 489, **3981**

JOURNAL OF BIOCHEMISTRY (TOKYO) (JA/0021-924X) [01782512] **489**

JOURNAL OF BIOCHEMISTRY (TOKYO) (US/0021-924x) [05721687] **489**

JOURNAL OF BIOCOMMUNICATION, THE (US/0094-2499) [02239926] **3593**

JOURNAL OF BIOELECTRICITY **See** ELECTRO- AND MAGNETOBIOLOGY **454**

JOURNAL OF BIOENERGETICS AND BIOMEMBRANES (US/0145-479X) [02569757] **565**

JOURNAL OF BIOGEOGRAPHY (UK/0305-0270) [02240360] **2567**

JOURNAL OF BIOLOGICAL CHEMISTRY, THE (US/0021-9258) [01782222] **489**

JOURNAL OF BIOLOGICAL CONTROL (II/0970-5732) [25929984] **460**

JOURNAL OF BIOLOGICAL CURATION (UK/0958-7608) [21403467] 460, **4090**

JOURNAL OF BIOLOGICAL EDUCATION (UK/0021-9266) [01793228] 1897, **460**

JOURNAL OF BIOLOGICAL PHOTOGRAPHY (US/0274-497X) [06364814] **460**

JOURNAL OF BIOLOGICAL PHYSICS (NE/0092-0606) [01788732] **495**

JOURNAL OF BIOLOGICAL REGULATORS AND HOMEOSTATIC AGENTS (IT/0393-974X) [17597229] **460**

JOURNAL OF BIOLOGICAL RHYTHMS (US/0748-7304) [11000168] **460**

JOURNAL OF BIOLOGICAL SCIENCES RESEARCH (IQ/1010-3910) [11002316] **460**

JOURNAL OF BIOLOGICAL SCIENCES, THE (II/0021-9282) [01800332] **460**

●JOURNAL OF BIOLOGICAL SYSTEMS (SI/0218-3390) [28384826] **460**

JOURNAL OF BIOLUMINESCENCE AND CHEMILUMINESCENCE (UK/0884-3996) [12366428] **495**

JOURNAL OF BIOMATERIALS APPLICATIONS (US/0885-3282) [12617082] **3694**

JOURNAL OF BIOMECHANICAL ENGINEERING (US/0148-0731) [02833687] **3694**

JOURNAL OF BIOMECHANICS (US/0021-9290) [01754470] **582**

JOURNAL OF BIOMEDICAL ENGINEERING (UK/0141-5425) [04812517] **3694**

JOURNAL OF BIOMEDICAL MATERIALS RESEARCH (US/0021-9304) [01784387] **3593**

●JOURNAL OF BIOMEDICAL SCIENCE (SZ/1021-7770) [30039739] **3594**

JOURNAL OF BIOMOLECULAR NMR (NE/0925-2738) [24245932] 495, **461**

JOURNAL OF BIOMOLECULAR STRUCTURE & DYNAMICS (US/0739-1102) [09688706] 980, **461**

JOURNAL OF BIOPHARMACEUTICAL STATISTICS (US/1054-3406) [22850869] 461, **4310**

JOURNAL OF BIOSCIENCES (II/0250-5991) [05871960] **461**

JOURNAL OF BIOSOCIAL SCIENCE (UK/0021-9320) [01754471] **5205**

JOURNAL OF BIOSOCIAL SCIENCE. SUPPLEMENT (UK/0300-9645) [03583494] **5205**

JOURNAL OF BLACK POETRY **See** KITABU CHA JUA **3402**

JOURNAL OF BLACK PSYCHOLOGY, THE (US/0095-7984) [01798722] 2266, **4594**

JOURNAL OF BLACK STUDIES (US/0021-9347) [01799971] **2266**

JOURNAL OF BLACK THEOLOGY IN SOUTH AFRICA (SA/1015-2296) [I10152296] 2266, **4968**

JOURNAL OF BONE AND JOINT SURGERY. AMERICAN VOLUME (PRINT ED.) (US/0021-9355) [01754473] 3966, **3882**

JOURNAL OF BONE AND JOINT SURGERY. BRITISH VOLUME (UK/0301-620X) [01754474] 3882, **3966**

JOURNAL OF BONE AND JOINT SURGERY (COMPUTER FILE), THE (US/1058-2436) [24345961] **3966**

JOURNAL OF BONE AND JOINT SURGERY. QUINQUENNIAL INDEX (US) [07349986] **3966**

JOURNAL OF BONE AND JOINT SURGERY. SUBJECT BIBLIOGRAPHY (US) [07350216] **3966**

JOURNAL OF BONE AND MINERAL RESEARCH (US/0884-0431) [12298460] **3805**

●JOURNAL OF BOOK OF MORMON STUDIES, THE (US/1065-9366) [26797697] **4968**

JOURNAL OF BORDERLAND RESEARCH, THE (US/0897-0394) [11009141] **4241**

JOURNAL OF BORDERLANDS STUDIES (US/0886-5655) [12932204] **2740**

●JOURNAL OF BRAIN IMAGING AND BEHAVIOR (US) **3594**

JOURNAL OF BRAIN RESEARCH (GW) **3834**

JOURNAL OF BRITISH MUSIC THERAPY (UK/0951-5038) [17513092] 3594, **4125**

JOURNAL OF BRITISH PODIATRIC MEDICINE LONDON 1991 (UK/0961-6055) [I09616055] **3918**

JOURNAL OF BRITISH STUDIES, THE (US/0021-9371) [01783237] **2694**

JOURNAL OF BROADCASTING & ELECTRONIC MEDIA (US/0883-8151) [11850577] **1134**

●JOURNAL OF BRONCHOLOGY (US/1070-8030) [28471573] **3950**

JOURNAL OF BRYOLOGY (UK/0373-6687) [01784017] **515**

JOURNAL OF BUDDHIST PHILOSOPHY (US/0741-2193) [10125230] **5021**

JOURNAL OF BUILDING RESEARCH (IQ) **618**

JOURNAL OF BURN CARE & REHABILITATION, THE (US/0273-8481) [06989058] **3594**

JOURNAL OF BUSINESS (US) [13522006] **686**

JOURNAL OF BUSINESS ADMINISTRATION (DHAKA, BANGLADESH) (BG) [17530707] 873, **686**

JOURNAL OF BUSINESS ADMINISTRATION (VANCOUVER) (CN/0021-941X) [01754478] 1498, **686**

JOURNAL OF BUSINESS AND ECONOMIC PERSPECTIVES (US) [10986314] 1498, **686**

JOURNAL OF BUSINESS & ECONOMIC STATISTICS (US/0735-0015) [08854855] 1498, **1534**

JOURNAL OF BUSINESS AND ECONOMIC STUDIES / NORTHEAST BUSINESS AND ECONOMIC ASSOCIATION, THE (US) [25158355] 1498, **686**

JOURNAL OF BUSINESS AND ECONOMIC STUDIES, THE (US) [25003154] 1498, **686**

JOURNAL OF BUSINESS & ENTREPRENEURSHIP (US/1042-6337) [19097072] **686**

JOURNAL OF BUSINESS & FINANCE LIBRARIANSHIP (US/0896-3568) [17009734] 686, **3219**

JOURNAL OF BUSINESS & INDUSTRIAL MARKETING, THE (US/0885-8624) [12762674] **927**

JOURNAL OF BUSINESS AND PSYCHOLOGY (US/0889-3268) [13847167] 686, **4594**

JOURNAL OF BUSINESS AND SOCIAL STUDIES, THE (NR/0021-9428) [02447969] **686**

JOURNAL OF BUSINESS AND SOCIETY (CY/1012-2591) [21102447] **1569**

JOURNAL OF BUSINESS AND TECHNICAL COMMUNICATION (US/1050-6519) [18973702] **1114**

JOURNAL OF BUSINESS (CHICAGO, ILL.), THE (US/0021-9398) [01605755] **686**

JOURNAL OF BUSINESS COMMUNICATION (1973) (US/0021-9436) [08945725] 873, **1114**

●JOURNAL OF BUSINESS ECONOMICS (UK/0962-1369) 686, **1498**

JOURNAL OF BUSINESS ETHICS (NE/0167-4544) [08398838] 686, **2251**

JOURNAL OF BUSINESS FINANCE & ACCOUNTING (UK/0306-686X) [00989252] 793, **746**

JOURNAL OF BUSINESS FORECASTING METHODS & SYSTEMS, THE (US/0278-6087) [07845115] 927, **1592**

JOURNAL OF BUSINESS LAW, THE (UK/0021-9460) [01800097] **3101**

JOURNAL OF BUSINESS LOGISTICS (US/0735-3766) [04304746] 686, **5385**

JOURNAL OF BUSINESS RESEARCH (US/0148-2963) [03291849] **686**

JOURNAL OF BUSINESS (SINGAPORE) (SI/0377-0419) [01790735] **686**

JOURNAL OF BUSINESS STRATEGIES (US/0887-2058) [11793724] 873, **686**

JOURNAL OF BUSINESS STRATEGY, THE (US/0275-6668) [06848182] **686**

●JOURNAL OF BUSINESS-TO-BUSINESS MARKETING (US/1051-712X) [22095614] **927**

JOURNAL OF BUSINESS VALUATION, THE (CN/0703-1947) [03980134] **746**

JOURNAL OF BUSINESS VENTURING (US/0883-9026) [12252477] **686**

JOURNAL OF BYELORUSSIAN STUDIES (UK/0075-4161) [01783783] **3289**

JOURNAL OF C LANGUAGE TRANSLATION, THE (US/1042-5721) [19084893] **1279**

JOURNAL OF CALIFORNIA AND GREAT BASIN ANTHROPOLOGY (US/0191-3557) [04853558] **238**

JOURNAL OF CALIFORNIA LAW ENFORCEMENT (US/0449-5063) [02750892] **3167**

JOURNAL OF CALIFORNIA TAXATION, THE *CEASED.* (US/1046-400X) [20401623] **2987**

JOURNAL OF CAMEROON AFFAIRS (US/0093-8483) [01792423] **2640**

JOURNAL OF CANADIAN ART HISTORY (CN/0315-4297) [01794618] **323**

JOURNAL OF CANADIAN FICTION (CN/0047-2255) [01988792] **3399**

JOURNAL OF CANADIAN PETROLEUM TECHNOLOGY, THE (CN/0021-9487) [01780975] **4262**

JOURNAL OF CANADIAN POETRY (CN/0705-1328) [03963452] 3345, **3464**

JOURNAL OF CANADIAN STUDIES (CN/0021-9495) [00816138] **2740**

JOURNAL OF CANCER (IR/0378-2360) [02429264] **3819**

●JOURNAL OF CANCER CARE (UK/0960-9768) [25238396] **3819**

JOURNAL OF CANCER EDUCATION, THE (US/0885-8195) [12738724] **3819**

JOURNAL OF CANCER RESEARCH AND CLINICAL ONCOLOGY (GW/0171-5216) [04678452] **3819**

JOURNAL OF CARBOHYDRATE CHEMISTRY (US/0732-8303) [08436545] **1042**

●JOURNAL OF CARDIAC FAILURE (US/1071-9164) [28763263] **3706**

JOURNAL OF CARDIAC SURGERY (US/0886-0440) [12817127] **3966**

JOURNAL OF CARDIOLOGY (JA/0914-5087) [18305159] **3706**

JOURNAL OF CARDIOLOGY. SUPPLEMENT (JA) [20999663] **3706**

JOURNAL OF CARDIOPULMONARY REHABILITATION (US/0883-9212) [12159734] **3706**

JOURNAL OF CARDIOTHORACIC AND VASCULAR ANESTHESIA (US/1053-0770) [22448011] **3683**

●JOURNAL OF CARDIOVASCULAR DIAGNOSIS AND PROCEDURES (US/1073-7774) [29527152] **3694**

JOURNAL OF CARDIOVASCULAR ELECTROPHYSIOLOGY (US/1045-3873) [20086266] **3707**

JOURNAL OF CARDIOVASCULAR NURSING, THE (US/0889-4655) [13897469] 3707, **3858**

JOURNAL OF CARDIOVASCULAR PHARMACOLOGY (US/0160-2446) [03646254] 3707, **4310**

JOURNAL OF CARDIOVASCULAR SURGERY (IT/0021-9509) [01754485] 3707, **3966**

JOURNAL OF CARDIOVASCULAR TECHNOLOGY (NEW YORK, N.Y.) (US/1043-4356) [19467980] **3694**

JOURNAL OF CAREER ASSESSMENT (US/1069-0727) [27926913] 4594, **4205**

JOURNAL OF CAREER DEVELOPMENT (US/0894-8453) [11297198] **4206**

JOURNAL OF CAREER PLANNING & EMPLOYMENT (US/0884-5352) [12406394] **4206**

JOURNAL OF CARIBBEAN HISTORY, THE (BB/0047-2263) [01588454] **2741**

JOURNAL OF CARIBBEAN STUDIES (US/0190-2008) [06217126] **2741**

JOURNAL OF CARNIOMANDIBULAR DISORDERS, THE (US/0890-2739) [14191110] **3834**

●JOURNAL OF CASE MANAGEMENT (US/1061-3706) [25277522] **3787**

JOURNAL OF CASH MANAGEMENT (US/0731-1281) [08180463] **873**

JOURNAL OF CATALYSIS (US/0021-9517) [01783064] **1053**

JOURNAL OF CELL BIOLOGY, THE (US/0021-9525) [01390147] **537**

JOURNAL OF CELL SCIENCE (UK/0021-9533) [01754489] **537**

JOURNAL OF CELL SCIENCE. SUPPLEMENT (UK/0269-3518) [11844322] **537**

JOURNAL OF CELLULAR BIOCHEMISTRY (US/0730-2312) [07980584] **489**

JOURNAL OF CELLULAR BIOCHEMISTRY. SUPPLEMENT (US/0733-1959) [08237918] **489**

JOURNAL OF CELLULAR PHARMACOLOGY *CEASED.* (US) [24732206] 489, **4310**

JOURNAL OF CELLULAR PHYSIOLOGY (US/0021-9541) [01794205] 537, **582**

JOURNAL OF CELLULAR PLASTICS (US/0021-955X) [01754491] 980, **4455**

●JOURNAL OF CELTIC LINGUISTICS (UK/0962-1377) [25694065] **3289**

JOURNAL OF CENTRAL ASIA (PK) [05235246] 271, **2655**

JOURNAL OF CENTRE FOR ADVANCED TV STUDIES : JCATS (UK/0308-6801) [07616187] **1134**

JOURNAL OF CEPHALOPOD BIOLOGY *SUSPENDED.* (US/0843-6150) [21344544] **461**

JOURNAL OF CERAMIC HISTORY (UK/0449-5713) [03953023] **2591**

JOURNAL OF CEREAL SCIENCE (UK/0733-5210) [08603019] 5118, **176**

JOURNAL OF CEREBRAL BLOOD FLOW AND METABOLISM (US/0271-678X) [06680300] **582**

JOURNAL OF CHEMICAL AND BIOCHEMICAL KINETICS (US/1058-5834) [24334229] 489, **1054**

JOURNAL OF CHEMICAL AND ENGINEERING DATA (US/0021-9568) [01589690] **2014**

●JOURNAL OF CHEMICAL CRYSTALLOGRAPHY (US/1074-1542) [29608467] **1032**

JOURNAL OF CHEMICAL DEPENDENCY TREATMENT (US/0885-4734) [12676678] **1345**

JOURNAL OF CHEMICAL ECOLOGY (US/0098-0331) [02245984] 980, **2217**

JOURNAL OF CHEMICAL EDUCATION (US/0021-9584) [01754494] 1756, **980**

JOURNAL OF CHEMICAL EDUCATION. SOFTWARE, A *CEASED.* (US/1050-4281) [21487448] **980**

JOURNAL OF CHEMICAL EDUCATION. SOFTWARE, B (US/1050-429X) [20401837] 1288, **980**

JOURNAL OF CHEMICAL EDUCATION. SOFTWARE, C (US/1050-4303) [21487633] 1756, **980**

●JOURNAL OF CHEMICAL EDUCATION. SOFTWARE. D (US/1066-4157) [26943911] **980**

JOURNAL OF CHEMICAL ENGINEERING OF JAPAN (JA/0021-9592) [00818129] **2014**

JOURNAL OF CHEMICAL INDUSTRY AND ENGINEERING (CHINA) *CEASED.* (CC/1000-9027) [10016069] **2014**

JOURNAL OF CHEMICAL INFORMATION AND COMPUTER SCIENCES (US/0095-2338) [02241471] 1191, **980**

JOURNAL OF CHEMICAL NEUROANATOMY (UK/0891-0618) [14558761] **3834**

JOURNAL OF CHEMICAL PHYSICS, THE (US/0021-9606) [01782311] 1054, **4408**

JOURNAL OF CHEMICAL RESEARCH. INDEXES (UK) [04137647] **980**

JOURNAL OF CHEMICAL RESEARCH. MICROFICHE (UK) **980**

JOURNAL OF CHEMICAL RESEARCH. MINIPRINT (UK/0308-2350) [02943808] **980**

JOURNAL OF CHEMICAL RESEARCH. SYNOPSES (UK/0308-2342) [02943752] **980**

JOURNAL OF CHEMICAL SCIENCES (II/0377-8444) [02719706] **980**

JOURNAL OF CHEMICAL TECHNOLOGY AND BIOTECHNOLOGY (1986) (UK/0268-2575) [13284377] 3694, **1026**

JOURNAL OF CHEMICAL THERMODYNAMICS, THE (UK/0021-9614) [01243408] **1054**

JOURNAL OF CHEMICAL TRANSPORT & INDUSTRIAL HISTORY (US/1045-0637) [19990666] **1026**

●JOURNAL OF CHEMICAL VAPOR DEPOSITION (US/1056-7860) [23853118] **980**

JOURNAL OF CHEMOMETRICS (UK/0886-9383) [13041442] **980**

JOURNAL OF CHEMOTHERAPY (FLORENCE) (IT/1120-009X) [19584658] **3594**

JOURNAL OF CHEROKEE STUDIES (US/0146-2962) [02690846] 2741, **2266**

●JOURNAL OF CHICANA STUDIES (US/1065-4690) [26612230] **2741**

JOURNAL OF CHILD AND ADOLESCENT GROUP THERAPY (US/1053-0800) [22447918] **4594**

JOURNAL OF CHILD AND ADOLESCENT PSYCHIATRIC AND MENTAL HEALTH NURSING (US/0897-9685) [17680311] 3858, **3928**

●JOURNAL OF CHILD AND ADOLESCENT PSYCHIATRIC NURSING (US/1073-6077) [29487240] 3928, **3858**

JOURNAL OF CHILD AND ADOLESCENT PSYCHOPHARMACOLOGY (US/1044-5463) [19829651] 4594, **3928**

JOURNAL OF CHILD AND ADOLESCENT PSYCHOTHERAPY *CEASED.* (US/0748-8793) [11031825] **4594**

●JOURNAL OF CHILD & ADOLESCENT SUBSTANCE ABUSE (US/1067-828X) [27359350] **1345**

●JOURNAL OF CHILD AND FAMILY STUDIES (US/1062-1024) [25526090] **2281**

JOURNAL OF CHILD AND YOUTH CARE (CN/0840-982X) [19901113] **5291**

JOURNAL OF CHILD AND YOUTH CARE WORK (US/0741-9481) [10278616] **5291**

JOURNAL OF CHILD-CARE ADMINISTRATION (US/1066-1468) [10661468] 873, **5291**

JOURNAL OF CHILD LANGUAGE (UK/0305-0009) [00974793] **3289**

JOURNAL OF CHILD LAW, THE (UK/0955-4475) [20334075] **2987**

JOURNAL OF CHILD NEUROLOGY (US/0883-0738) [12041143] 3834, **3904**

JOURNAL OF CHILD PSYCHOLOGY AND PSYCHIATRY (UK/0373-8086) [03738086] **4594**

JOURNAL OF CHILD PSYCHOLOGY AND PSYCHIATRY AND ALLIED DISCIPLINES (UK/0021-9630) [01307942] 3904, **4594**

JOURNAL OF CHILD PSYCHOTHERAPY (UK/0075-417X) [01754498] **3928**

●JOURNAL OF CHILD SEXUAL ABUSE (US/1053-8712) [22683562] **5291**

JOURNAL OF CHILDHOOD COMMUNICATION DISORDERS (US/0735-3170) [06849737] **1880**

JOURNAL OF CHILDREN AND YOUTH *SUSPENDED.* (US) [09536371] **1756**

JOURNAL OF CHINESE GEOGRAPHY, THE (SI/0218-1444) [24417846] **2567**

JOURNAL OF CHINESE LAW (US/1041-7567) [14933747] **2987**

JOURNAL OF CHINESE LINGUISTICS (US/0091-3723) [01787085] **3289**

JOURNAL OF CHINESE MEDICINE, THE (UK/0143-8042) [07503477] **3594**

JOURNAL OF CHINESE PHILOSOPHY (US/0301-8121) [01792532] **4350**

JOURNAL OF CHINESE RELIGIONS (US/0737-769X) [09181452] **4968**

JOURNAL OF CHINESE STUDIES (US/0278-2847) [07076763] **2655**

JOURNAL OF CHINESE STUDIES (ALBUQUERQUE, N.M.) (US/0742-5929) [10382137] **2505**

JOURNAL OF CHIROPRACTIC (US/0744-9984) [08239735] **3594**

JOURNAL OF CHIROPRACTIC EDUCATION, THE (US/1042-5055) [19085455] **3805**

JOURNAL OF CHIROPRACTIC TECHNIQUE (US/1062-9920) [25545613] 4380, **3805**

JOURNAL OF CHRISTIAN CAMPING (US/0021-9649) [01696997] **4874**

JOURNAL OF CHRISTIAN COUNSELING (US/0146-0366) [02860202] **4968**

JOURNAL OF CHRISTIAN EDUCATION (AT/0021-9657) [03306795] 1756, **4968**

JOURNAL OF CHRISTIAN HEALING, THE (US/0738-2944) [09563408] **4968**

JOURNAL OF CHRISTIAN JURISPRUDENCE *SUSPENDED.* (US/0741-6075) [06780756] 4968, **2987**

JOURNAL OF CHRISTIAN NURSING (US/0743-2550) [10538989] 4968, **3858**

JOURNAL OF CHRISTIAN RECONSTRUCTION, THE (US/0360-1420) [02243886] **4968**

JOURNAL OF CHROMATOGRAPHIC SCIENCE (US/0021-9665) [01794207] **1016**

JOURNAL OF CHROMATOGRAPHY (NE/0021-9673) [00987924] **1016**

●JOURNAL OF CHROMATOGRAPHY. A (NE) [29336194] **1016**

●JOURNAL OF CHROMATOGRAPHY. B, BIOMEDICAL APPLICATIONS (NE/0378-4347) [29859296] **1017**

JOURNAL OF CHROMATOGRAPHY. BIOMEDICAL APPLICATIONS (NE/0378-4347) [02852944] **980**

JOURNAL OF CHROMATOGRAPHY LIBRARY (NE/0301-4770) [02134146] **981**

JOURNAL

Alphabetical Title Index

JOURNAL OF CHRONIC DISEASES AND THERAPEUTICS RESEARCH (UK/0141-3317) [04214785] **3594**

JOURNAL OF CHURCH AND STATE (US/0021-969X) [01586802] 4968, **4478**

JOURNAL OF CIRCUITS, SYSTEMS, AND COMPUTERS (SI/0218-1266) [24310702] **2068**

●JOURNAL OF CITRICULTURE (US) **176**

JOURNAL OF CIVIL DEFENSE (US/0740-5537) [03876781] **1073**

JOURNAL OF CLASSICAL PHYSICS, THE (US/0730-2886) [07985416] **4408**

JOURNAL OF CLASSIFICATION (US/0176-4268) [11242280] 461, **3512**

JOURNAL OF CLASSROOM INTERACTION, THE (US/0749-4025) [03838812] 4594, **1756**

JOURNAL OF CLASSROOM MANAGEMENT (US/1060-3174) [24930061] **1897**

JOURNAL OF CLEAN TECHNOLOGY AND ENVIRONMENTAL SCIENCES (US/1052-1062) [22187197] **2175**

●JOURNAL OF CLEANER PRODUCTION (UK/0959-6526) [29354752] **1613**

JOURNAL OF CLIMATE (US/0894-8755) [16275228] **1426**

JOURNAL OF CLINICAL AND EXPERIMENTAL GERONTOLOGY **CEASED.** (US/0192-1193) [04988818] **3753**

JOURNAL OF CLINICAL AND EXPERIMENTAL NEUROPSYCHOLOGY (NE/0168-8634) [11772612] 4594, **3834**

JOURNAL OF CLINICAL & LABORATORY IMMUNOLOGY (UK/0141-2760) [04254361] **3673**

JOURNAL OF CLINICAL ANESTHESIA (US/0952-8180) [16797247] **3683**

JOURNAL OF CLINICAL APHERESIS (US/0733-2459) [08542694] **3819**

JOURNAL OF CLINICAL BIOCHEMISTRY AND NUTRITION (JA/0912-0009) [14525916] 4193, **489**

JOURNAL OF CLINICAL CHILD PSYCHOLOGY (US/0047-228X) [01783926] **4594**

JOURNAL OF CLINICAL CHIROPRACTIC (US/0271-4817) [06596699] **4380**

JOURNAL OF CLINICAL COMPUTING (US/0090-1091) [01773908] 1191, **3787**

JOURNAL OF CLINICAL DENTISTRY, THE (US/0895-8831) [16851043] **1326**

JOURNAL OF CLINICAL ELECTROPHYSIOLOGY (US/0892-5070) [15214578] **582**

JOURNAL OF CLINICAL ENDOCRINOLOGY AND METABOLISM, THE (US/0021-972X) [07747175] **3731**

JOURNAL OF CLINICAL ENGINEERING (US/0363-8855) [03015476] **3694**

JOURNAL OF CLINICAL EPIDEMIOLOGY (UK/0895-4356) [16638324] **3735**

JOURNAL OF CLINICAL ETHICS, THE (US/1046-7890) [20521494] 3594, **2251**

JOURNAL OF CLINICAL FORENSIC MEDICINE (UK/1353-1131) **3741**

JOURNAL OF CLINICAL GASTROENTEROLOGY (US/0192-0790) [04817583] **3746**

●JOURNAL OF CLINICAL GEROPSYCHOLOGY (US) 3753, **4595**

JOURNAL OF CLINICAL HEMATOLOGY AND ONCOLOGY **CEASED.** (US/0162-9360) [02255378] 3819, **3772**

JOURNAL OF CLINICAL HYPNOTHERAPY AND HYPNOANALYSIS (US) **2858**

JOURNAL OF CLINICAL IMMUNOASSAY (US/0736-4393) [09125455] **3673**

JOURNAL OF CLINICAL IMMUNOLOGY (US/0271-9142) [06742940] **3673**

JOURNAL OF CLINICAL INVESTIGATION, THE (US/0021-9738) [01445593] **3594**

JOURNAL OF CLINICAL INVESTIGATION. [MICROFICHE], THE (US) **3594**

JOURNAL OF CLINICAL LABORATORY ANALYSIS, THE (US/0887-8013) [13352973] **3594**

JOURNAL OF CLINICAL LABORATORY ASSAY (US) **3594**

JOURNAL OF CLINICAL LASER MEDICINE & SURGERY (US/1044-5471) [19827917] **3967**

JOURNAL OF CLINICAL MICROBIOLOGY (US/0095-1137) [01799460] **565**

JOURNAL OF CLINICAL MONITORING (US/0748-1977) [10897663] **3594**

JOURNAL OF CLINICAL NEURO-OPHTHALMOLOGY (US/0272-846X) [07368366] **3875**

JOURNAL OF CLINICAL NEUROPHYSIOLOGY (US/0736-0258) [09069439] **3834**

JOURNAL OF CLINICAL NEUROSCIENCE (AT/0967-5868) **3594**

●JOURNAL OF CLINICAL NURSING (UK/0962-1067) [25492708] **3858**

JOURNAL OF CLINICAL NUTRITION & GASTROENTEROLOGY, THE **CEASED.** (SP/0214-2880) [15085387] 4193, **3746**

JOURNAL OF CLINICAL ONCOLOGY (US/0732-183X) [08320014] **3819**

JOURNAL OF CLINICAL ORTHODONTICS (US/0022-3875) [01778704] **1326**

JOURNAL OF CLINICAL PATHOLOGY (UK/0021-9746) [01680973] **3895**

JOURNAL OF CLINICAL PATHOLOGY. SUPPLEMENT. ROYAL COLLEGE OF PATHOLOGISTS SYMPOSIA (UK/0144-0330) [10455380] **3895**

JOURNAL OF CLINICAL PEDIATRIC DENTISTRY, THE (US/1053-4628) [22606133] 3904, **1326**

JOURNAL OF CLINICAL PERIODONTOLOGY (DK/0303-6979) [00972525] **1326**

JOURNAL OF CLINICAL PHARMACOLOGY, THE (US/0091-2700) [01580982] **4310**

JOURNAL OF CLINICAL PHARMACY (UK/0308-6593) [03217511] **4310**

JOURNAL OF CLINICAL PHARMACY AND THERAPEUTICS (UK/0269-4727) [15466105] **4310**

JOURNAL OF CLINICAL PRACTICE IN SEXUALITY, THE (US/0898-7386) [17251249] **5187**

JOURNAL OF CLINICAL PSYCHIATRY ADVANCES IN PSYCHIATRIC TREATMENT MONOGRAPH SERIES, THE (US/1056-2141) [23556716] **3928**

JOURNAL OF CLINICAL PSYCHIATRY, THE (US/0160-6689) [03661773] **3928**

●JOURNAL OF CLINICAL PSYCHOANALYSIS (US) [26147230] **3928**

JOURNAL OF CLINICAL PSYCHOLOGY (US/0021-9762) [01348731] **4595**

●JOURNAL OF CLINICAL PSYCHOLOGY IN MEDICAL SETTINGS (US/1068-9583) [27868884] **4595**

JOURNAL OF CLINICAL PSYCHOPHARMACOLOGY (US/0271-0749) [06541910] 4595, **4310**

JOURNAL OF CLINICAL READING: RESEARCH AND PROGRAMS (US) **1756**

●JOURNAL OF CLINICAL RESEARCH AND DRUG DEVELOPMENT (1993) (US/1066-7865) [27049298] **4310**

JOURNAL OF CLINICAL RESEARCH AND PHARMACOEPIDEMIOLOGY (US/1047-0336) [20585075] **4311**

●JOURNAL OF CLINICAL RHEUMATOLOGY (US/1076-1608) [30415935] **3594**

JOURNAL OF CLUSTER SCIENCE (US/1040-7278) [18516182] **981**

JOURNAL OF COAL QUALITY, THE (US/0732-8087) [08435012] **1948**

JOURNAL OF COASTAL RESEARCH (US/0749-0208) [11052665] **1357**

JOURNAL OF COATED FABRICS (US/0093-4658) [01800147] 981, **5353**

JOURNAL OF COFFEE RESEARCH (II/0374-8537) [02255761] **176**

JOURNAL OF COGNITIVE NEUROSCIENCE, THE (US/0898-929X) [17949603] **3835**

JOURNAL OF COGNITIVE PSYCHOTHERAPY, THE (US/0889-8391) [14091508] **4595**

JOURNAL OF COGNITIVE REHABILITATION, THE (US/1062-2969) [23688097] **3835**

JOURNAL OF COLD REGIONS ENGINEERING (US/0887-381X) [13202939] 618, **2025**

JOURNAL OF COLLECTIVE NEGOTIATIONS IN THE PUBLIC SECTOR (US/0047-2301) [01784643] **1682**

JOURNAL OF COLLEGE ADMISSIONS, THE (US/0734-6670) [08693360] **1832**

JOURNAL OF COLLEGE AND ADULT READING AND LEARNING (US/1066-0941) [23934888] **1832**

●JOURNAL OF COLLEGE & UNIVERSITY FOODSERVICE (US/1053-8739) [22683546] 1832, **2345**

JOURNAL OF COLLEGE AND UNIVERSITY LAW, THE (US/0093-8688) [01792838] 1832, **2987**

JOURNAL OF COLLEGE AND UNIVERSITY STUDENT HOUSING, THE (US/0161-827X) [03714601] **1832**

JOURNAL OF COLLEGE MANAGEMENT (UK) 1865, **1832**

JOURNAL OF COLLEGE READING AND LEARNING (US) [11557366] **1832**

JOURNAL OF COLLEGE SCIENCE TEACHING (US/0047-231X) [01783456] 1832, **5118**

JOURNAL OF COLLEGE STUDENT DEVELOPMENT (US/0897-5264) [17539103] **1832**

JOURNAL OF COLLEGE STUDENT PSYCHOTHERAPY (US/8756-8225) [11664095] **4595**

JOURNAL OF COLLOID AND INTERFACE SCIENCE (US/0021-9797) [01793620] **1054**

●JOURNAL OF COMBINATORIAL DESIGNS (US/1063-8539) [26150211] 5329, **3512**

JOURNAL OF COMBINATORIAL THEORY. SERIES A (US/0097-3165) [01644967] **3512**

JOURNAL OF COMBINATORIAL THEORY. SERIES B (US/0095-8956) [00899380] 5118, **3512**

JOURNAL OF COMBINATORICS, INFORMATION & SYSTEM SCIENCES (II/0250-9628) [03727676] **3512**

JOURNAL OF COMMERCE AND COMMERCIAL **See** IMPORT BULLETIN **839**

JOURNAL OF COMMERCE & INDUSTRY **See** JOURNAL OF COMMERCE, INDUSTRY & TRANSPORTATION **842**

JOURNAL OF COMMERCE. EXPORT BULLETIN (NEW YORK, N.Y. : 1978) (US) [13685995] **842**

JOURNAL OF COMMERCE, INDUSTRY & TRANSPORTATION (LB/0303-9293) [01798664] 1613, **842**

JOURNAL OF COMMERCE TRANSPORTATION TELEPHONE TICKLER, THE **See** TRANSPORTATION TELEPHONE TICKLER **5397**

JOURNAL OF COMMERCE (VANCOUVER) (CN/0709-1230) [05385341] **842**

JOURNAL OF COMMERCIAL BANK LENDING **See** JOURNAL OF COMMERCIAL LENDING, THE **793**

●JOURNAL OF COMMERCIAL LENDING, THE (US/1062-6271) [25162070] **793**

JOURNAL OF COMMON MARKET STUDIES (UK/0021-9886) [01587552] **1569**

JOURNAL OF COMMONWEALTH & COMPARATIVE POLITICS, THE (UK/0306-3631) [02240097] **4478**

JOURNAL OF COMMONWEALTH LITERATURE (UK/0021-9894) [01623556] **3399**

JOURNAL OF COMMUNICABLE DISEASES (II/0019-5138) [01680814] 3714, **4786**

JOURNAL OF COMMUNICATION (US/0021-9916) [01754508] **1114**

JOURNAL OF COMMUNICATION AND RELIGION, THE (US/0894-2838) [15692372] **4968**

●JOURNAL OF COMMUNICATION AND TRANSFORMATIONAL MYTH (US/1064-752X) [26388210] 3399, **2321**

JOURNAL OF COMMUNICATION DISORDERS (US/0021-9924) [01037366] **3835**

JOURNAL OF COMMUNICATION INQUIRY, THE (US/0196-8599) [04047986] **1114**

JOURNAL OF COMMUNICATION THERAPY (US/0734-4368) [08731016] 1114, **4595**

JOURNAL OF COMMUNICATIONS TECHNOLOGY (US/1047-0492) [20589091] **1159**

●JOURNAL OF COMMUNICATIONS TECHNOLOGY & ELECTRONICS (US/1064-2269) [26279469] **2068**

JOURNAL OF COMMUNIST STUDIES **See** JOURNAL OF COMMUNIST STUDIES AND TRANSITION POLITICS, THE **4542**

JOURNAL OF COMMUNIST STUDIES AND TRANSITION POLITICS, THE (UK) **4542**

JOURNAL OF COMMUNIST STUDIES, THE (UK/0268-4535) [12639747] **4542**

JOURNAL OF COMMUNITY AND APPLIED SOCIAL PSYCHOLOGY (UK/1052-9284) [22416060] 4595, **5249**

JOURNAL OF COMMUNITY COMMUNICATION, THE (US/0194-2158) [05343905] 5249, **1114**

JOURNAL OF COMMUNITY EDUCATION **CEASED.** (UK/0263-5909) [102635909] **1756**

JOURNAL OF COMMUNITY GARDENING (US/0738-632X) [09659905] **2421**

●JOURNAL OF COMMUNITY GUIDANCE AND RESEARCH (II/0970-1346) [27980158] **4595**

JOURNAL OF COMMUNITY HEALTH (US/0094-5145) [02244911] **4786**

JOURNAL OF COMMUNITY HEALTH NURSING (US/0737-0016) [09298236] **3858**

Alphabetical Title Index — JOURNAL

JOURNAL OF COMMUNITY NURSING (UK) **3858**

●JOURNAL OF COMMUNITY PRACTICE (US/1070-5422) [28403957] **2826**

JOURNAL OF COMMUNITY PSYCHOLOGY (US/0090-4392) [01785233] **4595**

JOURNAL OF COMPARATIVE CULTURES, THE *CEASED.* (US/0363-6666) [01775578] **5249**

JOURNAL OF COMPARATIVE ECONOMICS (US/0147-5967) [03201654] **1592**

JOURNAL OF COMPARATIVE FAMILY STUDIES (CN/0047-2328) [01792159] **2281**

JOURNAL OF COMPARATIVE LITERATURE & AESTHETICS (II/0252-8169) [08714643] 3399, **354**

JOURNAL OF COMPARATIVE NEUROLOGY (1911) (US/0021-9967) [01697212] **3835**

JOURNAL OF COMPARATIVE PATHOLOGY (UK/0021-9975) [01641333] 5513, **3895**

JOURNAL OF COMPARATIVE PHYSICAL EDUCATION AND SPORT / ISCPES, INTERNATIONAL SOCIETY ON COMPARATIVE PHYSICAL EDUCATION AND SPORT (GW/1010-8262) [23245200] 4901, **1856**

JOURNAL OF COMPARATIVE PHYSIOLOGY. A, SENSORY, NEURAL, AND BEHAVIORAL PHYSIOLOGY (GW/0340-7594) [10697832] 3835, **582**

JOURNAL OF COMPARATIVE PHYSIOLOGY. B, BIOCHEMICAL, SYSTEMIC, AND ENVIRONMENTAL PHYSIOLOGY (GW/0174-1578) [10697806] **582**

JOURNAL OF COMPARATIVE PSYCHOLOGY (1983) (US/0735-7036) [08997203] **4595**

JOURNAL OF COMPENSATION AND BENEFITS (US/0893-780X) [12407824] **1682**

JOURNAL OF COMPLEXITY (US/0885-064X) [12561539] **3512**

JOURNAL OF COMPOSITE MATERIALS (US/0021-9983) [01754514] **2103**

JOURNAL OF COMPOSITES TECHNOLOGY & RESEARCH (US/0884-6804) [12170326] **2103**

JOURNAL OF COMPREHENSIVE HEALTH IN SOUTH AFRICA (SA) **4786**

JOURNAL OF COMPUTATIONAL ACOUSTICS (SI/0218-396X) **4452**

JOURNAL OF COMPUTATIONAL AND APPLIED MATHEMATICS (NE/0377-0427) [02246023] **3512**

●JOURNAL OF COMPUTATIONAL AND GRAPHICAL STATISTICS (US/1061-8600) [25481718] **5329**

●JOURNAL OF COMPUTATIONAL BIOLOGY (US/1066-5277) [26981925] **461**

JOURNAL OF COMPUTATIONAL CHEMISTRY (US/0192-8651) [05081734] **981**

JOURNAL OF COMPUTATIONAL MATHEMATICS (CC/0254-9409) [10987539] **3512**

JOURNAL OF COMPUTATIONAL NEUROSCIENCE (NE/0929-5313) **3835**

JOURNAL OF COMPUTATIONAL PHYSICS (US/0021-9991) [01640027] 3512, **4408**

JOURNAL OF COMPUTER ABSTRACTS AND RESEARCH (US/1077-6265) [30842834] 1191, **1209**

JOURNAL OF COMPUTER AIDED MATERIALS DESIGN (NE/0928-1045) **1191**

JOURNAL OF COMPUTER-AIDED MOLECULAR DESIGN (NE/0920-654X) [15036814] 1234, 1282, **1229**

●JOURNAL OF COMPUTER AND SOFTWARE ENGINEERING (US/1069-5451) [28095457] **1230**

JOURNAL OF COMPUTER AND SYSTEM SCIENCES (US/0022-0000) [01754515] 3512, **1247**

●JOURNAL OF COMPUTER AND SYSTEMS SCIENCES INTERNATIONAL (US/1064-2307) [26271520] **1191**

JOURNAL OF COMPUTER ASSISTED LEARNING (UK/0266-4909) [10970768] **1223**

JOURNAL OF COMPUTER-ASSISTED MICROSCOPY (US/1040-7286) [18516208] **1223**

JOURNAL OF COMPUTER ASSISTED TOMOGRAPHY (US/0363-8715) [02986385] **3942**

JOURNAL OF COMPUTER-BASED INSTRUCTION (US/0098-597X) [02242252] **1223**

JOURNAL OF COMPUTER INFORMATION SYSTEMS, THE (US/0887-4417) [12829623] **1260**

JOURNAL OF COMPUTER SCIENCE AND TECHNOLOGY (CC/1000-9000) [20699620] **1191**

JOURNAL OF COMPUTER SCIENCE EDUCATION (US) 1756, **1192**

JOURNAL OF COMPUTER SECURITY (NE/0926-227X) **1227**

JOURNAL OF COMPUTERS IN MATHEMATICS AND SCIENCE TEACHING, THE (US/0731-9258) [08272789] 1897, **1224**

JOURNAL OF COMPUTING & SOCIETY *CEASED.* (US/1044-0755) [19681690] **5205**

JOURNAL OF COMPUTING IN CHILDHOOD EDUCATION (US/1043-1055) [19300114] 1804, **1224**

JOURNAL OF COMPUTING IN CIVIL ENGINEERING (US/0887-3801) [13202903] 1192, **2025**

JOURNAL OF COMPUTING IN HIGHER EDUCATION (US/1042-1726) [18963913] 1224, **1832**

JOURNAL OF COMPUTING IN TEACHER EDUCATION (US/1040-2454) [18356494] 1192, **1897**

JOURNAL OF CONCHOLOGY (UK/0022-0019) [06988449] **5587**

JOURNAL OF CONFEDERATE HISTORY *See* JOURNAL OF CONFEDERATE HISTORY SERIES **2741**

●JOURNAL OF CONFEDERATE HISTORY SERIES (US) [26758517] **2741**

JOURNAL OF CONFLICT RESOLUTION, THE (US/0022-0027) [01623560] **4527**

●JOURNAL OF CONFLICT STUDIES (CN/1198-8614) **4527**

JOURNAL OF CONFUCIUS, THE GRAND MASTER OF ALL AGES, THE (HK) [10973096] **433**

JOURNAL OF CONSTITUTIONAL AND PARLIAMENTARY STUDIES (II/0022-0043) [01754517] 4478, **2987**

JOURNAL OF CONSTRUCTION ACCOUNTING & TAXATION (US/1054-3007) [22835628] 746, **618**

JOURNAL OF CONSTRUCTION ENGINEERING AND MANAGEMENT (US/0733-9364) [08675438] 618, **2025**

JOURNAL OF CONSTRUCTIONAL STEEL RESEARCH (UK/0143-974X) [07422277] 2025, **618**

●JOURNAL OF CONSTRUCTIVIST PSYCHOLOGY (US/1072-0537) [28855385] **4595**

JOURNAL OF CONSULTING AND CLINICAL PSYCHOLOGY (US/0022-006X) [01590721] **4595**

JOURNAL OF CONSUMER AFFAIRS, THE (US/0022-0078) [01754518] **1297**

JOURNAL OF CONSUMER MARKETING, THE (UK/0736-3761) [09113615] **927**

JOURNAL OF CONSUMER POLICY (NE/0168-7034) [09601413] 2987, **1297**

●JOURNAL OF CONSUMER PSYCHOLOGY: OFFICIAL JOURNAL OF THE SOCIETY FOR CONSUMER PSYCHOLOGY (US/1057-7408) [24111393] 1297, **761**

JOURNAL OF CONSUMER RESEARCH, THE (US/0093-5301) [01794673] **927**

JOURNAL OF CONSUMER SATISFACTION, DISSATISFACTION, AND COMPLAINING BEHAVIOR (US/0899-8620) [18241276] **1297**

JOURNAL OF CONSUMER STUDIES AND HOME ECONOMICS (UK/0309-3891) [03616619] 2791, **1298**

JOURNAL OF CONTAMINANT HYDROLOGY (NE/0169-7722) [13775695] **1415**

JOURNAL OF CONTEMPLATIVE PSYCHOTHERAPY (US/0894-8577) [16274743] **3928**

JOURNAL OF CONTEMPORARY AFRICAN STUDIES : JCAS (SA/0258-9001) [08662402] 5206, **2848**

JOURNAL OF CONTEMPORARY ART (US/0897-2400) [17432962] **354**

JOURNAL OF CONTEMPORARY ASIA (UK/0047-2336) [01586065] 5206, **2655**

JOURNAL OF CONTEMPORARY CRIMINAL JUSTICE (US/1043-9862) [06155314] **3167**

JOURNAL OF CONTEMPORARY ETHNOGRAPHY (US/0891-2416) [14687529] 238, **5249**

JOURNAL OF CONTEMPORARY HEALTH LAW AND POLICY, THE (US/0882-1046) [11745921] **2987**

JOURNAL OF CONTEMPORARY HISTORY (UK/0022-0094) [01783199] **2621**

JOURNAL OF CONTEMPORARY LAW (US/0097-9937) [01205166] **2987**

JOURNAL OF CONTEMPORARY LEGAL ISSUES (US/0896-5595) [17198153] **2987**

JOURNAL OF CONTEMPORARY MATHEMATICAL ANALYSIS (US/1068-3623) [25645442] **3512**

JOURNAL OF CONTEMPORARY PHYSICS (US/1068-3372) [25678517] **4408**

JOURNAL OF CONTEMPORARY PSYCHOTHERAPY (US/0022-0116) [01790808] **4595**

JOURNAL OF CONTEMPORARY THOUGHT (II) [24866391] **2505**

●JOURNAL OF CONTINGENCIES AND CRISIS MANAGEMENT (UK/0966-0879) [28637696] **873**

JOURNAL OF CONTINUING EDUCATION IN HOSPITAL & CLINICAL PHARMACY, THE (US/0163-481X) [04398344] **4311**

JOURNAL OF CONTINUING EDUCATION IN NURSING, THE (US/0022-0124) [01783530] **3858**

JOURNAL OF CONTINUING EDUCATION IN THE HEALTH PROFESSIONS, THE (CN/0894-1912) [15863225] **3594**

JOURNAL OF CONTINUING HIGHER EDUCATION, THE (US/0737-7363) [09348566] **1832**

JOURNAL OF CONTINUING MEDICAL EDUCATION (CN/0712-9912) [09096394] 1756, **3594**

JOURNAL OF CONTINUING SOCIAL WORK EDUCATION (US/0276-0878) [07312805] 5291, **1756**

JOURNAL OF CONTRACT LAW (AT/1030-7230) [18060232] **2987**

JOURNAL OF CONTROLLED RELEASE (NE/0168-3659) [11301964] **981**

JOURNAL OF COOPERATIVE EDUCATION (US/0022-0132) [01754522] **1756**

JOURNAL OF COORDINATION CHEMISTRY (US/0095-8972) [01754523] **981**

JOURNAL OF COPTIC STUDIES (BE/1016-5584) [24612988] **2640**

JOURNAL OF CORPORATE ACCOUNTING AND FINANCE (US/1044-8136) [19909880] **746**

JOURNAL OF CORPORATE DISCLOSURE AND CONFIDENTIALITY *CEASED.* (US/1052-3405) [20896752] **3101**

JOURNAL OF CORPORATE FINANCE (NE/0929-1199) **793**

●JOURNAL OF CORPORATE MANAGEMENT, THE (AT/1038-2410) [I10382410] 873, **3101**

JOURNAL OF CORPORATE TAXATION, THE (US/0094-0593) [01793612] **4734**

JOURNAL OF CORPORATION LAW, THE (US/0360-795X) [01723653] **3101**

JOURNAL OF CORRECTIONAL EDUCATION (1974) (US/0740-2708) [07109772] **3167**

JOURNAL OF COST ANALYSIS, THE (US/0882-3871) [11161242] **747**

●JOURNAL OF COST MANAGEMENT (US) [25500412] **3482**

JOURNAL OF COST MANAGEMENT FOR THE MANUFACTURING INDUSTRY (US/0899-5141) [16766963] 3482, **873**

JOURNAL OF COUNSELING AND DEVELOPMENT (US/0748-9633) [11046863] **1913**

JOURNAL OF COUNSELING AND HUMAN SERVICE PROFESSIONS (US/0887-5502) [13306623] **4595**

JOURNAL OF COUNSELING PSYCHOLOGY (US/0022-0167) [01782942] **4595**

JOURNAL OF COUNTRY MUSIC, THE (US/0092-0517) [01788743] **4126**

JOURNAL OF COUPLES THERAPY (US/0897-4446) [17501848] 4596, **2281**

JOURNAL OF CRANIO-MAXILLO-FACIAL SURGERY (GW/1010-5182) [15347571] **3967**

JOURNAL OF CRANIOFACIAL GENETICS AND DEVELOPMENTAL BIOLOGY (DK/0270-4145) [06411603] **3805**

JOURNAL OF CRANIOFACIAL GENETICS AND DEVELOPMENTAL BIOLOGY. SUPPLEMENT (US/0890-6661) [12616123] **582**

JOURNAL OF CRANIOFACIAL SURGERY, THE (CN/1049-2275) [21186847] **3967**

JOURNAL OF CRANIOMANDIBULAR DISORDERS *See* JOURNAL OF OROFACIAL PAIN **3837**

JOURNAL OF CREATIVE BEHAVIOR, THE (US/0022-0175) [01714749] **4596**

●JOURNAL OF CREATIVE VISUAL LEARNING, THE (US/1061-8694) [25484890] **1756**

●JOURNAL OF CREATIVE WRITING AND BIBLIOTHERAPY, THE (US/1065-755X) [26716480] 3399, **2921**

JOURNAL OF CRIME & JUSTICE (US/0735-648X) [08420063] **3167**

JOURNAL OF CRIMINAL JUSTICE (US/0047-2352) [01788590] **3167**

JOURNAL — Alphabetical Title Index

JOURNAL OF CRIMINAL JUSTICE EDUCATION (US/1051-1253) [21878534] **3167**

JOURNAL OF CRIMINAL LAW & CRIMINOLOGY (US/0091-4169) [01038922] **3107**

JOURNAL OF CRIMINAL LAW & CRIMINOLOGY. [MICROFILM], THE (US/0091-4169) [05816671] **3107**

JOURNAL OF CRIMINAL LAW (HERTFORD) (UK/0022-0183) [01754526] **3107**

JOURNAL OF CRITICAL ANALYSIS, THE *CEASED.* (US/0022-0213) [01800050] **1756**

JOURNAL OF CRITICAL CARE (US/0883-9441) [12257697] **3594**

JOURNAL OF CRITICAL ILLNESS, THE (US/1040-0257) [14037293] **3595**

JOURNAL OF CROATIAN STUDIES (US/0075-4218) [01783040] **3289**

JOURNAL OF CROSS-CULTURAL GERONTOLOGY (NE/0169-3816) [12823676] **3753**

JOURNAL OF CROSS-CULTURAL PSYCHOLOGY (US/0022-0221) [01587107] 238, **4596**

JOURNAL OF CRUSTACEAN BIOLOGY (US/0278-0372) [07639032] **555**

JOURNAL OF CRYPTOLOGY (US/0933-2790) [18181851] **3512**

JOURNAL OF CRYSTAL GROWTH (NE/0022-0248) [01604674] **1032**

JOURNAL OF CRYSTALLOGRAPHIC AND SPECTROSCOPIC RESEARCH (US/0277-8068) [07645712] **1032**

●JOURNAL OF CULINARY PRACTICE *SUSPENDED.* (US/1052-9241) [22411285] **2346**

●JOURNAL OF CULTURAL DIVERSITY (US/1071-5568) [28678808] **5206**

JOURNAL OF CULTURAL ECONOMICS (NE/0885-2545) [04706319] 1498, **323**

JOURNAL OF CULTURAL GEOGRAPHY (US/0887-3631) [06826289] **2567**

JOURNAL OF CUNEIFORM STUDIES (US/0022-0256) [01782513] **3290**

JOURNAL OF CURRENT BIOSCIENCES (II/0256-0011) [11585556] 461, **489**

●JOURNAL OF CURRENT ISSUES AND RESEARCH IN ADVERTISING (US/1064-1734) [25864037] **761**

JOURNAL OF CURRENT LASER ABSTRACTS (CN/0022-0264) [06534334] 4435, **4426**

JOURNAL OF CURRENT PODIATRIC MEDICINE, THE *CEASED.* (US/0893-2034) [14077134] **3918**

JOURNAL OF CURRENT SOCIAL ISSUES (US/0041-7211) [02240706] **4968**

JOURNAL OF CURRICULUM AND SUPERVISION (US/0882-1232) [11769028] **1897**

JOURNAL OF CURRICULUM STUDIES (UK/0022-0272) [01754529] **1898**

JOURNAL OF CURRITUCK COUNTY HISTORICAL SOCIETY, THE (US/0091-9640) [01786729] **2741**

●JOURNAL OF CUSTOMER SERVICE IN MARKETING & MANAGEMENT (US/1069-2533) [27965159] 927, **873**

JOURNAL OF CUTANEOUS AGING & COSMETIC DERMATOLOGY *CEASED.* (US/0894-0061) [15724850] **3721**

JOURNAL OF CUTANEOUS PATHOLOGY (DK/0303-6987) [00972411] 3895, **3721**

JOURNAL OF CYTOLOGY AND GENETICS, THE (II/0253-7605) [05118989] 548, **537**

JOURNAL OF DAIRY RESEARCH, THE (UK/0022-0299) [01754531] **195**

JOURNAL OF DAIRY SCIENCE (US/0022-0302) [01800266] **195**

●JOURNAL OF DAIRYING FOODS & HOME SCIENCES (II) **196**

JOURNAL OF DANISH ARCHAEOLOGY (DK/0108-464X) [09388292] **271**

JOURNAL OF DATA & COMPUTER COMMUNICATIONS *CEASED.* (US/1054-089X) [18329216] 1159, **1260**

JOURNAL OF DATABASE ADMINISTRATION (US/1047-9430) [20818541] **1192**

●JOURNAL OF DATABASE MANAGEMENT (US/1063-8016) [26139845] **1254**

JOURNAL OF DAY CARE ADMINISTRATION (US) 873, **5291**

JOURNAL OF DECORATIVE AND PROPAGANDA ARTS, THE (US/0888-7314) [13728363] **373**

JOURNAL OF DEMOCRACY (US/1045-5736) [20333981] **4478**

JOURNAL OF DENTAL EDUCATION (US/0022-0337) [01800296] **1326**

JOURNAL OF DENTAL HYGIENE (US/1043-254X) [18792954] **1326**

JOURNAL OF DENTAL RESEARCH (US/0022-0345) [01754534] **1326**

JOURNAL OF DENTISTRY (UK/0300-5712) [01778716] **1326**

JOURNAL OF DENTISTRY FOR CHILDREN (US/0022-0353) [01586413] **1326**

JOURNAL OF DEPRESSION & STRESS (US) 4596, **3928**

●JOURNAL OF DERIVATIVES, THE (US/1074-1240) [28599438] **904**

JOURNAL OF DERMATOLOGIC SURGERY AND ONCOLOGY *See* DERMATOLOGIC SURGERY **3719**

JOURNAL OF DERMATOLOGIC SURGERY AND ONCOLOGY, THE (US/0148-0812) [03060181] 3721, **3967**

JOURNAL OF DERMATOLOGICAL SCIENCE (NE/0923-1811) [21319893] **3721**

JOURNAL OF DERMATOLOGICAL TREATMENT, THE (UK/0954-6634) [20763077] **3721**

JOURNAL OF DERMATOLOGY, THE (JA/0385-2407) [01781899] **3721**

JOURNAL OF DESIGN AND MANUFACTURING (UK/0962-4694) [25529900] 1982, **3482**

JOURNAL OF DESIGN HISTORY (UK/0952-4649) [18336226] **2099**

JOURNAL OF DEVELOPING AREAS, THE (US/0022-037X) [01624404] 1569, **2910**

JOURNAL OF DEVELOPING SOCIETIES (NE/0169-796X) [13047827] **2621**

JOURNAL OF DEVELOPMENT AND ADMINISTRATIVE STUDIES, THE (NP) [05791323] 4658, **1613**

JOURNAL OF DEVELOPMENT COMMUNICATION, THE (MY/0128-3863) [23609941] 2921, **1114**

JOURNAL OF DEVELOPMENT ECONOMICS (NE/0304-3878) [01292659] **1569**

JOURNAL OF DEVELOPMENT PLANNING (US/0085-2392) [01754535] 1569, **1637**

JOURNAL OF DEVELOPMENT STUDIES, THE (UK/0022-0388) [01754536] **1569**

JOURNAL OF DEVELOPMENTAL AND BEHAVIORAL PEDIATRICS (US/0196-206X) [05780657] 3928, **3904**

JOURNAL OF DEVELOPMENTAL AND PHYSICAL DISABILITIES (US/1056-263X) [23606603] **4389**

JOURNAL OF DEVELOPMENTAL DISABILITIES, THE *SUSPENDED.* (US/0097-8892) [01799462] **4389**

JOURNAL OF DEVELOPMENTAL EDUCATION (US/0894-3907) [11173908] **1756**

JOURNAL OF DEVELOPMENTAL PHYSIOLOGY (UK/0141-9846) [05152455] 582, **3763**

JOURNAL OF DHARMA (II/0253-7222) [02350712] 4350, **4968**

●JOURNAL OF DIABETES AND ITS COMPLICATIONS (US/1056-8727) [23882563] **3731**

JOURNAL OF DIABETES MANAGEMENT (US/0895-0652) [16438548] **3731**

JOURNAL OF DIABETIC COMPLICATIONS *See* JOURNAL OF DIABETES AND ITS COMPLICATIONS **3731**

JOURNAL OF DIAGNOSTIC MEDICAL SONOGRAPHY (US/8756-4793) [11570399] **3595**

JOURNAL OF DIETETIC SOFTWARE *SUSPENDED.* (US/0742-826X) [10462325] **4193**

JOURNAL OF DIFFERENTIAL EQUATIONS (US/0022-0396) [01754537] **3512**

JOURNAL OF DIFFERENTIAL GEOMETRY (US/0022-040X) [01796299] **3512**

JOURNAL OF DIGITAL IMAGING (US/0897-1889) [17429647] **3942**

JOURNAL OF DIRECT MARKETING (US/0892-0591) [15071375] **927**

JOURNAL OF DISABILITY (US/1047-1448) [20612441] **4389**

JOURNAL OF DISABILITY POLICY STUDIES, THE (US/1044-2073) [19730450] **4389**

JOURNAL OF DISPERSION SCIENCE AND TECHNOLOGY (US/0193-2691) [05156318] **4428**

JOURNAL OF DISPUTE RESOLUTION (US/1052-2859) [18929963] **2987**

JOURNAL OF DISTANCE EDUCATION / REVUE DE L'ENSEIGNEMENT A DISTANCE (CN/0830-0445) [15482793] **1756**

JOURNAL OF DIVORCE & REMARRIAGE (US/1050-2556) [21431397] 3121, **2281**

JOURNAL OF DOCUMENT AND TEXT MANAGEMENT (UK) 3219, **1192**

JOURNAL OF DOCUMENTATION (UK/0022-0418) [01754538] **3219**

JOURNAL OF DOCUMENTATION PROJECT MANAGEMENT *CEASED.* (US/0891-5865) [14918704] **1192**

JOURNAL OF DRAMATIC THEORY AND CRITICISM (US/0888-3203) [13452245] **5365**

JOURNAL OF DRUG DEVELOPMENT (UK/0952-9500) [17958950] **4311**

JOURNAL OF DRUG EDUCATION (US/0047-2379) [01022664] **1345**

JOURNAL OF DRUG ISSUES (US/0022-0426) [01754539] **1346**

JOURNAL OF DRUG RESEARCH (UA/0368-1866) [02254228] **4311**

●JOURNAL OF DRUG TARGETING (US/1061-186X) [25218475] **4311**

●JOURNAL OF DRUG THERPAY IN NEUROLOGICAL DISORDERS (US) 4311, **3835**

JOURNAL OF DURASSIAN STUDIES (US/1059-0196) [23251416] **3399**

●JOURNAL OF DYNAMIC AND CONTROL SYSTEMS (US) **2118**

JOURNAL OF DYNAMIC SYSTEMS, MEASUREMENT, AND CONTROL (US/0022-0434) [01585805] **1982**

JOURNAL OF DYNAMICS AND DIFFERENTIAL EQUATIONS (US/1040-7294) [18516267] **3512**

JOURNAL OF EARLY ADOLESCENCE, THE (US/0272-4316) [06842183] **4596**

●JOURNAL OF EARLY CHRISTIAN STUDIES (US/1067-6341) [27316330] **4968**

JOURNAL OF EARLY INTERVENTION (US/1053-8151) [19753071] 1804, **1880**

JOURNAL OF EARLY SOUTHERN DECORATIVE ARTS (US/0098-9266) [03164140] **373**

JOURNAL OF EARTH SCIENCES, NAGOYA UNIVERSITY, THE (JA/0022-0442) [01588646] **1357**

JOURNAL OF EAST AND WEST STUDIES (KO) [01790358] **4479**

JOURNAL OF EAST ASIAN AFFAIRS, THE (KO/1010-1608) [07718220] **2655**

●JOURNAL OF EAST ASIAN LINGUISTICS (NE/0925-8558) [25986900] **3290**

JOURNAL OF EAST TENNESSEE HISTORY (US) **2741**

JOURNAL OF EAST TENNESSEE HISTORY, THE (US/1058-2126) [23044540] **2741**

●JOURNAL OF EAST-WEST BUSINESS (US/1066-9868) [27117143] **686**

JOURNAL OF EASTERN AFRICAN RESEARCH & DEVELOPMENT (KE/0251-0405) [02205669] **2640**

JOURNAL OF ECCLESIASTICAL HISTORY, THE (UK/0022-0469) [01604275] **4968**

JOURNAL OF ECOBIOLOGY (II/0970-9037) [21438867] **2217**

JOURNAL OF ECOLOGY, THE (UK/0022-0477) [01754541] **515**

JOURNAL OF ECONOMETRICS (NE/0304-4076) [01788577] **1592**

●JOURNAL OF ECONOMIC AND SOCIAL INTELLIGENCE (UK) [27697737] **5206**

JOURNAL OF ECONOMIC AND SOCIAL MEASUREMENT (US/0747-9662) [10842209] **5206**

JOURNAL OF ECONOMIC AND TAXONOMIC BOTANY (II/0250-9768) [07717713] **515**

JOURNAL OF ECONOMIC ARCHAEOLOGY, THE (US/1050-3986) [21474974] **2781**

JOURNAL OF ECONOMIC BEHAVIOR & ORGANIZATION (NE/0167-2681) [06974696] **1498**

JOURNAL OF ECONOMIC COOPERATION AMONG ISLAMIC COUNTRIES (TU) [08332773] **1498**

JOURNAL OF ECONOMIC DEVELOPMENT (KO/0254-8372) [06022672] **1498**

JOURNAL OF ECONOMIC DYNAMICS & CONTROL (NE/0165-1889) [05380104] **1499**

JOURNAL OF ECONOMIC EDUCATION, THE (US/0022-0485) [01251432] **1499**

JOURNAL OF ECONOMIC ENTOMOLOGY (US/0022-0493) [01782240] 4245, **5610**

JOURNAL OF ECONOMIC GROWTH *CEASED.* (US/0897-1862) [16503616] **1499**

JOURNAL OF ECONOMIC HISTORY, THE (US/0022-0507) [01782353] **1569**

●JOURNAL OF ECONOMIC INTEGRATION (KO/1015-356X) [27365434] **1637**

JOURNAL

JOURNAL OF ECONOMIC LITERATURE (US/0022-0515) [01788942] 1499, **1535**

JOURNAL OF ECONOMIC PERSPECTIVES, THE (US/0895-3309) [16474127] **1499**

JOURNAL OF ECONOMIC PSYCHOLOGY (NE/0167-4870) [07754472] **1593**

JOURNAL OF ECONOMIC REFORM AND TRANSFORMATION **CEASED.** (UK/0964-0428) **1637**

JOURNAL OF ECONOMIC STUDIES (BRADFORD) (UK/0144-3585) [01001112] **1499**

JOURNAL OF ECONOMIC SURVEYS (UK/0950-0804) [16274457] **1570**

JOURNAL OF ECONOMIC THEORY (US/0022-0531) [01754545] 3512, **1593**

JOURNAL OF ECONOMICS (US/0361-6576) [02247103] **1499**

JOURNAL OF ECONOMICS AND BUSINESS (US/0148-6195) [01754546] 687, **1499**

JOURNAL OF ECONOMICS AND FINANCE (US/1055-0925) [21120643] 794, **1499**

JOURNAL OF ECONOMICS AND INTERNATIONAL RELATIONS **SUSPENDED.** (HK/1013-1809) [17763052] **1570**

●JOURNAL OF ECONOMICS & MANAGEMENT STRATEGY (US/1058-6407) [24345288] **873**

JOURNAL OF ECONOMICS (VIENNA, AUSTRIA) (AU/0931-8658) [13896849] **1593**

●JOURNAL OF ECOTOXICOLOGY & ENVIRONMENTAL MONITORING : INTERNATIONAL JOURNAL FOR SCIENTIFIC RESEARCH ON TOXICOLOGY AND POLLUTIONS (II) [25584195] **2233**

JOURNAL OF ECUMENICAL STUDIES (US/0022-0558) [01754547] **4968**

JOURNAL OF EDUCATION & PSYCHOLOGY (II/0022-0590) [01782870] 1756, **4596**

JOURNAL OF EDUCATION AND SOCIAL CHANGE (II/0970-3500) [18452092] **1756**

JOURNAL OF EDUCATION (BOSTON, MASS.) (US/0022-0574) [06468040] **1756**

JOURNAL OF EDUCATION FINANCE (US/0098-9495) [02242897] **1865**

JOURNAL OF EDUCATION FOR BUSINESS (US/0883-2323) [12093834] 1756, **687**

JOURNAL OF EDUCATION FOR LIBRARY AND INFORMATION SCIENCE (US/0748-5786) [10967687] **3220**

JOURNAL OF EDUCATION (HALIFAX) (CN/0022-0566) [01782665] **1756**

JOURNAL OF EDUCATION IN MUSEUMS (UK) **4090**

JOURNAL OF EDUCATION POLICY (UK/0268-0939) [13755428] **1756**

JOURNAL OF EDUCATIONAL ADMINISTRATION AND HISTORY (UK/0022-0620) [01251379] **1865**

JOURNAL OF EDUCATIONAL ADMINISTRATION, THE (AT/0022-0639) [01754554] **1865**

●JOURNAL OF EDUCATIONAL AND BEHAVIORAL STATISTICS (US/1076-9986) [30674665] 1757, **1795**

JOURNAL OF EDUCATIONAL AND PSYCHOLOGICAL CONSULTATION (US/1047-4412) [20695240] **1757**

JOURNAL OF EDUCATIONAL COMPUTING RESEARCH (US/0735-6331) [08962433] **1224**

JOURNAL OF EDUCATIONAL GERONTOLOGY **See** EDUCATION & AGEING **3750**

JOURNAL OF EDUCATIONAL GERONTOLOGY (UK/0268-9987) [I02689987] **3753**

JOURNAL OF EDUCATIONAL ISSUES OF LANGUAGE MINORITY STUDENTS (US) 2266, **1757**

JOURNAL OF EDUCATIONAL MEASUREMENT (US/0022-0655) [01783080] **1757**

●JOURNAL OF EDUCATIONAL MULTIMEDIA AND HYPERMEDIA (US/1055-8896) [23364063] 1898, **1224**

JOURNAL OF EDUCATIONAL PHILOSOPHY AND HISTORY : AN ANNUAL PUBLICATION OF THE SOUTHWESTERN PHILOSOPHY OF EDUCATION SOCIETY (US) [29949281] **1757**

JOURNAL OF EDUCATIONAL PSYCHOLOGY (US/0022-0663) [01754557] 1757, **4596**

JOURNAL OF EDUCATIONAL PUBLIC RELATIONS (US/0741-3653) [10134558] 761, **1757**

JOURNAL OF EDUCATIONAL RESEARCH (PK) [05757534] **1757**

JOURNAL OF EDUCATIONAL RESEARCH AND EXTENSION (II/0022-068X) [01716708] **1898**

JOURNAL OF EDUCATIONAL RESEARCH (WASHINGTON, D.C.), THE (US/0022-0671) [01695843] **1757**

JOURNAL OF EDUCATIONAL STATISTICS (US/0362-9791) [02398276] 1757, **1795**

JOURNAL OF EDUCATIONAL TECHNOLOGY SYSTEMS (US/0047-2395) [01785037] 1898, **1224**

JOURNAL OF EDUCATIONAL TELEVISION (UK/0260-7417) [08836701] 1115, **1757**

JOURNAL OF EDUCATIONAL THOUGHT (CN/0022-0701) [01754559] **1757**

JOURNAL OF EGYPTIAN ARCHAEOLOGY, THE (UK/0075-4234) [01641765] **271**

JOURNAL OF ELASTICITY (NE/0374-3535) [01754560] **4428**

JOURNAL OF ELASTOMERS AND PLASTICS, THE (US/0095-2443) [01794056] 5076, **4456**

JOURNAL OF ELDER ABUSE & NEGLECT (US/0894-6566) [16162582] 5180, **5291**

JOURNAL OF ELECTRICAL AND ELECTRONICS ENGINEERING, AUSTRALIA (AT/0725-2986) [07678714] **2068**

JOURNAL OF ELECTRICAL ENGINEERING (CH) [01785161] **2068**

●JOURNAL OF ELECTROANALYTICAL CHEMISTRY (SZ) [25777323] **1034**

JOURNAL OF ELECTROANALYTICAL CHEMISTRY AND INTERFACIAL ELECTROCHEMISTRY (NE/0022-0728) [01793683] **1034**

JOURNAL OF ELECTROANALYTICAL CHEMISTRY (LAUSANNE, SWITZERLAND) **See** BIOELECTROCHEMISTRY AND BIOENERGETICS **2036**

JOURNAL OF ELECTROCARDIOLOGY (US/0022-0736) [01754562] **3707**

JOURNAL OF ELECTROMAGNETIC WAVES AND APPLICATIONS (NE/0920-5071) [15688154] **2068**

JOURNAL OF ELECTROMYOGRAPHY AND KINESIOLOGY (UK/1050-6411) [21569220] **3805**

JOURNAL OF ELECTRON MICROSCOPY (JA/0022-0744) [01754563] **572**

JOURNAL OF ELECTRON MICROSCOPY TECHNIQUE **See** MICROSCOPY RESEARCH AND TECHNIQUE **573**

JOURNAL OF ELECTRON SPECTROSCOPY AND RELATED PHENOMENA (NE/0368-2048) [01138887] **4435**

JOURNAL OF ELECTRONIC DEFENSE (US/0192-429X) [05053486] **4048**

JOURNAL OF ELECTRONIC ENGINEERING : JEE (JA/0385-4507) [02386068] **2068**

●JOURNAL OF ELECTRONIC IMAGING (US/1017-9909) [23553442] **2068**

JOURNAL OF ELECTRONIC MATERIAL APPLICATIONS **CEASED.** (US/0968-2783) **2068**

JOURNAL OF ELECTRONIC MATERIALS (US/0361-5235) [02059833] **2068**

JOURNAL OF ELECTRONIC PACKAGING (US/1043-7398) [19452008] **2069**

JOURNAL OF ELECTRONIC TESTING (US/0923-8174) [22270507] **2069**

JOURNAL OF ELECTRONICS (CHINA) (CC/0217-9822) [02179822] **2069**

JOURNAL OF ELECTRONICS MANUFACTURING (UK/0960-3131) [25517721] **2069**

JOURNAL OF ELECTROPHYSIOLOGICAL TECHNOLOGY (UK/0307-5095) [01731072] 582, **3595**

JOURNAL OF ELECTROPHYSIOLOGY (US/0892-1059) [15080158] **2069**

JOURNAL OF ELECTROSTATICS (NE/0304-3886) [02240842] **2069**

JOURNAL OF ELEMENTARY SCIENCE EDUCATION (US) [19504309] 5118, **1898**

JOURNAL OF EMERGENCY MEDICINE, THE (US/0736-4679) [09159685] **3725**

JOURNAL OF EMERGENCY NURSING (US/0099-1767) [02243381] 3725, **3858**

JOURNAL OF EMERGENCY SURGERY AND INTENSIVE CARE, THE (IT/1120-8708) [11208708] 3725, **3967**

●JOURNAL OF EMOTIONAL AND BEHAVIORAL DISORDERS (US/1063-4266) [26024532] **4596**

●JOURNAL OF EMOTIONAL AND BEHAVIORAL PROBLEMS (US/1064-7023) [26461243] **4596**

●JOURNAL OF EMPIRICAL FINANCE (NE/0927-5398) [28316773] **794**

JOURNAL OF EMPIRICAL THEOLOGY : JET (NE/0922-2936) [19616028] **4969**

JOURNAL OF EMPLOYEE OWNERSHIP LAW AND FINANCE, THE (US/1046-7491) [20504934] **1682**

JOURNAL OF EMPLOYMENT COUNSELING (US/0022-0787) [01783485] **4206**

●JOURNAL OF END USER COMPUTING (US/1063-2239) [25931248] **1192**

JOURNAL OF ENDOCRINOLOGICAL INVESTIGATION (IT/0391-4097) [04595726] **3731**

JOURNAL OF ENDOCRINOLOGY, THE (UK/0022-0795) [01754564] **3731**

JOURNAL OF ENDODONTICS (US/0099-2399) [01705956] **1327**

JOURNAL OF ENDOTOXIN RESEARCH (UK/0968-0519) **3595**

JOURNAL OF ENDOUROLOGY (US/0892-7790) [15261808] **3990**

●JOURNAL OF ENDOVASCULAR SURGERY (US/1074-6218) [29765730] **3967**

JOURNAL OF ENERGETIC MATERIALS (JOEM) (US/0737-0652) [09307970] **4431**

●JOURNAL OF ENERGETICS AND FLUIDS ENGINEERING **SUSPENDED.** (US/1051-3248) [21927075] 4431, **2091**

JOURNAL OF ENERGY AND DEVELOPMENT, THE (US/0361-4476) [01981677] **1948**

JOURNAL OF ENERGY & NATURAL RESOURCES LAW (UK/0264-6811) [09874604] 1948, 2196, **2987**

JOURNAL OF ENERGY ENGINEERING (US/0733-9402) [08674500] 1948, **2118**

JOURNAL OF ENERGY, HEAT AND MASS TRANSFER (II/0970-9991) [25764640] **4431**

JOURNAL OF ENERGY, NATURAL RESOURCES & ENVIRONMENTAL LAW (US/1053-377X) [22283262] **3113**

JOURNAL OF ENGINEERING AND APPLIED SCIENCES **CEASED.** (UK/0191-9539) [04965207] **1982**

JOURNAL OF ENGINEERING AND TECHNOLOGY MANAGEMENT (NE/0923-4748) [20770489] **1982**

JOURNAL OF ENGINEERING DESIGN (UK/0954-4828) [22694455] **2099**

JOURNAL OF ENGINEERING EDUCATION IN SOUTHEAST ASIA (NZ/0377-7472) [02240294] **1982**

●JOURNAL OF ENGINEERING EDUCATION (WASHINGTON, D.C.) (US/1069-4730) [27365510] **1982**

JOURNAL OF ENGINEERING FOR GAS TURBINES AND POWER (US/0742-4795) [10356681] **2118**

JOURNAL OF ENGINEERING FOR INDUSTRY (US/0022-0817) [01696421] **1982**

JOURNAL OF ENGINEERING FOR INTERNATIONAL DEVELOPMENT (CN/1183-7667) [25796575] **1982**

JOURNAL OF ENGINEERING GEOLOGY (II/0970-5317) [01754567] **1982**

JOURNAL OF ENGINEERING MATERIALS AND TECHNOLOGY (US/0094-4289) [01775150] 2103, **2118**

JOURNAL OF ENGINEERING MATHEMATICS (NE/0022-0833) [01911360] 3512, **1982**

JOURNAL OF ENGINEERING MECHANICS (US/0733-9399) [08675461] **2118**

JOURNAL OF ENGINEERING PHYSICS **See** JOURNAL OF ENGINEERING PHYSICS AND THERMOPHYSICS **4408**

●JOURNAL OF ENGINEERING PHYSICS AND THERMOPHYSICS (US/1062-0125) [25504191] 1982, **4408**

JOURNAL OF ENGINEERING RESEARCH, SEOUL NATIONAL UNIVERSITY (KO) **1982**

JOURNAL OF ENGINEERING SCIENCES (SU/0377-9254) [10049877] **1982**

JOURNAL OF ENGINEERING TECHNOLOGY (US/0747-9964) [10853866] **1982**

JOURNAL OF ENGLISH AND FOREIGN LANGUAGES (II/0970-8332) [I09708332] **3290**

JOURNAL OF ENGLISH AND GERMANIC PHILOLOGY, THE (US/0363-6941) [02192801] **3290**

JOURNAL OF ENGLISH LANGUAGE AND LITERATURE, THE (KO) [08598179] 3399, **3290**

JOURNAL OF ENGLISH LANGUAGE TEACHING (INDIA), THE (II/0022-0876) [04989370] 1898, **3290**

JOURNAL OF ENGLISH LINGUISTICS (US/0075-4242) [01783217] **3290**

JOURNAL OF ENGLISH STUDIES (WARANGAL), THE (II/0970-6232) [01790468] **3290**

JOURNAL — Alphabetical Title Index

- JOURNAL OF ENHANCED HEAT TRANSFER: AN INTERNATIONAL JOURNAL OF THEORY AND APPLICATION IN HIGH-PERFORMANCE HEAT AND MASS TRANSFER (US/1065-5131) [26621474] **4431**

- JOURNAL OF ENTERPRISING CULTURE (SI/0218-4958) [30698060] **687**

JOURNAL OF ENTOMOLOGICAL RESEARCH (II/0378-9519) [03994497] 5610, **5587**

JOURNAL OF ENTOMOLOGICAL SCIENCE (US/0749-8004) [11198824] **5610**

- JOURNAL OF ENTREPRENEURSHIP, THE (II/0971-3557) [27964884] **687**

- JOURNAL OF ENVIRONMENT & DEVELOPMENT, THE (US/1070-4965) [26268045] 2175, **1499**

JOURNAL OF ENVIRONMENTAL BIOLOGY (II/0254-8704) [08981068] 461, **2233**

JOURNAL OF ENVIRONMENTAL ECONOMICS AND MANAGEMENT (US/0095-0696) [01796173] 2233, **1499**

JOURNAL OF ENVIRONMENTAL EDUCATION, THE (US/0095-8964) [01800009] **2175**

- JOURNAL OF ENVIRONMENTAL ENGINEERING (US/1056-2702) [23603863] **1982**

JOURNAL OF ENVIRONMENTAL ENGINEERING (NEW YORK N.Y.) (US/0733-9372) [08675387] 1982, **2233**

JOURNAL OF ENVIRONMENTAL HEALTH (US/0022-0892) [05271897] 4786, **2175**

JOURNAL OF ENVIRONMENTAL HORTICULTURE (US/0738-2898) [09424057] **2421**

- JOURNAL OF ENVIRONMENTAL HYDROLOGY (US/1058-3912) [24291359] **1416**

JOURNAL OF ENVIRONMENTAL LAW (UK/0952-8873) [17786560] **3113**

JOURNAL OF ENVIRONMENTAL LAW AND LITIGATION (US/1049-0280) [13326045] **3113**

JOURNAL OF ENVIRONMENTAL LAW AND PRACTICE (CN/1181-7534) [22606901] **3113**

JOURNAL OF ENVIRONMENTAL MANAGEMENT (UK/0301-4797) [01786927] **2175**

JOURNAL OF ENVIRONMENTAL PATHOLOGY, TOXICOLOGY AND ONCOLOGY (US/0731-8898) [08266212] **3819**

- JOURNAL OF ENVIRONMENTAL PERMITTING (US/1058-1367) [24226507] **2987**

- JOURNAL OF ENVIRONMENTAL PLANNING AND MANAGEMENT (UK/0964-0568) [26089803] **2826**

- JOURNAL OF ENVIRONMENTAL POLYMER DEGRADATION (US/1064-7546) [26391406] 2175, **981**

JOURNAL OF ENVIRONMENTAL PSYCHOLOGY (UK/0272-4944) [06855117] 2175, **4596**

JOURNAL OF ENVIRONMENTAL QUALITY (US/0047-2425) [01800003] 100, **2217**

JOURNAL OF ENVIRONMENTAL QUALITY MANAGEMENT (US/1055-7547) [23302402] **2175**

JOURNAL OF ENVIRONMENTAL QUALITY (NEW YORK, N.Y.) (US/1055-7563) [23302418] **2175**

JOURNAL OF ENVIRONMENTAL RADIOACTIVITY (UK/0265-931X) [11752594] **2233**

JOURNAL OF ENVIRONMENTAL REGULATION (US/1055-758X) [23302489] **2175**

JOURNAL OF ENVIRONMENTAL SCIENCE AND HEALTH. PART A, ENVIRONMENTAL SCIENCE AND ENGINEERING (US/0360-1226) [01832278] **1982**

JOURNAL OF ENVIRONMENTAL SCIENCE AND HEALTH. PART B, PESTICIDES, FOOD CONTAMINANTS, AND AGRICULTURAL WASTES (US/0360-1234) [02093648] 3981, 4245, **2176**

JOURNAL OF ENVIRONMENTAL SCIENCE AND HEALTH. PART C, ENVIRONMENTAL CARCINOGENESIS & ECOTOXICOLOGY REVIEWS (US/1059-0501) [24465089] **2234**

JOURNAL OF ENVIRONMENTAL SCIENCE LABORATORY (JA/0915-6194) [I09156194] **2176**

JOURNAL OF ENVIRONMENTAL SCIENCES (CHINA) (CC/1001-0742) [23258889] **2234**

- JOURNAL OF ENVIRONMENTAL STATISTICS (US/1065-7568) [26716510] **2176**

JOURNAL OF ENVIRONMENTAL SYSTEMS (US/0047-2433) [01783879] **2176**

JOURNAL OF ENZYME INHIBITION (SZ/8755-5093) [11332414] **461**

JOURNAL OF EPIDEMIOLOGY AND COMMUNITY HEALTH (1979) (UK/0143-005X) [05385322] 4786, **3735**

JOURNAL OF EPILEPSY (US/0896-6974) [17256789] **3835**

JOURNAL OF EPSILON PI TAU, THE (US/0887-9532) [05292954] 5118, **1757**

JOURNAL OF EQUINE MEDICINE AND SURGERY, THE (US/0147-0833) [03075300] 5513, **2800**

JOURNAL OF EQUINE VETERINARY SCIENCE (US/0737-0806) [07643410] 5513, **2800**

JOURNAL OF EQUIPMENT LEASE FINANCING, THE (US/0740-008X) [09839021] **873**

JOURNAL OF ERIE STUDIES (US/0090-1938) [01784708] **2741**

JOURNAL OF ERITREAN STUDIES *CEASED.* (US/1048-597X) [15272124] **2848**

JOURNAL OF ESSENTIAL OIL RESEARCH, THE (US/1041-2905) [18710125] 515, **1026**

JOURNAL OF ESTHETIC DENTISTRY (CN/1040-1466) [18334839] **1327**

JOURNAL OF ET NURSING *See* JOURNAL OF WOUND, OSTOMY, AND CONTINENCE NURSING **3860**

JOURNAL OF ET NURSING *See* JOURNAL OF THE WOCN **3860**

JOURNAL OF ET NURSING (US/1055-3045) [23132987] **3858**

JOURNAL OF ETHIOPIAN LAW (ET/0022-0914) [01754576] **2987**

JOURNAL OF ETHIOPIAN STUDIES (ET/0304-2243) [01779437] **2640**

JOURNAL OF ETHNIC STUDIES, THE *CEASED.* (US/0091-3219) [01775152] **2266**

JOURNAL OF ETHNOBIOLOGY (US/0278-0771) [07636827] **238**

JOURNAL OF ETHNOLOGY & SOCIOLOGY *See* JOURNAL OF SOCIOLOGY **5250**

JOURNAL OF ETHNOPHARMACOLOGY (SZ/0378-8741) [04649997] **4311**

JOURNAL OF ETHOLOGY (JA/0289-0771) [11244761] **239**

- JOURNAL OF EUKARYOTIC MICROBIOLOGY, THE (US/1066-5234) [26981898] **5587**

JOURNAL OF EURO MARKETING (US/1049-6483) [21269716] 843, **927**

JOURNAL OF EUROPEAN BUSINESS, THE (US/1044-002X) [19643523] **1613**

JOURNAL OF EUROPEAN ECONOMIC HISTORY, THE (IT/0391-5115) [01784022] **1570**

JOURNAL OF EUROPEAN INDUSTRIAL TRAINING (UK/0309-0590) [03425832] **873**

JOURNAL OF EUROPEAN PUBLIC POLICY (UK/1350-1763) **4658**

JOURNAL OF EUROPEAN SOCIAL POLICY (UK/0958-9287) [I09589287] 5206, **2518**

JOURNAL OF EUROPEAN STUDIES (UK/0047-2441) [01796625] **2694**

JOURNAL OF EUROPEAN STUDIES (KARACHI) (PK/0258-9680) [12155036] **2694**

JOURNAL OF EVERETT & SNOHOMISH COUNTY HISTORY *CEASED.* (US/0273-4966) [07062643] **2741**

JOURNAL OF EVOLUTIONARY BIOCHEMISTRY AND PHYSIOLOGY (US/0022-0930) [01800055] 489, **582**

JOURNAL OF EVOLUTIONARY BIOLOGY (SZ/1010-061X) [17884292] **548**

JOURNAL OF EVOLUTIONARY ECONOMICS (GW/0936-9937) [24102551] **1593**

JOURNAL OF EVOLUTIONARY PSYCHOLOGY (US/0737-4828) [09368834] 4596, **3399**

JOURNAL OF EXPERIENTIAL EDUCATION, THE (US/1053-8259) [04982252] **1880**

JOURNAL OF EXPERIMENTAL AESTHETICS (CN/0318-8558) [03436708] **354**

JOURNAL OF EXPERIMENTAL & CLINICAL CANCER RESEARCH : CR (IT/0392-9078) [10009183] **3819**

JOURNAL OF EXPERIMENTAL & THEORETICAL ARTIFICIAL INTELLIGENCE (UK/0952-813X) [20911086] **1214**

- JOURNAL OF EXPERIMENTAL AND THEORETICAL PHYSICS (US/1063-7761) [26140718] **4409**

JOURNAL OF EXPERIMENTAL ANIMAL SCIENCE (1991) (GW/0939-8600) [23274746] **5513**

JOURNAL OF EXPERIMENTAL BIOLOGY (UK/0022-0949) [01754580] **582**

JOURNAL OF EXPERIMENTAL BOTANY (UK/0022-0957) [01783178] **515**

JOURNAL OF EXPERIMENTAL CHILD PSYCHOLOGY (US/0022-0965) [01431145] **4596**

JOURNAL OF EXPERIMENTAL EDUCATION, THE (US/0022-0973) [01641618] **1898**

JOURNAL OF EXPERIMENTAL MARINE BIOLOGY AND ECOLOGY (NE/0022-0981) [01783316] **555**

JOURNAL OF EXPERIMENTAL MEDICINE, THE (US/0022-1007) [01390073] **3673**

JOURNAL OF EXPERIMENTAL PATHOLOGY *CEASED.* (US/0730-8485) [08071430] **3895**

JOURNAL OF EXPERIMENTAL PSYCHOLOGY : ANIMAL BEHAVIOR PROCESSES (US/0097-7403) [02441504] **4596**

- JOURNAL OF EXPERIMENTAL PSYCHOLOGY. APPLIED (US/1076-898X) [30635181] **4596**

JOURNAL OF EXPERIMENTAL PSYCHOLOGY : GENERAL (US/0096-3445) [02441503] **4596**

JOURNAL OF EXPERIMENTAL PSYCHOLOGY : HUMAN PERCEPTION AND PERFORMANCE (US/0096-1523) [02441505] **4597**

JOURNAL OF EXPERIMENTAL PSYCHOLOGY. LEARNING, MEMORY, AND COGNITION (US/0278-7393) [07949766] **4597**

JOURNAL OF EXPERIMENTAL PSYCHOLOGY. LEARNING, MEMORY, AND COGNITION [MICROFORM] (US/0278-7393) [09200900] **4597**

JOURNAL OF EXPERIMENTAL SOCIAL PSYCHOLOGY (US/0022-1031) [01754583] 5249, **4597**

JOURNAL OF EXPERIMENTAL ZOOLOGY. SUPPLEMENT (US/1059-8324) [15915780] **5587**

JOURNAL OF EXPERIMENTAL ZOOLOGY, THE (US/0022-104X) [01696224] **5587**

JOURNAL OF EXPLOSIVES ENGINEERING, THE (US/0889-0668) [12148721] **1982**

JOURNAL OF EXPOSURE ANALYSIS AND ENVIRONMENTAL EPIDEMIOLOGY (US/1053-4245) [22529149] 3735, **2176**

- JOURNAL OF EXPRESSIVE THERAPY (US/1057-7432) [24111592] **4597**

JOURNAL OF EXTENSION (US/0022-0140) [01714173] **1914**

JOURNAL OF EXTENSION SYSTEMS (II) [16734797] **100**

JOURNAL OF EXTRA-CORPOREAL TECHNOLOGY, THE (US/0022-1058) [03497615] **3772**

JOURNAL OF FAMILY AND CULTURE, THE (US) [12812986] 2281, **5249**

- JOURNAL OF FAMILY AND ECONOMIC ISSUES (US/1058-0476) [24203047] **2281**

JOURNAL OF FAMILY ISSUES (US/0192-513X) [05035642] **2282**

JOURNAL OF FAMILY LAW (US/0022-1066) [01754585] **3121**

JOURNAL OF FAMILY LAW *See* UNIVERSITY OF LOUISVILLE JOURNAL OF FAMILY LAW **3122**

- JOURNAL OF FAMILY NURSING (US/1074-8407) [29859620] **3858**

JOURNAL OF FAMILY PRACTICE, THE (US/0094-3509) [01793919] **3738**

JOURNAL OF FAMILY PSYCHOLOGY (US/0893-3200) [15471832] 2282, **4597**

JOURNAL OF FAMILY PSYCHOTHERAPY (US/0897-5353) [17534086] 4597, **2282**

- JOURNAL OF FAMILY SOCIAL WORK (US/1052-2158) [22222421] **5291**

JOURNAL OF FAMILY THERAPY (UK/0163-4445) [04392881] 2282, **3928**

JOURNAL OF FAMILY VIOLENCE (US/0885-7482) [12712841] 5292, **2282**

JOURNAL OF FAMILY WELFARE, THE (II/0022-1074) [01774521] **589**

- JOURNAL OF FAR EASTERN BUSINESS (UK/1351-0363) [I13510363] **687**

JOURNAL OF FARMING SYSTEMS RESEARCH-EXTENSION (US/1051-6786) [22044949] **100**

JOURNAL OF FEMINIST FAMILY THERAPY (US/0895-2833) [16545991] 5559, 4597, **2282**

JOURNAL OF FEMINIST STUDIES IN RELIGION (US/8755-4178) [11309512] 5559, **4969**

JOURNAL OF FERMENTATION AND BIOENGINEERING (JA/0922-338X) [19468128] **565**

JOURNAL OF FERROCEMENT (TH/0125-1759) [05635773] 618, **632**

Alphabetical Title Index — JOURNAL

JOURNAL OF FERTILIZER ISSUES *CEASED.* (US/0748-4690) [10958744] **176**

JOURNAL OF FIELD ARCHAEOLOGY (US/0093-4690) [01798634] **271**

JOURNAL OF FIELD ORNITHOLOGY (US/0273-8570) [06290256] **5618**

JOURNAL OF FILM AND VIDEO (US/0742-4671) [10354585] **4073**

JOURNAL OF FINANCE & DEVELOPMENT (BG) [07041991] **794**

JOURNAL OF FINANCE (NEW YORK), THE (US/0022-1082) [01782429] **794**

● JOURNAL OF FINANCIAL ABSTRACTS (US) **794**

JOURNAL OF FINANCIAL AND QUANTITATIVE ANALYSIS (US/0022-1090) [01754589] **794**

JOURNAL OF FINANCIAL & STRATEGIC DECISIONS (US/1065-1853) [20687870] **4734**

JOURNAL OF FINANCIAL ECONOMICS (NE/0304-405X) [01780979] 904, **794**

JOURNAL OF FINANCIAL EDUCATION *SUSPENDED.* (US/0093-3961) [01792349] **794**

● JOURNAL OF FINANCIAL ENGINEERING, THE (US/1062-8924) [25793961] **1982**

JOURNAL OF FINANCIAL INTERMEDIATION (US/1042-9573) [19258619] 794, **904**

JOURNAL OF FINANCIAL MANAGEMENT AND ANALYSIS (II/0970-4205) [18767483] **794**

JOURNAL OF FINANCIAL PLANNING (DENVER, COLO.) (US/1040-3981) [18316803] **794**

JOURNAL OF FINANCIAL RESEARCH, THE (US/0270-2592) [04647611] **794**

JOURNAL OF FINANCIAL SERVICES RESEARCH (US/0920-8550) [16996700] **794**

JOURNAL OF FIRE PROTECTION ENGINEERING (US/1042-3915) [19032224] 1982, **2291**

JOURNAL OF FIRE SCIENCES (US/0734-9041) [08822978] **2291**

JOURNAL OF FISH BIOLOGY (UK/0022-1112) [01754591] **2306**

JOURNAL OF FISH DISEASES (UK/0140-7775) [03862290] **2306**

JOURNAL OF FISHERIES & AQUACULTURE *CEASED.* (PH/0115-690X) [09408069] **2306**

JOURNAL OF FIXED INCOME, THE (US/1059-8596) [24772799] **904**

● JOURNAL OF FLOW VISUALIZATION AND IMAGE PROCESSING (US/1065-3090) [26570199] **2091**

JOURNAL OF FLUENCY DISORDERS (US/0094-730X) [01795295] **3595**

JOURNAL OF FLUID CONTROL, THE (US/8755-8564) [10932367] **2091**

JOURNAL OF FLUID MECHANICS (UK/0022-1120) [01782778] **2091**

JOURNAL OF FLUIDS AND STRUCTURES (UK/0889-9746) [14109168] **2092**

JOURNAL OF FLUIDS ENGINEERING (US/0098-2202) [02239834] **2092**

JOURNAL OF FLUORESCENCE (US/1053-0509) [22439996] **4435**

JOURNAL OF FLUORINE CHEMISTRY (SZ/0022-1139) [01786333] **981**

JOURNAL OF FOETAL MEDICINE (IT/0392-9507) [11320316] **3763**

JOURNAL OF FOLKLORE RESEARCH (US/0737-7037) [09444482] **2321**

JOURNAL OF FOOD & AGRICULTURE (NR/0794-7194) [25667576] 100, **2346**

JOURNAL OF FOOD BIOCHEMISTRY (US/0145-8884) [02917846] **2346**

JOURNAL OF FOOD COMPOSITION AND ANALYSIS (US/0889-1575) [13800268] **1026**

JOURNAL OF FOOD DISTRIBUTION RESEARCH (US/0047-245X) [02550025] **2346**

JOURNAL OF FOOD ENGINEERING (UK/0260-8774) [08927217] **2346**

● JOURNAL OF FOOD LIPIDS (US/1065-7258) [26710264] 981, **2346**

JOURNAL OF FOOD PROCESS ENGINEERING (US/0145-8876) [02924831] **2346**

JOURNAL OF FOOD PROCESSING AND PRESERVATION (US/0145-8892) [03082583] **2346**

● JOURNAL OF FOOD PRODUCTS MARKETING (US/1045-4446) [20113582] 927, **2346**

JOURNAL OF FOOD PROTECTION (US/0362-028X) [02771676] **2346**

JOURNAL OF FOOD QUALITY (US/0146-9428) [03252366] 4786, **2346**

JOURNAL OF FOOD SAFETY (US/0149-6085) [03531563] 4786, **2346**

JOURNAL OF FOOD SCIENCE (US/0022-1147) [01680911] **2346**

JOURNAL OF FOOD SCIENCE AND TECHNOLOGY (II/0022-1155) [01800339] 2346, **4193**

JOURNAL OF FOODSERVICE SYSTEMS (US/0196-4283) [05814665] **2347**

● JOURNAL OF FOOT AND ANKLE SURGERY, THE (US/1067-2516) [27182191] 3882, **3967**

JOURNAL OF FOOT SURGERY *See* JOURNAL OF FOOT AND ANKLE SURGERY, THE **3967**

JOURNAL OF FOOT SURGERY, THE (US/0449-2544) [03711674] **3918**

JOURNAL OF FORAMINIFERAL RESEARCH (US/0096-1191) [00870235] **5588**

JOURNAL OF FORECASTING (UK/0277-6693) [07625627] 687, **5249**

JOURNAL OF FOREIGN EXCHANGE AND INTERNATIONAL FINANCE (II) [16468552] **794**

JOURNAL OF FORENSIC ECONOMICS (US/0898-5510) [17687420] **1499**

JOURNAL OF FORENSIC IDENTIFICATION (US/0895-173X) [16507764] **3741**

JOURNAL OF FORENSIC ODONTO-STOMATOLOGY, THE (AT/0258-414X) [10614789] **1327**

JOURNAL OF FORENSIC PSYCHIATRY, THE (UK/0958-5184) [24379100] **3928**

JOURNAL OF FORENSIC SCIENCES (US/0022-1198) [01754597] **3741**

JOURNAL OF FOREST ENGINEERING (CN/0843-5243) [20781830] **2385**

JOURNAL OF FORESTRY (US/0022-1201) [01782263] **2385**

JOURNAL OF FORTH APPLICATION AND RESEARCH, THE (US/0738-2022) [09543511] **1279**

● JOURNAL OF FOURIER ANALYSIS AND APPLICATIONS, THE (US/1069-5869) [28122903] 5118, **3512**

JOURNAL OF FRENCH LANGUAGE STUDIES (UK/0959-2695) [23435771] **3290**

JOURNAL OF FRESHWATER BIOLOGY (II/0970-9517) [21431555] **555**

JOURNAL OF FRESHWATER ECOLOGY (US/0270-5060) [06458917] **2218**

● JOURNAL OF FRICTION AND WEAR (US/1068-3666) [27658735] **1982**

● JOURNAL OF FRUIT AND ORNAMENTAL PLANT RESEARCH (PL) [30382412] **176**

JOURNAL OF FRUIT SCIENCE (CC/1001-7364) [26565616] 2347, **100**

JOURNAL OF FUNCTIONAL ANALYSIS (US/0022-1236) [01784383] **3513**

JOURNAL OF FUNCTIONAL PROGRAMMING (UK/0956-7968) [23534135] **1279**

JOURNAL OF FURTHER AND HIGHER EDUCATION (UK/0309-877X) [03487122] **1832**

JOURNAL OF FUSION ENERGY (US/0164-0313) [04556672] 2156, **1949**

JOURNAL OF FUTURES MARKETS, THE (US/0270-7314) [06493305] **904**

JOURNAL OF GAMBLING STUDIES (US/1050-5350) [21533381] **5292**

JOURNAL OF GARDEN HISTORY (UK/0144-5170) [07132577] **2421**

● JOURNAL OF GASTROENTEROLOGY (JA/0944-1174) [30102704] **3747**

JOURNAL OF GASTROENTEROLOGY AND HEPATOLOGY (AT/0815-9319) [14037025] **3747**

JOURNAL OF GASTROINTESTINAL MOTILITY (US/1043-4518) [19480841] **3747**

JOURNAL OF GASTRONOMY, THE (US/0747-7368) [10788540] **2347**

JOURNAL OF GAY & LESBIAN PSYCHOTHERAPY (US/0891-7140) [14978121] 4597, **2794**

● JOURNAL OF GAY & LESBIAN SOCIAL SERVICES (US/1053-8720) [22683509] 5292, **2794**

JOURNAL OF GEM INDUSTRY (II/0022-1244) [10258156] **2915**

JOURNAL OF GEMMOLOGY AND PROCEEDINGS OF THE GEMMOLOGICAL ASSOCIATION OF GREAT BRITAIN (UK/0022-1252) [02323560] **1440**

JOURNAL OF GEMMOLOGY, THE (UK) [06076324] **1440**

JOURNAL OF GENDER STUDIES (UK/0958-9236) [24317037] **5559**

JOURNAL OF GENDER STUDIES (SOUTH PORTLAND, ME.) (US/1062-6751) [25695569] 5559, **3995**

JOURNAL OF GENERAL AND APPLIED MICROBIOLOGY, THE (JA/0022-1260) [01782890] **565**

JOURNAL OF GENERAL CHEMISTRY OF THE USSR (US/0022-1279) [01782505] **981**

JOURNAL OF GENERAL CHEMISTRY OF THE USSR *See* RUSSIAN JOURNAL OF GENERAL CHEMISTRY **992**

JOURNAL OF GENERAL EDUCATION (UNIVERSITY PARK, PA.), THE (US/0021-3667) [01754601] **1757**

JOURNAL OF GENERAL INTERNAL MEDICINE (US/0884-8734) [12486900] **3798**

JOURNAL OF GENERAL MANAGEMENT (UK/0306-3070) [01793821] **873**

JOURNAL OF GENERAL MEDICINE, THE (II) [22178174] **3738**

JOURNAL OF GENERAL MICROBIOLOGY *See* MICROBIOLOGY **567**

JOURNAL OF GENERAL MICROBIOLOGY, THE (UK/0022-1287) [01754602] **565**

JOURNAL OF GENERAL ORTHODONTICS (US/1048-1990) [20865120] **1327**

JOURNAL OF GENERAL PHYSIOLOGY, THE (US/0022-1295) [01390169] **582**

JOURNAL OF GENERAL PSYCHOLOGY, THE (US/0022-1309) [01782300] **4597**

JOURNAL OF GENERAL VIROLOGY, THE (UK/0022-1317) [01754603] **565**

JOURNAL OF GENETIC AND DEVELOPMENTAL TOXICOLOGY (US/1052-1070) [22187224] **3981**

● JOURNAL OF GENETIC COUNSELING (US/1059-7700) [24728238] **548**

JOURNAL OF GENETIC PSYCHOLOGY, THE (US/0022-1325) [01639282] **4597**

JOURNAL OF GENETICS (II/0022-1333) [01643134] **548**

JOURNAL OF GENETICS & BREEDING (IT/0394-9257) [19719646] 100, **548**

JOURNAL OF GEOCHEMICAL EXPLORATION (NE/0375-6742) [01784019] **2141**

JOURNAL OF GEODYNAMICS (UK/0264-3707) [10537114] **1384**

JOURNAL OF GEOGRAPHY (HOUSTON) (US/0022-1341) [01754604] **2567**

JOURNAL OF GEOGRAPHY IN HIGHER EDUCATION (UK/0309-8265) [03782055] 1832, **2567**

JOURNAL OF GEOLOGICAL EDUCATION (US/0022-1368) [01754605] 1757, **1384**

JOURNAL OF GEOLOGY, THE (US/0022-1376) [01608377] **1385**

JOURNAL OF GEOMAGNETISM AND GEOELECTRICITY (JA/0022-1392) [01782911] **1407**

JOURNAL OF GEOMANCY *See* ANCIENT MYSTERIES **4240**

JOURNAL OF GEOMETRIC ANALYSIS, THE (US/1050-6926) [21574354] **3513**

JOURNAL OF GEOMETRY (SZ/0047-2468) [01787475] **3513**

JOURNAL OF GEOMETRY AND PHYSICS (NE/0393-0440) [11541027] 3513, **4409**

JOURNAL OF GEOPHYSICAL RESEARCH (US/0148-0227) [02396688] **1407**

JOURNAL OF GEOPHYSICAL RESEARCH. ATMOSPHERES (US) 1426, **1408**

JOURNAL OF GEOPHYSICAL RESEARCH. OCEANS (US) 1450, **1408**

JOURNAL OF GEOPHYSICAL RESEARCH. PLANETS : JGR (US) [24364419] **1408**

JOURNAL OF GEOPHYSICAL RESEARCH. SOLID EARTH : JGR (US) [24424753] **1408**

JOURNAL OF GEOPHYSICAL RESEARCH. SPACE PHYSICS (US) 396, **1408**

JOURNAL OF GEOTECHNICAL ENGINEERING (US/0733-9410) [08674396] 2025, **1385**

JOURNAL OF GERIATRIC DRUG THERAPY (US/8756-4629) [11566939] 4311, **3753**

JOURNAL OF GERIATRIC PSYCHIATRY (US/0022-1414) [01149695] 3753, **3928**

JOURNAL OF GERIATRIC PSYCHIATRY AND NEUROLOGY (US/0891-9887) [15051229] 3929, **3753**

JOURNAL OF GERONTOLOGICAL NURSING (US/0098-9134) [02243369] **3858**

JOURNAL OF GERONTOLOGICAL NURSING (US/0098-9134) [08450131] **3858**

JOURNAL OF GERONTOLOGICAL SOCIAL WORK (US/0163-4372) [04392786] 5180, **5292**

JOURNAL — Alphabetical Title Index

JOURNAL OF GERONTOLOGY (KIRKWOOD) (US/0022-1422) [01608055] 4597, **3753**

●JOURNAL OF GERONTOLOGY: PSYCHOLOGICAL SCIENCES AND SOCIAL SCIENCES, THE (US) **3753**

JOURNAL OF GLACIOLOGY, THE (UK/0022-1430) [01782640] **1416**

JOURNAL OF GLASS STUDIES (US/0075-4250) [01605749] **2591**

●JOURNAL OF GLAUCOMA (US/1057-0829) [23932664] **3876**

JOURNAL OF GLOBAL BUSINESS (HARRISONBURG, VA.) (US/1053-7287) [22619421] **687**

JOURNAL OF GLOBAL BUSINESS : JGB (US/1050-6284) [21567117] **687**

●JOURNAL OF GLOBAL INFORMATION MANAGEMENT (US/1062-7375) [25723350] **3220**

JOURNAL OF GLOBAL MARKETING (US/0891-1762) [14639823] **927**

JOURNAL OF GLOBAL OPTIMIZATION : AN INTERNATIONAL JOURNAL DEALING WITH THEORETICAL AND COMPUTATIONAL ASPECTS OF SEEKING GLOBAL OPTIMA AND THEIR APPLICATIONS IN SCIENCE, MANAGEMENT AND ENGINEERING (NE/0925-5001) [23918897] 1983, **3513**

JOURNAL OF GNATHOLOGY, THE (US/0891-8171) [12180237] **1327**

JOURNAL OF GOVERNMENT AND POLITICAL STUDIES (II) [05088872] **4479**

●JOURNAL OF GOVERNMENT INFORMATION (UK/1352-0237) [29785232] **4658**

JOURNAL OF GRAPH THEORY (US/0364-9024) [03057169] **3513**

JOURNAL OF GREAT LAKES RESEARCH (US/0380-1330) [03044239] **1416**

JOURNAL OF GROUP PSYCHOTHERAPY, PSYCHODRAMA AND SOCIOMETRY (US/0731-1273) [08119999] **3929**

●JOURNAL OF GROUP THEORY IN PHYSICS (US/1070-2458) [28309942] **4409**

JOURNAL OF GUIDANCE, CONTROL, AND DYNAMICS (US/0731-5090) [08156828] **26**

JOURNAL OF GUITAR ACOUSTICS (US/0735-4371) [08260790] **4126**

JOURNAL OF GYNAECOLOGICAL ENDOCRINOLOGY (IT) [12391538] **3763**

JOURNAL OF GYNECOLOGIC SURGERY (US/1042-4067) [19036651] **3763**

●JOURNAL OF GYNECOLOGIC TECHNIQUES (US/1069-2673) [27965952] **3763**

JOURNAL OF H.M. CUSTOMS AND EXCISE, THE (UK) [04171477] **4704**

JOURNAL OF HALACHA AND CONTEMPORARY SOCIETY (US/0730-2614) [07757050] **5050**

JOURNAL OF HAND SURGERY, BRITISH VOLUME (UK/0266-7681) [10496492] **3967**

JOURNAL OF HAND SURGERY (ST. LOUIS, MO.), THE (US/0363-5023) [02429344] **3967**

JOURNAL OF HAND THERAPY (US/0894-1130) [15797995] **4380**

JOURNAL OF HARD MATERIALS (UK/0954-027X) [22156813] **5118**

JOURNAL OF HAZARDOUS MATERIALS (NE/0304-3894) [02246095] 4786, **2234**

JOURNAL OF HEAD & NECK PATHOLOGY *CEASED.* (BE/0770-9471) [10170166] **3595**

JOURNAL OF HEAD TRAUMA REHABILITATION, THE (US/0885-9701) [12793733] **4380**

JOURNAL OF HEALTH ADMINISTRATION EDUCATION, THE (US/0735-6722) [08968524] **4786**

JOURNAL OF HEALTH & HEALING (WILDWOOD, GA.) (US/1044-2790) [19731129] **2599**

JOURNAL OF HEALTH AND HOSPITAL LAW : A PUBLICATION OF THE AMERICAN ACADEMY OF HOSPITAL ATTORNEYS OF THE AMERICAN HOSPITAL ASSOCIATION (US/1046-4360) [17999014] 3787, **2987**

JOURNAL OF HEALTH AND HUMAN RESOURCES ADMINISTRATION (US/0160-4198) [03678098] 4658, 4786, **5292**

●JOURNAL OF HEALTH AND PLACE (UK/1353-8292) **4786**

JOURNAL OF HEALTH AND SAFETY, THE (UK/0954-576X) [I0954576X] **4786**

JOURNAL OF HEALTH AND SOCIAL BEHAVIOR (US/0022-1465) [01695738] 4597, **4786**

JOURNAL OF HEALTH & SOCIAL POLICY (US/0897-7186) [17604917] **5292**

JOURNAL OF HEALTH CARE BENEFITS (US/1057-5073) [24043045] 4786, **2885**

JOURNAL OF HEALTH CARE CHAPLAINCY (US/0885-4726) [12680040] 3787, **4969**

JOURNAL OF HEALTH CARE FINANCE (US) 3787, **794**

JOURNAL OF HEALTH CARE FOR THE POOR AND UNDERSERVED (US/1049-2089) [21175275] **4786**

JOURNAL OF HEALTH CARE MARKETING (US/0737-3252) [07480207] 4786, **927**

JOURNAL OF HEALTH ECONOMICS (NE/0167-6296) [08834820] **1499**

JOURNAL OF HEALTH EDUCATION. ASSOCIATION FOR THE ADVANCEMENT OF HEALTH EDUCATION (US/1055-6699) [23065182] **4786**

●JOURNAL OF HEALTH INFORMATION MANAGEMENT RESEARCH, THE (US/1060-5657) [25037568] **4787**

JOURNAL OF HEALTH OCCUPATIONS EDUCATION (US/0890-6874) [14516136] **3595**

JOURNAL OF HEALTH, PHYSICAL EDUCATION, RECREATION, AND DANCE : JOURNAL OF WVAHPERD (US) [09763996] **1856**

JOURNAL OF HEALTH POLITICS, POLICY AND LAW (US/0361-6878) [02115780] 3595, **2987**

JOURNAL OF HEALTHCARE EDUCATION AND TRAINING (US/0898-2740) [13848484] **3595**

JOURNAL OF HEALTHCARE MATERIAL MANAGEMENT (US/0889-2482) [12742916] **3787**

JOURNAL OF HEALTHCARE PROTECTION MANAGEMENT (US/0891-7930) [12351839] **3787**

●JOURNAL OF HEALTHCARE RISK MANAGEMENT : THE JOURNAL OF THE AMERICAN SOCIETY FOR HEALTHCARE RISK MANAGEMENT (US) [27248047] **873**

JOURNAL OF HEART AND LUNG TRANSPLANTATION, THE (US/1053-2498) [22486861] **3967**

●JOURNAL OF HEART VALVE DISEASE, THE (UK/0966-8519) [27141420] **3707**

JOURNAL OF HEAT TRANSFER (US/0022-1481) [01782922] 4409, **1983**

JOURNAL OF HEAT TREATING (US/0190-9177) [04781590] **4006**

JOURNAL OF HELLENIC STUDIES (UK/0075-4269) [01754613] **1078**

JOURNAL OF HELMINTHOLOGY (UK/0022-149X) [01754614] **5588**

●JOURNAL OF HEMATOTHERAPY (US/1061-6128) [25380549] **3798**

JOURNAL OF HEPATO-BILIARY-PANCREATIC SURGERY (GW/0944-1166) **3967**

JOURNAL OF HEPATOLOGY (NE/0168-8278) [11460329] **3798**

●JOURNAL OF HERBS, SPICES & MEDICINAL PLANTS (US/1049-6475) [21269692] **2421**

JOURNAL OF HEREDITY, THE (US/0022-1503) [01724935] **548**

JOURNAL OF HERPETOLOGY (US/0022-1511) [01783314] **5588**

JOURNAL OF HETEROCYCLIC CHEMISTRY (US/0022-152X) [01783072] **1042**

JOURNAL OF HIGH RESOLUTION CHROMATOGRAPHY : HRC (GW/0935-6304) [19502754] **1017**

JOURNAL OF HIGH SPEED NETWORKS (NE/0926-6801) **1242**

JOURNAL OF HIGH TECHNOLOGY MANAGEMENT RESEARCH (US/1047-8310) [20790634] **1614**

JOURNAL OF HIGH TEMPERATURE CHEMICAL PROCESSES (FR) **4409**

JOURNAL OF HIGHER EDUCATION (II) [02418990] **1832**

JOURNAL OF HIGHER EDUCATION (AT/1034-3350) [I10343350] **1832**

JOURNAL OF HIGHER EDUCATION (COLUMBUS), THE (US/0022-1546) [01590640] **1833**

JOURNAL OF HIMALAYAN GEOLOGY (II) [28036635] **1385**

JOURNAL OF HIMALAYAN STUDIES & REGIONAL DEVELOPMENT (II) [07086235] **2218**

JOURNAL OF HISPANIC LATINO THEOLOGY (US) 2266, **4969**

JOURNAL OF HISPANIC PHILOLOGY (US/0147-5460) [02733970] 3399, **3290**

JOURNAL OF HISPANIC POLICY *See* HARVARD JOURNAL OF HISPANIC POLICY **2262**

JOURNAL OF HISTOCHEMISTRY AND CYTOCHEMISTRY, THE (US/0022-1554) [01800247] **537**

JOURNAL OF HISTORIC MADISON, INC. OF WISCONSIN, THE (US/0361-574X) [02247061] **2741**

JOURNAL OF HISTORICAL GEOGRAPHY (UK/0305-7488) [02243260] **2567**

JOURNAL OF HISTORICAL RESEARCH (II/0022-1562) [01716990] **2655**

JOURNAL OF HISTORICAL REVIEW, THE (US/0195-6752) [05584935] **2621**

JOURNAL OF HISTORICAL SOCIOLOGY (UK/0952-1909) [18102209] **5249**

JOURNAL OF HISTORY AND POLITICS (US/0228-6939) [20379044] 4479, **2621**

JOURNAL OF HISTORY, THE (PH) [01783145] **2621**

JOURNAL OF HISTOTECHNOLOGY (US/0147-8885) [03456694] **538**

●JOURNAL OF HIV/AIDS PREVENTION & EDUCATION FOR ADOLESCENTS & CHILDREN (US/1069-837X) [28166202] 1757, **4787**

JOURNAL OF HOLISTIC NURSING (US/0898-0101) [12391430] **3858**

●JOURNAL OF HOME & CONSUMER HORTICULTURE (US/1054-4682) [22901359] **2421**

JOURNAL OF HOME ECONOMICS EDUCATION (CN/0705-7830) [04249915] **2791**

JOURNAL OF HOME ECONOMICS. INSTITUTE OF AUSTRALIA (AT) **2791**

JOURNAL OF HOME ECONOMICS (WASHINGTON) (US/0022-1570) [01782239] **2791**

JOURNAL OF HOME HEALTH CARE PRACTICE (US/0897-8018) [17628469] **5292**

JOURNAL OF HOMOSEXUALITY (US/0091-8369) [01790856] 5187, **2795**

JOURNAL OF HOROLOGICAL INSTITUTE OF JAPAN (JA) **2916**

JOURNAL OF HORTICULTURAL SCIENCE, THE (UK/0022-1589) [07382220] **2421**

JOURNAL OF HOSPITAL INFECTION, THE (US/0195-6701) [05585087] **3714**

JOURNAL OF HOSPITAL MARKETING (US/0883-7570) [12221286] 928, **3787**

●JOURNAL OF HOSPITALITY & LEISURE MARKETING (US/1050-7051) [21574618] 928, **4851**

JOURNAL OF HOUSING (1979) (US/0272-7374) [05819400] **2826**

JOURNAL OF HOUSING ECONOMICS (US/1051-1377) [21878213] 1499, **2826**

JOURNAL OF HOUSING FOR THE ELDERLY (US/0276-3893) [07374810] 5180, **2826**

JOURNAL OF HOUSING RESEARCH (US/1052-7001) [22354165] **2826**

JOURNAL OF HUMAN BEHAVIOR AND LEARNING *See* NEW DIRECTIONS FOR EDUCATION REFORM : A PUBLICATION OF THE COLLEGE OF EDUCATION AND BEHAVIORAL SCIENCES, WESTERN KENTUCKY UNIVERSITY **1767**

JOURNAL OF HUMAN ECOLOGY (DELHI) (II/0970-9274) [22378278] **2218**

JOURNAL OF HUMAN ERGOLOGY (JA/0300-8134) [01789959] **583**

JOURNAL OF HUMAN EVOLUTION (UK/0047-2484) [01783947] **239**

JOURNAL OF HUMAN HYPERTENSION (UK/0950-9240) [18713785] **3707**

JOURNAL OF HUMAN JUSTICE, THE (CN/0847-2971) [21416690] **2987**

JOURNAL OF HUMAN LACTATION (US/0890-3344) [14247077] **3763**

JOURNAL OF HUMAN MOVEMENT STUDIES (UK/0306-7297) [01950920] **583**

JOURNAL OF HUMAN MUSCLE PERFORMANCE *CEASED.* (US/1053-2137) [22480004] **3805**

JOURNAL OF HUMAN NUTRITION AND DIETETICS (UK/0952-3871) [18608310] **4193**

JOURNAL OF HUMAN RESOURCES, THE (US/0022-166X) [01604126] **1914**

JOURNAL OF HUMANISM & ETHICAL RELIGION (US/0899-7691) [18211831] **2251**

JOURNAL OF HUMANISTIC EDUCATION *CEASED.* (US/0890-0493) [07854418] **1898**

JOURNAL OF HUMANISTIC EDUCATION AND DEVELOPMENT, THE (US/0735-6846) [08847684] **1898**

JOURNAL OF HUMANISTIC PSYCHOLOGY, THE (US/0022-1678) [01783229] **4597**

JOURNAL OF HUMANITIES (ZOMBA, MALAWI) (MW) [16243895] **2848**

JOURNAL OF HYDRAULIC ENGINEERING (NEW YORK, N.Y.) (US/0733-9429) [08672558] **2092**

JOURNAL

Alphabetical Title Index

JOURNAL OF HYDRAULIC ENGINEERING (WASHINGTON, D.C.) **CEASED.** (US/1051-2705) [21899702] **2092**

JOURNAL OF HYDRAULIC RESEARCH (NE/0022-1686) [03910556] **2092**

JOURNAL OF HYDROBIOLOGY (II/0970-3594) [16777551] **461**

JOURNAL OF HYDRODYNAMICS (CC/1001-6058) [I10016058] **2092**

JOURNAL OF HYDROLOGICAL SCIENCES (PL/0324-8372) [02243104] **1416**

JOURNAL OF HYDROLOGY (AMSTERDAM) (NE/0022-1694) [01783126] **1416**

JOURNAL OF HYDROLOGY, NEW ZEALAND (NZ/0022-1708) [01754623] **1416**

JOURNAL OF HYDROSCIENCE AND HYDRAULIC ENGINEERING / COMMITTEE ON HYDRAULICS, JAPAN SOCIETY OF CIVIL ENGINEERS (JA) [10065659] **2092**

JOURNAL OF HYGIENE, EPIDEMIOLOGY, MICROBIOLOGY, AND IMMUNOLOGY (XR/0022-1732) [01696965] 3735, **4787**

●JOURNAL OF HYMENOPTERA RESEARCH (US/1070-9428) [28308627] **5610**

JOURNAL OF HYPERBARIC MEDICINE *See* UNDERSEA & HYPERBARIC MEDICINE **3697**

JOURNAL OF HYPERBARIC MEDICINE (US/0884-1225) [12308219] **3595**

JOURNAL OF HYPERTENSION (US/0263-6352) [09766054] **3707**

JOURNAL OF HYPERTENSION. SUPPLEMENT (UK/0952-1178) [11876404] **3707**

JOURNAL OF ICHTHYOLOGY (US/0032-9452) [01798162] **2307**

JOURNAL OF IMA, THE (US/0899-8299) [18265352] **3595**

JOURNAL OF IMAGING SCIENCE *See* JOURNAL OF IMAGING SCIENCE AND TECHNOLOGY, THE **5118**

●JOURNAL OF IMAGING SCIENCE AND TECHNOLOGY, THE (US/1062-3701) [25324639] **5118**

JOURNAL OF IMAGING TECHNOLOGY *See* JOURNAL OF IMAGING SCIENCE AND TECHNOLOGY, THE **5118**

JOURNAL OF IMMUNOASSAY (US/0197-1522) [05972176] **3673**

JOURNAL OF IMMUNOLOGICAL METHODS (NE/0022-1759) [01783876] **3673**

JOURNAL OF IMMUNOLOGICAL RESEARCH : JIR : THE JOURNAL OF THE ITALIAN FEDERATION OF IMMUNOLOGICAL SOCIETIES **CEASED.** (IT/1120-3765) [26850634] **3673**

JOURNAL OF IMMUNOLOGY (1950), THE (US/0022-1767) [01778718] **3673**

JOURNAL OF IMMUNOTHERAPY *See* JOURNAL OF IMMUNOTHERAPY WITH EMPHASIS ON TUMOR IMMUNOLOGY : OFFICIAL JOURNAL OF THE SOCIETY FOR BIOLOGICAL THERAPY **3674**

JOURNAL OF IMMUNOTHERAPY (US/1053-8550) [22684095] **3674**

●JOURNAL OF IMMUNOTHERAPY WITH EMPHASIS ON TUMOR IMMUNOLOGY : OFFICIAL JOURNAL OF THE SOCIETY FOR BIOLOGICAL THERAPY (US/1067-5582) [27262736] **3674**

JOURNAL OF IMPERIAL AND COMMONWEALTH HISTORY, THE (UK/0308-6534) [01089553] **2695**

JOURNAL OF IN VITRO FERTILIZATION AND EMBRYO TRANSFER *See* JOURNAL OF ASSISTED REPRODUCTION AND GENETICS **3763**

JOURNAL OF INCLUSION PHENOMENA AND MOLECULAR RECOGNITION IN CHEMISTRY (NE/0923-0750) [19889316] **1054**

JOURNAL OF INCOME AND WEALTH, THE (II) [07361144] **794**

JOURNAL OF INCOME DISTRIBUTION (UK) **794**

●JOURNAL OF INDEPENDENT RESEARCH (US/1055-8888) [23363990] 323, **1757**

JOURNAL OF INDEPENDENT SOCIAL WORK *See* JOURNAL OF ANALYTIC SOCIAL WORK **5291**

JOURNAL OF INDIAN ASSOCIATION FOR ENVIRONMENTAL MANAGEMENT (II/0970-8480) [25800037] **2234**

JOURNAL OF INDIAN COUNCIL OF PHILOSOPHICAL RESEARCH (II) [10714088] **4350**

JOURNAL OF INDIAN EDUCATION (II/0377-0435) [02244691] **1757**

JOURNAL OF INDIAN HISTORY (II/0022-1775) [01773643] **2655**

JOURNAL OF INDIAN ORTHODONTIC SOCIETY, THE (II/0301-5742) [01330448] **1327**

JOURNAL OF INDIAN PHILOSOPHY (NE/0022-1791) [01783390] **4350**

JOURNAL OF INDIAN PSYCHOLOGY (II/0379-3885) [04204928] **4597**

JOURNAL OF INDIAN SCHOOL OF POLITICAL ECONOMY (II) [21469876] 4479, **1499**

JOURNAL OF INDIAN WATER RESOURCES SOCIETY / IWRS (II) [15122553] **5535**

JOURNAL OF INDIAN WATER WORKS ASSOCIATION (II/0970-275X) [09201672] **5535**

JOURNAL OF INDIAN WRITING IN ENGLISH, THE (II/0302-1319) [02239636] **3400**

JOURNAL OF INDIGENOUS STUDIES, THE (CN/0838-4711) [19758199] **2741**

●JOURNAL OF INDIVIDUAL EMPLOYMENT RIGHTS (US/1055-7512) [23298068] **1682**

JOURNAL OF INDIVIDUAL PSYCHOLOGY (US/0022-1805) [01715632] **4597**

JOURNAL OF INDO-EUROPEAN STUDIES : MONOGRAPH SERIES (US/0895-7258) [06415854] **5206**

JOURNAL OF INDO-EUROPEAN STUDIES, THE (US/0092-2323) [01786142] 239, **3290**

JOURNAL OF INDUSTRIAL AFFAIRS (UK/0143-084X) [I0143084X] **687**

JOURNAL OF INDUSTRIAL ECONOMICS, THE (UK/0022-1821) [01782867] **1614**

JOURNAL OF INDUSTRIAL IRRADIATION TECHNOLOGY **CEASED.** (US/0735-7923) [08996599] **981**

JOURNAL OF INDUSTRIAL MICROBIOLOGY (NE/0169-4146) [13509063] **565**

JOURNAL OF INDUSTRIAL POLLUTION CONTROL (II/0970-2083) [14756019] **2234**

JOURNAL OF INDUSTRIAL RELATIONS, THE (AT/0022-1856) [01783211] **1682**

JOURNAL OF INDUSTRIAL TEACHER EDUCATION (US/0022-1864) [01604142] **1914**

JOURNAL OF INDUSTRIAL TECHNOLOGY / THE NATIONAL ASSOCIATION OF INDUSTRIAL TECHNOLOGY (US/0882-6404) [11930413] **5118**

JOURNAL OF INDUSTRY, THE (AT/0022-1872) [01782894] **1614**

JOURNAL OF INFECTION, THE (UK/0163-4453) [04392967] **3714**

●JOURNAL OF INFECTIOUS DISEASE PHARMACOTHERAPY (US/1068-7777) [27805602] 3595, **4311**

JOURNAL OF INFECTIOUS DISEASES, THE (US/0022-1899) [01754628] **3714**

JOURNAL OF INFERENTIAL AND DEDUCTIVE BIOLOGY (US/0883-1378) [12143576] **461**

●JOURNAL OF INFLAMMATORY BOWEL DISEASE (US) **3747**

JOURNAL OF INFORMATION & OPTIMIZATION SCIENCES (II/0252-2667) [07685228] **3513**

●JOURNAL OF INFORMATION ETHICS (US/1061-9321) [25489800] 3220, **2251**

JOURNAL OF INFORMATION MANAGEMENT **SUSPENDED.** (US/0198-9839) [06267046] **2885**

JOURNAL OF INFORMATION NETWORKING (UK/0966-9248) [28434143] 3220, **1242**

JOURNAL OF INFORMATION PROCESSING **CEASED.** (JA/0387-6101) [04087221] **1260**

JOURNAL OF INFORMATION PROCESSING AND CYBERNETICS (GW/0863-0593) [15783215] **1251**

JOURNAL OF INFORMATION RECORDING MATERIALS (1985) (GW/0863-0453) [16066393] **4371**

JOURNAL OF INFORMATION SCIENCE (NE/0165-5515) [05094715] **3220**

●JOURNAL OF INFORMATION SCIENCE AND TECHNOLOGY (II/0971-1988) [I09711988] **3220**

JOURNAL OF INFORMATION SYSTEMS (UK/0959-2954) [23596842] **1248**

JOURNAL OF INFORMATION SYSTEMS EDUCATION (US/1055-3096) [23136569] **1192**

JOURNAL OF INFORMATION SYSTEMS (OXFORD, ENGLAND) *See* INFORMATION SYSTEMS JOURNAL **1247**

JOURNAL OF INFORMATION SYSTEMS, THE (US/0888-7985) [13721495] 1192, **747**

●JOURNAL OF INFORMATION TECHNOLOGY FOR TEACHER EDUCATION (UK/0962-029X) [I0962029X] **1757**

JOURNAL OF INFORMATION TECHNOLOGY : JIT (UK/0268-3962) [16205068] 3220, **1192**

JOURNAL OF INFORMATION TECHNOLOGY MANAGEMENT (US/1042-1319) [22095836] **873**

●JOURNAL OF INFRASTRUCTURE SYSTEMS (US/1076-0342) [30374253] **2025**

JOURNAL OF INFUSIONAL CHEMOTHERAPY, THE (US/1060-0051) [24879081] **3819**

JOURNAL OF INHERITED METABOLIC DISEASE (UK/0141-8955) [05845444] **3798**

JOURNAL OF INORGANIC AND ORGANOMETALLIC POLYMERS (US/1053-0495) [22440002] **981**

JOURNAL OF INORGANIC BIOCHEMISTRY (US/0162-0134) [04082308] **489**

JOURNAL OF INSECT BEHAVIOR (US/0892-7553) [15255607] **5610**

JOURNAL OF INSECT PHYSIOLOGY (UK/0022-1910) [01782777] 583, **5610**

JOURNAL OF INSTITUTE OF ECONOMIC RESEARCH (II/0020-2851) [01640961] **1570**

JOURNAL OF INSTITUTIONAL AND THEORETICAL ECONOMICS : JITE (GW/0932-4569) [19674264] 1499, 4479, **5206**

JOURNAL OF INSTRUCTIONAL PSYCHOLOGY (US/0094-1956) [01793698] 1757, **4597**

JOURNAL OF INSTRUMENTATION & CONTROL / INSTITUTE OF INSTRUMENTATION AND CONTROL, AUSTRALIA (AT) [10713121] **2069**

JOURNAL OF INSURANCE ISSUES (US) [23446016] **2885**

JOURNAL OF INSURANCE MEDICINE (NEW YORK, N.Y.) (US/0743-6661) [10551296] **2885**

JOURNAL OF INSURANCE REGULATION (US/0736-248X) [08838801] **2885**

JOURNAL OF INTEGRAL EQUATIONS AND APPLICATIONS, THE (US/0897-3962) [17485776] **3513**

JOURNAL OF INTEGRATIVE AND ECLECTIC PSYCHOTHERAPY (US/0729-8579) [16637580] **3929**

●JOURNAL OF INTELLECTUAL DISABILITY RESEARCH (UK/0964-2633) [25322048] **4598**

●JOURNAL OF INTELLIGENT & FUZZY SYSTEMS (US/1064-1246) [26210459] **5118**

JOURNAL OF INTELLIGENT & ROBOTIC SYSTEMS (NE/0921-0296) [18197178] 1214, **1220**

●JOURNAL OF INTELLIGENT CONTROL, NEUROCOMPUTING AND FUZZY LOGIC (US) **1214**

JOURNAL OF INTELLIGENT INFORMATION SYSTEMS: INTEGRATING ARTIFICIAL INTELLIGENCE AND DATABASE TECHNOLOGIES (US/0925-9902) 1254, **1214**

JOURNAL OF INTELLIGENT MANUFACTURING (UK/0956-5515) [21997513] **1214**

JOURNAL OF INTELLIGENT MATERIAL SYSTEMS AND STRUCTURES (US/1045-389X) [20109871] **5118**

JOURNAL OF INTELLIGENT SYSTEMS (UK/0334-1860) [17021841] **1214**

JOURNAL OF INTENSIVE CARE MEDICINE (US/0885-0666) [12565680] **3595**

JOURNAL OF INTENSIVE ENGLISH STUDIES (US/0899-885X) [18261599] **3290**

JOURNAL OF INTER-AMERICAN MEDICINE, THE (US/0363-2768) [02376314] **3595**

JOURNAL OF INTERACTIVE INSTRUCTION DEVELOPMENT (US/1040-0370) [18296835] **1192**

JOURNAL OF INTERAMERICAN STUDIES AND WORLD AFFAIRS (US/0022-1937) [02239844] **4527**

JOURNAL OF INTERCULTURAL STUDIES (AT/0725-6868) [08144941] 2266, **1919**

JOURNAL OF INTERCULTURAL STUDIES (HIRAKATA, OSAKA) (JA/0388-0508) [02745703] **239**

JOURNAL OF INTERDISCIPLINARY CYCLE RESEARCH (NE/0022-1945) [01754631] **461**

JOURNAL OF INTERDISCIPLINARY ECONOMICS (UK/0260-1079) [13172100] **1499**

JOURNAL OF INTERDISCIPLINARY HISTORY, THE (US/0022-1953) [01799976] **2621**

JOURNAL OF INTERDISCIPLINARY LITERARY STUDIES (NE/1044-8985) [19964547] 2266, **3400**

JOURNAL OF INTERDISCIPLINARY STUDIES (US/0890-0132) [14127017] **4969**

JOURNAL — Alphabetical Title Index

JOURNAL OF INTERFERON RESEARCH (US/0197-8357) [06135612] **565**

JOURNAL OF INTERGROUP RELATIONS (US/0047-2492) [01775154] **5250**

●JOURNAL OF INTERIOR DESIGN (US/1071-7641) [28236006] **2901**

JOURNAL OF INTERIOR DESIGN EDUCATION AND RESEARCH (US/0147-0418) [03081870] **2901**

JOURNAL OF INTERLIBRARY LOAN & INFORMATION SUPPLY (US/1042-4458) [19050720] **3220**

●JOURNAL OF INTERLIBRARY LOAN, DOCUMENT DELIVERY & INFORMATION SUPPLY (US/1072-303X) [28905312] **3220**

JOURNAL OF INTERMOUNTAIN ARCHEOLOGY (US/0738-2030) [09363481] 239, 2741, **271**

JOURNAL OF INTERNAL MEDICINE (UK/0954-6820) [19214370] **3798**

JOURNAL OF INTERNAL MEDICINE. SUPPLEMENT (UK/0955-7873) [19588004] **3799**

●JOURNAL OF INTERNATIONAL ACCOUNTING AUDITING & TAXATION (US/1061-9518) [25493389] **747**

JOURNAL OF INTERNATIONAL AFFAIRS (BALTIMORE, MD.) *See* TOWSON STATE JOURNAL OF INTERNATIONAL AFFAIRS **4536**

JOURNAL OF INTERNATIONAL AFFAIRS (NEW YORK) (US) [03756446] **4527**

JOURNAL OF INTERNATIONAL AND COMPARATIVE SOCIAL WELFARE (US/0898-5847) [12380388] **5292**

JOURNAL OF INTERNATIONAL ARBITRATION (SZ/0255-8106) [10863392] **3131**

JOURNAL OF INTERNATIONAL BANKING LAW (UK/0267-937X) [13290550] **3087**

JOURNAL OF INTERNATIONAL BUSINESS STUDIES (CN/0047-2506) [01604487] 1500, **687**

JOURNAL OF INTERNATIONAL CONSUMER MARKETING (US/0896-1530) [16929104] **928**

JOURNAL OF INTERNATIONAL DEVELOPMENT (UK/0954-1748) [19495246] **1500**

JOURNAL OF INTERNATIONAL ECONOMIC INTEGRATION (KO) [15799441] **1637**

JOURNAL OF INTERNATIONAL ECONOMIC STUDIES (JA/0911-1247) [20684356] **794**

JOURNAL OF INTERNATIONAL ECONOMICS (NE/0022-1996) [01797961] **1637**

JOURNAL OF INTERNATIONAL FINANCIAL MANAGEMENT & ACCOUNTING (UK/0954-1314) [19931743] **747**

JOURNAL OF INTERNATIONAL FINANCIAL MARKETS, INSTITUTIONS & MONEY (US/1042-4431) [19050648] 794, **1637**

JOURNAL OF INTERNATIONAL FOOD & AGRIBUSINESS MARKETING (US/0897-4438) [17501809] 100, **2347**

JOURNAL OF INTERNATIONAL MARKETING AND MARKETING RESEARCH (UK) [17645430] **928**

JOURNAL OF INTERNATIONAL MARKETING (EAST LANSING, MICH.) (US/1069-031X) [26897890] **928**

JOURNAL OF INTERNATIONAL MEDICAL RESEARCH, THE (UK/0300-0605) [02319495] **3595**

JOURNAL OF INTERNATIONAL MONEY AND FINANCE (UK/0261-5606) [08608679] **795**

JOURNAL OF INTERNATIONAL PHYSICIANS (US/0161-7702) [03997317] **3595**

JOURNAL OF INTERNATIONAL SECURITIES MARKETS, THE (UK) [17003741] **1500**

JOURNAL OF INTERNATIONAL TAXATION (US/1049-6378) [21268452] **4734**

JOURNAL OF INTERNATIONAL TRADE AND ECONOMIC DEVELOPMENT (UK/0963-8199) 843, **1637**

JOURNAL OF INTERPERSONAL VIOLENCE (US/0886-2605) [12879051] **5292**

JOURNAL OF INTERPRETATION (SILVER SPRING, MD.) *CEASED.* (US/0882-7893) [11985805] **5292**

●JOURNAL OF INTERPROFESSIONAL CARE (UK) [25270898] 5292, **3775**

JOURNAL OF INTERVENTIONAL CARDIOLOGY (US/0896-4327) [17152753] **3707**

JOURNAL OF INTERVENTIONAL RADIOLOGY (UK/0268-0882) [14933634] **3942**

JOURNAL OF INTRAVENOUS NURSING (US/0896-5846) [17204351] **3858**

JOURNAL OF INTRAVENOUS THERAPY (LOS ANGELES) (US/0194-1658) [05355681] **3595**

JOURNAL OF INVASIVE CARDIOLOGY, THE (US/1042-3931) [19034338] **3707**

JOURNAL OF INVERSE AND ILL-POSED PROBLEMS (NE/0928-0219) 4409, **3513**

JOURNAL OF INVERTEBRATE PATHOLOGY (US/0022-2011) [01754635] 3895, **5611**

JOURNAL OF INVESTIGATIONAL ALLERGOLOGY & CLINICAL IMMUNOLOGY (SP/1018-9068) [23902761] **3674**

JOURNAL OF INVESTIGATIVE DERMATOLOGY, THE (US/0022-202X) [00988051] **3721**

●JOURNAL OF INVESTIGATIVE MEDICINE (US) **3595**

JOURNAL OF INVESTIGATIVE SURGERY (US/0894-1939) [15863360] **3967**

●JOURNAL OF INVESTING, THE (US/1068-0896) [27424869] **904**

●JOURNAL OF INVITATIONAL THEORY AND PRACTICE (US/1060-6041) [25043919] 4598, **1898**

JOURNAL OF IRISH ARCHAEOLOGY, THE (IE/0268-537X) [10782518] **271**

JOURNAL OF IRISH LITERATURE, THE *CEASED.* (US/US/0047-2514) [00974150] **3400**

JOURNAL OF IRREPRODUCIBLE RESULTS, THE (US/0022-2038) [01783378] **5118**

JOURNAL OF IRRIGATION AND DRAINAGE ENGINEERING (US/0733-9437) [08672531] **2092**

JOURNAL OF IRRIGATION ENGINEERING AND RURAL PLANNING (JA/0287-8607) [09677207] 2092, **176**

JOURNAL OF ISLAMIC BANKING & FINANCE : QUARTERLY PUBLICATION OF THE INTERNATIONAL ASSOCIATION OF ISLAMIC BANKS, KARACHI (ASIAN REGION) (PK) [12434027] **795**

JOURNAL OF ISLAMIC STUDIES (OXFORD, ENGLAND) (UK/0955-2340) [22521955] **5043**

JOURNAL OF ISRAELI HISTORY, THE (UK) **2769**

JOURNAL OF ITALIAN FOOD & WINE (US/1073-3124) [29382107] **2347**

JOURNAL OF J J GROUP OF HOSPITALS AND GRANT MEDICAL COLLEGE (II/0520-5085) [01779387] **3787**

JOURNAL OF JAPAN FOUNDRYMAN'S SOCIETY (JA) **4006**

JOURNAL OF JAPANESE LINGUISTICS (JA) [22723090] **3290**

JOURNAL OF JAPANESE STUDIES, THE (US/0095-6848) [01798633] **2655**

JOURNAL OF JAPANESE TRADE & INDUSTRY (JA/0285-9556) [08152747] 1500, **687**

JOURNAL OF JASTRO : THE OFFICIAL JOURNAL OF THE JAPANESE SOCIETY FOR THERAPEUTIC RADIOLOGY AND ONCOLOGY, THE (JA/1040-9564) [18591911] **3819**

JOURNAL OF JAZZ DISCOGRAPHY (UK) [04683084] **4126**

JOURNAL OF JEWISH COMMUNAL SERVICE (US/0022-2089) [02509312] **2266**

●JOURNAL OF JEWISH EDUCATION (US) [30901914] **5050**

JOURNAL OF JEWISH MUSIC AND LITURGY (US/0197-0100) [04079294] 5050, **4126**

JOURNAL OF JEWISH STUDIES, THE (UK/0022-2097) [01782554] **5050**

JOURNAL OF JEWISH THOUGHT & PHILOSOPHY, THE (SZ/1053-699X) [22610014] **5050**

JOURNAL OF JUDICIAL ADMINISTRATION (AT/1036-7918) [24841820] **2987**

JOURNAL OF JURISTIC PAPYROLOGY, THE (PL/0075-4277) [01754640] **2988**

JOURNAL OF JUVENILE LAW (US/0160-2098) [03367760] **3121**

JOURNAL OF KANSAS PHARMACY, THE (US/0194-5106) [11418593] **4311**

JOURNAL OF KENTUCKY STUDIES, THE (US/8755-4208) [11299805] **3400**

JOURNAL OF KERALA STUDIES (II/0377-0443) [01780980] **2655**

JOURNAL OF KEW GUILD (UK) **2421**

JOURNAL OF KING SAUD UNIVERSITY. SCIENCE (SU) [22538064] **5119**

●JOURNAL OF KNOT THEORY AND ITS RAMIFICATIONS (SI/0218-2165) [25645810] **3513**

JOURNAL OF KOREAN AFFAIRS (US/0047-2522) [01783585] **2655**

JOURNAL OF KOREAN APPLIED ECOLOGY (KO/1012-0408) [I10120408] **2218**

JOURNAL OF KOREAN MEDICAL SCIENCE (KO/1011-8934) [15484284] **3595**

JOURNAL OF KOREAN STUDIES (SEATTLE, WASH. : 1979), THE (US/0731-1613) [05735985] **2655**

JOURNAL OF LABELLED COMPOUNDS & RADIOPHARMACEUTICALS (UK/0362-4803) [02339476] **1054**

JOURNAL OF LABOR ECONOMICS (US/0734-306X) [08722806] 1682, **1500**

JOURNAL OF LABOR RESEARCH (US/0195-3613) [05460716] 1500, **1682**

JOURNAL OF LABORATORY AND CLINICAL MEDICINE, THE (US/0022-2143) [01716105] **3595**

JOURNAL OF LAND USE & ENVIRONMENTAL LAW (US/0892-4880) [11687340] **3113**

JOURNAL OF LANGUAGE AND SOCIAL PSYCHOLOGY (US/0261-927X) [09016161] 4598, **3290**

JOURNAL OF LANGUAGE ARTS AND COMMUNICATION (J.L.A.C.) (NR) [08278698] 1115, **3290**

JOURNAL OF LANGUAGE FOR INTERNATIONAL BUSINESS, THE (US/8755-0504) [11093084] 687, **3290**

JOURNAL OF LAPAROENDOSCOPIC SURGERY (US/1052-3901) [22282876] **3967**

JOURNAL OF LARYNGOLOGY AND OTOLOGY (UK/0022-2151) [01754643] **3889**

JOURNAL OF LARYNGOLOGY AND OTOLOGY. SUPPLEMENT, THE (UK/0144-2945) [04558974] **3889**

JOURNAL OF LASER APPLICATIONS (US/1042-346X) [19017225] **4435**

JOURNAL OF LATIN AMERICAN LORE (US/0360-1927) [01845716] **2321**

JOURNAL OF LATIN AMERICAN STUDIES (UK/0022-216X) [01800137] **2741**

JOURNAL OF LATIN COMMUNITY HEALTH, THE (US/0740-2279) [09634888] **4787**

JOURNAL OF LAUGHTER IN TEACHING/TRAINING : JOLT, THE (US/1018-5666) [24383674] **1898**

JOURNAL OF LAW AND COMMERCE, THE (US/0733-2491) [07942474] 843, **2988**

JOURNAL OF LAW & ECONOMICS, THE (US/0022-2186) [01607223] 1500, **2988**

JOURNAL OF LAW & EDUCATION (US/0275-6072) [01797968] 2988, **1865**

JOURNAL OF LAW AND EDUCATION / BRIGHAM YOUNG UNIVERSITY (US) [25679032] **2988**

JOURNAL OF LAW AND ETHICS IN DENTISTRY *CEASED.* (US/0894-8879) [16286814] 2251, **1327**

JOURNAL OF LAW AND HEALTH (US/1044-6419) [12489576] **3741**

JOURNAL OF LAW AND INFORMATION SCIENCE (AT/0729-1485) [08962639] 1227, 3220, **2988**

JOURNAL OF LAW & POLITICS (US/0749-2227) [10199244] 4479, **2988**

JOURNAL OF LAW AND RELIGION, THE (US/0748-0814) [10032671] 4969, **2988**

JOURNAL OF LAW AND SOCIETY (UK/0263-323X) [08833836] 5250, **2988**

JOURNAL OF LAW, ECONOMICS & ORGANIZATION (US/8756-6222) [11613201] 1500, **2988**

●JOURNAL OF LAW, MEDICINE & ETHICS, THE (US/1073-1105) [28649728] 2251, 3595, **2988**

JOURNAL OF LEARNING DISABILITIES (US/0022-2194) [01604299] **1880**

JOURNAL OF LEARNING SKILLS, THE (US/0740-5715) [09102434] **1757**

JOURNAL OF LEATHER RESEARCH (NR/0189-5222) [14179854] **3184**

JOURNAL OF LEEDS UNIVERSITY MINING SOCIETY, THE (UK) [02278635] **2141**

JOURNAL OF LEGAL ASPECTS OF SPORT (US/1072-0316) [25118975] 4901, **2988**

JOURNAL OF LEGAL ECONOMICS (US/1054-3023) [22835741] **1500**

JOURNAL OF LEGAL EDUCATION (US/0022-2208) [01754647] **2988**

JOURNAL OF LEGAL HISTORY, THE (UK/0144-0365) [07028583] **2988**

JOURNAL OF LEGAL MEDICINE (CHICAGO. 1979), THE (US/0194-7648) [04997813] **3741**

JOURNAL OF LEGAL PLURALISM AND UNOFFICIAL LAW (US/0732-9113) [07725943] **2988**

JOURNAL OF LEGAL STUDIES EDUCATION, THE (US/0896-5811) [11306837] **2988**

JOURNAL OF LEGAL STUDIES, THE (US/0047-2530) [01754648] **2988**

JOURNAL OF LEGAL THOUGHTS (PK) [07519827] **2989**

JOURNAL OF LEGISLATION (US/0146-9584) [02888973] **2989**

JOURNAL OF LEISURABILITY (1980) (CN/0711-222X) [06575702] 4851, **4389**

JOURNAL OF LEISURE RESEARCH (US/0022-2216) [01783376] **4851**

JOURNAL OF LEUKOCYTE BIOLOGY (US/0741-5400) [10186822] **3799**

JOURNAL OF LIBERTARIAN STUDIES, THE (US/0363-2873) [02921225] **5206**

JOURNAL OF LIBRARIANSHIP AND INFORMATION SCIENCE (UK/0961-0006) [23295081] **3220**

JOURNAL OF LIBRARY ADMINISTRATION (US/0193-0826) [05139880] **3220**

JOURNAL OF LIBRARY AND INFORMATION SCIENCE (DELHI) (II/0970-714X) [02879875] **3220**

JOURNAL OF LIBRARY SERVICE (II) [01784104] **3220**

●JOURNAL OF LIE THEORY (GW) **3513**

JOURNAL OF LIGHT & VISUAL ENVIRONMENT (JA/0387-8805) [08757480] **4436**

JOURNAL OF LIGHT CONSTRUCTION (NATIONAL ED.), THE (US/1056-828X) [23859442] **618**

JOURNAL OF LIGHT CONSTRUCTION (NEW ENGLAND ED), THE (US/1050-2610) [21433165] **618**

JOURNAL OF LIGHTWAVE TECHNOLOGY (US/0733-8724) [08648989] **4436**

JOURNAL OF LINGUISTIC ANTHROPOLOGY (US/1055-1360) [23092195] 3290, **239**

JOURNAL OF LINGUISTICS (UK/0022-2267) [01754651] **3290**

JOURNAL OF LIPID MEDIATORS (NE/0921-8319) [20224609] **1042**

●JOURNAL OF LIPID MEDIATORS AND CELL SIGNALLING (NE/0929-7855) [30302539] **1042**

JOURNAL OF LIPID RESEARCH (US/0022-2275) [01589637] **583**

JOURNAL OF LIPOSOME RESEARCH (US/0898-2104) [17743119] **538**

JOURNAL OF LIQUID CHROMATOGRAPHY (US/0148-3919) [03527306] **1017**

JOURNAL OF LITERARY CRITICISM (II) [12146726] **3345**

JOURNAL OF LITERARY SEMANTICS (NE/0341-7638) [00974146] 3400, **3290**

JOURNAL OF LITERARY STUDIES (PRETORIA, SOUTH AFRICA) (SA/0256-4718) [12857964] **3345**

JOURNAL OF LITERATURE AND AESTHETICS (II) [09185946] 354, **3400**

JOURNAL OF LITHOTRIPSY & STONE DISEASE See JOURNAL OF STONE DISEASE, THE **3968**

JOURNAL OF LIVESTOCK AND AGRICULTURE See ST. JOSEPH JOURNAL OF LIVESTOCK AND AGRICULTURE **222**

JOURNAL OF LOGIC AND COMPUTATION (UK/0955-792X) [22480617] **1214**

●JOURNAL OF LOGIC, LANGUAGE, AND INFORMATION (NE/0925-8531) [26231379] 3291, **4350**

JOURNAL OF LOGIC PROGRAMMING, THE (US/0743-1066) [10510063] **1280**

JOURNAL OF LONG TERM CARE ADMINISTRATION, THE (US/0093-4445) [01793613] **3787**

JOURNAL OF LONG-TERM EFFECTS OF MEDICAL IMPLANTS (US/1050-6934) [21574387] **3595**

JOURNAL OF LOSS PREVENTION IN THE PROCESS INDUSTRIES (UK/0950-4230) [17457254] **2099**

JOURNAL OF LOW FREQUENCY NOISE AND VIBRATION (UK/0263-0923) [09708000] **2234**

JOURNAL OF LOW TEMPERATURE PHYSICS (US/0022-2291) [00844607] **4409**

JOURNAL OF LUMINESCENCE (NE/0022-2313) [01640731] **4436**

JOURNAL OF MACHINERY MANUFACTURE AND RELIABILITY (US/1052-6188) [22337843] 1220, **2118**

JOURNAL OF MACROECONOMICS (US/0164-0704) [04572345] **1500**

JOURNAL OF MACROMARKETING (US/0276-1467) [07317157] **928**

JOURNAL OF MACROMOLECULAR SCIENCE. CHEMISTRY See JOURNAL OF MACROMOLECULAR SCIENCE. PURE AND APPLIED CHEMISTRY **1042**

JOURNAL OF MACROMOLECULAR SCIENCE. PHYSICS (US/0022-2348) [19700913] **4409**

●JOURNAL OF MACROMOLECULAR SCIENCE. PURE AND APPLIED CHEMISTRY (US/1060-1325) [24877750] **1042**

JOURNAL OF MACROMOLECULAR SCIENCE. REVIEWS IN MACROMOLECULAR CHEMISTRY (US/0022-2356) [01783201] **1042**

JOURNAL OF MACROMOLECULAR SCIENCE. REVIEWS IN MACROMOLECULAR CHEMISTRY AND PHYSICS (US/0736-6574) [09201882] **981**

JOURNAL OF MAGIC HISTORY, THE (US/0192-9917) [05094422] **4862**

JOURNAL OF MAGNETIC RESONANCE (US/0022-2364) [01783377] **4444**

JOURNAL OF MAGNETIC RESONANCE IMAGING (US/1053-1807) [22469246] **3942**

●JOURNAL OF MAGNETIC RESONANCE. SERIES A (US/1064-1858) [26224216] **4444**

●JOURNAL OF MAGNETIC RESONANCE. SERIES B (US/1064-1866) [26224244] **4444**

JOURNAL OF MAGNETISM AND MAGNETIC MATERIALS (NE/0304-8853) [02322040] **4444**

JOURNAL OF MAGNETOHYDRODYNAMICS & PLASMA RESEARCH (US) 4444, **2069**

JOURNAL OF MAHARASHTRA AGRICULTURAL UNIVERSITIES (II/0378-2395) [02942501] **176**

●JOURNAL OF MAINTENANCE IN THE ADDICTIONS (US) **1346**

JOURNAL OF MALTESE STUDIES (MM/0075-4285) [02287037] 3291, **3400**

●JOURNAL OF MAMMALIAN EVOLUTION (US/1064-7554) [26391434] **239**

JOURNAL OF MAMMALOGY (US/0022-2372) [01800234] **5588**

JOURNAL OF MANAGEMENT (US/0149-2063) [03450558] **873**

JOURNAL OF MANAGEMENT ACCOUNTING RESEARCH (US/1049-2127) [21148637] 873, **747**

JOURNAL OF MANAGEMENT CONSULTING (AMSTERDAM) (US/0168-7778) [09310182] **873**

JOURNAL OF MANAGEMENT DEVELOPMENT, THE (UK/0262-1711) [08735092] **943**

JOURNAL OF MANAGEMENT EDUCATION : A PUBLICATION OF THE ORGANIZATIONAL BEHAVIOR TEACHING SOCIETY (US) [23135974] **1757**

JOURNAL OF MANAGEMENT EDUCATION (NEWBURY PARK, CALIF.) (US/1052-5629) [22303862] 1898, **873**

●JOURNAL OF MANAGEMENT HISTORY (UK/1355-2546) **874**

JOURNAL OF MANAGEMENT IN ENGINEERING (US/0742-597X) [10381678] **1983**

JOURNAL OF MANAGEMENT IN MEDICINE (UK/0268-9235) [15904061] **3596**

JOURNAL OF MANAGEMENT IN PRACTICE (US/1042-1300) [18945510] **874**

JOURNAL OF MANAGEMENT INFORMATION SYSTEMS (US/0742-1222) [10260798] **3220**

●JOURNAL OF MANAGEMENT INQUIRY (US/1056-4926) [23725363] **874**

JOURNAL OF MANAGEMENT SCIENCE & POLICY ANALYSIS (US/1042-7309) [19117140] **4658**

JOURNAL OF MANAGEMENT STUDIES, THE (UK/0022-2380) [01783076] **874**

JOURNAL OF MANAGEMENT SYSTEMS, THE (US/1041-2808) [18706554] **943**

JOURNAL OF MANAGERIAL ISSUES (US/1045-3695) [20110604] **874**

JOURNAL OF MANAGERIAL PSYCHOLOGY (UK/0268-3946) [15465626] 874, **4598**

JOURNAL OF MANIPULATIVE AND PHYSIOLOGICAL THERAPEUTICS (US/0161-4754) [03957827] **4380**

●JOURNAL OF MANUAL & MANIPULATIVE THERAPY, THE (US/1066-9817) [27117055] **3882**

JOURNAL OF MANUAL MEDICINE CEASED. (GW/0935-6339) [20351081] **3596**

JOURNAL OF MANUFACTURING SYSTEMS (US/0278-6125) [07853568] **3482**

JOURNAL OF MANUFACTURING, THE CEASED. (US/1041-4673) [18774610] **3482**

JOURNAL OF MARINE ARCHAEOLOGY (II) [24256827] **271**

●JOURNAL OF MARINE BIOTECHNOLOGY, THE (US) [28523618] 3694, **555**

JOURNAL OF MARINE EDUCATION See SEA WORLD **557**

●JOURNAL OF MARINE ENVIRONMENTAL ENGINEERING (SZ/1061-026X) [25161139] **2176**

JOURNAL OF MARINE RESEARCH (US/0022-2402) [01782330] **555**

JOURNAL OF MARINE SCIENCES CEASED. (CC) **555**

JOURNAL OF MARINE SYSTEMS See JOURNAL OF THE EUROPEAN ASSOCIATION OF MARINE SCIENCES AND TECHNIQUES **1450**

JOURNAL OF MARINE SYSTEMS (NE/0924-7963) [24497443] **1450**

JOURNAL OF MARITAL AND FAMILY THERAPY (US/0194-472X) [04613511] **2282**

JOURNAL OF MARKETING (US/0022-2429) [01782320] **928**

JOURNAL OF MARKETING CHANNELS (US/1046-669X) [20484835] **928**

●JOURNAL OF MARKETING COMMUNICATIONS (UK/1352-7266) **928**

JOURNAL OF MARKETING EDUCATION (US/0273-4753) [05733672] **928**

JOURNAL OF MARKETING FOR HIGHER EDUCATION (US/0884-1241) [12308299] 928, **1833**

JOURNAL OF MARKETING FOR MENTAL HEALTH (US/0883-7589) [12221340] **4787**

JOURNAL OF MARKETING MANAGEMENT (UK/0267-257X) [13616717] **928**

●JOURNAL OF MARKETING PRACTICE : APPLIED MARKETING SCIENCE (UK/1355-2538) **928**

JOURNAL OF MARKETING RESEARCH (US) [01978245] **928**

JOURNAL OF MARRIAGE AND THE FAMILY (US/0022-2445) [01641520] **2282**

JOURNAL OF MARTIAL ARTS (US) **4901**

JOURNAL OF MASS MEDIA ETHICS (US/0890-0523) [13338929] **2251**

●JOURNAL OF MASS SPECTROMETRY. PART A (UK/1076-5174) [30505598] 1042, **1017**

JOURNAL OF MATERIALS CHEMISTRY (UK/0959-9428) [23295112] **981**

JOURNAL OF MATERIALS EDUCATION, THE (US/0738-7989) [09437783] **2103**

JOURNAL OF MATERIALS ENGINEERING (US/0931-7058) [15736270] **2103**

JOURNAL OF MATERIALS ENGINEERING See JOURNAL OF MATERIALS ENGINEERING AND PERFORMANCE **2118**

●JOURNAL OF MATERIALS ENGINEERING AND PERFORMANCE (US/1059-9495) [24820669] **2118**

JOURNAL OF MATERIALS IN CIVIL ENGINEERING (US/0899-1561) [18026017] **2025**

●JOURNAL OF MATERIALS MANUFACTURING AND PROCESSING SCIENCE (US/1062-0656) [25517123] **3482**

JOURNAL OF MATERIALS PROCESSING TECHNOLOGY (NE/0924-0136) [21058561] 1282, **2103**

JOURNAL OF MATERIALS RESEARCH (US/0884-2914) [12358170] **2103**

JOURNAL OF MATERIALS SCIENCE (UK/0022-2461) [01754660] **4006**

JOURNAL OF MATERIALS SCIENCE & TECHNOLOGY (US/1005-0302) **5119**

JOURNAL OF MATERIALS SCIENCE LETTERS (UK/0261-8028) [08163319] **2103**

JOURNAL OF MATERIALS SCIENCE. MATERIALS IN ELECTRONICS (UK/0957-4522) [21581688] **2069**

JOURNAL OF MATERIALS SCIENCE. MATERIALS IN MEDICINE (UK/0957-4530) [21929562] **3694**

JOURNAL OF MATERIALS SHAPING TECHNOLOGY See JOURNAL OF MATERIALS ENGINEERING AND PERFORMANCE **2118**

●JOURNAL OF MATERIALS SYNTHESIS AND PROCESSING (US/1064-7562) [26391464] **2104**

JOURNAL OF MATERNAL-FETAL INVESTIGATION : THE OFFICIAL JOURNAL OF FRENCH SOCIETY OF ULTRASOUND IN MEDICINE AND BIOLOGY ... [ET AL.] (US/0939-6322) [26688474] **3763**

●JOURNAL OF MATERNAL-FETAL MEDICINE, THE (US/1057-0802) [23932765] **3763**

JOURNAL OF MATHEMATICAL ANALYSIS AND APPLICATIONS (US/0022-247X) [01800257] **3513**

JOURNAL

Alphabetical Title Index

JOURNAL OF MATHEMATICAL AND PHYSICAL SCIENCES (II/0047-2557) [01783499] 4409, **3513**

JOURNAL OF MATHEMATICAL BEHAVIOR, THE (US/0732-3123) [07704522] 1898, **3513**

JOURNAL OF MATHEMATICAL BIOLOGY (AU/0303-6812) [01794831] 3513, **461**

JOURNAL OF MATHEMATICAL CHEMISTRY (NE/0259-9791) [17319203] **981**

JOURNAL OF MATHEMATICAL ECONOMICS (NE/0304-4068) [01983975] 3513, **1500**

JOURNAL OF MATHEMATICAL IMAGING AND VISION (US/0924-9907) **3513**

JOURNAL OF MATHEMATICAL PHYSICS (US/0022-2488) [01800258] 3513, **4409**

JOURNAL OF MATHEMATICAL PSYCHOLOGY (US/0022-2496) [01783082] 3513, **4598**

JOURNAL OF MATHEMATICAL RESEARCH AND EXPOSITION (CC/1000-9191) [I10009191] **3513**

●JOURNAL OF MATHEMATICAL SCIENCES (US/1072-3374) [28916588] **3513**

JOURNAL OF MATHEMATICAL SCIENCES (II/0449-2757) [01754663] **3514**

JOURNAL OF MATHEMATICAL SOCIOLOGY, THE (US/0022-250X) [01783908] 3514, **5250**

JOURNAL OF MATHEMATICAL SYSTEMS, ESTIMATION, AND CONTROL (US/1052-0600) [22173480] **3514**

JOURNAL OF MATHEMATICS OF KYOTO UNIVERSITY (JA/0023-608X) [01783327] **3514**

JOURNAL OF MATHEMATICS, TOKUSHIMA UNIVERSITY (JA/0075-4293) [01767564] **3514**

JOURNAL OF MATHEMATICS / UNIVERSITY OF THE PUNJAB (PK) [15133586] **3514**

JOURNAL OF MAYAN LINGUISTICS (US/0195-475X) [04205735] 239, **3291**

JOURNAL OF MECHANOCHEMISTRY & CELL MOTILITY (US/0091-6552) [01783878] **538**

JOURNAL OF MECHNICAL DESIGN (1990) (US/1050-0472) [21319125] **2118**

JOURNAL OF MEDECINE NUCLEAIRE ET BIOPHYSIQUE (FR/0992-3039) [18581867] 3848, **495**

JOURNAL OF MEDIA ECONOMICS (US/0899-7764) [18128413] **1115**

JOURNAL OF MEDICAL AND HEALTH LABORATORY TECHNOLOGY, MALAYSIA (MY/0126-7752) [06288559] **3596**

JOURNAL OF MEDICAL AND PHARMACEUTICAL MARKETING **SUSPENDED.** (NR/0331-0124) [I03310124] **4311**

JOURNAL OF MEDICAL AND VETERINARY MYCOLOGY (UK/0268-1218) [13369100] **575**

●JOURNAL OF MEDICAL BIOGRAPHY (UK/0967-7720) [27919322] **3967**

JOURNAL OF MEDICAL COLLEGES OF PLA (CC/1000-9094) [15923412] **3596**

JOURNAL OF MEDICAL EDUCATION TECHNOLOGIES (US/1056-2478) [23600468] **3596**

JOURNAL OF MEDICAL ENGINEERING & TECHNOLOGY (UK/0309-1902) [02778165] **3694**

JOURNAL OF MEDICAL ENTOMOLOGY (US/0022-2585) [01783323] 5513, 4787, **5611**

JOURNAL OF MEDICAL ETHICS (UK/0306-6800) [01838186] 2251, **3596**

JOURNAL OF MEDICAL GENETICS (UK/0022-2593) [01640533] **549**

JOURNAL OF MEDICAL HUMANITIES, THE (US/1041-3545) [18731853] 2848, **3596**

JOURNAL OF MEDICAL MICROBIOLOGY (UK/0022-2615) [01797958] **565**

JOURNAL OF MEDICAL PRACTICE MANAGEMENT, THE (US/8755-0229) [11248524] **3914**

JOURNAL OF MEDICAL PRIMATOLOGY (SZ/0047-2565) [01783975] **5513**

JOURNAL OF MEDICAL SCREENING (UK) 4787, **3596**

●JOURNAL OF MEDICAL SPEECH-LANGUAGE PATHOLOGY (US/1065-1438) [26514546] **4390**

JOURNAL OF MEDICAL SYSTEMS (US/0148-5598) [03321484] **3787**

JOURNAL OF MEDICAL VIROLOGY (US/0146-6615) [02988328] **565**

JOURNAL OF MEDICINAL CHEMISTRY (US/0022-2623) [01754668] 4311, **490**

JOURNAL OF MEDICINE AND PHILOSOPHY, THE (NE/0360-5310) [01909882] 4350, **3596**

JOURNAL OF MEDICINE (WESTBURY) (US/0025-7850) [01357589] **3596**

JOURNAL OF MEDIEVAL AND RENAISSANCE STUDIES, THE (US/0047-2573) [00817176] **2695**

JOURNAL OF MEDIEVAL HISTORY (NE/0304-4181) [02338020] **2695**

JOURNAL OF MEDIEVAL HISTORY MICROFORM (SZ/0304-4181) [17285895] **2695**

●JOURNAL OF MEDIEVAL LATIN : A PUBLICATION OF THE NORTH AMERICAN ASSOCIATION OF MEDIEVAL LATIN, THE (BE/0778-9750) [25502694] **3291**

JOURNAL OF MEDITERRANEAN ANTHROPOLOGY & ARCHAEOLOGY (GR/0253-6625) [08612289] 271, **239**

JOURNAL OF MEDITERRANEAN ARCHAEOLOGY (UK/0952-7648) [18799927] **271**

JOURNAL OF MEDITERRANEAN STUDIES (UK) **2848**

JOURNAL OF MEDITERRANEAN STUDIES (MM/1016-3476) [24102518] **2848**

JOURNAL OF MEMBRANE BIOLOGY, THE (US/0022-2631) [01799894] **538**

JOURNAL OF MEMBRANE SCIENCE (NE/0376-7388) [02145503] **5119**

JOURNAL OF MEMORY AND LANGUAGE (US/0749-596X) [11148687] 3291, **4598**

JOURNAL OF MENNONITE STUDIES (CN/0824-5053) [10669089] **4969**

●JOURNAL OF MEN'S STUDIES, THE (US/1060-8265) [25065810] 5250, **3995**

JOURNAL OF MENTAL DEFICIENCY RESEARCH **See** JOURNAL OF INTELLECTUAL DISABILITY RESEARCH **4598**

●JOURNAL OF MENTAL HEALTH (UK/0963-8237) [26585830] **3929**

JOURNAL OF MENTAL HEALTH ADMINISTRATION (US/0092-8623) [01771078] **5292**

JOURNAL OF MENTAL HEALTH COUNSELING (US/1040-2861) [16265327] **5292**

JOURNAL OF METAMORPHIC GEOLOGY (UK/0263-4929) [09535341] **1458**

JOURNAL OF METEOROLOGY (UK/0307-5966) [03353417] **1426**

JOURNAL OF MEXICAN AMERICAN HISTORY, THE **CEASED.** (US/0047-2581) [01754673] **2741**

JOURNAL OF MICROBIAL BIOTECHNOLOGY (II/0256-8551) [14756106] **3694**

JOURNAL OF MICROBIOLOGICAL METHODS (NE/0167-7012) [09403833] **566**

JOURNAL OF MICROBIOLOGY AND BIOTECHNOLOGY (KO/1017-7825) [27919305] **566**

JOURNAL OF MICROCOLUMN SEPARATIONS, THE (US/1040-7685) [18519551] **981**

JOURNAL OF MICROCOMPUTER APPLICATIONS (UK/0745-7138) [09235894] **1268**

JOURNAL OF MICROCOMPUTER SYSTEMS MANAGEMENT **See** JOURNAL OF END USER COMPUTING **1192**

JOURNAL OF MICROCOMPUTER SYSTEMS MANAGEMENT (US/1043-6464) [19506270] **1192**

●JOURNAL OF MICROELECTROMECHANICAL SYSTEMS (US/1057-7157) [24103550] **2069**

●JOURNAL OF MICROELECTRONIC SYSTEMS INTEGRATION (US/1070-0056) [28230043] **1248**

JOURNAL OF MICROENCAPSULATION (UK/0265-2048) [10736323] 3596, **4311**

JOURNAL OF MICROMECHANICS AND MICROENGINEERING : STRUCTURES, DEVICES, AND SYSTEMS (UK/0960-1317) [23664365] 2118, 4409, **2069**

JOURNAL OF MICROPALEONTOLOGY (UK/0262-821X) [09322660] **4227**

JOURNAL OF MICROSCOPY (OXFORD) (UK/0022-2720) [01644311] **572**

JOURNAL OF MICROWAVE POWER AND ELECTROMAGNETIC ENERGY, THE (US/0832-7823) [12644830] **2069**

JOURNAL OF MIDDLE ATLANTIC ARCHAEOLOGY (US/0883-9697) [12267366] **271**

●JOURNAL OF MILITARY AVIATION (US/1057-8307) [24124307] 4048, **26**

JOURNAL OF MILITARY HISTORY, THE (US/0899-3718) [18078225] **4048**

JOURNAL OF MIND AND BEHAVIOR, THE (US/0271-0137) [06543005] 4350, **4598**

JOURNAL OF MINERAL LAW & POLICY (US/0892-9017) [12593208] 2141, **2989**

JOURNAL OF MINES, METALS & FUELS (II/0022-2755) [05713051] **2141**

JOURNAL OF MINING AND GEOLOGY (NR/0022-2763) [02246733] 1385, **2141**

●JOURNAL OF MINING RESEARCH (II) [27653691] **2141**

●JOURNAL OF MINING SCIENCE (US/1062-7391) [25723475] **2142**

●JOURNAL OF MINISTRY IN ADDICTION & RECOVERY (US/1053-8755) [22683447] 4969, **1346**

●JOURNAL OF MINISTRY MARKETING & MANAGEMENT (US/1057-1523) [23958820] 874, **928**

JOURNAL OF MINORITY AGING, THE (US/0742-6291) [05329814] 2266, **5180**

JOURNAL OF MINORITY BUSINESS FINANCE (US/0735-0643) [08902983] **795**

JOURNAL OF MINORITY EMPLOYMENT (US/0890-1163) [14183876] **1682**

JOURNAL OF MISSISSIPPI HISTORY, THE (US/0022-2771) [01782329] **2741**

JOURNAL OF MMINERAL LAW & POLICY **See** JOURNAL OF NATURAL RESOURCES & ENVIRONMENTAL LAW **3113**

JOURNAL OF MODERN AFRICAN STUDIES, THE (UK/0022-278X) [01783128] **2640**

JOURNAL OF MODERN GREEK STUDIES (US/0738-1727) [09537018] **2695**

JOURNAL OF MODERN HELLENISM (US/0743-7749) [10670145] **2266**

JOURNAL OF MODERN HISTORY, THE (US/0022-2801) [01782294] **2621**

●JOURNAL OF MODERN ITALIAN STUDIES (UK/1354-571X) 2518, **3291**

JOURNAL OF MODERN KOREAN STUDIES, THE (US/8756-2235) [11249357] **2655**

JOURNAL OF MODERN LITERATURE (US/0022-281X) [00949853] **3345**

JOURNAL OF MOLECULAR AND CELLULAR CARDIOLOGY (UK/0022-2828) [01783531] **3707**

JOURNAL OF MOLECULAR BIOLOGY (UK/0022-2836) [01782923] **461**

JOURNAL OF MOLECULAR CATALYSIS (SZ/0304-5102) [02244168] **1054**

JOURNAL OF MOLECULAR CATALYSIS B : ENZYMATIC (NE/1381-1177) **1054**

JOURNAL OF MOLECULAR ELECTRONICS **See** ADVANCED MATERIALS FOR OPTICS AND ELECTRONICS **5080**

JOURNAL OF MOLECULAR ENDOCRINOLOGY (UK/0952-5041) [18271261] **3731**

JOURNAL OF MOLECULAR EVOLUTION (GW/0022-2844) [01784021] 982, **549**

JOURNAL OF MOLECULAR GRAPHICS (UK/0263-7855) [09492250] 982, **1234**

JOURNAL OF MOLECULAR LIQUIDS (NE/0167-7322) [09461972] **982**

JOURNAL OF MOLECULAR MEDICINE (GW/0946-2716) **3596**

JOURNAL OF MOLECULAR NEUROSCIENCE (US/0895-8696) [16835283] 461, **3835**

JOURNAL OF MOLECULAR SPECTROSCOPY (US/0022-2852) [01782810] **4436**

JOURNAL OF MOLECULAR STRUCTURE (NE/0022-2860) [01136815] **1054**

JOURNAL OF MOLECULAR STRUCTURE. THEOCHEM (NE/0166-1280) [07073454] **1054**

JOURNAL OF MOLLUSCAN STUDIES (UK/0260-1230) [02573904] **5588**

JOURNAL OF MOLLUSCAN STUDIES. SUPPLEMENT, THE **CEASED.** (UK) [04558857] **5588**

JOURNAL OF MONETARY ECONOMICS (NE/0304-3932) [01314426] **1500**

JOURNAL OF MONEY, CREDIT, AND BANKING (US/0022-2879) [01783384] **795**

JOURNAL OF MORAL EDUCATION (UK/0305-7240) [01783973] 2251, **1758**

JOURNAL OF MORMON HISTORY (US/0094-7342) [02242494] **4969**

JOURNAL OF MORPHOLOGY (1931) (US/0362-2525) [02200304] **583**

JOURNAL OF MORPHOLOGY. SUPPLEMENT (US/0898-9249) [15531270] **461**

JOURNAL OF MOTOR BEHAVIOR (US/0022-2895) [01783382] **583**

JOURNAL OF MOTOR VEHICLE LAW (CN/0840-7754) [19915923] 5418, **2989**

JOURNAL OF MULTI-CULTURAL AND CROSS-CULTURAL RESEARCH IN ART EDUCATION (US/0740-1833) [09888835] **354**

●JOURNAL OF MULTICRITERIA ANALYSIS (UK/1057-9214) [24221823] **4598**

JOURNAL OF MULTICULTURAL COUNSELING AND DEVELOPMENT (US/0883-8534) [12199656] **4598**

JOURNAL OF MULTICULTURAL LIBRARIANSHIP See MULTICULTURAL REVIEW **2268**

JOURNAL OF MULTICULTURAL SOCIAL WORK (US/1042-8224) [19225114] **5292**

JOURNAL OF MULTILINGUAL AND MULTICULTURAL DEVELOPMENT (UK/0143-4632) [06286264] **3291**

JOURNAL OF MULTINATIONAL FINANCIAL MANAGEMENT (US/1042-444X) [19050676] **1637**

JOURNAL OF MULTINATIONAL STRATEGIES, THE *CEASED.* (US/1049-7722) [21308720] **687**, **1637**

JOURNAL OF MULTISTATE TAXATION, THE (US/1054-8394) [22994228] **4734**

JOURNAL OF MULTIVARIATE ANALYSIS (US/0047-259X) [01783582] **3514**

JOURNAL OF MULTIVARIATE EXPERIMENTAL PERSONALITY AND CLINICAL PSYCHOLOGY See MULTIVARIATE EXPERIMENTAL CLINICAL RESEARCH **4605**

JOURNAL OF MUSCLE FOODS (US/1046-0756) [20323541] **2347**

JOURNAL OF MUSCLE RESEARCH AND CELL MOTILITY (UK/0142-4319) [06517602] **538**

JOURNAL OF MUSCLE SHOALS HISTORY, THE (US/0094-8039) [01795446] **2741**

JOURNAL OF MUSCULOSKELETAL MEDICINE (US/0899-2517) [11341434] **3805**

●JOURNAL OF MUSCULOSKELETAL PAIN (US/1058-2452) [24243628] **3805**

JOURNAL OF MUSEUM EDUCATION, THE (US/1059-8650) [12232131] **4090**

JOURNAL OF MUSEUM ETHNOGRAPHY / MUSEUM ETHNOGRAPHERS' GROUP (UK/0954-7169) [26595933] **4090**, **239**

JOURNAL OF MUSIC TEACHER EDUCATION (US/1057-0837) [23932596] **1898**, **4126**

JOURNAL OF MUSIC THEORY (US/0022-2909) [01783233] **4126**

JOURNAL OF MUSIC THEORY PEDAGOGY, THE (US/0891-7639) [14984048] **4126**

JOURNAL OF MUSIC THERAPY (US/0022-2917) [02308498] **3596**, **4126**

JOURNAL OF MUSICOLOGICAL RESEARCH, THE (US/0141-1896) [06273983] **4126**

JOURNAL OF MUSICOLOGY (ST. JOSEPH, MICH.), THE (US/0277-9269) [07659180] **4126**

●JOURNAL OF MUTUAL FUND SERVICES, THE (US/1071-846X) [28739983] **904**

JOURNAL OF MYCOPATHOLOGICAL RESEARCH (II/0971-3719) [I09713719] **575**

JOURNAL OF MYOCARDIAL ISCHEMIA, THE (US/1045-7984) [20236044] 3773, **3707**

JOURNAL OF NANJING UNIVERSITY (CH/0253-4932) [I02534932] **1833**

JOURNAL OF NARRATIVE AND LIFE HISTORY (US/1053-6981) [22610085] **3400**

JOURNAL OF NARRATIVE TECHNIQUE, THE (US/0022-2925) [02217492] **3400**

JOURNAL OF NATAL AND ZULU HISTORY (SA/0259-0123) [04452563] **2640**

JOURNAL OF NATIONAL ACADEMY OF MATHEMATICS, INDIA (II) [18354984] **3514**

JOURNAL OF NATIONAL BLACK NURSES' ASSOCIATION : JNBNA (US/0885-6028) [12675158] **3859**

JOURNAL OF NATURAL DISASTER SCIENCE *CEASED.* (JA) [13782418] **5119**

JOURNAL OF NATURAL GEOMETRY (UK/0963-2654) [I09632654] **3514**

JOURNAL OF NATURAL HISTORY (UK/0022-2933) [01783312] **4166**

JOURNAL OF NATURAL PRODUCTS (US/0163-3864) [04359563] **1043**

●JOURNAL OF NATURAL RESOURCES & ENVIRONMENTAL LAW (US/1070-4833) [27828994] **3113**

●JOURNAL OF NATURAL RESOURCES AND LIFE SCIENCES EDUCATION (US/1059-9053) [24804539] **100**

JOURNAL OF NATURAL RUBBER RESEARCH (MY/0127-7065) [14151484] **5076**

JOURNAL OF NATURAL SCIENCES AND MATHEMATICS (PK/0022-2941) [01642599] **5119**

●JOURNAL OF NATURAL TOXINS (US/1058-8108) [24384628] **4311**

●JOURNAL OF NATURAL TOXINS (US/1058-8108) [23364925] **3981**

JOURNAL OF NATURE CONSERVATION (II/0970-5945) [I09705945] 2196, **2218**

JOURNAL OF NATUROPATHIC MEDICINE, THE (US/1047-7837) [20788909] **3596**

JOURNAL OF NAVAJO EDUCATION (US/1042-3265) [18924480] 2266, **1758**

JOURNAL OF NAVIGATION, THE (UK/0373-4633) [01783951] **4177**

JOURNAL OF NEAR-DEATH STUDIES (US/0891-4494) [14781775] **4241**

JOURNAL OF NEAR EASTERN STUDIES (US/0022-2968) [01754689] **3291**

JOURNAL OF NEAR INFRARED SPECTROSCOPY (UK) **4436**

JOURNAL OF NEGRO EDUCATION, THE (US/0022-2984) [01782303] 2266, **1758**

JOURNAL OF NEGRO HISTORY, THE (US/0022-2992) [01782257] **2741**

JOURNAL OF NEMATOLOGY (US/0022-300X) [01797954] **5588**

●JOURNAL OF NEOPLATONIC STUDIES, THE (US/1065-5840) [26639418] **4350**

JOURNAL OF NEPAL CHEMICAL SOCIETY, NEPAL CHEMICAL SOCIETY (NP/1012-8611) [13259139] **982**

JOURNAL OF NEPAL GEOLOGICAL SOCIETY (NP) [08720928] **1385**

JOURNAL OF NEPHROLOGY (IT) [22238699] **3991**

JOURNAL OF NERVOUS AND MENTAL DISEASE, THE (US/0022-3018) [01754691] 3929, **3835**

●JOURNAL OF NETWORK AND SYSTEMS MANAGEMENT (US/1064-7570) [26391499] **1242**

JOURNAL OF NEURAL TRANSMISSION. GENERAL SECTION : JNT (AU/0300-9564) [20283490] **3835**

JOURNAL OF NEURAL TRANSMISSION. PARKINSON'S DISEASE AND DEMENTIA SECTION (AU/0936-3076) [20080821] **3835**

JOURNAL OF NEURAL TRANSMISSION. SUPPLEMENTUM (AU/0303-6995) [00972418] **3835**

JOURNAL OF NEURAL TRANSPLANTATION & PLASTICITY (UK/0792-8483) [23170154] **3835**

●JOURNAL OF NEURO-AIDS (US/1069-7438) [28166083] 3674, **3835**

JOURNAL OF NEURO-ONCOLOGY (US/0167-594X) [09414459] 3835, **3819**

●JOURNAL OF NEURO-OPHTHALMOLOGY (US/1070-8022) [28471510] **3876**

JOURNAL OF NEUROBIOLOGY (US/0022-3034) [01799888] 461, **3835**

JOURNAL OF NEUROCHEMISTRY (US/0022-3042) [01782775] **3836**

JOURNAL OF NEUROCYTOLOGY (UK/0300-4864) [01785119] **538**

JOURNAL OF NEUROENDOCRINOLOGY (UK/0953-8194) [20225561] **3836**

JOURNAL OF NEUROGENETICS (SZ/0167-7063) [10004179] 3836, **549**

JOURNAL OF NEUROIMAGING (US/1051-2284) [21896793] **3836**

JOURNAL OF NEUROIMMUNOLOGY (NE/0165-5728) [07629351] **3836**

JOURNAL OF NEUROLINGUISTICS (UK/0911-6044) [13715239] **3291**

JOURNAL OF NEUROLOGIC REHABILITATION (US/0888-4390) [13573374] **3836**

JOURNAL OF NEUROLOGICAL & ORTHOPAEDIC MEDICINE & SURGERY, THE (US/0890-6599) [12092859] 3836, 3882, **3967**

JOURNAL OF NEUROLOGY (GW/0340-5354) [00938795] **3836**

JOURNAL OF NEUROLOGY, NEUROSURGERY AND PSYCHIATRY (UK/0022-3050) [01783362] 3929, **3836**

JOURNAL OF NEUROLOGY SUPPLEMENT (GW/0939-1517) [I09391517] **3836**

JOURNAL OF NEUROPATHOLOGY AND EXPERIMENTAL NEUROLOGY (US/0022-3069) [01754695] **3836**

JOURNAL OF NEUROPHYSIOLOGY (US/0022-3077) [01695642] 583, **3836**

JOURNAL OF NEUROPSYCHIATRY AND CLINICAL NEUROSCIENCES, THE (US/0895-0172) [16402144] 3836, **3929**

JOURNAL OF NEURORADIOLOGY (FR/0150-9861) [03260562] **3942**

JOURNAL OF NEUROSCIENCE METHODS (NE/0165-0270) [04929303] **3837**

JOURNAL OF NEUROSCIENCE NURSING, THE (US/0888-0395) [13107404] 3837, **3859**

JOURNAL OF NEUROSCIENCE RESEARCH (US/0360-4012) [02244695] **3837**

JOURNAL OF NEUROSCIENCE, THE (US/0270-6474) [06476199] **3836**

JOURNAL OF NEUROSURGERY (US/0022-3085) [01800316] 3967, **3837**

JOURNAL OF NEUROSURGICAL ANESTHESIOLOGY (US/0898-4921) [17823956] **3967**

JOURNAL OF NEUROSURGICAL SCIENCES (IT/0390-5616) [01020283] **3968**

JOURNAL OF NEUROTRAUMA (US/0897-7151) [17603118] **3837**

●JOURNAL OF NEUROVIROLOGY (UK) **3837**

JOURNAL OF NEW GENERATION COMPUTER SYSTEMS (GW/0863-0445) [18664196] **1192**

JOURNAL OF NEW JERSEY POETS (US/0363-4205) [02456139] **3464**

JOURNAL OF NEW MUSIC RESEARCH (NE/0929-8215) **4126**

JOURNAL OF NEW ZEALAND LITERATURE : JNZL (NZ/0112-1227) [10444036] **3400**

JOURNAL OF NEWSPAPER AND PERIODICAL HISTORY *CEASED.* (UK/0265-5942) [11719092] **2921**

JOURNAL OF NIH RESEARCH, THE (US/1043-609X) [19496183] 5119, **461**

JOURNAL OF NIHON UNIVERSITY SCHOOL OF DENTISTRY (JA/0029-0432) [01760382] **1327**

JOURNAL OF NON-CLASSICAL LOGIC See JOURNAL OF APPLIED NON-CLASSICAL LOGICS **3511**

JOURNAL OF NON-CRYSTALLINE SOLIDS (NE/0022-3093) [01783540] **2591**

JOURNAL OF NON-EQUILIBRIUM THERMODYNAMICS (GW/0340-0204) [02884069] **4431**

JOURNAL OF NON-NEWTONIAN FLUID MECHANICS (NE/0377-0257) [02477749] **2092**

JOURNAL OF NONDESTRUCTIVE EVALUATION (US/0195-9298) [05702860] **2104**

JOURNAL OF NONLINEAR BIOLOGY (US/1047-1200) [20609153] **495**

JOURNAL OF NONLINEAR SCIENCE (US/0938-8974) [22379097] **5119**

JOURNAL OF NONPARAMETRIC STATISTICS (US/1048-5252) [20967664] **5329**

JOURNAL OF NONPROFIT & PUBLIC SECTOR MARKETING (US/1049-5142) [21245626] **928**

JOURNAL OF NONVERBAL BEHAVIOR (US/0191-5886) [04967863] 1115, **4598**

JOURNAL OF NORTHEAST-AFRICAN STUDIES, THE (US/1062-5038) [25643288] **2640**

JOURNAL OF NORTHEAST ASIAN STUDIES (US/0738-7997) [08636881] **4479**

JOURNAL OF NORTHEAST FORESTRY UNIVERSITY (CC) **2386**

JOURNAL OF NORTHERN LUZON (PH/0115-2408) [02242906] 5206, **1758**

JOURNAL OF NORTHWEST ATLANTIC FISHERY SCIENCE (CN/0250-6408) [07289445] **2307**

JOURNAL OF NORTHWEST SEMITIC LANGUAGES (NE/0085-2414) [01783903] **3291**

JOURNAL OF NUCLEAR AGRICULTURE AND BIOLOGY (II/0379-5489) [02366281] **100**

JOURNAL OF NUCLEAR BIOLOGY AND MEDICINE : OFFICIAL PUBLICATION OF THE ITALIAN ASSOCIATION OF NUCLEAR MEDICINE (AIMN), THE (IT) [24172485] **3942**

●JOURNAL OF NUCLEAR CARDIOLOGY (US/1071-3581) [28626290] **3707**

JOURNAL OF NUCLEAR MATERIALS (NE/0022-3115) [01782975] **2156**

JOURNAL OF NUCLEAR MEDICINE (1978), THE (US/0161-5505) [03945779] **3848**

JOURNAL OF NUCLEAR MEDICINE. SUPPLEMENT (US/0075-4315) [01778728] **3848**

JOURNAL OF NUCLEAR MEDICINE TECHNOLOGY (US/0091-4916) [01787380] 3943, **3848**

JOURNAL OF NUCLEAR SCIENCE AND TECHNOLOGY (JA/0022-3131) [02251715] **2156**

JOURNAL OF NUMBER THEORY (US/0022-314X) [01800049] **3514**

JOURNAL

Alphabetical Title Index

JOURNAL OF NUMERICAL LINEAR ALGEBRA WITH APPLICATIONS **CEASED**. (SI/0129-3281) [26368997] **3514**

JOURNAL OF NURSE-MIDWIFERY (US/0091-2182) [04618369] 3763, **3859**

JOURNAL OF NURSING (CH/0047-262X) **3859**

JOURNAL OF NURSING ADMINISTRATION, THE (US/0002-0443) [01783395] **3859**

JOURNAL OF NURSING CARE QUALITY (US/1057-3631) [24020317] **3859**

JOURNAL OF NURSING EDUCATION, THE (US/0148-4834) [01644709] 1758, **3859**

JOURNAL OF NURSING ETHICS, THE **SUSPENDED**. (US) [04585654] 3859, **2251**

JOURNAL OF NURSING JOCULARITY (US/1055-3088) [23137517] **3859**

●JOURNAL OF NURSING MANAGEMENT (UK/0966-0429) [27673423] **3859**

●JOURNAL OF NURSING MEASUREMENT (US/1061-3749) [25277470] **3859**

JOURNAL OF NURSING RESEARCH (US/1046-4972) [20429850] **3859**

JOURNAL OF NURSING STAFF DEVELOPMENT : JNSD (US/0882-0627) [11730498] **3859**

JOURNAL OF NUTRITION EDUCATION (US/0022-3182) [01799886] **4193**

JOURNAL OF NUTRITION FOR THE ELDERLY (US/0163-9366) [04538227] 5180, **4193**

●JOURNAL OF NUTRITION IN RECIPE & MENU DEVELOPMENT (US/1055-1379) [23092231] **4193**

JOURNAL OF NUTRITION, THE (US/0022-3166) [01782301] **4193**

JOURNAL OF NUTRITIONAL BIOCHEMISTRY, THE (US/0955-2863) [21104658] **4193**

●JOURNAL OF NUTRITIONAL IMMUNOLOGY (US/1049-5150) [21245729] 3674, **4193**

JOURNAL OF NUTRITIONAL MEDICINE (UK/0955-6664) [22133463] **4193**

JOURNAL OF NUTRITIONAL SCIENCE AND VITAMINOLOGY (JA/0301-4800) [02105431] **4193**

JOURNAL OF OBJECT-ORIENTED PROGRAMMING (US/0896-8438) [17305956] **1280**

JOURNAL OF OBJECTIVE STUDIES (II) [21401356] **5043**

JOURNAL OF OBSTETRIC, GYNECOLOGIC, AND NEONATAL NURSING : JOGNN (US/0884-2175) [11738525] 3763, **3859**

JOURNAL OF OBSTETRICS AND GYNAECOLOGY (UK/0144-3615) [07865410] **3763**

JOURNAL OF OBSTETRICS AND GYNAECOLOGY OF INDIA (II/0022-3190) [01644376] **3763**

●JOURNAL OF OCCUPATIONAL AND ENVIRONMENTAL MEDICINE (US/1076-2752) [30446507] **3596**

●JOURNAL OF OCCUPATIONAL AND ORGANIZATIONAL PSYCHOLOGY (UK/0963-1798) [25416838] **4598**

JOURNAL OF OCCUPATIONAL HEALTH AND SAFETY, AUSTRALIA AND NEW ZEALAND, THE (AT/0815-6409) [14690884] **2864**

JOURNAL OF OCCUPATIONAL MEDICINE (US/0096-1736) [01236007] **2864**

●JOURNAL OF OCCUPATIONAL MEDICINE AND TOXICOLOGY (US/1054-044X) [22725237] **3981**

JOURNAL OF OCCUPATIONAL PSYCHOLOGY **See** JOURNAL OF OCCUPATIONAL AND ORGANIZATIONAL PSYCHOLOGY **4598**

JOURNAL OF OCCUPATIONAL REHABILITATION (US/1053-0487) [22439949] **2864**

●JOURNAL OF OCEANOGRAPHY (JA/0916-8370) [26165313] **1450**

JOURNAL OF OCULAR PHARMACOLOGY (US/8756-3320) [11545195] 4311, **3876**

JOURNAL OF OCULAR THERAPY & SURGERY (US/0730-0883) [07950712] **3876**

JOURNAL OF OFFENDER MONITORING (US/1043-500X) [19477162] **3167**

JOURNAL OF OFFENDER REHABILITATION (US/1050-9674) [21727463] 5292, 4598, **3167**

JOURNAL OF OFFICIAL STATISTICS (SW/0282-423X) [11960555] **5329**

●JOURNAL OF OFFSHORE FINANCE AND TAX (US/1078-1161) [30997737] 4734, **795**

JOURNAL OF OFFSHORE MECHANICS AND ARCTIC ENGINEERING (US/0892-7219) [15249271] **2092**

JOURNAL OF OFFSHORE TECHNOLOGY (UK) **1983**

JOURNAL OF OILSEEDS RESEARCH (II/0970-2776) [12771047] **176**

JOURNAL OF OMAN STUDIES : SCIENTIFIC RESULTS OF THE ROYAL GEOGRAPHICAL SOCIETY (UK/0379-0703) **2567**

JOURNAL OF OMAN STUDIES, THE (MK/0378-8180) [03874222] **2655**

JOURNAL OF ONCOLOGY MANAGEMENT, THE (US/1061-9364) [25489467] **3819**

JOURNAL OF ONE-DAY SURGERY (UK/0963-5386) [10963 5386] **3968**

JOURNAL OF ONE-NAME STUDIES, THE (UK/0262-4842) [11811701] **2455**

JOURNAL OF OPERATIONAL PSYCHIATRY (US/0047-2638) [01789571] **3929**

JOURNAL OF OPERATIONS MANAGEMENT (US/0272-6963) [06904059] **1614**

JOURNAL OF OPERATOR THEORY (RM/0379-4024) [05031487] **3514**

JOURNAL OF OPHTHALMIC NURSING & TECHNOLOGY (US/0744-7132) [08508044] 3876, **3859**

JOURNAL OF OPHTHALMIC PHOTOGRAPHY, THE (US/0198-6155) [06175607] **3876**

JOURNAL OF OPTICAL COMMUNICATIONS (GW/0173-4911) [07385357] **4436**

●JOURNAL OF OPTICAL TECHNOLOGY (US/1070-9762) [28523107] **4436**

JOURNAL OF OPTICS (US/0150-536X) [02928356] **4436**

JOURNAL OF OPTICS RESEARCH (US) **4436**

●JOURNAL OF OPTIMAL NUTRITION, THE (US/1061-2130) [25214856] **4193**

JOURNAL OF OPTIMIZATION THEORY AND APPLICATIONS (US/0022-3239) [01754705] 5119, **3514**

JOURNAL OF OPTOMETRIC EDUCATION (US/0098-6917) [01512164] **4216**

JOURNAL OF OPTOMETRIC VISION DEVELOPMENT (1976) (US/0149-886X) [03560256] **4216**

JOURNAL OF ORAL AND MAXILLOFACIAL SURGERY (US/0278-2391) [07757702] 1327, **3968**

JOURNAL OF ORAL IMPLANTOLOGY, THE (US/0160-6972) [03693079] **1327**

JOURNAL OF ORAL PATHOLOGY & MEDICINE (DK/0904-2512) [19787126] **1327**

JOURNAL OF ORAL REHABILITATION (UK/0305-182X) [01020760] **1327**

JOURNAL OF ORANGE COUNTY STUDIES **SUSPENDED**. (US) [19113090] **2741**

JOURNAL OF ORGANIC CHEMISTRY (US/0022-3263) [01782318] **1043**

JOURNAL OF ORGANIC CHEMISTRY OF THE USSR (US/0022-3271) [01783240] **1043**

●JOURNAL OF ORGANIC CHEMISTRY OF THE USSR (US/1070-4280) [28365085] **1043**

JOURNAL OF ORGANIZATIONAL BEHAVIOR (UK/0894-3796) [16060737] **4598**

JOURNAL OF ORGANIZATIONAL BEHAVIOR MANAGEMENT (US/0160-8061) [03271654] 874, **4599**

JOURNAL OF ORGANIZATIONAL CHANGE MANAGEMENT (UK/0953-4814) [19758283] **874**

JOURNAL OF ORGANIZATIONAL COMPUTING (US/1054-1721) [22773826] 1115, **874**

JOURNAL OF ORGANOMETALLIC CHEMISTRY (SZ/0022-328X) [01783208] **1043**

JOURNAL OF ORGANOMETALLIC CHEMISTRY LIBRARY (NE/0378-5203) [03257222] **1043**

JOURNAL OF ORGONOMY, THE (US/0022-3298) [01754708] **3596**

JOURNAL OF ORIENTAL RESEARCH, MADRAS, THE (II/0022-3301) [01754710] **3291**

JOURNAL OF ORIENTAL RESEARCH OF THE UNIVERSITY OF MADRAS **See** ANNALS OF ORIENTAL RESEARCH / UNIVERSITY OF MADRAS **2645**

JOURNAL OF ORIENTAL STUDIES (HONG KONG) (HK/0022-331X) [01639703] **2655**

JOURNAL OF ORISSA MATHEMATICAL SOCIETY (II) [13807904] **3514**

●JOURNAL OF OROFACIAL PAIN (US/1064-6655) [26368188] **3837**

JOURNAL OF ORTHOMOLECULAR MEDICINE (CN/0834-4825) [15726974] **3929**

JOURNAL OF ORTHOPAEDIC AND SPORTS PHYSICAL THERAPY, THE (US/0190-6011) [04733348] 3954, **3882**

JOURNAL OF ORTHOPAEDIC MEDICINE (CN) **3882**

JOURNAL OF ORTHOPAEDIC RESEARCH (US/0736-0266) [09069401] **3882**

JOURNAL OF ORTHOPAEDIC RHEUMATOLOGY (UK/0951-9580) [19272553] **3882**

●JOURNAL OF ORTHOPAEDIC SURGERY (HK/1022-5536) [30638153] 3968, **3882**

JOURNAL OF ORTHOPAEDIC SURGERY, THE **CEASED**. (FR) [30772138] 3968, **3882**

JOURNAL OF ORTHOPAEDIC SURGICAL TECHNIQUES, THE (UK/0334-0236) [12752745] 3968, **3882**

●JOURNAL OF ORTHOPAEDIC TECHNIQUES (US/1056-7437) [23833720] **3882**

JOURNAL OF ORTHOPAEDIC TRAUMA (US/0890-5339) [14257379] **3882**

●JOURNAL OF ORTHOPAEDICS (UK/1353-3258) **3882**

JOURNAL OF OSAKA DENTAL UNIVERSITY (JA/0475-2058) [02254887] **1327**

JOURNAL OF OSAKA UNIVERSITY DENTAL SCHOOL, THE (JA/0473-4599) [01226769] **1327**

JOURNAL OF OSTEOPATHIC SPORTS MEDICINE : JOSM **CEASED**. (US/0893-3871) [15529657] **3954**

JOURNAL OF OTOLARYNGOLOGY. SUPPLEMENT, THE (CN/0707-7270) [03827242] **3889**

JOURNAL OF OTOLARYNGOLOGY, THE (CN/0381-6605) [02604347] **3889**

JOURNAL OF OUTDOOR EDUCATION (US/0022-3336) [01754711] 4874, **1758**

JOURNAL OF PACIFIC HISTORY, THE (AT/0022-3344) [01784547] **2669**

JOURNAL OF PACIFIC STUDIES (FJ/1011-3029) [02208346] **2669**

JOURNAL OF PACKAGING TECHNOLOGY (US/0892-029X) [15062864] **4219**

JOURNAL OF PAEDIATRICS AND CHILD HEALTH (AT/1034-4810) [21266318] **3905**

JOURNAL OF PAEDIATRICS, OBSTETRICS, AND GYNAECOLOGY (HK/1012-8875) [11258314] 3764, **3905**

JOURNAL OF PAIN AND SYMPTOM MANAGEMENT (US/0885-3924) [12629494] 4599, **3596**

JOURNAL OF PALEOLIMNOLOGY (NE/0921-2728) [18594885] **461**

JOURNAL OF PALEONTOLOGY (US/0022-3360) [01754714] **4227**

JOURNAL OF PALEOPATHOLOGY (IT) [18025983] 239, **3895**

JOURNAL OF PALESTINE STUDIES (US/0377-919X) [01784372] **2655**

JOURNAL OF PALLIATIVE CARE (CN/0825-8597) [13770237] **5292**

JOURNAL OF PALYNOLOGY (II/0022-3379) [01754715] **515**

JOURNAL OF PAN AFRICAN STUDIES, THE (US/0888-6601) [13683769] **5206**

JOURNAL OF PARALEGAL EDUCATION AND PRACTICE (US/0895-6219) [16705300] **2989**

JOURNAL OF PARALLEL AND DISTRIBUTED COMPUTING (US/0743-7315) [10658446] **1260**

JOURNAL OF PARAMETRICS (US/1015-7891) [18510850] **747**

JOURNAL OF PARAPSYCHOLOGY, THE (US/0022-3387) [01588544] **4241**

JOURNAL OF PARASITOLOGY, THE (US/0022-3395) [01606759] **5588**

JOURNAL OF PARENTERAL SCIENCE AND TECHNOLOGY (US/0279-7976) [07263963] **4311**

JOURNAL OF PARK AND RECREATION ADMINISTRATION (US/0735-1968) [08895725] **4706**

JOURNAL OF PARLIAMENTARY INFORMATION, THE (II/0447-9408) [01773645] **4658**

JOURNAL OF PARTIAL DIFFERENTIAL EQUATIONS (CC/1000-940X) [21145406] **3514**

JOURNAL OF PARTNERSHIP TAXATION (US/0749-4513) [10586016] **4734**

JOURNAL OF PASTORAL CARE, THE (US/0022-3409) [01754717] 4599, **4969**

JOURNAL OF PASTORAL COUNSELING, THE (US/0449-508X) [07231275] **4969**

JOURNAL OF PASTORAL PRACTICE **See** JOURNAL OF BIBLICAL COUNSELING, THE **4968**

JOURNAL OF PASTORAL PRACTICE, THE (US/0196-9072) [04283375] **5017**

JOURNAL OF PASTORAL PSYCHOTHERAPY (US/0886-5477) [12929601] **4599**

JOURNAL OF PASTORAL THEOLOGY (US/1064-9867) [23997115] **4969**

JOURNAL OF PATHOLOGY (UK/0022-3417) [01754718] **3895**

JOURNAL OF PAY & REWARD MANAGEMENT (UK/1351-6051) **874**

JOURNAL OF PEACE RESEARCH (NO/0022-3433) [01607337] **4527**

JOURNAL OF PEASANT STUDIES, THE (UK/0306-6150) [01799425] **5250**

JOURNAL OF PEDIATRIC & PERINATAL NUTRITION *CEASED.* (US/8756-6206) [11613735] 4193, 3764, **3905**

JOURNAL OF PEDIATRIC ENDOCRINOLOGY, THE (UK/0334-018X) [12862055] 3731, **3905**

JOURNAL OF PEDIATRIC GASTROENTEROLOGY AND NUTRITION (US/0277-2116) [07520467] 4193, **3905**

JOURNAL OF PEDIATRIC HEALTH CARE (US/0891-5245) [14878057] **3905**

●JOURNAL OF PEDIATRIC HEMATOLOGY / ONCOLOGY (US) 3819, **3773**

JOURNAL OF PEDIATRIC NURSING (US/0882-5963) [11892752] 3905, **3859**

JOURNAL OF PEDIATRIC ONCOLOGY NURSING (US/1043-4542) [19471182] 3905, 3819, **3859**

JOURNAL OF PEDIATRIC OPHTHALMOLOGY AND STRABISMUS (US/0191-3913) [03951436] 3876, **3905**

●JOURNAL OF PEDIATRIC ORTHOPEDICS. PART B (US/1060-152X) [24886124] **3882**

JOURNAL OF PEDIATRIC PSYCHOLOGY (US/0146-8693) [03042988] 3905, **4599**

JOURNAL OF PEDIATRIC SURGERY (US/0022-3468) [01608086] 3905, **3968**

JOURNAL OF PEDIATRICS, THE (US/0022-3476) [01754720] **3905**

JOURNAL OF PELVIC SURGERY (US/1077-2847) **3968**

●JOURNAL OF PENSION BENEFITS (US/1069-4064) [28034524] **2885**

JOURNAL OF PENSION PLANNING AND COMPLIANCE (US/0148-2181) [03128450] 2989, **904**

●JOURNAL OF PENTECOSTAL THEOLOGY (UK/0966-7369) [27278373] 2251, **5062**

●JOURNAL OF PEPTIDE SCIENCE (UK/1075-2617) [29986337] **1043**

JOURNAL OF PERFORMANCE OF CONSTRUCTED FACILITIES (US/0887-3828) [13202979] **2025**

JOURNAL OF PERINATAL & NEONATAL NURSING, THE (US/0893-2190) [15465213] 3764, **3859**

●JOURNAL OF PERINATAL EDUCATION, THE (US/1058-1243) [24223184] **3764**

JOURNAL OF PERINATAL MEDICINE (GW/0300-5577) [02105671] **3764**

JOURNAL OF PERINATAL MEDICINE SUPPLEMENT (GW/0936-174X) [I0936174X] **3764**

JOURNAL OF PERINATOLOGY (US/0743-8346) [10681421] **3764**

JOURNAL OF PERIODONTAL RESEARCH (DK/0022-3484) [01754721] **1327**

JOURNAL OF PERIODONTOLOGY (1970) (US/0022-3492) [02105859] **1327**

●JOURNAL OF PERSONAL INJURY LITIGATION (UK) **2989**

JOURNAL OF PERSONAL SELLING & SALES MANAGEMENT, THE (US/0885-3134) [07410012] **928**

JOURNAL OF PERSONALITY (US/0022-3506) [01353902] **4599**

JOURNAL OF PERSONALITY AND CLINICAL STUDIES (II) [15703819] **4599**

JOURNAL OF PERSONALITY AND SOCIAL PSYCHOLOGY (US/0022-3514) [01783133] **4599**

JOURNAL OF PERSONALITY ASSESSMENT (US/0022-3891) [01799623] **4599**

JOURNAL OF PERSONALITY DISORDERS (US/0885-579X) [12676327] **4599**

JOURNAL OF PESTICIDE REFORM (US/0893-357X) [15529579] 2234, **4245**

JOURNAL OF PESTICIDE SCIENCE (TOKYO, 1975) (JA/0385-1559) [02459982] **4245**

JOURNAL OF PETROLEUM GEOLOGY (UK/0141-6421) [04611690] 1385, **4262**

JOURNAL OF PETROLEUM MARKETING : JPM / PMAA, THE (US/1055-5056) [23193084] **4262**

JOURNAL OF PETROLEUM RESEARCH (IQ/1012-8603) [14170853] **4262**

JOURNAL OF PETROLEUM SCIENCE & ENGINEERING (NE/0920-4105) [16655734] **4262**

JOURNAL OF PETROLEUM TECHNOLOGY (US/0149-2136) [02725566] **4262**

JOURNAL OF PETROLOGY (UK/0022-3530) [01782966] **1458**

JOURNAL OF PHARMACEUTICAL AND BIOMEDICAL ANALYSIS (UK/0731-7085) [08237858] **4311**

●JOURNAL OF PHARMACEUTICAL CARE IN AIDS/HIV TREATMENT (US/1065-1799) [26520106] **3674**

●JOURNAL OF PHARMACEUTICAL CARE IN PAIN & SYMPTOM CONTROL (US/1056-4950) [23725514] **4311**

JOURNAL OF PHARMACEUTICAL MARKETING & MANAGEMENT (US/0883-7597) [12223333] **4311**

JOURNAL OF PHARMACEUTICAL MEDICINE : THE OFFICIAL JOURNAL OF THE SOCIETY OF PHARMACEUTICAL MEDICINE (UK/0958-0581) [26023376] **4312**

JOURNAL OF PHARMACEUTICAL SCIENCE AND TECHNOLOGY (US/1076-397X) [30054061] **4312**

JOURNAL OF PHARMACEUTICAL SCIENCE AND TECHNOLOGY (US) **4312**

JOURNAL OF PHARMACEUTICAL SCIENCES (US/0022-3549) [01754726] **4312**

JOURNAL OF PHARMACOBIO-DYNAMICS (JA/0386-846X) [04759874] **4312**

JOURNAL OF PHARMACOEPIDEMIOLOGY (US/0896-6966) [17256720] **3596**

JOURNAL OF PHARMACOKINETICS AND BIOPHARMACEUTICS (US/0090-466X) [01786688] **4312**

●JOURNAL OF PHARMACOLOGICAL AND TOXICOLOGICAL METHODS (US/1056-8719) [23882530] 3981, **4312**

JOURNAL OF PHARMACOLOGICAL METHODS *See* JOURNAL OF PHARMACOLOGICAL AND TOXICOLOGICAL METHODS **4312**

JOURNAL OF PHARMACOLOGY AND EXPERIMENTAL THERAPEUTICS, THE (US/0022-3565) [01606914] **4312**

JOURNAL OF PHARMACY (PK/0253-8288) [09868576] **4312**

●JOURNAL OF PHARMACY & LAW, THE (US/1062-4546) [25625319] 2989, **4312**

JOURNAL OF PHARMACY AND PHARMACOLOGY (UK/0022-3573) [01754728] **4312**

JOURNAL OF PHARMACY AND PHARMACOLOGY. SUPPLEMENT (US) [01754729] **4312**

JOURNAL OF PHARMACY PRACTICE (US/0897-1900) [17429589] **4312**

JOURNAL OF PHARMACY TEACHING (US/1044-0054) [19643702] 1833, **4312**

JOURNAL OF PHARMACY TECHNOLOGY, THE (US/8755-1225) [11240953] **4313**

JOURNAL OF PHASE EQUILIBRIA (US/1054-9714) [23041780] **4006**

JOURNAL OF PHENOMENOLOGICAL PSYCHOLOGY (US/0047-2662) [02240975] **4599**

JOURNAL OF PHILIPPINE DEVELOPMENT (PH/0115-9143) [09278458] **1614**

JOURNAL OF PHILIPPINE LIBRARIANSHIP (PH/0022-359X) [02235100] **3220**

JOURNAL OF PHILIPPINE STATISTICS (PH/0022-3603) [02228201] **5329**

JOURNAL OF PHILOSOPHICAL LOGIC (NE/0022-3611) [01783936] 4350, **3291**

JOURNAL OF PHILOSOPHICAL RESEARCH (US/1053-8364) [21948591] **4350**

JOURNAL OF PHILOSOPHY AND THE VISUAL ARTS (UK/0956-2834) [I09562834] 354, **4350**

JOURNAL OF PHILOSOPHY OF EDUCATION (UK/0309-8249) [04353786] **1898**

JOURNAL OF PHILOSOPHY, THE (US/0022-362X) [06415579] **4350**

JOURNAL OF PHONETICS (UK/0095-4470) [01787666] **3291**

JOURNAL OF PHOTOCHEMISTRY AND PHOTOBIOLOGY. A, CHEMISTRY (SZ/1010-6030) [16862352] **1054**

JOURNAL OF PHOTOCHEMISTRY AND PHOTOBIOLOGY. B, BIOLOGY (SZ/1011-1344) [16877735] **1054**

JOURNAL OF PHOTOGRAPHIC SCIENCE, THE (UK/0022-3638) [01782892] **4371**

JOURNAL OF PHOTOPOLYMER SCIENCE AND TECHNOLOGY (JA/0914-9244) [I09149244] **5119**

JOURNAL OF PHYCOLOGY (US/0022-3646) [01783379] **515**

JOURNAL OF PHYSICAL AND CHEMICAL REFERENCE DATA (US/0047-2689) [01754733] 982, **4409**

JOURNAL OF PHYSICAL CHEMISTRY (1952) (US/0022-3654) [01681052] **1054**

JOURNAL OF PHYSICAL CHEMISTRY. SUPPLEMENTARY MATERIAL, THE (US) [04765100] **1055**

JOURNAL OF PHYSICAL EDUCATION AND SPORT SCIENCES : A BI-ANNUAL PUBLICATION OF SPORTS AUTHORITY OF INDIA (II) [21914864] 4901, **1856**

●JOURNAL OF PHYSICAL EDUCATION NEW ZEALAND (NZ/1172-5958) [28901683] **1856**

JOURNAL OF PHYSICAL EDUCATION, RECREATION & DANCE (US/0730-3084) [07374247] 1313, **1856**

JOURNAL OF PHYSICAL OCEANOGRAPHY (US/0022-3670) [01783916] **1450**

JOURNAL OF PHYSICAL ORGANIC CHEMISTRY (UK/0894-3230) [16014922] **1043**

JOURNAL OF PHYSICS. A : MATHEMATICAL AND GENERAL (UK/0305-4470) [02242691] **4409**

JOURNAL OF PHYSICS AND CHEMISTRY OF SOLIDS, THE (UK/0022-3697) [02392502] 982, **4409**

JOURNAL OF PHYSICS. B : ATOMIC, MOLECULAR, AND OPTICAL PHYSICS (UK/0953-4075) [17570920] **4409**

JOURNAL OF PHYSICS. CONDENSED MATTER : AN INSTITUTE OF PHYSICS JOURNAL (UK/0953-8984) [19068764] **4409**

JOURNAL OF PHYSICS. D : APPLIED PHYSICS (UK/0022-3727) [01772505] **4410**

JOURNAL OF PHYSICS. G: NUCLEAR AND PARTICLE PHYSICS (UK/0954-3899) [19033035] **4448**

JOURNAL OF PHYSICS OF THE EARTH (JA/0022-3743) [01754741] **1408**

JOURNAL OF PHYSIOLOGY AND PHARMACOLOGY : AN OFFICIAL JOURNAL OF THE POLISH PHYSIOLOGICAL SOCIETY (PL) [24515696] 4313, **583**

JOURNAL OF PHYSIOLOGY (LONDON) (UK/0022-3751) [01754742] **583**

●JOURNAL OF PHYSIOLOGY, PARIS (FR/0928-4257) [27457309] **583**

JOURNAL OF PHYTOLOGICAL RESEARCH (II/0970-5767) [24565261] **515**

JOURNAL OF PHYTOPATHOLOGY 1986 (GW/0931-1785) [I09311785] **100**

JOURNAL OF PIDGIN AND CREOLE LANGUAGES (NE/0920-9034) [14765516] **3291**

JOURNAL OF PIERRE FAUCHARD ACADEMY. INDIA SECTION (II/0970-2199) [17251093] **1327**

JOURNAL OF PINEAL RESEARCH (DK/0742-3098) [10315536] **583**

JOURNAL OF PLANKTON RESEARCH (US/0142-7873) [05138160] **5588**

JOURNAL OF PLANNING AND ENVIRONMENT LAW (UK/0307-4870) [01785309] **3113**

JOURNAL OF PLANNING EDUCATION AND RESEARCH (US/0739-456X) [08399085] **2826**

JOURNAL OF PLANNING LITERATURE (US/0885-4122) [12627034] 2826, **2840**

JOURNAL OF PLANT ANATOMY AND MORPHOLOGY (II/0256-436X) [11653681] **515**

JOURNAL OF PLANT AND MACHINERY (II/0449-5721) [01800032] **2118**

JOURNAL OF PLANT BIOLOGY (KO) **515**

JOURNAL OF PLANT GROWTH REGULATION (US/0721-7595) [07579900] **515**

JOURNAL OF PLANT NUTRITION (US/0190-4167) [04710420] **515**

JOURNAL OF PLANT PHYSIOLOGY (GW/0176-1617) [11063615] **516**

JOURNAL OF PLANT PROTECTION IN THE TROPICS (MY/0127-6883) [13783498] **100**

●JOURNAL OF PLANT RESEARCH (JA/0918-9440) [28013509] **516**

JOURNAL OF PLANT SCIENCE RESEARCH, THE (II/0970-2539) [16320413] **516**

JOURNAL OF PLANTATION CROPS (II/0304-5242) [02245591] **176**

JOURNAL OF PLASMA PHYSICS (UK/0022-3778) [01754745] **4410**

JOURNAL OF PLASTIC FILM & SHEETING (US/8756-0879) [11463860] **4456**

JOURNAL OF PODIATRIC MEDICAL EDUCATION *CEASED.* (US/0093-7339) [00966167] **3918**

JOURNAL OF POETRY THERAPY (US/0889-3675) [13855297] 3464, **4599**

JOURNAL
Alphabetical Title Index

JOURNAL OF POLICE AND CRIMINAL PSYCHOLOGY (US/0882-0783) [11735084] **3167**

JOURNAL OF POLICY ANALYSIS AND MANAGEMENT (US/0276-8739) [07442272] **4479**

JOURNAL OF POLICY HISTORY (US/0898-0306) [17693262] **4479**

JOURNAL OF POLICY MODELING (US/0161-8938) [04058752] **5206**

JOURNAL OF POLISH SCIENCE **CEASED.** (PL) **5119**

JOURNAL OF POLITICAL ECONOMY, THE (US/0022-3808) [01754747] **1500**

●JOURNAL OF POLITICAL PHILOSOPHY (US/0963-8016) [28383473] **4350**

JOURNAL OF POLITICAL SCIENCE (CLEMSON) (US/0098-4612) [02241340] **4479**

JOURNAL OF POLITICAL STUDIES (II/0047-2700) [01587455] **4479**

JOURNAL OF POLITICS, THE (US/0022-3816) [01590736] **4479**

JOURNAL OF POLLUTION PREVENTION (US/1052-1550) [22196843] **2234**

JOURNAL OF POLYGRAPH SCIENCE, THE (US/0893-4827) [15599119] **3167**

JOURNAL OF POLYGRAPH STUDIES *See* JOURNAL OF POLYGRAPH SCIENCE, THE **3167**

JOURNAL OF POLYMER ENGINEERING (IS/0334-6447) [12563515] **2104**

JOURNAL OF POLYMER MATERIALS (II/0970-0838) [11340157] **982**

JOURNAL OF POLYMER SCIENCE. PART A, POLYMER CHEMISTRY (US/0887-624X) [13379035] **1043**

JOURNAL OF POLYMER SCIENCE. PART B, POLYMER PHYSICS (US/0887-6266) [13378941] **1043**

JOURNAL OF POLYMORPHOUS PERVERSITY (US/0737-1195) [09311019] 3929, **4599**

JOURNAL OF POPULAR CULTURE (US/0022-3840) [01754751] **2741**

JOURNAL OF POPULAR FILM AND TELEVISION, THE (US/0195-6051) [04652347] **4073**

JOURNAL OF POPULAR LITERATURE **CEASED.** (US/0897-3075) [13991095] **3400**

JOURNAL OF POPULATION AND SOCIAL STUDIES (TH) **4554**

JOURNAL OF POPULATION ECONOMICS (GW/0933-1433) [18597923] **4554**

JOURNAL OF POROUS MATERIALS (NE/1380-2224) **5119**

JOURNAL OF PORTFOLIO MANAGEMENT (US/0095-4918) [01796505] **904**

JOURNAL OF POST ANESTHESIA NURSING (US/0883-9433) [12257669] **3859**

JOURNAL OF POST KEYNESIAN ECONOMICS (US/0160-3477) [03671902] **1593**

JOURNAL OF POSTGRADUATE MEDICINE (BOMBAY) (II/0022-3859) [01587263] **3597**

JOURNAL OF POSTGRADUATE PHARMACY. COMMUNITY EDITION, THE (US/0163-3759) [04359788] **4313**

JOURNAL OF POSTGRADUATE PHARMACY. HOSPITAL EDITION, THE (US/0163-3910) [04359833] **4313**

JOURNAL OF POTASSIUM RESEARCH (II/0257-4993) [18426347] **176**

●JOURNAL OF POTATO PRODUCTION & POSTHARVEST HANDLING (US) **176**

JOURNAL OF POWDER & BULK SOLIDS TECHNOLOGY **CEASED.** (UK/0147-698X) [03215606] **2014**

JOURNAL OF POWER SOURCES (SZ/0378-7753) [02664681] **2118**

JOURNAL OF PRACTICAL APPLICATIONS OF SPACE (US/1046-8757) [20550214] **26**

JOURNAL OF PRACTICAL APPROACHES TO DEVELOPMENTAL HANDICAP (CN/0707-7807) [04205133] 1881, **4390**

●JOURNAL OF PRACTICAL HYGIENE, THE (US/1072-7965) [29203255] **1327**

JOURNAL OF PRACTICAL NURSING, THE (US/0022-3867) [06139186] **3860**

JOURNAL OF PRAGMATICS (NE/0378-2166) [03197305] **3291**

JOURNAL OF PRE-COLLEGE PHILOSOPHY, THE (US/0162-9662) [04258182] **4351**

JOURNAL OF PRE-RAPHAELITE AND AESTHETIC STUDIES *See* JOURNAL OF PRE-RAPHAELITE STUDIES (1992), THE **2848**

●JOURNAL OF PRE-RAPHAELITE STUDIES (1992), THE (US/1060-149X) [24881855] **2848**

JOURNAL OF PRECISION TEACHING (US/0271-8200) [06688289] **1898**

JOURNAL OF PREHISTORIC RELIGION (SW/0283-8486) [16927236] **4969**

JOURNAL OF PRESSURE VESSEL TECHNOLOGY (US/0094-9930) [01472102] **2118**

JOURNAL OF PREVENTIVE MEDICINE AND HYGIENE (IT/1121-2233) [26850652] **4787**

JOURNAL OF PREVENTIVE PSYCHIATRY AND ALLIED DISCIPLINES **CEASED.** (US/1049-6343) [21268344] 5206, **3929**

JOURNAL OF PRIMARY PREVENTION, THE (US/0278-095X) [07721550] 4599, **4787**

JOURNAL OF PRISON & JAIL HEALTH **CEASED.** (US/0731-8332) [08261167] 3597, **3167**

JOURNAL OF PRISONERS ON PRISONS (CN/0838-164X) [18936120] **3167**

JOURNAL OF PRIVATE ENTERPRISE, THE (US/0890-913X) [14578002] **687**

JOURNAL OF PROBATION AND PAROLE : THE JOURNAL OF THE NEW YORK STATE PROBATION OFFICERS ASSOCIATION (US/0278-1042) [05747858] **3167**

JOURNAL OF PROCESS CONTROL (UK/0959-1524) [23479161] **3482**

●JOURNAL OF PRODUCT & BRAND MANAGEMENT, THE (UK/1061-0421) [25167950] **761**

JOURNAL OF PRODUCT INNOVATION MANAGEMENT, THE (US/0737-6782) [09425135] **687**

JOURNAL OF PRODUCTION AGRICULTURE (US/0890-8524) [14402895] **176**

JOURNAL OF PRODUCTIVITY ANALYSIS (US/0895-562X) [16688174] **1614**

●JOURNAL OF PRODUCTS AND TOXICS LIABILITY (US/0967-2680) [26286727] **2989**

JOURNAL OF PRODUCTS LIABILITY (US/0363-0404) [02867947] **2989**

JOURNAL OF PROFESSIONAL BOOKKEEPING AND MANAGEMENT *See* JOURNAL OF ACCOUNTING, TAXATION AND FINANCE FOR BUSINESS, THE **746**

JOURNAL OF PROFESSIONAL BOOKKEEPING AND MANAGEMENT, THE (US/1056-8662) [23887110] **747**

JOURNAL OF PROFESSIONAL ISSUES IN ENGINEERING EDUCATION AND PRACTICE (US/1052-3928) [22282992] **2026**

JOURNAL OF PROFESSIONAL LEGAL EDUCATION, THE (AT/0810-9729) [10232638] **2989**

JOURNAL OF PROFESSIONAL NURSING (US/8755-7223) [11400859] **3860**

JOURNAL OF PROFESSIONAL SERVICES MARKETING (US/0748-4623) [10947393] **929**

JOURNAL OF PROFESSIONAL STUDIES (US) [04843058] **1833**

●JOURNAL OF PROGRAMMING LANGUAGES (UK/0963-9306) **1280**

JOURNAL OF PROGRESSIVE HUMAN SERVICES (US/1042-8232) [19225078] **5292**

JOURNAL OF PROGRESSIVE LEGAL THOUGHT (US/1053-8445) [20763798] **2989**

JOURNAL OF PROMOTION MANAGEMENT (US/1049-6491) [21269746] **874**

JOURNAL OF PROPERTY FINANCE (UK/0958-868X) [23722022] **4839**

JOURNAL OF PROPERTY MANAGEMENT (US/0022-3905) [03931985] **4839**

JOURNAL OF PROPERTY RESEARCH (UK/0959-9916) [24091092] 1500, **4839**

JOURNAL OF PROPERTY TAX MANAGEMENT (US) [22658582] **4734**

JOURNAL OF PROPERTY TAXATION (US/1041-4797) [18778006] **4734**

JOURNAL OF PROPERTY VALUATION & INVESTMENT (UK/0960-2712) [23198995] **4839**

JOURNAL OF PROPRIETARY RIGHTS, THE (US/1041-3952) [18757754] 1305, **2989**

JOURNAL OF PROPULSION AND POWER (US/0748-4658) [10947338] **26**

JOURNAL OF PROSTHETIC DENTISTRY, THE (US/0022-3913) [01782559] **1327**

JOURNAL OF PROSTHETICS AND ORTHOTICS (US/1040-8800) [18564121] **3597**

●JOURNAL OF PROSTHODONTICS (US/1059-941X) [24833150] **1327**

JOURNAL OF PROTECTIVE COATINGS & LININGS (US/8755-1985) [11284340] **5119**

JOURNAL OF PROTEIN CHEMISTRY (US/0277-8033) [07646306] **490**

JOURNAL OF PROTOZOOLOGY *See* JOURNAL OF EUKARYOTIC MICROBIOLOGY, THE **5587**

JOURNAL OF PROTOZOOLOGY RESEARCH (JA/0917-4427) [26617268] **462**

JOURNAL OF PROTOZOOLOGY, THE (US/0022-3921) [01716181] **5588**

JOURNAL OF PSYCHIATRIC AND MENTAL HEALTH NURSING (UK/1351-0126) 3860, **3929**

JOURNAL OF PSYCHIATRIC RESEARCH (UK/0022-3956) [01754759] **3929**

JOURNAL OF PSYCHIATRY & LAW, THE (US/0093-1853) [01791885] 3929, **2989**

JOURNAL OF PSYCHIATRY & NEUROSCIENCE (CN/1180-4882) [23861822] 3837, **3929**

JOURNAL OF PSYCHOACTIVE DRUGS (US/0279-1072) [07565359] **1346**

JOURNAL OF PSYCHOEDUCATIONAL ASSESSMENT (US/0734-2829) [08722578] 1758, **4599**

JOURNAL OF PSYCHOHISTORY, THE (US/0145-3378) [02428996] **4599**

JOURNAL OF PSYCHOLINGUISTIC RESEARCH (US/0090-6905) [01800203] 4600, **3291**

JOURNAL OF PSYCHOLOGICAL RESEARCHES (II/0022-3972) [01754761] **4600**

JOURNAL OF PSYCHOLOGICAL TYPE (US/0895-8750) [12384630] **4600**

JOURNAL OF PSYCHOLOGY AND CHRISTIANITY (US/0733-4273) [08404774] 4600, **4969**

JOURNAL OF PSYCHOLOGY & HUMAN SEXUALITY (US/0890-7064) [14361639] 5187, **4600**

JOURNAL OF PSYCHOLOGY AND JUDAISM (US/0700-9801) [03324195] 5050, **4600**

JOURNAL OF PSYCHOLOGY AND THEOLOGY (US/0091-6471) [01787711] 4969, **4600**

JOURNAL OF PSYCHOLOGY, THE (US/0022-3980) [01782317] **4600**

JOURNAL OF PSYCHOPATHOLOGY AND BEHAVIORAL ASSESSMENT (US/0882-2689) [11793643] **4600**

JOURNAL OF PSYCHOPHARMACOLOGY **CEASED.** (US/0449-3044) [02166877] 4600, **4313**

JOURNAL OF PSYCHOPHARMACOLOGY (OXFORD, ENGLAND) (UK/0269-8811) [19962867] 4600, **4313**

JOURNAL OF PSYCHOPHYSIOLOGY (UK/0269-8803) [16513165] 583, **4600**

JOURNAL OF PSYCHOSOCIAL NURSING AND MENTAL HEALTH SERVICES (US/0279-3695) [07816794] 3929, **3860**

JOURNAL OF PSYCHOSOCIAL ONCOLOGY (US/0734-7332) [08799194] **3819**

JOURNAL OF PSYCHOSOMATIC OBSTETRICS AND GYNAECOLOGY (NE/0167-482X) [10009972] **3764**

JOURNAL OF PSYCHOSOMATIC RESEARCH (UK/0022-3999) [01782774] 4600, **3597**

JOURNAL OF PSYCHOTHERAPY INTEGRATION (US/1053-0479) [22439881] 3929, **4600**

●JOURNAL OF PSYCHOTHERAPY PRACTICE AND RESEARCH, THE (US/1055-050X) [23065306] **3929**

JOURNAL OF PUBLIC ADMINISTRATION RESEARCH AND THEORY (US/1053-1858) [22469315] **4659**

JOURNAL OF PUBLIC AND INTERNATIONAL AFFAIRS **CEASED.** (US/0195-6000) [05468983] **5206**

JOURNAL OF PUBLIC ECONOMICS (NE/0047-2727) [01798094] **4734**

JOURNAL OF PUBLIC HEALTH DENTISTRY (US/0022-4006) [01793457] **1328**

JOURNAL OF PUBLIC HEALTH MEDICINE (UK/0957-4832) [21663362] 4787, **3597**

JOURNAL OF PUBLIC HEALTH POLICY (US/0197-5897) [06077515] **4787**

JOURNAL OF PUBLIC POLICY (UK/0143-814X) [07858865] **4479**

JOURNAL OF PUBLIC POLICY & MARKETING (US/0743-9156) [10339729] 4659, **929**

●JOURNAL OF PUBLIC RELATIONS RESEARCH (US/1062-726X) [25177902] **761**

JOURNAL OF PUBLIC SAFETY COMPUTING, THE **CEASED.** (US/1058-8663) [24413189] 1192, **4787**

JOURNAL OF PULP AND PAPER SCIENCE (CN/0826-6220) [10670824] **4234**

Alphabetical Title Index — JOURNAL

JOURNAL OF PURE AND APPLIED ALGEBRA (NE/0022-4049) [01800179] **3514**

JOURNAL OF PURE AND APPLIED SCIENCES (ANKARA) (TU/0022-4057) [02263070] **5119**

JOURNAL OF PURE AND APPLIED SCIENCES BAHAWALPUR (PK/0255-3643) [I02553643] **5119**

JOURNAL OF QUALITY ASSURANCE See JOURNAL FOR HEALTHCARE QUALITY **3858**

JOURNAL OF QUALITY ASSURANCE See JOURNAL FOR HEALTHCARE QUALITY: PROMOTING EXCELLENCE IN HEALTHCARE **4786**

JOURNAL OF QUALITY ENVIRONMENTAL MANAGEMENT (US/1055-7555) [23302411] **2176**

●JOURNAL OF QUALITY IN CLINICAL PRACTICE (AT) [30137699] **3597**

●JOURNAL OF QUALITY IN MAINTENANCE ENGINEERING (UK/1355-2511) **874**

JOURNAL OF QUALITY TECHNOLOGY (US/0022-4065) [01800135] **874**, **5119**

JOURNAL OF QUANTITATIVE ANTHROPOLOGY (NE/0922-2995) [19133469] **239**

JOURNAL OF QUANTITATIVE CRIMINOLOGY (US/0748-4518) [10945712] **3167**

JOURNAL OF QUANTITATIVE ECONOMICS : JOURNAL OF THE INDIAN ECONOMETRIC SOCIETY (II) [12791593] **1500**

JOURNAL OF QUANTITATIVE LINGUISTICS (NE/0929-6174) **3291**

JOURNAL OF QUANTITATIVE SPECTROSCOPY & RADIATIVE TRANSFER (UK/0022-4073) [01783070] **4436**

●JOURNAL OF QUANTUM NONLINEAR PHENOMENA (US/1062-7944) [25749118] **4410**

●JOURNAL OF QUESTIONED DOCUMENT EXAMINATION (US/1061-3455) [25258029] **3167**

JOURNAL OF RADIATION CURING AND RADIATION CURING (US/1057-5715) [23113543] **4436**

JOURNAL OF RADIATION RESEARCH (JA/0449-3060) [01783177] **4436**

JOURNAL OF RADIOANALYTICAL AND NUCLEAR CHEMISTRY (SZ/0236-5731) [10540203] **1017**

JOURNAL OF RADIOANALYTICAL AND NUCLEAR CHEMISTRY (SZ/0236-5731) [10396163] **1017**

JOURNAL OF RADIOANALYTICAL AND NUCLEAR CHEMISTRY. LETTERS (SZ/0236-5731) [10540344] **1017**

JOURNAL OF RADIOLOGICAL PROTECTION (UK/0952-4746) [18265885] **4436**

JOURNAL OF RAILWAY TANK CARS (US/1045-067X) [19991183] **5432**

JOURNAL OF RAKUNO GAKUEN UNIVERSITY. NATURAL SCIENCE (JA) [20500534] **4166**

JOURNAL OF RAMAN SPECTROSCOPY (UK/0377-0486) [01787090] **4436**

JOURNAL OF RANGE MANAGEMENT (US/0022-409X) [01782570] **100**

●JOURNAL OF RAPID METHODS AND AUTOMATION IN MICROBIOLOGY (US/1060-3999) [24987430] **4194**, **2347**

JOURNAL OF RAPTOR RESEARCH, THE (US/0892-1016) [15078979] **5588**

JOURNAL OF RARE OLD BOOKS, THE (CN/0826-1067) [11734469] **4829**

JOURNAL OF RATIONAL-EMOTIVE AND COGNITIVE-BEHAVIOR THERAPY (US/0894-9085) [16307814] **4600**

JOURNAL OF READING (US/0022-4103) [01754770] **1898**

JOURNAL OF READING BEHAVIOR (US/0022-4111) [01263454] **1758**

JOURNAL OF READING EDUCATION (US/0886-5701) [11200030] **1758**

JOURNAL OF READING, WRITING AND LEARNING DISABILITIES INTERNATIONAL See READING & WRITING QUARTERLY **1884**

JOURNAL OF REAL ESTATE & CONSTRUCTION (SI) [26826209] **4839**

JOURNAL OF REAL ESTATE FINANCE AND ECONOMICS, THE (US/0895-5638) [16688275] **795**, **4839**

JOURNAL OF REAL ESTATE LITERATURE (US/0927-7544) **4839**, **3400**

JOURNAL OF REAL ESTATE RESEARCH, THE (US/0896-5803) [15220526] **4839**

JOURNAL OF REAL ESTATE TAXATION (US/0093-5107) [01792269] **4839**, **4734**

JOURNAL OF REALITY THERAPY (US/0743-0493) [09662645] **4600**

JOURNAL OF RECENT ADVANCES IN APPLIED SCIENCES (II/0970-1990) [15273198] **5119**, **462**

JOURNAL OF RECEPTOR RESEARCH (US/0197-5110) [06061073] **538**

JOURNAL OF RECONSTRUCTIVE MICROSURGERY (US/0743-684X) [10643595] **3968**

JOURNAL OF RECREATIONAL MATHEMATICS (US/0022-412X) [01588561] **3514**

JOURNAL OF REFRACTIVE & CORNEAL SURGERY (US) **3876**

●JOURNAL OF REFRACTIVE AND CORNEAL SURGERY (US/0883-0444) [30372788] **3597**

JOURNAL OF REFUGEE STUDIES (UK/0951-6328) [18854800] **1919**

JOURNAL OF REGIONAL HISTORY (II) [08756636] **2769**

JOURNAL OF REGIONAL SCIENCE (US/0022-4146) [01682251] **2567**, **1500**

JOURNAL OF REGRESSION THERAPY, THE (US/1054-0830) [22741395] **4600**

JOURNAL OF REGULATION AND SOCIAL COSTS **CEASED.** (US/1054-8939) [23011871] **687**, **1500**

JOURNAL OF REGULATORY ECONOMICS (US/0922-680X) [20107653] **843**

JOURNAL OF REHABILITATION (US/0022-4154) [01640621] **5292**

JOURNAL OF REHABILITATION ADMINISTRATION (US/0148-3846) [03295025] **943**, **4390**

JOURNAL OF REHABILITATION AND HEALTH (US/1068-9591) [27870214] **3597**

JOURNAL OF REHABILITATION IN ASIA, THE **CEASED.** (II/0022-4162) [01800336] **4380**

JOURNAL OF REHABILITATION RESEARCH AND DEVELOPMENT (US/0748-7711) [10988482] **4380**

JOURNAL OF REHABILITATION SCIENCES (NE/0923-0211) [20626737] **4390**

JOURNAL OF REINFORCED PLASTICS AND COMPOSITES (US/0731-6844) [08228265] **2104**

JOURNAL OF RELIGION AND HEALTH (US/0022-4197) [01783067] **3929**, **4969**

JOURNAL OF RELIGION AND PSYCHICAL RESEARCH, THE (JS/0731-2148) [08135828] **4242**, **4969**

JOURNAL OF RELIGION AND THE APPLIED BEHAVIORAL SCIENCES (US/0275-1402) [07087643] **4600**, **4970**

JOURNAL OF RELIGION IN AFRICA (NE/0022-4200) [01754773] **4970**

●JOURNAL OF RELIGION IN DISABILITY & REHABILITATION (US/1059-9258) [24814488] **4390**, **4970**

●JOURNAL OF RELIGION IN PSYCHOTHERAPY (US/1045-5876) [20150956] **4970**, **3929**

JOURNAL OF RELIGION, THE (US/0022-4189) [01590720] **4969**

●JOURNAL OF RELIGIOUS & THEOLOGICAL INFORMATION (US/1047-7845) [20789044] **4970**, **3220**

JOURNAL OF RELIGIOUS ETHICS, THE (US/0384-9694) [01590034] **2251**

JOURNAL OF RELIGIOUS GERONTOLOGY (US/1050-2289) [21426735] **4970**, **5180**

JOURNAL OF RELIGIOUS HISTORY, THE (AT/0022-4227) [01783012] **4970**

JOURNAL OF RELIGIOUS STUDIES (II/0047-2735) [01800031] **4970**

JOURNAL OF RELIGIOUS STUDIES (CLEVELAND, OHIO) (US/0193-3604) [05057629] **4970**

JOURNAL OF RELIGIOUS THOUGHT, THE (US/0022-4235) [01754775] **4970**

JOURNAL OF RENAL NUTRITION (US/1051-2276) [21896802] **3991**

JOURNAL OF REPRINTS FOR ANTITRUST LAW AND ECONOMICS, THE (US/0022-4243) [01754776] **3101**

JOURNAL OF REPRINTS OF DOCUMENTS AFFECTING WOMEN (US/0362-062X) [03054932] **5559**, **2989**

JOURNAL OF REPRODUCTION & FERTILITY (UK/0022-4251) [01783013] **583**, **3597**

JOURNAL OF REPRODUCTION & FERTILITY. ABSTRACT SERIES / SOCIETY FOR THE STUDY OF FERTILITY (UK/0954-0725) [18409458] **583**

JOURNAL OF REPRODUCTION AND FERTILITY. SUPPLEMENT (UK/0449-3087) [01639439] **3597**

JOURNAL OF REPRODUCTIVE AND INFANT PSYCHOLOGY (UK/0264-6838) [10960360] **4600**, **3764**

JOURNAL OF REPRODUCTIVE IMMUNOLOGY (NE/0165-0378) [05044067] **3674**

JOURNAL OF REPRODUCTIVE MEDICINE (US/0024-7758) [01796754] **3764**

JOURNAL OF RESEARCH AND DEVELOPMENT IN EDUCATION (US/0022-426X) [01754777] **1758**

JOURNAL OF RESEARCH AND EDUCATION IN INDIAN MEDICINE, THE (II) [13278832] **3597**

JOURNAL OF RESEARCH AND TRAINING, THE (US/0092-3931) [01788755] **3929**

JOURNAL OF RESEARCH APAU, THE (II) [12932276] **100**

JOURNAL OF RESEARCH / ASSAM AGRICULTURAL UNIVERSITY (II/0258-1728) [09617321] **100**

JOURNAL OF RESEARCH IN AYURVEDA & SIDDHA (II/0254-3478) [08049831] **4185**

JOURNAL OF RESEARCH IN CHILDHOOD EDUCATION (US/0256-8543) [12019948] **1758**

JOURNAL OF RESEARCH IN CRIME AND DELINQUENCY, THE (US/0022-4278) [03983442] **3167**

JOURNAL OF RESEARCH IN CRIME AND DELINQUENCY, THE (US/0022-4278) [01783073] **3167**

JOURNAL OF RESEARCH IN MUSIC EDUCATION (US/0022-4294) [01782663] **4126**

JOURNAL OF RESEARCH IN PERSONALITY (US/0092-6566) [01788573] **4601**

JOURNAL OF RESEARCH IN PHARMACEUTICAL ECONOMICS (US/0896-6621) [17242403] **4313**

JOURNAL OF RESEARCH IN READING (UK/0141-0423) [04417636] **3291**, **1898**

JOURNAL OF RESEARCH IN RURAL EDUCATION (US/1062-4228) [23303099] **1758**

JOURNAL OF RESEARCH IN SCIENCE TEACHING (US/0022-4308) [01783131] **5119**

JOURNAL OF RESEARCH IN SINGING AND APPLIED VOCAL PEDAGOGY (US) [15242782] **386**, **4126**

JOURNAL OF RESEARCH OF THE AMERICAN FEDERATION OF ASTROLOGERS (US/0882-4517) [11843694] **390**

JOURNAL OF RESEARCH OF THE NATIONAL INSTITUTE OF STANDARDS AND TECHNOLOGY (US/1044-677X) [19017279] **4031**

JOURNAL OF RESEARCH ON ADOLESCENCE (US/1050-8392) [21653571] **1881**, **4601**

●JOURNAL OF RESEARCH ON CHRISTIAN EDUCATION (US/1065-6219) [26656409] **4970**

JOURNAL OF RESEARCH ON COMPUTING IN EDUCATION (US/0888-6504) [13696457] **1224**

JOURNAL OF RESEARCH ON THE LEPIDOPTERA, THE (US/0022-4324) [01754781] **5611**

JOURNAL OF RESEARCH (ORISSA UNIVERSITY OF AGRICULTURE AND TECHNOLOGY) (II) [09680618] **100**

JOURNAL OF RESEARCH, PUNJAB AGRICULTURAL UNIVERSITY (II/0048-6019) [01605116] **100**

JOURNAL OF RESEARCH RANCHI (II/0971-1724) [I09711724] **100**

JOURNAL OF RESOURCE MANAGEMENT AND TECHNOLOGY, THE (US/0745-6999) [09406024] **2234**

JOURNAL OF RESPIRATORY DISEASES, THE (US/0194-259X) [05368655] **3950**

●JOURNAL OF RESTAURANT & FOODSERVICE MARKETING (US/1052-214X) [22222339] **2347**, **5071**

JOURNAL OF RETAIL BANKING (US/0195-2064) [05365080] **929**, **795**

JOURNAL OF RETAILING (US/0022-4359) [01782289] **955**

JOURNAL OF RETAILING AND CONSUMER SERVICES (UK/0969-6989) **955**

JOURNAL OF RHEOLOGY (NEW YORK, N.Y.) (US/0148-6055) [03526986] **4428**

JOURNAL OF RHEUMATOLOGY. SUPPLEMENT, THE (CN/0380-0903) [02443336] **3805**

JOURNAL OF RHEUMATOLOGY, THE (CN/0315-162X) [01181728] **3805**

JOURNAL OF RISK AND INSURANCE, THE (US/0022-4367) [01800182] **2885**

JOURNAL OF RISK AND UNCERTAINTY (US/0895-5646) [16689184] **4601**, **1500**

JOURNAL OF RITUAL STUDIES (US/0890-1112) [14153910] **4970**

JOURNAL OF ROBOTIC SYSTEMS (US/0741-2223) [10125153] **1214**

JOURNAL OF ROBOTICS AND MECHATRONICS (JA/0915-3942) [I09153942] **1220**, **1214**

JOURNAL — Alphabetical Title Index

JOURNAL OF ROCKINGHAM COUNTY HISTORY AND GENEALOGY, THE (US/0363-1656) [02420614] 2455, **2741**

JOURNAL OF ROMAN ARCHAEOLOGY (US/1047-7594) [18999240] **271**

JOURNAL OF ROMAN STUDIES MONOGRAPHS (UK) [10884837] **2695**

JOURNAL OF ROMAN STUDIES, THE (UK/0075-4358) [01782277] **1078**

JOURNAL OF ROOT CROPS (II/0378-2409) [03062847] 176, **100**

JOURNAL OF RTC REAL ESTATE *CEASED*. (US/1055-4211) [23169279] **4839**

JOURNAL OF RURAL AND SMALL SCHOOLS *CEASED*. (US/0890-9520) [14563193] **1758**

JOURNAL OF RURAL COMMUNITY PSYCHOLOGY *CEASED*. (US/0276-2285) [07116817] **4601**

JOURNAL OF RURAL COOPERATION (IS/0377-7480) [01799162] **1542**

JOURNAL OF RURAL DEVELOPMENT (KO/1013-0764) [05502227] **100**

JOURNAL OF RURAL DEVELOPMENT AND ADMINISTRATION (PK/0047-2751) [08537498] **4659**

JOURNAL OF RURAL DEVELOPMENT (HYDERABAD, INDIA) (II/0970-3357) [08408303] **5206**

JOURNAL OF RURAL HEALTH, THE (US/0890-765X) [12020952] **4787**

JOURNAL OF RURAL RECONSTRUCTION (II) [30442184] **2826**

JOURNAL OF RURAL STUDIES (UK/0743-0167) [10490841] **5250**

●JOURNAL OF RUSSIAN AND EAST EUROPEAN PSYCHIATRY (US/1061-0413) [25167906] **3929**

●JOURNAL OF RUSSIAN AND EAST EUROPEAN PSYCHOLOGY (US/1061-0405) [25167865] **4601**

●JOURNAL OF RUSSIAN LASER RESEARCH (US/1071-2836) [28601544] **4436**

●JOURNAL OF RUSSIAN TECHNOLOGY (US/1065-7304) [26710029] **5119**

JOURNAL OF S C C J (JA/0387-5253) [I03875253] **1026**

JOURNAL OF S CORPORATION TAXATION (US/1045-1471) [20025562] **4735**

JOURNAL OF SAFE MANAGEMENT OF DISRUPTIVE AND ASSAULTIVE BEHAVIOR *See* CPI NATIONAL REPORT **4583**

●JOURNAL OF SAFE MANAGEMENT OF DISRUPTIVE AND ASSAULTIVE BEHAVIOR, THE (US/1065-3341) [26573654] **3168**

JOURNAL OF SAFETY RESEARCH (US/0022-4375) [01800052] **2864**

JOURNAL OF SAN DIEGO HISTORY, THE (US/0022-4383) [07920794] **2742**

●JOURNAL OF SCHOLARLY PUBLISHING (CN) [30471520] **4816**

JOURNAL OF SCHOOL HEALTH, THE (US/0022-4391) [01782350] 1758, **4787**

JOURNAL OF SCHOOL LEADERSHIP (US/1052-6846) [22350025] **1865**

JOURNAL OF SCHOOL NURSING, THE (US/1059-8405) [24758374] **3860**

●JOURNAL OF SCHOOL PSYCHOLOGY (US) **4601**

JOURNAL OF SCHOOL PSYCHOLOGY (US/0022-4405) [01783330] 1758, **4601**

JOURNAL OF SCHOOL SOCIAL WORK, THE (US/0098-9584) [02240047] **1865**

JOURNAL OF SCIENCE AND MATHEMATICS EDUCATION IN SOUTHEAST ASIA (MY/0126-7663) [06977384] 5119, **1758**

JOURNAL OF SCIENCE AND TECHNOLOGY (PK/0250-5339) [04356119] **5119**

●JOURNAL OF SCIENCE EDUCATION AND TECHNOLOGY (US/1059-0145) [24458783] **5119**

JOURNAL OF SCIENCE OF THE HIROSHIMA UNIVERSITY. SERIES A. PHYSICS AND CHEMISTRY (1971) (JA/0386-3034) [06589756] 982, **4410**

JOURNAL OF SCIENCE OF THE HIROSHIMA UNIVERSITY. SERIES B. DIVISION 1. ZOOLOGY (JA/0368-4113) [01606497] **5588**

JOURNAL OF SCIENCE OF THE HIROSHIMA UNIVERSITY. SERIES B. DIVISION 2. BOTANY (JA/0075-4366) [01605507] **516**

JOURNAL OF SCIENCE TEACHER EDUCATION (US/1046-560X) [20471037] 5119, **1898**

JOURNAL OF SCIENCES, ISLAMIC REPUBLIC OF IRAN (IR/1016-1104) [22466672] **5119**

JOURNAL OF SCIENTIFIC AND APPLIED PHOTOGRAPHY AND CINEMATOGRAPHY (US) [09471597] **4371**

JOURNAL OF SCIENTIFIC & INDUSTRIAL RESEARCH (II) [13019626] **5119**

JOURNAL OF SCIENTIFIC COMPUTING (US/0885-7474) [12712802] **5120**

JOURNAL OF SCIENTIFIC EXPLORATION (US/0892-3310) [15153049] **5120**

JOURNAL OF SCIENTIFIC RESEARCH (BHOPAL) (II/0253-7230) [05534115] **5120**

JOURNAL OF SCOUTING HISTORY (US) 2621, **5232**

●JOURNAL OF SECOND LANGUAGE WRITING (US/1060-3743) [24947684] **3291**

JOURNAL OF SECONDARY AND ADULT READING (US/0732-1791) [08311817] **1898**

JOURNAL OF SECONDARY GIFTED EDUCATION : JSGE, THE (US/1077-4610) [30808734] 1065, **1881**

JOURNAL OF SECURITY ADMINISTRATION (US/0195-9425) [05711993] **3168**

JOURNAL OF SEDIMENTARY PETROLOGY (US/0022-4472) [01715304] **1458**

●JOURNAL OF SEDIMENTARY RESEARCH. SECTION A, SEDIMENTARY PETROLOGY AND PROCESSES (US/1073-130X) [29338004] **1459**

●JOURNAL OF SEDIMENTARY RESEARCH. SECTION B, STRATIGRAPHY AND GLOBAL STUDIES (US/1073-1318) [29338035] **1459**

JOURNAL OF SEED TECHNOLOGY (US/0146-3071) [03252954] **176**

●JOURNAL OF SEISMIC EXPLORATION (FR/0963-0651) [25862080] **1408**

JOURNAL OF SEMANTICS (NIJMEGEN) (NE/0167-5133) [09983557] **3291**

JOURNAL OF SEMI-CUSTOM ICS (UK/0264-3375) [11870309] **2069**

JOURNAL OF SEMITIC STUDIES (UK/0022-4480) [01782837] 3292, **2266**

JOURNAL OF SENSORY STUDIES (US/0887-8250) [13392864] **2347**

JOURNAL OF SEPARATION PROCESS TECHNOLOGY *CEASED*. (UK/0260-6275) [07368873] **982**

●JOURNAL OF SEROTONIN RESEARCH (UK) **3597**

JOURNAL OF SERVICES MARKETING, THE (US/0887-6045) [13306854] 950, **929**

JOURNAL OF SEX & MARITAL THERAPY (US/0092-623X) [02246185] 3929, 2282, **5187**

JOURNAL OF SEX EDUCATION AND THERAPY (US/0161-4576) [03900884] **5187**

JOURNAL OF SEX RESEARCH, THE (US/0022-4499) [04872050] **5187**

JOURNAL OF SEX RESEARCH, THE (US/0022-4499) [01783365] **5187**

JOURNAL OF SEXUAL HEALTH (UK/0963-6757) [I09636757] 2599, **5187**

JOURNAL OF SHELLFISH RESEARCH (US/0730-8000) [08065878] **2307**

JOURNAL OF SHIP PRODUCTION, THE (US/8756-1417) [11481958] **4177**

JOURNAL OF SHIP RESEARCH (US/0022-4502) [01782995] **4177**

JOURNAL OF SHIPPING, CUSTOMS & TRANSPORT LAWS (II/0377-0494) [02245629] **3181**

JOURNAL OF SHIVAJI UNIVERSITY. SCIENCE (II/0250-5347) [11175645] **5120**

●JOURNAL OF SHOULDER AND ELBOW SURGERY (US/1058-2746) [24252465] **3968**

JOURNAL OF SIKH STUDIES (II/0379-8194) [02246229] 4351, **4970**

●JOURNAL OF SLAVIC LINGUISTICS (US/1068-2090) [27471390] **3292**

●JOURNAL OF SLAVIC MILITARY STUDIES, THE (UK) [28178039] **4048**

●JOURNAL OF SLEEP RESEARCH (UK/0962-1105) [25772760] **3597**

JOURNAL OF SMALL ANIMAL PRACTICE, THE (UK/0022-4510) [01754797] 4286, **5513**

JOURNAL OF SMALL BUSINESS AND ENTREPRENEURSHIP (CN/0827-6331) [13319394] **687**

JOURNAL OF SMALL BUSINESS FINANCE, THE (US/1057-2287) [23983737] **687**

JOURNAL OF SMALL BUSINESS MANAGEMENT (US/0047-2778) [01800008] **874**

JOURNAL OF SMALL EXOTIC ANIMAL MEDICINE (US) [24370276] **5513**

●JOURNAL OF SMALL FRUITS & VITICULTURE (US/1052-0015) [22164536] **100**

JOURNAL OF SMOKING-RELATED DISORDERS, THE (UK/0959-2431) [25866110] 5373, **3981**

JOURNAL OF SMOOTH MUSCLE RESEARCH (JA/0916-8737) [26500144] **3805**

JOURNAL OF SOCIAL AND ADMINISTRATIVE PHARMACY : JSAP (SW/0281-0662) [10170821] **4313**

JOURNAL OF SOCIAL AND BEHAVIORAL SCIENCES (US) [02246247] **5206**

JOURNAL OF SOCIAL AND BIOLOGICAL STRUCTURES *See* JOURNAL OF SOCIAL AND EVOLUTIONARY SYSTEMS **5250**

JOURNAL OF SOCIAL AND CLINICAL PSYCHOLOGY (US/0736-7236) [09199268] **4601**

JOURNAL OF SOCIAL AND ECONOMIC STUDIES (NEW DELHI, INDIA) (II/0377-0508) [10890710] **5206**

●JOURNAL OF SOCIAL AND EVOLUTIONARY SYSTEMS (US/1061-7361) [25426051] **5250**

JOURNAL OF SOCIAL AND PERSONAL RELATIONSHIPS (UK/0265-4075) [10643317] 5250, **4601**

JOURNAL OF SOCIAL BEHAVIOR AND PERSONALITY (US/0886-1641) [12847972] **4601**

JOURNAL OF SOCIAL DEVELOPMENT IN AFRICA (RH) [14260818] **5206**

●JOURNAL OF SOCIAL DISTRESS AND THE HOMELESS (US/1053-0789) [22447873] 5250, **5293**

JOURNAL OF SOCIAL HISTORY (US/0022-4529) [01799887] **5206**

JOURNAL OF SOCIAL ISSUES, THE (US/0022-4537) [01782412] 4601, **5206**

JOURNAL OF SOCIAL PHILOSOPHY (US/0047-2786) [02245897] 4351, **5206**

JOURNAL OF SOCIAL POLICY (UK/0047-2794) [00986734] **5293**

JOURNAL OF SOCIAL PSYCHOLOGY, THE (US/0022-4545) [01782304] **4601**

JOURNAL OF SOCIAL RECONSTRUCTION *SUSPENDED*. (US/0196-2000) [05843984] **5207**

JOURNAL OF SOCIAL RESEARCH (RANCHI) (II/0449-315X) [01956967] **239**

JOURNAL OF SOCIAL SCIENCE (MW) [01793343] **5207**

JOURNAL OF SOCIAL SCIENCE TEACHERS *See* JOURNAL OF SOCIAL AND BEHAVIORAL SCIENCES **5206**

JOURNAL OF SOCIAL SCIENCES & HUMANITIES (PK) [12349710] 2849, **5207**

JOURNAL OF SOCIAL SCIENCES AND HUMANITIES (SEOUL) (KO/0023-4044) [02468580] **2849**

●JOURNAL OF SOCIAL SECURITY LAW (UK) **2989**

JOURNAL OF SOCIAL SERVICE RESEARCH (US/0148-8376) [03736259] **5293**

JOURNAL OF SOCIAL STUDIES RESEARCH (US/0885-985X) [04888184] **5207**

JOURNAL OF SOCIAL STUDIES, THE (BG) [06314653] **5207**

JOURNAL OF SOCIAL THEORY IN ART EDUCATION, THE (US/1057-0292) [21207773] 323, 1898, **354**

JOURNAL OF SOCIAL TRANSFORMATION, THE (II) [04817264] **5250**

JOURNAL OF SOCIAL WELFARE & FAMILY LAW (UK/0141-8033) [23466742] 5293, **3121**

JOURNAL OF SOCIAL WORK & HUMAN SEXUALITY (US/0276-3850) [07378748] 5187, **5293**

JOURNAL OF SOCIAL WORK AND POLICY IN ISRAEL (IS/0334-9977) [17846418] **5293**

JOURNAL OF SOCIAL WORK EDUCATION (US/1043-7797) [11773132] 1758, **5293**

JOURNAL OF SOCIAL WORK PRACTICE (UK/0265-0533) [13551349] **5293**

JOURNAL OF SOCIO-ECONOMICS (US/1053-5357) [22548607] **1570**

JOURNAL OF SOCIOLOGICAL STUDIES, THE (II) [09104525] **5250**

JOURNAL OF SOCIOLOGY (CH) **5250**

JOURNAL OF SOCIOLOGY AND SOCIAL WELFARE (US/0191-5096) [01107708] **5293**

JOURNAL OF SOCIOLOGY (CLEVELAND) (US/0069-0864) [01792092] **5250**

JOURNAL OF SOFTWARE MAINTENANCE (UK/1040-550X) [18446004] **1288**

JOURNAL OF SOIL AND WATER CONSERVATION (US/0022-4561) [01782825] **2196**

Alphabetical Title Index — JOURNAL

JOURNAL OF SOIL AND WATER CONSERVATION IN INDIA (II/0022-457X) [01604717] **2196**

JOURNAL OF SOIL BIOLOGY & ECOLOGY (II) [09873843] **176**

●JOURNAL OF SOIL CONTAMINATION (US/1058-8337) [24402087] **176**

JOURNAL OF SOIL SCIENCE *See* EUROPEAN JOURNAL OF SOIL SCIENCE **171**

JOURNAL OF SOIL SCIENCE, THE (UK/0022-4588) [01782536] **176**

JOURNAL OF SOL-GEL SCIENCE AND TECHNOLOGY (US/0928-0707) **5120**

JOURNAL OF SOLAR ENERGY ENGINEERING (US/0199-6231) [06054906] **1949**

JOURNAL OF SOLAR ENERGY RESEARCH / SOLAR ENERGY RESEARCH CENTER, SCIENTIFIC RESEARCH COUNCIL, BAGHDAD (IQ/0256-7911) [14180765] **1949**

JOURNAL OF SOLAR SCIENCES (US/0276-3486) [07343081] **1949**

JOURNAL OF SOLID STATE CHEMISTRY (US/0022-4596) [01783527] **982**

●JOURNAL OF SOLID WASTE (US/1056-2575) [23603787] **2234**

JOURNAL OF SOLUTION CHEMISTRY (US/0095-9782) [01784642] 462, **1055**

JOURNAL OF SOUND AND VIBRATION (UK/0022-460X) [01783075] **4452**

JOURNAL OF SOURCES IN EDUCATIONAL HISTORY (UK/0140-671X) [04264600] **1758**

JOURNAL OF SOUTH AMERICAN EARTH SCIENCES (UK/0895-9811) [16883694] **1357**

JOURNAL OF SOUTH ASIAN AND MIDDLE EASTERN STUDIES (US/0149-1784) [03436931] **2769**

JOURNAL OF SOUTH ASIAN LITERATURE (US/0091-5637) [01627749] **3400**

JOURNAL OF SOUTHEAST ASIA BUSINESS (US/1055-2073) [23121009] **687**

JOURNAL OF SOUTHEAST ASIAN EARTH SCIENCES (UK/0743-9547) [10728291] **1357**

JOURNAL OF SOUTHEAST ASIAN STUDIES (SINGAPORE) (SI/0022-4634) [01784403] **2655**

JOURNAL OF SOUTHEAST UNIVERSITY (CC) [21145875] **5120**

JOURNAL OF SOUTHERN AFRICAN AFFAIRS (US/0275-5327) [03098465] **4479**

JOURNAL OF SOUTHERN AFRICAN STUDIES (UK/0305-7070) [01799424] **2641**

JOURNAL OF SOUTHERN HISTORY, THE (US/0022-4642) [01782314] **2742**

JOURNAL OF SOUTHWEST GEORGIA HISTORY, THE (US/0739-1943) [09700850] **2742**

JOURNAL OF SOVIET LASER RESEARCH (US/0270-2010) [06353310] **4437**

JOURNAL OF SOVIET MATHEMATICS (US/0090-4104) [01628196] **3514**

JOURNAL OF SOVIET MILITARY STUDIES *See* JOURNAL OF SLAVIC MILITARY STUDIES, THE **4048**

JOURNAL OF SOVIET MILITARY STUDIES, THE (UK/0954-254X) [19232239] **4048**

JOURNAL OF SOVIET NATIONALITIES *CEASED.* (US/1043-7916) [19564139] **2266**

JOURNAL OF SPACE ABSTRACTS AND RESEARCH (US) 26, **41**

JOURNAL OF SPACE LAW (US/0095-7577) [01796565] 26, **2989**

JOURNAL OF SPACECRAFT AND ROCKETS (US/0022-4650) [01783074] **26**

JOURNAL OF SPECIAL EDUCATION TECHNOLOGY (US/0162-6434) [04184761] **1881**

JOURNAL OF SPECIAL EDUCATION, THE (US/0022-4669) [01783202] **1881**

JOURNAL OF SPECTROSCOPY (TU) [22504891] **4437**

JOURNAL OF SPECULATIVE PHILOSOPHY, THE (US/0891-625X) [01754812] **4351**

JOURNAL OF SPEECH AND HEARING RESEARCH (US/0022-4685) [01754814] **4390**

JOURNAL OF SPEECH-LANGUAGE-HEARING ASSOCIATION OF VIRGINIA (US) [23104213] **3889**

JOURNAL OF SPEECH-LANGUAGE PATHOLOGY AND AUDIOLOGY (CN/0848-1970) [19735939] **4390**

JOURNAL OF SPELEAN HISTORY, THE (US/0022-4693) [06783033] **1357**

JOURNAL OF SPICES AND AROMATIC CROPS (II) [l09713328] **177**

JOURNAL OF SPINAL DISORDERS (US/0895-0385) [16414201] **3805**

JOURNAL OF SPINE RESEARCH *CEASED.* (US/1058-1588) [24231617] **3597**

JOURNAL OF SPIRITUAL FORMATION *CEASED.* (US) [29699199] **4970**

JOURNAL OF SPORT & EXERCISE PSYCHOLOGY (US/0895-2779) [16534632] **4901**

JOURNAL OF SPORT AND SOCIAL ISSUES (US/0193-7235) [04233486] 4902, **5250**

JOURNAL OF SPORT BEHAVIOR (US/0162-7341) [03850194] **4902**

JOURNAL OF SPORT HISTORY (US/0094-1700) [01793987] **4902**

JOURNAL OF SPORT MANAGEMENT (US/0888-4773) [13609168] 874, **4902**

●JOURNAL OF SPORT REHABILITATION (US/1056-6716) [23819570] **3954**

JOURNAL OF SPORTS MEDICINE AND PHYSICAL FITNESS (IT/0022-4707) [01590778] **3954**

JOURNAL OF SPORTS PHILATELY (US/0447-953X) [08875617] **2785**

JOURNAL OF SPORTS SCIENCES (UK/0264-0414) [10088912] **4902**

JOURNAL OF SPORTS TRAUMATOLOGY AND RELATED RESEARCH (IT/1120-3137) [l11203137] **4902**

JOURNAL OF ST. LUKE'S HEART INSTITUTE (US/0748-8238) [11010220] **3707**

JOURNAL OF STAFF DEVELOPMENT, THE (US/0276-928X) [07271402] **1801**

JOURNAL OF STAFF, PROGRAM & ORGANIZATION DEVELOPMENT, THE (US/0736-7627) [09209637] **1898**

JOURNAL OF STAINED GLASS : THE JOURNAL OF THE BRITISH SOCIETY OF MASTER GLASS PAINTERS, THE (UK) [12873791] **2591**

JOURNAL OF STATE GOVERNMENT *See* SPECTRUM (LEXINGTON, KY.) **4686**

JOURNAL OF STATE GOVERNMENT, THE (US/1043-2248) [13775213] **4479**

JOURNAL OF STATE TAXATION (US/0744-6713) [08463874] **4735**

JOURNAL OF STATISTICAL COMPUTATION AND SIMULATION (US/0094-9655) [01793216] 5329, **1282**

JOURNAL OF STATISTICAL PHYSICS (US/0022-4715) [01783387] **4410**

JOURNAL OF STATISTICAL PLANNING AND INFERENCE (NE/0378-3758) [03185135] **3514**

JOURNAL OF STATISTICAL RESEARCH - UNIVERSITY OF DACCA. INSTITUTE OF STATISTICAL RESEARCH AND TRAINING (BG/0256-422X) [01588632] 3514, **5329**

JOURNAL OF STEROID BIOCHEMISTRY AND MOLECULAR BIOLOGY, THE (UK/0960-0760) [22512922] 982, **462**

JOURNAL OF STEWARDSHIP (US/0891-0235) [03894366] **4970**

JOURNAL OF STONE DISEASE, THE *SUSPENDED.* (US/1059-9509) [24821004] **3968**

JOURNAL OF STORED PRODUCTS RESEARCH (UK/0022-474X) [01783139] **2347**

JOURNAL OF STRAIN ANALYSIS FOR ENGINEERING DESIGN, THE (UK/0309-3247) [02514610] **2118**

JOURNAL OF STRATEGIC AND SYSTEMIC THERAPIES, THE (CN/0711-5075) [09099715] **3929**

●JOURNAL OF STRATEGIC CHANGE (US/1057-9265) [24223075] **687**

JOURNAL OF STRATEGIC INFORMATION SYSTEMS, THE (UK/0963-8687) [25762617] **1248**

●JOURNAL OF STRATEGIC MARKETING (UK/0965-254X) 874, **929**

JOURNAL OF STRATEGIC STUDIES, THE (UK/0140-2390) [04918920] **4048**

JOURNAL OF STRATEGIC THERAPIES *See* JOURNAL OF SYSTEMIC THERAPIES **3597**

●JOURNAL OF STRENGTH AND CONDITIONING RESEARCH (US/1064-8011) [26407413] 2599, **4902**

JOURNAL OF STROKE AND CEREBROVASCULAR DISEASES (US/1052-3057) [22248418] **3837**

JOURNAL OF STRUCTURAL BIOLOGY (US/1047-8477) [20794033] **462**

JOURNAL OF STRUCTURAL CHEMISTRY (US/0022-4766) [01782985] **1055**

JOURNAL OF STRUCTURAL ENGINEERING (II/0970-0137) [01790507] **2026**

JOURNAL OF STRUCTURAL ENGINEERING (NEW YORK, N.Y.) (US/0733-9445) [08675516] **2026**

JOURNAL OF STRUCTURAL GEOLOGY (UK/0191-8141) [04967864] **1385**

JOURNAL OF STRUCTURAL LEARNING (US/0022-4774) [01800054] **1758**

JOURNAL OF STRUCTURAL LEARNING AND INTELLIGENT SYSTEMS (UK) **1898**

JOURNAL OF STUDENT FINANCIAL AID, THE (US/0884-9153) [01799936] **1758**

JOURNAL OF STUDIES IN JUSTICE (AT/1031-8313) **5250**

JOURNAL OF STUDIES IN TECHNICAL CAREERS (US/0163-3252) [04381548] **1914**

JOURNAL OF STUDIES IN THE BHAGAVADGITA, THE (CN/0706-6449) [07855003] **5041**

JOURNAL OF STUDIES ON ALCOHOL (US/0096-882X) [01261091] **1346**

JOURNAL OF SUBMICROSCOPIC CYTOLOGY AND PATHOLOGY (IT) [17540157] **538**

JOURNAL OF SUBSTANCE ABUSE (US/0899-3289) [18804126] **1346**

JOURNAL OF SUBSTANCE ABUSE TREATMENT (US/0740-5472) [09965265] **1346**

●JOURNAL OF SUDDEN INFANT DEATH SYNDROME AND INFANT MORTALITY (US) **3905**

JOURNAL OF SUGAR BEET RESEARCH (US/0899-1502) [18008217] **177**

●JOURNAL OF SUNG-YUAN STUDIES (US/1059-3152) [24565424] **2505**

JOURNAL OF SUPERCOMPUTING, THE (US/0920-8542) [16654116] **1192**

JOURNAL OF SUPERCONDUCTIVITY (US/0896-1107) [16914037] 2104, **2069**

JOURNAL OF SUPERCRITICAL FLUIDS, THE (US/0896-8446) [17306028] **1017**

●JOURNAL OF SUPERHARD MATERIALS (US/1063-4576) [26040296] **4006**

JOURNAL OF SUPERVISION AND TRAINING IN MINISTRY (US/0160-7774) [03758171] **4970**

JOURNAL OF SUPREME COURT HISTORY (US/1059-4329) [23157394] **4659**

JOURNAL OF SURFACE MOUNT TECHNOLOGY (US) **1983**

JOURNAL OF SURFACE SCIENCE AND TECHNOLOGY (II/0970-1893) [14988172] **5120**

JOURNAL OF SURGICAL ONCOLOGY (US/0022-4790) [01799890] 3968, **3820**

JOURNAL OF SURGICAL ONCOLOGY. SUPPLEMENT (US/1046-7416) [20226007] **3820**

JOURNAL OF SURGICAL RESEARCH, THE (US/0022-4804) [01783129] **3968**

JOURNAL OF SURVEYING ENGINEERING (US/0733-9453) [08674896] **2026**

JOURNAL OF SUSTAINABLE AGRICULTURE (US/1044-0046) [19643640] **100**

●JOURNAL OF SUSTAINABLE FORESTRY (US/1054-9811) [23041634] **2386**

JOURNAL OF SUSTAINABLE TOURISM (UK/0966-9582) [28536725] **5481**

JOURNAL OF SWIMMING RESEARCH, THE (US/0747-5993) [10756214] **4902**

JOURNAL OF SYMBOLIC COMPUTATION (UK/0747-7171) [10791050] 1192, **3514**

JOURNAL OF SYMBOLIC LOGIC, THE (US/0022-4812) [01782331] **3515**

JOURNAL OF SYNAGOGUE MUSIC (US/0449-5128) [02441470] 5050, **4126**

JOURNAL OF SYNTHETIC METHODS (UK/0260-8847) [03793803] **1043**

JOURNAL OF SYSTEMIC THERAPIES (US/0711-7075) **3597**

JOURNAL OF SYSTEMS AND SOFTWARE, THE (US/0164-1212) [04583109] 1288, **1280**

JOURNAL OF SYSTEMS ENGINEERING (US/0938-7706) **1983**

JOURNAL OF SYSTEMS INTEGRATION (US/0925-4676) [25443749] **1192**

JOURNAL OF SYSTEMS MANAGEMENT (US/0022-4839) [01794211] **687**

JOURNAL OF TAIWAN MUSEUM (CH/0256-257X) [10256497] **4166**

JOURNAL OF TAMIL STUDIES (II/0022-4855) [01773647] **2849**

JOURNAL OF TAXATION DIGEST *See* WGL TAX JOURNAL DIGEST, THE **4758**

JOURNAL OF TAXATION DIGEST, THE (US/8755-6049) [08059457] **4735**

JOURNAL — Alphabetical Title Index

JOURNAL OF TAXATION OF ESTATES & TRUSTS, THE **CEASED.** (US/1044-9418) [19951818] **3118**

JOURNAL OF TAXATION OF EXEMPT ORGANIZATIONS, THE (US/1043-0539) [19288930] **4735**

JOURNAL OF TAXATION OF INVESTMENTS (US/0747-9115) [10202539] **904**

JOURNAL OF TAXATION OF S CORPORATIONS, THE **CEASED.** (US/1040-502X) [18434250] **795**

JOURNAL OF TAXATION, THE (US/0022-4863) [01782768] **4735**

JOURNAL OF TEACHER DEVELOPMENT (UK/0964-0606) **1899**

JOURNAL OF TEACHER EDUCATION (US/0022-4871) [01782535] **1865**

JOURNAL OF TEACHING IN INTERNATIONAL BUSINESS (US/0897-5930) [17559857] **1637, 688**

JOURNAL OF TEACHING IN PHYSICAL EDUCATION (US/0273-5024) [07062604] **1856**

JOURNAL OF TEACHING IN SOCIAL WORK (US/0884-1233) [12308254] **1899, 5293**

JOURNAL OF TEACHING PRACTICE (AT/1030-407X) [I1030407X] **1899**

JOURNAL OF TEACHING WRITING (US/0735-1259) [08872753] **1899, 3292**

JOURNAL OF TECHNICAL PHYSICS (PL/0324-8313) [02243606] **4410**

JOURNAL OF TECHNICAL WRITING AND COMMUNICATION (US/0047-2816) [01800187] **1899, 1115**

●JOURNAL OF TECHNOLOGY AND TEACHER EDUCATION (US/1059-7069) [24681049] **5120, 1758**

JOURNAL OF TECHNOLOGY EDUCATION (US/1045-1064) [20001913] **5120**

JOURNAL OF TECHNOLOGY IN ADDICTION & RECOVERY (US/0882-3375) [11808746] **1346**

JOURNAL OF TECHNOLOGY IN MATHEMATICS **CEASED.** (US/1055-789X) [23324046] **3515**

JOURNAL OF TECHNOLOGY TRANSFER, THE (US/0892-9912) [06370978] **5120**

●JOURNAL OF TELEMEDICINE AND TELECARE (UK) **3597**

JOURNAL OF TELUGU STUDIES : RESEARCH QUARTERLY OF TELUGU UNIVERSITY (II) [18969968] **3400**

JOURNAL OF TERRAMECHANICS (UK/0022-4898) [01783299] **2026**

JOURNAL OF TERTIARY EDUCATIONAL ADMINISTRATION (AT/0157-6038) [11942429] **1758**

JOURNAL OF TESTING AND EVALUATION (US/0090-3973) [01785173] **1983**

JOURNAL OF TEXAS CATHOLIC HISTORY AND CULTURE / TEXAS CATHOLIC HISTORICAL SOCIETY, THE (US/1048-2431) [20876278] **2742, 5031**

JOURNAL OF TEXTILE INDUSTRY (PK) [01784297] **5353**

JOURNAL OF TEXTURE STUDIES (US/0022-4901) [01800057] **4313, 2347**

JOURNAL OF THE ABRAHAM LINCOLN ASSOCIATION (US/0898-4212) [17635815] **2742**

JOURNAL OF THE ACADEMY FOR EVANGELISM IN THEOLOGICAL EDUCATION (US/0894-9034) [14286142] **4970**

JOURNAL OF THE ACADEMY OF FLORIDA TRIAL LAWYERS (US/0515-2046) [04954928] **2989**

JOURNAL OF THE ACADEMY OF MARKETING SCIENCE (US/0092-0703) [01788738] **929**

JOURNAL OF THE ACADEMY OF REHABILITATIVE AUDIOLOGY (US/0149-8886) [03529398] **3889**

JOURNAL OF THE ACOUSTICAL SOCIETY OF AMERICA, THE (US/0001-4966) [01226792] **4452**

JOURNAL OF THE ACOUSTICAL SOCIETY OF INDIA (II/0253-7257) [09179324] **4410**

JOURNAL OF THE ACOUSTICAL SOCIETY OF JAPAN (E), THE (JA/0388-2861) [07057795] **4453**

JOURNAL OF THE ADELAIDE BOTANIC GARDENS (AT/0313-4083) [03440508] **516**

JOURNAL OF THE ADHESIVE AND SEALANT COUNCIL, THE (US/0149-3108) [03472235] **4456, 1026**

JOURNAL OF THE AERONAUTICAL SOCIETY OF INDIA, THE (II/0001-9267) [03189799] **26**

JOURNAL OF THE AFRICAN ASSOCIATION FOR LITERACY AND ADULT EDUCATION (KE) [15094450] **1801**

JOURNAL OF THE AFRO-AMERICAN HISTORICAL AND GENEALOGICAL SOCIETY (US/0272-1937) [06757902] **2266, 2455**

JOURNAL OF THE AGRICULTURAL SOCIETY OF TRINIDAD & TOBAGO **SUSPENDED.** (TR/0368-1327) [02386993] **101**

JOURNAL OF THE AIR & WASTE MANAGEMENT ASSOCIATION (US/1047-3289) [20666358] **2196**

JOURNAL OF THE ALABAMA ACADEMY OF SCIENCE, THE (US/0002-4112) [01226818] **5120**

JOURNAL OF THE ALABAMA DENTAL ASSOCIATION, THE (US/0002-4198) [02257111] **1328**

JOURNAL OF THE ALASKA GEOLOGICAL SOCIETY (US/0277-1918) [07514618] **1385**

JOURNAL OF THE ALL INDIA INSTITUTE OF SPEECH AND HEARING, THE (II/0377-0524) [03908382] **3889**

JOURNAL OF THE ALLEGHENIES (US/0276-7449) [02263096] **2742**

JOURNAL OF THE AMERICAN ACADEMY FOR THE PRESERVATION OF OLD-TIME COUNTRY MUSIC, THE (US/1054-3872) [22875077] **4126**

JOURNAL OF THE AMERICAN ACADEMY OF AUDIOLOGY (CN/1050-0545) [21387755] **3889**

JOURNAL OF THE AMERICAN ACADEMY OF CHILD AND ADOLESCENT PSYCHIATRY (US/0890-8567) [14404226] **3929**

JOURNAL OF THE AMERICAN ACADEMY OF DERMATOLOGY (US/0190-9622) [04781711] **3721**

JOURNAL OF THE AMERICAN ACADEMY OF MATRIMONIAL LAWYERS, THE (US/0882-6714) [11925215] **3121**

JOURNAL OF THE AMERICAN ACADEMY OF NURSE PRACTITIONERS (US/1041-2972) [18711432] **3860**

JOURNAL OF THE AMERICAN ACADEMY OF PHYSICIAN ASSISTANTS (US/0893-7400) [15635769] **3597**

JOURNAL OF THE AMERICAN ACADEMY OF PSYCHIATRY AND NEUROLOGY (US/0362-4870) [02381084] **3930**

JOURNAL OF THE AMERICAN ACADEMY OF PSYCHOANALYSIS, THE (US/0090-3604) [01784970] **3930**

JOURNAL OF THE AMERICAN ACADEMY OF RELIGION (US/0002-7189) [02592504] **4970**

JOURNAL OF THE AMERICAN ANALGESIA SOCIETY (US/0002-7243) [02101864] **1328, 3597**

JOURNAL OF THE AMERICAN ANIMAL HOSPITAL ASSOCIATION, THE (US/0587-2871) [01479286] **5513**

JOURNAL OF THE AMERICAN ASSOCIATION OF VARIABLE STAR OBSERVERS, THE (US/0271-9053) [03296591] **396**

JOURNAL OF THE AMERICAN BOARD OF FAMILY PRACTICE, THE (US/0893-8652) [15679932] **3738**

JOURNAL OF THE AMERICAN CERAMIC SOCIETY (US/0002-7820) [01479639] **2591**

JOURNAL OF THE AMERICAN CHAMBER OF COMMERCE IN JAPAN / ACCJ, THE (JA/0002-7847) [06322829] **820**

JOURNAL OF THE AMERICAN CHEMICAL SOCIETY (US/0002-7863) [01226990] **982**

JOURNAL OF THE AMERICAN COLLEGE OF CARDIOLOGY (US/0735-1097) [08909559] **3707**

JOURNAL OF THE AMERICAN COLLEGE OF DENTISTS, THE (US/0002-7979) [01083170] **1328**

JOURNAL OF THE AMERICAN COLLEGE OF NUTRITION (US/0731-5724) [08227639] **4194**

●JOURNAL OF THE AMERICAN COLLEGE OF SURGEONS (US/1072-7515) [29192491] **3968**

JOURNAL OF THE AMERICAN COLLEGE OF TOXICOLOGY (US/0730-0913) [07942475] **3982**

JOURNAL OF THE AMERICAN CREATIVITY ASSOCIATION (US) **1758**

JOURNAL OF THE AMERICAN DEAFNESS AND REHABILITATION ASSOCIATION : JADARA (US/0899-9228) [18141357] **4390**

JOURNAL OF THE AMERICAN DENTAL ASSOCIATION (USA ED.), THE (US/0002-8177) [01777821] **1328**

JOURNAL OF THE AMERICAN DIETETIC ASSOCIATION (US/0002-8223) [01083209] **4194**

JOURNAL OF THE AMERICAN GERIATRICS SOCIETY (US/0002-8614) [01084746] **3753**

●JOURNAL OF THE AMERICAN HEALTH CARE, THE (US/1078-6856) [31157478] **5293**

JOURNAL OF THE AMERICAN HELICOPTER SOCIETY (US/0002-8711) [01827576] **26**

JOURNAL OF THE AMERICAN HISTORICAL SOCIETY OF GERMANS FROM RUSSIA (US/0162-8283) [04200235] **2695**

JOURNAL OF THE AMERICAN HOLISTIC VETERINARY MEDICAL ASSOCIATION (US) [20764512] **5513**

JOURNAL OF THE AMERICAN INSTITUTE FOR CONSERVATION (US/0197-1360) [03064874] **323**

JOURNAL OF THE AMERICAN INSTITUTE OF HOMEOPATHY (US/0002-8967) [05395485] **3775**

JOURNAL OF THE AMERICAN KILLIFISH ASSOCIATION, THE (US/0002-967X) [11287596] **2307**

JOURNAL OF THE AMERICAN LEATHER CHEMISTS ASSOCIATION, THE (US/0002-9726) [01480261] **3184**

JOURNAL OF THE AMERICAN LISZT SOCIETY (US/0147-4413) [03162965] **4126**

JOURNAL OF THE AMERICAN MATHEMATICAL SOCIETY (US/0894-0347) [15735952] **3515**

JOURNAL OF THE AMERICAN MEDICAL ASSOCIATION EN ARGENTINA (AG/0325-9226) [06370920] **3597**

●JOURNAL OF THE AMERICAN MEDICAL INFORMATICS ASSOCIATION (US/1067-5027) [27252647] **3597**

JOURNAL OF THE AMERICAN MEDICAL WOMEN'S ASSOCIATION (1972) (US/0098-8421) [01793622] **3914, 3597**

JOURNAL OF THE AMERICAN MOSQUITO CONTROL ASSOCIATION (US/8756-971X) [11730964] **4245**

JOURNAL OF THE AMERICAN MOSQUITO CONTROL ASSOCIATION. SUPPLEMENT (US/1046-3607) [19856592] **3741**

JOURNAL OF THE AMERICAN MUSICAL INSTRUMENT SOCIETY (US/0362-3300) [02280059] **4126**

JOURNAL OF THE AMERICAN MUSICOLOGICAL SOCIETY (US/0003-0139) [01480473] **4126**

JOURNAL OF THE AMERICAN OIL CHEMISTS' SOCIETY (US/0003-021X) [06885827] **1043**

JOURNAL OF THE AMERICAN OPTOMETRIC ASSOCIATION (US/0003-0244) [01033855] **4216**

JOURNAL OF THE AMERICAN ORIENTAL SOCIETY (US/0003-0279) [01480509] **3292**

JOURNAL OF THE AMERICAN OSTEOPATHIC ACADEMY ORTHOPEDICS **SUSPENDED.** (US/0740-0926) [09741056] **3883**

JOURNAL OF THE AMERICAN OSTEOPATHIC ASSOCIATION, THE (US/0098-6151) [01081714] **3598**

JOURNAL OF THE AMERICAN PARAPLEGIA SOCIETY (US/0195-2307) [05389769] **3598**

JOURNAL OF THE AMERICAN PLANNING ASSOCIATION (US/0194-4363) [04626214] **2826**

JOURNAL OF THE AMERICAN PODIATRIC MEDICAL ASSOCIATION (US/8750-7315) [11700519] **3918**

JOURNAL OF THE AMERICAN PORTUGUESE SOCIETY, THE **SUSPENDED.** (US/0098-4981) [02240484] **2695**

JOURNAL OF THE AMERICAN PSYCHIATRIC NURSING ASSOCIATION (US) **3860**

JOURNAL OF THE AMERICAN PSYCHOANALYTIC ASSOCIATION (US/0003-0651) [01034344] **4601**

JOURNAL OF THE AMERICAN PSYCHOANALYTIC ASSOCIATION. MONOGRAPH SERIES (US) [06933727] **4601**

●JOURNAL OF THE AMERICAN REAL ESTATE AND URBAN ECONOMICS ASSOCIATION (US/1067-8433) [26846250] **4839**

JOURNAL OF THE AMERICAN RESEARCH CENTER IN EGYPT (US/0065-9991) [01480668] **2641**

JOURNAL OF THE AMERICAN ROMANIAN ACADEMY OF ARTS AND SCIENCES (US/0896-1018) [12123709] **2518**

●JOURNAL OF THE AMERICAN SHETLAND PONY CLUB (US) [30088128] **2800**

JOURNAL OF THE AMERICAN SOCIETY FOR HORTICULTURAL SCIENCE (US/0003-1062) [01772171] **2421**

JOURNAL OF THE AMERICAN SOCIETY FOR INFORMATION SCIENCE (US/0002-8231) [01798118] **3220**

JOURNAL OF THE AMERICAN SOCIETY FOR MASS SPECTROMETRY (US/1044-0305) [19650595] **1017**

Alphabetical Title Index — JOURNAL

JOURNAL OF THE AMERICAN SOCIETY FOR PREVENTIVE DENTISTRY (US/0093-4518) [02243596] **1328**

JOURNAL OF THE AMERICAN SOCIETY FOR PSYCHICAL RESEARCH (1932) (US/0003-1070) [01224084] **4242**

JOURNAL OF THE AMERICAN SOCIETY OF BREWING CHEMISTS (US/0361-0470) [02002998] **982**

JOURNAL OF THE AMERICAN SOCIETY OF CLU & CHFC (US/1052-2875) [14699798] 795, **2886**

JOURNAL OF THE AMERICAN SOCIETY OF ECHOCARDIOGRAPHY (US/0894-7317) [16198043] **3707**

JOURNAL OF THE AMERICAN SOCIETY OF FARM MANAGERS AND RURAL APPRAISERS (US/0003-116X) [01480809] **101**

JOURNAL OF THE AMERICAN SOCIETY OF NEPHROLOGY (US/1046-6673) [20484750] **3991**

JOURNAL OF THE AMERICAN SOCIETY OF OCULARISTS, THE (US/1055-5161) [23197540] **3876**

JOURNAL OF THE AMERICAN SPORTING BOOK COLLECTOR, THE (US/0736-7724) [09220654] 4902, **2774**

JOURNAL OF THE AMERICAN STATISTICAL ASSOCIATION (US/0162-1459) [01480864] **5329**

JOURNAL OF THE AMERICAN STUDIES ASSOCIATION OF TEXAS (US/0587-5064) [02574543] 3400, **2742**

JOURNAL OF THE AMERICAN TAXATION ASSOCIATION, THE (US/0198-9073) [06262525] **4735**

JOURNAL OF THE AMERICAN VETERINARY MEDICAL ASSOCIATION (US/0003-1488) [01084791] **5513**

JOURNAL OF THE AMERICAN VIOLA SOCIETY (US/0898-5987) [12533148] **4126**

JOURNAL OF THE ANATOMICAL SOCIETY OF INDIA (II/0003-2778) [01033749] **3679**

JOURNAL OF THE ANCIENT NEAR EASTERN SOCIETY, THE (US/0897-6074) [12393888] **2621**

JOURNAL OF THE ANDAMAN SCIENCE ASSOCIATION (II/0970-4183) [I09704183] **5120**

JOURNAL OF THE ANDHRA HISTORICAL RESEARCH SOCIETY (II) [08514314] **2655**

JOURNAL OF THE ANNUAL CONVENTION - EPISCOPAL CHURCH. DIOCESE OF BETHLEHEM (US/0730-6938) [04822881] **5062**

JOURNAL OF THE ANTHROPOLOGICAL SURVEY OF INDIA, THE (II/0970-3411) [27341900] **239**

JOURNAL OF THE ARIZONA-NEVADA ACADEMY OF SCIENCE (US/0193-8509) [03980789] **1357**

JOURNAL OF THE ARKANSAS MEDICAL SOCIETY, THE (US/0004-1858) [01064443] **3598**

JOURNAL OF THE ARMS & ARMOUR SOCIETY, THE (UK/0004-2439) [08744995] **4048**

JOURNAL OF THE ARNOLD ARBORETUM. SUPPLEMENTARY SERIES / HARVARD UNIVERSITY (US) [24662051] **2421**

JOURNAL OF THE ARNOLD SCHOENBERG INSTITUTE (US/0146-5856) [02987368] **4126**

JOURNAL OF THE ARTISTS' CHOICE MUSEUM, THE (US/0882-8504) [09789098] 354, **4090**

JOURNAL OF THE ASIATIC SOCIETY (II/0368-3303) [07102772] **2505**

JOURNAL OF THE ASIATIC SOCIETY OF BANGLADESH (BG/0377-0540) [02239639] **5232**

JOURNAL OF THE ASIATIC SOCIETY OF BOMBAY (II/0004-9709) [01514453] **5232**

JOURNAL OF THE ASSAM SCIENCE SOCIETY (II/0587-1921) [08041514] **5120**

JOURNAL OF THE ASSOCIATION FOR ACADEMIC MINORITY PHYSICIANS (US/1048-9886) [21101738] **3914**

JOURNAL OF THE ASSOCIATION FOR COMPUTING MACHINERY (US/0004-5411) [01514518] **1192**

JOURNAL OF THE ASSOCIATION FOR PERSONS WITH SEVERE HANDICAPS, THE (US/0749-1425) [10586552] **1881**

JOURNAL OF THE ASSOCIATION OF AVIAN VETERINARIANS (US/1044-8314) [19900883] 5618, **5513**

JOURNAL OF THE ASSOCIATION OF CHILDREN'S PROSTHETIC-ORTHOTIC CLINICS *CEASED.* (US/0884-8424) [12488246] **3883**

JOURNAL OF THE ASSOCIATION OF FOOD AND DRUG OFFICIALS (US/0898-4131) [17212478] 2347, **4787**

JOURNAL OF THE ASSOCIATION OF MILITARY DERMATOLOGISTS (US/0360-4020) [01874997] **3721**

JOURNAL OF THE ASSOCIATION OF NURSES IN AIDS CARE, THE (US/1055-3290) [23155223] 3674, **3860**

JOURNAL OF THE ASSOCIATION OF OBSTETRIC AND GYNAECOLOGICAL PHYSIOTHERAPISTS (UK/0955-2839) [I09552839] **3764**

JOURNAL OF THE ASSOCIATION OF OFFICIAL ANALYTICAL CHEMISTS *See* JOURNAL OF AOAC INTERNATIONAL **1016**

JOURNAL OF THE ASSOCIATION OF PHYSICIANS OF INDIA (II) [11487052] **3799**

JOURNAL OF THE ASSOCIATION OF PUBLIC ANALYSTS *CEASED.* (UK/0004-5780) [01029604] **4787**

JOURNAL OF THE ASSOCIATION OF SURVEYORS OF PAPUA NEW GUINEA, THE (PP) [06044486] **2026**

JOURNAL OF THE ASSOCIATION OF TEACHERS OF JAPANESE, THE (US/0885-9884) [04398443] 1899, **3292**

JOURNAL OF THE ASTRONAUTICAL SCIENCES, THE (US/0021-9142) [07231351] **26**

JOURNAL OF THE ATLANTIC PROVINCES LINGUISTIC ASSOCIATION *See* LINGUISTICA ATLANTICA : JOURNAL OF THE ATLANTIC PROVINCES LINGUISTIC ASSOCATION **3299**

JOURNAL OF THE ATMOSPHERIC SCIENCES (US/0022-4928) [01754829] **1427**

JOURNAL OF THE AUSTRALASIAN CERAMIC SOCIETY (SZ) [23993596] **2591**

JOURNAL OF THE AUSTRALIAN CATHOLIC HISTORICAL SOCIETY (AT/0084-7259) [09916951] **5031**

JOURNAL OF THE AUSTRALIAN ENTOMOLOGICAL SOCIETY (AT/0004-9050) [01518797] **5588**

JOURNAL OF THE AUSTRALIAN MATHEMATICAL SOCIETY. SERIES A : PURE MATHEMATICS AND STATISTICS (AT/0263-6115) [07230097] **3515**

JOURNAL OF THE AUSTRALIAN MATHEMATICAL SOCIETY. SERIES B : APPLIED MATHEMATICS, THE (AT/0334-2700) [02071076] **3515**

JOURNAL OF THE AUSTRALIAN NAVAL INSTITUTE (AT/0312-5807) [I03125807] **4178**

JOURNAL OF THE AUSTRALIAN POPULATION ASSOCIATION (AT/0814-5725) [I08145725] **4554**

JOURNAL OF THE AUSTRALIAN POPULATION ASSOCIATION (AT) [20555340] **4562**

JOURNAL OF THE AUSTRALIAN WAR MEMORIAL (AT/0729-6274) [11477770] **4048**

JOURNAL OF THE AUTONOMIC NERVOUS SYSTEM (NE/0165-1838) [05867295] **3837**

JOURNAL OF THE BAHRAIN MEDICAL SOCIETY (BA/1015-6321) [I10156321] **3598**

JOURNAL OF THE BALINT SOCIETY (UK/0307-4765) [01029587] **3930**

JOURNAL OF THE BANGLADESH CHEMICAL SOCIETY (BG) [21351923] **982**

JOURNAL OF THE BARBADOS MUSEUM AND HISTORICAL SOCIETY, THE (BB/0005-5891) [01519178] **4090**

JOURNAL OF THE BOMBAY NATURAL HISTORY SOCIETY (II/0006-6982) [01536710] **4166**

JOURNAL OF THE BRAXTON HISTORICAL SOCIETY (US/1064-2595) [06607423] **2742**

JOURNAL OF THE BRAZILIAN CHEMICAL SOCIETY (BL/0103-5053) [25044578] **982**

JOURNAL OF THE BRISTOL AND AVON FAMILY HISTORY SOCIETY (UK/0308-4183) [I03084183] **2455**

JOURNAL OF THE BRITISH ARCHAEOLOGICAL ASSOCIATION (UK/0068-1288) [01537130] **272**

JOURNAL OF THE BRITISH ASSOCIATION FOR IMMEDIATE CARE, THE (UK) [08897794] **3725**

JOURNAL OF THE BRITISH ASSOCIATION OF TEACHERS OF THE DEAF, THE (UK/0266-4062) [10497947] 4390, **1881**

JOURNAL OF THE BRITISH ASTRONOMICAL ASSOCIATION (UK/0007-0297) [01537134] **396**

JOURNAL OF THE BRITISH CONTACT LENS ASSOCIATION (UK/0141-7037) [06740115] **3876**

JOURNAL OF THE BROMELIAD SOCIETY (US/0090-8738) [02445503] **516**

JOURNAL OF THE BURMA RESEARCH SOCIETY (BR/0304-2227) [01537852] **2656**

JOURNAL OF THE BUTLER SOCIETY (IE) [10105558] **2455**

JOURNAL OF THE CALIFORNIA DENTAL ASSOCIATION (US/1043-2256) [18933472] **1328**

JOURNAL OF THE CAMBRIDGESHIRE FAMILY HISTORY SOCIETY (UK/0309-5800) [I03095800] **2455**

JOURNAL OF THE CANADIAN ASSOCIATION FOR YOUNG CHILDREN *See* CANADIAN CHILDREN **1803**

JOURNAL OF THE CANADIAN ATHLETIC THERAPISTS ASSOCIATION, THE *SUSPENDED.* (CN/0225-9877) [08555810] **3954**

JOURNAL OF THE CANADIAN CERAMIC SOCIETY (CN/0068-8444) [I00688444] **2591**

JOURNAL OF THE CANADIAN CHIROPRACTIC ASSOCIATION, THE (CN/0008-3194) [06939872] **3805**

JOURNAL OF THE CANADIAN CHURCH HISTORICAL SOCIETY (CN/0008-3208) [01553067] **4970**

JOURNAL OF THE CANADIAN HISTORICAL ASSOCIATION (CN/0847-4478) [24014937] **2742**

JOURNAL OF THE CERAMIC SOCIETY OF JAPAN (JA/0912-9200) [20547262] **2591**

JOURNAL OF THE CHARLES H. TWEED INTERNATIONAL FOUNDATION (US/0885-3517) [10891826] **1328**

JOURNAL OF THE CHEMICAL SOCIETY, CHEMICAL COMMUNICATIONS (UK/0022-4936) [01553996] **982**

JOURNAL OF THE CHEMICAL SOCIETY. FARADAY TRANSACTIONS (UK/0956-5000) [20905692] **1055**

JOURNAL OF THE CHEMICAL SOCIETY OF PAKISTAN (PK/0253-5106) [06571343] **982**

JOURNAL OF THE CHEROKEE STRIP (US) [04654499] **2742**

JOURNAL OF THE CHESTERFIELD HISTORICAL SOCIETY OF VIRGINIA (US/0731-3020) [08163153] **2742**

JOURNAL OF THE CHINA SOCIETY (CH/0578-154X) [02306591] **5232**

JOURNAL OF THE CHINESE BIOCHEMICAL SOCIETY (CH/0379-7368) [07937979] **490**

JOURNAL OF THE CHINESE CHEMICAL SOCIETY (TAIPEI) (CH/0009-4536) [02259342] **982**

JOURNAL OF THE CHINESE INSTITUTE OF CHEMICAL ENGINEERS (CH/0368-1653) [01554361] **2014**

JOURNAL OF THE CHINESE LANGUAGE TEACHERS ASSOCIATION (US/0009-4595) [01554364] 1899, **3292**

JOURNAL OF THE CHINESE LANGUAGE TEACHERS ASSOCIATION / CHUNG WEN CHIAO SHIH HSUEH HUI HSUEH PAO (US) [18778142] 1759, **3292**

JOURNAL OF THE CHRISTIAN MEDICAL ASSOCIATION OF INDIA (II) [01588000] 4970, **3598**

JOURNAL OF THE CHRISTIAN MEDICAL FELLOWSHIP (UK) **4970**

●JOURNAL OF THE CHRONIC FATIGUE SYNDROMES (US/1057-3321) [24014075] **3598**

JOURNAL OF THE CLAN CAMPBELL SOCIETY (UNITED STATES OF AMERICA) (US/0731-955X) [08216939] 2621, **2455**

●JOURNAL OF THE CLINICAL ORTHOPAEDIC SOCIETY (US/1069-6970) [28141725] **3883**

JOURNAL OF THE COIN LAUNDRY AND DRYCLEANING INDUSTRY, THE (US/1062-8088) [25750002] 1614, **1026**

JOURNAL OF THE COLLEGE OF EDUCATION FOR ON CAMPUS STUDENTS AND FACULTY (US) **1759**

JOURNAL OF THE COLORADO-WYOMING ACADEMY OF SCIENCE, THE (US) [08784442] **5175**

JOURNAL OF THE COMMUNICATIONS RESEARCH LABORATORY (JA/0914-9260) [19060599] **1159**

JOURNAL OF THE COMMUNITY DEVELOPMENT SOCIETY (US/0010-3829) [01564519] **5250**

JOURNAL OF THE CONDUCTORS' GUILD (US/0734-1032) [08450789] **4127**

JOURNAL OF THE ... CONVENTION - NATIONAL WOMAN'S RELIEF CORP (US) [04794129] **5559**

JOURNAL OF THE COOLING TOWER INSTITUTE *See* CTI JOURNAL **2112**

JOURNAL OF THE COPYRIGHT SOCIETY OF THE U.S.A (US/0886-3520) [08107929] **1305**

JOURNAL OF THE CORK HISTORICAL AND ARCHAEOLOGICAL SOCIETY (IE/0010-8731) [01771310] 272, **2695**

JOURNAL
Alphabetical Title Index

JOURNAL OF THE COUNTY KILDARE ARCHAEOLOGICAL SOCIETY (IE/0332-0782) [01771323] **272**

JOURNAL OF THE COUNTY LOUTH ARCHAEOLOGICAL AND HISTORICAL SOCIETY (IE/0070-1327) [04568004] **272**

● JOURNAL OF THE CZECH GEOLOGICAL SOCIETY (XR/0008-7378) [29686236] **1385**

JOURNAL OF THE DAGUERREIAN SOCIETY (US) **4371**

JOURNAL OF THE DALIAN INSTITUTE OF TECHNOLOGY (CC) **5120**

JOURNAL OF THE DECORATIVE ARTS SOCIETY 1890-1940 (UK/0260-9568) [04397558] **373**

JOURNAL OF THE DENTAL ASSOCIATION OF THAILAND, THE (TH/0045-9917) [01034370] **1328**

JOURNAL OF THE DEPARTMENT OF ENGLISH (UNIVERSITY OF CALCUTTA. DEPT. OF ENGLISH) (II) [06969423] **3400**

JOURNAL OF THE DEPARTMENT OF PHILOSOPHY (II) [03405737] **4351**

JOURNAL OF THE DIABETIC ASSOCIATION OF INDIA (II/0304-4513) [01388853] **3731**

JOURNAL OF THE DIABETIC ASSOCIATION OF INDIA. SCIENTIFIC SECTION (II/0970-4027) [I09704027] **3731**

JOURNAL OF THE EARLY REPUBLIC (US/0275-1275) [07088630] **2742**

JOURNAL OF THE EARTH AND SPACE PHYSICS (IR/0378-1046) [04531701] **4410**

JOURNAL OF THE EAST AFRICA NATURAL HISTORY SOCIETY AND NATIONAL MUSEUM (KE/0012-8317) [05813454] **4166**

JOURNAL OF THE ECONOMIC AND SOCIAL HISTORY OF THE ORIENT (NE/0022-4995) [06009613] **2656**

JOURNAL OF THE EGYPTIAN MEDICAL ASSOCIATION (UA/0013-2411) [09812227] **3598**

JOURNAL OF THE EGYPTIAN PUBLIC HEALTH ASSOCIATION, THE (UA/0013-2446) [01029403] **4787**

JOURNAL OF THE EGYPTIAN SOCIETY OF PARASITOLOGY (UA/0253-5890) [07020734] **462**

JOURNAL OF THE EGYPTIAN VETERINARY MEDICAL ASSOCIATION (UA/0379-3044) [03610675] **5513**

JOURNAL OF THE EIGHTEEN NINETIES SOCIETY (UK/0144-008X) [03954119] **3400**

JOURNAL OF THE ELECTROCHEMICAL SOCIETY (US/0013-4651) [01029376] **1034**

JOURNAL OF THE ELECTROCHEMICAL SOCIETY OF INDIA (II/0013-466X) [01567738] **1026**

JOURNAL OF THE ELISHA MITCHELL SCIENTIFIC SOCIETY (US/0013-6220) [01567791] **5120**

JOURNAL OF THE ENGINEERS' CLUB OF ST. LOUIS. A MONTHLY PERIODICAL DEVOTED TO THE INTERESTS OF THE ENGINEERING PROFESSION IN ST. LOUIS (US/0013-8150) [01567926] **1983**

JOURNAL OF THE ENGLISH LITERARY CLUB, THE (PK) [12155088] 3400, **3465**

JOURNAL OF THE ENTOMOLOGICAL SOCIETY OF BRITISH COLUMBIA (CN/0071-0733) [02247409] **5611**

JOURNAL OF THE ENTOMOLOGICAL SOCIETY OF SOUTHERN AFRICA (SA/0013-8789) [01568026] **5589**

● JOURNAL OF THE EUROPEAN ACADEMY OF DERMATOLOGY AND VENEREOLOGY : JEADV (NE/0926-9959) [27009031] **3721**

JOURNAL OF THE EUROPEAN ASSOCIATION OF MARINE SCIENCES AND TECHNIQUES (NE/0924-7963) **1450**

JOURNAL OF THE EUROPEAN CERAMIC SOCIETY (UK/0955-2219) [20139950] **2591**

● JOURNAL OF THE EUROPEAN OPTICAL SOCIETY, PART B, QUANTUM OPTICS (UK) [25991501] **4437**

JOURNAL OF THE EVANGELICAL THEOLOGICAL SOCIETY (US/0360-8808) [02244860] **4970**

JOURNAL OF THE EXPERIMENTAL ANALYSIS OF BEHAVIOR (US/0022-5002) [01782917] **4601**

JOURNAL OF THE FACULTY OF AGRICULTURE. HOKKAIDO UNIVERSITY (JA/0018-344X) [06472883] **101**

JOURNAL OF THE FACULTY OF AGRICULTURE, KYUSHU UNIVERSITY (JA/0023-6152) [09802493] **101**

JOURNAL OF THE FACULTY OF AGRICULTURE, TOTTORI UNIVERSITY (JA/0082-5360) [01586865] **101**

JOURNAL OF THE FACULTY OF ENGINEERING. SHINSHU UNIVERSITY (JA/0037-3818) [10463538] **1983**

JOURNAL OF THE FACULTY OF ENGINEERING, UNIVERSITY OF TOKYO. SERIES A, ANNUAL REPORT (JA/0563-7945) [02148799] **1983**

JOURNAL OF THE FACULTY OF ENGINEERING, UNIVERSITY OF TOKYO. SERIES B (JA/0563-7937) [02148806] **1983**

JOURNAL OF THE FACULTY OF MEDICINE, BAGHDAD (IQ/0041-9419) [01641533] **3598**

JOURNAL OF THE FACULTY OF PHARMACY GAZI UNIVERSITY (TU) **4313**

JOURNAL OF THE FACULTY OF SCIENCE, HOKKAIDO IMPERIAL UNIVERSITY. SERIES 5, BOTANY *See* JOURNAL OF THE FACULTY OF SCIENCE, HOKKAIDO UNIVERSITY, SERIES 5, BOTANY **516**

JOURNAL OF THE FACULTY OF SCIENCE, HOKKAIDO UNIVERSITY. SERIES 4. GEOLOGY AND MINERALOGY (JA/0018-3474) [02254560] **1357**

JOURNAL OF THE FACULTY OF SCIENCE, HOKKAIDO UNIVERSITY, SERIES 5, BOTANY (JA/0368-2145) [22740375] **516**

JOURNAL OF THE FACULTY OF SCIENCE, HOKKAIDO UNIVERSITY. SERIES VII. GEOPHYSICS (JA/0441-067X) [06712523] **1408**

JOURNAL OF THE FACULTY OF SCIENCE, UNIVERSITY OF TOKYO. SECTION 3, BOTANY (JA/0368-2196) [09232386] **516**

JOURNAL OF THE FACULTY OF SCIENCE, UNIVERSITY OF TOKYO. SECTION III : BOTANY (JA/0371-7712) [01642747] **5120**

JOURNAL OF THE FACULTY OF SCIENCE, UNIVERSITY OF TOKYO. SECTION V, ANTHROPOLOGY (JA/0373-4722) [01767585] **239**

JOURNAL OF THE FACULTY OF SCIENCE, UNIVERSITY OF TOKYO. SECTION V, ANTHROPOLOGY / TOKYO DAIGAKU RIGAKUBU KIYO. DAI 5-RUI, JINRUIGAKU (JA/0373-4722) [09225141] **239**

JOURNAL OF THE FACULTY OF VETERINARY MEDICINE UNIVERSITY ANKARA (TU) **5513**

JOURNAL OF THE FANTASTIC IN THE ARTS *CEASED.* (US/0897-0521) [17376518] 354, **3400**

JOURNAL OF THE FARMERS' CLUB *See* FARMERS' CLUB JOURNAL (LONDON, ENGLAND) **85**

JOURNAL OF THE FLAGSTAFF INSTITUTE (US/0146-1958) [02882501] 3482, **1637**

JOURNAL OF THE FLORIDA MEDICAL ASSOCIATION (1974) (US/0015-4148) [01224114] **3598**

JOURNAL OF THE FLORIDA MOSQUITO CONTROL ASSOCIATION (US/1055-355X) [23158151] 4245, **4787**

JOURNAL OF THE FLUORESCENT MINERAL SOCIETY (US/0160-0958) [03618221] **1440**

JOURNAL OF THE FOOD MARKETING CENTRE (II/0302-9808) [01797692] **2347**

JOURNAL OF THE FOREIGN POLICY RESEARCH ASSOCIATION OF THE UNIVERSITY OF REDLANDS (US) [01827312] **4527**

JOURNAL OF THE FORMOSAN MEDICAL ASSOCIATION / TAI-WAN I CHIH (HK/0929-6646) [26850468] **3598**

JOURNAL OF THE FRANKLIN INSTITUTE (US/0016-0032) [01331857] **5120**

JOURNAL OF THE FRESHMAN YEAR EXPERIENCE (US/1053-203X) [19112355] **1833**

JOURNAL OF THE FRIENDS' HISTORICAL SOCIETY, THE (UK/0071-9587) [01570227] **5062**

JOURNAL OF THE GALWAY ARCHAEOLOGICAL AND HISTORICAL SOCIETY (IE/0332-415X) [I0332415X] 2621, **272**

JOURNAL OF THE GANGANATHA JHA KENDRIYA SANSKRIT VIDYAPEETHA (II/0377-0575) [04202002] **3292**

JOURNAL OF THE GENERAL CONVENTION OF THE NEW JERUSALEM (US) [04634859] **5062**

JOURNAL OF THE ... GENERAL SYNOD / ANGLICAN CHURCH OF CANADA (CN/0826-3205) [11762370] 5031, **5062**

JOURNAL OF THE GEOGRAPHICAL ASSOCIATION OF TANZANIA *CEASED.* (TZ/0016-738X) [02024527] **2567**

JOURNAL OF THE GEOLOGICAL SOCIETY (UK/0016-7649) [01934542] **1385**

● JOURNAL OF THE GEOLOGICAL SOCIETY OF CHINA (CH/1018-7057) [25862483] **1385**

JOURNAL OF THE GEOLOGICAL SOCIETY OF INDIA (II/0016-7622) [01570703] **1385**

JOURNAL OF THE GEOLOGICAL SOCIETY OF IRAQ (IQ/0533-8301) [02383550] **1385**

JOURNAL OF THE GLASS ASSOCIATION, THE (UK) [13219263] **2592**

JOURNAL OF THE GRASSLAND SOCIETY OF SOUTHERN AFRICA *See* AFRICAN JOURNAL OF RANGE AND FORAGE SCIENCE **45**

JOURNAL OF THE GRASSLAND SOCIETY OF SOUTHERN AFRICA, THE (SA/0256-6702) [11189979] **101**

JOURNAL OF THE GREATER HOUSTON DENTAL SOCIETY, THE (US/1062-0265) [20698991] **1328**

JOURNAL OF THE GYPSY LORE SOCIETY (US/0017-6087) [01751670] **2321**

JOURNAL OF THE HELLENIC DIASPORA (US/0364-2976) [02585622] **2695**

JOURNAL OF THE HELMINTHOLOGICAL SOCIETY OF WASHINGTON (US/1049-233X) [21171214] **5589**

JOURNAL OF THE HERALDRY SOCIETY OF SCOTLAND (UK) [05855590] **2455**

JOURNAL OF THE HERPETOLOGICAL ASSOCIATION OF AFRICA (SA/0441-6651) [03472004] **5589**

JOURNAL OF THE HISTORIC FARM BUILDINGS GROUP (UK/0952-5513) [19117925] **618**

JOURNAL OF THE HISTORICAL SOCIETY OF NIGERIA *SUSPENDED.* (NR/0018-2540) [02160057] **2641**

JOURNAL OF THE HISTORICAL SOCIETY OF SOUTH AUSTRALIA (AT/0312-9640) [05295154] **2669**

JOURNAL OF THE HISTORY OF BIOLOGY (NE/0022-5010) [01783306] 4351, **462**

JOURNAL OF THE HISTORY OF COLLECTIONS (UK/0954-6650) [19984120] **4090**

JOURNAL OF THE HISTORY OF ECONOMIC THOUGHT (US/1053-8372) [21616035] **1500**

JOURNAL OF THE HISTORY OF IDEAS (US/0022-5037) [01591903] **4351**

JOURNAL OF THE HISTORY OF MEDICINE AND ALLIED SCIENCES (US/0022-5045) [01800317] **3598**

JOURNAL OF THE HISTORY OF PHILOSOPHY (US/0022-5053) [01783132] **4351**

JOURNAL OF THE HISTORY OF SEXUALITY (US/1043-4070) [19451600] **5187**

JOURNAL OF THE HISTORY OF THE BEHAVIORAL SCIENCES (US/0022-5061) [01783134] 5207, **4601**

● JOURNAL OF THE HISTORY OF THE NEUROSCIENCES (UK/0964-704X) [28180217] **490**

JOURNAL OF THE HISTORY SOCIETY (1979) (SI/0217-913X) [03878973] **2621**

JOURNAL OF THE HOME ECONOMICS ASSOCIATION OF AUSTRALIA (AT/0158-6912) [I01586912] **2791**

JOURNAL OF THE HONG KONG ARCHAEOLOGICAL SOCIETY (HK) [02465191] **272**

JOURNAL OF THE HONG KONG BRANCH OF THE ROYAL ASIATIC SOCIETY (HK/0085-5774) [01764576] **5232**

JOURNAL OF THE HONG KONG MEDICAL ASSOCIATION (HK/1010-8424) [14137098] **3598**

JOURNAL OF THE HOSPITAL FOR SPECIAL SURGERY, THE (US/0362-0727) [02441343] **3968**

JOURNAL OF THE HOUSE OF REPRESENTATIVES OF THE ... REGULAR SESSION OF THE GENERAL ASSEMBLY OF THE STATE OF IOWA (US) [06125796] **4659**

JOURNAL OF THE HOUSE OF REPRESENTATIVES OF THE ... SESSION OF THE ... GENERAL ASSEMBLY OF THE STATE OF SOUTH CAROLINA (US) [09519057] **4659**

JOURNAL OF THE HUMANITIES AND SOCIAL SCIENCES (US/0361-5154) [02399179] 5207, **2849**

JOURNAL OF THE IDAHO ACADEMY OF SCIENCE (US/0536-3012) [06441090] **5120**

JOURNAL OF THE IES (US/1052-2883) [21106092] **2176**

JOURNAL OF THE ILLINOIS OPTOMETRIC ASSOCIATION (US/0279-6422) [07134013] **4216**

JOURNAL OF THE ILLINOIS SPEECH & THEATRE ASSOCIATION (US/0145-5516) [02761223] **5365**

JOURNAL OF THE ILLUMINATING ENGINEERING INSTITUTE OF JAPAN (JA) **1983**

JOURNAL OF THE ILLUMINATING ENGINEERING SOCIETY (US/0099-4480) [00875785] **2069**

JOURNAL OF THE INDIAN ACADEMY OF APPLIED PSYCHOLOGY (II/0019-4247) [01642119] **4602**

JOURNAL OF THE INDIAN ACADEMY OF FORENSIC SCIENCES (II/0579-4749) [01586494] **3741**

JOURNAL OF THE INDIAN ACADEMY OF MATHEMATICS, THE (II/0970-5120) [06518653] **3515**

JOURNAL OF THE INDIAN ACADEMY OF PHILOSOPHY, THE (II/0019-4271) [01605935] **4351**

JOURNAL OF THE INDIAN ACADEMY OF WOOD SCIENCE (II/0379-5497) [07754932] **2402**

JOURNAL OF THE INDIAN ANTHROPOLOGICAL SOCIETY (II/0019-4387) [01752830] **239**

JOURNAL OF THE INDIAN BOTANICAL SOCIETY, THE (II/0019-4468) [01752836] **516**

JOURNAL OF THE INDIAN CHEMICAL SOCIETY (II/0019-4522) [01029434] **982**

JOURNAL OF THE INDIAN DENTAL ASSOCIATION (II/0019-4611) [05150864] **1328**

JOURNAL OF THE INDIAN FISHERIES ASSOCIATION (II/0971-1422) [I09711422] **2307**

JOURNAL OF THE INDIAN GEOPHYSICAL UNION (II/0257-7968) [02668760] **1408**

JOURNAL OF THE INDIAN INSTITUTE OF ARCHITECTS (II/0019-4913) [01752884] **302**

JOURNAL OF THE INDIAN INSTITUTE OF BANKERS (II/0019-4921) [01774647] **795**

JOURNAL OF THE INDIAN INSTITUTE OF SCIENCE (II/0019-4964) [01291143] 1983, **5120**

JOURNAL OF THE INDIAN INSTITUTE OF SCIENCE 1960 (II/0970-4140) [I09704140] **5120**

JOURNAL OF THE INDIAN INSTITUTE OF SCIENCE. SECTION A: ENGINEERING AND TECHNOLOGY (II) [04209249] 1983, **5120**

JOURNAL OF THE INDIAN INSTITUTE OF SCIENCE. SECTION B: PHYSICAL AND CHEMICAL SCIENCES (II) [04209265] **5121**

JOURNAL OF THE INDIAN INSTITUTE OF SCIENCE. SECTION C: BIOLOGICAL SCIENCES (II/0368-2684) [04209293] **5121**

JOURNAL OF THE INDIAN LEATHER TECHNOLOGISTS' ASSOCIATION (II/0019-5758) [09443658] **3184**

JOURNAL OF THE INDIAN MATHEMATICAL SOCIETY, THE (II/0019-5839) [07080586] **3515**

JOURNAL OF THE INDIAN MEDICAL ASSOCIATION (II/0019-5847) [01034358] **3598**

JOURNAL OF THE INDIAN MEDICAL PROFESSION (II/0022-507X) [01696889] **3598**

JOURNAL OF THE INDIAN MERCHANTS' CHAMBER (II/0019-5901) [02692539] **843**

JOURNAL OF THE INDIAN MUSICOLOGICAL SOCIETY (II/0251-012X) [01645834] **4127**

JOURNAL OF THE INDIAN POTATO ASSOCIATION : OFFICIAL JOURNAL OF THE INDIAN POTATO ASSOCIATION, CENTRAL POTATO RESEARCH INSTITUTE (II) [11141206] **177**

JOURNAL OF THE INDIAN SOCIETY FOR COTTON IMPROVEMENT (II/0970-308X) [I0970308X] **177**

JOURNAL OF THE INDIAN SOCIETY OF AGRICULTURAL STATISTICS (II/0019-6363) [01752980] **154**

JOURNAL OF THE INDIAN SOCIETY OF ORIENTAL ART (II/0970-6070) [01752981] **354**

JOURNAL OF THE INDIAN SOCIETY OF SOIL SCIENCE (II/0019-638X) [01752983] **177**

JOURNAL OF THE INDIAN STATISTICAL ASSOCIATION (II/0537-2585) [01604579] **5330**

JOURNAL OF THE INDIANA DENTAL ASSOCIATION (US/0019-6568) [09981163] **1328**

JOURNAL OF THE INLAND FISHERIES SOCIETY OF INDIA (II/0379-3435) [03357610] **2307**

JOURNAL OF THE INSTITUTE FOR THE NEW MAN (US/0743-8532) [10685545] **5250**

JOURNAL OF THE INSTITUTE OF ACTUARIES (UK/0020-2681) [06832973] **2886**

JOURNAL OF THE INSTITUTE OF ACTUARIES STUDENTS' SOCIETY *CEASED.* (UK/0020-269X) [08546985] **1759**

JOURNAL OF THE INSTITUTE OF AGRICULTURE AND ANIMAL SCIENCE (NP) [21288721] **101**

JOURNAL OF THE INSTITUTE OF ASIAN STUDIES (II/0970-2814) [16151736] **2656**

JOURNAL OF THE INSTITUTE OF BANGLADESH STUDIES, THE (BG) [03178942] **2656**

JOURNAL OF THE INSTITUTE OF BREWING (UK/0046-9750) [08423749] **2368**

JOURNAL OF THE INSTITUTE OF CHARTERED ACCOUNTANTS OF SRI LANKA (CE/1015-0005) [05540855] **747**

JOURNAL OF THE INSTITUTE OF CIVIL DEFENSE AND DISASTER STUDIES *See* EMERGENCY **1073**

JOURNAL OF THE INSTITUTE OF ENERGY (UK/0144-2600) [05037385] **1949**

JOURNAL OF THE INSTITUTE OF GEOLOGY, VIKRAM UNIVERSITY (II/0368-251X) [02174065] **1385**

JOURNAL OF THE INSTITUTE OF HEALTH EDUCATION (UK/0307-3289) [I03073289] **4787**

JOURNAL OF THE INSTITUTE OF HEALTH RECORD INFORMATION & MANAGEMENT (UK) **3598**

JOURNAL OF THE INSTITUTE OF MEDICINE (NP) [08832086] **3598**

JOURNAL OF THE INSTITUTE OF MINE SURVEYORS OF SOUTH AFRICA (SA/0020-2983) [09688899] **2142**

JOURNAL OF THE INSTITUTE OF PUBLIC ADMINISTRATION (II) [09680702] **4659**

JOURNAL OF THE INSTITUTE OF WOOD SCIENCE (UK/0020-3203) [01753255] **2402**

JOURNAL OF THE INSTITUTION ENGINEERS (INDIA). AEROSPACE ENGINEERING DIVISION (II/0257-3423) [18727445] **26**

JOURNAL OF THE INSTITUTION OF CHEMISTS, CALCUTTA (II/0020-3254) [09743916] **983**

JOURNAL OF THE INSTITUTION OF ELECTRONICS AND TELECOMMUNICATION ENGINEERS (II/0377-2063) [01790590] 2070, **1159**

JOURNAL OF THE INSTITUTION OF ENGINEERS, BANGLADESH (BG/0379-4318) [11231438] **1983**

JOURNAL OF THE INSTITUTION OF ENGINEERS (INDIA) *See* JOURNAL OF THE INSTITUTION OF ENGINEERS (INDIA). COMPUTER ENGINEERING DIVISION **1230**

JOURNAL OF THE INSTITUTION OF ENGINEERS (INDIA) *See* JOURNAL OF THE INSTITUTION OF ENGINEERS (INDIA). MARINE ENGINEERING DIVISION **2092**

JOURNAL OF THE INSTITUTION OF ENGINEERS (INDIA) (II/0020-3386) [01753270] **2070**

JOURNAL OF THE INSTITUTION OF ENGINEERS (INDIA). AGRICULTURAL ENGINEERING DIVISION (II/0257-3431) [19585999] 1983, **101**

JOURNAL OF THE INSTITUTION OF ENGINEERS (INDIA). CIVIL ENGINEERING DIVISION (II/0373-1995) [01606766] **2026**

JOURNAL OF THE INSTITUTION OF ENGINEERS (INDIA). COMPUTER ENGINEERING DIVISION (II/0020-3386) [18727438] **1230**

JOURNAL OF THE INSTITUTION OF ENGINEERS (INDIA). ELECTRONICS & TELECOMMUNICATION ENGINEERING DIVISION (II/0251-1096) [01753271] **2070**

JOURNAL OF THE INSTITUTION OF ENGINEERS (INDIA). INTERDISCIPLINARY PANELS (II/0970-9843) [15077964] **1983**

JOURNAL OF THE INSTITUTION OF ENGINEERS (INDIA). MARINE ENGINEERING DIVISION (II) [18727455] **2092**

JOURNAL OF THE INSTITUTION OF ENGINEERS (INDIA). MECHANICAL ENGINEERING DIVISION (II/0020-3408) [01644690] **2118**

JOURNAL OF THE INSTITUTION OF ENGINEERS (INDIA). MINING ENGINEERING (II/0257-442X) [14345288] **2142**

JOURNAL OF THE INSTITUTION OF ENGINEERS. INDIA. PART CH: CHEMICAL ENGINEERING DIVISION (II/0020-3351) [01589659] **2014**

JOURNAL OF THE INSTITUTION OF ENGINEERS (INDIA). PART EN CALCUTTA, ENVIRONMENTAL ENGINEERING DIVISION, THE (II/0251-110X) [02810372] 1983, **2176**

● JOURNAL OF THE INTERAMERICAN MEDICAL AND HEALTH ASSOCIATION (US/1060-3085) [24924180] **3598**

JOURNAL OF THE INTERDENOMINATIONAL THEOLOGICAL CENTER, THE (US/0092-6558) [01791227] **4971**

JOURNAL OF THE INTERNATIONAL ACADEMY OF HOSPITALITY RESEARCH, THE (US/1052-6099) [22332842] **1501**

JOURNAL OF THE INTERNATIONAL ASSOCIATION OF BUDDHIST STUDIES, THE (US/0193-600X) [04904093] **5021**

JOURNAL OF THE INTERNATIONAL ASSOCIATION OF PUPIL PERSONNEL WORKERS, THE (US/0020-6016) [02336749] **1759**

JOURNAL OF THE INTERNATIONAL ASSOCIATION OF ZOO EDUCATORS (AT/1040-5208) [16532157] **5589**

JOURNAL OF THE INTERNATIONAL COUNCIL FOR HEALTH, PHYSICAL EDUCATION, AND RECREATION *See* ICHPER JOURNAL : THE OFFICIAL MAGAZINE OF THE INTERNATIONAL COUNCIL FOR HEALTH, PHYSICAL EDUCATION, AND RECREATION **1855**

JOURNAL OF THE INTERNATIONAL COUNCIL FOR HEALTH, PHYSICAL, EDUCATION, AND RECREATION (US/1046-3380) [18898517] **1856**

JOURNAL OF THE INTERNATIONAL FEDERATION OF CLINICAL CHEMISTRY (US/1051-2292) [21914629] **983**

JOURNAL OF THE INTERNATIONAL LISTENING ASSOCIATION : JILA (US) [23822101] **1115**

JOURNAL OF THE INTERNATIONAL NEUROPSYCHOLOGICAL SOCIETY (UK/1355-6177) **4602**

● JOURNAL OF THE INTERNATIONAL OAK SOCIETY (US) [26124032] **2421**

JOURNAL OF THE INTERNATIONAL PHONETIC ASSOCIATION (UK/0025-1003) [02157736] **3292**

JOURNAL OF THE INTERNATIONAL SOCIETY FOR RESPIRATORY PROTECTION (US/0892-6298) [15249685] **1983**

JOURNAL OF THE IOWA ACADEMY OF SCIENCE, THE (US/0896-8381) [17303957] **5121**

JOURNAL OF THE IOWA ARCHEOLOGICAL SOCIETY (US/0535-5729) [01608245] **272**

JOURNAL OF THE IRISH COLLEGES OF PHYSICIANS AND SURGEONS (IE/0374-8405) [01588760] 1833, **3598**

JOURNAL OF THE IRISH DENTAL ASSOCIATION, THE (IE/0021-1133) [06381341] **1328**

JOURNAL OF THE IRISH FAMILY HISTORY SOCIETY (IE/0790-7060) [15729682] **2455**

JOURNAL OF THE IRISH SOCIETY FOR EUROPEAN LAW *See* IRISH JOURNAL OF EUROPEAN LAW **2985**

JOURNAL OF THE IRISH SOCIETY FOR LABOUR LAW (IE/0790-0473) [11105845] **3150**

JOURNAL OF THE JAPAN SOCIETY FOR AERONAUTICAL AND SPACE SCIENCES (JA/0021-4663) [10116692] **26**

JOURNAL OF THE JAPANESE AND INTERNATIONAL ECONOMIES (US/0889-1583) [13800330] **1637**

JOURNAL OF THE JAPANESE SOCIETY OF COMPUTATIONAL STATISTICS (JA/0915-2350) [22590151] 5330, **3515**

JOURNAL OF THE JOHANNES SCHWALM HISTORICAL ASSOCIATION, INC (US/8755-3805) [08705184] 2695, **2742**

JOURNAL OF THE JOHANNESBURG HISTORICAL FOUNDATION (SA) [06185832] **2641**

JOURNAL OF THE K.R. CAMA ORIENTAL INSTITUTE (II/0970-0609) [03901021] **4971**

JOURNAL OF THE KAFKA SOCIETY OF AMERICA (US/0894-6388) [12181740] **3345**

JOURNAL OF THE KANAWHA VALLEY GENEALOGICAL SOCIETY, THE (US/0270-4064) [06229814] **2455**

JOURNAL OF THE KANSAS BAR ASSOCIATION, THE (US/0022-8486) [02441132] **2989**

JOURNAL OF THE KANSAS DENTAL ASSOCIATION (US/0888-7063) [11176502] **1328**

JOURNAL OF THE KANSAS ENTOMOLOGICAL SOCIETY (US/0022-8567) [01783294] **5611**

JOURNAL OF THE KARNATAK UNIVERSITY. SCIENCE (II/0075-5168) [02313390] **5121**

JOURNAL OF THE KENTUCKY MEDICAL ASSOCIATION, THE (US/0023-0294) [01779029] **3598**

JOURNAL OF THE KOREAN INSTITUTE OF ELECTRICAL ENGINEERS (KO/0374-4876) [04844684] **2070**

JOURNAL OF THE KOREAN INSTITUTE OF SURFACE ENGINEERING (KO) **1983**

JOURNAL OF THE KOREAN MATHEMATICAL SOCIETY (KO/0304-9914) [09287865] **3515**

JOURNAL OF THE KOREAN NUCLEAR SOCIETY (KO/0372-7327) [10115525] **4448**

JOURNAL OF THE KOREAN PHYSICAL SOCIETY (KO/0374-4884) [06095045] **4410**

JOURNAL OF THE KOREAN SOCIETY OF FOOD AND NUTRITION (KO) 2347, **4194**

JOURNAL OF THE KUWAIT MEDICAL ASSOCIATION, THE (KU/0023-5776) [01029197] **3598**

JOURNAL OF THE KYUSHU DENTAL SOCIETY. ENGLISH ABSTRACTS, THE (JA) [06467683] **1328**

JOURNAL OF THE LANCASHIRE & CHESHIRE BRANCH OF THE WESLEY HISTORICAL SOCIETY (UK) [09008503] **2695**

JOURNAL OF THE LANCASHIRE DIALECT SOCIETY, THE (UK/0075-7799) [03617888] **3292**

JOURNAL OF THE LANCASTER COUNTY HISTORICAL SOCIETY (US/0023-7477) [02297909] **2742**

JOURNAL OF THE LANGUAGE ASSOCIATION OF EASTERN AFRICA (KE/0251-0421) [02855906] **3292**

JOURNAL OF THE LAW SOCIETY OF SCOTLAND, THE (UK/0458-8711) [01606496] **2989**

JOURNAL OF THE LEARNING SCIENCES, THE (US/1050-8406) [21653645] **1759**

JOURNAL OF THE LEGAL PROFESSION, THE (US/0196-7487) [02802368] **2989**

JOURNAL OF THE LEGISLATIVE ASSEMBLY OF THE PROVINCE OF PRINCE EDWARD ISLAND (CN/0319-4973) [02443908] **4659**

JOURNAL OF THE LEPIDOPTERISTS' SOCIETY (US/0024-0966) [07654420] **5589**

JOURNAL OF THE LINCOLN ASSASSINATION (US) **2742**

JOURNAL OF THE LINGUISTIC ASSOCIATION OF NIGERIA : JOLAN (NR/0189-5680) [10450271] **3292**

JOURNAL OF THE LONDON MATHEMATICAL SOCIETY (UK/0024-6107) [01756133] **3515**

JOURNAL OF THE LONDON SOCIETY, THE (UK/0024-6158) [04343537] 302, **354**

JOURNAL OF THE LOUISIANA STATE MEDICAL SOCIETY, THE (US/0024-6921) [10035081] **3599**

JOURNAL OF THE LUTE SOCIETY OF AMERICA, INC (US/0076-1524) [02088599] **4127**

JOURNAL OF THE LYCOMING COUNTY HISTORICAL SOCIETY, THE (US/0887-543X) [04208698] **2742**

JOURNAL OF THE MADHYA PRADESH ITIHASA PARISHAD (II) [03249687] **2656**

JOURNAL OF THE MADRAS UNIVERSITY. SECTION A, HUMANITIES (II) [01640088] **2849**

JOURNAL OF THE MAGOFFIN COUNTY HISTORICAL SOCIETY, THE (US/0893-5416) [15371381] **2456**

JOURNAL OF THE MAHARAJA SAYAJIRAO UNIVERSITY OF BARODA (II/0025-0422) [01696081] **1759**

JOURNAL OF THE MALACOLOGICAL SOCIETY OF AUSTRALIA (AT/0085-2988) [02448405] **5589**

JOURNAL OF THE MALAYSIAN BRANCH OF THE ROYAL ASIATIC SOCIETY (SI/0126-7353) [05350783] **2656**

JOURNAL OF THE MALAYSIAN VETERINARY MEDICAL ASSOCIATION *See* MALAYSIAN VETERINARY JOURNAL, THE **5516**

JOURNAL OF THE MAMMALOGICAL SOCIETY OF JAPAN (JA/0914-1855) [19694553] **5589**

JOURNAL OF THE MAMMILLARIA SOCIETY, THE (UK/0464-8072) [06247621] **516**

JOURNAL OF THE MANAGEMENT PROFESSIONALS ASSOCIATION (II/0970-0447) [I09700447] **874**

JOURNAL OF THE MARINE BIOLOGICAL ASSOCIATION OF INDIA (II/0025-3146) [01756689] **555**

JOURNAL OF THE MARINE BIOLOGICAL ASSOCIATION OF THE UNITED KINGDOM (UK/0025-3154) [01756690] **555**

JOURNAL OF THE MARKET RESEARCH SOCIETY (UK/0025-3618) [05593182] **929**

JOURNAL OF THE MARYLAND STATE DENTAL ASSOCIATION (US/0025-4355) [01332644] **1328**

JOURNAL OF THE MASSACHUSETTS ASSOCIATION OF HEALTH, PHYSICAL EDUCATION, RECREATION AND DANCE (US) **1856**

JOURNAL OF THE MASSACHUSETTS DENTAL SOCIETY (US/0025-4800) [01332697] **1328**

JOURNAL OF THE MATHEMATICAL SOCIETY OF JAPAN (JA/0025-5645) [01696554] **3515**

JOURNAL OF THE MECHANICAL BEHAVIOR OF MATERIALS (UK/0334-8938) [18424198] **2119**

JOURNAL OF THE MECHANICS AND PHYSICS OF SOLIDS (UK/0022-5096) [01782726] **2104**

JOURNAL OF THE MEDICAL ASSOCIATION OF GEORGIA (US/0025-7028) [01756971] **3599**

JOURNAL OF THE MEDICAL ASSOCIATION OF THAILAND (TH/0025-7036) [01778905] **3599**

JOURNAL OF THE METEOROLOGICAL SOCIETY OF JAPAN (JA/0026-1165) [02244312] **1427**

JOURNAL OF THE MICHIGAN DENTAL ASSOCIATION, THE (US/0026-2102) [01029180] **1328**

JOURNAL OF THE MIDWEST FINANCE ASSOCIATION *CEASED.* (US/0272-6637) [01644391] 795, **905**

JOURNAL OF THE MIDWEST HISTORY OF EDUCATION SOCIETY (US/0092-2986) [01788440] **1759**

JOURNAL OF THE MIDWEST MODERN LANGUAGE ASSOCIATION, THE (US/0742-5562) [10363564] **3292**

● JOURNAL OF THE MILITARY HISTORY SOCIETY OF MANITOBA (CN/1188-164X) [30456421] 2742, **4048**

JOURNAL OF THE MILKING SHORTHORN AND ILLAWARRA BREEDS (US/0145-8264) [01443128] **213**

JOURNAL OF THE MINE MEDICAL OFFICERS' ASSOCIATION OF SOUTH AFRICA (SA) [18713648] **2142**

JOURNAL OF THE MINE VENTILATION SOCIETY OF SOUTH AFRICA (SA/0368-3206) [02397940] **2142**

JOURNAL OF THE MINNESOTA ACADEMY OF SCIENCE (US/0026-539X) [01333118] **5121**

JOURNAL OF THE MISSISSIPPI ACADEMY OF SCIENCES (US/0076-9436) [01643758] **5121**

JOURNAL OF THE MISSISSIPPI STATE MEDICAL ASSOCIATION (US/0026-6396) [01758369] **3599**

JOURNAL OF THE MISSOURI BAR (US/0026-6485) [01209885] **2989**

JOURNAL OF THE MISSOURI WATER AND SEWERAGE CONFERENCE (US/0096-4255) [01461698] 5535, **2234**

JOURNAL OF THE MODOC COUNTY HISTORICAL SOCIETY (US/0196-2019) [06154446] **2742**

JOURNAL OF THE MOSCOW PATRIARCHATE, THE (RU/0201-7318) [01791410] **5039**

JOURNAL OF THE MOSCOW PHYSICAL SOCIETY : JMPS (UK/0960-0175) [24202370] **4410**

JOURNAL OF THE MUHYIDDIN IBN ARABI SOCIETY (UK/0266-2183) [11861851] **5043**

JOURNAL OF THE MUSEUM OF FINE ARTS, BOSTON (US/1041-2433) [18691473] **4090**

JOURNAL OF THE MUSIC ACADEMY, MADRAS, THE (II) [01641279] 1313, **4127**

JOURNAL OF THE N.J. ASSOCIATION OF OSTEOPATHIC PHYSICIANS AND SURGEONS, THE (US/0892-0249) [12244454] **3599**

JOURNAL OF THE NATIONAL AGRICULTURAL SOCIETY OF CEYLON (CE/0547-3616) [01586207] **101**

JOURNAL OF THE NATIONAL ASSOCIATION OF ADMINISTRATIVE LAW JUDGES (US/0735-0821) [08261108] **3093**

JOURNAL OF THE NATIONAL ASSOCIATION OF DOCUMENT EXAMINERS (US/8755-1020) [11258380] **3168**

JOURNAL OF THE NATIONAL BOTANICAL SOCIETY (II/0971-2976) [I09712976] **516**

JOURNAL OF THE NATIONAL BUILDINGS ORGANISATION (II/0027-8815) [02679337] **618**

JOURNAL OF THE NATIONAL CANCER INSTITUTE (US/0027-8874) [01064763] **3820**

JOURNAL OF THE NATIONAL CANCER INSTITUTE MONOGRAPHS *See* MONOGRAPHS NATIONAL CANCER INSTITUTE **3821**

JOURNAL OF THE NATIONAL INSTITUTE OF PLANTATION MANAGEMENT (CE) [08604521] **101**

JOURNAL OF THE NATIONAL INTEGRATED MEDICAL ASSOCIATION (II/0377-0621) [01598143] **3599**

JOURNAL OF THE NATIONAL MEDICAL ASSOCIATION (US/0027-9684) [01064483] **3599**

JOURNAL OF THE NATIONAL RESEARCH COUNCIL OF THAILAND (TH/0028-0011) [02109267] **5121**

JOURNAL OF THE NATIONAL REYE'S SYNDROME FOUNDATION *SUSPENDED.* (US/0276-2293) [06297767] **3599**

JOURNAL OF THE NATIONAL SCIENCE COUNCIL OF SRI LANKA (CE/0300-9254) [01797709] **5121**

JOURNAL OF THE NATIONAL TECHNICAL ASSOCIATION (US/0271-776X) [06680493] **5121**

JOURNAL OF THE NEPAL MEDICAL ASSOCIATION : JNMA (NP) [13849075] **4787**

JOURNAL OF THE NEPAL RESEARCH CENTRE : NJRC (GW) [05969496] **2695**

JOURNAL OF THE NEUROLOGICAL SCIENCES (NE/0022-510X) [01783295] **3837**

● JOURNAL OF THE NEUROMUSCULOSKELETAL SYSTEM (US/1067-8239) [27360715] 3837, **3805**

JOURNAL OF THE NEW BRUNSWICK MUSEUM (CN/0703-0606) [03883134] **4090**

JOURNAL OF THE NEW ENGLAND GARDEN HISTORY SOCIETY (US/1053-2617) [22495581] **2421**

JOURNAL OF THE NEW ENGLAND LUTHERAN HISTORICAL SOCIETY (US/1051-0605) [10389006] **4971**

JOURNAL OF THE NEW ENGLAND WATER ENVIRONMENT ASSOCIATION (US) **2234**

JOURNAL OF THE NEW ENGLAND WATER POLLUTION CONTROL ASSOCIATION (US/0548-4502) [06328243] **2234**

JOURNAL OF THE NEW ENGLAND WATER WORKS ASSOCIATION (US/0028-4939) [01759782] 5535, **4761**

JOURNAL OF THE NEW HAVEN COLONY HISTORICAL SOCIETY (US/0548-4987) [01590368] **2742**

JOURNAL OF THE NEW JERSEY DENTAL ASSOCIATION (US/0093-7347) [03932578] **1328**

JOURNAL OF THE NEW JERSEY SPEECH AND HEARING ASSOCIATION *CEASED.* (US/0028-5935) [05659490] **4390**

JOURNAL OF THE NEW YORK ENTOMOLOGICAL SOCIETY (US/0028-7199) [01334066] **5589**

JOURNAL OF THE NEW YORK INSTITUTE OF LEGAL RESEARCH, THE (US/1049-5304) [21247884] **2989**

JOURNAL OF THE NEW YORK STATE NURSES ASSOCIATION, THE (US/0028-7644) [02014914] **3860**

JOURNAL OF THE NEW ZEALAND SOCIETY OF PERIODONTOLOGY (NZ/0111-1485) [04683620] **1328**

JOURNAL OF THE NIGERIAN MATHEMATICAL SOCIETY (NR/0189-8965) [09448981] **3515**

JOURNAL OF THE NORTH AMERICAN BENTHOLOGICAL SOCIETY (US/0887-3593) [13196288] **2218**

JOURNAL OF THE NORTH AMERICAN FALCONERS' ASSOCIATION, THE (US/0097-6253) [01799131] 4902, **4874**

JOURNAL OF THE NORTH AMERICAN WOLF SOCIETY (US/0740-0152) [04734350] **5589**

JOURNAL OF THE NORTH-EAST INDIA COUNCIL FOR SOCIAL SCIENCE RESEARCH, THE (II) [05146120] **5207**

JOURNAL OF THE NORTH EASTERN COUNCIL (II) [04842003] **1570**

JOURNAL OF THE NORTH MIDDLESEX FAMILY HISTORY SOCIETY (UK/0141-9544) [15040952] **2456**

JOURNAL OF THE NORTH MISSISSIPPI CONFERENCE OF THE UNITED METHODIST CHURCH ... : SESSION SINCE MERGER OF THE UPPER MISSISSIPPI CONFERENCE (ORGANIZED IN 1891) AND THE NORTH MISSISSIPPI CONFERENCE (ORGANIZED IN 1870) (US) [07374482] **5062**

JOURNAL OF THE NUMISMATIC ASSOCIATION OF AUSTRALIA (AT) [18691349] **2781**

JOURNAL OF THE NUMISMATIC SOCIETY OF INDIA, THE (II/0029-6066) [01624274] **2781**

JOURNAL OF THE NUTRITIONAL ACADEMY (US/0197-0666) [05915155] **4194**

JOURNAL OF THE OCEANOLOGICAL SOCIETY OF KOREA (KO/0374-8049) [08611721] **1450**

JOURNAL OF THE OIL TECHNOLOGISTS' ASSOCIATION OF INDIA, THE (II) [03253228] **4262**

JOURNAL OF THE OLD DROGHEDA SOCIETY (IE) [10385317] **5232**

JOURNAL OF THE ONTARIO SOCIETY FOR EDUCATION THROUGH ART (CN/0842-8417) [19568672] **354**

JOURNAL OF THE OPERATIONAL RESEARCH SOCIETY, THE (UK/0160-5682) [03685489] 5121, **3515**

JOURNAL OF THE OPERATIONS RESEARCH SOCIETY OF JAPAN (JA/0453-4514) [01755058] **5121**

Alphabetical Title Index — JOURNAL

JOURNAL OF THE OPTICAL SOCIETY OF AMERICA (US/0039-3941) [01642072] **4437**

JOURNAL OF THE OPTICAL SOCIETY OF AMERICA. A, OPTICS AND IMAGE SCIENCE (US/0740-3232) [09921721] **4437**

●JOURNAL OF THE OPTICAL SOCIETY OF AMERICA. A, OPTICS, IMAGE SCIENCE, AND VISION (US) [28755048] **4437**

JOURNAL OF THE OPTICAL SOCIETY OF AMERICA. B, OPTICAL PHYSICS (US/0740-3224) [09921588] **4437**

JOURNAL OF THE ORDER OF BUDDHIST CONTEMPLATIVES, THE (US/0891-1177) [14578021] **5021**

JOURNAL OF THE ORDERS AND MEDALS SOCIETY OF AMERICA, THE (US) [27121939] **2781**

JOURNAL OF THE OREGON DENTAL ASSOCIATION, THE (US/0030-4670) [01334372] **1329**

JOURNAL OF THE ORIENTAL INSTITUTE, M.S. UNIVERSITY OF BARODA (II/0030-5324) [01774243] **2505**

JOURNAL OF THE ORIENTAL SOCIETY OF AUSTRALIA, THE (AT/0030-5340) [01761508] **2656**

JOURNAL OF THE OTO-LARYNGOLOGICAL SOCIETY OF AUSTRALIA *See* AUSTRALIAN JOURNAL OF OTO-LARYNGOLOGY : THE OFFICIAL JOURNAL OF THE AUSTRALIAN SOCIETY OF OTO-LARYNGOLOGY HEAD AND NECK SURGERY **3887**

JOURNAL OF THE OTTO RANK ASSOCIATION (US/0030-6711) [01761580] **4602**

●JOURNAL OF THE OUGHTRED SOCIETY, THE (US/1061-6292) [25381084] **3515**

JOURNAL OF THE PAKISTAN HISTORICAL SOCIETY (PK/0030-9796) [01761751] **2656**

JOURNAL OF THE PAKISTAN MEDICAL ASSOCIATION *SUSPENDED.* (PK/0030-9982) [01081664] **3599**

JOURNAL OF THE PALAEONTOLOGICAL SOCIETY OF INDIA (II/0552-9360) [01761777] **4227**

JOURNAL OF THE PATENT AND TRADEMARK OFFICE SOCIETY (US/0882-9098) [11733610] **1305**

JOURNAL OF THE PENNSYLVANIA ACADEMY OF SCIENCE (US/1044-6753) [18783191] **5121**

JOURNAL OF THE PENNSYLVANIA OSTEOPATHIC MEDICAL ASSOCIATION, THE (US/0479-9534) [08179733] **3599**

JOURNAL OF THE PENNSYLVANIA SPEECH-LANGUAGE-HEARING ASSOCIATION, THE (US) [11942955] **4390**

JOURNAL OF THE PHILADELPHIA ASSOCIATION FOR PSYCHOANALYSIS (US/0094-1476) [01793889] **3930**

JOURNAL OF THE PHILADELPHIA COUNTY DENTAL SOCIETY (US) [10858772] **1329**

JOURNAL OF THE PHILIPPINE PHARMACEUTICAL ASSOCIATION (PH/0368-3826) [l03683826] **4313**

JOURNAL OF THE PHILOSOPHICAL SOCIETY (SA) [05061839] **4351**

JOURNAL OF THE PHILOSOPHY OF SPORT (US/0094-8705) [01795819] **4902**

JOURNAL OF THE PHYSICAL SOCIETY OF JAPAN (JA/0031-9015) [01762332] **4410**

●JOURNAL OF THE PHYSICIANS ASSOCIATION FOR AIDS CARE (US/1074-2395) [29630770] 3715, **3674**

JOURNAL OF THE PLAINSONG & MEDIAEVAL MUSIC SOCIETY *See* PLAINSONG AND MEDIEVAL MUSIC **4146**

JOURNAL OF THE PLAYING-CARD SOCIETY (UK/0305-2133) [I03052133] 2774, **4862**

JOURNAL OF THE POLITICAL SCIENCE SOCIETY (SI) [02043611] **4479**

JOURNAL OF THE POLYNESIAN SOCIETY (NZ/0032-4000) [01762632] 239, **3292**

JOURNAL OF THE PRINT WORLD (US/0737-7436) [06619954] **4566**

JOURNAL OF THE PRINTING HISTORICAL SOCIETY (UK/0079-5321) [01642888] **3292**

JOURNAL OF THE PROCEEDINGS OF THE ... ANNUAL CONVENTION OF THE PROTESTANT EPISCOPAL CHURCH IN THE DIOCESE OF BETHLEHEM *See* JOURNAL OF THE ANNUAL CONVENTION - EPISCOPAL CHURCH. DIOCESE OF BETHLEHEM **5062**

JOURNAL OF THE RAMANUJAN MATHEMATICAL SOCIETY (II/0970-1249) [16913475] **3515**

JOURNAL OF THE RESEARCH SOCIETY OF PAKISTAN (PK/0034-5431) [01641070] 2849, **5207**

JOURNAL OF THE RIO GRANDE VALLEY HORTICULTURAL SOCIETY (US/0485-2044) [02123640] **2421**

JOURNAL OF THE ROCKY MOUNTAIN MEDIEVAL AND RENAISSANCE ASSOCIATION (US/0195-8453) [05638248] 323, **2621**

JOURNAL OF THE ROYAL AGRICULTURAL SOCIETY OF ENGLAND (UK/0080-4134) [01716163] **101**

JOURNAL OF THE ROYAL ANTHROPOLOGICAL INSTITUTE, THE (UK) **239**

JOURNAL OF THE ROYAL ARMY MEDICAL CORPS (UK/0035-8665) [01029165] 4048, **3599**

JOURNAL OF THE ROYAL ARTILLERY, THE (UK) [08433089] **4048**

JOURNAL OF THE ROYAL ASIATIC SOCIETY OF GREAT BRITAIN & IRELAND (UK/0035-869X) [01764574] **2769**

JOURNAL OF THE ROYAL ASTRONOMICAL SOCIETY OF CANADA, THE (CN/0035-872X) [01586913] **396**

JOURNAL OF THE ROYAL AUSTRALIAN HISTORICAL SOCIETY (AT/0035-8762) [03832170] **2670**

JOURNAL OF THE ROYAL COLLEGE OF PHYSICIANS AND SURGEONS OF THE UNITED STATES OF AMERICA : JRCP&S (US) [30040001] 3986, **3968**

JOURNAL OF THE ROYAL COLLEGE OF PHYSICIANS OF LONDON (UK/0035-8819) [01064771] **3599**

JOURNAL OF THE ROYAL COLLEGE OF SURGEONS OF EDINBURGH (UK/0035-8835) [01064687] **3968**

JOURNAL OF THE ROYAL INSTITUTION OF CORNWALL (UK) [01772115] **2695**

JOURNAL OF THE ROYAL MUSICAL ASSOCIATION (UK/0269-0403) [16 46836] **4127**

JOURNAL OF THE ROYAL NAVAL MEDICAL SERVICE (UK/0035-9033) [01064702] **3599**

JOURNAL OF THE ROYAL SIGNALS INSTITUTION (UK/0374-3519) [I03743519] **5232**

JOURNAL OF THE ROYAL SOCIETY OF ANTIQUARIES OF IRELAND, THE (IE/0035-9106) [06906544] 272, **2695**

JOURNAL OF THE ROYAL SOCIETY OF HEALTH (UK/0264-0325) [09402371] **4787**

JOURNAL OF THE ROYAL SOCIETY OF MEDICINE (UK/0141-0768) [03722674] **3599**

JOURNAL OF THE ROYAL SOCIETY OF MEDICINE. SUPPLEMENT (UK) [10461570] **3599**

JOURNAL OF THE ROYAL SOCIETY OF NEW ZEALAND (NZ/0303-6758) [02301786] 1357, **5121**

JOURNAL OF THE ROYAL SOCIETY OF WESTERN AUSTRALIA (AT/0035-922X) [07520165] **4166**

JOURNAL OF THE ROYAL STATISTICAL SOCIETY. SERIES A (GENERAL) (UK/0035-9238) [01764625] **5330**

JOURNAL OF THE ROYAL STATISTICAL SOCIETY. SERIES A: (STATISTICS IN SOCIETY) (UK) [18305542] **5330**

JOURNAL OF THE ROYAL STATISTICAL SOCIETY. SERIES B (METHODOLOGICAL) (UK/0035-9246) [01346117] **5330**

JOURNAL OF THE ROYAL UNITED SERVICES INSTITUTE OF AUSTRALIA (AT/0728-1188) [08926160] **4048**

JOURNAL OF THE RUTGERS UNIVERSITY LIBRARY, THE (US/0036-0473) [01764696] **3221**

JOURNAL OF THE SAN JUAN ISLANDS (US/0734-3809) [08582787] **5761**

JOURNAL OF THE SCIENCE OF FOOD AND AGRICULTURE (UK/0022-5142) [01782672] 101, **2347**

JOURNAL OF THE SCIENCE SOCIETY OF THAILAND (TH/0303-8122) [02754366] **5121**

JOURNAL OF THE SCOTTISH ROCK GARDEN CLUB, THE (UK) [05245940] **2422**

JOURNAL OF THE SENATE OF THE GENERAL ASSEMBLY OF THE STATE OF SOUTH CAROLINA (US) [10140163] **4659**

JOURNAL OF THE SENATE OF THE UNITED STATES OF AMERICA (US) [07913890] **4479**

JOURNAL OF THE SENATE, STATE OF FLORIDA (US) [12890900] **2990**

JOURNAL OF THE SERBIAN CHEMICAL SOCIETY (YU/0352-5139) [13377317] **983**

JOURNAL OF THE SHAW HISTORICAL LIBRARY, THE (US/0889-0277) [13775733] **3221**

JOURNAL OF THE SIAM SOCIETY, THE (TH) [02981679] **2656**

JOURNAL OF THE SIERRA LEONE MEDICAL & DENTAL ASSOCIATION (SL/0253-8482) [06513642] **1329**

JOURNAL OF THE SIMPLIFIED SPELLING SOCIETY (UK/0950-9585) [l09509585] **1759**

JOURNAL OF THE SINGAPORE NATIONAL ACADEMY OF SCIENCE (SI/0129-3729) [02033157] **5121**

JOURNAL OF THE SOCIETY FOR ACCELERATIVE LEARNING AND TEACHING, THE (US/0273-2459) [07037317] **1881**

JOURNAL OF THE SOCIETY FOR ARMENIAN STUDIES (US/0747-9301) [10837066] **2656**

JOURNAL OF THE SOCIETY FOR ARMY HISTORICAL RESEARCH (UK/0037-9700) [01644191] **4048**

●JOURNAL OF THE SOCIETY FOR GYNECOLOGIC INVESTIGATION (US/1071-5576) [28678798] **3764**

JOURNAL OF THE SOCIETY FOR HEALTH SYSTEMS (US/1043-1721) [19331141] **4788**

●JOURNAL OF THE SOCIETY FOR INFORMATION DISPLAY (US/0734-1768) [27328193] **3221**

JOURNAL OF THE SOCIETY FOR ITALIC HANDWRITING, THE (UK/0037-9743) [04141958] **380**

JOURNAL OF THE SOCIETY FOR PSYCHICAL RESEARCH (UK/0037-9751) [01641860] **4242**

JOURNAL OF THE SOCIETY FOR STUDY OF STATE GOVERNMENTS (II) [01680846] **4659**

JOURNAL OF THE SOCIETY FOR UNDERWATER TECHNOLOGY (UK/0141-0814) [07337006] **1450**

JOURNAL OF THE SOCIETY OF ARCHER-ANTIQUARIES (UK/0560-6152) [01955587] **4902**

JOURNAL OF THE SOCIETY OF ARCHITECTURAL HISTORIANS (US/0037-9808) [02392510] **302**

JOURNAL OF THE SOCIETY OF ARCHIVISTS (UK/0037-9816) [01586854] **2482**

JOURNAL OF THE SOCIETY OF AUTOMOTIVE ENGINEERS OF JAPAN (JA/0385-7298) [09446370] **5418**

JOURNAL OF THE SOCIETY OF BASQUE STUDIES IN AMERICA (US/1042-3834) [18966784] **2695**

JOURNAL OF THE SOCIETY OF COMMUNITY MEDICINE HONG KONG (HK/0379-3176) [I03793176] **3599**

JOURNAL OF THE SOCIETY OF COSMETIC CHEMISTS (US/0037-9832) [01086504] **1026**

JOURNAL OF THE SOCIETY OF DAIRY TECHNOLOGY (UK/0037-9840) [02487510] **196**

JOURNAL OF THE SOCIETY OF DYERS AND COLOURISTS (UK/0037-9859) [01765919] **1026**

JOURNAL OF THE SOCIETY OF LEATHER TECHNOLOGISTS AND CHEMISTS (UK/0144-0322) [10971764] 1026, **3184**

JOURNAL OF THE SOCIETY OF LEATHER TRADES'S CHEMISTS *See* JOURNAL OF THE SOCIETY OF LEATHER TECHNOLOGISTS AND CHEMISTS **3184**

JOURNAL OF THE SOCIETY OF LOGISTICS ENGINEERING (US) **1983**

JOURNAL OF THE SOCIETY OF OCCUPATIONAL MEDICINE *See* OCCUPATIONAL MEDICINE **3623**

JOURNAL OF THE SOMERSET INDUSTRIAL ARCHAEOLOGICAL SOCIETY *CEASED.* (UK/0307-1723) [05389012] **272**

JOURNAL OF THE SOUTH AFRICAN INSTITUTE OF MINING & METALLURGY (SA/0038-223X) [02395243] 4006, **2142**

JOURNAL OF THE SOUTH AFRICAN INSTITUTION OF CIVIL ENGINEERS / JOERNAAL VAN DIE SUID-AFRIKAANSE INSTITUUT VAN SIVIELE INGENIEURS (SA/1021-2019) [28622970] **2026**

JOURNAL OF THE SOUTH AFRICAN VETERINARY ASSOCIATION (SA/0301-0732) [01390932] **5513**

JOURNAL OF THE SOUTH CAROLINA BAPTIST HISTORICAL SOCIETY (US/0146-0196) [02830010] **5062**

JOURNAL OF THE SOUTH CAROLINA MEDICAL ASSOCIATION (1975) (US/0038-3139) [09770937] **3599**

JOURNAL OF THE SOUTH SEAS SOCIETY (SI) [02055011] 5207, **2656**

JOURNAL OF THE SOUTHERN CALIFORNIA DENTAL HYGIENISTS' ASSOCIATION (US/0038-3899) [01391312] **1329**

●JOURNAL OF THE SOUTHERN ORTHOPAEDIC ASSOCIATION (US/1059-1052) [24479695] **3883**

JOURNAL — Alphabetical Title Index

JOURNAL OF THE SOUTHWEST (US/0894-8410) [15876763] **2742**

JOURNAL OF THE SPORTS TURF RESEARCH INSTITUTE, THE (UK/0561-6832) [02500872] **4902**

JOURNAL OF THE SRI LANKA BRANCH OF THE ROYAL ASIATIC SOCIETY (CE/1013-9818) [05049193] **2656**

JOURNAL OF THE ST. CLAIR COUNTY HISTORICAL SOCIETY (US/0095-3911) [01796762] **2742**

JOURNAL OF THE STATISTICAL AND SOCIAL INQUIRY SOCIETY OF IRELAND (IE/0081-4776) [09130837] **5330**

JOURNAL OF THE STATISTICAL INSTITUTE OF JAMAICA (JM) [19225800] **5330**

JOURNAL OF THE STEWARD ANTHROPOLOGICAL SOCIETY (US/0039-1344) [01766516] **239**

JOURNAL OF THE STUDENT NATIONAL MEDICAL ASSOCIATION (US/1044-1654) [19697846] **3599**

JOURNAL OF THE SUFFOLK ACADEMY OF LAW (US/0888-2142) [06463704] **2990**

JOURNAL OF THE SWAMY BOTANICAL CLUB, THE (II) [12616054] **516**

JOURNAL OF THE TANZANIA ASSOCIATION OF FORESTERS (TZ/0856-0269) [15012100] **2386**

JOURNAL OF THE TENNESSEE ACADEMY OF SCIENCE (US/0040-313X) [01767277] **5121**

JOURNAL OF THE TENNESSEE DENTAL ASSOCIATION, THE (US/0040-3385) [01391373] **1329**

JOURNAL OF THE TENNESSEE MEDICAL ASSOCIATION (US/0040-3318) [01224423] **3600**

JOURNAL OF THE TEXTILE ASSOCIATION (II/0368-4636) [01784117] **5353**

JOURNAL OF THE TEXTILE INSTITUTE (UK/0040-5000) [01767380] **5353**

JOURNAL OF THE TEXTILE MACHINERY SOCIETY OF JAPAN (JA/0040-5043) [04340626] **5353**

JOURNAL OF THE TILES & ARCHITECTURAL CERAMICS SOCIETY (UK/0264-5157) [I02645157] **302**

JOURNAL OF THE TOKYO UNIVERSITY OF FISHERIES (JA/0040-9014) [01782481] **2307**

JOURNAL OF THE TRANSPORTATION RESEARCH FORUM (US/1046-1469) [17285821] **5385**

JOURNAL OF THE UNITED SERVICE INSTITUTION OF INDIA, THE (II/0041-770X) [10440414] **4048**

JOURNAL OF THE UNIVERSITY OF BOMBAY (II) [01774264] **1833**

JOURNAL OF THE UNIVERSITY OF BOMBAY, SCIENCE: PHYSICAL SCIENCES, MATHEMATICS, BIOLOGICAL SCIENCES AND MEDICINE (II/0368-4644) [I03684644] **5121, 3515**

JOURNAL OF THE UNIVERSITY OF KUWAIT, SCIENCE, THE (KU/0376-4818) [02991328] **5121**

JOURNAL OF THE UNIVERSITY OF POONA, SCIENCE AND TECHNOLOGY (II/0551-4932) [01774402] **5122**

JOURNAL OF THE URBAN AND REGIONAL INFORMATION SYSTEMS ASSOCIATION (US/1045-8077) [20244292] **2826**

JOURNAL OF THE US ARMY MEDICAL DEPARTMENT, THE (US) [21020000] **4048, 3600**

JOURNAL OF THE VIOLA DA GAMBA SOCIETY OF AMERICA (US/0507-0252) [02159011] **4127**

JOURNAL OF THE VIOLIN SOCIETY OF AMERICA (US/0148-6845) [02757386] **4127**

JOURNAL OF THE VIRGIN ISLANDS ARCHAEOLOGICAL SOCIETY (VI/0363-1168) [02243684] **272**

JOURNAL OF THE VIVEKANANDA INSTITUTE OF MEDICAL SCIENCES (II/0970-4396) [17251033] **3600**

JOURNAL OF THE WALTER ROTH MUSEUM OF ARCHAEOLOGY AND ANTHROPOLOGY (GY) [06656514] **272, 239**

JOURNAL OF THE WALTERS ART GALLERY (US/0083-7156) [01769377] **354, 4090**

JOURNAL OF THE WARBURG AND COURTAULD INSTITUTES (UK/0075-4390) [08364251] **2518**

JOURNAL OF THE WASHINGTON ACADEMY OF SCIENCES (US/0043-0439) [01769417] **5122**

JOURNAL OF THE WEST (US/0022-5169) [01783221] **2742**

JOURNAL OF THE WEST VIRGINIA HISTORICAL ASSOCIATION, THE (US/0270-4765) [06412779] **2743**

JOURNAL OF THE WESTERN PACIFIC ORTHOPAEDIC ASSOCIATION See JOURNAL OF ORTHOPAEDIC SURGERY **3882**

JOURNAL OF THE WESTERN PACIFIC ORTHOPAEDIC ASSOCIATION, THE (HK/0043-4019) [01086490] **3883**

JOURNAL OF THE WESTERN SOCIETY OF PERIODONTOLOGY / PERIODONTAL ABSTRACTS, THE (US/0148-4893) [03295168] **1329**

JOURNAL OF THE WILLIAM MORRIS SOCIETY, THE (UK/0084-0254) [01681324] **373**

JOURNAL OF THE WOCN (US) **3860**

JOURNAL OF THE WORCESTER POLYTECHNIC INSTITUTE See WPI JOURNAL **5171**

JOURNAL OF THE WORLD AQUACULTURE SOCIETY (US/0893-8849) [15704671] **2307**

JOURNAL OF THE WRITERS GUILD OF AMERICA. WEST (US/1055-1948) [21053603] **1682, 3400**

JOURNAL OF THE YUGOSLAV FOREIGN TRADE (YU/0022-5452) [02263123] **4527**

JOURNAL OF THE ZOOLOGICAL SOCIETY OF INDIA (II/0049-8769) [01607220] **5589**

JOURNAL OF THEOLOGICAL STUDIES (UK/0022-5185) [01782539] **4971**

JOURNAL OF THEOLOGY (US/0361-1906) [01907424] **4971**

JOURNAL OF THEOLOGY FOR SOUTHERN AFRICA (SA/0047-2867) [01789723] **4971**

JOURNAL OF THEOLOGY (UNITED THEOLOGICAL SEMINARY) (US) **4971**

JOURNAL OF THEORETICAL BIOLOGY (UK/0022-5193) [01783069] **462**

JOURNAL OF THEORETICAL GRAPHICS AND COMPUTING *SUSPENDED.* (US/1040-7847) [18529033] **1234**

JOURNAL OF THEORETICAL POLITICS (UK/0951-6298) [19571198] **4479**

JOURNAL OF THEORETICAL PROBABILITY (US/0894-9840) [16388986] **3515**

JOURNAL OF THERAPEUTIC HORTICULTURE (US) [15744402] **1881, 2422**

JOURNAL OF THERMAL ANALYSIS (UK/0368-4466) [01799891] **1055**

JOURNAL OF THERMAL BIOLOGY (UK/0306-4565) [02246186] **462**

JOURNAL OF THERMAL ENGINEERING, THE (II/0253-7265) [08521921] **2119**

JOURNAL OF THERMAL INSULATION (US/0148-8287) [03386436] **2606**

● JOURNAL OF THERMAL INSULATION AND BUILDING ENVELOPES (US/1065-2744) [26562542] **618**

● JOURNAL OF THERMAL SPRAY TECHNOLOGY (US/1059-9630) [24820790] **4006**

JOURNAL OF THERMAL STRESSES (UK/0149-5739) [03522573] **2119**

JOURNAL OF THERMOPHYSICS AND HEAT TRANSFER (US/0887-8722) [13392807] **4431**

JOURNAL OF THERMOPLASTIC COMPOSITE MATERIALS (US/0892-7057) [15239474] **1026**

JOURNAL OF THETA ALPHA KAPPA (US/8756-4785) [11564548] **4971**

● JOURNAL OF THIRD WORLD SPECTRUM (US/1072-5040) [28988476] **4527**

JOURNAL OF THIRD WORLD STUDIES (US/8755-3449) [11280312] **1637**

JOURNAL OF THORACIC AND CARDIOVASCULAR SURGERY (US/0022-5223) [01754847] **3707, 3968**

JOURNAL OF THORACIC IMAGING (US/0883-5993) [12174382] **3600**

JOURNAL OF THOUGHT (US/0022-5231) [01783310] **1759**

JOURNAL OF THROMBOSIS AND THROMBOLYSIS (NE/0929-5305) **3600**

JOURNAL OF TIME SERIES ANALYSIS (UK/0143-9782) [07367448] **3516**

JOURNAL OF TISSUE CULTURE METHODS (NE/0271-8057) [06694043] **538**

JOURNAL OF TISSUE VIABILITY (UK/0965-206X) [28146264] **3721, 538**

JOURNAL OF TONGJI MEDICAL UNIVERSITY (CC/0257-716X) [13644389] **3600**

JOURNAL OF TOURISM STUDIES, THE (AT/1035-4662) [22883232] **843, 5481**

JOURNAL OF TOXICOLOGIC PATHOLOGY (JA/0914-9198) [I09149198] **3896**

JOURNAL OF TOXICOLOGY AND ENVIRONMENTAL HEALTH (US/0098-4108) [02244935] **2865, 3982**

JOURNAL OF TOXICOLOGY. CLINICAL TOXICOLOGY (US/0731-3810) [08175535] **3982**

JOURNAL OF TOXICOLOGY. CUTANEOUS AND OCULAR TOXICOLOGY (US) [08179128] **3982**

JOURNAL OF TOXICOLOGY. TOXIN REVIEWS (US/0731-3837) [08178961] **3982**

JOURNAL OF TRACE AND MICROPROBE TECHNIQUES (US/0733-4680) [08592424] **1017**

JOURNAL OF TRACE ELEMENTS AND ELECTROLYTES IN HEALTH AND DISEASE (GW/0931-2838) [18352545] **3600**

JOURNAL OF TRACE ELEMENTS IN EXPERIMENTAL MEDICINE, THE (US/0896-548X) [17195944] **3600**

JOURNAL OF TRADITIONAL ACUPUNCTURE, THE (US/0270-661X) [06433120] **3600**

JOURNAL OF TRADITIONAL CHINESE MEDICINE (CC/0254-6272) [08676745] **3600**

JOURNAL OF TRAFFIC MEDICINE (SW/0345-5564) [11198060] **4788, 3600**

JOURNAL OF TRAFFIC SAFETY EDUCATION (US/0164-1344) [04579964] **5441**

JOURNAL OF TRAINING & PRACTICE IN PROFESSIONAL PSYCHOLOGY, THE *CEASED.* (US/0895-7673) [16792702] **4602**

JOURNAL OF TRANSCULTURAL NURSING (US/1043-6596) [19524392] **3860**

● JOURNAL OF TRANSLATION AND TEXTLINGUISTICS (US/1055-4513) [23188125] **3292**

● JOURNAL OF TRANSNATIONAL LAW & POLICY (US/1067-8182) [26210308] **3131**

● JOURNAL OF TRANSNATIONAL MANAGEMENT DEVELOPMENT (US/1068-6061) [27720388] **874**

JOURNAL OF TRANSPERSONAL PSYCHOLOGY, THE (US/0022-524X) [01800053] **4602**

JOURNAL OF TRANSPLANT COORDINATION : OFFICIAL PUBLICATION OF THE NORTH AMERICAN TRANSPLANT COORDINATORS ORGANIZATION (NATCO) (DK/0905-9199) [24317976] **3799**

JOURNAL OF TRANSPORT ECONOMICS AND POLICY (UK/0022-5258) [00856156] **5385**

● JOURNAL OF TRANSPORT GEOGRAPHY (UK/0966-6923) [28452206] **2567**

JOURNAL OF TRANSPORT HISTORY, THE (UK/0022-5266) [01754849] **1570, 5385**

JOURNAL OF TRANSPORTATION ENGINEERING (US/0733-947X) [08674831] **5385, 2026**

JOURNAL OF TRAUMA, THE (US/0022-5282) [01783002] **3969**

JOURNAL OF TRAUMATIC STRESS (US/0894-9867) [16389067] **3930, 4602**

● JOURNAL OF TRAVEL AND TOURISM MARKETING (US/1054-8408) [22994251] **929, 5482**

JOURNAL OF TRAVEL MEDICINE (CN/1195-1982) **3600**

JOURNAL OF TRAVEL RESEARCH (US/0047-2875) [02532184] **5482**

● JOURNAL OF TREE FRUIT PRODUCTION (US/1055-1387) [23092250] **101, 177**

JOURNAL OF TREE SCIENCES (II) [10945417] **2422, 2386**

JOURNAL OF TRIBOLOGY (US/0742-4787) [10379677] **2119**

JOURNAL OF TROPICAL & GEOGRAPHICAL NEUROLOGY : THE OFFICIAL JOURNAL OF THE RESEARCH GROUP ON TROPICAL NEUROLOGY OF THE WORLD FEDERATION OF NEUROLOGY *CEASED.* (UK/0963-0880) [26320151] **3986, 3837**

JOURNAL OF TROPICAL ECOLOGY (UK/0266-4674) [12958594] **2218**

JOURNAL OF TROPICAL FOREST SCIENCE (MY/0128-1283) [20340114] **2386**

JOURNAL OF TROPICAL FORESTRY (II/0970-1494) [14290767] **2386**

JOURNAL OF TROPICAL MEDICINE AND HYGIENE (UK/0022-5304) [01639249] **3986**

JOURNAL OF TROPICAL PEDIATRICS (1980) (UK/0142-6338) [06328278] **3986, 3905**

JOURNAL OF TRUE EDUCATION See JOURNAL OF ADVENTIST EDUCATION, THE **1897**

JOURNAL OF TSINGHUA UNIVERSITY (CC) **2026**

JOURNAL OF TUNG-CHI UNIVERSITY (CC) [08710274] **302**

JOURNAL OF TURBOMACHINERY (US/0889-504X) [12741561] **2119**

Alphabetical Title Index — JOURNAL

JOURNAL OF TURFGRASS MANAGEMENT (US/1070-437X) [28361050] **2422**

JOURNAL OF TURKISH PHYTOPATHOLOGY, THE (TU/0378-8024) [03836286] **516**

JOURNAL OF TURKISH STUDIES (US/0743-0019) [03637349] **5207**

JOURNAL OF UFO STUDIES, THE (US/0730-5478) [08027111] **26**

JOURNAL OF UGANDAN LIBRARIES (UG) [11662887] **3221**

JOURNAL OF UKRAINIAN GRADUATE STUDIES (CN/0701-1792) [03436225] 3400, **2695**

JOURNAL OF UKRAINIAN STUDIES (CN/0228-1635) [06744531] 5207, **2849**

JOURNAL OF ULTRASOUND IN MEDICINE (US/0278-4297) [07828058] **3943**

JOURNAL OF UNCONVENTIONAL HISTORY (US) [20708286] **2621**

JOURNAL OF UNDERGRADUATE ECONOMICS, THE (US/0146-1664) [02878793] **1501**

JOURNAL OF UNDERGRADUATE MATHEMATICS (US/0022-5339) [01754853] **3516**

JOURNAL OF UNDERGRADUATE PSYCHOLOGICAL RESEARCH (US/0096-1337) [01798557] **4602**

JOURNAL OF UNDERGRADUATE RESEARCH IN PHYSICS, THE (US/0731-3764) [08178885] **4410**

JOURNAL OF UOEH (JA/0387-821X) [05826451] 2865, **4788**

JOURNAL OF URBAN AFFAIRS (US/0735-2166) [08261798] **2826**

JOURNAL OF URBAN AND CULTURAL STUDIES (US/1054-1802) [22775741] 5250, **1759**

JOURNAL OF URBAN ECONOMICS (US/0094-1190) [01793720] **1501**

JOURNAL OF URBAN HISTORY (US/0096-1442) [01798556] 2826, **2621**

JOURNAL OF URBAN PLANNING AND DEVELOPMENT (US/0733-9488) [08674763] 2826, **2026**

●JOURNAL OF URBAN TECHNOLOGY, THE (US/1063-0732) [25851022] **2826**

JOURNAL OF UROGENITAL PATHOLOGY (US/1054-8734) [23004317] **3991**

●JOURNAL OF UROLOGIC PATHOLOGY (US/1067-1919) [27159029] **3991**

JOURNAL OF UROLOGICAL NURSING (US/0738-7350) [09652070] 3860, **3991**

JOURNAL OF UROLOGY, THE (US/0022-5347) [01754854] **3991**

JOURNAL OF VACUUM SCIENCE & TECHNOLOGY. A: VACUUM, SURFACES, AND FILMS (US/0734-2101) [08697396] **4410**

JOURNAL OF VACUUM SCIENCE & TECHNOLOGY. B, MICROELECTRONICS AND NANOMETER STRUCTURES PROCESSING, MEASUREMENT AND PHENOMENA (US/1071-1023) [23276603] 983, **4410**

●JOURNAL OF VAISNAVA STUDIES, THE (US/1062-1237) [25528895] **4971**

JOURNAL OF VALUE INQUIRY, THE (NE/0022-5363) [01754856] **4351**

JOURNAL OF VASCULAR AND INTERVENTIONAL RADIOLOGY (US/1051-0443) [21769279] **3943**

●JOURNAL OF VASCULAR INVESTIGATION (UK/1353-8012) 3707, **3600**

JOURNAL OF VASCULAR MEDICINE AND BIOLOGY *CEASED.* (US/1042-5268) [19075517] **462**

JOURNAL OF VASCULAR NURSING (US/1062-0303) [22592800] 3707, **3860**

●JOURNAL OF VASCULAR RESEARCH (SZ/1018-1172) [25568995] **3707**

JOURNAL OF VASCULAR SURGERY (US/0741-5214) [10161047] **3969**

JOURNAL OF VASCULAR TECHNOLOGY, THE (US/1044-4122) [17505542] **3708**

●JOURNAL OF VEGETABLE CROP PRODUCTION (US/1049-6467) [21269665] **177**

JOURNAL OF VEGETATION SCIENCE (SW/1100-9233) [21277157] **516**

JOURNAL OF VERTEBRATE PALEONTOLOGY (US/0272-4634) [06842311] **4227**

JOURNAL OF VESTIBULAR RESEARCH (US/0957-4271) [23174919] **3889**

JOURNAL OF VETERINARY ANAESTHESIA (UK) [24421845] **5514**

JOURNAL OF VETERINARY AND ANIMAL SCIENCES (II/0971-0701) [25467196] **5514**

JOURNAL OF VETERINARY DENTISTRY (US/0898-7564) [16118468] **5514**

JOURNAL OF VETERINARY DIAGNOSTIC INVESTIGATION (US/1040-6387) [18477067] **5514**

JOURNAL OF VETERINARY EMERGENCY AND CRITICAL CARE (SANTA BARBARA, CALIF.) (US/1056-6392) [23816117] **5514**

JOURNAL OF VETERINARY INTERNAL MEDICINE (US/0891-6640) [14948161] **5514**

JOURNAL OF VETERINARY MEDICAL EDUCATION (US/0748-321X) [02156481] **5514**

JOURNAL OF VETERINARY MEDICAL SCIENCE (JA/0916-7250) [23597950] **5514**

JOURNAL OF VETERINARY MEDICINE. SERIES A (GW/0931-184X) [I0931184X] **5514**

JOURNAL OF VETERINARY MEDICINE. SERIES B (GW/0931-1793) [I09311793] **5514**

JOURNAL OF VETERINARY PARASITOLOGY (II/0971-1031) [20351119] **5514**

JOURNAL OF VETERINARY PHARMACOLOGY AND THERAPEUTICS (UK/0140-7783) [04580359] **5514**

JOURNAL OF VETERINARY PHYSIOLOGY AND ALLIED SCIENCES (II) [14560310] **5514**

JOURNAL OF VIBRATION AND ACOUSTICS (US/1048-9002) [21012339] 2099, **4453**

JOURNAL OF VIBRATION AND CONTROL (US) [30832327] **1983**

JOURNAL OF VIETNAMESE STUDIES (AT/1030-6390) [20032896] **2656**

JOURNAL OF VINYL TECHNOLOGY (US/0193-7197) [05232422] **4456**

●JOURNAL OF VIRAL HEPATITIS (UK/1352-0504) **3600**

JOURNAL OF VIROLOGICAL METHODS (NE/0166-0934) [06403038] **566**

JOURNAL OF VIROLOGY (US/0022-538X) [01783311] **566**

JOURNAL OF VISION REHABILITATION (LINCOLN, NEB.) (US/1041-0384) [16112828] 4216, **3876**

JOURNAL OF VISUAL COMMUNICATION AND IMAGE REPRESENTATION (US/1047-3203) [20665542] **1234**

JOURNAL OF VISUAL IMPAIRMENT & BLINDNESS (US/0145-482X) [02736747] **4390**

JOURNAL OF VISUAL LANGUAGES AND COMPUTING (UK/1045-926X) [20284708] **1192**

JOURNAL OF VISUAL LITERACY (US/1051-144X) [20547023] **3292**

JOURNAL OF VISUALIZATION AND COMPUTER ANIMATION, THE (UK/1049-8907) [21344150] **1234**

JOURNAL OF VITAL CHRISTIANITY *See* VITAL CHRISTIANITY (1994) **5008**

JOURNAL OF VITAL CHRISTIANITY, A (US/1046-543X) [20447836] **4971**

JOURNAL OF VLSI SIGNAL PROCESSING (US/0922-5773) [19026663] **2070**

JOURNAL OF VOCATIONAL AND TECHNICAL EDUCATION (US/0888-8639) [11908438] **1914**

JOURNAL OF VOCATIONAL BEHAVIOR (US/0001-8791) [01783396] 1914, **4602**

JOURNAL OF VOCATIONAL EDUCATION RESEARCH, THE (US/0739-3369) [03395445] **1914**

JOURNAL OF VOCATIONAL HOME ECONOMICS EDUCATION (US) [09589605] **2791**

JOURNAL OF VOCATIONAL REHABILITATION (US/1052-2263) [22218190] **4380**

JOURNAL OF VOICE (US/0892-1997) [15106737] **3600**

JOURNAL OF VOLCANOLOGY AND GEOTHERMAL RESEARCH (NE/0377-0273) [02335670] **1408**

JOURNAL OF VOLUNTEER ADMINISTRATION, THE (US/0733-6535) [08634796] **5293**

JOURNAL OF WATER BORNE COATINGS (US/0163-4526) [04380593] **4224**

●JOURNAL OF WATER CHEMISTRY AND TECHNOLOGY (US/1063-455X) [26040111] 5535, **2234**

JOURNAL OF WATER RESOURCES (IQ/0255-0148) [09248369] **5535**

JOURNAL OF WATER RESOURCES PLANNING AND MANAGEMENT (US/0733-9496) [08674714] 2026, **5535**

JOURNAL OF WATER SUPPLY RESEARCH AND TECHNOLOGY - AQUA (UK/0003-7214) [20064631] **5535**

JOURNAL OF WATERWAY, PORT, COASTAL, AND OCEAN ENGINEERING (US/0733-950X) [08674675] 2026, **2092**

JOURNAL OF WAVE-MATERIAL INTERACTION (US/0887-0586) [13077189] **2104**

JOURNAL OF WEATHER MODIFICATION, THE (US/0739-1781) [06429694] **1427**

JOURNAL OF WEST AFRICAN LANGUAGES, THE (UK/0022-5401) [00844072] **3292**

JOURNAL OF WEST INDIAN LITERATURE (BB/0258-8501) [15211499] **3400**

JOURNAL OF WILD CULTURE, THE (CN/0833-0018) [17883916] **2196**

JOURNAL OF WILDERNESS MEDICINE (UK/0953-9859) [21281452] **3600**

JOURNAL OF WILDLIFE DISEASES (US/0090-3558) [01587351] **5514**

JOURNAL OF WILDLIFE MANAGEMENT, THE (US/0022-541X) [01782497] **2196**

●JOURNAL OF WILDLIFE REHABILITATION (US/1071-2232) [28576800] **2196**

JOURNAL OF WIND ENGINEERING AND INDUSTRIAL AERODYNAMICS (NE/0167-6105) [06561918] **1983**

JOURNAL OF WINE RESEARCH / THE INSTITUTE OF MASTERS OF WINE (UK/0957-1264) [22780303] **2368**

JOURNAL OF WOMEN & AGING (US/0895-2841) [16546320] 5180, 5293, **5559**

JOURNAL OF WOMEN AND RELIGION (US/0888-5621) [07863169] **4971**

●JOURNAL OF WOMEN'S HEALTH (US/1059-7115) [24681378] 5559, **3600**

JOURNAL OF WOMEN'S HISTORY (US/1042-7961) [19219902] **5559**

JOURNAL OF WOMEN'S MINISTRIES (US/1064-1084) [10735359] 5559, **4971**

JOURNAL OF WOOD CHEMISTRY AND TECHNOLOGY (US/0277-3813) [07580150] 4234, 2402, **1055**

JOURNAL OF WORKERS COMPENSATION, THE (US/1059-4167) [24584686] **2886**

JOURNAL OF WORLD EDUCATION (SNEDSTED, DENMARK) (DK/0904-3063) [11968790] **1759**

JOURNAL OF WORLD FOREST RESOURCE MANAGEMENT (UK/0261-4286) [11815411] **2386**

JOURNAL OF WORLD HISTORY (US/1045-6007) [20155374] **2621**

JOURNAL OF WORLD PEACE, THE *SUSPENDED.* (US/8756-8691) [11672023] **4527**

JOURNAL OF WORLD PREHISTORY (US/0892-7537) [15255571] **272**

JOURNAL OF WORLD TRADE (SZ/1011-6702) [17661898] **843**

●JOURNAL OF WOUND CARE (UK/0969-0700) [I09690700] **3600**

●JOURNAL OF WOUND, OSTOMY, AND CONTINENCE NURSING (US/1071-5754) [28679185] **3860**

JOURNAL OF X-RAY SCIENCE AND TECHNOLOGY (US/0895-3996) [16628609] **3943**

JOURNAL OF XIAN MEDICAL UNIVERSITY (CC/0258-0659) [21577411] **3600**

JOURNAL OF YOUTH AND ADOLESCENCE (US/0047-2891) [01783955] **5207**

JOURNAL OF YOUTH SERVICES IN LIBRARIES (US/0894-2498) [15901512] **3221**

JOURNAL OF ZOO AND WILDLIFE MEDICINE : OFFICIAL PUBLICATION OF THE AMERICAN ASSOCIATION OF ZOO VETERINARIANS (US/1042-7260) [19115490] **5514**

JOURNAL OF ZOOLOGY (1987) (UK/0952-8369) [15264754] **5589**

JOURNAL OFFICIEL (CG) [01788417] **2990**

JOURNAL OFFICIEL DE LA REPUBLIQUE ALGERIENNE DEMOCRATIQUE ET POPULAIRE (AE) [17001668] **2990**

JOURNAL OFFICIEL DE LA REPUBLIQUE ET CANTON DU JURA (SZ) [08037043] **2990**

JOURNAL OFFICIEL DE LA REPUBLIQUE FRANCAISE. AVIS ET RAPPORTS DU CONSEIL ECONOMIQUE ET SOCIAL (FR) [09857365] **1501**

JOURNAL OFFICIEL DE LA REPUBLIQUE FRANCAISE. DEBATS PARLEMENTAIRES, ASSEMBLEE NATIONALE (CUMULATIF) (FR/0429-3088) [06468368] **4479**

JOURNAL OFFICIEL DE LA REPUBLIQUE FRANCAISE. DEBATS PARLEMENTAIRES, ASSEMBLEE NATIONALE. QUESTIONS ECRITES ET REPONSES DES MINISTRES (FR/0242-6757) [13297733] **4659**

JOURNAL

Alphabetical Title Index

JOURNAL OFFICIEL DE LA REPUBLIQUE FRANCAISE. DEBATS PARLIAMENTAIRES, ASSEMBLEE NATIONALE. COMPTE RENDU INTEGRAL (FR/0242-6765) [13297651] **4659**

JOURNAL OFFICIEL DE LA REPUBLIQUE FRANCAISE DEBATS SENAT COMPTE RENDU (FR) **4659**

JOURNAL OFFICIEL DE LA REPUBLIQUE FRANCAISE DEBATS SENAT QUESTIONS ECRITES (FR) **4659**

JOURNAL OFFICIEL DE LA REPUBLIQUE FRANCAISE. EDITION DES LOIS ET DECRETS : NUMERO COMPLEMENTAIRE (FR) [04816881] **2990**

JOURNAL OFFICIEL DE LA REPUBLIQUE FRANCAISE LES LOIS ET DECRETS. TABLES (FR) **2990**

JOURNAL OFFICIEL DE LA REPUBLIQUE POPULAIRE DU CONGO (CF) [06326674] **2990**

JOURNAL OFFICIEL DES COMMUNAUTES EUROPEENNES : COMMUNICATIONS ET INFORMATIONS (FR/0449-5152) [01754864] **26**

JOURNAL OFFICIEL DU BURKINA FASO (UV) [16507436] **4659**

JOURNAL OFFICIEL. LOIS ET DECRETS (FR) [01713593] **2990**

JOURNAL (OGDENSBURG, N.Y.), THE (US/0893-5149) [10906085] **5717**

JOURNAL / OHIO SCHOOL BOARDS ASSOCIATION (US/0893-5289) [11165554] **1865**

JOURNAL - OKLAHOMA STATE MEDICAL ASSOCIATION (US/0030-1876) [09571262] **3601**

JOURNAL ON EXCELLENCE IN COLLEGE TEACHING (US/1052-4800) [22294409] **1833**

JOURNAL - ONTARIO ASSOCIATION OF CHILDREN'S AID SOCIETIES (CN/0030-283X) [03082346] **5293**

JOURNAL - ONTARIO OCCUPATIONAL HEALTH NURSES ASSOCIATION (CN/0828-542X) [12069429] **3860**

JOURNAL-OPINION (US/0746-1674) [07503088] **5757**

JOURNAL OPTION GLOBALE (CN/0710-2143) [08192774] **323**

JOURNAL - OSWEGO COUNTY HISTORICAL SOCIETY (US/0092-9549) [01791709] **2743**

JOURNAL / PAKISTAN BAR COUNCIL (PK) [07035442] **2990**

JOURNAL : PAPER OF THE NATIONAL UNION OF CIVIL AND PUBLIC SERVANTS (UK/0957-8978) [26571172] 1682, **4704**

JOURNAL-PATRIOT, THE (US) [11801152] **5723**

JOURNAL (PENETANGUISHENE) (CN/1184-5139) [25589835] **5787**

JOURNAL PERIODIQUE (CN/0826-2322) [11096342] **396**

JOURNAL / PHILADELPHIA SOCIAL STUDIES COUNCIL, THE (US/1051-7103) [22095473] **5207**

JOURNAL, PHYSICAL THERAPY EDUCATION (US/0899-1855) [18025611] **4380**

JOURNAL PLUS, LE (CN/1182-2589) [22426354] 1065, **5232**

JOURNAL PRATIQUE DE DROIT FISCAL ET FINANCIER See JOURNAL DE DROIT FISCAL **2986**

JOURNAL - PROVINCIAL ASSOCIATION OF CATHOLIC TEACHERS (CN/0848-9025) [21486879] 5031, **1759**

JOURNAL / Q.F.M.A (CN/0712-9262) [08867895] 3482, **2906**

JOURNAL QUEBEC QUILLES, LE (CN/0849-1623) [23295859] **4902**

JOURNAL RECORD (HAMILTON, AL.) (US) [15363887] **5627**

JOURNAL RECORD (OKLAHOMA CITY, OKLA.), THE (US/0737-5468) [09382886] **688**

JOURNAL REGIONAL (QUEBEC) (CN/0706-3318) [06859002] **5787**

JOURNAL REGIONAL (SAINT-JEAN) (CN/0821-414X) [09796182] **5787**

JOURNAL-REVIEW (US) [11422721] **5665**

JOURNAL REVIEWS FOR SCHOOL ADMINISTRATORS (US/1056-408X) [23720417] **1865**

●JOURNAL / RHODE ISLAND BAR ASSOCIATION (US/1073-8800) [29542373] **2990**

JOURNAL ROBOTIQUE, LE See JOURNAL ROBOTIQUE INFORMATIQUE INDUSTRIELLE, LE **2119**

JOURNAL ROBOTIQUE INFORMATIQUE INDUSTRIELLE, LE (FR) **2119**

JOURNAL - ROYAL BRITISH LEGION (UK/0308-4949) [01785446] **5232**

JOURNAL (ROYAL HISTORICAL SOCIETY OF QUEENSLAND : 1985) (AT) [13392610] **2670**

JOURNAL (ROYAL INSTITUTE OF BRITISH ARCHITECTS : OVERSEAS ED.) See RIBA JOURNAL **308**

JOURNAL (ROYAL INSTITUTE OF BRITISH ARCHITECTS : OVERSEAS ED.) (UK/0953-6973) [17285107] **302**

JOURNAL RPF (FR/0337-2693) [03822167] **2606**

JOURNAL - RUBBER RESEARCH INSTITUTE OF SRI LANKA (CE/0379-1130) [03715237] **177**

JOURNAL (SANGEET RESEARCH ACADEMY (CALCUTTA, INDIA)) (II) [09103911] **4127**

JOURNAL / SASKATCHEWAN MATHEMATICS TEACHERS' SOCIETY (CN/0714-7082) [09201121] 1899, **3516**

JOURNAL : SCIENCE (II) [05243409] **5122**

JOURNAL : SCIENCE, TECHNOLOGY & MEDICINE (II/0970-4116) [01790512] **5122**

JOURNAL SEAMUS : THE JOURNAL OF THE SOCIETY FOR ELECTRO-ACOUSTIC MUSIC IN THE UNITED STATES (US/0897-6473) [16375650] **4127**

JOURNAL - SEATTLE-KING COUNTY DENTAL SOCIETY (US) [01391407] **1329**

JOURNAL SILVER SOCIETY (UK) **4006**

JOURNAL - SINGAPORE COMPUTER SOCIETY (SI) [01784316] **1261**

JOURNAL - SOCIAL HISTORY CURATORS GROUP (UK/0962-7871) [l09627871] **4090**

JOURNAL - SOCIETY FOR THE STUDY OF BLACK PHILOSOPHY (U.S.), THE (US/0741-627X) [10222375] **4351**

JOURNAL / SOUTHERN CALIFORNIA DENTAL ASSISTANTS ASSOCIATION (US/0738-7970) [09702893] **1329**

JOURNAL ST-LOUIS (CN/0710-2186) [08458532] **5787**

JOURNAL - STANSTEAD COUNTY HISTORICAL SOCIETY (CN/0081-4369) [02247180] **2743**

JOURNAL STAR, THE (US) [08807680] **5660**

●JOURNAL SUBSCRIPTION CATALOG / THE ASSOCIATION OF AMERICAN UNIVERSITY PRESSES (US/1064-5470) [26326018] **4821**

JOURNAL SUBSCRIPTION PRICE LIST / COMMONWEALTH AGRICULTURAL BUREAUX (UK) [08735242] **101**

JOURNAL SUISSE DE HORLOGERIE ET DE BIJOUTERIE (SZ/0368-4172) [I03684172] **2915**

JOURNAL SUPER-MERITAS, LE (CN/1183-3084) [25314215] **2536**

JOURNAL - SUPREME COURT OF THE UNITED STATES (US/0270-9805) [02641607] **3141**

JOURNAL - TEXAS SOCIETY FOR ELECTRON MICROSCOPY (US/0196-5662) [05840713] **572**

JOURNAL, THE (US) [18120434] **5729**

JOURNAL, THE (US) [27801867] **5742**

●JOURNAL, THE (US) [26059950] **5660**

JOURNAL, THE (US) [25642196] **5654**

JOURNAL / THE CANADIAN ASSOCIATION FOR HEALTH, PHYSICAL EDUCATION AND RECREATION (CN/0834-1915) [13696948] **1856**

JOURNAL / THE CANADIAN FOUNDATION FOR ILEITIS AND COLITIS (CN/0827-4681) [12874069] **3747**

JOURNAL - THE ENGLISH PLACE-NAME SOCIETY (UK) [01567971] **2695**

JOURNAL - THE INSTITUTION OF ENGINEERS, SINGAPORE (SI/0377-7464) [01790737] **1984**

JOURNAL - THE INTERNATIONAL NETSUKE COLLECTORS SOCIETY (US/0095-2591) [01796401] **373**

●JOURNAL : THE JOURNAL OF THE AMERICAN BLOOD RESOURCES ASSOCIATION, THE (US) [26585935] 3799, **3773**

JOURNAL : THE LITERARY MAGAZINE OF THE OHIO STATE UNIVERSITY, THE (US/1045-084X) [15732743] **3400**

JOURNAL - THE LOS ANGELES INSTITUTE OF CONTEMPORARY ART CEASED. (US/0094-8985) [01795540] **354**

JOURNAL : THE MAGAZINE OF THE INDIANA SCHOOL BOARDS ASSOCIATION, THE (US) [26206799] **1865**

JOURNAL : THE OFFICIAL PUBLICATION OF THE GEORGIA PHARMACEUTICAL ASSOCIATION (US) [28146923] **4313**

JOURNAL - THE PETER WILLCOCKS SOCIETY (US) [04306346] **2456**

JOURNAL / THE WISCONSIN ASSOCIATION FOR HEALTH, PHYSICAL EDUCATION, RECREATION, AND DANCE, WAHPERD (US/0889-3535) [13877725] **1856**

JOURNAL (THIRTIES SOCIETY (LONDON, ENGLAND)) (UK/0265-2625) [08872532] **302**

JOURNAL - TIMBER DEVELOPMENT ASSOCIATION OF INDIA (II/0377-936X) [01639013] **2402**

JOURNAL TIMES, THE (US/0746-2867) [09926347] **5768**

JOURNAL/TRIBUNE, THE (US) [27827987] **5742**

JOURNAL - TRINITY COLLEGE OF QUEZON CITY (PH) [01794468] **1833**

JOURNAL - UNITED ASSOCIATION OF JOURNEYMEN AND APPRENTICES OF THE PLUMBING AND PIPE FITTING INDUSTRY (US) [01474204] **1682**

JOURNAL - UNITED REFORMED CHURCH HISTORY SOCIETY (UK/0049-5433) [02163048] **5062**

JOURNAL - UNIVERSITIES ART ASSOCIATION OF CANADA (CN/0315-940X) [02210254] **355**

JOURNAL WATCH (US/0896-7210) [17283612] 3601, **3660**

●JOURNAL WATCH (SOUND RECORDING) (US/1063-1887) [25929475] **5317**

JOURNAL WEST (DUNDAS) (CN/0229-7817) [08319803] **5787**

JOURNAL - WESTERN NEW YORK GENEALOGICAL SOCIETY (US/0890-6858) [01795593] **2456**

JOURNAL - WISCONSIN STATE READING ASSOCIATION (US/0160-9270) [03574416] **1899**

JOURNAL - WORLD PHEASANT ASSOCIATION (UK) [02732988] **2196**

JOURNAL / WORLD RESOURCES INSTITUTE CEASED. (US/0883-8100) [12225812] **5293**

JOURNAL - ZAMBIA LIBRARY ASSOCIATION (ZA/0049-853X) [03247081] **3221**

JOURNALEN SYKEPLEIEN (NO) [21901047] **3860**

JOURNALISM ABSTRACTS See JOURNALISM & MASS COMMUNICATION ABSTRACTS **2921**

JOURNALISM & MASS COMMUNICATION ABSTRACTS (US/1077-694X) **2921**

JOURNALISM & MASS COMMUNICATION DIRECTORY (US/0895-6545) [13576584] **2921**

JOURNALISM & MASS COMMUNICATION EDUCATOR (US/1077-6958) **2921**

JOURNALISM & MASS COMMUNICATION MONOGRAPHS (US/1077-6966) **2921**

JOURNALISM & MASS COMMUNICATION QUARTERLY (US/1077-6990) **2921**

JOURNALISM EDUCATOR See JOURNALISM & MASS COMMUNICATION EDUCATOR **2921**

JOURNALISM HISTORY (US/0094-7679) [01795320] **2921**

JOURNALISM MONOGRAPHS See JOURNALISM & MASS COMMUNICATION MONOGRAPHS **2921**

JOURNALISM QUARTERLY See JOURNALISM & MASS COMMUNICATION QUARTERLY **2921**

JOURNALISM SCHOLARSHIP GUIDE (US/0449-3354) [02252786] **2921**

JOURNALISM STUDIES REVIEW (UK) [03374482] **2921**

JOURNALISME (FR/0449-3370) [04977914] **2921**

JOURNALISMUS (GW) [01784756] **2921**

JOURNALIST (UK/0022-5541) [05301989] **2921**

JOURNALIST, DE (NE/0022-555X) [01782859] **2921**

JOURNALIST (EDMONTON) (CN/0823-1672) [09938410] **1092**

JOURNALIST. PAO JEN. WARTAWAN, THE (SI) [06932935] **2921**

JOURNALISTE DU TOURISME, LE (BE) **5482**

JOURNALISTEN-HANDBUCH (GW) [02240571] **2921**

JOURNALISTS' AFFAIRS (XR) [04261406] **2921**

JOURNALS IN TRANSLATION (UK) [04836972] **3221**

JOURNALS OF GERONTOLOGY (US) **3753**

●JOURNALS OF GERONTOLOGY: BIOLOGICAL SCIENCES AND MEDICAL SCIENCES, THE (US) **3753**

JOURNALS OF THE SENATE / THE PARLIAMENT OF THE COMMONWEALTH OF AUSTRALIA (AT) [01518752] **4659**

JOURNEE VINICOLE, LA (FR) [04055421] **2368**

JOURNEES ANNUELLES DE DIABETOLOGIE DE L'HOTEL-DIEU (FR/0075-4439) [01695829] **3731**

JOURNEES DE LA RECHERCHE OVINE ET CAPRINE *CEASED.* (FR/0243-0088) [03767317] **213**

JOURNEES DE LA RECHERCHE PORCINE EN FRANCE (FR/0767-9874) [03184974] **2347, 5515**

JOURNEES DE LA SOCIETE DE LEGISLATION COMPAREE (FR) [07490991] **3131**

JOURNEES EQUATIONS AUX DERIVEES PARTIELLES (FR) [06233272] **3516**

JOURNEES PARISIENNES DE PEDIATRIE (FR/0399-029X) [11332335] **3905**

JOURNEY (KITCHENER) (CN/0820-8832) [09981995] **380**

JOURNEY (LYNCHBURG, VA.) (US/0887-8854) [13441290] **4971**

JOURNEYMEN (CANDIA, N.H.) (US/1061-8538) [24582948] **3995**

●JOURNEYS (BLOOMINGTON, ILL.) (US/1063-729X) [26133706] **4862**

JOWITT'S DICTIONARY OF ENGLISH LAW (UK) **2990**

JOY OF HERBS, THE *CEASED.* (US/1040-8134) [18542491] **2422**

JOYAS & JOYEROS (SP/0213-120X) [I0213120X] **2915**

JOYCE (FR/0982-6904) [I09826904] **3400**

JOYCE STUDIES ANNUAL (US/1049-0809) [21122366] **3400**

JOYCE STUDIES IN ITALY (IT) [20059553] **3400**

JOYFUL CHILD JOURNAL (US/1045-5205) [20136231] **2282**

JOYFUL WOMAN MAGAZINE, THE (US/0885-8004) [12733907] **5559**

JOYSTICK : HOW TO WIN AT VIDEO GAMES *CEASED.* (US) [08778077] **4862**

JP AIRLINE-FLEETS INTERNATIONAL (SZ) [09055557] **26**

JPC. JOURNAL OF PLANAR CHROMATOGRAPHY, MODERN TLC (GW/0933-4173) [17979300] **983**

JPEN, JOURNAL OF PARENTERAL AND ENTERAL NUTRITION (US/0148-6071) [03334533] **4194**

JPG LETTER (JA/0916-7781) [I09167781] **2505**

JPL PUBLICATION (US/0892-9661) [05865406] 2119, **26**

JPMA : JOURNAL OF THE PHILIPPINE MEDICAL ASSOCIATION (PH) [11028766] **3601**

JPMS; JOURNAL OF POLITICAL & MILITARY SOCIOLOGY (US/0047-2697) [01786872] **5250**

JPRS REPORT (US) [22095191] **2505**

●JPRS REPORT. CENTRAL EURASIA. MILITARY AFFAIRS / FOREIGN BROADCAST INFORMATION SERVICE (US) [25761329] **4048**

JPRS REPORT EPIDEMIOLOGY (US) [16635345] **3735**

●JPRS REPORT. SCIENCE & TECHNOLOGY. CENTRAL EURASIA. CHEMISTRY [MICROFORM] / FOREIGN BROADCAST INFORMATION SERVICE (US) [27015489] 5122, **983**

●JPRS REPORT. SCIENCE & TECHNOLOGY. CENTRAL EURASIA. ENGINEERING & EQUIPMENT [MICROFORM] / FOREIGN BROADCAST INFORMATION SERVICE (US) [27017348] 5122, **1984**

●JPRS REPORT. SCIENCE & TECHNOLOGY. CENTRAL EURASIA. LIFE SCIENCES (US) [26487462] **3694**

●JPRS REPORT. SCIENCE & TECHNOLOGY. CENTRAL EURASIA. SPACE (US) [26191122] **26**

JPRS REPORT. SCIENCE & TECHNOLOGY. CHINA (US) [16679179] **5122**

JPRS REPORT. SCIENCE & TECHNOLOGY. EUROPE (US) [18218903] **5122**

●JPRS REPORT. SCIENCE & TECHNOLOGY. EUROPE/INTERNATIONAL (US) [28855429] **5122**

JPRS REPORT. SCIENCE & TECHNOLOGY. JAPAN. MICROFORM (US) [19997561] **5122**

JPRS REPORT. SCIENCE & TECHNOLOGY. USSR. CHEMISTRY (US) [21999493] **983**

JPRS REPORT. SCIENCE AND TECHNOLOGY. USSR. CHEMISTRY *See* JPRS REPORT. SCIENCE & TECHNOLOGY. CENTRAL EURASIA. CHEMISTRY [MICROFORM] / FOREIGN BROADCAST INFORMATION SERVICE **983**

JPRS REPORT. SCIENCE & TECHNOLOGY. USSR. COMPUTERS (US) [20434326] **1192**

JPRS REPORT. SCIENCE & TECHNOLOGY. USSR. EARTH SCIENCES (US) [17623131] **5122**

JPRS REPORT. SCIENCE & TECHNOLOGY. USSR. ENGINEERING & EQUIPMENT (US) [22098422] **1984**

JPRS REPORT. SCIENCE & TECHNOLOGY. USSR. LIFE SCIENCES (US/0898-3690) [17356290] **5122**

JPRS REPORT. SCIENCE & TECHNOLOGY. USSR. SPACE *See* JPRS REPORT. SCIENCE & TECHNOLOGY. CENTRAL EURASIA. SPACE **26**

JPRS REPORT. SCIENCE & TECHNOLOGY. USSR: SPACE BIOLOGY & SPACE MEDICINE *CEASED.* (US) [16946082] **3601**

JPRS REPORT. SOVIET UNION. ECONOMIC AFFAIRS *See* FBIS REPORT. SOVIET UNION. REPUBLIC AFFAIRS **1132**

JPRS REPORT. SOVIET UNION. EKO : ECONOMICS & ORGANIZATION OF INDUSTRIAL PRODUCTION (US) [16676798] **1614**

JPRS REPORT. SOVIET UNION. MILITARY POLICY *See* JPRS REPORT. CENTRAL EURASIA. MILITARY AFFAIRS / FOREIGN BROADCAST INFORMATION SERVICE **4048**

JPRS REPORT. SOVIET UNION. POLITICAL AFFAIRS *See* FBIS REPORT. SOVIET UNION. REPUBLIC AFFAIRS **1132**

JPRS REPORT. TELECOMMUNICATIONS. MICROFORM (US) [19998095] **1159**

JPS, JURNAL PENELITIAN SOSIAL (IO) [03018985] **5207**

JPT. ANNUAL REVIEW AND MEMBERSHIP DIRECTORY *See* SPE MEMBERSHIP DIRECTORY **4279**

JQS. JOURNAL OF QUATERNARY SCIENCE (UK/0267-8179) [14397228] **1385**

JR. AMERICAN MODELER (US/0090-4937) [01785213] **27**

JR. HIGH MINISTRY (US/1055-1409) [23093059] **4971**

JR; JUVENTUD REBELDE (CU) [03797732] **5799**

JR. (PETERBOROUGH, N.H.) (US/0742-6607) [10412847] **1268**

JR. RIDER, THE (CN/0381-1050) [03409442] **2800**

JRE STUDIES IN RELIGIOUS ETHICS (US/0145-2797) [02721891] **2252**

JREA (JA/0447-2322) [11832495] **5432**

JSAE REVIEW (JA/0389-4304) [06664983] **5418**

JSE HANDBOOK / JOHANNESBURG STOCK EXCHANGE, THE (SA) [24100840] **905**

JSE HANDBOOK, THE (SA) [24031379] **688**

JSL, JOURNAL OF THE SCHOOL OF LANGUAGES *SUSPENDED.* (II/0377-0648) [01790599] **3293**

JSME INTERNATIONAL JOURNAL. SERIES 2, FLUIDS ENGINEERING, HEAT TRANSFER, POWER, COMBUSTION, THERMOPHYSICAL PROPERTIES (JA/0914-8817) [17852357] **2119**

JSME INTERNATIONAL JOURNAL. SERIES 3, VIBRATION, CONTROL ENGINEERING, ENGINEERING FOR INDUSTRY (JA/0914-8825) [17852388] **2119**

●JSME INTERNATIONAL JOURNAL. SERIES A, MECHANICS AND MATERIAL ENGINEERING (JA) [27651526] **2104**

JSME INTERNATIONAL JOURNAL. SERIES B, FLUIDS AND THERMAL ENGINEERING (JA) [27801904] **2119**

JSME INTERNATIONAL JOURNAL. SERIES C, DYNAMICS, CONTROL, ROBOTICS, DESIGN AND MANUFACTURING (JA) [27968700] **2119**

JSME INTERNATIONAL JOURNAL. SERIES I, SOLID MECHANICS, STRENGTH OF MATERIALS (JA/0914-8809) [17852335] **2119**

JSN INTERNATIONAL (JA) [10331194] **5353**

JSW. JOURNAL OF STUDENT WRITING (CN/0711-7671) [14473522] **3400**

JTA DAILY NEWS BULLETIN (US/0021-3772) [01782366] **5050**

JTA WEEKLY NEWS DIGEST (US/0021-6763) [04060574] **2266**

JTN (JA) [03988566] **5353**

JTS INFORMA (PR) [09097355] **2990**

JU BU SAENG HWAL (KO) **5559**

JUA NAN NUNG YEH TA HSUEH HSUEH PAO (CC) [13531926] **101**

JUBILEE (GORRIE) (CN/0316-8417) [02247228] **3400**

JUBILEE INTERNATIONAL (US/0736-9662) [09285953] **4971**

JUBILEE (MISSISSAUGA) (CN/0824-5347) [10805656] **3168**

JUCUNDA LAUDATIO; RASSEGNA DI MUSICA ANTICA (IT/0022-5711) [01713623] **4127**

JUDAICA (SZ/0022-572X) [01782431] **5050**

JUDAICA BOHEMIAE (XR/0022-5738) [03983424] **5050**

JUDAICA BOOK NEWS *CEASED.* (US/0022-5754) [01783635] **5013**

JUDAICA LIBRARIANSHIP (US/0739-5086) [09748447] **3221**

JUDAISM (US/0022-5762) [01782703] **5050**

JUDEA, SAMARIA, AND GAZA AREA STATISTICS QUARTERLY (IS) [17293623] **5330**

JUDGE DREDD (US/1043-4135) [15501128] **2489**

JUDGE, THE (US) [01754874] **3141**

JUDGEMENTS OF THE UNITED NATIONS ADMINISTRATIVE TRIBUNAL (US) [05068235] **3131**

JUDGES' JOURNAL, THE (US/0047-2972) [01783479] **3141**

JUDGES' RETIREMENT SYSTEM : ANNUAL FINANCIAL REPORT AND REPORT OF OPERATIONS FOR THE FISCAL YEAR ENDED JUNE 30 ... / ADMINISTERED BY THE BOARD OF ADMINISTRATION, PUBLIC EMPLOYEES' RETIREMENT SYSTEM (US) [08137625] **3141**

JUDGMENTS OF THE ADMINISTRATIVE TRIBUNAL OF THE INTERNATIONAL LABOUR ORGANISATION: ORDINARY SESSION (SZ/0378-7362) [06116006] **3150**

JUDICATURE (US/0022-5800) [01754878] **3141**

JUDICIAL & LEGAL DIRECTORY (MY) [09897938] **3141**

JUDICIAL CONDUCT REPORTER (US/0193-7367) [05140296] **3141**

JUDICIAL FELLOWS PROGRAM, THE (US/0270-0654) [06035809] **3141**

JUDICIAL FUNCTION OUTLINE (US/0148-4982) [03305047] **2990**

JUDICIAL HIGHLIGHTS BULLETIN (US/0449-5519) [05095019] **2990**

JUDICIAL REVIEW (UK) **2990**

JUDICIAL STAFF DIRECTORY (US) [13238092] **3141**

●JUDISCHER ALMANACH (GW) [29293882] **2695**

JUDO *SUSPENDED.* (UK/0022-5819) [01782838] **2599**

JUDO (FRANCE) (FR) **4902**

JUDO JOURNAL (US/1066-6257) [27017722] **4902**

JUENES ANNEES *See* JEUNES ANNEES. AGES 3 TO 6 **1065**

JUEVES DE EXCELSIOR *CEASED.* (MX) [02689555] **2489**

JUGEND UND BUCH *See* 1000 UND 1 BUCH **1059**

JUGENDBUCH HEUTE / ARBEITSGEMEINSCHAFT VON JUGENDBUCHVERLEGERN (GW/0723-8991) [11772533] **1065**

JUGENDBUCHMAGAZIN (GW/0177-4247) [I01774247] **3400**

JUGENDHILFE (GW) [06174384] **5293**

JUGENDHILFE IN NORDRHEIN WESTFALEN, DIE (GW) [19004520] **5293**

JUGENDWOHL (GW/0022-5975) [I00225975] **1065**

JUGGLERS' WORLD (US/1019-4835) [I10194835] **4902**

JUGHEAD (MAMARONECK, ILL.) (US/0022-5991) [09379341] **4862**

JUGHEAD WITH ARCHIE (US/8750-0639) [10957117] **4862**

JUGOSHI NOTO / ONNATACHI NO IMA O TOU KAI (JA) [09398958] **5559**

JUGOSLAVENSKA AKADEMIJA ZNANOSTI I UMJETNOSTI *See* FILOLOGIJA **3281**

JUGOSLAVENSKA AKADEMIJA ZNANOSTI I UMJETNOSTI, RAZRED ZA LIKOVNE UMJETNOSTI *See* BULLETIN - JUGOSLAVENSKA ADAKEMIJA ZNANOSTI I UMJETNOSTI, RAZRED ZA LIKOVNE UMJETNOSTI **345**

JUGOSLAVENSKA GINEKOLOGIJA I PERINATOLOGIJA (YU/0352-5562) [13175936] **3764**

JUGOSLAVENSKA — Alphabetical Title Index

JUGOSLAVENSKA MEDICINSKA BIOKEMIJA (CI/0352-1311) [I03521311] **3694**

JUGOSLAVENSKA PEDIJATRIJA (CI/0448-0171) [I04480171] **3905**

JUGOSLOVENSKA REVIJA ZA KRIMINOLOGIJU I KRIVICNO PRAVO (YU) [04996276] **3107**

JUGOSLOVENSKI ISTORIJSKI CASOPIS (YU/0350-2902) [01783153] **2695**

JUGOSLOVENSKI PREGLED; INFORMATIVNO DOKUMENTARNI PRIRUCNIK O JUGOSLAVIJI (YU/0022-6114) [01782821] **5207**

JUGOSLOVENSKI SEMINAR ZA STRANE SLAVISTE : YUS (YU) [18119091] **3293**

JUGOSLOVENSKO VOCARSTVO. JOURNAL OF YUGOSLAV POMOLOGY (YU/0350-2155) [03763595] **177**

JUGUETECNICA (SP) **2774**

JUGUETES Y JUEGOS DE ESPANA (SP/0022-6157) [I00226157] **2584**

JUIFS EN URSS, LES (FR) [22096679] **5050**

JUILLIARD JOURNAL, THE (US/1064-1580) [26235410] **386**

JUKE BLUES (UK) [18185857] **4127**

JUKEBOX COLLECTOR (US/1053-6884) [22610281] **4127**

JUKEBOX COLLECTOR NEWSLETTER See JUKEBOX COLLECTOR **4127**

JULES VERNE (FR) [02855707] **3400**

JULESBURG ADVOCATE (US) [03547397] **5643**

JULIEN GRACQ (FR) [25139711] **3400**

JULIET ART MAGAZINE (IT) **355**

JULIT (GW/0938-202X) [I0938202X] **3401**

JUMA. DAS JUGENDMAGAZIN (GW/0940-4961) [I09404961] **1759**

JUMBO FLASH REPORTS (US) 795, **929**

JUMBO GUIDE TO RHODESIA (RH) [01788945] **5482**

JUMELLO, LE (CN/0823-776X) [10785407] **2282**

JUMIN KATSUDO (JA) [01790140] **2176**

JUMIN KIHON DAICHO ROPPO / JICHISHO GYOSEIKYOKU KANSHU (JA) [10240788] **2990**

JUMP CUT (US/0146-5546) [02971578] **1115**

JUNCTION EAGLE, THE (US) [13244657] **5751**

JUND UMAN (MK) [02962400] **4048**

JUNEAU EMPIRE (US) [09611310] **5629**

JUNELI (II) [08621379] **3401**

JUNG SHU WEN HSUEH TSUNG KAN (CC) [07120848] **3401**

JUNGE KIRCHE; EINE ZEITSCHRIFT EUROPAISCHER CHRISTEN (GW/0022-6319) [01773914] **4971**

JUNGE LITERATUR AUS OSTERREICH (AU) [09031719] **3401**

JUNGE UNION DEUTSCHLANDS See JAHRBUCH - JUNGE UNION DEUTSCHLANDS **2281**

JUNGE WELT (GW) [01782511] **1065**

JUNIATA NEWS (US) [12295338] **5737**

JUNIATA SENTINEL (MIFFLINTOWN, PA. : 1955) (US) [14388977] **5737**

JUNIOR BOOK AWARDS (US) [06370018] **3458**

JUNIOR BOOKSHELF (UK/0022-6505) [01782381] **1072**

JUNIOR BOWLER (US/0273-9100) [01783325] **4902**

JUNIOR CHAMBER OF COMMERCE FOR LONDON See ANNUAL REVIEW - THE JUNIOR CHAMBER OF COMMERCE FOR LONDON **818**

JUNIOR EDUCATION (UK) **1759**

JUNIOR EDUCATION SPECIAL See JUNIOR PROJECTS **1899**

JUNIOR (HAGERSTOWN, MD.) (US/0748-6928) [11000155] **4971**

JUNIOR HIGH CREATIVE TEACHING AIDS (US/0190-2644) [04681973] **1899**

JUNIOR HIGH MAGAZINE ABSTRACTS CEASED. (US/1045-5493) [20143572] 1759, **1795**

JUNIOR HIGH SCHOOL LIBRARY CATALOG (US) [02263136] **418**

JUNIOR HIGH, SENIOR YOUTH TEACHER See LIFELINES FOR YOUTH TEACHER **4973**

JUNIOR HIGH TEACHER (US/0744-8813) [08623268] **1899**

JUNIOR HISTORIAN See TEXAS HISTORIAN, THE **2763**

JUNIOR HOCKEY ACTION (CN/0826-4279) [11193127] **4902**

JUNIOR LEAGUE REVIEW CEASED. (US/0274-8584) [06657033] **5559**

JUNIOR MODE (CN/1183-6547) [25066577] **2282**

JUNIOR PHILATELIC SOCIETY, LONDON See STAMP LOVER, THE **2787**

JUNIOR PROJECTS (UK) **1899**

JUNIOR SCHOLASTIC (US/0022-6688) [01782333] **1065**

JUNIOR SEARCH See MIDDLE SEARCH **1795**

JUNIOR SEARCH. [COMPUTER FILE] (US) **1759**

JUNIOR STUDENT (US/0277-917X) [07703250] **4971**

●JUNIOR STUDENT GUIDE (US/1059-3373) [24568241] 1759, **4971**

●JUNIOR TEACHER GUIDE (US/1059-3322) [24568106] 1759, **4971**

JUNIOR TEACHER (SPRINGFIELD, MO.) (US/0277-9161) [07712283] **1899**

●JUNIOR TENNIS (US/1074-0554) [29601262] **4902**

JUNIOR TRAIL (US) 1065, **5062**

JUNIOR TRAILS (US/0022-6718) [04074386] **4971**

JUNKAN SEIGYO (JA/0389-1844) [I03891844] **3601**

JUNNAN NUIDAIJI (KO/0253-6250) [08983951] **3601**

JUNSHIN GAKUHO (JA/0911-0682) [I09110682] **2849**

JUNTA DE ESTUDIOS HISTORICOS DE ENTRE RIOS See REVISTA - JUNTA DE ESTUDIOS HISTORICOS DE ENTRE RIOS **2758**

JUNTA DE ESTUDIOS HISTORICOS DE MENDOZA See REVISTA DE LA JUNTA DE ESTUDIOS HISTORICOS DE MENDOZA **4171**

JUNTA TRIBUNE-DEMOCRAT, LA (US/1056-4616) [21427442] **5636**

JUNTENDO IGAKU (JA/0022-6769) [09938055] **3601**

JURA : JURISTISCHE AUSBILDUNG (GW/0170-1452) [05896190] **2990**

JURA (SWITZERLAND) See JOURNAL OFFICIEL DE LA REPUBLIQUE ET CANTON DU JURA **2990**

JURIDICA (MX) [02253811] **2990**

JURIDICAL REVIEW, THE (UK/0022-6785) [01782259] **2990**

JURIDISCHE BIBLIOTHECARIS, DE (NE/0167-8477) [08200877] **3221**

JURIMETRICS (CHICAGO, ILL.) (US/0897-1277) [05266384] 5122, **2990**

JURIS (US/0022-6807) [01783426] **2990**

JURIS-CLASSEUR : BAIL A LOYER (FR) **2990**

JURIS-CLASSEUR COLLECTIVITES LOCALES (FR/0758-671X) [I0758671X] **2990**

JURIS-CLASSEUR DE DROIT COMPARE (FR) [01754904] **3131**

JURIS-CLASSEUR DE DROIT INTERNATIONAL (FR/0750-8239) [I07508239] **3131**

JURIS-CLASSEUR DE LA SECURITE SOCIALE (FR/0750-8387) [I07508387] **2990**

JURIS-CLASSEUR : DROIT COMMERCIAL. TRAITE DES SOCIETES (FR) **2990**

JURIS-CLASSEURS. DROIT CIVIL See RECUEIL PERIODIQUE DES JURIS-CLASSEURS : DROIT CIVIL **3091**

JURIS NEWSLETTER (US) [03305270] **2990**

JURIS QUAESITOR (US/0146-2709) [02905300] **2990**

JURISCA DECISIONS DE LA COMMISSION DES AFFAIRS SOCIALES (CN) **4659**

JURISCIVEL DO S.T.F (BL) [01796541] **3090**

JURISDOCS (US/0162-3079) [04150561] **2990**

JURISELECTION (QUEBEC) (CN/1180-341X) [23659461] **2990**

JURISFEMME (OTTAWA) (CN/0835-0892) [16850330] 5559, **2990**

JURISPRUDENCE DU CONSEIL D'ETAT See EXECUTION DES DECISIONS DES JURISDICTIONS ADMINISTRATIVES **4647**

JURISPRUDENCE DU PORT D'ANVERS (BE) [02239882] **3181**

JURISPRUDENCE DU PORT D'ANVERS ET DES AUTRES VILLES COMMERCIALES ET INDUSTRIELLES DE LA BELGIQUE See JURISPRUDENCE DU PORT D'ANVERS **3181**

JURISPRUDENCE EN DROIT DU TRAVAIL. DECISIONS DES COMMISSAIRES DU TRAVAIL (CN/0707-2775) [08548705] **3150**

JURISPRUDENCE EXPRESS (CN/0705-3061) [04880292] **2991**

JURISPRUDENCE LOGEMENT (CN/0830-0380) [12366806] **2991**

JURISPRUDENCE (SCARBOROUGH, ONT.) See CASE LAW DIGESTS **2949**

JURISPRUDENCIA ARGENTINA (AG) [01639933] **2991**

JURISPRUDENCIA BRASILEIRA (BL) [08557186] **3090**

JURISPRUDENCIA BRASILEIRA CRIMINAL (BL) [09206526] **3107**

JURISPRUDENCIA CATARINENSE (BL) [02239895] **2991**

JURISPRUDENCIA DE SEGURIDAD SOCIAL Y SANIDAD (SP) [06832246] **2991**

JURISPRUDENCIA DEL TRIBUNAL SUPREMO DE PUERTO RICO (PR) [07821089] **2991**

JURISPRUDENTIE VOOR GEMEENTEN (NE/0924-4824) [I09244824] **4659**

JURIST (BADEN-BADEN, GERMANY) (GW) [07702583] **2991**

JURIST (WASHINGTON), THE (US/0022-6858) [01754914] 2991, **5031**

JURISTAT (CN/0715-271X) [09242077] 3168, **3081**

JURISTE (MONCTON) (CN/0829-5476) [13816880] 2991, **1092**

JURISTEN & KONOMEN See JURISTEN / DANMARKS JURIST- OG KONOMFORBUND **2991**

JURISTEN / DANMARKS JURIST- OG KONOMFORBUND (DK/0107-699X) [09925144] **2991**

JURISTENZEITUNG (GW/0022-6882) [01782801] **2991**

JURISTISCHE ABHANDLUNGEN (GW) [01587249] **2991**

JURISTISCHE ARBEITSBLATTER (GW) [04315341] **2991**

JURISTISCHE BLATTER (AU/0022-6912) [01639219] **2991**

JURISTISCHE RUNDSCHAU (GW/0022-6920) [01754917] **2991**

JURISTISCHE WOCHENSCHRIFT. See DEUTSCHES RECHT **2960**

JURISUTO (JA) [12491658] **2991**

JURNAL ANTROPOLOGI DAN SOSIOLOGI (MY/0126-5016) [05060783] 5250, **239**

JURNAL BAHASA MODEN : JURNAL PUSAT BAHASA, UNIVERSITI MALAYA (MY/0127-3957) [11229878] **3293**

JURNAL DEMOKRASI (IO) [25248411] **4510**

JURNAL DEWAN BAHASA (MY) [20981473] **3401**

JURNAL FILSAFAT (IO/0853-4454) [25361275] **4351**

JURNAL FIZIK MALAYSIA (MY) [11965553] **4410**

JURNAL INSTITUSI JURUTERA MALAYSIA (MY/0126-513X) [13568340] **1984**

JURNAL KEPENDIDIKAN (IO/0125-992X) [22687900] **1899**

JURNAL PENDIDIK DAN PENDIDIKAN : / JOURNAL TERBITAN PUSATT PENGAJIAN ILMU PENDIDIKAN / EDUCATORS AND EDUCATION : JOURNAL OF SCHOOL OF EDUCATIONAL STUDIES (MY) [22469581] **1759**

JURNAL PENELITIAN DAN PENGEMBANGAN KEHUTANAN (IO/0216-9525) [I02169525] **2386**

JURNAL PENELITIAN PASCA PANEN PERIKANAN (IO/0216-8316) [18334993] **2307**

JURNAL PENELITIAN PERIKANAN LAUT (IO/0216-7727) [13692615] **2307**

JURNAL PENYELIDIKAN MARDI (MY/0128-0686) [22337426] **101**

JURNAL PERKEMBANGAN PRODUKSI & TEKHNOLOGI INDUSTRI (IO) [08212222] 3482, **1614**

JURNAL SAINS - INSTITUT PENYELIDIKAN GETAH MALAYSIA (MY/0126-9569) [08542187] **5122**

JURNAL SAINS NUKLEAR MALAYSIA (MY) [16236490] **4448**

JURNAL SEJARAH MELAKA (MY/0126-8988) [04219542] **2656**

JURNAL STUDI AMERIKA / UNIVERSITAS INDONESIA, PROGRAM PASCASARJANA KAJIAN WILAYAH AMERIKA (IO) [24222316] **2743**

JURNAL VETERINAR MALAYSIA (MY) [22343623] **5515**

JURONG INDUSTRIES DIRECTORY (SI) [09368868] **1614**

JURUPA THIS WEEK (US) **5636**

JURY: A HANDBOOK OF LAW AND PROCEDURE, THE (CN) **2991**

JURY (NEW YORK, N.Y.) (US) [11552971] **2991**

JURY TRIALS AND TRIBULATIONS, INC (US/0889-6003) [14102941] **2991**

JURY VERDICTS WEEKLY (US/0888-0646) [08095336] **2991**

JUS (PE) [02241963] **2991**

JUS GENTIUM (IT/0022-6963) [01754921] **3131**

JUS. JURISTISCHE SCHULUNG (GW/0022-6939) [01783212] **2991**

JUS MEDICUM (BE/0775-0803) [12155454] **2991**, **3741**

JUS (MILAN, ITALY) (IT/0022-6955) [01754920] **1833**

JUSER (LOS ANGELES, CALIF.) (US/0888-9007) [13447411] **2769**

JUSHO KAJIN SHIRIZU (JA) [01797300] **3465**

JUSQU'A LA MORT ACCOMPAGNER LA VIE (FR/0768-6625) [I07686625] **3601**

JUSSENS VENNER (NO/0022-6971) [I00226971] **2991**

JUST A BITE (UK) [06438564] **5071**

JUST ABOUT MUSIC (CN) [04259259] **4127**

JUST BETWEEN FRIENDS (CN/0849-5718) [21348880] **2489**

JUST BETWEEN US (US/1052-3758) [22271281] **3465**

JUST B'TWX US *CEASED.* (US/0075-4587) [01773915] **3221**

JUST CAUSE (CN/0824-281X) [10156746] **4390**, **2991**

JUST COMPENSATION (US/0738-6494) [01754951] **4840**, **2991**

JUST CROSSSTITCH (US/0883-0797) [12048160] **5184**

JUST GO! *See* ECO TRAVELER **5469**

JUST GO! (US/1050-639X) [21569159] **5482**

JUST HORSIN' AROUND (US/1041-2786) [18706415] **2800**

JUST-IN-TIME & QUICK RESPONSE NEWS (US/1061-6888) [25406307] **843**

JUST NEWS (CN/1182-4301) [22768586] **4659**

JUST PEACE (WASHINGTON, D.C.) (US/1062-6255) [25419430] **4479**, **5559**

JUSTICE (CN/0225-4115) [06473954] **3168**

JUSTICE (JM) [01784043] **4971**

JUSTICE & PEACE REVIEW (PH/0116-6360) [21208492] **4510**

JUSTICE EXPENDITURE AND EMPLOYMENT EXTRACTS : DATA FROM THE ANNUAL GENERAL FINANCE AND EMPLOYMENT SURVEYS (US) [13001237] **3168**

JUSTICE FOR CHILDREN *CEASED.* (US/0888-9120) [13222920] **3121**

JUSTICE INSTITUTE OF BRITISH COLUMBIA *See* ANNUAL REPORT - JUSTICE INSTITUTE OF BRITISH COLUMBIA **2934**

JUSTICE INSTITUTE OF BRITISH COLUMBIA. LIBRARY *See* AUDIO VISUAL CATALOGUE / LIBRARY, JUSTICE INSTITUTE OF BRITISH COLUMBIA **408**

JUSTICE LEAGUE INTERNATIONAL (US/0896-3282) [17008710] **4862**

JUSTICE (NEW YORK, N.Y. 1919) (US/0022-7013) [02277370] **1682**

●JUSTICE OF THE PEACE & LOCAL GOVERNMENT LAW (UK/1351-5756) [29978607] **2991**, **4659**

JUSTICE OF THE PEACE (CHICHESTER) (UK/0141-5859) [01783893] **2991**

JUSTICE OF THE PEACE REPORTS (CHICHESTER, WEST SUSSEX) (UK/0264-3731) [09428463] **2991**

JUSTICE PROFESSIONAL, THE (US/0888-4315) [13570635] **2991**

JUSTICE QUARTERLY (US/0741-8825) [10232906] **2991**

JUSTICE (QUEBEC) *CEASED.* (CN/0707-8501) [08941190] **2991**

JUSTICE REPORT (CN/0823-9436) [12782284] **3168**

JUSTICE REPORT (CN/0823-9436) [12782287] **3168**

JUSTICE RESEARCH NOTES (CN/1181-9243) [23659081] **2991**

JUSTICE (SOCIETY) *See* ANNUAL REPORT / JUSTICE SOCIETY **2934**

JUSTICE SYSTEM JOURNAL, THE (US/0098-261X) [02241130] **3141**

JUSTICE TRENDS (AT/0157-6011) [I01576011] **4510**

JUSTICE (WASHINGTON, D.C.) (US/1056-8905) [23444099] **2992**

JUSTICE WATCH / COMMITTEE FOR PUBLIC JUSTICE, INC *SUSPENDED.* (US/0891-9224) [08342260] **2992**

JUSTICIA (NEW YORK) (US/0195-3737) [05436809] **1682**

JUSTICIA Y PAZ (MX) [16521598] **4510**

JUSTICIA Y PAZ / COMITE PRO JUSTICIA Y PAZ DE GUATEMALA (MX) [18937798] **4510**

JUSTICIELE KINDERBESCHERMING (NE/0168-5783) [05809968] **3168**, **3081**

JUSTIFICATIONS OF APPROPRIATION ESTIMATES FOR COMMITTEES ON APPROPRIATIONS - UNITED STATES DEPT. OF EDUCATION (US/8756-2979) [10246451] **1865**

JUSTIN G. SCHILLER, LTD *See* CHAPBOOK MISCELLANY **3374**

JUSTINIAN (AT/0157-5317) [I01575317] **2992**

JUSTIS [COMPUTER FILE] : CELEX, OFFICIAL LEGAL DATABASE OF THE EUROPEAN COMMUNITIES (UK) [23154064] **2992**

JUSTITIA (US) [04314720] **3141**

JUSTITIELE VERKENNINGEN (NE) [02322910] **3107**

JUSTUF; DAS JURAMAGAZIN (GW) **2992**

JUTAKU KINYU KOKO *See* JUTAKU KINYU KOKO NEMPO **795**

JUTAKU KINYU KOKO NEMPO (JA) [02811894] **795**

JUTAKU SANGYO HANDOBUKKU (JA) [03718436] **618**

JUTA'S SOUTH AFRICAN AND RHODESIAN INCOME TAX SERVICE : INCOME TAX TABLES AND COMPUTATIONS FOR REPUBLIC OF SOUTH AFRICA, SOUTH WEST AFRICA, UNITED KINGDOM, RHODESIA (SA) [01792955] **4735**

JUTA'S SOUTH AFRICAN INCOME TAX SERVICE. INCOME TAX TABLES, RATES, REBATES AND COMPUTATIONS FOR REPUBLIC OF SOUTH AFRICA, SOUTH WEST AFRICA, FEDERATION OF RHODESIA AND NYASALAND, UNITED KINGDOM *See* JUTA'S SOUTH AFRICAN AND RHODESIAN INCOME TAX SERVICE : INCOME TAX TABLES AND COMPUTATIONS FOR REPUBLIC OF SOUTH AFRICA, SOUTH WEST AFRICA, UNITED KINGDOM, RHODESIA **4735**

JUTE AND JUTE FABRICS, BANGLADESH (BG/1010-3791) [04600104] **5353**

JUTE DEVELOPMENT JOURNAL (II) [08789900] **101**

JUTE MARKETS & PRICES *See* WORLD FIBRE NEWS **5360**

JUVENILE AND ADULT CORRECTIONAL DEPARTMENTS, INSTITUTIONS, AGENCIES, AND PAROLING AUTHORITIES, UNITED STATES AND CANADA *See* DIRECTORY, JUVENILE & ADULT CORRECTIONAL DEPARTMENTS, INSTITUTIONS, AGENCIES & PAROLING AUTHORITIES / AMERICAN CORRECTIONAL ASSOCIATION **3163**

JUVENILE & FAMILY COURT JOURNAL (US/0161-7109) [03932682] **3121**

JUVENILE AND FAMILY COURT NEWSLETTER (US/0162-9859) [04251312] **3121**

●JUVENILE AND FAMILY JUSTICE TODAY (US/1062-2926) [25569067] **2992**

JUVENILE AND FAMILY LAW DIGEST (US/0279-2257) [07646369] **3121**

JUVENILE COURT REPORT (LINCOLN) (US/0362-918X) [05254973] **3121**

JUVENILE COURT STATISTICS (US) [01795308] **3168**

JUVENILE COURT STATISTICS AND ADOPTION PETITIONS IN KANSAS (US) [01783993] **3081**

JUVENILE COURT STATISTICS (WASHINGTON) (US/0091-3278) [01786924] **3168**, **3081**

JUVENILE JUSTICE AND DELINQUENCY PREVENTION PLAN (US) [08081890] **3168**

JUVENILE JUSTICE DIGEST (US/0094-2413) [03783468] **3168**

JUVENILE JUSTICE INFORMATION SYSTEM : (JJIS) / KANSAS BUREAU OF INVESTIGATION, STATISTICAL ANALYSIS CENTER (US) [10540256] **3168**

JUVENILE LAW NEWSLETTER (US/0095-697X) [01796709] **3121**

JUVENILE LAW REPORTS (US/0276-9603) [05794657] **3121**

JUVENILE MERCHANDISING (US/0022-7161) [04122455] **929**

JUVENILE SERVICES ADMINISTRATION ANNUAL REPORT (US) [22928703] **3168**

JUVENTUD TECNICA (CU/0449-4555) [02628249] **5122**

JUZEN IGAKKAI ZASSHI (JA/0022-7226) [09726097] **3601**

JUZNOSLOVENSKI FILOLOG (YU/0350-185X) [01605317] **3293**

JW PLUS (CN/0823-1346) [10061637] **2915**

JYLLANDS-POSTEN (DK/0109-1182) [I01091182] **5799**

JYOTISHA-KALPA (II) [01783507] **390**

JYOTSNA (II) [04078094] **3401**

JYVASKYLA CROSS-LANGUAGE STUDIES (FI/0358-6464) [I03586464] **3293**

K.A.R.D. FILES DYE DATA, THE (US/0899-1723) [11886399] **2456**

K.A.R.D. FILES PRESENTS ABSHIRE ABSTRACTS, THE (US/0899-1685) [16865441] **2456**

K.A.R.D. FILES PRESENTS BLAKELEY BANDWAGON, THE (US/0899-1715) [18033159] **2456**

K.A.R.D. FILES PRESENTS LUTTRELL LINEAGES & DATA, THE (US/0899-1731) [18032605] **2456**

K.A.R.D. FILES PRESENTS RAMBO REFERENCES, THE (US/0899-174X) [10905669] **2456**

K & I.E. EN C. KUNST EN CULTUUR (BE/0022-7277) [03100543] **323**

K & K (DK) [22750186] **3293**, **3401**

K.G.M.T.I. KOZLEMENYEI (HU/0302-8720) [01793765] **4006**, **1984**

K. HUMANISTIKA VETENSKAPSSAMFUNDET I UPPSALA *See* ARSBOK / KUNGL. HUMANISTISKA VETENSKAPS-SAMFUNDET I UPPSALA **2842**

K : INTERNATIONAL CERAMICS MAGAZINE (IT/1120-2343) [22037646] **2592**

K-PLASTIC- & KAUTSCHUK-ZEITUNG EXPORT ISSUE (GW/0177-0608) [I01770608] **5076**

K.R. CAMA ORIENTAL INSTITUTE *See* JOURNAL OF THE K.R. CAMA ORIENTAL INSTITUTE **4971**

K-THEORY (NE/0920-3036) [15320999] **3516**

K.V.P. MANITOBA NEWS (CN/0828-5942) [12093224] **3896**

K.V.S.A. GUIDE TO THE NORTH SEA CANAL, AMSTERDAM, YMIUDEN, VELSEN, BEVERWYK, ZAANSTAD, AND SCHIPOL AIRPORT (NE) [18294632] **5482**

KABBALAH (IS/0334-6994) [13577240] **4242**

KABLAN VEHA-BONEH, HA- (IS) [01798548] **618**

KABOTAJ VE ULUSLARARAS DENIZ TASMAS ISTATISTIKLERI (TU) [18804239] **5450**

KABUKA SORAN (JA) [03233320] **905**

KABUKI (JA) [04038461] **4527**

KABUPATEN DAERAH TINGKAT II KENDAL DALAM ANGKA *See* KABUPATEN KENDAL DALAM ANGKA **5330**

KABUPATEN GRESIK DALAM ANGKA (IO) [09727397] **5330**

KABUPATEN KENDAL DALAM ANGKA (IO) [11977941] **5330**

KABUPATEN KLATEN DALAM ANGKA *See* KLATEN DALAM ANGKA **5330**

KACHESTVO PROMYSHLENNOI PRODUKTSII (RU) [20942955] **1614**

KACHIKU HANSHOKUGAKU ZASSHI (TOKYO. 1977) (JA/0385-9932) [06849183] **5589**

KACHIKU KOKINZAI KENKYUKAIHO (JA/0911-4319) [I09114319] **5515**

KADAMBINI (II) [01642702] **3401**

KADMOS (GW/0022-7498) [01754936] **272**

KADO: ART OF FLOWER ARRANGEMENT (JA) **2774**, **2435**

KADUNA, NIGERIA (STATE) *See* GAZETTE - KADUNA STATE OF NIGERIA **2973**

KAEBYOK UI SORI (KO) [08648440] **2505**

KAEDORIK TAEHAKKYO HANIN TONGMUNHOE *See* HOEBO **1750**

KAEHYOK SINANG (KO) [07718507] **4971**

KAEKSOK (KO) [10707197] **386**

KAEN KASET (TH/0125-0485) [I01250485] **101**

KAENJU (JA) [02802582] **1570**

KAET MAGAZINE (US/1045-5744) [19945536] **1134**

KAGAKU GIJUTSU BUNKEN SOKUHO. BUTSURI, OYO BUTSURI-HEN (JA/0011-3336) [I00113336] **4410**, **4426**

KAGAKU GIJUTSU BUNKEN SOKUHO. KAGAKU. KAGAKU KOGYO HEN : KOKUNAI-HEN (JA/0011-3271) [06796058] **983**, **2014**, **2005**

KAGAKU GIJUTSU BUNKEN SOKUHO: KANKYO KOGAI HEN (JA) [02245148] **2234**, **2184**

KAGAKU

KAGAKU GIJUTSU KENKYU CHOSA HOKOKU / HENSHU SORIFU TOKEIKYOKU (JA) [04399351] **5122**

KAGAKU GIJUTSU KENKYU CHOSA NI FUTAISURU ENERUGI KENKYU CHOSA HOKOKU / HENSHU, SORIFU TOKEIKYOKU (JA) [09122439] **1949**

KAGAKU GIJUTSU KENKYUJO HOKOKU / JOURNAL OF THE NATIONAL CHEMICAL LABORATORY FOR INDUSTRY (JA/0388-3213) [09546022] **983**

KAGAKU GIJUTSU ROPPO / HENSHU KAGAKU GIJUTSUCHO (JA) [08909682] **5122**

KAGAKU GIJUTSUCHO MUKI ZAISHITSU KENKYUJO YORAN CEASED. (JA) [02247073] **1984**

KAGAKU GIJUTSUCHO SHIGEN CHOSAJO KIHO. / THE QUARTERLY REPORT OF [THE] NATIONAL INSTITUTE OF RESOURCES (JA) [03819709] **2197**

KAGAKU KEISATSU KENKYUJO See KAGAKU KEISATSU KENKYUJO NEMPO **3168**

KAGAKU KEISATSU KENKYUJO NEMPO (JA) [02497056] **3168**

KAGAKU KEIZAI (JA/0453-0683) [09600103] **1026**

KAGAKU KOGAKU (JA/0375-9253) [09486742] **2014**

KAGAKU KOGAKU RONBUNSHU (JA/0386-216X) [04258947] **2014**

KAGAKU KOGYO (JA/0451-2014) [09719734] **2014**

KAGAKU KYOIKU (JA) [10280235] **983**

KAGAKU (KYOTO) (JA/0451-1964) [02243893] **983**

KAGAKU/NINGEN (JA/07901551] **5232**

KAGAKU RYOHO NO RYOIKI (1987) (JA/0913-2384) [27464907] **3601**

KAGAKU: SCIENCE (JA) **5122**

KAGAKU SHINBUN (JA) [09950340] **5122**

KAGAKU SHOHO (JA) [03093476] **983**

KAGAKU SOCHI (JA/0368-4849) [08702745] **1026**

KAGAKU TO KOGYO (TOKYO) (JA/0022-7684) [09544572] **983**

KAGAKU TO SEIBUTSU (JA/0453-073X) [09448182] **101**, **490**

KAGAKUHIN TORIHIKI YORAN (JA) [01797071] **1614**

KAGAKUSHI KENKYU (JA/0022-7692) [01754939] **5122**

KAGAN CABLE TV FINANCIAL DATABOOK, THE (US) [16348427] 795, **1134**

KAGAN CENSUS OF CABLE AND PAY TV. UPDATE, THE (US/0736-7015) [09169873] **1134**

KAGAN MEDIA INDEX, THE (US/0893-2700) [15481089] **1614**

KAGAWA DAIGAKU. KYOIKUGAKUBU See KAGAWA DAIGAKU KYOIKUGAKUBU KENKYU HOKOKU : GEIJUTSU SAKUHIN SHU **355**

KAGAWA DAIGAKU KYOIKUGAKUBU KENKYU HOKOKU : GEIJUTSU SAKUHIN SHU (JA) [04879321] **355**

KAGAWA DAIGAKU. NOGAKUBU See KAGAWA DAIGAKU NOGAKUBU KIYO **102**

KAGAWA DAIGAKU. NOGAKUBU See KAGAWA DAIGAKU NOGAKUBU GAKUZYUTU HOKOKU **101**

KAGAWA DAIGAKU NOGAKUBU GAKUZYUTU HOKOKU (JA/0368-5128) [09733728] **101**

KAGAWA DAIGAKU NOGAKUBU GAKUZYUTU HOKOKU (JA/0368-5128) [01771517] **101**

KAGAWA DAIGAKU NOGAKUBU KIYO (JA/0453-0764) [04610402] **102**

KAGENNA CEASED. (SA) **2499**

KAGOSHIMA DAIGAKU KYOIKUGAKUBU KYOIKU KENKYUJO KENKYU KIYO See KENKYU KIYO. SHIZEN KAGAKU HEN / NATURAL SCIENCE. BULLETIN OF THE FACULTY OF EDUCATION, KAGOSHIMA UNIVERSITY. KAGOSHIMA DAIGAKU KYOIKUGAKUBU **5123**

KAGOSHIMA DAIGAKU NOGAKUBU GAKUJUTSU HOKOKU (JA/0453-0845) [01641503] **102**

KAGOSHIMA DAIGAKU SUISANGAKUBU KIYO (JA/0453-087X) [07633708] **2307**

KAGOSHIMA, JAPAN (PREFECTURE) See KANKYO HAKUSHO **2234**

KAGOSHIMA-KEN CHAGYO SHIKENJO KENKYU HOKOKU (JA/0911-4785) [l09114785] 2368, **102**

KAGOSHIMA-KEN EISEI KENKYUJOHO (1983) (JA/0289-7512) [27456977] **4788**

KAGOSHIMA-KEN KANKYO SENTA SHOHO (JA/0910-5158) [27475249] **2176**

KAGOSHIMA-KEN KOGYO GIJUTSU SENTA KENKYU HOKOKU (JA/0916-3905) [l09163905] **5122**

KAGOSHIMA-KEN KOGYO SHIKENJO See NEMPO **5132**

KAGOSHIMA-KEN NOGYO SHIKENJO See KAGOSHIMA-KEN NOGYO SHIKENJO KENKYU HOKOKU **102**

KAGOSHIMA-KEN NOGYO SHIKENJO KENKYU HOKOKU (JA/0388-8215) [03356173] **102**

KAHANE (US/0276-2714) [04999224] **2266**

KAHANI (II) [01784287] **3401**

KAHOL VE-LAVAN (IS) [06637003] **2656**

KAHPER JOURNAL (RICHMOND, KY.) (US/0022-7269) [07526268] **1856**

KAHPERD JOURNAL (BOWLING GREEN, KY.) (US/1071-2577) [11673061] **1856**

KAHPERD JOURNAL (PITTSBURG, KAN.) (US/0893-3316) [11429801] **1857**

KAHTOU (CN/0827-2077) [11762366] **2536**

KAIBOGAKU ZASSHI (JA/0022-7722) [07511738] **3679**

KAICHU KOEN JOHO (JA) [04853738] **462**

KAIGAI DENKI TSUSHIN (JA) [07381082] **1159**

KAIGAI GENGOGAKU JOHO (JA) [08696025] **3293**

KAIGAI KENSETSU KYORYOKUKAI See JAPAN'S CONSTRUCTION TODAY **618**

KAIGAI KENSETSU KYORYOKUKAI. JAPAN'S CONSTRUCTION See JAPAN'S CONSTRUCTION TODAY **618**

KAIGAI KOGYO JIJO CHOSA HOKOKUSHO: INDO, PAKISUTAN, BANGURADISSHU (JA) [02441478] **1614**

KAIGAI KOGYO JIJO CHOSA HOKOKUSHO: MADAGASUKARU, SUWAJIRANDO (JA) [02441477] **1614**

KAIGAI KOGYO JIJO CHOSA HOKOKUSHO. MARESHIA, TAI OKOKU, CHIRI KYOWAKOKU, EKUADORU KYOWAKOKU, TANZANIA RENGO KYOWAKOKU, EJIPUTO ARABU KYOWAKOKU / HENSHU, KINZOKU KOGYO JIGYODAN SHIRYO SENTA (JA) [10004323] **1440**

KAIGAI KOGYO JIJO CHOSA HOKOKUSHO: NAIJERIA, GANA, KOTO JIBOARU (JA) [02805653] **1614**

KAIGAI KOGYO JUJO CHOSA HOKOKUSHO : AMERIKA, MARESHIA, SURIRANKA, TAI, KANKOKU (JA) [06913466] **1440**

KAIGAI SEIKATSU NO TEBIKI (JA) [01790136] **1984**

KAIGAI SHAKAI HOSHO JOHO (JA/0911-484X) [08985245] **5294**

KAIGAI SHIJO HAKUSHO. DAI 1 BUNSATSU: SEKAI BOEKI NO GENJO (JA) [01796930] **1637**

KAIGAI SHRIYO RISUTO (JA) [05760218] **2142**

KAIGAI TOSHI KENKYUJO HO (JA) [06898776] **905**

KAIGAI TOZAN KENKYUKAI See KAIGAI TOZAN KENKYUKAI SHIRYO **2567**

KAIGAI TOZAN KENKYUKAI SHIRYO (JA) [01790320] **2567**

KAIGAN SHOKO KENCHI SENTA CHOI NEMPO (JA) [03677052] **1451**

KAIGAN SHOKO KENSHI SENTA See KAIGAN SHOKO KENSHI SENTA CHOI NEMPO **1451**

KAIGI DAIGAKKO See KAIGI DAIGAKKO KENKYU HOKOKU **1833**

KAIGI DAIGAKKO KENKYU HOKOKU (JA/0288-3708) [04698255] **1833**

KAIHATSU KOHO (JA) [02245318] **2826**

KAIHATSU RONSHU (JA) [01797389] **2826**

KAIHATSU TO KENSHU (JA) [07243981] 5560, **4206**

KAIHATSU TO KOGAI (JA) [04900213] **2197**

KAIHO (JA/0372-7785) [02830156] 2386, **102**

KAIHO - DAIGAKU KIJUN KYOKAI (JA) [06794842] **1833**

KAIHO - KANTO GAKUIN DAIGAKU KOGAKUBU KOGAKKAI (JA/02245297] **5122**

KAIHO NO HI O MOYASE (JA) [01790154] **5250**

KAIIN JITTAI CHOSA (JA) [04821173] **3860**

KAIIN MEIBO - BANKOKU NIHONJIN SHOKO KAIGISHO. / LIST OF MEMBERS - JAPANESE CHAMBER OF COMMERCE, BANGKOK (JA) [05091021] **820**

KAIJO HOAN DAIGAKKO KENKYU HOKOKU. RIKOGAKU-KEI (JA/0287-2951) [l02872951] 1984, **5122**

KAIJO HOAN TOKEI NEMPO (JA) [02441327] **5450**

KAIKU (TORONTO) (CN/1187-3949) [25314120] **2266**

KAILASH (NP/0377-7499) [01790576] **239**

KAINAN TOKEI NENPO (JA) [02245290] **4178**

KAINDL-ARCHIV : MITTEILUNGEN DER RAIMUND FRIEDRICH KAINDL GESELLSCHAFT (GW) [10088289] **3708**

KAIROS (FR/1148-9227) [21437393] **4351**

KAIROS (OAKLAND, CALIF.) (US/0277-710X) [07632993] **3345**

KAIROS : REVISTA PUBLICADA POR EL SEMINARIO TEOLOGICO CENTROAMERICANO (GT) [21792432] **5017**

KAIROS; ZEITSCHRIFT FUER RELIGIONSWISSENSCHAFT UND THEOLOGIE (AU/0022-7757) [01783032] **4971**

KAIROSHITSU GIHO - TOKYO DAIGAKU GENSHIKAKU KENKYUJO KAIROSHITSU (JA) [03493926] **2156**

KAISETSU KYOIKU ROPPO (JA) [04259970] **2992**

KAITE, EL (US/0741-1766) [10090001] **380**

KAIYO KAGAKU GIJUTSU SENTA See SHOZO GIJUTSU JOHO SHIRYO ICHIRAN **1457**

KAIYO KAGAKU GIJUTSU SENTA SHIKEN KENKYU HOKOKU (JA/0387-382X) [08672394] **1451**

KAIYO KAIHATSU KANKEI SHIRYO SOMOKUROKU (JA) [03208739] **1451**

KAIYO KAIHATSU NO GENJO TO TEMBO (JA) [01797303] **1416**

KAJAKS TRACK AND FIELD CLUB See ANNUAL - KAJAKS TRACK AND FIELD CLUB **4883**

KAJIAN MALAYSIA : JOURNAL OF MALAYSIAN STUDIES (MY/0127-4082) [11789732] 5207, **2656**

KAJOK KYEHOEK NONJIP (KO) [05189393] **589**

KAJONG CHOSON (KO) [11831499] **2505**

KAJU BYOGAICHU BOJO HANDOBUKKU (JA) [01799702] 4245, **2422**

KAJU SHIKENJO, HIRATSUKA, JAPAN See BULLETIN OF THE FRUIT TREE RESEARCH STATION. SERIES B. (OKITSU) **69**

KAJU SHIKENJO NYUSU (JA) [05189284] **2422**

KAJU SHIKENJO. OKITSU SHIJO See SHIKEN KENKYU NEMPO : BYOGAI, CHUGAI HEN **186**

KAKAO + ZUCKER (GW/0022-7838) [04818835] **2347**

KAKATIYA JOURNAL OF ENGLISH STUDIES (II) [03246825] **3401**

KAKEI CHOSA NENPO (JA) [07162626] **1501**

●KAKO (NEW YORK, N.Y.), LES (US/1061-351X) [25259759] **2536**

KAKTEEN UND ANDERE SUKKULENTEN (GW/0022-7846) [04068681] 2422, **516**

KAKU (JA) [05720518] **3401**

KAKU IGAKU (JA/0022-7854) [03735427] **3848**

KAKURIKEN KEDKYU HOKOKU (JA/0385-2105) [04621042] 1055, **4448**

KAKUSHOCHO KOHO YOTEI JIKO (JA) [04057829] **4659**

KAL KAN VIDEO FORUM (US) **5515**

KALAKSHETRA QUARTERLY (II) [06009454] **323**

KALAMA (II) [10453557] **3401**

KALAMA (CALCUTTA, INDIA) See KALAMA **3401**

KALAMAZOO COLLEGE QUARTERLY (US/8750-5746) [11544380] **1833**

KALAMAZOO GAZETTE (1916) (US) [09940379] **5692**

KALAMAZOO LABOR MARKET REVIEW See KALAMAZOO'S LABOR MARKET NEWS **1682**

KALAMAZOO NATURE CENTER See NATURE CENTER NEWS **2200**

KALAMAZOO VALLEY FAMILY NEWSLETTER, THE CEASED. (US/0888-7861) [01784038] **2456**

●KALAMAZOO'S LABOR MARKET NEWS (US) [25954178] **1682**

KALATHOS : REVISTA DEL SEMINARIO DE ARQUEOLOGIA Y ETNOLOGIA TUROLENSE, COLEGIO UNIVERSITARIO DE TERUEL (SP) [08407687] 2266, **272**

KALAVRITT / KALAVRTTA (II) [08621592] **355**

●KALBOTYRA / VILNIUSSKII UNIVERSITET (LI/0202-3296) [30531800] **3293**

KALE (TZ) [01784718] **2641**

KALEIDOSCOPE / A SPECTRUM OF ARTICLES FOCUSING ON FAMILIES (US) **2282**

KALEIDOSCOPE (AKRON, OHIO), THE (US/0748-8742) [10224877] **3401**

KALEIDOSCOPE (BOSTON) (US/0095-5213) [01796786] **1759**

KALEIDOSCOPE (MADISON, WIS.) (US/0893-6226) [15604769] **1759**

KALEIDOSCOPE REGINA (CN/0848-0893) [I08480893] 4090, **5122**

KALENDAR (US) [21129775] **2266**

KALENDAR HOLOSU SPASYTELJA (CN/0381-5110) [02587842] **5039**

KALENDAR KANADSKEJ SLOVENSKEJ LIGY (CN/0410-935X) [07966364] **2695**

KALENDAR KSL (1980) (CN/0229-6152) [07966360] **2695**

KALENDAR SVITLA (CN/0380-0962) [02578638] **5031**

KALENDAR ZNAMENATELNYKH I PAMIATNYKH DAT (RU/0130-2051) [07962408] **2621**

KALENDARZ DZIENNIKA POLSKIEGO (UK) [13106544] **196**

KALENDARZ POLSKI NA ROK ... (US) [07675016] **1927**

KALENDER FUER DEN BIOGARTEN (GW/0931-380X) [I0931380X] **462**

KALENDER / OSTERREICHISCHER KAMERADSCHAFTSBUND (AU) [11481923] **4048**

KALEVALASEURAN VUOSIKIRJA (FI/0355-0311) [01782476] **3401**

KALFOU (CN/0820-8417) [10105582] **2743**

KALI UND STEINSALZ (GW/0022-7951) [01587345] **1440**

KALIFORNIISKII VESTNIK (US) [09170570] **2266**

KALIKASAN, THE PHILIPPINE JOURNAL OF BIOLOGY (PH/0115-0553) [02990220] **462**

KALIMANTAN SELATAN. KANTOR SENSUS DAN STATISTIK *See* INDIKATOR EKONOMI KALIMANTAN SELATAN **1567**

KALINANGAN (PH) [02363035] **2656**

KALIS SHOPPING CENTER LEASING DIRECTORY (US/0899-8930) [18252513] **1501**

KALISPELL'S WEEKLY NEWS (US) [12871032] **5705**

KALKI (ORADELL) **CEASED**. (US/0022-7994) [02603716] **3345**

KALLIOPE (US/0735-7885) [08981808] 5560, **323**

KALMIOPSIS (ASHLAND, OR.) (US/1055-419X) [23169114] **516**

KALO SURAJA (II) [09648652] **3465**

KALONA NEWS, THE (US) [15803144] **5671**

KALORI; JOURNAL OF THE MUSEUMS ASSOCIATION OF AUSTRALIA (AT/0047-312X) [06781046] 355, **4090**

KALOS (US/0145-2398) [02421089] 5187, **2795**

KALTE UND KLIMATECHNIK (GW/0343-2246) [03739490] **2606**

KALULU (MW) [03217203] **2321**

KAMAAINA'S GUIDE TO HAWAII'S DIVE SHOPS & TOUR OPERATIONS (US/1056-3385) [23669613] **5482**

KAMAI FORUM (US/1066-9353) [27095481] **5636**

KAMAR DAGANG DAN INDUSTRI JAWA BARAT DAFTAR ANGGOTA KAMAR DAGANG DAN INDUSTRI DI JAWA BARAT **818**

KAMENA (PL) [01784002] **3401**

KAMENNYI POIAS / KURGANSKAIA, ORENBURGSKAIA, CHELIABINSKAIA PISATELSKIE ORGANIZATSII (RU) [20341290] **3401**

KAMER VAN KOOPHANDEL EN FABRIEKEN VOOR AMSTERDAM *See* VERSLAG / KAMER VAN KOOPHANDEL EN FABRIEKEN VOOR AMSTERDAM **856**

KAMERA UND SCHULE (GW/0022-8109) [09074528] **4371**

KAMERUN : EINFUHRPROGRAMM (GW) [04339309] **843**

KAMERUN : ENERGIEWIRTSCHAFT (GW) [05064424] **1949**

KAMERUN : WIRTSCHAFTLICHE ENTWICKLUNG (GW) [02520040] **1570**

KAMGYUL (KO) [04940775] **2422**

KAMI PA GIKYOSHI (JA/0022-815X) [06585066] **4234**

KAMI, PARUPU GIJUTSU TAIMUSU (JA/0453-1507) [10285990] **4234**

KAMI PARUPU KOGYO SETSUBI CHOSA HOKOKUSHO (JA) [02243597] **4234**

KAMI PARUPU KOGYO SETSUBI SHOSA HOKOKUSHO *See* KAMI PARUPU SEIZO SETSUBI CHOSA HOKOKUSHO / TSUSHO SANGYO DAIJIN KAMBO CHOSA TOKEIBU HEN **4234**

KAMI PARUPU SEIZO SETSUBI CHOSA HOKOKUSHO / TSUSHO SANGYO DAIJIN KAMBO CHOSA TOKEIBU HEN (JA) [07436209] **4234**

KAMI STRATEGIC ASSUMPTIONS (US) **1501**

KAMLOOPS LIVING **CEASED**. (CN/1191-0135) [25589890] **5482**

KAMMER DER GEWERBLICHEN WIRTSCHAFT FUR TIROL *See* BERICHT - KAMMER DER GEWERBLICHEN WIRTSCHAFT FUR TIROL **1548**

KAMMER DER GEWERBLICHEN WIRTSCHAFT FUR WIEN (AUSTRIA) WIEN *See* STATISTIK - KAMMER DE GEWERBLICHEN WIRTSCHAFT FUR WIEN **5342**

KAMMER DER TECHNIK. BEZIRKSVERBAND SUHL *See* TAGUNGSBAND - KAMMER DER TECHNIK SUHL **5161**

KAMMER FUER ARBEITER UND ANGESTELLTE FUER VORARLBERG *See* TATIGKEITSBERICHT / KAMMER FUER ARBEITER UND ANGESTELLTE FUER VORARLBERG **1713**

KAMMER FUR ARBEITER UND ANGESTELLTE FUR NIEDEROSTERREICH. JAHRESBERICHT *See* JAHRBUCH DER KAMMER FUR ARBEITER UND ANGESTELLTE FUER NIEDEROSTERREICH **1681**

KAMMER FUR ARBEITER UND ANGESTELLTE FUR NIEDEROSTERRICH *See* JAHRBUCH DER KAMMER FUER ARBEITER UND ANGESTELLTE FUER NIEDEROSTERREICH **1681**

KAMMER FUR LAND- UND FORSTWIRTSCHAFT IN SALZBURG *See* BERICHT - KAMMER FUR LAND- UND FORSTWIRTSCHAFT IN SALZBURG **65**

KAMOURASKA (LA POCATIERE) (CN/0707-7157) [04746998] **5787**

KAMPANA (NEW YORK, N.Y.) (US/0022-8206) [03098868] **2266**

KAMPANJE! (NO) [06565780] 950, **929**

KAN (JA) [01790282] **2656**

KAN-CHIANG CHING CHI (CC) [11948214] **1501**

KAN-SU CHIAO YU (CH) [08912545] **1759**

KAN-SU HUA PAO GANSUHUABAO (CC) [11654366] **2656**

KANABEC COUNTY TIMES (US) [01754957] **5696**

KANADA EXPLORER (CN/1183-5877) [25423266] **5482**

KANADA KURIER (ALBERTA AUSG.) (CN/0712-8878) [08858310] **5787**

KANADA KURIER (AUSGABE FUER BRITISH COLUMBIA) (CN/0712-8886) [08724207] **5787**

KANADA KURIER (MANITOBA AUSG.) (CN/0712-8894) [08858294] **5787**

KANADA KURIER (MONTREAL AUSG.) (CN/0712-8908) [08724200] **5787**

KANADA KURIER (ONTARIO AUSGABE) (CN/0712-8916) [08730541] **5787**

KANADA KURIER (OTTAWA AUSG.) (CN/0712-8924) [08858312] **5787**

KANADA KURIER (SASKATCHEWAN AUSG.) (CN/0712-8932) [08858306] **5787**

KANADA KURIER (TORONTO AUSGABE) (CN/0712-8940) [08777612] **5788**

KANADA, WIRTSCHAFT IN ZAHLEN / BUNDESSTELLE FUR AUSSENHANDELSINFORMATION (GW) [09345553] **1570**

KANADA : WIRTSCHAFTLICHE ENTWICKLUNG (GW) [03527939] **1501**

KANADAN SUOMALAINEN (CN/0827-9012) [11919031] **2536**

KANADIER (GW/0175-6346) [11690806] **5801**

KANADSKE LISTY (TORONTO. 1973) (CN/0449-7368) [01606315] **5788**

KANAGAWA DAIGAKU KOGAKU KOGAKU KENKYUJO SHOHO (JA/0387-0324) [10462831] 1984, **5122**

KANAGAWA DAIGAKU KOGAKUBU KENKYU HOKOKU (JA/0368-5381) [10279742] **1984**

KANAGAWA-KEN EISEI KENKYUJO KENKYU HKOKU (JA/0303-0350) [01328740] **4788**

KANAGAWA-KEN KOGAI SENTA *See* KANAGAWA-KEN KOGAI SENTA NEMPO **2234**

KANAGAWA-KEN KOGAI SENTA KENKYU HOKOKU (JA/0389-9365) [10337816] **2176**

KANAGAWA-KEN KOGAI SENTA NEMPO (JA) [02246304] **2234**

KANAGAWA-KEN NOGYO SOGO KENKYUJO KENKYU HOKOKU (JA/0388-8231) [10927144] **102**

KANAGAWA-KEN SANGYO SENTA *See* KANAGAWA-KEN SANGYO SENTA SHIKEN KENKYU KOKOKU **5589**

KANAGAWA-KEN SANGYO SENTA SHIKEN KENKYU KOKOKU (JA) [01797138] **5589**

KANAGAWA-KEN SUISAN SHIKENJO KENKYU HOKOKU (JA) [07474031] **2307**

KANAGAWA-KEN TAIKI OSEN CHOSA KENKYU HOKOKU (JA) [10282952] **2234**

KANAGAWA-KEN TANSUIGYO ZOSHOKU SHIKENJO *See* KANAGAWA-KEN TANSUIGYO ZOSHOKU SHIKENJO HOKOKUSHO **2307**

KANAGAWA-KEN TANSUIGYO ZOSHOKU SHIKENJO HOKOKUSHO (JA) [05791137] **2307**

KANAGAWA KENRITSU EISEI TANKI DAIGAKU KIYO (JA/0388-6042) [I03886042] **3914**

KANAGAWA KENRITSU HAKUBUTSUKAN KENKYU HOKOKU. SHIZEN KAGAKU (JA/0453-1906) [01961060] **4166**

KANAGAWA KENRITSU MAIZO BUNKAZAI SENTA NENPO (JA) [10398688] **2656**

KANAGAWA KENSHI KENKYU / KANAGAWA KENSHI HENSHU IINKAI HEN (JA) [07982490] **2656**

KANAGAWA SHIGAKU : KANAGAWA SHIKA DAIGAKU GAKKAI ZASSHI (JA/0454-8302) [10333195] **1329**

KANARENINSTITUT *See* I.C. NACHRICHTEN **269**

KANATA SOSIG (CN/0228-0221) [06757593] **5788**

KANAVA (HELSINKI. 1973) (FI/0355-0303) [01640377] **3345**

KANAWA MAGAZINE FOR RECREATIONAL PADDLING IN CANADA (CN/1189-5152) [26758158] **4874**

KANAWHA VALLEY GENEALOGICAL SOCIETY *See* JOURNAL OF THE KANAWHA VALLEY GENEALOGICAL SOCIETY, THE **2455**

KANAZAWA DAIGAKU BUNGAKUBU RONSHU. BUNGAKUKA HEN (JA) [08861947] **3293**

KANAZAWA DAIGAKU BUNGAKUBU RONSHU. KODO KAGAKUKA HEN (JA) [08861889] **5232**

KANAZAWA DAIGAKU BUNGAKUBU RONSHU. SHIGAKUKA HEN (JA) [08861904] **2621**

KANAZAWA DAIGAKU KEIZAI GAKUBU RONSHU (JA) [08863561] **1593**

KANAZAWA DAIGAKU KEIZAI RONSHU (JA/0289-0615) [07105682] **1501**

KANAZAWA DAIGAKU. KYOIKU GAKUBU *See* KANAZAWA DAIGAKU KYOIKUGAKUBU KIYO : KYOIKU KAGAKU JIMBUN KAGAKU SHAKAI KAGAKU HEN **1833**

KANAZAWA DAIGAKU KYOIKUGAKUBU *See* KANAZAWA DAIGAKU KYOIKUGAKUBU KIYO : SHIZEN KAGAKU HEN **1833**

KANAZAWA DAIGAKU. KYOIKUGAKUBU. KANAZAWA DAIGAKU DAIGAKU KYOIKUGAKUBU KIYO *See* KANAZAWA DAIGAKU KYOIKUGAKUBU KIYO : SHIZEN KAGAKU HEN **1833**

KANAZAWA DAIGAKU KYOIKUGAKUBU KIYO : JIMBUN SHAKAI KAGAKU *See* KANAZAWA DAIGAKU KYOIKUGAKUBU KIYO : KYOIKU KAGAKU JIMBUN KAGAKU SHAKAI KAGAKU HEN **1833**

KANAZAWA DAIGAKU KYOIKUGAKUBU KIYO : KYOIKU KAGAKU JIMBUN KAGAKU SHAKAI KAGAKU HEN (JA) [01790146] **1833**

KANAZAWA DAIGAKU KYOIKUGAKUBU KIYO : SHIZEN KAGAKU HEN (JA/0387-0995) [01790145] 5122, **1833**

KANAZAWA DAIGAKU. KYOYOBU *See* KANAZAWA DAIGAKU KYOYOBU RON SHU: JIMBUN KAGAKU HEN **2849**

KANAZAWA DAIGAKU KYOYOBU RON SHU: JIMBUN KAGAKU HEN (JA) [01799674] **2849**

KANAZAWA IKA DAIGAKU ZASSHI (JA/0385-5759) [04677178] **3601**

KANAZAWA KOKUZEIKYOKU TOKEISHO (JA) [01799701] **4735**

●KANCH. NEW DELHI (II) [I09713751] **1984**

KANCHI KENCHIKU (JA/0301-9934) [01796948] **618**

KANCHO EIZEN (JA) [03535190] **618**

KANE : HITOTSUBASHI DAIGAKU FUZOKU TOSHOKAN HO (JA/0387-8783) [07860187] **3221**

KANE REPUBLIC (KANE, PA. : 1912) (US) [14961502] **5737**

KANE'S BEVERAGE WEEK (US/0882-2573) [12349167] **2368**

KANG CHAN WEN I YEN CHIU (CC) [09934929] **323**

KANG SHENG SU (CC/0254-6116) [09552421] **4313**

KANGO GIJUTSU: JAPANESE JOURNAL OF NURSING ART (JA) **3860**

KANGO TENBO (JA/0385-549X) [04690088] **3860**

KANHISTIQUE (US/0738-9736) [07516769] 251, **2743**

KANI HOKEN YUBIN NENKIN FUKUSHI JIGYODAN *See* JIGYO YORAN - KANI HOKEN YUBIN NENKIN FUKUSHI JIGYODAN **1681**

KANI SEIMEI HOKEN NO SHIBORITSU SHOGAI HASSEIRITSU NI KANSURU CHOSA (JA) [01797212] **2886**

KANINA (CR/0378-0473) [03618682] **323**

KANKAKEE DAILY JOURNAL (US) **5660**

KANKAKEE VALLEY NEWS-POST, THE (US) [15000995] **5665**

KANKAVATI (II) [02246617] **3401**

KANKO RODO (JA) [06004057] **1682**

KANKYO GIJUTSU (JA/0388-9459) [10333253] 1984, **2197**

KANKYO HAKUSHO (AOMORI-KEN, JAPAN) (JA) [08147157] **2235**

KANKYO HAKUSHO (EHIME-KEN, JAPAN) (JA) [09123193] **2235**

KANKYO HAKUSHO (FUKUSHIMA-KEN, JAPAN. KOGAI KISEIKA) (JA) [07808711] **2235**

KANKYO HAKUSHO (NAGANO-SHI, JAPAN) (JA) [10105597] **1570**

KANKYO HAKUSHO (SHIZUOKA-KEN, JAPAN) (JA) [07846390] **2235**

KANKYO HENIGEN KENKYU (JA/0910-0865) [27475186] **2176**

KANKYO HOZEN NO GENKYO TO TAISAKU (JA) [04509590] **2335**

KANKYO IGAKU KENKYUJO NENPO (JA/0369-3570) [10461656] **3601**

KANKYO KAGAKU SOGO KENKYUJO NENPO (JA/0285-5895) [09580525] **2176**

KANKYO KOGAI NENKAN (JA) [01797093] **3113**

KANKYO TO KOGYO O MUSUBU KAI *See* DNIAS ANNUAL REPORT + 1 **5101**

KANO. NIGERIA (STATE) *See* ESTIMATES OF THE GOVERNMENT - KANO. NIGERIA (STATE) **4722**

KANO STUDIES (NR/0567-4840) [02232838] **2499**

KANON : YEARBOOK OF THE SOCIETY OF THE LAW OF THE ORIENTAL CHURCHES (AU) [05534006] **5039**

KANOZOIKUM UND BRAUNKOHLEN DER TURKEI (GW) [02694252] **1385**

KANPUR UNIVERSITY RESEARCH JOURNAL (SCIENCE) (II) [18300016] **5122**

KANSAI BYOCHUGAI KENKYUKAI HO (JA/0387-1002) [10335293] **2422**

KANSAI DAIGAKU, OSAKA. KOGAKUBU *See* TECHNOLOGY REPORTS OF KANSAI UNIVERSITY **1998**

KANSAI DAIGAKU, OSAKA KOGYO GIJUTSU KENKYUJO *See* KOGIKEN NYUSU **5124**

KANSAI IKA DAIGAKU *See* KANSAI IKA DAIGAKU ZASSHI **3601**

KANSAI IKA DAIGAKU ZASSHI (JA/0022-8400) [09419609] **3601**

KANSAI UNIVERSITY REVIEW OF LAW AND POLITICS (JA/0388-886X) [07123186] 4479, **2992**

KANSAI ZOSEN KYOKAI SHI / JOURNAL OF THE KANSAI SOCIETY OF NAVAL ARCHITECTS, JAPAN (JA/0389-9101) [29191004] **5450**

KANSALLIS-OSAKE-PANKKI *See* ECONOMIC REVIEW - KANSALLIS-OSAKE-PANKKI **1558**

KANSANEDUSTAJAIN VAALIT (FI) [03249128] **4659**

KANSANELAKELAITOKSEN JULKAISUJA. AL (FI/0355-4813) [21076850] **3601**

KANSANELAKELAITOKSEN JULKAISUJA. M (FI/0355-4821) [06301751] 3601, **2886**

KANSANELAKELAITOKSEN JULKAISUJA. ML (FI/0355-483X) [06299695] **5294**

KANSANTALOUDELLINEN AIKAKAUSKIRJA (FI/0022-8427) [01782480] 688, **1501**

KANSANTALOUS (FI) [20144900] **4735**

KANSAS *See* KANSAS EMPLOYMENT SECURITY LAW, G.S. 1949 ..., THE **3150**

KANSAS (US/0022-8435) [01789265] **2536**

KANSAS *See* KANSAS STATUTES ANNOTATED **2992**

KANSAS. ADULT AUTHORITY *See* BIENNIAL REPORT - KANSAS ADULT AUTHORITY **3158**

KANSAS ADVISORY COUNCIL ON AGING *See* ANNUAL REPORT / KANSAS ADVISORY COUNCIL ON AGING **3749**

KANSAS AGRICULTURAL EXPERIMENT STATION *See* AGRICULTURAL RESEARCH IN KANSAS **51**

KANSAS AGRICULTURE (US) [21461593] **102**

KANSAS ANNUAL FINANCIAL REPORT FOR PERIOD JULY 1, ... TO JUNE 30, ... / STATE OF KANSAS, DEPARTMENT OF ADMINISTRATION, DIVISION OF ACCOUNTS AND REPORTS (US) [21656201] **4735**

KANSAS ANTHROPOLOGIST, THE (US/1069-0379) [21137064] **239**

KANSAS ASSOCIATION FOR HEALTH, PHYSICAL EDUCATION AND RECREATION. K.A.H.P.E.R. JOURNAL *See* KAHPERD JOURNAL (PITTSBURG, KAN.) **1857**

KANSAS BANKER, THE (US/0022-8478) [04074467] **795**

KANSAS BAR ASSOCIATION *See* JOURNAL OF THE KANSAS BAR ASSOCIATION, THE **2989**

KANSAS. BUREAU OF HEALTH EDUCATION *See* FILM AND PAMPHLET CATALOG **4810**

KANSAS. BUREAU OF REGISTRATION AND HEALTH STATISTICS *See* MONTHLY SUMMARY OF VITAL STATISTICS **4810**

KANSAS BUSINESS NEWS *SUSPENDED.* (US/0199-3607) [05802894] **688**

KANSAS BUSINESS REVIEW (LAWRENCE. 1977) (US/0164-8632) [04859956] **688**

KANSAS BUSINESS TEACHER / KANSAS BUSINESS TEACHERS ASSOCIATION, THE (US) [01641484] 1759, **688**

KANSAS CHIEF, THE (US) [11086868] **5676**

KANSAS CITY AVIATION (US/0273-9895) [07051058] **27**

KANSAS CITY BUSINESS JOURNAL (US/0734-2748) [08722326] **688**

KANSAS CITY COMMERCE (US/1056-6015) [23744827] **820**

KANSAS CITY GENEALOGIST, THE (US/0451-3991) [01783300] **2456**

KANSAS CITY GRAIN MARKET REVIEW *CEASED.* (US/0738-7296) [04527146] 202, **1501**

KANSAS CITY GRAIN REPORTER *See* KANSAS CITY GRAIN MARKET REVIEW **1501**

KANSAS CITY HOMES & GARDENS (US) **2422**

KANSAS CITY JEWISH CHRONICLE (US/0022-8524) [04083614] **5676**

KANSAS CITY KANSAN, THE (US) [08776666] **5676**

KANSAS CITY MAGAZINE & THE TOWN SQUIRE (US/0896-8292) [17303465] **2743**

● KANSAS CITY METRO BUSINESS DIRECTORY (US/1069-6334) [26134050] **688**

KANSAS CITY, MO. CITY MANAGER *See* MESSAGE OF THE CITY MANAGER TO THE CITY COUNCIL SUBMITTING THE EXECUTIVE BUDGET **4737**

● KANSAS CITY SMALL BUSINESS MONTHLY (US/1068-2422) [27482776] **688**

KANSAS CITY STAR, THE (US/0745-1067) [03555868] **5703**

KANSAS. COMMISSION ON ALCOHOLISM *See* KANSAS STATE PLAN FOR COMPREHENSIVE ALCOHOL ABUSE AND ALCOHOLISM PREVENTION, TREATMENT AND REHABILITATION **1346**

KANSAS COURT RULES AND PROCEDURE (US/0748-5255) [10338586] **3141**

KANSAS. DEPT. OF ADMINISTRATION. DIVISION OF ACCOUNTS AND REPORTS *See* KANSAS ANNUAL FINANCIAL REPORT FOR PERIOD JULY 1, ... TO JUNE 30, ... / STATE OF KANSAS, DEPARTMENT OF ADMINISTRATION, DIVISION OF ACCOUNTS AND REPORTS **4735**

KANSAS. DEPT. OF ADMINISTRATION. DIVISION OF ACCOUNTS AND REPORTS *See* COMPREHENSIVE MANAGEMENT REPORT **741**

KANSAS. DEPT. OF HEALTH AND ENVIRONMENT *See* BALANCED PERSPECTIVE ON : THE HEALTH OF KANSANS **4768**

KANSAS. DEPT. OF SOCIAL AND REHABILITATION SERVICES *See* KANSAS FINAL COMPREHENSIVE SOCIAL SERVICE PLAN, TITLE XX SOCIAL SECURITY ACT **5294**

KANSAS DIRECTORY (US/0190-5171) [01494154] **4659**

KANSAS DIRECTORY OF COMMERCE, THE (US/1042-0355) [18661968] **820**

KANSAS DIRECTORY OF PUBLIC OFFICIALS *See* DIRECTORY OF KANSAS PUBLIC OFFICIALS **4643**

KANSAS DIRECTORY. SUPPLEMENT (US/0360-6252) [02240777] **4659**

KANSAS. DIVISION OF PROPERTY VALUATION *See* STATISTICAL REPORT OF PROPERTY ASSESSMENT AND TAXATION **4848**

KANSAS. DIVISION OF THE BUDGET *See* GOVERNOR'S BUDGET REPORT, PREPARED BY THE DIVISION OF THE BUDGET, THE **4729**

KANSAS ECONOMIC INDICATORS (US) [02666419] 688, **1501**

KANSAS. ECONOMIC OPPORTUNITY OFFICE *See* YEAR END REPORT - KANSAS ECONOMIC OPPORTUNITY OFFICE **1528**

KANSAS EDUCATIONAL DIRECTORY (US/0099-0728) [02239904] **1759**

● KANSAS EMPLOYMENT LAW LETTER (US/1074-0422) [29583228] **3150**

KANSAS EMPLOYMENT SECURITY LAW, G.S. 1949 ..., THE (US) [01782452] **3150**

KANSAS ENGLISH (US/0739-0157) [09680960] **1899**

KANSAS ENTOMOLOGICAL SOCIETY *See* JOURNAL OF THE KANSAS ENTOMOLOGICAL SOCIETY **5611**

KANSAS ENVIRONMENT (US/0279-5078) [06575825] **2235**

KANSAS FARMER (US/0022-8583) [04152266] **102**

KANSAS FINAL COMPREHENSIVE SOCIAL SERVICE PLAN, TITLE XX SOCIAL SECURITY ACT (US) [03285976] 2886, **5294**

KANSAS FOLKLORE SOCIETY *See* NEWSLETTER - KANSAS FOLKLORE SOCIETY **2323**

KANSAS GEOGRAPHER, THE *SUSPENDED.* (US) [01645497] **2567**

KANSAS GEOLOGICAL SURVEY *See* GROUND-WATER SERIES (LAWRENCE, KAN.) **1414**

KANSAS GEOLOGICAL SURVEY *See* STORIES OF RESOURCE-FULL KANSAS **1398**

KANSAS GOVERNMENT JOURNAL (US/0022-8613) [04083802] **4659**

KANSAS. GOVERNOR *See* GOVERNOR'S LEGISLATIVE MESSAGE AND BUDGET REPORT, THE **4652**

● KANSAS HEALTH CARE IN PERSPECTIVE (US/1065-4186) [26605147] **4788**

● KANSAS HERITAGE (US) [27210012] **2743**

KANSAS HIGHWAY & TRAFFIC STATISTICS / GOVERNOR'S COMMITTEE ON CRIMINAL ADMINISTRATION, STATISTICAL ANALYSIS CENTER (US) [08357298] **5401**

KANSAS. HIGHWAY SAFETY COORDINATING OFFICE *See* MERGE **5441**

KANSAS HISTORY (US/0149-9114) [03578697] **2743**

KANSAS IN PERSPECTIVE (US/1065-545X) [25070887] **5330**

● KANSAS INSURANCE AGENT & BROKER (US/1069-1847) [27955408] **2886**

KANSAS. INSURANCE DEPT *See* REPORT OF THE COMMISSIONER OF INSURANCE - KANSAS **2892**

KANSAS. INSURANCE DEPT *See* ANNUAL REPORT OF THE KANSAS INSURANCE DEPARTMENT **2873**

KANSAS-IOWA ENVIRONMENTAL LAW LETTER (US/1057-4174) [24033393] **3113**

KANSAS JOURNAL (US) [09844249] **5232**

KANSAS JOURNAL OF LAW & PUBLIC POLICY, THE (US/1055-8942) [23369008] **2992**

KANSAS KIN (US/0451-4084) [01755014] **2456**

KANSAS LEGAL DIRECTORY, THE (US) [01783927] **2992**

KANSAS LEGISLATIVE HANDBOOK (US) **4659**

KANSAS. LEGISLATURE. HOUSE OF REPRESENTATIVES *See* RULES AND DIRECTORY **4684**

KANSAS. LEGISLATURE. LEGISLATIVE COORDINATING COUNCIL *See* REPORT ON KANSAS LEGISLATIVE INTERIM STUDIES TO THE LEGISLATURE **3038**

KANSAS. LEGISLATURE. LEGISLATIVE DIVISION OF POST AUDIT *See* BIENNIAL REPORT / LEGISLATIVE POST AUDIT COMMITTEE AND LEGISLATIVE DIVISION OF POST AUDIT **739**

KANSAS. LEGISLATURE. LEGISLATIVE RESEARCH DEPT *See* APPROPRIATIONS REPORT / KANSAS LEGISLATIVE RESEARCH DEPARTMENT **4711**

KANSAS MEDICINE (US/8755-0059) [11241715] **3601**

KANSAS MUSIC REVIEW (US/0022-8702) [01782555] **4127**

KANSAS, NEBRASKA ZIP+4 STATE DIRECTORY (US) [11647412] **1145**

KANSAS NURSE, THE (US/0022-8710) [01280310] **3860**

KANSAS. OFFICE OF CONSUMER CREDIT COMMISSIONER *See* REPORT ON KANSAS UNIFORM CONSUMER CREDIT CODE **808**

KANSAS. OFFICE OF JUDICIAL ADMINISTRATION *See* EXECUTIVE SUMMARY OF THE KANSAS JUDICIAL BRANCH / OFFICE OF JUDICIAL ADMINISTRATION, AN **3140**

KANSAS. OFFICE OF THE OMBUDSMAN FOR CORRECTIONS *See* ANNUAL REPORT TO THE CITIZENS' ADVISORY BOARD ON CORRECTIONS **3157**

KANSAS OPTOMETRIC ASSOCIATION *See* KANSAS OPTOMETRIC JOURNAL **4216**

KANSAS OPTOMETRIC JOURNAL (US/1063-1623) [07241771] **4216**

KANSAS ORNITHOLOGICAL SOCIETY *See* BULLETIN - KANSAS ORNITHOLOGICAL SOCIETY **5616**

KANSAS PUBLISHER, THE (US/0022-8737) [04089497] **2921**

KANSAS QUARTERLY (US/0022-8745) [01755018] 2849, **2536**

KANSAS REALTOR (US/0279-9960) [07420184] **4840**

KANSAS REGISTER (US/0744-2254) [08073290] **4659**

KANSAS RESTAURANT (US/0022-8753) [04089585] 2347, **5071**

KANSAS SCHOOL NATURALIST *CEASED.* (US/0022-877X) [01755019] **1899**

KANSAS SPORTS (US/0894-4431) [16080931] **4902**

KANSAS. STATE ADVISORY COUNCIL FOR VOCATIONAL EDUCATION *See* ANNUAL EVALUATION OF VOCATIONAL EDUCATION IN KANSAS **1910**

KANSAS. STATE BIOLOGICAL SURVEY *See* TECHNICAL PUBLICATIONS OF THE STATE BIOLOGICAL SURVEY OF KANSAS **474**

KANSAS STATE BOARD OF AGRICULTURE *See* KANSAS AGRICULTURE **102**

KANSAS. STATE BOARD OF ENGINEERING EXAMINERS *See* REPORT AND ROSTER : REGISTERED LAND SURVEYORS **2030**

KANSAS. STATE BOARD OF INDIGENTS' DEFENSE SERVICES *See* ANNUAL REPORT TO THE GOVERNOR AND LEGISLATURE - STATE BOARD OF INDIGENTS' DEFENSE SERVICES (KANSAS) **4035**

KANSAS. STATE CONSERVATION COMMISSION *See* CONSERVATION IN KANSAS **2190**

KANSAS. STATE DEPT. OF EDUCATION *See* TITLE VI-B, EDUCATION OF THE HANDICAPPED ACT : ANNUAL PROGRAM PLAN **1886**

KANSAS. STATE DEPT. OF EDUCATION *See* ANNUAL PROGRAM PLAN FOR FISCAL YEARS - KANSAS. STATE DEPT. OF EDUCATION **1725**

KANSAS. STATE DEPT. OF EDUCATION *See* ANNUAL PROGRAM PLAN : TITLE I, ESEA - KANSAS. STATE DEPT. OF EDUCATION **1875**

KANSAS STATE DEPT. OF EDUCATION *See* STATE PLAN FOR VOCATIONAL EDUCATION **1916**

KANSAS. STATE DEPT. OF EDUCATION. STATISTICAL SERVICES SECTION. SELECTED SCHOOL STATISTICS *See* PUBLIC SCHOOL REPORT (TOPEKA, KAN. : 1978) **1776**

KANSAS. STATE DEPT. OF PUBLIC INSTRUCTION *See* TEXTBOOKS SUITABLE FOR USE IN KANSAS SCHOOLS **1787**

KANSAS. STATE DEPT. OF SOCIAL WELFARE *See* JUVENILE COURT STATISTICS AND ADOPTION PETITIONS IN KANSAS **3081**

KANSAS STATE HISTORICAL SOCIETY MIRROR *See* KANSAS HERITAGE **2743**

KANSAS STATE PLAN FOR COMPREHENSIVE ALCOHOL ABUSE AND ALCOHOLISM PREVENTION, TREATMENT AND REHABILITATION (US/0098-003X) [03336392] **1346**

KANSAS. STATE REGISTRATION AND EXAMINING BOARD FOR ARCHITECTS *See* REPORT - KANSAS. STATE REGISTRATION AND EXAMINING BOARD FOR ARCHITECTS **307**

KANSAS STATE UNIVERSITY. COOPERATIVE EXTENSION SERVICE *See* EXTENSION ENGINEERING IN KANSAS; R **1542**

KANSAS. STATE UNIVERSITY OF AGRICULTURE AND APPLIED SCIENCE, MANHATTAN. CENTER FOR ENERGY STUDIES *See* REPORT - CENTER FOR ENERGY STUDIES, KANSAS STATE UNIVERSITY **1994**

KANSAS STATISTICAL ABSTRACT (US/0453-2600) [01167610] **5330**

KANSAS STATUTES ANNOTATED (US) [01754971] **2992**

KANSAS STOCKMAN, THE (US/0022-8826) [04089701] **213**

KANSAS TOO (US) **2536**

KANSAS. UNIVERSITY *See* UNIVERSITY OF KANSAS PALEONTOLOGICAL CONTRIBUTIONS. ARTICLE **4231**

KANSAS. UNIVERSITY. MEDICAL CENTER *See* BULLETIN - UNIVERSITY OF KANSAS MEDICAL CENTER, THE **3777**

KANSAS VETERINARIAN (US) [01644622] **5515**

KANSAS VOCATIONAL EDUCATION *See* STATE PLAN FOR VOCATIONAL EDUCATION **1916**

KANSAS WAGE SURVEY / RESEARCH AND ANALYSIS SECTION, DEPARTMENT OF HUMAN RESOURCES, DIVISION OF POLICY AND MANAGEMENT ANALYSIS (US) [03804153] **1682**

KANSAS WILDLIFE & PARKS (US/0898-6975) [17864734] **2197**

KANSAS WORKING PAPERS IN LINGUISTICS (US/1043-3805) [05106933] **3293**

KANSAS WORKS (US) **5676**

KANSAS WRITER'S MARKET (US/0146-3217) [02923465] **3401**

KANSATIETEELLINEN ARKISTO ... (FI/0355-1830) [04378145] **240**

KANSEN, ENSHO, MENEKI (JA/0387-1010) [10278811] **3674**

KANSENSHOGAKU ZASSHI (JA/0387-5911) [10335385] **4788**

KANT-STUDIEN (GW/0022-8877) [01782290] **4351**

KANTO GAKUIN DAIGAKU. KOGAKKAI *See* KANTO GAKUIN DAIGAKU KOGAKUBU KOGAKKAI KOEN ROMBUN SHU **1984**

KANTO GAKUIN DAIGAKU KOGAKUBU *See* KENKYU HOKOKU - KANTO GAKUIN DAIGAKU KOGAKUBU **1984**

KANTO GAKUIN DAIGAKU KOGAKUBU KOGAKKAI *See* KAIHO - KANTO GAKUIN DAIGAKU KOGAKKAI **5122**

KANTO GAKUIN DAIGAKU KOGAKUBU KOGAKKAI KOEN ROMBUN SHU (JA) [04980581] **1984**

KANTO GAKUIN DAIGAKU. OSAWA KINEN KENCHIKU SETSUBI KOGAKU KENKYJO *See* KENCHIKU SETSUBI KOGAKU KENKYUJO HO **2606**

KANTO KO-SHIN-ETSU-SEI CHIIKI KEIZAI GAIKAN (JA) [02243340] **1570**

KANTO RINBOKU IKUSHUJO NENPO (JA/0288-6510) [102886510] **2386**

KANTO SEIKEI SAIGAI GEKA GAKKAI ZASSHI (JA/0389-7087) [10335505] **3883**

KANTO SHIN-ETSU KOKUZEIKYOKU TOKEISHO (JA) [03054850] **4735**

KANTO YUSEIKYOKU TOKEI NEMPO (JA) [01797416] **1145**

KANTON BERN (N.G.) LEERWOHNUNGSBESTAND ... / AMT FUR STATITISK DES KANTONS BERN (SZ) [10686720] **2826**

KANTOOR EN EFFICIENCY (NE) **4212**

KANTOORMACHINE-INDUSTRIE / CENTRAAL BUREAU VOOR DE STATISTIEK, HOOFDAFDELING STATISTIEKEN VAN INDUSTRIE EN BOUWNIJVERHEID (NE) [10528205] **1570**

KANTOORMANAGEMENT (AMSTERDAM) (NE/0925-6032) [I09256032] **874**

KANTOVSKII SBORNIK / MINISTERSTVO VYSSHEGO I SREDNEGO SPETSIALNOGO OBRAZOVANIIA RSFSR, KALININGRADSKII GOSUDARSTVENNYI UNIVERSITET (RU/0207-6918) [08980177] **4351**

KANTSTUDIEN. ERGANZUNGSHEFTE / IM AUFTRAGE DER KANT-GESELLSCHAFT (GW) [01929555] **4351**

KANTU (PE) [15730958] **323**

KANZA ... / PITTSBURG STATE UNIVERSITY (US) [04954494] **1833**

KANZEI CHUO BUNSEKISHOHO (JA/0286-1933) [102861933] **5122**

KANZEI KANKEI KOBETSU TSUTATSU SHU (JA) [05055810] **843**

KANZO (TOKYO, JAPAN : 1960) (JA/0451-4203) [10278870] **3601**

KANZUME JIHO (JA) [11411377] **2347**

KAO CHA YU YEN CHIU / SHANG-HAI TZU JAN PO WU KUAN (CC) [11047742] **4167**

KAO-HSIUNG I HSUEH KO HSUEH TSA CHIH (CH/0257-5655) [13469191] **3601**

KAO-HSIUNG SHIH CHENG FU ... SHIH CHENG CHI HUA / KAO-HSIUNG SHIH CHENG FU PIEN (CH) [08268894] **4660**

KAO-HSIUNG SHIH (TAIWAN) *See* KAO-HSIUNG SHIH CHENG FU ... SHIH CHENG CHI HUA / KAO-HSIUNG SHIH CHENG FU PIEN **4660**

KAO KU (CC/0453-2899) [01586773] **272**

KAO KU HSUEH CHI KAN / KAO KU PIEN CHI PU PIEN (CH) [08868835] **272**

KAO KU JEN LEI HSUEH KAN / KUO LI TAIWAN TA HSUEH (CH/0077-5843) [01755028] **240**

KAO KU YU WEN WU (CC) [07130144] **272**

KAO YUAN SHENG WU HSUEH CHI KAN (CC) [09181376] **462**

KAOGU XUEBAO (CC/0453-2902) [01640680] **272**

KAOGU YU WENWU (CC/1000-7830) [I10007830] **272**

KAPITAALGOEDERENVOORRAAD / CENTRAAL BUREAU VOOR DE STATISTIEK, HOOFDAFDELING STATISTIEKEN VAN KAPITAALGOEDERENVOORRAAD EN BALANSEN (NE/0923-9669) [25699032] **905**

KAPITAL (NO/0332-5423) [I03325423] **795**

KAPITAL DATA (NO/0800-3173) [I08003173] **688**

KAPITALIZM (PL) [03620781] **1570**

● KAPITALMARKTSTATISTIK / DEUTSCHE BUNDESBANK (GW/0943-8769) [28005514] 795, 5330, **730**

KAPPA ALPHA JOURNAL, THE (US/0888-8868) [01782223] 1102, **5232**

KAPPA ALPHA (SOUTHERN ORDER) *See* KAPPA ALPHA JOURNAL, THE **5232**

KAPPA DELTA PI (HONOR SOCIETY) *See* KAPPA DELTA PI RECORD **1759**

KAPPA DELTA PI RECORD (US/0022-8958) [01755030] **1759**

KAPU (HU/0238-888X) [19816021] **2695**

KAR INTERNATIONAL (US/0732-1074) [08333678] **4480**

KARACHI. UNIVERSITY. DEPT. OF LIBRARY SCIENCE *See* REPORT OF THE LIBRARY SCIENCE DEPARTMENT **3245**

KARACHI UNIVERSITY JOURNAL OF SCIENCE (PK/0250-5363) [06784104] **5122**

KARADA NO KAGAKU (JA) [10335618] **3601**

KARAI OLI (CE) [03485836] **2656**

KARAMU (CHARLESTON, ILL.) (US/0022-8990) [02263195] 3465, **3401**

KARANKAWA KOUNTRY : A PUBLICATION OF CALHOUN COUNTY GENEALOGICAL SOCIETY (US) [15649912] **2456**

KARATE AND ORIENTAL ARTS (UK) [01794193] **4902**

KARATE, BUSHIDO (FR/1243-3853) [I12433853] **4902**

KARATE KEBEC (CN/0383-6517) [02915611] 2599, **4902**

KARATE, KUNG-FU ILLUSTRATED (US/0888-031X) [13227683] **4902**

KARATE MAGAZINE & ORIENTAL ARTS *See* KARATE AND ORIENTAL ARTS **4902**

KARATE PROFILES MADE IN AMERICA (US/1062-3558) [25595929] **4903**

● KARBO, ENERGOCHEMIA, EKOLOGIA (PL) [26134857] 1949, **1440**

KARD FILES ADAMSON ANCESTRY, THE (US/0899-1693) [18030764] **2456**

KARDIOLOGIA POLSKA (1957) (PL/0022-9032) [06522927] **3708**

KARDIOLOGIJA (RU/0022-9040) [01755033] **3708**

KARIKAZO *CEASED.* (US/0164-2537) [04610943] **2321**

KARJATALOUS (FI/0047-3251) [02313290] **196**

KARKA (TEL AVIV) (IS/0302-6566) [01784366] **2197**

KARL-MAY-GESELLSCHAFT   Alphabetical Title Index

KARL-MAY-GESELLSCHAFT *See* JAHRBUCH DER KARL-MAY-GESELLSCHAFT **3398**

KARLSRUHER BEITRAEGE (GW/0721-4979) [12544083] **2695**

KARLSRUHER JURISTISCHE BIBLIOGRAPHIE (GW/0453-3283) [01779454] **3081**

KARLSRUHER MANUSKRIPTE ZUR MATHEMATISCHEN UND THEORETISCHEN WIRTSCHAFTS- UND SOZIALGEOGRAPHIE (GW/0344-7073) [I03447073] **2567**

KARLSTAD NORTH STAR NEWS (US) [01755036] **5696**

KARMEL (BEIRUT, LEBANON) (SY) [08392368] **3401**

KARNATAK UNIVERSITY, DHARWAR, INDIA *See* JOURNAL OF THE KARNATAK UNIVERSITY. SCIENCE **5121**

KARNATAKA, INDIA. DEPT. OF ANIMAL HUSBANDRY AND VETERINARY SERVICES *See* ANNUAL REPORT OF THE DEPARTMENT OF ANIMAL HUSBANDRY AND VETERINARY SERVICES IN KARNATAKA, INDO-DANISH PROJECT HESSARGHATTA AND BANGALORE DAIRY, BANGALORE **5503**

KARNATAKA, INDIA. DEPT. OF PRISONS *See* ANNUAL REPORT - PRISONS DEPARTMENT (INDIA) **3157**

KARNATAKA, INDIA. LEGISLATURE. COMMITTEE ON THE WELFARE OF SCHEDULED CASTES AND SCHEDULED TRIBES *See* REPORT - KARNATAKA LEGISLATURE, COMMITTEE ON THE WELFARE OF SCHEDULED CASTES & SCHEDULED TRIBES **5305**

KARNATAKA, INDIA. LEGISLATURE. LEGISLATIVE ASSEMBLY. COMMITTEE OF PRIVILEGES *See* REPORT - KARNATAKA LEGISLATIVE ASSEMBLY, COMMITTEE OF PRIVILEGES **4680**

KARNATAKA, INDIA. PLANNING DEPT *See* ANNUAL PLAN - GOVERNMENT OF KARNATAKA, PLANNING DEPARTMENT **1546**

KARNATAKA, INDIA. PUBLIC WORKS DEPT. CHIEF ENGINEER, COMMUNICATIONS AND BUILDINGS *See* BUILDINGS STATISTICS IN KARNATAKA STATE **632**

KARNATAKA (INDIA). PUBLIC WORKS DEPT. STATISTICAL UNIT *See* ROAD STATISTICS IN KARNATAKA STATE **5402**

KARNATAKA LAW JOURNAL. SUPPLEMENT, THE (II) [03603723] **2992**

KARNATAKA STATE FINANCIAL CORPORATION *See* ANNUAL REPORT AND ACCOUNTS - KARNATAKA STATE FINANCIAL CORPORATION **770**

KARNATAKA STATE ROAD TRANSPORT CORPORATION *See* ADMINISTRATION REPORT - KARNATAKA STATE ROAD TRANSPORT CORPORATION **5375**

KARNES CITATION (KARNES CITY, TEX. : 1978) (US) [14442813] **5751**

KARNTNER HEIMATLEBEN (AU/0022-7560) [01783253] **2695**

KARNTNER MUSEUMSSCHRIFTEN (GW/0022-7587) [02219534] **4090**

KARNTNER SCHULVERSUCHSINFORMATIONEN (AU) [01794769] **1759**

KAROGS (RIGA) (LV/0132-6295) [01782659] **2518**

KAROLINSKA FORBUNDET, STOCKHOLM *See* KAROLINSKA FORBUNDETS ARSBOK **2518**

KAROLINSKA FORBUNDETS ARSBOK (SW/0348-9833) [01782420] **2518**

KARPATALJA : A KARPATALJAI MAGYAR KULTURALIS SZOVETSEG LAPJA (UN) [24357074] **2696**

KARSTENIA (FI/0453-3402) [01755037] **575**

KARSTOLOGIA (FR) [09523979] **1408**

KARSZT ES BARLANG (HU/0324-6221) [07149412] **1408**

KART OG PLAN (NO/0047-3278) [01783464] **2567**

KART SPORT (US/0744-5962) [08423211] **5418**

KART-TECH (US/0279-8816) [07332048] **4903**

KARTEI DER PRAKTISCHEN MEDIZIN (GW/0022-9113) [I00229113] **3601**

KARTEN (GW/0937-597X) [I0937597X] **795**

KARTER NEWS (US/0096-3216) [01798864] 5418, **4903**

KARTHAGO (FR/0453-3429) [01782958] **272**

KARTING (UK/0022-913X) **4903**

KARTING DIGEST (US/0192-1134) [04950440] **5418**

KARTINI (IO) [04249822] **5560**

KARTKATALOG / NORGES GEOGRAFISKE OPPMALING (NO) [10999487] **2580**

KARTOFEL I OVOSHCHI (RU/0022-9148) [03772762] **177**

KARTOFFELBAU (GW/0022-9156) [03772775] **177**

KARTOFFELFORSCHUNG AKTUELL (GW) **102**

KARTOGRAFISCH TIJDSCHRIFT (NE) [02401141] **2582**

KARTOGRAPHISCHE NACHRICHTEN (GW/0022-9164) [01782858] **2582**

KARTOPLIARSTVO (RU) [09844716] **2422**

KARUNUNGAN (PH) [13857523] **4351**

KARWEI (NE) 3995, **2901**

KARYA-KARYA GEREJA KATOLIK INDONESIA (IO) [03154651] **5031**

KARYOKU GENSHIRYOKU HATSUDEN (JA/0387-1029) [10356885] **4448**

KASAI : NIHON KASAI GAKKAISHI (JA/0449-9042) [10282906] **2291**

KASARINLAN (PH/0116-0923) [13077486] **2656**

KASEKI (JA/0022-9202) [09544997] **4227**

KASEN GEPPO (JA/0368-475X) [04030197] **5353**

KASEN SHOROPPO (JA) [03081148] **1416**

KASETSART UNIVERSITY. FACULTY OF FISHERIES *See* KASETSART UNIVERSITY FISHERY RESEARCH BULLETIN **2307**

KASETSART UNIVERSITY. FACULTY OF FORESTRY *See* FOREST RESEARCH BULLETIN **2381**

KASETSART UNIVERSITY FISHERY RESEARCH BULLETIN (TH/0453-3453) [01290574] **2307**

KASHANAH (IR) [12064928] **2505**

KASHRUS MAGAZINE (US/1074-3502) [26926746] 2266, **2347**

KASHSHAF AL-AHRAM (UA) [03502550] **418**

KASHSHAF AL-THAWRAH AL-SHAHRI (IQ) [10153973] **418**

KASHU MAINICHI (US/0893-8962) [12815123] **5636**

KASMERA (VE/0075-5222) [I00755222] **3601**

KASOKUKI KAGAKU TOKYO (JA/0912-7305) [I09127305] **5123**

KASSEI SANSO, FURI RAJIKARU (JA/0915-8847) [I09158847] **983**

KASSEL. DEUTSCHES MUSIKGESCHICHTLICHES ARCHIV *See* KATALOG DER FILMSAMMLUNG **4127**

KASSELER ARBEITEN ZUR SPRACHE UND LITERATUR (GW/0170-8805) [I01708805] 3401, **3293**

KASSELER BEITRAGE ZUR VOR- UND FRUHGESCHICHTE (GW) [01755045] **240**

KASUMIGAURA CHIIKI KENKYU HOKOKU (JA) [10436785] **1570**

KASUN RE'O BEDTIME STORIES (US/1054-3015) [22835680] **3401**

KASVATUS (FI/0022-927X) [06219025] **1759**

KASVATUSNEUVOLATOIMINTA. VERKSAMHETEN VID RADGIVNINGSBYRAER FOR UPPFOSTRINGSFRAGOR (FI) [06785686] **5294**

KATAHDIN TIMES (US/1064-0657) [26207412] **5685**

KATALIZ I KATALIZATORY; RESPUBLIKANSKII MEZHVEDOMSTVENNYI SBORNIK (UN) [05020605] **1055**

KATALOG (DK/0904-2334) [23917424] **4371**

KATALOG (MY) [09788234] **5330**

KATALOG BINA DESA (IO) [08578563] **5250**

KATALOG DER BIBLIOTHEK FUER INTERNATIONALE SCHULE ZEITSCHRIFTEN (GW) [19739145] **2795**

KATALOG DER FILMSAMMLUNG (GW) [01755043] **4127**

KATALOG FAUNY POLSKI (PL) [01762601] **5589**

KATALOG KNIG IZDATELSTVA NAUKA (RU) [09471972] **4816**

KATALOG NA SUVETSKITE REFERATIVNI I INFORMATSIONNI SPISANIIA ZA ... GODINA (BU) [19254113] **5123**

KATALOG OVER NORSKE SJKART OG NAUTISKE PUBLIKASJONER (NO) [05626872] **4185**

KATALOG OVER PERSONAL, INSTITUTIONER OCH SEKTIONER (SW) [20135588] **843**

KATALOG PERATURAN PERUNDANG-UNDANGAN REPUBLIK INDONESIA (IO) [02245655] **2992**

KATALOG RADIATSIONNYKH DANNYKH (RU) **1427**

KATALOG ROZPRAW DOKTORSKICH I HABILITACYJNYCH (PL/0453-3674) [01755047] **418**

KATALOG SADOVOE ZAVEDENIE "SINOP" E I.V. VELIKAGO KNIAZIA ALEKSANDRA MIKHAILOVICHA (RU) [12088732] **2422**

KATALOG (SWEDEN. POSTENS FRIMARKSAVDELNING) (SW) [10278776] **2785**

KATALOG ZABYTKOW SZTUKI POLSCE (PL) [05281546] **355**

KATALOGE (GW/0588-3431) [01564103] **355**

KATAPULT (SZ) **4903**

KATAR : WIRTSCHAFTLICHE ENTWICKLUNG (GW) [03530045] **1570**

KATATHESE (GR) [02241138] **3401**

KATECHETA (PL/0209-1291) [I02091291] **4971**

KATEI GAHO (JA) **2791**

KATEI SEIKATSU (JA) [01797074] **2282**

KATES KIN (US/0741-2045) [08892236] **2456**

KATHA PRIZE STORIES (II) [25749589] **3401**

KATHALAKSHMI (II) [01588160] **3401**

KATHANA (II) [08620560] **3401**

KATHARINE DEXTER MCCORMICK LIBRARY *See* CURRENT LITERATURE IN FAMILY PLANNING **2287**

KATHMANDU REVIEW (NP) [08383303] 4480, **1501**

KATHMANDU VALLEY TELEPHONE DIRECTORY (NP) [25584483] **1115**

KATHOLIEK DOCUMENTATIE CENTRUM *See* JAARBOEK VAN HET KATHOLIEK DOCUMENTATIE CENTRUM **5030**

KATHOLIEKE UNIVERSITEIT TE LEUVEN. INSTITUUT VOOR TOEGEPASTE LINGUÄISTIK *See* ITL. INSTITUUT VOOR TOEGEPASTE LINGUISTIK **3288**

KATHOLIEKE VERENIGING GEHANDICAPTEN (BE) **4390**

KATHOLISCHEN MISSIONEN, DIE (GW) [03988310] **5031**

KATHOLISCHES LEBEN UND KAEMPFEN IN ZEITALTER DER GLAUBENSSPALTUNG *See* KATHOLISCHES LEBEN UND KIRCHENREFORM IN ZEITALTER DER GLAUBENSSPALTUNG **5031**

KATHOLISCHES LEBEN UND KIRCHENREFORM IN ZEITALTER DER GLAUBENSSPALTUNG (GW) [05024535] **5031**

KATIB (JERUSALEM) (IS) [12077064] **2992**

KATIPUNAN (OAKLAND, CALIF. : 1987) *CEASED.* (US/0895-0032) [16396920] **2656**

KATOEN- EN WOLINDUSTRIE / CENTRAAL BUREAU VOOR DE STATISTIEK, HOOFDAFDELING STATISTIEKEN VAN INDUSTRIE EN BOUWNIJVERHEID (NE) [10608091] **1570**

KATOLICKY TYDENIK (XR) [23743501] **5031**

KATOLSK ARSSKRIFT (SW) [02962428] **4971**

KATORIKKU KENKYU (JA) [04967259] **5031**

KATORIKKU SHINGAKU *See* KATORIKKU KENKYU **5031**

KATSUYO RODO TOKEI (JA) [17436194] **1682**

KATUNDI YNE (IT) [03093687] **2696**

KATXA-TA (CK) [03926718] **2743**

KATY KEENE *CEASED.* (US/0886-4748) [12629588] **4862**

KAUAI (US/0895-9382) [16859010] **5482**

KAUAI UPDATE, THE (US/0898-1418) [17728896] **5482**

KAUCHUK I REZINA (RU/0022-9466) [06231955] **5076**

KAUFMAN KOUNTY KONNECTIONS (US/0884-7525) [10635642] **2456**

KAUKAUNA TIMES (US) [10714643] **5768**

KAUPPA- JA TEOLLISUUSMINISTERION ENERGIAOSASTON JULKAISUJA SARJA B, ENERGIATALOUDELLISET SELVITYKSET (FI) [17006090] **1949**

KAUPPALEHTI (FI) **5800**

KAUPPAMERENKULUN SEKA HUOLINTA- JA AHTAUSTOIMINNAN TASETILASTO (FI) [02239723] **5451**

KAUPPAREKISTERI *See* KAUPPAREKISTERILEHTI **688**

KAUPPAREKISTERILEHTI (FI/0022-9504) [08227560] **688**

Alphabetical Title Index

KELLNER'S

KAUTSCHUK + GUMMI KUNSTSTOFFE (GW/0022-9520) [02448107] **5076**

KAVAK VE HIZLI GELISEN YABANCI TUR ORMAN AGACLARI ARASTIRMA ENSITUSU *See* YILLIK BULTENI - KAVAK VE HIZLI GELISEN YABANCI TUR ORMAN AGACLARI ARASTIRMA ENSITUSU **2398**

KAVAKA (II/0379-5179) [02339907] **575**

KAVANGO (NAMIBIA) *See* JAARVERSLAG / ADMINISTRASIE VIR KAVANGO'S **1681**

KAVANGO (NAMIBIA). LEGISLATIVE ASSEMBLY *See* DEBATTE VAN DIE ... SESSIE VAN DIE WETGEWENDE VERGADERING VAN DIE KAVANGO **4642**

KAVI *See* KAVI INDIA **3465**

KAVI INDIA (II) [08522222] **3465**

KAVILOKA (II) [02240203] **3465**

KAVITA (NEPALA RAJAKIYA PRAJNA-PRATISHTHANA : 1979) (NP) [08364799] **3465**

KAVKAZ I VIZANTIIA (AI/0203-4883) [06306652] **2696**

KAWA TO HAKIMONO (JA) [02441432] **3184**

KAWASAKI IGAKKAISHI (JA/0386-5924) [04761271] **3601**

KAWASAKI JUKOGYO KABUSHIKI KAISHA *See* ANNUAL REPORT / KAWASAKI HEAVY INDUSTRIES, LTD **1597**

KAWASAKI MEDICAL JOURNAL (JA/0385-0234) [02156479] **3601**

KAWASAKI SEITETSU GIHO (JA/0368-7236) [10284383] **4006**

KAWASAKI-SHI KYOIKU KENKYUJO *See* KAWASAKI-SKI KYOIKU KENKYUJO KENKYU HOKOKUSHO **1759**

KAWASAKI-SKI KYOIKU KENKYUJO KENKYU HOKOKUSHO (JA) [05671958] **1759**

KAWASAKI STEEL TECHNICAL REPORT (TOKYO. 1980) (JA/0388-9475) [07629531] 3482, **4006**

KAWEAH RIVER FLOWS, DIVERSIONS AND STORAGE (US/0149-189X) [03440184] **1416**

KAYAK (SANTA CRUZ) (US/0022-9555) [02241964] **3465**

KAYHAN (UK) **4480**

KAYHAN-I FARHANGI (IR) [11192035] **5043**

KAYHAN-I HAV (IR) [13323013] **5803**

KAYHAN-I VARZISHI (IR) [11218404] **4903**

●KAYHAN URDU (IR) [26187504] **5803**

KAZAKHSTANSKAIA PRAVDA : ORGAN TSENTRALNOGO KOMITETA KOMMUNISTICHESKOI PARTII KAZAKHSTANA (KZ) [19218671] **5805**

KAZAN (JA/0453-4360) [04049017] **1408**

KAZAN FUNKA YOCHI RENRAKUKAI *See* KAZAN FUNKA YOCHI RENRAKUKAI KAIHO **1408**

KAZAN FUNKA YOCHI RENRAKUKAI KAIHO (JA) [02246556] **1408**

KAZAN, RUSSIA (CITY). UNIVERSITET *See* SBORNIK ASPIRANTSKIKH RABOT: TEORIIA PLASTIN I OBOLOCHEK **1995**

KAZANSKIJ MEDICINSKIJ ZURNAL (RU/0368-4814) [07599949] **3601**

KAZE DAYORI (JA) [02468702] **3221**

KAZOKUSHI KENKYU / KAZOKUSHI KENKYU HENSHU IINKAI HEN (JA) [07244068] **2282**

KBENHAVNS LUFTHAVN, ARSRAPPORT (DK) [02242882] **27**

KBENHAVNS LUFTHAVNSVEN (DENMARK) *See* KBENHAVNS LUFTHAVN, ARSRAPPORT **27**

KBENHAVNS SPORVEJE *See* BERETNING OG REGNSKAB - KBENHAVNS SPORVEJE **5377**

KBENHAVNS UNIVERSITET. GEOLOGISK CENTRALINSTITUT *See* ARSBERETNING - GEOLOGISK CENTRALINSTITUT (KBENHAVN) **1366**

KBENHAVNS UNIVERSITET. INSTITUT FOR GRSK OG LATINSK MIDDELALDERFILOLOGI *See* CAHIERS DE L'INSTITUT DU MOYENAGE GREC ET LATIN / UNIVERSITE DE COPENHAGUE **3271**

KBM. KANTOORMARKT (NE/0169-7285) [I01697285] **4212**

KCSA NEWSLETTER (US) [24705135] **102**

KDI PUNGIBYOL KYONGJE CHONMANG / QUARTERLY ECONOMIC OUTLOOK (KO) [08903555] **1570**

KEA NEWS (US/0164-3959) [04708998] **1759**

KEADAAN ANGKATAN KERJA DI INDONESIA (IO/0126-3919) [08433212] **1682**

KEADAAN ANGKATEN KERJA DI INDONESIA : ANGKA SEMENTARA (IO) [04455490] **1682**

KEADAAN KESEHATAN ANAK DAN IBU : HASIL SURVEI SOSIAL EKONOMI NASIONAL (IO) [08756650] **3764**

KEARNEY DAILY HUB, THE (US) [13412897] **5706**

KEATS-SHELLEY JOURNAL (US/0453-4387) [01800245] **3401**

KEATS-SHELLEY REVIEW (UK) [15995233] **3401**

KEBEK KOMIK (CN/0700-9054) [03348839] **4862**

KEBIJAKSANAAN OPERASIONIL DAN RENCANA KERJA ROUTINE & PEMBANGUNAN (IO) [01797923] **1682**

●KEE PRODUCTIONS PRESENTS THE INTERCESSORY BIBLE JOURNAL (US/1061-4958) [25324233] **5017**

KEEL JA KIRJANDUS (ER/0022-9601) [01782947] 1078, **3293**

●KEEN ON NEW YORK SURVEY OF TOP-RATED SERVICES, THE (JS/1058-6652) [24351085] 5560, **3995**

KEENE SENTINEL, THE (US) [21349675] **5708**

KEENELAND (US) **2800**

KEEP FLORIDA BEAUTIFUL (US/1059-342X) [24575585] **2235**

KEEP THE FAITH (US) **4971**

KEEPER'S LOG (US/0883-0061) [11843875] **2026**

KEEPER'S VOICE (US/0274-4872) [06347107] **3168**

KEEPING CURRENT (US/0889-0560) [11593740] **2886**

KEEPING POSTED. TEACHER'S/LEADER'S EDITION (NEW YORK) (US/0163-352X) [04350986] 5050, **1759**

KEEPING SCORE (US/0738-7229) [09655288] **1501**

KEEPING TRACK (CN/1199-1836) **159**

KEEPING UP (US/0890-1422) [14159444] **5207**

KEEPING UP WITH KODALY CONCEPTS IN MUSIC EDUCATION (US/0098-0668) [01799175] 1899, **4127**

KEEPSAKE MAGAZINE FOR BRIDES (US/0740-5154) [09960321] **2282**

KEEPSAKE SERIES (US) [01536740] **3401**

KEESINGS HISTORISCH ARCHIEF (NE) [13385844] **2622**

KEESING'S RECORD OF WORLD EVENTS (UK/0950-6128) [15359635] **4480**

KEESING'S UK RECORD (UK/0952-195X) [I0952195X] **4527**

KEFAR HABAD : SHEVUON TSEIRE AGUDAT HABAD BE-E. HA-K (US) [11410296] **5050**

KEGIATAN L.S.D. SELURUH INDONESIA (IO) [02156348] **5207**

KEGON (JA) [05163093] **5232**

KEHITYSVAMMAISTEN ERITYISHUOLTO (FI) [19301101] **5294**

KEHRWIEDER (GW/0176-473X) [02436505] **5451**

KEIEI KAGAKU KYOKAI *See* JOURNAL OF THE OPERATIONS RESEARCH SOCIETY OF JAPAN **5121**

KEIEI ROMU NO SHISHIN (JA) [01790102] **943**

KEIEI SHISU HAND BUKKU : SANGYOBETSU HEN (JA) [04472809] **795**

KEIEI TOSHO SOMOKUROKU (JA) [02244820] **1614**

KEIKAKU GYOSEI / NIHON KEIKAKU GYOSEI GAKKAI (JA/0387-2513) [10732856] **2826**

KEIKINZOKU (JA/0451-5994) [09598718] **4006**

KEIKINZOKU KOGYO TOKEI NEMPO (JA) [01796837] **4025**

KEIKINZOKU YOSETSU (JA/0368-5306) [10290898] 618, **4027**

KEILSCHRIFTBIBLIOGRAPHIE (GW) **418**

KEILSCHRIFTURKUNDEN AUS BOGHAZKOEI (GW) [01782730] **3401**

KEIO BUSINESS REVIEW (JA/0453-4557) [02226835] **688**

KEIO COMMUNICATION REVIEW (JA/0388-7596) [07450957] **1115**

KEIO ECONOMIC STUDIES (JA/0022-9709) [02229970] **1570**

KEIO GIJUKU DAIGAKU GENGO BUNKA KENKYUJO KIYO (JA) [04698377] **1833**

KEIO GIJUKU DAIGAKU, TOKYO. GENGO BUNKA KENKYUJO *See* KEIO GIJUKU DAIGAKU GENGO BUNKA KENKYUJO KIYO **1833**

KEIO GIJUKU DAIGAKU, TOKYO JOHO KAGAKU KENKYUJO *See* KOHO - KEIO GIJUKU DAIGAKU JOHO KAGAKU KENKYUJO **1261**

KEIO IGAKU (JA/0368-5179) [10284444] **3601**

KEIO JOURNAL OF MEDICINE (JA/0022-9717) [01755059] **3601**

KEIO SCIENCE AND TECHNOLOGY REPORTS (JA/0286-4215) [08466094] **1984**

KEIRYO KENKYUJO NEMPO (JA) [01799735] **5123**

KEIRYO KOKUGOGAKU (JA) [01640365] **3516**

KEISEI GEKA (JA/0021-5228) [I00215228] **3969**

KEISOKU JIDO SEIGYO GAKKAI ROMBUNSHI. TRANSACTIONS OF THE SOCIETY OF INSTRUMENT AND CONTROL ENGINEERS (JA) [11445161] **1984**

KEISOKU TO SEIGYO (JA/0453-4662) [09489799] **1984**

KEITH CALLARD LECTURES (CN/0541-623X) [02341933] **3401**

KEITHWOOD DIRECTORY OF HOSPITAL & SURGICAL SUPPLY DEALERS (US/0162-9840) [04254327] **3602**

KEIZAI CHOSA KYOKAI *See* SHIRYO KANKO ANNAI **1584**

KEIZAI DOKO GEPPO / TSUSHO SANGYOSHO SANGYO SEISAKUKYOKU CHOSAKA KANSHU (JA) [08982928] **1570**

KEIZAI GAKKAI HO (JA) [09365049] **1501**

KEIZAI HENDO KANSOKU SHIRYONEMPO (JA) [12034755] **688**

KEIZAI KEIEI KENKYU (JA) [07330505] **1501**

KEIZAI KENKYU / HITOTSUBASHI DAIGAKU KEIZAI KENKYUJO HEN (JA/0022-9733) [01755061] **1501**

KEIZAI KENKYUJO HO / KEIZAI DOYUKAI KEIZAI KENKYUJO (JA) [10842238] **688**

KEIZAI KISHODAI / ASAHI SHINBUN KEIZAIBU HEN (JA/11699086] **1570**

KEIZAI RIRON (JA) [05671350] **1501**

KEIZAI SHINGO JITEN (JA/0450-0040) [04048715] **1593**

KEIZAI SHIRIN (JA/0022-9741) [I00229741] **1501**

KEIZAI TOKEI GEPPO. ECONOMIC STATISTICS MONTHLY (JA) [05872406] **1535**

KEIZAI TOKEI NEMPO (JA) [04510859] **1501**

KEIZAI TOKEI NEMPO (JA) [02245228] **1501**

KEIZAI TOKEI NENKAN (JA) [03217989] 1570, **1535**

KEIZAIGAKU RONSAN (JA) [05083235] **1593**

KEIZAIGAKU RONSO KYOTO. 1949 (JA/0387-3021) [I03873021] **1501**

KEIZAIGAKU ZASSHI (JA/0451-6281) [21654181] **1501**

KEKKAKU (JA/0022-9776) [01624153] **3950**

KELETKUTATAS (HU) [03265157] 2518, **2696**

KELLER'S INDUSTRIAL SAFETY REPORT (US/1053-3826) [22521947] **2865**

KELLEY BLUE BOOK ADVANCE SHEETS (US) **5418**

KELLEY BLUE BOOK CO *See* TRAVEL TRAILERS, 5TH WHEEL TRAILERS, CAMPING TRAILERS RV GUIDE, NEW & USED VALUES **5397**

KELLEY BLUE BOOK CO *See* MOBILE HOME & RV TRAILER GUIDE, NEW & USED VALUES **5387**

KELLEY BLUE BOOK EARLY MODEL CAR GUIDE (US) **5385**

KELLEY BLUE BOOK MANUFACTURED HOUSING USED VALUE GUIDE (US/1063-0074) [18435023] **2826**

KELLEY BLUE BOOK MOTORCYCLE GUIDE (US) **5385**

KELLEY BLUE BOOK NEW CAR PRICE MANUAL (US/0897-6171) [08524076] **5418**

KELLEY BLUE BOOK, OFFICIAL GUIDE FOR OLDER CARS (US) [05979751] **5418**

KELLEY BLUE BOOK. RESIDUAL VALUE GUIDE (US) [13449127] **5418**

KELLEY BLUE BOOK. RV MOTOR HOME GUIDE (US) [13401683] **5418**

KELLEY BLUE BOOK. RV TRAILER GUIDE (US) [07966040] **5418**

KELLNER'S MONEYGRAM (US/0162-3702) [04170935] **4371**

KELLOGG — Alphabetical Title Index

KELLOGG EVENING NEWS, THE (US) [13142996] **5657**

● KELLY INSURANCE DIRECTORY: NATIONWIDE HOSPITAL INSURANCE BILLING DIRECTORY (US) [23747081] **2886**

● KELLY'S (UK/1350-4150) [29195843] **843**

KELLY'S BUSINESS DIRECTORY (UK/0269-9265) [14447947] **843**

KELLY'S POST OFFICE LONDON BUSINESS DIRECTORY *CEASED.* (UK/0266-3791) [12206981] **688**

KELLY'S U.K. EXPORTS *CEASED.* (UK/0268-3105) [14375371] **843**

KELOWNA CITY DIRECTORY. (1958. BUSINESS EDITION) (CN/0319-0013) [02441987] **2567**

KELOWNA TODAY (CN/0227-3489) [06858262] **5788**

KELTICA (US/0192-1207) [04988866] 3401, **2696**

KEMBLE OCCASIONAL, THE *CEASED.* (US/0453-4867) [03350183] 4816, **4566**

KEMENATE, DIE (GW) **2282**

KEMIA (FI/0355-1628) [01794767] **1027**

KEMIA UJABB EREDMENYEI, A (HU/0075-5397) [01787720] **983**

KEMIAI KOEZLEMENYEK (HU/0022-9814) [04068883] **983**

KEMIAN TEOLLISUUS (FINLAND. TILASTOKESKUS) (FI/0786-0048) [19489222] **1570**

KEMIJA U INDUSTRIJI (CI/0022-9830) [01782813] **983**

KEMIKARU ENGINIYARINGU (JA/0387-1037) [09600081] **2014**

KEMISK TIDSKRIFT (SW/0039-6605) [01794192] **983**

● KEMIVARLDEN (SW/1102-6650) [25576245] 843, **1055**

KEMMERER GAZETTE, THE (US) [12292754] **5772**

KEMPER COUNTY MESSENGER (US) [15079471] **5701**

KEMPE'S ENGINEER'S YEAR-BOOK (UK/0075-5400) [02148465] **1984**

KEMPE'S ENGINEERS YEAR-BOOK FOR ... (UK/0075-5400) [07448829] **1984**

KEMPS INTERNATIONAL FILM & TELEVISION YEAR BOOK (UK) [04423012] **4073**

KEMPS INTERNATIONAL MUSIC BOOK (UK) [21580063] **4127**

KEN-CUR REPORT, THE (CN/0823-7042) [10199126] **905**

KEN GERBINO'S SMART INVESTING (US/1059-6674) [24662601] **905**

KEN-TON BEE (US/0745-6875) [09396185] **5717**

KENA (US) 404, **5560**

KENCHIKU BUNKA (JA/0003-8490) [02667802] **302**

KENCHIKU JISSHI SEKKEI REI SHIRYO (JA) [02247020] **302**

KENCHIKU SETSUBI KOGAKU KENKYUJO HO (JA) [04426918] **2606**

KENDALL COUNTY RECORD (YORKVILLE, ILL. : 1864 : WEEKLY) (US) [11445706] **5660**

KENDELSER OM FAST EJENDOM (DK) [02246859] **2992**

KENDRICK GAZETTE, THE (US) [20311511] **5657**

KENENKEN DAYORI / HENSHU, KENENKEN KAKURITSU O MEZASU HITOBITO NO KAI JIMUKYOKU (JA) [11360711] **4788**

KENIA : ENERGIEWIRTSCHAFT (GW) [05064439] **1949**

KENIA: WIRTSCHAFTSDATEN UND WIRTSCHAFTSDOKUMENTATION (GW) [06225435] **1570**

KENILWORTH LEADER (US/8750-8664) [11874050] **5710**

KENKO HOKEN KUMIAI JIGYO NEMPO (JA) [02247107] **2886**

KENKY KIYO - TOYOTA KOGYO KOTO SEMMON GAKKO (JA) [05724214] **1833**

KENKYU HOKOKU (JA) [08323366] **2307**

KENKYU HOKOKU / BULLETIN OF THE INDUSTRIAL RESEARCH CENTER OF EHIME PREFECTURE. EHIME-KEN KOGYO GIJUTSU SENTA (JA) [10263176] **5123**

KENKYU HOKOKU - GIFU DAIGAKU KYOIKUGAKUBU FUZOKU SHOGAKKO (JA) [05277377] **1899**

KENKYU HOKOKU / HYOGO KENRITSU CHIKUSAN SHIKENJO (JA/0388-3116) [10326093] **102**

KENKYU HOKOKU / KANKYO KAGAKU KENKYUJO (JA/0287-5071) [10388989] **2235**

KENKYU HOKOKU - KANTO GAKUIN DAIGAKU KOGAKUBU (JA/0368-5373) [02245414] **1984**

KENKYU HOKOKU / NAGASAKI DAIGAKU KOGAKUBU (JA/0286-0902) [10444517] **1984**

KENKYU HOKOKU.--NIHON SEMBAI KOSHA CHUO KENKYUJO (JA/0369-4372) [01797291] **5373**

KENKYU HOKOKU. RESEARCH BULLETINS OF THE COLLEGE EXPERIMENT FORESTS, HOKKAIDO UNIVERSITY (JA) [03531528] **2386**

KENKYU HOKOKU SHU - KOKURITSU KOKUGO KENKYUJO (JA) [05671261] **3293**

KENKYU HOKOKU SHU - TOKYO-TO SHINSHIN SHOGAISHA FUKUSHI SENTA (JA) [02972298] 4390, **5294**

KENKYU HOKOKU SHUROKU (JA) [05713973] **1760**

KENKYU HOKOKU TOHOKU NOGYO SHIKENJO (JA/0495-7318) [02609659] **102**

KENKYU HOKOKUSHO (KISHO KENKYUJO (JAPAN) (JA) [09293317] **1427**

KENKYU KIYO - AKASHI KOGYO KOTO SEMMON GAKKO (JA) [07015345] **5123**

KENKYU KIYO - AKITA KOGYO KOTO SENMON GAKKO (JA/0285-5364) [10244048] **5123**

KENKYU KIYO - HIROSHIMA DAIGAKU KYOIKUGAKUBU GAKUBU FUZOKU KYODO KENKYU TAISEI (JA) [04430681] **1760**

KENKYU KIYO / KAGOSHIMA JOSHI DAIGAKU (JA/0389-1623) [07954175] **1833**

KENKYU KIYO - KENRITSU NIIGATA JOSHI TANKI DAIGAKU (JA) [01797388] **1833**

KENKYU KIYO - KUNITACHI ONGAKU DAIGAKU (JA) [02612527] **4127**

KENKYU KIYO - MUSASHINO BIJUTSU DAIGAKU (JA) [02245325] **323**

KENKYU KIYO / RESEARCH REPORTS OF THE ANAN TECHNICAL COLLEGE. ANAN KOGYO KOTO SENMON GAKKO (JA/0570-006X) [10339496] **5123**

KENKYU KIYO - RISSHO JOSHI DAIGAKU TANKI DAIGAKUBU (JA) [02329747] **5232**

KENKYU KIYO. SHIZEN KAGAKU HEN / NATURAL SCIENCE. BULLETIN OF THE FACULTY OF EDUCATION, KAGOSHIMA UNIVERSITY. KAGOSHIMA DAIGAKU KYOIKUGAKUBU (JA) [10283879] 1092, **5123**

KENKYU KIYO - SHIZUOKA JOSHI TANKI DAIGAKU (JA) [04928456] **1833**

KENKYU KIYO / TOKUGAWA RINSEISHI KENKYUJO (JA/0386-9032) [10809550] **2386**

KENKYU KIYO / TOKUSHIMA BUNRI DAIGAKU (JA) [10448341] **1092**

KENKYU KIYO - TOKYO-TO ROJIN SOGO KENKYUJO, TOKYO-TO YOIKUIN FUZOKU BYOIN *See* TOKYO-TO ROJIN SOGO KENKYUJO NEMPO **3755**

KENKYU KIYO / TOKYO TORITSU JOHO SHORI KYOIKU SENTA (JA/0385-1753) [07902260] **1760**

KENKYU NEMPO - NIIGATA DAIGAKU SEKISETSU CHIIKI SAIGAI KENKYU SENTA (JA) [07336980] 1408, **1385**

KENKYU NEMPO - TOYAMA DAIGAKU NIHONKAI KEIZAI KENKYUJO (JA) [03189672] **1570**

KENKYU NENKAN (JA/0302-8801) [01796947] **3293**

KENKYU NENPO / NIHON DAIGAKU BUNRI GAKUBU (MISHIMA) (JA/0388-4821) [10871739] **5123**

KENKYU NENPO (TAKUSHOKU DAIGAKU. KENKYUJO) (JA/0289-0747) [10978972] **5207**

KENKYU REPOTO - SAN PAURO JIMBUN KAGAKU KENKYUJO (BL) [02244216] **2743**

KENKYU ROMBUN SHOROKU SHU (JA) [03678287] **4428**

KENKYU SEIKA NENPO (JA) [10592085] **2119**

KENKYU SHUROKU (JA) [01797397] **1899**

KENKYUSHITSU IHO (JA) [06952961] **5250**

KENMARE NEWS (US) [02252787] **5725**

KENNEBEC JOURNAL (AUGUSTA, ME. : 1975) (US/0745-2039) [08814143] **5685**

KENNEBECASIS VALLEY POST (CN/0228-7897) [08063794] **5788**

KENNEDY INSTITUTE OF ETHICS JOURNAL (US/1054-6863) [22939052] **2252**

KENNEDY LIBRARY QUARTERLY, EASTERN WASHINGTON UNIVERSITY (US/1055-8977) [23366833] **3221**

KENNEDY SCHOOL CASE CATALOG, THE (US/1052-9020) [18777664] **875**

KENNEDY'S CAREER STRATEGIST (US/0891-2572) [14264301] **4206**

KENNEL GAZETTE, THE (UK) [09846263] **4286**

KENNEL HEALTHLINE *CEASED.* (US/1061-9976) [20191172] **5515**

KENNEL REVIEW (US/0164-4289) [03431528] **4287**

KENNER/METAIRIE LIVING (US/1051-0591) [21818220] **5684**

KENNESAW NEIGHBOR, THE (US/0191-7072) [04960707] **5654**

KENNETH COLEMAN'S REALITY THEORY NEWSLETTER (US/0739-3563) [09748197] **4602**

KENNETH NEBENZAHL, INC *See* RARE AMERICANA **423**

KENNIS EN METHODE (NE/0165-1773) [05225918] **4351**

KENOSHA NEWS (US/0749-713X) [11167392] **5768**

KENRITSU NIIGATA JOSHI TANKI DAIGAKU *See* KENKYU KIYO - KENRITSU NIIGATA JOSHI TANKI DAIGAKU **1833**

KENSA TO GIJUTSU (JA/0301-2611) [01357027] **3602**

KENSEI KANKEI SHIMBUN KIJI KIRINUKI SAKUIN (JA) [02532432] **5805**

KENSETSU TOKEI GEPPO (JA) [02245396] **618**

KENSETSUGYO ANZEN EISEI HOREI HYAKKA (JA) [02441099] **618**

KENSETSUGYO HOREI TSUTATSU ZENSHO (JA) [03116713] **618**

KENSETSUSHO SETCHI HO KANKEI HOREISHU / KENSETSU DAIJIN KANBO BUNSHOKA KANSHU (JA) [10240469] **2992**

KENT ARCHAEOLOGICAL REVIEW (UK/0023-0014) [01783620] **272**

KENT COLLECTOR, THE (US/0163-1861) [04303638] **355**

KENT COUNTY DAILY TIMES, THE (US) [26083618] **5741**

KENT COUNTY NEWS (US) [18952694] **5686**

KENT DIRECTORY (CN/0828-5543) [12178001] **2567**

KENT FAMILY HISTORY SOCIETY *See* KENT FAMILY HISTORY SOCIETY JOURNAL **2456**

KENT FAMILY HISTORY SOCIETY JOURNAL (UK/0305-9359) [05045605] **2456**

KENT RECUSANT HISTORY (UK/0044-4018) [07683154] **5031**

KENTAVR (RU) [25206216] **2992**

KENTON COUNTY RECORDER, THE (US) [24685526] **5681**

KENTON TIMES, THE (US) [10112155] **5729**

KENTRON EPISTEMONIKON EREUNON *See* EPETERIS **2650**

KENTUCKY *See* ACTS OF THE GENERAL ASSEMBLY OF THE COMMONWEALTH OF KENTUCKY **4624**

KENTUCKY ACADEMY OF SCIENCE *See* TRANSACTIONS OF THE KENTUCKY ACADEMY OF SCIENCE **5166**

KENTUCKY ADMINISTRATIVE REGULATIONS SERVICE : CONTAINING REGULATIONS PROMULGATED BY ADMINISTRATIVE AGENCIES OF THE COMMONWEALTH OF KENTUCKY IN EFFECT AS OF ... (US) [05766146] **4660**

KENTUCKY ADVANCED TECHNOLOGY DIRECTORY, THE (US/1045-3415) [20075024] **5123**

● KENTUCKY AFIELD (US/1059-9177) [24807858] **4874**

KENTUCKY AGRI-NEWS (US/8750-9792) [11977395] **102**

KENTUCKY AIRPORT DIRECTORY (US) [01782450] **27**

KENTUCKY ALUMNUS (US/0732-6297) [08398823] **1102**

KENTUCKY ANCESTORS (US/0023-0103) [00849378] **2456**

KENTUCKY AND TENNESSEE LEGAL DIRECTORY, THE (US/0450-089X) [01782616] **3141**

KENTUCKY. ATTORNEY GENERAL'S OFFICE *See* OPINIONS OF THE ATTORNEY GENERAL OF KENTUCKY FOR THE PERIOD JANUARY 1, 1968-JOHN B. BRECKINRIDGE, ATTORNEY GENERAL, 1968-1972 **3142**

KENTUCKY. ATTORNEY GENERAL'S OFFICE *See* ATTORNEY GENERAL'S OPINIONS **3139**

KENTUCKY. ATTORNEY GENERAL'S OFFICE *See* OPINIONS OF THE ATTORNEY GENERAL OF KENTUCKY **3142**

KENTUCKY. ATTORNEY GENERAL'S OFFICE *See* BIENNIAL REPORT / ATTORNEY GENERAL **3139**

KENTUCKY BEEKEEPERS' QUARTERLY (US) [06652198] **102**

Alphabetical Title Index — KENYA

KENTUCKY BENCH & BAR (US/0164-9345) [01197275] **2992**

KENTUCKY. BUREAU OF HIGHWAYS. DIVISION OF ACCOUNTS *See* FINANCIAL REPORT TO MANAGEMENT **5440**

KENTUCKY BUSINESS DIRECTORY (US/1048-728X) [13460733] **688**

KENTUCKY CHECKLIST OF STATE PUBLICATIONS **CEASED.** (US/1054-2841) [22419665] **418**

KENTUCKY CITY (1968), THE (US/0453-5677) [07962449] **4660**

KENTUCKY CLUBWOMAN, THE (US/0740-6185) [09983478] **5232**

KENTUCKY COLLEGE AND UNIVERSITY ENROLLMENTS (US) [06177742] **1833**, **1795**

KENTUCKY COLLEGES AND UNIVERSITIES : DEGREES CONFERRED (US/0145-9120) [02821246] **1833**

KENTUCKY COMMERCE (US/1046-9257) [20557938] **820**

KENTUCKY COMMISSION ON HUMAN RIGHTS *See* KENTUCKY DIRECTORY OF BLACK ELECTED OFFICIALS **4660**

KENTUCKY CONVERSATION NEWS / DIVISION OF CONSERVATION (US) [08658983] **2235**

KENTUCKY. COUNCIL ON PUBLIC HIGHER EDUCATION *See* KENTUCKY COLLEGES AND UNIVERSITIES : DEGREES CONFERRED **1833**

KENTUCKY CROP & LIVESTOCK REPORTING SERVICE *See* SURVEY ANNOUNCEMENT - KENTUCKY CROP & LIVESTOCK REPORTING SERVICE **222**

KENTUCKY DENTAL JOURNAL (US/0744-396X) [08244980] **1329**

KENTUCKY. DEPT. FOR HUMAN RESOURCES. DIVISION FOR RESEARCH AND SPECIAL PROJECTS *See* WORKERS COVERED BY KENTUCKY UNEMPLOYMENT INSURANCE LAW BY COUNTY **2896**

KENTUCKY. DEPT. FOR LOCAL GOVERNMENT *See* KENTUCKY LOCAL DEBT REPORT **4735**

KENTUCKY. DEPT. OF AERONAUTICS *See* KENTUCKY AIRPORT DIRECTORY **27**

KENTUCKY. DEPT. OF CHILD WELFARE *See* ANNUAL REPORT **5272**

KENTUCKY. DEPT. OF ECONOMIC SECURITY *See* REPORT - KENTUCKY. DEPT. OF ECONOMIC SECURITY **5305**

KENTUCKY. DEPT. OF EDUCATION. BUREAU OF ADMINISTRATION AND FINANCE *See* PROFILES OF KENTUCKY PUBLIC SCHOOLS **1775**

KENTUCKY. DEPT. OF EDUCATION. BUREAU OF ADMINISTRATION AND FINANCE *See* SUMMARY OF KENTUCKY EDUCATION **1798**

KENTUCKY. DEPT. OF EDUCATION. BUREAU OF ADMINISTRATION AND FINANCE *See* SCHOOL BUS PURCHASES **1871**

KENTUCKY. DEPT. OF HEALTH *See* REPORT - KENTUCKY. DEPT OF HEALTH **4798**

KENTUCKY. DEPT. OF HIGHWAYS *See* REPORT **5443**

KENTUCKY. DEPT. OF LAW *See* BIENNIAL REPORT OF THE DEPARTMENT OF LAW TO ... GOVERNOR, COMMONWEALTH OF KENTUCKY FOR THE BIENNIAL PERIOD ... AS REQUIRED BY KRS 15.080 **3139**

KENTUCKY. DEPT. OF LAW. BIENNIAL REPORT OF THE DEPARTMENT OF LAW TO ... GOVERNOR, COMMONWEALTH OF KENTUCKY FOR THE BIENNIAL PERIOD ... AS REQUIRED BY KRS 15.080 *See* BIENNIAL REPORT / ATTORNEY GENERAL **3139**

KENTUCKY. DEPT. OF REVENUE *See* REPORT - KENTUCKY. DEPT. OF REVENUE **4745**

KENTUCKY DIRECTORY OF BLACK ELECTED OFFICIALS (US) [04706312] **4660**

KENTUCKY DIRECTORY OF MANUFACTURERS (US/0075-5494) [04309050] **3482**

KENTUCKY ECONOMIC STATISTICS (US) [07368691] **1501**, **1535**

KENTUCKY EDUCATION ASSOCIATION *See* KEA NEWS **1759**

KENTUCKY EMPLOYMENT LAW LETTER (US/1052-4371) [22293427] **3150**

KENTUCKY ENGINEER (US/0746-2255) [02448110] **1984**

KENTUCKY ENGLISH BULLETIN (US/0023-0197) [03603521] **3293**, **3401**

KENTUCKY EXPLORER, THE (US/0890-8362) [14473227] **2743**

KENTUCKY FAMILY RECORDS (US) [05045761] **2456**

KENTUCKY FARM BUREAU FEDERATION *See* KENTUCKY FARM BUREAU NEWS **102**

KENTUCKY FARM BUREAU NEWS (US/0023-0200) [04089875] **102**

KENTUCKY FARMER, THE (US/0023-0219) [04090152] **102**

KENTUCKY GAME & FISH (US/0889-3802) [13865876] **4874**

KENTUCKY. GENERAL ASSEMBLY. LEGISLATIVE RESEARCH COMMISSION *See* FINAL REPORTS OF INTERIM JOINT AND SPECIAL COMMITTEES **2970**

KENTUCKY HAPPY HUNTING GROUND (US/0023-0235) [01782642] **2197**, **4874**

● KENTUCKY HEALTH CARE IN PERSPECTIVE (US/1065-4194) [26605650] **4788**

KENTUCKY HOSPITAL FACTS (US) [06350554] **3787**

KENTUCKY HOSPITAL RESEARCH AND EDUCATION FOUNDATION *See* HOSPITAL WAGE, SALARY, AND BENEFITS SURVEY **3785**

KENTUCKY HOSPITALS MAGAZINE (US) [25716022] **3787**

KENTUCKY IN PERSPECTIVE (US/1065-5468) [25703445] **5330**

KENTUCKY JOURNAL (LEXINGTON, KY.) (US/1063-9357) [19996490] **2536**

KENTUCKY JOURNAL OF COMMERCE AND INDUSTRY, THE (US/0279-5388) [C7090067] **843**

KENTUCKY JOURNAL OF ECONOMICS AND BUSINESS, THE (US/0734-4058) [05519248] **688**, **1501**

KENTUCKY LABOR NEWS (US/0023-0251) [04090175] **1682**

KENTUCKY LAW JOURNAL (US/0023-026X) [01755105] **2992**

KENTUCKY LAW SUMMARY (US/1042-9212) [07992963] **2992**

KENTUCKY LEGAL DIRECTORY, THE (US/0145-658X) [02771146] **2992**

KENTUCKY. LEGISLATIVE RESEARCH COMMISSION *See* KENTUCKY ADMINISTRATIVE REGULATIONS SERVICE : CONTAINING REGULATIONS PROMULGATED BY ADMINISTRATIVE AGENCIES OF THE COMMONWEALTH OF KENTUCKY IN EFFECT AS OF ... **4660**

KENTUCKY LIBRARIES (US/0732-5452) [07189344] **3221**

KENTUCKY LIVING (US/1043-853X) [19581640] **2536**

KENTUCKY LOCAL DEBT REPORT (US/0095-1498) [03332038] **4735**

KENTUCKY LOCAL OFFICIALS (US) [01800021] **4660**

KENTUCKY MANPOWER DEVELOPMENT, INC *See* ANNUAL REPORT - KENTUCKY MANPOWER DEVELOPMENT, INC **3913**

KENTUCKY MANUFACTURERS REGISTER (US/0741-9031) [10232277] **3482**

KENTUCKY MARQUEE (US/0892-4899) [15239464] **5365**

KENTUCKY MEDICAL ASSOCIATION *See* JOURNAL OF THE KENTUCKY MEDICAL ASSOCIATION, THE **3598**

KENTUCKY NEW ERA (HOPKINSVILLE, KY. : DAILY) (US) [14064300] **5681**

KENTUCKY NURSE (US/0742-8367) [09619240] **3860**

KENTUCKY. OFFICE FOR LOCAL GOVERNMENT. KENTUCKY LOCAL DEBT REPORT *See* KENTUCKY LOCAL DEBT REPORT **4735**

KENTUCKY PARKS **CEASED.** (US/0892-1350) [12244421] **2197**

KENTUCKY PHARMACIST, THE (US/0194-567X) [02263212] **4313**

KENTUCKY PHILOLOGICAL REVIEW (US) [18614583] **3401**

KENTUCKY PIONEER GENEALOGY AND RECORDS (US/0748-5565) [05511452] **2456**

KENTUCKY POETRY REVIEW **CEASED.** (US/0889-647X) [03354696] **3345**

KENTUCKY POST (CONVINGTON KY. : 1974) (US) [12111874] **5729**

KENTUCKY PRIMARY AND GENERAL ELECTION (US/0095-6856) [01796051] **4480**

KENTUCKY. PUBLIC RECORDS DIVISION *See* KENTUCKY CHECKLIST OF STATE PUBLICATIONS **418**

KENTUCKY QUERIES *See* TENNESSEE & KENTUCKY QUERIES **2474**

KENTUCKY QUERIES (US/0899-1359) [17639191] **2456**

KENTUCKY. REGISTRY OF ELECTION FINANCE *See* KENTUCKY PRIMARY AND GENERAL ELECTION **4480**

KENTUCKY REVIEW (LEXINGTON. 1979), THE (US/0191-1031) [04790142] **2849**

KENTUCKY RULES OF COURT. FEDERAL : INCLUDING AMENDMENTS RECEIVED THROUGH OCTOBER 1 ... (US/1058-3211) [22871104] **2992**

KENTUCKY RULES OF COURT. STATE (US/1058-322X) [22871140] **2992**

KENTUCKY SCHOOL DIRECTORY, THE (US/0091-0775) [01785542] **1760**

KENTUCKY STANDARD, THE (US/8750-0760) [10960238] **5681**

KENTUCKY. STATE BOARD OF EXAMINERS AND REGISTRATION OF LANDSCAPE ARCHITECTS *See* ROSTER OF REGISTERED LANDSCAPE ARCHITECTS, COMMONWEALTH OF KENTUCKY **2430**

KENTUCKY. STATE PARK COMMISSION *See* REPORTS AND RECOMMENDATIONS ... / KENTUCKY. STATE PARK COMMISSION **4708**

KENTUCKY STATE PENITENTIARY *See* POPULATION MOVEMENT **3173**

KENTUCKY TRAVEL GUIDE (US/0453-5812) [07095045] **5482**

KENTUCKY. UNIVERSITY. DEPT. OF FORESTRY *See* FOR **2379**

KENTUCKY WARBLER, THE (US/0160-5070) [01623554] **5618**

KENTUCKY, WEST VIRGINIA ZIP+4 STATE DIRECTORY (US) [11586436] **1145**

KENTUCKY'S GROWING GOLD (US) [03582173] **2386**

KENTWOOD LEDGER, THE (US/0890-8087) [14401764] **5684**

KENTWOOD NEWS (US) [17502293] **5684**

KENYA *See* ESTIMATES OF RECURRENT EXPENDITURE OF THE GOVERNMENT OF KENYA **4646**

KENYA *See* KENYA GAZETTE, THE **2992**

KENYA (KE/0378-2158) [07724004] **2641**

KENYA *See* CATALOGUE OF GOVERNMENT PUBLICATIONS **412**

KENYA ADVANCED CERTIFICATE OF EDUCATION, REGULATIONS AND SYLLABUSES (KE) [11008751] **1760**

KENYA AGRICULTURAL ABSTRACTS. CURRENT SERIES / PREPARED AND ISSUED BY KENYA AGRICULTURAL DOCUMENTATION CENTRE, MINISTRY OF AGRICULTURE (KE) [11715791] **102**

KENYA AGRICULTURAL RESEARCH INSTITUTE. AGRICULTURAL RESEARCH DEPT *See* RECORD OF RESEARCH **125**

KENYA AGRICULTURAL RESEARCH INSTITUTE. VETERINARY RESEARCH DEPT *See* ANNUAL REPORT / KENYA AGRICULTURAL RESEARCH INSTITUTE, VETERINARY RESEARCH DEPARTMENT **5503**

KENYA BUILDER, THE (KE) [05167264] **618**

KENYA BUSINESS DIRECTORY (KE) [09342824] **688**

KENYA BUSINESS SPOTLIGHT (KE) [11231197] **1501**

KENYA. CENTRAL BUREAU OF STATISTICS *See* MIGRATION AND TOURISM STATISTICS **5500**

KENYA CERTIFICATE OF BUSINESS EDUCATION. REGULATIONS AND SYLLABUSES (KE) **1899**

KENYA CERTIFICATE OF EDUCATION, REGULATIONS AND SYLLABUSES / KENYA NATIONAL EXAMINATIONS COUNCIL (KE) [11008781] **1899**

KENYA CERTIFICATE OF SECONDARY EDUCATION, REGULATIONS AND SYLLABUSES (KE) **1899**

KENYA CERTIFICATE OF TECHNICAL EDUCATION. REGULATIONS AND SYLLABUSES (KE) **1899**

KENYA COFFEE (KE/1010-3481) [09498566] **177**

KENYA. COURT OF APPEAL *See* DIGEST OF DECISIONS OF THE COURT **2961**

KENYA ENGINEER : JOURNAL OF THE INSTITUTION OF ENGINEERS OF KENYA (KE) [11270038] **1984**

KENYA ENTERPRISE, THE (KE) [04071712] **843**

KENYA EXPORT DIRECTORY (KE) [03645633] **843**

KENYA EXPORT NEWS (1976) **SUSPENDED.** (KE/0453-6460) [02986438] **843**

KENYA GAZETTE, THE (KE) [03156440] **2992**

KENYA HIGH COURT DIGEST (KE) [05774626] **2992**

KENYA JOURNAL OF EDUCATION (KE) [15078742] **1760**

KENYA

Alphabetical Title Index

KENYA JOURNAL OF SCIENCES. SERIES B, BIOLOGICAL SCIENCES (KE/0250-8257) [21547862] **462**

KENYA LITERATURE BUREAU See COMPLETE CATALOGUE FROM KENYA LITERATURE BUREAU **413**

KENYA MEDIA ADVERTISING REVIEW (KE) [02541168] **761**

KENYA. METEOROLOGICAL DEPT See ANNUAL REPORT ON THE KENYA METEOROLOGICAL DEPARTMENT FOR THE PERIOD 1ST JULY ... TO 30TH JUNE ... **1420**

KENYA. MINISTRY OF COMMERCE AND INDUSTRY See GUIDE TO INDUSTRIAL INVESTMENT, A **900**

KENYA. MINISTRY OF LABOUR See ANNUAL REPORT - KENYA. MINISTRY OF LABOUR **1649**

KENYA NATIONAL ARCHIVES. NATIONAL DOCUMENTATION AND INFORMATION RETRIEVAL SERVICES See ACCESSIONS LIST / MINISTRY OF HOME AFFAIRS AND NATIONAL HERITAGE, DEPARTMENT OF KENYA NATIONAL ARCHIVES, NATIONAL DOCUMENTATION AND INFORMATION RETRIEVAL SERVICES **2478**

KENYA NATIONAL BIBLIOGRAPHY (KE) [09997044] **418**

KENYA NATIONAL LIBRARY SERVICE. NATIONAL REFERENCE & BIBLIOGRAPHIC DEPT See KENYA NATIONAL BIBLIOGRAPHY **418**

KENYA NATIONAL PARK'S TRUSTEES See REPORT **2203**

KENYA PAST AND PRESENT (KE/0257-8301) [01784015] **2641**

KENYA. PUBLIC SERVICE COMMISSION See REPORT ON THE WORKING OF THE PUBLIC SERVICE COMMISSION OF KENYA **4682**

KENYA RAILWAYS See ANNUAL REPORT / KENYA RAILWAYS **4627**

KENYA RECORD (KE) [07579161] **2641**

KENYA REVIEW (KE/1010-3716) [02246951] **1571**

KENYA STATISTICAL DIGEST (KE) [08299464] **5330**

KENYA TEA DEVELOPMENT AUTHORITY See ANNUAL REPORT AND STATEMENT OF ACCOUNTS / KENYA TEA DEVELOPMENT AUTHORITY **822**

KENYA TUBERCULOSIS AND RESPIRATORY DISEASES RESEARCH CENTRE See ANNUAL REPORT / KENYA TUBERCULOSIS AND RESPIRATORY DISEASES RESEARCH CENTRE **3948**

KENYAN PERIODICALS DIRECTORY (KE) [12043064] **418**

KENYATTA UNIVERSITY See CALENDAR / KENYATTA UNIVERSITY **1813**

KENYATTA UNIVERSITY COLLEGE See DIRECTORY OF RESEARCH WHICH IS BEING CONDUCTED BY KENYATTA UNIVERSITY COLLEGE STAFF, A **1821**

KENYON LEADER (US) [01755116] **5696**

KENYON REVIEW, THE (US/0163-075X) [01782352] **3345**

KEOSAUQUA EAGLE (US) [11252503] **5671**

KEOWEE COURIER (US) [10744200] **5742**

KEP ES HANGTECHNIKA (HU/0023-0480) [01782969] **4437**

KEPADATAN PERUSAHAAN INDUSTRI DAN TENAGA KERJA DI SEKTOR INDUSTRI BERDASARKAN JUMLAH PENDUDUK DI TIAP-TIAP PROPINSI, KABUPATEN, KOTA MADYA (IO) [02473538] **1682**

KEPES IFJUSAG (YU) [01786782] **2696**

KEPI BLANC (FR) [06771819] **4048**

KEPI, THE (US) [09962695] **2743**

KEPLER JOHANNES GESAMMELTE WERKE (GW) **5123**

KEPNER TREGOE BUSINESS REVIEW (US/0897-4217) [16988448] **875**

KERALA HIGH COURT NOTES, THE (II) [01784087] **2992**

KERALA (INDIA) See CATALOGUE OF PUBLICATIONS STOCKED IN GOVERNMENT PRESSES, TRIVANDRUM, ERNAKULAM AND SHORANUR **413**

KERALA (INDIA). ANIMAL HUSBANDRY DEPARTMENT See ADMINISTRATION REPORT OF THE ANIMAL HUSBANDRY DEPARTMENT FOR THE YEAR ... **44**

KERALA, INDIA (STATE). BUREAU OF ECONOMICS AND STATISTICS See DISTRICT INCOME OF KERALA **1480**

KERALA, INDIA (STATE). LEGISLATIVE ASSEMBLY. BUSINESS ADVISORY COMMITTEE See REPORT - KERALA, INDIA (STATE). LEGISLATIVE ASSEMBLY. BUSINESS ADVISORY COMMITTEE **3038**

KERALA PRODUCTIVITY JOURNAL (II) [01784181] **875**

KERALA SOCIOLOGIST (II) [04766817] **5250**

KERAMIEK (NE) **2592**

KERAMIK AUGSBURG (GW/0173-6760) [01736760] **2592**

KERAMISCHE ZEITSCHRIFT (GW/0023-0561) [01783036] **2592**

KERAMOS (BONN) (GW/0453-7580) [01800006] **373**

KERAULOPHON, THE (US/0735-8660) [09047481] **4127**

KERESKEDELMI SZEMLE (HU) [06180657] **1501**

KERK EN THEOLOGIE (NE/0450-1489) [07101051] **4972**

KERKELIJK JAARBOEKJE DER GEREFORMEERDE GEMEENTEN (NE) [21020793] **4972**

KERKHISTORISCHE BIJDRAGEN (NE/0169-8451) [01698451] **4972**

KERKHOVEN BANNER, THE (US) [01755131] **5696**

KERMAN NEWS, THE (US) [28493535] **5636**

KERMES : ARTE E TECNICA DEL RESTAURO (IT) [20282691] **355**

KERN-GEN, THE (US/0453-7637) [04187576] **2456**

KERN REPORT, THE (US/1055-5544) [23236066] 1159, **688**

KERNFORSCHUNGSANLAGE JULICH. INSTITUT FUR FESTKORPERFORSCHUNG See IFF BULLETIN **4428**

KERNOS (BE) [18786524] **4972**

KERNTECHNIK (1987) (GW/0932-3902) [15802940] **2156**

KEROUAC CONNECTION (US/0954-2965) [109542965] **3401**

KERRANG! (UK/0262-6624) [l02626624] **1298**

KERR'S COST DATA FOR LANDSCAPE CONSTRUCTION (US/1062-0745) [21061441] **2422**

KERRVILLE MOUNTAIN SUN (US) [14190507] **5751**

KERRVILLE TIMES, THE (US) [14366504] **5751**

KERRYMAN (IE) **5803**

KERSHNER KINFOLK (US/0736-0886) [09054688] **2456**

KERTESZET ES SZOLESZET (HU/0023-0677) [09846402] **2422**

KERTESZETI ES ELELMISZERIPARI EGYETEM KOEZLEMENYEI / PUBLICATIONS UNIVERSITATIS HORTICULTURAE INDUSTRIAEQUE ALIMENTARIAE, A (HU/0238-6852) [21024495] **2422**

KERTHA PATRIKA (IO) [06271834] **2992**

KERUX (US/0888-3513) [13562720] **4972**

KERYGMA (OTTAWA) (CN/0023-0693) [02049580] **4972**

KERYGMA UND DOGMA (GW/0023-0707) [01783850] **4972**

KERYGMA UND DOGMA. BEIHEFT (GW/0453-7726) [08327886] **4972**

KES : ZEITSCHRIFT FUER KOMMUNIKATIONS UND EDV SICHERHEIT (GW/0177-4565) **1115**

KESAFIM (IS) [07289645] **795**

KESATUAN PEKERJA P2 S PENGANGKUTAN See TRIENNIAL REPORT - TRANSPORT WORKERS UNION **1715**

KESEHATAN MASJARAKAT See KESEHATAN MASYARAKAT **4788**

KESEHATAN MASYARAKAT (IO/0126-0979) [01799434] **4788**

KESENIAN MASYARAKAT (SI) [02908977] **3401**

KESIN HESAPLAR, BELEDIYELER, IL OZEL IDARELERI (TU) [17653086] **4660**

KESKEYTTAMISET AMMATILLISISSA OPPILAITOKSISSA SEKA KANSANOPISTOISSA JA-KORKEAKOULUISSA (FI) [03939801] **1760**

KESKIASTEEN KOULUNUUDISTUS. REFORMERINGEN AV MELLANSTADIEUTBILDNINGEN (FI) [05590043] **1760**

KESKIASTEEN KOULUTUKSEN KEHITTAMISOHJELMA VUOSILLE (FI) [19070551] **1760**

KESS TAX PRACTICE REPORT CEASED. (US/0162-7511) [02256545] **4735**

KESTER'S WILD GAME FOOD NURSERIES See ATTRACT WILDLIFE, IMPROVE OUR ENVIRONMENT **2187**

KESTNER-MUSEUM See JAHRESBERICHT / KESTNER-MUSEUM **4089**

KETAHANAN NASIONAL (IO/0303-4992) [01793688] **4048**

KETSUEKI TO MYAKUKAN (JA/0386-9717) [10278623] **3773**

KETSUGO SOSHIKI (JA/0389-7079) [10408710] **3805**

KETTENWIRK-PRAXIS (GW/0047-3405) [l00473405] **5353**

KETTERING-OAKWOOD TIMES, THE (US/8750-8141) [11799146] **5729**

KETTERING REPORT (US/0743-8478) [10674125] **5207**

KETTERING REVIEW (US/0748-8815) [11025917] 1760, **4660**

KETTLE RIVER ECHO, THE (CN/0715-5360) [09538852] **5788**

KEUANGAN (IO) [06468625] **795**

KEUANGAN NEGARA (IO) [01794240] **4735**

KEVO NOTES (FI/0356-861X) [25643689] **462**

KEW BULLETIN (UK/0075-5974) [07024976] **516**

KEW MAGAZINE See CURTIS'S BOTANICAL MAGAZINE **508**

KEW MAGAZINE, THE (UK/0265-3842) [10901458] **516**

KEW RECORD OF TAXONOMIC LITERATURE RELATING TO VASCULAR PLANTS FOR ... / ROYAL BOTANIC GARDENS, KEW, THE (UK) [03570679] **516**

KEW RICHMOND (UK/0961-4141) [l09614141] **516**

KEWA (CN/0228-4111) [08315777] **272**

KEWASKUM STATESMAN (US) [13549906] **5768**

KEWAUNEE ENTERPRISE (US) [11673966] **5768**

KEWAUNEE STAR, THE (US) [11779494] **5768**

KEXUE FAZHAN (CH/0250-1651) [01799753] **5123**

KEXUE TONGBAO (SCIENTIA) (US/0097-7411) [01796436] **5123**

KEY ABSTRACTS. ADVANCED MATERIALS (UK/0950-4753) [17191758] 2104, **2005**

KEY ABSTRACTS. ANTENNAS & PROPAGATION (UK/0950-4761) [17010659] 2070, **2005**

KEY ABSTRACTS. ARTIFICIAL INTELLIGENCE (UK/0950-477X) [16107617] 1214, 2070, **2005**

KEY ABSTRACTS. BUSINESS AUTOMATION (UK/0954-9153) [19645155] 1220, 1268, **2005**

KEY ABSTRACTS. COMPUTER COMMUNICATIONS & STORAGE (UK/0950-4788) [17010712] 1192, **2005**

KEY ABSTRACTS. COMPUTING IN ELECTRONICS AND POWER (UK/0950-4796) [16634622] 2070, **2005**

KEY ABSTRACTS. ELECTRONIC CIRCUITS (UK/0306-557X) [06371533] 2070, **2005**

KEY ABSTRACTS. ELECTRONIC INSTRUMENTATION (UK/0950-480X) [15353522] 2070, **2005**

KEY ABSTRACTS. FACTORY AUTOMATION (UK) 1220, **1209**

KEY ABSTRACTS. HIGH-TEMPERATURE SUPERCONDUCTORS (UK/0953-1262) [18609765] 2070, **2005**

KEY ABSTRACTS. HUMAN-COMPUTER INTERACTION (UK) 1192, **1209**

KEY ABSTRACTS. MACHINE VISION (UK/0952-7052) [18518786] 1214, 1220, **1209**

KEY ABSTRACTS. MEASUREMENTS IN PHYSICS (UK/0950-4818) [15353475] 4410, **4426**

KEY ABSTRACTS. MICROELECTRONICS AND PRINTED CIRCUITS (UK/0952-7060) [18609736] 2070, **2005**

KEY ABSTRACTS. MICROWAVE TECHNOLOGY (UK/0952-7079) [18609683] 2070, **2005**

KEY ABSTRACTS. NEURAL NETWORKS (UK) 1192, **1209**

KEY ABSTRACTS. OPTOELECTRONICS (UK/0950-4826) [17010833] 2070, **2006**

KEY ABSTRACTS. POWER SYSTEMS AND APPLICATIONS (UK/0950-4834) [15995198] 1193, **1209**

KEY ABSTRACTS. ROBOTICS & CONTROL (UK/0950-4842) [16107543] 1214, 2099, **1209**

KEY ABSTRACTS. SEMICONDUCTOR DEVICES (UK/0950-4850) [17064558] 2070, **2006**

KEY ABSTRACTS. SOFTWARE ENGINEERING (UK/0950-4869) [17157674] 1230, **1209**

KEY ABSTRACTS. TELECOMMUNICATIONS (UK/0950-4877) [17064377] 1159, **1125**

Alphabetical Title Index — KIDNEY

KEY BRITISH ENTERPRISES : KBE / COMPILED AND PUBLISHED BY PUBLICATIONS DIVISION, DUN & BRADSTREET LIMITED (UK/0142-5048) [03734028] 843, **688**

KEY BUSINESS DIRECTORY OF AUSTRALIA : KBD *CEASED.* (AT/0726-0288) [08731631] **688**

KEY BUSINESS RATIOS (US/0708-1553) [04879558] 688, **731**

KEY (CALGARY) (CN/0846-3913) [25127748] **5788**

KEY CARDIOLOGY (US/0899-8019) [18229181] **3708**

KEY COMPANY DIRECTORY, U.S. MANUFACTURING *CEASED.* (US) [07387722] **3482**

KEY ENGINEERING MATERIALS (SZ/1013-9826) [14050315] **2104**

KEY FINDER (US/0741-5338) [10149919] **2456**

KEY (GOREVILLE) (US/0160-8932) [03782916] 761, **929**

KEY INDICATORS (UK/0953-8348) [I09538348] **2307**

KEY INDICATORS OF DEVELOPING ASIAN AND PACIFIC COUNTRIES (PH/0116-3000) [23167916] **1571**

KEY INDICATORS (PORT-VILA, VANUATU) (NN) [09175796] **1571**

KEY INTERVENTIONAL RADIOLOGY *CEASED.* (US/1040-8479) [18550096] **3943**

KEY NEUROLOGY AND NEUROSURGERY (US/0886-8018) [12994100] 3969, **3837**

KEY NOTES MUSICAL LIFE IN THE NETHERLANDS (NE) **4127**

KEY NOTES (YPSILANTI, MICH.) (US/0887-1825) [13189108] **1760**

KEY OBSTETRICS AND GYNECOLOGY (US/0896-4467) [17154633] **3764**

KEY OFFICERS OF FOREIGN SERVICE POSTS (US/0023-0790) [01783120] **3131**

KEY OFFICIALS HANDBOOK (SJ) [01785133] **4660**

KEY OPTHALMOLOGY (US/0886-8026) [12994022] **3876**

KEY PERSONNEL DIRECTORY (LAW SOCIETY OF ALBERTA) (CN/0229-9089) [08091247] **2992**

KEY POPULATION AND VITAL STATISTICS. LOCAL AND HEALTH AUTHORITY AREAS / OFFICE OF POPULATION CENSUSES AND SURVEYS (UK) [17887866] 4788, **4554**

KEY REPORTER, THE (US/0023-0804) [01645168] **1092**

●KEY SOLUTIONS (US/1064-2145) [26232021] **1984**

KEY STATISTICS / DEPARTMENT OF STATISTICS, NEW ZEALAND (NZ/0114-2119) [19681874] **5330**

KEY STATISTICS, ELEMENTARY AND SECONDARY EDUCATION IN ONTARIO (CN/1180-4998) [24152214] **1760**

KEY. THIS WEEK IN MIAMI BEACH (US/0192-3536) [05065768] **5482**

KEY TO CHRISTIAN EDUCATION (US/0023-0839) [04090214] 1760, **4972**

KEY TO INCOME TAX (UK) [07848798] **4735**

KEY TO ROUTING NUMBERS (US/1064-5349) [14175484] **795**

KEY TO THE BUDGET DOCUMENTS (II) [02411878] **4735**

KEY (VICTORIA) (CN/1187-5216) [25352079] **4660**

KEY VIVE (AT/0310-8260) [05044866] **4127**

KEY WEST CITIZEN, THE (US) [02701762] **5650**

KEY-WORD-INDEX OF WILDLIFE RESEARCH (SZ) [02352926] 2197, **2184**

●KEY WORDS (US/1064-1211) [26210275] **3221**

KEYBOARD (UK) [01789010] **4127**

KEYBOARD ARTS *CEASED.* (US/0090-3361) [01784961] **4127**

KEYBOARD CLASSICS (US/1044-3266) [09375479] **4127**

●KEYBOARD CLASSICS & PIANO STYLIST (US/1069-4285) [27673059] **4127**

KEYBOARD COMPANION (US) **4127**

KEYBOARD (CUPERTINO, CALIF.) (US/0730-0158) [07628273] **4128**

KEYBOARD MUSICA Y TECNOLOGIA (SP) **4128**

KEYBOARD STUDIES (NE) [22514641] **4128**

KEYBOARD WORLD *SUSPENDED.* (US/0199-3313) [04409322] **4128**

KEYBOARDS (GW/0178-4641) [I01784641] **4128**

KEYES ENCYCLOPEDIC DICTIONARY OF PROCUREMENT LAW (US) [04559002] **2992**

KEYHOLE (US) [04721787] **2456**

KEYING IN (US) 1914, **688**

KEYNOTE (BOMBAY, INDIA) (II) [09228512] **2505**

KEYNOTE (VANCOUVER) (CN/0317-5855) [02248252] **4128**

KEYNOTES (DALLAS, TEX.) (US/0277-0792) [07471847] **2812**

KEYNOTES PRESCRIBED PHARMACEUTICALS (UK) **4313**

KEYS (NORTHFIELD, ILL.) (US/0895-948X) [16858986] **4128**

KEYS TO HEALTH (CN/0823-9827) [11564277] **3602**

KEYSTONE COAL BUYERS MANUAL *See* KEYSTONE NEWS BULLETIN **2142**

KEYSTONE COAL INDUSTRY MANUAL (US) [01198149] **2142**

KEYSTONE FOLKLORE *SUSPENDED.* (US/0149-8444) [01172984] **2321**

KEYSTONE GAZETTE (BELLEFONTE, PA. : 1989) (US/1052-8547) [20816311] **5737**

KEYSTONE NEWS BULLETIN *CEASED.* (US/0149-5801) [03527129] **2142**

KEYSTONE (PITTSBURGH, PA. 1968), THE (US/0744-4036) [07294960] **5432**

KEYSTONE SEEKERS GENEALOGICAL QUARTERLY (US/0737-2868) [09343147] **2456**

●KEYSTONE WATER QUALITY MANAGER (US/1069-0212) [27301389] 2235, **5535**

KEYWORD INDEX TO SERIAL TITLES (UK/0143-9553) [06729730] **2489**

KEYWORDS (US/0197-7342) [06103033] **1287**

KFKI (HU/0368-5330) [08163997] **4411**

KFRI INFORMATION BULLETIN (II) [11189317] **2422**

KFRI RESEARCH REPORT (II/0970-8103) [14547193] **2386**

KFZ I.E. KRAFTFAHRZEUG-BETRIEB UND AUTOMARKT (GW/0047-3049) [01783940] **5418**

KGST MITTEILUNGEN / KOMMUNALE GEMEINSCHAFTSSTELLE FUER VERWALTUNGSVEREINFACHUNG (GW) [07000374] **4660**

KHADI GRAMODYOG (II/0023-1029) [01586266] **1614**

KHALG GAZETI (AJ) [30101909] **5778**

KHANG CHIEN (US) **2266**

KHAOUA (CN/0700-9496) [03291566] **5031**

KHARCHOVA PROMYSLOVIST (UN/0554-2081) [01788395] **2347**

KHARKIVSKYI DERZHAVNYI UNIVERSYTET IMENI O.M. HORKOHO *See* PRIKLADNAIA MATEMATIKA I MEKHANIKA **3527**

KHARKIVSKYI DERZHAVNYI UNIVERSYTET IMENI O.M. HORKOHO *See* NAUKOVYI KOMUNIZM **1693**

KHARKIVSKYI DERZHAVNYI UNIVERSYTET IMENI O.M. HORKOHO *See* MATEMATIKA **3518**

KHARKIVSKYI POLITEKHNICHNYI INSTYTUT IMENI V. I. LENINA *See* RUSSIAN CASTINGS TECHNOLOGY **4018**

KHARKIVSKYI POLITEKHNICHNYI INSTYTUT IMENI V. I. LENINA *See* LITEJNOE PROIZVODSTVO **4007**

KHARKOV. UNIVERSYTET *See* FILOLOHIIA **3281**

KHARKOV. UNIVERSYTET. SERIIA FILOLOHICHNA *See* FILOLOHIIA **3281**

KHAVATIN DAIJIST (PK) [02239400] **3401**

KHETI (II/0023-1088) [09846834] **102**

KHIDROLOGIIA I METEOROLOGIIA (BU/0450-2078) [03267276] **1427**

KHIMIA I TEKHNOLOGIIA VODY. ENGLISH. SOVIET JOURNAL OF WATER CHEMISTRY AND TECHNOLOGY *See* JOURNAL OF WATER CHEMISTRY AND TECHNOLOGY **2234**

KHIMICHESKAIA FIZIKA (US/0733-2831) [08560637] **1055**

KHIMIIA I FIZICHESKAIA KHIMIIA POLIMEROV (KZ) [06653707] **1043**

KHIMIIA I KHIMICHESKAIA TEKHNOLOGIIA (BW) [02243509] **983**

KHIMIIA I TEKHNOLOGIIA VODY (US/0734-1679) [08558750] 5535, **2235**

KHIMIIA PLAZMY (RU) [01799394] **983**

KHIMIIA PRIRODNYKH SOEDINENII (UZ/0023-1150) [04084324] **1043**

KHIMIIA V SHKOLE (RU/0368-5632) [09490320] 1760, **983**

KHIPU (GW/0170-0391) [07604091] 2849, **323**

KHIRURGICHESKAIA I ORTOPEDICHESKAIA STOMATOLOGIIA (RU) [05639642] 1329, **3969**

KHLEBOPRODUKTY : EZHEMESIACHNYI TEORETICHESKII I NAUCHNO-PRAKTICHESKII ZHURNAL MINISTERSTVA KHLEBOPRODUKTOV SSSR I GOSUDARSTVENNOGO AGROPROMYSHLENNOGO KOMITETA SSSR (RU/0235-2508) [18282072] **2347**

KHLIBOROB UKRAINY *See* ZEMLIA I LIUDY UKRAINY **148**

KHLIBOROB UKRAINY. (KHLEBOROB UKRAINY) (RU/0131-7482) [04084463] **177**

KHLOPOK (RU/0235-2567) [18186994] **177**

KHOA HOC KY THUAT *See* TAP CHI KHOA HOC KY THUAT **5161**

KHOLODILNAIA TEKHNIKA (RU) [04084519] **2606**

KHOSANA : THE BULLETIN OF THE THAILAND/LAOS/CAMBODIA STUDIES GROUP OF THE SOUTHWEST ASIA COUNCIL, ASSOCIATION FOR ASIAN STUDIES (US/0898-1930) [03898235] **2505**

KHOZIAIN (RU/0868-7188) [24020636] **102**

KHOZIAIN (BW/0869-1479) [24042047] **102**

KHOZIAISTVO I PRAVO (RU) [06339107] **2992**

KHOZRASCHET, FINANSY I KREDIT (UN) [02662665] **795**

KHRANITELNA PROMISHLENOST (BU) [04154687] **2235**

KHRISTIANIN (RU) [24031483] **5062**

KHRONIKA KHUDOZHESTVENNOI ZHIZNI (RU) [02244058] **355**

KHRONIKA ZASHCHITY PRAV V SSSR (US/0892-9165) [01793638] **4510**

KHUDOZHESTVENNOE NASLEDIE: KHRANENIE, ISSLEDOVANIE, RESTAVRATSIIA (RU) [03244200] **355**

KHUDOZHESTVENNOE TVORCHESTVO / AKADEMIIA NAUK SSSR, NAUCHNYI SOVET PO ISTORII MIROVOI KULTURY, KOMISSIIA KOMPLEKSNOGO IZUCHENIIA KHUDOZHESTVENNOGO TVORCHESTVA (RU) [08803442] **3401**

KHUDOZHNIK (RU) [06181439] **355**

KI KLIMA KAELTE HEIZUNG *See* KI LUFT UND KAELTETECHNIK **618**

KI LUFT UND KAELTETECHNIK (GW/0945-0459) **618**

KIA (KO) [10400164] **1571**

KIABARA (NR/0331-8168) [06407235] **2849**

KIANJA (MG) [01787503] **2499**

KIBBUTZ TRENDS (IS/5792-7290) [23957417] **4542**

KIBERNETIKA, AUTOMATIZACIJA POSLOVANJA : MESECNI CASOPIS ZAVODA ZA EKONOMSKI EKSPERTIZE (YU) [08001702] **5123**

KIBERNETIKA I SISTEMNYI ANALIZ : KSA / INSTITUT KIBERNETIKI IM. V.M. GLUSHKOVA AN USSR (UN) [25502409] **1251**

KIBERNETIKA I VYCHISLITELNAIA TEKHNIKA. ENGLISH (US/0739-8417) [09823067] **1251**

KIBERNETIKA I VYCISLITELNAJA TEHNIKA (KIEV) (UN/0454-9910) [09490324] **1252**

KIBERNETIKA NA MORSKOM TRANSPORTE (UN) [04469195] **5451**

KIBUTS, HA- (IS) [02242665] **4542**

KICHO KWAHAK YONGU (KO) [08663875] **5123**

KICHO KWAHAK YONGUSO NONMUNJIP (KO) [12959915] **5123**

KICK ILLUSTRATED *See* INSIDE KARATE **4900**

KICK IT OVER (CN/0823-6526) [09929609] **4542**

KICK (NEW YORK, N.Y. 1983) (US/0882-8180) [11993766] **4903**

KICKER SPORTMAGAZIN (GW) [03796265] **4903**

KID (IT) **1865**

KID CARE MAGAZINE (US/0894-8720) [16274673] **5294**

KID CITY (US/0899-4293) [18093337] 1760, **1065**

KID PROOF (CN/0843-0284) [20001769] **1065**

●KIDDIE BAZAAR (US/1057-3011) [24004260] **1065**

KIDDIE KARE MAGAZINE (US/0887-350X) [13228406] **1760**

KIDMA *SUSPENDED.* (IS/0334-2212) [01951924] **1571**

●KIDNEY: A CURRENT SURVEY OF WORLD LITERATURE (US/0940-7936) [26672051] **3991**

KIDNEY Alphabetical Title Index

KIDNEY DISEASE (US/0270-062X) [06248299] **3991**

KIDNEY INTERNATIONAL (US/0085-2538) [01624467] **3991**

KIDNEY INTERNATIONAL. SUPPLEMENT (US/0098-6577) [01506985] **3991**

KIDNEY, THE *SUSPENDED*. (US/0023-1304) [01779032] **3991**

KIDNEY, UROLOGY, AND HEMATOLOGY *CEASED*. (US) [12380527] 3773, **3991**

KIDO (JA) [02554314] **4862**

KIDO (SEOUL, KOREA) (KO) [11411630] **4972**

KIDOKKYO SASANG (KO) [05523789] **4972**

KIDORUI (JA/0910-2205) [I09102205] **1357**

KIDOU *CEASED*. (SZ) **4851**

KIDRON NEWS THE DALTON GAZETTE, THE (US) [17892999] **5729**

KIDS (UK) [01788474] **5294**

KIDS (US/0023-1312) [01834183] **1065**

KIDS CAN READ (LONDON, ONT.) *CEASED*. (CN/0836-298X) [16861239] **3221**

KIDS CHAT (US) **1065**

KIDS CLUB MAGAZINE (US/1048-8839) [21058308] **1065**

KIDS COOKING NEWSLETTER (US/0889-843X) [14086676] **2791**

●KIDS COPY (US/1063-9659) [26206925] **1065**

KIDS CREATIONS (CN) **1085**

●KIDS CUE (US/1071-0620) [28540870] **5643**

KIDS DISCOVER (US/1054-2868) [22832169] **1065**

KIDS FASHIONS MAGAZINE (US/0362-6660) [02339811] **1085**

KIDS, KIDS, KIDZ MAGAZINE (US) **2282**

KIDS PARADE (CN/1183-4501) [23295242] **1085**

KIDS' PUZZLE EXPRESS (US) 4862, **1065**

KIDS (STORRS, CONN.) (US/1057-2996) [22164300] **5294**

KIDS' TIME OUT (US/1053-2420) [22485585] **1065**

KIDS TORONTO (CN/0826-9696) [13448793] **4851**

KIDS TORONTO DIRECTORY, THE (CN/0842-6023) [19611385] **1065**

KIDS VANCOUVER DIRECTORY, THE (CN/0842-4241) [19462164] **1065**

KIDSART NEWS (US/0892-8991) [15293203] 355, **1065**

KIDSCIENCE (MANKATO, MINN.) (US/1041-1798) [18674830] **1804**

KIDSNET (WASHINGTON, D.C.) (US/1064-1114) [26206983] **1134**

KIDSPORTS (ARLINGTON, VA.) *CEASED*. (US/1054-7002) [22942365] 4903, **1065**

KIDSPRINT TIMES (US/1065-3872) [26611441] **1804**

●KIDSTAR 1250 (US/1064-2056) [26229878] **1065**

KIDSTUFF (US/0278-632X) [07856452] **1065**

KIDTECH NEWS (US) **1224**

●KIEFERORTHOPAEDIE : DIE ZEITSCHRIFT FUER DIE PRAXIS (GW/0945-7917) [30643515] **1329**

KIEL TRI COUNTY RECORD (US) [15200117] **5768**

KIEL. UNIVERSITAT. INSTITUT FUR MEERESKUNDE *See* JAHRESBERICHT - INSTITUT FUER MEERESKUNDE AN DER UNIVERSITAT KIEL **1450**

KIEL. UNIVERSITAT. INSTITUT FUR WELTWIRTSCHAFT *See* BERICHT DES PRASIDENTEN UBER DIE TATIGKEIT DES INSTITUTS **1633**

KIELER ARBEITSPAPIERE (GW/0342-0787) [17168960] **1501**

KIELER GEOGRAPHISCHE SCHRIFTEN (GW) [03806390] **2567**

KIELER HISTORISCHE STUDIEN (GW/0453-8471) [01605188] **2622**

KIELER MEERESFORSCHUNGEN. SONDERHEFT (GW/0172-7893) [04628542] **555**

KIELER MILCHWIRTSCHAFTLICHE FORSCHUNGSBERICHTE (GW/0023-1347) [06188170] **196**

KIELER STUDIEN (GW/0340-6989) [01755142] **1571**

KIELER STUDIEN ZUR DEUTSCHEN LITERATURGESCHICHTE (GW/0453-8501) [01587626] **3401**

KIERKEGAARDIANA (DK/0075-6032) [01782991] **4351**

KIEV. POLITEKHNICHNYI INSTYTUT *See* VESTNIK KIEVSKOGO POLITEKHNICHESKOGO INSTITUTA. SERIIA PRIBOROSTROENIIA **3489**

KIEV. UNIVERSYTET *See* VISNYK KYIVSKOHO UNIVERSYTETU. SERIIA FIZYKY **4424**

KIGYO HAKUSHO (JA) [11931514] **1571**

KIGYO KAIKEI KISOKUSHU / OKURASHO SHOKENKYOKU KIGYO ZAIMUKA KANSHU (JA) [10787020] 795, **747**

KIGYO KEIRETSU SORAN (JA) [03459339] **1614**

KIGYOBETSU GAISHI DONYU SORAN : JOJO KIGYO HEN (JA) [02245151] **795**

KIITO KENSA KENKYU HOKOKU (JA/0285-0567) [09579305] **5353**

KIJI NO UCHIGAWA / ASAHI SHINBUNSHA HEN (JA) [10903625] **2921**

KIJK OP HET NOORDEN (NE/0023-1363) [01784552] **1501**

KIJK UIT (BE) **795**

KIKAI GIJUTSU (JA/0451-9396) [10290936] **2119**

KIKAI GIJUTSU KENKYUJO *See* BULLETIN OF MECHANICAL ENGINEERING LABORATORY **2111**

KIKAI GIJUTSU KENKYUJO SHOHO (JA/0388-4252) [09847039] **5123**

KIKAI KIGU RYUTSU NO DOKO: CHOSA NO YOSHI TO SONO KEKKA (JA) [01797384] **1614**

KIKAI SEKKEI (JA/0387-1045) [I03871045] **2119**

KIKAI TO KOGU (JA/0387-1053) [10279793] 3482, **2119**

KIKAIKA NOGYO (JA) [08595752] **159**

KIKAIKA NOGYO (JA/0023-1371) [I00231371] **159**

KIKAN ANIMA (JA) [02246452] **4167**

KIKAN GENDAI KYOIKU SHINRI (JA) [02244190] **4602**

KIKAN JICHITAIGAKU KENKYU (JA) [08054069] **4660**

KIKAN JINJI GYOSEI (JA) [03666192] **4704**

KIKAN KAGAKU SOSETSU / NIHON KAGAKKAI HEN (JA) [24728847] **983**

KIKAN KEIZAI KENKYU (JA/0387-1789) [09227366] **1571**

KIKAN KOKKAI GIIN (JA) [06714742] **4660**

KIKAN KYOIKU UNDO (JA) [04372741] **1760**

KIKAN KYOSHOKU KATEI (JA) [02243454] **1760**

KIKAN NIHON KEIZAI SHIHYO *CEASED*. (JA) [16797632] **1593**

KIKAN NIHON SHISO SHI (JA) [02749922] **2656**

KIKAN RIRON-KEIZAIGAKU (JA/0557-109X) [01799687] **1501**

KIKAN RODOHO (JA) [19346899] **3150**

KIKAN SHAKAI HOSHO KENKYU (JA/0387-3064) [05671705] **5294**

KIKAN YUSO TEMBO (JA) [02556221] **843**

KIKANSHI; BANKOKU BUKKYOTO REMMEI KEN SEITO KOKUGO UNDO (JA) [04276688] **5021**

KILDESKATTELEKSIKON (DK) [02242125] **4735**

KILGORE NEWS HERALD, THE (US) [14369436] **5751**

KILIMO NEWS : NEWSLETTER OF THE MINISTRY OF AGRICULTURE (KE) [07231925] **102**

KILK (IR) [23675833] 355, **3401**

KILLAM WORLD (CN/0821-249X) [10051981] **1833**

KILLEEN DAILY HERALD (US) [14353839] **5751**

KILLERS AND CRIPPLERS, THE (US) [03007479] **3602**

KILLSHOT (CN/0711-7094) [08724020] **4862**

KILLSHOT (PADUCAH, KY.) (US/1069-2614) [25099723] **4903**

KILOMBERO SUGAR COMPANY *See* ANNUAL REPORT - KILOMBERO SUGAR COMPANY **2327**

KILT AND HARP, THE (US/0882-6811) [11926916] **4128**

KIMBALL TRI-COUNTY NEWS (US) [01606417] **5696**

KIMBERLY DAILY BULLETIN (CN) **5788**

KIMBERLY DIRECTORY / PREPARED BY THE OFFICE OF REGIONAL ADMINISTRATION AND THE NORTH WEST (AT) [07309979] **1501**

KIME'S INTERNATIONAL LAW DIRECTORY (UK/0075-6040) [03874378] **3131**

KIMIA (MY/0126-9070) [01790674] **983**

KIMYA SANAYI (TU/0368-7163) [I03687163] 5123, **983**

KIN HUNTERS (US/1064-9999) [19087482] **2456**

KIN IN LINN (US/0737-6987) [09415302] **2457**

KIN KOLLECTING (US/1069-207X) [16782240] **2457**

KIN MAGAZINE (CN/0822-9201) [11046535] **2457**

KINAADMAN. WISDOM (PH) [05301527] 2849, **2656**

KINATUINAMOT ILLENGAJUK / LABRADOR GENDAI INUIT ASSOCIATION (CN/0715-4437) [09159573] **2536**

KINCARDINE INDEPENDENT, THE (CN/0834-6674) [18047188] **5788**

KIND EN ADOLESCENT (NE) 4602, **1065**

KIND NEWS JR (US/1050-821X) [21719447] **2197**

KIND TEACHER (US/1049-9482) [21056764] **1760**

KINDAI CHUGOKU (JA) [03170039] **2657**

KINDAI CHUGOKU KENKYU IHO / HENSHUSHA, TOYO BUNKO KINDAI CHUGOKU KENKYU IINKAI (JA) [06227409] **2657**

KINDER (IT) **1760**

KINDER (GW) **1804**

KINDERARZT, DER (GW/0340-5877) [I03405877] **3602**

KINDERARZTLICHE PRAXIS (GW/0023-1495) [01755154] **3906**

KINDERBOOK NEWSLETTER, THE (US/0896-1336) [16932496] **3401**

KINDERCENTRA / CENTRAAL BUREAU VOOR DE STATISTIEK (NE) [05319125] **5294**

KINDEREN (NE) 2282, **1065**

KINDERGARTEN CLASS PACKET, THE (US/0160-4279) [03686601] **1760**

KINDERGARTEN CREATIVE TEACHING AIDS (US/0190-261X) [04681726] **1899**

KINDERGARTEN HEUTE (GW/0344-3949) [I03443949] **1804**

KINDERGARTEN PROGRAM HELPS (US/0163-8718) [04520245] 1899, **5062**

KINDERGARTEN TEACHER (US/0745-8258) [08717768] **4972**

●KINDERGARTEN TEACHER GUIDE (US/1072-1444) [28872311] **4972**

KINDERHEILKUNDE UND JUGENDMEDIZIN (GW/0932-6596) [15697910] **3906**

KINDERKRANKENSCHWESTER (GW/0723-2276) [09821910] **3906**

KINDEROPVANG (NE) 1760, **1066**

KINDEX (US/0733-8937) [02706013] 2992, **3081**

●KINDHEIT UND ENTWICKLUNG (GW) [30548890] **4602**

KINDRED SPIRIT (US) [04887540] **4972**

KINDRED SPIRIT NETWORK NEWSLETTER *See* COMMON BOUNDARY, THE **4582**

KINDRED SPIRITS (CN/0823-3837) [11734497] **2457**

KINDRED SPIRITS OF P.E.I (CN/1184-7603) [24256731] **3401**

KINEDIT (CN/0824-2402) [10008028] **5788**

KINEMA JUMPO. / KINEJUN: MOTION PICTURE TIMES (JA) [03281818] **4073**

KINEMATIKA I FIZIKA NEBESNYH TEL (UN/0233-7665) [11941046] **4411**

KINEMATIKA I FIZIKA NEBESNYKH TEL (US/0884-5913) [12406513] **396**

KINEMATOGRAPH FRANKFURT (GW/0936-3777) [I09363777] **4073**

KINESIOLOGY AND MEDICINE FOR DANCE (US/1058-7438) [20586517] **1313**

KINESIOLOGY (WASHINGTON) (US/0093-6960) [01792593] **583**

KINESIS (CARBONDALE, ILL.) (US/0023-1568) [02280301] **4351**

KINESIS REPORT, THE (US/0193-1911) [05138912] 1115, **4602**

KINESIS (VANCOUVER) (CN/0317-9095) [01721050] **5560**

KINESIS (WHITEFISH, MONT.) (US/1056-781X) [23853468] **3402**

KINESITHERAPEUTE PRATICIEN (FR/0297-6005) [I02976005] **3806**

KINESITHERAPIE SCIENTIFIQUE (FR/0023-1576) [04869210] **4381**

KINETICS AND CATALYSIS (US/0023-1584) [01783016] **1044**

KINETIKA I KATALIZ (RU/0453-8811) [02448129] **1055**

KINETOSCOPIO, EL (CK/0121-3776) [23127099] **4073**

KINFOLK (US/0556-9796) [05050673] **2457**

KINFOLKS (LAKE CHARLES, LA.) (US/0742-7654) [10422056] **2457**

KING (IT) **2489**

KING ABDULAZIZ MEDICAL JOURNAL (SU/0254-413X) [08158198] **3602**

KING TOWNSHIP WEEKLY, THE (CN/0380-3686) [02443364] **5788**

KINGBIRD, THE (US/0023-1606) [01782741] **5618**

KINGDOM BUILDER / BAPTIST TRAINING UNION, THE (US/0746-6889) [10223252] **5062**

KINGFISHER (BERKELEY, CALIF.) (US) [15691760] **3402**

KINGFISHER FREE PRESS, THE (US) [12239699] **5732**

KING'S COAL EXPORT REPORT (US/1047-4269) [20690122] **2142**

KING'S COALSTATS. COAL EXPORT REPORT (US/1050-172X) [21414612] **2142**

KING'S COALSTATS. COAL PRODUCTION REPORT (US/1050-1665) [22459390] **2142**

KING'S COALSTATS. ELECTRIC UTILITIES REPORT (US/1050-1525) [21403821] **2142**

KING'S COALSTATS. FOB MINE PRICES (US/1050-1649) [21404253] **2142**

KING'S COALSTATS. GRAIN EXPORT REPORT (US/1050-169X) [21404318] **843**

KING'S COALSTATS. INTERNATIONAL COAL TRADE (US/1050-1703) [21404376] **2142**

KING'S COALSTATS. MONTHLY COAL GUIDE (US/1050-1533) [21403269] **2142**

KING'S COALSTATS. MONTHLY COAL GUIDE. ELECTRIC UTILITIES REPORT (US/1050-1495) [21402064] 2070, **2142**

KING'S COALSTATS. MONTHLY COAL GUIDE. MINE PRICE REPORT (US/1050-1509) [21402642] **2142**

KING'S COALSTATS. MONTHLY COAL GUIDE. MINE PRODUCTION REPORT (US/1050-1517) [21402760] **2142**

KING'S COALSTATS. PETROLEUM COKE EXPORT REPORT (US/1050-1711) [21404403] **2142**

KING'S GAZETTE (UK/0085-2546) [05026567] **3602**

KING'S INTERNATIONAL COAL TRADE & WORLD COAL STATISTICS (US/0749-9043) [11190008] **2142**

KING'S LETTER, THE (US/0147-1384) [03131492] **4128**

KING'S NORTHERN COAL (US/0749-1719) [11103921] **1614**

KING'S PETROLEUM COKE REPORT (US/1047-4285) [20690147] **2142**

KING'S SOUTHERN COAL (US/0749-1697) [11104096] **1614**

KING'S THEOLOGICAL REVIEW **CEASED.** (UK/0143-5922) [06718306] **4972**

KING'S WESTERN COAL (US/0749-1700) [11103931] **1614**

KINGSMAN See KING'S THEOLOGICAL REVIEW **4972**

KINGSTON CITY DIRECTORY (US) [15200665] **2567**

KINGSTON COMMERCE (CN/0711-3358) [08469692] **843**

KINGSTON LAW REVIEW, THE **CEASED.** (UK/0453-8854) [01783912] **2992**

KINGSTON PUBLIC LIBRARY INQUIRER, THE (CN/1193-9540) [28061942] **3221**

KINGSTON RELATIONS (CN/1188-1089) [11881089] **2457**

KINGSTON THIS WEEK (CN/0712-9068) [08867632] **5788**

KINGSTON WOMEN'S CENTRE See KINGSTON WOMEN'S CENTRE NEWSLETTER **5560**

KINGSTON WOMEN'S CENTRE NEWSLETTER (CN/0383-9915) [02915634] **5560**

KINH-TE TAP-SAN (VM) [01795033] **1571**

KINISTINO POST [MICROFORM], THE (CN) [15467411] **5788**

KINJIN KENKYUJO KENKYU HOKOKU (JA/0388-8266) [01194597] **575**

KINJIN KENKYUSHO See KINJIN KENKYUJO KENKYU HOKOKU **575**

KINJO GAKUIN DAIGAKU RONSHU, KASEIGAKU HEN (JA/0286-8237) [11580127] **2791**

KINKI ARUMINIUMU HYOMEN SHORI KENKYUKAI KAISHI (JA/0285-6689) [10292777] **4006**

KINKI CHIIKI TSUSHO SANGYO TOKEI YORAN / OSAKA TSUSHO SANGYOKYOKU HEN (JA) [08720505] **1571**

KINKI DAIGAKU GENSHIRYOKU KENKYUJO NENPO (JA) [10279841] 1949, **4411**

KINKI DAIGAKU IGAKU ZASSHI (JA/0385-8367) [05045846] **3602**

KINKI DAIGAKU KOGAKUBU KENKYU HOKOKU (JA/0386-491X) [10339973] **1984**

KINKI DAIGAKU KYUSHU KOGAKUBU KENKYU HOKOKU. RIKOGAKU-HEN (JA/0288-738X) [l0288738X] **1984**

KINKI DAIGAKU NOGAKUBU KIYO (JA/0453-8889) [01755165] **102**

KINKI DAIGAKU RIKOGAKUBU KENKYU HOKOKU (JA/0386-4928) [10410858] **5123**

KINKI NORIN SUISAN TOKEI (JA) [02246476] **102**

KINKI ZAISEI KEIZAI TOKEI NEMPO (JA) [03140154] **1571**

KINO (PL/0023-1673) [01783563] **4073**

KINO (GW) [18043818] **4073**

KINO (BU/0861-4393) [24185297] **4073**

KINO : GERMAN FILM (GW) **4073**

KINO I VREMIA (RU) [05140527] **4073**

KINO; OBRAZKOVY FILMOVY CRTNACTIDENIK (XR) [06181475] **4073**

KINO ZAIRYO (JA/0286-4835) [09288752] **1984**

KINOBUCH (GW) [03357050] **4073**

KINOPANORAMA (RU) [04865356] **4073**

KINOSCHRIFTEN : JAHRBUCH DER GESELLSCHAFT FUER FILMTHEORIE (AU) [19651444] **4073**

KINOSHI KENKYUKAI SHI / ANNALS OF THE HIGH PERFORMANCE PAPER SOCIETY, JAPAN (JA/0288-5867) [11605416] **4235**

KINOSTSENARII; ALMANAKH (RU) [02240817] **3402**

KINSHIP (US/0023-1703) [04090304] **5294**

KINSHIP KRONICLE (US/0882-9802) [10635900] **2457**

KINSMAN COURIER, THE (US) [10079019] **2457**

KINXIONS (RICHMOND) (CN/1183-2312) [24265678] **2457**

KINYU SHOROPPO (JA) [02712550] **795**

KINZOKU (JA/0368-6337) [09936548] **4006**

KINZOKU HAKUBUTSUKAN KIYO (JA/0285-8452) [10603220] **4006**

KINZOKU KOGYO JIGYODAN See SEIMITSU CHOSA HOKOKUSHO: JOZANKEI CHIIKI **2151**

KINZOKU KOGYO JIGYODAN. CHISHITSU KAISEKI IINKAI See CHISHITSU KAISEKI IINKAI HOKOKUSHO **2136**

KINZOKU KOGYO JIGYODAN SHIRYO SENTA See KAIGAI KOGYO JUJO CHOSA HOKOKUSHO : AMERIKA, MARESHIA, SURIRANKA, TAI, KANKOKU **1440**

KINZOKU KOGYO JIGYODAN SHIRYO SENTA See KAIGAI KOGYO JIJO CHOSA HOKOKUSHO: MADAGASUKARU, SUWAJIRANDO **1614**

KINZOKU KOGYO JIGYODAN SHIRYO SENTA See KAIGAI KOGYO JIJO CHOSA HOKOKUSHO: INDO, PAKISUTAN, BANGURADISSHU **1614**

KINZOKU KOGYO JIGYODAN SHIRYO SENTA See KAIGAI KOGYO JIJO CHOSA HOKOKUSHO: NAIJERIA, GANA, KOTO JIBOARU **1614**

KINZOKU ZAIRYO GIJUTSU KENKYUJO (JAPAN) See KINZOKU ZAIRYO GIJUTSU KENKYUJO NEMPO **4006**

KINZOKU ZAIRYO GIJUTSU KENKYUJO NEMPO (JA) [07486945] **4006**

KIOPCHE YONGAM (KO) [08794383] **1614**

KIOWA COUNTY SIGNAL (GREENSBURG, KAN. : 1936) (US) [11666641] **5676**

KIOWA INDIAN NEWS (US) [08800814] **5732**

KIOWA NEWS (KIOWA, KAN. : 1983) (US) [09614770] **5676**

KIPLING JOURNAL (UK/0023-1738) [01782296] **3402**

KIPLINGER AGRICULTURE LETTER, THE (US/0023-1746) [13545322] **102**

KIPLINGER CALIFORNIA LETTER, THE (US/0453-9249) [04093118] **905**

KIPLINGER FLORIDA LETTER See KIPLINGERS FLORIDA BUSINESS LETTER **905**

KIPLINGER FLORIDA LETTER, THE (US/0023-1754) [02448134] **905**

KIPLINGER TAX LETTER, THE (US/0023-1762) [02251019] **4735**

KIPLINGER WASHINGTON LETTER, THE (US/0023-1770) [01642252] 688, **4480**

KIPLINGERS FLORIDA BUSINESS LETTER (US) [29209175] **905**

KIPLINGER'S PERSONAL FINANCE MAGAZINE (US/1056-697X) [23819939] **795**

KIPLINGER'S PERSONAL FINANCE MAGAZINE [MICROFORM] (US/1056-697X) [24357349] **795**

●KIPLINGER'S RETIREMENT REPORT (US/1075-6671) [30107831] **4480**

KIPLINGER'S SURE WAYS TO CUT YOUR TAXES (US) **4735**

KIPPING CHESS CLUB MAGAZINE, THE (UK) [04154381] **4862**

KIPS BOOK, THE (US/0192-5334) [05021075] **1274**

KIPU (EC) [10504645] 240, **5250**

KIRATI YUGA (II) [02399722] **1682**

KIRBYVILLE BANNER (US) [17368986] **5751**

KIRCHE IM OSTEN (GW/0453-9273) [02235431] **5039**

KIRCHE IM OSTEN. MONOGRAPHIENREIHE (GW/0453-9281) [02276164] **5062**

KIRCHE IN NOT (GW) [02216389] **5031**

KIRCHE UND ISRAEL (GW/0179-7239) [17010964] **5050**

KIRCHE UND KONFESSION (GW/0453-929x) [02270727] **4972**

KIRCHE UND RECHT (AU) [05058446] **4972**

KIRCHENCHOR, DER (GW/0023-1800) [07526662] **4128**

KIRCHENMUSIKALISCHES JAHRBUCH (GW/0075-6199) [01624291] **4128**

KIRCHENMUSIKER, DER (GW/0023-1819) [04711688] **4128**

KIRCHLICHE ZEITGESCHICHTE (GW/0932-9951) [20309483] **4972**

KIRCHLICHES AMTSBLATT DER EVANGELISCHEN KIRCHE IM RHEINLAND (GW) [03786452] **4972**

KIRCHLICHES JAHRBUCH FUER DIE EVANGELISCHE KIRCHE IN DEUTSCHLAND (GW/0075-6210) [06979970] **5062**

KIRCHLICHES MONATSBLATT FUER DAS EVANGELISCH-LUTHERISCHE HAUS (US) [01714590] **5062**

KIRGIZIIA V PECHATI SSSR I ZARUBEZHNYKH SOTSIALISTICHESKIKH STRAN (KG/0204-0670) [19174754] **418**

KIRISUTOKYO KAGAKU KOTARI. SEISHO KYOKA (US/0145-7527) [02775293] **5062**

KIRISUTOKYO KAGAKU SAKIGAKE (US/0145-8019) [02779043] **4972**

KIRJALLISUUDENTUTKIJAIN SEURAN VUOSIKIRJA (FI/0355-0176) [01782477] **3402**

KIRJASTOLEHTI (FI/0023-1843) [01604608] **3221**

KIRJASTOTIEDE JA INFORMATIIKKA (FI/0358-9803) [l03589803] **3221**

KIRKE OG KULTUR (NO/0023-186X) [08418585] **4972**

KIRKEHISTORISKE SAMLINGER (DK/0450-3171) [l04503171] **2622**

KIRKIA (RH) [04186906] 102, **516**

KIRKLAND'S ROCKY MOUNTAIN PETROLEUM DIRECTORY See ROCKY MOUNTAIN PETROLEUM DIRECTORY **4277**

KIRKUS CHILDRENS (US) 1066, **3345**

KIRKUS REVIEWS (US) [24199017] **3345**

KIRKWOOD HISTORICAL REVIEW (US/0451-9949) [16708904] **2743**

KIROGI (KO) [04375604] **2505**

KIROKU (JA) [05698535] **2921**

KIRON, LE (CN/0709-8456) [08071386] **4903**

KIRSCHNER'S INSURANCE DIRECTORIES. NORTHERN CALIFORNIA (US/1071-8230) [19347988] **2886**

KIRSCHNER'S INSURANCE DIRECTORIES. PACIFIC NORTHWEST (US/1071-8222) [25644416] **2886**

KIRSCHNER'S INSURANCE DIRECTORY. SOUTHERN CALIFORNIA (US/1071-8249) [18888387] **2886**

KIRTLANDIA (US/0075-6245) [01554907] **4167**

KIRUTAYUKAM (CE) [08721531] **3402**

KIRYAT SEFER (IS/0023-1851) [01755169] **5050**

KISAENGCHUNGHAK CHAPCHI **See** KOREAN JOURNAL OF PARASITOLOGY, THE **3715**

KISALFOLDI KONYVTAROS (HU/0209-7788) [I02097788] **3221**

KISARAZU KOGYO KOTO SEMMON GAKKO **See** KISARAZU KOGYO KOTO SEMMON GAKKO KIYO **5232**

KISARAZU KOGYO KOTO SEMMON GAKKO KIYO (JA) [02243439] **5232**

KISEICHUGAKU ZASSHI (JA/0021-5171) [04525172] **462**

KISEKI (JA) [01790322] **3465**

KISERLETES ORVOSTUDOMANY (HU/0023-1878) [06177008] **3602**

KISHO EISEI SENTA GIJUTSU HOKOKU (JA) [07417684] **1427**

KISHO KENKYU NOTO (JA) [02749802] **1408, 1427**

KISHO KENKYUJO (JAPAN) **See** KISHO KENKYUJO KENKYU GYOSEKI GAIYO SHU **1427**

KISHO KENKYUJO KENKYU GYOSEKI GAIYO SHU (JA/0303-013X) [01797217] **1427**

KISHOCHO GEPPO : ZENKOKU KISHOHYO (JA) [06148603] **1427**

KISHOCHO HARO KANSOKU SHIRYO. / THE RESULTS OF SEA WAVES OBSERVATIONS (JA) [05080202] **1451**

KISHOCHO KAIYO KISHO BUI ROBOTTO KANSOKU SHIRYO. / DATA FROM OCEAN DATA BUOY STATIONS (JA) [04177241] **1427**

KISHOCHO NENPO: ZENKOKU KISHOHYO. ANNUAL REPORT OF THE JAPAN METEOROLOGICAL AGENCY: METEOROLOGICAL OBSERVATIONS (JA) [04486222] **1427**

KISHU KEIZAISHI BUNKASHI KENKYUJO KIYO (JA) [08858950] **1571**

KISHWAUKEE GENEALOGISTS (US) **2457**

KISKERESKEDELEM ES A FOGYASZTASI SZOLGALTATASOK ... BAN / KOZPONTI STATISZTIKAI HIVATAL, A (HU) [20881707] **955**

KISKERESKEDELMI ARALAKULAS (HU) [01789603] **1593**

KISO, KANKYO KAGAKU KENKYU (JA/0285-6905) [07878736] **1357**

KISO SEIBUTSUGAKU KENKYUJO (JAPAN) **See** SEIBUTSU KAGAKU SOGO KENKYU KIKO KISO SEIBUTSUGAKU KENKYUJO YORAN **472**

KISO SEIBUTSUGAKU KENKYUJO NENPO (JA) [10103498] **462**

KISO SHINRIGAKU KENKYU (JA/0287-7651) [I02877651] **4602**

KISS **CEASED.** (US/0161-2735) [03918732] **5074**

KISTENYESZTOK LAPJA (HU/0133-4565) [02560584] **5589**

KISUL SIDAE (KO) [09198390] **5123**

KISWAHILI (TZ/0856-048X) [01787500] **3402, 3293**

KIT AB' AL -ILM' (CN/1188-052X) [25796517] **3221**

KIT - ASSOCIATION OF RESEARCH LIBRARIES. SYSTEMS AND PROCEDURES EXCHANGE CENTER (US/0160-3582) [03065585] **3221**

●KIT CAR (US/1072-7981) [29203924] **5418**

KIT CAR ILLUSTRATED (US/1062-9610) [25820952] **5418, 2774**

KIT GUNS & HOBBY GUNSMITHING (US/0882-7362) [11900985] **4006, 2774**

KITA CHOSEN KENKYU (JA) [03478496] **2657**

KITA KANTO IGAKU (JA/0023-1908) [09947159] **3602**

KITA NIHON BYOGAICHU KENKYUKAIHO (JA/0368-623X) [I0368623X] **102**

KITA NIPPON BYOGAICHU KENKYUKAI **See** KITA NIPPON BYOGAICHU KENKYUKAI HO **102**

KITA NIPPON BYOGAICHU KENKYUKAI HO (JA) [04589962] **102**

KITAB AL-ARABI FI LUBNAN / AL-NADI AL-THAQAFI AL-ARABI (LE) [07621650] **418**

KITAB AL-SANAWI (MUASSASAH AL-ARABIYAN LIL-DIRASAT WA-AL-NASHR) (LE) [11474333] **2657**

KITABAT (BA) [11477221] **3465, 3402**

KITABNAMAH-I RAHAVARD (US/0747-9034) [10820934] **3402**

KITABU CHA JUA (US) [02241663] **3402**

KITAKYUSHU DAIGAKU HOSEI RONSHU (JA) [04829551] **2992**

KITAKYUSHU DAIGAKU SHOKEI RONSHU (JA) [06898032] **5207**

KITAKYUSHU KOGYO KOTO SENMON GAKKO KENKYU HOKOKU (JA/0285-5283) [10279931] **1092, 5123**

KITANOMARU; KOKURITSU KOBUNSHOKAN HO (JA) [02245415] **2482**

KITASATO ARCHIVES OF EXPERIMENTAL MEDICINE, THE **CEASED.** (JA/0023-1924) [01755170] **3602**

KITASATO IGAKU (JA/0385-5449) [10279870] **3602**

KITCHEN & BATH BUSINESS (US/0730-2487) [07948941] **2901**

KITCHEN & BATH CONCEPTS (US/8750-9504) [11950890] **2902**

KITCHEN & BATH DESIGN NEWS (US/8750-345X) [11269792] **2902**

KITCHEN AND BATH IDEAS (US/0731-5600) [08201383] **2902**

KITCHEN & BATH SOURCE BOOK (US) [22283316] **2902**

KITCHEN AND FAMILY ROOM IDEAS (US) [01783913] **2902**

KITCHEN GARDEN (NEWARK, DEL.), THE (US/0883-7333) [12221209] **2422**

KITCHENER-WATERLOO RECORD (CN/0824-5150) [11085182] **5788**

KITELINES (US/0192-3439) [03904284] **4851**

KITH AND KIN OF BOONE COUNTY, WEST VIRGINIA (US/0273-0391) [06321097] **2457**

KITH 'N KIN (FREMONT, OHIO) (US/1053-5837) [22631696] **2457**

KITPLANES (US/0891-1851) [12960382] **27**

KITSUENSHITSU (JA) [11767380] **4788**

KITTSON COUNTY ENTERPRISE (US) [01755172] **5696**

KIUN CHOSA WOLBO (KO) [07939162] **1614**

KIVA (TUSCON, ARIZ.), THE (US/0023-1940) [01782335] **272**

KIWANIS (US/0162-5276) [04171174] **5232**

KIWON (KO) [05721720] **3402**

KIYO (JA) [07745419] **2657**

KIYO - CHUO DAIGAKU BUNGAKUBU (JA) [02243457] **5232**

KIYO - HIROSAKI DAIGAKU IRYO GIJUTSU TANKI DAIGAKUBU (JA) [04165532] **5232**

KIYO (ISHIKAWA KENRITSU KYODO SHIRYOKAN) **See** KIYO **2657**

KIYO - KYORITSU JOSHI TANKI DAIGAKU. BUNKA (JA/0388-3647) [I03883647] **1092, 3402**

KIYO - TOBA SHOSEN KOTO SEMMON GAKKO (JA) [06653478] **1833**

KIYO - YUGE SHOSEN KOTO SEMMON GAKKO (JA) [06225785] **4178**

KIYWWNIYM (IS/0334-472X) [05367257] **5050**

KJEMI (NO/0023-1983) [01790998] **1027**

KKL STRASBOURG **See** ALMANACH - K.K.L. STRASBOURG **2609**

KKUMIM (KO) [04765247] **373**

KLACTO JAZZ MAGAZINE (US) [10220441] **4128**

KLAGE : KOLNER LINGUISTISCHE ARBEITEN, GERMANISTIK (GW) [14583989] **3293**

KLAGENFURTER BEITRAEGE ZUR SPRACHWISSENSCHAFT (AU) [03679935] **3293**

KLANSMAN, THE (US/0749-0763) [06967634] **2266**

KLANWATCH INTELLIGENCE REPORT : A PROJECT OF THE SOUTHERN POVERTY LAW CENTER (US) [07560969] **4510**

KLASGIDS (SA/1010-3465) [11587469] **3402, 3293**

KLASINGS BOOTSMARKT INTERNATIONAL (GW) [06721580] **4178**

KLASSIFIKATORY I DOKUMENTY V ASU / GOSUDARSTVENNYI KOMITET STANDARTOV SOVETA MINISTROV SSSR, VSESOIUZNYI NAUCHNO-ISSLEDOVATELSKII INSTITUT TEKHNICHESKOI INFORMATSII, KLASSIFIKATSII I KODIROVANIIA) (RU) [09321478] **875, 1193**

KLATEN DALAM ANGKA (IO) [09689784] **5330**

KLAUS-GROTH-GESELLSCHAFT (GERMANY) **See** JAHRESGABE - KLAUS-GROTH-GESELLSCHAFT **3398**

KLEBEN UND DICHTEN (0943-1454) [I09431454] **1055**

KLEI, GLAS, KERAMIEK (NE/0167-5001) [06436170] **2592**

KLEINE DEUTSCHE PROSADENKMALER DES MITTELALTERS (GW/0075-6318) [02236438] **3345**

KLEINE HEFTE ZUR STADTGESCHICHTE (GW) [21016044] **2696**

KLEINE PHILOSOPHISCHE BIBLIOGRAPHIEN (GW/0420-0985) [02233507] **4365**

KLEINE SCHRIFTEN (GW/0588-344X) [03211761] **4090**

KLEINE SCHRIFTEN (GW/0524-0379) [02618448] **3221**

KLEINE SCHRIFTEN DER GESELLSCHAFT FUER THEATERGESCHICHTE (GW/0176-8905) [01751184] **5365**

KLEINE TEXTE FUER VORLESUNGEN UND UEBUNGEN (GW) [06870185] **3402, 3293**

KLEINE ZEITUNG (AU) [20070867] **5778**

KLEINHEUBACHER BERICHTE (GW/0343-5725) [05052825] **396**

KLEINTIER-PRAXIS (GW/0023-2076) [01755177] **5515**

KLEIO (SA/0023-2084) [02270107] **2641**

KLERONOMIA : PERIODIKON DEMODIEUMA TOU PATRIARCHIKOU HIDRYMATOS PATERIKON MELETON (GR) [02352966] **4972**

●KLIATT (WELLESLEY, MASS.) (US/1065-8602) [26779299] **3221**

KLIATT YOUNG ADULT PAPERBACK BOOK GUIDE **See** KLIATT (WELLESLEY, MASS.) **3221**

KLIK (NE) **3602**

KLIK PHOTO SHOWCASE (US) **4371**

KLIMA-EILINFORMATION (GW) **1427**

KLIMA, KALTE, HEIZUNG (GW/0172-1984) [06687513] **2606**

KLIMAATBEHEERSING (NE) **2606**

KLIMAT I GIDROLOGIIA SIBIRI I DALNEGO VOSTOKA (RU/0130-2272) [03943212] **1416**

KLIMATOLOGISCHE WERTE (GW) **1427**

KLINICESKAJA HIRURGIJA (KIEV) (UN/0023-2130) [01605338] **3969**

KLINICESKAJA MEDICINA (RU/0023-2149) [01713561] **3602**

●KLINICHESKAIA LABORATORNAIA DIAGNOSTIKA (RU/0869-2084) [30431410] **983, 3896**

KLINIKA OCZNA (PL/0023-2157) [07099988] **3876**

KLINIKARZT, DER (GW/0341-2350) [02096126] **3602**

KLINISCH-ONKOLOGISCHES SEMINAR (GW/0344-595X) [03512235] **3820**

KLINISCH-RADIOLOGISCHES SEMINAR (GW/0342-443X) [04644162] **3943**

KLINISCHE ANASTHESIOLOGIE UND INTENSIVTHERAPIE (GW/0341-5023) [00983302] **3683**

KLINISCHE CHEMIE IN EINZELDARSTELLUNGEN (GW/0176-4829) [05999477] **984**

KLINISCHE MONATSBLATTER FUER AUGENHEILKUNDE (GW/0023-2165) [04174460] **3876**

KLINISCHE NEURORADIOLOGIE **CEASED.** (GW/0939-7116) [I09397116] **3943**

KLINISCHE PADIATRIE (GW/0300-8630) [01716817] **3906**

KLINISCHE PSYCHOLOGIE UND PSYCHOPATHOLOGIE (GW/0343-9429) [04647718] **3930, 4602**

KLINISCHE UND EXPERIMENTELLE UROLOGIE (GW/0174-2752) [07339401] **3991**

KLINISCHE WOCHENSCHRIFT **See** CLINICAL INVESTIGATOR, THE **3565**

KLINISCHE WOCHENSCHRIFT **See** CLINICAL INVESTIGATION **3796**

KLINISCHES LABOR (GW/0941-2131) [25776633] **5123**

KLINISK SYGEPLEJE (DK/0902-2767) [I09022767] **3602**

KLINKII : THE JOURNAL OF THE FORESTRY SOCIETY OF THE PAPUA NEW GUINEA UNIVERSITY OF TECHNOLOGY (PP) [07289509] **2386**

KLIO (LEIPZIG, GERMANY : 1906) (GW/0075-6334) [05661538] **2622**

KLM (AIRLINE) **See** ANNUAL REPORT KLM ROYAL DUTCH AIRLINES **11**

KLOSTERNEUBURG, AUSTRIA (MONASTERY OF AUGUSTINIAN CANONS) **See** JAHRBUCH DES STIFTES KLOSTERNEUBURG. NEUE FOLGE **5030**

KLUB (MOSCOW, R.S.F.S.R. : 1989) (RU/0235-5043) [20750221] **5207**

KLUCZE DO OZNACZANIA KREGOWCOW POLSKI (PL/0075-6342) [01447080] **5589**

KLUWER INTERNATIONAL SERIES IN ENGINEERING AND COMPUTER SCIENCE, THE (US) [14405758] **1193, 1984**

KMETIJSKI INSTITUT SLOVENIJE **See** RAZISKAVE IN STUDIJE - KMETIJSKI INSTITUT SLOVENIJE **125**

KMI. BUEROWIRTSCHAFT, LEHRE UND PRAXIS (GW/0178-594X) [I0178594X] **1899**

KMT (SAN FRANCISCO, CALIF.) (US/1053-0827) [22448205] **272**

KNARR-KNERR-KNORR FAMILY NEWSLETTER (US) [23244165] **2457**

KNAUTH'S BENEDICT ON ADMIRALTY (US) [01519515] **3181**

●KNEE SURGERY, SPORTS TRAUMATOLOGY, ARTHROSCOPY (GW/0942-2056) [29184098] **3969**

●KNEE, THE (UK/0968-0160) [30370397] **3806**

KNIFE WORLD (US/0276-9042) [07445131] **2774**

KNIGA I ISKUSSTVO V SSSR (RU) [05592084] **418**

KNIGA. ISSLEDOVANIA I MATERIALY (RU/0134-837X) [I0134837X] **2622**

KNIGHT LETTER (CHARLOTTESVILLE) (US/0193-886X) [04042368] **2457**

KNIGHT LETTER (FORT WORTH, TEX.) (US/0454-8973) [04853210] **2457**

●KNIGHT-RIDDER CRB COMMODITY YEARBOOK STATISTICAL SUPPLEMENT, THE (US) [29376144] **905**

KNIGHT'S BUILDING REGULATIONS (UK) **618**

KNIGHTS ENVIRONMENT & PUBLIC HEALTH ACTS (UK) **4788**

KNIGHT'S LOCAL GOVERNMENT AND MAGISTERIAL REPORTS, WITH STATUTES, STATUTORY INSTRUMENTS, & C (UK) [01751436] **4660**

KNIGI GLAVNOI REDAKTSII VOSTOCHNOI LITERATURY IZDATELSTVA NAUKA (RU) [07937338] **4816**

KNIHY (XR) [24851287] **5799**

KNIP (NE) **5184**

KNIPSELKRANT ECONOMIE (BE/0771-1522) [I07711522] **1502**

KNIPSELKRANT PSYCHIATRIE (NE) **3930**

KNIPSELKRANT VOOR GEESTELIJKE GEZONDHEIDSZORG (BE) **3930**

KNIT & CHAT (CN/0711-639X) [08499734] **5184**

KNIT FABRIC PRODUCTION (US/0145-4900) [07909311] **5353**

KNIT SANOP / KNITTING INDUSTRY (KO) [10061699] **5184**

KNITKING MAGAZINE (US) 2774, **5184**

KNITOVATIONS (US/0160-6336) [03712075] **5353**

KNITTERS (US/0747-9026) [10821083] **5184**

KNITTER'S JOURNAL (US/0090-8215) [01786107] **5184**

KNITTING DIGEST (US/1072-7167) [29187563] **5184**

KNITTING ELEGANCE *CEASED.* (US/8750-9768) [11967759] **5184**

KNITTING INTERNATIONAL (UK/0266-8394) [05054252] **5353**

KNITTING TIMES (US/0023-2300) [01794210] **5184**

KNITTING WORLD (SEABROOK, N.H.) (US/0194-8083) [05033149] **5184**

KNIVES (US/0277-0725) [07395639] **4007**

KNIVES ILLUSTRATED (US/0898-8943) [17947098] **2774**

KNIZHKA PARTIINOGO AKTIVISTA (RU/0302-8445) [01793230] **4660**

KNIZHNAIA LETOPIS. DOPOLNITELNYI VYPUSK. KNIGI I BROSHIURY / GOSUDARSTVENNYI KOMITET SSSR PO DELAM IZDATELSTV, POLIGRAFII I KNIZHNOI TORGOVLI, VSESOIUZNAIA ORDENA "ZNAK POCHETA" KNIZHNAIA PALATA (RU/0130-2329) [07850611] **418**

KNIZHNAIA TORGOVLIA. BIBLIOGRAFICHESKAIA INFORMATSIIA; NOVOSTI LITERATURY (RU) [01799401] **4829**

KNIZHNAIA TORGOVLIA. OPYT, PROBLEMY, ISSLEDOVANIIA (RU/0320-1244) [10262151] **4829**

KNIZHNAIA TORGOVLIA. REFERATIVNAIA INFORMATSIIA (RU/0131-4122) [01799400] **4829**

KNIZHNOE OBOZRENIE (RU/0023-2378) [01964882] **5809**

KNIZNA REVUE (XO) [25209422] **5810**

KNIZNICE A INFORMACIE (XO) [25000762] **3221**

KNIZNICE ODBORNYCH A VEDECKYCH SPISU VYSOKEHO UCENI TECHNICKEHO V BRNE. SVAZEK A (XR/0231-5394) [10042236] **5123**

KNIZNY MAGAZIN (XO) [01800018] **4816**

KNJIZEVNA ISTORIJA (YU/0350-6428) [01462590] **3402**

KNJIZEVNA KRITIKA (YU/0350-4123) [11032581] **3402**

KNJIZEVNA SMOTRA (CI/0455-0463) [01783388] **3402**

KNJIZEVNE NOVINE : ORGAN SAVEZA KNJIZEVNIKA JUGOSLAVIJE (YU/0023-2416) [01782899] **5813**

KNJIZEVNOST I JEZIK (YU/0454-0689) [02107721] **3293**

KNJIZNICA (XV/0023-2424) [01783106] **3221**

KNOW NEWS ... IS GOOD NEWS (US) **1193**

KNOW YOUR WORLD EXTRA (US/0163-4844) [04387051] **1899**

KNOWLEDGE (UK) **4073**

KNOWLEDGE ACQUISITION (UK/1042-8143) [19218762] **1214**

KNOWLEDGE AND POLICY (US/0897-1986) [22684432] 5123, **1115**

KNOWLEDGE AND SOCIETY, STUDIES IN THE SOCIOLOGY OF CULTURE PAST AND PRESENT (US/0278-1557) [07714680] **5251**

KNOWLEDGE-BASED SYSTEMS (GUILDFORD, SURREY) (UK/0950-7051) [17340817] **1193**

KNOWLEDGE (BEVERLY HILLS, CALIF.) (US/0164-0259) [04556737] **5207**

KNOWLEDGE (BEVERLY HILLS, CALIF.) *See* SCIENCE COMMUNICATION **5151**

KNOWLEDGE CENTER COURSEWARE LIBRARY (US/0895-0008) [16396630] **1193**

KNOWLEDGE ENGINEERING REVIEW, THE (UK/0269-8889) [18341769] **1214**

KNOWLEDGE (FORT WORTH, TEX.) (US/0738-8640) [08599391] **3345**

KNOWLEDGE INDUSTRY PUBLICATIONS 200 (US) [17565035] **1115**

KNOWLEDGE INDUSTRY PUBLICATIONS, INC *See* INSTRUCTIONAL MATERIALS ADOPTION DATA FILE **1896**

KNOWLEDGE MATTERS (US/0886-4063) [12897732] **4351**

●KNOWLEDGE ORGANIZATION : KO (GW/0943-7444) [27958157] **3221**

KNOWLEDGE, THE (UK/0966-3371) **1134**

KNOX COUNTY CAPITAL IMPROVEMENTS PROGRAM (US) [05262133] **2827**

KNOX COUNTY DAILY NEWS (BICKNELL, IND. : 1991) (US/1060-6173) [22964792] **5665**

KNOX COUNTY, ILLINOIS GENEALOGICAL SOCIETY QUARTERLY (US/0741-7284) [05053360] **2457**

KNOX COUNTY, KENTUCKY KINFOLK (US/0276-4857) [07355950] **2457**

KNOX COUNTY NEWS, THE (US) [14191309] **5751**

KNOXVILLE GAZETTE (US) [05948398] **2536**

KNOXVILLE JOURNAL *See* EAST TENNESSEE'S WEEKEND JOURNAL **5745**

KNOXVILLE JOURNAL (KNOXVILLE, TENN. : 1925) (US) [11989592] **5745**

KNOXVILLE NEWS-SENTINEL, THE (US) [12008657] **5745**

KNV-KORTOM (AMSTERDAM) *See* INZET AMSTERDAM **2910**

KNYGOTYRA (LI/0204-2061) [03702122] **3221**

KO HSUEH HSUEH YU KO HSUEH CHI SHU KUAN LI SCIENTOLOGY AND MANAGEMENT OF S. & T (CC) [10049796] **5123**

KO HSUEH HUA PAO (CC) [05771466] **5123**

KO HSUEH SHIH TAI (CH) [09330677] **5123**

KO HSUEH TAN SO (CC) [22982487] **5123**

KO, KONSUMENTOMBUDSMANNEN. TIDSKRIFTEN (SW) [02336979] **1571**

KO MING SHIH TZU LIAO / CHUNG-KUO JEN MIN CHENG CHIH HSIEH SHANG HUI I CHUAN KUO WEI YUAN HUI, WEN SHIH TZU LIAO YEN CHIU WEI YUAN HUI PIEN (CH) [08142391] **2657**

KO MUNHWA (KO) [06587303] **272**

KOATSU GASU (JA/0452-2311) [09534320] **1984**

KOBE DAIGAKU IGAKUBU KIYO (JA/0075-6431) [09913445] **3602**

KOBE DAIGAKU. KEIEIGAKUBU *See* ANNALS OF THE SCHOOL OF BUSINESS ADMINISTRATION, KOBE UNIVERSITY, THE **638**

KOBE DAIGAKU. KOGAKUBU *See* MEMOIRS OF THE FACULTY OF ENGINEERING, KOBE UNIVERSITY **1987**

KOBE DAIGAKU. NOGAKU-BU *See* KOBE DAIGAKU NOGAKU-BU KENKYU HOKOKU. SCIENCE REPORTS OF FACULTY OF AGRICULTURE, KOBE UNIVERSITY **102**

KOBE DAIGAKU NOGAKU-BU KENKYU HOKOKU. SCIENCE REPORTS OF FACULTY OF AGRICULTURE, KOBE UNIVERSITY (JA/0454-2370) [03333063] **102**

KOBE ECONOMIC & BUSINESS REVIEW (JA/0075-6407) [01782752] **1571**

KOBE GAKUIN KEIZAIGAKU RONSHU (JA) [03648199] **1502**

KOBE JOURNAL OF MATHEMATICS (JA/0289-9051) [11605279] **3516**

KOBE JOURNAL OF MEDICAL SCIENCES (JA/0023-2513) [06988460] **3602**

KOBE KAIYO KISHODAI *See* MEMOIRS OF THE KOBE MARINE OBSERVATORY, THE **1452**

KOBE SHOSEN DAIGAKU KIYO. DAI 2-RUI, SHOSEN, RIKOGAKU HEN (JA/0450-609X) [10152677] **4178**

KOBE UNIVERSITY ECONOMIC REVIEW (JA/0454-1111) [01782993] **1571**

KOBE ZEIKAN. / KOBE CUSTOMS (JA) [03304969] **5268**

KOBELCO TECHNOLOGY REVIEW (JA/0913-4794) [18610712] **5123**

KOBENHAVNS UNIVERSITET. MUSIKVIDENSKABELIGT INSTITUT *See* MUSIK & FORSKNING **4137**

KOBIE. ARTE EDERRAK *See* KOBIE. BELLAS ARTES / DIPUTACION FORAL DE BIZKAIA **355**

KOBIE. BELLAS ARTES / DIPUTACION FORAL DE BIZKAIA (SP/0214-7955) [25395397] **355**

KOBIJUTSU (JA/0454-112X) [01755201] **355**

KOBRIN LETTER, THE (US/0271-1990) [06562724] **3345**

KOBUNKAZAI NO KAGAKU (JA/0368-6272) [08007634] 251, **355**

KOBUNSHI (JA/0454-1138) [02448146] **1044**

KOBUNSHI GAKKAI *See* KOBUNSHI KAGAKU NO TEMBO **4456**

KOBUNSHI KAGAKU NO TEMBO (JA) [01796855] **4456**

KOBUNSHI KAKO (JA/0368-6426) [07004206] **4456**

KOBUNSHI RONBUNSHU (TOKYO) (JA/0386-2186) [01512483] **984**

KOBUTSUGAKU ZASSHI (JA/0454-1146) [09733642] **1440**

KOCHI DAIGAKU GAKUJUTSU KENKYU HOKOKU. NOGAKU (JA/0389-0473) [10401041] **102**

KOCHI DAIGAKU GAKUJUTSU KENKYU HOKOKU. SHIZEN KAGAKU (JA/0389-0244) [09304619] 1092, **5124**

KOCHI DAIGAKU. HOKEN KANRI SENTA *See* KOCHI DAIGAKU HOKEN KANRI SENTA NEMPO **1899**

KOCHI DAIGAKU HOKEN KANRI SENTA NEMPO (JA) [07801526] **1899**

KOCHI DAIGAKU KYOIKU GAKUBU KENKYU HOKOKU. AI 1-BU (JA) [10214843] **1760**

KOCHI DAIGAKU KYOIKU GAKUBU KENKYU HOKOKU. DAI 2-BU (JA) [10214050] **2849**

KOCHI DAIGAKU KYOIKU GAKUBU KENKYU HOKOKU. DAI 3-BU (JA/0389-0449) [09405322] **5124**

KOCHI DAIGAKU RIGAKUBU KIYO. KAGAKU (JA/0389-0279) [07935846] **984**

KODAE TOSOGWAN PO (KO) [07395777] **3222**

KODAI (JA/0452-2516) [12036398] **272**

KODAI CHUSEI KOKUBUNGAKU (JA) [11937390] **3402**

KODAI MATHEMATICAL JOURNAL (JA/0386-5991) [04250606] **3516**

KODAI ROSHIA KENKYU (JA) [09649912] 2696, **3293**

KODAK HIGHLIGHTS (US) [01638934] **4371**

KODAK LABORATORY CHEMICALS BULLETIN (US/0270-4986) [06455301] **984**

KODAK TECH BITS (US/0452-2591) [09687744] **4371**

KODAKERY (US) [06039489] **1614**

KODALY ENVOY (US) [02240937] **1899**

KODALY — Alphabetical Title Index

KODALY MUSICAL TRAINING INSTITUTE See BULLETIN - KODALY MUSICAL TRAINING INSTITUTE INC **4106**

KODI (SZ) **4851**

KODIAK DAILY MIRROR, THE (US/0740-2112) [09898603] **5629**

KODIKAS (GW/0171-0834) [05877046] **3293**

KODIKAS EPITHEORESEOS ERGATIKOU DIKAIOU (GR) [11058466] **3150**

KODINHOITOAPU (FI) [03921036] **5294**

KODOMO NO HONDANA (JA) [06636529] **1066**

KODOMO NO TOMO (JA) [12218992] **1066**, **3402**

KODRY (MV/0130-2337) [08082123] **3402**

KOEBSTADMUSEET "DEN GAMLE BY" (AARHUS, DENMARK) See AARBOG / KOEBSTADMUSEET "DEN GAMLE BY" **2671**

KOEDOE (SA/0075-6458) [01615272] **5589**

KOEI KIGYO KINYU KOKO See KOEI KIGYO KINYU KOKO **689**

KOEI KIGYO KINYU KOKO (JA) [02988042] **689**

KOENERUGI BUTSURIGAKU KENKYUJO See KOENERUGIKEN GEPPO **4448**

KOENERUGI BUTSURIGAKU KENKYUJO (JAPAN) See ANNUAL REPORT **4445**

KOENERUGIKEN GEPPO (JA) [02652838] **4448**

KOEPEL VIJF (BE/0771-7172) [07717172] **1760**

KOERPERERZIEHUNG (GW/0323-4916) [03234916] **2599**

KOERS (SA/0023-270X) [05054722] **4351**

KOESTSU SHIKENJO KENKYU BUNKEN HOROKUSHU See KOSETSU SHIKENJO KENKYU SEIKA SHOROKUSHU **5124**

KOETUSSELOSTUS - VAKOLA (FI/0428-4372) [18042227] **102**

KOEZLEKEDESTUDOMANYI SZEMLE (HU/0023-4362) [01782706] **5385**

KOGAI (JA/0454-9015) [10425872] **2235**

KOGAI HAKUSHO (FUKUSHIMA-KEN, JAPAN) See KANKYO HAKUSHO (FUKUSHIMA-KEN, JAPAN. KOGAI KISEIKA) **2235**

KOGAI KANKEI TOSHO MOKUROKU. TSUIROKU (JA) [01790161] **2235**

KOGAI KANKEI ZASSHI KIJI SAKUIN (JA) [01797141] **2235**

KOGAI KENKYU NEMPO (JA) [03061358] **2235**

KOGAI NO ARAMASHI (JA) [05842713] **2235**

KOGAI SHIGEN KENKYOJO HIJO See SHIGEN TO TANKYO **2205**

KOGAI SHIGEN KENKYUJO See KOGAI SHIGENKEN NYUSU **2235**

KOGAI SHIGEN KENKYUJO See KOGAI SHIGEN KENKYUJO IHO **5124**

KOGAI SHIGEN KENKYUJO HOKOKU (JA/0368-685X) [10038778] **2235**

KOGAI SHIGEN KENKYUJO IHO (JA) [02245363] **5124**

KOGAI SHIGENKEN NYUSU (JA) [06830713] **2235**

KOGAKKAN DAIGAKU See KOGAKKAN DAIGAKU KIYO **5233**

KOGAKKAN DAIGAKU KIYO (JA) [02972104] **5233**

KOGAKU (JA/0389-6625) [10425985] **4437**

KOGAKU SHOTOKUSHA MEIBO; KANTO-BAN (JA) [02243587] **4735**

KOGEI NOSAKUBUTSU TOKEI NEMPO (JA) [02245302] **177**

KOGIKEN NYUSU (JA) [05458808] **5124**

KOGNITIONSWISSENSCHAFT (GW/0938-7986) [24184922] **3293**, **4602**

KOGO MISUL (KO) [06872463] **272**, **355**

KOGYO GIJUTSU (JA) [02243522] **5124**

KOGYO GIJUTSU ZASSHI NENKAN (JA) [01797365] **5124**

KOGYO GIJUTSUIN BISEIBUTSU KOGYO GIJUTSU KENKYUSHO KENKYU HOKOKU (JA/0368-5365) [01196223] **2347**, **1027**

KOGYO GIJUTSUIN (JAPAN) See AGENCY OF INDUSTRIAL SCIENCE AND TECHNOLOGY : AIST **5081**

KOGYO GIJUTSUIN (JAPAN). DENSHI GIJUTSU SOGO KENKYUGO See SUMMARIES OF REPORTS OF THE ELECTROTECHNICAL LABORATORY **2082**

KOGYO GIJUTSUIN (JAPAN). DENSHI GIJUTSU SOGO KENKYUJO See DENSHI GIJUTSU SOGO KENKYUJO YORAN **2041**

KOGYO GIJUTSUIN (JAPAN). DENSHI GIJUTSU SOGO KENKYUJO See DENSHI GIJUTSU SOGO KENKYUJO HOKOKURUI ICHIRAN **2040**

KOGYO GIJUTSUIN (JAPAN). DENSHI GIJUTSU SOGO KENKYUJO See DENSHI GIJUTSU SOGO KENKYUJO KENKYU HOKOKU **2041**

KOGYO GIJUTSUIN KEIRYO KENKYUJO (JAPAN) See KEIRYO KENKYUJO NEMPO **5123**

KOGYO GIJUTSUIN SHIKEN KENKYUJO KENKYU KEIKAKU (JA) [02247108] **5124**

KOGYO GIJUTSUIN SHOKAI (JA) [03191476] **5124**

KOGYO GIJUTSUIN TOKKYO SHOROKUSHU (JA) [02243584] **1305**

KOGYO KANETSU (JA/0454-1499) [10418864] **2606**

KOGYO KAYAKU (JA/0368-6450) [09533880] **2143**

KOGYO REAMETARU (JA/0368-654X) [10474502] **4007**

KOGYO TOKEI HYO. KOGYO CHIKU HEN / TSUSHO SANGYO DAIJIN KANBO CHOSA TOKEIBU (JA) [10958119] **1682**

KOGYO TOSO (JA/0286-6943) [10340878] **5124**, **984**

KOGYO YOSUI (JA/0454-1545) [09392084] **2093**, **5535**

KOGYO ZAIRYO (JA/0452-2834) [10461918] **1984**

KOHA (YU) [06686613] **2696**

KOHASZATI ES ONTESZETI SZAKIRODALMI TAJEKOZTATO (HU/0231-0708) [02310708] **4007**

KOHO - KEIO GIJUKU DAIGAKU JOHO KAGAKU KENKYUJO (JA) [04996340] **1261**

KOI USA (US/0748-7320) [10992857] **2422**

KOINONIA (PRINCETON, N.J.) (US/1047-1057) [20607482] **4972**

KOINONIKOS PROYPOLOGISMOS ETOUS ... / HYPOURGEIO HYGEIAS, PRONOIAS, KAI KOINONIKON ASPHALISEON, GENIKE GRAMMATEIA KOINONIKON ASPHALISEON, D/NSE EPITHEORESES (GR) [20273576] **4735**, **5294**

KOINOS - GRUPPO E FUNZIONE ANALITICA (IT) **4602**

KOJIN JUTAKU, IPPAN KASHITSUKE, KENSETSU SHIKIN RIYOSHA CHOSA HOKOKU (JA) [07902298] **796**

KOJIN KIGYO EIGYO CHOSA HOKOKU (JA) [05690649] **1614**

KOJO (JA) [05721635] **3402**

KOJO KANRI (JA/0023-2777) [I00232777] **875**

KOKAI KUNRENJO See CHOSA KENKYU JIHO - KOKAI KUNRENJO **4175**

KOKALOS : STUDI PUBBLICATI DALL'ISTITUTO DI STORIA ANTICA DELL'UNIVERSITA DI PALERMO (IT/0454-1596) [01755211] **1078**

KOKETSUATSU See HYPERTENSION RESEARCH, CLINICAL AND EXPERIMENTAL **3706**

KOKKA (JA/0023-2785) [01588205] **355**

KOKKA GAKKAI ZASSHI (JA/0023-2793) [01643429] **5207**, **4480**

KOKKA OMUIN SAIGAI HOSHO KANKEI HOREI SHU (JA) [03738428] **1682**

KOKKAIDO KOGAI BOSHI KENKYUJO HO (JA/0286-0945) [02441431] **2235**

KOKOGAKU ZASSHI (JA/0003-8075) [01696225] **272**

KOKOGYO SHISU NEMPO (JA) [02623310] **1571**

KOKOKU KAGAKU (JA) [08924079] **761**

KOKOMO TRIBUNE (KOKOMO, IND. : 1966) (US/0746-2034) [08801387] **5665**

KOKOTSUGAKU (JA) [03019779] **3402**

KOKS I HIMIJA (RU/0023-2815) [02448155] **1044**

KOKS, SMOA, GAZ See KARBO, ENERGOCHEMIA, EKOLOGIA **1440**

KOKU EISEI GAKKAI ZASSHI (JA/0023-2831) [01196287] **1329**

KOKU GIJUTSU KENKYUJO YORAN See KOKU UCHU GIJUTSU KENKYUJO **27**

KOKU IGAKU JIKKENTAI KENKYU SEIKA GAIYO (JA) [02245368] **3799**

KOKU NENKAN. / AVIATION ANNUAL OF JAPAN (JA) [04473594] **27**

KOKU UCHU GIJUTSU KENKYUJO See NAL; NATIONAL AEROSPACE LABORATORY, JAPAN **29**

KOKU UCHU GIJUTSU KENKYUJO (JA) [02246172] **27**

KOKU YUSO TOKEI NENPO (JA) [01797080] **27**

KOKUBO MONDAI KENKYUKAI KOENROKUSHU (JA) [09457995] **4048**

KOKUBUNGAKU KAISHAKU TO KANSHO (JA) [01755214] **3345**

KOKUBUNGAKU KENKYU SHIRYOKAN See KOKUBUNGAKU KENKYU SHIRYOKAN ZO MAIKURO SHIRYO MOKUROKU / HENSHU, KOKUBUNGAKU KENKYU SHIRYOKAN SEIRI ETSURANBU **3458**

KOKUBUNGAKU KENKYU SHIRYOKAN See KOKUBUNGAKU KENKYU SHIRYOKAN KIYO **3402**

KOKUBUNGAKU KENKYU SHIRYOKAN See KOKUBUNGAKU KENKYU SHIRYOKAN ZO CHIKUJI KANKOBUTSU MOKUROKU **3458**

KOKUBUNGAKU KENKYU SHIRYOKAN See KOKUBUNGAKU KENKYU SHIRYOKAN HO **3293**

KOKUBUNGAKU KENKYU SHIRYOKAN HO (JA) [05765398] **3402**, **3293**

KOKUBUNGAKU KENKYU SHIRYOKAN KIYO (JA) [02564634] **3402**

KOKUBUNGAKU KENKYU SHIRYOKAN ZO CHIKUJI KANKOBUTSU MOKUROKU (JA) [07036691] **3458**

KOKUBUNGAKU KENKYU SHIRYOKAN ZO MAIKURO SHIRYO MOKUROKU / HENSHU, KOKUBUNGAKU KENKYU SHIRYOKAN SEIRI ETSURANBU (JA) [10686111] **3458**

KOKUBUNGAKU NENJIBETSU RONBUNSHU. CHUKO / HENSHU, GAKUJUTSU BUNKEN (JA) [09967858] **3402**

KOKUBUNGAKU NENJIBETSU RONBUNSHU. CHUSEI / GAKUJUTSU BUNKEN FUKYUKAI (JA) [09548202] **3402**

KOKUBUNGAKU NENJIBETSU RONBUNSHU. JODAI / GAKUJUTSU BUNKEN FUKYUKAI (JA) [09548245] **3402**

KOKUBUNGAKU NENJIBETSU RONBUNSHU. KINDAI / GAKUJUTSU BUNKEN KANKOKAI (JA) [10590993] **3402**

KOKUBUNGAKU NENJIBETSU RONBUNSHU. KINSEI / GAKUJUTSU BUNKEN FUJYUKAI (JA) [09548194] **3402**

KOKUBUNGAKU NENJIBETSU RONBUNSHU. KOKUBUNGAKU IPPAN / GAKUJUTSU BUNKEN FUKYUKAI (JA) [09548255] **3402**

KOKUBYO GAKKAI See KOKUBYO GAKKAI ZASSHI **3602**

KOKUBYO GAKKAI ZASSHI (JA/0300-9149) [01425535] **3602**

KOKUDO CHIRIIN See BULLETIN OF THE GEOGRAPHICAL SURVEY INSTITUTE **2557**

KOKUDO RIYO HAKUSHO / KOKUDOCHO HEN (JA) [10801399] **5535**, **4840**

KOKUDO TOKEI YORAN (JA) [05958469] **1502**

KOKUFU BONSAI TEN (JA) [04546350] **2422**

KOKUGAKUIN DAIGAKU. DAIGAKUIN See KOKUGAKUIN DAIGAKU KEIZAIGAKU KENKYU **1502**

KOKUGAKUIN DAIGAKU KEIZAIGAKU KENKYU (JA) [07675499] **1502**

KOKUGAKUIN DAIGAKU NIHON BUNKA KENKYUJO HO (JA) [03341963] **4972**

KOKUGAKUIN DAIGAKU. NIHON BUNKA KENKYUJO See KOKUGAKUIN DAIGAKU NIHON BUNKA KENKYUJO HO **4972**

KOKUGO KYOIKY KENKYUJO See KENKYU NENKAN **3293**

KOKUGO TO KOKUBUNGAKU (JA/0387-3110) [01755216] **3402**, **3293**

KOKUGOGAKU (JA) [01585910] **3293**

KOKUMIN KEIZAI KEISAN NEMPO. ANNUAL REPORT ON NATIONAL ACCOUNTS (JA) [05345276] **1502**

KOKUNAISAN HATABAKO KAISETSUSHO (JA) [03460120] **5373**

KOKURITSU BOSAI KAGAKU GIJUTSU SENTA, TOKYO See YORAN - KOKURITSU BOSAI KAGAKU GIJUTSU SENTA **2579**

KOKURITSU EISEI SHIKENJO See CHOSA GEPPO **4771**

KOKURITSU EISEI SHIKENJO See KOKURITSU EISEI SHIKENJO YORAN **4788**

KOKURITSU EISEI SHIKENJO See EISEI SHIKENJO HOKOKU **4774**

KOKURITSU EISEI SHIKENJO YORAN (JA) [05885805] **4788**

KOKURITSU GAN SENTA See KOKURITSU GAN SENTA NEMPO **3820**

KOKURITSU GAN SENTA NEMPO (JA) [02914652] **3820**

KOKURITSU GEKIJO ENGEIJO (JA) [12014414] **5365**

KOKURITSU IDENGAKU KENKYUJO (JAPAN) See REPORT OF THE NATIONAL INSTITUTE OF GENETICS 551

KOKURITSU IDENGAKU KENKYUJO, MISHIMA, JAPAN See KOKURITSU IDENGAKU KENKYUJO NEMPO 549

KOKURITSU IDENGAKU KENKYUJO NEMPO (JA) [02971672] 549

KOKURITSU JUNKANKIBYO SENTA GYOSEKI NEMPO (JA) [07486335] 3708

KOKURITSU KAGAKU HAKUBUTSUKAN See BULLETIN OF THE NATIONAL SCIENCE MUSEUM. SERIES B, BOTANY 505

KOKURITSU KAGAKU HAKUBUTSUKAN (JAPAN) See BULLETIN OF THE NATIONAL SCIENCE MUSEUM. SERIES D, ANTHROPOLOGY 233

KOKURITSU KAGAKU HAKUBUTSUKAN (JAPAN) See KOKURITSU KAGAKU HAKUBUTSUKAN NYUSU 5124

KOKURITSU KAGAKU HAKUBUTSUKAN NYUSU (JA) [02240173] 5124

KOKURITSU KOBUNSHOKAN See KITANOMARU; KOKURITSU KOBUNSHOKAN HO 2482

KOKURITSU KOGAI KENKYUJO KENKYU HOKOKU (JA) [10341225] 2235

KOKURITSU KOKKAI TOSHOKAN GEPPO (JA/0027-9153) [01755220] 3222

KOKURITSU KOKKAI TOSHOKAN (JAPAN) See KOKURITSU KOKKAI TOSHOKAN SHOKUIN MEIBO 3222

KOKURITSU KOKKAI TOSHOKAN (JAPAN) See KOKURITSU KOKKAI TOSHOKAN GEPPO 3222

KOKURITSU KOKKAI TOSHOKAN. SEIRIBU See CHUGOKUGO CHOSENGO TOSHO SOKUHO 413

KOKURITSU KOKKAI TOSHOKAN SHOKUIN MEIBO (JA) [02452903] 3222

KOKURITSU KOKUGO KENKYUJO See KENKYU HOKOKU SHU - KOKURITSU KOKUGO KENKYUJO 3293

KOKURITSU KOSHU EISEIIN (JAPAN) See KOKURITSU KOSHU EISEIIN NEMPO 4788

KOKURITSU KOSHU EISEIIN NEMPO (JA) [02458548] 4788

KOKURITSU KOSHU EISEIIN, TOKYO See YORAN - KOKURITSU KOSHU EISEIIN 4808

KOKURITSU KYOGIJO YORAN (JA) [05057232] 1857

KOKURITSU KYOIKU KENKYUJO KENKYU SHUROKU (JA/0285-0125) [08873038] 1760

KOKURITSU KYOKUCHI KENKYUJO See KYOKUCHIKEN NYUSU 5125

KOKURITSU KYOKUCHI KENKYUJO See KOKURITSU KYOKUCHI KENKYUJO YORAN 5124

KOKURITSU KYOKUCHI KENKYUJO YORAN (JA) [02246547] 5124

KOKURITSU KYOTO BYOIN See BYOIN NEMPO 4770

KOKURITSU KÂOSHÂU EISEIIN (JAPAN) See JIGYO YORAN - KOKURITSU KOSHU EISEIIN 4786

KOKURITSU MINZOKUGAKU HAKUBUTSUKAN See KOKURITSU MINZOKUGAKU HAKUBUTSUKAN KENKYU HOKOKU 240

KOKURITSU MINZOKUGAKU HAKUBUTSUKAN KENKYU HOKOKU (JA/0385-180X) [03436190] 240

KOKURITSU MINZOKUGAKU HAKUBUTSUKAN KENKYU HOKOKU. BESSATSU (JA) [10790155] 240

KOKURITSU MUSASHI RYOYOJO (JAPAN). SHINKEI SENTA See KOKURITSU MUSASHI RYOYOJO SHINKEI SENTA NENPO 3837

KOKURITSU MUSASHI RYOYOJO SHINKEI SENTA NENPO (JA) [08922036] 3930, 3837

KOKURITSU REKISHI MINZOKU HAKUBUTSUKAN KENKYU HOKOKU (JA/0286-7400) [10232352] 4090

KOKURITSU RYOYOJO YORAN (JA) [06831699] 3787

KOKURITSU SEIYO BIJUTSUKAN See KOKURITSU SEIYO BIJUTSUKAN NEMPO. BULLETIN ANNUEL DU MUSEE NATIONAL D'ART OCCIDENTAL 355

KOKURITSU SEIYO BIJUTSUKAN NEMPO. BULLETIN ANNUEL DU MUSEE NATIONAL D'ART OCCIDENTAL (JA) [05329729] 355

KOKURITSU TAMA KENKYUJO See KOKURITSU TAMA KENKYUJO NEMPO 3602

KOKURITSU TAMA KENKYUJO NEMPO (JA) [02520075] 3602

KOKURITSU YOBO EISEI KENKYUJO (JAPAN) See KOKURITSU YOBO EISEI KENKYUJO NEMPO 4788

KOKURITSU YOBO EISEI KENKYUJO NEMPO (JA) [02621596] 4788

KOKUSAI JIJO (JA) [01790141] 5233

KOKUSAI JINJI KOSHINROKU : ZENKOKUHEN (JA) [01799697] 433

KOKUSAI JOYAKUSHU (JA) [11508774] 3132

KOKUSAI KANKEI-GAKU KENKYU (JA) [03054436] 4527

KOKUSAI KANKEI GAKUBU KENKYU NENPO (JA/0388-4279) [08391628] 4527

KOKUSAI KANKEI KENKYU. KOKUSAI BUNKA-HEN (JA/0916-3654) [I09163654] 4527

KOKUSAI KANKEI KENKYU. KOKUSAI KANKEI-HEN (JA/0916-3646) [I09163646] 4527

KOKUSAI KANKEI KENKYU (MISHIMA-SHI, JAPAN) (JA/0389-2603) [10603671] 4528

KOKUSAI KOGYO SHOYUKEN HOGO KYOKAI, NIHON BUKAI GEPPO (JA/0385-6909) [11635305] 1305

KOKUSAI KORYU KIKIN See KOKUSAI KORYU KIKIN FERO ICHIRAN 2657

KOKUSAI KORYU KIKIN See KOKUSAI KORYU KIKIN NEMPO 2657

KOKUSAI KORYU KIKIN See KOKUSAI KORYU KIKIN BUNKAJIN TANKI SHOHEISHA ICHIRAN 2657

KOKUSAI KORYU KIKIN BUNKAJIN TANKI SHOHEISHA ICHIRAN (JA) [08248746] 2657

KOKUSAI KORYU KIKIN FERO ICHIRAN (JA) [08248764] 2657

KOKUSAI KORYU KIKIN NEMPO (JA) [04440436] 2657

KOKUSAI KORYU KIKIN NYUSU / HENSHU, KOKUSAI KORYU KIKIN SOMUBU SOMUKA (JA) [09067729] 2657

KOKUSAI KORYU KIKIN. TORONTO OFFICE See JAPAN FOUNDATION PROGRAMS AVAILABLE IN CANADA, THE 2654

KOKUSAI KOTSU ANZEN GAKKAI See IATSS RESEARCH 5441

KOKUSAI KRYU (JA) [01797409] 5251

KOKUSAI KYORYOKU JIGYODAN See KOKUSAI KYORYOKU JIGYODAN NEMPO 1571

KOKUSAI KYORYOKU JIGYODAN NEMPO (JA) [02979002] 1571

KOKUSAI MONDAI SHIRYO (JA) [01790142] 4528

KOKUSAI NIHON BUNGAKU KENKYU SHUKAI KAIGIROKU (JA/0387-7280) [07039136] 3402

KOKUSAI SEIKEI JOHO (JA) [11439136] 4528

KOKUSAI SHIGEN (JA) [02243667] 843

KOKUSAIHO GAIKO ZASSHI (JA/0023-2866) [01643043] 3132

KOKUSHIGAKU (JA) [02243698] 2657

KOKUSHIKAN DAIGAKU KYOYO GAKKI See KOKUSHIKAN DAIGAKU KYOYO RON SHU 2505

KOKUSHIKAN DAIGAKU KYOYO RON SHU (JA) [02469208] 2505

KOKUYU RINYA JIGYO TOKEISHO (JA) [02541526] 2386

KOKYO JIGYO TO YOSAN / KENSETSUSHO KOKYO JIGYO YOSAN KENKYUKAI HEN (JA) [09951617] 4735

KOKYO SENTAKU NO KENKYU (JA) [12028297] 1502

KOKYO SHIKEN KENKYU KIKAN ANNAI : RIKOGAKU TEMA HEN (JA) [06932040] 5124

KOKYU (JA/0286-9314) [I02869314] 3950

KOKYU TO JUNKAN (JA/0452-3458) [10102231] 3799

KOL LUBLIN (IS) [04864390] 2266

KOL YAAKOV (CN/0228-2577) [06860236] 5050

KOL YISRAEL (IS) [07624587] 5050

KOLAHAL (II) [12573302] 4128

KOLEOPTEROLOGISCHE RUNDSCHAU (AU/0075-6547) [04742580] 5589

KOLLOIDNYJ ZURNAL (RU/0023-2912) [01589163] 1055

KOLNER BEITRAGE ZUR MUSIKFORSCHUNG (GW) [06923926] 4128

KOLNER DOMBLATT (GW/0450-6413) [05261438] 302

KOLNER JAHRBUCH FUER VOR- UND FRUHGESCHICHTE (GW/0075-6512) [02271123] 2696

KOLNER MUSEUMS-BULLETIN (GW/0933-257X) [16810132] 355, 4090

KOLNER ROMANISTISCHE ARBEITEN (SZ/0075-6520) [01755204] 3402

KOLNER SCHRIFTEN ZUM EUROPARECHT (GW) [01755205] 2992

KOLNER SCHRIFTEN ZUR POLITISCHEN WISSENSCHAFT (GW/0075-6539) [02277766] 4480

KOLNER ZEITSCHRIFT FUER SOZIOLOGIE UND SOZIALPSYCHOLOGIE (GW/0023-2653) [07508362] 5251

KOLUMBIEN : ENERGIEWIRTSCHAFT (GW) [04865174] 1949

KOLUMBIEN : WIRTSCHAFTLICHE ENTWICKLUNG (GW) [02355833] 1571

KOLUMNA (MV/0236-1485) [22418302] 3402

KOMABANO: KAMPO (JA) [07965238] 3458

KOMAROVSKIE CHTENIIA (RU) [03746157] 517

KOMAZAWA DAIGAKU BUKKYO GAKUBU RON SHU (JA) [02243653] 5021

KOMAZAWA DAIGAKU, TOKYO. BUKKYO GAKUBU See KOMAZAWA DAIGAKU BUKKYO GAKUBU RON SHU 5021

KOMAZAWA DAIGAKU, TOKYO. GAIKOKUGOBU See RON SSHU - KOMAZAWA DAIGAKU GAIKOKUGOBU 3318

KOMBA (KE) [11128941] 5590

KOMBIKORMOVAIA PROMYSHLENNOST (RU/0235-2605) [25366336] 202

KOMBINATORNYI ANALIZ (RU/0321-4729) [04333790] 3516

KOMETNYI TSIRKULIAR / GRUPPA PO ISSLEDOVANIIU KOMET -I KIEVSKII UNIVERSITET IM. T.G. SHEVCHENKO (RU) [06099924] 396

KOMETY I METEORY (TA/0568-6199) [01755227] 396

KOMITET NORMALIZACJI I MIAR See BIULETYN POLSKIEGO KOMITETU NORMALIZACJI I MIAR 4029

KOMMANDO See PARATUS 4053

KOMMENTAR ZUM ALTEN TESTAMENT CEASED. (GW) 4972

KOMMENTAR ZUM SCHWEIZERISCHEN ZIVILGESETZBUCH (SZ) [01641385] 2992

KOMMENTARE ZUM ARZNEIBUCH DER DEUTSCHEN DEMOKRATISCHEN REPUBLIK (GW/0138-5798) [06866320] 4313

●KOMMENTARII (RU) [26888632] 3402

KOMMENTARII ARBITRAZHNOI PRAKTIKI (RU) [03512067] 2992

KOMMENTARII SUDEBNOI PRAKTIKI ZA ... GOD / VSESOIUZNYI NAUCHNO-ISSLEDOVATELSKII INSTITUT SOVETSKOGO ZAKONODATELSTVA (RU) [03189792] 2992

KOMMERCHESKII VESTNIK (RU) [05063082] 843, 689

●KOMMERSANT DAILY (RU) [27207111] 5809

KOMMERSANT : ORGAN SOIUZA OBEDINENNYKH KOOPERATIVOV SSSR (RU) [23729743] 5251

KOMMISSION FUER ZEITGESCHICHTE See VEROFFENTLICHUNGEN DER KOMMISSION FUER ZEITGESCHICHTE. REIHE B: FORSCHUNGEN 5038

KOMMISSION FUR ZEITGESCHICHTE See VEROFFENTLICHUNGEN DER KOMMISSION FUR ZEITGESCHICHTE. REIHE A : QUELLEN 5038

KOMMUNAL HANDBOGEN (DK) [27247423] 4480, 4660

KOMMUNAL HANDBOGEN MED INDKBSBOGEN See KOMMUNAL HANDBOGEN 4660

KOMMUNAL LITTERATUR (SW/0023-3056) [11139863] 4698

KOMMUNALE GEMEINSCHAFTSSTELLE FUER VERWALTUNGSVEREINFACHUNG See KGST MITTEILUNGEN / KOMMUNALE GEMEINSCHAFTSSTELLE FUER VERWALTUNGSVEREINFACHUNG 4660

KOMMUNALE TAL FRA INDENRIGSMINISTERIET ... SKN (DK/0901-0319) [19644841] 4735

KOMMUNALIS ELLAS FONTOSABB ADATAI (HU) [16932999] 4660

KOMMUNALTEKNIKK (NO) [05070364] 2827

KOMMUNALVALGENE I KOMMUNER OG AMTSKOMMUNER (DK/0904-339X) [20276293] 4480

KOMMUNALWIRTSCHAFT (GW/0450-7169) [01782857] 4660

KOMMUNERNAS FINANSER (SW/0347-7290) [01695293] 4735

KOMMUNEVALGET   Alphabetical Title Index

KOMMUNEVALGET (NO) [01785874] **4698**

KOMMUNIKATION (SZ) [07329734] **1159**

KOMMUNIST (AU) [03392606] **4542**

KOMMUNIST (LI/0321-2114) [05629374] **4542**

KOMMUNIST SOVETSKOJ LATVII *CEASED.* (LV/0321-2092) [05654388] **4542**

KOMMUNISTISCHER BUND WESTDEUTSCHLAND. ZENTRALES KOMITEE *See* POLITISCHER BERICHT DES ZENTRALEN KOMITEES DES KOMMUNISTISCHEN BUNDES WESTDEUTSCHLAND AN DIE ORDENTLICHE DELEGIERTENKONFERENZ **2703**

KOMPAS (IO/0452-3970) [06484313] **5803**

KOMPASS (UK/0075-6733) [02230810] **689**

KOMPASS; AUSTRALIA (AT) [04155531] **731**

KOMPASS (BOCHUM), DER (GW/0342-0809) [05067421] 2143, **2886**

KOMPASS DENMARK (DK) **1614**

KOMPASS DIRECTORY OF AMERICAN BUSINESS IN SINGAPORE (SI) [13369159] **689**

KOMPASS-FRANCE (FR) [09492648] **1571**

KOMPASS; INDEKS OVER NORGES INDUSTRI OG NRINGSLIV (NO/0075-6709) [03569098] **1571**

KOMPASS: INFORMATIONSWERK UBER AUSGEWAHLTE DEUTSCHE FIRMEN (GW) [03647832] **1614**

KOMPASS JAPAN *CEASED.* (AT) **689**

KOMPASS; MANUEL D'INFORMATIONS SUR L'ECONOMIE DE LA BELGIQUE ET DU GRAND-DUCHE DE LUXEMBOURG (BE/0075-6636) [01783023] **1502**

KOMPASS NATIONAL (CN/1180-0488) [22425001] **689**

KOMPASS NATIONAL. KOMPASS CANADA : REGISTER OF CANADIAN INDUSTRY AND TRADE *CEASED.* (CN/1180-0488) [22424987] **689**

KOMPASS PHILIPPINES (AT) **689**

KOMPASS; REGISTER OF INDUSTRY AND COMMERCE OF SWITZERLAND AND LIECHTENSTEIN (SZ) [05109234] **3482**

KOMPASS; REGISTER OF SINGAPORE INDUSTRY AND COMMERCE (SI) [04248569] 843, **1615**

KOMPASS; REGISTER OF SPANISH INDUSTRY AND COMMERCE (AT) [04151976] 843, **1615**

KOMPASS; REGISTER OF TAIWAN INDUSTRY AND COMMERCE (CH) [02245516] 843, **1615**

KOMPASS; REPERTORIO GENERALE DELL'ECONOMIA ITALIANA; REGISTER OF ITALIAN INDUSTRY AND COMMERCE (IT/0075-6687) [01783142] **843**

KOMPASS: SPECIAL SERVICES (FR) [04683169] **1615**

KOMPASS-SVERIGE (SW) [12889825] **1615**

KOMPILASI DATA OUTPUT & [I.E. DAN] INPUT USAHA TANI PADI INTENSIFIKASI PER KABUPATEN DI JAWA-MADURA (IO) [04661596] **177**

KOMPLEKSNOE ISPOLZOVANIE MINERALNOGO SYRIA (RU) [06032157] **2143**

KOMPLEKSNYE METALLOORGANICESKIE KATALIZATORY POLIMERIZACII OLEFINOV (RU/0203-8722) [I02038722] **4007**

KOMPLEKTOVANIE I ISPOLZOVANIE KNIZKNYKH FONDOV MASSOVYKH BIBLIOTEK (RU) [06351641] **3222**

KOMPOZITSIONNYE POLIMERNYE MATERIALY / AKADEMIIA NAUK UKRAINSKOI SSR, INSTITUT KHIMII VYSOKOMOLEKULIARNYKH SOEDINENII (UN/0203-3275) [08456247] **1044**

KOMPUTER W SZKOLE (PL/0866-9619) [I08669619] **1224**

KOMPYUTO CHONGNAM (KO) [06782963] **1261**

KOMPYUTO PIJON (KO) [10248742] **1193**

KOMPYUTOPIA / COMPUTOPIA (JA) [07334540] **1193**

KOMSOMOLSKAIA PRAVDA : ORGAN TSENTRALNOGO KOMITETA VLKSM (RU) [01755232] **5809**

KOMU KONGHAKHOE CHI (KO) [04910751] **5076**

KOMUNALNI FONDOVI U GRADSKIM NASELJIMA (YU) [02241469] 4761, **4698**

KOMUNIKA (IO/0126-2491) [08743183] **3293**

KOMUNIST UKRAINY (UN/0130-2434) [07404852] **4542**

KOMUNISTYCHNA PARTIIA UKRAIENY. TSENTRALAVI KOMITET *See* REPORT OF THE CENTRAL COMMITTEE OF THE COMMUNIST PARTY OF UKRAINE TO THE CONGRESS OF THE COMMUNIST PARTY OF UKRAINE **4546**

KOMUNISTYCHNA PARTIIA UKRAINY. ZIZD *See* MATERIALY ... ZIZDU KOMUNISTYCHNOI PARTII UKRAINY **4543**

KOMYUUNIKEISYON KWAHAK (KO) [08202585] **1115**

KON POLSKI (PL) [02286143] **2800**

KONAN DAIGAKU *See* MEMOIRS OF THE KONAN UNIVERSITY. SCIENCE SERIES **5128**

KONAN JOSHI DAIGAKU KENKYU KIYO (JA/0386-4405) [03864405] **1092**

KONAPI (NP) [08352817] **2657**

KONBATEKKU (JA/0911-2316) [27463109] **4235**

KONCHU (JA/0013-8770) [10359800] **5611**

KONDITOREI UND CAFE (GW/0023-3234) [I00233234] **2347**

KONFEDERACJA 76 I.E. SIEDEMDZIESIAT SZESC (US) [04651624] **2696**

KONFERENCJA NAUKOWO-TECHNICZNA. RENTGENOGRAFIA STOSOWANA *See* CONFERENCE ON APPLIED CRYSTALLOGRAPHY. PROCEEDINGS **1031**

KONFERENCJE (PL) [05637427] **2027**

KONFERENTSII, SOVESHCHANIIA, SIMPOZIUMY I VYSTAVKI, PROVODIMYE V STRANAKH-CHLENAKH TSENTRA (RU) [01791332] **5124**

KONGANG SAENGHWAL (KO) [09350943] **4788**

KONGANG SIDAE (KO) [10568900] **4788**

KONGELIGE BIBLIOTEK (DENMARK) *See* FUND OG FORSKNING I DET KONGELIGE BIBLIOTEKS SAMLINGER **3211**

KONGELIGE DANSKE BALLET *See* KONGELIGE DANSKE BALLET : PROGRAM, DEN **1313**

KONGELIGE DANSKE BALLET : PROGRAM, DEN (DK) [20292135] **1313**

KONGELIGE DANSKE VIDENSKABERNES SELSKAB. BIOLOGISKE SKRIFTER (DK/0366-3612) [01565922] **462**

KONGELIGE DANSKE VIDENSKABERNES SELSKAB. MATEMATISK-FYSISKE MEDDELELSER (DK/0023-3323) [01565926] 4411, **3516**

KONGELIGE DANSKE VIDENSKABERNES SELSKAB MATHEMATISK FYSISKE MEDDELESER (DK) 4411, **3516**

KONGELIGE NORSKE VIDENSKABERS SELSKAB *See* FORHANDLINGER - DET KONGELIGE NORSKE VIDENSKABERS SELSKAB **5105**

KONGELIGE VETERINR- OG LANDBOHJSKOLE (DENMARK). AFDELINGEN FOR PLANTERNES ERNRING *See* BERETNING FOR PERIODEN ... **501**

KONGERIGET DANMARKS HANDELS-KALENDER (COPENHAGEN, DENMARK : 1965) *See* EXPORT DENMARK : KONGERIGET DANMARKS HANDELS- OG EKSPORTKALENDER **834**

KONGETSU NO NOYAKU (JA/0023-334X) [10426210] **984**

KONGGAE TUKHO KONGBO (KO) [10160796] **1305**

KONGGAN (KO/0454-3114) [04340935] **323**

KONGGI CHOHWA, NAENGDONG NONGHAK (KO) [10265928] **2606**

KONGHAK NONJIP (KO) [20664614] 5124, **1985**

● KONGHAK YON'GU POGO (KO) [30562915] **1985**

KONGJIAN KEXUE XUEBAO (CC/0254-6124) [10345588] **27**

KONGLIGA SVENSKA VETENSKAPS-AKADEMIENS HANDLINGAR (SW) [08263718] **5124**

KONGOP KISUL (KO) [10386235] **5124**

KONGOP KISUL KYOYUK (KO) [09330245] **1914**

KONGOP KISUL YONGU (KO) [10007986] **5124**

KONGRES IPADI (IO) [02972675] **1593**

KONGRES POLONII KANADYJSKIEJ (CN/0824-4650) [10620187] **2743**

KONGRES UKRAJINCIV KANADY (CN/0318-9678) [02441967] **2743**

KONGRES WANITA INDONESIA *See* BERITA KOWANI **5551**

KONGSANKWON KYONGJE (KO) [11505884] **1502**

KONGZHI LILUN YU YINGYONG (CC/1000-8152) [11095920] **1985**

KONIEC WIEKU (PL) [21573621] **3402**

KONINKLIJK INSTITUUT VOOR DE TROPEN *See* REVIEW OF AGRICULTURAL PROGRAMMES AND ADVISORY ACTIVITIES / ROYAL TROPICAL INSTITUTE **128**

KONINKLIJK INSTITUUT VOOR TAAL-, LAND- EN VOLKENKUNDE (NETHERLANDS). CARAIBISCHE AFDELING *See* CARIBBEAN ABSTRACTS / EDITED AND PUBLISHED BY THE DEPARTMENT OF CARIBBEAN STUDIES OF THE ROYAL INSTITUTE OF LINGUISTICS AND ANTHROPOLOGY **5227**

KONINKLIJK MUSEUM VOOR SCHONE KUNSTEN (BELGIUM) *See* JAARBOEK VAN HET KONINKLIJK MUSEUM VOOR SCHONE KUNSTEN **353**

KONINKLIJKE ACADEMIE VOOR GENEESKUNDE VAN BELGIE *See* VERHANDELINGEN - KONINKLIJKE ACADEMIE VOOR GENEESKUNDE VAN BELGIE **3649**

KONINKLIJKE ACADEMIE VOOR NEDERLANDSE TAAL- EN LETTERKUNDE *See* JAARBOEK **3288**

KONINKLIJKE ACADEMIE VOOR NEDERLANDSE TAAL- EN LETTERKUNDE *See* VERSLAGEN EN MEDEDELINGEN - KONINKLIJKE ACADEMIE VOOR NEDERLANDSE TAAL - EN LETTERKUNDE **3331**

KONINKLIJKE BIBLIOTHEEK (NETHERLANDS) *See* CENTRALE CATALOGUS VAN PERIODIEKEN EN SERIEWERKEN IN NEDERLANDSE BIBLIOTHEKEN (CCP). CUMULATIEF SUPPLEMENT **413**

KONINKLIJKE NEDERLANDSE AKADEMIE VAN WETENSCHAPPEN. CENTRAAL BUREAU VOOR SCHIMMELCULTURES *See* LIST OF CULTURES **566**

KONINKLIJKE NETHERLANDS VLIEGTUIGENFABRIEK FOKKER, N.V *See* ANNUAL REPORT / N.V. KONINKLIJKE NEDERLANDS VLIEGTUIGENFABRIEK FOKKER **1597**

KONINKRIJK DER NEDERLANDEN IN DE TWEEDE WERELDOORLOG (NE) **2622**

KONJUNKTUR IM HANDWERK, DIE (GW) [02380716] **1615**

KONJUNKTUR VON MORGEN (GW/0023-3439) [I00233439] **1615**

KONJUNKTURBERICHT (AU) [03257415] **1502**

KONJUNKTURBERICHTE UBER DAS HANDWERK *See* KONJUNKTUR IM HANDWERK, DIE **1615**

KONJUNKTURPOLITIK (GW/0023-3498) [01783320] **1571**

KONJUNTURBERICHT *See* KONJUNKTURBERICHT **1502**

KONKRET (GW/0023-3528) [01783841] **2518**

KONKRETY (PL/0137-4680) [I01374680] **2518**

KONKURITO KOGAKU (JA/0387-1061) [10341345] **619**

● KONKURRENS/ UITGAVEN AV STATENS PRIS- OCH KONKURRENSVERK I SAMARBETE MED NARINGSFRIHETSOMBUDSMANNEN OCH MARKNADSDOMSTOLEN (SW/1102-6065) [25777202] **1502**

KONKURSSITIEDOTE (FI/0355-2292) [19232818] **796**

KONNICHI NO KANKOKU (JA) [04478291] **2657**

KONNICHI NO NIHONGA: YAMATANE BIJUTSUKAN SHO TEN (JA) [03930028] **355**

KONOMISK REVY (NO) [04909538] **1571**

KONOMISK UTSYN (NO/0078-1924) [01203808] **1535**

KONOMISKE ANALYSER (NO) [10058143] **1502**

KONOMISKE RAD (DENMARK). FORMANDSKABET *See* DANSK OKONOMI **1479**

KONSERVATIV HEUTE (GW) [02241886] **4480**

KONSOL CHONGNAM (KO) [04511392] 619, **2027**

KONSTHISTORISK TIDSKRIFT (SW/0023-3609) [01782446] **355**

KONSTPERSPEKTIV (SW/0347-4453) [I03474453] **355**

KONSTRUIEREN + GIESSEN (GW/0341-6615) [10114481] **2119**

KONSTRUIROVANIE I TEKHNOLOGIIA PROIZVODSTVA SELSKOKHOZIAISTVENNYKH MASHIN (UN) [02244326] **2120**

KONSTRUKCIJU ILGAAMZIS KUMO IR STIPRUMO PRADIDINIMAS (LI) **619**

KONSTRUKCIONNYE MATERIALY NA OSNOVE UGLERODA (RU/0134-9392) [03459323] **619**

KONSTRUKSI : DIRECTORY PERUSAHAAN DKI JAKARTA (IO) [04680144] **619**

KONSTRUKTION (1981) (GW/0720-5953) [07235795] **2120**

KONSTRUKTIONSPRAXIS (GW/0937-4167) [I09374167] **2120**

KONSTRUKTIVER IGENIEURBAU (GW/0023-3633) [05078514] **2027**, **619**

KONSTRUKTIVNAIA TEROIIA FUNKTSII I FUNKTSIONALNYI ANALIZ (RU/0206-6548) [07398370] **3516**

KONSULARISCHE VERTRETUNGEN UND ANDERE VERTRETUNGEN IN DER BUNDESREPUBLIK DEUTSCHLAND UND BERLIN (WEST) (GW) [02534243] **3132**

KONSULARISCHEN VERTRETUNGEN IN DER BUNDESREPUBLIK DEUTSCHLAND UND IM LAND BERLIN *See* KONSULARISCHE VERTRETUNGEN UND ANDERE VERTRETUNGEN IN DER BUNDESREPUBLIK DEUTSCHLAND UND BERLIN (WEST) **3132**

KONSULTATSII I OTVETY NA VOPROSY. V POMOSHCH RABOTNIKAM SOVETOV I DEPUTATAM (RU) [02604120] **4660**

KONSUMENT (AU) **1298**

KONSUMENTRATT & I.E. OCH EKONOMI (SW) [05194009] **1502**

KONSUMENTVERKETS FOERFATTNINGSSAMLING (SW) [04960885] **2993**

KONTAKT (PARIS, FRANCE) (FR) [09492349] **2696**

KONTAKT (TORONTO) (CN/0023-365X) [01783375] **2567**

KONTAKTE (GW/0172-8717) [06434865] **2070**

KONTANT (BERLIN, GERMANY) (GW) [07715003] **1066**

KONTEKST (RU/0259-4412) [02239444] **3402**

KONTENRAHMEN DER VOLKSEIGENEN INDUSTRIE MIT ERLAUTERUNGEN, BUCHUNGSANWEISUNGEN UND BUCHUNGSBEISPIELEN *See* KONTENRAHMEN INDUSTRIE MIT ERLAUTERUNGEN, BUCHUNGSANWEISUNGEN UND BUCHUNGSBEISPIELEN **747**

KONTENRAHMEN FUR VOLKSEIGENE BETRIEBE UND KOMBINATE MIT VEREINFACHTEN ANFORDERUNGEN AN RECHNUNGSFUHRUNG UND STATISTIK (GW) [03718407] **747**

KONTENRAHMEN INDUSTRIE MIT ERLAUTERUNGEN, BUCHUNGSANWEISUNGEN UND BUCHUNGSBEISPIELEN (GW) [02241772] **747**

KONTINENT *CEASED*. (GW) [02441313] **2518**

KONTINENT (BERLIN, GERMANY) (GW/0176-4179) [11135370] **4480**

KONTINENZ (GW/0940-9092) [I09409092] **3747**

KONTRAST; TIDSSKRIFT FOR POLITIKK, KULTUR, KRITIKK (NO) [05097927] **2518**

KONTRASTE FREIBURG. 1992 (GW/0942-136X) [I0942136X] **5031**

KONTRASTE, IMPULS *See* KONTRASTE FREIBURG. 1992 **5031**

KONTROLLEN MED KONSUMMAELKPRODUKTER (DK) [07324001] **196**

KONTROLLEN MED KONSUMMLKPRODUKTER *See* RAPPORT OM KONTROLLEN MED KONSUMMLKPRODUKTER FOR ARET **198**

KONTYNENTY (PL/0023-3765) [06191955] **2567**

KONYVTARI FIGYELO (HU/0023-3773) [04051801] **3222**

KONYVTARI JEGYZESEK (HU/0209-4894) [I02094894] **3222**

KONYVTARI LEVELEZO/LAP (HU/0865-1329) [I08651329] **3222**

KONYVTAROS (HU/0450-7886) [04060689] **3222**

KONZEPTE DER SPRACH- UND LITERATURWISSENSCHAFT (GW/0344-6735) [02236187] **3402**, **3293**

KONZERNE IN SCHAUBILDERN (GW/0935-0241) [I09350241] **689**

KONZERTE / PHILHARMONISCHES ORCHESTER DER STADT DORTMUND (GW) [19783629] **4128**

KONZERTIERTE AKTION; BERICHT UEBER DIE ERFAHRUNGEN SEIT IHREM BESTEHEN (GW) [01786759] **1502**

KONZERV- ES PAPRIKAIPAR (HU) [02342753] **2347**, **2791**

KOOKS MAGAZINE (US/1045-103X) **4242**

KOON GAKKAISHI (JA/0387-1096) [10474244] **4007**

KOOPERATION (LIESSEM, WACHTBERG, GERMANY) (GW) [18116758] **2518**

KOORDINACIJSKI ODBOR HRVATA TORONTO *See* GLAS K O H T-A **3578**

KOORDINACIONNAJA HIMIJA (RU/0132-344X) [02241580] **1055**

KOORDINATOR VISTI UKRAJINSKOJ KREDYTOVOJ KOOPERACIJI (CN/0384-8566) [03264455] **796**

KOORDINATSIONNAIA KHIMIIA. ENGLISH. SOVIET JOURNAL OF COORDINATION CHEMISTRY *See* RUSSIAN JOURNAL OF COORDINATION CHEMISTRY **992**

KOORI MAIL (AT) **5777**

KOOTENAY GRAPEVINE, THE (CN/0715-4593) [09223242] **5788**

KOOTENAY WEEKLY EXPRESS, THE (CN/1184-6224) [24266487] **4851**

KOPENHAGENER BEITRAEGE ZUR GERMANISTISCHEN LINGUISTIK (DK/0105-0257) [01775819] **3293**

KOPFSCHMERZ (GW/0723-5364) [10278505] **3602**

KOREA & WORLD AFFAIRS (KO/0251-3072) [03860590] **4528**

KOREA ANNUAL (KO) [01048667] **2657**

KOREA BRIEFING (US/1053-4806) [22537782] **2506**

KOREA BRIEFING (US) [24170965] **2657**

KOREA BUSINESS WORLD (KO) [13854902] **689**

KOREA CENTRAL DAILY (U.S. EDITION) (US) [12961925] **5636**

KOREA DIRECTORY, THE (KO) [01772526] **2657**

KOREA ECONOMIC REPORT (KO) [19402863] **1571**

KOREA ECONOMIC WEEKLY, THE (KO) [25491988] **1502**

KOREA HERALD, THE (KO) [01781426] **5805**

KOREA JOURNAL (KO/0023-3900) [01755247] **2657**

KOREA JOURNAL OF POPULATION AND DEVELOPMENT (KO) [23932147] **5251**

KOREA NEWSREVIEW (US/0146-9657) [03093349] **2506**

KOREA NON-LIFE INSURANCE INDUSTRY (KO) [07155038] **2886**

KOREA OBSERVER (KO) [01789330] **2849**

KOREA PHOTO NEWS (KO) [03943425] **2657**

KOREA PICTORIAL (KO) [02229871] **2657**

KOREA PRODUCTS & CATALOGUES DIRECTORY (KO) [04049792] **843**

KOREA REPORT (US/1048-2539) [19275137] **4480**

KOREA (REPUBLIC). KWAHAK KISULCHO *See* KOMPYUTO CHONGNAM **1261**

KOREA SHIPPING GAZETTE (KO) [05275246] **5451**

KOREA STATISTICAL HANDBOOK (KO) [05252200] **5330**

KOREA TIMES. TORONTO EDITION (CN/0712-1733) [08734000] **5788**

KOREA TODAY (KO) [01783885] **2506**

KOREA TODAY (PYONGYANG) (KN/0454-4072) [08797015] **2657**

KOREA TRADE REVIEW (KO) [05542383] **843**

KOREA/UPDATE (US) [09901589] **4510**

KOREA WEEK (US/0023-3951) [01797956] **2657**

KOREAM JOURNAL (US) [25926141] **2266**

KOREAN AND KOREAN-AMERICAN STUDIES BULLETIN (US/0749-7970) [11198960] **2657**

KOREAN BUSINESS DIRECTORY (KO/0454-4102) [01783220] **689**

KOREAN BUSINESS REVIEW (KO) [12740071] **689**

KOREAN CHURCH DIRECTORY OVERSEAS (US/0197-7776) [06103761] **4972**

KOREAN CULTURE & ARTS FOUNDATION, THE (KO) [04820481] **323**

KOREAN CULTURE (LOS ANGELES) (US/0270-1618) [06348960] **2657**

KOREAN DAILY NEWS / KOREAN CENTRAL NEWS AGENCY (JA) [09183925] **2489**

KOREAN DIRECTORY (JA) **929**

KOREAN ECONOMIST, THE (US) [01586733] **1502**

KOREAN FOREIGN TRADE *See* FOREIGN TRADE OF THE DEMOCRATIC PEOPLE'S REPUBLIC OF KOREA **836**

KOREAN INDEX OF MEDICAL SPECIALITIES (SI) **3602**

KOREAN JOURNAL OF BIOCHEMISTRY (KO/0378-8512) [07483085] **490**

KOREAN JOURNAL OF BOTANY, THE *See* JOURNAL OF PLANT BIOLOGY **515**

KOREAN JOURNAL OF CHEMICAL ENGINEERING, THE (KO/0256-1115) [13213645] **2014**

KOREAN JOURNAL OF COMPARATIVE LAW (KO/0377-0729) [02241662] **2993**

KOREAN JOURNAL OF DEFENSE ANALYSIS (KO) [21015849] **4048**

KOREAN JOURNAL OF INTERNATIONAL STUDIES, THE (KO/0377-0451) [02241538] **4528**

KOREAN JOURNAL OF OPHTHALMOLOGY : KJO (KO) [17800552] **3876**

KOREAN JOURNAL OF PARASITOLOGY (KO/0023-4001) [02478555] **3715**

● KOREAN JOURNAL OF PARASITOLOGY, THE (KO) [30898903] **3715**

KOREAN JOURNAL OF PHARMACOLOGY : OFFICIAL JOURNAL OF THE SOCIETY OF PHARMACOLOGY, REPUBLIC OF KOREA, THE (KO) [13554932] **4313**

KOREAN JOURNAL OF PSYCHOLOGY (KO) **4602**

KOREAN JOURNAL OF TOXICOLOGY, THE (KO/0258-2368) [I02582368] **3982**

KOREAN NATURE (KO/0023-4036) [01716358] **2197**

KOREAN REVIEW, THE (US/0163-0229) [04261641] **2657**

KOREAN SCIENTIFIC ABSTRACTS (KO/0023-4052) [04241561] **1985**, **5124**

KOREAN SIGNAL (KO) [02030028] **4480**

KOREAN SOCIAL SCIENCE JOURNAL (KO) [11167589] **5207**

KOREAN STAMPS (KO) [09565269] **2785**

KOREAN STUDIES (US/0145-840X) [03618266] **2657**

KOREAN TOURISM ANNUAL REPORT (KO) [11920658] **843**

KOREAN TRADE DIRECTORY (KO) [02148571] **843**

KOREANA (KO) [17220991] **2849**, **355**

KOREIA SEGODNIA (KO) [02243262] **2657**

KORESPONDENCE POMEMBNIH SLOVENCEV / EPISTULAE SLOVENORUM ILLUSTRIUM / ACADEMIA SCIENTIARUM ET ARTIUM SLOVENICA, CLASSIS II: PHILOLOGIA ET LITTERAE (XV) [11484247] **3402**

KORHAZ- ES ORVOSTECHNIKA (HU/0139-4509) [07371787] **3602**

KORIA SWIPOJU CHONOL (KO) [10126477] **5451**

KORIAN-OMERIKAN (US/0732-7250) [08434852] **2743**

KORIGU : HIROSHIMA DAIGAKU KYOIKU KENKYU SENTA TSUSHIN (JA/0388-6913) [08878871] **1833**

KORION PIPUL (US/0743-2577) [10539146] **2266**

KORKEAKOULUISSA SUORITETUT TUTKINNOT (FI) [03352993] **1833**

KORKEAKOULUOPETTAJIEN LUKUMAARA (FI) [03585324] **1760**

KORKEAKOULUT (FI) [04944144] **1833**

KORKOTILASTOA (FI) [05823258] **796**

KORMA (RU/0130-2515) [01636681] **103**

KORMOVYE KULTURY (RU/0235-2540) [18197373] **202**

KORN/FERRY INTERNATIONAL (FIRM) *See* BOARD OF DIRECTORS ANNUAL STUDY **861**

KORNYEZETSTATISZTIKAI ADATGYUJTEMENY (HU) [05764688] **2176**

KORNYEZETVEDELMI SZAKIRODALMI TAJEKOZTATO (HU/0231-0716) [I02310716] **2218**

KOROSE A OCHRANA MATERIALU (XR/0452-599X) [09510884] **984**

KOROSKI SLOVENEC (AU) [20400207] **5778**

KOROT (IS/0023-4109) **3602**

KOROTH (JERUSALEM : 1951) (IS) [07602880] **3602**

KORPI *See* MAJALAH BULANAN KORPRI **1689**

KORRESPONDENZ — Alphabetical Title Index

KORRESPONDENZ ABWASSER : KA (GW/0341-1540) [09787246] **2235**

KORRESPONDENZBLATT DES VEREINS FUER NIEDERDEUTSCHE SPRACHFORSCHUNG (GW/0342-0752) [01244751] **3293**

KORROSION (GW) [05082979] **984**

KORROSJONS-NYTT (NO) [05082821] **4007**

KORROZIOS FIGYELO (HU/0133-2546) [10596676] **4007**

KORT BESTEK (NE/0168-9045) [l01689045] **4660**

KORT SAGT ! (DK/0902-7270) [l09027270] **3222**

KORTARS (HU/0023-415X) [01782979] **3402**

KORTBEGRIP VAN LANDBOUSTATISTIEK / AFDELING LANDBOUBEMARKINGSNAVORSING (SA) [02495368] 103, **154**

KORTTERMYN EKONOMIESE AANWYSERS / REPUBLIEK VAN SUID-AFRIKA, BURO VIR STATISTIEK (SA) [01798698] **1571**

KORUNK (RM) [01783143] **2849**

KORYO INSAM HAKHOE *See* KORYO INSAM HAKHOE CHI **2422**

KORYO INSAM HAKHOE CHI (KO) [05238331] **2422**

KORYO TAEHAKKYO. CHUNGANG TOSOGWAN *See* KODAE TOSOGWAN PO **3222**

KORYO TAEHAKKYO. UIKWA TAEHAK *See* KORYO TAEHAKKYO UIKWA TAEHAK NONMUNJIP. KOREA UNIVERSITY MEDICAL JOURNAL **3602**

KORYO TAEHAKKYO UIKWA TAEHAK NONMUNJIP. KOREA UNIVERSITY MEDICAL JOURNAL (KO) [05045409] **3602**

KOS : RIVISTA DI CULTURA E STORIA DELLE SCIENZE MEDICHE, NATURALI E UMANE DIRETTA DA MASSIMO PIATTELLI PALMARINI (IT) [10957282] 2849, **5124**

KOSA (Il) [01784177] **2506**

KOSAKU KIKAI SETSUBI TO TOKEI CHOSA HOKOKUSHO (JA) [02441392] **1615**

KOSALA : JOURNAL OF THE INDIAN RESEARCH SOCIETY OF AVADH (II) [08620766] **2657**

KOSANKINBYO KENKYUSHO ZASSHI (JA/0910-6073) [l09106073] **3602**

KOSEI HODO *See* DAIGAKU TO GAKUSEI / MOMBUSHO DAIGAKUKYOKU GALISEOLA HEN **1734**

KOSEN KYOIKU (JA) [06484708] **1914**

KOSETSU SHIKENJO GIJUTSU SHIDO JIREI RISUTO (JA) [07243221] **5124**

KOSETSU SHIKENJO KENKYU BUNKEN SHOROKUSHU (JA) [07242948] **5124**

KOSETSU SHIKENJO KENKYU SEIKA SHOROKUSHU (JA) [08405854] **5124**

KOSHER BUSINESS *CEASED.* (US/1061-8473) [25480577] **1615**

KOSHER GOURMET MAGAZINE, THE (US/0888-4811) [13577229] **2791**

KOSHU EISEI KENKYU (JA/0916-6823) [26064259] **4788**

KOSHU EISEI NI KANSURU KENKYU HOKOKU (JA) [04677252] **4788**

KOSI WOLBO (KO) [11353506] **4704**

KOSICE, CZECHOSLOVAK REPUBLIC. VYSOKA SKOLA TECHNICKA *See* SBORNIK VEDECKYCH PRAC **1995**

KOSMETIEK (NE/0165-2192) [l01652192] **404**

KOSMETIK INTERNATIONAL (GW) [04319020] **404**

KOSMICESKIE ISSLEDOVANIJA (RU/0023-4206) [03281515] 1408, **27**

KOSMICHESKAIA BIOLOGIIA I AVIAKOSMICHESKAIA MEDITSINA *See* AVIAKOSMICHESKAIA I EKOLOGICHESKAIA MEDITSINA **3554**

KOSMICHESKIE LUCHI. COSMIC RAYS (RU/0368-6485) [03722662] **4437**

KOSMORAMA (DK/0023-4222) [05162166] **4073**

KOSMOS + OEKUMENE (NE) [07109399] 5207, **4972**

KOSMOS (STOCKHOLM) (SW/0368-6213) [01782526] **5124**

KOSMOS (STUTTGART) (GW/0023-4230) [04084824] **5124**

KOSMOS (TORRANCE, CALIF.) (US/0278-8101) [05097959] **390**

KOSMOS (WARSAW, POLAND) (PL/0023-4249) [17934511] **462**

KOSMOSOPHIE (GW/0454-448X) [l0454448X] **4351**

KOSOY'S TRAVEL GUIDE TO EUROPE (CN/0711-4680) [08499937] **5482**

KOSOY'S TRAVEL GUIDE TO FLORIDA AND THE SOUTH (CN/0711-4702) [08507474] **5482**

KOSSUTH LAJOS TUDOMANYEGYETEM *See* STUDIA ROMANICA. SERIES LINGUISTICA **3325**

KOSSUTH LAJOS TUDOMANYEGYETEM *See* STUDIA ROMANICA. SERIES LITTERARIA **3441**

KOSSUTH LAJOS TUDOMANYEGYETEM. MATEMATIKAI INTEZET *See* PUBLICATIONES MATHEMATICAL (DEBRECEN) **3529**

KOSTEN EN FINANCIERING VAN DE GEZONDHEIDSZORG / CENTRAAL BUREAU VOOR DE STATISTIEK, HOOFDAFDELING GEZONDHEIDSSTATISTIEKEN (NE/0075-6954) [10760997] **4788**

KOSZALINSKIE ZESZYTY MUZEALNE (PL/0137-5261) [l01375261] **4090**

KOTAI BUTSURI. A SHIRIZU (JA) [10426351] **4411**

KOTAIGUN SEITAI GAKKAI KAIHO (JA/0386-4561) [12028094] 462, **4554**

KOTHARI'S INDUSTRIAL DIRECTORY OF INDIA (II) [16137637] **905**

KOTIMAAN VESILIIKENNE (FI/0782-5315) [19560572] **5385**

KOTITALOUSESINEIDEN KORJAUS (FI) [02437138] **2812**

KOTO SAIBANSHO KEIJI SAIBAN SOKUHO SHU / HOMU DAIJIN KANBO SHIHO HOSEI CHOSABU HEN (JA) [10345397] **3107**

KOTOIPARI SZEMLE (HU) [06806321] 5353, **1085**

KOTOSH / INSTITUTO NACIONAL DE CULTURA - FILIAL HUANUCO (PE) [04413128] **2743**

KOTSU ANZEN KOGAI KENKYUJO *See* KOTSU ANZEN KOGAI KENKYUJO NEMPO **5385**

KOTSU ANZEN KOGAI KENKYUJO NEMPO (JA) [01790323] 5418, **5385**

KOTSU IGAKU (JA/0022-5274) [10454144] **3602**

KOTSU SHOROPPO (JA) [01790068] **5385**

KOTSUGAKU KENKYU: KENKYU NEMPO (JA) [05021818] **5385**

KOUDE MAGAZINE (NE/0925-6318) [22965497] **2606**

● KOULUTUS (FI/1236-4746) [30374315] **1760**

KOULUTUSLUOKITUS (FI) [06577189] **1899**

KOUNTRY KORRAL MAGAZINE (SW) [01788646] **4128**

KOUQIANG YIXUE (CH/0254-0061) [06459418] **1329**

KOVCHEG (FR) [04816973] **3402**

KOVELS' ANTIQUES & COLLECTIBLES PRICE LIST, THE (US/0738-2405) [08980033] **251**

KOVELS' COMPLETE ANTIQUES PRICE LIST, THE (US/0192-2351) [02998420] **251**

KOVELS ON ANTIQUES AND COLLECTIBLES (US/0741-6091) [10161134] 2774, **251**

KOVETS KEREM SHELOMOH (US) [06498456] **5050**

KOVETS NOAM HA-TORAH (US) [24955332] **5050**

KOVETS YAGDIL TORAH (BROOKLYN, NEW YORK, N.Y. : 1976) (US) [07519807] **5050**

KOVOEXPORT (XR/0023-4311) [01782840] **843**

KOVOVE MATERIALY (XO/0023-432X) [02448170] **4007**

KOWAN GIJUTSU KENKYUJO *See* GUIDE **2090**

KOWAN GIJUTSU KENKYUJO HOKOKU (JA) [07414784] **5535**

KOWAN GIJUTSU KENKYUJO KOENKAI KOEN SHU (JA) [03470915] **2093**

KOY. KORROSION OCH YTSKYDD (SW) [01786930] **1985**

KOYO DOKO CHOSA KEKKA NO GAIYO (JA) [01797046] **1682**

KOYO KANRI CHOSA HOKOKU (JA) [01797386] **943**

KOYU (JA) [04605736] **2657**

KOZA (UN) [25000414] **5811**

KOZAN (JA/0287-9840) [10454263] **2143**

KOZARSTVI (XR/0023-4338) [01782932] **3184**

KOZERDEKU TAJEKOZTATO ES HIRDETESEK (HU) [02245127] **3482**

KOZGAZDASAGI SZEMLE (HU/0023-4346) [01782811] 1502, **689**

KOZHEVENNO-OBUVNAIA PROMYSHLENNOST (RU/0023-4354) [09467182] **3184**

KOZUTI KOZLEKEDESI SZAKIRODALMI TAJEKOZTATO (HU/0231-0724) [l02310724] **5441**

KOZUTI KOZLEKEDESI SZAKIRODALMI TAJEKOZTATO. UTUGYI SZAKKIADAS (HU/0237-2576) [l02372576] **5441**

KPA BULLETIN *See* KENTUCKY PHILOLOGICAL REVIEW **3401**

KPFA PROGRAM FOLIO (US) [02378135] **1134**

KPFK (RADIO STATION : LOS ANGELES, CALIF.) KPFK FOLIO *See* FOLIO (NORTH HOLLYWOOD) **1132**

KPFK (RADIO STATION : LOS ANGELES, CALIFORNIA) *See* FOLIO (NORTH HOLLYWOOD) **1132**

KPSS -- RUKOVODIASHCHAIA SILA SOVETSKOGO OBSHCHESTVA (RU) [19913429] **418**

KPSS XXVI SEZDI QARORLARINI HAETGA TATBIQ ETISHDA UZBEKISTON MATBUOTI (UZ/0206-314X) [14229413] **5251**

K+R KERAMISCHE RUNDSCHAU KLIMA + RAUM (AU) **373**

KR-TIEDOTE / SISAASIAINMINISTERIO, KAAVOITUS- JA RAKENNUSOSASTO (FI) [04970111] **2827**

KRAFTARET : SVENSKA KRAFTVERKSFORENINGENS VERKSAMHETSBERATTELSE (SW) [11658854] **2070**

KRAFTFAHRZEUGTECHNIK (GW/0023-4419) [01782872] **5418**

KRAFTFUTTER (GW/0023-4427) [03772858] **202**

KRAGOZORI (CN/0226-8566) [06860086] **2696**

KRAI NASH IUZHNOURALSKII (RU) [06768795] **2696**

KRAJ RAD; RADZIECKI TYGODNIK ILUSTROWANY (PL) [06203162] **2518**

KRAJSKE KULTURNI STREDISKO V BRNE *See* ROCENKA - KRAJSKE KULTURNI STREDISKO V BRNE **2707**

KRAKOW. WYZSZA SZKOTA PEDAGOGICZNA *See* PRACE MATEMATYCZNE **3527**

KRAKS BLA BOG (DK/0900-1476) [01604584] **433**

KRANKENDIENST (GW/0023-4486) [l00234486] **3602**

KRANKENGYMNASTIK (GW/0023-4494) [04119530] **4381**

KRANKENHAUS-HYGIENE + INFEKTIONSVERHUTUNG (GW/0720-3373) [08897932] **4788**

KRANKENHAUS (WIEN) (AU/0075-7063) [01984332] **3787**

KRANKENHAUSPHARMAZIE (GW/0173-7597) [07561788] **4313**

KRANKENHAUSPSYCHIATRIE (GW/0937-289X) [l0937289X] **3930**

KRANKENHAUSTECHNIK (GW/0720-3977) [l07203977] **3787**

KRANKENHAUSUMSCHAU (GW/0023-4508) [l00234508] **3787**

KRANKENPFLEGE (SZ/0253-0465) [05951168] **3861**

KRANKENPFLEGE JOURNAL (GW/0174-108X) [06571453] **3861**

KRANKENVERSICHERUNG (BERLIN), DIE (GW/0301-4835) [01783111] **2886**

KRAS I SPELEOLOGIA (PL/0137-5482) [04863105] **1385**

KRASNAIA ZVEZDA (RU) [02263299] **4048**

KRASNOYARSK, SIBERIA. INSTITUT TSVETNYKH METALLOV *See* LITEINCE PROIZVODSTVO, METALLOVEDENIE I OBRABOTKA METALLOV DAVLENIEM **4007**

KRATKAIA LITERATURNAIA ENTSIKLOPEDIA (RU) **3402**

KRATKIE SOOBSCENIA PO FIZIKE (RU/0455-0595) [06348318] **4411**

KRATKIE SOOBSENIA - INSTITUT ARHEOLOGII (RU/0130-2620) [l01302620] **272**

KRATKIE SOOBSHCHENIIA - AKADEMIIA NAUK SSSR, INSTITUT ARKHEOLOGII (RU) [05623195] **272**

KRATYLOS (GW/0023-4567) [01783319] **3293**

KRAUS CURRICULUM DEVELOPMENT LIBRARY (US/0740-1868) [09905779] **1899**

KRAUS CURRICULUM DEVELOPMENT LIBRARY. CUMULATIVE SUBJECT INDEX (US) [10842014] **3222**

KRAUS HEFTE *CEASED.* (GW) [03993945] **3403**

KREATIVE KIDS KOPY FUNLETTERS (US/8756-5404) [11589164] **4862**

KREBSBEKAMPFUNG (GW/0342-8907) [04840433] **3820**

KREDIETBANK (BRUSSELS, BELGIUM) *See* ANNUAL REPORT - KREDIETBANK, N. V., BRUSSELS **771**

KREDIT- OCH VALUTAMARKNADEN (SW) [18309084] **796**

KREDIT UND KAPITAL (GW/0023-4591) [04052159] **796**

KREDITPRAXIS 1979 (GW/0172-7400) [I01727400] **796**

KREDYTOVA KOOPERATYVA BUDUCHNIST' (CN/0380-2159) [02583266] **1542**

KREFELD IMMIGRANTS AND THEIR DESCENDANTS (US/0883-7961) [12223595] **2457**

KREISFREIE STADTE UND LANDKREISE IN ZAHLEN (GW) [10158780] **5330**

KREISSTANDARDZAHLEN (GW) [03641741] **5330**

KREMS AN DER DONAU, AUSTRIA (CITY) STADTARCHIV *See* MITTEILUNGEN DES KREMSER STADTARCHIVS **2699**

KREPLAN (DK) [01792010] **5432**

KRESGE ART MUSEUM BULLETIN (US/0887-9222) [12873340] 4090, **355**

KRESS LIBRARY OF BUSINESS AND ECONOMICS *See* PUBLICATION OF THE KRESS LIBRARY OF BUSINESS AND ECONOMICS **705**

KRESTANSKA AKADEMIA *See* STUDIE **5000**

KREUZER (GW) [26815579] **323**

KRIDER NURSERIES *See* ILLUSTRATED GARDEN BOOK / KRIDER'S **2420**

KRIEG UND LITERATUR (GW/0935-9060) [21890894] 3403, **2696**

KRIEGBAUM HERITAGE, THE (US/0743-2763) [10513851] **2457**

KRIGSHISTORISK TIDSSKRIFT (DK) [06096418] **2622**

KRIMINALIST, DER (GW) [02242524] **3168**

KRIMINALISTIK (GW/0023-4699) [09511409] **3168**

KRIMINALSOZIOLOGISCHE BIBLIOGRAPHIE (AU) [04993645] 5251, **3168**

KRIMINOLOGISCHE SCHRIFTENREIHE (GW) [01755285] **3168**

KRIMINOLOGISCHES BULLETIN (SZ) [07699689] **3168**

KRIMINOLOGISCHES JOURNAL (GW) [03550622] **3168**

KRISHI CHAYANIKA (II) **177**

KRISHI SAMEEKSHA (II) **2910**

KRISIS (INTERNATIONAL CIRCLE FOR RESEARCH IN PHILOSOPHY) (US/0894-5233) [12875896] **4351**

KRISTALLIZATSIIA I SVOISTVA KRISTALLOV; MEZHVUZOVSKII SBORNIK (RU) [03336371] **1032**

KRISTALLOGRAFIJA (RU/0023-4761) [02001989] **1032**

KRISTEN VIDENSKABS HEROLD (US/0145-7551) [02776844] **4972**

KRISTEN VIDENSKABS KVARTALSHEFTE. BIBELSTUDIER (US/0145-739X) [02775617] **5017**

KRISTEN VITENSKAPS KVARTALSHEFTE. BIBELSTUDIER (US/0145-7381) [02774717] **5017**

KRITERION (BL/0100-512X) [02284725] **4351**

KRITIK (MY) [02698925] **2657**

KRITIK (SI) [06285357] **4351**

KRITIK (KBENHAVN) (DK/0454-5354) [01607846] **3403**

KRITIKA I MUZYKOZNANIE (RU) [07680818] **4128**

KRITIKA PHYLLA (GR) [05097128] **3403**

KRITIKAS GADAGRAMATA (LV) [05166300] **3403**

KRITIKK JOURNALEN (NO) [15349358] **3403**

KRITIKON LITTERARUM (GW) [01785793] **3293**

KRITISCH AKKOORD (BE) [04051853] **3403**

KRITISCHE BERICHTE (GW/0340-7403) [01964601] **355**

KRITISCHE JUSTIZ (GW/0023-4834) [01606477] **2993**

KRITISCHE STUDIEN ZUR GESCHICHTSWISSENSCHAFT (GW) [02270771] **2622**

KRITISCHE VIERTELJAHRESSCHRIFT FUER GESETZGEBUNG UND RECHTSWISSENSCHAFT (GW/0179-2830) [19107909] **2993**

KRITISCHES LEXIKON ZUR DEUTSCHSPRACHIGEN GEGENWARTSLITERATUR (GW) **1927**

KRMIVA (CI/0023-4850) [03776610] **103**

KRMIVARSTVI A SLUZBY (XR) [04849173] **202**

KROEBER ANTHROPOLOGICAL SOCIETY *See* SPECIAL PUBLICATIONS - KROEBER ANTHROPOLOGICAL SOCIETY **246**

KROEBER ANTHROPOLOGICAL SOCIETY *See* PAPERS - KROEBER ANTHROPOLOGICAL SOCIETY **243**

KROKODIL (RU/0130-2671) [01755292] **3345**

KROLIKOVODSTVO I ZVEROVODSTVO (RU/0023-4885) [09510971] **3184**

KROLOWA APOSTOOW (PL) [24661442] **5031**

KRONIEK VAN HET REMBRANDTHUIS, DE (NE/0166-0381) [05115468] **355**

KRONIKA (PL) [01790932] **2696**

KRONIKA; CASOPIS ZA SLOVENSKO KRAJENO ZGODOVINO (XV/0023-4923) [01783098] **2696**

KRONIKA (TORONTO) (CN/0704-4380) [06272731] **2536**

KRONOS (SA/0259-0190) [15178283] **2641**

KRONOS (US/0361-6584) [02247102] **2622**

KROVOOBRASCENIE (AI/0368-6736) [01350494] **3708**

KRP. KOSTENRECHNUNGSPRAXIS 1977 (GW/0931-9077) [I09319077] **689**

KRUSE REPORT (US/0192-5458) [05047078] 251, **5418**

KRYLIA RODINY (RU/0130-2701) [05110303] **27**

KRYSTALINIKUM (XR/0454-5524) [01755293] **1386**

KRYTYKA (PL/0867-5244) [08415843] **2696**

KRZEPNIECIE METALI I STOPOW (PL/0208-9386) [08247618] **4007**

KRZYZOWKA (PL/0137-7663) [I01377663] **4862**

KS PYOSI SANGPUM MONGNOK (KO) [16829443] **4031**

KSU ECONOMIC AND BUSINESS REVIEW (JA/0387-2955) [01799589] **1571**

KTAV NEWSPAPER (AT/0729-5162) [I07295162] **1804**

KTAVET (RM) **2266**

KTB (FOX LAKE, FLA.) (US/1046-7335) [20306027] **2622**

KTBL-ARBEITSPAPIER (GW) [10814188] **103**

KTEMA (FR/0221-5896) [04049074] 273, **1078**

KTS ZEITSCHRIFT FUER INSOLVENZRECHT : KONKURS, TREUHAND, SANIERUNG (GW/0934-6724) [20381636] **2993**

KU FENG (CC) [09030207] **3403**

KU HSIANG JEN (CH) [11380089] **2657**

KU KLUX KLAN (1915-) *See* PAPERS READ AT THE MEETING OF GRAND DRAGONS, KNIGHTS OF THE KU KLUX KLAN **5235**

KU KUNG HSUEH SHU CHI KAN / KUO LI KU KUNG PO WU YUN PIEN CHI (CH) [11409618] **4090**

KU KUNG PO WU YUAN YUAN KAN (CC) [01755294] **4090**

KU KUNG WEN WU YUEH KAN (CH) [10975331] **355**

KU SHIH HUI (CC) [06519998] **3403**

KU TAI WEN HSUEH LI LUN YEN CHIU / CHUNG-KUO KU TAI WEN HSUEH LI LUN HSUEH HUI PIEN (CC) [07799723] **3403**

KU TI LI HSUEH PAO (CC) [08913331] **2120**

KU TIEN WEN HSUEH / CHUNG-KUO KU TIEN WEN HSUEH YEN CHIU HUI CHU PIEN (CH) [07801128] **3403**

KU TIEN WEN HSUEH LUN TSUNG (CC) [08630890] **3403**

KU TIEN WEN HSUEH LUN TSUNG (CHI LU SHE) (CC) [09688978] **3403**

KUALA LUMPUR BANKERS DIRECTORY (MY) [04122126] **796**

KUAN CHA CHIA (HK) [04110289] **2506**

KUAN HUAI (CH) [08319874] **2657**

KUAN KUANG TUNG CHI NIEN PAO (CH) [01797611] **5482**

KUAN KUANG TZU LIAO (CH) [01797598] **5482**

KUAN KUANG YUEH PAO *See* KUAN KUANG TZU LIAO **5482**

KUANG CHIAO CHING (HK) [01790380] **2506**

KUANG-HSI WEN HSUEH (CC) [09146975] **3403**

KUANG KAO TSA CHIH (CH) [25539564] **761**

KUANG-TUNG FU NU (CC) [08968537] **5560**

KUANG-TUNG HUA PAO (CC) [22253410] **2506**

KUANG-TUNG HUA YUAN CHI KAN (CH) [10256871] **355**

KUANG-TUNG WEN SHIH TZU LIAO (CC) [07182662] **2657**

KUANG YE JI SHU (CH/0300-3760) [01427097] **2143**

KUANGCHAN ZONGHE LIYONG (CC/1000-6532) [I10006532] **1441**

KUANGCHUANG DIZHI (CC/0258-7106) [09639627] **1441**

KUANGCHUANG DIZHI KEXUEYUAN, KUANGCHUANG DIZHI YANJIUSUO SUOKAN (CC/0254-6132) [10377293] **1386**

KUANGWU XUEBAO (CC/1000-4734) [09220165] **1441**

KUANGYE GONGCHENG (CC/0253-6099) [09674669] **2143**

KUBA : WIRTSCHAFTLICHE ENTWICKLUNG (GW) [06605857] **1571**

KUBBEALT AKADEMI MECMUAS (TU) [02242029] **323**

KUCHE (GW/0344-4376) [I03444376] **2348**

KUCHING WATER BOARD *See* ANNUAL REPORT - KUCHING WATER BOARD **4759**

KUDZU (CAYCE) (US/0194-424X) [04121627] **5485**

KUEI-CHOU SHE HUI KO HSUEH (CC) [09247144] **5208**

KUEI-CHOU WEN SHIH TZU LIAO HSUAN CHI / CHUNG-KUO JEN MIN CHENG CHIH HSIEH SHANG HUI I KUEI-CHOU SHENG WEI YUAN HUI, WEN SHIH TZU LIAO YEN CHIU WEI YUAN HUI PIEN (CC) [08779528] **2657**

KUEI SUAN YEN HSUEH PAO (CC/0454-5648) [10485373] **1037**

KUEI-YANG SHIH YUAN HSUEH PAO. SHE HUI KO HSUEH PAN (CC) [09856334] **5233**

KUELGAZDASAG (HU) [01783922] **843**

KUENSTLER (MUENCHEN) (GW/0934-1730) [20944859] **323**

KUENSTLERGILDE; EIN MITTEILUNGSBLATT FUER UNSERE MITGLIEDER, DIE (GW) **355**

KUESTE (GW/0452-7739) [01782766] **2093**

KUGANG SAENGMURHAK YONGU (KO) [08352245] **1329**

KUGO KUNGMUNHAK YONGAM / KUGO KUNGMUN HAKHOE YOKKUM (KO) [08503891] **3293**

●KUHN-ARCHIV (GW/0940-3507) [28607141] **177**

KUJAWY I POMORZE (PL/0867-4248) [I08674248] **2518**

KUKA (NR/0331-4545) [12116414] 3403, **3465**

KUKCHAEK YONGU (KO) [11309030] **4480**

KUKCHE CHONGBO CHARYO (KO) [09087097] **2622**

KUKCHE HAKSUL KANGYONHOE NONMUNJIP (KO) [05003129] **5233**

KUKCHE HAKSUL TAEHOE NONMUNJIP (KO) [14287073] **5233**

KUKCHE KORAE KONSOLTONTU (KO) [09243189] **1637**

KUKCHE KWANGWANG KONGSA *See* KOREAN TOURISM ANNUAL REPORT **843**

KUKCHE MUNJE (KO) [05189746] **4528**

KUKHOE UIWON CHONGNAM (KO) [10039190] **4660**

KUKHOE UIWON TONGUHOE *See* KUKHOE UIWON CHONGNAM **4660**

KUKI CHOWA EISEI KOGAKKAI *See* TRANSACTIONS OF SHASE JAPAN **2608**

KUKI CHOWA EISEI KOGAKKAI RONBUNSHU (JA) [03616575] **619**

KUKI SEIJO (JA/0023-5032) [05098155] **2235**

KUKILA (IO/0126-9223) [12963835] **5618**

KUKKA KOSI (KO) [11382233] **4704**

KUKTO KAEBAL YONGU (KO) [08466781] **1571**

KUKTO WA KONSOL (KO) [11778769] 619, **1615**

KUKURUZA (RU) [09848850] **177**

KUKURUZA I SORGO (RU/0233-7770) [13340630] **177**

KUL : MANEDSBULLETIN (LU) [04161403] **1615**

KULBRINTER (LU) [04299684] **4262**

KULFOLDI MAGYAR NYELVU KIADVANYOK (HU/0133-333X) [03642501] **418**

KULFOLDI TARSADALOMTUDOMANYI KEZIKONYVEK (HU/0133-5839) [11087568] **5227**

KULL AL-FUNUN (LY) [03156418] **323**

KULLO POKCHI (KO) [11385814] **1682**

KULLOJA (KO) [05235716] **1683**

KULTTUURIN JULKINEN RAHOITUS (FI) [20949149] **4735**

KULTUR & TECHNIK (GW/0344-5690) [04753575] **4090**

KULTUR CHRONIK (GW/0724-343X) [11280892] **2849, 323**

KULTUR ISTATISTIKLERI (TU) [18024338] **323, 334**

KULTUR UND FREIZEIT (SZ) [02243656] **323**

KULTUR UND GESELLSCHAFT (GW) [01784028] **4528**

KULTURA (YU/0023-5164) [05124228] **2518**

KULTURA FIZYCZNA (PL) [01784582] **1857**

KULTURA I KULTURNOE STROITELSTVO (RU) [03045518] **2849**

KULTURA I RELIGIIA *CEASED.* (RU) [27096545] **4972**

KULTURA I SPOECZENSTWO (PL/0023-5172) [02315271] **2849**

KULTURA I ZHIZN (RU/0023-5199) [01771095] **4528**

KULTURA (PARIS) (FR/0023-5148) [01755308] **3403**

KULTURA (PRAGUE, CZECHOSLOVAKIA) (XR) [19463610] **3403, 5799**

KULTURA SLOVA (XO/0023-5202) [02315460] **3293**

KULTURA, UMETNOST, INFORMACIJE / ZAVOD SR SLOVENIJE ZA STATISTIKO (XV) [08228899] **2696**

KULTURBAUTEN (GW/0233-2337) [I02332337] **302**

KULTURELLES LEBEN (GW/0451-0410) [02315436] **1683**

KULTUREN (SW/0454-5915) [02243005] **2622**

KULTURENS VARLD (SW/0282-5902) [19046657] **2696**

KULTURGEOGRAFISKE SKRIFTER (DK/0416-7066) [04443546] **2567**

KULTURGESCHICHTE DER ANTIKEN WELT (GW) [08137645] **323, 273**

KULTURKATALOGEN (SW) [20949510] **2518**

KULTURNO-PROSVETITELNAIA RABOTA (RU/0454-5990) [04226046] **1881**

KULTURNO-UMETNISKA IN PROSVETNA DEJAVNOST (XV) [06495906] **5330**

KULTUROS BARAI (LI/0134-3106) [02340885] **2518**

KULTURPFLANZE (GW/0075-7209) [02448179] **177**

KULTURPFLANZE : BEIHEFT. BERICHTE UND MITTEILUNGEN AUS DEM INSTITUT FUER KULTURPFLANZENFORSCHUNG DER DEUTSCHEN AKADEMIE DER WISSENSCHAFTEN ZU BERLIN IN GATERSLEBEN KRS. ASCHERLEBEN, DIE (GW/0454-6032) [05268994] **5351**

KULTURRADET : STATENS KULTURRAD INFORMERAR (SW/0283-1899) [19712698] **2696**

KULTUUR JA ELU (ER/0452-814X) [01782980] **2536**

KULTUURLEVEN (BE/0023-5288) [I00235288] **5251**

KUMAMOTO DAIGAKU. KOGAKUBU *See* MEMOIRS OF THE FACULTY OF ENGINEERING, KUMAMOTO UNIVERSITY **1987**

KUMAMOTO JOSHI DAIGAKU GAKUJUTSU KIYO (JA/0368-5837) [09913564] **1092**

KUMAMOTO JOURNAL OF MATHEMATICS (JA/0914-675X) [18299795] **3516**

KUMAMOTO-KEN EISEI KOGAI KENKYUJO *See* KUMAMOTO-KEN EISEI KOGAI KENKYUJO HO **4788**

KUMAMOTO-KEN EISEI KOGAI KENKYUJO HO (JA) [01797360] **4788**

KUMAMOTO-KEN SUISAN SHIKENJO *See* KUMAMOTO-KEN SUISAN SHIKENJO KENKYU HOKOKU **2307**

KUMAMOTO-KEN SUISAN SHIKENJO KENKYU HOKOKU (JA) [06909853] **2307**

KUMAMOTO KOGYO DAIGAKU KENKYU HOKOKU (JA/0385-132X) [10279707] **5124**

KUMAMOTO KOKUZEIKYOKU TOKEISHO (JA) [02849715] **4735**

KUMAMOTO MEDICAL JOURNAL, THE (JA/0023-5326) [01755311] **3660**

KUMHYONG, KONGGU (KO) [11898724] **1615**

KUML (DK/0454-6245) [02263321] **2696**

KUMPULAN KERTAS KARYA - DEPARTEMEN TENAGA KERJA, TRANSMIGRASI DAN KOPERASI, TEAM POLICY RESEARCH (IO) [02246253] **1683**

KUMPULAN PIDATO MENTERI KESEHATAN RI (IO) [09539699] **4788**

KUMSONG TONGSIN (KO) [10502016] **1615**

KUMYUNG KYONGJE (KO) [10631569] **796**

KUN CHUNG CHIH SHIH (CC/0452-8255) [09256950] **5611**

KUN CHUNG FEN LEI HSUEH PAO (CC) [07322012] **5611**

K'UN CH'UNG HSUEH PAO (CC/0454-6296) [02310913] **5611**

KUN CHUNG HSUEH YEN CHIU CHI KAN / CHUNG-KUO KO HSUEH YUAN SHANG-HAI KUN CHUNG YEN CHIU SO PIEN (CC) [09396304] **5590**

KUN CHUNG TIEN TI (CC) [19582000] **5611**

KUNA-MELBA NEWS (US) [18927319] **5657**

KUNAPIPI (DK/0106-5734) [05285131] **324, 3403**

KUNCHONGXUE YANJIU JIKAN (CH/1002-0926) [I10020926] **5611**

KUNG CHENG CHI HSIEH (CH) [09179159] **619**

KUNG CHI TUNG LI HSUEH HSUEH PAO (CC/0258-1825) [21730088] **27, 4411**

KUNG CHU CHI SHU (CH) [08995314] **5124**

●KUNG FU MASTERS (US/1068-7645) [27802264] **4903**

KUNG FU MI AO (HK) [02246214] **4903**

KUNG LUN (CH) [09147797] **2657**

KUNG YEH CHI SHU YEN CHIU YUAN. KUANG YEH YEN CHIU SO *See* M.R.S.O. REPORT **2143**

KUNG YEH CHING YING KUAN LI CHING YEN HSUAN PIEN / KUO CHIA CHING WEI CHI YEH KUAN LI CHU PIEN (CC) [09535175] **1615**

KUNG YEH WU JAN FANG CHIH / CHING CHI PU KUNG YEH WU JAN FANG CHIH CHI SHU FU TAO HSIAO TSU PIEN (CH) [09938505] **2235**

KUNG YEH YUEH KAN (HK) [02245535] **5124**

KUNGL. KRIGSVETENSKAPSAKADEMIEN (SWEDEN) *See* HANDLINGAR OCH TIDSKRIFT **4045**

KUNGL. MUSIKALISKA AKADEMIEN (SWEDEN) *See* MATRIKEL **4130**

KUNGL. SKOGS- OCH LANTBRUKSAKADEMIENS TIDSKRIFT (SW/0023-5350) [09598765] **2386, 103**

KUNGL. SKYTTEANSKA SAMFUNDETS HANDLINGAR (SW/0560-2416) [01765615] **2696**

KUNGL. TEKNISKA HOGSKOLAN HOGSKOLAN *See* STUDIEHANDBOK **5160**

KUNGL. VITTERHETS-, HISTORIE- OCH ANTIKVITETSAKADEMIENS ARSBOK (SW/0083-6796) [I00836796] **2849**

KUNGLIGA SVENSKA VETENSKAPSAKADEMIEN *See* KONGLIGA SVENSKA VETENSKAPS-AKADEMIENS HANDLINGAR **5124**

KUNGLIGA SVENSKA VETENSKAPSAKADEMIEN *See* VETENSKAPSAKADEMIEN **5169**

KUNGMIN MUNHAK (JA) [10156809] **3403**

KUNGMIN SAENGHWAL SIGAN CHOSA (KO) [09227816] **5251**

KUNGMIN UNHAENG *See* YONCHA POGOSO - KUNGMIN UNHAENG **817**

KUNGMIN YULLI YONGU (KO) [09147831] **2252**

KUNGNIP CHUNGANG TOSOGWAN (SEOUL, KOREA) *See* TOSOGWAN HWICHONG **3253**

KUNGNIP KONGOP PYOJUN SIHOMSO *See* YON'GU POGO - KUNGNIP K ONGOP PYOJUN SIHOMSO **5172**

KUNGNIP KONGWON (KO) [08835416] **2197**

KUNI NO KAIYO KAGAKU GIJUTSU KAIHATSU NO GENJO TO KONGO NO HOKO / KAIYO KAGAKU GIJUTSU KAIHATSU SUISHIN RENRAKU KAIGI HEN (JA) [07845000] **1451**

KUNI NO SHIKEN KENKYU GYOMU KEIKAKU (JA) [03641807] **5124**

KUNITACHI ONGAKU DAIGAKU *See* KENKYU KIYO - KUNITACHI ONGAKU DAIGAKU **4127**

KUNNALLINEN VIRKALUETTELO (FI/0786-3624) [19548482] **4660**

KUNNALLISTALOUDEN ENNAKKOTILASTO (FI) [02242851] **4735**

KUNNALLISTEN VIRANHALTIJOIDEN JA KUUKAUSIPALKKAISTEN TYONTEKIJOIDEN JA TOIMIHENKILOIDEN PALKAT (FI) [07051823] **4660**

KUNNALLISTIETEELLINEN AIKAKAUSKIRJA (FI/0356-3669) [I03563669] **4660**

KUNST & ANTIQUITATEN (GW/0341-4159) [08998073] **251, 355**

KUNST & KOMMUNIKATION DANSK UDG (DK/0902-8099) [I09028099] **1115, 355**

KUNST & MUSEUMJOURNAAL (DUTCH EDITION) (NE/0924-5251) [20409012] **355**

KUNST & MUSEUMJOURNAAL (ENGLISH EDITION) (NE/0924-526X) [20859786] **356**

KUNST BULLETIN (SZ) **356**

KUNST EN BELEID IN NEDERLAND (NE/0921-4755) [20989920] **356**

KUNST- EN CULTUURAGENDA *See* K & I.E. EN C. KUNST EN CULTUUR **323**

KUNST + HANDWERK *See* KUNSTHANDWERK & DESIGN **373**

KUNST IN HESSEN UND AM MITTELRHEIN (GW/0452-8514) [02292231] **356**

KUNST OG KULTUR (NO/0023-5415) [01589324] **373**

KUNST OG MUSEUM (DK/0454-6520) [I04546520] **4090, 356**

KUNST UND ALTERTUM AM RHEIN (GW/0075-725X) [02280374] **356**

KUNST UND DAS SCHONELTEIM, DIE (GW/0023-5423) [01782251] **356**

KUNST UND KIRCHE (AU/0023-5431) [04109854] **302, 356**

KUNST UND LITERATUR *CEASED.* (GW/0023-544X) [01924742] **356**

KUNST + UNTERRICHT (GW/0023-5466) [06160517] **4351**

KUNST + UNTERRICHT 1985 (GW/0931-7112) [I09317112] **356**

KUNSTAKADEMIET (DENMARK). ARKITEKTSKOLEN *See* STUDIEINFORMATION **309**

●KUNSTARBOK ART YEARBOOK, NORWAY (NO/0803-6160) [26037001] **356**

KUNSTAUKTION (AU) [04743043] **356**

KUNSTCHRONIK (GW/0023-5474) [01589769] **356**

KUNSTDENKMALER DER SCHWEIZ, DIE (SZ) [02286297] **356**

KUNSTERZIEHUNG : ZEITSCHRIFT FUR LEHRER UND JUGENDERZIEHER (SZ/0451-0887) [08715250] **1760, 324**

KUNSTFORUM INTERNATIONAL (GW/0177-3674) [02710706] **356**

KUNSTGESCHICHTLICHE GESELLSCHAFT ZU BERLIN *See* SITZUNGSBERICHTE / KUNSTGESCHICHTLICHE GESELLSCHAFT ZU BERLIN **364**

KUNSTHANDEL, DER (GW/0023-5504) [04115410] **356**

●KUNSTHANDWERK & DESIGN (GW) [25405853] **373**

KUNSTHANDWERK IN EUROPA (GW) [09093692] **373**

KUNSTHARZ NACHRICHTEN (GW/0170-0693) [11309466] **4456**

KUNSTHAUS LEMPERTZ, COLOGNE *See* ALTE KUNST **335**

KUNSTHISTORIKER (AU/1015-0129) [I10150129] **356**

KUNSTHISTORISCHES INSTITUT IN FLORENZ *See* MITTEILUNGEN DES KUNSTHISTORISCHES INSTITUTES FLORENZ **358**

KUNSTHISTORISCHES JAHRBUCH GRAZ (AU/1010-3856) [05158411] **356**

KUNSTJAHRBUCH DER STADT LINZ (AU/0454-6601) [04106092] **356**

KUNSTMAGAZIN (GW/0343-0456) [04408379] **356**

KUNSTMESTSTOFFENINDUSTRIE / CENTRAAL BUREAU VOOR DE STATISTIEK, HOOFDAFDELING STATISTIEKEN VAN INDUSTRIE EN BOUWNIJVERHEID (NE) [10421459] **1615**

KUNSTPREISJAHRBUCH (GW/0174-3511) [08916691] **356**

KUNSTREPORT (GW/0172-7265) [02661937] **356**

KUNSTSPIEGEL (GW/0172-8350) [09026295] **324**

KUNSTSTOF EN RUBBER (NE/0167-9597) [09593570] **5076**

KUNSTSTOFF INFORMATION (GW) **5076**

KUNSTSTOFF-JOURNAL (GW/0047-3766) [05249193] **4456**

KUNSTSTOFF WOCHENDIENST (GW) 5076

KUNSTSTOFFBERATER (1979) (GW/0172-6374) [07514724] 4456

KUNSTSTOFFE (GW/0023-5563) [02448196] 4456

KUNSTSTOFFE EUROPE See PLAST EUROPE : PE : KUNSTSTOFFE 4457

KUNSTSTOFFE EUROPE See PE. PLAST EUROPE 4457

KUNSTSTOFFE FEUR DIE ELEKTRONIK UND OPTIK (GW/0932-6138) [I09326138] 5076

KUNSTSTOFFE IN OSTERREICH (AU) [01785847] 4456

KUNSTSTOFFE PLASTICS (MONATLICH AUSG.) See KUNSTSTOFFE SYNTHETICS 4456

KUNSTSTOFFE-PLASTICS (SOLOTHURN) (SZ/0023-5598) [02311632] 4456

KUNSTSTOFFE SYNTHETICS (SZ/1021-0601) [I10210601] 4456

KUNSTSTOFVERWERKENDE INDUSTRIE / CENTRAAL BUREAU VOOR DE STATISTIEK, HOOFKAFDELING STATISTIEKEN VAN INDUSTRIE EN BOUWNIJVERHEID (NE/0168-4418) [11881719] 1615

KUNSTVERSTEIGERUNG (AU) [04743036] 356

KUNSTWISSENSCHAFTLICHE STUDIEN (GW) [01624102] 356

KUNTAINLIITTOJEN TALOUS (FI) [02241839] 4735

KUNTASEKTORIN KUUKAUSIPALKAT / TILASTOKESKUS (FI/0784-9370) [19531940] 4660

KUNTIEN JA KUNTAINLIITTOJEN SOSIAALITOIMEN KAYTTOMENOT JA TULOT (FI) [19245443] 4660

KUNTIEN TALOUS: KUNNITTAISET TIEDOT. KOMMUNERNAS EKONOMI: UPPGIFTER ENLIGT KOMMUN (FI) [03351907] 4735

KUNTSBEELD (NE) 356

KUO CHI HANG KUNG / GUOJI HANGKONG (CC) [05655631] 27

KUO CHI HSING SHIH NIEN CHIEN / SHANG-HAI KUO CHI WEN TI YEN SHIU SO PIEN (CH) [09289628] 4528

KUO CHI HUO I (CC/1002-5030) [11204238] 843

KUO CHI KUAN HSI HSUEH PAO (CH) [04162377] 4528

KUO CHI NAN SHE HSUEH HUI TSUNG KAN / KUO CHI NAN SHE HSUEH HUI PI SHU CHU PIEN (HK) [23185487] 3403

KUO CHI WEN TI YEN CHIU (CC) [10788062] 4528

KUO CHIA I HSUEH TSA CHIH (CH) [11508510] 3603

KUO CHIAO FU TAO / TAI-WAN SHENG LI TAI-CHUNG SHIH FAN CHUAN KO HSUEH HSIAO (CH) [08912622] 1760

KUO LI CHUNG HSING TA HSUEH LI KUNG HSUEH PAO / KUO LI CHUNG HSING TA HSUEH LI KUNG HSUEH PAO PIEN CHI WEI YUAN HUI (CC) [21664295] 1985

KUO LI CHUNG YANG TU SHU KUAN (CHINA) See NATIONAL CENTRAL LIBRARY NEWSLETTER 3233

KUO LI KU KUNG PO WU YUAN See NEWSLETTER & GALLERY GUIDE / NATIONAL PALACE MUSEUM 4094

KUO LI TAI-WAN SHIH FAN TA HSUEH. YING YU HSI See STUDIES IN ENGLISH LITERATURE & LINGUISTICS 3325

KUO LI TAI-WAN TA HSUEH FA HSUEH LUN TSUNG (CH) [12374493] 2993

KUO LI TAI-WAN TA HSUEH KUNG CHENG HSUEH KAN (CH/0404-5360) [02146948] 1985

KUO SHIH PING LUN (HK) [23259999] 2657

KUO WAI KUNG SSU FEN LEI CHIH NAN CLASSIFIED INTERNATIONAL BUSINESS DIRECTORY FOR CHINA (CC) [08853923] 689

KUO WAI WEN HSUEH (CC) [09178861] 3345

KUO WEN HSUEH PAO (CH) [01646036] 3403

KUORMA-AUTO LINJALIIKENNE (FI) [02241632] 5418

KUOYUK PYONNGNON (KO) [05156849] 1760

KUPRIAKAI SPOUDAI (CY/0081-1580) [01696868] 2696

KURANTY (RU) [17572820] 5809

KURASHI NO TAME NO HORITSU (JA) [10703418] 2993

KURASHI NO TECHO (JA) [31470748] 1985

KURASHI NO TOKEI / KOKUMIN SEIKATSU SENTA HEN (JA) [09651115] 1683

KURDISH LIFE (US/1061-8457) [25479154] 2266, 2769

KURDISH STUDIES (US/1070-0870) [28203254] 2769

KURDISH TIMES See KURDISH STUDIES 2769

KURIER LUBELSKI (PL/0137-9224) [I01379224] 5808

KURIER (ORANGE, VA), DER (US/1059-9762) [15232222] 2457

KURIER SZCZECINSKI (PL/0137-9240) [I01379240] 5808

KURIHAMA TSUSHIN (JA) [04742300] 1881

KURINIKARU SUTADI (JA/0388-5585) [09493914] 3861

KURISUCHYON HEROLDU (US/0749-0143) [11061278] 5636

KURORTOLOGIIA I FIZIOTERAPIIA (RU) [05758442] 4381

KURORTOLOGIIA I FIZIOTERAPIIA (BU/0368-7066) [09490333] 2599

KURSBUCH (GW/0023-5652) [01755336] 2518

KURSBUCH - DEUTSCHE BUNDESBAHN (GW) [02358756] 5432

KURSBUCH: INTERNATIONALER + I.E. UND BINNENVERKEHR (GW) [03990589] 5432

KURSCHNERS DEUTSCHER GELEHRTEN-KALENDER (GW) [01924160] 418

KURSCHNERS DEUTSCHER LITERATUR-KALENDER (GW) [07896644] 3403

KURT WEILL NEWSLETTER (US/0899-6407) [10645527] 4128

KURTRIERISCHES JAHRBUCH (GW/0452-9081) [02280458] 2696

KURUKSHETRA (II/0023-5660) [01773665] 5251

KURUME DAIGAKU RONSO (JA/0368-5144) [03584534] 2506

KURUME DAIGAKU. SHOGAKUBU See KURUME DAIGAKU RONSO 2506

KURUME MEDICAL JOURNAL (JA/0023-5679) [01755337] 3603

KURYER ZJEDNOCZENIA (US/0744-8910) [08634515] 5729

KURZBERICHT UBER LATEINAMERIKA (GW) [07525568] 844, 1502

KURZBERICHTE AUS DEN PAPYRUSSAMMLUNGEN / BIBLIOTHEK DER JUSTUS LIEBIG-HOCHSCHULE (GW) [03898559] 1078

KURZBERICHTE / INSTITUT FUER ARBEITSMARKT- UND BERUFSFORSCHUNG (GW/0173-6574) [10738698] 1683

KURZDARSTELLUNG DER DOKUMENTATIONS-LEITSTELLE MODERNER ORIENT UND TATIGKEITSBERICHT (GW) [04040072] 3222

KURZWEIL REPORT, THE (US/0190-1656) [04611121] 4390

KUSIRI NO CHISHIKI (JA/0287-6485) [10341581] 4313

KUTATASSZERVEZESI TAJEKOZTATO (HU/0866-5192) [24357783] 5124

KUTLWANO (BS/0023-5733) [02263345] 2641

KUTUB WA-MAQALAT / MAHAD AL-INMA AL-ARABI, WAHDAT AL-TAWTHIQ WA-AL-TAHRIR (LE) [10173393] 418

KUUKAUSIKATSAUS SUOMEN ILMASTOON (FI/0303-2485) [01793441] 1427

KUUMBA (LOS ANGELES, CALIF.) (US/1049-328X) [21206745] 3403

KUWAIT See AL-KUWAYT AL-YAWM 2929

KUWAIT BULLETIN OF MARINE SCIENCE (KU/0250-362X) [08872407] 1451

KUWAIT PETROLEUM CORPORATION See ANNUAL REPORT / KUWAIT PETROLEUM CORPORATION 4250

KUWAIT (STATE). AL-IDARAH AL-MARKAZIYAH LIL-IHSA See STATISTICAL ABSTRACT - CENTRAL STATISTICAL OFFICE 5339

KUWAIT TIMES (KU) 5806

KUWAIT (WASHINGTON, D.C.) (US) [10159829] 2657

KUWAIT, WIRTSCHAFTLICHE ENTWICKLUNG, HANDELSSTELLE FUR AUSSENHANDELSINFORMATION (GW) [09047723] 1571

KUWAIT : WIRTSCHAFTSDATEN UND WIRTSCHAFTSDOKUMENTATION (GW) [05947789] 1571

KUWAITI DIGEST, THE (KU) [02306024] 2506

KUZNECNO-STAMPOVOCNOE PROIZVODSTVO (1959) (RU/0201-7296) [09490305] 4007

KVANTOVAIA ELEKTRONIKA (UN/0368-7155) [02621049] 2070

KVANTOVAJA ELEKTRONIKA (MOSKVA) (RU/0368-7147) [24041929] 2070

KVASNY PRUMYSL (XR/0023-5830) [04084943] 2368

KVETY (XR/0023-5849) [01782759] 2518

KVINNOVETENSKAPLIG TIDSKRIFT (SW/0348-8365) [09813336] 3764

KW HEUTE (GW/0937-6186) [I09376186] 689, 4007

KW MAGAZINE (CN/0822-8140) [10450974] 2536

KWAHAK SEDAE / KWAHAK SEDAE YOKKUM (KO) [25521396] 5124

KWALITEIT IN BEDRIJF (NE/0169-9261) [I01699261] 929, 689

KWANDONG (JA) [10039036] 1092

KWANGGO CHONGBO (KO) [11252060] 761

KWANGSAN CHIJIL (KO) [05629398] 2143

KWANGWANG CHONGBO (KO) [10263870] 5482

KWANSEI GAKUIN UNIVERSITY ANNUAL STUDIES (JA/0454-7306) [02265143] 1833

KWARTA (PL/0239-6629) [I02396629] 3403

KWARTAALBERICHT NIEUW BURGELIJK WETBOEK (NE) 2993

KWARTAALOVERZICHT VAN DE ECONOMIE (BE/0773-3666) [19463432] 905

KWARTAALSCHRIFT / RIJKS PSYCHOLOGISCHE DIENST (NE) [11103969] 4788

KWARTALNIK ARCHITEKTURY I URBANISTYKI (PL/0023-5865) [02690156] 302

KWARTALNIK ELEKTRONIKI I TELEKOMUNIKACJI (PL) [26627358] 2070

KWARTALNIK GEOLOGICZNY (PL/0023-5873) [01661703] 1386

KWARTALNIK HISTORII I TEORII RUCHU ZAWODOWEGO (PL/0860-9357) [20777615] 1683

KWARTALNIK HISTORII KULTURY MATERIALNEJ (PL/0023-5881) [01782835] 2696

KWARTALNIK HISTORII NAUKI I TECHNIKI (PL/0023-589X) [02263350] 5124

KWARTALNIK HISTORII PRASY POLSKIEJ (PL/0137-2998) [03573378] 4816

KWARTALNIK HISTORYCZNY (PL/0023-5903) [01782466] 2622

KWARTALNIK NEOFILOLOGICZNY (PL/0023-5911) [01782905] 3294

KWARTALNIK OPOLSKI (PL/0023-592X) [02263352] 2696

KWARTALNIK PEDAGOGICZNY (PL/0023-5938) [01782896] 1760

KWIC INDEX TO KNOW YOUR GOVERNMENT (CN) 4660

KWOC LIST OF PETROLEUM ABSTRACTS' THESAURUS, AND NEW E & P TERMS (US/0892-4465) [15193836] 4263

KWOC LIST OF PETROLEUM ABSTRACTS' GEOGRAPHIC THESAURUS AND GEOGRAPHIC THESAURUS. SUPPLEMENTAL DESCRIPTORS (US/0896-6141) [17236273] 1386

KY THUAT IEN LC (VM) [05017926] 2070

KYBERNETES (UK/0368-492X) [01591609] 1252

KYBERNETIKA (XR/0023-5954) [01783260] 1252

KYESONG MUNHAK (JA) [09169072] 3403

●KYIVSKA STAROVYNA (UN/0869-3595) [26332044] 3403

KYIVSKYI DERZHAVNYI UNIVERSYTET IM. T.H. SHEVCHENKA See VISNIK KIIVSKOGO UNIVERSITETU. SERIJA HIMII 995

KYIVSKYI POLITEKHNICHNYI INSTYTUT See VESTNIK KIEVSKOGO POLITEKHNICHESKOGO INSTITUTA. SERIIA RADIOELEKTRONIKA 4442

KYKLOS (SZ/0023-5962) [01782461] 5208

KYNGGI CHONMANG CHOSA (KO) [08164908] 1571

KYOBO MUNGO (KO) [09059680] 4829

KYODAN NEWS LETTER (JA) [01921768] 4972

KYODO KANKEI SHIMBUN KIJI SAKUIN (JA) [04286269] 2526

KYODO KENKYU KATSUDO HOKOKUSHI (JA) [09290744] 2849, 5208

KYODO SHIRYOKAN DAYORI (JA) [04426506] 2657

KYOHOE WA YOKSA (KO) [12004378] **4972**

KYOHOESA YON'GU (KO) [05190057] **5031**

KYOIKU (JA) [02368163] **1760**

KYOIKU SEISAKU KENKYU (JA) [04221343] **1760**

KYOIKU SHAKAIGAKU KENKYU (JA/0387-3145) [05792974] **5251, 1760**

KYOIKU SHINRIGAKU KENKYU (JA/0021-5015) [04426248] **4602**

KYOIKUGAKUBU KENKYU HOKOKU. SHIZEN KAGAKU (GIFU) (JA/0533-9529) [07907387] **5124**

KYOIKUSHI HIKAKU KYOIKU RONKO (JA) [09345346] **1760**

KYOKA PURASUCHIKKUSU (JA/0452-9685) [09733669] **4456**

KYOKAN KENKYU GYOSEKI ICHIRAN (JA) [03866099] **5124**

KYOKAN KENKYU YOROKU (JA) [03753819] **5125**

KYOKUCHIKEN NYUSU (JA) [02175219] **5125**

KYONGGI PUKPU SANGUI (KO) [10269673] **844**

KYONGGI YONGAM (KO) [08690981] **2657**

KYONGHYANG CHAPCHI (KO) [05529413] **5031**

KYONGJE NONJIP (KO) [04856317] **1593**

KYONGJE NONJIP (CHUNGNAM TAEHAKKYO. PUSOL KYONGYONG KYONGJE YONGUSO) (KO) [14907414] **1502**

KYONGJE PURIPUSU (KO) [07759497] **1571**

KYONGJE RIBYU (KO) [04979956] **1571**

KYONGJE RIBYU (SOUL UNHAENG) *See* KYONGJE RIBYU **1571**

KYONGNAM MUNHAK (KO) [11335096] **3294**

KYONGSANG NONJIP (CHUNGNAM TAEHAKKYO. PUSOL KUONGYONG KYONGJE YONGUSO) (KO) [10398867] **1593**

KYONGSANT NONJIP (TAEGU TAEHAKKYO. KYONGSANG MUNJE YONGUSO) (KO) [09446312] **1593**

KYONGYONG KWA KOMPYUTO (KO) [05021881] **1193**

KYONGYONG KWA NODONG (KO) [05160132] **3150**

KYONGYONG NONCHONG (YONGNAM TAEHAKKYO. PUSOL KYONGYONG YONGUSO) (KO) [08293932] **1615**

KYONGYONG NONJIP (CHUNGNAM TAEHAKKYO. PUSOL KYONGYONG KYONGJE YONGUSO) (KO) [14907288] **875**

KYONGYONG NONJIP (SOUL TAEHAKKYO. KYONGYONG YONGUSO) (KO/0023-369X) [04587725] **1615**

KYONGYONG SARYE YON'GU (KO) [05060133] **875**

KYONGYONG YONGU (CHOSON TAEHAKKYO. KYONGYONG YONGUSO) (KO) [08352285] **1615, 875**

KYONGYONGHAK YON'GU (KO) [05703915] **875**

KYORE UI KIL (KO) [25496870] **2506**

KYORIN IGAKKAI ZASSHI (JA/0368-5829) [10283771] **3603**

KYORITSU JOSHI DAIGAKU KASEI GAKUBU KIYO (JA/0388-3612) [I03883612] **2791**

KYORITSU JOSHI TANKI DAIGAKU SEIKATSU KAGAKUKA KIYO (JA/0917-2300) [I09172300] **462**

KYORITSU YAKKA DAIGAKU KENKYU NENPO (JA/0452-9731) [09787087] **4313**

KYOSHIN SOKUHO (JA) [02245377] **1408**

KYOSHOBA SOGO KENKYUJO HOKOKU (JA/0386-4634) [07325988] **2800**

KYOTO DAIGAKU *See* JOURNAL OF MATHEMATICS OF KYOTO UNIVERSITY **3514**

KYOTO DAIGAKU. ABUYAMA JISHIN KANSOKUJO *See* SEISMOLOGICAL BULLETIN OF ABUYAMA SEISMOLOGICAL OBSERVATORY, KYOTO UNIVERSITY **1410**

KYOTO DAIGAKU. BOSAI KENKYUJO *See* BULLETIN OF THE DISASTER PREVENTION RESEARCH INSTITUTE **2019**

KYOTO DAIGAKU. GENSHIRO JIKKENJO *See* ANNUAL REPORTS OF THE RESEARCH REACTOR INSTITUTE, KYOTO UNIVERSITY **4446**

KYOTO DAIGAKU. GENSHIRO JIKKENJO. GAKUJUTSU KOENKAI *See* HOBUNSHU / KYOTO DAIGAKU GENSHIRO JIKKENJO GAKUJUTSU KOENKAI **1053**

KYOTO DAIGAKU. JIMBUN KAGAKU KENKYUJO *See* TOYOGAKU BUNKEN RUIMOKU **2666**

KYOTO DAIGAKU. KAGAKU KENKYUJO *See* BULLETIN OF THE INSTITUTE FOR CHEMICAL RESEARCH, KYOTO UNIVERSITY **963**

KYOTO DAIGAKU KEKKAKU KYOBU SHIKKAN KENKYUJO KIYO (JA/0009-3378) [01778865] **3799**

KYOTO DAIGAKU. KEKKUKU KYOBU SHIKKAN KENKYUJO *See* KYOTO DAIGAKU KEKKAKU KYOBU SHIKKAN KENKYUJO KIYO **3799**

KYOTO DAIGAKU. KOGAKUBU *See* MEMOIRS OF THE FACULTY OF ENGINEERING, KYOTO UNIVERSITY **1987**

KYOTO DAIGAKU NIHON KAGAKU SENI KENKYUJO KOENSHU (JA/0368-6280) [09994607] **5353**

KYOTO DAIGAKU. NOGAKUBU *See* MEMOIRS OF THE COLLEGE OF AGRICULTURE, KYOTO UNIVERSITY **108**

KYOTO DAIGAKU NOGAKUBU ENSHURIN HOKOKU (JA/0368-511X) [09623265] **2386**

KYOTO DAIGAKU. RIGAKUBU *See* MEMOIRS OF THE FACULTY OF SCIENCE, KYOTO UNIVERSITY. SERIES OF PHYSICS, ASTROPHYSICS, GEOPHYSICS AND CHEMISTRY **4412**

KYOTO DAIGAKU. RIGAKUBU *See* MEMOIRS OF THE FACULTY OF SCIENCE, KYOTO UNIVERSITY. SERIES OF BIOLOGY **464**

KYOTO DAIGAKU TONAN AJIA KENKYU SENTA *See* KYOTO DAIGAKU TONAN AJIA KENKYU SENTA YORAN **2506**

KYOTO DAIGAKU TONAN AJIA KENKYU SENTA YORAN (JA) [06108385] **2506**

KYOTO DAIGAKU. UEDA ATSUSHI KENKYUSHITSU *See* KYOTO DAIGAKU UEDA ATSUSHI KENKYUSHITSU KENKYU ROMBUN SHU **1683**

KYOTO DAIGAKU UEDA ATSUSHI KENKYUSHITSU KENKYU ROMBUN SHU (JA) [02478567] **1683**

KYOTO-FU EISEI KENKYUJO *See* KYOTO-FU EISEI KENKYUJO NENPO **4788**

KYOTO-FU EISEI KENKYUJO NENPO (JA/0389-5041) [08364568] **2176, 4788**

KYOTO-FU SHIGAKU KENKYU RONSHU (JA) [07505561] **1833**

KYOTO FURITSU DAIGAKU *See* KYOTO FURITSU DAIGAKU GAKUJUTSU HOKOKU. RIGAKU, SEIKATSU KAGAKU. SCIENTIFIC REPORTS OF THE KYOTO PREFECTURAL UNIVERSITY. NATURAL SCIENCE AND LIVING SCIENCE. SER. A: NATURAL SCIENCE. A-KEIRETSU: RIGAKU **463**

KYOTO FURITSU DAIGAKU GAKUJUTSU HOKOKU, NOGAKU (JA/0075-7373) [I00757373] **103**

KYOTO FURITSU DAIGAKU GAKUJUTSU HOKOKU. RIGAKU, SEIKATSU KAGAKU. SCIENTIFIC REPORTS OF THE KYOTO PREFECTURAL UNIVERSITY. NATURAL SCIENCE AND LIVING SCIENCE. SER. A: NATURAL SCIENCE. A-KEIRETSU: RIGAKU (JA) [04707613] **463**

KYOTO FURITSU DAIGAKU. NOGAKUBU *See* KYOTO FURITSU DAIGAKU. NOGAKUBU GAKUJUTSU HOKOKU **103**

KYOTO FURITSU DAIGAKU NOGAKUBU ENSHURIN HOKOKU (JA) [07833900] **2386**

KYOTO FURITSU DAIGAKU. NOGAKUBU GAKUJUTSU HOKOKU (JA) [01755354] **103**

KYOTO FURITSU DAIGAKU. SEIKATSU BUNKA SENTA *See* KYOTO FURITSU DAIGAKU SEIKATSU BUNKA SENTA NEMPO **2506**

KYOTO FURITSU DAIGAKU SEIKATSU BUNKA SENTA NEMPO (JA) [03610494] **2506**

KYOTO FURITSU IKA DAIGAKU ZASSHI (JA) [09726103] **3603**

KYOTO FURITSU KAIYO SENTA KENKYU RONBUN (JA) [09005065] **2307**

KYOTO GAIKOKUGO DAIGAKU *See* KYOTO GAIKOKUGO DAIGAKU KENKYU RONSO **2506**

KYOTO GAIKOKUGO DAIGAKU KENKYU RONSO (JA) [03571757] **2506**

KYOTO JOSHI DAIGAKU SHOKUMOTSU GAKKAI SHI (JA/0289-3827) [01196315] **2348**

KYOTO KOKURITSU HAKUBUTSUKAN *See* GAKUSO - KYOTO KOKURITSU HAKUBUTSUKAN **4088**

KYOTO PASTEUR KENKYUJO KENKYU HOKOKU (JA/0914-2177) [I09142177] **5125**

KYOTO SANGYO DAIGAKU KEIZAI KEIEI GAKKAI *See* KSU ECONOMIC AND BUSINESS REVIEW **1571**

KYOTO-SHI KANKO CHOSA NEMPO (JA) [08458465] **5482**

KYOTO-SHI REKISHI SHIRYOKAN KIYO (JA/0910-1349) [12093867] **2657**

KYOWVA GENEALOGICAL SOCIETY NEWS LETTER (US/1049-863X) [16314677] **2457**

KYOYO RONSO (JA) [03225306] **2849**

KYOYOBU KENKYU HOKOKU / GIFU DAIGAKU (JA) [10427874] **1092**

KYOYUK (KO) [04856503] **1760**

KYOYUK KAEBAL (KO) [10053713] **1760**

KYOYUK NONCHONG (TONGGUK TAEHAKKYO. KYOYUK TAEHAGWON) (KO) [08941525] **5233**

KYOYUK TONGGYE YONBO (KO) [25747700] **1760**

KYOYUK YONGU (CHOSON TAEHAKKYO. KYOYUK YONGUSO) (KO) [08365025] **1760**

KYRIAKATIKA NEA (US/0746-4479) [10049317] **2266, 5689**

KYRKOHISTORISK AARSSKRIFT (SW/0085-2619) [01755362] **4972**

KYRKOMUSIKERNAS TIDNING (SW/0281-286X) [13160880] **4128**

KYUJIN TO JITTAI CHOSA HOKOKU (JA) [01797075] **1683**

KYUKYU SHOROPPO / SHOBOCHO YOBO KYUKYUKA HEN (JA) [08868018] **5294**

KYUNGPOOK MATHEMATICAL JOURNAL (KO/0454-8124) [01284187] **3516**

KYUSHU AMERICAN LITERATURE (JA/0454-8132) [01285454] **3403**

KYUSHU BYOGAICHU KENKYUKAI *See* KYUSHU BYOGAICHU KENKYUKAIHO **517**

KYUSHU BYOGAICHU KENKYUKAIHO (JA/0385-6410) [03793408] **517**

KYUSHU DAIGAKI, FUKUOKA JAPAN. TOKYO RIKIGAKU KENKYUJO *See* KENKYU ROMBUN SHOROKU SHU **4428**

KYUSHU DAIGAKU DAIGAKUIN SOGO RIKOGAKU KENKYUKA HOKOKU (JA/0388-1717) [21996793] **1985**

KYUSHU DAIGAKU. FUKUOKA, JAPAN *See* BULLETIN OF THE KYUSHU UNIVERSITY FORESTS **2376**

KYUSHU DAIGAKU, FUKUOKA, JAPAN. OYO RIKIGAKU KENKYUJO *See* REPORTS OF RESEARCH INSTITUTE FOR APPLIED MECHANICS, KYUSHU UNIVERSITY **1994**

KYUSHU DAIGAKU KINO BUSSHITSU KAGAKU KENKYUJO HOKOKU (JA/0914-3793) [18825961] **2104**

KYUSHU DAIGAKU KOGAKU SHUHO (JA/0023-2718) [09787070] **1985**

KYUSHU DAIGAKU NOGAKUBU FUZOKU SUISAN JIKKENJO HOKOKU (JA/0285-6921) [03290901] **2307**

KYUSHU DAIGAKU NOGAKUBU GAKUGEI ZASSHI (JA/0368-6264) [04531614] **5125**

KYUSHU DAIGAKU NOGAKUBU GAKUGEI ZASSHI (JA/0368-6264) [09534377] **103**

KYUSHU DAIGAKU. NOGAKUBU. SUISAN JIKKENJO *See* KYUSHU DAIGAKU NOGAKUBU FUZOKU SUISAN JIKKENJO HOKOKU **2307**

KYUSHU DAIGAKU. RIGAKUBU *See* MEMOIRS OF THE FACULTY OF SCIENCE, KYUSHU UNIVERSITY. SERIES C. CHEMISTRY **985**

KYUSHU DAIGAKU RIGAKUBU KENKYU HOKOKU. CHIKYU WAKUSEI KAGAKU (JA/0916-7315) [24918937] **1386**

KYUSHU DENKI GASU NENKAN *See* KYUSHU DENKI NENKAN **4660**

KYUSHU DENKI NENKAN (JA) [02714850] **4660**

KYUSHU GEIJUTSU KOKA DAIGAKU. TOSHOKAN *See* KYUSHU GEIJUTSU KOKA DAIGAKU ZOKA TOSHO NOKUROKU **3222**

KYUSHU GEIJUTSU KOKA DAIGAKU ZOKA TOSHO NOKUROKU (JA) [03214153] **3222**

●KYUSHU JOURNAL OF MATHEMATICS (JA) [30653229] **3516**

KYUSHU KAKUKEN KANKOBUTSU MOKUROKU *See* KYUSHU KANKOCHO KANKOBUTSU MOKUROKU **418**

KYUSHU KANKOCHO KANKOBUTSU MOKUROKU (JA) [02952070] **418**

KYUSHU KEIZAI CHOSA KYOKAI *See* KYUSHU KEIZAI HAKUSHO **4840**

KYUSHU KEIZAI HAKUSHO (JA) [02809019] **4840**

KYUSHU KOGYO DAIGAKU *See* KYUSHU KOGYO DAIGAKU KENKYU HOKOKU, KOGAKU **5125**

KYUSHU KOGYO DAIGAKU KENKYU HOKOKU, KOGAKU (JA/0453-0357) [04269987] **5125**

LABOR

KYUSHU KOGYO GIJUTSU SHIKENJC HOKOKU. TOKUSHUGO (JA/0286-2018) [08246688] **5125**

KYUSHU KYORITSU DAIGAKU KENKYU HOKOKU. KOGAKUBU (JA/0911-9485) [I09119485] **1985**

KYUSHU NOGYO JOSEI HOKOKU (JA) [02823889] **103**

KYUSHU NOGYO SHIKENJO HOKOKU (JA/0376-0685) [06713178] **103**

KYUSHU NOGYO SHIKENJO NOGYO SHIKENJO See KYUSHU NOGYO SHIKENJO HOKOKU **103**

KYUSHU NOSHI NEMPO (JA) [03903168] **103**

KYUSHU SANGYO DAIGAKU KOGAKUBU KENKYU HOKOKU (JA/0286-7826) [10341717] **1985**

KYUSHU SANGYO DAIGAKU SHOKEI RONSO (JA) [03085103] **1593**

KYUSHU SEKITAN KOKUSU TOKEI NENKAN (JA) [02744567] **2143**

KYUSHU SHIKA GAKKAI ZASSHI (JA/0368-6833) [I03686833] **1329**

KYUSHU SHINKEI SEISHIN IGAKU (JA/0023-6144) [09770263] **3930**

KYUSHU TEIKOKU DAIGAKU NOGAKUBU GAKUGEI ZASSHI See KYUSHU DAIGAKU NOGAKUBU GAKUGEI ZASSHI **103**

KYUSHU TOKAI DAIGAKU KIYO. KOGAKUBU (JA/0286-4002) [18618045] **1985**

KYUSHU TOKAI DAIGAKU NOGAKUBU KIYO (JA) [08925702] **103**

KYUSHU TSUSHO SANGYO NEMPO (JA) [04985736] **1571**

KYUSHU UNYU YORAN. RIKUUN HEN (JA) [23007208] **5385**

KYUSHU YUSEIKYOKU TOKEI NEMPO (JA) [01797418] **1145**

L.A. 411 (US/1062-6603) [10522729] **4073**

L. A. ARCHITECT (US/0885-7377) [04343269] **302**

L.A.E. LA LETTRE AFRIQUE ENERGIES (FR/0754-5215) [I07545215] **1949**

L.A. MAGAZINE See LOS ANGELES **2537**

L.A. PARENT (US/0740-3437) [09994350] **1066**

L.A.S.I.E (AT/0047-3774) [01184420] **3222**

L.A. STYLE *CEASED.* (US/0895-3465) [13072865] **1085**

L. A. W. G. LETTER (CN/0316-3393) [02813756] **4480**

L.A. WEEKLY (US/0192-1940) [05133328] **5636**

L & S LEATHER BUYERS GUIDE AND LEATHER TRADE MARKS FOR SHOE AND ACCESSORY LEATHERS See LEATHER BUYERS GUIDE **3185**

L.C. CLASSIFICATION: ADDITIONS AND CHANGES (US/0041-7912) [02748014] **3222**

L.C.D. STAMP CO See PUBLIC STAMP AUCTION **2787**

L.C. SUBJECT HEADINGS WEEKLY LISTS (US) [28226762] **3222**

L.C. SUBJECT HEADINGS WEEKLY LISTS (DETROIT, MICH.) (US/8755-366X) [11274610] **3222**

L.E.A (BL) [05886000] **2657**

L.E.R.S. MONOGRAPH SERIES (US/0742-3896) [09475139] **3708**

L.-F. CELINE (FR) [02244324] **3403**

L.O.H. CENTRAL CALIFORNIA INDUSTRIAL DIRECTORY, THE (US/8756-5102) [11555934] **1615**

L. RAY BUCKENDALE LECTURE (US/0458-5526) [02708637] **2120**

L.S.B. BULLETIN (US/0440-4904) [06852169] 103, **1386**

L UNION VICTORIAVILLE CANADA (CN) **5788**

L5 NEWS (TUCSON, ARIZ. : 1986) (US/8756-5331) [14136357] **27**

LA-BAS (US/0193-7820) [03355561] **3465**

LA BELLE STAR, THE (US) [13501316] **5703**

LA/C BUSINESS BULLETIN (US) [23280049] **2993**

LA CROSSE COUNTY COUNTRYMAN (US) [06642316] **5768**

LA CROSSE TRIBUNE (US/0745-9793) [01755375] **5768**

LA ESPANA MEDIEVAL, EN (SP/0214-3038) [26018652] **2696**

LA FAYETTE (US) [07760539] **2457**

LA FERIA NEWS, THE (US) [14353927] **5751**

LA FILE (US/0733-0642) [08278918] **2422**

LA MARQUE TIMES, THE (US) [14369280] **5751**

LA-MATHIL (US) [01793776] **3294**

LA MESA COURIER (US/0744-8759) [08623368] **5636**

LA MIRADA LAMPLIGHTER (US/0192-0324) [05010810] **5636**

●LA POINTE, A (US/1063-889X) [26173908] **2457**

LA PORTE HERALD-ARGUS, THE (US) [08786946] **5665**

●LA RECORD (UK) [25605160] **3222**

LA TRIBUNE DE L'EXPANSION See TRIBUNE PARIS. 1992, LA **855**

LA TROBE LIBRARY See LA TROBE LIBRARY JOURNAL **3222**

LA TROBE LIBRARY JOURNAL (AT/0041-3151) [02303102] 2670, **3222**

LA VERNE MAGAZINE (US/0199-347X) [05803867] **2536**

LA WOMAN / LOS ANGELES CITY COMMISSION ON THE STATUS OF WOMEN (US) [23361088] **5560**

LA YOUTH (US) **1066**

LAAKARIT (FI/0780-1785) [09921971] 3914, **1329**

LAB 2000 (SP/0213-7275) [I02137275] **5125**

LAB ANIMAL (US/0093-7355) [02255388] **5125**

LAB-INSTRUMENTEN AMSTERDAM (NE/0368-7368) [I03687368] **3603**

●LAB LAW REPORTER (US/1065-7576) [26716543] **2993**

LAB PRODUCTS INTERNATIONAL. BRUSSELS (BE/0775-602X) [I0775602X] **463**

LAB REPORT (US/1045-7313) [20213304] **3603**

LAB (RIDGEWOOD) (US/0192-7698) [05026694] **3603**

LAB TALK (AT/0159-2033) 1899, **5125**

LABCHOWS DIGEST (US/0190-2474) [04647791] **5515**

LABDATA (US/0730-5672) [07023721] **1615**

LABDEV. PART A, PHYSICAL SCIENCES (II/0368-7430) [04651204] **5125**

LABELS & LABELLING INTERNATIONAL (UK/0143-2192) [I01432192] **4219**

LABEO; RASSEGNA DI DIRETTO ROMANO (IT/0023-6462) [04173021] **2993**

LABIRINT/EKSTSENTR (RU) [25864500] **3403**

LABIRINTI (IT) **2827**

LABMEDICA (WILTON, CONN.) (US/1054-0970) [17383177] **3603**

LABOR (BE) [02448212] **1683**

LABOR AND DEVELOPMENT (TG) [03998186] **1683**

LABOR & EMPLOYMENT LAW (US/0193-5739) [05092489] **3150**

LABOR AND EMPLOYMENT LAW ANTHOLOGY *SUSPENDED.* (US) **3150**

LABOR AND EMPLOYMENT LAW NEWSLETTER (US/8756-792X) [10863666] **3150**

LABOR & INVESTMENTS *CEASED.* (US/0279-0467) [07479153] 905, **1683**

LABOR ARBITRATION AWARDS (US/0023-6500) [02253691] **1683**

LABOR ARBITRATION IN GOVERNMENT (US/0047-3839) [05157451] **3150**

LABOR ARBITRATION INDEX (ANNUAL SUMMARY) (US/1043-5964) [06575009] **3150**

LABOR ARBITRATION INFORMATION SYSTEM (US/0744-5253) [08232616] **3150**

LABOR AREA SUMMARIES (US) **1683**

LABOR AREA SUMMARY. MONTHLY STATISTICAL REPORT See LABOR AREA SUMMARY. STATISTICAL REPORT **1683**

●LABOR AREA SUMMARY. STATISTICAL REPORT (US) [26485979] **1683**

LABOR AREA TRENDS IN SUPPLY AND DEMAND : BROCKTON, MASSACHUSETTS, STANDARD METROPOLITAN STATISTICAL AREA (US) [05133023] **1683**

LABOR AREA TRENDS IN SUPPLY AND DEMAND : LAWRENCE-HAVERHILL, STANDARD METROPOLITAN STATISTICAL AREA (US) [05152479] **1683**

LABOR AREA TRENDS IN SUPPLY AND DEMAND: MASSACHUSETTS/BOSTON AREA (US) [05133081] **1683**

LABOR CENTER REPORTER *CEASED.* (US) [09068664] **1683**

LABOR CONTRACT LAW BULLETIN (US/8755-7886) [11264248] **3150**

LABOR EDITION TRADE ACTION : MONTHLY REVIEW ON TRADE-UNION INFORMATION AND TRAINING, EDITED BY THE W.C.L. WORLD SECRETARIAT FOR TRADE ACTION (BE) [11567463] **1683**

LABOR EDUCATION NEWS / UCLA INSTITUTE OF INDUSTRIAL RELATIONS (US) [25385133] **1683**

LABOR FORCE AND EMPLOYMENT IN WASHINGTON STATE (US) [17283041] **1683**

LABOR FORCE STATISTICS (HONOLULU) (US/0147-4758) [03172533] **1535**

LABOR FORCE STATUS OF INDIANA RESIDENTS (US/0362-3793) [02312009] **1683**

LABOR HISTORY (US/0023-656X) [01755402] **1683**

LABOR HOSPITALARIA (SP/0211-8262) [02118262] **3787**

LABOR LAW (US) [02970161] **3150**

LABOR LAW ANTHOLOGY *SUSPENDED.* (US/0892-4449) [15192893] **3150**

LABOR LAW JOURNAL (CHICAGO) (US/0023-6586) [01755405] **3150**

LABOR LAW REPORT (US/0193-1628) [05120896] **3150**

LABOR LAW REPORTER (US) [04031354] **3150**

LABOR LAWS OF INDIANA (US) [05952687] **3150**

LABOR LAWS OF MAINE (US) [06070848] **3150**

LABOR LAWYER, THE (US/8756-2995) [11541843] **3150**

LABOR-MANAGEMENT RELATIONS IN STATE AND LOCAL GOVERNMENTS (US/0272-3689) [03076431] 4660, **1683**

LABOR-MANAGEMENT RELATIONS IN THE PUBLIC SERVICE (US/0730-5486) [05191433] 943, **1683**

LABOR-MANAGEMENT RELATIONS ISSUES IN STATE AND LOCAL GOVERNMENTS (US) [04171914] 4660, **1683**

LABOR MARKET INFORMATION DIRECTORY (US/1063-3804) [24006351] **1683**

LABOR MARKET INFORMATION DIRECTORY FOR VIRGINIA EMPLOYMENT COMMISSION (US/0149-9254) [03562658] **1683**

LABOR MARKET INFORMATION FOR AFFIRMATIVE ACTION PROGRAMS (US) [05794407] **1683**

LABOR MARKET INFORMATION FOR AFFIRMATIVE ACTION PROGRAMS (VIRGINIA EMPLOYMENT COMMISSION. MANPOWER RESEARCH DIVISION) (US) [07066166] **1684**

LABOR MARKET INFORMATION NEWSLETTER (US) [24775785] **1684**

LABOR MARKET INFORMATION REVIEW: BROCKTON, MASSACHUSETTS, STANDARD METROPOLITAN STATISTICAL AREA (US) [04406839] **1684**

LABOR MARKET INFORMATION REVIEW : COMMONWEALTH OF MASSACHUSETTS (US) [04406760] **1684**

LABOR MARKET INFORMATION REVIEW : LABOR MARKET AREA, FALL RIVER, MASSACHUSETTS-RHODE ISLAND (US) [04406792] **1684**

LABOR MARKET INFORMATION REVIEW : LABOR MARKET AREA, NEW BEDFORD, MASSACHUSETTS (US) [04406995] **1684**

LABOR MARKET INFORMATION REVIEW : LABOR MARKET AREA, PITTSFIELD, MASSACHUSETTS (US) [04406772] **1684**

LABOR MARKET INFORMATION REVIEW: LABOR MARKET AREA, SPRINGFIELD-CHICOPEE-HOLYOKE, MASSACHUSETTS (US) [04406806] **1684**

LABOR MARKET INFORMATION REVIEW : LABOR MARKET AREA, WORCESTER, MASSACHUSETTS (US) [04406786] **1684**

LABOR MARKET INFORMATION REVIEW : STANDARD METROPOLITAN STATISTICAL AREA, BOSTON, MASSACHUSETTS (US) [04407082] **1684**

LABOR MARKET INFORMATION REVIEW : STANDARD METROPOLITAN STATISTICAL AREA, FITCHBURG-LEOMINSTER, MASSACHUSETTS (US) [04406956] **1684**

LABOR MARKET INFORMATION REVIEW : STANDARD METROPOLITAN STATISTICAL AREA, LAWRENCE-HAVERHILL, MASSACHUSETTS (US) [04406899] **1684**

LABOR — Alphabetical Title Index

LABOR MARKET INFORMATION REVIEW : STANDARD METROPOLITAN STATISTICAL AREA, LOWELL, MASSACHUSETTS (US) [04407106] **1684**

LABOR MARKET PLANNING INFORMATION : WISCONSIN STATE-LEVEL STATISTICAL REPORT / WISCONSIN DEPARTMENT OF INDUSTRY, LABOR AND HUMAN RELATIONS, DIVISION OF EMPLOYMENT AND TRAINING POLICY, LABOR MARKET INFORMATION BUREAU (US) [24773379] **1684**

LABOR MARKET REVIEW *See* VIRGINIA LABOR MARKET REVIEW / VIRGINIA EMPLOYMENT COMMISSION, ECONOMIC INFORMATION SERVICES DIVISION **1716**

LABOR MARKET REVIEW AND PLANNING INFORMATION (US) [07894123] **1684**

LABOR MARKET REVIEW: SALINAS-SEASIDE-MONTEREY STANDARD METROPOLITAN STATISTICAL AREA (US/0192-9844) [05090598] **1684**

LABOR MARKET REVIEW : SAN FRANCISCO-OAKLAND STANDARD METROPOLITAN STATISTICAL AREA (US/0192-8295) [05069784] **1684**

LABOR MARKET REVIEW : SAN JOSE STANDARD METROPOLITAN STATISTICAL AREA (US/0192-9739) [05090104] **1684**

LABOR MARKET REVIEW: SANTA CRUZ STANDARD METROPOLITAN STATISTICAL AREA (US) [04926532] **1684**

LABOR MARKET REVIEW : SANTA ROSA STANDARD METROPOLITAN STATISTICAL AREA (US) [04926631] **1684**

LABOR MARKET REVIEW: VALLEJO-FAIRFIELD-NAPA STANDARD METROPOLITAN STATISTICAL AREA (US) [04926711] **1684**

LABOR MARKET REVIEW : VIRGINIA'S LABOR FORCE AND UNEMPLOYMENT ESTIMATES AND EMPLOYMENT, HOURS AND EARNINGS / VIRGINIA EMPLOYMENT COMMISSION, ECONOMIC INFORMATION SERVICES DIVISION (US) [18067088] **1684**

LABOR-MEDIZIN (GIT-VERLAG GIEBELER) (GW/0170-205X) [11718696] **3603**

LABOR MILITANT (US/0892-4902) [15266902] **1684**

LABOR NOTES (DETROIT, MICH.) (US/0275-4452) [06002978] **1684**

LABOR OFFICES IN THE UNITED STATES AND CANADA (US) [01784590] **1685**

LABOR OFFICES IN THE UNITED STATES AND IN CANADA *See* LABOR OFFICES IN THE UNITED STATES AND CANADA **1685**

LABOR PAGE, THE (US/8755-1284) [10005819] **1685**

LABOR RELATIONS AND PUBLIC POLICY SERIES (US/0075-7470) [02290775] **1685**

LABOR RELATIONS MASTER TABLE OF CASES (US) [04790660] **3151**

LABOR RELATIONS REFERENCE MANUAL (US/1043-5506) [01755409] **3151**

LABOR RELATIONS REPORTER (US/0148-7981) [08128294] **3151**

LABOR RELATIONS TODAY (WASHINGTON, D.C.) (US) [16143761] **1685**

LABOR RELATIONS WEEK (US/0891-4141) [14765982] **1685**

LABOR RESEARCH REPORT (ALBANY) (US/0093-5034) [01792491] **1685**

LABOR RESEARCH REVIEW (US/0885-4238) [10639159] **1685**

LABOR + SPRECHSTUNDE / SCHWEIZERISCHER VERBAND DER ARZTGEHILFINNEN (SZ/1012-8956) [11249501] **1685**

LABOR STUDIES JOURNAL (US/0160-449X) [03714657] **1685**

LABOR SURPLUS AREAS (US/0882-0279) [11718489] 950, **1685**

LABOR TRENDS (SOUTHFIELD, MICH.) (US/0023-6659) [06081829] 943, **1685**

LABOR UNITY (U.S. ED.) (US/0890-6041) [08538208] **1685**

LABOR WORLD, THE (US/0023-6667) [01696219] **1685**

LABORATOIRE ASSOCIE AU C.N.R.S. NO 132 ETUDES GEOLOGIQUES OUEST-AFRICAINES *See* RAPPORT BISANNUEL D'ACTIVITE - LABORATOIRE ASSOCIE AU C.N.R.S NO 132 ETUDES GEOLOGIQUES OUEST-AFRICAINES **1393**

LABORATOIRE CENTRAL DES PONTS ET CHAUSSEES *See* RAPPORT GENERAL D'ACTIVITE - LABORATOIRE CENTRAL DES PONTS ET CHAUSSEES **2030**

LABORATOIRES ET CENTRES DE RECHERCHE : RAPPORT D'ACTIVITE / ECOLE POLYTECHNIQUE (FR) [20211794] **5125**

LABORATORIO 2000 (IT/1120-8376) [11208376] 463, **984**

LABORATORIO 2000 : RIVISTA DEL RICERCATORE CHEMICO E BIOCHIMICO (IT) **984**

LABORATORIO DE ARTE : REVISTA DEL DEPARTAMENTO DE HISTORIA DEL ARTE (SP/1130-5762) [25836196] **356**

LABORATORIO DE CARRETERAS Y GEOTECNIA (SPAIN) *See* BOLETIN DE INFORMACION DEL LABORATORIO DE CARRETERAS Y GEOTECNIA **5439**

LABORATORIO MUSICA *CEASED.* (IT) **4128**

LABORATORIO NACIONAL DE INVESTIGACAO VETERINARIA *See* REPOSITORIO DE TRABALHOS DO L.N.I.V **5520**

LABORATORIO POLITICA INDUSTRIALE (IT) **4528**

LABORATORIUM PRAKTIJK (NE) **463**

LABORATORIUMSMEDIZIN (GW/0342-3026) [04454370] **3603**

LABORATORNOE DELO *See* KLINICHESKAIA LABORATORNAIA DIAGNOSTIKA **3896**

LABORATORY AND RESEARCH METHODS IN BIOLOGY AND MEDICINE *CEASED.* (US/0160-8584) [03783682] 3603, **463**

LABORATORY ANIMAL HANDBOOKS (UK/0458-5933) [01755412] **3603**

LABORATORY ANIMAL SCIENCE (CHICAGO) (US/0023-6764) [01755413] **5515**

LABORATORY ANIMALS (LONDON) (UK/0023-6772) [01641209] **5515**

LABORATORY AUTOMATION AND INFORMATION MANAGEMENT (NE) **5125**

LABORATORY BUYERS GUIDE (CN/0381-6729) [03031711] **5125**

LABORATORY CENTRE FOR DISEASE CONTROL (CANADA). BUREAU OF EPIDEMIOLOGY. CANADA DISEASES WEEKLY REPORT *See* CANADA COMMUNICABLE DISEASE REPORT **4770**

LABORATORY EQUIPMENT (US/0023-6810) [02448223] 5125, **950**

● LABORATORY EQUIPMENT BUYERS GUIDE (UK/0967-389X) [27192086] **5125**

LABORATORY EQUIPMENT DIGEST (UK/0023-6829) [02785077] **5125**

LABORATORY EQUIPMENT DIRECTORY (UK/0141-8963) [08338203] **5125**

LABORATORY EQUIPMENT DIRECTORY & BUYERS GUIDE (UK) [01788638] **5125**

LABORATORY HAZARDS BULLETIN (UK/0261-2917) [08367759] 2865, **2872**

● LABORATORY INDUSTRY REPORT (US/1060-5118) [25014315] **1615**

LABORATORY INVESTIGATION (US/0023-6837) [01755414] **3896**

LABORATORY MEDICINE (US/0007-5027) [01605929] **3603**

LABORATORY MEDICINE ABSTRACT AND COMMENT *CEASED.* (US/1050-9658) [21726071] **3603**

LABORATORY MICROCOMPUTER (UK/0262-2955) [10880890] **1268**

LABORATORY NEWS (UK/0266-7169) [27716133] **463**

LABORATORY NEWS (AT) 984, 1357, **463**

LABORATORY PC USER *SUSPENDED.* (US/0897-0130) [14257732] **1268**

LABORATORY PRACTICE (UK/0023-6853) [01643316] **5125**

LABORATORY PRIMATE NEWSLETTER (US/0023-6861) [01755416] **5515**

LABORATORY PRODUCT NEWS (CN/0047-3855) [01986605] **5125**

LABORATORY PRODUCTS TECHNOLOGY (UK) **5125**

LABORATORY REGULATION MANUAL (US/0272-3778) [03722594] 5125, **2993**

LABORATORY REGULATION NEWS (US/1048-0706) [20845704] 226, **5125**

LABORATORY ROBOTICS AND AUTOMATION (US/0895-7533) [16786644] 1220, **1214**

LABORATORY TECHNIQUES IN BIOCHEMISTRY AND MOLECULAR BIOLOGY (NE/0075-7535) [01641625] **490**

LABORDOC [ONLINE DATABASE] (SZ) 1685, **1535**

LABOREGISTER, THE *CEASED.* (US/0149-8495) [03562893] **1685**

LABOREO (SP/0210-1718) [I02101718] **1685**

LABORER (WASHINGTON), THE (US/0023-6888) [02448225] **1685**

LABORERS' BENEFITS REVIEW (US) [18933749] **5294**

LABORES DEL HOGAR (SP/0047-3863) [I00473863] **4851**

LABORPRAXIS (GW/0344-1733) [11312232] **3603**

LABORPRAXIS IN DER MEDIZIN (GW/0171-4279) [07612980] **3603**

LABOR'S HERITAGE (US/1041-5904) [18732561] **1685**

LABORSCOPE (SZ) **1985**

LABORWATCH (US) 2993, **943**

LABOUR ADVOCATE (ST. CATHARINES) (CN/0711-3889) [08730673] **1685**

LABOUR AND EMPLOYMENT POLICIES IN ITALY (IT) [20975437] **1685**

LABOUR & INDUSTRY (AT) [20474666] **1685**

LABOUR AND MANPOWER REPORT / MINISTRY OF LABOUR AND MANPOWER (MY/0127-0362) [07970630] **1685**

LABOUR ARBITRATION CASES (CN/0023-690X) [02049928] **3151**

LABOUR ARBITRATION (VANCOUVER, B.C.) (CN/0821-2635) [09456936] **3151**

LABOUR CAPITAL AND SOCIETY (CN/0706-1706) [05511221] **1685**

LABOUR CHRONICLE (II) [01773669] **1685**

LABOUR COMMENTARY (CN/0226-2290) [08185689] **1685**

● LABOUR ECONOMICS (NE/0927-5371) [28773230] **1685**

LABOUR EDUCATION (SZ/0378-5467) [02304013] **1685**

LABOUR FOCUS ON EASTERN EUROPE (UK) [05905548] 2696, **1685**

LABOUR FORCE (AT) 5330, **1686**

LABOUR FORCE ANNUAL AVERAGES (CN/1181-6627) [24624017] 1686, **1535**

LABOUR FORCE BY SEX (TR) [01789550] 1686, **1535**

LABOUR FORCE / DEPARTMENT OF STATISTICS, THE (JM) [01784568] **1686**

LABOUR FORCE INFORMATION (CN/0708-3157) [04441530] 1686, **1535**

LABOUR FORCE (MONTHLY ED.) (CN/0380-6804) [01783963] 1686, **1535**

LABOUR FORCE STATISTICS (FR/0474-5515) [02813674] **1686**

LABOUR FORCE STATUS AND OTHER CHARACTERISTICS OF FAMILIES / AUSTRALIAN BUREAU OF STATISTICS (AT) [10199993] 1686, **1535**

LABOUR FORCE SURVEY (IRELAND. CENTRAL STATISTICS OFFICE) (IE) [08382833] **1686**

LABOUR (HALIFAX) (CN/0700-3862) [03400132] **1686**

LABOUR (HALIFAX) (CN/0700-3862) [02483378] **1686**

LABOUR HISTORY (CANBERRA) (AT/0023-6942) [08118863] **1686**

LABOUR HISTORY REVIEW (UK) [21878068] **1686**

LABOUR INSPECTION : REPORT FOR ... OF THE INDUSTRIAL INSPECTORATE AND GENERAL INSPECTORATE OF LABOUR (IE) [11692829] **2865**

LABOUR LAW DOCUMENTS (SZ/1014-7071) [21991848] **3151**

LABOUR LAW JOURNAL (II/0023-6977) [02903312] **3151**

LABOUR LAW UPDATE (CN/0848-5917) [23247998] **3151**

LABOUR-MANAGEMENT RELATIONS SERIES (SZ/0538-8325) [04303482] 875, **1686**

LABOUR MARKET AND SOCIAL POLICY OCCASIONAL PAPERS / ORGANISATION FOR ECONOMIC CO-OPERATION AND DEVELOPMENT (FR) [22444217] **1686**

LABOUR MARKET DEVELOPMENTS (CN/1187-4457) [25314245] **1686**

LABOUR MARKET QUARTERLY REPORT. GREAT BRITAIN (UK/0952-2506) [I09522506] **1686**

LABOUR MARKET REVIEW (IE) [24048285] **1686**

LABOUR NETWORK (AT) **1686**

LABOUR NEWS & GRAPHICS (CN/0832-6223) [15493006] **1686**

LABOUR PARTY ANNUAL REPORT (UK) 4660, **4480**

LABOUR RELATIONS BULLETIN (CN) 3787, **1686**

LABOUR RESEARCH (LONDON) (UK/0023-7000) [02904804] **1686**

LABOUR REVIEW / ST. CATHARINES AND DISTRICT LABOUR COUNCIL (CN/0229-2726) [08770456] **1686**

LAKE

LABOUR ROMA (IT/1121-7081) [I11217081] **1686**

LABOUR (ROME, ITALY) (IT) [17391416] **1686**

LABOUR SCENE, THE (CN/0709-0862) [05362418] **1686**

LABOUR STANDARDS IN CANADA (CN/0576-1123) [03222379] **1686**

LABOUR STATISTICS (CY/0255-8386) [24617587] **1686**

LABOUR STATISTICS ... AUSTRALIA (AT/0314-2779) [12028255] **1686, 1535**

LABOUR STATISTICS : WAGE RATES, EARNINGS AND AVERAGE HOURS WORKED IN THE PRINTING AND NEWSPAPER INDUSTRY, ENGINEERING INDUSTRY, BUILDING INDUSTRY AND COMMERCE (SA) [02242518] **1686, 1535**

LABOUR STUDIES BRIEFING (AT/0817-8798) [I08178798] **1687, 4528**

LABOUR SURVEY (SOCIETY OF THE PLASTICS INDUSTRY OF CANADA) (CN/0229-4567) [08368428] **4456, 1687**

LABOUR TIMES (CN/0823-1494) [09964694] **3151**

LABRADOR CRAFT PRODUCERS ASSOCIATION *See* ATUAGATSANGA / LABRADOR CRAFT PRODUCERS ASSOCIATION **370**

LABRADOR QUARTERLY : LQ, THE (US/8750-3557) [11269016] **4287**

LABRADORIAN, THE (CN/0715-4941) [09543091] **5788**

LABYRINT (XR) [24336532] **5799**

LABYRINTH (BOSTON, MASS.) (US/1053-2625) [22495599] **2422**

LABYRINTH (WATERLOO) (CN/0318-8450) [02443229] **1078**

LABYRINTHOS (IT/0393-0807) [09639787] **356**

LAC MANUAL SERIES (UK/0144-0314) [03858583] **5515**

LAC NEWS (UK/0308-9568) [04617681] **5515**

LACE COLLECTOR, THE *CEASED.* (US) [25512288] **5184**

LACERTA (NE/0023-7051) [02486408] **5590**

LACERTANIEUWS *See* LACERTA **5590**

LACEY BEACON (US/0747-4377) [10866026] **5710**

LACIO DROM : RIVISTA BIMESTRALE DI STUDI ZINGARI (IT/0394-2791) [23997317] **2321**

LACKAWANNA JURIST (US/0023-7078) [01755427] **2993**

LACMA PHYSICIAN (US/0162-7163) [04220329] **3914**

LACON HOME JOURNAL (LACON, ILL. : 1866 : WEEKLY) (US) [08814732] **5660**

LACROSSE (BALTIMORE, MD.) (US/0194-7893) [05022409] **4903**

LACROSSE (LONDON, ENG.) (UK/0023-7086) [09072161] **4903**

LACROSSE MAGAZINE (US/1069-5893) [28119191] **4903**

●LACROSSE TALK (UK) **4903**

LACTATION REVIEW, THE *SUSPENDED.* (US/0362-3173) [02207482] **3764**

L'ACTION AUTOMOBILE *See* ACTION AUTOMOBILE ET TOURISTIQUE, L' **5403**

LACTUCA (SUFFERN, N.Y.) (US/0896-8705) [16632987] **3403**

LACUS FORUM (US/0195-377X) [04240905] **3294**

LAD (MEMPHIS, TENN.) (US/0893-5262) [15562688] **5062**

LAD WARSZAWA (PL/0208-7723) [I02087723] **4972**

LADDER (WASHINGTON, D.C.), THE (US/0882-1828) [11769861] **3294**

LADENBAU (SZ/0458-6123) [05177451] **619, 302**

LADIES' HOME JOURNAL (US/0023-7124) [01624448] **2791, 5560**

LADINIA (SZ) [07856868] **3465**

LADOC (PE/0360-3350) [02172582] **4972**

LADY (UK/0023-7167) [I00237167] **2518**

●LADY ARCANE (US/1057-2929) [24004099] **380**

LADY GOLFER (SCOTTSDALE) (US/0092-8909) [01791795] **4903**

LADYBUG (PERU, ILL.) (US/1051-4961) [21982650] **1066**

LADY'S CIRCLE (US/0023-7191) [04090671] **5560**

LADY'S CIRCLE 1,001 CHRISTMAS IDEAS (US/0731-9959) [07878422] **374**

LADY'S CIRCLE HOME MAKING CRAFT IDEAS (US/0731-9983) [08291501] **374**

LADY'S CIRCLE KNITTING & CROCHET CREATIVE IDEAS (US/0732-9504) [08483629] **5184**

LADY'S CIRCLE PATCHWORK QUILTS (US/0731-9916) [08290530] **5184**

LADY'S CIRCLE PATCHWORK QUILTS PRESENTS QUILT CRAFT (US/1057-7971) [24118071] **5184**

LADYSMITH NEWS (LADYSMITH, WIS. : 1927) (US/0749-7059) [11165244] **5768**

LAE NEWS (US/0162-3052) [03757342] **1760**

LAEKARMATRIKELN (SW/0282-633X) [20407617] **3914**

LAENDERBERICHT. TSCHAD / STATISTISCHES BUNDESAMT (GW/0939-690X) [29809669] **5330**

LAFAYETTE BUSINESS DIGEST (US/1048-2822) [11934985] **689**

LAFAYETTE COUNTY HERITAGE NEWS (US/1064-5527) [26326734] **2457**

LAFAYETTE LEADER (LAFAYETTE, IND. : 1952) (US) [15926097] **5665**

LAFTA'S NEWSLETTER *See* NEWSLETTER - LATIN AMERICAN FREE TRADE ASSOCIATION **847**

LAG & [I.E. OCH] AVTAL (SW) [06352502] **3151**

LAGASCALIA (SP/0210-7708) [04368738] **517**

LAGEBERICHT DER NIEDEROSTERREICHISCHEN LAND- UND FORSTWIRTSCHAFT (AU) [02475760] **103**

LAGEN OM ALLMAN FORSAKRING OCH ANDRA FORFATTNINGAR OM SOCIALFORSAKRING M.M (SW) [06352788] **2886, 5294**

LAGERKATALOG (GW) [01788349] **418**

LAGNIAPPE (US/0193-7588) [05242944] **3403**

LAGNIAPPE LETTER (US/1040-3175) [11994662] **1637**

LAGNIAPPE QUARTERLY MONITOR (US/1040-3183) [18374778] **1615**

LAGOS CITY DIRECTORY (NR) [03342756] **2567**

LAGOS STATE (NIGERIA). HIGH COURT *See* SELECTED JUDGEMENTS OF THE HIGH COURT OF LAGOS STATE **3047**

LAGOS STATE (NIGERIA). MINISTRY OF EDUCATION AND COMMUNITY DEVELOPMENT *See* STATISTICS OF EDUCATION IN LAGOS STATE **1798**

LAGRANGE STANDARD (US) [11122094] **5665**

(LAGUNA), A (US/0147-7196) [03233833] **3403**

LAHAINA NEWS, THE (US) [09126808] **5656**

LAHEY CLINIC HEALTH LETTER (US) **4788**

LAHONTAN VALLEY NEWS AND FALLON EAGLE STANDARD (US) [13958263] **5707**

LAHORE CHAMBER OF COMMERCE & INDUSTRY *See* CLASSIFIED DIRECTORY OF MEMBERS - LAHORE CHAMBER OF COMMERCE & INDUSTRY **819**

LAHORE CHAMBER OF COMMERCE & INDUSTRY. RESEARCH AND STATISTICAL DEPT *See* STATISTICAL REPORT **733**

LAI NOTES / THE UNIVERSITY OF NEW MEXICO LATIN AMERICAN INSTITUTE (US) [06985849] **1833**

LAIETANIA (SP/0212-8985) [08788316] **2622, 273**

LAIFS (US/0146-910X) [03058071] **2422**

LAIKS (BROOKLYN, N.Y. : 1949) (US) [11324925] **5717**

LAISSEZ-FAIRE *CEASED.* (UK) [24488468] **4480**

LAISVE, I (US/0094-498X) [01793420] **2696**

LAIT ET NOUS, LE (BE/0770-2515) [03271121] **196**

LAIT, LE (FR/0023-7302) [01696711] **196**

LAKARTIDNINGEN (SW/0023-7205) [01755460] **3603**

LAKASKULTURA (HU) [02937173] **2902**

LAKE ALFRED PRESS (US) **5650**

LAKE AND RESERVOIR MANAGEMENT (US/1040-2381) [17486705] **5535, 2235**

LAKE CHARLES AMERICAN-PRESS (US/0739-1196) [09689352] **5684**

LAKE CHELAN MIRROR (US) [23184372] **5761**

LAKE CITIES SUN, THE (US) [17659553] **5751**

LAKE CITY GRAPHIC (US) [01755472] **5696**

LAKE CITY SILVER WORLD (US) [23118013] **5643**

LAKE COUNTRY REPORTER (US) [12198093] **5768**

LAKE COUNTY (IL) GENEALOGICAL SOCIETY *See* LAKE COUNTY (IL) GENEALOGICAL SOCIETY QUARTERLY **2457**

LAKE COUNTY (IL) GENEALOGICAL SOCIETY QUARTERLY (US/0736-4059) [09107733] **2457**

LAKE COUNTY NEWS-CHRONICLE (US) [20449629] **5696**

LAKE COUNTY RECORD-BEE (US/0746-4304) [10036834] **5636**

LAKE COUNTY STAR (CROWN POINT, IND.) (US) [15503922] **5665**

LAKE COUNTY STAR, THE (US) [12219612] **5692**

LAKE CRYSTAL TRIBUNE (US) [01755478] **5696**

LAKE EFFECT (US/0887-4492) [13231153] **5681**

LAKE ELSINORE VALLEY SUN-TRIBUNE (US/0745-1350) [08859701] **5636**

LAKE ERIE COLLEGE *See* ALUMNAE/I DIRECTORY / LAKE ERIE COLLEGE **1097**

LAKE ERIE WASTEWATER MANAGEMENT STUDY PUBLIC INFORMATION FACT SHEET (US) [03455405] **2235**

LAKE EUFAULA WORLD (US/0745-9017) [09553931] **5732**

LAKE FORESTER (US/0744-7973) [08556760] **5661**

LAKE GENEVA REGIONAL NEWS, THE (US) [15257302] **5768**

LAKE GEORGE MIRROR (LAKE GEORGE, N.Y. : 1890) (US) [11306031] **5717**

LAKE GEORGE PARK COMMISSION *See* NEWSLETTER - LAKE GEORGE PARK COMMISSION **2200**

LAKE HAVASU CITY HERALD (US/1068-1884) [27464108] **5630**

LAKE LILLIAN CRIER (US) [01755480] **5696**

LAKE LOG CHIPS (US/0270-5680) [04232813] **5451, 844**

LAKE MARTIN LIVING MAGAZINE (US/1070-8103) [28473515] **4851**

LAKE MICHIGAN WATER QUALITY REPORT (US/0361-8188) [02247133] **5535**

LAKE MILLS GRAPHIC, THE (US) [16151477] **5671**

LAKE MILLS HEADER (US) [15146114] **5768**

LAKE NEWS, THE (US/8750-3689) [11349025] **5681**

LAKE OCONEE FREE PRESS, THE (US/1064-6876) [23149606] **5654**

LAKE ONTARIO REGIONAL LIBRARY SYSTEM *See* TALKING BOOKS CATALOGUE / LAKE ONTARIO REGIONAL LIBRARY SYSTEM **426**

LAKE ONTARIO REGIONAL LIBRARY SYSTEM *See* DIRECTORY - LAKE ONTARIO REGIONAL LIBRARY SYSTEM **3206**

LAKE OSWEGO REVIEW (US/0889-2369) [13819679] **5733**

LAKE PARK JOURNAL (US) [01714944] **5696**

LAKE PARK NEWS (LAKE PARK, IOWA : 1976) (US) [16409617] **5671**

LAKE PLACID NEWS (US) [13511395] **5717**

LAKE POWELL CHRONICLE (US) [13362077] **5630**

LAKE POWELL FISHERIES INVESTIGATIONS (US/0736-5586) [09136429] **2307**

LAKE POWELL POST-IMPOUNDMENT INVESTIGATIONS *See* LAKE POWELL FISHERIES INVESTIGATIONS **2307**

LAKE STATION HERALD (US/1044-2839) [17255368] **5665**

LAKE STEVENS JOURNAL (US) [21390219] **5761**

LAKE STREET REVIEW, THE *CEASED.* (US/0889-6410) [03464146] **3403**

LAKE SUPERIOR MAGAZINE (US/0890-3050) [14199789] **2537**

LAKE SURVEY CENTER *See* CHART CATALOG, GREAT LAKES, CONNECTING WATERS, NEW YORK CANALS, LAKE WINNEBAGO, MINNESOTA-ONTARIO BORDER LAKES, LAKE CHAMPLAIN, INLAND ROUTE-MICHIGAN **2580**

LAKE UNION HERALD (US/0194-908X) [02937401] **5062**

LAKE VIEW RESORT (LAKE VIEW, IOWA : 1910) (US) [17022717] **5671**

LAKE WALES DAILY, THE (US) [23660572] **5650**

LAKE WORTH HERALD, THE (US) [02734405] **5650**

LAKEFIELD — Alphabetical Title Index

LAKEFIELD STANDARD (US) [01755490] **5696**

LAKEFIELD, THE CHRONICLE (CN/0821-4816) [09586318] **5788**

LAKEHEAD FOREST : A NEWSLETTER FROM THE SCHOOL OF FORESTRY, LAKEHEAD UNIVERSITY, THE (CN/1183-2894) [24257122] **2386**

LAKEHEAD UNIVERSITY *See* LAKEHEAD UNIVERSITY SUMMER SESSION **1834**

LAKEHEAD UNIVERSITY. SCHOOL OF LIBRARY TECHNOLOGY *See* LUSOLT TALK **3229**

LAKEHEAD UNIVERSITY SUMMER SESSION (CN/0316-8166) [02247160] **1834**

LAKELAND BOATING (1982) (US/0744-9194) [08650127] **594**

LAKELAND TIMES (US/0746-4274) [10036524] **5768**

LAKER, THE (US) [01779477] **5696**

LAKES AND RESERVOIRS (AT/1320-5331) **5535**

LAKES DISTRICT NEWS (CN) **5788**

LAKES LETTER (CN/0709-0013) [05257239] **1416**

LAKESHORE CHRONICLE (US) [12390671] **5768**

LAKESIDE LEADER (CN/0821-3372) [09543125] **5788**

LAKEVILLE JOURNAL, THE (US) [11561623] **5645**

LAKEWOOD JEFFERSON SENTINEL (1991), THE (US/1060-5215) [25014932] **5643**

LAKEWOOD SENTINEL (1990) (US/1053-6337) [22599919] **5643**

LAKEWOOD SENTINEL (DENVER, COLO. : 1990) *See* LAKEWOOD JEFFERSON SENTINEL (1991), THE **5643**

LAKIMIES (FI/0023-7353) [11715443] **2993**

LAKOKRASOCHNYE MATERIALY I IKH PRIMENENIE (RU/0023-737X) [02448231] **4224**

LAKOTA TIMES *See* INDIAN COUNTRY TODAY **5743**

LAKOTA TIMES, THE (US/0744-2238) [08116671] **5744**

LAL-BAUGH; JOURNAL OF THE MYSORE HORTICULTURAL SOCIETY, THE (II/0023-7388) [01771531] **2422**

LALAHAN HAYVANCILIK ARASTIRMA ENSTITUSU DERGISI (TU) [26844784] **213**

LALIES : ACTES DES SESSIONES DE LINGUISTIQUE ET DE LITTERATURE (FR) [08506491] **3294**

LALIT KALA (II/0458-6506) [01624395] **324**

LALIT KALA CONTEMPORY (II/0023-7396) [01714807] **356**

LALOGGIA'S SPECIAL SITUATION REPORT AND STOCK MARKET FORECAST (US/0890-8079) [14398672] **796**

LALU LINTAS ANGKUTAN ANTAR PULAU MENURUT GOLONGAN BARANG, DAERAH ASAL, DAN TUJUAN (IO) [07855846] **5451**

LAM-MISPAHA (US/0894-9816) [03916355] **5050**

LAMAR DAILY NEWS AND HOLLY CHIEFTAIN, THE (US) [21360872] **5643**

LAMAR DEMOCRAT (US/0745-9300) [09613011] **5703**

LAMAR DEMOCRAT AND THE SULLIGENT NEWS. (VERNON, AL.), THE (US) [14996314] **5627**

LAMAR JOURNAL OF THE HUMANITIES (US/0275-410X) [04725715] **2849**

LAMAR-MERIFIELD, GEOLOGISTS *See* TECHNICAL REPORT - LAMAR-MERIFIELD **1399**

LAMATCHIL (US) **2266**

LAMAZE IN ONTARIO (CN/0714-3680) [11422277] **3764**

LAMB COUNTY LEADER-NEWS (US) [14195779] **5751**

LAMB CROP & WOOL / IOWA CROP AND LIVESTOCK REPORTING SERVICE (US) [06203967] **213**

LAMBDA ALPHA JOURNAL OF MAN (US/0047-3928) [01775582] **240**

LAMBDA BOOK REPORT (US/1048-9487) [21076801] 3345, **2795**

LAMBDA RISING NEWS (US/1053-363X) [22517404] **4829**

LAMBERT/LAMBERTH ASSOCIATION *See* NEWSLETTER OF THE LAMBERT-LAMBERTH ASSOCIATION **2463**

LAMBERTON NEWS (US) [01755496] **5696**

LAMBERT'S COMMUNICATIONS DIRECTORY, WASHINGTON-BALTIMORE (US/0741-689X) [10176451] **1115**

LAMBI, LE (CN/0707-8927) [08967890] **2266**

LAMB'S PASTURES (US/0883-7708) [12224513] **2457**

LAMBTON COLLEGE *See* FOR YOUR CAREER INFORMATION **1824**

LAMBTON COLLEGE *See* FOR YOUR CAREER INFORMATION **1824**

LAMBTON COUNTY GAZETTE, THE (CN/0383-8080) [03248501] **5788**

LAMESA PRESS-REPORTER (US) [15123258] **5751**

LAMIERA (IT/0391-5891) [05194419] **4007**

LAMMERGEYER, THE (SA/0075-7780) [01755498] **4167**

LAMONI CHRONICLE, THE (US) [15326103] **5671**

LAMONT-DOHERTY GEOLOGICAL OBSERVATORY *See* TECHNICAL REPORT - LAMONT-DOHERTY GEOLOGICAL OBSERVATORY **1399**

LAMONT-DOHERTY GEOLOGICAL OBSERVATORY *See* LAMONT-DOHERTY GEOLOGICAL OBSERVATORY OF COLUMBIA UNIVERSITY : [REPORT] **1386**

LAMONT-DOHERTY GEOLOGICAL OBSERVATORY OF COLUMBIA UNIVERSITY : [REPORT] (US) [14390880] **1386**

LAMOURE CHRONICLE (US) [01755499] **5725**

LAMP (NEW YORK), THE (US/0023-7418) [01755500] **4263**

LAMP OF DELTA ZETA, THE (US/0887-2554) [02349567] **1834**

LAMP, THE (AT/0047-3936) [01437794] **3861**

LAMPADA (UK/0266-8769) [12960735] **3861**

LAMPAS (NE/0165-8204) [05215204] **3294**

LAMPASAS DISPATCH RECORD (US/8750-1759) [11081763] **5751**

LAMPLIGHTER (CHICAGO, ILL.) (US/1044-8756) [19943905] **3182**

LAMY COMMERCIAL (FR) [09988155] **3101**

LAMY DEHOVE (FR) 2993, **2348**

LAMY DROIT COMMERCIAL (FR) **2993**

LAMY DROIT DE L'INFORMATIQUE (FR/0983-6802) [19854251] **2993**

LAMY DROIT DU FINANCEMENT (FR) **2993**

LAMY DROIT ECONOMIQUE (FR) [19821725] **1502**

LAMY FISCAL (FR) [07028837] 4735, **2993**

LAMY FORMULAIRES. REGROUPEMENT DROIT DE SOCIETES (FR) **2993**

LAMY PROTECTION SOCIALE (FR) **3101**

LAMY SOCIAL (FR) 689, **2993**

LAMY SOCIETIES COMMERCIALES (FR) [18272288] **3101**

LAMY TRANSPORT (SERVICES LAMY) *See* LAMY TRANSPORT (SOCIETE LAMY) **2993**

LAMY TRANSPORT (SOCIETE LAMY) (FR) [08312283] 5385, **2993**

LAN CHIU / CHUNG-KUO LAN CHIU HSIEH HUI CHU PAN (CC) [11500739] **4903**

LAN-CHOU HSUEH KAN LAN ZHOU XUE KAN (CC) [10621123] **5233**

LAN-CHOU TA HSUEH HSUEH PAO. SHE HUI KO HSUEH PAN (CC/1000-2804) [08833512] **5208**

LAN COMPUTING (US/1055-1808) [23059465] **1193**

LAN MAGAZINE (NE) **1242**

LAN REPORTER *CEASED.* (US/1051-4066) [21952848] **1242**

●LAN (SAN FRANCISCO, CALIF.) (US/1069-5621) [27395364] **1242**

LAN TECHNOLOGY *CEASED.* (US/1042-4695) [19068525] 1268, **1242**

LAN TIMES (US/1040-5917) [18081253] 1268, **1242**

LANAIAN (LANAI CITY, HAWAII : 1978) (US) [08801731] **5656**

LANARK, LEEDS AND GRENVILLE COMMUNITY INFORMATION DIRECTORY (CN/0715-4739) [09313042] **5294**

LANBOOK (US) [19121912] **1242**

LANCASHIRE AND CHESHIRE ANTIQUARIAN SOCIETY *See* TRANSACTIONS OF THE LANCASHIRE AND CHESHIRE ANTIQUARIAN SOCIETY **2713**

LANCASHIRE LIFE (UK) [05194425] **2518**

LANCASTER BEE (US/0746-4487) [10049405] **5717**

LANCASTER CONFERENCE NEWS (US/0747-2706) [10682296] **5062**

LANCASTER COUNTY CONNECTIONS (US/0748-1071) [10871801] **2457**

LANCASTER COUNTY HERITAGE *CEASED.* (US/0890-8893) [11031188] **2457**

LANCASTER COUNTY (PA.) HISTORICAL SOCIETY *See* JOURNAL OF THE LANCASTER COUNTY HISTORICAL SOCIETY **2742**

LANCASTER EAGLE-GAZETTE (US) [11859821] **5729**

LANCASTER FARMING (US/0023-7485) [04090706] **103**

LANCASTER INDEPENDENT PRESS *See* LIP (LANCASTER, PA.) **3346**

LANCASTER LABOUR LAW REPORTS. 2, LABOUR LAW NEWS (CN) [20030789] **3151**

LANCASTER LIVESTOCK REPORTER (US/0738-730X) [08433935] **214**

LANCASTER NEW ERA (US) [09398280] **5737**

LANCASTER NEWS (LANCASTER, TEX.) *See* TODAY LANCASTER **5755**

LANCASTER NEWS, THE (US/0745-7421) [09420408] **5742**

●LANCASTER'S CONSTRUCTION INDUSTRY EMPLOYMENT LAW NEWS (CN/1194-4552) [28395806] 619, **3151**

●LANCASTER'S EMPLOYMENT EQUITY REPORTER (CN/1194-6237) [28474032] **1687**

●LANCASTER'S WRONGFUL DISMISSAL EMPLOYMENT LAW NEWS (CN/1194-398X) [28277531] **3151**

LANCE K. LERAY'S BAKERY WORLD OF CANADA (CN/0710-569X) [08713508] **2348**

LANCET (BRITISH EDITION) (UK/0140-6736) [01755507] **3603**

LANCET ED. FRANCAISE *CEASED.* (NE/0923-7577) [10923757] **3603**

LANCET EDIZIONE ITALIANA, THE (IT/0393-0637) [l03930637] **3603**

LANCET NIHONGO-BAN, THE (JA/0916-6386) [10916638] **3603**

LANCET (NORTH AMERICAN EDITION), THE (US/0099-5355) [02141608] **3603**

LANCET (SPANISH EDITION), THE (SP) **3604**

LAND AGRARWIRTSCHAFT UND GESELLSCHAFT (GW/0176-2389) [13297492] **103**

LAND, AIR & WATER (US) **2235**

LAND AND HUMAN SETTLEMENTS (CN/0715-3023) [10092687] **2910**

LAND AND MINERALS SURVEYING *CEASED.* (UK/0265-4210) [10807659] 2568, **2027**

LAND & NATURAL RESOURCES DIVISION JOURNAL (US) [02387252] **2197**

LAND & SEA-BASED ELECTRONICS FORECAST (US) **2070**

LAND AND WATER (FORT DODGE) (US/0192-9453) [02305816] 5536, **2197**

LAND & WATER INTERNATIONAL (NE/0023-7604) [02263421] **2093**

LAND AND WATER LAW REVIEW (US/0023-7612) [09463093] **3113**

LAND AND WATER REPORT (US/0272-6068) [06190568] **2197**

LAND AND WATER RESEARCH NEWS (AT/1033-1360) [l10331360] 5536, **1357**

LAND AND WATER ROME (IT/0254-6280) [l02546280] **5536**

LAND AREAS OF THE NATIONAL FOREST SYSTEM (US/0196-7878) [03792604] **2386**

LAND ASSESSMENT/SALES RATIO STUDY AND EQUALIZED ASSESSMENTS (CN/0228-4278) [04441892] **4660**

LAND BANK OF THE PHILIPPINES *See* ANNUAL REPORT - LAND BANK OF THE PHILIPPINES **771**

LAND CLAIMS NEWSLETTER (CN/1185-040X) [23659435] **2993**

LAND COMPENSATION BOARD INDEX TO APPLICATIONS DISPOSED OF (CN/0704-5808) [04955048] **2993**

LAND COMPENSATION REPORTS (CN/0380-4208) [01755514] **2993**

LAND CONTAMINATION & RECLAMATION (UK/0967-0513) [l09670513] **2176**

LAND DEGRADATION AND REHABILITATION (UK/0898-5812) [17853557] 2197, **177**

LAND DEVELOPMENT DIGEST (MY/0126-6160) [05330716] **4840**

LAND ECONOMICS (US/0023-7639) [01604370] **103**

LAND ECONOMIST (CN/0820-7240) [09519490] **1502**

LAND INFORMATION DIRECTORY / SPONSORED BY LAND INFORMATION SYSTEMS ADVISORY COMMITTEE (AT) [08566867] **4660**

LAND INVESTMENT NEWS (US/0891-7337) [15011425] **4840, 905**

LAND JUGEND (AU) [09858574] **103**

LAND LETTER : THE NEWSLETTER FOR NATURAL RESOURCE PROFESSIONALS (US) **689**

LAND LETTER (WASHINGTON, D.C.) (US/0890-7625) [09109608] **2197**

LAND MANAGEMENT AND ENVIRONMENTAL LAW REPORT See ENVIRONMENTAL LAW AND MANAGEMENT **3111**

LAND MANAGEMENT AND ENVIRONMENTAL LAW REPORT : LME LAW REPORT (UK/0955-6354) [20428508] **3113**

LAND MANAGEMENT HANDBOOKS / PROVINCE OF BRITISH COLUMBIA, MINISTRY OF FORESTS (CN/0229-1622) [10290584] **2386**

LAND MANAGEMENT REPORT (CN/0702-9861) [09141763] **2218, 2386**

LAND (MANKATO, MINN.), THE (US/0279-1633) [03558549] **103**

LAND MOBILE RADIO NEWS (US/1070-6593) [28448809] **1134**

LAND REFORM, LAND SETTLEMENT AND COOPERATIVES (IT/0251-1894) [01785568] **103, 1542**

LAND REPORT, THE (US) [12676064] **103**

LAND RESOURCE STUDY (UK/0436-399X) [01981967] **1502**

LAND RESOURCES LABORATORY SERIES (US/0275-6161) [07164561] **2197**

LAND RESOURCES MANAGEMENT : DIVISIONAL REPORT FROM THE CSIRO DIVISION OF LAND RESOURCES MANAGEMENT / CSIRO, DIVISION OF LAND RESOURCES MANAGEMENT, PERTH, WESTERN AUSTRALIA (AT) [09170720] **2197**

LAND RIG NEWSLETTER, THE (US/1043-7312) [10607272] **4263**

LAND RIGHTS NEWS (AT/0313-6353) [05207698] **4840**

LAND, THE (AT) [09856951] **5777**

LAND TRENDS (NEW YORK, N.Y.) (US/0739-6376) [08354857] **4840**

LAND- UND FORSTWIRTSCHAFLICHE BETRIEB, DER (AU) [09857812] **2386**

LAND- UND FORSTWIRTSCHAFT, DIE (GW) [02580143] **103, 154**

LAND- UND FORSTWIRTSCHAFT, FISCHEREI. REIHE 3.1.6, ANBAU VON ZIERPFLANZEN / HERAUSGEBER : STATISTISCHES BUNDESAMT (GW) [08596162] **2422**

LAND- UND FORSTWIRTSCHAFT, FISCHEREI. REIHE 2.1.1 : BETREIBSGROSSENSTRUKTUR (GW) [03486505] **103**

LAND- UND FORSTWIRTSCHAFT, FISCHEREI. REIHE 4.3.1 : SCHLACHTTIER- UND FLEISCHBESCHAU (GW) [03702237] **3482**

LAND- UND FORSTWIRTSCHAFT, FISCHEREI. REIHE 4.2.1, SCHLACHTUNGEN UND FLEISCHGEWINNUNG / HERAUSGEBER : STATISTISCHES BUNDESAMT (GW) [08690370] **1615, 214**

●LAND- UND FORSTWIRTSCHAFT, FISCHEREI. REIHE 3.2.3, WEINBESTAENDE / STATISTISCHES BUNDESAMT (GW) [30993144] **2368**

LAND- UND FORSTWIRTSCHAFT, FISCHEREI. REIHE 3.2.3, WEINBESTAENDE UND LAGERBEHAELTER See LAND- UND FORSTWIRTSCHAFT, FISCHEREI. REIHE 3.2.3, WEINBESTAENDE / STATISTISCHES BUNDESAMT **2368**

LAND- UND FORSTWIRTSCHAFT, FISCHEREI. REIHE 3.2.2, WEINERZEUGUNG (GW) [20569581] **2368**

LAND- UND FORSTWIRTSCHAFT, FISCHEREI. REIHE 3, LANDWIRTSCHAFTLICHE BODENNUTZUNG UND PFLANZLICHE ERZEUGUNG / STATISTISCHES BUNDESAMT (GW) [27184541] **103**

LAND- UND FORSTWIRTSCHAFT, FISCHEREI. REIHE 3 : PFLANZLICHE ERZENGUNG (GW) [03567360] **103**

LAND- UND FORSTWIRTSCHAFT, FISCHEREI. REIHE 3 : VIEHWIRTSCHAFT (GW/0072-3665) [03048248] **2307**

LAND- UND FORSTWIRTSCHAFT, FISCHEREI. REIHE 3.2, HEUERNTE / HERAUSGEBER STATISTISCHES BUNDESAMT (GW) [09344826] **103**

LAND- UND FORSTWIRTSCHAFT, FISCHEREI. REIHE 3.2, WACHSTUMSTAND FUR WINTERGETREIDE UND WINTEROLFRUCHTE / HERAUSGEBER STATISTISCHES BUNDESAMT (GW) [09242076] **104**

LAND- UND FORSTWIRTSCHAFT, FISCHEREI. REIHE 4.3, FLEISCHUNTERSUCHUNG (GW) [19250179] **1615**

LAND- UND FORSTWIRTSCHAFTLICHE See BETRIEBSERGEBNISSE VON UMSTELLUNGS- UND BESITZFESTIGUNGSBETRIEBEN **66**

LAND- UND FORSTWIRTSCHAFTLICHE See BETRIEBSWIRTSCHAFTLICHE ERGEBNISSE VON LANDWIRTSCHAFTLICHEN BETRIEBEN IN DER STEIERMARK **66**

LAND UND FORSTWIRTSCHAFTLICHE BETRIEB, DER See AGRO BONUS **2373**

LAND UPDATE : A PUBLICATION OF THE NATIONAL LAND COMMITTEE (SA) [27764871] **2197**

●LAND USE & ENVIRONMENT FORUM (US/1072-7973) [29203837] **3114**

LAND USE & ENVIRONMENT LAW REVIEW (US/0192-8309) [04379640] **3114**

LAND USE DIGEST (US/0023-768X) [01755520] **2827, 4840**

LAND USE FORUM (US/1058-7012) [24358758] **2993**

LAND USE LAW & ZONING DIGEST (US/0094-7598) [01795344] **4840, 2993**

LAND USE LAW REPORT (US/1064-0401) [24596371] **2993**

LAND USE PLANNING IN NEBRASKA (US/0145-8620) [02791131] **4840**

LAND USE POLICY (UK/0264-8377) [10378501] **1502**

LAND + WATER / MILIEUTECHNIEK (NE) **2027**

LANDARBEITERKAMMER FUR TIROL See TATIGKEITSBERICHT DER LANDARBEITERKAMMER FUR TIROL **139**

LANDBAUFORSCHUNG VOLKENRODE (GW/0458-6859) [05156758] **104**

LANDBAUFORSCHUNG VOLKENRODE, SONDERHEFT (GW/0376-0723) [27140611] **104**

LANDBOTE, DER (GW) [04085262] **104**

LANDBOUW-ECONOMISCH INSTITUUT, AFDELING LANDBOUW: PUBLIKATIE (NE) [07984651] **104**

LANDBOUW-ECONOMISCH INSTITUUT. AFDELING STATISTIEK See AGRARISCH WEEKOVERZICHT **46**

LANDBOUW-ECONOMISCH INSTITUUT. AFDELING STRUCTUURONDERZOEK See PUBLIKATIE 2 / LANDBOUW-ECONOMISCH INSTITUUT, AFDELING STRUCTUURONDERZOEK **123**

LANDBOUW-ECONOMISCH INSTITUUT (NETHERLANDS) See MEDELINGEN - LANDBOUW-ECONOMISCH INSTITUUT **107**

LANDBOUWCIJFERS (NE/0436-5569) [01209626] **154**

LANDBOUWLEVEN (BE/0772-7240) [07727240] **104**

LANDBOUWMACHINE-INDUSTRIE / CENTRAAL BUREAU VOOR DE STATISTIEK, HOOFDAFDELING STATISTIEKEN VAN INDUSTRIE EN BOUWNIJVERHEID (NE) [10290516] **159**

LANDBOUWMECHANISATIE (NE/0023-7795) [03772916] **159**

LANDBOUWSTATISTIEKEN (BE) [02356820] **104, 154**

LANDBOUWTIJDSCHRIFT (1988) (BE/0776-2143) [07762143] **104**

LANDBRUGETS PRISFORHOLD (DK/0106-519X) [09086813] **104**

LANDBRUGSMARKEDER. FORKLARINGER, PRISER (BE) [07436532] **104**

LANDBRUGSREGNSKABSSTATISTIK (DK/0107-5675) [09069600] **104**

LANDBRUGSSTATISTIK (DK) [05818425] **104, 154**

LANDBRUGSSTATISTIK HERUNDER GARTNERI OG SKOVBRUG See LANDBRUGSSTATISTIK **154**

LANDBRUKS KONOMISK FORUM (NO/0800-5974) [08005974] **1502, 104**

LANDBRUKSDIREKTRENS ARSMELDING (NO) [01786032] **104**

LANDEIGENAAR (NE/0166-5839) [01665839] **4840**

LANDENDOCUMENTATIEMAPPEN (NE/0922-4939) [09224939] **2568**

LANDER WYOMING STATE JOURNAL (US) [26205972] **5772**

LANDERBANK ECONOMIC BULLETIN (AU/0377-0788) [02851047] **1502**

LANDERBANK REPORT : REPORT ON THE AUSTRIAN ECONOMY (AU) [11749579] **689, 1502**

LANDERBERICHT. AFGHANISTAN / [STATISTISCHES BUNDESAMT] (GW/0938-5398) [21530703] **5331**

LANDERBERICHT. ANGOLA / STATISTISCHES BUNDESAMT (GW) [25323064] **5331**

LANDERBERICHT. BAHRAIN / STATISTISCHES BUNDESAMT (GW) [25932981] **1571, 1535**

LANDERBERICHT. BANGLADESCH (GW) [23222332] **2506**

LANDERBERICHT. BIRMA (GW/0937-7824) [23268050] **2506**

LANDERBERICHT. BOLIVIEN / STATISTISCHES BUNDESAMT (GW) [25323292] **5331**

LANDERBERICHT. BRASILIEN / STATISTISCHES BUNDESAMT (GW/0940-0907) [25327791] **5331**

LANDERBERICHT. BULGARIEN / STATISTISCHES BUNDESAMT (GW) [25327180] **5331**

LANDERBERICHT. COTE D'IVOIRE / STATISTISCHES BUNDESAMT (GW) [25323401] **5331**

LANDERBERICHT. DOMINIKANISCHE REPUBLIK (GW) [23384392] **2512**

LANDERBERICHT : GABUN (GW) [06166517] **5331**

LANDERBERICHT. GOLFSTAATEN / STATISTISCHES BUNDESAMT (GW) [24271851] **5331**

LANDERBERICHT. GRIECHENLAND / STATISTISCHES BUNDESAMT (GW) [24226491] **5331**

LANDERBERICHT. GUATEMALA / [STATISTISCHES BUNDESAMT] (GW/0937-7794) [23223073] **2551**

LANDERBERICHT. HAITI (GW/0937-082X) [23273949] **2512**

LANDERBERICHT. INDIEN / STATISTISCHES BUNDESAMT (GW) [25323503] **5331**

LANDERBERICHT. INDONESIEN (GW/0938-4472) [23264374] **5331**

LANDERBERICHT. IRAN / STATISTISCHES BUNDESAMT (GW) [27253404] **5331**

LANDERBERICHT. JAMAIKA (GW/0937-7816) [23223189] **2512**

LANDERBERICHT. JAPAN (GW/0939-3773) [23277488] **2506**

LANDERBERICHT. KAMBODSCHA / STATISTISCHES BUNDESAMT (GW) [25323618] **5331**

LANDERBERICHT. KOREA, DEMOKRATISCHE VOLKSREPUBLIK (GW/0937-9975) [23230354] **5331**

LANDERBERICHT. LESOTHO / STATISTISCHES BUNDESAMT (GW) [25323756] **5331**

LANDERBERICHT. LIBYEN (GW/0937-7859) [23235887] **2499**

LANDERBERICHT. MADAGASKAR / STATISTISCHES BUNDESAMT (GW) [25324006] **5331**

LANDERBERICHT. MALAYSIA / STATISTISCHES BUNDESAMT (GW/0937-7972) [24227345] **5331**

LANDERBERICHT. MALI / STATISTISCHES BUNDESAMT (GW) [24227863] **5331**

LANDERBERICHT. MAROKKO (GW) [23279310] **2499**

LANDERBERICHT. NICARAGUA / STATISTISCHES BUNDESAMT (GW) [25328417] **5331**

LANDERBERICHT. NIEDERLANDE / STATISTISCHES BUNDESAMT (GW/0938-474X) [24226368] **5331**

LANDERBERICHT. NORWEGEN / STATISTISCHES BUNDESAMT (GW) [25323912] **5331**

LANDERBERICHT. OSTASIATISCHE STAATEN / STATISTISCHES BUNDESAMT (GW) [25695919] **5331**

LANDERBERICHT. PARAGUAY / [STATISTISCHES BUNDESAMT] (GW/0937-7948) [23274279] **2551**

LANDERBERICHT. PHILIPPINEN (GW/0937-7921) [23276897] **2506**

LANDERBERICHT. SOMALIA / STATISTISCHES BUNDESAMT (GW) [25329520] **5331**

LANDERBERICHT. STAATEN MITTEL- UND OSTEUROPAS / EUROSTAT [UND] STATISTISCHES BUNDESAMT (GW) [24210878] **5331**

●LANDERBERICHT. SUDAMERIKANISCHE STAATEN / STATISTISCHES BUNDESAMT (GW) [25781512] **5331**

LANDERBERICHT. THAILAND (GW/0939-6896) [23381935] **2506**

LANDERBERICHT. TOGO / EUROSTAT [UND] STATISTISCHES BUNDESAMT (GW) [25330273] **5331**

LANDERBERICHT. TURKEI (GW/0937-7891) [23274186] **2506**

LANDERBERICHT — Alphabetical Title Index

LANDERBERICHT : UNGARN (GW) [06428431] **5331**

LANDERBERICHT. VEREINIGTE ARABISCHE EMIRATE (GW/0938-4707) [23260525] **2506**

LANDERBERICHT. ZAIRE (GW/0939-3854) [23276262] **2499**

LANDERBERICHTE. CHILE (GW) [02410103] **2552**

LANDERBERICHTE DES STATISTISCHEN BUNDESAMTES (GW) **4660**

LANDERGBERICHT. VEREINIGTE STAATEN (GW/0937-7913) [23273283] **2537**

LANDERKURZBERICHT : BELIZE (GW) [06372698] **1572**

LANDERKURZBERICHT : NAMIBIA (SUDWESTAFRIKA) (GW) [06163671] **5331**

LANDERKURZBERICHT : VIETNAM (GW) [06163537] **1572**

LANDERKURZBERICHTE : BAHAMAS (GW) [01798418] **5331**

LANDERKURZBERICHTE : BAHRAIN, KATAR (GW) [01785841] **5331**

LANDERKURZBERICHTE : BOLIVIEN (GW) [02378931] **5331**

LANDERKURZBERICHTE : FRANZ.-GUAYANA (GW) [04965755] **5331**

LANDERKURZBERICHTE : HONG KONG (GW) [02534707] **5332**

LANDERKURZBERICHTE : JORDANIEN (GW) [04961594] **5332**

LANDERKURZBERICHTE : KONGO (GW) [01796255] **5332**

LANDERKURZBERICHTE: KONGO (BRAZZAVILLE) See LANDERKURZBERICHTE : KONGO **5332**

LANDERKURZBERICHTE: KUBA (GW/0072-2871) [02376706] **5332**

LANDERKURZBERICHTE : NEPAL (GW) [04961369] **5332**

LANDERKURZBERICHTE : PANAMA (GW) [02376697] **5332**

LANDERKURZBERICHTE : PERU (GW/0072-3274) [02376461] **5332**

LANDERKURZBERICHTE : REPUBLIK KOREA (GW) [04965692] **5332**

LANDERKURZBERICHTE : VENEZUELA (GW/0072-369X) [02376632] **5332**

LANDERKURZBERICHTE : ZYPERN (GW) [04924424] **5332**

LANDERS FILM & VIDEO REVIEWS CEASED. (US/1050-2041) [20496288] **4073**

LANDESAMT FUR DATENVERARBEITUNG UND STATISTIK NORDRHEIN-WESTFALEN See GEMEINDEN NORDRHEIN-WESTFALEN, DIE **5327**

LANDESAMT FUR DATENVERARBEITUNG UND STATISTIK NORDRHEIN-WESTFALEN See BEHORDENVERZEICHNIS NORDRHEIN-WESTFALEN / LANDESAMT FUER DATENVERARBEITUNG UND STATISTIK NORDRHEIN-WESTFALEN **4632**

LANDESAMT FUR DATENVERARBEITUNG UND STATISTIK NORDRHEIN-WESTFALEN See AUSFUHR NORDRHEIN-WESTFALENS, DIE **824**

LANDESAMT FËUR DATENVERARBEITUNG UND STATISTIK NORDRHEIN-WESTFALEN See VEROFFENTLICHUNGEN DES LANDESAMTES FUER DATENVERARBEITUNG UND STATISTIK NORDRHEIN-WESTFALEN **5346**

LANDESARBEITSAMT HESSEN See ARBEITSMARKT IN HESSEN : JAHRESZAHLEN, DER **1651**

LANDESARBEITSAMT TIROL See JAHRESBERICHT DES LANDESARBEITSAMTES TIROL **1681**

LANDESARBEITSGEMEINSCHAFT ZUR BEKAMPFUNG DER GESCHLECHTSKRANKHEITEN UND FUR GESCHLECHTSERZIEHUNG NORDRHEIN-WESTFALEN See SONDERHEFT **4803**

LANDESHAUSHALT (AU) [10572880] **4660**

LANDESJUGENDPLAN : DURCHFUHRUNGSPLAN (GW) [02879289] **5294**

LANDESVEREINIGUND DER INDUSTRIELLEN ARBEITGEBERVERBANDE NORDRHEIN-WESTFALENS See ARBEITGEBER NRW **1651**

LANDESVERTEIDIGUNGSAKADEMIE (AUSTRIA). INSTITUT FUER MILITAERISCHE GRUNDLAGENFORSCHUNG See STUDIENMATERIAL - INSTITUT FUER MILITAERISCHE GRUNDLAGENFORSCHUNG **4058**

LANDFALL (NZ/0023-7930) [01755523] **3403**

LANDFORM (AT/0816-3405) [I08163405] **1386**

LANDINRICHTING UTRECHT (NE/0922-6419) [I09226419] **4660**

LANDINSPEKTREN; TIDSSKRIFT FOR OPMALINGSOG MATRIKELVAESEN (DK/0105-4570) [05685784] **2027**

LANDIS' LANDINGS (US/1048-2059) [20833062] **2457**

LANDLINE WELLINGTON (NZ/0114-7579) [I01147579] **1386**

LANDLORD TENANT LAW BULLETIN (US/0271-5228) [06634422] 2827, **2993**

LANDLORD-TENANT RELATIONS REPORT (US/1050-3196) [11852712] 4840, **2827**

LANDLORD VS. TENANT/NYC (US/0883-0746) [12056967] 2827, **2993**

LANDMAN (FT. WORTH) (US/0457-088X) [03136909] **4263**

LANDMARK (US) [06386075] **796**

LANDMARK BRIEFS AND ARGUMENTS OF THE SUPREME COURT OF THE UNITED STATES : CONSTITUTIONAL LAW (US/0194-4010) [04180932] **3093**

LANDMARK (CALGARY) (CN/0843-459X) [20603227] **2422**

LANDMARK (EL MONTE), THE (US/0271-5414) [04254823] **2743**

LANDMARK (PLATTE CITY, MO.) (US) [13571936] **5703**

LANDMARK, THE (US) [20362767] **5689**

LANDMARKS AND NEW HORIZONS IN CONTINUING EDUCATION (US) [01641947] **1801**

LANDMARKS OBSERVER (US/0272-1384) [06771281] **2743**

LANDMARKS (SEATTLE, WASH.) SUSPENDED. (US/0734-4007) [08485300] **2743**

LANDMEN'S DIRECTORY (US/0272-8370) [11439689] **4263**

LANDOUNUUS / AGRICULTURAL NEWS (US) [10669053] **104**

LANDSAT NON-U.S. STANDARD CATALOG (US/0364-7587) [02585978] **27**

LANDSAT U.S. STANDARD CATALOG (US/0364-7560) [02585907] **27**

LANDSCAPE ALBERTA NURSERY TRADES ASSOCIATION See MEMBERSHIP DIRECTORY, PLANT SOURCE LIST **2424**

LANDSCAPE ALBERTA NURSERY TRADES ASSOCIATION. MEMBERSHIP ROSTER See MEMBERSHIP DIRECTORY, PLANT SOURCE LIST **2424**

LANDSCAPE AND GARDEN CONTRACTOR (UK) **2422**

LANDSCAPE & IRRIGATION (US/0745-3795) [09113725] 177, **2422**

●LANDSCAPE & NURSERY DIGEST (US/1071-3697) [28622897] **2422**

LANDSCAPE AND URBAN PLANNING (NE/0169-2046) [13491237] **2827**

LANDSCAPE ARCHITECT & SPECIFIER NEWS (US/1060-9962) [25152637] **2422**

LANDSCAPE ARCHITECTURAL REVIEW CEASED. (CN/0228-6963) [07857879] **2422**

LANDSCAPE ARCHITECTURE (US/0023-8031) [01755527] **2423**

LANDSCAPE ARCHITECTURE. HOME LANDSCAPE (US/0278-8373) [07871373] **2423**

LANDSCAPE ARCHITECTURE NEWS DIGEST (US/0023-754X) [02251471] **2423**

LANDSCAPE AUSTRALIA (AT/0310-9011) [06578502] **2423**

LANDSCAPE (BERKELEY, CALIF.) (US/0023-8023) [01589006] **2568**

LANDSCAPE CONTRACTOR, THE (US/0194-7257) [04978916] **2423**

LANDSCAPE DESIGN (UK/0020-2908) [01606022] **2423**

LANDSCAPE DESIGN (VAN NUYS, CALIF.) (US/1070-3853) [28357800] **2423**

LANDSCAPE ECOLOGY (NE/0921-2973) [16947265] **2218**

LANDSCAPE HISTORY (UK/0143-3768) [07122596] 2568, **2423**

LANDSCAPE INSTITUTE See LANDSCAPE INSTITUTE YEARBOOK AND DIRECTORY **302**

LANDSCAPE INSTITUTE YEARBOOK AND DIRECTORY (UK/0265-4199) [17008441] **302**

LANDSCAPE JOURNAL (US/0277-2426) [07534225] **2423**

LANDSCAPE MANAGEMENT (US/0894-1254) [15559976] **2423**

LANDSCAPE RESEARCH (UK/0142-6397) [04266219] **2423**

LANDSCAPE RESEARCH. EXTRA (UK) [19283656] **2423**

LANDSCAPE SCOTLAND QUARTERLY (UK/0266-0954) [I02660954] **2423**

LANDSCAPE SYSTEMS (UK/0195-489X) [05514527] **2423**

LANDSCAPE, THE CEASED. (NZ/0110-1439) [04904111] 302, **2422**

LANDSCAPE TRADES (CN/0225-6398) [06054463] **2423**

LANDSCAPER (AT) **2423**

LANDSCAPING HOMES & GARDENS GARDEN PLANS (US/0737-1632) [09298566] **2423**

LANDSCAPING, LAWNS AND GARDENS (US/0271-9126) [06690912] **2423**

LANDSCHAFTSARCHITEKTUR (GW/0323-3162) [03136771] **2423**

LANDSCOPE (AT/0815-4465) [12755558] **2197**

LANDSKAB (DK/0023-8066) [07525367] **2423**

LANDSLAGET FOR BYGDE- OG BYHISTORIE See SKRIFTER **2709**

LANDSLIDE (EUREKA) (US/0093-0679) [01791405] **1386**

LANDSMEN (WASHINGTON, D.C.) (US/1055-4661) [23175509] 2266, **2457**

LANDSORGANISATIONEN I DANMARK See LO-BLADET **1688**

LANDSORGANISATIONEN I SVERIGE See LO I.E. LANDSORGANISATIONEN I SVERIGE TIDNINGEN **1572**

LANDSTINGENS PLANER (SW) [06571702] **5294**

LANDSTINGSVARLDEN (SW/0282-4485) [I0282A485] **4661**

LANDTECHNIK, DIE (GW/0023-8082) [02500979] **159**

LANDTECHNISCHE ZEITSCHRIFT (GW/0011-5010) [03992887] **104**

LANDWATCH (REDLANDS, CALIF.) (US/1060-8826) [25106006] **4840**

LANDWIRTSCHAFT IN NORDRHEIN-WESTFALEN, DIE (GW) [02474729] **104**

LANDWIRTSCHAFT SCHWEIZ (SZ) [19348063] **104**

LANDWIRTSCHAFTLICHES JAHRBUCH DER SCHWEIZ. ANNUAIRE AGRICOLE DE LA SUISSE (SZ/0023-8171) [01604944] **104**

LANDWIRTSCHAFTLICHES WOCHENBLATT FUR WESTFALEN UND LIPPE (GW) [04085378] **104**

LANDWIRTSCHAFTLICHES WOCHENBLATT : LWBW (GW) [26266852] **104**

LANDWIRTSCHAFTLICHES ZENTRALBLATT. ABTEILUNG IV. VETERINARMEDIZIN (SZ/0023-821X) [01755532] **5515**

LANDWIRTSCHAFTSKAMMER RHEINLAND. ABTEILUNG ERZEUGUNG. GRUPPE GARTENBAU See GARTENBAULICHE VERSUCHSBERICHTE **2416**

LANDWIRTSCHAFTSKAMMER SCHLESWIG-HOLSTEIN See BETRIEBSERGEBNISSE : DURCHSCHNITTSERGEBNISSE **66**

LANDWIRTSCHAFTSKRANKENKASSE FUR STEIERMARK See JAHRESBERICHT **1681**

LANDWORKER, THE (UK) [03139667] 104, **1687**

LANE COUNTY HISTORIAN (US/0458-7227) [02298962] **2743**

●LANE GUIDE (WESTERN ED.) (US/1062-8932) [25793975] **796**

LANE REPORT, THE (US/1063-925X) [23251023] **689**

LANG CLASSICAL STUDIES (US/0891-4087) [14766172] **1078**

LANG VAN (CN/0832-1922) [15646372] **2489**

LANGAGE ET L'HOMME, LE (BE/0458-7251) [04901096] 4602, **3294**

LANGAGE ET SOCIETE (FR/0181-4095) [05261034] **3294**

LANGAGES (PARIS) (FR/0458-726X) [01695353] **3294**

LANGENBECKS ARCHIV FEUR CHIRURGIE. SUPPLEMENT. KONGRESSBAND (GW) [25007411] **3969**

LANGENBECKS ARCHIV FUER CHIRURGIE (GW/0023-8236) [01642973] **3969**

LANGENSCHEIDT'S SPRACH-ILLUSTRIERTE (GW/0023-8252) [01755535] **3294**

LANGE'S HANDBOOK OF CHEMISTRY (US/0748-4585) [02307440] **984**

LANGFORD BUGLE, THE (US) [12814140] **5744**

LANGFORD TO COLWOOD TELEGRAM (CN/0380-4607) [02443261] **5788**

LANGFRISTIGE KREDIT, DER (GW) [05194433] **905**

LANGHALI (KATHMANDU, NEPAL) (NP) [11985267] **3294**

LANGLEY TIMES (CN/0711-7450) [08700940] **5788**

LANGMUIR (US/0743-7463) [10666233] **1055**

LANGSTON HUGHES REVIEW, THE (US/0737-0555) [09273146] **3345**

LANGUAGE (SI) [01790693] **3294**

LANGUAGE ABUSE FORUM (CN/1183-1316) [24690507] **3294**

LANGUAGE ACQUISITION (US/1048-9223) [21070311] **3294**

LANGUAGE AND COGNITIVE PROCESSES (UK/0169-0965) [12849677] **3294**

LANGUAGE & COMMUNICATION (UK/0271-5309) [06663991] 1115, **3294**

LANGUAGE AND COMPUTERS (NE/0921-5034) [20786175] **3294**

LANGUAGE AND COMPUTERS: STUDIES IN PRACTICAL LINGUISTICS (NE) **3294**

LANGUAGE AND EDUCATION (UK/0950-0782) [17316721] 1760, **3294**

LANGUAGE AND LANGUAGE EDUCATION (AT/1036-6709) 1760, **3294**

LANGUAGE AND LANGUAGE LEARNING (UK/0458-7294) [05586939] **3294**

LANGUAGE AND LEARNING (UK) 3294, **1899**

LANGUAGE AND LINGUISTICS IN MELANESIA : JOURNAL OF THE LINGUISTIC SOCIETY OF PAPUA NEW GUINEA (PP) [09188672] **3294**

LANGUAGE AND LITERACY NEWS (UK/0958-8140) [25325330] 3294, **1899**

●LANGUAGE AND LITERATURE (UK/0963-9470) [27029473] 3403, **3294**

LANGUAGE AND LITERATURE (SAN ANTONIO, TEX.) (US/1057-6037) [09172304] 3403, **3294**

LANGUAGE AND SOCIETY (CN/0709-7751) [06026370] **3295**

LANGUAGE AND SPEECH (UK/0023-8309) [01755538] **3295**

LANGUAGE AND STYLE (US/0023-8317) [01755539] **3295**

LANGUAGE ARTS (US/0360-9170) [02244875] 3295, **1804**

LANGUAGE ASSOCIATION BULLETIN (US/0889-6917) [08622743] 3295, **1899**

LANGUAGE ASSOCIATION OF EASTERN AFRICA See JOURNAL OF THE LANGUAGE ASSOCIATION OF EASTERN AFRICA **3292**

●LANGUAGE AWARENESS (UK/0965-8416) [26288703] **3295**

LANGUAGE (BALTIMORE) (US/0097-8507) [01361911] **3295**

LANGUAGE CENSUS REPORT FOR CALIFORNIA PUBLIC SCHOOLS (US) [20721405] **3295**

LANGUAGE, CULTURE, AND CURRICULUM (UK/0790-8318) [18366198] 1899, **3295**

●LANGUAGE FORUM (UK/1351-024X) **3295**

LANGUAGE FORUM (II/0253-9071) [04082882] **3295**

LANGUAGE IN EDUCATION (US) [04389157] 3295, **1760**

LANGUAGE IN FOCUS (MISSISSAUGA, ONT.) (CN/0823-4159) [11360481] **3295**

LANGUAGE IN SOCIETY (UK/0047-4045) [01642172] **3295**

LANGUAGE INTERNATIONAL (NE/0923-182X) [20028639] **3295**

LANGUAGE INTERVENTION SERIES (US/0190-0382) [04595793] **3295**

LANGUAGE LEARNING (US/0023-8333) [01640701] **3295**

LANGUAGE LEARNING JOURNAL : THE JOURNAL OF THE ASSOCIATION OF LANGUAGE LEARNING (UK/0957-1736) [21263174] **3295**

LANGUAGE OF DANCE SERIES (US/0888-1286) [13484466] **1313**

LANGUAGE OF DEFENSE : HANDBOOK OF ACRONYMS AND TERMINOLOGY **CEASED.** (US/1050-7310) [21583797] **4048**

LANGUAGE PROBLEMS & LANGUAGE PLANNING (US/0272-2690) [06802740] **3295**

LANGUAGE PROJECTS' REVIEW (SA/1018-3442) [10183442] **3295**

LANGUAGE QUARTERLY / PUBLISHED AT THE UNIVERSITY OF SOUTH FLORIDA UNDER THE AUSPICES OF THE DIVISION OF LANGUAGE (US) [22151215] **3295**

LANGUAGE RESEARCH (KO/0254-4474) [02437098] **3296**

LANGUAGE RESEARCH BULLETIN / ICU (JA/0913-3615) [16187338] **3296**

LANGUAGE SCIENCES (OXFORD) (UK/0388-0001) [04986705] **3296**

LANGUAGE, SPEECH & HEARING SERVICES IN SCHOOLS (US/0161-1461) [02280683] **1881**

LANGUAGE TEACHER / JAPAN ASSOCIATION OF LANGUAGE TEACHERS, THE (JA/0289-7938) [11393225] **3296**

LANGUAGE TEACHING (UK/0261-4448) [08321333] 1899, 3296, **3336**

LANGUAGE TESTING (UK/0265-5322) [11309224] **3296**

LANGUAGE TRAINING (UK) [12267788] **689**

LANGUAGE VARIATION AND CHANGE (US/0954-3945) [19133382] **3296**

●LANGUAGES IN EUROPE (UK/0965-240X) [I0965240X] 3296, **1761**

LANGUAGES OF ASIA AND AFRICA (UK/0261-0116) [09150626] **3296**

●LANGUAGES OF DESIGN (NE/0927-3034) [27026673] **3296**

LANGUAGES OF SOUTH INDIA (CN/0316-7429) [06965843] **3296**

●LANGUAGES OF THE WORLD (GW/0940-0788) [24637076] **3296**

LANGUAGES OF THE WORLD. CD-ROM (US) **3296**

LANGUE ET CULTURES (SZ) **3296**

LANGUE ET LITTERATURE FRANCAISES AU CANADA (1970) (CN/0384-5710) [02569828] 3403, **3296**

LANGUE FRANCAISE (FR/0023-8368) [01303744] **3296**

LANGUES ET LINGUISTIQUE (CN/0226-7144) [08809928] **3296**

LANGUES MODERNES, LES (FR/0023-8376) [01755544] 1899, **3296**

LANGUES NEO-LATINES, LES (FR/0184-7570) [01955212] **3296**

LANGUES ORIENTALES ANCIENNES PHILOLOGIE ET LINGUISTIQUE (BE/0987-7738) [18854730] **3296**

LANIERA (IT) **5354**

LANIGAN ADVISOR (CN) **5788**

LANKA GUARDIAN (CE) [07413127] **2658**

LANLINE (GW) **1242**

LANS & INTERNETWORKING (UK) **1115**

LANSDOWNE LETTER, THE (CN/0821-6649) [09796229] **619**

LANSDOWNE'S CONSTRUCTION COSTS HANDBOOK (CN/0820-8794) [09551509] **619**

LANSING LABOR MARKET REVIEW See LANSING'S LABOR MARKET NEWS **1687**

LANSING METROPOLITAN QUARTERLY (US) **2622**

LANSING STATE JOURNAL (US/0274-9742) [06678181] **5692**

●LANSING'S LABOR MARKET NEWS (US) [25954343] **1687**

LANTBRUKSARET / LRF (SW) [10158497] **104**

LANTERN (US) [25004885] **1092**

LANTERN (SA/0023-8422) [02361847] **2499**

LANTERN (BAYTOWN, TEX.) (US) [17188235] **5751**

LANTERN'S CORE, THE (US/0047-4053) [04154188] **3222**

LANTERNU : GUIA PA NOS HISTORIA (NE) [10164189] **2622**

LANTHORN (HOUGHTON COLLEGE) (US) [08815065] **1092**

LANTMANNEN (SW) [03772994] **104**

LANTZVILLE LOG, THE (CN/0710-5487) [08713639] **5788**

LANZHOU DAXUE XUEBAO. ZIRAN ZIRAN KEXUE BAN (CC/0455-2059) [04337280] **5125**

LAO TUNG PAO HU (CH) [09038711] **2865**

LAO TUNG WEI SHENG YU HUAN CHING I HSUEH LABOUR HEALTH AND ENVIRONMENTAL MEDICINE (CC) [11008637] **2865**

LAOGRAPHIA (GR/1010-7266) [04265422] **2321**

LAOGRAPHIKE KYPROS (CY) [01792076] **2321**

●LAPAROSCOPIC SURGERY (CN/1188-0252) [26923468] **3969**

●LAPAROSCOPIC SURGERY UPDATE (US/1067-2036) [27160935] **3604**

LAPEER COUNTY PRESS See COUNTY PRESS (LAPEER, MICH.) **5691**

LAPEL PIN POTPOURRI (US/0738-2936) [09563331] 374, **5184**

LAPIDARY JOURNAL, THE (US/0023-8457) [01755549] **2915**

LAPIDUS LETTER, THE **CEASED.** (US/0742-7972) [10446456] **2537**

LAPIN AU QUEBEC, LE (CN/0381-7415) [02412041] **2537**

●LAPIN MAGAZINE (CN/1188-8717) [26715090] **5515**

LAPIN TUTKIMUSASEMA KEVO See REPORTS FROM THE KEVO SUBARCTIC RESEARCH STATION **4171**

LAPIS (MILAN, ITALY) (IT) [19006231] **5560**

LAPIS (MUNCHEN) (GW/0342-2933) [03462089] **1357**

LAPIZ : REVISTA MENSUAL DE ARTE (SP/0212-1700) [14961409] **356**

LAPORAN DEPARTEMEN TENAGA KERJA, TRANSMIGRASI DAN KOPERASI (IO) [01797859] **1687**

LAPORAN DINAS PERINDUSTRIAN DAERAH ISTIMEWA YOGYAKARTA (IO) [03130381] **1572**

LAPORAN DIREKTORAL JENDERAL INDUSTRI KIMIA (IO) [02989583] **984**

LAPORAN - KANTOR WILAYAH DEPARTEMEN PERDAGANGAN PROPINSI JAWA TIMUR (IO) [02416064] **844**

LAPORAN - KANTOR WILAYAH DEPARTEMEN PERINDUSTRIAN DAERAH ISTIMEWA YOGYAKARTA (IO) [04698607] **1572**

LAPORAN KEGIATAN DEPARTEMEN SOSIAL (IO) [02245660] **5251**

LAPORAN KEGIATAN - DEWAN PIMPINAN PUSAT, HIMPUNAN NELAYAN SELURUH INDONESIA (IO) [04276718] **1687**

LAPORAN KEGIATAN KANTOR WILAYAH DEP. SOSIAL & DINAS SOSIAL PROPINSI DAERAH TINGKAT I LAMPUNG (IO) [02659403] **5294**

LAPORAN KEGIATAN YAYASAN TENAGA KERJA INDONESIA (IO) [04689674] **1687**

LAPORAN KEPALA KANTOR SENSUS DAN STATISTIK DKI JAKARTA (IO) [06463349] **5332**

LAPORAN KERJA PENGURUS BESAR PERSATUAN GURU REPUBLIK INDONESIA (IO) [03376654] **1761**

LAPORAN KERJA - PERWAKILAN DEPARTEMEN SOSIAL DAERAH TINGKAT I SUMATERA SELATAN (IO) [02412797] **5294**

LAPORAN / LEMBAGA STUDI PEMBANGUNAN (IO) [10510912] **1572**

LAPORAN METEOROLOGI DAN GEOFISIKA (IO) [18361182] 1408, **1427**

LAPORAN PASARAN HARTA (IO) [07254950] **4840**

LAPORAN PELAKSANAAN KULIAH KERJA NYATA, K.K.N (IO) [03210996] **1834**

LAPORAN PELAKSANAAN KULIAH KERJA NYATA MAHASISWA UNIVERSITAS SRIWIJAYA (IO) [05332227] **1834**

LAPORAN PELAKSANAAN TUGAS-TUGAS & I.E. DAN PEDOMAN PELAKSANAAN TUGAS-TUGAS (IO) [06515463] **5294**

LAPORAN PENELITIAN PERIKANAN LAUT See JURNAL PENELITIAN PERIKANAN LAUT **2307**

LAPORAN PERUSAHAAN - BIRO KLASIFIKASI INDONESIA (IO) [01800406] **5451**

LAPORAN REKTOR PADA DIES NATALIS UNIVERSITAS INDONESIA (IO) [02239644] **1834**

LAPORAN STATISTIK BRI (IO) [03301065] 796, **731**

LAPORAN STATISTIK BULANAN - BAGIAN PENGUMPULAN DAN PENGOLAHAN DATA, BIRO PERENCANAAN, DEPARTEMEN TENAGA KERJA, TRANSMIGRASI DAN KOPERASI (IO) [04402352] 1687, **1535**

LAPORAN - SURVEY AGRO EKONOMI INDONESIA (IO) [03296815] **104**

LAPORAN TAHUN ANGGARAN DIREKTORAT JENDERAL TRANSMIGRASI (IO) [03134977] **1502**

LAPORAN TAHUNAN (IO) [05116817] **1572**

LAPORAN TAHUNAN (IO) [08499989] **463**

LAPORAN TAHUNAN (IO) [05325003] **2386**

LAPORAN TAHUNAN (IO) [23659325] **796**

LAPORAN TAHUNAN BIRO PROYEK KHUSUS BKKBN (IO) [03942374] **589**

LAPORAN TAHUNAN - DEPALINDO (IO) [04144207] **5451**

LAPORAN TAHUNAN - DEPARTEMEN PEKERJAAN UMUM DAN TENAGA LISTRIK, BIRO VII : UMUM (IO) [04413070] **1615**

LAPORAN Alphabetical Title Index

LAPORAN TAHUNAN / DEPARTEMEN PERDAGANGAN DAN KOPERASI, KANTOR WILAYAH PERDAGANGAN PROPINSI JAWA TIMUR (IO) [09563821] **844**

LAPORAN TAHUNAN - DINAS KEHUTANAN PROPINSI SUMATERA UTARA (IO) [02468425] **2386**

LAPORAN TAHUNAN / DINAS SOSIAL DAERAH TINGKAT I SUMATERA UTARA (IO) [23375563] **5294**

LAPORAN TAHUNAN DINAS TENAGA KERJA DAERAH ISTIMEWA YOGYAKARTA (IO) [01790726] **1687**

LAPORAN TAHUNAN - DIREKTORAT JENDERAL HUBUNGAN EKONOMI LUAR NEGERI (IO) [02245661] **844**

LAPORAN TAHUNAN / DIREKTORAT JENDERAL PERHUBUNGAN LAUT, KANTOR WILAYAH II, PELABUHAN DUMAI (IO) [09872785] **1615**

LAPORAN TAHUNAN DIREKTORAT NAVIGASI (IO) [01790758] **5451**

LAPORAN TAHUNAN DIREKTORAT PERLINDUNGAN DAN PENGAWETAN ALAM (IO) [02465585] **4167**

LAPORAN TAHUNAN - INSPEKTORAT PERKEBUNAN BESAR DAERAH IV RIAU (IO) [05758742] **104**

LAPORAN TAHUNAN - KANTOR WILAYAH DEPARTEMEN PERINDUSTRIAN PROPINSI BALI (IO) [04869976] **1572**

LAPORAN TAHUNAN - KANTOR WILAYAH DEPARTEMEN PERINDUSTRIAN PROPINSI SULAWESI TENGAH (IO) [03011377] 1572, **1535**

LAPORAN TAHUNAN KEGIATAN USAHA PERTAMBANGAN SWASTA NASIONAL DAN PERUSAHAAN PERTAMBANGAN DAERAH (IO) [04427801] **1615**

LAPORAN TAHUNAN ... KETUA PENGARAH INSURANS (MY/0126-8252) [09289348] **2886**

LAPORAN TAHUNAN PUSAT DOKUMENTASI ILMIAH NASIONAL (IO) [02605096] **396**

LAPORAN TAHUNAN PUSAT PENELITIAN DAN PENGEMBANGAN GEOLOGI (IO) [07994692] **1386**

LAPORAN TAHUNAN - YAYASAN PENGURUSAN MALAYSIA (MY) [02243227] **875**

LAPORAN TENTANG PELAKSANAAN PROYEK-PROYEK PEMBANGUNAN YANG DIPERTANGGUNG JAWABKAN PADA DEPARTEMEN TENAGA KERJA, TRANSMIGRASI DAN KOPERASI R.I (IO) [02240281] **1687**

LAPORAN TRIWULAN - DIREKTORAT JENDERAL PAJAK (IO) [03199905] **4735**

LAPORAN TRIWULAN - PERWAKILAN DEPARTEMEN PERDAGANGAN PROPINSI DJAWA-TIMUR (IO) [01784323] **844**

LAPORAN - WALIKOTA JAKARTA PUSAT (IO) [01797858] **4661**

LAPORAN - WALIKOTA JAKARTA TIMUR (IO) [01795916] **4661**

LAPORTE-BAYSHORE SUN See BAYSHORE SUN, THE **5747**

LAPSILISA (FI) [19247065] **5294**

LAPURAN TAHUN DAN KIRA-KIRA See LAPURAN TAHUNAN ... BAGI TAHUN BERAKHIR 31HB MAC **1615**

LAPURAN TAHUN DAN KIRA-KIRA - MALAYSIA INDUSTRIAL ESTATES SENDIRIAN BERHAD (MY) [03235319] 4840, **1502**

LAPURAN TAHUNAN ... BAGI TAHUN BERAKHIR 31HB MAC (MY) [06643292] **1615**

LAPURAN TAHUNAN - JABATAN PELAJARAN MELAKA (MY) [02245939] **1761**

LAPURAN TAHUNAN - JABATAN PERTANIAN NEGERI PAHANG (MY) [03244551] **104**

LAPURAN TAHUNAN / JABATAN TELEKOM MALAYSIA (MY) [08909210] **1159**

LAPURAN TAHUNAN - MAJLIS PENGELUAR-PENGELUAR GETAH MALAYSIA (MY/0126-8309) [01799334] **5076**

LAPURAN TAHUNAN - MAKTAB KERJASAMA MALAYSIA (MY) [03511979] **1615**

LAPURAN TAHUNAN - PERSATUAN KELAB-KELAB BELIA MALAYSIA (MY) [03161544] **2282**

LAPURAN TAHUNAN - SURUHANJAYA PERKHIDMATAN AWAM NEGERI SABAH (MY) [02027025] **4704**

LAPURAN TAHUNAN SURUHANJAYA PERKHIDMATAN AWAM NEGERI SABAH (MY) [01790739] **4661**

LARAMIE DAILY BOOMERANG (LARAMIE, WYO. : 1957) (US) [14928921] **5772**

LAREDO MORNING TIMES (US/0740-5227) [09978613] **5751**

LARES (FIRENZE) (IT) [02295440] 2321, **240**

LARGE ANIMAL VETERINARIAN COVERING HEALTH & NUTRITION (US/1043-7533) [18603490] **5515**

LARGE ANIMAL VETERINARY REPORT (US/1069-1774) [22216385] **5515**

LARGE CLASS I HOUSEHOLD GOODS CARRIERS SELECTED EARNINGS DATA (US) [05187336] 5441, **5385**

LARGE CLASS I MOTOR CARRIERS OF PROPERTY SELECTED EARNINGS DATA (US) [04176276] 844, **5385**

LARGE CORPORATE BANKING (US/0197-4181) [04850084] **796**

LARGE EMPLOYERS IN MASSACHUSETTS, THE (US/0145-8760) [02806094] **1687**

LARGE PRINT BOOKS / GEORGIAN BAY REGIONAL LIBRARY SYSTEM (CN/0229-4370) [07966327] **4829**

LARGE-PRINT SCORES AND BOOKS CATALOG (US/0363-8472) [04525695] 4390, 3403, **4128**

LARGE SPACE STRUCTURES & SYSTEMS IN THE SPACE STATION ERA (US) [23671748] **27**

LARGO CONSUMO (IT) 1502, **929**

LARIMORE PIONEER, THE (US) [20706999] **5725**

LARKSPUR REPORT, THE (US/0895-8505) [16824604] **4480**

LARMAC CONSOLIDATED INDEX TO THE CONSTITUTION AND LAWS OF CALIFORNIA (US) [07062314] **2993**

LAROUCO / GRUPO ARQUEOLOXICO LAROUCO (SP) [25066170] 240, **273**

LARU STUDIES (CN/0704-1217) [04296416] **4661**

LARUE COUNTY HERALD NEWS, THE (US) [13868284] **5681**

LARVICULTURE & ARTEMIA NEWSLETTER (BE/0779-1119) [07791119] **2307**

LARY CREWS THEATRE GRAPEVINE See SUNCOAST THEATRE GRAPEVINE, THE **5369**

LARYNGO- RHINO- OTOLOGIE (GW/0935-8943) [19683992] **3889**

LARYNGOSCOPE. SUPPLEMENT, THE (US) [04292933] **3889**

LARYNGOSCOPE, THE (US/0023-852X) [01755551] **3889**

LAS AMERICAS (US/1045-1013) [20065090] **2543**

LAS AMERICAS JOURNAL (US/0891-0650) [14577049] **4480**

LAS CRUCES BULLETIN (US/0885-8527) [12764876] **5814**

LAS CRUCES SUN-NEWS (US) [11302799] **5712**

LAS VEGAN (US/0199-7254) [06104554] **2537**

LAS VEGAN CITY MAGAZINE (US) [22104803] **2537**

LAS VEGAS See LAS VEGAS INTERNATIONALE **2537**

●LAS VEGAS BUSINESS PRESS (US/1071-2186) [27567137] **5708**

●LAS VEGAS CASINO JOURNAL (US) [26187303] **4862**

LAS VEGAS INSIDER, THE (US/0271-0145) [06544260] **2537**

LAS VEGAS INTERNATIONALE (US/0886-165X) [12862476] **2537**

LAS VEGAS OPTIC (US) [07880971] **5712**

LAS VEGAS REVIEW-JOURNAL (US) [08079993] **5707**

LAS VEGAS SUN (US) [10033184] **5707**

LAS VIRGENES ENTERPRISE (US/0193-9904) [05282935] **5636**

LASA FORUM / LATIN AMERICAN STUDIES ASSOCIATION (US/0890-7218) [10005251] 5208, **2743**

LASER AND PARTICLE BEAMS (UK/0263-0346) [09427416] **4437**

LASER & TECHNOLOGY (IT) [25007261] **4437**

LASER: APPLICAZIONI INDUSTRIALI TECHNOLOGIE MERCATO (IT) **5125**

LASER CHEMISTRY (SZ/0278-6273) [07853790] **984**

LASER DISC NEWSLETTER, THE (US/0749-5250) [11136006] **5317**

LASER DISC REVIEW (UK/0267-9671) [02679671] **5125**

LASER FOCUS MID-MONTH REPORT See LASER REPORT **4437**

LASER FOCUS WORLD (US/1043-8092) [19045940] **4437**

LASER FOCUS WORLD BUYERS' GUIDE (US) [18977457] **4437**

LASER INTERACTION AND RELATED PLASMA PHENOMENA (US/0148-0987) [03267396] **4411**

LASER NURSING (US/0888-6075) [13664099] **3861**

LASER PHYSICS (RU/1054-660X) [22937678] **4411**

LASER-PRAXIS (GW/0937-7069) [21968179] **4437**

LASER-RAMAN & INFRARED SPECTROSCOPY ABSTRACTS (UK) [02484874] **4437**

LASER REPORT (US/0023-8600) [04723220] **4437**

LASER THERAPY (UK/0898-5901) [17855745] **4437**

LASER UND OPTOELEKTRONIK (GW/0722-9003) [08835679] **4411**

LASERJET JOURNAL CEASED. (US/1054-3724) [15498330] **4566**

LASERMEDIZIN : ORGAN DER DEUTSCHEN GESELLSCHAFT FUER LASERMEDIZIN (GW/0938-765X) [25007204] **3969**

LASERS AND LIGHT IN OPHTHALMOLOGY (NE/0922-5307) [20052191] **3876**

LASERS & OPTRONICS (US/0892-9947) [15310584] **4438**

LASERS IN ENGINEERING (US/0898-1507) [17729761] **1985**

LASERS IN MEDICAL SCIENCE (UK/0268-8921) [13165306] **3604**

LASERS IN MEDICINE CEASED. (NE/0925-8434) [24375446] **3604**

LASERS IN SURGERY AND MEDICINE (US/0196-8092) [05899718] **3969**

LASERS IN THE LIFE SCIENCES (SZ/0886-0467) [12817842] **4438**

LASERTONE NEWS (US) **4566**

LASHON VE-IVRIT CEASED. (IS) [22389509] **3296**

LASSALETTER (CN/0820-8700) [10082662] **1761**

LASSEN COUNTY TIMES (US) **5636**

LAST GASP (CN/0710-6920) [08469644] **2177**

LAST OG BUSS (NO/0802-7870) [08027870] **5418**

LAST RIGHTS (CN/1198-3922) [30801470] **2252**

LAST WORD (FRIENDSWOOD, TEX.), THE (US/1057-0055) [23906839] 3403, **2922**

LASTECHNIEK (NE/0023-8694) [05179864] **4027**

LATAH COUNTY GENEALOGICAL SOCIETY CEASED. (US/0747-6663) [10764958] **2458**

LATAX REPORT (US/0745-4449) [09178823] **4736**

LATE IMPERIAL CHINA (US/0884-3236) [12271932] **2658**

LATEINAMERIKA (GW/0176-2818) [11586013] **2743**

LATEINAMERIKA-KURIER (SZ) 1502, **689**

LATEINAMERIKA NACHRICHTEN (SZ) [04755079] **1572**

LATEINAMERIKA STUDIEN (GW/0343-3781) [04521560] **2743**

LATENT IMAGE (US/0198-585X) [04608374] **302**

LATER YEARS (LAFAYETTE, IND.), THE SUSPENDED. (US/0892-6921) [15246616] **5294**

LATERANUM (VC/1010-7215) [02298919] **4972**

LATEST COMPOSITE FEATURE RELEASE SCHEDULE (US/0889-4566) [14073142] **324**

LATEST EDITIONS OF U.S. AIR FORCE AERONAUTICAL CHARTS (US/0364-6793) [02572557] 27, **4048**

LATEST INFORMATION ON NATIONAL ACCOUNTS OF DEVELOPING COUNTRIES. INFORMATIONS RECENTES SUR LES COMPTES NATIONAUX DES PAYS EN DEVELOPPEMENT (FR) [05805834] **1502**

LATEST SCOOP, THE (US/0732-0620) [04781509] **2348**

●LATEST WORD (PHILADELPHIA, PA.), THE (US/1067-716X) [27329411] **3604**

LATHAM LETTER, THE (US/0740-5820) [08682361] **2177**

LATIN AMERICA AND CARIBBEAN CONTEMPORARY RECORD (US/0736-9700) [09121535] **2743**

LATIN AMERICA AND THE CARIBBEAN : SELECTED ECONOMIC AND SOCIAL DATA (US) [24393811] **2911**

LATIN AMERICA BIBLIOGRAPHY SERIES (US) [05470716] **418**

LATIN AMERICA COMMENTARY (US) [23712762] **2743**

LATIN AMERICA CONSENSUS FORECASTS (UK/0957-0950) [09684972] 1637, **1502**

LATIN AMERICA EVANGELIST (US) [01777018] **4973**

Alphabetical Title Index — LAURENS

LATIN AMERICA FINANCE **SUSPENDED.** (US/0887-882X) [13438622] **796**

LATIN AMERICA MONITOR. ANDEAN GROUP (UK) [24857304] **1572**

LATIN AMERICA MONITOR. CENTRAL AMERICA (UK) [25002969] **1502**

LATIN AMERICA MONITOR. MEXICO & BRAZIL (UK) [24998757] **1503**

LATIN AMERICA MONITOR. SOUTHERN CONE (UK) [24857299] **1503**

LATIN AMERICA PETROLEUM DIRECTORY (US/0193-8738) [04048921] **4263**

LATIN AMERICA REGIONAL REPORTS. ANDEAN GROUP (UK/0143-5248) [05777828] **1572**

LATIN AMERICA REGIONAL REPORTS. BRAZIL (UK/0143-5272) [05712375] **1572**

LATIN AMERICA REGIONAL REPORTS. CARIBBEAN (UK/0143-523X) [05761483] **1572**

LATIN AMERICA REGIONAL REPORTS. MEXICO & CENTRAL AMERICA **CEASED.** (UK/0143-5264) [05758727] **1572**

LATIN AMERICA REGIONAL REPORTS. SOUTHERN CONE (UK/0143-5256) [05804606] **1572**

LATIN AMERICA (WASHINGTON) (US/0092-4148) [01789268] **2743**

LATIN AMERICAN ADVISOR, THE (US/1062-4651) [25636058] **1503**

LATIN AMERICAN ANTHROPOLOGY REVIEW, THE (US/1045-7577) [20252631] **240**

LATIN AMERICAN ANTIQUITY (US/1045-6635) [20181183] **273**

LATIN AMERICAN APPLIED RESEARCH / PESQUISA APLICADA LATINO AMERICANA / INVESTIGACION APLICADA LATINOAMERICANA (AG/0327-0793) [19614122] **2014**

LATIN AMERICAN ART (US/1042-9808) [19275113] **356**

LATIN AMERICAN BUSINESS ADVISOR / UNIVERSITY OF MIAMI (US) [25303006] **1503**

LATIN AMERICAN ECONOMIC OUTLOOK (US/8756-1301) [10932357] **1572**

LATIN AMERICAN ECONOMY & BUSINESS (UK/0960-8702) [22655583] **1637**

LATIN AMERICAN EVANGELICAL CENTER FOR PASTORAL STUDIES *See* OCCASIONAL ESSAYS **4983**

LATIN AMERICAN HISTORICAL DICTIONARIES (US) [02298937] **2743**

LATIN AMERICAN INDEX (US/0090-9416) [03832395] **4480**

LATIN AMERICAN INDEX, LTD *See* LATIN AMERICAN INDEX **4480**

LATIN AMERICAN INDIAN LITERATURES JOURNAL (US/0888-5613) [12169447] **3403**

LATIN AMERICAN ISSUES (US/0741-3378) [10157705] **2743**

LATIN AMERICAN JEWISH STUDIES ASSOCIATION *See* LATIN AMERICAN JEWISH STUDIES NEWSLETTER (1983) **5050**

LATIN AMERICAN JEWISH STUDIES NEWSLETTER (1983) (US/0738-1379) [09534990] **5050**

●LATIN AMERICAN LAW & BUSINESS REPORT (US/1065-7428) [26709734] **3101**

LATIN AMERICAN LITERARY REVIEW (US/0047-4134) [01784953] **3345**

LATIN AMERICAN MINING LETTER (UK/0267-5099) [09515686] **2143**

LATIN AMERICAN MONITOR. CARIBBEAN (UK) [25005884] **1572**

LATIN AMERICAN NEWSLINE (UK) [I09696660] **2512**

LATIN AMERICAN PERSPECTIVES (US/0094-582X) [01794709] **4542**

LATIN AMERICAN POPULATION HISTORY BULLETIN (US/1050-2351) [20951089] **4554, 2743**

LATIN AMERICAN REGIONAL REPORTS. BRAZIL *See* BRAZIL REPORT **1549**

LATIN AMERICAN RESEARCH REVIEW (US/0023-8791) [01588206] **2743**

LATIN AMERICAN RESERVE FUND *See* ANNUAL REPORT / LATIN AMERICAN RESERVE FUND **771**

LATIN AMERICAN REVIEW (LEXINGTON, MASS.) (US/0732-6270) [08379748] **1572**

LATIN AMERICAN ROUNDUP (FR) [04146975] **2744**

LATIN AMERICAN SATELLITE DIRECTORY (US) **1159**

LATIN AMERICAN SERIALS LIST / U.T. AUSTIN, GENERAL LIBRARIES, BENSON COLLECTION (US) [10186972] **3222**

LATIN AMERICAN SPECIAL REPORTS (UK/0264-2867) [10189330] **2512**

LATIN AMERICAN SPECIAL REPORTS (UK/0264-2867) [15356310] **2552**

LATIN AMERICAN STUDIES CENTER MONOGRAPH SERIES (US/0076-8189) [01757310] **2744**

LATIN AMERICAN STUDIES IN THE UNIVERSITIES AND POLYTECHNICS OF THE UNITED KINGDOM (UK) [22190916] **2552**

LATIN AMERICAN STUDIES (SAKURA-MURA, IBARAKI-KEN, JAPAN) (JA/0285-3582) [07938075] **2744**

LATIN AMERICAN STUDIES WORKING PAPERS (US) [01781376] **2744**

●LATIN AMERICAN TELECOM REPORT (US/1062-3884) [25603027] **1115**

LATIN AMERICAN THEATRE REVIEW (US/0023-8813) [01639559] **5372, 5365**

LATIN AMERICAN TIMES (BOGOTA) (US/0265-0886) [04968943] **2744**

LATIN AMERICAN TRAVEL & PAN AMERICAN HIGHWAY GUIDE (US/0075-8159) [01783248] **5441, 5482**

LATIN AMERICAN UURBAN RESEARCH (US/0075-8167) [00994533] **2827**

LATIN AMERICAN WEEKLY REPORT (UK/0143-5280) [14087111] **2489**

LATIN AMERICAN WORKING GROUP *See* L. A. W. G. LETTER **4480**

LATIN AMERICAN YEARLY REVIEW, THE (FR) [02673471] **3346**

●LATIN MASS, THE (US/1064-556X) [26327441] **5031**

LATIN MUSIC YEARBOOK, THE (US/0278-7989) [07860423] **4128**

LATIN N.Y (US) [08889933] **2267**

LATINAMERICA PRESS (PE) [03547208] **2744**

LATINAMERICAN FORESTRY BIBLIOGRAPHY / INSTITUTO FORESTAL LATINOAMERICANO (VE/0798-1945) [12934855] **517, 2386**

LATINAMERIKA-INSTITUTET I STOCKHOLM *See* INFORME ANUAL / INSTITUTO DE ESTUDIOS LATINOAMERICANOS. UNIVERSIDAD DE ESTOCOLMO **2739**

LATINFINANCE (CORAL GABLES, FLA.) (US/1048-535X) [19214829] **796**

LATINGRAFICA (SP) [03286104] **380, 4566**

LATINITAS (VC/0023-883X) [01642567] **3296**

LATINO AMERICA (MX/0460-1955) [02289827] **2267**

LATINO DATA BULLETIN (US) [24959970] **2267**

LATINO STUDIES JOURNAL (US/1066-1344) [19637169] **2267**

●LATINO STUDIES JOURNAL / NORTHEASTERN UNIVERSITY (US) [30410462] **2267**

LATINOAMERICANA (STOCKHOLM) (SW) [05040568] **2512**

LATINOGRAMA **CEASED.** (US/0890-863X) [05688109] **2267**

LATINSKAIA AMERIKA (RU/0044-748X) [24851214] **2744**

LATINSKAIA AMERIKA (KHUDOZHESTVENNAIA LITERATURA (FIRM)) (RU) [12783934] **3403**

LATIUM (IT/0393-6813) [15814166] **2849**

LATOHATAR (HU) [01792282] **3346**

LATOMUS (BE/0023-8856) [01755564] **3296, 3404**

LATROBE BULLETIN (US) [13379254] **5737**

LATTE 1976, IL (IT/0392-6060) [I03926060] **196**

LATTICE (US) **1441**

LATVIA (LV) [02322986] **2696**

LATVIA - BALTIC STATE (LV) **2518**

●LATVIAN DIMENSIONS (US/1062-9505) [25820437] **2267**

LATVIAN JOURNAL OF PHYSICS AND TECHNICAL SCIENCES (LV/0868-8257) [25910323] **4411**

LATVIESU INZENIERU APVIENIBA *See* TECHNIKAS APSKATS - LATVIESU INZENIERU APVIENIBA **1998**

LATVIESU VALODAS KULTURAS JAUTAJUMI (LV/0130-0059) [08694504] **3296**

●LATVIIAS LAIKS (LV) [25759473] **5806**

LATVIJAS EV.-LUT. BAZNICAS GADA GRAMATA UN KALENDARS (US) [04080584] **4973**

LATVIJAS EVAN *See* LATVIJAS EV.-LUT. BAZNICAS GADA GRAMATA UN KALENDARS **4973**

LATVIJAS KIMIJAS ZURNALS (LV/0868-8249) [23954696] **984**

LATVIJAS PADOMJU SOCIALISTISKAS REPUBLIKAS ZINATNU AKADEMIJA. RADIOASTROFIZIKAS OBSERVATORIJA *See* BIULLETEN RADIOASTROFIZICHESKOI OBSERVATORII AKADEMII NAUK LATVIISKOI **3296**

LATVIJAS PSR PRESES HRONIKA; LATVIJAS PSR VALSTS REGISTRACIJAS UN ANALITISKAS BIBLIOGRAFIJAS ORGANS (LV/0023-8910) [01641084] **418**

LATVIJAS ZINATNU AKADEMIJAS VESTIS (LV/0868-6556) [22635827] **5125**

LATVIJSKIJ MATEMATICESKIJ EZEGODNIK (LV/0321-2270) [01956929] **3516**

LATVJU MAKSLA (US/0362-7047) [02320017] **356**

LAUGH COMICS DIGEST MAGAZINE (US/8750-0612) [10956832] **4862**

LAUGH FACTORY (US/0748-3090) [10920985] **2537**

LAUGH (MAMARONECK, N.Y.) **CEASED.** (US/0023-8945) [17012023] **4863**

LAUGHING BEAR NEWSLETTER (US/1056-0327) [03356505] **4816**

LAUGHING MATTERS (US/0731-1788) [08139627] **4863**

LAUNDRY AND DRY CLEANING WAGE SURVEY, BALTIMORE, MD. / U.S. DEPARTMENT OF LABOR, BUREAU OF LABOR STATISTICS (US) [08125530] **1687**

LAUNDRY AND DRY CLEANING WAGE SURVEY, DETROIT, MICH. / U.S. DEPARTMENT OF LABOR, BUREAU OF LABOR STATISTICS (US) [08464074] **1687**

LAUNDRY AND DRY CLEANING WAGE SURVEY, MIDDLESEX, MONMOUTH, AND OCEAN COUNTIES, N.J. / U.S. DEPARTMENT OF LABOR, BUREAU OF LABOR STATISTICS (US) [08463108] **1687**

LAUNDRY AND DRY CLEANING WAGE SURVEY, MONTANA / U.S. DEPARTMENT OF LABOR, BUREAU OF LABOR STATISTICS (US) [08462655] **1687**

LAUNDRY AND DRY CLEANING WAGE SURVEY, PORTLAND, OREG.-WASH. / U.S. DEPARTMENT OF LABOR, BUREAU OF LABOR STATISTICS (US) [08463952] **1687**

LAUNDRY AND DRY CLEANING WAGE SURVEY, PORTSMOUTH-CHILLICOTHE-GALLIPOLIS, OHIO / U.S. DEPARTMENT OF LABOR, BUREAU OF LABOR STATISTICS (US) [09288845] **1687**

LAUNDRY AND DRY CLEANING WAGE SURVEY, PUERTO RICO / U.S. DEPARTMENT OF LABOR, BUREAU OF LABOR STATISTICS (US) [09288962] **1687**

LAUNDRY AND DRY CLEANING WAGE SURVEY, SOUTHEASTERN MASSACHUSETTS / U.S. DEPARTMENT OF LABOR, BUREAU OF LABOR STATISTICS (US) [08123969] **1687**

LAUNDRY AND DRY CLEANING WAGE SURVEY, TUCSON-DOUGLAS, ARIZ. / U.S. DEPARTMENT OF LABOR, BUREAU OF LABOR STATISTICS (US) [08463501] **1687**

LAUNDRY AND DRY CLEANING WAGE SURVEY, WASHINGTON, D.C.-MD.-VA. / U.S. DEPARTMENT OF LABOR, BUREAU OF LABOR STATISTICS (US) [08466483] **1687**

LAUNDRY AND DRY CLEANING WAGE SURVEY, WESTERN AND NORTHERN MASSACHUSETTS / U.S. DEPARTMENT OF LABOR, BUREAU OF LABOR STATISTICS (US) [08462745] **1687**

LAUNDRY AND DRY CLEANING WAGE SURVEY, WICHITA, KAN. / U.S. DEPARTMENT OF LABOR, BUREAU OF LABOR STATISTICS (US) [08463825] **1687**

LAUNDRY NEWS (US/0164-5765) [04508166] **1027, 5354**

LAUREATY LENINSKOGO KOMSOMOLA (RU) [01799920] **3404**

LAUREL LEADER (US/0748-528X) [10960357] **5686**

LAUREL LEADER-CALL (LAUREL, MISS. : 1936) (US) [10307959] **5701**

LAUREL MESSENGER (US/0023-8988) [04090763] **2458, 2744**

LAUREL OUTLOOK (US) [13842507] **5705**

LAUREL REVIEW / WEST VIRGINIA WESLEYAN COLLEGE, THE (US/0023-9003) [02263449] **3404**

LAURENCE WITTEN. CATALOGUE *See* CATALOGUE - LAURENCE WITTEN RARE BOOKS **4827**

LAURENCE WITTEN RARE BOOKS *See* CATALOGUE - LAURENCE WITTEN RARE BOOKS **4827**

LAURENS COUNTY ADVERTISER, THE (US) [28173657] **5742**

LAURENTIAN — Alphabetical Title Index

LAURENTIAN SUN (CN/1182-8323) [23230486] **5788**

LAURENTIAN UNIVERSITY OF SUDBURY See GAZETTE - LAURENTIAN UNIVERSITY **1825**

LAURENTIANUM (IT/0023-902X) [05066099] **5031**

LAURIER CAMPUS (CN/0700-5105) [03279425] **1834**

LAURISTON S. TAYLOR LECTURES IN RADIATION PROTECTION AND MEASUREMENTS (US/0277-9196) [07659335] **4788**

LAVAGGIO INDUSTRIALE (IT) **1615**

LAVAL THEOLOGIQUE ET PHILOSOPHIQUE (CN/0023-9054) [05768296] **4352, 4973**

LAVAL THEOLOGIQUE ET PHILOSOPHIQUE (CN/0023-9054) [01755569] **4352, 4973**

LAVAL UNIVERSITY. FOREST RESEARCH FOUNDATION See NOTE TECHNIQUE - LE FONDS DE RECHERCHES FORESTIERES DE L'UNIVERSITE LAVAL **2390**

LAVALIN (CN/0704-5689) [05787732] **1985**

LAVALIN (ENGLISH EDITION) (CN/0227-7964) [06703447] **1985**

LAVALIN INC See LAVALIN (ENGLISH EDITION) **1985**

LAVALIN INC See LAVALIN **1985**

LAVANT - SCENE DU THEATRE (FR) [07098730] **4073**

LAVENDER LINE, THE (US) [09209494] **2458**

LAVENTHOL & HORWATH PERSPECTIVE CEASED. (US/0147-2208) [03128741] **747**

LAVORO 80. QUADERNI (IT) [13202058] **3151**

LAVORO CRITICO (IT) [02370228] **3404**

LAVORO E DIRITTO (IT) [18933757] **3151**

LAVORO E MEDICINA (IT/0391-3147) [I03913147] **3604**

LAVORO E PREVIDENZA OGGI (IT/0390-251X) [02242204] **3151**

LAVORO E SICUREZZA SOCIALE (IT) [05210863] **5494**

LAVORO E SINDACATO CEASED. (IT/0390-0991) [02852444] **1687**

LAVORO INFORMAZIONE (IT) **1687**

LAVORO NELLA GIURISPRUDENZA, IL (IT) **2993**

LAVORO SICURO (IT/0390-2528) [I03902528] **2865**

LAVORO SICURO (IT) **1687**

LAVOROSOCIETA SUSPENDED. (IT) **1687**

LAVOURA ARROZEIRA (BL/0023-9143) [06621106] **104**

LAW ALMANAC (AT) [01755574] **2993**

●LAW ALUMNI DIRECTORY, ST. MARY'S UNIVERSITY SCHOOL OF LAW (US) [25606211] **2993**

LAW ALUMNI JOURNAL, THE (US/0458-8428) [02742761] **2993, 1102**

LAW & ANTHROPOLOGY (AU/0259-0816) [15295484] **240, 2993**

LAW & BUSINESS DIRECTORY OF BANKRUPTCY ATTORNEYS (US/1064-0371) [16804435] **3087**

LAW & BUSINESS DIRECTORY OF CORPORATE COUNSEL (US/0272-4065) [06321324] **3101**

●LAW & BUSINESS DIRECTORY OF ENVIRONMENTAL ATTORNEYS (US/1064-0363) [24680057] **3114**

LAW & BUSINESS DIRECTORY OF LITIGATION ATTORNEYS (US/1062-2470) [20505671] **3090**

LAW AND CONTEMPORARY PROBLEMS (US/0023-9186) [01606534] **2994**

LAW AND CRITIQUE (UK/0957-8536) [18410327] **2994**

LAW AND ETHICS OF THE VETERINARY PROFESSION (US) [21170639] **5515, 2994**

LAW AND HISTORY REVIEW (US/0738-2480) [09548757] **2994**

LAW & HOUSING JOURNAL (US/0193-8290) [03702137] **2827, 2994**

LAW AND HUMAN BEHAVIOR (US/0147-7307) [03173559] **5251, 2994**

LAW & INEQUALITY (US/0737-089X) [09306912] **2994**

LAW AND INTERNATIONAL AFFAIRS (BG) [02679232] **3132**

LAW & JUSTICE (UK/0269-817X) [02441288] **2994**

LAW AND LEGAL INFORMATION DIRECTORY (US/0740-090X) [07151879] **2994**

LAW AND LEGISLATION IN THE GERMAN DEMOCRATIC REPUBLIC CEASED. (GW/0458-8460) [01755577] **2994**

LAW AND MENTAL HEALTH CEASED. (US/0890-5037) [14373183] **4788, 2994**

LAW AND ORDER (US/0023-9194) [02250430] **3168**

LAW AND PHILOSOPHY (NE/0167-5249) [08454773] **4352, 2994**

LAW & POLICY (UK/0265-8240) [10761514] **2994**

LAW AND POLICY IN INTERNATIONAL BUSINESS (US/0023-9208) [01755578] **3101**

LAW AND POLITICS BOOK REVIEW (US/1062-7421) [25724298] **4480, 2994**

LAW AND POPULATION PROGRAMME NEWSLETTER (US/0148-6136) [01781546] **4554, 2994**

LAW & PSYCHOLOGY REVIEW (US/0098-5961) [02241415] **2994**

LAW & SEXUALITY (US/1062-0680) [24611882] **2494, 2795**

LAW & SOCIAL INQUIRY (US/0897-6546) [17590005] **5251, 2994**

LAW AND SOCIETY NEWSLETTER See LAW AND SOCIETY QUARTERLY **2994**

LAW & SOCIETY NEWSLETTER (DENVER, COLO.) (US/8755-7088) [01640520] **2994**

LAW AND SOCIETY QUARTERLY (II/0377-0869) [01790633] **2994**

LAW & SOCIETY REVIEW (US/0023-9216) [01755580] **5208, 2994**

LAW AND STATE CEASED. (GW/0341-6151) [04630023] **4480, 3132**

LAW AND THE WORKPLACE (US/0747-6469) [10748759] **3151**

LAW ASSOCIATION FOR ASIA AND THE WESTERN PACIFIC See LAWASIA **2997**

LAW BOOKS IN PRINT / EDITED AND COMPILED BY J. MYRON JACOBSTEIN AND MEIRA G. PIMSLEUR (US) [08842126] **4829, 2995**

LAW BOOKS IN REVIEW (US/0886-0408) [01244757] **2995**

LAW BOOKS PUBLISHED (US/0023-9240) [03879465] **4829, 2995**

LAW BULLETIN (UNIVERSITY OF ZAMBIA. LAW ASSOCIATION) See LEGALITY : A JOURNAL OF THE UNIVERSITY OF ZAMBIA LAW ASSOCIATION **3001**

LAW CALENDAR (AT) [03251141] **2995**

LAW COMPUTERS AND ARTIFICIAL INTELLIGENCE (UK) **2995, 1214**

LAW DAY U.S.A. PLANNING GUIDE AND PROGRAM MANUAL (US) [06615941] **2995**

LAW DEPARTMENT MANAGEMENT ADVISER (US/1052-2972) [22249052] **875**

LAW DIGEST (RICHMOND, VA.) (US) [16160397] **3141**

LAW ENFORCEMENT BULLETIN (US) [04532766] **3168**

LAW ENFORCEMENT INTELLIGENCE ANALYSIS DIGEST (US/0895-3945) [16627150] **3168**

LAW ENFORCEMENT LEGAL REPORTER INCORPORATED, THE (US/0195-0290) [05225674] **3168**

LAW ENFORCEMENT LEGAL REVIEW (US/1070-9967) [07878776] **3107**

LAW ENFORCEMENT LEGAL SUMMARIES (US) [01784770] **3169**

LAW ENFORCEMENT LEGISLATIVE BUY-FUND : BIENNIUM REPORT (US) [08102011] **3169**

LAW ENFORCEMENT NEWS (US/0364-1724) [02566252] **3169**

LAW ENFORCEMENT OFFICERS KILLED AND ASSAULTED (US/0747-7961) [10083958] **3169**

LAW ENFORCEMENT REPORT See LAW ENFORCEMENT REPORT **3169**

LAW ENFORCEMENT REPORT (US/0094-8438) [02241262] **3169**

LAW ENFORCEMENT TECHNOLOGY (US/0747-3680) [10773609] **3169**

●LAW FIRM BENEFITS (US/1061-9410) [25489364] **2995**

LAW FIRM MARKETING AND PROFIT REPORT CEASED. (US) [29343070] **929, 2995**

LAW FIRM PARTNERSHIP REPORT (US/1056-2028) [23542132] **2995**

LAW FIRM PROFIT REPORT (US/0895-9412) [16859051] **2995**

LAW FIRMS YELLOW BOOK (US/1054-4054) [22877182] **2995, 1927**

LAW FOR BUSINESS (UK/0954-2809) [I09542809] **3101**

LAW FORUM SERIES (US) [01606418] **2995**

LAW GROUP DOCKET See DOCKET : A JOURNAL OF THE INTERNATIONAL HUMAN RIGHTS LAW GROUP **4507**

LAW GROUP DOCKET, THE (US) [07668602] **4510**

LAW HANDBOOK - REDFERN LEGAL CENTRE (AT/0814-4788) [I08144788] **2995**

LAW IN AMERICAN SOCIETY (US/0197-3886) [01642565] **2995**

LAW IN CONTEXT (BUNDOORA, VIC.) (AT/0811-5796) [10592404] **2995**

LAW IN EASTERN EUROPE (NE/0075-823X) [01589255] **2995**

LAW IN JAPAN (JA/0458-8584) [01604755] **2995**

LAW INFORMANT, THE (CN/1185-2534) [24368110] **2995**

LAW INSTITUTE JOURNAL (AT/0023-9267) [01755591] **2995**

LAW JOURNAL See LAW JOURNAL OF MARUT BUNNAG INTERNATIONAL LAW OFFICE **2995**

LAW JOURNAL OF MARUT BUNNAG INTERNATIONAL LAW OFFICE (TH) [03084651] **2995**

LAW JOURNAL / QUEENSLAND INSTITUTE OF TECHNOLOGY (AT/0816-4800) [14367218] **2995**

LAW JOURNAL QUEENSLAND UNIVERSITY OF TECHNOLOGY (AT) **2995**

LAW LETTER & JOURNAL (US/0883-0959) [11000476] **2995**

LAW LIBRARIAN (LONDON) (UK/0023-9275) [01437728] **2995, 3222**

LAW LIBRARIANS' SOCIETY OF WASHINGTON, D. C See UNION LIST OF LEGAL PERIODICALS, DISTRICT OF COLUMBIA AREA **3067**

LAW LIBRARY INFORMATION REPORTS (UK/0268-8336) [09311505] **2995, 3222**

LAW LIBRARY JOURNAL (US/0023-9283) [01642568] **2995, 3222**

LAW LIBRARY LIGHTS (US/0457-2483) [07211028] **2995, 3222**

LAW LIBRARY NEWSLETTER (US/0147-1376) [03117285] **2995, 3222**

LAW LINES (US/0148-0553) [03266540] **2995, 3222**

LAW, MEDICINE & HEALTH CARE (US/0277-8459) [07646525] **3604, 2995**

LAW NOTES (LONDON, ENGLAND) CEASED. (UK) [06913216] **2995**

LAW NOW (CN/0841-2626) [20183910] **2995**

LAW OF BANK DEPOSITS, COLLECTIONS, AND CREDIT CARDS, THE (US) [04379100] **3087**

LAW OF LENDER LIABILITY (US) **2995**

LAW OF LIABILITY INSURANCE (US) [01695321] **2886, 2996**

LAW OF MODERN COMMERCIAL PRACTICES, THE (US) [02255539] **2996, 844**

LAW OF OIL AND GAS LEASES (US) [01537473] **4263, 2996**

LAW OF THE HANDICAPPED : REPORTER AND COMMENTATOR, THE (US/0733-6233) [08425616] **4390, 2996**

LAW OF THE LAND (US/0271-2032) [06557880] **3179**

LAW OF THE SEA BULLETIN (US) [10788375] **3181**

LAW OF THE SEA INSTITUTE. CONFERENCE See PROCEEDINGS OF THE ANNUAL CONFERENCE OF THE LAW OF THE SEA INSTITUTE **3182**

LAW OF THE SEA INSTITUTE: OCCASIONAL PAPERS (US/0080-2808) [01117504] **3132, 2307, 1451**

LAW OF THE SEA INSTITUTE: WORKSHOP BOOKS (US) **3181**

LAW OF WORKMEN'S COMPENSATION (US) [01696117] **3151**

●LAW OFFICE ADMINISTRATOR (US/1071-7242) [28536071] **875**

LAW OFFICE AUTOMATOR, THE (US/1056-5698) [23740206] **2996**

LAW OFFICE COMPUTING (US/1055-128X) [23092346] **1193, 2996**

LAW OFFICE ECONOMICS AND MANAGEMENT (US/0458-8630) [01755604] **2996, 875**

LAW OFFICE EMPLOYMENT BULLETIN. COMPLIANCE AND LITIGATION (US) [29490304] **2996**

LAW OFFICE GUIDE IN COMPUTERS CEASED. (US/0739-5132) [09745827] **1268, 2996**

LAW OFFICE INFORMATION SERVICE CEASED. (US/0164-5390) [04525538] **2996, 3081**

LAW OFFICE MANAGEMENT (1981) (US/0883-0525) [08672234] **875, 2996**

LAW OFFICE MANAGEMENT & ADMINISTRATION REPORT (US/0735-4843) [08938938] **875, 2996**

LAW OFFICE MANAGEMENT JOURNAL (CN/0843-7076) [21102078] **2996**

Alphabetical Title Index — LAWYERS

LAW OFFICE TECHNOLOGY REVIEW (US/1047-6482) [20769769] 2996, **1193**

LAW OFFICER'S BULLETIN, THE (US/0145-6571) [02771527] **3107**

LAW PRACTICE MANAGEMENT (CN/0829-2094) [13369173] **2996**

LAW PRACTICE MANAGEMENT (CHICAGO, ILL.) (US/1045-9081) [20285898] **2996**

LAW QUARTERLY REVIEW, THE (UK/0023-933X) [01755607] **2996**

LAW REFERENCER, THE (II) [01586260] **2996**

LAW REFORM COMMISSION OF BRITISH COLUMBIA *See* ANNUAL REPORT OF THE LAW REFORM COMMISSION OF BRITISH COLUMBIA **2935**

LAW REFORM COMMISSION OF CANADA *See* ANNUAL REPORT - LAW REFORM COMMISSION OF CANADA **2934**

●LAW-RELATED CD-ROM UPDATE (US/1065-9285) [26795233] 1277, **2996**

LAW RELATING TO TRADE DESCRIPTIONS (UK) **2996**

LAW REPORTER (WASHINGTON, D.C.) (US/1052-4649) [12212915] **2996**

LAW REPORTS. CHANCERY DIVISION (1972) (UK/0264-1097) [15069740] **2996**

LAW REPORTS. CHANCERY DIVISION, FAMILY DIVISION (UK/0265-1211) [01643930] **3121**

LAW REPORTS. FAMILY DIVISION (UK/0264-1119) [15069909] **3121**

LAW REPORTS. HOUSE OF LORDS (UK/0264-1135) [01755611] **2996**

LAW REPORTS. INDEX, THE (UK/0265-1238) [11956417] **2996**

LAW REPORTS OF NIGERIA, THE (NR) [07090471] **2996**

●LAW REPORTS OF THE COMMONWEALTH (UK) [30558760] **3093**

LAW REPORTS OF THE COMMONWEALTH. COMMERCIAL LAW REPORTS *See* LAW REPORTS OF THE COMMONWEALTH **3093**

LAW REPORTS OF THE COMMONWEALTH. CONSTITUTIONAL AND ADMINISTRATIVE LAW REPORTS (UK/0951-0699) [12794104] **3093**

LAW REPORTS OF THE COMMONWEALTH. CRIMINAL LAW REPORTS (UK) [13490130] **3107**

LAW REPORTS. QUEEN'S BENCH DIVISION, AND ON APPEAL THEREFROM IN THE COURT OF APPEAL, AND DECISIONS IN THE COURT OF APPEAL CRIMINAL DIVISION AND EMPLOYMENT APPEAL TRIBUNAL, THE (UK) [07525873] **2996**

LAW REPORTS, WEEKLY LAW REPORTS, AND RESTRICTIVE PRACTICES REPORTS. CONSOLIDATED INDEX *See* LAW REPORTS. INDEX, THE **2996**

LAW REVIEW (UK) **2996**

LAW REVIEW JOURNAL (US/0734-1938) [04730747] **2996**

LAW REVIEW (WELLINGTON) (US/0042-5117) [01696098] **2996**

LAW SCHOOL ADMINISTRATOR'S JOURNAL (US/0741-1170) [10084642] 1865, **2996**

LAW SCHOOL JOURNAL (US/0737-2590) [07289755] 1834, **2996**

LAW SCHOOL NEWS *See* MINNESOTA LAW ALUMNI NEWS **1102**

LAW SCHOOL RECORD (US/0529-097X) [01755617] **2997**

LAW SCHOOL TRANSCRIPT, THE (US/0737-1152) [03908482] **2997**

LAW SEMINAR JOURNAL (US/0892-7073) [15239711] **2997**

LAW SOCIETY BULLETIN (AT/0157-8952) [I01578952] **2997**

LAW SOCIETY (GREAT BRITAIN) *See* LEGAL AID: ANNUAL REPORTS OF THE LAW SOCIETY AND OF THE LORD CHANCELLOR'S ADVISORY COMMITTEE **3179**

LAW SOCIETY JOURNAL (SYDNEY, N.S.W. : 1982) (AT) [09818257] **2997**

LAW SOCIETY OF ALBERTA *See* KEY PERSONNEL DIRECTORY (LAW SOCIETY OF ALBERTA) **2992**

LAW SOCIETY OF ALBERTA *See* NEWSLETTER - LAW SOCIETY OF ALBERTA **3017**

LAW SOCIETY OF SCOTLAND *See* REPORT OF THE LAW SOCIETY OF SCOTLAND ON THE LEGAL AID SCHEME **3180**

LAW SOCIETY OF SCOTLAND. REPORT ON THE LEGAL AID SCHEME *See* REPORT OF THE LAW SOCIETY OF SCOTLAND ON THE LEGAL AID SCHEME **3180**

LAW SOCIETY OF UPPER CANADA *See* OCCASIONAL REPORT - LAW SOCIETY OF UPPER CANADA **3020**

LAW SOCIETY OF UPPER CANADA *See* SPECIAL LECTURES OF THE LAW SOCIETY OF UPPER CANADA **3058**

LAW SOCIETY OF UPPER CANADA *See* GAZETTE - THE LAW SOCIETY OF UPPER CANADA **2973**

LAW SOCIETY'S GAZETTE (UK/0262-1495) [I02621495] **2997**

LAW TALK (WELLINGTON, N.Z.) (NZ) [15078658] **2997**

LAW TEACHER, THE (UK/0306-9400) [01786290] **2997**

LAW TEACHER'S JOURNAL (US/0741-1197) [10084683] **2997**

LAW/TECHNOLOGY (US/0278-3916) [07231557] **5125**

LAW TECHNOLOGY PRODUCT NEWS (US/1071-9121) [28763127] 5125, **2997**

LAW TIMES, THE (SI) [02251474] **2997**

LAW UNDER REVIEW : QUARTERLY BULLETIN OF LAW REFORM PROJECTS (UK) [20141867] **2997**

LAW UNION NEWS (TORONTO) (CN/0824-4421) [11382101] 4510, **2997**

LAW WEEK'S SUMMARY & ANALYSIS OF CURRENT LAW (US/0190-5252) [04724453] **2997**

LAWASIA (AT) [01784004] **2997**

LAWASIA HUMAN RIGHTS BULLETIN (AT) [08881828] **4510**

LAWFUL RESERVOIR MARKET DEMAND FOR PRORATED GAS FIELDS (US) **4263**

LAWG REPORT (CN/0848-1679) [21103164] **4510**

LAWINENEREIGNISSE UND WITTERUNGSABLAUF IN OSTERREICH (AU/0377-0877) [01784887] 1427, **1386**

LAWLAB JOURNAL *See* EXPERT WITNESS JOURNAL **2968**

LAWMARK (US/0737-8971) [09478973] **2997**

LAWN AND GARDEN MARKETING *CEASED.* (US) [08443639] **2423**

LAWN & GARDEN TRADE (CN/0705-212X) [03991860] **2423**

LAWN & LANDSCAPE MAINTENANCE (US/1046-154X) [20267904] **2423**

LAWN, GARDEN, AND FARM TRACTOR TRADE-IN GUIDE *CEASED.* (US/1043-089X) [17436664] **159**

LAWN, GARDEN AND HOME SHOWTIME *CEASED.* (US/0148-7906) [03721717] **2423**

LAWN TENNIS ALMANACK, THE (UK) [02946381] **4903**

LAWRENCE. ALUMNI EDITION (US/0091-2034) [01786716] **1092**

LAWRENCE ALUMNUS *See* LAWRENCE. ALUMNI EDITION **1092**

LAWRENCE BERKELEY LABORATORY. ENERGY AND ENVIRONMENT DIVISION *See* ENERGY AND ENVIRONMENT ANNUAL REPORT **1939**

LAWRENCE BERKELEY LABORATORY. ENERGY AND ENVIRONMENT DIVISION *See* COMBUSTION RESEARCH **1935**

LAWRENCE BERKELEY LABORATORY. ENVIRONMENTAL INSTRUMENTATION GROUP *See* INSTRUMENTATION FOR ENVIRONMENTAL MONITORING **2174**

LAWRENCE COUNTY ADVOCATE (US/0883-6531) [12178047] **5745**

LAWRENCE COUNTY CENTENNIAL (US/8750-3352) [11256520] **5744**

LAWRENCE COUNTY HISTORICAL SOCIETY BULLETIN (US) **2744**

LAWRENCE DAILY JOURNAL-WORLD (US) [08807303] **5677**

LAWRENCE EAGLE-TRIBUNE (US) [13742983] **5689**

LAWRENCE LEDGER, THE (US/0746-1771) [09832919] **5710**

LAWRENCE LIVERMORE LABORATORY. MECHANICAL ENGINEERING DEPT. RESEARCH ENGINEERING DIVISION *See* MECHANICAL ENGINEERING DEPARTMENT, RESEARCH ENGINEERING DIVISION ACTIVITIES HIGHLIGHTS REPORT **2122**

LAWRENCE REVIEW OF NATURAL PRODUCTS, THE (US/0734-4961) [08771132] **4313**

LAWRENCE TIMES, THE (US) [16145806] **5665**

LAWRENCE TOWNSHIP JOURNAL, THE (US) [16119227] **5665**

●LAWRENCE'S DEALER PRINT PRICES (US/1059-3187) [24562952] **356**

LAWS, ETC. LAWS OF ANTIGUA *See* LAWS OF ANTIGUA AND BARBUDA **2997**

LAWS OF ANGUILLA (AM) [11098659] **2997**

LAWS OF ANTIGUA AND BARBUDA (AQ) [11063734] **2997**

LAWS OF FLORIDA (US) [01569416] **2997**

LAWS OF MEXICO (US) **2997**

LAWS OF PUERTO RICO ANNOTATED (US) [09573634] **2997**

LAWS OF ST. CHRISTOPHER, NEVIS & ANGUILLA (AM) [11055538] **2997**

LAWS OF THE GAME AND UNIVERSAL GUIDE FOR REFEREES (SZ) [04082488] 4903, **2997**

LAWS OF THE GAME, FORESTATION AND PARKS COMMISSION OF STATE OF NEBRASKA *See* LAWS OF THE STATE OF NEBRASKA PERTAINING TO THE GAME AND PARKS COMMISSION **3114**

LAWS OF THE GAME OF RUGBY FOOTBALL WITH INSTRUCTIONS AND NOTES FOR GUIDANCE OF REFEREES (UK) [01791141] **4903**

LAWS OF THE REGENTS, UNIVERSITY OF COLORADO (US) [09344010] **4661**

LAWS OF THE STATE OF NEBRASKA PERTAINING TO THE GAME AND PARKS COMMISSION (US) [02242188] **3114**

LAWS RELATED TO THE DEPARTMENT OF SOCIAL SERVICES, PASSED DURING THE LEGISLATIVE SESSION (US/0148-4494) [03306875] 5294, **2997**

LAWS RELATING TO FIRES AND FIREMEN, STATE OF CALIFORNIA (US) [06297691] 2291, **2997**

LAWS RELATING TO STATE BANKS AND TRUST COMPANIES, SAVINGS BANKS, INDUSTRIAL BANKS, SAVINGS BANK LIFE INSURANCE, BUILDING OR SAVINGS AND LOAN ASSOCIATIONS (US) [03488628] **3087**

LAWS RELATING TO THE MINNESOTA PUBLIC SCHOOL SYSTEM (US) [01757876] 1865, **2997**

LAWS RELATING TO THE PRACTICE OF OPTOMETRY, WITH RULES AND REGULATIONS (US/0160-1326) [03620880] 4216, **2997**

LAWTON CONSTITUTION, THE (US/0889-566X) [12239552] **5732**

LAWTON MORNING PRESS *CEASED.* (US/0746-3235) [09930878] **5732**

LAWYER (UK) **2997**

LAWYER DIRECTORY (ROCKVILLE, MD.) (US/0276-6108) [07372627] **2997**

LAWYER GUIDE & DIRECTORY, LOS ANGELES COUNTY (US) [03880556] **2997**

LAWYER HIRING & TRAINING REPORT (US/0739-1706) [09616599] **2997**

LAWYER INTERNATIONAL (IE/0791-7481) **2997**

LAWYER-PILOTS BAR ASSOCIATION *See* LPBA JOURNAL **3005**

LAWYER REFERRAL NETWORK (US/0890-7765) [14089035] **2997**

LAWYER, THE (TR) [04233464] **2997**

LAWYER-TO-LAWYER CONSULTATION PANEL (US/0091-0430) [01786374] **2997**

LAWYER'S ALERT (US/0278-9817) [07938072] **2998**

LAWYER'S ALMANAC, THE (US/0277-9544) [10600388] **2998**

LAWYERS AND THE ARTS COMMITTEE NEWSLETTER *See* ARTS, ENTERTAINMENT & SPORTS LAW NEWS **2937**

LAWYERS AND THE ARTS COMMITTEE NEWSLETTER / AMERICAN BAR ASSOCIATION, YOUNG LAWYERS DIVISION (US) [26906664] 357, **2998**

LAWYERS' ARBITRATION LETTER (US) [05593509] **2998**

LAWYER'S BRIEF, THE (US/0898-9966) [04844997] **2998**

LAWYERS DIARY AND MANUAL *See* MASSACHUSETTS LAWYERS DIARY AND MANUAL : INCLUDING BAR DIRECTORY **3007**

LAWYERS DIARY AND MANUAL INCLUDING BAR DIRECTORY OF NEW JERSEY (US) [02943825] **2998**

LAWYERS' EUROPE (UK/0967-6562) [I09676562] **2998**

LAWYERS' EUROPE (UK) **2998**

LAWYERS FACT BOOK (UK) **2998**

LAWYERS FOR THE ARTS NEWSLETTER *See* LAWYERS AND THE ARTS COMMITTEE NEWSLETTER / AMERICAN BAR ASSOCIATION, YOUNG LAWYERS DIVISION **2998**

LAWYERS' GUIDE TO MEDICAL PROOF (US) [04554031] 3604, **2998**

LAWYERS IN EUROPE (UK/0959-0889) [21481856] **3132**

LAWYERS JOB BULLETIN BOARD (US) **2998**

LAWYERS
Alphabetical Title Index

LAWYERS LETTER / JUDICIAL ADMINISTRATION DIVISION, AMERICAN BAR ASSOCIATION, LAWYERS CONFERENCE (US/0740-0519) [09796856] **3141**

LAWYERS' LIABILITY REVIEW (US/0896-7075) [15364189] **2998**

LAWYER'S MEDICAL DIGEST (US/8755-5891) [11271900] 3604, **2998**

LAWYER'S MICROCOMPUTER, THE (US/0732-0922) [08316597] 1268, **2998**

LAWYER'S MONTHLY CATALOG (US/1044-7660) [19870619] **2998**

LAWYERS MONTHLY CATALOG, ANNUAL (US/1049-7978) [21310613] **2998**

LAWYER'S PC, THE (US/0740-0942) [09879865] 1268, **2998**

LAWYER'S REGISTER INTERNATIONAL BY SPECIALTIES AND FIELDS OF LAW INCLUDING A DIRECTORY OF CORPORATE COUNSEL (US/1061-7272) [23200871] **3101**

LAWYER'S REMEMBRANCER (UK) **2998**

LAWYER'S REMEMBRANCER (UK/0142-7490) [I01427490] **2998**

LAWYERS TITLE NEWS (US/0272-7161) [04722486] **2998**

LAWYERS WEEKLY GUIDEBOOK (US/0732-4901) [04563199] **2998**

LAWYERS WEEKLY (SCARBOROUGH) (CN/0830-0151) [15372946] **2998**

●LAWYER'S WEEKLY USA (US/1069-7837) [27930193] **2998**

LAWYER'S WORD : A NEWSLETTER FOR LAWYERS USING MICROSOFT WORD AND OTHER MICROSOFT PRODUCTS, THE *CEASED.* (US/1056-1226) [23469864] 2998, **1288**

LAX (GLENDALE, CALIF.) (US/1044-4785) [19803586] **1193**

LAXTON'S NATIONAL BUILDING PRICE BOOK (UK) [15504426] **619**

LAYERS AND EGG PRODUCTION (US/1057-7866) [15809449] **214**

●LAZARILLO (SP) [27408702] **2696**

●LAZARILLO SALAMANCA (SP/1131-9151) [I11319151] **3296**

LAZAROA (SP/0210-9778) [07962922] **517**

LBA BANKER NEWSLETTER, THE (US) **796**

LBI NEWS (NEW YORK, N.Y.) (US/0023-625X) [02802406] **2696**

LBL RESEARCH REVIEW (US/0882-1305) [11769081] **4448**

LC & YOU (US/8755-4313) [11308360] 1085, **404**

LC FOLK ARCHIVE FINDING AID (US/0736-4903) [09143250] 2267, 3222, **5269**

LC FOLK ARCHIVE REFERENCE AID (US/0736-4911) [09143376] **2325**

LC GC (US/0888-9090) [13573955] **984**

LC GC INTERNATIONAL (US/0895-5441) [16665711] **984**

LC-MS UPDATE (UK/0964-1645) [I09641645] **5125**

LC SCIENCE TRACER BULLET (US/0090-5232) [03315419] 5125, **5175**

LCOMM NEWS / LIBRARY COUNCIL OF METROPOLITAN MILWAUKEE (US) [08671293] **3222**

LCPA BROADSIDE (US/0736-296X) [09114617] **3223**

LCPA'S INDEX TO LIBRARY OF CONGRESS INFORMATION BULLETIN (US/0882-6374) [11989757] **3223**

LDA JOURNAL (US/0092-4458) [04170872] **1329**

LDA NEWSBRIEFS (US) **1881**

LDB INTERIOR TEXTILES (US/0892-743X) [15249831] 2906, **5354**

LDC DEBT REPORT (US) [18143521] **796**

LDI MANAGEMENT DISCUSSION PAPER (US) [18917173] **3787**

LDRC 50-STATE SURVEY / PREPARED BY LEADING MEDIA ATTORNEYS AND LAW FIRMS IN ALL FIFTY STATES AND THE U.S. TERRITORIES (US) [09386377] **2998**

LDRC BULLETIN (US/0737-8130) [09461575] **2998**

LE CENTER LEADER (US) [01755650] **5696**

LE ROY INDEPENDENT, THE (US) [01641548] **5696**

LE SUEUR NEWS-HERALD (US) [20518792] **5696**

LE-TORAH VE-HORA AH (US/0094-5625) [01793986] **5050**

LEABHARLANN, AN (IE/0023-9542) [06100542] **3223**

LEACHTAI CHOLM CILLE (IE) [22142298] 3297, **3404**

LEAD ABATEMENT NEWS *CEASED.* (US/1060-6653) [25053110] **5294**

LEAD AND ZINC IN THE 1990'S - WORLD AND LATIN AMERICA (UK) **4007**

LEAD AND ZINC INDUSTRY (US/0570-9369) [01122349] **4007**

LEAD AND ZINC STATISTICS (UK/0023-9577) [02448261] 4007, **4025**

LEAD AND ZINC (UNITED STATES. PRESIDENT) (US) [01291889] **1441**

LEAD BELLY LETTER (US/1056-5329) [23236157] **4128**

LEAD DAILY CALL (US) [09423033] **5744**

LEAD DETECTION & ABATEMENT REPORT (US/1059-4930) [24607244] **4788**

●LEAD POISONING REPORT (US/1075-0665) [29926004] **4788**

LEAD / U.S. DEPARTMENT OF THE INTERIOR, BUREAU OF MINES (US) [26241826] 2143, **4007**

LEADER *See* J.C.I. NEWS **5232**

LEADER (1993), THE (US/1072-1568) [28876984] **5647**

LEADER AND STATE REGISTER *See* LEADER (1993), THE **5647**

LEADER (ANDERSON, IND.) (US/1055-2626) [23129300] **4973**

LEADER (CORNING, N.Y.), THE (US/1050-1983) [21454838] **5717**

LEADER COURIER, THE (US) [11681098] **5677**

LEADER ENTERPRISE, THE (US) [16959079] **5729**

LEADER (GARFIELD HEIGHTS, OHIO), THE (US/8750-8095) [11799724] **5729**

LEADER (GLOUCESTER) *CEASED.* (CN/0713-7761) [08985154] **4851**

LEADER-HERALD, THE (US) [10928015] **5717**

LEADER IN ACTION (US/8755-2620) [11242842] 4480, **1834**

LEADER IN THE CHURCH SCHOOL TODAY (US/0895-1403) [16508052] **4973**

LEADER (LANSING, KAN.), THE (US/1050-5806) [12091518] **5677**

LEADER (MORRISBURG) (CN/0834-6666) [16581977] **5788**

LEADER / NATIONAL WILDLIFE FEDERATION, THE (US/0738-1492) [09535478] **2197**

LEADER-NEWS (WASHBURN, N.D.), THE (US/0888-0220) [13451536] **5725**

LEADER-OBSERVER, THE (US) [11386323] **5718**

LEADER (OTTAWA. 1976) (CN/0711-5377) [08534458] **4851**

LEADER (PHILADELPHIA, PA.) (US) [12632813] **5737**

LEADER (POINT PLEASANT BEACH, N.J.) (US/0745-6816) [09397597] **5710**

LEADER-RECORD, THE (US) [01641716] **5696**

LEADER (RESEARCH TRIANGLE PARK, N.C.), THE (US/0195-0622) [04988776] **5723**

LEADER-TELEGRAM (US/0891-0227) [07464862] **5768**

LEADER-TIMES (US) [15080095] **5737**

LEADER (TREMONTON, UTAH), THE (US/0747-1416) [10569439] **5756**

LEADER-TRIBUNE (FORT VALLEY, GA.), THE (US/8750-250X) [11171893] **5654**

LEADER-VINDICATOR, THE (US) [14813682] **5737**

LEADERS (US/0163-3635) [04343990] **1572**

LEADER'S DIGEST *See* LEADERS MAGAZINE (LEXINGTON) **2886**

LEADER'S EQUIPMENT LEASING NEWSLETTER (US/0733-4303) [08582296] **2998**

LEADER'S EUROPE 1992 LAW & STRATEGY (US/1047-2827) [20652034] **2998**

●LEADER'S EUROPEAN MARKET LAW REPORT (US) [27330983] **2998**

LEADER'S LEGAL TECH NEWSLETTER (US/0738-0186) [09491942] 1193, **2998**

LEADERS MAGAZINE (LEXINGTON) (US/0023-9631) [06656642] **2886**

LEADERS OF AMERICAN SECONDARY EDUCATION (US) [01783685] **1761**

LEADERS OF MODERN ANTHROPOLOGY SERIES (US) [01696029] **240**

LEADER'S PRODUCT LIABILITY LAW AND STRATEGY (US/0733-513X) [15274331] **2999**

●LEADERSHIP (US) [27865928] **5294**

LEADERSHIP & ORGANIZATION DEVELOPMENT JOURNAL (UK/0143-7739) [07803578] **875**

LEADERSHIP (CAROL STREAM) (US/0199-7661) [05956624] **4973**

●LEADERSHIP DIRECTORIES ON CD-ROM (US/1075-3869) [30045105] **689**

LEADERSHIP EDUCATION (US/1062-1474) [25533034] **875**

LEADERSHIP FOR STUDENT ACTIVITIES (US/1040-5399) [18441066] **1761**

LEADERSHIP (FORT WORTH, TEX.) (US/1055-9108) [23378566] **5294**

LEADERSHIP IN ACTION *See* CHRISTIAN EDUCATION INFORMER, THE **4944**

●LEADERSHIP IN HEALTH SERVICES (CN/1188-3669) [25312281] **3787**

LEADERSHIP MEDICA (IT) **3604**

LEADERSHIP QUARTERLY, THE (US/1048-9843) [21097969] **875**

LEADERSHIP (WASHINGTON) (US/0195-9204) [05712131] **875**

●LEADERSHIP WITH A HUMAN TOUCH (US/1057-4816) [24048776] **875**

LEADING EDGE LIGHTHOUSE (US/0887-9095) [13414930] **689**

LEADING EDGE (PROVO, UTAH), THE (US/1049-5983) [20152558] **3404**

●LEADING EDGE (TULSA, OKLA.) (US/1070-485X) [27206867] **1408**

LEADLINE, THE (CN/0705-6931) [04129887] **2592**

LEADSCAN (UK/0950-1584) [14982446] 4007, **4025**

LEADSOURCE. AKRON/CANTON (US) [18033054] **689**

LEADSOURCE. CHICAGO METRO CENTRAL (US) [17847794] **689**

LEADSOURCE. CHICAGO METRO NORTH (US) [17847662] **689**

LEADSOURCE. CHICAGO METRO SOUTH (US) [17893937] **689**

LEADSOURCE. CHICAGO METRO WEST (US) [17846738] **689**

LEADSOURCE. CLEVELAND METRO EAST (US/0893-651X) [15612305] **689**

LEADSOURCE. CLEVELAND METRO WEST (US/0893-6528) [15612355] **689**

LEADSOURCE. DETROIT METRO NORTH (US) [16566608] **690**

LEADSOURCE. DETROIT METRO SOUTHEAST (US) [16570786] **690**

LEADSOURCE. DETROIT METRO WEST (US) [16571212] **690**

LEADSOURCE. METRO PHOENIX (US) [17666656] **690**

LEADSOURCE. METRO TUCSON *See* INSIDE CONTACTS U.S.A. METRO TUCSON MARKETING DIRECTORY **682**

LEADVILLE HERALD DEMOCRAT (US) [22538506] **5643**

LEAF-CHRONICLE, THE (US/0745-7367) [09421144] **5745**

LEAF (FORT COLLINS, COLO.), THE (US/1064-0185) [26191647] 2218, **2197**

LEAFLET (GREAT BRITAIN. AGRICULTURAL DEVELOPMENT AND ADVISORY SERVICE) (UK) [08085043] **105**

LEAFLET, THE (US/0023-964X) [01791978] 3297, **1761**

LEAFLETS, FOLDERS, ETC. - DEPT. OF HUMAN RESOURCES (CN) [02442710] **4661**

LEAGUE BULLETIN (US) [06141245] **2744**

LEAGUE OF ACTION SERVICE (US) 4510, **5560**

LEAGUE OF ARAB STATES. MISSAO NO BRASIL *See* L.E.A **2657**

LEAGUE OF ARAB STATES. MISSAO NO BRASIL. REVISTA DA L.E.A *See* L.E.A **2657**

LEAGUE OF ARIZONA CITIES AND TOWNS *See* MUNICIPAL POLICY STATEMENT - LEAGUE OF ARIZONA CITIES & TOWNS **4687**

LEAGUE OF CANADIAN POETS *See* NEWSLETTER - EXECUTIVE COMMITTEE, LEAGUE OF CANADIAN POETS **3467**

LEAGUE OF NATIONS. CHILD WELFARE INFORMATION CENTRE *See* ANNUAL REPORT ON CHILD WELFARE, FOR THE ... SESSION OF THE ADVISORY COMMITTEE ON SOCIAL QUESTIONS **5272**

LEAGUE OF RED CROSS SOCIETIES *See* BIENNIAL REPORT - LEAGUE OF RED CROSS SOCIETIES **5274**

LEAGUE OF WOMEN VOTERS OF NEW JERSEY *See* NJ VOTER **4669**

LEAGUER, THE (US/0023-9666) [04090805] **1761**

Alphabetical Title Index — LECTURES

LEANDER MCCORMICK OBSERVATORY See PUBLICATIONS OF THE LEANDER MCCORMICK OBSERVATORY OF THE UNIVERSITY OF VIRGINIA **399**

LEARN See SERVICE CIRCULAR - LEARN **1783**

LEARN ENGLISH IN CANADA (CN/0711-1509) [10220691] 1761, **3297**

●LEARN FOR YOURSELF (UK/0969-9015) **1801**

LEARNED PUBLISHING (UK/0953-1513) [20181459] **4816**

LEARNING AND INDIVIDUAL DIFFERENCES (US/1041-6080) [18810223] **1761**

LEARNING AND INSTRUCTION : THE JOURNAL OF THE EUROPEAN ASSOCIATION FOR RESEARCH ON LEARNING AND INSTRUCTION (UK/0959-4752) [24183065] **1899**

●LEARNING & MEMORY (COLD SPRING HARBOR, N.Y.) (US/1072-0502) [28855213] **4602**

LEARNING AND MEMORY / ISSUED BY UNIVERSITY OF SHEFFIELD BIOMEDICAL INFORMATION SERVICE (UK/0143-7534) [08273532] **3930**

LEARNING AND MOTIVATION (US/0023-9690) [01755679] **4602**

LEARNING CENTER DIGEST, THE (US/1042-7996) [19219667] **1761**

LEARNING CHANNEL MONTHLY PROGRAM GUIDE See TLC MONTHLY **2494**

LEARNING DISABILITIES (PITTSBURGH, PA.) (US/1046-6819) [20310978] **1881**

LEARNING DISABILITIES RESEARCH AND PRACTICE (US/0938-8982) [22378988] **1881**

LEARNING DISABILITY QUARTERLY (US/0731-9487) [04783529] **1881**

LEARNING ENGLISH IN BRITAIN (UK) [18996528] **3297**

LEARNING EXCHANGE (AT/0310-3242) [I03103242] **1761**

LEARNING LETTER (US) **1761**

●LEARNING ORGANIZATION, THE (UK) 690, 1503, **943**

LEARNING (PALO ALTO, CALIF.) (US/0090-3167) [01785013] **1900**

LEARNING RESOURCES JOURNAL (UK/0268-2125) [I02682125] **1834**

LEARNING RESOURCES JOURNAL / UNIVERSITY OF MINNESOTA HEALTH SCIENCES (US) [25200047] 2599, **1900**

LEARNING (ROCKVILLE) (US/0361-9990) [02376402] **1761**

LEARNING VACATIONS CEASED. (US) [06622091] **5482**

LEARNING WITH COMPUTERS (SCARBOROUGH, ONT.) (CN/0821-3623) [09951464] **1224**

LEAR'S (NEW YORK, N.Y.) CEASED. (US/0897-0149) [17367107] **5560**

LEASIDE VILLAGER, THE (CN/0715-4631) [09166875] **5788**

LEASING AND FINANCIAL SERVICES MONITOR, THE (US/0888-8981) [13754543] 1503, **690**

LEASING DIGEST See ASSET FINANCE & LEASING DIGEST **773**

LEASING OPPORTUNITIES (1983) (US/0732-9237) [08471856] **690**

LEASING SOURCEBOOK (US/1045-2508) [18410785] **1615**

LEAST DEVELOPED COUNTRIES ... REPORT / PREPARED BY THE UNCTAD SECRETARIAT, THE (US/0257-7550) [12306299] **1572**

LEATHER AND ALLIED PRODUCTS INDUSTRIES (CN/0828-9859) [15159177] **3184**

LEATHER AND FOOTWEAR IN ASIA (UK) **3185**

LEATHER BUYERS GUIDE CEASED. (US/0075-8345) [01796216] **3185**

LEATHER CONSERVATION NEWS (US/0898-0128) [13447153] **3185**

LEATHER CRAFTERS JOURNAL, THE (US/1056-4225) [23716286] **374**

LEATHER GUIDE See INTERNATIONAL LEATHER GUIDE **3184**

LEATHER IN ASIA See LEATHER AND FOOTWEAR IN ASIA **3185**

LEATHER IN ASIA (UK/0269-1418) [I02691418] **3185**

LEATHER (LONDON) (UK/0023-9739) [01789212] **3185**

LEATHER MANUFACTURER, THE (US/0023-9763) [02448265] **3185**

LEATHER SCIENCE ABSTRACTS : LESA (II) [20621756] **3185**

LEATHER SCIENCE (MADRAS) SUSPENDED. (II/0023-9771) [10842292] **3185**

LEATHER TODAY (US/0884-660X) [12424987] **3185**

LEATHER WARE (II) [23280563] **3185**

LEATHERNECK (US/0023-981X) [01755682] **4049**

LEAVEN (FRANKLIN PARK, ILL.) (US/8750-2011) [11110647] **2282**

LEAVEN (KANSAS CITY), THE (US/0194-9799) [05168232] **5677**

LEAVENWORTH ECHO, THE (US) [16996294] **5761**

LEAVENWORTH TIMES LEAVENWORTH, KAN. : 1878) (US) [08807992] **5677**

LEAVES OF TWIN OAKS, THE CEASED. (US/0023-9836) [03686189] **5269**

LEAWOOD SUN, THE (US) [11919765] **5677**

LEB (CN/0227-0242) [08405156] **1834**

LEBA (PO) [07445095] **273**

LEBANESE MEDICAL JOURNAL (LE/0023-9852) [05227741] **3604**

LEBANESE PHARMACEUTICAL JOURNAL. LA REVUE PHARMACEUTIQUE LIBANAISE, THE (LE) [20316309] **4314**

LEBANON DEMOCRAT AND WILSON COUNTY NEWS, THE (US) [19213655] **5745**

LEBANON ENTERPRISE, THE (US) [14106618] **5681**

LEBANON EXPRESS (US) **5733**

LEBANON FILE / COUNCIL OF LEBANESE AMERICAN ORGANIZATIONS (US/1059-4698) [24601215] **2658**

LEBANON LIGHT (US/1075-8852) **1093**

LEBANON NEWS (WASHINGTON, D.C. 1978) (US/0742-9665) [08363516] **2489**

LEBANON TIMES, THE (US) [12704128] **5677**

LEBARON RUSSELL BRIGGS PRIZE HONORS ESSAYS IN ENGLISH (US/0075-8396) [01755686] **3404**

LEBEN (CLAYTON, MO.), DAS (US/0893-7443) [15635945] **3297**

LEBEN UND UMWELT (GW/0303-4283) [01041855] 2218, **463**

LEBENDE SPRACHEN (GW/0023-9909) [02955742] **3297**

LEBENDIGE SEELSORGE (GW) [02354002] **4973**

LEBENSBILDER AUS SCHWABEN UND FRANKEN (GW) [02299521] **433**

LEBENSBILDER ZUR GESCHICHTE DER BOHMISCHEN LANDER / HERAUSGEGEBEN IM AUFTRAG DEG COLLEGIUM CAROLINUM (GW) [08211192] 2696, **433**

LEBENSMITTEL-GROSSHANDEL See FOOD + I.E. UND NONFOOD **2337**

LEBENSMITTEL-INDUSTRIE, DIE SUSPENDED. (SZ/0024-0028) [02955252] **2791**

LEBENSMITTEL PRAXIS (GW) [04089480] **2348**

LEBENSMITTEL TECHNOLOGIE (SZ) [02158909] **2348**

LEBENSMITTEL- UND BIOTECHNOLOGIE (AU/0254-9298) [20041492] **2348**

LEBENSMITTEL-WISSENSCHAFT + I.E. UND TECHNOLOGIE (UK/0023-6438) [02407016] **2348**

LEBENSMITTEL-ZEITUNG (GW/0024-0001) [01782904] **2348**

LEBENSMITTELCHEMIE : ZEITSCHRIFT DER LEBENSMITTELCHEMISCHEN GESELLSCHAFT, FACHGRUPPE IN DER GESELLSCHAFT DEUTSCHER CHEMIKER (GW/0937-1478) [23835670] **2348**

LEBENSMITTELTECHNIK (GW/0047-4290) [I00474290] **2348**

LEBENSMITTELTIERARZT See ARCHIV FUER LEBENSMITTELHYGIENE **2327**

LEBER, MAGEN, DARM (GW/0300-8622) [01778875] **3747**

LEBLANC BELL (US) **4128**

LEBO ENTERPRISE, THE (US) [10254032] **5677**

LEBRETON (CN/0703-9581) [04040041] **2827**

LECCIONES CHRISTIANAS PARA JOVENES. ALUMNO (US/1050-5393) [21531733] **4973**

LECCIONES CRISTIANAS (US/0149-8363) [03563688] **4973**

LECCIONES CRISTIANAS PARA JOVENES. LIBRO DEL MAESTRO (US/1050-5385) [21531701] **4973**

LECCIONES DE LA ESCUELA SABATICA (US/8750-4448) [11422846] **4973**

LECOURT (US/0147-3190) [03139839] **2999**

L'ECOUTE, A (CN/0700-3900) [03264681] **4128**

LECTERN RESOURCE (US/0746-763X) [10259329] **4973**

LECTINS, BIOLOGY, BIOCHEMISTRY, CLINICAL BIOCHEMISTRY (GW/0723-8878) [08567212] **463**

LECTINS SHEFFIELD (UK/0143-4217) [I01434217] **490**

LECTIONARY HOMILETICS (US/1043-2310) [19356753] **4973**

●LECTOR (US) **5031**

LECTOR (BERKELEY, CALIF.) (US/0732-8001) [08434187] **3346**

●'LECTRIC AUTO NEWS (US/1061-4052) [25301944] **5418**

LECTURA DANTIS (CHARLOTTESVILLE, VA.) (US/0897-5280) [16730997] **3404**

LECTURA Y VIDA (US/0325-8637) [08680530] **1900**

LECTURAS (SP) **1761**

LECTURAS DE ECONOMIA (CK/0120-2596) [08184329] **1572**

LECTURAS DE HISTORIA DEL ARTE (SP) [26912504] **357**

LECTURAS MATEMATICAS (CK/0120-1980) [I01201980] **3516**

LECTURE FAITE (CN/0714-8216) [09084930] **2999**

LECTURE JEUNE (FR) **1066**

LECTURE JEUNESSE (FR/0152-8505) [I01528505] **1066**

LECTURE JEUNESSE See LECTURE JEUNE **1066**

LECTURE NOTES IN ARTIFICIAL INTELLIGENCE (GW) [19230794] **1214**

LECTURE NOTES IN BIOMATHEMATICS (GW/0341-633X) [00939245] 3516, **463**

LECTURE NOTES IN CHEMISTRY (GW/0342-4901) [03093622] **984**

LECTURE NOTES IN COMPUTER SCIENCE (GW/0302-9743) [03719235] **1214**

LECTURE NOTES IN CONTROL AND INFORMATION SCIENCES (GW/0170-8643) [04248306] **3223**

LECTURE NOTES IN EARTH SCIENCES (GW/0930-0317) [12890170] **1357**

LECTURE NOTES IN ECONOMICS AND MATHEMATICAL SYSTEMS (GW/0075-8442) [01589790] 3516, **1503**

LECTURE NOTES IN ENGINEERING (US/0176-5035) [09907999] **1985**

LECTURE NOTES IN MEDICAL INFORMATICS (GW/0172-7788) [04986547] 3223, **3604**

LECTURE NOTES IN PHYSICS (GW/0075-8450) [01606610] **4411**

LECTURE NOTES IN PHYSICS. NEW SERIES M, MONOGRAPHS (GW) [24814834] **4411**

LECTURE NOTES IN PURE AND APPLIED MATHEMATICS (US) [01755690] **3516**

LECTURE NOTES IN STATISTICS (US) [08264024] **3516**

LECTURE NOTES-MONOGRAPH SERIES (US/0749-2170) [10242368] **5332**

LECTURE NOTES SERIES - AARHUS, DENMARK. UNIVERSITET. MATEMATISK INSTITUT (DK/0065-017X) [01460514] **3516**

LECTURE NOTES SERIES (UNIVERSITY OF WATERLOO. CONSTRUCTION MANAGEMENT GROUP) (CN/0711-2564) [08462307] **619**

LECTURE SERIES - HAN'GUK SONBAK YON'GUSO (US) [05044801] **875**

LECTURE SERIES - VON KARMAN INSTITUTE FOR FLUID DYNAMICS (BE/0377-8312) [02850797] 4428, **2093**

LECTURES (IT) [09673720] **3404**

LECTURES - DALLAS. SOUTHERN METHODIST UNIVERSITY. CASUALTY AND PROPERTY INSURANCE INSTITUTE (US) [01561690] **2886**

LECTURES GIVEN AT THE STUD MANAGERS COURSE (US) [05958978] **2800**

LECTURES IN ANAESTHESIOLOGY CEASED. (UK/0267-0003) [12429124] **3683**

LECTURES IN APPLIED MATHEMATICS (US/0075-8485) [04054378] **3516**

LECTURES IN MEMORY OF LOUISE TAFT SEMPLE (US/0578-2775) [02309511] **3404**

LECTURES LIEGE (BE/0251-7388) [I02517388] **3346**

LECTURES ON GAS CHROMATOGRAPHY (US/0075-8515) [01755696] **984**

LECTURES — Alphabetical Title Index

LECTURES ON MATHEMATICS AND PHYSICS (II/0970-6313) [I09706313] 4411, **3516**

LECTURES ON MATHEMATICS IN THE LIFE SCIENCES (US/0075-8523) [01755697] 463, **3516**

● LED LAMPS & DISPLAYS (US/1063-4002) [26001142] **2070**

LEDARSKAP, EKONOMEN (SW/0280-7823) [09958798] **1503**

LEDER (GW/0024-0176) [02955692] **3185**

LEDER UND HAUTEMARKT (GW/0342-7641) [11313173] **3185**

LEDERINDUSTRIE / CENTRAAL BUREAU VOOR DE STATISTIEK, HOOFDAFDELING STATISTIEKEN VAN INDUSTRIE EN BOUWNIJVERHEID (NE/0168-471X) [11880998] **3185**

LEDERWARENINDUSTRIE, EXCL. KLEDING / CENTRAAL BUREAU VOOR DE STATISTIEK, HOOFDAFDELING STATISTIEKEN VAN INDUSTRIE EN BOUWNIJVERHEID (NE/0168-5139) [11876309] **3185**

LEDGE, THE (US/1046-2724) [19532068] **3465**

LEDGER-INDEPENDENT, THE (US) [13571371] **5681**

LEDGER (LAKELAND), THE (US/0163-0288) [04277984] **5650**

LEDGER (RIDGEFIELD, CONN.), THE (US/0888-3017) [11517150] **5645**

LEDGER-STAR (US/0889-6135) [13970092] **5759**

LEDGER, THE (US) **5677**

LEE COUNTY EAGLE, THE (US/1050-3846) [21472766] **5627**

LEE COUNTY OBSERVER (US) [28483687] **5742**

LEE SAYLOR, INC *See* CURRENT CONSTRUCTION COSTS **612**

LEEDS ARTS CALENDAR (UK/0024-0257) [05432397] **357**

LEEDS, ENGLAND. CHAMBER OF COMMERCE *See* CLASSIFIED TRADE DIRECTORY OF MEMBERS (LEEDS CHAMBER OF COMMERCE) **819**

LEEDS NEWS, THE (US) [14245485] **5627**

LEEDS PHILOSOPHICAL AND LITERARY SOCIETY *See* PROCEEDINGS OF THE LEEDS PHILOSOPHICAL AND LITERARY SOCIETY. SCIENTIFIC SECTION **2852**

LEEDS PHILOSOPHICAL AND LITERARY SOCIETY *See* PROCEEDINGS OF THE LEEDS PHILOSOPHICAL AND LITERARY SOCIETY, LITERARY AND HISTORICAL SECTION **5235**

LEEDS STUDIES IN ENGLISH (UK/0075-8566) [01755705] **3297**

LEEDS TEXTS AND MONOGRAPHS (UK/0075-8574) [05979289] 3404, **3297**

LEER (SP) [15502000] **3404**

LEESVILLE DAILY LEADER (US) [17689062] **5684**

LEETOWN NEWS (US) [15650594] **5671**

LEFSETZ LETTER, THE (US/0892-1830) [15143925] **4128**

LEFT BANK (US/1056-7429) [23835781] **3404**

LEFT BUSINESS OBSERVER (US/1042-0134) [17870305] 796, **1503**

LEFT CURVE (US/0160-1857) [02303188] **4480**

● LEFT HISTORY (CN/1192-1927) [28857188] 5208, **4480**

LEFT INDEX (US/0733-2998) [08574892] 4543, **4502**

LEFT REVIEW (KENT) (US/0195-7333) [02941416] **4543**

LEFTWARD (CN/0381-7350) [03209994] **4543**

LEG SHOW (US/0734-4295) [08739758] **3995**

LEGA NAZIONALE DELLE COOPERATIVE E DELLE MUTUE *See* ANNUARIO DELLA COOPERAZIONE ITALIANA **1546**

LEGACY (US/1045-3423) [20075120] **2744**

LEGACY (AMHERST, MASS.) (US/0748-4321) [10881450] 5560, **3404**

LEGACY (FORT COLLINS, COLO.) (US/1052-3774) [22271781] **4706**

LEGACY (LOS ANGELES, CALIF.) (US/0898-6444) [17401503] **5050**

LEGACY (MONROEVILLE, ALA.) (US/1064-9743) [25505146] **2458**

LEGAL 500 : THE MAJOR LAW FIRMS IN ENGLAND, WALES AND SCOTLAND, THE (UK) [18265265] **2999**

LEGAL ACTION (UK/0266-3953) [10590385] **2999**

LEGAL ACTION IN NEW SOUTH WALES (AT) [06704180] **2999**

LEGAL AID: ANNUAL REPORTS OF THE LAW SOCIETY AND OF THE LORD CHANCELLOR'S ADVISORY COMMITTEE (UK) [03997204] **3179**

LEGAL AID COMMISSION OF WESTERN AUSTRALIA *See* HEARSAY : LEGAL AID PRACTICE NOTES AND INFORMATION BULLETIN OF THE LEGAL AID COMMISSION OF WESTERN AUSTRALIA **3179**

LEGAL AID NEWS (NEW YORK), THE (US/0147-9458) [03183597] **3180**

LEGAL ALERT (US) **2999**

LEGAL ALERT (CN/0712-841X) [08996197] **3101**

● LEGAL AND CRIMINOLOGICAL PSYCHOLOGY (UK/1355-3259) **3169**

LEGAL ASPECTS OF MEDICAL PRACTICE (US/0190-2350) [03786297] 3604, **2999**

LEGAL ASPECTS OF PHARMACY PRACTICE (US/0191-8516) [04922159] 4314, **2999**

LEGAL ASPECTS OF PSYCHIATRIC PRACTICE (US/0883-0924) [11891853] 3930, **2999**

LEGAL ASSISTANCE OF NORTH DAKOTA, INC *See* LAW OF THE LAND **3179**

LEGAL ASSISTANCES NOTEBOOK (US) **3180**

LEGAL ASSISTANT TODAY (1990) (US/1051-3663) [21653861] **2999**

● LEGAL ASSISTANT'S NOTEBOOK (NORTHERN CALIFORNIA ED.), THE (US/1062-8959) [25796268] **2999**

● LEGAL ASSISTANT'S NOTEBOOK. VOL. 1, SOUTHERN CALIFORNIA ED, THE (US/1062-8940) [25796185] **2999**

LEGAL ASSISTANTS: UPDATE (US/0272-1961) [06766138] **2999**

LEGAL BIBLIOGRAPHIC DATA SERVICE : WEEKLY LISTING (US/0360-7151) [02243726] **3081**

LEGAL BIBLIOGRAPHY JOURNAL (US/0741-1189) [10084659] **3081**

LEGAL BRIEFS FOR EDITORS, PUBLISHERS, AND WRITERS (US/0149-1695) [03434013] 4816, **2999**

LEGAL BRIEFS FOR THE CONSTRUCTION INDUSTRY *CEASED.* (US/0730-952X) [08107485] 619, **2999**

LEGAL BULLETIN - UNITED STATES LEAGUE OF SAVINGS INSTITUTIONS (US/1049-376X) [12877790] **3087**

LEGAL BULLETIN (WASHINGTON) (US/0547-7794) [01796525] **3087**

LEGAL BUSINESS (UK/0958-4609) [I09584609] **2999**

LEGAL CIRCLE, THE (US/0145-2851) [02720756] **2999**

LEGAL COMPILATION (US) [02233765] **3114**

LEGAL CONNECTION; CORPORATIONS & LAW FIRMS, THE *CEASED.* (US/0270-3424) [05713772] **3101**

LEGAL CONSIDERATIONS IN DENTISTRY (US) [07092688] 1329, **2999**

LEGAL DATE (AT) 1761, **2999**

LEGAL DIRECTORY OF WASHINGTON STATE (US/0741-5036) [10187156] **2999**

LEGAL EAGLE, THE (US) [03061886] **2999**

LEGAL EDGE, THE (US/1063-9888) [17206950] **2999**

LEGAL EDUCATION REVIEW (AT/1033-2839) [19659528] **2999**

LEGAL EXECUTIVE, THE (UK/0024-0362) [01755724] 690, **2999**

LEGAL FOR LIFE (CN/1189-3257) [25796291] 905, **796**

LEGAL HANDBOOK FOR ARCHITECTS, ENGINEERS AND CONTRACTORS (US/0887-1183) [12865754] 302, 619, **2999**

LEGAL HISTORY (II/0377-0907) [02241708] **2999**

LEGAL INFORMATION ALERT (US/0883-1297) [10474392] **3081**

LEGAL INFORMATION MANAGEMENT INDEX (US/0747-9298) [10765349] 2999, 3223, **3082**

LEGAL INFORMATION MANAGEMENT REPORTS (US) [19016140] **2999**

LEGAL INFORMATION SERVICE - NATIVE LAW CENTRE (CN/0225-2287) [06054512] 2267, **2999**

LEGAL INFORMATION SERVICE (TEHRAN, IRAN) (IR) [09796111] **2999**

LEGAL INTELLIGENCER, THE (US/0277-495X) [06913244] **2999**

LEGAL INVESTIGATOR, THE (US/0741-417X) [10125127] **3000**

LEGAL ISSUES IN RECREATION ADMINISTRATION (US/1062-6719) [25695412] **4706**

LEGAL ISSUES OF EUROPEAN INTEGRATION (NE/0377-0915) [02859544] **3132**

LEGAL JOURNALS INDEX (UK/0950-4206) [16721926] **3000**

LEGAL LC SUBJECT HEADINGS -WEEKLY LISTS (US) **3000**

LEGAL-LEGISLATIVE REPORTER NEWS BULLETIN (US/0458-9599) [02860250] **3151**

LEGAL LOOSELEAFS IN PRINT (US/0275-4088) [07139482] **3082**

LEGAL MALPRACTICE REVIEW (US/0148-2750) [03280802] 2886, **3000**

LEGAL MANAGEMENT (US/1043-7355) [19048666] **3000**

LEGAL MEMORANDUM (RESTON), A (US/0192-6152) [02088629] 1865, **3000**

LEGAL NEWSLETTER (SPRINGFIELD, ILL.) (US/0732-4537) [07601082] **4704**

LEGAL NEWSLETTER (WASHINGTON, D.C.) (US/0739-5183) [09739964] **3000**

LEGAL NEWSLETTERS IN PRINT (US/8755-416X) [11299533] **3082**

LEGAL NOTES (US) [04995012] **3000**

LEGAL NOTES FOR EDUCATION (US/0093-397X) [01792350] 1761, **3000**

LEGAL NOTES FOR INSURANCE (US/0094-0623) [01793592] 2886, **3000**

LEGAL NOTES (WASHINGTON) (US/0147-9490) [03254086] **3087**

LEGAL OPINION LETTER / WASHINGTON LEGAL FOUNDATION (US/1056-1137) [23467614] **3000**

LEGAL OPINIONS OF THE OFFICE OF GENERAL COUNSEL - UNITED STATES. DEPT. OF HOUSING AND URBAN DEVELOPMENT (US/0272-7129) [05361519] **3000**

LEGAL PERIODICALS IN ENGLISH (US) [02046770] **3082**

LEGAL PERSPECTIVES *SUSPENDED.* (CN/0840-190X) [18998443] **3000**

LEGAL PUBLISHER, THE (US/1056-196X) [23528803] 3000, **4816**

LEGAL PUBLISHING PREVIEW *CEASED.* (US/0000-1333) [21362119] **3000**

LEGAL QUARTERLY DIGEST OF MINE SAFETY AND HEALTH DECISIONS (US/1051-533X) [21986612] 2865, 2143, **3000**

LEGAL REFERENCE SERVICES QUARTERLY (US/0270-319X) [06389554] 3223, **3000**

LEGAL REFORMER, THE (US) [18679712] **3000**

LEGAL REGISTER, METROPOLITAN WASHINGTON, THE (US/8756-2006) [06652059] **3000**

LEGAL REPORTER, THE (AT/0159-2483) [15926719] **3000**

LEGAL REQUIREMENTS FOR BUSINESS RECORDS (US) **3101**

LEGAL RESEARCH AND LAW LIBRARY MANAGEMENT. SUPPLEMENT / JULIUS J. MARKE, RICHAD SLOANE (US) [11935846] **3000**

LEGAL RESEARCH JOURNAL (US/0146-0382) [02905249] **3000**

LEGAL RESEARCH UPDATE (CN/0835-6009) [17462392] **3000**

LEGAL RESEARCHER'S DESK REFERENCE, THE (US/1050-3056) [21455280] **3000**

LEGAL RESOURCE INDEX (US/0272-9296) [06534211] 3000, **3082**

LEGAL RESPONSE : CHILD ADVOCACY AND PROTECTION *See* CHILDREN AND THE LAW COMMITTEE NEWSLETTER **5278**

LEGAL SECTION PROCEEDINGS / THE ... ANNUAL MEETING OF THE LEGAL SECTION OF THE AMERICAN COUNCIL OF LIFE INSURANCE (US) [22394317] 3000, **2886**

LEGAL SERIES (AU/0074-1868) [01753404] **1949**

LEGAL SERVICE BULLETIN *See* ALTERNATIVE LAW JOURNAL **3179**

LEGAL SHOCK (CN/0225-5391) [06285004] 4973, **3000**

LEGAL STUDIES FORUM, THE (US/0894-5993) [12005788] **3000**

LEGAL STUDIES (LONDON. 1981) (UK/0261-3875) [07708936] **3000**

LEGAL SUPPORT STAFF NEWSLETTER (CN/0229-5393) [07888602] 875, **3001**

LEGAL THEORY (UK/1352-3252) **3001**

LEGAL TIMES (US/0732-7536) [08239967] **3001**

LEGAL VIDEO REVIEW (US/0898-9427) [12257128] **3001**

LEGAL WRITING JOURNAL (US/0732-4529) [07289824] **3001**

LEGAL WRITING : THE JOURNAL OF THE LEGAL WRITING INSTITUTE (US) [25783718] **3001**

Alphabetical Title Index
LEICA

LEGALIDAD SOCIALISTA : BOLETIN DE INFORMACION JURIDICA EDITADO POR LA FISCALIA GENERAL DE LA REPUBLICA (CU/0138-7669) [09099592] **3001**

LEGALITA E GIUSTIZIA (IT) [15024939] **3001**

LEGALITY : A JOURNAL OF THE UNIVERSITY OF ZAMBIA LAW ASSOCIATION (ZA) [07972412] **3001**

LEGALITY OF MICROFILM (US) **1277**

LEGALTRAC [COMPUTER FILE] (US) **3001, 3082**

LEGEND (WASHINGTON, D.C.) (US/1058-1847) [24236799] **3404**

LEGENDA (BL) [06494904] **2552**

LEGENDE (CN/0226-7764) [06515211] **1761**

LEGENDS SPORTS MEMORABILIA (US/1067-4748) [27243030] **4903**

LEGGERE (IT) [20404273] **3404**

LEGGERE DONNA (IT) [17939853] **3404, 5560**

LEGGI D'ITALIA (IT) **3001**

LEGGI, LE (IT) **3001**

LEGGI NUOVE *CEASED.* (IT) **3001**

LEGGI PER LA CASA (IT) **3001**

LEGGI REGIONALI TOSCANA (IT) **3001**

LEGI SOCIAL (FR/0223-4726) [09705513] **3151**

LEGION (CN/0024-0435) [02049993] **4049**

LEGION OF SUPER-HEROES (US) [21765810] **4863**

LEGION, THE (UK) [06713572] **2518**

LEGIONNAIRES DISEASE UPDATE SERVICE (UK) **4788**

LEGIPRESSE (FR/0751-9478) [07519478] **3001**

LEGIS BANCOS INFORMATIVO CVM / COMISSAO DA VALORES MOBILIARIOS (BL) [07163377] **3001**

LEGIS BANCOS INFORMATIVO. IMPOSTO DE RENDA : IR (BL) [09313780] **3001**

LEGISLACAO DE ENSINO DE 1O. E 2O. GRAUS. FEDERAL (BL) [09764539] **1761, 3001**

LEGISLACAO DO DISTRITO FEDERAL (BL) [02239311] **3001**

LEGISLACAO DO ESTADO DE MATO GROSSO DO SUL / SECRETARIA DE ADMINISTRACAO (BL) [08072870] **3001**

LEGISLACAO DO ESTADO DO RIO DE JANEIRO (BL) [03125213] **3001**

LEGISLACAO DO ESTADO DO RIO DE JANEIRO / SECRETARIA DE ESTADO DE JUSTICA, DIVISAO DE DIVULGACAO (BL/0100-378X) [08018986] **3001**

LEGISLACAO DO TRABALHO *See* REVISTA LTR **3153**

LEGISLACAO FEDERAL E MARGINALIA (BL) [08868139] **3001**

LEGISLACAO LISBOA. (1991) (PO/0871-9497) [08719497] **4480**

LEGISLACAO MINEIRA *See* REVISTA JURIDICA LEMI. EDICAO NACIONAL **3042**

LEGISLACION ECONOMICA (CK) [06621121] **1503**

LEGISLACION VENEZOLANA (VE) [09901824] **3001**

LEGISLATIEF (IO) [02241168] **3001**

LEGISLATION AFFECTING SOUTH DAKOTA MUNICIPALITIES (US/0093-2280) [05512388] **4661**

LEGISLATION CHECK LIST (US/0095-8220) [01798018] **3001**

LEGISLATION DIGEST (CN) **2369**

LEGISLATION DU TRAVAIL (CN/0848-5925) [23247997] **1615**

LEGISLATION (SCARBOROUGH) (CN/1183-062X) [23304544] **3001**

LEGISLATIVE ACTIONS AFFECTING HIGHER EDUCATION, WASHINGTON STATE LEGISLATURE (US) [04023033] **1865**

LEGISLATIVE ALERT (US) **4661**

LEGISLATIVE ALERT (US) **4661, 3001**

LEGISLATIVE APPROPRIATIONS REPORT (US/0160-1245) [03617102] **3001**

LEGISLATIVE ASSEMBLY OF ALBERTA (CN/1182-7823) [23264549] **4661**

LEGISLATIVE ASSEMBLY REPORT ON APPROPRIATIONS AND ESTIMATED REVENUES (US) [05465051] **4736**

LEGISLATIVE BUDGET BOOK : A PUBLICATION OF THE LEGISLATIVE BUDGET OFFICE / JOINT SENATE FINANCE-HOUSE APPROPRIATIONS COMMITTEE (US) [10540728] **4661**

LEGISLATIVE BUDGET ESTIMATES (US/0495-2499) [02144361] **4661, 4736**

LEGISLATIVE BULLETIN - ASSOCIATION OF WASHINGTON CITIES (US/0740-4204) [09948654] **4661, 3001**

LEGISLATIVE BULLETIN - FLORIDA (US/0426-570X) [01387182] **3001**

LEGISLATIVE BULLETIN - NEW YORK STATE SCHOOL BOARDS ASSOCIATION (US/1048-2733) [04866803] **1865**

LEGISLATIVE BULLETIN / OHIO CITIZENS' COUNCIL (US/0739-0130) [09680384] **3001**

LEGISLATIVE BULLETIN, THE (US) [07511891] **3001**

LEGISLATIVE CALENDAR / COMMITTEE ON ENERGY AND COMMERCE (US) [07849197] **4661**

LEGISLATIVE CALENDAR / SELECT COMMITTEE ON INTELLIGENCE, UNITED STATES SENATE (US) [09966548] **4661**

LEGISLATIVE CALENDAR / UNITED STATES HOUSE OF REPRESENTATIVES, COMMITTEE ON BANKING, FINANCE, AND URBAN AFFAIRS (US/0190-5473) [04719229] **796, 4661**

LEGISLATIVE CALENDAR / UNITED STATES HOUSE OF REPRESENTATIVES, COMMITTEE ON RULES (US/0190-5805) [01368238] **4661**

LEGISLATIVE CALENDAR / UNITED STATES HOUSE OF REPRESENTATIVES, COMMITTEE ON THE BUDGET (US/0147-3638) [03145476] **4736**

LEGISLATIVE CALENDAR / UNITED STATES HOUSE OF REPRESENTATIVES, COMMITTEE ON VETERAN AFFAIRS (US/0364-4200) [02552192] **4049, 4661**

LEGISLATIVE CALENDAR - UNITED STATES SENATE. COMMITTEE ON AGRICULTURE, NUTRITION, AND FORESTRY (US/0147-4103) [03160214] **4661**

LEGISLATIVE CALENDAR - UNITED STATES SENATE. COMMITTEE ON GOVERNMENTAL AFFAIRS (US/0147-6572) [03214304] **4661**

LEGISLATIVE CONFERENCE REPORT (US) [25334529] **2267**

LEGISLATIVE DIGEST ALASKA (US) [29205709] **4661**

LEGISLATIVE DIGEST (ASSOCIATION OF WASHINGTON CITIES) *See* LEGISLATIVE BULLETIN - ASSOCIATION OF WASHINGTON CITIES **3001**

LEGISLATIVE DIGEST (CN) **2369**

LEGISLATIVE DIGEST : BILLS OF LABOR INTEREST PASSED BY THE NEW YORK STATE LEGISLATURE (US) [07020414] **3151**

LEGISLATIVE FISCAL REPORT (CARSON CITY) (US/0363-2121) [02433439] **3001**

LEGISLATIVE FISCAL REPORT TO THE JOINT SENATE FINANCE-HOUSE APPROPRIATIONS COMMITTEE *See* IDAHO LEGISLATIVE FISCAL REPORT TO THE JOINT SENATE FINANCE-HOUSE APPROPRIATIONS COMMITTEE : A PUBLICATION OF THE LEGISLATIVE BUDGET OFFICE **4655**

LEGISLATIVE HISTORY OF CAB REGULATIONS (US) [04506541] **27, 3002**

LEGISLATIVE HISTORY OF TITLES I-XX OF THE SOCIAL SECURITY ACT (US/0732-6394) [08006388] **5294, 3002**

LEGISLATIVE INFORMATION SERVICE (US) **4661**

LEGISLATIVE MANUAL - GENERAL ASSEMBLY OF SOUTH CAROLINA (US/0362-272X) [01766093] **4661**

LEGISLATIVE MANUAL (NORTH CAROLINA. GENERAL ASSEMBLY. LEGISLATIVE SERVICES OFFICE) (US) [06599914] **3141**

LEGISLATIVE MANUAL OF THE NEVADA LEGISLATURE *See* LEGISLATIVE MANUAL, STATE OF NEVADA **3002**

LEGISLATIVE MANUAL, STATE OF NEVADA (US) [01380265] **3002**

LEGISLATIVE MANUAL, STATE OF WASHINGTON (US) [19650695] **4661**

LEGISLATIVE MEMORANDUM (US) [04855086] **3002**

LEGISLATIVE NETWORK FOR NURSES (US/8756-0054) [11455768] **3861, 3002**

LEGISLATIVE NEWS ALERT (US/0889-4574) [14073936] **4698, 4661**

LEGISLATIVE REPORT - COUNCIL ON BLACK MINNESOTANS (US) [09449184] **2267, 3002**

LEGISLATIVE REPORT (EDMONTON) (CN/0709-5333) [05529022] **3002**

LEGISLATIVE REPORT / MICHIGAN COUNCIL FOR THE ARTS (US) [07137981] **324, 3002**

LEGISLATIVE REPORT ON JUVENILE PROBATION SUBSIDY (US/0364-5649) [02665568] **3169**

LEGISLATIVE REPORTER (LINCOLN) *CEASED.* (US/0092-1505) [01787480] **3108**

LEGISLATIVE REPORTING SERVICE / COMMERCE CLEARING HOUSE (US) [08776884] **4661**

LEGISLATIVE REVIEW (US/0145-8604) [02791439] **3002**

LEGISLATIVE REVIEW ACTIVITY - UNITED STATES. CONGRESS. SENATE. COMMITTEE ON LABOR AND HUMAN RESOURCES (US/0730-2649) [07960963] **3002**

LEGISLATIVE STATUS REPORT (NATIONAL ASSOCIATION OF COMMUNITY HEALTH CENTERS) (US/0739-7690) [09714359] **4789, 3002**

LEGISLATIVE STATUS REPORT - UNITED STATES. VETERANS ADMINISTRATION (US/8755-4410) [08374098] **3002**

LEGISLATIVE STUDIES QUARTERLY (US/0362-9805) [02398192] **4480**

LEGISLATIVE SUMMARY - CONNECTICUT. DEPT. ON AGING (US) [05757316] **3002**

LEGISLATIVE SUMMARY - DEPARTMENT OF COMMUNITY AND REGIONAL AFFAIRS, DIVISION OF COMMUNITY AND RURAL DEVELOPMENT (US/0147-9644) [03252344] **3002**

LEGISLATIVE SYNOPSIS AND DIGEST ... GENERAL ASSEMBLY, STATE OF ILLINOIS (US) [12429807] **4661**

LEGISLATIVE UPDATE - ALABAMA COUNCIL FOR SCHOOL ADMINISTRATION AND SUPERVISION (US/1056-7569) [23845835] **1866**

LEGISLATIVE UPDATE / CONGRESSIONAL HISPANIC CAUCUS (US) [22616861] **2267**

LEGISLATOR'S GUIDE, A (US) [08164968] **4661**

LEGISLATOR'S HANDBOOK (DETROIT, MICH.), THE (US/0278-1352) [05739150] **4736**

LEGISLATURE OF ONTARIO DEBATES. OFFICIAL REPORT (HANSARD). STANDING COMMITTEE ON REGULATIONS AND OTHER STATUTORY INSTRUMENTS (CN/0711-9682) [10425687] **3002**

LEGISLAZIONE ITALIANA, LA (IT) [16573374] **3002**

LEGISLAZIONE PENALE (IT/0393-134X) [0393134X] **3169**

LEGISLAZIONE PENALE (IT) **3002**

LEGISLAZIONE PENALE TRIBUTARIA (IT) **3002**

LEGISLAZIONE PER LA SICUREZZA E L IGIENE DEL LAVORO (IT) **4789**

LEGISLAZIONE VALUTARIA ITALIANA (IT) **844, 690**

LEGISLETTER (US/8756-5587) [10568406] **3002**

LEGISTATIVE QUICK REPORT (US) [21431824] **4661**

LEGNO, IL (IT) [04089573] **844**

LEGO DACTA DEALER NEWS (US/1056-4837) [23723476] **1615**

LEGON JOURNAL OF THE HUMANITIES (GH) [02303238] **2849**

LEGON OBSERVER, THE (GH/0024-0540) [03889842] **2641**

LEGUME RESEARCH (II/0250-5371) [04402524] **105**

LEGUMES FRAIS, FRANCE: STATISTIQUES DE COMMERCE EXTERIEUR (FR) [04374202] **1616**

LEHI FREE PRESS (US/8750-4669) [11461448] **5756**

LEHIGH COUNTY HISTORICAL SOCIETY *See* PROCEEDINGS OF THE LEHIGH COUNTY HISTORICAL SOCIETY **2755**

LEHRBUCH DER DIFFERENTIELLEN PSYCHOLOGIE (GW) [06111071] **4602**

LEHRBUCHER UND MONOGRAPHIEN ZUR DIDAKTIK DER MATHEMATIK (GW) [15278044] **3516**

LEHREN UND LERNEN (GW/0341-8294) [02432020] **1761**

LEHRLINGSSTATISTIK / KAMMER DER GEWERBLICHEN WIRTSCHAFT FUER STEIERMARK (AU) [01792271] **1687**

LEI (MILANO. 1976) *See* GLAMOUR MILANO **5557**

LEI MILANO. 1976 (IT/1120-7736) [11207736] **5560**

LEIA (SAO PAULO, BRAZIL) *SUSPENDED.* (BL) [12030786] **418**

LEIBESUEBUNGEN-LEIBESERZIEHUNG (AU) **2599**

LEIBNIZ : SAEMTLICHE SCHRIFTEN UND BRIEFE (GW) **4352**

LEICA-FOTOGRAFIE (GW/0024-0621) [03067795] **4371**

LEICA FOTOGRAFIE INTERNATIONAL (GW/0937-3977) [19619581] **4371**

LEICA MANUAL (US/0093-9374) [01793937] **4371**

LEICESTER Alphabetical Title Index

LEICESTER, ENGLAND. UNIVERSITY. DEPT. OF ENGLISH LOCAL HISTORY *See* OCCASIONAL PAPERS - DEPT. OF ENGLISH LOCAL HISTORY, LEICESTER UNIVERSITY **2701**

LEICHHARDT HISTORICAL JOURNAL (AT) [02312758] **2670**

LEICHTATHLET, DER *See* LEICHTATHLETIK **4903**

LEICHTATHLET BERLIN, DDR. 1953 (GW/0323-4134) [I03234134] **4903**

LEICHTATHLETIK (GW) [15142031] **4903**

LEIDEN BOTANICAL SERIES (NE) [03149516] **517**

LEIDEN JOURNAL OF INTERNATIONAL LAW (NE/0922-1565) [18978561] **3132**

LEIDINGGEVEN & ORGANISEREN (NE) **875**

LEIDS KUNSTHISTORISCH JAARBOEK (NE/0169-4855) [09379203] 302, **357**

LEIDSE GERMANISTISCHE EN ANGLISTISCHE REEKS (NE/0458-9971) [02300455] 3297, **3404**

LEIDSE ROMANTISCHE REEKS (NE/0075-8647) [01716925] 3297, **3404**

LEIF : LIFE AND EDUCATION IN FINLAND (FI/0788-2211) [24069480] 1761, **1801**

LEIPZIG. DEUTSCHE ZENTRALBUCHEREI FUR BLINDE *See* HORBUCHVERZEICHNIS **5266**

LEIPZIG. MUSEUM FUR VOLKERKUNDE *See* MITTEILUNGEN - MUSEUM FUER VOLKERKUNDE ZU LEIPZIG **4091**

LEIPZIG. UNIVERSITAT. MUSIKINSTRUMENTEN-MUSEUM *See* AUFSATZE UND JAHRESBERICHT - KARL-MARX-UNIVERSITAT MUSIKINSTRUMENTEN-MUSEUM **4101**

LEISTUNGSSPORT (GW/0341-7387) [05200152] **3954**

●LEISURE AND FAMILY FUN: LAFF (US/1053-4814) [22538270] **4851**

LEISURE AND PERSONAL SERVICES (CN/0838-2174) [20938341] **1616**

LEISURE & RECREATION (JA/0915-1729) [I09151729] **4851**

LEISURE AND RECREATION STATISTICS ESTIMATES (UK) [06687596] **4856**

LEISURE ARTS (US/0890-6386) [14294123] **324**

LEISURE BEVERAGE INSIDER NEWSLETTER (US/1040-3736) [10485693] **2369**

LEISURE FORUM (CN/0704-643X) [03887256] **4851**

LEISURE INDUSTRY REPORT (US) [17531628] **4851**

LEISURE INFORMATION QUARTERLY / NEW YORK UNIVERSITY, SCHOOL OF EDUCATION, HEALTH, NURSING AND ARTS PROFESSIONS, DEPT. OF RECREATION, LEISURE STUDIES, PHYSICAL EDUCATION & SPORT (US) [10032170] **4851**

LEISURE LINES (SACRAMENTO, CALIF.) (US/0733-5377) [07934126] **4706**

LEISURE MANAGEMENT (UK/0266-9102) [10059727] **4852**

LEISURE MANAGER : THE JOURNAL OF THE INSTITUTE OF LEISURE & AMENITY MANAGEMENT, THE (UK/0267-3754) [11929610] **4852**

LEISURE NEWSLETTER (CN/0701-1334) [03436326] **5251**

LEISURE OPPORTUNITIES (UK/0952-8210) [24352855] **4852**

LEISURE OPTIONS (AT/1036-0573) [I10360573] **4852**

LEISURE PAINTER AND CRAFTSMAN (UK) 374, **4224**

LEISURE, RECREATION, AND TOURISM ABSTRACTS (UK/0261-1392) [07379122] 5482, 4852, **4856**

LEISURE SCIENCES (US/0149-0400) [03421956] 4852, **5208**

LEISURE STUDIES (UK/0261-4367) [08419589] **4852**

LEISURE TIME ELECTRONICS *CEASED*. (US/0273-6586) [06798848] **2070**

LEISURE TODAY, SELECTED READINGS (US) [06719283] **4852**

●LEISURE WATCH CANADA (CN/1189-4873) [26714727] **4707**

LEISURE WHEELS (CN/0709-7093) [05840801] **5385**

LEISURE WORLD (CN/1184-146X) [23598656] 4852, **5482**

LEISURE WORLD NEWS (US/0745-5011) [09242511] **2537**

LEISUREWAYS (CN/0712-5747) [09318451] 5482, **4852**

LEITENDE ANGESTELLTE (GW) [06674938] **943**

LEITENDE MANNER UND FRAUER DER WIRTSCHAFT (GW) [05260360] 1503, **433**

LEITERPLATTEN (GW/0177-1205) [I01771205] **1193**

LEITFADEN DER ANGEWANDTEN MATHEMATIK UND MECHANIK (GW/0459-021X) [11217515] **3516**

LEITUNG UND PLANUNG VON WISSENSCHAFT UND TECHNIK (SZ) [03259740] **5126**

LEJEUNIA (BE/0457-4184) [04872250] **517**

LEJOTIEK BRUSSEL (BE/0777-3455) [I07773455] **5251**

LEKARSKY OBZOR (XO/0457-4214) [09451697] **3604**

LEKARZ WOJSKOWY (PL/0024-0745) [01778877] **3604**

LEKTUURGIDS; BIBLIOGRAFICH TIJDSCHRIFT (BE) [05216588] **418**

LELIRE ET L'ECRIRE (CN/0824-2712) [10082750] **5788**

LEMBAGA (IO) [03098385] **3297**

LEMBAGA BIOLOGI NASIONAL *See* LAPORAN TAHUNAN **463**

LEMBAGA EKONOMI DAN KEMASYARAKATAN NASIONAL. PERPUSTAKAAN *See* DAFTAR TAMBAHAN KOLEKSI PERPUSTAKAAN LEKNAS **1531**

LEMBAGA ILMU PENGETAHUAN INDONESIA *See* BULLETIN **5090**

LEMBAGA ILMU PENGETAHUAN INDONESIA. BERITA L.I.P.I *See* BERITA ILMU PENGETAHUAN DAN TEKNOLOGI **5088**

LEMBAGA PEMASARAN PERTANIAN PERSEKUTUAN *See* QUARTERLY COMMODITY STATISTICS - LEMBAGA PEMASARAN PERTANIAN PERSEKUTUAN **1537**

LEMBAGA PENDIDIKAN DAN PEMBINAAN MANAJEMEN *See* REPORT - INSTITUTE FOR MANAGEMENT EDUCATION AND DEVELOPMENT **884**

LEMBAGA STUDI PEMBANGUNAN (INDONESIA) *See* LAPORAN / LEMBAGA STUDI PEMBANGUNAN **1572**

LEMBARAN PUBLIKASI PUSAT PENGEMBANGAN TEKNOLOGI MINYAK DAN GAS BUMI LEMIGAS (IO/0125-9644) [06638906] **4263**

LEMEL (AT/0729-5898) [I07295898] 4007, **2915**

LEMKIVSCINA (US/0888-2436) [10239750] **2696**

LEMKIVSKYJ KALENDAR (CN/0317-2910) [02248055] **2744**

LEMON-AID (US) [06008958] **5684**

LEMON-AID (1985) (CN/0834-2423) [16320148] **5418**

LEMON-AID NEW CAR GUIDE (CN/0714-5861) [09029951] **5418**

LEMONT METROPOLITAN (US/8750-6998) [11686757] **5661**

LEMOUZI (FR/0024-0761) [08607259] 3459, **2321**

LEMOYNE-TILLY 735-KV LINE (CN/1186-7043) [24402167] **1985**

LEMOYNE-TILLY LIGNE A 735 KV (CN/1186-7035) [24402164] **2197**

LEMPESIS REPORT ON PERSONAL COMPUTING *CEASED*. (US/1054-5166) [22904764] **1193**

LEN BUCKWALTER'S NORTH AMERICAN CB CHANNEL DIRECTORY (US/0148-0189) [03256311] **1159**

LENAU-FORUM (AU/0024-0788) [01434265] **3404**

LENDEMAINS (GW) [04525547] 3297, **3404**

LENDER LIABILITY LAW REPORT (US/1045-1463) [16349314] **3087**

LENDER LIABILITY LITIGATION REPORTER (US/1042-5764) [19019352] **3087**

LENDER LIABILITY NEWS (US/0898-7645) [17894435] **3087**

LENDING LAW FORUM, THE (US/0098-891X) [02242563] **3087**

LENDING TRANSACTIONS AND THE BANKRUPTCY REFORM ACT (US/0733-0049) [06509461] **3087**

LENGAS (FR/0153-0313) [04289865] **3297**

LENGTH OF STAY BY DIAGNOSIS AND OPERATION, NORTH CENTRAL REGION (US/0895-9846) [16883200] **3787**

LENGTH OF STAY BY DIAGNOSIS AND OPERATION, NORTHEASTERN REGION (US/0895-9838) [16883139] **3787**

LENGTH OF STAY BY DIAGNOSIS AND OPERATION, SOUTHERN REGION (US/0895-9854) [16883240] **3787**

LENGTH OF STAY BY DIAGNOSIS AND OPERATION, UNITED STATES (US/0895-982X) [16882259] **3787**

LENGTH OF STAY BY DIAGNOSIS AND OPERATION, WESTERN REGION (US/0895-9862) [16883271] **3788**

LENGTH OF STAY IN PAS HOSPITALS, UNITED STATES, EASTERN REGION (US/0096-1329) [01332580] **3788**

LENGUAJE (CK) [05250902] **3297**

LENGUAJE CALI (CK/0120-3479) [I01203479] **3297**

LENGUAJE Y CIENCIAS (PE/0024-0796) [02093386] **3297**

LENGUAJES (AG) [02242831] **3297**

LENGUAS MODERNAS (VE/0503-8448) [01497284] **3297**

LENGUAS MODERNAS (SANTIAGO) (CL/0716-0542) [04609952] **3297**

LENINGRAD. GOSUDARSTVENNYI PEDAGOGICHESKII INSTITUT IMENI A.I. GERTSENA *See* GERTSENOVSKIE CHTENIIA: INOSTRANNYE IAZYKI **3284**

LENINGRAD. GOSUDARSTVENNYI RUSSKII MUZEI *See* SOOBSHCHENIIA **364**

LENINGRAD. INSTITUT VODNOGO TRANSPORTA. GIDROTEKHNICHESKAIA LABORATORIIA *See* MATERIALY **2093**

LENINGRAD, RUSSIAN S. F. S. R. STATISTICHESKOE UPRAVLENIE *See* NARODNOE KHOZIAISTVO LENINGRADA I LENINGRADSKOI OBLASTI **5334**

LENINGRAD. UNIVERSITET. FILOLOGICHESKII FAKUKTET *See* VOPROSY FILOLOGII **3332**

LENINGRAD. UNIVERSITET. LESOSTEPNAIA NAUCHNO-ISSLEDOVATEL'SKAIA STANTSIIA *See* TRUDY LESOSTEPNOI NAUCHNO-ISSLEDOVATEL'SKOI STANTSII LENINGRADSKOGO UNIVERSITETA "LES NA VORSKLE." **2397**

LENINGRAD. UNIVERSITET. MATEMATIKO-MEKHANICHESKII FAKULTET *See* PRIKLADNAIA MEKHANIKA **2125**

LENINGRAD. VSESOIUZNYI INSTITUT ZASHCHITY RASTENII *See* BIULLETEN VSESOIUZNOGO NAUCHNO-ISSLEDOVATELSKOGO INSTITUTA ZASHCHITY RASTENII **502**

LENINGRADSKII GOSUDARSTVENNYI PEDAGOGICHESKII INSTITUT IMENI A. I. GERTSENA *See* GERTSENOVSKIE CHTENIIA; KHIMIIA **976**

LENINIST (LONDON, ENGLAND) *CEASED*. (UK) [14190697] **4543**

LENINSKAIA TEORIIA OTRAZHENIIA I PROBLEMY PSIKHOLOGII (RU) [05718674] 4602, **583**

LENKURT DEMODULATOR *See* GTE LENKURT DEMODULATOR **2056**

LENOX TIME TABLE (US) [11241454] **5671**

LENS AND EYE TOXICITY RESEARCH (US/1042-6922) [19106905] **3604**

LENS : LENTIL EXPERIMENTAL NEWS SERVICE (CN/0828-1432) [06261960] **178**

LENS NEWSLETTER (SY) [19872178] **178**

LENT (VAN LENT) NEWSLETTER (US/0883-7406) [12223048] **2458**

LENTIL ABSTRACTS *CEASED*. (UK/0260-8464) [08363310] **105**

LEO BAECK INSTITUT BULLETIN *See* JUDISCHER ALMANACH **2695**

LEO BAECK INSTITUTE OF JEWS FROM GERMANY *See* LBI NEWS (NEW YORK, N.Y.) **2696**

LEOM, LEOM U-MASORET (IS) [01796424] **5050**

LEON COUNTY HISTORICAL COLLECTIONS (US/0731-8960) [08264452] **2744**

LEON HUNTERS DISPATCH, THE (US/8756-5595) [11565474] **2458**

LEON JOURNAL-REPORTER, THE (US) [15468357] **5671**

●LEONARDO ELECTRONIC ALMANAC (US/1071-4391) [28648107] 5126, **324**

LEONARDO (KISSING) (GW/0935-1108) [24394480] **302**

LEONARDO MUSIC JOURNAL : LMJ : JOURNAL OF THE INTERNATIONAL SOCIETY FOR THE ARTS, SCIENCES AND TECHNOLOGY (UK/0961-1215) [25225778] **4128**

LEONARDO (OXFORD) (UK/0024-094X) [01755782] **357**

LEONARD'S ANNUAL PRICE INDEX OF ART AUCTIONS (US/0747-6566) [09295343] **357**

●LEONARD'S ANNUAL PRICE INDEX OF PRINTS, POSTERS & PHOTOGRAPHS (US/1064-0452) [26200177] 357, **4371**

LEOPOLDIANUM (BL/0101-9635) [02243797] **1834**

LEOPOLDINA (GW) [01755783] **5126**

LEOTI STANDARD (US) [12727767] **5677**

Alphabetical Title Index — LETTERS

LEPIDOPTERA (DK/0075-8787) [03773082] **5590**

LEPIDOPTERISTS' SOCIETY *See* NEWS OF THE LEPIDOPTERISTS' SOCIETY **5592**

LEPRA REPORT (UK) [06317586] **3604**

LEPROSY RELIEF (CANADA) *See* LEPROSY RELIEF CANADA INC **4789**

LEPROSY RELIEF CANADA INC (CN/0382-7682) [02848030] **4789**

LEPROSY REVIEW (UK/0305-7518) [01715866] **3604**

LEPTA (RU) [24729998] **3404**

LEPTOSPIROSIS SURVEILLANCE, ANNUAL SUMMARY (1977) (US) [08569997] **4789**

LER HISTORIA (PO) [10757504] **2696**

LERCHE, DIE (GW) [17991528] **5590**

LERNFELD BETRIEB (GW/0930-4460) [09304460] 1503, **690**

LESBIAN AND GAY STUDIES NEWSLETTER : LGSN (CN/1064-5950) [20750504] **2795**

LESBIAN CONTRADICTION (US/1064-4776) [11086337] **2795**

LESBIAN ETHICS (US/8755-5352) [11337345] 2795, **2252**

LESBIAN-GAY LAW NOTES (US/8755-9021) [10938096] 2795, **3002**

LESBIAN HERSTORY ARCHIVES NEWSLETTER (US/1064-0819) [10758876] **2795**

LESBIAN NEWS (CANOGA PARK, CALIF.), THE (US/0739-1803) [05269194] 5560, **2795**

LESBIAN READER, THE (US/0361-5928) [02308540] **2795**

●LESBIAN REVIEW OF BOOKS, THE (US/1077-5684) [30835592] **2795**

LESBO (MONTREAL) *CEASED.* (CN/0712-8398) [08734094] **2795**

LESELAND (GW) [11299346] **4829**

LESHONENU (IS/0024-1091) [01695301] **3297**

LESHONENU LA-AM (IS) [01794650] **3297**

LESKOS INFO POWER (US) **3223**

LESKOVACKI ZBORNIK (YU/0459-1070) [05281092] 4090, **2696**

LESLIE COUNTY NEWS (HYDEN, KY.) (US) [15056955] **5681**

LESNAIA PROMYSHLENNOST (MOSKVA) (RU/0368-7619) [01755787] **2387**

LESNICKA PRACE (XR/0322-9254) [01780610] **2387**

LESNICKY CASOPIS (XO/0323-1046) [01713738] **2387**

LESNICTVI (XR/0024-1105) [07761609] **2387**

LESNOE KHOZAJSTVO (MOSKVA) (RU/0024-1113) [01755788] **2387**

LESOSECHNYE, LESOSKLADSKIE RABOTY I SUKHOPUTNYI TRANSPORT LESA : MEZHVUZOVSKII SBORNIK NAUCHNYKH TRUDOV / LENINGRADSKAIA LESOTEKHNICHESKAIA AKADEMIIA IMENI S.M. KIROVA (RU/0134-5710) [08942940] 2402, **2387**

LESOTHO BUSINESS DIRECTORY (LO) [01790012] **690**

LESOTHO EXPORT DIRECTORY (LO) [19711252] **844**

LESOTHO INDEX (LO) [20456410] **2499**

LESOTHO LAW JOURNAL (LO/0255-6472) [12207334] **3002**

LESOTHO STATISTICAL YEARBOOK / COMPILED AND ISSUED BY BUREAU OF STATISTICS (LO) [19031342] **5332**

LESOVEDEIE I LESNOE KHOZIAISTVO (RU/0132-8743) [09863873] **5126**

LESOVEDENIE (RU/0024-1148) [01755789] **2387**

LESOVEDENIE. ENGLISH. SOVIET FOREST SCIENCES *See* RUSSIAN FOREST SCIENCES **2394**

LESOVODSTVO I AGROLESOMELIORATSIIA (UN/0459-1216) [06108517] **2387**

LESOVODSTVO, LESNYE KULTURY I POCHVOVEDENIE (RU/0130-9099) [01793645] 178, **2387**

LESSING YEARBOOK (US/0075-8833) [01794961] **3346**

LESSOR'S GUIDE TO RESIDUAL VALUES - COMPUTER (US) **1245**

L'ESTAMPE, DE (CN/0712-6700) [09582051] **380**

LET THE PEOPLE WORSHIP (US/0891-3927) [14924890] **4973**

LETCHER COUNTY COMMUNITY NEWS-PRESS (US/0899-1820) [17946512] **5681**

LETECKY OBZOR (XR) [06205511] **27**

LETECTVI + I.E. A KOSMONAUTIKA (XR/0024-1156) [01782686] **27**

LETHAIA (NO/0024-1164) [02277593] **4227**

LETHBRIDGE HERALD MICROFORM, THE (CN/0839-4938) [10386367] **5788**

LETHBRIDGE MAGAZINE (CN/0821-5278) [09606636] **2537**

LETMINIMUM / KOZPONTI STATISZTIKAI HIVATAL (HU) [25857234] **5332**

LETNANY, CZECHOSLOVAK REPUBLIC. VYZKUMNY A ZKUSEBNI LETECKY USTAV *See* ZPRAVA VZLU **41**

LETNI PREGLED INVESTICIJ (XV) [09872888] **905**

LETNI PREGLED PROMETA IN ZVEZ (XV) [07042046] **5385**

LETNI PREGLED ZUNANJE TRGOVINE / ZAVOD SR SLOVENIJE ZA STATISTIKO (XV) [08000481] **844**

LETOPIS' GAZETNYKH STATEI (RU/0024-1172) [01714341] **5809**

LETOPIS IZOIZDANII (RU) [02731061] **357**

LETOPIS PECHATI SEVERNOI OSETII (RU) [11480787] **418**

LETOPIS PERIODICHESKIKH I PRODOLZHAIUSHCHIKHSIA IZDANII / GOSUDARSTVENNYI KOMITET SOVETA MINISTROV SSSR PO DELAM IZDATELSTV, POLIGRAFII I KNIZHNOI TORGOVLI [I] VSESOIUZNAIA KNIZHNAIA PALATA (RU) [05360588] **3404**

LETOPIS RETSENZII (RU) [09551076] **1927**

LETOPIS SLOVENSKE AKADEMIJE ZNANOSTI IN UMETNOSTI (XV/0374-0315) [01775075] **2849**

LETOPIS ZHURNALNYKH STATEI (RU/0024-1202) [01589828] **418**

LETOPISI I KHRONIKI (RU) [01796723] **2696**

LETOPISI : IZDANIE NA SUIUZA NA BULGARSKITE PISATELI (BU) [23729627] **3404**

LETRA (RIO DE JANEIRO, BRAZIL) (BL) [07211555] 3297, **3404**

LETRAS DE BUENOS AIRES (AG/0326-2928) [07699567] **3404**

LETRAS DE DEUSTO (SP/0210-3516) [04251089] **2849**

LETRAS DE HOJE (BL/0101-3335) [04927844] 3404, **3297**

LETRAS DEL ECUADOR (EC) [02263496] **1761**

LETRAS FEMENINAS (US/0277-4356) [03816008] 5560, **3404**

LETRAS PENINSULARES (US/0897-7542) [17616837] **3404**

LETRAS Y COLORES : A CULTURAL PUBLICATION BY EL CENTRO CULTURAL DE LA RAZA (US) [24229524] **2267**

LETRONER, DER (GW) **690**

LET'S CHEER (US/0733-9674) [08131766] **4903**

LET'S DANCE (US/0024-1253) [01755793] **1313**

LET'S GO. BUDGET GUIDE TO GREECE *See* LET'S GO. THE BUDGET GUIDE TO GREECE & TURKEY **5483**

LET'S GO. BUDGET GUIDE TO ISRAEL AND EGYPT (US) [17868554] **5482**

LET'S GO. BUDGET GUIDE TO SPAIN, PORTUGAL & MOROCCO *See* LET'S GO. THE BUDGET GUIDE TO SPAIN & PORTUGAL **5483**

●LET'S GO. BUDGET GUIDE TO USA & CANADA (US) **5482**

●LET'S GO RACIN' (CN/1188-5416) [26714630] **4903**

LET'S GO: THE BUDGET GUIDE TO BRITAIN AND IRELAND (US) [05142902] **5482**

LET'S GO. THE BUDGET GUIDE TO CALIFORNIA AND HAWAII INCLUDING RENO, LAS VEGAS, GRAND CANYON, AND BAJA CALIFORNIA (US/0898-8366) [17258026] **5482**

LET'S GO: THE BUDGET GUIDE TO EUROPE (US/0163-4585) [02086831] **5482**

LET'S GO: THE BUDGET GUIDE TO FRANCE (US) [04974365] **5482**

●LET'S GO: THE BUDGET GUIDE TO GREECE & TURKEY (US/1064-1009) [25127355] **5483**

LET'S GO. THE BUDGET GUIDE TO ITALY (INCLUDING TUNISIA) (US/1043-4690) [17416758] **5483**

LET'S GO. THE BUDGET GUIDE TO LONDON (US/1057-6274) [23007436] **5483**

LET'S GO. THE BUDGET GUIDE TO LONDON / WRITTEN BY HARVARD STUDENT AGENCIES, INC (US) [23011842] **5483**

LET'S GO. THE BUDGET GUIDE TO MEXICO (US) [12239721] **5483**

LET'S GO. THE BUDGET GUIDE TO NEW YORK CITY (US/1059-0412) [23011717] **5483**

LET'S GO. THE BUDGET GUIDE TO PACIFIC NORTHWEST, WESTERN CANADA, AND ALASKA INCLUDING ALBERTA AND BRITISH COLUMBIA--VANCOUVER, BANFF AND LAKE LOUISE, CALGARY, GLACIER/WATERTON NATIONAL PARKS (US/0898-6215) [17292226] **5483**

●LET'S GO. THE BUDGET GUIDE TO SPAIN & PORTUGAL (US) [27474576] **5483**

LET'S GO. THE BUDGET GUIDE TO THE USA (US/0275-9837) [07088264] **5483**

LET'S GO. THE BUDGET GUIDE TO THE USA *See* LET'S GO. BUDGET GUIDE TO USA & CANADA **5482**

●LET'S GO: THE BUDGET GUIDE TO WASHINGTON, D.C./ WRITTEN BY HARVARD STUDENT AGENCIES, INC (US) [24932726] **4736**

LET'S GO : THE STUDENT GUIDE TO THE UNITED STATES AND CANADA (US/0090-788X) [01785872] **5483**

LET'S HALT AWHILE IN GREAT BRITAIN (UK) [01785647] 5483, **2807**

LET'S HALT AWHILE IN IRELAND (UK) [06398329] **5483**

LET'S LIVE (US/0024-1288) [01775588] 3604, **4194**

LET'S PLAY HOCKEY (US/0889-4795) [14077779] **4903**

LET'S PRAY TOGETHER *CEASED.* (US/0740-9613) [10067613] 2282, **5031**

LET'S SQUARE DANCE (UK/0301-8881) [01792938] **1313**

LET'S START (IT) **1761**

LET'S TALK GREEN (CN/1188-3022) [25590064] **2177**

LET'S TALK GREEN (CN/1188-3022) [25590065] **2177**

LETTER EXCHANGE, THE (US/0882-3804) [11833321] **3404**

LETTER FROM CHILE, A (CL) [04975561] **2552**

LETTER FROM SIA (US) **905**

LETTER FROM TAIZE (US) [02915006] **4973**

LETTER (HOUSTON, TEX.) (US/0899-3017) [18060451] 1687, **875**

●LETTER OF CREDIT LAW AND ANNOTATIONS (US/1065-9072) [26790461] **3002**

LETTER OF CREDIT UPDATE (US/0883-0487) [12042145] **796**

LETTER OF THE LAA, THE (CN/0705-4890) [05018603] **3223**

LETTER TO LIBRARIES ONLINE [COMPUTER FILE] : A NEWSLETTER OF THE OREGON STATE LIBRARY (US/1059-3195) [24564891] **3223**

LETTERA DALL'ITALIA (IT/0393-6457) [14582209] **324**

LETTERA FINANZIARIA *CEASED.* (IT/0391-7711) [I03917711] **796**

LETTERA INTERNAZIONALE (IT) [17976340] **3404**

LETTERA MARKETING (IT) **929**

LETTERA QUOTIDIANA : SETTORE TESSILE I+C (IT) **5354**

LETTERATO (IT/0024-130X) [08773099] 3297, **3404**

LETTERATURA ITALIANA. AGGIORNAMENTO BIBLIOGRAFICO (IT/1121-0753) [I11210753] **3459**

LETTERATURA ITALIANA. STUDI E TESTI, LA (IT) [05979261] **3405**

LETTERATURE D'AMERICA (IT) [07587473] **3405**

LETTERATURE D'OLTRALPE E D'OLTREOCEANO. SAGGI E STUDI (IT) [02298474] **3405**

LETTERE ITALIANE (IT/0024-1334) [01755799] **3405**

LETTERHEADS (US) [03574492] **4212**

LETTERS (US) [05232471] **3405**

LETTERS AND NOTICES (UK) [07160915] **4973**

LETTERS & PAPERS ON THE SOCIAL SCIENCES *CEASED.* (US/0092-718X) [01791404] **5208**

LETTERS ARTS REVIEW (US) **380**

LETTERS, El (US) [23452740] **1985**

LETTERS IN APPLIED MICROBIOLOGY (UK/0266-8254) [12166978] **566**

LETTERS IN MATHEMATICAL PHYSICS (NE/0377-9017) [02453644] 3517, **4411**

LETTERS IN PEPTIDE SCIENCE (NE) **1044**

LETTERS OF CREDIT REPORT (US/0886-0459) [12817653] **796**

LETTERS OF DH LAWRENCE (UK) **3405**

LETTING

LETTING GO (US) [11055000] **1761**

LETTORE DI PROVINCIA, IL (IT/0024-1350) [01540363] **3405**

LETTRE (SJ) [01785396] **1761**

LETTRE 101, RECHERCHE INDUSTRIE ENERGIE *See* INDUSTRIES PARIS **1611**

LETTRE ADA, LA (FR) [I09810455] **1280**

LETTRE AFRICAINE, LA (CN/0820-0726) [10420464] **4528**

LETTRE AFRIQUE EXPANSION, LA (FR/0996-9888) [I09969888] **4480**

LETTRE BANQUE ET SECURITE, LA (FR) **1503**

LETTRE - C.A.F (FR/0766-883X) [I0766883X] **1503**

LETTRE DE BOURBON, LA (FR/0759-6677) [11108380] **2641**

LETTRE DE CLEO, LA (FR/0993-2801) [I09932801] **1224**

LETTRE DE CONJONCTURE (BRUSSELS, BELGIUM) (BE/0772-0831) [10865412] **1572**

LETTRE DE LA CONCURRENCE, LA (FR/0752-5168) [I07525168] **690**

LETTRE DE LA F.I.D.H *See* LETTRE HEBDOMADAIRE DE LA FIDH / FEDERATION INTERNATIONALE DES LIGUES DES DROITS DE L'HOMME, LA **4510**

LETTRE DE LA F.I.D.H. / FEDERATION INTERNATIONALE DES DROITS DE L'HOMME, LA (FR/0755-7876) [22992609] **4510**

LETTRE DE LA FRANCOPHONIE (FR/1168-3961) [24571030] **1761**

LETTRE DE LA SURETE DE FONCTIONNEMENT, LA (FR) **1616**

LETTRE DE L'ABBE GRAVEL, LA (CN/0380-0946) [02578559] **5062**

LETTRE DE L'AUTOMATIQUE, LA (FR) **2120**

LETTRE DE L'EDI PARIS, LA (FR/1145-9646) [I11459646] **1115**

LETTRE DE L'EQUIPEMENT ELECTRIQUE ET ELECTRONIQUE L. 3 E, LA (FR/0183-6552) [I01836552] **2070**

LETTRE DE L'EXPANSION, LA (FR/0399-8606) [I03998606] **1503**

LETTRE DE LIAISON POUR LA RECHERCHE EUROPEENNE EN COMMUNICATION *CEASED.* (FR) **1115**

LETTRE DE L'INFECTIOLOGUE, LA (FR/0296-9009) [I02969009] **3604**

LETTRE DE L'OIV (FR) **105**

LETTRE DE MICHEL DEBRE, LA (FR/0151-8801) [I01518801] **3405**

LETTRE DE QUEBEC, LA (CN/0713-3448) [08867759] **2744**

LETTRE DE REPORTERS SANS FRONTIERES, LA (FR/1148-3164) [I11483164] **2922**

LETTRE DE TELETEL, LA (FR/0766-5385) [20376309] **1115**

LETTRE DES AMIS : BULLETIN DES QUAKERS EN FRANCE (FR) [11995808] **4973**

LETTRE DES COMMUNICATIONS - CLAUDE PICHE COMMUNICATIONS (CN/0823-3926) [10862205] **1115**

LETTRE DES CUISINISTES, DES BAINISTES ET DES ELECTROMENAGISTES, LA (FR/0988-4343) [I09884343] **2791**

LETTRE DES MUSEES ET DES EXPOSITIONS (FR/0993-9067) **4090**

LETTRE DES SYSTEMES D'INFORMATIONS MEDICALISEES (FR) 1275, **3604**

LETTRE D'EUROPE AVENIR, LA (FR/0298-3958) [I02983958] **4480**

LETTRE D'INFORMATION - ANACT (FR/0399-449X) [05998927] **1687**

LETTRE D'INFORMATION DU C.E.E, LA (FR/0982-460X) [I0982460X] **1687**

LETTRE D'INFORMATION DU COMITE CONSULTATIF NATIONAL D'ETHIQUE POUR LES SCIENCES DE LA VIE ET DE LA SANTE (FR/0296-4074) [25545449] **2252**

LETTRE D'INFORMATION METAUX DE LA REVUE LA RECUPERATION (FR/0181-1223) [I01811223] **4007**

LETTRE D'INFORMATIONS - COMITE INTERNATIONAL OLYMPIQUE *See* REVUE OLYMPIQUE **4915**

LETTRE D'INFORMATIONS DU COMITE CONSULTATIF NATIONAL D ETHIQUE (FR) **2252**

LETTRE D'ORION MAGAZINE, LA (FR/0987-3872) [I09873872] **2915**

LETTRE DU C.E.P.I.I. / CENTRE D'ETUDES PROSPECTIVES ET D'INFORMATIONS INTERNATIONALES, LA (FR/0243-1947) [14561893] **1637**

LETTRE DU CARDIOLOGUE, LA (FR/0761-5035) [I07615035] **3708**

LETTRE DU CONTINENT : LC, LA (FR) [13785353] 4480, **1503**

LETTRE DU GROUPEMENT NATIONAL DE LA COOPERATION, LA (FR/0760-4211) [I07604211] **1638**

LETTRE DU GYNECOLOGUE, LA (FR/0759-1594) [I07591594] **3764**

LETTRE DU MANAGER (FR/0763-8515) [I07638515] **875**

LETTRE DU MEDECIN (FR) **3604**

LETTRE DU PHARMACOLOGUE, LA (FR) **4314**

LETTRE DU PSYCHIATRE, LA (FR) **3930**

LETTRE DU PSYCHIATRE PARIS, LA (FR/0223-9434) [I02239434] 3837, **3930**

LETTRE DU RHUMATOLOGUE (FR) **3806**

LETTRE EUROPEENNE DU PROGRES TECHNIQUE, LA (FR/0765-0094) [I07650094] **5126**

LETTRE - EUROSANTE, LA (FR/1148-9480) [I11489480] **4789**

LETTRE FISCALE QUEBECOISE (CN/1183-0050) [24266190] **4661**

LETTRE. FRENCH TV MARKET NEWSLETTER, LA (FR/0996-7826) [I09967826] **1159**

●LETTRE HEBDOMADAIRE DE LA FIDH / FEDERATION INTERNATIONALE DES LIGUES DES DROITS DE L'HOMME, LA (FR) [28601467] **4510**

LETTRE INTERNATIONALE *SUSPENDED.* (FR/0762-3690) [12307760] **3405**

LETTRE MEDICALE, LA *SUSPENDED.* (FR/0153-4742) [I01534742] **3604**

LETTRE MEDICALE SUR LES MEDICAMENTS ET LA THERAPEUTIQUE, LA (US) **4314**

LETTRE MENSUELLE DE FRANCE PHARMACIE LABORATOIRES, LA (FR/1145-4881) [I11454881] **4314**

LETTRE (PARIS, 1957) *SUSPENDED.* (FR) [I02948265] **4816**

LETTRE PHYTOTHERAPIQUE (FR) **4314**

LETTRE TOURISTIQUE PARIS, LA (FR/1146-1918) [I11461918] **5483**

LETTRES BOTANIQUES (PARIS) (FR/0181-1797) [05896835] **517**

LETTRES ET RENCONTRES DU CASIER POSTAL (CN/1183-7381) [25652280] **2537**

LETTRES MANUSCRITES OU COMMUNIQUES PUBLIES DANS L'ARCHIDIOCESE D'OTTAWA (CN/0820-6945) [09448445] **5031**

LETTRES QUEBECOISES (CN/0382-084X) [02624883] **3405**

LETTRES ROMANES / UNIVERSITE CATHOLIQUE DE LOUVAIN, LES (BE) [01208048] **3405**

LETTURE (IT/0024-144X) [04675628] **5365**

LETTURE CLASSENSI (IT/0459-1623) [02299716] **3405**

LETUNK (YU) [05280149] **2696**

LEUCAENA RESEARCH REPORTS (CH/0254-8364) [08926336] **105**

LEUCOCYTES (UK/0142-8160) [I01428160] **3674**

LEUKEMIA (UK/0887-6924) [13346687] **3820**

LEUKEMIA & LYMPHOMA (UK/1042-8194) [19226345] **3820**

●LEUKEMIA & LYMPHOMA REVIEWS (SZ/1060-6815) [25052499] **3820**

LEUKEMIA RESEARCH (UK/0145-2126) [03012893] **3820**

LEUKEMIA REVIEWS INTERNATIONAL (US/0737-7673) [09444114] **3820**

LEUMI MORTGAGE BANK *See* ANNUAL REPORT FOR ... / LEUMI MORTGAGE BANK LTD **771**

LEUVENSCHE BIJDRAGEN *See* LEUVENSE BIJDRAGEN **3297**

LEUVENSE BIJDRAGEN (BE/0024-1482) [05301522] **3297**

LEVANT (LONDON) (UK/0075-8914) [01036021] 2769, **273**

LEVANT (MONTPELLIER, FRANCE) (FR/0992-0757) [19285499] **2658**

LEVANTE (IT/0024-1504) [02100864] **2518**

LEVANTE AGRICOLA (SP) [04631437] **178**

LEVELLAND AND HOCKLEY COUNTY NEWS-PRESS (US) [15680828] **5751**

LEVELLAND LEADER (US/0746-8334) [10310403] **5751**

LEVELTARI KOEZLEMENYEK (HU/0024-1512) [11035195] 2482, **2622**

LEVELTARI SZEMLE (HU/0457-6047) [18343049] **2482**

LEVENDE BILLEDER (DK/0108-5697) [11980612] 1134, **4073**

LEVENDE NATUUR, DE (NE/0024-1520) [04089803] **2197**

LEVENDE TALEN (NE/0024-1539) [07938860] **3297**

LEVERAGED LEASING (US/0882-9950) [09060218] **3002**

LEVERNET (US/0749-8217) [11198364] **690**

LEVIATA (BL) [28059301] **324**

LEVIATAN (MADRID, SPAIN) (SP/0210-6337) [07910730] **4528**

LEVIATANO, IL (IT) [04250347] **4543**

LEVIATHAN & KINNIKINNIK (US/0360-1765) [02243934] **2537**

LEVIATHAN (DUSSELDORF) (GW/0340-0425) [01789347] **5208**

LEVINSON LETTER, THE (US/0738-9167) [09668182] **875**

LEVISON LETTER, THE (US/0743-9520) [10715257] **875**

LEVNADSFORHALLANDEN ARSBOK (SW) [02245165] **5251**

LEVRES URBAINES (CN/0823-5112) [10680877] **3465**

LEWIS COUNTY HERALD (US) [19467133] **5681**

LEWIS COUNTY HERALD (US) [14366632] **5681**

LEWIS COUNTY HISTORICAL SOCIETY *See* JOURNAL - LEWIS COUNTY HISTORICAL SOCIETY **2740**

LEWIS LIVING (US/0883-685X) [12193805] **105**

LEWISBORO LEDGER *See* LEDGER (RIDGEFIELD, CONN.), THE **5645**

LEWISBURG TRIBUNE (US) [18332930] **5745**

LEWISON JOURNAL (US) [22602025] **5696**

LEWISTON JOURNAL (US) [09235812] **5685**

LEWISTON MORNING TRIBUNE (US/0892-2586) [08782931] **5657**

LEWISTON - PORTER SENTINEL (US) **5718**

LEWISTOWN NEWS-ARGUS (US) [11338425] **5705**

LEWISVILLE DAILY LEADER (US/0745-6174) [09399270] **5751**

LEWISVILLE NEWS, THE (US) [17370326] **5752**

LEX : COLETANEA DE LEGISLACAO E JURISPRUDENCIA (BL) [02761793] **3002**

LEX COLLEGII (US/0749-9078) [05976368] **1834**

LEX (COLOMBO, SRI LANKA) (CE) [11694723] **3002**

LEX-INTERDOC (BE/0771-5102) [11011071] **3002**

LEX, JURISPRUDENCIA DO SUPREMO TRIBUNAL FEDERAL (BL) [06687156] **3002**

LEX; LEGISLAZIONE ITALIANA (IT/0024-1598) [01697227] **3002**

LEX (PANAMA, PANAMA) (PN) [08288544] **3002**

LEXICOGRAPHICA (GW) [12983772] **3297**

LEXICOGRAPHICA. SERIES MAIOR (GW/0175-9264) [14942554] **3297**

LEXICOM (CN/0823-6313) [09981839] **747**

LEXICON (US) **2458**

LEXIKON DES FRUHGRIECHISCHEN EPOS (GW) **3405**

LEXIKON DES MITTELALTERS (GW) **1927**

LEXINGTON GENEALOGICAL EXCHANGE (US/0747-6485) [10748696] **2458**

LEXINGTON HERALD-LEADER (US/0745-4260) [09146384] **5681**

LEXINGTON MINUTE-MAN (US) [13745576] **5689**

LEXINGTON PROGRESS, THE (US) [19110587] **5745**

LEXINGTON THEOLOGICAL QUARTERLY (US/0024-1628) [01172520] **4973**

LEXIQUE (LILLE) (FR/0756-7138) [10078054] **3297**

LEXIQUE - ONTARIO. MINISTERE DES SERVICES SOCIAUX ET COMMUNAUTAIRES (CN/1186-0367) [24280784] **5294**

LEXIS (PE/0254-9239) [04012868] **3297**

LEXPORT (II) [03443588] **3185**

LEXUS USA *CEASED.* (US/0743-1112) [10509338] 1220, 1292, **1288**

LEY DE PRESUPUESTO NACIONAL *See* DECRETO DEL PRESUPUESTO GENERAL DE LA NACION **4720**

LEY DE PRESUPUESTO PARA EL EJERCICIO FISCAL (VE) [07559232] **4736**

Alphabetical Title Index — LIBRARY

LEY DEL IMPUESTO GENERAL DE IMPORTACION : NUEVO SISTEMA ARMONIZADO (MX) **844**

LEY (FIRM) *See* IMPUESTOS : BOLETIN INFORMATIVO MENSUAL AL SERVICIO DE LOS CONTRIBUYENTES **4731**

LEY, REVISTA JURIDICA PARAGUAYA, LA (AG) [05654398] **3002**

LEYDEN STAR-SENTINEL (US/0195-2528) [05424176] **5661**

LEYES ... APROBADAS BAJO LA CONSTITUCION DE 1980 (CL) [08403147] **3002**

LEYES PROMULGADAS (UY) [03399988] **3002**

LEYTE-SAMAR STUDIES (PH/0024-1679) [02263515] **2658**

LEZ VALENCIENNES / UNIVERSITE DE VALENCIENNES (FR/0760-5641) [13297142] **3405**

LG ARGOMENTI : RIVISTA CENTRO STUDI LETTERATURA GIOVANILE (IT/0026-5748) [10634736] **3405**

LGA BILL OF PARTICULARS (US/0360-3156) [02171688] **3002**

LGB TELEGRAM (US/1056-893X) [23887995] **5385**

LGC LOCAL GOVERNMENT CHRONICLE (UK) [06936444] **4662**

LHAT BULLETIN (US) [20617688] 5365, **302**

L'HERITAGE (CHALMETTE) (US/0162-0851) [03766911] **2458**

LHRT NEWSLETTER *See* LIBRARY HISTORY ROUND TABLE NEWSLETTER **3225**

LI GUIDE TO DINING & WINING NEWSLETTER *CEASED.* (US/1070-9940) [28525201] **2348**

LI HSUEH CHIN CHAN (CC) [10125279] **4428**

LI HUA JIANYAN. HUAXUE FENCE (CC/1001-4020) [21274253] **4007**

LI KUNG HSUEH PAO *See* KUO LI CHUNG HSING TA HSUEH LI KUNG HSUEH PAO / KUO LI CHUNG HSING TA HSUEH LI KUNG HSUEH PAO PIEN CHI WEI YUAN HUI **1985**

LI SHIH HSUEH PAO (CH) [04941714] **2696**

LI SHIH TI LI / CHUNG-KUO TI LI HSUEH HUI LI SHIH TI LI CHUAN YEH WEI YUAN HUI, LI SHIH TI LI PIEN CHI WEI YUAN HUI PIEN (CC) [08682815] **2568**

LI SHIH WEI WU CHU I YEN CHIU (CC) [22716934] **4543**

LI SHIH WEN HSUEH (CC) [11508582] **3405**

LIABILITY LEDGER (US/0193-3388) [05152835] **3002**

LIABILITY OF ATTORNEYS AND ACCOUNTANTS FOR SECURITIES TRANSACTIONS / BY ROBERT J. HAFT (US) [24918425] 3002, **747**

LIABILITY REPORTER (US/0271-5481) [06628828] **3169**

LIABILITY RISK AND INSURANCE (UK) **2886**

LIAISON - AMIS DU JARDIN BOTANIQUE DE MONTREAL (CN/1193-767X) [27391213] **2423**

LIAISON BULLETIN BETWEEN DEVELOPMENT RESEARCH AND TRAINING INSTITUTES (PARIS, FRANCE : 1979) *CEASED.* (FR) [09203077] **1503**

LIAISON BULLETIN (WASHINGTON, D.C.) (US/0742-5430) [10381733] **1881**

LIAISON - CANADIAN ASSOCIATION OF LEGAL ASSISTANTS (CN/1187-4945) [25796492] **3003**

LIAISON - CANADIAN ASSOCIATION OF LEGAL ASSISTANTS (CN/1187-4945) [25796495] **3003**

LIAISON-CEICI (ENGLISH ED.) (CN/1183-3815) [24368147] **1761**

LIAISON (CIMENTS CANADA LAFARGE) (CN/0318-1340) [02585024] **1616**

● LIAISON / CONSEIL REGIONAL DE L'ENVIRONNEMENT CHAUDIERE-APPALACHES (CN/1188-8539) [26715162] **2197**

LIAISON - COUNCIL OF MINISTERS OF EDUCATION, CANADA *SUSPENDED.* (CN/0825-7868) [11539815] **1761**

LIAISON ENERGIE FRANCOPHONIE (CN/0840-7827) [20001019] **1949**

LIAISON II (CN/0702-3839) [05257400] **3223**

LIAISON - INTERGOVERNMENTAL COMMITTEE ON URBAN AND REGIONAL RESEARCH (CN/0843-5278) [20308943] **2827**

LIAISON (MONTREAL. 1975) (CN/0701-0532) [03406426] **4662**

LIAISON (OTTAWA) (CN/0380-9579) [03251250] **3223**

LIAISON (SHERBROOKE) (CN/0318-8418) [02036122] **1093**

LIAISON ST-LOUIS (CN/0704-6723) [06562913] **2537**

LIAISON (THEATRE-ACTION) (CN/0227-227X) [06563700] 324, **5365**

LIAISONS FINANCIERES EN FRANCE *See* LIAISONS FINANCIERES, LES **796**

LIAISONS FINANCIERES, LES (FR) [08818736] **796**

LIAISONS INTERNATIONALES / CENTRE OECUMENIQUE DE LIAISONS INTERNATIONALES (BE/0770-450X) [10067471] **4528**

LIAISONS (MONTREAL) *SUSPENDED.* (CN/0707-7726) [04784067] 1900, **3297**

LIAISONS PARIS. 1963 (FR/0024-1717) [00241717] **3169**

LIAISONS SOCIALES (FR) **5208**

LIAISONS SOCIALES. BREF SOCIAL (FR/0294-8168) [02948168] **5208**

LIAISONS SOCIALES. DOCUMENTS (FR/0417-870X) [0417870X] **5208**

LIAISONS SOCIALES. LEGISLATION SOCIALE (FR/0294-8176) [02948176] **3003**

LIAN HE RI BAO (US/0891-1436) [09926281] **5718**

LIAN HE TONG XUN (US/0892-5828) [15250544] **2658**

LIANHE WANBAO (SI) **5810**

LIANHE ZAO BOA (SI) **5810**

LIAO-NING HSU MU SHOU I (CC) [11690243] **5515**

LIAO-NING KUNG JEN (CC) [11535529] **1687**

LIAO WANG (PEKING, CHINA) (CC) [10765187] **2506**

LIAOWANG (INTERNATIONAL ED.) (US/8755-9358) [11423209] **2506**

LIAS (NE/0304-0003) [01798652] **2518**

LIAS NEWSLETTER (US/0147-8729) [03246271] **3003**

LIASON (CN) **324**

LIB TEC (AT/0814-5539) [I08145539] **3223**

LIBANON : WIRTSCHAFTLICHE ENTWICKLUNG (GW) [05140994] **1572**

LIBANON : WIRTSCHAFTSDATEN UND WIRTSCHAFTSDOKUMENTATION (GW) [06229699] **1572**

LIBER (UK) [21326584] **3346**

LIBER 25 (PO) [11101197] **4049**

LIBER ANNUUS - STUDIUM BIBLICUM FRANCISCANUM (IS) [02187376] **5017**

LIBER : LIBRI PER BAMBINI E RAGAZZI (IT) **4829**

LIBERA VOCE DI POLIZIA ITALIANA (IT) **3169**

LIBERACION Y DERECHO (AG) [01795746] **3003**

LIBERAL CATHOLIC (UK/0024-1792) [01776816] **5031**

LIBERAL DEMOCRATS NEWS : THE PAPER OF THE SOCIAL AND LIBERAL DEMOCRATS (UK) [20910398] **4543**

LIBERAL EDUCATION (WASHINGTON, D.C.) (US/0024-1822) [01755825] **1834**

LIBERAL OPINION WEEK (US/1051-6433) [21999507] **5671**

LIBERAL RELIGIOUS EDUCATION (US) **4973**

LIBERAL STAR *SUSPENDED.* (JA/0286-3553) [06528905] **2658**

LIBERATION (US) [01604560] **4480**

LIBERATION AND MARXISM (US/1051-7871) [22122185] **4543**

LIBERATION (LONDON) (UK/0024-1873) [02303255] **2622**

LIBERATION (MILTON) (CN/0227-2687) [06757695] **4973**

LIBERATION (MILTON. 1984) (CN/0829-0954) [16187620] **4973**

LIBERATION PARIS. 1973 (FR/0335-1793) [I03351793] **2849**

LIBERATOR (1988), THE (US/1040-3760) [18395602] 3995, **5251**

LIBERETA (IT) **5294**

LIBEREZ LES VACANCES (CN/0712-9599) [08867725] **5295**

LIBERIA *See* LIBERIAN CODE OF LAWS OF ... : ADOPTED BY THE LEGISLATURE OF THE REPUBLIC OF LIBERIA ... **3003**

LIBERIA ALERT (US) [14943576] **2641**

LIBERIA-FORUM (GW/0179-4515) [16506516] **2641**

LIBERIA HERALD, THE (LB) [11620648] **5806**

LIBERIA. MINISTRY OF PLANNING AND ECONOMIC AFFAIRS *See* EXTERNAL TRADE OF LIBERIA : EXPORTS **835**

LIBERIA. MINISTRY OF PLANNING AND ECONOMIC AFFAIRS *See* PUBLIC SECTOR ACCOUNTS OF LIBERIA **4743**

LIBERIA. MINISTRY OF PLANNING AND ECONOMIC AFFAIRS *See* ECONOMIC SURVEY OF LIBERIA **1558**

LIBERIA : WIRTSCHAFTLICHE ENTWICKLUNG (GW) [02515974] **1572**

LIBERIAN CODE OF LAWS OF ... : ADOPTED BY THE LEGISLATURE OF THE REPUBLIC OF LIBERIA ... (US) [08985012] **3003**

LIBERIAN ECONOMIC AND MANAGEMENT REVIEW, THE (LB) [02359780] 875, **1503**

LIBERIAN OUTLOOK, THE (LB) [04275540] **2641**

LIBERIAN STUDIES JOURNAL (US/0024-1989) [01755829] **2641**

LIBERIAN STUDIES RESEARCH WORKING PAPER (US) [02304172] **2641**

LIBERTA, LA (IT) **5804**

LIBERTARIAN ANALYSIS (US/0047-4509) [01785187] **4480**

LIBERTARIAN DIGEST, THE (US/0272-5959) [06873902] 4352, **4480**

LIBERTARIAN VOICE (CN/0713-021X) [08584529] **4480**

LIBERTAS (GW/0341-9762) [I03419762] **4480**

LIBERTAS (ENGLISH EDITION MONTREAL) (CN/1183-5249) [24368676] **4510**

LIBERTAS MATHEMATICA (US/0278-5307) [07823042] **3517**

LIBERTE (BRUSSELS, BELGIUM) (BE) [11202192] **2911**

LIBERTE (MONTREAL) (CN/0024-2020) [01755831] 3346, **3465**

LIBERTITRES (FR) [27667303] **3405**

LIBERTY BELL (REEDY, W. VA.) (US/0145-7667) [02772513] **4481**

LIBERTY GAZETTE (LIBERTY, TEX.) (US) **5752**

LIBERTY (PORT TOWNSEND, WASH.) (US/0894-1408) [15799355] **4481**

LIBERTY, THEN AND NOW (US/0360-3342) [02243673] **2537**

LIBERTY VINDICATOR *See* VINDICATOR (LIBERTY, TEX.) **5755**

LIBERTY (WASHINGTON. 1906) (US/0024-2055) [01640028] **5062**

LIBERTYVILLE REVIEW (US/0744-852X) [08598277] **5661**

LIBIDO (CHICAGO, ILL.) (US/0899-8272) [18234803] 5188, **3405**

LIBRAIRIE ILLUSTREE, LA (CN/0229-7221) [09067708] **324**

LIBRARIAN CAREER DEVELOPMENT: AN INTERNATIONAL JOURNAL (UK) **3223**

● LIBRARIANS AT LIBERTY (US/1069-0832) [27921487] **3223**

LIBRARIANS COLLECTION LETTER (US/1063-5386) [24878316] **3223**

LIBRARIANS' HANDBOOK (BIRMINGHAM) (US/0093-1888) [01377969] **3223**

LIBRARIANS' NEWSLETTER (US/0194-0112) [04298411] **3223**

LIBRARIAN'S WORLD (US/0739-0297) [06130920] **3223**

LIBRARIES ALONE *CEASED.* (AT/1032-1438) [I10321438] **3223**

LIBRARIES & CULTURE (US/0894-8631) [16275086] 3223, **4829**

LIBRARIES AND INFORMATION SERVICES TODAY : THE YEARLY CHRONICLE *CEASED.* (US/1055-3665) [23231627] **3223**

LIBRARIES DIRECTORY (UK/0961-4575) [23885229] **3223**

LIBRARIES FOR COLLEGE STUDENTS WITH HANDICAPS (US/0149-547X) [03499661] 4390, **3223**

LIBRARIES IN MAINE (US) [10225310] **3223**

LIBRARIES IN THE NEWS (US) [01640298] **3223**

LIBRARIES IN THE UNITED KINGDOM AND THE REPUBLIC OF IRELAND (UK) [05149129] **3223**

LIBRARIES, INFORMATION CENTERS AND DATABASES IN SCIENCE AND TECHNOLOGY : A WORLD GUIDE (GW/0176-7593) [11530111] **3258**

LIBRARIES OF MAINE *See* LIBRARIES IN MAINE **3223**

LIBRARIES TODAY. GENDAI NO TOSHOKAN (JA) **3223**

LIBRARIES (TULSA, OKLA.) (US/0748-2035) [10918715] **3223**

LIBRARIUM (SZ/0024-2152) [01645461] **4830**

LIBRARY (UK/0024-2160) [01755835] **418**

LIBRARY ACCESS : SERVICES FOR PEOPLE WITH DISABILITIES *CEASED.* (US) [24622252] 4390, **3223**

LIBRARY

Alphabetical Title Index

LIBRARY ACCESSIONS - ARCTIC INSTITUTE OF NORTH AMERICA (CN/0382-4284) [02275568] **3223**

LIBRARY ACCESSIONS LIST / UNESCO PRINCIPAL REGIONAL OFFICE FOR ASIA AND THE PACIFIC (TH) [18760790] **3223**

LIBRARY ACQUISITIONS : PRACTICE AND THEORY (US/0364-6408) [02946513] **3223**

LIBRARY ADMINISTRATION & MANAGEMENT (US/0888-4463) [13578074] **3224**

LIBRARY ADMINISTRATOR'S DIGEST (US/0746-6129) [09330609] **3224**

LIBRARY & ARCHIVAL SECURITY (US/0196-0075) [05579435] 2482, **3224**

LIBRARY AND INFORMATION NEWS (UK/0269-8161) [10131058] **3224**

LIBRARY AND INFORMATION RESEARCH NEWS (UK/0141-6561) [07919278] **3224**

LIBRARY AND INFORMATION RESEARCH REPORT (UK) [11241791] **3224**

LIBRARY AND INFORMATION SCIENCE (JA/0373-4447) [01714245] **3224**

LIBRARY & INFORMATION SCIENCE ABSTRACTS (UK/0024-2179) [02314876] **3224, 3258**

LIBRARY AND INFORMATION SCIENCE EDUCATION STATISTICAL REPORT (US/0739-506X) [09747607] **3224, 3258**

LIBRARY & INFORMATION SCIENCE RESEARCH (US/0740-8188) [09844287] **3224**

LIBRARY AND INFORMATION SCIENCE UPDATE (CN/0820-0521) [09375319] **3224**

LIBRARY AND INFORMATION SERVICE (CC/0252-3116) [06806323] **3224**

LIBRARY & INFORMATION SERVICES / NTIS *See* NTIS ALERT. LIBRARY & INFORMATION SCIENCES **3237**

LIBRARY AND INFORMATION TECHNOLOGY ASSOCIATION (U.S.) *See* LITA NEWSLETTER **3228**

LIBRARY & LIBRARIAN, THE (II) [04077965] **3224**

LIBRARY ARCHIVES AND INFORMATION STUDIES (IS) [19919178] 2482, **3224**

LIBRARY ASSOCIATION *See* PAMPHLETS **3240**

LIBRARY ASSOCIATION *See* PROCEEDINGS, PAPERS AND SUMMARIES OF DISCUSSIONS AT THE ... CONFERENCE **3242**

LIBRARY ASSOCIATION *See* YEAR BOOK / THE LIBRARY ASSOCIATION **3257**

LIBRARY ASSOCIATION OF ALBERTA *See* LETTER OF THE LAA, THE **3223**

LIBRARY ASSOCIATION OF ALBERTA OCCASIONAL PAPER, THE (CN/0075-904X) [08555338] **3224**

LIBRARY ASSOCIATION OF AUSTRALIA. SPECIAL LIBRARIES SECTION *See* SPECIAL LIBRARIES IN QUEENSLAND **3250**

LIBRARY ASSOCIATION RECORD *See* LA RECORD **3222**

LIBRARY AUTOMATION NEWS (US/0898-6118) [17859129] **3224**

LIBRARY BINDINGS (WEYBURN) (CN/0228-541X) [08071679] **3224**

LIBRARY BOARD OF QUEENSLAND *See* DIRECTORY OF STATE AND PUBLIC LIBRARY SERVICES IN QUEENSLAND **3208**

LIBRARY BOOK CATALOG (US) [10151454] 3169, **3224**

LIBRARY BOOKSELLER, THE (US/0024-2217) [01643639] **3224**

LIBRARY BULLETIN (AT) [05902171] 4128, **3224**

LIBRARY BULLETIN (UK) [01475440] **3224**

LIBRARY BULLETIN - AUSTRALIAN BROADCASTING TRIBUNAL (AT/0811-1359) [I08111359] **3224**

LIBRARY BULLETIN - BOREAL INSTITUTE FOR NORTHERN STUDIES (CN/0225-4484) [06563075] **3224**

LIBRARY BULLETIN - CENTER ON SOCIAL WELFARE POLICY AND LAW (US) [03115186] **3225, 5295**

LIBRARY BULLETIN / GEOLOGICAL SURVEY OF INDIA, CENTRAL LIBRARY (II) [07664100] **1386**

LIBRARY BULLETIN (INSTITUTE OF SOUTHEAST ASIAN STUDIES) (SI/0073-9723) [02141372] **3225**

LIBRARY BULLETIN - TEXAS DEPARTMENT OF WATER RESOURCES (US/0148-7876) [03376633] **3225, 5536**

LIBRARY CAT NEWSLETTER, THE (US/1071-2593) [22929351] **3225, 4287**

LIBRARY CATALOG OF THE MARTIN P. CATHERWOOD LIBRARY OF THE NEW YORK STATE SCHOOL OF INDUSTRIAL AND LABOR RELATIONS, CORNELL UNIVERSITY. SUPPLEMENT (US/0360-1080) [02243551] 1503, **1687**

LIBRARY CATALOGUE. SUPPLEMENT (US) [02510564] **418**

LIBRARY CHRONICLE OF THE UNIVERSITY OF TEXAS AT AUSTIN, THE (US/0024-2241) [02772131] **2849**

LIBRARY CHRONICLE (PHILADELPHIA, PA.), THE (US/0024-2233) [06675300] **418**

LIBRARY COMPENSATION REVIEW (US/0730-3785) [07996319] **3225**

LIBRARY COMPUTER SYSTEMS AND EQUIPMENT REVIEW *CEASED*. (US/0895-531X) [16665822] **3225**

LIBRARY CONSERVATION NEWS (UK/0265-041X) [12893811] **3225**

LIBRARY COUNCIL OF NEW SOUTH WALES *See* ANNUAL REPORT / LIBRARY COUNCIL OF NEW SOUTH WALES **3190**

LIBRARY CURRENTS (US/0741-4188) [10151361] **3225**

LIBRARY DEVELOPMENTS (AUSTIN, TEX.) (US/0145-5397) [02254869] **3225**

LIBRARY DIRECTIONS : A NEWSLETTER OF UNIVERSITY OF MANITOBA LIBRARIES (CN/1183-8701) [25314024] **3225**

LIBRARY DIRECTORY AND ... STATISTICAL REPORT (US) [16879904] **3225**

LIBRARY EMPLOYEE RELATIONS NEWSLETTER, THE (US/0363-8863) [02539989] **1688**

LIBRARY EQUIPMENT REPORT *CEASED*. (UK/0269-963X) [I0269963X] **3225**

LIBRARY FOOTNOTES (CN/0838-360X) [20996154] **3225**

LIBRARY HERALD (US) [06702247] **3225**

LIBRARY HERALD (II/0024-2292) [01643535] **3225**

LIBRARY HI TECH (US/0737-8831) [09477925] 1193, **3225**

LIBRARY HI TECH BIBLIOGRAPHY (US/1040-4333) [14289930] **3258**

LIBRARY HI TECH NEWS (US/0741-9058) [10232245] 1193, **3225**

LIBRARY HISTORY (UK/0024-2306) [01755852] **3225**

● LIBRARY HISTORY ROUND TABLE NEWSLETTER (US) [28160903] **3225**

LIBRARY HOTLINE (US/0740-736X) [09906452] **3225**

LIBRARY IMAGINATION PAPER, THE (US/0197-5587) [04554259] **3225**

LIBRARY INSTRUCTION ROUND TABLE NEWS (US/0270-6792) [04718633] **3225**

LIBRARY ISSUES (US/0734-3035) [07251238] **3225**

LIBRARY JOURNAL *See* REVIEWS-ON-CARDS **3246**

LIBRARY JOURNAL (1976) (US/0363-0277) [02351916] **3225**

LIBRARY LECTURES (KNOXVILLE) (US/0270-059X) [05190374] **3226**

LIBRARY LIFE : NEW ZEALAND LIBRARY ASSOCIATION NEWSLETTER (NZ/0110-4373) [07616633] **3226**

LIBRARY LIST (US) [01780522] 105, **3226**

LIBRARY LITERATURE (US/0024-2373) [04566866] 3226, **3258**

LIBRARY LITERATURE [COMPUTER FILE] (US) [22288950] **3259**

LIBRARY MANAGEMENT (MCB PUBLICATIONS (FIRM)) (UK/0143-5124) [08138387] 875, **3226**

LIBRARY MANAGEMENT QUARTERLY (US) [13172293] **3226**

LIBRARY MANAGER (UK) **3226**

LIBRARY MICROMATION NEWS *See* LIBRARY TECHNOLOGY NEWS LTN **3227**

LIBRARY MONITOR *CEASED*. (UK/0957-2791) [I09572791] **3226**

LIBRARY MONITOR, THE (KU) [13782232] **796**

LIBRARY MOSAICS (US/1054-9676) [21236074] **3226**

LIBRARY NETWORKS (US/0145-9627) [02811119] **3226**

LIBRARY NEWS (SZ/1017-6241) [24118599] **3226**

LIBRARY NEWS & ACQUISITIONS *See* OUR LIBRARY PRESENTS ... **3240**

LIBRARY NEWS - GEAC LIBRARY INFORMATION SYSTEM (CN/0847-9488) [20787089] **3226**

LIBRARY NEWS - LA TRABE UNIVERSITY LIBRARY (AT/0155-8471) [I01558471] **3226**

LIBRARY NOTES (CHAPEL HILL) (US/0468-5725) [06152827] **3226**

LIBRARY NOTES / SOCIAL SECURITY ADMINISTRATION (US) [12247468] **5295**

LIBRARY OF ANTHROPOLOGY (US/0141-1012) [07193809] **240**

LIBRARY OF ARABIC LINGUISTICS (UK) [13193313] **3297**

LIBRARY OF CONGRESS *See* NEAR EAST SERIES **2659**

LIBRARY OF CONGRESS *See* DIRECTORY / LIBRARY OF CONGRESS **3206**

LIBRARY OF CONGRESS *See* CDMARC BIBLIOGRAPHIC **413**

LIBRARY OF CONGRESS *See* LIBRARY OF CONGRESS SUBJECT HEADINGS IN MICROFORM **3226**

LIBRARY OF CONGRESS ACQUISITIONS. MANUSCRIPT DIVISION (US/0275-9616) [07264920] **3226**

LIBRARY OF CONGRESS ACQUISITIONS. RARE BOOK AND SPECIAL COLLECTIONS DIVISION (US/0739-7526) [09780202] **3226**

LIBRARY OF CONGRESS. CATALOG PUBLICATION DIVISION *See* NAME AUTHORITIES. CUMULATIVE MICROFORM EDITION **3232**

LIBRARY OF CONGRESS. CATALOGING DISTRIBUTION SERVICE *See* COMPLETE CATALOG - LIBRARY OF CONGRESS. CATALOGING DISTRIBUTION SERVICE, THE **3203**

LIBRARY OF CONGRESS. CATALOGING POLICY AND SUPPORT OFFICE *See* L.C. SUBJECT HEADINGS WEEKLY LISTS **3222**

LIBRARY OF CONGRESS. CATALOGING POLICY AND SUPPORT OFFICE *See* LIBRARY OF CONGRESS SUBJECT HEADINGS / PREPARED BY THE CATALOGING POLICY AND SUPPORT OFFICE, COLLECTIONS SERVICES **3226**

LIBRARY OF CONGRESS CLASSIFICATION SCHEDULES COMBINED WITH ADDITIONS AND CHANGES (US) [16883181] **3226**

LIBRARY OF CONGRESS. COLLECTIONS SERVICES *See* COLLECTIONS SERVICES NEWS **3203**

LIBRARY OF CONGRESS. CONGRESSIONAL RESEARCH SERVICE. AMERICAN LAW DIVISION *See* SUPPLEMENT TO CAMPAIGN FINANCE LAW **3061**

LIBRARY OF CONGRESS. COPYRIGHT OFFICE *See* CATALOG OF COPYRIGHT ENTRIES. FOURTH SERIES. PART 3. PERFORMING ARTS **1302**

LIBRARY OF CONGRESS. COPYRIGHT OFFICE *See* CATALOG OF COPYRIGHT ENTRIES, FOURTH SERIES. 4, MOTION PICTURES & FILMSTRIPS. MICROFORM **1302**

LIBRARY OF CONGRESS. COPYRIGHT OFFICE *See* CATALOG OF COPYRIGHT ENTRIES. FOURTH SERIES. PART 6. MAPS **1302**

LIBRARY OF CONGRESS. COPYRIGHT OFFICE *See* COMPENDIUM OF COPYRIGHT OFFICE PRACTICES **1303**

LIBRARY OF CONGRESS. COPYRIGHT OFFICE *See* CATALOG OF COPYRIGHT ENTRIES. FOURTH SERIES. PART 4, MOTION PICTURES & FILMSTRIPS MICROFORM **4065**

LIBRARY OF CONGRESS. COPYRIGHT OFFICE *See* CATALOG OF COPYRIGHT ENTRIES. FOURTH SERIES. PART 5. VISUAL ARTS **1302**

LIBRARY OF CONGRESS. COPYRIGHT OFFICE *See* CATALOG OF COPYRIGHT ENTRIES. FOURTH SERIES. PART 8. RENEWALS **1302**

LIBRARY OF CONGRESS. COPYRIGHT OFFICE *See* ANNUAL REPORT OF THE REGISTER OF COPYRIGHTS **1301**

LIBRARY OF CONGRESS. COPYRIGHT OFFICE *See* CATALOG OF COPYRIGHT ENTRIES. FOURTH SERIES. PART 7. SOUND RECORDINGS **1302**

LIBRARY OF CONGRESS. COPYRIGHT OFFICE *See* CATALOG OF COPYRIGHT ENTRIES. FOURTH SERIES. PART 2. SERIALS & PERIODICALS **1302**

LIBRARY OF CONGRESS. COPYRIGHT OFFICE *See* CATALOG OF COPYRIGHT EENTRIES, FOURTH SERIES. PART 1, NONDRAMATIC LITERARY WORKS [MICROFORM] **1302**

LIBRARY OF CONGRESS. DIVISION FOR THE BLIND AND PHYSICALLY HANDICAPPED. INSTRUCTIONAL CASSETTE RECORDINGS CATALOG *See* INSTRUCTIONAL CASSETTE RECORDINGS CATALOG **4122**

LIBRARY OF CONGRESS. EXCHANGE AND GIFT DIVISION *See* MONTHLY CHECKLIST OF STATE PUBLICATIONS **420**

LIBRARY OF CONGRESS INFORMATION BULLETIN (US/0041-7904) [02566556] **3226**

LIBRARY OF CONGRESS. LIBRARY OF CONGRESS OFFICE, BRAZIL *See* ACCESSIONS LIST, BRAZIL. CUMULATIVE LIST OF SERIALS / LIBRARY OF CONGRESS **406**

LIBRARY OF CONGRESS. LIBRARY OF CONGRESS OFFICE, CAIRO *See* ACCESSIONS LIST, MIDDLE EAST **406**

LIBRARY OF CONGRESS. LIBRARY OF CONGRESS OFFICE, JAKARTA *See* ACCESSIONS LIST, SOUTHEAST ASIA **406**

LIBRARY OF CONGRESS. LIBRARY OF CONGRESS OFFICE, JAKARTA *See* ACCESSIONS LIST, SOUTHEAST ASIA. CUMULATIVE LIST OF INDONESIAN SERIALS **406**

LIBRARY OF CONGRESS. LIBRARY OF CONGRESS OFFICE, JAKARTA *See* ACCESSIONS LIST, SOUTHEAST ASIA. CUMULATIVE LIST OF MALAYSIA, SINGAPORE AND BRUNEI SERIALS **406**

LIBRARY OF CONGRESS. LIBRARY OF CONGRESS OFFICE, JAKARTA. ACCESSIONS LIST, INDONESIA, MALAYSIA, SINGAPORE AND BRUNEI. CUMULATIVE LIST OF MALAYSIA, SINGAPORE, AND BRUNEI SERIALS *See* ACCESSIONS LIST, SOUTHEAST ASIA. CUMULATIVE LIST OF MALAYSIA, SINGAPORE AND BRUNEI SERIALS **406**

LIBRARY OF CONGRESS. LIBRARY OF CONGRESS OFFICE, NAIROBI, KENYA *See* QUARTERLY INDEX TO PERIODICAL LITERATURE, EASTERN AND SOUTHERN AFRICA **3427**

LIBRARY OF CONGRESS. LIBRARY OF CONGRESS OFFICE, NAIROBI, KENYA *See* ACCESSIONS LIST, EASTERN AFRICA **406**

LIBRARY OF CONGRESS. LIBRARY OF CONGRESS OFFICE, NAIROBI, KENYA *See* ACCESSIONS LIST, EASTERN AFRICA. ANNUAL SERIAL SUPPLEMENT **406**

LIBRARY OF CONGRESS. LIBRARY OF CONGRESS OFFICE, NAIROBI, KENYA *See* ACCESSIONS LIST, EASTERN AND SOUTHERN AFRICA **406**

LIBRARY OF CONGRESS. LIBRARY OF CONGRESS OFFICE, NAIROBI, KENYA. ACCESSIONS LIST, EASTERN AFRICA *See* ACCESSIONS LIST, EASTERN AND SOUTHERN AFRICA **406**

LIBRARY OF CONGRESS. LIBRARY OF CONGRESS OFFICE, NEW DELHI *See* ACCESSIONS LIST, SOUTHEAST ASIA. CUMULATIVE LIST OF SERIALS, BURMA, THAILAND AND LAOS **406**

LIBRARY OF CONGRESS. LIBRARY OF CONGRESS OFFICE, NEW DELHI *See* ACCESSIONS LIST. SOUTH ASIA **406**

LIBRARY OF CONGRESS. LIBRARY OF CONGRESS OFFICE, RIO DE JANEIRO *See* ACCESSIONS LIST, BRAZIL AND URUGUAY **406**

LIBRARY OF CONGRESS. MANUSCRIPT DIVISION *See* LIBRARY OF CONGRESS ACQUISITIONS. MANUSCRIPT DIVISION **3226**

LIBRARY OF CONGRESS. NATIONAL LIBRARY SERVICE FOR THE BLIND AND PHYSICALLY HANDICAPPED *See* CASSETTE BOOKS **4827**

LIBRARY OF CONGRESS. NATIONAL LIBRARY SERVICE FOR THE BLIND AND PHYSICALLY HANDICAPPED *See* BRAILLE SCORES CATALOG. ORGAN **4104**

LIBRARY OF CONGRESS. NATIONAL LIBRARY SERVICE FOR THE BLIND AND PHYSICALLY HANDICAPPED *See* BRAILLE SCORES CATALOG. INSTRUMENTAL **4104**

LIBRARY OF CONGRESS. NATIONAL LIBRARY SERVICE FOR THE BLIND AND PHYSICALLY HANDICAPPED *See* BRAILLE BOOKS **4827**

LIBRARY OF CONGRESS. NATIONAL LIBRARY SERVICE FOR THE BLIND AND PHYSICALLY HANDICAPPED *See* LARGE-PRINT SCORES AND BOOKS CATALOG **4128**

LIBRARY OF CONGRESS. NATIONAL LIBRARY SERVICE FOR THE BLIND AND PHYSICALLY HANDICAPPED *See* BRAILLE SCORES CATALOG. VOCAL **4105**

LIBRARY OF CONGRESS. NATIONAL LIBRARY SERVICE FOR THE BLIND AND PHYSICALLY HANDICAPPED *See* INSTRUCTIONAL CASSETTE RECORDINGS CATALOG **4122**

LIBRARY OF CONGRESS. NATIONAL LIBRARY SERVICE FOR THE BLIND AND PHYSICALLY HANDICAPPED *See* INSTRUCTIONAL DISC RECORDINGS CATALOG **4122**

LIBRARY OF CONGRESS. OFFICE FOR SUBJECT CATALOGING POLICY *See* LIBRARY OF CONGRESS SUBJECT HEADINGS **3226**

LIBRARY OF CONGRESS. OFFICE FOR SUBJECT CATALOGING POLICY *See* CDMARC SUBJECTS **3201**

LIBRARY OF CONGRESS. OFFICE FOR SUBJECT CATALOGING POLICY. LIBRARY OF CONGRESS SUBJECT HEADINGS *See* LIBRARY OF CONGRESS SUBJECT HEADINGS / PREPARED BY THE CATALOGING POLICY AND SUPPORT OFFICE, COLLECTIONS SERVICES **3226**

LIBRARY OF CONGRESS. OFFICE OF SUBJECT CATALOGING POLICY. L.C. SUBJECT HEADINGS WEEKLY LISTS *See* L.C. SUBJECT HEADINGS WEEKLY LISTS **3222**

LIBRARY OF CONGRESS. PROCESSING SERVICES *See* CATALOGING SERVICE BULLETIN **3200**

LIBRARY OF CONGRESS. PROFESSIONAL ASSOCIATION *See* INSIGHTS **3217**

LIBRARY OF CONGRESS PUBLICATIONS IN PRINT (US/0083-1603) [02561502] **419**

LIBRARY OF CONGRESS. PUBLICATIONS ISSUED BY THE LIBRARY SINCE 1897 *See* LIBRARY OF CONGRESS PUBLICATIONS IN PRINT **419**

LIBRARY OF CONGRESS. RARE BOOK AND SPECIAL COLLECTIONS DIVISION *See* LIBRARY OF CONGRESS ACQUISITIONS. RARE BOOK AND SPECIAL COLLECTIONS DIVISION **3226**

LIBRARY OF CONGRESS. SERIAL & GOVERNMENT PUBLICATIONS DIVISION *See* NEWSPAPERS RECEIVED CURRENTLY IN THE LIBRARY OF CONGRESS **5647**

LIBRARY OF CONGRESS. SUBJECT CATALOGING DIVISION *See* L.C. SUBJECT HEADINGS WEEKLY LISTS (DETROIT, MICH.) **3222**

LIBRARY OF CONGRESS. SUBJECT CATALOGING DIVISION *See* CDMARC SUBJECTS **3201**

LIBRARY OF CONGRESS. SUBJECT CATALOGING DIVISION *See* L.C. CLASSIFICATION: ADDITIONS AND CHANGES **3222**

LIBRARY OF CONGRESS. SUBJECT CATALOGING DIVISION *See* SUBJECT HEADINGS IN MICROFORM **3251**

LIBRARY OF CONGRESS SUBJECT HEADINGS (US/1048-9711) [22238028] **3226**

● LIBRARY OF CONGRESS SUBJECT HEADINGS IN MICROFORM (US) [28227135] **3226**

LIBRARY OF CONGRESS SUBJECT HEADINGS / PREPARED BY THE CATALOGING POLICY AND SUPPORT OFFICE, COLLECTIONS SERVICES (US) [28614917] **3226**

LIBRARY OF LIVING PHILOSOPHERS, THE (US/0075-9139) [01995203] **4352**

LIBRARY OF RELIGIOUS PHILOSOPHY (US) **4973, 4352**

LIBRARY OF THE AMERICAN HOSPITAL ASSOCIATION, ASA S. BACON MEMORIAL *See* CUMULATIVE INDEX OF HOSPITAL LITERATURE **3779**

LIBRARY OF THEORIA (SW) [01755857] **4352**

LIBRARY OUTREACH REPORTER (US/0895-1179) [16470940] **3226**

LIBRARY OWNER'S MANUAL (1980) (CN/0225-8307) [06515806] **3226**

LIBRARY PERSONNEL NEWS (US/0891-2742) [14686969] **943**

LIBRARY POCKETFUL, A (CN/0713-5386) [08981102] **3226**

LIBRARY PR NEWS (US/0164-9566) [03703202] **761, 3226**

LIBRARY PROGRESS (INTERNATIONAL) (II/0970-1052) [08938343] **3226**

LIBRARY PUBLICATION NUMBER ONE: PHILSOM, PERIODICAL HOLDINGS IN THE LIBRARY OF THE SCHOOL OF MEDICINE. WASHINGTON UNIVERSITY (ST. LOUIS, MO.). SCHOOL OF MEDICINE. LIBRARY *See* PHILSOM/S : PERIODICAL HOLDINGS IN THE LIBRARY OF THE SCHOOL OF MEDICINE BY SUBJECT **3241**

LIBRARY PUBLICATION NUMBER TWO: PHILSOMS, PERIODICAL HOLDINGS IN THE LIBRARY OF THE SCHOOL OF MEDICINE BY SUBJECT. WASHINGTON UNIVERSITY (ST. LOUIS, MO.). SCHOOL OF MEDICINE. LIBRARY *See* PHILSOM/S : PERIODICAL HOLDINGS IN THE LIBRARY OF THE SCHOOL OF MEDICINE BY SUBJECT **3241**

LIBRARY QUARTERLY (CHICAGO), THE (US/0024-2519) [01755858] **3226**

LIBRARY RESEARCH NEWS / MCMASTER UNIVERSITY (CN/0024-9270) [02545445] **3227**

LIBRARY RESOURCES & TECHNICAL SERVICES (US/0024-2527) [01696755] **3227**

LIBRARY RESOURCES FOR THE BLIND & PHYSICALLY HANDICAPPED (US/0364-1236) [02977219] **4390, 3227**

LIBRARY REVIEW (GLASGOW) (UK/0024-2535) [02312850] **3227**

LIBRARY REVIEW (LOUISVILLE, KY.) (US/0041-9788) [02263698] **3227**

LIBRARY SCIENCE WITH A SLANT TO DOCUMENTATION (II/0024-2543) [01755861] **3227**

LIBRARY SCIENTIST, THE (NR/0331-0132) [09163340] **3227**

LIBRARY SERIES / UNIVERSITY OF KANSAS LIBRARIES (US/0075-5001) [01606628] **3227**

LIBRARY SERVICE TO THE PEOPLE OF NEW YORK STATE (US) [06780658] **3227**

LIBRARY SERVICES AND CONSTRUCTION ACT ANNUAL PROGRAM (US) [08714187] **3227**

LIBRARY SERVICES BULLETIN (CO-OPERATIVE COLLEGE OF CANADA) (CN/0823-6828) [10052019] **1542**

LIBRARY SOFTWARE REVIEW (US/0742-5759) [10366937] **3227, 1288**

LIBRARY STATISTICS OF COLLEGES AND UNIVERSITIES IN THE PACIFIC NORTHWEST (US/8755-4267) [10860837] **3227, 3259**

LIBRARY STATISTICS OF ILLINOIS COLLEGES AND UNIVERSITIES (US/0094-2626) [05725480] **3227, 3259**

LIBRARY SYSTEMS (US/0277-0288) [07484071] **1193, 3227**

LIBRARY TALK (US/1043-237X) [18495382] **3227**

● LIBRARY TECHNOLOGY NEWS LTN (UK/0964-7627) [26463025] **3227**

LIBRARY TECHNOLOGY REPORTS (US/0024-2586) [02910540] **3227**

LIBRARY TIMES INTERNATIONAL (US/0743-4839) [10597606] **3227**

LIBRARY TRENDS (US/0024-2594) [02313195] **3227**

LIBRARY VIDEO MAGAZINE. VIDEORECORDING *CEASED*. (US/0895-2248) [14289335] **3228**

LIBRARY WORK *CEASED*. (UK/0953-9638) [I09539638] **3228**

LIBRARY WORKER (CN/0714-2862) [10224871] **3228, 1688**

LIBRE BELGIQUE, LA (BE) [11968450] **5778**

LIBRE COURS (CN/0315-4130) [02248071] **1834**

LIBRE EXPRESION (GT) [25736578] **1115**

LIBRE MONDIAL DES INVENTIONS, LE (FR) [21435456] **5126**

LIBRE POLITIQUE, ANTHROPOLOGIE, PHILOSOPHIE (FR) [03234069] **5208**

LIBRE SERVICE ACTUALITES (FR) **1115**

LIBRERIA *SUSPENDED*. (SP) [01791906] **4830**

LIBRES (KENT, OHIO) (US/1058-6768) [24355989] **3228**

LIBRESENS PARIS (FR/1157-7452) [I11577452] **5062**

LIBRI E DOCUMENTI, ARCHIVO STORICO CIVICO E BIBLIOTECA TRIVULZIANA (IT/0390-1009) [04552625] **2622**

LIBRI E RIVISTE D'ITALIA (IT/0024-2683) [02319889] **3405**

LIBRI (KBENHAVN) (DK/0024-2667) [01755866] **3228**

LIBRI NUOVI E USATI (IT) [24452932] **4830**

LIBRI ONCOLOGICI (CI/0300-8142) [01353295] **3820**

LIBRINOVITA (IT) **4830**

LIBRO DEL ANO (CHICAGO, ILL.) (US/1055-632X) [23246326] **1927**

LIBRO EN AMERICA LATINA Y EL CARIBE, EL (CK/0121-1242) [17947870] **4566, 4830**

LIBRO VERDE, EL (US/0270-2002) [06346601] **1616**

LIBRO Y EL PUEBLO, EL (MX/0186-3738) [02263554] **3259**

LIBROS *CEASED*. (CK) [02244896] **4830**

LIBROS AL DIA (VE) [02762286] **4830**

LIBROS EN ESPANOL ... TITULOS (MX) [10177320] **4830**

LIBROS EN VENTA EN HISPANOAMERICA Y ESPANA (PR/0075-918X) [04258438] **419**

LIBROS ESPANOLES EN VENTA, ISBN (SP) [12045842] **419**

LIBROS MEJOR EDITADOS, ESPANA (SP) [11246297] **4570**

LIBSAT (CN/0712-6115) [09336440] **3228**

LIBTECH NEWS (AT/0815-8428) [I08158428] **3228**

LIBYA

Alphabetical Title Index

LIBYA ANTIQUA / KINGDOM OF LIBYA, MINISTRY OF NATIONAL ECONOMY (LY/0459-2980) [04221464] 251, **273**

LIBYAN JOURNAL OF AGRICULTURE, THE (LY/1010-3740) [02733288] **105**

LIBYAN JOURNAL OF SCIENCE, THE (LY/0368-7481) [02918916] **5126**

LIBYAN STUDIES : ANNUAL REPORT OF THE SOCIETY FOR LIBYAN STUDIES (UK) [08784017] **2641**

LIBYEN : WIRTSCHAFTLICHE ENTWICKLUNG (GW) [03530016] **1572**

LICENCES ISSUED TO DRIVERS AND RIDERS OF MOTOR VEHICLES / BUREAU OF STATISTICS, KONEDOBU, PAPUA (PP) [07373622] **5418**

LICENSED ATTORNEYS OF NORTH DAKOTA (US/0091-9055) [01786632] **3003**

LICENSED BEVERAGE JOURNAL (US/0024-2764) [04046360] **2369**

LICENSED FUEL FACILITY STATUS REPORT *CEASED.* (US) [06187595] **1949**

LICENSED OPERATING REACTORS, STATUS SUMMARY REPORT (US/0278-3487) [07465682] **2156**

LICENSED PSYCHOLOGISTS (US) [15870762] **4602**

LICENSED SALARIES AND RELATED INFORMATION - MINNESOTA SCHOOL BOARDS ASSOCIATION (US) [06374031] **1866**

LICENSEE CONTRACTOR AND VENDOR INSPECTION STATUS REPORT (US/1056-9049) [04511705] **4662**

LICENSEE EVENT REPORT (LER) COMPILATION *CEASED.* (US/1056-9057) [09708277] 1949, **3003**

LICENSEES, DENTAL PRACTICE ACT (US) [06126325] **1329**

LICENSING BOOK, THE (US/0741-0107) [10077149] **4830**

LICENSING BUSINESS REVIEW (UK/1073-8983) [29546339] **1306**

LICENSING, COUNTERSIGNING, AND SURPLUS LINE LAWS FOR THE 50 STATES, DISTRICT OF COLUMBIA, PUERTO RICO, AND THE VIRGIN ISLANDS (US/0742-5120) [10501701] 2886, **3003**

LICENSING ECONOMICS REVIEW (US) **1503**

LICENSING EXECUTIVES SOCIETY (U.S.A.) *See* NOUVELLES, LES **1306**

LICENSING INTERNATIONAL (US/0889-9320) [12628065] **3003**

LICENSING JOURNAL, THE (US/1040-4023) [18398601] **1616**

LICENSING LAW AND BUSINESS INSTITUTE *See* ANNUAL LICENSING LAW AND BUSINESS INSTITUTE **3095**

LICENSING LAW AND BUSINESS REPORT (US/0162-5764) [04158867] **3101**

LICENSING LAWS OF NEW SOUTH WALES. LIQUOR ACT & REGULATIONS (UK) **3003**

LICENSING LETTER, THE (US/8755-6235) [11387453] **929**

LICENSING REPORT (US) **1306**

LICENSING REPORTER EUROPE (UK/1073-8991) [29546316] **1306**

LICENSING REVIEW (UK/0959-8421) [I09598421] **3003**

●LICENSING TODAY INTERNATIONAL (UK) [29546439] **1503**

LICHENOLOGIST (LONDON) (UK/0024-2829) [01755877] **517**

LICHT-FORSCHUNG (GW/0172-3286) [09271072] **4438**

LICHT (MUNCHEN) (GW/0171-5496) [05236327] **2070**

LICHTENBERG-JAHRBUCH (GW/0936-4242) [20716306] **3405**

LICKING LANTERN, THE (US/0748-1012) [10873047] **2458**

LICKING VALLEY COURIER (US) [14439130] **5681**

LICNI DOHOCI (YU/0300-2535) [01784847] **1535**

LICORNE, LA (FR/0398-9992) [04644300] **3405**

LICTON SPRINGS REVIEW / A NORTH SEATTLE COMMUNITY COLLEGE LITERARY GUILD PUBLICATION (US/1056-3113) [23659165] **3346**

LIDE A ZEME (XR/0024-2896) [02263564] **2568**

LIDIL : REVUE DE DIDACTIQUE DES LANGUES (FR) **3297**

LIDOVE NOVINY (XR/0862-5921) [21415895] **5799**

LIE GROUPS. HISTORY, FRONTIERS, AND APPLICATIONS (US/1045-6368) [09818172] **5208**

LIE GROUPS. SERIES B, SYSTEMS INFORMATION AND CONTROL *CEASED.* (US) [09615605] **1193**

LIEBIGS ANNALEN DER CHEMIE (GW/0170-2041) [04719928] **984**

LIECHTENSTEIN. AMT FUR VOLKSWIRTSCHAFT *See* IN VERKEHR GESETZTE NEUE MOTORFAHRZEUGE **5417**

LIECHTENSTEIN : PRINCIPALITY IN THE HEART OF EUROPE (LH) **2518**

LIEN ECONOMIQUE : BULLETIN DE LA CHAMBRE DE COMMERCE ET D'INDUSTRIE DE BASSE-TERRE, LE (GP/0396-9371) [05046144] 820, **1503**

LIEN HO PAO ... TUAN PIEN HSIAO SHUO CHIANG TSO PIN CHI (CH) [08256529] **3405**

LIEN HO WEN HSUEH (CH) [13189750] **3405**

LIEN HO YUEH KAN (CH) [09267635] **2506**

LIEN HOA (CN/0714-8038) [09054392] **2658**

LIEN HORTICOLE (FR/0293-6852) [09745285] **2424**

LIEN HUAN HUA LUN TSUNG LIAN HUAN HUA LUN CONG (CC) [11857616] **324**

LIEN (HULL) (CN/0711-7418) [09026013] **3861**

LIEN, LE (CN/0849-1577) [23242666] **2282**

LIEN, LE *CEASED.* (CN/0714-556X) [09086727] **1542**

LIEN (ORDRE DES TECHNICIENS EN RADIOLIGIE DU QUEBEC) (CN/0713-7621) [08985164] **3943**

LIES OF OUR TIMES (US/1046-7912) [20521236] 2922, **4481**

LIETUVIU DIENOS (US/0024-2950) [01713767] **2267**

LIETUVIU KALBOTYROS KLAUSIMAI (LI/0130-0172) [02147868] **3297**

LIETUVIU TAUTOS PRAEITIS (US/0091-4347) [01786997] **2696**

●LIETUVOS FIZIKOS ZURNALAS / LITHUANIAN JOURNAL OF PHYSICS / LITOVSKII FIZICHESKII ZHURNAL / LIETUVOS FIZIKU DRAUGIJA (LI) [29984150] **4411**

LIETUVOS ISTORIJOS METRASTIS (LI/0202-3342) [01785191] **2697**

LIETUVOS MOKSLU AKADEMIJA. EKSPERIMENTINE BIOLOGIJA (LI/0235-7232) [22995231] **463**

LIETUVOS TSR AUKSTUJU MOKYKLU MOKSLO DARBAI: BIOLOGIJA (LI/0459-3383) [01755892] **463**

LIETUVOS TSR AUKSTUJU MOKYKLU MOKSLO DARBAI, CHEMIJA IR CHEMINIS TECHNOLOGIJA (LI/0459-3391) [02900397] **984**

LIETUVOS TSR AUKSTUJU MOKYKLU MOKSLO DARBAI: GEOGRAFIJA (LI/0202-3288) [09185339] **2568**

LIETUVOS TSR AUKSTUJU MOKYKLU MOKSLO DARBAI: ISTORIJA (LI/0459-3456) [03723859] **2697**

LIETUVOS TSR AUKSTUJU MOKYKLU MOKSLO DARBAI. KALBOTYRA *See* KALBOTYRA / VILNIUSSKII UNIVERSITET **3293**

LIETUVOS TSR AUKSTUJU MOKYKLU MOKSLO DARBAI: LITERATURA (LI/0459-3472) [04340839] **3405**

LIETUVOS TSR AUKSTUJU MOKYKLU MOKSLO DARBAI: PEDAGOGIKA (LI/0202-3326) [12171026] 4602, **1761**

LIETUVOS TSR AUKSTUJU MOKYKLU MOKSLO DARBAI: PSICHOLOGIJA (LI/0202-3318) [07847666] **4602**

LIETUVOS VETERINARIJOS AKADEMIJOS MOKSLO DARBAI (RU/0202-3334) [I02023334] **5515**

LIETUVOS ZEMDIRBYSTES MOKSLINIO TYRIMO INSTITUTO DARBAI (LI) [I0320054X] **105**

LIEUX DE L'ENFANCE (FR/0767-0303) [19806178] **1066**

LIFE AFTER DEATH, AN ISLAMIC PERSPECTIVE (US/1053-2943) [22503914] **5043**

LIFE & HEALTH INSURANCE SALES (US/1053-2838) [21541265] **2886**

LIFE & LEISURE (KE) [12063098] **2641**

LIFE & PEACE REVIEW (SW/0284-0200) [I02840200] **4973**

LIFE AND WORK (UK/0024-306X) [04339310] **5062**

LIFE AND WORK LESSON ANNUAL *See* ADULT LIFE AND WORK LESSON ANNUAL **4932**

LIFE ASSOCIATION NEWS (US/0024-3078) [01623629] **2886**

LIFE AT KEN-CARYL (US/0899-6318) [18171732] **5643**

LIFE CHEMISTRY REPORTS (US/0278-6281) [07853635] 984, **490**

LIFE (CHICAGO) (US/0024-3019) [04267940] **2489**

LIFE COMPANY TAX NEWSLETTER (US/0047-4606) [01783683] 2886, **3003**

●LIFE DESIGNS (US/1064-217X) [26234138] 4602, **2599**

LIFE FORUM (PH) [09190972] 2282, **5031**

LIFE INSURANCE BUSINESS IN TAIWAN (CH) [12095994] **2886**

LIFE INSURANCE BUYING (US) [05971239] **2886**

LIFE INSURANCE FACT BOOK (US/0075-9406) [02315293] **2886**

LIFE INSURANCE IDEAS (US/0024-3116) [02660579] **2887**

LIFE INSURANCE INTERNATIONAL (IE/0956-327X) [21493554] **2887**

LIFE INSURANCE PLANNING (US/0024-3132) [02660595] **2887**

LIFE INSURANCE SELLING (US/0024-3140) [02906328] **2887**

LIFE INSURANCE TABLES (CN/0835-2933) [19491351] **2887**

LIFE LINE (US) **5704**

LIFE-LINE (NATIONAL HYDROCEPHALUS FOUNDATION) (US/1059-6593) [24661310] **3604**

LIFE LINES (LINCOLN, NEB.) (US/0744-0677) [04350495] **5180**

LIFE LINES : NEWSLETTER OF THE NATIONAL COALITION AGAINST THE DEATH PENALTY (US) [11367872] **3169**

LIFE POSITIVE! (US/1058-6636) [24350858] **875**

LIFE PURPOSE JOURNALS (US) **4973**

LIFE SAFETY CODE HANDBOOK (US/0192-1002) [04939039] **2291**

LIFE SCIENCE ADVANCES. BIOCHEMISTRY : A JOURNAL OF THE COUNCIL OF SCIENTIFIC RESEARCH INTEGRATION (II) [18943286] **490**

LIFE SCIENCE ADVANCES. EXPERIMENTAL AND CLINICAL ENDOCRINOLOGY : A JOURNAL OF THE COUNCIL OF SCIENTIFIC RESEARCH INTEGRATION (II) [18943282] **3731**

LIFE SCIENCE ADVANCES. GENERAL ENDOCRINOLOGY : A JOURNAL OF THE COUNCIL OF SCIENTIFIC RESEARCH INTEGRATION (II) [18943272] **3731**

LIFE SCIENCE ADVANCES. MOLECULAR GENETICS : A JOURNAL OF THE COUNCIL OF SCIENTIFIC RESEARCH INTEGRATION (II) [18943279] **549**

LIFE SCIENCE ADVANCES. PLANT PHYSIOLOGY : A JOURNAL OF COUNCIL OF SCIENTIFIC RESEARCH INTEGRATION (II) [18943266] **517**

LIFE SCIENCE BOOK REVIEW (US/1056-2672) [23613198] **5126**

LIFE SCIENCE LAB PRODUCTS (US/1056-0866) [23461198] 984, **463**

LIFE SCIENCES (US) [01459510] **5126**

LIFE SCIENCES CONTRIBUTIONS / ROYAL ONTARIO MUSEUM (CN/0384-8159) [01432199] 5590, **4090**

LIFE SCIENCES MISCELLANEOUS PUBLICATION (CN/0082-5093) [02441840] **5590**

LIFE SCIENCES OCCASIONAL PAPERS *CEASED.* (CN/0082-5107) [02441841] **5590**

LIFE SKILLS CENTER NEWS *See* LIFE SKILLS NEWS **2791**

LIFE SKILLS NEWS (US/0882-4452) [11837619] **2791**

LIFE STORIES *See* INTERNATIONAL YEARBOOK OF ORAL HISTORY AND LIFE STORIES **2620**

LIFE STYLES HEALTH SERIES (US/0277-545X) [05670559] **4789**

LIFE SUPPORT (CN/0383-8099) [03304105] **3604**

LIFE SUPPORT SYSTEMS *CEASED.* (UK/0261-989X) [09123340] **3604**

LIFE WITH ARCHIE *CEASED.* (US/0024-3248) [10677584] **4863**

LIFEFORCE ECOLOGY NEWS (US) [25324067] **2218**

LIFELINE - CANADIAN MEMORIAL CHIROPRACTIC COLLEGE (CN/0713-7974) [08996205] **5788**

LIFELINE (SEATTLE, WASH.) (US/0895-4127) [16634227] **1346**

LIFELINE (SORRENTO) (CN/0712-2462) [08734108] **4789**

LIFELINE (TORRANCE, CALIF.) (US/1051-9467) [22152747] **4194**

LIFELINER (US/0047-4630) [01785859] **2458**

LIFELINES (US) **2267**

●LIFELINES FOR YOUTH TEACHER (US/1063-794X) [26137265] **4973**

LIFELINES (PLATTSBURGH, N.Y.) (US/8755-920X) [11406642] **2458**

LIFELINES SASKATCHEWAN (1981) (CN/0711-4257) [08499607] **4789**

LIFELINES (SHERWOOD PARK. 1979) (CN/0225-6975) [06264518] 5560, 2282, **589**

LIFELONG LEARNING (BERKELEY, CALIF.) (US/0882-8482) [12026804] **1761**

LIFEPRINTS (US) **4390**

LIFERAFT (COLORADO SPRINGS, COLO.) (US/1064-3753) [23961073] **875**

LIFESTYLE (US/0095-1013) [01796162] **2537**

LIFESTYLE ASIA (PH) **2506**

LIFESTYLE MARKET ANALYST, THE (US/1067-182X) [19876190] **929**

LIFESTYLE ZIP CODE ANALYST, THE (US/1057-8080) [23372571] **1298**

LIFESTYLES (NEW YORK, N.Y.) See JOURNAL OF FAMILY AND ECONOMIC ISSUES **2281**

LIFESTYLES SEASON (AT) 2197, **4186**

LIFETIME DATA ANALYSIS (NE/1380-7870) **1193**

LIFETIME ENCYCLOPEDIA OF LETTERS (US) [08689590] **3297**

LIFLINE (US/0739-8638) [07221145] **3228**

LIFLINE See ALUMNAE MAGAZINE - SWEET BRIAR COLLEGE **1808**

LIFTOFF (GRAND RAPIDS, MICH.) See QUEST (GRAND RAPIDS, MICH.) **32**

LIFTOFF (GRAND RAPIDS, MICH.) (US/1060-7692) [25060829] **27**

LIGAND QUARTERLY NOTIZIE TECHNICHE (IT) **3604**

LIGAND REVIEW, THE (US/0197-4041) [06023387] **3674**

LIGEIA (FR/0989-6023) [21284589] **324**

LIGESTILLINGSARBEJDET I AF (DK) [11821551] **1688**

LIGHT (US) [03078778] 4390, **5295**

●LIGHT & ENGINEERING (US/1068-9761) [27875674] **2070**

●LIGHT & ISLAMIC REVIEW, THE (US/1060-4596) [25253218] **5043**

LIGHT AND LIFE (WINONA LAKE) (US/0024-3299) [01776489] **5062**

LIGHT AVIATION (UK) [06081947] **27**

LIGHT CHAMPION (US/0746-4142) [10029344] **5752**

●LIGHT (CHICAGO, ILL.) (US/1064-8186) [26384502] 3465, **3405**

LIGHT (COLUMBUS, OHIO) See LIGHT & ISLAMIC REVIEW, THE **5043**

LIGHT LIST (US/0565-1557) [02923471] **4178**

LIGHT, MEDIUM, HEAVY TRUCK SHOP MANUAL (US) [08298817] **5385**

LIGHT METAL AGE (US/0024-3345) [01755910] **4007**

LIGHT METALS (NEW YORK) (US/0147-0809) [01480067] **4007**

LIGHT 'N' HEAVY (US/0190-6569) [04998910] **4973**

LIGHT (NASHVILLE, TENN.) (US) [08641036] **4973**

LIGHT (NEW YORK. 1973) (US/0147-121X) [03110542] **3465**

LIGHT OF CONSCIOUSNESS (US/1040-7448) [18516513] **4973**

LIGHT OF LIFE (II/0970-2571) [I09702571] **4974**

LIGHT ON THE WORD. TEACHER (US/0277-139X) [07688592] **1900**

LIGHT PLANE MAINTENANCE (US/0278-8950) [07896152] **27**

LIGHT (TORONTO. 1978) (CN/0229-5636) [08770587] **5043**

LIGHT TRUCK EQUIPMENT NEWS (CN/0707-7939) [04747136] **5788**

LIGHT TRUCK REPAIR MANUAL MECHANICAL PARTS / LABOR ESTIMATING MANUAL (US) **5418**

LIGHT (WASHINGTON), THE (US/0456-0434) [04692539] **1688**

LIGHT YEAR (CLEVELAND, OHIO) *CEASED.* (US/0743-913X) [10436951] **3465**

LIGHTBEARER (UK) [05280251] **5062**

●LIGHTBULB/INVENT!, THE (US) [28012027] **1306**

LIGHTHOUSE (BURLINGTON) (CN/0711-5628) [08790788] **1357**

LIGHTHOUSE (CAMBRIDGE, MASS.) (US/1061-8732) [23099226] **5560**

●LIGHTHOUSE (UNIVERSITY PARK, PA.), THE (US/1070-6690) [28448105] **4128**

LIGHTING (AT) **2070**

●LIGHTING ANSWERS (US/1069-0050) [27879000] **619**

LIGHTING DESIGN (IT) **4438**

LIGHTING DESIGN & APPLICATION (US/0360-6325) [09663517] **2070**

LIGHTING DIMENSIONS (US/0191-541X) [03662625] **4074**

LIGHTING EQUIPMENT NEWS (UK/0024-3418) [11584328] **2071**

●LIGHTING HANDBOOK. REFERENCE & APPLICATION (US) [29371747] **2071**

LIGHTING IN AUSTRALIA (AT/0728-5639) [08687170] **2071**

LIGHTING JOURNAL (RUGBY, WARWICKSHIRE) (UK) [13816921] **2071**

LIGHTING RESEARCH & TECHNOLOGY (UK/0024-3426) [01755914] **2071**

LIGHTING + SOUND INTERNATIONAL (UK/0268-7429) **5126**

LIGHTNING FLASH (PITTSFIELD, MASS.), THE (US/0164-0011) [04553898] **1427**

LIGHTWAVE (US/0741-5834) [10179779] 1159, **4438**

LIGHTWAVE BUYERS GUIDE (US) **4438**

LIGHTWORKS (US/0161-4223) [03940893] 4371, **357**

LIGNE DE MASSE, LA (CN/0704-1969) [04518901] **4543**

LIGNINGSVEJLEDNINGEN. SELSKABER / STATSSKATTEDIREKTORATET, LIGNINGSAFDELINGEN, SELSKABSSKATTEKONTORET (DK/0106-5408) [09901793] **4736**

LIGONIER ECHO, THE (US) [13727087] **5737**

LIGUE CANADIENNE DE FOOTBALL See REGLEMENT OFFICIEL DE JEU POUR LA LIGUE CANADIENNE DE FOOTBALL **4914**

LIGUE CANADIENNE DE FOOTBALL See LIVRE OFFICIEL DES RECORDS - LIGUE CANADIENNE DE FOOTBALL **4903**

LIGUE HAITIENNE DES DROITS HUMAINS See BULLETIN - LIQUE HAITIENNE DES DROITS HUMAINS **4505**

LIGUORIAN (US/0024-3450) [01755916] 2282, **5031**

LIGURIA (ITALY). CONSIGLIO REGIONALE See NOTIZIARIO DEL CONSIGLIO REGIONALE DELLA LIGURIA **3019**

LIGURIA TRE / A CURA DEL CENTRO STUDI, UNIONE DELLE CAMERE DI COMMERCIO LIGURI (IT) [07627680] **1572**

LIHC MONTHLY REPORT (US) **2827**

LIIKENTEEN TILINPAATOSTILASTO (FI/0784-8463) [20871471] **5385**

LIIKETALOUDELLINEN AIKAKAUSKIRJA (FI/0024-3469) [04507064] **1503**

LIIKEVAIHTOVEROVELVOLLISET YRITYKSET (FI) [03499157] **4736**

LIIKUNNAN JA KANSANTERVEYDEN JULKAISUJA (FI/0357-2498)[I03572498] **2599**

LIIKUNTA JA TIEDE (FI/0358-7010) [I03587010] **4903**

LIJECNICKI VJESNIK (CI/0024-3477) [01778878] **3604**

LIJST VAN AANWINSTEN / UNIVERSITEITSBIBLIOTHEEK VAN AMSTERDAM (NE) [08429389] **3228**

LIJST VAN DOCENTEN IN DE NEERLANDISTIEK AAN BUITENLANDSE UNIVERSITEITEN EN LEDENLIJST IVN / INTERNATIONALE VERENIGING VOOR NEERLANDISTIEK (NE) [10746785] **1834**

●LIKARSKA SPRAVA (UN/1019-5297) [25785155] **3604**

LIKAS-YAMAN (PH) [12126753] **2197**

LIKEMBE; REVUE ZAIROISE DE MUSIQUE (CG) [01789142] **4128**

LIKHT SHTRALN (US) [01795969] **3405**

LIKUNDOLI : ENQUETES D'HISTOIRE ZAIROISE (CG) [02240891] **2641**

LILACS ON CD-ROM (US) **3660**

LILI, ZEITSCHRIFT FUER LITERATURWISSENSCHAFT UND LINGUISTIK (GW/0049-8653) [02852420] 3405, **3298**

LILIES AND OTHER LILIACEAE (UK/0075-949X) [01786375] **2424**

LILITH (FITZROY, VIC.) (AT/0813-8990) [16862367] **5560**

LILITH (NEW YORK) (US/0146-2334) [02694720] 5560, **5050**

LILLE MEDICAL (1987) (FR/0981-1095) [19484000] **3604**

LILLOA (AG/0075-9481) [01755920] **517**

LILLY DIGEST (US/0193-5097) [01773932] **4314**

LILLY DIGEST OF THE STATEMENTS OF ... RETAIL DRUG STORES (US) [03078265] 955, **4314**

LILLY (ELI) AND COMPANY. PHARMACEUTICAL DIVISION See LILLY DIGEST **4314**

LILRC NEWSLETTER AND CALENDAR (US/0887-3739) [13227305] **3228**

LILY YEARBOOK See LILY YEARBOOK OF THE NORTH AMERICAN LILY SOCIETY, INC, THE **2424**

LILY YEARBOOK OF THE NORTH AMERICAN LILY SOCIETY, INC, THE (US/0741-9910) [10263903] **2424**

LIMA NEWS, THE (US) [16619399] **5729**

LIMA TIMES (PE) [05092412] **2552**

LIMBA ROMANA (RM/0024-3523) [07942923] **3298**

LIMBA SI LITERATURA ROMANA / SOCIETATEA DE STIINTE FILOLOGICE (RM) [04026131] **3298**

LIMBA SI LITERATURA / SOCIETATEA DE STIINTE ISTORICE SI FILOLOGICE (RM) [01787596] **3298**

●LIMBAUGH LETTER, THE (US/1065-0377) [26491255] **4481**

LIMBURG (BE/0776-1325) [I07761325] **2519**

LIMBURG (NETHERLANDS) PROVINCIALE WATERSTAAT See JAARVERSLAG - PROVINCIALE WATERSTAAT IN LIMBURG **2025**

LIMBURGS GESCHIED- EN OUDHEIDKUNDIG GENOOTSCHAP See PUBLICATIONS DE LA SOCIETE HISTORIQUE ET ARCHEOLOGIQUE DANS LE LIMBOURG **306**

LIMBURGSE SOCIAAL EKONOMISCHE VERKENNING (NE) [18541372] **1503**

LIME SPRINGS HERALD (LIME SPRINGS, IOWA : 1932) (US) [15348630] **5671**

LIMELIGHT *CEASED.* (US) **324**

LIMERENCE FORUM (US/0731-3772) [08175160] **4603**

LIMESFORSCHUNGEN (GW/0459-4371) [02310894] **273**

LIMESTONE (WASHINGTON) (US/0547-0684) [01755926] **4007**

LIMITED INFINITY (US/1058-5656) [24386602] **3405**

LIMITED MOBILITY & IMMOBILIZED PATIENT PRODUCTS (US) **3605**

LIMITED OFFERING EXEMPTIONS: REGULATION D (US/0739-1889) [09703191] **3101**

LIMITED PARTNERS LETTER (US/0163-0652) [04290853] **3003**

LIMITED PARTNERSHIP INVESTMENT REVIEW *CEASED.* (US/0892-516X) [15217170] **690**

LIMITS IN THE SEAS (US/0092-6426) [01791347] **3181**

LIMNOBIOS (AG/0325-7592) [05304213] **555**

LIMNOLOGICA (GW/0075-9511) [01755929] **463**

LIMNOLOGICAL CONTRIBUTION (US/0730-2827) [07338146] **1416**

LIMNOLOGY AND OCEANOGRAPHY (US/0024-3590) [01755910] **1451**

LIMOI (CN/0704-0318) [08045879] **5233**

LIMOSA (NE/0024-3620) [01696932] **5618**

LIMOUSIN LEADER, THE (CN/0381-5552) [02585062] **214**

LIMOUSIN WORLD (US/8750-2127) [11108317] **214**

LIMOUSINE & CHAUFFEUR (US/8750-7374) [11723017] **5385**

LIMPEZA PUBLICA (BL) [02243798] **2235**

LIMRA'S MARKETFACTS (US/0889-0986) [13841536] 929, **2887**

LIN CHAN KUNG YEH (CC) [11341769] **2402**

LIN CHUANG I HSUEH (CH/0258-4697) [10328980] **3605**

LIN YEH K'O CHI TNG HSUN (CC) [08122250] **2387**

LIN YEH SHIH YEN SO YEN CHIU PAO KAO (CH) [17369545] **2387**

LIN YEH SHIH YEN SO YEN CHIU PAO KAO CHI KAN (CH/1010-5204) [18727511] **2387**

LINA : LITERATURINDEX NATURWISSENSCHAFTEN (GW) **5126**

LINACRE QUARTERLY, THE (US/0024-3639) [01588532] 3605, **2252**

LINC BELCONNEN (AT/1031-6574) [I10316574] **1386**

LINCHAN HUAXUE YU GONGYE (CC/0253-2417) [08862643] **2387**

LINCOLN CO. TENNESSEE PIONEERS (US) [04232876] **2458**

LINCOLN COLLEGE, LINCOLN, N.Z. AGRICULTURAL ECONOMICS RESEARCH UNIT See ECONOMIC SURVEY OF NEW ZEALAND WHEATGROWERS : FINANCIAL ANALYSIS, AN **81**

LINCOLN COUNTY JOURNAL (US) [20647151] **5657**

LINCOLN Alphabetical Title Index

LINCOLN COUNTY LEADER (US/0892-3353) [11702954] **5733**

LINCOLN COUNTY RECORD (PIOCHE, NEV. : 1968) (US/8755-3260) [11285049] **5707**

LINCOLN COURIER (LINCOLN, ILL. : 1968) *See* COURIER, THE **5659**

LINCOLN DAILY STAR, THE (US) [10319081] **5706**

LINCOLN HERALD (US/0024-3671) [05041025] **2744**

LINCOLN JOURNAL (US) [22174917] **5689**

LINCOLN JOURNAL (LINCOLN, NEB.) (US/1054-7983) [10522658] **5706**

LINCOLN LABORATORY JOURNAL, THE (US/0896-4130) [17064383] **5126**

LINCOLN LAW REVIEW (SAN FRANCISCO, CALIF.) (US/0024-368X) [01645222] **3003**

LINCOLN LIBRARY OF ESSENTIAL INFORMATION (COLUMBUS, OHIO : 1982), THE (US/0735-0813) [08853005] **3228**

LINCOLN LORE (US/0162-8615) [01755933] **2744**

LINCOLN PARKER, THE (US/0192-5768) [05047043] **5692**

LINCOLN RECORD SOCIETY *See* REPORT FOR THE YEAR ... / THE LINCOLN RECORD SOCIETY **2705**

LINCOLN REVIEW (US/0192-5083) [05015755] **2744**

LINCOLN SENTINEL-REPUBLICAN, THE (US) [11688878] **5677**

LINCOLNSHIRE FAMILY HISTORIAN (UK/0261-3565) [09594990] **2458**

LINCOLNSHIRE HISTORY AND ARCHAEOLOGY (UK/0459-4487) [02321474] 2622, **273**

LINCOLNSHIRE PAST & PRESENT (UK/0960-9555) [22839512] **2697**

LIND LEADER (LIND, WASH. : 1946) (US) [16993127] **5761**

LINDA HALL LIBRARY *See* LINDA HALL LIBRARY MISCELLANY **3228**

LINDA HALL LIBRARY MISCELLANY (US/0273-0227) [06986471] **3228**

LINDBERGIA (SW/0105-0761) [02096764] **517**

LINDEN LANE MAGAZINE (US/0736-1084) [08860122] 3405, **324**

LINDLEYANA : THE SCIENTIFIC JOURNAL OF THE AMERICAN ORCHID SOCIETY (US/0889-258X) [13435778] **517**

LINDSAY GAZETTE (US/1072-1800) [27053520] **5636**

LINDSAY THIS WEEK (CN/0228-0566) [06958906] **5788**

LINDSBORG NEWS-RECORD, THE (US) [11898056] **5677**

LINEA D'OMBRA (IT) [12544068] **3405**

LINEA EDP (IT) **1193**

LINEA INTIMA *See* LINEA INTIMA ITALIA **1085**

LINEA INTIMA ITALIA (IT) **1085**

LINEA TEATRALE (IT) [19964673] **5365**

LINEA VERDE (IT/0394-3704) [03943704] **2424**

LINEAGE (COMMACK, N.Y.) (US/0899-1871) [18028202] **2458**

LINEAGRAFICA (IT/0024-3744) [11626375] **380**

LINEAIRES (FR/0981-4183) [09814183] **5126**

LINEAPELLE (IT) 1085, **3185**

LINEAR ALGEBRA AND ITS APPLICATIONS (US/0024-3795) [01716586] **3517**

LINEAR AND MULTILINEAR ALGEBRA (US/0308-1087) [02245998] **3517**

LINEAR CIRCUITS DATA BOOK (US/0741-4226) [10151239] **2071**

LINEAR INTEGRATED CIRCUITS AND MOS DEVICES (US/0092-7201) [01791158] **2071**

LINEN HALL REVIEW (UK/0266-1500) [11703539] **3405**

LINER TRADE REPORT (NE) **844**

LINER'S INSURANCE MARKETING INSIDER (US/0892-1458) [15096982] **2887**

LINES AND BY-LINES (US) **2458**

LINES OF COMMUNICATION : THE INDEPENDENT VOICE FOR THE TELECOMS TRADE AND INDUSTRY (UK) [24572462] **1159**

LINES OF DESCENT (CN) **2458**

LINES REVIEW (UK/0459-4541) [06318952] **3346**

LINEUP (US) 2774, **5386**

LINFOLKB2S : MAGAZINE FOR THE LINCOLNSHIRE AND SOUTH HUMBERSIDE DISTRICT OF THE E.F.D.S.S (UK) [13182520] **4128**

LING NAN WEN SHIH (CC) [11455096] **3405**

LING NAN YIN YUEH (CC) [09351064] **4128**

LINGUA (AMSTERDAM, NETHERLANDS) (NE/0024-3841) [01755938] **3298**

LINGUA E LITERATURA (BL/0101-4862) [01604094] **3298**

LINGUA E NUOVA DIDATTICA : LEND (IT/0394-2813) [26922996] **3298**

LINGUA E STILE (IT/0024-385X) [02102994] **3298**

LINGUA FRANCA : THE REVIEW OF ACADEMIC LIFE (US/1051-3310) [21930326] **1834**

LINGUA, LETTERATURA, CIVILTA / UNIVERSITA DI PERUGIA (IT) [08216813] **3405**

LINGUA NOSTRA (IT/0024-3868) [02354631] **3298**

LINGUA POSNANIENSIS (PO/0079-4740) [01755939] **3298**

LINGUAGEM (RIO DE JANEIRO, BRAZIL) (BL) [10361589] **3298**

LINGUE DEL MONDO *CEASED.* (IT) [06045180] **3298**

LINGUIST (LONDON, ENGLAND : 1986) (UK/0268-5965) [13411010] **3298**

LINGUISTIC ANALYSIS (US/0098-9053) [02242565] **3298**

LINGUISTIC & LITERARY STUDIES IN EASTERN EUROPE (NE/0165-7712) [07578240] **3298**

LINGUISTIC ASSOCIATION OF CANADA AND THE UNITED STATES *See* LACUS FORUM **3294**

LINGUISTIC BIBLIOGRAPHY FOR THE YEAR ... AND SUPPLEMENT FOR THE YEARS ... (NE) [13385800] **3298**

LINGUISTIC CALCULATION *CEASED.* (NE) [11335278] **3298**

LINGUISTIC CIRCLE OF MANITOBA AND NORTH DAKOTA *See* PROCEEDINGS OF THE LINGUISTIC CIRCLE OF MANITOBA AND NORTH DAKOTA **3312**

LINGUISTIC INQUIRY (US/0024-3892) [01604261] **3298**

LINGUISTIC MODELS (NE) [13315497] **3298**

LINGUISTIC NOTES FROM LA JOLLA (US/0737-4720) [04629353] **3298**

LINGUISTIC REVIEW, THE (NE/0167-6318) [08028440] **3298**

LINGUISTICA (XV/0024-3922) [01789799] **3298**

LINGUISTICA ANTVERPIENSIA (BE/0304-2294) [02323794] **3299**

●LINGUISTICA ATLANTICA : JOURNAL OF THE ATLANTIC PROVINCES LINGUISTIC ASSOCATION (CN) [28600613] **3299**

LINGUISTICA BIBLICA (PL/0342-0884) [02106228] 3299, **4974**

LINGUISTICA COMPUTAZIONALE (IT/0392-6907) [10889211] **3299**

LINGUISTICA E LETTERATURA (IT) [03746463] **3299**

LINGUISTICA ESPANOLA ACTUAL (SP) [06960544] **3299**

LINGUISTICA EXTRANEA. STUDIA (US/0887-9958) [05256779] **3299**

●LINGUISTICA PRAGENSIA (XR) [24910340] **3299**

LINGUISTICA SILESIANA (PL/0208-4228) [02366298] **3299**

LINGUISTICA URALICA (ER/0132-0777) [22282675] **3299**

LINGUISTICA Y LITERATURA : REVISTA DEL DEPARTAMENTO DE ESPANOL (CK/0120-5587) [05285172] 3405, **3299**

LINGUISTICS (NE/0024-3949) [01755941] **3299**

LINGUISTICS ABSTRACTS (UK/0267-5498) [13146207] **3299**

LINGUISTICS AND EDUCATION (US/0898-5898) [17855807] 1761, **3299**

LINGUISTICS AND LANGUAGE BEHAVIOR ABSTRACTS (US/0888-8027) [12000062] 3299, **3336**

LINGUISTICS AND PHILOSOPHY (NE/0165-0157) [03127141] 4352, **3299**

LINGUISTICS IN THE NETHERLANDS (NE) [08140615] **3299**

LINGUISTICS OF THE TIBETO-BURMAN AREA (US/0731-3500) [04790670] **3299**

LINGUISTIK AKTUELL (NE/0166-0829) [13315444] **3299**

LINGUISTIQUE AFRICAINE (PARIS, FRANCE) (FR/0994-7744) [19548675] **3299**

LINGUISTIQUE ET SCIENCES HUMAINES *See* LINGUISTIQUE ET SCIENCES HUMAINES **3299**

LINGUISTIQUE ET SCIENCES HUMAINES (CG/1010-7274) [20341026] **3299**

LINGUISTIQUE ET SEMIOLOGIE (FR/0246-6341) [02466341] **3299**

LINGUISTIQUE (PARIS. 1965), LA (FR/0075-966X) [03087617] **3299**

LINGUISTIQUE SEMIOLOGIE (FR) **3299**

LINGUISTISCHE ARBEITEN TUBINGEN (GW/0344-6727) [03446727] **1688**

LINGUISTISCHE ARBEITEN UND BERICHTE (GW/0179-2180) [05508006] **3299**

LINGUISTISCHE BERICHTE (GW/0024-3930) [02319633] **3299**

LINGUISTISCHE REIHE (GW) [06702236] **3299**

LINGVISTICAE INVESTIGATIONES (NE/0378-4169) [03265622] **3299**

LINGVISTICAE INVESTIGATIONES. SUPPLEMENTA (NE/0165-7569) [06803516] **3300**

LINGVISTICHESKIE PROBLEMY FUNKTSIONALNOGO MODELIROVANIIA RECHEVOI DEIATELNOSTI (RU/0130-9277) [04389210] 3517, **3300**

LINGVISTIKA I PROBLEMY STILIA (RU) [05329904] **3300**

LINIE KOLN, DIE (GW/0344-5224) [03445224] **1085**

LINING OUT STOCK FOR ... / APPALACHIAN NURSERIES (US) [11521169] **2424**

LININGTON LINEUP (US/8756-5609) [11552202] **3405**

LINK (CN/0827-6978) [14259679] **2568**

LINK (IS/0792-9765) [24202919] 5126, **690**

LINK (II/0459-469X) [01642383] **2506**

LINK (ASHLAND, MASS.) (US/1040-3469) [18390322] **5295**

LINK (CLEVELAND, OHIO) (US/0733-8503) [04555569] **357**

●LINK (DURHAM, N.C.), THE (US/1065-5832) [26638867] 3605, **5295**

LINK FOR MCMASTER PART-TIME STUDENTS, THE (CN/0707-6932) [04747172] **1761**

LINK LINE (US/0735-8407) [09001767] 4789, **1761**

LINK (MISSISSAUGA. 1977) (CN/0703-7007) [03453093] **3228**

LINK (NEW YORK), THE (US/0024-4007) [02244248] **2658**

LINK (OTTAWA) (CN/0709-020X) [06082711] **1761**

LINK, THE (US/1049-4928) [21237848] **1193**

LINK TO THE ONTARIO SOCIETY OF OCCUPATIONAL THERAPISTS, THE (CN/1184-6828) [24267030] 1881, **3605**

LINK (TROY, MICH.) (US/1045-9723) [20306136] **761**

LINK-UP (AT/0158-5460) [01585460] 4390, **3228**

LINK-UP (MINNEAPOLIS, MINN. 1983) (US/0739-988X) [09846150] 1268, **1242**

LINK (VICTORIA) (CN/0383-0535) [02811285] **3228**

LINK (WINNIPEG. 1974) (CN/0380-299X) [02942546] **2658**

LINK (WOODLAND HILLS) (US) **3837**

LINK'AGE (TORONTO) (CN/1183-6091) [24368659] **5295**

LINKING RING, THE (US/0024-4023) [04046393] **4863**

LINKS BRISBANE *CEASED.* (AT/0156-1103) [01561103] **1804**

LINKS - ENVIRONMENTAL EDUCATORS' PROVINCIAL SPECIALIST ASSOCIATION (CN/0848-8754) [21344801] **2177**

LINKS MAGAZINE (US) **4903**

LINKS (NEW YORK, N.Y.) *SUSPENDED.* (US/0894-3036) [12591152] **4789**

LINKS (SACRAMENTO) (US/0163-2205) [04318993] **5295**

LINKS : SOZIALISTISCHE ZEITUNG (GW/0024-404X) [03087459] 1593, **4543**

LINN NEWS-LETTER (US) [12605529] **5671**

LINNAEAN SOCIETY OF NEW YORK *See* TRANSACTIONS OF THE LINNAEAN SOCIETY OF NEW YORK **529**

LINNEAN : NEWSLETTER AND PROCEEDINGS OF THE LINNEAN SOCIETY OF LONDON, THE (UK) [10581014] **463**

LINNEAN SOCIETY OF LONDON *See* LINNEAN : NEWSLETTER AND PROCEEDINGS OF THE LINNEAN SOCIETY OF LONDON, THE **463**

LINNEAN SOCIETY OF LONDON *See* ZOOLOGICAL JOURNAL OF THE LINNEAN SOCIETY **5601**

Alphabetical Title Index — LIST

LINNEAN SOCIETY OF LONDON *See* BIOLOGICAL JOURNAL OF THE LINNEAN SOCIETY **445**

LINNEAN SOCIETY OF NEW SOUTH WALES *See* PROCEEDINGS OF THE LINNEAN SOCIETY OF NEW SOUTH WALES **4170**

LINNEAN SOCIETY SYMPOSIUM SERIES (UK/0161-6366) [02320579] **5233**

LINNEANA BELGICA (BE/0024-4090) [06369298] **463**

LINNEEN, LE (CN/0227-2377) [07295172] **4167**

LINN'S STAMP NEWS (US/0161-6234) [01755951] **2785**

LINN'S U.S. STAMP YEARBOOK (US/0748-996X) [10979935] **2785**

LINN'S WORLD STAMP ALMANAC (US/0146-6887) [03008395] **2785**

LINQ (AT) [03358915] **3405**

LINSCOTT'S DIRECTORY OF IMMUNOLOGICAL AND BIOLOGICAL REAGENTS (US/0740-7394) [08913092] **3674**

LINTON REGISTER *See* LINTON TRAINER'S RESOURCE DIRECTORY, THE **943**

● LINTON TRAINER'S RESOURCE DIRECTORY, THE (US/1064-234X) [26235910] **943**

LINTUMIES / SUOMEN LINTUTIETEELLINEN YHDISTYS (FI/0357-3524) [09839142] **5618**

LINYE KE-JI (CH/1001-9499) [I10019499] 5126, **2387**

LINYE KEXUE (1979) (CC/1001-7488) [09004742] **2387**

LINYE KEXUE YANGJIU (CC/1001-1498) [20346319] **2387**

LINZER-ABENDBOTE (AU) [20115124] **5778**

LINZER MITTAGSPOST (AU) [20255993] **5778**

LINZER VOLKSBLATT (AU) [11968198] **5778**

LION AND THE UNICORN (BROOKLYN), THE (US/0147-2593) [03134351] **3346**

LION (UNITED STATES ED.), THE (US/0024-4163) [01644325] **5233**

LIONEL COHEN LECTURES *CEASED*. (IS/0075-9740) [01754262] **1761**

LIONS MAGAZINE (US/0744-8074) [08566557] **1093**

LIP (LANCASTER, PA.) *CEASED*. (US/0744-3722) [08223460] **3346**

LIP SERVICE (US/0893-620X) [15604660] **4129**

LIPID FILE *CEASED*. (UK/0951-9599) [I09519599] **3708**

LIPID REVIEW (UK/0950-5857) [15617105] **3708**

LIPID TECHNOLOGY (UK/0956-666X) [I0956666X] **984**

LIPIDS (US/0024-4201) [01643294] **583**

LIPIKA (II/0377-0982) [01783493] **386**

LIPOSOMES (UK/0264-9659) [I02649659] **490**

LIPP. LIBRARY INSIGHTS, PROMOTION & PROGRAMS *CEASED*. (US/0196-1977) [03431559] **3228**

● LIPPINCOTT'S ORAL AND MAXILLOFACIAL SURGERY (US/1064-6698) [26369024] **1329**

LIPPINCOTT'S REVIEWS. RADIOLOGY *CEASED*. (US/1059-2156) [24513872] **3943**

LIPS (MONTCLAIR, N.J.) (US/0278-0933) [07702264] **3465**

LIPSCOMBE REPORT (AT/0817-6191) [I08176191] 4263, **1949**

LIQUEFIED GAS DIRECTORY OF AMERICA INC. WESTERN REGION (US/8756-7091) [11605395] **4263**

LIQUEFIED PETROLEUM GASES HANDBOOK (US) 2291, **4263**

LIQUID CHEMICALS (UK/0951-5836) [20601410] **984**

LIQUID CHROMATOGRAPHY ABSTRACTS (UK/0306-2104) [01790991] **1017**

LIQUID CHROMATOGRAPHY LITERATURE, ABSTRACTS & INDEX *See* GAS & LIQUID CHROMATOGRAPHY LITERATURE, ABSTRACTS & INDEX **1011**

LIQUID CHROMATOGRAPHY LITERATURE, ABSTRACTS AND INDEX (US/0147-328X) [03140916] **1017**

LIQUID CHROMATOGRAPHY MASS SPECTROMETRY ABSTRACTS (UK/0262-4168) [08428507] **984**

LIQUID CRYSTALS (UK/0267-8292) [13907464] **1032**

LIQUID CRYSTALS AND ORDERED FLUIDS (US/0146-5597) [02971487] **1032**

LIQUID FOSSIL FUEL TECHNOLOGY, QUARTERLY TECHNICAL PROGRESS REPORT (US) [08165442] **4263**

LIQUID GAS CARRIER REGISTER (UK/0305-1803) [02241910] **4263**

LIQUIDS HANDLING (UK/0268-9219) [I02689219] **4263**

LIQUOR RETAILING HANDBOOK (AT) **2369**

LIQUOR STORE MONTHLY (SA) **2369**

LIRE (FR/0338-5019) [04730304] **3405**

LIRE, BULLETIN DE LA SOCIETE BIBLIOGRAPHIQUE ET ORGANE DU BUREAU D'INFORMATIONS BIBLIOGRAPHIQUES... (FR) [01607224] **419**

LIRICA NEL MONDO (IT) [03087798] **4129**

LISA PLUS [COMPUTER FILE] (UK/0966-8799) 3228, **3259**

LISAN AL-ARAB (CN/0833-3858) [15809619] **5788**

LISANDUSI MOTETE JA UUDISTE VABALE LEVIKULE EESTIS (LAANE VALJAANNE) (SW) [19645899] **2697**

LISCOMBE SHEEP BULLETIN (UK) [04711823] **214**

LISHI YANJIU (CC) [12125702] **2622**

LISP AND SYMBOLIC COMPUTATION (US/0892-4635) [15205015] **1280**

LISP NEWS (US) [20051914] 3228, **3003**

LISP POINTERS (US/1045-3563) [19499999] **1280**

LIST. LIBRARY AND INFORMATION SCIENCE TRENDS (AT/1039-3013) [I10393013] **3228**

LIST OF ACCEPTED ADHESIVE-TYPE NAMEPLATES (CN/0711-3676) [08649545] **1616**

LIST OF ACCREDITED HEALTH CARE FACILITIES (CN/0843-2457) [20372556] **3788**

LIST OF ADDITIONS, A (US) [01783978] **3259**

LIST OF ALBERTA PUBLICATIONS AND LEGISLATION (CN/0837-7375) [16837427] **4662**

LIST OF APPROPRIATIONS : MADE BY THE REGULAR SESSION OF THE ... GENERAL ASSEMBLY AND THE ... SPECIAL SESSION THEREOF FOR THE BIENNIUM (US) [20591120] **4736**

LIST OF ART NEEDLEWORK, YARN KNITTING STORES (US/0161-6218) [03973331] **5184**

LIST OF CERTIFICATED PILOT SCHOOLS (US) [05176001] **27**

LIST OF CERTIFICATED U.S. AIR CARRIERS (US) [06440011] **27**

LIST OF CERTIFIED ELECTRICAL EQUIPMENT (1988) (CN/0838-8539) [18248063] **2071**

LIST OF CERTIFIED HEALTH CARE PRODUCTS AND SERVICES (CN/0824-7536) [09859915] **3605**

LIST OF CERTIFIED OCCUPATIONAL HEALTH AND SAFETY PRODUCTS (CN/0833-899X) [I0833899X] **2865**

LIST OF CERTIFIED PLUMBING PRODUCTS (1983) (CN/0833-8973) [15299416] **2606**

LIST OF CLASSES OF UNITED STATES GOVERNMENT PUBLICATIONS AVAILABLE FOR SELECTION BY DEPOSITORY LIBRARIES (US/0882-4045) [05529709] **419**

LIST OF COMPANIES REGISTERED UNDER THE INVESTMENT COMPANY ACT OF 1940 (US/0098-9657) [02239234] **905**

LIST OF CSA CERTIFIED COMFORT CONDITIONING EQUIPMENT (CN/1200-006X) [30673762] **2606**

LIST OF CSA CERTIFIED ELEVATOR EQUIPMENT (CN/1186-6152) [24368265] **2120**

LIST OF CSA CERTIFIED HEALTH CARE PRODUCTS AND SERVICES (CN/1200-1678) [31000989] **3605**

LIST OF CULTURES (NE/0377-0990) [01518987] **566**

LIST OF CURRENT PERIODICAL PUBLICATIONS IN ETHIOPIA (ET/0459-5009) [02310709] **2635**

LIST OF DIPLOMATIC AND CONSULAR MISSIONS, TRADE AND INTERNATIONAL ORGANIZATIONS / [ISSUED BY PROTOCOL DIVISION, MINISTRY OF FOREIGN AFFAIRS] (TZ) [11226759] **3132**

LIST OF DIPLOMATIC CORPS - QATAR. PROTOCOL DEPT (QA) [03926749] **3132**

LIST OF DOCUMENTS AND PUBLICATIONS IN THE FIELD OF MASS COMMUNICATION *SUSPENDED*. (FR) [03647113] **1115**

LIST OF ELECTRODES CERTIFIED TO CSA W48 SERIES OF STANDARDS AND APPLICABLE AWS A5. SPECIFICATIONS (CN/0822-742X) [10840830] **4027**

LIST OF EQUIPMENT AND MATERIALS (CN/0319-2318) [02443283] **619**

LIST OF EUROPEAN VHF SOUND BROADCASTING STATIONS (BE) **1134**

LIST OF FISHING VESSELS - NORTHWEST ATLANTIC FISHERIES ORGANIZATION (CN/0250-7811) [09845370] **2307**

LIST OF GOVERNMENT AUTHORS (US) [05035069] **419**

LIST OF HOLDINGS - AUSTRALIAN NATIONAL UNIVERSITY, RESEARCH SCHOOL OF SOCIAL SCIENCES, ARCHIVES OF BUSINESS AND LABOUR (AT/0727-3924) [I07273924] **690**

LIST OF INSPECTED TANK BARGES & TANKSHIPS (US/0145-7705) [02781587] **5451**

LIST OF INTERCEPTED PLANT PESTS (US/0092-6825) [01796523] **2424**

LIST OF JOURNALS ABSTRACTED (NE/0923-5582) [09763145] 3605, **3660**

LIST OF JOURNALS ABSTRACTED (1983) *See* EMBASE LIST OF JOURNALS INDEXED **3657**

LIST OF JOURNALS INDEXED IN INDEX MEDICUS (US/0093-3821) [02760305] **3660**

LIST OF LEGAL INVESTMENTS FOR SAVINGS BANKS IN CONNECTICUT (US/0098-0005) [01798898] 796, **905**

LIST OF LEGAL INVESTMENTS FOR SAVINGS BANKS, SAVINGS DEPOSITS OF TRUST COMPANIES AND COOPERATIVE BANKS (US) [06689105] 796, **905**

LIST OF LICENCES UNDER THE EXCISE TAX ACT (CN/0527-7507) [08870108] 1503, **690**

LIST OF LIGHTS AND FOG SIGNALS (US/0096-1280) [06767321] **4178**

LIST OF LIGHTS AND FOG SIGNALS. BALTIC SEA WITH KATTEGAT, BELTS AND SOUND, AND GULF OF BOTHNIA (US) [11780314] **4178**

LIST OF LIGHTS AND FOG SIGNALS. BRITISH ISLES, ENGLISH CHANNEL, AND NORTH SEA (US) [10159106] **4178**

LIST OF LIGHTS, BUOYS AND FOG SIGNALS *See* LIST OF LIGHTS, BUOYS AND FOG SIGNALS. ATLANTIC COAST **4178**

LIST OF LIGHTS, BUOYS AND FOG SIGNALS. ATLANTIC COAST (CN/0590-9384) [04250016] **4178**

LIST OF LIGHTS, BUOYS AND FOG SIGNALS. PACIFIC COAST (CN/0382-1080) [03527668] **4178**

LIST OF LOCAL BOARDS OF THE SELECTIVE SERVICE SYSTEM (US/0094-4092) [01794081] **4049**

LIST OF MARGINABLE OTC STOCKS AS OF ... (LS) [11625679] **905**

LIST OF MATERIALS ACCEPTABLE FOR USE ON SYSTEMS OF REA ELECTRIFICATION BORROWERS / RURAL ELECTRIFICATION ADMINISTRATION, U.S. DEPARTMENT OF AGRICULTURE (US) [02239126] **2071**

LIST OF MATERIALS ACCEPTABLE FOR USE ON TELEPHONE SYSTEMS OF REA BORROWERS / UNITED STATES DEPARTMENT OF AGRICULTURE, RURAL ELECTRIFICATION ADMINISTRATION (US) [02714944] **1159**

LIST OF MEDICAL PRACTITIONERS CURRENTLY LICENSED TO PRACTISE IN THE PROVINCE / THE COLLEGE OF PHYSICIANS AND SURGEONS OF MANITOBA (CN/0823-6909) [10156742] **3914**

LIST OF MEMBER INSTITUTIONS - FEDERAL SAVINGS AND LOAN INSURANCE CORPORATION (US/0428-1365) [01789028] 796, **2887**

LIST OF MEMBERS AND FIRMS (UK) [06612359] **747**

LIST OF MEMBERS AND SPONSORS *See* IRG AND ITS MEMBERS AND SPONSORS **2402**

LIST OF MEMBERS AND SUBSCRIBERS / BOTANICAL SOCIETY OF THE BRITISH ISLES (UK) [09080351] **517**

LIST OF MEMBERS / AUCTIONEERS' ASSOCIATION OF ALBERTA (CN/0229-155X) [07869982] **929**

LIST OF MEMBERS / BALTIC AND INTERNATIONAL MARITIME CONFERENCE (DK) [05586151] **5451**

LIST OF MEMBERS / BIBLIOGRAPHICAL SOCIETY OF AMERICA (US/0737-0458) [09257716] **419**

LIST OF MEMBERS - BRITISH RECORDS ASSOCIATION (UK) [01793296] **2482**

LIST OF MEMBERS - CAMBRIDGE UNIVERSITY (UK) [04357916] **1834**

LIST OF MEMBERS / CHARTERED ASSOCIATION OF CERTIFIED ACCOUNTANTS (UK) [15194052] **747**

LIST OF MEMBERS / FRESHWATER BIOLOGICAL ASSOCIATION (UK/0308-6739) [07848968] **463**

LIST — Alphabetical Title Index

LIST OF MEMBERS - INTERNATIONAL FEDERATION FOR HOUSING AND PLANNING (NE) [01787561] **2827**

LIST OF MEMBERS - INTERNATIONAL INSTITUTE FOR STRATEGIC STUDIES (UK/0306-8390) [02239866] **4049**

LIST OF MEMBERS - INTERNATIONAL SOCIETY FOR JAZZ RESEARCH. MITGLIEDERLISTE - INTERNATIONALE GESELLSCHAFT FUER JAZZFORSHCUNG. LISTE OF MEMBRES - SOCIETE INTERNATIONALE DE RECHERCHES SCIENTIFIQUE POUR LE JAZZ (AU) [03921680] **4129**

LIST OF MEMBERS OF THE DIPLOMATIC CORPS / MINISTRY OF FOREIGN AFFAIRS OF THE ISLAMIC REPUBLIC OF IRAN (IR) [10974230] **4662**

LIST OF MEMBERS OF THE HOUSE OF COMMONS OF CANADA (CN/0316-1641) [02248384] **4662**

LIST OF MEMBERS OF THE INTERNATIONAL STATISTICAL INSTITUTE (NE) [03283604] **5332**

LIST OF MEMBERS - THE ASSOCIATION OF JAPANESE CONSULTING ENGINEERS (JA) [03356339] **2027**

LIST OF MEMBERS / THE HAKLUYT SOCIETY (UK) [13355238] **2568**

LIST OF MEMBERS - WORLD PEACE COUNCIL (FI) [06972422] **3132**

LIST OF NAUTICAL CHARTS AND ITS CORRECTIONS BY NOTICES TO MARINERS: PERMANENT, PRELIMINARY AND TEMPORARY (BL) [05252216] **4185**

LIST OF NURSERYMEN, FLORISTS & DEALERS AND PLANT INSPECTION AND QUARANTINE OFFICIALS (US/0737-1004) [09168632] **2435**

LIST OF PERIODICALS ABSTRACTED (SZ) [03154978] **2865**

LIST OF PLANTS OPERATING UNDER USDA POULTRY AND EGG GRADING AND EGG PRODUCTS INSPECTION PROGRAMS (US/0195-4776) [05434843] **214**

LIST OF PLANTS OPERATING UNDER USDA POULTRY AND EGG INSPECTION AND GRADING PROGRAMS *See* LIST OF PLANTS OPERATING UNDER USDA POULTRY AND EGG GRADING AND EGG PRODUCTS INSPECTION PROGRAMS **214**

LIST OF POLITICAL PRISONERS IN THE USSR (GW) [18709575] **4510**

LIST OF PROPRIETARY SUBSTANCES AND NONFOOD COMPOUNDS AUTHORIZED FOR USE UNDER USDA INSPECTION AND GRADING PROGRAMS (US/0748-3082) [08725108] **2348**

LIST OF PUBLICATIONS AND MAPS (US) [06541047] **1386**

LIST OF PUBLICATIONS / ARKANSAS GEOLOGICAL COMMISSION (US/8756-5986) [07632672] **1363**

LIST OF PUBLICATIONS / INTERNATIONAL TELECOMMUNICATION UNION (SZ) [07092754] **1159**

LIST OF PUBLICATIONS OF THE BUREAU OF MARINE SCIENCE & TECHNOLOGY, MARINE RESEARCH LABORATORY (US) [02240858] **555**

LIST OF PUBLICATIONS / TENNESSEE DIVISION OF GEOLOGY (US) [06527860] **1386**

LIST OF PUBLICATIONS - UNITED STATES. CONGRESSIONAL BUDGET OFFICE (US/0277-0776) [05849612] **4736**

LIST OF PUBLISHED SOIL SURVEYS (US) [04253590] **178**

LIST OF RECENT ACCESSIONS AND FOREIGN PATENT TRANSLATIONS OF THE SCIENTIFIC LIBRARY (US) [03457926] **1306**

LIST OF RECENT PERIODICAL ARTICLES (US/0885-4408) [05428953] 796, **1503**

LIST OF REGISTERED DOCTORS OF MEDICINE AND SURGERY, DOCTORS OF OSTEOPATHY LICENSED TO PRACTICE MEDICINE AND SURGERY, DOCTORS OF OSTEOPATHY LICENSED TO PRACTICE OSTEOPATHY, DOCTORS OF CHIROPRACTIC, DOCTORS OF PODIATRY (US/0276-2250) [04295342] **3914**

LIST OF RESEARCH WORKERS IN THE AGRICULTURAL SCIENCES IN THE COMMONWEALTH (UK) [05431500] **105**

LIST OF RESIDENTIAL CARE FACILITIES / STATISTICS CANADA, CANADIAN CENTRE FOR HEALTH INFORMATION (CN/1180-3045) [30502324] **5295**

LIST OF SCHOOLS, ADDRESSES AND STATISTICS (SA) [01785457] **1761**

LIST OF SCHOOLS IN MANITOBA (CN/0826-337X) [10232728] **1762**

LIST OF SELECTED WIPO MEETINGS (SZ) [20958613] **1306**

LIST OF SERIALS AVAILABLE IN CAMBRIDGE UNIVERSITY LIBRARY AND IN OTHER LIBRARIES CONNECTED WITH THE UNIVERSITY [MICROFORM] (UK) [15090328] **3228**

LIST OF SERIALS INDEXED FOR ONLINE USERS (US/0736-7139) [09199853] **3660**

LIST OF SHIPOWNERS / LLOYD'S REGISTER OF SHIPPING (UK) [11724617] **5451**

LIST OF SHIPS (CN/0833-5672) [13145699] **5451**

LIST OF SMALL BUSINESS CONCERNS INTERESTED IN PERFORMING RESEARCH AND DEVELOPMENT, A (US) [05152269] **690**

LIST OF SMALL BUSINESS INVESTMENT COMPANIES *See* DIRECTORY OF OPERATING SMALL BUSINESS INVESTMENT COMPANIES **896**

LIST OF STATUTORY INSTRUMENTS (UK) [06842707] **3003**

LIST OF TATTOOED REGISTERED HARNESS HORSES (US/0884-1284) [12168499] **2800**

LIST OF THE DIPLOMATIC CORPS AND CONSULAR, TRADE AND OTHER FOREIGN REPRESENTATIVES *See* DIPLOMATIC CORPS AND CONSULAR, TRADE, AND OTHER FOREIGN REPRESENTATIVES IN PAKISTAN / MINISTRY OF FOREIGN AFFAIRS **4520**

LIST OF THE MEMBERS OF THE ROYAL COLLEGES OF PHYSICIANS OF THE UNITED KINGDOM (UK/0307-7462) [01705942] **3915**

LIST OF THESES IN HISTORY OF SCIENCE IN BRITISH UNIVERSITIES IN PROGRESS OR RECENTLY COMPLETED, A (UK) [06484268] **1834**

LIST OF TRANSLATIONS IN THE LIBRARY OF THE GEOLOGICAL SURVEY OF CANADA (CN) [02902723] **1386**

LIST OF U.S. AIR CARRIERS *See* LIST OF CERTIFICATED U.S. AIR CARRIERS **27**

LIST OF VISITING SCHOLARS IN CANADA (CN/0319-6410) [02442994] **1762**

LIST OF WORKING DOCUMENTS (LU/0531-4348) [02240655] **4662**

LIST OF WORTHWHILE LIFE AND HEALTH INSURANCE BOOKS, A (US/0537-9350) [02244362] **2887**

LIST : PROGRAMMI PER IL TUO HOME COMPUTER ***SUSPENDED.*** (IT) 1234, 1268, **1280**

LIST (VERO BEACH, FLA.) ***CEASED.*** (US/0738-8543) [09660839] **1268**

LISTA DAS ESTACOES E POSTOS, CORREIO (PO) [09788382] **1145**

LISTA DE LIBROS Y FOLLETOS RECIBIDOS (VE) [01477639] **105**

LISTA DE LOS SENORES QUE FORMAN LOS EXPRESADOS COLEGIOS (SP) [04308682] **3141**

LISTA DE SENORES COLEGIADOS (SP) [01787521] **3003**

LISTA DE SENORES COLEGIADOS, GUIA JUDICIAL Y ADMINISTRATIVA (SP) [03307550] **3003**

LISTA DEL CUERPO DIPLOMATICO (SP) [07082873] **3132**

LISTA DIPLOMATICA (ECUADOR. MINISTERIO DE RELACIONES EXTERIORES) *See* LISTA DIPLOMATICA Y DE LOS ORGANISMOS INTERNACIONALES / DIRECCION GENERAL DE PROTOCOLO **4528**

LISTA DIPLOMATICA Y DE LOS ORGANISMOS INTERNACIONALES / DIRECCION GENERAL DE PROTOCOLO (EC) [08383053] **4528**

LISTA NACIONAL DE ARGENTINA (UY) [01780099] **3003**

LISTE ANNOTEE D'ARBITRES DE GRIEFS (CN/0229-9062) [06241106] **1688**

LISTE BIMESTRIELLE DES PUBLICATIONS DU GOUVERNEMENT DU QUEBEC (CN/0840-7908) [19750345] 4662, **4698**

LISTE D'ABREVIATIONS DE MOTS DES TITRES DE PUBLICATIONS EN SERIE (FR/0259-000X) [14089757] **3228**

LISTE D'ABREVIATIONS DE MOTS DES TITRES DE PUBLICATIONS EN SERIE. SUPPLEMENT (FR/0259-0018) [15027357] **3228**

LISTE DER AUSLANDISCHEN MILITARATTACHES (GW) [11203068] **4049**

LISTE DER DIPLOMATISCHEN MISSIONEN UND ANDEREN VERTRETUNGEN IN BONN (GW/0723-953X) [01799067] **4662**

●LISTE DES ACQUISITIONS / CENTRE D'ETUDES HIMALAYENNES (FR) [30395431] **419**

LISTE DES ACQUISITIONS - INFORMATHEQUE DE LINGUISTIQUE. UNIVERSITE D'OTTAWA (CN/0317-1981) [02248086] **3300**

LISTE DES BENEFICIAIRES D'UNE SUBVENTION DU FONDS NATIONAL DE LA RECHERCHE SCIENTIFIQUE OU D'UN DES TROIS FONDS ASSOCIES AVEC INDICATION DES RECHERCHES POURSUIVIES ET DE L'INSTITUTION D'ACCUEIL (BE) [01785926] **5126**

LISTE DES DIPLOMES INSTITUES SUR LE PLAN NATIONAL ET SANCTIONNANT UNE FORMATION PROFESSIONNELLE (FR) [06411892] **1834**

LISTE DES DISTANCES KILOMETRIQUES, AFFERENTES AUX PARCOURS TERRITORIAUX DES DEPECHES EN TRANSIT (SZ) [07491169] **1145**

LISTE DES FILMS VISES PAR CATEGORIES DE SPECTATEURS (CN/0713-3529) [08752094] **4074**

●LISTE DES FILMS VISES PAR CATEGORIES DE SPECTATEURS, DIFFUSION PRIVEE (CN/1191-7423) [27272224] **4074**

LISTE DES INDICATIFS D'APPEL ET DES IDENTITES NUMERIQUES DES STATIONS UTILISEES DANS LES SERVICES MOBILE MARITIME ET MOBILE MARITIME PAR SATELLITE (SZ) [19609254] **1159**

LISTE DES MEMBRES / ASSOCIATION INTERNATIONALE DE SIGNALISATION MARITIME (FR) [19615302] **4178**

LISTE DES MEMBRES DE LA SOCIETE GEOLOGIQUE DE FRANCE (FR) [20084062] **1386**

LISTE DES MEMBRES DE LA SOCIETE GEOLOGIQUE DE FRANCE AU (FR) [11554938] **1386**

LISTE DES MEMBRES DES CORPS DIPLOMATIQUE ET CONSULAIRE ET DES ORGANISATIONS INTERNATIONALES (NG) [04532851] **4528**

LISTE DES MEMBRES DU CLUB DES ORNITHOLOGUES DE SIC QUEBEC (CN/0228-2151) [06959309] **5618**

LISTE DES MEMBRES DU CORPS CONSULAIRE (SZ) [07715426] **4662**

LISTE DES MEMBRES DU CORPS CONSULAIRE, ISTANBUL (TU) [24781744] **4662**

LISTE DES MEMBRES - INSTITUT BELGE DE NORMALISATION (BE) [01786199] **4031**

LISTE DES NOUVEAUTES - COLLEGE DE L'ASSOMPTION. BIBLIOTHEQUE DU COLLEGIAL (CN/0826-1334) [10862184] **3228**

LISTE DES NOUVELLES ACQUISITIONS - HOPITAL SAINT-VINCENT, OTTAWA, ONT. BIBLIOTHEQUE (CN/1184-6038) [24265441] 3228, **3605**

LISTE DES PERIODIQUES / CENTRE D'INFORMATION SUR LE DEVELOPPEMENT (CN/0823-1729) [10105749] **2911**

LISTE DES PERIODIQUES REGULIEREMENT RECUS - UNIVERSITE DE MONTREAL. BIBLIOTHEQUE DES SCIENCES HUMAINES ET SOCIAL (CN/0226-0565) [06264810] **419**

LISTE DES PUBLICATIONS DU COMMISSARIAT A L'ENERGIE ATOMIQUE / CENTRE D'ETUDES NUCLEAIRES DE SACLAY, SERVICE DE DOCUMENTATION (FR/0398-9275) [07968738] **1949**

●LISTE DES RAPPORTS ANNUELS, BIBLIOTHEQUE PRINCIPALE JE (CN/1187-7154) [25590174] **4662**

●LISTE DES RAPPORTS ANNUELS, BIBLIOTHEQUE PRINCIPALE JE, LIST OF ANNUAL REPORTS, MAIN LIBRARY (JE) (CN/1187-7154) [25590173] 3228, **4662**

LISTE DES RELIGIEUX ET CATALOGUE DES MAISONS ET OEUVRES / CONGREGATION DE SAINTE-CROIX, SOCIETE DES PERES, LA PROVINCE CANADIENNE (CN/0845-4507) [20103932] **4974**

LISTE DES STATIONS DE TELEVISION. ZONE EUROPEENNE (BE) [06435414] **1134**

LISTE DES TRAVAUX ARACHNOLOGIQUES MONDIAUX *See* LISTE DES TRAVAUX ARACHNOLOGIQUES PARUS EN ... OU ACTUELLEMENT SOUS PRESSE **5590**

LISTE DES TRAVAUX ARACHNOLOGIQUES PARUS EN ... OU ACTUELLEMENT SOUS PRESSE (FR) [09540175] **5590**

LISTE DESCRIPTIVE DES ETABLISSEMENTS PUBLICS D'ENSEIGNEMENT DE SECOND DEGRE DISPENSANT UN ENSEIGNEMENT PROFESSIONNEL DE CYCLE COURT OU DE CYCLE LONG : TERRITOIRES D'OUTRE-MER (FR) [05320696] **1914**

LISTE D'IDENTIFICATION DES ENTOMOPHAGES (SZ) [01791479] **4245**

LISTE DIPLOMATIQUE - DEPARTEMENT DU PROTOCOLE (UA) [03475348] **3132**

Alphabetical Title Index — LITERATURE

LISTE DIPLOMATIQUE ET CONSULAIRE See LISTE DU CORPS DIPLOMATIQUE - REPUBLIQUE DU SENEGAL **3132**

LISTE DU CORPS DIPLOMATIQUE AU CAIRE (UA) [03477366] **3132**

LISTE DU CORPS DIPLOMATIQUE - REPUBLIQUE DU SENEGAL (SG) [02239923] **3132**

LISTE MENSUELLE (BE/0005-8521) [01519451] 1503, **1535**

LISTE OFFICIELLE DES NAVIRES DE MER BELGES ET DE LA FLOTTE DE LA FORCE NAVALE (BE) [02239787] **5451**

LISTE OVER GODKJENTE ENTREPRENRER (NO) [02481601] **1616**

LISTE OVER MDEDOKUMENTER (LU) [20049913] **3132**

LISTE PAR SECTEUR DES PRINCIPALES CONCENTRATIONS REALISEES DANS L'INDUSTRIE FRANCAISE (FR) [10054697] **1616**

LISTE QUINQUENNIALE DES ENTREES EN CARACTERES CYRILLIQUES (FR) [03304825] **419**

LISTE TEMOIN SUR LA PLANIFICATION FISCALE (CN/0821-0772) [10195133] **4736**

LISTEN (ENGLISH EDITION, OTTAWA) (CN/1183-1820) [24690696] **4390**

LISTEN (FRANKFURT AM MAIN, GERMANY) (GW/0179-7417) [20626015] **3346**

LISTEN (FRENCH EDITION, OTTAWA) (CN/1183-1820) [24690697] **4390**

LISTEN (MOUNTAIN VIEW, CALIF.) (US/0024-435X) [01776494] 1066, **1346**

●LISTEN (NEW YORK, N.Y. 1991) (US/1054-3104) [22840463] **4129**

LISTEN REAL LOUD **SUSPENDED.** (US/0893-8083) [15650651] **5560**

LISTENER WELLINGTON (NZ/0110-5787) [I01105787] **1134**

LISTENERS' GUIDE - WGMS (US/0147-0388) [03081760] **4129**

LISTENING POST (CITY OF INDUSTRY) (US/0148-3544) [01782104] 5317, **4129**

LISTENING (RIVER FOREST) (US/0024-4414) [01755960] 4352, **4974**

LISTENING (WASHINGTON) (US/0196-7258) [03661852] 5031, **4390**

LISTER HILL NATIONAL CENTER FOR BIOMEDICAL COMMUNICATIONS See REPORT TO THE CONGRESS - LISTER HILL NATIONAL CENTER FOR BIOMEDICAL COMMUNICATIONS **3633**

LISTES - ASSOCIATION CANADIENNE DES PRODUCTEURS DE PATES ET PAPIERS, SECTION TECHNIQUE (CN/0822-4811) [10216713] **4235**

LISTIN DE COLEGIADOS - COLEGIO OFICIAL DE APAREJADORES Y ARQUITECTOS TECNICOS DEL CENTRO DE ESPANA (SP) [01795472] 1834, **302**

LISTING OF AIRCRAFT ACCIDENTS-INCIDENTS BY MAKE AND MODEL, U.S. CIVIL AVIATION (US/0360-3954) [02243898] **27**

LISTING OF ELIGIBLE LABOR SURPLUS AREAS UNDER DEFENSE MANPOWER POLICY NO. 4A AND EXECUTIVE ORDER 10582 (US) [05153140] **1688**

LISTING OF PEER REVIEWERS USED BY NSF DIVISIONS (US/0146-6968) [02736744] **5126**

LISTING OF PRECEDENT DECISIONS THAT HAVE NOT BEEN PUBLISHED IN BOUND VOLUMES AS OF ... (US) [09911939] **1920**

LISTING OF SUPPLEMENTARY DOCUMENTS / STATISTICS CANADA, LIBRARY (CN/0228-5134) [08382710] 3228, **3259**

LISTING OF SUPPLEMENTARY DOCUMENTS, SUPPLEMENT / STATISTICS CANADA, LIBRARY (CN/0835-085X) [16410093] 3228, **3259**

LISTINO BORSA VALORI (IT) **820**

LISTINO DEI PREZZI ALL'INGROSSO SULLA PIAZZA DI MILANO (IT) [08248777] **1616**

LISTINO MENSILE PREZZI INGROSSO SULLA PIAZZA DI SIRACUSA (IT) **820**

LISTINO PREZZI ALL INGROSSO. FIRENZE (IT) **820**

LISTINO PREZZI PARTI RICAMBIO AUTOVETTURE E VEICOLI COMMERCIALI (IT) **844**

LISTINO PREZZI PARTI RICAMBIO MOTOVEICOLI E VEICOLI INDUSTRIALI (IT) **844**

LISTINO QUINDICINALE DEI PREZZI ALL'INGROSSO PRATICATI SULLA PIAZZA DI ROMA (IT) [07603779] **844**

LISTINO SETTIMANALE DEI PREZZI ALL'INGRESSO SULLA PIAZZA DI MILANO See LISTINO DEI PREZZI ALL'INGROSSO SULLA PIAZZA DI MILANO **1616**

LISTINO UFFICIALE BORSA VALORI ROMA (IT) **820**

LISTO (NEW YORK, N.Y.) **CEASED.** (US/1055-1204) [23086111] **2537**

LISTS OF LIGHTS, BUOYS AND FOG SIGNALS. INLAND WATERS (CN/0381-3401) [02952262] **4178**

LISTS OF PARTIES EXCLUDED FROM FEDERAL PROCUREMENT OR NONPROCUREMENT PROGRAMS (US/1057-5774) [18206428] **4662**

LISTY (IT) [01789835] **2697**

LISTY (BLATTER) (AU) [02240658] **4481**

LISTY CUKROVARNICKE See LISTY CUKROVARNICKE A REPARSKE **178**

●LISTY CUKROVARNICKE A REPARSKE (XR) [28083439] **178**

LISTY CUKROVARNICKI CASOPIS PRO PRUMSYL CUKROVARNICKY V CECHACH (XR) [06205007] **1027**

LISTY FILOLOGICKE (PRAGUE, CZECHOSLOVAKIA : 1946) (XR/0024-4457) [02962306] **3300**

LISWA NEWSLETTER (AT/1035-4816) [I10354816] **3228**

LISZT SAECULUM (SW) [05198743] **4129**

LISZT SOCIETY JOURNAL, THE (UK) [03567493] **4129**

LISZT SOCIETY (LONDON, ENGLAND) See LISZT SOCIETY JOURNAL, THE **4129**

LIT PAGE, THE (US/1047-6989) [20745674] **3228**

LIT-POT-HEC (CN/0822-7543) [10420460] **876**

LITA NEWSLETTER (US/0196-1799) [05757570] **3228**

LITALERT (VIENNA, VA.) (US/8756-9647) [11770179] **1306**

LITARATURA I MASTATSTVA (BW) [07207171] **3406**

LITCHFIELD COUNTY TIMES, THE (US/0744-6705) [08490099] **5645**

LITCHFIELD ENQUIRER (US) [10316028] **5645**

LITCHVILLE BULLETIN (US) [01755965] **5725**

LITE FLYER (US/1043-4968) [19476441] **27**

LITE FLYER SAFETY ALERT ACTIONGRAM (US/1043-495X) [19476343] **27**

LITEINCE PROIZVODSTVO, METALLOVEDENIE I OBRABOTKA METALLOV DAVLENIEM (RU/0302-9069) [05693053] **4007**

LITEJNOE PROIZVODSTVO (UN/0024-449X) [01783882] **4007**

LITERA (TU/0459-5106) [04122377] 3300, **3406**

LITERACY **CEASED.** (FR) [01491190] **1881**

LITERACY ADVANCE (US/0363-5481) [02464910] **1881**

LITERACY LINK (AT/0158-3026) [I01583026] **1881**

●LITERACY NEWS: A PUBLICATION OF THE NATIONAL INSTITUTE FOR LITERACY (US) [25897317] **1881**

LITERACY (TORONTO) (CN/0700-5369) [23686561] **1881**

LITERACY WORKS (CN/1183-3793) [24265934] **1762**

LITERARISCHER VEREIN IN STUTTGART See BIBLIOTHEK **3457**

LITERARNI ARCHIV (XR/0231-5904) [01755972] **3406**

LITERARNY TYZDENNIK : CASOPIS ZVAZU SLOVENSKYCH SPISOVATELOV (XO) [19248115] **3406**

LITERARY AGENTS OF NORTH AMERICA MARKETPLACE (US/8756-2219) [09964955] **2922**

LITERARY AND LINGUISTIC COMPUTING (UK/0268-1145) [14082151] 3300, **1193**

LITERARY CAVALCADE (CN) 3406, **1762**

LITERARY CAVALCADE (US/0024-4511) [04171185] 1900, **3406**

LITERARY CRITERION, THE (II/0024-452X) [01716590] **3406**

LITERARY CRITICISM REGISTER (US/0733-2165) [08534845] 3346, **3357**

LITERARY ENDEAVOUR, THE (II/0255-2779) [08383293] **3406**

LITERARY HALF-YEARLY, THE (II/0024-4554) [01642409] **3406**

●LITERARY IMAGE (US/1064-8062) [26407681] **3406**

LITERARY MAGAZINE REVIEW (US/0732-6637) [08382676] **3346**

LITERARY MARKET PLACE (1988) (US/0000-1155) [18891886] **4821**

LITERARY MARKET REVIEW (US/0198-151X) [06178892] **3406**

LITERARY ONOMASTICS STUDIES **CEASED.** (US/0160-8703) [03772973] **3406**

LITERARY READER (II) [01784077] **3406**

LITERARY RESEARCH **CEASED.** (US/0891-6365) [14938385] **3406**

LITERARY REVIEW (EDINBURGH) (UK/0144-4360) [08923475] **3346**

LITERARY REVIEW (LUCKNOW) (II/0304-1123) [01797779] **3346**

LITERARY REVIEW OF CANADA, THE (CN/1188-7494) [26245206] 4830, **3406**

LITERARY REVIEW (TEANECK), THE (US/0024-4589) [01645668] **3406**

LITERARY SCANNER (US/1058-8353) [24402208] **3346**

LITERARY SKETCHES (US/0024-4597) [01149623] **3406**

LITERAT, DER (GW/0024-4627) [05319172] **3406**

LITERATI CHICAGO (US/0895-9269) [16854902] **3406**

LITERATI INTERNAZIONALE (US/1054-9404) [23026675] **3406**

LITERATOR (SA/0258-2279) [26798876] **3406**

LITERATUR FUER LESER (GW/0343-1657) [05223581] **3406**

LITERATUR IN WISSENSCHAFT UND UNTERRICHT : LWU (GW/0024-4643) [0231503E] **3406**

LITERATUR-SCHNELLDIENST KUNSTSTOFFE, KAUTSCHUK, FASERN (GW/0932-7754) [I09327754] **5126**

LITERATUR UND WIRKLICHKEIT (GW/0075-9937) [01607531] **3406**

LITERATURA (PL/0137-2548) [09913506] **3406**

LITERATURA ARGENTINA; REVISTA BIBLIOGRAFICA, LA (AG) [02351175] **3459**

LITERATURA (BUDAPEST) (HU/0133-2368) [02243678] **3406**

LITERATURA, DITY, CHAS (UN) [07931231] **3406**

LITERATURA FOIRO (IT) [03780206] **3406**

LITERATURA I ISKUSSTVO (RU/0459-5351) [01756011] **3406**

LITERATURA IR MENAS (LI) [06498438] **3406**

LITERATURA LUDOWA (PL/0024-4708) [02104993] **2321**

LITERATURA MEXICANA (MX/0188-2546) [22258856] **3406**

LITERATURA NA SWIECIE (PL) [10056387] **3406**

LITERATURA O NARODONASELENII (RU) [18609208] **4554**

LITERATURA OB ULIANOVSKOI OBLASTI (RU) [05791993] **2635**

LITERATURA RADZIECKA (RU/0024-4716) [01756014] **3406**

LITERATURA V SHKOLE (RU/0024-4724) [04336168] **3406**

LITERATURA Y SOCIEDAD (SP) [10819102] **3407**

LITERATURBERICHTE UEBER WASSER, ABWASSER, LUFT UND FESTE ABFALLSTOFFE (GW/0340-4900) [02356257] **2235**

LITERATURDIENST / HERAUSGEBER ; BUND FUER LEBENSMITTELRECHT UND LEBENSMITTELKUNDE (GW/0343-6632) [07407638] **2348**

LITERATURDOKUMENTATION ZUR ARBEITSMARKT- UND BERUFSFORSCHUNG (GW) [01794962] **1688**

LITERATURE ABSTRACTS. CATALYSTS & CATALYSIS See LITERATURE ABSTRACTS. CATALYSTS / ZEOLITES **4284**

LITERATURE ABSTRACTS. CATALYSTS & CATALYSIS (US/1065-0539) [26523018] 4263, **4284**

●LITERATURE ABSTRACTS. CATALYSTS / ZEOLITES (US/1074-6870) [29779867] 4263, **4284**

●LITERATURE ABSTRACTS. HEALTH & ENVIRONMENT (US/1065-0490) [25587859] 2235, **2184**

●LITERATURE ABSTRACTS. PETROLEUM REFINING & PETROCHEMICALS (US/1065-0512) [25588044] 4263, **4284**

●LITERATURE ABSTRACTS. PETROLEUM SUBSTITUTES (US/1065-0504) [25595538] 1949, 4263, **4284**

●LITERATURE ABSTRACTS. TRANSPORTATION & STORAGE (US/1065-0520) [25595340] 4263, **4284**

LITERATURE — Alphabetical Title Index

LITERATURE ANALYSIS OF MICROCOMPUTER PUBLICATIONS : LAMP **CEASED**. (US/0735-9721) [09039363] 1268, **1209**

LITERATURE AND BELIEF (US/0732-1929) [08324773] 4974, **3407**

LITERATURE AND CONTEMPORARY REVOLUTIONARY CULTURE (US/0885-3274) [12616516] **3407**

LITERATURE & HISTORY (UK/0306-1973) [02244209] 2697, **3407**

LITERATURE AND MEDICINE (US/0278-9671) [07920375] 2849, **3605**

LITERATURE & PATENT ABSTRACTS. OILFIELD CHEMICALS **CEASED**. (US/1065-0547) [26530126] 1027, 4263, **4284**

LITERATURE AND PSYCHOLOGY (US/0024-4759) [01756017] 4603, **3407**

LITERATURE AND THE SCIENCES OF MAN (US/1040-7928) [18533043] **3407**

LITERATURE & THEOLOGY (UK/0269-1205) [16502653] 4974, **3407**

LITERATURE BASE **SUSPENDED**. (AT/1034-6244) [I10346244] **3407**

LITERATURE CRITICISM FROM 1400 TO 1800 (US/0740-2880) [09921331] **3346**

LITERATURE EAST & WEST (US/0024-4767) [01756018] **3407**

LITERATURE FILM QUARTERLY (US/0090-4260) [01784960] **4074**

●LITERATURE INDEX (US/1065-0431) [26065350] **4263**

LITERATURE, INTERPRETATION, THEORY (US/1043-6928) [19533748] **3407**

LITERATURE (NEW YORK, N.Y.) *See* LITERATURE INDEX **4263**

LITERATURE OF ART, THE (UK/0141-335X) [04359887] 357, **3407**

LITERATURE SCAN. ANESTHESIOLOGY **SUSPENDED**. (US/0892-2438) [15129792] **3683**

LITERATURE SCAN. TRANSPLANTATION (US/0883-8410) [12228436] **3969**

LITERATURE (WASHINGTON) (US/0197-8829) [03815298] **3407**

LITERATURE [MICROFORM] / NEWSBANK, INC (US) [11578157] **3407**

LITERATUREN ARKHIV / BULGARSKA AKADEMIIA NA NAUKITE, INSTITUT ZA BULGARSKA LITERATURA (BU/0459-5564) [01643406] **3407**

LITERATUREN FORUM (BU/0861-2153) [I08612153] **5779**

LITERATUREN ZBOR (XN/0024-4791) [02101314] **3407**

LITERATURINFORMATION TERRITORIALFORSCHUNG, TERRITORIALPLANUNG (GW) [07632072] **2568**

LITERATURMAGAZIN (GW/0934-6503) [02323730] **3407**

LITERATURNA MISL (BU/0324-0495) [01756019] **3407**

LITERATURNAIA CHECHENO-INGUSHETIIA (RU) [06149165] **3407**

LITERATURNAIA GRUZIIA (GS/0458-0311) [04314321] **3407**

LITERATURNAIA ROSSIIA : EZHENEDELNIK PRAVLENIIA SOIUZA PISATELEI RSFSR I PRAVLENIIA MOSKOVSKOGO OTDELENIIA SOIUZA PISATELEIA RSFSR (RU) [02263625] **3346**

LITERATURNAIA UCHEBA (RU) [04748636] **3407**

LITERATURNAJA ARMENIJA (AI/0130-3597) [04336082] **3346**

LITERATURNOE NASLEDSTVO (RU) [01756021] **3407**

LITERATURNOE OBOZRENIE (RU/0321-2904) [04282409] **3407**

LITERATURNYI AZERBAIDZHAN (AJ) [04314255] **3407**

LITERATURNYI KIRGIZSTAN (KG/0459-5637) [04328896] **3346**

LITERATURNYI KURER (US) [09567595] **3407**

LITERATURWISSENSCHAFT, GESELLSCHAFTSWISSENSCHAFT (GW) [04891453] **5208**

LITERATURWISSENSCHAFTLICHES JAHRBUCH (GW/0075-997X) [02323496] **3407**

LITERATURZUSAMMENSTELLUNGEN ... DER TECHNISCHEN INFORMATIONS- UND DOKUMENTATIONSSTELLE DES BWB (GW) [11093376] **4049**

LITERATUURBULLETIN GEESTELIJKE VOLKSGEZONDHEID (NE/0034-4621) **876**

LITERATUURINFORMATIE PERSONEELSBELEID EN ORGANISATIE (NE/0921-6154) [I09216154] **690**

LITFASS (GW) [03243326] **3407**

LITHIC TECHNOLOGY (US/0197-7261) [04319185] **273**

LITHIUM AND ANIMAL BEHAVIOR **CEASED**. (CN/0705-4718) [03963625] 4603, **5515**

LITHIUM (EDINBURGH) (UK/0954-1381) [I09541381] **4314**

LITHIUM RESEARCH REVIEW SERIES (US/0731-8065) [08252444] **4007**

LITHIUM THERAPY MONOGRAPHS **CEASED**. (SZ/1011-2928) [17367555] **3605**

LITHOCLASTIA (FR/0336-4933) [03695504] **619**

LITHOLOGY AND MINERAL RESOURCES (US/0024-4902) [01756025] 1386, **2143**

LITHOS (NO/0024-4937) [01265750] **1441**

LITHOWEEK (UK/0264-732X) [09163580] **4566**

●LITHUANIA BUSINESS PACK, THE (UK) **690**

LITHUANIAN AMERICAN COMMUNITY *See* VIOLATIONS OF HUMAN RIGHTS IN SOVIET OCCUPIED LITHUANIA, THE **4514**

LITHUANIAN MATHEMATICAL JOURNAL (US/0363-1672) [02422539] **3517**

●LITHUANIAN WEEKLY (LI) [27342460] **5806**

LITIGATING AN ANTITRUST CASE (US/0196-3317) [05781779] **3101**

LITIGATION (US) [04051626] **3003**

LITIGATION (US/0097-9813) [01799361] **3003**

LITIGATION AND ADMINISTRATIVE PRACTICE SERIES (US/8756-4548) [11564610] **3003**

LITIGATION APPLICATIONS (US/1055-4084) [23166652] **3003**

LITIGATION (CHICHESTER, ENGLAND) (UK/0263-2160) [08820622] **3003**

LITIGATION COMMITTEE NEWSLETTER (US/1072-9984) [20787769] **3003**

LITIGATION COURSE HANDBOOK SERIES (US/8756-4491) [05018001] **3003**

LITIGATION LETTER (UK/0268-0653) [I02680653] **3003**

LITIGATION NEWS (US/0147-9970) [02037315] **3003**

●LITIGATION SERVICES RESOURCE DIRECTORY (US/1061-3625) [25266724] **3003**

LITIGATION UNDER THE FEDERAL OPEN GOVERNMENT LAWS (US/1068-7149) [23907677] **4481**

●LITIGATOR, THE (UK) **3003**

LITIR NEWSLETTER OF VICTORIAN STUDIES (CN/0821-4077) [09823595] **3407**

LITIS (BL) [02243872] **3003**

LITMAG 500, THE (US) [20136345] **3407**

LITO **CEASED**. (IT) **2489**

LITO NEWSLETTER **CEASED**. (IT) **5126**

LITOLOGIA I POLEZNYE ISKOPAEMYE (RU/0024-497X) [04337259] **2143**

LITOLOGIJA I PALEOGEOGRAFIJA (RU/0131-1719) [02518257] **1459**

LITOPYS BOIKIVSHCHYNY (US) [01794314] **2697**

LITOPYS BRAZOTVORCHYKH VYDAN. LETOPIS IZOBRAZITELNYKH IZDANII (UN) [05539143] **419**

LITORAL (SP) [03020621] **3407**

LITOVSKII FIZICHESKII SBORNIK *See* LIETUVOS FIZIKOS ZURNALAS / LITHUANIAN JOURNAL OF PHYSICS / LITOVSKII FIZICHESKII ZHURNAL / LIETUVOS FIZIKU DRAUGIJA **4411**

LITOVSKII FIZICHESKII SBORNIK (US/1047-4064) [20687751] **4411**

LITOVSKIJ FIZICESKIJ SBORNIK (LI/0024-2969) [06123383] **4411**

LITOVSKIJ MATEMATICESKIJ SBORNIK (LI/0132-2818) [01756027] **3517**

LITT RESTAURANT GUIDE (NATIONAL ED.) (CN/0846-2984) [25314046] **5071**

LITT RESTAURANT GUIDE (QUEBEC ED.) (CN/0846-300X) [25314041] **5071**

LITT RESTAURANT GUIDE, THE (CN/0846-2992) [25314048] **5071**

LITT RESTAURANT GUIDE (WESTERN ED.) (CN/0846-3018) [25314054] **5071**

LITTERAE (GW) [02320760] **3346**

LITTERARIA PRAGENSIA (XR/0862-8424) [24395051] 2622, **3408**

LITTERATUR & SAMFUND (DK/0106-620X) [04725513] 3346, **3408**

LITTERATUR/PUBLICATIONS (SW) [05819997] **633**

LITTERATUR, TEATER, FILM (SW) [01645549] **324**

LITTERATURE AFRICAINE (FR/0459-5815) [02320824] **3408**

LITTERATURE, MEDECINE, SOCIETE (FR/0248-3521) [16986424] **3605**

LITTERATURE ORALE ARABO-BERBERE (FR/0336-5654) [04389284] **3408**

LITTERATURE (PARIS. 1971) (FR/0047-4800) [00986752] **3408**

LITTERATURES CLASSIQUES (FR/0992-5279) [19472009] **3408**

LITTERATURES DE LANGUES EUROPEENNES AU TOURNANT DU SIECLE, LECTURES D'AUJOURD'HUI. SERIE D, PERSPECTIVE CRITIQUE (CN) [11207711] **3346**

LITTERATURES (MONTREAL) (CN/0838-1453) [18305117] **3408**

LITTERATURES POPULAIRES DE TOUTES LES NATIONS, LES (FR) [02321829] **3408**

LITTERATURES (TOULOUSE) (FR/0563-9751) [07884043] **3408**

LITTEREALITE (CN/0843-4182) [20443474] **3408**

LITTLE BALKANS REVIEW, THE **SUSPENDED**. (US/0271-7735) [06684105] **357**

LITTLE BEND (CN/0316-6902) [02247747] **5788**

LITTLE BIG HORN ASSOCIATES *See* NEWSLETTER - LITTLE BIG HORN ASSOCIATES **2749**

LITTLE BIG HORN ASSOCIATES *See* RESEARCH REVIEW - LITTLE BIG HORN ASSOCIATES **2757**

LITTLE CANADA PRESS (US) **5696**

LITTLE LAMP, THE (US/0460-1297) [02109229] 4352, **4974**

LITTLE LEAGUE BASEBALL, INC *See* OFFICIAL REGULATIONS AND PLAYING RULES. LITTLE LEAGUE, SENIOR LEAGUE, BIG LEAGUE SOFTBALL **4910**

LITTLE MERMAID MAGAZINE, THE **CEASED**. (US/1060-8001) [25064233] **1066**

LITTLE NECK-GLEN OAKS LEDGER (US) [11628490] **5718**

LITTLE NECK LEDGER (US) **5718**

LITTLE PEOPLE'S PRESS, THE (US/1043-9595) [19619282] **2922**

LITTLE REVIEW, THE (US/0024-5054) [03359722] **3408**

LITTLE WORD MACHINE, THE (UK) [03359792] **3465**

LITTLEFORK TIMES (US) [01756037] **5697**

LITTLETON INDEPENDENT, THE (US/0744-7949) [08560474] **5689**

LITTLETON TIMES (US/0897-8395) [17640108] **5643**

LITUANISTICA / LIETUVOS MOKSLU AKADEMIJA (LI/0235-716X) [22857437] **2697**

LITUANISTIKA V SSSR: EKONOMIKA (RU) [06244732] **1503**

LITUANISTIKA V SSSR: ISKUSSTVOVEDENIE (LI/0207-1258) [06492732] **324**

LITUANISTIKA V SSSR: PRAVO (LI) [05809996] **3003**

LITUANISTIKOS DARBAI (US/0459-5947) [01782109] **2697**

LITUANUS (US/0024-5089) [01608200] **2697**

LITURGICAL CONFERENCE **CEASED**. (US) [01623589] **4974**

●LITURGICAL MINISTRY (US/1059-7786) [24767902] **4974**

LITURGIE (FR) **4974**

LITURGIE FOI ET CULTURE (CN) **4974**

LITURGIEWISSENSCHAFTLICHE QUELLEN UND FORSCHUNGEN (GW/0076-0048) [01696632] **4974**

LITURGISCHES JAHRBUCH (GW/0024-5100) [01773946] **4974**

LITURGY 90 (US/1046-9990) [20580145] **5031**

LITURGY DOCUMENTARY SERIES (US) [09247316] **4974**

LITURGY (WASHINGTON) (US/0458-063X) [07017885] **4974**

LIU CHUAN (CC) [09146977] **3408**

LIUMINESTSENTNYE MATERIALY I OSOBO CHISTYE VSHCHESTVA (RU) [01795967] **4438**

LIUTERIA MUSICA E CULTURA **CEASED**. (IT) **4129**

LIVE ANIMAL TRADE & TRANSPORT MAGAZINE (US/1043-1039) [19298633] **226**

LIVE ANIMALS REGULATIONS / IATA (CN/0256-4742) [07908800] **5386**

LIVE (LAVAL) (CN/0713-4991) [08903072] **4129**

LIVE LETTERS (US/1062-0087) [25503371] **3408**

LIVE LINES (NZ) [03113855] 690, **2071**

LIVE OAK (OAKLAND, CALIF. 1982), THE (US/0897-9839) [17682575] **2458**

LIVE POETS (US/1056-7089) [23825244] **3465**

LIVE/PRO LIGHT & SOUND (UK) [I09624856] **386**

LIVE REGISTER, MONTHLY AREA ANALYSIS DUBLIN (IE/0791-3206) [I07913206] 1688, **1503**

LIVE STEAM (US/0364-5177) [01588348] **5432**

LIVE STOCK AND ANIMAL PRODUCTS STATISTICS *See* LIVESTOCK STATISTICS / STATISTICS CANADA, AGRICULTURE DIVISION, LIVESTOCK AND ANIMAL PRODUCTS SECTION **154**

LIVE TO RIDE (AT) **4852**

LIVE WIRE / FAX SERVICE (US) **4212**

●LIVE WIRE (NEW YORK, N.Y. 1991) (US/1059-4809) [24639797] **4129**

LIVELY ARTS INFORMATION DIRECTORY, THE (US) [08524044] **386**

LIVER (COPENHAGEN) (DK/0106-9543) [07593887] **3799**

LIVER, NORMAL FUNCTION AND DISEASE (US/0163-9021) [04525987] **3799**

●LIVER TRANSPLANTATION AND SURGERY (US/1074-3022) [29667010] **3969**

LIVERMORE ROOTS TRACER *See* ROOTS TRACER **2471**

LIVERPOOL CLASSICAL MONTHLY : LCM (UK/0309-3700) [04044494] 3408, **251**

LIVERPOOL ECHO (UK) [18505532] **5812**

LIVERPOOL FAMILY HISTORIAN (UK/0260-759X) [I0260759X] **2458**

LIVERPOOL LAW REVIEW, THE (UK/0144-932X) [06767704] **3003**

LIVERPOOL MONOGRAPHS IN HISPANIC STUDIES (UK/0261-1538) [08724146] **3408**

LIVERPOOL SALINA CLAY REVIEW (US) **5718**

LIVESTOCK ADVISER (II/0970-3004) [02351183] **5515**

LIVESTOCK AND LIVESTOCK PRODUCTS, AUSTRALIA (AT/0812-2598) [10335827] 214, **154**

LIVESTOCK AND LIVESTOCK PRODUCTS : SOUTH AUSTRALIA (AT) [08247471] 214, **154**

LIVESTOCK AND LIVESTOCK PRODUCTS, WESTERN AUSTRALIA / AUSTRALIAN BUREAU OF STATISTICS, WESTERN AUSTRALIAN OFFICE (AT) [09936006] 214, **154**

LIVESTOCK AND MEAT AUTHORITY OF QUEENSLAND *See* ANNUAL REPORT / THE LIVESTOCK AND MEAT AUTHORITY OF QUEENSLAND **206**

LIVESTOCK AND MEAT STATISTICS. SUPPLEMENT (US/0190-5678) [01728146] **154**

LIVESTOCK & POULTRY INVENTORY, VALUE / IOWA CROP AND LIVESTOCK REPORTING SERVICE (US) [06203995] **214**

LIVESTOCK AND POULTRY UPDATE (US/1048-1605) [18676548] **214**

LIVESTOCK AND POULTRY UPDATE *See* LIVESTOCK, DAIRY AND POULTRY SITUATION AND OUTLOOK **105**

LIVESTOCK CONSERVATION INSTITUTE. MEETING *See* PROCEEDINGS / LIVESTOCK CONSERVATION INSTITUTE **219**

●LIVESTOCK, DAIRY AND POULTRY SITUATION AND OUTLOOK (US/1076-2183) [29824748] **105**

LIVESTOCK FACT SHEET (US) [01185429] **214**

LIVESTOCK MARKET DIGEST (US/0024-5208) [01587260] **214**

LIVESTOCK MARKET REVIEW (ANNUAL ED.) (CN/0068-7324) [03210301] **214**

LIVESTOCK, MEAT, WOOL MARKET NEWS (US) [04512121] **214**

LIVESTOCK PRODUCTION SCIENCE (NE/0301-6226) [02108259] **214**

LIVESTOCK PRODUCTS, AUSTRALIA / AUSTRALIAN BUREAU OF STATISTICS (AT) [12033143] 214, **154**

LIVESTOCK REPORT (1985) (CN/0828-3095) [13434701] **214**

LIVESTOCK REPORT (1985) *See* LIVESTOCK STATISTICS / STATISTICS CANADA, AGRICULTURE DIVISION, LIVESTOCK AND ANIMAL PRODUCTS SECTION **154**

LIVESTOCK RESEARCH FOR RURAL DEVELOPMENT [COMPUTER FILE] (US) [25321339] **214**

LIVESTOCK REVIEW / WISCONSIN (US) 105, **2348**

LIVESTOCK SLAUGHTER / IOWA CROP AND LIVESTOCK REPORTING SERVICE (US) [06203940] **214**

LIVESTOCK SLAUGHTER. SUMMARY (US/1057-7874) [13368770] **214**

LIVESTOCK SLAUGHTER (WASHINGTON, D.C.) (US/0499-0544) [02572342] **214**

●LIVESTOCK STATISTICS / STATISTICS CANADA, AGRICULTURE DIVISION, LIVESTOCK AND ANIMAL PRODUCTS SECTION (CN) [30463826] 214, **154**

LIVESTOCK STATISTICS, TASMANIA / AUSTRALIAN BUREAU OF STATISTICS (AT) [09869324] 214, **154**

LIVESTOCK (TOPEKA, KAN.) (US/0745-0842) [04173907] 196, **215**

LIVESTOCK WEEKLY (SAN ANGELO) (US/0162-5047) [03271370] **215**

LIVING ANEW (US/0743-0264) [10489820] **4603**

LIVING ARCHITECTURE (DK/0108-4135) [10600059] **302**

LIVING AUTHOR SERIES (US) [09806960] **3408**

LIVING BETTER (US/1059-2539) [09210417] **2791**

LIVING BIRD (1991) (US/1059-521X) [24618159] **5618**

LIVING BLUES (US/0024-5232) [03759004] **4129**

LIVING BLUES BLUES DIRECTORY (US/1044-1026) [19687372] **4129**

LIVING CHURCH (1942), THE (US/0024-5240) [03681962] **4974**

LIVING CITY (AT [03114651] **4662**

LIVING CITY (NEW YORK) (US/0193-5968) [05214914] **4974**

LIVING (DENVER ED.) (US/0741-5508) [10197978] **2537**

LIVING EARTH (BRISTOL) (UK/0954-1098) [19366814] **105**

LIVING (FLORIDA GULF COAST ED.) (US/0741-546X) [10191846] **2537**

LIVING HAND (FR) [02242734] **3408**

LIVING HISTORICAL FARMS BULLETIN (US/0047-4851) [02206859] **2622**

LIVING HISTORY LOCAL GUIDE (UK) [10288805] **2622**

LIVING HISTORY OF THE WORLD; YEARBOOK (US/0076-0072) [01783204] **2622**

LIVING (HOUSTON, ED.) (US/0741-5486) [10197882] **4840**

LIVING IN NORTH YORK (CN/0712-6360) [09230731] **2568**

LIVING IN SOUTH CAROLINA (US/0047-486X) [04046438] **1298**

LIVING IN VENEZUELA (VE) [19869266] **2552**

LIVING LIGHT, THE (US/0024-5275) [01639258] **5031**

LIVING MARXISM (UK/0955-2448) [27272315] **4543**

LIVING MUSEUM, THE (US/0024-5283) [01604159] 4167, **4090**

LIVING MUSIC (US/8755-092X) [10640596] **4129**

LIVING NOW (US) [03114600] **2902**

LIVING OFF THE LAND (US/0738-7687) [07348839] **2424**

LIVING ORTHODOXY (US/0279-8433) [07313878] **5039**

LIVING OUTDOORS *See* FIELD & STREAM (FAR WEST ED.) **4872**

LIVING OUTDOORS *See* FIELD & STREAM (WEST ED.) **4872**

LIVING OUTDOORS *See* FIELD & STREAM (NORTHEAST ED.) **4872**

LIVING PHYSICS (US/0893-8067) [15649747] **4411**

LIVING POETS LIBRARY (US) [02328349] **3465**

LIVING PRAYER (US/0890-5568) [14231148] **4974**

●LIVING PULPIT, THE (US/1059-2733) [24529866] **4974**

●LIVING SAFETY (CN/1200-2275) [31191631] **4789**

LIVING SAFETY FOR THE CANADIAN FAMILY (CN/0714-5896) [09804082] **4789**

LIVING (SOUTH FLORIDA ED.) (US/0741-3440) [10192626] **4840**

LIVING THE WORD. LEVEL 8, GRADES TEN-TWELVE STUDENT'S RESOURCE (US/0883-7236) [12220577] **4974**

LIVING TREE NEWS, THE (US/8755-9714) [07980806] **2458**

LIVING WELL WITH DIABETES (US/0895-397X) [16644573] **3731**

LIVING WITH CHILDREN (US/0456-3271) [04164170] **2282**

LIVING WITH CHRIST. COMPLETE EDITION (CN/0703-6752) [05359886] **4974**

LIVING WITH CHRIST. SUNDAY EDITION (CN/0703-6760) [05385118] **4974**

LIVING WITH PRESCHOOLERS (US/0162-4350) [04168526] 1804, **2282**

LIVING WITH TEENAGERS (US/0162-4261) [04171427] **2283**

LIVING WORD (SWAN RIVER) (CN/0229-5261) [08770519] **5018**

LIVING WORLD (LOS ANGELES, CALIF.) (US/0896-2154) [16968381] **2252**

LIVINGSTON COUNTY AGRICULTURAL NEWS (US/0024-5313) [04117247] **105**

LIVINGSTON COUNTY NEWS (GENESEO, N.Y.) (US/1046-8293) [19892004] **5718**

LIVINGSTON ENTERPRISE (US) [19106624] **5745**

LIVINGSTON ENTERPRISE (LIVINGSTON, MONT. : DAILY) (US) [13864916] **5705**

LIVINGSTON FAMILY NEWSLETTER (US/0742-4744) [10337003] **2458**

LIVINGSTON LEDGER (US) [14151574] **5681**

LIVINGSTON UNIVERSITY *See* ALUMNI DIRECTORY / LIVINGSTON UNIVERSITY ; COMPILED AND PUBLISHED BY COLLEGE & UNIVERSITY PRESS **1098**

LIVLEX TRABALHISTA (BL) [02240066] **3151**

LIVRE BLEU DES FUTURS CHEFS D'ETABLISSEMENT ET ADJOINTS, LE (FR) [20286015] **1866**

LIVRE DE L'ANNEE (CN/0380-8246) [02585288] **1927**

LIVRE DE REGLEMENTS ADMINISTRATIFS / FEDERATION QUEBECOISE DE HOCKEY SUR GLACE INC (CN/0821-4603) [09551528] **4903**

LIVRE DES FEUX, DES BOUEES ET DES SIGNAUX DE BRUME. EAUX INTERIEURES (CN/0381-3398) [02754885] **4178**

LIVRE DES FEUX, DES BOUEES ET DES SIGNAUX DE BRUME: EAUX INTERIEURES (A L'OUEST DE MONTREAL ET A L'EST DE LA COLOMBIE-BRITANNIQUE) (CN) [03198149] **4178**

LIVRE DES FEUX, DES BOUEES ET DES SIGNAUX DE BRUME. COTE DU PACIFIQUE (CN/0704-5417) [03527616] **4178**

LIVRE D'ICI (MENSUEL) (CN/0714-9948) [09938325] **4830**

LIVRE D'OR DE LA MOTO, LE (FR) [02970383] 4903, **4081**

LIVRE ET L'ESTAMPE, LE (BE/0024-533X) [02108387] **4830**

LIVRE INTERNATIONAL DES VENTES PARIS, LE (FR/1154-5445) [I11545445] **357**

LIVRE OFFICIEL DES RECORDS - LIGUE CANADIENNE DE FOOTBALL (CN/0225-7203) [06316298] **4903**

LIVRE SLOVENE, LE (XV/0459-6242) [06218262] **3408**

LIVRES (FR) **4816**

LIVRES DE FRANCE *CEASED*. (FR) [05703933] **419**

LIVRES DISPONIBLES CANADIENS DE LANGUE FRANCAISE (CN/0836-7078) [16834662] **4816**

LIVRES DISPONIBLES, LES (FR) [03584613] **4830**

LIVRES DU MOIS, LES (FR/0294-0027) [10768749] **4816**

LIVRES HEBDO (FR/0294-0000) [10768649] **419**

LIVRES JEUNES AUJOURD'HUI (FR/0223-4289) [I02234289] **3408**

LIVRET DE LA RECHERCHE / INSTITUT NATIONAL DES LANGUES ET CIVILISATIONS ORIENTALES (FR/0755-4796) [19825741] 3300, **2658**

LIVRET DES REGLEMENTS DE LA FEDERATION CANADIENNE DES ARCHERS (1974) (CN/0706-3180) [06515894] 4874, **4903**

LIVRET DU DEPARTEMENT DES LANGUES AFRICAINES ET LINGUISTIQUE (CM) [05259618] **3300**

LIVRETE TRIMESTRAL DA CIENCIA CRISTA. LICOES BIBLICAS (US/0145-7454) [02774604] **5018**

LIVRO DO ANO, O (BL) [01791989] **2622**

LIVROS EM PORTUGUES (CN/0710-5231) [09448367] **4830**

LIVRUSTKAMMAREN (SW/0024-5372) [03057568] **4049**

LIVSMEDELSTEKNIK (SW/0024-5399) [I00245399] **2348**

LIVSTEGN (NO/0801-1834) [18600402] **3300**

LIVYERE, THE (CN/0715-3015) [09340487] **2744**

LIWAYWAY (PH) [01799027] **2506**

LIXUE YU SHIJIAN (CC/1000-0879) [09039590] **4428**

LIZI JIAOHUAN YU XIFU (CH/1001-5493) [I10015493] **984**

LJUBLJANA. UNIVERZA. INSTITUT ZA GOZDNO IN LESNO GOSPODARSTVO *See* ZBORNIK GOZDARSTVA IN LESARSTVA **2398**

LJUSKULTUR (SW) [02972903] **2235**

LJZ : LIECHTENSTEINISCHE JURISTEN-ZEITUNG (LH) [09360552] **3004**

LLA BULLETIN (US/0196-3023) [02448335] **3228**

LLAFUR (UK/0306-0837) [04099256] **1688**

LLAMA BANNER (US/0899-6202) [18160907] **5515**, **105**

LLAMAS (US/0887-9923) [13409372] **5590**

LLANO ESTACADO HERITAGE *See* GREATER LLANO ESTACADO SOUTHEAST HERITAGE, THE **2735**

LLANO ESTACADO PLAYA LAKE WATER RESOURCES STUDY (US) [07339984] **5536**

LLANO NEWS (LLANO, TEX.) (US) [14473050] **5752**

LLEN CYMRU (UK/0076-0188) [04278219] **3346**

LLETRA DE CANVI (SP) [17854159] **3408**

LLEWELLYN'S ... DAILY PLANETARY GUIDE (US/0743-6408) [10630877] **390**

LLEWELLYN'S DAILY PLANETARY GUIDE & ASTROLOGER'S DATEBOOK (US/1061-7507) [25378840] **390**

LLEWELLYN'S MOON SIGN BOOK AND DAILY PLANETARY GUIDE *CEASED.* (US) [04982096] **390**

LLEWELLYN'S NEW WORLDS OF MIND AND SPIRIT (US) **4242**

LLIBRES INFANTILS, JUVENILS I DIDACTICS EN CATALA / ASSOCIACIO D'EDITORS EN LLENGUA CATALANA, GREMI D'EDITORS DE CATALUNYA, I.N.L.E (SP) [08788235] **1066**

LLOYD, DE (NE) **5386**

LLOYD'S AVIATION LAW (US) [10923421] **3181**

LLOYDS BANK ANNUAL REVIEW *CEASED.* (UK/0953-5004) [18647194] **1572**

LLOYD'S BANK ECONOMIC BULLETIN (UK/0261-0175) [I02610175] **796**

LLOYDS BANK REVIEW *CEASED.* (UK/0024-547X) [01756064] **796**

LLOYD'S CANADIAN CHEMICAL DIRECTORY *See* LLOYD'S CANADIAN CHEMICAL, PHARMACEUTICAL, AND PRODUCT DIRECTORY **4314**

LLOYD'S CANADIAN CHEMICAL, PHARMACEUTICAL, AND PRODUCT DIRECTORY *CEASED.* (CN/0068-8452) [03105871] **4314**

LLOYD'S CANADIAN ENGINEERING & INDUSTRIAL YEAR BOOK (CN/0068-8665) [03304054] 3482, **2099**

LLOYD'S CANADIAN FOOTWEAR AND LEATHER DIRECTORY (CN/0068-8762) [03681001] **3185**

LLOYD'S CANADIAN HARDWARE, ELECTRICAL AND BUILDING SUPPLY DIRECTORY (CN/0456-3867) [01783385] **619**

LLOYD'S CANADIAN JEWELLERY AND GIFTWARE DIRECTORY (CN/0068-9041) [04754699] 2584, **2915**

LLOYD'S CANADIAN MUSIC DIRECTORY (CN/0381-5730) [04635113] **4129**

LLOYD'S CANADIAN TEXTILE DIRECTORY (CN/0068-9858) [03199531] **5354**

LLOYD'S CANADIAN VARIETY MERCHANDISE DIRECTORY (CN/0068-9955) [04678049] **2584**

LLOYD'S CASUALTY WEEK (UK/0966-761X) [I0966761X] **5451**

LLOYD'S CONFIDENTIAL INDEX OF STEAM AND MOTOR VESSELS (UK) [07244317] **5451**

LLOYD'S (FIRM) *See* LLOYD'S MARITIME AND COMMERCIAL LAW QUARTERLY **3181**

LLOYD'S INSURANCE INTERNATIONAL (US) 3181, **2887**

LLOYD'S INTERNATIONAL MARINE EQUIPMENT GUIDE (UK) [19071874] **4178**

LLOYD'S LAW REPORTS (UK/0024-5488) [01756067] **3181**

LLOYD'S LIST (UK) **5451**

●LLOYD'S LIST MARITIME ASIA (HK/1015-227X) [27511814] **5451**

LLOYD'S LOADING LIST (UK) [02972844] **5386**

LLOYD'S MARITIME AND COMMERCIAL LAW QUARTERLY (UK/0306-2945) [01799264] **3181**

LLOYD'S MARITIME ASIA (HK/0217-1120) [12766095] **5451**

LLOYD'S MARITIME ATLAS (UK/0076-020X) [01012166] **5451**

LLOYD'S MARITIME DIRECTORY (UK/0268-327X) [08753156] **5451**

LLOYD'S MARITIME LAW (US) [13608008] **3181**

LLOYD'S MARITIME LAW NEWSLETTER (UK/0268-0696) [I02680696] **3181**

LLOYD'S MEXICAN ECONOMIC REPORT (MX/0188-1833) [02667825] **905**

LLOYD'S MONTHLY LIST OF LAID UP VESSELS (UK/0266-6189) [I02666189] **5451**

LLOYD'S NAUTICAL YEAR BOOK (UK) [04470306] **4178**

LLOYD'S PORTS OF THE WORLD (UK) [08564685] **5451**

LLOYD'S PROFESSIONAL LIABILITY TODAY (UK/0268-9669) [I02689669] **3004**

LLOYD'S REGISTER ANNUAL REPORT (UK) [14999220] **5451**

LLOYD'S REGISTER OF CLASSED YACHTS (UK) [07667939] **594**

LLOYD'S REGISTER OF SHIPPING *See* REGISTER OF OFFSHORE UNITS, SUBMERSIBLES & DIVING SYSTEMS **5455**

LLOYD'S REGISTER OF SHIPPING (UK/0261-2151) [02974897] **5451**

LLOYD'S REGISTER OF SHIPPING (FIRM : 1914-) *See* STATISTICAL TABLES **5457**

LLOYD'S REGISTER SHIPBUILDING RETURNS : MERCHANT SHIPS OF 100 TONS GROSS AND UPWARDS (UK) [08979771] **5451**

LLOYD'S SHIP MANAGER : LSM (UK/0265-2455) [22416466] **5452**

LLOYD'S SHIPBUILDING REVIEW (UK) [01794496] **5452**

LLOYD'S SHIPPING ECONOMIST (UK/0144-6673) [05773411] **5452**

LLOYD'S SHIPPING INDEX (UK/0144-4549) [07822013] **5452**

LLOYD'S VOYAGE RECORD (UK/0144-4557) [17671000] **5452**

LLOYD'S WEEKLY CASUALTY REPORTS (UK/0047-4908) [I00474908] **4178**

LLOYD'S WEEKLY CASUALTY REPORTS (UK) [11847370] **5452**

LLOYD'S WEEKLY LIST OF ALTERATIONS TO THE REGISTER OF SHIPS (UK) [21225539] **5452**

LLULL : BOLETIN DE LA SOCIEDAD ESPANOLA DE HISTORIA DE LAS CIENCIAS (SP/0210-8615) [07385991] **5126**

LMA BUSINESSLETTER, THE (US/1065-7444) [26710828] 929, **215**

LMC QUARTERLY RUBBER REPORTS SERVICE (UK) **5076**

LMH: LOGISTICS & MATERIALS HANDLING (AT) **1616**

LMI REVIEW / WASHINGTON STATE EMPLOYMENT SECURITY DEPARTMENT (US) [11718370] **1688**

LMS ALERT. NEUROPSYCHOTHERAPEUTICS *CEASED.* (NZ/1170-814X) [I1170814X] **4314**

LMT (NORWALK, CONN.) (US/1058-7845) [24386123] 876, **1329**

LNG DIGEST (US/0276-5918) [07387655] **4263**

LNG OBSERVER, THE (US/1053-6949) [22609904] **4263**

LNNINGER OG INNTEKTER (NO) [09563295] 1688, **1535**

LNNSSTATISTIKK FOR ANSATTE I FORRETNINGSMESSIG TJENESTEYTING OG I INTERESSEORGANISASJONER (NO) [08150241] 1688, **1535**

LNNSSTATISTIKK FOR ANSATTE I SKOLEVERKET (NO/0800-2843) [12823501] **1866**

LNNSSTATISTIKK FOR ANSATTE I VAREHANDEL (NO) [05346888] 1688, **1536**

LO-BLADET (DK/0105-032X) [01786421] **1688**

LO I.E. LANDSORGANISATIONEN I SVERIGE TIDNINGEN (SW) [06300615] **1572**

LO-POWER COMMUNITY TV (US/0279-4152) [07833200] **1134**

LO SPETTACOLO IN ITALIA (IT) [07192190] **4852**

LOADSTAR (US/0886-4144) [16003104] **1288**

LOADSTAR 128 QUARTERLY (US/1040-5542) [18443168] **1288**

LOAN GROWTH CREDIT RISK REVIEW (US/0160-5860) [03698815] **796**

LOANS & GRANTS FROM UNCLE SAM (US) **1834**

LOAVES & FISHES (TORONTO, ONT.) (CN/0714-7880) [09670631] **4974**

LOBBY DIGEST, THE *See* LOBBY DIGEST & PUBLIC AFFAIRS MONTHLY, THE **4662**

●LOBBY DIGEST & PUBLIC AFFAIRS MONTHLY, THE (CN/1193-4034) [27193656] **4662**

LOBBY MONITOR, THE (US/1057-0853) [23932516] **4481**

LOBBYING & INFLUENCE ALERT (US/1058-2762) [24252341] **4481**

LOBBYING IN THE FLORIDA HOUSE OF REPRESENTATIVES (US/0148-4354) [03308707] **4662**

●LOBBYING RESOURCE DIRECTORY (US/1057-0594) [23926347] **4662**

LOBBYISTS REGISTRATION ACT ANNUAL REPORT (CN/1184-0471) [23243154] 4662, **4481**

LOBLOLLY *CEASED.* (US/0361-3577) [02246108] **2744**

LOBSTER (UK) **4481**

LOCAL 1-FLM TEMPO (US/8750-8311) [11669804] **3185**

LOCAL 1-S NEWS (US/0011-8915) [05954431] **1688**

LOCAL 2 NEWS (US/0737-3678) [09367331] **2291**

LOCAL 824 BULLETIN (US) [06023818] **1688**

LOCAL AREA NETWORK MAGAZINE *See* LAN (SAN FRANCISCO, CALIF.) **1242**

LOCAL AREA NETWORK MAGAZINE : LAN, THE (US/0898-0012) [15483466] **1193**

LOCAL AREA NETWORKS (US/1051-1962) [21887412] **1193**

LOCAL AREA NETWORKS NEWSLETTER *See* LOCAL AREA NETWORKS **1193**

LOCAL AREA PERSONAL INCOME (US/0271-8588) [03622072] **1503**

LOCAL ARTS (UK) **324**

LOCAL AUTHORITIES PARTICIPATING IN LOW-RENT HOUSING PROGRAMS (US/0147-8974) [03113342] **2827**

LOCAL AUTHORITY ELECTION STATISTICS (NZ) [09755300] **4698**

LOCAL AUTHORITY LAW (UK/0963-1054) [I09631054] **3169**

●LOCAL AUTHORITY SOCIAL WORK EXPENDITURE (UK) **5295**

LOCAL AUTHORITY STATISTICS / NEW ZEALAND (NZ) [09088780] **4698**

LOCAL BODY REVIEW *See* NEW ZEALAND LOCAL GOVERNMENT **4669**

LOCAL CLIMATOLOGICAL DATA (US) [02782145] **1427**

LOCAL CLIMATOLOGICAL DATA. ABILENE, TEXAS, ANNUAL SUMMARY WITH COMPARATIVE DATA (US/0198-4888) [06261922] **1427**

LOCAL CLIMATOLOGICAL DATA. ABILENE, TEXAS, MONTHLY SUMMARY (US/0198-4896) [06267582] **1427**

LOCAL CLIMATOLOGICAL DATA. ALAMOSA, COLORADO, MONTHLY SUMMARY (US/0198-7739) [05515164] **1427**

LOCAL CLIMATOLOGICAL DATA. ALBUQUERQUE, NEW MEXICO, ANNUAL SUMMARY WITH COMPARATIVE DATA (US/0198-3474) [06264635] **1427**

LOCAL CLIMATOLOGICAL DATA. ANCHORAGE, ALASKA. ANNUAL SUMMARY WITH COMPARATIVE DATA (US/0197-954X) [06240911] **1427**

LOCAL CLIMATOLOGICAL DATA. ASHEVILLE, NORTH CAROLINA. MONTHLY SUMMARY (US/0198-3709) [06320869] **1427**

LOCAL CLIMATOLOGICAL DATA. AUGUSTA, GEORGIA. ANNUAL SUMMARY WITH COMPARATIVE DATA (US/0198-1587) [06264191] **1427**

LOCAL CLIMATOLOGICAL DATA. AVOCA, PENNSYLVANIA. ANNUAL SUMMARY WITH COMPARATIVE DATA (US/0198-4470) [06263206] **1427**

LOCAL CLIMATOLOGICAL DATA. BETHEL, ALASKA, ANNUAL SUMMARY WITH COMPARATIVE DATA (US/0197-9620) [06241069] **1427**

LOCAL CLIMATOLOGICAL DATA. BIRMINGHAM, ALABAMA, CITY OFFICE, ANNUAL SUMMARY WITH COMPARATIVE DATA (US/0275-1798) [07090818] **1428**

LOCAL CLIMATOLOGICAL DATA. BIRMINGHAM, ALABAMA, MUNICIPAL AIRPORT, ANNUAL SUMMARY WITH COMPARATIVE DATA (US/0275-178X) [06570540] **1428**

Alphabetical Title Index — LOCAL

LOCAL CLIMATOLOGICAL DATA. BIRMINGHAM, ALABAMA. NAT. WEATHER SERVICE FCST. OFC. MONTHLY SUMMARY (US/0197-9450) [06156184] **1428**

LOCAL CLIMATOLOGICAL DATA. BLOCK ISLAND, RHODE ISLAND, MONTHLY SUMMARY (US/0198-4586) [06254501] **1428**

LOCAL CLIMATOLOGICAL DATA. BLUE CANYON, CALIFORNIA, ANNUAL SUMMARY WITH COMPARATIVE DATA (US/0198-0874) [06281638] **1428**

LOCAL CLIMATOLOGICAL DATA. BOSTON, MASSACHUSSETS, ANNUAL SUMMARY WITH COMPARATIVE DATA (US/0198-2419) [06246450] **1428**

LOCAL CLIMATOLOGICAL DATA. BURLINGTON, VERMONT, ANNUAL SUMMARY WITH COMPARATIVE DATA (US/0198-5302) [06212934] **1428**

LOCAL CLIMATOLOGICAL DATA. BURLINGTON, VERMONT, MONTHLY SUMMARY (US/0198-5310) [00941980] **1428**

LOCAL CLIMATOLOGICAL DATA. BURNS, OREGON, MONTHLY SUMMARY (US/0198-4128) [06299865] **1428**

LOCAL CLIMATOLOGICAL DATA. CAIRO, ILLINOIS, MONTHLY SUMMARY (US/0198-1838) [06301730] **1428**

LOCAL CLIMATOLOGICAL DATA. CHEYENNE, WYOMING. MONTHLY SUMMARY (US/0198-5795) [05536488] **1428**

LOCAL CLIMATOLOGICAL DATA. CLEVELAND, OHIO, ANNUAL SUMMARY WITH COMPARATIVE DATA (US/0198-3938) [06308828] **1428**

LOCAL CLIMATOLOGICAL DATA. COLUMBIA, SOUTH CAROLINA, MONTHLY SUMMARY (US/0198-4659) [06257374] **1428**

LOCAL CLIMATOLOGICAL DATA. CONCORD, NEW HAMPSHIRE, MONTHLY SUMMARY (US/0198-3377) [00941985] **1428**

LOCAL CLIMATOLOGICAL DATA. DES MOINES, IOWA, MONTHLY SUMMARY (US/0198-2060) [06301172] **1428**

LOCAL CLIMATOLOGICAL DATA. DETROIT, MICHIGAN, METROPOLITAN AIRPORT, ANNUAL SUMMARY WITH COMPARATIVE DATA (US/0198-2532) [06246574] **1428**

LOCAL CLIMATOLOGICAL DATA. DODGE CITY, KANSAS, ANNUAL SUMMARY WITH COMPARATIVE DATA (US/0198-215X) [06255105] **1428**

LOCAL CLIMATOLOGICAL DATA. ELKINS, WEST VIRGINIA. MONTHLY SUMMARY (US/0198-5639) [06300192] **1428**

LOCAL CLIMATOLOGICAL DATA. ELKO, NEVADA, MONTHLY SUMMARY (US/0198-327X) [06319360] **1428**

LOCAL CLIMATOLOGICAL DATA. FAIRBANKS, ALASKA. ANNUAL SUMMARY WITH COMPARATIVE DATA (US/0197-9728) [06244633] **1428**

LOCAL CLIMATOLOGICAL DATA. FARGO, NORTH DAKOTA, MONTHLY SUMMARY (US/0198-3849) [06234832] **1428**

LOCAL CLIMATOLOGICAL DATA. FORT SMITH, ARKANSAS. MONTHLY SUMMARY (US/0198-0610) [06317626] **1428**

LOCAL CLIMATOLOGICAL DATA. FORT WAYNE, INDIANA, MONTHLY SUMMARY (US/0198-1978) [06301791] **1428**

LOCAL CLIMATOLOGICAL DATA. GRAND JUNCTION, COLORADO, ANNUAL SUMMARY WITH COMPARATIVE DATA (US/0198-7666) [06215590] **1428**

LOCAL CLIMATOLOGICAL DATA. GRAND RAPIDS, MICHIGAN, ANNUAL SUMMARY WITH COMPARATIVE DATA (US/0198-2575) [06244749] **1428**

LOCAL CLIMATOLOGICAL DATA. GREENSBORO, HIGH POINT, WINSTON-SALEM AP, N.C, MONTHLY SUMMARY (US/0198-3768) [06321954] **1428**

LOCAL CLIMATOLOGICAL DATA. GREENVILLE-SPARTANBURG AP. GREER, S.C., MONTHLY SUMMARY (US/0198-4675) [06184830] **1428**

LOCAL CLIMATOLOGICAL DATA. GULKANA, ALASKA, MONTHLY SUMMARY (US/0197-971X) [06247382] **1428**

LOCAL CLIMATOLOGICAL DATA. HARTFORD, CONNECTICUT, MONTHLY SUMMARY (US/0198-1161) [06317727] **1428**

LOCAL CLIMATOLOGICAL DATA. HUNTINGTON, WEST VIRGINIA. MONTHLY SUMMARY (US/0198-5655) [06300165] **1428**

LOCAL CLIMATOLOGICAL DATA. JACKSON, KENTUCKY, ANNUAL SUMMARY WITH COMPARATIVE DATA (US/0278-9140) [07907446] **1428**

LOCAL CLIMATOLOGICAL DATA. JACKSON, MISSISSIPPI, MONTHLY SUMMARY (US/0198-280X) [06211261] **1429**

LOCAL CLIMATOLOGICAL DATA. KEY WEST, FLORIDA, MONTHLY SUMMARY (US/0198-1374) [06203049] **1429**

LOCAL CLIMATOLOGICAL DATA. KNOXVILLE, TENNESSEE, ANNUAL SUMMARY WITH COMPARATIVE DATA (US/0198-4802) [06264429] **1429**

LOCAL CLIMATOLOGICAL DATA. LANSING, MICHIGAN, ANNUAL SUMMARY WITH COMPARATIVE DATA (US/0198-2613) [06244959] **1429**

LOCAL CLIMATOLOGICAL DATA. LAS VEGAS, NEVADA, MONTHLY SUMMARY (US/0198-3318) [06320285] **1429**

LOCAL CLIMATOLOGICAL DATA. LEWISTON, IDAHO, ANNUAL SUMMARY WITH COMPARATIVE DATA (US/0198-1781) [06299356] **1429**

LOCAL CLIMATOLOGICAL DATA. LITTLE ROCK, ARKANSAS, MONTHLY SUMMARY (US/0198-0629) [06317678] **1429**

LOCAL CLIMATOLOGICAL DATA. LYNCHBURG, VIRGINIA. MONTHLY SUMMARY (US/0198-5337) [06299411] **1429**

LOCAL CLIMATOLOGICAL DATA. MCGRATH, ALASKA, ANNUAL SUMMARY WITH COMPARATIVE DATA (US/0197-9841) [06245968] **1429**

LOCAL CLIMATOLOGICAL DATA. MIAMI, FLORIDA. ANNUAL SUMMARY WITH COMPARATIVE DATA (US/0198-1269) [06192700] **1429**

LOCAL CLIMATOLOGICAL DATA. MIDDLETOWN/HARRISBURG INTL. APT. MONTHLY SUMMARY (US/1059-7050) [24680881] **1429**

LOCAL CLIMATOLOGICAL DATA. MILWAUKEE, WISCONSIN. ANNUAL SUMMARY WITH COMPARATIVE DATA (US/0198-5744) [06297020] **1429**

LOCAL CLIMATOLOGICAL DATA. MOLINE, ILLINOIS, MONTHLY SUMMARY (US/0198-1870) [04091847] **1429**

LOCAL CLIMATOLOGICAL DATA. MONTGOMERY, ALABAMA, ANNUAL SUMMARY WITH COMPARATIVE DATA (US/0197-9523) [06307455] **1429**

LOCAL CLIMATOLOGICAL DATA. MONTGOMERY, ALABAMA, MONTHLY SUMMARY (US/0197-9531) [06317396] **1429**

LOCAL CLIMATOLOGICAL DATA. MOUNT SHASTA, CALIFORNIA, ANNUAL SUMMARY WITH COMPARATIVE DATA (US/0198-0939) [06281778] **1429**

LOCAL CLIMATOLOGICAL DATA. MOUNT WASHINGTON OBSERVATORY, GORHAM, NEW HAMPSHIRE. MONTHLY SUMMARY (US/0198-3393) [00941976] **1429**

LOCAL CLIMATOLOGICAL DATA. NORTH PLATTE, NEBRASKA. ANNUAL SUMMARY WITH COMPARATIVE DATA (US/0198-3156) [06244586] **1429**

LOCAL CLIMATOLOGICAL DATA. OAK RIDGE, TENNESSEE. MONTHLY SUMMARY (US/0198-487X) [06260635] **1429**

LOCAL CLIMATOLOGICAL DATA. OLYMPIA, WASHINGTON. MONTHLY SUMMARY (US/0198-5418) [06299669] **1429**

LOCAL CLIMATOLOGICAL DATA. OMAHA, NEBRASKA (NORTH). MONTHLY SUMMARY (US/0198-3202) [06247285] **1429**

LOCAL CLIMATOLOGICAL DATA. ORLANDO, FLORIDA, MONTHLY SUMMARY (US/0198-1390) [06202930] **1429**

LOCAL CLIMATOLOGICAL DATA. PADUCAH. KY., MONTHLY SUMMARY (US/8755-058X) [11243263] **1429**

LOCAL CLIMATOLOGICAL DATA. PENDLETON, OREGON, ANNUAL SUMMARY WITH COMPARATIVE DATA (US/0198-4179) [06262785] **1429**

LOCAL CLIMATOLOGICAL DATA. PHILADELPHIA, PENNSYLVANIA, MONTHLY SUMMARY (US/0198-4543) [04092362] **1429**

LOCAL CLIMATOLOGICAL DATA. PHOENIX, ARIZONA, MONTHLY SUMMARY (US/0198-0475) [06317440] **1429**

LOCAL CLIMATOLOGICAL DATA. PITTSBURGH, PENNSYLVANIA, GREATER PITTSBURGH AIRPORT. ANNUAL SUMMARY WITH COMPARATIVE DATA (US/0270-0514) [06321398] **1429**

LOCAL CLIMATOLOGICAL DATA. PITTSBURGH, PENNSYLVANIA. WEA. SVS. CONTRACT MET. OBSY. GREATER PITTSBURGH INTL. AP. MONTHLY SUMMARY (US/0270-0522) [06321569] **1429**

LOCAL CLIMATOLOGICAL DATA. PONAPE ISLAND, PACIFIC, ANNUAL SUMMARY WITH COMPARATIVE DATA (US/0198-4373) [06262911] **1429**

LOCAL CLIMATOLOGICAL DATA. PORT ARTHUR, TEXAS, ANNUAL SUMMARY WITH COMPARATIVE DATA (US/0198-5140) [06262100] **1429**

LOCAL CLIMATOLOGICAL DATA. RAPID CITY, SOUTH DAKOTA, ANNUAL SUMMARY WITH COMPARATIVE DATA (US/0198-4721) [06257273] **1430**

LOCAL CLIMATOLOGICAL DATA. ROANOKE, VIRGINIA. MONTHLY SUMMARY (US/0198-5396) [06299609] **1430**

LOCAL CLIMATOLOGICAL DATA. ROCHESTER, NEW YORK, MONTHLY SUMMARY (US/0198-3660) [06184570] **1430**

LOCAL CLIMATOLOGICAL DATA. ROCKFORD, ILLINOIS, MONTHLY SUMMARY (US/0198-1919) [06301711] **1430**

LOCAL CLIMATOLOGICAL DATA. SHERIDAN, WYOMING. MONTHLY SUMMARY (US/0198-5833) [06301035] **1430**

LOCAL CLIMATOLOGICAL DATA. SPOKANE, WASHINGTON. MONTHLY SUMMARY (US/0198-5493) [06299714] **1430**

LOCAL CLIMATOLOGICAL DATA. TALKEETNA, ALASKA, ANNUAL SUMMARY WITH COMPARATIVE DATA (US/0198-0521) [06246015] **1430**

LOCAL CLIMATOLOGICAL DATA. TUCSON, ARIZONA, MONTHLY SUMMARY (US/0198-0483) [06317508] **1430**

LOCAL CLIMATOLOGICAL DATA. WAKE ISLAND, PACIFIC, MONTHLY SUMMARY (US/0198-442X) [06301592] **1430**

LOCAL CLIMATOLOGICAL DATA. WASHINGTON, D.C., WASHINGTON NATIONAL AIRPORT, MONTHLY SUMMARY (US/0198-1188) [06168351] **1430**

LOCAL CLIMATOLOGICAL DATA. WICHITA FALLS, TEXAS. MONTHLY SUMMARY (US/0198-5256) [06270218] **1430**

LOCAL CLIMATOLOGICAL DATA. WINNEMUCCA, NEVADA, MONTHLY SUMMARY (US/0198-3350) [06320501] **1430**

LOCAL CLIMATOLOGICAL DATA. YUMA, ARIZONA, ANNUAL SUMMARY WITH COMPARATIVE DATA (US/0198-0653) [06308179] **1430**

LOCAL CLIMATOLOGICAL DATA. YUMA, ARIZONA. MONTHLY SUMMARY (US/0198-0602) [06317579] **1430**

LOCAL COUNCIL REVIEW (UK/0308-3594) [02244778] **4662**

LOCAL ECONOMY (UK/0269-0942) [16220717] **1573**

●LOCAL ENVIRONMENT JOURNAL, THE (UK) **2177**

LOCAL EXCHANGE, THE (CN/0706-7046) [04879798] **2537**

LOCAL GOVERNMENT (PK) [01781301] **4662**

●LOCAL GOVERNMENT AND ENVIRONMENTAL REPORTS OF AUSTRALIA, THE (AT/1039-7213) [28434071] 3114, **4662**

LOCAL GOVERNMENT APPEALS TRIBUNAL REPORTS OF NEW SOUTH WALES, THE (AT) [06767856] **3004**

LOCAL GOVERNMENT ATTORNEYS OF VIRGINIA *See* LGA BILL OF PARTICULARS **3002**

LOCAL GOVERNMENT BULLETIN (AT/1057-1796) [06936331] **4662**

LOCAL GOVERNMENT COMPANION (UK) [02324922] **4662**

LOCAL GOVERNMENT EMPLOYMENT (CN/0703-7392) [02248940] 4662, **1688**

LOCAL GOVERNMENT ENGINEERS ASSOCIATION OF NEW SOUTH WALES JOURNAL (AT/0810-5669) [I08105669] **1985**

LOCAL GOVERNMENT FINANCE, NEW SOUTH WALES (AT) [08096492] **4736**

LOCAL GOVERNMENT FINANCE REVENUE AND EXPENDITURE ASSETS AND LIABILITIES ACTUAL *SUSPENDED.* (CN/0703-2749) [01784983] **4736**

LOCAL GOVERNMENT FOCUS (AT/0819-470X) [I0819470X] **4662**

LOCAL GOVERNMENT IN SOUTHERN AFRICA (SA/1015-0048) [08752964] **4662**

LOCAL GOVERNMENT LAW BULLETIN (US/0362-5729) [02304205] **3004**

LOCAL GOVERNMENT MANAGEMENT (AT/0819-1212) [I08191212] **4662**

LOCAL GOVERNMENT MONITOR (US/1058-3491) [24270494] **4663**

LOCAL GOVERNMENT POLICY MAKING (UK/0264-2050) [11200051] **4663**

LOCAL GOVERNMENT QUARTERLY (II) [01784240] **4663**

LOCAL
Alphabetical Title Index

LOCAL GOVERNMENT REPORTS OF AUSTRALIA See LOCAL GOVERNMENT AND ENVIRONMENTAL REPORTS OF AUSTRALIA, THE **4662**

LOCAL GOVERNMENT REPORTS OF AUSTRALIA, THE (AT/0076-0242) [01782926] 3114, **4663**

LOCAL GOVERNMENT REVIEW (UK) [02253554] **4663**

LOCAL GOVERNMENT REVIEW IN JAPAN (JA/0288-7622) [06896034] **4663**

●LOCAL GOVERNMENT REVIEW REPORTS (UK/1351-5764) [29864393] **3004**

LOCAL GOVERNMENT STUDIES (UK/0300-3930) [01431088] **876**

LOCAL GOVERNMENTS OF AUSTRALIA (AT) **4663**

LOCAL HEALTH DEPARTMENTS IN OREGON (US/0146-1516) [02831362] **4789**

LOCAL HISTORIAN (COLUMBUS, OHIO) (US/0893-3340) [11870639] **2744**

LOCAL HISTORIAN (LONDON. 1968) (UK/0024-5585) [02263656] **2697**

LOCAL HISTORY (UK/0266-2698) [13385181] **2697**

LOCAL HISTORY RECORDS - BOURNE SOCIETY (UK/0520-6790) [01793078] 2622, **2482**

LOCAL HISTORY STUDIES (US/0276-4105) [05063426] **2744**

LOCAL ISSUES : A COMPTROLLER OF THE TREASURY PUBLICATION FOR LOCAL GOVERNMENT AND THE PUBLIC (US) [17286951] **4663**

LOCAL JEWISH HISTORICAL SOCIETY NEWS / AMERICAN JEWISH HISTORICAL SOCIETY (US) [18152884] **5050**

LOCAL POPULATION STUDIES (UK/0143-2974) [02324976] 2697, **4554**

LOCAL PROGRAMS (US) [15806313] **324**

LOCAL SCHOOL EXPENDITURES (US) [05655854] **1866**

LOCAL SERVICE CARRIERS PASSENGER ENPLANEMENTS (US/0146-7549) [03025568] **27**

LOCAL/STATE FUNDING REPORT / GIS, GOVERNMENT INFORMATION SERVICES (US/0741-3173) [10132927] **4663**

LOCAL STUDIES LIBRARIAN, THE (UK) [11763253] **3228**

●LOCAL TELECOM COMPETITION NEWS (US/1067-6333) [27316403] **1159**

LOCAL TRANSPORT TODAY (UK/0962-6220) [I09626220] **5386**

LOCALDOC / GROUPEMENT DE RECHERCHES COORDONNEES SUR L'ADMINISTRATION LOCALE; CENTRE D'ETUDE ET DE RECHERCHE SUR LA VIE LOCALE (FR/0769-2412) [19760796] **4663**

LOCALNETTER NEWSLETTER, THE (US/0886-2397) [12894426] **1193**

LOCANA (BANGALORE, INDIA) (II) [11799148] **3408**

LOCATE: LAW OFFICE COMPUTER APPLICATIONS TECHNIQUES AND EQUIPMENT (US) [09207215] 876, **3004**

LOCATION IDENTIFIERS (US/0364-5282) [02562806] **27**

LOCATION INDICATORS. INDICATEURS D'EMPLACEMENT. INDICADORES DE LUGAR (CN) [06211871] **27**

●LOCATION SCIENCE (UK/0966-8349) [28210884] **5208**

LOCATION UPDATE (US/1058-3238) [20460170] **4074**

LOCATOR (US) [03099188] **2120**

LOCATOR OF USED MACHINERY & EQUIPMENT (US/0740-3712) [09953133] **2120**

LOCAZIONI E CONDOMINIO : CASI E QUESTIONI (IT) **2827**

LOCK HAVEN REVIEW (US/0459-6730) [02448336] **1834**

LOCKE NEWSLETTER, THE (UK/0307-2606) [01642607] **4352**

LOCKHART POST-REGISTER (US) [14707863] **5752**

LOCKHEED AIRCRAFT CORPORATION (US/0273-432X) [07040686] 1688, **1536**

LOCKHEED HORIZONS (US/0459-6773) [02350930] **27**

LOCKNEY BEACON, THE (US) [14195939] **5752**

LOCKSMITH LEDGER INTERNATIONAL (US/1050-2254) [21438382] **2812**

LOCKWOOD-POST'S DIRECTORY OF THE PULP, PAPER AND ALLIED TRADES (US/1046-5359) [17243278] **4235**

LOCOMOTIVE & RAILWAY PRESERVATION (US/0891-7647) [13521114] **5432**

LOCOMOTIVE ENGINEER NEWSLETTER, THE (US/0898-8625) [17933232] 1985, **5432**

LOCOMOTIVE ENGINEERS JOURNAL (1987) (US/0894-3605) [16016614] **1688**

LOCOMOTIVE (HARTFORD, CONN.), THE (US/0741-8760) [01756084] **5432**

LOCOMOTIVE MAINTENANCE OFFICERS ASSOCIATION (U.S.) See ANNUAL PROCEEDINGS, PRE-CONVENTION REPORT - LOCOMOTIVE MAINTENANCE OFFICERS ASSOCIATION (U.S.) **5429**

LOCOMOTIVE MAINTENANCE OFFICERS ASSOCIATION (U.S.). ANNUAL PROCEEDINGS OF THE ANNUAL MEETING See ANNUAL PROCEEDINGS, PRE-CONVENTION REPORT - LOCOMOTIVE MAINTENANCE OFFICERS ASSOCIATION (U.S.) **5429**

LOCOMOTIVE MAINTENANCE OFFICERS ASSOCIATION (U.S.). PRE-CONVENTION REPORT See ANNUAL PROCEEDINGS, PRE-CONVENTION REPORT - LOCOMOTIVE MAINTENANCE OFFICERS ASSOCIATION (U.S.) **5429**

LOCOMOTIVE QUARTERLY (US/0276-6736) [03675918] **5432**

LOCUS (CAMBRIDGE, MASS.) (US/0047-4959) [02255782] 4816, **3408**

LOCUS (DENTON, TEX.) (US/0898-8056) [17913159] **2744**

LODE STAR, THE (US/0890-5207) [14254581] **2308**

LODGING AND RESTAURANT INDEX See HOSPITALITY INDEX, THE **869**

LODGING AND RESTAURANT INDEX (US/0894-5128) [13562076] 2807, **5483**

LODGING HOSPITALITY (US/0148-0766) [03265925] **2807**

LODGING MAGAZINE (US/1078-6503) [23265678] **2807**

LODGING OUTLOOK (US) [22173368] **5483**

LODI ENTERPRISE, THE (US) [13776880] **5768**

LODI NEWS-SENTINEL (US) [27481158] **5636**

LOEB RETAIL LETTER (US) **955**

LOEX NEWS (US/0739-0386) [04624946] **3228**

LOFTY TIMES (US) [05275193] **3465**

LOG ANALYST, THE (US/0024-581X) [02498024] 4263, **1949**

LOG (ANNAPOLIS), THE (US/0024-5801) [04232770] **4863**

LOG (BROOKLYN) (US/0160-2047) [03633886] **1688**

LOG (DESTIN, FLA.) (US/0892-2969) [15148077] **5650**

LOG (HAYES), THE (UK/0024-5798) [03136472] **28**

LOG HOME LIVING (US/1041-830X) [18860065] **302**

LOG HOME LIVING ANNUAL BUYER'S GUIDE (US) 4840, **634**

●LOG HOMES ILLUSTRATED (US/1072-6063) [29072465] **619**

LOG HOMES MAGAZINE DESIGN, CONSTRUCTION & FINANCE ISSUE (US/1069-0344) [278.:0435] **619**

LOG OF MYSTIC SEAPORT, THE (US/0024-5828) [01644506] **2744**

LOG/ON (LOUISVILLE, KY.) (US/8756-4149) [09311164] **1275**

LOG TRAIN, THE (US/0743-281X) [10509080] **5432**

LOGA. LOCAL GOVERNMENT ANNOTATIONS (UK/0023-6349) [04422835] **4663**

LOGAN BANNER (LOGAN, W. VA. : DAILY) (US/0746-0570) [09714987] **5764**

LOGAN COUNTY NEWS (CRESCENT, OKLA.) (US/0896-4661) [13663931] **5732**

LOGAN HERALD-OBSERVER (US) [12888372] **5671**

LOGAN LEADER (RUSSELLVILLE, KY.) (US) [13958057] **5681**

LOGAN LEADER (RUSSELLVILLE, KY.) See NEWS-DEMOCRAT & LEADER **5682**

LOGAN REPUBLICAN (LOGAN, KAN. : 1911) (US) [12377912] **5677**

LOGBUCH, DAS (GW/0175-7601) [I01756076] 5452, **2774**

LOGGER AND LUMBERMAN MAGAZINE, THE (US/0192-7124) [05077691] **2402**

●LOGGER (VANCOUVER) (CN/1193-5855) [27193887] **2402**

LOGGING & SAWMILLING JOURNAL (CN/0714-363X) [08471408] **2402**

LOGGING INDUSTRY (CN/0834-440X) [13418656] 2402, **2399**

LOGGING RESEARCH PROGRESS REPORT (CN/0318-2541) [02442135] **2402**

●LOGIA (FORT WAYNE, INDIANA) (US/1064-0398) [26229120] **4974**

LOGICIELS ET SERVICES (FR/0296-8754) [02968754] **1193**

LOGIK UND GRUNDLAGEN DER MATHEMATIK (GW) [06695879] **3517**

LOGIN BROTHERS HEALTH SCIENCES LIBRARY NEWSLETTER (US) **3605**

LOGIQUE ET ANALYSE (BE/0024-5836) [01756092] **3517**

LOGISTICA (IT) **5126**

LOGISTICA MANAGEMENT (IT/1120-3587) [I11203587] **876**

LOGISTICS AND TRANSPORTATION REVIEW, THE (CN/0047-4991) [02051585] **5386**

LOGISTICS INFORMATION MANAGEMENT (UK/0957-6053) [22199381] 876, **3229**

LOGISTICS OUTLOOK FOR SHIPPERS (US/0737-917X) [09471844] **844**

LOGISTICS SPECTRUM (US/0024-5852) [03136534] **5126**

LOGISTICS (STAMFORD) (UK/0955-8241) [I09558241] **950**

LOGISTICS TODAY (UK) [14063676] **2120**

LOGISTIK HEUTE (GW/0173-6213) [I01736213] 690, **5386**

LOGISTIQUES MAGAZINE (FR) **876**

LOGO EXCHANGE (US/0888-6970) [13695909] **1280**

LOGOPEDIA CONTEMPORANEA (IT) **3605**

LOGOPEDIE EN FONIATRIE (NE/0166-252X) [I0166252X] **4391**

LOGOPHILE CEASED. (UK/0309-6270) [09446800] **3300**

LOGOS (BL) [02242051] **5233**

LOGOS (UK/0957-9656) [22578098] **4830**

LOGOS (IT/0024-5887) [01799380] **4352**

LOGOS (ARGONNE, ILL.) (US/0748-2116) [10410839] **5126**

LOGOS (BUENOS AIRES) (AG) [02325033] **4352**

LOGOS (COLUMBO, SRI LANKA) (CE/0458-1725) [01604822] **2506**

LOGOS JOURNAL (US/0194-3820) [01780996] **4974**

LOGOS / LENINGRADSKII GOSUDARSTVENNYI UNIVERSITET (RU) [25566384] **5251**

LOGOS (MEXICO) (MX/0185-6375) [03926782] **4352**

LOGOS, NEUE FOLGE (GW/0941-9683) **4352**

LOGOS (SANTA CLARA, CALIF.) CEASED. (US/0276-5667) [07191500] **4352**

LOGOS, THE (US) [16834726] **5752**

LOGOTHERAPIA (GW) [19262057] **3889**

LOGSDON CONNECTIONS (US/0732-7595) [08401491] **2458**

LOHN + GEHALT (GW/0172-9047) [I01729047] 1503, **690**

LOHNE UND GEHALTER. REIHE 2. 1 : ARBEITSVERDIENSTE IN DER INDUSTRIE (GW) [04383167] **1688**

LOHNE UND GEHALTER. REIHE 5, LOHNE, GEHALTER UND ARBEITSKOSTEN IM AUSLAND / STATISTISCHES BUNDESAMT (GW) [25122639] **1688**

●LOIRE VALLEY INSIGHT GUIDES (US/1064-2900) [26244279] **5483**

LOIS DU QUEBEC (CN/0318-4447) [02441887] **3004**

LOIS DU TRAVAIL (CN/1184-7484) [24256636] 1688, **3004**

L'OISEAU MAGAZINE : REVUE DE LA LIGUE FRANCAISE POUR LA PROTECTION DES OISEAUX (FR/0297-5785) [19008463] **5618**

LOISIR ET SOCIETE (CN/0705-3436) [04079745] **4852**

LOISIR. INFORMATION (CN/0701-1342) [03412129] **4852**

LOISIR LONGUEUIL (CN/0711-3293) [08503271] **4852**

LOISIRAMA (BE) **4852**

LOISIRS-PRESSE (CN/0713-553X) [08932746] **4903**

LOISIRS SANTE (FR) [08922635] **4381**

LOJAS & I.E. E LOJISTAS (BL) [01795821] **955**

LOK AWAZ (PANJABI EDITION) (CN/0700-8147) [03406284] **2744**

LOK-MAGAZIN (GW) [03136408] **5432**

LOK SABHA. PARLIAMENTARY COMMITTEES. SUMMARY OF WORK (II/0445-6793) [01784263] **4663**

LOK UDYOG (II/0024-5925) [01756097] **690**

LOKALHISTORISK FORENING FOR SONDERHALD KOMMUNE *See* ARSSKRIFT - LOKALHISTORISK FORENING FOR SONDERHALD KOMMUNE **2676**

LOKAYAN BULLETIN (II) [19638324] **5295**

LOKOLE (CG) [01798677] **2641**

●LOKOMOTIV (RU) [29034544] **5432**

LOLLIPOPS (US/0890-3557) [14206205] **1900**

LOMA LINDA UNIVERSITY SURGEON *CEASED.* (US/0731-3063) [08150400] **3969**

LOMBARD (IT) [19503788] **796**

LOMBARDIA VERDE (IT) **2218**

LOMPOC RECORD, THE (US) [11528217] **5636**

LONDON AND MIDDLESEX ARCHAEOLOGICAL SOCIETY *See* TRANSACTIONS OF THE LONDON & MIDDLESEX ARCHAEOLOGICAL SOCIETY **284**

LONDON AND MIDDLESEX HISTORICAL SOCIETY (ONT.) *See* NEWSLETTER / LONDON AND MIDDLESEX COUNTY HISTORICAL SOCIETY **2749**

LONDON ARCHAEOLOGIST, THE (UK/0024-5984) [02328755] **273**

LONDON BIRD REPORT (UK) [04621498] **5590**

LONDON BOROUGH COUNCIL ELECTIONS (UK) [01783958] **4481**

LONDON BROADSIDE (CN/0316-1986) [03248147] **2744**

LONDON BUSINESS MONTHLY MAGAZINE (CN/0820-5698) [16850959] **690**

LONDON BUSINESS SCHOOL BIBLIOGRAPHY OF FINANCIAL MARKETS (UK) [16936955] **796**

LONDON CALLING (LONDON, ENGLAND : 1981) *See* BBC WORLDWIDE : THE BBC WORLD SERVICE MAGAZINE **1127**

LONDON COLLECTOR, THE (US) [02903770] **3408**

LONDON CORN CIRCULAR, THE (UK) [02903693] **202**

LONDON CURRENCY REPORT (UK/0307-0360) [06246834] **797**

LONDON DEFENCE STUDIES (UK/0961-8422) [27342373] **4049**

LONDON DIPLOMATIC LIST / FOREIGN OFFICE, THE (UK) [14686131] **3132**

LONDON DIRECTORY & INTERNATIONAL REGISTER OF COMMERCE, THE (UK) [01786194] **1638**

LONDON DIRECTORY FOR TRADE AND INDUSTRY, THE (UK/0952-8784) [18078151] 1616, **844**

LONDON (ENGLAND). COMMISSIONER OF POLICE *See* REPORT OF THE COMMISSIONER OF POLICE OF THE METROPOLIS FOR THE YEAR **3174**

LONDON ENVIRONMENTAL BULLETIN (UK/0264-5904) [I02645904] **2177**

LONDON FREE PRESS (MORNING : 1907) (CN/0839-0681) [18759022] **5788**

LONDON GAZETTE, THE (UK) [01464336] **5812**

LONDON GRADUATE SCHOOL OF BUSINESS STUDIES. CENTRE FOR ECONOMIC FORECASTING *See* ECONOMIC OUTLOOK (LONDON. 1977) **1483**

LONDON. INNER LONDON EDUCATION AUTHORITY *See* INNER LONDON EDUCATION STATISTICS **1795**

LONDON JOURNAL, THE (UK/0305-8034) [04300546] **2697**

LONDON. LABORATORY OF THE GOVERNMENT CHEMIST *See* REPORT OF THE GOVERNMENT CHEMIST **991**

LONDON LEAF (CN/0824-5304) [12093280] **2458**

LONDON LOG (UK) **5483**

LONDON LORE (UK) [10846441] **2322**

LONDON MAGAZINE (UK/0024-6085) [01680782] **3408**

LONDON MAGAZINE (LONDON, ONT.) (CN/0711-6233) [08489376] **2537**

LONDON MARKET NEWSLETTER (UK/0265-8356) [I02658356] **2887**

LONDON MATHEMATICAL SOCIETY *See* LONDON MATHEMATICAL SOCIETY NEWSLETTER, THE **3517**

LONDON MATHEMATICAL SOCIETY *See* JOURNAL OF THE LONDON MATHEMATICAL SOCIETY **3515**

LONDON MATHEMATICAL SOCIETY *See* BULLETIN OF THE LONDON MATHEMATICAL SOCIETY, THE **3498**

LONDON MATHEMATICAL SOCIETY *See* PROCEEDINGS OF THE LONDON MATHEMATICAL SOCIETY **3528**

LONDON MATHEMATICAL SOCIETY LECTURE NOTE SERIES (UK/0076-0552) [08088082] **3517**

LONDON MATHEMATICAL SOCIETY NEWSLETTER, THE (UK) [20433290] **3517**

LONDON MATHEMATICAL SOCIETY STUDENT TEXTS (UK) [13505171] **3517**

LONDON METROBULLETIN (CN/0824-4596) [10615660] **4663**

LONDON NATURALIST (UK/0076-0579) [09039498] **4167**

LONDON NEWS (LONDON. EAST ED.) *CEASED.* (CN/1194-0387) [27203017] **5788**

LONDON OIL REPORTS (UK/0143-0114) [05019564] **4263**

LONDON ORIENTAL BIBLIOGRAPHIES (UK/0458-2241) [02326235] **419**

LONDON ORIENTAL SERIES (UK/0076-0625) [02326263] **2622**

LONDON PASSENGER TRANSPORT (UK/0309-5428) [11558078] **5432**

LONDON PHILATELIST, THE (UK) [02448346] **2785**

LONDON POSTAL HISTORY GROUP NOTEBOOK (UK) **1145**

LONDON REGISTER OF REMARKABLE EVENTS, CONTAINING ACCOUNTS OF MURDERS, SUICIDES, INQUESTS, SHIPWRECKS, DESTRUCTIVE FIRES, ACCIDENTS, AND OTHER REMARKABLE OCCURRENCES IN VARIOUS PARTS OF THE GLOBE, THE (UK) [11218898] **2519**

LONDON REVIEW OF BOOKS, THE (UK/0260-9592) [05655695] **3346**

LONDON RISING TIDE, THE (UK) [02952420] **5251**

LONDON. ROYAL COLLEGE OF SURGEONS OF ENGLAND *See* HANDBOOK LONDON. ROYAL COLLEGE OF SURGEONS OF ENGLAND **3965**

LONDON SCHOOL OF ECONOMICS AND POLITICAL SCIENCE *See* RESEARCH AT LSE **1517**

LONDON SCHOOL OF ECONOMICS MONOGRAPHS ON SOCIAL ANTHROPOLOGY (UK) **240**

LONDON THEATRE GUIDE (UK) 5483, **5365**

LONDON THEATRE NEWS (US/1064-0312) [24335508] **5365**

LONDON TOPOGRAPHICAL RECORD (UK) [06945972] **2568**

LONDON TRIBUNE (CN/0710-281X) [08418971] **5789**

LONDON UKRAINIAN BUSINESS AGENCY *See* UKRAINE BUSINESS REVIEW **717**

LONDON. UNIVERSITY. INSTITUTE OF COMMONWEALTH STUDIES *See* COMMONWEALTH PAPERS **1090**

LONDON. UNIVERSITY. WARBURG INSTITUTE *See* STUDIES OF THE WARBURG INSTITUTE **2855**

LONDON'S WHO & WHY MAGAZINE (CN/0824-4529) [10441441] **433**

LONE STAR HORSE REPORT (US/0892-6271) [15249483] **2800**

LONE STAR HUMOR DIGEST, THE (US/8756-7369) [11657132] **4863**

●LONE STAR LITERARY QUARTERLY (US/1062-7790) [25739067] **3408**

LONE STAR SIERRAN (US/0195-1955) [03919453] 2218, **2177**

LONE TREE REPORTER (LONE TREE, IOWA : 1981) (US) [11988151] **5671**

LONERGAN REVIEW (CN) [29534271] **3346**

LONERGAN STUDIES NEWSLETTER (CN/0828-184X) [07789326] **4974**

LONERGAN WORKSHOP *See* LONERGAN WORKSHOP **4974**

LONERGAN WORKSHOP *SUSPENDED.* (US/0148-2009) [03957628] **4974**

LONG BEACH COMMUNITY NEWS (US) [12956337] **5636**

LONG BEACH PRESS-TELEGRAM (US) [11448123] **5636**

LONG DISTANCE BOOK. VOL. 2, GOVERNMENT DIRECTORY OF ADDRESSES AND TELEPHONE NUMBERS *See* GOVERNMENT DIRECTORY OF ADDRESSES AND TELEPHONE NUMBERS, THE **4651**

LONG DISTANCE BOOK. VOL. 2, GOVERNMENT DIRECTORY OF ADDRESSES AND TELEPHONE NUMBERS *See* LONG DISTANCE DIRECTORY OF GOVERNMENT ADDRESSES AND TELEPHONE NUMBERS **4663**

LONG DISTANCE DIRECTORY OF GOVERNMENT ADDRESSES AND TELEPHONE NUMBERS (US/1062-1466) [25532914] **4663**

LONG-DISTANCE LETTER, THE (US/0740-6851) [09992058] **1159**

LONG HOURS AND PREMIUM PAY (US) [04622679] **1688**

LONG ISLAND ASSOCIATION DIRECTORY OF DIVERSIFIED SERVICES (US/0882-3626) [11832258] **690**

LONG ISLAND ASSOCIATION (N.Y.) *See* LONG ISLAND BUSINESS DIRECTORY & BUYERS GUIDE, THE **690**

LONG ISLAND BUSINESS DIRECTORY & BUYERS GUIDE, THE (US/1052-8431) [18206046] **690**

LONG ISLAND BUSINESS NEWS (US/0894-4806) [16116374] **690**

LONG ISLAND DIRECTORY OF MANUFACTURERS (US/0882-3618) [07994523] **3482**

●LONG ISLAND EXPRESS QUARTERLY (US/1062-8223) [25760619] **4852**

LONG ISLAND FORUM (US/0024-628X) [02927202] **2744**

LONG ISLAND GARDENING (US) [13438850] **2424**

LONG ISLAND HERITAGE : A GUIDE TO AND A JOURNAL OF THE ISLAND'S HISTORY, ANTIQUES AND ARTS *CEASED.* (US) [08458370] **2744**

LONG ISLAND HISTORICAL JOURNAL, THE (US/0898-7084) [17885988] **2744**

LONG ISLAND JEWISH WEEK, THE (US/0745-5607) [09285891] **5051**

LONG ISLAND JEWISH WORLD (US/0199-2899) [05757455] **2267**

LONG ISLAND MENTAL HEALTH CLINICIAN : JOURNAL OF CENTRAL NASSAU GUIDANCE & COUNSELING SERVICES, INC (US/1040-2160) [18353402] **3930**

LONG ISLAND MONTHLY EXPRESS *See* LONG ISLAND EXPRESS QUARTERLY **4852**

LONG ISLAND POETRY COLLECTIVE *See* LONG ISLAND POETRY COLLECTIVE NEWSLETTER, THE **3465**

LONG ISLAND POETRY COLLECTIVE NEWSLETTER, THE (US) [03360374] **3465**

LONG ISLAND POSTAL HISTORIAN (US) **1145**

LONG ISLAND RECREATION & VISITORS GUIDE (US/0882-1895) [07480385] **5483**

LONG ISLAND SOUND STUDY UPDATE (US) **2537**

LONG ISLAND TRAVELER *See* LONG ISLAND TRAVELER, MATTITUCK WATCHMAN, THE **5718**

LONG ISLAND TRAVELER, MATTITUCK WATCHMAN, THE (US) [11048406] **5718**

LONG ISLAND UPDATE (US/1067-2079) [27161063] **2537**

LONG ISLAND'S NIGHTLIFE MAGAZINE (US/0744-7590) [08529492] **4852**

LONG LIFE MAGAZINE (US/0191-1864) [04761323] **3754**

LONG POINT BIRD OBSERVATORY *See* NEWSLETTER - LONG POINT BIRD OBSERVATORY **5618**

LONG POND REVIEW (US/8756-5099) [03363044] **3408**

LONG-RANGE ICE OUTLOOK: EASTERN ARCTIC *See* EASTERN ARCTIC ICE, THE SEASONAL OUTLOOK **1413**

LONG RANGE JUDICIAL FACILITY PLAN (US/0734-0524) [08663342] **3141**

LONG RANGE PLANNING (UK/0024-6301) [01756149] **876**

LONG RANGE PROGRAM FOR LIBRARY DEVELOPMENT IN ALASKA (US) [08547060] **3229**

LONG-RANGE PROGRAM FOR LIBRARY DEVELOPMENT IN MISSISSIPPI. SUPPLEMENT (US) [06034428] **3229**

LONG RANGE PROGRAM. LIBRARY DEVELOPMENT IN ALASKA *See* LONG RANGE PROGRAM FOR LIBRARY DEVELOPMENT IN ALASKA **3229**

LONG-RANGE PROGRAM ... UPDATE & EXTENSION AND ANNUAL PROGRAM / OKLAHOMA DEPARTMENT OF LIBRARIES (US) [10510068] **3229**

LONG-RANGE RESEARCH PLAN (US) [09658806] **2156**

LONG ROOM (IE/0024-631X) [01716662] **3229**

LONG STAPLE COTTON REVIEW (US/0565-2022) [02586011] 5354, **178**

LONG STORY, THE (US/0741-4242) [10155105] **3408**

LONG-TERM ALTERNATIVE SCENARIOS AND 25-YEAR EXTENSION (US) [14756279] **1573**

LONG-TERM — Alphabetical Title Index

LONG-TERM BENTHIC MONITORING PROGRAMS NEAR THE MORGANTOWN AND CALBERT CLIFFS POWER PLANTS (US/0882-8334) [11871195] **1949**

LONG TERM CARE (US/0192-7701) [05026737] **3788**

LONG-TERM CARE ADMINISTRATOR (US/0146-275X) [02887703] **3788**

LONG-TERM CARE EXECUTIVE NETWORK *CEASED.* (US/1062-2616) [25561743] **3605**

LONG TERM CARE MANAGEMENT (US/0743-1422) [10564192] **3605**

LONG TERM CARE MONITOR (CN/1180-2189) [22254293] **3605**

LONG-TERM CARE NEWS *See* CONTINUING CARE CONNECTION : LINKING LONG-TERM, HOME AND COMMUNITY CARE SYSTEMS **5280**

LONG-TERM CARE NEWS / HOSPITAL ASSOCIATION OF NEW YORK STATE (US) [20214971] 3605, **5295**

LONG-TERM CARE QUARTERLY *CEASED.* (US/0891-8104) [13757732] **3788**

LONG TERM ENERGY PLAN (US/0733-5903) [08609850] **1949**

LONG TERM ENERGY PLAN. APPENDICES (US/0733-592X) [08609873] **1949**

LONG TERM ENERGY PLAN. EXECUTIVE SUMMARY (US/0733-5911) [08609905] **1949**

LONG-TERM FORECAST (US/8755-1500) [11224063] **1573**

LONG-TERM SERVICE DATA BANKS (US/0749-923X) [11177692] **1573**

LONG TERM VALUES (US/0744-3846) [08247138] **905**

●LONG TERM VIEW, THE (US) [25626464] 4663, **4481**

LONGEVITY (NEW YORK, N.Y. : 1988) (US/0895-8254) [22482294] **3754**

LONGMAN WORLD ENERGY CD-ROM (UK) **1949**

LONGMEADOW NEWS (US/0746-3693) [09977473] **5645**

LONGSHORE NEWSLETTER PROCEDURE MANUAL (US) **1688**

LONGTON ELK CITY NEWS-SUN, THE (US) [11216084] **5677**

LONGVIEW SUNDAY NEWS-JOURNAL, THE (US) [14509384] **5752**

LONGWOOD GRADUATE PROGRAM SEMINARS, THE (USUS/1057-3224) [17371927] **2424**

LOOK AT FINLAND *CEASED.* (FI/0024-6379) [01644240] **2519**

LOOK AT LEISURE, A (CN/0715-2361) [09269448] **4852**

LOOK AT LONDON (CN/0227-8499) [07295250] **5483**

LOOK BACK AT BOB DYLAN (US/1049-4340) [21218273] **4129**

LOOK HEAR (UK) **1115**

LOOK HERE (US/0197-355X) [04423547] **1834**

LOOK INSIDE (CN/0226-9848) [08439975] **5065**

LOOK JAPAN (JA/0456-5339) [04975486] **2506**

LOOK (MONTREAL) (CN/0823-5635) [10451574] **1085**

LOOKEAST (TH) [02303270] **5483**

LOOKING AHEAD (VANCOUVER) (CN/1189-3540) [25796520] **4129**

LOOKING AHEAD (WASHINGTON, D.C. : 1982) (US/0747-525X) [09275463] **1638**

LOOKING EAST (PO) [05810269] **5039**

LOOKING FOR EMPLOYMENT IN FOREIGN COUNTRIES (US/1052-7664) [22212270] **690**

LOOKING FORWARD (SEATTLE, WASH.) (US/0896-7032) [17272701] **4789**

LOOKING OUT FOR YOUR LEGAL RIGHTS (US/0889-602X) [13539013] **3004**

●LOOKING TOWARD THE FUTURE: A FIVE YEAR PLAN FOR THE IOWA DEPARTMENT OF CORRECTIONS / PREPARED BY THE IOWA DEPARTMENT OF CORRECTIONS, BUREAU OF RESEARCH AND PLANNING (US) [22442980] **3169**

"LOOKING UP" TIMES, THE (US/0893-3898) [15540167] **3408**

LOOKINGFIT (US/0890-4189) [14233233] **2599**

LOOKOUT. FOODS (US/0740-3860) [09948481] **2348**

LOOKOUT (NEW YORK), THE (US/0024-6425) [01756157] 4974, **5295**

LOOKOUT. NON-FOODS (US/0740-3852) [09948413] **2348**

LOOKOUT (SIOUX LOOKOUT) (CN/0383-8102) [03264543] **5789**

LOOKOUT, THE (US) [02448352] **4974**

LOOKOUT, THE (SP) [05224455] **2519**

LOOKS LONDON (UK/0268-4969) [I02684969] **2489**

LOOMING (ER/0134-4536) [02987767] 3346, **3408**

LOOMIS CHAFFEE SCHOOL *See* ALUMNI DIRECTORY - LOOMIS CHAFFEE SCHOOL **1098**

LOON, THE (US/0024-645X) [01756158] **5618**

LOONFEATHER (US/0734-0699) [06586836] **3346**

LOONSTRUCTUURONDERZOEK *CEASED.* (NE) [02514018] 1688, **1536**

LOOSE CHANGE (US/0278-4114) [07786755] **2774**

LOOSE LEAF LECTIONARY (US) **5031**

LOOSELEAF REGULATIONS SYSTEM. SERVICE 1. INCOME TAX (US) [02778281] **4736**

LOOSELEAF REGULATIONS SYSTEM. SERVICE 2. ESTATE AND GIFT TAX (US) [02778237] **4736**

LOOSELEAF REGULATIONS SYSTEM. SERVICE 3. EMPLOYMENT TAX (US) [02778297] **4736**

LORD'S DAY LEADER *See* SUNDAY (ATLANTA, GA.) **5001**

LORE AND LANGUAGE (UK/0307-7144) [02337937] 3300, **2322**

LORE (MILWAUKEE, WIS.) (US/0276-475X) [01624123] **4090**

LORE, THE (II) [02245630] **2506**

LORIS (CE/0024-6514) [01756159] **2197**

LORRAIN, LE (CN/0715-8599) [09770564] **4663**

LORTON PAPERS (US) [25560421] **4543**

LOS ALAMOS MONITOR (US/0893-3456) [12186965] **5712**

LOS ALAMOS SCIENCE (US/0273-7116) [06818444] **5126**

LOS ALAMOS SCIENTIFIC LABORATORY. E-DIVISION *See* E-DIVISION SEMIANNUAL REPORT **1936**

LOS ALTOS TOWN CRIER (US/8750-4588) [11641777] **5636**

LOS ANGELES (US/0024-6522) [04046470] **2537**

LOS ANGELES AREA CHAMBER OF COMMERCE *See* CATALOG OF MEMBERSHIP PROGRAMS AND SERVICES **818**

LOS ANGELES BUSINESS JOURNAL (US/0194-2603) [05366014] **690**

LOS ANGELES (CALIF.) *See* CITY OF LOS ANGELES PLANNING AND ZONING CODE : CHAPTER 1 OF THE LOS ANGELES MUNICIPAL CODE **2818**

LOS ANGELES (CALIF.) *See* CITY OF LOS ANGELES BUILDING CODE **2950**

LOS ANGELES (CALIF.). CULTURAL AFFAIRS DEPT *See* CULTURAL AFFAIRS NEWS **318**

LOS ANGELES, CALIF. DEPT. OF CITY PLANNING *See* STATISTICAL SUMMARY OF DEPARTMENTAL ACTIONS **2840**

LOS ANGELES (CALIF). DEPT. OF SOCIAL SERVICE *See* STATISTICAL REPORT - CITY OF LOS ANGELES. SOCIAL SERVICE DEPARTMENT **5267**

LOS ANGELES (CALIF.). OFFICE OF THE MAYOR *See* BUDGET - LOS ANGELES **4714**

LOS ANGELES (CALIF.). POLICE DEPT *See* ANNUAL REPORT / LOS ANGELES POLICE DEPARTMENT **3157**

LOS ANGELES CO., CALIF *See* SALARY ORDINANCE OF THE COUNTY OF LOS ANGELES **4705**

LOS ANGELES CO., CALIF. DEPT. OF REGIONAL PLANNING *See* QUARTERLY BULLETIN - DEPARTMENT OF REGIONAL PLANNING, COUNTY OF LOS ANGELES, CALIFORNIA **2832**

LOS ANGELES COMMERCIAL DIRECTORY (US/0736-1971) [09033739] 955, **844**

LOS ANGELES COMPUTER CURRENTS (US/0897-9308) [17689568] **1193**

LOS ANGELES COUNTY ALMANAC (US/0092-1882) [01789133] **4663**

LOS ANGELES COUNTY AREA AGENCY ON AGING. ADVISORY COUNCIL *See* ANNUAL REPORT - LOS ANGELES COUNTY AREA AGENCY ON AGING, ADVISORY COUNCIL **5272**

LOS ANGELES COUNTY BAR ASSOCIATION *See* BARRISTERS NEWSLETTER **2940**

LOS ANGELES COUNTY (CALIF.). AUDITOR-CONTROLLER *See* COMPREHENSIVE ANNUAL FINANCIAL REPORT, COUNTY OF LOS ANGELES **4718**

LOS ANGELES COUNTY (CALIF.). BOARD OF SUPERVISORS *See* FINAL BUDGET / COUNTY OF LOS ANGELES **4724**

LOS ANGELES COUNTY FLOOD CONTROL DISTRICT *See* HYDROLOGIC REPORT (LOS ANGELES) **5534**

LOS ANGELES COUNTY MEDICAL ASSOCIATION *See* LACMA PHYSICIAN **3914**

LOS ANGELES COUNTY MEDICAL ASSOCIATION *See* DIRECTORY OF MEMBERS / LOS ANGELES COUNTY MEDICAL ASSOCIATION **3913**

LOS ANGELES COUNTY MUSEUM OF ART *See* LOS ANGELES COUNTY MUSEUM OF ART REPORT **4090**

LOS ANGELES COUNTY MUSEUM OF ART REPORT (US/0197-5021) [04676155] 357, **4090**

LOS ANGELES COUNTY POPULAR STREET ATLAS (CENSUS TRACT ED.) (US/0733-6918) [03825717] **2568**

LOS ANGELES COUNTY, WAGE RATE SURVEY (US) [20710353] **1688**

LOS ANGELES DAILY JOURNAL, THE (US/0362-3575) [04582698] **3004**

LOS ANGELES FLUTE NEWS NETWORK (US) [13641078] **4129**

LOS ANGELES INSTITUTE OF CONTEMPORARY ART *See* JOURNAL - THE LOS ANGELES INSTITUTE OF CONTEMPORARY ART **354**

LOS ANGELES INTERNATIONAL FERN SOCIETY *See* LAIFS **2422**

LOS ANGELES JOB BANK, THE (US) [18111499] **690**

LOS ANGELES (LAPORTE, PA.) (US/0893-7265) [15694678] **2537**

LOS ANGELES LAWYER (US/0162-2900) [03796877] **3004**

●LOS ANGELES LETTER, THE (US/1070-2938) [28312953] **4663**

LOS ANGELES MICRO-GEOGRAPHER, THE (US) [18343531] **2568**

LOS ANGELES NEWS CONSERVANCY (US) [10338916] **2537**

LOS ANGELES OBSERVER (US/0890-0949) [12962046] **2537**

LOS ANGELES OLYMPIC ORGANIZING COMMITTEE *See* ANNUAL REPORT / LOS ANGELES OLYMPIC ORGANIZING COMMITTEE **4883**

LOS ANGELES, ORANGE COUNTIES STREET ATLAS AND DIRECTORY (ZIP CODE EDITION) (US/0883-5136) [11514419] **2568**

LOS ANGELES READER (US/1046-2392) [20366200] **2537**

LOS ANGELES SENTINEL (US/0890-4340) [09505770] **5636**

LOS ANGELES. SOUTHWEST MUSEUM. FREDERICK WEBB HODGE ANNIVERSARY PUBLICATION FUND *See* PUBLICATIONS **279**

LOS ANGELES THEATRE & ENTERTAINMENT REVIEW (US/1040-2292) [18355122] **5365**

LOS ANGELES TIMES INDEX (US/0742-4817) [10379910] **5692**

LOS ANGELES TIMES, THE (US/0458-3035) [03638237] **5636**

LOS ANGELES. UNIVERSITY OF SOUTHERN CALIFORNIA. SCHOOL OF SOCIAL WORK *See* SOCIAL WORK PAPERS OF THE SCHOOL OF SOCIAL WORK, UNIVERSITY OF SOUTHERN CALIFORNIA **5309**

LOS ANGELES WESTSIDE GENEALOGICAL SOCIETY NEWSLETTER (US) [2458]

LOS BANOS ENTERPRISE, THE (US) [20400807] **5636**

LOS BEXARENOS GENEALOGICAL REGISTER (US) [16960175] **2458**

LOS CUATRO VIENTOS, DE (MX) [24057733] **4974**

LOS GATOS WEEKLY (US/0748-4704) [10958829] **5636**

LOSE WEIGHT NATURALLY NEWSLETTER (US/0892-7294) [15247955] **4194**

LOSS, GRIEF & CARE (US/8756-4610) [11566979] 5251, **4603**

LOSS PREVENTION (UK/0097-2312) [01448342] 2865, **2014**

LOSS PREVENTION BULLETIN (UK/0260-9576) [I02609576] 2014, **2865**

LOST AND FOUND TIMES (US) [03363165] 357, **3408**

LOST CREEK LETTERS (US/1048-2172) [20866234] **3408**

LOST GENERATION JOURNAL (US/0091-2948) [01786705] **3408**

LOST IN CANADA? *CEASED.* (US/0362-4293) [02289588] **2458**

LOST/STOLEN SECURITIES (CN/0820-7879) [10314566] **797**

LOST TREASURE (US/0195-2692) [05433838] **5074**

Alphabetical Title Index — LOUISIANA

●LOST TREASURE'S TREASURE CACHE (US/1063-1372) [25897604] **4852**

LOT OF BUNKUM, A (US) [08961279] **2458**

LOT OF BUNKUM. YEARBOOK, A (US/0882-2425) [11742502] **2458**

LOTO ATLANTIQUE (CANADA) See REVUE ANNUELLE - LOTO ATLANTIQUE, CANADA **4683**

LOTO-LIAISON (CN/0706-196X) [06300045] **4663**

LOT'S WIFE (MICROFICHE) (AT) [04089372] **5777**

LOTT FAMILY NEWSLETTER, THE (US/0740-9389) [10027572] **2458**

LOTTA CONTRO LA TUBERCOLOSI E LE MALATTIE POLMONARI SOCIALI (IT/0368-7546) [06403364] **3950**

LOTTERY & GAMING REVIEW (CN/0828-7503) [12577428] **4863**

LOTTERY PLAYER'S MAGAZINE (US/0277-5565) [07590144] **4863**

LOTTERY WORLD (US/0098-9177) [02242654] **4736**

LOTUS (CAIRO) (UA/0002-0664) [01794787] **3408**

LOTUS (CAMBRIDGE, MASS.) (US/8756-7334) [11638314] 690, **1288**

LOTUS (CAMBRIDGE, MASS.) See PC WORLD **1271**

LOTUS INTERNATIONAL (IT) [03076558] **302**

LOTUS (MUSKOGEE, ILL.) (US/1056-3954) [23703621] **4603**

LOTUS NEWSLETTER CEASED. (US/0316-0106) [02247931] **105**

LOTUS ON WINDOWS (US/1055-7504) [23297980] **1288**

LOTUS ONE SOURCE. CD/CORPORATE. U.S. PUBLIC COS (US/1060-2178) [24098500] **691**

●LOTUS WORKS REPORT, THE (US/1059-7344) [24704955] **1193**

LOU PROUVENCAU A L'ESCOLO (FR/0758-4938) [10013526] **3300**

LOU TERRAIRE (FR/0293-373X) [11553762] **2697**

LOUDOUN COUNTY HANDBOOK (US) [10863252] **2745**

LOUDOUN COUNTY HISTORICAL SOCIETY See BULLETIN OF THE LOUDOUN COUNTY HISTORICAL SOCIETY, INC **2725**

LOUDOUN TIMES-MIRROR (US/0740-4034) [09923549] **5759**

LOUGHTON REVIEW (UK/0305-1765) [103051765] **5812**

●LOUIS RUKEYSER'S WALL STREET (US/1060-9903) [25148071] **905**

LOUISA COUNTY HISTORICAL MAGAZINE (US) [05430247] **2745**

LOUISBURG HERALD, THE (US/8750-6378) [08810989] **5677**

LOUISIANA See WEST'S LOUISIANA STATUTES ANNOTATED **3074**

LOUISIANA See WEST'S LOUISIANA SESSION LAW SERVICE **3074**

LOUISIANA See STATE OF LOUISIANA, ACTS OF THE LEGISLATURE **3059**

LOUISIANA ACADEMY OF SCIENCES See PROCEEDINGS OF THE LOUISIANA ACADEMY OF SCIENCES, THE **5141**

LOUISIANA AGRICULTURAL EXPERIMENT STATION See BULLETIN OF THE AGRICULTURAL EXPERIMENT STATION OF THE LOUISIANA STATE UNIVERSITY AND A & M COLLEGE **69**

LOUISIANA AGRICULTURAL EXPERIMENT STATION See LSU FORESTRY NOTES **105**

LOUISIANA AGRICULTURAL EXPERIMENT STATION See CIRCULAR - LOUISIANA AGRICULTURAL EXPERIMENT STATION **74**

LOUISIANA AGRICULTURAL EXPERIMENT STATION. DEPARTMENT OF AGRONOMY See REPORT OF PROJECTS / LOUISIANA AGRICULTURAL EXPERIMENT STATION. DEPT. OF AGRONOMY **126**

LOUISIANA AGRICULTURAL EXPERIMENT STATION. DEPT. OF AGRONOMY See AGRONOMY RESEARCH REPORT **56**

LOUISIANA AGRICULTURAL EXPERIMENT STATION. SOUTHEAST RESEARCH STATION See ANNUAL PROGRESS REPORT / SOUTHEAST RESEARCH STATION, LOUISIANA AGRICULTURAL EXPERIMENT STATION **205**

LOUISIANA AGRICULTURE (US/0024-6735) [01642166] **105**

LOUISIANA. AIR CONTROL COMMISSION See PROGRAM AND PROJECT ACCOMPLISHMENTS (NEW ORLEANS) **2239**

LOUISIANA ALMANAC (US/0896-6206) [06410768] **1927**

LOUISIANA ANNUAL MILK MARKETING REPORT, THE (US/0085-2880) [01788799] **929**

LOUISIANA ANNUAL OIL AND GAS REPORT CEASED. (US/0735-0716) [05592495] **4263**

LOUISIANA ARCHAEOLOGICAL SOCIETY See LOUISIANA ARCHAEOLOGY **273**

LOUISIANA ARCHAEOLOGY (US/1071-7358) [04587620] **273**

LOUISIANA ASSOCIATION OF EDUCATORS See LAE NEWS **1760**

LOUISIANA BANKER (1989), THE (US/1050-379X) [21473322] **797**

LOUISIANA BAR JOURNAL (US/0459-8881) [01756224] **3004**

LOUISIANA. BOARD OF REGENTS See FACTBOOK ON PUBLIC HIGHER EDUCATION IN LOUISIANA **1823**

LOUISIANA CASES REPORTED IN SOUTHERN REPORTER, SECOND SERIES (US/0745-4589) [01783621] **3004**

LOUISIANA CIVIL CODE (US) [06419080] **3090**

LOUISIANA CIVIL LAW AND PROCEDURE NEWSLETTER (US) [06652593] **3090**

LOUISIANA COASTAL LAW (US) [06124357] **3114**

LOUISIANA CONSERVATIONIST (1948) (US/0024-6778) [01756225] **2197**

LOUISIANA CONTRACTOR (US/0195-7074) [05624749] **619**

LOUISIANA CORPORATE NEWSLETTER (US) [01783994] **3101**

LOUISIANA COUNTRY (US) [11793258] **105**

LOUISIANA. CRIMINAL JUSTICE INFORMATION SYSTEM DIVISION See CRIME IN LOUISIANA **3080**

LOUISIANA CROP-WEATHER SUMMARY (US/0273-8848) [06999144] **178**

LOUISIANA. DATA PROCESSING COORDINATING AND ADVISORY COUNCIL See DATA PROCESSING ANNUAL REPORT AND LONG-RANGE PLAN FOR FISCAL YEARS ... / STATE OF LOUISIANA **4641**

LOUISIANA DENTAL ASSOCIATION See LDA JOURNAL **1329**

LOUISIANA. DEPT. OF AGRICULTURE See ANALYSIS OF OFFICIAL PESTICIDE SAMPLES **4243**

LOUISIANA. DEPT. OF AGRICULTURE AND IMMIGRATION. ANALYSIS OF PESTICIDES See ANALYSIS OF OFFICIAL PESTICIDE SAMPLES **4243**

LOUISIANA. DEPT. OF ART, HISTORICAL AND CULTURAL PRESERVATION See REPORT OF ACTIVITIES FOR THE STATE DEPARTMENT OF ART, HISTORICAL AND CULTURAL PRESERVATION **2853**

LOUISIANA. DEPT. OF EDUCATION. BUREAU OF FOOD AND NUTRITION SERVICES See STATE PLAN OF SCHOOL NUTRITION PROGRAMS / BUREAU OF FOOD AND NUTRITION SERVICES **1872**

LOUISIANA. DEPT. OF HEALTH AND HUMAN RESOURCES See PROPOSED COMPREHENSIVE ANNUAL SERVICES PROGRAM PLAN **5302**

LOUISIANA. DEPT. OF OCCUPATIONAL STANDARDS See REPORT - LOUISIANA DEPT. OF OCCUPATIONAL STANDARDS **1706**

LOUISIANA. DEPT. OF STATE See PRIMARY AND GENERAL ELECTION RETURNS - LOUISIANA **4674**

LOUISIANA. DEPT. OF STATE See AGENTS OF FOREIGN CORPORATIONS - LOUISIANA. DEPT. OF STATE **1596**

LOUISIANA DIRECTORY OF CITIES, TOWNS, AND VILLAGES (US/0741-0867) [10070593] **2745**

LOUISIANA. DIVISION OF ACADEMIC PROGRAMS See LOUISIANA ESEA TITLE II STATE PLAN **1834**

LOUISIANA. DIVISION OF NATURAL RESOURCES AND ENERGY. PROJECT ENGINEERING SECTION See ENERGY CONSERVATION ANNUAL REPORT **1939**

LOUISIANA. DIVISION OF VOCATIONAL REHABILITATION See BIENNIAL REPORT - STAFF SERVICES SECTION, DIVISION OF VOCATIONAL REHABILITATION **1911**

LOUISIANA EDUCATION RESEARCH JOURNAL (US/0740-5235) [05588338] **1762**

●LOUISIANA EMPLOYMENT LAW LETTER (US/1059-5058) [24609781] **3151**

LOUISIANA ENGINEER (US/0024-6794) [04046758] **1985**

●LOUISIANA ENVIRONMENTAL COMPLIANCE UPDATE (US/1066-1115) [26860522] **3114**

LOUISIANA ESEA TITLE II STATE PLAN (US) [06894773] **1834**

LOUISIANA FARM REPORTER (US/0273-883X) [07000583] **105**

LOUISIANA FOLKLORE MISCELLANY (US/0090-9769) [01785377] **2322**

LOUISIANA FOREST PRODUCTS (US/8756-8314) [07787849] **2402**

LOUISIANA GAME & FISH (US/0744-3692) [08215046] **4874**

LOUISIANA GENEALOGICAL REGISTER, THE (US/0148-7655) [03381774] **2458**

LOUISIANA GEOLOGICAL SURVEY See FOLIO SERIES - LOUISIANA GEOLOGICAL SURVEY **1376**

LOUISIANA GEOLOGICAL SURVEY See PUBLICATIONS OF THE LOUISIANA GEOLOGICAL SURVEY **1392**

LOUISIANA GROCER, THE (US) [09870588] **2348**

LOUISIANA. HEALTH AND SOCIAL AND REHABILITATION SERVICES ADMINISTRATION See STATISTICAL REPORT - LOUISIANA, HEALTH AND SOCIAL AND REHABILITATION SERVICES ADMINISTRATION (ANNUAL) **3661**

●LOUISIANA HEALTH CARE IN PERSPECTIVE (US/1065-4208) [26605666] **4789**

LOUISIANA HIGHER EDUCATION FACILITIES (US) [01784047] **1834**

LOUISIANA. HIGHER EDUCATION FACILITIES COMMISSION See LOUISIANA HIGHER EDUCATION FACILITIES **1834**

LOUISIANA HISTORICAL QUARTERLY (US/0095-5949) [01782268] **2745**

LOUISIANA HISTORY (US/0024-6816) [01782994] **2745**

LOUISIANA HORSE (US/0747-1912) [10633233] **2800**

LOUISIANA IN PERSPECTIVE (US/1065-5476) [26655574] **5332**

LOUISIANA INDUSTRY ENVIRONMENTAL ALERT (US/1055-257X) [23129294] **2177**

LOUISIANA INSUROR (US/0024-6832) [04821595] **2887**

LOUISIANA INTERNATIONAL TRADE DIRECTORY (US/0147-4464) [03162973] **844**

LOUISIANA LABOR MARKET (US/0091-4711) [01787401] **1688**

LOUISIANA LAW REVIEW (US/0024-6859) [01756232] **3004**

LOUISIANA LEGAL DIRECTORY, THE (US/0278-4734) [06796686] **3004**

LOUISIANA. LEGISLATURE. SENATE See OFFICIAL JOURNAL OF THE PROCEEDINGS OF THE SENATE AND HOUSE OF REPRESENTATIVES OF THE STATE OF LOUISIANA AND THE LEGISLATIVE CALENDAR **4485**

LOUISIANA LIBRARY ASSOCIATION See LLA BULLETIN **3228**

LOUISIANA LIFE (1989) (US/1042-9980) [19279681] **2537**

LOUISIANA LITERATURE (US/0890-0477) [11229034] **3408**

●LOUISIANA MANUFACTURERS REGISTER (US/1053-8992) [22687033] **3482**

LOUISIANA. MIGRANT EDUCATION PROGRAM See ANNUAL EVALUATION REPORT - LOUISIANA. MIGRANT EDUCATION PROGRAM **1725**

LOUISIANA. MILK DIVISION See LOUISIANA ANNUAL MILK MARKETING REPORT, THE **929**

LOUISIANA MUNICIPAL REVIEW (US/0164-3622) [04633029] **4663**

LOUISIANA (MUSEUM) See LOUISIANA-REVY **324**

LOUISIANA. OFFICE OF CONSERVATION See SECONDARY RECOVERY AND PRESSURE MAINTENANCE OPERATIONS IN LOUISIANA **2150**

LOUISIANA. OFFICE OF CONSERVATION. ENGINEERING DIVISION See PETROLEUM ACTIVITY REPORT **4272**

LOUISIANA. OFFICE OF MENTAL HEALTH See LOUISIANA STATE PLAN FOR COMPREHENSIVE MENTAL HEALTH SERVICES **4789**

LOUISIANA. OFFICE OF PUBLIC HEALTH STATISTICS See PUBLIC HEALTH STATISTICS (NEW ORLEANS) **4811**

LOUISIANA. OFFICE OF THE GOVERNOR. DIVISION OF ADMINISTRATION See CAPITAL OUTLAY BUDGET (LOUISIANA) **4716**

LOUISIANA — Alphabetical Title Index

LOUISIANA OUT-OF-DOORS (US/0738-8098) [09692763] 2197, **4874**

LOUISIANA PEACE OFFICER (US) [05132228] **3169**

LOUISIANA PHARMACIST, THE (US/0192-3838) [02263693] **4314**

LOUISIANA PHILOSOPHY OF EDUCATION JOURNAL (US) [06008950] **1762**

LOUISIANA PLANNING DIRECTORY (US/0148-6160) [03225868] **2827**

LOUISIANA PRESS-JOURNAL, THE (US) [19418910] **5704**

●LOUISIANA QUERIES (US/1044-792X) [19913484] **2458**

LOUISIANA. RED RIVER VALLEY AGRICULTURAL EXPERIMENT STATION (BOSSIER CITY, LA.) *See* ANNUAL RESEARCH REPORT - RED RIVER VALLEY AGRICULTURAL EXPERIMENT STATION (BOSSIER CITY, LA.) **163**

LOUISIANA REGISTER (US/0098-8545) [02240926] **3004**

LOUISIANA-REVY (DK/0024-6891) [06160286] **324**

LOUISIANA RURAL ECONOMIST (US/8756-6273) [04692246] 1503, **105**

LOUISIANA SOCIAL STUDIES JOURNAL (US/1040-2748) [18367123] **5208**

LOUISIANA SPORTSMAN (US/8750-9016) [11921691] **4903**

LOUISIANA. STATE BANKING DEPT *See* BIENNIAL REPORT OF THE COMMISSIONER OF FINANCIAL INSTITUTIONS AND SUPERVISOR OF HOMESTEAD AND BUILDING AND LOAN ASSOCIATIONS **778**

LOUISIANA STATE BAR ASSOCIATION *See* ANNUAL REPORT - LOUISIANA STATE BAR ASSOCIATION **2934**

LOUISIANA STATE BAR ASSOCIATION *See* NEWS BRIEFS : A PUBLICATION OF THE LOUISIANA STATE BAR ASSOCIATION **3017**

LOUISIANA. STATE BOARD OF EXAMINERS FOR SPEECH PATHOLOGY AND AUDIOLOGY *See* DIRECTORY - LOUISIANA STATE BOARD OF EXAMINERS FOR SPEECH PATHOLOGY AND AUDIOLOGY **3887**

LOUISIANA STATE BOARD OF NURSING *See* ANNUAL REPORT TO THE GOVERNOR OF THE STATE OF LOUISANA **3851**

LOUISIANA. STATE DEPT. OF HOSPITALS. ANNUAL STATISTICAL REPORT *See* STATISTICAL REPORT - LOUISIANA, HEALTH AND SOCIAL AND REHABILITATION SERVICES ADMINISTRATION (ANNUAL) **3661**

LOUISIANA STATE PLAN FOR COMPREHENSIVE MENTAL HEALTH SERVICES (US/0162-8461) [04225951] **4789**

LOUISIANA. STATE PLANNING OFFICE *See* ISSUE PAPER - OFFICE OF STATE PLANNING **1568**

LOUISIANA STATE UNIVERSITY AND AGRICULTURAL AND MECHANICAL COLLEGE. COOPERATIVE EXTENSION SERVICE *See* FOREST PRODUCTS NEWS **2381**

LOUISIANA STATE UNIVERSITY, BATON ROUGE. COASTAL STUDIES INSTITUTE *See* TECHNICAL REPORT - COASTAL STUDIES INSTITUTE, CENTER FOR WETLAND RESOURCES, LOUISIANA STATE UNIVERSITY **2206**

LOUISIANA STATE UNIVERSITY (BATON ROUGE, LA.). RICE RESEARCH STATION *See* ANNUAL RESEARCH REPORT / RICE RESEARCH STATION **163**

LOUISIANA. STATE UNIVERSITY IN NEW ORLEANS. DIVISION OF BUSINESS AND ECONOMIC RESEARCH. RESEARCH STUDY *See* RESEARCH STUDY - DIVISION OF BUSINESS AND ECONOMIC RESEARCH, COLLEGE OF BUSINESS ADMINISTRATION, UNIVERSITY OF NEW ORLEANS **1581**

LOUISIANA. SUPREME COURT *See* RULES OF THE SUPREME COURT OF LOUISIANA, ADOPTED AUGUST 31, 1973, EFFECTIVE JANUARY 1, 1974 AS AMENDED ... **3143**

LOUISIANA. SUPREME COURT *See* LOUISIANA CASES REPORTED IN SOUTHERN REPORTER, SECOND SERIES **3004**

LOUISIANA TECH UNIVERSITY *See* LOUISIANA TECH UNIVERSITY FACULTY PUBLICATIONS. ANNUAL SUPPLEMENT **419**

LOUISIANA TECH UNIVERSITY FACULTY PUBLICATIONS. ANNUAL SUPPLEMENT (US/0099-1457) [02243129] **419**

LOUISIANA. UNIVERSITY OF SOUTHWESTERN LOUISIANA, LAFAYETTE *See* U S L HISTORY SERIES, THE **2764**

LOUISIANA WEEKLY, THE (US) [02263695] 2267, **5684**

LOUISVILLE (US/0024-6948) [04046814] **2537**

LOUISVILLE DEFENDER, THE (US) [10644972] **5681**

LOUISVILLE DIRECTORY OF MANUFACTURERS (US) [17913848] **3482**

LOUISVILLE LAW EXAMINER (US/0890-8605) [08834905] **3004**

LOUISVILLE MESSENGER, THE (US/0746-0961) [09747706] **5706**

LOUISVILLE PRESBYTERIAN THEOLOGICAL SEMINARY (1901-) LIBRARY *See* REPORT OF THE LIBRARIAN **3245**

LOUISVILLE REVIEW, THE (US/0148-3250) [03297083] **3408**

LOUISVILLE TIMES (US) [20570292] **5643**

LOUISVILLE. UNIVERSITY *See* UNIVERSITY OF LOUISVILLE STUDIES IN PALEONTOLOGY AND STRATIGRAPHY **4231**

LOUNAIS-HAMEEN LUONNONSUOJELUYHDISTYS *See* LOUNAIS-HAMEEN LUONTO **2197**

LOUNAIS-HAMEEN LUONTO (FI/0355-3728) [01756238] **2197**

●LOUPE (SANTA MONICA, CALIF.) (US/1062-8460) [25768415] **2915**

LOUSAVORITCH (CN/0228-2380) [06860052] **2745**

LOUVAIN BREWING LETTERS (BE/0777-8805) [I07778805] **2369**

LOUVAIN MEDICAL (BE/0024-6956) [06403451] **3605**

LOUVAIN STUDIES (BE/0024-6964) [01756242] **4974**

LOUVAIN. UNIVERSITE CATHOLIQUE *See* BIBLIOTHECA EPHEMERIDUM THEOLOGICARUM LOVANIENSIUM **4939**

LOUVAIN. UNIVERSITE CATHOLIQUE *See* SYLLOGE EXCERPTORUM E DISSERTATIONIBUS AD GRADUM DOCTORIS IN SACRA THEOLOGIA VEL IN IURE CANONICO CONSEQUENDUM CONSCRIPTIS **5037**

LOUVAIN. UNIVERSITE CATHOLIQUE. CENTRE D'HISTOIRE DE L'AFRIQUE *See* ENQUETES ET DOCUMENTS D'HISTOIRE AFRICAINE **2639**

LOUVAIN. UNIVERSITE CATHOLIQUE. INSTITUT SUPERIEUR DE PHILOSOPHIE *See* BIBLIOTHEQUE PHILOSOPHIQUE **4342**

LOUVAIN. UNIVERSITE CATHOLIQUE. SECTION D'ARCHEOLOGIE ET D'HISTOIRE DE L'ART *See* PUBLICATIONS **279**

LOV OG RETT (NO/0024-6980) [01756282] **3004**

LOVE LETTER, THE **CEASED.** (US/8750-8745) [11876791] **1762**

LOVE MAKES THE WORLD GO AWRY (CN/0227-5449) [08045892] **3409**

LOVE STORY (UK) **5074**

LOVECRAFT STUDIES (US/0899-8361) [06495965] **3409**

LOVEJOY'S COLLEGE GUIDE (US/0076-132X) [05168465] **1834**

LOVEJOY'S GUIDANCE DIGEST (US/0024-7022) [02327937] **1834**

LOVEJOY'S PREP AND PRIVATE SCHOOL GUIDE **CEASED.** (US) [06500553] **1762**

LOVELAND DAILY REPORTER-HERALD (US) [22832534] **5643**

LOVELOCK REVIEW-MINER (US) [13776846] **5707**

LOW INCOME HOME ENERGY ASSISTANCE PROGRAM (US/8756-9000) [11666435] **1949**

LOW-INCOME HOUSING TAX CREDIT ADVISOR (US/1065-3678) [22735301] **3004**

LOW-INCOME HOUSING TAX CREDIT HANDBOOK (US) [23807006] **4736**

●LOW INTENSITY CONFLICT AND LAW ENFORCEMENT (UK/0966-2847) [I09662847] **3169**

LOW PRICED STOCK SURVEY, THE (US/0273-7752) [06909672] **905**

LOW-RENT HOUSING HOMEOWNERSHIP OPPORTUNITES (US) [02932994] **2827**

LOW RIDER (US/0199-9362) [04670290] **5418**

LOW TEMPERATURE DIRECTORY : THE NEWSLETTER OF THE BRITISH CRYOGENICS COUNCIL (UK) **4411**

●LOW TEMPERATURE PHYSICS (US/1063-777X) [26140213] **4411**

LOW VISION ABSTRACTS (US/0362-4889) [02270192] **4391**

LOWDOWN 1982 (AT/0158-099X) [I0158099X] **386**

LOWE INVESTMENT & FINANCIAL LETTER (US/0193-9262) [05269473] **905**

LOWE MANAGEMENT CORPORATION *See* LOWE INVESTMENT & FINANCIAL LETTER **905**

LOWELL TRIBUNE, THE (US) [15504455] **5665**

LOWER AUSTRIA (AUSTRIA) *See* AUSZUG AUS DEN TATIGKEITSBERICHTEN DER GRUPPEN UND ABTEILUNGEN DES AMTES DER NO LANDESREGIERUNG, EIN **4631**

LOWER AUSTRIA (AUSTRIA) *See* NIEDEROSTERREICHISCHE SOZIALHILFE UND JUGENDWOHLFAHRTSPFLEGE **5299**

LOWER BUCKS COUNTY REAL ESTATE DIRECTORY (US/0146-3438) [02919882] **4840**

LOWER COLORADO RIVER AUTHORITY *See* ANNUAL REPORT - LOWER COLORADO RIVER AUTHORITY **2087**

LOWER COLUMBIA BUSINESS (US/1056-7070) [23825312] **691**

●LOWER EXTREMITY, THE (US/1068-6991) [27758319] **3883**

LOWERING YOUR CHOLESTEROL (US/1055-6028) [23237287] **2599**

LOWIEC POLSKI (PL/0137-1266) [I01371266] **4874**

LOWNDES SIGNAL, THE (US) [09238790] **5627**

LOWRY AIRMAN (US) [23231510] **5643**

LOWRY'S POWER AND VELOCITY RATINGS REPORT (US) 797, **905**

LOWRY'S WEEKLY MARKET TREND ANALYSIS (US) 797, **905**

LOYAL (GW/0343-0103) [I03430103] **4049**

LOYALIST GAZETTE, THE (CN/0047-5149) [02051839] **2745**

LOYOLA CONSUMER LAW REPORTER (US/1041-5114) [18790210] 1298, **3004**

LOYOLA EDUCATIONAL INDEX; A READERS' GUIDE TO EDUCATION AND PSYCHOLOGY (US) [01606410] 4603, **1762**

LOYOLA ENTERTAINMENT LAW JOURNAL (US/0740-9370) [10024788] 386, **3004**

LOYOLA LAW REVIEW (US/0192-9720) [01642662] **3004**

LOYOLA LECTURE SERIES IN POLITICAL ANALYSIS (US) **4481**

●LOYOLA OF LOS ANGELES ENTERTAINMENT LAW JOURNAL (US) [25267742] 3004, **324**

LOYOLA OF LOS ANGELES INTERNATIONAL AND COMPARATIVE LAW JOURNAL (US/0277-5417) [07590377] **3132**

LOYOLA OF LOS ANGELES LAW REVIEW (US/0147-9857) [03262904] **3004**

LOYOLA UNIVERSITY OF CHICAGO LAW JOURNAL (US/0024-7081) [04643808] **3005**

LOYOLA UNIVERSITY OF CHICAGO. SCHOOL OF LAW *See* LOYOLA UNIVERSITY OF CHICAGO LAW JOURNAL **3005**

LOZANIA (CK/0085-2899) [01714469] **5590**

LOZARSTVO I VINARSTVO (BU/0458-4244) [04095038] **2424**

LP-GAS (US/0024-7103) [01782747] **4263**

LP GAS REVIEW (UK) [05321161] **4263**

LPBA JOURNAL (US/0274-9319) [06871564] 28, **3005**

LPG IN WORLD MARKETS (UK) [10706705] **4263**

LPTV REPORT, THE **CEASED.** (US/0892-5585) [15246929] **1134**

LRA TRADE UNION ADVISOR (US/1058-0557) [18933742] **1688**

LRABER HASARAKAKAN GITUTYUNNERI (AI/0320-8117) [02505043] **5208**

LRA'S ECONOMIC NOTES (US/0895-5220) [15245811] **1688**

LRB SUMMARIES (KEW GARDENS, QUEENS, NEW YORK, N.Y.) (US/0740-2554) [08958780] 1920, **3005**

LRC NEWSBRIEFS (US/0899-563X) [17851181] **4736**

LRD BOOKLETS (UK) **1688**

LRE PROJECT EXCHANGE (US/0734-0990) [07996105] 1762, **3005**

LRE REPORT (US/0731-9711) [06714514] 1762, **3005**

LRIS NEWSLETTER (CN/0709-4590) [23659247] 3229, **2387**

LRRC LABOR UPDATE / LABOR RELATIONS AND RESEARCH CENTER, UNIVERSITY OF MASSACHUSETTS, AMHERST (US) [25756626] **1688**

●LS NEWSLETTER (CN/1193-2333) [26714936] **3229**

LSA ANNUAL MEETING HANDBOOKS (US) **3300**

LSA BULLETIN (US/0023-6365) [01101332] **3300**

LSA. LIBRE SERVICE ACTUALITES (FR/0024-2632) [I00242632] **955**

LSBA ... CONVENTION IN REVIEW / WRITTEN BY LOUISIANA SCHOOL PUBLIC RELATION ASSOCIATION (US) [08031296] **1762**

LSE MAGAZINE (UK/0023-639X) [21325164] **1503**

LSI JOURNAL (US/0741-7667) [10177190] 1268, **1280**

LSI RESIDENTIAL CONSTRUCTION COSTS / LEE SAYLOR, INC (US) [09691423] **619**

LSL; LEDER, SCHUKE, LEDERWAREN (SZ/0024-0192) [02970820] **3185**

LSU FORESTRY NOTES (US/0458-5682) [03567994] **105**

LSU WOOD UTILIZATION NOTES (US/0076-1109) [06730791] **2387**

LTA CONFERENCE (CN/0707-2147) [08936792] **3300**

LTBC : LIBRARY TECHNICIANS ASSOCIATION OF BRITISH COLUMBIA (CN/0715-7533) [10595521] **3229**

LTC PAPER (US/0084-0793) [13292634] **4663**

LTCB RESEARCH (JA/0287-2404) [04162505] 1503, **797**

LU HSUN YEN CHIU NIEN KAN / HSI PEI TA HSUEH LU HSUN YEN CHIU SHIH PIEN (CC) [08531488] **3409**

LU HSUN YEN CHIU TZU LIAO / PEI-CHING LU HSUN PO WU KUAN, LU HSUEN YEN CHIU SHIH PIEN (CC) [08501160] **3409**

LU HSUN YEN CHIU WEN TSUNG (CC) [08298267] **3409**

LU REES ARCHIVES (AT/0725-7015) [I07257015] 2482, **3229**

LU YU TIEN TI (SHANGHAI, CHINA) (CC) [09146628] **5483**

LU YU WEN HSUEH (CH) [10665362] **2568**

LUA MI (US/0891-1444) [14636974] **3409**

LUA NOVA (BL) [11952189] 5208, **4352**

LUAS & INTENSITAS SERANGAN HAMA & PENYAKIT DI INDONESIA (IO) [03806599] **2424**

LUAS TANAH MENURUT PENGGUNAANNYA DI JAWA & MADURA (IO) [08161583] **105**

LUAS TANAMAN, PRODUKSI, DAN PERSEDIAAN TANAMAN PERKEBUNAN YANG TERPENTING (IO) [05948475] **178**

LUBBOCK AVALANCHE-JOURNAL (US) [13990546] **5752**

LUBBOCK AVALANCHE-JOURNAL (LUBBOCK, TEX. : 1959 : MORNING ED.) **CEASED.** (US) [13990498] **5752**

LUBECKER SCHRIFTEN ZUR ARCHAOLOGIE UND KULTURGESCHICHTE / AMT FUER VOR- UND FRUHGESCHICHTE (BODENDENKMALPFLEGE) DER HANSESTADT LUBECK (GW/0721-3735) [05997514] 2622, **273**

LUBELSKIE TOWARZYSTWO NAUKOWE *See* BIULETYN LUBELSKIE TOWARZYSTWA NAUKOWEGO. MATEMATYKA, FIZYKA-CHEMIA **3497**

LUBRICATION ENGINEERING (US/0024-7154) [01756256] **2120**

LUBRICATION (NEW YORK, N.Y. : 1911) (US/0024-7146) [01586031] **2120**

LUBRICATION SCIENCE (UK/0954-0075) [I09540075] **1985**

LUCARNE (CN/0711-3285) [08605093] **302**

LUCAS (AT/1030-4428) [I10304428] **4975**

LUCAS-SYLVAN NEWS (US) [12544669] **5677**

LUCE E OMBRA; RIVISTA DI STUDI METAPSICHICI E DI PROBLEMI DELL'ANIMA E DEL PENSIERO (IT) [03128798] **4242**

LUCEAFARUL (US) [06440306] **3346**

LUCEAFARUL (RM/0458-435X) [02386130] **3409**

LUCEBNIK (XR) [03128717] **1688**

LUCENTUM (SP/0213-2338) [12241404] **273**

LUCH / ASSOCIATION OF BULGARIAN WRITERS AND ARTISTS IN EXILE (US) [08265276] **324**

LUCHA STRUGGLE (US/0885-4378) [08077690] 5062, **5208**

LUCHT EN OMGEVING (NE) **2177**

LUCHT- EN RUIMTEVAART TECHNIEK LITERATUUROVERZICHT / WETENSCHAPPELIJK EN TECHNIEK DOCUMENTATIE- EN INFORMATIECENTRUM VOOR DE KRIJGSMACHT (NE) [10214118] **28**

LUCHTVERONTREINIGING, METINGEN BUITENLUCHT / CENTRAAL BUREAU VOOR DE STATISTIEK, AFDELING MILIEUHYGIENE (NE) [09766480] **2235**

LUCIDITY (US/0897-6481) [17597562] **3465**

LUCKNOW LAW TIMES (II) [01756264] **3005**

LUCKNOW LIBRARIAN (II/0024-7219) [02232839] **3229**

LUCKNOW UNIVERSITY JOURNAL OF SOCIAL WORK (II) [01589120] **5295**

LUCRARI DE MUZICOLOGIE (RM) [02926096] **4129**

LUCRARI STIINTIFICE, INSTITUL AGRONOMIC "N. BALCESCU," BUCURESTI, SERIA D, ZOOTEHNIE (RM/0374-8898) [02256489] **5590**

LUCRARI STIINTIFICE. INSTITUTUL AGRONOMIC TIMISOARA, SERIA MEDICINA VETERINARA (RM/0563-5586) [01197043] **5515**

LUCRARI STIINTIFICE - INSTITUTUL AGRONOMIC ION IONESCU DE LA BRAD. SERIA ZOOTEHNIE - MEDICINA VETERINARA (RM) [06410813] **105**

LUCRARI STIINTIFICE - INSTITUTUL AGRONOMIC "NICOLAE BALCESCU," BUCURESTI, SERIA C, MEDICINA VETERINARA (RM/0254-0509) [03496633] **5515**

LUCRARI STIINTIFICE, INSTITUTUL AGRONOMIC TIMISOARA, SERIA AGRONOMIE (RM/0563-5578) [09590812] **105**

LUCRARI STIINTIFICE - INSTITUTUL DE CERCETARI PENTRU VALORIFICAREA LEGUMELOR SI FRUCTELOR (RM) [02882006] **178**

LUCRARI STIINTIFICE - INSTITUTUL DE CERCETARI SI PROIECTARI PENTRU VALORIFICAREA SI INDUSTRIALIZAREA LEGUMELOR SI FRUCTELOR (RM/1010-1349) [10101349] 2348, **105**

LUCRARI STIINTIFICE. ZOOTEHNIE (RM) [03919305] **5590**

LUCRARILE INSTITUTULUI DE CERCETARI VETERINARE SI BIOPREPARATE "PASTEUR" (RM/0368-7732) [04558093] **5515**

LUCRARILE SEMINARULUI DE MATEMATICA SI FIZICA AL INSTITUTULUI POLITEHNIC "TRAIAN VUIA" TIMISOARA (RM) [12037002] 4411, **3517**

LUCRURI NOI SI VECHI (US/8756-8012) [11666098] **4975**

LUCUARI STIINTIFICE - INSTITUTUL AGRONOMIC "NICOLAE BALESCU", BUCURESTI. SERIA E. IMBUNATATIRI FUNCIARE (RM/1015-2172) [09494768] **2568**

LUD (PL/0076-1435) [02924774] **2322**

LUDAS EVKONYV (HU/0133-9214) [21717383] **2519**

LUDAS MATYI (HU) [02926195] **2519**

LUDAS MATYI EVKONYVE *See* LUDAS EVKONYV **2519**

LUDOTECA (IT) **4903**

LUDOWICI NEWS, THE (US) [19500618] **5654**

LUDWIG SYMPOSIA (AT/0737-142X) [08150175] **3820**

LUFKIN DAILY NEWS, THE (US) [18269794] **5752**

LUFT UND KAELTETECHNIK *See* KI LUFT UND KAELTETECHNIK **618**

LUFT- UND KALETECHNIK (GW/0024-7251) [06175672] **619**

LUFT- UND RAUMFAHRT (GW/0173-6264) [09767371] **28**

LUFTFAHRT INTERNATIONAL (GW) [03321774] 28, **4049**

LUFTFAHRT-NORMEN-VERZEICHNIS (GW) [02989668] **28**

LUFTFARTSSTATISTIKK / CIVIL AVIATION STATISTICS NORWAY (NO/0800-4072) [11836336] **41**

LUFTFARTSVERKET (SW) [06428506] **28**

LUFTWAFFEN-FORUM (GW) **28**

LUGAR EM COMUNICACAO (BL) [01785106] **1115**

LUI PARIS **CEASED.** (FR/0750-3520) [I07503520] **3995**

LUISTER (NE/0024-7286) [I00247286] **4129**

LULLWATER REVIEW (US/1051-5968) [21994551] **3409**

LULU REVU (CN/0709-8030) [06183380] **3409**

LUMBER CO-OPERATOR, THE (US/0024-7294) [04013670] **2402**

LUMBER PRODUCTION AND MILL STOCKS (US/0276-5551) [03054373] **2402**

LUMBY REVIEW (CN/0715-4569) [09166898] **5789**

LUMEN (CN) 2622, **3409**

LUMEN VITAE (BE/0024-7324) [01756266] **4975**

LUMERA, LA (CN/0382-5280) [02624875] **2489**

LUMIERE D'ENCRE (CN/1184-8626) [24570939] **3409**

LUMIERE ET PAIX (CN/0705-6346) [04249893] **2252**

LUMIERE ET VIE (FR/0024-7359) [01773954] **4975**

LUMIERES (MONTREAL) **CEASED.** (CN/0835-4790) [17636423] **4074**

LUMINA (MONTREAL) (CN/1181-8212) [24266611] **3837**

LUMINANCE (MONTREAL) (CN/1183-935X) [25066716] **4975**

LUMINARY (MUNCY, PA.) (US) [14221579] **5737**

LUMINARY : THE NEWSLETTER OF THE MUSEUM OF EARLY SOUTHERN DECORATIVE ARTS, THE (US) [07310051] **374**

LUMINITA **CEASED.** (RM) [06190448] **2519**

LUMO (CN/0827-3154) [02051983] **3300**

LUNAR & PLANETARY INFORMATION BULLETIN (US/0891-4664) [06419397] **396**

LUNAR SAMPLE NEWSLETTER (US/0748-9781) [10264692] **396**

LUND ART PRESS **SUSPENDED.** (SW/1101-5462) [11015462] **303**

● LUND DISSERTATIONS IN SOCIOLOGY (SW/1102-4712) [11024712] **5251**

LUND ECONOMIC STUDIES (SW/0460-0029) [02371043] **1503**

LUND MONOGRAPHS IN SOCIAL ANTHROPOLOGY (SW/1101-9948) [11019948] 5208, **240**

LUND PAPERS IN ECONOMIC HISTORY (SW) [23957422] **1573**

LUND POLITICAL STUDIES (SW/0460-0037) [02339563] **4481**

LUND STUDIES IN ENGLISH (SW/0076-1451) [01715778] 3409, **3300**

● LUND STUDIES IN ETHICS AND THEOLOGY (SW/1102-769X) [I1102769X] 4975, **2252**

LUND STUDIES IN GEOGRAPHY. SERIES A. PHYSICAL GEOGRAPHY (SW/0076-146X) [01607285] **2568**

LUND STUDIES IN GEOGRAPHY. SERIES B. HUMAN GEOGRAPHY (SW/0076-1478) [01638943] **2568**

LUND. UNIVERSITET. HISTORISKA MUSEET *See* MEDDELANDEN FRAN LUNDS UNIVERSITETS HISTORISKA MUSEUM **274**

LUNDASTUDIER I NORDISK SPRAKVETENSKAP. SERIE A (SW) [02349481] **3300**

LUNDBERG LETTER (US/0195-4563) [05459410] **4263**

LUNDER GERMANISTISCHE FORSCHUNGEN (SW/0348-2146) [01756281] **3300**

LUNDI, LE (CN/0704-7886) [03890026] **5560**

LUNDIAN : AN INTERNATIONAL MAGAZINE, THE (SW) **2519**

LUNDS UNIVERSITET. GEOGRAFISKA INSTITUTIONEN *See* MEDDELANDEN FRAN LUNDS UNIVERSITETS GEOGRAFISKA INSTITUTION. AVHANDLINAR **2569**

LUNG (GW/0341-2040) [02888375] **3950**

LUNG & RESPIRATION (GW/0176-1749) [12862052] **3950**

LUNG BIOLOGY IN HEALTH AND DISEASE (US/0362-3181) [02205117] **3950**

LUNG CANCER (AMSTERDAM, NETHERLANDS) (NE/0169-5002) [13919021] **3820**

LUNG DISEASE WEEKLY (US/1078-2877) **3950**

LUNG INDIA (II/0970-2113) [10909385] **3950**

LUNG TSAI TIEN (CH) [09310557] **4242**

LUNGE + ATMUNG. A (GW/0720-0706) [I07200706] **3950**

LUONNON TUTKIJA (FI/0024-7383) [02970650] **4167**

LUPTA DE CLASA *See* ERA SOCIALISTA **4541**

LUPTONIAN, THE (US/0099-1791) [02242055] **2458**

LUPUS (UK/0961-2033) [25601279] **3721**

LUPUS NEWS (US/0732-0280) [08317966] **3721**

LUQMAN (IR) [15105715] 2769, **5043**

LURE OF THE LITCHFIELD HILLS, THE (US) [09842882] **2745**

LURELU

Alphabetical Title Index

LURELU (CN/0705-6567) [04098029] **1066**

LURZER'S INT'L ARCHIVE (US/0893-0260) [14159702] **762**

LUSAKA PROVINCE ANNUAL REPORT FOR THE YEAR ... / REPUBLIC OF ZAMBIA, OFFICE OF THE PRIME MINISTER (ZA) [09764151] **4663**

LUSAKA, ZAMBIA. ACTIVITIES OF CITY LIBRARY SECTION *See* ACTIVITIES OF THE LUSAKA CITY LIBRARIES **3187**

LUSAKA, ZAMBIA. CITY LIBRARIES SECTION *See* ACTIVITIES OF THE LUSAKA CITY LIBRARIES **3187**

LUSCOMBE ASSOCIATION NEWS (US/0889-4361) [14047459] **28**

LUSITANIA SACRA (PO/0076-1508) [01782984] 4975, **2622**

LUSITANO (CAMBRIDGE) (CN/0707-5324) [04635179] **5789**

LUSK'S ANNE ARUNDEL COUNTY REAL ESTATE DIRECTORY, PROPERTY TRANSFERS (US/0099-1686) [02243689] **4840**

LUSK'S BALTIMORE COUNTY REAL ESTATE DIRECTORY, PROPERTY TRANSFERS (US/0099-104X) [02243313] **4840**

LUSK'S CARROLL COUNTY REAL ESTATE DIRECTORY (US/0360-0874) [02243767] **4840**

LUSK'S DISTRICT OF COLUMBIA ASSESSMENT DIRECTORY SERVICE *See* LUSK'S DISTRICT OF COLUMBIA REAL ESTATE DIRECTORY SERVICE **4840**

LUSK'S DISTRICT OF COLUMBIA REAL ESTATE DIRECTORY SERVICE (US/0196-4119) [05806999] **4840**

LUSK'S EAST SUFFOLK COUNTY REAL ESTATE DIRECTORY (US/0363-0668) [02407133] **4840**

LUSK'S FAIRFAX COUNTY, VIRGINIA REAL ESTATE DIRECTORY SERVICE (US/0197-0305) [05951508] **4840**

LUSK'S MONTGOMERY COUNTY, MARYLAND, ASSESSMENT DIRECTORY (US/0557-4447) [05261138] 4736, **4840**

LUSK'S NORTHERN VIRGINIA REAL ESTATE GUIDE (US/0745-8878) [09541585] **4840**

LUSK'S PRINCE WILLIAM COUNTY REAL ESTATE DIRECTORY SERVICE (US/0094-8713) [01795333] **4840**

LUSO-BRAZILIAN REVIEW (US/0024-7413) [01756283] **1078**

● LUSOAMERICANO CALIFORNIA (US/1065-8262) [26755783] **5636**

LUSOAMERICANO (NEWARK, N.J.) (US/0898-9052) [10939653] **5710**

LUSOLT TALK (CN/0226-0115) [07294983] **3229**

LUSTRUM (GW/0024-7421) [01756285] **1078**

LUTE NEWS : THE LUTE SOCIETY NEWSLETTER (UK) [19864722] **4129**

LUTE SOCIETY OF AMERICA *See* JOURNAL OF THE LUTE SOCIETY OF AMERICA, INC **4127**

LUTE SOCIETY OF AMERICA QUARTERLY (US) [19855411] **4129**

LUTE : THE JOURNAL OF THE LUTE SOCIETY, THE (UK) [09344807] **5233**

LUTHER (GW/0340-6210) [01779499] **5062**

LUTHER FAMILY NEWSLETTER, THE (US/0896-4602) [16436942] **2458**

LUTHERAN AMBASSADOR, THE (US/0746-3413) [01588332] **5062**

LUTHERAN BROTHERHOOD BOND *See* BOND (MINNEAPOLIS, MINN.) **5057**

LUTHERAN (CHICAGO, ILL. : 1988) (US/0024-743X) [17500997] **5062**

LUTHERAN CHURCH DIRECTORY FOR THE UNITED STATES (US/0363-4051) [02439095] **5063**

LUTHERAN CHURCH IN AMERICA *See* YEARBOOK / LUTHERAN CHURCH IN AMERICA **5069**

LUTHERAN CHURCH IN AMERICA. EASTERN CANADA SYNOD. CONVENTION *See* MINUTES - ANNUAL CONVENTION OF THE EASTERN CANADA SYNOD, LUTHERAN CHURCH IN AMERICA **5064**

LUTHERAN COMMENTATOR (US/0894-0304) [15732425] **4975**

LUTHERAN COUNCIL IN THE U.S.A. NEWS BUREAU (NEWS RELEASE) (US/0361-8757) [01771118] **5063**

LUTHERAN COUNCIL IN THE UNITED STATES OF AMERICA. NEWS BUREAU *See* LUTHERAN COUNCIL IN THE U.S.A. NEWS BUREAU (NEWS RELEASE) **5063**

LUTHERAN DIGEST, THE (US/0458-497X) [01756294] **5063**

LUTHERAN EDUCATION (US/0024-7448) [01756295] 1762, **5063**

LUTHERAN EDUCATOR (US/0458-4988) [01589057] 5063, **1762**

LUTHERAN FORUM (US/0024-7456) [01585943] **5063**

LUTHERAN JOURNAL, THE (US/0360-6945) [02605705] **5063**

LUTHERAN LAYMAN, THE (US/0024-7464) [01681377] 5063, **4975**

LUTHERAN LIBRARIES (US/0024-7472) [01756299] 5063, **3229**

LUTHERAN PARTNERS (US/0885-9922) [12536706] **5063**

LUTHERAN PERSPECTIVE *CEASED*. (US/0279-4462) [07879415] **5063**

LUTHERAN QUARTERLY (GETTYSBURG. 1949) (US/0024-7499) [15995487] **4975**

LUTHERAN SCHOOL OF THEOLOGY AT CHICAGO *See* ALUMNI DIRECTORY / LUTHERAN SCHOOL OF THEOLOGY AT CHICAGO **1098**

LUTHERAN SENTINEL (US/0024-7510) [01715484] **5063**

LUTHERAN SPOKESMAN (US/0024-7537) [01756306] **5063**

LUTHERAN SYNOD QUARTERLY, THE (US/0360-9685) [01756308] **5063**

LUTHERAN, THE (AT) [01642392] **5062**

LUTHERAN THEOLOGICAL JOURNAL (AT/0024-7553) [01776505] **5063**

LUTHERAN THEOLOGICAL SEMINARY, GETTYSBURG, PA *See* BULLETIN - LUTHERAN THEOLOGICAL SEMINARY, GETTYSBURG **5057**

LUTHERAN VISTAS (US) [01645947] **5063**

LUTHERAN WITNESS REPORTER (US/0024-7588) [01756311] **5063**

LUTHERAN WITNESS (ST. LOUIS), THE (US/0024-757X) [01756310] **5063**

LUTHERAN WOMAN TODAY (US/0896-209X) [16954116] **5063**

LUTHERAN WOMEN'S MISSIONARY LEAGUE QUARTERLY ECHO *See* LWML QUARTERLY ECHO **4975**

LUTHERAN WOMEN'S MISSIONARY LEAGUE QUARTERLY ECHO / NEBRASKA DISTRICT SOUTH (US/8750-5207) [11486455] **5063**

LUTHERAN WORLD FEDERATION *See* LWF DOCUMENTATION **4975**

LUTHERAN WORLD FEDERATION. NEWS SERVICE *See* INFORMATION - LUTHERAN WORLD FEDERATION NEWS SERVICE **5061**

LUTHERANS ALERT, NATIONAL *CEASED*. (US/0361-2392) [01695896] **5063**

LUTHERISCHE KIRCHE (GW) [05808906] **5063**

LUTHERISCHE MONATSHEFTE (GW/0024-7618) [01585768] **4975**

LUTHERISCHE THEOLOGIE UND KIRCHE (GW) [03175179] **4975**

LUTHERJAHRBUCH (GW/0342-0914) [01756287] **4975**

LUTHERSK KIRKETIDENDE (NO/0332-5431) [01606782] **5063**

LUTRA (NE/0024-7634) [04687872] **5590**

LUTRIN (CN/0226-868X) [06859951] **4129**

LUTTE DE CLASSE 1986 (FR/0295-5385) [l02955385] **4543**

LUTTE OUVRIERE (MONTREAL) (CN/0701-8746) [04253179] **4543**

LUTTES URBAINES (CN/0228-684X) [07805553] **2827**

LUTUKKA (FI/0782-050X) [I0782050X] **2697**

LUVERNE JOURNAL (AND NEWS), THE (US) [12061522] **5627**

LUX BIBLICA : RIVISTA TEOLOGICA SEMESTRALE EDITA A CURA DI IBEI E VERITAS EDIZIONI (IT) **4975**

LUX; LA REVUE DE L'ECLAIRAGE (FR/0024-7669) [09542426] **2071**

LUXEMBOURG. SERVICE CENTRAL DE LA STATISTIQUE ET DES ETUDES ECONOMIQUES *See* CAHIERS ECONOMIQUES **1530**

LUXEMBOURG. SERVICE CENTRAL DE LA STATISTIQUE ET DES ETUDES ECONOMIQUES *See* BULLETIN DU STATEC / SERVICE CENTRAL DE LA STATISTIQUE ET DES ETUDES ECONOMIQUES **1530**

LUXEMBURG : ENERGIEWIRTSCHAFT (GW) [05064402] **1949**

LUXEMBURG. MINISTERE DE L'EDUCATION NATIONALE. SERVICE DES STATISTIQUES *See* STATISTIQUES DE L'ENSEIGNEMENT SECONDAIRE **1798**

LUXEMBURG. MINISTERE DE L'EDUCATION NATIONALE. SERVICE DES STATISTIQUES *See* INFORMATIONS STATISTIQUES - MINISTERE DE L'EDUCATION NATIONALE, SERVICE DES STATISTIQUES **1752**

LUXEMBURG. MINISTERE DES FINANCES *See* BUDGET DE L'ETAT - MINISTERE DES FINANCES **4714**

LUXEMBURG NEWS (US) [13776588] **5768**

LUXEMBURG : WIRTSCHAFT IN ZAHLEN UND WIRTSCHAFTSDOKUMENTATION (GW) [06261801] **1573**

LUZ (CLAYTON, MO.), LA (US/0886-179X) [05003646] **3300**

LUZ (NEW YORK) (US/0271-0846) [06545855] **5188**

LUZIFER-AMOR (GW/0933-3347) [19964761] 3930, **4603**

LVIVSKYI DERZHAVNYI UNIVERSYTET IM. IV. FRANKA *See* VISNYK. SERIIA FILOLOHICHNA **3332**

LVNW NIEUWS (NE) **5295**

LVOV. UNIVERSITET *See* VISNIK LVIVSKOGO ORDENA LENINA DERZARNOGO UNIVERSITETU IM. IV. FRANKA. SERIJA MEHANIKO-MATEMATICNA **3540**

LWF DOCUMENTATION (GW/0174-1756) [04609138] **4975**

● LWML QUARTERLY ECHO (US/1066-5749) [27001521] **4975**

● LYCEUM TECHNICAL JOURNAL (US/1048-8693) [21063874] **1985**

LYCEUM TIMES, THE (US/0897-9715) [17683149] **3409**

LYCHNOS (SW/0076-1648) [09859076] **5126**

LYCHNOS ARSBOK (SW) **5126**

LYCHNOS: LARDOMSHISTORISKA SAMFUNDETS ARSBOK (SW/0076-1648) [01782323] **5126**

LYCOMING COUNTY GENEALOGICAL SOCIETY NEWSLETTER (US) **2458**

LYCOMING HISTORICAL SOCIETY. JOURNAL *See* JOURNAL OF THE LYCOMING COUNTY HISTORICAL SOCIETY, THE **2742**

LYD & [I.E. OG] BILDE (NO) [06002573] **4129**

LYDIA (IT) **2489**

LYLE OFFICIAL ANTIQUES REVIEW, THE (US) [01791366] **251**

LYLE OFFICIAL ARMS AND ARMOUR REVIEW, THE (UK) [06874012] **4049**

LYLE OFFICIAL ARTS REVIEW, THE (UK) [03553378] **357**

LYLE OFFICIAL BOOKS REVIEW, THE (UK) [06873951] **419**

LYMAN COUNTY ADVOCATE *See* ADVOCATE-LEADER, THE **5743**

LYMAN COUNTY ARGUS-LEADER *See* ADVOCATE-LEADER, THE **5743**

LYMAN ENTOMOLOGICAL MUSEUM AND RESEARCH LABORATORY *See* LYMAN ENTOMOLOGICAL MUSEUM AND RESEARCH LABORATORY MEMOIR **4090**

LYMAN ENTOMOLOGICAL MUSEUM AND RESEARCH LABORATORY MEMOIR (CN/0318-6784) [02442202] 5611, **4090**

LYMPHOCYTES SHEFFIELD (UK/0142-8179) [I01428179] **490**

LYMPHOKINE AND CYTOKINE RESEARCH (US/1056-5477) [23707684] **538**

LYMPHOLOGY (US/0024-7766) [01756333] **3773**

LYNCH INTERNATIONAL INVESTMENT SURVEY, THE (US) [09036591] **905**

LYNCHBURG NEWS (US/8750-2674) [11197093] **5729**

LYNDEN TRIBUNE, THE (US) [17398139] **5761**

LYNDON B. JOHNSON SCHOOL OF PUBLIC AFFAIRS *See* POLICY RESEARCH PROJECT REPORT **4674**

LYNN/LINN LINEAGE QUARTERLY (US/0892-418X) [15187485] **2459**

LYNN RIVER REVIEW (CN/0821-1485) [09766558] **3346**

LYNX JAHRBUCH (GW) [01783873] **2519**

LYON CHIRURGICAL (SZ/0024-7782) [01756336] **3969**

LYON COUNTY NEWS (GEORGE, IOWA) (US) [16394117] **5671**

LYON COUNTY REPORTER (ROCK RAPIDS, IOWA : 1956) (US) [16221836] **5671**

LYON MEDITERRANEE MEDICAL. MEDECINE DU SUD-EST (FR/0766-5466) [I07665466] **3605**

LYON PHARMACEUTIQUE (FR/0024-7804) [09554684] **4314**

LYONS DAILY NEWS (1929) (US/1040-1504) [12407011] **5677**

LYONS TEACHER-NEWS (US/0093-0164) [01791105] **4129**

LYRA (GUTTENBERG, N.J.) (US/0897-6716) [17602582] **3409**

LYRIC (CHRISTIANSBURG, VA.), THE (US/0024-7820) [01756348] **3465**

LYRIC OPERA OF CHICAGO *See* LYRIC OPERA OF CHICAGO ANNUAL REPORT, THE **4129**

LYRIC OPERA OF CHICAGO ANNUAL REPORT, THE (US) [14637425] **4129**

LYRIKVANNEN (SW/0460-0762) [01775851] **3409**

LYSISTRATA (VICTORIA) (CN/0318-1480) [02441699] **5560**

LYSOSOMES *See* LYSOSOMES & ENDOCYTOSIS **3605**

LYSOSOMES & ENDOCYTOSIS (UK/1351-5322) 490, **3605**

LYSOSOMES IN BIOLOGY AND PATHOLOGY (NE) [11522968] **463**

M A A E BULLETIN (CN/0704-6189) [03790829] **357**

M.A.A.E. JOURNAL (CN/0229-7477) [08028131] **357**

M.A.C (US/0741-0379) [08085142] **2482**

M + A KALENDER *See* M + A MESSEPLANER **762**

M + A MESSEPLANER (GW) **762**

M + A MESSEPLANER FUR MESSEN UND AUSSTELLUNGEN INTERNATIONAL (GW) [15562741] **929**

M.A.N-ROLAND REVUE (GW) [09316274] **4566**

M-+-A-REPORT 1982 (GW/0723-3361) [I07233361] 844, **820**

M.A.S.B.O. NEWS (CN/1186-608X) [24279926] 691, **1762**

M & A EUROPE (SZ) [18767617] 797, **691**

M & A JAPAN (UK) **797**

M & B PHARMACEUTICAL BULLETIN (UK/0460-2390) [05318486] **4314**

M & C. MEETING & CONGRESSI (IT/0390-2692) [I03902692] **762**

M & M, D & D (FR/0266-0245) [15199847] **4314**

M & MD : MARKETING AND MEDIA DECISIONS (US) [21516561] **762**

M & S TIMES (US/0894-7473) [16218620] 1616, **5386**

M. B. E. T. A. NEWSLETTER (CN/0381-6788) [03031623] 1762, **691**

M B NEWS (US/0192-2491) [03826757] **357**

M BOOK (US) [05811345] **1834**

M.C.G.S. REPORTER (US/0740-1531) [06559263] **2459**

M/C HEALTH AND FITNESS NEWSLETTER (AT) [12849331] **4789**

M D A INFORMATION *CEASED*. (UK/0309-6653) [I03096653] **4091**

M.D. COMPUTING (US/0724-6811) [09798478] **1268**

M.D.P. MONOGRAFIAS DE PEDIATRIA (SP) **3906**

M D T, MOTORCYCLE DEALER & TRADE (CN/0705-2030) [03991807] **4081**

M/E/A/N/I/N/G (NEW YORK, N.Y.) (US/1040-8576) [17793001] **324**

M.E. MEETINGS & EXPOSITIONS (US/0093-0482) [01791791] **691**

M.E.N. ECONOMIC WEEKLY / MIDDLE EAST NEWS (UA) [04470915] **1503**

M.E.T.U. JOURNAL OF THE FACULTY OF ARCHITECTURE *SUSPENDED*. (TU) [02587583] **303**

M-G FINANCIAL WEEKLY. INDUSTRISCOPE EDITION, THE (US/0148-284X) [02563098] **905**

M.H.E.T.A. JOURNAL (CN/0315-9329) [02247560] 1900, **2791**

M I C MISSION NEWS (CN/0315-9655) [02443240] **4975**

M.I.M.S. IRELAND (IE/0300-8223) [10103434] **3605**

M.I. MONTAJES E INSTALACIONES (SP/0210-184X) [I0210184X] **2606**

M.I.R.L. REPORT (US/0362-1553) [02194410] 1441, **2143**

M. I. T. EAST ASIAN SCIENCE SERIES (US) [02377699] **5126**

M. MACINTOSH MAGAZINE (IT/1120-8465) [I11208465] 1277, **1264**

M (NEW YORK, N.Y. 1991) *CEASED*. (US/1063-9704) [24924830] **1085**

M.O.C.A. BULLETIN (AT/0819-9000) [I08199000] 4091, **357**

M P & P, METAL-WORKING PRODUCTION & PURCHASING (CN/0383-090X) [02754689] **4007**

M/R (US/0885-470X) [12680069] **2537**

M.R.S.O. REPORT (CH/0377-1571) [01797614] **2143**

M.R.S. REPORT (UK) [09877847] **196**

M; REVIJA (YU) [01794925] **2519**

M.S.L.A.V.A. JOURNAL (CN/0315-9124) [02060917] **3229**

M S ONTARIO (CN/0707-0934) [04631891] **3837**

M-SERIES MONOGRAPHS (AT) 1503, **5483**

M T P INTERNATIONAL REVIEW OF SCIENCE (UK) [02254892] **5126**

M5V MAGAZINE *CEASED*. (CN/1197-9704) [24860999] **324**

MA BERICHTSBAND (GW) [09070452] **5251**

MA CAISSE D'ECONOMIE (CN/0704-0881) [03980055] **1542**

MA-KO-SSU CHU I YEN CHIU TSUNG KAN / MAKESIZHUYIYANJIU (CC) [11604544] **4543**

MA REPORT (FAIRFAX, VA.), THE (US/1042-4075) [19038159] **3674**

MA TSUI HSUEH TSA CHIH *See* ACTA ANAESTHESIOLOGICA SINICA **3680**

MAA- JA METSATALOUS (FI/0357-5527) [10236140] 2387, **105**

MAA- JA METSATALOUS HELSINKI. 1988 (FI/0784-8404) [I07848404] 105, **154**

MAA NEWS (CN/0821-2422) [09511120] **357**

MAA NOTES (US) [11620788] **3517**

MAADHYAM : BIMONTHLY ABOUT FILMS, FILMMAKERS & FILM SOCIETIES (II) [08302519] **4074**

MAADINI (CG/0250-538X) [02239999] **2143**

MAALAISKUNTIEN JA KUNTAINLIITTOJEN TUNTIPALKKAISTEN TYONTEKIJOIDEN PALKAT (FI) [02243700] **4663**

MAALIM THAQAFIYAH (TS) [25382741] **2506**

MAALOT (IS) [06885558] **1762**

MAANDBERICHT GEZONDHEIDSSTATISTIEK (NE) [08843725] **4789**

MAANDBLAD VOOR ARBEIDSOMSTANDIGHEDEN *See* ARBEIDSOMSTANDIGHEDEN **2859**

MAANDBLAD VOOR BEDRIJFSADMINISTRATIE EN-ORGANISATIE (NE/0005-7622) [06685838] **4212**

MAANDBULLETIN BUITENLANDSE HANDEL EEG (NE) **5332**

MAANDELIJKSCH OVERSICHT DER WEERSGESTELDHEID (NE) [06420076] **1430**

MAANDELIJKSCH OVERSICHT DER WEERSGESTELDHEID IN NEDERLAND *See* MAANDOVERZICHT VAN HET WEER IN NEDERLAND / KONINKLIJK NEDERLANDS METEOROLOGISCH INSTITUUT **1430**

MAANDELIJKSE MEDEDELINGEN - INSPECTIE VOOR HET BRANDWEERWEZEN (NE) [02245010] **619**

MAANDOVERZICHT VAN HET WEER IN NEDERLAND / KONINKLIJK NEDERLANDS METEOROLOGISCH INSTITUUT (NE) [08376400] **1430**

MAANDSCHRIFT CBS (NE) **5332**

MAANDSCHRIFT ECONOMIE (NE/0013-0486) [06381337] **1503**

MAANDSTATISTIEK BOUWNIJVERHEID (NE/0166-9338) [01794362] 619, **633**

MAANDSTATISTIEK FINANCIEWEZEN (NE) [01794276] 797, **731**

MAANDSTATISTIEK INTERNATIONAL WEGVERVOER (NE) [25898175] **5386**

MAANDSTATISTIEK POLITIE EN JUSTITIE (NE/0548-1937) [02518269] 3005, **3082**

MAANDSTATISTIEK RECHTSBESCHERMING EN VEILIGHEID (NE/0169-9385) [13782817] 3169, **3082**

MAANDSTATISTIEK VAN BEVOLKING EN VOLKSGEZONDHEID (NE/0024-8711) [02518314] **4789**

MAANDSTATISTIEK VAN DE BINNELANDSE HANDEL EN DIENSTVERLENING (NE) [05040757] **844**

MAANDSTATISTIEK VAN DE BINNENLANDSE HANDEL EN DIENSTVERLENING (NE) [05096592] **1616**

MAANDSTATISTIEK VAN DE BOUWNIJVERHEID *See* MAANDSTATISTIEK BOUWNIJVERHEID **633**

MAANDSTATISTIEK VAN DE BUITENLANDSE HANDEL (NE/0923-1668) [20655231] **844**

MAANDSTATISTIEK VAN DE BUITENLANDSE HANDEL PER LAND (NE/0024-8746) [02582764] **844**

MAANDSTATISTIEK VAN DE INDUSTRIE (NE/0470-6684) [02562983] **3482**

MAANDSTATISTIEK VAN DE PRIJZEN (NE) [04486071] 1593, **1536**

MAANDSTATISTIEK VAN HET FINANCIEWEZEN *See* MAANDSTATISTIEK FINANCIEWEZEN **731**

MAANDSTATISTIEK VAN VERKEER EN VERVOER / CENTRAAL BUREAU VOOR DE STATISTIEK. DE (NE) [11562133] **5401**

MAANKAYTTO (FI) [02244699] **2027**

MAANMITTAUSINSINOORI *See* MAANKAYTTO **2027**

MAARAKENNUS JA KULJETUS (FI) [05624008] **2027**

MAARAV (US/0149-5712) [03522603] **3300**

MAARIF (IR) [13865011] **4352**

MAARIV (IS) [01680810] **5804**

MAAS JOURNAL OF ISLAMIC SCIENCE (II/0970-1672) [11742420] **5043**

MAASAAMUUTTO MUUTON SUUNNAN MUKAAN KUNNITTAIN ... (FI) [10161012] **4554**

MAASGOUW, DE (NE/0166-0314) [02344093] **2697**

MAATALOUSTILASTOLLINEN KUUKAUSIKATSAUS. MONTHLY REVIEW OF AGRICULTURAL STATISTICS (FI) [03375926] 106, **154**

MAATILAREKISTERI (FI/0785-7500) [11561372] **106**

MAATILATALOUDEN YRITYS- JA TULOTILASTO ... TULO- JA VEROTUSTIEDOT (FI) [10142023] **106**

MAATSCHAPPIJ BELANGEN (NE) **844**

MAATSCHAPPIJ DER NEDERLANDSE LETTERKUNDE TE LEIDEN *See* JAARBOEK - MAATSCHAPPIJ DER NEDERLANDSE LETTERKUNDE TE LEIDEN **5232**

MAATSTAF (NE/0024-8851) [02336535] 3409, **3300**

MAB 'S-GRAVENHAGE (NE/0924-6304) [I09246304] **747**

MAB TECHNICAL NOTES (FR/0251-981X) [06071897] **463**

MABLETON NEIGHBOR, THE (US/0192-2483) [04974671] **5654**

MABON (UK/0024-886X) [03363633] **324**

MABTON PRESS, THE (US) [17415809] **5761**

MABUE HA-NAHAL (IS) [07418239] **5051**

MAC/CHICAGO (CHICAGO, ILL.) (US/1045-5825) [20156884] **1193**

MAC FLYER *See* MAC FORUM: THE JOURNAL OF THE MILITARY AIRLIFT COMMAND, THE **4049**

MAC FORUM *See* MOBILITY FORUM : THE JOURNAL OF THE AIR MOBILITY COMMAND, THE **28**

MAC FORUM: THE JOURNAL OF THE MILITARY AIRLIFT COMMAND, THE (US) [25207664] 28, **4049**

MAC HOME JOURNAL (US) **1268**

MAC INFORMATIQUE (FR) **1193**

● MAC REVISTA (BL) [26970693] **324**

MAC SUBJECTS (US/0899-1642) [18054874] **1194**

MAC-TALLA - CLAN MACQUARRIE OF ATLANTIC CANADA (CN/0821-6290) [09751857] **2459**

MAC TITLES IN PRINT (US/0891-0243) [14543646] **1194**

MACACADEMY MENTOR *CEASED*. (US) **1194**

MACADAM NICE (FR/1164-4079) [I11644079] 2827, **5441**

MACADEMIC. CD-ROM (US) **1224**

MACAE ESPIRITA (BL) [05712598] **4975**

MACAN : WIRTSCHAFTLICHE ENTWICKLUNG (GW) [02356045] **1573**

MACAO. DIRECCAO DOS SERVICOS DE FINANCAS *See* ORCAMENTO GERAL PARA O ANO ECONOMICO DE ... / REPUBLICA PORTGUESA, GOVERNO DE MACAU, SERVICOS DE FINANCAS **4739**

MACAO. REPARTICAO DOS SERVICOS DE ESTATISTICA *See* BOLETIM MENSUAL DE ESTATISTICA **5323**

MACAO. REPARTICAO PROVINCIAL DOS SERVICOS DE FINANCAS. ORCAMENTO GERAL PARA O ANO ECONOMICO *See* ORCAMENTO GERAL PARA O ANO ECONOMICO DE ... / REPUBLICA PORTGUESA, GOVERNO DE MACAU, SERVICOS DE FINANCAS **4739**

MACAREUX (CANADIAN PARKS SERVICE) *See* JOURNAL LE MACAREUX **4706**

MACAREUX (SERVICE CANADIEN DES PARCS) *See* JOURNAL LE MACAREUX (FRENCH EDITION) **4706**

MACARONI

Alphabetical Title Index

MACARONI (MINNEAPOLIS, MINN.) (US/1054-8254) [22978963] **2537**

MACAULAY LAND USE RESEARCH INSTITUTE *See* ANNUAL REPORT / MACAULAY LAND USE RESEARCH INSTITUTE **163**

●MACAUTHORITY (LOUISVILLE, KY.), THE (US/1062-452X) [25625227] **1288**

●MACAUTHORITY SOFTWARE CONNECTION (US/1063-2700) [25955192] **1288**

MACAZINE *See* MACHACKER **1194**

MACBARGAIN CONNECTION NEWSLETTER : MONEY-SAVING NEWS AND INFO ABOUT APPLE MACINTOSH PRODUCTS AND SERVICES (US/1047-8221) [20805634] **1194**

MACCHINE (IT/0024-8959) **2120**

MACCHINE E MOTORI AGRICOLI (IT/0024-8967) [09880015] **159**

MACDONALD PHYSICS LABORATORY. STORMY WEATHER GROUP *See* SCIENTIFIC REPORT - MCGILL UNIVERSITY, STORMY WEATHER GROUP **1434**

MACDONALD PHYSICS LABORATORY. STORMY WEATHER GROUP *See* MCGILL UNIVERSITY. STORMY WEATHER GROUP. TECHNICAL REPORT **1430**

MACE DIALOGUE (CN/0713-6242) [08967724] **1801**

MACEDONIA (REPUBLIC). REPUBLICKI ZAVOD ZA STATISTIKA *See* OSNOVNI UCILISTA VO SRM SPORED GRADSKO-SELSKO PODRACJE **1796**

MACEDONIA (REPUBLIC). REPUBLICKI ZAVOD ZA STATISTIKA *See* IZBORI NA DELEGACII I DELEGATI ZA SOBORITE NA SOBRANIJATA **4698**

MACEDONIAE ACTA ARCHAEOLOGICA (XN/0350-1639) [07122512] **273**

MACEDONIAN REVIEW (XN/0350-3089) [02263737] **2849**

MACH (US) **2795**

MACHACKER (US) **1194**

MACHEN FAMILY COURIER (US/8755-7193) [11390315] **2459**

MACHI & SUMAI (JA/0287-0150) [12000655] **2827**

MACHIAVELLI STUDIES (US/1049-9776) [17373359] 4481, **3409**

MACHIKANEYAMA RONSO : BIGAKUHEN (JA) [03257664] **4352**

MACHIKANEYAMA RONSO : BUNGAKUHEN (JA) [01790189] **3300**

MACHIKANEYAMA RONSO: SHIGAKUHEN (JA) [01790190] 5208, **2850**

MACHIKANEYAMA RONSO: SHINRIGAKU, SHAKAIGAKU, KYOIKUGAKU HEN (JA) [01790192] **5233**

MACHIKANEYAMA RONSO : TETSUGAKUHEN (JA/0387-4818) [01790188] 4352, **2850**

MACHINE AND TOOL DIRECTORY (US) [01868074] **2120**

MACHINE BUILDING INDUSTRY (II/0541-6388) [06231011] **2120**

MACHINE DESIGN (US/0024-9114) [02111909] **2120**

MACHINE-INDUSTRIE / CENTRAAL BUREAU VOOR DE STATISTIEK, HOOFDAFDELING STATISTIEKEN VAN INDUSTRIE EN BOUWNIJVERHEID (NE) [10607970] **1573**

MACHINE INTELLIGENCE AND PATTERN RECOGNITION (NE/0923-0459) [14037359] 1248, **1215**

MACHINE INTELLIGENCE NEWS (UK/0267-0429) [12361744] **1215**

MACHINE KNITTERS SOURCE, THE (US/1049-3700) [21214551] **374**

MACHINE KNITTING MONTHLY (UK/0269-9761) [I02699761] **5184**

MACHINE KNITTING NEWS (UK/0266-8505) [I02668505] **5354**

MACHINE LEARNING (US/0885-6125) [12681958] **1215**

MACHINE MANUAL OF INSTRUCTIONS FOR JUDGES OF ELECTION. PRIMARY ELECTION (US/0272-8389) [06932054] **4663**

MACHINE-MEDIATED LEARNING (US/0732-6718) [08412752] 1900, **1224**

MACHINE OUTIL (FR/0024-9149) [01794493] **2120**

MACHINE TRANSLATION (NE/0922-6567) [20341793] **1194**

MACHINE VIBRATION (US/0939-7418) **2120**

MACHINE VISION AND APPLICATIONS (US/0932-8092) [17899117] **1252**

MACHINERIE LOURDE (CN/0319-3977) [02442864] **2120**

MACHINERY & EQUIPMENT MRO (CN/0831-8603) [15241420] **2120**

MACHINERY & EQUIPMENT PRICING GUIDE (US/0091-8377) [01783655] **2120**

MACHINERY AND PRODUCTION ENGINEERING (UK/0024-919X) [02355166] **2120**

MACHINERY BUYERS GUIDE (UK) [05849017] 2120, **950**

MACHINERY CLASSIFIED (UK) **2120**

MACHINERY INDUSTRIES, EXCEPT ELECTRICAL MACHINERY (1986) (CN/0835-0132) [18315427] **2121**

MACHINERY MARKET (UK/0024-9211) [I00249211] **2121**

MACHINERY OUTLOOK (US/8756-923X) [11742558] **1616**

MACHINERY'S ANNUAL BUYER'S GUIDE *See* MACHINERY BUYERS GUIDE **950**

MACHINERY'S HANDBOOK (US) [04525210] **2121**

MACHINES PRODUCTION PARIS (FR/0047-536X) [I0047536X] **2121**

MACHINING TECHNOLOGY QUARTERLY (US) **3482**

MACHINISME AGRICOLE TROPICAL *SUSPENDED.* (FR/0242-2565) [09880410] **159**

MACHINIST CANADA, THE (CN/0824-2453) [10032175] **1689**

MACHINIST, THE *CEASED.* (US/0047-5378) [01928326] **1688**

MACHINOEXPORT (RU) [07475646] **2121**

MACHLETT CATHODE PRESS (US/0008-7882) [01850516] **2071**

MACINTOSH ADVERTISING REPORT (US/1058-7411) [24404434] **762**

MACINTOSH-AIDED DESIGN *CEASED.* (US/1048-8995) [21066410] **1194**

MACINTOSH BUSINESS LETTER, THE (US/0894-9603) [16363786] **1194**

MACINTOSH BUSINESS REVIEW *CEASED.* (US/0899-725X) [18169862] 1194, **691**

MACINTOSH BUYER'S GUIDE, THE *CEASED.* (US/1041-8156) [15058964] **1194**

MACINTOSH CONSTRUCTION FORUM (US/1055-7350) [21020035] 303, **1194**

MACINTOSH DISCOUNT REPORTER NEWSLETTER, THE (US/1048-3535) [20927810] **1194**

MACINTOSH MAGAZINE (NE) **1194**

MACINTOSH MARKET REPORT (US/1044-131X) [19692187] **1194**

MACINTOSH MARKET REPORT : AD ANALYSIS *CEASED.* (US) **1194**

●MACINTOSH TIPS & TRICKS (PRINT) (US/1070-6720) [28447746] **1194**

MACINTOUCH (US/0887-9648) [13441416] **1194**

MACKAY PORT AUTHORITY *See* ANNUAL REPORT / MACKAY PORT AUTHORITY **5447**

MACKENZIE DELTA RESEARCH PROJECT *See* MDRP **2828**

MACKENZIE DRIFT (CN/0228-0558) [06758167] **5789**

MACKENZIE OUTREACH (CN/0824-6297) [11054292] **357**

MACKINAC, THE (US/0744-5288) [08333559] **2177**

MACKINTOSH YEARBOOK OF WEST EUROPEAN ELECTRONICS DATA *See* YEARBOOK OF WORLD ELECTRONICS DATA ... VOL. 1, WEST EUROPE **2086**

MACKLIN MIRROR (CN/0706-7240) [04955063] **5789**

MACKNIT *CEASED.* (US/0886-1188) [12871898] **5184**

MACKSVILLE ENTERPRISE (US) [12649586] **5677**

MACLAREN STANDARD, THE (US/0736-8445) [09234588] **2459**

MACLEAN-HUNTER RESEARCH BUREAU *See* BRAND RECOGNITION STUDY : OFFICE EQUIPMENT & METHODS **922**

MACLEAN-HUNTER RESEARCH BUREAU *See* MARKET RESEARCH FACTS AND TRENDS FROM MACLEAN-HUNTER RESEARCH BUREAU **1504**

MACLEAN'S (CN/0024-9262) [01756390] **2489**

MACMILLAN DIRECTORY OF INTERNATIONAL ADVERTISERS AND AGENCIES *See* STANDARD DIRECTORY OF INTERNATIONAL ADVERTISERS & AGENCIES **766**

MACMILLAN DIRECTORY OF LEADING PRIVATE COMPANIES *See* DIRECTORY OF LEADING PRIVATE COMPANIES, INCLUDING CORPORATE AFFILIATIONS **666**

MACNEIL/LEHRER REPORT. BROADCAST REVIEW AND INDEX, THE (US/0192-1460) [05002620] **4528**

MACNEWS *CEASED.* (IT) **1194**

MACNEWS *CEASED.* (US/0893-3480) [15501795] **691**

MACOLIN (SZ) **2850**

MACOMB COUNTY DENTAL SOCIETY (MICH.) *See* JOURNAL : MACOMB COUNTY DENTAL SOCIETY **1326**

MACOMB COUNTY LEGAL NEWS (US/0024-9289) [04049713] **3005**

MACOMB DAILY, THE (US/1071-1406) [26884283] **5692**

MACON BEACON (MACON, MISS. : 1860) (US) [10232493] **5701**

MACON COUNTY TIMES (US/0745-5976) [09355107] **5745**

MACON MAGAZINE (US) [21880900] **2537**

MACON TELEGRAPH (US/1054-2485) [22789733] **5654**

MACOUPIN COUNTY ENQUIRER (US) [17109005] **5661**

MACPLAS (IT/0394-3453) [I03943453] **4456**

MACPREPRESS (US/1058-6601) [24351784] **2489**

MACPUBLISHING *CEASED.* (UK) **1194**

MACRAE'S BLUE BOOK (1986) (US/0886-9189) [13034862] **1616**

MACRAE'S DIRECTORY OF FIRMS MARKETING THROUGH MANUFACTURERS' REPRESENTATIVES (US/0749-1093) [11080074] **3482**

MACRAE'S INDUSTRIAL DIRECTORY ARIZONA, NEW MEXICO (US/0739-8476) [09832274] **1616**

MACRAE'S INDUSTRIAL DIRECTORY. COLORADO, UTAH, NEVADA (US/0740-6126) [09965227] **1616**

MACRAE'S INDUSTRIAL DIRECTORY. IOWA, NEBRASKA (US/0740-428X) [09952675] **1616**

MACRAE'S INDUSTRIAL DIRECTORY. MARYLAND, D.C., DELAWARE (US/0740-2929) [09912080] 4007, **3483**

MACRAE'S INDUSTRIAL DIRECTORY. MICHIGAN (US/0740-6096) [09965224] **1616**

MACRAE'S INDUSTRIAL DIRECTORY. MISSOURI (US/0740-607X) [09965209] **1616**

MACRAE'S INDUSTRIAL DIRECTORY. OREGON (US/0740-610X) [09965230] **1616**

MACRAE'S INDUSTRIAL DIRECTORY. WASHINGTON STATE (US/0740-6134) [09965282] **1616**

MACRAE'S INDUSTRIAL DIRECTORY. WISCONSIN (US/0740-6053) [09965197] **1616**

MACRAE'S STATE INDUSTRIAL DIRECTORY. CONNECTICUT, RHODE ISLAND (US/1041-2638) [18702174] **1616**

MACRAE'S STATE INDUSTRIAL DIRECTORY. MAINE, NEW HAMPSHIRE, VERMONT (US/0891-4605) [13783179] **1616**

MACRAE'S STATE INDUSTRIAL DIRECTORY. MARYLAND, DISTRICT OF COLUMBIA, DELAWARE (US/0740-2929) [14517654] 4007, **3483**

MACRAE'S STATE INDUSTRIAL DIRECTORY. MASSACHUSETTS, RHODE ISLAND (US/0740-4689) [14708729] **1616**

MACRAE'S STATE INDUSTRIAL DIRECTORY. NEW JERSEY (US/0891-2629) [14151094] **1616**

MACRAE'S STATE INDUSTRIAL DIRECTORY. NEW YORK STATE (US/0885-033X) [12176653] **1616**

MACRAE'S STATE INDUSTRIAL DIRECTORY. NORTH CAROLINA, SOUTH CAROLINA, VIRGINIA (US/0888-3793) [13552725] **1616**

MACRAE'S STATE INDUSTRIAL DIRECTORY. PENNSYLVANIA (US/0740-4298) [14392927] **1617**

MACRO (NE) [01788117] **397**

MACROECONOMICS (GUILFORD, CONN.) (US) [09740317] **1503**

●MACROMEDIA USER JOURNAL (US/1065-3929) [26597480] **1115**

MACROMIND DEVELOPER LETTER *See* MACROMEDIA USER JOURNAL **1115**

MACROMOLECULAR ALTERATION AND REPAIR IN CARCINOGENESIS (US) [03458417] **3820**

●MACROMOLECULAR CHEMISTRY AND PHYSICS (SZ/1022-1352) [29693904] 4411, **985**

MACROMOLECULAR CHEMISTRY (ROYAL SOCIETY OF CHEMISTRY (GREAT BRITAIN)) (UK/0144-2988) [07218658] **1044**

●MACROMOLECULAR RAPID COMMUNICATIONS (SZ/1022-1336) [29608533] **985**

MACROMOLECULAR REPORTS (US/1060-278X) [24072830] 5126, **985**

MACROMOLECULAR STRUCTURES (UK/0963-6986) [25545551] **985**

●MACROMOLECULAR SYMPOSIA (GW/1022-1360) [29906321] **985**

MACROMOLECULAR SYNTHESES (US/0076-2091) [01756393] **985**

MACROMOLECULAR SYNTHESES. COLLECTIVE VOLUME (US/0163-6189) [04090352] **1044**

●MACROMOLECULAR THEORY AND SIMULATIONS (SZ/1022-1344) [29608471] **985**

MACROMOLECULES (US/0024-9297) [01268535] **1044**

MACROPHAGES SHEFFIELD (UK/0142-8195) [I01428195] 490, **3605**

MACT CHICAGO *See* MEN OF ALL COLORS TOGETHER CHICAGO : [NEWSLETTER] **2795**

MACTECH MAGAZINE (US/1067-8360) [27246054] **1280**

MACTIMES (US/0891-365X) [14714110] **1194**

MACTUTOR (US/8756-8810) [11693627] **1280**

MACTUTOR COMPANION SOURCE CODE DISKS (US) **1280**

MACUSER LONDON (UK/0269-3275) [I02693275] **1268**

MACUSER (NEW YORK, N.Y.) (US/0884-0997) [12305693] **1268**

MACWEEK (US/0892-8118) [15262373] **1238**

MACWORLD (LONDON) (UK/0957-2341) [25210671] **1194**

MACWORLD (SAN FRANCISCO, CALIF.) (US/0741-8647) [10221175] **1268**

MAD (NEW YORK, N.Y.) (US/0024-9319) [01775852] **4863**

MAD RIVER (US/1054-2655) [22806664] **3409**

MADAGASCAR RENOUVEAU (MG) [07118719] **2641**

MADAGASKAR : ENERGIEWIRTSCHAFT (GW) [05064432] **1950**

MADAME (GW/0024-936X) [I0024936X] 1085, **404**

MADAME AU FOYER (CN/0541-6620) [02400262] **5560**

MADAME FIGARO (FR) [09545056] **1085**

MADAME JOURS DE FRANCE (FR/1164-0359) [I11640359] **2519**

MADAMINA (US/0740-5812) [07818152] 386, **4129**

MADCHEN (GW) **1066**

MADDEN FAMILY NEWSLETTER (US/0883-556X) [12196262] **2459**

MADDUX REPORT, THE (US/0889-0838) [12205874] **691**

MADE IN BIELLA (IT) **844**

MADE IN CANADA. ARTISTS IN BOOKS (CN/0228-7749) [08916729] **357**

MADE IN EUROPE (GW) [02448386] **1617**

MADE IN THE USA (US) [21191479] **1298**

MADE IN TUNISIA (TI) [04066659] **1573**

MADE IN USA **SUSPENDED.** (US/0160-614X) [03725014] **844**

MADELIA TIMES-MESSENGER (US) [01756396] **5697**

MADEMOISELLE (NEW YORK, N.Y. 1935) (US/0024-9394) [01715227] 404, 1085, **5560**

MADERA COUNTY HISTORIAN, THE (US/0464-2910) [06322597] **2745**

MADERA HERITAGE QUARTERLY (US/1061-253X) [25221641] **2459**

MADERA TRIBUNE (US/8750-9571) [11964754] **5636**

MADERA Y SU USO, LA (MX) [21309822] **2402**

MADERPRESS BARCELONA (SP/1131-897X) [I1131897X] **634**

MADHUMATI (II) [03195624] **3409**

MADHYA PRADESH BUDGET IN BRIEF (II) [01606967] **4736**

MADHYA PRADESH (INDIA). DIRECTORATE OF ECONOMICS AND STATISTICS *See* MADHYA PRADESH BUDGET IN BRIEF **4736**

MADHYA PRADESH ITIHASA PARISHAD *See* JOURNAL OF THE MADHYA PRADESH ITIHASA PARISHAD **2656**

MADHYA PRADESH WEEKLY NOTES (II) [06827350] **3005**

MADHYAHNA (II) [03438293] **2506**

MADHYAPRADESA KA RTU EVAM PHASALA PRATIVEDANA / MADHYAPRADESA SASANA, BHU-ABHILEKHA MUKHYALAYA (II) [09519543] **178**

MADILL RECORD, THE (US) [13686183] **5732**

MADISON AVENUE HANDBOOK, THE (US/0076-2148) [01856375] **762**

MADISON CO. MUSINGS (US/1071-1937) [08850336] **2459**

MADISON COUNTY CARRIER (US) **5650**

MADISON COUNTY GENEALOGIST, THE (US/0090-5186) [01785231] **2459**

MADISON COUNTY HERALD (CANTON, MISS. : 1906) (US) [14868244] **5701**

MADISON COUNTY HERITAGE (US/0197-498X) [04582564] **2745**

MADISON COUNTY HISTORICAL SOCIETY (N.Y.) *See* ANNUAL TRADITIONAL CRAFT DAYS **370**

MADISON COUNTY RECORD (US/0889-4205) [14047343] **5627**

MADISON COURIER (MADISON, IND : 1892 : DAILY) (US) [12442598] **5665**

MADISON DAILY LEADER (US) **5744**

MADISON EAGLE, THE (US) [15794867] **5710**

MADISON INSTITUTE NEWSLETTER, THE (US/8755-8874) [11423073] **240**

MADISON MAGAZINE (US/0192-7442) [05105629] **2537**

MADISON MESSENGER (US/0891-2262) [14703669] **5729**

MADISON NEWS (MADISON, KAN. : 1915) (US) [11741958] **5677**

MADISON REVIEW, THE (US) [12800195] 3465, **3409**

MADISON WEEKLY HERALD (MADISON, IND. : 1940) *See* WEEKLY HERALD (MADISON, IND. : 1974) **5668**

MADISON WESTERN GUARD (US) [01623717] **5697**

MADISONIAN, THE (US) [19928349] **5654**

MADISON'S CANADIAN LUMBER DIRECTORY (CN/0316-6414) [02247671] **2402**

MADISON'S CANADIAN LUMBER REPORTER (CN/0715-5468) [09502268] **2402**

MADJALAH HYGIENE PERUSAHAAN, KESEHATAN-KESELAMATAN KERJA, DAN DJAMINAN SOSIAL *See* MAJALAH HYGIENE PERUSAHAAN, KESEHATAN-KESELAMATAN KERJA, DAN JAMINAN SOSIAL **2865**

MADJALAH KETAHANAN NASIONAL *See* KETAHANAN NASIONAL **4048**

MADOC NEWS, THE (CN/0706-7011) [04955127] **5789**

MADOC REVIEW (CN/0712-4910) [09159450] **2537**

MADOQUA (SA) [06121035] **2197**

MADOQUA (WINDHOEK. 1975) (SX/1011-5498) [04280496] **4167**

MADRAS AGRICULTURAL JOURNAL, THE (II/0024-9602) [01696960] **106**

MADRAS INSTITUTE OF DEVELOPMENT STUDIES *See* BULLETIN - MADRAS INSTITUTE OF DEVELOPMENT STUDIES **1549**

MADRAS LAW JOURNAL, THE (II) [06234585] **3005**

MADRAS PIONEER, THE (US) [11325179] **5733**

MADRAS VETERINARY COLLEGE *See* MADRAS VETERINARY COLLEGE ANNUAL, THE **5516**

MADRAS VETERINARY COLLEGE ANNUAL, THE (II/0379-0517) [01756407] 1834, **5516**

MADRES DE PLAZA DE MAYO : [BOLETIN] (AG) [11968015] **5295**

MADRID. BOLSA *See* ANUARIO - BOLSA DE MADRID **891**

MADRID. CASA DE VELAZQUEZ *See* MELANGES DE LA CASA DE VELAZQUEZ **2698**

MADRID FILATELICO (SP) [06382373] **2785**

MADRID (SPAIN). AYUNTAMIENTO *See* REVISTA DE LA BIBLIOTECA, ARCHIVO Y MUSEO DEL AYUNTAMIENTO DE MADRID **3246**

MADRID, UNE (SP/0213-9510) [I02139510] **3605**

MADRIDER MITTEILUNGEN (GW/0418-9744) [02349596] **273**

MADRIGALISTI DELL'ITALIA SETTENTRIONALE / UNIVERSITA DI BOLOGNA, INSTITUTO DI DISCIPLINE DELLA MUSICA (IT) [11742388] **4129**

MADRIKH LA-KASHRUT (US) [03528359] **5051**

MADRONA **CEASED.** (US/0047-5432) [02350570] **3465**

MADRONO (US/0024-9637) [01586614] **517**

MADUREZ (MX) [03603609] **3754**

MAEGYONG HOESA YONGAM (KO) [08203155] **691**

MAELEXO BINAFSI YA WAGOMBEA UBUNGE WA TAIFA VITI MAALUM VYA WANAWAKE (TZ) [19837328] 5560, **4481**

MAELKERITIDENDE (DK/0024-9645) [01716342] **106**

MAENAD (US/0275-5629) [07181679] **5560**

MAENNER-VOGUE (GW/0177-7246) [I01777246] **3995**

MAES ANNUAL REPORT (US) [31002126] **106**

MAESTRO, THE (US/0541-8771) [03262356] **4129**

MAFES RESEARCH HIGHLIGHTS (US/0091-4460) [02252167] 2387, **106**

MAFIA 67 (CN/0711-5504) [08898763] **4663**

MAG (YU) [01786883] **2121**

MAGA, LA (AG) [24959988] **324**

MAGALLA AL-AKADIMIYYA AL-ARABIYYA LI-N-NAQL AL-BAHRI (UA/0304-2855) [07268369] **4178**

MAGALLAT AL-BUHUT AL-ZIRAIYYAT WA-AL-MAWARID AL-MAIYYAT (IQ) [14171112] **106**

MAGALLAT AL-BUHUT AL-ZIRA'IYYAT WA-AL-MAWARID AL-MA'IYYAT. AL-INTAG AL-HAYAWANI (IQ/1012-3466) [I10123466] 5536, **106**

MAGALLAT AL-BUHUT AL-ZIRA'IYYAT WA-AL-MAWARID AL-MA'IYYAT. AL-INTAG AL-NABATI (IQ/1012-3474) [I10123474] 5536, **106**

MAGALLAT AL-BUHUT AL-ZIRA'IYYAT WA-AL-MAWARID AL-MA'IYYAT. AL-TURBAT WA-MASADIR AL-MIYAH (IQ/1012-3482) [I10123482] 178, 5536, **106**

MAGALLAT AL-DILTA LI-L-ULUM (UA/1012-5965) [17291442] **5126**

MAGALLAT AL-GAMIYYAT AL-KIMYAWIYAAT AL-IRAQIWAT (IQ/0379-8321) [03245690] **985**

MAGALLAT GAMIAT AL-MALIK SAUD. AL-ULUM AL-ZIRAIYYAT (SU/1018-3590) [I10183590] **106**

MAGALLAT MAGMA AL-LUGAT AL-ARABIYYAT BI-DIMASQ (SY/0258-1442) [I02581442] **1834**

MAGALLAT MATHAF AL-TARIH AL-TABII (BAGDAD) (IQ/1017-8678) [19666816] **4167**

MAGALLAT TIBB AL-ASNAN AL-URDUNNIYYAT (JO/0258-4638) [11320212] **1329**

MAGASIN AGRICOLE (PARIS) (FR/0763-8922) [I07638922] **106**

MAGASIN FRA DET KONGELIGE BIBLIOTEK (DK/0905-5533) [23926484] **3229**

MAGASIN FRA DET KONGELIGE BIBLIOTEK OG UNIVERSITETSBIBLIOTEKET I (DK/0901-7496) [15626369] **3229**

MAGAZETTE (SHREVEPORT, LA.), THE **CEASED.** (US/0897-8921) [17658556] **2538**

MAGAZIN CSN (XR/0862-7932) [24054603] **1617**

MAGAZIN FUER AMERIKANISTIK (GW/0170-2513) [04141323] **2745**

MAGAZIN ISTORIC (RM/0541-881X) [02263749] **2671**

MAGAZIN KUNST (GW/0024-9777) [01607833] **357**

MAGAZIN'ART (WESTMOUNT) (CN/0844-1707) [20001743] **324**

MAGAZINE (SZ/0460-5047) [06689249] **1617**

MAGAZINE (ABINGTON, PA.) (US/0890-6890) [14351563] **3409**

MAGAZINE AFFAIRES PLUS (CN/1187-0176) [24860657] **797**

MAGAZINE - ALABAMA GENEALOGICAL SOCIETY, INC (US/0568-806X) [06034931] **2459**

MAGAZINE & BOOKSELLER (US/0744-3102) [08177978] **4816**

MAGAZINE ANTIQUES (1971), THE (US/0161-9284) [04063090] **251**

MAGAZINE ARCHIMED **CEASED.** (CN/1188-3758) [25796382] **2482**

MAGAZINE ARTICLE SUMMARIES (CD-ROM ED.) (US/1041-1151) [18647030] 2489, **2497**

MAGAZINE ARTICLE SUMMARIES FULL TEXT ELITE (US/1060-6769) [25055225] 2489, **2497**

MAGAZINE ARTICLE SUMMARIES FULL TEXT SELECT (US/1058-0255) [24184109] 2489, **2497**

MAGAZINE ARTICLE SUMMARIES (PRINT ED.) **CEASED.** (US/0895-3376) [16571503] 2489, **2497**

MAGAZINE ASAP PLUS [COMPUTER FILE] (US) 2489, **2497**

MAGAZINE ASAP SELECT [COMPUTER FILE] (US) 2489, **2497**

MAGAZINE — Alphabetical Title Index

MAGAZINE / BANQUE DE LA REPUBLIQUE D'HAITI (HT/1012-3326) [25702957] **797**

MAGAZINE - CANADIAN ORNAMENTAL PHEASANT AND GAME BIRD ASSOCIATION (CN/0225-0721) [06136379] 5618, **2774**

● MAGAZINE CARGUIDE (CN/1187-9475) [26497723] **5418**

MAGAZINE (CENTRE GEORGES POMPIDOU) (FR) [21138348] **324**

MAGAZINE COLLECTION (US) **2489**

MAGAZINE - COLLEGE OF AGRICULTURE, NAGPUR (II) [04051271] **106**

MAGAZINE - COLLEGE OF ENGINEERING, TRIVANDRUM, INDIA (II) [05218534] **1985**

MAGAZINE CONTRE-JOUR (CN/0821-1329) [09766500] 5418, **4903**

MAGAZINE DE LA COMMUNICATION GRAPHIQUE, LE (CN/0835-9369) [17463639] **380**

MAGAZINE DES ARTS MARTIAUX DU QUEBEC, LE (CN/0713-4290) [09046712] **4903**

MAGAZINE DES UTILISATEURS FORTUNE 1000 (CN/1183-5451) [25313700] **876**

MAGAZINE DES VEHICULES UTILITAIRES ANCIENS, LE (CN/1186-7639) [24368603] **5386**

MAGAZINE DESIGN & PRODUCTION (US/0882-049X) [11730876] 4816, **2922**

MAGAZINE ENFANTS, LE (CN/1187-435X) [25652224] **1066**

MAGAZINE EQUESTRE (1984) (CN/0826-5682) [11355533] **2800**

MAGAZINE EXPRESS [COMPUTER FILE] (US) 2489, **2497**

MAGAZINE FOR CHRISTIAN YOUTH, THE (US/8756-4564) [11570268] 1066, **4975**

MAGAZINE FOR EVERY US VETERAN, THE (US/0364-5169) [02639063] **4049**

MAGAZINE / HUXFORD GENEALOGICAL SOCIETY, INC (US/0747-8445) [06156799] **2459**

MAGAZINE ILLUSTRE (CN/0709-5775) [05696750] **2538**

MAGAZINE INDEX. HOT TOPICS *See* HOT TOPICS **2535**

MAGAZINE INDEX PLUS [COMPUTER FILE] (US) 2489, **2497**

MAGAZINE INDEX SELECT MICROFICHE (US) 2489, **2497**

MAGAZINE INDEX SELECT [COMPUTER FILE] (US) 2489, **2497**

MAGAZINE INDEX, THE (US) [04169596] 2489, **2497**

MAGAZINE INFO TECH (CN) **5126**

MAGAZINE ISSUES (US/0899-7039) [18186317] **4816**

MAGAZINE LITTERAIRE (FR/0024-9807) [01641319] **3409**

● MAGAZINE LUMIERE (CN/1193-6924) [27202949] **4603**

MAGAZINE MARKETS & FEES (CN/1184-1516) [23598653] **4816**

MAGAZINE NCT, LE *See* CAHIERS DE LA NCT **5362**

MAGAZINE (NORTH VANCOUVER) (CN/0711-3692) [09864016] **2538**

MAGAZINE OF ALBEMARLE COUNTY HISTORY, THE (US/0076-2342) [11278685] **2745**

MAGAZINE OF AMERICA'S BEST RECIPES, THE (US/1048-8383) [21052331] 2791, **4194**

● MAGAZINE OF ARTIFICIAL INTELLIGENCE IN FINANCE, THE (US/1074-679X) [29773841] 797, **1194**

MAGAZINE OF BIBLIOGRAPHIES (US) [01785930] **419**

MAGAZINE OF CONCRETE RESEARCH (UK/0024-9831) [01820962] 619, **2027**

MAGAZINE OF HISTORY (US/0882-228X) [11780691] 1900, **2622**

MAGAZINE OF SPECULATIVE POETRY, THE (US/8755-8785) [11427442] **3465**

MAGAZINE OF THE JEFFERSON COUNTY HISTORICAL SOCIETY (US) [05512304] **2745**

MAGAZINE OF VIRGINIA GENEALOGY (US/0743-8095) [10674811] **2459**

MAGAZINE PAIN DE VIE (CN/0847-9380) [20787201] **3605**

MAGAZINE PEOPLE (US/8756-3827) [11056722] **4816**

● MAGAZINE PROVIGO (ED. FRANCAISE) (CN/1192-6929) [28955150] **2538**

● MAGAZINE PROVIGO (ENGLISH EDITION) (CN/1192-6937) [28955147] **2538**

MAGAZINE RACK [COMPUTER FILE] (US) [24235660] **3229**

MAGAZINE RECYCLING BENELUX (NE) **2236**

MAGAZINE SEARCH (US/1071-2739) [28599884] 2489, **2497**

MAGAZINE STOP (CN/0705-6869) [04249827] **2538**

MAGAZINE TREND REPORT (US/1044-6079) [06636867] **762**

MAGAZINE WEEK (UK) **2922**

MAGAZINES AND NEWSPAPERS - CALGARY PUBLIC LIBRARY (CN/1182-0691) [22378603] **5789**

MAGAZINES CAREER DIRECTORY (US/0889-8502) [14091659] **4816**

MAGAZINES FOR LIBRARIES (US/0000-0914) [04940202] **3229**

MAGAZINES FOR YOUNG PEOPLE (US/0000-1368) [23108961] **1066**

MAGAZINES / HALIFAX CITY REGIONAL LIBRARY (CN/0822-6512) [10339645] **419**

MAGAZINEWEEK (FRAMINGHAM, MASS.) *CEASED.* (US/0895-2124) [16512436] **4816**

MAGAZYN HISTORYCZNY (PL/0580-0943) [23807697] **2697**

MAGAZYN HUTNICZY (PL/0239-3611) [02393611] **4007**

MAGAZYN KRYMINALNY 997 (PL/0867-0404) [08670404] **4863**

MAGAZYN MODZIEZY (PL) [08937232] **1085**

MAGAZYN MUZYCZNY : MM (PL/0021-5600) [10979778] **4129**

MAGAZYN POMORZE, FAKTY I MYSLI (PL) [01785934] **2519**

MAGAZYN RODZINNY. MR (PL) [01795220] **2283**

MAGAZYN WILENSKI (LI) [27703642] **2519**

MAGAZZINI & TRASPORTILOGISTICA *See* LOGISTICA **5126**

MAGGLINGEN (SZ/0254-1246) [02541246] **4903**

MAGHREB CONFIDENTIEL PARIS (FR/1150-4447) [11504447] 1504, **4481**

MAGHREB-DEVELOPPEMENT (FR/0153-114X) [09062966] **1638**

MAGHREB, LE (TU/0330-9266) [07921713] **2641**

MAGHREB, MACHREK (FR) [04447342] **2641**

MAGHREB QUARTERLY (UK/0961-9836) **1573**

MAGHREB QUARTERLY REPORT (UK/0961-9836) [I09619836] 4481, **1573**

● MAGHREB REPORT (US/1071-7579) [28718579] **2499**

MAGHREB REVIEW, THE (UK/0309-457X) [04116541] **2641**

MAGHREB SELECTION (FR) **2499**

MAGIC CROCHET (US/0246-5957) [09141787] **5184**

... MAGIC DIRECTORY, THE (US/0736-704X) [09181362] **4863**

MAGIC (LAKEWOOD, CALIF.) (US/1062-2845) [25568113] **4863**

MAGIC MAGAZINE (NEW YORK) (US/0097-5176) [01799010] **4863**

MAGIC MAGAZINE (ORLANDO, FLA.) (US/1054-6723) [22935677] **4904**

MAGICAL BLEND (1989) (US/1073-5879) [23128345] **4242**

MAGICAL BLEND MAGAZINE (US/1040-4287) [18410765] **4242**

MAGICK CIRCLE DIRECTORY OF OCCULT GOODS AND SERVICES, THE (US/0742-8898) [10467168] **4242**

MAGILL (IE/0332-1754) [05325677] **2519**

MAGILL ANNUAL (IE) [16441269] **3409**

MAGILL BOOK REVIEW (US/0890-7722) [14391476] 3347, **4830**

MAGILL'S CINEMA ANNUAL (US/0739-2141) [09315435] **4074**

MAGILL'S LITERARY ANNUAL (US/0163-3058) [03644785] **4821**

● MAGILL'S SURVEY OF CINEMA (US/1065-6553) [26666837] **4074**

MAGISTER (ST-NICOLAS) (CN/0047-5483) [02056893] **1762**

MAGISTRA (CN) 5560, **5031**

MAGISTRATE (KAMPALA, UGANDA) (UG) [09542092] **3005**

MAGISTRATE NEWSLETTER *See* ALASKA COURT SYSTEM NEWSLETTER **3138**

MAGISTRATE, THE (UK) [02441440] **3169**

MAGLEV NEWS *See* HIGH SPEED TRANSPORT NEWS **4443**

MAGLEV NEWS (US/1065-6561) [26666539] **4444**

MAGLIE CALZE INDUSTRIA (IT/0024-9947) [I00249947] **1085**

MAGLIERIA (IT/0033-9067) [18435677] **1085**

MAGLIERIA ITALIANA (IT) **1085**

MAGMA (BLUE BELL, PA.) (US/1063-5122) [26048594] **3943**

MAGNA TIMES (MAGNA, UTAH : 1982) (US) [13028638] **5756**

MAGNES LECTURE SERIES (US) [11858858] **3605**

MAGNESIUM AND MAGNESIUM COMPOUNDS (US) [03025693] **4007**

MAGNESIUM AND TRACE ELEMENTS *CEASED.* (SZ/1015-3845) [21400675] **985**

MAGNESIUM-BULLETIN (GW/0172-908X) [06571492] **4007**

MAGNESIUM MILL PRODUCTS (US/0735-8466) [03092894] 844, **1617**

MAGNESIUM RESEARCH : OFFICIAL ORGAN OF THE INTERNATIONAL SOCIETY FOR THE DEVELOPMENT OF RESEARCH ON MAGNESIUM (UK/0953-1424) [19022703] 4194, **3605**

● MAGNET NEWSLETTER, THE (US/1065-6782) [26677560] **1804**

MAGNETIC AND ELECTRICAL SEPARATION (US/1055-6915) [23272946] **4444**

MAGNETIC FUSION ENERGY; PROGRAM SUMMARY DOCUMENT (US) [06568232] **1950**

MAGNETIC FUSION PROGRAM SUMMARY DOCUMENT (US) [04969085] **4444**

MAGNETIC MEDIA INTERNATIONAL NEWSLETTER (US/0738-923X) [11595967] **2071**

MAGNETIC NORTH *CEASED.* (US/0739-6481) [09805924] **4444**

MAGNETIC RESONANCE IMAGING (US/0730-725X) [08047251] **3943**

MAGNETIC RESONANCE IN CHEMISTRY : MRC (UK/0749-1581) [11079428] **1044**

MAGNETIC RESONANCE IN MEDICINE (US/0740-3194) [09922011] **3943**

MAGNETIC RESONANCE MATERIALS IN PHYSICS, BIOLOGY AND MEDICINE (US) **3943**

MAGNETIC RESONANCE QUARTERLY (US/0899-9422) [18270263] **3943**

MAGNETIC RESONANCE REVIEW (US/0097-7330) [01798883] **4444**

MAGNETIC SEPARATION NEWS (US/0731-3632) [08175411] **4444**

MAGNETISM (US/0464-4387) [02111195] **4444**

MAGNETOHYDRODYNAMICS (NEW YORK, N.Y. 1965) (US/0024-998X) [01756469] **4444**

MAGNETOHYDRODYNAMICS (NEW YORK, N.Y. 1989) (US/0891-9801) [15048928] **2071**

MAGNETS IN YOUR FUTURE *CEASED.* (US/0887-5707) [13312833] **3943**

MAGNITNAJA GIDRODINAMIKA (LV/0025-0015) [02448397] **4444**

MAGNITO-POLUPROVODNIKOVYE I ELEKTROMASHINNYE ELEMENTY AVTOMATIKI (RU) [02245145] 4444, **2071**

MAGNITOGORSKII GORNO-METALLURGICHESKII INSTITUT IM. G.I. NOSOVA *See* SBORNIK NAUCNYH TRUDOV - MAGNITOGORSKIJ GORNOMETALLURGICESKIJ INSTITUT IM. G. J. NOSOVA **4018**

MAGNITOSFERNYE ISSLEDOVANIIA (RU) [08817695] **1408**

MAGNOLIA GAZETTE (MAGNOLIA, MISS. : 1872) (US) [12868708] **5701**

MAGNOLIA (HAMMOND, LA.) (US/0738-3053) [06661128] **5233**

MAGNOLIA (WINSTON-SALEM, N.C.) (US/1054-9153) [18830093] **2424**

MAGOOK (CN/0702-6803) [03956713] **3409**

MAGOOK (EDITION FRANCAISE) (CN/0227-1346) [06689184] **1066**

MAGPIES (AT/0817-0088) [20603033] **3409**

MAGUARE : REVISTA DEL DEPARTAMENTO DE ANTROPOLOGIA DE LA UNIVERSIDAD NACIONAL DE COLOMBIA (CK/0120-3045) [09022703] **240**

MAGUNESHUMU KYOTO (JA/0913-4867) [I09134867] **985**

MAGYAR ALLATORVOSOK LAPJA (HU/0025-004X) [03773502] **5516**

MAGYAR ALUMINUM *CEASED.* (HU/0025-0058) [06793041] **4008**

MAGYAR BELORVOSI ARCHIVUM (1955) (HU/0025-0066) [07108757] **3605**

MAGYAR ELET (CN/0833-0883) [21401079] **5789**

MAGYAR EPITOMUVESZET
(BUDAPEST, 1952) (HU/0025-0082)
[02554823] **303**

MAGYAR EREMGYUJTOK
EGYESULETE CSONGRAD MEGYEI
SZERVEZETENEK KIADVANYAI, A
(HU/0230-788X) [I0230788X] **2781**

MAGYAR FOLDRAJZI TARSASAG *See*
FOLDRAJZI KOZLEMENYEK **2561**

MAGYAR GEOFIZIKA (HU/0025-0120)
[06577220] **1408**

MAGYAR GRAFIKA (HU/0479-480X)
[09456715] **380**

MAGYAR HIRADO (NEW BRUNSWICK,
N.J.) (US) [11940886] **5729**

MAGYAR HIRLAP (HU/0133-1906)
[24637053] **5802**

MAGYAR HIRMONDO (CALGARY)
(CN/0824-6300) [10831987] **2745**

MAGYAR JOG ES KULFOLDI JOGI
SZEMLE *See* MAGYAR JOG (MAGYAR
JOGASZ SZOVETSEG : 1982) **3005**

MAGYAR JOG (MAGYAR JOGASZ
SZOVETSEG : 1982) (HU/0025-0147)
[08934103] **3005**

MAGYAR KEMIAI FOLYOIRAT
(HU/0025-0155) [01856253] **985**

MAGYAR KEMIKUSOK LAPJA
(HU/0025-0163) [06772868] **985**

MAGYAR KERESKEDELMI ES
VENDEGLATOIPARI MUZEUM *See*
MAGYAR KERESKEDELMI ES
VENDEGLATOIPARI MUZEUM
EVKONYVE, A **844**

MAGYAR KERESKEDELMI ES
VENDEGLATOIPARI MUZEUM
EVKONYVE, A (HU) [03519898] **844**

MAGYAR KEVE (US) [03962154] **2519**

MAGYAR KOEZTARSASAG
ALLAMIGAZGATASI
HELYNEVKOENYVE *See* MAGYAR
KOEZTARSASAG HELYNEVKOENYVE
/ KOEZPONTI STATISZTIKAI HIVATAL,
A **4663**

●MAGYAR KOEZTARSASAG
HELYNEVKOENYVE / KOEZPONTI
STATISZTIKAI HIVATAL, A
(HU/1216-1993) [29606130] **4663**

MAGYAR KONYVSZEMLE
(HU/0025-0171) [01756473] 3229, **3259**

MAGYAR KONYVTARI
SZAKIRODALOM BIBLIOGRAFIAJA, A
(HU/0133-736X) [I0133736X] 3229, **3259**

MAGYAR MEZOGAZDASAG (HU)
[03773572] **106**

MAGYAR MEZOGAZDASAGI MUZEUM
KOZLEMENYEI, A (HU/0521-4238)
[18970978] **106**

MAGYAR MUEEMLE KVEDELEM
(HU/0580-4736) [01793346] **303**

MAGYAR MUHELY (FR/0025-0201)
[07207948] **3300**

MAGYAR NAPTAR (NEW YORK)
(US/0094-1484) [01792704] **2489**

MAGYAR NEMZET (HU/0133-185X)
[12013467] **5802**

MAGYAR NEMZETI BANK *See* ANNUAL
REPORT / NATIONAL BANK OF
HUNGARY **771**

MAGYAR NEMZETI BIBLIOGRAFIA:
IDOSZAKI KIADVANYOK
BIBLIOGRAFIAJA (HU/0231-4592)
[10418181] **419**

MAGYAR NEMZETI BIBLIOGRAFIA.
IDOSZAKI KIADVANYOK
REPERTORIUMA (HU/0133-6894)
[03645408] **419**

MAGYAR NEMZETI GALERIA
EVKONYVE (HU) [03019215] **357**

MAGYAR NEMZITI GALERIA *See*
MAGYAR NEMZETI GALERIA
EVKONYVE **357**

MAGYAR NOORVOSOK LAPJA
(HU/0025-021X) [06523393] **3764**

MAGYAR NYELV (HU/0025-0228)
[04354941] **3300**

MAGYAR NYELVJARASOK
(HU/0541-9298) [01812233] **3409**

MAGYAR NYELVOR (HU/0025-0236)
[04358578] **3300**

MAGYAR OLAJIPARI MUZEUM *See*
MAGYAR OLAJIPARI MUZEUM
EVKONYVE, A **4263**

MAGYAR OLAJIPARI MUZEUM
EVKONYVE, A (HU) [02280686] **4263**

MAGYAR OLIMPIAI AKADEMIA
EVKONYVE, A (HU/0238-0412)
[20176288] **4904**

MAGYAR ONKOLOGIA (HU/0025-0244)
[06306459] **3820**

MAGYAR ORVOSI BIBLIOGRAFIA
(HU/0025-0252) [01902330] **3660**

MAGYAR PEDAGOGIA (HU/0025-0260)
[01855331] **1762**

MAGYAR PEDIATER (HU/0303-5042)
[00967448] **3906**

MAGYAR PSZICHOLOGIAI SZEMLE
(HU/0025-0279) [01855503] **4603**

MAGYAR RESTAURALAS
(HU/0866-4013) [24359037] **357**

MAGYAR SZO NAPTARA, A (YU)
[01795060] **2519**

MAGYAR TALALKOZO *See* A MAGYAR
TALALKOZO KRONIKAJA **2671**

MAGYAR TEXTILTECHNIKA
(HU/0025-0309) [04095080] **5354**

MAGYAR TRAUMATOLOGIA,
ORTHOPAEDIA ES HELYREALLIT
SEBESZET (HU/0025-0317) [14206967]
3969

MAGYAR TUDOMANY (HU/0025-0325)
[09542283] **5126**

MAGYAR UROLOGIA (HU/0864-8921)
[I08648921] **3991**

MAGYAR ZENE (HU/0025-0384)
[01842684] **4129**

MAH KEDAI (IS) [03249784] **2791**

MAHA BODHI, THE (II/0025-0406)
[08151071] **5021**

MAHAD AL-JAZAIRI LIL-TAWHID
AL-SINAI WA-AL-MILKIYAH
AL-SINAIYAH *See* BULLETIN DE
L'INSTITUT ALGERIEN DE
NORMALISATION ET DE PROPRIETE
INDUSTRIELLE **1302**

MAHADIR AL-JALSAT (UA) [04355128]
3300

MAHANADI REVIEW, THE (II)
[08713948] **3409**

MAHARASHTRA BAR COUNCIL
JOURNAL (II) [02422833] **3005**

MAHARASHTRA (INDIA) *See* OUTLINE
OF ACTIVITIES - GOVERNMENT OF
MAHARASHTRA **4672**

MAHARASHTRA (INDIA) *See*
PERFORMANCE BUDGET:
IRRIGATION AND POWER
DEPARTMENT **4740**

MAHARASHTRA, INDIA (STATE).
BOARD OF SECONDARY EDUCATION
See VARSHIKA VRTTANTA -
MAHARASHTRA RAJYA MADHYAMIKA
SIKSHANA MANDALA **1789**

MAHARASHTRA, INDIA (STATE).
DIRECTORATE OF ECONOMICS AND
STATISTICS *See* HANDBOOK OF
BASIC STATISTICS OF
MAHARASHTRA STATE **5328**

MAHARASHTRA, INDIA (STATE). FOOD
AND DRUG ADMINISTRATION *See*
ANNUAL ADMINISTRATION REPORT -
FOOD AND DRUG ADMINISTRATION,
MAHARASHTRA STATE **4626**

MAHARASHTRA, INDIA (STATE).
LEGISLATURE. LEGISLATIVE
COUNCIL. COMMITTEE ON
GOVERNMENT ASSURANCES *See*
ASVASANA SAMITI
(VIDHANAPARISHAD) AHAVALA **4631**

MAHARASHTRA, INDIA (STATE).
LEGISLATURE. LEGISLATIVE
COUNCIL. COMMITTEE ON
GOVERNMENT ASSURANCES.
REPORT *See* ASVASANA SAMITI
(VIDHANAPARISHAD) AHAVALA **4631**

MAHARASHTRA, INDIA (STATE).
RURAL DEVELOPMENT DEPT *See*
CONSOLIDATED FINANCE AND
REVENUE ACCOUNTS OF ZILLA
PARISHADS AND PANCHAYAT
SAMITIS IN THE STATE OF
MAHARASHTRA **4718**

MAHARASHTRA JOURNAL OF
EXTENSION EDUCATION (II)
[09438756] **106**

MAHARASHTRA TAIMSA VARSHIKA (II)
[02239632] **2506**

MAHARDDHIKA PRADIPTA
(IO/0542-092X) [01798283] **240**

MAHASAGAR (II/0542-0938) [01606581]
1451

MAHASHEVET (IS) [04701164] **5051**

MAHD BULLETIN (US/1064-5608)
[04607731] **3229**

MAHFIL (TUNIS, TUNISIA) (TI)
[09594571] **3465**

MAHJUBAH (IR) [08921072] 5560, **5043**

MAHNAMAH-I PASDAR-I ISLAM /
DAFTAR-I TABLIGHAT-I ISLAMI (IR)
[10154827] **5043**

MAHNAMAH-I SHAHID (IR) [10074695]
2658

MAHNAMAH RAH-I ISLAM (II)
[25585129] **5043**

MAHNOMEN PIONEER, THE (US)
[01756494] **5697**

MAHONING MEANDERINGS /
MAHONING COUNTY CHAPTER OF
THE OHIO GENEALOGICAL SOCIETY
(US) [16934354] **2459**

MAHUT (IS/0333-838X) [22973799]
5051, **3409**

MAI NAP (HU/0239-0639) [I02390639]
5802

MAIA (IT/0025-0538) [01756496] **1078**

MAIEUTICS *CEASED.* (CN/0226-2428)
[10768832] **5208**

MAIGETSU KINRO TOKEI TOKUBETSU
CHOSA HOKOKU (JA) [01797191] **1689**

MAIGETSU KINRO TOKEI YORAN /
RODO DAIJIN KANBO SEISAKU
CHOSABU HEN (JA) [12850559] **1689**

MAIGRIR MEDECINE BEAUTE
(CN/0714-3761) [09099669] **4194**

MAIKURO SOPUTUWEO (KO)
[10568960] 1268, **1238**

MAIL-JOURNAL, THE (US) [15472040]
5665

MAIL (MILFORD, PA.) (US/1053-0703)
[20585877] **1145**

MAIL ON SUNDAY (UK/0263-8878)
[I02638878] **5812**

MAIL ORDER BUSINESS DIRECTORY :
A COMPLETE GUIDE TO THE MAIL
ORDER MARKET (US/0085-2953)
[04333146] **691**

MAIL ORDER CONNECTION *See*
DIRECT RESPONSE SPECIALIST **2532**

MAIL ORDER PRODUCT GUIDE
(US/1040-1296) [18330563] **691**

MAILBOX (GREENSBORO), THE
(US/0199-6045) [06046703] **1900**

MAILBOX LIBRARY SERVICE
(CN/0848-7456) [23598731] **3229**

MAILBOX NEWS (US/0889-4884)
[08374512] 374, **2791**

MAILBOX, THE (US) [11643596] **1900**

MAILBOX, THE (US) [11643628] **1804**

MAILING LIST COMPANIES AND
CATAGORIES ... DIRECTORY
(US/1043-4372) [19470910] **1145**

MAILING LIST TIDBITS (US) **929**

MAILLON, LE (CN/0383-7297)
[03258683] **5295**

MAIMONIDEAN STUDIES
(US/1050-1630) [21402405] **4352**

MAIN (US/0147-1201) [03093189] **4186**

MAIN CURRENTS IN MODERN
THOUGHT (US/0025-0570) [01756498]
2538

MAIN DE L'AGE D'OR, LA
(CN/0824-1503) [11807882] **5180**

MAIN ECONOMIC INDICATORS
(FR/0474-5523) [00958143] **1573**

MAIN ECONOMIC INDICATORS.
HISTORICAL STATISTICS /
ORGANISATION FOR ECONOMIC
CO-OPERATION AND DEVELOPMENT
(FR/0474-5442) [01606299] **1573**

MAIN ESTIMATES - BUDGET BUREAU
(CN/0844-6695) [20031401] **4736**

MAIN ESTIMATES - FINANCIAL
MANAGEMENT SECRETARIAT
(YELLOWKNIFE. 1987) (CN/0844-6725)
[19967545] **4663**

MAIN ESTIMATES, HIGHLIGHTS BY
MINISTRY (CN/0848-5933) [23248993]
4663

MAIN ESTIMATES OF CURRENT
EXPENDITURE OF THE PROVINCE OF
MANITOBA (CN/0704-1748) [04250333]
4736

MAIN GROUP METAL CHEMISTRY
(UK/0334-7575) [17157595] **4008**

MAIN LINE TIMES (US) [13983454]
5737

MAIN RECOMMENDATIONS,
PROCEEDINGS AND AGENDA NOTES
(II/0589-090X) [01605606] **2827**

MAIN SCIENCE AND TECHNOLOGY
INDICATORS (FR/1011-792X)
[17947575] **5126**

MAIN SHEET (US/0025-0600)
[04049742] **594**

MAIN STREET MEMORANDUM, THE
(US) **5295**

MAIN STREET MESSAGE
(US/1057-0381) [23915871] **5483**

MAIN STREET NEWS (US/0897-2559)
[15811975] **2827**

MAIN TITLE (US/0360-1935) [02244095]
4129

MAINAKE (SP/0212-078X) [I0212078X]
4228, 2622, **273**

MAINE *See* MAINE REVISED
STATUTES ANNOTATED / MAINE
LEGISLATIVE SERVICE **844**

MAINE *See* LABOR LAWS OF MAINE
3150

MAINE AGRICULTURAL AND FOREST
EXPERIMENT STATION *See* ANNUAL
REPORT / MAINE AGRICULTURAL AND
FOREST EXPERIMENT STATION,
UNIVERSITY OF MAINE **60**

MAINE AGRICULTURAL EXPERIMENT
STATION *See* MAES ANNUAL REPORT
106

MAINE AGRICULTURAL EXPERIMENT
STATION. ANNUAL REPORT *See* MAES
ANNUAL REPORT **106**

MAINE AGRICULTURAL EXPERIMENT
STATION. MAES ANNUAL REPORT *See*
ANNUAL REPORT / MAINE
AGRICULTURAL AND FOREST
EXPERIMENT STATION, UNIVERSITY
OF MAINE **60**

●MAINE AGRICULTURAL REPORT
(US/1062-2691) [25563791] **106**

MAINE ALUMNUS *See* MAINE (ORONO,
ME.) **1102**

MAINE-ANJOU INTERNATIONAL
(CN/0823-4604) [10339663] **215**

MAINE — Alphabetical Title Index

MAINE ANTIQUE DIGEST (US/0147-0639) [03078878] **251**

MAINE ARCHAEOLOGICAL SOCIETY *See* BULLETIN / MAINE ARCHAEOLOGICAL SOCIETY **263**

MAINE (AUBURN, ME.) (US/1046-6053) [20468488] **2745**

MAINE BAR JOURNAL (US/0885-9973) [12792453] **3005**

MAINE BIRDLIFE (US/8756-9620) [11764329] **5590**, **4167**

MAINE. BUREAU OF FORESTRY *See* FINANCIAL REPORT AND PROGRESS REPORT ON SPRUCE BUDWORM PROGRAMS **2379**

MAINE. BUREAU OF LABOR AND INDUSTRY *See* BLI BULLETIN **1655**

MAINE. BUREAU OF LABOR. RESEARCH AND STATISTICS DIVISION *See* DIRECTORY OF MAINE LABOR ORGANIZATIONS **1663**

MAINE. BUREAU OF LABOR. RESEARCH AND STATISTICS DIVISION *See* CHARACTERISTICS OF WORK- RELATED INJURIES AND ILLNESSES IN MAINE **2860**

MAINE. BUREAU OF PUBLIC LANDS *See* BIENNIAL REPORT TO LEGISLATURE - BUREAU OF PUBLIC LANDS **4632**

MAINE. BUREAU OF TAXATION *See* REVENUE REPORT - MAINE **4747**

MAINE. BUREAU OF VOCATIONAL EDUCATION *See* MAJOR GOALS OF VOCATIONAL EDUCATION IN MAINE **1914**

MAINE BUSINESS AND EMPLOYMENT LAW (US/0748-3120) [10947163] **3151**, **3101**

MAINE BUSINESS DIRECTORY (US/1048-7115) [21013005] **691**

MAINE BUSINESS INDICATORS (US/0025-0619) [04410954] **1573**

MAINE CATALOG, THE (US/0090-2128) [01784832] **2538**

MAINE. COUNCIL ON DEVELOPMENTAL DISABILITIES *See* MAINE'S STATE PLAN ON DEVELOPMENTAL DISABILITIES **5295**

MAINE. COURTS *See* MAINE RULES OF COURT, WITH AMENDMENTS **3141**

MAINE. DEPARTMENT OF INLAND FISHERIES AND GAME. INFORMATION AND EDUCATION DIVISION *See* PAMPHLET - MAINE DEPARTMENT OF INLAND FISHERIES AND GAME, INFORMATION AND EDUCATION DIVISION **2201**

MAINE. DEPT. OF AGRICULTURE, FOOD, AND RURAL RESOURCES *See* REPORT OF ... COMMISSIONER OF AGRICULTURE, FOOD AND RURAL RESOURCES TO THE ... REGULAR SESSION OF THE ... MAINE STATE LEGISLATURE **126**

MAINE. DEPT. OF AGRICULTURE. REPORT OF THE COMMISSIONER OF AGRICULTURE *See* REPORT OF ... COMMISSIONER OF AGRICULTURE, FOOD AND RURAL RESOURCES TO THE ... REGULAR SESSION OF THE ... MAINE STATE LEGISLATURE **126**

MAINE. DEPT. OF MANPOWER AFFAIRS. ANNUAL PLANNING INFORMATION *See* ANNUAL PLANNING INFORMATION / STATE OF MAINE **1648**

MAINE. DEPT. OF MARINE RESOURCES *See* ANNUAL REPORT - MAINE. DEPT. OF MARINE RESOURCES **442**

MAINE. DEPT. OF MENTAL HEALTH AND CORRECTIONS *See* MAINE MENTAL HEALTH PLAN **4789**

MAINE. DEPT. OF MENTAL HEALTH AND CORRECTIONS *See* AFFIRMATIVE ACTION PLAN - MAINE. DEPT. OF MENTAL HEALTH AND CORRECTIONS **4763**

MAINE. DEPT. OF MENTAL HEALTH AND MENTAL RETARDATION *See* MENTAL HEALTH PLAN (AUGUSTA, ME.) **4790**

MAINE. DEPT. OF TRANSPORTATION. BRIDGE DESIGN SECTION *See* ANNUAL REPORT / MAINE DEPARTMENT OF TRANSPORTATION, BRIDGE DESIGN SECTION **5438**

MAINE. DEPT. OF TRANSPORTATION. BUREAU OF PLANNING *See* HIGHWAY SUFFICIENCY REPORT **5441**

MAINE DIRECTORY OF NATURAL RESOURCE ORGANIZATIONS (US/0148-0359) [03264235] **2197**

MAINE EDUCATIONAL DIRECTORY (US/0460-6949) [01781040] **1762**

●MAINE ENTRY, THE (US) [25265722] **3229**

MAINE ENVIRONMENT (US/0898-7742) [14176317] **2197**

MAINE FIELD NATURALIST *See* MAINE NATURALIST (STEUBEN, ME.) **4167**

MAINE FISH AND WILDLIFE (US/0360-005X) [02243021] **4874**, **2308**

MAINE GEOLOGIST, THE (US/0270-8345) [04545721] **1386**

●MAINE HEALTH CARE IN PERSPECTIVE (US/1065-4216) [26605682] **4789**

MAINE HEALTH FACILITIES, RESOURCES, AND UTILIZATION / PREPARED BY BUREAU OF HEALTH PLANNING AND DEVELOPMENT, MAINE DEPARTMENT OF HUMAN SERVICES (US) [08616050] **3788**

MAINE HISTORICAL SOCIETY *See* NEWSLETTER / MAINE HISTORICAL SOCIETY **2749**

MAINE HISTORICAL SOCIETY QUARTERLY (US/0163-1152) [02263768] **2745**

MAINE HOSPITAL WAGE SURVEY / MAINE DEPARTMENT OF LABOR, BUREAU OF EMPLOYMENT SECURITY, DIVISION OF ECONOMIC ANALYSIS AND RESEARCH (US) [10250744] **1689**

MAINE IN PERSPECTIVE (US/1065-5484) [26655659] **5332**

MAINE. LABOR MARKET EVALUATION AND PLANNING SECTION *See* ANNUAL PLANNING INFORMATION / STATE OF MAINE **1648**

MAINE. LAW ENFORCEMENT PLANNING & ASSISTANCE AGENCY *See* PROGRESS REPORT - MAINE LAW ENFORCEMENT PLANNING AND ASSISTANCE AGENCY **3173**

MAINE LAW REVIEW (1963) (US/0025-0651) [04546677] **3005**

MAINE LEGIONNAIRE, THE (US/0161-584X) [03970279] **5233**

MAINE LIBRARY ASSOCIATION *See* MONTHLY MEMO - MAINE LIBRARY ASSOCIATION AND MAINE STATE LIBRARY **3232**

MAINE. LIBRARY COMMISSION *See* REPORT OF THE LIBRARY COMMISSION OF MAINE **3245**

MAINE-LY AGRICULTURE *See* MAINE AGRICULTURAL REPORT **106**

MAINE-LY LIBRARIES *See* MAINE ENTRY, THE **3229**

MAINE. MANPOWER RESEARCH DIVISION *See* WOMEN AND MINORITY MANPOWER STATISTICS **1540**

MAINE. MANPOWER RESEARCH DIVISION *See* MAINE OCCUPATIONAL WAGES AND FRINGE BENEFITS BY INDUSTRY IN MANUFACTURING **1689**

MAINE. MANPOWER RESEARCH DIVISION *See* ANNUAL PLANNING INFORMATION FOR AROOSTOOK COUNTY **1646**

MAINE. MANPOWER RESEARCH DIVISION *See* ANNUAL PLANNING REPORT: MAINE, BALANCE OF STATE **1648**

MAINE. MANPOWER RESEARCH DIVISION *See* ANNUAL PLANNING INFORMATION FOR YORK COUNTY **1646**

MAINE. MANPOWER RESEARCH DIVISION *See* ANNUAL PLANNING INFORMATION FOR CUMBERLAND COUNTY **1646**

MAINE. MANPOWER RESEARCH DIVISION *See* ANNUAL PLANNING INFORMATION FOR PENOBSCOT CONSORTIUM **1646**

MAINE MANUFACTURING DIRECTORY (US/1045-6317) [13986080] **3483**

MAINE MENTAL HEALTH PLAN (US/0147-2585) [03134402] **5295**, **4789**

MAINE MONTHLY LOCAL CLIMATOLOGICAL DATA. MICROFILM (US) [10833432] **1430**

MAINE MUNICIPAL ASSOCIATION *See* MUNICIPAL DIRECTORY (AUGUSTA) **4667**

●MAINE NATURALIST (STEUBEN, ME.) (US/1063-3626) [25990314] **4167**

MAINE, NEW HAMPSHIRE, VERMONT ZIP+4 STATE DIRECTORY (US/8756-9841) [11537407] **1145**

MAINE NURSE, THE (US/0025-0767) [15796393] **3861**

MAINE OCCUPATIONAL WAGES AND FRINGE BENEFITS BY INDUSTRY IN MANUFACTURING (US) [04456208] **1689**

MAINE OCCUPATIONAL WAGES IN MANUFACTURING INDUSTRIES / OCCUPATIONAL OUTLOOK AND JOB INFORMATION SECTION (US) [08205317] **1689**

MAINE OCCUPATIONAL WAGES IN NONMANUFACTURING INDUSTRIES / OCCUPATIONAL OUTLOOK AND JOB INFORMATION SECTION (US) [08257023] **1689**

MAINE ORGANIC FARMER & GARDENER, THE (US/0891-9194) [03950626] **106**

MAINE (ORONO, ME.) (US) [17492151] **1102**

MAINE PROSECUTOR BULLETIN, THE (US/0094-5439) [01794407] **3108**

MAINE PROSECUTOR, CRIMINAL LEGISLATION MANUAL, THE (US/0098-079X) [01798771] **3169**

MAINE. PUBLIC UTILITIES COMMISSION *See* REPORT TO THE JOINT STANDING COMMITTEE ON PUBLIC UTILITIES, MAINE LEGISLATURE **4682**

MAINE REGISTER, STATE YEAR-BOOK AND LEGISLATIVE MANUAL (US/0145-9597) [01247632] **4663**

MAINE REVISED STATUTES ANNOTATED / MAINE LEGISLATIVE SERVICE (US) [01756507] **844**

MAINE RULES OF COURT, WITH AMENDMENTS (US) [01590125] **3141**

MAINE SCHOLAR, THE (US/1052-018X) [19889240] **2850**

MAINE SCHOOL MANAGEMENT ASSOCIATION *See* SALARIES & WAGES IN MAINE PUBLIC SCHOOLS **1870**

MAINE SCHOOL STATISTICS (US/0542-1098) [02245883] **1762**, **1795**

MAINE SCIENCE & TECHNOLOGY REPORT : A PUBLICATION OF THE MAINE SCIENCE AND TECHNOLOGY COMMISSION (US) [21665240] **5126**

MAINE SNOWMOBILER (US/0195-2870) [05458191] **4904**

MAINE. SOIL AND WATER CONSERVATION COMMISSION *See* BIENNIAL REPORT - MAINE, SOIL AND WATER CONSERVATION COMMISSION **2188**

MAINE SPORTSMAN, THE (US/0199-0365) [05530078] **4904**

MAINE STATE BOARD FOR REGISTRATION OF ARCHITECTS AND LANDSCAPE ARCHITECTS *See* ROSTER OF REGISTERED ARCHITECTS AND LANDSCAPE ARCHITECTS YEAR ENDING JUNE 30 ... / MAINE STATE BOARD FOR REGISTRATION OF ARCHITECTS AND LANDSCAPE ARCHITECTS **308**

MAINE. STATE EMPLOYMENT AND TRAINING COUNCIL *See* ANNUAL PLANNING INFORMATION FOR STATE OF MAINE **1646**

MAINE. STATE EMPLOYMENT AND TRAINING COUNCIL *See* CETA ACTIVITY IN THE STATE OF MAINE, FISCAL YEAR ... / STATE EMPLOYMENT AND TRAINING COUNCIL **1658**

MAINE STATE HARNESS RACING COMMISSION *See* REPORT OF THE ... RACING SEASON / MAINE STATE HARNESS RACING COMMISSION **4915**

MAINE STATE LIBRARY *See* GOVERNMENT PUBLICATIONS CHECKLIST / MAINE STATE LIBRARY **416**

MAINE STATE LIBRARY. CHECKLIST OF STATE OF MAINE PUBLICATIONS RECEIVED BY THE MAINE STATE LIBRARY *See* GOVERNMENT PUBLICATIONS CHECKLIST / MAINE STATE LIBRARY **416**

MAINE. STATE PLANNING OFFICE *See* ANNUAL REPORT - STATE PLANNING OFFICE. EXECUTIVE DEPARTMENT. STATE OF MAINE **2815**

MAINE. STATE PLANNING OFFICE *See* SURVEY OF MUNICIPAL PLANNING AND REGULATORY ACTIVITY, A **2836**

MAINE TEACHER, THE (US/0025-0775) [01903934] **1762**

MAINE TIMES (US/0025-0783) [02253782] **2177**, **5685**

MAINE TOWNSMAN, THE (US/0025-0791) [01903966] **4664**

MAINE TRAIL, THE (US/0047-5548) [01756526] **5386**

MAINE UNITED METHODIST, THE (US/0745-0273) [08732311] **5063**

MAINE, VERMONT, NEW HAMPSHIRE DIRECTORY OF MANUFACTURERS (US/0197-1220) [05700168] **3483**

MAINE WATER QUALITY STATUS (US/0147-4596) [03173411] **2236**, **5536**

MAINE WATER UTILITIES ASSOCIATION *See* JOURNAL - MAINE WATER UTILITIES ASSOCIATION **4761**

MAINELINE (CN/0316-8581) [02247251] **215**

MAINE'S STATE PLAN ON DEVELOPMENTAL DISABILITIES (US/0161-3979) [03896007] **5295**

MAINSTREAM (US) [02123570] **1093**

MAINFRAME CLIENT/SERVER (UK) **1288**

MAINFRAME COMMUNICATIONS *CEASED.* (US) **1194**

MAINFRAME COMPUTERS (US) [09554507] **1194**

MAINFRAME MARKET MONTHLY (US) **1245**

MAINFRAME REPORT (US) **1194**

MAINFRANKISCHES JAHRBUCH FUER GESCHICHTE UND KUNST (GW/0076-2725) [02354604] **2697**, **357**

MAINICHI DAILY NEWS (JA) [12789311] **5805**

Alphabetical Title Index

MAJOITUSTILASTO

MAINICHI NYUSU JITEN (JA) [02239556] **1927**

MAINICHI SHINBUN (JA) [10684368] **5805**

MAINLINE MODELER (US/0199-5421) [05978560] **5432**

MAINLINES (INDIANAPOLIS, IND.) (US/0278-9450) [07939000] **3861**

●MAINSHEET (SAN FRANCISCO, CALIF.) (US/1064-1688) [26222879] **594**

MAINSTREAM (II) [01588771] **4528**

MAINSTREAM AMERICA (US/0749-2391) [10437481] **4481**

MAINSTREAM NEWS (US/1046-6355) [20479515] **4391**

MAINSTREAM (SACRAMENTO, CALIF.) (US/0891-088X) [04683681] **226**

MAINSTREAM (SAN DIEGO, CALIF.) (US/0278-8225) [07907053] **4391**

MAINTAINER (VANCOUVER) (CN/0827-5637) [13435685] **876**

MAINTENANCE & ENTREPRISE PARIS (FR/1154-6433) [I11546433] **1985**

MAINTENANCE EXECUTIVE (US/1055-9663) [24252664] **1617**

MAINTENANCE FARNHAM (UK/0953-2110) [I09532110] 3483, **1985**

MAINTENANCE MANAGEMENT INTERNATIONAL (NE/0167-5389) [08691740] **876**

MAINTENANCE (NEWSLETTER FOR PROFESSIONAL TRUCK DRIVER/OWNERS) (US/0890-1791) [14163045] **5386**

MAINTENANCE (NEWSLETTER FOR PROFESSIONAL TRUCK EQUIPMENT MANAGERS) (US/0890-1775) [14163002] 1985, **5386**

MAINTENANCE (NEWSLETTER FOR PROFESSIONAL TRUCK EQUIPMENT SUPERVISORS) (US/0890-1783) [14163028] **5386**

MAINTENANCE SUPERVISOR'S BULLETIN (US/0194-5912) [04867974] **876**

MAINTENANCE SUPERVISOR'S DEVELOPMENT PROGRAM (US) **876**

MAINTENANCE SUPPLIES (US/0025-0929) [04172376] **2236**

MAINTENANCE TECHNOLOGY (US/0899-5729) [18144285] **619**

MAINTENANCE : THE NEWSLETTER FOR PROFESSIONAL TRUCK EQUIPMENT EXECUTIVES (US/0890-1767) [14162987] 1985, **5386**

MAINTENANCE UPDATE (SZ) **619**

MAINZER PHILOSOPHISCHE FORSCHUNGEN (GW/0076-2776) [02349778] **4352**

MAINZER REIHE, DIE (GW/0076-2784) [05168526] **3465**

MAINZER STUDIEN ZUR AMERIKANISTIK (GW/0170-9135) [I01709135] 3300, **3409**

MAINZER ZEITSCHRIFT (GW/0076-2792) [01413993] **357**

MAIRENA (RIO PIEDRAS, SAN JUAN, P.R.) (PR/1050-835X) [08312580] **3465**

●MAIS-GRAIN, RESULTATS D'ESSAIS ..., HYBRIDES RECOMMANDES EN ... / CONSEIL DES PRODUCTIONS VEGETALES DU QUEBEC (CN/1193-3046) [26776170] **106**

MAISON & JARDIN (FR/0025-0945) [04453719] 2424, **2902**

MAISON DES SCIENCES DE L'HOMME (PARIS, FRANCE) See MATERIAUX POUR L'ETUDE DE L'EXTREME-ORIENT MODERNE ET CONTEMPORAIN. TRAVAUX **2658**

MAISON DES SCIENCES DE L'HOMME (PARIS, FRANCE) See MATERIAUX POUR L'ETUDE DE L'EXTREME-ORIENT MODERNE ET CONTEMPORAIN. ETUDES LINGUISTIQUES **3301**

MAISON-DIEU, LA (FR/0025-0937) [01608201] **5032**

MAISON ET TRAVAUX (FR) **2792**

MAISON FRANCAISE, LA (FR/0025-0953) [01756533] **2792**

●MAISON FRANCE ISRAEL / CHAMBRE DE COMMERCE FRANCE-ISRAEL (FR/1165-0265) [27953393] **844**

MAISON INDIVIDUELLE, LA (FR/0150-6439) [I01506439] **4206**

MAISON MAGAZINE, ANTILLES : M (MQ) [19301295] 374, **303**

MAISONS D'ICI (CN/0226-6857) [06473592] **2827**

MAITHILI AKADAMI PATRIKA (II) [10879788] 3409, **3300**

MAITRE ELECTRICIEN, LE (CN/0025-0988) [02430001] **2071**

MAITRE FRIGORISTE (CN/0823-5198) [11463198] **2071**

MAITRE IMPRIMEUR, LE (CN/0025-0996) [02057185] **4566**

MAITRES *CEASED*. (CN) [19230640] **3005**

MAITRES (MONTREAL) *CEASED*. (CN/0842-9960) [19991161] **3005**

MAITRISE DE L'ENERGIE (MONTREAL) (CN/0831-4667) [15997038] **1950**

MAITRISE PARIS (FR/1157-6049) [I11576049] **4206**

MAIZE ABSTRACTS (UK/0267-2987) [12385518] 106, **154**

MAIZE GENETICS COOPERATION NEWS LETTER (US) [01590070] **106**

MAIZE NEWS (SA) [07982738] **106**

MAIZO BUNKAZAI HAKKUTSU CHOSA HOKOKU (JA) [01799692] **273**

MAJALAH ARKITEK (MY) [25540122] **303**

MAJALAH BANK NEGARA INDONESIA 1946 (IO) [02430097] **797**

MAJALAH BIMAS KATOLIK (IO) [03489047] **5032**

MAJALAH BPPT / BADAN PENKAJIAN DAN PENERAPAN TEKNOLOGI (IO) [09544488] **5127**

MAJALAH BULANAN KORPRI (IO/0216-4051) [08226656] **1689**

MAJALAH DEMOGRAFI INDONESIA (IO/0126-0251) [02245653] **4554**

MAJALAH FAKULTAS HUKUM UNIVERSITAS AIRLANGGA (IO) [07471996] **3005**

MAJALAH HYGIENE PERUSAHAAN, KESEHATAN-KESELAMATAN KERJA, DAN JAMINAN SOSIAL (IO) [01795393] **2865**

MAJALAH ILMIAH FAKULTAS ILMU SOSIAL UNIVERSITAS AIRLANGGA (IO) [08734519] **5208**

MAJALAH ILMU-ILMU SASTRA INDONESIA (IO/0541-721X) [02263745] **5251**

MAJALAH IPI (IO) [03028409] **3229**

MAJALAH KEBUDAYAAN MINANGKABAU (IO) [01797875] **2658**

MAJALAH KEDOKTERAN INDONESIA (IO/0377-1121) [01405598] **3606**

MAJALAH KESEHATAN MASYARAKAT (IO/0126-0979) [21265763] **4789**

MAJALAH KEUANGAN *See* KEUANGAN **795**

MAJALAH PEMBINAAN BAHASA INDONESIA (IO/0126-4737) [07184578] **3300**

MAJALAH PERPUSTAKAAN (IO) [06687492] **3229**

MAJALAH PERPUSTAKAAN MALAYSIA (MY/0126-7809) [06181201] **3229**

MAJALAH PERUSAHAAN GULA (IO/0541-7406) [03726060] **106**

MAJALAH RISDA (MY) [01797883] **5076**

MAJALAH TEKHNIS PARIWISATA (IO) [03405642] **2568**

MAJALAH UNIVERSITAS SUMATERA UTARA (IO) [03448718] **1834**

MAJALLA (LONDON), AL (UK/0261-0876) [07859703] **2489**

MAJALLAH (SY) [01756539] **3300**

MAJALLAH AL-ASKARIYAH AL-FILASTINIYAH (TUNIS, TUNISIA) (TI) [10536778] **4049**

MAJALLAH-I DANISHKADAH-I DARUSAZI (IR/0254-4547) [I02544547] **4314**

MAJALLAH-I FIZIK (IR) [10982790] **4411**

MAJALLAH-I NIZAM-I PIZISHKI-I IRAN (IR/0254-4571) [02096270] **3606**

MAJALLAH-I NUR-I ILM : NASHRIYAH-I JAMIAH-I MUDARRISIN-I HAWZAH-I ILMIYAH-I QUM (IR) [11799671] **5043**

MAJALLAH-I ZABANSHINASI (IR/0259-9082) [14106890] **3301**

MAJALLAH PERANGKAAN BERKENAAN PERUSAHAAN PERLOMBONGAN MALAYSIA (MY) [02247118] **2143**

MAJALLAN AL ARABIYAH LIL BUHUTH AL TARBAWIYAH, AL *See* ARAB JOURNAL OF EDUCATION **1726**

MAJALLAT AL-AKADEMIYAH AL-ARABIYAH LIL-NAQL AL-BAHARI (UA) [05238606] **4178**

MAJALLAT AL-BUHUTH ABTARIKHIYAH (LY) [06690608] **2641**

MAJALLAT AL-BUHUTH AL-TARIKHIYAN (LY) [06855826] **2641**

MAJALLAT AL-BUHUTH WA-AL-DIRASAT AL-ARABIYAH (UA) [05268681] **2658**

MAJALLAT AL-FIKR AL-ISLAMI / TUSDIRUHA JAMAAT AL-FIKR WA-AL-THAQAFAH AL-ISLAMIYAH BI-AL-KHARTUM (SJ) [11055927] **5043**

MAJALLAT AL-FIKR AL-MUASIR (LE) [01799111] **2506**

MAJALLAT AL-IQTISAD WA-AL-IDARAH (SU) [03428980] **1617**

MAJALLAT AL-KHADAMAT AL-SIHHIYAH LI-IQLIM SHARQ AL-BAHR AL-MUTAWASSIT (UA) [21372222] 4789, **3606**

MAJALLAT AL-NIL / TASDURU AN MARKAZ AL-NIL LIL-ILAM WA-AL-TALIM WA-AL-TADRIB (UA) [12119261] **1801**

MAJALLAT AL-NUR AL-URTHUDHUKSIYAH (LE) [07627591] **5039**

MAJALLAT AL-QUWAT AL-MUSALLAHAH AL-MALAKIYAH (MR) [04066574] **4049**

MAJALLAT AL-SALAM (US/0882-9756) [11926899] **5039**

MAJALLAT AL-SHABIBAH AL-SAHRAWIYAH (MR) [06065062] **2499**

MAJALLAT AL-SHARQ AL-AWSAT (UA) [02914532] **2769**

MAJALLAT AL-SHIR (TI) [09143390] **3465**

MAJALLAT AL-SHURTAH (MR) [02641968] **3169**

MAJALLAT AL-SIYASAH WA-AL-ISTIRATIJIYAH (SJ) [09512007] **4481**

MAJALLAT AL-TALIM AL-ALI WA-AL-BAHTH AL-ILMI (IO) [02641508] **1834**

MAJALLAT AL-TARBIYAH WA-AL-TALIM (MR) [09631991] **1762**

MAJALLAT AL-TAWTHIQ AL-TARBAWI (SU) [02556107] **1762**

MAJALLAT AL-TIJARAH WA-AL-SINAAH, DUBAYY (TS) [05508132] **1573**

MAJALLAT AL-ULUM AL-IJTIMAIYAH (KU/0253-1097) [10565043] **5208**

MAJALLAT AWWAL NUFIMBIR (AE) [06010906] **2641**

MAJALLAT DAR AL-NIYABAH (MR) [11097626] **2641**

MAJALLAT DIRASAT AL-KHALIJ WA-AL-JAZIRAH AL-ARABIYAH (KU) [03295574] **2769**

MAJALLAT GHURFAT TIJARAT WA-SINAAT ABU ZABY (TS) [08158435] **844**

MAJALLAT JAMIAT AL-IMARAT AL-ARABIYAH AL-MUTTAHIDAH (TS) [11423779] **1835**

MAJALLAT KULLIYAT AL-ADAB, JAMIAT AL-MALIK SAUD (SU) [12570490] 1093, **357**

MAJALLAT KULLIYAT AL-ADAB WA-AL-ULUM AL-INSANIYAH (SU) [09138345] **2850**

MAJALLAT KULLIYAT AL-ADAB WA-AL-ULUM AL-INSANIYAH BI-AL-RABAT (MR) [04914619] **5233**

MAJALLAT KULLIYAT AL-MALIK KHALID AL-ASKARIYAH (SU) [10221552] **4049**

MAJALLAT KULLIYAT AL-SHARIAH (UA) [05698700] 5043, **3005**

MAJALLAT KULLIYAT AL-TARBIYAH, JAMIAT AL-BASRAH (IQ) [07483567] **1835**

MAJALLAT KULLIYAT ULUM AL-BIHAR (SU) [09496510] **1451**

MAJALLAT KULLIYAT USUL AL-DIN / TUSDIRUHA KULLIYAT USUL AL-DIN (SU) [07376753] **5043**

MAJALLAT MAHAD AL-MAKHTUTAT AL-ARABIYAH / JAMIAT (KU/0575-1454) [01538094] **3301**

MAJALLAT MAJMA AL-LUGHAH AL-ARABIYAH (UA) [01645363] **3301**

MAJALLAT MARKAZ AL-BUHUTH (SU) [12000341] **5233**

MAJALLAT MUSTAQBAL AL-SHABAB AL-MAGHRIBI (MR) [09897701] **2641**

MAJALLAT TARIKH AL-MAGHRIB (MR) [08439758] **2641**

●MAJESTAS (GW/0945-1439) **2622**

MAJESTY (UK) [12202645] **2519**

MAJI REVIEW (TZ/0377-113X) [02245990] **2093**

MAJLIS PENGELUAR-PENGELUAR GETAH MALAYSIA *See* LAPURAN TAHUNAN - MAJLIS PENGELUAR-PENGELUAR GETAH MALAYSIA **5076**

MAJMA AL-LUGHAH AL-ARABIYAH BI-DIMASHQ *See* MAJALLAH **3300**

MAJMA AL-LUGHAH AL-ARABIYAH (CAIRO, EGYPT) *See* MAHADIR AL-JALSAT **3300**

MAJMA AL-LUGHAH AL-ARABIYAH (CAIRO, EGYPT) *See* MAJALLAT MAJMA AL-LUGHAH AL-ARABIYAH **3301**

MAJOITUSLIIKKEIDEN KAPASITEETTI (FI) [03680534] 2807, **5071**

MAJOITUSTILASTO, MAJOITUSLIIKKEIDEN KAPASITEETIN KAYTTO (FI) [02245138] **2807**

MAJOLLAH-'I BASTANSHINASI VA-TARIKH (IR/1015-2830) [I10152830] 2769, **273**

MAJOR ACTIVITY ANNOUNCEMENTS (US) **1689**

MAJOR AIRLINES ANALYSIS OF FULL YEAR ... FINANCIAL AND OPERATING RESULTS (US/8756-9019) [11578719] **28**

MAJOR BUSINESS ORGANISATIONS OF EASTERN EUROPE AND THE SOVIET UNION (UK) [24262891] **691**

MAJOR CAPITAL PROJECTS INVENTORY (CN/0715-6448) [09354760] **797**

MAJOR CHANGES IN STATE MEDICAID PROGRAMS (US/1061-6764) [25168040] **5295**

MAJOR CHEMICAL AND PETROCHEMICAL COMPANIES OF EUROPE (NE) [21428542] **4263**

MAJOR COMPANIES OF ARGENTINA, BRAZIL, MEXICO, AND VENEZUELA *CEASED.* (UK) [08107829] **1617**

MAJOR COMPANIES OF EUROPE (UK) [08377695] **691**

MAJOR COMPANIES OF NIGERIA (UK) [05046927] **844**

MAJOR COMPANIES OF THE ARAB WORLD (UK/0144-0594) [03622187] **691**

MAJOR COMPANIES OF THE FAR EAST AND AUSTRALASIA (UK/0961-3226) [22369466] **691**

●MAJOR CONCEPTS IN POLITICS AND POLITICAL THEORY (US/1059-3535) [24577555] **4481**

MAJOR DEVELOPMENT ANNOUNCEMENTS ANNUAL REPORT / ATLANTA REGIONAL COMMISSION (US) [08999567] **2827**

MAJOR DEVELOPMENT ANNOUNCEMENTS IN THE ATLANTA REGION *See* MAJOR ACTIVITY ANNOUNCEMENTS **1689**

MAJOR DEVELOPMENT TRENDS IN THE ATLANTA REGION *See* MAJOR DEVELOPMENT ANNOUNCEMENTS ANNUAL REPORT / ATLANTA REGIONAL COMMISSION **2827**

●MAJOR DONORS (US/1061-1266) [25184503] **4338**

MAJOR EMPLOYERS, CENTRAL PUGET SOUND (US) [25646625] 1689, **691**

MAJOR EMPLOYERS DIRECTORY, CENTRAL PUGET SOUND REGION *See* MAJOR EMPLOYERS, CENTRAL PUGET SOUND **691**

MAJOR EMPLOYERS, METROPOLITAN CHICAGO (US) [07509774] **691**

MAJOR EMPLOYMENT ANNOUNCEMENTS IN THE ATLANTA REGION *See* MAJOR ACTIVITY ANNOUNCEMENTS **1689**

MAJOR EMPLOYMENT ANNOUNCEMENTS IN THE ATLANTA REGION / ATLANTA REGIONAL COMMISSION (US) [17461667] **1689**

MAJOR ENERGY COMPANIES OF EUROPE (UK) [21508994] **1950**

MAJOR EVENTS (CN/1184-0498) [23659137] **5483**

MAJOR FINANCIAL INSTITUTIONS OF CONTINENTAL EUROPE *See* MAJOR FINANCIAL INSTITUTIONS OF EUROPE **797**

MAJOR FINANCIAL INSTITUTIONS OF EUROPE (UK/0268-232X) [25308735] **797**

MAJOR GOALS OF VOCATIONAL EDUCATION IN MAINE (US/0090-8428) [01785941] **1914**

MAJOR HISTOCOMPATIBILITY COMPLEX, THE (US) [03455740] **538**

MAJOR HOME APPLIANCE INDUSTRY FACT BOOK (US) [23587992] **2812**

MAJOR HOUSEHOLD APPLIANCES (US/0744-2130) [03057238] **2812**

MAJOR INDUSTRIES OF INDIA ANNUAL (II/0460-7368) [01773705] **1617**

MAJOR LEAGUE BASEBALL OFFICIAL ... PREVIEW (US) [21414832] **4904**

MAJOR MANUFACTURING AND MINING INVESTMENT PROJECTS (AT/0158-6335) [I01586335] 2143, **3483**

MAJOR MASS MARKET MERCHANDISERS (US/1074-1682) [28742588] **1085**

MAJOR MATTERS BEFORE THE FEDERAL COMMUNICATIONS COMMISSION (US) [06438599] **4664**

MAJOR MEDICAL PLANS : SELECTED COLLECTIVE BARGAINING AGREEMENTS, CALIFORNIA (US/0090-6506) [01785777] 3606, **2887**

MAJOR NONDEPOSIT FUNDS OF COMMERCIAL BANKS (US) [08624644] **797**

MAJOR PROBLEMS IN DERMATOLOGY *CEASED.* (UK/0301-7842) [01001407] **3721**

MAJOR PROBLEMS IN NEUROLOGY (UK/0301-5602) [01695263] **3837**

MAJOR PROBLEMS IN OPHTHALMOLOGY *CEASED.* (UK/0309-2410) [02469571] **3876**

MAJOR PROBLEMS IN PATHOLOGY (US/0076-2881) [01770834] **3896**

MAJOR PROBLEMS IN VETERINARY MEDICINE *CEASED.* (US/0741-5575) [08089931] **5516**

MAJOR PROGRAMS, BUREAU OF LABOR STATISTICS (US/0160-2985) [03322222] 1689, **1536**

MAJOR REGIONAL PROJECT, GEOLOGY FOR DEVELOPMENT, THE PRECAMBRIAN OF AFRICA (UNESCO) *See* NEWSLETTERS / UNESCO, MAJOR REGIONAL PROJECT, GEOLOGY FOR DEVELOPMENT **1389**

MAJOR REPORT - CENTRE FOR URBAN AND COMMUNITY STUDIES, UNIVERSITY OF TORONTO (CN/0319-4620) [02442888] **2827**

MAJOR TAX PLANNING (US/1055-5498) [06445788] **4736**

●MAJOR UK COMPANIES HANDBOOK (UK/1355-7939) [13557939] **844**

MAJOR WAGE SETTLEMENTS (CN/0848-6433) [24280031] **1689**

MAKAI (US/0745-2896) [08491534] **1451**

MAKALAH STAF LPEM (IO) [11633203] **1573**

MAKARIM AL-AKHLAQ AL-ISLAMIYAH (UA) [05772236] **5043**

MAKE IT NOW - BAKE IT LATER! (US) [05508198] **2792**

MAKEDONIKA (THESSALONIKA) (GR/0076-289X) [01756541] 2697, **2850**

MAKEDONSKA TRIBUNA (US/0024-9009) [04049666] **5665**

MAKEDONSKI ARHIVIST (XN/0350-1728) [01791696] **2482**

MAKEDONSKI FOLKLOR (XN/0542-2108) [05467965] **2322**

MAKEDONSKI JAZIK (XN/0025-1089) [04440978] **3301**

MAKERERE ADULT EDUCATION JOURNAL (UG) [03674025] **1801**

MAKERERE UNIVERSITY *See* HANDBOOK FOR THE FACULTY OF ARTS AND FACULTY OF SOCIAL SCIENCES **1827**

MAKERERE UNIVERSITY *See* REPORT - MAKERERE UNIVERSITY **1844**

MAKERERE UNIVERSITY. DEPT. OF RELIGIOUS STUDIES AND PHILOSOPHY *See* OCCASIONAL RESEARCH PAPERS - DEPARTMENT OF RELIGIOUS STUDIES AND PHILOSOPHY, MAKERERE UNIVERSITY **4983**

MAKERERE UNIVERSITY. GRANTS COMMITTEE *See* REPORT OF THE UNIVERSITY GRANTS COMMITTEE **1844**

MAKERERE UNIVERSITY. SCIENCE FACULTY *See* HANDBOOK - MAKERERE UNIVERSITY. SCIENCE FACULTY **5109**

MAKHON HA-YISREELI LE-HEKER HA-SAPANUT *See* YEDION **5458**

MAKHON LI-YEHASIM BENLEUMIYIM AL-SHEM LEONARD DAIVIS *See* ANNUAL REPORT OF ACTIVITIES / THE LEONARD DAVIS INSTITUTE FOR INTERNATIONAL RELATIONS **4515**

MAKING CITIES LIVABLE NEWSLETTER (US/0891-8821) [15025524] **2827**

MAKING THE GRADE IN COLLEGE (US) [21333406] **1835**

MAKING WAVES (PASADENA, CALIF.) (US/0883-5616) [12102434] **5233**

MAKING WAVES (PORT ALBERNI) (CN/1192-2427) [27165331] **1504**

MAKROMOLEKULARE CHEMIE *See* MACROMOLECULAR CHEMISTRY AND PHYSICS **985**

MAKROMOLEKULARE CHEMIE (BASEL, SWITZERLAND : 1981) (SZ/0025-116X) [07455073] **1044**

MAKROMOLEKULARE CHEMIE. MACROMOLECULAR SYMPOSIA, DIE (SZ/0258-0322) [13430804] 1055, **1044**

MAKROMOLEKULARE CHEMIE. MACROMOLECULAR SYMPOSIA *See* MACROMOLECULAR SYMPOSIA **985**

MAKROMOLEKULARE CHEMIE. RAPID COMMUNICATIONS *See* MACROMOLECULAR RAPID COMMUNICATIONS **985**

MAKROMOLEKULARE CHEMIE. RAPID COMMUNICATIONS, DIE (SZ/0173-2803) [06241230] **1044**

MAKROMOLEKULARE CHEMIE. THEORY AND SIMULATIONS *See* MACROMOLECULAR THEORY AND SIMULATIONS **985**

MAKROMOLEKULARE CHEMIE: THEORY AND SIMULATIONS, DIE (SZ/1018-5054) [25268798] **985**

MAKTAB AL-ABHATH WA-AL-MUSAHAMAT AL-MADINIYAH (RABAT, MOROCCO) *See* BUREAU DE RECHERCHES ET DE PARTICIPATIONS MINIERES : RAPPORT **1421**

MAKTAB AL-ABHATH WA-AL-MUSAHAMAT AL-MADINIYAH (RABAT, MOROCCO) *See* ACTIVITIES / BUREAU DE RECHERCHES ET DE PARTICIPATIONS MINIERES **2132**

MAKTAB KERJASAMA MALAYSIA *See* LAPURAN TAHUNAN - MAKTAB KERJASAMA MALAYSIA **1615**

MAKTABA (KE/0253-5971) [01794691] **3229**

MAKTABA AFRIKANA SERIES (US/0146-8553) [03063149] **2641**

MAKTABAT AL-IDARAH (SU) [05080537] **3229**

MAKTABDA UZBEK, RUS TILLARI VA ADABIETI (UZ/0320-2887) [24162840] **3301**

MAKU (JA/0385-1036) [10427827] **463**

MAKUNAGI (JA) [04149571] **5590**

MAL DE BLOCS (CN/0228-7838) [08023703] **3005**

MAL-I-MIC (1979) (CN/0229-012X) [07970384] **2745**

MAL SORI (KO) [07940891] **3301**

MALACCA AND SINGAPORE STRAITS TIDE TABLES (US) [07359077] **4178**

MALACOLOGIA (US/0076-2997) [01696513] **5590**

MALACOLOGICAL REVIEW (US/0076-3004) [01680739] **5590**

MALACOLOGICAL SOCIETY OF AUSTRALIA *See* JOURNAL OF THE MALACOLOGICAL SOCIETY OF AUSTRALIA **5589**

MALACOLOGY DATA NET (US/0892-6506) [13586254] **5590**

MALADIES CHRONIQUES AU CANADA (CN/0228-8702) [07822777] 4789, **3606**

MALADIES METABOLIQUES. E81 (FR) **3606**

MALADJUSTMENT AND THERAPEUTIC EDUCATION *See* THERAPEUTIC CARE AND EDUCATION : THE JOURNAL OF THE ASSOCIATION OF WORKERS FOR CHILDREN WITH EMOTIONAL AND BEHAVIOURAL DIFFICULTIES **4620**

MALAGASY REPUBLIC. MINISTERE DU DEVELOPPEMENT RURAL ET DE LA REFORME AGRAIRE *See* GAZATIM-BAOVAO - MINISTERAN'NY FAMPANDROSOANA NY AMBANIVOHITRA SY NY FANAVAOZANA NY FIZAKAN-TANY **89**

MALAGASY REPUBLIC. SERVICE GEOLOGIQUE *See* CATALOGUE DES PUBLICATIONS - SERVICE GEOLOGIQUE DE MADAGASCAR **1371**

MALAHAT REVIEW, THE (CN/0025-1216) [01756543] **3409**

MALAKOLOGIAI TAJEKOZTATO (HU/0230-0648) [19609828] **5590**

MALAKOLOGISCHE ABHANDLUNGEN (GW/0070-7260) [04520614] **5590**

MALARIA SURVEILLANCE : ANNUAL SUMMARY / NATIONAL COMMUNICABLE DISEASE CENTER (US) [01036044] 4789, **3715**

MALAWI (MW) [01789093] **2499**

MALAWI *See* MALAWI GOVERNMENT GAZETTE, THE **4664**

MALAWI BUYERS GUIDE / COMPILED AND PUBLISHED BY THE MALAWI EXPORT PROMOTION COUNCIL (MW) [09719342] 844, **950**

MALAWI DEVELOPMENT CORPORATION *See* ANNUAL REPORT - MALAWI DEVELOPMENT CORPORATION **1597**

MALAWI DEVELOPMENT CORPORATION. REPORT AND ACCOUNTS *See* ANNUAL REPORT - MALAWI DEVELOPMENT CORPORATION **1597**

MALAWI ECONOMIC BRIEF (MW) [11989994] **1504**

MALAWI : ENERGIEWIRTSCHAFT (GW) [05064452] **1950**

MALAWI. GEOLOGICAL SURVEY DEPT *See* MEMOIR - MALAWI GEOLOGICAL SURVEY DEPARTMENT **1387**

MALAWI GOVERNMENT GAZETTE, THE (MW) [11422405] **4664**

MALAWI JOURNAL OF SCIENCE (MW) [02553766] **5127**

MALAWI JOURNAL OF SCIENCE & TECHNOLOGY (MW/1019-7079) [I10197079] **5127**

MALAWI. MINISTRY OF AGRICULTURE AND NATURAL RESOURCES *See* HIGHLIGHTS **92**

MALAWI MONTHLY STATISTICAL BULLETIN (MW) [08840696] **5332**

MALAWI. NATIONAL STATISTICAL OFFICE *See* TOURIST REPORT - MALAWI. NATIONAL STATISTICAL OFFICE **5494**

Alphabetical Title Index — MALUKU

MALAWI. SELECT COMMITTEE ON PUBLIC ACCOUNTS See FIRST REPORT OF THE PUBLIC ACCOUNTS COMMITTEE TO THE NATIONAL ASSEMBLY, THE **4726**

MALAWI STATISTICAL YEARBOOK (MW) [01785186] **5332**

MALAWI : WIRTSCHAFTLICHE ENTWICKLUNG (GW) [02520102] **1573**

MALAWIAN GEOGRAPHER, THE (MW/1010-5549) [02784749] **2568**

MALAWIAN WRITERS SERIES (MW) [07588505] **3409**

MALAYA (FEDERATION). DEPT. OF SOCIAL WELFARE See REPORT - MALAYA (FEDERATION) DEPT. OF SOCIAL WELFARE **5305**

MALAYALAM LITERARY SURVEY (II) [04602396] **3465**

MALAYAN AGRICULTURAL PRODUCERS ASSOCIATION See ANNUAL REPORT - MALAYAN AGRICULTURAL PRODUCERS ASSOCIATION **60**

MALAYAN LAW JOURNAL See SINGAPORE LAW REPORTS, THE **3055**

MALAYAN LAW JOURNAL (BILINGUAL ED.) (SI/0025-1283) [01756553] **3005**

MALAYAN NATURALIST (MY/0127-0206) [08093913] **4167**

MALAYAN NATURE JOURNAL, THE (MY/0025-1291) [02357237] **4167**

MALAYANG PILIPINO / FREE FILIPINO (PH) [09678110] **2769**

MALAYSIA See OFFICIAL YEAR BOOK - MALAYSIA **2507**

MALAYSIA See SENARAI PERJAWATAN DI KEMENTERIAN-KEMENTERIAN DAN JABATAN-JABATAN DALAM ANGGARAN PERBELANJAAN PERSEKUTUAN **4685**

MALAYSIA AGRICULTURAL DIRECTORY & INDEX (MY) [11892241] **106**

MALAYSIA. BAHAGIAN INSURAN See LAPORAN TAHUNAN ... KETUA PENGARAH INSURANS **2886**

MALAYSIA. BAHAGIAN PARIT DAN TALIAIR See PENYATA TAHUNAN BAHAGIAN PARIT DAN TALIAIR, KEMENTERIAN PERTANIAN MALAYSIA BAGI TAHUN ... **2094**

MALAYSIA. BAHAGIAN PERANCANG DAN PENYELIDIKAN PELAJARAN See JERNAL BAHAGIAN PERANCANG DAN PENYELIDIKAN PELAJARAN **1755**

MALAYSIA. BAHAGIAN PERIKANAN See PERANGKAAN TAHUNAN PERIKANAN **2317**

MALAYSIA EXPORTERS (MY) [05810256] **844**

MALAYSIA INDUSTRIAL DIGEST (MY/0542-3937) [02359357] **1573**

MALAYSIA INTER-RELIGIOUS ORGANISATION See SUARA **5001**

MALAYSIA. JABATAN PENYIASATAN KAJIBUMI See DISTRICT MEMOIR / GEOLOGICAL SURVEY OF WEST MALAYSIA **1373**

MALAYSIA. JABATAN PERANGKAAN See BUKU MAKLUMAT PERANGKAAN GETAH BAGI MALAYSIA. RUBBER STATISTICS HANDBOOK OF MALAYSIA **5078**

MALAYSIA. JABATAN PERANGKAAN See KATALOG **5330**

MALAYSIA. JABATAN PERANGKAAN See SIARAN PERANGKAAN TAHUNAN, SABAH. ANNUAL BULLETIN OF STATISTICS, SABAH **5338**

MALAYSIA. JABATAN PERANGKAAN. KATALOK See KATALOG **5330**

MALAYSIA. JABATAN TELEKOM See LAPURAN TAHUNAN / JABATAN TELEKOM MALAYSIA **1159**

MALAYSIA. KEMENTERIAN BURUH DAN TENAGA RAKYAT See MONTHLY REPORT - MINISTRY OF LABOUR & MANPOWER (KUALA LUMPUR) **1691**

MALAYSIA. KEMENTERIAN KEWANGAN See ECONOMIC REPORT - MALAYSIA. KEMENTERIAN KEWANGAN **1557**

MALAYSIA. KEMENTERIAN PELAJARAN See JOURNAL - KEMENTERIAN PELAJARAN MALAYSIA **1756**

MALAYSIA. KEMENTERIAN PERTANIAN DAN TANAH See BULLETIN OF STATISTICS RELATING TO THE MINING INDUSTRY OF MALAYSIA **2002**

MALAYSIA. KEMENTERIAN PERUSAHAAN UTAMA See MAJALLAH PERANGKAAN BERKENAAN PERUSAHAAN PERLOMBONGAN MALAYSIA **2143**

MALAYSIA. KENENTARIAN KEWANGAN See BUDGET SPEECH AND TAX PROPOSALS **4715**

MALAYSIA MASA KINI (MY) [11206905] **2658**

MALAYSIA. PIHAK BERKUASA KEMAJUAN PEKEBUN KECIL PERUSAHAAN GETAH See MAJALAH RISDA **5076**

MALAYSIA SHOWCASE (MY) [07364894] **1573**

MALAYSIA : WIRTSCHAFTLICHE ENTWICKLUNG (GW) [03527911] **1504**

MALAYSIA : WIRTSCHAFTSDATEN UND WIRTSCHAFTSDOKUMENTATION (GW) [06260128] **1573**

MALAYSIA, WIRTSCHAFTSSTRUKTUR / BUNDESSTELLE FUR AUSSENHANDELSINFORMATION (GW) [07699030] **1573**

MALAYSIAN AGRICULTURAL JOURNAL, THE (MY/0025-1321) [01756561] **106**

MALAYSIAN APPLIED BIOLOGY (MY/0126-8643) [04625076] **106, 463**

MALAYSIAN BUILDING & CONSTRUCTION (MY/0377-1148) [02242813] **619**

MALAYSIAN BUSINESS (MY) [01784327] **691**

MALAYSIAN CHINESE ASSOCIATION. GENERAL ASSEMBLY See SECRETARY-GENERAL'S REPORT **4685**

MALAYSIAN FINANCE & DEVELOPMENT (MY) [01785333] **1573**

MALAYSIAN FORESTER, THE (MY/0302-2935) [01793177] **2387**

MALAYSIAN GEOGRAPHERS (MY/0126-642X) [07286855] **2568**

MALAYSIAN INDUSTRIAL ESTATES LTD See LAPURAN TAHUN DAN KIRA-KIRA - MALAYSIA INDUSTRIAL ESTATES SENDIRIAN BERHAD **1502**

MALAYSIAN INDUSTRIAL ESTATES LTD. ANNUAL REPORT AND ACCOUNTS See LAPURAN TAHUN DAN KIRA-KIRA - MALAYSIA INDUSTRIAL ESTATES SENDIRIAN BERHAD **1502**

MALAYSIAN INDUSTRIAL ESTATES SENDIRIAN BERHAD See LAPURAN TAHUNAN ... BAGI TAHUN BERAKHIR 31HB MAC **1615**

MALAYSIAN INSTITUTE OF MANAGEMENT See LAPORAN TAHUNAN - YAYASAN PENGURUSAN MALAYSIA **875**

MALAYSIAN JOURNAL OF AGRICULTURAL ECONOMICS, THE (MY) [12697898] **107**

MALAYSIAN JOURNAL OF ECONOMIC STUDIES : JOURNAL OF THE MALAYSIAN ECONOMIC ASSOCIATION AND THE FACULTY OF ECONOMICS AND ADMINISTRATION, UNIVERSITY OF MALAYA (MY) [20998516] **2911**

MALAYSIAN JOURNAL OF PATHOLOGY, THE (MY/0126-8635) [07349079] **3896**

MALAYSIAN JOURNAL OF SCIENCE (MY/0126-7906) [01785419] **5127**

MALAYSIAN JOURNAL OF TROPICAL GEOGRAPHY (MY/0127-1474) [07255443] **2568**

MALAYSIAN MANAGEMENT REVIEW (MY/0025-1348) [02359468] **691**

MALAYSIAN MATHEMATICAL SOCIETY See BULLETIN OF THE MALAYSIAN MATHEMATICAL SOCIETY **3498**

MALAYSIAN RUBBER REVIEW (MY/0127-2969) [14955162] **5076**

MALAYSIAN VETERINARY JOURNAL, THE CEASED. (MY/0126-5652) [07594595] **5516**

MALCHUS : THE NATION'S LESBIAN & GAY CHRISTIAN MONTHLY (US) **2795**

MALCOLM BALDRIGE NATIONAL QUALITY AWARD NEWSLETTER (US) **4031**

MALCOLM HULKE STUDIES IN CINEMA AND TELEVISION (US/0884-6944) [12412142] **4074**

MALCOLM LOWRY REVIEW, THE (CN/0828-5020) [11733187] **3347**

MALCONTENT, THE (US/1062-9173) [25805911] **3409**

MALDEN, MASS. PUBLIC LIBRARY See ANNUAL REPORT OF THE MALDEN PUBLIC LIBRARY **3191**

MALDOROR (UY) [05433028] **3409**

MALECKI ON INSURANCE (US/1059-6186) [24647573] **2887**

MALEDICTA (US/0363-3659) [03188018] **2322, 3301**

MALEDICTA PRESS PUBLICATIONS (US/0363-9037) [02540925] **3301**

MALEMA RIBHOLUSANA PAOJELA (II) [12094239] **4543**

MALEZAS / ASOCIACION ARGENTINA PARA EL CONTROL DE MALEZAS (AG) [08521387] **2424, 517**

MALI (FR) [01795565] **1573**

MALI (REPUBLIC). SERVICE DE LA STATISTIQUE GENERALE ET DE LA COMPTABILITE ECONOMIQUE NATIONALE See BULLETIN MENSUEL DE STATISTIQUE / REPUBLIQUE DU MALI, MINISTERE D'ETAT CHARGE DU PLAN ET DE LA COORDINATION DES AFFAIRES ECONOMIQUES ET FINANCIERES, SERVICE DE LA STATISTIQUE GENERALE ET DE LA COMPTABILITE ECONOMIQUE NATIONALE **5324**

MALI WIRTSCHAFTLICHE ENTWICKLUNG / BUNDESSTELLE FUR AUSSENHANDELSINFORMATION (GW) [07377856] **1573**

MALIBU SURFSIDE NEWS, THE (US/0191-7307) [04960829] **5636**

MALIBU TIMES (US/1050-4931) [11570745] **5637**

MALINI (US/0737-8688) [09276200] **3409, 2267**

MALL OG MINNE (NO/0024-855X) [02108499] **2322, 3301**

MALLAS JA OLUT (FI/0356-3014) [03342229] **2369**

MALLET, THE CEASED. (US/0162-8879) [04241329] **634**

MALLORN (UK/0308-6674) [03364461] **3409**

MALMGREN'S WORLD TRADE OUTLOOK (US/0162-640X) [04196932] **845**

MALONE SOCIETY See COLLECTIONS - MALONE SOCIETY, LONDON **3376**

MALONE TELEGRAM (US) [22186885] **5718**

● MALONEY'S ANTIQUES & COLLECTIBLES RESOURCE DIRECTORY (US) [28951364] **251**

MALPRACTICE BI-WEEKLY NEWSLETTER INDEX OF FRAUD, MEDICAL MISTAKES, DIAGNOSTIC ERRORS, AND ADVERSE REACTIONS, INCLUDING ILLNESSES AND DISEASES CAUSED BY DOCTORS (US/1056-4748) [23719332] **3741**

MALPRACTICE DIGEST (US/0094-6133) [01794870] **3005**

MALPRACTICE PREVENTION FOR HOSPITALS (US/0193-6166) [05222557] **3005**

MALPRACTICE PREVENTION FOR PHYSICIANS (US/0276-0495) [07260687] **3915, 3005**

MALPRACTICE PREVENTION REPORTER (US/0739-6031) [09752410] **3005**

MALPRACTICE REPORTER. ANESTHESIOLOGY, THE (US/0738-1018) [09503841] **3683, 3005**

MALPRACTICE REPORTER. HOSPITALS, THE (US/0738-1956) [09515984] **3606, 3005**

MALPRACTICE REPORTER. OB/GYN, THE (US/0738-1948) [09516038] **3764, 3005**

MALPRACTICE REPORTER. PODIATRY, THE (US/0749-3495) [11123601] **3606, 3005**

MALPRACTICE REPORTER. SURGERY : MPR, THE (US) [16713667] **3969, 3005**

MALPRACTICE REPORTER, THE (US/0738-1026) [08716870] **3915, 3005**

MALT NEWSLETTER (CN/0710-3417) [12064679] **3229**

MALTA. DEPT. OF INFORMATION. REPORT ON THE WORKING OF GOVERNMENT DEPARTMENTS See REPORTS ON THE WORKING OF GOVERNMENT DEPARTMENTS FOR THE YEAR ... **4682**

MALTA. INFORMATION DIVISION See REPORTS ON THE WORKING OF GOVERNMENT DEPARTMENTS FOR THE YEAR ... **4682**

MALTA. MINISTRY OF FOREIGN AFFAIRS See EXTERNAL AFFAIRS SERVICE LIST **2968**

MALTA. OFFICE OF STATISTICS See QUARTERLY DIGEST OF STATISTICS **5337**

MALTA. OFFICE OF STATISTICS See ANNUAL ABSTRACTS OF STATISTICS - CENTRAL OFFICE OF STATISTICS (VALLETTA) **5321**

MALTA. OFFICE OF STATISTICS. STATISTICAL ABSTRACT OF THE MALTESE ISLANDS See ANNUAL ABSTRACTS OF STATISTICS - CENTRAL OFFICE OF STATISTICS (VALLETTA) **5321**

MALTA TRADE DIRECTORY (UK) [03216770] **845**

MALTA, WIRTSCHAFT IN ZAHLEN / BUNDESSTELLE FUR AUSSENHANDELSINFORMATION (GW) [09351330] **1573**

MALTESE DIRECTORY : CANADA, UNITED STATES (CN/0317-6983) [02308198] **2745**

MALTON PILOT, THE (CN/0700-8082) [03400010] **5789**

MALUKU, INDONESIA. KANTOR SENSUS DAN STATISTIK See INVENTARISASI AKOMODASI PROPINSI MALUKU **5071**

MALVERN — Alphabetical Title Index

MALVERN DAILY RECORD (US) [12959730] **5631**

MALVERN LEADER (MALVERN, IOWA : 1883) (US) [12257312] **5671**

MALY ROCZNIK STATYSTYCZNY (PL/0079-2608) [01078700] **5332**

MAM/FA NEWSLETTER (US) [23877848] **357**

MAMMAL REVIEW (UK/0305-1838) [01785925] **5590**

MAMMALIA DEPICTA (GW/0301-2778) [15235973] **5590**

MAMMALIA (PARIS) (FR/0025-1461) [01449590] **5590**

MAMMALIAN GENOME (US/0938-8990) [22379127] **463**

MAMMALIAN SPECIES (US/0076-3519) [01756570] **464**

MAMMALS : A MULTIMEDIA ENCYCLOPEDIA (US) 1927, **5591**

MAMMARY GLAND (UK/0964-7600) **464**

MAMMILLARIA SOCIETY *See* JOURNAL OF THE MAMMILLARIA SOCIETY, THE **516**

●MAMMOGRAPH ABSTRACTS : BREAST CANCER SCREENING REFERENCES (UK/0962-0605) [24543536] **3820**

MAMMOTH TRUMPET (US/8755-6898) [10987796] 240, **273**

MAN AND CULTURE IN OCEANIA (JA) [14342511] 240, **2267**

MAN & DEVELOPMENT (II/0258-0438) [06289025] **1617**

MAN & ENVIRONMENT (II/0258-0446) [03318347] 240, **1386**

MAN AND LIFE (II) [03217890] **240**

MAN AND MEDICINE (US/0145-9783) [02831480] 3606, **2252**

MAN AND NATURE (CN/0824-3298) [12168420] **2622**

MAN AND WORLD (NE/0025-1534) [01241935] **4352**

MAN AT ARMS (US/0191-3522) [04853326] **4049**

MAN! (AUSTIN, TEX.) *CEASED.* (US/1056-5175) [23734408] **3995**

MAN (BOSTON, MASS.) (US/1057-5383) [24072209] **1194**

●MAN (CHICAGO, ILL.) (US/1062-2543) [25559548] 357, **2267**

MAN-ENVIRONMENT SYSTEMS (US/0025-1550) [01789193] 5251, **303**

MAN IN INDIA (II/0025-1569) [01605851] **240**

MAN IN SOUTHEAST ASIA (AT/0580-5287) [02365247] **240**

MAN IN THE NORTHEAST (US/0191-4138) [02263799] **240**

MAN, ISLE OF. TREASURY. ECONOMICS SECTION *See* ISLE OF MAN DIGEST OF ECONOMIC AND SOCIAL STATISTICS **1534**

MAN (LONDON) (UK/0025-1496) [01756573] **240**

MAN-MADE FIBERS OF JAPAN (JA/0303-7215) [01793831] **5354**

MAN-MADE TEXTILES IN INDIA (II/0377-7537) [01790567] **5354**

MAN MAGNUM (SA) [09798340] **4904**

MAN. MUSEUM ARCHAEOLOGISTS NEWS (UK/0959-4272) [09594272] **273**

MAN TO MAN (OTTAWA) (CN/0825-3498) [11807710] 3995, **5251**

MAN UNDERWATER (CN/0383-7777) [03232850] **4904**

MANA (FJ) [05296244] **3409**

MANA (ALEXANDRIA, VA.) (US/0464-8145) [02383634] **2519**

MANA ANNUAL OF CREATIVE WRITING, THE (PO/0377-1164) [02241180] **3409**

MANA, MANNHEIMER ANALYTIKA *CEASED.* (GW/0176-1226) [15080033] **324**

MANA MEMBERS DIRECTORY OF MANUFACTURERS' SALES AGENCIES (US/0890-7641) [14227579] **3483**

MANAB MON (II/0025-1615) [01790477] 464, 5251, **4603**

MANABAMANA (II) [03231567] **4603**

MANADSJOURNALEN (SW/0349-4225) [08773262] **3229**

MANAGE (US/0025-1623) [01909229] **876**

MANAGE IT (US/1047-7926) [20788488] **5127**

MANAGED ACCOUNT REPORTS (UK) **797**

MANAGED CARE ALERT *See* HEALTH ALLIANCE ALERT **2881**

MANAGED CARE INSIGHTS (US/1049-457X) [21256446] **3606**

●MANAGED CARE (LANGHORNE, PA.) (US/1062-3388) [25589518] **3788**

MANAGED CARE LAW OUTLOOK (US/1042-4091) [19036724] 2887, **3006**

MANAGED CARE OUTLOOK (US/0896-6567) [17241183] **3788**

●MANAGED CARE QUALITY (US/1064-5454) [26326048] 5295, **1617**

MANAGED CARE UPDATE (US) **4789**

MANAGED CARE WEEK (US/1056-7461) [23835718] **3788**

MANAGED HEALTH CARE DIRECTORY (US/1072-2815) [24094760] **3788**

MANAGED HEALTHCARE (US/1060-1392) [29925470] **4789**

MANAGED HEALTHCARE NEWS (US/1060-1392) [24881059] **4789**

MANAGEMENT (IT) **876**

MANAGEMENT ABSTRACTS (II/0377-1172) [02239392] **876**

MANAGEMENT ACCOUNTANT (PK) **747**

MANAGEMENT ACCOUNTANT, THE (II/0025-1674) [01590232] **747**

MANAGEMENT ACCOUNTING (LONDON) (UK/0025-1682) [04567633] 876, **747**

MANAGEMENT ACCOUNTING (NEW YORK, N.Y.) (US/0025-1690) [02245037] **747**

MANAGEMENT ACCOUNTING RESEARCH (UK/1044-5005) [19817960] **747**

MANAGEMENT ADVISORY SERVICES: GUIDELINE SERIES (US/0065-8766) [01480038] 748, **876**

MANAGEMENT & COMPUTER (GW) 1194, **876**

MANAGEMENT & COORDINATION (JA/0914-9007) [20873205] **876**

●MANAGEMENT & DOCTORS (US/1071-3255) [27766528] **3915**

MANAGEMENT AND LABOUR STUDIES (II/0258-042X) [06168461] 1689, **943**

MANAGEMENT AND MARKETING ABSTRACTS (UK/0308-2172) [04104163] 691, **731**

MANAGEMENT AUCKLAND (NZ/0025-1658) [I00251658] **876**

MANAGEMENT AWARENESS PROGRAM (US/0360-7542) [02245098] **876**

MANAGEMENT BIBLIOGRAPHIES & REVIEWS (UK/0309-0582) [03170422] 876, **731**

MANAGEMENT BULLETINS (US) **876**

MANAGEMENT COMMUNICATION QUARTERLY (US/0893-3189) [15482759] 876, **1115**

MANAGEMENT COMPENSATION IN CANADA (CN/0315-5420) [02441522] **943**

MANAGEMENT COMPENSATION IN CANADIAN BANKING & FINANCE (CN/0383-7874) [03248366] 797, **876**

MANAGEMENT COMPENSATION IN THE RAILROAD INDUSTRY *See* MANAGEMENT COMPENSATION, RAILROADS **5432**

MANAGEMENT COMPENSATION, RAILROADS (US/0273-0332) [06984338] **5432**

MANAGEMENT COMPENSATION SURVEY / CONDUCTED AND PUBLISHED BY SIBSON & COMPANY (US) [08665962] **943**

MANAGEMENT COMPENSATION SURVEY OF THE INSURANCE INDUSTRY (US/8756-6001) [11565987] 2887, **1689**

MANAGEMENT CONSULTANCY (UK) **876**

MANAGEMENT CONSULTANT INTERNATIONAL (IE/0956-3253) [21493519] **876**

MANAGEMENT CONSULTING (BOSTON, MASS.) (US/0741-3092) [08512052] 876, **4206**

MANAGEMENT CONTENTS *CEASED.* (US/0360-2400) [01866138] 876, **731**

MANAGEMENT CONTENTS [ONLINE DATABASE] (US) 876, **731**

MANAGEMENT DAN USAHAWAN INDONESIA (IO/0302-9859) [09149316] **876**

MANAGEMENT DATA LIST (ML) BASIC NAVY MICROFORM (US) [07430908] **4178**

MANAGEMENT DECISION (UK/0025-1747) [01756583] **877**

MANAGEMENT DEVELOPMENT GUIDE *See* AMA GUIDE TO MANAGEMENT DEVELOPMENT & TRAINING COURSES / AMERICAN MANAGEMENT ASSOCIATION, THE **859**

MANAGEMENT DEVELOPMENT REVIEW (UK) [29452834] **877**

MANAGEMENT DEVELOPMENT SERIES (US) [06026808] **877**

MANAGEMENT (DUBLIN) (IE/0025-164X) [11445823] **877**

MANAGEMENT E INFORMATICA *CEASED.* (IT) **1194**

MANAGEMENT EDUCATION AND DEVELOPMENT (UK/0047-5688) [01788812] 877, **1617**

MANAGEMENT ET CONJONCTURE SOCIALE PARIS (FR/1157-5662) [11575662] **877**

MANAGEMENT ET TECHNOLOGIES ALIMENTAIRES *CEASED.* (FR) [21614516] **1617**

MANAGEMENT HEUTE (GW) [05667394] **877**

MANAGEMENT HORIZONS (US) [03008733] **877**

MANAGEMENT IMPROVEMENT AND COST REDUCTION GOALS (US) [01783557] 877, **4664**

MANAGEMENT IN EDUCATION (UK/0892-0206) [15062206] **1762**

MANAGEMENT IN GOVERNMENT (II/0047-570X) [01756585] **4664**

MANAGEMENT IN GOVERNMENT (LONDON, ENGLAND) (UK/0263-4678) [08370152] **4704**

MANAGEMENT IN PRACTICE (NEWPORT NEWS, VA.) (US/1067-9391) [27122358] **943**

MANAGEMENT INFO (NE) **877**

MANAGEMENT INFORMATION GUIDE *CEASED.* (US/0076-3632) [01756587] **877**

MANAGEMENT INFORMATION REPORT / OFFICE OF FINANCIAL MANAGEMENT (US) [11770895] **877**

MANAGEMENT INFORMATION SERVICE (II/0300-2667) [01784132] **877**

MANAGEMENT INFORMATION SYSTEMS QUARTERLY (US/0276-7783) [03681309] **1194**

MANAGEMENT INTERNATIONAL REVIEW (GW/0025-181X) [06838229] **877**

MANAGEMENT JAPAN (JA/0025-1828) [02287860] **877**

MANAGEMENT JOURNAL (UY/0300-2144) [01784735] **877**

MANAGEMENT (KENYA INSTITUTE OF MANAGEMENT) (KE) [08843710] **877**

MANAGEMENT LAURETES: A COLLECTION OF AUTOBIOGRAPHICAL ESSAYS (US) **877**

●MANAGEMENT LEARNING (UK/1350-5076) [30101233] 877, **1617**

MANAGEMENT MATTERS (PLANTATION, FLA.) (US/1054-4275) [22913424] **943**

MANAGEMENT MEMO (US) **877**

MANAGEMENT MEMO (BE) **877**

MANAGEMENT MONITOR / NCD (NE) [08366707] **877**

MANAGEMENT NEWS (BRITISH INSTITUTE OF MANAGEMENT) *See* PROFESSIONAL MANAGER **883**

MANAGEMENT NEWS : THE NEWSPAPER OF THE BRITISH INSTITUTE OF MANAGEMENT (UK/0025-1844) [10176723] **877**

MANAGEMENT OF HOUSING (US/0147-3433) [03145043] **2827**

MANAGEMENT OF VOLUNTARY ORGANISATIONS (UK) 877, **4338**

MANAGEMENT PAKISTAN, THE (PK) [05044963] **877**

MANAGEMENT PARTNER (NE) **877**

MANAGEMENT PAY REVIEW (UK/1351-4954) **1689**

MANAGEMENT PLAN / PRIVATE COLLEGES ACCREDITATION BOARD *CEASED.* (CN/1182-7890) [22929038] **1866**

●MANAGEMENT POLICIES AND PERSONNEL LAW (US) [25072705] **3151**

MANAGEMENT PORTFOLIO (US/1050-2114) [21427005] 4566, **877**

MANAGEMENT QUARTERLY (US/0025-1860) [02254047] 930, **877**

MANAGEMENT REPORT (US) [01480579] **2402**

MANAGEMENT REPORT FOR NONUNION ORGANIZATIONS (US) **1689**

MANAGEMENT REPORT - GENERAL SERVICES ADMINISTRATION (US/0091-6242) [01786961] 878, **4664**

MANAGEMENT REPORT (NEW YORK, N.Y.) (US/0745-4880) [09228295] **944**

MANAGEMENT RESEARCH NEWS : MRN (UK/0140-9174) [10068933] **878**

MANAGEMENT RESULTS *See* CDA/WIESENBERGER MUTUAL FUNDS UPDATE **894**

MANAGEMENT REVIEW (US) [04621471] **878**

MANAGEMENT REVIEW (SARANAC LAKE) (US/0025-1895) [04590611] **944**

MANAGEMENT S.A (AT) **878**

MANAGEMENT SCIENCE (US/0025-1909) [01641131] **878**

MANAGEMENT SCIENCES TRAINING CENTER (US) [06653584] **944**

MANAGEMENT SELECTION AND DEVELOPMENT, ANNUAL STATUS REPORT (US) [01787515] **4664**

MANAGEMENT SERIES (INDIANAPOLIS) (US/0095-1676) [01795088] **2198**

MANAGEMENT SERVICES AND PRODUCTION ABSTRACTS *See* OPERATIONS & PRODUCTION MANAGEMENT ABSTRACTS **2006**

MANAGEMENT SERVICES ASSOCIATES, AUSTIN, TEX *See* MSA TAX CORRESPONDENT **4737**

MANAGEMENT SERVICES (ENFIELD) (UK/0307-6768) [03160058] **878**

MANAGEMENT STRATEGY (US/0889-9444) [04015565] **4707**

MANAGEMENT STUDY ABROAD *CEASED.* (US) [20332692] **878**

MANAGEMENT SUMMARY (US/0748-6316) [10960196] 878, **2887**

MANAGEMENT SUMMARY (PERTH, W.A.) (AT) [10983013] 4664, **2198**

MANAGEMENT TECHNOLOGY (NEW YORK, N.Y. : 1983) (US/0736-5225) [09156874] **5127**

MANAGEMENT TODAY (UK/0025-1925) [00820307] **878**

MANAGEMENT-WISSEN (GW/0340-4137) [I03404137] **878**

MANAGER GENT (BE/0771-9833) [I07719833] **878**

MANAGER MAGAZIN (GW/0341-4418) [06067605] **878**

MANAGER NEWSLETTER (CN/1187-4147) [25590152] **1145**

MANAGER NEWSLETTER (CN/1187-4147) [25590153] **878**

MANAGER UPDATE (UK/0957-4212) [20808960] **1689**

MANAGERIAL ACCOUNTING (US) 691, **748**

MANAGERIAL AUDITING JOURNAL (UK/0268-6902) [18340122] **748**

MANAGERIAL FINANCE (UK/0307-4358) [01692375] 878, **797**

MANAGERIAL LAW (UK/0309-0558) [05043519] **3151**

MANAGERIAL PSYCHOLOGY (II) [11164476] **4603**

MANAGERS AS LEADERS (US) **878**

MANAGER'S DEVELOPMENT PROGRAM (US) **878**

MANAGER'S INTELLIGENCE REPORT (US) **878**

MANAGER'S LEGAL BULLETIN (US/0889-4493) [13992649] **3151**

MANAGER'S MAGAZINE (US/0025-1968) [01904827] **2887**

MANAGERS (NEW YORK) (US/0092-4407) [01784482] **906**

MANAGER'S TROUBLESHOOTER, THE (US) [21335788] **944**

MANAGING AUTOMATION (US/0895-3805) [15465583] 878, **1234**

MANAGING CLINICAL DIRECTORATES (UK) **3788**

MANAGING CORROSION WITH PLASTICS (US/0197-3967) [06018993] **2014**

MANAGING DIVERSITY (US) [27345488] **1689**

●MANAGING EMPLOYEE HEALTH BENEFITS (US/1065-3937) [26602620] 2887, **878**

MANAGING END-USER COMPUTING *CEASED.* (US/1048-6933) [15533132] **1268**

MANAGING FOR HEALTH *CEASED.* (US/0897-7607) [17616849] 878, **4789**

MANAGING HOUSING LETTER (US/0193-6808) [05251275] **2827**

●MANAGING INFORMATION (UK/1352-0229) [29915815] **878**

MANAGING INFORMATION (US) [07524578] **3229**

MANAGING INFORMATION TECHNOLOGY / DATAPRO (US) [24350102] **1194**

MANAGING INTELLECTUAL PROPERTY (UK/0960-5002) [I09605002] **1306**

●MANAGING OFFICE TECHNOLOGY (US/1070-4051) [28270179] 4212, **878**

MANAGING (PITTSBURGH) *CEASED.* (US/0162-3346) [05246221] **878**

●MANAGING SENIORCARE (US/1063-035X) [25845168] 3754, **5295**

MANAGING SERVICE QUALITY (UK) [29572105] **691**

MANAGING SERVICE QUALITY (UK) **878**

MANAGING SOLID WASTE IN OREGON (US/0737-2957) [08561735] **2236**

●MANAGING SYSTEM DEVELOPMENT (US) [27464774] **1261**

●MANAGING TECHNOLOGY TODAY (US/1062-3310) [25587599] **878**

MANAGING THE CIVILIAN WORK FORCE. A GUIDE FOR MILITARY MANAGER (US) **1689**

MANAGING THE ENVIRONMENT (UK) **2177**

MANAGING THE HUMAN CLIMATE (US/0277-7398) [07303313] **762**

MANAGING THE NATION'S PUBLIC LANDS : A PROGRAM REPORT PREPARED PURSUANT TO REQUIREMENTS OF THE FEDERAL LAND POLICY AND MANAGEMENT ACT OF 1976 (US) [08920900] 4664, **878**

MANAGING TODAY'S FAMILY *CEASED.* (US/1059-5120) [24609450] **2283**

●MANAGING VOICE NETWORKS (US) [25423843] **1159**

MANAGING WITH COMPUTERS *CEASED.* (US/0895-6162) [16704193] **1194**

MANAJEMEN (IO) [07935602] **1617**

MANANAM PUBLICATION SERIES (US) [21666142] **4975**

MANAOCAI (II) [11798679] **3301**

MANAR AL-ISLAM (TS) [03927879] **5043**

MANAR (JIDDAH, SAUDI ARABIA) (SU) [09160131] **5233**

MANAS (II/0025-1984) [02380041] **4603**

MANASA SAMACARA *See* MANASABHARATI : SRI RAMACARITAMANASA CATUSSATABDI SAMAROHA SAMITI, MADHYAPRADESA, BHOPALA KI MASIKA MUKHAPATRIKA **3409**

MANASABHARATI : SRI RAMACARITAMANASA CATUSSATABDI SAMAROHA SAMITI, MADHYAPRADESA, BHOPALA KI MASIKA MUKHAPATRIKA (II) [09319972] 4975, **3409**

MANASAMANI (II/0377-9505) [01784411] **5041**

MANAV (II) [11776363] **240**

MANCHESTER BUSINESS SCHOOL (UNIVERSITY OF MANCHESTER) *See* MBA COURSE, THE DPBA COURSE, THE **1835**

MANCHESTER CHAMBER OF COMMERCE AND INDUSTRY YEARBOOK *See* MANCHESTER CHAMBER OF COMMERCE AND INDUSTRY YEARBOOK **820**

MANCHESTER CHAMBER OF COMMERCE AND INDUSTRY YEARBOOK (UK/0306-5758) [01798884] **820**

MANCHESTER ENTERPRISE (US) [12259814] **5692**

MANCHESTER ENTERPRISE, THE (US) [15058738] **5681**

MANCHESTER FOLK DIRECTORY (UK) [02441439] **4129**

MANCHESTER GEOGRAPHER : JOURNAL OF THE MANCHESTER GEOGRAPHICAL SOCIETY, THE (UK/0260-5503) [08279029] **2568**

MANCHESTER GUARDIAN WEEKLY (UK/0025-200X) [06124621] **5812**

MANCHESTER GUARDIAN WEEKLY (1985) (UK/0959-3608) [07918511] **5812**

MANCHESTER JOURNAL (MANCHESTER, VT.), THE (US/1062-5070) [09735891] **5708**

MANCHESTER MEMOIRS / MANCHESTER LITERARY AND PHILOSOPHICAL SOCIETY (UK) [09314878] **3301**

MANCHESTER PRESS, THE (US) [10954831] **5671**

MANCHESTER REGION HISTORY REVIEW (UK) [20467289] **2697**

MANCHESTER SCHOOL OF ECONOMIC AND SOCIAL STUDIES, THE (UK/0025-2034) [04567626] 5208, **1504**

MANCHESTER STAR-MERCURY (US) [19933368] **5654**

MANCHESTER WORKING PAPERS IN AGRICULTURAL ECONOMICS (UK) [16843914] **107**

MANCHETE ESPORTIVA (BL) [05653385] **4904**

MANCUNION : THE OFFICIAL NEWSPAPER OF MANCHESTER UNIVERSITY STUDENTS UNION (UK) **1093**

M&A AND CORPORATE GOVERNANCE LAW REPORTER *See* BANK AND CORPORATE GOVERNANCE LAW REPORTER **774**

MANDAN NEWS (US) [23194281] **5725**

MANDAT (WILLOWDALE. 1991) (CN/1187-4619) [25652354] **691**

MANDATE (TORONTO. 1979) (CN/0225-7068) [06299222] **4975**

MANDATORY AIRCRAFT MODIFICATIONS AND INSPECTIONS SUMMARY (UK) **28**

M&O (NE/0165-1722) [04580934] **1617**

MANDOLIN WORLD NEWS (US/0199-6533) [06069889] **4129**

M&R. MARINE AND RECREATION NEWS *CEASED.* (US/0025-312X) [04050103] 5386, **594**

MANEDS BRSEN (DK) [05959765] **691**

MANEDSSTATISTIKK OVER UTENRIKSHANDELEN (NO/0332-6403) [01760789] **1536**

MANEJO INTEGRADO DE PLAGAS (CR/1016-0469) [I10160469] **107**

MANG CHUNG (CC) [10648732] **3409**

MANG-NON *See* VAN NGHE TRE **2274**

MANGAJIN (ATLANTA, GA.) (US/1051-8177) [22140277] **380**

MANGANESE LITERATURE REVIEW (FR/0398-1657) [I03981657] **1357**

MANHATTAN BOOK HOUND (US/0198-9960) [06290528] **4830**

MANHATTAN LAND USE DIRECTORY (US) [09345871] **4736**

MANHATTAN LAWYER *CEASED.* (US/0893-8911) [15713892] **3006**

MANHATTAN MEDICINE (US/0744-4966) [08364736] **3606**

MANHATTAN MEDICINE *See* MM NEWS **3617**

MANHATTAN MENUS (US/0197-5099) [06029997] **5071**

MANHATTAN MERCURY (MANHATTAN, KAN. : 1954) (US) [12431284] **5677**

MANHATTAN OFFICE BUILDINGS. DOWNTOWN (US/0886-2737) [12109917] **4840**

MANHATTAN OFFICE BUILDINGS. MIDTOWN (US/0886-3725) [12964303] **4840**

MANHATTAN OFFICE BUILDINGS. MIDTOWN SOUTH (US/1046-8943) [20538919] **4840**

MANHATTAN POETRY REVIEW (US/0885-9205) [12774398] **3465**

MANHATTAN REVIEW (NEW YORK, N.Y. : 1980), THE (US/0275-6889) [07235836] **3465**

●MANHATTAN USER'S GUIDE (US/1062-0141) [25504834] **2568**

MANI DI FATA (IT) **5560**

MANIE DES JEUX, LA (CN/0829-3848) [13171949] **4863**

MANIFEST : A NEWSLETTER TO THE ASSOCIATES OF THE JAMES FORD BELL LIBRARY, WILSON LIBRARY, UNIVERSITY OF MINNESOTA, THE (US/0542-5174) [01756604] **419**

MANIFESTO (IT/0025-2158) [I00252158] **5804**

MANILA BULLETIN (PH) [13647440] **5807**

MANILA CHRONICLE, THE (PH) [23660448] **5807**

MANILA STOCK EXCHANGE JOURNAL (PH) [08942579] **906**

MANILA TIMES INTERNATIONAL (US/1044-4416) [19791033] **5637**

MANILA TIMES, USA, THE (US/0898-5642) [17850429] **2490**

MANIPULATOR, THE (GW/0178-3556) [12561510] **5801**

MANIPUR (INDIA). DEPT. OF STATISTICS *See* ECONOMIC AND FUNCTIONAL CLASSIFICATION OF THE MANIPUR GOVERNMENT BUDGET, AN **4721**

MANIPUR (INDIA). DEPT. OF STATISTICS *See* BUDGET IN BRIEF - MANIPUR (INDIA). DEPT. OF STATISTICS **4714**

MANISHA (BHAGALPUR, INDIA) (II) [11818247] **1835**

MANITOBA *See* BUDGET DES DEPENSES PRINCIPAL DE LA PROVINCE DU MANITOBA **4714**

MANITOBA *See* MANITOBA AND SASKATCHEWAN SUCCESSION DUTY AND GIFT TAX LEGISLATION **4736**

MANITOBA AGRICULTURE STATISTICS (CN/0713-3359) [08752078] 107, **154**

MANITOBA AND SASKATCHEWAN SUCCESSION DUTY AND GIFT TAX LEGISLATION (CN/0317-0306) [02247618] **4736**

MANITOBA ARCHAEOLOGICAL JOURNAL (CN/1188-5424) [26090961] **273**

MANITOBA ARCHAEOLOGICAL QUARTERLY (CN/0705-2669) [04079579] **273**

MANITOBA ASSOCIATION FOR ART EDUCATION *See* M A A E BULLETIN **357**

MANITOBA — Alphabetical Title Index

MANITOBA ASSOCIATION OF PRINCIPALS *See* PRINCIPAL ISSUE **1868**

MANITOBA ASSOCIATION OF SCHOOL TRUSTEES *See* NEWSLETTER - MANITOBA ASSOCIATION OF SCHOOL TRUSTEES **1867**

MANITOBA ASSOCIATION OF SCHOOL TRUSTEES *See* MAST. MANITOBA ASSOCIATION OF SCHOOL TRUSTEES **4664**

MANITOBA. BUREAU OF STATISTICS *See* RETAIL FOOD PRICE INDEXES **956**

MANITOBA BUREAU OF STATISTICS *See* MANITOBA STATISTICAL REVIEW **1504**

MANITOBA BUSINESS (CN/0709-2423) [05375508] **691**

MANITOBA BUSINESS EDUCATION TEACHERS ASSOCIATION *See* M. B. E. T. A. NEWSLETTER **691**

MANITOBA CAMPING DIRECTORY (CN/0823-8588) [11453897] **4874**

MANITOBA CANADA VACATION HANDBOOK *See* MANITOBA VACATION GUIDE **5483**

MANITOBA CEC NEWS (CN/1184-1133) [23598511] **1882**

MANITOBA CHAMBERS OF COMMERCE *See* PRESENTATION TO THE PREMIER AND PROVINCIAL CABINET **1579**

MANITOBA CHINESE POST (CN/0708-9457) [05257144] **5789**

MANITOBA. CIVIL SERVICE COMMISSION. EMPLOYEE BENEFITS AND OTHER PAYMENTS *See* SUPPLEMENTARY INFORMATION FOR LEGISLATIVE REVIEW, EXPENDITURE ESTIMATES - MANITOBA., CIVIL SERVICE COMMISSION. EMPLOYEE BENEFITS AND OTHER PAYMENTS **4689**

MANITOBA CO-OPERATOR (CN/0025-2239) [02435287] **5789**

MANITOBA COMMUNITY REPORTS (CN) [01786607] **2827**

MANITOBA COMPOSERS' ASSOCIATION (CN/0824-7358) [11873836] **4129**

MANITOBA CONSTITUTIONAL TASK FORCE *See* MANITOBA CONSTITUTIONAL TASK FORCE **4664**

MANITOBA CONSTITUTIONAL TASK FORCE (CN/1185-3948) [24571317] **4664**

MANITOBA CONSTRUCTION & RESOURCE INDUSTRIES (CN/0712-2594) [09000497] **619**

MANITOBA CONSUMER (1985) (CN/0848-1989) [21103150] **1298**

MANITOBA CROP INSURANCE CORPORATION *See* ANNUAL REPORT - MANITOBA CROP INSURANCE CORPORATION **2873**

MANITOBA CURLING REVIEW (CN/0823-8448) [11360494] **4904**

●MANITOBA DAIRYMAN (CN) [28954886] **196**

MANITOBA DATA SERVICES *See* INFORM (WINNIPEG) **1188**

MANITOBA DATA SERVICES *See* ANNUAL REPORT / MANITOBA DATA SERVICES **1235**

MANITOBA DECISIONS, CIVIL AND CRIMINAL CASES (CN/0380-0008) [02627327] **3006**

MANITOBA DENTAL ASSOCIATION *See* BULLETIN - MANITOBA DENTAL ASSOCIATION **1318**

MANITOBA DENTAL ASSOCIATION *See* DIRECTORY / MANITOBA DENTAL ASSOCIATION **1322**

MANITOBA. DEPARTMENT OF LABOR *See* WAGE AND SALARY SURVEY. ANNUAL **1717**

MANITOBA. DEPT. OF EDUCATION. LIBRARY *See* ACQUISITIONS LIST / MANITOBA, DEPT. OF EDUCATION, LIBRARY **1792**

MANITOBA. DEPT. OF FINANCE *See* MAIN ESTIMATES OF CURRENT EXPENDITURE OF THE PROVINCE OF MANITOBA **4736**

MANITOBA. DEPT. OF FINANCE *See* FINANCIAL REPORT - MANITOBA DEPARTMENT OF FINANCE **4725**

MANITOBA. DEPT. OF NATURAL RESOURCES *See* PUBLICATIONS LIST - MANITOBA. DEPARTMENT OF NATURAL RESOURCES **2202**

MANITOBA. DEPT. OF RENEWABLE RESOURCES AND TRANSPORTATION SERVICES *See* HOOK N' COOK **4654**

MANITOBA. DIRECTION DES RESSOURCES EDUCATIVES FRANCAISES *See* DIRECTION DES RESSOURCES EDUCATIVES FRANCAISES EN ACTION, LA **1735**

MANITOBA DIRECTORY OF LEGAL SERVICES *See* MANITOBA LEGAL SERVICES DIRECTORY **3180**

MANITOBA. ENVIRONMENTAL COUNCIL *See* ANNUAL REPORT - MANITOBA ENVIRONMENTAL COUNCIL **2160**

MANITOBA FARM LANDS OWNERSHIP BOARD *See* ANNUAL REPORT / THE MANITOBA FARM LANDS OWNERSHIP BOARD **61**

MANITOBA FOOD PRODUCTS DIRECTORY (CN/0228-8966) [07822827] **2348**

MANITOBA GAZETTE, THE (CN/0706-3350) [02249463] **4481**

MANITOBA GOVERNMENT PUBLICATIONS (MONTHLY ED.) (CN/0318-1200) [02249877] **4664**

MANITOBA HEALTH RESEARCH COUNCIL *See* ANNUAL REPORT - MANITOBA HEALTH RESEARCH COUNCIL **3550**

MANITOBA HIGH SCHOOLS ATHLETIC DIRECTORY (CN/0225-9273) [06272214] **4904**

MANITOBA HISTORICAL SOCIETY NEWSLETTER (CN/0226-5036) [09137857] **2745**

MANITOBA HISTORY (CN/0226-5044) [06742462] **2745**

MANITOBA HOME AND SCHOOL NEWS (CN/0714-4733) [09033881] **1762**

MANITOBA HOME ECONOMICS TEACHERS' ASSOCIATION *See* M.H.E.T.A. JOURNAL **2791**

MANITOBA HYDRO *See* ANNUAL REPORT - THE MANITOBA HYDRO-ELECTRIC BOARD **4759**

MANITOBA. IMPRIMEUR DE LA REINE *See* STATUTORY PUBLICATIONS, PRICE LIST - MANITOBA. OFFICE OF THE QUEEN'S PRINTER (FRENCH EDITION) **3059**

MANITOBA INSECT CONTROL GUIDE (CN/0228-7927) [07817906] **107**

MANITOBA JOURNAL OF COUNSELLING : MJC (CN/0831-3245) [15059988] **1882**

MANITOBA JOURNAL OF TECHNOLOGY EDUCATION (CN/0843-7823) [20665354] **5127**

MANITOBA LABOUR MARKET INFORMATION BULLETIN (CN/0711-6411) [08574709] **1689**

MANITOBA. LAND VALUE APPRAISAL COMMISSION *See* ANNUAL REPORT OF THE LAND VALUE APPRAISAL COMMISSION **4834**

MANITOBA LAW JOURNAL (1966) (CN/0076-3861) [01639394] **3006**

MANITOBA. LAWS, STATUTES, ETC *See* STATUTES OF THE PROVINCE OF MANITOBA **3059**

●MANITOBA LEGAL SERVICES DIRECTORY (CN/1187-8754) [26497500] **3180**

MANITOBA. LEGISLATIVE ASSEMBLY *See* DEBATES AND PROCEEDINGS - LEGISLATIVE ASSEMBLY OF MANITOBA **4641**

MANITOBA. LEGISLATIVE ASSEMBLY *See* VOTES AND PROCEEDINGS OF THE LEGISLATIVE ASSEMBLY OF MANITOBA **4694**

MANITOBA. LEGISLATIVE LIBRARY *See* SELECTED NEW TITLES / LEGISLATIVE LIBRARY OF MANITOBA **424**

MANITOBA LIBRARY ASSOCIATION *See* NEWSLINE - MANITOBA LIBRARY ASSOCIATION **3236**

MANITOBA LOTTERIES FOUNDATION *See* ANNUAL REPORT / MANITOBA LOTTERIES FOUNDATION **4627**

MANITOBA. MANITOBA ENVIRONMENT *See* STATE OF THE ENVIRONMENT, REPORT FOR MANITOBA **2221**

MANITOBA. MANITOBA ENVIRONMENT AND WORKPLACE SAFETY AND HEALTH *See* ANNUAL REPORT - MANITOBA ENVIRONMENT AND WORKPLACE SAFETY AND HEALTH **2160**

MANITOBA. MANITOBA FINANCE *See* SUPPLEMENTARY INFORMATION FOR LEGISLATIVE REVIEW, REVENUE ESTIMATES **813**

MANITOBA. MANITOBA INDUSTRY, TRADE AND TOURISM *See* DEPARTMENT OF INDUSTRY, TRADE AND TOURISM AND LOTTERIES FUNDED PROGRAMS, FITNESS AND SPORT DIRECTORATES, SUPPLEMENTARY INFORMATION FOR LEGISLATIVE REVIEW, ... EXPENDITURE ESTIMATES **4720**

MANITOBA. MANITOBA NATURAL RESOURCES *See* ANNUAL REPORT - MANITOBA NATURAL RESOURCES **2133**

MANITOBA MEDICAL REVIEW (MICROFICHE) (CN/0025-2255) [03230224] **3606**

MANITOBA MEDICINE (CN/0832-6096) [16955854] **3606**

MANITOBA. MINERALS DIVISION *See* REPORT OF ACTIVITIES - MINERALS DIVISION (WINNIPEG) **1394**

MANITOBA MODERN LANGUAGE JOURNAL *CEASED.* (CN/0820-6066) [09414391] **3301**

MANITOBA MUSIC EDUCATOR (CN/0315-9116) [13138059] 1900, **4130**

MANITOBA. OFFICE OF THE QUEEN'S PRINTER *See* STATUTORY PUBLICATIONS, PRICE LIST - MANITOBA. OFFICE OF THE QUEEN'S PRINTER (ENGLISH EDITION) **3059**

●MANITOBA PARKS AND WILDERNESS (CN/1189-4407) [26714636] **4707**

MANITOBA PHYSICAL EDUCATION TEACHERS' ASSOCIATION *See* MANITOBA PHYSICAL EDUCATION TEACHERS' ASSOCIATION **1857**

MANITOBA PHYSICAL EDUCATION TEACHERS' ASSOCIATION (CN/0706-0882) [06141363] **1857**

MANITOBA PRODUCTION STATISTICS REPORT (CN/1187-2942) [25590192] 1617, **1536**

MANITOBA PROFESSIONAL ENGINEER (CN/0025-2271) [01971383] **1985**

MANITOBA PSYCHOLOGIST (CN/0711-1533) [08581293] **4603**

MANITOBA. PUBLIC LIBRARY SERVICES *See* PUBLIC LIBRARY SERVICES NEWSLETTER **3243**

MANITOBA REPORTS (FREDERICTON, N.B. : BOUND CUMULATION) (CN/0713-7109) [09096446] **3006**

MANITOBA RESEARCH COUNCIL *See* ANNUAL REPORT / MANITOBA RESEARCH COUNCIL **4464**

MANITOBA RESTAURANT NEWS (CN/1184-1605) [23238160] **5071**

MANITOBA SCHOOL LIBRARY AUDIO VISUAL ASSOCIATION *See* M.S.L.A.V.A. JOURNAL **3229**

MANITOBA SCHOOL LIBRARY AUDIO VISUAL ASSOCIATION. M.S.L.A.V.A. JOURNAL *See* MSLA JOURNAL **3232**

MANITOBA SCIENCE TEACHER (CN/0315-9159) [02061320] **5127**

MANITOBA SOCIAL SCIENCE TEACHER, THE (CN/0316-6473) [02247684] 1900, **5208**

MANITOBA SOCIAL WORKER (CN/0715-3481) [09128334] **5295**

MANITOBA SPECTRA (CN/0318-2118) [02441711] **691**

MANITOBA STATISTICAL REVIEW (CN/0700-2971) [03424891] 1536, **1504**

MANITOBA STATUTES AND RULES OF COURT JUDICIALLY CONSIDERED, INCLUDING ALL AMENDMENTS TO THE STATUTES AND RULES SINCE THE LAST CONSOLIDATIONS IN EACH CASE (CN) [05965986] **3006**

MANITOBA TEACHER (CN/0025-228X) [02061347] **1762**

MANITOBA. TEACHERS' RETIREMENT ALLOWANCES FUND BOARD *See* REPORT TO MEMBERS - MANITOBA TEACHERS' RETIREMENT ALLOWANCES FUND **1870**

MANITOBA TRADE DIRECTORY *CEASED.* (CN/0076-390X) [01715962] **845**

MANITOBA UNDERWATER COUNCIL *See* NEWSLETTER - MANITOBA UNDERWATER COUNCIL **4908**

MANITOBA UNDERWATER COUNCIL. NEWSLETTER *See* MAN UNDERWATER **4904**

MANITOBA VACATION GUIDE (CN/0703-6248) [03236110] **5483**

MANITOBA. WASTE REDUCTION AND PREVENTION BRANCH *See* STRATEGY REPORT - MANITOBA. WASTE REDUCTION AND PREVENTION BRANCH **2244**

MANITOBA WATER SERVICES BOARD *See* ANNUAL REPORT OF THE MANITOBA WATER SERVICES BOARD **5529**

MANITOBA, WINNIPEG AND VICINITY CHINESE TELEPHONE DIRECTORIES (CN/0849-0619) [22135414] **1159**

MANITOBA WINNIPEG BUILDING AND CONSTRUCTION TRADES COUNCIL YEARBOOK (CN/0714-3222) [09336385] 620, **1689**

MANITOBAN (CN) [01714064] **5789**

MANITOU SPRINGS JOURNAL *See* PIKES PEAK JOURNAL, THE **5644**

MANITOULIN EXPOSITOR (CN/0834-6682) [16581901] 2267, **5789**

MANJARI (II/0304-1247) [02246649] **3409**

MANKIND QUARTERLY (US/0025-2344) [00820324] **240**

MANLEY FAMILY NEWSLETTER (US/0883-7805) [12223706] **2459**

MANLY SIGNAL (MANLY, IOWA : 1921) (US) [16141003] **5671**

●MANN FANTASY BASEBALL GUIDE, THE (US/1072-3595) [28916877] **4904**

MANN-MALLIN FANTASY BASEBALL GUIDE *See* MANN FANTASY BASEBALL GUIDE, THE **4904**

●MANN-MALLIN FANTASY BASEBALL GUIDE, THE (US) [25362115] 4863, **4904**

Alphabetical Title Index — MANUFACTURING

MANN-MALLIN FANTASY BASEBALL GUIDE, THE (US/1056-5108) [23728283] **4904**

MANNAM (KO) [10296938] **5063**

MANNERING REPORT, THE (US) **5208**

MANNHEIMER GEOGRAPHISCHE ARBEITEN (GW) [06523430] 1504, 2218, **2568**

MANNHEIMER SOZIALWISSENSCHAFTLICHE STUDIEN (GW) [02363200] **5251**

MANNING MONITOR (US) [09426975] **5671**

MANNING TIMES, THE (US) [13611767] **5742**

MANNLICHER COLLECTOR, THE (US/0883-6949) [12573592] **251**

MANNVILLE REFLECTIONS (CN/0228-054X) [06958960] **5789**

MANO EN EL CAJON, LA (SP/0303-1152) [01793895] **3465**

MANOA (US/1045-7909) [20237037] **3347**

MANORAMA YEAR BOOK (II/0542-5778) [02376638] **1927**

MANOTICK NEWS, THE (CN/0700-8058) [03399996] **5789**

MANPOWER AND APPLIED PSYCHOLOGY *CEASED.* (IE/0025-2409) [05025127] **4603**

MANPOWER AND HUMAN RESOURCES STUDIES (US/0149-080X) [03428472] 944, **1689**

MANPOWER & MIGRATION SERIES / UNIVERSITY OF DURHAM, CENTRE FOR MIDDLE EASTERN AND ISLAMIC STUDIES (UK) [11058716] **1920**

MANPOWER ARGUS (NE) **1689**

MANPOWER DOCUMENTATION (II/0047-5793) [02353005] **1689**

MANPOWER INCOME REPORT (TR) [02244237] **1689**

MANPOWER INFORMATION FOR AFFIRMATIVE ACTION PROGRAMS (US/0099-1104) [02243566] **1689**

MANPOWER INFORMATION SERVICE. SUPPLEMENT (US) [03007714] **1689**

MANPOWER JOURNAL (II/0542-5808) [01773713] **1689**

MANPOWER PLANNING AND UTILIZATION (US/0147-4766) [03173611] **1689**

MANPOWER PLANNING DATA (WASHINGTON) (US/0094-4106) [01794420] 4664, **944**

MANPOWER RESEARCH (US/0565-3061) [01250724] **1689**

MANPOWER TRAINING NEEDS, PUERTO RICO (PR/0147-8281) [03233254] **1689**

MANSFIELD NEWS-MIRROR (US/0746-3847) [10012843] **5752**

MANTAP : MAJALAH ILMIAH PKMI : JOURNAL OF THE INDONESIAN ASSOCIATION FOR SECURE CONTRACEPTION (IO) [08504967] **589**

MANTATOPHOROS (NE/0306-0020) [04939157] **3301**

MANTECA BULLETIN (US/0745-2748) [09012700] **5637**

MANTEIA (FR/0025-2492) [01756655] **3410**

MANTENIMIENTO BARCELONA (SP/0214-4344) [I02144344] **4008**

MANTETSUKAI HO (JA) [06706094] **5432**

MANTETSUKAI (JAPAN) *See* MANTETSUKAI HO **5432**

MANTHANA (II) [07237567] **2506**

MANTHANA (KATHMANDU, NEPAL) (NP) [08500859] **3410**

MANTI MESSENGER (MANTI, UTAH : 1981) (US) [12799584] **5756**

MANUAL & DIRECTORY - ONTARIO JOINT FICTION RESERVE (CN/0319-406X) [02443002] **3229**

MANUAL DE CONSULTAS TRIBUTARIAS / ASSOCIACION NACIONAL DE INSPECTORES DE IMPUESTOS INTERNOS (CL) [08376304] 4736, **3006**

MANUAL DE ESTADISTICA AGRARIA (SP) [05686094] 107, **154**

MANUAL DE LA ORGANIZACION DEL GOBIERNO DE CHILE--MICROFORM / DEPARTAMENTO DE ESTUDIOS FINANCIEROS, MINISTERIO DE HACIENDA (UK) [09989331] **4664**

MANUAL FOR COMPLEX AND MULTIDISTRICT LITIGATION (US) [01768398] **3006**

MANUAL FOR LABORATORY WORKLOAD RECORDING METHOD (US) **3896**

MANUAL FOR PENNSYLVANIA TAX COLLECTORS *See* TAX COLLECTORS MANUAL **4752**

MANUAL FOR THE GENERAL COURT (US/0196-4585) [01605177] **4664**

MANUAL FOR THE USE OF THE LEGISLATURE OF THE STATE OF NEW YORK (US) [01760145] **3006**

MANUAL - INSTITUTO FORESTAL, CHILE (CL/0581-6386) [01779916] **2387**

MANUAL. NEW YORK BUILDING LAWS (US) [04648680] 620, **3006**

MANUAL OF ACCEPTABLE PRACTICES (US) [03112012] 620, **2827**

MANUAL OF CLASSIFICATION (US) [04859604] **1306**

MANUAL OF CRITERIA FOR MEDICAL AUTHORIZATION /INCLS UPDATES (US) **3915**

MANUAL OF ENVIRONMENTAL POLICY: THE EC & BRITAIN (UK) **2177**

MANUAL OF EXAMINATION AND INSURANCE REFERENCE GUIDE FOR ILLINOIS INSURANCE AGENTS AND BROKERS *See* HANSON'S MANUAL OF EXAMINATION AND INSURANCE LAW HANDBOOK **2976**

MANUAL OF LEGISLATIVE ACTS RULES AND GUIDANCE NOTES CONCERNING NORTH SEA OFFSHORE DEVELOPMENTS (UK) **4263**

MANUAL OF MANAGEMENT ASSUMPTIONS FOR PLANNING BUSINESS STRATEGIES (US/0149-8258) [03555822] **879**

MANUAL OF MATERIALS HANDLING : BUYERS' GUIDE TO STORAGE-HANDLING-DISTRIBUTION EQUIPMENT-COMPONENTS & SERVICES (UK) [06388124] **950**

MANUAL OF MEDICAL THERAPEUTICS / DEPARTMENT OF MEDICINE, WASHINGTON UNIVERSITY SCHOOL OF MEDICINE (US) [07435260] **3606**

MANUAL OF ORGANIZATION STRUCTURE *See* ORGANIZATION OF THE GOVERNMENT OF ALBERTA **4671**

MANUAL OF PATENT EXAMINING PROCEDURE (US/0364-2453) [01768632] **1306**

MANUAL OF REGULATIONS AND PROCEDURES FOR FEDERAL RADIO FREQUENCY MANAGEMENT (US) [05523177] **1134**

MANUAL OF REGULATIONS AND PROCEDURES FOR RADIO FREQUENCY MANAGEMENT (US) [02990543] 1159, **879**

MANUAL OF SOCIAL SERVICES IN MANITOBA (CN/0318-5427) [02583366] **5295**

MANUAL OF TARIFF COORDINATING CONFERENCES RESOLUTIONS--PASSENGER; TC23/TC123 RESOLUTIONS, EUROPE/MIDDLE EAST-JAPAN/KOREA (SZ) [06083898] **845**

MANUAL OF THE AMERICAN RAILWAY ENGINEERING ASSOCIATION (US/0065-9940) [01480649] **5432**

MANUAL OF THE GENERAL ASSEMBLY OF THE STATE OF GEORGIA (US/0098-8103) [02242099] **4664**

MANUAL OF THE LEGISLATURE OF NEW JERSEY (US/0890-3832) [02540430] **4664**

MANUAL OF THE SENATE AND HOUSE OF DELEGATES (US/0363-1184) [01253731] **4664**

MANUAL ON UNIFORM TRAFFIC CONTROL DEVICES FOR STREETS AND HIGHWAYS (US) [05003294] **5441**

MANUAL PARA LA REPARACION DE AUTOMOVILES Y CAMIONES, GUIA DEL COMERCIO Y LA INDUSTRIA AUTOMOTOR (AG) [02648888] **5418**

MANUAL PRACTICO DEL AHORRISTA Y DEL INVERSIONISTA (PE) [05686620] **906**

MANUAL PRACTICO DEL IMPORTADOR (UY) [05010485] **845**

MANUAL - THE STATE OF RHODE ISLAND AND PROVIDENCE PLANTATIONS (US/0197-4238) [03012834] **4664**

MANUAL - UNITED NATIONS EDUCATIONAL, SCIENTIFIC AND CULTURAL ORGANIZATION. GENERAL CONFERENCE (US) [01491384] **5233**

MANUALE DEL REGISTRO (IT) **4664**

MANUALE DISCIPLINA ECONOMICA SCAMBI ESTERO (IT) **845**

MANUALS AND REPORTS ON ENGINEERING PRACTICE (US/0734-7685) [01480782] **2027**

MANUEL - ASSOCIATION CANADIENNE DE BADMINTON (CN/0227-5996) [08064028] **4904**

MANUEL DE PRATIQUE DE L'ARCHITECTURE (CN/0228-8222) [07966276] **303**

MANUEL D'EXPLOITATION FORESTIERE DES TERRES DE LA COURONNE (CN/1185-9075) [25883321] **2387**

MANUEL D'INTERPRETATION ET D'APPLICATION DE LA CONVENTION COLLECTIVE F.I.I.Q. ... EN VIGUEUR DANS LES CENTRES D'ACCUEIL MEMBRES DE L'ASSOCIATION DES CENTRES D'ACCUEIL DU QUEBEC (CN/1189-041X) [23658919] **1689**

MANUEL D'INTERPRETATION ET D'APPLICATION DES CONVENTIONS COLLECTIVES F.T.Q. (U.E.S. LOCAL 298 ET S.C.F.P.) ... EN VIGUEUR DANS LES CENTRES D'ACCUEIL MEMBRES DE L'ASSOCIATION DES CENTRES D'ACCUEIL DU QUEBEC (CN/1184-6577) [23686612] **1690**

MANUEL POUR LA PREPARATION DES DECLARATIONS D'IMPOT DES CORPORATIONS (CN/0824-3158) [10156976] **4736**

MANUEL PRATIQUE DES DOUANES C.F.T.C (FR/0222-8599) [19010927] **1920**

MANUELLE MEDIZIN (GW/0025-2514) [07601920] **3606**

MANUFACTURED HOME MERCHANDISER (US/1047-2967) [20658803] 1617, **2827**

MANUFACTURED HOMES APPRAISAL GUIDE, OFFICIAL VALUATION GUIDE (US/0276-1645) [07301437] **2827**

MANUFACTURED HOUSING DEALER. ANNUAL DIRECTORY & BUYER'S GUIDE (US/0277-7924) [04796009] **2827**

MANUFACTURED HOUSING INDUSTRY ... BUYER'S MANUAL (US/0733-2351) [08525359] **2828**

MANUFACTURED HOUSING NEWSLETTER (US/0197-1816) [05972312] **2828**

MANUFACTURED HOUSING QUARTERLY *CEASED.* (US) [11075126] **2828**

MANUFACTURER NZ (NZ) **3483**

MANUFACTURER (WELLINGTON. 1988) *See* NEW ZEALAND MANUFACTURER 1992 **3485**

MANUFACTURERS' AGENTS NATIONAL ASSOCIATION (U.S.) *See* MANA MEMBERS DIRECTORY OF MANUFACTURERS' SALES AGENCIES **3483**

MANUFACTURERS AND PROCESSORS DIRECTORY, SOUTH DAKOTA (US/1049-3050) [20437419] **3483**

MANUFACTURERS DIRECTORY, WINDSOR-ESSEX COUNTY, ONTARIO, CANADA (CN/0826-7413) [12045257] **3483**

MANUFACTURERS GUIDE : OHIO (US/0197-2723) [05848829] **3483**

MANUFACTURERS HANOVER ECONOMIC REPORT, THE (US/0885-4149) [08598608] **1504**

MANUFACTURERS HANOVER FINANCIAL DIGEST, THE (US) [02250448] **797**

MANUFACTURERS' MONTHLY (AT/0025-2530) [I00252530] **3483**

MANUFACTURERS OF ELECTRIC WIRE AND CABLE (PRELIMINARY ED.) (CN/0700-0774) [05072390] 2071, **3483**

MANUFACTURERS OF SMALL ELECTRIC APPLIANCES (CN) [01695741] **3483**

MANUFACTURERS' SHIPMENTS, INVENTORIES, AND ORDERS (US/0364-1880) [02548418] **3483**

● MANUFACTURING & PROCESS AUTOMATION (CN/1192-5973) [28166277] **1220**

MANUFACTURING AND PROCESS ENGINEERING ABSTRACTS *CEASED.* (US/1063-7354) [26133847] 2177, **1985**

MANUFACTURING AUTOMATION (US/1060-2712) [24924546] 5127, **3483**

MANUFACTURING BREAKTHROUGH (UK/0964-2366) [26190429] **3483**

MANUFACTURING CHEMIST (LONDON: 1981) (UK/0262-4230) [10443345] 3483, **985**

MANUFACTURING CLOTHIER (LONDON) (UK/0025-2565) [06979281] **1085**

MANUFACTURING CONFECTIONER, THE (US/0163-4364) [04373387] **3483**

MANUFACTURING ENGINEERING (US/0361-0853) [02245700] 3483, **1986**

MANUFACTURING ENGINEERING AND MATERIALS PROCESSING (US) [12114559] **1986**

MANUFACTURING HANDBOOK AND BUYERS' GUIDE / PLASTICS TECHNOLOGY (US) [09840215] **4456**

MANUFACTURING IN MINNESOTA (US/0149-9521) [03581813] **3483**

MANUFACTURING INDUSTRIES OF CANADA, NATIONAL AND PROVINCIAL AREAS (CN/0382-4144) [02946570] **3483**

MANUFACTURING INDUSTRIES OF CANADA. SUB-PROVINCIAL AREAS *CEASED.* (CN/0382-4012) [02438729] **3483**

MANUFACTURING — Alphabetical Title Index

MANUFACTURING MANAGEMENT SERIES (US/0076-4256) [04375287] **3483, 879**

MANUFACTURING MARKET INSIDER (US/1072-8651) [29228691] **3484**

MANUFACTURING + MARKETING OPPORTUNITIES; BULLETIN (CN/0706-0084) [05324736] 930, **3484**

MANUFACTURING OPERATIONS (US/0743-023X) [10494225] **3484**

MANUFACTURING OPPORTUNITIES (CN) [02244876] **3484**

MANUFACTURING RESOURCE PLANNING *CEASED.* (US/0736-8313) [09231419] **1617**

MANUFACTURING REVIEW (US/0896-1611) [16934379] **3484**

MANUFACTURING SERIES C. DEPARTMENT OF STATISTICS. NO. 4, MANUFACTURE OF PAPER AND PAPER PRODUCTS, PRINTING, AND PUBLISHING (NZ) [07938580] 4008, **1617**

MANUFACTURING SUCCESS *See* CONTINUOUS IMPROVEMENT **3477**

MANUFACTURING SYSTEMS (US/0748-948X) [11036477] 1220, 3484, **1617**

MANUFACTURING TECHNOLOGY / NTIS *See* NTIS ALERT. MANUFACTURING TECHNOLOGY **3485**

MANUFACTURING TODAY (US/0164-968X) [04300471] **3484**

MANUFACTURING USA (US/1044-7024) [19869738] **3484**

MANUSCRIPT LETTERS OR COMMUNIQUES PUBLISHED IN THE ARCHDIOCESE OF OTTAWA (CN/0820-6937) [09448440] **5032**

MANUSCRIPT REPORT SERIES - MARINE SCIENCES AND INFORMATION DIRECTORATE (CN/0710-667X) [07821513] **1451**

MANUSCRIPT REPORTS - INTERNATIONAL DEVELOPMENT RESEARCH CENTRE (CN/0826-6433) [I08266433] **107**

MANUSCRIPT SOCIETY NEWS, THE (US/0195-7813) [05664496] 2622, **2774**

MANUSCRIPT SOCIETY (U.S.) *See* DIRECTORY OF MEMBERS / THE MANUSCRIPT SOCIETY **2773**

MANUSCRIPT SOCIETY (U.S.). MS DIRECTORY *See* DIRECTORY OF MEMBERS / THE MANUSCRIPT SOCIETY **2773**

MANUSCRIPTA GEODAETICA (GW/0340-8825) [04163502] **1408**

MANUSCRIPTA MATHEMATICA (GW/0025-2611) [01756669] **3517**

MANUSCRIPTA (ST. LOUIS, MO.) (US/0025-2603) [01756668] **2850**

MANUSCRIPTS FOR TUBA SERIES (US/0363-6585) [02496411] **4130**

MANUSCRIPTS (NEW YORK, N.Y.) (US/0025-262X) [04619231] **2774**

MANUSCRIPTS OF THE MIDDLE EAST (NE/0920-0401) [15645008] **4830**

MANUSCRIPTUM (RM/1010-5492) [04366183] **3410**

MANUSCRITO (BL/0100-6045) [04759049] **4352**

MANUSCRITOS POETICOS (SP) **3465**

MANUSCRITS (SP/0213-2397) [22149039] **2697**

MANUSHI (II/0257-7305) [06713863] **5560**

MANUSIA DAN MASYARAKAT (MY/0303-3171) [02239418] **240**

MANUSIA INDONESIA (IO) [03592412] **240**

MANUSKRIPTE (AU/0025-2638) [02380123] **3410**

MANUSKRIPTE ZUR KUNSTWISSENSCHAFT IN DER WERNERSCHEN VERLAGSGESELLSCHAFT (GW) [14076373] **324**

MANUTENCION Y ALMACENAJE (SP/0025-2646) [I00252646] **5127**

MANUTENTION-EMBALLAGES (BE) [05955472] **4219**

MANUTENZIONE : TECNICA E MANAGEMENT (IT) **5127**

MANVILLE NEWS, THE (US/1058-6857) [15649366] **5710**

MANX LAW REPORTS (UK/0267-534X) [12793998] **3006**

MANY CORNERS (US) [02254239] **3347**

● MANY PATHS (US) **4975**

MANY VOICES (US/1042-2277) [18974242] **4603**

MANYO (JA) [04253519] **3465**

MANZANA MORDIDA, LA (PE) [04219482] **3466**

MAO PI TUNG WU SSU YANG (CC) [18148317] **5591**

MAO TSE-TUNG WEN I SSU HSIANG YEN CHIU / CHUAN KUO MAO TSE-TUNG WEN I SSU HSIANG YEN CHIU HUI PIEN (CC) [11890970] **324**

MAOPOLSKA KRAKOW (PL/0867-0064) [I08670064] **2519**

MAOR, HA- (US) [07855153] **5051**

MAP AND CHART SERIES (US/0097-3793) [01379870] **1357**

MAP COLLECTOR, THE (UK/0140-427X) [06524436] **2582**

MAP LIBRARY (MAPPING AND CHARTING ESTABLISHMENT RE (GREAT BRITAIN)) *See* GREAT BRITAIN. DIRECTORATE OF MILITARY SURVEY. MAP LIBRARY. SELECTED ACCESSIONS **2565**

MAP, MONITORING ATTITUDES OF THE PUBLIC (US/0161-2174) [03854718] **2887**

MAP ONLINE USERS GROUP *See* NEWSLETTER / MAP ONLINE USERS GROUP **3235**

MAP REPORT (KANKAKEE, ILL.), THE (US/1065-6324) [25144943] **2582**

MAP SERIES (TALLAHASSEE, FLA.) (US/0085-0624) [01397609] **2582**

MAP TECHNICAL REPORTS SERIES / MEDITERRANEAN ACTION PLAN, MED POL, UNITED NATIONS ENVIRONMENT PROGRAMME (GR) [14288492] **2177**

MAPA MUNDI; RENAISSANCE PERFORMING SCORES. SERIES A: SPANISH CHURCH MUSIC (UK) [06719963] **4130**

MAPAN. JOURNAL OF METROLOGY SOCIETY OF INDIA (II/0970-3950) [I09703950] **1430**

MAPICS THE MAGAZINE (US/0891-7973) [15033461] 5127, **879**

MAPLE LAKE MESSENGER (US) [01624272] **5697**

MAPLE SHADE PROGRESS (US) [12393164] **5710**

MAPLE SYRUP JOURNAL, THE (US/8750-9881) [11990638] **2348**

MAPLE TECHNICAL NEWSLETTER, THE (US/1061-5733) [25400729] **1280**

MAPLEWOOD REVIEW (US) [01714900] **5697**

MAPLINE (US/0196-0881) [02712600] **2582**

MAPLINE. SPECIAL NUMBER (US) [05584012] **2582**

MAPNETTER NEWSLETTER, THE *CEASED.* (US/0888-6989) [13692968] **1194**

MAPPE, DIE (GW/0025-2697) [06381461] **2902**

MAPPEMONDE (FR/0764-3470) [14158228] **2582**

MAPPI DEI FORNITORI DI IMPIANTI SPORTIVI RICREATIVI (IT) **4904**

MAPPING AWARENESS (UK/0954-7126) [I09547126] 2582, **1194**

MAPPING AWARENESS & GIS EUROPE (UK/0954-712636) [23258424] **1242**

MAPPING SCIENCES AND REMOTE SENSING (US/0749-3878) [11120779] **2582**

MAPPS NEWSLETTER (MY/0127-0192) [I01270192] **517**

MAPS ALBERTA *See* CATALOGUE / MAPS ALBERTA **2581**

MAPS AND PUBLICATIONS ... PRICE LIST (US/0278-9655) [07906058] **2582**

MAPS NEWS (US) **4975**

MAPS ON FILE (US/0275-8083) [07240499] **2582**

MAPUTO ANTES DE INDEPENDENCIA: GEOGRAFIA DE UMA CIDADE COLONIAL (PO) [15054083] **2828**

MAQUIGNON DE LEVRARD (CN/0228-2763) [07314095] **2538**

MAQUILA (EL PASO, TEX.) (US/1050-6497) [21371453] **1617**

MAQUINARIA PARA PLASTICOS (US/0730-9120) [08094078] 4456, **930**

MAR Y PESCA *SUSPENDED.* (CU/0025-2735) [01791939] **2308**

MARANATHA (ST-HYACINTHE) (CN/0318-9147) [03258566] **4975**

MARANDU (PY) [25716292] **1346**

MARANHAO, BRAZIL (STATE). COMPANHIA DE DESENVOLVIMENTO DE DISTRITOS INDUSTRIAIS *See* RELATORIO DA DIRETORIA EXECUTIVA - COMPANHIA DE DESENVOLVIMENTO DE DISTRITOS INDUSTRIAIS DO MARANHAO **1580**

MARANHAO, BRAZIL (STATE). DEPARTAMENTO DE ESTRADAS DE RODAGEM *See* PLANO RODOVIARIO ESTADUAL **5442**

MARATHI PRAKASANA VARSHIKA ANI PRAKASANA DAYARI (II) [11793427] **4830**

MARATHON BALLINAMORE, CO. LEITRIM (IE/0047-5874) [I00475874] **2538**

MARATHON HANDBOOK (US/0360-9928) [02245742] **4904**

MARATHWADA UNIVERSITY, AURANGABAD, INDIA *See* MARATHWADA UNIVERSITY JOURNAL **1835**

MARATHWADA UNIVERSITY JOURNAL (II/0025-2751) [02383620] **1835**

MARAYA (LE) [09595113] **2658**

MARBLEHEAD MAGAZINE (US/0274-6115) [06453291] **2538**

MARBURGER BEITRAGE ZUR MUSIKFORSCHUNG (GW/0542-6502) [01971093] **4130**

MARBURGER GELEHRTEN GESELLSCHAFT *See* ABHANDLUNGEN **3337**

MARBURGER GEOGRAPHISCHE SCHRIFTEN (GW/0341-9290) [01714367] **2568**

MARBURGER INDEX : INVENTORY OF ART IN GERMANY : USERS MANUAL (GW) [11810410] **357**

MARBURGER JAHRBUCH FUER KUNSTWISSENSCHAFT (GW/0342-121X) [01756675] **357**

MARBURGER THEOLOGISCHE STUDIEN (GW/0542-657X) [02377651] **4975**

MARC : TAPE, CD-ROM FOR RETROSPECTIVE CONVERSION (US) [22742454] **3230**

MARCAS DE FABRICA, COMERCIO Y AGRICULTURA (AG) [01799505] **1306**

MARCH FOR LIFE (US/1069-7098) [28138507] **589**

MARCH FOR LIFE PROGRAM/JOURNAL (US/0364-0019) [04625272] **2252**

MARCH OF DIMES BIRTH DEFECTS FOUNDATION *See* ANNUAL REPORT / MARCH OF DIMES BIRTH DEFECTS FOUNDATION **3551**

MARCH OF FAITH (US/0461-0636) [03792661] **4975**

MARCHE BYWARD (CN/0227-8138) [06958749] **5483**

MARCHE DE L'ACIER EN ..., LE (INT/0497-9486) [I04979486] **1617**

MARCHE DU TRAVAIL (QUEBEC) (CN/0226-2576) [12148312] **1690**

MARCHE INTERNATIONAL (PIERREFONDS) (CN/0226-1995) [06299620] **2911**

MARCHE MONDIAL DE L'AUDIOVISUEL, LE (BE) 5317, **4371**

MARCHE (MONTREAL) (CN/1187-4775) [25652309] **4904**

MARCHE (OTTAWA-CARLETON ONTARIO). DEPARTEMENT DE L'URBANISME. GROUPE DE PARTICIPATION PUBLIQUE), EN (CN) [08469765] **2828**

MARCHE ROMANE (BE/0542-6669) [02106279] **3301**

MARCHEMOS (EL PASO, TEX.) (US/0731-2741) [08157200] **3230**

MARCHES AFRICAINS PARIS. 1988 (FR/0984-9521) [I09849521] **845**

MARCHES AGRICOLES, ALIMENTAIRES ET FONCIERS (FR) [01789858] **107**

MARCHES AGRICOLES ET ALIMENTAIRES *See* MARCHES AGRICOLES, ALIMENTAIRES ET FONCIERS **107**

MARCHES ARABES (FR) **845**

MARCHES EST EUROPEENS (FR) **1504**

MARCHES PUBLICS (FR/0542-6685) [06392225] **4664**

MARCHES TROPICAUX ET MEDITERRANEENS (FR/0025-2859) [08883142] **845**

MARCO POLO (IT) **3347**

MARCO POLYMER NOTES (US) **2015**

MARCOLIAN, THE (US/0025-2867) [04050084] **1093**

MARCONI'S INTERNATIONAL REGISTER (US/0076-4418) [01773961] 1927, **1116**

MARCONI'S INTERNATIONAL REGISTER (US/0076-4418) [05107580] **1159**

MARDOM NAMEH. JAHRBUCH ZUR GESCHICHTE UND GESELLSCHAFT DES MITTLEREN ORIENTS (GW) [06746880] **2658**

MARE BALTICUM (GW/0542-6758) [01587324] **4481**

MAREES TERRESTRES BULLETIN D'INFORMATIONS (BE/0542-6766) [04120784] **1357**

MARFA INDEPENDENT AND THE BIG BEND SENTINEL, THE (US/0747-119X) [10554786] **5752**

MARINE

MARFY *CEASED.* (IT) **2490**

MARG (II/0025-2913) [01756680] **357**

MARGA (CE/0047-5912) [01756681] **1573**

MARGARET GEE'S MEDIA GUIDE (AT) **1116**

MARGARET SANGER PAPERS PROJECT NEWSLETTER (US/1062-6573) [25425718] **589**

MARGARETOLOGIST, THE (US/0892-1989) [13398596] **2915**

MARGARINE- EN OLIEFABRIEKEN / CENTRAAL BUREAU VOOR DE STATISTIEK, HOOFDAFDELING STATISTIEKEN VAN INDUSTRIE EN BOUWNIJVERHEID (NE/0168-5716) [10467649] **1617**

MARGARINE- EN OLIEFABRIEKEN PRODUKTIESTATISTIEKEN *See* MARGARINE- EN OILEFABRIEKEN / CENTRAAL BUREAU VOOR DE STATISTIEK, HOOFDAFDELING STATISTIEKEN VAN INDUSTRIE EN BOUWNIJVERHEID **1617**

●MARGEM (BL/0103-8915) [27155517] 5251, **5208**

MARGENES (PE) [16894399] **2552**

MARGENES (PUEBLA, MEXICO) (MX) [10060718] **3410**

MARGES, ELS (SP) [05116434] **3301**

MARGIN (II/0025-2921) [01756683] **1573**

MARGIN : A QUARTERLY MAGAZINE FOR IMAGINATIVE WRITING AND IDEAS (US) **3410**

MARGIN (COLORADO SPRINGS, COLO.), THE *SUSPENDED.* (US/0887-851X) [13428681] **1504**

MARGINALIEN (GW/0025-2948) [02349178] **419**

MARGINALITA E SOCIETA (IT) [21429690] **5251**

MARGRIET (NE/0025-2956) [01080717] **2519**

MARI : ANNALES DES RECHERCHES INTERDISCIPLINAIRES (FR) [09680120] **273**

MARI BOARD CONVERTING NEWS (US) **4219**

MARIAGES (FR/0025-2980) [I00252980] **2283**

MARIAN STUDIES (US/0464-9680) [01756684] **5032**

MARIANUM: EPHEMERIDES MARIOLOGIAE (IT) [01770843] **4975**

MARICHEM (UK/0264-2697) [09460877] **5386**

MARICOPA COUNTY LABOR MARKET REVIEW (US) [03885084] **1690**

MARIE CLAIRE EN ESPANOL (MX/0188-2724) [I01882724] **1085**

MARIE CLAIRE (ITALIAN EDITION) (IT) **5561**

MARIE-CLEMENT STAUB, A.A., SKETCHES OF HIS LIFE AND WORK (CN/1187-5402) [25423748] **4975**

MARIE-EVE (CN/0704-058X) [07818090] **2538**

MARIE FRANCE *CEASED.* (FR) **5561**

MARIE-FRANCE (FR/0025-3057) [I00253057] **1086**

MARIE-PIER (CN/0823-6356) [09859923] **5561**

MARIE SELBY BOTANICAL GARDENS *See* BULLETIN - THE MARIE SELBY BOTANICAL GARDENS **505**

MARIEL (MIAMI, FLA. : 1986) (US/0892-7820) [15115866] **2745**

MARIETTA DAILY JOURNAL (MARIETTA, GA.), THE (US/8750-4618) [11461340] **5654**

MARIETTA TIMES (1977) (US) [17063607] **5729**

MARIGOLD LIBRARY SYSTEM *See* MARIGOLD LIBRARY SYSTEM DIRECTORY **3230**

MARIGOLD LIBRARY SYSTEM DIRECTORY (CN/0714-895X) [09313152] **3230**

MARIGOLD REPORT (CN/0226-5737) [06461827] **3230**

MARIN COUNTY COURT REPORTER (US/0745-8959) [09551979] **3006**

MARIN INDEPENDENT JOURNAL (US/0891-5164) [14879653] **5637**

MARIN KIN TRACER, THE (US/0277-8718) [05063792] **2459**

MARINA DOCK AGE (US) **594**

MARINA ITALIANA (IT) **4049**

MARINA MERCANTE IBEROAMERICANA / INSTITUTO DE ESTUDIOS DE LA MARINA MERCANTE, LA (AG) [06383758] **5452**

MARINA MERCANTILE, LA *SUSPENDED.* (IT/0025-3103) [06236246] **5452**

MARINA NEWS *See* M&R. MARINE AND RECREATION NEWS **594**

MARINA NEWS (LONG BEACH, CALIF.) (US/0746-4320) [10037334] **5637**

MARINA YEARBOOK (UK/0302-0983) [01792669] **594**

MARINE (GW) [04697100] **4178**

MARINE ACCIDENT REPORTS. SUMMARY FORMAT / NATIONAL TRANSPORTATION SAFETY BOARD (US) [08270403] **4178**

MARINE ADVISORY BULLETIN (US) [04095899] 556, **1451**

MARINE AFFAIRS BIBLIOGRAPHY (CN/0226-8361) [06550967] **3181**

MARINE & AVIATION INSURANCE REPORT (UK/0265-8410) [I02658410] **2887**

MARINE AND INSURANCE NEWS (CN/0228-8923) [07822647] **2887**

MARINE AND PETROLEUM GEOLOGY (UK/0264-8172) [10584686] 4264, **1386**

MARINE BEHAVIOUR AND PHYSIOLOGY (US/0091-181X) [01789191] **583**

MARINE BIOLOGICAL ASSOCIATION OF INDIA *See* JOURNAL OF THE MARINE BIOLOGICAL ASSOCIATION OF INDIA **555**

MARINE BIOLOGICAL ASSOCIATION OF THE UNITED KINGDOM *See* JOURNAL OF THE MARINE BIOLOGICAL ASSOCIATION OF THE UNITED KINGDOM **555**

MARINE BIOLOGICAL LABORATORY (WOODS HOLE, MASS.) *See* INFORMATIONAL BULLETIN - MARINE BIOLOGICAL LABORATORY **554**

MARINE BIOLOGY (GW/0025-3162) [01713888] **556**

MARINE BLUE BOOK (OVERLAND PARK, KAN.) (US/1061-6772) [24601647] **594**

MARINE BRIEFS (US/0735-7486) [05626573] **1451**

MARINE BUYERS' DIRECTORY (CN/0318-3017) [02441844] **5452**

MARINE CHEMISTRY (NE/0304-4203) [01775862] **1451**

MARINE CORPS GAZETTE (LS/0025-3170) [02276114] **4049**

MARINE DEVELOPMENT IN JAPAN (JA) [02242977] **1451**

MARINE DIGEST AND TRANSPORTATION NEWS (US/1059-2970) [18067517] **845**

MARINE DIRECTORY (US) [04814877] **5452**

MARINE DOCK AGE (US) **594**

MARINE ECOLOGY (BERLIN, WEST) (GW/0173-9565) [07528529] **2218**

MARINE ECOLOGY. PROGRESS SERIES (HALSTENBEK) (GW/0171-8630) [05696404] **2218**

MARINE ENGINEERING DIGEST *SUSPENDED.* (CN/0824-734X) [11283971] **1986**

MARINE ENGINEERING SOCIETY IN JAPAN *See* BULLETIN OF THE MARINE ENGINEERING SOCIETY IN JAPAN **1967**

MARINE ENVIRONMENTAL RESEARCH (UK/0141-1136) [04268046] **2177**

MARINE EQUIPMENT CATALOG (US/0882-1984) [11040703] **4179**

MARINE EQUIPMENT DIRECTORY (CN/0824-8729) [02441743] **4179**

MARINE FISH MANAGEMENT (US/0195-4555) [05455867] **2308**

MARINE FISH MONTHLY (US/1045-3555) [20084219] **2308**

MARINE FISHERIES MANAGEMENT REPORTER *CEASED.* (US/0730-3394) [07988606] **2308**

MARINE FISHERIES RESEARCH DEPARTMENT ANNUAL REPORT (SI) [07385511] **2308**

MARINE FISHERIES REVIEW (US/0090-1830) [01716848] 556, **2308**

MARINE GEODESY (US/0149-0419) [03045235] **1358**

MARINE GEOLOGY (NE/0025-3227) [01756692] **1386**

MARINE GEOPHYSICAL RESEARCHES (NE/0025-3235) [01607617] **1451**

●MARINE GEORESOURCES & GEOTECHNOLOGY (US/1064-119X) [26208273] 1386, **1986**

MARINE GEOTECHNOLOGY (US/0360-8867) [02244971] **1451**

MARINE INDUSTRY FAX DIRECTORY (US) [17967937] **1159**

MARINE INDUSTRY NEWS (AT) **1617**

MARINE INSURANCE INTERNATIONAL (UK/0268-1927) [20021694] **2887**

MARINE JOURNAL (WASHINGTON, D.C.) *See* MARINE OFFICER **4049**

MARINE LABORATORY (ABERDEEN, SCOTLAND) *See* ANNUAL REVIEW / MARINE LABORATORY ABERDEEN **1446**

●MARINE LIFE (FR) [27096489] **556**

MARINE LOG : A PUBLICATION OF THE FLORIDA SEA GRANT COLLEGE (US) [09505418] **1451**

MARINE LOG (NEW YORK, N.Y.) (US/0897-0491) [17156061] **5452**

MARINE MAMMAL NEWS (US) **5591**

MARINE MAMMAL SCIENCE (US/0824-0469) [12006236] **1452**

MARINE MARCHANDE EN ..., LA (FR/0755-365X) [01795598] **5452**

MARINE MICROBIAL FOOD WEBS (FR/0297-8148) [13258184] **566**

MARINE MICROPALEONTOLOGY (NE/0377-8398) [02779140] **4228**

MARINE MINING *See* MARINE GEORESOURCES & GEOTECHNOLOGY **1986**

MARINE NEWS (UK) [08782985] **5452**

MARINE OBSERVER, THE (UK/0025-3251) [01914275] **1430**

MARINE OFFICER (US/1075-9069) [30211876] **4049**

MARINE ORNITHOLOGY (SA) [23117088] **5618**

MARINE POLICY (UK/0308-597X) [02884687] **1452**

MARINE POLICY REPORTS (US/0735-5912) [20380970] **3181**

MARINE POLLUTION BULLETIN (UK/0025-326X) [01338294] **2236**

MARINE POLLUTION RESEARCH TITLES (UK) [02580724] **2236**

MARINE PRODUCTS EXPORT DEVELOPMENT AUTHORITY *See* MARINE PRODUCTS EXPORT REVIEW **845**

MARINE PRODUCTS EXPORT REVIEW (IT) [02378041] **845**

MARINE PROPULSION INTERNATIONAL (UK/0143-3709) [09208342] **5452**

MARINE RECREATIONAL FISHERIES (US/0161-522X) [03953576] **2308**

MARINE RECREATIONAL FISHERY STATISTICS SURVEY. PACIFIC COAST (US) [11689613] 2308, **2317**

MARINE RESEARCH IN INDONESIA (IO/0079-0435) [03950321] 1452, **556**

MARINE RESEARCH LABORATORY, ST. PETERSBURG *See* CONTRIBUTION - FLORIDA DEPARTMENT OF NATURAL RESOURCES MARINE RESEARCH LABORATORY **1448**

MARINE RESEARCH LABORATORY, ST. PETERSBURG, FLA *See* LIST OF PUBLICATIONS OF THE BUREAU OF MARINE SCIENCE & TECHNOLOGY, MARINE RESEARCH LABORATORY **555**

MARINE RESOURCE BULLETIN (US/0196-2515) [05785984] **1452**

MARINE RESOURCE ECONOMICS (US/0738-1360) [09535422] **2308**

MARINE RESPONSE BULLETIN : WEST COAST OIL SPILL PREVENTION AND RESPONSE (US/1059-0641) [24469564] **4264**

MARINE SAFETY MANUAL (US) [04481871] **4179**

MARINE SCIENCE CONTENTS TABLES. ACTUALITES DES SCIENCES DE LA MER. INDICES DE REVISTAS SOBRE CIENCIAS MARINAS (IT/0025-3308) [01714356] 1452, **1363**

MARINE SCIENCE (PLENUM) (US/0160-273X) [03655158] **1452**

MARINE SCIENCES (NEW YORK, N.Y. : 1982) (US/0732-7137) [08405607] **1452**

MARINE SCIENCES RESEARCH LABORATORY TECHNICAL REPORT (CN/0316-1633) [02247970] **556**

MARINE SERVICE CENTER (US) **594**

●MARINE SOCIETY VIEWS (US/1060-2607) [24899376] **4049**

MARINE STORES INTERNATIONAL (UK) [03667015] 4179, **1617**

MARINE STRUCTURES (UK/0951-8339) [18711448] **4179**

MARINE TECHNOLOGY AND SNAME NEWS (US) [18508579] **1452**

MARINE TECHNOLOGY NEWS (US/1071-1333) [28555771] **4179**

MARINE TECHNOLOGY SOCIETY *See* MARINE TECHNOLOGY SOCIETY JOURNAL **1452**

MARINE TECHNOLOGY SOCIETY JOURNAL (US/0025-3324) [01623789] **1452**

MARINE TEXTILES (US/0885-9949) [12792523] **5354**

MARINE TRADES (1978) (CN/0705-8993) [04448704] 594, **845**

MARINE WEEK MARINE DESIGN INTERNATIONAL (UK) [01794433] **4179**

MARINEBLAD   Alphabetical Title Index

MARINEBLAD (NE/0025-3340) [06880852] **4179**

MARINER (VANCOUVER, B.C.) *SUSPENDED.* (CN/0829-545X) [13490296] **5452**

MARINER'S CATALOG, THE (US/0198-9618) [03522314] **4179**

MARINER'S MIRROR (UK/0025-3359) [01587947] **4179**

MARINERS' (SINGAPORE) (SI/0303-4445) [02245937] **4179**

MARINERS WEATHER LOG (US/0025-3367) [01781430] **4179, 1430**

MARINES (WASHINGTON, D.C.) (US/1056-9073) [09741236] **4049**

MARINETTE EAGLE-STAR, THE (US) [14509074] **5768**

MARINNYTT (SW/0025-3375) [06352146] **4179**

MARIOLOGICAL SOCIETY OF AMERICA. NATIONAL CONVENTION *See* MARIAN STUDIES **5032**

MARION ADVERTISER, THE (US) [14686835] **5768**

MARION COUNTY, ALABAMA TRACKS (US/0748-2795) [10899175] **2459**

MARION COUNTY DEED REPORT (US) **691**

MARION COUNTY RECORD (MARION, KAN. : 1957) (US) [11822156] **5677**

MARION RECORD (MARION, S.D.) (US) [12814275] **5744**

MARION STAR AND MULLINS ENTERPRISE (US) [28436784] **5743**

MARION TIMES-STANDARD, THE (US) [09140298] **5627**

MARION ZIMMER BRADLEY'S FANTASY MAGAZINE (US/0897-9286) [17669543] **3410**

MARIONNETTES PARIS (FR/0761-9529) [I07619529] **4852**

MARIPOSA FOLK FESTIVAL (CN/0712-6263) [09318443] 324, **4130**

MARIPOSA WEEKLY GAZETTE AND MINER (US) [27316897] **5637**

MARISIA / COMITETUL DE CULTURA SI EDUCATIE SOCIALISTA AL JUDETULUI MURES, MUSEUL JUDETEAN MURES (RM) [05218179] **2697**

MARITAL STATUS AND LIVING ARRANGEMENTS (US/0146-4213) [02943248] **2283**

MARITIM KONTAKT (DK/0106-7818) [10493215] **4179**

MARITIME ABSTRACTS (US/1045-3296) [15472453] **5452**

MARITIME ADVISOR. COURT CASE DIGEST, THE (US/0894-668X) [16181713] **3181**

MARITIME ANTHROPOLOGICAL STUDIES : MAST *CEASED.* (NE/0922-1476) [18373977] **241**

MARITIME ART ASSOCIATION *See* MAA NEWS **357**

MARITIME DEFENCE (UK/0950-558X) [10838324] **4179**

MARITIME GUIDE / LLOYD'S REGISTER OF SHIPPING (UK/0264-6420) [10909920] **5452**

MARITIME INFORMATION REVIEW (NE/0920-1610) [I09201610] **3181**

MARITIME LAW REPORTER (US) [16835389] **3181**

MARITIME NEWSLETTER (US/0161-9373) [02989688] 5452, **1690**

MARITIME PATROL AVIATION (CN) **28**

MARITIME POLICY AND MANAGEMENT (UK/0308-8839) [02899960] 1504, **5452**

MARITIME RESEARCH INFORMATION SERVICE *See* MRIS ABSTRACTS **4179**

MARITIME STUDIES AND MANAGEMENT (UK) [02580887] **5452**

MARITIME STUDIES CURRENT AWARENESS BULLETIN (UK) **4179**

MARITIME SURVEY (UK) [03527744] **4179**

MARITIME TRANSPORT (FR/0474-5884) [01761469] **5452**

MARITIME WORKER (AT) [05518349] 4179, **1690**

MARITIMER (AMHERST) (CN/0704-0652) [04746685] **4391**

MARITIMES (US/0025-3472) [02112792] **1452**

MARITIMEWEEK (ARLINGTON, VA.) (US/1054-383X) [22874457] **3181**

MARJORIE KINNAN RAWLINGS JOURNAL OF FLORIDA LITERATURE, THE (US/1060-3409) [23587708] **3410**

MARK (FI) [05959977] **930**

MARK LEIBOVIT'S THE VOLUME REVERSAL SURVEY (US/8755-3406) [11274880] **797**

MARK SKOUSEN'S FORECASTS & STRATEGIES ON INFLATION, TAXES AND GOVERNMENT CONTROLS (US/0272-0868) [06805271] **4736**

●MARK SPIVAK'S FLORIDA WINE BULLETIN (US/1062-1032) [25526044] **2369**

MARK TWAIN JOURNAL (1954) (US/0025-3499) [04635029] 3347, **433**

MARK TWAIN SOCIETY BULLETIN (US/0272-6378) [06185858] 433, **3410**

MARK-UP / WASHINGTON OFFICE, NATIONAL COUNCIL OF CHURCHES (US) [10213774] **4975**

MARKA, ACTUALIDAD Y ANALISIS (PE) [02422839] **2552**

MARKAZ AL-KUWAYT LIL-MALUMAT WA-AL-MIKRUFILM *See* DALIL AL-KUWAYT AL-YAWM / WIZARAT AL-TAKHTIT, MARKAZ AL-KUWAYT LIL-MALUMAT WA-AL-MIKRUFILM **2959**

MARKAZ AL-QAWMI LIL-TANMIYAH WA-AL-TADRIB AL-TAAWUNI (SUDAN) *See* AL-BARNEAMAJ AL-SANAWI / AL-MARKAZ AL-QAWMI LIL-TANMIYAH WA-AL-TADRIB AL-TAAWUNI **1643**

MARKAZ TADRIB MALAKAT MAHW AL-UMMIYAH WA-TALIM AL-KIBAR *See* DAWRIYAT MALUMAT / TASDURU AN MARKAZ TADRIB MALAKAT MAHW AL-UMMIYAH WA-TALIM AL-KIBAR, TARABULUS **1734**

MARKEE (SANFORD, FLA.) (US/1073-8924) [25287211] 4371, **4074**

MARKER (NEW YORK, N.Y.), THE (US/0882-3634) [11822517] **3606**

MARKERS (US/0277-8726) [06690897] 2459, **357**

MARKESAN HERALD (US) [14713382] **5768**

MARKET ABSORPTION OF APARTMENTS (US/0363-8286) [02456937] **2828**

●MARKET. ASIA PACIFIC (US/1059-275X) [24529939] **930**

MARKET CHARTS *See* MARKET CHARTS INC **1504**

MARKET CHARTS INC (US/1071-1740) [28564003] **1504**

MARKET CHRONICLE, THE (US/0360-1773) [02243560] **906**

MARKET COMMENTARY *See* AGRI-FOOD PERSPECTIVES **47**

●MARKET DATA RETRIEVAL'S CIC SCHOOL DIRECTORY. ALABAMA (US/1067-6430) [25334846] **1762**

●MARKET DATA RETRIEVAL'S CIC SCHOOL DIRECTORY. ARKANSAS (US/1067-960X) [25334894] **1866**

●MARKET DATA RETRIEVAL'S CIC SCHOOL DIRECTORY. DISTRICT OF COLUMBIA (US/1067-957X) [25334967] **1762**

●MARKET DATA RETRIEVAL'S CIC SCHOOL DIRECTORY. IDAHO (US/1067-6538) [25335000] **1762**

●MARKET DATA RETRIEVAL'S CIC SCHOOL DIRECTORY. INDIANA (US/1067-6554) [25335023] **1762**

●MARKET DATA RETRIEVAL'S CIC SCHOOL DIRECTORY. MAINE (US) [25335069] **1762**

●MARKET DATA RETRIEVAL'S CIC SCHOOL DIRECTORY. MASSACHUSETTS (US) [25224864] **1762**

●MARKET DATA RETRIEVAL'S CIC SCHOOL DIRECTORY. MINNESOTA (US/1067-6643) [25335099] **1762**

●MARKET DATA RETRIEVAL'S CIC SCHOOL DIRECTORY. MISSISSIPPI (US/1067-6651) [25335105] **1763**

●MARKET DATA RETRIEVAL'S CIC SCHOOL DIRECTORY. NEW HAMPSHIRE (US) [25335145] **1763**

●MARKET DATA RETRIEVAL'S CIC SCHOOL DIRECTORY. PENNSYLVANIA (US/1067-6791) [25335232] **1763**

●MARKET DATA RETRIEVAL'S CIC SCHOOL DIRECTORY. RHODE ISLAND (US) [25335248] **1763**

●MARKET DATA RETRIEVAL'S CIC SCHOOL DIRECTORY. VERMONT (US) [25335318] **1763**

MARKET DATA RETRIEVAL'S CIC SCHOOL DIRECTORY. WISCONSIN (US/1067-6899) [25335353] **1763**

MARKET DATA RETRIEVAL'S SALES MANAGER'S GUIDE TO THE U.S. SCHOOL MARKET (US/1071-7471) [25335390] **1763**

MARKET DEVELOPMENT CENTRE *See* ANNUAL REPORT - MARKET DEVELOPMENT CENTRE **921**

MARKET--EUROPE (US/1050-9410) [21717696] **845**

MARKET FORECAST, ELECTRIC ENERGY REQUIREMENTS IN THE NORTHWEST TERRITORIES *See* UPDATE, MARKET FORECAST, ELECTRIC ENERGY REQUIREMENTS IN THE NORTHWEST TERRITORIES **1959**

MARKET FORECAST, ELECTRIC ENERGY REQUIREMENTS IN THE YUKON TERRITORY *See* UPDATE, MARKET FORECAST, ELECTRIC ENERGY REQUIREMENTS IN YUKON **4762**

MARKET GUIDE, LATIN AMERICA (US/0278-6192) [07842220] **1574**

MARKET GUIDE (NEW YORK, N.Y.) (US/0278-6524) [12685326] 906, **797**

MARKET GUIDE, THE (US/1046-2171) [23744613] **906**

MARKET HISTORY REPORTS (US) [26776607] **4840**

●MARKET INFORMATION (UK/0966-212X) [I0966212X] **906**

MARKET INFORMATION SERIES (II) [01784105] **845**

MARKET INSIDER BULLETIN (CN/1182-4166) [23302374] **1504**

MARKET INTELLIGENCE BULLETIN (II) **691**

MARKET INTEREST RATE FOR PROJECT MORTGAGE INSURANCE (US) [03114847] **2887**

●MARKET LATIN AMERICA (US/1066-7024) [27032731] 930, **691**

MARKET LETTER (UK/0951-3175) [I09513175] 3606, **4314**

MARKET LETTER (BUDAPEST, HUNGARY) *See* MONTHLY REPORT / NATIONAL BANK OF HUNGARY **800**

MARKET LOGIC FROM THE INSTITUTE FOR ECONOMETRIC RESEARCH (US/0162-6817) [04215307] **906**

MARKET MONITOR (TORONTO) (CN/1186-0928) [24266123] **906**

MARKET MONTH (US/0890-023X) [14121303] **906**

MARKET MOVES *CEASED.* (US/0882-1496) [11790020] **1238**

MARKET NEWS. LIVESTOCK, MEAT, GRAIN AND SEED DIVISION (US/0279-4543) [07894788] **107**

MARKET NEWS (RICHMOND) (US/0507-066X) [02438630] 845, **107**

MARKET NICHES IN ... (US/1059-1923) [24499082] **692**

MARKET OF VEGETABLE OILS AND OILSEED MEALS (AG) [24681412] **5777**

MARKET PRICE AND INDEX (US) **930**

MARKET PROFILES (UK/0967-6384) **906**

MARKET REPORT & NEWSLETTER (US/0747-4121) [10833400] **215**

MARKET REPORT - YAITYOPYA NEGD BANK (ET) [02534767] **1574**

MARKET RESEARCH ABSTRACTS (UK/0025-3596) [04014152] 930, **731**

MARKET RESEARCH EUROPE (UK/0308-3446) [04735914] 930, **731**

MARKET RESEARCH FACTS AND TRENDS FROM MACLEAN-HUNTER RESEARCH BUREAU *CEASED.* (CN/0025-360X) [01988766] **1504**

MARKET RESEARCH GREAT BRITAIN (UK) [06832930] 845, **930**

MARKET RESEARCH HANDBOOK (CN/0590-9325) [02443720] **930**

MARKET RESEARCH IN GREAT BRITAIN (UK) [08525799] **930**

MARKET RESEARCH REPORT (II) [05135331] **1617**

MARKET RESEARCH REPORTER (UK/0963-7257) [I09637257] **906**

MARKET RESEARCH SOCIETY *See* JOURNAL OF THE MARKET RESEARCH SOCIETY **929**

MARKET SHARE REPORTER (US/1052-9578) [22423852] **930**

MARKET SHARE REPORTS CATALOG (US) [03151103] **692**

MARKET SITUATION FOR LEAD, THE (UK) **4008**

MARKET SITUATION FOR ZINC, THE (UK) **4008**

MARKET STATISTICS (US/0146-731X) [03022622] **906**

MARKET TECHNICIANS ASSOCIATION JOURNAL (US/0734-502X) [08744678] **906**

MARKET (TORONTO) (CN/0227-6062) [08010203] **2121**

MARKET TRENDS FOR SELECTED CHEMICAL PRODUCTS ... AND PROSPECTS TO ... / ECONOMIC COMMISSION FOR EUROPE (US) [18851855] 985, **1638**

MARKET WATCH (NEW YORK, N.Y.) (US/0277-9277) [07659272] **2369**

MARKETER, THE (US/1050-186X) [21420347] **930**

MARKETERS FORUM MAGAZINE (US/0888-3327) [13587056] **930**

MARKETER'S GUIDE TO MEDIA (US/1061-7159) [25417369] **1116**

MARKETFACT DIGEST (AT) **930**

MARKETING (AT) **930**

MARKETING (BL) [06381843] **930**

MARKETING ACTION PLANNER (US) [10867121] **930**

MARKTFORSCHUNG

MARKETING AND ADVERTISING NEWS **SUSPENDED.** (UK/0306-3615) [01794190] 762, **930**

MARKETING AND ADVERTISING REFERENCE SERVICE [ONLINE DATABASE] (US) 762, **731**

MARKETING & P. R. CONSULTANTS (ASIA) *See* REPORT ON FINANCE, COMMERCE, INDUSTRY - SOUTHEAST ASIA **707**

MARKETING AND RESEARCH TODAY : THE JOURNAL OF THE EUROPEAN SOCIETY FOR OPINION AND MARKETING RESEARCH (NE/0923-5957) [19819805] 930, **731**

MARKETING & SALES CAREER DIRECTORY (US/0889-8510) [14091620] 762, **930**

MARKETING ASPARAGUS FROM CALIFORNIA *See* MARKETING CALIFORNIA ASPARAGUS **2349**

MARKETING BREAKTHROUGHS (UK/0955-4785) [09554785] **930**

MARKETING BRIEFING **CEASED.** (US/1051-2799) [21322515] **930**

MARKETING BUDAPEST (HU/0237-1995) [I02371995] **930**

MARKETING BULLETIN - DEPARTMENT OF MARKETING, MASSEY UNIVERSITY (NZ/0113-6895) [I01136895] **930**

MARKETING BULLETIN (SYRACUSE) (US/0093-2736) [05050105] **930**

MARKETING CALIFORNIA AND ARIZONA MELONS, INCLUDES CANTALOUPS-HONEYDEWS-WATERMELONS (US) [11761833] **2348**

MARKETING CALIFORNIA APRICOTS (US) [03313687] **2348**

MARKETING CALIFORNIA ARTICHOKES (US/0098-7360) [02242172] **2348**

MARKETING CALIFORNIA ASPARAGUS (US) [06311129] **2349**

MARKETING CALIFORNIA BROCCOLI (US/0148-4966) [03308332] **2349**

MARKETING CALIFORNIA CARROTS (US/0146-0676) [02871617] **2349**

MARKETING CALIFORNIA CELERY (US/0148-4974) [03308317] **2349**

MARKETING CALIFORNIA CHERRIES (US) [06547658] **2349**

MARKETING CALIFORNIA CHERRIES FOR FRESH MARKET *See* MARKETING CALIFORNIA CHERRIES **2349**

MARKETING CALIFORNIA, COLORADO, IDAHO, NEW MEXICO, OREGON, AND WASHINGTON ONIONS (US) [26323015] **107**

MARKETING CALIFORNIA DRIED FRUITS (US/0094-2510) [01793902] **2349**

MARKETING CALIFORNIA ONIONS (US) [01783345] **2349**

MARKETING CALIFORNIA PEARS (US/0277-1489) [07498938] **2349**

MARKETING CALIFORNIA PEARS FOR FRESH MARKET *See* MARKETING CALIFORNIA PEARS **2349**

MARKETING CALIFORNIA PLUMS (US) [02960057] **2349**

MARKETING CALIFORNIA POTATOES (US) [03799547] **2349**

MARKETING CALIFORNIA POTATOES, FEATURING THE KERN DISTRICT (US) [14222913] **2349**

MARKETING CALIFORNIA POTATOES FROM THE KERN DISTRICT AND STOCKTON DELTA DISTRICT (US/0363-7964) [02545023] **2349**

MARKETING CALIFORNIA TOMATOES (US) [03313584] **2349**

MARKETING CLASSES FOR ADULTS *See* COURSE TRENDS **1734**

MARKETING COMMUNICATIONS (UNITED BUSINESS PUBLICATIONS) *See* POTENTIALS IN MARKETING **935**

MARKETING COMPUTERS (US/0895-5697) [16689599] **1194**

MARKETING + DISTRIBUTION ABSTRACTS (UK) [06434765] 930, **731**

MARKETING EASTERN NORTH CAROLINA VEGETABLES ... CROP / FEDERAL STATE MARKET NEWS SERVICE (US) [08598149] **2349**

MARKETING ECONOMICS INSTITUTE *See* MEI MARKETING ECONOMICS GUIDE **933**

MARKETING EDUCATION REVIEW (US/1052-8008) [22390535] **930**

MARKETING EDUCATORS' JOURNAL (US) [12673266] **930**

MARKETING ERDGAS (GW) [20104887] **930**

MARKETING ESPANSIONE **CEASED.** (IT) [10007656] **930**

MARKETING EXECUTIVE REPORT **CEASED.** (US/1054-2388) [22786154] **930**

MARKETING FLORIDA AVOCADOS, LIMES, MANGOS (US/0160-0370) [03590299] **2349**

MARKETING FLORIDA TROPICAL FRUITS & VEGETABLES (US/0732-9768) [08481332] **2349**

MARKETING FLORIDA VEGETABLES : SUMMARY (US/0193-242X) [01377616] **2349**

MARKETING FOR LAWYERS (US/0893-7788) [15641607] **3006**

MARKETING GLOBE (AT) **931**

MARKETING (GUILFORD, CONN.) (US/0730-2606) [06999261] **931**

MARKETING HIGHER EDUCATION (US/0896-7156) [17281499] 1835, **931**

MARKETING IN EUROPE (BE/0025-3723) [02256551] **931**

MARKETING IN NIGERIA (NR) [08922334] **931**

MARKETING INFORMATION (US/0732-7331) [08414299] **931**

MARKETING INTELLIGENCE & PLANNING (UK/0263-4503) [11908336] **931**

MARKETING INTELLIGENCE. FIBEROPTIC (UK/0728-9358) [11036517] 931, **1159**

MARKETING-JOURNAL (GW/0025-3774) [I00253774] **762**

MARKETING LETTER MILSONS POINT (AT/0815-4384) [I08154384] **931**

MARKETING LETTERS (US/0923-0645) [21315262] **931**

MARKETING LETTUCE FROM IMPERIAL VALLEY AND BLYTHE DISTRICTS (US) [03307825] 931, **178**

MARKETING LETTUCE FROM SALINAS-WATSONVILLE-KING CITY AND OTHER CENTRAL CALIFORNIA DISTRICTS *See* MARKETING LETTUCE FROM SALINAS-WATSONVILLE, OTHER CENTRAL CALIFORNIA DISTRICTS AND COLORADO **2349**

MARKETING LETTUCE FROM SALINAS-WATSONVILLE, OTHER CENTRAL CALIFORNIA DISTRICTS AND COLORADO (US/0732-7625) [09401516] **2349**

MARKETING LIBRARY SERVICES (US/0896-3908) [17061891] 931, **3230**

MARKETING (LONDON) (UK/0025-3650) [02448438] **931**

●MARKETING MAGAZINE (TORONTO) (CN/1196-4650) [29322776] **931**

●MARKETING MANAGEMENT (CHICAGO, ILL.) (US/1061-3846) [25278592] **931**

MARKETING MAN'S GUIDE TO KENYA, A (KE) [11124788] **931**

MARKETING MICHIGAN APPLES, PEACHES, AND PRUNES (US) [10572977] **2349**

MARKETING MICHIGAN ONIONS AND POTATOES (US) [07500301] **2349**

MARKETING MICHIGAN VEGETABLES (US) [03306097] **2349**

MARKETING MIX DIGEST (NE/0025-3782) [I00253782] **931**

MARKETING MIX (JOHANNESBURG, SOUTH AFRICA) (SA) [08125329] **931**

MARKETING MUNCHEN (GW/0344-1369) [I03441369] **931**

MARKETING NEWS (US/0025-3790) [02448442] **931**

... MARKETING NEWS INTERNATIONAL DIRECTORY OF THE AMERICAN MARKETING ASSOCIATION AND MARKETING SERVICES GUIDE, THE (US) [25126038] **931**

... MARKETING NEWS INTERNATIONAL DIRECTORY OF THE AMERICAN MARKETING ASSOCIATION AND THE MARKETING YELLOW PAGES, THE (US) [27291732] **931**

MARKETING NORTHWEST APPLES (US) [03792494] **107**

MARKETING OPTIONS (CN/0822-3998) [11830284] 2887, **931**

MARKETING ORC INDEX (US/0739-8212) [09801382] **931**

MARKETING PULSE, THE (US/1065-9994) [26822983] **931**

MARKETING REHABILITATION SERVICES (US) **932**

●MARKETING REPORT, THE (US/1064-3893) [26273592] **932**

MARKETING RESEARCH (CHICAGO, ILL.) (US/1040-8460) [18549487] **932**

MARKETING RESEARCH IN EUROPE (NE) [02899534] **932**

MARKETING RESEARCH REPORT (US/0082-9781) [01380703] **932**

MARKETING RESULTS (NE) **932**

MARKETING REVIEW (US) [06290208] **932**

MARKETING REVIEW (MARKETING ASSOCIATION OF PAKISTAN) (PK) [08522216] **932**

MARKETING SCIENCE (PROVIDENCE, R.I.) (US/0732-2399) [08337960] **932**

MARKETING SELECTED CALIFORNIA VEGETABLES (US) [08162974] **2349**

MARKETING SOCIAL (CN/0380-0180) [02062326] **932**

MARKETING STRATEGY LETTER *See* STRATEGIC DIRECTION **713**

MARKETING SUCCESS (UK/0961-7752) [09617752] **932**

MARKETING SURVEYS INDEX (UK/0964-0142) [09640142] **932**

MARKETING TECHNOLOGY (US/8756-2855) [11520883] **932**

MARKETING TO DOCTORS (US/1043-5417) [19483833] **932**

MARKETING TO DOCTORS *See* MANAGEMENT & DOCTORS **3915**

MARKETING TO KIDS REPORT (US) **932**

MARKETING TO WOMEN (1989) (US/1047-1677) [19805560] 932, **5561**

MARKETING (TORONTO) (CN/0025-3642) [02499973] **932**

MARKETING TREASURES (US/0895-1799) [16511713] **932**

MARKETING TRENDS (DEUTSCHE AUSG.) (US/0882-4770) [11853495] **932**

MARKETING TRENDS (ED. ESPANOLA) (US/0882-4789) [11853200] **932**

MARKETING TRENDS (ED. FRANCAISE) (US/0882-4762) [11851221] **932**

MARKETING TRENDS (ED. ITALIANA) (US/0882-4797) [11852947] **932**

MARKETING TRIBUNE (IT) **692**

MARKETING UPDATE (CLEVELAND, OHIO) **CEASED.** (US/0732-555X) [08384324] **932**

MARKETING WEEK (UK) [13556100] **932**

MARKETING WEEK (UK/0141-9285) [I01419285] **932**

MARKETING WESTERN POTATOES (US) **107**

MARKETIPS : A NEWSLETTER FOR FSS CUSTOMERS (US) [08021349] **1298**

MARKETLETTER (MARKET ED.) (UK/0891-589X) [14909317] **2435**

MARKETNEWS (CN/0714-7422) [09457189] **5317**

MARKETOLOGY (II) [10063850] **932**

MARKETONS BV (NE) **1238**

MARKETOOLS (HERNDON, VA.) (US/1059-8200) [24778972] **932**

MARKETPLACE MAGAZINE (US/1054-2264) [20639555] **692**

MARKETPLACE (SCOTTDALE), THE (US/0199-7130) [06099223] **1504**

MARKETPLACE (TORONTO) (CN/1180-4696) [23231185] **845**

MARKETS YEAR BOOK (UK) [09885670] **5127**

MARKETSCAN INTERNATIONAL (US) **932**

MARKETSCORE (US) **4840**

MARKETSEARCH / COMPILED BY ARLINGTON MANAGEMENT PUBLICATIONS LIMITED IN ASSOCIATION WITH THE BRITISH OVERSEAS TRADE BOARD (UK) [13688122] 932, **731**

MARKETSOURCE (CHICAGO, ILL.) (US/1055-5579) [23235850] **1504**

MARKHAM MONTH (CN/0715-4461) [09336364] **2538**

MARKHAM STAR-TRIBUNE *See* STAR (HARVEY-MARKHAM AREA ED.), THE **5662**

MARKING INDUSTRY MAGAZINE (US/0164-4939) [04757840] **933**

MARKSCHEIDEWESEN, DAS (GW/0174-1357) [05213104] **2143**

MARKSISTSKO-LENINSKAIA ETIKA / AKADEMIIA NAUK SSSR, INSTITUT NAUCHNOI INFORMATSII PO OBSHCHESTVENNYM NAUKAM (RU) [05639485] **2252**

MARKSIZM-LENINIZM I NASHE VREMIA (XR) [02241755] **4481**

MARKSMAN (AT) **4904**

MARKT & TECHNIK (GW/0344-8843) [I03448843] **2071**

MARKT, DER (AU) [06957808] 879, **933**

MARKT INTERN ELEKTROHANDEL (GW) 950, **933**

MARKT INTERN MOEBELHANDEL (GW) **2906**

MARKT KOMMUNIKATION (GW) [02918553] 933, **1116**

MARKTBERICHT: MILCH (GW) [09885864] **196**

MARKTFORSCHUNG & MANAGEMENT (GW/0933-7105) [20424590] **879**

MARKTINFORMATIONEN — Alphabetical Title Index

MARKTINFORMATIONEN FUR INDUSTRIE UND AUSSENHANDEL DER DDR MIT ERGANZUNGEN ZUR AUSSENHANDELSPRAXIS (GW) [01789496] **845**

MARKWICK MIDDEN (CN/0821-3275) [10330285] **2459**

MARLBORO HERALD-ADVOCATE (US) [27920407] **5743**

MARLEY ORGANIZATION See TMO UPDATE **4033**

MARLIN (US/0749-2006) [11092774] **2308**

MARLIN DEMOCRAT (1989) (US/1046-1752) [20344580] **5752**

MARMAC GUIDE TO ATLANTA, A (US/0735-827X) [09026038] **5483**

MARMAC GUIDE TO HOUSTON AND GALVESTON, A (US/0735-8261) [09025998] **5483**

MARMAC GUIDE TO LOS ANGELES, A (US/0736-8119) [09228623] **2568**

MARMAC GUIDE TO NEW ORLEANS, A (US/0736-8135) [09232491] **5483**

MARMAC GUIDE TO PHILADELPHIA, A (US/0736-8127) [09232397] **5483**

MARMARA UNIVERSITESI ECZACILIK DERGISI (TU/1011-3398) [I10113398] **4314**

MARMORA HERALD (CN) **5789**

MARO PROGRESSIVE LEARNING SYSTEMS See BULLETIN - MARO PROGRESSIVE LEARNING SYSTEMS **1803**

MAROC (FR) [02650089] **5484**

MAROC MEDICAL (MR/0025-388X) [05086253] **3606**

MAROC REPRESSION (FR) [16991059] **4481**

MAROKKO, ALLGEMEINES EINFUHRPROGRAMM / BUNDESSTELLE FUER AUSSENHANDELSINFORMATION (GW) [11361504] **845**

MAROKKO, ERZBERGBAU / BUNDESSTELLE FUER AUSSENHANDELSINFORMATION (GW) [11361736] **1617**

MARPLE'S BUSINESS NEWSLETTER (US/0279-960X) [07386451] **692**

MARQUEE (NORWALK), THE (US/0364-815X) [02662641] **4130**

MARQUEE (TORONTO) (CN/0700-5008) [03348933] **4074**

MARQUEE (WASHINGTON, D.C.) (US) [01756706] 303, **5365**

MARQUES INTERNATIONALES : ORGANE OFFICIEL DU BUREAU INTERNATIONAL DE L'UNION POUR LA PROTECTION DE LA PROPRIETE INDUSTRIELLE, LES (SZ) [02448444] **1306**

MARQUETTE COUNTY TRIBUNE, THE (US) [15033023] **5768**

MARQUETTE LAW REVIEW (US/0025-3987) [01695814] **3006**

MARQUETTE SPORTS LAW JOURNAL (US/1057-6029) [23026085] 4904, **3006**

MARQUETTE TRIBUNE (MILWAUKEE), THE (US/0025-3995) [04050120] **5768**

MARQUIS WHO'S WHO DIRECTORY OF COMPUTER GRAPHICS (US/8756-0690) [11349615] **1234**

MARQUIS WHO'S WHO DIRECTORY OF ONLINE PROFESSIONALS (US/0884-044X) [11658472] **1275**

MARQUIS WHO'S WHO INDEX TO WHO'S WHO BOOKS (US/0884-7118) [12056673] 1927, **433**

MARRIAGE & DIVORCE (US/0093-6146) [01792399] **2283**

MARRIAGE & FAMILY (US/0272-7897) [06536474] **2283**

MARRIAGE AND FAMILY NEWSLETTER (US/0362-9341) [02256162] **2283**

MARRIAGE & FAMILY REVIEW (US/0149-4929) [03504015] **2283**

MARRIAGE CONNECTION (US/1045-3407) [20080726] 1195, **2283**

MARRIAGE ENCOUNTER See MARRIAGE (SAINT PAUL, MINN.) **2283**

MARRIAGE PARTNERSHIP (US/0897-5469) [17004667] 2283, **4975**

●MARRIAGE (SAINT PAUL, MINN.) (US/1063-1054) [25881651] **2283**

MARRIAGES, AUSTRALIA (AT) [09289151] 2283, **2287**

MARRIAGES / STATISTICS CANADA, CANADIAN CENTRE FOR HEALTH INFORMATION (CN/1195-4140) [29411249] 2283, **2287**

MARRS, JANET KAY See BELL FAMILY NEWSLETTER, THE **2439**

MARS DAILY SENTINEL, LE (US) [12929004] **5671**

MARS EXCHANGE (US/0736-2498) [09075068] **2459**

MARS EXCHANGE NEWSLETTER See MARS EXCHANGE **2459**

MARS UNDERGROUND NEWS (US) [24097499] **397**

MARSEILLAISE, LA (FR) [20988755] **5800**

MARSEILLE INFORMATIONS (FR) [12060270] **2519**

MARSH & MAPLE (CN/0384-093X) [03248141] **3466**

MARSHALL COUNTY HISTORICAL QUARTERLY (US/0738-7571) [07993046] **2745**

MARSHALL EVENING MESSENGER See MARSHALL NEWS MESSENGER **5752**

MARSHALL ISLANDS JOURNAL (1980) (XE/0892-2098) [06962426] **5806**

MARSHALL LOEB'S MONEY GUIDE (US/8755-1586) [11218235] **797**

MARSHALL MORNING NEWS See MARSHALL NEWS MESSENGER **5752**

MARSHALL NEWS MESSENGER (US/1046-5502) [13684676] **5752**

MARSHALL UNIVERSITY See ALUMNI DIRECTORY / MARSHALL UNIVERSITY **1098**

MARSHFIELD MAIL, THE (US) [13723292] **5704**

MARSHFIELD NEWS-HERALD (US) [13781678] **5769**

MARSH'S CALIFORNIA CORPORATION LAW (US) **3101**

MARSYAS PARIS (FR/0985-3286) [I09853286] **358**

MART JOURNAL (CN/0711-7922) [08659319] **1763**

MART (MONTREAL) (CN/0319-2709) [02442190] **2121**

MARTELLO PAPERS (CN/1183-3661) [24486918] **4528**

MARTHA'S KIDLIT NEWSLETTER (US/1045-4292) [20122992] 3410, **1066**

MARTHA'S VINEYARD (US/1052-5785) [22332196] 2369, **107**

MARTHA'S VINEYARD TIMES, THE (US/8750-1449) [11035733] **5689**

MARTH'S FLORIDA GUIDE (US) [27785997] **1116**

MARTIAL ARTS TRAINING (US/0898-4786) [17825497] **4904**

MARTIN BROWER'S ORANGE COUNTY REPORT (US/0882-0589) [11741597] **692**

MARTIN CENTRE FOR ARCHITECTURAL AND URBAN STUDIES See TRANSACTIONS OF THE MARTIN CENTRE FOR ARCHITECTURAL & URBAN STUDIES **310**

MARTIN COUNTY NEWS (US/0885-5102) [12649488] **5752**

MARTIN FAMILY QUARTERLY (US/0099-1864) [02243393] **2459**

●MARTIN LUTHER KING, JR. MEMORIAL STUDIES IN RELIGION, CULTURE, AND SOCIAL DEVELOPMENT (US/1052-181X) [22205213] 4976, **5251**

MARTIN P. CATHERWOOD LIBRARY See LIBRARY CATALOG OF THE MARTIN P. CATHERWOOD LIBRARY OF THE NEW YORK STATE SCHOOL OF INDUSTRIAL AND LABOR RELATIONS, CORNELL UNIVERSITY. SUPPLEMENT **1687**

MARTINDALE-HUBBELL BAR REGISTER, THE (US/1051-5518) [21358540] **3006**

MARTINDALE-HUBBELL CANADIAN LAW DIRECTORY (US) **3006**

●MARTINDALE-HUBBELL DISPUTE RESOLUTION DIRECTORY (US) **3006**

MARTINDALE-HUBBELL INTERNATIONAL LAW DIRECTORY (US) [23266418] **3006**

MARTINDALE-HUBBELL LAW DIGEST (US) [22923929] **3006**

MARTINDALE-HUBBELL LAW DIRECTORY (PRINT) (US/0191-0221) [01645529] **3006**

MARTINELLA See VOCE DI MILANO, LA **2495**

MARTINEZ NEW GAZETTE (US) **5637**

MARTINIQUE. CONSEIL GENERAL See RAPPORT DE PRESENTATION ET EXPOSE DES MOTIFS DE LA DECISION MODIFICATIVE ... / REPUBLIQUE FRANCAISE, DEPARTEMENT DE LA MARTINIQUE. CONSEIL GENERAL **4744**

MARTIN'S ANNUAL CRIMINAL CODE (CN/0527-7892) [02247257] **3108**

●MARTIN'S ONTARIO CRIMINAL PRACTICE (CN/1188-9640) [27203151] **3108**

MARTIN'S RELATED CRIMINAL STATUTES (CN/0710-1805) [08327357] **3108**

MARTYRDOM AND RESISTANCE (US/0892-1571) [04732326] **2267**

MARUNI (NE) [02239384] **2506**

MARUT BUNNAG INTERNATIONAL LAW OFFICE See LAW JOURNAL OF MARUT BUNNAG INTERNATIONAL LAW OFFICE **2995**

MARVEL AGE CEASED. (US/8750-4367) [11401154] **4863**

MARVEL COMICS PRESENTS (US/1044-7180) [19876406] **4863**

MARVEL FANFARE (NEW YORK, N.Y.) (US/0746-7664) [10259450] **4863**

MARVEL TALES (CHICAGO, ILL.) (US) [09787739] **4863**

MARXISM AND THE MASS MEDIA (US/0098-9509) [02240809] **4502**

MARXISM TODAY CEASED. (UK/0025-4118) [02378832] 5251, 4481, **2519**

MARXISMO OGGI (IT) [19287868] **4543**

MARXIST REVIEW. LONDON (UK/0965-9749) [I09659749] **4543**

MARXIST REVIEW, THE (II/0542-7762) [01695650] **4543**

MARXISTISCHE BLATTER (GW/0542-7770) [01715283] **4543**

MARXISTISK ANTROPOLOGI (DK/0106-5173) [08029502] **241**

MARYKNOLL (US/0025-4142) [05803058] **5032**

MARYLAND. ADMINISTRATIVE OFFICE OF THE COURTS See STATISTICAL COMPILATION - ADMINISTRATIVE OFFICE OF THE COURTS (ANNAPOLIS) **3083**

MARYLAND. ADMINISTRATIVE OFFICE OF THE COURTS See AMICUS CURIARUM **3138**

MARYLAND ADVANCE REPORTS (US/0199-0926) [05583233] **3006**

MARYLAND. ADVISORY COUNCIL ON ALCOHOLISM CONTROL See ANNUAL REPORT - MARYLAND. ADVISORY COUNCIL ON ALCOHOLISM CONTROL **1341**

MARYLAND AGRI-ECONOMICS (US/0542-8297) [05515392] 1504, **107**

MARYLAND AGRI-FACTS (US/0747-301X) [10691343] **178**

MARYLAND AGRI-VIEWS (US/0745-4317) [01069691] **107**

MARYLAND AGRICULTURAL EXPERIMENT STATION See ANNUAL REPORT - MARYLAND AGRICULTURAL EXPERIMENT STATION **61**

MARYLAND AGRICULTURAL STATISTICS SUMMARY FOR... (US) [26102526] 107, **154**

MARYLAND. ALCOHOLISM CONTROL ADMINISTRATION See ANNUAL REPORT OF THE ALCOHOLISM CONTROL ADMINISTRATION FOR ... - MARYLAND **1341**

MARYLAND AND DELAWARE GENEALOGIST, THE CEASED. (US/0025-4150) [01756753] **2459**

MARYLAND ANGLER, THE (US/0195-007X) [05192287] **2308**

MARYLAND ARCHEOLOGY (US/0148-6012) [08563986] **273**

MARYLAND BANK MONITOR (US/0146-230X) [02908367] **797**

MARYLAND BAR JOURNAL, THE (US/0025-4177) [01644662] **3006**

●MARYLAND BEVERAGE JOURNAL (US/1058-935X) [24439184] **2369**

MARYLAND BICENTENNIAL COMMISSION See ANNUAL REPORT OF THE MARYLAND BICENTENNIAL COMMISSION TO THE GOVERNOR, THE GENERAL ASSEMBLY, AND THE SECRETARY, DEPARTMENT OF ECONOMIC AND COMMUNITY DEVELOPMENT **2720**

MARYLAND BICENTENNIAL STUDIES (US) [01781041] **2745**

MARYLAND BIRDLIFE (US/0147-9725) [03257656] **5618**

MARYLAND. BOARD OF PHARMACY See ANNUAL REPORT OF THE MARYLAND BOARD OF PHARMACY **4291**

MARYLAND. BOARD OF REVENUE ESTIMATES See REPORT OF THE MARYLAND BOARD OF REVENUE ESTIMATES ON ESTIMATED MARYLAND REVENUES **4746**

MARYLAND. BOARD OF REVENUE ESTIMATES. REPORT ON ESTIMATED MARYLAND REVENUES See REPORT OF THE MARYLAND BOARD OF REVENUE ESTIMATES ON ESTIMATED MARYLAND REVENUES **4746**

MARYLAND BUSINESS & LIVING (US/0747-0320) [10501934] **692**

MARYLAND BUSINESS DIRECTORY (US/1048-7123) [21010791] **692**

MARYLAND CLUB WOMAN, THE (US/0279-3490) [06241409] **5561**

MARYLAND COMMISSION ON HEREDITARY DISORDERS See ANNUAL REPORT / MARYLAND COMMISSION ON HEREDITARY DISORDERS **542**

Alphabetical Title Index — MARYLAND

MARYLAND. COMPTROLLER'S OFFICE *See* SUPPLEMENTAL FINANCIAL DATA FOR THE FISCAL YEAR ENDED JUNE 30 ... / STATE OF MARYLAND **4751**

MARYLAND. COMPTROLLER'S OFFICE *See* COMPREHENSIVE ANNUAL FINANCIAL REPORT FOR THE YEAR ENDED ... - COMPTROLLER'S OFFICE, COMPTROLLER OF THE TREASURY OF MARYLAND **4718**

MARYLAND. COOPERATIVE EXTENSION SERVICE *See* MARYLAND AGRI-ECONOMICS **107**

MARYLAND. COUNCIL FOR HIGHER EDUCATION *See* HIGHER EDUCATION DATA BOOK **1828**

MARYLAND. COURT OF APPEALS *See* MARYLAND ADVANCE REPORTS **3006**

MARYLAND. CRIMINAL INJURIES COMPENSATION BOARD *See* ANNUAL REPORT - STATE OF MARYLAND. CRIMINAL INJURIES COMPENSATION BOARD **3157**

MARYLAND. DEPT. OF ECONOMIC AND COMMUNITY DEVELOPMENT *See* MARYLAND STATISTICAL ABSTRACT **5332**

MARYLAND. DEPT. OF ECONOMIC AND COMMUNITY DEVELOPMENT *See* MARYLAND ECONOMY, THE **1504**

MARYLAND. DEPT. OF ECONOMIC AND COMMUNITY DEVELOPMENT. MARYLAND STATISTICAL ABSTRACT *See* MARYLAND STATISTICAL ABSTRACT **1504**

MARYLAND. DEPT. OF ECONOMIC AND EMPLOYMENT DEVELOPMENT *See* MARYLAND STATISTICAL ABSTRACT **1504**

MARYLAND. DEPT. OF EMPLOYMENT AND SOCIAL SERVICES *See* PAMPHLET - DEPARTMENT OF EMPLOYMENT AND SOCIAL SERVICES (BALTIMORE) **5300**

MARYLAND. DEPT. OF EMPLOYMENT AND SOCIAL SERVICES *See* INFORMATION PAMPHLET - DEPARTMENT OF EMPLOYMENT AND SOCIAL SERVICES (BALTIMORE) **5290**

MARYLAND. DEPT. OF HEALTH AND MENTAL HYGIENE *See* ANNUAL STATISTICAL SUMMARY OF THE STATE OF MARYLAND FAMILY PLANNING PROGRAM **2287**

MARYLAND. DEPT. OF HEALTH AND MENTAL HYGIENE. LABORATORIES ADMINISTRATION *See* STATISTICAL AND ACCOUNTING REPORT **4811**

MARYLAND. DEPT. OF LABOR AND INDUSTRY. ANNUAL REPORT *See* ANNUAL REPORT - DIVISION OF LABOR AND INDUSTRY (MARYLAND) **1649**

MARYLAND. DEPT. OF STATE PLANNING *See* NEWSLETTER - MARYLAND DEPARTMENT OF STATE PLANNING **2829**

MARYLAND. DEPT. OF STATE PLANNING *See* CATALOG OF STATE ASSISTANCE PROGRAMS **4637**

MARYLAND. DEPT. OF STATE PLANNING *See* CAPITAL PROJECTS **4716**

MARYLAND. DEPT. OF STATE PLANNING. CATALOG OF STATE ASSISTANCE PROGRAMS *See* CATALOG OF STATE ASSISTANCE PROGRAMS **2908**

MARYLAND. DEPT. OF TRANSPORTATION *See* TWENTY YEAR HIGHWAY NEEDS STUDY **5446**

MARYLAND. DIVISION OF CORRECTION *See* SPECIAL REPORT - DIVISION OF CORRECTION, A **3177**

MARYLAND. DIVISION OF CORRECTION *See* REPORT - MARYLAND DIVISION OF CORRECTION **3174**

MARYLAND. DIVISION OF LABOR AND INDUSTRY *See* ANNUAL REPORT - DIVISION OF LABOR AND INDUSTRY (MARYLAND) **1649**

MARYLAND. DIVISION OF LIBRARY DEVELOPMENT AND SERVICES *See* ANNUAL REPORT / DIVISION OF LIBRARY DEVELOPMENT AND SERVICES **3190**

MARYLAND. DIVISION OF SPECIAL EDUCATION *See* ANNUAL SUMMARY / DIVISION OF SPECIAL EDUCATION **1875**

MARYLAND. DIVISION OF VOCATIONAL-TECHNICAL EDUCATION *See* MARYLAND STATE PLAN FOR VOCATIONAL-TECHNICAL EDUCATION **1914**

MARYLAND DOCUMENTS (US/0195-3443) [05425680] **419**

MARYLAND ECONOMY, THE (US/0465-1057) [03318025] **1504**

MARYLAND EMPLOYMENT LAW LETTER (US/1049-9377) [21356972] **3151**

MARYLAND ENTOMOLOGIST (US/0275-8652) [03655707] **5591**

● MARYLAND ENVIRONMENTAL LAW LETTER (US/1062-7960) [25744698] **3114**

MARYLAND FARM ECONOMICS *See* MARYLAND AGRI-ECONOMICS **107**

MARYLAND FARMER (BALTIMORE, MD. : 1979) (US/0279-7895) [07261127] **107**

MARYLAND. FOSTER CARE REVIEW BOARD *See* ANNUAL REPORT / FOSTER CARE REVIEW BOARD **5272**

MARYLAND FRUIT GROWER, THE (US/0025-4223) [02432995] **178**

MARYLAND GENEALOGICAL SOCIETY *See* MEMBERSHIP DIRECTORY / MARYLAND GENEALOGICAL SOCIETY **2460**

MARYLAND GENEALOGICAL SOCIETY *See* MARYLAND GENEALOGICAL SOCIETY BULLETIN **2459**

MARYLAND GENEALOGICAL SOCIETY BULLETIN (US) [05746214] **2459**

MARYLAND. GENERAL ASSEMBLY *See* ROSTER AND LIST OF COMMITTEES OF THE GENERAL ASSEMBLY OF MARYLAND **4684**

MARYLAND. GENERAL ASSEMBLY. STATE DEPT. OF LEGISLATIVE REFERENCE. LIBRARY DIVISION *See* MARYLAND DOCUMENTS **419**

MARYLAND GEOGRAPHER, THE (US/0090-9300) [01785949] **2568**

MARYLAND GEOLOGICAL SURVEY *See* INFORMATION CIRCULAR (MARYLAND GEOLOGICAL SURVEY) **1382**

MARYLAND GRAPEVINE, THE (US/1052-6161) [14286579] **178**

● MARYLAND HEALTH CARE IN PERSPECTIVE (US/1065-4224) [26605697] **4789**

MARYLAND HERPETOLOGICAL SOCIETY *See* BULLETIN OF THE MARYLAND HERPETOLOGICAL SOCIETY **5579**

MARYLAND HIGH BLOOD PRESSURE COMMISSION *See* ANNUAL REPORT - MARYLAND HIGH BLOOD PRESSURE COMMISSION **3699**

MARYLAND HIGH-TECH DIRECTORY (US/1047-6423) [19952431] **5127**

MARYLAND HIGHER EDUCATION LOAN CORPORATION *See* ANNUAL REPORT **1809**

MARYLAND HIGHER EDUCATION LOAN CORPORATION *See* ANNUAL REPORT TO THE GOVERNOR AND THE GENERAL ASSEMBLY OF MARYLAND **1809**

MARYLAND HISTORIAN, THE (US/0025-424X) [02385885] **2622**

MARYLAND HISTORICAL MAGAZINE (US/0025-4258) [01756756] **2459**, **2745**

MARYLAND HISTORICAL TRUST *See* ANNUAL REPORT - MARYLAND HISTORICAL TRUST **2720**

MARYLAND HOUSING FUND *See* ANNUAL REPORT / MARYLAND HOUSING FUND **2873**

MARYLAND IN PERSPECTIVE (US/1065-5492) [26479868] **5332**

MARYLAND. INCOME TAX DIVISION *See* SUMMARY REPORT, INDIVIDUAL INCOME TAX RETURNS FILED **4751**

MARYLAND. INCOME TAX DIVISION. SUMMARY REPORT, RESIDENT INDIVIDUAL INCOME TAX RETURNS FILED FOR THE YEAR . *See* SUMMARY REPORT, INDIVIDUAL INCOME TAX RETURNS FILED **4751**

MARYLAND INDUSTRIAL DEVELOPMENT FINANCING AUTHORITY *See* ANNUAL REPORT ... / THE MARYLAND INDUSTRIAL DEVELOPMENT FINANCING AUTHORITY **4629**

MARYLAND INDUSTRIAL DEVELOPMENT FINANCING AUTHORITY *See* FINANCIAL REPORT / MARYLAND INDUSTRIAL DEVELOPMENT FINANCING AUTHORITY **1607**

MARYLAND JOCKEY CLUB *See* PREAKNESS, THE **2801**

MARYLAND JOURNAL OF CONTEMPORARY LEGAL ISSUES (US) [21878898] **3006**

MARYLAND JOURNAL OF HEALTH, PHYSICAL EDUCATION, RECREATION AND DANCE (US) **1857**

MARYLAND JOURNAL OF INTERNATIONAL LAW AND TRADE (US/0884-9331) [11538756] **3132**

MARYLAND JUVENILE SERVICES ADMINISTRATION *See* JUVENILE SERVICES ADMINISTRATION ANNUAL REPORT **3168**

MARYLAND LAW REVIEW (1936) (US/0025-4282) [01756758] **3006**

MARYLAND LAWYERS' MANUAL (US) [01787781] **3007**

MARYLAND MAGAZINE (1988) (US/1040-7936) [18534172] **2745**

MARYLAND MANUAL (US/0094-4491) [00992069] **4664**

● MARYLAND MANUFACTURERS DIRECTORY (EVANSTON, ILL.) (US/1065-2507) [26537760] **3484**

MARYLAND MEDICAL JOURNAL (1985) (US/0886-0572) [11680834] **3606**

MARYLAND. MENTAL HYGIENE ADMINISTRATION *See* ANNUAL REPORT - MENTAL HYGIENE ADMINISTRATION **4766**

MARYLAND MUSIC EDUCATOR (US) [06805473] 1763, **4130**

MARYLAND-NATIONAL CAPITAL PARK AND PLANNING COMMISSION *See* PROPOSED BUDGET FOR THE MARYLAND-NATIONAL CAPITAL PARK AND PLANNING COMMISSION. MONTGOMERY COUNTY PROGRAMS, A **4707**

MARYLAND NATURALIST, THE (US/0096-4158) [01375630] **4167**

MARYLAND NONPUBLIC SCHOOLS AND INSTITUTIONS (US) [18202932] **1763**

MARYLAND NURSE, THE (US/0047-6080) [04510177] **3861**

MARYLAND NUTRITION CONFERENCE FOR FEED MANUFACTURERS *See* PROCEEDINGS - MARYLAND NUTRITION CONFERENCE FOR FEED MANUFACTURERS **121**

MARYLAND. OFFICE OF RECREATION AND LEISURE SERVICES *See* COUNTY AND MUNICIPAL RECREATION AND PARK SERVICES STUDY (MARYLAND) **4849**

MARYLAND. OFFICE OF THE PUBLIC DEFENDER *See* REPORT OF THE OFFICE OF THE PUBLIC DEFENDER FOR THE STATE OF MARYLAND **3108**

MARYLAND PHARMACIST, THE (US/0025-4347) [02263873] **4314**

MARYLAND POETRY REVIEW (BROOKLANDVILLE, MD.) (US/0892-807X) [15287891] 3410, **3466**

MARYLAND POLICE AND CORRECTIONAL TRAINING COMMISSIONS REPORT TO THE GOVERNOR, THE SECRETARY OF PUBLIC SAFETY AND CORRECTIONAL SERVICES, AND MEMBERS OF THE GENERAL ASSEMBLY (US/0148-2602) [03280762] **3169**

MARYLAND. POLICE TRAINING COMMISSION *See* MARYLAND POLICE AND CORRECTIONAL TRAINING COMMISSIONS REPORT TO THE GOVERNOR, THE SECRETARY OF PUBLIC SAFETY AND CORRECTIONAL SERVICES, AND MEMBERS OF THE GENERAL ASSEMBLY **3169**

MARYLAND. PORT ADMINISTRATION *See* FOREIGN COMMERCE STATISTICAL REPORT : PORT OF BALTIMORE AND OTHER MARYLAND PORTS **729**

● MARYLAND PROCUREMENT REPORT, THE (US/1066-2251) [26904099] **4664**

MARYLAND PROSECUTOR, THE (US/0748-2957) [10909331] **3108**

MARYLAND PUBLIC & PRIVATE POST SECONDARY EDUCATION INSTITUTIONS, AGENCIES, AND BOARDS. DIRECTORY (US/0190-9983) [04511489] **1835**

MARYLAND PUBLIC TV (US/0732-8125) [08416098] **1134**

● MARYLAND QUERIES (US/1044-7938) [19913506] **2459**

MARYLAND REGISTER (US/0360-2834) [02243687] **3007**

● MARYLAND REGISTER CONTRACT WEEKLY (US/1061-2696) [25224632] **4664**

MARYLAND RESEARCHER, THE (US/0047-6099) [04050237] **3007**

MARYLAND SALES AND USE TAX REVENUES COLLECTED IN MONTGOMERY COUNTY COMPARED WITH COLLECTIONS STATEWIDE AND IN OTHER MAJOR SUBDIVISIONS *See* ANALYSIS OF MARYLAND SALES AND USE TAX ... REVENUES COLLECTED IN MONTGOMERY COUNTY / MONTGOMERY COUNTY GOVERNMENT, DEPARTMENT OF FINANCE **4709**

MARYLAND. SOCIAL SERVICES ADMINISTRATION *See* INCIDENTS OF SUSPECTED CHILD ABUSE IN MARYLAND **5289**

MARYLAND STANDARDS AND SPECIFICATIONS FOR SOIL EROSION AND SEDIMENT CONTROL (US/8756-9205) [11633980] **178**

MARYLAND. STATE BOARD FOR COMMUNITY COLLEGES *See* SELECTED STATISTICAL DATA - MARYLAND STATE BOARD FOR COMMUNITY COLLEGES **1797**

MARYLAND. STATE BOARD FOR COMMUNITY COLLEGES *See* STATE PLAN FOR COMMUNITY COLLEGES IN MARYLAND **1848**

MARYLAND. STATE BOARD FOR HIGHER EDUCATION *See* ANNUAL EQUAL POSTSECONDARY EDUCATIONAL OPPORTUNITY STATUS REPORT FOR THE PERIOD ... (MARYLAND) **1809**

MARYLAND
Alphabetical Title Index

MARYLAND. STATE DEPT. OF EDUCATION. OFFICE OF MANAGEMENT INFORMATION SYSTEMS See FEDERAL PROGRAM EXPENDITURES FOR MARYLAND PUBLIC SCHOOLS **1746**

MARYLAND. STATE DEPT. OF LEGISLATIVE REFERENCE See SYNOPSIS OF LAWS ENACTED BY THE STATE OF MARYLAND **3062**

MARYLAND. STATE HIGHWAY ADMINISTRATION See STATE HIGHWAY IMPROVEMENT PROGRAM: PRIMARY SYSTEM **2031**

MARYLAND STATE PLAN FOR VOCATIONAL-TECHNICAL EDUCATION (US) [20150148] **1914**

MARYLAND STATE TEACHERS' ASSOCIATION See MSTA HANDBOOK **1900**

MARYLAND. STATE WATER QUALITY ADVISORY COMMITTEE See ANNUAL REPORT / STATE WATER QUALITY ADVISORY COMMITTEE **5530**

MARYLAND STATE YEARLY AIR QUALITY DATA REPORT (US/0191-2194) [04403557] **28**

MARYLAND STATEWIDE PLAN FOR POSTSECONDARY EDUCATION (US) [06077865] **1835**

MARYLAND STATISTICAL ABSTRACT (US/0580-9029) [04265246] **5332**

MARYLAND STATISTICAL ABSTRACT (US/0580-9029) [18271698] 1763, 4554, **1504**

MARYLAND TECHNOLOGY RESOURCE GUIDE (US/1056-4055) [23719489] **5127**

MARYLAND TIMES-PRESS (US) [20764748] **5686**

MARYLAND TRAVEL SCENE (US/0300-7502) [01372841] **5484**

MARYLAND. UNIVERSITY. NATURAL RESOURCES INSTITUTE See CONTRIBUTION - UNIVERSITY OF MARYLAND, NATURAL RESOURCES INSTITUTE **2191**

MARYLAND-WASHINGTON BEVERAGE JOURNAL (MARYLAND ED.) See MARYLAND BEVERAGE JOURNAL **2369**

MARYLAND-WASHINGTON BEVERAGE JOURNAL (WASHINGTON, D.C. ED.) See WASHINGTON BEVERAGE JOURNAL **2372**

MARYLAND. WATER RESOURCES ADMINISTRATION See MARYLAND STANDARDS AND SPECIFICATIONS FOR SOIL EROSION AND SEDIMENT CONTROL **178**

MARYLAND WHOLESALE FRUIT & VEGETABLE REPORT (US/0744-3196) [08188408] **178**

MARYSVILLE ADVOCATE, THE (US) [08801258] **5677**

MARYSVILLE JOURNAL-TRIBUNE (US/1069-2207) [18102443] **5729**

MARYVILLE-ALCOA DAILY TIMES (US) [12653129] **5745**

MARZBLATT (GW) [04424727] **3410**

MAS DEL PERU Y DEL MUNDO (PE) [03931217] **1574**

MAS (NEW YORK, N.Y.) CEASED. (US/1046-5634) [20541425] **2267**

MASABEY 'ENWS (IS/0792-0970) [I07920970] 944, **1690**

MASALAH-MASALAH INTERNASIONAL MASAKINI (IO) [03415479] **4528**

MASB JOURNAL (US/1052-2824) [15238795] **1866**

MASCA RESEARCH PAPERS IN SCIENCE AND ARCHAEOLOGY (US/1048-5325) [19912922] **274**

MASCHINE, DIE (GW/0340-5737) [06381382] **2121**

MASCHINE DOKUMENTATION, DIE (GW) [01785915] **2121**

MASCHINEN-INDUSTRIE IM DEUTSCHEN REICH, DIE (GR) [20292103] **2121**

MASCHINEN SCHADEN, DER (GW/0025-4517) [06381512] **2121**

MASCHINENBAU (SZ) [03214309] **2121**

MASCHINENBAUTECHNIK CEASED. (SZ/0025-4495) [01914667] **2121**

MASCHINENMARKT (GW/0025-4509) [11515448] **1986**

MASCHINENSCHADEN, DER (GW/0025-4517) [04174480] **2121**

MASCHINENWELT ELEKTROTECHNIK CEASED. (AU/0025-4533) [07031420] **2121**

MASCOUCHOIS (CN/0838-5513) [19573665] **4852**

●MASCULINITIES : OFFICIAL PUBLICATION OF THE MEN'S STUDIES ASSOCIATION, NATIONAL ORGANIZATION FOR MEN AGAINST SEXISM (US/1072-8538) [27878630] **3995**

MASENO JOURNAL OF EDUCATION, ARTS AND SCIENCE (KE) [I1019360X] 324, 5127, **1763**

MASHINOSTROENE (BU/0025-455X) [09622898] **2121**

MASHINY I APPARATY KHIMICHESKOI TEKHNOLOGII (RU) [03189519] **1027**

MASHPRIBORINTORG (RU) [03496897] **3484**

MASHRU AL-MIZANIYAH AL-AMMAH WA-MIZANIYAT AL-TANMIYAH LIL-AM AL-MALI ... (SJ) [08402827] **4736**

MASIKA ANKARA SARA. MONTHLY ABSTRACT OF STATISTICS (II) [06135738] **5332**

MASINY I TEHNOLOGIJA TORFJANOGO PROIZVODSTVA (BW/0134-9570) [02484118] **2143**

MASK BLACKBURN (AT/0726-9072) [I07269072] 1763, **386**

MASKAN : ARKHITEKTURA I STROITELSTVO UZBEKISTANA, AZERBAIDZHANA, KYRGYZSTANA, TADZHIKISTANA, TURKMENISTANA (UZ) [25910184] **303**

MASKE UND KOTHURN (AU/0025-4606) [01756769] **3410**

MASKS (STANFORD) (US/0360-2192) [02244244] **2538**

MASON COUNTY GENEALOGICAL SOCIETY NEWSLETTER, THE (US/0885-4459) [12645401] **2459**

MASON COUNTY NEWS (US) [14208523] **5752**

MASON FAMILY NEWSLETTER (US/0895-4496) [16693271] **2459**

MASON MEMORIES CEASED. (US/0735-4754) [08948216] **2745**

MASON VALLEY NEWS (US) [13755049] **5707**

MASONRY (US/0025-4681) [04796727] **620**

MASONRY INTERNATIONAL (UK/0950-2289) [11927100] **620**

MASONRY SOCIETY JOURNAL, THE (US/0741-1294) [08106542] **620**

MASORET (NEW YORK, N.Y.) (US/1063-0015) [25749875] **5051**

MASS BAY ANTIQUES (US) **251**

MASS COM PERIODICAL LITERATURE INDEX (SI/0217-1287) [10328498] **1116**

MASS COMM REVIEW (US/0193-7707) [03489331] 2922, **1116**

MASS ENTERTAINMENT BUYERS GUIDE (US/0748-1675) [10884397] **4863**

MASS HIGH TECH (US/8750-2100) [09376749] **5127**

MASS MARKET RETAILERS (US/0743-5258) [10609831] **955**

MASS MEDIA IN INDIA / RESEARCH AND REFERENCE DIVISION, MINISTRY OF INFORMATION AND BROADCASTING, GOVERNMENT OF INDIA (II) [05861535] **1116**

MASS MEDIA : RIVISTA BIMESTRALE DELLA COMUNICAZIONE (IT) [17628707] **1116**

MASS RETAILING MERCHANDISER (US) [02245077] **879**

MASS SPECTROMETRY (UK/0305-9987) [01605804] **1017**

MASS SPECTROMETRY BULLETIN (UK/0025-4738) [01756780] 1017, **1011**

MASS SPECTROMETRY REVIEWS (US/0277-7037) [07626296] **1017**

MASS TRANSIT (WASHINGTON, D.C.) (US/0364-3484) [01794668] **5386**

MASSA (MY) [11069685] **2506**

MASSACHUSETTS ADMINISTRATIVE LAW LIBRARY ON CD-ROM [COMPUTER FILE] / SOCIAL LAW LIBRARY (US) [23201891] **3007**

MASSACHUSETTS ADVOCACY CENTER See ANNUAL REPORT - MASSACHUSETTS ADVOCACY CENTER **2934**

MASSACHUSETTS AGRICULTURAL STATISTICS (US/0092-9794) [01791467] 107, **155**

MASSACHUSETTS AGRICULTURE (US/0739-8867) [09810513] **107**

MASSACHUSETTS APPELLATE TAX BOARD REPORTER (US/0732-0825) [08302015] **4736**

MASSACHUSETTS ARCHAEOLOGICAL SOCIETY See BULLETIN OF THE MASSACHUSETTS ARCHAEOLOGICAL SOCIETY **264**

MASSACHUSETTS ATTORNEY DISCIPLINE REPORTS : DECISIONS OF THE SUPREME JUDICIAL COURT OF MASSACHUSETTS / COMPILED BY BOARD OF BAR OVERSEERS (US) [09709164] **3007**

MASSACHUSETTS AUXILIARE, THE (US/0746-8725) [10351520] **5233**

MASSACHUSETTS BAY TRANSPORTATION AUTHORITY. BUDGET COMMITTEE See MBTA BUDGET, REPORT OF ADVISORY BOARD BUDGET COMMITTEE **5386**

MASSACHUSETTS BUSINESS DIRECTORY (OMAHA, NEB.) (US/1048-7131) [21010848] **692**

MASSACHUSETTS. CIVIL DEFENSE AGENCY AND OFFICE OF EMERGENCY PREPAREDNESS See BIENNIAL REPORT OF THE MASSACHUSETTS CIVIL DEFENSE AGENCY AND OFFICE OF EMERGENCY PREPAREDNESS TO THE GOVERNOR AND GENERAL COURT **1072**

MASSACHUSETTS. COMMISSION ON INDIAN AFFAIRS See REPORT OF THE MASSACHUSETTS COMMISSION ON INDIAN AFFAIRS **4681**

MASSACHUSETTS. COMMISSION ON JUDICIAL CONDUCT See ANNUAL REPORT OF THE MASSACHUSETTS COMMISSION ON JUDICIAL CONDUCT **3139**

MASSACHUSETTS. COMMISSION ON JUDICIAL CONDUCT. ANNUAL REPORT OF THE COMMISSION ON JUDICIAL CONDUCT See ANNUAL REPORT OF THE MASSACHUSETTS COMMISSION ON JUDICIAL CONDUCT **3139**

MASSACHUSETTS. COMMISSIONER OF VETERANS' SERVICES See REPORT - MASSACHUSETTS. COMMISSIONER OF VETERANS' SERVICES **4055**

MASSACHUSETTS. COMMITTEE ON CRIMINAL JUSTICE See COMPREHENSIVE CRIMINAL JUSTICE PLAN, CRIMINAL JUSTICE PROGRAMS **3160**

MASSACHUSETTS, CONNECTICUT, RHODE ISLAND VERDICT REPORTER, THE (US/1050-852X) [21652107] **3090**

MASSACHUSETTS COUNCIL ON THE ARTS AND HUMANITIES See GUIDE TO PROGRAMS & SERVICES / THE MASSACHUSETTS COUNCIL ON THE ARTS AND HUMANITIES **321**

MASSACHUSETTS CPA REVIEW (US/0025-4770) [03422098] **748**

MASSACHUSETTS. CRIMINAL HISTORY SYSTEMS BOARD See COMBINED ANNUAL REPORTS FOR FISCAL YEAR ... **3160**

MASSACHUSETTS DAILY COLLEGIAN, THE (US/0890-0434) [14126051] 1835, **5689**

MASSACHUSETTS DECISIONS REPORTED IN NORTH EASTERN REPORTER, SECOND SERIES (US/0744-818X) [08581699] **3007**

MASSACHUSETTS. DEPT. OF COMMUNITY AFFAIRS. BUREAU OF REGIONAL PLANNING See REGIONAL PROFILES **5255**

MASSACHUSETTS. DEPT. OF CORRECTION See REVIEW OF CURRENT RESEARCH **3175**

MASSACHUSETTS. DEPT. OF EDUCATION See DISTRIBUTION OF HIGH SCHOOL GRADUATES **1736**

MASSACHUSETTS. DEPT. OF EDUCATION See PROGRAM DIRECTORY / MASSACHUSETTS DEPARTMENT OF EDUCATION **1775**

MASSACHUSETTS. DEPT. OF EDUCATION. DIVISION OF RESEARCH AND STATISTICS See RESEARCH BULLETIN - COMMONWEALTH OF MASSACHUSETTS, DEPARTMENT OF EDUCATION, DIVISION OF RESEARCH AND STATISTICS **1796**

MASSACHUSETTS. DEPT. OF FOOD AND AGRICULTURE See DIRECTORY - MASSACHUSETTS DEPARTMENT OF FOOD AND AGRICULTURE **79**

MASSACHUSETTS. DEPT. OF FOOD AND AGRICULTURE See MASSACHUSETTS AGRICULTURE **107**

MASSACHUSETTS. DEPT. OF FOOD AND AGRICULTURE. ANNUAL REPORT See MASSACHUSETTS AGRICULTURE **107**

MASSACHUSETTS. DEPT. OF PUBLIC WORKS See STATE AID TO MUNICIPALITIES FOR HIGHWAYS AND STREETS (BOSTON) **5444**

MASSACHUSETTS. DEPT. OF REVENUE See BIENNIAL REPORT OF THE COMMISSIONER OF REVENUE SUBMITTING AN EQUALIZATION AND PROPORTIONMENT UPON THE SEVERAL CITIES AND TOWNS OF THE AMOUNT OF PROPERTY AND THE PROPORTION OF EVERY ONE THOUSAND DOLLARS OF STATE AND COUNTY TAX WHICH SHOULD BE ASSESSED UPON EACH CITY AND TOWN **4713**

MASSACHUSETTS. DEPT. OF REVENUE See ANNUAL REPORT / COMMONWEALTH OF MASSACHUSETTS, DEPARTMENT OF REVENUE **4710**

MASSACHUSETTS. DEPT. OF SOCIAL SERVICES See ANNUAL REPORT / MASSACHUSETTS DEPARTMENT OF SOCIAL SERVICES **5272**

MASSACHUSETTS. DEPT. OF THE STATE AUDITOR. ANNUAL REPORT See STATE AUDITOR'S OFFICE ANNUAL REPORT, FISCAL YEAR ENDED JUNE 30 ... (MASSACHUSETTS), THE **4749**

Alphabetical Title Index — MASSACHUSETTS

MASSACHUSETTS. DEPT. OF THE STATE SECRETARY. STATE BOOKSTORE CATALOGUE *See* SECRETARY OF STATE'S BOOKSTORE CATALOG, THE **424**

MASSACHUSETTS DIRECTORY OF MANUFACTURERS (US/0195-5810) [05464788] **3484**

MASSACHUSETTS DISCRIMINATION LAW REPORTER (US/0199-5235) [05918256] 4510, **3007**

MASSACHUSETTS. DIVISION OF BANKS AND LOAN AGENCIES. ANNUAL CALL REPORT FOR ALL CREDIT UNIONS *See* ANNUAL CREDIT UNION CALL REPORT / THE COMMONWEALTH OF MASSACHUSETTS, OFFICE OF THE COMMISSIONER OF BANKS **770**

MASSACHUSETTS. DIVISION OF EMPLOYMENT SECURITY *See* LABOR AREA TRENDS IN SUPPLY AND DEMAND: MASSACHUSETTS/BOSTON AREA **1683**

MASSACHUSETTS. DIVISION OF EMPLOYMENT SECURITY *See* LABOR AREA TRENDS IN SUPPLY AND DEMAND : BROCKTON, MASSACHUSETTS, STANDARD METROPOLITAN STATISTICAL AREA **1683**

MASSACHUSETTS. DIVISION OF EMPLOYMENT SECURITY *See* LABOR AREA TRENDS IN SUPPLY AND DEMAND : LAWRENCE-HAVERHILL, STANDARD METROPOLITAN STATISTICAL AREA **1683**

MASSACHUSETTS. DIVISION OF EMPLOYMENT SECURITY. RESEARCH DEPT *See* MASSACHUSETTS ECONOMIC ASSUMPTIONS **1504**

MASSACHUSETTS ECONOMIC ASSUMPTIONS (US/0360-5744) [02244826] **1504**

MASSACHUSETTS ELECTION STATISTICS / COMPILED IN THE ELECTIONS DIVISION, DEPARTMENT OF THE STATE SECRETARY (US) [05938794] **4502**

MASSACHUSETTS ENVIRONMANAGEMENT REPORT (US) **2177**

●MASSACHUSETTS ENVIRONMENTAL COMPLIANCE UPDATE (US/1064-2374) [26238151] **3114**

MASSACHUSETTS. EXECUTIVE OFFICE OF HUMAN SERVICES *See* BUDGET RECOMMENDATIONS. EXECUTIVE SUMMARY / MASSACHUSETTS EXECUTIVE OFFICE OF HUMAN SERVICES **5275**

MASSACHUSETTS FACTS (US/0894-3427) [15997644] **2538**

MASSACHUSETTS FAMILY LAW JOURNAL, THE (US) [09667762] **3121**

MASSACHUSETTS FRUIT GROWERS' ASSOCIATION *See* NEW ENGLAND FRUIT MEETINGS **111**

MASSACHUSETTS GENERAL HOSPITAL *See* ANNUAL REPORT **3776**

●MASSACHUSETTS HEALTH CARE IN PERSPECTIVE (US/1065-4232) [26605734] **4789**

MASSACHUSETTS HERPETOLOGICAL SOCIETY *See* MHS REVIEW **5591**

MASSACHUSETTS HISTORICAL SOCIETY *See* COLLECTIONS OF THE MASSACHUSETTS HISTORICAL SOCIETY **2728**

MASSACHUSETTS HISTORICAL SOCIETY *See* PROCEEDINGS OF THE MASSACHUSETTS HISTORICAL SOCIETY **2755**

MASSACHUSETTS HOME MORTGAGE FINANCE AGENCY *See* ANNUAL REPORT - MASSACHUSETTS HOME MORTGAGE FINANCE AGENCY **771**

MASSACHUSETTS IN PERSPECTIVE (US/1065-5506) [26655985] **5332**

MASSACHUSETTS INDUSTRIAL FINANCE AGENCY *See* ANNUAL REPORT - MASSACHUSETTS INDUSTRIAL FINANCE AGENCY **771**

MASSACHUSETTS INSTITUTE OF TECHNOLOGY *See* M. I. T. EAST ASIAN SCIENCE SERIES **5126**

MASSACHUSETTS INSTITUTE OF TECHNOLOGY. ENERGY LABORATORY *See* E-LAB **1936**

MASSACHUSETTS INSTITUTE OF TECHNOLOGY. LIBRARIES *See* SERIALS M.I.T. LIBRARIES **3249**

MASSACHUSETTS INSTITUTE OF TECHNOLOGY. RESEARCH LABORATORY OF ELECTRONICS *See* RLE PROGRESS REPORT **2079**

MASSACHUSETTS INSTITUTE OF TECHNOLOGY. SEA GRANT PROGRAM *See* QUARTERLY REPORT - MIT SEA GRANT PROGRAM **5143**

MASSACHUSETTS INSTITUTE OF TECHNOLOGY. SEA GRANT PROJECT OFFICE *See* REPORT MITSG **1456**

MASSACHUSETTS INTERSCHOLASTIC ATHLETIC ASSOCIATION *See* MIAA NEWSLETTER, THE **4904**

MASSACHUSETTS. LABOR AREA RESEARCH DEPT *See* LABOR MARKET INFORMATION REVIEW: LABOR MARKET AREA, SPRINGFIELD-CHICOPEE-HOLYOKE, MASSACHUSETTS **1684**

MASSACHUSETTS. LABOR AREA RESEARCH DEPT *See* LABOR MARKET INFORMATION REVIEW: BROCKTON, MASSACHUSETTS, STANDARD METROPOLITAN STATISTICAL AREA **1684**

MASSACHUSETTS. LABOR AREA RESEARCH DEPT *See* ANNUAL PLANNING INFORMATION REPORT, FISCAL YEAR ... BOSTON, MASSACHUSETTS STANDARD METROPOLITAN STATISTICAL AREA / PREPARED BY EDWARD F. KAZONCHA, LABOR MARKET ECONOMIST (DIVISION OF EMPLOYMENT SECURITY, JOB MARKET RESEARCH, LABOR AREA RESEARCH) **1647**

MASSACHUSETTS. LABOR AREA RESEARCH DEPT *See* LABOR MARKET INFORMATION REVIEW : LABOR MARKET AREA, NEW BEDFORD, MASSACHUSETTS **1684**

MASSACHUSETTS. LABOR AREA RESEARCH DEPT *See* LABOR MARKET INFORMATION REVIEW : STANDARD METROPOLITAN STATISTICAL AREA, BOSTON, MASSACHUSETTS **1684**

MASSACHUSETTS. LABOR AREA RESEARCH DEPT *See* LABOR MARKET INFORMATION REVIEW : LABOR MARKET AREA, WORCESTER, MASSACHUSETTS **1684**

MASSACHUSETTS. LABOR AREA RESEARCH DEPT *See* LABOR MARKET INFORMATION REVIEW : STANDARD METROPOLITAN STATISTICAL AREA, LOWELL, MASSACHUSETTS **1684**

MASSACHUSETTS. LABOR AREA RESEARCH DEPT *See* LABOR MARKET INFORMATION REVIEW : STANDARD METROPOLITAN STATISTICAL AREA, LAWRENCE-HAVERHILL, MASSACHUSETTS **1684**

MASSACHUSETTS. LABOR AREA RESEARCH DEPT *See* LABOR MARKET INFORMATION REVIEW : LABOR MARKET AREA, FALL RIVER, MASSACHUSETTS-RHODE ISLAND **1684**

MASSACHUSETTS. LABOR AREA RESEARCH DEPT *See* LABOR MARKET INFORMATION REVIEW : LABOR MARKET AREA, PITTSFIELD, MASSACHUSETTS **1684**

MASSACHUSETTS. LABOR AREA RESEARCH DEPT *See* ANNUAL PLANNING REPORT : FALL RIVER, MASSACHUSETTS-RHODE ISLAND LABOR MARKET AREA **1648**

MASSACHUSETTS. LABOR AREA RESEARCH DEPT *See* LABOR MARKET INFORMATION REVIEW : STANDARD METROPOLITAN STATISTICAL AREA, FITCHBURG-LEOMINSTER, MASSACHUSETTS **1684**

MASSACHUSETTS. LABOR AREA RESEARCH DEPT *See* LABOR MARKET INFORMATION REVIEW : COMMONWEALTH OF MASSACHUSETTS **1684**

MASSACHUSETTS. LABOR RELATIONS COMMISSION *See* MLRC NEWS **1691**

MASSACHUSETTS. LABOR RELATIONS COMMISSION *See* ANNUAL REPORT - MASSACHUSETTS LABOR RELATIONS COMMISSION **3144**

MASSACHUSETTS LABOR RELATIONS COMMISSION. REPORT OF THE ACTIVITIES OF THE MASSACHUSETTS LABOR RELATIONS COMMISSION FOR THE FISCAL YEAR . *See* ANNUAL REPORT - MASSACHUSETTS LABOR RELATIONS COMMISSION **3144**

MASSACHUSETTS LANDINGS, ANNUAL SUMMARY (US/0095-3334) [01796325] **2308**

MASSACHUSETTS LAW REVIEW (US/0163-1411) [03829364] **3007**

MASSACHUSETTS LAWYERS DIARY AND MANUAL : INCLUDING BAR DIRECTORY (US/0738-369X) [07989294] **3007**

MASSACHUSETTS LAWYERS WEEKLY (US/0196-7509) [05877581] **3007**

MASSACHUSETTS LEGAL DIRECTORY, WITH RHODE ISLAND SECTION (US/0195-5845) [04845047] **3007**

MASSACHUSETTS LEGISLATIVE DIRECTORY / MASSACHUSETTS TAXPAYERS FOUNDATION, INC (US) [03716223] **4664**

MASSACHUSETTS MEDICAL NEWS (US/0273-8929) [07025084] **3606**

MASSACHUSETTS MUNICIPAL PERSONNEL ASSOCIATION *See* MUNICIPAL SALARY SURVEY : BENCH-MARK JOBS **1692**

MASSACHUSETTS MUNICIPAL PROFILES (US/0888-6083) [13664068] **5332**

MASSACHUSETTS MUSIC NEWS (US/0147-2550) [03122362] **4130**

MASSACHUSETTS NURSE, THE (US/0163-0784) [02285840] **3861**

MASSACHUSETTS. OCCUPATION/INDUSTRY RESEARCH DEPT *See* UNFILLED JOB OPENINGS **1715**

MASSACHUSETTS. OCCUPATION/INDUSTRY RESEARCH DEPT *See* ANNUAL SUMMARY, CHARACTERISTIC OF THE INSURED UNEMPLOYED (MASSACHUSETTS) **1650**

MASSACHUSETTS. OCCUPATIONAL/INDUSTRY RESEARCH DEPT *See* LARGE EMPLOYERS IN MASSACHUSETTS, THE **1687**

MASSACHUSETTS. OFFICE FOR CHILDREN *See* ANNUAL REPORT - COMMONWEALTH OF MASSACHUSETTS, OFFICE FOR CHILDREN **4627**

MASSACHUSETTS. OFFICE OF THE COMMISSIONER OF BANKS *See* ANNUAL REPORT OF THE COMMISSION OF BANKS RELATING TO CREDIT UNIONS FOR THE YEAR ENDED ... FINANICIAL STATEMENT **771**

MASSACHUSETTS. OFFICE OF THE COMMISSIONER OF BANKS *See* ANNUAL REPORT OF THE COMMISSIONER OF BANKS RELATING TO CREDIT UNIONS FOR THE YEAR ENDED ... OFFICERS **771**

MASSACHUSETTS. OFFICE OF THE COMMISSIONER OF BANKS *See* ANNUAL CREDIT UNION CALL REPORT / THE COMMONWEALTH OF MASSACHUSETTS, OFFICE OF THE COMMISSIONER OF BANKS **770**

MASSACHUSETTS. OFFICE OF THE SECRETARY OF STATE *See* SECRETARY OF STATE'S BOOKSTORE CATALOG, THE **424**

MASSACHUSETTS PHARMACY JOURNAL (US/1052-6986) [22352683] **4314**

MASSACHUSETTS POLITICAL ALMANAC, THE (US/0277-1314) [07345696] **4664**

MASSACHUSETTS PRIMER / MASSACHUSETTS TAXPAYERS FOUNDATION, INC, A (US/1046-3216) [14814747] **4737**

MASSACHUSETTS QUERIES (US/0897-7739) [17623793] **2459**

MASSACHUSETTS REGISTER (BOSTON, MASS. 1976) (US) [04109606] **3007**

MASSACHUSETTS REHABILITATION COMMISSION *See* EXPENDITURES REPORT OF THE MASSACHUSETTS REHABILITATION COMMISSION **1668**

MASSACHUSETTS REVIEW, THE (US/0025-4878) [01640212] **2850**

MASSACHUSETTS. STATE AUDITOR'S OFFICE *See* STATE AUDITOR'S OFFICE ANNUAL REPORT, FISCAL YEAR ENDED JUNE 30 ... (MASSACHUSETTS), THE **4749**

MASSACHUSETTS. STATE EMPLOYMENT AND TRAINING COUNCIL *See* ANNUAL REPORT TO THE GOVERNOR ON EMPLOYMENT AND TRAINING. MASSACHUSETTS **1650**

MASSACHUSETTS STATE ETHICS COMMISSION *See* RULINGS ENFORCEMENT ACTIONS, ADVISORY OPINIONS / STATE ETHICS COMMISSION **3045**

MASSACHUSETTS STATE LABOR COUNCIL *See* NEWSLETTER - MASSACHUSETTS STATE LABOR COUNCIL **1695**

MASSACHUSETTS STATE PUBLICATIONS (US) [05932792] **419**

MASSACHUSETTS STATE PUBLICATIONS, CHECKLIST (US) [19861471] **3230**

MASSACHUSETTS STUDIES IN ENGLISH *CEASED.* (US/0047-6161) [01695590] **3347**

MASSACHUSETTS. SUPREME JUDICIAL COURT *See* OFFICIAL OPINIONS FROM THE SUPREME JUDICIAL COURT OF MASSACHUSETTS EDITION **3021**

MASSACHUSETTS. SUPREME JUDICIAL COURT *See* MASSACHUSETTS ATTORNEY DISCIPLINE REPORTS : DECISIONS OF THE SUPREME JUDICIAL COURT OF MASSACHUSETTS / COMPILED BY BOARD OF BAR OVERSEERS **3007**

MASSACHUSETTS TAXPAYERS FOUNDATION *See* STATE BUDGET TRENDS **4749**

MASSACHUSETTS TECHNOLOGY DEVELOPMENT CORPORATION *See* ANNUAL REPORT / MASSACHUSETTS TECHNOLOGY DEVELOPMENT CORPORATION **5084**

MASSACHUSETTS   Alphabetical Title Index

●MASSACHUSETTS TECHNOLOGY RESOURCE GUIDE (US/1060-1554) [24881354] **5127**

MASSACHUSETTS. UNIVERSITY. FERNALD ENTOMOLOGICAL CLUB *See* FERNALD CLUB YEARBOOK **5583**

MASSACHUSETTS VOTER / LEAGUE OF WOMEN VOTERS OF MASSACHUSETTS, THE (US) [22974887] **4481**

MASSACHUSETTS. WATER QUALITY AND RESEARCH SECTION *See* SUMMARY OF WATER QUALITY **5540**

MASSACHUSETTS WILDLIFE (US/0025-4924) [01756842] **4874, 2198**

MASSACHUSETTS ZIP+4 STATE DIRECTORY (US) [11525922] **1145**

MASSACOMMUNICATIE (NE) **1116**

MASSAGE (DAVIS, CALIF.) (US/1057-378X) [24021400] **2599**

MASSAPEQUA POST (US) [24222049] **5718**

MASSCITIZEN (US/8750-8516) [09710270] **3007**

MASSE (MONTREAL) (CN/0705-0615) [04039598] **1690**

MASSES OUVRIERES (FR/0181-057X) [11921797] **4976, 1690**

MASSIMARIO DEL FORO ITALIANO; RACOLTA DELLE MASSIME DELLE SENTENZE DELLA CASSAZIONE CIVILE, IL (IT) [01590282] **3007**

MASSIMARIO DELLA GIURISPRUDENZA ITALIANA (IT/0025-4940) [I00254940] **3007**

MASSIMARIO DI GIURISPRUDENZA DEL LAVORO (IT) [05439523] **3151**

MASSIMARIO PENALE COMPLETO DELLA CORTE SUPREMA DI CASSAZIONE (IT/0392-6354) [I03926354] **3007**

MASSOG (US/0738-1549) [04224017] **2459**

MASSON MONOGRAPHS IN DENTISTRY (US/0277-4445) [07002195] **1329**

MASSON MONOGRAPHS IN DIAGNOSTIC PATHOLOGY (US/0733-4265) [07101066] **3896**

MASSON MONOGRAPHS IN PEDIATRIC HEMATOLOGY/ONCOLOGY (US/0736-0088) [07557750] 3820, **3906**

MASSON PUBLISHING USA *See* MASSON TODAY **4816**

MASSON TODAY (US/0272-5541) [06877405] **4816**

MAST (MADISON, WIS.) (US/1051-824X) [20986095] **1145**

MAST. MANITOBA ASSOCIATION OF SCHOOL TRUSTEES (CN/0381-9531) [03956413] **4664**

MASTER : AMMINISTRAZIONE E FINANZA (IT) **797**

MASTER BAKERS' HANDBOOK AND BUYERS GUIDE (UK/0142-7571) [I01427571] **2349**

MASTER CARD (US) **2490**

MASTER DETECTIVE (US/0025-5017) [04050401] **2538**

MASTER DRAWINGS (US/0025-5025) [01608040] **380**

MASTER FEDERAL TAX MANUAL *See* RESEARCH INSTITUTE MASTER FEDERAL TAX MANUAL WITH FEDERAL TAX COORDINATOR 2D REFERENCES **3039**

MASTER INDEX TO DIRECTORY OF CORPORATE AFFILIATIONS, INTERNATIONAL DIRECTORY OF CORPORATE AFFILIATIONS, LEADING PRIVATE COMPANIES (US/1058-0042) [23200555] **692**

MASTER LECTURE SERIES, THE (US/0892-0060) [09146155] **4603**

MASTER PHOTOGRAPHER (UK) **4371**

MASTER PLAN FOR HIGHER EDUCATION IN LOUISIANA--A PROGRESS REPORT, THE (US) [07243888] **1835**

MASTER PLAN FOR TRANSPORTATION (TRENTON) (US/0092-1254) [01784615] **5386**

MASTER PRODUCTION SCHEDULING *CEASED.* (US/0736-8259) [09231356] **1617**

MASTER SALESMANSHIP (US/0199-3887) [05838750] **933**

MASTER SERMON SERIES *CEASED.* (US/0362-0808) [02106567] **4976**

MASTER SHOE REBUILDER, THE (US/0275-1992) [06246133] **1086**

MASTER TAPE LIST OF EDUCATIONAL TEXTS FOR THE VISUALLY AND PHYSICALLY HANDICAPPED ... (CN/0229-8066) [08071991] 4391, **1882**

MASTER TEACHER, THE (US/0889-6259) [06253805] **1900**

MASTER THOUGHTS (US) 4352, **5018**

MASTERA KHUDOZHESTVENNOGO SLOVA (RU) [19504425] **1116**

MASTERBUILDER, THE (JM) [06246010] **620**

MASTERGUIDE. CENTRAL (US/8756-2812) [11520261] **303**

●MASTERING CLINICAL PEDIATRIC DENTISTRY (US/1076-7428) [30602743] **1329**

MASTERING FOOD ALLERGIES (US) **2349**

MASTERING PEDIATRIC DENTISTRY (US/1065-741X) [26709680] **1329**

MASTERPLOTS II (US) **3410**

MASTERS AND MONUMENTS OF THE RENAISSANCE (US/8756-0828) [07542839] **4130**

MASTERS (AUGUSTA) (US/0191-8117) [04917514] **4904**

MASTERS CURRICULA IN EDUCATIONAL COMMUNICATIONS AND TECHNOLOGY *See* GRADUATE CURRICULA IN EDUCATIONAL COMMUNICATIONS AND TECHNOLOGY **1826**

MASTER'S SEMINARY JOURNAL, THE (US/1066-3959) [I10663959] **4976**

●MASTER'S THESES DIRECTORIES (US/1072-5903) [29041416] **1835**

MASTER'S THESES DIRECTORIES. ARTS AND SOCIAL SCIENCES *See* MASTER'S THESES DIRECTORIES **1835**

MASTER'S THESES DIRECTORIES. EDUCATION (US/1072-5911) [25207341] **1835**

MASTER'S THESES DIRECTORIES. NATURAL AND TECHNICAL SCIENCES *See* MASTER'S THESES DIRECTORIES **1835**

MASTER'S THESES DIRECTORIES. THE ARTS AND SOCIAL SCIENCES (US/1066-9795) [25597308] 5208, 1835, **324**

MASTERS THESES IN THE PURE AND APPLIED SCIENCES ACCEPTED BY COLLEGES AND UNIVERSITIES OF THE UNITED STATES AND CANADA (US/0736-7910) [02442861] 1835, **5127**

MASTERSKAIA (RU) [02244869] **3410**

MASTHEAD (MISSISSAUGA) (CN/0832-512X) [17748601] **4816**

MASTHEAD, THE (US/0025-5122) [02574589] **2922**

MASTIKA (MY) [02541633] **2658**

MASUI (JA/0021-4892) [01778897] **3683**

MASUI TO SOSEI (JA/0385-1664) [05578968] **3683**

MASYARAKAT INDONESIA (IO) [01826571] **5208**

MASYARAKAT KITA (IO) [04518852] **5208**

MASYARAKAT SEJARAWAN INDONESIA *See* BERITA KOMUNIKASI MASYARAKAT SEJARAWAN INDONESIA **2647**

MAT SPECIAL ISSUE (TZ) [02852254] **3517**

MATAJUR *See* NOVI MATAJUR **2701**

MATATU (NE/0932-9714) [18404258] **3410**

MATCH (MULHEIM) (GW/0340-6253) [04385649] 3517, **985**

MATCH WEEKLY (UK/0262-5601) [I02625601] **1298**

MATCHING GIFT DETAILS (US/1052-9098) [13356599] **4338**

MATCHING GIFT NOTES : NOTES OF INTEREST FROM CASE, THE NATIONAL CLEARINGHOUSE FOR CORPORATE MATCHING GIFT INFORMATION (US) [11065653] 692, **1763**

MATEKON (US/0025-1127) [02240112] 3517, **1504**

MATEMAATTISTEN AINEIDEN AIKAKAUSKIRJA (FI/0025-5149) [06297266] **3517**

MATEMATICA APLICADA E COMPUTACIONAL (US/0101-8205) [10157467] **3517**

MATEMATICESKIJ SBORNIK (MOSKVA) (RU/0368-8666) [01756854] **3517**

MATEMATICHESKAIA FIZIKA I NELINEINAIA MEKHANIKA (UN/0233-7568) [11225285] **4412**

MATEMATICHESKIE ZAMETKI (RU/0025-567X) [01641292] **3517**

MATEMATICHESKOE MODELIROVANIE (RU/0234-0879) [19881659] **3517**

MATEMATICKI VESNIK (YU/0025-5165) [04087161] **3518**

MATEMATIKA (UN) [05702136] **3518**

MATEMATIKAI LAPOK (HU/0025-519X) [03335687] **3518**

MATEMATYKA (PL) [04837773] **3518**

MATERIA (IT) **303**

MATERIA MEDICA POLONA (ENGLISH EDITION) (PL/0025-5246) [03439912] 3606, **4314**

MATERIAL CULTURE (US/0883-3680) [10955057] 2568, **241**

MATERIAL CULTURE DIRECTORIES (US/0743-7528) [10662528] **5251**

MATERIAL ENGINEERING (US) [05621032] 2104, **2099**

MATERIAL HANDLING ENGINEERING (US/0025-5262) [03975106] **2104**

MATERIAL HANDLING ENGINEERING. HANDBOOK DIRECTORY (US/0025-5262) [01756856] **2104**

MATERIAL HANDLING PRODUCT NEWS (US/0195-2366) [05395909] **2104**

MATERIAL HISTORY REVIEW (CN/1183-1073) [23926488] **2745**

MATERIAL INFORMATION (US/1057-0160) [23914081] **5354**

MATERIAL MATTERS (UK) **2121**

MATERIAL MATTERS (UK/0309-7471) [I03097471] 3230, **1066**

MATERIAL PERFORMANCE: CORROSION ENGINEERING BUYER'S GUIDE *See* NACE CORROSION ENGINEERING BUYER'S GUIDE : OFFICIAL PUBLICATION OF NACE **2015**

MATERIAL REQUIREMENTS PLANNING *CEASED.* (US/0736-8321) [09231247] **1618**

MATERIAL SAFETY DATA SHEETS SERVICE (US) [11991221] **2865**

MATERIAL UND ORGANISMEN (GW/0025-5270) [06367139] **1986**

MATERIAL UND ORGANISMEN; BEIHEFT (GW/0025-5270) [01589856] 490, **1017**

MATERIALANGEBOT, DAS (GW) [05305829] **692**

MATERIALE DE CONSTRUCTII (RM/0253-0201) [11427833] **620**

MATERIALE PLASTICE (RM/0025-5289) [09561890] **4456**

MATERIALES DE CONSTRUCCION (MADRID) (SP/0465-2746) [06388023] **620**

MATERIALI E CONTRIBUTI PER LA STORIA DELLA NARRATIVA GRECO-LATINA (IT) [03136620] 3410, **3301**

MATERIALI E DISCUSSIONI PER L'ANALISI DEI TESTI CLASSICI (IT/0392-6338) [05939156] **1078**

MATERIALI E STRUTTURE (IT) [23862366] **303**

MATERIALI PER UNA STORIA DELLA CULTURA GIURIDICA (IT) [02365398] **3007**

MATERIALIA TURCICA (GW) [03610316] 2267, **2658**

MATERIALIEN DES FORSCHUNGSINSTITUTS FUR DIE ZAHNARZTLICHE VERSORGUNG (GW/0175-7326) [11253359] **1329**

●MATERIALIEN / LANDESUMWELTAMT (GW) **2177**

MATERIALIEN ZUR GESCHICHTE DER RAMANUJA-SCHULE (AU) [06843759] **4352**

MATERIALIEN ZUR POLITISCHEN BILDUNG (GW/0340-0476) [10452806] **4481**

MATERIALIEN ZUR VOR- UND FRUHGESCHICHTE VON HESSEN (GW) [03260510] **274**

MATERIALKUNDLICH-TECHNISCHE REIHE (GW/0170-589X) [11320860] **5127**

MATERIALOZNANIE I TEKNOLOGIYA (BU/0204-7535) [01794757] 2104, **4008**

MATERIALPRUFUNG (GW/0025-5300) [06314582] **2104**

MATERIALS & DESIGN (UK/0264-1275) [09062775] 2099, **2104**

MATERIALS AND PROCESSING REPORT *See* MATERIALS TECHNOLOGY (NEW YORK, N.Y.) **2106**

MATERIALS AND PROCESSING REPORT (US/0887-1949) [13133732] **2104**

●MATERIALS AND STRUCTURES / INTERNATIONAL UNION OF TESTING AND RESEARCH LABORATORIES FOR MATERIALS AND STRUCTURES (RILEM) (UK) [25492750] 2027, **620**

MATERIALS AT HIGH TEMPERATURES (UK/0960-3409) [23746010] **2105**

MATERIALS AUSTRALIA (AT/1037-7107) [26323162] **4008**

MATERIALS CHARACTERIZATION (US/1044-5803) [19834236] **4008**

MATERIALS CHEMISTRY AND PHYSICS (SZ/0254-0584) [09440329] **1055**

MATERIALS EDGE (UK/0952-5211) [16800940] **4008**

MATERIALS ENGINEERING (IT) **2105**

MATERIALS ENGINEERING *CEASED.* (US/0025-5319) [04624772] 2099, **2105**

MATERIALS ENGINEERING MODENA (IT/1120-7302) [I11207302] **2105**

MATERIALS ENGINEERING SERIES (US) **1986**

MATERIALS EVALUATION (US/0025-5327) [01804783] **2105**

MATERIALS FOR THE STUDY OF ALASKA HISTORY (CN) [02381280] **2745**

MATERIALS FORUM (AT/0883-2900) [12101152] **1986**

MATERIALS HANDBOOK (US) [02252969] **2105**

MATERIALS HANDLING NEWS (UK/0025-5351) [03773862] **2121**

MATERIALS INFORMATION ENGINEERED MATERIALS SEARCH-IN-PRINT SERIES (US) **2105**

MATERIALS ISSUES IN ART AND ARCHAEOLOGY (US) [23846424] 274, **358**

MATERIALS LETTERS (NE/0167-577X) [08812706] **2105**

MATERIALS MANAGEMENT AND DISTRIBUTION (CN/0025-5343) [01587116] **1618**

MATERIALS MANAGEMENT & PHYSICAL DISTRIBUTION ABSTRACTS (US/0196-8211) [05904709] **879**

●MATERIALS MANAGEMENT IN HEALTH CARE (US/1059-4531) [24595550] 879, **3788**

MATERIALS-MANAGEMENT JOURNAL OF INDIA (II) [01774522] **692**

MATERIALS PERFORMANCE (US/0094-1492) [01794130] **2105**

MATERIALS PERFORMANCE : CORROSION ENGINEERING BUYER'S GUIDE (US/0148-0529) [03263914] 2105, **2015**

MATERIALS PROCESSING, THEORY AND PRACTICES (NE/0167-790X) [11825082] **2105**

MATERIALS RECLAMATION HANDBOOK (UK/0956-2982) [I09562982] **2105**

MATERIALS RECOVERY AND RECYCLING YEARBOOK : DIRECTORY & GUIDE (US) [21187505] **2236**

MATERIALS RECYCLING WEEKLY (UK) **2236**

MATERIALS RESEARCH BULLETIN (US/0025-5408) [01645091] **2105**

MATERIALS RESEARCH SOCIETY *See* MATERIALS RESEARCH SOCIETY SYMPOSIA PROCEEDINGS **2071**

MATERIALS RESEARCH SOCIETY SYMPOSIA PROCEEDINGS (US/0272-9172) [06979489] 4412, **2071**

MATERIALS SCIENCE & ENGINEERING. A, STRUCTURAL MATERIALS : PROPERTIES, MICROSTRUCTURE AND PROCESSING (SZ/0921-5093) [18235725] **2105**

MATERIALS SCIENCE AND ENGINEERING ABSTRACTS *CEASED.* (US/1063-732X) [26133800] 2105, **2006**

MATERIALS SCIENCE & ENGINEERING. B, SOLID-STATE MATERIALS FOR ADVANCED TECHNOLOGY (SZ/0921-5107) [18373948] **2105**

MATERIALS SCIENCE & ENGINEERING. C, BIOMIMETIC MATERIALS, SENSORS AND SYSTEMS (SZ/0928-4931) **1986**

MATERIALS SCIENCE AND ENGINEERING : R-REPORTS (SZ/0927-796X) [28356512] **1986**

MATERIALS SCIENCE AND TECHNOLOGY (UK/0267-0836) [11741814] 4008, **2105**

●MATERIALS SCIENCE CITATION INDEX (US/1062-5496) [25669188] **5127**

MATERIALS SCIENCE FORUM (SZ/0255-5476) [11834143] **2106**

MATERIALS SCIENCE MONOGRAPHS (NE/0166-6010) [06895816] **1986**

●MATERIALS SCIENCE (NEW YORK, N.Y.) (US/1068-820X) [27820516] **2106**

MATERIALS SCIENCE REPORTS (NE/0920-2307) [14434780] **2106**

MATERIALS SCIENCE RESEARCH (US/0076-5201) [01834210] **5127**

MATERIALS SCIENCES PROGRAMS (US/0198-7798) [04648027] **2106**

MATERIALS TECHNOLOGY (COLUMBUS) (US/0272-4170) [06825993] **2106**

●MATERIALS TECHNOLOGY (NEW YORK, N.Y.) (US/1066-7857) [27049263] **2106**

MATERIALS TRANSACTIONS, JIM (JA/0916-1821) [19503783] **4008**

●MATERIALS WORLD : THE JOURNAL OF THE INSTITUTE OF MATERIALS (UK/0967-8638) [27344978] **2106**

MATERIALWISSENSCHAFT UND WERKSTOFFTECHNIK (GW/0933-5137) [17735700] **2106**

MATERIALY (RU) [05593695] **2093**

MATERIALY BADAWCZE - INSTYTUT METEOROLOGII I GOSPODARKI WODNEJ. SERIA, HYDROLOGIA I OCEANOLOGIA (PL/0239-6297) [I02396297] 1452, **1416**

MATERIALY BADAWCZE. SERIA: GOSPODARKA WODNA I OCHRONA WOD (PL) [03154642] 2236, **5536**

MATERIALY BADAWCZE. SERIA: METEOROLOGIA (PL) **1430**

MATERIALY DO ZVODU PAMIATOK ISTORII TA KULTURY NARODIV SRSR PO UKRAINSKII RSR (UN) [19880990] **2623**

MATERIALY I ISSLEDOVANIA - GOSUDARSTVENNYE MUZEI MOSKOVSKOGO KREMLA (RU/0202-6538) [I02026538] **4091**

MATERIALY I ISSLEDOVANIIA - GOSUDARSTVENNYE MUZEI MOSKOVSKOGO KREMLIA (RU) [05792115] **2697**

MATERIALY I ISSLEDOVANIIA PO FOLKLORU BASHKIRII I URALA (RU) [02475775] **2322**

MATERIALY I OPRACOWANIA STATYSTYCZNE (PL/0867-0846) **5332**

MATERIALY KRAEVOI EPIDEMIOLOGII I GIGIENY (KG) [05176201] 4789, **3735**

MATERIALY NAUCNOJ STUDENCESKOJ KONFERENCII (RU/0301-1933) [01353340] **5127**

MATERIALY OGNIOTRWALE (PL) **2106**

MATERIALY OKEANOLOGICHESKIKH ISSLEDOVANII (RU) [20366711] **1452**

MATERIALY PO ARHEOLOGII EVROPEJSKOGO SEVERO-VOSTOKA (RU/0130-3740) [I01303740] **274**

MATERIALY PO ARKHEOLOGII EVROPEISKOGO SEVERO-VOSTOKA (RU/0465-3238) [04048589] **274**

MATERIALY PO ISTORII AZERBAIDZHANA (AJ/0408-2621) [02255229] **2658**

MATERIALY PO ISTORII KIRGIZOV I KIRGIZII (RU/0302-9107) [01793131] **2697**

MATERIALY PO ISTORII KOMMUNISTICHESKOI PARTII TADZHIKISTANA (TA) [05656321] **4481**

MATERIALY PO MATEMATICHESKOMU OBESPECHENIIU EVM. SERIIA FORTRAN (RU) [20366580] **3518**

MATERIALY PROBLEMNOI KOMISSII AKADEMII MEDITSINSKIKH NAUK SSSR "KOR', VIRUSNYE ENTSEFALITY, POLIOMIELIT" / AKADEMIA MEDITSINSKIKH NAUK SSSR, INSTITUT POLIOMIELITA I VIRUSNYKH ENTSEFALITEV (RU) [07474162] **3606**

MATERIALY - RESPUBLIKANSKA ONOMASTYCHNA (HIDRONIMICHNA) NARADA (UN) [04617051] **4664**

MATERIALY SEZDA PROFESSIONALNYKH SOIUZOV SSSR (RU) [05256269] **1690**

MATERIALY SIMPOZIUMOV PO OBSHCHEI IMMUNOLOGII / AKADEMIIA MEDITSINSKIKH NAUK SSSR, INSTITUT EPIDEMIOLOGII I MIKROBIOLOGII IM. N.F. GAMALEI (RU) [06007978] **3674**

MATERIALY ... VERKHOVNOGO SOVETA SSSR (RU) [11223784] **4481**

MATERIALY ... ZIZDU KOMUNISTYCHNOI PARTII UKRAINY (UN) [09495353] **4543**

MATERIARU RAIFU (JA/0915-3594) [I09153594] **2106**

MATERIAUX ET CONSTRUCTIONS *See* MATERIALS AND STRUCTURES / INTERNATIONAL UNION OF TESTING AND RESEARCH LABORATORIES FOR MATERIALS AND STRUCTURES (RILEM) **620**

MATERIAUX ET ORGANISMES (GW/0543-0119) [02254613] **464**

MATERIAUX ET TECHNIQUES (FR/0032-6895) [06384428] **2106**

MATERIAUX POUR LA CARTE GEOLOGIQUE DE LA SUISSE (SZ/0365-9798) [04102915] **1386**

MATERIAUX POUR L'ETUDE DE L'EXTREME-ORIENT MODERNE ET CONTEMPORAIN. ETUDES LINGUISTIQUES (US/0076-5252) [02350601] **3301**

MATERIAUX POUR L'ETUDE DE L'EXTREME-ORIENT MODERNE ET CONTEMPORAIN. TRAVAUX (US/0076-5279) [02350580] **2658**

MATERIAUX POUR L'HISTOIRE DE NOTRE TEMPS (FR/0769-3206) [14087808] **2623**

MATERIAY BADAWCZE. SERIA: INZYNIERIA WODNA (PL) [02273667] **2093**

MATERIAY ELEKTRONICZNE (PL/0209-0058) [11501546] **2071**

MATERIAY I PRACE ANTROPOLOGICZNE (PL/0076-521X) [02973427] **241**

MATERIAY / INSTYTUT POLSKI I MUZEUM IM. GENERRA SIKORSKIEGO (UK) [19248156] **2623**

MATERIAY MUZEUM BUDOWNICTWA LUDOWEGO W SANOKU (PL/0137-320X) [I0137320X] **4091**

MATERIAY ZACHODNIO POMORSKIE (PL/0076-5236) [03828759] **2697**

MATERIE PLASTICHE ED ELASTOMERI (IT/0025-5459) [06386105] **4456**

MATERIE PLASTICHE : PRODOTTI PROCESSI MERCATI. SERVIZI DOCUMONT (IT) [10433965] **4456**

MATERIEL DIDACTIQUE AGREE PAR LE MINISTERE DE L'EDUCATION POUR LES ECOLES PRIMAIRES ET SECONDAIRES DE LANGUE FRANCAISE. SUPPLEMENT (CN/0226-9376) [08878579] **1866**

MATERINSTVO I DETSTVO *See* ROSSIISKII VESTNIK PERINATOLOGII I PEDIATRII / MINISTERSTVO ZDRAVOOKHRANENIIA ROSSIISKOI FEDERATSII, MOSKOVSKII NII PEDIATRII I DETSKOI KHIRURGII, MOSKOVSKII OBLASTNOI NII AKUSHERSTVA I GINEKOLOGII **3911**

MATERINSTVO I DETSTVO / MINISTERSTVO ZDRAVOOKHRANENIIA ROSSIISKOI FEDERATSII (RU/0869-2114) [30684325] **3906**

MATERNAL & CHILD HEALTH (RICHMOND, SURREY) (UK/0262-0200) [07695329] 3906, 3764, **3738**

MATERNAL AND CHILD HEALTH STATISTICS : NORTH CAROLINA (US) [04893225] 3764, **3660**

MATERNAL-CHILD NURSING JOURNAL (US/0090-0702) [01268456] 3906, 3764, **3861**

MATERNAL HEALTH NEWS (CN/0820-6465) [09428044] **3764**

MATERNAL/NEWBORN ADVOCATE *CEASED.* (US/0190-0757) [03734534] 3906, **3764**

●MATH HORIZONS (US/1072-4117) [28941388] **3518**

MATH JOURNAL, THE (CN/1184-8952) [24368409] 1900, **3518**

MATH NOTEBOOK (US/0272-8885) [06970759] 3518, **1882**

MATHEMATICA & PAEDAGOGIA *See* MATHEMATIQUE ET PEDAGOGIE **3522**

MATHEMATICA BALKANICA *CEASED.* (YU/0350-2007) [01713551] **3518**

MATHEMATICA BOHEMICA / CZECHOSLOVAK ACADEMY OF SCIENCES (XR/0862-7959) [23709665] **3518**

MATHEMATICA IN EDUCATION (US/1065-2965) [26566859] 3518, **1763**

MATHEMATICA JAPONICA (JA/0025-5513) [01642792] **3518**

MATHEMATICA JOURNAL, THE (US/1047-5974) [20729051] **3518**

MATHEMATICA NUMERICA SINICA (CC) [08215324] **3518**

MATHEMATICA PANNONICA (AU/0865-2090) [26136628] **3518**

MATHEMATICA SCANDINAVICA (DK/0025-5521) [01713617] **3518**

MATHEMATICA SLOVACA (XO/0139-9918) [02172151] **3518**

MATHEMATICA / SOCIETATEA DE STIINTE MATEMATICE SI FIZICE (RM) [22253171] **3518**

MATHEMATICAE NOTAE (AG/0025-553X) [03960265] **3518**

MATHEMATICAL AND COMPUTER MODELLING (UK/0895-7177) [16753450] 1195, **3518**

MATHEMATICAL AND DYNAMICAL ASTRONOMY SERIES (BL/0102-4914) [11160849] **397**

MATHEMATICAL ASSOCIATION *See* NEWS LETTER / MATHEMATICAL ASSOCIATION **3524**

MATHEMATICAL ASSOCIATION *See* REPORT OF COUNCIL **3531**

MATHEMATICAL ASSOCIATION OF TANZANIA *See* MAT SPECIAL ISSUE **3517**

MATHEMATICAL BIOSCIENCES (US/0025-5564) [01681432] 3518, **464**

MATHEMATICAL CHEMISTRY (US/1049-2801) [21191848] 3518, **985**

MATHEMATICAL CHRONICLE *See* NEW ZEALAND JOURNAL OF MATHEMATICS **3524**

●MATHEMATICAL COGNITION (UK/1354-6791) **3518**

MATHEMATICAL CONCEPTS AND METHODS IN SCIENCE AND ENGINEERING (US/0885-9418) [07759900] 2071, **3518**

MATHEMATICAL ECONOMICS TEXTS (US/0076-5325) [01979191] 3518, **1504**

MATHEMATICAL — Alphabetical Title Index

MATHEMATICAL EDUCATION FOR TEACHING (UK) **3518**

MATHEMATICAL ENGINEERING IN INDUSTRY (NE/0169-121X) [16882082] 1986, **3518**

MATHEMATICAL FINANCE : AN INTERNATIONAL JOURNAL OF MATHEMATICS, STATISTICS AND FINANCIAL THEORY (UK/0960-1627) [24203118] 797, **3518**

MATHEMATICAL GAZETTE (UK/0025-5572) [01585913] **3519**

MATHEMATICAL GEOLOGY (US/0882-8121) [11985061] **1386**

MATHEMATICAL JOURNAL OF OKAYAMA UNIVERSITY (JA/0030-1566) [01865630] **3519**

MATHEMATICAL LINGUISTICS. KEIYRKO KOKUGOGAKU (JA) [26483565] 3519, **3301**

MATHEMATICAL LOG, THE (US/0025-5580) [01586091] **3519**

●MATHEMATICAL LOGIC QUARTERLY (GW/0942-5616) [27820247] **3519**

MATHEMATICAL MEDLEY (SI/0217-2976) [05280296] **3519**

MATHEMATICAL METHODS IN THE APPLIED SCIENCES (GW/0170-4214) [04935107] 1986, **3519**

MATHEMATICAL METHODS OF OPERATIONS RESEARCH (HU/0209-6137) [11701592] **3519**

●MATHEMATICAL METHODS OF STATISTICS (US/1066-5307) [26982230] **3519**

MATHEMATICAL MODELING (US/1054-6634) [22937493] **3519**

●MATHEMATICAL MODELING AND COMPUTATIONAL EXPERIMENT (US/1061-7590) [25442694] **3519**

●MATHEMATICAL MODELLING AND SCIENTIFIC COMPUTING (US/1067-0688) [27128040] 1195, **3519**

MATHEMATICAL MODELLING OF SYSTEMS (NE/1381-2424) **3519**

MATHEMATICAL MODELS & METHODS IN APPLIED SCIENCES : MP3SAS (SI/0218-2025) [24707803] 5127, **3519**

MATHEMATICAL NOTES (US) [06322904] **3519**

MATHEMATICAL NOTES (US) [06324164] **3519**

MATHEMATICAL NOTES OF THE ACADEMY OF SCIENCES OF THE USSR **See** MATHEMATICAL NOTES (ROSSIISKAIA AKADEMIIA NAUK) **3519**

●MATHEMATICAL NOTES (ROSSIISKAIA AKADEMIIA NAUK) (US/1067-9073) [27160088] **3519**

MATHEMATICAL PHYSICS AND APPLIED MATHEMATICS (NE/0165-2419) [11482463] 4412, **3519**

MATHEMATICAL PHYSICS STUDIES (NE/0921-3767) [06544788] 3519, **4412**

MATHEMATICAL POPULATION STUDIES (US/0889-8480) [14086866] **4554**

MATHEMATICAL PROCEEDINGS OF THE CAMBRIDGE PHILOSOPHICAL SOCIETY (UK/0305-0041) [02241860] **3519**

MATHEMATICAL PROGRAMMING MASTER INDEX (NE) [03581670] **3519**

MATHEMATICAL PROGRAMMING. SERIES A : A PUBLICATION OF THE MATHEMATICAL PROGRAMMING SOCIETY (NE) [17447276] **3519**

MATHEMATICAL REPORTS (CHUR, SWITZERLAND) **CEASED.** (SZ/0275-7214) [07208090] **3520**

MATHEMATICAL REPORTS OF COLLEGE OF GENERAL EDUCATION, KYUSHU UNIVERSITY (JA/0287-9980) [02879980] **3520**

MATHEMATICAL RESEARCH (GW/0138-3019) [08420625] **3520**

●MATHEMATICAL RESEARCH LETTERS (US/1073-2780) [29380880] **3520**

MATHEMATICAL RESEARCH REPORT (CC/0255-7789) [I02557789] **3520**

MATHEMATICAL REVIEWS (US/0025-5629) [01756873] 3520, **3542**

MATHEMATICAL SCIENCES PROFESSIONAL DIRECTORY (US/0737-4356) [09345752] **3520**

MATHEMATICAL SCIENTIST (AT/0312-3685) [03307264] **3520**

MATHEMATICAL SOCIAL SCIENCES (NE/0165-4896) [07346213] 3520, **5208**

MATHEMATICAL SPECTRUM (UK/0025-5653) [01586472] **3520**

MATHEMATICAL SURVEYS AND MONOGRAPHS (US/0885-4653) [10906839] **3520**

MATHEMATICAL SYSTEMS IN ECONOMICS (GW/0344-3302) [02406327] 1593, **3520**

MATHEMATICAL SYSTEMS THEORY (US/0025-5661) [01756874] **3520**

MATHEMATICAL WORLD (US/1055-9426) [23370072] **3520**

MATHEMATICHESKIE VOPROSY KIBERNETIKI (RU) [19110136] **1252**

MATHEMATICIANS OF OUR TIME **CEASED.** (US) [02253100] **3520**

MATHEMATICS AND COMPUTER EDUCATION (US/0730-8639) [08075457] 1224, **3520**

MATHEMATICS AND COMPUTERS IN SIMULATION (NE/0378-4754) [03468975] 3520, **1282**

MATHEMATICS AND ITS APPLICATIONS (US/0543-0941) [02253101] **3520**

MATHEMATICS AND SCIENCES BULLETIN (CN/0848-7499) [23263605] 5127, **3520**

MATHEMATICS AND STATISTICS RESEARCH DEPARTMENT PROGRESS REPORT (US) [05873022] 3520, **3542**

MATHEMATICS COUNCIL NEWSLETTER (1983) (CN/0823-1117) [10082583] 1900, **3520**

MATHEMATICS EDUCATION RESEARCH JOURNAL (AT/1033-2170) [I10332170] 1900, **3520**

MATHEMATICS EDUCATION, THE (II/0047-6269) [04981180] **3520**

MATHEMATICS IN SCHOOL (UK/0305-7259) [03422040] 1763, **3520**

MATHEMATICS IN SCIENCE AND ENGINEERING (US/0076-5392) [01756876] 1986, 5127, **3521**

MATHEMATICS INTERNATIONAL (US/0091-7214) [08714989] **3521**

MATHEMATICS JOURNAL OF TOYAMA UNIVERSITY (JA/0916-6009) [23114710] **3521**

MATHEMATICS LECTURE SERIES (US) [06637403] **3521**

MATHEMATICS MAGAZINE (US/0025-570X) [01756877] **3521**

MATHEMATICS OF COMPUTATION (US/0025-5718) [01590115] **3521**

MATHEMATICS OF CONTROL, SIGNALS, AND SYSTEMS : MCSS (US/0932-4194) [17389638] 3521, **1986**

MATHEMATICS OF FINITE ELEMENTS AND APPLICATIONS, THE (US/0271-1982) [06569595] 1986, **3521**

MATHEMATICS OF OPERATIONS RESEARCH (US/0364-765X) [02404005] **3521**

MATHEMATICS OF THE USSR : IZVESTIJA (US/0025-5726) [01639300] **3521**

MATHEMATICS OF THE USSR : SBORNIK (US/0025-5734) [01681277] **3521**

MATHEMATICS REVIEW **CEASED.** (UK/0957-1280) [I09571280] **3521**

MATHEMATICS STUDENT (AHMEDABAD), THE (II/0025-5742) [01342578] **3521**

MATHEMATICS TEACHER, THE (US/0025-5769) [01756879] 1900, **3521**

MATHEMATICS TEACHING (UK/0025-5785) [01756880] 1900, **3521**

●MATHEMATICS TEACHING IN THE MIDDLE SCHOOL (US/1072-0839) [28856592] 1900, **3521**

MATHEMATICS TODAY (II) [13192179] **3521**

MATHEMATIKA (UK/0025-5793) [01696232] **3521**

MATHEMATIKUNTERRICHT (GW/0025-5807) [I00255807] 1900, **3521**

MATHEMATIQUE 3031, DEFINITION DU DOMAINE, EXAMENS DE FIN D'ETUDES SECONDAIRES, DE JANVIER ... ET JUIN (CN/1187-4821) [25352061] **3521**

MATHEMATIQUE 3032, DEFINITION DU DOMAINE, EXAMENS DE FIN D'ETUDES SECONDAIRES, DE JANVIER ... ET JUIN (CN/1187-483X) [25352065] **3521**

MATHEMATIQUE ET PEDAGOGIE (BE) [06805756] **3522**

MATHEMATIQUES, INFORMATIQUE ET SCIENCES HUMAINES / CENTRE D'ANALYSE ET DE MATHEMATIQUE SOCIALES, LABORATOIRE MIXTE DE L'ECOLE DES HAUTES ETUDES EN SCIENCES SOCIALES ET DU CENTRE NATIONAL DE LA RECHERCHE SCIENTIFIQUE (FR) [18810134] **3522**

MATHEMATISCHE ANNALEN (GW/0025-5831) [01639684] **3522**

MATHEMATISCHE LEHRBUECHER UND MONOGRAPHIEN. ABTEILUNG 1. MATHEMATISCHE LEHRBUECHER (GW/0076-5430) [01756886] **3522**

MATHEMATISCHE LEHRBUECHER UND MONOGRAPHIEN. ABTEILUNG 2. MATHEMATISCHE MONOGRAPHIEN (GW/0076-5430) [01756885] **3522**

MATHEMATISCHE NACHRICHTEN (GW/0025-584X) [01756887] **3522**

MATHEMATISCHE SCHULERBUCHEREI (GW/0076-5449) [I00765449] **3522**

MATHEMATISCHE SEMESTERBERICHTE (GW/0720-728X) [07714312] **3522**

MATHEMATISCHE ZEITSCHRIFT (GW/0025-5874) [01715585] **3522**

MATHEWS' C A T V (CN/0703-2765) [06141378] **1134**

MATHNEWS (CN/0705-0410) [08315782] **3522**

MATHS & STATS (UK/0959-3950) [I09593950] 1835, **3522**

MATHSCI DISC [COMPUTER FILE] (US) [20439005] **3522**

●MATHUSER (US/1062-7030) [25701962] **3522**

MATI (TEL-AVIV) (IS/0025-5912) [01792752] **2027**

●MATICA : CASOPIS HRVATSKE MATICE ISELJENIKA (CI) [28397576] **3347**

MATILDA ZIEGLER MAGAZINE FOR THE BLIND (US/0025-5955) [06956890] **4391**

MATIPANI (II) [11175514] **3410**

MATKAILUMAAILMA **See** SUOMEN MATKAILU **2523**

MATKAILUN EDISTAMISKESKUS. HOTELLILUOKITTELUTY ORYHMA **See** HOTELLILUOKITTELUTY ORYHMA : MUISTIO **2806**

MATO GROSSO (BRAZIL : STATE). COORDENADORIA DE PLANEJAMENTO E ORCAMENTACAO **See** ORCAMENTO DO ESTADO **4739**

MATO GROSSO (BRAZIL : STATE). DEPARTAMENTO DE ORCAMENTO E ADMINISTRACAO GERAL. ORCAMENTO DO ESTADO **See** ORCAMENTO DO ESTADO **4739**

MATO GROSSO (BRAZIL : STATE). SECRETARIA DE FAZENDA **See** BOLETIM INFORMATIVO DA SECRETARIA DE FAZENDA **4713**

MATO GROSSO, BRAZIL (STATE). TRIBUNAL DE JUSTICA **See** ANAIS FORENSES DO ESTADO DE MATO GROSSO **2933**

MATO GROSSO DO SUL (BRAZIL) **See** LEGISLACAO DO ESTADO DE MATO GROSSO DO SUL / SECRETARIA DE ADMINISTRACAO **3001**

MATO GROSSO DO SUL (BRAZIL). SECRETARIA DE INFRA-ESTRUTURA REGIONAL E URBANA **See** RELATORIO DE ATIVADADES - SECRETARIA DE INFRA-ESTRUTURA REGIONAL E URBANA **1624**

MATO GROSSO DO SUL (BRAZIL). TRIBUNAL DE JUSTICA **See** REVISTA DE JURISPRUDENCIA DO TRIBUNAL DE JUSTICA DE MATO GROSSO DO SUL / RESPONSABILIDADE DE COMISSAO TECNICA PERMANENTE DE BIBLIOTECA E PUBLICACOES **3041**

MATRA : MAJALAH TREND PRIA (IO) [14876217] **2283**

MATRIART (TORONTO) (CN/1182-6169) [23296399] 5561, **358**

MATRICULE ZERO (CN/0712-3914) [08898751] **1835**

MATRIKEL (SW) [03942340] **4130**

MATRIKEL / STOCKHOLMS HANDELSKAMMARE (SW) [11711781] **845**

MATRIMONIAL DECISIONS OF GREAT BRITAIN AND IRELAND FOR ... (UK) [12635351] 2283, **4976**

MATRIMONIAL LAW REPORTER, THE (II) [06893344] **3121**

MATRIMONIAL STRATEGIST, THE (US/0736-4881) [09142507] **3121**

MATRIX : A REVIEW FOR PRINTERS AND BIBLIOPHILES (UK/0261-3093) [08682905] **334**

MATRIX AND TENSOR QUARTERLY, THE **CEASED.** (UK/0025-5998) [01779833] **3522**

●MATRIX BIOLOGY : JOURNAL OF THE INTERNATIONAL SOCIETY FOR MATRIX BIOLOGY (GW/0945-053X) [30091752] **464**

MATRIX (LENNOXVILLE) (CN/0318-3610) [02441909] **3410**

MATRIX NEWS (US/1059-0749) [24137593] **1242**

MATRIX (STUTTGART) (GW/0934-8832) [19411805] **3606**

MATRIX (STUTTGART, GERMANY) **See** MATRIX BIOLOGY : JOURNAL OF THE INTERNATIONAL SOCIETY FOR MATRIX BIOLOGY **464**

MATRIX (URBANA, ILL.) (US/8755-7266) [11451795] **3466**

MATRIX (WASHINGTON, D.C. 1992) **CEASED.** (US/1064-1343) [26215399] 1618, **1220**

MATSUMOTO SHIGAKU (JA/0385-1613) [10341915] **1329**

MATSUYAMA DAIGAKU RONSHU (JA/0461-4593) [21063203] **5209**

MATSYA (II/0253-9314) [03519512] **2308**

MATTAWA RECORDER [MICROFORM], THE (CN/0834-6828) [16582032] **5789**

MATTER OF FACT : DIGEST OF CURRENT FACTS WITH CITATIONS TO SOURCES *See* MATTER OF FACT : STATEMENTS CONTAINING STATISTICS ON CURRENT SOCIAL, ECONOMIC AND POLITICAL ISSUES **5209**

MATTER OF FACT : STATEMENTS CONTAINING STATISTICS ON CURRENT SOCIAL, ECONOMIC AND POLITICAL ISSUES (US) **5209**

MATTERS OF HEALTH (US) **3915**

MATTHAY NEWS, THE (US/0360-8484) [02244193] **4130**

MATTHEWS' CATV *See* MATTHEWS' CATV DIRECTORY **1134**

MATTHEWS' CATV DIRECTORY (CN) **1134**

MATTHEWS' LIST (CN/0380-4437) [02062475] **1116**

● MATTHEWS MEDIA DIRECTORY (CN/1193-9575) [28061887] **1116**

MATTINO DI PADOVA (IT) **5804**

MATTINO (NAPLES, ITALY : 1950) (IT) [22616503] **5804**

MATTITUCK WATCHMAN *See* LONG ISLAND TRAVELER, MATTITUCK WATCHMAN, THE **5718**

MATTOON JOURNAL GAZETTE (US) [21488780] **5661**

MATTRESSES AND FOUNDATIONS (US/0276-6418) [07376677] **3484**

MATURE GROUP TRAVELER (US/1062-2772) [25576767] **5484**

MATURE HEALTH *CEASED*. (US/0891-9232) [15042424] **4789**

MATURE INVESTOR, THE (US/1040-323X) [18374446] **906**

MATURE LIVING (NASHVILLE) (US/0162-427X) [04165523] **5180**

MATURE MARKET REPORT (US/0894-2609) [15986525] **933**

MATURE OUTLOOK (US/0742-0935) [10282366] **5180**

MATURE OUTLOOK NEWSLETTER (US/0748-4003) [10935540] **5180**

MATURE STUDENTS' HANDBOOK (UK) [20493483] **1763**

MATURE TRAVELER (US/1043-2280) [19357962] **5484**

MATURE YEARS (US/0025-6021) [01792781] 5180, **4976**

MATURITAS (IE/0378-5122) [04124775] **3754**

MATURITE (CN/0836-0081) [18603677] **5295**

MATURITY DISTRIBUTION OF OUTSTANDING NEGOTIABLE TIME CERTIFICATES OF DEPOSIT *See* MATURITY DISTRIBUTION OF OUTSTANDING NEGOTIABLE TIME CERTIFICATES OF DEPOSIT AT LARGE COMMERCIAL BANKS AS OF ... **797**

MATURITY DISTRIBUTION OF OUTSTANDING NEGOTIABLE TIME CERTIFICATES OF DEPOSIT AT LARGE COMMERCIAL BANKS AS OF ... (US) [05527242] **797**

MAUDSLEY MONOGRAPHS (UK/0076-5465) [01777783] **3930**

MAUI (US/0895-9609) [16865626] **5484**

MAUI NEWS, THE (US/8750-457X) [08807554] **5656**

MAUI UPDATE, THE (US/0895-9390) [16857018] **5484**

MAUL : MIYAGI-KEN DAIGAKU TOSHOKAN KYOKAI KAIHO (JA) [06601904] **3230**

MAUM (KO) [04894816] **4352**

MAURICE (MF) [08320880] **2642**

MAURICE EWING SERIES (US/0197-6346) [03695238] **1358**

MAURITANIA. DIRECTION DE LA STATISTIQUE ET DES ETUDES ECONOMIQUES *See* AL-NASHRAH AL-SHAHRIYAH LIL-IHSA - IDARAT AL-IHSAAT WA-AL-DIRASAT AL-IQTISADIYAH **5320**

MAURITIAN INTERNATIONAL (UK/0265-444X) [20054982] **2642**

MAURITIUS *See* GOVERNMENT GAZETTE OF MAURITIUS, THE **4651**

MAURITIUS. AUDIT DEPT *See* REPORT OF THE DIRECTOR OF AUDIT ON THE ACCOUNTS OF MAURITIUS FOR THE YEAR ENDED 30 JUNE ... **4746**

MAURITIUS. AUDIT DEPT. REPORT OF THE DIRECTORY OF AUDIT *See* REPORT OF THE DIRECTOR OF AUDIT ON THE ACCOUNTS OF MAURITIUS FOR THE YEAR ENDED 30 JUNE ... **4746**

MAURITIUS COMMERCIAL BANK LIMITED *See* REPORT & ACCOUNTS FOR THE YEAR ENDED 30TH APRIL ... / THE MAURITIUS COMMERCIAL BANK LIMITED **807**

MAURITIUS LAW REVIEW REVUE DE DROIT, DE DOCTRINE, ET DE JURISPRUDENCE MAURICIENNE (MF) [08425491] **3007**

MAURITIUS. MINISTRY OF COOPERATIVES AND COOPERATIVE DEVELOPMENT *See* REPORT OF THE MINISTRY OF CO-OPERATIVES AND CO-OPERATIVE DEVELOPMENT FOR PERIOD ... **1543**

MAURITIUS. MINISTRY OF FINANCE *See* BUDGET SPEECH - MINISTER OF FINANCE **4715**

MAURITIUS. POLICE DEPT. ANNUAL REPORT ON THE MAURITIUS POLICE FORCE AND ON CRIME *See* ANNUAL REPORT OF THE MAURITIUS POLICE FORCE **3157**

MAURITIUS. POLICE FORCE *See* ANNUAL REPORT OF THE MAURITIUS POLICE FORCE **3157**

MAURITIUS POLICE MAGAZINE, THE (MF) [10344701] **3169**

MAURITIUS. PUBLIC SERVICE COMMISSION *See* REPORT OF THE PUBLIC AND POLICE SERVICE COMMISSIONS **4681**

MAURITIUS. PUBLIC SERVICE COMMISSION *See* REPORT OF THE PUBLIC SERVICE COMMISSION **4681**

MAURITIUS SUGAR SYNDICATE *See* REPORT AND STATEMENT OF ACCOUNT / THE MAURITIUS SUGAR SYNDICATE **4680**

MAURITIUS : WIRTSCHAFTSDATEN UND WIRTSCHAFTSDOKUMENTATION (GW) [06225421] **1574**

MAUSAM (II/0252-9416) [05898036] 1408, **1430**

MAVERICK GUIDE TO AUSTRALIA, THE (US/0730-0018) [06057934] **5484**

MAVERICK GUIDE TO HAWAII, THE (US/0278-6613) [04707533] **5484**

● MAVERICK GUIDE TO MALAYSIA AND SNGAPORE / LEN RUTLEDGE (US) [24859181] **5484**

MAVERICK GUIDE TO NEW ZEALAND, THE (US/0278-5501) [07826879] **5484**

MAVERICK GUIDE TO THAILAND (US) [22904989] **5484**

MAWA REVIEW (US/0742-9738) [10494373] **3410**

MAWAS DIRI (IO/0302-9646) [01792668] **2506**

MAWEWI (MAHWAH, N.J.) (US/1053-4423) [22532804] **2538**

MAWQIF AL-ARABI (NICOSIA, CYPRUS) (CY) [11104187] **2658**

MAWQIF (BEIRUT, LEBANON) (LE) [11952785] **2658**

● MAWSUAT AL-SADIRAT AL-MISRIYAH (UA) [26139763] **845**

MAX (MILAN, ITALY) (IT) [13740289] **1086**

MAX-PLANCK-GESELLSCHAFT *See* JAHRBUCH - MAX-PLANCK-GESELLSCHAFT **5117**

MAX-PLANCK-INSTITUT FUER AERONOMIE *See* MITTEILUNGEN AUS DEM MAX-PLANCK-INSTITUT FUER AERONOMIE **1431**

MAX - PLANCK - INSTITUT FUER GESCHICHTE *See* VEROFFENTLICHUNGEN - MAX-PLANCK-INSTITUT FUER GESCHICHTE **2632**

MAX-PLANCK-INSTITUT FUER PLASMAPHYSIK GARCHING BEI MUNCHEN (GW/0340-8914) [11580942] **4412**

MAX-PLANCK-INSTITUT FUER STROMUNGSFORSCHUNG *See* MITTEILUNGEN AUS DEM MAX-PLANCK-INSTITUT FUER STROMUNGSFORSCHUNG UND DER AERODYNAMISCHEN VERSUCHSANSTALT **28**

MAX-PLANCK-INSTITUT FUR KERNPHYSIK *See* JAHRESBERICHT / MAX-PLANCK-INSTITUT FUER KERNPHYSIK **4448**

MAX-PLANCK-INSTITUT FUR STROMUNGSFORSCHUNG *See* BERICHT - MAX-PLANCK-INSTITUT FUER STROMUNGSFORSCHUNG **2087**

MAXI-LOISIR (CN/0711-0502) [08649568] **386**

MAXIMA (PO) **1086**

MAXIMUM CONCENTRATIONS AT THE WORKPLACE AND BIOLOGICAL TOLERANCE VALUES FOR WORKING MATERIALS (GW) [15104890] **3982**

MAXIMUM ROCKNROLL (US/0743-3530) [10553172] **4130**

MAXIMUM TRAVEL PER DIEM ALLOWANCES FOR FOREIGN AREAS (US/1058-000X) [12444737] **5484**

MAXINE'S PAGES (US/1055-8489) [23359760] **2538**

MAXWELL COMPACT LIBRARIES. AIDS (US/1061-5458) [25345497] **3674**

MAXWELL MACMILLAN CHESS MONTHLY *See* CHESS (OXFORD) **4858**

MAXWELL REVIEW (US/0025-6110) [02241249] **5209**

MAXWELL SCIENTIFIC INTERNATIONAL *See* INTERNATIONAL GUIDE TO PERIODICALS & REFERENCE WORKS **5115**

MAY DAY PICTORIAL NEWS *CEASED*. (US/0025-6129) [04940643] **5452**

MAY MODELARZ (PL/0137-883X) [0137883X] **2774**

MAY ROCZNIK FILMOWY (PL) [07131951] **4074**

MAY ROCZNIK STATYSTYKI MIEDZYNARODOWEJ (PL) [01789540] **5332**

MAYA MARATHI (II/0303-3066) [02239571] **3410**

MAYAB (MADRID) (SP/1130-6157) [14209890] **5209**

MAYAN LINGUISTICS (US) **3301**

MAYAN LINGUISTICS NEWSLETTER (US/1062-1288) [24398328] **3301**

MAYAPADA (IO) [01795461] **2506**

MAYBERRY GAZETTE, THE (US/1043-2639) [19453404] **1134**

MAYDICA (IT/0025-6153) [01716147] **107**

MAYFAIR LONDON (UK/0025-6161) [I00256161] **3995**

MAYFIELD MESSENGER (MAYFIELD, KY. : 1923) (US) [12603677] **5681**

MAYFLOWER DESCENDANT : A MAGAZINE OF PILGRIM GENEALOGY AND HISTORY, THE (US/8756-3959) [01605029] 2745, **2459**

MAYFLOWER DIGEST (GW) [14758340] **2490**

MAYFLOWER PILGRIM *See* MAYFLOWER DIGEST **2490**

MAYFLOWER QUARTERLY, THE (US/0148-5032) [01590096] **2745**

MAYGAMV (II) [09698161] **3301**

MAYIBUYE : JOURNAL OF THE AFRICAN NATIONAL CONGRESS (SA) [24054553] **2642**

MAYNOOTH REVIEW, THE (IE) [11707581] **3410**

MAYO ALUMNI (US) **1102**

MAYO ALUMNUS *See* MAYO ALUMNI **1102**

MAYO CLINIC *See* MAYO CLINIC PROCEEDINGS **3799**

MAYO CLINIC HEALTH LETTER (ENGLISH ED.) (US/0741-6245) [10204452] **4789**

MAYO CLINIC HEALTH LETTER (GERMAN ED.) (GW/0933-9914) [17807078] **4790**

MAYO CLINIC PROCEEDINGS (US/0025-6196) [00822709] **3799**

MAYORS MANAGEMENT REPORT (US) **879**

MAYOR'S MANAGEMENT REPORT. SUPPLEMENT, THE (US) [07591754] **4664**

MAYOR'S MANAGEMENT REPORT, THE (US) [04714811] **4737**

MAYORS OF AMERICA'S PRINCIPAL CITIES, THE (US) [04340416] **4790**

MAYURQA (SP/0301-8296) [04355011] **2697**

MAYVILLE MONITOR (US) **5692**

MAYVILLE NEWS, THE (US/0749-7105) [11178103] **5769**

MAYVILLE SENTINEL (US) [26715323] **5718**

MAZAL U'BRACHA (IS/0334-6838) [26596866] **1618**

MAZAMA (US/0275-6226) [01756900] **5233**

MAZINGIRA (EDICION EN ESPANOL) (UK/0145-5729) [03349092] **2177**

MAZINGIRA (EDITION FRANCAISE) (UK/0145-5710) [03349156] **2177**

MAZOWIECKI OSRODEK BADAN NAUKOWYCH *See* PRACE **1702**

MAZPUTNINS (US/0025-6218) [08353534] **1066**

MAZUIXEE ZAZHII (CH/0254-1319) [08360822] **3606**

MB : MONTI E BOSCHI (IT/0390-6736) [09564542] **2387**

MB NEWS (NEW YORK, N.Y.) (US/0743-1279) [10496895] **1134**

MB PRODUCTIETECHNIEK (NE) 5317, **1195**

MBA COURSE, THE DPBA COURSE, THE (UK) [11346982] 692, **1835**

MBA EMPLOYMENT GUIDE *CEASED*. (US/0738-2200) [02882732] **692**

MBA NEWSLETTER, THE (US/1055-0534) [23065406] **692**

MBA PROGRAM AT WESTERN *See* WESTERN MBA PROGRAM, THE **719**

MBA REVIEW *CEASED*. (UK/0954-4836) [20739501] 692, **1835**

MBB : BELASTINGBESCHOUWINGEN (NE/0005-8335) [18147846] 3007, **4737**

MBEA TODAY (US/0892-9831) [10588015] 692, **1763**

MBI. MEDICO-BIOLOGIC INFORMATION (BU/0324-119X) [06885345] **3606**

MBI MUSIC BUSINESS INFORMATIONS (UK/0768-8172) [I07688172] **4130**

MBI'S INDIAN INDUSTRIES ANNUAL (II/0541-5357) [01645853] **1618**

MBL LECTURES IN BIOLOGY (US/0275-8679) [07251448] **464**

MBROJTJA KOMBETARE (US) [03905440] **2697**

MBS REPORTS *See* MORTGAGE MARKETPLACE, THE **800**

MBSI NEWS BULLETIN *See* NEWS BULLETIN / THE MUSICAL BOX SOCIETY INTERNATIONAL **4140**

MBTA BUDGET, REPORT OF ADVISORY BOARD BUDGET COMMITTEE (US) [05464847] **5386**

MC/B MANUFACTURING CHEMISTS (FIRM) *See* CHEMICAL REFERENCE MANUAL **1014**

MC COMPUTERPRAXIS FUER TECHNISCHE ANWENDER (GW) **1269**

MC : DIE MIKROCOMPUTER-ZEITSCHRIFT (GW/0720-4442) [15674899] **1269**

MC. MENSA CANADA COMMUNICATIONS (CN/0820-4217) [16656385] **5233**

MC : MICROCOMPUTER (IT) **1269**

MC : THE MODERN CHURCHMAN (UK/0025-7597) [09879720] **4976**

MCALESTER NEWS-CAPITAL, THE (US) [18420240] **5732**

MCCALL'S (US/0024-8908) [04171150] 404, 2792, 2283, **5561**

MCCALL'S BOOK FOR BRIDES (US/0270-0050) [06299163] **2283**

MCCALL'S CHRISTMAS KNIT & CROCHET (US/0276-6671) [07377896] **5185**

MCCALL'S COUNTRY DECORATING (US/0272-4499) [06825871] **374**

MCCALL'S CROCHET PATTERNS (US/1065-0288) [26157338] **5185**

MCCALL'S DECORATING BOOK (US/0272-1562) [06744828] **2906**

MCCALL'S EARLY AMERICAN DECORATING & CRAFTS (US) [06280777] 374, **2902**

MCCALL'S NEEDLEWORK (US/1069-2894) [28036733] **5185**

MCCALL'S NEEDLEWORK & CRAFTS (US/0024-8924) [04117390] **5185**

MCCALL'S (PATTERN BOOK) (US/0198-2478) [06132868] **5185**

MCCALL'S PATTERNS (US/0198-6457) [06181212] **5185**

● MCCALL'S QUILTING (US/1072-8295) [29208626] 374, **5185**

MCCARTHY TETRAULT REGULATORY REPORTER (US) **1160**

MCCARVILLE REPORT, THE (US/0732-0205) [08278226] **4481**

MCCAUSLAND'S ORDER OF DIVINE SERVICE (CN/0831-6074) [14555438] **4976**

MCCLAIN CO. OK HISTORICAL AND GENEALOGICAL SOCIETY QUARTERLY NEWSLETTER (US/1066-8446) [12857197] **2459**

MCCLURE CENTER MAGAZINE *CEASED.* (US/0743-4111) [10528481] **1195**

MCCONNAUGHEY BULLETIN (MCCONNAUGHEY AND VARIANTS) OF THE MCCONNAUGHEY SOCIETY OF AMERICA, INC, THE (US/0196-2078) [05785028] **5233**

MCCONNAUGHEY SOCIETY OF AMERICA *See* MCCONNAUGHEY BULLETIN (MCCONNAUGHEY AND VARIANTS) OF THE MCCONNAUGHEY SOCIETY OF AMERICA, INC, THE **5233**

MCCOOK DAILY GAZETTE (US) [13412916] **5706**

MCCORMICK MESSENGER (US) [28235144] **5743**

MCCOY'S HAZARDOUS WASTE REGULATORY UPDATE SERVICE *See* HAZARDOUS WASTE UPDATE SERVICE, THE **2231**

MCCREARY COUNTY RECORD (US) [14199952] **5681**

MCCURTAIN GAZETTE (US) [12110732] **5732**

MCCUTCHEON'S DETERGENTS & EMULSIFIERS : FUNCTIONAL MATERIALS (US/0145-6911) [02776728] **985**

MCCUTCHEON'S DETERGENTS & EMULSIFIERS. NORTH AMERICAN EDITION (US/0145-7055) [02773598] **1044**

MCCUTCHEON'S EMULSIFIERS & DETERGENTS (INTERNATIONAL EDITION) (US/0734-0567) [07721176] **1027**

MCCUTCHEON'S FUNCTIONAL MATERIALS. NORTH AMERICAN EDITION (US/0734-0559) [08652025] **1027**

MCD. MIDDLE ATLANTIC EDITION (US/0733-6012) [08349991] **5386**

MCD WAREHOUSING DISTRIBUTION DIRECTORY (US/1075-0517) [06012100] **845**

MCDONALD QUARTERLY (CN/1183-8329) [25423219] **5295**

MCDOWELL EXPRESS, THE (US/0199-8137) [06217284] **5723**

MCDUFFIE PROGRESS, THE (US) [21434758] **5654**

MCELROY FAMILY NEWSLETTER, THE (US/0147-992X) [03251696] **2459**

MCFARLAND COMMUNITY LIFE (US/0883-6566) [11948664] **5769**

MCGEORGE MAGAZINE / UNIVERSITY OF THE PACIFIC, MCGEORGE SCHOOL OF LAW (US) [11781393] **3007**

MCGEORGE SCHOOL OF LAW *See* MCGEORGE MAGAZINE / UNIVERSITY OF THE PACIFIC, MCGEORGE SCHOOL OF LAW **3007**

MCGILL JOURNAL OF EDUCATION (CN/0024-9033) [01641918] **1763**

MCGILL JOURNAL OF POLITICAL ECONOMY, THE (CN/0712-1148) [07315273] 797, **1504**

MCGILL LAW JOURNAL (CN/0024-9041) [01756910] **3132**

MCGILL MEDICAL JOURNAL *CEASED.* (CN/0024-905X) [01778900] **3606**

MCGILL MEDICAL UNDERGRADUATE JOURNAL *See* MCGILL MEDICAL JOURNAL **3606**

MCGILL NEWS, THE (CN/0024-9068) [02349628] **1093**

MCGILL REPORTER (CN/0848-8436) [21340912] **1835**

MCGILL SUB-ARCTIC RESEARCH PAPERS (CN/0076-1982) [01756919] 1387, **2568**

MCGILL UNIVERSITY *See* GENERAL ANNOUNCEMENT - MCGILL UNIVERSITY, MONTREAL **1825**

MCGILL UNIVERSITY *See* CALENDAR / MCGILL UNIVERSITY **1813**

MCGILL UNIVERSITY. CENTRE FOR DEVELOPING-AREA STUDIES *See* KEITH CALLARD LECTURES **3401**

MCGILL UNIVERSITY. CENTRE FOR EAST ASIAN STUDIES *See* CENTRE FOR EAST ASIAN STUDIES OCCASIONAL PAPERS **2648**

MCGILL UNIVERSITY. COMPUTING CENTRE *See* NEWS LETTER - MCGILL UNIVERSITY COMPUTING CENTRE **1197**

MCGILL UNIVERSITY. FACULTY OF DENTISTRY *See* MCGILL UNIVERSITY. FACULTY OF DENTISTRY **1329**

MCGILL UNIVERSITY. FACULTY OF DENTISTRY (CN/0316-8336) [02247174] **1329**

MCGILL UNIVERSITY. GRADUATE SCHOOL OF LIBRARY AND INFORMATION STUDIES *See* NEWSLETTER / MCGILL UNIVERSITY GRADUATE SCHOOL OF LIBRARY AND INFORMATION STUDIES **1837**

MCGILL UNIVERSITY. INSTITUTE OF OCEANOGRAPHY *See* BIENNIAL REPORT / INSTITUTE OF OCEANOGRAPHY, MCGILL UNIVERSITY **1446**

MCGILL UNIVERSITY. STORMY WEATHER GROUP. TECHNICAL REPORT (CN/0460-332X) [02247895] **1430**

MCGILL WORKING PAPERS IN LINGUISTICS (CN/0824-5282) [10832053] **3301**

MCGOLDRICK'S CANADIAN CUSTOMS TARIFF HARMONIZED SYSTEM (CN/1183-3246) [17393972] **845**

MCGRAW-HILL BOOK COMPANY *See* MCGRAW-HILL DICTIONARY OF SCIENTIFIC AND TECHNICAL TERMS **1927**

MCGRAW-HILL BOOK COMPANY *See* MCGRAW-HILL MANAGEMENT AWARENESS PROGRAM **879**

MCGRAW-HILL DICTIONARY OF SCIENTIFIC AND TECHNICAL TERMS (US/05979862) 5127, **1927**

● MCGRAW-HILL DIRECTORY OF MANAGEMENT FACULTY, THE (US/1062-1989) [25157656] **879**

MCGRAW-HILL ENCYCLOPEDIA OF SCIENCE & TECHNOLOGY (US) [08325500] 5127, **1927**

MCGRAW-HILL HAZARDOUS WASTE MONITOR (US/0894-2374) [15876214] **2236**

MCGRAW-HILL HEALTH LETTER (US/1056-1129) [23467383] **2599**

MCGRAW-HILL HOMEBOOK, THE (US/0162-8151) [04254671] **2902**

MCGRAW-HILL INFORMATION SYSTEMS COMPANY *See* MCGRAW-HILL'S DODGE CONSTRUCTION SYSTEMS COSTS **620**

MCGRAW-HILL MANAGEMENT AWARENESS PROGRAM (US) [02360865] **879**

MCGRAW-HILL PUBLICATIONS COMPANY. ECONOMICS DEPT *See* ANNUAL MCGRAW-HILL SURVEY : BUSINESS' SPENDING PLANS FOR PLANTS AND EQUIPMENT **1546**

● MCGRAW-HILL WORLD FUTURES AND OPTIONS DIRECTORY / COMPILED BY NICK BATTLEY (UK) [23764591] **797**

MCGRAW-HILL YEARBOOK OF SCIENCE AND TECHNOLOGY (US/0076-2016) [01681201] **5127**

● MCGRAW-HILL'S CANCER & GENETICS REPORT (US/1070-597X) [28406545] **3820**

MCGRAW-HILL'S COMPUTER CAREERS (US/0882-3979) [11826514] 1195, **4206**

MCGRAW-HILL'S DODGE CONSTRUCTION SYSTEMS COSTS (US) [07326601] **620**

● MCGRAW-HILL'S FEDERAL TECHNOLOGY REPORT (US/1066-873X) [27075333] **1618**

MCGRAW-HILL'S HEALTH BUSINESS (US/0888-9805) [13765514] **4790**

MCGRAW-HILL'S MEDICAL UTILIZATION REVIEW (US/0734-1970) [08702283] **3606**

MCGRAW-HILL'S NATIONAL ELECTRICAL CODE HANDBOOK *CEASED.* (US/0277-6758) [05383200] **2071**

MCGRAW-HILL'S TECH TRANSFER REPORT (US/1042-9158) [19257320] **1618**

MCGRAW-HILL'S UTILITY ENVIRONMENT REPORT (US/1053-9379) [22695358] **4761**

MCGREGOR FUND *See* MCGREGOR FUND REPORT **797**

MCGREGOR FUND REPORT (US/0197-7229) [04347813] **797**

MCGREGOR MIRROR AND THE CRAWFORD SUN, THE (US/1044-0348) [14442617] **5752**

MCGREGOR'S WHO OWNS WHOM (SA) [18129553] **692**

MCGUFFEY WRITER, THE (US/0891-1673) [14687468] **1066**

MCHENRY COUNTY ILLINOIS CONNECTION QUARTERLY (US/0885-8314) [10701925] **2460**

MCIC NEWS (CN/0710-457X) [10634811] **4528**

MCINTOSH GALLERY (CN/0227-0609) [08028261] **358**

MCINTOSH TIMES, THE (US) [01640630] **5697**

MCKEAN COUNTY MINER (SMETHPORT, PA. : 1974) (US) [16873157] **5737**

MCKEE-BERGER-MANSUETO *See* BUILDING COST FILE. WESTERN EDITION **603**

MCKEES ROCKS GAZETTE *See* SUBURBAN GAZETTE **5739**

MCKINNEY MAZE, THE (US/0736-2420) [09078483] **2460**

MCKINNEY'S NEW YORK RULES OF COURT (US/0747-7872) [09088487] **3141**

MCKINNEY'S SESSION LAWS OF NEW YORK (US) [01587852] **3007**

MCKINSEY AND COMPANY *See* MCKINSEY QUARTERLY, THE **879**

MCKINSEY QUARTERLY, THE (US/0047-5394) [04403951] **879**

MCKNIGHT'S LONG-TERM CARE NEWS (US/1048-3314) [20921062] 3788, **5295**

MCLEAN COUNTY INDEPENDENT (US) [01756929] **5725**

MCLEAN COUNTY JOURNAL AND TURTLE LAKE WAVE, THE (US) [20005994] **2490**

MCLEAN COUNTY NEWS (US) [13958464] **5681**

MCLEAN HOSPITAL *See* MCLEAN HOSPITAL JOURNAL **3930**

MCLEAN HOSPITAL JOURNAL (US/0363-0226) [02336555] **3930**

MCLEAN PROVIDENCE JOURNAL AND FAIRFAX HERALD, THE (US) [13765246] **5759**

MCM (IT/0393-8190) [14263738] **324**

MCMAHON HEAVY CONSTRUCTION COST GUIDE (US/1050-270X) [20161512] **2027**

Alphabetical Title Index — MEAT

MCMASTER ASSOCIATION OF PART-TIME STUDENTS **See** LINK FOR MCMASTER PART-TIME STUDENTS, THE **1761**

MCMASTER COURIER, THE (CN/0820-7984) [09562938] **5789**

MCMASTER JOURNAL OF THEOLOGY **CEASED.** (CN/0849-0899) [22159247] **4976**

MCMASTER SYMPOSIUM ON IRON AND STEELMAKING (CN/0227-5503) [02256164] **4008**

MCMASTER UNIVERSITY ASSOCIATION FOR 18TH CENTURY STUDIES **See** PUBLICATIONS OF THE MCMASTER UNIVERSITY ASSOCIATION FOR 18TH CENTURY STUDIES **2626**

MCN (US) [23706075] **1234**

MCN, THE AMERICAN JOURNAL OF MATERNAL CHILD NURSING (US/0361-929X) [02134192] 3906, **3861**

MCNEESE REVIEW, THE (US/0885-467X) [01937295] **3347**

MCPS OVERSEAS AND STATESIDE UPDATES/MICRO COMPUTERS PROCESSING SYSTEM (US) **1269**

MCVILLE MESSENGER (US/8750-5436) [11491572] **5725**

MD (US) [17966832] **2106**

MD ANDERSON ONCOLOG / THE UNIVERSITY OF TEXAS, MD ANDERSON CANCER CENTER (US) [24547539] **3820**

MD LEINFELDEN (GW/0343-0642) [l03430642] **2902**

MD, MATERIALDIENST DES KONFESSIONSKUNDLICHEN INSTITUTS (GW) [05758037] **4976**

MD/PC (US/0735-4436) [08909332] 3788, **3007**

MDA NEWSMAGAZINE **See** MDA REPORTS **3606**

MDA NEWSMAGAZINE / MUSCULAR DYSTROPHY ASSOCIATION (US/8750-2321) [11141033] **3806**

●MDA REPORTS (US/1061-4370) [25308486] **3606**

MDE. MANAGERIAL AND DECISION ECONOMICS (UK/0143-6570) [06522705] **1504**

MDI MANAGEMENT JOURNAL (II/0970-6623) [24337119] 879, **692**

MDR WATCH (US/0890-7587) [14374024] **3606**

MDRP (CN/0576-2944) [01283057] **2828**

MDR'S CIC SCHOOL DIRECTORY : NATIONAL SET (US) [06593922] **1900**

ME DE MIRU HOKKAIDO SANGYO (JA) [02977397] **1574**

ME, MEHANIZACIA I ELEKTRIFIKACIA SELSKOGO HOZAISTVA (MOSKVA) (RU/0206-572X) [08077479] **107**

ME. MUSIC EXPRESS MAGAZINE **CEASED.** (CN/0848-9645) [21665353] **4130**

ME NAISET (FI/0025-6277) [06318366] **5561**

MEA VILLA : REVISTA DA BIBLIOTECA PUBLICA MUNICIPAL DE V.N. DE GAIA (PO) [19806557] **3410**

MEAD JOHNSON ADVANCES IN THERAPEUTICS (UK/0264-1410) [08516993] **3606**

MEAD JOHNSON SYMPOSIUM ON PERINATAL AND DEVELOPMENTAL MEDICINE **CEASED.** (US/0190-0749) [02254617] **3606**

MEADE COUNTY MESSENGER (BRANDENBURG, KY. : 1987) (US) [16286727] **5681**

MEADOW LAKE PROGRESS (CN) **5789**

MEADOW RIVER POST (US) [12789453] **5764**

●MEADOWLARK (EVANSTON, ILL.) (US/1065-2043) [26528979] **5618**

MEADVILLE TRIBUNE (1955) (US/0747-2412) [02263938] **5737**

MEAFORD CENTENNIAL, THE (CN/0319-1672) [02442224] **5789**

MEAGHER COUNTY NEWS (WHITE SULPHUR SPRINGS, MONT. : 1934) (US) [13336945] **5705**

MEALEY'S EUROPEAN ENVIRONMENTAL LAW REPORT (US/1050-897X) [21696261] **3114**

MEALEY'S LITIGATION REPORT. ASBESTOS PROPERTY ACTIONS (US/1040-0192) [18316685] **3007**

MEALEY'S LITIGATION REPORT. REINSURANCE (US/1049-5347) [21248120] **3007**

MEALEY'S LITIGATION REPORT. TOBACCO (US/0886-0122) [12792409] 5373, **3007**

●MEALEY'S LITIGATION REPORTS. AMERICANS WITH DISABILITIES ACT (US/1068-5405) [27701177] 4391, **3007**

MEALEY'S LITIGATION REPORTS. ASBESTOS (US/0742-4647) [10356413] 2865, **3007**

MEALEY'S LITIGATION REPORTS. BAD FAITH (US/0893-1011) [15348329] 2887, **3007**

MEALEY'S LITIGATION REPORTS. BANKING INSOLVENCY (US/1057-1000) [23949834] 3008, **797**

●MEALEY'S LITIGATION REPORTS. BREAST IMPLANTS (US/1067-0246) [27058266] **3008**

●MEALEY'S LITIGATION REPORTS. D&O LIABILITY (US/1068-414X) [27670201] **3008**

MEALEY'S LITIGATION REPORTS. INSURANCE (US/8755-9005) [11446805] 2887, **3008**

●MEALEY'S LITIGATION REPORTS. INSURANCE FRAUD (US/1075-380X) [30042292] **2887**

MEALEY'S LITIGATION REPORTS. INSURANCE INSOLVENCY (US/1043-8416) [19579726] 2887, **3008**

●MEALEY'S LITIGATION REPORTS. INTELLECTUAL PROPERTY (US/1065-9390) [26812453] 1306, **3008**

MEALEY'S LITIGATION REPORTS. IRANIAN CLAIMS **CEASED.** (US/0742-4655) [10354431] **3132**

MEALEY'S LITIGATION REPORTS. LEAD (US/1059-4116) [24522326] **3008**

●MEALEY'S LITIGATION REPORTS. PATENTS (US/1070-4043) [28358520] **3008**

MEALEY'S LITIGATION REPORTS. PREMISES LIABILITY (US/1070-4035) [28358502] **3008**

MEALEY'S LITIGATION REPORTS. PUNITIVE DAMAGES & TORT REFORM (US/1055-307X) [23137133] 3101, **2887**

MEALEY'S LITIGATION REPORTS. SUPERFUND (US/0897-3407) [17465357] 2236, **3114**

●MEALEY'S LITIGATION REPORTS. TOXIC TORTS (US/1064-1475) [25636327] 2236, **3008**

MEAN MOUNTAIN MUSIC (US/0195-6191) [05505567] 5317, **4130**

MEANDER (PL/0025-6285) [01924923] **1078**

MEANING OF LIFE, THE (US/1071-328X) [27451591] **4352**

MEANJIN (PARKVILLE, VIC.) (AT/0815-953X) [03972868] **3410**

MEANS ASSEMBLIES COST DATA (US/0894-4342) [12957096] **620**

●MEANS BUILDING CONSTRUCTION COST DATA (US/1066-0240) [26536124] **620**

MEANS COLORADO DIRECTORY, THE (US/0273-3803) [07037760] **4074**

●MEANS CONCRETE & MASONRY COST DATA (US/1075-0274) [29578518] **620**

MEANS CONCRETE COST DATA (US/1075-0533) [15255807] **620**

MEANS CONSTRUCTION COST INDEXES (US/0361-9591) [02156627] **620**

MEANS ELECTRICAL CHANGE ORDER COST DATA (US/1044-2812) [19731802] **2071**

MEANS ELECTRICAL COST DATA (US/0748-7002) [10511731] 2072, **620**

●MEANS FACILITIES CONSTRUCTION COST DATA (US/1075-0789) [29614302] **620**

MEANS FACILITIES COST DATA (US/0888-6709) [13688504] **303**

●MEANS FACILITIES MAINTENANCE & REPAIR COST DATA (US/1074-0953) [29593140] **620**

MEANS HEAVY CONSTRUCTION COST DATA (US/0893-5602) [15585859] **620**

MEANS HISTORICAL COST INDEXES (US/0277-8610) [07637005] **620**

MEANS INTERIOR COST DATA (US) [17445122] **620**

MEANS LABOR RATES FOR THE CONSTRUCTION INDUSTRY (US) [17642043] 1690, **620**

MEANS LANDSCAPE COST DATA **See** MEANS SITE WORK & LANDSCAPE COST DATA **621**

MEANS LIGHT COMMERCIAL COST DATA (US/0896-7601) [17310421] **620**

MEANS MECHANICAL CHANGE ORDER COST DATA **CEASED.** (US/1054-4798) [22902196] **620**

MEANS MECHANICAL COST DATA (US/0748-2698) [10501552] **620**

MEANS OPEN SHOP BUILDING CONSTRUCTION COST DATA (US) [17641902] **620**

MEANS PLUMBING CHANGE ORDER COST DATA **CEASED.** (US/1054-478X) [22902175] **2606**

MEANS PLUMBING COST DATA (US/1042-3850) [18995894] **2607**

MEANS REPAIR & REMODELING COST DATA (US/0898-5006) [17285120] **620**

MEANS RESIDENTIAL COST DATA (US/0896-8624) [17285112] **621**

●MEANS SITE WORK & LANDSCAPE COST DATA (US/1064-5128) [25002153] **621**

MEANS SITE WORK COST DATA **See** MEANS SITE WORK & LANDSCAPE COST DATA **621**

MEANS SQUARE FOOT COSTS : RESIDENTIAL, COMMERCIAL, INDUSTRIAL, INSTITUTIONAL (US/0732-815X) [08262612] **621**

MEASEF (MEKHON HA-KETAV (JERUSALEM)) (IS) [10906953] **2507**

MEASLES SURVEILLANCE REPORT (US/0198-6899) [01770688] **4790**

MEASLEY'S LITIGATION REPORTS TOBACCO **See** MEALEY'S LITIGATION REPORTS. TOXIC TORTS **3008**

MEASURE OF EXCELLENCE / LAURANCE D. LINFORD, A (US/1060-1309) [24877640] **2745**

MEASUREMENT AND CONTROL (UK/0020-2940) [04518800] **2121**

MEASUREMENT & CONTROL NEWS (US/0194-1461) [05344634] **4031**

MEASUREMENT AND EVALUATION IN COUNSELING AND DEVELOPMENT (US/0748-1756) [10874466] 4603, **1763**

MEASUREMENT : JOURNAL OF THE INTERNATIONAL MEASUREMENT CONFEDERATION (UK/0263-2241) [10193209] **4031**

MEASUREMENT SCIENCE & TECHNOLOGY (UK/0957-0233) [20943814] **4412**

MEASUREMENT TECHNIQUES (US/0543-1972) [01590428] **2121**

MEASUREMENTS & CONTROL (US/0148-0057) [03262759] **5127**

MEASURING & CONTROL DEVICES (US) **1986**

MEASURING MORMONISM (US/0094-5633) [01794669] **4976**

MEAT AND DAIRY PRODUCTS **CEASED.** (UK) [06257268] 196, **215**

●MEAT & LIVESTOCK REVIEW / PRODUCED BY THE AUSTRALIAN MEAT AND LIVESTOCK CORPORATION, MARKETING INTELLIGENCE UNIT (AT) [25391603] 215, **2349**

MEAT & POULTRY (US/0892-6077) [15149795] 215, **2349**

●MEAT & POULTRY FACTS (US) [27462924] **215**

MEAT AND POULTRY INSPECTION (US/0093-4364) [08366429] **215**

MEAT AND POULTRY INSPECTION DIRECTORY (US/0740-8609) [03260420] **215**

MEAT AND POULTRY INSPECTION MANUAL (US) [04512081] **215**

MEAT AND POULTY INSPECTION REGULATIONS (US) [04506608] **215**

MEAT ANIMALS, PRODUCTION, DISPOSITION, AND INCOME (US/0748-0318) [10827083] **215**

MEAT BALANCES IN OECD COUNTRIES / BILANS DE LA VIANDE DANS LES PAYS DE L'OCDE (FR) [11034417] 845, **215**

MEAT BOARD REPORTS [ANNUAL REPORT] (US) [01249485] **215**

MEAT BUSINESS MAGAZINE (US/1049-5908) [21274696] **2349**

MEAT FACTS **See** MEAT & POULTRY FACTS **215**

MEAT FOCUS INTERNATIONAL (UK/0961-2076) [09612076] **215**

MEAT HYGIENIST, THE (UK/0308-7050) [12016722] 4790, **2349**

MEAT INDUSTRY BULLETIN, THE (AT) [09887705] **215**

MEAT INDUSTRY DIGEST (AT) **2349**

MEAT PRICE OUTLOOK (US/0747-6019) [10768276] **215**

MEAT PRICE RELATIONSHIPS (US/0882-3065) [06515318] **1618**

MEAT PROBE (CN/0826-4554) [11193172] **2349**

MEAT PROCESSING (US/0025-6390) [04969319] **2349**

●MEAT PROCESSING INTERNATIONAL (US) [29397297] **215**

MEAT REPORT FROM THE UNIVERSITY OF ILLINOIS AT URBANA-CHAMPAIGN (US) [08630356] 215, **2349**

MEAT RESEARCH NEWSLETTER (AT/0815-676X) [03297403] 2350, **215**

MEAT SCIENCE (UK/0309-1740) [02954367] 2350, **215**

MEAT SCIENCE INSTITUTE **See** PROCEEDINGS. ANNUAL MEAT SCIENCE INSTITUTE **2353**

MEAT SHEET, THE (US/0889-3608) [10731067] **2350**

MEAT — Alphabetical Title Index

MEAT SOURCE **CEASED.** (US/0887-9214) [13412598] 5071, **2350**

MEAT TRADES JOURNAL (UK) [09889703] **2350**

MECANICA POPULAR (US/0025-6420) [04050448] **2538**

MECANIQUE ET ACOUSTIC (FR) **4453**

● MECANIQUE INDUSTRIELLE ET MATERIAUX : REVUE DU GAMI (FR) [28118697] **2121**

MECANIQUE, MATERIAUX, ELECTRICITE (FR/0025-6439) [01789911] **2121**

MECANIZAREA AGRICULTURII (RM) [17930789] **159**

MECC PERSPECTIVES - MIDDLE EAST COUNCIL OF CHURCHES (SZ) [20087269] **5039**

MECCA (NEW ORLEANS) (US/0094-0321) [01793591] **4130**

MECCANICA (MILAN) (NE/0025-6455) [01756941] **4428**

MECCANICA OGGI (IT/1121-2047) [11212047] **2121**

MECH (US/0025-6471) [02566698] **4179**

MECHA-PRESS (CN/1183-5443) [24368127] **1313**

MECHANICAL BUYER & SPECIFIER. HVAC/REFRIGERATION (CN/1183-9015) [25652247] **2607**

MECHANICAL BUYER & SPECIFIER. PLUMBING, PIPING & HEATING (CN/1183-9007) [25652250] **2607**

MECHANICAL/ELECTRICAL ... COSTBOOK / BNI, BUILDING NEWS (US/1061-3374) [24305087] **621**

● MECHANICAL ENGINEERING ABSTRACTS (US/1063-7311) [26133758] 2121, **2006**

MECHANICAL ENGINEERING BULLETIN (II/0379-5527) [04815767] **2121**

MECHANICAL ENGINEERING DEPARTMENT, RESEARCH ENGINEERING DIVISION ACTIVITIES HIGHLIGHTS REPORT (US) [05927404] **2122**

MECHANICAL ENGINEERING (MARCEL DEKKER, INC.) (US/0899-3858) [08592214] **2122**

MECHANICAL ENGINEERING (NEW YORK, N.Y. 1919) (US/0025-6501) [01756943] **2122**

MECHANICAL ENGINEERING NEWS (FAYETTEVILLE, ARK.) (US/0025-651X) [00850989] **2122**

MECHANICAL INCORPORATED ENGINEER (UK/0954-6529) [18657857] **2122**

MECHANICAL LABOR ESTIMATING GUIDE (US) [19538773] **5418**

MECHANICAL MUSIC (US/1045-795X) [20064057] **4130**

MECHANICAL PARTS/LABOR ESTIMATING GUIDE. DOMESTIC GLASS (US/0884-0156) [12158355] **5418**

MECHANICAL PARTS/LABOR ESTIMATING GUIDE. TRANSMISSION (US) [16310486] **1986**

MECHANICAL PRODUCTS CATALOG **See** HUTTON CONSTRUCTION CATALOG : MECHANICAL PRODUCTS **2115**

MECHANICAL SYSTEMS AND SIGNAL PROCESSING (UK/0888-3270) [13562314] **2122**

MECHANICAL TRADE CONTRACTORS (CN/0835-1031) [16520123] **621**

MECHANICAL WORKING & STEEL PROCESSING (US/0147-7781) [02280069] **4008**

MECHANICAL WORKING OF STEEL **See** MECHANICAL WORKING & STEEL PROCESSING **4008**

MECHANICS ANALYSIS **CEASED.** (NE/0924-2147) [09242147] **2106**

MECHANICS & HOME REPAIR (US/0271-2210) [06561856] **621**

MECHANICS AND MATHEMATICAL METHODS SECOND SERIES, THERMAL STRESSERS (NE/0921-9749) [09219749] **4428**

MECHANICS AND MATHEMATICAL METHODS. THIRD SERIES, ACOUSTIC, ELECTROMAGNETIC, AND ELASTIC WAVE SCATTERING (NE/0921-9331) [25177213] **4428**

MECHANICS AND PHYSICS OF DISCRETE SYSTEMS (NE/0926-9282) [09269282] **4429**

MECHANICS, DYNAMICAL SYSTEMS (NE) [19532119] **2106**

MECHANICS OF COMPOSITE MATERIALS (US/0191-5665) [04967889] **2106**

MECHANICS OF COMPOSITE MATERIALS AND STRUCTURE (UK/1075-9417) [30331049] **2106**

MECHANICS OF CREEP BRITTLE MATERIALS (UK/0959-5864) [09595864] **2106**

MECHANICS OF ELASTIC AND INELASTIC SOLIDS **CEASED.** (NE) [10836493] **2106**

MECHANICS OF ELASTIC STABILITY **CEASED.** (NE) [12782355] **2106**

MECHANICS OF MATERIALS (NE/0167-6636) [08260838] **2106**

MECHANICS OF SOLIDS (US/0025-6544) [04473597] **4412**

MECHANICS OF STRUCTURAL SYSTEMS (NE/0924-2139) [09242139] **4429**

MECHANICS OF STRUCTURES AND MACHINES (US/0890-5452) [14261536] 2122, **2106**

MECHANICS OF SURFACE STRUCTURES (NE) [17614346] **1986**

MECHANICS RESEARCH COMMUNICATIONS (US/0093-6413) [01792785] **4429**

MECHANICS (URBANA) (US/0076-5783) [02942156] **2122**

MECHANIK (PL/0025-6552) [07028726] **2122**

MECHANIKA I BUDOWNICTWO (PL) [02244395] **2122**

MECHANIKA I KOMPUTER / POLSKA AKADEMIA NAUK, INSTYTUT PODSTAWOWYCH PROBLEMOW TECHNIKI (PL/0137-5067) [07372659] **2107**

MECHANIKA TEORETYCZNA I STOSOWANA (PL/0079-3701) [04567077] **4429**

MECHANISM AND MACHINE THEORY (UK/0094-114X) [01756949] **2122**

MECHANISMS OF AGEING AND DEVELOPMENT (SZ/0047-6374) [02239471] 3754, **584**

MECHANISMS OF DEVELOPMENT (IE/0925-4773) [22927690] **464**

MECHANISMS OF DEVELOPMENT. SUPPLEMENT (IE) **538**

MECHANISMS OF INORGANIC AND ORGANOMETALLIC REACTIONS (US/0740-8900) [09909702] **1037**

MECHANIZACE ZEMEDELSTVI (XR/0373-6776) [09542527] **143**

MECHANIZACJA I AUTOMATYZACJA GORNICTWA (PL/0208-7448) [02714081] **2143**

MECHANIZACJA ROLNICTWA (PL/0461-5220) [04095205] **160**

MECHANO BUYERS DIRECTORY. NORTHERN CALIFORNIA (US) [08136706] **3484**

MECHATRONIC SYSTEMS ENGINEERING (NE/0924-3992) [24236430] 1986, **1220**

MECHATRONICS (OXFORD) (UK/0957-4158) [22714631] **1195**

MECHELECIV (US/0047-6382) [05702309] **5127**

MECKLENBURG GAZETTE, THE (US) [27377077] **5723**

MECKLENBURG TIMES (US) **5723**

MECKLER'S BIBLIOGRAPHIES OF BATTLES AND LEADERS **See** BIBLIOGRAPHIES OF BATTLES AND LEADERS **4061**

MED AD NEWS (US/1067-733X) [27341448] **4314**

MED BIL I EUROPA (NO) [02504525] **2697**

MED DEV (US/0883-1750) [12210687] **3607**

MED-REC AUTOMATION & MANAGEMENT REPORT (US) **3788**

MED-REPORT (GW/0934-3148) [09343148] **3607**

MED-SURG NURSING QUARTERLY **CEASED.** (US/1062-7537) [25730048] **3861**

MED TEC INTERNATIONAL (NZ) [23181309] **3607**

MEDAL COLLECTOR **See** JOURNAL OF THE ORDERS AND MEDALS SOCIETY OF AMERICA, THE **2781**

MEDAL COLLECTOR BULLETIN **See** MEDAL COLLECTOR, THE **2774**

MEDAL COLLECTOR, THE (US/0025-6633) [10818028] **2774**

MEDAL LONDON (UK/0263-7707) [10634993] **2781**

MEDAL NEWS HINDHEAD. 1989 (UK/0958-4986) [09584986] 4049, **2781**

MEDALIST FLASHBACK NOTEBOOK (US/0743-6580) [06795269] **4904**

MEDALLION (AUSTIN, TEX.) (US/0890-7595) [02584348] **2745**

MEDALS YEARBOOK (US/0737-6529) [09409760] **4049**

MEDAN, INDONESIA. UNIVERSITAS SUMATERA UTARA **See** MAJALAH UNIVERSITAS SUMATERA UTARA **1834**

MEDAN, INDONESIA. UNIVERSITAS SUMATERA UTARA. FAKULTAS PERTANIAN **See** ALUMNI FAKULTAS PERTANIAN UNIVERSITAS SUMATERA UTARA **1100**

MEDBOOKS (SZ) [04650677] **4830**

MEDDELANDE / FORSKNINGSSTIFTELSEN SKOGSARBETEN (SW/0532-2499) [10969181] **2387**

MEDDELANDE - JORDBRUKSTEKNISKA INSTITUTET (SW/0368-3419) [01754337] 1987, **107**

MEDDELANDEN **See** STATISTISKA MEDDELANDEN **5344**

MEDDELANDEN FRAN INSTITUTIONEN FOR NORDISKA SPRAK VID STOCKHOLMS UNIVERSITET: MINS (SW/0348-3568) [07228767] **3301**

MEDDELANDEN FRAN LUNDS UNIVERSITETS GEOGRAFISKA INSTITUTION. AVHANDLINAR (SW/0346-6787) [01624232] **2569**

MEDDELANDEN FRAN LUNDS UNIVERSITETS HISTORISKA MUSEUM (SW/0458-4767) [04584767] **274**

MEDDELANDEN FRAN LUNDS UNIVERSITETS HISTORISKA MUSEUM **CEASED.** (SW) [05658588] **274**

MEDDELANDEN FRAN SVENSKA RIKSARKIVET (SW/0282-762X) [19035230] **2482**

MEDDELANDEN / SVENSKA FORSKNINGSINSTITUTET I ISTANBUL (SW/0347-8068) [07686764] **2623**

MEDDELANDEN / SVENSKA TRAASKYDDSINSTITUTET / REPORTS / THE SWEDISH WOOD PRESERVATION INSTITUTE (SW/0346-7090) [03046226] **2402**

MEDDELELSER **See** RESERVEOFFICEREN **4055**

MEDDELELSER FRA NY CARLSBERG GLYPTOTEK (DK/0085-3208) [03621352] **358**

MEDDELELSER FRA SKOGFORSK / NORSK INSTITUTT FOR SKOGFORSKNING, INSTITUTT FOR SKOGFAG, NLH (NO/0803-2866) [23981696] **2387**

MEDDELELSER FRA STATSSKATTEDIREKTORATET OG LIGNINGSRADET (DK) [03745049] **4737**

MEDDELELSER FRA THORVALDSENS MUSEUM (DK/0085-7262) [03621405] **358**

MEDDELELSER / NORSK PALARINSTITUTT (NO/0373-5605) [01652000] **5127**

MEDDELELSER OM GRNLAND. BIOSCIENCE (DK/0106-1054) [06517677] 5127, **464**

MEDDELELSER OM GRNLAND. GEOSCIENCE (DK/0106-1046) [06517659] **1358**

MEDDELELSER OM GRNLAND. MAN & SOCIETY (DK/0106-1062) [07393930] **2519**

MEDDELELSER OM KONSERVERING (DK/0106-469X) [06444292] **358**

MEDDELELSER / UNIVERSITET I OSLO, SLAVISK-BALTISK AVDELING (NO) [22530424] **3301**

MEDECIN BIOPATHOLOGISTE PARIS, LE (FR/0999-6338) [09996338] **3607**

MEDECIN DU QUEBEC (CN/0025-6692) [02062830] **3607**

MEDECIN VETERINAIRE DU QUEBEC, LE (CN/0225-9591) [06473633] **5516**

MEDECINE AERONAUTIQUE ET SPATIALE (FR/0294-0817) [08651589] **3607**

MEDECINE & CHIRURGIE DIGESTIVES (FR/0047-6412) [01641241] **3969**

MEDECINE, BIOLOGIE, ENVIRONNEMENT (BE/0302-0800) [02239823] **464**

MEDECINE D'AFRIQUE NOIRE (SG/0465-4668) [04654668] **3607**

MEDECINE DE L'HOMME PARIS (FR/0543-2243) [05432243] **3607**

MEDECINE DOUCE (FR) **3607**

MEDECINE DU SPORT (FR/0025-6722) [02584421] **3955**

MEDECINE ET ARMEES (FR/0300-4937) [01586937] 3607, **4049**

MEDECINE ET CHIRURGIE DU PIED (FR/0759-2280) [16863612] **3918**

MEDECINE ET DROIT (FR/1246-7391) 3008, **3607**

MEDECINE ET HYGIENE (SZ/0025-6749) [06268860] **3607**

MEDECINE ET MALADIES INFECTIEUSES (FR/0399-077X) [I0399077X] **3607**

MEDECINE ET NUTRITON (FR/0398-7604) [02185016] 4194, **3607**

MEDECINE FOETALE ET ECHOGRAPHIE EN GYNECOLOGIE (FR/1150-5966) [11505966] **3607**

MEDECINE HOSPITALIERE, LA **CEASED.** (FR) **3607**

MEDECINE INFANTILE, LA *CEASED.* (FR/0025-6773) [04552819] **3906**

MEDECINE MODERNE, RAPPORT SPECIAL (CN/1182-1507) [22378711] **3607**

MEDECINE NUCLEAIRE (FR) **3848**

MEDECINE SCIENCES : M/S (FR/0767-0974) [16920879] 3607, **464**

MEDECINE SCOLAIRE ET UNIVERSITAIRE (FR/0765-9547) [17346819] **4790**

MEDECINE TRADITIONNELLE CHINOISE ET ACUPUNCTURE (CN/0228-409X) [08465702] **3607**

MEDECINE TROPICALE (FR/0025-682X) [01778902] **3986**

MEDECINES NOUVELLES (QUEBEC) (CN/0838-2433) [18452617] **4314**

MEDECONOMICS (UK/0144-4271) [I01444271] **3607**

MEDEDELING (SR/1015-6941) [06006023] **1387**

MEDEDELING - INSTITUUT VOOR CULTUURTECHNIEK EN WATERHUISHOUDING (NE/0074-0411) [01634237] 5536, **178**

MEDEDELING (INSTITUUT VOOR RATIONELE SUIKERPRODUCTIE) (NE) [19365030] **178**

MEDEDELING / PROVINCIAAL ONDERZOEK- EN VOORLICHTINGSCENTRUM VOOR LAND- EN TUINBOUW, BEITEM-ROESELARE (BE) [08537562] **107**

MEDEDELINGEN DER ZITTINGEN - KONINKLIJKE ACADEMIE VOOR OVERZEESE WETTENSCHAPEN (BE/0001-4176) [01415166] **5127**

MEDEDELINGEN RIJKS GEOLOGISCHE DIENST (NE) [04831623] **1387**

MEDEDELINGEN VAN DE AFDELING LETTERKUNDE / KONINKLIJKE NEDERLANDSE AKADEMIE VAN WETENSCHAPPEN (NE) [22742972] **1835**

MEDEDELINGEN VAN DE GESCHIED- EN OUDHEIDKUNDIGE KRING VOOR LEUVEN EN OMGEVING (BE) [06212725] 274, **2697**

MEDEDELINGEN VAN DE HYDROBIOLOGISCHE VERENIGING *See* HYDROBIOLOGICAL BULLETIN **457**

MEDEDELINGEN VAN DE KONINKLIJKE ACADEMIE VOOR WETENSCHAPPEN, LETTEREN EN SCHONE KUNSTEN VAN BELGIE, KLASSE DER LETTEREN (BE) [03189847] **2850**

MEDEDELINGEN VAN DE KONINKLIJKE ACADEMIE VOOR WETENSCHAPPEN, LETTEREN EN SCHONE KUNSTEN VAN BELGIËE, KLASSE DER SCHONE KUNSTEN (BE) [01800839] **2850**

MEDEDELINGEN VAN DE NEDERLANDSE VERENIGING VOOR INTERNATIONAAL RECHT (NE) [01753617] **3132**

MEDEDELINGEN VAN DE WERKGROEP VOOR TERTIAIRE EN KWARTAIRE GEOLOGIE (NE/0165-280X) [09472179] 4228, **1387**

MEDEDELINGEN VAN HET NEDERLANDS INSTITUUT TE ROME (NE/0169-6572) [02255437] **358**

MEDEDELINGEN VAN HET P.J. MEERTENS-INSTITUUT (NE) [07985944] 3301, **2322**

MEDEDELINGEN VAN HET RIJKSSTATION VOOR LANDBOUWTECHNICK (BE/0303-9056) [I03039056] **107**

MEDEDELINGENBLAD - NEDERLANDSE VERENIGING VAN VRIENDEN VAN DE CERAMIEK *See* VORMEN UIT VUUR **2595**

MEDEDELINGEN VAN DE FACULTEIT LANDBOUWWETENSCHAPPEN, RIJKSUNIVERSITEIT, GENT (BE/0368-9697) [04689424] 107, **3694**

MEDELHAVSMUSEET (STOCKHOLM, SWEDEN) *See* BULLETIN - MEDELHAVSMUSEET **263**

MEDELINGEN - LANDBOUW-ECONOMISCH INSTITUUT (NE/0166-8129) [03235141] **107**

MEDELLIN (CK) [03691940] **5032**

MEDEQUIP *CEASED.* (AU/0253-7419) [09572873] **3607**

MEDEX (BE) **3607**

MEDI PAGES (US) **3607**

MEDI-US (CN/0382-8808) [03219729] **3607**

MEDIA (HK) [04348609] **2922**

MEDIA (CN) **2922**

●MEDIA AND FILM (US/1061-0316) [25161285] **325**

MEDIA & MARKETING EUROPE (UK) **933**

MEDIA & MARKETING EUROPE (UK) 933, **1116**

MEDIA AND METHODS (US/0025-6897) [00817432] **1900**

●MEDIA AND THE LAW (GREENWICH, CONN.) (US/1065-965X) [26820430] 3008, **1134**

MEDIA & VALUES (US/0149-6980) [04027720] 5251, **1116**

MEDIA ASIA (SI/0129-6612) [02240297] **1116**

MEDIA AUDIT. CORPUS CHRISTI, TEXAS. QUARTERLY REPORT, THE (US/0749-9868) [10476643] **4554**

MEDIA BOND INVESTOR *CEASED.* (US/1055-3541) [23157883] **906**

MEDIA BOX *CEASED.* (BE) **4852**

MEDIA BULLETIN / EUROPEAN INSTITUTE FOR THE MEDIA (UK/0267-5382) [14949238] **1116**

MEDIA BUSINESS (US/1045-716X) [20190529] **1116**

MEDIA, CULTURE & SOCIETY (UK/0163-4437) [04393549] **5251**

MEDIA CULTURE REVIEW (US) 2922, **1116**

MEDIA DATEN, FACHZEITSCHRIFTEN (GW/0170-4192) [08115514] **1116**

MEDIA DATEN. OESTERREICHS. WERBE AGENDA (GW) **933**

MEDIA DATEN. SCHWEIZ (GW) **1116**

MEDIA DATEN, ZEITSCHRIFTEN MIT AUSLANDSTEIL (GW/0170-4176) [08119288] **1116**

MEDIA DATEN ZEITUNGEN, ANZEIGENBLATTER (GW/0170-4184) [15866838] **4816**

MEDIA DEVELOPMENT (UK) [06610374] 4976, **1116**

MEDIA DIGEST (FINKSBURG) (US/0146-2091) [02880992] **1763**

MEDIA DUEMILA (IT/0393-0599) [I03930599] **1195**

MEDIA FILM (BE) **4074**

MEDIA FILM INDONESIA (IO) [09482653] **4074**

MEDIA FIVE BULLETIN, THE (CN/0713-0317) [08584604] **325**

MEDIA FORUM (IT/0394-9575) [I03949575] **762**

MEDIA FREE TIMES (CN/0316-1447) [03348793] **2538**

MEDIA GENERAL FINANCIAL SERVICES *See* INDUSTRISCOPE (RICHMOND) **901**

MEDIA GENERAL INDUSTRISCOPE *CEASED.* (US) [07548877] **906**

MEDIA GENERAL INDUSTRY SCOPE (US) **692**

MEDIA GENERAL MARKET DATAGRAPHICS (US/0279-1277) [07470524] **906**

MEDIA GUIDE INTERNATIONAL. EDITION : BUSINESS/PROFESSIONAL PUBLICATIONS (US/0164-1743) [04606299] **762**

MEDIA HISTORY DIGEST *CEASED.* (US/0195-6779) [05585069] **2922**

MEDIA IMPACT (CN) [02726556] **1116**

MEDIA INDUSTRY NEWSLETTER (US/0024-9793) [01623634] **1116**

MEDIA INFORMATION AUSTRALIA (AT/0312-9616) [03782005] 1134, **1116**

●MEDIA INFORMATION FOR THE ... IIHF WORLD JUNIOR HOCKEY CHAMPIONSHIPS / PREPARED BY THE CANADIAN HOCKEY LEAGUE (CN/1191-3991) [26497596] **4904**

MEDIA INFORMATION FOR THE ... WORLD JUNIOR HOCKEY CHAMPIONSHIPS *See* MEDIA INFORMATION FOR THE ... IIHF WORLD JUNIOR HOCKEY CHAMPIONSHIPS / PREPARED BY THE CANADIAN HOCKEY LEAGUE **4904**

MEDIA INTERNATIONAL (UK/0266-8688) [04722514] **762**

MEDIA JAYA (IO) [02554122] **1574**

MEDIA KEY SYNTHESIS (IT) **1116**

MEDIA KOMUNIKASI & INFORMASI (IO) [08182771] **845**

MEDIA LAW NOTES (US/0736-1750) [05244874] 1116, **3008**

MEDIA LAW REPORTER (US/0148-1045) [03264060] **3008**

MEDIA LETTER (CORAL GABLES, FLA.) (US/1054-6952) [22940329] **845**

MEDIA MANAGER : A PUBLICATION OF THE ASSOCIATION OF MEDIA MANAGERS, THE (CN/1188-1577) [25796325] **1116**

MEDIA MAP : THE EUROPEAN MEDIA YEARBOOK (UK) **762**

MEDIA MARKET GUIDE (NEW YORK, N.Y.) (US) [07846254] **762**

MEDIA MARKET GUIDE. TOP 100 MARKETING AREAS (US/0149-7626) [02763517] **762**

MEDIA MARKETING NEWS (BE) **933**

MEDIA MEMO (ENGLEWOOD, COLO.) *CEASED.* (US/0747-0908) [10541772] **1116**

MEDIA MERGERS & ACQUISITIONS (US/0895-4550) [16688460] 4737, **692**

MEDIA MONITOR (US) [23162866] **2922**

●MEDIA MONITOR (DANVILLE, CALIF.) (US/1061-9267) [25492866] **1116**

MEDIA MONITOR (NEW DELHI, INDIA) (II) [14245624] **1117**

MEDIA NEWS KEYS *CEASED.* (US/0033-3913) [09801048] **1117**

MEDIA PEOPLE (N.S.W./A.C.T. ED.) (AT/0815-5615) [I08155615] 1117, **1125**

MEDIA PERSPEKTIVEN (GW/0170-1754) [17064982] **1117**

MEDIA PRODUCTION (IT/1120-5784) [I11205784] **1117**

MEDIA PROFILES. THE CAREER DEVELOPMENT EDITION *CEASED.* (US/0740-1906) [09702228] **944**

MEDIA PROFILES. THE HEALTH SCIENCES EDITION (US/0740-1892) [09487423] **4790**

MEDIA REPORT TO WOMEN (US/0145-9651) [02360896] 5561, **1117**

MEDIA REVIEW (NR/1115-4489) [26494132] **1134**

MEDIA REVIEW DIGEST (US/0363-7778) [00988629] 4074, **4080**

MEDIA SCANDINAVIA (DK/0076-5821) [05149805] **4816**

MEDIA SCIENCE NEWSLETTER (US/0194-1607) [05327440] **1117**

MEDIA SELECTION (GW/0934-4217) [I09344217] **692**

MEDIA SPECTRUM (US/0731-3675) [02360304] **3230**

MEDIA SPORTS BUSINESS (US/0889-0951) [13842835] **1134**

MEDIA STUDIES JOURNAL (US/1057-7416) [24111474] **1117**

MEDIA WATCH. LOS ANGELES/ORANGE COUNTY (US/0741-2983) [10115888] **1117**

MEDIA WEEK (UK) **1117**

MEDIA WEST (CN/0228-1554) [07313877] **5251**

MEDIABOOK (IT) **762**

MEDIAEVAL SCANDINAVIA (DK/0076-5864) [01112520] **2697**

MEDIAEVAL SCANDINAVIA SUPPLEMENTS (DK/0106-102X) [07500206] **2697**

MEDIAEVAL STUDIES (CN/0076-5872) [02247258] 3410, **2697**

MEDIAEVALIA (BINGHAMTON) (US/0361-946X) [02157383] **2697**

MEDIAEVALIA HISTORICA BOHEMICA (XR/0862-979X) [25975321] **2698**

MEDIAEVALIA PHILOSOPHICA POLONORUM (PL/0076-5880) [02690867] **4352**

MEDIAEVISTIK (GW/0934-7453) [21833622] **2623**

MEDIAFILE (US/0885-4610) [09106102] 1134, **2922**

MEDIAFOKUS / TSMV (SA) [24931661] 1900, **1117**

MEDIAGUIDE (MORRISTOWN, N.J.) (US/1042-2129) [14370473] **2922**

MEDIAMARK RESEARCH BEER, WINE & LIQUOR REPORT (US) [18903349] **2369**

MEDIAMARKT (NE/0168-8235) [I01688235] **933**

MEDIAMARKT (NE) [18805222] **1117**

MEDIAMARKT. BIJLAGE (NE) [18805331] **1117**

MEDIAPLUSNEWS (IT/1120-1932) [I11201932] 5128, **692**

MEDIAPOLIS NEWS (MEDIAPOLIS, IOWA : 1984) (US/0747-3591) [10782003] **5671**

MEDIAQUEST (BOSTON, MASS.) (US/1051-7731) [22106536] **5252**

MEDIAS (FR) **3607**

MEDIAS (IT) 1117, **2922**

MEDIAS HEBDO (FR) **3607**

MEDIASCOPE. CHICAGO MARKET & MEDIA PLANNER (US/1064-5764) [26181082] **762**

MEDIASCOPE. SOUTHERN CALIFORNIA MARKET & MEDIA PLANNER (US/1064-5772) [26335318] **762**

MEDIASPOUVOIRS (FR/0762-5642) [17391638] **1117**

MEDIATEUR, LE (CN/0714-4520) [09084905] **325**

MEDIATION QUARTERLY (US/0739-4098) [09728166] **3121**

●MEDIATORS OF INFLAMMATION (UK/0962-9351) [26501563] **3607**

MEDIAWATCH — Alphabetical Title Index

MEDIAWATCH (ALEXANDRIA, VA.) (US/1053-8321) [22200576] **1117**

MEDIAWEEK (NEW YORK, N.Y.) (US/1055-176X) [23001039] **933**

MEDIAWEEK'S GUIDE TO MEDIA (US) [13763994] **1117**

MEDIC. METODOLOGIA E DIDATTICA CLINICA (US) **3607**

MEDICA JADERTINA (CI/0351-0093) [I03510093] **3607**

MEDICA (STUTTGART) (GW/0172-9160) [09714593] **3607**

MEDICAID TRENDS IN ALABAMA *See* ALABAMA MEDICAID **2872**

MEDICAL 911 (US/0275-2735) [07106715] **3725**

MEDICAL 911 SOURCEBOOK (US) **3725**

MEDICAL ABBREVIATIONS - 8600 CONVENIENCES AT THE EXPENSE OF COMMUNICATIONS AND SAFETY (US) **3607**

MEDICAL ABSTRACTS NEWSLETTER (US/0730-7810) [08090060] **3607**, **3660**

MEDICAL ADVERTISING NEWS (US/0745-0907) [08809107] **3607**, **762**

MEDICAL ALMANAC (US/0543-2480) [06476973] **3607**

MEDICAL & BIOLOGICAL ENGINEERING & COMPUTING (UK/0140-0118) [02861374] **3695**

MEDICAL AND DENTAL DEFENCE UNION OF SCOTLAND *See* ANNUAL REPORT / THE MEDICAL AND DENTAL DEFENCE UNION OF SCOTLAND LIMITED **3551**

MEDICAL AND HEALTH ANNUAL (US/0363-0366) [02917350] 4790, **3607**, **1927**

MEDICAL AND HEALTH CARE BOOKS AND SERIALS IN PRINT (US/0000-085X) [12129147] **3660**

MEDICAL AND HEALTH INFORMATION DIRECTORY (US/0749-9973) [03781345] 4790, **3608**

MEDICAL AND PEDIATRIC ONCOLOGY (US/0098-1532) [02244878] 3820, **3906**

MEDICAL AND PEDIATRIC ONCOLOGY. SUPPLEMENT (US/0740-8226) [09295526] 3821, **3906**

●MEDICAL & PHARMACEUTICAL BIOTECHNOLOGY ABSTRACTS (US/1063-1178) [25866552] **3695**, **3660**

MEDICAL AND SURGICAL DERMATOLOGY (US) **3721**

●MEDICAL & SURGICAL DERMATOLOGY : A CRITICAL GUIDE TO THE WORLD LITERATURE (US/0944-5196) [29873121] **3721**

MEDICAL AND VETERINARY ENTOMOLOGY (UK/0269-283X) [15645989] 5516, **5611**

MEDICAL ANTHROPOLOGY (US/0145-9740) [03411793] 3608, **241**

MEDICAL ANTHROPOLOGY QUARTERLY (US/0745-5194) [09250614] 3608, **241**

MEDICAL ASPECTS OF HUMAN SEXUALITY *CEASED*. (US/0025-7001) [00850501] **5188**

MEDICAL ASSISTANCE, MEDICAID (LANSING) (US/0193-9483) [03556283] 2887, **5295**

MEDICAL ASSISTANCE PROGRAM (US) [19904381] **5295**

MEDICAL ASSOCIATION OF GEORGIA *See* JOURNAL OF THE MEDICAL ASSOCIATION OF GEORGIA **3599**

MEDICAL AUDIT NEWS (UK/0959-2903) [I09592903] **748**

MEDICAL BENEFITS (US/0743-8079) [10675049] 692, **2887**

MEDICAL BOARD OF CALIFORNIA *See* ACTION REPORT / MEDICAL BOARD OF CALIFORNIA **3912**

MEDICAL BOOK GUIDE (US/0091-7877) [02242855] **3608**

MEDICAL BUSINESS JOURNAL *See* HEALTH BUSINESS **925**

MEDICAL BUSINESS JOURNAL, THE (US/0889-5538) [11319830] **3608**

MEDICAL CARE (US/0025-7079) [01606851] **3608**

MEDICAL CARE PRODUCTS (US/1066-825X) [27057766] **3788**

MEDICAL CARE REVIEW (US/0025-7087) [01604433] **3608**

MEDICAL CENTER (US/0745-4910) [08426314] **3788**

MEDICAL CHINA. NEWSFILE / CHUNG-KUO I HSUEH. NEWSFILE *SUSPENDED*. (HK) [18350087] 4790, **3608**

MEDICAL CLINICS OF NORTH AMERICA, THE (US/0025-7125) [01756980] **3608**

MEDICAL COMPUTING SERIES (US/0162-2382) [04119162] 1195, **3608**

MEDICAL CORPS INTERNATIONAL *CEASED*. (GW/0179-1826) [18306803] 4049, **3608**

MEDICAL DECISION MAKING (US/0272-989X) [06979671] 3608, **1215**

MEDICAL DEVICE & DIAGNOSTIC INDUSTRY (US/0194-844X) [05052569] **3608**

●MEDICAL DEVICE APPROVAL LETTER (US/1060-8338) [25069508] **3608**

MEDICAL DEVICE REGISTER : SUPPLEMENT (US/1068-9311) [22532497] **3608**

MEDICAL DEVICE TECHNOLOGY (US/1048-6690) [21016049] **3608**

MEDICAL DEVICE TRACKING (US) **3608**

MEDICAL DEVICES (US) [08067898] **3608**

MEDICAL DEVICES BULLETIN (US/0888-7136) [11140793] **3608**

MEDICAL DEVICES, DIAGNOSTICS & INSTRUMENTATION REPORTS (US/0163-2426) [04325889] **3608**

MEDICAL DEVICES REPORT (US/0748-4852) [10958583] 1306, **3608**

MEDICAL DEVISE REGISTER (US/0278-808X) [07822111] **3788**

MEDICAL DIGEST. CARDIOLOGIA (SP) **3708**

MEDICAL DIGEST. DERMATOLOGIA (SP) **3721**

MEDICAL DIGEST. GINECOLOGIA. OBSTETRICA (SP) **3765**

MEDICAL DIGEST. OFTALMOLOGIA (SP) **3876**

MEDICAL DIGEST. PSIQUIATRIA (SP) **3930**

MEDICAL DIGEST, THE (SA) **3608**

MEDICAL DIGEST. UROLOGIA (SP) **3991**

MEDICAL DIMENSIONS (US/0047-648X) [01535549] **3915**

MEDICAL DIRECTIONS (MERCER ISLAND, WASH.) (US/1052-0325) [22169588] **3608**

MEDICAL DIRECTORY (UK/0305-3342) [01776051] **3915**

MEDICAL DIRECTORY - COLLEGE OF PHYSICIANS AND SURGEONS OF ALBERTA (CN/0702-7826) [03519961] **3915**

MEDICAL DIRECTORY OF AUSTRALIA (AT) [05045326] **3915**

MEDICAL DIRECTORY OF AUSTRALIA, NEW ZEALAND, ETC *See* MEDICAL DIRECTORY OF AUSTRALIA **3915**

MEDICAL DIRECTORY OF NEW YORK STATE (US/0273-0561) [04673700] **3608**

MEDICAL DIRECTORY (VANCOUVER) (CN/0069-5726) [02247550] **3915**

MEDICAL DIRECTORY (WATERVILLE) (US/0145-5583) [02749313] 3008, **3915**

MEDICAL DOSIMETRY : OFFICIAL JOURNAL OF THE AMERICAN ASSOCIATION OF MEDICAL DOSIMETRISTS (US) [19743847] **3943**

MEDICAL ECONOMICS (US/0025-7206) [01756983] **3608**

MEDICAL ECONOMICS FOR SURGEONS (US/0744-4206) [08256650] **3969**

MEDICAL EDUCATION (UK/0308-0110) [02328585] **3609**

MEDICAL ELECTRONIC PRODUCTS (US/0194-147X) [03617497] **3609**

MEDICAL ELECTRONICS & EQUIPMENT NEWS (US/0361-4174) [02067378] **3609**

MEDICAL ELECTRONICS NEWS *See* MEDICAL ELECTRONICS & EQUIPMENT NEWS **3609**

MEDICAL ELECTRONICS (PITTSBURGH, PA.) (US/0149-9734) [03422818] **3609**

●MEDICAL ENGINEERING & PHYSICS (UK/1350-4533) [29693720] **3695**

MEDICAL EQUIPMENT CLASSIFIED, THE (US/0162-816X) [04440010] **3609**

MEDICAL EQUIPMENT JOURNAL OF JAPAN (JA/0025-8830) **3609**

MEDICAL ETHICS ADVISOR (US/0886-0653) [12827770] 3609, **2252**

MEDICAL EXAMINATION REVIEW BOOK. NEUROLOGY SPECIALTY BOARD REVIEW (US/0090-7073) [05693020] **3837**

MEDICAL EXAMINATION REVIEW BOOK. OBSTETRICS AND GYNECOLOGY SPECIALTY BOARD REVIEW (US/0091-4223) [05692973] **3765**

MEDICAL EXAMINATION REVIEW BOOK. PATHOLOGY SPECIALTY BOARD REVIEW (US/0090-7065) [05692887] **3896**

MEDICAL EXAMINATION REVIEW BOOK. VOLUME 11. PEDIATRICS (US/0090-7030) [05694196] **3906**

MEDICAL EXECUTIVE COMMITTEE REPORTER, THE (US/1060-3131) [24926700] **4790**

MEDICAL FOCUS (WURZBURG, GERMANY) (GW/0724-8172) [11868962] **3609**

MEDICAL FORUM (OXFORD, OXFORDSHIRE) *CEASED*. (UK/0261-3646) [09651185] **3609**

MEDICAL FRAUD AND OVERSERVICING / THE PARLIAMENT OF THE COMMONWEALTH OF AUSTRALIA, JOINT COMMITTEE OF PUBLIC ACCOUNTS (AT) [16918537] **3609**, **3008**

MEDICAL GROUP MANAGEMENT JOURNAL (US/0899-8949) [17236907] **3609**

MEDICAL GROUP MANAGEMENT MARKETERS GUIDEPOST (US/1049-880X) [21326753] **933**

MEDICAL GROUP MANAGEMENT WASHINGTON REPORT (US/1040-2306) [18357751] **3788**

MEDICAL GROUP NEWS *CEASED*. (US/0025-7265) [02254846] **3609**

MEDICAL HISTORY (UK/0025-7273) [01645179] **3609**

MEDICAL HISTORY. SUPPLEMENT (UK/0950-5571) [08294144] **3609**

MEDICAL HOTLINE *SUSPENDED*. (US/0274-614X) [06453036] **3609**

MEDICAL HUMANITIES REVIEW (US/0892-2772) [15146298] 2850, **3609**

MEDICAL HYPNOANALYSIS JOURNAL (US/0894-5098) [16122590] 3930, **4603**

MEDICAL HYPOTHESES (UK/0306-9877) [01357097] **3609**

MEDICAL IMAGING (US/0149-6727) [03512274] **3943**

MEDICAL IMAGING AND MONITORING (AT) **3609**

●MEDICAL IMAGING (PORTSMOUTH, R.I.) (US/1073-1202) [29333530] **3609**

MEDICAL IMMUNOLOGY (JA/0910-3740) [I09103740] **3674**

MEDICAL INDEXES (SI) **3609**

MEDICAL INDUSTRY ANALYSIS SERVICE (US/0275-1461) [07064368] **3609**

●MEDICAL INDUSTRY EXECUTIVE (US/1060-5193) [25014900] **3609**

MEDICAL INFORMATICS (UK/0307-7640) [03439422] 3609, **1261**

MEDICAL INNOVATION AT THE CROSSROADS (US) [22466121] **3609**

MEDICAL INTERFACE (US/0896-4831) [17164077] **3609**

MEDICAL JOURNAL (CN) [01767627] **3609**

MEDICAL JOURNAL, ARMED FORCES INDIA (II/0377-1237) [01940944] 4049, **3609**

MEDICAL JOURNAL OF AUSTRALIA (AT/0025-729X) [01640702] **3610**

MEDICAL JOURNAL OF BASRAH UNIVERSITY, THE (IQ/0253-0759) [04677294] **3610**

MEDICAL JOURNAL OF EGE UNIVERSITY (TU/1017-7698) [I10177698] **3610**

MEDICAL JOURNAL OF MALAYSIA (MY/0300-5283) [01642281] **3610**

MEDICAL JOURNAL OF ZAMBIA (ZA/0047-651X) [11429896] **3610**

MEDICAL JOURNAL - UNIVERSITY OF TORONTO (CN/0833-2207) [I08332207] **3610**

MEDICAL LABORATORY SCIENCES (UK/0308-3616) [02302078] **3610**

MEDICAL LABORATORY SCIENCES. SUPPLEMENT (UK/0950-0294) [I09500294] **3610**

MEDICAL LABORATORY SCIENTIFIC OFFICERS REGISTER, THE (UK/0263-8568) [06990241] **3610**

MEDICAL LABORATORY WORLD (UK/0140-3028) [03821780] **3610**

MEDICAL LASER BUYERS' GUIDE (US/0896-0275) [16885240] 3610, **1618**

MEDICAL LASER INDUSTRY REPORT (US/0892-3108) [15158216] 3610, **1618**

MEDICAL LASER REPORT (US) [29706095] 3610, **1618**

MEDICAL LAW LETTER FOR PHYSICIANS, SURGEONS & HEALTH PROFESSIONALS, THE (US/0098-4833) [02241354] 3610, **3008**

MEDICAL LAW REPORTS (UK/0957-9346) [I09579346] 3610, **3008**

●MEDICAL LAW REVIEW (UK/0967-0742) [28552435] 3610, **3008**

MEDICAL LETTER (SP/0025-732X) **3610**

MEDICAL LETTER HANDBOOK OF ADVERSE DRUG INTERACTIONS, THE (US/0897-5418) [12649591] **4314**

MEDICAL LETTER ON DRUGS AND THERAPEUTICS EDITION FRANCAISE, THE (SZ/0253-8512) [I02538512] **4314**

MEDICARE

MEDICAL LETTER ON DRUGS AND THERAPEUTICS (ENGLISH ED.), THE (US/0025-732X) [01756997] **4315**

MEDICAL LIABILITY MONITOR (US/0732-9636) [07874431] **3008**

MEDICAL LIABILITY REPORTER (US/0199-1833) [05695007] 3915, **3008**

MEDICAL LIBRARY ASSOCIATION See BULLETIN OF THE MEDICAL LIBRARY ASSOCIATION **3198**

MEDICAL LIBRARY ASSOCIATION See DIRECTORY **3206**

MEDICAL LIBRARY ASSOCIATION. HOSPITAL LIBRARY SECTION See NATIONAL NETWORK (DALLAS, TEX.) **3619**

●MEDICAL LITIGATION ALERT (US/1067-1269) [27140688] 3610, **3008**

MEDICAL MALPRACTICE (US) [01756182] 3610, **2887**

MEDICAL MALPRACTICE DEFENSE REPORTER, THE **CEASED.** (US/0893-8229) [15649581] 3610, **3008**

MEDICAL MALPRACTICE LAW & STRATEGY (US/0747-8925) [10939929] **3008**

MEDICAL MALPRACTICE LITIGATION (US/0277-7266) [07476382] 3915, **3008**

MEDICAL MALPRACTICE LITIGATION REPORTER (US/0882-8555) [11976937] 3915, **3008**

MEDICAL MALPRACTICE - OB/GYN LITIGATION REPORTER (US/1056-4098) [23658668] 3765, **3741**

MEDICAL MALPRACTICE PREVENTION **SUSPENDED.** (US/0885-744X) [12712679] 3610, **3008**

MEDICAL MALPRACTICE VERDICTS, SETTLEMENTS & EXPERTS (US/0888-658X) [12333368] 3915, **3008**

MEDICAL MARKETING & MEDIA (US/0025-7354) [01796746] 3610, **933**

MEDICAL MEETINGS (US/0093-1314) [02360927] **3610**

MEDICAL MEETINGS ANNUAL DIRECTORY (US) [07600073] **3610**

MEDICAL MICROBIOLOGY (UK/0739-5868) [09296993] **566**

MEDICAL MICROBIOLOGY AND IMMUNOLOGY (GW/0300-8584) [01189481] 3674, **566**

●MEDICAL MICROBIOLOGY LETTERS : AN INTERNATIONAL JOURNAL FOR RAPID COMMUNICATIONS ON ALL ASPECTS OF MEDICAL AND CLINICAL MICROBIOLOGY (SZ/1018-4627) [26585709] **566**

MEDICAL MONITOR (US/1055-5951) [23236021] **3610**

MEDICAL-MORAL NEWSLETTER, THE (US/0025-7397) [01714098] 2252, **3610**

MEDICAL NETWORKS (CN/0846-1309) [24257002] **3610**

MEDICAL NEWS REPORT (US/1054-3066) [22836933] **3610**

MEDICAL OFFICE MANAGER (US/1052-4894) [22348431] 879, **3788**

MEDICAL OFFICE REPORT (US/0895-4313) [16638246] **3610**

MEDICAL ONCOLOGY AND TUMOR PHARMACOTHERAPY (UK/0736-0118) [09073224] 4315, **3821**

MEDICAL OPINION (NEW YORK, N.Y.) (US/0090-1474) [04597638] **3610**

●MEDICAL OUTCOMES & GUIDELINES ALERT (US/1067-4195) [27206541] **3610**

MEDICAL OUTCOMES & GUIDELINES SOURCEBOOK (US) **3610**

MEDICAL PHYSICS HANDBOOKS (UK/0143-0203) [06317691] 3610, **4412**

MEDICAL PHYSICS (LANCASTER) (US/0094-2405) [01794379] 3610, **4412**

MEDICAL PHYSICS MONOGRAPH (US/0163-1802) [04411670] 3611, **4412**

MEDICAL POST, THE (CN/0025-7435) [01988714] **3611**

MEDICAL PRACTICE FOR TRIAL LAWYERS (US) **3008**

●MEDICAL PRACTICE MANAGEMENT NEWS (US/1069-1944) [27952198] **3788**

MEDICAL PRINCIPLES AND PRACTICE (SZ/1011-7571) [19461661] **3611**

MEDICAL PROBLEMS OF PERFORMING ARTISTS (US/0885-1158) [12567861] **3611**

MEDICAL PRODUCT MANUFACTURING NEWS (US/0893-6250) [15604122] **3611**

MEDICAL PRODUCTS MARKETERS DIRECTORY (US/0275-4940) [07121675] **3695**

MEDICAL PRODUCTS SALES (US/0279-4802) [07905243] **3611**

MEDICAL PROGRESS (HONG KONG) (HK/0377-9963) [02887211] **4315**

MEDICAL PROGRESS THROUGH TECHNOLOGY (NE/0047-6552) [02263977] **3695**

MEDICAL PSYCHOTHERAPY **CEASED.** (CN/0835-3069) [18047419] 4603, **3611**

MEDICAL RADIOGRAPHY AND PHOTOGRAPHY **CEASED.** (US/0025-746X) [01757008] **3943**

●MEDICAL RECORD RISKS, CLAIMS & LITIGATION (US/1061-4192) [25305531] 3788, **3008**

MEDICAL RECORDS BRIEFING (US/1052-4924) [17011224] **3788**

MEDICAL REFERENCE SERVICES QUARTERLY (US/0276-3869) [07374943] 3611, **3230**

MEDICAL REGISTER, THE (UK) [06218870] **3915**

MEDICAL REMARKETER, THE (US/0887-0691) [13108203] **1618**

MEDICAL RESEARCH COUNCIL ANNUAL REPORT (UK/0141-2256) [11980785] **3611**

MEDICAL RESEARCH COUNCIL (CANADA) See DECISIONS - MEDICAL RESEARCH COUNCIL (CANADA) **3571**

MEDICAL RESEARCH COUNCIL (CANADA) See NEWSLETTER - MEDICAL RESEARCH COUNCIL (OTTAWA) **3621**

MEDICAL RESEARCH COUNCIL (CANADA) See REPORT OF THE PRESIDENT - MEDICAL RESEARCH COUNCIL (OTTAWA) **3633**

MEDICAL RESEARCH COUNCIL (CANADA) See REPORT - MEDICAL RESEARCH COUNCIL **3633**

MEDICAL RESEARCH COUNCIL (CANADA) See GRANTS AND AWARDS GUIDE - MEDICAL RESEARCH COUNCIL **3579**

MEDICAL RESEARCH COUNCIL (GREAT BRITAIN) See MEDICAL RESEARCH COUNCIL HANDBOOK **3611**

MEDICAL RESEARCH COUNCIL (GREAT BRITAIN) See MEDICAL RESEARCH COUNCIL ANNUAL REPORT **3611**

MEDICAL RESEARCH COUNCIL (GT. BRIT.). LABORATORY ANIMALS CENTRE See LAC NEWS **5515**

MEDICAL RESEARCH COUNCIL HANDBOOK (UK/0309-0132) [06280985] **3611**

MEDICAL RESEARCH COUNCIL OF CANADA See REPORT OF THE PRESIDENT - MEDICAL RESEARCH COUNCIL OF CANADA **3633**

MEDICAL RESEARCH FUNDING BULLETIN (US) [03227473] **3611**

MEDICAL RESEARCH FUNDING NEWS **CEASED.** (US/1052-9152) [22409817] **3611**

MEDICAL RESEARCH IN THE VETERANS' ADMINISTRATION (US/0083-3541) [02242278] **3611**

MEDICAL RESEARCH INDEX (UK) [06621057] **3611**

MEDICAL REVIEW OF MEETINGS & LISTINGS, THE (CN/1186-2858) [24860210] **3611**

MEDICAL ROUNDS **CEASED.** (US/0892-3736) [15172711] **3611**

MEDICAL SCHOOL ADMISSION REQUIREMENTS, UNITED STATES AND CANADA (US/0738-6060) [03600521] 3611, **1835**

MEDICAL SCIENCE RESEARCH (UK/0269-8951) [15617763] **3611**

MEDICAL SCIENCES BULLETIN (US/0199-4905) [05934162] 3611, **4315**

MEDICAL SCIENCES INTERNATIONAL WHO'S WHO (UK) [16940478] **3915**

MEDICAL SECTION PROCEEDINGS : THE ... ANNUAL MEETING OF THE MEDICAL SECTION OF THE AMERICAN COUNCIL OF LIFE INSURANCE (US) [11143450] **2888**

MEDICAL SERIES, BULLETIN (US/0073-7518) [02262285] **3611**

MEDICAL SOCIETY OF LONDON See TRANSACTIONS OF THE MEDICAL SOCIETY **3647**

●MEDICAL SOFTWARE REVIEWS (US/1059-907X) [24807606] **3611**

MEDICAL STAFF BRIEFING (US) 3915, **3788**

MEDICAL STAFF COUNSELOR, THE **CEASED.** (US/0899-8981) [15996820] **3915**

MEDICAL STAFF DIRECTORY (US/0730-1448) [06959467] 3915, **1330**

MEDICAL STAFF FORUM (US/0735-2514) [08901033] **3788**

MEDICAL STAFF LEADER (US/1041-6501) [18819899] **3611**

MEDICAL STUDENT (DARIEN) (US/0360-7623) [01931884] **3611**

MEDICAL SUBJECT HEADINGS (US/0565-811X) [02482950] **3230**

MEDICAL SUBJECT HEADINGS. ANNOTATED ALPHABETIC LIST (US/0147-5711) [06392946] 3611, **3230**

MEDICAL SUBJECT HEADINGS. SUPPLEMENTARY CHEMICAL RECORDS (US/0891-3994) [09379687] 3611, **3230**

MEDICAL SUBJECT HEADINGS. TREE ANNOTATIONS (US/0161-3278) [03864224] **3611**

MEDICAL SUBJECT HEADINGS. TREE STRUCTURES (US/0147-099X) [01778210] 3611, **3230**

●MEDICAL SUPPLY CATALOG / U.S. PUBLIC HEALTH SERVICE (US) [26321690] **3611**

MEDICAL TEACHER (UK/0142-159X) [05133070] 1763, **3611**

MEDICAL TECHNOLOGIST AND SCIENTIST, THE **CEASED.** (UK/0309-2666) [02324504] **3612**

●MEDICAL TECHNOLOGISTS AND TECHNICIANS CAREER DIRECTORY (US/1070-7271) [28513973] **3915**

MEDICAL TECHNOLOGY (US/0899-3092) [18075708] **3612**

MEDICAL TECHNOLOGY STOCK LETTER (US/1065-996X) [17397281] 3695, **906**

MEDICAL TECHNOLOGY (TOKYO. 1973) (JA/0389-1887) [01083320] 5128, **3612**

MEDICAL TEXTILES (NE/0266-2078) [12862051] 5354, **3612**

●MEDICAL TOXICOLOGY (US) [28689663] **3982**

MEDICAL TRIAL TECHNIQUE QUARTERLY (US/0025-7591) [01757032] **3742**

MEDICAL TRIAL TECHNIQUE QUARTERLY ANNUAL (US/0161-3251) [03875777] **3009**

MEDICAL TRIBUNE (1980) (US/0279-9340) [07367813] **3612**

●MEDICAL TRIBUNE FOR THE FAMILY PHYSICIAN (US) [29264039] **3612**

MEDICAL TRIBUNE FOR THE INTERNIST & CARDIOLOGIST (US) [29264107] **3612**

MEDICAL TRIBUNE. GERMAN EDITION (GW) **3612**

MEDICAL TRIBUNE. MICROFORM (US/0279-9340) [13663594] **3612**

MEDICAL TRIBUNE NEW YORK See MEDICAL TRIBUNE FOR THE INTERNIST & CARDIOLOGIST **3612**

MEDICAL TRIBUNE (NEW YORK, N.Y. : 1980) See MEDICAL TRIBUNE FOR THE FAMILY PHYSICIAN **3612**

MEDICAL UPDATE (US) [06234989] **3612**

MEDICAL UPDATE (CHICAGO, ILL.) (US/0732-0183) [08102910] **3612**

MEDICAL USES OF STATISTICS (US) 3612, **3660**

●MEDICAL UTILIZATION MANAGEMENT (US) [29700175] **3612**

MEDICAL UTILIZATION REVIEW See MEDICAL UTILIZATION MANAGEMENT **3612**

MEDICAL UTILIZATION REVIEW DIRECTORY (US/1050-9984) [21743345] **3612**

●MEDICAL WASTE ANALYST (US/1072-6039) [29045228] **3612**

MEDICAL WASTE MANAGEMENT See OCCUPATIONAL HEALTH AND SAFETY HEALTH FACILITIES REPORT **2866**

MEDICAL WASTE MONITOR (US/1058-2711) [24261356] **3612**

MEDICAL WASTE NEWS (US/1048-4493) [20950157] 2236, **3612**

MEDICAL WORLD AND NEWSLETTER (UK) **3612**

MEDICAL WORLD ANNUAL (US) [01588201] **3612**

MEDICAL WORLD (LONDON, ENGLAND : 1969) (UK) [10063718] **3612**

MEDICAL WORLD MAGAZINE (CN/0828-3575) [13778260] **3612**

MEDICAL WORLD NEWS **SUSPENDED.** (US/0025-763X) [01757036] 464, **3612**

MEDICAL WORLD NEWS REVIEW (US/0094-5811) [01794038] **3612**

MEDICAMENTOS DE ACTUALIDAD (SP/0025-7656) [01714032] **4315**

MEDICAMENTS D'AUJOURD'HUI (CN/0702-8970) [03948051] **4315**

MEDICAMUNDI **CEASED.** (US/0025-7664) [01778926] **3612**

MEDICARE ADVISOR (US/0897-9634) [17682542] **5295**

MEDICARE AND MEDICAID DATA BOOK, THE (US/0743-5959) [08471985] 2888, **5295**

●MEDICARE AND MEDICAID LAW BULLETIN (US/1068-1019) [27425387] 5295, **2888**

MEDICARE AND MEDICAID LAW REPORTER **CEASED.** (US/1060-5355) [25031778] 5295, **3009**

MEDICARE COMPLIANCE ALERT (US/1047-1863) [20620710] 1690, **2888**

MEDICARE — Alphabetical Title Index

MEDICARE COVERAGE ISSUES MANUAL (US) [24663471] **5295**

MEDICARE EXPLAINED (US/0733-4672) [07224745] 5295, **2888**

MEDICARE, HEALTH INSURANCE FOR THE AGED AND DISABLED. SUMMARY-UTILIZATION AND REIMBURSEMENT BY PERSON (US/0730-143X) [07888092] 2888, **5295**

MEDICARE HOME HEALTH AGENCY MANUAL (US) [25984324] **5296**

MEDICARE HOSPITAL MANUAL (US) [24663818] 3788, **2888**

MEDICARE MANAGER (US/1068-2465) [27482407] **2888**

MEDICARE/MEDICAID NURSING HOME INFORMATION. NEW JERSEY (US) [19861330] **3788**

MEDICARE-MEMORANDUM (OUTPATIENT CLINIC ED.) (US/0896-4815) [17164381] 2888, **5296**

MEDICARE PART A INTERMEDIARY MANUAL. PART 3, CLAIMS PROCESS, HCFA PUBLICATION, 13 3 (US) [29234085] **5296**

MEDICARE PROGRAM STATISTICS. SELECTED STATE DATA / HEALTH CARE FINANCING ADMINISTRATION (US) [12932257] 5296, **5266**

MEDICARE PROVIDER REIMBURSEMENT MANUAL (US) [26060278] **5296**

MEDICARE REIBURSEMENT MANUAL FOR CLINICAL LABORATORIES (US) 4664, **3612**

MEDICARE SKILLED NURSING FACILITY MANUAL (US) [28776556] **5296**

MEDICARE, USE OF SKILLED NURSING FACILITIES (US/0730-7942) [06493792] 3861, **2888**

MEDICASSETTE. RADIOLOGY *CEASED*. (US/0887-0675) [15517193] **3943**

MEDICINA (JA/0025-7699) [10427963] **3612**

MEDICINA & HISTORIA (SP/0300-8169) [10333341] **3612**

MEDICINA (BUENOS AIRES) (AG/0025-7680) [01778928] **3613**

MEDICINA CLINICA (SP/0025-7753) [01778929] **3613**

MEDICINA CUTANEA IBERO-LATINO-AMERICANA (PO/0210-5187) [01924559] **3721**

MEDICINA DE EMPRESA (SP) **3613**

MEDICINA DE POSTGRADO *CEASED*. (MX/0300-3833) [01425354] **3613**

MEDICINA DE REHABILITACION *SUSPENDED*. (SP/0214-8714) [02148714] **4381**

MEDICINA DEL LAVORO (IT/0025-7818) [01778931] **3613**

MEDICINA DELLO SPORT (IT) [05936665] **3955**

MEDICINA DEMOCRATICA (IT) **3613**

MEDICINA DI LABORATORIO, LA (IT) **3613**

MEDICINA E INFORMATICA (IT/1120-3773) [I11203773] **3613**

MEDICINA E MORALE (IT/0025-7834) [13116282] 2252, **3613**

MEDICINA GERIATRICA (IT/0391-4844) [10706680] **3754**

MEDICINA INTEGRAL (SP) **3613**

MEDICINA INTENSIVA / SOCIEDAD ESPANOLA DE MEDICINA INTENSIVA Y UNIDADES CORONARIAS (SP/0210-5691) [25865090] **3613**

MEDICINA INTERNA (BUCHAREST, ROMANIA : 1991) (RM) **3799**

MEDICINA MILITAR (SP) **3613**

MEDICINA MODERNA (IT) **3613**

MEDICINA OGGI (IT/0392-4548) [I03924548] **3613**

MEDICINA ORTOPEDICA (IT) **3883**

MEDICINA OSPEDALIERA ROMANA (IT/0391-7231) [07371869] **3613**

MEDICINA PSICOSOMATICA (IT/0025-7893) [03418927] **3613**

MEDICINA RIBEIRAO PRETO (BL/0076-6046) [I00766046] **3613**

MEDICINA SOCIALE (IT/0025-7915) [I00257915] **3613**

MEDICINA TERMALE E CLIMATOLOGIA *CEASED*. (IT/0580-9320) [01778936] **3613**

MEDICINA TORACICA (IT) [19485180] **3950**

●MEDICINA VETERINARA SI CRESTEREA ANIMALELOR (RM) [27335739] **5516**

MEDICINA VETERINARIA (BARCELONA, SPAIN) (SP/0212-8292) [11648296] **5516**

MEDICINA Y CIRUGIA DE GUERRA *See* REVISTA DE SANIDAD MILITAR **3635**

MEDICINA Y ETICA (MX/0188-5022) [I01885022] **2252**

MEDICINA Y SEGURIDAD DEL TRABAJO (SP/0465-546X) [01811542] **2865**

MEDICINAL & AROMATIC PLANTS ABSTRACTS (II/0250-4367) [05795734] **517**

MEDICINAL CHEMISTRY RESEARCH (US/1054-2523) [22831625] 985, **4315**

MEDICINAL PLANTS OF THE WORLD (US) [10642742] **517**

MEDICINAL RESEARCH (US/0076-6062) [01757041] **4315**

MEDICINAL RESEARCH REVIEWS (US/0198-6325) [06190031] **4315**

MEDICINE (US) [04448376] **3799**

MEDICINE & BIOLOGY *See* NTIS ALERT. MEDICINE & BIOLOGY **3623**

MEDICINE AND GLOBAL SOCIETY (UK) **3613**

MEDICINE AND GLOBAL SURVIVAL (UK) 3613, **4790**

MEDICINE AND LAW (GW/0723-1393) [08755784] **3742**

MEDICINE AND SCIENCE IN SPORTS AND EXERCISE (US/0195-9131) [05700789] **3955**

MEDICINE AND SPORT SCIENCE (SZ/0254-5020) [10636865] **3955**

MEDICINE AND WAR (UK/0748-8009) [11011172] 4528, **3613**

MEDICINE (BALTIMORE) (US/0025-7974) [01716220] **3613**

MEDICINE BIOLOGIE ENVIRONMENT (BE) 464, **3613**

MEDICINE D'AFRIQUE NOIRE (FR) [07558076] **3613**

MEDICINE DIGEST (UK) [04092341] **3613**

MEDICINE DIGEST. ASIA (HK) [29427566] **3613**

●MEDICINE, EXERCISE, NUTRITION, AND HEALTH (US/1057-9354) [24171251] 4194, **3613**

MEDICINE IN PRACTICE (UK/0260-2342) [11472418] **3738**

MEDICINE INTERNATIONAL. THE MONTHLY ADD-ON JOURNAL. UK EDITION (UK/0144-0403) [07810579] **3613**

MEDICINE INTERNATIONAL. THE QUARTERLY ADD-ON JOURNAL (UK/0144-0411) [I01440411] **3613**

●MEDICINE (NEW YORK, N.Y. 1993) (US/1066-4149) [26943658] **3614**

MEDICINE NORTH AMERICA (CN/0225-3895) [06688733] **3614**

MEDICINE, SCIENCE, AND THE LAW (UK/0025-8024) [01757043] **3742**

MEDICINE (SPANISH EDITION) (SP) **3614**

MEDICINE. TRATADO DE MEDICINA INTERNA (SP) **3799**

MEDICINSK FDSELS- OG MISDANNELSESSTATISTIK / SUNDHEDSSTYRELSEN (DK/0904-1966) [19637812] **3765**

MEDICINSK TEKNIK (SW/0346-542X) [I0346542X] **3614**

MEDICINSKA ISTRAZIVANJA. SUPPLEMENTUM (YU/0301-083X) [01353482] **3614**

MEDICINSKAJA PARAZITOLOGIJA I PARAZITARNYE BOLEZNI (RU/0025-8326) [01757056] **3986**

MEDICINSKAJA RADIOLOGIJA (RU/0025-8334) [01757057] **3943**

MEDICINSKAJA SESTRA (RU/0025-8342) [01778942] **3861**

MEDICINSKAJA TEHNIKA (RU/0025-8075) [07600175] **3614**

MEDICINSKI ANALI (CI/0352-602X) [16239175] **3614**

MEDICINSKI CASOPIS (YU/0350-1221) [01354356] **3614**

MEDICINSKI PREGLED (YU/0025-8105) [02943611] **3614**

MEDICINSKI RAZGLEDI (XV/0025-8121) [02943399] **3614**

MEDICO D'ITALIA (IT) **3614**

MEDICO E BAMBINO (IT) [18713421] **3906**

MEDICO E PAZIENTE (IT/0390-0347) [03900347] **3614**

MEDICO INTERAMERICANO (US/0278-9779) [07960819] 3969, **3614**

MEDICO-LEGAL JOURNAL, THE (UK/0025-8172) [01640970] **3742**

MEDICO MADRID, EL (SP/0214-6363) [I02146363] **3614**

MEDICOLEGAL-GRAM / OFFICE OF THE CHIEF MEDICAL EXAMINER (US) [07498974] **3742**

MEDICOLEGAL LIBRARY (GW/0176-7151) [11131618] **3742**

MEDICOM (NR/0253-0961) [07239335] **3614**

MEDICOR NEWS (HU/0209-732X) [03183048] **3944**

MEDICOS IMPRESOS *See* TARIFAS Y DATOS: MEDIOS IMPRESOS **767**

MEDICUS *CEASED*. (IT) **3614**

MEDIE MENSILI ED ANNUALE DELLE QUOTAZIONI RIPORTATE NEI LISTINI SETTIMANALI DEI PREZZI ALL'INGROSSO SULLA PIAZZA DI MILANO PER L'ANNO (IT) [20500699] **1593**

MEDIEN-BULLETIN (GW/0723-2128) [I07232128] **1134**

MEDIEN + ERZIEHUNG (GW/0341-6860) [07985950] **1117**

MEDIEN IN FORSCHUNG + UNTERRICHT. SERIE A (GW) [11759172] **3410**

MEDIEN KONKRET (GW/0931-9808) [I09319808] **1117**

MEDIENSPIEGEL (GW/0179-5724) [I01795724] **2490**

MEDIENWISSENSCHAFT, REZENSIONEN (GW/0176-4241) [13310994] **1117**

MEDIEVAL ACADEMY BOOKS (US) [18607470] **3410**

●MEDIEVAL AND EARLY MODERN MYSTICISM (US/1056-7917) [23853575] **4242**

MEDIEVAL AND LATER POTTERY IN WALES : BULLETIN OF THE WELSH MEDIEVAL POTTERY RESEARCH GROUP (UK) [12843002] **2592**

MEDIEVAL & RENAISSANCE DRAMA IN ENGLAND (US/0731-3403) [08162140] 3347, **5366**

MEDIEVAL AND RENAISSANCE MONOGRAPH SERIES (US/0892-9718) [07943396] **2698**

MEDIEVAL AND RENAISSANCE STUDIES (DURHAM) (US/0584-4150) [02461535] **2698**

MEDIEVAL & RENAISSANCE TEXTS AND STUDIES (US) [09494747] **2698**

MEDIEVAL ARCHAEOLOGY (UK/0076-6097) [01607565] 2698, **274**

MEDIEVAL CERAMICS (UK) [09114008] **2592**

●MEDIEVAL ENCOUNTERS (NE/1380-7854) **2623**

MEDIEVAL ENGLISH THEATRE (UK/0143-3784) [06466204] **5366**

MEDIEVAL ENGLISH THEATRE MODERN SPELLING TEXTS (UK/0264-2786) [I02642786] **3301**

MEDIEVAL FOLKLORE (US/1048-857X) [21068191] **2322**

MEDIEVAL HISTORY (UK/0960-0752) [23602354] **2698**

MEDIEVAL IBERIAN PENINSULA. TEXTS AND STUDIES (NE/0076-6100) [06257962] **2698**

MEDIEVAL PHILOSOPHY AND THEOLOGY (US/1057-0608) [23926124] 4976, **4352**

MEDIEVAL PROSOPOGRAPHY (US/0198-9405) [06285170] **2698**

MEDIEVAL SERMON STUDIES NEWSLETTER (UK/0140-1211) [04968730] **4976**

MEDIEVALES (FR/0751-2708) [12673123] **2623**

MEDIEVALIA ET HUMANISTICA (US/0076-6127) [01587726] 1078, **2698**

MEDIEVALIA / INSTITUTO UNIVERSITARIO DE ESTUDIOS MEDIEVALES (SP/0211-3473) [09022522] **2698**

MEDIFACTS [SOUND RECORDING] (CN/0317-7017) [08581161] **3738**

MEDIFAX ROMA (IT/1121-2810) [I11212810] **3614**

MEDIFO *CEASED*. (NE) **3614**

MEDIGRAM (EAST LANSING, MICH. : 1985) (US/8750-9741) [11612687] 3915, **3614**

MEDIGUIDE TO CARDIOLOGY (US/0738-2979) [09587411] **3708**

●MEDIGUIDE TO DEPRESSION IN PRIMARY CARE (US/1065-0725) [26506284] **3614**

MEDIGUIDE TO INFECTIOUS DISEASES (US/0737-6030) [08291395] **3715**

MEDIGUIDE TO OB/GYN (US/0738-2987) [09142309] **3765**

MEDIGUIDE TO ONCOLOGY (US/0278-2480) [07643151] **3821**

MEDIGUIDE TO ORTHOPAEDICS (US/0737-6073) [09142534] **3883**

MEDIGUIDE TO PAIN (US/0738-2995) [09142680] **3614**

MEDIGUIDE TO PEDIATRICS (US/0897-9774) [17681137] **3906**

MEDIGUIDE TO RHEUMATOLOGY (US/0738-3002) [09586993] **3806**

MEDIGUIDE TO SKIN CONDITIONS (US/0737-6081) [08527025] **3722**

MEDIGUIDE TO SPECIAL PROBLEMS IN OPHTHALMOLOGY (US/1056-330X) [23664169] **3876**

MEDIKA (IO/0126-0901) [03219187] 3614, **4315**

MEDIKO-BIOLOGICESKAJA INFORMACIJA (BU/0204-6725) [11271202] 464, **3614**

MEDIKO-BIOLOGICNI PROBLEMI (BU/0323-9802) [01249672] 3614, **464**

MEDIKON (BE/0304-4823) [04406087] **3614**

MEDILAG (NR) [01778941] **3614**

MEDIMARK RESEARCH MAGAZINE QUALITATIVE AUDIENCES REPORT (US/1048-3225) [18902662] **933**

MEDIMARK RESEARCH MAGAZINE TOTAL AUDIENCES REPORT (US/1048-3217) [18903030] **933**

MEDINA COUNTY GAZETTE (MEDINA, OHIO : 1982) (US) [10651586] **5729**

MEDINA COUNTY STORY (US/0884-8068) [12412796] **2460**

MEDIO AMBIENTE Y URBANIZACION (AG) [18392094] **2828**

MEDIOEVO (IT/0391-2566) [04486266] **4352**

MEDIOEVO E RINASCIMENTO : ANNUARIO DEL DIPARTIMENTO DI STUDI SUL MEDIOEVO E IL RINASCIMENTO DELL'UNIVERSITA DI FIRENZE (IT/0394-7858) [17830990] **2698**

MEDIOEVO LATINO (IT) [08045004] 2623, **2635**

MEDIOEVO ROMANZO (IT/0390-0711) [02245190] **3301**

MEDIOS AUDIO-VISUALES (SP) [04028682] 5317, **4074**

MEDIOS PUBLICITARIOS MEXICANOS; TARIFAS E INFORMACION *CEASED*. (US) [06687619] **762**

MEDIQUIZ ANNUAL (US/0363-3926) [02379750] **3614**

MEDISCH CONTACT (NE) **3614**

MEDISCH-FARMACEUTISCHE MEDEDELINGEN (NE/0168-7670) [I01687670] **4315**

MEDISCH JAAR, HET (NE/0167-6601) [05536362] **3614**

MEDISCHE INSTRUMENTEN- EN ORTHOPEDISCHE ARTIKELENINDUSTRIE, TANDTECHNISCHE WERKPLAATSEN / CENTRAAL BUREAU VOOR DE STATISTIEK, HOOFDAFDELING STATISTIEDEN VAN INDUSTRIE EN BOUWNIJVERHEID (NE/0924-2554) [10640219] **3614**

MEDISTAT / WORLD MEDICAL MARKET ANALYSIS (UK) **3614**

MEDIT (IT/1120-6403) [I11206403] **107**

MEDITERRANEA (SP) [03701026] 464, **5591**

MEDITERRANEAN HISTORICAL REVIEW (UK) [14124152] **2698**

MEDITERRANEAN JOURNAL OF SOCIAL PSYCHIATRY / MEDITERRANEAN SOCIOPSYCHIATRIC ASSOCIATION (YU/0351-4501) [19668192] 4603, **3930**

MEDITERRANEAN LANGUAGE REVIEW (GW/0724-7567) [10762334] **3301**

MEDITERRANEAN QUARTERLY (US/1047-4552) [20704333] **4528**

MEDITERRANEAN STUDIES (MM) [05544411] **2850**

MEDITERRANEE (FR/0025-8296) [01757055] **2698**

MEDITERRANEE MEDICALE (FR/0302-9263) [04585506] **3614**

MEDITSINSKA TEKHNIKA / MA-TSENTR ZA NAUCHNA INFORMATSIIA PO MEDITSINA I ZDRAVEOPAZVANE S TSENTRALNA MEDITSINSKA BIBLIOTEKA (BU/0324-1440) [10417777] **3614**

MEDITSINSKAJA GAZETA (RU/0025-8318) [06285939] **4790**

●MEDITSINSKAIA POMOSHCH / MEDICAL CARE / MINISTERSTVO ZDRAVOOKHRANENIA RF (RU/0869-7760) [30454443] **3614**

MEDITSINSKII ZHURNAL UZBEKISTANA (UZ/0025-830X) [09614865] **3614**

MEDIUM AEVUM (UK/0025-8385) [01607862] 3410, 2698, **3301**

MEDIUM AEVUM (MUNICH) (GW/0543-3533) [01757060] **3347**

MEDIUM (BOTHELL, WASH.) (US/0889-0773) [05421462] **3230**

MEDIUM COMPANIES OF EUROPE (UK/0960-1449) [22496296] **692**

MEDIUM (FRANKFURT) (GW/0025-8350) [05330335] 5209, **1117**

MEDIUM (SASKATOON) (CN/0025-8377) [02065497] **1763**

MEDIUM-TERM CORPORATE TOTAL RATE-OF-RETURN INDEXES (US/0749-5404) [10164662] **797**

MEDIUM-TERM OUTLOOK *See* MEDIUM-TERM REVIEW / THE ECONOMIC AND SOCIAL RESEARCH INSTITUTE **1574**

MEDIUM-TERM PLANNING GUIDELINES (CN/0828-4334) [11527000] **1950**

●MEDIUM-TERM REVIEW / THE ECONOMIC AND SOCIAL RESEARCH INSTITUTE (IE/0790-9470) [17868008] **1574**

MEDIZIN AKTUELL (GW/0323-5386) [02832324] **3615**

MEDIZIN, GESELLSCHAFT, UND GESCHICHTE : JAHRBUCH DES INSTITUTS FUER GESCHICHTE DER MEDIZIN DER ROBERT BOSCH STIFTUNG (GW/0939-351X) [26653282] 4315, **3615**

MEDIZIN IN RECHT UND ETHIK (GW/0176-4284) [10104417] **3742**

MEDIZIN IN WEST-BERLIN, DIE (GW) [03474455] **3915**

MEDIZIN OHNE NEBENWIRKUNGEN (GW/0939-6292) [09396292] **4315**

MEDIZIN UND GESELLSCHAFT (GW/0323-6153) [04565860] **3615**

MEDIZINHISTORISCHES JOURNAL (GW/0025-8431) [01641794] **3615**

MEDIZINISCHE KLINIK (MUNCHEN. 1983) (GW/0723-5003) [09718705] **3615**

MEDIZINISCHE KLINIK. SUPPLEMENT (GW) [14760976] **3615**

MEDIZINISCHE LANDERKUNDE (GW/0076-6151) [01777784] **3615**

MEDIZINISCHE MONATSSCHRIFT FUER PHARMAZEUTEN (GW/0342-9601) [04138421] **4315**

MEDIZINISCHE MONATSSCHRIFT (STUTTGART) (GW/0025-8474) [01757064] **3615**

MEDIZINISCHE WELT (GW/0025-8512) [01696274] **3615**

MEDIZINPRODUKTE JOURNAL (GW/0944-6885) **3615**

MEDIZINRECHT (GW/0723-8886) [10111258] **3742**

MEDIZINTECHNIK (STUTTGART) (GW/0344-9416) [04450102] **3615**

MEDJUNARODNA POLITIKA (CI) **4481**

MEDLARS (US) 464, **3615**

MEDLEMSFORTECKNING (SW) [C1791909] **3410**

MEDLINE KNOWLEDGE FINDER. / MODEL UM-11 (US) 3230, **3615**

MEDLINE KNOWLEDGE FINDER. UM-5 (US) 3230, **3615**

MEDLINE [COMPUTER FILE] (US) [22289463] 3230, **3615**

MEDOC *CEASED*. (US/0097-9732) [01375549] 3615, **3660**

MEDPRO MONTH (US) [25130036] **3789**

MEDSTAT REPORT *CEASED*. (US) **3661**

MEDSUBHYP (FR/0294-1007) [I02941007] **3615**

●MEDSURG NURSING : OFFICIAL JOURNAL OF THE ACADEMY OF MEDICAL- SURGICAL NURSES (US) [27184946] **3969**

MEDTRONIC NEWS (US) **3708**

MEDUCATION INTERNATIONAL *See* PHYSIFAX **3627**

MEDVIN P-H-C- TRADELETTER (US) 692, **2607**

MEDWAY VALLEY NEWS (1978) (CN/0711-1754) [10032080] **2198**

MEDWELT COMPACT (GW/0941-682X) [25790982] **3615**

MEDYCYNA DOSWIADCZALNA I MIKROBIOLOGIA (PL/0025-8601) [01930736] **3615**

MEDYCYNA PRACY (PL/0465-5893) [04023543] **3615**

MEDYCYNA WETERYNARYJNA (PL/0025-8628) [04451841] **5516**

MEDYK WARSZAWA (PL/0867-3055) [I08673055] **3615**

MEED (UK/0047-7230) [14363775] **1574**

MEEKER HERALD, THE (US) [11154129] **5643**

MEELFABRIEKEN, GORT- EN RIJSTPELLERIJEN E.D. / CENTRAAL BUREAU VOOR DE STATISTIEK, HOOFDAFDELING STATISTEIKEN VAN INDUSTRIE EN BOUWNIJVERHEID (NE/0168-5066) [10420744] **202**

MEER & YACHTEN (FR) **594**

MEERESFORSCHUNG *CEASED*. (GW/0341-6836) [04048873] **1452**

MEERESTECHNIK (GW/0025-8644) [05430215] **2093**

MEESFAX (CY) **4264**

MEET- EN REGELAPPARATEN- EN OVERIGE INSTRUMENTENINDUSTRIE / CENTRAAL BUREAU VOOR DE STATISTIEK, HOOFDAFDELING STATISTIEKEN VAN INDUSTRIE EN BOUWNIJVERHEID (NE) [11884303] **4031**

MEET THE PRESS : AMERICA'S PRESS CONFERENCE OF THE AIR (US/0543-3754) [01757068] **2746**

MEETING - ASSOCIATION OF ISLAND MARINE LABORATORIES OF THE CARIBBEAN (US) [04241228] **1452**

MEETING - INTER-AFRICAN CONFERENCE ON RURAL WELFARE (US/0538-2793) [06351704] **5296**

MEETING INVITATION, ANNUAL REPORT, HISTORICAL NOTES / INSTITUTE FOR REWRITING INDIAN HISTORY (II) [07777483] **2769**

MEETING MANAGER, THE (US/8750-7218) [11308876] **692**

MEETING NEWS (US/0145-630X) [02762963] **692**

MEETING OF THE TECHNICAL COMMITTEE - CINTERFOR (UY) [03146531] **1690**

MEETING PAPERS ON MICROFICHE (US) [12849721] **2015**

MEETING PLANNERS ALERT (US/0743-3832) [10569847] **944**

●MEETING REPORTS, CARDIOVASCULAR (US/1063-2468) [25936634] **3708**

MEETINGS AND CONVENTIONS (US/0025-8652) [09715788] **692**

MEETINGS & INCENTIVE TRAVEL (CN/0225-8285) [06473912] **5484**

MEETINGS CANADA (CN/0226-7500) [06512223] **5233**

MEETINGS INMED (US/1046-6983) [20495298] **3615**

MEETINGS MONTHLY, NEWS BULLETIN (CN/0841-9663) [19105447] **5484**

MEETINGS (NEW YORK, N.Y. 1980) (US/8755-1810) [08018451] **3230**

MEETINGS ON ATOMIC ENERGY (AU/0047-6641) [01757069] **1950**

●MEETINGS REPORTS. CNS (US/1063-245X) [25936445] **3838**

●MEGABUCKING (STERLING HEIGHTS, MICH.) (US/1048-0528) [20844340] **692**

MEGADRILOGICA (CN/0380-9633) [02851936] **5591**

MEGAFON *SUSPENDED*. (AG) [04044110] **3410**

MEGAMOT / MOSAD SOLD LEMAAN HA-YELED VEHA-NOAR (IS/0025-8679) [05462377] **5209**

MEGAPOLIS EXPRESS (RU/0868-5827) [23729679] **5809**

MEGATRENDS AKTUELL *See* TRENDLETTER MEGATRENDS AKTUELL **1524**

MEGHALAYA (INDIA) *See* BUDGET SPEECH - MEGHALAYA (INDIA) **4715**

MEGHALAYA (INDIA) *See* CIVIL LIST OF GAZETTED EMPLOYEES UNDER THE GOVERNMENT OF MEGHALAYA, AS ON 1ST JANUARY ... **4638**

MEGHALAYA (INDIA) *See* MEMORANDUM ON THE BUDGET ESTIMATES WITH DEMANDS FOR GRANTS AND ANNUAL FINANCIAL STATEMENT **4737**

MEGHALAYA (INDIA) *See* ESTIMATE OF EXPENDITURE IN RESPECT OF WHICH A VOTE-ON-ACCOUNT IS REQUIRED **4721**

MEGHALAYA (INDIA). DEPT. OF AGRICULTURE *See* PERFORMANCE BUDGET **119**

MEGHALAYA (INDIA). LEGISLATIVE ASSEMBLY *See* RESUME OF BUSINESS TRANSACTED DURING SESSION OF THE MEGHALAYA LEGISLATIVE ASSEMBLY, ASSEMBLED UNDER THE DEMOCRATIC CONSTITUTION OF INDIA **4494**

MEGHALAYA, INDIA. LEGISLATIVE ASSEMBLY. COMMITTEE ON PETITIONS *See* REPORT - MEGHALAYA LEGISLATIVE ASSEMBLY, COMMITTEE ON PETITIONS **5305**

MEGHALAYA INDUSTRIAL DEVELOPMENT CORPORATION *See* ANNUAL REPORT - MEGHALAYA INDUSTRIAL DEVELOPMENT CORPORATION LIMITED **1597**

MEGHALAYA YEAR BOOK, THE (II/0377-127X) [02243326] **2658**

MEGIDDO MESSAGE (US/0194-7826) [01773971] **5018**

MEH LADY (US/0090-9408) [05141018] 5561, **1835**

MEHANIKA KOMPOZITNYH MATERIALOV (LV/0203-1272) [05575475] **2107**

MEHANIKA TVERDOGO TELA (KIEV) (UN/0321-1975) [11774646] **4429**

MEHKERE — Alphabetical Title Index

MEHKERE HA-MERKAZ LE-HEKER HA-FOLKLOR (IS) [06523137] **2322**

MEHKERE YERUSHALAYIM BE-FOLKLOR YEHUDI / HA-UNIVERSITAH HA-IVRIT BI-YERUSHALAYIM, HA-FAKULTAH LE-MADAE HA-RUAH, HA-MAKHON LE-MADAE HA-YAHADUT (IS/0333-7030) [08217332] 3410, **2322**

MEHKERE YERUSHALAYIM BE-MAHASHEVET YISRAEL / HA-UNIVERSITAH HA-IVRIT BI-YERUSHALAYIM, HA-FAKULTAH LE-MADAE HA-RUAH, HA-MAKHON LE-MADAE HA-YAHADUT (IS/0333-7081) [08217363] **5051**

MEHKERE YERUSHALAYIM BE-SIFRUT IVRIT / HA-UNIVERSITAH HA-IVRIT BI-YERUSHALAYIM, HA-FAKULTAH LE-MADAE HA-RUAH, HA-MAKHON LE-MADAE HA-YAHADUT (IS/0333-693X) [08217305] **3410**

MEHRAN UNIVERSITY RESEARCH JOURNAL OF ENGINEERING AND TECHNOLOGY (PK/0254-7821) [10713164] **1987**

MEI CHIA HSUEH HSUN / MERICA NEWS (US) [08758700] **2267**

MEI HSUEH / CHUNG-KUO SHE HUI KO HSUEH YUAN CHE HSUEH YEN CHIU SO MEI HSUEH YEN CHIU SHIH, SHANG-HAI WEN I CHU PAN SHE WEN I LI LUN PIEN CHI SHIH HO PIEN (CC) [08147974] **325**

MEI HSUEH SHU LIN / LIU KANG-CHI, WU YUEH PIEN (CC) [11893223] **4352**

MEI-KUO CHU PAN CHIH CHUNG-KUO YEN CHIU LUN CHU HSUAN CHAI (US) [23677612] **4830**

MEI MARKETING ECONOMICS GUIDE (US/0092-4857) [01789897] 1504, **933**

MEI SHU (CC) [01757071] **358**

MEI SHU CHIA (HK) [04341123] **358**

MEI SHU SHIH LUN TSUNG KAN / CHUNG-KUO I SHU YEN CHIU YUAN MEI SHU YEN CHIU SO, "MEI SHU SHIH LUN" TSUNG KAN PIEN CHI PU PIEN (CC) [08682669] **358**

MEI SHU TSUNG HENG / CHUNG-KUO MEI SHU CHIA HSIEH HUI CHIANG-SU FEN HUI PIEN (CC) [11831431] **358**

MEI SHU YEN CHIU (CC) [05392872] **358**

MEI TI YEN CHIU YU HSIN SHANG / HSI NAN SHIH FAN HSUEH YUAN CHUNG WEN HSI, CHUNG-CHING SHIH WEN HSUEH I SHU CHIEH LIEN HO HUI, CHUNG-CHING CHU PAN SHE PIEN CHI PU, CHU PAN (CC) [11844551] **4352**

MEIDEN REVIEW. INTERNATIONAL EDITION (JA/0387-5385) [03875385] **2072**

MEIE ELU OUR LIFE (CN/0047-665X) [01779176] **5789**

MEIE ELU, TAHTRAAMAT (CN/0461-6871) [05018193] **2267**

MEIE TEE, AMEERIKA EESTLASTE AJAKIRI *CEASED.* (US) [01681314] **2746**

MEIERIPOSTEN (NO/0025-8776) [03773611] **196**

MEIER'S ADRESSBUCH INTERNATIONALER EINKAUFSFUHRER (GW) [24788205] **845**

MEIJERBERGS ARKIV FOR SVENSK ORDFORSKNING (SW/0348-7741) [01781044] **3302**

MEIJI DAIGAKU *See* MEIJI DAIGAKU KYOYO RONSHU **1835**

MEIJI DAIGAKU. KEIJI HAKUBUTSUKAN *See* MEIJI DAIGAKU KEIJI HAKUBUTSUKAN SHIRYO **4840**

MEIJI DAIGAKU. KEIJI HAKUBUTSUKAN *See* MEIJI DAIGAKU KEIJI HAKUBUTSUKAN MOKUROKU **3009**

MEIJI DAIGAKU KEIJI HAKUBUTSUKAN MOKUROKU (JA) [06132808] **3009**

MEIJI DAIGAKU KEIJI HAKUBUTSUKAN NEMPO (JA) [06167340] **3009**

MEIJI DAIGAKU KEIJI HAKUBUTSUKAN SHIRYO (JA) [04863454] **4840**

MEIJI DAIGAKU KYOYO RONSHU (JA) [05146039] **1835**

MEIJI DAIGAKU RIKO GAKUBU KENKYU HOKOKU (JA) [22748376] **5128**

MEIJI DAIGAKU SHAKAI KAGAKU KENKYUJO KIYO (JA) [05076838] **5209**

MEIJI DAIGAKU, TOKYO. MEIJI HAKUBUTSUKAN *See* MEIJI DAIGAKU KEIJI HAKUBUTSUKAN NEMPO **3009**

MEIJI DAIGAKU, TOKYO. SHAKAI KAGAKU KENKYUJO *See* ANNUAL REPORT OF THE INSTITUTE OF SOCIAL SCIENCES, MEIJI UNIVERSITY **5191**

MEIJI DAIGAKU, TOKYO. SHAKAI KAGAKU KENKYUJO *See* MEIJI DAIGAKU SHAKAI KAGAKU KENKYUJO KIYO **5209**

MEIJI DAIGAKU, TOKYO. TOSHOKAN *See* MEIJI DAIGAKU TOSHOKAN SHOZO CHIKUJI KANKOBUTSU MOKUROKU: WA-OBUNHEN **419**

MEIJI DAIGAKU TOSHOKAN SHOZO CHIKUJI KANKOBUTSU MOKUROKU: WA-OBUNHEN (JA) [05398795] **419**

MEIJI SEIKA KENKYU NENPO (JA) [10448215] **5128**

MEIJO DAIGAKU RIKO GAKUBU KENKYU HOKOKU (JA/0386-4952) [10446082] **5128**

MEIKAI DAIGAKU SHIGAKU ZASSHI (JA) [19107142] **1330**

MEILLEURES ADRESSES DE LA FONDERIE PARIS, LES (FR/1164-1711) [11641711] **845**

MEILLEURES ADRESSES DES TRAITEMENTS DE SURFACE, LES (FR/1240-9863) [112409863] 1504, **692**

MEILLEURES ADRESSES DES TRAITEMENTS THERMIQUES, LES (FR/0992-2164) [109922164] 1504, **693**

MEIN SCHONER GARTEN (GW) [04102206] **2424**

MEINE FAMILIE & ICH (GW/0933-081X) [10933081X] **2519**

MEINUNGEN ZUR AGRAR- UND UMWELTPOLITIK (GW) [15313411] **107**

MEISEI DAIGAKU KENKYU KIYO. RIKO GAKUBU (JA/0388-130X) [10422190] 1987, **5128**

MEISEI DAIGAKU. TOSHOKAN *See* CATALOGUE OF RARE BOOKS **4827**

MEISTERWERKE DER MUSIK (GW) [06502486] **4130**

MEITAN KEXUE JISHU (CC/0253-2336) [08864238] **2143**

MEJ : MEDIA EDUCATION JOURNAL (UK) 1117, **1763**

MEKEEL'S WEEKLY STAMP NEWS (US) [07106173] **2785**

MEKHANIKA (RU) [04402215] **2122**

MEKHANIKA GORNYKH POROD I GORNOE DAVLENIE (RU) [03443615] **1459**

MEKHANIZATSIIA I AVTOMATIZATSIIA BIBLIOTECHNO-BIBLIOGRAFICHESKI KH PROTSESSOV (RU) [01794764] **3230**

MEKHANIZATSIIA I ELEKTRIFIKASIIA SEL'SKOGO KHOZIAISTVA (RU/0202-1927) [09898989] **1987**

MEKHANIZATSIIA STROITELSTVA (RU/0025-8903) [08242497] **2027**

MEKHON HA-TEKANIM HA-YISREELI *See* MATI (TEL-AVIV) **2027**

MELA NOTES (US/0364-2410) [02577555] **3230**

MELAKA, MALAYSIA (STATE). JABATAN PELAJARAN *See* LAPURAN TAHUNAN - JABATAN PELAJARAN MELAKA **1761**

MELANCHITHON-SCHRIFTEN DER STADT BRETTEN (GW) [20288095] **5252**

MELANDERIA (PULLMAN, WASH.) (US/0076-6224) [01757074] **5611**

MELANESIAN JOURNAL OF THEOLOGY : JOURNAL OF THE MELANESIAN ASSOCIATION OF THEOLOGICAL SCHOOLS (PP) [12850412] **4976**

MELANESIAN LAW JOURNAL (AT/0254-0657) [01757075] **3009**

MELANGES - CENTRE DE RECHERCHES ET D'APPLICATIONS PEDAGOGIQUES EN LANGUES (FR/0077-2712) [08835861] **3302**

MELANGES CHINOIS ET BOUDDHIQUES (BE) [01757076] **5021**

MELANGES DE LA BIBLIOTHEQUE DE LA SORBONNE (FR/0293-2148) [09638239] **419**

MELANGES DE LA CASA DE VELAZQUEZ (FR/0076-230X) [01795975] **2698**

MELANGES DE L'ECOLE FRANCAISE DE ROME. ANTIQUITE (IT/0223-5102) [02292798] **2698**

MELANGES DE L'ECOLE FRANCAISE DE ROME. ITALIE ET MEDITERRANEE (IT) [24145921] **2623**

MELANGES DE L'ECOLE FRANCAISE DE ROME. MOYEN AGE (IT) [22142259] **274**

MELANGES DE L'UNIVERSITE SAINT-JOSEPH (LE/0253-164X) [07155703] **1078**

MELANGES DE SCIENCE RELIGIEUSE (FR/0025-8911) [01640672] **4976**

MELANGES - INSTITUT DOMINICAIN D'ETUDES ORIENTALES DU CAIRE (UA/0575-1330) [03076076] **3302**

MELANIE KLEIN AND OBJECT RELATIONS (CN/0848-8479) [21340543] **4603**

MELANOMA RESEARCH (UK/0960-8931) [24024301] **3821**

MELBOURNE HISTORICAL JOURNAL (AT/0076-6232) [02264009] **2670**

MELBOURNE JOURNAL OF POLITICS (AT/0085-3224) [04372527] **4481**

MELBOURNE NOTES ON AGRICULTURAL EXTENSION *CEASED.* (AT) [01903076] **107**

MELBOURNE PSYCHOLOGY MONOGRAPHS (AT/0814-3757) [I08143757] **4603**

MELBOURNE UNIVERSITY LAW REVIEW (AT/0025-8938) [01714379] **3009**

MELBOURNE. UNIVERSITY. LIBRARY *See* REPORT - MELBOURNE. UNIVERSITY. LIBRARY **3245**

MELBOURNE. UNIVERSITY. SCHOOL OF AGRICULTURE AND FORESTRY *See* AGRICULTURAL ECONOMICS REPORT **49**

MELBURNER BLETER (AT) [04224765] **3410**

MELDING / NORGES LANDBRUKSHGSKOLE, INSTITUTT FOR KONOMI OG SAMFUNNSFAG (NO/0802-9210) [25635410] 1504, **107**

MELDING / NORGES LANDBRUKSHGSKOLE, INSTITUTT FOR LANDBRUKSKONOMI (NO) [09219766] **107**

MELIBEA (PE) [02316274] **3410**

MELIORACE (XR) [25519364] **178**

MELIORATSIIA I VODNOE KHOZIAISTVO (MOSCOW, R.S.F.S.R.) (RU/0235-2524) [18188681] **2093**

MELITA THEOLOGICA (MM/1012-9588) [01587122] **4976**

MELK (NE) **196**

MELKKOEIEN (NE) [05356830] **196**

MELLEMFOLKELIGT SAMVIRKE *See* MS BIBLIOTEKSNYT **4529**

MELLIAND-TEXTILBERICHTE (1976) (GW/0341-0781) [07250859] **5354**

MELLON ECONOMIC BRIEFING *CEASED.* (US/0734-3558) [08429464] 797, **1504**

MELODIE (GW) [04388477] **4130**

MELODIE UND RHYTHMUS (GW/0025-9004) [09709584] **4130**

MELODY MAKER (LONDON) (UK/0025-9012) [01606149] **4130**

MELPOMENE (MINNEAPOLIS, MINN.) (US/1043-8734) [19588208] **5561**

MELROSE BEACON (US) [01757089] **5697**

MELROSE PARK HERALD WITH NEWS OF STONE PARK (US/0745-3744) [09108877] **5661**

MELSHEIMER ENTOMOLOGICAL SERIES (US/0076-6321) [01152963] **5591**

MELTING POT, THE (US) [06401409] **2460**

MELTON JOURNAL, THE (US/0891-7116) [08413684] 5051, **1763**

MELTS *CEASED.* (US/0895-7738) [16797288] **4412**

MELUS (US/0163-755X) [04417668] **3410**

MELUSINE (FR) [08044961] **325**

MELVILLE ADVANCE (CN) **5789**

MELVILLE SOCIETY *See* MELVILLE SOCIETY EXTRACTS **3411**

MELVILLE SOCIETY EXTRACTS (US/0193-8991) [04130073] 433, **3411**

MELYEPITESI ES VIZEPITESI SZAKIRODALMI TAJEKOZTATO (HU/0231-0732) [102310732] **2027**

MEMBER BANK CONDITION, TENTH FEDERAL RESERVE DISTRICT (US/0091-2549) [01786905] **797**

MEMBER BANK OPERATING RATIOS, FOURTH FEDERAL RESERVE DISTRICT (US) [01351082] **797**

MEMBER DIRECTORY (US) [16119429] **1835**

MEMBER DIRECTORY - AMERICAN HISTORICAL PRINT COLLECTORS SOCIETY (US/1067-8980) [27364900] **358**

MEMBER DIRECTORY - FINANCIAL EXECUTIVES INSTITUTE (US) [06765736] **693**

● MEMBER NEWS / MINNESOTA HISTORICAL SOCIETY (US/1064-5675) [26330473] **2746**

MEMBER NEWSLETTER - FOREST PRODUCTS RESEARCH SOCIETY (US) [01780588] **2388**

MEMBER ROSTER - ROBERT MORRIS ASSOCIATES (US/0195-5985) [05468186] **797**

MEMBERS & CARS (CN/0714-8569) [09145844] 251, **5418**

MEMBERS AND FIRMS / THE STOCK EXCHANGE (UK) [10075156] **906**

MEMBERS CALENDAR - MUSEUM OF MODERN ART (US/0195-105X) [06386047] 358, **4091**

MEMBERS' COMPUTERIZED DATA EXCHANGE (US/0741-0565) [10063190] **2460**

Alphabetical Title Index — MEMBERSHIP

MEMBERS' DIGEST - ONTARIO FEDERATION OF AGRICULTURE *CEASED.* (CN/0225-0985) [06245481] **107**

MEMBERS' DIRECTORY / FEDERATION OF HONG KONG INDUSTRIES (HK) [08254134] **1618**

MEMBERS DIRECTORY / THE INSTITUTION OF ENVIRONMENTAL HEALTH OFFICERS (UK/0264-5947) [08837426] **4790**

MEMBERS' GUIDE TO THE BCTF (CN/0316-8182) [02247179] **1900**

●MEMBERS' HANDBOOK & BUYERS' GUIDE : THE GREEN BOOK / THE INSTITUTION OF AGRICULTURAL ENGINEERS (UK/0965-867X) [26234180] **160**

MEMBERS' HANDBOOK - AUTOMOBILE ASSOCIATION OF KENYA (KE) [06535357] **5418**

MEMBER'S HANDBOOK / SOCIETY OF BIBLICAL LITERATURE (US) [07094090] **5018**

MEMBERS' HANDBOOK - THE ALBERTA TEACHERS' ASSOCIATION (CN/0706-9839) [04589527] **1866**

MEMBERS IN GOOD STANDING AS OF ... / SOCIETY FOR ITALIAN HISTORICAL STUDIES (US/0276-7228) [07298243] **2698**

MEMBERS - INTERNATIONAL FOLK MUSIC COUNCIL (CN/0250-765X) [06960325] **4130**

MEMBERS' REGISTER (SZ) [27988595] **906**

MEMBERS' REGISTER / AIBD, THE ASSOCIATION OF INTERNATIONAL BOND DEALERS (SZ) [16989951] **906**

MEMBER'S YEAR BOOK - AMERICAN SOCIETY OF CORPORATE SECRETARIES (US/0742-986X) [09185413] **879**

MEMBERSHIP AND STATISTICAL DIRECTORY - NEW ENGLAND GAS ASSOCIATION (US/0741-112X) [10075233] 4264, **4284**

MEMBERSHIP/COMMITTEE DIRECTORY - BUILDING OWNERS AND MANAGERS ASSOCIATION INTERNATIONAL (US/0192-9909) [05094178] **4840**

MEMBERSHIP/COMMITTEE DIRECTORY - NATIONAL ASSOCIATION OF MEAT PURVEYORS (U.S.) (US/0884-1101) [12094145] **2350**

MEMBERSHIP DIRECTORY (GT) [20406287] **845**

MEMBERSHIP DIRECTORY (US/1055-3010) [20180413] **4130**

MEMBERSHIP DIRECTORY (US) [05150371] **3915**

●MEMBERSHIP DIRECTORY (US) [26408039] **3230**

MEMBERSHIP DIRECTORY (US) [25512246] **464**

MEMBERSHIP DIRECTORY (US) [21120718] **2599**

MEMBERSHIP DIRECTORY (US) [20225732] **4603**

●MEMBERSHIP DIRECTORY (US) [29785960] **3789**

MEMBERSHIP DIRECTORY (US) [12357682] **906**

MEMBERSHIP DIRECTORY / AACSB (US) [10378796] 693, **1835**

MEMBERSHIP DIRECTORY / ACCIS (CN/1184-1834) [23686574] **1835**

MEMBERSHIP DIRECTORY / ALOA, ASSOCIATED LOCKSMITHS OF AMERICA, INC (US/1054-7355) [22943444] **4206**

MEMBERSHIP DIRECTORY - AMERICAN ASSOCIATION OF EQUINE PRACTITIONERS (US/1068-0810) [18484467] 2800, **5516**

MEMBERSHIP DIRECTORY / AMERICAN ASSOCIATION OF EXPORTERS AND IMPORTERS (US) [08329516] **845**

MEMBERSHIP DIRECTORY - AMERICAN ASTRONOMICAL SOCIETY (1984) (US/1061-9038) [10188465] **397**

MEMBERSHIP DIRECTORY - AMERICAN CHAMBER OF COMMERCE IN EGYPT (UA) [11304695] **820**

MEMBERSHIP DIRECTORY - AMERICAN CHAMBER OF COMMERCE OF GUATEMALA (GT) [07543559] **820**

MEMBERSHIP DIRECTORY / AMERICAN CHIROPRACTIC ASSOCIATION (US/0747-8372) [09882724] **3615**

●MEMBERSHIP DIRECTORY / AMERICAN COLLEGE OF OCCUPATIONAL AND ENVIRONMENTAL MEDICINE (US) [27807918] **3615**

MEMBERSHIP DIRECTORY / AMERICAN COLLEGE OF OCCUPATIONAL MEDICINE (US) [23019110] **3615**

MEMBERSHIP DIRECTORY / AMERICAN COLLEGE OF PHYSICIANS (US/1053-0967) [22448266] 3615, **1927**

MEMBERSHIP DIRECTORY - AMERICAN COMPENSATION ASSOCIATION (US) [04419822] **944**

MEMBERSHIP DIRECTORY / AMERICAN INSTITUTE OF PROFESSIONAL GEOLOGISTS (US/0275-4991) [07124244] **1387**

MEMBERSHIP DIRECTORY / AMERICAN MEDICAL WRITERS ASSOCIATION (US) [09/94209] 3615, **5233**

MEMBERSHIP DIRECTORY - AMERICAN SOCIETY FOR PUBLIC ADMINISTRATION, NATIONAL CAPITAL AREA CHAPTER (US/0145-2223) [01251651] **4664**

MEMBERSHIP DIRECTORY - AMERICAN SOCIETY FOR PUBLIC ADMINISTRATION, WASHINGTON D.C. CHAPTER *See* MEMBERSHIP DIRECTORY - AMERICAN SOCIETY FOR PUBLIC ADMINISTRATION, NATIONAL CAPITAL AREA CHAPTER **4664**

MEMBERSHIP DIRECTORY / AMERICAN SOCIETY OF CIVIL ENGINEERS (US) [11223255] **2027**

MEMBERSHIP DIRECTORY AND AMERICAN CORRESPONDENTS OVERSEAS (US/0360-5752) [02244119] **2922**

●MEMBERSHIP DIRECTORY AND BUSINESS PAGES FOR THE CHAMBER OF COMMERCE OF ST. JOSEPH COUNTY (US) [25173801] **820**

MEMBERSHIP DIRECTORY AND BUYERS GUIDE *See* MEMBERSHIP DIRECTORY AND BUSINESS PAGES FOR THE CHAMBER OF COMMERCE OF ST. JOSEPH COUNTY **820**

MEMBERSHIP DIRECTORY & BUYERS GUIDE (US) [10863395] **820**

MEMBERSHIP DIRECTORY AND BUYERS' GUIDE - AMERICAN FROZEN FOOD INSTITUTE (US/0361-0888) [02245026] **2350**

MEMBERSHIP DIRECTORY & BUYERS' GUIDE / ONTARIO HOTEL AND MOTEL ASSOCIATION (CN/0849-3685) [23238145] **2807**

MEMBERSHIP DIRECTORY AND CERTIFICATION REGISTRY (US/0271-5082) [06654853] **2198**

MEMBERSHIP DIRECTORY AND HANDBOOK (US/0840-819X) [20108736] **3230**

MEMBERSHIP DIRECTORY AND HANDBOOK / BOTANICAL SOCIETY OF AMERICA (US) [15003812] **517**

MEMBERSHIP DIRECTORY AND HANDBOOK / INDIANA LIBRARY DERATION (US) [24057623] **3230**

MEMBERSHIP DIRECTORY AND SURVIVAL GUIDE / INTERNATIONAL DOCUMENTARY ASSOCIATION (US) [22924265] **1134**

MEMBERSHIP DIRECTORY - APPRAISERS ASSOCIATION OF AMERICA, INC (US/0148-9348) [03400422] **4840**

MEMBERSHIP DIRECTORY - ASSOCIATION FOR INVESTMENT MANAGEMENT AND RESEARCH (US/1056-6074) [21667635] **906**

MEMBERSHIP DIRECTORY - CANADIAN ASSOCIATION FOR INFORMATION SCIENCE (CN/0705-6834) [04079893] **3230**

MEMBERSHIP DIRECTORY - CANADIAN ASSOCIATION OF COLLEGE AND UNIVERSITY STUDENT SERVICES (CN/1183-3734) [24257207] **1835**

MEMBERSHIP DIRECTORY - CANADIAN ASSOCIATION OF COLLEGE AND UNIVERSITY STUDENT SERVICES (CN/1183-3734) [24257208] **1835**

MEMBERSHIP DIRECTORY - CANADIAN PSYCHIATRIC ASSOCIATION. REPERTOIRE DES MEMBRES - ASSOCIATION DES PSYCHIATRES DU CANADA (CN/0576-5986) [02443138] **3930**

MEMBERSHIP DIRECTORY / CANADIAN SOCIETY FOR CHEMICAL ENGINEERING (CN/1184-0218) [23230866] **2015**

MEMBERSHIP DIRECTORY / CANADIAN SOCIETY FOR INDUSTRIAL SECURITY (CN/1186-8058) [24623480] **2865**

MEMBERSHIP DIRECTORY / CANADIAN SOCIETY FOR INDUSTRIAL SECURITY (CN/1186-8058) [24623473] **2865**

MEMBERSHIP DIRECTORY / CHAMBER MUSIC AMERICA (US/0277-4054) [07412381] **4130**

MEMBERSHIP DIRECTORY CLASSIFIED BY SPECIALTY (US/0147-1953) [03113609] **906**

MEMBERSHIP DIRECTORY / EL PASO COUNTY HISTORICAL SOCIETY (US) [17896858] **2746**

MEMBERSHIP DIRECTORY - FLORIDA LIBRARY ASSOCIATION (US/0270-4595) [01410887] **3230**

MEMBERSHIP DIRECTORY - FOREST HISTORY SOCIETY (US) [02452303] **2388**

MEMBERSHIP DIRECTORY / GEOLOGICAL SOCIETY OF AMERICA (US/0277-5816) [03850151] **1387**

MEMBERSHIP DIRECTORY / GOLF COURSE SUPERINTENDENTS ASSOCIATION OF AMERICA *See* WHO'S WHO IN GOLF COURSE MANAGEMENT : DIRECTORY & SOURCE BOOK **4929**

MEMBERSHIP DIRECTORY / GUILD OF BOOK WORKERS (US) [14960436] **4830**

MEMBERSHIP DIRECTORY - GYPSY LORE SOCIETY, NORTH AMERICAN CHAPTER (US/0193-1598) [05120435] 241, **2322**

MEMBERSHIP DIRECTORY - INDUSTRIAL DEVELOPERS ASSOCIATION OF CANADA (CN/0845-8618) [20659421] **1618**

MEMBERSHIP DIRECTORY - INSTITUTE OF PAPER CONSERVATION (UK) [04387763] **4235**

MEMBERSHIP DIRECTORY / INTERNATIONAL ASSOCIATION OF AQUATIC AND MARINE SCIENCE LIBRARIES AND INFORMATION CENTERS (US/1021-495X) [27477582] **1452**

MEMBERSHIP DIRECTORY - INTERNATIONAL ASSOCIATION OF ASSESSING OFFICERS (1977) (US/0538-446X) [06961018] 3009, **4737**

MEMBERSHIP DIRECTORY - INTERNATIONAL ASSOCIATION OF ASSESSING OFFICERS. PERSONAL PROPERTY SECTION (US/0737-4267) [08225298] 4840, **4737**

MEMBERSHIP DIRECTORY / INTERNATIONAL ASSOCIATION OF MARINE SCIENCE LIBRARIES AND INFORMATION CENTERS (CN/0255-8114) [12178015] **3230**

MEMBERSHIP DIRECTORY / INTERNATIONAL ASSOCIATION OF RESIDENTIAL AND COMMUNITY ALTERNATIVES (US) [22257147] **5296**

MEMBERSHIP DIRECTORY / INTERNATIONAL SOCIETY OF APPRAISERS (US/8755-4356) [11313258] **693**

MEMBERSHIP DIRECTORY / INTERNATIONAL TRUMPET GUILD (US/8755-5964) [05161445] **4130**

MEMBERSHIP DIRECTORY / MARYLAND GENEALOGICAL SOCIETY (US/1056-0394) [23304352] **2460**

MEMBERSHIP DIRECTORY / MEDICAL SOCIETY OF NEW JERSEY (US) **3615**

MEMBERSHIP DIRECTORY - METROPOLITAN WASHINGTON BOARD OF TRADE (US/0362-3807) [02311995] **845**

MEMBERSHIP DIRECTORY - NATIONAL ABORTION FEDERATION (US/0196-3163) [05781196] **3765**

MEMBERSHIP DIRECTORY / NATIONAL ASSOCIATION FOR MUSIC THERAPY (US/8755-2892) [11247342] 3615, **4130**

MEMBERSHIP DIRECTORY / NATIONAL ASSOCIATION OF BUSINESS ECONOMISTS (US) [10591825] **1504**

MEMBERSHIP DIRECTORY - NATIONAL ASSOCIATION OF CEMETERIES *See* DIRECTORY OF MEMBERS, LOT EXCHANGE, MAUSOLEUM CRYPT EXCHANGE, DOLLAR CREDIT PLANS **2407**

MEMBERSHIP DIRECTORY - NATIONAL ASSOCIATION OF COLLEGE ADMISSIONS COUNSELORS (US/0090-3965) [01785344] **1835**

MEMBERSHIP DIRECTORY - NATIONAL COUNCIL FOR RESOURCE DEVELOPMENT (US/0162-0339) [04082640] **1763**

MEMBERSHIP DIRECTORY - NATIONAL ROOFING CONTRACTORS' ASSOCIATION (US/1053-8305) [22651708] **621**

MEMBERSHIP DIRECTORY - NATIONAL SOCIETY FOR PERFORMANCE AND INSTRUCTION (US/0730-7675) [04273708] 1900, **1224**

MEMBERSHIP DIRECTORY - NATIONAL SOCIETY OF FUND RAISING EXECUTIVES (US/0195-6795) [05528757] **798**

MEMBERSHIP DIRECTORY / NORTH AMERICAN LAKE MANAGEMENT SOCIETY (US) [22637185] **1505**

MEMBERSHIP DIRECTORY OF THE AMERICAN PSYCHOLOGICAL SOCIETY (US/1051-1830) [21885324] **4603**

MEMBERSHIP DIRECTORY - OREGON STATE BAR (US) [18261967] **3009**

MEMBERSHIP DIRECTORY / OSLA (CN/0845-8995) [20777051] **3889**

MEMBERSHIP DIRECTORY - PHILATELIC TRADERS' SOCIETY (UK/0305-3245) [03053245] **2785**

●MEMBERSHIP DIRECTORY, PLANT SOURCE LIST (CN/1191-3363) [26714614] **2424**

MEMBERSHIP — Alphabetical Title Index

MEMBERSHIP DIRECTORY - SOCIETY FOR NEUROSCIENCE (US/1052-9764) [06623930] **4603**

MEMBERSHIP DIRECTORY - SOCIETY OF AMERICAN ARCHIVISTS (US/0145-6490) [02770264] **2482**

MEMBERSHIP DIRECTORY / SOCIETY OF ARCHITECTURAL HISTORIANS (US) [23805027] **303**

MEMBERSHIP DIRECTORY / SOCIETY OF COSMETIC CHEMISTS (US/0730-7756) [08048236] **1027**

MEMBERSHIP DIRECTORY - SUBURBAN NEWSPAPERS OF AMERICA (US/0270-4641) [06408235] **5661**

MEMBERSHIP DIRECTORY / THE AMERICAN BELL ASSOCIATION (US) [15691732] **4130**

MEMBERSHIP DIRECTORY / THE BETTER BUSINESS BUREAU OF SOUTHEASTERN VIRGINIA (US) [10211374] **693**

MEMBERSHIP DIRECTORY / THE CANADIAN SOCIETY OF ANIMAL SCIENCE (CN/1185-9334) [25423392] **5516**

MEMBERSHIP DIRECTORY - THE FINANCIAL ANALYSTS FEDERATION (US/0430-4756) [01774921] **906**

MEMBERSHIP HANDBOOK (US) [28143401] **4130**

MEMBERSHIP LIST - AMERICAN MENSA LIMITED (US/0363-3616) [02457447] **5233**

MEMBERSHIP LIST - CANADIAN ASSOCIATION OF MUSIC LIBRARIES (1984) (CN/0828-7007) [12227600] **4130, 3231**

MEMBERSHIP LIST / CAPAC (CN/0823-955X) [11607629] **4130**

MEMBERSHIP LIST - ROYAL COLLEGE OF PSYCHIATRISTS (UK/0142-5447) [04596359] **3930**

MEMBERSHIP LIST - THE GALPIN SOCIETY (UK) [05257231] **4130**

MEMBERSHIP LIST / THE QUINTE BRANCH, O.G.S (CN/0714-4458) [09050443] **2460**

MEMBERSHIP LIST - VIRGINIA GENEALOGICAL SOCIETY (US/0196-4976) [05819271] **2460**

MEMBERSHIP ORGANIZATIONS NEWSLETTER *See* NON-PROFIT LEGAL & TAX LETTER **4739**

MEMBERSHIP ROSTER / ALBERTA REGISTERED DIETITIANS ASSOCIATION (CN/1184-8928) [24368405] **4194**

MEMBERSHIP ROSTER - AMERICAN ACADEMY OF PSYCHOANALYSIS (US/0736-4385) [08406047] **4603**

MEMBERSHIP ROSTER - AMERICAN SOCIETY OF TRAVEL AGENTS INC (US/0360-6597) [02640367] **5484**

MEMBERSHIP ROSTER - AUDIT BUREAU OF CIRCULATIONS (US) [07318543] **762**

MEMBERSHIP ROSTER - AUTOMOTIVE RETAILERS ASSOCIATION (WINNIPEG) (CN/1187-3469) [25589926] **955**

MEMBERSHIP ROSTER / CANADIAN PETROLEUM TAX SOCIETY (CN/0846-1023) [24256967] **4737**

MEMBERSHIP ROSTER - INTERNATIONAL CONFERENCE OF BUILDING OFFICIALS (US) [03136998] **621**

MEMBERSHIP SURNAME LIST (US/0882-4231) [11750452] **2460**

MEMBERSHIP-TEAM DIRECTORY (US) [19884982] **3970**

MEMBERSHIP UPDATE / CORRECTIONAL EDUCATION ASSOCIATION (US) [15989835] **3169**

MEMBRANCE SEPARATION ENGINEERING *CEASED.* (US/0890-5444) [14261606] 2015, **2027**

MEMBRANE & SEPARATION TECHNOLOGY NEWS (US/0737-8483) [09481061] **985**

MEMBRANE BIOCHEMISTRY (US/0149-046X) [03784284] **490**

MEMBRANE LIPIDS (UK/0952-0422) [109520422] **490**

MEMBRANE PROTEINS (UK/0143-4233) [I01434233] **490**

MEMBRANE PROTEINS (NEW YORK, N.Y.) (US/0161-2883) [03507085] **464**

MEMBRANE QUARTERLY (US/1052-0953) [22189848] **1027**

MEMBRANE SCIENCE AND DESALINATION (NE) [02360944] **5128**

MEMBRANE STRUCTURE AND FUNCTION (US) [06818559] **538**

MEMBRANE TECHNOLOGY (UK/0958-2118) [25786515] **3695**

MEMBRES DE L'ASSOCIATION NATIONALE DE LA RECHERCHE TECHNIQUE ET LEURS TRAVAUX, LES (FR) [13742288] **5128**

MEMENTO DE STATISTIQUE AGRICOLE : DORDOGNE (FR) [02242934] 5332, **155**

MEMENTO PRATIQUE DES SOCIETES COMMERCIALES *See* MEMENTO PRATIQUE FRANCIS LEFEBVRE: SOCIETES COMMERCIALES **3101**

MEMENTO PRATIQUE FRANCIS LEFEBVRE : AGRICULTURE (FR) [07386668] 107, **3009**

MEMENTO PRATIQUE FRANCIS LEFEBVRE. COMPTABLE (FR) [09072756] **748**

MEMENTO PRATIQUE FRANCIS LEFEBVRE: FISCAL (FR) [06300897] **3009**

MEMENTO PRATIQUE FRANCIS LEFEBVRE: SOCIAL (FR) [06319962] **3152**

MEMENTO PRATIQUE FRANCIS LEFEBVRE: SOCIETES COMMERCIALES (FR) [07668798] **3101**

MEMMINGER GESCHICHTSBLATTER (GW/0539-2896) [05881660] **2698**

MEMNONIA : BULLETIN EDITE PAR L'ASSOCIATION POUR LA SAUVEGARDE DU RAMESSEUM (FR) [25474293] **2642**

MEMO (LE) [13747973] **1505**

MEMO - AMERICAN INSTITUTE OF ARCHITECTS (1971) (US/0001-1487) [02520596] **303**

MEMO (CINCINNATI) (US/0190-3144) [04693017] **1690**

MEMO - CORPORATION FOR PUBLIC BROADCASTING *See* CPB REPORT **1130**

MEMO FROM PROBE (CN/0708-0735) [04875803] **5252**

MEMO PAD (US) **303**

MEMO (QUEBEC) (CN/0848-0877) [20985121] **693**

MEMO SCRIPT *See* PHARMA TECHNOLOGIE JOURNAL **4319**

MEMO TO MAILERS (US) [04508624] **1145**

MEMO: TO THE PRESIDENT (US/0047-6692) [03618804] **1835**

MEMO'ART (CN/0835-4588) [16886951] **358**

MEMOIR (ANTHROPOLOGICAL SURVEY OF INDIA) (II/0536-6712) [01771493] **241**

MEMOIR (CANADIAN SOCIETY OF PETROLEUM GEOLOGISTS) (CN/0703-1130) [02926639] 4264, **1387**

MEMOIR (CYPRUS. GEOLOGICAL SURVEY DEPT.) (CY/0574-8259) [04353765] **1387**

MEMOIR / GEOLOGICAL SOCIETY OF AMERICA (US/0072-1069) [01570694] **1387**

MEMOIR / GEOLOGICAL SOCIETY OF INDIA (II/0435-4001) [07929110] **1387**

MEMOIR - GEOLOGICAL SURVEY OF CANADA (CN/0068-7634) [01685573] **1387**

MEMOIR - GEOLOGICAL SURVEY OF NAMIBIA (SA/1018-4325) [I10184325] **1387**

MEMOIR - GEOLOGICAL SURVEY OF VICTORIA (AT/0369-0040) [01291934] **1387**

MEMOIR - GEOLOGICAL SURVEY OF WYOMING (US/0512-493X) [01642055] **1387**

MEMOIR - GEOLOGICAL SURVEY. SOUTH AFRICA (SA/0373-6938) [01343451] **1387**

MEMOIR - MALAWI GEOLOGICAL SURVEY DEPARTMENT (MW/0076-3136) [04208360] **1387**

MEMOIR (MONTANA BUREAU OF MINES AND GEOLOGY) (US/0077-1120) [01586794] 1387, **2143**

MEMOIR - NEW MEXICO BUREAU OF MINES & MINERAL RESOURCES (US/0548-5975) [01759893] **2143**

MEMOIR ... OF THE ASSOCIATION OF AUSTRALASIAN PALAEONTOLOGISTS (AT/0810-8889) [10032959] **4228**

MEMOIR - PACIFIC TROPICAL BOTANICAL GARDEN (US) [02841540] **517**

MEMOIR / THE PALEONTOLOGICAL SOCIETY (US/0078-8597) [03440131] **4228**

MEMOIRE AUX GOUVERNEMENTS CANADIEN ET QUEBECOIS (CN/0317-9303) [02248327] **2792**

MEMOIRE DE LA SOCIETE MATHEMATIQUE DE FRANCE (FR/0249-633X) [10748493] **3522**

MEMOIRE DE TRAME (FR/0987-3090) [I09873090] **3231**

MEMOIRE HORS-SERIE ... DE LA SOCIETE GEOLOGIQUE DE FRANCE (FR/0249-6410) [10698078] **1387**

MEMOIRE PRESENTE AU GOUVERNEMENT DU CANADA PAR LE CONGRES DU TRAVAIL DU CANADA (CN/0316-5906) [02247594] **1618**

MEMOIRE SUR LA TARIFICATION PROPOSEE POUR . *See* PROPOSITION TARIFAIRE **1513**

MEMOIRES (FR/1157-075X) [10051368] **2850**

MEMOIRES - ACADEMIE DES SCIENCES, BELLES LETTRES ET ARTS D'ANGERS (FR/0182-628X) [I0182628X] **2850**

MEMOIRES - ACADEMIE ROYALE DE BELGIQUE. CLASSE DES BEAUX-ARTS. COLLECTION IN 8 (BE/0378-7923) [I03787923] **325**

MEMOIRES C.E.R.E.S (FR/0025-9195) [04386556] **2027**

MEMOIRES DE BIOSPEOLOGIE (FR/0184-0266) [05919427] 5591, **464**

MEMOIRES DE LA CLASSE DES LETTRES. COLLECTION IN-8 (BE) [01460690] **3411**

MEMOIRES DE LA COMMISSION DES ANTIQUITES DU DEPARTEMENT DE LA COTE-D'OR (FR/0249-6747) [12185677] 325, **2850**

MEMOIRES DE LA SOCIETE ARCHEOLOGIQUE DU MIDI DE LA FRANCE (FR/0373-1901) [03007921] **274**

MEMOIRES DE LA SOCIETE ARCHEOLOGIQUE ET HISTORIQUE DE NANTES ET DE LOIRE-ATLANTIQUE (FR/0240-8260) [17738221] 2698, **274**

MEMOIRES DE LA SOCIETE D'AGRICULTURE, COMMERCE, SCIENCES ET ARTS DU DEPARTEMENT DE LA MARNE (FR) [02995038] 845, **107**

MEMOIRES DE LA SOCIETE DES SCIENCES NATURELLES ET ARCHEOLOGIQUES DE LA CREUSE (FR/0249-664X) [I0249664X] **274**

MEMOIRES DE LA SOCIETE D'HISTOIRE ET D'ARCHEOLOGIE DE BRETAGNE (FR/0750-1420) [01765806] 2698, **274**

MEMOIRES DE LA SOCIETE D'HISTOIRE ET D'ARCHEOLOGIE DE CHALON-SUR-SAONE (FR/1149-8080) [03078664] 2698, **274**

MEMOIRES DE LA SOCIETE ENTOMOLOGIQUE DU QUEBEC *CEASED.* (CN/0071-0784) [06596403] **5591**

MEMOIRES DE LA SOCIETE GENEALOGIQUE CANADIENNE-FRANCAISE (CN/0037-9387) [02208362] **2460**

MEMOIRES DE LA SOCIETE GEOLOGIQUE DU NORD (FR/0767-7375) [01696174] **1358**

MEMOIRES DE LA SOCIETE GEOLOGIQUE ET MINERALOGIQUE DE BRETAGNE (FR/0370-9892) [03422410] **1358**

MEMOIRES DE LA SOCIETE HISTORIQUE ET ARCHEOLOGIQUE DE L'ARRONDISSEMENT DE PONTOISE ET DU VEXIN *See* MEMOIRES DE LA SOCIETE HISTORIQUE ET ARCHEOLOGIQUE DE PONTOISE, DU VAL-D'OISE ET DU VEXIN **2698**

MEMOIRES DE LA SOCIETE HISTORIQUE ET ARCHEOLOGIQUE DE PONTOISE, DU VAL-D'OISE ET DU VEXIN (FR) [03620433] **2698**

MEMOIRES DE LA SOCIETE LINNEENNE DE NORMANDIE. SECTION BOTANIQUE (FR) [05056333] **517**

MEMOIRES DE LA SOCIETE NATIONALE DES ANTIQUAIRES DE FRANCE (FR) [14203231] **2698**

MEMOIRES DE LA SOCIETE NEOPHILOLOGIQUE DE HELSINKI (FI/0355-0192) [07856814] **3302**

MEMOIRES DE LA SOCIETE POUR L'HISTOIRE DU DROIT ET DES INSTITUTIONS DES ANCIENS PAYS BOURGUIGNONS, COMTOIS ET ROMANDS (FR/01952641] **3009**

MEMOIRES DE LA SOCIETE ROYALE D'HISTOIRE ET D'ARCHEOLOGIE DE TOURNAI (BE/1148-8093) [08915460] 2698, **274**

MEMOIRES DE LA SOCIETE VAUDOISE DES SCIENCES NATURELLES (SZ/0037-9611) [01645912] **5128**

MEMOIRES DE L'ACADEMIE DE METZ (FR/1149-0349) [11016983] **1078**

MEMOIRES DE L'ACADEMIE DES SCIENCES, ARTS ET BELLES LETTRES DE DIJON (FR/0755-3617) [09004380] **178**

MEMOIRES DE L'ACADEMIE DES SCIENCES, INSCRIPTIONS ET BELLES-LETTRES DE TOULOUSE (FR/0369-1896) [08906506] 325, **2850**

MEMOIRES DE L'ACADEMIE ROYALE DES SCIENCES, DES LETTRES ET DES BEAUX-ARTS DE BELGIQUE (BE) [08492162] **5233**

MEMOIRES DE L'INSTITUT DE GEOLOGIE DU BASSIN D'AQUITAINE (FR/0397-9520) [02673266] **1387**

Alphabetical Title Index — MEMORIA

MEMOIRES DE L'INSTITUT FONDAMENTAL D'AFRIQUE NOIRE (SG/0373-5338) [01642430] **2499**

MEMOIRES DE L'INSTITUT OCEANOGRAPHIQUE (MC/0304-5714) [03760279] **1452**

MEMOIRES. DEUXIEME SERIE (BRUXELLES) (BE) [01376258] **4167**

● MEMOIRES DU MUSEUM NATIONAL D'HISTOIRE NATURELLE (FR/1243-4442) [28682363] **4167**

MEMOIRES DU MUSEUM NATIONAL D'HISTOIRE NATURELLE. SERIE A, ZOOLOGIE (FR/0078-9747) [01411069] **5591**

MEMOIRES DU MUSEUM NATIONAL D'HISTOIRE NATURELLE. SERIE D, SCIENCES PHYSICO-CHIMIQUES (FR) [06125891] **4167**

MEMOIRES ET DOCUMENTS - COMMISSION D'HISTOIRE ECONOMIQUE ET SOCIALE DE LA REVOLUTION FRANCAISE (FR) [01314308] **1505**

MEMOIRES ET DOCUMENTS (FRANCE. SERVICE DE DOCUMENTATION ET DE CARTOGRAPHIE GEOGRAPHIQUES) (FR) [06698888] **2569**

MEMOIRES ET DOCUMENTS PUBLIES PAR LA SOCIETE D'HISTOIRE ET D'ARCHEOLOGIE DE GENEVE (SZ) [01772465] **2482**

MEMOIRES ET DOCUMENTS SUR ROME ET L'ITALIE MERIDIONALE (IT) [18493421] **2698**

MEMOIRES ET ETUDES SCIENTIFIQUES DE LA REVUE DE METALLURGIE (FR/0245-8292) [06850528] **4008**

MEMOIRES ET PUBLICATIONS DE LA SOCIETE DES SCIENCES, DES ARTS ET DES LETTRES DU HAINAUT (BE/0373-7667) [01624430] **2850, 325**

MEMOIRES - FEDERATION DES SOCIETES D'HISTOIRE ET D'ARCHEOLOGIE DE L'AISNE (FR) [I04281535] **2698, 274**

MEMOIRES HORS SERIE DE LA SOCIETE GEOLOGIQUE DE FRANCE (FR/0369-2027) [06925640] **1387**

MEMOIRES NOUVELLE. SERIE DE LA SOCIETE GEOLOGIQUE DE FRANCE (FR) **1387**

MEMOIRES OPTIQUES & SYSTEMES (FR/0990-7939) [I09907939] **1277**

MEMOIRES / SOCIETE D'HISTOIRE ET D'ARCHEOLOGIE DE BEAUNE (COTE-D'OR) (FR/0248-6644) [11701107] **2623, 274**

● MEMOIRES VIVES MONTREAL (CN/1188-8296) [I11888296] **303**

● MEMOIRES VIVES (MONTREAL) (CN/1188-8296) [29552037] **274**

MEMOIRS - HARVARD UNIVERSITY / UNIVERSITY LABORATORY OF PHYSICAL CHEMISTRY (US) [01839148] **1055**

MEMOIRS OF FACULTY OF TECHNOLOGY, TOKYO METROPOLITAN UNIVERSITY (JA/0082-4747) [01767592] **1987**

MEMOIRS OF NATIONAL INSTITUTE OF POLAR RESEARCH. SERIES E : BIOLOGY AND MEDICAL SCIENCE (JA) [04049253] **3616, 464**

MEMOIRS OF THE AMERICAN ACADEMY IN ROME (IT/0065-6801) [01479252] **1078**

MEMOIRS OF THE AMERICAN ENTOMOLOGICAL INSTITUTE (US/0065-8162) [01479818] **5611**

MEMOIRS OF THE AMERICAN ENTOMOLOGICAL SOCIETY (US/0065-8170) [01479819] **5611**

MEMOIRS OF THE AMERICAN MATHEMATICAL SOCIETY (US/0065-9266) [01480365] **3522**

MEMOIRS OF THE AMERICAN PHILOSOPHICAL SOCIETY HELD AT PHILADELPHIA FOR PROMOTING USEFUL KNOWLEDGE (US/0065-9738) [01480556] **4352**

MEMOIRS OF THE ASTRONOMICAL SOCIETY OF INDIA (II/0970-5295) [06102716] **397**

MEMOIRS OF THE BOTANICAL SURVEY OF SOUTH AFRICA (SA) [12230314] **517**

MEMOIRS OF THE COLLEGE OF AGRICULTURE, KYOTO UNIVERSITY **CEASED.** (JA/0388-2330) [01782618] **108**

MEMOIRS OF THE COLLEGE OF MEDICINE OF THE NATIONAL TAIWAN UNIVERSITY (CH) [06777105] **3616**

MEMOIRS OF THE COLORADO ARCHAEOLOGICAL SOCIETY (US) [09482084] **274**

MEMOIRS OF THE CONNECTICUT ACADEMY OF ARTS AND SCIENCES (US/0069-8970) [01564846] **2850**

MEMOIRS OF THE ENTOMOLOGICAL SOCIETY OF CANADA (CN/0071-075X) [10643452] **5591**

MEMOIRS OF THE ENTOMOLOGICAL SOCIETY OF CANADA (CN/0071-075X) [01447567] **5612**

MEMOIRS OF THE FACULTY OF AGRICULTURE, KAGOSHIMA UNIVERSITY (JA/0453-0853) [04602605] **108**

MEMOIRS OF THE FACULTY OF ENGINEERING (JA/0475-0071) [18810192] **1987**

MEMOIRS OF THE FACULTY OF ENGINEERING AND DESIGN, KYOTO INSTITUTE OF TECHNOLOGY. SERIES OF SCIENCE AND TECHNOLOGY (JA/0911-0305) [12073007] **5128**

MEMOIRS OF THE FACULTY OF ENGINEERING, HIROSHIMA UNIVERSITY (JA/0073-2311) [07826245] **1987**

MEMOIRS OF THE FACULTY OF ENGINEERING, HOKKAIDO UNIVERSITY (JA/0368-9379) [01588457] **1987**

MEMOIRS OF THE FACULTY OF ENGINEERING, KOBE UNIVERSITY (JA/0368-9638) [01787734] **1987**

MEMOIRS OF THE FACULTY OF ENGINEERING, KUMAMOTO UNIVERSITY (JA/0023-5334) [01696569] **1987**

MEMOIRS OF THE FACULTY OF ENGINEERING, KYOTO UNIVERSITY (JA/0023-6063) [06978900] **1987**

MEMOIRS OF THE FACULTY OF ENGINEERING KYUSHU UNIVERSITY (JA/0023-6160) [02264023] **1987**

MEMOIRS OF THE FACULTY OF ENGINEERING, NAGOYA UNIVERSITY (JA/0027-7657) [01758973] **1987**

MEMOIRS OF THE FACULTY OF ENGINEERING, OSAKA CITY UNIVERSITY (JA/0078-6659) [C1761545] **5128, 1987**

MEMOIRS OF THE FACULTY OF FISHERIES, HOKKAIDO UNIVERSITY (JA/0018-3466) [01696937] **2308**

MEMOIRS OF THE FACULTY OF SCIENCE, KOCHI UNIVERSITY. SERIES A, MATHEMATICS (JA/0389-0252) [07677960] **3522**

MEMOIRS OF THE FACULTY OF SCIENCE, KYOTO UNIVERSITY. SERIES OF BIOLOGY (JA/0454-7802) [02244406] **464**

MEMOIRS OF THE FACULTY OF SCIENCE, KYOTO UNIVERSITY. SERIES OF PHYSICS, ASTROPHYSICS, GEOPHYSICS AND CHEMISTRY (JA/0368-9689) [02241785] **4412**

MEMOIRS OF THE FACULTY OF SCIENCE KYUSHU UNIVERSITY. SERIES A (JA) [02263376] **1093**

MEMOIRS OF THE FACULTY OF SCIENCE, KYUSHU UNIVERSITY. SERIES A, MATHEMATICS (JA/0373-6385) [08380129] **3522**

MEMOIRS OF THE FACULTY OF SCIENCE, KYUSHU UNIVERSITY. SERIES C. CHEMISTRY (JA/0085-2635) [01755367] **985**

MEMOIRS OF THE FACULTY OF SCIENCE, KYUSHU UNIVERSITY. SERIES D, EARTH AND PLANETARY SCIENCES (JA/0916-7390) [23946988] **1387**

MEMOIRS OF THE FACULTY OF TECHNOLOGY, KANAZAWA UNIVERSITY (JA) **5128**

MEMOIRS OF THE GEOLOGICAL SURVEY OF NEW SOUTH WALES. PALAEONTOLOGY (AT/0077-8699) [04671509] **4228**

MEMOIRS OF THE HOURGLASS CRUISES (US/0085-0683) [01784606] **556**

MEMOIRS OF THE INSTITUTE OF SCIENTIFIC AND INDUSTRIAL RESEARCH, OSAKA UNIVERSITY (JA/0369-0369) [02676234] **5128**

MEMOIRS OF THE KOBE MARINE OBSERVATORY, THE (JA) [07668743] **1452**

MEMOIRS OF THE KONAN UNIVERSITY. SCIENCE SERIES (JA/0452-4160) [06210856] **5128**

MEMOIRS OF THE MUSEUM OF ANTHROPOLOGY, UNIVERSITY OF MICHIGAN (US/0076-8375) [01757335] **241**

MEMOIRS OF THE MUSEUM OF VICTORIA (AT) [11628078] **4091**

MEMOIRS OF THE MUSEUM OF VICTORIA. ANTHROPOLOGY AND HISTORY (AT/1035-4247) [I10354247] **4091**

MEMOIRS OF THE NATIONAL DEFENSE ACADEMY. MATHEMATICS, PHYSICS, CHEMISTRY, AND ENGINEERING (JA/0388-4112) [08374040] **4412, 3522**

MEMOIRS OF THE NATURAL HISTORY FOUNDATION OF ORANGE COUNTY (US/0749-1743) [11093738] **4167**

MEMOIRS OF THE NEW YORK BOTANICAL GARDEN (US/0077-8931) [01760027] **517**

MEMOIRS OF THE PACIFIC COAST ENTOMOLOGICAL SOCIETY (US/0475-3208) [02092459] **5591**

MEMOIRS OF THE PEABODY MUSEUM OF ARCHAEOLOGY AND ETHNOLOGY, HARVARD UNIVERSITY (US) [09128360] **4091, 274**

MEMOIRS OF THE QUEENSLAND MUSEUM (AT/0079-8835) [01362342] **4167**

MEMOIRS OF THE RESEARCH DEPARTMENT OF THE TOYO BUNKO (THE ORIENTAL LIBRARY) (JA/0082-562X) [01696054] **1835**

MEMOIRS OF THE SCHOOL OF SCIENCE AND ENGINEERING. WASEDA UNIVERSITY (JA/0369-1950) [01647228] **985, 1987**

MEMOIRS OF THE SOCIETY FOR ENDOCRINOLOGY (UK/0081-136X) [01765881] **3731**

MEMOIRS OF THE SOUTHERN CALIFORNIA ACADEMY OF SCIENCES (US/0097-2622) [01357339] **5128**

MEMOIRS OF THE TOKYO UNIVERSITY OF AGRICULTURE (JA/0372-0322) [01715414] **108**

MEMOIRS OF THE TORREY BOTANICAL CLUB (US/0097-3807) [01767639] **518**

MEMOIRS OF THE ZOOLOGICAL SURVEY OF INDIA (II) [03456905] **5591**

MEMOPRESS (SZ) [13992346] **4481**

MEMORABILIA ZOOLOGICA (PL/0076-6372) [01762604] **5591**

MEMORANDA SOCIETATIS PRO FAUNA ET FLORA FENNICA (FI/0373-6873) [01684972] **518**

MEMORANDUM - AMERICAN LIBRARY ASSOCIATION. OFFICE FOR INTELLECTUAL FREEDOM (US/0734-3086) [02513570] **1306**

MEMORANDUM - AMERICAN NEWSPAPER PUBLISHERS ASSOCIATION (US/0270-9864) [06514457] **4816**

MEMORANDUM EXPLANATORY OF THE BUDGET See ANNUAL FINANCIAL STATEMENT AND EXPLANATORY MEMORANDUM ON THE BUDGET OF THE PUNJAB GOVERNMENT **4709**

MEMORANDUM FROM INSTITUTE OF ECONOMIC RESEARCH, FACULTY OF ECONOMICS, UNIVERSITY OF GRONINGEN (NE) [07122020] **1505**

MEMORANDUM FROM TAX MANAGEMENT (US/0521-8098) [01767171] **4737**

MEMORANDUM ON ENTRY REQUIREMENTS TO COURSES OF TEACHER TRAINING IN SCOTLAND / SCOTTISH EDUCATION DEPARTMENT (UK) [06105601] **1900**

MEMORANDUM ON THE BUDGET ESTIMATES WITH DEMANDS FOR GRANTS AND ANNUAL FINANCIAL STATEMENT (II) [01784189] **4737**

MEMORANDUM OPINION AND ORDER (US/0364-8052) [02582154] **1117**

MEMORANDUM TO THE GOVERNMENT OF CANADA BY THE CANADIAN LABOUR CONGRESS (CN/0316-5892) [02247595] **1690**

MEMORIA (AG) [01787926] **1593**

MEMORIA (MX/0188-1744) [26705226] **358**

MEMORIA - ALIDE (PE) [03353664] **798**

MEMORIA AMERICANA (AG/0327-5752) [I03275752] **241**

MEMORIA ANUAL / COMISION CHILENA DEL COBRE (CL) [08757561] **4008**

MEMORIA ANUAL DEL CENTRO DOMINICANO DE PROMOCION DE EXPORTACIONES (DR) [02675913] **845**

MEMORIA ANUAL - INSTITUTO ARGENTINO DE OCEANOGRAFIA (AG) [05901827] **1452**

MEMORIA ANUAL / INSTITUTO NACIONAL DEL CAFE, INCAFE (ES) [19807124] **1618, 178**

MEMORIA ANUAL - SOCIEDAD DE FOMENTO FABRIL (CH) [03468310] **1914**

MEMORIA / BANCO CENTRAL DE LA REPUBLICA DOMINICA (DR) [15465143] **798**

MEMORIA / BANCO DE CREDITO AGRICOLA (MICROFORM) (SP) [08236851] **108, 798**

MEMORIA - CENTRAL DE COOPERATIVAS AGRARIAS DE PRODUCCION AZUCARERA DEL PERU LTDA. NO. 69 (PE) [03422235] **1542**

MEMORIA - CONSEJO SUPERIOR DE INVESTIGACIONES CIENTIFICAS (SP) [01697113] **5128**

MEMORIA / CORPORACION ANDINA DE FOMENTO (VE) [20062434] **798**

MEMORIA - CORPORACION FINANCIERA NACIONAL (EC) [06854831] **798**

MEMORIA DE ACTIVIDADES (SP) [08732645] **798**

MEMORIA DE EL COLEGIO NACIONAL (MX/0185-0539) [01555040] **1835**

MEMORIA DE LABORES (GT) [01791810] **798**

MEMORIA
Alphabetical Title Index

MEMORIA DE LABORES / PETROLEOS MEXICANOS (MX) [23752176] **4264**

MEMORIA DE LABORES - PETROLEOS MEXICANOS (MX) [04881372] **4264**

MEMORIA DE PAPEL (MX/0188-4824) [24234307] **325**

MEMORIA DEL CONGRESO INTERNACIONAL DE LITERATURA IBEROAMERICANA (PE) [04232799] **3347**

MEMORIA DEL ... FORO NACIONAL DE NOTARIADO Y REGISTRO (CK) [09700919] **3009**

MEMORIA DEL GERENTE GENERAL DEL BANCO CENTRAL DEL ECUADOR (EC/0067-3277) [01240618] **798**

MEMORIA DEL ICONA (SP) **108**

MEMORIA / DEPARTAMENTO NACIONAL DE PLANEACION (CK) [11540587] **1574**

MEMORIA - DESCO (PE) [03476067] **5209**

MEMORIA - EMPRESA NACIONAL DE FUNDICIONES (BO) [06470837] **4008**

MEMORIA - FINANCIERA NACIONAL DE CUBA (CU/0428-4119) [01370539] **798**

MEMORIA GENERAL - INSTITUTO GEOLOGICO Y MINERO DE ESPANA (SP) [01320799] 2144, **1387**

MEMORIA-INFORME / UNIVERSIDAD DE ZARAGOZA, BIBLIOTECA UNIVERSITARIA (SP) [21025249] **3231**

MEMORIA - INSTITUTO NACIONAL DE RACIONALIZACION Y NORMALIZACION. COMISION TECNICA DE TRABAJO NO. 53 INDUSTRIAS DE PLASTICS (SP) [01789707] **4456**

MEMORIA / INSTITUTO NACIONAL DEL CAFE, INCAFE, UNIDAD DE ESTUDIOS ESPECIALES *See* MEMORIA ANUAL / INSTITUTO NACIONAL DEL CAFE, INCAFE **178**

MEMORIA / OBSERVATORIO ASTRONOMICO NACIONAL (SP) [08798518] **397**

MEMORIA QUE PRESENTA EL CONSEJO DIRECTIVO DE LA SOCIEDAD DE FOMENTO FABRIL *See* MEMORIA ANUAL - SOCIEDAD DE FOMENTO FABRIL **1914**

MEMORIA QUE PRESENTA EL DIRECTOR GENERAL ... A LA HONORABLE ASAMBLEA DE REPRESENTANTES DE CORREGIMIENTOS (PN) [08637819] **5296**

MEMORIA - REUNION LATINOAMERICANA DE PRODUCCION ANIMAL (MX) [09902339] **2746**

MEMORIA - SOCIEDAD DE CIENCIAS NATURALES LA SALLE (VE) [04926454] **5128**

●MEMORIA STORICA : RIVISTA DEL CENTRO DI STUDI STORICI TERNI (IT) [28761642] **2698**

MEMORIA TECNICA - CONGRESO LATINAMERICANO DE SIDERURGIA (CL/0589-2813) [02242780] **4008**

MEMORIA (TURIN, ITALY) *CEASED.* (IT/0392-4564) [09427307] 5561, **2623**

MEMORIA Y BALANCE (AG) [01785975] **1690**

MEMORIA Y BALANCE GENERAL (AG) [07052989] **108**

MEMORIA Y BALANCE GENERAL (AG) [01792795] **1574**

MEMORIA Y CUENTA (VE) [15364255] **4194**

MEMORIA Y CUENTA (VE) [03249750] **1835**

MEMORIA Y CUENTA DE LA ASOCIACION DE INDUSTRIALES METALURGICOS Y DE MINERIA DE VENEZUELA (VE) [02608568] **4008**

MEMORIA Y CUENTA QUE EL MINISTERIO DE LA DEFENSA DE LA REPUBLICA DE VENEZUELA PRESENTA AL CONGRESO NACIONAL *See* MEMORIA Y CUENTA ... QUE EL MINISTRO DE LA DEFENSA PRESENTA AL CONGRESO NACIONAL / REPUBLICA DE VENEZUELA, MINISTERIO DE LA DEFENSA **4049**

MEMORIA Y CUENTA ... QUE EL MINISTRO DE LA DEFENSA PRESENTA AL CONGRESO NACIONAL / REPUBLICA DE VENEZUELA, MINISTERIO DE LA DEFENSA (VE) [07570883] **4049**

MEMORIA Y ESTADOS CONTABLES / ETERNIT ARGENTINA S.A (AG) [08643032] **693**

MEMORIAL JOURNAL OFFICIOL DU GRAND DUCHE DE LUXEMBOURG (LU) **1574**

MEMORIAL SOCIETY ASSOCIATION OF CANADA *See* NEWSLETTER - MEMORIAL SOCIETY ASSOCIATION OF CANADA **2407**

MEMORIAL UNIVERSITY OF NEWFOUNDLAND. CENTRE FOR COLD OCEAN RESOURCES ENGINEERING *See* C-C O R E NEWS **1967**

MEMORIAL UNIVERSITY OF NEWFOUNDLAND. DEPT. OF COMPUTING AND COMMUNICATIONS *See* COMPUTING & COMMUNICATIONS NEWSLETTER **1180**

MEMORIAL UNIVERSITY OF NEWFOUNDLAND. LIBRARY *See* SERIAL HOLDINGS IN NEWFOUNDLAND LIBRARIES **3249**

MEMORIAL UNIVERSITY OF NEWFOUNDLAND OCCASIONAL PAPERS IN BIOLOGY (CN/0702-0007) [09084977] **464**

MEMORIAL UNIVERSITY OF NEWFOUNDLAND. OFFICE OF RESEARCH *See* RESEARCH INVENTORY / MEMORIAL UNIVERSITY OF NEWFOUNDLAND, OFFICE OF RESEARCH **1845**

MEMORIAL UNIVERSITY OF NEWFOUNDLAND. OFFICE OF RESEARCH *See* RESEARCH DIRECTORY - MEMORIAL UNIVERSITY OF NEWFOUNDLAND. OFFICE OF RESEARCH **1845**

MEMORIALS - GEOLOGICAL SOCIETY OF AMERICA (US/0091-5041) [01784422] **1387**

MEMORIAL'S SENIOR HEALTH UPDATE (US/1057-7114) [24102969] **4790**

MEMORIAS (SP/0368-8283) [11198711] **5209**

MEMORIAS AL CONGRESO NACIONAL / REPUBLICA DE COLOMBIA, MINISTERIO DE MINAS Y ENERGIA (CK) [25836739] **2144**

MEMORIAS DA ACADEMIA DAS CIENCIAS DE LISBOA. CLASSE DE LETRAS (PO/0378-116X) [01460610] **5233**

MEMORIAS DA SOCIEDADE BROTERIANA (PO/0081-0665) [01645787] **518**

MEMORIAS DE HISTORIA ANTIGUA (SP) [07611302] **2623**

MEMORIAS DE LA ACADEMIA MEXICANA DE LA HISTORIA (MX/0378-0724) [01460623] **2746**

MEMORIAS DE LOS MUSEOS ARQUEOLOGICOS PROVINCIALES. (EXTRACTOS) (SP) [02882845] **4091**

MEMORIAS DEL MUSEO DE HISTORIA NATURAL JAVIER PRADO (PE/0457-9151) [01385622] **4167**

MEMORIAS DEL MUSEO DE HISTORIA NATURAL. UNIVERSIDAD NACIONAL MAYOR DE SAN MARCOS (PE) **4167**

MEMORIAS DO INSTITUTO BUTANTAN (SAO PAULO) (BL/0073-9901) [01397014] 5591, **3674**

MEMORIAS DO INSTITUTO DE BIOCIENCIAS (RECIFE) (BL/0100-2007) [01228519] **464**

MEMORIAS DO INSTITUTO DE INVESTIGACAO CIENTIFICA DE MOCAMBIQUE. SERIES C, CIENCIAS HUMANAS (MZ/0076-1184) [01397019] **5209**

MEMORIAS DO INSTITUTO DE INVESTIGACAO CIENTIFICA TROPICAL (PO/0870-0036) **5128**

MEMORIAS DO INSTITUTO OSWALDO CRUZ (BL/0074-0276) [01197361] **464**

MEMORIE / ACCADEMIA NAZIONALE DEI LINCEI, CLASSE DI SCIENZE MORALI, STORICHE E FILOLOGICHE (IT) [17217391] **3302**

MEMORIE / CLASSE DI SCIENZE FISICHE, MATEMATICHE E NATURALI (IT) [05574533] **5128**

MEMORIE DELLA SOCIETA ASTRONOMICA ITALIANA (IT/0037-8720) [01773396] **397**

MEMORIE DELLA SOCIETA ENTOMOLOGICA ITALIANA (IT/0037-8747) [01696242] **5612**

MEMORIE DELLA SOCIETA GEOGRAFICA ITALIANA (IT) [01772450] **2569**

MEMORIE DELLA SOCIETA GEOLOGICA ITALIANA (IT) **1387**

MEMORIE DELL'ACCADEMIA ITALIANA DI STUDI FILATELICI E NUMISMATICI (IT) [19644703] 2781, **1145**

MEMORIE DI BIOGEOGRAFIA ADRIATICA (IT/0505-2009) [02731530] **2569**

MEMORIE DI BIOLOGIA MARINA E DI OCEANOGRAFIA (IT/0390-492X) [03269510] 1452, **556**

MEMORIE DOMENICANE (PISTOIA : 1970) (IT) [08515748] 4976, **2698**

MEMORIE E RENDICONTI (ACCADEMIA DI SCIENZE, LETTERE E BELLE ARTE DI ACIREALE) *See* MEMORIE E RENDICONTI / ACCADEMIA DI SCIENZE, LETTERE E BELLE ARTI DEGLI ZELANTI E DEI DAFNICI **5128**

MEMORIE E RENDICONTI / ACCADEMIA DI SCIENZE, LETTERE E BELLE ARTI DEGLI ZELANTI E DEI DAFNICI (IT) [05461880] **5128**

MEMORIE LINCEE. MATEMATICA E APPLICAZIONI / CLASSE DI SCIENZE FISICHE, MATEMATICHE E NATURALI (IT) [23158049] **3522**

MEMORIE STORICHE FOROGIULIESI (IT/0392-1496) [04363398] **2698**

MEMORIES OF THE JEWISH MIDWEST (US) [15250733] **2267**

●MEMORIES PLUS (US/1062-9556) [25814668] 1801, **5180**

MEMORIILE SECTIEI DE STIINTE FILOLOGICE, LITERATURA SI ARTE (RM) [07729854] 3411, **3302**

MEMORIILE SECTIEI DE STIINTE ISTORICE (RM/0256-5293) [I02565293] **2698**

MEMORIILE SECTIILOR STIINTIFICE / ACADEMIA REPUBLICII SOCIALISTE ROMANIA (RM/0254-8607) [07720890] **5128**

●MEMORY (UK/0965-8211) [27809620] **4603**

MEMORY & COGNITION (US/0090-502X) [01788000] **4603**

MEMORY AND MICROCOMPUTERS (US/0733-2394) [08542747] **1269**

MEMORY CARD SYSTEMS & DESIGN (US/1055-5188) [23197677] **1195**

MEMORY DISCONTINUED DEVICES (US) [16639934] **2072**

MEMORY JOGGER (US) **693**

MEMORY LANE (LEIGH-ON-SEA, ESSEX) (UK/0266-8033) [09988914] **4130**

MEMOS (SPRINGFIELD, MO.) (US/0885-7776) [12748096] **4976**

MEMPHIS (US/0162-282X) [04146221] **2538**

MEMPHIS BUSINESS JOURNAL (US/0747-167X) [10617361] **693**

MEMPHIS ECONOMY / BUREAU OF BUSINESS & ECONOMIC RESEARCH, MEMPHIS STATE UNIVERSITY (US) [07392821] **1505**

MEMPHIS FLYER, THE (US) **2490**

MEMPHIS MUSIC DIRECTORY, THE (US/0272-8214) [06394297] **4130**

MEMPHIS PRESS-SCIMITAR (US) [13175061] **5745**

MEMPHIS STATE UNIVERSITY LAW REVIEW (US/0047-6714) [01757101] **3009**

MEMPHIS THEOLOGICAL SEMINARY JOURNAL (US) **4976**

MEN OF ACHIEVEMENT (UK/0306-3666) [01795299] **433**

MEN OF ALL COLORS TOGETHER CHICAGO : [NEWSLETTER] (US) [24450245] **2795**

MEN ONLY (UK) [04648380] **2519**

MENA STAR, THE (US/0747-1513) [10579675] **5632**

MENARA PERKEBUNAN (IO/0125-9318) [02256554] **108**

MENARD NEWS AND MESSENGER, THE (US) [17163997] **5752**

MENAS MONOGRAPH (UK) [10008264] **2642**

MENCKENIANA (US/0025-9233) [01604595] **3411**

MENDELEEV CHEMISTRY JOURNAL (US/0025-925X) [00850930] **985**

MENDELEEV COMMUNICATIONS / ROYAL SOCIETY OF CHEMISTRY, [AKADEMIIA NAUK SSSR] (RU/0959-9436) [23678108] **985**

MENDELSSOHN STUDIEN (GW) [01786321] **4131**

MENDOCINO BEACON, THE (US) [27879378] **5637**

●MENDOCINO COUNTY OUTLOOK (US/1065-8416) [26775815] **5637**

MENDOZA, ARGENTINE REPUBLIC (CITY). UNIVERSIDAD NACIONAL DE CUYO. FACULTAD DE CIENCIAS ECONOMICAS *See* REVISTA DE LA FACULTAD DE CIENCIAS ECONOMICAS **1595**

MENDY AND THE GOLEM (US/0278-4432) [07806992] **5018**

MEN'EKI YAKURI SHINPOJUMU (JA/0289-3371) [I02893371] 3674, **4315**

MENG YA (CC) [10854683] **3411**

MENIAIO DELTIO EMPORIKOU KAI VIOMECHANIKOU EPIMELETERIOU THESSALONIKES *See* DELTIO EMPORIKOU KAI VIOMECHANIKOU EPIMELETERIOU THESSALONIKES **1555**

MENIAIO STATISTIKO DELTIO - TRAPEZA TES HELLADOS (GR/1105-0519) [02268685] 798, **731**

MENNESKER OG RETTIGHETER (NO/0800-0735) [19467737] **4510**

MENNINGER CLINIC *See* BULLETIN OF THE MENNINGER CLINIC **3922**

●MENNINGER LETTER, THE (US/1066-937X) [27096351] **3930**

MENNINGER PERSPECTIVE (US/0025-9292) [01589811] **3930**

MENNOGESPRACH *See* ONTARIO MENNONITE HISTORY **4983**

Alphabetical Title Index — MERCADO

MENNOGESPRACH (WATERLOO) (CN/0824-5673) [10768375] **5063**

MENNONITE (1936), THE (US/0025-9330) [07580839] **5063**

MENNONITE BRETHREN HERALD (CN/0025-9349) [01697281] **5063**

MENNONITE BUSINESS AND PROFESSIONAL PEOPLE'S DIRECTORY (US) [02710971] **693**

MENNONITE CENTRAL COMMITTEE. PEACE SECTION TASK FORCE ON WOMEN IN CHURCH AND SOCIETY *See* REPORT - MENNONITE CENTRAL COMMITTEE. PEACE SECTION TASK FORCE ON WOMEN IN CHURCH AND SOCIETY **4992**

MENNONITE CONFERENCE OF EASTERN CANADA *See* DIRECTORY / MENNONITE CONFERENCE OF EASTERN CANADA **5059**

MENNONITE FAMILY HISTORY (US/0730-5214) [08035550] **2460**

MENNONITE HERITAGE (US) [04705786] **2460**

MENNONITE HISTORIAN (CN/0700-8066) [03399894] **5064**

MENNONITE HISTORICAL BULLETIN (US/0025-9357) [01713995] **5064**

MENNONITE LIBRARIAN AND ARCHIVIST, THE *CEASED.* (US/0889-5600) [13979724] **3231**

MENNONITE LIFE (US/0025-9365) [01757111] **5064**

MENNONITE MEDICAL MESSENGER (WINNIPEG, MAN.) (CN/0824-3093) [10195375] **3616**

MENNONITE QUARTERLY REVIEW, THE (US/0025-9373) [01638991] **5064**

MENNONITE REPORTER (CN/0380-0121) [01777032] **5789**

MENNONITE WEEKLY REVIEW (US/0889-2156) [01777033] **5677**

MENNONITE YEARBOOK & DIRECTORY (US/0275-1178) [01780998] **5064**

MENNONITISCHE GESCHICHTSBLATTER (GW/0342-1171) [01590558] **5064**

MENNONITISCHE POST (CN/0705-4041) [03900266] **5064**

MENNONITISCHES GEMEINDEBLATT, BRUCKE (GW) [14210317] **4976**

MENOMINEE HERALD-LEADER, THE (US) [09798511] **5692**

MENOMINEE TRIBAL NEWS (US) [06188781] **2267**

MENOMONEE FALLS NEWS, THE (US) [14956145] **5769**

●MENOPAUSE MANAGEMENT (US/1062-7332) [25719692] **5561**

●MENOPAUSE (NEW YORK, N.Y.) (US/1072-3714) [28934287] **3616**

MENOPAUSE NEWS (US/1061-4397) [25308176] **3765**

MENORES : REVISTA DE LA DIRECCION GENERAL DE PROTECCION JURIDICA DEL MENOR (SP) [13695903] **4790**

MEN'S AD REVIEW (US/0279-8999) [07344844] **762**

MENS & MELODIE (NE/0025-9462) [08755058] **4131**

MEN'S AWARENESS NETWORK *See* NEWSLETTER - MEN'S AWARENESS NETWORK **3931**

MEN'S BAZAAR ITALIA *See* UOMO HARPER'S BAZAAR **1088**

●MEN'S CONFIDENTIAL (US/1066-5706) [27001015] **3995**

MENS EN MAATSCHAPPIJ (NE/0025-9454) [09234364] **5209, 5252**

MENS EN WETENSCHAP (NE) **5128**

MEN'S EXERCISE (US/1059-9169) [24806821] **2599**

MEN'S GUIDE TO FASHION (US/0887-5219) [13308175] **1086**

MEN'S HEALTH (EMMAUS, PA. 1985) (US/0747-8461) [10810562] **3616**

MEN'S HEALTH (MAGAZINE) (US/1054-4836) [22901977] 3995, **2599**

MEN'S HEALTH (NEWSLETTER) *See* MEN'S CONFIDENTIAL **3995**

●MEN'S JOURNAL (NEW YORK, N.Y.) (US/1063-4657) [26042385] **3996**

MEN'S NEWS MAGAZINE (US/0748-5913) [09378825] **3996**

MEN'S STUDIES REVIEW *See* MASCULINITIES : OFFICIAL PUBLICATION OF THE MEN'S STUDIES ASSOCIATION, NATIONAL ORGANIZATION FOR MEN AGAINST SEXISM **3995**

MEN'S WEAR OF CANADA (CN/0025-9535) [01988686] **1086**

MEN'S WORKOUT (US/1058-3041) [24261658] **3996**

MENSA BULLETIN (US/0025-9543) [02546344] **5233**

MENSA CANADA SOCIETY *See* REGISTRE-ANNUAIRE - MENSA CANADA **5236**

MENSAJE ECONOMICO FINANCIERO (VE) [04707340] **1574**

MENSAJE (SANTIAGO, CHILE) (CL/0025-956X) [03659595] 5252, **4976**

MENSAJERO DEL CORAZON DE JESUS, EL (MX) [06682871] **4976**

MENSAJERO (SAN FRANCISCO, CALIF.), EL (US/1040-5712) [17895175] **2746**

MENSALOHA (US/8750-4529) [11486960] **4603**

MENSARIO DO CONTABILISTA (BL) [02648993] **748**

MENSCH & BUERO (GW/0933-8241) [I09338241] **4212**

MENSCH + RECHT : QUARTALSZEITSCHRIFT DER SCHWEIZERISCHEN GESELLSCHAFT FUR DIE EUROPAISCHE MENSCHENRECHTSKONVENTION (SGEMKO) / HERAUSGEBERIN SGEMKO (SZ) [09363103] **4510**

MENSCH UND BUERO (GW/0933-8241) **4212**

MENSUALISATION DES OUVRIERS DU BATIMENT, LA (FR) [01792059] **1690**

MENSUEL DE LACHUTE, LE (CN/0824-9040) [11431379] **5789**

MENSUEL DE STE-DOROTHEE, LE (CN/0823-6941) [10032106] **5789**

●MENSUEL DU CINEMA, LE (FR/1242-0492) [28131001] **4074**

MENTAL AND PHYSICAL DISABILITY LAW REPORTER (US/0883-7902) [10503120] 4391, 4604, **3009**

MENTAL HANDICAP : JOURNAL OF THE BRITISH INSTITUTE OF MENTAL HANDICAP (UK/0261-9997) [08654450] 4604, **5296**

MENTAL HANDICAP RESEARCH (UK/0952-9608) [18518192] **3930**

●MENTAL HEALTH AND SOCIAL WORK CAREER DIRECTORY (US/1070-7298) [28514087] 5296, **3915**

MENTAL HEALTH ANNUAL REPORT / DEPARTMENT OF HEALTH AND SOCIAL SERVICES, DIVISION OF MENTAL HEALTH AND DEVELOPMENTAL DISABILITIES (US) [07969145] **4790**

MENTAL HEALTH AUDIT CRITERIA SERIES (US/0190-1672) [04611177] **4790**

MENTAL HEALTH (BOCA RATON) (US/0272-9962) [04451602] 4604, **4790**

MENTAL HEALTH COMMISSION OF NEW BRUNSWICK *See* ANNUAL REPORT / MENTAL HEALTH COMMISSION OF NEW BRUNSWICK **4766**

MENTAL HEALTH COMMISSION OF NEW BRUNSWICK. REGION II *See* ANNUAL REPORT - MENTAL HEALTH COMMISSION OF NEW BRUNSWICK. REGION II **3920**

MENTAL HEALTH FUNDING NEWS *See* MENTAL HEALTH NEWS ALERT **5296**

MENTAL HEALTH-HUMAN RESOURCES CONFERENCE GUIDE (US/1064-685X) [20505074] **3616**

MENTAL HEALTH IN AUSTRALIA (1973) (AT/0310-5776) [01664056] **4790**

MENTAL HEALTH LAW NEWS (US/0889-017X) [13812422] 4790, **3009**

MENTAL HEALTH LAW PROJECT *See* SUMMARY OF ACTIVITIES - MENTAL HEALTH LAW PROJECT **3060**

MENTAL HEALTH LAW REPORTER (US/0741-5141) [10139336] **3009**

MENTAL HEALTH MANUAL (US) **3930**

●MENTAL HEALTH NEWS ALERT (US) 3930, **5296**

MENTAL HEALTH NEWS BULLETIN (CN/0827-2700) [11739658] **4790**

MENTAL HEALTH NURSING (UK) 3930, **3861**

MENTAL HEALTH PLAN (AUGUSTA, ME.) (US/0743-9113) [10681660] **4790**

MENTAL HEALTH PROGRAM REPORTS (US/0083-2154) [02264054] **4790**

●MENTAL HEALTH RAP (US/1065-7525) [26716269] 4790, **5296**

MENTAL HEALTH REPORTS (US/0191-6750) [04927619] **4790**

MENTAL HEALTH, RETARDATION AND HOSPITALS (CRANSTON) (US/0094-291X) [01791811] **3789**

MENTAL HEALTH SERVICE SYSTEM REPORTS. SERIES AN, EPIDEMIOLOGY (US/0276-6884) [07228158] 4790, **3736**

MENTAL HEALTH SERVICE SYSTEM REPORTS. SERIES CN, MENTAL HEALTH NATIONAL STATISTICS (US/0278-6877) [07228260] **4810**

MENTAL HEALTH SERVICE SYSTEM REPORTS. SERIES DN. HEALTH / MENTAL HEALTH RESEARCH (US/0730-1588) [07228221] **4604**

MENTAL HEALTH SERVICE SYSTEM REPORTS. SERIES EN, MENTAL HEALTH ECONOMICS (US/0733-9852) [08398186] **4790**

MENTAL HEALTH SERVICE SYSTEM REPORTS. SERIES GN, METHODOLOGY / U.S. DEPARTMENT OF HEALTH AND HUMAN SERVICES, PUBLIC HEALTH SERVICE, ALCOHOL, DRUG ABUSE, AND MENTAL HEALTH ADMINISTRATION, NATIONAL INSTITUTE OF MENTAL HEALTH (US/0273-3498) [07029427] **3930**

MENTAL HEALTH SPECIAL INTEREST SECTION NEWSLETTER (US/0279-4136) [07841287] **4790**

MENTAL HEALTH STATE PLAN (US/0146-7905) [03025900] **5296**

MENTAL HEALTH STATISTICAL NOTE (US/0361-9311) [02134065] 3930, **4790**

MENTAL HEALTH STATISTICS (JEFFERSON CITY) (US/0196-562X) [05304368] **4810**

MENTAL HEALTH SYSTEM DESCRIPTION AND BUDGET REQUESTS FOR THE STATE OF OKLAHOMA / OKLAHOMA STATE DEPARTMENT OF MENTAL HEALTH (US) [07772067] **4791**

MENTAL HEALTH SYSTEMS SOFTWARE DIRECTORY *CEASED.* (US/0883-3443) [12123279] 1215, **3616**

MENTAL HEALTH (TORONTO. 1979) (CN/0821-3305) [10027578] **3930**

MENTAL HEALTH (TORONTO. 1979) (CN/0821-3305) [10027575] **5296**

MENTAL HEALTH, UNITED STATES (US/0892-0664) [10720813] **4604**

MENTAL HEALTH WEEKLY (US/1058-1103) [24223238] 3931, **4604**

MENTAL HEALTH YEARBOOK/DIRECTORY, THE (US/0195-766X) [05514710] **4791**

MENTAL HOSPITALS *See* HOSPITAL & COMMUNITY PSYCHIATRY. MICROFILM **3926**

MENTAL HYGIENE LAW (NEW YORK) (US/0164-2650) [04578645] **3009**

... MENTAL MEASUREMENTS YEARBOOK, THE (US/0076-6461) [01537855] **1763**

MENTAL RETARDATION AND THE LAW (US/0098-8111) [02241456] **3009**

MENTAL RETARDATION (WASHINGTON) (US/0047-6765) [01713511] **1882**

MENTALIS (US/0360-7232) [01920022] **1330**

MENTALITIES (NZ/0111-8854) [09526436] **4604**

MENTOR MANAGEMENT DIGEST (UK) **879**

MENTOR (SINGAPORE) (SI) [08945820] 1690, **1763**

MENTORING INTERNATIONAL *CEASED.* (CN/0843-5405) [19674538] 944, **4604**

MENTZELIA (US) [04788708] **2424**

MENUS OF THE VALLEY'S FINEST RESTAURANTS (US/0148-4133) [03313659] **5071**

MER & BATEAUX PARIS (FR/0999-7148) [I09997148] **594**

MER ET BATEAUX *See* MEER & YACHTEN **594**

MER. MARINE ENGINEERS REVIEW (UK/0047-5955) [01820566] 4179, **1987**

MER (TOKYO, JAPAN) (JA/0503-1540) [09310032] **1452**

MERCADO (AG/0325-0687) [01798083] **1574**

MERCADO ASEGURADOR (AG) **2888**

MERCADO COMUM BRASILEIRO (BL) [02658583] **845**

MERCADO COMUM BRASILEIRO : BRASILIA, GOIAS, MINAS GERAIS (BL) [01798624] **846**

MERCADO COMUM BRASILEIRO : GUANABARA, ESPIRITO SANTO, RIO DE JANEIRO (BL) [01798831] **846**

MERCADO COMUM BRASILEIRO : PARANA, RIO GRANDE DO SUL, SANTA CATARINA (BL) [02243796] **693**

MERCADO COMUM BRASILEIRO : SAO PAULO (BL/0100-2570) [01798537] **846**

MERCADO DE CAFE NOS ESTADOS UNIDOS E NO CANADA. THE COFFEE MARKET IN THE UNITED STATES AND CANADA, O (US) [05839044] **2369**

MERCADO DE VALORES, EL (MX/0025-9756) [02264066] **798**

MERCADO EM ANALISE (BL) [02471396] **108**

MERCADO (MADRID, SPAIN) (SP/0210-9344) [18246627] **798**

MERCADO MUNDIAL. WORLD MARKET (SP) [06715336] **846**

MERCADOS — Alphabetical Title Index

MERCADOS AGRARIOS. PRECIOS / COMISION DE LAS COMUNIDADES EUROPEAS / LANDBRUGSMARKEDER. PRISER / KOMMISSIONEN FOR DE EUROPAEISKE FAELLESSKABER / AGRICULTURAL MARKETS. PRICES / COMMISSION OF THE EUROPEAN COMMUNITIES (LU/1014-8159) [29150129] 108, **155**

MERCADOS AGRICOLAS : INFORMACOES (BL) [06545994] **108**

MERCANTILE AGENT (AT) **846**

MERCANTILE GAZETTE (NZ) [08097630] **3102**

MERCATI AGRICOLI : PREZZI (IT) **108**

MERCATO METALSIDERURGICO (IT) **4008**

MERCED SUN-STAR (US) [20681689] **5637**

MERCER BULLETIN, THE (CN/0714-6914) [09250139] **1690**

MERCER BUSINESS : A PUBLICATION OF MERCER COUNTY CHAMBER (US/0194-9101) [05103759] **693**

MERCER COUNTY CHRONICLE (COLDWATER, OHIO : 1959) (US) [17359185] **5729**

●MERCER GUIDE TO SOCIAL SECURITY AND MEDICARE (US) [25678110] 1690, **2888**

MERCER ISLAND REPORTER (US) [17239081] **5761**

MERCER LAW REVIEW (US/0025-987X) [01757130] **3009**

MERCER MESSENGER (US/0747-3222) [10740341] **5710**

MERCER PENSION MANUAL, THE (CN) [18878578] **2888**

MERCHANDISING ... STATISTICAL AND MARKETING REPORT (US) [05903800] 933, **731**

MERCHANT EXPLORER, THE (US/0543-5056) [02225885] **846**

MERCHANT FLEETS OF THE WORLD / U.S. DEPARTMENT OF COMMERCE, MARITIME ADMINISTRATION (US) [02223151] **5453**

MERCHANT (HARRISBURG), THE (US/0164-5102) [04582385] **5737**

MERCHANT MAGAZINE, THE (US/0739-9723) [04204388] 693, **2402**

MERCHANTS AND MANUFACTURERS ASSOCIATION See ADMINISTRATIVE AND TECHNICAL SALARY SURVEY **1642**

MERCHANTS AND MANUFACTURERS ASSOCIATION See ENGINEERING, SCIENTIFIC AND TECHNICAL SALARY SURVEY **1974**

MERCHANTS AND MANUFACTURERS ASSOCIATION See SUPERVISORY AND MIDDLE MANAGEMENT SALARY SURVEY (LOS ANGELES) **1713**

MERCIAN GEOLOGIST (UK/0025-990X) [01716381] **1387**

MERCK INDEX; AN ENCYCLOPEDIA OF CHEMICALS AND DRUGS, THE (US/0076-6518) [01757135] **4315**

MERCK MANUAL OF DIAGNOSIS AND THERAPY, THE (US/0076-6526) [02630128] **3616**

MERCK VETERINARY MANUAL, THE (US/0076-6542) [01770866] **5516**

MERCREDI SOIR, LE (CN/0710-3794) [08716766] **5789**

MERCURIO, EL (CL) [05242664] **5798**

MERCURY IN ... (US) [09313294] **2144**

MERCURY IN WATER (US/0363-5015) [02430473] **420**

MERCURY (LOS ANGELES, CALIF.) (US/0025-9969) [04053438] **4904**

MERCURY (POTTSTOWN, PA.) (US) [15349778] **5737**

MERCURY-REGISTER (US) [27480706] **5637**

MERCURY (SAN FRANCISCO) (US/0047-6773) [01019048] **397**

MERCURY (UNITED STATES. BUREAU OF MINES) (US/0364-7919) [02256321] 4008, 2144, **4026**

MERCY COLLEGE See ALUMNI DIRECTORY / MERCY COLLEGE **1098**

MERDEKA (IO) [06492495] **5803**

MEREDITH MEMORIAL LECTURES (1975) (CN/0821-3690) [09467679] **3009**

MEREDITH NEWS, THE (US) [11145577] **5708**

MERENKULKU. KAUPPALAIVASTO (FI/0430-5574) [03283518] **5453**

MERENKULKU. MERILIIKENNE SUOMEN JA ULKOMAIDEN VALILLA (FI/0430-5582) [03318386] **5453**

MERENTUTKIMUSLAITOS See TOIMINTAKERTOMUS / MERENTUTKIMUSLAITOS **1457**

MERES ES AUTOMATIKA (HU/0025-9993) [11349393] **4031**

MERGE (US/0364-2518) [02613811] 4791, **5441**

MERGER AND ACQUISITION SOURCEBOOK (US/0742-602X) [09810846] **693**

●MERGER YEARBOOK, THE (US/1076-3600) [28312968] **693**

●MERGERS + ACQUISITIONS INTERNATIONAL (US) [26936835] **798**

MERGERS & ACQUISITIONS (US/0026-0010) [01606802] 879, **798**

MERGERS & ACQUISITIONS ABSTRACTS / ANBAR (UK/0959-7441) [23475481] **693**

MERGERS AND ACQUISITIONS IN CANADA (RICHMOND HILL, ONT.) (CN/0843-5421) [16220365] **693**

MERGERS & ACQUISITIONS INTERNATIONAL (UK) [20011043] **693**

MERGERS & ACQUISITIONS (LONDON, ENGLAND) (UK) [09777887] **1618**

MERGERS & ACQUISITIONS REPORT (US) **693**

MERGERS AND FEDERAL POLICY See CAMBRIDGE REPORT ON CORPORATE MERGERS AND CORPORATE POLICY, THE **782**

MERGERSTAT REVIEW (US/1071-4065) [08443270] **693**

MERIAN (HAMBURG, GERMANY) (GW/0026-0029) [01607228] **2519**

MERIDA, MEXICO. UNIVERSIDAD DE YUCATAN. ESCUELA DE CIENCIAS ANTROPOLOGICAS See BOLETIN DE LA ESCUELA DE CIENCIAS ANTROPOLOGICAS DE LA UNIVERSIDAD DE YUCATAN **232**

MERIDIAN (US) [07620044] **3466**

MERIDIAN (BUNDOORA, VIC.) (AT/0728-5914) [10157888] **3347**

MERIDIAN (LOS ANGELES) (US/0093-0997) [05452294] **3616**

MERIDIAN - MAP & GEOGRAPHY ROUND TABLE (AMERICAN LIBRARY ASSOCIATION) (US/1040-7421) [18508074] 3231, 2569, **2582**

MERIDIAN POETRY MAGAZINE (UK/0306-3461) [01794752] **3466**

MERIDIAN SOFTWARE ANALYSIS BULLETIN (US/0891-5318) [14879850] **2490**

MERIDIAN STAR (1914), THE (US/1064-9549) [10362622] **5701**

MERIDIANA (IT/0394-4115) [27141837] **5209**

MERIDIANI (IT) [22942061] **5484**

MERIDIANO 70 I.E. SETENTA (US) [02263813] **3411**

MERIDIES (PO) [14340396] **2267**

MERIDIONAL-LA FRANCE, LE (FR) [20926363] **5800**

MERIGAL (AT/0725-8739) [I07258739] **226**

MERI'S MONTHLY CIRCULAR (JA/0026-6809) [04622989] **1574**

MERIT SYSTEMS PROTECTION BOARD SERVICE. INCLUDES INDEX DIGEST AND ANALYSIS OF DECISIONS (US) **3090**

MERITE AGRICOLE ET MERITE DU DEFRICHEUR (CN) [06176874] **108**

MERIWETHER CONNECTIONS (US/1045-3199) [09567142] **2460**

MERIWETHER VINDICATOR, THE (US) [19899135] **5654**

MERIYASU KONGOP YONBO (KO) [04709828] 5185, **5354**

MERKAZ LE-TIKHNUN U-FITUAH HAKLAI VE-HITYASHVUTI, HA- See SEDAROT STATISTIYOT **156**

MERKBLATTER - KOMMISSION FUR EINBANDFRAGEN VEREINS DEUTSCHER BIBLIOTHEKARE (GW) [02512586] **4830**

●MERKBLATTER / LANDESUMWELTAMT (GW) 2177, **2236**

MERKENBLAD - BUREAU VOOR DE INDUSTRIELE EIGENDOM, NEDERLANDSE ANTILLEN (NE) [02239851] **1306**

MERKUR (GW/0026-0096) [01607817] **3347**

MERLYN'S PEN (US/0882-2050) [11778077] **1066**

MERLYN'S PEN SENIOR EDITION GRADES 9-12 (US) **1066**

MEROITICA (GW) [02472223] **846**

MERRIAM SUN, THE (US) [11920072] **5677**

MERRILL LYNCH EUROMONEY DIRECTORY See CEDEL EUROMONEY DIRECTORY, THE **782**

MERRILL LYNCH EUROMONEY DIRECTORY, THE (UK) [15987754] **798**

MERRILL-PALMER QUARTERLY (1960) (US/0272-930X) [08798266] **4604**

MERRILL'S ILLINOIS LEGAL TIMES (US/1063-3014) [15902212] **3009**

MERRILLVILLE HERALD, THE (US/1043-9587) [15651356] **5665**

MERSEYSIDE CHAMBER OF COMMERCE AND INDUSTRY See MERSEYSIDE CHAMBER OF COMMERCE AND INDUSTRY DIRECTORY **820**

MERSEYSIDE CHAMBER OF COMMERCE AND INDUSTRY DIRECTORY (UK/0302-4148) [01792624] **820**

MERTON ANNUAL, THE (US/0894-4857) [16115406] **4976**

MERTON SEASONAL OF BELLARMINE COLLEGE, THE (US/0899-4927) [11015570] **2490**

MERVEILLES & CONTES (US/0898-154X) [17735522] **3411**

MERVYN PEAKE REVIEW, THE (SZ/0309-1309) [05458099] **3411**

MES CONFIDENCES EROTIQUES (FR/0985-9861) [I09859861] **5188**

MESA REPORT (US/0097-6105) [02335532] **1452**

MESA SAFETY REVIEWS (US/0097-9368) [02254099] **2865**

MESA TRIBUNE (US) **5630**

MESA VERDE RESEARCH SERIES (US) [08057091] **4091**

MESABI DAILY NEWS (US) [01607656] **5697**

MESNE ZAJEDNICE (YU) [01798776] **4664**

MESOAMERICA (ANTIGUA, GUATEMALA) (GT/0252-9963) [07141215] **2746**

MESOAMERICA (INSTITUTE FOR CENTRAL AMERICAN STUDIES (COSTA RICA)) (CR) [08419218] **2512**

MESOAMERICAN STUDY GROUP NEWSLETTER, THE (US) [25302976] **2746**

MESOLITHIC MISCELLANY (US/0259-3548) [08029529] **274**

MESOPOTAMIA (IT/0391-4135) [02474894] **274**

MESOPOTAMIA JOURNAL OF AGRICULTURE (IQ/0379-7791) [04678919] **108**

MESPA PRINCIPAL (US) [09836523] **1866**

MESQUITE MESSENGER (US) **2402**

MESQUITE NEWS, THE (US/0746-4126) [10029405] **5752**

MESSAGE (GW) [02538842] **1764**

●MESSAGE (1993) (US/1071-5215) [28449771] **5043**

MESSAGE (CHERRY HILL), THE (US/0271-5732) [06268467] **4976**

●MESSAGE IN THE MUSIC (US/1056-554X) [23737643] **4131**

MESSAGE INTERNATIONAL (JAMAICA, NEW YORK, N.Y.) See MESSAGE (1993) **5043**

MESSAGE (NASHVILLE, TENN.) (US/0026-0231) [04170540] 2267, **5064**

MESSAGE OF THE CITY MANAGER TO THE CITY COUNCIL SUBMITTING THE EXECUTIVE BUDGET (US) [01783574] **4737**

MESSAGE OF THE CROSS (US) [01777034] **4976**

MESSAGE OLYMPIQUE (SZ/1011-405X) [08783080] **4904**

MESSAGER DE LA MINGANIE, LE (CN/0713-6862) [08977547] **5789**

MESSAGER DORVAL, LE (CN/0821-4174) [09547377] **5789**

MESSAGER EUROPEEN, LE (FR) [17561886] **2698**

MESSAGER EVANGELIQUE, LE (FR) [05950743] **4976**

MESSAGES DES POSTES ET TELECOMMUNICATIONS (FR) [04177474] **1160**

MESSAGES DES PTT (FR/0245-6001) [08226518] **1145**

MESSAGGERO DI LUCCA, IL (IT) [01773980] **5804**

MESSAGGERO VENETO (IT/1120-608X) [I1120608X] **5804**

MESSEN & PRUFEN (1990) (GW/0937-3446) [I09373446] **1987**

MESSENGER (FORT DODGE, IOWA), THE (US/0740-6991) [10027533] **5671**

MESSENGER INQUIRER (US) [13991290] **5681**

MESSENGER (KITCHENER) (CN/0381-5293) [03887113] **4976**

MESSENGER (MADISON, N.C.) (US/0892-1814) [15144065] **5723**

MESSENGER (MADISONVILLE, KY.) (US) [14124782] **5681**

MESSENGER OF THE CHESTERFIELD HISTORICAL SOCIETY OF VIRGINIA, THE (US/0731-3012) [08163251] **2746**

MESSENGER OF TRUTH (MOUNDRIDGE, KAN.) (US/0892-6662) [15266767] **4976**

MESSENGER-PRESS (US) [12317712] **5710**

MESSENGER (SCARBOROUGH) (CN/0228-2828) [06965922] **5789**

MESSENGER (STEINBACK) (CN/0701-3299) [03365675] **4976**

MESSENGER, THE (US) **4976**

MESSENGER, THE (US/0279-3911) [01757164] **2538**

MESSENGER (TROY, ALA.), THE (US/1044-0070) [16942287] **5627**

MESSENGER (WASAGA BEACH) (CN/0229-7833) [08401441] **4481**

●MESSIANIC JEW (AND HEBREW CHRISTIAN) / INTERNATIONAL MESSIANIC JEWISH (HEBREW CHRISTIAN) ALLIANCE, THE (UK) [26462810] **4976**

MESSIANIC OUTREACH, THE (US/0278-2782) [07767677] **5051**

MESSIEURS, MES AMOURS (CN/0704-5719) [03900656] **3466**

MESSINA. UNIVERSITA. ISTITUTO DI STORIA DELLARTE MEDIOEVALE E MODERNA See QUADERNI DELL ISTITUTO DI STORIA DELL ARTE MEDIEVALE E MODERNA, FACOLTA DI LETTERE E FILOSOFIA, UNIVERSITA DI MESSINA **362**

MESSING ABOUT IN BOATS (US) **4904**

MESTER (LOS ANGELES) (US/0160-2764) [01780999] 3302, **3411**

MESTSTOFFEN (NE/0169-2267) [17234856] **2424**

MESUESI (AA) [07324728] **1764**

MESURE ET EVALUATION EN EDUCATION (CN/0823-3993) [10638947] **1764**

MESURES GLOBALES DE PRODUCTIVITE (1989) (CN/1183-8620) [25883312] **1690**

MESURES (PARIS, FRANCE : 1983) (FR/0755-219X) [10254049] **1987**

MET GOLFER, THE (US/1042-7678) [19176457] **4904**

MET GROTTO NEWS (US) [04649920] **1408**

MET-MAR (FR/0222-5123) [09336450] **1430**

MET, MIDDLE EAST TRANSPORTATION (UK) [06640351] **5386**

META (MONTREAL) (CN/0026-0452) [05314805] **3302**

META (MONTREAL) (CN/0026-0452) [02063548] **3302**

META (TORONTO) (CN/0702-8415) [03439488] **4543**

METAAL & KUNSTSTOF (NE/0026-0460) [l00260460] **4008**

METAAL EN TECHNIEK (NE) **4008**

METAALPRODUKTENINDUSTRIE, EXCL. MACHINES EN TRANSPORTMIDDELEN / CENTRAAL BUREAU VOOR DE STATISTIEK, HOOFDAFDELING STATISTIEKEN VAN INDUSTRIE EN BOUWNIJVERHEIDI (NE/0168-6429) [11885835] 1618, **4008**

METABOLIC ASPECTS OF CARDIOVASCULAR DISEASE (NE/0167-725X) [07643721] **3708**

METABOLIC BRAIN DISEASE (US/0885-7490) [12712938] **3838**

METABOLIC, PEDIATRIC AND SYSTEMIC OPHTHALMOLOGY (1985) (US/0882-889X) [12001721] **3876**

METABOLISM, CLINICAL AND EXPERIMENTAL (US/0026-0495) [01757171] **3674**

METABOLISMO *CEASED.* (IT/0026-0509) [01929067] **3799**

METABOLISMO OGGI (IT) **3799**

METADATA'S LEGALGRAM FOR THE COMMUNICATIONS INDUSTRY (US/0197-7458) [06108754] 1117, **3009**

METAFORA VERDE (IT) **2218**

METAGAME (SOMERVILLE, MASS.) (US/1061-3811) [25278972] **3411**

METAI : LIETUVOS RASYTOJU SAJUNGOS MENRASTIS (LI/0134-3211) [24237619] **3411**

METAL (MX/0539-4457) [05306698] **4009**

METAL ARCHITECTURE (US/0885-5781) [12656949] **303**

●METAL-BASED DRUGS (UK/0793-0291) 4009, 4315, **4009**

METAL BULLETIN MONTHLY (UK/0373-4064) [02448544] **4009**

METAL BULLETIN SURVEYS : COPPER EDITION See WORLD COPPER DATABOOK **4024**

METAL BULLETIN, THE (UK/0026-0533) [02448543] **4009**

●METAL CD (UK/0967-442X) [I0967442X] **4131**

METAL/CENTER NEWS (US/0539-4511) [02448555] **4009**

METAL CONSTRUCTION NEWS (US/8756-2014) [11488088] **621**

METAL DISTRIBUTION (US/0098-2210) [02241043] **4009**

METAL EDGE (US/1068-2872) [24704178] **4131**

METAL FABRICATING NEWS (US/0026-055X) [04947140] 4009, **3484**

METAL FABRICATOR, THE *CEASED.* (US/0026-0568) [04454053] **4009**

METAL FINISHING (US/0026-0576) [01757174] **4009**

●METAL HEAT TREATING (US/1075-5594) [30082965] **4009**

METAL INDUSTRY INDICATORS / BUREAU OF MINES (US) [24236498] **2144**

METAL IONS IN BIOLOGICAL SYSTEMS (US/0161-5149) [01248175] **490**

METAL IONS IN BIOLOGY (US/0271-2911) [06311402] **490**

METAL K.O (CN/0824-7056) [11096334] **4131**

METAL MANIACS (US) 1066, **4131**

METAL MUSCLE (US/1045-6392) [20178391] **4131**

METAL POWDER REPORT (UK/0026-0657) [06276589] **4009**

METAL STAMPING (US/1040-967X) [18577821] **4027**

METAL STATISTICS (FRANKFURT) (GW/0170-9933) [00971498] **4026**

METAL STATISTICS (NEW YORK, N.Y.) (US/0076-6658) [01209689] **4026**

METAL STOCKHOLDING SERVICES & EQUIPMENT (UK/0301-9314) [01793043] **1505**

METAL TRENDS (CN/0824-7471) [11807705] 2144, **1618**

METALETTER (US/0047-6870) [01757180] **4009**

METALL (BERLIN) (GW/0026-0746) [04649390] **4009**

METALL. DAS MAGAZIN DER IG METALL (GW) [06101248] **4009**

METALLBEWERKING (NE) [06298564] 3484, **4009**

METALLE (GW) [03523145] **4009**

METALLI (IT) **4009**

METALLIC MATERIALS (UK/0264-7303) [09779334] **4009**

METALLICA 2000 (UK) 1441, **4009**

METALLITEOLLISUUS (FI/0785-0530) [19488981] **4009**

METALLOBERFLACHE (GW/0026-0797) [02448563] **4009**

METALLOFIZIKA (KIEV) (UN/0204-3580) [06821848] **4009**

METALLOGRAPHIC REVIEW, THE (US/0090-2098) [01784787] **4009**

METALLOORGANICHESKAIA KHIMIIA / AKADEMIIA NAUK SSSR (RU/0235-0114) [18203325] **1044**

METALLOREZHUSCHIE STANKI (UN) [03143092] **2122**

METALLOVEDENIE I TERMICESKAJA OBRABOTKA (KALININ) (RU/0026-0819) [03027086] **4009**

METALLOVEDENIE I TERMICHESKAYA OBRABOTKA METALLOV (US/0026-0673) [02083637] **4010**

METALLOVEDENIE I TERMICHESKAYA OBRABOTKA METALLOV. ENGLISH. METAL SCIENCE AND HEAT TREATMENT OF METALS See METALLOVEDENIE I TERMICHESKAYA OBRABOTKA METALLOV **4010**

METALLSTATISTIK (GW/0076-6682) [11714180] **4010**

METALLURG (RU/0026-0827) [01935638] **4010**

METALLURGIA (1978) (UK/0141-8602) [05326930] **4010**

METALLURGIA ITALIANA, LA (IT/0026-0843) [02448568] **4010**

●METALLURGICAL AND MATERIALS TRANSACTIONS. B, PROCESS METALLURGY AND MATERIALS PROCESSING SCIENCE (US/1073-5615) [29464178] **4010**

●METALLURGICAL AND MATERIALS TRANSACTIONS. PHYSICAL METALLURGY AND MATERIALS SCIENCE (US/1073-5623) [29464215] **4010**

METALLURGICAL JOURNAL (UK/0951-0869) [20465321] **4010**

METALLURGICAL PLANT AND TECHNOLOGY INTERNATIONAL : MPT (GW/0935-7254) [25222715] **4010**

METALLURGICAL PLANT AND TECHNOLOGY : MPT (GW/0171-4511) [08522012] **4010**

METALLURGICAL SCIENCE AND TECHNOLOGY (IT) [11526240] **4010**

METALLURGICAL SOCIETY OF AIME See TMS PAPER SELECTION **4022**

METALLURGICAL TRANSACTIONS. A. PHYSICAL METALLURGY AND MATERIALS SCIENCE (US/0360-2133) [01201312] **4010**

METALLURGICAL TRANSACTIONS. B, PROCESS METALLURGY (US/0360-2141) [01348596] **4010**

METALLURGICESKAJA TEPLOTEHNIKA (RU/0130-2884) [08039727] **4010**

METALLURGICSKAJA I GORNORUDNAJA PROMYSLENNOST (UN/0543-5749) [09614846] **4010**

METALLURGIE. LEXIQUE (FR/0154-036X) [07087622] 3231, **4010**

METALLURGIE (MONS) (BE/0543-5757) [06445232] **4010**

METALLURGIST (NEW YORK) (US/0026-0894) [01928486] **4010**

METALLURGY/MATERIALS EDUCATION YEARBOOK (US/0094-5447) [01794201] **4011**

METALLVERARBEITUNG (GW/0026-0908) [11092745] **4011**

METALLY / AKADEMIIA NAUK SSSR (RU) [25184441] **4011**

METALOZNAWSTWO, OBROBKA CIEPLNA, INZYNIERIA POWIERZCHNI (PL/0860-7583) [22572735] **4011**

METALS ABSTRACTS (UK/0026-0924) [01757191] 4011, **4026**

METALS ABSTRACTS INDEX (UK/0026-0932) [02251736] 4011, **4026**

METALS ANALYSIS AND OUTLOOK (UK/0143-0637) [09563001] **4011**

METALS AND CERAMICS DIVISION ANNUAL PROGRESS REPORT (US) [06263921] **4011**

METALS AND MATERIALS (BURY ST. EDMONDS) (UK/0266-7185) [11862221] **4011**

METALS AND MATERIALS (LONDON, ENGLAND : 1985) See MATERIALS WORLD : THE JOURNAL OF THE INSTITUTE OF MATERIALS **2106**

METALS & MINERALS ANNUAL REVIEW (UK) [22355289] 4011, **2144**

METALS AND MINERALS REVIEW (II/0026-0959) [02694269] **4011**

METALS ECONOMICS GROUP STRATEGIC REPORT (CN/0847-0197) **2144**

METALS FINANCE (UK) **4011**

METALS INDUSTRY NEWS (UK/0265-8321) [11615189] **4011**

METALS MATERIALS AND PROCESSES (II/0970-423X) [I0970423X] 4011, **2107**

METALS WEEK (US/0026-0975) [01757193] **4011**

METALS WEEK PRICE HANDBOOK (US/0363-1702) [01781000] **4011**

METALSMITH (US/0270-1146) [06343831] **374**

●METALURGIA & MATERIAIS / ABM (BL) [27668793] **4011**

METALURGIA (BUCURESTI) (RM/0461-9579) [02062737] **4011**

METALURGIA (LIMA, PERU) (PE) [08466895] **4011**

METALURGIA (SAO PAULO) (BL/0026-0983) [06354507] **4011**

METALURGIA Y ELECTRICIDAD (SP/0026-0991) [02448583] **4011**

METALURGIJA : CASOPIS FAKULTETA, INSTITUTA I ZELJEZARE SISAK (YU/0543-5846) [22335476] **4011**

METALWORKING AUSTRALIA (AT) **4011**

METALWORKING DIGEST (US/0026-1009) [04964490] **4011**

METALWORKING DISTRIBUTOR, THE *CEASED.* (US/1051-1407) [21879308] 1618, **4011**

METALWORKING, ENGINEERING AND MARKETING (JA/0911-9647) [I09119647] 1987, **4011**

METALWORKING MACHINERY (US/0885-3827) [02713453] 1618, **4012**

METALWORKING MACHINERY (US/0885-3827) 1618, **4012**

METALWORKING PRODUCTION (UK/0026-1033) [02448586] **4012**

METALWORKING SALES LEADS (US/0275-6943) [07207979] **4012**

METAPHILOSOPHY (UK/0026-1068) [01606437] **4352**

METAPHOR AND SYMBOLIC ACTIVITY (US/0885-7253) [12709758] **3411**

METAPHOR (SAN JOSE, CALIF.) (US/1055-0984) [23072282] **1093**

METAPHYSICAL REVIEW, THE (AT/0814-8805) [12259632] **3411**

METASCIENCE — Alphabetical Title Index

METASCIENCE (AT/0815-0796) [13342094] **5128**

METAUX, CORROSION - INDUSTRIE *SUSPENDED.* (FR/0026-1084) [07036794] **2015**

METAUX. CORROSION INDUSTRIE (FR/0026-1084) [01794361] **4012**

METEOR (CRYSTAL SPRINGS, MISS. : 1889) (US) [15076249] **5701**

METEOR NEWS (US/0146-9959) [03060987] **397**

METEORITICS (US/0026-1114) [01757198] **1387**

METEORITIKA (RU/0369-2507) [05225004] **397**

METEORNYE ISSLEDOVANIIA (RU) [06929194] **397**

●METEOROLOGICAL & GEOASTROPHYSICAL ABSTRACTS (US/1066-2707) [26909701] 1430, **1363**

METEOROLOGICAL AND GEOASTROPHYSICAL ABSTRACTS (US/0026-1130) [02487639] **1363**

METEOROLOGICAL MAGAZINE (UK/0026-1149) [07145433] **1430**

METEOROLOGICAL MONOGRAPHS (AMERICAN METEOROLOGICAL SOCIETY) (US/0065-9401) [01480421] **1431**

METEOROLOGICAL TRANSLATIONS (CN/0068-7782) [02442600] **1431**

METEOROLOGICKE ZPRAVY (XR/0026-1173) [03929356] **1431**

METEOROLOGIE, LA (FR/0026-1181) [05530456] **1431**

METEOROLOGIIA I GIDROLOGIIA; NAUCHNO-TEKHNICHESKII ZHURNAL (RU/0130-2906) [03215535] **1431**

METEOROLOGISCHE BEOBACHTUNGEN VON DEUTSCHEN FEUERSCHIFFEN DER NORDSEE (BUNDESREPUBLIK) (GW) [19371124] **1431**

METEOROLOGISCHE RUNDSCHAU *See* METEOROLOGISCHE ZEITSCHRIFT / HERAUSGEGEBEN VON DER DEUTSCHEN METEOROLOGISCHEN GESELLSCHAFT, OSTERREICHISCHEN GESELLSCHAFT FEUR METEOROLOGIE, SCHWEIZERISCHEN GESELLSCHAFT FUER GEOPHYSIK **1431**

●METEOROLOGISCHE ZEITSCHRIFT / HERAUSGEGEBEN VON DER DEUTSCHEN METEOROLOGISCHEN GESELLSCHAFT, OSTERREICHISCHEN GESELLSCHAFT FEUR METEOROLOGIE, SCHWEIZERISCHEN GESELLSCHAFT FUER GEOPHYSIK (GW/0941-2948) [25829182] **1431**

METEOROLOGISCHES OBSERVATORIUM HOHENPEISSENBERG *See* ERGEBNISSE DER AEROLOGISCHEN UND BODENNAHEN OZONMESSUNGEN **1425**

METEOROLOGISCHES OBSERVATORIUM HOHENPEISSENBERG. ERGEBNISSE DER AEROLOGISCHEN OZONSONDIERUNGEN UND DER GESAMTOZONMESSUNGEN *See* ERGEBNISSE DER AEROLOGISCHEN UND BODENNAHEN OZONMESSUNGEN **1425**

METEOROLOGY AND ATMOSPHERIC PHYSICS (AU/0177-7971) [14075380] **1431**

METEOROLOGY AND HYDROLOGY BUCURESTI *CEASED.* (RM/1015-3640) [I10153640] 1416, **1431**

METEOROLOGY; INTERNATIONAL STANDARDS AND RECOMMENDED PRACTICES. ANNEX 3 TO THE CONVENTION ON INTERNATIONAL CIVIL AVIATION (CN) [01753447] **28**

METEOROS (BOGOTA) (CK/0303-5093) [01793618] **1431**

METEOSAT IMAGE BULLETIN (GW) **1431**

METHANOL MONTHLY NEWSLETTER (UK) **986**

METHOD & THEORY IN THE STUDY OF RELIGION (CN) [20334559] **4977**

METHOD (LOS ANGELES, CALIF.) (US/0736-7392) [09433706] 4977, **4353**

METHODEN UND VERFAHREN DER MATHEMATISCHEN PHYSIK (GW/0170-9321) [I01709321] 4412, **3523**

METHODES ET TECHNIQUES DE L'INGENIEUR PARIS (FR/1152-0647) [I11520647] **1987**

METHODIKA *CEASED.* (GW/0932-6510) [16856393] **5209**

METHODIST CHURCH (SWEDEN) *See* METODISTKYRKANS I SVERIGE ARSBOK **5064**

METHODIST CHURCH (U.S.) *See* GENERAL MINUTES OF THE ANNUAL CONFERENCES OF THE UNITED METHODIST CHURCH **5060**

METHODIST HISTORY (US/0026-1238) [01714380] **5064**

METHODIST HOSPITALS OF DALLAS *See* BULLETIN OF THE MEDICAL STAFF OF THE METHODIST HOSPITALS OF DALLAS **3777**

METHODIST RECORDER (UK) [06719153] **5064**

METHODOLOGICAL SURVEYS IN BIOCHEMISTRY AND ANALYSIS (UK/0748-6715) [10251797] **490**

METHODOLOGY AND SCIENCE (NE/0543-6095) [02264088] **5209**

METHODOLOGY REPORTS (US/0098-4949) [02432626] **4810**

METHODS AND FINDINGS IN EXPERIMENTAL AND CLINICAL PHARMACOLOGY (SP/0379-0355) [05586831] **4315**

METHODS AND MODELS IN THE SOCIAL SCIENCES (GW/0076-6828) [02411476] **5209**

METHODS AND PHENOMENA (NE/0377-9025) [I03779025] **5128**

●METHODS & TECHNIQUES FOR THE CLINICAL LABORATORY (US/1065-2760) [26562462] **3616**

METHODS FOR THE EXAMINATION OF WATERS AND ASSOCIATED MATERIALS (UK/0141-075X) [10971528] **2236**

METHODS IN CELL BIOLOGY (US/0091-679X) [01791819] **538**

METHODS IN ENZYMOLOGY (US/0076-6879) [02239135] **490**

METHODS IN EXPLORATION SERIES (US/0743-0531) [10541527] **4264**

METHODS IN GENE TECHNOLOGY (UK) [24242127] **3695**

METHODS IN GEOCHEMISTRY AND GEOPHYSICS (NE/0076-6895) [01757212] **1408**

METHODS IN HEMATOLOGY *CEASED.* (US/0277-8599) [07627503] **3773**

METHODS IN MICROBIOLOGY (UK/0580-9517) [01644929] **566**

METHODS IN MOLECULAR AND CELLULAR BIOLOGY (US/0898-7750) [17898285] **464**

METHODS IN NEUROSCIENCES (US/1043-9471) [19612633] **3838**

METHODS IN ORGANIC SYNTHESIS (UK/0265-4245) [10634959] 1044, **1012**

METHODS IN PHARMACOLOGY (US/0091-3030) [00924315] **4315**

METHODS IN PLANT BIOCHEMISTRY (UK/1059-7522) [22140886] 986, **518**

METHODS IN SUBNUCLEAR PHYSICS (US/0097-1065) [01451832] **4448**

METHODS OF BIOCHEMICAL ANALYSIS (US/0076-6941) [01757215] **986**

METHODS OF CELL SEPARATION (US) [04374872] **538**

METHODS OF EXPERIMENTAL PHYSICS (US/0076-695X) [02195301] **4412**

METHODS OF INFORMATION IN MEDICINE (GW/0026-1270) [01643482] **3616**

●METHODS OF LOGIC IN COMPUTER SCIENCE (US/1075-0924) [29933336] **1195**

METHODS OF OPERATIONS RESEARCH (1980) (GW/0173-752X) [06719544] **1987**

METHODS (SAN DIEGO, CALIF.) (US/1046-2023) [20349833] **490**

METHOTREXATE UPDATE (US/0738-856X) [09660590] **3616**

METHOW VALLEY NEWS (US) [17320091] **5761**

METIERS DE LA PETITE ENFANCE (FR/1258-780X) **3616**

METIS (PARIS, FRANCE) (FR/0995-3310) [16140180] **3302**

METIS : REVUE D'ANTHROPOLOGIE DU MONDE GREC ANCIEN (GR) **241**

METIVTA, HA- (US/0094-9701) [01795882] **5051**

METLFAX (US/0026-1297) [05139489] **4012**

METMENYS (US/0543-615X) [01782116] **3411**

METODI & RICERCHE (IT/0394-6460) [15621164] **2698**

METODIKY PRO ZAVADENI VYSLEDKU VYZKUMU DO ZEMEDELSKE PRAXE (XR/0231-9470) [10465793] **108**

METODISTKYRKANS I SVERIGE ARSBOK (SW) [02246498] **5064**

METODOLOGICHESKIE I ISTORIOGRAFICHESKIE VOPROSY ISTORICHESKOI NAUKI (RU) [04267042] **2623**

METODOLOGICHESKIE VOPROSY FIZIKI (ER) [03428407] **4412**

METODY DISKRETNOGO ANALIZA V ...; SBORNIK TRUDOV (RU/0136-1228) [03410217] **3523**

METODY I PRAKTIKA OPREDELENI EFFEKTIVNOSTI KAPITALNYH VLOZENII I NOVOJ TEHNIKI (RU/0543-6222) [07190109] **906**

METOIKOS (CN/0712-2713) [08818725] **2267**

METRIC CONSTRUCTION PRODUCTS FILE (CN/0711-8015) [08605173] **621**

METRIC FACT SHEET (CN/0383-9184) [03222108] **4031**

METRIC MONITOR (CN/0700-2408) [02385666] **4031**

METRIC NEWS (US/0093-3708) [01791934] **4031**

METRIC STEEL. BULLETIN (CN/0705-2081) [04079562] **4012**

METRIC TODAY (US/1050-5628) [21540241] **4031**

METRICA (IT) [05386648] **3411**

METRIKA (GW/0026-1335) [01757217] **3523**

METRO BUSINESS (US/0194-7575) [04998828] **693**

METRO CALIFORNIA MEDIA (US/0889-2776) [04240992] **1117**

METRO CHICAGO REAL ESTATE (US/0893-0775) [15344786] **4841**

METRO GUIDE (MONTREAL, QUEBEC) (CN/0714-4776) [09046610] **5386**

METRO HANDBOOK AND DIRECTORY OF MEMBERS (US/0887-1973) [12706252] **3231**

●METRO IN VIEW (CN/1188-1941) [25882941] **1574**

METRO JACKSON BUSINESS NEWS (US) [21432450] **693**

METRO MAGAZINE (US/1057-8196) [12292871] **5386**

METRO MATIN (CN/0709-4663) [05696994] **5789**

METRO (MELBOURNE) (AT/0312-2654) [11977681] 1900, **4074**

METRO MISCELLANEOUS PUBLICATION (US/0732-801X) [07311890] **3231**

METRO NEW YORK DIRECTORY OF MANUFACTURERS (US/0731-7417) [08148956] **3484**

METRO NEWARK *CEASED.* (US/0194-2425) [05361466] **820**

●METRO PHOENIX MARKETING DIRECTORY (US/1059-6720) [24099003] **933**

METRO PLANNING REVIEW (CN/0829-9153) [15492415] **2828**

METRO PRESS (US) [16835412] **5729**

METRO (SAN JOSE, CALIF.) (US/0882-4290) [11831028] **2538**

METRO SPORTS MAGAZINE (US) **4904**

METRO-SUD (CN/0381-5080) [02587898] **5789**

METRO TELECASTER (1977) (CN/0708-2568) [05018430] **1134**

METRO TELECASTER (1977) *See* METRO WEEKLY TELECASTER **1134**

METRO TIMES (DETROIT, MICH.), THE (US/0746-4045) [10024235] **5692**

METRO WEEKLY TELECASTER (CN/1191-7962) [I11917962] **1134**

METRO (WINTER PARK, FLA.) (US/1058-7233) [24362971] **2902**

METROCREST NEWS, THE (US/8750-5606) [11514444] **5752**

METROECONOMICA (IT/0026-1386) [01749269] **1505**

METROLOGIA (GW/0026-1394) [01587275] **4031**

METROLOGIA APLICATA (1975) (RM/0377-8134) [02735643] **4031**

METROLOGIE ET APPAREILLAGE EN PHYSIQUE ET PHYSICOCHIMIE. E32 (FR) **1056**

METROLOGIE PRATIQUE ET LEGALE (FR/1161-4951) [28470019] **4031**

METROLOGIIA / GOSUDARSTVENNYI KOMITET SSSR PO STANDARTAM (RU/0132-4713) [09770083] **4031**

METROLOGISCHE ABHANDLUNGEN (GW/0232-3915) [09209471] **4031**

METRON (IT/0026-1424) [01605830] **5332**

METROPARKS EMERALD NECKLACE (US) [04012017] 2198, 4852, **4874**

METROPLAN *See* OVERALL PROGRAM DESIGN FOR COMPREHENSIVE METROPOLITAN PLANNING AND DECISION MAKING **2830**

METROPOLIS (CN/0844-3637) [19730354] **325**

METROPOLIS (NEW YORK, N.Y.) (US/0279-4977) [07750778] **358**

METROPOLIS (PARIS) (FR/0223-5633) [03853866] **2828**

METROPOLITAIN (ARLINGTON, VA.) (US/1058-1715) [24235890] **3411**

Alphabetical Title Index

MEXICO

METROPOLITAN ALMANAC (1989) (US/1045-5108) [20128208] **2538**

METROPOLITAN AREA GUIDE TO SERIALS *SUSPENDED.* (US/0739-1560) [03475250] **420**

METROPOLITAN ATLANTA BUSINESS DIRECTORY (US/0091-9756) [01788921] **693**

METROPOLITAN ATLANTA CONGENITAL DEFECTS PROGRAM *See* CONGENITAL MALFORMATIONS SURVEILLANCE **3759**

METROPOLITAN BOROUGH COUNCIL ELECTIONS *See* LONDON BOROUGH COUNCIL ELECTIONS **4481**

METROPOLITAN BUSINESS NEWS (US) [05046787] **693**

METROPOLITAN COUNCIL ... ANNUAL REPORT (US) [01156692] **4665**

METROPOLITAN HOME (US/0273-2858) [07045895] **2902**

METROPOLITAN HOME. (UK EDITION) (UK) **2902**

METROPOLITAN MUSEUM JOURNAL (US/0077-8958) [01760043] 358, **4091**

METROPOLITAN MUSEUM OF ART (NEW YORK, N.Y.) *See* BULLETIN - METROPOLITAN MUSEUM OF ART **4085**

METROPOLITAN MUSEUM OF ART (NEW YORK, N.Y.) *See* METROPOLITAN MUSEUM JOURNAL **4091**

METROPOLITAN NETWORK NEWS *See* U.S. TELECOMMUNICATIONS **1168**

●METROPOLITAN NEW YORK BUSINESS AND MARKET GUIDE, THE (US/1055-4165) [23168957] **693**

METROPOLITAN NEW YORK JOB BANK, THE (US) [15244585] 693, **4206**

METROPOLITAN NEWS-ENTERPRISE (US/0897-2281) [17446511] 3009, **5637**

METROPOLITAN OPERA BOX (US/0736-4229) [09120794] **4131**

METROPOLITAN OPERA SEASON ANNUAL SOUVENIR BOOK (US) **4131**

METROPOLITAN (PERTY) PASSENGER TRANSPORT TRUST *See* REPORT AND STATEMENT OF ACCOUNTS FOR THE YEAR ENDED 30TH JUNE, ... / METROPOLITAN (PERTH) PASSENGER TRANSPORT TRUST **5391**

METROPOLITAN PLANNING COMMISSION OF KNOXVILLE AND KNOX COUNTY, TENNESSEE *See* KNOX COUNTY CAPITAL IMPROVEMENTS PROGRAM **2827**

METROPOLITAN PURCHASOR *SUSPENDED.* (US/0192-7973) [04649962] **950**

METROPOLITAN REVIEW (CHICAGO, ILL.) (US/0893-8490) [15670354] 303, **2828**

METROPOLITAN RICHMOND APARTMENTS FOR RENT (US/1061-981X) [25498522] **2828**

METROPOLITAN (SAN JOSE, CALIF.) (US/1055-0992) [23072494] **1801**

METROPOLITAN SANITARY DISTRICT OF GREATER CHICAGO. BOARD OF COMMISSIONERS *See* BUDGET AS ADOPTED BY THE BOARD OF COMMISSIONERS **4634**

METROPOLITAN STAR (US/0026-1580) [04053543] **2267**

METROPOLITAN TORONTO ... ANNUAL VISITORS GUIDE (CN/0836-4443) [17236831] **5484**

METROPOLITAN TORONTO BUSINESS JOURNAL, THE (CN/0709-003X) [06363879] **693**

METROPOLITAN TORONTO CENTRAL LIBRARY *See* BULLETIN OF OUTSTANDING ACQUISITIONS OF THE METROPOLITAN TORONTO CENTRAL LIBRARY **3198**

METROPOLITAN TORONTO CITY DIRECTORY (1988) (CN/0839-0452) [18809604] **2538**

METROPOLITAN TORONTO LIBRARY BOARD *See* BOOKS IN FRISIAN (1980) **4826**

METROPOLITAN TORONTO LIBRARY BOARD *See* BOOKS IN ESTONIAN (1980) **4825**

METROPOLITAN TORONTO LIBRARY BOARD *See* BOOKS IN HUNGARIAN (1980) **4826**

METROPOLITAN TORONTO LIBRARY BOARD *See* BOOKS IN CHINESE (1980) **4825**

METROPOLITAN TORONTO LIBRARY BOARD *See* BOOKS IN GREEK (1980) **4826**

METROPOLITAN TORONTO LIBRARY BOARD *See* BOOKS IN ARABIC (1980) **4825**

METROPOLITAN TORONTO LIBRARY BOARD *See* BOOKS IN PERSIAN (1980) **4826**

METROPOLITAN TORONTO LIBRARY BOARD *See* BOOKS IN URDU (1980) **4826**

METROPOLITAN TORONTO LIBRARY BOARD *See* BOOKS IN VIETNAMESE (1980) **4826**

METROPOLITAN TORONTO LIBRARY BOARD *See* BOOKS IN DUTCH (1980) **4825**

METROPOLITAN TORONTO LIBRARY BOARD *See* BOOKS IN BENGALI (1980) **4825**

METROPOLITAN TORONTO LIBRARY BOARD *See* BOOKS IN UKRAINIAN (1980) **4826**

METROPOLITAN TORONTO LIBRARY BOARD *See* BOOKS IN POLISH (1980) **4826**

METROPOLITAN TORONTO LIBRARY BOARD *See* BOOKS IN GERMAN (1980) **4826**

METROPOLITAN TORONTO LIBRARY BOARD *See* BOOKS IN CROATIAN **4825**

METROPOLITAN TORONTO LIBRARY BOARD *See* BOOKS IN SPANISH (1980) **4826**

METROPOLITAN TORONTO LIBRARY BOARD *See* BOOKS IN YIDDISH **4826**

METROPOLITAN TORONTO LIBRARY BOARD *See* BOOKS IN HINDI (1980) **4826**

METROPOLITAN TORONTO LIBRARY BOARD *See* BOOKS IN FINNISH (1980) **4825**

METROPOLITAN TORONTO LIBRARY BOARD *See* BOOKS IN ITALIAN **4826**

METROPOLITAN TORONTO LIBRARY BOARD *See* BOOKS IN PORTUGUESE (1980) **4826**

METROPOLITAN TORONTO LIBRARY BOARD *See* BOOKS IN PANJABI (1980) **4826**

METROPOLITAN TORONTO LIBRARY BOARD *See* BOOKS IN GUJARATI **4826**

METROPOLITAN TORONTO LIBRARY BOARD *See* BOOKS IN TAGALOG (1980) **4826**

METROPOLITAN TORONTO LIBRARY BOARD. LANGUAGES CO-ORDINATOR *See* LANGUAGES OF SOUTH INDIA **3296**

METROPOLITAN TORONTO LIBRARY BOARD. LANGUAGES CO-ORDINATOR *See* BOOKS IN ARMENIAN **4825**

METROPOLITAN TORONTO LIBRARY BOARD. LANGUAGES CO-ORDINATOR *See* BOOKS IN DANISH **4825**

METROPOLITAN TORONTO LIBRARY BOARD. LANGUAGES CO-ORDINATOR *See* BOOKS IN JAPANESE **4826**

METROPOLITAN TORONTO LIBRARY BOARD. LANGUAGES CO-ORDINATOR *See* BOOKS IN MARATHI **4826**

METROPOLITAN TORONTO LIBRARY BOARD. LANGUAGES CO-ORDINATOR *See* BOOKS IN LITHUANIAN **4826**

METROPOLITAN TORONTO LIBRARY BOARD. MUNICIPAL REFERENCE LIBRARY *See* MUNICIPAL REFERENCE LIBRARY ACQUISITIONS **3232**

METROPOLITAN TORONTO LIBRARY. GENERAL REFERENCE DEPT *See* ACQUISITIONS / METROPOLITAN TORONTO LIBRARY, GENERAL REFERENCE DEPARTMENT **3187**

METROPOLITAN TORONTO LIBRARY. MUSIC DEPT *See* ACQUISITIONS - METROPOLITAN TORONTO LIBRARY, MUSIC DEPARTMENT **4098**

METROPOLITAN TORONTO LIBRARY. SCIENCE & TECHNOLOGY DEPT *See* METROPOLITAN TORONTO LIBRARY. SCIENCE & TECHNOLOGY DEPT. ACQUISITIONS **3231**

METROPOLITAN TORONTO LIBRARY. SCIENCE & TECHNOLOGY DEPT. ACQUISITIONS (CN/0226-255X) [06859871] **3231**

METROPOLITAN TORONTO LIBRARY. SOCIAL SCIENCES DEPT *See* ACQUISITIONS / METROPOLITAN TORONTO LIBRARY, SOCIAL SCIENCES DEPARTMENT **5189**

METROPOLITAN TORONTO (ONT.) *See* OPERATING BUDGET AS ADOPTED BY THE METROPOLITAN COUNCIL ON ... **4739**

METROPOLITAN TRANSIT COMMISSION *See* ANNUAL REPORT - METROPOLITAN TRANSIT COMMISSION **5376**

METROPOLITAN UNIVERSITIES (US/1047-8485) [20794069] **1835**

METROPOLITAN WASHINGTON BOARD OF TRADE *See* MEMBERSHIP DIRECTORY - METROPOLITAN WASHINGTON BOARD OF TRADE **845**

METROPOLITAN WASHINGTON BOARD OF TRADE NEWS *See* GREATER WASHINGTON BOARD OF TRADE NEWS, THE **1564**

METROPOLITAN WASHINGTON REGIONAL DIRECTORY (US/0076-7115) [01235791] **4665**

METROPOLITAN WATER BOARD *See* ANNUAL REPORT - METROPOLITAN WATER BOARD **5529**

METROPOLITAN WATER DISTRICT OF SOUTHERN CALIFORNIA *See* ANNUAL REPORT FOR THE FISCAL YEAR JULY 1 ... TO JUNE 30 ... / THE METROPOLITAN WATER DISTRICT OF SOUTHERN CALIFORNIA **5529**

METROSTROI (RU) [01795081] **5386**

METROWEST BUSINESS REVIEW, THE (US/0887-8528) [13429396] **693**

METSAHALLITUKSEN VUOSIKERTOMUS (FI) [18266748] **2388**

METSANDUSLIKUD UURIMUSED (ER/0135-2466) [08611794] **2388**

METSANTUTKIMUSLAITOKSEN TIEDONONTOJA (FI/0358-4283) [24227499] **2388**

METSATEHON TIEDOTUS (FI/0356-7257) [I03567257] **2388**

METSATYONTEKIJOIDEN VUOSIANSIOT / TILASTOKESKUS (FI/0784-929X) [19566206] **5333**

METTALBEWERKINGSMACHINE - INDUSTRIE EN MACHINEGEREEDSCHAPPENFABRIEKEN / CENTRAAL BUREAU VOOR DE STATISTIED, HOOFDAFDELING STATISTIEKEN VAN INDUSTRIE EN BOUWNIJVERHEID (NE/0168-342X) [10339796] 4012, **2122**

METU KALENDORIUS - PRISIKELIMO PARAPIJA, EKONOMINE SEKCIJA (CN/0380-1373) [02578660] **2490**

METUCHEN, EDISON REVIEW (US/0747-2390) [10654027] **5710**

METZER ZEITUNG (METZ, FRANCE : 1916) (FR) [21009226] **5800**

MEUBEL (NE) **2902**

MEUBELECHO (BE/0772-6287) **2906**

MEVAKER, HA- (US) [08969234] **2526**

MEXIA DAILY NEWS, THE (US) [13781889] **5752**

MEXIA STATE SCHOOL *See* ANNUAL REPORT FOR THE YEAR ENDED ... / MEXIA STATE SCHOOL **3550**

MEXICAN BULLETIN OF STATISTICAL INFORMATION (MX) [25500722] **1505**

MEXICAN ECONOMY : ECONOMIC AND FINANCIAL DEVELOPMENTS IN ... POLICIES FOR ... / BANCO DE MEXICO, THE (MX) [06453593] **798**

●MEXICAN ENVIRONMENTAL BUSINESS (US/1075-9034) [30368671] 2177, **693**

●MEXICAN FORECAST (MX) [28121117] **798**

MEXICAN FORUM, THE (US/0730-2584) [07217308] **2538**

MEXICAN REVOLUTION REPORTER, THE (US/0272-6890) [06906103] **2746**

MEXICAN SPORTFISHING NEWS (US/0885-0674) [12561577] **4874**

MEXICAN STUDIES (US/0742-9797) [10485431] 5252, **1505**

MEXICAN WAR QUARTERLY (US/1062-5615) [25666941] **2746**

MEXICO & CENTRAL AMERICAN HANDBOOK (UK) [22579851] **5484**

MEXICO BUSINESS MONTHLY (US/1054-2663) [22806710] **906**

MEXICO (CITY). INSTITUTO POLITECNICO NACIONAL. ESCUELA NACIONAL DE CIENCIAS BIOLOGICAS *See* ANALES DE LA ESCUELA NACIONAL DE CIENCIAS BIOLOGICAS (MEXICO) **441**

MEXICO (CITY). MUSEO NACIONAL DE ANTROPOLOGIA. SERVICIOS EDUCATIVOS *See* COLECCION BREVE **234**

MEXICO (CITY). UNIVERSIDAD NACIONAL. INSTITUTO DE BIOLOGIA *See* ANALES DEL INSTITUTO DE BIOLOGIA, UNIVERSIDAD NACIONAL AUTONOMA DE MEXICO. SERIE BOTANICA **498**

MEXICO (CITY). UNIVERSIDAD NACIONAL. INSTITUTO DE GEOFISICA *See* MONOGRAFIAS **1408**

MEXICO (CITY). UNIVERSIDAD NACIONAL. INSTITUTO DE QUIMICA *See* BOLETIN / MEXICO (CITY). UNIVERSIDAD NACIONAL. INSTITUTO DE QUIMICA **963**

MEXICO COMPANY HANDBOOK (BL) [21109006] **693**

MEXICO. CONSEJO NACIONAL DE CIENCIA Y TECNOLOGIA. DEPARTAMENTO BOLSA DE TRABAJO *See* BOLETIN BOLSA DE TRABAJO **1656**

MEXICO — Alphabetical Title Index

MEXICO. DEPARTAMENTO DE INVESTIGACION DE LAS TRADICIONES POPULARES *See* BOLETIN DEL DEPARTAMENTO DE INVESTIGACION DE LAS TRADICIONES POPULARES **2318**

MEXICO DESCONOCIDO (MX) [09190615] **5484**

MEXICO. DIRECCION GENERAL DE ESTADISTICA *See* ANUARIO ESTADISTICO DEL COMERCIO EXTERIOR DE LOS ESTADOS UNIDOS MEXICANOS **5400**

MEXICO. DIRECCION GENERAL DE INVENCIONES Y MARCAS *See* GACETA DE INVENCIONES Y MARCAS **1304**

MEXICO EN EL ARTE (MEXICO CITY, MEXICO) (MX/0185-4569) [12782541] **358**

MEXICO (FEDERAL DISTRICT). PROCURADURIA GENERAL DE JUSTICIA *See* GACETA OFICIAL - PROCURADURIA GENERAL DE JUSTICIA DEL DISTRITO FEDERAL **3140**

MEXICO FINANCE & OIL REPORT, THE (MX) [11601887] **1505**

MEXICO FINANCIAL MONTHLY REPORT (MX/0185-4178) [11871909] **798**

MEXICO GEOGRAFICO (MX) [05239161] **2746**

MEXICO HOLSTEIN (MX) [06662514] **196**

MEXICO. INSTITUTO NACIONAL DE ANTROPOLOGIA E HISTORIA. DEPARTAMENTO DE PREHISTORIA *See* TECNOLOGIA **246**

MEXICO LEDGER (US) [20387097] **5704**

MEXICO (LONDON, ENGLAND) (UK/0267-9973) [12985087] **2490**

MEXICO MAGAZINE (CARBONDALE, COLO.) (US/0894-4652) [16104092] **2538**

MEXICO MARKET BOOKLET (US) [06860472] **846**

MEXICO (NEW YORK, N.Y. 1983) (US/0883-2625) [09372946] **5484**

MEXICO NOW : A MONTHLY REPORT FROM SOUTH OF THE BORDER (MX) [08793993] **5484**

MEXICO REPORT (EL PASO, TEX.) (US/0277-0946) [07495288] **1574**

MEXICO. SECRETARIA DE OBRAS PUBLICAS *See* SOP **1627**

MEXICO SERVICE (US/1044-6303) [19853273] **2512**

MEXICO (STATE). TRIBUNAL FISCAL *See* REVISTA DEL TRIBUNAL FISCAL DEL ESTADO DE MEXICO **4747**

MEXICO TRADE AND LAW REPORTER (US/1058-5702) [24333523] 3009, **846**

MEXICO TRAV'LER, THE (US/8756-1395) [11500988] **5484**

MEXICO-UNITED STATES INTERPARLIAMENTARY GROUP. DELEGATION FROM THE UNITED STATES *See* REPORT OF THE SENATE DELEGATION ON THE MEETING-MEXICO-UNITED STATES INTERPARLIAMENTARY GROUP. DELEGATION FROM THE UNITED STATES **4533**

MEXICON (GW/0720-5988) [05821915] 274, **2746**

MEXIKO-PROJEKT DER DEUTSCHEN FORSCHUNGSGEMEINSCHAFT, DAS (GW/0418-842X) [01566376] **2746**

MEXIKO : WIRTSCHAFTLICHE ENTWICKLUNG (GW) [02519762] **1574**

MEXIKO, WIRTSCHAFTSDATEN UND WIRTSCHAFTSDOKUMENTATION / BUNDESTELLE FUR AUSSENHANDELSINFORMATION (GW) [09400416] **1574**

MEXLETTER (MX/0026-1858) [06066343] **798**

MEYER MIRROR, THE (US/0276-4237) [07340832] **2460**

MEYER'S DIRECTORY OF GENEALOGICAL SOCIETIES IN THE U.S.A. AND CANADA (US/0732-3395) [08337399] **2460**

MEYIBO (MX) [04349324] **2552**

MEYLER AND PECK'S DRUG-INDUCED DISEASES (NE/0167-5885) [07417201] **3616**

MEYLER'S SIDE EFFECTS OF DRUGS (NE/0376-7396) [02469612] **4315**

MEYNIANA (GW/0076-7689) [03718876] 4228, **1388**

MEYSSEL, MIKESELL, MIXSELL FAMILY NEWSLETTER (US/0748-8521) [11004416] **2460**

MEZHDUNARODNAIA SISTEMA NAUCHNOI I TEKHNICHESKOI INFORMAISII PO SEL'SKOMU I LESNOMU KHOZIAISTVU *See* BIULLETEN' NAUCHNO-TEKHNICHESKOI INFORMATSII MS AGROINFORM **67**

MEZHDUNARODNAIA ZHIZN (RU/0026-1874) [01938538] **4528**

MEZHDUNARODNI OTNOSHENIIA (BU) [01788679] **4528**

MEZHDUNARODNOE EKONOMICHESKOE SOTRUDNICHESTVO (RU) [24019588] **2911**

MEZHDUNARODNYI FORUM PO INFORMATSII I DOKUMENTATSII (RU) [05860644] **3231**

MEZHDUNARODNYI TSENTR NAUCHNOI I TEKHNICHESKOI INFORMATSII *See* REGISTR PERIODICHESKIKH IZDANII STRAN-CHLENOV MTSNTI. CHAST I: NUMERATSIONNYI RIAD **423**

MEZHDUNARODNYI TSENTR NAUCHNOI I TEKHNICHESKOI INFORMATSII *See* REGISTR PERIODICHESKIKH IZDANII STRAN-CHLENOV MTSNTI. CHAST II: VSPOMOGATELNYE UKAZATELI **2924**

MEZHDUNARODNYI TSENTR NAUCHNOI I TEKHNICHESKOI INFROMATSIL *See* KONFERENTSII, SOVESHCHANIIA, SIMPOZIUMY I VYSTAVKI, PROVODIMYE V STRANAKH-CHLENAKH TSENTRA **5124**

MEZHUNARODNYI TSENTR INFORMATSII V SEL'SKOM I LESNOM KHOZIAISTVE. BIULLETEN *See* BIULLETEN' NAUCHNO-TEKHNICHESKOI INFORMATSII MS AGROINFORM **67**

MEZHVUZOVSKII SBORNIK NAUCHNYKH TRUDOV / PERMSKII POLITEKHNICHESKII INSTITUT (RU) [05823199] **5128**

MEZHVUZOVSKII TEMATICHESKII SBORNIK / MOSKOVSKII ORDENA LENINA I ORDENA OKTIABRSKOI REVOLIUTSII ENERGETICHESKII INSTITUT (RU) [17222891] **1950**

MEZOGAZDASAGI ELELMISZERIPARI STATISZTIKAI ZSEBKONYU / LOZPONTI STATISZTIKAI HIVATAL (HU/0238-7891) [19247582] **5333**

MEZOGAZDASAGI ERO- ES MUNKAGEPEK (HU) [11940289] **160**

MEZOGAZDASAGI ES ELELMISZERIPARI KONYVTAROSOK TAJEKOZTATOJA (HU/0133-4875) [I01334875] **3231**

MEZOGAZDASAGI GEPESITESI TANULMANYOK (HU/0521-422X) [03019251] **160**

MEZOGAZDASAGI GEPUZEMELTETES (HU/0230-2810) [I02302810] **108**

MEZOGAZDASAGI SZOVETKEZETEK GAZDALKODASA A SZAMOK TUKREBEN (HU) [04894890] **108**

MEZZOGIORNO D'EUROPA *SUSPENDED.* (IT/0392-9566) [09037146] **1574**

MEZZOGIORNO D'EUROPA (IT/0394-3933) [12929525] **1505**

● MFE COLLECTORS' BOOKLINE (US/1073-3027) [29384254] **3411**

MFM. MODERNE FOTOTECHNIK (GW/0024-8142) [I00248142] **4371**

MFOC NEWSLETTER *See* FIBER OPTICS BUSINESS NEWSLETTER **1155**

MG. MEDICINA GENERAL (SP) **3616**

MH, MARYLAND'S HEALTH (US) [02435134] **4791**

MHBG, MATERIALS HANDLING BUYER'S GUIDE (UK) [03795416] **4220**

MHFA UPDATE (US/1061-9607) [24582044] **2828**

MHLA BULLETIN (CN/0831-2249) [15217153] **3231**

MHLA NEWS (CN/0848-9009) [21486510] 3616, **3231**

MHQ (NEW YORK, N.Y.) (US/1040-5992) [18462176] **4049**

MHS REVIEW (US/0093-9560) [01793187] **5591**

MHT DIRECTORY OF CONNECTICUT & RHODE ISLAND HIGH TCH CMPANIES *See* DIRECTORY OF CONNECTICUT AND RHODE ISLAND HIGH TECHNOLOGY COMPANIES, THE **1604**

MI GLOBO (US/0897-148X) [17417274] **1804**

MI MENSILE : IL MERCATO DELL INFORMAZIONE (IT) **762**

MIA CASA (IT) **2906**

MIAA NEWSLETTER, THE (US/0273-6683) [06800085] **4904**

MIAMI BUSINESS REVIEW (US/0026-1947) [01820887] **693**

MIAMI CHIEF (CANADIAN, TEX.) (US/0746-0082) [09670954] **5752**

● MIAMI DAILY BUSINESS REVIEW (US/1070-6437) [28249690] **5718**

● MIAMI HERALD ALMANAC OF FLORIDA POLITICS, THE (US/1069-3017) [27972399] **4481**

MIAMI HERALD (MIAMI, FLA.) (US/0898-865X) [02733685] **5650**

MIAMI HURRICANE, THE (US/1064-6442) [26347658] **5650**

MIAMI MALACOLOGICAL SOCIETY *See* QUARTERLY - MIAMI MALACOLOGICAL SOCIETY **5596**

MIAMI MEANDERINGS (US/0889-3640) [13854580] 2460, **2746**

MIAMI MEDICAL LETTER (US/1047-2509) [20681902] **3616**

MIAMI MEDICAL LETTER EN ESPANOL (US/1047-2495) [20682082] **3616**

MIAMI MEDICINE : THE OFFICIAL PUBLICATION OF THE DADE COUNTY MEDICAL ASSOCIATION (US) [06401138] **3616**

MIAMI MENSUAL (US/0273-9372) [07042499] 5484, **2538**

MIAMI NEWS-RECORD (US) [13676443] **5732**

MIAMI NEWS, THE *CEASED.* (US) [10000467] **5650**

MIAMI NEWSPAPERS INDEX *CEASED.* (US/0735-6064) [08175111] **5650**

MIAMI REPUBLICAN, THE (US) [11394898] **5677**

MIAMI REVIEW (US/0888-0263) [13451640] **5718**

MIAMI TIMES, THE (US/0739-0319) [02264129] **5650**

MIAMI TODAY (US/0889-2296) [13826579] **5650**

MIAMI, UNIVERSITY OF, CORAL GABLES, FLORIDA. INSTITUTE OF SCIENCE *See* PROCEEDINGS OF THE GULF AND CARIBBEAN FISHERIES INSTITUTE **2310**

MIBI-FNIM (IS) [04316417] **4543**

MIC/INFO (US) **1245**

MIC/SUB-APPLICATION DEVELOPMENT. [DISKETTE] (US) **1288**

MIC/SUB-IMAGING AND OFFICE SYSTEMS. [DISKETTE] (US) **1220**

MIC / TECH-COMPUTERS (US) **1248**

MIC/TECH-DATA COMMUNICATIONS (US) **1245**

MIC/TECH-MAINFRAME AND MINICOMPUTER (US) **1245**

MIC/TECH-MICROCOMPUTER AND WORKSTATION (US) **1245**

MIC/TECH-RETAIL AND BANKING (US) 798, **1248**

MIC-TECH-TELECOMMUNICATIONS (US) **1160**

MIC-TECH-UNIX (US) **1195**

MICAP RECAP (US/0889-3926) [13922984] **1346**

MICHAEL FIGHTING (CN/0227-0978) [08375615] **4977**

MICHAEL (ROUGEMONT) (CN/0317-8498) [02399183] **4481**

MICHAEL SINGER'S FILM DIRECTORS : A COMPLETE GUIDE / COMPILED AND EDITED BY MICHAEL SINGER (US) [22588959] **4074**

MICHEL BENELUX-KATALOG ... BELGIEN, NIEDERLANDE, LUXEMBURG (GW) [08605565] **2786**

MICHEL BRIEFE-KATALOG DEUTSCHLAND (GW) [08602281] **2786**

MICHEL BRIEFMARKENKATALOG: EUROPA *See* MICHEL EUROPA-KATALOG **2786**

MICHEL DEUTSCHLAND-SPEZIAL-KATALOG (GW) [07610419] **2786**

MICHEL EUROPA-KATALOG (GW/0301-6692) [01792730] **2786**

MICHEL GANZACHEN-KATALOG DEUTSCHLAND (GW) [07610600] **2786**

MICHEL GROSSBRITANNIEN-SPEZIAL-KATALOG (GW) [08602323] **2786**

MICHEL ITALIEN-KATALOG ... MIT MALTA, SAN MARINO UND VATIKANSTAAT (GW) [08598479] **2786**

MICHEL OSTERREICH-SPEZIAL-KATALOG (GW) [07610488] **2786**

MICHEL PRIVATGANZSACHEN-KATALOG BUNDESREPUBLIK DEUTSCHLAND, BERLIN, DEUTSCHE DEMOKRATISCHE REPUBLIK (GW) [07610575] **2786**

MICHEL SKANDINAVIEN-KATALOG (GW) [08602244] **2786**

MICHELIN GREAT BRITAIN AND IRELAND (UK) [01795924] **2807**

MICHELIN GREATER LONDON (UK) [01795707] 5072, **2807**

MICHELIN REIFENWERKE *See* DEUTSCHLAND **2685**

MICHELIN TYRE COMPANY, LTD *See* MICHELIN GREATER LONDON **2807**

MICHELIN TYRE COMPANY, LTD *See* MICHELIN GREAT BRITAIN AND IRELAND **2807**

MICHELIN TYRE COMPANY, LTD *See* AUSTRIA **5462**

Alphabetical Title Index **MICHIGAN**

MICHELIN TYRE COMPANY, LTD. TOURIST SERVICE *See* SPAIN **5491**

MICHI; A JOURNAL FOR CULTURAL EXCHANGE (JA) [06706682] **5252**

MICHIANA AREA HISTORIANS *See* PROCEEDINGS OF THE MICHIANA AREA HISTORIANS **2626**

MICHIANA SEARCHER (US/0736-5004) [08257473] **2460**

MICHIE COMPANY, CHARLOTTESVILLE, VIRGINIA *See* MICHIE ON BANKS AND BANKING **798**

MICHIE ON BANKS AND BANKING (US) [01643325] **798**

MICHIGAN *See* PUBLIC AND LOCAL ACTS OF THE LEGISLATURE OF THE STATE OF MICHIGAN **3032**

MICHIGAN *See* LAWS RELATED TO THE DEPARTMENT OF SOCIAL SERVICES, PASSED DURING THE LEGISLATIVE SESSION **2997**

MICHIGAN 4-H TODAY (US/1049-0175) [21110629] **5233**

MICHIGAN ACADEMICIAN (US/0026-2005) [01278369] **2850**

MICHIGAN AFL-CIO *See* MICHIGAN AFL-CIO NEWS **1690**

MICHIGAN AFL-CIO NEWS (US/0026-1998) [04053621] **1690**

MICHIGAN ALLEGAN-MUSKEGON-OTTAWA COUNTIES BUSINESS REGISTER (US/1057-3089) [24005281] **694**

MICHIGAN ALUMNUS (US/0746-2565) [03768310] **1102**

MICHIGAN ANNUAL AIR QUALITY REPORT (US/0275-2840) [07103148] **2236**

MICHIGAN APPELLATE DIGEST (US/0196-7649) [04245430] **3009**

MICHIGAN ARCHAEOLOGIST (US/0543-9728) [01757349] **274**

MICHIGAN ASSOCIATION OF SPEECH COMMUNICATION JOURNAL, THE (US) [11698958] **1117**

MICHIGAN. ATTORNEY GENERAL'S DEPARTMENT *See* REPORT OF THE ATTORNEY GENERAL **3142**

MICHIGAN BANKER (LANSING, MICH.) (US/1044-1948) [19707951] **798**

MICHIGAN BAR JOURNAL, THE (US/0164-3576) [04631048] **3009**

MICHIGAN BAY-MIDLAND-SAGINAW COUNTIES BUSINESS REGISTER (US/1057-3054) [24005163] **694**

MICHIGAN BEAN COMMISSION *See* BEAN COMMISSION JOURNAL, THE **164**

MICHIGAN BERRIEN-CASS-ST. JOSEPH BUSINESS REGISTER (US/1057-3097) [24005338] **694**

MICHIGAN BEVERAGE NEWS (US/0026-2021) [04053662] **2369**

MICHIGAN BOTANIST (US/0026-203X) [01757350] **518**

MICHIGAN BRANCH-HILLSDALE-LENAWEE-MONROE COUNTIES BUSINESS REGISTER (US/1057-3135) [24006487] **694**

MICHIGAN. BUREAU OF EMPLOYMENT AND TRAINING *See* MICHIGAN CETA ACTIVITY REPORT FOR ... **1690**

MICHIGAN. BUREAU OF THE BUDGET *See* ECONOMIC REPORT OF THE GOVERNOR (LANSING) **1484**

MICHIGAN BUSINESS EDUCATION ASSOCIATION *See* NEWS BULLETIN / MICHIGAN BUSINESS EDUCATION ASSOCIATION **699**

MICHIGAN BUSINESS LAW JOURNAL, THE (US/0899-9651) [18279434] **3102**

MICHIGAN BUSINESS (SOUTHFIELD, MICH. : 1984) (US/0886-5639) [11947718] **694**

MICHIGAN CALHOUN-KALAMAZOO COUNTIES BUSINESS REGISTER (US/1057-3100) [24005416] **694**

MICHIGAN CENTENNIAL FARMS DIRECTORY (US/0092-2250) [01786736] **108**

MICHIGAN CENTRAL REGION BUSINESS REGISTER (US/1057-3062) [24005206] **694**

MICHIGAN CETA ACTIVITY REPORT FOR ... (US/0731-2938) [08139384] **1690**

MICHIGAN CHRISTIAN ADVOCATE (US/0026-2072) [02393180] **4977**

MICHIGAN CHRONICLE, THE (US) [02264134] **5692**

MICHIGAN CITIZEN (US/1072-2041) [22836894] **5693**

MICHIGAN CITY OF DETROIT BUSINESS REGISTER (US/1057-3194) [24006586] **694**

MICHIGAN. CIVIL RIGHTS COMMISSION *See* CASE DIGEST (LANSING) **4505**

MICHIGAN CONTRACTOR & BUILDER (US) **621**

MICHIGAN COUNCIL FOR THE ARTS *See* LEGISLATIVE REPORT / MICHIGAN COUNCIL FOR THE ARTS **3002**

MICHIGAN COUNCIL ON PHYSICAL FITNESS AND HEALTH *See* MICHIGAN COUNCIL ON PHYSICAL FITNESS AND HEALTH ANNUAL REPORT TO THE MICHIGAN DEPARTMENT OF PUBLIC HEALTH **2599**

MICHIGAN COUNCIL ON PHYSICAL FITNESS AND HEALTH ANNUAL REPORT TO THE MICHIGAN DEPARTMENT OF PUBLIC HEALTH (US) [06549387] **2599**

MICHIGAN COUNTIES (US/0896-646X) [07851878] **4665**

MICHIGAN CPA, THE (US/0026-2064) [01775879] **748**

MICHIGAN CRITICAL MATERIALS REGISTER (US/0270-4579) [06379998] **2236**

MICHIGAN DAILY, THE (US/0745-967X) [09651208] **5693**

MICHIGAN DENTAL HYGIENISTS' ASSOCIATION *See* BULLETIN OF THE MICHIGAN DENTAL HYGIENISTS' ASSOCIATION, THE **1318**

MICHIGAN. DEPARTMENT OF COMMERCE *See* TECHNICAL REPORT - STATE RESOURCES PLANNING PROGRAM **1586**

MICHIGAN. DEPT. OF ADMINISTRATION *See* MICHIGAN STATE EMPLOYEES' RETIREMENT SYSTEM **4698**

MICHIGAN. DEPT. OF CIVIL SERVICE *See* ANNUAL REPORT - MICHIGAN DEPARTMENT OF CIVIL SERVICE **4701**

MICHIGAN. DEPT. OF COMMERCE *See* ANNUAL REPORT FOR THE YEAR ENDING JUNE 30 ... / STATE OF MICHIGAN, DEPARTMENT OF COMMERCE **823**

MICHIGAN. DEPT. OF EDUCATION *See* REPORT OF THE MICHIGAN EDUCATIONAL ASSESSMENT PROGRAM **1870**

MICHIGAN. DEPT. OF EDUCATION *See* MICHIGAN SCHOOL BOND LOAN PROGRAM : ANNUAL BULLETIN **1836**

MICHIGAN. DEPT. OF EDUCATION. RESEARCH, EVALUATION AND ASSESSMENT SERVICE *See* TECHNICAL REPORT : REPORT OF THE MICHIGAN EDUCATIONAL ASSESSMENT PROGRAM **1850**

MICHIGAN. DEPT. OF EDUCATION. RESEARCH, EVALUATION AND ASSESSMENT SERVICES *See* SCHOOL AND DISTRICT REPORTS. EXPLANATORY MATERIALS **1870**

MICHIGAN. DEPT. OF MENTAL HEALTH. RECIPIENT RIGHTS COMMITTEE *See* ANNUAL REPORT / MICHIGAN DEPARTMENT OF MENTAL HEALTH, RECIPIENT RIGHTS COMMITTEE **3920**

MICHIGAN. DEPT. OF NATURAL RESOURCES *See* BIENNIAL REPORT / STATE OF MICHIGAN, THE DEPARTMENT OF NATURAL RESOURCES **4632**

MICHIGAN. DEPT. OF PUBLIC HEALTH *See* PRIORITY HEALTH PROBLEMS OF MICHIGAN **4796**

MICHIGAN. DEPT. OF PUBLIC HEALTH *See* PROGRAM BUDGET STATEMENT **4796**

MICHIGAN. DEPT. OF SOCIAL SERVICES *See* PROPOSED MICHIGAN ANNUAL SOCIAL SERVICES PLAN **5302**

MICHIGAN. DEPT. OF SOCIAL SERVICES *See* PROGRAM STATISTICS - MICHIGAN DEPARTMENT OF SOCIAL SERVICES **5266**

MICHIGAN. DEPT. OF SOCIAL SERVICES *See* MIGRANT SERVICES STATISTICAL REPORT **1536**

MICHIGAN. DEPT. OF SOCIAL SERVICES. TITLE XX ADMINISTRATION DIVISION *See* PROPOSED MICHIGAN ANNUAL TITLE XX SERVICES PLAN **5302**

MICHIGAN. DEPT. OF STATE POLICE *See* UNIFORM CRIME REPORT FOR THE STATE OF MICHIGAN **3084**

MICHIGAN. DEPT. OF STATE POLICE *See* MICHIGAN SCHOOL BUS ACCIDENTS **5386**

MICHIGAN. DEPT. OF TRANSPORTATION *See* ANNUAL PROGRESS REPORT - MICHIGAN DEPARTMENT OF TRANSPORTATION **5376**

MICHIGAN DISCUSSIONS IN ANTHROPOLOGY (US/0193-7804) [03395465] **241**

MICHIGAN DISTRIBUTORS DIRECTORY (US/0890-4049) [14222558] **933**, **694**

●MICHIGAN DOCUMENTS / COMPILED BY DENISE K. GERMAIN-PETERS (US) [25902123] **3231**

MICHIGAN DOCUMENTS (MICROFICHE) *See* MICHIGAN DOCUMENTS / COMPILED BY DENISE K. GERMAIN-PETERS **3231**

MICHIGAN DRY BEAN DIGEST (US/0885-6060) [08375660] **178**

MICHIGAN EDUCATION DIRECTORY (US) [23808122] **1764**

MICHIGAN EMPLOYMENT LAW LETTER (US/1046-9109) [20584158] **3152**

MICHIGAN EMPLOYMENT SECURITY COMMISSION. DETROIT LABOR MARKET ANALYSIS UNIT. ANNUAL PLANNING REPORT, STATE OF MICHIGAN *See* ANNUAL PLANNING INFORMATION, FISCAL YEAR ... - MICHIGAN EMPLOYMENT SECURITY COMMISSION, BUREAU OF RESEARCH AND STATISTICS **1528**

●MICHIGAN ENVIRONMENTAL COMPLIANCE UPDATE (US/1073-9459) [29567712] **3114**

MICHIGAN ENVIRONMENTAL LAW LETTER (US/1046-9192) [20584236] **3114**

MICHIGAN. ENVIRONMENTAL PROTECTION BUREAU. ENVIRONMENTAL SERVICES DIVISION *See* MICHIGAN CRITICAL MATERIALS REGISTER **2236**

MICHIGAN ENVIRONMENTAL REPORT: (US/0747-735X) [10790652] **2177**

MICHIGAN FARMER (US/0026-2153) [08853479] **108**

MICHIGAN FARMER AND LIVESTOCK JOURNAL *See* MICHIGAN FARMER **108**

MICHIGAN FEMINIST STUDIES (US/1055-856X) [23364553] **5561**

MICHIGAN. FINANCIAL INSTITUTIONS BUREAU *See* MORTGAGE AND HOME IMPROVEMENT LENDING IN MICHICGAN PURSUANT TO THE ANTI-REDLINING ACT, ANNUAL REPORT **800**

MICHIGAN FINANCIAL JOURNAL (US/0742-8146) [10486552] **798**

MICHIGAN FIRE SERVICE NEWS (US) **2291**

MICHIGAN FISHERMAN, THE (US/0274-4783) [06346169] **2308**

MICHIGAN FLORIST, THE (US/0026-217X) [04054038] **2435**

MICHIGAN FORESTS (US) **2388**

MICHIGAN FOUNDATION DIRECTORY (US/0362-1561) [02275593] **4338**

MICHIGAN FREE PRESS (US/0147-7110) [03225095] **5693**

MICHIGAN GENESEE COUNTY BUSINESS REGISTER (US/1057-3151) [24006517] **694**

MICHIGAN GEOGRAPHICAL PUBLICATION (US/0076-7948) [02419410] **2569**

MICHIGAN. GEOLOGICAL SURVEY DIVISION *See* BULLETIN - MICHIGAN. GEOLOGICAL SURVEY DIVISION **1369**

MICHIGAN. GEOLOGICAL SURVEY DIVISION *See* ANNUAL DIRECTORY - DEPARTMENT OF NATURAL RESOURCES. GEOLOGICAL SURVEY DIVISION (LANSING) **1365**

MICHIGAN GERMANIC STUDIES (US/0098-8030) [01597960] **3411**, **3302**

MICHIGAN GOLFER (US) **4904**

MICHIGAN GOLFER (US/1071-2313) [18419542] **4904**

MICHIGAN HEALTH & SAFETY DIGEST (US/0746-0368) [09696664] **4791**

●MICHIGAN HEALTH CARE IN PERSPECTIVE (US/1065-4240) [26605756] **4791**

MICHIGAN HEALTH STATISTICS (US/0539-7413) [01794097] **4810**

MICHIGAN HISTORICAL REVIEW, THE (US/0890-1686) [13756240] **2746**

MICHIGAN HISTORY (US/0026-2196) [01757361] **2746**

MICHIGAN HIV REPORT / DEPARTMENT OF PUBLIC HEALTH (US) [25376056] **3674**, **3715**, **4791**

MICHIGAN HOSPITALS (US/0026-220X) [01757362] **3789**

MICHIGAN HOUSING MARKET INFORMATION SYSTEM MONOGRAPH SERIES, THE (US) [02245778] **2828**

MICHIGAN HUNTING & FISHING (US/1057-2856) [23997095] **4874**

MICHIGAN IN PERSPECTIVE (US/1065-5514) [25378406] **5333**

MICHIGAN INGHAM-JACKSON COUNTIES BUSINESS REGISTER (US/1057-3119) [24006414] **694**

●MICHIGAN INSURANCE HANDBOOK (US/1061-2610) [24394910] **2888**

MICHIGAN INSURANCE ISSUES HANDBOOK *See* MICHIGAN INSURANCE HANDBOOK **2888**

MICHIGAN JEWISH HISTORY (US/0543-9833) [01608359] **5051**

MICHIGAN — Alphabetical Title Index

MICHIGAN JOURNAL OF COUNSELING AND DEVELOPMENT (US/1044-2634) [15143303] **4604**

MICHIGAN JOURNAL OF INTERNATIONAL LAW (US/1052-2867) [19508503] **3132**

MICHIGAN JOURNAL OF POLITICAL SCIENCE (US/0733-4486) [07805339] **4481**

MICHIGAN KENT COUNTY BUSINESS REGISTER (US/1057-3143) [24006500] **694**

MICHIGAN LABOR MARKET REVIEW (US/0098-0307) [01799406] **1690**

MICHIGAN LAW REVIEW (US/0026-2234) [01757366] **3009**

MICHIGAN. LEGISLATIVE COUNCIL *See* MICHIGAN REGISTER **3010**

MICHIGAN. LEGISLATURE. SENATE. FISCAL AGENCY *See* APPROPRIATIONS REPORT (MICHIGAN) **4630**

MICHIGAN LIBRARIAN (1985) (US/0884-9919) [11645997] **3231**

MICHIGAN LICENSED OCCUPATIONS (US/0093-6421) [01792686] **4206**

MICHIGAN LIVING (US/0735-1798) [07954356] 5419, **5484**

MICHIGAN LIVINGSTON-WASHTENAW COUNTIES BUSINESS REGISTER (US/1057-3127) [24006450] 694, **1618**

MICHIGAN LODGING (US) [12588653] 4737, **748**

MICHIGAN MANUAL (US/0091-1933) [01643917] **4665**

MICHIGAN MANUFACTURERS DIRECTORY (US/0736-2889) [09097367] **3484**

MICHIGAN MATHEMATICAL JOURNAL, THE (US/0026-2285) [01757373] **3523**

MICHIGAN MEDICINE (US/0026-2293) [01589382] **3616**

MICHIGAN MIDDLE SCHOOL JOURNAL (US/0270-6571) [03699606] **1764**

MICHIGAN MILK MESSENGER (US/0026-2315) [04054061] **196**

MICHIGAN MINERAL PRODUCERS : ANNUAL DIRECTORY (US/0580-6143) [02253644] 1618, **1441**

MICHIGAN MONOGRAPHS IN CHINESE STUDIES (US) [09588982] **2658**

MICHIGAN. MUNICIPAL FINANCE COMMISSION *See* REPORT OF OUTSTANDING INDEBTEDNESS OF COUNTIES, CITIES, VILLAGES, TOWNSHIPS, SCHOOLS, SPECIAL DISTRICTS, AUTHORITIES, STATE BONDS **4745**

MICHIGAN MUNICIPAL LEAGUE AND MICHIGAN ASSOCIATION OF MUNICIPAL ATTORNEYS MONOGRAPH SERIES (US/1059-2105) [24516739] **3010**

MICHIGAN MUNICIPAL LIABILITY AND PROPERTY POOL BULLETIN (US/1058-4307) [24516766] **4665**

MICHIGAN MUNICIPAL REVIEW (US/0026-2331) [01608025] **4665**

MICHIGAN MUSIC (US/0160-9483) [03779557] **4131**

MICHIGAN NATURAL RESOURCES MAGAZINE, THE (US/0275-8180) [04158874] **2198**

MICHIGAN NORTH OAKLAND COUNTY BUSINESS REGISTER (US/1057-3178) [24006555] **694**

MICHIGAN NORTHEASTERN REGION COUNTIES BUSINESS REGISTER (US/1057-3046) [24005127] **694**

MICHIGAN NORTHWESTERN REGION BUSINESS REGISTER (US/1057-3038) [24005082] **694**

MICHIGAN NURSE (US/0026-2366) [02264141] **3861**

MICHIGAN NURSERY AND LANDSCAPE ASSOCIATION *See* VOICE, THE **2433**

MICHIGAN. OFFICE OF YOUTH SERVICES *See* PROGRESS REPORT - MICHIGAN DEPARTMENT OF SOCIAL SERVICES. OFFICE OF YOUTH SERVICES **5302**

MICHIGAN OPTOMETRIC ASSOCIATION *See* MICHIGAN OPTOMETRIST, THE **4216**

MICHIGAN OPTOMETRIST, THE (US/1071-1627) [07245721] **4216**

MICHIGAN OUT-OF-DOORS (US/0026-2382) [02759041] **2198**

MICHIGAN PAPERS ON SOUTH AND SOUTHEAST ASIA (US/0160-354X) [02593197] **2658**

MICHIGAN PHOTOGRAPHY JOURNAL : A PUBLICATION OF THE MICHIGAN FRIENDS OF PHOTOGRAPHY (US) [18376216] **4371**

MICHIGAN PROFESSIONAL ENGINEER (1990) (US/1054-5840) [22935242] **1987**

MICHIGAN PUBLIC EMPLOYEE REPORTER (US) **1690**

MICHIGAN. PUBLIC SCHOOL EMPLOYEES' RETIREMENT SYSTEM *See* FINANCIAL AND STATISTICAL REPORT - MICHIGAN. PUBLIC SCHOOL EMPLOYEES' RETIREMENT SYSTEM **1795**

MICHIGAN QUARTERLY REVIEW (US/0026-2420) [01757375] **3347**

MICHIGAN READING JOURNAL, THE (US/0047-7125) [02716438] **1900**

MICHIGAN REGISTER (US/0892-3124) [10503061] 4665, **3010**

MICHIGAN REPORT (US) **4665**

MICHIGAN RESTAURATEUR (1987) (US/0892-8231) [15175401] **5072**

MICHIGAN RETAILER, THE (US/0889-0439) [11544563] **879**

MICHIGAN ROMANCE STUDIES (US/0270-3629) [06395886] 3411, **3302**

MICHIGAN RUNNER, THE (US/0279-1773) [07606897] **4904**

MICHIGAN. RURAL DEVELOPMENT PROGRAM *See* RURAL ADVOCATE, THE **2834**

MICHIGAN SCHOOL BOND LOAN PROGRAM : ANNUAL BULLETIN (US/0148-4990) [03304944] **1836**

MICHIGAN SCHOOL BUS ACCIDENTS (US/0097-8744) [01788662] 4791, **5386**

MICHIGAN SLAVIC CONTRIBUTIONS (US/0076-8103) [01971037] **3302**

MICHIGAN SLAVIC MATERIALS (US/0543-9930) [01979208] **3302**

MICHIGAN SLAVIC TRANSLATIONS (US) [02420238] **3302**

MICHIGAN SNOWMOBILER (US/0746-2298) [09869659] **5386**

MICHIGAN. SOCIAL STUDIES TEXTBOOK REVIEW COMMITTEE *See* MICHIGAN SOCIAL STUDIES TEXTBOOK STUDY **1764**

MICHIGAN SOCIAL STUDIES TEXTBOOK STUDY (US/0277-0806) [07487143] 5209, **1764**

MICHIGAN SOCIOLOGICAL REVIEW (US) [05387705] **5252**

MICHIGAN SOUTH OAKLAND COUNTY BUSINESS REGISTER (US/1057-3186) [24006566] **694**

MICHIGAN SPEECH-LANGUAGE-HEARING ASSOCIATION JOURNAL / MSHA *SUSPENDED.* (US/0742-3284) [10292631] **4391**

MICHIGAN SPORTSMAN (OSHKOSH WIS.) (US/0539-8908) [06656700] **4874**

MICHIGAN. STATE ADVISORY COUNCIL FOR VOCATIONAL EDUCATION *See* BIENNIAL EVALUATION REPORT - MICHIGAN. STATE ADVISORY COUNCIL FOR VOCATIONAL EDUCATION **1911**

MICHIGAN. STATE BOARD OF EDUCATION *See* ANNUAL REPORT - MICHIGAN STATE BOARD OF EDUCATION **1725**

MICHIGAN. STATE BUILDING AUTHORITY *See* STATE BUILDING AUTHORITY, MICHIGAN **628**

MICHIGAN. STATE DEPT. OF CORRECTIONS *See* DIMENSIONS ... **3163**

MICHIGAN STATE EMPLOYEES' RETIREMENT SYSTEM (US/0092-9212) [01791006] **4698**

MICHIGAN STATE HORTICULTURAL SOCIETY *See* ANNUAL REPORT OF THE SECRETARY OF THE STATE HORTICULTURAL SOCIETY OF MICHIGAN **2409**

MICHIGAN STATE HOUSING DEVELOPMENT AUTHORITY *See* REPORT - MICHIGAN STATE HOUSING DEVELOPMENT AUTHORITY **2833**

●MICHIGAN STATE PLAN FOR VOCATIONAL-TECHNICAL EDUCATION (US) [23440193] **1914**

MICHIGAN. STATE TRANSPORTATION COMMISSION *See* ANNUAL REPORT, MICHIGAN TRANSPORTATION FUND **5376**

MICHIGAN STATE UNIVERSITY. AGRICULTURAL EXPERIMENT STATION *See* RESEARCH REPORT FROM THE MICHIGAN STATE UNIVERSITY AGRICULTURAL EXPERIMENT STATION, EAST LANSING **127**

MICHIGAN STATE UNIVERSITY. COLLEGE OF AGRICULTURE AND NATURAL RESOURCES *See* ALUMNI DIRECTORY / MICHIGAN STATE UNIVERSITY, COLLEGE OF AGRICULTURE AND NATURAL RESOURCES **1098**

MICHIGAN. STATE UNIVERSITY, EAST LANSING. ASIAN STUDIES CENTER *See* OCCASIONAL PAPERS. SOUTH ASIA SERIES **2661**

MICHIGAN STATE UNIVERSITY, EAST LANSING. COOPERATIVE EXTENSION SERVICE *See* EXTENSION BULLETIN - MICHIGAN. STATE UNIVERSITY, EAST LANSING. COOPERATIVE EXTENSION SERVICE **83**

MICHIGAN STATE UNIVERSITY. INSTITUTE OF WATER RESEARCH *See* TECHNICAL REPORT - INSTITUTE OF WATER RESEARCH (EAST LANSING) **5540**

MICHIGAN STATE UNIVERSITY. LATIN AMERICAN STUDIES CENTER *See* NEWSLETTER - MICHIGAN STATE UNIVERSITY, LATIN AMERICAN STUDIES CENTER **2750**

MICHIGAN STATE UNIVERSITY. PLACEMENT SERVICES *See* RECRUITING TRENDS (EAST LANSING) **1705**

MICHIGAN STUDIES IN THE HUMANITIES (US) [14199330] **2850**

MICHIGAN TAX LAWYER (US/0899-2460) [18044860] 4737, **3010**

MICHIGAN THEOLOGICAL JOURNAL (US/1048-2709) [20881951] **4977**

MICHIGAN THUMB REGION BUSINESS REGISTER (US/1057-3070) [24005231] **694**

MICHIGAN TOWNSHIP NEWS (US) **4665**

MICHIGAN TRIAL REPORTER, THE (US/0899-904X) [18261424] **3090**

MICHIGAN UPPER PENINSULA BUSINESS REGISTER (US/1057-302X) [24005048] **694**

MICHIGAN VETERANS TRUST FUND. BOARD OF TRUSTEES *See* ANNUAL REPORT - MICHIGAN VETERANS TRUST FUND. BOARD OF TRUSTEES **4035**

MICHIGAN VOTER, THE (US/0899-1545) [03511281] **4482**

MICHIGAN WASTE REPORT (US/0896-4246) [16746155] **2236**

MICHIGAN WESTERN WAYNE COUNTY BUSINESS REGISTER (US/1057-3208) [24006577] **694**

MICHIGAN. WOMEN'S COMMISSION *See* WOMEN'S PROGRAM **5571**

MICHIGAN WORKERS' COMP DIGEST *CEASED.* (US/0746-1461) [09537750] **3152**

MICHIGAN. WORKERS' COMPENSATION APPEAL BOARD *See* OPINIONS ON REVIEW FOR THE YEAR ... / STATE OF MICHIGAN, DEPARTMENT OF LABOR, WORKERS' COMPENSATION APPEAL BOARD AND APPELLATE COMMISSION **3153**

MICHIGAN WORKERS' COMPENSATION LAW REPORTER (US/0899-9090) [18012473] **3152**

MICHIGANA (US/0462-372X) [05854106] **2460**

●MICHIGAN'S LABOR MARKET NEWS (US) [25806996] **1690**

MICHIGAN'S OIL AND GAS FIELDS (US/0543-8470) [02253495] **4264**

MICHIGAN'S OIL & GAS NEWS (1983) (US/0746-5769) [10134494] **4264**

MICHMANIM / MIKHMANIM (IS/0334-7311) [14266670] **274**

MICIS NEWS (UK) **5128**

MICKLE STREET REVIEW, THE *CEASED.* (US/0194-1313) [05321986] **3411**

MICKY MAUS (GW) **1066**

MICMAC MALISEET NATION NEWS (CN/1184-6402) [24266630] **5789**

MICMAC NEWS *SUSPENDED.* (CN/0845-2555) [I08452555] **5789**

MICOLOGIA E VEGETAZIONE MEDITERRANEA (IT/0394-2597) [03942597] **575**

MICOLOGIA ITALIANA (IT/0390-0460) [01792236] **575**

MICOLOGIA NEOTROPICAL APLICADA (MX) [21481088] **575**

MICRO ABSTRACTS (UK/0958-4668) **1269**

MICRO & MACRO MARKETING (IT/1121-4228) [I11214228] **933**

MICRO AND PERSONAL COMPUTERS USED IN THE CONVENIENCE STORE INDUSTRY (US/8755-2132) [11208916] 1618, **1269**

MICRO COMPUTER COLLEG (GW/0177-5235) [14943648] **1195**

MICRO DECISION *CEASED.* (UK/0261-5142) [I02615142] **1269**

MICRO DISCOVERY (US/0732-9512) [08486252] **1269**

MICRO E PERSONAL COMPUTER (IT) **1269**

MICRO ECONOMICS / THE BOSTON COMPUTER SOCIETY (US/0883-4296) [12191645] 879, **694**

MICRO MAGAZINE *See* PC MICRO MAGAZINE **1271**

MICRO MAINFRAME CONNECTION (US/0748-8483) [11018424] **1269**

MICRO MONEY (US/0742-9398) [10478471] 1245, **1269**

MICRO MOONLIGHTER (US/0277-0059) [07475874] 1269, **1245**

MICRO MULTIMEDIA *CEASED.* (US) **1195**

MICRO ORDINATEUR / LE MENSUEL DE LA MICRO INFORMATIQUE ET DE SES UTILISATIONS (FR) **1269**

MICRO PUBLICATIONS, SOCIAL SCIENCE SERIES (DK/0901-0025) [I09010025] **5209**

MICRO-SCOPE AYLESBURY (UK/0264-3847) [I02643847] 1804, **1195**

MICRO SHOPPER (US) [06280776] **1269**

MICRO SOFTWARE MARKETING (US/0738-6354) [09655152] 933, **1288**

MICRO SOFTWARE REPORT *SUSPENDED.* (US/8755-5786) [10731226] 1288, **3231**

MICRO SYSTEMES PARIS. 1978 *CEASED.* (FR/0183-5084) [I01835084] **1269**

MICRO USER (UK) **1269**

MICRO WAVE NEWS (US/0275-6595) [07193171] **2350**

MICROBANKER (US/0738-7156) [09670674] **798**

MICROBANKER SOFTWARE BUYER'S GUIDE, THE (US) [17968350] **798**

MICROBEAM ANALYSIS (US/0278-1727) [07246538] 1018, **1012**

●MICROBEAM ANALYSIS (NEW YORK, N.Y.) (US/1061-3420) [25257880] **4438**

MICROBIAL BIOTECHNOLOGY *CEASED.* (UK) 3695, **566**

MICROBIAL CLEANUP *CEASED.* (UK/0966-6796) [I09666796] **566**

●MICROBIAL DRUG RESISTANCE, MECHANISMS, EPIDEMIOLOGY, AND DISEASE (US/1076-6294) [30567641] **3736**

MICROBIAL ECOLOGY (US/0095-3628) [02243116] 566, **2218**

MICROBIAL ECOLOGY IN HEALTH AND DISEASE (UK/0891-060X) [14559145] **3616**

MICROBIAL PATHOGENESIS (UK/0882-4010) [11821118] 566, **3715**

MICROBIAL RELEASES (GW) **566**

MICROBIAL RELEASES : VIRUSES, BACTERIA, FUNGI *CEASED.* (GW/0940-9653) [27264196] **566**

●MICROBIAL RESEARCH (GW/0944-5013) [30526530] **566**

MICROBIOLOGIA (MADRID) (SP/0213-4101) [16849850] **567**

MICROBIOLOGICA (IT/0391-5352) [04945105] **567**

MICROBIOLOGICAL REVIEWS (US/0146-0749) [03526643] **567**

MICROBIOLOGICAL UPDATE, THE (US/0889-3381) [11301891] **567**

MICROBIOLOGIE, ALIMENTS, NUTRITION (FR/0759-0644) [14694835] **108**

●MICROBIOLOGY (UK/1350-0872) [29693815] **567**

MICROBIOLOGY ABSTRACTS. SECTION A : INDUSTRIAL & APPLIED MICROBIOLOGY (US/0300-838X) [00936247] 567, **478**

MICROBIOLOGY ABSTRACTS. SECTION B, BACTERIOLOGY (US/0300-8398) [00936285] 567, **478**

MICROBIOLOGY ABSTRACTS. SECTION C, ALGOLOGY, MYCOLOGY & PROTOZOOLOGY (US/0301-2328) [00936291] 567, **478**

MICROBIOLOGY AND IMMUNOLOGY (JA/0385-5600) [02972418] 567, **3674**

MICROBIOLOGY EUROPE (GW/0945-8182) **567**

MICROBIOLOGY (NEW YORK) (US/0026-2617) [02431086] **567**

MICROBIOLOGY SERIES (US/0092-6027) [02196608] **567**

MICROBIOS (UK/0026-2633) [01643638] **567**

MICROBITS (CN/0823-5430) [10386267] **2072**

MICROCAD NEWS *See* DESIGNNET (AUSTIN, TEX.) **1233**

MICROCELL NEWS (US) **1160**

MICROCELL REPORT (US/1048-6976) [21015820] **1160**

MICROCHEMICAL JOURNAL (US/0026-265X) [01757385] **986**

MICROCIRCOLAZIONE OGGI (IT/1120-3811) [I11203811] **3616**

MICROCIRCULATION (UK/1350-4916) **3616**

MICROCIRCULATION, ENDOTHELIUM, AND LYMPHATICS (US/0740-9451) [10050756] **3616**

●MICROCOMPUTER ABSTRACTS (US/1074-3995) [29690201] **1269**

MICROCOMPUTER APPLICATIONS (ANAHEIM) (US/0820-0750) [09121410] **1269**

MICROCOMPUTER INDEX (US/8756-7040) [07821881] 1269, **1209**

MICROCOMPUTER INDUSTRY UPDATE (US/0741-6016) [10191281] 1269, **1209**

MICROCOMPUTER NEWS (AT/0726-352X) [I0726352X] **1195**

MICROCOMPUTER REVIEW (US/8755-7525) [09427335] 1264, **1269**

MICROCOMPUTER SOLUTIONS (U.S. ED.) (US/1041-8563) [17776743] **1269**

MICROCOMPUTER SYSTEMS *CEASED.* (US/0276-5098) [07389280] **1269**

MICROCOMPUTER TRAINER, THE (US/1055-3258) [23152896] **1269**

MICROCOMPUTER VENDOR DIRECTORY (US/0747-511X) [09787534] 1238, **1269**

MICROCOMPUTERS FOR INFORMATION MANAGEMENT (US/0742-2342) [10295058] 3231, **1269**

MICROCOMPUTERS FOR LIBRARIES (US/0743-0302) [10489672] **1269**

MICROCOMPUTERS IN CIVIL ENGINEERING (UK/0885-9507) [12793015] 1269, **2027**

MICROCOMPUTERS IN TRANSPORTATION. SOFTWARE AND SOURCE BOOK (US/0741-5451) [09983376] **5387**

MICROCONTAMINATION (US/0738-713X) [09670563] **2072**

MICROCOSM (LOUISVILLE SMSA EDITION) (US) [17504931] **694**

●MICROECONOMICS (US) [23600262] **1505**

MICROEDITIONS DE LA BIBLIOTHEQUE. CATALOGUE (CN/0707-848X) [06174118] **420**

MICROELECTRONIC ENGINEERING (NE/0167-9317) [10329408] **2072**

MICROELECTRONICS *See* SOVIET MICROELECTRONICS **2082**

MICROELECTRONICS (UK/0026-2692) [05877621] **2072**

MICROELECTRONICS AND RELIABILITY (UK/0026-2714) [06936575] **2072**

MICROELECTRONICS AND SIGNAL PROCESSING (UK/0736-6914) [09253182] 2072, **1195**

MICROELECTRONICS INTERNATIONAL (UK) **2072**

MICROELECTRONICS MANUFACTURING TECHNOLOGY *CEASED.* (US/1054-9668) [23036669] **2072**

MICROFAUNA MARINA (GW/0176-3296) [11820508] **465**

MICROFILM LIST (US) [06457482] **2482**

MICROFILMING CORPORATION OF AMERICA *See* CRIME AND JUVENILE DELINQUENCY : A BIBLIOGRAPHIC GUIDE TO THE DOCUMENTS UPDATE **3079**

MICROFILMING PROJECTS NEWSLETTER (US/0080-8857) [04186934] **3231**

MICROFORM MARKET PLACE (US/0362-0999) [01998426] **4822**

MICROFORM PUBLICATIONS BULLETIN : HEALTH, PHYSICAL EDUCATION AND RECREATION (US) [18102975] **1857**

MICROFORM REVIEW (US/0002-6530) [01757389] **3231**

MICROFORM REVIEW SERIES IN LIBRARY MICROGRAPHICS MANAGEMENT (US) [06534946] **3231**

MICROGRAPHICS AND OPTICAL STORAGE EQUIPMENT REVIEW *CEASED.* (US/0882-3294) [11808800] **1277**

MICROGRAPHICS INDEX. SUPPLEMENT, THE (US/0149-9882) [03586965] **4371**

MICROGRAPHICS INDEX, THE (US/0149-8975) [01984164] **4371**

MICROGRAPHICS NEWSLETTER (US/0883-9808) [01226802] **1195**

MICROGRAPHICS TODAY (US/0149-9300) [01912789] **4371**

MICROGRAVITY QUARTERLY (UK/0958-5036) [22454436] **4412**

MICROGRAVITY SCIENCE AND TECHNOLOGY (GW/0938-0108) [21815003] **4412**

MICROINFO, MICROFILM NEWS (UK) [15611748] **4566**

MICROINFO (TORONTO) (CN/0826-2705) [11734487] **1269**

MICROLEADS U.S. & CANADIAN DEALER DIRECTORY (US) **1245**

MICROLEADS VENDOR DIRECTORY (US/1056-0386) [19105361] **1245**

●MICROLITHOGRAPHY WORLD (US/1074-407X) [28982886] **2072**

MICROLOG, MICROFICHE COLLECTIONS (CN/0823-2113) [09981857] **420**

MICROLOG NEWSLETTER (CN/0708-790X) [05841403] **4816**

MICROLOGUE [MICROFORM] : [COMPLETE COLLEGE CATALOG COLLECTION ON MICROFICHE] (US) [08544206] **1836**

MICROMATH : A JOURNAL OF THE ASSOCIATION OF TEACHERS OF MATHEMATICS (UK/0267-5501) [14437719] 1900, **3523**

MICROMEGA (IT) [15805137] **4543**

MICROMEGAS (IT) [05205294] **1764**

MICROMEGAS (CEDAR FALLS, IOWA) (US/0026-2773) [02264163] **3466**

MICROMONTH (CN/0823-0234) [09822903] **1269**

MICRON AND MICROSCOPICA ACTA (UK/0739-6260) [09772845] **573**

●MICRON : THE INTERNATIONAL RESEARCH AND REVIEW JOURNAL FOR MICROSCOPY (UK/0968-4328) [27751008] **573**

MICRONESICA (GU/0026-279X) [02431494] **4167**

MICRONUTRIENT NEWS AND INFORMATION (UK/0957-4360) [I09574360] **4194**

MICROPALEONTOLOGY (US/0026-2803) [01645558] **4228**

MICROPALEONTOLOGY SPECIAL PUBLICATION (US/0160-2071) [02167020] **4228**

MICROPOROUS MATERIALS (NE/0927-6513) 2177, **986**

●MICROPRENEUR (NORTHWOOD, N.H.) (US/1065-6111) [26648675] **1269**

MICROPRO USERS' MONTHLY (US/0740-3526) [09921841] **1269**

MICROPROCESSING AND MICROPROGRAMMING (NE/0165-6074) [07324063] 1275, **1269**

MICROPROCESSOR REPORT (US/0899-9341) [18276055] **1270**

MICROPROCESSORS AND MICROSYSTEMS (UK/0141-9331) [04332259] **1230**

MICROPSYCH NETWORK *CEASED.* (US/0748-2051) [10908064] **4604**

MICROPUBLISHERS' TRADE LIST ANNUAL, THE (US/0361-2635) [02246315] **420**

MICROPUBLISHING REPORT (US/0889-9533) [13539379] 1195, **4816**

MICROQUEST REPORT (US/1065-9900) [I10659900] **5128**

MICROSCOPE (LONDON) (US/0026-282X) [07599737] 986, **573**

MICROSCOPE TECHNOLOGY & NEWS (US/1041-0716) [18622117] **573**

MICROSCOPIA ELECTRONICA Y BIOLOGIA CELULAR *See* BIOCELL **572**

MICROSCOPIA ELECTRONICA Y BIOLOGIA CELULAR : ORGANO OFICIAL DE LAS SOCIEDADES LATINOAMERICANAS DE MICROSCOPIA ELECTRONICA E IBEROAMERICANA DE BIOLOGIA CELULAR (AG/0326-3142) [13780642] **573**

MICROSCOPICA ACTA. SUPPLEMENT *SUSPENDED.* (GW/0342-958X) [05159369] **567**

MICROSCOPICAL SOCIETY OF CANADA *See* PROCEEDINGS OF THE MICROSCOPICAL SOCIETY OF CANADA **573**

MICROSCOPICAL SOCIETY OF CANADA *See* BULLETIN - MICROSCOPICAL SOCIETY OF CANADA **572**

MICROSCOPIE ELECTRONIQUE ET DIFFRACTION ELECTRONIQUE. E30 (FR) **5128**

MICROSCOPY (UK/0026-2838) [03353126] **573**

MICROSCOPY *See* QUEKETT JOURNAL OF MICROSCOPY, THE **573**

MICROSCOPY, MICROANALYSIS, MICROSTRUCTURES : MMM (FR) [22150184] **573**

●MICROSCOPY RESEARCH AND TECHNIQUE (US/1059-910X) [24807748] **573**

MICROSCOPY SOCIETY OF AMERICA BULLETIN *CEASED.* (US/1062-9785) [25839129] **573**

MICROSCOPY SOCIETY OF AMERICA PROCEEDINGS (US) **573**

●MICROSOFT C/C++ DEVELOPER'S JOURNAL (US/1068-5669) [27700956] **1288**

MICROSOFT CD-ROM YEARBOOK, THE (US/1042-0908) [18937926] **1195**

MICROSOFT MAGAZINE (UK/0964-0029) [I09640029] **1270**

●MICROSOFT MAGAZINE (US) **1195**

MICROSOFT — Alphabetical Title Index

MICROSOFT NETWORKING JOURNAL *CEASED.* (US/1052-8571) [22399147] **1288**

MICROSOFT-SYSTEM-JOURNAL (GW/0933-9434) [I09339434] **1195**

MICROSOFT SYSTEMS JOURNAL (US/0889-9932) [14109298] 1270, **1288**

MICROSOFT WORKS IN EDUCATION (US/1046-1981) [20348528] 1224, **1900**

MICROSOFTWARE NEWS FOR LOCAL GOVERNMENTS (US) **1195**

MICROSPIRIT (CN/0822-7268) [11734464] **1764**

MICROSTATE STUDIES (VI/0147-7935) [03230901] **4482**

MICROSTATION MANAGER (US/1057-9567) [24171396] **1195**

MICROSTRUCTURAL SCIENCE (US/0361-1213) [02245176] **4012**

MICROSURGERY (US/0738-1085) [09530514] **3970**

MICROSYSTEM TECHNOLOGIES (GW) **1195**

MICROSYSTEMES (FR) **1270**

MICROSYSTEMS COMPETITIVE REVIEW (US/0743-6343) [10625199] **1270**

●MICROSYSTEMS HANDBOOK (US/1063-1488) [25105611] **1270**

MICROTECNIC (SZ/0026-2854) [03817957] **4031**

MICROTIMES (PLEASANT HILL, CALIF.) (US/1065-0148) [14876196] 1238, **1270**

MICROVASCULAR RESEARCH (US/0026-2862) [01608379] **3773**

MICROVIEW (TORONTO) (CN/0836-5482) [13489079] 694, **1195**

MICROWAVE AND OPTICAL TECHNOLOGY LETTERS (US/0895-2477) [16520898] **2072**

MICROWAVE ENGINEERING EUROPE (UK/0960-667X) [25207143] **2072**

MICROWAVE JOURNAL (EURO-GLOBAL ED.) (US/0192-6217) [05108133] **2072**

MICROWAVE JOURNAL (INTERNATIONAL ED.) (US/0192-6225) [05108165] **4412**

MICROWAVE TIMES *See* COOKING CONNECTION **2789**

MICROWAVE TIMES, THE (US/0197-372X) [04485577] **2792**

MICROWAVE TUBE LIST *See* D.A.T.A.'S MICROWAVE TUBE **2040**

MICROWAVE WORLD (US/0276-7961) [06399014] **2072**

MICROWAVES AND FOOD (US) **2350**

MICROWAVES & RF (US/0745-2993) [09055160] **4438**

MICROWAVES & RF PRODUCT DATA DIRECTORY (US) [10524610] 4438, **2072**

MICROWAVES & RF PRODUCT EXTRA (US) 4438, **2072**

MICROWAVES PRODUCT DATA DIRECTORY (US/0194-7397) [04458415] **2072**

MID-AMERICA ASSOCIATION OF LAW LIBRARIES *See* NEWSLETTER - MID-AMERICA ASSOCIATION OF LAW LIBRARIES **3235**

MID-AMERICA (CHICAGO) (US/0026-2927) [01757398] 2746, **5032**

MID-AMERICA COMMERCE & INDUSTRY (US/0193-2047) [05167098] 3484, **950**

MID AMERICA FARMER GROWER, THE (US/1040-1423) [18336931] **108**

MID-AMERICA FOLKLORE (US/0275-6013) [05235296] **2322**

MID AMERICA INSURANCE (US/0026-2935) [04993190] **2888**

MID-AMERICA THEOLOGICAL JOURNAL (US/0734-9882) [08872523] **4977**

MID AMERICAN AUTO RACING NEWS (US/0199-2465) [05734462] 5419, **4904**

MID-AMERICAN JOURNAL OF BUSINESS (US/0895-1772) [13554905] **694**

MID-AMERICAN REVIEW (US/0747-8895) [10827798] **3411**

MID-AMERICAN REVIEW OF SOCIOLOGY (US/0732-913X) [02386091] **5252**

MID-ATLANTIC *See* FODOR'S MID-ATLANTIC **5472**

●MID-ATLANTIC ALMANACK, THE (US/1063-1763) [25909825] **2538**

MID-ATLANTIC ARCHIVIST, THE (US/0738-9396) [04042873] **2623**

MID-ATLANTIC COUNTRY (US/0888-1022) [12968073] **2538**

MID-ATLANTIC FOODSERVICE NEWS (US/0888-5311) [13645559] **2350**

MID-ATLANTIC GAME & FISH (US/1055-6540) [23249489] **4874**

MID-ATLANTIC JOURNAL OF BUSINESS, THE (US/0732-9334) [07680643] **694**

MID ATLANTIC PURCHASING (US/0745-1733) [08434921] **950**

MID-ATLANTIC SALES GUIDE TO HIGH-TECH COMPANIES (US/1040-0575) [18304576] **5128**

MID-ATLANTIC THOROUGHBRED (US/1056-3245) [23605626] **2800**

MID-CANADA OUTDOORS (CN/1185-2143) [24368493] **4874**

MID-CITIES NEWS, THE (US/1044-0089) [19683661] **5752**

MID-CONTINENT BANKER (NORTHERN EDITION) *See* BANK NEWS **775**

MID-CONTINENT BANKER (SOUTHERN EDITION) *See* BANK NEWS **775**

MID-CONTINENT BOTTLER (US/0026-2978) [05165133] **2369**

MID-COUNTY TIMES, THE (US/0749-8519) [11190278] **5769**

MID FRANKFURT (GW/0938-880X) [I0938880X] **5129**

MID-HUDSON LANGUAGE STUDIES (US/0272-717X) [04721243] **3302**

MID-ISLAND HERALD (PLAINVIEW-OLD BETHPAGE EDITION) (US/0894-0584) [15794405] **5718**

MID-ISLAND TIMES *See* MID-ISLAND TIMES & LEVITTOWN TIMES **5718**

MID-ISLAND TIMES & LEVITTOWN TIMES (US/0747-4741) [10904577] **5718**

MID-NORTH MONITOR, THE (CN/0227-3853) [06703371] **5789**

MID-PACIFIC REGION REPORT (US/0148-3811) [03295285] **2093**

MID-SESSION REVIEW OF THE ... BUDGET *See* MID-SESSION REVIEW : THE PRESIDENT'S BUDGET AND ECONOMIC GROWTH AGENDA OF THE ... BUDGET / EXECUTIVE OFFICE OF THE PRESIDENT, OFFICE OF MANAGEMENT AND BUDGET **4737**

●MID-SESSION REVIEW : THE PRESIDENT'S BUDGET AND ECONOMIC GROWTH AGENDA OF THE ... BUDGET / EXECUTIVE OFFICE OF THE PRESIDENT, OFFICE OF MANAGEMENT AND BUDGET (US) [26717725] **4737**

MID-SOUTH HUNTING & FISHING NEWS (US/0894-7767) [16220888] **4874**

MID SPORTS (US/1042-3516) [19017514] **4904**

MID-STREAM (INDIANAPOLIS) (US/0544-0653) [01895444] **4977**

MID-TERM ECONOMIC FORECAST (JA/0918-4422) [I09184422] **1505**

MID-TOWN/MT. PLEASANT REVUE (CN/0710-5363) [08716824] **5789**

MID WEEK PETROLEUM ARGUS (UK) **4264**

MID-WEST CONTRACTOR (US/0026-3044) [05165662] **621**

●MID-WESTERN EDUCATIONAL RESEARCHER (1991) (US/1056-3997) [23248503] **1764**

MID-WESTERN STATE, NIGERIA. MINISTRY OF ESTABLISHMENTS *See* STAFF LIST - MID-WESTERN STATE, NIGERIA. MINISTRY OF ESTABLISHMENTS **4687**

MID YEAR REVIEW OF THE ECONOMY (II) [20653219] **1505**

MID-YORK WEEKLY, THE (US) [14482378] **5718**

MIDAMERICA (EAST LANSING) (US/0190-2911) [02251221] **3411**

MIDCONTINENT OIL AND GAS WORLD (US/1071-4790) [28492923] **4264**

MIDCONTINENT OIL WORLD (US/0883-7325) [12225783] **4264**

MIDCONTINENT OIL WORLD PETROLEUM DIRECTORY *See* MIDCONTINENT PETROLEUM DIRECTORY **4264**

MIDCONTINENT PETROLEUM DIRECTORY (US) **4264**

MIDCONTINENTAL JOURNAL OF ARCHAEOLOGY, MCJA (US/0146-1109) [02198049] **274**

MIDDEN, THE (CN/0047-7222) [02066941] **274**

MIDDLE EAST, ABSTRACTS AND INDEX (US/0162-766X) [04213443] 2769, **2635**

MIDDLE EAST AND NORTH AFRICA, THE (UK/0076-8502) [01162440] **1927**

MIDDLE EAST & SOUTH ASIA FOLKLORE BULLETIN, THE (US/1074-0244) [28101348] **2322**

MIDDLE EAST AND SOUTH ASIA, THE (US/0084-2311) [02066457] 4482, **2769**

MIDDLE EAST AND WORLD CONSTRUCTION DIRECTORY (LE) **621**

MIDDLE EAST AND WORLD FOOD DIRECTORY (LE) **2350**

MIDDLE EAST ARCHITECTURAL DESIGN (UK/0142-0305) [19991377] **303**

MIDDLE EAST BUSINESS & BANKING (TU) [19242884] **1638**

MIDDLE EAST BUSINESS DIGEST *See* AFRICA-MIDDLE EAST BUSINESS DIGEST **637**

MIDDLE EAST BUSINESS INTELLIGENCE (US/0731-6305) [08225710] 879, **933**

MIDDLE EAST CIVIL AVIATION (US/1054-9838) [23041688] **28**

MIDDLE EAST CLIPBOARD, THE (US) [13912808] **2769**

MIDDLE EAST COMMUNICATIONS (UK/0269-9567) [I02699567] **1160**

MIDDLE EAST CONTEMPORARY SURVEY (US/0163-5476) [04146581] **2769**

MIDDLE EAST COUNCIL OF CHURCHES *See* MECC PERSPECTIVES - MIDDLE EAST COUNCIL OF CHURCHES **5039**

MIDDLE EAST CURRENCY REPORTS (UK/0307-0387) [11589240] **1638**

MIDDLE EAST DENTISTRY & ORAL HEALTH (UK/0266-8874) [13677754] **1330**

MIDDLE EAST DIARY. CD-ROM (US) **4528**

MIDDLE EAST ECONOMIC SURVEY (CY/0544-0424) [02264167] 798, **4264**

MIDDLE EAST ELECTRICITY (UK/0309-4707) [I03094707] **2072**

MIDDLE EAST EXECUTIVE REPORTS (US/0271-0498) [06550274] **3132**

MIDDLE EAST FOCUS *CEASED.* (CN/0705-8594) [04249958] **4528**

MIDDLE EAST FOOD TRADE & CATERING EQUIPMENT (UK/0265-6469) [I02656469] **2350**

MIDDLE EAST HEALTH (1981) (UK/0263-1016) [08400271] **3616**

MIDDLE EAST INDUSTRY & TRANSPORT *CEASED.* (UK/0261-1473) [07383537] **5387**

MIDDLE EAST INSIGHT (US/0731-9371) [08272529] **4482**

MIDDLE EAST INTERNATIONAL (UK/0047-7249) [01714066] **4528**

MIDDLE EAST JOURNAL OF ANESTHESIOLOGY (LE/0544-0440) [01778785] **3683**

MIDDLE EAST JOURNAL, THE (US/0026-3141) [01607025] 2769, **2635**

MIDDLE EAST LIBRARIANS ASSOCIATION *See* MELA NOTES **3230**

MIDDLE EAST (LONDON, ENGLAND : 1985) (UK/0305-0734) [12251136] 694, **1505**

MIDDLE EAST MILITARY BALANCE / JAFFEE CENTER FOR STRATEGIC STUDIES, THE (IS) [10359463] 4482, **4049**

MIDDLE EAST MONEY (UK) [13552008] **798**

MIDDLE EAST MONITOR (US/0026-315X) [01757412] 1638, **4482**

MIDDLE EAST (NEW YORK, N.Y.), THE (US/0271-3160) [06600126] **2658**

MIDDLE EAST OBSERVER. SPECIAL SERVICES, THE (UA) [10361687] **1574**

●MIDDLE EAST POLICY (US/1061-1924) [25216267] 2769, **4528**

MIDDLE EAST POLICY SURVEY (US/0276-5632) [07383628] **4482**

MIDDLE EAST QUARTERLY (US) **2526**

MIDDLE EAST REPORT (NEW YORK, N.Y. : 1988) (US/0899-2851) [17640394] **2526**

MIDDLE EAST REVIEW (SAFFRON WALDEN, ESSEX) (UK) [07153200] 694, **1638**

MIDDLE EAST SKETCH (LE) [01788400] **2769**

MIDDLE EAST STUDIES ASSOCIATION BULLETIN (US/0026-3184) [01645603] **2769**

MIDDLE EAST TRAVEL *SUSPENDED.* (UK/0140-8321) [10466602] **5484**

MIDDLE EAST WATER & SEWAGE (UK/0140-5098) [04446837] 2236, **5536**

MIDDLE EASTERN STUDIES (UK/0026-3206) [01644707] **2769**

MIDDLE ELEMENTARY CLASS PACKET, THE (US/0149-7723) [03569818] **1764**

MIDDLE ENGLISH DICTIONARY (US) **1927**

MIDDLE ENGLISH TEXTS (GW) [06781205] **3411**

MIDDLE JR. HIGH SCIENCE BULLETIN *See* SCIENCE SCOPE (WASHINGTON, D.C.) **5153**

MIDDLE MANAGEMENT PERSONNEL (US/0741-5443) [10157166] **944**

Alphabetical Title Index — MIGRATION

MIDDLE MARKET FINANCIAL MANAGEMENT; REPORT TO PARTICIPANTS (US) [06271966] 798, 879

MIDDLE MARKET FOCUS (US) 1505

MIDDLE SCHOOL JOURNAL (US/0094-0771) [01793788] 1764

MIDDLE SCHOOL WEEKLY (US) 1764

●MIDDLE SEARCH (US/1071-2755) [28599811] 1764, 1795

MIDDLE STATES ASSOCIATION OF COLLEGES AND SCHOOLS See GUIDE TO MIDDLE STATES SCHOOLS IN PENNSYLVANIA 1749

MIDDLE STATES ASSOCIATION OF COLLEGES AND SCHOOLS See GUIDE TO MIDDLE STATES SCHOOLS IN NEW YORK 1749

MIDDLE STATES ASSOCIATION OF COLLEGES AND SCHOOLS See GUIDE TO MIDDLE STATES SCHOOLS IN DELAWARE, DISTRICT OF COLUMBIA, MARYLAND, PUERTO RICO, CANAL ZONE, VIRGIN ISLANDS, OVERSEAS 1749

MIDDLE STATES ASSOCIATION OF COLLEGES AND SCHOOLS See GUIDE TO MIDDLE STATES SCHOOLS IN NEW JERSEY 1749

MIDDLE TENNESSEE GENEALOGY (US) 2460

MIDDLEBORO GAZETTE (MIDDLEBORO, MASS. : 1870) (US) [11674121] 5689

MIDDLEBURY COLLEGE MAGAZINE (US/0745-2454) [08338645] 1093

MIDDLEBURY INDEPENDENT (MIDDLEBURY, IND. : 1974) (US) [15650778] 5665

MIDDLEBURY STUDIES IN RUSSIAN LANGUAGE AND LITERATURE (US/0888-8752) [13739429] 3411, 3302

●MIDDLER & JUNIOR CHILDREN'S CHURCH TEACHER GUIDE (US/1059-3411) [24568357] 4977

MIDDLER STUDENT See MIDDLER STUDENT GUIDE 4977

●MIDDLER STUDENT GUIDE (US/1059-3314) [24568068] 4977

MIDDLER TEACHER (US/0277-9153) [07715387] 1900

●MIDDLER TEACHER GUIDE (US/1059-3306) [24568049] 1764, 4977

MIDDLESEX HOSPITAL JOURNAL See CHARLES BELL JOURNAL, THE 3778

MIDDLETOWN JOURNAL (US) 5729

MIDDLETOWN NEWS (MIDDLETOWN, IND. : 1913) (US) [13664550] 5665

MIDDLETOWN PRESS, THE (US) [08786309] 5645

MIDEAST DIRECTIONS (US/0731-8944) [08266131] 2769

MIDEAST MARKETS CEASED. (UK/0098-6461) [02241348] 933, 846

MIDEAST MIRROR (UK) 4482, 694

MIDEAST MONITOR CEASED. (US/0888-2460) [12921983] 2770

MIDEAST PRESS REPORT (US/0731-4655) [08197522] 4528

MIDEASTERN TOUR BOOK (US/0569-2865) [01168328] 5484

MIDF MELAPURKAN (MY) [01790770] 798

MIDGETS & MINI-SPRINTS RACING NEWS (US/0889-5279) [13915107] 4904

MIDI MEDIA (FR/0295-3943) [I02953943] 1117

MIDIA (BL) [04677709] 762

MIDIRS MIDWIFERY DIGEST (UK/0961-5555) [I09116555] 3765

MIDLAND ANCESTOR : JOURNAL OF THE BIRMINGHAM AND MIDLAND SOCIETY FOR GENEALOGY AND HERALDRY, THE (UK/0307-2851) [19109775] 2460

MIDLAND HISTORY (UK/0047-729X) [01757425] 2698

MIDLAND LOG (US) [03924267] 2746

MIDLAND REPORTER-TELEGRAM, THE (US/0890-5932) [14238795] 5752

MIDLAND TIMES (WYOMING, IOWA : 1973) (US) [12306552] 5671

MIDLANDS BUSINESS JOURNAL (US/0194-4525) [04657324] 694

MIDLIFE WELLNESS SUSPENDED. (US/0740-6150) [09979026] 3765

●MIDLIFE WOMAN (US/1061-348X) [25259961] 5561

MIDLOTHIAN MIRROR, THE (US) [16733784] 5752

MIDNIGHT (CN) [03406331] 2538

MIDNIGHT ENGINEERING (US/1050-0324) [21378461] 1987

MIDNIGHT HOROSCOPE (US/0199-7165) [06100896] 390

MIDNIGHT MARQUEE (US/0886-8719) [13041675] 386

MIDNIGHT ZOO (US/1058-2517) [24250703] 3411

MIDRANGE COMPUTING (US/1052-3561) [21758846] 1195

MIDRANGE SYSTEMS (US/1041-8237) [18858936] 1274

MIDSOUTH POLITICAL SCIENCE JOURNAL (US/1051-5054) [21984900] 4482

MIDSTREAM (NEW YORK) (US/0026-332X) [01714718] 5051

MIDTOWN NEWS (US/8750-5908) [11586357] 5732

MIDWEEK EAGLE (US) [20836898] 5725

MIDWEEK PLUS (US) [20836869] 5726

MIDWEEKER (US) [17060486] 5737

MIDWEST 4 WHEEL DRIVE ASSOCIATION See RULE BOOK - MIDWEST 4 WHEEL DRIVE ASSOCIATION 4915

MIDWEST AGRICULTURAL LAW JOURNAL (US/0738-6753) [09652516] 108, 3010

MIDWEST ALLIANCE IN NURSING JOURNAL / MAIN (US/1048-499X) [20959634] 3861

MIDWEST ANCESTREE QUARTERLY, THE (US/0198-9359) [06252890] 2460

MIDWEST ARCHIVES CONFERENCE See M.A.C 2482

MIDWEST AUTOMOTIVE NEWS (US/0026-3338) [04964824] 5419

MIDWEST ENGINEER (US/0026-3370) [01757432] 1987

MIDWEST FINANCE ASSOCIATION See JOURNAL OF THE MIDWEST FINANCE ASSOCIATION 905

MIDWEST FLYER MAGAZINE (US/0273-7515) [06884843] 28

MIDWEST FOODSERVICE NEWS (US) 2350

MIDWEST HISTORICAL AND GENEALOGICAL REGISTER (US/0271-8685) [06430410] 2460

MIDWEST HISTORY OF EDUCATION SOCIETY See JOURNAL OF THE MIDWEST HISTORY OF EDUCATION SOCIETY 1759

MIDWEST JEWISH WEEK, THE (US/1062-9521) [25814467] 5051

MIDWEST LANDSCAPING See LANDSCAPE CONTRACTOR, THE 2423

MIDWEST LIVING (US/0889-8138) [14086253] 2538

MIDWEST MEDICAL ETHICS See BIOETHICS FORUM 2249

MIDWEST MESSENGER (SOUTH EDITION) (US/0747-9565) [10846703] 1160

MIDWEST MOTORIST, THE (US/0026-3435) [04054165] 5484

MIDWEST MUSEUMS CONFERENCE NEWS BRIEF (US/1073-0893) 4091

MIDWEST OUTDOORS (US/0747-3648) [10775232] 4874

MIDWEST PLAN SERVICE See STRUCTURES AND ENVIRONMENT HANDBOOK 629

MIDWEST PLAN SERVICE See PROFESSIONAL DESIGN SUPPLEMENT 624

MIDWEST POETRY REVIEW (US/0745-8738) [09528234] 3466

●MIDWEST PUREBRED DOGPOST!, THE (US/1061-6586) [25390286] 226

MIDWEST QUARTERLY (PITTSBURG), THE (US/0026-3451) [01757446] 2538

MIDWEST RACING NEWS (US/0047-732X) [04054187] 5419, 4904

MIDWEST REAL ESTATE NEWS (US/0893-2719) [15071708] 4841

MIDWEST REGION LIBRARY NETWORK See ANNUAL REPORT - MIDWEST REGION LIBRARY NETWORK 3190

MIDWEST REGIONAL SOLAR ENERGY PLANNING VENTURE (US/0196-9064) [04285499] 1950

MIDWEST REVIEW (WAYNE, NEB. : 1975) (US/0740-3208) [05454649] 2746

MIDWEST SHARED NEWSLETTER (US) 2538

MIDWEST STUDIES IN PHILOSOPHY (US/0363-6550) [02489329] 4353

MIDWEST VOLLEYBALL MAGAZINE CEASED. (US/0893-3367) [15497269] 4905

MIDWESTERN ADVOCATE (US/0360-5094) [02244494] 3010

MIDWESTERN ARCHIVIST See ARCHIVAL ISSUES : JOURNAL OF THE MIDWEST ARCHIVES CONFERENCE 2479

MIDWESTERN DENTIST (US/0026-3478) [02264181] 1330

MIDWESTERN FOLKLORE (US/0894-4059) [16102373] 2322

MIDWESTERN MISCELLANY (US/0885-4742) [03723001] 3411

MIDWESTERN REGIONAL LIBRARY SYSTEM (ONT.) See TITLE LISTING - MIDWESTERN REGIONAL LIBRARY SYSTEM 426

MIDWESTERN REGIONAL LIBRARY SYSTEM (ONT.) See AUTHOR LISTING - MIDWESTERN REGIONAL LIBRARY SYSTEM 408

MIDWESTERN REGIONAL LIBRARY SYSTEM (ONT.) See 16MM FILM ADDENDUM - MIDWESTERN REGIONAL LIBRARY SYSTEM 4062

MIDWESTERN REGIONAL LIBRARY SYSTEM (ONT.) See SHELF LISTING - MIDWESTERN REGIONAL LIBRARY SYSTEM 5794

MIDWIFERY (UK/0266-6138) [12918279] 3765

MIDWIFERY TODAY (US/0891-7701) [14991213] 3765

●MIDWIFERY TODAY AND CHILDBIRTH EDUCATION (US) [28382829] 3765

MIDWIVES CHIRURGICAL NURSING See MIDWIVES CHRONICLE AND NURSING NOTES 3765

MIDWIVES CHRONICLE AND NURSING NOTES (UK/0026-3524) [02255073] 3765

MIDYEAR STATISTICS FOR FEDERALLY INSURED CREDIT UNIONS (US) [17556491] 798

MIE DAIGAKU KANKYO KAGAKU KENKYU KIYO (JA/0385-3381) [07370576] 2218

MIE DAIGAKU. KANKYO KAGAKU SOGO KENKYUSHITSU See MIE DAIGAKU KANKYO KAGAKU KENKYU KIYO 2218

MIE DAIGAKU SEIBUTSU SHIGEN GAKUBU KIYO (JA/0915-0471) [19654357] 2308

MIE MEDICAL JOURNAL (JA/0026-3532) [01606498] 3616

MIEJSKA BIBLIOTEKA PUBLICZNA W KRAKOWIE See BIBLIOGRAFIA KRAKOWA I WOJEWODZTWA MIEJSKIEGO KRAKOWSKIEGO ZA ROK ... / MIEJSKA BIBLIOTEKA PUBLICZNA W KRAKOWIE 408

MIELIENUUS See MAIZE NEWS 106

MIESIECZNIK LITERACKI (PL/0026-3567) [02106320] 3411

MIFAL, HA- (IS) [02241482] 1618

MIFAL HA-PAYIS See DIRECTORS' REPORT AND FINANCIAL STATEMENT 787

MIFAL HA-PAYIS See DUAH HA-DIREKTORYON U-MAAZAN 788

MIFFLIN COUNTY LEGAL JOURNAL (US) [01757455] 3010

MIFFLINBURG TELEGRAPH (US) [10365616] 5737

MIGHT'S COBOURG, PORT HOPE, ONTARIO, CITY DIRECTORY (CN/0317-6487) [02441744] 2569

MIGHT'S OAKVILLE ONTARIO CITY DIRECTORY (CN/0381-8578) [02587912] 2569

●MIGHTY MORPHIN POWER RANGERS (US) [30806629] 1066

MIGHTY THOR, THE (US/0274-533X) [06418265] 4863

MIGRACIJSKE TEME (CI/0352-5600) [18542164] 1920

MIGRANT ECHO (US/0047-7338) [01713713] 2623

MIGRANT EDUCATION: STATE EVALUATION REPORT (US) [05259707] 1764

MIGRANT HEALTH PROJECTS (US/0145-1340) [02663538] 4791

MIGRANT REPORT (US) [01787019] 1690

MIGRANT SERVICES REPORT See MIGRANT SERVICES STATISTICAL REPORT 1536

MIGRANT SERVICES STATISTICAL REPORT (US) [06048779] 1690, 1536

MIGRANT, THE (US/0026-3575) [01757456] 5618

MIGRATION ACTION (AT/0311-3760) [03113760] 1920

MIGRATION AND TOURISM STATISTICS (KE/0377-1385) [01794953] 5500

MIGRATION (BERLIN, WEST) (GW/0721-2887) [17304680] 1920

MIGRATION NEWS (SZ/0026-3583) [05439526] 1920

MIGRATION NEWS / INTERNATIONAL CATHOLIC EDUCATION COMMISSION CEASED. (SZ) [23957068] 1920

MIGRATION TODAY (SZ/0544-1188) [01757458] 1920

MIGRATION WORLD MAGAZINE (US/1058-5095) [14352974] 1920

MIGRATIONS — Alphabetical Title Index

MIGRATIONS (GENEVA, SWITZERLAND) (SZ) [16403417] **1920**

MIGRATIONS SANTE (FR/0335-7198) [I03357198] **4791**

MIGRATORY BIRDS CONVENTION ACT AND MIGRATORY BIRD REGULATIONS (CN) [02042843] 5618, **2198**

MIGUK PYONGNON (KO) [01790364] **2746**

MIGUKHAK AMERICAN STUDIES (KO) [08019473] **2746**

MIJN STOKPAARDJE (NE) **2786**

MIJU AN UI HAN'GUKIN (US) [05757702] **2746**

MIJU HAN'GUK ILBO (US/1041-7281) [18831257] **5647**

MIJU SAENGHWAL (US) [08094091] **2526**

MIKADO (FR/0758-4180) [I07584180] **1764**

MIKE BRUNO'S WHAT'S NEW(S) IN GRAPHIC COMMUNICATIONS (US/0737-6928) [09433438] **381**

MIKE SHAYNE MYSTERY MAGAZINE (US/0026-3621) [04055513] **5074**

MIKOLOGIAI KOZLEMENYEK (HU/0133-9095) [I01339095] **575**

MIKOLOGIJA I FITOPATOLOGIJA (RU/0026-3648) [04742672] **575**

MIKROBIOLOGICHESKII ZHURNAL (UN/0201-8462) [05671586] **567**

MIKROBIOLOGIIA (RU) [05434123] **567**

MIKROBIOLOGIJA (YU/0581-1538) [02896578] **567**

MIKROBIOLOGIJA (MOSKVA. 1932) (RU/0026-3656) [01589803] **567**

MIKROBIYOLOJI BULTENI (TU/0374-9096) [01262126] **567**

MIKROCHIMICA ACTA (AU/0026-3672) [01778788] **1018**

MIKROCHIMICA ACTA. SUPPLEMENTUM (1966) (GW/0076-8642) [03773795] **986**

MIKRODOK (BADEN-BADEN, GERMANY) (GW/0344-8010) [12327740] **1270**

MIKROELEKTRONIK (GW) [01792078] **2072**

MIKROELEKTRONIKA (RU/0544-1269) [07073192] **2072**

MIKROELEMENTY V SSSR : BIULLETEN VSESOIUZNOI KOORDINATSONNOI KOMISSII PO MIKROELEMENTAM / AKADEMIIA NAUK LATVIISKOI SSR, INSTITUT BIOLOGII (LV/0540-0163) [07603266] **465**

MIKROFILMEK CIMJEGYZEKE. MODERN NYOMTATVANYOK / ORSZAGOS SZECHENYI KONYVTAR (HU/0134-0352) [07386079] **3231**

MIKROKOSMOS (STUTTGART) (GW/0026-3680) [01606110] **573**

MIKRONIEK (NE/0026-3699) [I00263699] **465**

MIKROOEKOLOGIE UND THERAPIE (GW/0720-0536) [06391957] **3617**

MIKROWELLEN- & HF-MAGAZIN (GW/0936-9104) [I09369104] **2072**

MIKUNI'S CREDIT RATINGS (JA) **798**

MILAFF AL-ALAQAT AL-ARABIYAH AL-YABANIYAH / IDAD QISM AL-ALAQAT AL-DUWALIYAH (KU) [09789609] **2770**

MILAN. ISTITUTO SIEROTERAPICO MILANESE *See* BOLLETTINO DELL'INSTITUTO SIEROTERAPICO MILANESE **3667**

MILAN STANDARD WATSON JOURNAL, THE (US/0747-1734) [10621147] **5697**

MILAN. UNIVERSITA. ISTITUTO DI DIRITTO INTERNAZIONALE E STRANIERO *See* COMUNICAZIONI E STUDI **2955**

MILAN. UNIVERSITA. ISTITUTO DI PAPIROGOGIA *See* PAPIRI **278**

MILANO FINANZA : MF (IT) [22534402] **798**

MILANO MILANO (IT) **2490**

MILBANK HERALD ADVANCE (US) [12814379] **5744**

MILBANK QUARTERLY, THE (US/0887-378X) [13200708] **4791**

MILCH-MARKETING (GW) **196**

MILCH PRAXIX UND RINDERMAST, DIE (GW/0343-0200) [04105772] **215**

● MILCHRIND (GW/0941-1348) [26093942] **215**

MILCHWIRTSCHAFTLICHE BERICHTE AUS DEN BUNDESANSTALTEN WOLFPASSING UND ROTHOLZ (AU/0544-1706) [04105911] **196**

MILCHWISSENSCHAFT (GW/0026-3788) [01757471] 4194, **196**

MILE ZERO NEWS (CN/0228-037X) [06758241] **5789**

MILEPOST (WINNIPEG) (CN/0227-2458) [07313528] **5432**

MILES CITY STAR (US/0891-8988) [13080447] **5705**

MILES MESSENGER (US/0746-6668) [10214589] **5752**

● MILES TO GO (US/1061-7140) [25417439] **4905**

MILESTONE CAR, THE (US/01798715] **5419**

MILESTONES (US) **3789**

MILESTONES IN ANESTHESIA (US/1055-5137) [23195216] **3683**

MILFORD CABINET AND WILTON JOURNAL, THE (US) [21349587] **5708**

MILFORD CITIZEN, THE (US) [11488031] **5645**

MILFORD MAIL, THE TERRIL RECORD, THE (US) [16409613] **5671**

MILFORD SERIES, POPULAR WRITERS OF TODAY, THE (US/0163-2469) [04326095] **3411**

MILFORD TIMES, THE (US) [12221610] **5693**

MILIEU (NE) **2177**

MILIEU AANSPRAKELIJKHEID (NE) [20185523] 3010, **2198**

MILIEU DE VIE (CN/0708-9627) [05257114] **4852**

MILIEU MAGAZINE ALPHEN AAN DEN RIJN (NE/0924-6282) [I09246282] **2177**

MILIEU MANAGEMENT (NE) **2236**

MILIEU (OTTAWA) (CN/0835-1457) [20050187] **2236**

MILIEU (SAINTE-FOY) *SUSPENDED.* (CN/0380-2760) [05385676] **2198**

MILIEU THERAPY (US/0276-8887) [07441984] **4604**

MILIEUFACETTEN / CBS, CENTRAAL BUREAU VOOR DE STATISTIEK, MILIEUSTATISTIEKEN (NE) [19416328] **2236**

MILIEUMARKT (NE) **2177**

● MILIEUSTRATEGIE ALPHEN AAN DEN RIJN. 1994 (NE/0929-791X) [I0929791X] **2177**

MILITAERT TIDSSKRIFT (DK) **4050**

MILITAIRE SPECTATOR, DE (NE) [06299880] **4050**

MILITANT (UK) **4050**

MILITANT CHRETIEN INTERNATIONAL, LE (CN/0228-1171) [06959940] **5032**

MILITANT INTERNATIONAL REVIEW (UK) [05294062] **4050**

MILITANT (NEW YORK, N.Y. 1941), THE (US/0026-3885) [02264193] **5718**

MILITAR UND SOZIALWISSENSCHAFTEN (GW) [18366213] 4050, **5252**

MILITARGESCHICHTE (GW) [23926501] **4050**

MILITARGESCHICHTLICHE MITTEILUNGEN (GW/0026-3826) [06375295] **2698**

MILITARGESCHICHTLICHES BEIHEFT ZUR EUROPAISCHEN WEHRKUNDE WIHRWISSENSCHAFTLICHE RUNDSCHAU (GW/0932-0458) [18580093] **4050**

MILITARHISTORISK TIDSKRIFT (SW/0023-5369) [14122286] **4050**

MILITARIA AUCTION - TOREX (CN/0822-4943) [10007963] **2781**

MILITARIA BELGICA (BE) [05540840] **4050**

MILITARPOLITIK (GW/0171-9033) [10141406] **4050**

MILITARWISSENSCHAFTLICHE QUELLENKUNDE (GW) [08256772] **4062**

MILITARY AIRCRAFT FORECAST (US) 28, **4050**

MILITARY & AEROSPACE ELECTRONICS (US/1046-9079) [20569881] 28, **4050**

MILITARY & COMMERCIAL FIBER BUSINESS (US/1051-2470) [21898090] **4438**

MILITARY & POLICE UNIFORM ASSOCIATION NEWSLETTER, THE (US/1072-8112) [29210566] **2795**

MILITARY ASSISTANCE PROGRAM ADDRESS DIRECTORY (US/0278-3029) [03116251] **4050**

MILITARY BALANCE, THE (UK/0459-7222) [01779849] **4050**

MILITARY BUSINESS REVIEW *CEASED.* (US/0883-3427) [11956772] 4050, **950**

MILITARY CHAPLAIN, THE (US/0026-3958) [01757475] 4977, **4050**

MILITARY CHAPLAINS' REVIEW (US/0360-9693) [01641872] **4050**

MILITARY CLUB & HOSPITALITY (US/0886-8832) [13033412] 4050, **2350**

MILITARY CLUBS & RECREATION (US/0192-2718) [05025435] **4050**

MILITARY COLLECTOR & HISTORIAN (US/0026-3966) [01757476] **4050**

MILITARY COST HANDBOOK (US/1051-6069) [08501012] **4050**

MILITARY DEALERS AND COLLECTORS DIRECTORY AND HANDBOOK (US) [11124516] **4050**

MILITARY ELECTRONICS BRIEFING (US) 2072, **4050**

MILITARY ENGINEER, THE (US/0026-3982) [01645645] 4050, **1987**

MILITARY FIRE FIGHTER (UK) **2291**

MILITARY FIREFIGHTER (UK/0964-9700) [I09649700] **2291**

MILITARY GOVERNMENT JOURNAL AND NEWS LETTER *See* CIVIL AFFAIRS JOURNAL AND NEWSLETTER **4638**

MILITARY GROCER (US/1058-8620) [24411723] **4050**

MILITARY HISTORICAL SOCIETY (GREAT BRITAIN) *See* BULLETIN - MILITARY HISTORICAL SOCIETY **4038**

MILITARY HISTORY (HERNDON, VA.) (US/0889-7328) [11492012] **4050**

MILITARY HISTORY JOURNAL (SA/0026-4016) [02512522] 2623, **4050**

MILITARY HISTORY MAGAZINE PRESENTS GREAT BATTLES *See* GREAT BATTLES **2617**

MILITARY HISTORY OF THE SOUTHWEST *See* MILITARY HISTORY OF THE WEST **4050**

MILITARY HISTORY OF THE SOUTHWEST (US/0898-8064) [17913112] **4050**

● MILITARY HISTORY OF THE WEST (US/1071-2011) [28161744] **4050**

MILITARY ILLUSTRATED : PAST & PRESENT (UK/0268-8328) [15189054] 2623, **4050**

MILITARY IMAGES (US/1040-4961) [18433936] **4050**

MILITARY IMAGES MAGAZINE *See* MILITARY IMAGES **4050**

MILITARY INTELLIGENCE (US/0026-4024) [03454871] **4050**

MILITARY LAW REPORTER *CEASED.* (US/0193-3906) [05214401] **3183**

MILITARY LAW REVIEW (US/0026-4040) [01695128] **3183**

MILITARY LIFESTYLE (UNITED STATES EDITION) (US/0885-8403) [12736935] **4051**

MILITARY LIVING (US/0740-5065) [06059057] **4051**

MILITARY LIVING'S R & R REPORT (US/0740-5073) [09973109] **4051**

MILITARY MANPOWER STATISTICS (US/0741-1340) [07952852] 4051, **4062**

MILITARY MARKET (US/0026-4067) [01715023] **4051**

MILITARY MEDICINE (US/0026-4075) [01641787] 4051, **3617**

MILITARY MICROWAVES ANNUAL CONFERENCE PROCEEDINGS (UK) **4051**

MILITARY MODELER (US/0195-1467) [05306888] **4051**

MILITARY MODELLING (UK/0026-4083) [02253209] **2774**

MILITARY OPERATIONS RESEARCH (US/0275-5823) [07189064] **4051**

MILITARY PERSONNEL AND DEPENDENTS IN HAWAII (US/0363-8359) [02548232] 4051, **4062**

MILITARY POLICE (1987) (US/0895-4208) [16219915] **3169**

MILITARY PSYCHOLOGY (US/0899-5605) [18143648] **4051**

MILITARY RESEARCH LETTER *See* DEFENSE ACQUISITION REPORT **4040**

MILITARY REVIEW (US/0026-4148) [02558412] **4051**

MILITARY ROBOTICS (US/0896-0348) [16891365] 4051, **1215**

MILITARY (SACRAMENTO, CALIF.) (US/1046-2511) [12347097] **4051**

MILITARY SPACE (US/0743-7897) [10688088] 4051, **28**

MILITARY SPACE-A AIR OPPORTUNITIES AROUND THE WORLD (US) **4051**

MILITARY TECHNOLOGY (GW/0722-3226) [17718846] **4051**

MILITARY TOWN AND INSTALLATION (US/1041-6129) [18810962] **4051**

MILITARY VEHICLES (US/0893-3863) [15529731] **4051**

MILITARY VEHICLES FORECAST (US) **4051**

MILITARY YEAR-BOOK (II/0076-8782) [01774525] **4051**

MILITRT TIDSSKRIFT (DK/0026-3850) [I00263850] **4051**

MILK AND LIQUID FOOD TRANSPORTER (US/0199-2317) [03968565] **5387**

MILK AND MILK PRODUCTS BALANCES IN OECD COUNTRIES (FR) [11049857] 846, **196**

MILK FACTS (US/0740-9222) [03722451] **196**

MILK INDUSTRY (UK/0026-4172) [01757482] **196**

MILK / IOWA CROP & LIVESTOCK REPORTING SERVICE (US) [06204116] **196**

MILK MARKETER (US/0162-2781) [04146256] **197**

MILK PRODUCER *CEASED.* (UK/0026-4180) [04739107] **197**

MILK PRODUCTION (WASHINGTON) (US/0026-4202) [02635867] **197**

●MILKING SHORTHORN JOURNAL (1993) (US/1073-9394) [28552512] **215**

MILKING SHORTHORN YEAR BOOK (US) [03715086] **197**

MILKWEED CHRONICLE *CEASED.* (US/0275-8113) [07154512] **325**

MILL HUNK HERALD, THE *CEASED.* (US) [06546471] 1690, **3466**

MILL, THE (US) [03370826] **3412**

MILLAGE COMPARISON FOR ... (US) [17596048] **4737**

MILLARD COUNTY CHRONICLE PROGRESS (US/8750-3093) [11219875] **5757**

MILLARD COUNTY GAZETTE, THE (US) [12735169] **5757**

MILLAT-I BIDAR (US/8750-7145) [10172608] **2770**

MILLAT TRACTORS LIMITED *See* MILLAT TRACTORS LIMITED **160**

MILLAT TRACTORS LIMITED (PK) [11046818] **160**

MILLCREEK SUN, THE (US/0747-2943) [10687077] **5737**

MILLE LACS COUNTY TIMES (US) [01624283] **5697**

MILLE LACS MESSENGER, THE (US) [01757486] **5697**

MILLE PLUMES (CN/0705-0437) [04039601] **358**

MILLECANALI (IT) **4074**

MILLECONGRESSI (IT) **3617**

MILLELIBRI *CEASED.* (IT) [19234127] **3412**

MILLENNIUM (UK/0305-8298) [01794979] **4529**

MILLENNIUM FILM JOURNAL (US/1064-5586) [03765443] **4074**

MILLER COMPREHENSIVE GOVERNMENTAL GAAP GUIDE (US/0891-6918) [14960426] **748**

MILLER COMPREHENSIVE GOVERNMENTAL GAAP GUIDE UPDATE SERVICE (US) [16818819] **748**

MILLER MONITOR (US) [08515618] **2460**

MILLER PRESS, THE (US) [12862535] **5744**

MILLER PRODUCT LIABILITY SAFETY ENCYCLOPEDIA (UK) 4791, **3010**

MILLER'S COMPREHENSIVE GAAP GUIDE / MARTIN A. MILLER (US/0734-8355) [06057200] **748**

MILLER'S COMPREHENSIVE GAAP GUIDE. STUDENT EDITION (US/0736-8577) [09231439] **748**

MILLER'S COMPREHENSIVE GAAP GUIDE UPDATE (US) [08377949] **748**

MILLER'S SOLUTIONS TO THE UNIFORM CPA EXAM (US/0736-8542) [09234809] **748**

MILLERTON NEWS, THE (US) [13352476] **5718**

MILLETLERARAS HUKUK VE MILLETLERARAS OZEL HUKUK BULTENI : MHB (TU) [20324995] **3132**

MILLIKIN QUARTERLY (US/8750-7706) [11747938] **1836**

MILLIMAN & ROBERTSON, INC *See* ACTUARIAL VALUATION, NEBRASKA STATE PATROLMEN'S RETIREMENT SYSTEM **2872**

MILLIMETER (US/0164-9655) [02254737] **4074**

MILLIMETRO, IL (IT/0392-5498) [l03925498] **2922**

MILLING AND BAKING NEWS (US/0091-4843) [01771850] 2350, **202**

MILLING DIRECTORY BUYER'S GUIDE (US/1045-9030) [20033343] **202**

MILLION BAHT BUSINESS INFORMATION, THAILAND (TH) [06432076] **694**

MILLION BRIGHTON (UK/0960-832X) [l0960832X] **3412**

MILLION DOLLAR DIRECTORY (US/0070-7619) [01167732] **1505**

MILLION DOLLAR DIRECTORY, TOP 50,000 COMPANIES (US/1051-3442) [11959332] 1505, **695**

MILL'S PHARMACY STATE BOARD REVIEW (US/0163-8084) [04454503] **4315**

MILLTOWN STUDIES (IE/0332-1428) [08697903] **4977**

MILNE'S POULTRY DIGEST (AT/1032-3767) [l10323767] **215**

MILNE'S PRIME BEEF (AT/1037-0641) [l10370641] **215**

MILPITAS POST (US/0745-6212) [09313839] **5637**

MILSTRIP : MILITARY STANDARD REQUISITIONING & ISSUE PROCEDURES (US) [03028769] **4051**

MILSTRIP. SUPPLEMENT NO. 1 : ROUTING IDENTIFIER CODES (US) [03007473] **4051**

MILTON COURIER, THE (US) [14184544] **5769**

MILTON QUARTERLY (US/0026-4326) [01697097] **3347**

MILTON STANDARD, THE (US) [13922585] **5737**

MILTON STUDIES (US/0076-8820) [01757490] **3347**

MILTON WEEKLY TRIBUNE (CN/0706-683X) [06025574] **5789**

MILTONVALE RECORD, THE (US) [10193455] **5677**

MILTRONICS *CEASED.* (UK/0144-5243) [06765738] **4051**

MILWAUKEE (US/0026-4334) [01789565] **1574**

MILWAUKEE AREA MEDIA DIRECTORY (US/0196-8505) [05913595] **1117**

MILWAUKEE COUNTY TRANSIT BOARD *See* ANNUAL REPORT - MILWAUKEE COUNTY TRANSIT BOARD **5376**

MILWAUKEE COURIER (US/0026-4350) [04166496] **5769**

MILWAUKEE HISTORY (US/0163-7622) [04297571] **2746**

MILWAUKEE JOURNAL, THE (US/1052-4452) [01757504] **5769**

MILWAUKEE LABOR PRESS (US/0279-3741) [05385685] **1690**

MIL'WAUKEE LAWYER, THE *CEASED.* (US/0148-3242) [02845390] **3010**

MILWAUKEE MAGAZINE (US/0741-1243) [10102193] **2538**

MILWAUKEE PROFESSIONAL NURSE (US/0026-4369) [08758783] **3861**

MILWAUKEE. PUBLIC LIBRARY *See* MILWAUKEE READER **4830**

MILWAUKEE READER (US/0026-4377) [01781389] **4830**

MILWAUKEE SENTINEL (1883), THE (US/1052-4479) [11723897] **5769**

MILWAUKEE STAR (MILWAUKEE, WIS. : 1976) (US) [06706692] **5769**

MILWAUKEE (WFMR, INC. (RADIO STATION : MILWAUKEE)) *See* MILWAUKEE MAGAZINE **2538**

MIM (SAINT-AUGUSTIN-DE-DESMAURES, QUEBEC) (CN/0229-7507) [08143576] **4665**

MIMALAH (NP) [02240220] **3412**

MIMAR (SINGAPORE) *CEASED.* (SI/0129-8372) [08139833] 621, **303**

MIMARLIK FAKULTESI DERGISI (TU/0258-5316) [l02585316] **303**

MIMBAR *See* TRIBUN **2509**

MIMBAR AGAMA & BUDAYA / DIASUH OLEH LEMBAGA PENELITIAN IAIN JAKARTA (IO) [10463329] **5044**

MIMBAR PERMIAS. ENGLISH EDITION (US/0732-2267) [04369452] **1764**

MIME JOURNAL (US/0145-787X) [01915206] **5366**

MIME NEWS (US) [04119171] **386**

MIME NEWS (CLAREMONT, CALIF.) *See* MOVEMENT THEATRE QUARTERLY **5366**

MIMEOGRAPHED BIBLIOGRAPHY SERIES - INDUSTRIAL RELATIONS CENTRE. QUEEN'S UNIVERSITY (CN/0714-8887) [09088980] **420**

MIMOS : MITTEILUNGEN DER SCHWEIZERISCHEN GESELLSCHAFT FUER THEATERKULTUR (SZ) [20242023] **5366**

MIMPO SARON; ZUIHITSU (JA) [03266394] **2658**

MIMS (UK/0027-0431) [02448644] **4315**

MIMS AFRICA (UK/0140-4415) [03012634] **4315**

MIMS ANNUAL, AUSTRALIAN EDITION (AT/0725-4709) [06374074] **4315**

MIMS CARIBBEAN (UK) **4315**

MIMS COLOUR INDEX (UK) [01411292] **4315**

MIMS CROWS NEST (AT/1035-5723) [l10355723] **4315**

MIMS DESK REFERENCE (SA/0076-8847) [20116312] 3617, **4316**

MIMS DISEASE INDEX (AT/1035-5693) [l10355693] **3715**

MIMS HOSPITAL EQUIPMENT AND SUPPLIES (AT/0159-9100) [l01599100] **3789**

MIMS INDIA (II/0970-1036) [l09701036] 3617, **4316**

MIMS MAGAZINE (UK) [l03086550] **4316**

MIMS MEDICAL SPECIALTIES (SA/0027-0431) [18515411] **4316**

MIMS MIDDLE EAST (UK/0302-4172) [10103469] **3617**

MIMS UK (UK) **4316**

MIMSELA (II) [12075671] **3412**

MIN CHU TAI-WAN (US) [07431226] **2658**

MIN CHU YU FA CHIH (CC) [06656657] **2658**

MIN FAX (US/1047-1359) [06927063] **2828**

MIN I TSA CHIH (CH) [06905649] **5252**

MIN TSU HSUEH YEN CHIU / CHUNG-KUO MIN TSU HSUEH YEN CHIU HUI PIEN (CC) [10065595] **241**

MIN TSU WEN HSUEH YEN CHIU (CC) [11435100] **4482**

MIN TSU WEN HUA (CC) [11451546] **2658**

MIN TSU YU WEN (CC) [05337786] **3302**

MINAMI KYUSHU ZAIMUKYOKU YORAN (JA) [02953706] **4737**

MINAMI OSAKA BYOIN IGAKU ZASSHI (JA/0540-1259) [l05401259] **3617**

MINARET (LOS ANGELES, CALIF.), THE (US/0892-0559) [15080166] **5044**

MINARET, THE (UK) [03579227] **5044**

MINARET, THE (PK/0026-4415) [01607728] **5044**

MINARIA HELVETICA (SZ) [20242502] **2144**

MINAS GERAID (BRAZIL). SUPERINTENDENCIA DE ORCAMENTO *See* ORCAMENTO EMPRESAS **4671**

MINAS GERAIS (BRAZIL) *See* REVISTA JURIDICA LEMI. LEGISLACAO ESTADUAL. MINAS GERAIS **3042**

MINAS GERAIS (BRAZIL). CENTRO DE DOCUMENTACAO E INFORMACOES EDUCACIONAIS *See* BOLETIM INFORMATIVO - CENTRO DE DOCUMENTACAO E INFORMACOES EDUCACIONAIS **1728**

MINAS GERAIS (BRAZIL). SECRETARIA DE ESTADO DE ADMINISTRACAO *See* BOLETIM DO SERVIDOR **4702**

MINAS GERAIS, BRAZIL. UNIVERSIDADE CATOLICA. INSTITUTO DE DIRETITO DA ENERGIA *See* REVISTA DO INSTITUTO DE DIREITO DA ENERGIA **3042**

MINAS GERAIS, BRAZIL. UNIVERSIDADE FEDERAL. ESCOLA DE BIBLIOTECONOMIA *See* REVISTA DA ESCOLA DE BIBLIOTECONOMIA DA UFMG **3246**

MINAS GERAIS, BRAZIL. UNIVERSIDADE FEDERAL. INSTITUTO DE PESQUISAS RADIOATIVAS *See* RELATORIO ANUAL **4451**

MINATURE GOLF MAGAZINE *See* FAMILY ENTERTAINMENT CENTER **4861**

MINBAR AL-ISLAM (UA) [05370241] **5044**

MINCE ET SVELTE (CN/0226-7535) [06512173] **4194**

MINCHUNG SINMUN (CN/0225-1205) [06141345] **5789**

MIND (UK/0026-4423) [01594357] **4353**

MIND & LANGUAGE (UK/0268-1064) [13848820] **3302**

MIND BODY HEALTH DIGEST *CEASED.* (US/0898-3127) [17790209] **3799**

●MIND / BODY MEDICINE (CN/1195-1990) **3617**

MIND IN MOTION (US/8756-1549) [11482110] **3466**

●MIND MATTERS (US/1062-1806) [25535877] **4604**

MIND, THE MEETINGS INDEX. SERIES SEMT, SCIENCE, ENGINEERING, MEDICINE, TECHNOLOGY (US/0739-5914) [09773163] **5175**

MIND YOUR OWN BUSINESS (UK/0143-1374) [l01431374] **695**

MINDANAO ART AND CULTURE (PH) [07920773] **2322**

MINDANAO JOURNAL (PH/0115-2742) [02778917] **2658**

●MINDFIELD (NEW YORK, N.Y.) (US/1065-3848) [26604219] **4604**

MINDOLO ECUMENICAL FOUNDATION See ANNUAL REPORT - MINDOLO ECUMENICAL FOUNDATION **4935**

MINDS AND MACHINES (DORDRECHT) (NE/0924-6495) [23368454] **1215**

MINDSZENTY REPORT, THE (US/0026-4474) [04598074] 4543, **4977**

MINE AND QUARRY (UK/0369-1632) [01645297] **2144**

MINE AND QUARRY MECHANISATION CEASED. (AT/0085-3453) [01757518] **2144**

MINE DEVELOPMENT BIMONTHLY See METALS ECONOMICS GROUP STRATEGIC REPORT **2144**

MINE INJURIES AND WORKTIME (US) [04812070] **2865**

MINE LIFE (AT/1031-8380) [I10318380] **2144**

MINE PRODUCTION OF SILVER IN ... / THE SILVER INSTITUTE (US) [07468263] **2144**

MINE REGULATION REPORTER (US/1040-8223) [18542618] 2144, **3010**

MINE WATER AND THE ENVIRONMENT (AT) **1416**

MINEMET See ANNUAIRE MINEMET **2133**

MINER COUNTY PIONEER (US) [12814032] **5744**

MINERACAO METALURGIA (1968) (BL/0100-6908) [02448648] 2144, **4012**

MINERAL AND ELECTROLYTE METABOLISM (SZ/0378-0392) [03687147] 3731, **3799**

MINERAL & ENERGY INFORMATION SOURCES (US) [11940774] 1950, **2144**

MINERAL COMMODITY SUMMARIES (US/0160-5151) [03673088] 2144, **2006**

MINERAL COUNTY INDEPENDENT AND HAWTHORNE NEWS (US) [13775514] **5708**

MINERAL COUNTY MINER, THE (US/0745-791X) [09472451] **5643**

MINERAL ECONOMICS ABSTRACTS (US/0160-3779) [03665135] **2144**

MINERAL EXPLORATION, MINING, AND PROCESSING PATENTS (US/0544-2486) [01757523] **2144**

MINERAL INDUSTRY, EXPLORATION, PRODUCTION AND PROCESSING SURVEY (US/0275-9985) [07263298] **1441**

MINERAL INDUSTRY OF COLORADO IN ..., THE (US) [09457061] **1441**

MINERAL INDUSTRY OF TEXAS IN ..., THE (US) [09505174] **1618**

MINERAL INDUSTRY QUARTERLY (AT/0313-6086) [06575462] **2144**

● MINERAL INDUSTRY QUARTERLY REPORT (CN/1188-9004) [27725382] 4027, **1441**

MINERAL INDUSTRY REPORT. NORTHWEST TERRITORIES (CN/0707-3623) [02442665] 2144, **1618**

MINERAL INDUSTRY SURVEYS (US/0886-0564) [01777201] **2144**

MINERAL INDUSTRY SURVEYS. CADMIUM (US) [03027582] **2144**

MINERAL INDUSTRY SURVEYS. GRAPHITE, NATURAL IN ... (US/0739-2125) [09301957] **2144**

MINERAL INDUSTRY SURVEYS. POTASH IN CROP YEAR ... (US) [03045197] **1441**

MINERAL INFORMATION SERIES ADELAIDE (AT/0725-6221) [I07256221] **2144**

MINERAL INFORMATION SOURCES (US/0749-9876) [10315586] 1950, 2144, **1358**

MINERAL LAW NEWSLETTER (US/0897-6694) [11319791] 4264, 2144, **3010**

MINERAL LAW SERIES (US/0897-0122) [17368715] **3010**

MINERAL MATTERS (US/0889-6925) [09095477] **2144**

MINERAL METABOLISM : AN ADVANCED TREATISE (US) [01639572] **584**

MINERAL NEWS (COEUR D'ALENE, IDAHO) (US/0885-4327) [12636685] **1441**

MINERAL PERSPECTIVES (US/0270-9473) [03268031] **1441**

MINERAL PLANNING (UK/0267-1409) [I02671409] **1441**

MINERAL POLICY ISSUES OCCASIONAL PAPER (AT/0818-4968) [I08184968] **4012**

MINERAL POLICY SECTOR INTERNAL REPORT (CN/0713-7044) [07510720] **2144**

MINERAL PROCESSING AND EXTRACTIVE METALLURGY REVIEW (UK/0882-7508) [11961125] 4012, **2144**

MINERAL PRODUCTION, NEW SOUTH WALES (AT/0727-9272) [I07279272] **2144**

MINERAL RESEARCH (II) [01790430] **1441**

MINERAL RESOURCE CIRCULAR (US/0099-7749) [01375237] **1441**

MINERAL RESOURCE REPORT (HARRISBURG) (US/0160-824X) [01951720] 1416, **1388**

MINERAL RESOURCES (AT/0077-8737) [02053627] **2144**

MINERAL RESOURCES BULLETIN - GEOLOGICAL SURVEY OF WESTERN AUSTRALIA (AT/0373-2711) [01657839] **1388**

MINERAL RESOURCES DEVELOPMENT SERIES (TH/0082-8114) [01768051] **2144**

MINERAL RESOURCES DEVELOPMENT SERIES (US) [06680451] **2198**

MINERAL RESOURCES REPORT CANBERRA (AT/0312-3766) [I03123766] **1358**

MINERAL RESOURCES SERIES (LAWRENCE) (US/0271-0447) [04406778] **1441**

MINERAL REVENUES : THE ... REPORT ON RECEIPTS FROM FEDERAL AND INDIAN LEASES (US) [10410730] 1505, **2198**

MINERAL SANDS REPORT (UK) **4012**

MINERAL WELLS INDEX (US) [14442766] **5752**

MINERAL WOOL INCLUDING FIBROUS GLASS INSULATION (CN/0229-6098) [10859132] **621**

MINERALES (CL/0026-458X) [06188971] **2072**

MINERALIA SLOVACA (XO/0369-2086) [01793828] **1441**

MINERALIENFREUND (SZ/0379-5357) [04723783] **1441**

MINERALIUM DEPOSITA (GW/0026-4598) [01639255] **1441**

MINERALOGICA ET PETROGRAPHICA ACTA (IT/0540-1437) [05394665] 1388, **1441**

MINERALOGICAL ABSTRACTS (UK/0026-4601) [01586463] 1441, **1363**

MINERALOGICAL ASSOCIATION OF CANADA See NEWSLETTER - MINERALOGICAL ASSOCIATION OF CANADA **1443**

MINERALOGICAL JOURNAL (JA/0544-2540) [01715252] **1441**

MINERALOGICAL MAGAZINE (UK/0026-461X) [02363665] **1441**

MINERALOGICAL RECORD, THE (US/0026-4628) [01757528] **1441**

MINERALOGICAL SOCIETY BULLETIN (UK/0263-9513) [09026062] **1441**

MINERALOGICAL SOCIETY (GREAT BRITAIN) See MONOGRAPH - MINERALOGICAL SOCIETY **1442**

MINERALOGICAL SOCIETY (GREAT BRITAIN) See MINERALOGICAL SOCIETY BULLETIN **1441**

MINERALOGICESKIJ ZURNAL (UN/0204-3548) [05971114] **1442**

MINERALOGICHESKII SBORNIK (RU) [01617673] **1388**

MINERALOGY AND PETROLOGY (AU/0930-0708) [15305407] 1459, **1442**

MINERALOLTECHNIK (GW/0341-1893) [08757504] 1988, **1442**

MINERALS; A REPORT FOR THE REPUBLIC OF SOUTH AFRICA (SA/0560-9178) [01209001] **1442**

MINERALS & ENERGY JOURNAL / OFFICE OF MINERALS AND ENERGY (VICTORIA) (AT) [12884809] **1950**

MINERALS AND ENERGY RESEARCH INSTITUTE OF WESTERN AUSTRALIA See ANNUAL REPORT / MINERALS AND ENERGY RESEARCH INSTITUTE OF WESTERN AUSTRALIA **1932**

MINERALS AND ENERGY RESEARCH NEWS (AT/1031-556X) [I1031556X] 1950, **2144**

MINERALS & METALLURGICAL PROCESSING (US/0747-9182) [10842473] **4012**

MINERALS AND METALS TRADING CORPORATION OF INDIA LTD See MMTC NEWS **1618**

MINERALS AND MINERAL DEVELOPMENT, WESTERN AUSTRALIA (AT) [05531993] **2144**

MINERALS AND ROCKS (US) [02251225] 1459, **1442**

MINERALS ENGINEERING (UK/0892-6875) [15238580] **2144**

MINERALS EXPLORATION ALERT (US/0730-6474) [08044761] **1442**

MINERALS GAZETTE (AT) [I10374930] **2145**

MINERALS HANDBOOK (LONDON, ENGLAND) (UK/0265-3923) [11759276] **2145**

MINERALS HEALTH AND SAFETY CONTRACT RESEARCH, DEVELOPMENT, AND DEMONSTRATION IN FISCAL YEAR ... / BY STAFF, DIVISION OF MINERALS HEALTH AND SAFETY TECHNOLOGY (US) [06549448] **2865**

MINERALS IN THE ECONOMY OF FLORIDA (US/0190-874X) [04014593] **1442**

MINERALS IN THE ECONOMY OF MAINE (US/0190-9061) [04251879] **1618**

MINERALS IN THE ECONOMY OF NEW MEXICO (US/0190-8758) [04014589] **1442**

MINERALS INDUSTRY INTERNATIONAL : BULLETIN OF THE INSTITUTION OF MINING AND METALLURGY (UK/0955-2847) [19695066] **1442**

MINERALS INDUSTRY SURVEY (AT/0727-3800) [I07273800] **4012**

MINERALS PROCESSING (US/0026-4644) [01606234] **1442**

MINERALS QUARTERLY (AT) **2145**

MINERALS REPORT (US/0584-3448) [01969164] **1442**

MINERALS RESEARCH IN CSIRO (AT) [06899887] **2145**

MINERALS TODAY CEASED. (US/1057-9745) [21099091] **1442**

MINERALS TRANSPORTATION (US/0094-7466) [01799903] 5387, **1442**

MINERALS YEARBOOK (US/0076-8952) [01847412] **1442**

MINERALS YEARBOOK (US) [23075076] **1442**

MINERALS YEARBOOK. MINERAL INDUSTRIES OF THE BALKAN COUNTRIES (US) [23528112] **1442**

MINERAUX ET FOSSILES, LE GUIDE DU COLLECTIONNEUR (FR/0335-6566) [03785379] **1358**

MINERIA EN CUBA, LA (CU/0253-5653) [04179114] **2145**

MINERIA Y PETROLEO (PE/0379-170X) [04822569] **4264**

MINER'S NEWS (US/0890-6157) [14349029] **2145**

MINERVA (UK) 274, **358**

MINERVA AEROSPAZIALE (IT/0026-4709) [I00264709] **28**

MINERVA ANESTESIOLOGICA (IT/0375-9393) [01642709] **3683**

MINERVA ANGIOLOGICA (IT/0391-3627) [11116092] **3799**

MINERVA (ARLINGTON, VA.) (US/0736-718X) [09201074] 5561, **4051**

MINERVA BIOTECHNOLOGICA (IT/1120-4826) [28141624] **465**

MINERVA CARDIOANGIOLOGICA (IT/0026-4725) [06522872] **3708**

MINERVA CHIRURGICA (IT/0026-4733) [01639835] **3970**

MINERVA ENDOCRINOLOGICA (IT/0391-1977) [11116173] **3731**

MINERVA GASTROENTEROLOGICA E DIETOLOGICA (IT) [24147683] 4194, **3747**

MINERVA GINECOLOGICA (IT/0026-4784) [01696021] **3765**

MINERVA HISTORICAL SOCIETY QUARTERLY (US/1067-7380) [27335490] **2623**

MINERVA (LONDON) (UK/0026-4695) [02225648] 1836, **5129**

MINERVA (LONDON. 1989) (UK/0957-7718) [21732204] **275**

MINERVA MEDICA (IT/0026-4806) [01757536] **3799**

MINERVA MEDICOLEGALE : ORGANO UFFICIALE DELLA SOCIETA ITALIANA DI MMEDICINA LEGALE E DELLE ASSICURAZIONI (IT/0026-4849) [01757539] **3742**

MINERVA OFTALMOLOGICA (IT/0026-4903) [07599766] **3876**

MINERVA ORTOGNATODONTICA (IT/0394-168X) [18466937] **1330**

MINERVA ORTOPEDICA E TRAUMATOLOGICA (IT) [15263873] **3883**

MINERVA PEDIATRICA (IT/0026-4946) [01605460] **3906**

MINERVA PSICHIATRICA (IT/0391-1772) [03570649] 4604, **3931**

MINERVA : REVISTA DE FILOLOGIA CLASICA (SP/0213-9634) [17889456] **1078**

MINERVA STOMATOLOGICA (IT/0026-4970) [01644794] **1330**

MINERVA UROLOGICA E NEFROLOGICA (IT/0393-2249) [11889848] **3991**

MINERVA'S BULLETIN BOARD (US/0897-6104) [17567132] **4051**

MINERVE DE SAINT-LAURENT, LA (CN/1184-7247) [24266853] **1836**

MINERVE PNEUMOLOGICA (IT/0026-4954) [I00264954] **3950**

Alphabetical Title Index — MINNESOTA

MINES & CARRIERES (FR/0994-2556) [20126041] **2145**

MINES AND ENERGY REVIEW (AT/1034-8794) [22404039] 1388, **2145**

MINES AND MINERAL RESOURCES (CN/0821-2538) [06351873] **1358**

MINES AND MINERALS INFORMATION CIRCULAR (CN/1184-6518) [23686713] **2145**

MINES BRANCH MONOGRAPH (OTTAWA) (CN/0068-7863) [02443595] **2145**

MINES DE CHARBON (CN) [01773830] 1950, 2145, **2006**

MINES DIRECTORY (US/0197-9965) [06153447] **2145**

MINES, GEOLOGIE ET ENERGIE (MR/0251-4079) [07344769] **1358**

MINES MAGAZINE (US/0096-4859) [04590645] 2145, **1442**

MINES (TORONTO) (CN/0317-9524) [02813788] **2145**

MINETECH (II) [09360140] **2145**

MINFO (AT/0812-0293) [I08120293] **2145**

MING JEN (CH) [10854676] **2658**

MING SHIH TZU LIAO TSUNG KAN / CHUNG-KUO SHE HUI KO HSUEH YUAN LI SHIH YEN CHIU SO MING SHIH SHIH PIEN (CC) [08459528] **2658**

MING SHIH YEN CHIU LUN TSUNG / CHUNG-KUO SHE HUI KO HSUEH YUAN LI SHIH YEN CHIU SO MING SHIH YEN CHIU SHIH PIEN (CH) [10674562] **2658**

MING STUDIES *SUSPENDED.* (US/0147-037X) [02434815] **2658**

MINGAN KYONGJE PAEKSO (KO) [09406443] **1574**

MINGAY'S ELECTRICAL RETAILER (AT) 2073, **955**

MINGAY'S PRODUCT SERVICE *See* MINGAY'S RETAIL GUIDE **955**

MINGAY'S RETAIL GUIDE (AT) **955**

MINI BRIEFCASE (US) **4264**

MINI-JEUX, LES (CN/0711-3307) [08507263] **4863**

MINI JOURNAL, LE (CN/0225-5529) [06136573] **1804**

MINI LAB FOCUS (US) **4371**

MINI MICROCOMPUTER, DE (NE) **1195**

MINI MONITOR / WORLD HUNGER YEAR (US) [12482706] **108**

MINI MOUTH MAGAZINE (CN/0319-5309) [02442302] **1066**

MINI RECREATION (CN/0714-489X) [09046656] **4863**

MINI-RECUEIL DE RENSEIGNEMENTS FISCAUX (CN/0821-0799) [10195210] **3010**

MINI STORAGE MESSENGER, THE (US/0273-5822) [07083115] **695**

MINI TOKEI HANDO BUKKU (JA) [09329028] **5333**

MINIATIURNYE KNIGI SSSR / THE USSR MINIATURE BOOKS (RU) [08558286] **420**

MINIATURA / A CURA DELLA SOCIETA DI STORIA DELLA MINIATURA (IT) [19496095] **4830**

MINIATURE BOOK SOCIETY NEWSLETTER, THE (US/0894-5489) [16157764] **4830**

MINIATURE COLLECTOR (US/0199-9184) [06289058] **2774**

MINIATURE ELECTRONIC COMPONENTS DATA ANNUAL *See* EUROPEAN MINIATURE ELECTRONIC COMPONENTS AND ASSEMBLIES DATA : INCLUDING SIX-LANGUAGE GLOSSARIES OF ELECTRONIC COMPONENT AND MICROELECTRONICS TERMS **2054**

MINIATURE HORSE JOURNAL, THE (US/0279-4985) [07912623] **2801**

MINIATURE PATTERNS & PRODUCTS MAGAZINE (US/0732-3697) [08342113] **374**

MINIATURE QUILTS (US/1065-0245) [24842090] **5185**

MINIATURE WARFARE *See* MINIATURE WARFARE & MODEL SOLDIERS **4051**

MINIATURE WARFARE & MODEL SOLDIERS (UK) [01789491] **4051**

MINIATURE WARGAMES (UK) 2623, **2774**

MINIATURES DEALER (CLIFTON, VA. : 1985) *CEASED.* (US/0882-9187) [11896928] **2774**

MINIATURES SHOWCASE *CEASED.* (US/0896-7288) [17283402] **2775**

MINIBUS LONDON (UK/0959-0218) [I09590218] **1078**

MINILAB DEVELOPMENTS (US/1052-4142) [22286101] **1618**

MINIMALLY INVASIVE NEUROSURGERY (GW) 3970, **3838**

●MINIMALLY INVASIVE SURGICAL NURSING (US/1068-5685) [27736678] 3970, **3861**

MINIMALLY INVASIVE THERAPY (UK/0961-625X) [25383553] **3970**

MINIMIS, DE (US/0418-4432) [02242958] **3010**

MINIMUM PROPERTY STANDARDS FOR CARE-TYPE HOUSING (US) [03454225] **2828**

MINIMUM PROPERTY STANDARDS FOR MULTIFAMILY HOUSING (US) [03454283] **2828**

MINIMUM PROPERTY STANDARDS FOR ONE-AND TWO-FAMILY DWELLINGS (US) [03454366] **2828**

MINIMUM WAGE AND MAXIMUM HOURS STANDARDS UNDER THE FAIR LABOR STANDARDS ACT (US/0093-5611) [01783851] **1690**

MINING AND ENGINEERING (RH/0254-0304) [08006022] **2145**

MINING AND METALLURGICAL INSTITUTE OF JAPAN *See* JOURNAL - MINING AND METALLURGICAL INSTITUTE OF JAPAN **4006**

MINING AND MINERAL PROCESSING OPERATIONS IN CANADA (CN/0825-219X) [09243101] **2145**

M NING AND PUBLIC LANDS REPORT (US/0748-2027) [10900315] **2145**

MINING ANNUAL REVIEW (UK/0076-8995) [01757549] **2145**

MINING BUSINESS DIGEST (US/1055-9957) [23441566] **2145**

MINING DATABASE (UK) 4012, **2145**

MINING DEPARTMENT MAGAZINE (UK/0307-9066) [05879845] 1442, **2145**

MINING DIRECTORY, THE (UK/0262-7965) [22329115] **2145**

MINING ENGINEER (LONDON) (UK/0026-5179) [01757551] **2145**

MINING ENGINEERING (US/0026-5187) [01757552] **2145**

MINING ENVIRONMENTAL MANAGEMENT (UK/0969-4218) [29368070] **1408**

MINING EXPLAINED (CN) **2145**

MINING EXPLORATION AND DEVELOPMENT REVIEW, BRITISH COLUMBIA AND YUKON TERRITORY (CN/0318-1766) [01794405] **2145**

MINING IN ZIMBABWE (RH) [07188926] **2146**

MINING INDUSTRY OF BRITISH COLUMBIA AND THE YUKON, THE (CN) [01406136] **2146**

MINING JOURNAL (1954) (US/0898-4964) [09729223] **5693**

MINING JOURNAL GOLD SERVICE (UK) **2146**

MINING JOURNAL (LONDON. 1908) (UK/0026-5225) [02438984] **2146**

MINING MACHINERY AND MINERAL PROCESSING EQUIPMENT (US/0276-9786) [06662930] **2146**

MINING MAGAZINE (LONDON) (UK/0308-6631) [01757555] **2146**

MINING MIRROR (US) [05932896] **2146**

MINING MONTHLY *See* AUSTRALIA'S MINING MONTHLY **2134**

MINING PERSONNEL PRACTICES SURVEY (US/0192-5032) [05015960] **1690**

●MINING QUARTERLY (AT/1320-3770) **2146**

MINING RECORD (1968), THE (US/0026-5241) [03220237] **2146**

MINING RESEARCH REVIEW (US/0197-906X) [04562595] **2146**

MINING REVIEW CANBERRA 1977 (AT/0314-4607) [I03144607] **2146**

MINING REVIEW (NORTH VANCOUVER) (CN/0711-3277) [08454731] **2146**

MINING SOURCE BOOK (CN/0840-6723) [19076963] **2146**

MINING STATISTICS : NORTH OF 60 (CN) [01784939] 2146, **2006**

MINING SURVEY (JOHANNESBURG) (SA/0026-5268) [01788586] **2146**

MINING TASMANIA (AT) [06491828] 2146, **2006**

MINING TECHNOLOGY (MANCHESTER) (UK/0026-5276) [02246103] **2146**

MINING (TORONTO) (CN/0317-9508) [02871847] **2146**

MINING, WESTERN AUSTRALIA / AUSTRALIAN BUREAU OF STATISTICS, WESTERN AUSTRALIAN OFFICE (AT) [07763038] 2146, **2006**

MINING WORLD NEWS (US/1047-7551) [20780159] **2146**

MINISISTEMI *CEASED.* (IT/1120-5164) [I11205164] **1195**

MINISTERE DU ROYAUME POUR LE CANADA, LE (CN/0823-2555) [10052142] **5064**

MINISTERIAL FORMATION (SZ/0255-8777) [04283012] **4977**

MINISTERIO PUBLICO (VENEZUELA. MINISTERIO PUBLICO) *See* REVISTA DEL MINISTERIO PUBLICO : ORGANO DE DIVULGACION DEL MINISTERIO PUBLICO DE LA REPUBLICA DE VENEZUELA **3042**

MINISTERO DEL REGNO PER IL CANADA, IL (CN/0823-2571) [10220927] **5064**

MINISTRIES TODAY (US/0891-5725) [14515156] **4977**

MINISTRY CURRENTS *CEASED.* (US/1069-1766) [24278084] **4977**

MINISTRY DEVELOPMENT JOURNAL *CEASED.* (US/0895-9056) [09746661] **5064**

MINISTRY IN ACTION NEWSLETTER (US) **4977**

MINISTRY (WASHINGTON, D.C.) (US/0026-5314) [07949287] **4977**

MINITRUCKIN' (ANAHEIM, CALIF.) (US/1052-0961) [22189862] 5419, **4905**

MINIVAN, PICKUP, AND 4X4 BOOK, THE (US/1062-2578) [25561715] **5419**

MINJOK KYOYUK YONGU (KO) [08702429] **1764**

MINJOK MUNHWA (MINJOK MUNHWA CHUJINHOE) (KO) [09631061] **2659**

MINJU KONGHWADANG *See* DRP BULLETIN **4472**

MINK (US/0749-8683) [04066762] **1618**

MINKAN TOKEI CHOSA SHIRYO ICHIRAN (JA) [01783593] **420**

MINNA NO TOSHOKAN (JA) [04276637] **3231**

MINNEAPOLIS AREA REALTOR (US/1054-9684) [23035621] **4841**

MINNEAPOLIS. BOARD OF EDUCATION *See* SCHOOL BULLETIN, MINNEAPOLIS PUBLIC SCHOOLS **1782**

MINNEAPOLIS COLLEGE OF ART AND DESIGN *See* ALUMNI DIRECTORY / MINNEAPOLIS COLLEGE OF ART AND DESIGN **1098**

MINNEAPOLIS GRAIN EXCHANGE *See* STATISTICAL ANNUAL - MINNEAPOLIS GRAIN EXCHANGE **156**

MINNEAPOLIS INSTITUTE OF ARTS *See* MINNEAPOLIS INSTITUTE OF ARTS BULLETIN, THE **325**

MINNEAPOLIS INSTITUTE OF ARTS BULLETIN, THE (US/0076-910X) [03139157] **325**

MINNEAPOLIS LABOR REVIEW, THE (US/0274-9017) [01757634] **1690**

MINNEAPOLIS MESSENGER (US) [08801497] **5677**

MINNEAPOLIS REALTOR (US/0745-3906) [01588006] **4841**

MINNEAPOLIS SPOKESMAN (US) [01715036] **2267**

MINNEAPOLIS/ST. PAUL CITYBUSINESS (US/0883-3044) [12111328] **695**

MINNEAPOLIS STAR AND TRIBUNE INDEX (MINNEAPOLIS, MINN.) (US/0738-9868) [08813995] **5697**

MINNELLA'S POCKET-GUIDE TO COPIERS (US/0883-4377) [11775525] **4212**

MINNEOLA RECORD (MINNEOLA, KAN. : 1976) (US) [10102111] **5677**

MINNESOTA *See* MINNESOTA MOTOR VEHICLE LAW **3010**

MINNESOTA *See* LAWS RELATING TO THE MINNESOTA PUBLIC SCHOOL SYSTEM **2997**

MINNESOTA AACR 2 TRAINERS SERIES (US/1056-0033) [23303792] **3231**

MINNESOTA ADMINISTRATIVE RULES AND REGULATIONS (US) [01641595] **4665**

MINNESOTA. ADVISORY COMMITTEE OF EXAMINERS IN MORTUARY SCIENCE *See* BIENNIAL REPORT OF EXAMINING AND LICENSING BOARDS / ADVISORY COMMITTEE OF EXAMINERS IN MORTUARY SCIENCE (MINNESOTA) **4768**

MINNESOTA AG MANUAL, THE (US/0883-4385) [11525334] **108**

MINNESOTA AGRICULTURAL ECONOMIST (US/0885-4874) [01758095] **108**

MINNESOTA AID TO FAMILIES WITH DEPENDENT CHILDREN FOR FISCAL YEAR ... (US) [08659724] **5296**

MINNESOTA ALCOHOL PROGRAMS FOR HIGHWAY SAFETY (US/0093-2558) [01792051] 3169, **4791**

MINNESOTA — Alphabetical Title Index

MINNESOTA ALMANAC, THE (US/0363-289X) [02850304] **2746**

MINNESOTA AND ENVIRONS WEATHER ALMANAC (US/0095-7348) [01790834] **1431**

MINNESOTA ANNUAL REPORT : MUNICIPAL REVENUE BONDS (US) [05340093] 1505, **906**

MINNESOTA ARCHAEOLOGIST, THE (US/0026-5403) [01645423] **275**

MINNESOTA ARTS DIRECTORY (US/1060-3107) [23664793] **358**

MINNESOTA. BANKING DIVISION *See* REPORT OF THE COMMISSIONER OF BANKS OF DEBT PRORATE COMPANIES LICENSED UNDER MINNESOTA STATUTES, CHAPTER 332 **807**

MINNESOTA. BANKING DIVISION *See* CONSOLIDATED ANNUAL REPORT FOR THE YEAR ENDING DECEMBER 31 ... / DEPARTMENT OF COMMERCE, BANKING DIVISION **784**

MINNESOTA. BOARD OF ANIMAL HEALTH *See* MINNESOTA. LIVESTOCK SANITARY BOARD. ANNUAL REPORT **5516**

MINNESOTA. BOARD OF ASSESSORS *See* BIENNIAL REPORT OF EXAMINING AND LICENSING BOARDS / BOARD OF ASSESSORS **4713**

MINNESOTA. BOARD OF BARBER EXAMINERS *See* BIENNIAL REPORT OF EXAMINING AND LICENSING BOARDS / BOARD OF BARBER EXAMINERS **402**

MINNESOTA. BOARD OF DENTISTRY *See* BIENNIAL REPORT - MINNESOTA BOARD OF DENTISTRY **1317**

MINNESOTA. BOARD OF EXAMINERS FOR NURSING HOME ADMINISTRATORS *See* BIENNIAL REPORT OF EXAMINING AND LICENSING BOARDS - MINNESOTA. BOARD OF EXAMINERS FOR NURSING HOME ADMINISTRATORS **4768**

MINNESOTA BOARD OF NURSING *See* BIENNIAL REPORT OF EXAMINING AND LICENSING BOARDS - MINNESOTA BOARD OF NURSING **3852**

MINNESOTA BOARD OF PODIATRY *See* BIENNIAL REPORT OF EXAMINING AND LICENSING BOARDS / MINNESOTA BOARD OF PODIATRY **3556**

MINNESOTA. BOARD OF PSYCHOLOGY *See* BIENNIAL REPORT OF EXAMINING AND LICENSING BOARDS / MINNESOTA BOARD OF PSYCHOLOGY **4577**

MINNESOTA BOARD OF TEACHING *See* BIENNIAL REPORT OF EXAMINING AND LICENSING BOARDS / MINNESOTA BOARD OF TEACHING **1889**

MINNESOTA BOARD ON JUDICIAL STANDARDS *See* ANNUAL REPORT, MINNESOTA BOARD ON JUDICIAL STANDARDS FOR THE CALENDAR YEAR ... / MINNESOTA BOARD ON JUDICIAL STANDARDS **3139**

MINNESOTA BUSINESS JOURNAL *CEASED.* (US/0192-5504) [05037979] **695**

MINNESOTA CALENDAR OF EVENTS (US) [04686412] **5484**

MINNESOTA CALLS *CEASED.* (US) **2539**

MINNESOTA CHEMIST, THE (US/0026-5411) [01758117] **986**

MINNESOTA CHILDREN UNDER STATE GUARDIANSHIP AS DEPENDENT/NEGLECTED, YEAR ENDING JUNE 30 ... ANNUAL REPORT (US) [08684540] **5296**

MINNESOTA CITIES (US/0148-8546) [03596157] **4665**

MINNESOTA COMMERCIAL FLOWER GROWERS ASSOCIATION BULLETIN (US) [26559444] **2435**

MINNESOTA CORPORATION INCOME TAX (US) [04450237] **4737**

MINNESOTA COUNTIES (US) [01779869] **2539**

MINNESOTA DAILY, THE (US) [01588350] **5697**

MINNESOTA. DEPARTMENT OF ADMINISTRATION *See* MINNESOTA ADMINISTRATIVE RULES AND REGULATIONS **4665**

MINNESOTA. DEPT. OF ADMINISTRATION. DIVISION OF PROCUREMENT *See* MN SMALL BUSINESS PROCUREMENT PROGRAM FOR SOCIALLY OR ECONOMICALLY DISADVANTAGED VENDORS F.Y. ... ANNUAL REPORT / DEPARTMENT OF ADMINISTRATION, DIVISION OF PROCUREMENT **4666**

MINNESOTA. DEPT. OF CIVIL SERVICE *See* BIENNIAL REPORT - STATE OF MINNESOTA, DEPARTMENT OF CIVIL SERVICE **4701**

MINNESOTA. DEPT. OF CONSERVATION. BIENNIAL REPORT *See* BIENNIAL REPORT - MINNESOTA DEPARTMENT OF NATURAL RESOURCES **2188**

MINNESOTA. DEPT. OF CORRECTIONS *See* BIENNIAL REPORT / MINNESOTA DEPARTMENT OF CORRECTIONS **3158**

MINNESOTA. DEPT. OF CORRECTIONS. DIVISION OF RESEARCH AND PLANNING *See* WORK RELEASE FOR MISDEMEANANTS IN MINNESOTA **3179**

MINNESOTA. DEPT. OF ECONOMIC DEVELOPMENT *See* MINNESOTA ANNUAL REPORT : MUNICIPAL REVENUE BONDS **906**

MINNESOTA. DEPT. OF ECONOMIC DEVELOPMENT *See* MINNESOTA TAX GUIDE **4737**

MINNESOTA. DEPT. OF ECONOMIC DEVELOPMENT. RESEARCH DIVISION *See* MINNESOTA NEW AND EXPANDING INDUSTRY **1618**

MINNESOTA. DEPT. OF ECONOMIC DEVELOPMENT. RESEARCH DIVISION *See* MINNESOTA STATISTICAL PROFILE **5333**

MINNESOTA. DEPT. OF ECONOMIC DEVELOPMENT. RESEARCH DIVISION *See* MANUFACTURING IN MINNESOTA **3483**

MINNESOTA. DEPT. OF ECONOMIC SECURITY *See* REPORT TO THE LEGISLATURE - MINNESOTA. DEPT. OF ECONOMIC SECURITY **1707**

MINNESOTA. DEPT. OF FINANCE *See* COMPREHENSIVE ANNUAL FINANCIAL REPORT FOR THE YEAR ENDED JUNE 30, ... (MINNESOTA) **4718**

MINNESOTA. DEPT. OF HEALTH *See* BIENNIAL REPORT - MINNESOTA DEPARTMENT OF HEALTH **4768**

MINNESOTA. DEPT. OF JOBS AND TRAINING *See* ANNUAL REPORT / MINNESOTA DEPARTMENT OF JOBS AND TRAINING **1649**

MINNESOTA. DEPT. OF MILITARY AFFAIRS *See* BIENNIAL REPORT - STATE OF MINNESOTA, DEPARTMENT OF MILITARY AFFAIRS **4037**

MINNESOTA. DEPT. OF NATURAL RESOURCES *See* BIENNIAL REPORT - MINNESOTA DEPARTMENT OF NATURAL RESOURCES **2188**

MINNESOTA. DEPT. OF PUBLIC SERVICE *See* BIENNIAL REPORT - STATE OF MINNESOTA DEPARTMENT OF PUBLIC SERVICE **4632**

MINNESOTA. DEPT. OF PUBLIC SERVICE. REPORT FOR THE BIENNIUM *See* BIENNIAL REPORT - STATE OF MINNESOTA DEPARTMENT OF PUBLIC SERVICE **4632**

MINNESOTA. DEPT. OF PUBLIC WELFARE *See* PROPOSED COMPREHENSIVE ANNUAL SERVICES PROGRAM PLAN **5302**

MINNESOTA. DEPT. OF PUBLIC WELFARE *See* PUBLIC ASSISTANCE FOR MINNESOTA INDIANS **2271**

MINNESOTA. DEPT. OF PUBLIC WELFARE. OPERATIONS REVIEW DIVISION. REPORTS AND STATISTICS *See* MINNESOTA MEDICAL ASSISTANCE (TITLE XIX) FOR FISCAL YEAR ... **5296**

MINNESOTA. DEPT. OF PUBLIC WELFARE. RESEARCH AND STATISTICS DIVISION. INCOME MAINTENANCE SECTION *See* MINNESOTA MEDICAL ASSISTANCE BIENNIAL REPORT DATA **5296**

MINNESOTA. DEPT. OF REVENUE *See* REAL ESTATE ASSESSMENT/SALES RATIO STUDY **4843**

MINNESOTA. DEPT. OF REVENUE *See* BIENNIAL REPORT - STATE OF MINNESOTA, DEPARTMENT OF REVENUE **4713**

MINNESOTA. DEPT. OF TRANSPORTATION *See* ANNUAL SUMMARY OF SPEED LIMIT 55 MONITORING PROGRAM / MINNESOTA, DEPARTMENT OF TRANSPORTATION **5377**

MINNESOTA. DEPT. OF TRANSPORTATION *See* VEHICLE WEIGHT AND USE DATA COLLECTED ON MINNESOTA ROADS **5399**

MINNESOTA. DEPT. OF VETERANS' AFFAIRS *See* BIENNIAL REPORT - STATE OF MINNESOTA, DEPARTMENT OF VETERANS AFFAIRS **4038**

MINNESOTA DIRECTORY OF MANUFACTURERS (US) [08642398] **3484**

MINNESOTA. DIVISION OF VOCATIONAL REHABILITATION *See* ANNUAL BOOKLET - MINNESOTA, DIVISION OF VOCATIONAL REHABILITATION, DEPARTMENT OF EDUCATION **1644**

MINNESOTA DRAMA EDITIONS *CEASED.* (US/0076-9142) [01645080] **5366**

MINNESOTA ELECTED OFFICIALS ... (US) [05588751] **4665**

MINNESOTA. ELECTION DIVISION *See* MINNESOTA ELECTION RESULTS : PRIMARY AND GENERAL ELECTIONS **4665**

MINNESOTA ELECTION RESULTS : PRIMARY AND GENERAL ELECTIONS (US) [05260026] **4665**

MINNESOTA EMPLOYMENT LAW LETTER (US/1054-6367) [22923800] **3152**

MINNESOTA ENGLISH JOURNAL (US) [01758146] 3302, 3412, **1900**

●MINNESOTA ENVIRONMENTAL COMPLIANCE UPDATE (US/1072-916X) [29236711] **3114**

MINNESOTA. ENVIRONMENTAL HEALTH SPECIALIST/SANITARIAN ADVISORY COUNCIL *See* BIENNIAL REPORT OF EXAMINING AND LICENSING BOARDS - MINNESOTA. ENVIRONMENTAL HEALTH SPECIALIST/SANITARIAN ADVISORY COUNCIL **2225**

MINNESOTA. ENVIRONMENTAL QUALITY BOARD *See* EQB MONITOR **2230**

MINNESOTA ENVIRONMENTAL QUALITY BOARD *See* REPORT OF ACTIVITIES. MINNESOTA ENVIRONMENTAL QUALITY BOARD **2241**

MINNESOTA FAMILY LAW JOURNAL (US/0278-761X) [07886852] **3122**

MINNESOTA. FINANCE AND INTERNATIONAL TRADE DIVISION *See* BIENNIAL REPORT AND OVERVIEW OF MINNESOTA MUNICIPAL REVENUE BONDS **892**

MINNESOTA FIRE CHIEF (US/0026-5470) [01642872] **2291**

MINNESOTA FLYER (US/0889-4809) [01589111] **28**

MINNESOTA FOOD GUIDE *See* MINNESOTA GROCER **2350**

MINNESOTA GENEALOGIST (US/0581-0086) [01758168] **2460**

MINNESOTA GENERAL ASSISTANCE AND WORK READINESS ANNUAL REPORT, FISCAL YEAR ... (US) [15914486] **5296**

MINNESOTA GENERAL ASSISTANCE ANNUAL REPORT *See* MINNESOTA GENERAL ASSISTANCE AND WORK READINESS ANNUAL REPORT, FISCAL YEAR ... **5296**

MINNESOTA GENERAL ELECTION RESULTS *See* MINNESOTA ELECTION RESULTS : PRIMARY AND GENERAL ELECTIONS **4665**

MINNESOTA GEOLOGICAL SURVEY *See* GUIDEBOOK SERIES-MINNESOTA GEOLOGICAL SURVEY **1382**

MINNESOTA. GEOLOGICAL SURVEY *See* INFORMATION CIRCULAR - MINNESOTA GEOLOGICAL SURVEY **1382**

MINNESOTA GEOLOGICAL SURVEY *See* BULLETIN - MINNESOTA GEOLOGICAL SURVEY **1370**

MINNESOTA GOVERNMENT REPORT, THE TWICE-WEEKLY NEWSLETTER ON STATE GOVERNMENT (US) [04028131] **4665**

MINNESOTA. GOVERNOR *See* GOVERNOR'S REPORT ON ENVIRONMENTAL QUALITY, THE **2172**

MINNESOTA. GOVERNOR *See* ANNUAL REPORT ON THE QUALITY OF THE ENVIRONMENT (ST. PAUL) **2161**

MINNESOTA GROCER (US) [13154470] **2350**

MINNESOTA GUIDEBOOK TO STATE AGENCY SERVICES (US/1061-0987) [04204760] **4665**

●MINNESOTA HEALTH CARE IN PERSPECTIVE (US/1065-4259) [26605771] **4791**

MINNESOTA HEALTH STATISTICS (US/0094-5641) [01794689] **4791**

MINNESOTA HIGHER EDUCATION COORDINATING BOARD *See* HECB ADVISORY COMMITTEES, STATUS REPORT / PREPARED BY THE STAFF OF THE MINNESOTA HIGHER EDUCATION COORDINATING BOARD **1827**

MINNESOTA. HIGHER EDUCATION COORDINATING COMMISSION. PLANNING REPORT *See* PLANNING REPORT - MINNESOTA HIGHER EDUCATION COORDINATING BOARD **1841**

MINNESOTA. HIGHER EDUCATION COORDINATION BOARD *See* PLANNING REPORT - MINNESOTA HIGHER EDUCATION COORDINATING BOARD **1841**

MINNESOTA. HIGHWAY SAFETY AND RESEARCH STATION *See* MINNESOTA ALCOHOL PROGRAMS FOR HIGHWAY SAFETY **4791**

MINNESOTA HISTORIC SITES PAMPHLET SERIES (US/0544-3571) [02432522] **2746**

MINNESOTA HISTORICAL ARCHAEOLOGY SERIES (US/0076-9193) [01758175] **2746**

MINNESOTA HISTORICAL SOCIETY. STATE HISTORIC PRESERVATION OFFICE *See* ANNUAL PRESERVATION PROGRAM - MINNESOTA HISTORICAL SOCIETY. STATE HISTORIC PRESERVATION OFFICE, THE **2720**

MINNESOTA HISTORY (US/0026-5497) [01758179] 5209, **2746**

MINNESOTA HISTORY NEWS *See* MEMBER NEWS / MINNESOTA HISTORICAL SOCIETY **2746**

MINNESOTA HOCKEY (US/1050-740X) [21194361] **4905**

MINNESOTA HORTICULTURIST, THE (US/0026-5500) [04166469] **2424**

MINNESOTA IN PERSPECTIVE (US/1065-5522) [26656102] **5333**

MINNESOTA INSURANCE (US/0740-8366) [10028577] **2888**

MINNESOTA INTERNATIONAL TRADE DIRECTORY (US) [05233016] **1638**

MINNESOTA JOURNAL (US/0741-9449) [10292134] **4665**

MINNESOTA. JUDICIAL COUNCIL *See* BIENNIAL REPORT / THE JUDICIAL COUNCIL OF THE STATE OF MINNESOTA **2941**

MINNESOTA LABOR MARKET REVIEW (US) [15217847] **1690**

MINNESOTA LAKE TRIBUNE (US) [01758196] **5697**

MINNESOTA LAND MANAGEMENT INFORMATION CENTER *See* NEWSLETTER - LAND MANAGEMENT INFORMATION CENTER **4669**

MINNESOTA LAW ALUMNI NEWS (US/0540-2239) [01605704] 3010, **1102**

MINNESOTA LAW REVIEW (US/0026-5535) [01758198] **3010**

MINNESOTA LEGAL DIRECTORY, THE (US/0749-0224) [09359747] **3010**

MINNESOTA LEGAL REGISTER (US/0026-5543) [01758201] **3141**

MINNESOTA LEGISLATIVE MANUAL (US) [01245717] **4665**

MINNESOTA. LEGISLATURE. COMMISSION ON TAXATION AND PRODUCTION OF IRON ORE AND OTHER MINERALS *See* REPORT OF THE COMMISSION ON TAXATION AND PRODUCTION OF IRON ORE AND OTHER MINERALS **4745**

MINNESOTA. LEGISLATURE. HOUSE OF REPRESENTATIVES *See* WEEKLY WRAP-UP / MINNESOTA HOUSE OF REPRESENTATIVES **3073**

MINNESOTA. LEGISLATURE. HOUSE OF REPRESENTATIVES. WEEKLY NEWS WRAP-UP *See* WEEKLY WRAP-UP / MINNESOTA HOUSE OF REPRESENTATIVES **3073**

MINNESOTA. LEGISLATURE. LEGISLATIVE COMMISSION ON MINNESOTA RESOURCES *See* BIENNIAL REPORT TO THE LEGISLATURE / LEGISLATIVE COMMISSION ON MINNESOTA RESOURCES **4632**

MINNESOTA LEGISLATURE. OFFICE OF THE LEGISLATIVE AUDITOR. FINANCIAL AUDITS DIVISION *See* STATE OF MINNESOTA FINANCES **4749**

MINNESOTA LITERATURE NEWSLETTER (US/0890-0566) [02255414] **3412**

MINNESOTA. LIVESTOCK SANITARY BOARD. ANNUAL REPORT (US) [06912703] **5516**

MINNESOTA MANUFACTURERS REGISTER (US/0738-1514) [09529692] **3484**

MINNESOTA MEDIA DIRECTORY (MIDWEST ED.) (US/1057-3240) [23716302] **1117**

MINNESOTA MEDIA DIRECTORY (TWIN CITIES ED. 1991) (US/1056-6465) [23752473] **1117**

MINNESOTA MEDICAL ASSISTANCE BIENNIAL REPORT DATA (US/0085-347X) [03392658] **5296**

MINNESOTA MEDICAL ASSISTANCE (TITLE XIX) FOR FISCAL YEAR ... (US) [09223873] 4791, **5296**

MINNESOTA MEDICINE (US/0026-556X) [01758212] **3617**

MINNESOTA MONTHLY (COLLEGEVILLE, MINN.) (US/0739-8700) [02256805] **2539**

MINNESOTA ... MOTOR VEHICLE CRASH FACTS (MINNESOTA. DEPT. OF PUBLIC SAFETY. OFFICE OF TRAFFIC SAFETY : 1982) (US) [10340452] **5419**

MINNESOTA MOTOR VEHICLE LAW (US) [01757883] 5387, **3010**

MINNESOTA NEW AND EXPANDING INDUSTRY (US/0148-6233) [03341958] **1618**

MINNESOTA NURSES ASSOCIATION *See* MNA ACCENT **3862**

MINNESOTA NUTRITION CONFERENCE (US/0271-1893) [06584242] **5516**

MINNESOTA. OFFICE OF CRIME VICTIMS OMBUDSMAN *See* BIENNIAL REPORT OF THE OFFICE OF CRIME VICTIMS OMBUDSMAN **3158**

MINNESOTA. OFFICE OF THE GOVERNOR *See* PROPOSED BIENNIAL BUDGET PRESENTED BY GOVERNOR TO LEGISLATURE **4742**

MINNESOTA. OFFICE OF THE LEGISLATIVE AUDITOR. FINANCIAL AUDITS DIVISION *See* INTERNAL CONTROL REPORT TO THE STATE LEGISLATURE **4732**

MINNESOTA OUT-OF-DOORS (US/0026-5608) [01758227] **4874**

MINNESOTA PHARMACIST (US/0026-5616) [01605585] **4316**

MINNESOTA POLICE JOURNAL (US/0026-5624) [01758233] **3169**

MINNESOTA POLITICAL ACTION REPORT (US/1056-4667) [23716214] **4482**

MINNESOTA. POLLUTION CONTROL AGENCY *See* DAMMING THE SOLID WASTE STREAM : THE BEGINNING OF SOURCE REDUCTION IN MINNESOTA **2227**

MINNESOTA POLLUTION CONTROL AGENCY *See* MINNESOTA WATER QUALITY WORK PLAN FY ... / MINNESOTA POLLUTION CONTROL AGENCY **2236**

MINNESOTA POLLUTION CONTROL AGENCY. AIR QUALITY DIVISION. TECHNICAL SERVICES SECTION *See* AIR QUALITY IN MINNESOTA **2223**

MINNESOTA PREHISTORIC ARCHAEOLOGY SERIES (US) [01781107] **275**

MINNESOTA PROGRAM FOR VICTIMS OF SEXUAL ASSAULT *See* ANNUAL REPORT ... / MINNESOTA PROGRAM FOR VICTIMS OF SEXUAL ASSAULT, MINNESOTA DEPARTMENT OF CORRECTIONS **5272**

MINNESOTA REAL ESTATE DIRECTORY (US/0360-8077) [02245016] **4841**

MINNESOTA REAL ESTATE JOURNAL (US/0893-2255) [11718391] **4841**

MINNESOTA REAL ESTATE LAW JOURNAL (US/0278-7628) [07889406] 4841, **3010**

MINNESOTA REALTOR (US/0195-1963) [05350979] **4841**

MINNESOTA REPORT (UNIVERSITY OF MINNESOTA. AGRICULTURAL EXPERIMENT STATION) (US) [08768316] **108**

MINNESOTA. RESIDENTIAL UTILITY CONSUMER UNIT *See* ANNUAL REPORT / RESIDENTIAL UTILITY CONSUMER UNIT, OFFICE OF CONSUMER SERVICES, MINNESOTA DEPARTMENT OF COMMERCE **4629**

MINNESOTA REVIEW (NEW YORK, N.Y.) (US/0026-5667) [01779874] **3347**

MINNESOTA SCHOOL BOARDS ASSOCIATION *See* LICENSED SALARIES AND RELATED INFORMATION - MINNESOTA SCHOOL BOARDS ASSOCIATION **1866**

MINNESOTA. SCHOOL FOR THE DEAF, FARIBAULT *See* COMPANION **4385**

MINNESOTA SCIENCE (US/0026-5675) [03596167] 2218, **108**

MINNESOTA. SECTION OF FISHERIES *See* SPECIAL PUBLICATION - DIVISION OF FISH AND WILDLIFE, SECTION OF FISHERIES **2313**

MINNESOTA. SECTION OF WILDLIFE *See* WILDLIFE RESEARCH **2209**

MINNESOTA SPORTSMAN (US/0274-8622) [04936045] **4874**

MINNESOTA (ST. PAUL. 1978) (US/0164-9450) [04324222] **1102**

MINNESOTA STATE ADVISORY COUNCIL FOR VOCATIONAL EDUCATION *See* ANNUAL EVALUATION REPORT / MINNESOTA STATE ADVISORY COUNCIL FOR VOCATIONAL EDUCATION **1910**

MINNESOTA. STATE AUDITOR *See* REPORT OF THE STATE AUDITOR OF MINNESOTA ON THE REVENUES, EXPENDITURES, AND DEBT OF THE CITIES AND VILLAGES IN MINNESOTA **4746**

MINNESOTA. STATE BOARD OF ACCESSORS. BIENNIAL REPORT OF EXAMINING AND LICENSING BOARDS *See* BIENNIAL REPORT OF EXAMINING AND LICENSING BOARDS / BOARD OF ASSESSORS **4713**

MINNESOTA STATE BOARD OF CHIROPRACTIC EXAMINERS *See* BIENNIAL REPORT OF EXAMINING AND LICENSING BOARDS **4379**

MINNESOTA STATE BOARD OF CHIROPRATIC EXAMINERS *See* BIENNIAL REPORT OF EXAMINING AND LICENSING BOARDS **3803**

MINNESOTA. STATE BOARD OF ELECTRICITY *See* BIENNIAL REPORT OF EXAMINING AND LICENSING BOARDS - MINNESOTA. STATE BOARD OF ELECTRICITY **2036**

MINNESOTA STATE INDIVIDUAL INCOME TAX, THE (US) [05907124] **4737**

MINNESOTA STATE PLANNING AGENCY. DEVELOPMENTAL DISABILITIES PLANNING OFFICE *See* DEVELOPMENTAL DISABILITIES STATE PLAN **5282**

MINNESOTA STATE PLANNING AGENCY. OFFICE OF LOCAL AND URBAN AFFAIRS *See* MINNESOTA STATISTICAL ABSTRACT **5333**

MINNESOTA STATE REGISTER, THE (US) [23003065] **4665**

MINNESOTA STATE RETIREMENT SYSTEM *See* COMPREHENSIVE ANNUAL FINANCIAL REPORT OF THE HIGHWAY PATROLMENS' RETIREMENT FUND FOR THE FISCAL YEAR ENDING JUNE 30 ... - (MINNESOTA) **3160**

MINNESOTA STATE RETIREMENT SYSTEM *See* HIGHWAY PATROLMEN'S FUND, STATEMENT TO EMPLOYEES **5287**

MINNESOTA STATISTICAL ABSTRACT (US/0093-9668) [01793268] **5333**

MINNESOTA STATISTICAL PROFILE (US) [03440387] **5333**

MINNESOTA STUDIES IN THE PHILOSOPHY OF SCIENCE (US/0076-9258) [01758283] **5129**

MINNESOTA STUDIES IN VOCATIONAL REHABILITATION (US/0094-8047) [03526832] **1690**

MINNESOTA SYMPOSIA ON CHILD PSYCHOLOGY (US/0076-9266) [01758284] **4604**

MINNESOTA TAX COURT DECISIONS (US/0734-7707) [08803712] **4737**

MINNESOTA TAX GUIDE (US) [03440341] **4737**

MINNESOTA TAX JOURNAL *CEASED.* (US/0734-7537) [08799103] **4737**

MINNESOTA TECHNOLOGY (US/1060-8281) [23751440] **5129**

MINNESOTA THOROUGHBRED JOURNAL (US/0894-5632) [16138136] **2801**

MINNESOTA UNITED METHODIST LEADER (US) **5697**

MINNESOTA UNITED METHODIST REPORTER (US/0893-4142) [15537510] **5697**

MINNESOTA VENTURES (US/1058-3653) [20782441] **695**

MINNESOTA VETERINARIAN, THE (US) [01586920] **5516**

MINNESOTA VOCATIONAL ASSOCIATION *See* MVA VIEWPOINTS **1765**

MINNESOTA VOLUNTEER, THE (US/0196-593X) [01608258] **2198**

MINNESOTA VOTER, THE (US) [01758302] 5561, **4665**

MINNESOTA VOTER, THE (US/0740-1191) [09872397] **4482**

MINNESOTA WATER QUALITY WORK PLAN FY ... / MINNESOTA POLLUTION CONTROL AGENCY (US) [07043577] **2236**

MINNESOTA WELLNESS JOURNAL *See* WELLNESS JOURNAL, THE **4807**

MINNESOTA WILDLIFE REPORT (US/1040-0680) [14874409] **2198**

MINNESOTA WOMAN'S YEARBOOK (US/0198-9898) [03899956] 5561, **5296**

MINNESOTA WRITING PROJECT (US/1061-6535) [25387877] **3412**

MINNESOTA'S JOURNAL OF LAW AND POLITICS (US) 4665, **3010**

MINNIE 'N ME, THE BEST FRIENDS COLLECTION (US/1053-6280) [22590355] **1066**

MINOLTA MIRROR (JA) [05020542] **4371**

MINOR NONMETALS (US) [04171482] **2146**

MINOR ORES AND MINERALS (UK/0951-0680) [18471731] **2146**

MINOR PLANET BULLETIN, THE (US/1052-8091) [04263320] **397**

MINOR PLANET CIRCULARS/MINOR PLANETS AND COMETS (US/0736-6884) [05622733] **397**

MINORANZE (IT) [08543847] **5209**

MINORE GIUSTIZIA (IT) **3010**

MINORITE INVISIBLE *CEASED.* (CN/0847-5636) [22154968] **4391**

MINORITIES & SUCCESS (US/1058-6318) [24341288] **879**

MINORITIES & WOMEN IN BUSINESS *CEASED.* (US/1053-2749) [12404890] 2267, **5561**

MINORITIES AND WOMEN IN HIGHER EDUCATION (US) [17616733] 5561, **4510**

MINORITIES IN BUSINESS INSIDER (US/1050-3463) [21467918] **1690**

MINORITY — Alphabetical Title Index

MINORITY AND FEMALE MEMBERSHIP IN REFERRAL UNIONS See EQUAL EMPLOYMENT OPPORTUNITY REPORT. MINORITIES AND WOMEN IN APPRENTICESHIP PROGRAMS AND REFERRAL UNIONS **1667**

MINORITY AND SECOND LANGUAGE EDUCATION. ELEMENTARY AND SECONDARY LEVELS (CN/0706-3717) [04441611] **1764**

MINORITY & WOMEN DOCTORAL DIRECTORY (US/1066-9507) [25533343] 2276, **1836**

MINORITY BIOMEDICAL SUPPORT PROGRAM : A DIRECTORY OF THE RESEARCH PROJECTS (US) [04956089] **3617**

MINORITY BUILDER (US/0090-855X) [01785672] **621**

●MINORITY BUILDER GAZETTE, THE (US/1056-7828) [23853351] **621**

MINORITY BUSINESS ENTREPRENEUR (US/1048-0919) [18788065] **695**

MINORITY BUSINESS NEWS U.S.A (US) 2267, **695**

MINORITY BUSINESS REVIEW (HEMPSTEAD, N.Y.) (US/1041-0864) [18631134] 1618, **695**

MINORITY BUSINESS TODAY (US) [11506947] **695**

MINORITY EDUCATION *CEASED.* (US/0730-0034) [07405878] 2267, **1764**

MINORITY ENGINEER : ME, THE (US/0884-1829) [08705081] **1988**

MINORITY ENTRPRENEUR. A CLEARINGHOUSE FOR BUSINESS DEVELOPMENT (US) **695**

MINORITY/ETHNIC MEDIA GUIDE, USA (US/0730-5141) [06307042] 2267, **1117**

MINORITY FUNDING REPORT (US/1047-3300) [20666549] **5296**

MINORITY LITERARY EXPO (US/1055-0690) [23067833] 2267, **3347**

●MINORITY LITERARY EXPO (BIRMINGHAM, ALA.) (US/1061-2246) [25216415] 2267, **3347**

MINORITY MARKETS ALERT (US/1041-7524) [18839361] **906**

MINORITY MBA (US/1040-1547) [18335831] **695**

●MINORITY NURSE NEWSLETTER (US/1071-9946) [28823528] **3861**

MINORITY ORGANIZATIONS: A NATIONAL DIRECTORY (US/0162-9034) [04266184] **2267**

MINORITY PUPILS AND STAFF IN THE CONNECTICUT PUBLIC SCHOOLS (US) [06458246] 2267, **1764**

MINORITY REVIEW, THE *See* JOBS IN HIGHER EDUCATION **4205**

MINORITY STUDENT OPPORTUNITIES IN UNITED STATES MEDICAL SCHOOLS (US/0085-3488) [04401746] 3617, **1836**

MINORITY TRENDSLETTER *See* THIRD FORCE (1993) **4513**

MINORITY TRENDSLETTER : A PUBLICATION FROM THE CENTER FOR THIRD WORLD ORGANIZING, THE (US) [18285060] **4510**

MINORITY VOICES *SUSPENDED.* (US/0148-1037) [03263896] **358**

MINORITY/WOMEN'S BUSINESS ENTERPRISES DIRECTORY (US/0743-7366) [10648721] 695, **1618**

MINOS (SP/0544-3733) [01758322] **3302**

MINOSEG ES MEGBIZHATOSAG (HU/0580-4485) [06796793] **4220**

MINOT DAILY NEWS, THE (US/0885-3053) [01758323] **5726**

MINPROC : MINERAL PROCESSING ABSTRACTS *CEASED.* (CN/0828-8461) [18121321] 2146, **2006**

MINSA PALLYE YONGU / MINSA PALLYE YONGUHOE PYON (KO) [12031044] 3010, **4510**

MINSEI IIN JIDO IIN NO TEBIKI (JA) [05515019] **5296**

MINSHOHO ZASSHI (JA) [19052037] **3090**

MINTEC : MINING TECHNOLOGY ABSTRACTS *CEASED.* (CN/0823-0773) [10356082] 2146, **2006**

MINTEK BULLETIN (SA/1012-5299) [I10125299] **2146**

MINTEK RESEARCH DIGEST (SA) [10136444] **4012**

MINTEL LEISURE INTELLIGENCE (UK) 5484, **4852**

MINTEL MARKET INTELLIGENCE (UK) 950, **933**

MINTEL PERSONAL FINANCE INTELLIGENCE (UK) **798**

MINTETSU TOKEI NEMPO (JA) [03686408] **5432**

MINTIS (UK) [01791149] **2699**

MINUTE LA FRANCE *See* MINUTE PARIS. 1993 **1764**

●MINUTE PARIS. 1993 (FR/1243-7751) [I12437751] **1764**

MINUTEMAN (US) [05974931] **1836**

MINUTES (CN) [09743114] **28**

MINUTES - ANNUAL CONVENTION OF THE EASTERN CANADA SYNOD, LUTHERAN CHURCH IN AMERICA (CN/0317-9583) [02443263] **5064**

MINUTES : LEGISLATIVE ASSEMBLY OFFICIAL REPORT (CJ) [05218744] **4665**

MINUTES / OCIC (BE/0771-0461) [20033678] 4131, **4074**

MINUTES OF ANNUAL MEETING - BRITISH COLUMBIA ASSOCIATION OF HOSPITALS AND HEALTH ORGANIZATIONS (CN/0384-9481) [02070795] **3789**

MINUTES OF EVIDENCE (UK) [20139638] **1145**

MINUTES OF MEETING / NATIONAL ADVISORY EYE COUNCIL (US/0192-771X) [05035149] **3876**

MINUTES OF PROCEEDINGS AND EVIDENCE OF SUB-COMMITTEE B OF THE SPECIAL COMMITTEE ON EMPLOYMENT OPPORTUNITIES FOR THE '80S (CN/0825-0677) [08659901] 4665, **1691**

●MINUTES OF PROCEEDINGS AND EVIDENCE OF THE ABORIGINAL LIAISON COMMITTEE OF THE SPECIAL JOINT COMMITTEE ON A RENEWED CANADA (ENGLISH EDITION) (CN/1189-3672) [26497962] **2746**

●MINUTES OF PROCEEDINGS AND EVIDENCE OF THE ABORIGINAL LIAISON COMMITTEE OF THE SPECIAL JOINT COMMITTEE ON A RENEWED CANADA (FRENCH EDITION) (CN/1189-3672) [26497966] **2747**

MINUTES OF PROCEEDINGS AND EVIDENCE OF THE SPECIAL COMMITTEE ON A NORTHERN GAS PIPELINE (CN/0707-3216) [05018681] **4264**

MINUTES OF PROCEEDINGS AND EVIDENCE OF THE SPECIAL COMMITTEE ON CANADA-UNITED STATES AIR TRANSPORT SERVICES (CN/0848-791X) [23248952] **28**

●MINUTES OF PROCEEDINGS AND EVIDENCE OF THE SPECIAL COMMITTEE ON ELECTORAL REFORM (CN/1193-1043) [26497974] **4482**

●MINUTES OF PROCEEDINGS AND EVIDENCE OF THE SPECIAL COMMITTEE ON ELECTORAL REFORM (FRENCH EDITION) (CN/1193-1043) [26497977] **4482**

MINUTES OF PROCEEDINGS AND EVIDENCE OF THE SPECIAL COMMITTEE ON PENSION REFORM (CN/0825-0138) [10037294] 2888, **1691**

MINUTES OF PROCEEDINGS AND EVIDENCE OF THE SPECIAL COMMITTEE ON REGULATORY REFORM (CN/0710-6327) [08192850] **3010**

MINUTES OF PROCEEDINGS AND EVIDENCE OF THE SPECIAL COMMITTEE ON SUBJECT MATTER OF BILL C-80 (FIREARMS) (CN/0848-7928) [23248943] **4665**

MINUTES OF PROCEEDINGS AND EVIDENCE OF THE SPECIAL COMMITTEE ON THE ACT RESPECTING CUSTOMS (CN/1187-4430) [25314249] **4737**

MINUTES OF PROCEEDINGS AND EVIDENCE OF THE SPECIAL COMMITTEE ON THE ACT RESPECTING CUSTOMS (CN/1187-4430) [25314251] **4665**

MINUTES OF PROCEEDINGS AND EVIDENCE OF THE SPECIAL COMMITTEE ON THE FEDERAL-PROVINCIAL FISCAL ARRANGEMENTS (CN/0710-9733) [08379004] **4665**

MINUTES OF PROCEEDINGS AND EVIDENCE OF THE SPECIAL COMMITTEE ON TRENDS IN FOOD PRICES (CN) [02248504] **2350**

MINUTES OF PROCEEDINGS AND EVIDENCE OF THE SPECIAL JOINT COMMITTEE OF THE SENATE AND OF THE HOUSE OF COMMONS ON IMMIGRATION POLICY (CN) [02242551] **1920**

MINUTES OF PROCEEDINGS AND EVIDENCE OF THE SPECIAL JOINT COMMITTEE OF THE SENATE AND OF THE HOUSE OF COMMONS ON SENATE REFORM (CN/0825-0251) [10036750] **4665**

MINUTES OF PROCEEDINGS AND EVIDENCE OF THE SPECIAL JOINT COMMITTEE OF THE SENATE AND THE HOUSE OF COMMONS ON PROCESS FOR AMENDING THE CONSTITUTION OF CANADA (CN/1186-0375) [24280137] **4482**

MINUTES OF PROCEEDINGS AND EVIDENCE OF THE STANDING COMMITTEE ON HOUSE MANAGEMENT (CN/1187-2462) [25066928] **4665**

MINUTES OF PROCEEDINGS AND EVIDENCE OF THE STANDING COMMITTEE ON MANAGEMENT AND MEMBERS' SERVICES (CN/0228-0825) [06758379] **3010**

MINUTES OF PROCEEDINGS AND EVIDENCE OF THE STANDING COMMITTEE ON MULTICULTURALISM AND CITIZENSHIP (CN/0846-9423) [26791155] **2539**

MINUTES OF PROCEEDINGS AND EVIDENCE OF THE STANDING COMMITTEE ON NORTHERN PIPELINES (CN/0707-8978) [04879978] **4264**

MINUTES OF PROCEEDINGS AND EVIDENCE OF THE STANDING COMMITTEE ON OFFICIAL LANGUAGES (CN/1187-2896) [25066982] **3302**

MINUTES OF PROCEEDINGS AND EVIDENCE OF THE SUB-COMMITTEE OF THE STANDING COMMITTEE ON AGRICULTURE ON FARM CREDIT ARRANGEMENTS (CN/0825-0146) [09998795] **108**

MINUTES OF PROCEEDINGS AND EVIDENCE OF THE SUB-COMMITTEE ON DEVELOPMENT AND HUMAN RIGHTS OF THE STANDING COMMITTEE ON EXTERNAL AFFAIRS AND INTERNATIONAL TRADE (CN/1187-4414) [25314265] **4510**

MINUTES OF PROCEEDINGS AND EVIDENCE OF THE SUB-COMMITTEE ON DEVELOPMENT AND HUMAN RIGHTS OF THE STANDING COMMITTEE ON EXTERNAL AFFAIRS AND INTERNATIONAL TRADE (CN/1187-4414) [25314267] **4510**

MINUTES OF PROCEEDINGS AND EVIDENCE OF THE SUB-COMMITTEE ON DREE PROGRAMMES (QUEBEC) OF THE STANDING COMMITTEE ON REGIONAL DEVELOPMENT (CN/0713-651X) [08916748] **4665**

MINUTES OF PROCEEDINGS AND EVIDENCE OF THE SUB-COMMITTEE ON FINANCIAL INSTITUTIONS LEGISLATION OF THE STANDING COMMITTEE ON FINANCE (CN/1187-452X) [25314263] **798**

MINUTES OF PROCEEDINGS AND EVIDENCE OF THE SUB-COMMITTEE ON FINANCIAL INSTITUTIONS LEGISLATION OF THE STANDING COMMITTEE ON FINANCE (CN/1187-452X) [25314260] **3087**

MINUTES OF PROCEEDINGS AND EVIDENCE OF THE SUB-COMMITTEE ON HEALTH ISSUES OF THE STANDING COMMITTEE ON HEALTH AND WELFARE, SOCIAL AFFAIRS, SENIORS AND THE STATUS OF WOMEN (CN/1187-4406) [25314254] **4791**

MINUTES OF PROCEEDINGS AND EVIDENCE OF THE SUB-COMMITTEE ON HEALTH ISSUES OF THE STANDING COMMITTEE ON HEALTH AND WELFARE, SOCIAL AFFAIRS, SENIORS AND THE STATUS OF WOMEN (CN/1187-4406) [25314256] **4791**

MINUTES OF PROCEEDINGS AND EVIDENCE OF THE SUB-COMMITTEE ON INDIAN WOMEN AND THE INDIAN ACT OF THE STANDING COMMITTEE ON INDIAN AFFAIRS AND NORTHERN DEVELOPMENT (CN/0825-012X) [09705106] **2267**

MINUTES OF PROCEEDINGS AND EVIDENCE OF THE SUB-COMMITTEE ON INTERNATIONAL DEVELOPMENT OF THE STANDING COMMITTEE ON EXTERNAL AFFAIRS AND NATIONAL DEFENSE (CN) [02244522] **2911**

●MINUTES OF PROCEEDINGS AND EVIDENCE OF THE SUB-COMMITTEE ON INTERNATIONAL FINANCIAL INSTITUTIONS OF THE STANDING COMMITTEE ON FINANCE (CN/1193-2643) [26758130] **799**

●MINUTES OF PROCEEDINGS AND EVIDENCE OF THE SUB-COMMITTEE ON INTERNATIONAL FINANCIAL INSTITUTIONS OF THE STANDING COMMITTEE ON FINANCE (ENGLISH EDITION) (CN/1193-2643) [26758134] **799**

MINUTES OF PROCEEDINGS AND EVIDENCE OF THE SUB-COMMITTEE ON INTERNATIONAL TRADE OF THE STANDING COMMITTEE ON EXTERNAL AFFAIRS AND INTERNATIONAL TRADE (CN/1187-6492) [25590042] **846**

MINUTES OF PROCEEDINGS AND EVIDENCE OF THE SUB-COMMITTEE ON NATIONAL SECURITY OF THE STANDING COMMITTEE ON JUSTICE AND THE SOLICITOR GENERAL (CN/1187-6514) [25590052] **4666**

MINUTES OF PROCEEDINGS AND EVIDENCE OF THE SUB-COMMITTEE ON NORAD OF THE STANDING COMMITTEE ON EXTERNAL AFFAIRS AND INTERNATIONAL TRADE (CN/0848-7936) [23248976] **846**

Alphabetical Title Index   **MISCELLANEOUS**

MINUTES OF PROCEEDINGS AND EVIDENCE OF THE SUB-COMMITTEE ON PRIVATE MEMBERS BUSINESS OF THE STANDING COMMITTEE ON HOUSE MANAGEMENT (CN/1187-2470) [25066939] **4666**

MINUTES OF PROCEEDINGS AND EVIDENCE OF THE SUB-COMMITTEE ON PRIVATE MEMBERS BUSINESS OF THE STANDING COMMITTEE ON HOUSE MANAGEMENT (CN/1187-2470) [25066937] **4666**

MINUTES OF PROCEEDINGS AND EVIDENCE OF THE SUB-COMMITTEE ON THE BANK OF CANADA OF THE STANDING COMMITTEE ON FINANCE (CN/1187-6506) [25590048] **799**

MINUTES OF PROCEEDINGS AND EVIDENCE OF THE SUB-COMMITTEE ON THE BANK OF CANADA OF THE STANDING COMMITTEE ON FINANCE (CN/1187-6506) [25590046] **799**

MINUTES OF PROCEEDINGS AND EVIDENCE OF THE SUB-COMMITTEE ON THE PENITENTIARY SYSTEM IN CANADA (CN) [03254551] **3169**

●MINUTES OF PROCEEDINGS AND EVIDENCE OF THE SUB-COMMITTEE ON THE ST. LAWRENCE SEAWAY OF THE STANDING COMMITTEE ON TRANSPORT (CN/1193-2651) [26758136] **5387**

●MINUTES OF PROCEEDINGS AND EVIDENCE OF THE SUB-COMMITTEE ON THE ST. LAWRENCE SEAWAY OF THE STANDING COMMITTEE ON TRANSPORT (FRENCH EDITON) (CN/1193-2651) [26758141] **5387**

MINUTES OF PROCEEDINGS AND EVIDENCE OF THE SUB-COMMITTEE ON THE STATUS OF WOMEN OF THE STANDING COMMITTEE ON HEALTH AND WELFARE, SOCIAL AFFAIRS, SENIORS AND ON THE STATUS OF WOMEN (CN/1184-1451) [23248137] **4666, 5561**

MINUTES OF PROCEEDINGS - COUNCIL OF EUROPE, PARLIAMENTARY ASSEMBLY (FR) [02395956] **4666**

MINUTES OF PROCEEDINGS OF THE ANNUAL CONFERENCE - ASSOCIATION OF SUPERINTENDENTS OF INSURANCE OF THE PROVINCES OF CANADA (CN/0315-7253) [02442012] **2888, 3010**

MINUTES OF THE ANNUAL CONFERENCE ON DOBLE CLIENTS *See* MINUTES OF THE ... ANNUAL INTERNATIONAL CONFERENCE OF DOBLE CLIENTS **2073**

MINUTES OF THE ... ANNUAL INTERNATIONAL CONFERENCE OF DOBLE CLIENTS (US/0730-9775) [08073118] **2073**

MINUTES OF THE ANNUAL MEETING OF THE FIRST CATHOLIC SLOVAK UNION OF THE UNITED STATES OF AMERICA AND CANADA (US/0275-6145) [07143602] **2747**

MINUTES OF THE FLORIDA OUTDOOR RECREATIONAL DEVELOPMENT COUNCIL, FLORIDA OUTDOOR RECREATIONAL PLANNING COMMITTEE (US/0428-6472) [01399298] **4874**

MINUTES OF THE MEETING - ARKANSAS-WHITE-RED BASINS INTER-AGENCY COMMITTEE (US/0403-1911) [01182810] **108, 5536**

MINUTES OF THE MEETING - ASSOCIATION OF RESEARCH LIBRARIES (US/0044-9652) [01518448] **3231**

MINUTES OF THE ... MEETING / CENTRAL COMMITTEE OF THE WORLD COUNCIL OF CHURCHES (SZ) [06469422] **4977**

MINUTES OF THE MEETING - NORTHEASTERN RESOURCES COMMITTEE (US) [01149980] **2198**

MINUTES OF THE MEETING OF THE EXECUTIVE COMMITTEE OF THE COUNCIL - AMERICAN LAW INSTITUTE (US) [05260465] **695**

MINUTES OF THE REGULAR ANNUAL CONGRESS ... / FEDERATION INTERNATIONALE DES SOCIETES D'AVIRON (FR) [17454051] **2519**

MINUTES OF THE SEMI-ANNUAL MEETING OF THE BOARD OF DIRECTORS OF THE FIRST CATHOLIC SLOVAK UNION OF THE UNITED STATES AND CANADA (US/0275-6250) [07143900] **5032**

MINUTES OF THE ... SESSION OF THE GOVERNING BODY / INTERNATIONAL LABOUR OFFICE (SZ) [01753601] **1691**

MINUTES OF THE TRUSTEES OF THE COLLEGE, ACADEMY AND CHARITABLE SCHOOLS, UNIVERSITY OF PENNSYLVANIA (US/0148-2564) [03284091] **1866**

MINUTES / THE ... GENERAL SYNOD OF THE UNITED CHURCH OF CHRIST (US) [08155797] **5064**

MINUTES - UNITED PRESBYTERIAN CHURCH IN THE U.S.A (US/0082-8548) [01517997] **5064**

MINWA NO TECHO (JA) [05592117] **2322**

MINZOKU SHUKYO KENKYU (JA) [08057119] **4977**

MINZOKUGAKU KENKYU (JA) [01758325] **241**

MINZOKUGAKU RONSO (JA) [07096434] **2322**

MINZUXUE YANJIUSUO JIKAN, ZHONGYANG YANJIUYUAN (CH/0001-3935) [02259370] **5252, 241**

MIO CONNECTION (US) **2460**

MIORITA (US/0110-0068) [02370069] **2699**

●MIR ISKUSSTV (RU) [26435524] **325**

MIR. MANAGEMENT INTERNATIONAL REVIEW 1990 (GW/0938-8249) [I09388249] **879, 695**

MIR MUZEIA (RU/0869-8171) [29762483] **4091**

MIR (PHILADELPHIA, PA.) (US) [11642002] **3412**

●MIR ZHENSHCHINY (RU/0869-494X) [25585873] **5561**

MIRA (SAN FRANCISCO, CALIF.) *SUSPENDED.* (US/1056-2915) [23110663] **3675**

MIRABEL-- A VOL D'OISEAU (CN/0229-3285) [08072186] **4666**

MIRABEL, LE (CN/0316-9103) [02247393] **5789**

MIRABEL (SAINT-EUSTACHE) (CN/0711-3781) [08649750] **5790**

MIRABELLA (NEW YORK, N.Y.) (US/1044-5153) [19822963] **5561**

MIRACLES MAGAZINE (US/1061-3927) [25285361] **4977**

MIRADA, LA (AG) [24557178] **2747**

MIRAERUL MUNNUNDA (KO) [01790362] **2623**

MIRD PAMPHLETS (US/0361-0497) [02003252] **3944**

MIRIAD (CN/0713-6722) [08967814] **3412**

MIRKIN REPORT (US/1048-910X) [21095455] **2600**

MIRO : MUSIC INDUSTRY RESEARCH ORGANISATION (UK) **4131**

MIROIR DE L'HISTOIRE (FR/0988-0321) [05386050] **2623**

MIROIR DU CYCLISME 1960 *SUSPENDED.* (FR/0397-569X) [I0397569X] **429**

MIROVAJA EKONOMIKA I MEZDUNARODNYE OTNOSENIJA (RU/0026-5829) [01935606] **1574**

MIRROR *CEASED.* (US/0730-0808) [07937963] **1330**

MIRROR (LO) [22337628] **5806**

MIRROR (1984) (US/1072-1037) [22502013] **3169**

MIRROR (DAWSON CREEK) (CN/0712-1105) [08690458] **5790**

MIRROR-EXAMINER (CN/1196-071X) [28395720] **5790**

MIRROR (LONDON, ONT.) (CN/0711-5911) [09156985] **2623, 1093**

MIRROR MONTREAL. 1990 (CN/1182-5812) [11825812] **2539**

MIRROR NEWS (US/0191-4677) [04902448] **933, 3484**

MIRROR, THE (US/0738-7237) [02254380] **2747, 4977**

MIRRORS : INTERNATIONAL HAIKU FORUM (US) **3466**

MIS (PL/0137-7698) [I01377698] **1066**

MIS INTERRUPT (CN/0710-9679) [08415768] **1764, 879**

●MIS MANAGEMENT REVIEW (US/1060-3565) [24946011] **1195**

MIS REPORT (US) [10662914] **4666**

MISA DOMINICAL CASTILIAN (SP) **4977**

MISA DOMINICAL CATALONIAN (SP) **4977**

MISAENGMUL HAKHOE CHI (RU/0440-2413) [10827224] **567**

MISAENGMUL KWA PARHYO (KO) [10187936] **567**

MISAHAH AL-JIYULUJIYAH AL-MISRIYAH *See* ANNALS OF THE GEOLOGICAL SURVEY OF EGYPT **1365**

MISC (US) [24649646] **5233**

MISCELANEA ANTROPOLOGICA ECUATORIANA (EC/0254-7678) [08854360] **2267, 241**

MISCELANEA COMILLAS (SP/0210-9522) [05433472] **4977**

MISCELANEA DE ESTUDIOS ARABES Y HERBAICOS (SP/0544-408X) [04286120] **3302**

MISCELANEA - FUNDACION MIGUEL LILLO (AG/0074-025X) [02379606] **4167**

MISCELANEA MEDIEVAL MURCIANA (SP/0210-4903) [08518238] **2699**

MISCELANEA ODDELENI RUKOPISU A VZACNYCH TISKU / STATNI KNIHOVNA CESKE SOCIALISTICKE REPUBLIKY, NOSITELKA RADU REPUBLIKY (XR) [19690692] **4830**

MISCELLANEA ARCHIVISTICA (BE) [04732881] **2482**

MISCELLANEA BAVARICA MONACENSIA (GW/0581-0124) [02434896] **2699**

MISCELLANEA FRANCESCANA (IT) [10395952] **5032**

MISCELLANEA FRANCESCANA DI STORIA, DI LETTERE, DI ARTI *See* MISCELLANEA FRANCESCANA **5032**

MISCELLANEA HISTORIAE PONTIFICIAE (IT) [01764507] **4977**

MISCELLANEA MEDIAEVALIA (GW/0544-4128) [02433682] **2699**

MISCELLANEA MUSICOLOGICA (ADELAIDE) (AT/0076-9355) [01758333] **4131**

MISCELLANEA STORICA DELLA VALDELSA (IT/0026-5888) [04391223] **2699**

MISCELLANEA ZOOLOGICA HUNGARICA *SUSPENDED.* (HU/0230-9017) [11184405] **5591**

MISCELLANEOUS BULLETIN (NEW SOUTH WALES. DIVISION OF AGRICULTURAL SERVICES) (AT/0815-7162) [20332900] **108**

MISCELLANEOUS INFORMATION, THE TOKYO UNIVERSITY FORESTS (JA/0493-4326) [01714579] **2388**

MISCELLANEOUS PAPERS / HISTORY OF MEDICINE SOCIETY OF APPALACHIA (US) [23664621] **3617**

MISCELLANEOUS PAPERS - LANDBOUWHOGESCHOOL WAGENINGEN (NE/0083-6990) [01635734] **109**

MISCELLANEOUS PAPERS - TEXAS MEMORIAL MUSEUM (US/0082-3082) [03902277] **4091**

MISCELLANEOUS PUBLICATION (US) [02739510] **4264, 1388**

MISCELLANEOUS PUBLICATION OF THE TOHOKU NATIONAL AGRICULTURAL EXPERIMENT STATION (JA) [05638653] **109**

MISCELLANEOUS PUBLICATION - TALL TIMBERS RESEARCH STATION (US/0496-764X) [01421350] **465**

MISCELLANEOUS PUBLICATION - TEXAS AGRICULTURAL EXPERIMENT STATION (US/0097-6334) [02625018] **109**

MISCELLANEOUS PUBLICATION - UNITED STATES DEPARTMENT OF AGRICULTURE (US/0097-0212) [01740185] **109**

MISCELLANEOUS PUBLICATION - UNIVERSITY OF KANSAS, MUSEUM OF NATURAL HISTORY (US/0075-5028) [01308500] **4167**

MISCELLANEOUS PUBLICATION - WESTERN AUSTRALIA DEPARTMENT OF AGRICULTURE (AT/0725-847X) [24386318] **109**

MISCELLANEOUS PUBLICATIONS - FLORIDA. AGRICULTURAL EXPERIMENT, GAINESVILLE. LIBRARY (US/0428-6103) [01375351] **109**

MISCELLANEOUS PUBLICATIONS - MUSEUM OF ZOOLOGY, UNIVERSITY OF MICHIGAN (US/0076-8405) [01607508] **4167, 5591**

MISCELLANEOUS REPORT - BUREAU OF FISHERIES LABORATORY (US) [05932626] **2308**

MISCELLANEOUS REPORT - CENTRE FOR OVERSEAS PEST RESEARCH (UK/0307-9058) [01173285] **109**

MISCELLANEOUS REPORT (GEOLOGICAL SURVEY OF CANADA) (CN/0068-7642) [01552912] **1388**

MISCELLANEOUS REPORT - GREAT LAKES FORESTRY CENTRE (CN/0832-7130) [I08327130] **2388**

MISCELLANEOUS REPORT - STATE OF OHIO, DEPARTMENT OF NATURAL RESOURCES, DIVISION OF GEOLOGICAL SURVEY (US/0361-0519) [02003207] **1388**

MISCELLANEOUS REPORT - U.S. ARMY, CORPS OF ENGINEERS, COASTAL ENGINEERING RESEARCH CENTER (US/0193-5992) [02469093] **2093**

MISCELLANEOUS REPORT - U. S. LAKE STATES FOREST EXPERIMENT STATION, ST. PAUL (US) [01540252] **2388**

MISCELLANEOUS REPORT (UNIVERSITY OF MINNESOTA. AGRICULTURAL EXPERIMENT STATION) *See* MINNESOTA REPORT (UNIVERSITY OF MINNESOTA. AGRICULTURAL EXPERIMENT STATION) **108**

MISCELLANEOUS REPORTS - MINISTRY OF AGRICULTURE AND NATURAL RESOURCES. AGRICULTURAL RESEARCH INSTITUTE (CY/0253-6749) [16270372] **109**

MISCELLANEOUS — Alphabetical Title Index

MISCELLANEOUS SERIES - DEPARTMENT OF GEOGRAPHY, UNIVERSITY OF HULL (UK/0441-4004) [02084987] **2569**

MISCELLANEOUS SERIES - NEW ZEALAND GEOGRAPHICAL SOCIETY (NZ/0078-0022) [I00780022] **2569**

MISCELLANEOUS SERIES (NORTH DAKOTA GEOLOGICAL SURVEY) (US/0078-1576) [01308266] **1388**

MISCELLANIA ZOOLOGICA (SP/0211-6529) [08102411] **5591**

MISCELLANY (US) [05262105] **1836**

MISCELLANY OF THE SCOTTISH HISTORY SOCIETY (UK) [07825653] **2699**

MISE A JOUR DE LA LISTE DES MEMBRES DU CIEE AU ... (CN/0820-6309) [09452686] **2699**

MISE A JOUR EN DROIT D'AUTEUR, LA (FR/1163-1651) [I11631651] **3010**

MISES A JOUR CARDIOLOGIQUES (FR/0300-0702) [10138652] **3708**

MISES AU POINT DE BIOCHIMIE PHARMACOLOGIQUE (FR/0294-0671) [04556944] **4316**

MISHA (RU) **1066**

MISHAWAKA ENTERPRISE (MISHAWAKA, IND. : 1985) (US/8750-829X) [11848002] **5665**

MISHKAN (IS) [12337710] **4977**

MISHPACHA (VIENNA, VA.) (US/1050-9348) [12318857] **5051**

MISHPATIM (IS) [01758342] **1836**

MISINFORMATION (US) **1195**

MISION (BUENOS AIRES, ARGENTINA) (AG) [08768256] **4977**

MISIONES EXTRANJERAS (SP) [02245051] **4977**

MISKOLCI HERMAN OTTO MUZEUM KOZLEMENYEI, A (HU/0540-3391) [21381125] 358, **4091**

●MISNOMER (PRESTONBURG, KY.) (US/1061-5296) [25343809] **3466**

MISS B ENGLISH ED (GW/0937-3543) [I09373543] **1086**

MISSET WORLD POULTRY (NE) [22963119] **215**

MISSETS DISTRIFOOD NIEUWSBLAD (NE) **5806**

MISSETS MILIEU MAGAZINE (NE) **2177**

MISSETS MILIEU NIEUWSBRIEF (NE) **4220**

MISSETS PAKBLAD (NE) **4220**

MISSILE FORECAST (US) **4051**

MISSILE MONITOR (US/1060-8273) [25067313] **4051**

MISSILE/ORDNANCE LETTER *See* DEFENSE ACQUISITION REPORT **4040**

MISSING LINKS *See* CAR-DEL SCRIBE **2441**

MISSIO APOSTOLICA : JOURNAL OF THE LUTHERAN SOCIETY FOR MISSIOLOGY (US/1068-3151) [27644739] **4977**

MISSIOLOGY (US/0091-8296) [01787681] **4977**

MISSION (DK) [03505886] **4978**

MISSION (AT) **5064**

MISSION AND MINISTRY (US/1058-0565) [09833699] 5018, **5064**

MISSION (DEPARTEMENT EVANGELIQUE FRANCAIS D'ACTION APOSTOLIQUE) (FR/0760-2626) [21925657] **5064**

MISSION-FOCUS *CEASED*. (US/0164-4696) [04741527] **5064**

MISSION FRONTIERS (US/0889-9436) [08630362] **4978**

MISSION HAND BOOK (US/0095-2036) [01796259] **4978**

MISSION HANDBOOK. USA/CANADA PROTESTANT MINISTRIES OVERSEAS (US/1050-771X) [21096388] **4978**

MISSION IMPOSSIBLE (CN/0822-9619) [10680871] **5296**

MISSION INN MUSUEM JOURNAL (US/1052-3030) [22248320] **4091**

MISSION INTERCOM *CEASED*. (US) [04445034] **4978**

●MISSION: JOURNAL OF MISSION STUDIES (CN/1198-0400) [31235241] **4978**

MISSION (QUEBEC) (CN/0708-9813) [05257312] **5032**

MISSION (ST-LAMBERT, QUEBEC), EN (CN/0822-837X) [11734474] **4978**

MISSION STUDIES (NE/0168-9789) [11125083] **4978**

MISSION UPDATE (US) **5032**

MISSIONALIA (SA/0256-9507) [02250882] 4978, **5013**

MISSIONALIA HISPANICA *CEASED*. (SP/0211-5492) [01695390] **5032**

MISSIONARY EVANGEL (US/0273-6780) [06804458] **4978**

MISSIONARY HERALD (LONDON, ENGLAND : 1921) (UK) [01588233] **5064**

MISSIONARY MONTHLY (US/0161-7133) [04010267] **4978**

MISSIONARY MONTHLY REFORMED REVIEW *See* MISSIONARY MONTHLY **4978**

MISSIONARY NEWS *See* MISSION **5064**

MISSIONARY NEWS SERVICE *CEASED*. (US/0026-6051) [06552698] **4978**

MISSIONARY SEER (US) **4978**

MISSIONARY SISTERS OF THE IMMACULATE CONCEPTION *See* M I C MISSION NEWS **4975**

MISSIONARY TIDINGS (WINONA LAKE, IND.) (US/1043-0725) [09055353] **4978**

MISSIONGRAMS / BEREAN MISSION (US) [08550492] **4978**

MISSIONI CATTOLICHE *See* MONDO E MISSIONE **5032**

MISSIONNAIRES CATHOLIQUES CANADIENS, STATISTIQUES (CN/0225-3801) [06156831] 5032, **5013**

MISSIONNAIRES ENSEMBLE (CN/0838-7052) [18242430] **4978**

MISSIONS ADVANCED RESEARCH AND COMMUNICATION CENTER *See* NEWSLETTER - MISSIONS ADVANCED RESEARCH AND COMMUNICATIONS CENTER **4982**

MISSIONS DES FRANCISCAINS (CN/0700-4192) [03403129] **5032**

MISSIONS DES ILES (CN/0229-0928) [08079397] **4978**

MISSIONS ETRANGERES (CN/0026-6116) [04433113] **4978**

MISSIONS TODAY (MEMPHIS, TENN.) (US/1051-3345) [21928499] **4978**

MISSIONS USA (US/0279-5345) [07090278] **5064**

MISSIONSWISSENSCHAFTLICHE FORSCHUNGEN (GW/0076-9428) [02433708] **4978**

MISSISSAUGA BUSINESS REPORT (CN) **695**

MISSISSAUGA BUSINESS TIMES (CN/1185-2186) [24570933] **695**

MISSISSAUGA NEWS (CN) **5790**

MISSISSINEWA GENEALOGICAL QUARTERLY (US/0091-3189) [01786710] **2460**

MISSISSIPPI *See* MISSISSIPPI CODE 1972, ANNOTATED : ADOPTED AS THE OFFICIAL CODE OF THE STATE OF MISSISSIPPI BY THE 1972 SESSION OF THE LEGISLATURE **3010**

MISSISSIPPI 4-H NEWS (US) [05158967] **5233**

MISSISSIPPI ACADEMY OF SCIENCES *See* JOURNAL OF THE MISSISSIPPI ACADEMY OF SCIENCES **5121**

MISSISSIPPI. AGRICULTURAL AND FORESTRY EXPERIMENT STATION *See* INFORMATION SHEET - MISSISSIPPI STATE UNIVERSITY. AGRICULTURAL AND FORESTRY EXPERIMENT STATION **96**

MISSISSIPPI AGRICULTURAL AND FORESTRY EXPERIMENT STATION *See* MAFES RESEARCH HIGHLIGHTS **106**

MISSISSIPPI AGRICULTURAL AND FORESTRY EXPERIMENT STATION *See* TECHNICAL BULLETIN - MISSISSIPPI AGRICULTURAL AND FORESTRY EXPERIMENT STATION **139**

MISSISSIPPI. AGRICULTURAL AND FORESTRY EXPERIMENT STATION MISSISSIPPI STATE *See* INFORMATION BULLETIN - MISSISSIPPI. AGRICULTURAL AND FORESTRY EXPERIMENT STATION, MISSISSIPPI STATE **96**

MISSISSIPPI. AIR & WATER POLLUTION CONTROL COMMISSION *See* ANNUAL REPORT - MISSISSIPPI AIR AND WATER POLLUTION CONTROL COMMISSION **2224**

MISSISSIPPI ARCHAEOLOGY (US/0738-775X) [06993746] **275**

MISSISSIPPI ARMCHAIR RESEARCHER, THE (US/0743-1856) [10509061] **2460**

MISSISSIPPI ARTS COMMISSION *See* ANNUAL REPORT - MISSISSIPPI ARTS COMMISSION **312**

MISSISSIPPI BANK DIRECTORY (US) **799**

MISSISSIPPI BANKER, THE (US/0026-6159) [04059308] **799**

MISSISSIPPI BIBLE AND CEMETERY RECORDS (US/0742-499X) [10352454] **2460**

MISSISSIPPI. BOARD OF MISSISSIPPI LEVEE COMMISSIONERS *See* REGULAR MEETING - BOARD OF MISSISSIPPI LEVEE COMMISSIONERS **4679**

MISSISSIPPI BOARD OF WATER COMMISSIONERS *See* BULLETIN - MISSISSIPPI BOARD OF WATER COMMISSIONERS **5531**

MISSISSIPPI. BUREAU OF GEOLOGY *See* BULLETIN - MISSISSIPPI DEPARTMENT OF ENVIRONMENTAL QUALITY, BUREAU OF GEOLOGY **1370**

MISSISSIPPI BUSINESS DIRECTORY (US/1046-056X) [18827150] **695**

MISSISSIPPI BUSINESS EDUCATION ASSOCIATION JOURNAL (US) 1764, **695**

MISSISSIPPI BUSINESS JOURNAL, THE (US/0195-0002) [05184368] **695**

MISSISSIPPI CEMETERY AND BIBLE RECORDS *See* MISSISSIPPI BIBLE AND CEMETERY RECORDS **2460**

MISSISSIPPI CERTIFIED PUBLIC ACCOUNTANT : YEARBOOK, THE (US) [07703005] **748**

MISSISSIPPI COAST *CEASED*. (US/1045-1021) [20058913] **2539**

MISSISSIPPI COAST HISTORICAL & GENEALOGICAL SOCIETY (US/1053-8216) [09568990] **2461**

MISSISSIPPI CODE 1972, ANNOTATED : ADOPTED AS THE OFFICIAL CODE OF THE STATE OF MISSISSIPPI BY THE 1972 SESSION OF THE LEGISLATURE (US) [09819221] **3010**

MISSISSIPPI COLLEGE LAW REVIEW (US/0277-1152) [04338905] **3010**

MISSISSIPPI COLLEGE. SCHOOL OF LAW *See* MISSISSIPPI COLLEGE LAW REVIEW **3010**

MISSISSIPPI CONSTRUCTION *CEASED*. (US/1059-4620) [24601006] **621**

MISSISSIPPI COVERED EMPLOYMENT & WAGES (US/0090-5321) [01785295] **1691**

MISSISSIPPI. CRIMINAL JUSTICE PLANNING COMMISSION *See* JUVENILE JUSTICE AND DELINQUENCY PREVENTION PLAN **3168**

MISSISSIPPI DENTAL ASSOCIATION JOURNAL (US/0098-4329) [01446625] **1330**

MISSISSIPPI. DEPT. OF ARCHIVES AND HISTORY *See* ANNUAL REPORT OF THE MISSISSIPPI DEPARTMENT OF ARCHIVES AND HISTORY **2479**

MISSISSIPPI. DEPT. OF WILDLIFE CONSERVATION *See* ANNUAL REPORT - MISSISSIPPI. DEPT. OF WILDLIFE CONSERVATION **2186**

MISSISSIPPI. DIVISION OF MEDICAID *See* ANNUAL REPORT / OFFICE OF THE GOVERNOR, DIVISION OF MEDICAID **2873**

MISSISSIPPI. DIVISION OF VOCATIONAL REHABILITATION *See* VOCATION REHABILITATION ANNUAL REPORT FOR ... **1716**

MISSISSIPPI. DIVISION OF VOCATIONAL REHABILITATION. REPORT *See* VOCATION REHABILITATION ANNUAL REPORT FOR ... **1716**

MISSISSIPPI. DRIVER SERVICES DIVISION. STATISTICAL BUREAU *See* SUMMARY OF ALL REPORTED MOTOR VEHICLE TRAFFIC ACCIDENTS AND ACTIVITIES OF ALL FIELD PERSONNEL AND DRIVER SERVICES DIVISION IN THE STATE OF MISSISSIPPI **5445**

MISSISSIPPI EDUCATIONAL DIRECTORY *See* EDUCATIONAL DIRECTORY OF MISSISSIPPI SCHOOLS **1741**

MISSISSIPPI EDUCATOR, THE (US/0164-8683) [04272765] **1764**

MISSISSIPPI EMPLOYMENT *CEASED*. (US) [06547064] **1691**

●MISSISSIPPI EMPLOYMENT LAW LETTER (US/1074-0430) [29583234] **3152**

MISSISSIPPI. EMPLOYMENT SECURITY COMMISSION *See* MISSISSIPPI COVERED EMPLOYMENT & WAGES **1691**

MISSISSIPPI ENTERPRISE, THE (US) [15339733] **5701**

MISSISSIPPI FARM BUREAU NEWS (US/0026-6205) [04117512] **109**

MISSISSIPPI. FEED AND FERTILIZER CONTROL DIVISION *See* TONNAGE OF FERTILIZER SOLD IN MISSISSIPPI **141**

MISSISSIPPI FINANCIAL STATISTICS FOR HIGHWAY PLANNING ON STATE HIGHWAYS COUNTY ROADS CITY STREETS (US/0096-333X) [01798838] **5401**

MISSISSIPPI FOLKLORE REGISTER (US/0026-6248) [02438621] **2322**

MISSISSIPPI FRINGE BENEFIT SURVEY (US/0731-1494) [08116050] **1691**

MISSISSIPPI GAME & FISH (MARIETTA, GA.) (US/0744-4192) [08256751] **4874**

Alphabetical Title Index — MISSOURI

MISSISSIPPI GENEALOGICAL EXCHANGE (US/0540-3995) [04448417] **2461**

MISSISSIPPI GEOLOGY (US/0275-8555) [07019908] 4228, **1388**

MISSISSIPPI. GOVERNOR'S OFFICE OF INTERGOVERNMENTAL PERSONNEL *See* ANNUAL PROGRESS REPORT ... / GOVERNOR'S OFFICE OF INTERGOVERNMENTAL PERSONNEL (MISSISSIPPI) **4701**

MISSISSIPPI GUIDE TO LABOR MARKET INFORMATION / MISSISSIPPI EMPLOYMENT SECURITY COMMISSION (US) [04714409] **1691**

MISSISSIPPI HEALTH CARE COMMISSION *See* ANNUAL REPORT - MISSISSIPPI HEALTH CARE COMMISSION **4766**

● MISSISSIPPI HEALTH CARE IN PERSPECTIVE (US/1065-4267) [26605788] **4791**

MISSISSIPPI HIGHWAY TRAFFIC REPORT / PREPARED BY THE MISSISSIPPI STATE HIGHWAY DEPARTMENT, TRANSPORTATION PLANNING DIVISION ; IN COOPERATION WITH U.S. DEPARTMENT OF TRANSPORTATION, FEDERAL HIGHWAY ADMINISTRATION (US) [05541755] **5441**

MISSISSIPPI IN PERSPECTIVE (US/1065-5530) [26657191] **5333**

MISSISSIPPI (JACKSON, MISS. 1982) (US/0747-1602) [10114972] **2539**

MISSISSIPPI KITE, THE **SUSPENDED.** (US/0737-0393) [09293102] **5591**

MISSISSIPPI LANDINGS, ANNUAL SUMMARY (US/0098-0803) [01799507] **2308**

MISSISSIPPI LAW JOURNAL (US/0026-6280) [01588099] **3011**

MISSISSIPPI LAW JOURNAL. CUMULATIVE TEN-YEAR INDEX FOR VOLUMES 41-50 (US) [09520860] **3011**

MISSISSIPPI LAWYER, THE (US/0462-8551) [02255084] **3011**

MISSISSIPPI LEGAL DIRECTORY, THE (US/0738-2235) [07810317] **3011**

MISSISSIPPI LEGION'AIRE (US/0026-6299) [04120670] **5233**

MISSISSIPPI LIBRARIES (US/0194-388X) [04849546] **3231**

MISSISSIPPI MAGAZINE (JACKSON) (US/0199-5677) [06008693] **2539**

MISSISSIPPI MANUFACTURERS DIRECTORY (US) [07413169] **3484**

MISSISSIPPI MARINE RESOURCES COUNCIL *See* ANNUAL REPORT - MISSISSIPPI MARINE RESOURCES COUNCIL **1446**

MISSISSIPPI MEMORIES (US/1056-1587) [23478384] **2461**

MISSISSIPPI MORBIDITY REPORT (US/0745-2535) [08983404] **5333**

MISSISSIPPI MUD, THE (US/0739-0424) [03371150] **325**

MISSISSIPPI MUNICIPALITIES (US/0026-6337) [04618308] **4666**

MISSISSIPPI OFFICIAL AND STATISTICAL REGISTER (US/0196-4755) [01243227] 4666, **4698**

MISSISSIPPI OIL & GAS PRODUCTION REPORT (US/0274-6980) [06513198] **4264**

MISSISSIPPI ORNITHOLOGICAL SOCIETY *See* MOS NEWSLETTER **5592**

MISSISSIPPI OUTDOORS (1987) (US/1041-9306) [17238359] **4874**

MISSISSIPPI PHARMACIST (US/0161-3189) [03901739] **4316**

MISSISSIPPI PRESS (PASCAGOULA, MISS.), THE (US/1059-7166) [16221097] **5701**

MISSISSIPPI PUBLIC ROAD MILEAGE AS OF DECEMBER 31 / PREPARED BY MISSISSIPPI STATE HIGHWAY DEPARTMENT, TRANSPORTATION PLANNING DIVISION IN COOPERATION WITH U.S. DEPARTMENT OF TRANSPORTATION, FEDERAL HIGHWAY ADMINISTRATION (US) [06284912] **5441**

MISSISSIPPI QUARTERLY, THE (US/0026-637X) [01758368] 5209, **2850**

MISSISSIPPI RAG, THE (US/0742-4612) [03442159] **4131**

MISSISSIPPI RECORDS **CEASED.** (US/1064-0320) [26202190] **2461**

MISSISSIPPI RESEARCH AND DEVELOPMENT CENTER *See* R&D REVIEW (JACKSON, MISS.) **5144**

MISSISSIPPI REVIEW (US/0047-7559) [02458266] **3412**

MISSISSIPPI RIVER PARKWAY COMMISSION (ILL.) *See* REPORT OF THE MISSISSIPPI RIVER PARKWAY COMMISSION TO THE ... GENERAL ASSEMBLY OF ILLINOIS / MISSISSIPPI RIVER PARKWAY COMMISSION **5443**

MISSISSIPPI RIVER PARKWAY COMMISSION OF MINNESOTA *See* REPORT OF THE MISSISSIPPI RIVER PARKWAY COMMISSION OF MINNESOTA **4681**

MISSISSIPPI RN, THE (US/0026-6388) [01445313] **3861**

MISSISSIPPI SAXOPHONE (US/1061-7019) [25422492] **4131**

MISSISSIPPI SCHOOL FOR THE BLIND *See* ANNUAL REPORT / MISSISSIPPI SCHOOL FOR THE BLIND **4383**

MISSISSIPPI SOCIETY OF CERTIFIED PUBLIC ACCOUNTANTS *See* MISSISSIPPI CERTIFIED PUBLIC ACCOUNTANT : YEARBOOK, THE **748**

MISSISSIPPI. STATE BOARD FOR VOCATIONAL EDUCATION *See* STATE PLAN FOR THE ADMINISTRATION OF VOCATIONAL EDUCATION UNDER THE VOCATIONAL EDUCATION AMENDMENTS OF 1976. PUBLIC LAW 94-482, MISSISSIPPI : ANNUAL PLAN FOR FISCAL YEAR ... **1916**

MISSISSIPPI STATE BOARD OF ARCHITECTURE *See* ROSTER OF REGISTERED ARCHITECTS / MISSISSIPPI STATE BOARD OF ARCHITECTURE **308**

MISSISSIPPI STATE BOARD OF ARCHITECTURE. ANNUAL REPORT *See* ROSTER OF REGISTERED ARCHITECTS / MISSISSIPPI STATE BOARD OF ARCHITECTURE **308**

MISSISSIPPI STATE BOARD OF CONTRACTORS *See* ROSTER OF LICENSED CONTRACTORS IN THE STATE OF MISSISSIPPI **627**

MISSISSIPPI. STATE DEPT. OF HEALTH *See* ANNUAL REPORT / MISSISSIPPI, STATE DEPARTMENT OF HEALTH **4766**

MISSISSIPPI. STATE GAME AND FISH COMMISSION *See* BIENNIAL REPORT OF THE STATE GAME AND FISH COMMISSION TO THE REGULAR SESSION OF THE MISSISSIPPI LEGISLATURE **2297**

MISSISSIPPI STATE GOVERNMENT PUBLICATIONS (US/0148-1843) [03269545] **420**

MISSISSIPPI. STATE HOSPITAL COMMISSION *See* REPORT OF THE MISSISSIPPI STATE HOSPITAL COMMISSION **3792**

MISSISSIPPI STATE LIBRARY COMMISSION *See* MISSISSIPPI STATE GOVERNMENT PUBLICATIONS **420**

MISSISSIPPI. STATE LIBRARY COMMISSION *See* LONG-RANGE PROGRAM FOR LIBRARY DEVELOPMENT IN MISSISSIPPI. SUPPLEMENT **3229**

MISSISSIPPI STATE MEDICAL ASSOCIATION *See* JOURNAL OF THE MISSISSIPPI STATE MEDICAL ASSOCIATION **3599**

MISSISSIPPI STATE MEDICAL ASSOCIATION DIRECTORY (US) **3617**

MISSISSIPPI STATE OIL & GAS BOARD BULLETIN *See* MISSISSIPPI OIL & GAS PRODUCTION REPORT **4264**

MISSISSIPPI STATE PLAN FOR CONSTRUCTION OF HOSPITALS AND MEDICAL FACILITIES (US) [12922746] **3789**

MISSISSIPPI STATE UNIVERSITY. COOPERATIVE EXTENSION SERVICE *See* INFORMATION SHEET - MISSISSIPPI STATE UNIVERSITY. COOPERATIVE EXTENSION SERVICE **1542**

MISSISSIPPI. STATE VETERANS AFFAIRS BOARD *See* REPORT - MISSISSIPPI. STATE VETERANS AFFAIRS BOARD **4055**

MISSISSIPPI STATISTICAL ABSTRACT (US) [02254636] **5333**

MISSISSIPPI SUPERVISOR AND CHANCERY CLERK, CIRCUIT CLERK, TAX ASSESSOR & COLLECTOR (US/0738-727X) [09655021] **4666**

MISSISSIPPI. TRANSPORTATION PLANNING DIVISION *See* TRUCK WEIGHT STUDY (JACKSON) **5398**

MISSISSIPPI WEEKLY WEATHER & CROP REPORT (US) [05306630] **178**

MISSISSIPPI WILDLIFE (US/1044-0062) [19681856] **4874**

MISSISSIPPI WORKERS' COMPENSATION REPORTER (US/1052-7869) [21064337] 1691, **2888**

MISSISSIPPI'S BUSINESS POPULATION (US/0544-4969) [05589833] **695**

MISSISSIPPI'S BUSINESS (UNIVERSITY, MISS.) **CEASED.** (US/0026-6442) [01585521] **695**

MISSISSIPPI'S HEALTH (US) [01758375] **4791**

MISSOULIAN (MISSOULA, MONT. 1961) (US/0746-4495) [10049426] **5693**

MISSOURI. ABANDONED MINE LAND SECTION *See* MISSOURI'S ABANDONED MINED LANDS ... ANNUAL REPORT **2146**

MISSOURI ACADEMY OF SCIENCE *See* OCCASIONAL PAPER - MISSOURI ACADEMY OF SCIENCE **5135**

MISSOURI ACADEMY OF SCIENCE *See* TRANSACTIONS OF THE MISSOURI ACADEMY OF SCIENCE **5166**

MISSOURI AIRPORT DIRECTORY (US/0160-4562) [03672691] **28**

MISSOURI ALUMNUS (US/0745-0583) [06240369] **1102**

MISSOURI ARCHAEOLOGICAL SOCIETY QUARTERLY (US/0743-7641) [10665327] 2267, **275**

MISSOURI ARCHAEOLOGIST, THE (US/0076-9576) [01758405] **275**

MISSOURI AREA LABOR TRENDS (US/0148-4214) [03047001] **1691**

MISSOURI BAR ASSOCIATION *See* REPORT OF THE PROCEEDINGS OF THE ANNUAL MEETING OF THE ... MISSOURI BAR ASSOCIATION **3038**

MISSOURI BAR BULLETIN (US) [16915860] **3011**

MISSOURI BEEF CATTLEMAN (US/0192-3056) [04993228] **216**

MISSOURI BOTANICAL GARDEN *See* ANNALS OF THE MISSOURI BOTANICAL GARDEN **499**

MISSOURI BOTANICAL GARDEN BULLETIN (US/0026-6507) [02457743] **518**

MISSOURI C.H.P. IN RETROSPECT (US/0094-0429) [01793215] **4791**

MISSOURI CASES REPORTED IN SOUTH WESTERN REPORTER, SECOND SERIES (US/0745-7642) [04647028] **3011**

MISSOURI CENTER FOR HEALTH STATISTICS *See* MISSOURI VITAL STATISTICS **5333**

MISSOURI. COMMISSION ON HIGHER EDUCATION *See* ANNUAL REPORT TO THE GOVERNOR AND MEMBERS OF THE GENERAL ASSEMBLY - MISSOURI COMMISSION ON HIGHER EDUCATION **1809**

MISSOURI. COMMISSION ON HUMAN RIGHTS *See* REPORT - MISSOURI. COMMISSION ON HUMAN RIGHTS **4512**

MISSOURI COMPREHENSIVE STATE PLAN FOR DRUG ABUSE PREVENTION AND TREATMENT (US/0362-8388) [02349202] **1346**

MISSOURI CONSERVATIONIST (US/0026-6515) [01758407] **2198**

MISSOURI DECISIONS REPORTED IN SOUTH WESTERN REPORTER, SECOND SERIES *See* MISSOURI CASES REPORTED IN SOUTH WESTERN REPORTER, SECOND SERIES **3011**

MISSOURI DENTAL JOURNAL (JEFFERSON CITY, MO.) (US/0887-4646) [11821468] **1330**

MISSOURI. DEPT. OF CORRECTIONS. REPORT *See* BIENNIAL REPORT - MISSOURI DIVISION OF CORRECTIONS **3158**

MISSOURI. DEPT. OF EDUCATION *See* STATISTICS OF MISSOURI NONPUBLIC ELEMENTARY AND SECONDARY SCHOOLS **1798**

MISSOURI. DEPT. OF LABOR AND INDUSTRIAL RELATIONS *See* ANNUAL REPORT - MISSOURI. DEPT. OF LABOR AND INDUSTRIAL RELATIONS **1649**

MISSOURI. DEPT. OF MENTAL HEALTH *See* MENTAL HEALTH STATISTICS (JEFFERSON CITY) **4810**

MISSOURI. DEPT. OF MENTAL HEALTH *See* CONSOLIDATED PLAN / MISSOURI DEPARTMENT OF MENTAL HEALTH **4772**

MISSOURI. DEPT. OF MENTAL HEALTH *See* CONSOLIDATED PLAN. APPENDICES / MISSOURI DEPARTMENT OF MENTAL HEALTH **4772**

MISSOURI. DEPT. OF REVENUE *See* FINANCIAL REPORT OF THE MISSOURI DEPARTMENT OF REVENUE **4725**

MISSOURI. DEPT. OF SOCIAL SERVICES *See* MISSOURI TITLE XX PROPOSED COMPREHENSIVE SERVICE PLAN **5296**

MISSOURI. DEPT. OF SOCIAL SERVICES. DIVISION OF DATA PROCESSING *See* ANNUAL REPORT - DEPARTMENT OF SOCIAL SERVICES, DIVISION OF DATA PROCESSING (MISSOURI) **5272**

MISSOURI DIRECTORY OF MANUFACTURERS (1988) (US/0895-2469) [16521753] **3484**

MISSOURI. DISASTER PLANNING AND OPERATIONS OFFICE, CIVIL DEFENSE *See* NEWSLETTER - DISASTER OPERATIONS OFFICE, STATE OF MISSOURI **1073**

MISSOURI — Alphabetical Title Index

MISSOURI. DIVISION OF ALCOHOLISM AND DRUG ABUSE See MISSOURI STATE PLAN ON ALCOHOL AND DRUG ABUSE PREVENTION AND TREATMENT **1346**

MISSOURI. DIVISION OF ALCOHOLISM AND DRUG ABUSE See MISSOURI STATE PLAN FOR THE IMPLEMENTATION OF THE COMPREHENSIVE ALCOHOL ABUSE AND ALCOHOLISM PREVENTION, TREATMENT AND REHABILITATION ACT OF 1970 **1346**

MISSOURI. DIVISION OF BUDGET AND PLANNING See MISSOURI OVERALL PROGRAM DESIGN AND ANNUAL WORK PROGRAM **2828**

MISSOURI. DIVISION OF CORRECTIONS See BIENNIAL REPORT - MISSOURI DIVISION OF CORRECTIONS **3158**

MISSOURI. DIVISION OF EMPLOYMENT SECURITY See ANNUAL PLANNING INFORMATION FOR SPRINGFIELD SMSA **1646**

MISSOURI. DIVISION OF EMPLOYMENT SECURITY See ANNUAL PLANNING INFORMATION FOR COLUMBIA SMSA **1528**

MISSOURI. DIVISION OF EMPLOYMENT SECURITY See MISSOURI OCCUPATIONAL STAFFING PATTERNS OF SELECTED NON-MANUFACTURING INDUSTRIES SURVEYED **4206**

MISSOURI. DIVISION OF FAMILY SERVICES See FINAL COMPREHENSIVE ANNUAL SOCIAL SERVICE PROGRAM PLAN **5285**

MISSOURI. DIVISION OF FISHERIES See ABSTRACTS OF FISHERY RESEARCH REPORTS **2293**

MISSOURI. DIVISION OF INSURANCE See ANNUAL REPORT AND STATISTICAL DATA - DIVISION OF INSURANCE (MISSOURI) **2897**

MISSOURI. DIVISION OF MENTAL HEALTH See MISSOURI COMPREHENSIVE STATE PLAN FOR DRUG ABUSE PREVENTION AND TREATMENT **1346**

MISSOURI ECONOMIC INDICATORS (US/0195-6159) [03159081] **1574**

MISSOURI. ELECTIONS COMMISSION See ANNUAL REPORT - MISSOURI ELECTIONS COMMISSION **4628**

MISSOURI EMPLOYMENT LAW LETTER (US/1054-6375) [22923844] **3152**

MISSOURI ENTERPRISE (US/0279-3261) [07759878] **2539**

MISSOURI ENVIRONMENTAL COMPLIANCE UPDATE (US) [30332404] **3114**

MISSOURI ENVIRONMENTAL LAW LETTER (US/1057-4166) [24033372] **3114**

MISSOURI FACTS (US/1056-9596) [23903927] **2747**

MISSOURI FARMER See TODAY'S FARMER **141**

MISSOURI FB NEWS (US/0026-6574) [04055566] **109**

MISSOURI FOLKLORE SOCIETY JOURNAL (US/0731-2946) [05980419] **2322**

MISSOURI FOREST PEST REPORT (US/0739-893X) [06350545] **2388**

MISSOURI GAME & FISH (US/0889-3799) [13865859] **4875**

MISSOURI. GENERAL ASSEMBLY. COMMITTEE ON LEGISLATIVE RESEARCH See CLASSIFIED INDEX, TRULY AGREED TO AND FINALLY PASSED HOUSE AND SENATE BILLS **2951**

MISSOURI. GENERAL ASSEMBLY. COMMITTEE ON STATE FISCAL AFFAIRS See STATUTORY SALARIES, MISSOURI STATE OFFICIALS **4689**

MISSOURI. GENERAL ASSEMBLY. COMMITTEE ON STATE FISCAL AFFAIRS See APPROPRIATIONS REPORT / COMMITTEE ON STATE FISCAL AFFAIRS **4711**

MISSOURI. GENERAL ASSEMBLY. COMMITTEE ON STATE FISCAL AFFAIRS. APPROPRIATION SUMMARY See APPROPRIATIONS REPORT / COMMITTEE ON STATE FISCAL AFFAIRS **4711**

MISSOURI GEOCODE LIST (US/0196-5239) [05826088] **2569**

MISSOURI. GOVERNOR'S ADVISORY COUNCIL ON COMPREHENSIVE HEALTH PLANNING See MISSOURI C.H.P. IN RETROSPECT **4791**

● MISSOURI HEALTH CARE IN PERSPECTIVE (US/1065-4275) [26605806] **4791**

MISSOURI HEALTH MANPOWER (US/0196-5247) [03789532] **3915**

MISSOURI HIGHWAY AND TRANSPORTATION COMMISSION See ANNUAL REPORT / MISSOURI HIGHWAY & TRANSPORTATION COMMISSION **5438**

MISSOURI HISTORICAL REVIEW (US/0026-6582) [01758409] **2747**

MISSOURI HOME HEALTH AGENCY PROFILES (US) [16751691] **4791**

MISSOURI HOSPITAL PROFILES (US/0192-6543) [04991163] **3789**

MISSOURI IN PERSPECTIVE (LAWRENCE, KAN.) (US/1065-5549) [26657344] **5333**

MISSOURI JEWISH POST & OPINION CEASED. (US/0746-1291) [09787945] **2268**

MISSOURI JOURNAL OF HEALTH, PHYSICAL EDUCATION, RECREATION AND DANCE (US/1058-6288) [13765160] **4905, 1857**

MISSOURI JOURNAL OF MATHEMATICAL SCIENCES (US/0899-6180) [18160132] **3523**

MISSOURI JOURNAL OF RESEARCH IN MUSIC EDUCATION (US/0085-350X) [02844806] **1764, 4131**

MISSOURI JUDICIAL REPORT (US) [09614697] **3011**

MISSOURI. LAND RECLAMATION COMMISSION See BIENNIAL REPORT - LAND RECLAMATION COMMISSION **2225**

MISSOURI LAW FINDER (US) [10160444] **3011**

MISSOURI LAW REVIEW (US/0026-6604) [01758411] **3011**

MISSOURI LEGAL DIRECTORY, THE (US) [06239165] **3011**

MISSOURI LIBRARIES (US/0899-6458) [18161083] **3231**

MISSOURI MAGAZINE (SAINT LOUIS, MO.) (US/1047-6830) [20510570] **2539**

MISSOURI MANUFACTURERS REGISTER (US/0893-2816) [15472129] **3484**

MISSOURI MEDICINE (US/0026-6620) [01758413] **3617**

MISSOURI MINERAL INDUSTRY NEWS See MISSOURI MINERAL NEWS **1442**

MISSOURI MINERAL NEWS (US/0091-052X) [01785461] **2146, 1442**

MISSOURI MUNICIPAL REVIEW (US/0026-6647) [01758414] **4666**

MISSOURI, NEW AND EXPANDING INDUSTRY (US/0898-3925) [16988715] **1618**

MISSOURI NEWS (US/0746-827X) [10306876] **4978**

MISSOURI NURSE, THE (US/0026-6655) [04055570] **3861**

MISSOURI NURSING HOME AND RESIDENTIAL CARE FACILTIY [I.E. FACILITY] PROFILES / MISSOURI DEPARTMENT OF HEALTH, STATE CENTER FOR HEALTH STATISTICS (US) [13549336] **3789**

MISSOURI NUTRITION EDUCATION & TRAINING PROGRAM (US) [07850937] **4194**

MISSOURI OCCUPATIONAL STAFFING PATTERNS OF SELECTED NON-MANUFACTURING INDUSTRIES SURVEYED (US/0148-1851) [03269966] **4206**

MISSOURI. OFFICE OF ADMINISTRATION. DIVISION OF ACCOUNTING See COMPREHENSIVE ANNUAL FINANCIAL REPORT, STATE OF MISSOURI **4718**

MISSOURI. OFFICE OF ADMINISTRATION. DIVISION OF ACCOUNTING See INDEX FOR FISCAL YEAR APPROPRIATIONS **4731**

MISSOURI. OFFICE OF STATE COURTS ADMINISTRATOR See MISSOURI JUDICIAL REPORT **3011**

MISSOURI. OFFICE OF THE PUBLIC COUNSEL See REPORT OF THE OFFICE OF THE PUBLIC COUNSEL, STATE OF MISSOURI **4681**

MISSOURI. OFFICE OF THE SECRETARY OF STATE See ANNUAL STATISTICAL REPORT OF EXPENDITURES MADE IN CONNECTION WITH ELECTIONS, THE **4501**

MISSOURI. OFFICE OF THE SECRETARY OF STATE See MISSOURI REGISTER **3011**

MISSOURI OVERALL PROGRAM DESIGN AND ANNUAL WORK PROGRAM (US/0149-9610) [03148731] **2828**

MISSOURI PHARMACISTS (US/0026-6663) [04055605] **4316**

MISSOURI PHILOLOGICAL ASSOCIATION See PUBLICATIONS OF THE MISSOURI PHILOLOGICAL ASSOCIATION **3313**

MISSOURI POPULATION ESTIMATES, BY COUNTY, BY AGE, BY SEX (US/0734-032X) [03932260] **4554**

MISSOURI PRESS NEWS (US/0026-6671) [02277679] **4817**

MISSOURI. PUBLIC DEFENDER COMMISSION See MISSOURI'S PUBLIC DEFENDER AND APPOINTED COUNSEL PROGRAMS **3108**

MISSOURI PUBLIC SERVICE COMMISSION See REGULATED ELECTRIC STUDY (JEFFERSON CITY) **4679**

MISSOURI PUBLIC SERVICE COMMISSION. OFFICE OF ECONOMIC RESEARCH See WATER INDUSTRY STATISTICAL PROFILE, A **5549**

MISSOURI QUERIES (US/1041-6552) [16647068] **2461**

MISSOURI REGISTER (US/0149-2942) [03457432] **3011**

MISSOURI RESOURCE REVIEW (US) [15171929] **2198**

MISSOURI REVIEW, THE (US/0191-1961) [04225276] **3412**

MISSOURI RIVER BASIN COMMISSION See STATUS OF ELECTRIC POWER IN THE MISSOURI RIVER BASIN **2082**

MISSOURI RIVER BASIN REGION, WATER RESOURCES RESEARCH INSTITUTES (US) [03787453] **5536**

MISSOURI RIVER BASIN, STATE AND FEDERAL WATER AND RELATED LAND RESOURCE PROGRAMS (US/0161-4118) [03915817] **2093**

MISSOURI RULES OF COURT, STATE AND FEDERAL (US/0732-6556) [04918163] **3141**

MISSOURI RURALIST (US/0026-668X) [04152073] **109**

MISSOURI SCHOOL MUSIC MAGAZINE (US) [10851836] **4131**

MISSOURI SCHOOLS (US/0745-1237) [03395621] **1764**

MISSOURI STATE ECONOMY IN REVIEW (US) [04567425] **1574**

MISSOURI STATE EXECUTIVE BRANCH DIRECTORY (US) [03154401] **4666**

MISSOURI STATE GENEALOGICAL ASSOCIATION JOURNAL (US/0747-5667) [08147765] **2461**

MISSOURI STATE HEALTH PLAN (US) [06054274] **4791**

MISSOURI STATE PLAN FOR HIGH BLOOD PRESSURE CONTROL (US/0742-1354) [06931184] **3708**

MISSOURI STATE PLAN FOR THE IMPLEMENTATION OF THE COMPREHENSIVE ALCOHOL ABUSE AND ALCOHOLISM PREVENTION, TREATMENT AND REHABILITATION ACT OF 1970 (US/0148-7752) [03367686] **1346**

MISSOURI STATE PLAN ON ALCOHOL AND DRUG ABUSE PREVENTION AND TREATMENT (US/0273-205X) [06993775] **1346**

MISSOURI. STATEWIDE HEALTH COORDINATING COUNCIL See MISSOURI STATE HEALTH PLAN **4791**

MISSOURI. SUPREME COURT See MISSOURI CASES REPORTED IN SOUTH WESTERN REPORTER, SECOND SERIES **3011**

MISSOURI TEAMSTER (US/0026-6728) [04055621] **1691**

MISSOURI TITLE XX PROPOSED COMPREHENSIVE SERVICE PLAN (US) [08134142] **5296**

MISSOURI UNION LIST OF SERIAL PUBLICATIONS (US/0164-0496) [04572647] **3231**

MISSOURI VALLEY ECONOMIC ASSOCIATION See JOURNAL OF ECONOMICS **1499**

MISSOURI VALLEY TIMES-NEWS (US) [16750029] **5671**

MISSOURI VETERINARIAN See VETERINARY MEDICAL REVIEW (COLUMBIA, MO.) **5525**

MISSOURI VITAL STATISTICS (US/0098-1974) [02241063] **5333**

MISSOURI WATER AND SEWERAGE CONFERENCE See MISSOURI WATER AND WASTEWATER CONFERENCE **5536**

MISSOURI WATER AND WASTEWATER CONFERENCE (US) 2236, **5536**

MISSOURI WATER QUALITY REPORT (US/0195-752X) [04018681] **1416**

MISSOURI WILDLIFE (US) 2198, **2218**

MISSOURI WORKERS' COMP LAW REPORTER (US) **3087**

MISSOURI ZIP+4 STATE DIRECTORY / PREPARED BY THE ADDRESS INFORMATION SYSTEMS DIVISION, DELIVERY SERVICES DEPARTMENT (US) [11636316] **1145**

MISSOURI'S ABANDONED MINED LANDS ... ANNUAL REPORT (US) [14993575] **2146**

MISSOURI'S ENVIRONMENT (US) [04172125] **2177**

MISSOURI'S PUBLIC DEFENDER AND APPOINTED COUNSEL PROGRAMS (US) [06281839] **3108**

MISTER X (CN/0827-3812) [12782133] **4863**

MISTLETOE LEAVES (US) [04659147] **2747**

MISTRAL (CN/0318-2088) [02441817] **3466**

Alphabetical Title Index   MITTEILUNGEN

MISUL CHARYO (KO/0540-4568) [04146213] **374**

MISUL SEGYE (KO) [11750365] **358**

MISURE CRITICHE (IT/0392-6397) [05278224] **3412**

MIT KELL TUDNI AZ ... EVI NEPGAZDASAGI TERVROL? (HU) [19609708] **1574**

MIT PRESS SERIES IN HEALTH AND PUBLIC POLICY (US/0277-8637) [07566464] **5296**

MIT PRESS SERIES IN INFORMATION SYSTEMS (US/0891-4702) [14871924] **1195**

MIT PRESS SERIES IN SIGNAL PROCESSING, OPTIMIZATION, AND CONTROL, THE (US/0885-9434) [05344425] **4412**

MIT PRESS SERIES ON THE REGULATION OF ECONOMIC ACTIVITY (US) [07885081] **1505**

MIT REPORT (CAMBRIDGE, MASS. : 1981), THE *CEASED.* (US/0744-2505) [08134490] **5129**

MIT WORKING PAPERS IN LINGUISTICS (US/1049-1058) [06680070] **3302**

MITA GAKKAI ZASSHI (JA/0026-6760) [23076916] **1505**

MITA SHOGAKU KENKYU / KEIO GIJUKU DAIGAKU SHOGAKKAI (JA) [02264272] **695**

MITARBEIT, DIE *CEASED.* (GW/0026-6779) [01714141] **4978**

MITCHELL COLLISION ESTIMATING AND REPAIR MANUAL. DOMESTIC VEHICLE DIMENSIONS. VDD (US) **5419**

MITCHELL COLLISION ESTIMATING AND REPAIR MANUAL. IMPORT VEHICLE DIMENSIONS. VDI (US) **5419**

MITCHELL COUNTY PRESS-NEWS, THE (US/0746-7540) [10253565] **5671**

MITCHELL DAILY REPUBLIC (US) **5744**

MITCHELL DOMESTIC LIGHT TRUCKS AND VANS SERVICE AND REPAIR (US) [23671432] **5387**

MITCHELL GUIDE. NEW YORK CITY, THE (US/0748-8556) [10195652] **5296**

MITCHELL GUIDE TO FOUNDATIONS, CORPORATIONS, AND THEIR MANAGERS : NEW JERSEY, THE (US) [18571221] **4338**

MITCHELL GUIDE TO PROFESSIONAL ESTIMATING (US) **5419**

MITCHELL MANUALS, INC *See* AUTOMOTIVE AIR CONDITIONING AND HEATING SERVICE MANUAL : BOOK SUPPLEMENT **5406**

MITCHELL MANUALS, INC *See* HEAVY TRUCK COLLISION ESTIMATING GUIDE: CHEVROLET, DIAMOND REO, DODGE, FORD, FREIGHTLINER, GMC, INTERNATIONAL, KENWORTH, MACK, PETERBILT, WHITE **5383**

MITCHELL-NOBLE OFFICIAL CATALOG OF BUREAU PRECANCELS *See* NOBLE OFFICIAL CATALOG OF BUREAU PRECANCELS, THE **2786**

MITCHELL SERVICE AND REPAIR MANUAL. ANNUAL DATA: TUNE-UP / ELECTRICAL / MECHANICAL (US) **5419**

MITCHELL TECH SERVICE BULLETIN (US/8755-4453) [09506734] **5419**

MITCHELL TECHNICAL SERVICE BULLETIN, COLLISION (US/0276-2382) [07325936] **5419**

MITCHELL TRIBUNE, THE (US) [13451335] **5665**

MITEKUFAT HAEVEN (IS) **275**

MITGLIEDER DER DEUTSCHEN GESELLSCHAFT FUR INNERE MEDIZIN (GW) [02563820] **3617**

MITGLIEDER-VERZEICHNIS / DEUTSCHE ORIENT-GESELLSCHAFT (GW) [05698392] **2659**

MITGLIEDER-VERZEICHNIS MIT UBERSICHT DER ARBEITS-, LANDES-, REGIONAL- UND STADTGRUPPEN / DEUTSCHE GESELLSCHAFT FUER HERPETOLOGIE UND TERRARIENKUNDE E.V (GW) [27972962] **3617**

MITGLIEDERVERZEICHNIS (GW) [01785968] **1442, 1388**

MITGLIEDERVERZEICHNIS DER GESELLSCHAFT FUER SCHLESWIG-HOLSTEINISCHE GESCHICHTE (GW) [12086855] **1574**

MITGLIEDERVERZEICHNIS - GESELLSCHAFT FUR NUCLEARMEDIZIN (GW) [03622326] **3944**

MITHILA-BHARATI (II) [05260289] **3302**

MITIGATION AND ADAPTATION STRATEGIES FOR GLOBAL CHANGE (NE/1381-2386) **4482**

MITOCHONDRIA / ISSUED MONTHLY BY UNIVERSITY OF SHEFFIELD BIOMEDICAL INFORMATION SERVICE (UK/0142-8217) [17653842] **491, 3617**

MITRE CORPORATION *See* MITRE TECHNICAL REPORT **5129**

MITRE TECHNICAL REPORT (US/0364-3972) [02589611] **5129**

MITROPOLIA ARDEALULUI (RM/1013-4204) [I10134204] **5032**

MITROPOLIA MOLDOVEI SI SUCEVEI : REVISTA OFICIALA A ARHIEPISCOPIEI IASILOR SI A EPISCOPIEI ROMANULUI SI HUSILOR (RM) [23064290] **5032**

MITSPEH (IS) [01793835] **2659**

MITSUBACHI KAGAKU / HONEYBEE SCIENCE (JA/0388-2217) [07431206] **109**

MITSUBISHI DENKI GIHO (JA/0369-2302) [02448681] **2073**

MITSUBISHI ELECTRIC ADVANCE (JA/0386-5096) [14206760] **2073**

MITSUBISHI GENSHIRYOKU GIHO (JA/0388-3396) [10343824] **5129**

MITSUBISHI JUKO GIHO (JA/0387-2432) [10342551] **5129**

MITSUBISHI KEIZAI KENKYUJO *See* MERI'S MONTHLY CIRCULAR **1574**

MITSUI ZOSEN GIHO (JA/0026-6825) [09590818] **1988**

MITTEILUNG (DEUTSCHE FORSCHUNGSGEMEINSCHAFT. KOMMISSION FUR WASSERFORSCHUNG) (GW/0933-2022) [16166936] **5536**

MITTEILUNGEN (GW) [02828586] **621**

MITTEILUNGEN (GW) [20737548] **28**

MITTEILUNGEN (GW) [29329418] **3231**

MITTEILUNGEN ARBEITSGEMEINSCHAFT FUER KLINISCHE NEPHROLOGIE (GW) **3617**

MITTEILUNGEN - ARBEITSGEMEINSCHAFT FUR JUGENDHILFE (GW) [01787981] **5296**

MITTEILUNGEN - ARBEITSGEMEINSCHAFT FUR JURISTISCHES BIBLIOTHEKS- (GERMANY) (GW) [01784667] **3011**

MITTEILUNGEN AUS DEM AUSSCHUSS FUER PULVERMETALLURGIE (GW/0722-7736) [09408706] **4012**

MITTEILUNGEN AUS DEM GEBIETE DER LEBENSMITTELUNTERSUCHUNG UND HYGIENE (SZ/0026-6841) [01586175] **491**

MITTEILUNGEN AUS DEM GEOLOGISCH-PALAEONTOLOGISCHEN INSTITUT DER UNIVERSITAET HAMBURG (GW/0072-1115) [C1751718] **1388**

MITTEILUNGEN AUS DEM HAMBURGISCHEN ZOOLOGISCHEN MUSEUM UND INSTITUT (GW/0072-9612) [03251769] **5591**

MITTEILUNGEN AUS DEM INSTITUT FUER ALLGEMEINE BOTANIK HAMBURG (GW/0344-5615) [04507832] **518**

MITTEILUNGEN AUS DEM INSTITUT FUER SEEFISCHEREI DER BUNDESFORSCHUNGSANSTALT FUER FISCHEREI (GW/0436-6425) [01973234] **2308**

MITTEILUNGEN AUS DEM MAX-PLANCK-INSTITUT FUER AERONOMIE (GW/0075-9546) [01964892] **1431**

MITTEILUNGEN AUS DEM MAX-PLANCK-INSTITUT FUER STROMUNGSFORSCHUNG UND DER AERODYNAMISCHEN VERSUCHSANSTALT (GW/0374-1257) [05693653] **28**

MITTEILUNGEN AUS DEM MUSEUM FUER VOLKERKUNDE HAMBURG (GW/0072-9469) [15743646] **241**

MITTEILUNGEN AUS DEM MUSEUM FUER VOLKERKUNDE ZU LEIPZIG (GE) [02448273] **241**

MITTEILUNGEN AUS DEM ZOOLOGISCHEN MUSEUM IN BERLIN (GW/0373-8493) [09938158] **5591**

MITTEILUNGEN AUS DER ARBEITSMARKT- UND BERUFSFORSCHUNG (GW/0340-3254) [05230256] **1691**

MITTEILUNGEN AUS DER BIOLOGISCHEN BUNDESANSTALT FUER LAND- UND FORSTWIRTSCHAFT, BERLIN-DAHLEM (GW/0067-5849) [09813792] **2388**

MITTEILUNGEN DER ABTEILUNG FUER GEOLOGIE, PALAONTOLOGIE UND BERGBAU AM LANDESMUSEUM JOANNEUM (AU) [05352122] **1388**

MITTEILUNGEN DER ABTEILUNG FUER GEOLOGIE, PALAONTOLOGIE UND BERGBAU AM LANDESMUSEUM JOANNEUM. SH (AU/0379-1432) [03250021] **4228, 1388**

MITTEILUNGEN DER ABTEILUNG FUER MINERALOGIE AM LANDESMUSEUM JOANNEUM (AU/0257-4217) [15500850] **1442**

MITTEILUNGEN DER ANTHROPOLOGISCHEN GESELLSCHAFT IN WIEN (AU/0066-4693) [01719321] **241**

MITTEILUNGEN DER ANTIQUARISCHEN GESELLSCHAFT IN ZURICH (SZ) [01588165] **2699**

MITTEILUNGEN DER ARBEITSGEMEINSCHAFT FUER MITTELRHEINISCHE MUSIKGESCHICHTE (GW) [06868270] **4131**

MITTEILUNGEN DER ARBEITSSTELLE FUR ETHNOMEDIZIN (GW) [06479898] **3617**

MITTEILUNGEN DER ASTRONOMISCHEN GESELLSCHAFT (GW/0374-1958) [01845963] **397**

MITTEILUNGEN DER BAYERISCHE (GW/0077-2070) [01793648] **1388, 4228**

MITTEILUNGEN DER BERLINER GESELLSCHAFT FUER ANTHROPOLOGIE, ETHNOLOGIE UND URGESCHICHTE (GW/0178-7896) [04540955] **241**

MITTEILUNGEN DER BOTANISCHEN STAATSSAMMLUNG MUNCHEN (GW/0006-8179) [01590119] **518**

MITTEILUNGEN DER BUNDESFORSCHUNGSANSTALT FUER FORST- UND HOLZWIRTSCHAFT REINBEK BEI HAMBURG (GW/0368-8798) [01763649] **2388**

MITTEILUNGEN DER DEUTSCHEN BODENKUNDLICHE GESELLSCHAFT (GW/0343-107X) [04658597] **178**

MITTEILUNGEN DER DEUTSCHEN GESELLSCHAFT FUER ALGEMEINE UND ANGEWANDTE ENTOMOLOGIE (GW/0344-9084) [10169606] **5612**

MITTEILUNGEN DER DEUTSCHEN GESELLSCHAFT FUER MUSIK DES ORIENTS (GW/0417-2051) [01792361] **4131**

MITTEILUNGEN DER DEUTSCHEN ORIENT-GESELLSCHAFT ZU BERLIN (GW/0342-118X) [01268274] **275, 2659**

MITTEILUNGEN DER DEUTSCHEN PATENTANWALTE (GW/0026-6884) [I00266884] **1306**

MITTEILUNGEN DER EIDGENOSSISCHEN FORSCHUNGSANSTALT FUER WALD, SCHNEE UND LANDSCHAFT (SZ/1016-3158) [24438463] **2424, 2388**

MITTEILUNGEN DER ENTOMOLOGISCHEN GESELLSCHAFT BASEL (SW) [02945088] **5612**

MITTEILUNGEN DER FORSTLICHEN BUNDES-VERSUCHSANSTALT WIEN (AU/0374-9037) [08840361] **2388**

MITTEILUNGEN DER FORSTLICHEN VERSUCHS- UND FORSCHUNGSANSTALT BADEN-WRTTEMBERG (GW/0178-3165) [03350430] **2388**

MITTEILUNGEN DER GEODATISCHEN INSTITUTE DER TECHNISCHEN UNIVERSITAT GRAZ (AU/0255-3074) [09356325] **1388**

MITTEILUNGEN DER GEOGRAPHISCHEN GESELLSCHAFT IN HAMBURG (GW/0374-9061) [01604285] **2569**

MITTEILUNGEN DER GEOGRAPHISCHEN GESELLSCHAFT IN MUNCHEN (GW/0072-0941) [01570672] **2569**

MITTEILUNGEN DER GESELLSCHAFT FUER PFLANZENBAUWISSENSCHAFTEN (GW/0934-5116) [I09345116] **518**

MITTEILUNGEN DER GESELLSCHAFT FUER SALZBURGER LANDESKUNDE (AU) [02408140] **2670**

MITTEILUNGEN DER GESELLSCHAFT FUER VERGLEICHENDE KUNSTFORSCHUNG IN WIEN (AU) [08882772] **358**

MITTEILUNGEN DER HANS PFITZNER-GESELLSCHAFT (GW/0440-2863) [02489369] **4131**

MITTEILUNGEN DER INTERNATIONALEN STIFTUNG MOZARTEUM (AU/0541-2331) [04595607] **4131**

MITTEILUNGEN DER KARL-MAY-GESELLSCHAFT (GW/0941-7842) [I09417842] **3412**

MITTEILUNGEN DER MATHEMATISCHEN GESELLSCHAFT IN HAMBURG (GW/0340-4358) [06757647] **3523**

MITTEILUNGEN DER MUNCHNER ENTOMOLOGISCHEN GESELLSCHAFT (GW/0340-4943) [01645059] **5591**

MITTEILUNGEN DER OSTERREICHICHEN NUMISMATISCHEN GESELLSCHAFT (AU/0029-9359) [I00299359] **2781**

MITTEILUNGEN DER OSTERREICHISCHEN GALERIE (AU/0083-615X) [01640236] **358**

MITTEILUNGEN DER OSTERREICHISCHEN GEOGRAPHISCHEN GESELLSCHAFT (AU) [05357492] **2569**

MITTEILUNGEN DER OSTERREICHISCHEN GEOLOGISCHEN GESELLSCHAFT (AU/0378-8199) [04480155] **1388**

MITTEILUNGEN — Alphabetical Title Index

MITTEILUNGEN DER OSTERREICHISCHEN GESELLSCHAFT FUER MUSIKWISSENSCHAFT (AU) [01794435] **4131**

MITTEILUNGEN DER SCHWEIZERISCHEN ENTOMOLOGISCHEN GESELLSCHAFT (SZ/0036-7575) [01586648] **5612**

MITTEILUNGEN : DER STUDIENGEMEINSCHAFT FUER GESCHICHTE DER EVANGELISCH METHODISTISCHEN KIRCHE (GW) **5064**

MITTEILUNGEN DER VERSUCHSANSTALT FUER PILZANBAU DER LANDWIRTSCHAFTSKAMMER RHEINLAND, KREFELD-GROSSHUTTENHOF (GW/0171-2446) [24905211] 2218, **2388**

MITTEILUNGEN DER VERSUCHSANSTALT FUER WASSERBAU, HYDROLOGIE UND GLAZIOLOGIE (SZ/0374-0056) [02185870] **1416**

MITTEILUNGEN DER VERSUCHSSTATION FUER DAS GARUNGSGEWERBE IN WIEN (AU) [02720916] **1027**

MITTEILUNGEN DES AMTES FUR STANDARDISIERUNG, MESSWESEN UND WARENPRUFUNG (GW) [02241116] **5129**

MITTEILUNGEN DES BAYERISCHEN NOTARVEREINS, DER NOTARKASSE UND DER LANDESNOTARKAMMER BAYERN (GW/0941-4193) [I09414193] **2519**

MITTEILUNGEN DES DEUTSCHEN ARCHAEOLOGISCHEN INSTITUTS, ROEMISCHE ABTEILUNG (GW/0342-1287) [04820596] **275**

MITTEILUNGEN DES DEUTSCHEN ARCHAEOLOGISCHEN INSTITUTS (GW/0342-1279) [03693390] **275**

MITTEILUNGEN DES DEUTSCHEN ARCHAOLOGISCHEN INSTITUTS, ATHENISCHE ABTEILUNG (GW/0342-1295) [08426386] **275**

MITTEILUNGEN DES DEUTSCHEN ARCHAEOLOGISCHEN INSTITUTS, ATHENISCHE ABTEILUNG (GW) [01565503] **275**

MITTEILUNGEN DES DEUTSCHEN GERMANISTENVERBANDES (GW/0418-9426) [01566482] **1764**

MITTEILUNGEN DES HISTORISCHEN VEREINS DER PFALZ (GW/0073-2680) [01696248] **2699**

MITTEILUNGEN DES INSTITUTS FUER OESTERREICHISCHE GESCHICHTSFORSCHUNG. ERGAENZUNGSBAND (AU) [06316027] **2699**

MITTEILUNGEN DES INSTITUTS FUER OSTERREICHISCHE GESCHICHTSFORSCHUNG (AU/0073-8484) [18544072] **2699**

MITTEILUNGEN DES KREMSER STADTARCHIVS (AU/0452-7070) [04067898] **2699**

MITTEILUNGEN DES KUNSTHISTORISCHES INSTITUTES FLORENZ (IT/0342-1201) [01569388] **358**

MITTEILUNGEN DES NATURWISSENSCHAFTLICHEN VEREINES FUER STEIERMARK (AU/0369-1055) [01759521] **5129**

MITTEILUNGEN DES OBEROSTERREICHISCHEN LANDESARCHIVS (AU/0259-4137) [01814904] **2699**

MITTEILUNGEN DES OBSTBAUVERSUCHSRINGES DES ALTEN LANDES (GW/0178-2916) [05300746] **2424**

MITTEILUNGEN DES OSTERREICHISCHEN STAATSARCHIVS (AU) [01518883] **2482**

MITTEILUNGEN DES SONDERFORSCHUNGSBEREICHS 79 FUER WASSERFORSCHUNG IM KUSTENBEREICH DER TECHNISCHEN UNIVERSITAT HANNOVER (GW/0340-7098) [02813437] **1452**

MITTEILUNGEN DES SUDETENDEUTSCHEN ARCHIVS (GW) [05049699] **2699**

MITTEILUNGEN DES VEREINIGUNG SCHWEIZERISCHER VERSICHERUNGSMATHEMATIKER (SZ/0042-3815) [09372834] 3523, **2888**

MITTEILUNGEN DES VEREINS DEUTSCHER EMAILFACHLEUTE E.V. (1990) (GW/0938-9865) [I09389865] **4224**

MITTEILUNGEN DES VEREINS DEUTSCHER EMAILFACHLEUTE E.V. UND DES DEUTSCHEN EMAIL ZENTRUSM E.V (GW/0723-886X) [07972709] **2592**

MITTEILUNGEN DES VEREINS FUER FORSTLICHE STANDORTSKUNDE UND FORSTPFLANZENZUCHTUNG (GW/0506-7049) [I05067049] **2388**

MITTEILUNGEN DES VEREINS FUR GESCHICHTE DER STADT NURNBERG (US/0083-5579) [15686873] **2623**

MITTEILUNGEN - DEUTSCHE AKADEMIE FUER STADTEBAU UND LANDESPLANUNG (GW/0011-9822) [04870075] **2828**

MITTEILUNGEN - DEUTSCHE FORSCHUNGSGESELLSCHAFT FUER DRUCK- UND REPRODUKTIONSTECHNIK E.V (GW/0175-6869) [01756869] **4566**

MITTEILUNGEN - DEUTSCHE GESELLSCHAFT FUR PHARMAKOLOGIE UND TOXIKOLOGIE (GW/0934-4640) [I09344640] 3982, **4316**

MITTEILUNGEN (DEUTSCHER VEREIN FUR VERMESSUNGSWESEN. LAANDESVEREIN HESSEN) See DVW HESSEN MITTEILUNGEN **2022**

MITTEILUNGEN FU BERLIN : AMTSBLATT DER FREIEN UNIVERSITAT BERLIN (GW/0723-0745) [06931715] **1093**

MITTEILUNGEN FUER DIE VIEH- UND FLEISCHWIRTSCHAFT (GW) **216**

MITTEILUNGEN - GESELLSCHAFT DEUTSCHER CHEMIKER, FACHGRUPPE GESCHICHTE DER CHEMIE (GW/0934-8506) [I09348506] **986**

MITTEILUNGEN / GESELLSCHAFT FUER ANGEWANDTE MATHEMATIK UND MECHANIK (GW) [26336228] 4429, **3523**

MITTEILUNGEN / HANDELSKAMMER HAMBURG See HAMBURGER WIRTSCHAFT : ZEITSCHRIFT DER HANDELSKAMMER HAMBURG **838**

MITTEILUNGEN (IFO-INSTITUT FUR WIRTSCHAFTSFORSCHUNG. ABTEILUNG ENTWICKLUNGSLANDER) (GW) [07754203] **1574**

MITTEILUNGEN - INSTITUT FUER BAUTECHNIK (GW/0172-3006) [I01723006] **621**

MITTEILUNGEN - INTERNATIONALEN VEREINIGUNG FUER THEORETISCHE UND ANGEWANDTE LIMNOLOGIE (GW/0538-4680) [01689404] **1416**

MITTEILUNGEN KLOSTERNEUBURG : REBE UND WEIN, OBSTBAU UND FRUCHTEVERWERTUNG (AU/0007-5922) [06411795] 178, **2369**

MITTEILUNGEN - LEICHTWEISS-INSTITUT FUER WASSERBAU DER TECHNISCHEN UNIVERSITAT BRAUNSCHWEIG (GW/0343-1223) [06933930] **2093**

MITTEILUNGEN - MUSEUM FOLKWANG ESSEN (GW/0935-2422) [I09352422] **4091**

MITTEILUNGEN - MUSEUM FUER VOLKERKUNDE ZU LEIPZIG (GW) [03929025] **4091**

MITTEILUNGEN / NAMIBIA WISSENSCHAFTLICHE GESELLSCHAFT (SX) [23449048] **4168**

MITTEILUNGEN OESTERREICHISCHEN GESELLSCHAFT TROPENMEDIZIN UND PARASITOLOGIE (AU) **3799**

MITTEILUNGEN (OSTERREICHISCHER ALPENVEREIN (1950)- (AU) [09055826] **4875**

MITTEILUNGEN (OSTERREICHISCHER ALPENVEREIN (1950)-. AKADEMISCHE SEKTION) See MITTEILUNGEN (OSTERREICHISCHER ALPENVEREIN (1950)- **4875**

MITTEILUNGEN / OSTERREICHISCHES GETRANKE INSTITUT (AU) [24233144] **5129**

MITTEILUNGEN - PTB (GW/0030-834X) [11905671] 4412, **5129**

MITTEILUNGEN - RHEINISCH-WESTFALISCHES INSTITUT FEUR WIRTSCHAFTSFORSCHUNG ESSEN See RWI-MITTEILUNGEN **3637**

MITTEILUNGEN UND FORSCHUNGSBEITRAGE DER CUSANUS-GESELLSCHAFT (GW/0590-451X) [01565717] **4353**

MITTEILUNGSBLATT / CHEMISCHE GESELLSCHAFT DER DEUTSCHEN DEMOKRATISCHEN REPUBLIK (GW/0411-8987) [07446119] **986**

MITTEILUNGSBLATT DER ARBEITSGEMEINSCHAFT KATHOLISCH-THEOLOGISCHER BIBLIOTHEKEN, AKTHB (GW/0177-8358) [I01778358] **3231**

MITTEILUNGSBLATT DER BUNDESANSTALT FUER FLEISCHFORSCHUNG, KULMBACH (GW/0721-099X) [I0721099X] **216**

MITTEILUNGSBLATT DER BUNDESANSTALT FUER WASSERBAU (GW/0572-5801) [07665292] **2093**

MITTEILUNGSBLATT DES AMTES FUR SCHULE (GW) [05738384] **1764**

MITTEILUNGSBLATT DES BUNDES DER EVANGELISCHEN KIRCHEN IN DER DEUTSCHEN DEMOKRATISCHEN REPUBLIK (GW) [05289224] **5064**

MITTEILUNGSBLATT / GESELLSCHAFT DEUTSCHER CHEMIKER, FACHGRUPPE CHEMIE-INFORMATION (GW/0178-4927) [25996173] **986**

MITTEILUNGSBLATT - MUSEUMSVERBAND FUER NIEDERSACHSEN UND BREMEN E.V (GW/0931-4857) [I09314857] **4091**

MITTEILUNGSBLATT - VERBAND DER BIBLIOTHEKEN DES LANDES NORDRHEIN WESTFALEN (GW/0042-3629) [02269175] **3232**

MITTELLATEINISCHE STUDIEN UND TEXTE (NE/0076-9754) [01971044] **3412**

MITTELLATEINISCHES JAHRBUCH (GW/0076-9762) [01800884] **3302**

MITTELLATEINISCHES WORTERBUCH BIS ZUM AUSGEHENDEN 13 JAHRHUNDERT (GW) **1927**

MITTELMAN LETTER, THE (US/0739-0963) [09301816] **1330**

MITTELNIEDERDEUTSCHES HANDWORTERBUCH (GW) **3302**

MIV: MUSEERNE I VIBORG AMT (DK/0107-9328) [01791852] 4091, **2699**

MIX (BERKELEY, CALIF.), THE (US/0164-9957) [04300405] **5317**

MIXED MOSS (UK) **3412**

MIXER AND SERVER See CATERING INDUSTRY EMPLOYEE **1658**

MIXING AND SEPARATION TECHNOLOGY ABSTRACTS (UK/0955-7059) [20847790] **2015**

MIXTUUR, DE (NE) [10217972] **4131**

MIYAGI, JAPAN (PREFECTURE). SEIKATSU KANKYOBU See KANKYO HAKUSHO **2234**

MIYAGI-KEN DAIGAKU TOSHOKAN KYOKAI See MAUL : MIYAGI-KEN DAIGAKU TOSHOKAN KYOKAI KAIHO **3230**

MIYAGI-KEN GEIJUTSU NENKAN (JA) [03698612] **325**

MIYAGI-KEN NOGYO TANKI DAIGAKU GAKUJUTSU HOKOKU (JA/0540-4894) [I05404894] **109**

MIYAGI-KEN NOGYO TANKI DAIGAKU KIYO (JA/0386-8370) [10407965] **109**

MIYAGI KOGYO KOTO SENMON GAKKO KENKYU KIYO (JA/0286-3707) [10339835] **5129**

MIYAGI KYOIKU DAIGAKU KIYO. DAI 2-BUNSATSU, SHIZEN KAGAKU, KYOIKU KAGAKU (JA/0289-4424) [27456552] **1358**

MIYAZAKI DAIGAKU KOGAKUBU KENKYU HOKOKU (JA/0540-4932) [09937906] **1988**

MIYAZAKI DAIGAKU KYOIKU GAKUBU KIYO. GEIJUTSU, HOKEN TAIIKU, KASEI, GIJUTSU (JA/0285-8592) [10028328] **1764**

MIYAZAKI DAIGAKU. KYOIKUGAKUBU See MIYAZAKI DAIGAKU KYOIKUGAKUBU KIYO : JIMBUN KAGAKU **1866**

MIYAZAKI DAIGAKU. KYOIKUGAKUBU See MIYAZAKI DAIGAKU KYOIKUGAKUBU KIYO : SHIZEN KAGAKU **1866**

MIYAZAKI DAIGAKU. KYOIKUGAKUBU See MIYAZAKI DAIGAKU KYOIKUGAKUBU KIYO : SHAKAI KAGAKU **1866**

MIYAZAKI DAIGAKU KYOIKUGAKUBU KIYO : JIMBUN KAGAKU (JA) [02244818] **1866**

MIYAZAKI DAIGAKU KYOIKUGAKUBU KIYO : SHAKAI KAGAKU (JA) [02244819] **1866**

MIYAZAKI DAIGAKU KYOIKUGAKUBU KIYO : SHIZEN KAGAKU (JA/0285-8576) [02244843] **1866**

MIYAZAKI DAIGAKU. NOGAKUBU See MIYAZAKI DAIGAKU NOGAKUBU KENKYU JIHO **109**

MIYAZAKI DAIGAKU NOGAKUBU KENKYU JIHO (JA/0544-6066) [01590079] **109**

MIYONG SAENGHWAL (KO) [10841775] **404**

MIZAH HE-HADASH (IS/0017-7083) [02270322] **2770**

MIZU SHIGEN KAIHATSU BENRAN (JA) [02243007] **109**

MIZU SHIGEN KAIHATSU KODAN (JAPAN) See MIZU SHIGEN KAIHATSU BENRAN **109**

MIZU SHORI GIJUTSU (JA/0026-7015) [10462033] **5536**

MIZUE A MONTHLY REVIEW OF THE FINE ARTS (JA) **325**

MIZUNAMI-SHI KASEKI HAKUBUTSUKAN KENKYU HOKOKU (JA/0385-0900) [02515687] **4228**

MIZUSAWA KANSOKU SENTA GIHO (JA/0915-3780) [21768002] **1358**

MIZUSHIGEN KAIHATSU KODAN. SHIKENJO See SHIKENJO NENPO **2095**

MIZZ (UK) **5561**

MIZZOU INTERNATIONAL DIRECTORY (US/1041-1887) [18674075] **1836**

MJP. MONTREAL JOURNAL OF POETICS (CN/0823-1605) [09977292] **3466**

MJSA ARBOK (NO) [10265358] **2699**

MK. MOBEL-KULTUR (GW/0047-7796) [I00477796] **2906**

ML. GUIA DEL MATERIAL DE LABORATORIO (SP) **986**

ML NEWSLETTER (AT) 1764, **3303**

MLA DIRECTORY OF PERIODICALS (US/0197-0380) [05350432] **3259**

●MLA DIRECTORY OF SCHOLARLY PRESSES IN LITERATURE AND LANGUAGE (US/1057-2899) [24001007] **3412**

MLA HANDBOOK FOR WRITERS OF RESEARCH PAPERS (US) **2922**

MLA INDEX AND BIBLIOGRAPHY SERIES (US/0094-6478) [03817617] **4131**

MLA INTERNATIONAL BIBLIOGRAPHY (US/1063-3316) [22217225] **3303**

MLA INTERNATIONAL BIBLIOGRAPHY OF BOOKS AND ARTICLES ON THE MODERN LANGUAGES AND LITERATURES (COMPLETE ED.) (US/0024-8215) [14202426] 3303, **3336**

MLA INTERNATIONAL BIBLIOGRAPHY OF BOOKS AND ARTICLES ON THE MODERN LANGUAGES AND LITERATURES (OPTION B) *CEASED.* (US/0740-8730) [09678154] 3303, **3412**

MLA INTERNATIONAL BIBLIOGRAPHY OF BOOKS AND ARTICLES ON THE MODERN LANGUAGES AND LITERATURES (OPTION C) (US/0740-8722) [09609785] 3412, **3303**

MLA INTERNATIONAL BIBLIOGRAPHY OF BOOKS AND ARTICLES ON THE MODERN LANGUAGES AND LITERATURES. VOLUME 5, FOLKLORE (US) [10280172] **2322**

MLA JOB INFORMATION LIST. ENGLISH ED (US) [04009367] 3303, **4206**

MLA JOB INFORMATION LIST. FOREIGN LANGUAGE EDITION (US) [11368281] **4206**

MLA NEWS (US/0541-5489) [05235804] 3617, **3232**

MLA NEWS LETTER - MINNESOTA LIBRARY ASSOCIATION (US/0748-9285) [01590808] **3232**

MLA NEWSLETTER (NEW YORK) (US/0160-5720) [02565642] **3303**

MLA REPORT, THE (US/0742-762X) [09888040] **3182**

MLA TECHNICAL REPORTS (US) [09706296] **4131**

MLADA KULTURA (YU) [01791697] **3412**

MLADEZH I OBSHTESTVO / NAUCHNOIZSLEDOVATELSKI INSTITUT ZA MLADEZHTA PRI TSK NA DKMS (BU) [21112668] **2283**

MLADY SVET (XR/0323-2042) [18235702] **1066**

MLBD NEWSLETTER (II/0970-1435) [09701435] **3232**

MLBD SERIES IN LINGUISTICS (II) [09599027] **3303**

MLC ECONOMIC INFORMATION SERVICE. MEAT DEMAND TRENDS (UK/0140-6388) [I01406388] **216**

MLC UPDATE (US/0275-7583) [07231481] **3232**

MLD, A WOMEN'S MAILING LIST DIRECTORY (US) [23186420] **5561**

MLD CANADIAN TRAVELLER (CN/1185-216X) [24368431] **5484**

MLJEKARSTVO (CI/0026-704X) [09448178] **197**

MLLE-ACTUALITE (CN/0380-4372) [02443309] **2539**

MLM NEWS *CEASED.* (US/0894-2692) [15963286] **762**

MLM SUCCESS See UPLINE (CHARLOTTESVILLE, VA.) **717**

MLN (US/0026-7910) [01756365] **3303**

MLO, MEDICAL LABORATORY OBSERVER (US/0580-7247) [02535940] **3617**

MLRC NEWS (US) [07001043] **1691**

MLYNSKO-PEKARENSKY PRUMYSL A TECHNIKA SKLADOVANI OBILI (XR/0026-7058) [09917181] **202**

MM (DK/0105-6972) [01789054] **4131**

MM NEWS (US) **3617**

●MMAP LOG (US/1059-8065) [24773077] **275**

●MMC : MEDIAS MAGNETIQUES CANADA (CN/1191-2693) [26497734] **4444**

MMD 1,000, THE (US/0883-0495) [08055567] 799, **933**

MMG, MEDIZIN, MENSCH, GESELLSCHAFT *CEASED.* (GW/0340-8183) [02897891] **3617**

MMI PRESS POLYMER MONOGRAPH SERIES (US/0275-7265) [07227716] **986**

MMI PRESS SYMPOSIUM SERIES (US/0195-3966) [05434731] **986**

MMPI (IO) [09482583] **4074**

MMR, MINERALS & METALS REVIEW (II/0378-6366) [03434008] 2146, **4012**

MMTC NEWS (II/0377-1482) [01797728] 4012, **1618**

MMU, DER MATHEMATISCHE UND NATURWISSENSCHAFTLICHE UNTERRICHT (GW/0025-5866) [06599615] **3523**

MMW. MUNCHENER MEDIZINISCHE WOCHENSCHRIFT (GW/0341-3098) [02790147] **3617**

MN SMALL BUSINESS PROCUREMENT PROGRAM FOR SOCIALLY OR ECONOMICALLY DISADVANTAGED VENDORS F.Y. ... ANNUAL REPORT / DEPARTMENT OF ADMINISTRATION, DIVISION OF PROCUREMENT (US) [09272335] **4666**

MNA ACCENT (US/0026-5586) [01758224] **3862**

MNEMOSUNE (ATHENAI) (GR/1105-1019) [04602748] **1078**

MNEMOSYNE (NE/0026-7074) [01189611] **3303**

MNEMOSYNE. SUPPLEMENTUM (NE/0169-8958) [01695217] **1078**

MO FENLI KEXUE YU JISHU (CC/0254-6140) [10345257] **5129**

MO HU SHU HSUEH (CC) [09144066] **3523**

MO INFO (US/0884-2205) [11818678] **3232**

MO TENG CHIA TING. MODERN HOME (HK) [03430555] **2902**

MOBIELE TELECOMMUNICATIE (NE) **1160**

MOBIL FARM FUTURE (US) [03225981] **160**

MOBIL OIL CORPORATION. WHOLESALE PROGRAMS DEPT See MOBIL FARM FUTURE **160**

MOBIL ROAD ATLAS AND TRIP PLANNING GUIDE, UNITED STATES, CANADA, AND MEXICO (US/0899-6806) [18181056] 5484, **2569**

MOBIL TRAVEL GUIDE : CALIFORNIA AND THE WEST (US/0076-9827) [03172490] **5484**

MOBIL TRAVEL GUIDE. FREQUENT TRAVELERS' GUIDE TO MAJOR CITIES (US/1075-5926) [23154132] 2808, **5484**

MOBIL TRAVEL GUIDE. GREAT LAKES AREA (US/0076-9789) [01615291] **5485**

MOBIL TRAVEL GUIDE : MIDDLE ATLANTIC STATES (US/0076-9797) [03532201] **5485**

MOBIL TRAVEL GUIDE. NORTHEAST (US/1040-1075) [18333340] 2808, **5485**

MOBIL TRAVEL GUIDE. NORTHWEST AND GREAT PLAINS STATES (US/0076-9819) [01144108] **5485**

MOBIL TRAVEL GUIDE. SOUTHEAST (US/1040-1067) [18333313] **5485**

MOBIL TRAVEL GUIDE. SOUTHWEST AND SOUTH CENTRAL AREA (US/0076-9843) [02782406] **5485**

MOBIL TRAVEL GUIDE. WASHINGTON, D.C (US/1040-3507) [18389456] **5485**

MOBIL WORLD (US/0885-5056) [06634649] **4264**

MOBILCOM FUNKSCHAU (GW) **1160**

MOBILE & CELLULAR (UK) [25196269] **1160**

MOBILE & HOLIDAY HOMES (UK) [10318880] **2828**

MOBILE & SATELLITE (UK) **1117**

MOBILE BAY MONTHLY (US) [13047747] **2539**

MOBILE BEACON & ALABAMA CITIZEN, THE (US) [02666053] **5627**

●MOBILE BEAT INTERNATIONAL (US/1058-0212) [24182685] **4131**

MOBILE BUSINESS (UK/0957-4980) [I09574980] **695**

MOBILE COMMUNICATIONS DIRECTORY See WIRELESS INDUSTRY DIRECTORY **1169**

MOBILE COMMUNICATIONS DIRECTORY See CELLULAR / MOBILE COMMUNICATIONS DIRECTORY, THE **1151**

MOBILE COMMUNICATIONS FOR UK COMMERCE & INDUSTRY *SUSPENDED.* (UK) **846**

MOBILE DATA REPORT (US/1040-7022) [18504899] **1242**

MOBILE EUROPE (UK/1350-7362) [I13507362] **1160**

MOBILE HOME AND HOLIDAY CARAVAN See MOBILE & HOLIDAY HOMES **2828**

MOBILE HOME & RV TRAILER GUIDE, NEW & USED VALUES (US/1054-8076) [02674872] **5387**

MOBILE HOME LIVING (US/8750-0655) [10957061] **2828**

MOBILE IDEAS (US) [08041797] **4830**

MOBILE/MANUFACTURED HOME BLUE BOOK (US/0733-6497) [08613602] **3484**

MOBILE MILANO, IL (IT/0026-7112) [I00267112] **2906**

MOBILE OFFICE (US/1047-1952) [20621123] 1160, **695**

MOBILE OFFICE MAGAZINE'S CELLULAR BUYERS' GUIDE (US/1062-6638) [23470629] **1117**

MOBILE PHONE NEWS (US/0737-5077) [09405112] **1160**

MOBILE PRODUCT NEWS (US/1044-1190) [19687832] **1160**

MOBILE PRODUCTS INTERNATIONAL (US/1055-5285) [23199949] **1117**

MOBILE RADIO REPORTS See INDUSTRIAL COMMUNICATIONS **1113**

MOBILE RADIO TECHNOLOGY (US/0745-7626) [09434253] **1135**

MOBILE REGISTER, THE (US) [04049192] **5627**

MOBILE SATELLITE NEWS (POTOMAC, MD.) (US/1046-5286) [20436855] **1160**

MOBILE SATELLITE REPORTS (US/1046-6061) [20464644] **1160**

MOBILE TELECOMMUNICATIONS NEWS (UK/0267-1255) [I02671255] **1160**

MOBILES (AT) **1160**

MOBILFUNK HEIDELBERG (GW/0941-7494) [I09417494] **1117**

MOBILIA (AMSTERDAM) (NE/0165-5302) [I01655302] 303, **2906**

MOBILITEIT VAN DE NEDERLANDSE BEVOLKING IN ... / CENTRAAL BUREAU VOOR DE STATISTIEK, HOOFDAFDELING STATISTIEKEN VAN VERKEER EN VERVOER, DE (NE) [10339920] **4554**

●MOBILITY FORUM : THE JOURNAL OF THE AIR MOBILITY COMMAND, THE (US) [26480994] 4051, **28**

MOBILITY OF UNDERGRADUATE COLLEGE STUDENTS BETWEEN WASHINGTON COLLEGES AND UNIVERSITIES (US/0148-267X) [03279489] **1836**

MOBILITY TRENDS (US) [02251024] **5387**

MOBILITY (WASHINGTON) (US/0195-8194) [05661339] 4841, **695**

MOBIUS (ALEXANDRIA, VA.) (US/0734-3108) [08722624] 1298, **695**

MOCCASIN TELEGRAPH (US) [01751384] **695**

MOCI; MONITEUR DU COMMERCE INTERNATIONAL, LE (FR/0026-9719) [05327774] 846, **3011**

MOCT MOST : ECONOMIC JOURNAL ON EASTERN EUROPE & SOVIET UNION (IT) **1638**

MOCT-MOST: ECONOMIC POLICY IN TRANSITIONAL ECONOMIES (NE/1120-7388) [23466653] 879, **1505**

MOD CONTRACTS BULLETIN (UK/0269-0365) [I02690365] 4051, **695**

MODA (IT) 5561, **1086**

MODA E BIJOUX *SUSPENDED.* (IT) **2915**

MODA IN (IT/1120-1967) [I11201967] **2490**

MODA ITALIA See MODA **1086**

MODA VIVA (IT) **1086**

●MODAL ANALYSIS (US/1066-0763) [26834792] **2122**

MODAN MEDIA (JA) [02243142] **568**

MODASPORT VACANZE (IT) **1086**

MODE AUSTRALIA (AT/0155-4611) [I01554611] 5561, **1086**

MODE EN PEINTURE *SUSPENDED.* (FR) **1086**

MODE ET MODE (JA) **1086**

MODE FOR BRIDES (AT/0729-5081) [I07295081] 5561, **2283**

MODE INTERNATIONAL (US/0162-1378) [04111680] **1086**

MODE MAGAZINE TRIBUNE (BE) **1086**

MODEHELLAS. HOME BEACH EDITION (GR) **1086**

MODEL AIRPLANE NEWS (US/0026-7295) [01758435] 2775, **28**

MODEL AUTO REVIEW (UK/0267-2715) [12125338] 5419, **2775**

MODEL AVIATION (US/0744-5059) [06240283] **2775**

MODEL AVIATION CANADA (CN/0317-7831) [02248112] 2775, **28**

MODEL BOATS (UK/0144-2910) [06699066] **594**

MODEL BUILDER (1981) (US/0731-4795) [08182841] **2775**

MODEL CALL / RICHARD POIRIER MODEL & TALENT AGENCY (US/1061-4737) [25314306] **1086**

MODEL CARS MONTHLY See RADIO CONTROL MODEL CARS **2777**

MODEL CITIES BULLETIN (US/0091-1038) [01786133] **1764**

MODEL ENGINEER, THE (UK/0026-7325) [05543672] **2775**

MODEL ENGINEERS' WORKSHOP (UK/0959-6909) [I09596909] **2775**

MODEL (NEW YORK, N.Y.) (US/0898-4980) [17826121] **762**

MODEL RAILROAD BUYERS GUIDE (US) [02316202] **5433**

MODEL RAILROAD CRAFTSMAN See RAILROAD MODEL CRAFTSMAN **2777**

MODEL RAILROADER (US/0026-7341) [01696545] **2775**

MODEL RAILROADING (US/0199-1914) [05703708] **2775**

MODEL RAILWAYS (1987) (UK/0953-0584) [I09530584] **2775**

MODEL RETAILER (CLIFTON, VA.) (US/0191-6904) [04926939] **2775**

MODEL SHIP BUILDER (US/0199-7068) [06096212] **4179**

MODEL SHIPWRIGHT (UK) [08119872] **2775**

MODEL SHOPPER (US/0892-2780) [15143735] **2775**

MODEL T TIMES (US/0891-6187) [14939413] **5387**

MODELE MAGAZINE (FR) 1086, **404**

MODELES LINGUISTIQUES (FR/0249-6267) [06468215] **3303**

MODELI I SISTEMY OBRABOTKI INFORMATSII (UN/0203-5650) [13416244] **3232**

MODELING AND SIMULATION (US/0198-0092) [04612683] **1282**

MODELING, IDENTIFICATION AND CONTROL (NO/0332-7353) [07957395] **3523**

●MODELING OF GEO-BIOSPHERE PROCESSES (GW/0938-9563) [I09389563] **1358**

MODELING ON MICROS AND WORKSTATIONS : PROCEEDINGS OF THE SCS MULTICONFERENCE ON MODELING ON MICROS AND WORKSTATIONS (US) [23161057] 1270, **1282**

MODELIROVANIE I OPTIMIZATSIIA KHIMICHESKIKH PROTSESSOV (RU) [04723105] **1027**

MODELIROVANIE V MEKHANIKE / AKADEMIIA NAUK SSSR, SIBIRSKOE OTDELENIE, VYCHISLITELNYI TSENTR [I] INSTITUT TEORETICHESKOI I PRIKLADNOI MEKHANIKI (RU/0201-8268) [19880936] **4429**

MODELLANALYSEN LITERATUR (GW) [10625126] **3412**

MODELLEISENBAHNER, DER (GW) [06375299] **5433**

MODELLHUT 1975 (GW/0723-7839) [I07237839] **1086**

MODELLINA MILANO (IT/1121-8290) [I11218290] **1086**

MODELLING & SIMULATION IN MATERIALS SCIENCE AND ENGINEERING (UK) **2107**

MODELLING, SIMULATION & CONTROL. B (FR/0761-2516) [25207038] **2122**

MODELLISTICA (IT/0392-4076) [I03924076] **2775**

MODELL'S DRUGS IN CURRENT USE AND NEW DRUGS (US/1044-0704) [17938825] **4316**

MODELOS Y DISENOS INDUSTRIALES (AG) [01795925] **1306**

MODELS IN DERMATOLOGY CEASED. (SZ/0259-1340) [16567377] **3722**

MODELTEC (US/0742-7107) [10426649] **5129**

MODEM & TELECOMUNICAZIONI (IT) **1160**

MODEM NOTES (US/0741-580X) [10204511] **1264**

MODENA See MODENA ECONOMICA **846**

MODENA ECONOMICA (IT) [02244664] **846**

MODERN AFRICA (UK/0264-8067) [03383357] **696**

MODERN AGE (CHICAGO) (US/0026-7457) [01758440] **2539**

MODERN AGING RESEARCH CEASED. (US/0275-360X) [07118976] **3754**

MODERN AGRICULTURE AND INDUSTRY (PH) [02339447] **109**

MODERN AMERICA (US/0076-9894) [02437316] **2539**

MODERN & CONTEMPORARY FRANCE (UK/0963-9489) [12300070] **5209**

MODERN APPLICATIONS NEWS (US/0277-9951) [07684973] 3484, **4012**

MODERN APPROACHES TO THE DIAGNOSIS AND INSTRUCTION OF MULTI-HANDICAPPED CHILDREN (NE) [01781343] **3838**

MODERN ARTS CRITICISM CEASED. (US/1052-1712) [22202613] **358**

MODERN ASIAN STUDIES (UK/0026-749X) [01606245] **2659**

MODERN ASPECTS OF ELECTROCHEMISTRY (US/0076-9924) [00933141] **1034**

MODERN ASTRONOMY (BUFFALO) (US/0091-1046) [01785998] **397**

MODERN ATHLETE AND COACH (AT) [06385501] **4905**

MODERN AUSTRIAN LITERATURE (US/0026-7503) [01877535] 2850, **3412**

MODERN AVIATION LIBRARY (US/0196-1527) [05736828] 3232, **29**

MODERN BAKING (US/0897-6201) [17571997] **2350**

MODERN BELIEVING (UK) **4978**

MODERN BLACK MEN CEASED. (US/0883-296X) [12100417] **3996**

MODERN BOATING 1980 (AT/0811-0697) [08110697] **594**

MODERN BREWERY AGE (US/0026-7538) [06392377] **2369**

MODERN BREWERY AGE BLUE BOOK (US) [03957065] **2369**

MODERN BRIDE (US/0026-7546) [01758443] **2283**

MODERN CASTING (US/0026-7562) [06140445] **4012**

MODERN CELL BIOLOGY (US/0745-3000) [09072164] **538**

MODERN CHINA (US/0097-7004) [01799219] 5209, **2659**

MODERN CHINESE LITERATURE (US/8755-8963) [11455288] **3412**

MODERN CHLOR-ALKALI TECHNOLOGY (US/0747-7406) [10763707] **986**

MODERN CHURCHMAN See MODERN BELIEVING **4978**

MODERN CHURCHMAN, THE (UK/0026-7597) [01639695] **4978**

MODERN CONCEPTS IN IMMUNOLOGY (US/0891-3676) [11951794] **3675**

MODERN CONSTITUTIONAL LAW (US) [04623442] **3093**

MODERN DAIRY (CN/0026-7651) [02442820] **197**

MODERN DENTAL PRACTICE CEASED. (US/0894-7953) [16244470] **1330**

MODERN DISTRIBUTION MANAGEMENT (US/0544-6538) [14576767] **879**

MODERN DRAMA (CN/0026-7694) [01716920] 3412, **5366**

MODERN DRAMATISTS RESEARCH AND PRODUCTION SOURCEBOOKS (US/1055-999X) [23443043] **3412**

MODERN DRUMMER (US/0194-4533) [04660723] **4131**

MODERN ELEKTRONIK (SW) **2073**

●MODERN ENGLISH TEACHER (UK/0308-0587) [25740814] **1900**

MODERN FIBRES (II/0377-1490) [02240194] **5354**

MODERN FICTION STUDIES (US/0026-7724) [01645443] **3347**

MODERN FINISHING METHODS (CN/0380-2299) [02443369] **4012**

MODERN FISHING (AT/0026-7732) [I00267732] 4875, **4905**

MODERN FOOD SERVICE NEWS (US/0888-7829) [20495918] **5072**

●MODERN GENETICS (US/1056-4497) [23712016] **549**

MODERN GEOLOGY (US/0026-7775) [01280911] **1388**

MODERN GERMAN STUDIES (GW) [12183684] 3303, **3412**

MODERN GOLD COINAGE (US/0149-4279) [03485440] **2781**

MODERN GOVERNMENT/NATIONAL DEVELOPMENT (US/0360-7941) [02244977] **4666**

MODERN GREEK SOCIETY (US/0147-0779) [01449214] **5209**

MODERN GREEK STUDIES ASSOCIATION See BULLETIN OF THE MODERN GREEK STUDIES ASSOCIATION **2681**

MODERN GREEK STUDIES YEARBOOK (US/0884-8432) [12488176] **2699**

MODERN GROCER (US/0026-7805) [04055630] **2350**

MODERN HAIKU (US/0026-7821) [03371275] **3466**

MODERN HEALTHCARE (1977) (US/0160-7480) [03346252] **3789**

MODERN HEBREW LITERATURE (IS/0334-4266) [01534248] **3412**

MODERN HI-FI AND MUSIC (US/0097-2533) [01799084] 4131, **5317**

MODERN HI-FI & STEREO GUIDE (QUARTERLY) See MODERN HI-FI AND MUSIC **5317**

MODERN HISTORY REVIEW (UK/0956-0726) [I09560726] **2623**

MODERN HUMANITIES RESEARCH ASSOCIATION See ANNUAL BULLETIN OF THE MODERN HUMANITIES RESEARCH ASSOCIATION **2842**

MODERN HUMANITIES RESEARCH ASSOCIATION See PUBLICATIONS **2852**

MODERN INDIAN SHORT STORIES (II) [02861630] **3412**

MODERN INTERNATIONAL DRAMA (US/0026-7856) [01758460] 5366, **3412**

MODERN IRISH PLAYS (IE) [11839549] **5366**

MODERN JEWELER (1981) (US/0744-2513) [08134534] **2915**

MODERN JEWELER (NATIONAL EXECUTIVE EDITION) See MODERN JEWELER (1981) **2915**

MODERN JEWISH STUDIES ANNUAL (US/0270-9406) [05296534] **3412**

MODERN JUDAISM (US/0276-1114) [07316976] **5051**

MODERN LANGUAGE ASSOCIATION OF AMERICA See MLA DIRECTORY OF PERIODICALS **3259**

MODERN LANGUAGE ASSOCIATION OF AMERICA See MLA NEWSLETTER (NEW YORK) **3303**

MODERN LANGUAGE JOURNAL (BOULDER, COLO.), THE (US/0026-7902) [01642244] **3303**

MODERN LANGUAGE QUARTERLY (SEATTLE) (US/0026-7929) [01758463] **3347**

MODERN LANGUAGE REVIEW, THE (UK/0026-7937) [01587205] **3303**

MODERN LANGUAGE STUDIES (US/0047-7729) [03718093] 3348, **3303**

MODERN LAW REPORTS, EMBODYING CASES DECIDED BY THE SUPREME COURT OF THE REPUBLIC OF SRI LANKA (CE) [02619290] **3011**

MODERN LAW REVIEW (UK/0026-7961) [01587508] **3011**

MODERN LITURGY (US/0363-504X) [02437451] **4978**

MODERN LOGIC (US/1047-5982) [20729602] **3523**

MODERN MACHINE SHOP (US/0026-8003) [01758467] **2122**

MODERN MACHINE SHOP NC/CAM GUIDEBOOK See MODERN MACHINE SHOP NC/CIM GUIDEBOOK **2122**

MODERN MACHINE SHOP NC/CIM GUIDEBOOK (US) [15354302] **2122**

MODERN MANAGEMENT (COLLINGWOOD, VIC.) (AT) [17532208] **109**

MODERN MANAGEMENT : JOURNAL OF THE INSTITUTE OF SUPERVISORY MANAGEMENT AND INSTITUTION OF INDUSTRIAL MANAGERS (UK) [15143274] **944**

MODERN MASTERS SERIES (US/0738-0429) [I09506859] 2623, **358**

MODERN MATERIALS HANDLING (US/0026-8038) [01758470] 4220, **3484**

MODERN MATURITY (US/0026-8046) [01758471] **5180**

MODERN MATURITY (NRTA ED.) (US/0747-6302) [08255338] **5180**

MODERN MEDICINE (BECKENHAM) (UK/0262-4273) [06769216] **367**

MODERN MEDICINE (MINNEAPOLIS) (US/0026-8070) [01044700] 3617, **3661**

MODERN MEDICINE (NEDERLANDSE ED.) (NE/0929-0141) [I09290141] **3617**

MODERN MEDICINE OF IRELAND (UK/0306-6657) [06718267] **3618**

MODERN METALS (US/0026-8127) [01758473] **4013**

MODERN METHODS IN PHARMACOLOGY (US/0732-7218) [08407857] **4316**

MODERN METHODS OF PLANT ANALYSIS (1985) (GW/0937-8340) [01761705] **518**

MODERN MICROBIOLOGICAL METHODS (UK/1048-6593) [20989931] **568**

MODERN MIDDLE EAST SERIES (NEW YORK) (US/0077-0027) [02453563] **2770**

MODERN MONOGRAPHS IN ANALYTICAL CHEMISTRY (US) [08859620] **1018**

MODERN MOTOR See MOTOR **5387**

MODERN NURSING HOME DIRECTORY OF NURSING HOMES IN THE UNITED STATES, U.S. POSSESSIONS AND CANADA (US/0093-9900) [01793880] **3789**

Alphabetical Title Index

MOLECULAR

MODERN OFFICE TECHNOLOGY (US/0746-3839) [10008833] **4212**

MODERN PAINT AND COATINGS (US/0098-7786) [02240427] **4224**

MODERN PAINTERS (LONDON, ENGLAND) (UK/0953-6698) [18302256] **358**

MODERN PATHOLOGY (US/0893-3952) [15506806] **3896**

MODERN PHARMACOLOGY-TOXICOLOGY (US/0098-6925) [01512448] **4316**

MODERN PHILOLOGY (US/0026-8232) [01758480] **3303**

MODERN PHOTOGRAPHY ANNUAL (US/0580-8162) [01789790] **4371**

MODERN PHOTOGRAPHY'S GUIDE TO THE WORLD'S BEST CAMERAS (US/0197-5986) [05640935] **4371**

MODERN PHYSICS LETTERS A (SI/0217-7323) [13645127] **4448**

MODERN PHYSICS LETTERS. B, CONDENSED MATTER PHYSICS, STATISTICAL PHYSICS, APPLIED PHYSICS (SI/0217-9849) [16698973] **4412**

MODERN PLASTICS (US/0026-8275) [04696134] **4456**

MODERN PLASTICS ENCYCLOPEDIA (1954) (US/0085-3518) [04185627] **4457**

MODERN PLASTICS INTERNATIONAL (SZ/0026-8283) [03544158] **4457**

MODERN PLASTICS INTERNATIONAL ENCYCLOPEDIA (US) **2107**

MODERN POETS IN TRANSLATION SERIES (US) [14080751] **3466**

MODERN POWER SYSTEMS (UK/0260-7840) [07102694] **1950**

MODERN PROBLEMS OF PHARMACOPSYCHIATRY (SZ/0077-0094) [00972460] **4316**, **3931**

MODERN PSYCHOANALYSIS (US/0361-5227) [02078669] **4604**

MODERN PSYCHOTHERAPY (US/0163-2841) [04321012] **4604**

MODERN PUBLICITY (UK) [04586434] **762**, **381**

MODERN PURCHASING (CN/0026-833X) [02068363] **950**

MODERN QUATERNARY RESEARCH IN SOUTHEAST ASIA (NE/0168-6151) [03658286] **275**, **4228**

MODERN RAILWAYS (UK/0026-8356) [01758487] **5433**

MODERN RATIONALIST, THE (II/0304-1727) [02239566] **4978**

MODERN RECORDING & MUSIC **SUSPENDED.** (US/0273-8511) [06477680] **4131**, **5317**

MODERN RECORDING & MUSIC'S BUYER'S GUIDE (US/0276-9239) [07167256] **4131**, **5317**

MODERN REFORMATION (US) **5065**

MODERN REVIEW (CALCUTTA), THE (II/0026-8380) [01681145] **2507**

MODERN REVIEW, THE (UK) [25354771] **1135**, **4074**

MODERN ROMANCES (US/0026-8399) [04055645] **5074**

MODERN SALES TECHNOLOGY (US/0739-3725) [09736125] **933**

MODERN SALON (US/0148-4001) [03301099] **404**

MODERN SCHOOLMAN, THE (US/0026-8402) [01758490] **4353**

MODERN SCIENCE AND VEDIC SCIENCE (US/0891-5989) [14922047] **4186**

MODERN SCOTTISH PAINTERS **CEASED.** (UK) [10386442] **358**

●MODERN SCREEN'S COUNTRY MUSIC (US/1070-5104) [28395500] **4131**

MODERN SCREEN'S COUNTRY MUSIC SPECIAL **See** MODERN SCREEN'S COUNTRY MUSIC **4131**

MODERN SHORT STORIES **SUSPENDED.** (US/1040-9068) [18574283] **3412**

MODERN SILVER COINAGE (US/0149-7707) [03544327] **2782**

MODERN STEEL CONSTRUCTION (US/0026-8445) [02251245] **621**

MODERN SYNTHETIC METHODS (GW/0176-7615) [10387770] **1027**

MODERN TECHNIQUES IN STRUCTURING PARTNERSHIP AGREEMENTS (US) [29843045] **3102**

MODERN THEOLOGY (UK/0266-7177) [11538889] **4978**

MODERN TIRE DEALER (US/0026-8496) [04455675] **5419**

MODERN TRENDS IN OPHTHALMOLOGY (UK) [04053363] **3876**

MODERN TRENDS IN ORTHOPAEDICS (US/0077-0159) [03990577] **3883**

MODERN UNIONIST, THE **CEASED.** (AT) [13726007] **1691**

MODERN VETERINARY PRACTICE (1973) (US/0362-8140) [02308852] **5516**

MODERN WOODWORKING (US/1055-4440) [23030029] **634**

MODERN WOODWORKING DIRECTORY AND BUYERS GUIDE (US) **634**

MODERNA SPRAK (SW/0026-8577) [01758512] **3303**

MODERNE KUECHE, DIE (GW) [06367221] **2906**

MODERNE MATHEMATIK IN ELEMENTARER DARSTELLUNG (GW) [01644105] **3523**

MODERNE RONTGENFOTOGRAFIE / ORWO (GW/0138-2934) [12114877] **3944**

MODERNE SPRACHEN (AU/0026-8666) [04430150] **3303**

●MODERNISM/MODERNITY (BALTIMORE, MD.) (US/1071-6068) [28689804] **3412**

MODES & TECHNIQUES INTERNATIONAL (FR/0992-5597) [l09925597] **1086**

MODES & TECHNIQUES VETIR (FR) [14708164] **1086**

MODES ET TRAVAUX (FR/0026-8739) [l00268739] **325**

MODESTO BEE, THE (US) [28464207] **5637**

MODIFICATION AU TARIF (CN/1193-1051) [26497978] **846**

MODIFICATION DE LA LIGNE RIVIERE-DU-LOUP-SAINT-CLEMENT (CN/1187-5666) [25468323] **2198**

MOD'S IV DETALJERTE VIRKNINGSTABELLER FOR ... (NO) [11335761] **1574**

MODO DESIGN MAGAZINE (IT/0391-3635) [06782825] **303**, **2902**

MODOC COUNTY HISTORICAL SOCIETY **See** JOURNAL OF THE MODCC COUNTY HISTORICAL SOCIETY **2742**

MODOC COUNTY RECORD, THE (US) [28103482] **5637**

MODSPIL (DK/0105-9238) [17164544] **4131**

MODULAR HI-FI COMPONENTS SERVICE DATA (US/0730-1197) [07208881] **2073**

MODULE D'AUTOFORMATION (CN/0825-0464) [11607492] **1764**, **3618**

MODULES/HYBRIDS **CEASED.** (US/0734-5178) [08767679] **2073**

MODULO (IT/0390-1025) [l03901025] **621**

MODULO (BL) [02448712] **358**

MODULUS (US/0191-4022) [01639578] **303**

MODUS (UK/0264-9683) [15588147] **2792**

MODY TECHNIK (PL/0462-9760) [l04629760] **5129**

MOEBIUS (CN/0225-1582) [08079026] **3412**

MOEDA E FINANCAS (BL) [01788322] **799**

MOER (NE/0166-3755) [l01663755] **1764**

MOFTUL ROMAN (RM) [23748164] **3348**

MOGUCNOSTI (CI/0544-7267) [02141277] **3413**

MOHAIR AUSTRALIA (AT) [04255328] **5354**

MOHAN ROPPO (JA) [03048607] **3011**

MOHAVE COUNTY MINER AND OUR MINERAL WEALTH **See** MOHAVE COUNTY MINER (KINGMAN, ARIZ. : 1931) **5630**

MOHAVE COUNTY MINER (KINGMAN, ARIZ. : 1931) (US) [08793635] **5630**

MOHAVE DAILY MINER AND KINGMAN DAILY MINER, THE (US/0746-9764) [10280798] **5630**

MOHAVE VALLEY NEWS (US/0164-9078) [04232890] **5630**

MOHAWK, THE (US/0740-9699) [10068336] **2461**

MOHR-KURIER (GW) **4830**

MOI AUVERGNE, A (FR/0220-6765) [09190564] **2461**

MOIS, LE (SZ/0304-2162) [01795563] **799**

MOJAVE DESERT NEWS, THE (US/1065-1152) [26509381] **5637**

MOJE LEKTURY (PL/0867-4329) [l08674329] **1066**

MOKCHAE KONGHAK (KO) [08558025] **2402**

MOKCHAE KONGOP **See** MOKCHAE KONGHAK **2402**

MOKSLAS IR GYVENIMAS (LI) [02505438] **5129**

MOKUZAI GAKKAISHI (JA/0021-4795) [01780664] **2403**

MOKUZAI KENKYU SHIRYO (JA/0285-7049) [02245268] **634**

MOKUZAI RYUTSU KOZO HOKOKUSHO (JA) [03801500] **2403**

MOL (JA/0386-5495) [09617448] **2015**

MOLASSES MARKET NEWS (US/0145-0662) [02600155] **933**, **109**

MOLDOVA I MIR (MV) [25620951] **4482**

MOLDOVA SI LUMEA (MV/0132-6627) [26288580] **4543**

MOLE (CN/0827-2387) [11734392] **4131**

MOLECULAR AND BIOCHEMICAL PARASITOLOGY (NE/0166-6851) [06293731] **465**

MOLECULAR AND CELLULAR BIOCHEMISTRY (NE/0300-8177) [01787431] **491**

MOLECULAR AND CELLULAR BIOLOGY (US/0270-7306) [06492263] **539**, **568**

●MOLECULAR AND CELLULAR DIFFERENTIATION (US/1065-3074) [26570093] **986**, **465**

MOLECULAR AND CELLULAR ENDOCRINOLOGY (IE/0303-7207) [01144080] **3732**

MOLECULAR AND CELLULAR NEUROSCIENCES (US/1044-7431) [19879705] **3838**

MOLECULAR AND CELLULAR PROBES (UK/0890-8508) [14402545] **465**

MOLECULAR AND CHEMICAL NEUROPATHOLOGY (US/1044-7393) [19855597] **3838**

MOLECULAR & GENERAL GENETICS : MGG (GW/0026-8925) [01758517] **549**

MOLECULAR ASPECTS OF CELLULAR REGULATION (NE/0167-6970) [07398437] **539**

MOLECULAR ASPECTS OF MEDICINE (UK/0098-2997) [01456613] **3618**

MOLECULAR BIOLOGY AND EVOLUTION (US/0737-4038) [09364605] **465**

MOLECULAR BIOLOGY, BIOCHEMISTRY, AND BIOPHYSICS (US/0077-0221) [01758519] **465**

MOLECULAR BIOLOGY (NEW YORK) (US/0026-8933) [00819101] **465**

●MOLECULAR BIOLOGY OF THE CELL (US/1059-1524) [24486692] **539**

MOLECULAR BIOLOGY REPORTS (NE/0301-4851) [01787363] **465**

MOLECULAR BIOLOGY TECHNIQUES (UK/1356-1324) **491**, **3618**

●MOLECULAR BIOTECHNOLOGY (US/1073-6085) [29487200] **3695**

MOLECULAR BIOTHERAPY **CEASED.** (US/0952-8172) [16797236] **465**

MOLECULAR BRAIN RESEARCH (NE/0169-328X) [19645119] **465**, **3838**

MOLECULAR BREEDING (NE/1380-3743) **986**

MOLECULAR CARCINOGENESIS (US/0899-1987) [18028363] **465**

MOLECULAR COMPARATIVE PHYSIOLOGY **CEASED.** (SZ) [28180214] **584**

MOLECULAR COMPLEXES (US/0091-0082) [01783688] **1056**

MOLECULAR CRYSTALS AND LIQUID CRYSTALS. LETTERS SECTION (1991) (US/1055-5218) [23197787] **1032**

MOLECULAR CRYSTALS AND LIQUID CRYSTALS. LETTERS SECTION (NEW YORK, N.Y. : 1991) (US) [23197789] **1032**

MOLECULAR CRYSTALS AND LIQUID CRYSTALS (NEW YORK, N.Y. : 1991) **See** MOLECULAR CRYSTALS AND LIQUID CRYSTALS SCIENCE AND TECHNOLOGY SECTION C, MOLECULAR MATERIALS **1033**

MOLECULAR CRYSTALS AND LIQUID CRYSTALS (NEW YORK, N.Y. : 1991) **See** MOLECULAR CRYSTALS AND LIQUID CRYSTALS SCIENCE AND TECHNOLOGY: SECTION A, MOLECULAR CRYSTALS AND LIQUID CRYSTALS **1032**

MOLECULAR CRYSTALS AND LIQUID CRYSTALS (NEW YORK, N.Y. : 1991) **See** MOLECULAR CRYSTALS AND LIQUID CRYSTALS SCIENCE AND TECHNOLOGY SECTION D, DISPLAY AND IMAGING **4438**

●MOLECULAR CRYSTALS AND LIQUID CRYSTALS SCIENCE AND TECHNOLOGY: SECTION A, MOLECULAR CRYSTALS AND LIQUID CRYSTALS (US/1058-725X) [24363825] **1032**

●MOLECULAR CRYSTALS AND LIQUID CRYSTALS SCIENCE AND TECHNOLOGY SECTION B, NONLINEAR OPTICS (US/1058-7268) [24364035] **4438**

MOLECULAR

● MOLECULAR CRYSTALS AND LIQUID CRYSTALS SCIENCE AND TECHNOLOGY SECTION C, MOLECULAR MATERIALS (US/1058-7276) [24363964] **1033**

● MOLECULAR CRYSTALS AND LIQUID CRYSTALS SCIENCE AND TECHNOLOGY SECTION D, DISPLAY AND IMAGING (US/1058-7284) [24364003] 1033, **4438**

MOLECULAR CRYSTALS AND LIQUID CRYSTALS. SUPPLEMENT SERIES (UK/0731-7689) [08249310] **1033**

MOLECULAR DYNAMICS NEWS (US/1046-5219) [12306857] **986**

● MOLECULAR ECOLOGY (UK/0962-1083) [25447413] **2218**

MOLECULAR ENDOCRINOLOGY (BALTIMORE, MD.) (US/0888-8809) [13739260] **3732**

MOLECULAR ENGINEERING (NE/0925-5125) [24374421] **1988**

MOLECULAR GENETIC MEDICINE (US/1057-2805) [23996929] 3618, **549**

MOLECULAR GENETICS, MICROBIOLOGY AND VIROLOGY (US/0891-4168) [14766467] 549, **568**

MOLECULAR IMMUNOLOGY (UK/0161-5890) [03979267] **3675**

MOLECULAR MARINE BIOLOGY AND BIOTECHNOLOGY (US/1053-6426) [22600878] 3695, **556**

MOLECULAR MATERIAL (US/1056-1935) [23528692] **986**

● MOLECULAR MEDICINE (CAMBRIDGE, MASS.) (US/1076-1551) [30416048] **3618**

MOLECULAR MEMBRANE BIOLOGY (US/0968-7688) **491**

MOLECULAR MICROBIOLOGY (UK/0950-382X) [15473109] **568**

MOLECULAR NEUROBIOLOGY (US/0893-7648) [15640289] **3838**

MOLECULAR NEUROPHARMACOLOGY *CEASED.* (UK/0959-5244) [23902673] 4316, **3838**

MOLECULAR PHARMACOLOGY (US/0026-895X) [01680861] **4316**

● MOLECULAR PHYLOGENETICS AND EVOLUTION (US/1055-7903) [23325059] **549**

MOLECULAR PHYSICS (UK/0026-8976) [01696284] **1056**

MOLECULAR PLANT-MICROBE INTERACTIONS (US/0894-0282) [15732242] **518**

MOLECULAR REPRODUCTION AND DEVELOPMENT (US/1040-452X) [18422591] **541**

MOLECULAR SIMULATION (US/0892-7022) [15239251] **4429**

MOLECULES AND CELLS (KO/1016-8478) [l10168478] **539**

MOLEKULIARNAIA BIOLOGIIA (UN/0375-9415) [01316924] **465**

MOLEKULIARNAIA FIZIKA I BIOFIZIKA VODNYKH SISTEM (RU) [05637687] **986**

MOLEKULIARNAIA GENETIKA, MIKROBIOLOGIIA I VIRUSOLOGIIA (RU/0208-0613) [17207692] **568**

MOLEKULIARNAIA SPEKTROSKOPIIA (RU) [02367332] **4438**

MOLEKULJARNAJA BIOLOGIJA (MOSKVA) (RU/0026-8984) [01210433] **568**

MOLEKULJARNAJA GENETIKA I BIOFIZIKA (UN/0136-491X) [03568776] **549**

MOLENAAR, DE (NE) [09917372] 216, **202**

MOLINE ADVANCE (MOLINE, KAN. : 1978) (US) [11216735] **5677**

MOLINERIA Y PANADERIA (SP/0026-900X) [04048221] **155**

MOLINI D'ITALIA (IT/0026-9018) [09554696] **202**

MOLINO DE PIMIENTA, EL (AG) [11966169] **3413**

MOLISE ECONOMICO (IT) **1505**

MOLKEREI-ZEITUNG; WELT DER MILCH, DIE (GW) [05119811] **197**

MOLKEREITECHNIK *CEASED.* (GW/0540-6021) [04925067] **197**

MOLLUSCAN RESEARCH (AT) **5591**

MOLOCHNAIA I MIASNAIA PROMYSHLENNOST *See* MOLOCHNAIA PROMYSHLENNOST **197**

● MOLOCHNAIA PROMYSHLENNOST (RU) [26281671] **197**

MOLOCHNOE I MIASNOE SKOTOVODSTVO (RU/0026-9034) [07161925] 197, **216**

MOLODA UKRAINA (CN/0026-9042) [01639742] **2519**

MOLODAIA GVARDIIA (RU) [19127772] **3466**

MOLODAIA POEZIIA (RU) [20860596] **3466**

MOLODEZHNAIA ESTRADA (RU) [04469890] **1066**

MOLTEN SALTS BULLETIN (FR) **1442**

MOLY CORROSION INHIBITORS (US/0730-9155) [08122425] **2015**

MOLYBDENUM MOSAIC (US/0163-1888) [04314140] **4013**

MOM ... GUESS WHAT ... ! (US) [06686091] **2795**

MOMA (NEW YORK, N.Y.) (US/0893-0279) [01145859] 4091, **358**

MOMBASA (KENYA). MUNICIPAL EDUCATION OFFICE *See* ANNUAL REPORT, MUNICIPAL EDUCATION DEPARTMENT, FOR THE YEAR ... **1725**

MOMBASA (KENYA). SOCIAL SERVICES AND HOUSING DEPT *See* ANNUAL REPORT OF THE DIRECTOR OF SOCIAL SERVICES & HOUSING FOR THE YEAR - MOMBASA KENYA **5272**

● MOMBERGER AIRPORT INFORMATION (GW/0942-3478) [l09423478] **29**

MOMBUSHO TOSHOKAN YORAN (JA) [02802856] **3232**

MOME (IT) **1764**

MOMENT (NEW YORK) (US/0099-0280) [02242489] **5051**

MOMENT (TORONTO) (CN/0838-8083) [18116068] **5252**

MOMENTUM (JOHANNESBURG, SOUTH AFRICA) *CEASED.* (SA) [12245220] **5387**

MOMENTUM (WASHINGTON) (US/0026-914X) [01758524] **4978**

MOMOYAMA GAKUIN DAIGAKU. SOGO KENKYUJO *See* KYODO KENKYU KATSUDO HOKOKUSHO **5208**

MOMOYAMA GAKUIN DAIGAKU. SOGO KENKYUJO HO *See* SOGO KENKYUJO HO **2508**

MON FRERE ET MOI (CN/0316-0785) [02468419] **4978**

MON JOURNAL LAURIER DES LAURENTIDES (CN/0225-0969) [06131754] **5790**

MON-KHMER STUDIES (US/0147-5207) [02727383] **3303**

MON MEILLEUR (CN/0228-0663) [07295260] **2801**

MON SEXE (CN/0383-6185) [03222678] **5188**

MONAHANS NEWS (MONAHANS, TEX. : 1931) (US) [14509460] **5752**

● MONALDI ARCHIVES FOR CHEST DISEASE. ARCHIVIO MONALDI PER LE MALATTIE DEL TORACE / FONDAZIONE CLINICA DEL LAVORO, IRCCS [AND] ISTITUTO DI CLINICA TISIOLOGICA E MALATTIE APPARATO RESPIRATORIO, UNIVERSITA DI NAPOLI, SECONDO ATENEO (IT) [28078860] **3950**

MONARCH NOTES. CD-ROM (US) **3413**

MONARCHY CANADA (CN/0319-4019) [01887674] **4482**

MONASH NINETEENTH-CENTURY DRAMA SERIES (AT/0157-471X) [l0157471X] **5366**

MONASH PAPERS ON SOUTHEAST ASIA (AT) [02472243] **2659**

MONASH PUBLICATIONS IN GEOGRAPHY (AT) [02253496] **2569**

MONASH PUBLICATIONS IN HISTORY (AT/0818-0032) [l08180032] **2623**

MONASH SOFTWARE LETTER (US/1062-0451) [25510879] **1288**

MONASH UNIVERSITY *See* RESEARCH REPORT - MONASH UNIVERSITY **1845**

MONASH UNIVERSITY. COUNCIL *See* REPORT OF THE COUNCIL **1844**

MONASH UNIVERSITY. FACULTY OF LAW *See* MONASH UNIVERSITY LAW REVIEW **3011**

MONASH UNIVERSITY LAW REVIEW (AT/0311-3140) [02250467] **3011**

MONASTERIOLOGIA (GR) [19112352] **5039**

MONASTIC STUDIES (CN/0026-9190) [01774005] **5032**

MONATLICHER WITTERUNGSBERICHT (GW/0435-7965) [l04357965] **1431**

MONATSBERICHTE - OESTERREICHISCHES INSTITUT FUER WIRTSCHAFTSFORSCHUNG (AU/0029-9898) [01769112] **1505**

MONATSBERICHTE UBER DIE OSTERREICHISCHE LANDWIRTSCHAFT / AGRARWIRTSCHAFTLICHES INSTITUT DES BUNDESMINISTERIUMS FUER LAND- UND FORSTWIRTSCHAFT (AU/0567-1248) [08456528] **109**

MONATSBEZUEGE DER ANGESTELLTEN IN DER INDUSTRIE OSTERREICHS (AU) [04995455] **1691**

MONATSBLATTER (SZ) [24331163] **5333**

MONATSHEFT DER OSTERREICHISCHEN HOLZAUSFUHR-STATISTIK (AU) [06508165] **2403**

MONATSHEFTE FUER CHEMIE (US/0026-9247) [02362046] **986**

MONATSHEFTE FUER EVANGELISCHE KIRCHENGESCHICHTE DES RHEINLANDES (GW) [05061307] **4979**

MONATSHEFTE FUER MATHEMATIK (AU/0026-9255) [04731576] **3523**

MONATSHEFTE FUER VETERINAERMEDIZIN (GW/0026-9263) [01639793] **5516**

MONATSHEFTE (MADISON, 1946) (US/0026-9271) [01758529] **3303**

MONATSSCHRIFT FUER BRAUWISSENSCHAFT (GW/0723-1520) [09360165] **2369**

MONATSSCHRIFT FUER DEUTSCHES RECHT (GW/0340-1812) [01758533] **3011**

MONATSSCHRIFT FUER KINDERHEILKUNDE (GW/0026-9298) [07106930] **3906**

MONATSSCHRIFT FUER KRIMINOLOGIE UND STRAFRECHTSREFORM (GW/0026-9301) [09818055] **3169**

MONATSSTATISTIK DES AUSSENHANDELS DER SCHWEIZ. STATISTIQUE MENSUELLE DU COMMERCE EXTERIEUR DE LA SUISSE (SZ) [03101757] **846**

● MONCTON CITY DIRECTORY (1992) (CN/1191-9310) [27809650] **2569**

MONCTON, NEW BRUNSWICK, CITY DIRECTORY, INCLUDING DIEPPE AND RIVERVIEW *See* MONCTON CITY DIRECTORY (1992) **2569**

MONDAY DEVELOPMENTS (US/1043-8157) [19609304] **5296**

MONDAY MAGAZINE (1983) (CN/0832-4719) [16948587] **696**

MONDAY MORNING. AL-SHIRA. ACH-CHIRAH (LE) [03823452] **2507**

MONDAY MORNING (INDIANAPOLIS, IND.) (US/0360-6171) [01903933] **5065**

MONDAY MORNING REPORT (US/0891-8651) [15049572] **5296**

MONDAY REPORT (US) **3789**

MONDAY REPORT ON RETAILERS (CN/0700-3528) [03248577] **955**

MONDAY REPORT (TALLAHASSEE, FLA.), THE (US/0733-9089) [01400161] **1866**

MONDE A BICYCLETTE, LE (CN/0823-5570) [10611110] **429**

MONDE ALPHABETIQUE / LE REGROUPEMENT DES GROUPES POPULAIRES EN ALPHABETISATION DU QUEBEC, LE (CN/1183-515X) [25066784] **1764**

MONDE ALPIN ET RHODANIEN, LE (FR) [02481201] 2322, **5269**

MONDE AQUATIQUE (CN/0705-4149) [03956575] **2308**

MONDE ARABE PARIS (FR/1241-5294) [l12415294] **4482**

MONDE CYCLISTE (IT) **429**

MONDE DE LA BIBLE, LE (FR/0154-9049) [03922562] **5018**

MONDE DE LA MUSIQUE, LE (FR/0181-7949) [13346342] **4132**

MONDE DE L'AUTOMOBILE (FR) **5419**

MONDE DE L'EDUCATION, LE (FR/0337-9213) [02380898] **1900**

MONDE DE L'ELECTRICITE, LE (CN/0026-9379) [02068568] **2073**

MONDE DIPLOMATIQUE, LE (FR/0026-9395) [01787978] **4529**

MONDE DIPLOMATIQUE, LE *CEASED.* (MX) [07156222] **4529**

MONDE. DOSSIERS ET DOCUMENTS, LE (FR/0153-419X) [09306997] **2519**

MONDE D'OUTRE-MER, PASSE ET PRESENT (FR/0077-0310) [02481255] **2623**

MONDE DU LOISIR ET DES SPORTS AU QUEBEC (CN/1183-4846) [25423719] **4905**

MONDE DU RENSEIGNEMENT 1988, LE (FR/0997-7139) [l09977139] 4666, **4051**

MONDE DU ROCK (CN/0823-0498) [10441302] 5317, **4132**

MONDE DU RUGBY, LE (FR) [02610429] **4905**

MONDE. ENGLISH EDITION *See* MANCHESTER GUARDIAN WEEKLY **5812**

MONDE ET LES MINERAUX, LE *CEASED.* (FR/0153-9167) [02757452] **1442**

MONDE. INDEX ANALYTIQUE, LE (UK) [02747227] **4817**

Alphabetical Title Index — MONOCLONAL

MONDE INFORMATIQUE, LE (FR/0242-5769) [I02425769] **1195**

MONDE JUIF, LE (FR/0026-9425) [01667302] **2699**

MONDE JURIDIQUE, LE (CN/0828-4989) [11873845] **3011**

MONDE, LE (FR/0395-2037) [01758539] **5800**

MONDE, LE (FR/0395-2037) [02527734] **5800**

MONDE NOUVEAU (THURSO) (CN/0226-0891) [06265071] **2283**

MONDE. REIMPRESSION EN MINIFORMAT, LE (FR/0153-789X) [04771029] **5800**

MONDE. SELECTION HEBDOMADAIRE, LE (FR/0026-9360) [03945430] **5801**

MONDES EN DEVELOPPEMENT (FR/0302-3052) [01792927] **1505**

MONDES ET CULTURES : COMPTES RENDUS TRIMESTRIELS DES SEANCES DE L'ACADEMIE DES SCIENCES D'OUTRE-MER (FR/0221-0436) [07074834] **5129**

MONDES NOUVEAUX (CN/0318-8280) [02729187] **5209**

MONDIAL: BULLETIN OF TENDER ANNOUNCEMENTS (TU) **2526**

MONDO AGRICOLO (IT) [09917441] **109**

MONDO APERTO *CEASED.* (IT/0026-9492) [04048502] **1638**

MONDO ARCHEOLOGICO (IT) [04140935] **275**

MONDO AUTOCAD (IT) **1195**

MONDO BANCARIO (IT/0026-9506) [26387018] **799**

MONDO BARCA (IT) **594**

MONDO CINESE (IT/0390-2811) [01796186] **2507**

MONDO DEL LATTE, IL (IT/0368-9123) [04748056] **197**

MONDO DEL NUOTO (IT) **4905**

MONDO DELLA BIBBIA, IL (IT/1120-7353) [I11207353] **5018**

MONDO DELLA CALZATURA : DESIGN E PRODUZIONE (IT) **3185**

MONDO E MISSIONE (IT/0026-6094) [01798081] **5032**

MONDO ECONOMICO (IT/0026-9522) [02130416] **1574**

MONDO GIUDIZIARIO, IL (IT) [03024092] **3011**

MONDO, IL (IT/0391-6855) [06385458] **2519**

MONDO LADINO : BOLLETTINO DELL'ISTITUTO CULTURALE LADINO (IT) [15621040] 5074, **3304**

MONDO LEGNO (IT/0392-6443) [I03926443] **634**

MONDO ODONTOSTOMATOLOGICO *CEASED.* (IT/0026-9565) [02362058] **1330**

MONDO OPERAIO *See* MONDOPERAIO **4543**

MONDO ORTODONTICO (IT/0391-2000) [03010154] **1330**

MONDO SANITARIO COMMISSIONI GRUPPI STUDI E LAVORO (IT) **3789**

MONDO SOMMERSO (IT) **5536**

MONDO UOMO (IT/0393-8085) [I03938085] **3996**

MONDO VITA *CEASED.* (IT) **4168**

MONDOPERAIO *CEASED.* (IT) [03398415] **4543**

MONDOVI HERALD-NEWS, THE (US) [15021001] **5769**

MONEDA : REVISTA DEL BANCO CENTRAL DE RESERVA DEL PERU (PE) [19968492] **799**

MONEDA Y CREDITO (SP/0026-959X) [04886021] **1593**

MONEDAS (MX) [04177185] **2782**

MONETA E CREDITO (IT/0026-9611) [06385521] **799**

MONETARIA (MX/0185-1136) [04701125] **799**

MONETARY INDICATORS (US) [01644045] **1574**

MONETARY MONOGRAPHS (NE) [15923725] **799**

MONETARY POLICY REPORT FROM THE COMMITTEE ON BANKING, HOUSING, AND URBAN AFFAIRS, UNITED STATES SENATE (US/0270-4005) [05211234] 2828, **799**

MONETARY TRENDS (US/0430-1978) [01716703] **1505**

MONEY AFFAIRS / CEMLA, CENTRE FOR LATIN AMERICAN MONETARY STUDIES (MX) [18677424] **1506**

MONEY AND BANKING (GUILFORD, CONN.) (US) [20765919] **799**

MONEY & REAL ESTATE (US/8756-9124) [11697640] **4841**

MONEY (BOCA RATON) (US/0272-9970) [04451532] **1574**

MONEY (CHICAGO, ILL.) (US/0149-4953) [01588464] **906**

MONEY DIGEST (US/0364-2429) [02981397] **799**

MONEY DIGEST (BATH) (CN/0833-3432) [15645064] **907**

MONEY FINDER (US/0273-8015) [06952946] **799**

MONEY-FINDER REPORTS *See* MONEY FINDER **799**

● MONEY FUND REPORT (US) [29125291] 799, **907**

MONEY INCOME AND POVERTY STATUS OF FAMILIES AND PERSONS IN THE UNITED STATES (US) [08691124] 1506, **4554**

MONEY INCOME OF HOUSEHOLDS, FAMILIES, AND PERSONS IN THE UNITED STATES (US) [08717339] **4554**

● MONEY INCOME TAX HANDBOOK, THE (US/1065-125X) [26513273] **4737**

MONEY LAUNDERING ALERT (US/1046-3070) [20378633] **3087**

MONEY LAUNDERING LAW REPORT (US/1050-4826) [21499797] **3011**

MONEY MACHINE (US/0892-5445) [15246788] **1195**

MONEY MAKING OPPORTUNITIES (US/0192-9399) [05134120] **696**

MONEY MANAGEMENT (UK) **799**

MONEY MANAGEMENT FOR PHYSICIANS *CEASED.* (US/0162-6507) [04201899] **799**

MONEY MANAGEMENT LETTER (US) **907**

MONEY MANAGEMENT UNITHOLDER (UK) **799**

MONEY MANAGER INTERVIEWS (US) [27374035] **907**

MONEY MANAGER PREVIEWS (US/0895-3635) [16572884] **799**

MONEY MANAGER REVIEW (US/1063-2301) [25932876] **907**

MONEY MARKET DIRECTORY OF TAX-EXEMPT ORGANIZATIONS, THE (US/1070-5228) [28397668] **4338**

MONEY MARKET FUND SURVEY'S COMPLETE DIRECTORY OF MONEY MARKET FUNDS (US/0730-949X) [08120239] **907**

MONEY MARKETING (UK) **907**

MONEY OAK, THE (US/8756-3185) [11541235] **799**

MONEY REPORTER (CN) **907**

MONEY STOCK, LIQUID ASSETS, AND DEBT MEASURES / BOARD OF GOVERNORS OF THE FEDERAL RESERVE SYSTEM (US) [10755885] **799**

MONEY TRENDS (SKANEATELES, N.Y.) (US/0731-2776) [08146442] **799**

MONEY WATCH (WASHINGTON, D.C.) *SUSPENDED.* (US/0898-1671) [17735033] 799, **1506**

MONEY WEEK (UK/0951-4767) [I09514767] **696**

MONEYLETTER (CN/0703-7163) [03453062] 799, **907**

MONEYPAPER, THE (US/0745-9858) [09658313] **696**

MONEYPLU$ NEWS (US/1055-9787) [23436422] **799**

MONEYTALK (US/0745-7146) [09394980] **2490**

MONEYWI$E (US/0749-6028) [11171214] **799**

MONEYWORLD (US) **799**

MONGOLIA SOCIETY NEWSLETTER (1985), THE (US/0894-6523) [13780024] **2659**

MONGOLIA SOCIETY OCCASIONAL PAPERS, THE (US/0077-0396) [01589349] **2659**

MONGOLIA SOCIETY SPECIAL PAPERS, THE (US/0896-0925) [18190277] **2659**

MONGOLIAN STUDIES (US/0190-3667) [01416164] **2659**

MONGOLSKAIA *See* SEZD MONGOLSKOI NARODNO-REVOLIUTSIONNOI PARTII **4546**

MONI TALK (US/0896-9884) [17365643] **1619**

MONIST, THE (US/0026-9662) [01758549] **4353**

MONITA NENPO (JA) [10631029] **4666**

MONITEUR AFRICAIN, LE (SG) [02242790] **846**

MONITEUR ARCHITECTURE AMC, LE (FR/0998-4194) [20121566] **303**

MONITEUR BELGE. BELGISCH STAATSBLAD (US) [04507096] **3011**

MONITEUR CONGOLAIS *See* JOURNAL OFFICIEL **2990**

MONITEUR DE L'AUTOMOBILE, LE (BE) **5419**

MONITEUR DES AFFAIRES ET DE LA FINANCE, LE (CN/0226-2894) [06460918] **907**

MONITEUR DES PHARMACIES ET DES LABORATOIRES (FR/0026-9689) [I00269689] **4316**

MONITEUR DES TRAVAUX PUBLICS ET DU BATIMENT, LE (FR/0026-9700) [I00269700] **621**

MONITEUR DU FILM EN BELGIQUE, LE (BE/0771-4874) [I07714874] **4074**

MONITEUR HOSPITALIER, LE (FR/0993-9199) [I09939199] **3789**

MONITEUR INTERNAT PARIS, LE *CEASED.* (FR/0994-4478) [I09944478] **4316**

MONITEUR PROFESSIONNEL DE L'ELECTRICITE, LE (FR) [06445138] **2073**

MONITIN (IS) [05181673] **2507**

MONITOIRES DU CYMBALUM PATAPHYSICUM (FR/0339-7203) [15620005] **4353**

MONITOR (US) [06260293] **2865**

MONITOR (AT) [05918040] 1117, **2073**

MONITOR (UK) [07429092] 1242, 1275, **1277**

MONITOR (IT) [03611768] 2123, **621**

MONITOR (UK) [13351182] **4264**

MONITOR ABINGDON (UK/0260-6666) [I02606666] 1263, **1275**

MONITOR (ATLANTA, GA.), THE (US/0897-1153) [15814200] **4482**

MONITOR (CHARLOTTETOWN) (CN/0703-1513) [03781812] **5790**

MONITOR (CLEARWATER, FLA.) *CEASED.* (US/0895-8777) [16847715] **933**

MONITOR DE LA FARMACIA Y DE LA TERAPEUTICA, EL (SP) [06024247] **4316**

MONITOR ECONOMIA (IT) **1506**

MONITOR-HERALD, THE (US) [14817973] **5701**

MONITOR (LIDGERWOOD, N.D. : 1981) *See* RICHLAND COUNTY NEWS-MONITOR **5726**

MONITOR (MCALLEN, TEX.), THE (US/8750-524X) [11478197] **5752**

MONITOR POLSKI : DZIENNIK URZEDOWY RZECZYPOSPOLITEJ POLSKIEJ (PL) [05933923] **3011**

MONITOR (RICHMOND HILL) (CN/1183-5389) [24368125] **1619**

MONITOR (ROCKVILLE, MD.) (US/1070-2792) [28311781] 1242, 1248, **1270**

MONITOR (STOCKHOLM, SWEDEN) (SW) [11387106] **2236**

MONITOR (TORONTO) (CN/1183-9473) [25423262] **5790**

MONITOR (TRENTON, N.J.), THE (US/0746-8350) [10310959] **5710**

MONITOR WEEKLY, THE (UK) [09257695] **2623**

MONITORE ZOOLOGICO ITALIANO. MONOGRAFIA (IT/0391-1632) [03442275] **5591**

MONITORING & REPORTING PROJECT / GOVERNOR'S TASK FORCE FOR HANDICAPPED CITIZENS (US) [10969723] **4391**

MONITORING FONOVOGO ZAGRIAZNENI!A PRIRODNYKH SRED / GOSUDARSTVENNYI KOMITET SSSR PO GIDROMETEOROLOGII I KONTROLIU PRIRODNOI SREDY, AKADEMIIA NAUK SSSR, LABORATORIIA MONITORINGA PRIRODNOI SREDY I KLIMATA (RU/0234-9140) [09461165] **1431**

MONITORING OF CONCORDE OPERATIONS AT DULLES INTERNATIONAL AIRPORT (US) [03457655] **29**

MONITORING REPORT, THE (US) [06442668] **1135**

MONITORING THE FUTURE (US/0190-9185) [04770475] **5209**

MONITORING TIMES (US/0889-5341) [13943620] **1135**

MONITORUL OFICIAL AL ROMANIEI. PATRTEA 1. PUBLICATII SI ANUNTURI (RM) [22434305] **4666**

MONK (SAN FRANCISCO, CALIF.) (US/0899-6059) [18183102] **4604**

MONKEYSHINES ON AMERICA (US) 2569, **2747**

MONKEYSHINES ON HEALTH AND SCIENCE (US) 2600, **5129**

MONKEYSHINES ON YOU! (US/0899-8116) [18230435] **4863**

● MONMOUTH'S EARLY REPORT (US/1065-7797) [26734245] **1691**

MONOCLONAL ANTIBODIES (UK/0261-4960) [I02614960] **3675**

MONOCLONAL Alphabetical Title Index

MONOCLONAL ANTIBODIES BIBLIOGRAPHY (US) [11894183] **5129**

MONOCLONAL ANTIBODIES (NEW YORK, N.Y.) (US/1047-871X) [20803633] **539**

MONOGRAFIA DEL COLEGIO IBERO-LATINO-AMERICANO DE DERMATOLOGIA (SP/0210-5268) [03991724] **3722**

MONOGRAFIA - FUNDACAO GETULIO VARGAS (BL/0532-8381) [01390487] **5233**

MONOGRAFIA - POLITECHNIKA KRAKOWSKA IM. TADEUSZA KOSCIUSZKI (PL/0860-097X) [I0860097X] **5129**

MONOGRAFIAS (MX) [06141178] **1408**

MONOGRAFIAS DE DERMATOLOGIA : M.D.D (SP/0214-4220) [24910203] **3722**

MONOGRAFIAS DE DIAGNOSTICO POR IMAGEN : MDI (SP) **3944**

MONOGRAFIAS DE LA ACADEMIA NACIONAL DE CIENCIAS EXACTAS, FISICAS Y NATURALES (AG/0327-5426) [I03275426] **5129**

MONOGRAFIAS DE MATEMATICA (BL/0100-0934) [01758556] **3523**

MONOGRAFIAS DEL INSTITUTO DE MATEMATICAS. UNIVERSIDAD NACIONAL AUTONOMA DE MEXICO (MX/0187-4780) [07381083] **3523**

MONOGRAFIAS DEL INSTITUTO EDUARDO TORROJA DE LA CONSTRUCCION Y DEL CEMENTO (SP) [01963755] **621**

MONOGRAFIAS DEL INSTITUTO NACIONAL DE CARDIOLOGIA (MX) [24317903] **3708**

MONOGRAFIAS I.N.I.A (SP) [01166623] **109**

MONOGRAFIAS (INSTITUTO DE PESQUISAS TECNOLOGICAS) (BL/0102-1958) [07756234] **5129**

MONOGRAFIAS - MUSEO ETNOGRAFICO MUNICIPAL "DAMASO ARCE" (AG/0326-7903) [I03267903] **241**

MONOGRAFIE DE IL LAVORO NEUROPSICHIATRICO, LE *CEASED.* (IT/0394-0101) [00929263] **3931**

MONOGRAFIE DI ARCHEOLOGIA LIBICA (IT/0077-4093) [02527296] **275**

MONOGRAFIE MATEMATYCZNE (PL/0077-0507) [01758558] **3523**

MONOGRAM REPORTS (US) **5129**

MONOGRAM, THE (US) [02256439] **4264**

MONOGRAPH (US/0435-4419) [01433225] **5234**

MONOGRAPH - AMERICAN DANCE THERAPY ASSOCIATION (US/0097-627X) [01798631] 1313, **1882**

MONOGRAPH - AMERICAN FISHERIES SOCIETY (US/0362-1715) [02196818] **2308**

MONOGRAPH / AMERICAN HEART ASSOCIATION (US/0891-320X) [13757741] **3708**

MONOGRAPH AND RESEARCH SERIES (UNIVERSITY OF CALIFORNIA, LOS ANGELES. INSTITUTE OF INDUSTRIAL RELATIONS) (US/0739-439X) [08545261] **5209**

MONOGRAPH / ANTIQUARIAN HOROLOGICAL SOCIETY (UK/0518-0333) [07104260] **2916**

MONOGRAPH (ASSOCIATION OF SEXOLOGISTS) (US) [09120261] **5188**

MONOGRAPH / AUSTRALIAN INSTITUTE OF FAMILY STUDIES (AT) [18346233] **2283**

MONOGRAPH. BRITISH SOCIETY FOR PLANT GROWTH REGULATION (UK) [22700603] **109**

MONOGRAPH / BRITISH SOCIETY FOR PLANT GROWTH REGULATION (UK) [23734333] **2424**

MONOGRAPH - CANMET (CN/0821-8234) [11015186] **2146**

MONOGRAPH - CENTRE FOR MANAGEMENT IN AGRICULTURE, INDIAN INSTITUTE OF MANAGEMENT (II) [05318678] 879, **109**

MONOGRAPH - CHILDREN'S PSYCHIATRIC RESEARCH INSTITUTE (CN/0227-8561) [02250093] **3931**

MONOGRAPH / COMMITTEE FOR MONETARY RESEARCH AND EDUCATION (US/0734-0486) [08036111] **799**

MONOGRAPH / EUROPEAN BREWERY CONVENTION (GW/0255-7045) [10586988] **2369**

MONOGRAPH - GEOLOGICAL SURVEY OF ALABAMA (US/0886-7526) [01478907] **1388**

MONOGRAPH - INDIANA ACADEMY OF SCIENCE (US) [04873642] **5129**

MONOGRAPH / INSTITUTE OF APPLIED SOCIAL AND ECONOMIC RESEARCH (PP) [05072302] **5209**

MONOGRAPH: LEGAL AND ADMINISTRATIVE SERIES (SZ) [05698936] 1135, **3011**

MONOGRAPH (MAXWELL GRADUATE SCHOOL OF CITIZENSHIP AND PUBLIC AFFAIRS. METROPOLITAN STUDIES PROGRAM) (US/0738-3207) [09582604] 1506, **4666**

MONOGRAPH - MINERALOGICAL SOCIETY (UK/0144-1485) [11274428] **1442**

MONOGRAPH - NEW YORK PSYCHOANALYTIC INSTITUTE. ERNST KRIS STUDY GROUP (US/0077-9008) [03767752] **4604**

MONOGRAPH OF THE DEPARTMENT OF GEOLOGY AND GEOGRAPHY, ST. LAWRENCE UNIVERSITY (US) [03916829] 2569, **1388**

MONOGRAPH ... OF THE SOCIETY FOR ASIAN AND COMPARATIVE PHILOSOPHY (US) [02998909] **4353**

MONOGRAPH / ONTARIO ASSOCIATION GEOGRAPHIC ENVIRONMENTAL EDUCATION, THE (CN/0048-1793) [02069592] **2569**

MONOGRAPH SERIES (US) [02915320] **3011**

MONOGRAPH SERIES (UK) [01587523] **5018**

MONOGRAPH SERIES (AT) [01518660] **2147**

MONOGRAPH SERIES - AMERICAN ASSOCIATION OF CEREAL CHEMISTS (US/0065-7107) [01479356] **2350**

MONOGRAPH SERIES / AMERICAN GROUP PSYCHOTHERAPY ASSOCIATION (US/0742-3187) [09455770] **3931**

MONOGRAPH SERIES (AUSTRALIA. DEPT. OF HEALTH. POLICY AND PLANNING DIVISION) (AT/0157-5503) [09561580] **4791**

MONOGRAPH SERIES - COLT ARCHAEOLOGICAL INSTITUTE (UK/0588-5132) [03258185] **275**

MONOGRAPH SERIES - CRIMINAL LAW EDUCATION AND RESEARCH CENTER (US/0590-0875) [01565431] **3108**

MONOGRAPH SERIES - DELAWARE MUSEUM OF NATURAL HISTORY (US/0084-9650) [01683487] **4168**

MONOGRAPH SERIES - FACULTY OF COMMERCE AND BUSINESS ADMINISTRATION, UNIVERSITY OF BRITISH COLUMBIA (CN/0572-6972) [01537202] 1506, **696**

MONOGRAPH SERIES (GREAT BRITAIN. PUBLIC HEALTH LABORATORY SERVICE) *CEASED.* (UK/0300-5666) [01645951] **4791**

MONOGRAPH SERIES IN ETHNOMUSICOLOGY (US) [10410445] 2268, **4132**

MONOGRAPH SERIES IN WORLD AFFAIRS (US/0077-0582) [01566255] **4529**

MONOGRAPH SERIES - INSTITUTE FOR PALESTINE STUDIES (LE) [05982393] **4529**

MONOGRAPH SERIES (JAMES COOK UNIVERSITY OF NORTH QUEENSLAND. DEPARTMENT OF GEOGRAPHY) (AT/0158-8273) [06713468] **2569**

MONOGRAPH SERIES OF THE EUROPEAN ORGANIZATION FOR RESEARCH ON TREATMENT OF CANCER (US/0146-0447) [02833745] **3821**

MONOGRAPH SERIES OF THE WEED SCIENCE SOCIETY OF AMERICA (US/1052-6129) [13165634] **178**

MONOGRAPH SERIES ON DENTAL MATERIALS AND THERAPEUTICS / AMERICAN DENTAL ASSOCIATION [AND] COUNCIL ON DENTAL THERAPEUTICS [AND] COUNCIL ON DENTAL MATERIALS, INSTRUMENTS, AND EQUIPMENT (US) [22444890] **1330**

MONOGRAPH SERIES ON MINERAL DEPOSITS (GW/0341-6356) [02163369] **1442**

MONOGRAPH SERIES - ONTARIO INSTITUTE FOR STUDIES IN EDUCATION (CN/0078-5016) [02955100] **1764**

MONOGRAPH SERIES - REGIONAL SCIENCE RESEARCH INSTITUTE (US/0080-0627) [03735157] 2569, **1506**

MONOGRAPH SERIES / SOCIETY FOR NEW TESTAMENT STUDIES (UK) [25054451] **4979**

MONOGRAPH SERIES / SOCIETY FOR THE SCIENTIFIC STUDY OF RELIGION (US) [05166104] **4979**

MONOGRAPH SERIES - UNITED STATES HISTORICAL SOCIETY (US/0146-5651) [01639629] **2747**

MONOGRAPH SERIES (UNIVERSITY OF CALIFORNIA, SAN DIEGO. CENTER FOR U.S.-MEXICAN STUDIES) (US) [10154013] **2747**

MONOGRAPH SERIES - UNIVERSITY OF TULSA (US/0885-761X) [01608056] **3348**

MONOGRAPH - SIGMA THETA TAU (US/0147-5223) [03179057] **3862**

MONOGRAPH - STUDENT PERSONNEL ASSOCIATION FOR TEACHER EDUCATION (US/0562-2174) [05711610] **1836**

MONOGRAPH - UNIVERSITY OF CALIFORNIA, LOS ANGELES. CHICANO STUDIES CENTER (US) [03081981] **2747**

MONOGRAPH / UNIVERSITY OF CAMBRIDGE, DEPT. OF APPLIED ECONOMICS (UK) [07526461] **1506**

MONOGRAPH - UNIVERSITY OF FLORIDA. AGRICULTURAL EXPERIMENT STATION (US/0899-3874) [15966427] **109**

MONOGRAPH - UNIVERSITY OF WASHINGTON. CENTER FOR SOCIAL WORK RESEARCH (US/0883-7643) [12225312] **5296**

MONOGRAPH / [WORLD REHABILITATION FUND] (US/0738-128X) [09438434] 4391, **4381**

MONOGRAPHIAE BIOLOGICAE (NE/0077-0639) [01589565] **465**

MONOGRAPHIAE BOTANICAE (PL/0077-0655) [01758559] **518**

MONOGRAPHIC REVIEW (US/0885-7512) [12712634] **3413**

MONOGRAPHIC SUPPLEMENT ... TO CATALOGING & CLASSIFICATION QUARTERLY *CEASED.* (US/0898-008X) [17688776] **420**

MONOGRAPHIE ... DE L'ENSEIGNEMENT MATHEMATIQUE (SZ/0425-0818) [05884841] **3523**

MONOGRAPHIE - ECOLE DE RELATIONS INDUSTRIELLES, UNIVERSITE DE MONTREAL (CN/0708-9945) [05375340] 1691, **944**

MONOGRAPHIE - INSTITUT INTERUNIVERSITAIRE DES SCIENCES NUCLEAIRES (BE/0534-1299) [01596799] **4448**

MONOGRAPHIEN AUS DEM GESAMTGEBIETE DER PSYCHIATRIE (GW/0077-0671) [01639429] 3931, **3838**

MONOGRAPHIEN ZUR GESCHICHTE DES MITTELALTERS (GW/0026-9832) [01758561] **2699**

MONOGRAPHIEN ZUR PHILOSOPHISCHEN FORSCHUNG (GW) [02630497] **4353**

MONOGRAPHIEN ZUR SCHWEIZER GESCHICHTE (SZ/0581-0353) [02513718] **2699**

MONOGRAPHIEN ZUR VOLKERKUNDE (GW/0440-1522) [02062708] **241**

MONOGRAPHIES FRANCAISES DE PSYCHOLOGIE (FR/0077-071X) [02504858] **4604**

MONOGRAPHIES TECHNIQUES SUR L'UTILISATION DES ACIERS SPECIAUX (FR/0544-8379) [11199166] **4013**

MONOGRAPHS (US) [05290971] **29**

MONOGRAPHS - ACADEMY OF NATURAL SCIENCES OF PHILADELPHIA (US/0096-7750) [01382830] **4168**

MONOGRAPHS AND TEXTBOOKS IN PHYSICAL SCIENCE (US) **5129**

MONOGRAPHS FOR TEACHERS (UK) [01784834] **986**

MONOGRAPHS FOR TEACHERS OF FRENCH *See* FRENCH MONOGRAPHS **3283**

MONOGRAPHS IN ALLERGY (SW/0077-0760) [01758564] **3675**

MONOGRAPHS IN CLINICAL CYTOLOGY (SZ/0077-0809) [01758565] **539**

MONOGRAPHS IN CLINICAL PEDIATRICS (US/1044-4882) [19815996] **3906**

MONOGRAPHS IN CONTEMPORARY AUDIOLOGY (US/0892-1873) [06263343] **3889**

MONOGRAPHS IN DEVELOPMENT ANTHROPOLOGY (US) **241**

MONOGRAPHS IN DEVELOPMENTAL BIOLOGY (SZ/0077-0825) [01770885] **466**

MONOGRAPHS IN DEVELOPMENTAL PEDIATRICS (US/0162-6906) [04130197] **3906**

MONOGRAPHS IN ECONOMIC ANTHROPOLOGY (US/0895-9994) [11284011] **241**

MONOGRAPHS IN EDUCATION (WINNIPEG) (CN/0709-6313) [05694944] **1765**

MONOGRAPHS IN ELECTROANALYTICAL CHEMISTRY AND ELECTROCHEMISTRY SERIES (US) **986**

MONOGRAPHS IN EPIDEMIOLOGY AND BIOSTATISTICS (US/0740-0845) [09585207] **3736**

MONOGRAPHS IN ETHIOPIAN LAND TENURE (ET) [02250468] 1506, **109**

Alphabetical Title Index — MONTANA

MONOGRAPHS IN FETAL PHYSIOLOGY (NE/0165-196X) [02263940] **584**

MONOGRAPHS IN HUMAN GENETICS (SZ/0077-0876) [01777788] **549**

MONOGRAPHS IN INTERNATIONAL STUDIES. AFRICA SERIES (US/1052-0481) [11998945] **2642**

MONOGRAPHS IN INTERNATIONAL STUDIES. SOUTHEAST ASIA SERIES (US/1040-9599) [11998915] **2659**

●MONOGRAPHS IN LINGUISTICS (US/1056-5019) [23725663] **3304**

●MONOGRAPHS IN LINGUISTICS AND THE PHILOSOPHY OF LANGUAGE (US/1065-9528) [26813991] **3304**

MONOGRAPHS IN MATHEMATICS (SZ) [10232261] **3523**

MONOGRAPHS IN NEURAL SCIENCES (SZ/0300-5186) [02824976] **3838**

MONOGRAPHS IN ORAL SCIENCE (SZ/0077-0892) [01770886] **1330**

MONOGRAPHS IN ORGANIZATIONAL BEHAVIOR AND INDUSTRIAL RELATIONS (US) [10661071] **1691**

●MONOGRAPHS IN P/M SERIES (US/1061-6071) [25378595] **4013**

MONOGRAPHS IN PATHOLOGY (US/0077-0922) [01781335] **3896**

MONOGRAPHS IN POPULATION BIOLOGY (US/0077-0930) [01758569] **466**

MONOGRAPHS IN PRIMATOLOGY (US/0740-9729) [09438474] 241, **5591**

MONOGRAPHS IN PSYCHOBIOLOGY (US/0749-1190) [11079188] **466**

MONOGRAPHS IN PSYCHOBIOLOGY AND DISEASE (US/0270-0131) [05733838] 4604, **466**

MONOGRAPHS IN SYSTEMATIC BOTANY FROM THE MISSOURI BOTANICAL GARDEN (US/0161-1542) [03861431] **518**

MONOGRAPHS IN TOXICOLOGY : ENVIRONMENTAL AND SAFETY ASPECTS (UK/0273-2939) [07037398] 2177, **3982**

MONOGRAPHS IN UROLOGY *CEASED.* (US/0198-7577) [06230212] **3991**

MONOGRAPHS IN VIROLOGY (SZ/0077-0965) [01758571] **568**

MONOGRAPHS IN WORLD ARCHAEOLOGY (US/1055-2316) [23123611] **275**

MONOGRAPHS NATIONAL CANCER INSTITUTE (US) **3821**

MONOGRAPHS - NATIONAL CANCER INSTITUTE (U.S.) (US/1052-6773) [21986096] **3821**

MONOGRAPHS OF MARINE MOLLUSCA (US/0162-8321) [04236017] **5591**

MONOGRAPHS OF THE AMERICAN ASSOCIATION ON MENTAL RETARDATION (US/0895-8009) [16800142] **1882**

MONOGRAPHS OF THE AMERICAN COLLEGE OF NUTRITION (US/0164-0585) [04552241] **4194**

MONOGRAPHS OF THE AMERICAN JEWISH ARCHIVES (US/0002-905X) [02406178] **2268**

MONOGRAPHS OF THE ASSOCIATION FOR ASIAN STUDIES (US) [03376153] **2659**

MONOGRAPHS OF THE HEBREW UNION COLLEGE (US/0190-5627) [04732999] **5051**

MONOGRAPHS OF THE HIGH/SCOPE EDUCATIONAL RESEARCH FOUNDATION (US/0149-242X) [03526615] **1765**

MONOGRAPHS OF THE JOURNAL OF THE AMERICAN ACADEMY OF CHILD PSYCHIATRY (US/0065-6852) [02264330] 3931, **3906**

MONOGRAPHS OF THE MARIO NEGRI INSTITUTE FOR PHARMACOLOGICAL RESEARCH (US/0085-3100) [03681647] **4316**

MONOGRAPHS OF THE PESHITTA INSTITUTE, LEIDEN (NE) [22375270] **4979**

MONOGRAPHS OF THE PHYSIOLOGICAL SOCIETY (UK/0079-2020) [01624464] **584**

MONOGRAPHS OF THE PHYSIOLOGICAL SOCIETY OF PHILADELPHIA (US/0148-4427) [03338201] **584**

MONOGRAPHS OF THE RUTGERS CENTER OF ALCOHOL STUDIES (US/0080-4983) [00972407] **1346**

MONOGRAPHS OF THE SOCIETY FOR RESEARCH IN CHILD DEVELOPMENT (US/0037-976X) [01765889] **4604**

MONOGRAPHS OF THE WESTERN FOUNDATION OF VERTEBRATE ZOOLOGY (US/0097-0387) [01334783] **5592**

MONOGRAPHS ON APPLIED OPTICS (US/0077-0973) [01776326] **4438**

MONOGRAPHS ON APPROPRIATE INDUSTRIAL TECHNOLOGY (US) [06163187] **1619**

MONOGRAPHS ON ASTRONOMICAL SUBJECTS (US/0141-1128) [05620723] **397**

MONOGRAPHS ON CRYOGENICS (UK/0265-2994) [09966340] **4431**

MONOGRAPHS ON EDUCATION (FR/0503-4221) [01597182] **1765**

MONOGRAPHS ON ENDOCRINOLOGY (US/0077-1015) [01758574] **3732**

MONOGRAPHS ON FRAGRANCE RAW MATERIALS (UK/0276-704X) [06349530] **404**

MONOGRAPHS ON MUSIC IN HIGHER EDUCATION (US/0093-6642) [01792664] 1836, **4132**

MONOGRAPHS ON OCEANOGRAPHIC METHODOLOGY (FR/0077-104X) [03890164] **1452**

MONOGRAPHS ON STATISTICS AND APPLIED PROBABILITY (UK/0960-6696) [I09606696] **5333**

MONOGRAPHS ON THE ANCIENT NEAR EAST (US/0732-6491) [05430494] **2659**

MONOGRAPHS - ROYAL ASIATIC SOCIETY OF GREAT BRITAIN AND FINLAND. MALAYSIAN BRANCH (SI/0557-384X) [01715710] **2659**

MONOGRAPHS. SOCIAL SCIENCES - UNIVERSITY OF FLORIDA (US) [01996589] **5209**

MONOLITH (US/0147-6653) [03214867] **4132**

MONROE COUNTY BEACON, THE (US) [17165861] **5729**

MONROE COUNTY DEMOCRAT (SPARTA, WIS. : 1895) (US) [13572554] **5769**

MONROE COUNTY GENEALOGICAL SOCIETY NEWS (US/0893-5718) [15585821] **2461**

MONROE COUNTY NEWS (ALBIA, IOWA : 1902) (US) [15213497] **5671**

MONROE COURIER (US) [26890226] **5645**

MONROE EVENING TIMES (MONROE, WIS. 1898) (US/1068-5820) [14758242] **5769**

MONROE JOURNAL, THE (US/0884-8750) [12491130] **5627**

MONROE LEGACY, THE (US) **5671**

MONROE LEGAL REPORTER *SUSPENDED.* (US/0275-0791) [01644321] **3011**

MONROE MIRROR, THE *See* MONROE LEGACY, THE **5671**

MONROE MONITOR/VALLEY NEWS (US/0890-2879) [14205315] **5761**

MONROE WATCHMAN, THE (US) [13090897] **5764**

MONROEVILLE SPECTATOR, THE (US) [10009370] **5729**

MONROVIA, LIBERIA. UNIVERSITY OF LIBERIA. DIVISION OF SCIENCE *See* U. L. SCIENCE MAGAZINE **5167**

MONSALVAT *CEASED.* (SP/0210-4083) [02242024] **4132**

MONSTER WORLD *See* FAMOUS MONSTERS **4068**

MONT FOLLICK SERIES (UK) [02465154] **3304**

MONT-LAURIER (QUEBEC) *See* BULLETIN / VILLE DE MONT-LAURIER **4635**

MONT-ROLLAND (QUEBEC) *See* INFORMATION MONT-ROLLAND **4656**

MONTAG-FRUHBLATT WIENER NEUESTE NACHRICHTEN (AU) [20359632] **5778**

MONTAGE (ROCKVILLE, MD.) (US/0883-5438) [12063617] **2539**

MONTAGE (TORONTO. 1981) (CN/0710-0159) [08469683] **5234**

MONTAGNA OGGI (IT) **2490**

MONTAGNE ET ALPINISME, LA (FR/0047-7923) [02469840] **4875**

MONTAGNES MAGAZINE GRENOBLE (FR/0184-2595) [I01842595] **4875**

MONTAGSPRESSE (AU) [20070618] **5778**

MONTAGUE BURTON LECTURE ON INTERNATIONAL RELATIONS (UK) [01758578] **4529**

MONTAGUE'S MODERN BOTTLE IDENTIFICATION AND PRICE GUIDE (US/0192-3900) [04997917] **2592**

MONTAIGNE STUDIES (US/1049-2917) [21201718] **3413**

MONTALBAN (VE/0252-9076) [02377959] **2699**

MONTANA *See* MONTANA MAGAZINE **2539**

MONTANA (US/0026-9891) [02438980] **2747**

MONTANA *See* MONTANA CODE ANNOTATED **3011**

MONTANA ACADEMY OF SCIENCES *See* PROCEEDINGS OF THE MONTANA ACADEMY OF SCIENCES **5141**

MONTANA. AGING SERVICES BUREAU *See* MONTANA AGING SERVICES PROGRAM BOOK **5296**

MONTANA AGING SERVICES PROGRAM BOOK (US/0270-3823) [06383845] **5296**

MONTANA AGRESEARCH (US/0895-1489) [11035473] **110**

MONTANA AGRICULTURAL STATISTICS (US) [04799233] 110, **155**

MONTANA AGRICULTURAL STATISTICS BULLETIN (US) **155**

MONTANA AIR QUALITY DATA AND INFORMATION SUMMARY FOR ... (US/0732-2801) [08320228] **2236**

MONTANA. BOARD OF CRIME CONTROL *See* MONTANA COMPREHENSIVE PLAN FOR CRIMINAL JUSTICE IMPROVEMENT **3170**

MONTANA. BOARD OF CRIME COUNCIL *See* ANNUAL ACTION PROGRAMS - MONTANA. BOARD OF CRIME COUNCIL **3156**

MONTANA. BOARD OF INVESTMENTS *See* FISCAL YEAR REPORT - STATE OF MONTANA. BOARD OF INVESTMENTS **899**

MONTANA. BOARD OF MILK CONTROL *See* ANNUAL REPORT - MONTANA. BOARD OF MILK CONTROL **192**

MONTANA. BOARD OF OIL AND GAS CONSERVATION *See* MONTANA OIL AND GAS STATISTICAL BULLETIN / BOARD OF OIL AND GAS CONSERVATION **4264**

MONTANA BUREAU OF MINES AND GEOLOGY *See* GEOLOGIC MAP - MONTANA BUREAU OF MINES AND GEOLOGY **1377**

MONTANA BUREAU OF MINES AND GEOLOGY *See* SPECIAL PUBLICATION - STATE OF MONTANA, BUREAU OF MINES AND GEOLOGY **1398**

MONTANA BUSINESS QUARTERLY (US/0026-9921) [01758606] 696, **1506**

MONTANA CASE NAMES CITATOR (US) **3011**

MONTANA CATHOLIC, THE (US/0883-7899) [12211042] **5032**

MONTANA CODE ANNOTATED (US) [08003126] **3011**

MONTANA CODE ANNOTATED STATUTES TEXT (US) **3012**

MONTANA COMPREHENSIVE PLAN FOR CRIMINAL JUSTICE IMPROVEMENT (US) [03283554] **3170**

MONTANA CPA (US) **748**

MONTANA. CRIMINAL JUSTICE DATA CENTER *See* CRIME IN MONTANA **3080**

MONTANA CROP & LIVESTOCK REPORTER (US/0279-0394) [07471819] 216, **178**

MONTANA DAV NEWS (US) [03366777] **4052**

MONTANA. DEPT. OF ADMINISTRATION. ACCOUNTING DIVISION *See* MONTANA SUPPLEMENTAL FINANCIAL SCHEDULES **4737**

MONTANA. DEPT. OF AGRICULTURE *See* ANNUAL REPORT OF THE DEPARTMENT OF AGRICULTURE (MONTANA) **61**

MONTANA. DEPT. OF BUSINESS REGULATION *See* ANNUAL REPORT OF THE DEPARTMENT OF BUSINESS REGULATION (HELENA) **823**

MONTANA. DEPT. OF HEALTH AND ENVIRONMENTAL SCIENCES *See* MONTANA STATE PLAN FOR ALCOHOL ABUSE AND ALCOHOLISM PREVENTION, TREATMENT, AND REHABILITATION, THE **1347**

MONTANA. DEPT. OF HEALTH AND ENVIRONMENTAL SCIENCES. BUREAU OF RECORDS & STATISTICS *See* MONTANA VITAL STATISTICS **4562**

MONTANA. DEPT. OF MILITARY AFFAIRS *See* ANNUAL REPORT OF THE DEPARTMENT OF MILITARY AFFAIRS TO THE GOVERNOR OF MONTANA **4035**

MONTANA. DEPT. OF PUBLIC INSTRUCTION *See* DESCRIPTIVE REPORT OF PROGRAM ACTIVITIES FOR VOCATIONAL EDUCATION **1912**

MONTANA. DEPT. OF SOCIAL AND REHABILITATION SERVICES *See* ANNUAL REPORT OF THE DEPARTMENT OF SOCIAL AND REHABILITATION SERVICES TO THE GOVERNOR OF MONTANA **5272**

MONTANA — Alphabetical Title Index

MONTANA DIRECTORY OF TRADE AND TECHNICAL ASSOCIATIONS *See* MONTANA DIRECTORY OF TRADE, TECHNICAL, AND SELECTED PROFESSIONAL ASSOCIATIONS **846**

MONTANA DIRECTORY OF TRADE, TECHNICAL, AND SELECTED PROFESSIONAL ASSOCIATIONS (US) [06702458] **846**

MONTANA. DIVISION OF EMPLOYMENT SECURITY RESEARCH AND ANALYSIS SECTION *See* ANNUAL PLANNING INFORMATION FOR MONTANA, RURAL CEP AREA, BALANCE-OF-THE-STATE, BILLINGS SMSA, GREAT FALLS SMSA **1646**

MONTANA. DIVISION OF EMPLOYMENT SECURITY. RESEARCH AND ANALYSIS SECTION *See* MONTANA ECONOMIC INDICATORS **1574**

MONTANA ECONOMIC INDICATORS (US/0146-4302) [02942670] **1574**

MONTANA ENVIRONMENTAL QUALITY COUNCIL *See* ANNUAL REPORT - ENVIRONMENTAL QUALITY COUNCIL **2160**

MONTANA ENVIRONMENTAL SCIENCES (US/0193-8126) [05243570] **2236**

MONTANA FARMER-STOCKMAN (US/1041-1674) [02251248] **216**

MONTANA. FIRE MARSHAL BUREAU *See* ANNUAL REPORT - MONTANA. FIRE MARSHAL BUREAU **5272**

MONTANA. FISH AND GAME DEPARTMENT *See* SPECIAL REPORT - MONTANA FISH AND GAME DEPARTMENT **2313**

MONTANA FOOD DISTRIBUTOR (US/0047-7931) [04055680] **2350**

MONTANA GEOLOGICAL SOCIETY *See* NEWS LETTER / MONTANA GEOLOGICAL SOCIETY **1389**

MONTANA GRAIN NEWS (US/1046-6088) [20480601] **203**

●MONTANA HEALTH CARE IN PERSPECTIVE (US/1065-4283) [26605830] **4791**

MONTANA HEALTH SYSTEMS AGENCY *See* GRANT APPLICATION FOR CONTINUATION OF FULL DESIGNATION **4777**

MONTANA HISTORICAL ENERGY STATISTICS (US) [06176940] 1950, **1963**

MONTANA HUMAN SERVICES DIRECTORY (US/0160-595X) [03691836] **5297**

MONTANA IN PERSPECTIVE (US/1065-5557) [26659732] **5333**

MONTANA LAW REVIEW (US/0026-9972) [01605472] **3012**

MONTANA LAW WEEK (US) **3012**

MONTANA LAWYER, THE (US/0276-3788) [05039377] **3012**

MONTANA. LEGISLATIVE ASSEMBLY. ADMINISTRATIVE CODE COMMITTEE *See* BIENNIAL REPORT TO THE LEGISLATURE - MONTANA LEGISLATIVE ASSEMBLY. ADMINISTRATIVE CODE COMMITTEE **2941**

MONTANA. LEGISLATIVE ASSEMBLY. ADMINISTRATIVE CODE COMMITTEE *See* ADMINISTRATIVE CODE COMMITTEE BIENNIAL REPORT TO THE ... LEGISLATURE **4461**

MONTANA. LEGISLATIVE ASSEMBLY. ADMINISTRATIVE CODE COMMITTEE. BIENNIAL REPORT TO THE LEGISLATURE *See* ADMINISTRATIVE CODE COMMITTEE BIENNIAL REPORT TO THE ... LEGISLATURE **4461**

MONTANA. LEGISLATIVE ASSEMBLY. HOUSE OF REPRESENTATIVES. HOUSE JOURNAL *See* HOUSE JOURNAL OF THE ... LEGISLATURE OF THE STATE OF MONTANA **4476**

MONTANA. LEGISLATIVE ASSEMBLY. OFFICE OF THE LEGISLATIVE AUDITOR *See* STATE OF MONTANA, DEPARTMENT OF LABOR AND INDUSTRY, WORKMEN'S COMPENSATION DIVISION, REPORT ON REVIEW OF CERTAIN INSURANCE AND DISABILITY COMPENSATION OPERATIONS **1712**

MONTANA. LEGISLATIVE ASSEMBLY. SENATE. SENATE JOURNAL *See* SENATE JOURNAL OF THE ... LEGISLATURE OF THE STATE OF MONTANA **4495**

MONTANA. LEGISLATURE *See* SENATE AND HOUSE JOURNALS OF THE ... LEGISLATURE OF THE STATE OF MONTANA COMMENCING IN SPECIAL SESSION ... AND ENDING ... **4495**

MONTANA. LEGISLATURE. HOUSE OF REPRESENTATIVES *See* HOUSE JOURNAL OF THE ... LEGISLATURE OF THE STATE OF MONTANA **4476**

MONTANA. LEGISLATURE. LEGISLATIVE COUNCIL *See* LEGISLATIVE REVIEW **3002**

MONTANA. LEGISLATURE. SENATE *See* SENATE JOURNAL OF THE ... LEGISLATURE OF THE STATE OF MONTANA **4495**

MONTANA LIBRARY DIRECTORY, WITH STATISTICS OF MONTANA PUBLIC LIBRARIES (US/0094-873X) [01795318] 3232, **3259**

MONTANA MAGAZINE (US/0274-9955) [06846181] **2539**

MONTANA MANUFACTURERS & PRODUCTS DIRECTORY *See* MONTANA MANUFACTURERS DIRECTORY **3485**

●MONTANA MANUFACTURERS DIRECTORY (US/1057-6681) [24092078] **3485**

MONTANA MINING DIRECTORY (US) [24916765] **2147**

MONTANA MORBIDITY REPORT (US/0745-5429) [09273142] **4554**

MONTANA ... NETWORK REVIEW (US/0883-4458) [12068579] **2236**

MONTANA NEWSPAPER RATES AND DATA (US) **5705**

MONTANA. OFFICE OF THE GOVERNOR *See* GOVERNOR'S BIENNIAL REPORT (MONTANA) **4652**

MONTANA. OFFICE OF THE GOVERNOR *See* BUDGET AMENDMENT REPORT **4714**

MONTANA. OFFICE OF THE LEGISLATIVE AUDITOR *See* STATE OF MONTANA DEPARTMENT OF NATURAL RESOURCES AND CONSERVATION : REPORT ON EXAMINATION OF FINANCIAL STATEMENT **2206**

MONTANA. OFFICE OF THE LEGISLATIVE AUDITOR *See* STATE OF MONTANA OFFICE OF THE SUPERINTENDENT OF PUBLIC INSTRUCTION AND BOARD OF PUBLIC EDUCATION : REPORT ON AUDIT **4688**

MONTANA. OFFICE OF THE LEGISLATIVE AUDITOR *See* STATE OF MONTANA, BOARD OF EXAMINERS, REPORT ON EXAMINATION OF FINANCIAL STATEMENTS **4749**

MONTANA. OFFICE OF THE LEGISLATIVE AUDITOR *See* REPORT OF EVALUATION OF STUDENT FINANCIAL AID (HELENA) **1844**

MONTANA. OFFICE OF THE STATE CO-ORDINATOR OF INDIAN AFFAIRS *See* REPORT - OFFICE OF THE STATE CO-ORDINATOR OF INDIAN AFFAIRS (MONTANA) **2272**

MONTANA. OIL AND GAS CONSERVATION DIVISION *See* ANNUAL REVIEW FOR THE YEAR RELATING TO OIL AND GAS **4250**

MONTANA OIL AND GAS STATISTICAL BULLETIN / BOARD OF OIL AND GAS CONSERVATION (US) [07246388] **4264**

MONTANA OIL JOURNAL (1953) (US/0047-794X) [02251250] **4264**

MONTANA OUTDOORS (US/0027-0016) [01758613] **4875**

MONTANA PLAN FOR CRIMINAL JUSTICE IMPROVEMENT *See* MONTANA COMPREHENSIVE PLAN FOR CRIMINAL JUSTICE IMPROVEMENT **3170**

MONTANA POSTAL CACHE (US/0146-5368) [02969399] **1145**

MONTANA SCIENCE & TECHNOLOGY ALLIANCE *See* BIENNIAL REPORT / MONTANA SCIENCE & TECHNOLOGY ALLIANCE **5088**

MONTANA SOCIAL SERVICE, HEALTH AND RECREATIONAL DIRECTORY *See* MONTANA HUMAN SERVICES DIRECTORY **5297**

MONTANA STATE AGING SERVICES BUREAU RESOURCE BOOK *See* MONTANA AGING SERVICES PROGRAM BOOK **5296**

MONTANA STATE ARCHITECTURAL REVIEW (US/0741-6849) [09789090] **303**

MONTANA. STATE BUREAU OF MINES AND GEOLOGY *See* REPORT - MONTANA STATE BUREAU OF MINES AND GEOLOGY **1394**

MONTANA STATE HEALTH PLAN (US) [06100217] **4791**

MONTANA. STATE LIBRARY, HELENA *See* WEEKLY LIST OF MONTANA STATE PUBLICATIONS RECEIVED BY MONTANA STATE LIBRARY **4694**

MONTANA STATE PLAN FOR ALCOHOL ABUSE AND ALCOHOLISM PREVENTION, TREATMENT, AND REHABILITATION, THE (US/0090-3809) [01784902] **1347**

MONTANA STATE UNIVERSITY *See* ALUMNI DIRECTORY / MONTANA STATE UNIVERSITY **1098**

MONTANA. STATEWIDE HEALTH COORDINATING COUNCIL *See* MONTANA STATE HEALTH PLAN **4791**

MONTANA SUPPLEMENTAL FINANCIAL SCHEDULES (US) [11570765] **4737**

MONTANA SUPREME COURT PREVIEWS (US) **3012**

MONTANA TAXATION (US) [18398812] **4737**

MONTANA TAXATION (US) [03369195] **4737**

MONTANA TAXPAYER'S ASSOCIATION *See* MONTANA TAXATION **4737**

MONTANA. UNIVERSITY, MISSOULA. COLLEGE OF ARTS AND SCIENCES *See* CAS FORUM **1814**

MONTANA. UNIVERSITY, MISSOULA. DEPT. OF ANTHROPOLOGY *See* UNIVERSITY OF MONTANA CONTRIBUTIONS TO ANTHROPOLOGY **247**

MONTANA VITAL STATISTICS (US/0077-1198) [01785077] **4562**

MONTANA WATER POLLUTION CONTROL PROGRAM PLAN (US/0149-8509) [03565217] **5536**

MONTANA. WATER QUALITY BUREAU *See* MONTANA WATER POLLUTION CONTROL PROGRAM PLAN **5536**

MONTANA. WATER RESOURCES DIVISION *See* PROGRESS REPORT OF THE MONTANA STATE WATER PLAN **2095**

MONTANA WILDLIFE (BOZEMAN, MONT.) (US/0746-9896) [10447602] **2198**

MONTANA WOOLGROWER (US/0027-0024) [03281349] **216**

MONTANARO D'ITALIA, MONTI E BOSCHI *See* MONTANARO D'ITALIA (TORINO, ITALY) **2388**

MONTANARO D'ITALIA (TORINO, ITALY) (IT) [15482562] **2388**

MONTCLAIR JOURNAL OF SOCIAL SCIENCES AND HUMANITIES, THE *SUSPENDED.* (US/0093-5778) [05672538] 2850, **5209**

MONTCLAIR TIMES, THE (US) [13200616] **5710**

MONTE CARLO METHODS AND APPLICATIONS (NE/0929-9629) **5129**

MONTE VISTA JOURNAL, THE (US) [21096821] **5643**

MONTECITO LIFE (US/8750-4863) [11434492] **5637**

MONTEDISON GROUP *See* FACTS AND FIGURES (MONTEDISON GROUP) **675**

MONTEFIORE MEDICINE (US/0149-6735) [03066966] **3618**

MONTEMORA (US) [02917482] **3413**

MONTEREY LIFE *SUSPENDED.* (US/0274-8770) [06669394] **2539**

MONTEREY, MEXICO. INSTITUTO TECNOLOGICO Y DE ESTUDIOS SUPERIORES. DIVISION DE CIENCIAS AGROPECUARIAS Y MARITIMAS *See* INFORME DE INVESTIGACION - DIVISION DE CIENCIAS AGROPECUARIAS Y MARITIMAS, INSTITUTO TECNOLOGICO DE MONTEREY **96**

MONTESANO GRAYS HARBOR COUNTY VIDETTE, THE (US/0745-7383) [09421054] **5761**

MONTESSORI LIFE (US/1054-0040) [21889616] **1882**

MONTESSORI NEWS / IMS (US/0889-6720) [14077642] **1765**

MONTESSORI OBSERVER / IMS, THE (US/0889-5643) [13983524] **1765**

MONTEVALLO TODAY (US/1052-3634) [22256674] **1102**

MONTEVIDEO. BIBLIOTECA DEL PODER LEGISLATIVO. DEPARTAMENTO DE SELECCION Y REGISTRO DE MATERIAL BIBLIOGRAFICO *See* BOLETIN BIBLIOGRAFICO - DEPARTAMENTO DE SELECCION Y REGISTRO DE MATERIAL BIBLIOGRAFICO **411**

MONTEVIDEO, UNIVERSIDAD. FACULTAD DE HUMANIDADES Y CIENCIAS. SECCION HISTORIA DE LA CULTURA *See* FUENTES PARA LA HISTORIA SOCIAL Y ECONOMICA DEL RIO DE LA PLATA **2734**

MONTEZUMA VALLEY JOURNAL (US) [03547277] **5643**

MONTFORT A LA UNE (CN/1182-1574) [22378784] **5297**

MONTGOMERY ADVERTISER (1987), THE (US/0892-4457) [15155895] **5627**

MONTGOMERY BUSINESS (US/0889-4442) [13895424] **696**

MONTGOMERY CO., MD. OFFICE OF INFORMATION *See* REPORT ON ACTIVITIES OF THE COUNTY GOVERNMENT DURING THE FISCAL YEAR, A **4681**

MONTGOMERY COUNTY BUSINESS DIRECTORY (US/1060-4898) [23831964] **696**

MONTGOMERY COUNTY GENEALOGICAL SOCIETY QUARTERLY (US/1041-777X) [09301638] **2461**

MONTGOMERY COUNTY LAW REPORTER (US) [01715588] **3012**

MONTGOMERY COUNTY (MD.). DEPT. OF FINANCE *See* COMPREHENSIVE ANNUAL FINANCIAL REPORT MONTGOMERY COUNTY, MARYLAND **4718**

Alphabetical Title Index — MONTHLY

MONTGOMERY COUNTY (MD.). DEPT. OF FINANCE. OFFICE OF THE DIRECTOR *See* REVENUE COMPARISON WITH FY ... AND FY ... ESTIMATES **4746**

MONTGOMERY COUNTY REAL ESTATE REPORT (US) **4841**

MONTGOMERY COUNTY SENTINEL (US) [19232398] **5686**

MONTGOMERY COUNTY STORY, THE (US) [10965147] **2747**

MONTGOMERY HERALD, THE (US) [12776088] **5764**

MONTGOMERY INDEPENDENT, THE (US) [14279902] **5627**

MONTGOMERY JOURNAL, THE (US/0162-2080) [04122588] **5759**

MONTGOMERY MESSENGER (US) [01713770] **5697**

MONTGOMERYSHIRE COLLECTIONS (UK/0144-0071) [04856504] **2699**

MONTH AT UNESCO, THE (FR/1014-9759) [06270768] **4979**

MONTH (LONDON. 1882), THE (UK/0027-0172) [01589103] **4979**

MONTHLY ALERT / INFOSOUTH (US) [21111228] **2388**

MONTHLY & SEASONAL WEATHER OUTLOOK (US/1057-9664) [08686468] **1431**

MONTHLY BENEFIT STATISTICS (CHICAGO) (US/0364-7129) [02653115] **1691**, **1536**

MONTHLY BIBLIOGRAPHY. PART II, SELECTED ARTICLES / UNITED NATIONS, LIBRARY (SZ/0251-6624) [04635247] **4529**

MONTHLY BIBLIOGRAPHY. PT 1 : BOOKS, OFFICIAL DOCUMENTS, SERIALS (SZ/0251-6616) [05022250] **420**

MONTHLY BULLETIN (MY/0126-5865) [10859894] **5076**

MONTHLY BULLETIN / BANCO DE PORTUGAL, RESEARCH AND STATISTICS DEPARTMENT (PO/0871-0783) [19743356] **799**

MONTHLY BULLETIN CONSTRUCTION INDICES FOR USE WITH NATIONAL ECONOMIC DEVELOPMENT OFFICE PRICE ADJUSTMENT FORMULA. CIVIL ENGINEERING WORKS *See* MONTHLY BULLETIN OF INDICES PRICE ADJUSTMENT FORMULAE FOR CONSTRUCTION CONTRACTS **633**

MONTHLY BULLETIN (KREDIETBANK (BRUSSELS, BELGIUM)) (BE) [17567286] **907**, **1506**

MONTHLY BULLETIN NORTH SEA (NE/0168-8332) [I01688332] **1358**

MONTHLY BULLETIN / OAPEC, ORGANIZATION OF ARAB PETROLEUM EXPORTING COUNTRIES *SUSPENDED.* (KU) [19508077] **4264**

MONTHLY BULLETIN OF INDICES. PRICE ADJUSTMENT FORMULAE FOR BUILDING CONTRACTS *See* MONTHLY BULLETIN OF INDICES PRICE ADJUSTMENT FORMULAE FOR CONSTRUCTION CONTRACTS **633**

MONTHLY BULLETIN OF INDICES PRICE ADJUSTMENT FORMULAE FOR CONSTRUCTION CONTRACTS (UK/0964-4571) [I09644571] **633**

MONTHLY BULLETIN OF STATISTICS, THE REPUBLIC OF CHINA (CH/0256-2324) [03150891] **5333**

MONTHLY BULLETIN OF STATISTICS - UNITED NATIONS (US/0041-7432) [01713528] **5333**

MONTHLY BULLETIN OF THE MINISTRY OF HEALTH & THE PUBLIC HEALTH LABORATORY SERVICE *See* HEALTH TRENDS **4781**

MONTHLY BULLETIN, PORT OF CHITTAGONG (BG) [06825757] **5453**

MONTHLY BUSINESS ANALYSIS (CN/0047-8024) [02069647] **696**

MONTHLY BUSINESS & TAX BULLETIN (PH/0115-1657) [02242638] **3102**

● MONTHLY BUSINESS FAILURES / THE DUN & BRADSTREET CORPORATION (US) [28260688] **696**

MONTHLY BUSINESS REVIEW - FEDERAL RESERVE BANK OF DALLAS (US) [01332279] **1506**

MONTHLY CATALOG OF UNITED STATES GOVERNMENT PUBLICATIONS (US/0362-6830) [02264351] **4666**

MONTHLY CATALOG OF UNITED STATES GOVERNMENT PUBLICATIONS (US) [16403500] **420**

MONTHLY CATALOG PREVIEWS : A MONTHLY INDEX TO U.S. GOVERNMENT PUBLICATIONS DISTRIBUTED TO DEPOSITORY LIBRARIES IN PRINT OF MICROFICHE FOR ... *CEASED.* (US) [25771746] **420**

MONTHLY CHECKLIST OF STATE PUBLICATIONS (US/0027-0288) [02553426] **420**

MONTHLY CLIMATIC DATA FOR THE WORLD (US/0027-0296) [04512269] **1431**

MONTHLY COFFEE STATISTICS (US/0730-3254) [06912935] 2369, **2362**

MONTHLY COLDS STORAGE REPORT (CHICAGO, ILL.) (US/0744-2998) [08173384] **216**

MONTHLY COLLECTOR (SUDBURY) (CN/0707-2937) [04635204] **2786**

MONTHLY COMMENTARY AND OUTLOOK (CN/1182-8919) [23659541] **110**

MONTHLY COMMENTARY ON INDIAN ECONOMIC CONDITIONS (II/0027-030X) [01758636] **1574**

MONTHLY COMMODITY PRICE BULLETIN (SZ/0251-6438) [07303332] **110**

MONTHLY COTTON LINTERS REVIEW *See* MONTHLY COTTON LINTERS REVIEW **179**

MONTHLY COTTON LINTERS REVIEW (US/0027-0318) [05979000] 5354, **179**

MONTHLY CRUDE STEEL PRODUCTION (BE) **1619**

MONTHLY DIGEST OF STATISTICS (SI) [02045976] **5333**

MONTHLY DIGEST OF STATISTICS (ZA/0027-0377) [01477712] **5333**

MONTHLY DIGEST OF STATISTICS (UK/0017-3622) [01751426] **5333**

MONTHLY DIGEST OF TAX ARTICLES, THE (US/0027-0385) [01758639] **4737**

MONTHLY DIGESTS OF SOVIET ELECTRONICS PAPERS (US/1054-8483) [22917867] **2073**

MONTHLY DIRECTORY OF S. ASIAN ASSOCIATIONS & BUSINESSES, THE (CN/0700-3471) [03279382] **696**

MONTHLY ECONOMIC LETTER - PRIVATE DEVELOPMENT CORPORATION OF THE PHILIPPINES (PH) [02514303] **799**

MONTHLY ECONOMIC REPORT - NATIONAL DEVELOPMENT FINANCE CORPORATION. ECONOMIC RESEARCH & PROJECT DIVISION (PK) [02468705] **1575**

MONTHLY ECONOMIC REVIEW (JA/0005-5255) [02265124] **799**

MONTHLY ECONOMIC REVIEW (OTTAWA) (CN/0712-4791) [09313044] **1506**

MONTHLY ECONOMIC SURVEY (UK) **110**

MONTHLY ECONOMIC SURVEY - INTERNATIONAL COMMERCIAL BANK OF CHINA (CH/1013-9893) [01604893] 799, **1506**

MONTHLY EMPLOYMENT AND QUARTERLY WAGES OF WORKERS COVERED BY THE MISSISSIPPI EMPLOYMENT SECURITY LAW, BY COUNTY, BY INDUSTRY *See* MISSISSIPPI COVERED EMPLOYMENT & WAGES **1691**

MONTHLY ENERGY INDICATORS *See* MONTHLY ENERGY REVIEW **1950**

MONTHLY ENERGY REVIEW (US/0095-7356) [01798576] **1950**

MONTHLY ENERGY REVIEW DATABASE [COMPUTER FILE] (US) [24124135] **1950**

MONTHLY EX.-IM. OPPORTUNITIES (CN/0384-6032) [03304189] **846**

MONTHLY EXPORT TRENDS (PK) [15161305] **846**

MONTHLY F.O.B. PRICE SUMMARY PAST SALES. INLAND MILLS (US/0195-9409) [05711339] **2403**

MONTHLY FOREIGN TRADE STATISTICS OF PAKISTAN (PK/0552-8267) [01774038] 1506, **1536**

MONTHLY GAS UTILITY STATISTICAL REPORT (US) [01715406] **4698**

MONTHLY GUIDE TO RECORDED MUSIC, THE (UK) [10075279] **4132**

MONTHLY IMPORT DETENTION LIST / DEPT. OF HEALTH AND HUMAN SERVICES, FOOD AND DRUG ADMINISTRATION (US) [12043967] **2350**

MONTHLY INDEX TO THE FINANCIAL TIMES (UK) [09503324] **1506**

MONTHLY INDICATORS OF CURRENT ECONOMIC SITUATION OF BANGLADESH (BG) [17257944] **1575**

MONTHLY INDICATORS - WOOD GUNDY LIMITED (CN/0826-7758) [12199529] **1506**

MONTHLY INFORMATION REVIEW - BANQUE MAROCAINE DU COMMERCE EXTERIEUR (MR/0851-0202) [03807163] **846**

MONTHLY JOB SERVICE STATISTICS (US) [15128310] **2888**

MONTHLY LABOR REVIEW (US/0098-1818) [05345258] **1691**

MONTHLY LAW DIGEST, THE (II) [10941349] **3012**

MONTHLY LETTER ABOUT EVANGELISM. LETTRE MENSUELLE SUR L'EVANGELISATION, A (SZ/0540-8059) [01777718] **4979**

MONTHLY MARKET STATISTICS (HK) **5333**

MONTHLY MASTER/MONTHLY RETURNS (US/1052-3464) [13577406] **907**

MONTHLY MEMO (US) [05300958] **696**

MONTHLY MEMO - MAINE LIBRARY ASSOCIATION AND MAINE STATE LIBRARY (US) [05666347] **3232**

MONTHLY MIGRATION AND TOURIST STATISTICS FOR ... (RH) [08287542] **5500**

MONTHLY MINI-LESSONS IN CARE OF THE AGING (US/0889-4744) [13900390] **5180**

MONTHLY MLS STATISTICAL SURVEY (CN/0839-6361) [19095499] **4841**

MONTHLY MOTOR FUEL REPORTED BY STATES (US) [12247594] **4264**

MONTHLY MUSIC REPORT (US/1056-2877) [23612828] **4132**

MONTHLY NEW FOOD PRODUCTS IN JAPAN (JA) [05637744] **2350**

MONTHLY NEWS BULLETIN (II/0581-300X) [01695726] **3413**

MONTHLY NEWS LETTER / MAINE MERCHANTS ASSOCIATION (US/0744-9208) [08656295] **696**

MONTHLY NEWS - MULTICULTURAL COUNCIL OF WINDSOR AND ESSEX COUNTY (CN/0710-9695) [08454672] **2268**

MONTHLY NEWSLETTER - AMERICAN ASSOCIATION OF THEOLOGICAL SCHOOLS (US) [02071788] **4979**

MONTHLY NEWSLETTER FOR THE DATACOMM'S INDUSTRY (UK/0952-5475) **1238**

MONTHLY NEWSLETTER - INDIAN INVESTMENT CENTRE (II/0019-4999) [01797754] 799, **907**

MONTHLY NEWSLETTER (UNITED STATES. NAVY DEPT. BUREAU OF SUPPLIES AND ACCOUNTS) *See* NEWSLETTER - UNITED STATES. NAVY. SUPPLY CORPS **4181**

MONTHLY NEWSPRINT STATISTICAL REPORT (US/0889-7565) [07141500] **4566**

MONTHLY NEWSPRINT STATISTICS / CANADIAN PULP AND PAPER ASSOCIATION (CN/0709-602X) [05765580] 4235, **4240**

MONTHLY NOTES OF THE ASTRONOMICAL SOCIETY OF SOUTHERN AFRICA (SA/0024-8266) [01712338] **397**

MONTHLY NOTICES OF THE ROYAL ASTRONOMICAL SOCIETY (UK/0035-8711) [02450289] **397**

MONTHLY OIL AND GAS PRODUCTION REPORT (CN/0228-5622) [05987308] **4264**

MONTHLY OIL AND GAS STATISTICS (FR) **4284**

MONTHLY OIL REPORT (UK) **4264**

MONTHLY OPERATIONAL SUMMARY (US/0379-8674) [25613739] **1506**

MONTHLY PETROLEUM INFORMATION (NR/0549-2513) [05022955] **4265**

MONTHLY POULTRY SUGGESTIONS / DEPARTMENT OF ANIMAL SCIENCE, COLLEGE OF AGRICULTURE, UNIVERSITY OF ILLINOIS AT URBANA-CHAMPAIGN (US) [08633722] **216**

MONTHLY PRESCRIBING REFERENCE (US/0883-0266) [12055122] **3618**

MONTHLY PRODUCT ANNOUNCEMENT / U.S. DEPARTMENT OF COMMERCE, BUREAU OF THE CENSUS (US) [07372650] **4554**

MONTHLY PRODUCTION OF PIG IRON IN 54 IISI COUNTRIES (BE) **1619**

MONTHLY PRODUCTION OF SELECTED INDUSTRIES OF INDIA (II) [02960156] 1619, **1536**

MONTHLY PRODUCTION OF SOFT DRINKS (CN/0527-575X) [02443763] **2369**

MONTHLY PRODUCTION REPORT (US) 1619, **4265**

MONTHLY PUBLIC OPINION SURVEYS (II) [I03039943] **4482**

MONTHLY PUBLIC OPINION SURVEYS (II/0537-1848) [01774648] **2526**

MONTHLY/QUARTERLY TRADE BULLETIN (UG) [03214275] **846**

MONTHLY RADIATION SUMMARY *CEASED.* (CN/0027-0482) [02593834] **1431**

MONTHLY RAINFALL REVIEW. AUSTRALIA (AT/0819-3592) [I08193592] **1431**

MONTHLY RECORD (CANADA. ATMOSPHERIC ENVIRONMENT SERVICE : 1983) (CN) [11095158] **1431**

MONTHLY RECORD: METEOROLOGICAL OBSERVATIONS IN CANADA (CN) [01774861] **1431**

MONTHLY — Alphabetical Title Index

MONTHLY RECORD. METEOROLOGICAL OBSERVATIONS IN CANADA. SUPPLEMENT (CN/0225-3739) [05460885] **1431**

MONTHLY RECORD OF THE FREE CHURCH OF SCOTLAND, THE (UK) [05528449] **5065**

MONTHLY REPORT - ASSOCIATION OF AMERICAN PUBLISHERS (US/0748-8173) [11011043] **4817**

MONTHLY REPORT (CARACAS, VENEZUELA) (VE) [13675607] **1575**

MONTHLY REPORT - CENTRAL BANK OF NIGERIA, LAGOS (NR) [02369722] 1575, **799**

MONTHLY REPORT - MINISTRY OF LABOUR & MANPOWER (KUALA LUMPUR) (MY/0301-8288) [01792774] **1691**

●MONTHLY REPORT / NATIONAL BANK OF HUNGARY (HU) [26227431] **800**

MONTHLY REPORT OF ACTIVITIES / U.S. DEPARTMENT OF COMMERCE, NATIONAL OCEANIC AND ATMOSPHERIC ADMINISTRATION, NATIONAL OCEAN SURVEY (US) [07983755] **846**

MONTHLY REPORT OF THE DEUTSCHE BUNDESBANK (GW/0418-8292) [01723718] **1575**

MONTHLY REPORT OF THE IRON & STEEL STATISTICS (JA/0497-1140) [07567017] 4013, **4026**

MONTHLY REPORT OF WATER TEMPERATURES, TEMPERATURES IN DEGREES C. FOR SELECTED STATIONS IN THE PACIFIC NORTHWEST (US) [03455466] **1416**

●MONTHLY REPORT ON EUROPE (BE/1021-4224) [I10214224] **2519**

MONTHLY REPORT ON THE NUCLEAR FUEL MARKET *See* NUEXCO REVIEW **2157**

MONTHLY REPORT ON THE NUCLEAR FUEL MARKET (US/0742-4582) [10371835] **2156**

MONTHLY REPORT ON TOURISM, REPUBLIC OF CHINA (CH) **5485**

MONTHLY REVIEW (CN) **1432**

MONTHLY REVIEW. (BANGKOK BANK) (TH) [02111328] **800**

MONTHLY REVIEW / CT (US) **2539**

MONTHLY REVIEW (NEW YORK. 1949) (US/0027-0520) [01758661] 1506, **4543**

MONTHLY REVIEW OF CANADIAN FISHERIES STATISTICS (CN) [02249271] 2308, **2317**

MONTHLY SHIPPING REVIEW : SS&Y RESEARCH SERVICES LTD (UK) **5453**

MONTHLY STATEMENT (US) [08242541] **748**

MONTHLY STATEMENT - INSTITUTE OF CHARTERED ACCOUNTANTS OF ALBERTA, A (CN/0316-6546) [02247702] **748**

MONTHLY STATEMENT OF THE PUBLIC DEBT OF THE UNITED STATES (US/0364-1015) [05514941] **4737**

MONTHLY STATISTICAL BULLETIN (MW) [21892047] **5333**

MONTHLY STATISTICAL BULLETIN / MAJLIS PENGELUAR-PENGELUAR GETAH MALAYSIA (MY/0126-5865) [06078682] **5078**

MONTHLY STATISTICAL BULLETIN OF BANGLADESH (BG/0377-1555) [01790623] **5333**

MONTHLY STATISTICAL DIGEST, WEST BENGAL (II/0043-308X) [01797724] **1536**

MONTHLY STATISTICAL REPORT *See* MONTHLY STATISTICAL REPORT - NEW YORK (CITY). HUMAN RESOURCES ADMINISTRATION **5266**

MONTHLY STATISTICAL REPORT - AMERICAN PETROLEUM INSTITUTE. STATISTICS DEPT (US) [03236521] 4265, **4284**

MONTHLY STATISTICAL REPORT / JAMAICA TOURIST BOARD (JM) [24234279] **5485**

MONTHLY STATISTICAL REPORT - NEW YORK (CITY). HUMAN RESOURCES ADMINISTRATION (US) [05266138] 5297, **5266**

MONTHLY STATISTICAL REVIEW - SASKATCHEWAN. BUREAU OF STATISTICS (1978) (CN/0837-8649) [04312055] **5333**

MONTHLY STATISTICAL SUMMARY REPORT - STATE OF OHIO, DEPARTMENT OF MENTAL HEALTH AND MENTAL RETARDATION, DIVISION OF BUSINESS ADMINISTRATION, BUREAU OF STATISTICS (US/0090-7456) [01908419] 4791, **4810**

MONTHLY STATISTICAL SUMMARY, WESTERN AUSTRALIA *See* MONTHLY SUMMARY OF STATISTICS : WESTERN AUSTRALIA **4698**

MONTHLY STATISTICS. ALBERTA COAL INDUSTRY (CN/0382-2168) [02732355] 1950, **1963**

MONTHLY STATISTICS. ALBERTA ELECTRIC ENERGY INDUSTRY (CN/0319-3705) [02443866] **1950**

MONTHLY STATISTICS OF EMPLOYMENT *See* MONTHLY STATISTICS OF EMPLOYMENT **1536**

MONTHLY STATISTICS OF EMPLOYMENT (NZ) [05149198] 1691, **1536**

MONTHLY STATISTICS OF FOREIGN TRADE / OECD DEPARTMENT OF ECONOMICS AND STATISTICS (FR) [09263727] **731**

MONTHLY STOCK CHARTS (CN/0828-8178) [12577478] **907**

MONTHLY STOCK REVIEW (US/0734-4880) [08483379] **907**

MONTHLY SUMMARY OF JUTE AND GUNNY STATISTICS (II) [01414830] **155**

MONTHLY SUMMARY OF JUTE GOODS STATISTICS (BG) [01789544] **5333**

MONTHLY SUMMARY OF STATISTICS (AT) [02243818] **4698**

MONTHLY SUMMARY OF STATISTICS, AUSTRALIA (AT) [05869294] **5333**

MONTHLY SUMMARY OF STATISTICS, NEW SOUTH WALES (AT) [06467562] 4666, **4698**

MONTHLY SUMMARY OF STATISTICS, SOUTH AUSTRALIA (AT/0047-8032) [01799158] 4666, **4698**

MONTHLY SUMMARY OF STATISTICS, TASMANIA / AUSTRALIAN BUREAU OF STATISTICS (AT/0314-2094) [08073758] **5333**

MONTHLY SUMMARY OF STATISTICS : WESTERN AUSTRALIA (AT) [06047091] 4666, **4698**

MONTHLY SUMMARY OF VITAL STATISTICS (US/0449-7732) [04864278] **4810**

MONTHLY SUMMARY - UNITED STATES. AGRICULTURAL MARKETING SERVICE. POULTRY DIVISION. MARKET NEWS BRANCH (US/0891-8309) [15033445] **110**

MONTHLY SURVEY OF LIFE INSURANCE SALES IN THE UNITED STATES (1986) (US/1047-9961) [13940729] **2888**

MONTHLY SURVEY OF MANUFACTURING (CN/0840-8238) [19061356] **3485**

MONTHLY TRADE BULLETIN *See* MONTHLY TRADE BULLETIN - MINISTRY OF FINANCE, PLANNING AND ECONOMIC DEVELOPMENT, STATISTICS DIVISION **731**

MONTHLY TRADE BULLETIN - MINISTRY OF FINANCE, PLANNING AND ECONOMIC DEVELOPMENT, STATISTICS DIVISION (UG) [01795321] 846, **731**

MONTHLY TREASURY STATEMENT OF RECEIPTS AND OUTLAYS OF THE UNITED STATES GOVERNMENT FOR PERIOD FROM ... (US/0364-1007) [02520295] **800**

MONTHLY VITAL STATISTICS REPORT (US/0364-0396) [01685363] 2283, **4562**

MONTHLY WEATHER REPORT (UK/0027-0636) [I00270636] **1432**

MONTHLY WEATHER REVIEW (US/0027-0644) [01796375] **1432**

MONTHLY WEATHER REVIEW : NEW SOUTH WALES (AT) [01378272] **1432**

MONTHLY WEATHER REVIEW. NORTHERN TERRITORY / COMMONWEALTH OF AUSTRALIA, BUREAU OF METEOROLOGY, DEPARTMENT OF THE INTERIOR (AT) [09923396] **1432**

MONTHLY WEATHER REVIEW : QUEENSLAND (AT) [01253160] **1432**

MONTHLY WEATHER REVIEW : SOUTH AUSTRALIA (AT) [02246877] **1432**

MONTHLY WEATHER REVIEW : TASMANIA (AT) [05704214] **1432**

MONTHLY WEATHER REVIEW : WESTERN AUSTRALIA (AT) [01378299] **1432**

MONTICELLO EXPRESS (US) [10963501] **5671**

MONTICELLO NEWS (MONTICELLO, FLA.) (US/0746-5297) [10124570] **5650**

MONTICELLO UNLIMITED NEWS (US) [22446791] **5718**

MONTMORENCY (CN/0227-5341) [08045811] **1836**

MONTREAL & AREA AIRPORT BUSINESS DIRECTORY *See* MONTREAL & AREA AVIATION BUSINESS DIRECTORY (FRENCH EDITION) **29**

MONTREAL & AREA AIRPORT BUSINESS DIRECTORY *See* MONTREAL & AREA AVIATION BUSINESS DIRECTORY **29**

●MONTREAL & AREA AVIATION BUSINESS DIRECTORY (CN/1188-6676) [26715142] **29**

●MONTREAL & AREA AVIATION BUSINESS DIRECTORY (FRENCH EDITION) (CN/1188-6676) [26715143] **29**

MONTREAL BOARD OF TRADE *See* INDEX COMMERCIAL DE MONTREAL **839**

MONTREAL BOTANICAL GARDEN *See* DELECTUS SEMINUM ET SPORARUM QUAE HORTUS BOTANICUS MONTIS-REGII PRO MUTUA COMMUTATIONE OFFERT **508**

MONTREAL CE MOIS-CI *CEASED.* (CN/0316-8530) [02247231] **4852**

MONTREAL CUISINE (CN/0823-2857) [10052038] **5072**

MONTREAL GAZETTE, THE *See* GAZETTE (MONTREAL) **5785**

MONTREAL HUMANIST *See* HUMANIST IN CANADA **4348**

MONTREAL INTERNATIONAL BOOK FAIR *See* BULLETIN D'INFORMATION - FOIRE INTERNATIONALE DU LIVRE DE MONTREAL **4827**

MONTREAL JOINT HOSPITAL INSTITUTE *See* NEWSLETTER - MONTREAL JOINT HOSPITAL INSTITUTE **5298**

MONTREAL MAGAZINE (CN/0831-5213) [15373038] **4863**

MONTREAL-NORD (QUEBEC) *See* BULLETIN MUNICIPAL / VILLE DE MONTREAL-NORD **4634**

MONTREAL NOW! (CN/0823-8944) [11873841] **3466**

MONTREAL PASSIONS (CN/1183-2142) [24256700] **2747**

MONTREAL PASSIONS (CN/1183-2142) [24256696] **5485**

MONTREAL PEOPLE'S YELLOW PAGES (CN/0700-4222) [03304177] **2569**

MONTREAL (QUEBEC) *See* BUDGET / VILLE DE MONTREAL **4715**

MONTREAL (QUEBEC). CITY COUNCIL. BUDGET *See* BUDGET / VILLE DE MONTREAL **4715**

MONTREAL, QUEBEC. SERVICE DE L'HABITATION ET DE L'URBANISME *See* RAPPORT D'ACTIVITIES - SERVICE DE L'HABITATION ET DE L'URBANISME. VILLE DE MONTREAL **4678**

MONTREAL REVIEW (CN/0707-9656) [05528176] **2747**

MONTREAL SCOP (CN/0709-065X) [09086748] **386**

MONTREAL TRIBUNE (1990) (CN/1186-2165) [24368255] **5790**

MONTREAL WRITERS' FORUM (CN/0707-5316) [04754804] **3413**

MONTREALITES (CN/0821-4573) [09796139] **4666**

MONTROSE DAILY PRESS (US) [21533587] **5643**

MONTSERRAT CONSOLIDATED INDEX OF STATUTES AND SUBSIDIARY LEGISLATION TO 1ST JANUARY ... (BB) [13919655] **3132**

MONUMENT BUILDERS OF NORTH AMERICA *See* M B NEWS **357**

MONUMENTA AMERICANA (GW/0077-1384) [01586949] **275**

MONUMENTA ARCHAEOLOGICA (LOS ANGELES) (US/0363-7565) [02509827] **275**

MONUMENTA GERMANIAE ACUSTICA (GW) [04401248] **3304**

MONUMENTA GERMANIAE HISTORICA (GW) [04393780] **2699**

MONUMENTA GERMANIAE HISTORICA (DEUTSCHES INSTITUT FUR ERFORSCHUNG DES MITTELALTERS) *See* SCHRIFTEN DER MONUMENTA GERMANIAE HISTORICA (DEUTSCHES INSTITUT FUR ERFORSCHUNG DES MITTELALTERS) **2708**

MONUMENTA HENRICINA (PO) [07110058] **2699**

MONUMENTA HISPANIAE SACRA. SERIE LITURGICA / CONSEJO SUPERIOR DE INVESTIGACIONES CIENTIFICAS (SP) [09238556] **4979**

MONUMENTA HISTORICA SOCIETATIS IESU (IT) [01758683] **5032**

MONUMENTA IURIS CANONICI. SERIES A : CORPUS GLOSSATORUM (US) [07355113] **5032**

MONUMENTA MONODICA MEDII AEVI. HRSG. IM AUFTRAG DES INSTITUTS FUER MUSIKFORSCHUNG REGENSBURG MIT UNTERSTUTZUNG DER MUSIKGESCHICHTLICHEN KOMMISSION VON BRUNO STABLEIN (GW/0544-9987) [01981588] 5032, **4132**

MONUMENTA MUSICAE SACRAE (FR/0545-0004) [01997476] **4132**

MONUMENTA MUSICAE SVECICAE / SVENSKA SAMFUNDET FOR MUSIKFORSKNING (SW/0077-1473) [05003579] **4132**

MONUMENTA NIPPONICA (JA/0027-0741) [01640509] 2851, **2659**

Alphabetical Title Index — MORNINGSTAR

MONUMENTA NIPPONICA MONOGRAPHS (JA) [01775464] **2507**

MONUMENTA ORDINIS FRATRUM PRAEDICATORUM HISTORICA (IT) [06678102] **4979**

MONUMENTA SERICA (GW/0254-9948) [I02549948] 4353, 4979, **2623**

MONUMENTAL NEWS-REVIEW See STONE IN AMERICA **365**

MONUMENTEN (NE) 2623, **621**

MONUMENTEN EN LANDSCHAPPEN : M & L (BE/0770-4984) [11109299] **303**

MONUMENTET (AA/0253-1607) [03460148] 358, **303**

MONUMENTI ANTICHI. SERIE MISCELLANEA (IT/0391-8084) [01639940] 359, 2699, **303**

MONUMENTI ANTICHI. SERIE MONOGRAFICA / ACCADEMIA NAZIONALE DEI LINCEI (IT/0391-8092) [06441055] 359, 2699, **303**

MONUMENTI ETRUSCHI (IT/0545-008X) [02503116] **2699**

MONUMENTOS DE LA MUSICA ESPANOLA (SP) [09886976] **4132**

MONUMENTS ET MEMOIRES PARIS (FR/1148-6023) [I11486023] **275**

MONUMENTS ET SITES DE SEINE-ET-MARNE : REVUE DES AMIS DES MONUMENTS ET SITES DE SEINE-ET-MARNE (FR) [07786087] **2699**

MONUMENTS HISTORIQUES (1980) (FR/0242-830X) [07828711] **304**

MONUMENTS HISTORIQUES DE SEINE ET MARNE (FR/0540-8539) [I05408539] 359, 2699, **304**

MONUMENTS OF RENAISSANCE MUSIC (US/0077-1503) [02253212] **4132**

MOODY (CHICAGO, ILL.) (US/1052-2271) [22222875] **4979**

MOODY COUNTY ENTERPRISE (FLANDREAU, S.D. : 1938) (US) [12813885] **5744**

MOODY COURIER, THE (US) [14442748] **5752**

MOODY STREET IRREGULARS (US/0196-2604) [04227833] 434, **3413**

MOODY'S ANALYSES OF INVESTMENTS. BANK AND FINANCE SECTION. MONTHLY REPORTS See MOODY'S BANK & FINANCE NEWS REPORTS **800**

MOODY'S ... ANNUAL BOND RECORD (US/1050-0820) [21389482] **907**

MOODY'S BANK AND FINANCE MANUAL (US/0545-0152) [01758686] **800**

MOODY'S BANK & FINANCE NEWS REPORTS (US/0027-0814) [01758687] 907, **800**

MOODY'S BOND RECORD (US/0148-1878) [04153749] **907**

MOODY'S BOND SURVEY (US/0027-0822) [01758689] **907**

MOODY'S COMPLETE CORPORATE INDEX (US/0147-3093) [02807629] **696**

MOODY'S CREDIT OPTIONS. FINANCIAL INSTITUTIONS/SOVEREIGNS (US) [17833071] **800**

MOODY'S DIVIDEND RECORD (US/0192-7019) [01758690] **907**

MOODY'S DIVIDEND RECORD. ANNUAL CUMULATIVE ISSUE (US) [03995982] **907**

MOODY'S HANDBOOK OF COMMON STOCKS (US/0027-0830) [02784264] **907**

MOODY'S HANDBOOK OF DIVIDEND ACHIEVERS (US/0737-1586) [09297185] **907**

●MOODY'S HANDBOOK OF NASDAQ STOCKS (US/1059-8057) [24772987] **907**

MOODY'S HANDBOOK OF OTC STOCKS See MOODY'S HANDBOOK OF NASDAQ STOCKS **907**

MOODY'S INDUSTRIAL MANUAL (US/0545-0217) [01758691] **907**

MOODY'S INDUSTRIAL NEWS REPORTS (US/0027-0849) [01758692] **907**

MOODY'S INDUSTRY REVIEW (US/1047-3114) [10410625] **907**

MOODY'S INTERNATIONAL MANUAL (US/0278-3509) [07793423] **907**

MOODY'S INTERNATIONAL NEWS REPORTS (US/0278-3517) [07793318] **907**

MOODY'S MUNICIPAL & GOVERNMENT MANUAL (US/0545-0233) [01358961] **907**

MOODY'S MUNICIPAL ISSUES (US) [12014852] **907**

MOODY'S OTC INDUSTRIAL MANUAL (US/0192-7167) [01715294] **907**

MOODY'S OTC UNLISTED MANUAL (US/0890-5282) [14053026] **908**

MOODY'S PUBLIC UTILITY MANUAL (US/0545-0241) [01235242] **908**

MOODY'S STOCK SURVEY (US/0097-6997) [01799350] **908**

MOODY'S TRANSPORTATION MANUAL (US/0545-025X) [01758696] **5387**

MOODY'S UNIT INVESTMENT TRUST MANUAL (US) [18711782] **908**

MOODY'S UNIT INVESTMENT TRUSTS (US/1053-6175) [22589577] **908**

MOON FAMILY NEWSLETTER, THE (US/0738-8276) [09186829] **2461**

MOONS AND LION TAILES (US/0099-0264) [01646241] **3466**

MOORE AMERICAN, THE (US/0747-1947) [10633125] **5732**

MOORE COUNTY NEWS-PRESS, THE (US) [15148304] **5752**

MOOREA : THE JOURNAL OF THE IRISH GARDEN PLANT SOCIETY (IE/0332-4273) [09522817] 518, **2424**

MOOREANA : JOURNAL OF THE PALMETUM (AT/1037-1842) [25294315] 2424, **518**

MOOREFIELD EXAMINER AND HARDY COUNTY NEWS, THE (US/0740-2651) [09921953] **5764**

MOORES & ROWLAND'S ORANGE TAX GUIDE (UK/0951-8223) [I09518223] **4737**

MOORES & ROWLAND'S YELLOW TAX GUIDE (UK/0951-8231) [I09518231] **4737**

MOORE'S AND ROWLAND'S YELLOW TAX GUIDE (UK) **4737**

MOORE'S MANUAL; FEDERAL PRACTICE FORMS (US) [01758702] **3012**

MOOSE JAW TIMES-HERALD (CN) **5790**

MOOSE LAKE STAR GAZETTE (1983) (US/0746-2980) [09927783] **5697**

MOOSEHEAD ANTHOLOGY (CN/0842-1765) [18434053] **3413**

MOOT COURT CASEBOOK (US) [09884099] **3012**

MOOTTORIAJONEUVO- JA KUMIKORJAAMOT (FI) [02243046] **5419**

MOP : GEBAEUDEUNTERHALT & REINIGUNG (SZ) 1691, **621**

MOPED BIKING (US/0160-1806) [03724975] **4081**

MOPED DEALER (US/0161-4320) [03939940] **4081**

MORA FERENC MUZEUM EVKONYVE, A (HU/0563-0525) [10651071] 359, **4091**

MORAL EDUCATION FORUM (US/0163-6480) [04174710] 2252, **1765**

MORALIA (SP/0210-0581) [04927482] **5209**

MORALITY (US/0733-2424) [08271765] **2252**

MORALITY IN MEDIA, INC See MORALITY IN MEDIA INC. NEWSLETTER **3170**

MORALITY IN MEDIA INC. NEWSLETTER (US/0027-1004) [04055701] **3170**

MORAROJI KENKYU (JA) [02243315] **2252**

MORAVIA REPUBLICAN REGISTER (US) [11191966] **5718**

MORAVIAN (1989), THE (US/1041-0961) [18631357] **4979**

MORAVIAN HISTORICAL SOCIETY See TRANSACTIONS OF THE MORAVIAN HISTORICAL SOCIETY **5068**

MORAVIAN MUSIC JOURNAL (US/0278-0763) [07360352] **4132**

MORAVIAN THEOLOGICAL SEMINARY See BULLETIN - MORAVIAN THEOLOGICAL SEMINARY, THE **4941**

MORAVSKA LIRA (YU) [01795122] **3413**

MORBIDITY AND MORTALITY WEEKLY REPORT (US/0149-2195) [03454113] **4792**

MORBIDITY AND MORTALITY WEEKLY REPORT. CDC SURVEILLANCE SUMMARIES (US/0892-3787) [11086137] **4792**

●MORE FREE STUFF FOR KIDS (US/1065-5093) [26621742] **1066**

MORE FROM THE SHORE (US/1067-7402) [20575052] **2461**

MORE MINNESOTA GUIDE MAGAZINE (US/0277-0482) [07484365] **2539**

MORE POWER (US/0899-5834) [18144015] **1988**

MOREANA (FR/0047-8105) [01644152] **3413**

MOREHA LE-MOREH (CN/0820-7976) [09471568] **2659**

MORFOGEN ASSOCIATES NEWS (US/0895-8246) [16816295] **325**

MORFOGENEZ I REGENERATSIIA (UN/0368-9727) [01334500] **466**

●MORFOLOGIIA (RU) [28460941] **3679**

MORGAN COUNTY NEWS (US) [12248944] **5757**

MORGAN DIRECTORY REVIEWS / MDR CEASED. (US/0899-4560) [18098919] **3232**

MORGAN HILL TIMES, SAN MARTIN NEWS (US) [27019893] **5637**

MORGAN HORSE, THE (US/0027-1098) [02256681] **2801**

MORGAN MESSENGER (BERKELEY SPRINGS, W. VA.) (US/0895-1594) [12637249] **5764**

MORGAN MESSENGER, THE (US) [20821906] **5697**

MORGAN REPORT ON DIRECTORY PUBLISHING (US/0890-9512) [14583014] 762, **4817**

MORGAN STANLEY CAPITAL INTERNATIONAL PERSPECTIVE (MONTHLY) (US/1052-9713) [13652837] **908**

MORGAN STANLEY CAPITAL INTERNATIONAL PERSPECTIVE (QUARTERLY) (SZ/1052-9721) [13447291] **908**

MORGEN, DER (GW) [11975198] **5801**

MORGUARD REPORT (CN/0712-9769) [09639275] **4841**

MORI (JA) [05759582] **2388**

MORIARTY ON EXECUTIVE PENSIONS CEASED. (CN/1183-4692) [24267125] **879**

MORICHES BAY TIDE (US) [10947938] **5718**

MORINVILLE MIRROR (CN/0711-3811) [08770654] **5790**

MORNING ADVERTISER (UK) [18505319] **5812**

MORNING ADVOCATE (BATON ROUGE, LA.) (US/1056-2125) [09992163] **5684**

MORNING ADVOCATE (BATON ROUGE, LA.) See ADVOCATE (BATON ROUGE, LA.), THE **5683**

MORNING CALL (ALLENTOWN, PA.), THE (US/0884-5557) [09741200] **5737**

MORNING CHRONICLE (HALIFAX. TRI-WEEKLY ED.) CEASED. (UK/1186-5393) [10615600] **5812**

MORNING COFFEE CHAPBOOK SERIES (US/0882-147X) [11795902] **3466**

MORNING FAX, THE (US/0899-8108) [18230349] **1160**

MORNING GLORY (US/0745-5968) [01758721] **4979**

MORNING HERALD, THE (US) [09623455] **5686**

●MORNING (NEW YORK, N.Y.) (US/1061-8341) [25473296] **325**

MORNING NEWS (BLACKFOOT, IDAHO), THE (US/0893-3812) [13211080] **5657**

MORNING NEWS (ERIE, PA.) (US) [14813560] **5737**

MORNING NEWS (SPRINGDALE, ARK.), THE (US/1053-9689) [22457236] **5632**

MORNING NEWS TRIBUNE (US/1042-3621) [17470426] **5761**

MORNING STAR (US) [24839460] **5723**

MORNING STAR (LONDON, ENGLAND) (UK) [16310485] **5812**

MORNING STAR PEOPLE, THE (US/0047-8121) [03858528] **2268**

MORNING STAR, THE (UK) [06397972] **5812**

MORNING SUN (US) [22378715] **5693**

MORNING SUN, THE (US) [08799621] **5677**

MORNING WATCH (ST. JOHN'S) (CN/0384-5028) [03227433] **1765**

MORNINGSTAR 500 SOURCEBOOK (US) **908**

MORNINGSTAR ADR (US) **908**

MORNINGSTAR CLOSED END FUND SOURCEBOOK (AN) [27317072] **800**

MORNINGSTAR CLOSED-END FUNDS (US/1059-1419) [24490094] **908**

MORNINGSTAR JAPAN CEASED. (US/1061-1886) [25216461] **696**

MORNINGSTAR MUTUAL FUND 500 (US/1067-6228) [27317091] **908**

MORNINGSTAR MUTUAL FUND SOURCEBOOK CEASED. (US) [27899802] **908**

MORNINGSTAR MUTUAL FUNDS (US/1059-1443) [24361985] **908**

MORNINGSTAR MUTUAL FUNDS ONDISC (US/1059-1427) [24487836] **908**

MORNINGSTAR NO LOAD (US) **800**

MORNINGSTAR VARIABLE ANNUITIES / LIFE (US) **2888**

MORNINGSTAR VARIABLE ANNUITY/LIFE SOURCEBOOK CEASED. (US/1076-2167) [28482406] 2888

MOROCCO. AL-QUWAT AL-MUSALLAHAH AL-MALAKIYAH See MAJALLAT AL-QUWAT AL-MUSALLAHAH AL-MALAKIYAH 4049

MOROCCO BOUND (AT/0159-7191) [I01597191] 2775, 4830

MOROCCO COURIER, THE (US/1060-5231) [14867002] 5665

MORPHE / UNIVERSIDAD AUTONOMA DE PUEBLA, MAESTRIA EN CIENCIAS DEL LENGUAJE (MX) [17238634] 3304

MORPHOLOGIA MEDICA (GW/0172-9187) [08428917] 584, 3679

MORPHOLOGIAI ES IGAZSAGUGYI ORVOSI SZEMLE CEASED. (HU/0540-889X) [01785700] 466

MORRELL, MORRILL FAMILIES ASSOCIATION NEWSLETTER (US/0889-7247) [14107103] 2461

MORRIS AREA GENEALOGY SOCIETY NEWSLETTER (US) [19652520] 2461

MORRIS SUN (US) [01607107] 5697

MORRIS SUN-TRIBUNE (US) 5697

MORRIS TRIBUNE See MORRIS SUN-TRIBUNE 5697

MORRISON ENVIRONMENTAL DIRECTORY (US/1060-488X) [22869100] 2177, 1988

MORRISONS COVE HERALD (US) [15309790] 5737

MORROW COUNTY SENTINEL (MOUNT GILEAD, OHIO : 1859) (US) [12067588] 5729

MORSKOI GIDROFIZICHESKII ZHURNAL (UN/0233-7584) [11940993] 1452

MORSKOI GIDROFIZICHESKII ZHURNAL (NE/0920-5047) [17847762] 1453

MORSKOI GIDROFIZICHESKII ZHURNAL. ENGLISH. SOVIET JOURNAL OF PHYSICAL OCEANOGRAPHY See PHYSICAL OCEANOGRAPHY 1455

MORSKOI SBORNIK (RU/0134-9236) [08270012] 4179

MORTALITY STATISTICS (UK) [08864442] 4555

MORTALITY STATISTICS. PERINATAL AND INFANT : SOCIAL AND BIOLOGICAL FACTORS (UK) [08864502] 4555, 4562

MORTALITY, SUMMARY LIST OF CAUSES / STATISTICS CANADA, CANADIAN CENTRE FOR HEALTH INFORMATION (CN/1195-4108) [29407643] 4555

MORTGAGE AND HOME IMPROVEMENT LENDING IN MICHICGAN PURSUANT TO THE ANTI-REDLINING ACT, ANNUAL REPORT (US) [10901426] 800

MORTGAGE AND REAL ESTATE EXECUTIVES REPORT, THE (US/0047-813X) [02505425] 4841

MORTGAGE AND REAL ESTATE INVESTMENT GUIDE (US/0545-0659) [10330011] 4841

MORTGAGE BACKED SECURITIES LETTER (US) 800

MORTGAGE BANKERS ASSOCIATION OF AMERICA. ECONOMICS AND RESEARCH DEPT See NATIONAL DELINQUENCY SURVEY 800

MORTGAGE BANKING (US/0730-0212) [07639429] 800

MORTGAGE BROKER (CN/0712-2284) [08737658] 908

MORTGAGE CREDIT ANALYSIS FOR MORTGAGE INSURANCE ON ONE TO FOUR FAMILY PROPERTIES (US) [04169761] 2888

MORTGAGE CREDIT ANALYSIS FOR PROJECT MORTGAGE INSURANCE (US) [02924296] 2888

MORTGAGE FINANCE MONTHLY (UK/0957-1388) [I09571388] 800

MORTGAGE GUARANTY (US) [07937255] 2888

MORTGAGE INSURANCE COMPANIES OF AMERICA See FACTBOOK AND MEMBERSHIP DIRECTORY / MORTGAGE INSURANCE COMPANIES OF AMERICA 2879

MORTGAGE INSURANCE COMPANIES OF AMERICA. FACTBOOK AND DIRECTORY See FACTBOOK AND MEMBERSHIP DIRECTORY / MORTGAGE INSURANCE COMPANIES OF AMERICA 2879

MORTGAGE INSURANCE FOR THE PURCHASE OR REFINANCING OF EXISTING MULTIFAMILY HOUSING PROJECTS (US) [03115124] 2828, 2888

MORTGAGE MARKETPLACE, THE (US/0744-3927) [08243527] 800

MORTGAGE SERVICING DIRECTORY, THE (US) 800

MORTICIANS OF THE SOUTHWEST (US/0739-0289) [01758732] 2407

MORTON ARBORETUM See MORTON ARBORETUM QUARTERLY, THE 518

MORTON ARBORETUM QUARTERLY, THE (US/0027-125X) [01586577] 518

MORTON GROVE CHAMPION (US/0193-7251) [05237890] 5661

MORTON GROVE LIFE (US/0194-9381) [05133207] 5661

MORTON JOURNAL (MORTON, WASH. : 1988) (US) [18770797] 5761

MORTON TRIBUNE (US) [14220232] 5752

MORTUARY MANAGEMENT (US/0027-1268) [01758735] 2407

MOS NEWSLETTER (US) [07200675] 5592

MOSAIC (BLOOMINGTON, IND.) (US/1059-8197) [24775244] 2747

MOSAIC (WASHINGTON) CEASED. (US/0027-1284) [01758736] 5129

MOSAIC (WINNIPEG) (CN/0027-1276) [01607246] 3413

MOSAMBIK : ENERGIEWIRTSCHAFT (GW) [05064409] 1950

MOSASAUR, THE (US/0736-3907) [09116802] 4228

MOSCOSOA : CONTRIBUCIONES CIENTIFICAS DEL JARDIN BOTANICO NACIONAL "DR. RAFAEL M. MOSCOSO" (DR/0254-6442) [06153376] 518

MOSCOW BUSINESS TODAY (RU) 696

MOSCOW INTERNATIONAL BUSINESS CEASED. (US/1046-9621) [20575000] 696

MOSCOW MAGAZINE (NE) [22949748] 2490

MOSCOW. MUZEI MOSKOVSKOGO KREMLIA See MATERIALY I ISSLEDOVANIIA - GOSUDARSTVENNYE MUZEI MOSKOVSKOGO KREMLIA 2697

MOSCOW NEWS (RU/0027-1306) [01695248] 5809

MOSCOW. PUBLICHNAIA BIBLIOTEKA. NAUCHNO-ISSLEDOVATELSKII OTDEL BIBLIOTEKOVEDENIIA I TEORII BIBLIOGRAFII See PROGNOZIROVANIE RAZVITIIA BIBLIOTECHNOGO DELA V SSSR 3242

MOSCOW PULLMAN DAILY NEWS (US/1061-8597) [25480531] 5657

MOSCOW. TSENTRALNYI AERO-GIDRODINAMICHESKII INSTITUT See UCENYE ZAPISKIE CAGI 38

MOSCOW. UNIVERSITET See VESTNIK MOSKOVSKOGO UNIVERSITETA. SERIIA X : ZHURNALISTIKA 2925

MOSCOW. UNIVERSITET. BIBLIOTEKA See RUKOPISNAIA I PECHATNAIA KNIGA V FONDAKH 424

MOSCOW. UNIVERSITET. KAFEDRA GRUNTOVEDENIIA I INZHENERNOI GEOLOGII See VOPROSY INZHENERNOI GEOLGII I GRUNTOVEDENIIA 2000

MOSCOW UNIVERSITY BIOLOGICAL SCIENCES BULLETIN (US/0096-3925) [01245905] 466

MOSCOW UNIVERSITY CHEMISTRY BULLETIN (US/0027-1314) [02716932] 987

MOSCOW UNIVERSITY GEOLOGY BULLETIN (US/0145-8752) [02810189] 1388

MOSCOW UNIVERSITY MATHEMATICS BULLETIN (US/0027-1322) [01586983] 3523

MOSCOW UNIVERSITY MECHANICS BULLETIN (US/0027-1330) [02223115] 4429

MOSCOW UNIVERSITY PHYSICS BULLETIN (US/0027-1349) [01642222] 4412

MOSCOW UNIVERSITY SOIL SCIENCE BULLETIN (US/0147-6874) [02621924] 179

MOSCOW. VSESOIUZNYI NAUCHNO-ISSLEDOVATELSKII INSTITUT PO PERERABOTKE NEFTI I GAZA I POLUCHENIIU ISKUSSTVENNOGO ZHIDKOGO TOPLIVA. TRUDY See TRUDY - VSESOIUZNYI NAUCHNO-ISSLEDOVATELSKII INSTITUT PO PERERABOTKE NEFTI 4280

MOSELLA (FR) [05420800] 2569

MOSELLE FRUIT (FR) 2350

MOSINEE TIMES, THE (US/0748-8297) [11014164] 5769

MOSKOVSKIE NOVOSTI MICROFORM : MN : EZHENEDELNAIA GAZETA SOIUZA SOVETSKIKH OBSHCHESTV DRUZHBY I KULTURNOI SVIAZI S ZARUBEZHNYMI STRANAMI I AGENTSTVA PECHATI NOVOSTI (RU) [19504276] 5809

MOSKOVSKIE NOVOSTI : MN : EZHENEDELNAIA GAZETA SOIUZA SOVETSKIKH OBSHCHESTV DRUZHBY I KULTURNOI SVIAZI S ZARUBEZHNYMI STRANAMI I AGENTSTVA PECHATI NOVOSTI (RU) [27479399] 5809

MOSKOVSKII GOSUDARSTVENNYI UNIVERSITET See VESTNIK MOSKOVSKOGO UNIVERSITETA. SERIIA XV : VYCHISLITELNAIA MATEMATIKA I KIBERNETIKA 1262

MOSKOVSKII GOSUDARSTVENNYI UNIVERSITET IM. M.V. LOMONOSOVA See MOSCOW UNIVERSITY CHEMISTRY BULLETIN 987

MOSKOVSKII GOSUDARSTVENNYI UNIVERSITET IM. M.V. LOMONOSOVA See VESTNIK MOSKOVSKOGO UNIVERSITETA. SERIA 16. BIOLOGIA 475

MOSKOVSKII GOSUDARSTVENNYI UNIVERSITET IM. M. V. LOMONOSOVA See MOSCOW UNIVERSITY MATHEMATICS BULLETIN 3523

MOSKOVSKII GOSUDARSTVENNYI UNIVERSITET IM. M. V. LOMONOSOVA See VESTNIK MOSKOVSKOGO UNIVERSITETA. SERIIA XIV : PSIKHOLOGIIA 4621

MOSKOVSKII GOSUDARSTVENNYI UNIVERSITET IM. M. V. LOMONOSOVA See VESTNIK MOSKOVSKOGO UNIVERSITETA. SERIIA II. KHIMIIA 995

MOSKOVSKII GOSUDARSTVENNYI UNIVERSITET IM. M.V. LOMONOSOVA See MOSCOW UNIVERSITY SOIL SCIENCE BULLETIN 179

MOSKOVSKII GOSUDARSTVENNYI UNIVERSITET IM. M.V. LOMONOSOVA See VESTNIK MOSKOVSKOGO UNIVERSITETA. SERIIA VIII: ISTORIIA 2632

MOSKOVSKII GOSUDARSTVENNYI UNIVERSITET IM. M. V. LOMONOSOVA See MOSCOW UNIVERSITY MECHANICS BULLETIN 4429

MOSKOVSKII GOSUDARSTVENNYI UNIVERSITET IM. M.V. LOMONOSOVA See VESTNIK MORKOVSKOGO UNIVERSITETA. SERIIA XI : PRAVO 3071

MOSKOVSKII GOSUDARSTVENNYI UNIVERSITET IM. M.V. LOMONOSOVA See VESTNIK MOSKOVSKOGO UNIVERSITETA. SERIIA VII : FILOSOFIIA 4364

MOSKOVSKII GOSUDARSTVENNYI UNIVERSITET IM. M.V. LOMONOSOVA See MOSCOW UNIVERSITY PHYSICS BULLETIN 4412

MOSKOVSKII GOSUDARSTVENNYI UNIVERSITET IM. M.V. LOMONOSOVA See MOSCOW UNIVERSITY GEOLOGY BULLETIN 1388

MOSKOVSKII GOSUDARSTVENNYI UNIVERSITET IM. M. V. LOMONOSOVA See VESTNIK MOSKOVSKOGO UNIVERSITETA. SERIA IX : FILOLOGIIA 3331

MOSKOVSKII OBLASTNOI NAUCHNO-ISSLEDOVATELSKII INSTITUT AKUSHERSTVA I GINEKOLOGII See SBORNIK NAUCHNYKH TRUDOV MONIIAG 5149

MOSKOVSKII UNIVERSITET. ZOOLOGICHESKII MUZEI See SBORNIK TRUDOV ZOOLOGICHESKOGO MUZEIA 5597

MOSKOVSKII ZHURNAL (RU/0868-7110) [23954850] 359, 304

MOSKOVSKIÊI GOSUDARSTVENNYÊI UNIVERSITET IM. M.V. LOMONOSOVA See MOSCOW UNIVERSITY BIOLOGICAL SCIENCES BULLETIN 466

MOSKOVSKOE MATEMATICHESKOE OBSHCHESTVO See TRANSACTIONS OF THE MOSCOW MATHEMATICAL SOCIETY 3539

MOSKOVSKOE OBSHCHESTVO ISPYTATELEI PRIRODY See BJULLETEN MOSKOVSKOGO OBSCESTVA ISPYTATELEJ PRIRODY. OTDEL GEOLOGICESKIJ 1367

MOSKOVSKOE OBSHCHESTVO ISPYTATELEI PRIRODY See BIULLETEN. OTDEL BIOLOGICHESKII 448

MOSKOVSKOE OBSHCHESTVO ISPYTATELEI PRIRODY See BJULLETEN MOSKOVSKOGO OBSCESTVA ISPYTATELEJ PRIRODY. OTDEL BIOLOGICESKIJ 448

MOSKVA (RU/0131-2332) [02264420] 3413

MOSKVA V CIFRAH (RU/0259-5133) [06048124] 5333

MOSONMAGYAROVARI AGRARTUDOMANYI FOISKOLA KOZLEMENYEI See MOSONMAGYAROVARI MEZOGAZDASAGTUDOMANYI KAR KOZLEMENYEI, A 110

MOSONMAGYAROVARI MEZOGAZDASAGTUDOMANYI KAR KOZLEMENYEI, A (HU/0324-5705) [01264134] 110

MOSQUITO BORNE DISEASES BULLETIN (TH/0857-0817) [12005965] 4792

MOSQUITO SYSTEMATICS (US/0091-3669) [01696783] 2177

MOSSBAUER EFFECT DATA INDEX (US/0544-7259) [02031464] 2073

Alphabetical Title Index — MOTORCYCLE

MOSSBAUER EFFECT REFERENCE AND DATA JOURNAL (US/0163-9587) [03662980] **4426**

MOSSBAUER HANDBOOK (US/0272-2755) [06830184] 987, **1012**

MOSSBAUER SPECTROSCOPY ABSTRACTS (UK/0141-9064) [03924677] **4438**

MOSSE SWISS ADRESS (SZ) [07957426] **696**

MOSSTYPE CORPORATION See MOSSTYPER, THE **4566**

MOSSTYPER, THE (US/0148-5539) [03333533] **4566**

MOST (LAUSANNE) (US/0027-1438) [03334763] **3413**

MOST-PRESCRIBED DRUGS (US/8755-3082) [11275188] **4316**

MOSTOVI (BELGRADE) (YU/0350-6525) [07149400] 3413, **3304**

MOT See MOT AUTO-JOURNAL **5419**

MOT A MOT (QUEBEC) (CN/0227-8715) [07295286] **4529**

MOT A TROUVER MYSTERIEUX (CN/0228-569X) [08010220] **4863**

MOT AUTO-JOURNAL (GW) [01789855] **5419**

MOT : DIE AUTOZEITSCHRIFT (GW) [23736815] **5419**

MOT MYSTERE (CN/0228-5681) [08003243] **4863**

MOTA (US/0149-4902) [03506027] **4091**

MOTC'S NOTEBOOK (US/8756-9965) [12272693] 5269, **2283**

MOTEL ECONOMY GUIDE : FLORIDA & I-95 (US/0161-1925) [03854983] **2808**

MOTEL OCCUPANCY IN VERMONT (US) [08867821] **2808**

MOTHER & BABY (AT) **2283**

MOTHER & CHILD (LAHORE) (PK/0379-2617) [03940300] 3618, **2283**

MOTHER OF THYME (CN/1181-6074) [23598417] **5561**

MOTHER ROAD JOURNAL, THE (US/1056-3393) [23669693] **4905**

(M)OTHER TNGUES (CN/1180-5781) [24368181] **3413**

MOTHERING (US/0733-3013) [04093519] **2283**

MOTHEROOT JOURNAL **SUSPENDED**. (US/0739-5272) [05280133] 4817, **4830**

MOTHERS AND CHILDREN (WASHINGTON) (US/0272-6912) [06904090] **2283**

MOTHER'S MAGAZINE AND FAMILY CIRCLE (MICROFORM), THE (US) [25294537] 4979, **1765**

MOTHERS TODAY (US/0745-8371) [09497213] **3765**

MOTIF (COLUMBUS, OHIO) **SUSPENDED**. (US/0278-2286) [07753818] 3413, **2322**

MOTIF (SPRINGFIELD) (US/0273-2114) [06997720] 5065, **4132**

MOTION CONTROL (US/1053-4644) [22533054] **2123**

MOTION PICTURE ANNUAL, THE (US) [18261569] 4372, **4074**

MOTION PICTURE GUIDE, THE (US) [15997679] **4074**

MOTION PICTURE INVESTOR (US/0742-8839) [10510574] 4074, **908**

MOTION PICTURE THEATRES AND FILM DISTRIBUTORS (CN/0380-6294) [02585806] 4074, **4080**

●MOTIV (GW) [25330349] **4132**

MOTIVATION AND EMOTION (US/0146-7239) [02861856] **4604**

MOTIVATIONSFORSCHUNG (GW/0173-3532) [05261354] **4604**

MOTO JOURNAL (CN/0319-2865) [02075408] **4081**

MOTO REVUE (FR) 4082, **429**

MOTOCICLISMO (IT/0027-1961) **4082**

MOTOCROSS ACTION MAGAZINE (US/0146-3292) [02908016] **4082**

MOTOCULTURE MAGAZINE NEUILLY-SUR-SEINE (FR/0998-495X) [I0998495X] **2424**

MOTOCYCLISTE (MONTREAL) **SUSPENDED**. (CN/0832-1132) [16056036] **4082**

MOTON GUIDE TO AMERICAN COLLEGES WITH A BLACK HERITAGE See NEW MOTON GUIDE TO AMERICAN COLLEGES WITH A BLACK HERITAGE, THE **1837**

MOTONEIGE QUEBEC (CN/0836-7264) [17748338] **4905**

MOTOR (NE) 4905, **4082**

MOTOR See MOTOR IMPORTED CAR REPAIR MANUAL. PROFESSIONAL SERVICE TRADE EDITION **5419**

MOTOR (AT) **5387**

MOTOR 16 (SP/0212-9000) [I02129000] **5419**

MOTOR ACCIDENTS IN NEW ZEALAND (NZ/0550-5089) [02239303] 4792, **5387**

MOTOR AGE MECHANICS NEWSLETTER (US/0278-9418) [07921514] **5419**

MOTOR AUTO REPAIR MANUAL (US/0098-1745) [02240952] **5419**

MOTOR BOAT AND YACHTING (UK/0027-1780) [25488134] **594**

MOTOR BOATING & SAILING (US/0027-1799) [01785756] **594**

MOTOR CARRIER ANNUAL REPORTS (US/0160-4570) [03674593] **5387**

MOTOR CARRIER FREIGHT FORWARDER DIGEST SERVICE. INCLUDES SUPPLEMENTS (US) 846, **5387**

MOTOR CARRIER STATISTICAL SUMMARY (US/0196-5352) [03971223] **5401**

MOTOR COACH AGE (US/0739-117X) [06243094] **5387**

MOTOR CRASH ESTIMATING GUIDE (US/0194-9411) [05134274] 4792, **5419**

MOTOR CYCLE NEWS PETERBOROUGH (UK/0027-1853) [I00271853] **5387**

MOTOR-CYCLE SPORT (UK) [18843612] **4905**

MOTOR DOMESTIC WIRING DIAGRAM & MANUAL (US) **5419**

MOTOR EARLY MODEL CRASH ESTIMATING GUIDE (US/0160-1644) [03616743] **5419**

MOTOR EMISSION CONTROL MANUAL (US/0743-1031) [10492554] **5419**

MOTOR EQUIPMENT NEWS (AT) **5419**

MOTOR FREIGHT CIRCULAR AND ORDERS (US) **4265**

MOTOR FREIGHT CONTROLLER (US/0886-8778) [12297195] **5387**

MOTOR FUEL TAXES, AMOUNTS DISTRIBUTED TO CITIES, AND TO ALL LOCAL GOVERNMENTS BY COUNTY, CALENDAR YEAR ... / OHIO DEPARTMENT OF TAXATION (US) [06782501] **4737**

MOTOR HANDBOOK (US/0094-1514) [01793892] **5419**

MOTOR HOME & TRUCK CAMPER TRADE-IN GUIDE See INTERTEC RECREATIONAL VEHICLE TRADE-IN GUIDE **5481**

MOTOR HOME TRADE-IN GUIDE (US/0742-8073) [10436765] **2828**

MOTOR HOMES, CAMPERS, VAN CONVERSIONS, SURFER VANS (US) [01795319] 4852, **5387**

MOTOR IMPORTED CAR CRASH ESTIMATING GUIDE (US/0164-6346) [01794846] **5419**

MOTOR IMPORTED CAR REPAIR MANUAL (US/0090-1563) [04077311] **5419**

MOTOR IMPORTED CAR REPAIR MANUAL. PROFESSIONAL SERVICE TRADE EDITION (US/0163-9110) [04509567] **5419**

MOTOR IMPORTED ENGINE TUNE UP & ELECTRONICS MANUAL (US) [13305105] **5419**

MOTOR IMPORTED WIRING DIAGRAM & MANUAL (US) [20584110] **5419**

MOTOR IN CANADA **SUSPENDED**. (CN/0027-190X) [02075443] **5420**

MOTOR INDUSTRY JOURNAL (AT/0729-0799) [I07290799] **5420**

MOTOR INDUSTRY OF GREAT BRITAIN, THE (UK) [02080133] **5387**

MOTOR INDUSTRY OF GREAT BRITAIN ..., WORLD AUTOMOTIVE STATISTICS (UK) [15158036] **5420**

MOTOR INDUSTRY OF JAPAN (TOKYO, JAPAN : 1985) (JA) [13449124] **5420**

MOTOR INDUSTRY YEAR BOOK (NZ) [03172754] **5420**

●MOTOR INSURANCE MARKET (UK/0965-8629) [I09658629] **2888**

MOTOR ITALIA (IT) [06445411] **5420**

MOTOR LIGHT TRUCK TUNE UP & REPAIR MANUAL (US) [14253699] **5387**

MOTOR MATERIAL : M.M (JA) [09309899] **5420**

MOTOR MINIATURES (CN/0229-6128) [08302567] **5420**

MOTOR MUNDIAL (SP/0210-5969) [I02105969] 594, **5420**

MOTOR (NEW YORK) (US/0027-1748) [01758772] **5420**

MOTOR (NEW YORK) See MOTOR VACUUM & WIRING DIAGRAM DIAGNOSTIC MANUAL. PROFESSIONAL SERVICE TRADE EDITION **5420**

MOTOR NEWS (CHICAGO) (US/0194-8520) [05058554] **4082**

MOTOR NORTH (US/0300-6301) [01334644] **5420**

MOTOR PARTS AND TIME GUIDE (US/0098-1656) [01799536] **5420**

MOTOR RACING YEAR, THE (US/0090-2144) [01783532] 5420, **4905**

MOTOR REISEN REVUE (GW) [03075084] **5420**

MOTOR REPORT INTERNATIONAL **CEASED**. (UK/0306-6274) [I03066274] **5420**

MOTOR RUNDSCHAU See MOT AUTO-JOURNAL **5419**

MOTOR SERVICE (CHICAGO, ILL. : 1951) (US/0027-1977) [07631379] **5420**

MOTOR SHIP (UK/0027-2000) [07260964] **5453**

MOTOR SHIP DIRECTORY OF SHIPOWNERS & SHIPBUILDING See MOTOR SHIP DIRECTORY, THE **5453**

MOTOR SHIP DIRECTORY OF SHIPOWNERS & SHIPBUILDING, THE (UK) [20589326] **5453**

MOTOR SHIP DIRECTORY, THE (UK) [28560801] **5453**

MOTOR SPECIFICATIONS AND PRICES (UK) [06241877] **5387**

MOTOR SPORT (UK/0027-2019) [01932346] **4905**

MOTOR SPORT YEARBOOK (US/0091-8822) [01788489] 5420, **4905**

MOTOR SPORTS CAR ROAD TESTS, THE (UK) [19415994] 5420, **4905**

MOTOR TRADE JOURNAL (AT) 955, **5420**

MOTOR TRADER (UK/0027-2043) [I00272043] **5420**

MOTOR TRANSPORT [MICROFORM] (US/0027-206X) [15268313] **5387**

MOTOR TRAVEL See AAA TRAVELER. MUSKINGUM AAA EDITION, THE **5403**

MOTOR TREND (US/0027-2094) [01696683] 4905, **5420**

MOTOR TREND NEW CAR BUYER'S GUIDE (US/0160-8886) [03776509] **5420**

MOTOR TRUCK (CN/0027-2108) [02624982] **5387**

MOTOR TRUCK REPAIR MANUAL (US/0098-3624) [02241061] **5420**

MOTOR VACUUM & WIRING DIAGRAM DIAGNOSTIC MANUAL. PROFESSIONAL SERVICE TRADE EDITION (US/0273-1029) [06986102] **5420**

MOTOR VEHICLE CENSUS, TASMANIA (AT) [06958610] **5420**

MOTOR VEHICLE DATA BOOK (CN/0316-6198) [02441626] **5420**

MOTOR VEHICLE IDENTIFICATION (US/0736-8437) [06957001] **5420**

MOTOR VEHICLE REPORTS (CN/0709-5341) [06296118] 5441, **3012**

MOTOR VEHICLE SAFETY STANDARDS, WITH AMENDMENTS AND INTERPRETATIONS See FEDERAL MOTOR VEHICLE SAFETY STANDARDS AND REGULATIONS **4648**

MOTOR VEHICLE STATISTICS. ACCIDENT, LICENSE AND REGISTRATION STATISTICAL DATA (US) [22236278] 5420, **5441**

MOTOR VEHICLE TRAFFIC ACCIDENTS **CEASED**. (CN) [01789573] 4792, **5442**

●MOTOR WORLD (LOS ANGELES, CALIF.) (US/1055-8233) [23352090] **5420**

MOTORBOAT & EQUIPMENT DIRECTORY (US/0148-8740) [03611244] **594**

MOTORCAMPING HANDBOOK (US) [01785721] **4875**

MOTORCYCLE AND ATV MARKET REVIEW (US) [13452667] **5387**

MOTORCYCLE BLUE BOOK (US/0091-3774) [01785997] **4082**

●MOTORCYCLE CONSUMER NEWS (US/1073-9408) [29562597] **4082**

MOTORCYCLE DEALERNEWS MERCHANDISER (US/8755-4720) [11282589] **4082**

MOTORCYCLE DRAG RACING (US/0883-7228) [12219197] 4905, **4082**

MOTORCYCLE INDUSTRY BUSINESS JOURNAL, THE **CEASED**. (US/0731-3470) [08167580] **4082**

MOTORCYCLE INDUSTRY MAGAZINE : MI (US/0884-626X) [12405781] **4082**

MOTORCYCLE INTERNATIONAL (UK/0268-7151) [I02687151] **4082**

MOTORCYCLE, MOPED & ALL TERRAIN VEHICLE TRADE-IN GUIDE (US) [11446785] **4082**

MOTORCYCLE PRODUCT NEWS (US/0164-8349) [04315557] **4082**

MOTORCYCLE RED BOOK (US/0736-6116) [09167997] **4082**

MOTORCYCLE — Alphabetical Title Index

MOTORCYCLE RIDER'S GUIDE (US/0092-3095) [01792042] **4082**

MOTORCYCLE ROAD RACER ILLUSTRATED (US/1056-1455) [23601086] **4082**

MOTORCYCLE STATISTICAL ANNUAL (US/0149-3027) [03458152] **4082, 4083**

MOTORCYCLE TOURING (US/1041-5734) [18802539] **4082, 5485**

MOTORCYCLIST (LOS ANGELES, CALIF. 1912) (US/0027-2205) [01714454] **4082**

MOTORCYCLIST'S POST, THE (US/0164-9256) [04239742] **4905, 5387**

MOTORFAHRZEUGBESTAND IN DER SCHWEIZ NACH KANTONEN UND ORTSCHAFTEN (SZ) [03285820] **5420**

MOTORHOME (US/0744-074X) [08014439] **4852, 5387**

MOTORI (IT) [13652802] **5420**

MOTORIK (GW/0170-5792) [06191672] **4792**

MOTORING NEWS LONDON (UK/0027-2264) [I00272264] **5420, 4905**

MOTORISATION (PARIS) (FR/1156-1556) [24089503] **160**

MOTORIST See OHIO MOTORIST **5422**

MOTORIST (ALLENTOWN, PA.) (US/1056-2532) [23600843] **5420**

MOTORISTS GUIDE TO NEW & USED CAR PRICES (UK/0027-2302) [I00272302] **5421**

MOTORIZZAZIONE, LA (IT/1120-415X) [I1120415X] **5387**

MOTORLAND (US/0027-2310) [04059518] **5421**

MOTORRAD, DAS (GW) [06375291] **4082**

MOTORS AND GENERATORS (US/0736-2110) [03054569] **2073**

MOTOR'S AUTO REPAIR MANUAL See MOTOR AUTO REPAIR MANUAL **5419**

MOTOR'S HANDBOOK See MOTOR HANDBOOK **5419**

MOTOR'S IMPORTED CAR REPAIR MANUAL See MOTOR IMPORTED CAR REPAIR MANUAL **5419**

MOTOR'S PARTS AND TIME GUIDE See MOTOR PARTS AND TIME GUIDE **5420**

MOTORSPORTS MARKETING NEWS (US) **4905, 762**

MOTORSPORTS WEEKLY (US/1063-0422) [25851169] **4905**

MOTORYACHT (US/0735-5483) [08932996] **594**

MOTOSPRINT (IT) **4082**

MOTOTECNICA (IT) **2123**

MOTPOL (SW/0347-0989) [05984093] **3618**

MOTRICITE CEREBRALE, READAPTATION, NEUROLOGIE DU DEVELOPPEMENT (FR/0245-5919) [06828327] **3838**

MOTRIX (US/0027-2396) [09602863] **5421**

MOTS (FR/0243-6450) [07163007] **3304, 4482**

MOTS A TROUVER POPULAIRES (CN/0228-6475) [07818076] **4863**

MOTS A TROUVER RG (CN/0823-7123) [10179186] **4863**

MOTS CACHES J'AIME, LES (CN/0826-4740) [11193105] **4863**

MOTS CACHES SUPERMAGAZINE (CN/0822-4145) [09796274] **4863**

MOTS CROISES DE POCHE (FR) **2519**

MOTS CROISES ECLAIR (EDITION SEMESTRIELLE) (CN/0384-8191) [03400150] **4863**

MOTS CROISES FRANCAIS ANGLAIS (CN/0822-8728) [10676861] **4863**

MOTS CROISES POUR TOUT L'MONDE (CN/0712-5631) [09223160] **4863**

MOTS CROISES T V HEBDO (CN/0319-7115) [02578202] **4863**

MOTS ENTRE-CROISES POPULAIRES (CN/0228-6483) [07818063] **4863**

● MOTS ET DE CRAIE, DE (CN/1188-3766) [25796406] **1765**

MOTT PIONEER PRESS (US) [01758776] **5726**

● MOULES ZEBREES, ALERTE (CN/1188-4584) [26758296] **5592**

MOULTON ADVERTISER (1933), THE (US/1071-0337) [11990899] **5627**

MOULTON TRIBUNE (MOULTON, IOWA : 1981) (US) [15673894] **5671**

MOULTRIE COUNTY HERITAGE (US/8756-0836) [05773881] **2461**

MOULTRIE OBSERVER, THE (US) [19717762] **5654**

MOUND FACILITY See ANNUAL ENVIRONMENTAL MONITORING REPORT. MOUND FACILITY **2160**

MOUNDRIDGE JOURNAL (US) [11898472] **5677**

MOUNDSVILLE DAILY ECHO, THE (US) [13148366] **5764**

MOUNT AYR RECORD-NEWS (US) [13477448] **5671**

MOUNT BRYDGES BULLETIN, THE (CN/0316-0254) [02247315] **5790**

MOUNT DESERT ISLAND BIOLOGICAL LABORATORY See BULLETIN - MOUNT DESERT ISLAND BIOLOGICAL LABORATORY (1934) **450**

MOUNT HOLYOKE COLLEGE See ALUMNAE REGISTER / MOUNT HOLYOKE COLLEGE **1097**

MOUNT HOREB MAIL (US/0749-7091) [11181815] **5769**

MOUNT OLIVE HERALD, THE (US/0747-458X) [10889392] **5661**

MOUNT OLIVE REVIEW (US/0893-8288) [15681937] **3413**

MOUNT PLEASANT JOURNAL (MOUNT PLEASANT, PA.) (US) [11859705] **5737**

MOUNT PLEASANT NEWS, THE (US) [13908739] **5671**

MOUNT PROSPECT TIMES (US/0747-2595) [10684041] **5661**

MOUNT SHASTA HERALD (US/1064-6477) [26348236] **5637**

MOUNT SINAI JOURNAL OF MEDICINE, NEW YORK, THE (US/0027-2507) [01758779] **3618**

MOUNT UNION TIMES (MOUNT UNION, PA. : 1873) (US) [14136352] **5737**

MOUNT VERNON COLLEGE See ALUMNAE DIRECTORY / MOUNT VERNON COLLEGE **1096**

MOUNTAIN ADVOCATE (BARBOURVILLE, KY.) (US) [15598798] **5681**

MOUNTAIN & CITY BIKING (US/1046-4875) [20426271] **429**

MOUNTAIN BIKE (US/0897-5213) [24238829] **4905**

MOUNTAIN BIKE ACTION (US/0895-8467) [16823680] **4905**

● MOUNTAIN BIKE ACTION PARTS AND ACCESSORIES GUIDE (US/1062-7111) [25702369] **429**

● MOUNTAIN BIKE ACTION TRAVEL GUIDE (US/1062-7103) [25702348] **5485**

MOUNTAIN BIKING (1992) (US/1062-2918) [25569156] **429**

MOUNTAIN CITIZEN (US) [23605540] **2490**

MOUNTAIN COUNTRY : A NEWS MAGAZINE OF THE MOUNTAINS CONSERVANCY (US) [25598413] **2569**

MOUNTAIN COURIER-NEWS (US/0745-6220) [09313943] **5637**

MOUNTAIN DEMOCRAT AND PLACERVILLE TIMES (US) [27733285] **5637**

MOUNTAIN DIGGINGS (US/0146-8855) [03059952] **2747**

MOUNTAIN EAGLE (TANNERSVILLE, N.Y.), THE (US/1052-1356) [17718420] **5718**

MOUNTAIN EAGLE, THE (US) [06045754] **5681**

MOUNTAIN EAR (UK/0959-3160) [I09593160] **4875**

MOUNTAIN EMPIRE GENEALOGICAL QUARTERLY, THE (US/0882-4266) [11751782] **2461**

MOUNTAIN GAZETTE (US/0160-726X) [03764950] **4905**

MOUNTAIN GEOLOGIST, THE (US/0027-254X) [03404575] **1388**

MOUNTAIN HOME NEWS (US) [12292773] **5657**

MOUNTAIN MAIL (US) [20716596] **5643**

MOUNTAIN MESSENGER, THE (US/0278-4394) [07808380] **5637**

MOUNTAIN MOVERS (US/0164-7253) [04405621] **4979**

MOUNTAIN MUSIC See AMERICAN COONER **4882**

MOUNTAIN MUSIC AND WHERE TO FIND IT (US/0149-8096) [03552385] **4132**

MOUNTAIN NEWS AND MOUNTAINEER (US) **5637**

MOUNTAIN, PLAIN AND GARDEN (US/1057-5049) [21426829] **2424, 518**

MOUNTAIN PLAINS LIBRARY ASSOCIATION See MPLA NEWSLETTER (1975) **3232**

MOUNTAIN PRESS (SEVIERVILLE, TENN.), THE (US/0894-2218) [15925457] **5745**

MOUNTAIN RECORD (US/0896-8942) [17316849] **5021**

MOUNTAIN RESEARCH AND DEVELOPMENT (US/0276-4741) [07370570] **241**

MOUNTAIN STATE GEOLOGY (US/0163-2825) [03812205] **1388**

MOUNTAIN STATES BANKER See BANK NEWS **775**

MOUNTAIN STATES EMPLOYERS COUNCIL See MINING PERSONNEL PRACTICES SURVEY **1690**

MOUNTAIN STATES EMPLOYERS COUNCIL See BANK OFFICERS SALARY SURVEY **1654**

MOUNTAIN STATES EMPLOYERS COUNCIL See NORTH CENTRAL NEW MEXICO SALARY SURVEY **1695**

MOUNTAIN STATES MINING SURVEY (US/0275-9438) [07235181] **2147, 1442**

MOUNTAIN STATESMAN (GRAFTON, W. VA.) (US/0745-1334) [08852246] **5764**

MOUNTAIN TROUBADOUR, THE (US/0027-2604) [03374035] **3466**

MOUNTAIN VACATION & TRAVEL GUIDE COVERING WESTERN NORTH CAROLINA (US/0162-6523) [04185719] **5485**

MOUNTAINEER-HERALD, THE (US) [12685181] **5737**

MOUNTAINEER POSTMASTER (US/0194-536X) [04799851] **2539**

MOUNTAINEER. ROCKY MOUNTAIN HOUSE (CN) **4875**

MOUNTAINEER (SEATTLE, WASH.) (US/0027-2620) [01696082] **4875**

MOUNTAINEER (VEDDER CROSSING) (CN/0319-5562) [03222598] **4052**

MOUNTAINTOP EAGLE, THE (US) [15648080] **5737**

MOUNTAINWEST MAGAZINE (US/0191-9482) [04603651] **2539**

MOUNTRAIL COUNTY PROMOTER (US) [01758787] **5726**

MOUNTRAIL COUNTY RECORD (US) [01588146] **5726**

MOUSAION (PRETORIA, SOUTH AFRICA: 1983) (SA/0027-2639) [10155957] **3232**

MOUSE (IT) **2490**

MOUSE GENOME (UK/0959-0587) [21169006] **466**

MOUSEION GOULANDRE PHYSIKES HISTORIAS See ANNALES MUSEI GOULANDRIS **4161**

MOUSQUETON, LE (CN/0712-3817) [08898876] **4875**

MOUTH (US/1071-5657) [03374070] **4391**

MOUTH OF THE DRAGON (US/0145-0042) [01928864] **3466**

MOUTHPIECE (US) [22785950] **2775, 5618**

MOUTHPIECE (TORONTO) (CN/0380-0601) [02075532] **4132**

MOUTON, LE (FR) **3618**

MOUTON NOIR (CN/0826-2748) [11085198] **5790**

MOUVEMENT (OTTAWA) (CN/0705-6532) [11377311] **1542**

MOUVEMENT SOCIAL, LE (FR/0027-2671) [05380209] **5209, 2623**

MOUVEMENTS CEASED. (CN/0823-5651) [10643449] **1691**

MOVEMENT AND DANCE : MAGAZINE OF THE LABAN GUILD (UK) [08677636] **1314**

MOVEMENT DISORDERS (US/0885-3185) [12616375] **3838**

MOVEMENT OF CALIFORNIA FRUITS AND VEGETABLES BY RAIL, TRUCK, AND AIR (US/0094-2790) [01793901] **110, 846**

MOVEMENT THEATRE QUARTERLY (US/1065-1519) [26516120] **5366**

MOVEMENTS OF PUPILS IN POST-PRIMARY EDUCATION (AT) [16929278] **1765**

MOVIE (BOMBAY, INDIA) (II) [08756734] **4074**

MOVIE COLLECTOR'S WORLD (US/8750-5401) [11489736] **4075, 2775**

MOVIE GUIDE (CHICAGO, ILL.) (US/1057-0276) [23931159] **4075**

MOVIE (LONDON) (UK/0027-268X) [02361518] **4075**

MOVIE MAKER (US/1049-3859) [21213968] **4075**

MOVIE MARKETPLACE (US/1051-5488) [21992627] **4075, 4372**

MOVIE MIRROR (US/0027-271X) [04059566] **4075**

MOVIE STATS (US/1046-7858) [20534105] **1135, 1125**

MOVIE/TV MARKETING (JA) [06166375] **4075, 933**

MOVIE WORKS WEEKLY, THE (CN/0705-9175) [04256069] **4075**

Alphabetical Title Index — MT

MOVIE X (US/0090-2039) [01784789] **5188**

MOVIELINE (LOS ANGELES, CALIF.) (US/1055-0917) [21539429] **4075**

MOVIES (NEW YORK, N.Y.), THE **SUSPENDED.** (US/0742-4116) [10292448] **4075**

MOVIES ON TV AND VIDEOCASSETTE (US/1053-5314) [19094907] **4372, 1135**

MOVIES USA **CEASED.** (US/1044-1336) [19691994] **4075**

MOVIMENTO (IT) **4905, 4604**

MOVIMENTO BRASILEIRO DE ALFABETIZACAO. SETOR DE DOCUMENTACAO **See** BOLETIM BIBLIOGRAFICO SEDOC **410**

MOVIMENTO REGISTRO DITTE E ALBO IMPRESE ARTIGIANE **CEASED.** (IT) **820**

MOVIMENTO SINDICAL (BL) [01791758] **1691**

MOVIMIENTO DE HORTALIZAS, TUBERCULOS Y FRUTAS INGRESADOS A LIMA POR EL MERCADO MAYORISTA **See** MOVIMIENTO DE PRODUCTOS AGRICOLAS ALIMENTICIOS INGRESADOS A LIMA METROPOLITANA **110**

MOVIMIENTO DE PRODUCTOS AGRICOLAS ALIMENTICIOS INGRESADOS A LIMA METROPOLITANA (PE/0302-9409) [01792903] **110**

"MOVIN" (CN/0704-1500) [05789918] **5433**

MOVING AHEAD (CHICAGO, ILL.) (US/1046-137X) [20387063] **3618**

MOVING AND STORAGE WAGE SURVEY, ATLANTA, GA. / U.S. DEPARTMENT OF LABOR, BUREAU OF LABOR STATISTICS (US) [08463133] **1691**

MOVING AND STORAGE WAGE SURVEY, COLORADO SPRINGS, COLO. / U.S. DEPARTMENT OF LABOR, BUREAU OF LABOR STATISTICS (US) [09305748] **1691**

MOVING AND STORAGE WAGE SURVEY, MOBILE-PENSACOLA-PANAMA CITY, ALA.-FLA. / U.S. DEPARTMENT OF LABOR, BUREAU OF LABOR STATISTICS (US) [08126371] **1692**

MOVING AND STORAGE WAGE SURVEY, NASSAU-SUFFOLK, N.Y. / U.S. DEPARTMENT OF LABOR, BUREAU OF LABOR STATISTICS (US) [08463392] **1692**

MOVING AND STORAGE WAGE SURVEY, NORTHWEST TEXAS / U.S. DEPARTMENT OF LABOR, BUREAU OF LABOR STATISTICS (US) [08126165] **1692**

MOVING AND STORAGE WAGE SURVEY, OXNARD-SIMI VALLEY-VENTURA, CALIF. / U.S. DEPARTMENT OF LABOR, BUREAU OF LABOR STATISTICS (US) [09388287] **1692**

MOVING AND STORAGE WAGE SURVEY, PATERSON-CLIFTON PASSAIC, N.J. / U.S. DEPARTMENT OF LABOR, BUREAU OF LABOR STATISTICS (US) [08463257] **1692**

MOVING AND STORAGE WAGE SURVEY, RICHMOND, VA. / U.S. DEPARTMENT OF LABOR, BUREAU OF LABOR STATISTICS (US) [09313422] **1692**

MOVING AND STORAGE WAGE SURVEY, SAN ANTONIO, TEX. / U.S. DEPARTMENT OF LABOR, BUREAU OF LABOR STATISTICS (US) [08464319] **1692**

MOVING AND STORAGE WAGE SURVEY, UTICA-ROME, N.Y. / U.S. DEPARTMENT OF LABOR, BUREAU OF LABOR STATISTICS (US) [09491065] **1692**

MOVING AND STORAGE WAGE SURVEY, WESTERN AND NORTHERN MASSACHUSETTS / U.S. DEPARTMENT OF LABOR, BUREAU OF LABOR STATISTICS (US) [08463319] **1692**

MOVING AND STORAGE WAGE SURVEY, WICHITA, KAN. / U.S. DEPARTMENT OF LABOR, BUREAU OF LABOR STATISTICS (US) [08466140] **1692**

MOVING AND STORAGE WAGE SURVEY, WILMINGTON, DEL- N.J.-MD. / U.S. DEPARTMENT OF LABOR, BUREAU OF LABOR STATISTICS (US) [08463175] **1692**

MOVING FORCE (US/0195-7511) [05578391] **3012**

MOVING FORWARD : THE NATIONAL NEWSPAPER FOR PEOPLE WITH DISABILITIES (US/1056-7240) [23823370] **4391**

MOVING HOUSE AND HOME (NEW YORK, N.Y.) (US/0279-0971) [07537963] **5387**

MOVING IMAGE REVIEW (US/0897-0769) [17392285] **4075**

MOVING OUT (US) [05157262] **5561, 3413**

MOVING TECHNOLOGY (II/0970-6704) [I09706704] **5130**

MOVING TO & AROUND ALBERTA (CN/0713-8369) [09071351] **4841**

MOVING TO & AROUND HAMILTON, C.T.T., BRANTFORD, BURLINGTON & NIAGARA (CN/0843-9214) [24368205] **4841**

MOVING TO & AROUND SASKATCHEWAN (CN/0713-8385) [09074901] **4841**

MOVING TO & AROUND TORONTO & AREA (CN/0713-8377) [09086737] **4841**

MOVING TO & AROUND VANCOUVER & B.C (CN/0713-8407) [09071375] **4841**

MOVING TO & AROUND WINNIPEG & MANITOBA (CN/0715-7053) [09822885] **4841**

MOVING TO MONTREAL (CN/0702-9225) [03436466] **4841**

MOVING TO OTTAWA/HULL (1978) (CN/0226-7837) [06515613] **4841**

MOVING TO THE SAN FRANCISCO BAY AREA AND GREATER SACRAMENTO (CN/0828-4601) [18452320] **4841**

MOVOZNAVSTVO (KIEV) (RU/0027-2833) [02264439] **3304**

MOVOZNAVSTVO; NAUKOVI ZAPYSKY (UN/0027-2833) [01714083] **3304**

MOWIA WIEKI 1992 (PL/1230-4018) [I12304018] **2699**

MOYANGCHON (KO) [11855700] **3466**

MOYEN-AGE (FR/0027-2841) [02131368] **3304**

MOYEN FRANCAIS (CN/0226-0174) [05316962] **3413**

MOYEN ORIENT & OCEAN INDIEN, XVIE-XIXE (FR/0764-5562) [15187880] **2642**

MOZAMBIQUE. DIRECCAO DOS SERVICOS DE SAUDE E ASSISTENCIA. SECCAO DE ESTATISTICA **See** RELATORIO - DIRECCAO PROVINCIAL DOS SERVICOS DE SAUDE E ASSISTENCIA **4798**

MOZAMBIQUEFILE : A MOZAMBIQUE NEWS AGENCY MONTHLY / AIM (MZ) [20291632] **2642, 4482**

MOZART-JAHRBUCH (GW/0077-1805) [01758799] **4160, 4132**

MOZNAYIM (IS/0027-2892) [04430163] **3413**

MOZNAYIM (IS/0027-2892) [01758800] **3413**

MP (BL) [01789528] **3012**

MPE JOURNAL (IT) [01789024] **4457**

MPENAKEION PHYTOPATHOLOGIKON INSTITOUTON **See** ANNALES DE L'INSTITUT PHYTOPATHOLOGIQUE BENAKI **499**

MPG SPIEGEL (GW/0341-7727) [08751945] **5130**

MPH LIVING (SI) [05953912] **2792**

MPLA NEWSLETTER (1975) (US/0145-6180) [01915005] **3232**

MPLS. ST. PAUL (US/0162-6655) [03883465] **2747**

MPS IN THE NEWS (CN/0704-0377) [08071474] **3012**

MPTOZOAROP / EDILIZIA RESIDENZA PUBBLICA (IT) **2828**

MPWH BULLETIN : OFFICIAL QUARTERLY PUBLICATION OF THE MINISTRY OF PUBLIC WORKS AND HIGHWAYS **SUSPENDED.** (PH) [10181002] **4666**

MR. COGITO (US/0740-1205) [03375663] **3466**

MR (NORWALK, CONN.) (US/1049-6726) [21276400] **955**

MR (SAN FRANCISCO, CALIF.) (US/1055-6273) [23245268] **3944**

MR (UNIVERSITY OF CALIFORNIA, LOS ANGELES. INSTITUTE OF GOVERNMENT AND PUBLIC AFFAIRS) (US) [04480672] **4666**

MRA BLUE BOOK, RESEARCH SERVICES DIRECTORY (US) [26379930] **933**

MRAN MA NUIN NAM SUTESANA A SN **See** MYANMA NAING NGAN THUTEITHANA ATHIN GYANE. THE JOURNAL OF THE BURMA RESEARCH SOCIETY **2659**

MRAX INFORMATION (BE/0024-8320) **5209**

MRC NEWS (UK/0143-0130) [I01430130] **3618**

MRCR, MINING RESEARCH CONTRACT REVIEW (US) [06161967] **2147**

MRI BANKERS' GUIDE TO FOREIGN CURRENCY (US/1055-3851) [23162374] **800**

●MRI CLINICS OF NORTH AMERICA (US/1064-9689) [26478136] **3848, 3944**

MRI DECISIONS (US/0896-0704) [16898984] **3944**

MRI INFORMATIVO (VE) [05131308] **4666**

MRIS ABSTRACTS (US/0147-572X) [03198106] **5453, 4179**

MRL BULLETIN (US/0415-505X) [04871058] **3232**

MRL BULLETIN OF RESEARCH AND DEVELOPMENT (CH/1010-2744) [24579590] **1988**

MRL TECHNICAL NOTE (AT) [27160581] **5130**

MRO ALERT (US/1051-9661) [22161020] **3618, 3012**

MRQ (US/0731-8197) [08261523] **2775**

MRS BULLETIN (US/0883-7694) [12225171] **2107**

MRS RELAY (UK) **4265**

MRZ. MEDITSINSKII REFERATIVNYI ZHURNAL (RU) [05951830] **3618**

MS (US/0047-8318) [22202699] **5561**

MS & T : MILITARY SIMULATION & TRAINING (UK/0937-6348) [25757461] **4052**

MS BIBLIOTEKSNYT (DK) [02336903] **4529**

MS CANADA (CN/0315-1131) [02052011] **3838**

MS-DOS COLLECTION (US/1051-8592) [22148435] **1288**

MS QUARTERLY **See** MS QUARTERLY REPORT **3838**

MS QUARTERLY REPORT (US/0738-3967) [09592584] **3838**

MS TORONTO (1991) (CN/1187-466X) [25652231] **4391**

MS. TREE (US/0826-2586) [11852309] **5074**

MSA PROFILE (US/1043-8629) [19586750] **1506**

MSA TAX CORRESPONDENT (US/0364-250X) [02613840] **4737**

MSBA IN BRIEF (US/0884-1667) [12323028] **3012**

MSC/NASTRAN APPLICATION MANUAL. IBM EDITION (US/0741-8035) [10205892] **1195**

MSCS (CAMBRIDGE) (UK/0960-1295) [23727065] **1195**

MSF FINANCE NEWS (UK) [20975454] **1692**

MSF HEALTH NEWS (UK) [20971793] **1692**

MSF : MANUFACTURING, SCIENCE, FINANCE (UK) [19054813] **846**

MSHDA REVIEW **See** REPORT - MICHIGAN STATE HOUSING DEVELOPMENT AUTHORITY **2833**

●MSL LAW REVIEW (US/1066-1085) [26860719] **3012**

●MSLA JOURNAL (CN/1189-7163) [29874029] **3232**

MSM **See** SERVICE & SUPPORT MANAGEMENT **710**

MSOS JOURNAL (CN/0831-3040) [14879574] **5180**

MSPB ALERT (US/1065-0091) [26493335] **3012**

MSPB/FLRA CASE DECISIONS (US/0749-4637) [10357027] **3152**

MSRB REPORTS (US/0277-0911) [07496611] **3012**

MSRRT NEWSLETTER (US) **3232**

MST ENGLISH QUARTERLY, THE (PH/0047-5289) [04565698] **1900, 3304**

MSTA HANDBOOK (US/0191-3638) [05047403] **1900**

MSU-DOE PLANT RESEARCH LABORATORY **See** ANNUAL REPORT ... - MSU-DOE PLANT RESEARCH LABORATORY **499**

MSU INTERNATIONAL DEVELOPMENT PAPERS : REPRINT (US) [14921698] **110**

MSW MANAGEMENT (US/1053-7899) [22646653] **2236**

MSX-MS-DOC COMPUTER MAGAZINE (NE) **1196**

MT MAQUINAS Y TRACTORES AGRICOLAS **See** VIDA RURAL **144**

MT. MAQUINAS Y TRACTORES AGRICOLAS (SP/0214-9206) [I02149206] **160**

MT : MEDICAL TOP **SUSPENDED.** (IT) **3618**

MT. OLIVE CHRONICLE (US/0195-2498) [05424276] **5710**

MT. PLEASANT DAILY NEWS **See** MOUNT PLEASANT NEWS, THE **5671**

MT. PLEASANT FREE PRESS **See** MOUNT PLEASANT NEWS, THE **5671**

MT. PLEASANT REPUBLICAN (MOUNT PLEASANT, IOWA : 1899) **See** MOUNT PLEASANT NEWS, THE **5671**

MT. STERLING ADVOCATE, THE (US) [15111673] **5681**

MT   Alphabetical Title Index

MT TODAY (US/1060-7609) [25058355] **3618**

MT. VERNON OPTIC-HERALD (US) [16669774] **5752**

MTA (GW/0930-4622) [14690866] **3915**

MTA. MEDICINA INTERNA (SP/0212-1514) [I02121514] **3799**

MTA. PEDIATRIA (SP/0210-8135) [I02108135] **3906**

MTL. MONTREAL *CEASED*. (CN/0833-0026) [17236885] **2539**

MTLA QUARTERLY (US) [23864881] **3012**

MTM, MOTORCOACH TOUR MART (US/0161-9551) [04061265] **5485**

MTO PUBLICATION *See* PUBLICATION - MIDDLE TENNESSEE SECTION, TENNESSEE STATE PLANNING OFFICE **2832**

MTS=IP2S, INNOVATORS & INNOVATIONS (US/1059-0366) [24476357] **1765**

MTZ. MOTORTECHNISCHE ZEITSCHRIFT (GW/0024-8525) [01756370] **2123**

MU KARA SANI NOUVELLE FORMULE : BULLETIN D'INFORMATION ET DE LIAISON DE L'INSTITUT DE RECHERCHES EN SCIENCES HUMAINES L'UNIVERSITE DE NIAMEY (NG) [10328588] **5210**

MU PHI EPSILON *See* TRIANGLE OF MU PHI EPSILON, THE **4157**

MUANYAG ES GUMI (HU/0027-2914) [09435834] 5076, **4457**

MU'ASSASAT AL-DIRASAT AL-FILASTINIYAH *See* MONOGRAPH SERIES - INSTITUTE FOR PALESTINE STUDIES **4529**

MUASSASAT RISALAT AL-BATRUL AL-ARABI *See* RISALAT AL-BATRUL AL-ARABI **4277**

MUCAI GONGYE (CH/1001-8654) [I10018654] **2403**

MUCCHIO SELVAGGIO, IL (IT) [06003046] **4132**

MUCHACHA *SUSPENDED*. (CU/0864-0327) [08139762] **5561**

MUCHACHOS (IT) **1765**

MUCKRAKER : JOURNAL OF THE CENTER FOR INVESTIGATIVE REPORTING (US) [25472602] **2922**

●MUCOSAL IMMUNOLOGY UPDATE : OFFICIAL PUBLICATION OF THE SOCIETY FOR MUCOSAL IMMUNOLOGY (US/1068-7629) [27783839] **3675**

MUDDY ROOTS (US/8756-4327) [11535470] **2461**

MUEBLE, EL (SP/0027-2930) [I00272930] **2906**

MUECKE (GW/0930-7818) [I09307818] **1765**

MUEHLE + MISCHFUTTERTECHNIK, DIE (GW/0027-2949) [04426764] **203**

MUELLERIA (AT/0077-1813) [01641190] **518**

MUEMLEKVEDELEM (HU/0541-2439) [02980761] 304, **275**

MUENCHENER TEXTE UND UNTERSUCHUNGEN ZUR DEUTSCHEN LITERATUR DES MITTELALTERS (GW/0580-1362) [02475063] **3413**

MUENCHENER THEOLOGISCHE ZEITSCHRIFT (GW/0580-1400) [01774008] **5032**

MUFON UFO JOURNAL, THE (US/0270-6822) [04159230] **29**

MUGENDAI (JA) [11147716] **2851**

MUGWUMPS *SUSPENDED*. (US/0149-8517) [03562576] **4132**

MUHAMMADIYAH (ORGANIZATION) *See* ALMANAK MUHAMMADIYAH **5042**

MUHIBBAH (IO) [02537855] **5130**

MUHTVIERTLER BOTE (AU) [20126451] **5778**

MUIN (YE) [09753397] **2507**

MUIR'S ORIGINAL LOG HOME GUIDE FOR BUILDERS AND BUYERS (US/0844-3459) [19059598] **621**

MUISTIO (FINLAND. TILASTOKESKUS) (FI/0357-6507) [19032843] **5333**

MUJER/FEMPRESS / UNIDAD DE COMMUNICACION ALTERNATIVA DE LA MUJER, ILET (CL) [14873563] **5536**

MUJERES (CU) [02264458] **5561**

MUJERES (MADRID, SPAIN) (SP) [12955362] **5561**

MUJTAMA AL-BATRUL (TS) [10286477] **4265**

MUJTAMA WA-UMRAN (TI) [09159782] **304**

MUKI ZAISHITSU KENKYUJO *See* KAGAKU GIJUTSUCHO MUKI ZAISHITSU KENKYUJO YORAN **1984**

MUKI ZAISHITSU KENKYUJO KENKYU RONBUNSHU (JA) [10075523] **1037**

MUKWONAGO CHIEF, THE (US) [15071473] **5769**

MUKYOKAISHUGI NO JIKO TENKEN (JA) [04509679] **5065**

MULBERRY (US/0090-4953) [01785175] **3466**

MULBERRY PRESS (US) **5650**

MULCH (US/0027-3112) [01912814] **3413**

MULESHOE JOURNAL, THE (US) [14472812] **5752**

MULGA RESEARCH CENTRE JOURNAL (AT/0818-8238) [24298354] 2219, 2388, **41**

MULIKA (TZ) [01784374] **3413**

MULINO, IL (IT/0027-3120) [01641727] **3348**

MULKA SISE (KO) [11341399] **1575**

MULKA TONGGYE (KO) [21737720] **1575**

MULKEY JOURNAL (US/0148-6683) [03340978] **2461**

MULL UND ABFALL (GW/0027-2957) [I00272957] **4792**

MULLENS ADVOCATE, THE (US/1064-6132) [13805394] **5764**

MULLMAGAZIN (GW/0934-3482) [I09343482] **2236**

MULTI-BIBLE IBM. CD-ROM (US) **4979**

MULTI-COUNTY STAR (US/0194-2050) [05356354] **5654**

●MULTI-FACT (CN/1193-1884) [26758185] **3708**

MULTI-HOUSING MAINSTREAM (US/0744-169X) [08077079] **2828**

MULTI-HOUSING NEWS (US/0146-0919) [02850415] **2828**

MULTI-HOUSING NEWSLETTER (US) [25081839] **2828**

MULTI-INDUSTRY DEVELOPMENTS (US/0887-4093) [20684744] **1619**

MULTI-LEVEL MARKETING TAX AND FINANCIAL NEWSLETTER / MLM (US/0730-9171) [08122484] 4738, **933**

MULTI MEDIA BIRDS OF AMERICA *See* MULTIMEDIA AUDUBONS BIRDS **5618**

MULTI MEDIA BIRDS OF AMERICA. CD-ROM (US) **5618**

MULTI-MEDIA COMPUTING (NE/0923-8182) [I09238182] **1196**

●MULTI MEDIA TOOLS AND APPLICATIONS (NE/1380-7501) [26758185] **1288**

MULTI-UNIT AGREEMENTS IN THE FEDERAL GOVERNMENT (US) [04173474] **4666**

MULTI-USER COMPUTING (UK/0954-6561) **1242**

MULTI-YEAR PLAN - HUMBER COLLEGE OF APPLIED ARTS AND TECHNOLOGY (CN/0707-1248) [06859379] **1836**

MULTICHANNEL NEWS (US/0276-8593) [07398798] **1135**

MULTICULTURAL EDUCATION ABSTRACTS (UK/0260-9770) [08673922] 1765, **1795**

MULTICULTURAL EDUCATION COUNCIL NEWSLETTER OF THE ALBERTA TEACHERS' ASSOCIATION (CN/0829-9137) [16636813] **1765**

MULTICULTURAL EDUCATION JOURNAL (CN/0823-6283) [09816233] **1765**

MULTICULTURAL EDUCATION REVIEW (AT/1033-6281) **1765**

MULTICULTURAL EDUCATION REVIEW (BIRMINGHAM, ENGLAND) (UK) **1765**

●MULTICULTURAL EDUCATION (SAN FRANCISCO, CALIF.) (US/1068-3844) [27667643] **1765**

MULTICULTURAL LEADER (US/0896-5269) [17197007] **1765**

MULTICULTURAL LIBRARIES NEWSLETTER (AT/0158-9431) [I01589431] **3232**

●MULTICULTURAL REVIEW (US/1058-9236) [24433867] **2268**

MULTICULTURAL TEACHING TO COMBAT RACISM IN SCHOOL AND COMMUNITY (UK/0263-0869) [11811656] **1901**

MULTICULTURALISM (CN/0701-2586) [03791084] **5252**

MULTICULTURALISM IN EDUCATION NEWSLETTER (AT/0818-8823) [I08188823] 2268, **1765**

MULTIDIMENSIONAL SYSTEMS AND SIGNAL PROCESSING (US/0923-6082) [21508199] **1196**

MULTIDISCIPLINAR. REVISTA DO ICNPF (BL/0100-185X) [02245927] **1765**

MULTIDISCIPLINARY RESEARCH (US/0098-8553) [02240610] **4605**

MULTIHULL INTERNATIONAL (UK) 5453, **1988**

MULTIHULLS (US/0749-4122) [10414489] **4905**

MULTILATERAL TREATIES DEPOSITED WITH THE SECRETARY-GENERAL (US) [08463770] **3132**

MULTILATERAL TREATIES : INDEX AND CURRENT STATUS. CUMULATIVE SUPPLEMENT (UK) [22377353] **3133**

MULTILINGUA (NE/0167-8507) [09009426] **3304**

MULTILINGUAL COMPUTING (US/1065-7657) [26725858] **1196**

MULTILINGUAL COMPUTING AND BUYERS GUIDE *See* MULTILINGUAL COMPUTING MAGAZINE **1196**

MULTILINGUAL COMPUTING MAGAZINE (US) **1196**

MULTILINGUAL MATTERS (UK) [12381183] **3304**

MULTIMEDIA (IT) **1117**

... MULTIMEDIA & CD DIRECTORY, THE (US) [29526828] **1277**

MULTIMEDIA & TEXT *CEASED*. (US) **1196**

MULTIMEDIA AND VIDEODISC COMPENDIUM FOR EDUCATION AND TRAINING (US) [28903806] **1801**

MULTIMEDIA & VIDEODISC MONITOR (US/1054-7258) [22964371] **1619**

●MULTIMEDIA AUDUBONS BIRDS (US) **5618**

MULTIMEDIA BUSINESS AND LAW INTERNATIONAL (UK) 3012, **696**

●MULTIMEDIA BUSINESS REPORT (US/1065-8300) [26756630] 696, **1117**

MULTIMEDIA COMPUTING AND PRESENTATION *See* MULTIMEDIA BUSINESS REPORT **1117**

MULTIMEDIA COMPUTING & PRESENTATIONS (US/1051-953X) [22164755] **908**

... MULTIMEDIA DIRECTORY, THE (US) [24418009] **1248**

MULTIMEDIA INTERNATIONAL (UK) **1196**

MULTIMEDIA MARKETS (US) **933**

MULTIMEDIA MARKETS : INTERNATIONAL FORECAST SUPPLEMENT (US) **934**

●MULTIMEDIA MONITOR (US/1071-0698) [28539925] **1619**

●MULTIMEDIA NETWORK TECHNOLOGY REPORT (US/1077-4440) [30830488] **1196**

MULTIMEDIA REVIEW *CEASED*. (US/1046-3550) [20388603] **1196**

●MULTIMEDIA SCHOOLS (US/1075-0479) [29926033] 1901, **1196**

MULTIMEDIA SYSTEMS (GW/0942-4962) **1118**

MULTIMEDIA TECHNOLOGIES AND SYSTEMS (US) **1118**

●MULTIMEDIA WEEK (US/1064-6639) [26368110] **1118**

●MULTIMEDIA WORLD (US/1073-4759) [29410755] **1196**

MULTIMEDIA WORLD FACTBOOK. CD-ROM (US) **4482**

MULTIMIND (UK) **1901**

MULTINATIONAL BUSINESS (US/0300-3922) [01445808] **1638**

MULTINATIONAL CORPORATION REGULATORY GUIDEBOOK, THE (US/0273-0057) [06987458] **3012**

MULTINATIONAL EMPLOYER (UK/0953-7929) [I09537929] **944**

MULTINATIONAL ENVIRONMENTAL OUTLOOK *See* WORLD ENVIRONMENT REPORT **2248**

MULTINATIONAL EXECUTIVE TRAVEL COMPANION (US/0093-7487) [01792971] **5485**

MULTINATIONAL INDUSTRIAL RELATIONS SERIES (US/0149-0818) [03428432] 3133, **1692**

MULTINATIONAL MONITOR (US/0197-4637) [06018571] **846**

MULTINATIONAL SERVICE (INT/1021-4186) [I10214186] **846**

MULTINATIONALE SERVICE (BE) **696**

MULTIPHASE SCIENCE AND TECHNOLOGY (US/0276-1459) [07317066] **5130**

MULTIPLE IMAGING PROCEDURES (US/0195-9557) [05582694] **3944**

MULTIPLE JOBHOLDERS (US) [04298314] **1692**

MULTIPLE LINEAR REGRESSION VIEWPOINTS (US/0195-7171) [04304147] **3523**

MULTIPLE RISK FACTOR INTERVENTION TRIAL. PUBLIC ANNUAL REPORT (US/0164-0577) [03967016] **3708**

●MULTIPLE SCLEROSIS (UK) **3838**

MULTIPLE SCLEROSIS RESEARCH REPORTS (US/0897-0270) [15123732] **3838**

MULTIPLE SCLEROSIS SOCIETY REPORT *See* MS TORONTO (1991) **4391**

MULTIRACIAL EDUCATION (UK/0260-0226) [I02600226] **1765**

MULTIRACIAL SCHOOL (UK/0260-0226) [01788727] 2268, **1765**

MULTIROD BURST TEST PROGRAM PROGRESS REPORT FOR ... - U.S. NUCLEAR REGULATORY COMMISSION, OFFICE OF NUCLEAR REGULATORY RESEARCH (US) [08328065] **2156**

MULTISTATE BAR REVIEW MANUAL (US/0098-4671) [02239302] **3012**

MULTISTATE BAR REVIEW SERIES (US/0160-1334) [03616792] **3012**

MULTISTATE CORPORATE TAX GUIDE (US/1051-1555) [20848940] 748, **4738**

MULTISTATE LEGAL STUDIES, INC *See* MULTISTATE BAR REVIEW SERIES **3012**

MULTISTATE PART-YEAR NONRESIDENT RETURN GUIDE (US) **4738**

MULTISTATE TAX ANALYST (US/0892-4678) [13711019] **4738**

MULTISTATE TAX COMMISSION REVIEW (US) [09569704] **4738**

●MULTIVAC UPDATE (US/1061-1606) [25195266] **4413**

MULTIVARIATE BEHAVIORAL RESEARCH (US/0027-3171) [01292018] **4605**

MULTIVARIATE EXPERIMENTAL CLINICAL RESEARCH (US/0147-3964) [03091847] **4605**

MULTUNK : AZ MSZMP KOZPONTI BIZOTTSAGA PARTTORTENETI INTEZETENEK FOLYOIRATA (HU) [20743163] **4543**

MULVANE NEWS, THE (US) [12674593] **5677**

●MUMPS COMPUTING (US/1060-7684) [25059660] **1196**

MUMPS USER'S GROUP QUARTERLY (US) **1270**

MUNAIVAN (II) [11801383] **2659**

MUNAZZAMAT AL-AMAL AL-ARABIYAH *See* ANB MUNAZZAMAT AL-AMAL AL-ARABIYAH **1643**

MUNCA DE PARTID *CEASED.* (RM) [01787477] **4667**

MUNCHENER BEITRAEGE ZUR MEDIAVISTIK UND RENAISSANCE-FORSCHUNG (GW/0930-1127) [02481096] 3413, **3304**

MUNCHENER GEOGRAPHISCHE ABHANDLUNGEN (GW/0343-706X) [02155870] **2569**

MUNCHENER GEOGRAPHISCHE ABHANDLUNGEN REIHE B (GW/0932-3147) [I09323147] **2569**

MUNCHENER OSTASIATISCHE STUDIEN (GW/0170-3668) [01758811] 3304, **3413**

MUNCHENER PAPIERE ZUR LINGUISTIK *See* PAPIERE ZUR LINGUISTIK **3309**

MUNCHENER ROMANISTISCHE ARBEITEN (GW) [02475078] **3348**

MUNCHENER STUDIEN ZUR SPRACHWISSENSCHAFT (GW/0077-1910) [02515992] **3304**

MUNCHNER BEITRAEGE ZUR ABWASSER-, FISCHEREI- UND FLUSSBIOLOGIE (GW/0368-8275) [05332680] **556**

MUNCHNER EDITIONEN ZUR MUSIKGESCHICHTE (GW) [08447636] **4132**

MUNCHNER ENTOMOLOGISCHE GESELLSCHAFT *See* MITTEILUNGEN DER MUNCHNER ENTOMOLOGISCHEN GESELLSCHAFT **5591**

MUNCHNER GEOWISSENSCHAFTLICHE ABHANDLUNGEN. REIHE A, GEOLOGIE UND PALAONTOLOGIE (GW/0177-0950) [18125609] **1389**

MUNCHNER GEOWISSENSCHAFTLICHE ABHANDLUNGEN. REIHE B, ALLGEMEINE UND ANGEWANDTE GEOLOGIE (GW/0931-8739) [I09318739] **1389**

MUNCHNER GERMANISTISCHE BEITRAEGE (GW/0077-1872) [01696741] **3348**

MUNCHNER JAHRBUCH DER BILDENDEN KUNST (GW/0077-1899) [01716068] **359**

MUNCHNER VEROFFENTLICHUNGEN ZUR MUSIKGESCHICHTE (GW) [01589009] **4132**

MUNCHNER ZEITSCHRIFT FUER BALKANKUNDE (GW/0170-8929) [05784326] **2699**

MUNCIE EVENING PRESS (US) [11378678] **5665**

MUNCIE STAR, THE (US) [09293344] **5665**

MUNDA : REVISTA DO GRUPO DE ARQUEOLOGIA E ARTE DO CENTRO (PO/0871-0996) [10256153] 359, **275**

MUNDAY COURIER, THE (US/8750-6750) [11682373] **5752**

MUNDELEIN NEWS (US/0746-8938) [10378320] **5661**

MUNDELEIN REVIEW (US/0744-8538) [08598244] **5661**

MUNDO CIENTIFICO (SP/0211-3058) [I02113058] **5130**

MUNDO CRISTIANO (SP/0027-3252) [I00273252] **5032**

MUNDO DA ARTE (PO/0870-6190) [08903862] **359**

MUNDO ECONOMICO, POLITICO & I.E. E SOCIAL (BL) [02247105] **1575**

MUNDO EJECUTIVO (MX) [08562705] 1506, **800**

MUNDO ELECTRONICO. EDICION INTERNACIONAL (SP/0300-3787) [01786169] **2073**

MUNDO ELETRICO *SUSPENDED.* (BL) [05347211] **2073**

MUNDO FINANCIERO (SP/0300-3884) [01448411] 800, **1506**

MUNDO GANADERO (SP) 197, **216**

MUNDO HISPANICO (ATLANTA, GA.) (US/1051-4147) [21368913] 2268, **5654**

MUNDO HISPANO (AUSTIN, TEX.), EL (US/0739-8603) [05367311] **2268**

MUNDO LATINO, EL (US) [24048442] **2268**

MUNDO MECANICO *SUSPENDED.* (BL) [02722283] **2123**

MUNDO NUEVO (VE/0379-6922) [05283980] 5210, **4529**

MUNDO OBRERO (MADRID, SPAIN) (SP) [09116858] **1692**

MUNDO POLICIAL (BL) [03067980] **3170**

MUNDO SHUAR. SERIE C (EC) [04603558] **2747**

●MUNDO TEXTIL (US) **5354**

MUNDUS ARABICUS (US/8755-4925) [08573019] **3413**

MUNGUBO (KO) [10259143] **1619**

MUNHAK KWA CHISONG (KO) [05088968] **3413**

MUNHAK : KYONGBUSON (KO) [04913612] **3466**

MUNHAK SASANG (KO) [05084512] **3413**

MUNHAK UI SIDAE (KO) [11075549] **3414**

MUNHON CHONGBO / THE LITERARY INFORMATION (KO/1225-0090) [04710401] **3459**

MUNHON CHONGBOHAK PO (KO) [11063497] **3232**

MUNHWA OYON (KO) [10616630] **3304**

MUNHWA YESUL (KO) [13799867] **325**

MUNHWAO HAKSUP (KO) [06122213] **3304**

MUNICH. BOTANISCHE STAATSSAMMLUNG MUNCHEN *See* MITTEILUNGEN DER BOTANISCHEN STAATSSAMMLUNG MUNCHEN **518**

MUNICH. OSTEUROPA-INSTITUT *See* VEROFFENTLICHUNGEN DES OSTEUROPA-INSTITUTES MUNCHEN. REIHE: WIRTSCHAFT UND GESELLSCHAFT **1588**

MUNICH. UNIVERSITAT. MATHEMATISCHES INSTITUT *See* ALGEBRA-BERICHTE **3491**

MUNICIPAL ADMINISTRATION AND ENGINEERING *See* LOCAL GOVERNMENT IN SOUTHERN AFRICA **4662**

MUNICIPAL & INDUSTRIAL WATER & POLLUTION CONTROL (CN/0820-4446) [13556334] **2236**

MUNICIPAL AND PLANNING LAW REPORTS (CN/0702-7206) [03409205] 2828, **3012**

MUNICIPAL ASSOCIATION OF SOUTH CAROLINA *See* MUNICIPAL WAGE AND SALARY SURVEY **1692**

MUNICIPAL ATTORNEY, THE (US/0027-3449) [01714294] **3012**

MUNICIPAL ATTORNEYS' OPINIONS (US/0277-6294) [04997037] **3012**

MUNICIPAL BOND COMMISSION OF WEST VIRGINIA *See* ANNUAL SUMMARY OF RECEIPTS AND DISBURSEMENTS / MUNICIPAL BOND COMMISSION OF WEST VIRGINIA **891**

MUNICIPAL CODE OF CHICAGO (US) [01554107] **3012**

MUNICIPAL CORPORATIONS (US) [01773081] **4667**

MUNICIPAL COUNSELLOR *SUSPENDED.* (CN/0703-2412) [03959378] **4667**

MUNICIPAL/COUNTY EXECUTIVE DIRECTORY (US/0743-6211) [10975832] **4667**

MUNICIPAL/COUNTY EXECUTIVE DIRECTORY ANNUAL (US/0743-6211) [24641726] **4667**

MUNICIPAL DIRECTORY (AUGUSTA) (US/0272-4596) [06826810] **4667**

MUNICIPAL DIRECTORY (TORONTO) (CN/0318-0743) [02441884] **4667**

MUNICIPAL ENGINEER (INSTITUTION OF CIVIL ENGINEERS (GREAT BRITAIN)) *See* PROCEEDINGS OF THE INSTITUTION OF CIVIL ENGINEERS, TRANSPORT **2029**

MUNICIPAL ENGINEER (INSTITUTION OF CIVIL ENGINEERS (GREAT BRITAIN)) *See* PROCEEDINGS OF THE INSTITUTION OF CIVIL ENGINEERS. CIVIL ENGINEERING **2029**

MUNICIPAL ENGINEER (INSTITUTION OF CIVIL ENGINEERS (GREAT BRITAIN)) *See* PROCEEDINGS OF THE INSTITUTION OF CIVIL ENGINEERS. MUNICIPAL ENGINEER **2029**

MUNICIPAL ENGINEER (INSTITUTION OF CIVIL ENGINEERS (GREAT BRITAIN)) *See* PROCEEDINGS OF THE INSTITUTION OF CIVIL ENGINEERS. STRUCTURES AND BUILDINGS **2029**

MUNICIPAL ENGINEER (INSTITUTION OF CIVIL ENGINEERS (GREAT BRITAIN)) *See* PROCEEDINGS OF THE INSTITUTION OF CIVIL ENGINEERS. WATER, MARITIME AND ENERGY **2094**

MUNICIPAL ENGINEERS JOURNAL, THE (US/0027-3465) [01644442] **2237**

MUNICIPAL ENVIRONMENTAL JOURNAL (US/1058-1332) [24225767] **2178**

MUNICIPAL ENVIRONMENTAL RESEARCH LABORATORY *See* REPORT OF PROGRESS - MERL **2241**

MUNICIPAL EXECUTIVE DIRECTORY (US/0742-1710) [10270830] **4667**

MUNICIPAL FINANCE JOURNAL (US/0199-6134) [05987859] **4738**

MUNICIPAL FINANCE OFFICERS ASSOCIATION OF THE UNITED STATES AND CANADA *See* DIRECTORY OF MEMBERS - MUNICIPAL FINANCE OFFICERS ASSOCIATION **4720**

MUNICIPAL FINANCE OFFICERS ASSOCIATION OF THE UNITED STATES AND CANADA *See* SPECIAL BULLETIN - MUNICIPAL FINANCE OFFICERS ASSOCIATION OF THE UNITED STATES AND CANADA **4748**

MUNICIPAL GOVERNMENT WAGE SURVEY, CHICAGO, ILLINOIS / U.S. DEPARTMENT OF LABOR, BUREAU OF LABOR STATISTICS, NORTH CENTRAL REGION (US) [04007554] **1692**

MUNICIPAL GOVERNMENT WAGE SURVEY, COLUMBUS, OHIO / U.S. DEPARTMENT OF LABOR, BUREAU OF LABOR STATISTICS, NORTH CENTRAL REGION V (US) [03951402] **1692**

MUNICIPAL GOVERNMENT WAGE SURVEY, DETROIT, MICHIGAN / U.S. DEPARTMENT OF LABOR, BUREAU OF LABOR STATISTICS, NORTH CENTRAL REGION V (US) [06956335] **1692**

MUNICIPAL HANDBOOK : THE CITY OF CALGARY (CN/0384-840X) [03790678] **4667**

MUNICIPAL INSTRUCTORS' SECTION NEWS (US/0739-4918) [09765172] **4667**

MUNICIPAL JOURNAL (LONDON. 1970) (UK/0143-4187) [07003941] **4667**

MUNICIPAL LAW COURT DECISIONS (US/0027-3503) [01771635] **3012**

MUNICIPAL LAW REPORTER *See* CHROSTWAITE'S PENNSYLVANIA MUNICIPAL LAW REPORTER **2950**

MUNICIPAL LAW SECTION NEWSLETTER (US/0196-5778) [05836453] **3012**

MUNICIPAL LITIGATION REPORTER (US/0278-1301) [07715282] **3012**

MUNICIPAL MANAGEMENT *SUSPENDED.* (US/0164-7296) [04169812] **4667**

MUNICIPAL MANAGER, QUEENSLAND (AT/1036-2185) [I10362185] **4667**

MUNICIPAL MARKET DEVELOPMENTS *CEASED.* (US) [04616663] **908**

MUNICIPAL MARYLAND (US/0196-9986) [01779898] **4667**

MUNICIPAL NEWS (SEATTLE) (US/0027-352X) [04111040] **4667**

MUNICIPAL OFFICIALS OF MANITOBA (CN/0715-6804) [02248379] **4667**

MUNICIPAL POLICY STATEMENT - LEAGUE OF ARIZONA CITIES & TOWNS (US/0090-6875) [01785025] **4667**

MUNICIPAL PROGRESS (US/0146-8758) [03058232] **4667**

MUNICIPAL RECREATION & PARK SERVICES STUDY (US/0360-6716) [02243930] **4707**

MUNICIPAL Alphabetical Title Index

MUNICIPAL REFERENCE LIBRARY ACQUISITIONS (CN/0226-2533) [06688537] **3232**

MUNICIPAL REPORTER (SANTE FE, N.M.), THE (US/0028-6257) [04130991] **4667**

MUNICIPAL RESEARCH AND SERVICES CENTER OF WASHINGTON *See* DIGEST OF CITY LAWS (SEATTLE, WASH.) **2961**

MUNICIPAL RESEARCH AND SERVICES CENTER OF WASHINGTON *See* WASHINGTON MUNICIPAL SALARIES AND FRINGE BENEFITS **1717**

MUNICIPAL RESEARCH AND SERVICES CENTER OF WASHINGTON *See* RESEARCH MEMORANDUM - MUNICIPAL RESEARCH AND SERVICES CENTER OF WASHINGTON (SEATTLE) **4683**

MUNICIPAL REVIEW & AMA NEWS (UK/0027-3562) [07386722] **4667**

MUNICIPAL SALARY SURVEY (US/0363-1729) [02428386] **4667**

MUNICIPAL SALARY SURVEY : BENCH-MARK JOBS (US/0542-9676) [01783393] **4667**, **1692**

MUNICIPAL SOUTH (US/0027-3570) [02264471] **4667**

MUNICIPAL WAGE AND SALARY SURVEY (US/0199-9850) [06287551] **1692**

MUNICIPAL WORKER LAW BULLETIN (US/0893-8172) [15649550] **3152**

MUNICIPAL WORLD (CN/0027-3589) [01758841] **879**

MUNICIPAL YEAR BOOK AND PUBLIC SERVICES DIRECTORY, THE (UK/0305-5906) [02505411] **4667**

MUNICIPAL YEAR BOOK, KERALA (II) [06100086] **5333**

MUNICIPAL YEAR BOOK (WASHINGTON), THE (US/0077-2186) [01239357] **4667**

MUNICIPAL YELLOW BOOK (US/1054-4062) [22877218] **4667**, **1927**

MUNICIPALITE (1982) (CN/0713-4800) [09363035] **4667**

MUNICIPALITIES AND CORPORATION CASES (II/0377-757X) [01797744] **3012**

MUNICIPALITIES IN THE UNITED STATES SUPREME COURT (US) [13461776] **3012**

MUNICIPALITY (1916), THE (US/0027-3597) [07428383] **4667**

MUNICIPALITY OF SHUNIAH (CN/0319-4167) [02443071] **4667**

MUNICIPIO PAULISTA : ASPECTOS JURIDICOS (BL) [02970617] **3102**

MUNISING NEWS (US) [09359703] **5693**

MUNSTER. LANDESMUSEUM FUR NATURKUNDE *See* ABHANDLUNGEN AUS DEM LANDESMUSEUM FUR NATURKUNDE ZU MUNSTER IN WESTFALEN **4083**

MUNSTER (MUNCHEN), DAS (GW/0027-299X) [01713502] **359**

MUNSTERS & THE ADDAMS FAMILY REUNION, THE (US) **1135**

MUNTADA (BEIRUT, LEBANON) (LE) [11999222] **4979**

MUNTAKHAB AFSANE (II) [04444609] **3414**

MUNTU *SUSPENDED*. (GO/0768-9403) [13133175] **3304**

MUNYE CHINHUNG (KO) [04850180] **325**

MUNZEN REVUE (SZ) [09138299] **2782**

MUNZENSAMMLER MIT DEM MUNZENMARKT, DER (GW) [08376497] **2782**

MUOTO / TEOLLISUUSTAITEEN LIITTO ORNAMO (FI/0358-3511) [23950010] **304**

MUPPET MAGAZINE *CEASED*. (US/0737-6855) [09433847] **1066**

MUQARNAS (US/0732-2992) [08339076] **304**

MUR VIVANT, LE (FR) [21347678] **304**

MURAL CONSERVANCY OF LOS ANGELES JOURNAL (US) **359**

●MURKY AT BEST (US/1062-838X) [25764315] **325**

MURORAN CHIHOSHI KENKYU (JA) [03943134] **2659**

MURPHY MATES (US/1059-3713) [24523013] **2461**

MURRAY EAGLE (US) [12902128] **5757**

MURRAY LEDGER & TIMES, THE (US) [14170007] **5681**

MURRAY MATTERS (CN/1183-3726) [24265983] **2461**

MURRYSVILLE AREA STAR (US) [14207708] **5737**

MURZILKA (RU) [04925094] **1066**

MUSAG (IS) [03101580] **2507**

MUSASHINO BIJUTSU DAIGAKU *See* KENKYU KIYO - MUSASHINO BIJUTSU DAIGAKU **323**

MUSCATINE JOURNAL (MUSCATINE, IOWA: 1960) (US) [15669018] **5671**

MUSCLE & FITNESS (FR/0989-1013) [I09891013] **2600**

MUSCLE & NERVE (US/0148-639X) [03526488] **3838**

MUSCLE BUILDER (AT) **2600**

MUSCLE CAR REVIEW (US/0891-4796) [14870846] **5421**

MUSCLE CARS OF THE ... (US/0898-5820) [21021501] **2775**, **5421**

MUSCLE MAG INTERNATIONAL (CN/0317-087X) [02247704] **2600**

●MUSCLE MEDIA 2000 (US) [26645809] **2600**

MUSCLE MUSTANGS & FAST FORDS (US/1054-8912) [23011546] **5421**

MUSCLE POWER (US/1047-1960) [20621066] **2600**

MUSCLE WEST (CN/0824-4480) [10513427] **2600**

MUSCLECAR CLASSICS (US/0899-1421) [18005480] **5421**

MUSCLECARS (HACKENSACK, N.J.) (US/0897-0963) [17396557] **5421**

MUSCOGIANA (COLUMBUS, GA.) (US/1042-3419) [19011643] **2461**

MUSCULAR DEVELOPMENT (US/0047-8415) [03453867] **2600**

●MUSCULOSKELETAL MANAGEMENT (UK/1355-3224) **3806**

MUSCULOSKELETAL UPDATE (US/0277-3007) [07534528] **3806**

MUSE. ARTS AND ENTERTAINMENT IN CANBERRA (AT/0158-9571) [I01589571] **359**

MUSE (COLUMBIA) (US/0077-2194) [01758850] **275**, **359**, **4091**

MUSE (GRAHAM, N.C.) (US/0898-2392) [17756436] **3414**

MUSE, MUSIC SEARCH (US/1054-2639) [22807024] **4132**

MUSE NEWS *See* MUSEUM NATIONAL **4092**

MUSE (NSUKKA) (NR/0331-3468) [05342192] **3414**

MUSE (OTTAWA) (CN/0820-0165) [09938407] **4091**

MUSE (OTTAWA) (CN/0820-0165) [09938404] **4091**

MUSEE CONDE (FR/0767-7243) [I07677243] **359**, **4091**

MUSEE D'ARMES : [BULLETIN], LE (BE) [08693725] **4052**

MUSEE DE LA VIE WALLONNE (LIEGE, BELGIUM) *See* ENQUETES DU MUSEE DE LA VIE WALLONNE **2615**

MUSEE GALLIERA *See* CATALOGUE DE VENTE - PARIS. MUSEE GALLIERA **347**

MUSEE NATIONAL D'ART MODERNE (FRANCE) *See* CAHIERS DU MUSEE NATIONAL D'ART MODERNE **346**

MUSEE NATIONAL DES SCIENCES ET DE LA TECHNOLOGIE (CANADA) *See* RAPPORT ANNUEL - MUSEE NATIONAL DES SCIENCES ET DE LA TECHNOLOGIE (OTTAWA) **5144**

MUSEE NEUCHATELOIS (SZ) [04603709] **2268**, **2699**

MUSEEN IN BAYERN (GW) [17702011] **4091**

MUSEES (CN/0706-098X) [07317019] **4091**

MUSEES DE GENEVE (SZ/0027-3821) [02489474] **4091**

MUSEES ET COLLETIONS PUBLIQUES DE FRANCE (FR/0027-383X) [04980782] **4091**

MUSEES ROYAUX D'ART ET D'HISTOIRE (BELGIUM) *See* BULLETIN DES MUSEES ROYAUX D'ART ET D'HISTOIRE **4085**

MUSEES ROYAUX DES BEAUX-ARTS DE BELGIQUE *See* BULLETIN - MUSEES ROYAUX DES BEAUX-ARTS DE BELGIQUE **345**

MUSEES STRASBOURG (FR/0987-0210) [I09870210] **4091**

MUSEI FERRARESI (IT/0391-4399) [01359908] **325**

MUSELETTER (ST. ALBERT, ALTA.) (CN/0835-3220) [16688013] **4091**

MUSELETTER (WASHINGTON, D.C.) (US/0736-6949) [09167080] **4132**

MUSEO ARCHEOLOGICO NAZIONALE DI CIVIDALE DEL FRIULI *See* FORUM IULII **268**

MUSEO CANARIO, EL (SP/0211-450X) [07018982] **4091**

MUSEO CIVICO DI STORIA NATURALE DI VENEZIA *See* BOLLETTINO DEL MUSEO CIVICO DI STORIA NATURALE DI VENEZIA **4163**

MUSEO CIVICO DI STORIA NATURALE DI VERONA *See* BOLLETTINO DEL MUSEO CIVICO DI STORIA NATURALE DI VERONA **4085**

MUSEO DE HISTORIA NATURAL DE VALPARAISO *See* ANALES DEL MUSEO DE HISTORIA NATURAL DE VALPARAISO **4161**

MUSEO DE HISTORIA NATURAL "JAVIER PRADO." *See* MEMORIAS DEL MUSEO DE HISTORIA NATURAL JAVIER PRADO **4167**

MUSEO DE HISTORIA NATURAL (URUGUAY) *See* COMUNICACIONES ANTROPOLOGICAS DEL MUSEO DE HISTORIA NATURAL DE MONTEVIDEO **4087**

MUSEO DEL HOMBRE DOMINICANO *See* BOLETIN DEL MUSEO DEL HOMBRE DOMINICANO **2724**

MUSEO DEL PRADO *See* BOLETIN DEL MUSEO DEL PRADO **4085**

MUSEO HELSINKI (FI/0781-0032) [I07810032] **4091**

MUSEO HISTORICO (EC/0378-2018) [02264477] **2747**

MUSEO HISTORICO REGIONAL *See* REVISTA DEL MUSEO HISTORICO REGIONAL **4095**

MUSEO MUNICIPAL DE CIENCIAS NATURALES DE MAR DEL PLATA LORENZO SCAGLIA *See* PUBLICACIONES DEL MUSEO MUNICIPAL DE CIENCIAS NATURALES LORENZO SCAGLIA **4095**

MUSEO NACIONAL "DAVID J. GUZMAN." *See* ANALES DEL MUSEO NACIONAL "DAVID J. GUZMAN." **1724**

MUSEO NACIONAL DE HISTORIA NATURAL (URUGUAY) *See* ANALES - MUSEO NACIONAL DE HISTORIA NATURAL (URUGUAY) **4161**

MUSEOGRAMME (CN/0380-4623) [02076585] **4091**

MUSEOLOGIA (IT/0392-5528) [01798159] **4091**

MUSEOLOGIA (AMSTERDAM) (NE/0301-6463) [01792957] **4168**

MUSEOLOGIA SCIENTIFICA (IT) **4092**

MUSEOLOGY / TEXAS TECH UNIVERSITY (US/0196-0237) [04685644] **4092**

MUSEON, LE (BE/0771-6494) [06309161] **420**

MUSEOS (SP/0212-2820) [I02122820] **4092**

MUSE'S MILL (US) **3414**

MUSEU DA CASA BRASILEIRA *See* SEMINARIOS DO MUSEU DA CASA BRASILEIRA: BOLETIM **4096**

MUSEU NACIONAL (BRAZIL) *See* ARQUIVOS DO MUSEU NACIONAL **4084**

MUSEU PAULISTA *See* ANAIS DO MUSEU PAULISTA **2720**

MUSEUM (JA) **4092**

MUSEUM (US) [02892752] **4092**

MUSEUM ABSTRACTS (UK/0267-8594) [16623491] **4098**

MUSEUM ABSTRACTS INTERNATIONAL *CEASED*. (UK/0960-0183) [I09600183] **4092**

MUSEUM AFRICUM (NR) [02552146] **4092**

MUSEUM ANTHROPOLOGY (US/0892-8339) [15014641] **242**

MUSEUM (BRAUNSCHWEIG) *CEASED*. (GW/0341-8634) [11059279] **4092**

MUSEUM BRIEFS (US/0580-6976) [02659651] **4092**

MUSEUM CRITICUM *CEASED*. (IT) [03042799] **4092**

MUSEUM DESIGN (UK/0268-9855) [I02689855] **4092**

MUSEUM DEVELOPMENT (UK/0958-1758) **4092**

MUSEUM ED. FRANCAISE (FR/0304-3002) [I03043002] **4092**

MUSEUM (ENGLISH ED.) (UK/0027-3996) [01758859] **4092**

MUSEUM FUER VOLKERKUNDE UND SCHWEIZERISCHES MUSEUM FUER VOLKSKUNDE BASEL *See* BERICHT UBER DAS BASLER MUSEUM FUER VOLKERKUNDE UND SCHWEIZERISCHE MUSEUM FUER VOLKSKUNDE FUER DAS JAHR ... **232**

MUSEUM FUR UR- UND FRUHGESCHICHTE POTSDAM *See* VEROFFENTLICHUNGEN DES MUSEUMS FUER UR- UND FRUHGESCHICHTE POTSDAM **285**

MUSEUM HELVETICUM (SZ/0027-4054) [01152494] **275**

●MUSEUM INTERNATIONAL (UK/1350-0775) [27525955] **4092**

MUSEUM JOURNAL (LUBBOCK), THE (US/0580-261X) [01758868] **4092**

MUSEUM MANAGEMENT AND CURATORSHIP (1990) (UK/0964-7775) [21548198] **4092**

MUSIC

MUSEUM MATTERS (AT/1320-2677) **4092**

●MUSEUM NATIONAL (AT) [I10381694] **4092**

MUSEUM NATIONAL D'HISTOIRE NATURELLE (FRANCE) *See* ANNUAIRE DU MUSEUM NATIONAL D'HISTOIRE NATURELLE POUR L'ANNEE **4162**

MUSEUM NATIONAL D'HISTOIRE NATURELLE (FRANCE) *See* TRAVAUX ET ACQUISITIONS DU MUSEUM NATIONAL D'HISTOIRE NATURELLE **4173**

MUSEUM NEWS & VIEWS FROM THE NOVA SCOTIA MUSEUM COMPLEX *See* MUSEUMNEWS (HALIFAX) **4093**

MUSEUM NEWS LONDON (UK/0955-2057) [I09552057] **4092**

MUSEUM NEWS - UKRAINIAN MUSEUM OF CANADA (CN/0710-1228) [08327360] **4092**

MUSEUM NEWS (WASHINGTON) (US/0027-4089) [01758869] **4092**

MUSEUM NOTES (LONDON) (CN/0709-2725) [06757778] **4092**

MUSEUM NOTES (PROVIDENCE, R.I.) *SUSPENDED.* (US/0027-4097) [02234930] **359**

MUSEUM NOTES (VANCOUVER) (CN/0228-2364) [06860035] **4092**

MUSEUM OF CALIFORNIA, THE (US) [04391711] 359, **4092**

MUSEUM OF FINE ARTS, BOSTON *See* MUSEUM YEAR, THE **4092**

MUSEUM OF MANKIND. LIBRARY *See* ANTHROPOLOGICAL INDEX TO CURRENT PERIODICALS IN THE LIBRARY OF THE ROYAL ANTHROPOLOGICAL INSTITUTE **248**

MUSEUM OF MODERN ART (NEW YORK, N.Y.) *See* MOMA (NEW YORK, N.Y.) **358**

MUSEUM OF MODERN ART (NEW YORK, N.Y.) *See* MEMBERS CALENDAR - MUSEUM OF MODERN ART **4091**

MUSEUM OF MODERN ART (NEW YORK, N.Y.). LIBRARY *See* ANNUAL BIBLIOGRAPHY OF MODERN ART / THE MUSEUM OF MODERN ART LIBRARY, NEW YORK **333**

MUSEUM OF TEMPORARY ART *See* MOTA **4091**

MUSEUM OF THE FUR TRADE *See* QUARTERLY - MUSEUM OF THE FUR TRADE **2756**

MUSEUM OF THE FUR TRADE *See* QUARTERLY - THE MUSEUM OF THE FUR TRADE **3185**

MUSEUM OF THE GREAT PLAINS *See* MUSEUM OF THE GREAT PLAINS NEWSLETTER **4092**

MUSEUM OF THE GREAT PLAINS NEWSLETTER (US/0198-7763) [02898103] **4092**

MUSEUM PHILOLOGUM LONDINIENSE (NE) [03093763] **3304**

MUSEUM PROGRAM GUIDELINES (US/0090-9890) [01785509] **4092**

MUSEUM QUARTERLY (TORONTO, ONT.) *See* ONTARIO MUSEUM ANNUAL **4095**

MUSEUM REPORTER (UK/0954-0423) [I09540423] **4092**

MUSEUM ROUND-UP (CN/0045-3005) [02036982] **4092**

MUSEUM SOURCE MARKETPLACE (US) **4092**

MUSEUM STORE (US/1040-6999) [18504053] **4092**

MUSEUM STUDIES (CHICAGO, ILL.) (US/0069-3235) [01554088] **359**

MUSEUM TRAINING INSTITUTE *See* MUSEUM TRAINING INSTITUTE NEWS **4092**

MUSEUM TRAINING INSTITUTE NEWS (UK) [22572328] **4092**

MUSEUM YEAR, THE (US/0740-0403) [06275614] 325, **4092**

MUSEUMEDIA (MILWAUKEE, WISC.) (US/1055-8624) [23362006] **4093**

MUSEUMLEVEN / NEDERLANDTALIGE AFDELING VAN DE BELGISCHE MUSEUMVERENIGING (BE) [06492171] **4093**

●MUSEUMNEWS (HALIFAX) (CN/1191-0925) [26290505] **4093**

MUSEUMS AND ART GALLERIES IN GREAT BRITAIN AND IRELAND (UK/0141-6723) [04786433] **4093**

MUSEUMS AND GALLERIES COMISSION ANNUAL REPORTS (UK) **4093**

MUSEUMS ASSOCIATION *See* ANNUAL REPORT OF THE MUSEUMS ASSOCIATION FOR THE YEAR **4084**

MUSEUMS DOCUMENTATION ASSOCIATION (GREAT BRITAIN) *See* M D A INFORMATION **4091**

MUSEUMS IN INDIA (II) [15184284] **4093**

MUSEUMS IN NOVA SCOTIA (CN/0225-5235) [06133143] **4093**

MUSEUMS JOURNAL (UK/0027-416X) [01606681] **4093**

MUSEUMS / NATIONAL ENDOWMENT FOR THE ARTS (US/0737-7665) [02933312] 359, **4093**

MUSEUMS OF MALAWI *See* NDIWULA : THE ANNUAL NEWSLETTER OF THE MUSEUMS OF MALAWI **4093**

MUSEUMS YEARBOOK (UK/0307-7675) [02651536] **4093**

MUSEUMSKUNDE (GW/0027-4178) [01758877] **4093**

MUSEUMSNYTT (NO/0027-4186) [02512853] **4093**

MUSEUMSTRIP (BE/0774-1286) [I07741286] **4093**

MUSEUMVISIE (NE/0166-2074) [I01662074] **4093**

MUSEUS, DE (SP) [22755419] **4093**

MUSHING (ESTER, ALASKA) (US/0895-9668) [16876404] **4905**

MUSHIR (RAWALPINDI, PAKISTAN) (PK) [01776079] **4979**

MUSHIRO-BATA (JA) [08479101] **110**

MUSHROOM JOURNAL (UK/0144-0551) [02256561] **2424**

MUSHROOM JOURNAL FOR THE TROPICS *SUSPENDED.* (HK) [15810409] **575**

MUSHROOM (MOSCOW, IDAHO) (US/0740-8161) [10053958] **575**

MUSHROOM NEWS (US/0541-3869) [04578589] **179**

MUSHROOMS (US/0197-6281) [03599239] **179**

MUSI-STAFF [02247086] **4132**

MUSIC (UK/0960-6033) **4132**

MUSIC '91 (VANCOUVER) (CN/1186-2378) [24267032] **4132**

MUSIC ACADEMY (MADRAS, INDIA) *See* JOURNAL OF THE MUSIC ACADEMY, MADRAS, THE **4127**

MUSIC ALIVE (US/1051-8975) [08933133] 1765, **4132**

MUSIC ANALYSIS (UK) [08889408] **4132**

MUSIC & AUTOMATA (UK/0262-8260) [10293180] **4132**

MUSIC AND COMMUNICATION (IT) [01770900] 1118, **4132**

MUSIC & LETTERS (UK/0027-4224) [01758884] **4132**

MUSIC AND LITURGY (UK/0305-4438) [01587576] **4133**

MUSIC & MEDIA (NE) **4133**

MUSIC & MUSICIANS. INSTRUCTIONAL DISC RECORDINGS CATALOG *See* INSTRUCTIONAL DISC RECORDINGS CATALOG **4122**

MUSIC AND RECORDINGS (US) [04296451] 5317, **4133**

MUSIC & SOUND BUYER'S GUIDE (US) [09319252] **4133**

MUSIC & SOUND RETAILER, THE (US/0894-1238) [15046482] 5317, **4133**

MUSIC AND THE TEACHER (AT/0047-8431) [I00478431] **4133**

MUSIC ARTICLE GUIDE (US/0027-4240) [01590184] 4133, **4160**

MUSIC AT YALE (US/0146-096X) [02029674] **4133**

MUSIC BOOK GUIDE (US/0360-1943) [02244027] **4133**

MUSIC BOX, THE (UK) [02550221] 251, **4133**

MUSIC BUSINESS DIRECTORY (US/0747-6655) [10764274] **4133**

MUSIC BUSINESS INTERNATIONAL (FR) [30417486] **4133**

MUSIC CAPITOL NEWS. COUNTRYWIDE (US/0092-1041) [01788973] **4133**

MUSIC CATALOG (WASHINGTON, D.C.), THE (US/1055-5536) [23209415] 5317, **4133**

MUSIC CATALOG. [COMPUTER FILE] (US) [29585225] 4133, **420**

MUSIC CATALOGING BULLETIN (US/0027-4283) [01758886] 3232, **4133**

MUSIC CIRCULAR (US/0278-9051) [07864184] 4391, **4133**

MUSIC CITY NEWS (US/0027-4291) [04104657] **4133**

●MUSIC CITY NEWS (1994) (US/1078-5558) [31119052] **4133**

MUSIC CLUBS MAGAZINE (1963) (US/0161-2654) [02505384] **4133**

MUSIC, COMPUTERS & SOFTWARE (US/0896-4750) [16886386] 4133, **1240**

MUSIC CONNECTION (US) **4133**

MUSIC CRITICS ASSOCIATION (U.S.) *See* NEWSLETTER OF THE MUSIC CRITICS ASSOCIATION, INC **4141**

MUSIC DIRECTORY CANADA (CN/0820-0416) [09766559] **4133**

MUSIC EDUCATION REVIEW (UK) [04233484] 1901, **4133**

MUSIC EDUCATORS JOURNAL (US/0027-4321) [01639434] 1901, **4133**

MUSIC FOR THE LOVE OF IT (US/0898-8757) [17940832] **4133**

MUSIC FORUM, THE (US/0885-503X) [02264273] **4133**

MUSIC FROM CHINA NEWSLETTER (US/1071-2801) [28600010] **4133**

MUSIC HALL (UK) [06897841] **4133**

MUSIC IN NEW ZEALAND (NZ/0113-7441) [26430054] **4133**

MUSIC-IN-PRINT SERIES (US/0146-7883) [03015515] **4133**

MUSIC IN THE MEDIA : IMZ BULLETIN (AU) [22852441] **4133**

MUSIC IN TIME (IS) [11986041] **4133**

MUSIC IN WORSHIP (UK) [07341070] **4134**

MUSIC INC (US/1050-1681) [21416114] **4134**

MUSIC INDEX ON CD-ROM, THE (US/1066-1514) [24444443] **4134**

MUSIC INDEX, THE (US/0027-4348) [01643737] 4134, **4160**

MUSIC INDUSTRY BULLETIN (US/0270-3203) [06389439] **4134**

MUSIC INDUSTRY PRODUCTS (US/0740-3755) [09925748] **4134**

MUSIC INTERNATIONAL (RUSSIAN ED.) (US/1048-1494) [20860327] **4134**

MUSIC K 8 (US) **4134**

MUSIC LEADER, THE (US/0027-4372) [01586509] 4979, **4134**

MUSIC LIBRARIAN (US/1065-1179) [26509554] **4134**

MUSIC LIBRARY ASSOCIATION *See* MLA INDEX AND BIBLIOGRAPHY SERIES **4131**

MUSIC LIBRARY ASSOCIATION *See* NOTES. SUPPLEMENT FOR MEMBERS **4142**

MUSIC LIBRARY ASSOCIATION *See* NOTES (PHILADELPHIA, PA.) **4142**

MUSIC LIBRARY ASSOCIATION *See* MEMBERSHIP HANDBOOK **4130**

MUSIC LIBRARY ASSOCIATION JOB LIST (US) **4134**

MUSIC LIBRARY ASSOCIATION. MEMBERSHIP DIRECTORY *See* MEMBERSHIP HANDBOOK **4130**

MUSIC LIBRARY. MUSICAL SOUND RECORDINGS (US/1048-2741) [20905127] **5317**

●MUSIC MADNESS MAGAZINE (US/1061-8376) [25472851] **4134**

MUSIC MAKERS (NASHVILLE) (US/0162-4377) [01781117] **4134**

MUSIC MASTER (UK) [09505349] 4134, **5318**

MUSIC MCGILL (CN/0702-9012) [03436753] 1836, **4134**

MUSIC. MUSIC PROFESSIONAL TRAINING, CAREER DEVELOPMENT ORGANIZATIONS, MUSIC RECORDING, SERVICES TO COMPOSERS, CENTERS FOR NEW MUSIC RESOURCES, SPECIAL PROJECTS (US) [13030479] **4134**

MUSIC NEWS FROM PRAGUE (XR/0027-4410) [02255809] **4134**

MUSIC NOW (US/0027-4437) [04574232] **4134**

MUSIC OCLC USERS GROUP *See* NEWSLETTER - MUSIC OCLC USERS GROUP **4141**

●MUSIC OF THE BABA ALLAUDDIN GHARANA AS TAUGHT BY ALI AKBAR KHAN AT THE ALI AKBAR COLLEGE OF MUSIC, THE (US/1057-0934) [23937465] **4134**

MUSIC OF THE SPHERES (US/0892-2721) [15140862] 4134, **4186**

MUSIC PAPER, THE (US) [16119230] **4134**

MUSIC PERCEPTION (US/0730-7829) [08070327] **4134**

MUSIC PERFORMANCE RESOURCES *CEASED.* (US/0896-1352) [16929009] **4134**

... MUSIC RADIO DIRECTORY, THE *SUSPENDED.* (US) [15996002] 1135, **4134**

MUSIC REFERENCE COLLECTION, THE (US/0736-7740) [09210056] **4134**

●MUSIC REFERENCE SERVICES QUARTERLY (US/1058-8167) [24384124] **4134**

MUSIC RESEARCH FORUM (US/1042-1262) [13421049] **4134**

MUSIC RESEARCH NEWS (CN/0700-3838) [03400001] **4134**

MUSIC RESEARCHER'S EXCHANGE, THE (US/0271-5163) [04444970] 1765, **4134**

MUSIC — Alphabetical Title Index

MUSIC RETAILING (US/1051-1822) [21885302] 955, **4134**

MUSIC REVELATION (US/0882-8229) [11989555] **4134**

MUSIC REVIEW, THE (UK/0027-4445) [01758893] **4134**

MUSIC ROW (US/0745-5054) [09247172] **4135**

MUSIC SCENE (DIETIKON, SWITZERLAND) (SZ) [08580441] **4135**

MUSIC SCORE CATALOGUE - CARLETON UNIVERSITY (CN/0823-1338) [10763829] **4160**

MUSIC TEACHER (UK/0027-4461) [07050241] **4135**

MUSIC TECHNOLOGY (ELY) (UK/0957-6606) [24835173] **4135**

MUSIC TEMPO (US/0027-447X) [05276242] **4135**

MUSIC THEORY SPECTRUM (US/0195-6167) [05154569] **4135**

MUSIC THEORY TRANSLATION SERIES (US/0541-4024) [02046926] **4135**

MUSIC THERAPY (NEW YORK, N.Y.) (US/0734-7367) [08803871] 4605, **4135**

MUSIC THERAPY PERSPECTIVES (US/0734-6875) [08777846] 3618, **4135**

MUSIC TRADES (US/0027-4488) [01640823] **4135**

MUSIC TRADES INTERNATIONAL (UK) [01796810] **4135**

MUSIC TRADES INTERNATIONAL DIRECTORY (UK/0307-8523) [02161563] **4135**

MUSIC TRADES INTERNATIONAL YEARBOOK (UK) [01789056] **4135**

MUSIC USA (US/0197-4173) [05087618] **4135**

●MUSIC VIDEO MAGAZINE (US/1065-0229) [26483987] 1135, **4135**

MUSIC VIDEO RETAILER (US/8750-569X) [07972928] **4135**

MUSIC WEEK (1983) (UK/0265-1548) [09936275] 5318, **4135**

MUSIC WEEK DIRECTORY (UK/0267-3290) [11979398] **4135**

MUSIC WEEK INDUSTRY YEAR BOOK (UK) [03829059] **4135**

MUSIC WORKS (SAN FRANCISCO, CALIF.) (US/0193-5127) [05201590] **4135**

MUSIC WORLD MAGAZINE (LOS ANGELES) (US/0090-3663) [01784714] **4135**

MUSIC WORLD YEAR BOOK (UK) [12091117] **4135**

MUSICA (GW/0027-4518) [02362604] **4135**

MUSICA (IT) [05909505] **4135**

MUSICA ANTIQUA : ACTUELE INFORMATIE OVER OUDE MUZIEK (BE/0771-7016) [16504780] **4135**

MUSICA ASIATICA (UK/0140-6078) [03577479] **4135**

MUSICA BRITANNICA (UK/0580-2954) [01770901] **4135**

MUSICA (CASA DE LAS AMERICAS: 1980) (CU) [07910631] **4135**

MUSICA DISCIPLINA (IT/0077-2461) [05959556] **4135**

MUSICA DOMANI : ORGANO DELLA SOCIETA ITALIANA PER L'EDUCAZIONE MUSICALE (IT/0391-4380) [10000362] 1765, **4135**

MUSICA E DOSSIER *CEASED.* (IT) [16818856] **4136**

MUSICA (HILVERSUM, NETHERLANDS) *CEASED.* (NE) [10523331] **4136**

MUSICA HISPANA. SER. A: CANCION POPULAR (SP) [03036695] **4136**

MUSICA HISPANA. SER. B: POLIFONIA (SP) [03036664] **4136**

MUSICA HISPANA. SER. C: MUSICA DE CAMARA (SP) [03036647] **4136**

MUSICA IN URSS. (ITALIAN EDITION) (IT) **4136**

MUSICA JAZZ (IT/0027-4542) [09510794] **4136**

MUSICA JUDAICA (US/0147-7536) [03228452] 5051, **4136**

MUSICA MEDII AEVI (PL/0077-247X) [04398175] **4136**

MUSICA POPOLARE, LA (IT) [03679940] **4136**

MUSICA (ROME, ITALY : 1985) *SUSPENDED.* (IT) [17247072] **4136**

MUSICAE SACRAE MINISTERIUM (ROME) (IT) [09639944] 5032, **4136**

MUSICAL AMERICA (1987) (US/1042-3443) [15189010] **4136**

MUSICAL AMERICA. INTERNATIONAL DIRECTORY OF THE PERFORMING ARTS (US/0735-7788) [06541948] 4136, **386**

MUSICAL AMERICA'S FESTIVALS *CEASED.* (US) [23860633] **4136**

MUSICAL BOX SOCIETY INTERNATIONAL, MORGANTOWN, IND *See* DIRECTORY OF MEMBERS & MUSEUMS **4114**

MUSICAL DENMARK (US/0027-4585) [04376610] **4160**

MUSICAL HERITAGE REVIEW (US/0192-8627) [04272265] **4136**

MUSICAL INSTRUMENT COLLECTIONS OF THE WORLD (NE) **4136**

MUSICAL MAINSTREAM, THE (US/0364-7501) [03009857] 4391, 3232, **4136**

MUSICAL MERCHANDISE REVIEW (US/0027-4615) [02448828] **4136**

MUSICAL NEWS (SAN FRANCISCO, CALIF.) (US/0748-9293) [06257735] **4136**

MUSICAL NEWS (TORONTO) (CN/0709-7174) [05840837] 5318, **4136**

MUSICAL OPINION (UK/0027-4623) [01758905] **4136**

●MUSICAL PERFORMANCE (SZ/1049-8869) [21342400] **4136**

MUSICAL QUARTERLY, THE (US/0027-4631) [01642493] **4136**

MUSICAL SALVATIONIST, THE (UK) [06587310] **4136**

MUSICAL SOURCES (IE) [09170701] **4136**

MUSICAL TIMES (LONDON, ENGLAND : 1957) (UK/0027-4666) [05472115] **4136**

MUSICAL TIMES (LONDON, ENGLAND : 1957) *See* CHOIR & ORGAN **4109**

MUSICAL TRADITIONS (UK/0265-5063) [10806039] **4137**

MUSICAL WOMAN, THE (US/0737-0032) [09287454] 5561, **4137**

MUSICALIA LUCCA (IT/1121-0494) [I11210494] **4137**

MUSICIAN (GLOUCESTER, MASS.) (US/0733-5253) [08480685] **4137**

●MUSICIAN MAGAZINE SPECIAL EDITION SERIES (US/1064-5411) [26326292] **4137**

MUSICIAN OF THE SALVATION ARMY IN AUSTRALIA (AT) [01772543] **4137**

MUSICIAN'S GUIDE (BOSTON) (US/0362-2959) [02279076] **4137**

●MUSICIANS GUIDE TO TOURING & PROMOTION, THE (US/1062-4759) [25638279] **4137**

MUSICK (CN/0226-8620) [07295296] **4137**

MUSICOLOGICA AUSTRIACA (AU) [05586186] **4137**

MUSICOLOGICAL SOCIETY OF AUSTRALIA *See* NEWSLETTER / MUSICOLOGICAL SOCIETY OF AUSTRALIA **4141**

MUSICOLOGICAL STUDIES & DOCUMENTS (GW/0077-2496) [07064823] **4137**

MUSICOLOGY (US/0275-5866) [18517374] **4137**

MUSICOLOGY AND ETHNOMUSICOLOGY AT YORK (CN/0846-426X) [14979622] **4137**

MUSICOLOGY AUSTRALIA (AT/0814-5857) [12714872] **4137**

MUSICUS (SA) [05049859] **4137**

MUSICWORKS (CN/0225-686X) [06245226] **4137**

MUSICWORLD (NEW YORK, N.Y.) (US/1042-6736) [17546323] **4137**

MUSIGRAM / NATIONAL SHEET MUSIC SOCIETY (US) [23826042] **4137**

MUSIIKKI (FI) [04606403] **4137**

MUSIK-ALMANACH (KASSEL, GERMANY) (GW/0930-8954) [16441846] **4137**

MUSIK & FORSKNING (DK/0903-188X) [03989684] **4137**

MUSIK & THEATER (SAINT GALL, SWITZERLAND) (SZ) [07999804] 5366, **4137**

MUSIK DES OSTENS (GW/0580-3225) [04595650] **4137**

MUSIK EXPRESS/SOUNDS (SZ) [19293948] **4137**

MUSIK IN BAYERN : HALBJAHRESSCHRIFT DER GESELLSCHAFT FUER BAYERISCHE MUSIKGESCHICHTE E.V (GW) [05804086] **4137**

MUSIK IN DER SCHULE (GW/0027-4704) [02196017] **4137**

MUSIK-INFORMATION; BIBLIOGRAPHISCHE TITELUBERSICHT (GW) [01789182] **4160**

MUSIK-KONZEPTE (GW/0931-3311) [I09313311] **4137**

MUSIK MAGAZIN (GW/0930-7591) [15925416] **4137**

MUSIK PSYCHOLOGIE : JAHRBUCH DER DEUTSCHEN GESELLSCHAFT FUER MUSIKPSYCHOLOGIE (GW/0177-350X) [11856127] 4605, **4137**

MUSIK REPORT; DAS KRITISCHE HANDBUCH DER KLASSISCHEN MUSIKSCHALLPLATTE (GW) [01788289] 5318, **4137**

MUSIK-, TANZ- UND KUNSTTHERAPIE (GW/0933-6885) [I09336885] 3618, **4138**

MUSIK UND BILDUNG (GW/0027-4747) [02649663] **4138**

MUSIK UND GESELLSCHAFT (BERLIN, DDR) (SZ/0027-4755) [01758911] **4138**

MUSIK UND GOTTESDIENST (SZ/1015-6798) [06399339] **4138**

MUSIK UND KIRCHE (GW/0027-4771) [01624389] **4138**

MUSIK UND UNTERRICHT : ZEITSCHRIFT FUER MUSIKPADAGOGIK (GW) [22772299] **4138**

MUSIKALIER I DANSKE BIBLIOTEKER (DK) [06957870] 3232, **4138**

MUSIKALISCHE DENKMALER (GW/0077-2526) [03037460] **4138**

●MUSIKALNAIA AKADEMIIA (RU) [28580745] **4138**

MUSIKBRANCHENS ARBOG (DK) [10393167] **4138**

MUSIKERN (SW/0027-478X) [06298728] **4138**

MUSIKERZIEHUNG (AU/0027-4798) [01772545] **4138**

MUSIKETHNOLOGISCHE SAMMELBANDE (GW) [05885117] 2268, **4138**

MUSI*KEY (US/0895-1543) [16560399] **4138**

MUSIKFORSCHUNG (GW/0027-4801) [02669982] **4138**

MUSIKFORUM (GW/0323-5106) [04348856] **4138**

MUSIKFORUM : REFERATE UND INFORMATIONEN DES DEUTSCHEN MUSIKRATES (GW/0935-2562) [20575295] **4138**

MUSIKHANDEL (GW) [06395896] **4138**

MUSIKINSTRUMENT, DAS (GW/0027-4828) [06013056] **4138**

MUSIKMARKT, DER (GW/0047-8474) [02609892] **4138**

MUSIKREVY (SW/0027-4844) [03242904] **4138**

MUSIKTEXTE (GW) [10841661] **4138**

MUSIKTHEATER (GW) [06479632] 386, **4138**

MUSIKTHEORIE (GW/0177-4182) [13514790] **4138**

MUSIKTHERAPEUTISCHE UMSCHAU (GW/0172-5505) [10088351] **4138**

MUSIKTIDNINGEN (SW) [03155429] **4138**

MUSIKWISSENSCHAFTLICHE STUDIENBIBLIOTHEK (GW) [01758915] **4138**

MUSIL-FORUM (GW) [04914962] **3414**

MUSIQUE ET CULTURE STRASBOURG (FR/0750-2079) [I07502079] **4138**

MUSIQUE ET INSTRUMENTS (FR) [05458048] **4139**

MUSIQUE PERIODIQUE (CN/0702-9160) [03439485] **4139**

MUSIQUE SACREE 1947, LA (FR/1141-5177) [I11415177] **4139**

MUSIQUE VIVANTE (CN/1188-1496) [25883045] **4139**

MUSK-OX, THE *CEASED.* (CN/0077-2542) [01643318] 2623, **2569**

MUSKEGO SUN (US) [14869053] **5769**

MUSKEGON CHRONICLE, THE (US) [09802456] **5693**

MUSKEGON LABOR MARKET REVIEW *See* MUSKEGON'S LABOR MARKET NEWS **1692**

●MUSKEGON'S LABOR MARKET NEWS (US) [25954510] **1692**

MUSKIE : THE OFFICIAL PUBLICATION OF MUSKIES, INC (US) [08338086] **4875**

MUSKINGUM CLIMATE RESEARCH CENTER, NEW PHILADELPHIA, O *See* PRECIPATION ON THE MUSKINGUM RIVER WATERSHED, OHIO, BY 30 MINUTE PERIODS **1433**

MUSKOGEE COUNTY GENEALOGICAL SOCIETY QUARTERLY (US) **2461**

MUSKOGEE DAILY PHOENIX AND TIMES-DEMOCRAT (US) [12230536] **5732**

MUSKOGEE-PHOENIX (US) [0016040] **5732**

MUSKOKA FREE PRESS (CN/0701-1199) [03406543] **5790**

MUSKY HUNTER MAGAZINE (US/1041-6366) [18818282] **4875**

MUSLIM EDUCATION QUARTERLY (UK/0267-615X) [12046236] **1765**

MUSLIM HERALD (UK) **5044**

MUSLIM INDIA (II) [09438856] **5044**

MUSLIM (JAMAAH AL-ISLAMIYAH (LIBIYA)) (TR) [09201875] **5044**

MUSLIM JOURNAL (US/0883-816X) [12063707] **5044**

MUSLIM SCIENTIST (US/0148-0995) [03267364] **5210**

MUSLIM WORLD BOOK REVIEW, THE (UK/0260-3063) [07531434] **5044**

MUSLIM WORLD (HARTFORD), THE (US/0027-4909) [01758916] **5044**

MUSLIM WORLD LEAGUE JOURNAL, THE (SU) [09273501] **5044**

MUSLIMS OF THE SOVIET EAST (US/0203-5936) [10498423] **4979**

●MUSSELMAN'S ORIGINAL PRO BASKETBALL SCOUTING HANDBOOK (US/1062-9513) [25815503] **4905**

MUST See MUSEUM STORE **4092**

MUSTANG! (US/1043-2590) [19365230] **2801**

MUSTANG & FORDS (US/1059-5368) [24620347] **5421**

MUSTANG ILLUSTRATED (US/0898-8994) [17944262] **5421**

MUSTANG (LOS ANGELES, CALIF.) (US/0894-5179) [16119500] **4905, 5421**

MUSTANG MONTHLY MAGAZINE (US/0274-8460) [06827033] **5421**

MUSTANG TIMES (US/0744-2572) [08151073] **5421**

MUSTAQBAL AL-TARBIYAH (UA) [06158321] **1765**

MUSTARD SEED (CN/0711-1843) [08415788] **5065**

MUSU ZINIOS (US) [01795049] **4979**

MUSZAKI EGYETEMI KONYVTAROS (HU) [02959196] **3232**

MUSZAKI EGYETEMI KONYVTAROS (HU/0027-3015) [I00273015] **3232**

MUSZAKI INFORMACIO. KORSZERU MUNKAFELTETELEK, MUNKAVEDELEM (HU/0230-2896) [09991789] **2865**

MUTABLE DILEMMA, THE (US/0892-5429) [15246591] **4242**

MUTAGENESIS (UK/0267-8357) [12788607] **549**

MUTANTIA : ZONA DE LUCIDEZ IMPLACABLE (AG) [08333520] **5252**

MUTATION BREEDING NEWSLETTER (AU) [10450326] **110**

MUTATION BREEDING REVIEW (AU) [16795333] **518**

MUTATION RESEARCH (NE/0027-5107) [01590350] **549**

MUTATION RESEARCH. DNA REPAIR (NE/0921-8777) [21004184] **466**

MUTATION RESEARCH. DNAGING : GENETIC INSTABILITY AND AGING (NE/0921-8734) [19465484] **550**

MUTATION RESEARCH. ENVIRONMENTAL MUTAGENESIS AND RELATED SUBJECTS (NE) [12055035] **550**

MUTATION RESEARCH. FUNDAMENTAL AND MOLECULAR MECHANISMS OF MUTAGENESIS (NE) [20379572] **466**

MUTATION RESEARCH. GENETIC TOXICOLOGY (NE) **3982, 550**

MUTATION RESEARCH. GENETIC TOXICOLOGY TESTING See MUTATION RESEARCH. GENETIC TOXICOLOGY **550**

MUTATION RESEARCH. GENETIC TOXICOLOGY TESTING AND BIOMONITORING OF ENVIRONMENTAL OR OCCUPATIONAL EXPOSURE (NE) [21884403] **3982**

MUTATION RESEARCH. MUTATION RESEARCH LETTERS (NE/0165-7992) [07356055] **550**

MUTATION RESEARCH. REVIEWS IN GENETIC TOXICOLOGY (NE/0165-1110) [05971646] **550, 3982**

MUTISIA (CK/0027-5123) [01717939] **518**

MUTTERSPRACHE (WIESBADEN) (GW/0027-514X) [01642203] **3304**

MUTUAL AID (US/0734-9998) [08871582] **879, 4792**

MUTUAL FUND ADVISOR (US/1050-656X) [21589338] **908**

●MUTUAL FUND BUYER'S GUIDE (US/1067-1358) [27141816] **908**

MUTUAL FUND CHARTIST (US/0889-0064) [13787202] **800**

MUTUAL FUND DIRECTORY (US) [04144384] **908**

MUTUAL FUND FACT BOOK (US/0077-2550) [01753827] **908**

MUTUAL FUND FORECASTER (US/8755-9889) [11447603] **908**

MUTUAL FUND LETTER, THE (US/0742-9657) [10493093] **908**

●MUTUAL FUND MARKET NEWS (US/1070-3373) [28321021] **908**

MUTUAL FUND MONITOR, THE (US/8755-4291) [11308464] **800**

MUTUAL FUND MONTHLY (US/1064-0843) [26224162] **1506, 800**

MUTUAL FUND NEWS (US) **908**

MUTUAL FUND PERFORMANCE REPORT (US/1046-8773) [20550334] **908**

MUTUAL FUND PORTFOLIO DEVELOPER (US) **800**

MUTUAL FUND REPORT (US) **908**

MUTUAL FUND REPORTER (MONTHLY ED.) (US/8755-8319) [11451804] **800**

MUTUAL FUND REPORTER QUARTERLY ED.) (US/8755-8327) [11452046] **800**

MUTUAL FUND SOURCEBOOK (US/8755-4151) [11299605] **908**

MUTUAL FUND SOURCEBOOK (TORONTO) (CN/0835-4669) [16753835] **908**

MUTUAL FUND SPECIALIST, THE *CEASED.* (US/0741-1278) [09697670] **908**

MUTUAL FUND STRATEGIST (US) **908**

MUTUAL FUND TRENDS (US) **909**

MUTUAL FUND WEEKLY (US) **909**

MUTUAL FUNDS MAGAZINE (US) **909**

MUTUAL FUNDS ONFLOPPY (US) **909**

MUTUAL FUNDS PANORAMA See CDA/WIESENBERGER MUTUAL FUNDS PANORAMA **894**

MUTUAL MAGAZINE (PHILADELPHIA, PA. : 1980), THE (US/0740-672X) [09966670] **1692, 5433**

MUTUAL SECURITY PROGRAM FOR FISCAL YEAR 1952-, THE (US/0498-1367) [02480587] **4052**

MUTUALITE SOCIALE AGRICOLE EN ... / MSA, MUTUALITE SOCIALE AGRICOLE, LA (FR) [20225937] **110**

MUTUALITE SOCIALE AGRICOLE (FRANCE) See MUTUALITE SOCIALE AGRICOLE EN ... / MSA, MUTUALITE SOCIALE AGRICOLE, LA **110**

MUTUALITE SOCIALE AGRICOLE, STATISTIQUES, LA (FR) [03828810] **1692, 5297**

MUUSIKKO (FI) [06399447] **4139**

MUVESZETTORTENETI ERTESITO (HU/0027-5247) [04583631] **325**

MUVHIGO WA MULAULI NA MUTOLAMUVHALELANO MUHULU NGA HA MBALELANO DZA MUVHUSO WA VENDA NA WA MBALELANO DZA MIVHUSO MITUKU VHUPONI HAWO DZA NWAHA (SA) [02243536] **4738**

MUWASAFAT / AL-MAHAD AL-QAWMI LIL-MUWASAFAT WA-AL-MILKIYAH AL-SINAIYAH (TI/0330-8596) [12111149] **4031**

MUWOP : MUSEOLOGICAL WORKING PAPERS (SW) [09453461] **4093**

MUY INTERESANTE (SP) **5210**

MUYOK (KO) [10075219] **846**

MUYOK TAERIJOM CHONGNAM (KO) [09040055] **846**

●MUZE / EBSCO CD-ROM (US) **4139**

MUZEALNICTWO (PL/0464-1086) [I04641086] **4093**

MUZEI (RU) [07996274] **359**

MUZEI I PAMETNITSI NA KULTURATA / KOMITET ZA KULTURA *CEASED.* (BU/0324-1793) [08076306] **4093**

MUZEINOE DELO V SSSR (RU) [19247955] **4093**

MUZEJ (RU/0258-8064) [I02588064] **4093**

MUZEJNI A VLASTIVEDNA PRACE (XR) [04453495] **4093**

MUZEON YISRAEL (JERUSALEM) See ISRAEL MUSEUM JOURNAL, THE **4089**

MUZEUL DE ISTORIE AL TRANSILVANIEI See ACTA MUSEI NAPOCENSIS **2672**

MUZEUL JUDETEAN DE ISTORIE SI ARTA BACAU See CARPICA **2683**

MUZEUL REGIONAL ALBA IULIA See APULUM : ACTA MUSEI APULENSIS **2675**

MUZEUL TARII CRISURILOR See BIHAREA **232**

MUZEUL TARII CRISURILOR See NYMPHAEA **1359**

MUZEUM ARCHEOLOGICZNE I ETNOGRAFICZNE W LODZI See PRACE I MATERIAY MUZEUM ARCHEOLOGICZNEGO I ETNOGRAFICZNEGO W LODZI. SERIA ARCHEOLOGICZNA **278**

MUZEUM BRATISLAVA (XO/0027-5263) [I00275263] **4093**

MUZEUM ETNOGRAFICZNE W KRAKOWIE See ROCZNIK MUZEUM ETNOGRAFICZNEGO W KRAKOWIE **245**

MUZEUM NARODOWE W KIELCACH See ROCZNIK MUZEUM NARODOWEGO W KIELCACH **4096**

MUZEUM NARODOWE W WARSZAWIE See BULLETIN DU MUSEE NATIONAL DE VARSOVIE **4085**

MUZEUMI KOZLEMENYEK - MUVELODESI MINISZTERIUM MUZEUMI OSZTALY (HU/0133-4921) [I01334921] **4093**

MUZICA (RM/0580-3713) [02182919] **4139**

MUZIEK & DANS (NE/0166-0535) [04837405] **1314, 4139**

MUZIKOLOSKI ZBORNIK (YU/0580-373X) [04595708] **4139**

MUZIUM BRUNEI See BRUNEI MUSEUM JOURNAL **4085**

MUZSAK (HU/0133-2392) [I01332392] **4093**

MUZSIKA (HU/0027-5336) [04587456] **4139**

MUZUNAMI-SHI KASEKI HAKUBUTSUKAN See MIZUNAMI-SHI KASEKI HAKUBUTSUKAN KENKYU HOKOKU **4228**

MUZYKA (1956) (PL/0027-5344) [12139399] **4139**

MUZYKA I ZIZN (RU/0303-5689) [01793701] **4139**

MUZYKA (KIEV, UKRAINE) (UN/0131-2367) [19359703] **4139**

MUZYKA RELIGIJNA W POLSCE : MATERIAY I STUDIA (PL) [08014011] **5032, 4139**

MUZYKALNAIA FOLKLORISTIKA (RU) [01796009] **4139**

MUZYKALNAIA ZHIZN (RU/0131-2383) [04595503] **4139**

MUZYKALNOE VOSPITANIE Y SHKOLE (RU) [01793240] **1765, 4139**

MUZYKALNYI SOVREMENNIK (RU) [03717775] **4139**

MUZZLE BLASTS (US) [06639243] **4905**

MUZZLELOADER, THE (US/0274-5720) [06413337] **4905**

MUZZLELOADERS' ANNUAL (US/0146-6143) [02998661] **3485**

MVA VIEWPOINTS (US/0464-2082) [01756371] **1765**

MVMA MOTOR VEHICLE FACTS & FIGURES (US/0272-3395) [04216659] **5421**

MVP (CN/0829-6146) [13241478] **4905**

MVP-BERICHTE (GW/0173-0452) [09651224] **4792**

●MVP VIDEO JOURNAL OF GENERAL SURGERY (US/1058-1650) [24233871] **3970**

MVR (US/0270-3521) [06333626] **3414**

MVS UPDATE (UK) **1280**

MW : MEN'S WEAR OF CANADA (CN/0834-0064) [15609279] **1086**

MW NEWSLETTER, THE (US/0198-9340) [06254774] **2461**

MW-Q (CN/1186-091X) [24266137] **800**

MWETI (CF) **5799**

MY BROTHER AND I (CN/0316-8913) [02624596] **4979**

MY COUNTRY (US/0580-3772) [03098322] **2747**

MY DAILY VISITOR (US) **5032**

MY DEVOTIONS (US/0027-5387) [04104950] **1066, 4979**

MY FIRST MAGAZINE *CEASED.* (US/1057-1558) [23958932] **1066**

MY FRIEND (US/0164-3568) [04630435] **5032, 1066**

MY GUY (UK) **2490**

MY LITTLE SALESMAN TRUCK CATALOG (US/0192-7027) [05085594] **5421**

MY PET (CN/0707-4360) [05258137] **4287**

MY WEEKLY (UK) **5561**

MY WEEKLY READER. SUMMER EDITION A (US/1050-7647) [21587903] **1066**

MYANMA NAING NGAN THUTEITHANA ATHIN GYANE. THE JOURNAL OF THE BURMA RESEARCH SOCIETY (BR) [02416469] **2659**

MYCOBACTERIA (UK/1351-5292) **491, 3618**

MYCOLOGIA (US/0027-5514) [01640733] **575**

MYCOLOGIA HELVETICA (SZ/0256-310X) [10870273] **575**

MYCOLOGIA MEMOIR (GW/0580-3829) [01417060] **575**

MYCOLOGICAL PAPERS. COMMONWEALTH MYCOLOGICAL INSTITUTE (UK/0027-5522) [09713009] **575**

MYCOLOGICAL RESEARCH (UK/0953-7562) [19073320] **575**

MYCOLOGICAL — Alphabetical Title Index

MYCOLOGICAL SOCIETY OF AMERICA See INOCULUM (ITHACA, N.Y.) **5114**

MYCOLOGICAL SOCIETY OF AMERICA. NEWSLETTER See INOCULUM (ITHACA, N.Y.) **5114**

MYCOLOGIST, THE (UK/0269-915X) [15186143] **576**

MYCOLOGY SERIES (US/0730-9597) [08090378] **576**

MYCOPATHOLOGIA (1975) (NE/0301-486X) [01342728] **576**

MYCOPLASMATALES (US/0097-5249) [01295094] **568**

MYCORRHIZA (GW/0940-6360) [25807492] **518**

●MYCOSCIENCE (JA/1340-3540) [30989356] **518**

MYCOSES (GW/0933-7407) [17849088] **576**

MYCOSYSTEMA : ANNUAL REPORT OF SYSTEMATIC MYCOLOGY & LICHENOLOGY LABORATORY, INSTITUTE OF MICROBIOLOGY, ACADEMIA SINICA (CC) [19493670] **576**

MYCOTAXON (US/0093-4666) [01798491] 568, **518**

MYCOTOXIN RESEARCH (GW/0178-7888) [13977773] **519**

MYERS' FINANCE & ENERGY (US/0376-6454) [02587239] 800, **1950**

MYERS OF AMERICA (US/0883-2706) [12019690] **2461**

MYFOREST (II) [01758926] **2388**

MYKOLOGICKY SBORNIK (XR/0374-9436) [04048861] **519**

MYONNETYT RAKENNUSLUVAT (FI/0355-2314) [03499127] **621**

MYOTIS (GW/0580-3896) [04739659] **5592**

MYRA (UK) [12625135] **4863**

MYRA WALDO'S RESTAURANT GUIDE TO NEW YORK CITY AND VICINITY (US/0196-0032) [05739142] **5072**

MYRA WALDO'S TRAVEL GUIDE TO SOUTH AMERICA CEASED. (US/0196-0024) [05739154] **5485**

MYRA WALDO'S TRAVEL GUIDE TO SOUTHERN EUROPE (US/0196-3651) [05810796] **5485**

MYRA WALDO'S TRAVEL GUIDE TO THE ORIENT AND ASIA (US/0195-7759) [05664721] **5485**

MYRA WALDO'S TRAVEL GUIDE TO THE ORIENT AND THE PACIFIC See MYRA WALDO'S TRAVEL GUIDE TO THE ORIENT AND ASIA **5485**

MYRA WALDO'S TRAVEL GUIDE TO THE SOUTH PACIFIC CEASED. (US/0195-7767) [05664607] **5485**

MYRTLE BEACH JOURNAL, THE CEASED. (US/0745-8584) [09512434] **5637**

MYSL NARODOWA POLSKA (PL/0867-0072) [I08670072] **4482**

MYSORE. DEPT. OF ANIMAL HUSBANDRY AND VETERINARY SCIENCE. ANNUAL REPORT See ANNUAL REPORT OF THE DEPARTMENT OF ANIMAL HUSBANDRY AND VETERINARY SERVICES IN KARNATAKA, INDO-DANISH PROJECT HESSARGHATTA AND BANGALORE DAIRY, BANGALORE **5503**

MYSORE (INDIA : STATE) See DETAILED ESTIMATES OF IRRIGATION, ELECTRICITY AND PUBLIC WORKS FOR ... **2041**

MYSORE JOURNAL OF AGRICULTURAL SCIENCES (II/0047-8539) [01758934] **110**

MYSORE. LEGISLATURE. LEGISLATIVE ASSEMBLY. COMMITTEE OF PRIVILEGES. REPORT See REPORT - KARNATAKA LEGISLATIVE ASSEMBLY, COMMITTEE OF PRIVILEGES **4680**

MYSORE. PUBLIC WORKS DEPT. (COMMUNICATIONS AND BUILDINGS). ROAD STATISTICS IN MYSORE STATE See ROAD STATISTICS IN KARNATAKA STATE **5402**

MYSORE STATE TRADE AND INDUSTRIAL DIRECTORY (II) [01797674] **847**

MYSTERY FANCIER, THE CEASED. (US/0146-3160) [02904675] **3414**

MYSTERY MAGAZINE (US) [01604080] **3414**

MYSTERY NEWS (US/0734-9076) [08888062] **3348**

MYSTERY READERS JOURNAL (US/1043-3473) [19407886] **3414**

●MYSTERY REVIEW, THE (CN/1192-8700) [28395859] **3414**

MYSTERY SCENE (US) [19094671] **5074**

MYSTIC TRIANGLE See ROSICRUCIAN DIGEST **4243**

MYSTICS QUARTERLY (IOWA CITY, IOWA) (US/0742-5503) [10361923] **3414**

MYSTIQUE (TORONTO) (CN/0710-1988) [08418973] **5188**

MYTHES, CROYANCES ET RELIGIONS DANS LE MONDE ANGLO-SAXON (FR) [18006084] 3414, **4979**

MYTHIC SOCIETY, BANGALORE, INDIA See QUARTERLY JOURNAL OF THE MYTHIC SOCIETY (BANGALORE), THE **4989**

MYTHLORE (US/0146-9339) [02494503] **3414**

MYTHOS : A NEWSLETTER ABOUT STORY TELLING (AT) **2322**

MYTHPRINT (US/0146-9347) [02255810] **3414**

MYTHS AND FACTS (US/0894-6442) [11023975] **4529**

N 3 NEWS See OMEGA 3 NEWS **4794**

N.A.C.W.P.I JOURNAL (US/0027-576X) [01793034] 1765, **4139**

N.A.D.A. LARGE BOAT APPRAISAL GUIDE (US/1055-1972) [22341296] **594**

N.A.D.A. MOBILE HOME MANUFACTURED HOUSING APPRAISAL GUIDE (US/0742-9274) [08458780] **3485**

N. A. D. A. MOTORCYCLE & MOPED APPRAISAL GUIDE (US/0197-1980) [05961744] **4082**

N.A.D.A. MOTORCYCLE APPRAISAL GUIDE See N. A. D. A. MOTORCYCLE & MOPED APPRAISAL GUIDE **4082**

N.A.D.A. MOTORCYCLE, SNOWMOBILE, ATV, AND PERSONAL WATERCRAFT APPRAISAL GUIDE (US) [17360248] **5387**

N.A.D.A. OFFICIAL OLDER USED CAR GUIDE : AN OFFICIAL N.A.D.A. VALUE GUIDE (US) [13138952] **5388**

N.A.D.A. OFFICIAL USED CAR GUIDE (US/0027-5794) [05342279] **5421**

●N.A.D.A. OFFICIAL USED CAR GUIDE (RETAIL CONSUMER ED.) (US/1061-9054) [25487606] **5421**

N.A.D.A. RECREATION VEHICLE APPRAISAL GUIDE (US/0092-4601) [01788232] **5388**

N.A.D.A. SMALL BOAT APPRAISAL GUIDE (US/1055-1964) [22342341] **594**

N.A.D.A. TITLE AND REGISTRATION BOOK / THE OFFICIAL TITLE AND REGISTRATION BOOK OF THE NATIONAL AUTOMOBILE DEALERS ASSOCIATION (US) [08385600] **5421**

N.A.M.M. MUSIC RETAILER NEWS (US/0027-5913) [01789842] **4139**

N.A.R.D. JOURNAL (US/0162-1602) [04102933] **4316**

N.A.V.A. NEWS (US) **2623**

N.A. WAY MAGAZINE, THE (US/1046-5421) [20442567] **1347**

N & M. NATUR OG MILJ (NO/0802-4618) [I08024618] **2198**

N.B.I.A. NEWSLETTER (1989) (CN/0848-8851) [21400814] **110**

N. B. NATURALIST (CN/0047-9551) [02468793] **4168**

N.B.O. ABSTRACTS (II) [04583674] **621**

N.C. ... ANNUAL REPORT OF HAZARDOUS WASTE GENERATED, STORED, TREATED OR DISPOSED (US) [09071283] **2237**

●N-COMPASS (LINCOLN, NEB.) (US/1075-9719) [30106455] **3232**

●N.D.A. (SKOKIE, ILL.), THE (US/1064-9786) [26484230] **4316**

N.E.O.N., NATAL EDUCATION. ONDERWYS IN NATAL (SA/0377-1717) [01795780] **1765**

N.E.S.F.A. INDEX TO SHORT SCIENCE FICTION (US) [19503768] **3414**

N.H.C.A. BULLETIN / NATIONAL HAIRDRESSERS & COSMETOLOGISTS' ASSOCIATION, INC (US) [15919794] **404**

N I M RESEARCH DIGEST (SA) [01780258] **4013**

N.J. ANGLERS NEWS See ANGLERS' NEWS **2294**

N.J. STATE BAR ASSOCIATION (US/0145-5044) [02743065] **3012**

N.J. VASA HOME FAMILY (US/0744-8384) [08592893] **2283**

N.L.R.B ELECTION REPORT. CASES CLOSED (US/0270-9732) [02620756] **1692**

N (MINNEAPOLIS, MINN.) CEASED. (US/0893-3472) [14000274] **2922**

'N OORSIG VAN DIE REKENINGS VAN MYNMAATSKAPPYE (SA) [01789683] **1443**

N.P.B.A. GAZETTE (UK) [09982479] **216**

N. P. K. S. PROCESS & PLANT SUPPLIERS WORLD DIRECTORY (UK) **1027**

N.P.N. MEDECINE (FR/0248-9635) [09144344] **3618**

N.R.S., LA NOUVELLE REVUE SOCIALISTE (FR) [04302684] **4543**

N. S. TRAPPER'S NEWSLETTER (CN/0705-4831) [04080395] **2388**

N.S.U.C. UNDERWATER NEWS (CN/0711-3986) [08499851] **4905**

N.S.W. MASTER PLUMBER (AT/0819-1824) [08191824] **2607**

N.S.W. REALTY AUCTIONEER (AT/0727-0062) [I07270062] **4841**

N-SCALE (EDMONDS, WASH.) (US/1045-5140) [20138242] **5433**

N T A-T I A BOOKSHELF (US) [01641243] **4738**

N W EUROPE PETROLEUM DATABASE (UK) **4265**

N W S ACTION (US) **5561**

N.Y. CIVIL LIBERTIES (US/0746-0201) [04363792] **4511**

N.Y. COUNTY LAWYER / NEW YORK COUNTY LAWYERS' ASSOCIATION (US) [07711628] **3012**

N.Y. HABITAT (US/0745-0893) [08809252] 879, **4841**

N.Y. JOURNAL JAPAN (US/0742-8170) [10463374] 696, **4529**

N.Y. LETTER CARRIERS' OUTLOOK (US/0028-7342) [04090566] **1145**

N.Z.A.S.I.A.N (NZ/0110-0343) [04710457] **2659**

N.Z. SOIL SURVEY REPORT (NZ/0110-2079) [02359036] **179**

NA EKRANAKH MIRA (RU) [01783286] **4075**

NA HAKHOE CHI (KO) [08293304] **4792**

NA STRAZY (PL) [07054580] **5018**

NA SVIETLYI PRAZDNIK : PODAROK KHOZIAINA RABOTNIKU (RU) [19711739] **110**

NAACOG NEWSLETTER (US/0889-0579) [08942462] 3765, **3862**

NAACOG'S CLINICAL ISSUES IN PERINATAL AND WOMEN'S HEALTH NURSING (US/1046-7475) [20504464] **3765**

NAACOG'S WOMEN'S HEALTH NURSING SCAN (US/1055-3533) [23158303] **3862**

NAAM (US/0147-4618) [03173471] **4139**

NAAMAT (IS) [03215170] 2283, **5562**

NA'AMAT WOMAN (US/0888-191X) [13509229] **2770**

NAAMBOEK VAN OFFICIEREN DER KONINKLIJKE MARINE (NE) [07357274] **4179**

NAAMKUNDE (NE/0167-5257) [02416945] **3304**

NAAMLIJSTEN VOOR DE STATISTIEK VAN DE BUITENLANDSE HANDEL (NE/0168-4094) [I01684094] **696**

NAAMLOOZE VENNOOTSCHAP, DE (NE) [04542581] **696**

NAATI NEWS (AT/1031-5411) [I10315411] **3304**

NAAWP NEWS : PUBLICATION OF THE NATIONAL ASSOCIATION FOR THE ADVANCEMENT OF WHITE PEOPLE (US) [07641419] **5684**

NAB CLEARINGHOUSE QUARTERLY (US/0747-5837) [10756904] **1692**

NAB RADIO FINANCIAL REPORT See RADIO FINANCIAL REPORT / NAB **1137**

NABE JOURNAL See BILINGUAL RESEARCH JOURNAL **1728**

NABE NEWS (CLEVELAND, OHIO) (US/0745-3205) [09067889] 696, **1506**

NABET NEWS. INTERNATIONAL EDITION (US/0027-5697) [04105034] **1135**

NABLIUDENIIA ISKUSSTVENNYKH NEBESNYKH TEL (RU/0130-6863) [05540848] **29**

NABOKOVIAN, THE (US/0894-7120) [11607551] **3414**

NABP NEWSLETTER (US/8756-4483) [03876989] **4316**

NABTE REVIEW (US/0148-5784) [03337695] 1914, **696**

NACA NEWS (US) **226**

NACAC BULLETIN (US/1046-2929) [10743642] **1866**

NACADA JOURNAL (US/0271-9517) [16712184] **762**

NACADA JOURNAL / NATIONAL ACADEMIC ADVISING ASSOCIATION (US/0271-9517) [06712184] **1836**

NACAE ANNUAL REPORT (US) [02480610] **1801**

NACAO E DEFESA (PO) [14121453] **4482**

NACD CONVENTION See PROCEEDINGS OF THE ANNUAL NACD CONVENTION **2202**

NACE CORROSION ENGINEERING BUYER'S GUIDE : OFFICIAL PUBLICATION OF NACE (US) [07242504] **2015**

NACF MAGAZINE (UK) [14148155] **359**

NACHDRUCKVERZEICHNIS VON EINZELWERKEN, SERIEN UND ZEITSCHRIFTEN AUS ALLEN WISSENSGEBIETEN (REPRINT) (GW) [05358647] **420**

NACHRICHTEN AUS CHEMIE, TECHNIK UND LABORATORIUM (GW/0341-5163) [03244003] **987**

NACHRICHTEN AUS DEM KARTEN-UND VERMESSUNGSWESEN. REIHE II (GW/0469-4244) [18898603] **2582**

NACHRICHTEN AUS DEM KARTEN- UND VERMESSUNGSWESEN. REIHE I (GW/0071-920X) [01570073] **2569**

NACHRICHTEN AUS DEM KARTEN- UND VERMESSUNGSWESEN. SONDERHEFT (GW/0344-5879) [I03445879] **2569**

NACHRICHTEN AUS DEM OFFENTLICHEN VERMESSUNGSDIENST NORDRHEIN-WESTFALEN (GW) [02241032] **2027**

NACHRICHTEN AUS NIEDERSACHSENS URGESCHICHTE (GW) [04520157] **275**

NACHRICHTEN DER AKADEMIE DER WISSENSCHAFTEN IN GOTTINGEN. II, MATHEMATISCH-PHYSIKALISCHE KLASSE (GW/0065-5295) [04327156] **3523, 5130**

NACHRICHTEN DER AKADEMIE DER WISSENSCHAFTEN IN GOTTINGEN. PHILOLOGISCH-HISTORISCHE KLASSE (GW/0065-5287) [09238680] **3304**

NACHRICHTEN DER GESELLSCHAFT FUER NATUR- UND VOLKERKUNDE OSTASIENS/HAMBURG (GW/0016-9080) [01454519] **2623**

NACHRICHTEN DER NIEDERSACHSISCHEN VERMESSUNGS- UND KATASTERVERWALTUNG (GW) [02241033] **2582**

NACHRICHTEN FUER DOKUMENTATION (GW/0027-7436) [03759506] **3232**

NACHRICHTEN (GESELLSCHAFT FUR NATUR- UND VOLKERKUNDE OSTASIENS) See NACHRICHTEN DER GESELLSCHAFT FUER NATUR- UND VOLKERKUNDE OSTASIENS/HAMBURG **2623**

NACHRICHTENBLATT DER BAYERISCHEN ENTOMOLOGEN (GW/0027-7452) [01696869] **5612**

NACHRICHTENBLATT DER VERMESSUNGS- UND KATASTERVERWALTUNG RHEINLAND-PFALZ (GW/0939-2378) [01785927] **2027**

NACHRICHTENBLATT DES DEUTSCHEN PFLANZENSCHUTZDIENSTES (GW/0027-7479) [01772792] **519**

NACHRICHTENDIENST (GW/0012-1185) [05033997] **5297**

NACHRICHTENTECHNIK - ELEKTRONIK (GW/0323-4657) [01791223] **2073, 1160**

NACHSCHLAGEWERK DES BUNDESARBEITSGERICHTS (GW) [01752377] **3012**

NACION, LA (AG) [04942587] **5777**

NACIONAL (CARACAS, VENEZUELA) (VE) [04723193] **5813**

●NACLA REPORT ON THE AMERICAS (1993) (US/1071-4839) [28330375] **1506**

NACM BANKRUPTCY REORGANIZATION GUIDE (US/1055-8381) [23352958] **800**

NACOI FORUM (CN/0708-5249) [06025545] **2268**

NACORE'S ... COMPENSATION & BENEFITS SURVEY (US/1044-8799) [19959253] **2888**

NACS CAMPUS FOCUS (US/0896-0488) [16892136] **1836**

NACS WEEKLY BULLETIN (US/0895-7789) [16812042] **879**

NACTA JOURNAL (US/0149-4910) [01941493] **110**

NACUBO BUSINESS OFFICER (US/0147-877X) [03283132] **1866, 696**

NAD BROADCASTER, THE (US) [06804640] **4391**

NAD WARTA BODZ (PL/0208-6786) [I02086786] **2519**

NADA MANUFACTURED HOUSING APPRAISAL GUIDE (US) **2828**

NADA NEWSLETTER (US/0164-3592) [04631136] **5421**

NADA RETAIL AIRCRAFT APPRAISAL GUIDE (US) **29**

NADA VAN CONVERSION LIMOUSINE APPRAISAL GUIDE (US) **5421**

NADEZHNOST I DOLGOVECHNOST MASHIN I SOORUZHENII / AKADEMIIA NAUK UKRAINSKOI SSR, INSTITUT PROBLEM PROCHNOSTI (UN) [10158993] **2123**

NADEZHNOST I KONTROL KACHESTVA (RU/0130-6898) [06388477] **4220**

NADI AL-QISSAH (ALEXANDRIA, EGYPT) (UA) [10377621] **3414**

NADI AL-SAYYARAT WAL-AL-RIHLAT AL-MISRI See TOURIST GUIDE BOOK **5494**

NADIE AUSTRALIA JOURNAL, THE (AT/1037-700X) [I1037700X] 386, **1765**

NAE WASHINGTON INSIGHT (NEWSLETTER ED.) (US/0199-3038) [05768306] **4979**

NAEA NEWS (US/0160-6395) [01955811] **1765, 359**

NAEB BULLETIN (US/0161-7990) [04024725] **950**

NAECON (US/0547-3578) [01961416] **2073, 29**

NAEDA EQUIPMENT DEALER (US/1074-5017) [29717592] **160**

NAEN BULLETIN (US/0270-6881) [05250227] **1692, 1766**

NAFED DIRECTORY (US/0363-7131) [02529569] **2291**

NAFSA DIRECTORY OF INSTITUTIONS AND INDIVIDUALS IN INTERNATIONAL EDUCATIONAL EXCHANGE (US/0736-4660) [09135235] **1836**

NAFSA GOVERNMENT AFFAIRS BULLETIN (US/0889-9363) [14104778] **1920**

NAFSA STUDIES AND PAPERS. ENGLISH LANGUAGE SERIES (US) [05250710] **3304**

NAFT AL-ARAB (KU) [03488385] **847, 4265**

●NAFTA DIGEST / NORTH AMERICAN FREE TRADE AGREEMENT INFORMATION CENTER, THE GRADUATE SCHOOL OF INTERNATIONAL TRADE & BUSINESS ADMINISTRATION, LAREDO STATE UNIVERSITY (US/1075-9050) [25534504] **847**

NAFTA (ZAGREB, CROATIA) (CI) [19080299] **4265**

NAFTILIAKI (GR) [05185077] **5453**

●NAFTOVA I HAZOVA PROMYSLOVIST (UN) [27041027] **4265**

NAG HAMMADI STUDIES (NE) [02624573] **4979**

NAGA, THE ICLARM QUARTERLY (PH/0116-290X) [14191204] **2308**

NAGALAND BUDGET. SOME FACTS AND CHARTS (II/0303-8505) [01797755] **4738, 4699**

NAGALAND (INDIA) See EXPLANATORY MEMORANDUM ON THE BUDGET OF THE GOVERNMENT OF NAGALAND FOR ... **4723**

NAGALAND (INDIA). DIRECTORATE OF ECONOMICS AND STATISTICS See NAGALAND BUDGET. SOME FACTS AND CHARTS **4699**

NAGALAND, INDIA. PLANNING AND CO-ORDINATION DEPT See DRAFT ANNUAL PLAN - GOVERNMENT OF NAGALAND, PLANNING AND COORDINATION DEPT **1605**

NAGANO-KEN EISEI KOGAI KENKYUJO KENKYU HOKOKU (JA/0387-9070) [10343964] **2237, 4792**

NAGANO-KEN SHOKUHIN KOGYO SHIKENJO KENKYU HOKOKU (JA/0286-102X) [10343983] **2350**

NAGAOKA GIJUTSU KAGAKU DAIGAKU KENKYU HOKOKU (JA/0388-5631) [07610687] **5130**

NAGAOKA KOGYO KOTO SENMON GAKKO KENKYU KIYO (JA/0027-7568) [09989259] **5130**

NAGARLOK (II/0027-7584) [02621673] **4667**

NAGASAKI BUNKEN SOSHO (JA) [01796867] **2659**

NAGASAKI DAIGAKU KYOIKU GAKUBU KYOKA KYOIKUGAKU KENKYU HOKOKU (JA/0388-2810) [12485014] **1901**

NAGASAKI-KEN EISEI KOGAI KENKYUJO HO (JA) [08981502] **4792**

NAGASAKI KENRITSU NAGASAKI TOSHOKAN See ISHIDATAMI **3218**

NAGASAKI (PREFECTURE) See KANKYO HAKUSHO **2234**

NAGELS MUSIK-ARCHIV (GW) [05282179] **4139**

NAGOYA DAIGAKU. KOGAKUBU See MEMOIRS OF THE FACULTY OF ENGINEERING, NAGOYA UNIVERSITY **1987**

NAGOYA DAIGAKU KYOIKUGAKUBU KIYO See NAGOYA DAIGAKU KYOIKUGAKUBU KIYO. KYOIKUGAKKA **1766**

NAGOYA DAIGAKU KYOIKUGAKUBU KIYO. KYOIKUGAKKA (JA) [07990573] **1766**

NAGOYA DAIGAKU. OGATA KEISANKI SENTA See NAGOYA DAIGAKU OGATA KEISANKI SENTA NYUSU **1261**

NAGOYA DAIGAKU OGATA KEISANKI SENTA NYUSU (JA) [05951221] **1261**

NAGOYA DAIGAKU. SUIKEN KAGAKU KENKYUJO See NAGOYA DAIGAKU SUIKEN KAGAKU KENKYUJO NEMPO **2570**

NAGOYA DAIGAKU SUIKEN KAGAKU KENKYUJO NEMPO (JA) [02519617] **2570**

NAGOYA, JAPAN. SHIKAI. JIMUKYOKU. CHOSAKA See CHOSA SHIRYO **1469**

NAGOYA JOURNAL OF MEDICAL SCIENCE (JA/0027-7622) [01758974] **3618**

NAGOYA KOGYO DAIGAKU FUZOKU TOSHOKAN GAIYO (JA) [06142292] **3232**

NAGOYA KOGYO DAIGAKU GAKUHO (JA/0369-3171) [10462351] **5130**

NAGOYA KOGYO DAIGAKU KOGAKUBU FUZOKU YOGYO GIJUTSU KENKYU SHISETSU NEMPO (JA) [02246983] **2592**

NAGOYA KOGYO DAIGAKU. KOGAKUBU. YOGYO GIJUTSU KENKYU SHISETSU See NAGOYA KOGYO DAIGAKU KOGAKUBU FUZOKU YOGYO GIJUTSU KENKYU SHISETSU NEMPO **2592**

NAGOYA KOGYO DAIGAKU. TOSHOKAN See NAGOYA KOGYO DAIGAKU FUZOKU TOSHOKAN GAIYO **3232**

NAGOYA KOGYO GIJUTSU SHIKENJO See NAGOYA KOGYO GIJUTSU SHIKENJO NEMPO **5130**

NAGOYA KOGYO GIJUTSU SHIKENJO HOKOKU (JA/0027-7614) [10462306] **1619**

NAGOYA KOGYO GIJUTSU SHIKENJO NEMPO (JA) [02244913] **5130**

NAGOYA MATHEMATICAL JOURNAL (JA/0027-7630) [01758975] **3523**

NAGOYA MEDICAL JOURNAL (JA/0027-7649) [01778751] **3618**

NAGOYA-SHI EISEI KENKYUJO See NAGOYA-SHI EISEI KENKYUJO HO **4792**

NAGOYA-SHI EISEI KENKYUJO HO (JA) [06871816] **4792**

NAGOYA-SHI EISEI KENKYUJO KENKYU HOKOKU (JA/0369-3333) [09505771] **1619**

NAGOYA SHIRITSU DAIGAKU IGAKKAI ZASSHI. JOURNAL OF THE NAGOYA CITY UNIVERSITY MEDICAL ASSOCIATION (JA/0027-7606) [07611171] **3618**

NAGOYA SHIRITSU DAIGAKU. YAKUGAKUBU See NAGOYA SHIRITSU DAIGAKU YAKUGAKUBU KENKYU NENPO **4316**

NAGOYA SHIRITSU DAIGAKU YAKUGAKUBU KENKYU NENPO (JA/0369-5611) [09707827] **4316**

NAGOYA SHOKA DAIGAKU RONSHU (JA) [08007653] **1506**

NAGOYA UNIVERSITY. RESEARCH INSTITUTE OF ATMOSPHERICS See PROCEEDINGS OF THE RESEARCH INSTITUTE OF ATMOSPHERICS, NAGOYA UNIVERSITY **1433**

NAGPUR UNIVERSITY See JOURNAL : SCIENCE **5122**

NAGRA INFORMIERT (SZ/1012-8778) [14987859] **2237**

NAGWS SOFTBALL GUIDE (US) [15579229] **4905**

NAGWS VOLLEYBALL GUIDE (US) [16319448] **4905**

NAGYVILAG (HU) [01606135] **3414**

NAHAM MANAGEMENT JOURNAL, THE (US/1057-3526) [23110641] **3789**

NAHC WILD GAME COOKBOOK (US/8755-1713) [11220939] **2792**

●NAHE (WESTWOOD, MASS.) (US/1064-6078) [26339413] **1766, 4792**

NAHNU AL-ARAB (UA) [03679437] **2507**

NAHOST JAHRBUCH (GW) [18540612] **2519**

NAHRO ROSTER (US/0363-6453) [02531671] **1506, 2829**

NAHRUNG, DIE (GW/0027-769X) [01758978] **4192**

NAHT GUIDE TO SCHOOL MANAGEMENT (UK) **1866**

NAHUATZEN, EL (US/0162-9085) [04252977] **3466**

NAHVERKEHR, DER (GW/0722-8287) [I07228287] **5442**

NAIA NEWS (US/0740-5995) [04781565] **4905**

NAIC MALPRACTICE CLAIMS (US/0146-5481) [03523304] **2888**

NAIC NEWS, THE (US/0741-0727) [10081044] **2888**

NAIGAI — Alphabetical Title Index

NAIGAI TOKUSHU KYOIKU KANKYU KIKAN TO ICHIRAN (JA) [03676478] **4391**

NAIHUO CAILIAO (CC/1001-1935) [I10011935] **4013**

NAIKA (JA/0547-1729) [01338433] **3800**

NAIKA HOKAN (JA/0021-4809) [06380862] **3800**

NAIKAI BUNKA KENKYU KIYO (JA) [01797290] **2659**

NAILPRO (VAN NUYS, CALIF.) (US/1049-4553) [21255968] **405**

NAILS (US/0896-193X) [16513559] **2792**

NAIROBI (KENYA). CITY COUNCIL. HOUSING DEVELOPMENT DEPT *See* ANNUAL REPORT OF THE DIRECTOR, HOUSING DEVELOPMENT AND MANAGEMENT DEPARTMENT FOR THE YEAR.../CITY COUNCIL OF NAIROBI **2814**

NAIROBI (KENYA). DANDORA COMMUNITY DEVELOPMENT PROJECT DEPT. ANNUAL REPORT *See* ANNUAL REPORT OF THE DIRECTOR, HOUSING DEVELOPMENT AND MANAGEMENT DEPARTMENT FOR THE YEAR.../CITY COUNCIL OF NAIROBI **2814**

NAIROBI STOCK EXCHANGE *See* OFFICIAL YEAR BOOK **910**

NAIS MEMBER SCHOOL TUITION FEES, FACULTY SALARIES, AND ADMINISTRATIVE SALARIES (US/0161-1097) [03832181] **1866**

NAISSANCE & PETITE ENFANCE (FR) [24914291] **3765**

NAKSSI CHUNCHU (KO) [11361038] **2309**

NAL; NATIONAL AEROSPACE LABORATORY, JAPAN (JA) [02298016] **29**

NAL NEWS LETTER (II) [02732725] **29**

NALC RETIREE (US/8750-863X) [11874225] **1692**

NALS DOCKET *See* DOCKET, THE **2963**

NAM PUSAN CHONGNYON HOEUISO (KO) [09374453] **847**

NAM YANGJU MUNHWA (KO) [09538871] **3800**

NAMA KONKURITO TOKEI NEMPO (JA) [01790184] 621, **633**

NAMAH-I DANISHKADAH-I DAMPIZISHKI (IR/0042-0123) [02250579] **5516**

NAMAH-I JIBHAH-I NAJAT-I IRAN (FR) [20625392] **4482**

NAMARI TO AEN / LEAD AND ZINC. NIHON NAMARI AEN JUYO KENKYUKAI (JA/0027-772X) [10463662] **1443**

NAME AUTHORITIES. CUMULATIVE MICROFORM EDITION (US/0195-9093) [05996698] **3232**

NAME GLEANER (CN/0700-9445) [03403194] **3304**

NAME OF APPLICANTS FOR THE REGISTRATION OF TRADE MARKS / PATENT, TRADE MARKS, AND DESIGNS OFFICE, CANBERRA, A.C.T (AT) [08289687] **1306**

NAMENS ZWOLLE *CEASED.* (NE/0920-0223) [I09200223] **1506**

NAMES (US/0027-7738) [01695186] **2461**

NAMES AND ADDRESSES OF INSURANCE COMPANIES LISTED IN NEW YORK STATE ISSUED BY THE NEW YORK INSURANCE DEPT *See* DIRECTORY OF INSURANCE COMPANIES LICENSED IN NEW YORK STATE **2878**

NAMES IN SOUTH CAROLINA *CEASED.* (US/0077-2690) [02251259] **2570**

NAMES IN THE NEWS (US/0737-397X) [09360412] **434**

NAMES OF BUILDINGS (WITH ADDRESSES) / RATING AND VALUATION DEPARTMENT, HONG KONG (HK) [26776242] 621, **4667**

NAMI (JA) [07301187] **3414**

NAMIBIA, A SUMMARY OF FACTS AND FIGURES (ZA) [14876933] **1506**

NAMIBIA ABSTRACTS (ZA) [12038409] 1506, **4482**

NAMIBIA BULLETIN (US/0377-7588) [01794975] **3133**

NAMIBIA DEVELOPMENT BRIEFING / NAMIBIA SUPPORT COMMITTEE (SX) [25563176] **1506**

NAMIBIA YOUTH : OFFICIAL BULLETIN OF THE SWAPO YOUTH LEAGUE (AO) [11546363] **4482**

NAMIBIAN STRUGGLE, THE (SX) [09618953] **2499**

NAMIBIAN, THE (SX) **5806**

NAMIBIANA (SX/0259-2010) [07324806] **2642**

NAMIT JOURNAL (US/0163-612X) [04267383] **4139**

NAMN OCH BYGD (SW/0077-2704) [01758981] **2570**

NAN-CHING SHIH YUAN HSUEH PAO. CHE HSUEH SHE HUI KO HSUEH PAN (CH) [11149924] **5234**

NAN FANG CHIEN CHU. NANFANG JIANZHU / CHUNG-KUO CHIEN CHU HSUEH HUI KUANG-TUNG FEN HUI CHU PIEN (CC) [10719339] **304**

NAN KAI SHIH HSUEH / NAN KAI TA HSUEH LI SHIH HSI HSUEH SHU WEI YUAN HUI (CC) [11311844] **2623**

NAN-YANG CHIAO YU (SI) [01797570] **1766**

NAN-YANG HSUEH HUI, SINGAPORE *See* JOURNAL OF THE SOUTH SEAS SOCIETY **2656**

NANAIMO DIRECTORY (BUSINESS EDITION) (CN/0317-8838) [02248232] **2570**

NANCY DREW MYSTERY STORIES (US) [03765187] **3414**

NANDANA (II) [10513351] **3414**

N&GC : JOURNAL OF THE HORTICULTURAL TRADES ASSOCIATION (UK/0029-6430) [14470571] **2424**

N&GC NURSERYMAN & GARDEN CENTRE (UK) [14051433] **2424**

NANJING DAXUE XUEBAO. ZIRAN KEXUE (CC/0469-5097) [07887148] **5130**

NANJING HANGKONG XUEYUAN XUEBAO (CC/1000-1956) [I10001956] **29**

NANJING LINYE DAXUE XUEBAO (CC/1000-2006) [15161306] **2388**

NANJING NONGYE DAXUE XUEBAO (CC/1000-2030) [14288724] **110**

NANJING QIXIANG XUEYUAN XUEBAO (CH/1000-2022) [I10002022] **1432**

NANJING YIXUEYUAN XUEBAO (CC/1000-5331) [21664690] **3618**

NANKAIKEN KIYO (JA/0389-5351) [10527090] **2670**

NANKYOKU SHIRYO (JA/0085-7289) [01481548] **2570**

NANNY TIMES (US) [20653962] **2283**

●NANOBIOLOGY : JOURNAL OF RESEARCH ON NANOSCALE LIVING SYSTEMS (UK/0958-3165) [26430185] 3695, **539**

●NANOSTRUCTURED MATERIALS (US/0965-9773) [25608659] **2107**

NANOTECHNOLOGY (BRISTOL) (UK/0957-4484) [22150204] 3618, **1988**

NAN'S KNIT-KNACKS (CN/0705-3681) [03900119] **5354**

NANSEI KAIKU SUISAN KENKYUJO CHOSA HOKOKU (JA) [05511705] **2309**

NANSEI KAIKU SUISAN KENKYUJO (JAPAN) *See* NANSEI KAIKU SUISAN KENKYUJO KENKYU HOKOKU **2309**

NANSEI KAIKU SUISAN KENKYUJO (JAPAN) *See* NANSEI KAIKU SUISAN KENKYUJO CHOSA HOKOKU **2309**

NANSEI KAIKU SUISAN KENKYUJO KENKYU HOKOKU (JA/0388-841X) [02099268] **2309**

NANTO NO CHIMEI / NANTO CHIMEI KENKYU SENTA (JA) [12184399] **2570**

NANTUCKET JOURNAL (NANTUCKET, MASS. 1987) (US/1056-2265) [23606837] **2747**

NANTY-GLO JOURNAL, THE (US/0746-4037) [10024174] **5737**

NANZAN INSTITUTE FOR RELIGION AND CULTURE *See* BULLETIN - NANZAN INSTITUTE FOR RELIGION AND CULTURE **4941**

NANZAN REVIEW OF AMERICAN STUDIES : A JOURNAL OF CENTER FOR AMERICAN STUDIES, NANZAN UNIVERSITY (JA) [05684670] **5210**

NAO (AG) [13608977] **5234**

NAO REVISTA DE LA CULTURA DEL MEDITERRANEO (AG) **5210**

NAOS (ENGLISH ED.) (US/0889-342X) [11475028] **3304**

NAPA COUNTY RECORD AND NAPA VALLEY NEWS (US/0744-6942) [08515516] **5637**

NAPA VALLEY REGISTER, THE (US) [27716818] **5637**

NAPF PENSIONS LEGISLATION SERVICE (UK) **3013**

NAPJAINK (WEST-HILL) (CN/0821-5995) [10330261] **4979**

NAPL SPECIAL REPORT (US/0893-4975) [04675548] **4566**

NAPLES MONITOR, THE (US) [14563873] **5752**

NAPO NEWS (CN/0820-7364) [09938423] **5297**

NAPOLEON HOMESTEAD (US) [02251260] **5726**

NAPOLI NOBILISSIMA (IT/0027-7835) [01758998] 304, 2829, **325**

NAPPANEE ADVANCE-NEWS (US) [15649036] **5665**

NAPRALERT [ONLINE DATABASE] (US) 4316, **4334**

NAPSAC DIRECTORY OF ALTERNATIVE BIRTH SERVICES AND CONSUMER GUIDE (US/0273-3730) [07039458] **3765**

NAPSAC NEWS (US/0192-1223) [04964787] 1067, **589**

NAQSH (PK) [04444895] **3414**

NARA IGAKU ZASSHI (JA/0469-5550) [09533847] **3618**

NARA-KEN NOGYO SHIKENJO KENKYU HOKOKU (JA/0388-8371) [10383374] **110**

NARA KOGYO KOTO SENMON GAKKO KENKYU KIYO (JA/0387-1150) [10339890] 1093, **5130**

NARA KOKURITSU HAKUBUTSUKAN NEMPO (JA) [02245333] **4093**

NARA KYOIKU DAIGAKU KIYO. SHIZEN KAGAKU (JA/0547-2407) [09534386] **5130**

NARA NEWS (US/0730-014X) [05748854] **1135**

NARA PYLON : OFFICIAL PUBLICATION OF THE NATIONAL AIR RACING ASSOCIATION (US/1059-745X) [24706197] **4905**

NARAS JOURNAL (US/1051-5097) [21984638] **5318**

NARAYANGANJ CHAMBER OF COMMERCE AND INDUSTRY *See* CHAMBER NEWS - NARAYANGANJ CHAMBER OF COMMERCE & INDUSTRY **818**

NARC (KITCHENER) (CN/1185-880X) [25423236] **325**

NARC OFFICER, THE (US/0889-7794) [12882655] **3170**

●NARCOMAFIE (IT) **3170**

NARCOTIC DRUGS : ESTIMATED WORLD REQUIREMENTS FOR ..., STATISTICS FOR ... (US/1013-3453) [19498070] **4316**

NARCOTICS AND DRUG ABUSE (US/0094-3991) [01794145] **1347**

NARCOTICS CONTROL DIGEST *See* NARCOTICS ENFORCEMENT & PREVENTION DIGEST **1347**

NARCOTICS DEMAND REDUCTION *See* NARCOTICS ENFORCEMENT & PREVENTION DIGEST **1347**

●NARCOTICS ENFORCEMENT & PREVENTION DIGEST (US) 3013, **1347**

NARCOTICS LAW BULLETIN (US/8755-8289) [07182033] 1347, **3013**

NARCOTICS PROGRESS REPORT (HK) [01788235] **1347**

NARD JOURNAL (US/0027-5972) [01695474] **4317**

NARDA NEWS (US/0047-8717) [03249595] **2812**

NAREIF HANDBOOK OF MEMBER TRUSTS *See* REIT HANDBOOK OF MEMBER TRUSTS **912**

NARENDRA DEVA JOURNAL OF AGRICULTURAL RESEARCH (II/0970-230X) [23249809] **110**

NARF LEGAL REVIEW, THE (US/0739-862X) [09820585] **3013**

NARINGSFORSKNING *See* SCANDINAVIAN JOURNAL OF NUTRITION NARINGSFORSKNING **4199**

NARINGSFORSKNING. SUPPLEMENT (SW/0346-7104) [02336652] **4194**

NARITA: NARITASAN REIKOKAN SHIRYOKAN HO (JA) [04486212] **2659**

NARITASAN BUKKYO KENKYUJO KIYO (JA) [03931313] **5021**

NARKOSTATISTIK (DK) [19419788] **1347**

NARKOTIKAUTVECKLINGEN (SW/0346-5632) [10078696] **1347**

●NAROD I DEMOKRATIIA (UZ/0869-0685) [26143967] **4482**

NAROD POLSKI (US/0027-7894) [04129015] **5032**

NARODEN ARKHEOLOGICHESKI MUZEI *See* RAZKOPKI I PROUCHVANIIA. FOUILLES ET RECHERCHES **280**

NARODNA ARMIJA (YU/0027-7908) [06386222] **4052**

NARODNA BANKA FNRJ. CENTRALA ZA LR SLOVENIJO *See* BANCNI VESTNIK **774**

NARODNA BIBLIOTEKA SR SRBIJE *See* GODISNJAK - NARODNA BIBLIOTEKA SRBIJE **3212**

NARODNA OBRODA (XO) [21989238] **5810**

NARODNA TVORCHIST TA ETNOGRAFIIA (UN/0130-6936) [02111261] 2322, **374**

NARODNA UMJETNOST (CI) [02264534] **2322**

NARODNA VOLYA (US) **2519**

NARODNA ZDRAVSTVENA KULTURA U SR SRBIJI (YU/0351-7462) [05972659] **3618**

NARODNAIA HAZETA : ORHAN VIARKHOUNAHA SAVETA BELARUSKAI SSR (BW) [24297630] **5779**

NARODNI KNIHOVNA (XR/0862-7487) [23749837] **3232**

NARODNO STVARALASTVO. FOLKLOR (YU/0027-8017) [03617337] **2322**

NARODNO ZEMEDELSKO ZNAME (US/8755-9706) [11432697] **4482**

NARODNOE HOZAJSTVO UKRAINSKOJ SSR. STATISTICESKIJ EZEGODNIK (UN/0258-0780) [03178843] **5334**

NARODNOE KHOZIAISTVO LATVIISKOI SSR (LV/01795946] **800**

NARODNOE KHOZIAISTVO LENINGRADA I LENINGRADSKOI OBLASTI (RU) [04082100] **5334**

NARODNOE KHOZIAISTVO SOTSIALISTICHESKIKH STRAN V ... GODU : SOOBSHCHENIIA TSSU / INSTITUT EKONOMIKI MIROVOI SOTSIALISTICHESKOI SISTEMY AN SSSR, SEKTOR STATISTIKI (RU) [01607952] **5334**

NARODNOE KHOZIAISTVO SSSR / TSENTRALNOE STATISTICHESKOE UPRAVLENIE PRI SOVETE MINISTROV SSSR (RU/0469-5941) [01216180] **1536**

NARODNOE KHOZIAISTVO SSSR V *See* STRANY CHLENY SODRUZHESTVA NEZAVISIMYHK GOSUDARSTV **1540**

NARODNOE OBRAZOVANIE (RU/0027-8033) [01759000] **1766**

NARODNY FRONT SLOVENSKEJ SOCIALISTICKEJ REPUBLIKY. USTREDNY VYBOR *See* BULLETIN USTREDNEHO VYBORU NARODNEHO FRONTU SLOVENSKEJ SOCIALISTICKEJ REPUBLIKY **4635**

NARODNYI DEPUTAT (RU/0236-0918) [21313586] **4668**

NARODOPISNA REVUE (XR/0862-8351) [24255660] **242**

NARODY AZII I AFRIKI (URR/0027-8041) [01695516] **2642**

NARRAGANSETT TIMES (WAKEFIELD, R.I. : 1889) *See* CHARIHO TIMES (1993), THE **5741**

NARRANGANSETT MARINE LABORATORY *See* OCCASIONAL PUBLICATION - NARRAGANSETT MARINE LABORATORY **1453**

●NARRATIVE (COLUMBUS, OHIO) (US/1063-3685) [25993282] **3414**

NARRIA (SP) [06125856] **2322**

NARROW FABRICS (US/0149-032X) [03092544] 5354, **3485**

NARROW GAUGE AND SHORT LINE GAZETTE (US/0148-2122) [03282994] **5433**

NARTE NEWS (US/0898-0373) [17716817] **1160**

NARTY KRAKOW (PL/0860-9519) [I08609519] **4905**

NARU SIJIP / NARU MUNHAKHOE (KO) [09167528] **3466**

NAS GOLOS (US/0744-737X) [03523573] **2268**

NAS JEZIK (YU/0027-8084) [02264549] **3305**

NAS SOVREMENNIK (RU/0027-8238) [04895482] **3348**

NASA CONFERENCE PUBLICATION (US/0191-7811) [03619988] **29**

NASA CONTRACTOR REPORT (US/0565-7059) [02176408] **29**

NASA EARTH RESOURCES SURVEY PROGRAM *CEASED*. (US/0364-6440) [02576110] **1358**

NASA GAZETA (CN/0832-1329) [15310249] **2922**

NASA GEODYNAMICS PROGRAM ANNUAL REPORT FOR ... / GEODYNAMICS PROGRAM OFFICE, NASA OFFICE OF SPACE AND TERRESTRIAL APPLICATIONS (US) [09461140] **29**

NASA MAGAZINE *CEASED*. (US) [24813648] **29**

NASA/MSFC FY- ... ATMOSPHERIC PROCESSES RESEARCH REVIEW (US) [10171842] **1432**

NASA/MSFC FY ... GLOBAL SCALE ATMOSPHERIC PROCESSES RESEARCH PROGRAM REVIEW (US) [25154486] **29**

NASA NADA (US/0164-470X) [04750316] **5665**

NASA PATENT ABSTRACTS BIBLIOGRAPHY (US) [24342715] **29**

NASA REFERENCE PUBLICATION (US/0148-8589) [03301182] **29**

NASA SPACE SYSTEMS TECHNOLOGY MODEL (US/0273-4362) [07040166] **29**

NASA SPECIAL PUBLICATIONS / NATIONAL AERONAUTICS AND SPACE ADMINISTRATION, U.S.A (US) [10553995] **29**

NASA TECH BRIEFS (WASHINGTON, D.C. 1976) (US/0145-319X) [02600819] **5130**

NASA TECHNICAL MEMORANDUM (US/0499-9320) [11202069] **29**

NASA TECHNICAL PAPER (US/0148-8341) [03302098] **29**

NASA TECHNICAL REPORT (US/0077-314X) [01628039] **29**

NASA TECHNICAL TRANSLATION (US/0499-9355) [02172821] **30**

NASA TOTAL QUALITY MANAGEMENT ... ACCOMPLISHMENT REPORT (US/1051-225X) [21896508] **30**

NASADAD ALCOHOL AND DRUG ABUSE REPORT. MONTHLY REPORT (US/0270-2770) [06390987] **1347**

NASADAD ALCOHOL AND DRUG ABUSE REPORT. SPECIAL REPORT (US/0270-2789) [06398490] **1347**

NASA'S UNIVERSITY PROGRAM (US/0566-9847) [01768507] 1836, **30**

NASBA DIGEST OF STATE ACCOUNTANCY LAWS AND STATE BOARD REGULATIONS (US/0161-4290) [03916713] 748, **3013**

NASBO NEWSLETTER (US/0363-4965) [02466579] **4738**

NASC CONFERENCE REPORTER (US) [01783700] **1766**

NASCAR NEWS (US) [19758040] **5421**

NASCERE (IT) **2922**

NASCITA ATTIVA (IT) **3789**

NASDAQ FACT BOOK & COMPANY DIRECTORY (US) [23553524] **696**

NASDAQ YELLOW BOOK *CEASED*. (US/1058-2886) [24255550] **696**

NASE DEJINY *CEASED*. (US/0745-239X) [08968705] **2461**

NASE GRADEVINARSTVO (YU) **621**

NASE LIECIVE RASTLINY (XO) [06458470] **4317**

NASE REC (XR/0027-8203) [02980565] **3305**

NASE RODINA (SAINT PAUL, MINN.) (US/1045-8190) [20289764] **2461**

NASE SNAHY, CASOPIS STALEJ KONFERENCIE SLOVENSKYCH DEMOKRATICKYCH EXULANTOV (US/0547-3128) [01681286] **1920**

NASE STARINE (BN/0547-3136) [06058524] 359, 2699, **304**

NASE ZAJEDNISTVO (CN/0824-3522) [10420486] **4979**

NASE ZITTJA (US/0740-0225) [06406324] **5562**

NASELENIE (BU/0205-0617) [15181845] **4555**

NASFAA NEWSLETTER (US/0882-4630) [11891123] **1866**

NASH & CIBINIC REPORT, THE (US/0891-9291) [15032757] 3013, **4668**

●NASH DAGESTAN (RU) [25798654] 2268, **2699**

NASH DOM : [IZDANIE NA KOMITETA ZA KULTURA] (BU/0204-5060) [10199423] **2902**

NASH NOTATIONS (US/8756-4726) [11564532] **2461**

NASH SVIT (US/0027-8246) [02264560] **2747**

NASHARA AL-GHADA'ID AL-ALAMIYYAH (ARABIC ED.) (CN/0821-4964) [09981942] **4482**

NASHE SLOVO (WARSAW, POLAND) (PL) [11063670] **2268**

NASHI DEBIUTANTY (RU) [11983542] **5366**

NASHR-I DANISH (IR/0259-9090) [10153141] **5044**

NASHR-I RIYAZI (IR/1015-2857) [10152857] **3523**

NASHRAH AL-IKHBARIYAH (RESEARCH CENTRE FOR ISLAMIC HISTORY, ART, AND CULTURE) (TU) [11093439] 2851, **325**

NASHRAH (NICOSIA, CYPRUS) (CY) [11325519] **4483**

NASHRAT MAHAD SHUUN AL-AQALLIYAT AL-MUSLIMAH, JAMIAT AL-MALIK ABD AL-AZIZ BI-JIDDAH (SU) [06634819] **5044**

NASHRAT MARKAZ AL-ABHATH WA-AL-DIRASAT AL-ARABIYAH (LE) [11476575] **3305**

NASHRAT MUNAZZAMAT AL-AQTAR AL-ARABIYA AL-MUSADDIRAH LIL-BITRUL (KU) [05199395] **1619**

NASHRIYAH AL-IHSAIYAH AL-SANAWIYAH LIL-MAGHRIB *See* ANNUAIRE STATISTIQUE DU MAROC (RABAT, MOROCCO : 1982) **5321**

NASHRIYAH-I ANJUMANHA-YI DANISHJUYAN-I MUSALMAN, URUPA VA AMRIKA (FR) [21066329] **4543**

NASHRIYYAH-I SHIMI VA-MUHANDISI-I SHIMI-I IRAN (IR/1011-3509) [19300904] 2015, **987**

NASHUA DAILY TELEGRAPH (US) [11253677] **5708**

NASHUA REPORTER AND WEEKLY NASHUA POST, THE (US) [13910281] **5672**

NASHVILLE AREA CHAMBER OF COMMERCE BUSINESS DIRECTORY (US/0278-3223) [05742413] **696**

NASHVILLE BANNER (US) [09426483] **5745**

NASHVILLE BUSINESS AND LIFESTYLES (US/1052-4215) [22287515] **2490**

NASHVILLE BUSINESS JOURNAL (US/0889-2873) [13832200] **696**

NASHVILLE CABLEGUIDE (US/1058-1782) [24233292] **1135**

NASHVILLE CITY GUIDE (US/0278-6036) [07831775] **2747**

NASHVILLE INDEX (US/1056-2664) [23612361] **2539**

NASHVILLE RECORD, THE (US) [19252515] 3013, **696**

NASHVILLE WEST (US) [02244438] **4139**

NASHWAUK HERALD *See* EASTERN ITASCAN, THE **5695**

NASIG NEWSLETTER, THE (US/0892-1733) [13087404] **3232**

NASLEDSTVO (BU) [25858366] **2700**

NASPA JOURNAL (US/0027-6014) [03235174] **1866**

NASPO NEWSLETTER (US/0469-7928) [04582017] **950**

NASSA NEWS (US/8756-0925) [09443652] **325**

NASSAU COUNTY BAR ASSOCIATION ANNUAL DIRECTORY (US/0197-0968) [04327042] **3013**

NASSAU COUNTY HISTORICAL JOURNAL *See* NASSAU COUNTY HISTORICAL SOCIETY JOURNAL, THE **2747**

NASSAU COUNTY HISTORICAL SOCIETY *See* NASSAU COUNTY HISTORICAL SOCIETY JOURNAL, THE **2747**

NASSAU COUNTY HISTORICAL SOCIETY JOURNAL, THE (US/0094-9450) [01795470] **2747**

NASSAU GUARDIAN AND BAHAMA ISLANDS ADVOCATE AND INTELLIGENCER *See* NASSAU GUARDIAN, THE **5778**

NASSAU GUARDIAN, THE (BF) [09953020] **5778**

NASSAU LITERARY REVIEW, THE (US/0883-2374) [11884552] **1093**

NASSAU REVIEW, THE (US/0077-2879) [02264570] **2851**

NASSAUISCHE ANNALEN (GW/0077-2887) [02531330] **2700**

NASSP BULLETIN (US/0192-6365) [04248543] **1866**

NASSP NATIONAL ADVISORY LIST OF CONTESTS AND ACTIVITIES (US) [14712025] **1766**

NASSP NEWSLEADER (US/0278-0569) [07688570] **1866**

NASTAWGAN (CN/0828-1327) [12847239] 4875, **594**

NASTOLATKI WARSZAWA (PL/0867-4787) [I08674787] **1067**

NASW NEWS (US/0027-6022) [08734715] **5297**

NASW REGISTER OF CLINICAL SOCIAL WORKERS (US/0277-0695) [02676444] **5297**

NASZE PROBLEMY (PL) [02244304] **4817**

NATA DIRECTORY SYDNEY (AT/0311-8185) [I03118185] **2123**

NATA NEWS SYDNEY (AT/0311-662X) [I0311662X] **2123**

NATAL. AUDIT OFFICE *See* PROVINSIALE OUDITEUR SE VERSLAG VOOR DIE MIDDELEREKENINGS EN DIE FINANSIEREKENINGS, DIE **4742**

NATAL. AUDIT OFFICE. FINANCE ACCOUNTS (INCLUDING TRUST, HOUSING LOAN AND VILLAGE WATER SUPPLY ACCOUNTS) TEACHERS' PENSION AND PROVIDENT FUNDS ACCOUNTS AND APPROPRIATION ACCOUNTS ... WITH THE PROVINCIAL AUDITOR'S REPORTS THEREON *See* PROVINSIALE OUDITEUR SE VERSLAG VOOR DIE MIDDELEREKENINGS EN DIE FINANSIEREKENINGS, DIE **4742**

NATAL MUSEUM JOURNAL OF HUMANITIES (SA/1015-0935) [20864354] **2851**

NATAL MUSEUM, PIETERMARITZBURG *See* ANNALS OF THE NATAL MUSEUM, PIETERMARITZBURG **4162**

NATAL PROVINCIAL LIBRARY SERVICE *See* ANNUAL REPORT - NATAL PROVINCIAL LIBRARY SERVICE AND MUSEUM SERVICES **3190**

NATAL (SOUTH AFRICA). DEVELOPMENT AND SERVICES BOARD *See* ANNUAL REPORT FOR PERIOD ... / DEVELOPMENT AND SERVICES BOARD (NATAL) **4765**

NATAL (SOUTH AFRICA). DEVELOPMENT AND SERVICES BOARD. ANNUAL REPORT OF THE MEDICAL OFFICER OF HEALTH *See* ANNUAL REPORT FOR PERIOD ... / DEVELOPMENT AND SERVICES BOARD (NATAL) **4765**

NATALIA (SA/0085-3674) [02505893] **2642**

NATASHA. [CD-ROM] (US) **3765**

NATATION (PARIS) (FR/1169-8152) [11698152] **4852**

NATAT'S REPORTER (US/0735-9691) [09047048] **4668**

NATCHEZ DEMOCRAT (1916), THE (US/0888-8744) [09150665] **5701**

NATCHEZ TRACE NEWSLETTER (US/0739-1412) [07633923] **2461**

NATCHEZ TRACE TRAVELER (US/0738-985X) [09057346] **2461**

NATCHITOCHES GENEALOGIST, THE (US/0742-5872) [07427613] **2461**

NATCHITOCHES TIMES, THE (US) [08784594] **5684**

NATCON (CN/0319-9495) [10356009] **1692**

NATE NEWS HUDDERSFIELD (UK/0143-4136) [I01434136] 1901, **3305**

NATFHE HANDBOOK, THE (UK) [18479719] **1836**

NATFHE JOURNAL (UK/0308-1907) [I03081907] **1836**

NATHANIEL HAWTHORNE REVIEW : THE OFFICIAL PUBLICATION OF THE NATHANIEL HAWTHORNE SOCIETY, THE (US/0890-4197) [13638862] **3348**

NATICK BULLETIN (1982) (US/0895-7681) [16848736] **5689**

NATION (TH) **5811**

NATION AND THE WORLD (II) [25130404] **4529**

NATION DJIBOUTI, LA (FT) [25311882] **5799**

NATION, LA (DM) [24648473] **5778**

NATION (NEW YORK, N.Y.), THE (US/0027-8378) [01643268] **3348**

NATION ROUMAINE B.-ORGANE DU CONSEIL DES PARTIS POLITIQUES ROUMAINS (FR) [02264572] **4483**

NATION THIS MONTH *See* NATION THIS QUARTER / GOVERNMENT INFORMATION SERVICE, THE **2747**

●NATION THIS QUARTER / GOVERNMENT INFORMATION SERVICE, THE (XM) [26712822] **2747**

NATIONAL 5-PIN BOWLERS NEWS (CN/0705-7423) [04233425] **4906**

NATIONAL ABORTION FEDERATION (U.S.) *See* MEMBERSHIP DIRECTORY - NATIONAL ABORTION FEDERATION **3765**

NATIONAL ACAC JOURNAL (US/0027-8599) [01641382] **1836**

NATIONAL ACADEMY OF ARBITRATORS. MEETING *See* PROCEEDINGS OF THE ANNUAL MEETING - NATIONAL ACADEMY OF ARBITRATORS. MEETING **2868**

NATIONAL ACADEMY OF MEDICAL SCIENCES (INDIA) *See* ANNALS OF THE NATIONAL ACADEMY OF MEDICAL SCIENCES (INDIA) **3550**

NATIONAL ACADEMY OF SCIENCES, INDIA *See* NATIONAL ACADEMY SCIENCE LETTERS **5130**

NATIONAL ACADEMY OF SCIENCES, INDIA *See* ANNUAL NUMBER / NATIONAL ACADEMY OF SCIENCES, INDIA **5083**

NATIONAL ACADEMY OF SCIENCES PUBLICATION (US) [05723021] **5130**

NATIONAL ACADEMY OF SCIENCES (U.S.) *See* PROCEEDINGS OF THE NATIONAL ACADEMY OF SCIENCE OF THE UNITED STATES OF AMERICA **5141**

NATIONAL ACADEMY OF SCIENCES (U.S.) *See* REPORT OF THE TREASURER FOR THE FISCAL YEAR ENDED JUNE 30 ... / NATIONAL ACADEMY OF SCIENCES, INCLUDING NATIONAL ACADEMY OF ENGINEERING, NATIONAL RESEARCH COUNCIL AND INSTITUTE OF MEDICINE **5146**

NATIONAL ACADEMY OF SCIENCES (U.S.) *See* BIOGRAPHICAL MEMOIRS **430**

NATIONAL ACADEMY SCIENCE LETTERS (II/0250-541X) [04389308] **5130**

NATIONAL ACCIDENT SAMPLING SYSTEM (US/0741-1723) [10082632] **5401**

NATIONAL ACCOUNTS ESA, AGGREGATES (LU) [04042845] **4738**

NATIONAL ACCOUNTS STATISTICS (AM) [19660044] 1575, **1536**

NATIONAL ACCOUNTS STATISTICS. ANALYSIS OF MAIN AGGREGATES (US) [12260297] **1506**

NATIONAL ACCOUNTS STATISTICS. MAIN AGGREGATES AND DETAILED TABLES (US) [12148091] 1506, **1536**

NATIONAL ACCOUNTS STATISTICS (PORT MORESBY, PAPUA NEW GUINEA (PP) [04106265] 1507, **1536**

NATIONAL ACCOUNTS. VOL. 1, MAIN AGGREGATES / OCED, DEPARTMENT OF ECONOMICS AND STATISTICS (FR) [11049119] **1638**

NATIONAL AD SEARCH, THE (US/0744-7140) [08507973] **4206**

NATIONAL ADVERTISING DIVISION CASE REPORT (US) [09635347] **1298**

NATIONAL ADVERTISING INVESTMENTS IN NEWSPAPERS (US/0732-541X) [05854098] **762**

NATIONAL ADVERTISING INVESTMENTS ON MEDIA RECORDS NEWSPAPERS *See* NATIONAL ADVERTISING INVESTMENTS IN NEWSPAPERS **762**

NATIONAL ADVISORY BOARD FOR WILD FREE-ROAMING HORSES AND BURROS *See* PROCEEDINGS - NATIONAL ADVISORY BOARD FOR WILD FREE-ROAMING HORSES & BURROS **2801**

NATIONAL ADVISORY COUNCIL ON ADULT EDUCATION (U.S.) *See* NACAE ANNUAL REPORT **1801**

NATIONAL ADVISORY COUNCIL ON MATERNAL, INFANT, AND FETAL NUTRITION ... BIENNIAL REPORT (US) [07792234] **3765**

NATIONAL ADVISORY COUNCIL ON THE EDUCATION OF DISADVANTAGED CHILDREN (U.S.) *See* ANNUAL REPORT TO THE PRESIDENT AND THE CONGRESS - NATIONAL ADVISORY COUNCIL ON THE EDUCATION OF DISADVANTAGED CHILDREN **1875**

NATIONAL ADVISORY ENVIRONMENTAL HEALTH SCIENCES COUNCIL *See* ANNUAL REPORT - NATIONAL ADVISORY ENVIRONMENTAL HEALTH SCIENCES COUNCIL, NATIONAL INSTITUTES OF HEALTH **2161**

NATIONAL ADVISORY EYE COUNCIL (U.S.). MEETING *See* MINUTES OF MEETING / NATIONAL ADVISORY EYE COUNCIL **3876**

NATIONAL AERONAUTICS (US/0005-2116) [01786116] 4906, **30**

NATIONAL AEROSPACE STANDARDS (US) [06839065] **5130**

NATIONAL AEROSPACE STANDARDS COMMITTEE (U.S.) *See* NATIONAL AEROSPACE STANDARDS **5130**

NATIONAL AGRICULTURAL LIBRARY (U.S.) *See* LIBRARY LIST **3226**

NATIONAL AGRICULTURAL LIBRARY (US) *See* QUICK BIBLIOGRAPHY SERIES - NATIONAL AGRICULTURAL LIBRARY **124**

NATIONAL AGRICULTURAL PLASTICS CONFERENCE. PROCEEDINGS ... NATIONAL AGRICULTURAL PLASTICS CONFERENCE *See* PROCEEDINGS OF THE ... NATIONAL AGRICULTURAL PLASTICS CONGRESS **4459**

NATIONAL AGRICULTURAL RESEARCH PROGRAMME (TZ) [03954447] **110**

NATIONAL AGRICULTURAL SOCIETY OF CEYLON *See* JOURNAL OF THE NATIONAL AGRICULTURAL SOCIETY OF CEYLON **101**

NATIONAL AIDS BULLETIN / AUSTRALIAN FEDERATION OF AIDS ORGANISATIONS INC (AT/1030-5289) [20351147] **3715**

NATIONAL AIDS INFORMATION CLEARINGHOUSE CONFERENCE CALENDAR (US) [23595268] 3715, **3675**

NATIONAL AIR AND SPACE MUSEUM OCCASIONAL PAPER SERIES (US/1059-6127) [24647455] **30**

NATIONAL AIR POLLUTION SURVEILLANCE *CEASED.* (CN) [02248818] **2237**

NATIONAL AIR POLLUTION SURVEILLANCE. ANNUAL SUMMARY (CN/0381-2995) [02244663] **2237**

NATIONAL AIRCRAFT STANDARDS *See* NATIONAL AEROSPACE STANDARDS **5130**

NATIONAL AIRPORT SYSTEM PLAN (US/0161-3103) [03895345] **30**

NATIONAL AIRSPACE SYSTEM PLAN. ENGINEERING AND DEVELOPMENT (US/0747-976X) [10811881] **30**

NATIONAL ALLIANCE (US/0027-8513) [01776083] 4668, **1692**

NATIONAL ALUMNI DIRECTORY - ITHACA COLLEGE (US/0737-6596) [07613354] **1102**

NATIONAL AMATEUR ASTRONOMY NEWS (US/1044-7059) [19869643] **397**

NATIONAL-AMERICAN WHOLESALE GROCERS' ASSOCIATION *See* NAWGA DIRECTORY OF MEMBERS **2351**

NATIONAL AND FEDERAL LEGAL EMPLOYMENT REPORT, THE (US/0733-3285) [08566476] **3013**

NATIONAL AND INTERNATIONAL RELIGION REPORT (US) **4980**

NATIONAL APPLE NEWS / INTERNATIONAL APPLE INSTITUTE (US) [04912205] **2424**

NATIONAL APPLIANCE AND RADIO-TV DEALERS ASSOCIATION *See* NARDA NEWS **2812**

NATIONAL AQUATICS JOURNAL (US) [19211093] **4906**

NATIONAL AQUATICS JOURNAL (US) **4906**

NATIONAL ARCHIVES NEWSLETTER (CN/0824-8907) [11180172] **2482**

NATIONAL ARCHIVES OF CANADA *See* INTERFAX (OTTAWA) **4657**

NATIONAL ARCHIVES OF CANADA *See* STRATEGIC APPROACHES OF THE NATIONAL ARCHIVES OF CANADA **2484**

NATIONAL ARCHIVES OF RHODESIA *See* REPORT OF THE DIRECTOR OF NATIONAL ARCHIVES **2483**

NATIONAL ART-COLLECTIONS FUND (GREAT BRITAIN) *See* NATIONAL ART-COLLECTIONS FUND REVIEW **359**

NATIONAL ART-COLLECTIONS FUND (GREAT BRITAIN) *See* NACF MAGAZINE **359**

NATIONAL ART-COLLECTIONS FUND REVIEW (UK) [10193316] **359**

NATIONAL ARTIST SURVEY (US/1043-9900) [19580043] **359**

NATIONAL ARTS & CRAFTS NETWORK *See* SAC NEWS MONTHLY **5684**

NATIONAL ARTS FOUNDATION OF RHODESIA *See* ANNUAL REPORT AND BALANCE SHEET AND REVENUE AND EXPENDITURE ACCOUNT **312**

NATIONAL ASIAN PACIFIC AMERICAN BAR ASSOCIATION *See* DIRECTORY / NATIONAL ASIAN PACIFIC AMERICAN BAR ASSOCIATION **2961**

NATIONAL ASSOCIATION FOR BUSINESS TEACHER EDUCATION *See* NABTE REVIEW **696**

NATIONAL ASSOCIATION FOR FOREIGN STUDENT ADVISERS. NAFSA STUDIES AND PAPERS. ENGLISH LANGUAGE SERIES *See* NAFSA STUDIES AND PAPERS. ENGLISH LANGUAGE SERIES **3304**

NATIONAL ASSOCIATION FOR FOREIGN STUDENT AFFAIRS *See* NAFSA STUDIES AND PAPERS. ENGLISH LANGUAGE SERIES **3304**

NATIONAL ASSOCIATION FOR GIRLS & WOMEN IN SPORT *See* NAGWS SOFTBALL GUIDE **4905**

NATIONAL ASSOCIATION FOR GIRLS & WOMEN IN SPORT *See* OFFICIAL VOLLEYBALL RULES FOR GIRLS AND WOMEN **4910**

NATIONAL ASSOCIATION FOR GIRLS & WOMEN IN SPORT *See* NATIONAL ASSOCIATION FOR GIRLS & WOMEN IN SPORT **4906**

NATIONAL ASSOCIATION FOR GIRLS & WOMEN IN SPORT *See* NAGWS VOLLEYBALL GUIDE **4905**

NATIONAL ASSOCIATION FOR GIRLS & WOMEN IN SPORT (US) [15097000] 5562, **4906**

NATIONAL ASSOCIATION FOR LAW PLACEMENT MEMBERSHIP DIRECTORY (US/0272-6025) [06865871] **3013**

NATIONAL ASSOCIATION FOR LAW PLACEMENT (U.S.) *See* NATIONAL ASSOCIATION FOR LAW PLACEMENT MEMBERSHIP DIRECTORY **3013**

NATIONAL ASSOCIATION FOR MUSIC THERAPY *See* MEMBERSHIP DIRECTORY / NATIONAL ASSOCIATION FOR MUSIC THERAPY **4130**

NATIONAL ASSOCIATION FOR OLMSTED PARKS (US/0895-819X) [07010898] **4707**

NATIONAL ASSOCIATION FOR THE ADVANCEMENT OF WHITE PEOPLE *See* NAAWP NEWS : PUBLICATION OF THE NATIONAL ASSOCIATION FOR THE ADVANCEMENT OF WHITE PEOPLE **5684**

NATIONAL ASSOCIATION OF ACADEMIES OF SCIENCE (U.S.) *See* PROCEEDINGS, DIRECTORY AND HANDBOOK OF THE NATIONAL ASSOCIATION OF ACADEMIES OF SCIENCE, THE **5140**

NATIONAL ASSOCIATION OF ACADEMIES OF SCIENCE (U.S.) *See* DIRECTORY, PROCEEDINGS, AND HANDBOOK **5100**

NATIONAL ASSOCIATION OF ACADEMIES OF SCIENCE (U.S.). PROCEEDINGS, DIRECTORY AND HANDBOOK OF THE NATIONAL ASSOCIATION OF ACADEMIES OF SCIENCE *See* DIRECTORY, PROCEEDINGS, AND HANDBOOK **5100**

NATIONAL ASSOCIATION OF ADVISORS FOR THE HEALTH PROFESSIONS See DIRECTORY OF THE NATIONAL ASSOCIATION OF ADVISORS FOR THE HEALTH PROFESSIONS 3913

NATIONAL ASSOCIATION OF ADVISORS FOR THE HEALTH PROFESSIONS See ANNUAL MEMBERSHIP DIRECTORY - NATIONAL ASSOCIATION OF ADVISORS FOR THE HEALTH PROFESSIONS 3913

NATIONAL ASSOCIATION OF ADVISORS FOR THE HEALTH PROFESSIONS. DIRECTORY OF THE NATIONAL ASSOCIATION OF ADVISORS FOR THE HEALTH PROFESSIONS See ANNUAL MEMBERSHIP DIRECTORY - NATIONAL ASSOCIATION OF ADVISORS FOR THE HEALTH PROFESSIONS 3913

NATIONAL ASSOCIATION OF ATTORNEYS GENERAL. COMMITTEE ON THE OFFICE OF ATTORNEY GENERAL See SELECTED STATISTICS ON THE OFFICE OF ATTORNEY GENERAL 3083

NATIONAL ASSOCIATION OF AWARENESS IN MUSIC See NAAM 4139

NATIONAL ASSOCIATION OF BOARDS OF PHARMACY See PROCEEDINGS OF THE ANNUAL MEETING 4325

NATIONAL ASSOCIATION OF BROADCAST EMPLOYEES AND TECHNICIANS See NABET NEWS. INTERNATIONAL EDITION 1135

NATIONAL ASSOCIATION OF BUSINESS ECONOMISTS (U.S.) See MEMBERSHIP DIRECTORY / NATIONAL ASSOCIATION OF BUSINESS ECONOMISTS 1504

NATIONAL ASSOCIATION OF BUSINESS ECONOMISTS (U.S.) See BUSINESS ECONOMICS. MEMBERSHIP DIRECTORY 1466

NATIONAL ASSOCIATION OF CANADIANS OF ORIGINS IN INDIA See NACOI FORUM 2268

NATIONAL ASSOCIATION OF CEMETERIES See DIRECTORY OF MEMBERS, LOT EXCHANGE, MAUSOLEUM CRYPT EXCHANGE, DOLLAR CREDIT PLANS 2407

NATIONAL ASSOCIATION OF COLLEGE ADMISSIONS COUNSELORS See GOVERNANCE DIRECTORY 1825

NATIONAL ASSOCIATION OF COLLEGE ADMISSIONS COUNSELORS See NATIONAL ACAC JOURNAL 1836

NATIONAL ASSOCIATION OF COLLEGE ADMISSIONS COUNSELORS See MEMBERSHIP DIRECTORY - NATIONAL ASSOCIATION OF COLLEGE ADMISSIONS COUNSELORS 1835

NATIONAL ASSOCIATION OF COLLEGE AND UNIVERSITY BUSINESS OFFICERS See FEDERAL REGULATIONS AND THE EMPLOYMENT PRACTICES OF COLLEGES AND UNIVERSITIES 1669

NATIONAL ASSOCIATION OF COLLEGE AND UNIVERSITY BUSINESS OFFICERS See NACUBO BUSINESS OFFICER 696

NATIONAL ASSOCIATION OF COLLEGE WIND AND PERCUSSION. INSTRUCTORS See N.A.C.W.P.I JOURNAL 4139

NATIONAL ASSOCIATION OF COLLEGES AND TEACHERS OF AGRICULTURE See NACTA JOURNAL 110

NATIONAL ASSOCIATION OF CONGREGATIONAL CHRISTIAN CHURCHES See YEARBOOK - NATIONAL ASSOCIATION OF CONGREGATIONAL CHRISTIAN CHURCHES, THE 5010

NATIONAL ASSOCIATION OF CONSERVATION DISTRICTS. PROCEEDINGS OF THE ANNUAL CONVENTION See PROCEEDINGS OF THE ANNUAL NACD CONVENTION 2202

NATIONAL ASSOCIATION OF CONSUMER AGENCY ADMINISTRATORS NEWS (US/0270-2835) [04816274] 1298

NATIONAL ASSOCIATION OF DESKTOP PUBLISHERS FORUM, THE (US/0897-4764) [17513200] 1196, 4817

NATIONAL ASSOCIATION OF DESKTOP PUBLISHERS JOURNAL (US) [29396883] 1196, 4817

NATIONAL ASSOCIATION OF EDUCATIONAL BUYERS See NAEB BULLETIN 950

NATIONAL ASSOCIATION OF EDUCATIONAL NEGOTIATORS (U.S.) See NAEN BULLETIN 1766

NATIONAL ASSOCIATION OF ELEMENTARY PRINCIPALS (US/0090-4805) [01784712] 1867

NATIONAL ASSOCIATION OF ELEMENTARY SCHOOL PRINCIPALS. (FOUNDED 1970) See NATIONAL ASSOCIATION OF ELEMENTARY PRINCIPALS 1867

NATIONAL ASSOCIATION OF FIRE EQUIPMENT DISTRIBUTORS (U.S.) See NAFED DIRECTORY 2291

NATIONAL ASSOCIATION OF FRIENDSHIP CENTRES See NEWSLETTER - NATIONAL ASSOCIATION OF FRIENDSHIP CENTRES 5298

NATIONAL ASSOCIATION OF FURNITURE MANUFACTURERS See FIRA NAFM 2905

NATIONAL ASSOCIATION OF HOME AND WORKSHOP WRITERS NEWSLETTER (US) 634

NATIONAL ASSOCIATION OF HOME MANUFACTURERS See GUIDE TO MANUFACTURED HOMES 615

NATIONAL ASSOCIATION OF HOUSING AND REDEVELOPMENT OFFICIALS See NAHRO ROSTER 2829

NATIONAL ASSOCIATION OF INDEPENDENT SCHOOLS See NAIS MEMBER SCHOOL TUITION FEES, FACULTY SALARIES, AND ADMINISTRATIVE SALARIES 1866

NATIONAL ASSOCIATION OF INDEPENDENT SCHOOLS See ANNUAL REPORT - NATIONAL ASSOCIATION OF INDEPENDENT SCHOOLS 1725

NATIONAL ASSOCIATION OF INDEPENDENT SCHOOLS. NAIS MEMBER SCHOOL TUITION FEES, FACULTY SALARIES, AND ADMINISTRATIVE SALARIES See TUITIONS AND SALARIES 1873

NATIONAL ASSOCIATION OF INSURANCE COMMISSIONERS See NAIC MALPRACTICE CLAIMS 2888

NATIONAL ASSOCIATION OF INSURANCE COMMISSIONERS See FINANCIAL REVIEW OF ALIEN INSURERS 2880

NATIONAL ASSOCIATION OF INSURANCE COMMISSIONERS. MEETING See PROCEEDINGS OF THE NATIONAL ASSOCIATION OF INSURANCE COMMISSIONERS 2890

NATIONAL ASSOCIATION OF INSURANCE COMMISSIONERS. SECURITIES VALUATION OFFICE See VALUATIONS OF SECURITIES 918

NATIONAL ASSOCIATION OF INTERCOLLEGIATE ATHLETICS See NAIA NEWS 4905

NATIONAL ASSOCIATION OF MANUFACTURERS OF THE UNITED STATES OF AMERICA. POSTWAR COMMITTEE See REPORT - NATIONAL ASSOCIATION OF MANUFACTURERS OF THE UNITED STATES OF AMERICA. POSTWAR COMMITTEE 3487

NATIONAL ASSOCIATION OF MEAT PURVEYORS (U.S.) See MEMBERSHIP/COMMITTEE DIRECTORY - NATIONAL ASSOCIATION OF MEAT PURVEYORS (U.S.) 2350

NATIONAL ASSOCIATION OF METAL FINISHERS See DIRECTORY OF THE LEADING FIRMS IN THE JOB PLATING AND ENAMELING INDUSTRY 4001

NATIONAL ASSOCIATION OF MUSIC MERCHANTS (U.S.) See N.A.M.M. MUSIC RETAILER NEWS 4139

NATIONAL ASSOCIATION OF MUSICAL INSTRUMENT TECHNICIANS See NAMIT JOURNAL 4139

NATIONAL ASSOCIATION OF PARENTS & PROFESSIONALS FOR SAFE ALTERNATIVES IN CHILDBIRTH See NAPSAC DIRECTORY OF ALTERNATIVE BIRTH SERVICES AND CONSUMER GUIDE 3765

NATIONAL ASSOCIATION OF PARENTS & PROFESSIONALS FOR SAFE ALTERNATIVES IN CHILDBIRTH See NAPSAC NEWS 589

NATIONAL ASSOCIATION OF PARLIAMENTARIANS See BLUE BOOK - NATIONAL ASSOCIATION OF PARLIAMENTARIANS 4633

NATIONAL ASSOCIATION OF PERSONNEL CONSULTANTS (U.S.) See NATIONAL DIRECTORY OF PERSONNEL CONSULTANTS BY SPECIALIZATION 4206

NATIONAL ASSOCIATION OF PURCHASING MANAGEMENT See PURCHASING MANAGERS REPORT ON BUSINESS 1623

NATIONAL ASSOCIATION OF REAL ESTATE INVESTMENT TRUSTS See DIRECTORY OF MEMBERS / THE NATIONAL ASSOCIATION OF REAL ESTATE INVESTMENT TRUSTS, INC 4836

NATIONAL ASSOCIATION OF REAL ESTATE INVESTMENT TRUSTS See REIT HANDBOOK OF MEMBER TRUSTS 912

NATIONAL ASSOCIATION OF REALTORS See OPERATIONS MANUAL OF THE NATIONAL ASSOCIATION OF REALTORS 4842

NATIONAL ASSOCIATION OF REALTORS See WHO'S WHO (CHICAGO) 436

NATIONAL ASSOCIATION OF REALTORS. DEPT. OF ECONOMICS AND RESEARCH See HOME SALES YEARBOOK 4838

NATIONAL ASSOCIATION OF REALTORS. DEPT. OF ECONOMICS AND RESEARCH See EXISTING HOME SALES 4837

NATIONAL ASSOCIATION OF REGULATORY UTILITY COMMISSIONERS. ANNUAL REPORT ON UTILITY AND CARRIER REGULATION OF THE NATIONAL ASSOCIATION OF REGULATORY UTILITY COMMISSIONERS See UTILITY REGULATORY POLICY IN THE UNITED STATES AND CANADA : COMPILATION ... OF THE NATIONAL ASSOCIATION OF REGULATORY UTILITY COMMISSIONERS 4693

NATIONAL ASSOCIATION OF REGULATORY UTILITY COMMISSIONERS. CONVENTION AND REGULATORY SYMPOSIUM See PROCEEDINGS / ANNUAL CONVENTION AND REGULATORY SYMPOSIUM, NATIONAL ASSOCIATION OF REGULATORY UTILITY COMMISSIONERS 4675

NATIONAL ASSOCIATION OF RETAIL DRUGGISTS (U.S.) See N.A.R.D. JOURNAL 4316

NATIONAL ASSOCIATION OF SCHOOL PSYCHOLOGISTS See COMMUNIQUE (KENT) 4582

NATIONAL ASSOCIATION OF SCHOOLS OF ART See HANDBOOK / NATIONAL ASSOCIATION OF SCHOOLS OF ART AND DESIGN 351

NATIONAL ASSOCIATION OF SCHOOLS OF ART AND DESIGN (U.S.) See DIRECTORY / NATIONAL ASSOCIATION OF SCHOOLS OF ART AND DESIGN 319

NATIONAL ASSOCIATION OF SCHOOLS OF DANCE (U.S.) See HANDBOOK / NATIONAL ASSOCIATION OF SCHOOLS OF DANCE 1313

NATIONAL ASSOCIATION OF SCHOOLS OF MUSIC See HANDBOOK - NATIONAL ASSOCIATION OF SCHOOLS OF MUSIC 4120

NATIONAL ASSOCIATION OF SCHOOLS OF MUSIC See DIRECTORY - NATIONAL ASSOCIATION OF SCHOOLS OF MUSIC 4114

NATIONAL ASSOCIATION OF SCHOOLS OF MUSIC. MEETING See PROCEEDINGS OF THE ANNUAL MEETING - NATIONAL ASSOCIATION OF SCHOOLS OF MUSIC 4147

NATIONAL ASSOCIATION OF SCHOOLS OF THEATRE (U.S.) See HANDBOOK - NATIONAL ASSOCIATION OF SCHOOLS OF THEATRE (U.S.) 5364

NATIONAL ASSOCIATION OF SECONDARY SCHOOL PRINCIPALS (U.S.) See LEGAL MEMORANDUM (RESTON), A 3000

NATIONAL ASSOCIATION OF SECONDARY SCHOOL PRINCIPALS (U.S.) See NASSP BULLETIN 1866

NATIONAL ASSOCIATION OF SECONDARY SCHOOL PRINCIPALS (U.S.). NATIONAL COMMITTEE ON CONTESTS AND ACTIVITIES See NASSP NATIONAL ADVISORY LIST OF CONTESTS AND ACTIVITIES 1766

NATIONAL ASSOCIATION OF SECRETARIES OF STATE See NATIONAL ASSOCIATION OF SECRETARIES OF STATE HANDBOOK 4668

NATIONAL ASSOCIATION OF SECRETARIES OF STATE HANDBOOK (US/0547-4221) [01589417] 4668

NATIONAL ASSOCIATION OF SOCIAL WORKERS See NASW NEWS 5297

NATIONAL ASSOCIATION OF SOCIAL WORKERS See NASW REGISTER OF CLINICAL SOCIAL WORKERS 5297

NATIONAL ASSOCIATION OF SOCIAL WORKERS. WASHINGTON STATE CHAPTER See NEWSLETTER - NATIONAL ASSOCIATION OF SOCIAL WORKERS. WASHINGTON STATE CHAPTER 5299

NATIONAL ASSOCIATION OF STATE ALCOHOL AND DRUG ABUSE DIRECTORS See NASADAD ALCOHOL AND DRUG ABUSE REPORT. SPECIAL REPORT 1347

NATIONAL ASSOCIATION OF STATE ALCOHOL AND DRUG ABUSE DIRECTORS See NASADAD ALCOHOL AND DRUG ABUSE REPORT. MONTHLY REPORT 1347

NATIONAL ASSOCIATION OF STATE BOARDS OF ACCOUNTANCY See NASBA DIGEST OF STATE ACCOUNTANCY LAWS AND STATE BOARD REGULATIONS 3013

NATIONAL ASSOCIATION OF STATE BUDGET OFFICERS See FISCAL SURVEY OF THE STATES 4726

NATIONAL ASSOCIATION OF STATE BUDGET OFFICERS See NASBO NEWSLETTER 4738

NATIONAL — Alphabetical Title Index

NATIONAL ASSOCIATION OF STATE BUDGET OFFICERS. QUARTERLY NEWSLETTER *See* NASBO NEWSLETTER **4738**

NATIONAL ASSOCIATION OF STATE PURCHASING OFFICIALS *See* SUMMARY - ANNUAL MEETING - NATIONAL ASSOCIATION OF STATE PURCHASING OFFICIALS **952**

NATIONAL ASSOCIATION OF STATE PURCHASING OFFICIALS *See* NASPO NEWSLETTER **950**

NATIONAL ASSOCIATION OF STATE SCHOLARSHIP AND GRANT PROGRAMS (U.S.) *See* ANNUAL SURVEY - NATIONAL ASSOCIATION OF STATE SCHOLARSHIP AND GRANT PROGRAMS **1809**

NATIONAL ASSOCIATION OF STUDENT COUNCILS *See* NASC CONFERENCE REPORTER **1766**

NATIONAL ASSOCIATION OF STUDENT PERSONNEL ADMINISTRATORS (U.S.) *See* NASPA JOURNAL **1866**

NATIONAL ASSOCIATION OF SYNAGOGUE ADMINISTRATORS *See* PROCEEDINGS OF THE ANNUAL CONVENTION OF THE NATIONAL ASSOCIATION OF SYNAGOGUE ADMINISTRATORS **5052**

NATIONAL ASTRONOMICAL OBSERVATORY REPRINT (JA/0915-0021) **397**

NATIONAL AUCTION BULLETIN (US/0739-327X) [09719612] **2775**

● NATIONAL AUCTIONS & SALES (US/1055-8268) [23352200] 955, **1298**

NATIONAL AURICULA AND PRIMULA SOCIETY. SOUTHERN SECTION *See* YEAR BOOK - NATIONAL AURICULA & PRIMULA SOCIETY (SOUTHERN SECTION) **2434**

NATIONAL AUSTRALIA BANK *See* ANNUAL REPORT / NATIONAL AUSTRALIA BANK LIMITED **771**

NATIONAL AUTOMATION CONFERENCE. PROCEEDINGS *See* NATIONAL OPERATIONS AND AUTOMATION CONFERENCE PROCEEDINGS, THE **801**

NATIONAL AUTOMOBILE DEALERS ASSOCIATION *See* N.A.D.A. RECREATION VEHICLE APPRAISAL GUIDE **5388**

NATIONAL AUTOMOBILE DEALERS ASSOCIATION *See* N.A.D.A. OFFICIAL USED CAR GUIDE **5421**

NATIONAL AUTOMOBILE DEALERS ASSOCIATION *See* NADA NEWSLETTER **5421**

NATIONAL AUTOMOBILE DEALERS ASSOCIATION *See* N. A. D. A. MOTORCYCLE & MOPED APPRAISAL GUIDE **4082**

NATIONAL AVERAGE REPORT, COMMERCIAL BANKS (US) [18660048] **800**

NATIONAL AVIATION SYSTEM PLAN, THE (US/0566-6775) [03188373] **30**

NATIONAL AVIATION SYSTEM PLANNING REVIEW CONFERENCE. SUMMARY REPORT *See* CONFERENCE SUMMARY REPORT - AVIATION REVIEW CONFERENCE **17**

NATIONAL BALANCE SHEET ACCOUNTS (CN/0825-9216) [13200345] **4738**

NATIONAL BALLET MAGAZINE (CN/0845-4639) [19901164] **386**

NATIONAL BAND ASSOCIATION (U.S.) *See* DIRECTORY - NATIONAL BAND ASSOCIATION **4114**

NATIONAL BANK NEWS REVIEW (II) [16667708] **1575**

NATIONAL BANK OF GREECE REPORT (GR) [09815260] **800**

NATIONAL BANKING LAW REVIEW (CN/0822-1081) [09925311] **3087**

NATIONAL BANKRUPTCY REPORTER (US/0275-0252) [07077902] **3087**

NATIONAL BAPTIST CONVENTION OF THE UNITED STATES OF AMERICA. SPIRITUAL LIFE COMMISSION *See* NATIONAL BAPTIST WOMEN CLERGY DIRECTORY, THE **5065**

NATIONAL BAPTIST PREACHERWOMAN SERMON SERIES, THE (US/1058-5907) [24335581] **5065**

NATIONAL BAPTIST WOMEN CLERGY DIRECTORY, THE (US/1061-6225) [25276696] **5065**

NATIONAL BAR ASSOCIATION MAGAZINE (US/0741-0115) [10110859] **3013**

NATIONAL BAR BULLETIN, THE (US) [01776086] **3013**

NATIONAL BASEBALL HALL OF FAME AND MUSEUM *See* NATIONAL BASEBALL HALL OF FAME AND MUSEUM YEARBOOK **4906**

NATIONAL BASEBALL HALL OF FAME AND MUSEUM YEARBOOK (US/0278-1867) [07706203] **4906**

NATIONAL BIBLIOGRAPHY OF BARBADOS (BB) [03838928] **420**

NATIONAL BIBLIOGRAPHY OF BOTSWANA, THE (BS/0027-8777) [01588720] **420**

NATIONAL BIBLIOGRAPHY OF NIGERIA, THE (NR/0331-0019) [02380101] **420**

NATIONAL BIBLIOGRAPHY OF ZAMBIA, THE (ZA/0377-1636) [01798487] **420**

NATIONAL BILLIARD NEWS, THE (US/0747-3265) [05066148] **4906**

NATIONAL BIOGRAPHIC, THE (US) [05467687] **879**

NATIONAL BLACK LAW JOURNAL (US/0896-0194) [15539513] 2268, **3013**

NATIONAL BLOOD EXCHANGE (U.S.) *See* DIRECTORY FOR THE NATIONAL BLOOD EXCHANGE : A PROGRAM OF THE AMERICAN ASSOCIATION OF BLOOD BANKS **3771**

NATIONAL BLUEGRASS MUSIC NEWS, THE (US/0147-9938) [03251905] **4139**

NATIONAL BOARD EXAMINER, THE (US/0027-8785) [01641040] **3618**

NATIONAL BOARD INSPECTION CODE; A MANUAL FOR BOILER AND PRESSURE VESSEL INSPECTORS (US) [04181346] **2865**

NATIONAL BOARD OF BOILER AND PRESSURE VESSEL INSPECTORS *See* NATIONAL BOARD INSPECTION CODE; A MANUAL FOR BOILER AND PRESSURE VESSEL INSPECTORS **2865**

NATIONAL BOARD OF MEDICAL EXAMINERS *See* ANNUAL REPORT - NATIONAL BOARD OF MEDICAL EXAMINERS **3913**

NATIONAL BOAT BOOK (US/0363-1354) [02401035] **594**

NATIONAL BOOK CENTRE OF PAKISTAN *See* BAI **4824**

● NATIONAL BOOK OF LISTS, THE (US/1060-8435) [25071688] **1619**

NATIONAL BOYCOTT NEWS (US/1068-0845) [22167900] **1298**

NATIONAL BRAILLE ASSOCIATION *See* BULLETIN OF THE NATIONAL BRAILLE ASSOCIATION, INC **1876**

NATIONAL BUDGET FOR FINLAND (FI) [04701276] **4738**

NATIONAL BUDGET, THE (NO) [17657345] **4738**

NATIONAL BUILDER (LONDON) *CEASED.* (UK/0027-8807) [06299777] **621**

NATIONAL BUILDING CODE OF CANADA (CN/0700-1207) [03506659] **622**

NATIONAL BUILDINGS ORGANISATION (INDIA) *See* JOURNAL OF THE NATIONAL BUILDINGS ORGANISATION **618**

NATIONAL BULLETIN / MECHANICAL CONTRACTORS ASSOCIATION OF CANADA (CN/1186-9216) [24690421] **2027**

NATIONAL BULLETIN OF LITURGY (CN/0084-8425) [03243686] **4980**

NATIONAL BULLETIN ON POLICE MISCONDUCT (US/1042-5810) [18665270] **3170**

NATIONAL BUREAU OF ECONOMIC RESEARCH *See* ANNUAL REPORT - NATIONAL BUREAU OF ECONOMIC RESEARCH **1462**

NATIONAL BUREAU OF ECONOMIC RESEARCH *See* NBER REPORTER **1507**

NATIONAL BUREAU OF ECONOMIC RESEARCH *See* NBER WORKING PAPER SERIES **1507**

NATIONAL BUREAU OF STANDARDS MONOGRAPH (US/0083-1832) [01278275] **4413**

NATIONAL BUS TRADER (US/0194-939X) [05133147] **5388**

NATIONAL BUSINESS ASSOCIATION *See* NATIONAL BUSINESS ASSOCIATION **697**

NATIONAL BUSINESS ASSOCIATION (US/0191-5223) [04888683] **697**

NATIONAL BUSINESS EDUCATION YEARBOOK (1987) (US/1049-0256) [16164915] 1914, **697**

NATIONAL BUSINESS OUTLOOK (NZ/1172-3300) [I11723300] **800**

NATIONAL BUSINESS REVIEW (NZ/0110-6813) [01106813] **697**

NATIONAL BUSINESS REVIEW (NZ) [01106813] **697**

NATIONAL BUSINESS WOMAN (US/0027-8831) [04731580] 697, **5562**

NATIONAL BUTTON BULLETIN, THE (US/0027-884X) [07263855] **2775**

NATIONAL BUYERS' GUIDE TO INDUSTRIAL PRODUCTS AND BUSINESS SERVICES, THE (IO) [04212983] **847**

NATIONAL CABLE TELEVISION ASSOCIATION *See* CABLE SERVICES REPORT **1129**

NATIONAL CALENDAR OF OPEN COMPETITIVE ART EXHIBITIONS (US/0889-003X) [05880418] **374**

NATIONAL CAMPAIGN NEWS *See* AMERICAN SPIRIT / TAKE PRIDE IN AMERICA **2186**

NATIONAL CANCER INSTITUTE. DIAGNOSTIC RESEARCH ADVISORY COMMITTEE *See* ANNUAL REPORT - DIAGNOSTIC RESEARCH ADVISORY GROUP, NATIONAL INSTITUTES OF HEALTH **3808**

NATIONAL CANCER INSTITUTE. TOBACCO WORKING GROUP *See* ANNUAL REPORT - TOBACCO WORKING GROUP, NATIONAL INSTITUTES OF HEALTH **5372**

NATIONAL CANCER INSTITUTE (U.S.) *See* NCI FACT BOOK **3821**

NATIONAL CANCER INSTITUTE (U.S.). DIVISION OF CANCER CONTROL AND REHABILITATION *See* ANNUAL REPORT - DIVISION OF CANCER CONTROL AND REHABILITATION **3808**

NATIONAL CANCER INSTITUTE (U.S.). DIVISION OF CANCER PREVENTION AND CONTROL *See* ANNUAL REPORT - NATIONAL CANCER INSTITUTE (U.S.). DIVISION OF CANCER PREVENTION AND CONTROL **3808**

NATIONAL CANCER INSTITUTE (U.S.). DIVISION OF CANCER TREATMENT *See* ANNUAL REPORT / NATIONAL CANCER INSTITUTE, DIVISION OF CANCER TREATMENT **3808**

NATIONAL CANCER INSTITUTE (U.S.). DIVISION OF EXTRAMURAL ACTIVITIES *See* ANNUAL REPORT - NATIONAL CANCER INSTITUTE (U.S.). DIVISION OF EXTRAMURAL ACTIVITIES **3808**

NATIONAL CANCER INSTITUTE U.S. FIELD STUDIES AND STATISTICS PROGRAM *See* ANNUAL REPORT - NATIONAL CANCER INSTITUTE (U.S.). FIELD STUDIES AND STATISTICS PROGRAM **3808**

NATIONAL CANDY WHOLESALER *See* CANDY WHOLESALER **2330**

NATIONAL CAPITAL PHARMACIST, THE (US/0027-8890) [02264620] **4317**

NATIONAL CATHOLIC EDUCATIONAL ASSOCIATION. RESEARCH DEPT. CATHOLIC SCHOOLS IN THE UNITED STATES *See* NCEA-GANLEY'S CATHOLIC SCHOOLS IN AMERICA **5033**

NATIONAL CATHOLIC FORESTER (US/0745-5127) [09246476] **5032**

NATIONAL CATHOLIC REGISTER (US/0027-8920) [07785613] **5032**

NATIONAL CATHOLIC REPORTER (US/0027-8939) [01759105] **5033**

NATIONAL CATTLE FEEDLOT, MEAT PACKER AND GRAIN DEALERS DIRECTORY (US/0882-5149) [06227467] 203, **216**

NATIONAL CATTLEMEN (US/0885-7679) [12710739] **216**

NATIONAL CENTER FOR A BARRIER FREE ENVIRONMENT *See* REPORT OF THE PROCEEDINGS - NATIONAL CENTER FOR A BARRIER FREE ENVIRONMENT, A **2181**

NATIONAL CENTER FOR AGRICULTURAL LAW RESEARCH AND INFORMATION (U.S.) *See* NCALRI NEWSLETTER **111**

NATIONAL CENTER FOR ATMOSPHERIC RESEARCH (U.S.) *See* INFORMATION BULLETIN - NATIONAL CENTER FOR ATMOSPHERIC RESEARCH **1426**

NATIONAL CENTER FOR EDUCATION INFORMATION. NCEI. FULL SERVICE (US) **1766**

NATIONAL CENTER FOR EDUCATION STATISTICS *See* PROJECTS, PRODUCTS, AND SERVICES OF THE NATIONAL CENTER FOR EDUCATIONAL STATISTICS **1796**

NATIONAL CENTER FOR EDUCATION STATISTICS *See* INSTITUTIONAL CHARACTERISTICS OF COLLEGES AND UNIVERSITIES **1830**

NATIONAL CENTER FOR EDUCATION STATISTICS *See* FINANCIAL STATISTICS OF INSTITUTIONS OF HIGHER EDUCATION: CURRENT FUNDS, REVENUES AND EXPENDITURES SUMMARY DATA **1795**

NATIONAL CENTER FOR HEALTH SERVICES RESEARCH *See* SUMMARY OF GRANTS AND CONTRACTS ACTIVE ON ... **4804**

NATIONAL CENTER FOR HEALTH SERVICES RESEARCH AND DEVELOPMENT *See* PUBLICATIONS REPORT - NATIONAL CENTER FOR HEALTH SERVICES RESEARCH AND DEVELOPMENT **4811**

NATIONAL CENTER FOR HEALTH SERVICES RESEARCH AND DEVELOPMENT *See* FOCUS **2597**

NATIONAL CENTER FOR HEALTH STATISTICS (U.S.) *See* HEALTH IN THE UNITED STATES **4780**

NATIONAL CENTER FOR HEALTH STATISTICS (U.S.) *See* CATALOG OF PUBLICATIONS OF THE NATIONAL CENTER FOR HEALTH STATISTICS **4809**

NATIONAL CENTER FOR HEALTH STATISTICS (U.S.) *See* UNITED STATES LIFE TABLES **4560**

Alphabetical Title Index — NATIONAL

NATIONAL CENTER FOR HEALTH STATISTICS (U.S.) *See* CATALOG OF UNIVERSITY PRESENTATIONS **4771**

NATIONAL CENTER FOR JUVENILE JUSTICE *See* JUVENILE COURT STATISTICS (WASHINGTON) **3081**

NATIONAL CENTER FOR RESOURCE RECOVERY *See* ANNUAL REPORT - NATIONAL CENTER FOR RESOURCE RECOVERY **2224**

NATIONAL CENTER FOR SOCIAL STATISTICS *See* HEARINGS IN PUBLIC ASSISTANCE **5287**

NATIONAL CENTER FOR SOCIAL STATISTICS *See* EXPENDITURES FOR STAFF DEVELOPMENT AND TRAINING ACTIVITIES **5285**

NATIONAL CENTER FOR STATE COURTS *See* SURVEY OF JUDICIAL SALARIES **3143**

NATIONAL CENTER FOR STATE COURTS *See* ANNUAL REPORT - NATIONAL CENTER FOR STATE COURTS **3139**

NATIONAL CENTER FOR STATE COURTS *See* REPORT - NATIONAL CENTER FOR STATE COURTS **3142**

NATIONAL CENTER FOR STATE COURTS *See* REPORT, SURVEY OF METROPOLITAN JUVENILE COURTS / NATIONAL CENTER FOR STATE COURTS **3038**

NATIONAL CENTER FOR THE STUDY OF COLLECTIVE BARGAINING IN HIGHER EDUCATION AND THE PROFESSIONS (U.S.). CONFERENCE *See* PROCEEDINGS, ANNUAL CONFERENCE - NATIONAL CENTER FOR THE STUDY OF COLLECTIVE BARGAINING IN HIGHER EDUCATION AND THE PROFESSIONS (U.S.). CONFERENCE **1842**

NATIONAL CENTRAL LIBRARY NEWSLETTER (CH/0034-5016) [02254142] **3233**

NATIONAL CHART (CN/1193-4069) [I1934069] **4139**

NATIONAL CHART MAGAZINE *See* CHART MAGAZINE **4109**

NATIONAL CHILDREN'S BUREAU *See* ANNUAL REVIEW - NATIONAL CHILDREN'S BUREAU **5273**

NATIONAL CHILDREN'S BUREAU /ALL EXCEPT UK AND WALES /REGUALR DELIVERY (UK) **5297**

NATIONAL CHILDREN'S BUREAU. ANNUAL REPORT *See* ANNUAL REVIEW - NATIONAL CHILDREN'S BUREAU **5273**

NATIONAL CHRISTIAN REPORTER, THE (US/0279-8913) [07335174] **4980**

NATIONAL CHRONICLE (HAYDEN LAKE) (US/0027-898X) [04109027] **4483**

NATIONAL CHRONICLE (WASHINGTON, D.C.), THE (US/1061-5881) [22339456] **5647**

NATIONAL CIVIC REVIEW (US/0027-9013) [01607237] **4668**

NATIONAL CLEARINGHOUSE FOR ALCOHOL INFORMATION *See* SELECTED PUBLICATIONS - NATIONAL CLEARINGHOUSE FOR ALCOHOL INFORMATION **1349**

NATIONAL CLIMATE PROGRAM : ANNUAL REPORT (US/0740-5650) [08286373] **1432**

NATIONAL CLIMATIC CENTER *See* CLIMATOLOGICAL DATA FOR AMUNDSEN-SCOTT, ANTARCTICA **1422**

NATIONAL CLIMATIC CENTER. SATELLITE DATA SERVICES DIVISION *See* SATELLITE DATA USERS BULLETIN **1434**

NATIONAL CLOTHESLINE (MIDWEST ED.), THE (US/0744-6306) [08463325] **5354**

NATIONAL COAL ASSOCIATION *See* INTERNATIONAL COAL **1636**

NATIONAL COAL ASSOCIATION. DEPT. OF ECONOMICS AND STATISTICS *See* COAL DATA **1935**

NATIONAL COAL LEADER (US) [27521985] **2865**

NATIONAL COLLEGE OF THE STATE JUDICIARY (US/0095-2028) [01793886] **3013**

NATIONAL COLLEGIATE ATHLETIC ASSOCIATION *See* NCAA MEN'S AND WOMEN'S SOCCER RULES **4907**

NATIONAL COLLEGIATE ATHLETIC ASSOCIATION *See* READ-EASY FOOTBALL RULES **4914**

NATIONAL COLLEGIATE ATHLETIC ASSOCIATION *See* NCAA MEN'S AND WOMEN'S BASKETBALL RULES AND INTERPRETATIONS **4907**

NATIONAL COLLEGIATE ATHLETIC ASSOCIATION *See* ANNUAL REPORTS OF THE NATIONAL COLLEGIATE ATHLETIC ASSOCIATION **4883**

NATIONAL COLLEGIATE ATHLETIC ASSOCIATION *See* NCAA DIRECTORY **4906**

NATIONAL COLLEGIATE ATHLETIC ASSOCIATION *See* NCAA MEN'S AND WOMEN'S CROSS COUNTRY AND TRACK AND FIELD RULES **4907**

NATIONAL COLLEGIATE ATHLETIC ASSOCIATION *See* NCAA MEN'S ICE HOCKEY RULES AND INTERPRETATIONS **4907**

NATIONAL COLLEGIATE ATHLETIC ASSOCIATION *See* OFFICIAL NATIONAL COLLEGIATE ATHLETIC ASSOCIATION BASKETBALL STATISTICIANS' MANUAL, THE **4856**

NATIONAL COLLEGIATE ATHLETIC ASSOCIATION *See* NCAA MANUAL **4907**

NATIONAL COLLEGIATE ATHLETIC ASSOCIATION *See* NCAA MEN'S WATER POLO RULES **4907**

NATIONAL COLLEGIATE ATHLETIC ASSOCIATION *See* NCAA SWIMMING; ANNUAL GUIDE **4907**

NATIONAL COLLEGIATE ATHLETIC ASSOCIATION *See* NATIONAL COLLEGIATE CHAMPIONSHIPS (1978) **4906**

NATIONAL COLLEGIATE ATHLETIC ASSOCIATION *See* OFFICIAL NATIONAL COLLEGIATE ATHLETIC ASSOCIATION BASKETBALL RULES & INTERPRETATIONS, THE **4909**

NATIONAL COLLEGIATE ATHLETIC ASSOCIATION *See* NCAA NEWS, THE **4907**

NATIONAL COLLEGIATE ATHLETIC ASSOCIATION *See* NCAA FOOTBALL RULES AND INTERPRETATIONS **4906**

NATIONAL COLLEGIATE ATHLETIC ASSOCIATION *See* NCAA ILLUSTRATED MEN'S AND WOMEN'S BASKETBALL RULES **4907**

NATIONAL COLLEGIATE ATHLETIC ASSOCIATION *See* PROCEEDINGS OF THE SPECIAL CONVENTION OF THE NATIONAL COLLEGIATE ATHLETIC ASSOCIATION **4913**

NATIONAL COLLEGIATE ATHLETIC ASSOCIATION *See* NCAA MEN'S AND WOMEN'S SKIING RULES **4907**

NATIONAL COLLEGIATE ATHLETIC ASSOCIATION *See* PROCEEDINGS OF THE ANNUAL CONVENTION OF THE NATIONAL COLLEGIATE ATHLETIC ASSOCIATION (1967) **4913**

NATIONAL COLLEGIATE ATHLETIC ASSOCIATION *See* NCAA BASEBALL RULES **4906**

NATIONAL COLLEGIATE ATHLETIC ASSOCIATION *See* NCAA MEN'S LACROSSE RULES **4907**

NATIONAL COLLEGIATE ATHLETIC ASSOCIATION *See* NCAA MEN'S AND WOMEN'S TRACK AND FIELD AND CROSS COUNTRY RULES **4907**

NATIONAL COLLEGIATE ATHLETIC ASSOCIATION *See* OFFICIAL ... NCAA FOOTBALL / NATIONAL COLLEGIATE ATHLETIC ASSOCIATION **4910**

NATIONAL COLLEGIATE ATHLETIC ASSOCIATION *See* READ-EASY BASKETBALL RULES **4914**

NATIONAL COLLEGIATE ATHLETIC ASSOCIATION *See* READ-EASY MEN'S AND WOMEN'S BASKETBALL RULES **4914**

NATIONAL COLLEGIATE ATHLETIC ASSOCIATION. NCAA MEN'S AND WOMEN'S CROSS COUNTRY AND TRACK AND FIELD RULES *See* NCAA MEN'S AND WOMEN'S TRACK AND FIELD AND CROSS COUNTRY RULES **4907**

NATIONAL COLLEGIATE ATHLETIC ASSOCIATION. READ-EASY MEN'S AND WOMEN'S BASKETBALL RULES *See* READ-EASY BASKETBALL RULES **4914**

NATIONAL COLLEGIATE CHAMPIONSHIPS (1978) (US/0190-4329) [04696648] **4906**

NATIONAL COLLEGIATE FENCING CHAMPIONSHIPS HANDBOOK (US) [04936774] **4906**

NATIONAL COLLEGIATE SPORTS SERVICES *See* COLLEGE FOOTBALL MODERN RECORD BOOK **4890**

NATIONAL COMMERCIAL BANK OF DOMINICA *See* ANNUAL REPORT AND STATEMENT OF ACCOUNTS FOR THE YEAR ENDED 30TH JUNE ... / NATIONAL COMMERCIAL BANK OF DOMINICA **770**

NATIONAL COMMERCIAL FINANCE ASSOCIATION (U.S.) *See* ANNUAL REPORT - NATIONAL COMMERCIAL FINANCE ASSOCIATION (U.S.) **771**

NATIONAL COMMITTEE ON VITAL AND HEALTH STATISTICS : [SUMMARY REPORT], THE (US) [08548847] **4810**

NATIONAL COMMUNICATIONS FORUM. PROCEEDINGS OF THE NATIONAL COMMUNICATIONS FORUM *See* ANNUAL REVIEW OF COMMUNICATIONS **1149**

NATIONAL COMMUNITY REPORTER *See* NATAT'S REPORTER **4668**

NATIONAL COMPUTER GRAPHICS ASSOCIATION (US). CONFERENCE AND EXPOSITION *See* PROCEEDINGS OF THE ... ANNUAL CONFERENCE AND EXPOSITION OF THE NATIONAL COMPUTER GRAPHICS ASSOCIATION, INC **1234**

NATIONAL CONDITIONS OF THE REPUBLIC OF CHINA (CH) [18132095] **1575**

NATIONAL CONFERENCE OF BAR FOUNDATIONS' FOUNDATION FORUM (US/1062-5631) [25666952] **3013**

NATIONAL CONFERENCE OF STANDARDS LABORATORIES *See* NCSL NEWSLETTER **4031**

NATIONAL CONFERENCE OF STATE LEGISLATIVE LEADERS *See* YEARBOOK OF THE NATIONAL CONFERENCE OF STATE LEGISLATIVE LEADERS **4695**

NATIONAL CONFERENCE ON RADIATION CONTROL (US/0160-2136) [03111910] **4438**

NATIONAL CONFERENCE PUBLICATION - INSTITUTION OF ENGINEERS, AUSTRALIA (AT/0313-6922) [02680479] **1988**

NATIONAL CONFERENCE TASK FORCE ON RECREATION USE AND RESOURCE MANAGEMENT / EDISON ELECTRIC INSTITUTE (US) [08807808] **4852**

NATIONAL CONGRESS OF PARENTS AND TEACHERS *See* PTA HANDBOOK, THE **1775**

NATIONAL CONSERVATION STRATEGY FOR AUSTRALIA. NCSA NEWSLETTER (AT/0729-8226) [I07298226] **2198**

NATIONAL CONSTRUCTION ESTIMATOR / EDITED BY CAL PACIFIC ESTIMATORS (US/0547-5511) [04507383] **622**

NATIONAL CONSULTOR (US/0271-9150) [04298865] **4738, 748**

NATIONAL CONSUMER FINANCE ASSOCIATION. EDUCATIONAL SERVICES DIVISION *See* SELECTED AND ANNOTATED BIBLIOGRAPHY OF REFERENCE MATERIAL IN CONSUMER FINANCE **811**

NATIONAL CONSUMERS LEAGUE *See* BULLETIN **1294**

NATIONAL CONTRACT MANAGEMENT JOURNAL (1979) (US/1045-1668) [05796198] **879**

NATIONAL COOPERATIVE HIGHWAY RESEARCH PROGRAM *See* SYNTHESIS OF HIGHWAY PRACTICE **5393**

NATIONAL COOPERATIVE HIGHWAY RESEARCH PROGRAM *See* SUMMARY OF PROGRESS - NATIONAL COOPERATIVE HIGHWAY RESEARCH PROGRAM **5445**

NATIONAL COOPERATIVE HIGHWAY RESEARCH PROGRAM *See* RESEARCH RESULTS DIGEST / NATIONAL COOPERATIVE HIGHWAY RESEARCH PROGRAM **5443**

NATIONAL COOPERATIVE HIGHWAY RESEARCH PROGRAM REPORT (US/0077-5614) [01604180] **5442**

NATIONAL COOPERATIVE OBSERVER, THE (US) [23897362] **1432**

NATIONAL CORPORATION REPORTER, THE (US) [01587388] **697**

NATIONAL COTTON COUNCIL OF AMERICA. UTILIZATION RESEARCH DIVISION. MARKET RESEARCH SECTION *See* COTTON COUNTS ITS CUSTOMERS **5349**

NATIONAL COUNCIL FOR AGRICULTURAL EDUCATION *See* PROCEEDINGS OF THE ANNUAL MEETING - NATIONAL COUNCIL FOR AGRICULTURAL EDUCATION **122**

NATIONAL COUNCIL FOR EDUCATIONAL TECHNOLOGY *See* ANNUAL REPORT - NATIONAL COUNCIL FOR EDUCATIONAL TECHNOLOGY **1725**

NATIONAL COUNCIL FOR INTERNATIONAL VISITORS *See* NEWSLETTER - NATIONAL COUNCIL FOR INTERNATIONAL VISITORS **2911**

NATIONAL COUNCIL FOR RESOURCE DEVELOPMENT (U.S.) *See* MEMBERSHIP DIRECTORY - NATIONAL COUNCIL FOR RESOURCE DEVELOPMENT **1763**

NATIONAL COUNCIL FOR THERAPY AND REHABILITATION THROUGH HORTICULTURE *See* NEWSLETTER - NATIONAL COUNCIL FOR THERAPY AND REHABILITATION THROUGH HORTICULTURE (U.S.) **2425**

NATIONAL COUNCIL NEWS (ROCKVILLE, MD.) (US/0738-9159) [09705897] **5297**

NATIONAL COUNCIL OF EDUCATIONAL RESEARCH AND TRAINING *See* NCERT NEWS-LETTER **1867**

NATIONAL COUNCIL OF ENGINEERING EXAMINERS *See* NCEE REGISTRATION BULLETIN **1988**

NATIONAL COUNCIL OF JEWISH WOMEN *See* NCJW JOURNAL **2268**

NATIONAL COUNCIL OF PHYSICAL DISTRIBUTION MANAGEMENT *See* SUPPLEMENT TO BIBLIOGRAPHY ON PHYSICAL DISTRIBUTION MANAGEMENT **734**

NATIONAL — Alphabetical Title Index

NATIONAL COUNCIL OF SAVINGS INSTITUTIONS (U.S.) *See* DIRECTORY - NATIONAL COUNCIL OF SAVINGS INSTITUTIONS (U.S.) **788**

NATIONAL COUNCIL OF TEACHERS OF ENGLISH *See* RESEARCH REPORT - NATIONAL COUNCIL OF TEACHERS OF ENGLISH **3315**

NATIONAL COUNCIL OF THE ARTS *See* MUSEUM PROGRAM GUIDELINES **4092**

NATIONAL COUNCIL OF THE PAPER INDUSTRY FOR AIR AND STREAM IMPROVEMENT *See* NCASI TECHNICAL REVIEW : BULLETIN **4235**

NATIONAL COUNCIL OF THE PAPER INDUSTRY FOR AIR AND STREAM IMPROVEMENT. NATIONAL COUNCIL TECHNICAL REVIEW : BULLETIN *See* NCASI TECHNICAL REVIEW : BULLETIN **4235**

NATIONAL COUNCIL OF WOMEN OF CANADA *See* YEARBOOK - NATIONAL COUNCIL OF WOMEN OF CANADA (MICROFICHE) **5572**

NATIONAL COUNCIL ON CRIME AND DELINQUENCY. RESEARCH CENTER *See* PAROLE IN THE UNITED STATES **3171**

NATIONAL COUNCIL ON FAMILY RELATIONS. CONFERENCE *See* ANNUAL CONFERENCE PROCEEDINGS - NATIONAL COUNCIL ON FAMILY RELATIONS **2276**

NATIONAL COUNCIL ON HEALTH CARE TECHNOLOGY (U.S.) *See* REPORT / NATIONAL COUNCIL ON HEALTH CARE TECHNOLOGY **3633**

NATIONAL COUNCIL ON RADIATION PROTECTION AND MEASUREMENTS. MEETING *See* PROCEEDINGS OF THE ... ANNUAL MEETING OF THE NATIONAL COUNCIL ON RADIATION PROTECTION AND MEASUREMENTS **3944**

NATIONAL COUNTERFEIT DETECTOR, THE (US) [06298420] **800**

NATIONAL COUNTRY LIFE. LIVESTOCK FARMING EDITION (AT) [10634671] **216**

NATIONAL CREDIT OFFICE, INC. MARKETING AND MANAGEMENT SERVICES *See* DISTRIBUTORS OF ELECTRONIC PARTS **2042**

NATIONAL CREDIT UNION ADMINISTRATION RULES AND REGULATIONS (US) [06643532] **800**

NATIONAL CREDITOR/DEBTOR REVIEW (CN/0829-2019) [15127858] **3087**

NATIONAL CRIMINAL JUSTICE THESAURUS (US/0198-6546) [05174157] **3170**

NATIONAL CULINARY REVIEW, THE (US/0747-7716) [08437244] **2350**

NATIONAL CYSTIC FIBROSIS RESEARCH FOUNDATION. REPORT *See* CYSTIC FIBROSIS FOUNDATION ANNUAL REPORT FOR THE FISCAL YEAR ... **3804**

NATIONAL DAIRY COUNCIL *See* DAIRY COUNCIL DIGEST **193**

NATIONAL DANCE ASSOCIATION'S DANCE SCHOLARSHIP GUIDE (US) [24367927] **1314**

NATIONAL DATA BOOK OF FOUNDATIONS *See* GUIDE TO U.S. FOUNDATIONS, THEIR TRUSTEES, OFFICERS, AND DONORS **4338**

NATIONAL DEAN'S LIST, THE (US/0191-8133) [04800740] **1836**

NATIONAL DEBATE, THE (II/0302-6973) [01797678] **4483**

NATIONAL DEFENSE AND PERKINS (NATIONAL DIRECT) STUDENT LOAN PROGRAM DIRECTORY OF DESIGNATED LOW-INCOME SCHOOLS FOR TEACHER CANCELLATION BENEFITS FOR ... (US) [19037399] **1867**

NATIONAL DEFENSE EXECUTIVE RESERVE ANNUAL REPORT TO THE PRESIDENT, THE (US/0198-6120) [06176411] **4052**

NATIONAL DEFENSE, NATIONAL DIRECT, AND PERKINS LOAN PROGRAMS DIRECTORY OF DESIGNATED LOW-INCOME SCHOOLS FOR TEACHER CANCELLATION BENEFITS FOR THE ... SCHOOL YEAR / DEPARTMENT OF EDUCATION, OFFICE OF POSTSECONDARY EDUCATION, OFFICE OF STUDENT FINANCIAL ASSISTANCE (US) [27466615] **1882, 1766**

NATIONAL DEFENSE UNIVERSITY *See* NATIONAL SECURITY MANAGEMENT PROGRAMS. ADMINISTRATIVE PROCEDURES **4052**

NATIONAL DEFENSE (WASHINGTON) (US/0092-1491) [01789167] **4052**

NATIONAL DELINQUENCY SURVEY (US/0197-7938) [04565943] **800**

NATIONAL DENTAL ASSOCIATION JOURNAL *SUSPENDED.* (US/1050-530X) [11042479] **1330**

NATIONAL DEVELOPMENT. ASIA (US/0738-3037) [09559496] **1507**

NATIONAL DEVELOPMENT BANK OF SRI LANKA *See* REPORT & ACCOUNTS / NATIONAL DEVELOPMENT BANK OF SRI LANKA **807**

NATIONAL DEVELOPMENT BANK, SIERRA LEONE *See* REPORT AND ACCOUNTS - NATIONAL DEVELOPMENT BANK, SIERRA LEONE **807**

NATIONAL DEVELOPMENT FINANCE CORPORATION. ECONOMIC RESEARCH & PROJECT DIVISION *See* MONTHLY ECONOMIC REPORT - NATIONAL DEVELOPMENT FINANCE CORPORATION. ECONOMIC RESEARCH & PROJECT DIVISION **1575**

NATIONAL DEVELOPMENT. MIDDLE EAST/AFRICA (US/0738-1670) [09518609] **1988, 622**

●NATIONAL DEVELOPMENT PROGRAMME / GOVERNMENT OF THE TURKS AND CAICOS ISLANDS, BRITISH WEST INDIES (TC) [21169963] **2911**

NATIONAL DEVELOPMENT (WESTPORT, CONN.) (US/0730-0123) [07903223] **1507**

NATIONAL DEVELOPMENT (WESTPORT, CONN.) *See* NATIONAL DEVELOPMENT. ASIA **1507**

NATIONAL DIGEST OF HEALTH AND MEDICINE (US/1055-6044) [23237461] **3618**

NATIONAL DIPPER, THE (US/0895-9722) [16878497] **2350**

NATIONAL DIRECTORY AND ATLAS OF BUDGET MOTELS (US/0272-8699) [06945706] **2808**

NATIONAL DIRECTORY / CANADIAN INSTITUTE OF FOOD SCIENCE AND TECHNOLOGY (CN/0823-2717) [10032152] **2350**

NATIONAL DIRECTORY FOR SOFTWARE ADAPTATION (CN/1183-3955) [25313725] **1288**

NATIONAL DIRECTORY, HOME HEATING PRODUCTS (CN/0825-8260) [11559769] **2607**

NATIONAL DIRECTORY OF ABORIGINAL AND TORRES STRAIT ISLANDER ORGANISATIONS (AT/1037-6917) **2268**

NATIONAL DIRECTORY OF ADDRESSES AND TELEPHONE NUMBERS (MARINA DEL REY, CALIF.), THE (US/1043-4143) [19460871] **1118**

NATIONAL DIRECTORY OF ADDRESSES AND TELEPHONE NUMBERS (NEW YORK, N.Y.), THE (US/0740-7203) [08154350] **697**

NATIONAL DIRECTORY OF AIDS CARE (US) [21897280] **4792**

NATIONAL DIRECTORY OF ART & ANTIQUE BUYERS & SPECIALISTS (US/0899-6172) [18159870] **251**

NATIONAL DIRECTORY OF ARTS INTERNSHIPS (US/1043-092X) [12109373] **325**

NATIONAL DIRECTORY OF BASEBALL CAMPS *CEASED.* (US) **4906**

NATIONAL DIRECTORY OF BASKETBALL CAMPS *CEASED.* (US) **4906**

NATIONAL DIRECTORY OF BLIND TEACHERS (US/0743-4081) [10553564] **4391, 1766**

NATIONAL DIRECTORY OF BUDGET MOTELS (US/0146-3950) [02937239] **2808**

NATIONAL DIRECTORY OF BULLETIN BOARD SYSTEMS *CEASED.* (US/0884-9536) [12531543] **1196**

NATIONAL DIRECTORY OF CATALOGS, THE (US/1050-5830) [21557925] **847**

NATIONAL DIRECTORY OF CATHOLIC HIGHER EDUCATION (US/0736-9476) [09040757] **5033, 1836**

●NATIONAL DIRECTORY OF CERTIFIED COUNSELORS *SUSPENDED.* (US/0898-1493) [17728376] **4605, 1882**

NATIONAL DIRECTORY OF CERTIFIED PUBLIC ACCOUNTANTS, THE *CEASED.* (US/0731-0625) [07747810] **748**

NATIONAL DIRECTORY OF CHILD ABUSE SERVICES AND INFORMATION (US/0097-479X) [01799080] **5297**

NATIONAL DIRECTORY OF CHILDREN & YOUTH SERVICES *See* NATIONAL DIRECTORY OF CHILDREN, YOUTH & FAMILIES SERVICES **5297**

●NATIONAL DIRECTORY OF CHILDREN, YOUTH & FAMILIES SERVICES (US/1072-902X) [24087657] **5297**

●NATIONAL DIRECTORY OF CHIROPRACTIC, THE (US) [24928544] **4381, 3806**

●NATIONAL DIRECTORY OF CHURCHES, SYNAGOGUES, AND OTHER HOUSES OF WORSHIP (US/1070-3314) [28318409] **4980**

NATIONAL DIRECTORY OF COLLEGE ATHLETICS (WOMEN'S EDITION), THE (US/0739-1226) [04157489] **4906**

NATIONAL DIRECTORY OF COMMUNICATION CUSTOMER PREMISE EQUIPMENT WIRING & EQUIPMENT INSTALLERS, WITH RATE INFORMATION BY CITY, STATE & REGION, THE (US/0743-7072) [10639833] **2073**

NATIONAL DIRECTORY OF COMMUNITY NEWSPAPERS (1992) (US/1066-0887) [25635692] **5697**

●NATIONAL DIRECTORY OF CORPORATE DISTRESS SPECIALISTS, THE (US/1060-6025) [25043732] **697**

NATIONAL DIRECTORY OF CORPORATE GIVING (US/1050-9852) [20835367] **4338**

NATIONAL DIRECTORY OF CORPORATE PUBLIC AFFAIRS (US/0749-9736) [09208958] **762**

NATIONAL DIRECTORY OF COUNTY PARK AGENCIES (US) [08313649] **2198**

NATIONAL DIRECTORY OF COURTS OF LAW, THE (US/1054-9471) [23031248] **3013**

NATIONAL DIRECTORY OF EDUCATIONAL PROGRAMS IN GERONTOLOGY AND GERIATRICS (US/0148-4508) [23353471] **1836, 3754**

●NATIONAL DIRECTORY OF FIRE CHIEFS, RESCUE & EMERGENCY DEPARTMENTS (US/1066-5609) [26091347] **2291**

NATIONAL DIRECTORY OF FOOTBALL & SOCCER CAMPS *CEASED.* (US) **4906**

NATIONAL DIRECTORY OF FREE TOURIST ATTRACTIONS (US) [03118131] **5485**

NATIONAL DIRECTORY OF HEAD INJURY REHABILITATION SERVICES (US/0892-6972) [15182438] **3839, 3618**

NATIONAL DIRECTORY OF HIGH SCHOOL COACHES, THE (US) [05747352] **4906**

NATIONAL DIRECTORY OF HISPANIC ELECTED AND APPOINTED OFFICIALS / CONGRESSIONAL HISPANIC CAUCUS (US) [08483712] **4668**

NATIONAL DIRECTORY OF HOLISTIC HEALTH PROFESSIONALS, THE (US/0739-6724) [09118920] **3618**

NATIONAL DIRECTORY OF HOME MORTGAGE LENDERS, THE (US/1044-6605) [19822168] **801**

NATIONAL DIRECTORY OF INTERNSHIPS, RESIDENCIES & REGISTRARSHIPS, AUSTRALIA *SUSPENDED.* (AT/0155-9567) [15123682] **3619**

NATIONAL DIRECTORY OF INVESTMENT NEWSLETTERS, THE (US/0735-035X) [08173116] **909**

NATIONAL DIRECTORY OF LAW ENFORCEMENT ADMINISTRATORS, CORRECTIONAL INSTITUTIONS, AND RELATED GOVERNMENTAL AGENCIES (US/1066-5595) [14580815] **3170**

NATIONAL DIRECTORY OF LOCAL RESEARCHERS (US/0742-9045) [08486813] **2462**

NATIONAL DIRECTORY OF MAGAZINES, THE (US/0895-4321) [16638179] **2539**

NATIONAL DIRECTORY OF MAILING LISTS, THE (US) **1927**

NATIONAL DIRECTORY OF MEDICARE HOME HEALTH AGENCIES (US/0147-3476) [03145013] **5297, 2889**

NATIONAL DIRECTORY OF MINORITY-OWNED BUSINESS FIRMS (US/0886-3881) [12898424] **697**

NATIONAL DIRECTORY OF MODULAR BUILDING MANUFACTURERS (US/0092-668X) [01784472] **622**

NATIONAL DIRECTORY OF MORTICIANS *See* REDBOOK (CHAGRIN FALLS, OHIO), THE **2407**

NATIONAL DIRECTORY OF NONPROFIT ORGANIZATIONS (US/1048-8154) [21067893] **4338**

NATIONAL DIRECTORY OF OCCUPATIONAL HEALTH PROVIDERS (US) **3789**

NATIONAL DIRECTORY OF ORGANIC WHOLESALERS (US/1066-2162) [24356531] **2350**

NATIONAL DIRECTORY OF PERSONNEL CONSULTANTS BY SPECIALIZATION (US/0899-0212) [15704937] **4206**

NATIONAL DIRECTORY OF PRIVATE SOCIAL AGENCIES (US) [01696346] **5297**

NATIONAL DIRECTORY OF PROGRESSIVE AND RANK & FILE LABOR LAWYERS (US/0160-2586) [03642809] **3152**

●NATIONAL DIRECTORY OF PUBLIC PRACTITIONERS / CGA CANADA (CN/1188-6153) [26714662] **748**

●NATIONAL DIRECTORY OF PUBLIC PRACTITIONERS / CGA CANADA (CN/1188-6153) [26714660] **748**

NATIONAL

NATIONAL DIRECTORY OF REAL ESTATE ATTORNEYS, THE (US/1053-7902) [22646679] **4841, 3013**

NATIONAL DIRECTORY OF RETIREMENT FACILITIES (US/1053-6825) [13083769] **5180**

NATIONAL DIRECTORY OF SAFETY CONSULTANTS (US/0361-7904) [02441109] **4792**

NATIONAL DIRECTORY OF SENIOR CENTERS *See* DIRECTORY OF SENIOR CENTERS AND CLUBS **5179**

NATIONAL DIRECTORY OF SERVICE PRODUCT PROVIDERS TO NONPROFIT ORGANIZATIONS AND RESOURCE CENTER CATALOG (US) [19600553] **697**

NATIONAL DIRECTORY OF SHORTHAND REPORTERS (US/0271-1133) [06534417] **3013**

NATIONAL DIRECTORY OF STATE & LOCAL GOVERNMENT TRAINERS (US/0192-4273) [05003015] **4668**

NATIONAL DIRECTORY OF STORYTELLERS *See* NATIONAL DIRECTORY OF STORYTELLING **2322**

NATIONAL DIRECTORY OF STORYTELLING (US) [14121359] **2322**

NATIONAL DIRECTORY OF TRANSLATORS, INTERPRETERS AND LANGUAGE AIDES (AT/0814-9879) [I08149879] **3305**

NATIONAL DIRECTORY OF WOMEN ELECTED OFFICIALS (US/0740-2813) [07751964] **5562, 4483**

NATIONAL DIRECTORY OF WOMEN-OWNED BUSINESS FIRMS (US/0886-389X) [12898477] **5562, 697**

NATIONAL DIRECTORY / SCOTTISH CHAMBERS OF COMMERCE (UK) [14158227] **820**

NATIONAL DISABILITY LAW REPORTER (US/1053-1084) [22455118] **4391, 3013**

NATIONAL DISEASE AND THERAPEUTIC INDEX (US/0145-689X) [02778699] **3619**

NATIONAL DISEASE AND THERAPEUTIC INDEX (NDTI). DIAGNOSIS / IMS AMERICA (US) [10919001] **3619**

NATIONAL DISEASE AND THERAPEUTIC INDEX (NDTI). DRUG NATIONAL ESTIMATES / IMS AMERICA (US) [10919835] **3619**

NATIONAL DISTRIBUTION DIRECTORY OF LOCAL CARTAGE-SHORT HAUL CARRIERS WAREHOUSING *See* MCD WAREHOUSING DISTRIBUTION DIRECTORY **845**

NATIONAL DOG (AT/0728-8727) [I07288727] **5516**

NATIONAL DOG REVIEW (US/1050-8457) [21663179] **4287**

NATIONAL DRAGSTER (US/0466-2199) [08165646] **4906**

NATIONAL DRILLERS BUYERS GUIDE (US/0279-7739) [07251420] **5536**

NATIONAL DRUG CODE DIRECTORY *CEASED.* (US) [01759180] **4317**

NATIONAL DRUG INTELLIGENCE ESTIMATE (CN/0848-4740) [20740832] **1347**

NATIONAL DUROC NEWS AND DUROC JOURNAL-BULLETIN *See* DUROC NEWS **210**

NATIONAL ECONOMIC AND SOCIAL COUNCIL *See* REPORT ON THE ECONOMY AND THE PROSPECTS **1581**

NATIONAL ECONOMIC PROJECTIONS *See* NATIONAL ECONOMIC PROJECTIONS SERIES **1619**

NATIONAL ECONOMIC PROJECTIONS SERIES (US/0547-8154) [01162984] **1619**

NATIONAL ECONOMIC REVIEW (AT/0813-9474) [17217952] **1507**

●NATIONAL ECONOMIC, SOCIAL, & ENVIRONMENTAL DATA BANK [COMPUTER FILE] : NESE DB / U.S. DEPT. OF COMMERCE (US) [25918230] **2178**

NATIONAL ECONOMIC TRENDS (US/0430-1986) [03524689] **1507**

NATIONAL EDUCATION ASSOCIATION OF THE UNITED STATES *See* HANDBOOK **1749**

NATIONAL EDUCATION ASSOCIATION OF THE UNITED STATES. DEPT. OF CLASSROOM TEACHERS. OFFICIAL REPORT *See* OFFICIAL REPORT - ASSOCIATION OF CLASSROOM TEACHERS **1868**

NATIONAL EDUCATION ASSOCIATION OF THE UNITED STATES. REPRESENTATIVE ASSEMBLY *See* PROCEEDINGS OF THE ... REPRESENTATIVE ASSEMBLY / NATIONAL EDUCATION ASSOCIATION OF THE UNITED STATES **1869**

NATIONAL EDUCATION ASSOCIATION OF THE UNITED STATES. RESEARCH DIVISION *See* TEACHER SUPPLY AND DEMAND IN UNIVERSITIES, COLLEGES, AND JUNIOR COLLEGES **1849**

NATIONAL EDUCATION ASSOCIATION--RESEARCH *See* RANKINGS OF THE STATES **1776**

NATIONAL EDUCATION GOALS REPORT, THE (US/1062-1962) [24491339] **1766**

NATIONAL EDUCATIONAL SECRETARY (US) [04788189] **1766**

NATIONAL EDUCATOR, THE (US/0739-1617) [09714820] **5637**

NATIONAL ELECTRIC RATE BOOK (US/0364-8095) [02252688] **2073**

NATIONAL ELECTRICAL CODE (US/0550-4406) [03743098] **2073, 2292**

NATIONAL ELECTRICAL CODE HANDBOOK (1978), THE (US/0193-7324) [04626040] **2073, 2292**

NATIONAL EMERGENCY TRAINING & INFORMATION GUIDE (US) **4792**

NATIONAL EMISSIONS DATA SYSTEM (NEDS) FUEL USE REPORT (US) [04626165] **4265**

NATIONAL EMISSIONS REPORT (US/0094-8748) [01795405] **2237**

NATIONAL EMPLOYMENT LISTING SERVICE FOR HUMAN SERVICES (US/0194-0775) [04555389] **1692**

NATIONAL EMPLOYMENT LISTING SERVICE FOR THE CRIMINAL JUSTICE SYSTEM. SPECIAL EDITION: EDUCATIONAL OPPORTUNITIES (US/0194-0805) [05321791] **1836, 4206**

NATIONAL EMPLOYMENT LISTING SERVICE (HUNTSVILLE, TEX.) *See* BULLETIN, NATIONAL EMPLOYMENT LISTING SERVICE FOR THE CRIMINAL JUSTICE SYSTEM **4201**

NATIONAL EMPLOYMENT OPPORTUNITIES NEWSLETTER. COMPUTER/ELECTRONIC FIELD ENGINEERING *CEASED.* (US/0895-5778) [16704258] **1692**

NATIONAL ENDOWMENT FOR THE ARTS *See* GUIDE TO PROGRAMS - NATIONAL ENDOWMENT FOR THE ARTS **321**

NATIONAL ENDOWMENT FOR THE ARTS *See* ANNUAL REPORT - NATIONAL ENDOWMENT FOR THE ARTS/NATIONAL COUNCIL ON THE ARTS **313**

NATIONAL ENDOWMENT FOR THE ARTS *See* FEDERAL-STATE PARTNERSHIP **320**

NATIONAL ENDOWMENT FOR THE ARTS *See* NEW MUSIC PERFORMANCE AND CHAMBER MUSIC / NATIONAL ENDOWMENT FOR THE ARTS **4140**

NATIONAL ENDOWMENT FOR THE HUMANITIES *See* NATIONAL ENDOWMENT FOR THE HUMANITIES ... ANNUAL REPORT **2851**

NATIONAL ENDOWMENT FOR THE HUMANITIES *See* RESEARCH PROGRAMS - NATIONAL ENDOWMENT FOR THE HUMANITIES **2853**

NATIONAL ENDOWMENT FOR THE HUMANITIES *See* RESIDENTIAL FELLOWSHIPS FOR COLLEGE TEACHERS. SEMINAR DESCRIPTIONS **1845**

NATIONAL ENDOWMENT FOR THE HUMANITIES ... ANNUAL REPORT (US/8755-5492) [07495160] **2851**

NATIONAL ENDOWMENT FOR THE HUMANITIES. DIVISION OF FELLOWSHIPS AND SEMINARS *See* SUMMER STIPENDS. GUIDELINES & APPLICATION FORM **1905**

NATIONAL ENDOWMENT FOR THE HUMANITIES. DIVISION OF FELLOWSHIPS AND SEMINARS *See* SUMMER SEMINARS FOR COLLEGE TEACHERS. GUIDELINES AND APPLICATION FORM FOR DIRECTORS / NATIONAL ENDOWMENT FOR THE HUMANITIES, DIVISION OF FELLOWSHIPS AND SEMINARS **1905**

NATIONAL ENDOWMENT FOR THE HUMANITIES. DIVISION OF PUBLIC PROGRAMS *See* PUBLIC LIBRARY PROGRAM GUIDELINES **3243**

NATIONAL ENDOWMENT FOR THE HUMANITIES (U.S.) *See* RESEARCH PROGRAMS GUIDELINES **329**

NATIONAL ENERGY JOURNAL, THE (US/0279-4357) [07879855] **1950**

NATIONAL ENGINEER, THE (US/0027-9218) [01587716] **1988**

NATIONAL ENGINEERING LABORATORY (U.S.) *See* INTERNATIONAL ACTIVITIES **1979**

NATIONAL ENQUIRER (NEW YORK, N.Y. 1957) (US/1056-3482) [16171641] **2539**

NATIONAL ENVIRONMENTAL ENFORCEMENT JOURNAL (US) [14053262] **3114**

NATIONAL ENVIRONMENTAL IMPACT PROJECTION (US/0195-9794) [05654581] **2237**

NATIONAL ENVIRONMENTAL JOURNAL, THE (US/1067-2583) [27051790] **2178**

NATIONAL ENVIRONMENTAL RESEARCH CENTER, CINCINNATI *See* ACTIVE RESEARCH TASKS REPORT (CINCINNATI) **2159**

NATIONAL ENVIRONMENTAL RESEARCH CENTER, (CORVALLIS OR.) *See* PUBLICATIONS - NATIONAL ENVIRONMENTAL RESEARCH CENTER **2180**

NATIONAL ENVIRONMENTAL SCORECARD, THE (US/1054-3287) [22222423] **2178**

NATIONAL ESTIMATOR (US/1040-2926) [18367180] **2889**

NATIONAL EXAMINER (US) [13919146] **5718**

NATIONAL EXTENSION HOMEMAKERS COUNCIL *See* HOMEMAKER OF THE NATIONAL EXTENSION HOMEMAKERS COUNCIL, THE **2791**

NATIONAL EYE INSTITUTE *See* ANNUAL REPORT / NATIONAL EYE INSTITUTE **3872**

NATIONAL FACTORY & EQUIPMENT NEWS (CN/0713-0236) [08720627] **160**

NATIONAL FACULTY DIRECTORY, THE (US/0077-4472) [01267836] **1836**

NATIONAL FARM TRACTOR AND IMPLEMENT BLUE BOOK *CEASED.* (US/0193-7642) [03588798] **160**

NATIONAL FARMERS ORGANIZATION (U.S.) *See* NFO REPORTER, THE **112**

NATIONAL FARMERS UNION (CANADA) *See* NEWSLETTER - NATIONAL FARMERS UNION **112**

NATIONAL FARMERS UNION (CANADA). REGION 1 *See* REGION 1 SUBMISSION TO THE GOVERNMENT OF PRINCE EDWARD ISLAND **125**

NATIONAL FARMERS UNION (CANADA). REGION 1 *See* SUBMISSION TO THE GOVERNMENT OF NEW BRUNSWICK / NATIONAL FARMERS UNION, REGION 1 **138**

NATIONAL FARMERS UNION (CANADA). REGION 8 *See* NATIONAL FARMERS UNION, REGION 8, SUBMISSION TO THE GOVERNMENT OF BRITISH COLUMBIA ... **110**

NATIONAL FARMERS UNION, REGION 8, SUBMISSION TO THE GOVERNMENT OF BRITISH COLUMBIA ... (CN/0822-7969) [10764036] **110**

NATIONAL FARMERS UNION WASHINGTON NEWSLETTER (US/0027-9226) [01639693] **110**

NATIONAL FAX DIRECTORY (US/1045-9499) [20150165] **1160**

NATIONAL FEDERATION HANDBOOK (US/0737-5204) [06474937] **4906**

NATIONAL FEDERATION NEWS (US) **4906**

NATIONAL FEDERATION OF FINANCIAL ANALYSTS SOCIETIES. DIRECTORY OF MEMBERSHIPS *See* MEMBERSHIP DIRECTORY - THE FINANCIAL ANALYSTS FEDERATION **906**

NATIONAL FEDERATION OF STATE HIGH SCHOOL ASSOCIATIONS *See* BASKETBALL RULES SIMPLIFIED AND ILLUSTRATED ... FOR OFFICIALS, COACHES, PLAYERS, SPECTATORS **4887**

NATIONAL FEDERATION OF STATE HIGH SCHOOL ASSOCIATIONS *See* OFFICIAL HIGH SCHOOL ICE HOCKEY RULES **4909**

NATIONAL FEDERATION OF STATE HIGH SCHOOL ASSOCIATIONS *See* GIRLS BASKETBALL RULES BOOK. NATIONAL FEDERATION EDITION **4896**

NATIONAL FEDERATION OF STATE HIGH SCHOOL ASSOCIATIONS *See* TRACK AND FIELD AND CROSS COUNTRY RULE BOOK **4926**

NATIONAL FEDERATION OF STATE HIGH SCHOOL ASSOCIATIONS *See* HIGH SCHOOL BASEBALL RULES **4898**

NATIONAL FEDERATION OF STATE HIGH SCHOOL ASSOCIATIONS *See* NATIONAL HIGH SCHOOL SPORTS RECORD BOOK **4906**

NATIONAL FEDERATION OF STATE HIGH SCHOOL ASSOCIATIONS *See* HIGH SCHOOL SWIMMING, DIVING, AND WATER POLO RULES **4898**

NATIONAL FEDERATION OF STATE HIGH SCHOOL ASSOCIATIONS *See* SWIMMING AND DIVING RULES **4925**

NATIONAL FEDERATION OF STATE HIGH SCHOOL ASSOCIATIONS *See* FOOTBALL HANDBOOK **4895**

NATIONAL FEDERATION OF STATE HIGH SCHOOL ASSOCIATIONS *See* OFFICIAL HIGH SCHOOL FOOTBALL RULES **4909**

NATIONAL FEDERATION OF STATE HIGH SCHOOL ASSOCIATIONS *See* VOLLEYBALL RULE BOOK **4928**

NATIONAL FEDERATION OF STATE HIGH SCHOOL ASSOCIATIONS *See* OFFICIAL NATIONAL FEDERATION BASKETBALL RULE BOOK **4909**

NATIONAL — Alphabetical Title Index

NATIONAL FEDERATION OF STATE HIGH SCHOOL ASSOCIATIONS *See* OFFICIAL HIGH SCHOOL BOYS GYMNASTICS RULES **4909**

NATIONAL FEDERATION OF STATE HIGH SCHOOL ASSOCIATIONS *See* GIRLS GYMNASTICS JUDGING MANUAL. NATIONAL FEDERATION EDITION **4896**

NATIONAL FEDERATION OF STATE HIGH SCHOOL ASSOCIATIONS *See* OFFICIAL HIGH SCHOOL BASEBALL RULES **4909**

NATIONAL FEDERATION OF STATE HIGH SCHOOL ASSOCIATIONS *See* SOCCER RULE BOOK **4919**

NATIONAL FEDERATION OF STATE HIGH SCHOOL ASSOCIATIONS *See* FIELD HOCKEY RULES. NATIONAL FEDERATION ED **4894**

NATIONAL FEDERATION OF STATE HIGH SCHOOL ASSOCIATIONS *See* HIGH SCHOOL GIRLS GYMNASTICS RULES AND MANUAL **4898**

NATIONAL FEDERATION OF STATE HIGH SCHOOL ASSOCIATIONS *See* HIGH SCHOOL SOFTBALL RULES **4898**

NATIONAL FEDERATION OF STATE HIGH SCHOOL ASSOCIATIONS *See* HIGH SCHOOL SOFTBALL UMPIRES MANUAL **4898**

NATIONAL FEDERATION OF STATE HIGH SCHOOL ASSOCIATIONS *See* HIGH SCHOOL WRESTLING RULES **4898**

NATIONAL FEDERATION OF STATE HIGH SCHOOL ASSOCIATIONS *See* NATIONAL FEDERATION HANDBOOK **4906**

NATIONAL FEDERATION OF STATE HIGH SCHOOL ASSOCIATIONS *See* OFFICIAL HIGH SCHOOL SPIRIT RULES BOOK **4909**

NATIONAL FEDERATION OF STATE HIGH SCHOOL ASSOCIATIONS *See* SOCCER RULES **4919**

NATIONAL FEDERATION OF STATE HIGH SCHOOL ASSOCIATIONS. OFFICIAL HANDBOOK *See* NATIONAL FEDERATION HANDBOOK **4906**

NATIONAL FEDERATION OF STATE HIGH SCHOOL ASSOCIATIONS. OFFICIAL HIGH SCHOOL GIRLS GYMNASTICS RULES AND MANUAL *See* HIGH SCHOOL GIRLS GYMNASTICS RULES AND MANUAL **4898**

NATIONAL FEDERATION OF STATE HIGH SCHOOL ASSOCIATIONS. OFFICIAL HIGH SCHOOL SOFTBALL CASE BOOK AND UMPIRES MANUAL *See* HIGH SCHOOL SOFTBALL UMPIRES MANUAL **4898**

NATIONAL FEDERATION OF STATE HIGH SCHOOL ASSOCIATIONS. OFFICIAL HIGH SCHOOL SOFTBALL RULES *See* HIGH SCHOOL SOFTBALL RULES **4898**

NATIONAL FEDERATION OF STATE HIGH SCHOOL ASSOCIATIONS. SOCCER RULE BOOK *See* SOCCER RULES **4919**

NATIONAL FEDERATION VOLLEYBALL RULES COMMITTEE *See* VOLLEYBALL CASE BOOK AND OFFICIALS MANUAL **4928**

NATIONAL FERTILIZER DEVELOPMENT CENTER (U.S.) *See* PROGRESS (MUSCLE SHOALS, ALA.) **123**

NATIONAL FILM BOARD OF CANADA *See* ZOOM ON THE NFB **4080**

NATIONAL FILM BOARD OF CANADA *See* ZOOM IN : NEW FILMS AND VIDEOS FROM THE NATIONAL FILM BOARD OF CANADA **4080**

NATIONAL FILM BOARD OF CANADA *See* COMMERCIAL PRICE LIST FOR STILL PHOTOGRAPHS **4368**

NATIONAL FILM BOARD OF CANADA. PHOTOTHEQUE *See* COMMERCIAL PRICE LIST - N.F.B. PHOTOTHEQUE **4067**

NATIONAL FILM BOARD OF CANADA. TECHNICAL AND PRODUCTION SERVICES BRANCH *See* PERFORATIONS **4076**

NATIONAL FINANCES, THE (CN/0077-4529) [02588518] **4738**

NATIONAL FINANCING LAW DIGEST (US) [19297479] **3013**

NATIONAL FIRE ACADEMY *See* NATIONAL FIRE ACADEMY ... RESIDENTIAL PROGRAM **2292**

NATIONAL FIRE ACADEMY *See* COURSE CATALOG / NATIONAL FIRE ACADEMY **2288**

NATIONAL FIRE ACADEMY. CATALOG OF RESIDENT COURSES *See* COURSE CATALOG / NATIONAL FIRE ACADEMY **2288**

NATIONAL FIRE ACADEMY ... RESIDENTIAL PROGRAM (US) [06645037] **2292**

NATIONAL FIRE ALARM CODE (US) **2292**

NATIONAL FIRE & ARSON REPORT, THE (US/1064-4814) [09026325] **3170**

NATIONAL FIRE CODE OF CANADA (CN/0700-124X) [08437726] **2292**

NATIONAL FIRE CODES (US/0077-4545) [01782321] **2292**

NATIONAL FIRE CODES. SUPPLEMENT (US) [04000172] **2292**

NATIONAL FIRE PROTECTION ASSOCIATION *See* LIFE SAFETY CODE HANDBOOK **2291**

NATIONAL FIRE PROTECTION ASSOCIATION *See* NATIONAL FIRE CODES. SUPPLEMENT **2292**

NATIONAL FIRE PROTECTION ASSOCIATION *See* NATIONAL ELECTRICAL CODE HANDBOOK (1978), THE **2292**

NATIONAL FIRE PROTECTION ASSOCIATION *See* NATIONAL FIRE CODES **2292**

NATIONAL FIRE PROTECTION ASSOCIATION *See* ANNUAL MEETING, TECHNICAL COMMITTEE REPORTS **2288**

NATIONAL FIRE PROTECTION ASSOCIATION *See* FALL MEETING, TECHNICAL COMMITTEE REPORTS **2288**

NATIONAL FIRE PROTECTION ASSOCIATION. TECHNICAL COMMITTEE REPORTS *See* FALL MEETING, TECHNICAL COMMITTEE REPORTS **2288**

NATIONAL FIRM RETAIL RR PRODUCTIVITY TRACKING REPORT (US) **934**

NATIONAL FISHERIES INSTITUTE *See* NFI BLUE BOOK **2309**

NATIONAL FISHERMAN (US/0027-9250) [01606161] **2309**

NATIONAL FIVE DIGIT ZIP CODE AND POST OFFICE DIRECTORY (US/0731-9185) [08135572] **1145**

NATIONAL FLUID POWER ASSOCIATION *See* ENCYCLOPEDIA OF FLUID POWER STANDARDS. VOL. A : COMMUNICATIONS, INCLUDING GRAPHIC SYMBOLS AND METRIC UNITS **2088**

NATIONAL FLUID POWER ASSOCIATION *See* ENCYCLOPEDIA OF FLUID POWER STANDARDS. VOL. B : PRESSURE RATING **2089**

NATIONAL FLUID POWER ASSOCIATION *See* ENCYCLOPEDIA OF FLUID POWER STANDARDS. VOL. C : PUMPS, MOTORS, POWER UNITS & RESERVOIRS **2089**

NATIONAL FLUID POWER ASSOCIATION *See* ENCYCLOPEDIA OF FLUID POWER STANDARDS. VOL. J : BIBLIOGRAPHIES **2004**

NATIONAL FLUID POWER ASSOCIATION *See* ENCYCLOPEDIA OF FLUID POWER STANDARDS. VOL. I : TESTING **2089**

NATIONAL FLUID POWER ASSOCIATION *See* FLUID POWER INDUSTRY OUTLOOK SURVEY **3479**

NATIONAL FLUID POWER ASSOCIATION *See* DIRECTORY - NATIONAL FLUID POWER ASSOCIATION **2113**

NATIONAL FLUID POWER ASSOCIATION *See* ENCYCLOPEDIA OF FLUID POWER STANDARDS. VOL. D : FILTRATION AND CONTAMINATION **2089**

NATIONAL FLUID POWER ASSOCIATION *See* SALARY & BENEFITS SURVEY **1709**

NATIONAL FLUID POWER ASSOCIATION *See* ENCYCLOPEDIA OF FLUID POWER STANDARDS. VOL. G : CYLINDERS AND ACCUMULATORS **2089**

NATIONAL FLUID POWER ASSOCIATION *See* ENCYCLOPEDIA OF FLUID POWER STANDARDS. VOL. F : CONTROL PRODUCTS/PNEUMATIC SYSTEMS **2089**

NATIONAL FLUID POWER ASSOCIATION *See* ENCYCLOPEDIA OF FLUID POWER STANDARDS. VOL. E : CONDUCTORS AND ASSOCIATED PRODUCTS **2089**

NATIONAL FLUORIDATION NEWS SUSPENDED. (US/0027-9269) [02448914] **3982**

NATIONAL FLYING FARMER *See* INTERNATIONAL FLYING FARMER **96**

NATIONAL FOOTBALL LEAGUE *See* OFFICIAL RULES FOR PROFESSIONAL FOOTBALL **4910**

NATIONAL FOOTBALL LEAGUE *See* OFFICIAL NATIONAL FOOTBALL LEAGUE GUIDE **4909**

NATIONAL FOOTBALL LEAGUE *See* OFFICIAL ... NATIONAL FOOTBALL LEAGUE RECORD & FACT BOOK **4909**

NATIONAL FOOTBALL LEAGUE RETIRED PLAYERS ASSOCIATION (U.S.) *See* BUSINESS DIRECTORY / NATIONAL FOOTBALL LEAGUE RETIRED PLAYERS ASSOCIATION **4888**

NATIONAL FOREIGN ASSESSMENT CENTER (U.S) *See* INTERNATIONAL ECONOMIC & ENERGY STATISTICAL REVIEW **1568**

NATIONAL FOREIGN TRADE COUNCIL *See* NOTICIAS - NATIONAL FOREIGN TRADE COUNCIL **848**

NATIONAL FORENSIC JOURNAL (US/0749-1042) [10231745] **3305, 3742**

NATIONAL FORESTS FIRE REPORT (US) [02580664] **2292, 2388**

NATIONAL FORUM (ANN ARBOR) (US/0162-1831) [04038562] **5210, 1836**

NATIONAL FORUM OF APPLIED EDUCATIONAL RESEARCH JOURNAL (US/0895-3880) [16617735] **1867**

NATIONAL FORUM OF EDUCATIONAL ADMINISTRATION AND SUPERVISION JOURNAL (US/0888-8132) [13727376] **1766**

NATIONAL FORUM OF SPECIAL EDUCATION JOURNAL (US/1043-2167) [19342335] **1882**

NATIONAL FOUNDATION FOR ADVANCEMENT IN THE ARTS (U.S.) *See* ANNUAL REPORT - NATIONAL FOUNDATION FOR ADVANCEMENT IN THE ARTS (U.S.) **313**

NATIONAL FOUNDATION FOR ARTS EDUCATION NEWSLETTER *See* ARTS EDUCATION : THE MAGAZINE OF THE NATIONAL FOUNDATION FOR ARTS EDUCATION **315**

NATIONAL FRESH WATER FISHING (US) **2309**

NATIONAL FUNERAL DIRECTOR AND EMBALMER (US) [01759222] **2407**

NATIONAL FUTURES ASSOCIATION (U.S.) *See* ANNUAL REVIEW - NATIONAL FUTURES ASSOCIATION (U.S.) **891**

NATIONAL GALLERIES OF SCOTLAND BULLETIN (UK) **4093**

NATIONAL GALLERIES OF SCOTLAND EDINBURGH. 1987 (UK/0953-024X) [0953024X] **4093**

NATIONAL GALLERY OF CANADA *See* FINE ART PUBLICATIONS ... / NATIONAL GALLERY OF CANADA **320**

NATIONAL GALLERY TECHNICAL BULLETIN (UK/0140-7430) [05858583] **359**

NATIONAL GAMING SUMMARY (US) [28311156] **697**

NATIONAL GARDENER, THE (US/0027-9331) [06298991] **2424**

NATIONAL GARDENING (US/1052-4096) [14471348] **2425**

NATIONAL GARDENING MAGAZINE'S ... GARDEN HANDBOOK (US) [23168496] **2425**

NATIONAL GARDENING SURVEY (US/0270-0816) [06320799] **2425**

NATIONAL GAS ASSOCIATION OF AUSTRALIA *See* STATISTICAL YEAR BOOK - THE AUSTRALIAN GAS INDUSTRY **4284**

NATIONAL GAS CONSUMERS' COUNCIL (GREAT BRITAIN) *See* ANNUAL REPORT / NATIONAL GAS CONSUMERS' COUNCIL (GREAT BRITAIN) **4628**

NATIONAL GAS CONSUMERS' COUNCIL (GREAT BRITAIN). REPORT OF THE NATIONAL GAS CONSUMERS' COUNCIL FOR THE YEAR ENDED MARCH 31 . *See* ANNUAL REPORT / NATIONAL GAS CONSUMERS' COUNCIL (GREAT BRITAIN) **4628**

NATIONAL GENEALOGICAL INQUIRER (US/0148-8554) [03388357] **2462**

NATIONAL GENEALOGICAL SOCIETY *See* NATIONAL GENEALOGICAL SOCIETY QUARTERLY **2462**

NATIONAL GENEALOGICAL SOCIETY QUARTERLY (US/0027-934X) [01759226] **2462**

NATIONAL GEODETIC SURVEY (U.S.) *See* PUBLICATIONS OF THE NATIONAL GEODETIC SURVEY **399**

NATIONAL GEOGRAPHER (II/0470-0929) [01790561] **2570**

NATIONAL GEOGRAPHIC (US/0027-9358) [06451257] **2570**

NATIONAL GEOGRAPHIC INDEX (US) [03549751] **2570**

NATIONAL GEOGRAPHIC TRAVELER (US/0747-0932) [10542124] **5485**

NATIONAL GEOGRAPHIC WORLD (US/0361-5499) [02255097] **1067, 2570**

NATIONAL GEOGRAPHICAL JOURNAL OF INDIA, THE (II/0027-9374) [01606287] **2570**

NATIONAL GOVERNORS' ASSOCIATION *See* POLICY POSITIONS **4674**

NATIONAL GOVERNORS' ASSOCIATION *See* POLICY POSITIONS. WINTER MEETING SUPPLEMENT **4674**

NATIONAL GRAIN POLICIES (US/0071-710X) [01772638] **203**

NATIONAL GRAINS UPDATE (EASTERN ED.) (CN/0848-7162) [23658998] **203**

NATIONAL GRAINS UPDATE (WESTERN ED.) (CN/0848-7170) [23658993] **203**

NATIONAL GREENHOUSE GARDENER (US/0883-8313) [12225733] **2425**

NATIONAL GUARD ALMANAC (US/0363-8618) [03264262] **4052**

NATIONAL GUARD (WASHINGTON. 1978) (US/0163-3945) [04361191] **4052**

NATIONAL GUARDIAN DIRECTORY OF THE SCOTTISH LICENSED TRADE, THE (UK) [01789042] **847**

NATIONAL GUIDE. SUPPLEMENT, THE **CEASED.** (US/0732-3026) [07701864] **1766**

NATIONAL GUIDE TO FUNDING IN HEALTH (US/1071-1201) [22883878] **3619**

NATIONAL GUIDE TO GOVERNMENT (AT/1030-6641) [19818067] **4668**

NATIONAL GUILD OF CATHOLIC PSYCHIATRISTS **See** BULLETIN OF THE NATIONAL GUILD OF CATHOLIC PSYCHIATRISTS, INC, THE **3922**

NATIONAL HAIRDRESSERS AND COSMETOLOGISTS ASSOCIATION **See** N.H.C.A. BULLETIN / NATIONAL HAIRDRESSERS & COSMETOLOGISTS' ASSOCIATION, INC **404**

NATIONAL HARDWOOD MAGAZINE (US/0194-0910) [05321296] **634**

NATIONAL HEAD INJURY FOUNDATION CATALOGUE OF EDUCATIONAL MATERIALS (US) **3619**

●NATIONAL HEAD INJURY FOUNDATION'S TBI CHALLENGE!, THE (US/1071-6262) [28693276] **3619**

NATIONAL HEALTH DIRECTORY (US/0147-2771) [02879201] **4792**

NATIONAL HEALTH INTERVIEW SURVEY [COMPUTER FILE] / U.S. DEPARTMENT OF HEALTH AND HUMAN SERVICES, PUBLIC HEALTH SERVICE, CENTERS FOR DISEASE CONTROL (US) [23062568] **4792**

NATIONAL HEALTH POLICY FORUM (US) **4792, 4668**

NATIONAL HEALTH SERVICE CORPS (U.S.) **See** NHSC HEALTH CARE PRACTITIONERS **3725**

NATIONAL HEALTH STATISTICS CENTRE (N.Z.) **See** INDEX OF STATISTICS PUBLISHED BY THE DEPARTMENT OF HEALTH / NATIONAL HEALTH STATISTICS CENTRE, DEPARTMENT OF HEALTH (NEW ZEALAND) **4810**

NATIONAL HEALTH STATISTICS CENTRE (N.Z.) **See** HOSPITAL AND SELECTED MORBIDITY DATA **4810**

NATIONAL HEALTH STATISTICS CENTRE (N.Z.) **See** PUBLICATIONS INDEX / NATIONAL HEALTH STATISTICS CENTRE **4811**

NATIONAL HEALTH SURVEY / FEDERAL BUREAU OF STATISTICS, STATISTICS DIVISION, GOVERNMENT OF PAKISTAN (PK) [15370260] **4810**

NATIONAL HEART AND LUNG INSTITUTE. MEDICAL DEVICES APPLICATIONS COMMITTEE **See** ANNUAL REPORT - MEDICAL DEVICES APPLICATIONS COMMITTEE, NATIONAL INSTITUTES OF HEALTH **3551**

NATIONAL HEART AND LUNG INSTITUTE. NATIONAL BLOOD RESOURCE PROGRAM ADVISORY COMMITTEE **See** ANNUAL REPORT - NATIONAL BLOOD RESOURCE PROGRAM ADVISORY COMMITTEE, NATIONAL INSTITUTES OF HEALTH **4766**

NATIONAL HEART, LUNG, AND BLOOD ADVISORY COUNCIL **See** REPORT OF THE NATIONAL HEART, LUNG, AND BLOOD ADVISORY COUNCIL **3710**

NATIONAL HEART, LUNG, AND BLOOD INSTITUTE **See** ANNUAL REPORT / NATIONAL HEART, LUNG, AND BLOOD INSTITUTE **3699**

NATIONAL HEART, LUNG, AND BLOOD INSTITUTE **See** REPORT OF THE DIRECTOR, NATIONAL HEART, LUNG, AND BLOOD INSTITUTE **4798**

NATIONAL HEART, LUNG, AND BLOOD INSTITUTE ARTERIOSCLEROSIS AND HYPERTENSION ADVISORY COMMITTEE **See** ANNUAL REPORT - ARTERIOSCLEROSIS AND HYPERTENSION ADVISORY COMMITTEE, NATIONAL INSTITUTES OF HEALTH **3698**

NATIONAL HEART, LUNG, AND BLOOD INSTITUTE. CLINICAL APPLICATIONS AND PREVENTION ADVISORY COMMITTEE **See** ANNUAL REPORT - CLINICAL APPLICATIONS AND PREVENTION ADVISORY COMMITTEE, NATIONAL INSTITUTES OF HEALTH **3550**

NATIONAL HEART, LUNG, AND BLOOD INSTITUTE. DIVISION OF HEART AND VASCULAR DISEASES **See** MULTIPLE RISK FACTOR INTERVENTION TRIAL. PUBLIC ANNUAL REPORT **3708**

NATIONAL HEART, LUNG, AND BLOOD INSTITUTE. LIPID METABOLISM ADVISORY COMMITTEE **See** ANNUAL REPORT - LIPID METABOLISM ADVISORY COMMITTEE, NATIONAL INSTITUTES OF HEALTH **4766**

NATIONAL HIGH SCHOOL SPORTS RECORD BOOK (US/0192-978X) [05085488] **4906**

NATIONAL HIGHWAY AND AIRWAY CARRIERS AND ROUTES (US/0275-3286) [05070317] **5401**

NATIONAL HIGHWAY CARRIERS DIRECTORY AND ROUTES, INCLUDING AIR CARGO TRANSPORTS **See** NATIONAL HIGHWAY AND AIRWAY CARRIERS AND ROUTES **5401**

NATIONAL HIKING WAY BOARD (SOUTH AFRICA) **See** REPORT OF THE NATIONAL HIKING WAY BOARD **4878**

NATIONAL HISPANIC JOURNAL **SUSPENDED.** (US/0734-9920) [08122545] **2268**

NATIONAL HIV/AIDS LEGAL LINK NEWSLETTER (AT/1037-6615) [l10376615] **3013**

NATIONAL HOCKEY LEAGUE **See** OFFICIAL GUIDE & RECORD BOOK / THE NATIONAL HOCKEY LEAGUE **4909**

NATIONAL HOCKEY LEAGUE **See** SCHEDULE & RULE BOOK - NATIONAL HOCKEY LEAGUE **4916**

NATIONAL HOG FARMER (US/0027-9447) [04992920] **216**

NATIONAL HOME CENTER NEWS (US/0192-6772) [05066627] **2792**

NATIONAL HOME ESTIMATOR **See** NATIONAL CONSTRUCTION ESTIMATOR / EDITED BY CAL PACIFIC ESTIMATORS **622**

NATIONAL HOME-WORK NEWS (US/1043-9838) [19231347] **879**

NATIONAL HONEY MARKET NEWS (US) [19756878] **2350, 110**

NATIONAL HOOKUP (US/0194-4754) [04692098] **4391**

NATIONAL HORSEMAN, THE (US/0027-9455) [01759242] **2801**

NATIONAL HOSPITAL DISCHARGE SURVEY. ANNUAL SUMMARY (US) [19918069] **3789**

NATIONAL HOT ROD ASSOCIATION **See** DRAG RULES **4893**

NATIONAL HOUSING REGISTER (US/1059-3071) [24562399] **2829**

NATIONAL HURRICANE OPERATIONS PLAN (US/0092-2056) [01787566] **1432**

NATIONAL HYDATIDS COUNCIL (N.Z.) **See** ANNUAL REPORT - NATIONAL HYDATIDS COUNCIL **5503**

NATIONAL INCOME ACCOUNTS, THE (PH) [02480622] **1575**

NATIONAL INCOME AND EXPENDITURE ACCOUNTS (CN/0318-708X) [01795875] **1575**

NATIONAL INCOME AND EXPENDITURE ACCOUNTS : THE ANNUAL ESTIMATES (CN/0703-0037) [03214757] **1575**

NATIONAL INCOME AND EXPENDITURE CANBERRA (AT/1031-2765) [l10312765] **4738**

NATIONAL INCOME AND PRODUCT (JM/0448-1933) [01754164] **1536**

NATIONAL INDEPENDENT COAL LEADER **See** NATIONAL COAL LEADER **2865**

NATIONAL INDEPENDENT STUDY CENTER FISCAL YEAR ... COURSE CATALOG (US) [05305811] **4668**

NATIONAL INDEPENDENT STUDY CENTER (U.S.) **See** NATIONAL INDEPENDENT STUDY CENTER FISCAL YEAR ... COURSE CATALOG **4668**

NATIONAL INDIAN BROTHERHOOD OF CANADA. LIBRARY **See** ACCESSION LIST - NATIONAL INDIAN BROTHERHOOD, LIBRARY **2254**

NATIONAL INDIAN LAW LIBRARY **See** CATALOGUE - NATIONAL INDIAN LAW LIBRARY **3079**

NATIONAL INDUSTRIAL COUNCIL **See** NATIONAL INDUSTRIAL COUNCIL DIRECTORY **1619**

NATIONAL INDUSTRIAL COUNCIL DIRECTORY (US/0194-0686) [05296722] **1619**

NATIONAL INFORMATION STANDARDS SERIES (US/1041-5653) [18802624] **3233**

NATIONAL INSOLVENCY REVIEW (CN/0822-2584) [10676935] **3087**

NATIONAL INSTITUTE ECONOMIC REVIEW (UK/0027-9501) [01759256] **1507**

NATIONAL INSTITUTE FOR COAL RESEARCH (SOUTH AFRICA) **See** ANNUAL REPORT / NATIONAL INSTITUTE FOR COAL RESEARCH **2133**

NATIONAL INSTITUTE FOR CRIME PREVENTION AND REHABILITATION OF OFFENDERS. NATIONAL COUNCIL **See** ANNUAL REPORT - NATIONAL COUNCIL, NICRO **3157**

NATIONAL INSTITUTE FOR GLOBAL ENVIRONMENTAL CHANGE **See** ANNUAL REPORT / NATIONAL INSTITUTE FOR GLOBAL ENVIRONMENTAL CHANGE **2161**

NATIONAL INSTITUTE FOR METALLURGY **See** N I M RESEARCH DIGEST **4013**

NATIONAL INSTITUTE FOR OCCUPATIONAL SAFETY AND HEALTH **See** JOINT NIOSH/OSHA CURRENT INTELLIGENCE BULLETIN **2864**

NATIONAL INSTITUTE FOR OCCUPATIONAL SAFETY AND HEALTH **See** NIOSH CURRENT INTELLIGENCE BULLETIN **2866**

NATIONAL INSTITUTE FOR OCCUPATIONAL SAFETY AND HEALTH. DIVISION OF TRAINING **See** COURSE ANNOUNCEMENT - DIVISION OF TRAINING. NATIONAL INSTITUTE FOR OCCUPATIONAL SAFETY AND HEALTH **2861**

NATIONAL INSTITUTE FOR PETROLEUM LANDMEN **See** PROCEEDINGS OF THE NATIONAL INSTITUTE FOR PETROLEUM LANDMEN **4275**

NATIONAL INSTITUTE FOR PRODUCTIVITY **See** ANNUAL REPORT AND ACCOUNTS - NATIONAL INSTITUTE FOR PRODUCTIVITY **1597**

NATIONAL INSTITUTE OF ALLERGY AND INFECTIOUS DISEASES. RESEARCH RESOURCES BRANCH **See** NIAID CATALOG OF TISSUE TYPING ANTISERA **568**

NATIONAL INSTITUTE OF ALLERGY AND INFECTIOUS DISEASES (U.S.) **See** ANNUAL REPORT OF INTRAMURAL ACTIVITIES - NATIONAL INSTITUTE OF ALLERGY AND INFECTIOUS DISEASES (U.S.) **3712**

NATIONAL INSTITUTE OF ARTHRITIS, METABOLISM, AND DIGESTIVE DISEASES **See** ARTHRITIS, RHEUMATIC DISEASES, AND RELATED DISORDERS **3803**

NATIONAL INSTITUTE OF ARTS AND LETTERS, AMERICAN ACADEMY OF ARTS AND LETTERS (US) [02222534] **325**

NATIONAL INSTITUTE OF CHILD HEALTH AND HUMAN DEVELOPMENT. ADULT DEVELOPMENT AND AGING RESEARCH COMMITTEE **See** ANNUAL REPORT - ADULT DEVELOPMENT AND AGING RESEARCH COMMITTEE, NATIONAL INSTITUTES OF HEALTH **3749**

NATIONAL INSTITUTE OF CHILD HEALTH AND HUMAN DEVELOPMENT (U.S.) **See** NICHD ANNUAL REPORT **3907**

NATIONAL INSTITUTE OF CORRECTIONS (U.S.) **See** ANNUAL PROGRAM PLAN FOR FISCAL YEAR ... / U.S. DEPARTMENT OF JUSTICE, NATIONAL INSTITUTE OF CORRECTIONS **3156**

NATIONAL INSTITUTE OF DENTAL RESEARCH PROGRAMS (US/0360-7763) [01917136] **1330**

NATIONAL INSTITUTE OF DENTAL RESEARCH (U.S.) **See** ANNUAL REPORT - NATIONAL INSTITUTE OF DENTAL RESEARCH (U.S.) **1316**

NATIONAL INSTITUTE OF ECONOMIC AND SOCIAL RESEARCH **See** REGIONAL PAPERS - NATIONAL INSTITUTE OF ECONOMIC AND SOCIAL RESEARCH **1516**

NATIONAL INSTITUTE OF EDUCATION **See** CAREER EDUCATION PROGRAM : PROGRAM PLAN **1911**

NATIONAL INSTITUTE OF EDUCATION. R & D SYSTEM SUPPORT DIVISION **See** DATABOOK - U.S. DEPT. OF HEALTH, EDUCATION, AND WELFARE, NATIONAL INSTITUTE OF EDUCATION, DISSEMINATION AND RESOURCES GROUP, R & D SYSTEM SUPPORT DIVISION **1892**

NATIONAL INSTITUTE OF EDUCATION (U.S.) **See** GRANTS FOR RESEARCH ON EDUCATION AND WORK **1913**

NATIONAL INSTITUTE OF EDUCATION (U.S.) **See** GRANTS FOR RESEARCH ON DESEGREGATION **1748**

NATIONAL INSTITUTE OF EDUCATION (U.S.) **See** GRANTS FOR RESEARCH ON LAW AND GOVERNMENT IN EDUCATION **1748**

NATIONAL INSTITUTE OF ENVIRONMENTAL HEALTH SCIENCES **See** RESEARCH PROGRAMS / NATIONAL INSTITUTE OF ENVIRONMENTAL HEALTH SCIENCES **2242**

NATIONAL INSTITUTE OF GENERAL MEDICAL SCIENCES (U.S.) **See** ANNUAL REPORT / NATIONAL INSTITUTE OF GENERAL MEDICAL SCIENCES **442**

NATIONAL — Alphabetical Title Index

NATIONAL INSTITUTE OF GENETICS (JAPAN) See ANNUAL REPORT / NATIONAL INSTITUTE OF GENETICS **542**

NATIONAL INSTITUTE OF JUSTICE CATALOG (US) [24993406] **3141**

● NATIONAL INSTITUTE OF JUSTICE JOURNAL (US/1067-7453) [26714688] **3170**

NATIONAL INSTITUTE OF JUSTICE REPORTS See NATIONAL INSTITUTE OF JUSTICE JOURNAL **3170**

NATIONAL INSTITUTE OF JUSTICE (U.S.) See PUBLICATIONS OF THE NATIONAL INSTITUTE OF JUSTICE. SUPPLEMENT **4677**

NATIONAL INSTITUTE OF JUSTICE (U.S.) See NIJ PROGRAM PLAN / NATIONAL INSTITUTE OF JUSTICE **3170**

NATIONAL INSTITUTE OF JUSTICE (U.S.) See RESEARCH AND EVALUATION PLAN / NATIONAL INSTITUTE OF JUSTICE **3175**

NATIONAL INSTITUTE OF JUSTICE (U.S.). EVALUATION PLAN See RESEARCH AND EVALUATION PLAN / NATIONAL INSTITUTE OF JUSTICE **3175**

NATIONAL INSTITUTE OF JUSTICE (U.S.). RESEARCH AND EVALUATION PLAN See NIJ PROGRAM PLAN / NATIONAL INSTITUTE OF JUSTICE **3170**

NATIONAL INSTITUTE OF JUSTICE (U.S.). RESEARCH PLAN See RESEARCH AND EVALUATION PLAN / NATIONAL INSTITUTE OF JUSTICE **3175**

NATIONAL INSTITUTE OF LAW ENFORCEMENT AND CRIMINAL JUSTICE. OFFICE OF RESEARCH PROGRAMS See OFFICE OF RESEARCH PROGRAMS LIST OF SELECTED PUBLICATIONS & RESEARCH PROJECTS IN PROGRESS **3171**

NATIONAL INSTITUTE OF MENTAL HEALTH (U.S.) See MENTAL HEALTH PROGRAM REPORTS **4790**

NATIONAL INSTITUTE OF MENTAL HEALTH (U.S.). DIVISION OF INTRAMURAL RESEARCH PROGRAMS See ANNUAL REPORT - NATIONAL INSTITUTE OF MENTAL HEALTH (U.S.). DIVISION OF INTRAMURAL RESEARCH PROGRAMS **3920**

NATIONAL INSTITUTE OF MUNICIPAL LAW OFFICERS (U.S.) See NIMLO MODEL ORDINANCE SERVICE **4669**

NATIONAL INSTITUTE OF MUNICIPAL LAW OFFICERS, WASHINGTON, D.C See MUNICIPAL LAW COURT DECISIONS **3012**

NATIONAL INSTITUTE OF NEUROLOGICAL AND COMMUNICATIVE DISORDERS AND STROKE See TRAINING AWARDS, FELLOWSHIP AWARDS ... DATA BOOK / NATIONAL INSTITUTE OF NEUROLOGICAL AND COMMUNICATIVE DISORDERS AND STROKE **3847**

NATIONAL INSTITUTE OF NEUROLOGICAL AND COMMUNICATIVE DISORDERS AND STROKE See NINCDS RESEARCH PROGRAM. MUSCULAR DYSTROPHY AND OTHER NEUROMUSCULAR DISORDERS, THE **3843**

NATIONAL INSTITUTE OF NEUROLOGICAL AND COMMUNICATIVE DISORDERS AND STROKE See NINCDS RESEARCH PROGRAM. EPILEPSY, THE **3843**

NATIONAL INSTITUTE OF NEUROLOGICAL AND COMMUNICATIVE DISORDERS AND STROKE See FACT BOOK / NATIONAL INSTITUTE OF NEUROLOGICAL AND COMMUNICATIVE DISORDERS AND STROKE **3833**

NATIONAL INSTITUTE OF NEUROLOGICAL AND COMMUNICATIVE DISORDERS AND STROKE See NINCDS NEUROMUSCULAR DISORDERS RESEARCH PROGRAM, THE **3843**

NATIONAL INSTITUTE OF NEUROLOGICAL AND COMMUNICATIVE DISORDERS AND STROKE. EPILEPSY ADVISORY COMMITTEE See ANNUAL REPORT - EPILEPSY ADVISORY COMMITTEE, NATIONAL INSTITUTES OF HEALTH **3827**

NATIONAL INSTITUTE OF RURAL DEVELOPMENT (INDIA) See ANNUAL REPORT / NATIONAL INSTITUTE OF RURAL DEVELOPMENT **2814**

NATIONAL INSTITUTE OF RURAL DEVELOPMENT (INDIA). ANNUAL REPORT FOR ... OF THE NATIONAL INSTITUTE OF RURAL DEVELOPMENT See ANNUAL REPORT / NATIONAL INSTITUTE OF RURAL DEVELOPMENT **2814**

NATIONAL INSTITUTE OF SCIENCES OF INDIA. BIOGRAPHICAL MEMOIRS OF FELLOWS See BIOGRAPHICAL MEMOIRS OF FELLOWS OF THE INDIAN NATIONAL SCIENCE ACADEMY **430**

NATIONAL INSTITUTE ON AGING See REPORT TO COUNCIL ON AGING **5305**

NATIONAL INSTITUTE ON AGING. PROGRAM ANALYSIS OFFICE See INDEX OF CURRENT RESEARCH GRANTS AND CONTRACTS ADMINISTERED BY THE NATIONAL INSTITUTE ON AGING **3752**

NATIONAL INSTITUTE ON DRUG ABUSE. DIVISION OF SCIENTIFIC AND PROGRAM INFORMATION See EXECUTIVE REPORT, DATA FROM THE NATIONAL DRUG ABUSE TREATMENT UTILIZATION SURVEY (NDATUS) **1344**

NATIONAL INSTITUTE ON DRUG ABUSE. DIVISION OF SCIENTIFIC AND PROGRAM INFORMATION See SUMMARY REPORT, DATA FORM THE NATIONAL DRUG ABUSE TREATMENT UTILIZATION SURVEY (NDATUS) **1349**

NATIONAL INSTITUTE ON DRUG ABUSE. RESOURCE CENTER See AUDIOVISUAL CATALOG - NIDA RESOURCE CENTER **1341**

NATIONAL INSTITUTE ON DRUG ABUSE STATISTICAL SERIES. SERIES (US/0731-2458) [08073130] **1347, 1350**

NATIONAL INSTITUTE ON DRUG ABUSE STATISTICAL SERIES. SERIES H (US/0896-1190) [09431814] **1347, 1350**

NATIONAL INSTITUTES OF HEALTH ANNUAL REPORT OF INTERNATIONAL ACTIVITIES (US/0146-6690) [02982336] **3619**

NATIONAL INSTITUTES OF HEALTH. GENERAL CLINICAL RESEARCH CENTERS COMMITTEE See ANNUAL REPORT - GENERAL CLINICAL RESEARCH CENTERS COMMITTEE, NATIONAL INSTITUTES OF HEALTH **3776**

NATIONAL INSTITUTES OF HEALTH INTERNATIONAL AWARDS FOR BIOMEDICAL RESEARCH AND RESEARCH TRAINING (US) [01783964] **5130**

NATIONAL INSTITUTES OF HEALTH RESEARCH PLAN (US/0278-6834) [07820489] **4792**

NATIONAL INSTITUTES OF HEALTH (U.S.) See ANALYSIS OF RESEARCH PUBLICATIONS SUPPORTED BY NIH AND NIAID **4765**

NATIONAL INSTITUTES OF HEALTH (U.S.) See TELEPHONE AND SERVICE DIRECTORY / NATIONAL INSTITUTES OF HEALTH **4804**

NATIONAL INSTITUTES OF HEALTH (U.S.) See ANALYSIS OF RESEARCH PUBLICATIONS SUPPORTED BY NIH AND NHLBI **4765**

NATIONAL INSTITUTES OF HEALTH (U.S.) See BULLETIN - NATIONAL INSTITUTES OF HEALTH (U.S.) **4769**

NATIONAL INSTITUTES OF HEALTH (U.S.) See NATIONAL INSTITUTES OF HEALTH RESEARCH PLAN **4792**

NATIONAL INSTITUTES OF HEALTH (U.S.) See CLINICAL ELECTIVES FOR MEDICAL AND DENTAL STUDENTS AT THE NATIONAL INSTITUTES OF HEALTH **4771**

NATIONAL INSTITUTES OF HEALTH (U.S.) See SCIENTIFIC DIRECTORY AND ANNUAL BIBLIOGRAPHY **5176**

NATIONAL INSTITUTES OF HEALTH (U.S.) See POSTDOCTORAL RESEARCH FELLOWSHIP OPPORTUNITIES / NATIONAL INSTITUTES OF HEALTH **3628**

NATIONAL INSTITUTES OF HEALTH (U.S.). BIOMEDICAL ENGINEERING AND INSTRUMENTATION BRANCH See ANNUAL REPORT - NATIONAL INSTITUTES OF HEALTH (U.S.). BIOMEDICAL ENGINEERING AND INSTRUMENTATION BRANCH **3685**

NATIONAL INSTITUTES OF HEALTH (U.S.). CLINICAL CENTER See MEDICAL STAFF DIRECTORY **1330**

NATIONAL INSTITUTES OF HEALTH (U.S.). CLINICAL CENTER See HANDBOOK FOR STAFF PHYSICIANS / CLINICAL CENTER, NATIONAL INSTITUTES OF HEALTH **3780**

NATIONAL INSTITUTES OF HEALTH (U.S.). COMMITTEE MANAGEMENT STAFF See NIH ADVISORY COMMITTEES **4794**

NATIONAL INSTITUTES OF HEALTH (U.S.). DIVISION OF PUBLIC INFORMATION See NIH ALMANAC **4794**

NATIONAL INSTITUTES OF HEALTH (U.S.). DIVISION OF RESEARCH GRANTS See SCHEDULE OF NIH CONFERENCES **3639**

NATIONAL INSTITUTES OF HEALTH (U.S.). DIVISION OF RESEARCH RESOURCES See PROGRAM HIGHLIGHTS **3630**

NATIONAL INSTITUTES OF HEALTH (U.S.). DIVISION OF RESEARCH SERVICES See ANNUAL REPORT - NATIONAL INSTITUTE OF HEALTH (U.S.). DIVISION OF RESEARCH SERVICES **3551**

NATIONAL INSTITUTES OF HEALTH (U.S.). EDITORIAL OPERATIONS BRANCH See NIH PUBLICATIONS LIST **4810**

NATIONAL INSTITUTES OF HEALTH (U.S.). NUTRITION COORDINATING COMMITTEE See ANNUAL REPORT OF THE NATIONAL INSTITUTES OF HEALTH. PROGRAM BEHAVIORAL NUTRITION RESEARCH AND TRAINING **4187**

NATIONAL INSTITUTES OF HEALTH (U.S.). POSTDOCTORAL RESEARCH FELLOWSHIP OPPORTUNITIES CATALOG See POSTDOCTORAL RESEARCH FELLOWSHIP OPPORTUNITIES / NATIONAL INSTITUTES OF HEALTH **3628**

NATIONAL INSURANCE LAW REVIEW (US/0743-7927) [10686576] **2889, 3013**

NATIONAL INSURANCE SCHEME : ANNUAL REPORT YEAR ENDING ... / MINISTRY OF LABOUR AND NATIONAL INSURANCE (JM) [24204663] **2889**

NATIONAL INTELLIGENCE REPORT. CLINICAL LABS/BLOOD BANKS (US/0270-6768) [06481335] **3619**

NATIONAL INTEREST, THE (US/0884-9382) [12532731] **4529**

● NATIONAL INTERNAL AUDITING LETTER, THE (CN/1193-8765) [27809686] **748**

NATIONAL INVENTORY OF ACADEMIC & TRAINING COURSES IN PROGRAM & PROJECT EVALUATION (CN/1184-6313) [23658932] **420**

NATIONAL INVESTMENT AND FINANCE (II) [01608366] **847, 909**

NATIONAL JAIL AND ADULT DETENTION DIRECTORY (US/0192-8228) [04798029] **3170**

NATIONAL JESUIT NEWS (US/0199-0284) [05521187] **4980**

NATIONAL JEWELER (US/0027-9544) [02850451] **2915**

NATIONAL JEWISH COMMUNITY RELATIONS ADVISORY COUNCIL (U.S.) See DIRECTORY OF CONSTITUENT ORGANIZATIONS **2259**

NATIONAL JEWISH LAW REVIEW *SUSPENDED.* (US/0897-2222) [13956506] **3013**

NATIONAL JEWISH LIFE, THE (US) [17197327] **2268**

NATIONAL JEWISH NEWS, THE (US/1043-2795) [19371598] **5051**

NATIONAL JEWISH POST & OPINION (INDIANAPOLIS, INC. : 1984) (US/0888-0379) [13448139] **5665**

NATIONAL JOB BANK, THE (US/1051-4872) [10493072] **4206**

NATIONAL JOB BULLETIN (US) **4707, 4206**

NATIONAL JOB MARKET *CEASED.* (US/0747-4296) [10363248] **4206**

NATIONAL JOURNAL (1975) (US/0360-4217) [02244202] **4483**

NATIONAL JOURNAL (ALLENTOWN, PA.) (US/0744-3889) [08243470] **2775, 2592**

NATIONAL JOURNAL OF CONSTITUTIONAL LAW (CN/1181-9340) [24267044] **3093**

NATIONAL JOURNAL OF CONSTITUTIONAL LAW (CN/1181-9340) [24208528] **3093**

● NATIONAL JOURNAL OF HOMOEOPATHY : NJH (II) [27965115] **3775**

NATIONAL JOURNAL OF MEDICINE & MEDICAL RESEARCH (US/0733-9844) [08625302] **3619**

NATIONAL JOURNAL OF SOCIOLOGY (US/0892-4287) [15189541] **5252**

NATIONAL JUNIOR COLLEGE ATHLETIC ASSOCIATION See J U C O REVIEW **4901**

NATIONAL JURY VERDICT REVIEW AND ANALYSIS, THE (US/0887-2899) [13047247] **3090**

NATIONAL KIDNEY FOUNDATION. COUNCIL OF NEPHROLOGY SOCIAL WORKERS See CNSW NEWSLETTER **3989**

NATIONAL KNIFE MAGAZINE, THE (US/1051-4600) [10977758] **2775**

NATIONAL LABOUR REVIEW *CEASED.* (CN/0835-8087) [17526633] **3152**

● NATIONAL LAMB & WOOL GROWER (US/1075-0231) [29423270] **110**

NATIONAL LAMPOON (US/0027-9587) [01788770] **2539**

NATIONAL LAW JOURNAL, THE (US/0162-7325) [04161259] **3013**

NATIONAL LAW REVIEW REPORTER (US/0276-7546) [06471608] **3013**

NATIONAL LAW SCHOOL JOURNAL (II) [23859018] **3013**

NATIONAL LAWYER'S GUILD PRACTITIONER (US) **3013**

NATIONAL LEAGUE FOR NURSING See STATE-APPROVED SCHOOLS OF NURSING, L.P.N./L.V.N **3869**

NATIONAL LEAGUE GREEN BOOK (US/0896-6400) [05210194] **4906**

NATIONAL LEAGUE OF INSURED SAVINGS ASSOCIATIONS. LEGAL BULLETIN See LEGAL BULLETIN (WASHINGTON) **3087**

NATIONAL LEAGUE OF PROFESSIONAL BASEBALL CLUBS See NATIONAL LEAGUE GREEN BOOK **4906**

NATIONAL LEGAL ASSISTANT CONFERENCE CENTER See PARA-LEGAL UPDATE **3025**

NATIONAL LEGAL CENTER NEWS (US/0275-9233) [07231055] **3013**

NATIONAL LEGAL EAGLE (AT/0813-9741) [I08139741] **3013**

NATIONAL LEGAL EXCHANGE (US/1055-1069) [20626312] **3013**

NATIONAL LEGISLATION AND REGULATIONS RELATING TO TRANSNATIONAL CORPORATIONS / CENTRE ON TRANSNATIONAL CORPORATIONS (US) [13512414] **1638**

NATIONAL LIBRARIAN : THE NLA NEWSLETTER (US/0191-359X) [04654592] **3233**

NATIONAL LIBRARY AND DOCUMENTATION SERVICE (ZIMBABWE). COUNCIL See ANNUAL REPORT OF THE CHAIRMAN OF THE COUNCIL OF THE NATIONAL LIBRARY AND DOCUMENTATION SERVICE FOR THE YEAR ENDED ... **3191**

NATIONAL LIBRARY NEWS (CN/0027-9633) [01653895] **3233**

NATIONAL LIBRARY OF AUSTRALIA See ANNUAL REPORT - NATIONAL LIBRARY OF AUSTRALIA **3190**

NATIONAL LIBRARY OF AUSTRALIA See GUIDE TO COLLECTIONS OF MANUSCRIPTS RELATING TO AUSTRALIA **416**

NATIONAL LIBRARY OF AUSTRALIA See ACQUISITIONS NEWSLETTER **3187**

NATIONAL LIBRARY OF AUSTRALIA See INDONESIAN ACQUISITIONS LIST **3215**

NATIONAL LIBRARY OF AUSTRALIA See CATALOGUE OF 16 MM. FILMS **4065**

NATIONAL LIBRARY OF AUSTRALIA NEWS (AT/1032-1829) [23858432] **3233**

NATIONAL LIBRARY OF CANADA See MADE IN CANADA. ARTISTS IN BOOKS **357**

NATIONAL LIBRARY OF CANADA See ANNUAL REPORT / NATIONAL LIBRARY OF CANADA / RAPPORT ANNUEL / BIBLIOTHEQUE NATIONALE DU CANADA **3190**

NATIONAL LIBRARY OF CANADA See NATIONAL LIBRARY NEWS **3233**

NATIONAL LIBRARY OF CANADA See FORTHCOMING BOOKS - NATIONAL LIBRARY OF CANADA **3211**

NATIONAL LIBRARY OF MEDICINE AUDIOVISUALS CATALOG *CEASED.* (US/0149-9939) [04108612] 3619, **3233**

NATIONAL LIBRARY OF MEDICINE CURRENT CATALOG *CEASED.* (US) [23985263] **3619**

NATIONAL LIBRARY OF MEDICINE PROGRAMS AND SERVICES (US/0163-4569) [04746049] 3619, **3233**

NATIONAL LIBRARY OF MEDICINE (U.S.) See HEALTH SCIENCES SERIALS **3213**

NATIONAL LIBRARY OF MEDICINE (U.S.) See CURRENT CATALOG PROOF SHEETS, SEMIWEEKLY PROOF **3205**

NATIONAL LIBRARY OF MEDICINE (U.S.) See NATIONAL LIBRARY OF MEDICINE CURRENT CATALOG **3619**

NATIONAL LIBRARY OF MEDICINE (U.S) See NATIONAL LIBRARY OF MEDICINE PROGRAMS AND SERVICES **3233**

NATIONAL LIBRARY OF MEDICINE (U.S.) See NATIONAL LIBRARY OF MEDICINE AUDIOVISUALS CATALOG **3233**

NATIONAL LIBRARY OF MEDICINE (U.S.) See HEALTH SCIENCES AUDIOVISUALS **4781**

NATIONAL LIBRARY OF MEDICINE (U.S.) See MEDICAL SUBJECT HEADINGS **3230**

NATIONAL LIBRARY OF NEW ZEALAND See REPORT OF THE TRUSTEES OF THE NATIONAL LIBRARY OF NEW ZEALAND AND OF THE NATIONAL LIBRARIAN **3245**

NATIONAL LIBRARY OF SCOTLAND NEWS (UK/0950-7086) [I09507086] **3233**

NATIONAL LIBRARY OF WALES See CYLCHGRAWN LLYFRGELL GENEDLAETHOL CYMRU **3205**

NATIONAL LIFELINER, THE (CN/0709-8677) [05842269] **5297**

NATIONAL LIMESTONE INSTITUTE (U.S.) See LIMESTONE (WASHINGTON) **4007**

NATIONAL LIQUOR NEWS (AT/0816-0430) [I08160430] **2369**

NATIONAL LIST OF ADVERTISERS (TORONTO) (CN/0077-5177) [02443342] **763**

NATIONAL LIST OF HISTORIC THEATRE BUILDINGS (US) [12709868] **304**

NATIONAL LIVE STOCK AND MEAT BOARD See MEAT BOARD REPORTS [ANNUAL REPORT] **215**

NATIONAL LOCKSMITH, THE (US/0364-3719) [02636469] **2812**

NATIONAL LONGITUDINAL SURVEY OF YOUTH, THE (US/1060-4960) [24919443] **5252**

NATIONAL LOSS PREVENTION (CN/0228-894X) [07821123] **880**

NATIONAL LUBRICATING GREASE INSTITUTE See NLGI SPOKESMAN **2123**

NATIONAL LUBRICATING GREASE INSTITUTE ANNUAL MEETING PAPERS (US) **3485**

NATIONAL MALL MONITOR See NMM WEEKLY **4842**

NATIONAL MANPOWER AND YOUTH COUNCIL (PHILIPPINES) See CALENDAR YEAR REPORT / NATIONAL MANPOWER AND YOUTH COUNCIL **1657**

NATIONAL MANUFACTURERS REGISTER (US/0163-2191) [04311729] **3485**

NATIONAL MARINE POLLUTION PROGRAM. SUMMARY OF FEDERAL PROGRAMS AND PROJECTS, FY ... UPDATE (US) [18652667] **2237**

NATIONAL MARINER, THE (US/0746-391X) [10014073] **1453**

NATIONAL MARKET PLACE NEWS (AT/1030-8784) **2350**

NATIONAL MASTITIS COUNCIL (U.S.). MEETING See ANNUAL MEETING - NATIONAL MASTITIS COUNCIL, INC **191**

NATIONAL MEASUREMENT LABORATORY (U.S.) See TECHNICAL HIGHLIGHTS - NATIONAL MEASUREMENT LABORATORY **4032**

NATIONAL MEASUREMENT LABORATORY (U.S.). REACTOR RADIATION DIVISION See NBS. REACTOR. SUMMARY OF ACTIVITIES **4448**

NATIONAL MEAT PACKER REFERENCE GUIDE (US/0743-3956) [10554494] 4220, **216**

NATIONAL MECHANICAL CONTRACTOR ESTIMATOR (US) **2107**

NATIONAL MEDICAL CARE UTILIZATION AND EXPENDITURE SURVEY. SERIES B, DESCRIPTIVE REPCRT (US/0895-2728) [11997057] **3789**

NATIONAL MEDICAL CARE UTILIZATION AND EXPENDITURE SURVEY. SERIES C, ANALYTICAL REPORT (US/0895-2671) [12940550] **3789**

NATIONAL MEDICAL JOURNAL OF INDIA, THE (II/0970-258X) [18467004] **3619**

NATIONAL MEDICAL-LEGAL JOURNAL (US/1052-309X) [22265521] 3619, **3013**

NATIONAL MEETING - AMERICAN CHEMICAL SOCIETY, DIVISION OF ENVIRONMENTAL CHEMISTRY (US/0270-3009) [06395528] **987**

NATIONAL MEETING; PROGRAM (US) [02251081] **2015**

NATIONAL MEMBERSHIP DIRECTORY - WOMEN IN COMMUNICATIONS, INC (US/0360-3296) [02244188] 5562, **1118**

NATIONAL METAL WORKING BLUE BOOK (US/0363-1737) [02430936] **4013**

NATIONAL METALLURGICAL LABORATORY (INDIA) See NML TECHNICAL JOURNAL **4013**

NATIONAL METEOROLOGICAL CENTER GRIDPOINT DATA SET, VERSION II. CD-ROM (US) **1432**

NATIONAL MIDWEEK *SUSPENDED.* (PH/0116-2470) [13845414] **2659**

NATIONAL MILK RECORDS. ANNUAL REPORT, ENGLAND & WALES (UK) [01645352] **197**

NATIONAL MINORITY BUSINESS INFORMATION SYSTEM (US/0730-6334) [07629078] 5562, **697**

NATIONAL MINORITY DIGEST (US) [03134209] **2268**

NATIONAL MINORITY POLITICS (US/1057-1655) [21392309] **2268**

NATIONAL MODEL RAILROAD ASSOCIATION See NMRA BULLETIN **5433**

NATIONAL MONTHLY BOND SUMMARY, THE (US) [04472324] **909**

NATIONAL MONTHLY CONDOMINIUM EXECUTIVE REPORT (US/0739-5647) [09780194] **4841**

NATIONAL MONTHLY STOCK SUMMARY, THE (US/0275-8326) [04175927] **909**

NATIONAL MORTGAGE NEWS (US/1050-3331) [21464986] **801**

NATIONAL MOTOR FREIGHT CLASSIFICATION (US) [05540284] **5388**

NATIONAL MOTORIST (US/0279-3083) [07748745] **5485**

NATIONAL MULTIPLE SCLEROSIS SOCIETY See ANNUAL REPORT - NATIONAL MULTIPLE SCLEROSIS SOCIETY **3827**

NATIONAL MUNICIPAL LEAGUE See STATE CONSTITUTIONAL CONVENTION STUDIES **4687**

NATIONAL MUNICIPAL POLICY / AMERICAN MUNICIPAL ASSOCIATION (US) [04838091] **4668**

NATIONAL MUSEUM ACT; GUIDELINES FOR GRANT PROGRAMS (US) [04173515] **4093**

NATIONAL MUSEUM OF AFRICAN ART (U.S.) See CALENDAR **346**

NATIONAL MUSEUM OF AUSTRALIA See ANNUAL REPORT / THE NATIONAL MUSEUM OF AUSTRALIA **4084**

NATIONAL MUSEUM OF MAN See PUBLICATIONS IN ARCHAEOLOGY (OTTAWA) **279**

NATIONAL MUSEUM OF NEW ZEALAND See RECORDS - NATIONAL MUSEUM OF NEW ZEALAND **4095**

NATIONAL MUSEUM OF NEW ZEALAND MISCELLANEOUS SERIES (NZ/0110-1447) [08160511] **4093**

NATIONAL MUSEUM OF SCIENCE AND TECHNOLOGY (CANADA) See CORPORATE PLAN SUMMARY, CAPITAL BUDGET SUMMARY, OPERATING BUDGET SUMMARY **5097**

NATIONAL MUSEUM OF SCIENCE AND TECHNOLOGY (CANADA) See ANNUAL REPORT - NATIONAL MUSEUM OF SCIENCE AND TECHNOLOGY (OTTAWA) **4083**

NATIONAL MUSEUM PAPERS (PH/0117-0686) [22894799] **4168**

NATIONAL MUSEUMS OF SCOTLAND See NATIONAL MUSEUMS OF SCOTLAND ... REPORT **4093**

NATIONAL MUSEUMS OF SCOTLAND ... REPORT (UK/0953-7007) [18473928] **4093**

NATIONAL NETWORK (CN/0848-9947) [21680201] **3862**

NATIONAL NETWORK (DALLAS, TEX.) (US/1075-3753) [21588913] **3619**

NATIONAL NETWORK DIRECTORY (US/0736-7341) [09365522] **359**

NATIONAL NETWORK NEWS (CN/1181-8107) [23230559] **4052**

NATIONAL NEW CAR PRICE GUIDE (US) [08385670] **5421**

NATIONAL NEWS - AMERICAN LEGION AUXILIARY (US/1062-4244) [05752462] **5234**

NATIONAL NEWS FOR THE YOUTH MOVEMENT FOR THE COUNTRYSIDE (UK) [03319318] **1067**

NATIONAL NEWS LETTER - FEDERATION OF MILITARY AND UNITED SERVICES INSTITUTES OF CANADA (CN/0713-0511) [08932783] 5297, **4052**

NATIONAL NEWS - NATIONAL PENSIONERS AND SENIOR CITIZENS FEDERATION (CN/0849-2115) [23236705] **5180**

NATIONAL NEWS REPORT *CEASED.* (US/0049-044X) [02255901] 4483, **2198**

NATIONAL NEWSLETTER (CN) [20777989] **4863**

NATIONAL NEWSLETTER - ASSOCIATED GENERAL CONTRACTORS OF AMERICA (US/1044-7598) [19898377] **1619**

NATIONAL NEWSLETTER - ASSOCIATION OF PART-TIME PROFESSIONALS (U.S.) (US/0739-2931) [09718743] **4206**

NATIONAL NEWSLETTER - CANADIAN ASSOCIATION OF SEXUAL ASSAULT CENTRES (CN/0824-5045) [10768387] **5297**

NATIONAL NEWSLETTER (CANADIAN PARENTS FOR FRENCH) (CN/0715-8904) [11250504] **3305**

NATIONAL NEWSLETTER - CANSPA (CN/0229-2866) [08091430] **622**

NATIONAL NEWSPAPER ASSOCIATION See NATIONAL NEWSPAPER ASSOCIATION DIRECTORY **4817**

NATIONAL NEWSPAPER ASSOCIATION DIRECTORY (US/0147-7528) [03228657] **4817**

NATIONAL NEWSPAPER INDEX (US/0273-3676) [08894033] **5814**

NATIONAL NEWSPAPER INDEX (MONTHLY) (US) [19101714] **5814**

NATIONAL NEWSPATCH, THE (US/0891-3064) [14756743] 4391, **1882**

NATIONAL NONCONVENTIONAL ENERGY RESOURCES DEVELOPMENT PROGRAM PROGRESS REPORT / MINISTRY OF ENERGY, THE (PH) [07425700] **1950**

NATIONAL NOTARY, THE (US/0894-7872) [05747789] **4668**

NATIONAL NOW TIMES (US/0149-4740) [03494944] **5562**

NATIONAL — Alphabetical Title Index

NATIONAL OBSERVER BOOK OF CROSSWORDS, THE (US/0192-6837) [05085901] **4863**

NATIONAL OBSERVER. NEWSPAPER INDEX, THE (US/0363-7832) [02515221] **5693**

NATIONAL OCEAN SURVEY See MONTHLY REPORT OF ACTIVITIES / U.S. DEPARTMENT OF COMMERCE, NATIONAL OCEANIC AND ATMOSPHERIC ADMINISTRATION, NATIONAL OCEAN SURVEY **846**

NATIONAL OCEAN SURVEY See COLLECTED REPRINTS - NATIONAL OCEAN SURVEY **1448**

NATIONAL OCEAN SURVEY See LATEST EDITIONS OF U.S. AIR FORCE AERONAUTICAL CHARTS **4048**

NATIONAL OCEAN SURVEY ANNUAL REPORT / NOS - OFFICE OF PROGRAM DEVELOPMENT AND MANAGEMENT, PHYSICAL SCIENCE SERVICES BRANCH (US) [09236875] **1453**

NATIONAL OCEAN SURVEY. PHYSICAL SCIENCE SERVICES BRANCH See NATIONAL OCEAN SURVEY ANNUAL REPORT / NOS - OFFICE OF PROGRAM DEVELOPMENT AND MANAGEMENT, PHYSICAL SCIENCE SERVICES BRANCH **1453**

NATIONAL OCEANOGRAPHIC FLEET OPERATING SCHEDULES FOR ... (US/0748-1063) [10862262] **1453**

NATIONAL OFFICE DIRECTORY (US/0897-5922) [17560105] **697**

NATIONAL OIL & LUBE NEWS, THE (US/1071-1260) [28555070] **4265**

NATIONAL ON-CAMPUS REPORT (US/0300-6646) [01343315] **1836**

NATIONAL OPERATIONS AND AUTOMATION CONFERENCE PROCEEDINGS, THE (US/0095-5396) [01784535] 1220, **801**

NATIONAL OPERATIONS/AUTOMATION SURVEY (US/0735-0058) [08731148] **801**

NATIONAL OPINION POLL (US/0148-8449) [03456718] **5252**

NATIONAL OPINION RESEARCH CENTER See NEWSLETTER - NATIONAL OPINION RESEARCH CENTER **5252**

NATIONAL OPPORTUNITES FOR ALLIED HEALTH (US) **3915**

NATIONAL OPTICAL ASTRONOMY OBSERVATORIES NEWSLETTER See GEMINI PROJECT NEWSLETTER **395**

●... NATIONAL ORGANIC DIRECTORY, THE (US/1073-0540) [29303870] **2350**

NATIONAL ORGANIZATION FOR BLACK CHEMISTS AND CHEMICAL ENGINEERS. NATIONAL CONFERENCE See PROCEEDINGS, NOBCCHE **989**

NATIONAL ORGANIZATION FOR WOMEN See NATIONAL NOW TIMES **5562**

NATIONAL ORGANIZATION ON LEGAL PROBLEMS OF EDUCATION See NOLPE NOTES **3017**

NATIONAL ORGANIZATIONS OF STATE GOVERNMENT OFFICIALS DIRECTORY (US/1051-6093) [11115509] **4668**

NATIONAL ORIENTATION DIRECTORS ASSOCIATION (U.S.) See DATA BANK : A PUBLICATION OF THE NATIONAL ORIENTATION DIRECTORS ASSOCIATION **1862**

NATIONAL OSTRICH/EXOTICS DIRECTORY See ... NATIONAL OSTRICH/RATITE DIRECTORY, THE **216**

... NATIONAL OSTRICH/EXOTICS DIRECTORY, THE (US/1050-9801) [20681077] **216**

NATIONAL OSTRICH/RATITE DIRECTORY See OSTRICH NEWS RATITE DIRECTORY, THE **5517**

... NATIONAL OSTRICH/RATITE DIRECTORY, THE (US/1050-981X) [21718297] **216**

NATIONAL OTC STOCK JOURNAL, THE (US/0745-7049) [09387712] **909**

NATIONAL (OTTAWA) (CN/0315-2286) [01795201] 697, **3013**

NATIONAL (OTTAWA. 1978) (CN/0709-1370) [05528265] **1882**

NATIONAL OUTLOOK SYDNEY (AT/0158-6270) [I01586270] 4483, 4980, **5252**

NATIONAL PACKING NEWS (US/1073-6948) [29513803] **2351**

NATIONAL PALACE MUSEUM BULLETIN (CH/0027-9846) [02263335] **4093**

NATIONAL PANORAMA OF AMERICAN YOUTH, THE (US/0360-0815) [02243669] **1766**

NATIONAL PARALEGAL REPORTER (US/1058-482X) [24305936] **3014**

NATIONAL PARALEGAL REPORTER (US/1058-482X) [09698124] **3014**

NATIONAL PARK GUIDE (NEW YORK, N.Y.) (US/0734-7960) [08382579] **4707**

NATIONAL PARK SERVICE INTERPRETIVE SERIES. HISTORY (US) [01128755] **2198**

NATIONAL PARK SERVICE SCIENTIFIC MONOGRAPH SERIES (US/0363-0722) [01887790] 519, **1389**

NATIONAL PARK SERVICE SOURCE BOOK SERIES (US/0083-2316) [01135197] **4852**

NATIONAL PARK STATISTICAL ABSTRACT (US/0278-1328) [05417622] 2198, **2185**

NATIONAL PARKS (JA) 2198, **4707**

NATIONAL PARKS JAPAN (JA) **2198**

NATIONAL PARKS JOURNAL (AT/0047-9012) **2198**

NATIONAL PARKS TODAY (UK/0265-0460) [I02650460] **4707**

NATIONAL PARKS (WASHINGTON, D.C.) (US/0276-8186) [07077425] 2198, **4707**

NATIONAL PARLIAMENTARIAN (US/8755-7592) [08298042] **4668**

NATIONAL PASTIME, THE (US/0734-6905) [08788448] **4906**

NATIONAL PATTERNS OF R&D RESOURCES (US) [19977542] 1988, **5130**

NATIONAL PEACH COUNCIL See PROCEEDINGS - NATIONAL PEACH COUNCIL **2353**

NATIONAL PEACH COUNCIL ANNUAL See PROCEEDINGS - NATIONAL PEACH COUNCIL **2353**

NATIONAL PEST CONTROL ASSOCIATION See TECHNICAL RELEASE - NATIONAL PEST CONTROL ASSOCIATION **4248**

NATIONAL PEST CONTROL ASSOCIATION. ROSTER OF MEMBERS See WHO'S WHO IN PROFESSIONAL PEST CONTROL **437**

NATIONAL PESTICIDE INFORMATION RETRIEVAL SYSTEM See NPIRS NEWS / NATIONAL PESTICIDE INFORMATION RETRIEVAL SYSTEM **4246**

NATIONAL PETROLEUM COUNCIL See NATIONAL PETROLEUM COUNCIL **4265**

NATIONAL PETROLEUM COUNCIL (US/0741-1464) [09641282] **4265**

NATIONAL PETROLEUM NEWS (US/0149-5267) [03507011] **4265**

NATIONAL PETROLEUM NEWS FACTBOOK See NATIONAL PETROLEUM NEWS. MARKET FACTS **4265**

NATIONAL PETROLEUM NEWS. MARKET FACTS (US) [26250422] **4265**

NATIONAL PHARMACEUTICAL ASSOCIATION See JOURNAL - NATIONAL PHARMACEUTICAL ASSOCIATION **4310**

NATIONAL PHYSICIAN ASSISTANT PROGRAM PROFILE, THE (US/0363-7174) [02529356] **3619**

●NATIONAL PLAN OF INTEGRATED AIRPORT SYSTEMS (US) [13246439] **30**

NATIONAL POLITICAL SCIENCE REVIEW (US/0896-629X) [17223548] **4483**

NATIONAL PORTRAIT GALLERY (SMITHSONIAN INSTITUTION) See PERMANENT COLLECTION ILLUSTRATED CHECKLIST **362**

NATIONAL PORTS COUNCIL BULLETIN *CEASED.* (UK/0305-5701) [07061158] **5453**

NATIONAL POTATO GERMPLASM EVALUATION AND ENHANCEMENT REPORT (US/8756-2626) [10165446] **179**

NATIONAL POULTRY IMPROVEMENT PLAN. DIRECTORY OF PARTICIPANTS HANDLING EGG-TYPE AND MEAT-TYPE CHICKENS AND TURKEYS (US/0271-793X) [06396999] **216**

NATIONAL POULTRY IMPROVEMENT PLAN. DIRECTORY OF PARTICIPANTS HANDLING WATERFOWL, EXHIBITION POULTRY, AND GAME BIRDS (US/0271-7948) [06396984] 5618, **216**

NATIONAL POWER NEWS (UK) **2073**

NATIONAL PR PITCH BOOK (US) **1298**

NATIONAL PRESCRIPTION AUDIT: THERAPEUTIC CATEGORY REPORT (US/0145-5451) [02750708] **4317**

NATIONAL PRESERVATION NEWS (US/0882-4339) [11830604] **3233**

NATIONAL PRISON PROJECT JOURNAL, THE (US/1076-769X) [23593691] **3170**

NATIONAL PRO-LIFE JOURNAL, THE *CEASED.* (US/0363-9614) [02567811] **589**

NATIONAL PRODUCTIVITY REVIEW (US/0277-8556) [07650302] **880**

NATIONAL PROGRAM LETTER (US/0027-9943) [05662938] **1766**

NATIONAL PROPERTY LAW DIGESTS (US/0363-8340) [02548544] **3014**

NATIONAL PROVISIONER, THE (US/0027-996X) [01604420] **2351**

NATIONAL PSORIASIS FOUNDATION (U.S.) See ANNUAL REPORT - NATIONAL PSORIASIS FOUNDATION (U.S.) **3717**

NATIONAL PSYCHOLOGICAL ASSOCIATION FOR PSYCHOANALYSIS See BULLETIN - NATIONAL PSYCHOLOGICAL ASSOCIATION FOR PSYCHOANALYSIS **4579**

NATIONAL PSYCHOLOGIST, THE (US/1058-6776) [24356012] **4605**

NATIONAL PUBLIC ACCOUNTANT (1957), THE (US/0027-9978) [07664456] **748**

NATIONAL PUBLIC EMPLOYMENT REPORTER (US/0194-889X) [04690740] **3152**

NATIONAL QUERIES FORUM, THE (US/1058-7020) [23036584] **2462**

NATIONAL RADIO GUIDE (CN/0849-3952) [22487445] **1135**

NATIONAL RADIO PUBLICITY DIRECTORY (US/0276-4520) [07369970] **1135**

NATIONAL RADIO PUBLICITY OUTLETS (US/0889-2784) [12919646] **1135**

NATIONAL RAILWAY BULLETIN (US/0885-5099) [03160895] **5433**

NATIONAL RAILWAYS OF ZIMBABWE (RH) [07507208] **5433**

NATIONAL RATE BOOK AND COLLEGE NEWSPAPER DIRECTORY (US) [06182021] **1093**

NATIONAL REAL ESTATE INDEX (US) [14370797] **4841**

NATIONAL REAL ESTATE INDEX. MARKET MONITOR (US) [27801321] **4842**

NATIONAL REAL ESTATE INVESTOR (US/0027-9994) [01759345] 4842, **909**

NATIONAL REAL ESTATE INVESTOR. DIRECTORY ISSUE (US/0731-8693) [07648552] **4842**

NATIONAL REAL PROPERTY LAW REVIEW (CN/1181-9359) [23302809] **4842**

●NATIONAL REFERRAL ROSTER (US/1075-1084) [29932161] **4842**

NATIONAL REGISTER BULLETIN (US) [15614794] **304**

NATIONAL REGISTER OF ACCOMMODATION See WHERE TO STAY IN SCOTLAND, BED AND BREAKFAST **2810**

●NATIONAL REGISTER OF COMMERCIAL REAL ESTATE, THE (US/1062-6352) [25686851] **4842**

NATIONAL REGISTER OF HEALTH SERVICE PROVIDERS IN PSYCHOLOGY (US/0099-2151) [01692593] **4605**

NATIONAL REGISTER OF HEALTH SERVICE PROVIDERS IN PSYCHOLOGY. SUPPLEMENT (US/0730-5540) [07971787] **4605**

NATIONAL REGISTER OF HISTORIC PLACES INDEX ON CD-ROM (US) **2747**

NATIONAL REGISTER OF NON-GOVERNMENT SECONDARY SCHOOLS OF AUSTRALIA (AT) **1766**

NATIONAL REGISTER OF PROMINENT AMERICANS AND INTERNATIONAL NOTABLES (US) [05113110] **434**

NATIONAL REGISTRY OF COMMUNITY MENTAL HEALTH SERVICES (US) [12791767] **5297**

NATIONAL RELOCATION AND REAL ESTATE MAGAZINE (US) **4842**

NATIONAL REMUNERATION CENTRE REPORT ON SALARIES AND EXECUTIVE REMUNERATION (AT) **697**

NATIONAL REPORT COMPUTERS AND HEALTH (US/0273-4974) [07062683] 3619, **1196**

NATIONAL REPORT FOR TRAINING AND DEVELOPMENT *CEASED.* (US/0749-9884) [08404384] **880**

NATIONAL REPORT ON INTERNATIONAL STUDENTS IN CANADA, THE (CN/0848-1431) [21102174] **1766**

NATIONAL REPORT ON SUBSTANCE ABUSE, THE (US/0891-5709) [14917039] **1347**

NATIONAL REPORT ON WORK & FAMILY (US/0896-3002) [16996610] **5297**

NATIONAL REPORTER (BIXBY) (US/0161-8016) [04024698] **5732**

NATIONAL REPORTER (FREDERICTON, N.B. : BOUND CUMULATION) (CN/0317-641X) [09099853] **3014**

NATIONAL REPORTER ON LEGAL ETHICS AND PROFESSIONAL RESPONSIBILITY (US) [08334052] 2252, **3014**

NATIONAL

NATIONAL RESEARCH COUNCIL. COMMITTEE ON NUCLEAR SCIENCE See NUCLEAR SCIENCE SERIES, REPORT **2157**

NATIONAL RESEARCH COUNCIL OF CANADA See REVIEW OF THE NATIONAL RESEARCH COUNCIL (OTTAWA) **573**

NATIONAL RESEARCH COUNCIL OF CANADA See REPORT - NATIONAL RESEARCH COUNCIL OF CANADA **5145**

NATIONAL RESEARCH COUNCIL OF CANADA. ASSOCIATE COMMITTEE ON GEOTECHNICAL RESEARCH See TECHNICAL MEMORANDUM - ASSOCIATE COMMITTEE ON GEOTECHNICAL RESEARCH (OTTAWA) **2032**

NATIONAL RESEARCH COUNCIL OF CANADA. ASSOCIATE COMMITTEE ON HYDROLOGY See HYDROLOGICAL EVENTS **1414**

NATIONAL RESEARCH COUNCIL OF CANADA. SPACE RESEARCH FACILITIES BRANCH See S R F B NEWSLETTER **34**

NATIONAL RESEARCH COUNCIL OF THE PHILIPPINES See NRCP RESEARCH BULLETIN **5135**

NATIONAL RESEARCH COUNCIL. PANEL ON GEOLOGY AND SOLID EARTH GEOPHYSICS See EARTH SCIENCE INVESTIGATIONS, UNITED STATES ANTARCTIC RESEARCH PROGRAM (USARP) **1354**

NATIONAL RESEARCH COUNCIL (U.S.). FOOD AND NUTRITION BOARD See DIRECTORY - NATIONAL RESEARCH COUNCIL (U.S.). FOOD AND NUTRITION BOARD (1982) **4190**

NATIONAL RESEARCH COUNCIL (U.S.). TRANSPORTATION RESEARCH BOARD See PUBLICATIONS CATALOG **5390**

NATIONAL RESEARCH COUNCIL (U.S.). TRANSPORTATION RESEARCH BOARD See DIRECTORY OF THE TRANSPORTATION RESEARCH BOARD **5381**

NATIONAL RESEARCH COUNCIL (U.S.). TRANSPORTATION RESEARCH BOARD See SPECIAL REPORT - TRANSPORTATION RESEARCH BOARD, NATIONAL RESEARCH COUNCIL **5393**

NATIONAL RESTAURANT NEWS See NATION'S RESTAURANT NEWS **5072**

NATIONAL RETAIL FLORAL INDEX SPECIAL CONSUMER STUDY (US) [08124236] **2425**

NATIONAL REVIEW FOR LITURGY (UK/0309-4308) [I03094308] **4980**

NATIONAL REVIEW (NEW YORK) (US/0028-0038) [01759389] **4483**

NATIONAL REVIEW OF CORPORATE ACQUISITIONS, THE (US/0097-6202) [01377919] **697**

NATIONAL RIGHT TO LIFE NEWS (US/0164-7415) [01776622] 5210, **589**

NATIONAL RIGHT TO WORK NEWSLETTER (US/0197-7032) [01759391] **1692**

● NATIONAL ROLLING PLAN (NR) [26294697] **4738**

NATIONAL ROOFING CONTRACTORS' ASSOCIATION See MEMBERSHIP DIRECTORY - NATIONAL ROOFING CONTRACTORS' ASSOCIATION **621**

NATIONAL ROSTER OF REALTORS (US/0090-1741) [01784636] **4842**

NATIONAL ROUND TABLE ON THE ENVIRONMENT AND THE ECONOMY (CANADA) See NATIONAL ROUND TABLE REVIEW, THE **1507**

NATIONAL ROUND TABLE REVIEW (CN/1188-0945) [25314242] **2178**

NATIONAL ROUND TABLE REVIEW, THE (CN/1188-0945) [25314239] **1507**

NATIONAL RUGBY POST (CN) **4906**

NATIONAL RURAL ELECTRIC COOPERATIVE ASSOCIATION See NRECA--APPA LEGAL REPORTING SERVICE **3020**

NATIONAL RURAL LETTER CARRIER, THE (US/0028-0089) [04109098] **1146**

NATIONAL SACRED HARP NEWSLETTER *CEASED*. (US) [15154892] **4139**

NATIONAL SAFETY COUNCIL See PRODUCT SAFETY UP TO DATE **4796**

NATIONAL SAFETY COUNCIL See ACCIDENT PREVENTION MANUAL FOR BUSINESS & INDUSTRY **2858**

NATIONAL SALES DEVELOPMENT INSTITUTE See SELLING KNACKS **957**

NATIONAL SANITATION FOUNDATION (U.S.) See NSF FOOD SERVICE EQUIPMENT STANDARDS **2351**

NATIONAL SAVINGS AND LOAN LEAGUE See LEGAL NOTES (WASHINGTON) **3087**

NATIONAL SAVINGS AND LOAN LEAGUE See LEGAL BULLETIN (WASHINGTON) **3087**

NATIONAL SCHOLARSHIP CENTER (PHILIPPINES) See DIRECTORY OF ALUMNI - NATIONAL SCHOLARSHIP CENTER (PHILIPPINES) **1101**

NATIONAL SCHOOL BOARDS ASSOCIATION See TRIENNIAL REPORT : A SURVEY OF PUBLIC EDUCATION IN THE NATION'S URBAN SCHOOL DISTRICTS, THE **1788**

NATIONAL SCHOOL BOARDS ASSOCIATION See REPORT : ANNUAL CONVENTION **1869**

NATIONAL SCHOOL BUS REPORT (US/0889-0749) [04571369] **5388**

NATIONAL SCHOOL MARKET INDEX (US/1069-4757) [05399655] **1901**

NATIONAL SCHOOL ORCHESTRA ASSOCIATION See NSOA BULLETIN **4142**

NATIONAL SCIENCE COUNCIL (IRELAND) See PROGRESS REPORT **5142**

NATIONAL SCIENCE COUNCIL OF SRI LANKA See JOURNAL OF THE NATIONAL SCIENCE COUNCIL OF SRI LANKA **5121**

NATIONAL SCIENCE FOUNDATION (U.S.) See ANNUAL SCIENCE AND TECHNOLOGY REPORT TO THE CONGRESS **5084**

NATIONAL SCIENCE FOUNDATION (U.S.) See SCIENTIFIC MANPOWER **5155**

NATIONAL SCIENCE FOUNDATION (U.S.) See GRADUATE SCIENCE EDUCATION STUDENT SUPPORT AND POSTDOCTORALS **5108**

NATIONAL SCIENCE FOUNDATION (U.S.) See GUIDE TO PROGRAMS / NATIONAL SCIENCE FOUNDATION **5108**

NATIONAL SCIENCE FOUNDATION (U.S.) See ANNUAL REPORT - NATIONAL SCIENCE FOUNDATION **5084**

NATIONAL SCIENCE FOUNDATION (U.S.) See U.S. SCIENTISTS AND ENGINEERS **5167**

NATIONAL SCIENCE FOUNDATION (U.S.) See NSF GRANT POLICY MANUAL **5135**

NATIONAL SCIENCE FOUNDATION (U.S.) See STATE AWARD SUMMARY, FISCAL YEAR / NATIONAL SCIENCE FOUNDATION **5160**

NATIONAL SCIENCE FOUNDATION (U.S.). DIVISION OF INTERGOVERNMENTAL SCIENCE & PUBLIC TECHNOLOGY See ABSTRACTS OF PUBLICATIONS - NATIONAL SCIENCE FOUNDATION U.S **5079**

NATIONAL SCIENCE FOUNDATION (U.S.). DIVISION OF SCIENCE EDUCATION DEVELOPMENT AND RESEARCH See SOURCE BOOK OF PROJECTS, SCIENCE EDUCATION DEVELOPMENT AND RESEARCH **1872**

NATIONAL SCIENCE FOUNDATION (U.S.). DIVISION OF SCIENCE RESOURCES STUDIES See PROJECT SUMMARIES - NATIONAL SCIENCE FOUNDATION (U.S.). DIVISION OF SCIENCE RESOURCES STUDIES **5142**

NATIONAL SCULPTURE SOCIETY, NEW YORK See ANNUAL EXHIBITION - NATIONAL SCULPTURE SOCIETY **336**

NATIONAL SEA GRANT COLLEGE PROGRAM (U.S.) See SEA GRANT BIENNIAL REPORT / U.S. DEPARTMENT OF COMMERCE, NATIONAL OCEANIC AND ATMOSPHERIC ADMINISTRATION, NATIONAL SEA GRANT COLLEGE PROGRAM **1456**

NATIONAL SECRETARY See SECRETARY, THE **710**

NATIONAL SECURITY AFFAIRS FORUM, THE (US/0146-244X) [02914877] **4052**

NATIONAL SECURITY LAW REPORT / AMERICAN BAR ASSOCIATION, STANDING COMMITTEE ON LAW AND NATIONAL SECURITY (US) [24815155] **3014**

NATIONAL SECURITY MANAGEMENT PROGRAMS. ADMINISTRATIVE PROCEDURES (US) [06011719] **4052**

NATIONAL SECURITY REVIEW, THE (PH) [01789077] **4052**

NATIONAL SENIOR CITIZENS LAW CENTER (U.S.) See NSCLC WASHINGTON WEEKLY **3020**

NATIONAL SERVICE NEWSLETTER (US/1059-4922) [07013102] 1067, **5297**

NATIONAL SEVERE STORMS LABORATORY See ANNUAL REPORT / NATIONAL SEVERE STORMS LABORATORY **1420**

NATIONAL SHEVCHENKO MUSICAL ENSEMBLE GUILD OF CANADA See BULLETIN - NATIONAL SHEVCHENKO MUSICAL ENSEMBLE GUILD OF CANADA **4106**

NATIONAL SHIPPERS COUNCIL OF CAMEROON See RAPPORT D'ACTIVITE / NATIONAL SHIPPERS COUNCIL OF CAMEROON **5455**

NATIONAL SHIPPING CORPORATION (PAKISTAN) See REPORT AND ACCOUNTS FOR THE YEAR ENDED 30TH JUNE ... / PAKISTAN NATIONAL SHIPPING CORPORATION **5455**

NATIONAL SHIPPING CORPORATION (PAKISTAN). _TREPORT AND ACCOUNTS -NATIONAL SHIPPING CORPORATION See REPORT AND ACCOUNTS FOR THE YEAR ENDED 30TH JUNE ... / PAKISTAN NATIONAL SHIPPING CORPORATION **5455**

NATIONAL SHUFFLER (US/0745-2276) [08943322] **4864**

NATIONAL SKI AREA NEWS See NSAA NEWS **4908**

NATIONAL SOCIAL SCIENCE SURVEY REPORT (AT) **5210**

NATIONAL SOCIAL SCIENCE SURVEY REPORT / RESEARCH SCHOOL OF SOCIAL SCIENCES, AUSTRALIAN NATIONAL UNIVERSITY (AT/1031-4067) [28644626] **5210**

NATIONAL SOCIALIST (ARLINGTON, VA.), THE (US/0740-9508) [10033041] **4543**

NATIONAL SOCIETY FOR CLEAN AIR See NSCA MEMBERS' HANDBOOK **2179**

NATIONAL SOCIETY FOR PERFORMANCE AND INSTRUCTION See MEMBERSHIP DIRECTORY - NATIONAL SOCIETY FOR PERFORMANCE AND INSTRUCTION **1224**

NATIONAL SOCIETY FOR THE STUDY OF EDUCATION See ... YEARBOOK OF THE NATIONAL SOCIETY FOR THE STUDY OF EDUCATION, THE **1792**

NATIONAL SOCIETY OF FUND RAISING EXECUTIVES See MEMBERSHIP DIRECTORY - NATIONAL SOCIETY OF FUND RAISING EXECUTIVES **798**

NATIONAL SOCIETY OF FUND RAISING EXECUTIVES See NSFRE JOURNAL **5299**

NATIONAL SOCIETY OF PUBLIC ACCOUNTANTS See YEARBOOK - NATIONAL SOCIETY OF PUBLIC ACCOUNTANTS **753**

NATIONAL SOCIETY OF UNITED STATES DAUGHTERS OF 1812 See NEWS-LETTER - NATIONAL SOCIETY OF UNITED STATES DAUGHTERS OF 1812 **5234**

NATIONAL SOCIETY TO PREVENT BLINDNESS See REPORT - NATIONAL SOCIETY TO PREVENT BLINDNESS **3878**

NATIONAL SOFT DRINK ASSOCIATION See DIRECTORY OF MEMBERS - NATIONAL SOFT DRINK ASSOCIATION **2366**

NATIONAL SOFT DRINK ASSOCIATION See NSDA SALES SURVEY OF THE SOFT DRINK INDUSTRY **2370**

NATIONAL SOFT DRINK ASSOCIATION See ANNUAL REPORT / NATIONAL SOFT DRINK ASSOCIATION **2363**

NATIONAL SPEED SPORT NEWS (US/0028-0208) [04109120] **4906**

NATIONAL SPELEOLOGICAL SOCIETY. MET GROTTO See MET GROTTO NEWS **1408**

NATIONAL SPELEOLOGICAL SOCIETY. SECTION OF CAVE GEOLOGY AND GEOGRAPHY See GEO2 **1376**

NATIONAL SPIRITUALIST (INDIANAPOLIS, IND.), THE (US/0882-1275) [11665329] **4980**

NATIONAL SPOKESMAN (US/0091-2387) [01759426] **3839**

NATIONAL SPORTING GOODS ASSOCIATION See NSGA BUYING GUIDE **4908**

NATIONAL SQUARE DANCE DIRECTORY (US/0196-0040) [05032123] **1314**

NATIONAL STAMPAGRAPHIC (US/0747-5527) [10766881] 2775, **381**

NATIONAL STANDARD REFERENCE DATA SERIES (US/0083-1840) [01346541] **4031**

NATIONAL STANDARDS ASSOCIATION See INDEX OF AIR FORCE-NAVY AERONAUTICAL (AN), AIR FORCE-NAVY AERONAUTICAL DESIGN (AND) AND MILITARY (MS) STANDARDS **4045**

NATIONAL STOCK DOG MAGAZINE (US/0028-0267) [06452963] 226, **4287**

NATIONAL STONE ASSOCIATION BUYER'S GUIDE (US) **2147**

NATIONAL STRENGTH AND CONDITIONING ASSOCIATION BULLETIN (US) **1857**

NATIONAL STRENGTH & CONDITIONING ASSOCIATION JOURNAL (US/0744-0049) [07911764] **1857**

NATIONAL STRIPPER WELL SURVEY (US/0470-3219) [01753810] 4265, **2147**

NATIONAL STUDY OF SUPERMARKET SHOPPERS. CENSUS PROFILE, THE (US/0734-8274) [07213531] **1298**

NATIONAL STUTTERING PROJECT See LETTING GO **1761**

NATIONAL SURVEY OF CONSERVATION TILLAGE PRACTICES (INCLUDING OTHER TILLAGE TYPES) (US) [25608583] **179**

NATIONAL — Alphabetical Title Index

NATIONAL SURVEY OF CORPORATE LAW DEPARTMENTS COMPENSATION AND ORGANIZATION PRACTICES (US/1048-6550) [16076282] 697, **3102**

NATIONAL SURVEY OF ENGINEERING MANPOWER (SI) [03262454] 1988, **1693**

NATIONAL SURVEY OF FISHING, HUNTING, AND WILDLIFE-ASSOCIATED RECREATION (US/0736-6450) [09101960] **4875**

NATIONAL SURVEY OF FISHING, HUNTING, AND WILDLIFE-ASSOCIATED RECREATION. ALASKA (US) [10951805] **4875**

NATIONAL SURVEY OF FISHING, HUNTING, AND WILDLIFE-ASSOCIATED RECREATION. ARKANSAS (US/0742-7174) [10409387] **4875**

NATIONAL SURVEY OF FISHING, HUNTING, AND WILDLIFE-ASSOCIATED RECREATION. CONNECTICUT (US/0742-7166) [10409367] **4875**

NATIONAL SURVEY OF FISHING, HUNTING, AND WILDLIFE-ASSOCIATED RECREATION. IDAHO (US) [10951882] **4875**

NATIONAL SURVEY OF FISHING, HUNTING, AND WILDLIFE-ASSOCIATED RECREATION. ILLINOIS (US/0742-7158) [10409342] **4875**

NATIONAL SURVEY OF FISHING, HUNTING, AND WILDLIFE-ASSOCIATED RECREATION. LOUISIANA (US/0742-714X) [10411499] **4875**

NATIONAL SURVEY OF FISHING, HUNTING, AND WILDLIFE-ASSOCIATED RECREATION. MICHIGAN (US) [11128348] **4875**

NATIONAL SURVEY OF FISHING, HUNTING, AND WILDLIFE-ASSOCIATED RECREATION. NEW YORK (US/0742-7190) [10409141] **4875**

NATIONAL SURVEY OF HOSPITAL AND MEDICAL SCHOOL SALARIES (US) [06054273] **3915**

NATIONAL SURVEY OF SALARIES AND WAGES IN PUBLIC SCHOOLS (US/0147-9385) [03226851] 1766, **1693**

NATIONAL SURVEY OF SCIENTIFIC MANPOWER (SI) [03095304] 5130, **1693**

NATIONAL TANK TRUCK CARRIER DIRECTORY (US/0077-586X) [01213210] **5388**

NATIONAL TAX ASSOCIATION-TAX INSTITUTE OF AMERICA *See* PROCEEDINGS OF THE ... ANNUAL CONFERENCE ON TAXATION HELD UNDER THE AUSPICES OF THE NATIONAL TAX ASSOCIATION-TAX INSTITUTE OF AMERICA **4742**

NATIONAL TAX ASSOCIATION-TAX INSTITUTE OF AMERICA AND FUND FOR PUBLIC POLICY RESEARCH *See* N T A-T I A BOOKSHELF **4738**

NATIONAL TAX JOURNAL (US/0028-0283) [01759436] **4738**

NATIONAL TAX TRAINING PROGRAM : TAX PRACTICE FUNDAMENTALS FOR NONTAX PROFESSIONALS (US/0149-323X) [03460905] **3102**

NATIONAL TEACHING & LEARNING FORUM, THE (US/1057-2880) [24000937] **1901**

NATIONAL TECHNICAL ASSOCIATION *See* NEWSLETTER - NATIONAL TECHNICAL ASSOCIATION **5133**

NATIONAL TECHNICAL ASSOCIATION *See* JOURNAL OF THE NATIONAL TECHNICAL ASSOCIATION **5121**

NATIONAL TECHNICAL INSTITUTIE FOR THE DEAF FOCUS (US/0739-9278) [05785568] **4391**

NATIONAL TECHNICAL REPORT (JA/0028-0291) [09432103] **5130**

NATIONAL TELEPHONE DIRECTORY / DEPARTMENT OF ENERGY (US) [08995052] 1950, **4668**

NATIONAL TELEPHONE DIRECTORY FOR BROKERS, DEALERS, BANKS, MUTUAL FUNDS (US/0730-3823) [07992295] **801**

NATIONAL THEATRE SCHOOL OF CANADA *See* NATIONAL THEATRE SCHOOL OF CANADA **5366**

NATIONAL THEATRE SCHOOL OF CANADA (CN/0383-1256) [03202310] 1766, **5366**

NATIONAL TICK SURVEILLANCE PROGRAM (US/0503-5090) [01786851] **5516**

NATIONAL TIMES, THE (US) **2539**

NATIONAL TIRE DEALERS AND RETREADERS ASSOCIATION *See* NTDRA DEALER NEWS **5076**

NATIONAL TOMBSTONE EPITAPH, THE (US/0890-068X) [08911802] **2747**

NATIONAL TOOL, DIE & PRECISION MACHINING ASSOCIATION *See* NTDPMA BUYERS GUIDE, THE **951**

NATIONAL TOOLING AND MACHINING ASSOCIATION (U.S.) *See* BUYERS GUIDE - NATIONAL TOOLING & MACHINING ASSOCIATION **949**

NATIONAL TORT LAW DIGESTS (US/0742-4388) [10178223] **3014**

NATIONAL TOXICOLOGY PROGRAM TECHNICAL REPORT SERIES (US/0888-8051) [08530672] **3983**

NATIONAL TOXICOLOGY PROGRAM (U.S.) *See* ANNUAL PLAN FOR FISCAL YEAR ... / NATIONAL TOXICOLOGY PROGRAM **3978**

NATIONAL TRADE AND PROFESSIONAL ASSOCIATIONS OF THE UNITED STATES (WASHINGTON, D.C. : 1982) (US/0734-354X) [08119666] **5234**

NATIONAL TRADE & TARIFF SERVICE (CN) **3014**

NATIONAL TRADE DATA BANK, THE (US/1064-9913) [24445375] **847**

NATIONAL TRADE-INDEX OF SOUTH AFRICA (SA/0077-5894) [03525706] **847**

NATIONAL TRADE INDEX OF SOUTH AFRICA AND RHODESIA (SA) [01623582] **2499**

NATIONAL TRADE POLICY AGENDA : MESSAGE FROM THE PRESIDENT OF THE UNITED STATES TRANSMITTING THE NATIONAL TRADE POLICY AGENDA FOR ... AND AN ADDENDUM TO THE ... ANNUAL REPORT ON THE TRADE AGREEMENTS PROGRAM ... PURSUANT TO PUBLIC LAW 100-418 SEC 1641 (US) [20340971] **847**

NATIONAL TRAINING INDEX (UK) [10969292] **1766**

NATIONAL TRANSPORTATION SAFETY BOARD DECISIONS (US/0094-761X) [01794956] 4792, **5388**

NATIONAL TRANSPORTATION STATISTICS (US/0161-8628) [03967204] **5401**

NATIONAL TRAVEL EXPENDITURE STUDY (US/0362-7829) [02329824] **5485**

●NATIONAL TRAVEL SURVEY SEASONAL REPORTS (US) **5485**

●NATIONAL TRIAL LAWYER (FLORIDA ED.) (US/1066-7733) [27045288] **3014**

NATIONAL TRIAL LAWYER (NATIONAL ED.) (US/1049-684X) [21264660] **3014**

●NATIONAL TRIAL LAWYER (NEW YORK ED.) (US/1060-9210) [25113969] **3014**

NATIONAL TRUCK CHARACTERISTIC REPORT (US/0148-222X) [03282469] **5388**

NATIONAL TRUST (UK/0266-8068) [04672694] **304**

NATIONAL TRUST FOR HISTORIC PRESERVATION IN THE UNITED STATES *See* ANNUAL REPORT / NATIONAL TRUST FOR HISTORIC PRESERVATION **2720**

NATIONAL TRUST FOR SCOTLAND *See* GUIDE TO OVER 100 PROPERTIES / NATIONAL TRUST FOR SCOTLAND **2690**

NATIONAL TRUST FOR SCOTLAND *See* ANNUAL REPORT / NATIONAL TRUST FOR SCOTLAND **2675**

NATIONAL TRUST OF AUSTRALIA (VICTORIA) *See* TRUST NEWS **2207**

NATIONAL TRUST OF AUSTRALIA (VICTORIA) *See* TRUST : A QUARTERLY FROM THE NATIONAL TRUST OF AUSTRALIA (VICTORIA) **2671**

NATIONAL TRUST OF AUSTRALIA (WESTERN AUSTRALIA) *See* ANNUAL REPORT - NATIONAL TRUST OF AUSTRALIA, W.A **4628**

NATIONAL TRUST STUDIES (UK/0142-3487) [04403576] **325**

NATIONAL TRUST YEARBOOK *See* NATIONAL TRUST STUDIES **325**

NATIONAL UNDERSEA RESEARCH PROGRAM PROGRAM SUMMARY. P.A SUMMARY OF RESEARCH ACTIVITIES (US) [20580675] **1453**

NATIONAL UNDERSEA RESEARCH PROGRAM (U.S.) *See* NATIONAL UNDERSEA RESEARCH PROGRAM PROGRAM SUMMARY. P.A SUMMARY OF RESEARCH ACTIVITIES **1453**

NATIONAL UNDERWRITER CITY INSURANCE TELEPHONE DIRECTORY (US) **2889**

NATIONAL UNDERWRITER COMPANY *See* SOCIAL SECURITY MANUAL **5308**

NATIONAL UNDERWRITER (LIFE, HEALTH / FINANCIAL SERVICES ED.) (US/0893-8202) [15037753] **2889**

NATIONAL UNDERWRITER PROFILES. HEALTH INSURERS (US/1050-6357) [21568495] **2889**

NATIONAL UNDERWRITER PROFILES. LIFE INSURERS (US/1050-5857) [21551062] **2889**

NATIONAL UNDERWRITER PROFILES. PROPERTY / CASUALTY INSURERS (US/1050-6365) [21568569] **2889**

NATIONAL UNDERWRITER (PROPERTY & CASUALTY / RISK & BENEFITS MANAGEMENT EDITION) (US/1042-6841) [19106506] **2889**

NATIONAL UNION CATALOG. LC CARD NUMBER INDEX, THE (US) [01795535] **3233**

NATIONAL UNION CATALOG. MOTION PICTURES AND FILMSTRIPS (US/0093-9676) [00933921] **3259**

NATIONAL UNION CATALOG OF MANUSCRIPT COLLECTIONS *CEASED.* (US/0090-0044) [01759448] **3233**

NATIONAL UNION CATALOG. REGISTER OF ADDITIONAL LOCATIONS. CUMULATIVE MICROFORM EDITION (US/0361-5251) [06524109] **420**

NATIONAL UNION OF HOSPITAL AND HEALTH CARE EMPLOYEES. DISTRICT 1199 *See* 1199 NEWS **1642**

NATIONAL UNION OF SOUTH AFRICAN STUDENTS *See* NUSAS NEWSLETTER **1838**

NATIONAL UNION OF STUDENTS *See* ANNUAL MEETING - NATIONAL UNION OF STUDENTS **1809**

NATIONAL UNION OF THE FOOTWEAR, LEATHER & ALLIED TRADES *See* JOURNAL & REPORT - NATIONAL UNION OF THE FOOTWEAR, LEATHER & ALLIED TRADES **3184**

NATIONAL UNIVERSITY CONTINUING EDUCATION ASSOCIATION (U.S.) *See* MEMBER DIRECTORY **1835**

NATIONAL UNIVERSITY OF SINGAPORE *See* DIRECTORY OF CURRENT RESEARCH / NATIONAL UNIVERSITY OF SINGAPORE **5100**

NATIONAL UNIVERSITY OF SINGAPORE. LIBRARY *See* CHECKLIST OF CURRENT PERIODICALS / NATIONAL UNIVERSITY OF SINGAPORE LIBRARY **413**

NATIONAL URBAN LEAGUE *See* STATE OF BLACK AMERICA, THE **2273**

NATIONAL URBAN LEAGUE. RESEARCH DEPT *See* URBAN LEAGUE REVIEW, THE **2274**

NATIONAL URBAN MASS TRANSPORTATION STATISTICS (US/0737-2981) [07580933] **5401**

NATIONAL UTILITY CONTRACTOR, THE (US/0192-0359) [05005233] 2237, **622**

NATIONAL UTILITY CONTRACTORS ASSOCIATION *See* NATIONAL UTILITY CONTRACTOR, THE **622**

NATIONAL VANGUARD (US/0897-4012) [05281067] **5252**

NATIONAL VIETNAM VETERANS REVIEW (US) [08919169] **4052**

●NATIONAL VOLUNTEERS IN PARKS DIRECTORY (U.S. ED.) (US/1058-8221) [24394687] **4875**

NATIONAL VOTER, THE (US/0028-0372) [01604351] **4483**

NATIONAL WATER CONDITIONS (US/0736-2609) [08705174] **5536**

NATIONAL WATER LINE (US/0271-0692) [06550220] **5536**

NATIONAL WATER QUALITY INVENTORY : REPORT TO CONGRESS / UNITED STATES ENVIRONMENTAL PROTECTION AGENCY, OFFICE OF WATER REGULATIONS AND STANDARDS (US) [02469418] **5536**

NATIONAL WATER SAFETY CONGRESS JOURNAL *See* WATER SAFETY JOURNAL **4807**

NATIONAL WATER SUPPLY IMPROVEMENT ASSOCIATION. CONFERENCE AND INTERNATIONAL TRADE FAIR *See* TECHNICAL PROCEEDINGS / ANNUAL CONFERENCE AND INTERNATIONAL TRADE FAIR OF THE NATIONAL WATER SUPPLY IMPROVEMENT ASSOCIATION **5540**

NATIONAL WATERSHED CONGRESS; PROCEEDINGS (US/0470-3480) [01187193] **5536**

NATIONAL WEATHER ASSOCIATION *See* NEWSLETTER / NATIONAL WEATHER ASSOCIATION **1432**

NATIONAL WEATHER DIGEST (US/0271-1052) [03190581] **1432**

NATIONAL WETLANDS NEWSLETTER (US/0164-0712) [04571695] **3114**

NATIONAL WILDLIFE FEDERATION SCIENTIFIC AND TECHNICAL SERIES (US/1044-4971) [12931459] **4875**

NATIONAL WILDLIFE FEDERATION'S CONSERVATION (US/0736-9522) [09263059] **3114**

NATIONAL WILDLIFE REFUGES (US) [01534407] **2199**

NATIONAL WILDLIFE REHABILITATORS' ASSOCIATION (U.S.). SYMPOSIUM *See* WILDLIFE REHABILITATION **2209**

NATIONAL WINTER STORMS OPERATIONS PLAN (US/0742-4043) [05722557] **1432**

NATIONAL WOMAN'S RELIEF CORPS **See** JOURNAL OF THE ... CONVENTION - NATIONAL WOMAN'S RELIEF CORP **5559**

NATIONAL WOMEN'S ADVISORY COUNCIL (AUSTRALIA) **See** ANNUAL REPORT OF THE NATIONAL WOMEN'S ADVISORY COUNCIL ... **5551**

NATIONAL WOMEN'S HEALTH REPORT (US/0741-9147) [10236256] 5562, **4792**

NATIONAL WOODLANDS (US/0279-9812) [07085730] **2388**

NATIONAL WOOL GROWER (US/0028-0410) [01759459] **110**

NATIONAL YELLOW BOOK OF FUNERAL DIRECTORS, THE (US/1054-8238) [22959792] **2407**

NATIONALE REKENINGEN / CENTRAAL BUREAU VOOR DE STATISTIEK (NE/0168-3489) [11768277] **4668**

NATIONALISM AND ETHNIC POLITICS (UK) 2268, **4483**

NATIONALITIES PAPERS (US/0090-5992) [01785151] **2268**

NATIONALKONOMISK TIDSSKRIFT (DK/0028-0453) [06388586] **1507**

NATIONALMUSEET (DENMARK) **See** DANMARKS KIRKER **4952**

NATIONALMUSEETS ARBEJDSMARK (DK/0084-9308) [05282993] **5234**

NATIONALMUSEUM (SWEDEN) **See** BULLETIN - NATIONALMUSEUM **317**

NATIONALRAKENSKAPER (SW) [09817507] **1507**

NATIONALRAT UND BUNDESRAT AMTLICHES VERZEICHNIS DER MITGLEIDER, AUSSCHUSSE UND KLUBS (AU) [03472608] **4668**

●NATIONS AND NATIONALISM (UK/1354-5078) **4483**

NATION'S BUILDING NEWS (US/8750-6580) [11619762] 4842, **622**

NATION'S BUSINESS (US/0028-047X) [01759465] **697**

NATION'S CITIES WEEKLY (US/0164-5935) [04523354] **4668**

NATION'S HEALTH (1971), THE (US/0028-0496) [01641981] **4792**

NATION'S RESTAURANT NEWS (US/0028-0518) [01759470] **5072**

NATIONWIDE DIRECTORY, GIFT, HOUSEWARES & HOME TEXTILES BUYERS (US) [18307565] **955**

NATIONWIDE DIRECTORY. MAJOR MASS MARKET MERCHANDISERS **See** MAJOR MASS MARKET MERCHANDISERS **1085**

NATIONWIDE DIRECTORY. MAJOR MASS MARKET MERCHANDISERS (US/0737-061X) [09262998] 950, **1086**

NATIONWIDE HOSPITAL INSURANCE BILLING DIRECTORY **See** KELLY INSURANCE DIRECTORY: NATIONWIDE HOSPITAL INSURANCE BILLING DIRECTORY **2886**

NATIONWIDE OVERNIGHT STABLING DIRECTORY (US/0886-5647) [12932196] **2801**

NATIONWIDE WOMEN'S & CHILDREN'S WEAR DIRECTORY (US) **1086**

NATIVE AERICAN TEXTS SERIES (US/0361-3399) [02051859] **2268**

NATIVE AGENDA, NEWS (CN/1185-9946) [25590157] **4668**

NATIVE AMERICAN, THE (US) [03454117] **2268**

●NATIVE AMERICANS INFORMATION DIRECTORY (US/1063-9632) [26183203] **2268**

NATIVE CORN REPORT / CORNELL AMERICAN INDIAN AGRICULTURE PROGRAM (US) [24785360] **111**

NATIVE MONTHLY READER (US/1061-7884) [22339526] **2747**

NATIVE NEVADAN, THE **CEASED.** (US/0028-0534) [01638994] **2539**

●NATIVE NORTH AMERICAN ALMANAC (US/1070-8014) [28471544] **2268**

NATIVE PEOPLES (US/0895-7606) [16786745] 242, 2268, **2747**

NATIVE SISTERHOOD (CN/0703-9190) [03951264] **2268**

NATIVE SPORTS & CULTURE NEWS (CN/1187-3523) [25589909] **2268**

NATIVE STUDIES IN COLLEGES AND UNIVERSITIES (CN/0381-4580) [03963168] 1766, **2268**

NATIVE STUDIES REVIEW (CN/0831-585X) [15128061] 2747, **2268**

NATIVE VOICE (CN/0028-0542) [02010156] **2539**

NATIVE WOMEN'S NEWS (CN/0827-3944) [12178005] 5562, **2268**

NATO ADVANCED STUDY INSTITUTES SERIES. SERIES C, MATHEMATICAL AND PHYSICAL SCIENCES **See** NATO ASI SERIES. SERIES C, MATHEMATICAL AND PHYSICAL SCIENCES **3524**

NATO ASI SERIES. SERIES A, LIFE SCIENCES (US/0258-1213) [11566960] **466**

NATO ASI SERIES. SERIES C, MATHEMATICAL AND PHYSICAL SCIENCES (NE/0258-2023) [09998026] **3524**

NATO ASI SERIES. SERIES E, APPLIED SCIENCE (US/0168-132X) [10362234] **5130**

NATO ASI SERIES. SERIES F, COMPUTER AND SYSTEM SCIENCES (GW/0258-1248) [12232849] **1196**

NATO ASI SERIES. SERIES G, ECOLOGICAL SCIENCES (GW/0258-1256) [10297036] **2219**

NATO ASI SERIES. SERIES H, CELL BIOLOGY (GW/1010-8793) [15866279] **539**

NATO CHALLENGES OF MODERN SOCIETY (US/0730-9600) [08090512] **2237**

NATO CONFERENCE SERIES. I. ECOLOGY (US/0197-4475) [06033236] **2219**

NATO CONFERENCE SERIES : III, HUMAN FACTORS (US/0149-9351) [03561105] **584**

NATO CONFERENCE SERIES. IV. MARINE SCIENCES (US/0164-2057) [04612430] 1453, **556**

NATO CONFERENCE SERIES : VI, MATERIALS SCIENCE (US/0197-5145) [05908731] **5130**

NATO HANDBOOK, THE (BE) [03663958] **3133**

NATO MUTUAL SUPPORT ACT, AS AMENDED (ACQUISITION AND CROSS SERVICING AGREEMENTS WITH NATO ALLIES AND OTHER COUNTRIES); REPORT OF AGREEMENTS AND TRANSACTIONS / DEPARTMENT OF DEFENSE (US) [26036410] 4062, **4052**

NATO RECOMMENDED PRODUCTS LIST / MILITARY COMMITTEE, COMMUNICATIONS SECURITY AND EVALUATION AGENCY (US) [16669159] **697**

NATO REVIEW (BE/0255-3813) [01387966] **4529**

NATO SCIENCE AND SOCIETY NEWSLETTER (BE) **5130**

NATO-WARSAW AND STRATEGIES (NP/0749-0674) [11078136] **4483**

NATOM. FARMACIA NATURALE (IT/1121-1350) [11211350] **3619**

NATO'S FIFTEEN NATIONS (GW/0027-6065) [01758947] **4529**

NATO'S SIXTEEN NATIONS (NE/0169-1821) [09439168] **4052**

NATOTAWIN (CN/0703-4733) [03453065] **2748**

NATS JOURNAL / NATIONAL ASSOCIATION OF TEACHERS OF SINGING JOURNAL, THE (US/0884-8106) [12438205] **4139**

NATSIONALNA BIBLIOGRAFIIA NA REPUBLIKA BULGARIIA. SERIIA 1, BULGARSKI KNIGOPIS. KNIGI, NOTNI, GRAFICHESKI I KARTOGRAFSKI IZDANIIA (BU) [25597529] 4817, **4822**

NATSIONALNA BIBLIOGRAFIIA NA REPUBLIKA BULGARIIA. SERIIA 2, BULGARSKI KNIGOPIS. SLUZHEBNI IZDANIIA I DISERTATSII (BU) [25598897] 1836, 4817, **4822**

NATSIONALNA BIBLIOGRAFIIA NA REPUBLIKA BULGARIIA. SERIIA 5, LETOPIS NA STATIITE OT BULGARSKITE SPISANIIA I SBORNITSI (BU) [25597005] **4817**

NATSIONALNA BIBLIOGRAFIIA NA REPUBLIKA BULGARIIA. SERIIA 6, LETOPIS NA STATIITE OT BULGARSKITE VESTNITSI (BU) [25588849] **5779**

NATSO TRUCKERS NEWS (US/1040-2284) [18354738] **5388**

NATTURUFRINGURINN (IC/0369-5921) [03773955] **4168**

NATUNA PRAWAHA (II) [03262101] **3414**

NATUNA PURUSHA (II) [02397290] **3414**

NATUR (GW) [09864917] **2199**

NATUR + I.E. UND RECHT (GW) [06952446] **3114**

NATUR-UND GANZHEITSMEDIZIN : NGM (GW/0934-7909) [24844638] **3619**

NATUR UND HEIMAT (GW/0028-0593) [03185123] **4168**

NATUR UND LAND (AU/0028-0607) [05655936] 2219, **2178**

NATUR UND LANDSCHAFT (STUTTGART) (GW/0028-0615) [05887234] 2199, **4168**

NATUR UND MUSEUM (FRANKFURT AM MAIN : 1962) (GW/0028-1301) [04769070] **4168**

NATUR- UND NATIONALPARKE (SZ) [08530476] **4168**

NATURA (BL) [03580025] **466**

NATURA (NE/0028-0631) [04794178] **4168**

NATURA & MED (GW/0931-1513) [25129685] **3775**

NATURA BRESCIANA (IT/0391-156X) [02441299] **4168**

NATURA E MONTAGNA (IT) [04048975] 2178, **1358**

NATURA JUTLANDICA (DK/0077-6033) [04962237] **5592**

NATURA (MILANO) (IT/0369-6243) [04794155] **4168**

NATURAL AND APPLIED SCIENCE BULLETIN (PH/0028-0682) [04788540] **5130**

NATURAL AREAS JOURNAL (US/0885-8608) [09398454] **2199**

NATURAL BODY & FITNESS **CEASED.** (US/1048-1532) [20906008] **2600**

●NATURAL BODYBUILDING AND FITNESS (US/1071-555X) [28678814] 2600, **4906**

NATURAL CONNECTION, THE (US) 697, **2219**

NATURAL FARMER : PUBLICATION OF THE NATURAL ORGANIC FARMERS ASSOCIATION, THE (US) [09569335] **111**

●NATURAL FIBERS FACT BOOK (US/1062-0648) [25517137] **5354**

NATURAL FIBERS UTILIZATION RESEARCH ANNUAL PROGRESS REPORT FOR THE PERIOD OF ... TO THE NATURAL FIBERS & FOOD PROTEIN COMMISSION OF TEXAS (US) [07051797] **2351**

NATURAL FOODS MERCHANDISER (US/0164-338X) [04621892] **2351**

NATURAL GAS ANNUAL (US/0736-9808) [08702847] **4265**

●NATURAL GAS EXPORTER (CN/1195-5287) [29206104] **4265**

NATURAL GAS FOCUS (US/1073-6417) **4265**

NATURAL GAS FOR INDUSTRY AND COMMERCE **CEASED.** (UK/0140-3222) [02642662] **4265**

NATURAL GAS FROM CALIFORNIA FIELDS (US/0272-4863) [06829354] **4265**

NATURAL GAS HANDBOOK **CEASED.** (US/0744-6500) [08466379] **4265**

NATURAL GAS INTELLIGENCE (US/0739-1811) [08029547] 1950, **4265**

NATURAL GAS LAWYER'S JOURNAL, THE (US/1052-3413) [13564734] 4265, **3014**

NATURAL GAS MARKET REPORT (CN/0827-6056) [14938350] **4265**

NATURAL GAS MARKET UPDATE (CN/1185-5304) [25067059] 4265, **847**

NATURAL GAS MARKETING. END USER DIRECTORY (US/0894-9018) [16318398] **4265**

NATURAL GAS MARKETING ... INDUSTRY DIRECTORY (US/0894-900X) [16318293] **4265**

NATURAL GAS MONTHLY (WASHINGTON, D.C.) (US/0737-1713) [09314116] **4265**

NATURAL GAS (NEW YORK, N.Y.) (US/0743-5665) [10603260] **4265**

NATURAL GAS PRODUCER PRICES (US/0891-4230) [13901413] **4265**

●NATURAL GAS STATISTICS SOURCEBOOK (US/1074-6730) [29774364] **4284**

●NATURAL GAS UTILITY DIRECTORY (CN) 4266, **4761**

NATURAL GAS WEEK (US/8756-3037) [11520352] **4266**

NATURAL GAS WEEK INTERNATIONAL (US) **4266**

NATURAL GAS WEEK'S BID WEEK REPORT (US) **4266**

NATURAL GAS WEEK'S DAILY PRICELINE (US) **4266**

NATURAL GRAPHITE IN ... (WASHINGTON D.C. : 1980) **See** MINERAL INDUSTRY SURVEYS. GRAPHITE, NATURAL IN ... **2144**

NATURAL HAZARD RESEARCH WORKING PAPER **See** WORKING PAPER / NATURAL HAZARDS RESEARCH AND APPLICATIONS INFORMATION CENTER, INSTITUTE OF BEHAVIORAL SCIENCE, UNIVERSITY OF COLORADO **1437**

NATURAL HAZARDS (DORDRECHT) (NE/0921-030X) [18689058] **2178**

NATURAL HAZARDS OBSERVER (US/0193-8355) [03775541] **1358**

NATURAL HEALING NEWSLETTER (US) **2600**

●NATURAL HEALTH (US/1067-9588) [27132660] **2600**

NATURAL — Alphabetical Title Index

NATURAL HEALTH: THE GUIDE TO WELL-BEING (US) **2490**

NATURAL HISTORY (US/0028-0712) [01759475] **4168**

NATURAL HISTORY BOOK REVIEWS *CEASED.* (UK) [02050021] **4174**

NATURAL HISTORY BULLETIN (BANGKOK) (TH/0080-9462) [02027078] **4168**

NATURAL HISTORY BULLETIN OF THE SIAM SOCIETY (TH/0080-9462) [07711619] **4168**

NATURAL HISTORY OF EGYPT, THE (UK) [17427814] 275, **4168**

NATURAL HISTORY RESEARCH (JA/0915-9444) [24185430] 5592, **2219**

NATURAL IMAGE, THE (US) 2219, **4372**

●NATURAL IMMUNITY (SZ/1018-8916) [25482135] **3675**

NATURAL IMMUNITY AND CELL GROWTH REGULATION *See* NATURAL IMMUNITY **3675**

NATURAL LANGUAGE AND LINGUISTIC THEORY (NE/0167-806X) [09665812] **3305**

NATURAL LANGUAGE ENGINEERING (UK/1351-3249) 1988, 3305, **1196**

NATURAL LANGUAGE SEMANTICS (US/0925-854X) **3305**

NATURAL LIFE MAGAZINE (CN/0830-0887) [14708520] **4194**

NATURAL LIFE (UNIONVILLE. 1991) (CN/0701-8002) [26497713] 5252, **2600**

NATURAL PHYSIQUE (US/1044-6583) [19863374] **4906**

●NATURAL PRODUCT LETTERS (UK/1057-5634) [24059272] **491**

NATURAL PRODUCT REPORTS (UK/0265-0568) [10601505] 1044, **491**

NATURAL PRODUCT UPDATES (UK/0950-1711) [15526999] 1027, **1012**

NATURAL RESOURCE MODELING (US/0890-8575) [14404446] **2199**

NATURAL RESOURCES AND DEVELOPMENT (GW/0340-2797) [02881266] **2199**

NATURAL RESOURCES & EARTH SCIENCES *CEASED.* (US/0163-1438) [03457774] 1358, **2199**

NATURAL RESOURCES & ENERGY (US/0251-723X) [05711491] 1950, **2199**

NATURAL RESOURCES & ENVIRONMENT (US/0882-3812) [11821907] 2199, **3114**

NATURAL RESOURCES (COLLEGE PARK, MD.) (US/1043-7460) [19545042] **2199**

NATURAL RESOURCES COMPUTER NEWSLETTER (US/0890-5673) [14353073] 1196, **2199**

NATURAL RESOURCES DEFENSE COUNCIL. INTERNATIONAL PROJECT *See* NRDC WORLD ENVIRONMENT ALERT **2201**

NATURAL RESOURCES, ENERGY, AND ENVIRONMENTAL LAW (US/1045-0580) [19567865] **3114**

NATURAL RESOURCES FORUM (NE/0165-0203) [03149330] **2199**

NATURAL RESOURCES FORUM LIBRARY (NE/0167-4110) [05869704] **2199**

NATURAL RESOURCES INFORMATION DIRECTORY FOR THE STATE OF CONNECTICUT AND LIST OF PUBLICATIONS FOR THE CONNECTICUT GEOLOGICAL AND NATURAL HISTORY SURVEY (US/0748-481X) [10684032] **2199**

NATURAL RESOURCES JOURNAL (US/0028-0739) [01759480] **3115**

NATURAL RESOURCES METABASE (US/1053-1394) [22461110] **2199**

NATURAL RESOURCES, SCIENCE AND TECHNOLOGY NEWSLETTER (US/0090-9483) [01786045] **2199**

NATURAL RESOURCES TAX REVIEW, THE (US/1050-1932) [18396591] **2199**

NATURAL RESOURCES/WATER SERIES (US/1010-397X) [02246111] **2199**

NATURAL RUBBER NEWS *CEASED.* (US/0028-0755) [02530778] **5076**

NATURAL SCIENCE CENTERS: DIRECTORY (US) [04068375] **5131**

NATURAL SCIENCE REPORT OF THE OCHANOMIZU UNIVERSITY (JA/0029-8190) [01605180] **5131**

NATURAL SCIENCES (PK/0253-830X) [06035905] **5131**

NATURAL SCIENCES AND ENGINEERING RESEARCH COUNCIL CANADA *See* REPORT OF THE PRESIDENT / NATURAL SCIENCES AND ENGINEERING RESEARCH COUNCIL CANADA **4681**

NATURAL STONE DIRECTORY : DIMENSION STONE SOURCES FOR BRITAIN AND IRELAND (UK) [18064798] **622**

NATURAL THERAPIST *CEASED.* (AT) **3619**

●NATURAL TOXINS (US/1056-9014) [23890741] **3983**

NATURALEZA Y GRACIA (SP/0470-3790) [04766974] **4980**

NATURALIA (SAO JOSE DO RIO PRETO) (BL/0101-1944) [04116469] **4168**

●NATURALIST (DANVILLE, VT.), THE (US/1060-9938) [25148216] 2219, **2199**

NATURALIST (LEEDS) (UK/0028-0771) [04286535] 1389, **4168**

NATURALIST PORT ELIZABETH, THE (SA/1013-6444) [I10136444] **4168**

NATURALIST REVIEW *CEASED.* (US/0888-6547) [13698255] **2199**

NATURALIST (TRINIDAD AND TOBAGO) (TR) [09367440] **4168**

NATURALISTE CANADIEN, LE *CEASED.* (CN/0028-0798) [06312227] **2219**

NATURALISTES BELGES (BE/0028-0801) [03783781] **4168**

NATURALISTS' DIRECTORY AND ALMANAC INTERNATIONAL. SUPPLEMENT, THE (US) [08021694] **4168**

NATURALISTS' DIRECTORY AND ALMANAC, INTERNATIONAL, THE (US/0277-609X) [04368276] **5131**

NATURE ALERT (CN/1185-8877) [25423241] **2199**

NATURE AND ENVIRONMENT SERIES (FR) [05016374] 2199, **2178**

NATURE AND HEALTH (AT/0815-7006) [I08157006] **2600**

NATURE AND RESOURCES (FR/0028-0844) [01759492] **2199**

NATURE AND SYSTEM *CEASED.* (US/0191-2941) [04888928] **4168**

NATURE CANADA (CN/0374-9894) [01771665] **2199**

NATURE CENTER NEWS (US) [03574774] **2200**

NATURE CONSERVANCY *See* INFORMATION BULLETIN - THE NATURE CONSERVANCY **2195**

NATURE CONSERVANCY *See* POLICY BULLETIN - THE NATURE CONSERVANCY **2202**

NATURE CONSERVANCY MAGAZINE (US) [16852411] **2200**

NATURE CONSERVANCY (U.S.). IOWA CHAPTER, THE *See* NEWSLETTER - THE NATURE CONSERVANCY (U.S.). IOWA CHAPTER **2200**

NATURE CONSERVATION COUNCIL (N.Z.) *See* REPORT OF THE NATURE CONSERVATION COUNCIL FOR THE YEAR ENDED 31 MARCH ... **2203**

NATURE CONSERVATION COUNCIL (N.Z.) *See* NEWSLETTER - NEW ZEALAND. NATURE CONSERVATION COUNCIL **2200**

NATURE ET PROGRES PARIS (FR/0182-7146) [I01827146] **111**

NATURE ET RESSOURCES (UK/0304-2995) [I03042995] **2200**

NATURE FRIEND MAGAZINE (US/0888-4862) [13609494] **2200**

●NATURE GENETICS (US/1061-4036) [25302333] **550**

NATURE (LONDON) (UK/0028-0836) [01586310] **5131**

NATURE (LONDON, ENGLAND) *See* NATURE GENETICS **550**

NATURE MALAYSIANA (MY/0126-5318) [02810304] **4169**

●NATURE MEDICINE (US) **3619**

NATURE NORTHWEST (CN/0836-4702) [16959396] **4169**

NATURE NOTEBOOK (US) [05518725] **466**

NATURE OF ILLINOIS, THE (US/1068-0969) [14922938] **2200**

NATURE PHOTOGRAPHER (US/1049-6602) [21270883] **4372**

NATURE, SOCIETY, AND THOUGHT (US/0890-6130) [14282029] 4353, **5210**

NATURE SOCIETY NEWS (US/0890-3735) [14227104] **5592**

NATURE SOUTH (US/1054-9641) [23035805] **4169**

●NATURE STRUCTURAL BIOLOGY (US/1072-8368) [29209845] **466**

NATURE STUDY - AMERICAN NATURE STUDY SOCIETY (US/0028-0860) [05069986] **2219**

NATURE WALKABOUT *CEASED.* (AT) [06328234] **4169**

NATURELLEMENT : JOURNAL DU MOUVEMENT NATIONAL DE LUTTE POUR L'ENVIRONNEMENT (FR) **2178**

NATUREN (NO/0028-0887) [01607905] **5131**

NATUREN (NO) [06352050] **5131**

NATURENS VERDEN (DK/0028-0895) [01759496] **5131**

NATURES-SCIENCES-SOCIETES (FR/1240-1307) [I12401307] **5131**

NATURESCAPE (US/0273-5709) [06385912] **466**

NATUREZA EM REVISTA (BL) [04683157] 519, **5592**

NATURFORSCHENDE GESELLSCHAFT, AUGSBURG *See* BERICHT DER NATURFORSCHENDEN GESELLSCHAFT AUGSBURG **4163**

NATURFORSCHENDE GESELLSCHAFT BAMBERG *See* BERICHT - NATURFORSCHENDE GESELLSCHAFT BAMBERG **2188**

NATURFORSCHENDE GESELLSCHAFT IN ZURICH *See* NEUJAHRSBLATT (ZURICH) **5132**

NATURFORSCHENDE GESELLSCHAFT ZU FREIBURG I. B *See* BERICHTE DER NATURFORSCHENDEN GESELLSCHAFT ZU FREIBURG I. BR **5088**

NATURHEILPRAXIS MIT NATURMEDIZIN (GW/0177-6754) [12255320] **3619**

NATURHISTORISCHE GESELLSCHAFT ZU HANNOVER *See* BERICHT DER NATURHISTORISCHEN GESELLSCHAFT HANNOVER **4163**

NATURHISTORISCHES MUSEUMS (AUSTRIA) *See* NEUE DENKSCHRIFTEN DES NATURHISTORISCHEN MUSEUMS IN WIEN **4228**

NATURMILJON I SIFFROR (SW/1101-3192) [13389761] **2200**

NATUROPA (ENGLISH EDITION) (FR/0250-7072) [02241778] **2200**

NATUROPATHIC PHYSICIAN / THE AMERICAN ASSOCIATION OF NATUROPATHIC PHYSICIANS, THE (US) [25023831] **3619**

NATURSCHUTZ UND LANDSCHAFTSPLANUNG (GW) [23866284] **2425**

NATURVETENSKAPLIGA FORSKNINGSRADET (SWEDEN) *See* VERKSAMHETSBERATTELSE **5168**

NATURVETENSKAPLIGA FORSKNINGSRADET (SWEDEN) *See* RADSRAPPORT **4171**

NATURVETENSKAPLIGA FORSKNINGSRADETS ARSBOK (SW) [03191791] **5131**

NATURWISSENSCHAFTEN, DIE (GW/0028-1042) [01759509] **5131**

NATURWISSENSCHAFTLICH-MEDIZINISCHER VEREIN IN INNSBRUCK *See* BERICHTE DES NATURWISSENSCHAFTLICH-MEDIZINISCHEN VEREINS IN INNSBRUCK **5088**

NATURWISSENSCHAFTLICHE RUNDSCHAU (GW/0028-1050) [01759508] **5131**

NATURWISSENSCHAFTLICHER VEREIN FUR STEIERMARK, GRAZ *See* MITTEILUNGEN DES NATURWISSENSCHAFTLICHEN VEREINES FUER STEIERMARK **5129**

NATUUR- EN MILIEUVOORLICHTING (NE) [22381412] **2237**

NATUUR EN TECHNIEK (NE/0028-1093) [06313225] **5131**

NATUURBEHOUD (NE) **2200**

NATUURHISTORISCH MAANBLAD : ORGAAN VAN HET NATUURHISTORISCH GENOOTSCHAP IN LIMBURG (NE) [04912189] **4169**

NATUURKUNDE RAPPORT (NE) [05819467] **1914**

NATUURSTEEN (NE) **304**

NATUURSTEENBEWERKINGSBEDRIJVEN / CENTRAAL BUREAU VOOR DE INDUSTRIE I.E. STATISTIEK, HOOFDAFDELING STATISTIEKEN VAN INDUSTRIE EN BOUWNIJVERHEID (NE) [10340995] **1619**

NATUURWETENSCHAPPELIJK TIJDSCHRIFT (BE/0770-1748) [09692139] **4169**

NATUURWETENSCHAPPELIJKE WERKGROEP NEDERLANDSE ANTILLEN *See* UITGAVEN VAN DE NATUURWETENSCHAPPELIJKE WERKGROEP NEDERLANDSE ANTILLEN **4173**

NATYAM : NATYA PARISHAD, SAGARA KA PRAKASANA (II) [11989199] **2322**

NAUCHEN TSENTUR ZA PLANIRANE *See* TRUDOVE NA NAUCHEN TSENTUR ZA PLANIRANE **1587**

NAUCHNAIA SESSIIA - GOSUDARSTVENNYI NAUCHNO-ISSLEDOVATELSKII INSTITUT VITAMINOLOGII (RU) [06008036] **4195**

NAUCHNI TRUDOVE - VISSH SELSKOSTOPANSKI INSTITUT "VASIL KOLAROV" PLOVDIV (BU/0204-6385) [05544416] **111**

NAUCHNO-ISSLEDOVATELSKII I PROEKTNO-KONSTRUKTORSKII INSTITUT OBOGASHCHENIIA TVERDYKH GORIUCHIKH ISKOPAEMYKH *See* PROBLEMY OBOGASHCHENIIA TVERDYKH GOEIUCHIKH ISKOPAEMYKH **2148**

NAUCHNO-ISSLEDOVATELSKII INSTITUT KLINICHESKOI I EKSPERIMENTALNOI KHIRURGII *See* TRUDY INSTITUTA - NAUCNO-ISSLEDOVATELSKIJ INSTITUT KLINICESKOJ I EKSPERIMENTALNOJ HIRURGII M.Z. S.S.S.R **3977**

NAUCHNO-ISSLEDOVATELSKII INSTITUT PROMYSHLENNOGO STROITELSTVA *See* TRUDY INSTITUTA - NAUCNO-ISSLEDOVATELSKIJ INSTITUT PROMYSLENNOGO STROITELSTVA **630**

NAUCHNO-TEKHNICHESKII BIULLETEN PO AGRONOMICHESKOI FIZIKE (RU) [02779110] **111**

NAUCHNO-TEKHNICHESKII BIULLETEN VSESOIUZNOGO ORDENA LENINA I ORDENA DRUZHBY NARODOV NAUCHNO-ISSELDOVATELSKOGO INSTITUTA RASTENIEVODSTVA IMENI N.I. VAVILOVA / VSESOIUZNAIA ORDENA LENTINA I ORDENA TRUDOGO KRASNOGO ZNAMENI AKADEMIIA SELSKOKHOZIAISTVENNYKH NAUK IMENI V.I. LENINA (RU/0202-5361) [11226557] **2425**

NAUCHNOE UPRAVLENIE OBSHCHESTVOM (RU/0548-0108) [04469981] **4543**

NAUCHNYE DOKLADY VYSSHEI SHKOLY. BIOLOGICHESKIE NAUKI (RU/0470-4606) [05285429] **466**

NAUCHNYE DOKLADY VYSSHEI SHKOLY. FILOLOGICHESKIE NAUKI *See* FILOLOGICHESKIE NAUKI **3281**

NAUCHNYE OSNOVY OKHRANY PRIRODY. SBORNIK STATEI (RU) [05666522] **2200**

NAUCHNYE SOOBSHCHENIIA (MOSCOW, R.S.R.S.R.) (RU) [10631120] **359**

NAUCHNYE TRUDY (RU/0579-8620) [11008565] **4013**

NAUCHNYE TRUDY (RU) [01793143] **1857**

NAUCHNYE TRUDY (KZ) [01789632] **2147**

NAUCHNYE TRUDY / GRUZINSKII POLITEKHNICHESKII INSTITUT IM. V.I. LENINA (RU) [11087279] **5131**

NAUCHNYE TRUDY ISEP AN SSSR / AKADEMIIA NAUK SSSR, LENINGRADSKII NAUCHNYI TSENTR, INSTITUT SOTSIALNO EKONOMICHESKIKH PROBLEM (RU) [19913520] **5210**

NAUCHNYE TRUDY / KARAGANDA. NAUCHNO-ISSLEDOVATELSKII UGOLNYI INSTITUT *See* NAUCHNYE TRUDY **2147**

NAUCHNYE TRUDY (MOSKOVSKII INSTITUT STALI I SPLAVOV) (RU/0131-5145) [01799403] **4013**

NAUCHNYE TRUDY / MOSKOVSKII LESOTEKHNICHESKII INSTITUT (RU/0540-9691) [09638591] 1988, **2388**

NAUCHNYE TRUDY / VSESOIUZNYI NAUCHNO-ISSLEDOVATELSKII INSTITUT FARMATSII (RU) [17222525] **4317**

NAUCHNYE TRUDY / VSESOIUZNYI SELEKTSIONNO-GENETICHESKII INSTITUT *See* SBORNIK NAUCHNYKH TRUDOV (VSESOIUZNYI) **551**

NAUCHNYI ATEIZM / MINISTERSTVO PROSVESCHENIIA RSFSR, PERMSKII GOSUDARSTVENNYI PEDAGOGICHESKII INSTITUT, KAFEDRA MARKSISTSKO-LENINSKOI FILOSOFII (RU) [08203151] **4353**

NAUCHNYI REFERATIVNYI SBORNIK: MUZEEVEDENIE I OKHRANA PAMIATNIKOV (RU) [05348180] **4093**

NAUCNI I STRUCNI SKUPOVI U JUGOSLAVIJI I U INOSTRANSTVU (YU) [05725427] **5131**

NAUCNI SKUPOVI U SFRJ I U INOSTRANSTVU (YU) [02244794] **697**

NAUCNO-TEHNICESKAA INFORMACIA. SERIA 1, ORGANIZACIA I METODIKA INFORMACIONNOJ RABOTY (RU/0548-0019) [04400314] **3233**

NAUCNO-TEHNICESKAJA INFORMACIJA. VSESOJUZNYJ INSTITUT NAUCNOJ I TEHNICESKOJ INFORMACII. SERIJA 2. INFORMACIONNYE PROCESSY I SISTEMY (RU/0548-0027) [04400334] **1243**

NAUCNO-TEHNICESKIJ BULLETEN' VSESOUZNOGO SELEKCIONNO-GENETICESKOGO INSTITUTA (RU/0374-9525) [03749525] 550, **519**

NAUCNYE OSNOVY RAZVITIA ZIVOTNOVODSTVA V BELORUSSII (BW/0130-9803) [03149477] **216**

NAUCNYE TRUDY - VSESOJUZNYJ NAUCNO-ISSLEDOVATELSKIJ INSTITUT FIZIOLOGII BIOHIMII I PITANIJA SELSKO-HOZJAJSTEVENNYH ZIVOTNYH (RU/0203-6827) [03084181] **5516**

NAUGATUCK DAILY NEWS (US) [22188200] **5646**

NAUJIENOS (US/0745-5445) [09273424] **5661**

NAUKA-FANTASTYKA (UN) [24020466] **5131**

NAUKA I CHELOVECHESTVO (RU/0548-0345) [04741388] **5131**

NAUKA I MY (LV/0236-2767) [21383307] **5131**

NAUKA I RELIGIJA (RU/0130-7045) [01715391] **4980**

NAUKA I ZIZN (RU/0028-1263) [01071452] **5131**

NAUKA O ZEMI. GEOLOGICA (XO/0548-040X) [06643617] **1389**

NAUKA POLSKA (PL/0028-1271) [01759524] **5132**

NAUKA SEGODNIA (RU) [02241842] **5132**

NAUKA U PRAKSI BEOGRAD (YU/0350-1388) [03501388] **5132**

NAUKA V SSSR. ENGLISH. SCIENCE IN USSR *See* SCIENCE IN RUSSIA / RUSSIAN ACADEMY OF SCIENCES **5152**

NAUKA ZA GORATA (BU/0861-007X) [22633380] **2388**

NAUKOVYI KOMUNIZM (UN) [02609846] **1693**

NAULO MUKTI (II) [08623865] **3414**

NAUNYN-SCHMIEDEBERG'S ARCHIVES OF PHARMACOLOGY (GW/0028-1298) [01771667] **4317**

NAUTICA (IT/0392-369X) [I0392369X] **4179**

NAUTICAL BRASS, ETC (US) [13294184] **4179**

NAUTICAL MAGAZINE (UK/0028-1336) [08405829] **4179**

NAUTICAL RESEARCH JOURNAL (US/0738-7245) [06328267] **4179**

NAUTILUS (PHILADELPHIA), THE (US/0028-1344) [01759527] **5592**

NAUTISK ALMANAK (DK) [09561665] **397**

NAUTOLOGIA (PL/0548-0523) [04240443] **4179**

NAVA NEWS / NORTH AMERICAN VEXILLOLOGICAL ASSOCIATION (US/1053-3338) [22517392] **2623**

NAVA-PATHA (II) [08721431] **3414**

NAVAJO AREA NEWSLETTER *CEASED.* (US) [04644567] **1766**

NAVAJO NATION MESSENGER, THE (US) [28682558] 2268, **5712**

NAVAJO TIMES (WINDOW ROCK, ARIZ. : 1987) (US) [16464595] **5630**

NAVAJO YEARBOOK (US/0466-6658) [01135486] **2268**

NAVAL AFFAIRS (US/0028-1409) [04123895] **4179**

NAVAL ARCHITECT, THE (UK/0306-0209) [06418620] **5453**

NAVAL ARCHITECTURE AND OCEAN ENGINEERING (JA/0387-5504) [04275630] 2093, **4179**

NAVAL AVIATION NEWS (US/0028-1417) [02577618] **30**

NAVAL CRYPTOLOGIC VETERANS ASSOCIATION NEWSLETTER *See* CRYPTOLOG **4176**

NAVAL ENGINEERS JOURNAL (US/0028-1425) [02240093] **4179**

NAVAL FORCES (UK/0722-8880) [08372123] **4180**

NAVAL HEALTH RESEARCH CENTER *See* NHRC REPORT **3621**

NAVAL HISTORY (US/1042-1920) [16311980] **4180**

NAVAL INSTITUTE GUIDE TO COMBAT FLEETS OF THE WORLD (US) [22497546] **4180**

NAVAL LAW REVIEW (US/1049-0272) [13771109] **3183**

NAVAL RESEARCH LABORATORY *See* SELECTED EDUCATIONAL OPPORTUNITIES **1915**

NAVAL RESEARCH LABORATORY (U.S.) *See* FACT BOOK - NAVAL RESEARCH LABORATORY (U.S.) **4176**

NAVAL RESEARCH LOGISTICS (US/0894-069X) [15338977] **4180**

NAVAL RESEARCH REVIEWS (US/0028-145X) [01768623] **4180**

NAVAL RESERVE ASSOCIATION *See* NRA. NAVAL RESERVE ASSOCIATION NEWS **4181**

NAVAL REVIEW (UK) **4180**

NAVAL REVIEW (ANNAPOLIS) (US/0077-6238) [01771669] **4180**

NAVAL STORES REVIEW *See* INTERNATIONAL YEARBOOK **4177**

NAVAL STORES REVIEW (1979) (US/0164-4580) [04741711] 1027, **2403**

NAVAL SURFACE WARFARE CENTER (U.S.) *See* TECHNICAL DIGEST / NAVAL SURFACE WARFARE CENTER **4184**

NAVAL WAR COLLEGE REVIEW (US/0028-1484) [01779130] **4180**

NAVALAKATHA (II/0028-1492) [01790497] **3414**

NAVARAGA (II) [08623928] **3414**

NAVI (JA/0289-6079) [I02896079] **4180**

NAVIGATION (AT/0077-6262) [01791681] **4180**

NAVIGATION AND VESSEL INSPECTION CIRCULAR / DEPARTMENT OF TRANSPORTATION, UNITED STATES COAST GUARD (US) [03499675] **4180**

NAVIGATION (PARIS) (FR/0028-1530) [06314578] 30, **4180**

NAVIGATION SEASON EXTENSION DEMONSTRATION PROGRAM. DRAFT ENVIRONMENTAL STATEMENT (US) [03831539] **4180**

NAVIGATION (WASHINGTON) (US/0028-1522) [02083741] 30, **4180**

NAVIGATOR (ENGLISH EDITION) (FI) [12629072] **4180**

NAVIGATOR (NORFOLK, VA.), THE (US/1064-0894) [20660046] **2462**

NAVIRES, PORTS & CHANTIERS (FR/0028-159X) [06314654] **4180**

NAVIS; ANNUAIRE DE LA MARINE MARCHANDE, DE LA CONSTRUCTION NAVALE ET DES PORTS MARITIMES (FR) [07269417] **4180**

NAVORD OD (US) [03510348] **4180**

NAVORD REPORT *See* NAVORD OD **4180**

NAVORSINGE VAN DIE NASIONALE MUSEUM (SA/0067-9208) [02570455] 4093, **242**

NAVRH A BYDLENI (XR) [09848369] **2829**

NAVSEA JOURNAL (US/0161-9411) [04060873] **4180**

NAVSO NEWS (US/1045-0394) [20008751] **5297**

NAVY ARMS MUZZLELOADERS' JOURNAL (US/0272-7854) [06905365] **2812**

NAVY CHAPLAIN, THE (US) [15132019] **4180**

NAVY CIVIL ENGINEER (US/0096-9419) [01759538] **2027**

NAVY CONTRACTING DIRECTIVES (US) [05204209] **4180**

NAVY INTERNATIONAL (UK/0144-3194) [05821410] **4180**

NAVY LIST *See* NAVY LIST, THE **4180**

NAVY LIST, THE (UK) [04688243] **4180**

NAVY MEDICINE (US/0895-8211) [15734740] **3619**

NAVY NEWS (US/0028-1670) **5759**

NAVY NEWS (US/0028-1662) [04123910] **4180**

NAVY NEWS & UNDERSEA TECHNOLOGY (US/8756-1700) [12353771] **4180**

NAVY PERSONNEL RESEARCH AND DEVELOPMENT CENTER (U.S.) *See* ANNUAL REPORT - NAVY PERSONNEL RESEARCH AND DEVELOPMENT CENTER (U.S.) **4035**

NAVY TECHNICAL DISCLOSURE BULLETIN / OFFICE OF NAVAL RESEARCH, DEPARTMENT OF THE NAVY (US/0364-3646) [02640156] **4180**

NAVY TIMES (US/0028-1697) [03511129] 4052, **4180**

NAWCC BULLETIN (US) [13483943] 2775, **251**

NAWGA DIRECTORY OF MEMBERS (US/0145-4218) [02734576] **2351**

NAWPA PACHA (US/0077-6297) [01605919] **275**

NAYA (II/0376-6578) [01784088] **3414**

NAYA PRATIKA (II) [02240188] **3414**

NAYAM KADAMA (NP) [01790469] **2526**

NAYI TALIMA (II) [01784217] **1766**

NAZARETH (COMBERMERE) (CN/1183-1863) [25066642] **5033**

NAZEER (US) [11242183] **4483**

NAZIONE (IT/0391-6863) [I03916863] **5804**

NB. NEW BUILDER (UK/0956-9081) [I09569081] **622**

NBA FAMILY TALK (US) **5297**

NBA REGISTER (US/0739-3067) [09484715] **4906**

NBC BRIEF (US/1040-9270) [18577453] **4052**

NBC NEWS, RAND MCNALLY WORLD ATLAS & ALMANAC *CEASED.* (US) [22919783] 2623, **4483**

NBC/NFC NEWS (CN/0848-600X) [23004585] **622**

NBER DIGEST, THE (US/0888-949X) [06385547] **1507**

NBER MACROECONOMICS ANNUAL (US/0889-3365) [13854108] **1593**

NBER REPORTER (US/0276-119X) [03610992] **1507**

NBER WORKING PAPER SERIES (US/0898-2937) [05531441] **1507**

NBER WORKING PAPER SERIES ON HISTORICAL FACTORS IN LONG-RUN GROWTH (US/1058-8450) [20063548] **1575**

NBPGR ANNUAL REPORT (II) [24588038] **550**

NBRI NEWSLETTER : A QUARTERLY HOUSE JOURNAL OF THE NATIONAL BOTANICAL RESEARCH INSTITUTE (II) [04819077] **519**

NBS HANDBOOK (US) [19216952] **4031**

NBS. REACTOR. SUMMARY OF ACTIVITIES (US/0148-4192) [03130487] **4448**

NBTA NEWS (CN/0317-5227) [02078629] **1766**

NC ARTS (US/0748-1934) [10897486] **325**

NC FERTIGUNG (GW) **3485**

NC HOME *CEASED.* (US/1059-3500) [24579478] **2902**

NC PRAXIS (GW) [09128618] **2123**

NC SHOPOWNER *SUSPENDED.* (US/0271-1079) [06546507] **2123**

NC STATE ECONOMIST (US) [19827255] **111**

NCA QUARTERLY (US/1043-3511) [19415046] **1766**

●NCA/TCS NEWSLETTER (US/0163-772X) [25532819] **539**

NCA TODAY (US/0027-6219) [04278752] **1837**

NCAA BASEBALL RULES (US/0736-5209) [09121887] **4906**

NCAA BASKETBALL (US/0276-1017) [05739272] **4906**

NCAA DIRECTORY (US/0162-1467) [03954047] **4906**

NCAA FOOTBALL RULES AND INTERPRETATIONS (US/0736-5160) [05089628] **4906**

NCAA MANUAL (US/1053-0886) [19596534] **4907**

NCAA MEN'S AND WOMEN'S BASKETBALL RULES AND INTERPRETATIONS (US/1042-3877) [16824502] **4907**

NCAA MEN'S AND WOMEN'S CROSS COUNTRY AND TRACK AND FIELD RULES (US/0882-3170) [10284115] **4907**

NCAA MEN'S AND WOMEN'S RIFLE RULES (US/0736-5144) [10291281] **4907**

NCAA MEN'S AND WOMEN'S SKIING RULES (US/0741-9279) [10116681] **4907**

NCAA MEN'S AND WOMEN'S SOCCER RULES (US/0735-0368) [19917722] **4907**

NCAA MEN'S AND WOMEN'S SWIMMING AND DIVING RULES (US/0736-5128) [08918707] **4907**

●NCAA MEN'S AND WOMEN'S TRACK AND FIELD AND CROSS COUNTRY RULES (US) [26962199] **4907**

NCAA MEN'S ICE HOCKEY RULES AND INTERPRETATIONS (US/0735-9195) [08832887] **4907**

NCAA MEN'S LACROSSE RULES (US/0742-4361) [10255587] **4907**

NCAA MEN'S WATER POLO RULES (US/0734-0508) [08417313] **4907**

NCAA NEWS, THE (US/0027-6170) [02396789] **4907**

NCAA SWIMMING; ANNUAL GUIDE (US/0272-8095) [05418057] **4907**

NCAE NEWS BULLETIN (US/0027-6189) [04078129] **1867**

NCAHF NEWSLETTER (US/0890-3417) [13994779] **1298**

NCAIR NEWS (US) [04850803] **1196**

NCALRI NEWSLETTER (US) [25479820] 3014, **111**

NCASI SPECIAL REPORT (US) [08777759] 2237, **4235**

NCASI TECHNICAL REVIEW : BULLETIN (US) [06400699] **4235**

NCB QUEST (II) [20104742] **622**

NCBA COOPERATIVE BUSINESS JOURNAL (US/1065-7207) [26705184] **697**

●NCBE FORUM (US/1072-2076) [28895763] **1766**

NCBHR COMMUNIQUE (CN/1181-8778) [24256408] **2252**

NCBL NOTES (US/0733-1851) [07562730] **3014**

NCCA ILLUSTRATED MEN'S AND WOMEN'S BASKETBALL RULES (US/1042-3869) [16862483] **4907**

NCCLS DOCUMENT (US/0896-6443) [17367266] 3619, **466**

NCCP NEWSLETTER (PH/0116-4252) [20447999] **4483**

NCEA-GANLEY'S CATHOLIC SCHOOLS IN AMERICA (US/0147-8044) [03228033] 1766, **5033**

NCECA JOURNAL (US/0739-1544) [08586739] **2592**

NCECA NEWSLETTER (US/0739-1552) [07506170] **2592**

NCEE REGISTRATION BULLETIN (US/0199-8994) [06192985] **1988**

NCEOA JOURNAL (US/0889-8405) [14084887] **1766**

NCERT NEWS-LETTER (II) [01797697] **1867**

NCGR JOURNAL (US) **390**

NCI FACT BOOK (US/0270-7950) [06359787] 3789, **3821**

NCI GRANTS AWARDED (US/0272-9695) [06950926] **3821**

NCI INVESTIGATIONAL DRUGS. CHEMICAL INFORMATION (US) [11184006] **4317**

NCIP NEWS (US) [13706088] **3233**

NCJW JOURNAL (US/0161-2115) [03876880] 5562, **2268**

NCLIS NEWS / U.S. NATIONAL COMMISSION ON LIBRARIES AND INFORMATION SCIENCE (US) [21475765] **3233**

NCO JOURNAL, THE (US/1058-9058) [23353677] **4052**

NCOA JOURNAL (SAN ANTONIO, TEX.) (US/0747-0150) [10473932] **4052**

NCOA NETWORKS (US/1045-9073) [20285850] **5180**

NCOSS NEWS (AT/0313-4133) **5297**

NCPC QUARTERLY (US/0743-4529) [10601966] **2829**

NCPHS NEWSLETTER (US/1054-9188) [20061860] **1146**

NCPI ASSOCIATES NEWSLETTER *See* NCPI HOTLINE **3170**

NCPI HOTLINE (US) [04319964] **3170**

NCR CONNECTION (US/1059-9983) [24842382] **697**

NCR MONTHLY *See* NCR CONNECTION **697**

NCREIF REAL ESTATE PERFORMANCE REPORT, THE (US) [23750101] **4842**

NCRP NEWS (US) [02254848] **4438**

NCRP REPORT (US/0083-209X) [01768548] **4793**

●NCRR REPORTER / NATIONAL CENTER FOR RESEARCH RESOURCES (US) [28582412] **3619**

NCRTL SPECIAL REPORT (US/1054-7673) [22969229] **1901**

NCSA NEWSLETTER *CEASED.* (CN/0824-4820) [10638964] **5297**

NCSC SUBSCRIPTION PACKAGE PLAN (US) **3141**

NCSL CONFERENCE REPORT (US/0899-5052) [13214033] **3141**

●NCSL LEGISBRIEF (US/1068-2716) [27261364] **4668**

NCSL NEWSLETTER (US/0194-5149) [04786724] **4031**

NCSL STATE LEGISLATIVE SUMMARY : LIABILITY INSURANCE *CEASED.* (US) [15737666] **2889**

NCSR/TR / NATIONAL COUNCIL FOR SCIENTIFIC RESEARCH, ZAMBIA (ZA) [04089559] **5132**

NCUA WATCH NEWSLETTER, THE (US) **801**

NCVO NEWS (UK/0955-2170) [09552170] **5297**

NDA PIPELINE, THE (US/0890-6610) [10750138] **4317**

NDAA BULLETIN / NATIONAL DISTRICT ATTORNEYS ASSOCIATION (US) [16702454] **3108**

NDC PAPER (UK/0306-5464) [01138680] **3619**

NDIWULA : THE ANNUAL NEWSLETTER OF THE MUSEUMS OF MALAWI (MW) [22118054] **4093**

NDOLA DIRECTORY (ZA) [07519179] **2642**

NDP ANTI-WAR NEWSLETTER (CN/0824-4456) [10513348] **4529**

NDT & E INTERNATIONAL : INDEPENDENT NONDESTRUCTIVE TESTING AND EVALUATION (UK/0963-8695) [24727585] **1988**

●NDT UPDATE (US/1063-3588) [25990682] 5132, **4052**

●NDTA NETWORK (US/1063-7664) [26135799] **3839**

NDZ. NEUE DELIWA-ZEITSCHRIFT (GW/0341-0323) [09411676] **1950**

NE-METALLE *See* METALLE **4009**

NEA-AKTIVIST (ANCHORAGE, ALASKA) (US/1068-2511) [16912673] **1766**

NEA ... ALMANAC OF HIGHER EDUCATION, THE (US/0743-670X) [10634910] **1837**

NEA ESTIA (GR/0028-1735) [01492852] **2519**

NEA HIGHER EDUCATION ADVOCATE (US) [10888033] **1837**

NEA NEWSLETTER (FR) [10594612] **1950**

NEA PAIDEIA (GR) [10125287] **1766**

NEA PATRIDA (CN/0225-0594) [06136326] **5790**

NEA POREIA : LOGOTECHNIKO PERIODIKO (GR) [10776913] **3414**

NEA TODAY (US/0734-7219) [08795264] **1767**

NEA TOY HAMILTON (CN/0715-4410) [09146007] **5790**

NEAL SPELCE AUSTIN LETTER, THE (US/1071-0612) [05284736] 697, **1507**

NEAR EAST ARCHAEOLOGICAL SOCIETY BULLETIN (US/0739-0068) [01714481] **275**

NEAR EAST REPORT (US/0028-176X) [01759544] **4529**

NEAR EAST SERIES (US/0196-3562) [05802661] **2659**

NEAR NORTH NEWS (US/0028-1778) [04123985] **5661**

NEARA JOURNAL (US/0149-2551) [03461963] **2748**

NEAS. NEWSLETTER OF ENGINEERING ANALYSIS SOFTWARE (US/0739-697X) [05898453] 1288, **1988**

NEBRASKA *See* REVISED STATUTES OF NEBRASKA, 1943 **3040**

NEBRASKA *See* OFFICIAL BRAND LAWS (LINCOLN) **3021**

NEBRASKA *See* LAWS OF THE STATE OF NEBRASKA PERTAINING TO THE GAME AND PARKS COMMISSION **3114**

NEBRASKA ACADEMY OF SCIENCES *See* TRANSACTIONS OF THE NEBRASKA ACADEMY OF SCIENCES AND AFFILIATED SOCIETIES **5167**

NEBRASKA. ACCOUNTING DIVISION *See* ANNUAL FISCAL REPORT YEAR ENDING JUNE 30 ... / STATE OF NEBRASKA **4709**

NEBRASKA AGRICULTURAL STATISTICS (US) [04179002] 111, **155**

NEBRASKA ANCESTREE (US/0270-4463) [06183383] **2462**

NEBRASKA ANNUAL HOUSING REPORT (US/0160-211X) [03633042] **2829**

NEBRASKA BEVERAGE ANALYST (US/0028-1808) [05034662] **2369**

NEBRASKA BIRD REVIEW, THE (US/0028-1816) [01606385] **5592**

NEBRASKA. BOARD OF EXAMINERS FOR COUNTY HIGHWAY AND CITY STREET SUPERINTENDENTS *See* ANNUAL REPORT OF THE BOARD OF EXAMINERS FOR COUNTY HIGHWAY AND CITY STREET SUPERINTENDENTS **5438**

NEBRASKA CATTLEMAN (US/1062-8274) [09932171] **216**

NEBRASKA. COMMISSION ON AGING *See* STATE PLAN ON AGING FOR THE STATE OF NEBRASKA **5311**

NEBRASKA COMMISSION ON LAW ENFORCEMENT AND CRIMINAL JUSTICE *See* CRIMINAL JUSTICE COMPREHENSIVE PLAN **3162**

NEBRASKA COMMISSION ON LAW ENFORCEMENT AND CRIMINAL JUSTICE *See* JUVENILE COURT REPORT (LINCOLN) **3121**

NEBRASKA COMMISSION ON LAW ENFORCEMENT AND CRIMINAL JUSTICE *See* NEBRASKA COMPREHENSIVE CRIMINAL JUSTICE PLAN **3170**

NEBRASKA COMMISSION ON LAW ENFORCEMENT AND CRIMINAL JUSTICE *See* ANNUAL REPORT - NEBRASKA COMMISSION ON LAW ENFORCEMENT AND CRIMINAL JUSTICE **3157**

NEBRASKA COMPREHENSIVE CRIMINAL JUSTICE PLAN (US) [06460930] **3170**

NEBRASKA CPA (US) **749**

NEBRASKA DAILY NEWS-PRESS (US) [13363802] **5706**

NEBRASKA DEPARTMENT OF AERONAUTICS : ANNUAL REPORT (US) [22999137] **30**

Alphabetical Title Index — NEDERLANDS

NEBRASKA. DEPT. OF AERONAUTICS See NEBRASKA DEPARTMENT OF AERONAUTICS : ANNUAL REPORT **30**

NEBRASKA. DEPT. OF ECONOMIC DEVELOPMENT. DIVISION OF RESEARCH See NEBRASKA ANNUAL HOUSING REPORT **2829**

NEBRASKA. DEPT. OF ECONOMIC DEVELOPMENT. DIVISION OF RESEARCH See NEBRASKA VISITOR SURVEY **1507**

NEBRASKA. DEPT. OF HEALTH See ANNUAL REPORT - STATE OF NEBRASKA. DEPARTMENT OF HEALTH **4767**

NEBRASKA. DEPT. OF PUBLIC INSTITUTIONS See DPI YELLOW PAGES **5284**

NEBRASKA. DEPT. OF PUBLIC INSTITUTIONS. RESEARCH AND STATISTICS SECTION See ANNUAL STATISTICAL REPORT. MENTAL HEALTH SERVICES. MENTAL RETARDATION SERVICES. VETERANS' HOMES SERVICE (NEBRASKA) **5266**

NEBRASKA. DEPT. OF PUBLIC WELFARE See FINAL NEBRASKA COMPREHENSIVE ANNUAL SERVICES PLAN **5285**

NEBRASKA. DEPT. OF WATER RESOURCES See BIENNIAL REPORT OF THE DEPARTMENT OF WATER RESOURCES **5531**

NEBRASKA DIGEST (US) [05813872] **3014**

NEBRASKA DIRECTORY OF MANUFACTURERS AND THEIR PRODUCTS (US/0898-7033) [14109403] **3485**

NEBRASKA. DIVISION OF COMMUNITY AFFAIRS See ANNUAL AMENDMENT - NUMBER 13 TO THE NEBRASKA STATE PLAN FOR TITLE 1A OF THE HIGHER EDUCATION ACT OF 1965 **1809**

NEBRASKA. DIVISION OF DRUG CONTROL See ACTIVITY SUMMARY DRUG AND NARCOTIC CASES **1338**

NEBRASKA. DIVISION OF EMPLOYMENT See ANNUAL PLANNING REPORT - NEBRASKA DEPARTMENT OF LABOR, DIVISION OF EMPLOYMENT **1648**

NEBRASKA. DIVISION OF HEALTH DATA AND STATISTICAL RESEARCH See NEBRASKA HEALTH MANPOWER REPORTS: NURSING HOME ADMINISTRATORS **3789**

NEBRASKA. DIVISION OF HEALTH DATA AND STATISTICAL RESEARCH See NEBRASKA STATISTICAL REPORT OF ABORTIONS **591**

NEBRASKA. DIVISION OF HEALTH DATA AND STATISTICAL RESEARCH See NEBRASKA HEALTH MANPOWER REPORTS : PHYSICIAN'S ASSISTANTS **4793**

NEBRASKA. DIVISION OF HEALTH DATA AND STATISTICAL RESEARCH See NEBRASKA HEALTH MANPOWER REPORTS : OPTOMETRISTS **4216**

NEBRASKA. DIVISION OF VOCATIONAL EDUCATION See NEBRASKA STATE PLAN FOR THE ADMINISTRATION OF VOCATIONAL EDUCATION **1914**

NEBRASKA. DIVISION ON ALCOHOLISM See NEBRASKA STATE PLAN FOR ALCOHOLISM, THE **1347**

NEBRASKA. DIVISION ON ALCOHOLISM See NEBRASKA NUMBERS **1347**

NEBRASKA ENGLISH AND LANGUAGE ARTS JOURNAL (US/1051-9823) [22162072] **3414**

NEBRASKA ENGLISH JOURNAL (US/1061-6993) [25406356] **1093**

NEBRASKA EPISCOPALIAN, THE (US/1061-4486) [25316848] **5065**

NEBRASKA FARMER, THE (US/1049-1880) [01695480] **111**

NEBRASKA FERTILIZER & AG-CHEMICAL DIGEST (US/0199-672X) [06075684] **111**

NEBRASKA GAME & FISH (US/0897-8999) [17657516] **4875**

NEBRASKA GEOLOGICAL SURVEY See FIELD GUIDE - NEBRASKA GEOLOGICAL SURVEY **1375**

NEBRASKA. GOVERNOR See EXECUTIVE BUDGET / STATE OF NEBRASKA ; SUBMITTED TO THE ... SESSION OF THE LEGISLATURE BY ... GOVERNOR ; PREPARED BY ... TAX COMMISSIONER AND BUDGET DIRECTOR **4723**

NEBRASKA. GOVERNOR See EXECUTIVE CAPITAL CONSTRUCTION BUDGET **4723**

● NEBRASKA HEALTH CARE IN PERSPECTIVE (US/1065-4291) [26605848] **4793**

NEBRASKA HEALTH MANPOWER REPORTS: NURSING HOME ADMINISTRATORS (US/0148-9321) [03400482] **3789**

NEBRASKA HEALTH MANPOWER REPORTS : OPTOMETRISTS (US/0149-9599) [03584357] **4216**

NEBRASKA HEALTH MANPOWER REPORTS : PHYSICIAN'S ASSISTANTS (US) [04271030] **4793**

NEBRASKA HEALTH MANPOWER REPORTS. PODIATRISTS, PHYSICAL THERAPISTS, CHIROPRACTORS, SPEECH PATHOLOGISTS, AUDIOLOGISTS, VETERINARIANS (US) [21193478] **3915**

NEBRASKA HISTORY (US/0028-1859) [03558293] **2748**

NEBRASKA IN PERSPECTIVE (US/1065-5565) [26659823] **5334**

NEBRASKA. INVESTMENT COUNCIL See REPORT / STATE OF NEBRASKA, INVESTMENT COUNCIL **4746**

NEBRASKA JOURNAL OF HEALTH, PHYSICAL EDUCATION, RECREATION AND DANCE (US) **1857**

NEBRASKA JUDICIAL NEWSLETTER (US/0364-233X) [02618527] **3141**

NEBRASKA JUVENILE COURT REPORT (US/1070-8316) [27485673] 3170, **5297**

● NEBRASKA LAW NEWSLETTER (US/1062-953X) [25814579] **3014**

NEBRASKA LAW REVIEW (US/0047-9209) [01759578] **3014**

NEBRASKA LEGAL DIRECTORY, THE (US/0748-2744) [09359824] **3014**

NEBRASKA. LEGISLATURE See UNICAMERAL UPDATE **4692**

NEBRASKA LIBRARIES (US/1043-8807) [11335460] **3233**

NEBRASKA LIBRARY ASSOCIATION QUARTERLY (US/0028-1883) [02407351] **3233**

NEBRASKA LIBRARY DIRECTORY / COMPILED AND PUBLISHED BY NEBRASKA LIBRARY COMMISSION (US) [24151809] **3233**

NEBRASKA LUTHERAN (US/0745-2705) [09008953] **5065**

NEBRASKA. MANPOWER SERVICES COUNCIL See REPORT TO THE GOVERNOR FROM THE MANPOWER SERVICES COUNCIL, THE **1707**

● NEBRASKA MANUFACTURERS REGISTER (US/1059-7727) [24728289] **3485**

NEBRASKA MEDICAL JOURNAL, THE (US/0091-6730) [01680837] **3619**

NEBRASKA MINERAL OPERATIONS REVIEW (US/0730-9821) [08073468] **1443**

NEBRASKA MORTAR & PESTLE (US/0028-1891) [02264766] **4317**

NEBRASKA MUNICIPAL REVIEW (US/0028-1905) [01641149] **4668**

NEBRASKA MUSIC EDUCATOR, THE (US/0732-1503) [04270122] **4139**

NEBRASKA. NATURAL RESOURCES COMMISSION See STATE WATER PLAN PUBLICATION (LINCOLN) **5539**

NEBRASKA. NATURAL RESOURCES COMMISSION See IMPLEMENTATION OF LITTLE BLUE RIVER BASIN WATER QUALITY MANAGEMENT PLAN **2232**

NEBRASKA NEWSPAPER (US/0028-1913) [04161077] **5706**

NEBRASKA NUMBERS (US/0364-5673) [02665661] **1347**

NEBRASKA NURSE (US/0028-1921) [02302073] **3862**

NEBRASKA. OFFICE OF ATHLETIC COMMISSIONER See REPORT - OFFICE OF ATHLETIC COMMISSIONER (LINCOLN) **4915**

NEBRASKA. PUBLIC SERVICE COMMISSION See BIENNIAL REPORT / NEBRASKA PUBLIC SERVICE COMMISSION **4632**

NEBRASKA RESOURCES (US) [04317644] **2200**

NEBRASKA RETAILER (US/0028-1948) [04946769] **955**

NEBRASKA REVIEW (FAIRBURY, NEB.) (US/0270-4412) [06429771] **1093**

NEBRASKA REVIEW (OMAHA, NEB.), THE (US/8755-514X) [11332257] **2851**

NEBRASKA SELECTED STATISTICS FOR ... (US) [14234355] **5442**

NEBRASKA SPEECH AND HEARING JOURNAL **CEASED.** (US/0470-570X) [04990581] **4391**

NEBRASKA. STATE BOARD OF EDUCATION AND STATE BOARD OF VOCATIONAL EDUCATION See ANNUAL REPORT OF THE STATE BOARD OF EDUCATION TO THE GOVERNOR AND LEGISLATURE OF THE STATE OF NEBRASKA FOR THE FISCAL YEAR COMMENCING JULY 1, AND ENDING JUNE 30 ..., THE **1725**

NEBRASKA. STATE BOARD OF EXAMINERS FOR PROFESSIONAL ENGINEERS AND ARCHITECTS See ANNUAL REPORT OF THE NEBRASKA STATE BOARD OF EXAMINERS FOR PROFESSIONAL ENGINEERS AND ARCHITECTS **1965**

NEBRASKA STATE HISTORICAL SOCIETY See HISTORICAL NEWS LETTER **2737**

NEBRASKA STATE HISTORICAL SOCIETY See PUBLICATIONS OF THE NEBRASKA STATE HISTORICAL SOCIETY **2755**

NEBRASKA. STATE INVESTMENT COUNCIL See ANNUAL REPORT - STATE INVESTMENT COUNCIL. STATE OF NEBRASKA **4710**

NEBRASKA. STATE INVESTMENT COUNCIL. ANNUAL REPORT See REPORT / STATE OF NEBRASKA, INVESTMENT COUNCIL **4746**

NEBRASKA. STATE OFFICE OF PLANNING AND PROGRAMMING See U.S. BUDGET RECOMMENDATIONS **4757**

NEBRASKA STATE PLAN FOR ALCOHOLISM, THE (US/0149-2101) [03443469] **1347**

NEBRASKA STATE PLAN FOR THE ADMINISTRATION OF VOCATIONAL EDUCATION (US/0097-7349) [01798713] **1914**

NEBRASKA STATE PUBLICATIONS CHECKLIST (US/0091-0406) [01786372] **420**

NEBRASKA STATISTICAL REPORT OF ABORTIONS (US/0095-3105) [03389515] **591**

NEBRASKA SYMPOSIUM ON MOTIVATION (US/0146-7875) [03015235] **4605**

NEBRASKA TRACTOR TEST (US/0093-1489) [05508854] **160**

NEBRASKA. UNIVERSITY. DEPT. OF AGRICULTURAL EDUCATION See DEPARTMENT OF AGRICULTURAL EDUCATION REPORT **78**

NEBRASKA VISITOR SURVEY (US/0149-9165) [03576975] **1507**

NEBRASKA WEATHER & CROPS (US/0745-0117) [08717441] **179**

NEBRASKA WHEAT COMMITTEE See ANNUAL REPORT ... / NEBRASKA WHEAT COMMITTEE **1597**

NEBRASKA. WHEAT COMMITTEE See NEBRASKA WHEAT COMMITTEE/WHEAT DIVISION ANNUAL REPORT **111**

NEBRASKA WHEAT COMMITTEE/WHEAT DIVISION ANNUAL REPORT (US) [06651369] **111**

NEBRASKA WORKMEN'S COMPENSATION REHEARING DECISIONS (US/0278-7636) [07886338] **3152**

NEBRASKALAND (US/0028-1964) [01605451] 2200, **4852**

NEBULA AWARDS, THE (US/0741-5567) [10127556] **3414**

NEBULA (NORTH BAY) **SUSPENDED.** (CN/0317-2104) [02247952] **3414**

NEC GIHO (JA/0285-4139) [08909878] **5132**

NEC RESEARCH & DEVELOPMENT (JA/0048-0436) [04685026] **2073**

NECNP NEWSLETTER (US/0738-9477) [09692705] **2237**

● NED BACKGROUNDER: A FORUM FOR THE STUDY OF THE NATIONAL ENDOWMENT FOR DEMOCRACY AND OTHER U.S. GOVERNMENT DEMOCRATIZATION PROGRAMS, THE (US/1062-6867) [25696317] **4483**

NED. GEREF. TEOLOGIESE TYDSKRIF (SA/0378-9888) [06204484] **4980**

NEDELIA (RU) [06460825] **5809**

NEDERLANDS ARCHIEF VOOR KERKGESCHIEDENIS (NE/0028-2030) [01606887] **4980**

NEDERLANDS BOSBOUW TIJDSCHRIFT (NE/0369-3651) [01604363] **2389**

NEDERLANDS INSTITUUT VOOR EFFICIENCY. PUBLICATIE See NIVE-PUBLICATIE **880**

NEDERLANDS INTERNATIONAAL PRIVATRECHT : REPERTORIUM OP VERDRAGENRECHT, WETGEVING, RECHTSPRAAK EN LITERATUUR (NE/0167-7594) [10804589] **3014**

NEDERLANDS JURISTENBLAD : TEVENS ORGAAN DER NED. JURISTEN VEREENIGING (NE) [01644351] **3014**

NEDERLANDS KUNSTHISTORISCH JAARBOEK (NE/0169-6726) [02556028] **359**

NEDERLANDS MELK- EN ZUIVELTIJSCHRIFT (NE/0028-209X) [03774635] 197, **5132**

NEDERLANDS MILITAIR GENEESKUNDIG TIJDSCHRIFT (NE) [06390426] **3619**

NEDERLANDS TANDARTSENBLAD (NE) **1330**

NEDERLANDS THEOLOGISCH TIJDSCHRIFT (NE/0028-212X) [01776626] **4980**

NEDERLANDS TIJDSCHRIFT VOOR ANESTHESIOLOGIE (NE/0921-8769) [I09218769] **3683**

NEDERLANDS — Alphabetical Title Index

NEDERLANDS TIJDSCHRIFT VOOR DE PSYCHOLOGIE EN HAAR GRENSGEBIEDEN (NE/0028-2235) [09640180] **4605**

NEDERLANDS TIJDSCHRIFT VOOR DERMATOLOGIE & VENEREOLOGIE (NE/0925-8604) [I09258604] **3722**

NEDERLANDS TIJDSCHRIFT VOOR DIETISTEN (NE) 4195, **3619**

NEDERLANDS TIJDSCHRIFT VOOR ERGOTHERAPIE (NE/0166-4751) [I01664751] **5297**

NEDERLANDS TIJDSCHRIFT VOOR FOTONICA (NE/0925-5338) [I09255338] **4413**

NEDERLANDS TIJDSCHRIFT VOOR FYSIOTHERAPIE (NE) **4381**

NEDERLANDS TIJDSCHRIFT VOOR GENEESKUNDE (NE/0028-2162) [01642618] **3619**

NEDERLANDS TIJDSCHRIFT VOOR NATUURKUNDE (AMSTERDAM. 1991) (NE/0926-4264) [23702889] 4413, **5132**

NEDERLANDS TIJDSCHRIFT VOOR OPVOEDING, VORMING EN ONDERWIJS (NE/0169-1872) [I01691872] **1767**

NEDERLANDS TIJDSCHRIFT VOOR TANDHEELKUNDE (NE/0028-2200) [07626195] **1330**

NEDERLANDS TIJDSCHRIFT VOOR ZWAKZINNIGENZORG (NE/0923-2370) [I09232370] **3931**

NEDERLANDS VAN NU (BE/0771-5080) [I07715080] **3305**

NEDERLANDS VERBOND VAN DRUKKERIJEN See JAARVERSLAG - KONINKLIJK NEDERLANDS VERBOND VAN DRUKKERIJEN **4566**

NEDERLANDSCH ARCHIEVENBLAD (NE/0028-2049) [01776061] **2482**

NEDERLANDSCHE BANK (AMSTERDAM, NETHERLANDS) See QUARTERLY STATISTICS - DE NEDERLANDSCHE BANK N.V **1537**

NEDERLANDSCHE BANK (AMSTERDAM, NETHERLANDS) See QUARTERLY BULLETIN / DE NEDERLANDSCHE BANK N.V **805**

NEDERLANDSCHE BANK (AMSTERDAM, NETHERLANDS). QUARTERLY STATISTICS See QUARTERLY BULLETIN / DE NEDERLANDSCHE BANK N.V **805**

NEDERLANDSCHE BANK (AMSTERDAM, NETHERLANDS). VERSLAG VAN DEN PRESIDENT EN VERSLAG VAN DE COMMISSARISSEN See JAARVERSLAG (NEDERLANDSCHE BANK (AMSTERDAM, NETHERLANDS)) **793**

NEDERLANDSCHE LEEUW; MAANDBLAD VAN HET KONINKLIJK NEDERLANDSCH GENOOTSCHAP VOOR GESLACHT- EN WAPENKUNDE, DE (NE) [04942029] **2462**

NEDERLANDSCHE SCHEEPVAART UNIE See JAARVERSLAG - NEDERLANDSCHE SCHEEPVAART UNIE **5385**

NEDERLANDSE BOEK (NE/0166-0586) [I01660586] **3348**

NEDERLANDSE BOEKEN (CN/0710-5207) [09448392] **4830**

NEDERLANDSE CENTRALE ORGANISATIE VOOR See VERSLAGEN EN MEDEDELINGEN - COMMISSIE VOOR HYDROLOGISCH ONDERZOEK T.N.O **1418**

NEDERLANDSE CENTRALE ORGANISATIE VOOR See JAARVERSLAG - TECHNISCH PHYSISCHE DIENST TNO-TH **4407**

NEDERLANDSE CENTRALE ORGANISATIE VOOR TOEGEPAST- NATUURWETENSCHAPPELIJK ONDERZOEK. TECHNISCH-PHYSISCHE DIENST. VERSLAG See JAARVERSLAG - TECHNISCH PHYSISCHE DIENST TNO-TH **4407**

NEDERLANDSE CHEMISCHE INDUSTRIE (NE/0470-6021) [06458347] **987**

NEDERLANDSE COURANT (WILLOWDALE) (CN/0316-9782) [24280063] **2268**

NEDERLANDSE ENERGIEHUISHOUDING / CENTRAAL BUREAU VOOR DE STATISTIEK, DE (NE) [06382522] 1950, **1963**

NEDERLANDSE FINANCIERINGS-MAATSCHAPPIJ VOOR ONTWIKKELINGSLANDEN See JAARVERSLAG - NEDERLANDSE FINANCIERINGS-MAATSCHAPPIJ VOOR ONTWIKKELINGSLANDEN **4734**

NEDERLANDSE GEOGRAFISCHE STUDIES (NE/0169-4839) [I01694839] **2570**

NEDERLANDSE HOUTBOND See JAARVERSLAG - NEDERLANDSE HOUTBOND EN AANGESLOTEN VERENIGINGEN **1613**

NEDERLANDSE JEUGD EN HAAR ONDERWIJS / CENTRAAL BUREAU VOOR DE STATISTIEK, HOOFDAFDELING STATISTIEKEN VAN ONDERWIJS EN WETENSCHAPPEN, DE (NE/0168-4809) [06401272] **1767**

NEDERLANDSE JURISPRUDENTIE INZAKE INTERNATIONAAL BELASTINGRECHT: DIRECTE BELASTINGEN VAN INTERNATIONAAL OPERERENDE ONDERNEMINGEN (NE) 749, **4738**

NEDERLANDSE MILIEULITERATUUR (NE/0925-1049) [I09251049] **2178**

NEDERLANDSE NATUURHISTORISCHE VERENIGING See WETENSCHAPPELIJKE MEDEDELINGEN KNNV **4174**

NEDERLANDSE ONDERNEMINGEN EN HUN FINANCIELE KENMERKEN (NE) [05215936] 1575, **697**

NEDERLANDSE VERENIGING VOOR INTERNATIONAAL RECHT See MEDEDELINGEN VAN DE NEDERLANDSE VERENIGING VOOR INTERNATIONAAL RECHT **3132**

NEDERLANDSE VERENIGING VOOR MANAGEMENT See NIVE-PUBLICATIE **880**

NEDJELJNA DALMACIJA (CI) [01786526] **5799**

NEDLLOYD PARADE (NE) 944, **4212**

NEED A LIFT? (US/0548-1384) [05022355] **1837**

NEED ANALYSIS REQUIREMENTS, PLUS THE COMPLETE CSS CODE LIST (US/0270-4250) [06388670] **1837**

NEED FOR WORKERS IN SELECTED OCCUPATIONS RELATED TO VOCATIONAL & TECHNICAL EDUCATION PROGRAMS. REGION 1 (US) [06928369] **1693**

NEED FOR WORKERS IN SELECTED OCCUPATIONS RELATED TO VOCATIONAL & TECHNICAL EDUCATION PROGRAMS. REGION 2 (US) [06928822] **1693**

NEED FOR WORKERS IN SELECTED OCCUPATIONS RELATED TO VOCATIONAL & TECHNICAL EDUCATION PROGRAMS. REGION 3 (US) [06928860] **1693**

NEED FOR WORKERS IN SELECTED OCCUPATIONS RELATED TO VOCATIONAL & TECHNICAL EDUCATION PROGRAMS. REGION 4 (US) [06928797] **1693**

NEED FOR WORKERS IN SELECTED OCCUPATIONS RELATED TO VOCATIONAL & TECHNICAL EDUCATION PROGRAMS. REGION 5 (US) [06928743] **1693**

NEED FOR WORKERS IN SELECTED OCCUPATIONS RELATED TO VOCATIONAL & TECHNICAL EDUCATION PROGRAMS. REGION 6 (US) [06928448] **1693**

NEED FOR WORKERS IN SELECTED OCCUPATIONS RELATED TO VOCATIONAL & TECHNICAL EDUCATION PROGRAMS. REGION 7 (US) [06990779] **1693**

NEED FOR WORKERS IN SELECTED OCCUPATIONS RELATED TO VOCATIONAL & TECHNICAL EDUCATION PROGRAMS. REGION 8 (US) [06990724] **1693**

NEED FOR WORKERS IN SELECTED OCCUPATIONS RELATED TO VOCATIONAL & TECHNICAL EDUCATION PROGRAMS. REGION 9 (US) [06990818] **1693**

NEED FOR WORKERS IN SELECTED OCCUPATIONS RELATED TO VOCATIONAL & TECHNICAL EDUCATION PROGRAMS. REGION 10 (US) [06990798] **1693**

NEED FOR WORKERS IN SELECTED OCCUPATIONS RELATED TO VOCATIONAL & TECHNICAL EDUCATION PROGRAMS. REGION 11 (US) [06968458] **3916**

NEED FOR WORKERS IN SELECTED OCCUPATIONS RELATED TO VOCATIONAL & TECHNICAL EDUCATION PROGRAMS. REGION 12 (US) [06968555] **1693**

NEED FOR WORKERS IN SELECTED OCCUPATIONS RELATED TO VOCATIONAL & TECHNICAL EDUCATION PROGRAMS. REGION 13 (US) [06968603] **1693**

NEED FOR WORKERS IN SELECTED OCCUPATIONS RELATED TO VOCATIONAL & TECHNICAL EDUCATION PROGRAMS. REGION 14 (US) [06968940] **1693**

NEEDED RESEARCH IN BUSINESS EDUCATION (US) [16738560] 1767, **697**

NEEDLE AND BOBBIN CLUB, NEW YORK See BULLETIN OF THE NEEDLE AND BOBBIN CLUB, THE **5183**

NEEDLE ARTS (US) [11732811] **5185**

NEEDLE, THE (US) [20488799] **3620**

NEEDLE TIPS (US) **3675**

NEEDLEPOINT PLUS CEASED. (US/1040-5518) [18448758] **5185**

NEERLANDIA (NE) **326**

NEERLANDICA EXTRA MUROS (NE) [03312779] **1882**

●NEFESH (US/1058-8213) [24394618] **5051**

NEFROLOGIA (SP/0211-6995) [09438825] **3991**

NEFT I GAZ (RU) [03697226] **4266**

NEFTEHIMIJA (RU/0028-2421) [05970761] **4266**

NEFTEPERERABOTKA I NEFTEHIMIJA (KAZAN) (RU/0320-0094) [02998490] **987**

NEFTEPERERABOTKA, NEFTEHIMIJA I SLANCEPERERABOTKA (RU/0131-1670) [02640824] **4266**

NEFTEPROMYSLOVOE DELO: BURENIE NEFTIANYKH I GAZOVYKH I SKVAZHIN, DOBYCHA NEFTI (RU) [04254034] **2147**

NEFTIANAIA I GAZOVAIA PROMYSHLENNOST See NAFTOVA I HAZOVA PROMYSLOVIST **4265**

NEFTIANAIA PROMYSHELNNOST. SERIIA NEFTEGAZOVAIA GEOLOGIIA I GEOFIZIKA (RU) [08803456] **1408**

NEFTIANAIA PROMYSHLENNOST. SERIIA NEFTEPROMYSLOVOE STROITELSTVO (RU) [10417516] **4266**

NEFTJANIK (RU/0028-243X) [06513159] **4266**

NEFTJANOE HOZJAJSTVO (RU/0028-2448) [10557501] **4013**

NEGACIONES (SP) [03636964] **5210**

NEGARA (MY/0127-0095) [08261094] **5210**

NEGARIT GAZETA (ET) [01568302] **3014**

NEGATIVE CAPABILITY (US/0277-5166) [07582910] **3414**

NEGISHI KEIBA KINEN KOEN See NEGISHI KEIBA KINEN KOEN NENPO **2801**

NEGISHI KEIBA KINEN KOEN NENPO (JA) [11147660] **2801**

NEGM : THE VOICE OF THE NEW ENGLAND FOOD INDUSTRY : THE NEW NEW ENGLAND GROCERY AND MARKET MAGAZINE (US) [09925757] **2351**

NEGOCIATIONS 79 (CN/0228-2593) [06965827] **1693**

NEGOCIO A NEGOCIO (SP) **1619**

NEGOCIOS AL DIA (UK/0960-8710) [I09608710] **698**

NEGOCIOS EM EXAME See EXAME (1983) **673**

NEGOCIOS Y BANCOS : REVISTA PARA EL EJECUTIVO (MX/0028-2456) [03973798] 4738, **801**

NEGOTIATED SETTLEMENTS-- IN NEW BRUNSWICK See COLLECTIVE BARGAINING IN NEW BRUNSWICK **1660**

NEGOTIATED WORKING CONDITIONS (VICTORIA) (CN/0703-0665) [04080334] **1693**

NEGOTIATION JOURNAL (US/0748-4526) [10945745] 3014, **4483**

NEGOTIATIONS (US/0197-5978) [06053772] **3152**

NEGOTIATIONS 79 (CN/0228-2607) [06965807] **1693**

NEGOTIATIONS NEWS & SCHOOL LAW REPORTER (US) [05588500] **1867**

NEGRO ALMANAC See AFRICAN-AMERICAN ALMANAC, THE **2254**

NEGRO DIRECTORY (CN/0381-9477) [03219681] **2269**

NEGRO EDUCATIONAL REVIEW, THE (US/0548-1457) [01624176] 2269, **1767**

NEGRO HISTORY BULLETIN (US/0028-2529) [01759606] **2748**

NEHEZIPARI MUSZAKI EGYETEM (HUNGARY) See PUBLICATIONS OF THE TECHNICAL UNIVERSITY FOR HEAVY INDUSTRY. SERIES B: METALLURGY **4017**

NEHGS NEXUS (US/0747-9891) [10864963] **2462**

NEHW HEALTH WATCH (US/8756-0356) [11452456] 2178, **3862**

NEI JAN CHI KUNG CHENG (CC) [09651079] **2123**

NEI MENG-KU FU NU (CC) [10583150] **5210**

NEI MENG-KU LIN YEH (CC) [11546454] **2389**

NEI MENG-KU NUNG MU CHANG (CC) [11546964] **111**

NEI MENG-KU SHE HUI KO HSUEH (CC) [11921990] **2660**

NEI MENG-KU TUAN PIEN HSIAO SHUO HSUAN / CHUNG-KUO TSO CHIA HSIEH HUI NEI MENG-KU FEN HUI PIEN (CC) [11529995] **3415**

NEIGE, LA (FR/0247-1906) [I02471906] **4907**

NEIGHBORHOOD HEALTH CENTERS : SUMMARY OF PROJECT DATA. REPORT (US/0161-4533) [02802135] **4793**

NEIGHBORHOOD IDEAS (US/0740-526X) [03789266] **2829**

NEIGHBORHOOD WORKS, THE (US/0193-791X) [05256382] **2829**

NEIGHBORS (US/0162-3974) [03947317] **2889**

● NEIL SPERRY'S GARDENS (US/1061-3994) [25235694] **2425**

NEIMENGGU DAXUE XUEBAO (ZIRAN KEXUE BAN) (CC/1000-1638) [11858581] **5132**

NEIRANJI GONGCHENG (CC/1000-0925) [I10000925] **2123**

NEIROKHIMIIA (SZ/0749-4300) [11129067] **3839**

NEIROKHIMIIA (AI/0203-493X) [10417231] **987**

NEISS DATA HIGHLIGHTS : NATIONAL ELECTRONIC INJURY SURVEILLANCE SYSTEM (US) [03457997] **4793**

NEJROFIZIOLOGIJA (KIEV, 1969) (UN/0028-2561) [06513133] **3839**

NEJROHIRURGIJA (UN/0131-6842) [01353556] 3839, **3970**

NEKI POKAZATELJI TEHNICKOG RAZVOJA PRIVREDE JUGOSLAVIJE (YU) [01784851] 1619, **1536**

NEKOTORYE FILOSOFSKIE VOPROSY SOVREMENNOGO ESTESTVOZNANIJA (RU/0301-5386) [05417599] 5132, **4353**

NEL MESE (IT) **2490**

NELB LINK (US/0362-1618) [02194732] **3233**

NELLA GALASSIA DELL'INFORMAZIONE (IT) [18251812] **1118**

NELSON COMPANY See NELSON'S LAW OFFICE DIRECTORY **3014**

NELSON COUNTY ARENA (MICHIGAN, N.D. : 1919) (US/0895-5344) [01759612] **5726**

NELSON'S 401(K) MARKETPLACE DIRECTORY *CEASED.* (US/1063-9721) [26183457] 1507, **698**

● NELSON'S DIRECTORY OF INSTITUTIONAL REAL ESTATE (US/1060-5789) [25037573] 909, **4842**

NELSON'S DIRECTORY OF INVESTMENT MANAGERS (US/0896-0143) [16885455] **909**

NELSON'S DIRECTORY OF INVESTMENT RESEARCH (US/0896-0135) [16885380] **909**

NELSON'S DIRECTORY OF 'NEGLECTED STOCK' OPPORTUNITIES *CEASED.* (US/1063-1399) [25898825] **909**

● NELSON'S DIRECTORY OF PLAN SPONSORS AND TAX-EXEMPT FUNDS (US/1053-0312) [22437053] **909**

NELSON'S DIRECTORY OF REAL ESTATE CONSULTANTS See NELSON'S DIRECTORY OF INSTITUTIONAL REAL ESTATE **4842**

NELSON'S DIRECTORY OF REAL ESTATE INVESTMENTS (US/1058-854X) [24402178] 909, **4842**

NELSON'S EARNINGS OUTLOOK (US/1049-3344) [21206886] **801**

NELSON'S GLOBAL RESEARCH See NELSON'S GUIDE TO INSTITUTIONAL RESEARCH **909**

● NELSON'S GUIDE TO INSTITUTIONAL RESEARCH (US/1059-9290) [24810552] **909**

NELSON'S GUIDE TO INVESTMENT CONSULTANTS *CEASED.* (US/1049-5630) [21255526] **909**

NELSON'S GUIDE TO 'NEGLECTED' STOCKS See NELSON'S DIRECTORY OF 'NEGLECTED STOCK' OPPORTUNITIES **909**

NELSON'S GUIDE TO PENSION FUND CONSULTANTS (US/1053-2536) [22487016] **909**

NELSON'S LAW OFFICE DIRECTORY (US/0548-1546) [06312116] 880, **3014**

● NELSON'S TECHRESOURCE (US/1065-2396) [26535637] **909**

NEMA NEWS (US) [05300300] **4093**

NEMAN (BW/0028-2588) [04719793] **3348**

NEMATOLOGIA BRASILEIRA (BL/0102-2997) [13385467] **5592**

NEMATOLOGIA MEDITERRANEA (IT/0391-9749) [02273693] **111**

NEMATOLOGICA (NE/0028-2596) [01607885] **466**

NEMATOLOGICAL ABSTRACTS (UK/0957-6797) [21477255] 519, **478**

NEMATOLOGY CIRCULAR (US/0360-7550) [01374235] **466**

NEMATOLOGY LITERATURE LIST (US/0364-7005) [02660477] **111**

NEMATOLOGY NEWSLETTER (US/0199-817X) [06184619] **5592**

NEMATROPICA (US/0099-5444) [04332666] **5592**

NEMET FILOLOGIAI TANULMANYOK (HU/0418-4580) [02519191] 3305, **3415**

NEMO *CEASED.* (US/0746-9438) [10406833] **359**

NEMOURIA (US/0085-3887) [01759614] **4169**

NEMPO (JA) [07808752] **5132**

NEMPO (JA) [07808879] **5132**

NEMPO (JA) [01797109] **1693**

NEMPO: NIHON DENSHIN DENWA KOSHA DENKI TSUSHIN KENKYUJO (JA) [01797392] **2073**

NEMPO - NORINSHO KANTO RINBOKU IKUSHUJO (JA) [02245308] **2425**

NEMPO - SHIMBUN GEPPO SHA (JA) [01797305] **2660**

NEMPO - TOKYO DAIGAKU OGATA KEISANKI SENTA (JA/0385-2814) [02849593] **1261**

NEMS NEWS (UK/0267-2618) [I02672618] **4093**

NEMZETKOZI VASUTI OESSZEZEKOETTETESEK KIVONATOS MENETRENDJE (HU/0300-2330) [01784710] **5433**

NENDO KAGAKU (JA/0470-6455) [02474320] **1443**

NENG YUAN CHI KAN (CH/0379-7376) [01797650] **1950**

NENKAN GENDAI SHISHU (JA) [05254986] **3466**

NENKAN NIHON NO IRASUTORESHON (JA) [01796854] **381**

NENKAN NIHON NO KOKOKU SHASHIN (JA) [08833759] 763, **4372**

NENKIN FUKUSHI JIGYODAN See NENKIN FUKUSHI JIGYODAN NEMPO **5297**

NENKIN FUKUSHI JIGYODAN NEMPO (JA) [04292620] 5180, **5297**

NENKIN KENKYU NENPO (JA) [08775826] 5180, **5297**

NENPAN SHINKAN ANNAI (JA) [09567736] **420**

NENPO (JA) [09128994] **3233**

NENPO KEIZAIGAKU (JA) [07044724] **1575**

NENPO (KENSETSU KOGYO KENKYU SHINKOKAI) (JA) [10292410] **1988**

NENRYO OYOBI NENSHO (JA/0369-3783) [09769027] **1950**

NENSHO KENKYU (JA/0286-6501) [10463269] **1951**

NENTORI See REVISTA LETRARO-ARTISTIKE **2522**

NEO RESTAURATION (FR) **4093**

NEO-RESTAURATION COLLECTIVITES HOTELLERIE See NEO RESTAURATION **4093**

NEO-TECH REPORT, THE (US/1056-5744) [23740716] **5132**

NEODESHA SUN-REGISTER, THE (US) [14955821] **5677**

NEODVISNI DNEVNIK (XV/0353-8184) [I03538184] **5810**

NEOELLINIKI PAIDEIA (GR) **1067**

NEOHELICON (BUDAPEST) (HU/0324-4652) [02987317] **3348**

NEOLEX (FREDERICTON) (CN/0849-2271) [23264608] **3141**

NEOLOGIE EN MARCHE (CN/0713-214X) [08745124] **3305**

NEOLOGY / EDMONTON SCIENCE FICTION AND COMIC ARTS SOCIETY (CN/0228-913X) [07865694] **3415**

NEONATAL INTENSIVE CARE (US/1062-2454) [21594833] 3906, **3765**

NEONATAL NETWORK (US/0730-0832) [07938261] 3862, **3906**

NEONATAL PHARMACOLOGY QUARTERLY *CEASED.* (US/1056-8956) [23887913] 3906, **4317**

NEONATOLOGICA INFERMIERISTICA (IT) **3862**

NEONATOLOGY LETTER (US/0747-6132) [10763730] **3765**

NEONATOLOGY (NORWALK, CONN.) (US/0897-6295) [17576812] **3765**

NEOPHILOLOGUS (NE/0028-2677) [01759615] **3305**

NEOPLASIA (SP/0212-9787) [I02129787] **3821**

NEOPLASMA (XO/0028-2685) [01695110] **3821**

NEORGANICHESKIE STEKLA, POKRYTIIA I MATERIALY (LV/0132-7267) [05770483] **2592**

NEOT KEDUMIM LTD See ALON HA-ONATI - NEOT QEDUMIM, HA- **5014**

NEOTERM : JOURNAL OF THE INTERNATIONAL ORGANIZATION FOR UNIFICATION OF TERMINOLOGICAL NEOLOGISMS, AND WORLD BANK OF INTERNATIONAL TERMS (PL/0239-8028) [18319887] **3305**

NEOTESTAMENTICA (SA/0254-8356) [I02548356] **4980**

NEOTROPICA (AG/0548-1686) [02449006] **5592**

NEPAL BANK See BULLETIN - NEPAL BANK LIMITED **781**

NEPAL. CENTRAL BUREAU OF STATISTICS See STATISTICAL POCKET BOOK, NEPAL **5340**

NEPAL DOCUMENTATION (NP) [01784238] **5210**

NEPAL JOURNAL OF MANAGEMENT (NP) [01784266] **880**

NEPAL. MINISTRY OF FINANCE See ARTHIKA VARSHA KO KARYAKRAMA VIVARANA **4711**

NEPAL MISCELLANEOUS SERIES (NP) [08909478] **3014**

NEPAL. NATIONAL COMMISSION FOR UNESCO See UNESCO BULLETIN **3137**

NEPAL. NATIONAL PANCHAYAT See RASHTRIYA PANCAYATA NIYAMAVALI **4678**

NEPAL NATURE CONSERVATION SOCIETY See NEWSLETTER - NEPAL NATURE CONSERVATION SOCIETY **2200**

NEPAL PRESS DIGEST (NP/0028-2723) [01759623] **2507**

NEPAL PRESS REPORT (NP/0028-2731) [06109752] **2507**

NEPAL. RASHTRIYA VIKASA PARISHAD See BAITHAKAKO KARYAVAHIKO SANKSHIPTA-VIVARANA **1547**

NEPAL RECORDER (NP) [07118291] **4668**

NEPAL THESIS ABSTRACTS (NP) [12763512] **111**

NEPAL TRADE DIRECTORY (II) [01774554] **847**

NEPAL TRAVELLER'S BUSINESS DIRECTORY (NP) [16388169] **847**

NEPAL : WIRTSCHAFTLICHE ENTWICKLUNG (GW) [05136260] **1575**

NEPALI AKADAMI PATRIKA (NP) [08837250] **3305**

NEPEGESZSEGUGY (HU/0369-3805) [06306672] **4793**

NEPENTHES (MONTREAL) (CN/1186-8945) [24690520] **3415**

NEPHROLOGIE (SZ/0250-4960) [07073894] **3991**

NEPHROLOGY (AT/1320-5358) **3992**

NEPHROLOGY, DIALYSIS, TRANSPLANTATION (UK/0931-0509) [15991387] **3992**

NEPHROLOGY EXCHANGE, THE (US/1054-1810) [22775818] **3992**

NEPHROLOGY NEWS & ISSUES (US/0896-1263) [16399066] **3992**

NEPHRON (SZ/0028-2766) [01759628] **3992**

NEPOLNOZNACHNYE SLOVA (RU) [05593538] **3305**

NEPRAJZ ES NYELVTUDOMANY (HU/0586-3716) [04618628] 2269, 3305, **242**

NEPRAJZI ERTESITO : NEPRAJZI MUZEUM EVKONYVE (HU/0077-6599) [16665352] 242, **2269**

NEPRAJZI MUZEUM (HUNGARY) See ANNUAL REPORT / ETHNOGRAPHICAL MUSEUM **228**

NEPRAJZI MUZEUM (HUNGARY) See NEPRAJZI ERTESITO : NEPRAJZI MUZEUM EVKONYVE **2269**

NEPSZABADSAG (HU/0133-1752) [08360020] **5802**

NEPTUNE YACHTING (FR) **594**

NEPTUNIA (FR) [02528094] **4181**

NEPTUNUS (BE) [07967712] **4181**

NERA ENERGY OUTLOOK (US/1042-5063) [19081112] **1507**

NERC NEWS / NATURAL ENVIRONMENT RESEARCH COUNCIL (UK/0951-5305) [15908805] 4169, **2219**

NERIM AND ALLIED FAMILIES NEWS (US/0737-7967) [09444796] **2462**

NERVE CELL BIOLOGY / UNIVERSITY OF SHEFFIELD BIOMEDICAL INFORMATION SERVICE (UK/0142-8225) [09709595] **466**

NERVENARZT (GW/0028-2804) [01759633] 3931, **3839**

NERVENHEILKUNDE (GW/0722-1541) [09651279] 3931, **3839**

NERVLINE. A MICROCOMPUTER INFORMATION RETRIEVAL SYSTEM IN THE CLINICAL NEUROSCIENCES (US) **3839**

NERVNAJA SISTEMA (RU/0470-6625) [01759634] **3839**

NERVOUS SYSTEM AND ELECTRIC CURRENTS : PROCEEDINGS OF THE ... ANNUAL NATIONAL CONFERENCE OF THE NEUROELECTRIC SOCIETY, THE (US) [06472684] **3839**

NERVURE PARIS (FR/0988-4068) [I09884068] **3931**

NES OG HELGYA (NO) [04688216] **2700**

NESBITT MEMORIAL LIBRARY JOURNAL (US/1053-4733) [22537029] **2624**

NESHOBA DEMOCRAT, THE (US) [16258277] **5701**

NESPAK PRICE INDEX : ESCALATION OF PRICES OF CONSTRUCTION INDUSTRY INPUTS (PK) [08756162] 622, **1988**

NESS COUNTY NEWS (US) [12169572] **5677**

NESTLE FOUNDATION PUBLICATION SERIES (SZ/0253-0457) [06985883] **4195**

NESTLE NUTRITION WORKSHOP SERIES (US/0742-2806) [10305671] **4195**

NESTLE RESEARCH NEWS *CEASED.* (SZ/1010-0970) [08618709] **4195**

NESTOR (US/0028-2812) [01759635] 275, **286**

● NET GUIDE (US/1077-4173) [30803533] **1275**

NET-LINK : NEWSLETTER OF THE NATIONAL NETWORK OF LIBRARIES OF MEDICINE, MIDCONTINENTAL REGION (US) [24853117] **3233**

NET. NACHRICHTEN ELEKTRONIK + TELEMATIK (1984) (GW/0177-5499) [19934841] **1160**

NET RESULTS (US/0270-4900) [06462085] **4980**

NETBALL MAGAZINE (UK/0959-1117) [I09591117] **4907**

NETCOM ISSY-LES-MOULINEAUX (FR/0987-6014) [I09876014] **1118**

● NETGUIDE (MANHASSET, N.Y.) (US/1078-4632) [31093142] **1196**

NETHERLANDS-AMERICA COMMUNITY ASSOCIATION *See* ANNUAL REPORT / THE NETHERLANDS-AMERICA COMMUNITY ASSOCIATION, INC **5239**

NETHERLANDS-AMERICAN TRADE DIRECTORY / AMERICAN CHAMBER OF COMMERCE IN THE NETHERLANDS (NE) [09739983] **847**

NETHERLANDS ANTILLES. BUREAU VOOR DE INDUSTRIELE EIGENDOM *See* MERKENBLAD - BUREAU VOOR DE INDUSTRIELE EIGENDOM, NEDERLANDSE ANTILLEN **1306**

NETHERLANDS. ARBEIDSINSPECTIE *See* JAARVERSLAG - ARBEIDSINSPECTIE **1613**

NETHERLANDS-BRITISH TRADE DIRECTORY (UK) [01788304] **847**

NETHERLANDS. CENTRAAL BUREAU VOOR DE STATISTIEK. HOOFDAFDELING STATISTIEKEN VAN INDUSTRIE EN BOUWNIJVERHEID *See* GOLFKARTON- EN KARTONNAGE-INDUSTRIE PRODUKTIESTATISTIEKEN **4233**

NETHERLANDS. CENTRAAL BUREAU VOOR DE STATISTIEK *See* MAANDSTATISTIEK VAN BEVOLKING EN VOLKSGEZONDHEID **4789**

NETHERLANDS. CENTRAAL BUREAU VOOR DE STATISTIEK *See* MAANDSTATISTIEK POLITIE EN JUSTITIE **3082**

NETHERLANDS. CENTRAAL BUREAU VOOR DE STATISTIEK *See* MAANDSTATISTIEK VAN DE BINNENLANDSE HANDEL EN DIENSTVERLENING **844**

NETHERLANDS. CENTRAAL BUREAU VOOR DE STATISTIEK *See* CONJUNCTUURTEST **1552**

NETHERLANDS. CENTRAAL BUREAU VOOR DE STATISTIEK *See* VERBRUIK BOUWMATERIALEN : NIEUWBOUW WONINGEN **2033**

NETHERLANDS. CENTRAAL BUREAU VOOR DE STATISTIEK *See* LOONSTRUCTUURONDERZOEK **1536**

NETHERLANDS. CENTRAAL BUREAU VOOR DE STATISTIEK *See* STATISTISCH BULLETIN - CENTRAAL BUREAU VOOR DE STATISTIEK **5343**

NETHERLANDS. CENTRAAL BUREAU VOOR DE STATISTIEK *See* KINDERCENTRA / CENTRAAL BUREAU VOOR DE STATISTIEK **5294**

NETHERLANDS. CENTRAAL BUREAU VOOR DE STATISTIEK *See* MAANDSTATISTIEK VAN DE INDUSTRIE **3482**

NETHERLANDS. CENTRAAL BUREAU VOOR DE STATISTIEK *See* MAANDSTATISTIEK VAN DE BUITENLANDSE HANDEL PER LAND **844**

NETHERLANDS. CENTRAAL BUREAU VOOR DE STATISTIEK *See* UITVOERINGSORGANEN BUURT- EN KLUBHUISWERK **4855**

NETHERLANDS. CENTRAAL BUREAU VOOR DE STATISTIEK *See* PRODUKTIESTATISTIEKEN. BIERBROUWERIJEN EN MOUTERIJEN **2370**

NETHERLANDS. CENTRAAL BUREAU VOOR DE STATISTIEK *See* INVENTARISATIE SPORTACCOMMODATIES **4901**

NETHERLANDS. CENTRAAL BUREAU VOOR DE STATISTIEK *See* MAANDSTATISTIEK VAN DE BINNENLANDSE HANDEL EN DIENSTVERLENING **1616**

NETHERLANDS. CENTRAAL BUREAU VOOR DE STATISTIEK *See* MAANDSTATISTIEK VAN DE PRIJZEN **1536**

NETHERLANDS. CENTRAAL BUREAU VOOR DE STATISTIEK *See* MAANDSTATISTIEK FINANCIEWEZEN **731**

NETHERLANDS. CENTRAAL BUREAU VOOR DE STATISTIEK *See* PER LEERLING BESCHIKBAAR GESTELDE BEDRAGEN VOOR HET LAGER ONDERWIJS **1772**

NETHERLANDS. CENTRAAL BUREAU VOOR DE STATISTIEK. FABRIEKEN VAN TANDWIELEN, LAGERS EN ANDERE DRIJFWERKELEMENTEN PRODUKTIESTATISTIEKEN *See* FABRIEKEN VAN TANDWIELEN, LAGERS EN ANDERE DRIJFWERKELEMENTEN / CENTRAAL BUREAU VOOR DE STATISTIEK, HOOFDAFDELING STATISTIEK I.E. STATISTIEKEN VAN INDUSTRIE EN BOUWNIJVERHEID **1606**

NETHERLANDS. CENTRAAL BUREAU VOOR DE STATISTIEK. GROFSMEDERIJEN, STAMP- EN PERSBEDRIJVEN PRODUKTIESTATISTIEKEN *See* GROFSMEDERIJEN, STAMP- EN PERSBEDRIJVEN / CENTRAAL BUREAU VOOR DE STATISTIEK, HOOFDAFDELING STATISTIEKEN VAN INDUSTRIE EN BOUWNIJVERHEID **1608**

NETHERLANDS. CENTRAAL BUREAU VOOR DE STATISTIEK. HOOFDAFDELING STATISTIEKEN VAN INDUSTRIE EN BOUWNIJVERHEID *See* ALCOHOLFABRIEKEN EN DISTILLEERDERIJEN, BIERBROUWERIJEN EN MOUTERIJEN, FRISDRANKENINDUSTRIE PRODUKTIESTATISTIEKEN **2363**

NETHERLANDS. CENTRAAL BUREAU VOOR DE STATISTIEK. HOOFDAFDELING STATISTIEKEN VAN ONDERWIJS EN WETENSCHAPPEN *See* STATISTIEK VAN HET VWO, HAVO EN MAVO : IN-, DOOR- EN UITSTROOM VAN DE LEERLINGEN **1785**

NETHERLANDS. CENTRAAL BUREAU VOOR DE STATISTIEK. HOOFDAFDELING STATISTIEKEN VAN VERKEER EN VERVOER *See* STATISTIEK VAN DE BINNENVLOOT **5457**

NETHERLANDS. CENTRAAL BUREAU VOOR DE STATISTIEK. KANTOORMACHINE-INDUSTRIE, PRODUKTIESTATISTIEKEN *See* KANTOORMACHINE-INDUSTRIE / CENTRAAL BUREAU VOOR DE STATISTIEK, HOOFDAFDELING STATISTIEKEN VAN INDUSTRIE EN BOUWNIJVERHEID **1570**

NETHERLANDS. CENTRAAL BUREAU VOOR DE STATISTIEK. KOSTEN EN FINANCIERING VAN DE GEZONDHEIDSZORG IN NEDERLAND *See* KOSTEN EN FINANCIERING VAN DE GEZONDHEIDSZORG / CENTRAAL BUREAU VOOR DE STATISTIEK, HOOFDAFDELING GEZONDHEIDSSTATISTIEKEN **4788**

NETHERLANDS. CENTRAAL BUREAU VOOR DE STATISTIEK. ONDERZOEK NAAR VAKANTIES EN UITGAAN *See* ONDERZOEK NAAR VAKANTIES EN UITGAAN, DAG- EN VERBLIJFSRECREATIE / CENTRAAL BUREAU VOOR DE STATISTIEK, HOOFDAFDELING SOCIAAL-CULTURELE STATISTIEKEN **1700**

NETHERLANDS. CENTRAAL BUREAU VOOR DE STATISTIEK. PRODUKTIESTATISTIEKEN: BASIS-METAALINDUSTRIE *See* BASIS-METAALINDUSTRIE / CENTRAAL BUREAU VOOR DE STATISTIEK, HOOFDAFDELING STATISTIEKEN VAN INDUSTRIE EN BOUWNIJVERHEID **3998**

NETHERLANDS. CENTRAAL BUREAU VOOR DE STATISTIEK. PRODUKTIESTATISTIEKEN: KUNSTSTOFVERWERKENDE INDUSTRIE *See* KUNSTSTOFVERWERKENDE INDUSTRIE / CENTRAAL BUREAU VOOR DE STATISTIEK, HOOFKAFDELING STATISTIEKEN VAN INDUSTRIE EN BOUWNIJVERHEID **1615**

NETHERLANDS. CENTRAAL BUREAU VOOR DE STATISTIEK. PRODUKTIESTATISTIEKEN: LANDBOUWMACHINE-INDUSTRIE *See* LANDBOUWMACHINE-INDUSTRIE / CENTRAAL BUREAU VOOR DE STATISTIEK, HOOFDAFDELING STATISTIEKEN VAN INDUSTRIE EN BOUWNIJVERHEID **159**

NETHERLANDS. CENTRAAL BUREAU VOOR DE STATISTIEK. PRODUKTIESTATISTIEKEN: TAPIJT- EN VLOERMATTENINDUSTRIE *See* TAPIJT- EN VLOERMATTENINDUSTRIE / CENTRAAL BUREAU VOOR DE STATISTIEK, HOOFDAFDELING STATISTIEKEN VAN INDUSTRIE EN BOUWNIJVERHEID **1586**

NETHERLANDS. CENTRAAL PLANBUREAU *See* CENTRAAL ECONOMISCH PLAN **1551**

NETHERLANDS. CENTRAL BUREAU VOOR DE STATISTIEK. PRODUKTIESTATISTIEKEN: BINDERIJEN *See* BINDERIFEN / CENTRAL BUREAU VOOR DE STATISTIEK, HOOFDAFDELING STATISTIEKEN VAN INDUSTRIE EN BOUWNIJVERHEID **4824**

NETHERLANDS. CENTRALE LANDINRICHTINGSCOMMISSIE *See* JAARVERSLAG **4839**

NETHERLANDS. COMMISSIE VOOR DE BESTUURSHERVORMING *See* VERSLAG VAN DE WERKZAAMHEDEN - COMMISSIE VOOR DE BESTUURSHERVORMING **1853**

NETHERLANDS. DELEGATIE NAAR DE WERELDGEZONDHEIDSVERGADERING *See* VERSLAG VAN DE DELEGATIE VAN HET KONINKRIJK DER NEDERLANDEN NAAR DE WERELDGEZONDHEIDSVERGADERING **4806**

NETHERLANDS DEVELOPMENT COOPERATION POLICY (NE) [05091060] **2911**

NETHERLANDS. GEOLOGISCHE DIENST *See* MEDEDELINGEN RIJKS GEOLOGISCHE DIENST **1387**

NETHERLANDS. HYDROGRAFISCH BUREAU *See* CATALOGUS VAN NEDERLANDSE ZEEKAARTEN EN ANDERE HYDROGRAFISCHE PUBLIKATICS **2558**

NETHERLANDS. INSPECTIE VOOR HET BRANDWEERWEZEN *See* MAANDELIJKSE MEDEDELINGEN - INSPECTIE VOOR HET BRANDWEERWEZEN **619**

NETHERLANDS INTERNATIONAL LAW REVIEW (NE/0165-070X) [02256192] **3133**

NETHERLANDS INTERNATIONAL LAW REVIEW, INDEX (NE) [22243071] **3133**

NETHERLANDS JOURNAL OF AGRICULTURAL SCIENCE (NE/0028-2928) [01589065] **111**

● NETHERLANDS JOURNAL OF AQUATIC ECOLOGY : JOURNAL OF THE NETHERLANDS SOCIETY OF AQUATIC ECOLOGY (NE) [27775184] 2219, **556**

NETHERLANDS JOURNAL OF CARDIOLOGY : THREE-MONTHLY ISSUE OF THE NETHERLANDS HEART FOUNDATION AND THE NETHERLANDS SOCIETY OF CARDIOLOGY, THE (NE/0921-5018) [20929733] **3708**

NETHERLANDS JOURNAL OF HOUSING AND ENVIRONMENTAL RESEARCH (NE/0920-1580) [17154456] **2829**

NETHERLANDS JOURNAL OF HOUSING AND THE BUILT ENVIRONMENT (NE) [25792475] **2829**

NETHERLANDS JOURNAL OF MEDICINE (NE/0300-2977) [02664273] **3800**

NETHERLANDS JOURNAL OF PLANT PATHOLOGY (NE/0028-2944) [11011593] **519**

NETHERLANDS JOURNAL OF SEA RESEARCH (NE/0077-7579) [01161762] **556**

NETHERLANDS' JOURNAL OF SOCIAL SCIENCES : A PUBLICATION OF THE NETHERLANDS' SOCIOLOGICAL AND ANTHROPOLOGICAL SOCIETY, THE (NE) [19937768] **5210**

NETHERLANDS JOURNAL OF ZOOLOGY *CEASED.* (NE/0028-2960) [01759637] **5592**

NETHERLANDS (KINGDOM, 1815-) CENTRAAL BUREAU VOOR DE STATISTIEK *See* PRODUKTIESTATISTIEKEN : BROOD-, BESCHUIT-, BANKET-, KOEKEN BISCUITFABRIEKEN (W.O. BROOD- EN BANKETBAKKERIJEN) **2354**

NETHERLANDS (KINGDOM, 1815-). CENTRAAL BUREAU VOOR DE STATISTIEK *See* GEVANGENISSTATISTIEK **3165**

NETHERLANDS (KINGDOM, 1815-). CENTRAAL BUREAU VOOR DE STATISTIEK *See* STATISTIEK VAN HET AUTOPARK **5402**

NETHERLANDS (KINGDOM, 1815-). CENTRAAL BUREAU VOOR DE STATISTIEK *See* MAANDSTATISTIEK BOUWNIJVERHEID **633**

NETHERLANDS (KINGDOM, 1815-). CENTRAL BUREAU VOOR DE STATISTIEK. HOOFDAFDELING STATISTIEKEN VAN CRIMINALIET EN RECHTSPLEGING *See* JUSTICIELE KINDERBESCHERMING **3081**

NETHERLANDS (KINGDOM, 1815-). COMMISSIE MODERNISERING LEERPLAN NATUURKUNDE *See* NATUURKUNDE RAPPORT **1914**

NETHERLANDS (KINGDOM, 1815-). DEPARTEMENT VAN BUITENLANDSE ZAKEN. VOORLICHTINGSDIENST ONTWIKKELINGSSAMENWERKING *See* NETHERLANDS DEVELOPMENT COOPERATION POLICY **2911**

NETHERLANDS (KINGDOM, 1815-). INTERDEPARTEMENTALE COMMISSIE KINDERMISHANDELING *See* JAARVERSLAG BETREFFENDE HET EXPERIMENT VERTROUWENSARTSEN INZAKE KINDERMISHANDELING **3166**

NETHERLANDS (KINGDOM, 1815-) LOONBUREAU *See* CAO'S IN NEDERLAND **939**

NETHERLANDS (KINGDOM, 1815-). METEOROLOGISCH INSTITUUT *See* MAANDELIJKSCH OVERSICHT DER WEERSGESTELDHEID **1430**

NETHERLANDS (KINGDOM, 1815-). METEOROLOGISCH INSTITUUT *See* SYNOPTIC AND UPPER AIR OBSERVATIONS IN THE NETHERLANDS **1435**

NETHERLANDS (KINGDOM, 1815-). MINISTERIE VAN LANDBOUW EN VISSERIJ. DIRECTIE ALGEMENE ZAKEN. AFDELING STATISTIEK EN DOCUMENTATIE *See* JAARSTATISTIEK VAN DE VEEVOEDERS **213**

NETHERLANDS (KINGDOM, 1815-). MINISTERIE VAN LANDBOUW EN VISSERIJ. DIRECTIE ALGEMENE ZAKEN. AFDELING STATISTIEK EN DOCUMENTATIE *See* AGRARISCHE BUITENLANDSE HANDEL VAN POLEN, DE **2326**

NETHERLANDS (KINGDOM, 1815-). NEDERLANDSE ORGANISATIE VOOR ZUIVER-WETENSCHAPPELIJK ONDERZOEK *See* ZWO : PLAATS EN PERSPECTIEF **5173**

NETHERLANDS (KINGDOM, 1815-). PERMANENTE COMMISSIE VOOR OVERHEIDSDOCUMENTATIE *See* JAARVERSLAG VAN DE PERMANENTE COMMISSIE VOOR OVERHEIDSDOCUMENTATIE **4658**

NETHERLANDS (KINGDOM, 1815-). PLANTENZIEKTENKUNDIGE DIENST *See* VERSLAGEN EN MEDEDELING - PLANTENZIEKTENKUNDIGE DIENST **144**

NETHERLANDS (KINGDOM, 1815-). SOCIALE VERZEKERINGSRAAD *See* JAARVERSLAG - SOCIALE VERZEKERINGSRAAAD **5291**

NETHERLANDS. MINISTERIE VAN CULTUUR, RECREATIE EN MAATSCHAPPELIJK WERK *See* VERSLAG VAN DE HOOFDCONSULENT VOOR DE MUSEA **4097**

NETHERLANDS. MINISTERIE VAN DEFENSIE *See* NAAMBOEK VAN OFFICIEREN DER KONINKLIJKE MARINE **4179**

NETHERLANDS. MINISTERIE VAN ONDERWIJS EN WETENSCHAPPEN *See* GEGEVENS BETREFFENDE HET NAUTISCH ONDERWIJS **4176**

NETHERLANDS. MINISTERIE VAN ONDERWIJS EN WETENSCHAPPEN *See* ONDERWIJSVERSLAG **1770**

NETHERLANDS. MINISTERIE VAN VOLKSGEZONDHEID EN MILIEUHYGIENE *See* VERSLAG LEVENSMIDDELEN EN KEURING VAN WAREN **2360**

NETHERLANDS. PLANTENZIEKTENKUNDIGE *See* VERZAMELDE OVERDRUKKEN - PLANTENZIEKTENKUNDIGE DIENST **2433**

NETHERLANDS. PRODUKTIESTATISTIEKEN KATOEN- EN WOLINDUSTRIE *See* KATOEN- EN WOLINDUSTRIE / CENTRAAL BUREAU VOOR DE STATISTIEK, HOOFDAFDELING STATISTIEKEN VAN INDUSTRIE EN BOUWNIJVERHEID **1570**

NETHERLANDS QUARTERLY OF HUMAN RIGHTS (NE) [20752421] **4511**

NETHERLANDS. RIJKSDIENST VOOR DE MONUMENTENZORG *See* JAARVERSLAG - RIJKSDIENST VOOR DE MONUMENTENZORG **2693**

NETHERLANDS. RIJKSPLANOLOGISCHE DIENST *See* AANWINSTENLIJST : LIJST VAN AANWINSTEN DER BIBLIOTHEKEN VAN DE RPD EN HET HIROV **2812**

NETHERLANDS. RIJKSWATERSTAAT *See* JAARBERICHT / RIJKSWATERSTAAT **2091**

NETHERLANDS. SOCIAAL EN CULTUREEL PLANBUREAU *See* SOCIAAL EN CULTUREEL RAPPORT **5258**

NETHERLANDS. SOCIAAL EN CULTUREEL PLANBUREAU *See* SOCIAL AND CULTURAL REPORT **5258**

NETHERLANDS YEARBOOK OF INTERNATIONAL LAW (NE/0167-6768) [01759647] **3133**

NETLINE (US/0892-9467) [15347164] **1196**

NETMANAGER (US/0886-2230) [12887864] **880**

NETSU KOKASEI JUSHI (JA/0388-4384) [10378808] **4457**

NETSU SHORI (JA/0288-0490) [10383149] **4013**

NETSUSOKUTEI (JA/0386-2615) [09278923] **4413**, **987**

NETTAI IGAKU (JA/0385-5643) [07704148] **3986**

NETTAI NOGYO (JA/0021-5260) [02108900] **111**

NETTAI NOKEN SHUHO (JA) [08402268] **111**

NETTAI RINGYO 1984 (JA/0910-5115) [09105115] **2389**

NETTAI RINGYO KANKEI BUNKEN BUNRUI MOKUROKU (JA) [03738526] **2389**

NETWARE ADVISOR *See* INSIDE NETWARE **1287**

NETWARE PROGRAMMER'S JOURNAL (US/1055-6923) [23273001] **1196**

NETWARE SOLUTIONS (US/1058-2800) [24252042] **1196**

NETWARE TECHNICAL JOURNAL *CEASED.* (US/1040-4503) [18422274] **1243**, **1288**

●NETWORK 2D (US/1063-9829) [26184803] **1196**, **3014**

●NETWORK ADMINISTRATOR (US/1073-1164) [29333611] **1243**

NETWORK ARMIDALE (AT/1036-5931) [I10365931] **1767**

NETWORK (BRISTOL) (UK/0954-898X) [21370403] **1196**

NETWORK (CHARLOTTE, N.C.), THE (US/0897-9847) [17682667] **2283**, **5297**

NETWORK COMPUTING (US/1046-4468) [20412206] **1243**

NETWORK COMPUTING (UK/0966-7873) **1243**

NETWORK COMPUTING NEWS *See* UNISYS WORLD OPEN SYSTEMS NEWS **1206**

NETWORK CONNECTION (US/1061-9615) [21366595] 5297, **4980**

NETWORK CONSULTANT QUARTERLY (UK) **1118**

NETWORK DATA MANAGEMENT, MARKET STRATEGY REPORT (US/1062-0710) [25480430] **1619**

●NETWORK ECONOMICS LETTER (US/1069-126X) [27941632] **4413**

NETWORK FOR PUBLIC SCHOOLS (US/1041-8520) [19095651] **1767**

NETWORK FORTY (US) **4139**

NETWORK (LONDON. 1985) (UK/0269-3089) [14947650] **1196**

NETWORK MANAGEMENT INFORMATION SERVICE (UK) **1118**

NETWORK MANAGEMENT SYSTEMS & STRATEGIES (US/1043-1217) [19320673] **1243**

NETWORK (MELBOURNE (VIC.) (AT/0159-7302) [10060795] **5433**

NETWORK MONITOR *See* DISTRIBUTED COMPUTING MONITOR **1241**

NETWORK MONITOR *CEASED.* (UK/0953-8402) [I09538402] **1196**

NETWORK (NEWARK, N.J.), THE (US/1054-3880) [22875381] **5044**

NETWORK NEWS & VIEWS (US/1043-0644) [19224135] **1767**

NETWORK NEWS (BLUFFTON, OHIO) (US/0745-418X) [09139386] **5065**

NETWORK NEWS / CONSERVATION INFORMATION NETWORK (US) [17245449] **359**

NETWORK NEWS / NATIONAL DAY CARE RESEARCH NETWORK (CN/0844-2959) [20001562] **5297**

NETWORK NEWS - NATIONAL WOMEN'S HEALTH NETWORK (U.S.) (US/8755-867X) [10086071] 5562, **4793**

NETWORK NEWS (STANFORD, CALIF.) (US/0278-6923) [07863295] **1118**

NETWORK NEWS (SUDBURY, MASS.) *See* ABUI NETWORK NEWS **636**

NETWORK NEWS (WASHINGTON, D.C. 1982) (US/0882-6331) [11277387] **4529**

NETWORK NEWSLETTER, EI (US) **1693**

NETWORK (NIAGARA FALLS) (CN/0827-2417) [11734734] **5298**

NETWORK OF SASKATCHEWAN WOMEN (1983) (CN/0826-4929) [11377315] **5562**

NETWORK PAPER (IRRIGATION MANAGEMENT NETWORK (OVERSEAS DEVELOPMENT INSTITUTE)) (UK) [20124532] **179**

NETWORK PAPER / ODI, AGRICULTURAL ADMINISTRATION (RESEARCH AND EXTENSION) NETWORK (UK/0951-1873) [20121528] **111**

●NETWORK PAPER / ODI, RURAL DEVELOPMENT FORESTRY NETWORK (UK/0968-2627) [28834050] **2389**

NETWORK PAPER (SOCIAL FORESTRY NETWORK (OVERSEAS DEVELOPMENT INSTITUTE)) *See* NETWORK PAPER / ODI, RURAL DEVELOPMENT FORESTRY NETWORK **2389**

NETWORK PLANNING PAPER (US/0160-9742) [03798314] **3233**

NETWORK (RESEARCH TRIANGLE PARK) (US/0270-3637) [05917558] 4793, **589**

NETWORK RESOURCE REPORT, THE (US/8755-2124) [10932292] 1619, **1160**

NETWORK (SALT LAKE CITY, UTAH) (US/0890-3530) [14229796] **5562**

NETWORK SECURITY NEWSLETTER (UK/1353-4858) **1196**

NETWORK STRATEGY SERVICE (US) **1196**

NETWORK (TEMPE) (US/0093-3341) [01793741] **3233**

NETWORK (TORONTO. 1984) (CN/0825-0324) [11283959] **2600**

NETWORK (TORONTO. 1987) (CN/0836-0197) [17361174] **386**

NETWORK USER *See* BUSINESS COMMUNICATIONS **646**

NETWORK WEEK (UK/0965-3031) [I09653031] **1160**

NETWORK WORLD (US/0887-7661) [13350973] **1243**

NETWORK WORLD CANADA (CN/1187-2985) [25314012] **1197**

●NETWORKER (ASHEVILLE, N.C.), THE (US/1070-762X) [28463851] **4186**

NETWORKING IN KENTUCKY (US) [12033257] **3233**

NETWORKING MANAGEMENT *CEASED.* (US/1052-049X) [19909145] **1243**

NETWORKING : THE TAFE LEARN NETWORK NEWSLETTER (AT/1034-3326) [I10343326] **1767**

NETWORKS IN-DEPTH (US/0895-5077) [16662726] **1160**

NETWORKS (NEW YORK) (US/0028-3045) [01606335] **5132**

NEU (IT) 3970, **3839**

NEU-BRAUNFELSER JAHRBUCH (US/0273-0359) [06984706] **2748**

NEUBURGER KOLLEKTANEENBLATT (GW) [01793015] **2700**

NEUDRUCKE DEUTSCHER LITERATURWERKE (GW/0077-7668) [01759648] **3415**

NEUE ARBEITERPRESSE (GW) 4543, **1693**

NEUE ARZNEIMITTEL (GW/0724-567X) [08897971] **4317**

NEUE ASPEKTE RADIOLOGISCHER DIAGNOSTIK UND THERAPIE : JAHRBUCH ... DER SCHWEIZERISCHEN GESELLSCHAFT FUR RADIOLOGIE UND NUKLEARMEDIZIN (SZ/1013-204X) [11739682] **3944**

NEUE AUSGABE SAEMTLICHER WERKE. FRANZ LISZT (GW) **4139**

NEUE AUSGABE SAEMTLICHER WERKE. HEINRICH SCHUTZ (GW) **4139**

NEUE AUSGABE SAEMTLICHER WERKE. WOLFGANG AMADEUS MOZART (GW) **4140**

NEUE AUSGABE SAMTLICHER WERKE JOHANN SEBASTIAN BACH (GW) **4140**

NEUE AUSGABE SAMTLICHER WERKE SCHUBERT (GW) **4140**

NEUE AUSGRABUNGEN UND FORSCHUNGEN IN NIEDERSACHSEN (GW/0548-2682) [01588347] 276, **2700**

NEUE

NEUE BEITRAEGE ZUR LITERATURWISSENSCHAFT (GW/0548-2712) [02530715] **3415**

NEUE BERGBAUTECHNIK (GW/0047-9403) [01608330] **2147**

NEUE BIENENZEITUNG (BERLIN, GERMANY) See DEUTSCHES BIENEN JOURNAL **78**

NEUE BILDENDE KUNST (GW/0941-6501) [I09416501] **359**

NEUE BUECHEREI, DIE (GW/0028-3126) [02264792] **3233**

NEUE CHINA, DAS (GW) [05912644] **2660**

NEUE DENKSCHRIFTEN DES NATURHISTORISCHEN MUSEUMS IN WIEN (AU) [06342613] 1389, **4228**

NEUE DEUTSCHE BIOGRAPHIE (GW) **434**

NEUE DEUTSCHE LITERATUR (GW/0028-3150) [01759665] **3415**

NEUE, DIE (SZ) [11844021] **2520**

NEUE ENTOMOLOGISCHE NACHRICHTEN (GW/0722-3773) [11646021] **5592**

NEUE FREIE ZEITUNG (AU) [01788220] **2520**

NEUE GERMANISTIK *CEASED*. (US/0730-1359) [07641320] 3305, **3415**

NEUE GESELLSCHAFT, FRANKFURTER HEFTE, DIE (GW/0177-6738) [11912329] **5210**

NEUE HEFTE FUER PHILOSOPHIE (GW) [02264793] **4353**

NEUE HEIMAT (GW/0548-2801) [01696436] **4529**

NEUE HEIMAT UND WELT (AT/0817-6922) [I08176922] **5777**

NEUE HOCHSCHULE, DIE (GW) [06403476] **1914**

NEUE HUTTE *CEASED*. (GW/0028-3207) [02449011] **4013**

NEUE JURISTISCHE WOCHENSCHRIFT (GW/0341-1907) [08071682] **3014**

NEUE JUSTIZ (GW/0028-3231) [01606199] **3014**

NEUE KERAMIK (GW/0933-2367) [23671561] 2592, **3466**

NEUE KRIMINALPOLITIK (GW/0934-9200) [24472762] **3108**

NEUE KUNST IN MUNCHEN (GW/0176-7062) [I01767062] **359**

NEUE LANDWIRTSCHAFT (GW) [25636803] **111**

NEUE LITERATUR (RM) [06420047] **3348**

NEUE MUNCHNER BEITRAGE ZUR GESCHICHTE DER MEDIZIN UND NATURWISSENSCHAFTEN. MEDIZINHISTORISCHE REIHE (GW/0300-8371) [03081819] **3620**

NEUE MUSEUMSKUNDE *CEASED*. (GW/0028-3282) [04634728] **4093**

NEUE MUSIK IN DER BUNDESREPUBLIK DEUTSCHLAND (GW/0548-2879) [01780263] **4140**

NEUE MUSIKZEITUNG (GW) [06419315] **4140**

NEUE ORDNUNG (AU) [02413240] **2520**

NEUE ORDNUNG, DIE (GW) [13148873] **4980**

NEUE POLITISCHE LITERATUR (GW/0028-3320) [02133442] **5210**

NEUE PRAXIS (GW/0342-9857) [06676972] **5298**

NEUE RUNDSCHAU (GW/0028-3347) [04545734] **5801**

NEUE SAMMLUNG (GW/0028-3355) [01588516] **1767**

NEUE STEIRISCHE ZEITUNG (AU) [20070846] **5778**

NEUE STUDIEN ZUR ANGLISTIK UND AMERIKANISTIK (SZ) [13036898] **3305**

NEUE TECHNIK (SZ/0028-3398) [04855311] **5132**

NEUE TECHNIK IM BURO *CEASED*. (SZ/0028-3401) [06456966] **698**

NEUE WERBUNG (GW) [06394912] **763**

NEUE ZEIT (GW) [11885371] **5802**

NEUE ZEIT (GW) [06636446] **2624**

NEUE ZEIT (LINZ, AUSTRIA : 1935) (AU) [20126489] **5778**

NEUE ZEITALTER (MICROFICHE), DAS (US) [04356764] **2520**

NEUE ZEITSCHRIFT FUER ARBEITS UND SOZIALRECHT *CEASED*. (GW) [11939878] **3152**

NEUE ZEITSCHRIFT FUER MISSIONSWISSENSCHAFT. NOUVELLE REVUE DE SCIENCE MISSIONAIRE (SZ/0028-3495) [01772324] **4980**

NEUE ZEITSCHRIFT FUER MUSIK (GW) [23703502] **4140**

NEUE ZEITSCHRIFT FUER SYSTEMATISCHE THEOLOGIE UND RELIGIONSPHILOSOPHIE (GW/0028-3517) [01589497] **4980**

NEUE ZEITSCHRIFT FUER WEHRRECHT (GW) [06395004] **3183**

NEUE ZURCHER ZEITUNG UND SCHWEIZERISCHES HANDELSBLATT (SZ) [11869865] **5811**

NEUEREN SPRACHEN, DIE (GW/0342-3816) [02264802] **3305**

NEUERWERBUNGEN SUDASIEN (GW) [05626863] **420**

NEUERWERBUNGEN THEOLOGIE UND ALLGEMEINE RELIGIONSWISSENSCHAFT (GW/0720-3772) [08047599] **4980**

NEUERWERBUNGEN VORDERER ORIENT / UNIVERSITATSBIBLIOTHEK TUBINGEN, ORIENTABTEILUNG (GW) [08331058] **420**

NEUES AUS ALT-VILLACH (AU/0258-8382) [I02588382] **4094**

NEUES DEUTSCHLAND / ZENTRALORGAN DER SOZIALISTISCHEN EINHEITSPARTEI DEUTSCHLANDS (GW) [08752020] **5802**

NEUES GLAS (GW/0723-2454) [07860696] **2592**

NEUES HOCHLAND : NH (GW) [01588622] **2520**

NEUES JAHRBUCH FUER GEOLOGIE UND PALAONTOLOGIE. ABHANDLUNGEN (GW/0077-7749) [01759691] 4228, **1389**

NEUES JAHRBUCH FUER GEOLOGIE UND PALAONTOLOGIE. MONATSHEFTE (GW/0028-3630) [01759692] 4228, **1389**

NEUES JAHRBUCH FUER MINERALOGIE. ABHANDLUNGEN (GW/0077-7757) [01639266] **1443**

NEUES JAHRBUCH FUER MINERALOGIE. MONATSHEFTE (GW/0028-3649) [01640414] **1443**

NEUES LEBEN (RU) [06396914] **4980**

NEUES MANUAL FUER DIE PRAKTISCHE PHARMAZIE (GW) [20919887] **4317**

NEUESTE ZEITUNG (AU) [20077479] **5778**

NEUF; ARCHITECTURES NOUVELLES, MATERIAUX NOUVEAUX (BE) [04669308] **304**

NEUINDISCHE STUDIEN (GW) [02541377] **3305**

NEUJAHRSBLATT (ZURICH) (SZ) [01695287] **5132**

NEUPHILOLOGISCHE MITTEILUNGEN (FI/0028-3754) [01759696] **3305**

NEUQUEN, ARGENTINE REPUBLIC (PROVINCE). CONSEJO PROVINCIAL DE EDUCACION See RESENA **1779**

NEURAL COMPUTATION (US/0899-7667) [18211733] **1215**

NEURAL COMPUTING & APPLICATIONS (UK/0941-0643) [28080674] **3839**

NEURAL NETWORK NEWS (US/1051-5410) [21988859] **1215**

NEURAL NETWORK WORLD (XR/1210-0552) [I12100552] **1243**

NEURAL NETWORKS (US/0893-6080) [15601895] **1215**

NEURAL NETWORKS TODAY (US) [22996176] **1215**

●NEURAL, PARALLEL AND SCIENTIFIC COMPUTATIONS (US/1061-5369) [25354686] **1197**

NEURAL TECHNOLOGY UPDATE (UK) **1243**

NEURALTHERAPIE NACH HUNEKE (GW/0172-9225) [04612963] **3620**

NEURO-CHIRURGIE (FR/0028-3770) [01759697] **3839**

NEURO-ELECTRIC SOCIETY See NERVOUS SYSTEM AND ELECTRIC CURRENTS : PROCEEDINGS OF THE ... ANNUAL NATIONAL CONFERENCE OF THE NEUROELECTRIC SOCIETY, THE **3839**

NEURO ENDOCRINOLOGY LETTERS (GW/0172-780X) [06828369] **3732**

NEURO-OPHTHALMOLOGY (AMSTERDAM : AEOLUS PRESS. 1980) (NE/0165-8107) [06911025] 3839, **3876**

NEURO-ORTHOPEDICS (AU/0177-7955) [13502422] 3883, **3839**

NEURO-PSY (FR/0296-3981) [16863610] 4605, **3839**

NEUROBIOLOGIA (RECIFE) (BL/0028-3800) [02264804] 3931, **3839**

●NEUROBIOLOGY (HU) [28441794] 466, **3839**

NEUROBIOLOGY OF AGING (US/0197-4580) [06035686] **3839**

●NEUROBIOLOGY OF DISEASE (UK/0969-9961) **3620**

●NEUROBIOLOGY OF LEARNING AND MEMORY (US/1074-7427) [29817352] 3839, **466**

NEUROCASE (UK/1355-4794) **3839**

NEUROCHEMICAL RESEARCH (US/0364-3190) [02628725] **3839**

NEUROCHEMISTRY INTERNATIONAL (US/0197-0186) [05937082] **3839**

NEUROCHEMISTRY SHEFFIELD (UK/0142-8403) [I01428403] **491**

NEUROCHIRURGIA (GW/0028-3819) [01759698] **3970**

NEUROCOMPUTERS (US/0893-1585) [15461787] **1197**

NEUROCOMPUTING (AMSTERDAM) (NE/0925-2312) [24351769] **1215**

●NEURODEGENERATION (PHILADELPHIA, PA.) (US/1055-8330) [23359182] **3839**

NEUROELECTRIC NEWS *SUSPENDED*. (US/0047-942X) [01842573] **584**

NEUROENDOCRINE PERSPECTIVES *CEASED*. (NE/0168-0617) [08089973] **3732**

NEUROENDOCRINOLOGY (SZ/0028-3835) [01759699] 3732, **3840**

NEUROEPIDEMIOLOGY (SZ/0251-5350) [08487314] **3840**

●NEUROGASTROENTEROLOGY & MOTILITY (UK) **3840**

NEUROHYPOPHYSIAL HORMONES (UK/0143-4276) [I01434276] **3732**

NEUROHYPOPHYSIAL HORMONES See OXYTOCIN AND VASOPRESSIN **3732**

●NEUROIMAGE (SAN DIEGO, CALIF.) (US/1053-8119) [22646807] **3840**

NEUROIMAGING CLINICS OF NORTH AMERICA (US/1052-5149) [22299096] **3840**

NEUROIMMUNOMODULATION (SZ/1021-7401) **3840**

NEUROLAW LETTER, THE (US/1058-4706) [24301782] **3015**

NEUROLINGUISTICS (AMSTERDAM) (NE/0301-6412) [05031224] **3305**

NEUROLINGUISTIK : ZEITSCHRIFT FUER APHASIEFORSCHUNG UND -THERAPIE (GW/0933-2715) [24466726] 3305, **4381**

NEUROLOGIA (BARCELONA, SPAIN) (SP/0213-4853) [21455198] **3840**

NEUROLOGIA CROATICA : GLASILO UDRUZENJA NEUROLOGA JUGOSLAVIJE, OFFICIAL JOURNAL OF YUGOSLAV NEUROLOGICAL ASSOCIATION (CI/0353-8842) [24146935] **3840**

NEUROLOGIA EN COLOMBIA (CK/0120-1034) [03946931] **3840**

NEUROLOGIA ET PSYCHIATRIA (GR/0253-9446) [05536489] 3931, **3840**

NEUROLOGIA I NEUROCHIRURGIA POLSKA (PL/0028-3843) [06403839] **3840**

NEUROLOGIA MEDICO-CHIRURGICA (JA/0470-8105) [01778764] **3840**

NEUROLOGIA PSICHIATRIA SCIENZE UMANE (IT) [11116446] 3840, **3931**

NEUROLOGIC CLINICS (US/0733-8619) [08649168] **3840**

NEUROLOGIC CLINICS (ITALIAN EDITION) (IT) **3840**

NEUROLOGIC ILLNESS: DIAGNOSIS & TREATMENT (US/0736-9263) [08738602] **3840**

NEUROLOGICAL DISEASE AND THERAPY (US/1058-7535) [20351382] **3840**

NEUROLOGICAL RESEARCH (NEW YORK) (UK/0161-6412) [03983345] **3840**

●NEUROLOGIST (BALTIMORE, MD.), THE (US/1074-7931) [29833084] **3840**

NEUROLOGIST, THE (US/1073-8584) [29539753] **3840**

NEUROLOGY (US/0028-3878) [01713610] **3840**

NEUROLOGY ALERT (US/0741-4234) [09987236] **3841**

NEUROLOGY AND NEUROBIOLOGY (US/0736-4563) [08516350] 466, **3841**

NEUROLOGY CHRONICLE (US/1060-4197) [24990753] **3841**

NEUROLOGY, INDIA (II/0028-3886) [06401325] **3841**

NEUROLOGY, PSYCHIATRY AND BRAIN RESEARCH *CEASED*. (GW/0941-9500) [27264176] **3841**

NEUROMETHODS (US/0893-2336) [12700508] **3841**

NEUROMUSCULAR DISEASES (UK/0261-8412) [03806] 3806, **3841**

NEUROMUSCULAR DISORDERS : NMD (UK/0960-8966) [24318845] 3841, **3806**

NEURON (CAMBRIDGE, MASS.) (US/0896-6273) [17223779] 3841, **466**

NEUROONCOLOGY (NE/0166-3518) [05592805] **3841**

Alphabetical Title Index — NEVADA

NEUROPATHOLOGY AND APPLIED NEUROBIOLOGY (UK/0305-1846) [02437846] 3841, **3896**

NEUROPATOLOGIA POLSKA (PL/0028-3894) [07626249] **3841**

NEUROPEDIATRIA LATINOAMERICANA (UY) [05189622] **3906**

NEUROPEDIATRICS (GW/0174-304X) [07030896] 3906, **3841**

NEUROPEPTIDES (EDINBURGH) (UK/0143-4179) [06856547] **3841**

NEUROPEPTIDES (SHEFFIELD) (UK/0142-8233) [11823641] **3841**

NEUROPHARMACOLOGY (UK/0028-3908) [01796748] **4317**

NEUROPHYSIOLOGIE CLINIQUE (NE/0987-7053) [17800723] 584, **3841**

NEUROPHYSIOLOGY (NEW YORK) (US/0090-2977) [01759702] **3841**

NEUROPHYSIOLOGY SHEFFIELD (UK/0142-8241) [01428241] **584**

●NEUROPROTOCOLS (ORLANDO, FLA.) (US/1058-6741) [24352300] **3841**

NEUROPSICHIATRIA (IT/0028-3916) [01778765] 3931, **3841**

NEUROPSICOFARMACOLOGIA DEL COMPORTAMENTO (IT/0394-9540) [I03949540] 3841, **4317**

NEUROPSYCHIATRIA CLINICA (US/0723-0931) [09832595] **3931**

NEUROPSYCHIATRIE (GW) 3841, **3931**

NEUROPSYCHIATRIE DE L'ENFANCE ET DE L'ADOLESCENCE (FR/0222-9617) [05200244] **3841**

NEUROPSYCHIATRY, NEUROPSYCHOLOGY, BEHAVIORAL NEUROLOGY (US/0894-878X) [16274588] 3931, **3841**

NEUROPSYCHOBIOLOGY (SZ/0302-282X) [01809731] 3931, **3842**

NEUROPSYCHOLOGIA (UK/0028-3932) [01759703] 4605, **3842**

NEUROPSYCHOLOGICAL REHABILITATION (UK/0960-2011) [24541595] 3842, **4605**

NEUROPSYCHOLOGY (US/0894-4105) [16087051] 3842, **4605**

NEUROPSYCHOLOGY DEVELOPMENT AND COGNITION (NE) **4605**

NEUROPSYCHOLOGY REVIEW (US/1040-7308) [18516298] 4605, **3842**

NEUROPSYCHOPHARMACOLOGY (NEW YORK, N.Y.) (US/0893-133X) [15360199] **3842**

NEUROPTERA INTERNATIONAL. SUPPLEMENTAL SERIES (FR) [15541342] **5592**

NEURORADIOLOGY (GW/0028-3940) [01759704] 3944, **3842**

NEUROREHABILITATION (READING, MASS.) (US/1053-8135) [22646902] 4391, **3842**

NEUROREPORT (UK/0959-4965) [22982547] **3842**

NEUROSCIENCE (UK/0306-4522) [01343846] **3842**

NEUROSCIENCE AND BEHAVIORAL PHYSIOLOGY (US/0097-0549) [01772326] 3842, **584**

NEUROSCIENCE AND BIOBEHAVIORAL REVIEWS (US/0149-7634) [03552135] 4605, **3842**

NEUROSCIENCE CITATION INDEX (US/1057-6096) [24080913] **3842**

NEUROSCIENCE FACTS (US/1056-7186) [22756271] **3842**

NEUROSCIENCE LETTERS (NE/0304-3940) [01874501] 3931, **3842**

NEUROSCIENCE LETTERS. SUPPLEMENT (IE/0167-6253) [05031527] **3842**

NEUROSCIENCE NEWSLETTER (US/0278-3738) [04485623] **4605**

●NEUROSCIENCE NEWSLETTER (COLLEGE STATION, TEX.) (US/1064-8712) [25896594] **3842**

NEUROSCIENCE RESEARCH (IE/0168-0102) [11053860] 3931, **3842**

NEUROSCIENCE RESEARCH COMMUNICATIONS (UK/0893-6609) [15609800] **3843**

NEUROSCIENCE RESEARCH. SUPPLEMENT (IE/0921-8696) [12573469] **3843**

NEUROSCIENCES (KOBE. 1975) (JA/0388-7448) [04761709] **3843**

NEUROSURGERY (US/0148-396X) [03301698] 3843, **3970**

NEUROSURGERY CLINICS OF NORTH AMERICA (US/1042-3680) [19027296] 3843, **3970**

NEUROSURGERY QUARTERLY (US/1050-6438) [21569277] 3843, **3970**

NEUROSURGICAL CONSULTATIONS *CEASED.* (US/1045-6694) [20186300] **3843**

NEUROSURGICAL OPERATIVE ATLAS (US/1051-1490) [21881040] 3843, **3970**

NEUROSURGICAL REVIEW (GW/0344-5607) [04650279] **3970**

NEUROTOXICOLOGY AND TERATOLOGY (US/0892-0362) [15063346] **3843**

NEUROTOXICOLOGY (PARK FOREST SOUTH) (US/0161-813X) [05034026] 3983, **3843**

NEUROUROL. URODYN (US/0733-2467) [08542817] 3992, **3843**

NEUSEELAND: ENERGIEWIRTSCHAFT (GW) [06597904] **2123**

NEUSEELAND, FORSCHUNGSPOLITIK UND FORSCHUNGSPRAXIS / BUNDESSTELLE FUER AUSSENHANDELSINFORMATION (GW) [11507593] **4483**

NEUSEELAND : WIRTSCHAFTLICHE ENTWICKLUNG (GW) [03529990] **1575**

NEUSPRACHLICHE MITTEILUNGEN AUS WISSENSCHAFT UND PRAXIS : NM (GW/0028-3983) [03116533] 3305, **1767**

NEUSSER JAHRBUCH (GW/0077-7862) [14323999] **326**

NEUTESTAMENTLICHE ABHANDLUNGEN (GW) [01776627] **5018**

NEUTRON ACTIVATION ANALYSIS ABSTRACTS (UK) [01787982] **1056**

NEUTRON NEWS (US/1044-8632) [19930628] **987**

NEUVA REVISTA DE POLITICA, CULTURA Y ARTE (SP/1130-0426) [22223765] 2851, **5210**

NEUVE EGLISE (CN/0228-2585) [06860287] **5234**

NEVA (RU/0028-4009) [02149443] **3415**

NEVADA AGRICULTURAL STATISTICS (US/0196-0636) [03111773] 111, **155**

NEVADA ANNUAL PROGRAM PLAN FOR VOCATIONAL EDUCATION AND FIVE-YEAR STATE PLAN MODIFICATIONS (US) [06256894] **1914**

NEVADA APPEAL (CARSON CITY, NEV. : 1968) (US) [10636455] **5708**

NEVADA APPEAL. CHRONICLE EDITION (US) [13499312] **5708**

NEVADA ARCHEOLOGICAL SURVEY *See* RESEARCH PAPER - NEVADA ARCHEOLOGICAL SURVEY **280**

NEVADA AREA LABOR REVIEW. ECONOMIC DEVELOPMENTS AND ... OUTLOOK (US) [11255952] **1693**

NEVADA. BANKING DIVISION *See* REPORT OF THE SUPERINTENDENT OF BANKS AND SMALL LOAN COMPANIES **808**

NEVADA BAPTIST, THE (US/0279-4535) [07887450] **4980**

NEVADA BEVERAGE ANALYST (US/1053-6345) [22600072] **2369**

NEVADA BEVERAGE INDEX (US/0191-4723) [04935228] **2369**

NEVADA BUREAU OF MINES AND GEOLOGY *See* BULLETIN - NEVADA BUREAU OF MINES AND GEOLOGY **1370**

NEVADA BUSINESS AND ECONOMIC INDICATORS (US) 1507, **698**

NEVADA BUSINESS JOURNAL (US) [14930138] **698**

NEVADA (CARSON CITY, NEV.) (US/0199-1248) [05633459] **2540**

NEVADA CASINO JOURNAL (US/1047-529X) [20719263] **4864**

NEVADA. COMMISSION ON CRIME, DELINQUENCY, AND CORRECTIONS *See* STATE OF NEVADA COMPREHENSIVE CRIMINAL JUSTICE PROGRESS REPORT **3177**

NEVADA. COMMISSION ON CRIME, DELINQUENCY, AND CORRECTIONS *See* NEVADA COMPREHENSIVE CRIMINAL JUSTICE PLAN **3170**

NEVADA COMPREHENSIVE CRIMINAL JUSTICE PLAN (US) [06137745] **3170**

NEVADA COUNTY PICAYUNE (US) [16882039] **5632**

NEVADA COUNTY PICAYUNE (PRESCOTT, ARK. : 1885) *See* TIMES-PICAYUNE, THE **5632**

NEVADA CROP AND LIVESTOCK REPORTING SERVICE *See* NEVADA AGRICULTURAL STATISTICS **155**

NEVADA. DEPARTMENT OF CONSERVATION AND NATURAL RESOURCES *See* INVENTORY SERIES - STATE OF NEVADA, DEPARTMENT OF CONSERVATION AND NATURAL RESOURCES **2195**

NEVADA. DEPT. OF HUMAN RESOURCES. WELFARE DIVISION *See* COMPREHENSIVE ANNUAL SERVICES PROGRAM PLAN - (NEVADA) **5280**

NEVADA. DEPT. OF LAW ENFORCEMENT ASSISTANCE *See* STATE OF NEVADA UNIFORM CRIME REPORTS ... ANNUAL REPORT **3177**

NEVADA. DEPT. OF MOTOR VEHICLES. HIGHWAY PATROL DIVISION *See* ANNUAL REPORT - STATE OF NEVADA, DEPARTMENT OF MOTOR VEHICLES, HIGHWAY PATROL DIVISION **3157**

NEVADA. DIVISION OF COLORADO RIVER RESOURCES *See* FINANCIAL REPORT - STATE OF NEVADA, DIVISION OF COLORADO RIVER RESOURCES **2089**

NEVADA. DIVISION OF GAME *See* TROPHY BIG GAME INVESTIGATIONS AND HUNTING SEASON RECOMMENDATIONS / STATE OF NEVADA, DEPARTMENT OF WILDLIFE, DIVISION OF GAME **4927**

NEVADA. DIVISION OF JUVENILE COMMUNITY SERVICES *See* LEGISLATIVE REPORT ON JUVENILE PROBATION SUBSIDY **3169**

NEVADA. DIVISION OF MENTAL HYGIENE AND MENTAL RETARDATION *See* ANNUAL REPORT - DIVISION OF MENTAL HYGIENE AND MENTAL RETARDATION **4765**

NEVADA. EMPLOYMENT SECURITY DEPT *See* ANNUAL AREA LABOR REVIEW **1644**

NEVADA. EMPLOYMENT SECURITY RESEARCH SECTION *See* NEVADA WAGE SURVEY **1693**

NEVADA ENGINEER, THE (US/0047-9454) [03761887] **1988**

NEVADA. ETHICS COMMISSION *See* HYPOTHETICAL ADVISORY OPINIONS **2251**

NEVADA GAMING ABSTRACT / STATE GAMING CONTROL BOARD (US) [04350076] 4864, **4668**

NEVADA GOLF AND TENNIS (US/1055-9604) [23375355] **4907**

NEVADA HEALTH (US) [01639398] **4793**

●NEVADA HEALTH CARE IN PERSPECTIVE (US/1065-4305) [26605867] **4793**

NEVADA HERALD, THE (US) [13510229] **5704**

NEVADA HISTORICAL REVIEW (US/0099-0892) [02243487] **2748**

NEVADA HISTORICAL SOCIETY QUARTERLY (1961) (US/0047-9462) [02969442] **2748**

NEVADA IN PERSPECTIVE (US/1065-559X) [26660106] **5334**

NEVADA INDIAN AFFAIRS COMMISSION *See* REPORT OF THE NEVADA INDIAN AFFAIRS COMMISSION **2272**

NEVADA INDIAN AFFAIRS COMMISSION. REPORT *See* BIENNIAL REPORT - NEVADA INDIAN COMMISSION **2256**

NEVADA. INDIAN COMMISSION *See* BIENNIAL REPORT - NEVADA INDIAN COMMISSION **2256**

NEVADA JOURNAL (NEVADA, IOWA) (US/0747-430X) [10843295] **5672**

●NEVADA LAWYER (US/1068-882X) [27290040] **3015**

NEVADA LEGAL NEWS (US/0744-8902) [08636078] **3015**

NEVADA. LEGISLATIVE AUDITOR *See* STATE OF NEVADA REVENUE SHARING TRUST FUND AUDIT REPORT **4749**

NEVADA. LEGISLATIVE AUDITOR *See* AUDIT REPORT, STATE OF NEVADA DEPARTMENT OF COMMERCE, DIRECTOR'S OFFICE **823**

NEVADA. LEGISLATIVE AUDITOR *See* STATE OF NEVADA, DEPARTMENT OF PAROLE AND PROBATION, AUDIT REPORT **3177**

NEVADA. LEGISLATIVE AUDITOR *See* STATE OF NEVADA BOND TRUST FUND AUDITOR REPORT **2894**

NEVADA. LEGISLATIVE AUDITOR *See* STATE OF NEVADA, CONSOLIDATED BOND AND INTEREST REDEMPTION FUND, AUDIT REPORT **4749**

NEVADA. LEGISLATIVE AUDITOR *See* AUDIT REPORT, STATE OF NEVADA DEPARTMENT OF COMMERCE, BANKING AND SAVINGS AND LOAN DIVISIONS **773**

NEVADA. LEGISLATIVE AUDITOR *See* STATE OF NEVADA, DEPARTMENT OF PAROLE AND PROBATION, RESTITUTION TRUST FUND, AUDIT REPORT **3177**

NEVADA. LEGISLATIVE AUDITOR *See* AUDIT REPORT, STATE OF NEVADA, OFFICE OF THE GOVERNOR **4631**

NEVADA. LEGISLATIVE AUDITOR *See* AUDIT REPORT, STATE OF NEVADA, CLARK COUNTY TAXICAB AUTHORITY **4631**

NEVADA. LEGISLATIVE AUDITOR *See* STATE OF NEVADA, COMPUTER ACQUISITION SINKING FUND, AUDIT REPORT **4749**

NEVADA Alphabetical Title Index

NEVADA. LEGISLATIVE AUDITOR *See* AUDIT REPORT, STATE OF NEVADA DEPARTMENT OF COMMERCE, STATE FIRE MARSHAL DIVISION **2288**

NEVADA. LEGISLATIVE AUDITOR *See* AUDIT REPORT, STATE OF NEVADA, DEPARTMENT OF COMMERCE, REAL ESTATE DIVISION **4631**

NEVADA. LEGISLATIVE AUDITOR *See* AUDIT REPORT, STATE OF NEVADA, DEPARTMENT OF COMMERCE, HOUSING DIVISION **4631**

NEVADA. LEGISLATIVE AUDITOR *See* AUDIT REPORT, STATE OF NEVADA, DEPARTMENT OF COMMERCE, REAL ESTATE EDUCATION RESEARCH AND RECOVERY FUND **4631**

NEVADA. LEGISLATIVE AUDITOR *See* BIENNIAL REPORT OF THE LEGISLATIVE AUDITOR (NEVADA) **4713**

NEVADA. LEGISLATIVE AUDITOR *See* STATE OF NEVADA, DEPARTMENT OF CONSERVATION AND NATURAL RESOURCES, DIVISION OF STATE PARKS AUDIT REPORT **2206**

NEVADA. LEGISLATIVE AUDITOR. REPORT *See* BIENNIAL REPORT OF THE LEGISLATIVE AUDITOR (NEVADA) **4713**

NEVADA. LEGISLATIVE COMMISSION *See* NEVADA LEGISLATURE FINAL REPORT: CONTINGENCY FUND, LEGISLATIVE FUND, THE **4738**

NEVADA. LEGISLATIVE COUNSEL BUREAU *See* AUDIT REPORT - STATE OF NEVADA. DEPARTMENT OF ADMINISTRATION. PERSONNEL DIVISION **4631**

NEVADA. LEGISLATIVE COUNSEL BUREAU *See* AUDIT REPORT - STATE OF NEVADA. DEPARTMENT OF CONSERVATION AND NATIONAL RESOURCES. DIVISION OF STATE PARKS **2187**

NEVADA. LEGISLATIVE COUNSEL BUREAU *See* AUDIT REPORT - STATE OF NEVADA. PUBLIC SERVICE COMMISSION **4631**

NEVADA. LEGISLATIVE COUNSEL BUREAU *See* LEGISLATIVE FISCAL REPORT (CARSON CITY) **3001**

NEVADA. LEGISLATIVE COUNSEL BUREAU *See* AUDIT REPORT - STATE OF NEVADA. NEVADA STATE COUNCIL ON THE ARTS **315**

NEVADA. LEGISLATIVE COUNSEL BUREAU. DIVISION OF FISCAL ANALYSIS *See* LEGISLATIVE APPROPRIATIONS REPORT **3001**

NEVADA. LEGISLATIVE COUNSEL BUREAU. RESEARCH DIVISION *See* SUMMARY OF LEGISLATION **3061**

NEVADA. LEGISLATURE *See* HANDBOOK OF THE NEVADA LEGISLATURE **4654**

NEVADA LEGISLATURE FINAL REPORT: CONTINGENCY FUND, LEGISLATIVE FUND, THE (US) [02618519] **4738**

NEVADA. LEGISLATURE. LEGISLATIVE AUDITOR *See* AUDIT REPORT, STATE OF NEVADA DEPARTMENT OF GENERAL SERVICES, PURCHASING DIVISION, DONATED COMMODITIES REVOLVING FUND **4712**

NEVADA. LEGISLATURE. LEGISLATIVE AUDITOR *See* STATE OF NEVADA, DEPARTMENT OF THE MILITARY, AUDIT REPORT **4057**

NEVADA. LEGISLATURE. LEGISLATIVE AUDITOR *See* AUDIT REPORT, STATE OF NEVADA DEPARTMENT OF PAROLE AND PROBATION, PAROLEE'S REVOLVING LOAN FUND; PRISONER'S WORK RELEASE REVOLVING LOAN FUND **3158**

NEVADA. LEGISLATURE. LEGISLATIVE COUNCIL BUREAU *See* AUDIT REPORT - STATE OF NEVADA. NEVADA STATE MUSEUM **4084**

NEVADA LIBRARY DIRECTORY AND STATISTICS (US) [03878504] 3233, **3259**

NEVADA MANPOWER PLANNING COUNCIL *See* COMPREHENSIVE MANPOWER PLAN **1660**

NEVADA PUBLIC AFFAIRS REVIEW (US/0196-7355) [05145798] **4668**

NEVADA REVIEW OF BUSINESS & ECONOMICS (US/0148-5881) [03321381] 1507, **698**

NEVADA REVIEW OF BUSINESS AND ECONOMICS *See* NEVADA BUSINESS AND ECONOMIC INDICATORS **698**

NEVADA RNFORMATION (US/0273-4117) [04813358] **3862**

NEVADA STATE ANNUAL PROGRAM PLAN AMENDMENT TO NEVADA STATE PLAN FOR COMMUNITY SERVICE AND CONTINUING EDUCATION PROGRAMS, TITLE I, HIGHER EDUCATION ACT, 1965 (US) [03923735] **1837**

NEVADA. STATE BOARD FOR VOCATIONAL EDUCATION *See* NEVADA ANNUAL PROGRAM PLAN FOR VOCATIONAL EDUCATION AND FIVE-YEAR STATE PLAN MODIFICATIONS **1914**

NEVADA. STATE BOARD FOR VOCATIONAL EDUCATION *See* NEVADA STATE PLAN FOR VOCATIONAL EDUCATION **1914**

NEVADA. STATE BOARD FOR VOCATIONAL EDUCATION *See* NEVADA STATE PLAN FOR CAREER EDUCATION **1914**

NEVADA. STATE COMPREHENSIVE EMPLOYMENT AND TRAINING OFFICE *See* ANNUAL PLAN FOR THE GOVERNOR'S SPECIAL GRANT / STATE COMPREHENSIVE EMPLOYMENT & TRAINING OFFICE **1645**

NEVADA. STATE DEPT. OF EDUCATION. FINANCE DIVISION. RESEARCH BULLETIN *See* RESEARCH BULLETIN - STATE OF NEVADA, DEPARTMENT OF EDUCATION, OFFICE OF TECHNICAL ASSISTANCE **1870**

NEVADA. STATE DEPT. OF EDUCATION. OFFICE OF TECHNICAL ASSISTANCE *See* RESEARCH BULLETIN - STATE OF NEVADA, DEPARTMENT OF EDUCATION, OFFICE OF TECHNICAL ASSISTANCE **1870**

NEVADA. STATE FIRE MARSHAL DIVISION *See* BIENNIAL REPORT - NEVADA STATE FIRE MARSHAL DIVISION **2288**

NEVADA. STATE GAMING CONTROL BOARD *See* QUARTERLY REPORT - STATE GAMING CONTROL BOARD **4677**

NEVADA. STATE GAMING CONTROL BOARD *See* G.C.B. BULLETIN **3165**

NEVADA. STATE GAMING CONTROL BOARD *See* QUARTERLY REPORT FOR THE QUARTER ENDED ... / GAMING CONTROL BOARD **3174**

NEVADA. STATE GAMING CONTROL BOARD. ECONOMIC RESEARCH UNIT *See* DIRECT LEVIES ON GAMING IN NEVADA **4720**

NEVADA. STATE GAMING CONTROL BOARD. QUARTERLY & FISCAL YEAR REPORT FOR ... OF ... AND YEAR-TO-DATE COMPARISONS ... COMPARATIVE FISCAL YEAR REPORT . *See* QUARTERLY REPORT FOR THE QUARTER ENDED ... / GAMING CONTROL BOARD **3174**

NEVADA. STATE MUSEUM *See* OCCASIONAL PAPERS - NEVADA STATE MUSEUM **4094**

NEVADA STATE PLAN FOR CAREER EDUCATION (US/0091-5106) [01786951] **1914**

NEVADA STATE PLAN FOR VOCATIONAL EDUCATION (US/0094-1123) [01791680] **1914**

NEVADA. STATE PLANNING BOARD *See* CATALOGUE OF STATE PROGRAMS (CARSON CITY) **1551**

NEVADA STATEWIDE WAGE SURVEY *See* NEVADA WAGE SURVEY **1693**

NEVADA STATISTICAL ABSTRACT (US) [04386060] **5334**

NEVADA WAGE SURVEY (US) [03754809] **1693**

NEVIPENS ROMANI : NOTICIAS GITANAS (SP) **2269**

NEVRAXE : REVUE DE NEUROLOGIE *CEASED.* (FR) **3843**

NEVROLOGIJA, PSIHIATRIJA I NEVROHIRURGIJA (BU/0548-3794) [07630856] 3931, **3843**

NEVSKII PROSPEKT (RU) [23060462] **5809**

NEW ABOLITIONIST : NEWSLETTER OF NUCLEAR FREE AMERICA, THE (US) [14080285] **4052**

NEW ACCENTS (US) 3415, **3305**

NEW ACCOUNTANT (US/0882-8067) [11984828] **749**

NEW ADVOCATE (BOSTON, MASS.), THE (US/0895-1381) [16511786] 1805, **3415**

NEW AFRICAN (LONDON. 1978) (UK/0142-9345) [03955328] **2499**

NEW AFRICAN YEARBOOK (LONDON, ENGLAND : 1987) (UK) [16350378] **2499**

NEW AGE ENCYCLOPEDIA (US/1047-2746) [20646957] **4186**

NEW AGE JOURNAL (1983) (US/0746-3618) [09978138] **4186**

NEW AGE LINK'S LETTER LINK : THE SPIRITUAL AWARENESS NETWORK (US/1052-8032) [22391464] **4186**

NEW AGE RETAILER (US/1042-6566) [19100188] **4186**

NEW AGE, THE (US) [01715026] **2490**

NEW AGE WEEKLY (II) [06308032] **5803**

NEW AGE WEEKLY (II/0047-9500) [02256193] 1507, **4483**

NEW ALASKA OUTDOORS, THE (US/1059-7484) [24706854] **4875**

NEW ALASKAN (US/0300-8959) [01377884] **2540**

NEW ALBANIA *CEASED.* (AA) [06335595] **2520**

NEW ALBANY (FLOYD COUNTY, IND.), JEFFERSONVILLE (CLARK COUNTY, IND.) AND CITY DIRECTORY (US) [08038893] **2540**

NEW ALBANY GAZETTE (NEW ALBANY, MISS.) (US) [16102605] **5701**

NEW AMBEROLA GRAPHIC, THE (US/0028-4181) [04507493] **5318**

NEW AMERICAN (BELMONT, MASS.), THE (US/0885-6540) [12618341] **4483**

●NEW AMERICAN FARMER (US/1056-2133) [23554434] **111**

NEW AMERICAN FICTION SERIES, THE (US) [12674048] **3415**

NEW AMERICAN GUIDE TO COLLEGES, THE (US) [02535735] **1837**

NEW AMERICAN NATION SERIES (US) [03598805] **2540**

NEW AMERICAN (NEW YORK, N.Y.) (US) [21399164] **2269**

NEW AMERICAN PLAYS (US) [04444479] 5366, **3415**

NEW AMERICAN PRESS, THE (US/1045-8093) [18236776] **5650**

NEW AMERICAN, THE (US) [21354282] 2269, **5718**

NEW AMERICAN VIEW (US) [20463595] **4529**

NEW AMERICAN WRITING (US/0893-7842) [15367987] **3415**

NEW & EMERGING TECHNOLOGY *CEASED.* (US/0882-6382) [11926006] **5132**

NEW AND EXPANDED INDUSTRIES ANNOUNCED IN ALABAMA (US/0091-1542) [01786543] **1619**

●NEW APPROACHES TO EMPLOYEE MANAGEMENT (US) [27835474] **944**

NEW APPROACHES TO SOCIAL SCIENCE HISTORY (US) [09567211] 2624, **5210**

NEW ART EXAMINER (US/0886-8115) [12996177] **359**

NEW ART INTERNATIONAL (FR) **359**

NEW ARTS *See* NEW ARTS REVIEW **326**

NEW ARTS REVIEW (US/0277-6138) [07612035] **326**

NEW ASIA REVIEW (US/1075-2951) **2507**

NEW ASIAN MARKET ATLAS, THE (HK) [20774626] **698**

NEW ATHENAEUM (LEWISTON, N.Y.) (US/1048-8545) [19890559] **4980**

NEW BAJAN, THE *CEASED.* (BB) [17885785] **2490**

NEW BEACON (UK/0028-4270) [I00284270] **4391**

NEW BEACON REVIEW (UK/0269-2414) [15481825] **3415**

NEW BEGINNINGS (FRANKLIN PARK, ILL.) (US/8756-9981) [12035129] **5562**

NEW BERLIN CITIZEN, THE (US) [12880285] **5769**

NEW BERLIN ENTERPRISE (US/1062-4856) [25642320] **5769**

NEW BIOLOGIST, THE *CEASED.* (US/1043-4674) [19481072] **467**

NEW BIOTECH BUSINE$$ CANADA *See* CANADIAN BIOTECH NEWS **3690**

NEW BIOTECH BUSINESS (CN) **5132**

NEW BLACKFRIARS (UK/0028-4289) [01759741] **4980**

NEW BOAT AND MOTOR PRICE GUIDE BLUE BOOK (US/0884-8378) [11528165] **594**

NEW BODY (US/0732-4782) [08364635] **2600**

NEW BODY SPECIAL INTEREST PUBLICATIONS (US) [23229719] **2600**

NEW BOOK ANNOUNCEMENTS. ANNUAL BOOK CATALOG (US) [03945167] **4830**

NEW BOOK NEWS FROM QUEBEC (CN/0709-0641) [05360173] **4817**

NEW BOOKBINDER, THE (UK/0261-5363) [08152885] **4830**

NEW BOOKS IN THE COMMUNICATIONS LIBRARY (US/0734-8142) [08662454] 4830, **1118**

NEW BOOKS ON WOMEN AND FEMINISM (US/0742-7123) [08784642] **5562**

NEW BOOKS QUARTERLY CHECKLIST SERIES : AFRO-AMERICAN HISTORY AND CULTURE (US/0091-4959) [01787350] **2748**

●NEW BOOKTALKER, THE (US/1064-7511) [26388145] **4830**

NEW BOTANIST (II/0377-1741) [01797717] **519**

NEW BRASS KEY (US/0892-4937) [15267321] **2462**

NEW BREED MICROFORM, THE (US) [08448713] 1767, **2269**

Alphabetical Title Index — NEW

NEW BREEZE (JA/0915-3160) [I09153160] **1118**

NEW BREWER, THE (US/0741-0506) [10076487] **2369**

NEW BRUNSWICK *See* ROYAL GAZETTE. NEW BRUNSWICK **4684**

NEW BRUNSWICK *See* STATUTES OF NEW BRUNSWICK **3059**

NEW BRUNSWICK ARTS BOARD *See* ANNUAL REPORT / NEW BRUNSWICK ARTS BOARD **313**

NEW BRUNSWICK BRANCH NEWS (CN/0828-7821) [12199488] **1507**

NEW BRUNSWICK COURIER (CN/0823-3934) [10156752] **5790**

NEW BRUNSWICK. DEPT. OF HEALTH AND COMMUNITY SERVICES *See* ANNUAL REPORT - HEALTH AND COMMUNITY SERVICES. NEW BRUNSWICK **4765**

NEW BRUNSWICK. DEPT. OF INTERGOVERNMENTAL AFFAIRS *See* ANNUAL REPORT - NEW BRUNSWICK. DEPT. OF INTERGOVERNMENTAL AFFAIRS **4628**

NEW BRUNSWICK. DEPT. OF THE ENVIRONMENT. LIBRARY *See* ENVIRONMENT LIBRARY ACQUISITIONS LIST - NEW BRUNSWICK. DEPT. OF THE ENVIRONMENT. LIBRARY **3209**

NEW BRUNSWICK. DIVISION OF TUBERCULOSIS CONTROL *See* ANNUAL REPORT: TUBERCULOSIS CONTROL IN THE PROVINCE OF NEW BRUNSWICK **4767**

NEW BRUNSWICK EDUCATIONAL ADMINISTRATOR (CN/0827-4851) [13843510] **1867**

NEW BRUNSWICK FEDERATION OF LABOUR. ANNUAL SUBMISSION TO THE PREMIER AND MEMBERS OF THE CABINET OF THE GOVERNMENT OF NEW BRUNSWICK (CN/0316-5795) [10235759] **1693**

NEW BRUNSWICK FEDERATION OF LABOUR. CONVENTION *See* PROCEEDINGS, ANNUAL CONVENTION - NEW BRUNSWICK FEDERATION OF LABOUR **1702**

NEW BRUNSWICK. LEGISLATIVE ASSEMBLY. STANDING COMMITTEE ON PUBLIC ACCOUNTS *See* TRANSCRIPT OF STANDING COMMITTEE ON PUBLIC ACCOUNTS **4756**

NEW BRUNSWICK LIBRARY SERVICE *See* FIVE LIBRARY REGIONS ..., PROVINCE OF NEW BRUNSWICK, THE **3211**

NEW BRUNSWICK MUSEUM *See* JOURNAL OF THE NEW BRUNSWICK MUSEUM **4090**

NEW BRUNSWICK. OFFICE OF THE ATTORNEY GENERAL *See* NEOLEX (FREDERICTON) **3141**

NEW BRUNSWICK. OFFICE OF THE AUDITOR-GENERAL *See* REPORT OF THE AUDITOR GENERAL TO THE LEGISLATIVE ASSEMBLY (FREDERICTON) **4745**

NEW BRUNSWICK REPORTS (1969) (CN/0713-8989) [01604914] **3015**

NEW BRUNSWICK SOIL SURVEY, REPORT (CN/0839-6523) [03520069] **111**

NEW BRUNSWICK TEACHERS' ASSOCIATION *See* NBTA NEWS **1766**

NEW BUSINESS (GW/0342-4006) [I03424006] **698**

NEW BUSINESS INCORPORATIONS (US) [13295120] **698**

NEW BUSINESS OPPORTUNITIES (IRVINE, CALIF.) (US/1041-3707) [18732901] **698**

NEW BUSINESS REGISTER (US) **698**

NEW BUSINESS REPORT *See* AD BUSINESS REPORT **753**

NEW CANAAN ADVERTISER (US) [26245442] **5646**

NEW CANAAN HISTORICAL SOCIETY ANNUAL, THE (US/0734-2802) [08725919] **2748**

NEW CANADIAN REVIEW *CEASED.* (CN/0832-932X) [16948290] 3466, **3415**

NEW CANADIAN SLOVENE DIARY, THE (CN/0707-5650) [04678029] **2269**

NEW CAR COST GUIDE (US/0731-4787) [08197307] **5421**

NEW CASTLE NEWS (US) [02264831] **5737**

NEW CASTLE RECORD, THE (US) [17206693] **5759**

NEW CASTLE STATE HOSPITAL *See* ANNUAL REPORT - NEW CASTLE STATE HOSPITAL **3776**

NEW CATALYST (CN/0834-969X) [16854637] **2540**

NEW CATHOLIC EXPLORER (US/1044-8322) [19944782] **5033**

NEW CHARLOTTE, THE *CEASED.* (US) [13753486] **2540**

NEW CHATTO POETS (UK) [20614849] **3466**

NEW CHEROKEE ADVOCATE, THE (US) [11032357] **5732**

NEW CHINA QUARTERLY *CEASED.* (HK) [15005095] **1507**

●NEW CHOICES FOR RETIREMENT LIVING (US/1061-2157) [25187029] **5298**

NEW CHOICES FOR THE BEST YEARS (US/1041-6277) [18804772] **5180**

NEW CHURCH LIFE (US/0275-0805) [01680975] **5065**

NEW CICADA (JA) **3466**

NEW CIVIL ENGINEER (UK/0307-7863) [01181339] **2027**

NEW CLASSIC (SA/1010-5565) [02245196] **3415**

NEW CLINICAL APPLICATIONS. NEPHROLOGY (NE) [23110492] **3992**

NEW COATINGS & SURFACES (UK/0959-6062) [I09596062] **1027**

NEW COIN POETRY (SA/0028-4459) [02530866] **3466**

NEW COLLAGE MAGAZINE (US/0028-4467) [02539501] **3466**

NEW COLLECTOR'S DIRECTORY, THE (US/0363-3284) [02499768] **2775**

NEW COMIC WORLD, THE (CN/0382-7313) [02729453] **4864**

NEW COMMUNITY (UK/0047-9586) [02535779] 5252, **2269**

NEW COMPREHENSIVE BIOCHEMISTRY (US/0167-7306) [07503501] **987**

NEW CONCEPTS (GW/0340-1073) [01795211] **1056**

NEW CONCEPTS IN CARDIAC IMAGING (US/0743-9237) [10702816] **3708**

NEW CONCEPTS IN URBAN TRANSPORTATION *CEASED.* (US/0148-8457) [01586497] **5388**

NEW CONSCIOUSNESS SOURCEBOOK (US) [09634692] **4242**

NEW CONSENSUS AND REVIEW OF THE LATEST ISSUES OF RECORDED CLASSICAL MUSIC, THE (UK) [01789086] **4140**

NEW CONSTRUCTION (INTERNATIONAL ED.) (US/0892-6264) [15243466] **622**

NEW CONSUMER (UK/0958-7349) **1298**

NEW CONTRAST (SA/1017-5415) [22189801] **3415**

NEW CONVERSATIONS (US/0360-0181) [01682811] **4980**

NEW CORPORATION BEGINNING ... AND ENDING ... / NEW MEXICO STATE CORPORATION COMMISSION, CORPORATION AND FRANCHISE TAX DEPARTMENTS (US) [11798214] **1619**

NEW COVENANT (ANN ARBOR, MICH.) (US/0744-8589) [01773468] **5033**

NEW CRITERION (NEW YORK, N.Y.), THE (US/0734-0222) [08672257] **326**

NEW DANCE REVIEW, THE (US/1040-8908) [18567561] 386, **1314**

NEW DAWN (NEW YORK) (US/0164-8381) [04315786] **2795**

NEW DAY HERALD, THE (US/1040-2047) [18352836] **4186**

NEW DAY (PHILADELPHIA) *SUSPENDED.* (US/0028-453X) [01644629] **4980**

NEW DEFINITION / THE CENTER FOR CASE MANAGEMENT, INC, THE (US) [29525040] **3620**

NEW DELHI (II) [06893445] **2660**

NEW DELTA REVIEW (US/1050-415X) [11300903] **3415**

NEW DEMOCRAT / DEMOCRATIC LEADERSHIP COUNCIL, THE (US) [23888183] **4483**

NEW DEMOCRATIC ALTERNATIVE (CN/1183-0247) [24256488] **4483**

NEW DEMOCRATIC ALTERNATIVE (CN/1183-0247) [24256491] **4483**

NEW DENTIST (THOROFARE, N.J.), THE *CEASED.* (US/1067-2354) [27166157] **1330**

NEW DEPARTURES (UK/0028-4580) [01641091] **326**

NEW DESIGNS FOR YOUTH DEVELOPMENT (US/0270-2541) [06397287] **1067**

NEW DEVELOPMENT IN BIOSCIENCES (GW/0935-1906) [11856654] **467**

NEW DEVELOPMENTS IN EMPLOYMENT DISCRIMINATION (US/0893-7133) [15633588] **3152**

●NEW DEVELOPMENTS IN MEDICINE & DRUG THERAPY (US/1063-360X) [25990369] **4317**

NEW DIMENSIONS (US) [07137592] **3415**

NEW DIMENSIONS (US) **1298**

NEW DIMENSIONS. EDITED BY ROBERT SILVERBERG (US) [05119946] **3415**

NEW DIMENSIONS IN GIVING (US) 4980, **4338**

NEW DIMENSIONS IN MENTAL HEALTH (US/0146-1451) [02826869] **4793**

NEW DIMENSIONS IN PSYCHIATRY (US/0148-7361) [03262973] **3931**

NEW DIMENSIONS SCIENCE FICTION (US/0099-0906) [02243533] **3415**

NEW DIPLOMAT (UK) [18619367] **5812**

NEW DIRECTION (LOS ANGELES, CALIF.) (US/1059-5902) [24646720] **4980**

NEW DIRECTION (TORONTO) (CN/0712-8096) [08781390] **5018**

NEW DIRECTIONS (US) [01714604] **4391**

NEW DIRECTIONS FOR ADULT AND CONTINUING EDUCATION (US/1052-2891) [21731396] **1801**

NEW DIRECTIONS FOR CHILD DEVELOPMENT (US/0195-2269) [05004926] **4605**

NEW DIRECTIONS FOR COMMUNITY COLLEGES (US/0194-3081) [01589318] **1837**

NEW DIRECTIONS FOR EDUCATION REFORM (US) **4605**

●NEW DIRECTIONS FOR EDUCATION REFORM : A PUBLICATION OF THE COLLEGE OF EDUCATION AND BEHAVIORAL SCIENCES, WESTERN KENTUCKY UNIVERSITY (US) [28478405] **1767**

NEW DIRECTIONS FOR HIGHER EDUCATION (US/0271-0560) [01780265] **1837**

NEW DIRECTIONS FOR INSTITUTIONAL RESEARCH (US/0271-0579) [02256194] **1767**

NEW DIRECTIONS FOR MENTAL HEALTH SERVICES (US/0193-9416) [05242765] **5298**

●NEW DIRECTIONS FOR PHILANTHROPIC FUNDRAISING (US/1072-172X) [28873594] **5298**

NEW DIRECTIONS FOR PROGRAM EVALUATION (US/0164-7989) [04328338] **5298**

NEW DIRECTIONS FOR STUDENT SERVICES (US/0164-7970) [04354985] **1767**

NEW DIRECTIONS FOR TEACHING AND LEARNING (US/0271-0633) [06541567] **1901**

NEW DIRECTIONS FOR WOMEN *CEASED.* (US/0160-1075) [03617120] **5562**

NEW DIRECTIONS IN INFORMATION MANAGEMENT (US/0887-3844) [13205092] **3233**

NEW DIRECTIONS IN PUBLIC ADMINISTRATION RESEARCH *CEASED.* (US) [20443831] **4668**

NEW DIRECTIONS (NEW YORK, N.Y. 1979) (US/1064-072X) [26204720] **1767**

NEW DIRECTIONS (SINGAPORE) (SI/0377-175X) [01798929] **2660**

NEW DIRECTIONS (VANCOUVER) (CN/0384-9147) [03264552] **2219**

NEW DIRECTIONS (VANCOUVER. 1985) *CEASED.* (CN/0827-6153) [14398405] **4483**

NEW DIRECTIONS (WINNIPEG) (CN/0712-2101) [08790879] **5298**

NEW DIRECTORY OF MEDICAL SCHOOLS, THE (US) [07494303] **3620**

NEW DISCIPLES TEACHER, THE (US/0746-7702) [10258942] **5065**

NEW "DIVERS SPEAK OUT" ... DIVE TRAVEL DIRECTORY, THE (US/1058-398X) [24159124] **5485**

NEW DOCTOR (AT/0313-2153) [28484103] **3916**

NEW DOMINION (ALEXANDRIA, VA.) *CEASED.* (US/0891-3501) [14709527] **2540**

NEW DRIVER (HIGHLAND PARK, ILL.) *CEASED.* (US/0279-6384) [07132486] **5421**

NEW DRUG BUYER, THE (US) **3620**

NEW DRUG COMMENTARY (US/0734-1989) [08702334] **4317**

NEW DRUG INFORMATION DIGEST (CN/0849-0902) [22154900] **1347**

NEW DRUGS AND NOVEL COMPOUNDS IN MEDICINE AND PHARMACOLOGY (UK/0958-9422) [23657459] 3620, **4317**

NEW DRUGS SURVEY *SUSPENDED.* (JA) **4317**

NEW DYNAMICS OF PREVENTIVE MEDICINE (US/0360-2613) [01831993] **3620**

NEW EARNINGS SURVEY (LONDON, 1970-) (UK) [01472950] **1693**

●NEW ECONOMY (LONDON, ENGLAND) (UK/1070-3535) [28329271] **1507**

NEW EDINBURGH NEWS (CN/0703-9042) [03951199] **5790**

NEW EDITION (CN/0824-1813) [11868904] **5210**

NEW EDITION OF THE COMPLETE WORKS OF HECTOR BERLIOZ (GW) **4140**

NEW EDUCATION (MELBOURNE, VIC.) (AT) [09101342] **1767**

NEW EGYPT PRESS, THE (US) [13200634] **5710**

NEW ELECTRIC RAILWAY JOURNAL, THE (US/1048-3845) [20863382] **5433**

NEW ELECTRONIC ENCYCLOPEDIA. [COMPUTER FILE], THE (US) [18706658] **1927**

NEW ELECTRONIC PRODUCTS DIRECTORY *See* ELECTRONIC NEW PRODUCT DIRECTORY, THE **2047**

NEW ELECTRONICS (UK/0047-9624) [09360235] **2073**

NEW ELECTRONICS (NZ) **2073**

●NEW ENERGY NEWS (US/1075-0045) [29916128] **1951**

NEW ENGINEER (US/0047-9632) [01780266] **1988**

NEW ENGLAND ANTIQUES JOURNAL (US/0897-5795) [17560423] **251**

NEW ENGLAND ANTIQUITIES RESEARCH ASSOCIATION *See* NEARA JOURNAL **2748**

NEW ENGLAND BAPTIST (NORTHBOROUGH, MASS.), THE (US/0891-3137) [11828242] **5065**

NEW ENGLAND BIENNIAL : [CATALOG] : A JURIED EXHIBITION OF NEW ENGLAND PHOTOGRAPHERS / ORGANIZED BY THE PHOTOGRAPHIC RESOURCE CENTER (US/1058-6970) [24358813] **4372**

NEW ENGLAND BRIDE (US/0744-6861) [08500900] **2283**

NEW ENGLAND BUSINESS *CEASED.* (US/0164-3533) [04631678] **698**

NEW ENGLAND CHRISTIAN *CEASED.* (US/1050-4214) [21480767] **4980**

NEW ENGLAND CONSERVATIONIST, THE (US/0277-4690) [05433432] **2200**

NEW ENGLAND CONSTRUCTION (US/0028-470X) [04922163] **622**

NEW ENGLAND COUNTRY FOLKS (US/0746-6692) [10214510] **2540**

NEW ENGLAND CROP AND LIVESTOCK REPORTING SERVICE *See* MASSACHUSETTS AGRICULTURAL STATISTICS **155**

NEW ENGLAND DIRECTORY FOR COMPUTER PROFESSIONALS *CEASED.* (US/0739-6120) [09287638] **1238**

NEW ENGLAND ECONOMIC ALMANAC (US/0545-106X) [07104447] **1507**

NEW ENGLAND ECONOMIC INDICATORS (US/0548-4448) [01588238] **1536**

NEW ENGLAND ECONOMIC REVIEW (US/0028-4726) [01759765] 1575, **801**

NEW ENGLAND ELECTRICAL BLUE BOOK (US) [05096372] **2073**

NEW ENGLAND ENGINEERING JOURNAL (US/0274-6484) [06030270] **1988**

NEW ENGLAND ENTERTAINMENT DIGEST (US/0896-1506) [12498316] 326, **5366**

NEW ENGLAND ENTERTAINMENT DIGEST [MICROFORM] (US) [10436844] 326, **5366**

NEW ENGLAND ENVIRONMENTAL NETWORK NEWS (US/0198-8476) [06245321] 2219, **2178**

NEW ENGLAND FARM BULLETIN & GARDEN GAZETTE (US) **2425**

NEW ENGLAND FARMER (ST. JOHNSBURY) (US/0193-0923) [05140870] **111**

NEW ENGLAND FINANCIAL DIGEST (US) [08911330] **801**

NEW ENGLAND FISHERMAN *See* FISHERMAN (NEW ENGLAND ED.), THE **2302**

NEW ENGLAND FOLK DIRECTORY, THE (US/0732-4820) [08383595] **4140**

NEW ENGLAND FRUIT MEETINGS (US/0099-426X) [02160877] **111**

NEW ENGLAND GAME & FISH (US/0897-8972) [17657567] **4875**

NEW ENGLAND GARDENER *CEASED.* (US/0896-8160) [13622722] **2425**

NEW ENGLAND GAS ASSOCIATION *See* MEMBERSHIP AND STATISTICAL DIRECTORY - NEW ENGLAND GAS ASSOCIATION **4284**

NEW ENGLAND GAS ASSOCIATION. MEMBERSHIP DIRECTORY *See* MEMBERSHIP AND STATISTICAL DIRECTORY - NEW ENGLAND GAS ASSOCIATION **4284**

NEW ENGLAND HISTORICAL AND GENEALOGICAL REGISTER, THE (US/0028-4785) [07030049] 2748, **2462**

NEW ENGLAND INTERSTATE WATER POLLUTION CONTROL COMMISSION *See* REPORT - NEW ENGLAND INTERSTATE WATER POLLUTION CONTROL COMMISSION **2241**

NEW ENGLAND JOURNAL MEDICINE, THE (US/0028-4793) [07857129] **3620**

NEW ENGLAND JOURNAL OF BLACK STUDIES (US/0747-4970) [10735289] 5210, **2269**

NEW ENGLAND JOURNAL OF HISTORY / NEW ENGLAND HISTORY TEACHERS ASSOCIATION, THE (US) [18176310] **5210**

NEW ENGLAND JOURNAL OF HUMAN SERVICES (US/0277-996X) [07418994] 3620, **5298**

NEW ENGLAND JOURNAL OF MEDICINE (OVERSEAS ED.) (US/0028-4793) [19585961] **3620**

NEW ENGLAND JOURNAL OF MEDICINE, THE (US/0028-4793) [01587974] **3620**

NEW ENGLAND JOURNAL OF OPTOMETRY (US/0028-4807) [04124047] **4216**

NEW ENGLAND JOURNAL OF PARAPSYCHOLOGY (US/0147-3395) [03144727] **4242**

NEW ENGLAND JOURNAL OF PUBLIC POLICY (US/0749-016X) [11052775] **4668**

NEW ENGLAND JOURNAL OF TRANSPORTATION *See* NORTHEAST JOURNAL OF TRANSPORTATION, THE **5388**

NEW ENGLAND JOURNAL ON CRIMINAL AND CIVIL CONFINEMENT (US/0740-8994) [09355506] **3170**

NEW ENGLAND JURY VERDICT REVIEW AND ANALYSIS (US/0886-2540) [12859472] **3090**

NEW ENGLAND LAW LIBRARY CONSORTIUM UNION CATALOG. CD-ROM (US) **3015**

NEW ENGLAND LAW REVIEW (US/0028-4823) [01759770] **3015**

NEW ENGLAND LIBRARIES (US/1063-5408) [24022897] **3233**

NEW ENGLAND LIBRARY BOARD *See* NELB LINK **3233**

NEW ENGLAND LIVING (US/0884-5166) [10401555] **2540**

NEW ENGLAND MINORITY NEWS (US) 4207, **2269**

NEW ENGLAND MUSEUM ASSOCIATION *See* NEMA NEWS **4093**

NEW ENGLAND MUSICIAN'S GUIDE, THE (US/0098-3381) [02240844] **4140**

NEW ENGLAND OFFSHORE *See* OFFSHORE (WEST NEWTON) **594**

NEW ENGLAND PRINTER AND LITHOGRAPHER *See* NEW ENGLAND PRINTER & PUBLISHER **4567**

NEW ENGLAND PRINTER & PUBLISHER (US/0162-8771) [04124052] **4567**

NEW ENGLAND PROGRESS MAGAZINE (US) **2607**

NEW ENGLAND PURCHASER (US/0028-4858) [05091585] **950**

NEW ENGLAND QUARTERLY, THE (US/0028-4866) [01759778] **2748**

NEW ENGLAND RAILROAD CLUB, BOSTON *See* PROCEEDINGS OF THE NEW ENGLAND RAILROAD CLUB **5434**

NEW ENGLAND READING ASSOCIATION *See* NEW ENGLAND READING ASSOCIATION JOURNAL **1901**

NEW ENGLAND READING ASSOCIATION JOURNAL (US/0028-4882) [04826039] **1901**

NEW ENGLAND REAL ESTATE JOURNAL (US/0028-4890) [04124072] **4842**

NEW ENGLAND REAL ESTATE NEWS (US/1042-9689) [19260188] **4842**

NEW ENGLAND REVIEW (1990) (US/1053-1297) [22458982] **3415**

NEW ENGLAND RUNNER (US/1041-4800) [18778166] **4907**

NEW ENGLAND SALES GUIDE TO HIGH-TECH COMPANIES (US/1040-0591) [18304615] **5132**

NEW ENGLAND SENIOR CITIZEN *CEASED.* (US/0163-2248) [04320661] **5180**

NEW ENGLAND-ST. LAWRENCE VALLEY GEOGRAPHICAL SOCIETY *See* PROCEEDINGS - NEW ENGLAND-ST. LAWRENCE VALLEY GEOGRAPHICAL SOCIETY **2573**

NEW ENGLAND STATES LIMITED, THE (US/0162-1599) [04102892] **5433**

NEW ENGLAND TALK SHOW DIRECTORY (US/0741-7225) [09865624] **1135**

NEW ENGLAND THEATRE JOURNAL (US/1050-9720) [21734190] 386, **5366**

NEW ENGLAND WATER POLLUTION CONTROL ASSOCIATION *See* JOURNAL OF THE NEW ENGLAND WATER ENVIRONMENT ASSOCIATION **2234**

NEW ENGLAND WATER POLLUTION CONTROL ASSOCIATION *See* JOURNAL OF THE NEW ENGLAND WATER POLLUTION CONTROL ASSOCIATION **2234**

NEW ENGLAND WATER WORKS ASSOCIATION *See* JOURNAL OF THE NEW ENGLAND WATER WORKS ASSOCIATION **4761**

NEW ENGLANDER, THE (US/0028-4947) [02539586] **2540**

NEW ENTOMOLOGIST (JA/0028-4955) [08349954] **5612**

NEW EQUIPMENT DIGEST (US/0028-4963) [02253788] 951, **2123**

NEW EQUIPMENT NEWS (CN/0028-4971) [02009888] **3485**

NEW ERA (BARRYTOWN, N.Y.) *CEASED.* (US/0277-3082) [07532176] **4981**

NEW ERA IN EDUCATION (UK/0028-5048) [18445070] **1767**

NEW ERA IN EDUCATION (UK/0957-0942) [I09570942] **1767**

NEW ERA (LANARK) (CN/0227-8030) [06858314] **5790**

NEW ERA LAUNDRY & CLEANING LINES (US/0028-5056) [05011252] **698**

NEW ERA (LONDON) *See* NEW ERA IN EDUCATION **1767**

NEW ERA NURSING IMAGE INTERNATIONAL (NR/0794-4373) [14933636] **3862**

NEW ERA OF TELECOMMUNICATIONS IN JAPAN (JA/0912-0076) [I09120076] **1160**

NEW ERA (PARKER, S.D.) (US) [10845754] **5744**

NEW ERA (SALT LAKE CITY), THE (US/0164-5285) [04561402] 1067, **4981**

NEW ETHICALS (AUCKLAND. 1976) (NZ/0111-0020) [04081833] **4317**

NEW ETHICALS CATALOGUE (NZ/0110-9510) [04353384] 4317, **4334**

NEW EUROPE *CEASED.* (UK) [01788794] **2700**

●NEW EUROPE LAW REVIEW (US/1069-3181) [27694863] **3015**

NEW EXPENDITURE (II/0441-7119) [05183744] **4738**

NEW EXPENDITURE FOR THE YEAR (II) [05924983] **4738**

NEW FARM, THE (US/0163-0369) [04287586] **111**

NEW FARMER AND GROWER (UK/0952-1402) [I09521402] **111**

NEW FARMER'S FINDER (CN/0824-3972) [10441136] **160**

NEW FEDERALIST (US/1043-2264) [17636742] **4484**

NEW FEDERATION, THE (CN/0842-3024) [19916001] **2540**

NEW FIRMS LISTING SERVICES / LONG ISLAND ASSOCIATION OF COMMERCE & INDUSTRY (US) [10056326] **698**

NEW FISHING (NEW YORK) (US/0092-1734) [01786943] **2309**

NEW FLORIDA (US/0193-3108) [05173479] **2748**

NEW FOCUS (US) [18343609] **1767**

●NEW FOOD & DRUG PACKAGING, THE (US/1075-3028) [29216555] **4220**

NEW FOR CONSUMERS (US/0364-6777) [02573762] **1298**

NEW FORESTS (NE/0169-4286) [14450965] 2200, **2389**

NEW FORMATIONS (UK/0950-2378) [16784849] **3348**

●NEW FORTUNES (US/1066-789X) [27049348] 698, **801**

NEW FOUNDATION PAPERS (US/0748-6804) [08697945] **4981**

NEW FOUNDATIONS (CN/0703-9263) [03960114] **1694**

NEW FREEDOM QUARTERLY (US/8755-0598) [11247032] **5366**

NEW FROM EUROPE *CEASED.* (US/0740-3569) [09956112] **5132**

NEW FROM U.S *CEASED.* (US/0740-3577) [09956088] **2540**

NEW FRONTIERS IN EDUCATION (II/0047-9705) [02540978] **1837**

NEW FRONTIERS (SEATTLE) (US/0095-5248) [01796566] **5252**

NEW FUELS REPORT (US) **4266**

NEW FUN RUNNER (AT) **4907**

NEW GARDENS NEWSLETTER (US/0197-5633) [06065900] **2425**

NEW GENERATING PLANTS (US/0744-1770) [05373449] **2073**

NEW GENERATION (UK/0263-5429) [I02635429] **4555**

NEW GENERATION COMPUTING (JA/0288-3635) [10152227] 1288, **1270**

Alphabetical Title Index — NEW

NEW GENERATION COMPUTING SERIES (US) **1197**

NEW GERMAN-AMERICAN STUDIES (US/1043-5808) [19491029] **2269**

NEW GERMAN CRITIQUE (US/0094-033X) [01793512] **3415**

NEW GERMAN REVIEW (US/0889-0145) [13812374] **3415**

NEW GERMAN STUDIES (UK/0307-2770) [01589003] 3415, **3305**

NEW GHANA, THE (GH) [01786978] **2642**

NEW GLASS REVIEW (US/0275-469X) [07148964] **2592**

●NEW GLASS REVIEW (PRAHA) (XR/1210-2741) [26962987] **2592**

NEW GOSPEL TREASURE SELECT-A-SONG (US/0362-7357) [02312106] **4140**

NEW GROUND (SA/1016-9075) [24438874] **2178**

NEW GUARD *CEASED*. (US/0028-5137) [01681107] **4484**

NEW GUN WEEK, THE (US/0195-1599) [05323328] **4907**

NEW HAMPSHIRE *See* NEW HAMPSHIRE SELECTED MOTOR VEHICLE AND BOATING LAWS **3015**

NEW HAMPSHIRE *See* NEW HAMPSHIRE CRIMINAL CODE : R.S.A. TITLE LXII, AS AMENDED THROUGH JULY 1975 **3108**

NEW HAMPSHIRE *See* NEW HAMPSHIRE REVISED STATUTES ANNOTATED **3015**

NEW HAMPSHIRE AFFIRMATIVE ACTION DATA (US/0149-9211) [03562614] **1536**

NEW HAMPSHIRE ARCHEOLOGIST, THE (US/0077-8346) [09159198] **276**

NEW HAMPSHIRE. BANK COMMISSIONER'S OFFICE *See* REPORT - NEW HAMPSHIRE. BANK COMMISSIONER'S OFFICE **807**

NEW HAMPSHIRE BAR JOURNAL (US/0548-4928) [01759809] **3015**

NEW HAMPSHIRE BAR NEWS (US/1051-4023) [21953263] **3015**

NEW HAMPSHIRE BEVERAGE JOURNAL (US/0192-6462) [05062695] **2369**

NEW HAMPSHIRE. BUREAU OF MARKETS *See* WEEKLY MARKET BULLETIN (CONCORD) **145**

NEW HAMPSHIRE BUSINESS AND PROFESSIONAL DIRECTORY (US) [23661865] **698**

NEW HAMPSHIRE BUSINESS DIRECTORY (US/1048-714X) [21010809] **698**

NEW HAMPSHIRE BUSINESS JOURNAL (US) [24112206] **5708**

NEW HAMPSHIRE BUSINESS REVIEW (US/0164-8152) [04326367] **698**

NEW HAMPSHIRE COLLEGE JOURNAL (US/0742-9347) [10480274] **1093**

NEW HAMPSHIRE COMPREHENSIVE LAW ENFORCEMENT PLAN (US/0094-7628) [02239911] **3170**

NEW HAMPSHIRE CRIMINAL CODE : R.S.A. TITLE LXII, AS AMENDED THROUGH JULY 1975 (US) [09583416] **3108**

NEW HAMPSHIRE. DEPT. OF EDUCATION. DIVISION OF ADMINISTRATION *See* SCHOOL TRANSPORTATION SUMMARY **1872**

NEW HAMPSHIRE. DEPT. OF EDUCATION. DIVISION OF ADMINISTRATION *See* DISTRIBUTION OF STATE FOUNDATION AID TO NEW HAMPSHIRE SCHOOL DISTRICTS **1862**

NEW HAMPSHIRE. DEPT. OF EDUCATION. VOCATIONAL-TECHNICAL DIVISION *See* NEW HAMPSHIRE STATE PLAN, THE ADMINISTRATION OF VOCATIONAL TECHNICAL EDUCATION **1914**

NEW HAMPSHIRE. DEPT. OF EMPLOYMENT SECURITY *See* NEW HAMPSHIRE AFFIRMATIVE ACTION DATA **1536**

NEW HAMPSHIRE. DEPT. OF EMPLOYMENT SECURITY *See* ECONOMIC CONDITIONS IN NEW HAMPSHIRE LOCAL OFFICE AREAS **1664**

NEW HAMPSHIRE. DEPT. OF EMPLOYMENT SECURITY. ECONOMIC ANALYSIS AND REPORTING SECTION *See* ANNUAL PLANNING INFORMATION, BELKNAP COUNTY **1645**

NEW HAMPSHIRE. DEPT. OF EMPLOYMENT SECURITY. ECONOMIC ANALYSIS AND REPORTING SECTION *See* ANNUAL PLANNING INFORMATION : HILLSBOROUGH COUNTY **1646**

NEW HAMPSHIRE. DEPT. OF EMPLOYMENT SECURITY. ECONOMIC ANALYSIS AND REPORTS SECTION *See* ANNUAL PLANNING INFORMATION, NEW HAMPSHIRE **1647**

NEW HAMPSHIRE ENVIRONMENTAL MONITOR (US) **2178**

NEW HAMPSHIRE FACTS (US/0895-8114) [16809724] **2540**

NEW HAMPSHIRE. FISH AND GAME DEPARTMENT *See* TECHNICAL CIRCULAR - NEW HAMPSHIRE FISH AND GAME DEPARTMENT **4879**

NEW HAMPSHIRE GENEALOGICAL RECORD, THE (US/1055-0763) [04054509] **2462**

NEW HAMPSHIRE. GOVERNOR'S COMMISSION ON CRIME AND DELINQUENCY *See* NEW HAMPSHIRE COMPREHENSIVE LAW ENFORCEMENT PLAN **3170**

●NEW HAMPSHIRE HEAALTH CARE IN PERSPECTIVE (US/1065-4313) [26605919] **4793**

NEW HAMPSHIRE HISTORICAL SOCIETY, CONCORD *See* NEW HAMPSHIRE HISTORICAL SOCIETY NEWSLETTER **2748**

NEW HAMPSHIRE HISTORICAL SOCIETY NEWSLETTER (US) [04843593] **2748**

NEW HAMPSHIRE IN PERSPECTIVE (US/1065-5581) [26660023] **5334**

NEW HAMPSHIRE LAW DIRECTORY & DAYBOOK (US/0730-6210) [02663301] **3015**

NEW HAMPSHIRE LIBRARY STATISTICS (US/0749-0313) [03654787] 3234, **3259**

NEW HAMPSHIRE. LIQUOR COMMISSION *See* ANNUAL STATEMENT / STATE OF NEW HAMPSHIRE, LIQUOR COMMISSION **2363**

NEW HAMPSHIRE MAGAZINE (DURHAM) (US/0199-0306) [05524355] **1093**

NEW HAMPSHIRE MANUFACTURING DIRECTORY (US) [14147390] **698**

NEW HAMPSHIRE MARKETING DIRECTORY (US/0276-2110) [07060350] **934**

NEW HAMPSHIRE MONITOR *See* NEW HAMPSHIRE ENVIRONMENTAL MONITOR **2178**

NEW HAMPSHIRE MONTHLY LOCAL CLIMATOLOGICAL DATA. MICROFORM (US) [10848010] **1432**

NEW HAMPSHIRE POLITICAL ALMANAC, THE (US/0276-9778) [07184859] **4484**

NEW HAMPSHIRE PREMIER (US/1050-5512) [21532038] **2540**

NEW HAMPSHIRE PROFILES *CEASED*. (US/0028-5307) [03901797] **2748**

NEW HAMPSHIRE PUBLIC UTILITIES COMMISSION *See* NEW HAMPSHIRE PUBLIC UTILITIES COMMISSION REPORTS **4668**

NEW HAMPSHIRE PUBLIC UTILITIES COMMISSION REPORTS (US) [11951340] **4668**

NEW HAMPSHIRE QUARTER NOTES (US/0028-5315) [01789055] **4140**

NEW HAMPSHIRE REGISTER, STATE YEAR-BOOK AND LEGISLATIVE MANUAL (US/0545-1671) [02539089] **4669**

NEW HAMPSHIRE REPORTS. CURRENT CASES, THE (US) [05105380] **3015**

NEW HAMPSHIRE REVISED STATUTES ANNOTATED (US) [01641077] **3015**

NEW HAMPSHIRE RULEMAKING REGISTER (US) [10810576] **3015**

NEW HAMPSHIRE SELECTED MOTOR VEHICLE AND BOATING LAWS (US) [21387825] 5388, **3015**

NEW HAMPSHIRE SOCIETY OF GENEALOGISTS. STRAFFORD COUNTY CHAPTER *See* GENEALOGICAL RECORD OF STRAFFORD COUNTY, THE **2450**

NEW HAMPSHIRE SPIRIT (US/0897-0319) [17390421] **4907**

NEW HAMPSHIRE STATE COUNCIL ON AGING *See* STATE PLAN FOR PROGRAMS ON AGING UNDER TITLE III AND TITLE VII OF THE OLDER AMERICANS ACT OF 1965 AS AMENDED FOR THE STATE OF NEW HAMPSHIRE **5311**

NEW HAMPSHIRE. STATE DEPT. OF EDUCATION. DIVISION OF ADMINISTRATION *See* TEACHER SALARY SCHEDULES, NEW HAMPSHIRE SCHOOL DISTRICTS / NEW HAMPSHIRE STATE DEPARTMENT OF EDUCATION, DIVISION OF ADMINISTRATION **1713**

NEW HAMPSHIRE STATE PLAN, THE ADMINISTRATION OF VOCATIONAL TECHNICAL EDUCATION (US/0148-8171) [03375474] **1914**

NEW HAMPSHIRE. STATE PLANNING PROJECT *See* REPORT - N.H. STATE PLANNING PROJECT **4854**

NEW HAMPSHIRE SUNDAY NEWS (US/0892-8703) [08597236] **5708**

NEW HAMPSHIRE. SUPREME COURT *See* NEW HAMPSHIRE REPORTS. CURRENT CASES, THE **3015**

NEW HAMPSHIRE TOWN AND CITY *See* NEW HAMPSHIRE TOWN & CITY **4669**

NEW HAMPSHIRE TOWN & CITY (US/0545-171X) [10067623] **4669**

NEW HAMPSHIRE. TREASURY DEPT *See* ANNUAL REPORT OF THE TREASURER (STATE OF NEW HAMPSHIRE) **4710**

NEW HAMPTON TRIBUNE (NEW HAMPTON, IOWA : 1937) (US) [16049984] **5672**

NEW HAVEN ADVOCATE (US/0192-8511) [05119951] **5646**

NEW HAVEN COLONY HISTORICAL SOCIETY, NEW HAVEN *See* JOURNAL OF THE NEW HAVEN COLONY HISTORICAL SOCIETY **2742**

NEW HAVEN REGISTER, THE (US) [09149711] **5646**

NEW HAVEN STUDIES IN INTERNATIONAL LAW AND WORLD PUBLIC ORDER, THE (US/0738-2812) [09552800] **3133**

NEW HEADLAND POETRY MAGAZINE (UK) [01785079] **3466**

NEW HEALTH STANDARD JOURNAL, THE (US/1055-8934) [23364953] **2600**

NEW HEAVEN, NEW EARTH *CEASED*. (US/0896-3150) [12670128] **5665**

NEW HEBRIDES. CONDOMINIUM TREASURER *See* ACCOUNTS - NEW HEBRIDES CONDOMINIUM. COMPTES - CONDOMINIUM DES NOUVELLES-HEBRIDES **4708**

NEW HEBRIDES. GEOLOGICAL SURVEY *See* ANNUAL REPORT OF THE GEOLOGICAL SURVEY. NEW HEBRIDES CONDOMINIUM **1365**

NEW HI-FI SOUND (UK) [10520339] **5318**

NEW HISTORICISM, THE (US/1054-0873) [17427735] **3415**

NEW HOLLAND NEWS (NEW HOLLAND, PA. : 1986) (US) [13897140] **111**

NEW HOLSTEIN REPORTER (US/0749-6982) [11165822] **5769**

NEW HOMES (US/0890-4723) [12007693] **4842**

NEW HOMES MAGAZINE (US/0192-4893) [02251748] **4842**

NEW HOPE GOLDEN VALLEY POSTNEWS (US) [22000461] **5697**

NEW HORIZON (JERSEY CITY) (US/0364-8184) [02662602] 2748, **2269**

NEW HORIZON (LONDON, ENGLAND) (UK/0955-095X) [19620987] **5044**

NEW HORIZONS (CN/0381-7253) [03202240] **242**

●NEW HORIZONS (BALTIMORE, MD.) (US/1063-7389) [26134035] **3620**

NEW HORIZONS (COLUMBIA) (US/0363-6976) [01589688] **4981**

NEW HORIZONS IN ADULT EDUCATION (US/1062-3183) [23865312] **1882**

NEW HORIZONS IN EDUCATION (SYDNEY, N.S.W.) (AT) [08881079] **1767**

NEW HORIZONS (MILWAUKEE, WIS.) (US/0889-5678) [13983166] **1767**

NEW HORIZONS (TORONTO. 1972) (CN/0225-8536) [06562729] **4242**

NEW HORIZONS WORLD GUIDE (US/0553-0601) [04551879] **5485**

NEW HUMANIST (LONDON, ENGLAND) (UK/0306-512x) [01588022] **4353**

NEW HUNGARIAN QUARTERLY, THE (HU) [06326564] **2700**

NEW IDEA MELBOURNE (AT/0028-249X) [I0028249X] 2425, **2792**

NEW IDEAS IN PSYCHOLOGY (UK/0732-118X) [08317101] **4605**

NEW ILLUSTRATOR *See* LIGHT ON THE WORD. TEACHER **1900**

NEW IMAGE OF MAN IN MEDICINE, A (US/0270-7748) [05935730] **3620**

NEW IMAGE, THE (US/0896-050X) [16893522] **4216**

NEW IN CHESS YEARBOOK (NE/0168-7697) [11732112] **4864**

NEW IN COMPUTING MAGAZINE AND BUYER'S GUIDE (US/0743-037X) [10495215] **1238**

NEW IN PRINTING (UK) [15078995] **4567**

NEW INDIA (II) [03267971] **2507**

NEW INDIA BULLETIN (CN/0706-8409) [02590651] **4484**

NEW INDUSTRIES AND PLANT EXPANSIONS REPORTED IN WISCONSIN (US/0160-2063) [03633161] **1619**

NEW INFORMATION NEWS (US/1055-9345) [23369294] **1118**

NEW INTERNATIONAL (NEW YORK, N.Y. : 1983) (US/0737-3724) [09363388] **4543**

NEW INTERNATIONALIST (UK/0305-9529) [01788099] **4529**

NEW IRELAND FORUM *See* REPORT OF PROCEEDINGS / NEW IRELAND FORUM **2705**

NEW IRISH ARCHITECTURE (IE) [19769458] **304**

NEW ISSUES ALERT (US/0743-3433) [10553880] **909**

NEW ISSUES (FORT LAUDERDALE, FLA.) (US/0162-9050) [04252545] **909**

NEW JERSEY *See* RULES GOVERNING THE COURTS OF THE STATE OF NEW JERSEY, 1969 REVISION, AS AMENDED **3143**

NEW JERSEY 50 PLUS (US) **5711**

NEW JERSEY ACADEMY OF SCIENCE *See* BULLETIN - NEW JERSEY ACADEMY OF SCIENCE, THE **5091**

NEW JERSEY. ADMINISTRATIVE OFFICE OF THE COURTS *See* ANNUAL REPORT / NEW JERSEY JUDICIARY **3139**

NEW JERSEY. ADMINISTRATIVE OFFICE OF THE COURTS *See* PROCEEDINGS IN THE MUNICIPAL COURTS **3082**

NEW JERSEY ADMINISTRATIVE REPORTS (US) [08960395] **3093**

NEW JERSEY AIRPORT DIRECTORY (US) [24942322] **30**

NEW JERSEY & NATIONAL REGISTERS OF HISTORIC PLACES AS OF ... (US) [15372541] **2624**

NEW JERSEY AND NEW YORK PORT HANDBOOK (US/0742-2695) [10269803] **5453**

NEW JERSEY AREA LIBRARY DIRECTORY (US/0362-2967) [02278669] **3234**

NEW JERSEY ASSOCIATION FOR HEALTH, PHYSICAL EDUCATION AND RECREATION *See* REPORTER - NEW JERSEY ASSOCIATION FOR HEALTH, PHYSICAL EDUCATION AND RECREATION, THE **4799**

NEW JERSEY BASIC SKILLS COUNCIL *See* REPORT TO THE BOARD OF HIGHER EDUCATION ON THE RESULTS OF THE NEW JERSEY COLLEGE BASIC SKILLS PLACEMENT TESTING AND RECOMMENDATIONS ON INSTRUCTION AND CURRICULUM DEVELOPMENT / NEW JERSEY BASIC SKILLS COUNCIL **1844**

NEW JERSEY BELL JOURNAL *CEASED.* (US/0195-7627) [04887396] **1160**

NEW JERSEY BELL TELEPHONE COMPANY *See* NEW JERSEY BELL JOURNAL **1160**

NEW JERSEY BEVERAGE JOURNAL (US/0028-5552) [05143748] **2369**

NEW JERSEY BOATER (US/0886-0955) [12819696] **594**

NEW JERSEY BRIDE (US) [21381666] **2283**

NEW JERSEY BUILDING PERMITS, ANNUAL SUMMARY (US) **2829**

NEW JERSEY. BUREAU OF AIR POLLUTION CONTROL *See* ANNUAL REPORT - BUREAU OF POLLUTION CONTROL. STATE OF NEW JERSEY. DEPARTMENT OF ENVIRONMENTAL PROTECTION **2224**

NEW JERSEY. BUREAU OF MEDICAL FACILITY CONSTRUCTION AND PLANNING *See* NEW JERSEY STATE PLAN FOR THE CONSTRUCTION AND MODERNIZATION OF HOSPITALS AND OTHER MEDICAL FACILITIES **3789**

NEW JERSEY. BUREAU OF STATISTICAL ANALYSIS AND SOCIAL RESEARCH *See* FIRST AND READMISSIONS TO STATE AND COUNTY PSYCHIATRIC HOSPITALS BY COUNTY, MUNICIPALITY OF RESIDENCE, AND SERVICE AREA **3780**

NEW JERSEY BUSINESS (US/0028-5560) [04130924] **698**

NEW JERSEY BUSINESS DIRECTORY (US/1048-7158) [21010819] **698**

NEW JERSEY BUSINESS SOURCE BOOK, THE (US/1049-2879) [15803081] **847, 698**

NEW JERSEY. CASINO CONTROL COMMISSION *See* ANNUAL REPORT - NEW JERSEY CASINO CONTROL COMMISSION **3157**

NEW JERSEY. CIVIL SERVICE COMMISSION *See* STATE OF NEW JERSEY COMPENSATION PLAN : HIGHER EDUCATION AND THE STATE COLLEGES; AN ALPHABETICAL LISTING OF CLASS TITLES AND RANGES, STANDARD WORK HOURS BY CLASS **1848**

NEW JERSEY COURT RULES (US) **3015**

NEW JERSEY. DEPT. OF AGRICULTURE *See* CIRCULAR - NEW JERSEY DEPARTMENT OF AGRICULTURE **74**

NEW JERSEY. DEPT. OF BANKING *See* ANNUAL REPORT - STATE OF NEW JERSEY, DEPARTMENT OF BANKING, COMMISSIONER OF BANKING **772**

NEW JERSEY. DEPT. OF CIVIL SERVICE *See* BUSINESS AND GOVERNMENT SALARY AND WAGE SURVEYS (NEW JERSEY) **1657**

NEW JERSEY. DEPT. OF CIVIL SERVICE *See* SEPARATIONS, STATE SERVICE **4705**

NEW JERSEY. DEPT. OF COMMUNITY AFFAIRS. MUNICIPAL INFORMATION SERVICE *See* MUNICIPAL SALARY SURVEY **4667**

NEW JERSEY. DEPT. OF HIGHER EDUCATION *See* COMMUNITY COLLEGE FINANCES **1817**

NEW JERSEY. DEPT. OF TRANSPORTATION *See* MASTER PLAN FOR TRANSPORTATION (TRENTON) **5386**

NEW JERSEY. DEPT. OF TRANSPORTATION *See* REPORT OF OPERATIONS : HIGHWAYS, BUSES, AERONAUTICS, RAILROADS **5391**

NEW JERSEY DIRECTORY OF MANUFACTURERS (US/0195-9352) [05668365] **3485**

NEW JERSEY DIVISION OF LABOR MARKET AND DEMOGRAPHIC RESEARCH POPULATION ESTIMATES FOR NEW JERSEY (US) **4555**

NEW JERSEY. DIVISION OF MEDICAL ASSISTANCE AND HEALTH SERVICES *See* ANNUAL REPORT - STATE OF NEW JERSEY, DEPARTMENT OF INSTITUTIONS AND AGENCIES, DIVISION OF MEDICAL ASSISTANCE AND HEALTH SERVICES-MEDICAID **2873**

NEW JERSEY. DIVISION OF MEDICAL ASSISTANCE AND HEALTH SERVICES. ANNUAL REPORT *See* ANNUAL REPORT - STATE OF NEW JERSEY, DEPARTMENT OF INSTITUTIONS AND AGENCIES, DIVISION OF MEDICAL ASSISTANCE AND HEALTH SERVICES-MEDICAID **2873**

NEW JERSEY. DIVISION OF TAXATION *See* CERTIFICATION OF AVERAGE RATIOS AND COMMON LEVEL RANGE FOR USE IN THE TAX YEAR ... / STATE OF NEW JERSEY, DEPARTMENT OF THE TREASURY, DIVISION OF TAXATION **4717**

NEW JERSEY. DIVISION OF TAXATION. LOCAL PROPERTY AND PUBLIC UTILITY BRANCH *See* REPORT OF DATA FROM FA-1 FORMS - NEW JERSEY. DIVISION OF TAXATION. LOCAL PROPERTY AND PUBLIC UTILITY BRANCH **4745**

NEW JERSEY. DIVISION OF TAXATION. RESEARCH AND STATISTICS SECTION *See* STATISTICS OF INCOME : INCOME TAX RETURNS **4700**

NEW JERSEY. DIVISION OF VOCATIONAL EDUCATION *See* DESCRIPTIVE REPORT OF ACTIVITIES IN THE FIELDS OF AGRICULTURE, TRADES AND INDUSTRY, VOCATIONAL & GENERAL HOME ECONOMICS, OCCUPATIONAL INFORMATION AND GUIDANCE, DISTRIBUTIVE EDUCATION, AND INDUSTRIAL ARTS **1912**

NEW JERSEY. DIVISION OF WATER RESOURCES *See* NEW JERSEY/USEPA REGION II WATER RESOURCES MANAGEMENT AGREEMENT **5536**

NEW JERSEY ECONOMIC INDICATORS (1976) (US/1064-5942) [04860392] **1575, 1536**

NEW JERSEY EDUCATION ASSOCIATION *See* BASIC STATISTICAL DATA OF NEW JERSEY SCHOOL DISTRICTS **1793**

NEW JERSEY EDUCATION ASSOCIATION *See* NJEA REVIEW **1769**

NEW JERSEY EDUCATION ASSOCIATION *See* EXTRA PAY FOR EXTRA SERVICES IN NEW JERSEY SCHOOL DISTRICTS **1863**

NEW JERSEY EDUCATION ASSOCIATION. RESEARCH DIVISION *See* ANALYSIS OF PROVISIONS IN SELECTED ARTICLES OF AGREEMENTS **1860**

NEW JERSEY EDUCATION LAW REPORT, THE (US/0279-8557) [07329850] **1767, 3015**

NEW JERSEY ELECTION LAW ENFORCEMENT COMMISSION *See* REPORT OF THE ELECTION LAW ENFORCEMENT COMMISSION **4493**

NEW JERSEY EMPLOYMENT AND THE ECONOMY. ATLANTIC COASTAL REGION (ATLANTIC, CAPE MAY, MONMOUTH, AND OCEAN COUNTIES) (US) [14184202] **1694**

NEW JERSEY EMPLOYMENT AND THE ECONOMY. NORTHERN NEW JERSEY REGION (BERGEN, ESSEX, HUDSON, HUNTERDON, MIDDLESEX, MORRIS, PASSAIC, SOMERSET, SUSSEX, UNION AND WARREN COUNTIES) (US) [14173209] **1694**

NEW JERSEY EMPLOYMENT AND THE ECONOMY. SOUTHERN NEW JERSEY REGION (BURLINGTON, CAMDEN, CUMBERLAND, GLOUCESTER, MERCER, AND SALEM COUNTIES) (US) [14177590] **1694**

●NEW JERSEY EMPLOYMENT LAW LETTER (US/1064-2390) [26238199] **3152**

●NEW JERSEY ENVIRONMENTAL LAW LETTER (US/1060-9954) [25148326] **3115**

NEW JERSEY FACTS (US/0898-5405) [16636876] **2540**

NEW JERSEY FATAL MOTOR VEHICLE ACCIDENTS AND FATALITIES REVIEW, COMPARATIVE DATA REPORT *See* FATAL MOTOR VEHICLE ACCIDENT COMPARATIVE DATA REPORT **5440**

●NEW JERSEY FIRE FOCUS : THE OFFICIAL NEWSLETTER OF THE NJ BUREAU OF FIRE SAFETY (US) [25958307] **2292**

NEW JERSEY FISHERMAN *See* FISHERMAN (NEW JERSEY, DELAWARE BAY ED.), THE **4894**

NEW JERSEY FOLKLIFE (US/0887-8048) [13355928] **2322**

NEW JERSEY GENESIS (US) [01715720] **2540**

●NEW JERSEY HEALTH CARE IN PERSPECTIVE (US/1065-4526) [26607031] **4793**

NEW JERSEY HERALD (1960), THE (US/0893-3677) [12198584] **5711**

NEW JERSEY HISTORICAL COMMISSION *See* NEW JERSEY HISTORICAL COMMISSION NEWSLETTER **2748**

NEW JERSEY HISTORICAL COMMISSION NEWSLETTER (US/0047-9772) [05774325] **2748**

NEW JERSEY HISTORY (US/0028-5757) [01605452] **2748**

NEW JERSEY IN PERSPECTIVE (US/1065-5573) [26659946] **5334**

NEW JERSEY INDEX (US) [10683428] **420**

NEW JERSEY INDUSTRY ENVIRONMENTAL ALERT (US/1055-2588) [23129337] **2178**

NEW JERSEY JOURNAL OF PHARMACY, THE (US/0028-5773) [01715509] **4317**

NEW JERSEY JURY VERDICT REVIEW AND ANALYSIS (US/8750-8060) [11779739] **3090**

NEW JERSEY. JUVENILE PROBATION MANAGEMENT INFORMATION SYSTEM *See* PROBATION ADMINISTRATIVE MANAGEMENT SYSTEM / JUVENILE PROBATION MANAGEMENT INFORMATION SYSTEM **3173**

NEW JERSEY LAKE SURVEY FISHING MAPS GUIDE (US/1054-4623) [22901933] **2309**

NEW JERSEY LAKE SURVEY MAP GUIDE (US/1043-6405) [19502473] **2570**

NEW JERSEY LAW JOURNAL, THE (US/0028-5803) [01759865] **3015**

NEW JERSEY LAWYER (MAGAZINE) (US/0195-0983) [05276194] **3015**

NEW JERSEY LAWYERS DIARY AND MANUAL (US/1053-1955) [11773839] **3015**

NEW JERSEY LEGISLATIVE INDEX (US/0271-8448) [04911867] **3015**

NEW JERSEY LEGISLATIVE MANUAL (US) [01759853] **4484**

NEW JERSEY LIBRARIES (US/0028-5811) [01759867] **3234**

NEW JERSEY LUSO-AMERICANO *See* LUSOAMERICANO (NEWARK, N.J.) **5710**

NEW JERSEY MEDIA GUIDE (US/1054-5190) [20281026] **934, 1118**

NEW JERSEY MEDICINE (US/0885-842X) [12423732] **3620**

NEW JERSEY MONTHLY (US/0273-270X) [04423163] **2540**

NEW JERSEY MOSQUITO CONTROL ASSOCIATION *See* PROCEEDINGS, ANNUAL MEETING - NEW JERSEY MOSQUITO CONTROL ASSOCIATION, INC **2239**

NEW JERSEY MOTOR TRUCK ASSOCIATION *See* BULLETIN - NEW JERSEY MOTOR TRUCK ASSOCIATION **5378**

NEW JERSEY MUNICIPAL DATA BOOK, THE (US/0277-9218) [07661680] **2829**

NEW JERSEY MUNICIPAL LAW NEWS (US/0735-4010) [08912551] **3015**

NEW JERSEY MUNICIPALITIES (US/0028-5846) [01759870] **4669**

Alphabetical Title Index — NEW

NEW JERSEY NETWORK (FIRM) See ANNUAL REPORT - NEW JERSEY NETWORK (FIRM) **1149**

NEW JERSEY NURSE (1978) (US/0196-4895) [05759126] **3862**

NEW JERSEY. OFFICE OF BUSINESS ECONOMICS See ANNUAL SUMMARY OF DWELLING UNITS AUTHORIZED BY BUILDING PERMITS (NEW JERSEY) **2815**

NEW JERSEY. OFFICE OF DEMOGRAPHIC AND ECONOMIC ANALYSIS See PERSONAL INCOME FOR UNITED STATES, NEW JERSEY, AND COUNTIES **1578**

NEW JERSEY. OFFICE OF THE GOVERNOR See ECONOMIC REPORT OF THE GOVERNOR / STATE OF NEW JERSEY, GOVERNOR **1557**

NEW JERSEY OUTDOORS (US/0028-5889) [03176825] 4875, **2200**

NEW JERSEY PARENT-TEACHER (US/0028-5897) [04130963] **1867**

NEW JERSEY. PINELANDS COMMISSION See ANNUAL REPORT / NEW JERSEY, PINELANDS COMMISSION **1462**

NEW JERSEY POLICE MANUAL (US) **3170**

NEW JERSEY POLITICAL ALMANAC (US/8756-2618) [04603029] **4669**

NEW JERSEY PUBLIC EMPLOYEE REPORTER (US) [12243490] **1694**

NEW JERSEY PUBLIC SCHOOL RACIAL/ETHNIC ENROLLMENTS AND DROPOUTS / STATE OF NEW JERSEY, DEPARTMENT OF EDUCATION (US) [04371340] 2269, **1767**

NEW JERSEY QUERIES (US/0899-1340) [16809333] **2462**

NEW JERSEY REALTOR (US/0028-5919) [04130976] **4842**

NEW JERSEY REGISTER (US/0300-6069) [01375930] **4669**

NEW JERSEY REPORTER (US/0195-3192) [05471767] **4669**

NEW JERSEY REPORTS AND NEW JERSEY SUPERIOR COURT REPORTS (US/8750-2658) [11197132] **3142**

NEW JERSEY RESTAURANT GUIDE (US) **5072**

●NEW JERSEY REVIEW OF LITERATURE, THE (US/1073-8576) [29539737] **3415**

●NEW JERSEY RULES OF COURT (US/1070-6364) [26671214] **3015**

NEW JERSEY SCHOOL LAW DECISIONS (INDEX) (US/0146-7603) [03172212] 1767, **3015**

NEW JERSEY SENSOR NEWS / DIVISION OF OCCUPATIONAL AND ENVIRONMENTAL HEALTH (US) [24632171] **2865**

NEW JERSEY SESSION LAW SERVICE (US) [01759851] **3015**

NEW JERSEY SPEECH AND HEARING ASSOCIATION See JOURNAL OF THE NEW JERSEY SPEECH AND HEARING ASSOCIATION **4390**

NEW JERSEY STATE AFL-CIO See NEW JERSEY STATE AFL-CIO NEWS **1694**

NEW JERSEY STATE AFL-CIO NEWS (US) [05958426] **1694**

NEW JERSEY. STATE AGENCY FOR SOCIAL SECURITY See ANNUAL REPORT - NEW JERSEY. STATE AGENCY FOR SOCIAL SECURITY **5272**

NEW JERSEY STATE BAR ASSOCIATION See OFFICIAL DIRECTORY - NEW JERSEY STATE BAR ASSOCIATION **3021**

NEW JERSEY STATE BAR ASSOCIATION See N.J. STATE BAR ASSOCIATION **3012**

NEW JERSEY STATE CHAMBER OF COMMERCE. DEPT. OF GOVERNMENTAL AND ECONOMIC RESEARCH See PROPERTY TAX DATA, NEW JERSEY TAXING DISTRICTS, TAX RATES, TAX LEVIES, ASSESSMENT RATIOS **4742**

NEW JERSEY. STATE DEPT. OF EDUCATION. BUREAU OF GRANTS MANAGEMENT See DIRECTORY OF FEDERAL PROGRAMS ADMINISTERED BY THE NEW JERSEY DEPARTMENT OF EDUCATION, A **1862**

NEW JERSEY. STATE DEPT. OF EDUCATION. OFFICE OF MANAGEMENT INFORMATION. BRANCH OF STATISTICS See NUMBER OF ADMINISTRATORS AND SUPERVISORS, CLASSROOM TEACHERS, AND SPECIAL SERVICES PERSONNEL EMPLOYED IN EACH NEW JERSEY PUBLIC SCHOOL DISTRICT BY COUNTY **1867**

NEW JERSEY. STATE DEPT. OF HEALTH See PROSPECTIVE REIMBURSEMENT SYSTEM BASED ON PATIENT CASE-MIX FOR NEW JERSEY HOSPITALS, A **3791**

NEW JERSEY. STATE FARMLAND EVALUATION ADVISORY COMMITTEE See REPORT OF THE STATE FARMLAND EVALUATION ADVISORY COMMITTEE **126**

NEW JERSEY. STATE LAW ENFORCEMENT PLANNING AGENCY See APPLICANTS GUIDE, JUVENILE JUSTICE PROGRAMS ..., VICTIMS OF CRIME ACT-VICTIM ASSISTANCE PROGRAM **2936**

NEW JERSEY. STATE LAW ENFORCEMENT PLANNING AGENCY See CRIMINAL JUSTICE PLAN FOR NEW JERSEY. APPLICANTS GUIDE **3162**

NEW JERSEY. STATE LEGISLATURE See NEW JERSEY LEGISLATIVE MANUAL **4484**

NEW JERSEY STATE LIBRARY IMPRESSIONS *SUSPENDED.* (US/0890-8346) [05931452] **2748**

NEW JERSEY STATE PLAN FOR THE CONSTRUCTION AND MODERNIZATION OF HOSPITALS AND OTHER MEDICAL FACILITIES (US) [01789824] **3789**

NEW JERSEY STATE PLAN FOR THE CONSTRUCTION OF HOSPITALS AND RELATED MEDICAL FACILITIES See NEW JERSEY STATE PLAN FOR THE CONSTRUCTION AND MODERNIZATION OF HOSPITALS AND OTHER MEDICAL FACILITIES **3789**

NEW JERSEY STATE RAIL PLAN. UPDATE (US) [13035034] **5433**

NEW JERSEY STATUTES - TITLE 18A EDUCATION (US) 1767, **3015**

NEW JERSEY SUCCESS *CEASED.* (US/0886-9995) [11694676] **698**

NEW JERSEY. SUPERIOR COURT See REPORTS OF CASES ARGUED AND DETERMINED IN THE SUPERIOR COURT, APPELLATE DIVISION, CHANCERY DIVISION, LAW DIVISION, AND IN THE COUNTY COURTS OF THE STATE OF NEW JERSEY **3038**

NEW JERSEY TAX HANDBOOK (US/0147-2844) [03139490] **4738**

NEW JERSEY TEACHER AND SPECIAL SERVICES PERSONNEL SALARIES (US) [05535402] 1767, **1694**

NEW JERSEY TEACHER SALARIES (US) [09871232] **1901**

NEW JERSEY TRACK (US) 4864, **2600**

NEW JERSEY TRAFFIC DIRECTORY (STATEWIDE ED.), THE (US/1059-8545) [24804412] **5442**

NEW JERSEY TRIAL LAWYER, THE (US/1051-8746) [17241249] **3015**

NEW JERSEY/USEPA REGION II WATER RESOURCES MANAGEMENT AGREEMENT (US/0730-6369) [06855205] **5536**

NEW JERSEY. VIOLENT CRIMES COMPENSATION BOARD See ANNUAL REPORT OF THE VIOLENT CRIMES COMPENSATION BOARD (NEWARK) **3157**

NEW JERSEY WATER SUPPLY AUTHORITY See ANNUAL REPORT / NEW JERSEY WATER SUPPLY AUTHORITY **5529**

NEW JERSEY WOMAN MAGAZINE (US) **5562**

NEW JERSEY ZIP+4 STATE DIRECTORY (US) [11525705] **1146**

NEW JOURNAL (NEW HAVEN, CONN.), THE (US/0028-6001) [02537380] **1093**

NEW JOURNAL OF CHEMISTRY (1987) (FR/1144-0546) [15723556] **987**

NEW JOURNALIST (AT/0310-365X) [06810977] **2922**

NEW JUDEA See SIYYON **5052**

NEW KIT CAR MONTHLY, THE (US/0745-5860) [09306139] **5421**

NEW KOREA (LOS ANGELES, CALIF.) *CEASED.* (US/1054-5891) [15032553] **5637**

NEW LANGUAGE PLANNING NEWSLETTER (II) [17207202] **3305**

NEW LAUREL REVIEW (US/0145-8388) [02409827] 359, **3415**

NEW LAW FOR SURVEYORS (UK/0264-8121) [02648121] 3015, **4842**

NEW LAW JOURNAL, THE (UK/0306-6479) [01759879] **3015**

NEW LEADER (NEW YORK, N.Y.), THE (US/0028-6044) [01643783] **4543**

NEW LEADERS, THE (US/1065-1306) [26513498] **880**

NEW LEFT REVIEW (UK/0028-6060) [01605213] **4544**

NEW LETTERS (US/0146-4930) [01759882] **3416**

NEW LETTERS REVIEW OF BOOKS *SUSPENDED.* (US) [16583470] **3416**

NEW LIBRARY SCENE, THE (US/0735-8571) [08888408] **3234**

NEW LIBRARY WORLD (UK/0307-4803) [01759883] **3234**

NEW LIFE (AT) **5777**

NEW LIFE (DENVER) *SUSPENDED.* (US/0363-6968) [02246971] **5065**

NEW LIFE (HOLLYWOOD, CALIF.) (US/8750-7196) [11693212] **2540**

NEW LINK (CN/0824-6076) [11046443] **2748**

NEW LITERARY HISTORY (US/0028-6087) [01296558] **3348**

NEW LITERATURE & IDEOLOGY (CN/0702-7532) [02670052] 4544, **3416**

NEW LITERATURE ON OLD AGE (UK/0140-2447) [12227977] **5180**

NEW LITERATURE REVIEW (AT/0314-7495) [05981023] **3348**

NEW LITURGY. BULLETIN OF THE NATIONAL SECRETARIAT, IRISH EPISCOPAL COMMISSION FOR LITURGY (IE) [01780272] **5033**

NEW LONDON JOURNAL, THE (US) [14055745] **5672**

NEW MAP OF THE EUROPEAN PULP & PAPER INDUSTRY (BE) **4235**

NEW MARITIMES (CN/0713-4789) [09340495] **5790**

NEW MATERIALS INTERNATIONAL (UK/0954-3538) [09543538] **1619**

NEW MATERIALS/JAPAN (UK/0265-3443) [10522945] **2107**

NEW MATERIALS KOREA (NE/0952-6196) [18348975] **2107**

NEW MATERIALS WORLD (UK/0955-4777) [09554777] **5132**

NEW MATERIALS WORLD (UK) **698**

NEW MATHEMATICAL LIBRARY (US/0548-5932) [09678175] **3524**

NEW MATURE WOMAN (US/1053-1351) [22460758] **5562**

NEW MEDIA IN EDUCATION & ENTERTAINMENT (US/1062-7839) [25739654] 1767, **763**

NEW MEDIA IN EDUCATION AND ENTERTAINMENT See MULTIMEDIA BUSINESS REPORT **1117**

NEW MEDIA MARKETS (UK) [19641802] **934**

NEW MEDIA NEWS (BOSTON, MASS.) (US/1046-8684) [19769765] **1197**

NEW MEDIA SHOWCASE (US/1063-6471) [25215995] **1234**

NEW MEDICAL SCIENCE (US/0748-8777) [11031773] **3620**

NEW MEDICINES IN DEVELOPMENT FOR CHILDREN / PRESENTED BY THE PHARMACEUTICAL MANUFACTURERS ASSOCIATION (US) [23364390] **4317**

NEW MENORAH (US/0883-0215) [12032666] **4981**

NEW MERCERSBURG REVIEW, THE (US/0895-7460) [13897197] **4981**

NEW METHODS IN DRUG RESEARCH (SP/0213-411X) [12626812] **4317**

NEW METHODS (SAN FRANCISCO, CALIF.) (US/0277-3015) [07532135] **5517**

NEW METRO NEWS (US) **5661**

NEW MEXICAN (SANTA FE, N.M. : 1951) See SANTA FE NEW MEXICAN, THE **5713**

NEW MEXICO AGRICULTURAL STATISTICS (US/0077-8540) [05627799] 112, **155**

NEW MEXICO ALMANAC, THE (US/0360-1048) [02243704] **4669**

NEW MEXICO ARCHITECTURE *SUSPENDED.* (US/0545-3151) [05669466] **304**

NEW MEXICO. ATTORNEY GENERAL'S OFFICE See OPINION / STATE OF NEW MEXICO, OFFICE OF THE ATTORNEY GENERAL, DEPARTMENT OF JUSTICE **3142**

NEW MEXICO. ATTORNEY GENERAL'S OFFICE See IN THE PUBLIC INTEREST / OFFICE OF THE ATTORNEY GENERAL (NEW MEXICO) **3165**

NEW MEXICO. ATTORNEY GENERAL'S OFFICE See ANNUAL REPORT / OFFICE OF THE ATTORNEY GENERAL, DEPARTMENT OF JUSTICE, STATE OF NEW MEXICO **3139**

NEW MEXICO. BEHAVIORAL HEALTH SERVICES DIVISION See FOCUS ON BEHAVIORAL HEALTH **4587**

NEW MEXICO BEVERAGE ANALYST (US/0194-813X) [05034681] **2370**

NEW MEXICO. BOARD OF NURSING See NEW MEXICO BOARD OF NURSING ANNUAL REPORT TO GOVERNOR **3862**

NEW MEXICO BOARD OF NURSING ANNUAL REPORT TO GOVERNOR (US/0362-7438) [02315814] **3862**

NEW MEXICO. BUREAU OF GEOLOGY *See* NEW MEXICO'S ENERGY RESOURCES ... : ANNUAL REPORT OF BUREAU OF GEOLOGY IN THE MINING AND MINERALS DIVISION OF NEW MEXICO ENERGY AND MINERALS DEPARTMENT / COMPILED BY EMERY C. ARNOLD, DIRECTOR, (MINING AND MINERALS DIVISION), AND JAMES M. HILL, CHIEF (BUREAU OF GEOLOGY) **1951**

NEW MEXICO. BUREAU OF MINES AND MINERAL RESOURCES *See* OPEN FILE REPORT (SOCORRO, N.M.) **2147**

NEW MEXICO. BUREAU OF MINES AND MINERAL RESOURCES *See* BULLETIN - NEW MEXICO BUREAU OF MINES & MINERAL RESOURCES **2135**

NEW MEXICO. BUREAU OF MINES AND MINERAL RESOURCES *See* MEMOIR - NEW MEXICO BUREAU OF MINES & MINERAL RESOURCES **2143**

NEW MEXICO BUSINESS CURRENT ECONOMIC REPORT (US/0889-5937) [07293658] **1507, 1536**

NEW MEXICO BUSINESS JOURNAL (US/0164-6796) [04408579] **698**

NEW MEXICO BUSINESS NEWS *See* NEW MEXICO BUSINESS WEEKLY **698**

NEW MEXICO BUSINESS WEEKLY (US) **698**

NEW MEXICO CIVIL TRIAL REPORTER (US/0276-8127) [06404736] **3090**

NEW MEXICO DENTAL JOURNAL (US/0028-6176) [01809711] **1330**

NEW MEXICO. DEPARTMENT OF GAME AND FISH *See* ANNUAL REPORT - NEW MEXICO DEPARTMENT OF GAME AND FISH **2294**

NEW MEXICO. DEPT. OF ALCOHOLIC BEVERAGE CONTROL. OFFICE OF DIRECTOR *See* REPORT OF ACTIVITIES - NEW MEXICO. DEPT. OF ALCOHOLIC BEVERAGE CONTROL **2370**

NEW MEXICO DIGEST (CLOVIS), THE (US/0145-2665) [02723677] **1575**

NEW MEXICO EDUCATIONAL PERSONNEL DIRECTORY (US) [01586835] **1867**

NEW MEXICO. ENVIRONMENTAL IMPROVEMENT DIVISION *See* ANNUAL EVALUATION - NEW MEXICO. ENVIRONMENTAL IMPROVEMENT DIVISION **2160**

NEW MEXICO EPIDEMIOLOGY REPORT (US/8750-4642) [10963702] **3736**

NEW MEXICO FARM AND RANCH (US/0028-6192) [04130984] **112**

NEW MEXICO FOLKLORE RECORD, THE (US/0160-2330) [02537455] **2323**

NEW MEXICO FOREST PRODUCTS DIRECTORY (US/0094-2782) [01793476] **2389**

NEW MEXICO. FORESTRY DIVISION *See* REPORT OF ACTIVITIES - NEW MEXICO FORESTRY DIVISION **2392**

NEW MEXICO GENEALOGIST (US) [07627924] **2462**

NEW MEXICO GEOLOGICAL SOCIETY *See* SPECIAL PUBLICATION - NEW MEXICO GEOLOGICAL SOCIETY **1398**

NEW MEXICO GEOLOGICAL SOCIETY *See* GUIDEBOOK - NEW MEXICO GEOLOGICAL SOCIETY **1382**

NEW MEXICO GEOLOGY (US/0196-948X) [04710331] **1389**

NEW MEXICO. GOVERNOR *See* CAPITAL BUDGET **4716**

NEW MEXICO. GOVERNOR'S COMMITTEE ON CONCERNS OF THE HANDICAPPED *See* ANNUAL REPORT / NEW MEXICO, GOVERNOR'S COMMITTEE ON CONCERNS OF THE HANDICAPPED **5272**

NEW MEXICO. GOVERNOR'S OFFICE OF EMPLOYMENT AND TRAINING ADMINISTRATION *See* ANNUAL REPORT TO GOVERNOR ... ON EMPLOYMENT AND TRAINING ACTIVITIES THROUGHOUT NEW MEXICO DURING FISCAL YEAR ... **1650**

●NEW MEXICO HEALTH CARE IN PERSPECTIVE (US/1065-4321) [26605939] **4793**

NEW MEXICO HIGHLANDS UNIVERSITY *See* ALUMNI DIRECTORY / NEW MEXICO HIGHLANDS UNIVERSITY **1099**

NEW MEXICO. HIGHLANDS UNIVERSITY, LAS VEGAS *See* JOURNAL - NEW MEXICO HIGHLANDS UNIVERSITY **1832**

NEW MEXICO ... HIGHWAY STATISTICS AND RELATED INFORMATION (US/0731-017X) [08078774] **5401**

NEW MEXICO HISTORICAL REVIEW (US/0028-6206) [01759913] **2748**

NEW MEXICO HUMANITIES REVIEW *CEASED.* (US/0738-9671) [04891866] **2851**

NEW MEXICO IN PERSPECTIVE (US/1065-5794) [26665986] **5334**

NEW MEXICO INDEPENDENT, THE (US/0193-5356) [05229325] **5712**

NEW MEXICO JOURNAL OF READING, THE (US/0889-4604) [08185636] **1767**

NEW MEXICO JOURNAL OF SCIENCE (US/0270-3017) [04940863] **5132**

NEW MEXICO. JUDICIAL COUNCIL *See* ANNUAL REPORT OF THE JUDICIAL COUNCIL OF NEW MEXICO **2934**

NEW MEXICO LABOR MARKET REVIEW (US) [05756159] **1694**

NEW MEXICO LAW REVIEW (US/0028-6214) [01759914] **3015**

NEW MEXICO LAWYER (US) **3016**

NEW MEXICO. LEGISLATURE. FINANCE COMMITTEE *See* BUDGET ANALYSES OF STATE AGENCIES : REPORT OF THE LEGISLATIVE FINANCE COMMITTEE TO THE ... LEGISLATURE **4714**

NEW MEXICO. LEGISLATURE. FINANCE COMMITTEE. BUDGET ANALYSES, SELECTED STATE AGENCIES *See* BUDGET ANALYSES OF STATE AGENCIES : REPORT OF THE LEGISLATIVE FINANCE COMMITTEE TO THE ... LEGISLATURE **4714**

NEW MEXICO LIBRARY ASSOCIATION *See* NEWSLETTER - NEW MEXICO LIBRARY ASSOCIATION **3235**

NEW MEXICO LIBRARY DIRECTORY (US) [04719496] **3234**

NEW MEXICO LIBRARY STATISTICS (US/0278-9329) [05826093] **3234, 3259**

NEW MEXICO LOCAL GOVERNMENTS AND THE PROPERTY TAX (US) [04896594] **4738**

NEW MEXICO MAGAZINE (SANTA FE, N.M. : 1974) (US/0028-6249) [01759915] **2540**

NEW MEXICO MILITARY INSTITUTE *See* ALUMNI DIRECTORY / NEW MEXICO MILITARY INSTITUTE **1099**

NEW MEXICO MUSICIAN, THE (US/0742-8278) [07897485] **4140**

NEW MEXICO NURSE (US/0028-6273) [04130996] **3862**

NEW MEXICO. OFFICE OF STATE GEOLOGIST. NEW MEXICO'S ENERGY RESOURCES *See* NEW MEXICO'S ENERGY RESOURCES ... : ANNUAL REPORT OF BUREAU OF GEOLOGY IN THE MINING AND MINERALS DIVISION OF NEW MEXICO ENERGY AND MINERALS DEPARTMENT / COMPILED BY EMERY C. ARNOLD, DIRECTOR, (MINING AND MINERALS DIVISION), AND JAMES M. HILL, CHIEF (BUREAU OF GEOLOGY) **1951**

NEW MEXICO. OFFICE OF STATE TREASURER *See* FINANCIAL REPORT / STATE OF NEW MEXICO, OFFICE OF STATE TREASURER **4725**

NEW MEXICO PROFESSIONAL ENGINEER (1977) (US/0149-1954) [03441709] **1988**

NEW MEXICO PROGRESS, THE (US/0896-6478) [04867451] **5298**

NEW MEXICO. PROPERTY TAX DIVISION *See* ANNUAL REPORT - TAXATION & REVENUE DEPARTMENT, PROPERTY TAX DIVISION **4710**

NEW MEXICO. PROPERTY TAX DIVISION *See* ASSESSMENT/SALES RATIO STUDY **4711**

NEW MEXICO QUARTER HORSE, THE (US/0886-4241) [12885905] **2801**

NEW MEXICO. REAL ESTATE COMMISSION *See* ANNUAL REPORT - NEW MEXICO. REAL ESTATE COMMISSION **4834**

NEW MEXICO REAL ESTATE LAW REPORTER (US/0951-547X) [18262159] **4842, 3016**

NEW MEXICO. REGULATION AND LICENSING DEPT *See* ANNUAL REPORT / STATE OF NEW MEXICO, REGULATION & LICENSING DEPARTMENT **4629**

NEW MEXICO RESEARCH AND DEVELOPMENT INSTITUTE *See* ANNUAL REPORT / NEW MEXICO RESEARCH AND DEVELOPMENT INSTITUTE **1932**

NEW MEXICO. SECRETARY OF STATE *See* STATE OF NEW MEXICO OFFICIAL RETURNS ... GENERAL AND PRIMARY RETURNS **4688**

NEW MEXICO STATE BOARD OF PSYCHOLOGIST EXAMINERS *See* ANNUAL REPORT TO THE GOVERNOR / NEW MEXICO STATE BOARD OF PSYCHOLOGIST EXAMINERS **4574**

NEW MEXICO. STATE ENGINEER *See* BIENNIAL REPORT OF THE STATE ENGINEER OF NEW MEXICO **2019**

NEW MEXICO. STATE HEALTH PLANNING AND DEVELOPMENT BUREAU *See* NEW MEXICO STATE MEDICAL FACILITIES PLAN **3620**

NEW MEXICO STATE LAND OFFICE *See* ANNUAL REPORT / NEW MEXICO STATE LAND OFFICE **4628**

NEW MEXICO STATE MEDICAL FACILITIES PLAN (US/0196-4852) [05759280] **3620**

NEW MEXICO. STATE PARK AND RECREATION COMMISSION *See* ANNUAL REPORT - STATE PARK AND RECREATION COMMISSION **4848**

NEW MEXICO STATE POLICE *See* UNIFORM CRIME REPORTING **3178**

NEW MEXICO STATE UNIVERSITY. AGRICULTURAL EXPERIMENT STATION *See* RESEARCH REPORT - AGRICULTURAL EXPERIMENT STATION **127**

NEW MEXICO STATISTICAL ABSTRACT *SUSPENDED.* (US/0077-8575) [04573358] **1536**

NEW MEXICO. SUPREME COURT *See* REPORT OF CASES DETERMINED IN THE SUPREME COURT AND COURT OF APPEALS OF THE STATE OF NEW MEXICO **3038**

NEW MEXICO. UNEMPLOYMENT INSURANCE DIVISION. ACTUARIAL RESEARCH SECTION *See* FACTS AND FIGURES: NEW MEXICO EMPLOYERS, INDUSTRY, SIZE, AND LOCATION **1669**

NEW MEXICO. UNIVERSITY. ART MUSEUM *See* BULLETIN - THE UNIVERSITY OF NEW MEXICO ART MUSEUM **4086**

NEW MEXICO. UNIVERSITY. DIVISION OF GOVERNMENT RESEARCH *See* PUBLICATIONS - NEW MEXICO. UNIVERSITY. DIVISION OF GOVERNMENT RESEARCH **1843**

NEW MEXICO. UNIVERSITY. GENERAL LIBRARY *See* SOURCES (ALBUQUERQUE) **3250**

NEW MEXICO. VETERANS' SERVICE COMMISSION *See* REPORT OF THE NEW MEXICO VETERANS' SERVICE COMMISSION **4681**

NEW MEXICO WATER RESOURCES RESEARCH INSTITUTE *See* WRRI REPORT **5549**

NEW MEXICO WILDLIFE (US/0028-6338) [01608350] **2200**

NEW MEXICO'S ENERGY RESOURCES ... : ANNUAL REPORT OF BUREAU OF GEOLOGY IN THE MINING AND MINERALS DIVISION OF NEW MEXICO ENERGY AND MINERALS DEPARTMENT / COMPILED BY EMERY C. ARNOLD, DIRECTOR, (MINING AND MINERALS DIVISION), AND JAMES M. HILL, CHIEF (BUREAU OF GEOLOGY) (US) [08269661] **1389, 1951**

NEW MIAMI (US/1059-4140) [24584567] **698**

NEW MILFORD TIMES, THE (US) [27154944] **5646**

NEW MISCELLANY, THE (II) [25806493] **3416**

NEW MOBILITY (US) **3970**

NEW MODEL MAGAZINE (JA) **2624**

NEW MODEL PRODUCT INFORMATION MANUAL, PONTIAC (US) [07381043] **5421**

●NEW MOTHER (1992) (CN/1193-9397) [28061937] **2284**

NEW MOTON GUIDE TO AMERICAN COLLEGES WITH A BLACK HERITAGE, THE (US/0882-9462) [09561049] **2269, 1837**

NEW MOTOR VEHICLE SALES (MONTHLY ED.) (CN/0705-5595) [15466038] **5421, 5401**

NEW MUSIC (CN/0706-7984) [05071915] **4140**

NEW MUSIC NEWS (US/0197-5994) [06054351] **4140**

NEW MUSIC PERFORMANCE AND CHAMBER MUSIC / NATIONAL ENDOWMENT FOR THE ARTS (US) [05350411] **4140**

NEW MUSICAL EXPRESS. MICROFORM, THE (UK/0028-6362) [19258465] **5812**

NEW MYSTERY (US/1048-8324) [21049955] **3416**

NEW MYTHS (US/1055-9868) [22871377] **3416**

NEW NATION, THE (SA) [23010855] **5810**

NEW NIGERIAN (NR) [02546926] **5807**

NEW NIGERIANA (NR) [01784738] **420**

●NEW NONWOVENS WORLD, THE (US/1065-5247) [26625922] **5354**

NEW NORWAY CURRENT *See* NORWAY CURRENT, THE **5693**

NEW OBSERVATIONS (US/0737-5387) [09410530] **326, 3416**

NEW OFFICIAL GUIDE: JAPAN, THE (JA/0077-8591) [02264892] **2660**

NEW

NEW ON THE CHARTS (US/0276-7031) [05050675] **4140**

NEW OPTIONS *CEASED.* (US/0890-1619) [12983146] 5252, **4529**

NEW ORCHIDS (JA/0914-3238) [I09143238] **2425**

NEW ORDER (LINCOLN, NEB.), THE (US/0740-3283) [06631486] **4544**

NEW ORLEANS ACADEMY OF OPHTHALMOLOGY *See* TRANSACTIONS OF THE NEW ORLEANS ACADEMY OF OPHTHALMOLOGY **3879**

NEW ORLEANS CITIBUSINESS (US/0279-4527) [07897948] **698**

NEW ORLEANS, FRESH FRUIT AND VEGETABLE WHOLESALE MARKET PRICES (US) [03595314] 934, **112**

NEW ORLEANS GENESIS, THE (US/0548-6424) [06281747] **2462**

NEW ORLEANS JAZZ STUDY NEWSLETTER / NATIONAL PARK SERVICE/DENVER SERVICE CENTER (US) [24602041] **4707**

NEW ORLEANS MAGAZINE (1988) (US/0897-8174) [17635299] **2540**

NEW ORLEANS MARDI GRAS GUIDE (US/0195-3605) [04122610] **5485**

NEW ORLEANS MENU, THE (US/8756-498X) [08758053] 5072, **2351**

NEW ORLEANS MUSIC (UK/0308-1990) [21116746] **4140**

NEW ORLEANS OIL DIRECTORY (US) **4266**

NEW ORLEANS REVIEW, THE (US/0028-6400) [01835581] **3348**

NEW ORLEANS SUBURBAN (JEFFERSON AND ST. BERNARD PARISHES, LA.) DIRECTORY (US) [05916262] **2570**

NEW OUTLOOK (UK) [01793908] **2520**

NEW OUTLOOK (TEL AVIV) *CEASED.* (IS/0028-6427) [01587013] **4529**

NEW OXFORD REVIEW (US/0149-4244) [03489884] **4981**

NEW PACIFIC (SEATTLE, WASH.), THE (US/1050-3080) [20998812] **2540**

NEW PAGES (US/0271-8197) [06685717] **4817**

NEW PALTZ NEWS COMBINED WITH THE WALLKILL VALLEY WORLD, THE (US) [23173249] **5718**

NEW PARADIGM DIGEST (US/1062-0443) [25510919] **5252**

NEW PARENT ADVISER (US/0278-0976) [07701662] **2284**

●NEW PARKS NORTH (CN/1189-4512) [26498108] **4707**

NEW PATRIOT (CHICAGO, ILL. 1988) (US/0047-9829) [19346231] **3348**

NEW PATRIOT, THE (US/0098-3314) [02239887] **4052**

NEW PATTERNS OF LEARNING (US/0275-9578) [07252433] **4605**

NEW PERFORMANCE (US/0277-514X) [06069614] **1314**

NEW PERSPECTIVE (HAMILTON) (CN/0715-4445) [09336399] **2269**

NEW PERSPECTIVES (ARMDALE) (CN/1180-4963) [23598345] **1901**

NEW PERSPECTIVES ON CHILE (US) [21582951] **1768**

NEW PERSPECTIVES ON TURKEY (TU/0896-6346) [17250535] **5210**

NEW PERSPECTIVES QUARTERLY (US/0893-7850) [14636448] **4484**

NEW PHILIPPINES (PH) [01793278] **1575**

NEW PHILOSOPHY, THE (US/0028-6443) [02138799] **4353**

NEW PHYSICIAN (US/0028-6451) [01759936] **3620**

NEW PHYTOLOGIST, THE (UK/0028-646X) [01759937] **519**

NEW PITTSBURGH COURIER (CITY ED.) (US/1047-8051) [07476291] **5738**

NEW PITTSBURGH COURIER (NATIONAL ED.) (US/1047-806X) [07163927] **5738**

●NEW PLANTSMAN, THE (UK/1352-4186) [30313544] **2425**

NEW POETRY (UK/0548-6505) [05980683] **3466**

NEW POETS (UK) [01784511] **3466**

NEW POET'S HANDBOOK / THE LEAGUE OF CANADIAN POETS (CN/0827-2425) [11734404] **3466**

NEW POETS SERIES, THE (US/0277-2752) [05343872] **3467**

NEW POLISH PUBLICATIONS *CEASED.* (PL/0028-6486) [01590666] **4817**

NEW POLITICAL SCIENCE (US/0739-3148) [05019879] **4484**

NEW POLITICS (US/0028-6494) [01604184] **4544**

NEW POLYMERIC MATERIALS (NE) [17536663] **987**

NEW PRESS (QUEENS, N.Y.), THE (US/0894-6078) [16145970] **3416**

NEW PRODUCT DEVELOPMENT *SUSPENDED.* (US/0733-8252) [08673372] **934**

NEW PRODUCT DIRECTORY OF NEW YORK STOCK EXCHANGE LISTED COMPANIES, THE (US/0094-8918) [01795794] **1619**

NEW PRODUCT, NEW BUSINESS DIGEST *CEASED.* (US/0161-0740) [03825089] **699**

NEW PRODUCT REPORT, THE (UK) **934**

NEW PRODUCTS REVIEW (UK) 934, **405**

●NEW PROFESSIONAL SURVEY, THE (US/1064-8267) [26409650] **4207**

●NEW PROFESSIONAL, THE (US/1064-8259) [26409637] **4207**

NEW PROPERTY CASES (UK) **3016**

NEW PSYCHOLOGIST (UK) [04259279] **4605**

NEW PUBLICATIONS OF THE BUREAU OF MINES (US) [15642233] **2147**

NEW PUBLICATIONS OF THE GEOLOGICAL SURVEY (US/0364-2461) [01768428] **1389**

NEW PUBLICATIONS (UNITED STATES. BUREAU OF MINES) (US/0364-1376) [01348790] **2147**

NEW QUARTERLY (CN/0227-0455) [08099429] **3416**

NEW QUARTERLY (NEW YORK), THE (US/0147-2720) [03127971] **2490**

NEW QUEST (II/0258-0381) [03969886] **5252**

NEW RAIN (US/0899-3440) [18068200] **3416**

NEW RAMBLER (UK/0028-6540) [01640235] **3416**

NEW RECORD MIRROR (UK) **4140**

NEW RELEASES / ENERGY INFORMATION ADMINISTRATION (US) [15000853] **1951**

NEW RELIGIONS NEWSLETTER (CN/0704-5883) [03304643] **4981**

NEW RELIGIOUS MOVEMENTS (US/1040-0974) [18320017] **4981**

NEW RENAISSANCE, THE (US/0028-6575) [02290784] 3416, **326**

NEW REPUBLIC (NEW YORK, N.Y.) (US/0028-6583) [01759945] **2851**

NEW RESEARCH CENTERS (US/0028-6591) [01153938] **5132**

NEW RESEARCH IN MENTAL HEALTH (US/8756-260X) [04645346] 3931, **4793**

NEW RESEARCH REPORTS (US/0895-5093) [16668197] **1619**

NEW REVIEW *See* CLACKAMAS COUNTY REVIEW, THE **5733**

NEW REVIEW OF EAST-EUROPEAN HISTORY (US/0381-9140) [02585423] **2700**

NEW REVIEW OF THE LOW PAY UNIT, THE (UK) [22367343] **1694**

NEW RIVER REVIEW (US/0360-1455) [02243928] **3416**

NEW RUSSIAN WORD (US) [01760884] **5718**

NEW SCANDINAVIAN TECHNOLOGY (SW/1100-956X) [I1100956X] **5132**

NEW SCHOLAR, THE (US/0028-6613) [01642814] **5210**

NEW SCHOOL OBSERVER, THE (US/0883-6248) [06414160] **1093**

●NEW SCHOOLS, NEW COMMUNITIES (US/1077-2936) **1768**

●NEW SCIENCE CENTERS SUPPORT PROGRAM INFORMATION SERVICE BULLETIN (US/1065-917X) [26791774] **5132**

NEW SCIENTIST (1971) (UK/0262-4079) [02378350] **5132**

NEW SENSE BULLETIN (US/1057-0705) [23882555] **4605**

NEW SERIAL TITLES (US/0028-6680) [01759958] **3234**

NEW SERIES (US) [12377316] **3416**

NEW SERIES (SA/0576-6842) [03013422] **1837**

NEW SERMON BUILDER *See* SERMON BUILDER, THE **4996**

NEW SERVICE STATION AND PARTS BUYER (UK/0264-2603) [I02642603] **699**

NEW SETTLER'S GUIDE FOR WASHINGTON, D.C. AND COMMUNITIES IN NEARBY MARYLAND AND VIRGINIA, THE (US/0097-8213) [01799500] **2829**

NEW SHARON STAR, THE (US) [11040598] **5672**

NEW SKILLS FOR PROGRESS : MDTA (US/0098-0021) [01799566] **1694**

NEW SOCIALIST (DENVER, COLO.), THE (US/0731-034X) [08102012] **4544**

NEW SOLIDARITY *CEASED.* (US/0028-6737) [02945463] **2540**

NEW SOLIDARITY INTERNATIONAL PRESS SERVICE WEEKLY NEWS *See* EXECUTIVE INTELLIGENCE REVIEW **1490**

NEW SOLUTIONS (US/1048-2911) [20909869] **4793**

NEW SOURCES OF GRANTS AND AID FOR BUSINESS IN THE UK (UK) [17262242] **699**

NEW SOUTH WALES *See* GOVERNMENT GAZETTE OF THE STATE OF NEW SOUTH WALES **4651**

NEW SOUTH WALES ACTS PAMPHLETS (AT) **4669**

NEW SOUTH WALES. BUSH FIRE COUNCIL. BULLETIN *See* SITREP **5307**

NEW SOUTH WALES COAL INDUSTRY PROFILE (AT/1030-4851) [I10304851] **2147**

NEW SOUTH WALES. DEPT. OF AGRICULTURE. DIVISION OF DAIRYING *See* OFFICIAL HERD RECORDING STATISTICS **155**

NEW SOUTH WALES. DEPT. OF AGRICULTURE. DIVISION OF DAIRYING *See* OFFICIAL PRODUCTION RECORDS OF PURE BRED REGISTERED DAIRY COWS IN NEW SOUTH WALES **217**

NEW SOUTH WALES. DEPT. OF AGRICULTURE. ENTOMOLOGY BRANCH *See* ENTOMOLOGY BRANCH INSECT PEST BULLETIN **4244**

NEW SOUTH WALES. DEPT. OF INDUSTRIAL RELATIONS *See* NEW SOUTH WALES INDUSTRIAL GAZETTE **3152**

NEW SOUTH WALES. DEPT. OF MAIN ROADS *See* ANNUAL REPORT / COMMISSIONER FOR MAIN ROADS **5438**

NEW SOUTH WALES. DEPT. OF MINERAL RESOURCES *See* ANNUAL REPORT FOR THE YEAR ENDING JUNE 30TH ... **2133**

NEW SOUTH WALES. DEPT. OF MINERAL RESOURCES AND DEVELOPMENT. ANNUAL REPORT *See* ANNUAL REPORT FOR THE YEAR ENDING JUNE 30TH ... **2133**

NEW SOUTH WALES. DEPT. OF WATER RESOURCES *See* ANNUAL REPORT / DEPARTMENT OF WATER RESOURCES **5529**

NEW SOUTH WALES. FORESTRY COMMISSION *See* TECHNICAL PUBLICATION **2396**

NEW SOUTH WALES. FORESTRY COMMISSION *See* TECHNICAL PAPER - FORESTRY COMMISSION OF NEW SOUTH WALES **2396**

NEW SOUTH WALES. FORESTRY COMMISSION *See* RESEARCH REPORT - FORESTRY COMMISSION OF N.S.W **2393**

NEW SOUTH WALES GOVERNMENT DEPARTMENT LIBRARIES (AT) [09106679] **3234**

NEW SOUTH WALES INDUSTRIAL GAZETTE (AT/0028-677X) [07494256] **3152**

NEW SOUTH WALES LAW REPORTS (AT/0312-1674) [01773475] **3016**

NEW SOUTH WALES. LOCAL GOVERNMENT APPEALS TRIBUNAL *See* LOCAL GOVERNMENT APPEALS TRIBUNAL REPORTS OF NEW SOUTH WALES, THE **3004**

NEW SOUTH WALES MINERAL INDUSTRY REVIEW (AT/0727-5757) [I07275757] **2147**

NEW SOUTH WALES. PARLIAMENT. *See* BUDGET ESTIMATES / PARLIAMENT OF NEW SOUTH WALES **4634**

NEW SOUTH WALES. PARLIAMENT. LIBRARY *See* CATALOGUE OF BOOKS ADDED TO THE NEW SOUTH WALES PARLIAMENTARY LIBRARY FROM THE ... WITH SUBJECT-INDEX **3200**

NEW SOUTH WALES PRODUCTION & MARKETING REPORT. PIGS (AT) [11835122] **216**

NEW SOUTH WALES. RURAL ASSISTANCE BOARD *See* REPORT OF THE RURAL ASSISTANCE BOARD **126**

NEW SOUTH WALES. SOIL CONSERVATION SERVICE *See* ANNUAL REPORT / SOIL CONSERVATION SERVICE OF NSW **163**

NEW SOUTH WALES. STATE EMERGENCY SERVICES. BULLETIN *See* SITREP **5307**

NEW SOUTH WALES. STATE FISHERIES *See* REPORT OF THE NEW SOUTH WALES STATE FISHERIES FOR THE YEAR ENDED ... **2311**

NEW SOUTH WALES. UNIVERSITY, KENSINGTON. FACULTY OF MEDICINE *See* HANDBOOK - FACULTY OF MEDICINE, UNIVERSITY OF NEW SOUTH WALES **3580**

NEW SOUTH WALES. WORKERS' COMPENSATION COMMISSION See WORKERS' COMPENSATION REPORTS **3076**

NEW SOUTH WALES YEAR BOOK (AT/0085-4441) [07957504] **2510**

NEW SOUTHERN LITERARY MESSENGER, THE (US/0730-515X) [08016195] **3416**

NEW SPEAKERS AND LECTURERS (US/0731-2466) [08144251] **3306**

NEW SPIRIT (US/0190-1168) [04629085] **5298**

NEW STATESMAN & SOCIETY (UK/0954-2361) [18076586] **5210**

NEW STATUTES AFFECTING THE CRIMINAL LAW (US) [06275340] **3108**

● NEW STEEL (US/1074-1690) [29043579] **4013**

NEW STEEL CONSTRUCTION (UK) **622**

NEW STRAITS TIMES (MY) [08372855] **5806**

NEW STRAITS TIMES ANNUAL, THE (MY) [02858465] **2660**

NEW STUDIES IN AESTHETICS (US/0893-6005) [15600283] 4353, **359**

NEW STUDIES IN ATHLETICS (UK/0961-933X) [I0961933X] **4907**

NEW STUDIES IN THEOLOGY (UK) [06856480] **4981**

NEW STUDIES ON THE LEFT (US/1059-7395) [21076142] **5210**

NEW SUNDAY TIMES, MALAYSIA (MY) [09947555] **5806**

NEW SURGICAL TRENDS AND INTEGRATED THERAPIES IN ENDOMETRIAL, VULVAR, TROPHOBLASTIC NEOPLASIAS, ACTUALITY OF SURGICAL STAGING IN GYNAECOLOGICAL MALIGNANCIES-A (II) **3765**

NEW SURGICAL TRENDS AND INTEGRATED THERAPIES IN GYNAECOLOGIC ONCOLOGY: OVARIAN CERVICAL BREAST CANCER-A (IT) **3765**

NEW SYNTHETIC METHODS (GW) [05859246] **1044**

NEW TECH NEWS (US/0897-1137) [17407053] **3234**

NEW TECH NEWS MUNICH (GW/0935-2694) [I09352694] **5133**

NEW TECHNICAL BOOKS (US/0028-6869) [01642674] **987**

NEW TECHNIQUES IN BIOPHYSICS AND CELL BIOLOGY (UK/0301-374X) [01644033] **495**

NEW TECHNOLOGIES BULLETIN / CAMPDEN FOOD & DRINK RESEARCH ASSOCIATION (UK) [23741835] **2351**

NEW TECHNOLOGY IN THE HUMAN SERVICES (UK) [19730074] 1197, **5252**

NEW TECHNOLOGY JAPAN (JA) [14251247] **5133**

NEW TECHNOLOGY WEEK (US/0894-0789) [15746721] **5133**

NEW TECHNOLOGY, WORK, AND EMPLOYMENT (UK/0268-1072) [14252093] 1619, **1694**

NEW TELECOM QUARTERLY (US) **1160**

NEW TESTAMENT ABSTRACTS (US/0028-6877) [01759980] 5018, **5013**

NEW TESTAMENT STUDIES (UK/0028-6885) [01713962] **5018**

NEW TESTAMENT TOOLS AND STUDIES (NE/0077-8842) [01589775] **5018**

NEW THEATRE QUARTERLY : NTQ (UK/0266-464X) [12440003] **5366**

NEW THEOLOGY REVIEW (US/0896-4297) [17152907] **4981**

NEW THOUGHT (SCOTTSDALE, ARIZ.) (US/0146-7832) [02251311] **4981**

NEW TIMES (RU/0206-1473) [04866398] **4529**

● NEW TIMES INTERNATIONAL (RU) [25902144] 4484, **4530**

NEW TIMES (MOBILE, ALA.), THE (US/0885-1662) [10487314] **5627**

NEW TIMES (MOSCOW, R.S.F.S.R.) See NEW TIMES INTERNATIONAL **4530**

NEW TIMES (PHOENIX, ARIZ.) (US/0279-3962) [07820414] **5630**

NEW TIMES (SEATTLE, WASH.) (US/1044-2782) [16913457] **4186**

NEW TIMES : THE JOURNAL OF DEMOCRATIC LEFT (UK/0960-748X) [27870982] **5210**

NEW TITLES IN BIOETHICS (US/0361-6347) [02087813] 2252, **3620**

NEW TONES (II) [01784115] **2507**

NEW TRADE NAMES IN THE RUBBER AND PLASTICS INDUSTRIES (UK/0747-4954) [08097392] 4457, **5076**

NEW TRAIL (1982) (CN/0824-8125) [10595790] **1102**

NEW TREND (BALTIMORE, MD.) (US/0732-1848) [08355209] 5044, **4530**

NEW TRENDS IN ARRHYTHMIAS (IT/0393-5302) [13175686] **3708**

NEW TRENDS IN BIOLOGY TEACHING (FR/0077-8877) [01784389] 1901, **467**

NEW TRENDS IN CHEMISTRY TEACHING (FR) [02239220] **987**

NEW TRENDS IN CLINICAL NEUROPHARMACOLOGY : OFFICIAL JOURNAL OF THE EUROPEAN ASSOCIATION FOR CLINICAL NEUROPHARMACOLOGY (IT/0393-5345) [16650100] 4317, **3843**

NEW TRENDS IN EXPERIMENTAL AND CLINICAL PSYCHIATRY (IT/0393-5310) [13278873] **3931**

NEW TRENDS IN INTEGRATED SCIENCE TEACHING (FR) [01759986] 1901, **5133**

NEW TRENDS IN LIPID MEDIATORS RESEARCH (SZ/1011-6672) [19478239] **467**

NEW TRENDS IN MATHEMATICS TEACHING (US/0077-8893) [02414459] 1901, **3524**

NEW TRENDS IN OPHTHALMOLOGY (IT) **3877**

NEW TRENDS IN PHYSICS TEACHING. TENDANCES NOUVELLES DE L'ENSEIGNEMENT DE LA PHYSIQUE (FR) [01759987] 1901, **4413**

NEW ULM ENTERPRISE (US) [14564023] **5752**

NEW UNIONIST (MINNEAPOLIS, MINN.) (US/1070-7727) [05230392] 4484, **1694**

NEW UNIVERSITY OF ULSTER See REPORT TO THE UNIVERSITY COURT **1844**

NEW USES FOR SULPHUR TECHNOLOGY SERIES (CN/0225-2643) [06136612] **1027**

NEW VICO STUDIES (US/0733-9542) [08675347] **4353**

NEW VIDEO CEASED. (US/0887-9451) [13458816] **4075**

● NEW VIEWS (FORREST CITY, ARK.) (US/1062-9378) [25812249] **2540**

NEW VIRGINIA REVIEW (US/0163-2299) [04320580] **3348**

NEW VISIONS (US) **2269**

NEW VISIONS OF AZTLAN (US) [22135831] **2269**

NEW VISTAS IN COUNSELING SERIES (US/0160-7162) [03725628] 4605, **3620**

NEW VISTAS IN DRUG RESEARCH (AU/0938-9245) [23657455] **4318**

NEW VOICE (LOUISVILLE, KY.) (US/0894-8100) [15503742] **5681**

NEW VOICES (DIEGO MARTIN, TRINIDAD AND TOBAGO) (TR/0387-4185) [05505433] **3416**

NEW VOICES IN AMERICAN POETRY (US/0735-4584) [04204336] **3467**

NEW VOICES IN POETRY AND PROSE (US/1054-9366) [23024550] **3416**

NEW VOICES (NEW PALTZ) (US/0094-4645) [01794300] **3416**

NEW WARRIORS, THE (US/1053-7325) [22620621] **4864**

NEW WASHINGTON HERALD (US) [10084502] **5729**

● NEW WAVE WRESTLING (US/1060-5908) [25039972] **4907**

NEW WAVES (US/0897-5094) [17513925] **5536**

NEW WAYS (EVANSTON, ILL.) (US) [18570273] **3931**

NEW WELSH REVIEW, THE (UK/0954-2116) [19074830] **3416**

NEW WILDERNESS LETTER CEASED. (US/0197-4874) [03381191] **4875**

NEW WOLCOTT ENTERPRISE, THE (US) [15187924] **5666**

NEW WOMAN (US/0028-6974) [02251312] **5562**

NEW WOMEN/NEW CHURCH (US/1043-2221) [06232248] 5562, **4981**

NEW WORDS DIGEST CEASED. (US/1044-8578) [19928025] **1882**

NEW WORLD (1989), THE (US/1043-3538) [19409433] **5033**

NEW WORLD ARCHAEOLOGICAL FOUNDATION See PAPERS OF THE NEW WORLD ARCHAEOLOGICAL FOUNDATION **278**

NEW WORLD JOURNAL (US/0272-6394) [04030840] **2748**

● NEW WORLD OF IRISH NURSING : OFFICIAL JOURNAL OF IRISH NURSES ORGANISATION AND NATIONAL COUNCIL OF NURSES, THE (IE) [28711860] **3862**

NEW WORLD OF TRAVEL, THE (US/0893-1895) [15434187] **5485**

NEW WORLD OUTLOOK (US/0043-8812) [02244899] **5065**

NEW WRITERS (NEW YORK) (US/0092-6698) [01791122] **3416**

NEW WYCLIF SOCIETY NEWSLETTER, THE (CN/0227-5422) [08027924] **4981**

NEW YORK (US) [05958506] **1837**

NEW YORK (1968) (US/0028-7369) [01760010] **2540**

NEW YORK ACADEMY OF MEDICINE. LIBRARY See SUBJECT CATALOG OF THE LIBRARY. SUPPLEMENT **3251**

NEW YORK AFRICAN STUDIES ASSOCIATION See NEW YORK AFRICAN STUDIES ASSOCIATION NEWSLETTER **2642**

NEW YORK AFRICAN STUDIES ASSOCIATION NEWSLETTER (US/0148-7264) [03354531] **2642**

NEW YORK AMSTERDAM NEWS (1962) (US/1059-1818) [13416782] **5718**

NEW YORK AND NEW JERSEY REGIONAL MEDICAL LIBRARY NEWS (US) [04847157] 3620, **3234**

NEW YORK ANNUAL PROGRAM SUMMARY (US/0148-0820) [03265145] **112**

NEW YORK ANTIQUE ALMANAC OF ART, ANTIQUES, INVESTMENTS & YESTERYEAR, THE (US/0738-8365) [09694504] **251**

NEW YORK APPAREL NEWS (US/0279-7844) [07260958] **1086**

NEW YORK ARCHITECTS (US) [23298069] **304**

NEW YORK AUTO REPAIR NEWS (US/0191-4979) [04936267] **5421**

NEW YORK BAPTIST, THE (US/0893-9063) [14995076] **4981**

NEW YORK BEACON (US) **5718**

NEW YORK BEIJING DIRECTORY, THE SUSPENDED. (US/1049-4200) [14226494] **4669**

NEW YORK BOTANICAL GARDEN See NEWSLETTER - NEW YORK BOTANICAL GARDEN **519**

NEW YORK BUSINESS ENVIRONMENT (US/1065-1888) [19301353] **3115**

NEW YORK CARIB NEWS, THE (US/1051-4031) [18335474] **5718**

NEW YORK CAVER See MET GROTTO NEWS **1408**

NEW YORK CHAMBER OF COMMERCE AND INDUSTRY See REPORT OF THE NEW YORK CHAMBER OF COMMERCE AND INDUSTRY **821**

NEW YORK CITY ARTS FUNDING GUIDE (US/8755-7347) [11423942] **326**

NEW YORK CITY CHARTER AND ADMINISTRATIVE CODE, ANNOTATED (US) [01605239] **3016**

NEW YORK (CITY). CHARTERS See NEW YORK CITY CHARTER AND ADMINISTRATIVE CODE, ANNOTATED **3016**

NEW YORK (CITY). CITY COMMISSION ON HUMAN RIGHTS See RESEARCH REPORT - NEW YORK CITY COMMISSION ON HUMAN RIGHTS **4512**

NEW YORK CITY COUNCIL ON ECONOMIC EDUCATION See FACT BOOK : TABLES AND CHARTS ON THE NEW YORK METROPOLITAN REGION **5327**

NEW YORK (CITY). CRIMINAL COURT See ANNUAL REPORT - CRIMINAL COURT OF THE CITY OF NEW YORK **3078**

NEW YORK (CITY). EXECUTIVE CAPITAL BUDGET See EXECUTIVE CAPITAL BUDGET AND CAPITAL PROGRAM - NEW YORK CITY **4723**

NEW YORK CITY FRUIT AND VEGETABLE REPORT (US/0744-317X) [08186500] **112**

NEW YORK CITY JEWISH TRAVEL GUIDE (US) 5051, **5485**

NEW YORK (CITY). MAYOR'S OFFICE OF MODEL CITIES See ANNUAL REPORT - CITY OF NEW YORK, MAYOR'S OFFICE OF MODEL CITIES **2814**

NEW YORK (CITY). OFFICE OF MANAGEMENT AND BUDGET See ADOPTED BUDGET - CITY OF NEW YORK **4624**

NEW YORK CITY POETRY CALENDAR (US/1071-1686) [28589269] **3466**

NEW YORK (CITY). PRACTICING LAW INSTITUTE See UNDERSTANDING FINANCIAL STATEMENTS **752**

NEW YORK (CITY). PUBLIC LIBRARY See NEW TECHNICAL BOOKS **987**

NEW YORK CITY SUBWAY GUIDE (US) **5485**

NEW YORK CITY WHOLESALE FRUIT AND VEGETABLE REPORT (US) [09856231] 112, **2362**

NEW YORK CIVIL LIBERTIES UNION See LEGISLATIVE MEMORANDUM **3002**

NEW YORK CIVIL MOTION CITATOR (US/1043-0628) [08399755] **3016**

NEW YORK CLIMATE (US/0749-4114) [10414487] **1432**

Alphabetical Title Index — NEW

NEW YORK COFFEE AND SUGAR EXCHANGE *See* DAILY MARKET REPORT - NEW YORK COFFEE AND SUGAR EXCHANGE **2332**

NEW YORK CONSTRUCTION NEWS (US/0028-7164) [04127155] **622**

NEW YORK CORPORATION LAW ... WHITEBOOK, WHITE CORPORATION LAW : BUSINESS CORPORATION LAW, NOT-FOR-PROFIT CORPORATION LAW, SELECTIONS FROM RELATED STATUTES AS AMENDED BY THE ... REGULAR LEGISLATIVE SESSION THROUGH ... (US) [23011178] **3102**

NEW YORK COUNTY LAWYERS' ASSOCIATION *See* YEARBOOK - NEW YORK COUNTY LAWYERS' ASSOCIATION **3077**

NEW YORK ... CPLR REDBOOK (US) [08363243] **3090**

NEW YORK CROP REPORTING SERVICE *See* CHERRIES (ALBANY, N.Y.) **166**

NEW YORK DOCTOR, THE (US/0898-6401) [17866156] **3620**

NEW YORK EDUCATION LAW REPORT (US/0896-4122) [17064439] 1768, **3016**

NEW YORK EDUCATORS ASSOCIATION *See* NYEA ADVOCATE **1769**

●NEW YORK EMPLOYMENT LAW LETTER (US/1072-9178) [29236743] **3152**

NEW YORK ENVIRONMENTAL COMPLLIANCE UPDATE (US) **3115**

NEW YORK ENVIRONMENTAL NEWS : NYEN (US/0273-6438) [04749363] **2178**

NEW YORK FAMILY LAW UPDATE (US/1049-6319) [21266364] **3122**

NEW YORK FAMILY PHYSICIAN (US/1065-061X) [03545290] **3738**

NEW YORK FILM ANNEX *See* NEW YORK FILM ANNEX **4075**

NEW YORK FILM ANNEX (US/0884-2744) [12226801] **4075**

NEW YORK FINE PRINT (US/0733-7809) [04408200] **2269**

NEW YORK FOLKLORE (US/0361-204X) [02246165] **2323**

NEW YORK GAME & FISH (US/0897-9189) [17664546] **4875**

NEW YORK GENEALOGICAL AND BIOGRAPHICAL RECORD, THE (US/0028-7237) [01760071] **2462**

NEW YORK GUARDIAN, THE (US/1060-0167) [24875415] **5711**

●NEW YORK HEALTH CARE IN PERSPECTIVE (US/1065-433X) [26605969] **4793**

NEW YORK HERALD TIMES CROSSWORD PUZZLES ONLY (US/0886-9936) [13133483] **4864**

NEW YORK HERALD TRIBUNE CROSSWORD & OTHER WORD GAMES *See* HERALD TRIBUNE CROSSWORDS & OTHER WORD GAMES **4862**

NEW YORK HERALD TRIBUNE CROSSWORD PUZZLES ONLY *See* HERALD TRIBUNE CROSSWORD PUZZLES ONLY **4862**

NEW YORK HERALD TRIBUNE CROSSWORD PUZZLES. POCKET SIZE *See* NEW YORK HERALD TIMES CROSSWORD PUZZLES ONLY **4864**

NEW YORK HERALD TRIBUNE LARGE PRINT CROSSWORDS (US/0892-0168) [15097204] **4864**

NEW YORK HISTORY (US/0146-437X) [04862461] **2748**

NEW YORK HOLSTEIN-FRIESIAN NEWS *See* NEW YORK HOLSTEIN NEWS **216**

NEW YORK HOLSTEIN NEWS (US/0279-8611) [07334844] **216**

NEW YORK IN PERSPECTIVE (US/1065-5603) [26660191] **5334**

NEW YORK INTERNATIONAL LAW REVIEW (US/1050-9453) [17640317] **3133**

NEW YORK IRISH HISTORY (US/1073-8339) [18424069] **2700**

NEW YORK JEWISH WEEK, THE (US/0745-5356) [09144716] **2269**

NEW YORK JURY VERDICT REPORTER (METROPOLITAN ED.), THE (US/0738-1697) [08291663] **3016**

NEW YORK LAND REPORT : A PROJECT OF THE NEW YORK LAND INSTITUTE *CEASED.* (US) [06714872] **3115**

NEW YORK LATINO (US/1050-5490) [21533727] **2269**

NEW YORK LAW FINDER (US/0277-0512) [05085705] **3082**

NEW YORK LAW JOURNAL (US/0028-7326) [02255104] **3016**

NEW YORK LAW JOURNAL DIGEST-ANNOTATOR (US/0745-4406) [09147294] 3016, **3082**

NEW YORK LAW SCHOOL *See* NEW YORK LAW SCHOOL LAW REVIEW **3016**

NEW YORK LAW SCHOOL JOURNAL OF HUMAN RIGHTS (US/1046-4328) [17937400] **4511**

NEW YORK LAW SCHOOL JOURNAL OF INTERNATIONAL AND COMPARATIVE LAW (US) [10603145] **3133**

NEW YORK LAW SCHOOL LAW REVIEW (US/0145-448X) [02737481] **3016**

NEW YORK LAWS AFFECTING CORPORATIONS (US) [24893513] **3102**

NEW YORK LAWYERS DIARY AND MANUAL (US) [04714151] **3016**

NEW YORK LAWYER'S LETTER (US/0275-7346) [05377624] **3016**

NEW YORK LEGISLATIVE SERVICE, INC *See* NEW YORK LEGISLATIVE SERVICE : REPORT **4669**

NEW YORK LEGISLATIVE SERVICE : REPORT (US) [04967327] **4669**

NEW YORK LIBRARY ASSOCIATION *See* NYLA BULLETIN **3238**

NEW YORK LITERARY FORUM *SUSPENDED.* (US/0149-1040) [03983321] 326, **3416**

NEW YORK MEDICAL QUARTERLY, THE (US/0196-6871) [05851787] **3620**

NEW YORK MERCANTILE EXCHANGE *See* STATISTICAL YEARBOOK - NEW YORK MERCANTILE EXCHANGE **733**

NEW YORK METRO SALES GUIDE TO HIGH-TECH COMPANIES (US/1040-0583) [18304592] **5133**

NEW YORK METS INSIDE PITCH (US/0887-5863) [13322426] **4907**

NEW YORK MILITARY ACADEMY *See* ALUMNI DIRECTORY / NEW YORK MILITARY ACADEMY **1099**

NEW YORK MILLS HERALD (US) [01760092] **5697**

NEW YORK MODEL (US/0749-6311) [11139092] **1507**

NEW YORK MOTORIST (US/0028-7385) [04090634] **5421**

NEW YORK (N.Y.) *See* GREEN BOOK : OFFICIAL DIRECTORY OF THE CITY OF NEW YORK, THE **2565**

NEW YORK (N.Y.) *See* CITY RECORD, THE **4638**

NEW YORK (N.Y.) HUMAN RESOURCES ADMINISTRATION *See* MONTHLY STATISTICAL REPORT - NEW YORK (CITY). HUMAN RESOURCES ADMINISTRATION **5266**

NEW YORK (N.Y.). HUMAN RESOURCES ADMINISTRATION. DIVISION OF POLICY AND ECONOMIC RESEARCH *See* SELECTED CHARACTERISTICS OF PUBLIC ASSISTANCE RECIPIENTS IN NEW YORK CITY BY COMMUNITY DISTRICT **5307**

NEW YORK (N.Y.) MAYOR *See* EXECUTIVE CAPITAL BUDGET AND CAPITAL PROGRAM - NEW YORK CITY **4723**

NEW YORK (N.Y.). OFFICE OF THE COMPTROLLER *See* COMPREHENSIVE ANNUAL FINANCIAL REPORT OF THE COMPTROLLER FOR THE YEAR ENDED JUNE 30 ... - NEW YORK STATE **4718**

NEW YORK NATIVE (US/0744-060X) [08002067] **2795**

NEW YORK NEWSREEL (US/1054-0652) [09651005] **4075**

NEW YORK NO-FAULT ARBITRATION REPORTS (US/0193-7693) [03463896] **3016**

NEW YORK OPERA NEWSLETTER, THE (US/1043-2361) [19359124] **386**

●NEW YORK OUTDOORS (US) [26650619] **4875**

NEW YORK PALEONTOLOGICAL SOCIETY *See* NOTES - NEW YORK PALEONTOLOGICAL SOCIETY **4228**

NEW YORK PEDIATRICIAN (US/0737-4216) [09367912] **3906**

NEW YORK-PENNSYLVANIA COLLECTOR, THE (US) [05718195] **251**

NEW YORK POWER AUTHORITY *See* ANNUAL REPORT FOR ... / NEW YORK POWER AUTHORITY **4759**

NEW YORK PROFESSIONAL ENGINEER (US/0028-7458) [04683813] **1988**

NEW YORK. PUBLIC LIBRARY *See* FILMS / A CATALOG OF THE FILM COLLECTION **4071**

NEW YORK PUBLIC LIBRARY. ART AND ARCHITECTURE DIVISION *See* BIBLIOGRAPHIC GUIDE TO ART AND ARCHITECTURE **334**

NEW YORK PUBLIC LIBRARY. DANCE COLLECTION *See* BIBLIOGRAPHIC GUIDE TO DANCE **1314**

NEW YORK PUBLIC LIBRARY DIRECTORY OF COMMUNITY SERVICES, THE (US/0191-6629) [04894009] **5298**

NEW YORK PUBLIC LIBRARY. MUSIC DIVISION *See* BIBLIOGRAPHIC GUIDE TO MUSIC **4160**

NEW YORK PUBLIC LIBRARY. RESEARCH LIBRARIES *See* BIBLIOGRAPHIC GUIDE TO BUSINESS AND ECONOMICS **726**

NEW YORK PUBLIC LIBRARY. RESEARCH LIBRARIES *See* BIBLIOGRAPHIC GUIDE TO TECHNOLOGY **5173**

NEW YORK PUBLIC LIBRARY. RESEARCH LIBRARIES *See* BIBLIOGRAPHIC GUIDE TO PSYCHOLOGY **4622**

NEW YORK PUBLIC LIBRARY. RESEARCH LIBRARIES *See* BIBLIOGRAPHIC GUIDE TO GOVERNMENT PUBLICATIONS - FOREIGN **4696**

NEW YORK PUBLIC LIBRARY. RESEARCH LIBRARIES *See* CATALOG OF THE THEATRE AND DRAMA COLLECTIONS **5362**

NEW YORK PUBLIC LIBRARY. RESEARCH LIBRARIES *See* BIBLIOGRAPHIC GUIDE TO THEATRE ARTS **5372**

NEW YORK PUBLIC LIBRARY. RESEARCH LIBRARIES *See* DICTIONARY CATALOG OF THE JEWISH COLLECTION. SUPPLEMENT **415**

NEW YORK PUBLICITY OUTLETS (US/0077-9024) [06264358] **763**

NEW YORK QUARTERLY : NYQ, THE (US/0028-7482) [01760102] **3467**

NEW YORK REAL ESTATE JOURNAL (US/1057-2104) [23967461] **4842**

NEW YORK REAL ESTATE LAW REPORTER (US/0894-4903) [15024457] **4842**

NEW YORK RED BOOK, THE (US/0196-4623) [01642672] **4484**

NEW YORK REGGAE TIMES (US/0887-7335) [13336552] **4140**

NEW YORK RETAILER, THE (US) [01605812] **955**

NEW YORK REVIEW OF SCIENCE FICTION, THE (US/1052-9438) [21801115] 3459, **3416**

NEW YORK ROCKER (US) [08150713] **4140**

NEW YORK RUNNING NEWS (US/0161-7338) [04015548] **4907**

NEW YORK SCHOOL DISTRICT LAW LETTER, THE (US/0545-6339) [04762930] 1768, **3016**

NEW YORK SOCIETY OF ARCHITECTS *See* MANUAL. NEW YORK BUILDING LAWS **3006**

NEW YORK SOCIETY OF CLINICAL PSYCHOLOGISTS *See* DIRECTORY - THE NEW YORK SOCIETY OF CLINICAL PSYCHOLOGISTS, INC **4585**

NEW YORK SPORTS (US/0740-2384) [09941019] **4907**

NEW YORK (STATE) *See* REAL PROPERTY LAW, REAL PROPERTY ACTIONS AND PROCEEDINGS LAW, AND RELATED MISCELLANEOUS STATUTES, AS AMENDED **3035**

NEW YORK (STATE) *See* NEW YORK ... CPLR REDBOOK **3090**

NEW YORK (STATE) *See* CRIMINAL LAW **3106**

NEW YORK (STATE) *See* WHITE, NEW YORK CORPORATIONS: BCL, N-PCL AND RELATED STATUTES **3104**

NEW YORK (STATE) *See* COMMERCIAL LAW. GOLD BOOK. BENDER PAMPHLET EDITION. NEW YORK UNIFORM COMMERCIAL CODE, GENERAL OBLIGATIONS LAW **3097**

NEW YORK (STATE) *See* GOULD'S CRIMINAL LAW HANDBOOK OF NEW YORK **3107**

NEW YORK (STATE) *See* GILBERT CRIMINAL LAW AND PROCEDURE OF NEW YORK **3107**

NEW YORK (STATE) *See* OFFICIAL COMPILATION OF THE CODES, RULES AND REGULATIONS OF THE STATE OF NEW YORK **3021**

NEW YORK (STATE) *See* VEHICLE AND TRAFFIC LAW **3070**

NEW YORK (STATE) *See* VILLAGE LAW **3071**

NEW YORK (STATE) *See* INSURANCE LAW **2983**

NEW YORK (STATE) *See* DEBTOR & CREDITOR. BENDER PAMPHLET EDITION **2959**

NEW YORK (STATE) *See* NEW YORK TAX LAW **3016**

NEW YORK (STATE) *See* CIVIL PRACTICE LAW & RULES OF THE STATE OF NEW YORK : CPLR **3089**

NEW YORK (STATE) *See* MCKINNEY'S SESSION LAWS OF NEW YORK **3007**

NEW YORK (STATE) *See* FAMILY LAW. BENDER PAMPHLET EDITION **3120**

NEW Alphabetical Title Index

NEW YORK (STATE) See BANKING LAW: NEW YORK BANKING LAW 3085

NEW YORK (STATE) See CIVIL PRACTICE ANNUAL OF NEW YORK 3089

NEW YORK (STATE) See NEW YORK CORPORATION LAW ... WHITEBOOK, WHITE CORPORATION LAW : BUSINESS CORPORATION LAW, NOT-FOR-PROFIT CORPORATION LAW, SELECTIONS FROM RELATED STATUTES AS AMENDED BY THE ... REGULAR LEGISLATIVE SESSION THROUGH ... 3102

NEW YORK (STATE) See NEW YORK LAWS AFFECTING CORPORATIONS 3102

NEW YORK STATE AGRICULTURAL EXPERIMENT STATION See SPECIAL REPORT - NEW YORK STATE AGRICULTURAL EXPERIMENT STATION 137

NEW YORK STATE ARCHIVES AND RECORDS ADMINISTRATION. LOCAL GOVERNMENT RECORDS BUREAU. GRANTS ADMINISTRATION UNIT See GRANTS-IN-AID APPLICATION AND REFERENCE MATERIALS 4653

NEW YORK STATE ASSOCIATION OF COUNTIES See NYAC NEWS 4670

NEW YORK STATE ASSOCIATION OF COUNTIES See NYSAC COUNTY DIRECTORY 4670

NEW YORK STATE BANKER, THE (US/0028-7539) [04090604] 801

NEW YORK (STATE). BANKING DEPT See WEEKLY BULLETIN - NEW YORK (STATE). BANKING DEPT 816

NEW YORK STATE BAR ASSOCIATION. BUSINESS LAW SECTION. MEETING See PROCEEDINGS OF THE BUSINESS LAW SECTION ANNUAL MEETING 3102

NEW YORK STATE BAR ASSOCIATION. COMMITTEE ON PROFESSIONAL ETHICS See FORMAL OPINIONS - COMMITTEE ON PROFESSIONAL ETHICS, NEW YORK STATE BAR ASSOCIATION 2972

NEW YORK STATE BAR ASSOCIATION. CONSTRUCTION & SURETY LAW DIVISION See CONSTRUCTION & SURETY LAW DIVISION NEWSLETTER 2956

NEW YORK STATE BAR ASSOCIATION. INSURANCE, NEGLIGENCE AND COMPENSATION LAW SECTION See INCL JOURNAL 2980

NEW YORK STATE BAR ASSOCIATION. MUNICIPAL LAW SECTION See MUNICIPAL LAW SECTION NEWSLETTER 3012

NEW YORK STATE BAR ASSOCIATION. REAL PROPERTY LAW SECTION See REAL PROPERTY LAW SECTION NEWSLETTER 4845

NEW YORK STATE BAR ASSOCIATION. YOUNG LAWYERS SECTION See PERSPECTIVE (ALBANY, N.Y. 1983) 3029

NEW YORK STATE BAR JOURNAL (US/0028-7547) [01760205] 3016

NEW YORK STATE BOARD OF ELECTIONS FORMAL OPINION / STATE OF NEW YORK, STATE BOARD OF ELECTIONS (US) [09668706] 3016

NEW YORK (STATE). BUREAU OF BUSINESS RESEARCH See BUSINESS STATISTICS, NEW YORK STATE 727

NEW YORK (STATE). BUREAU OF CONSUMER FRAUDS AND PROTECTION See CONSUMER ACTION 1294

NEW YORK STATE BUSINESS FACT BOOK (US) [24997945] 699

NEW YORK STATE BUSINESS STATISTICS. ANNUAL SUMMARY (US) [22225679] 699, 732

NEW YORK STATE BUSINESS STATISTICS. QUARTERLY SUMMARY (US) [21224431] 5334

NEW YORK STATE COMMISSION ON JUDICIAL CONDUCT See DETERMINATIONS OF THE NEW YORK STATE COMMISSION ON JUDICIAL CONDUCT 3140

NEW YORK (STATE). COMPTROLLER'S OFFICE See OPERATING REPORT, NEW YORK STATE COMPTROLLER : THE TAXPAYERS' WATCHDOG 4739

NEW YORK (STATE). COMPTROLLER'S OFFICE See OPINIONS OF THE NEW YORK STATE COMPTROLLER 3023

NEW YORK STATE CONSERVATION COUNCIL COMMENTS (US/0745-8835) [09525373] 2200

NEW YORK STATE CONTRACT REPORTER (US) [20101605] 4669

NEW YORK STATE COUNCIL ON VOCATIONAL EDUCATION See ANNUAL REPORT PRESENTED TO THE NEW YORK STATE BOARD OF REGENTS 1910

NEW YORK (STATE). CRIME VICTIMS BOARD See ANNUAL REPORT / CRIME VICTIMS BOARD 3157

NEW YORK STATE CRIMINAL LAW REVIEW (US/0271-6283) [05903512] 3108

NEW YORK STATE DENTAL JOURNAL (US/0028-7571) [01760208] 1330

NEW YORK (STATE). DEPT. OF AUDIT AND CONTROL See INDEX TO THE PUBLIC SCHOOLS (ALBANY) 1752

NEW YORK (STATE). DEPT. OF AUDIT AND CONTROL See SPECIAL REPORT ON MUNICIPAL AFFAIRS FOR LOCAL FISCAL YEARS ENDED IN ... 4748

NEW YORK (STATE). DEPT. OF COMMERCE See ANNUAL REPORT - NEW YORK STATE DEPARTMENT OF COMMERCE 823

NEW YORK (STATE). DEPT. OF ENVIRONMENTAL CONSERVATION See ANNUAL REPORT - DEPARTMENT OF ENVIRONMENTAL CONSERVATION 2186

NEW YORK (STATE). DEPT. OF HEALTH See ANNUAL REPORT OF THE STATE DEPARTMENT OF HEALTH OF NEW YORK 4766

NEW YORK (STATE). DEPT. OF LABOR See ANNUAL REPORT - NEW YORK (STATE). DEPT. OF LABOR 1649

NEW YORK (STATE). DEPT. OF LABOR See LEGISLATIVE DIGEST : BILLS OF LABOR INTEREST PASSED BY THE NEW YORK STATE LEGISLATURE 3151

NEW YORK (STATE). DEPT. OF LABOR See STATISTICS ON OPERATIONS 1539

NEW YORK (STATE). DEPT. OF LABOR. DIVISION OF RESEARCH AND STATISTICS See ANNUAL EVALUATION OF THE NEW YORK STATE UNEMPLOYMENT INSURANCE FUND 1645

NEW YORK (STATE). DEPT. OF LABOR. DIVISION OF RESEARCH AND STATISTICS See EMPLOYMENT REVIEW 1667

NEW YORK (STATE). DEPT. OF LABOR. DIVISION OF RESEARCH AND STATISTICS See ANNUAL PLANNING REPORT: ROCHESTER LABOR AREA 1648

NEW YORK (STATE). DEPT. OF LABOR. DIVISION OF RESEARCH AND STATISTICS See COLLECTIVE BARGAINING SETTLEMENTS IN NEW YORK STATE 1660

NEW YORK (STATE). DEPT. OF LABOR. DIVISION OF RESEARCH AND STATISTICS See WAGE BULLETIN 1717

NEW YORK (STATE). DEPT. OF MOTOR VEHICLES See ANNUAL REPORT - STATE OF NEW YORK, DEPARTMENT OF MOTOR VEHICLES 5403

NEW YORK (STATE). DEPT. OF MOTOR VEHICLES See TRIO. TRAFFIC RULINGS, INTERPRETATIONS, OPINIONS 5446

NEW YORK (STATE). DEPT. OF PUBLIC SERVICE See FINANCIAL STATISTICS OF THE MAJOR PRIVATELY OWNED UTILITIES IN NEW YORK STATE 4697

NEW YORK (STATE). DEPT. OF SOCIAL SERVICES See ADMINISTRATIVE DIRECTIVE - DEPARTMENT OF SOCIAL SERVICES 5270

NEW YORK (STATE). DEPT. OF SOCIAL SERVICES See INFORMATIONAL LETTER - NEW YORK (STATE). DEPT. OF SOCIAL SERVICES 5290

NEW YORK (STATE). DEPT. OF SOCIAL SERVICES See ANNUAL REPORT ON THE PROVISION OF CHILD WELFARE SERVICES IN NEW YORK STATE 5273

NEW YORK (STATE). DEPT. OF SOCIAL SERVICES See ANNUAL REPORT, STATISTICAL SUPPLEMENT / NEW YORK STATE DEPARTMENT OF SOCIAL SERVICES 5273

NEW YORK (STATE). DEPT. OF STATE See STATISTICAL ABSTRACT - NEW YORK STATE DEPARTMENT OF STATE 4699

NEW YORK (STATE). DEPT. OF STATE See MANUAL FOR THE USE OF THE LEGISLATURE OF THE STATE OF NEW YORK 3006

NEW YORK STATE DIRECTORY, THE (US/0737-1314) [09315695] 4669

NEW YORK (STATE). DIVISION OF AUDITS AND ACCOUNTS See AUDIT OF NEW YORK STATE AGENCIES 739

NEW YORK (STATE). DIVISION OF CRIMINAL JUSTICE SERVICES See STATE OF NEW YORK COMPREHENSIVE CRIME CONTROL PLAN 3177

NEW YORK (STATE). DIVISION OF EMPLOYMENT. RESEARCH AND STATISTICS OFFICE. WAGE BULLETIN See WAGE BULLETIN 1717

NEW YORK (STATE). DIVISION OF HOUSING AND COMMUNITY RENEWAL See STATISTICAL SUMMARY OF PROGRAMS / NEW YORK STATE DIVISION OF HOUSING AND COMMUNITY RENEWAL 2841

NEW YORK (STATE). DIVISION OF THE LOTTERY See ANNUAL REPORT / NEW YORK'S LOTTERY 4628

NEW YORK STATE ECONOMIC AND REVENUE FORECASTS / NEW YORK STATE ASSEMBLY WAYS AND MEANS COMMITTEE STAFF (US) [22141280] 1507

NEW YORK STATE EMPLOYMENT AND TRAINING COUNCIL See CETA ACTIVITY IN NEW YORK STATE / PREPARED BY THE STAFF OF THE NEW YORK STATE EMPLOYMENT AND TRAINING COUNCIL (SETC) 1658

NEW YORK STATE ENERGY RESEARCH AND DEVELOPMENT AUTHORITY See SEMIANNUAL REPORT / NEW YORK STATE ENERGY RESEARCH AND DEVELOPMENT AUTHORITY 1956

NEW YORK STATE ENVIRONMENT SUSPENDED. (US/0048-0053) [04090664] 2178

NEW YORK STATE GFOA NEWSLETTER (US/1064-0762) [19701013] 801

NEW YORK (STATE). GOVERNOR See STATE OF NEW YORK EXECUTIVE BUDGET BRIEFING BOOK 4749

NEW YORK (STATE). GOVERNOR See STATE OF NEW YORK EXECUTIVE BUDGET, AGENCY PRESENTATIONS 4749

NEW YORK (STATE). GOVERNOR See STATE OF NEW YORK EXECUTIVE BUDGET ... ANNUAL MESSAGE 4749

NEW YORK STATE HOUSING FINANCE AGENCY See ANNUAL REPORT - NEW YORK STATE HOUSING FINANCE AGENCY 2814

NEW YORK (STATE). INSURANCE DEPT See STATISTICAL TABLES FROM ANNUAL STATEMENTS 2898

NEW YORK STATE JOURNAL OF MEDICINE CEASED. (US/0028-7628) [01590239] 3621

NEW YORK STATE JOURNAL OF PHARMACY, THE (US/0279-8778) [07334169] 4318

NEW YORK STATE JURY VERDICT REVIEW AND ANALYSIS (US/8750-8044) [10541707] 3090

NEW YORK STATE LAW DIGEST (US/0028-7636) [01586149] 3016

NEW YORK (STATE). LAWS, STATUTES, ETC See MENTAL HYGIENE LAW (NEW YORK) 3009

NEW YORK STATE LEGISLATIVE ANNUAL (US/0197-3983) [01714337] 4669

NEW YORK (STATE). LEGISLATURE. ASSEMBLY. PUERTO RICAN/HISPANIC TASK FORCE See LEGISLATIVE CONFERENCE REPORT 2267

NEW YORK (STATE). LEGISLATURE. ASSEMBLY. STANDING COMMITTEE ON CHILDREN AND FAMILIES See ANNUAL REPORT / NEW YORK STATE ASSEMBLY, COMMITTEE ON CHILDREN & FAMILIES 3119

NEW YORK (STATE). LEGISLATURE. ASSEMBLY. STANDING COMMITTEE ON CONSUMER AFFAIRS AND PROTECTION See ANNUAL REPORT / NEW YORK STATE ASSEMBLY, COMMITTEE ON CONSUMER AFFAIRS & PROTECTION 1293

NEW YORK (STATE). LEGISLATURE. ASSEMBLY. STANDING COMMITTEE ON EDUCATION See ANNUAL REPORT / NEW YORK STATE ASSEMBLY, COMMITTEE ON EDUCATION 1725

NEW YORK (STATE). LEGISLATURE. ASSEMBLY. STANDING COMMITTEE ON GOVERNMENTAL OPERATIONS See ANNUAL REPORT / NEW YORK STATE ASSEMBLY, STANDING COMMITTEE ON GOVERNMENTAL OPERATIONS 4628

NEW YORK (STATE). LEGISLATURE. ASSEMBLY. STANDING COMMITTEE ON LABOR See ANNUAL REPORT / STANDING COMMITTEE ON LABOR, NEW YORK STATE ASSEMBLY 3144

NEW YORK (STATE). LEGISLATURE. ASSEMBLY. STANDING COMMITTEE ON VETERANS' AFFAIRS See ANNUAL REPORT / NEW YORK STATE ASSEMBLY, COMMITTEE ON VETERANS' AFFAIRS 4035

NEW YORK (STATE). LEGISLATURE. JOINT LEGISLATIVE COMMITTEE ON MOTOR VEHICLES, TRAFFIC, AND HIGHWAY SAFETY See REPORT OF THE JOINT LEGISLATIVE COMMITTEE ON MOTOR VEHICLES, HIGHWAY AND TRAFFIC SAFETY TO THE LEGISLATURE OF THE STATE OF NEW YORK 5391

NEW YORK (STATE). LEGISLATURE. LEGISLATIVE COMMISSION ON EXPENDITURE REVIEW See ANNUAL REPORT TO THE LEGISLATURE / LEGISLATIVE COMMISSION ON EXPENDITURE 4711

Alphabetical Title Index

NEW

NEW YORK (STATE). LEGISLATURE. SELECT COMMITTEE ON INSURANCE RATES, REGULATION AND RECODIFICATION OF THE INSURANCE LAW *See* REPORT OF THE SELECT COMMITTEE ON INSURANCE RATES, REGULATION AND RECODIFICATION OF THE INSURANCE LAW **3038**

NEW YORK (STATE). LEGISLATURE. SENATE. STANDING COMMITTEE ON INSURANCE *See* ANNUAL REPORT OF THE NEW YORK STATE SENATE STANDING COMMITTEE ON INSURANCE **2873**

NEW YORK STATE LIBRARY *See* SERIALS MASTER LIST **3249**

NEW YORK STATE LIBRARY *See* CHECKLIST OF OFFICIAL PUBLICATIONS OF THE STATE OF NEW YORK, A **413**

NEW YORK STATE MEDICAL CARE FACILITIES FINANCE AGENCY *See* ANNUAL REPORT - NEW YORK STATE MEDICAL CARE FACILITIES FINANCE AGENCY **3776**

NEW YORK STATE MUNICIPAL BULLETIN (US) [04866828] **4669**

NEW YORK STATE MUSEUM *See* BULLETIN - NEW YORK STATE MUSEUM (1976) **4086**

NEW YORK STATE MUSEUM MEMOIR (US/0749-1158) [10836836] **4228, 4169**

NEW YORK STATE NURSES ASSOCIATION *See* JOURNAL OF THE NEW YORK STATE NURSES ASSOCIATION, THE **3860**

NEW YORK STATE OCCUPATIONAL NEEDS (US) [19008995] **1694**

NEW YORK (STATE). OFFICE FOR THE AGING *See* PROGRAMS AND PROGRESS **5302**

NEW YORK (STATE). OFFICE OF ADVOCATE FOR THE DISABLED *See* ANNUAL REPORT / NEW YORK STATE, OFFICE OF ADVOCATE FOR THE DISABLED **4628**

NEW YORK (STATE). OFFICE OF COURT ADMINISTRATION *See* STATISTICAL REPORT - STATE OF NEW YORK OFFICE OF COURT ADMINISTRATION **3083**

NEW YORK (STATE). OFFICE OF HEALTH SYSTEMS MANAGEMENT *See* SAFE, EFFECTIVE AND THERAPEUTICALLY EQUIVALENT PRESCRIPTION DRUGS **4329**

NEW YORK (STATE). OFFICE OF PLANNING COORDINATION *See* PLANNING LEGISLATION IN NEW YORK STATE **3029**

NEW YORK (STATE). OFFICE OF THE STATE DEPUTY COMPTROLLER FOR THE CITY OF NEW YORK *See* FINANCIAL PLAN STATUS REPORT / OFFICE OF THE STATE DEPUTY COMPTROLLER FOR THE CITY OF NEW YORK **4725**

NEW YORK (STATE). OMBUDSMEN AND SMALL BUSINESS SERVICES DIVISION *See* OMBUDSMEN AND SMALL BUSINESS SERVICES NEWS **701**

NEW YORK STATE OPTOMETRY *See* PROSPECTUS **4217**

NEW YORK STATE PHARMACIST, CENTURY II (US/0739-7062) [09796872] **4318**

●NEW YORK STATE PLAN FOR COORDINATION OF TRAINING, EMPLOYMENT AND RELATED PROGRAMS (US) [23374685] **4207, 5298**

NEW YORK STATE PROJECT FINANCE AGENCY *See* ANNUAL REPORT - NYS PROJECT FINANCE AGENCY **4628**

NEW YORK (STATE). PUBLIC EMPLOYMENT RELATIONS BOARD *See* REPORT ON FRINGE BENEFITS AND RELATED PRACTICES AFFECTING POLICEMEN **3174**

NEW YORK (STATE). PUBLIC EMPLOYMENT RELATIONS BOARD *See* REPORT ON FRINGE BENEFITS AND RELATED PRACTICES AFFECTING GENERAL EMPLOYEES OF CITIES **4682**

NEW YORK (STATE). PUBLIC EMPLOYMENT RELATIONS BOARD *See* REPORT ON SALARIES, FRINGE BENEFITS, AND RELATED PRACTICES AFFECTING CLASSIFIED SERVICE EMPLOYEES OF NEW YORK STATE **1707**

NEW YORK (STATE). PUBLIC EMPLOYMENT RELATIONS BOARD *See* OFFICIAL DECISIONS, OPINIONS AND RELATED MATTERS OF THE PUBLIC EMPLOYMENT RELATIONS BOARD OF THE STATE OF NEW YORK **3021**

NEW YORK (STATE). PUBLIC EMPLOYMENT RELATIONS BOARD *See* REPORT ON SALARY SCHEDULES FOR FULL TIME NON-INSTRUCTIONAL EMPLOYEES OF SCHOOL DISTRICTS **1870**

NEW YORK (STATE). PUBLIC EMPLOYMENT RELATIONS BOARD *See* NEWS - NEW YORK STATE PUBLIC EMPLOYMENT RELATIONS BOARD **1694**

NEW YORK STATE PUBLIC HIGH SCHOOL ATHLETIC ASSOCIATION *See* HANDBOOK - NEW YORK STATE PUBLIC HIGH SCHOOL ATHLETIC ASSOCIATION **4898**

NEW YORK (STATE). PUBLIC SERVICE COMMISSION *See* REPORTS / NEW YORK STATE, PUBLIC SERVICE COMMISSION **4682**

NEW YORK STATE PUPIL EVALUATION PROGRAM : SCHOOL ADMINISTRATOR'S MANUAL (US) [05014612] **1867**

NEW YORK STATE QUERIES (US/1041-6560) [16948167] **2462**

NEW YORK STATE REGISTER, THE (US/0197-2472) [04877826] **4669**

NEW YORK STATE SCHOOL BOARDS ASSOCIATION *See* LEGISLATIVE BULLETIN - NEW YORK STATE SCHOOL BOARDS ASSOCIATION **1865**

NEW YORK (STATE). STATE BOARD OF ELECTIONS *See* NEW YORK STATE BOARD OF ELECTIONS FORMAL OPINION / STATE OF NEW YORK, STATE BOARD OF ELECTIONS **3016**

NEW YORK (STATE). STATE COMMISSION ON EMINENT DOMAIN AND REAL PROPERTY TAX ASSESSMENT REVIEW *See* REPORT OF THE STATE COMMISSION ON EMINENT DOMAIN AND REAL PROPERTY TAX ASSESSMENT REVIEW **4846**

NEW YORK (STATE). STATE EDUCATION DEPT *See* OFFICIAL NEW YORK STATE EDUCATION DEPARTMENT REPORTS **1770**

NEW YORK (STATE). STATE LABOR RELATIONS BOARD *See* DECISIONS **1662**

NEW YORK (STATE). STATE LABOR RELATIONS BOARD *See* DECISIONS AND ORDERS OF THE NEW YORK STATE LABOR RELATIONS BOARD **3146**

NEW YORK (STATE). STATE SCIENCE SERVICE *See* BIENNIAL REPORT OF THE NEW YORK STATE SCIENCE SERVICE **5088**

NEW YORK STATE STATISTICAL YEARBOOK (US/0077-9334) [01923453] **5334**

NEW YORK STATE STUDENT LEADER (US/1048-2202) [20870617] **1837**

NEW YORK (STATE). SUPREME COURT. APPELLATE DIVISION *See* REPORTS OF CASES DECIDED IN THE APPELLATE DIVISION OF THE SUPREME COURT, STATE OF NEW YORK **3039**

NEW YORK STATE TAX MONITOR (US/0737-5891) [09417858] **4738, 3016**

NEW YORK (STATE). TEMPORARY STATE COMMISSION ON THE WATER SUPPLY NEEDS OF SOUTHEASTERN NEW YORK *See* YEAR REPORT - TEMPORARY STATE COMMISSION ON THE WATER SUPPLY NEEDS OF SOUTHEASTERN NEW YORK **5549**

NEW YORK STATE THRUWAY AUTHORITY *See* RULES AND REGULATIONS OF THE NEW YORK STATE THRUWAY AUTHORITY **3045**

NEW YORK STATE UNIVERSITY CONSTRUCTION FUND *See* ANNUAL REPORT / THE STATE UNIVERSITY CONSTRUCTION FUND **598**

NEW YORK STATE WATER POLLUTION CONTROL REVOLVING FUND *See* DRAFT INTENDED USE PLAN, PROJECT PRIORITY SYSTEM, PROJECT PRIORITY LIST, FEDERAL FISCAL YEAR: NEW YORK STATE REVOLVING FUND FOR WATER POLLUTION CONTROL **2227**

NEW YORK STATE'S ... HIGHWAY SUFFICIENCY RATINGS (US) [08157414] **5442**

NEW YORK STOCK EXCHANGE *See* FACT BOOK - NEW YORK STOCK EXCHANGE **898**

NEW YORK STOCK EXCHANGE. DEPT. OF PUBLIC RELATIONS AND MARKET DEVELOPMENT. FACT BOOK *See* FACT BOOK - NEW YORK STOCK EXCHANGE **898**

NEW YORK STOCK EXCHANGE. OFFICE OF THE HEARING BOARD *See* HEARING BOARD DECISIONS AND SUMMARIES . [MICROFORM] **1493**

NEW YORK STYLE & DESIGN (US) **2540**

NEW YORK TAX CASES (BUFFALO, N.Y.) (US/0898-9117) [17944606] **4738**

NEW YORK TAX LAW (US) [05811040] **3016**

NEW YORK TAX UPDATE (US/1056-4829) [19537124] **749**

●NEW YORK TECHNOLOGY RESOURCE GUIDE (US/1065-8041) [26739527] **5133**

NEW YORK. TELEVISION STATION WPIX *See* WPIX EDITORIALS **1143**

NEW YORK THEATRE CRITICS' REVIEWS (US/0028-7784) [04892948] **5366**

NEW YORK TIMES ANNUAL REVIEW, THE (US/0197-8004) [06111745] **2624**

NEW YORK TIMES BIOGRAPHICAL SERVICE, THE (US/0161-2433) [01425589] **434**

NEW YORK TIMES BOOK REVIEW, THE (US/0028-7806) [06441787] **3349**

NEW YORK TIMES CROSSWORD PUZZLES, THE (US/0364-3700) [02629007] **4864**

NEW YORK TIMES CURRENT EVENTS EDITION, THE (US/0190-1990) [04657290] **2540**

NEW YORK TIMES CURRENT EVENTS INDEX, THE (US/0277-0989) [07465588] **2490**

NEW YORK TIMES DIRECTORY OF THE FILM, THE (US) [04911855] **4075**

NEW YORK TIMES FILE, CRITICAL ISSUES. RESEARCH GUIDE AND INDEX, THE (US/0732-0892) [12095765] **2922**

NEW YORK TIMES FILM REVIEWS, THE (US/0362-3688) [02293207] **4075**

NEW YORK TIMES INDEX, THE (US/0147-538X) [01760220] **5814**

NEW YORK TIMES MAGAZINE, THE (US/0028-7822) [01760221] **2540**

NEW YORK TIMES SCHOOL MICROFILM COLLECTION INDEX BY REELS, THE (US/0095-5663) [01798243] **5711**

NEW YORK TIMES SCHOOL WEEKLY, THE (US/0028-7830) [04235934] **1093**

NEW YORK TIMES, THE (US/0362-4331) [01645522] **5719**

NEW YORK TIMES THEATER REVIEWS, THE (US/0160-0583) [03418664] **5366**

NEW YORK UNIVERSITY *See* STUDIES IN COMPARATIVE LITERATURE **3441**

NEW YORK UNIVERSITY *See* NEW YORK UNIVERSITY REVIEW OF LAW AND SOCIAL CHANGE **3016**

NEW YORK UNIVERSITY. CRIMINAL LAW EDUCATION AND RESEARCH CENTER *See* MONOGRAPH SERIES - CRIMINAL LAW EDUCATION AND RESEARCH CENTER **3108**

NEW YORK UNIVERSITY. DIVISION OF GENERAL EDUCATION *See* INSTITUTE ON FEDERAL TAXATION **4732**

●NEW YORK UNIVERSITY ENVIRONMENTAL LAW JOURNAL (US/1061-8651) [25484826] **3115**

NEW YORK UNIVERSITY. INSTITUTE ON FEDERAL TAXATION *See* PROCEEDINGS OF NEW YORK UNIVERSITY ... ANNUAL INSTITUTE ON FEDERAL TAXATION **4741**

NEW YORK UNIVERSITY INTERNATIONAL LAW SOCIETY *See* NEW YORK UNIVERSITY JOURNAL OF INTERNATIONAL LAW & POLITICS **3133**

NEW YORK UNIVERSITY JOURNAL OF INTERNATIONAL LAW & POLITICS (US/0028-7873) [02251321] **4484, 3133**

NEW YORK UNIVERSITY LAW REVIEW (1950) (US/0028-7881) [04950416] **3016**

NEW YORK UNIVERSITY MAGAZINE (US) [13754673] **1093**

NEW YORK UNIVERSITY REVIEW OF LAW AND SOCIAL CHANGE (US/0048-7481) [01784748] **3016**

NEW YORK VOICE (JAMAICA, N.Y.) (US) [10975737] **5719**

NEW YORK WASTE REPORTER *CEASED.* (US/1070-9266) [25518394] **2237**

NEW YORK WOMAN *CEASED.* (US) [06994975] **5562**

NEW YORK WOMEN IN FILM (US) **4075**

NEW YORK WORKER'S COMPENSATION COMMENTS (US/0194-7354) [04978823] **3152**

NEW YORK WORKERS' COMPENSATION LAW REPORTER (US) [15158717] **3152**

NEW YORK ZIP+4 STATE DIRECTORY (US) [11530410] **1146**

NEW YORKER (NEW YORK, N.Y. : 1925) (US/0028-792X) [01760231] **2490**

NEW YORKER STAATS-ZEITUNG (1991) (US/1061-7604) [25450500] **5719**

NEW YORKER STUDIEN ZUR NEUEREN DEUTSCHEN LITERATURGESCHICHTE (US/0721-4030) [13238896] **3416**

NEW YORKIN UUTISET (US/0895-5549) [09335208] **5719**

NEW YORK'S FOOD AND LIFE SCIENCES BULLETIN (US/0099-5223) [02165905] **112**

NEW YORK'S FOOD & LIFE SCIENCES QUARTERLY *See* CORNELL FOCUS **77**

NEW YOUTH CONNECTIONS (US/0737-285X) [09336777] **1067**

NEW ZEALAND *See* STATUTES OF NEW ZEALAND (1947), THE **3059**

NEW ZEALAND *See* NEW ZEALAND GAZETTE, THE **4484**

NEW
Alphabetical Title Index

NEW ZEALAND *See* NEW ZEALAND EXTERNAL RELATIONS AND TRADE RECORD **847**

NEW ZEALAND *See* DEFENCE REVIEW **4040**

NEW ZEALAND *See* NEW ZEALAND FOREIGN AFFAIRS AND TRADE RECORD **847**

NEW ZEALAND ACCOMMODATION INVENTORY AND ROOM OCCUPANCY RATES *See* NEW ZEALAND HOTEL/MOTEL INVENTORY AND ROOM OCCUPANCY RATES (LICENSED) **2810**

NEW ZEALAND ADMINISTRATIVE REPORTS : NZAR (NZ/0110-1277) [03686598] **3016**

NEW ZEALAND AGRICHEMICAL AND PLANT PROTECTION MANUAL (NZ/0114-4022) [I01144022] **112**

NEW ZEALAND AGRICULTURAL AIRCRAFT ACCIDENT SUMMARY (NZ) [01785048] 112, **30**

NEW ZEALAND AGRICULTURAL SCIENCE (NZ/0549-0146) [01715220] **112**

NEW ZEALAND ANNUAL (NZ/0110-0831) [01786414] **2510**

NEW ZEALAND ANTARCTIC RECORD (NZ/0110-5124) [05387219] 5133, **2570**

NEW ZEALAND ASIAN STUDIES SOCIETY *See* N.Z.A.S.I.A.N **2659**

NEW ZEALAND BEEKEEPER, THE (NZ) [05291770] **112**

NEW ZEALAND BILATERAL ASSISTANCE PROGRAMME. PROGRAMME PROFILES *See* PROGRAMME PROFILES **1513**

NEW ZEALAND BIRD BANDING SCHEME *See* ANNUAL REPORT OF THE NEW ZEALAND BIRD BANDING SCHEME **5614**

NEW ZEALAND BOOKS (NZ/1170-9103) [I11709103] **4831**

NEW ZEALAND BOOKS IN PRINT / NEW ZEALAND BOOK PUBLISHERS ASSOCIATION (AT/0157-7662) [04915291] 3234, 4817, **4822**

NEW ZEALAND. BOTANY DIVISION *See* TRIENNIAL REPORT - BOTANY DIVISION **529**

NEW ZEALAND BUSINESS WHO'S WHO, THE (NZ/0071-9571) [02577744] **699**

NEW ZEALAND CARTOGRAPHY AND GEOGRAPHIC INFORMATION SYSTEMS : THE JOURNAL OF THE NEW ZEALAND CARTOGRAPHIC SOCIETY (NZ/0110-6007) [24341839] 2570, **2582**

NEW ZEALAND. CENSUS AND STATISTICS DEPT. CENSUS OF LIBRARIES *See* CENSUS OF LIBRARIES **3201**

NEW ZEALAND CENSUS OF FISHING (NZ) [09628394] **2309**

NEW ZEALAND. CHIEF OMBUDSMAN *See* COMPENDIUM OF CASE NOTES OF THE OMBUDSMEN **4639**

NEW ZEALAND COMMERCIAL GROWER : OFFICIAL JOURNAL OF THE NEW ZEALAND VEGETABLE AND PRODUCE GROWERS' FEDERATION (NZ) [09936813] **2425**

NEW ZEALAND COMPANY REGISTER, THE (NZ/0549-0200) [07033621] **699**

NEW ZEALAND CONCRETE CONSTRUCTION (NZ/0549-0219) [04545445] **622**

NEW ZEALAND COUNCIL FOR EDUCATIONAL RESEARCH *See* ANNUAL REPORT - NEW ZEALAND COUNCIL FOR EDUCATIONAL RESEARCH **1725**

NEW ZEALAND COUNCIL OF TRADE UNIONS *See* NZCTU DIRECTORY **848**

NEW ZEALAND CURRENT TAXATION (NZ/0545-7572) [03574589] **4738**

NEW ZEALAND DAIRY BOARD *See* NEW ZEALAND DAIRY BOARD ANNUAL REPORT **197**

NEW ZEALAND. DAIRY BOARD *See* NEW ZEALAND DAIRY INDUSTRY; A SURVEY, THE **197**

NEW ZEALAND DAIRY BOARD ANNUAL REPORT (NZ) [21959592] **197**

NEW ZEALAND DAIRY INDUSTRY; A SURVEY, THE (NZ) [01794863] **197**

NEW ZEALAND DENTAL JOURNAL (NZ/0028-8047) [02265036] **1330**

NEW ZEALAND. DEPT. OF HEALTH *See* REPORT - NEW ZEALAND. DEPT. OF HEALTH **4798**

NEW ZEALAND. DEPT. OF HEALTH. MANAGEMENT SERVICES AND RESEARCH UNIT *See* HEALTH MANPOWER RESOURCES **3914**

NEW ZEALAND. DEPT. OF HEALTH. MANAGEMENT SERVICES AND RESEARCH UNIT *See* ANNUAL REPORT / MANAGEMENT SERVICES AND RESEARCH UNIT, DEPARTMENT OF HEALTH (NEW ZEALAND) **4766**

NEW ZEALAND. DEPT. OF LABOUR RESEARCH AND PLANNING DIVISION *See* REDUNDANCY IN NEW ZEALAND **1705**

NEW ZEALAND. DEPT. OF LABOUR RESEARCH AND PLANNING DIVISION *See* MONTHLY STATISTICS OF EMPLOYMENT **1536**

NEW ZEALAND. DEPT. OF LANDS *See* REPORT OF THE DEPARTMENT OF LANDS FOR THE YEAR ENDED ... **1580**

NEW ZEALAND. DEPT. OF SCIENTIFIC AND INDUSTRIAL RESEARCH *See* REPORT OF THE DEPARTMENT OF SCIENTIFIC AND INDUSTRIAL RESEARCH **5145**

NEW ZEALAND. DEPT. OF SCIENTIFIC AND INDUSTRIAL RESEARCH. CROP RESEARCH DIVISION *See* CROP RESEARCH NEWS **169**

NEW ZEALAND. DEPT. OF SOCIAL WELFARE *See* ANNUAL REPORT / DEPT. OF SOCIAL WELFARE, NEW ZEALAND **5272**

NEW ZEALAND. DEPT. OF SOCIAL WELFARE. REPORT OF THE DEPARTMENT OF SOCIAL WELFARE FOR THE YEAR ENDED . *See* ANNUAL REPORT / DEPT. OF SOCIAL WELFARE, NEW ZEALAND **5272**

NEW ZEALAND. DEPT. OF STATISTICS *See* INTER-INDUSTRY STUDY OF THE NEW ZEALAND ECONOMY **1534**

NEW ZEALAND. DEPT. OF STATISTICS *See* STATISTICS PUBLICATIONS CATALOGUE **5342**

NEW ZEALAND. DEPT. OF STATISTICS *See* CENSUS OF LIBRARIES **3201**

NEW ZEALAND. DEPT. OF STATISTICS *See* COUNTRY ANALYSIS OF EXTERNAL TRADE **830**

NEW ZEALAND. DEPT. OF STATISTICS *See* SHEEP RETURNS **221**

NEW ZEALAND. DEPT. OF STATISTICS. EXTERNAL TRADE OF NEW ZEALAND; COUNTRY ANALYSIS *See* COUNTRY ANALYSIS OF EXTERNAL TRADE **830**

NEW ZEALAND. DEPT. OF SURVEY AND LAND INFORMATION *See* REPORT OF THE DEPARTMENT OF SURVEY AND LAND INFORMATION FOR THE YEAR ENDED ... **2030**

NEW ZEALAND. DEPT. OF TRADE AND INDUSTRY *See* IMPORT LICENSING SCHEDULE **839**

NEW ZEALAND DIETETIC ASSOCIATION *See* JOURNAL - NEW ZEALAND DIETETIC ASSOCIATION **4192**

NEW ZEALAND DISABLED (NZ) **4391**

NEW ZEALAND DUTIES TAX GUIDE (AT) **4738**

NEW ZEALAND ECONOMIC PAPERS (NZ/0077-9954) [02593651] **1507**

NEW ZEALAND EDUCATION GAZETTE (WELLINGTON, N.Z. : 1980) (NZ/0111-1582) [06756162] **1768**

NEW ZEALAND ELECTRONICS REVIEW *CEASED*. (NZ/0549-026X) [06388514] **2073**

NEW ZEALAND EMPLOYMENT MANAGEMENT INFORMATION SYSTEM (EMIS) EMPLOYMENT OPERATION STATISTICS, THE (NZ) [22337508] **1694**

NEW ZEALAND ENERGY JOURNAL (NZ/0110-1668) [07817192] **1951**

NEW ZEALAND ENGINEERING (NZ/0028-808X) [02265037] **1988**

NEW ZEALAND ENTOMOLOGIST, THE (NZ/0077-9962) [01587943] **5592**

NEW ZEALAND EXPORTER (NZ) [09225313] **847**

NEW ZEALAND EXTERNAL RELATIONS AND TRADE RECORD (NZ/1171-7092) [26748628] **847**

NEW ZEALAND FAMILY PHYSICIAN, THE (NZ/0110-022X) [01421033] **3738**

NEW ZEALAND FARMER, THE (NZ) [05205437] **112**

NEW ZEALAND FICTION (NZ/0077-9970) [02574920] **3416**

NEW ZEALAND FISHERIES DATA REPORT (NZ/0113-2288) [I01132288] **2309**

NEW ZEALAND FISHERIES OCCASIONAL PUBLICATION (NZ/0113-227X) [I0113227X] **2309**

NEW ZEALAND FISHERIES RESEARCH BULLETIN (NZ/0113-2261) [18317026] **2309**

NEW ZEALAND FISHERIES TECHNICAL REPORT (NZ/0113-2180) [17462388] **2309**

NEW ZEALAND FISHERMAN (NZ/0113-9606) [I01139606] 2309, **4908**

NEW ZEALAND FLIGHT SAFETY (NZ/0112-8949) [14628957] **30**

●NEW ZEALAND FOREIGN AFFAIRS AND TRADE RECORD (NZ/1172-7195) [29190358] **847**

NEW ZEALAND FOREST INDUSTRIES (NZ/0113-3128) [16313651] 2389, **2403**

NEW ZEALAND FORESTRY (NZ/0112-9597) [14108144] **2389**

NEW ZEALAND GARDENER (NZ/0028-8136) [I00288136] **2425**

NEW ZEALAND GAZETTE, THE *CEASED*. (NZ) [06371081] **4484**

NEW ZEALAND GENERAL PRACTICE *See* GP WEEKLY **3738**

NEW ZEALAND GEOGRAPHER (NZ/0028-8144) [01760275] **2570**

NEW ZEALAND GEOLOGICAL SURVEY *See* NEW ZEALAND GEOLOGICAL SURVEY BULLETIN **1389**

NEW ZEALAND GEOLOGICAL SURVEY BASIN STUDIES (NZ) [14639725] **1389**

NEW ZEALAND GEOLOGICAL SURVEY BULLETIN (NZ) [01876268] **1389**

NEW ZEALAND GEOLOGICAL SURVEY BULLETINS *See* INSTITUTE OF GEOLOGICAL AND NUCLEAR SCIENCES MONOGRAPHS **1383**

NEW ZEALAND GEOLOGICAL SURVEY PALEONTOLOGICAL BULLETIN (NZ) [10257462] 4228, **1389**

NEW ZEALAND. GOVERNMENT COMPUTING SERVICE *See* REPORT OF THE GOVERNMENT COMPUTING SERVICE FOR THE YEAR ENDED 31 MARCH - NEW ZEALAND **4681**

NEW ZEALAND GRASSLAND ASSOCIATION *See* PROCEEDINGS OF THE NEW ZEALAND GRASSLAND ASSOCIATION **122**

NEW ZEALAND HEALTH & HOSPITAL (NZ/0114-3727) [20103594] 4793, **3789**

NEW ZEALAND HEALTH REVIEW (NZ/0111-6304) [08734921] **4793**

NEW ZEALAND HERALD, THE (NZ/0112-8787) [11123090] **5807**

NEW ZEALAND HISTORIC PLACES (NZ) [22147053] 276, 304, 5485, **2670**

NEW ZEALAND HOME AND BUILDING (NZ/0110-098X) [I0110098X] **2902**

NEW ZEALAND HOTEL/MOTEL INVENTORY AND ROOM OCCUPANCY RATES (LICENSED) (NZ) [09598829] 2808, **2810**

NEW ZEALAND. INDUSTRIAL PROCESSING DIVISION *See* INDUSTRIAL PROCESS RESEARCH AND DEVELOPMENT DIVISIONAL ANNUAL REPORT / INDUSTRIAL PROCESSING DIVISION, DEPARTMENT OF SCIENTIFIC AND INDUSTRIAL RESEARCH, NEW ZEALAND **2099**

NEW ZEALAND INSTITUTE OF ARGRICULTURAL SCIENCE *See* PROCEEDINGS OF THE NEW ZEALAND INSTITUTE OF ARGRICULTURAL SCIENCE & THE NEW ZEALAND SOCIETY HORTICULTURAL SCIENCE ANNUAL CONVENTION **122**

NEW ZEALAND INTERNATIONAL BUSINESS (NZ/0113-8138) [I01138138] **699**

NEW ZEALAND INTERNATIONAL REVIEW (NZ/0110-0262) [03727729] **4530**

NEW ZEALAND JOURNAL OF ADULT LEARNING (NZ/0112-224X) [I0112224X] **1801**

NEW ZEALAND JOURNAL OF AGRICULTURAL RESEARCH (NZ/0028-8233) [01607564] **112**

NEW ZEALAND JOURNAL OF ARCHAEOLOGY (NZ/0110-540x) [05932748] **276**

NEW ZEALAND JOURNAL OF BOTANY (NZ/0028-825X) [01760278] **519**

NEW ZEALAND JOURNAL OF BUSINESS (NZ/0110-9596) [13020728] **699**

NEW ZEALAND JOURNAL OF COMPUTING (NZ/0114-4596) [I01144596] **1197**

NEW ZEALAND JOURNAL OF CROP AND HORTICULTURAL SCIENCE (NZ/0114-0671) [20346537] 179, **2425**

NEW ZEALAND JOURNAL OF ECOLOGY (NZ/0110-6465) [04670522] **2219**

NEW ZEALAND JOURNAL OF EDUCATIONAL STUDIES (NZ/0028-8276) [01788656] **1768**

NEW ZEALAND JOURNAL OF ENVIRONMENTAL HEALTH (NZ/0112-0212) [I01120212] 2178, **4793**

NEW ZEALAND JOURNAL OF FORESTRY SCIENCE (NZ/0048-0134) [01780692] **2389**

NEW ZEALAND JOURNAL OF FRENCH STUDIES (NZ/0110-7380) [08130599] **3416**

NEW ZEALAND JOURNAL OF GEOGRAPHY (NZ/0028-8292) [01798041] **2570**

NEW ZEALAND JOURNAL OF GEOLOGY AND GEOPHYSICS (NZ/0028-8306) [01608250] **1389**

NEW ZEALAND JOURNAL OF HEALTH, PHYSICAL EDUCATION & RECREATION (NZ/0028-8314) [11389766] **1857**

Alphabetical Title Index — NEWCOMEN

NEW ZEALAND JOURNAL OF HEALTH, PHYSICAL EDUCATION & RECREATION (1980) *See* JOURNAL OF PHYSICAL EDUCATION NEW ZEALAND **1856**

NEW ZEALAND JOURNAL OF HISTORY, THE (NZ/0028-8322) [02577696] **2670**

NEW ZEALAND JOURNAL OF INDUSTRIAL RELATIONS (NZ/0110-0637) [05824969] **1694**

NEW ZEALAND JOURNAL OF MARINE AND FRESHWATER RESEARCH (NZ/0028-8330) [01760281] **556**

● NEW ZEALAND JOURNAL OF MATHEMATICS (NZ) [26178177] **3524**

NEW ZEALAND JOURNAL OF MEDICAL LABORATORY SCIENCE (NZ/1171-0195) [24158290] **3621**

NEW ZEALAND JOURNAL OF OCCUPATIONAL THERAPY (NZ/1171-0462) [28300493] **2865**

NEW ZEALAND JOURNAL OF PHYSIOTHERAPY (NZ/0303-7193) [01150499] **4381**

NEW ZEALAND JOURNAL OF PSYCHOLOGY (CHRISTCHURCH. 1983) (NZ/0112-109X) [09817480] **4605**

NEW ZEALAND JOURNAL OF SPORTS MEDICINE, THE (NZ/0110-6384) [05672554] **3955**

NEW ZEALAND JOURNAL OF TIMBER CONSTRUCTION, THE (NZ) [15864237] **2403**

NEW ZEALAND JOURNAL OF ZOOLOGY (NZ/0301-4223) [01794419] **5592**

NEW ZEALAND JOURNAL, THE (UK) [19094419] **5812**

NEW ZEALAND LAW JOURNAL, THE (US/0028-8373) [01760288] **3016**

NEW ZEALAND LAW REPORTS, THE (NZ/0110-148x) [01586367] **3133**

NEW ZEALAND LAW SOCIETY *See* NEW ZEALAND LAW SOCIETY'S NEWS SHEET, THE **3016**

NEW ZEALAND LAW SOCIETY'S NEWS SHEET, THE (NZ) [02721621] **3016**

NEW ZEALAND. LAWS, STATUTES, ETC *See* STATUTORY REGULATIONS **3059**

NEW ZEALAND LEGACY : JOURNAL OF THE NEW ZEALAND FEDERATION OF HISTORICAL SOCIETIES (NZ/0114-4189) [21585753] **2670**

NEW ZEALAND LIBRARIES (NZ/0028-8381) [02416464] **3234**

NEW ZEALAND LISTENER (NZ) [06339856] **1135**

NEW ZEALAND LOCAL GOVERNMENT (NZ) [02468718] **4669**

NEW ZEALAND MANUFACTURER 1992 (NZ/1171-5375) [111715375] **3485**

NEW ZEALAND. MAORI AND ISLAND AFFAIRS DEPT *See* REPORTS ON NIUE AND THE TOKELAU ISLANDS **4682**

NEW ZEALAND MARINE SCIENCES NEWSLETTER (NZ) [05091307] **1453**

NEW ZEALAND MATHEMATICS MAGAZINE, THE (NZ/0549-0510) [06385374] **3524**

NEW ZEALAND MEAT PRODUCER : OFFICIAL JOURNAL OF THE NEW ZEALAND MEAT PRODUCERS, THE (NZ) [09936975] **2351**

NEW ZEALAND MEDIA GUIDE *CEASED.* (AT/1035-8714) [I10358714] **1118**

NEW ZEALAND MEDICAL JOURNAL (NZ/0028-8446) [01713584] **3621**

NEW ZEALAND MEDICAL REGISTER / MEDICAL COUNCIL OF NEW ZEALAND (NZ) [07935198] **3916**

NEW ZEALAND MEDICAL WORKFORCE STATISTICS ... (US/0112-8868) [14877224] 3916, **3661**

NEW ZEALAND. MINISTRY OF AGRICULTURE AND FISHERIES *See* REPORT OF THE MINISTRY OF AGRICULTURE AND FISHERIES **126**

NEW ZEALAND. MINISTRY OF AGRICULTURE AND FISHERIES. INFORMATION SERVICES *See* FACTS & FIGURES ON NEW ZEALAND AGRICULTURE **83**

NEW ZEALAND. MINISTRY OF EDUCATION *See* REPORT OF THE MINISTRY OF EDUCATION, TE TAHUHU O TE MATAURANGA FOR THE 9 MONTHS FROM ... **1778**

NEW ZEALAND. MINISTRY OF FOREIGN AFFAIRS *See* FLOW OF RESOURCES FROM NEW ZEALAND TO DEVELOPING COUNTRIES, THE **2909**

NEW ZEALAND. MINISTRY OF FOREIGN AFFAIRS *See* UNITED NATIONS HANDBOOK **4537**

NEW ZEALAND. MINISTRY OF RESEARCH, SCIENCE AND TECHNOLOGY *See* REPORT OF THE MINISTRY OF RESEARCH, SCIENCE AND TECHNOLOGY FOR THE ... MONTHS ENDED 30 JUNE ... **471**

NEW ZEALAND. MINISTRY OF TRANSPORT *See* REPORT OF THE MINISTRY OF TRANSPORT **5391**

NEW ZEALAND. MINISTRY OF TRANSPORT. ECONOMICS DIVISION *See* TRUCK OPERATING COSTS **5398**

NEW ZEALAND. MINISTRY OF WORKS AND DEVELOPMENT *See* EFFICIENCY AND ECONOMY REVIEW **1605**

NEW ZEALAND MONTHLY REVIEW 1986 (NZ/0112-9120) [I01129120] **2510**

NEW ZEALAND MOTOR TRADE YEAR BOOK *See* MOTOR INDUSTRY YEAR BOOK **5420**

NEW ZEALAND MUSEUMS JOURNAL (NZ/1171-445X) [I1171445X] **359**

NEW ZEALAND NATIONAL BIBLIOGRAPHY (WELLINGTON, N.Z. : 1983) (NZ/0028-8497) [10756728] **421**

NEW ZEALAND NATURAL SCIENCES (NZ/0113-7492) [18923494] **1358**

NEW ZEALAND. NEW ZEALAND EXTERNAL RELATIONS AND TRADE RECORD *See* NEW ZEALAND FOREIGN AFFAIRS AND TRADE RECORD **847**

NEW ZEALAND NEWS REVIEW *CEASED.* (NZ) [06565730] **1575**

NEW ZEALAND NEWS UK (UK/0028-8500) [09950431] 2510, **5812**

NEW ZEALAND NURSING FORUM (NZ/0110-7968) [03999798] **3862**

NEW ZEALAND NURSING JOURNAL *See* NURSING NEW ZEALAND **3864**

NEW ZEALAND NURSING JOURNAL, THE (NZ/0028-8535) [01443225] **3862**

NEW ZEALAND OCEANOGRAPHIC INSTITUTE *See* CONTRIBUTION - NEW ZEALAND OCEANOGRAPHIC INSTITUTE **1448**

NEW ZEALAND OCEANOGRAPHIC INSTITUTE MEMOIR (NZ/0083-7903) [01630245] 556, **1453**

NEW ZEALAND. OFFICE OF AIR ACCIDENTS INVESTIGATION *See* NEW ZEALAND AGRICULTURAL AIRCRAFT ACCIDENT SUMMARY **30**

NEW ZEALAND OFFICIAL DEVELOPMENT ASSISTANCE *See* PROGRAMME PROFILES **1513**

NEW ZEALAND OUTLOOK (NZ/0113-1982) [I01131982] **2510**

NEW ZEALAND. PARLIAMENT *See* PARLIAMENTARY DEBATES. HOUSE OF REPRESENTATIVES **4672**

NEW ZEALAND. PATENT OFFICE *See* PATENT OFFICE JOURNAL **1307**

NEW ZEALAND PHARMACY (NZ/0111-431X) [20052096] **4318**

NEW ZEALAND POCKET DIGEST OF STATISTICS *See* FACTS NEW ZEALAND **5327**

NEW ZEALAND POPULATION REVIEW (NZ/0111-199X) [08739240] **4555**

NEW ZEALAND PRINTER MAGAZINE (NZ/1171-0829) [I11710829] **4567**

NEW ZEALAND RAILWAY OBSERVER (NZ/0028-8624) [I00288624] **5433**

NEW ZEALAND RECENT LAW REVIEW (NZ/0114-0655) [19946208] **3016**

NEW ZEALAND REGISTER OF SPECIALISTS (NZ/0300-2217) [01784841] **3916**

NEW ZEALAND REPRESENTATIVES OVERSEAS (NZ/0110-201X) [02242143] **4530**

NEW ZEALAND. ROAD TRAFFIC SAFETY RESEARCH COUNCIL *See* ROAD TRAFFIC SAFETY RESEARCH COUNCIL REPORT **5444**

NEW ZEALAND SCIENCE REVIEW (NZ/0028-8667) [05177808] **5133**

NEW ZEALAND SHIPPING GAZETTE CHRISTCHURCH (NZ/0027-724X) [I0027724X] **5453**

NEW ZEALAND SLAVONIC JOURNAL (NZ) [04204469] 3306, **2851**

NEW ZEALAND SOCIETY OF ANIMAL PRODUCTION *See* PROCEEDINGS OF THE NEW ZEALAND SOCIETY OF ANIMAL PRODUCTION **219**

NEW ZEALAND SOCIOLOGY (NZ/0112-921X) [15481756] **5252**

NEW ZEALAND. SOIL BUREAU *See* BULLETIN - NEW ZEALAND. SOIL BUREAU **165**

NEW ZEALAND. SOIL BUREAU *See* BULLETIN - NEW ZEALAND. SOIL BUREAU **69**

NEW ZEALAND SOIL BUREAU BIBLIOGRAPHIC REPORT (NZ/0110-165X) [01795409] **155**

NEW ZEALAND SOIL BUREAU SCIENTIFIC REPORT (NZ/0304-1735) [01794679] **179**

NEW ZEALAND SOIL NEWS (NZ/0545-7904) [01792531] **179**

NEW ZEALAND SPEECH-LANGUAGE THERAPISTS' JOURNAL, THE (NZ/0110-571X) [10615082] **3889**

NEW ZEALAND SPORTSWOMAN (NZ/1171-3771) [I11713771] **4908**

NEW ZEALAND. STATE SERVICES COMMISSION *See* REVIEW OF THE NEW ZEALAND COUNCIL FOR RECREATION AND SPORT **4854**

NEW ZEALAND STATISTICIAN, THE (NZ/0111-9176) [18709579] **5334**

NEW ZEALAND STOCK EXCHANGE WEEKLY DIARY (NZ) **909**

NEW ZEALAND TIMBER TODAY (NZ) [20113631] **2403**

NEW ZEALAND TREE GROWER (NZ/0111-2694) [I01112694] **2389**

NEW ZEALAND UNIVERSITIES LAW REVIEW (NZ/0549-0618) [01645729] **3016**

NEW ZEALAND. UNIVERSITY GRANTS COMMITTEE *See* REPORTS OF THE UNIVERSITY GRANTS COMMITTEE AND UNIVERSITY INSTITUTIONS **1845**

NEW ZEALAND. UNIVERSITY GRANTS COMMITTEE. REPORT OF THE UNIVERSITY GRANTS COMMITTEE FOR THE YEAR . *See* REPORTS OF THE UNIVERSITY GRANTS COMMITTEE AND UNIVERSITY INSTITUTIONS **1845**

NEW ZEALAND. VALUATION DEPT *See* REAL ETATE MARKET IN NEW ZEALAND, THE **4845**

NEW ZEALAND. VALUATION DEPT *See* URBAN REAL ESTATE MARKET IN NEW ZEALAND **4848**

NEW ZEALAND VETERINARY JOURNAL (NZ/0048-0169) [01642558] **5517**

NEW ZEALAND VISITOR STATISTICS (NZ) [19502878] **5334**

NEW ZEALAND VISITOR STATISTICS. ASIA (NZ) [19502943] **5334**

NEW ZEALAND VISITOR STATISTICS. AUSTRALIA AND PACIFIC (NZ) [19502981] **5334**

NEW ZEALAND VISITOR STATISTICS. EUROPE (NZ) [19502912] **5334**

NEW ZEALAND VISITOR STATISTICS. TOTAL VISITORS (NZ) [19502821] **5334**

NEW ZEALAND WHOLE EARTH CATALOGUE (NZ) [01788153] **3485**

NEW ZEALAND WILDLIFE (NZ/0028-8802) [04743786] **4875**

NEW ZEALAND WINGS (NZ/0110-1471) [I01101471] **30**

NEW ZEALAND WOOL MARKET REVIEW *See* WOOL MARKET REVIEW **5360**

NEW ZEALAND WOOL MARKET REVIEW (NZ/0113-2792) [I01132792] **5354**

NEWARK MUSEUM *See* ANNUAL REPORT - NEWARK MUSEUM **4083**

NEWARK MUSEUM ASSOCIATION *See* NEWS NOTES - NEWARK MUSEUM **4094**

NEWARK POST, THE (US) [12646398] **5647**

NEWARK PRESS (US/0741-9317) [10262289] **2922**

NEWBERG ON CLASS ACTIONS (US) [05694323] **3017**

NEWBERRY NEWSLETTER, A (US/1074-3596) [01780283] **3234**

NEWBERRY OBSERVER AND HERALD AND NEWS, THE (US) [14961519] **5743**

NEWBURGH REGISTER (NEWBURGH, IND.) (US) [14284987] **5666**

NEWCASTLE FORGOTTEN FANTASY LIBRARY, THE (US/0163-6251) [04419241] **3416**

NEWCASTLE INDEPENDENT (1977) (CN/0710-0116) [08192583] **5790**

NEWCASTLE-UPON-TYNE. UNIVERSITY. LIBRARY *See* PUBLICATIONS **3243**

NEWCASTLE-UPON-TYNE. UNIVERSITY. PHILOSOPHICAL SOCIETY *See* PROCEEDINGS OF THE UNIVERSITY OF NEWCASTLE-UPON-TYNE PHILOSOPHICAL SOCIETY **4358**

NEWCOMEN BULLETIN / NEWCOMEN SOCIETY FOR THE STUDY OF THE HISTORY OF ENGINEERING AND TECHNOLOGY, THE (UK) [07066291] **5133**

NEWCOMEN SOCIETY FOR THE STUDY OF THE HISTORY OF ENGINEERING AND TECHNOLOGY, LONDON *See* TRANSACTIONS - NEWCOMEN SOCIETY FOR THE STUDY OF THE HISTORY OF ENGINEERING AND TECHNOLOGY **5166**

NEWCOMEN SOCIETY FOR THE STUDY OF THE HISTORY OF ENGINEERING AND TECHNOLOGY (LONDON, ENGLAND) *See* NEWCOMEN BULLETIN / NEWCOMEN SOCIETY FOR THE STUDY OF THE HISTORY OF ENGINEERING AND TECHNOLOGY, THE **5133**

NEWCOMER'S — Alphabetical Title Index

... NEWCOMER'S GUIDE TO FLORIDA BUSINESS, THE (US/1052-7338) [22363685] **699**

NEWCOMERSTOWN NEWS (1953) (US) [17415380] **5729**

NEWEST REVIEW, THE (CN) [02585055] 326, **3349**

NEWFIELD NEWS (US/0746-5289) [10124581] **5719**

NEWFOUNDLAND See STATUTES OF THE PROVINCE OF NEWFOUNDLAND **3059**

NEWFOUNDLAND ANCESTOR (CN/0838-049X) [18243161] **2462**

NEWFOUNDLAND AND LABRADOR (ACCOMMODATION GUIDE) See NEWFOUNDLAND AND LABRADOR. ACCOMMODATIONS **2808**

NEWFOUNDLAND AND LABRADOR. ACCOMMODATIONS (CN) [15169546] **2808**

NEWFOUNDLAND AND LABRADOR BUSINESS DIRECTORY AND BUYERS GUIDE (CN/0316-7798) [01786316] **699**

NEWFOUNDLAND & LABRADOR BUSINESS JOURNAL (CN) **699**

NEWFOUNDLAND AND LABRADOR : CAMPGROUND GUIDE (CN/0713-7745) [09091422] **4852**

NEWFOUNDLAND AND LABRADOR FEDERATION OF LABOUR See ANNUAL CONVENTION - NEWFOUNDLAND AND LABRADOR FEDERATION OF LABOUR **1644**

NEWFOUNDLAND & PRINCE EDWARD ISLAND REPORTS (BOUND CUMULATION) (CN/0715-4755) [01716185] **3017**

NEWFOUNDLAND CHURCHMAN (CN/0549-0898) [02398532] **4981**

NEWFOUNDLAND. DIVISION OF PROGRAM DEVELOPMENT See PROGRAM OF STUDIES - NEWFOUNDLAND. DIVISION OF PROGRAM DEVELOPMENT **1903**

NEWFOUNDLAND FARM PRODUCTS CORPORATION See ANNUAL REPORT / NEWFOUNDLAND FARM PRODUCTS CORPORATION **61**

NEWFOUNDLAND FISHERIES (CN/0576-0917) [01798478] **2309**

NEWFOUNDLAND GAZETTE, THE (CN/0028-8888) [02249473] **3017**

NEWFOUNDLAND. GEOLOGICAL SURVEY BRANCH See CURRENT RESEARCH - NEWFOUNDLAND. GEOLOGICAL SURVEY BRANCH **1439**

NEWFOUNDLAND HERALD, THE (CN/0824-3581) [10391988] **2490**

NEWFOUNDLAND. HOUSE OF ASSEMBLY See VERBATIM REPORT **4693**

NEWFOUNDLAND JOURNAL OF GEOLOGICAL EDUCATION, THE (CN/0709-4426) [05198282] **1389**

NEWFOUNDLAND LIBRARY ASSOCIATION BULLETIN (CN/0832-9249) [17314241] **3234**

NEWFOUNDLAND LIFESTYLE (CN/0827-3960) [12150547] **2748**

NEWFOUNDLAND MEDICAL DIRECTORY (CN/0078-0316) [02248190] **3916**

NEWFOUNDLAND. OFFICE OF THE PARLIAMENTARY COMMISSIONER (OMBUDSMAN) See ANNUAL REPORT OF THE PARLIAMENTARY COMMISSIONER. OMBUDSMAN **4628**

NEWFOUNDLAND QUARTERLY (1971) (CN/0380-5832) [02079388] **2748**

NEWFOUNDLAND SIGNAL, THE (CN/0317-2309) [02247981] **5790**

NEWFOUNDLAND SOCIAL AND ECONOMIC PAPERS (CN/0078-0332) [02659572] **5211**

NEWFOUNDLAND SPORTSMAN (CN) **4908**

NEWFOUNDLAND STUDIES (CN/0823-1737) [13448899] **2749**

NEWFOUNDLAND TV TOPICS (CN/0227-1532) [06562893] **1160**

NEWINGTON TOWN CRIER (US/0745-0796) [08803043] **5646**

NEWKIRK NOTES (US/0882-6773) [12004373] **2462**

NEWLETTER - WOMEN'S HEALTH AND REPRODUCTIVE RIGHTS INFORMATION CENTRE See WOMEN'S HEALTH **2602**

NEWLOOK (FR) **1086**

NEWMAN REPORT, THE (US/0898-5367) [17844882] **934**

NEWMARKET BUSINESS REPORT (CN/1186-0413) [24266317] **699**

NEWMEDIA (SAN MATEO, CALIF.) (US/1060-7188) [24484628] **1118**

NEWMONTH (US/0192-1142) [05019896] **4484**

NEWNAN TIMES-HERALD, THE (US/0883-2536) [12114390] **5654**

NEWORLD (US/0160-3736) [03381350] **326**

NEWPORT BEACH (US/0743-7161) [10649509] **2541**

NEWPORT DAILY NEWS *CEASED.* (US/1053-2560) [09882960] **5741**

NEWPORT HISTORY (US/0028-8918) [04090725] **2749**

NEWPORT MERCURY (US) [24290526] **5741**

NEWPORT MINER, THE (US/0892-6239) [15248685] **5761**

NEWPORT NAVALOG (US) [24881938] **5741**

NEWPORT REVIEW, THE (US/0276-5241) [07355435] **2541**

NEWPORT THIS WEEK (US) [24915222] **5741**

NEWS (US/1041-5971) [17717720] **1694**

NEWS (YU) [01795178] **4075**

NEWS (US) [05285156] **4793**

NEWS 3X/400 (US/1040-6093) [18460380] 1248, 1264, **1238**

NEWS - ADMINISTRATIVE CONFERENCE OF THE UNITED STATES (US/0197-2316) [04327246] **4669**

NEWS ADVERTISER (AJAX CANADA) (CN) **5790**

NEWS ADVERTISER (KITIMAT) (CN/0316-0238) [02247307] **5790**

NEWS - AFFILIATE ARTISTS *CEASED.* (US) [05920536] **326**

NEWS - AMERICAN IMMIGRATION AND CITIZENSHIP CONFERENCE (US/0193-4570) [05266624] **1920**

NEWS & CINE INDIA See NEWS INDIA (NEW YORK) **2269**

NEWS & CITIZEN (US) **5757**

NEWS & DAILY ADVANCE (US) [14913712] **5759**

NEWS & FARMER (US/0048-0215) [04127164] **112**

NEWS AND FEATURES FROM NIH See NIH NEWS & FEATURES / NATIONAL INSTITUTES OF HEALTH **3622**

NEWS & FEATURES FROM NIH (US) [04381802] **4793**

NEWS & INFO / FRIENDS FOR LONG ISLAND'S HERITAGE (US) [25575892] 4094, **4169**

NEWS AND ISSUES (NEW YORK, N.Y.) (US/1064-6493) [25562056] **5298**

NEWS AND JOURNAL (RIPLEY, MISS.) (US/8755-9854) [10065520] 2749, **2462**

NEWS AND LEADER See DE SMET NEWS, THE **5743**

NEWS & LETTERS (US/0028-8969) [01796331] 5562, 4484, **1508**

NEWS & NOTES - AMERICAN ASSOCIATION ON MENTAL RETARDATION (US/0895-8033) [16800728] **1882**

NEWS AND NOTES FROM ALL OVER, NEWSLETTER OF THE SOCIETY FOR THE ERADICATION OF TELEVISION (US) **2490**

NEWS & OBSERVER (RALEIGH, N.C. : 1894) (US) [11750106] **5724**

NEWS AND PRESS (DARLINGTON, S.C.) [13610124] **5743**

NEWS & RECORD (US/0747-2862) [10688267] **5759**

● NEWS & RECORD (GREENSBORO, N.C.) (US/1072-0065) [25383111] **5724**

NEWS AND REPORTER (US) [27950965] **5743**

NEWS AND ROUND TABLE (US) [08131570] **5298**

NEWS & VIEWS - CANADIAN FEDERATION OF INDEPENDENT BUSINESS (US/0849-2867) [23231467] **699**

NEWS & VIEWS OF THE SOUTH CAROLINA LIBRARY ASSOCIATION (US) [06401316] **3234**

NEWS & VIEWS - ONTARIO GENEALOGICAL SOCIETY, LEEDS & GRENVILLE BRANCH (CN/0708-6350) [05322928] **2462**

NEWS & VIEWS (PITTSBURGH, PA.) (US/1042-5160) [19075237] **5298**

NEWS AND VIEWS - SIMCOE COUNTY HISTORICAL ASSOCIATION (CN/0700-4427) [09223116] **2749**

NEWS AND VIEWS (WASHINGTON, D.C.) (US) [12252448] **3017**

NEWS & VIEWS (WORLD JEWISH CONGRESS) See WJC REPORT : WORLD JEWISH CONGRESS PUBLICATION, THE **5053**

NEWS / ART DECO SOCIETY OF NEW YORK (US/0743-3522) [10553228] **359**

NEWS - ASSISTANCE LEAGUE OF SOUTHERN CALIFORNIA (US/0736-1459) [08821810] **5298**

NEWS - ASSOCIATION OF COLLEGIATE SCHOOLS OF ARCHITECTURE (US/0149-2446) [03464468] 1837, **304**

NEWS. AVERAGE ANNUAL PAY BY STATE AND INDUSTRY / UNITED STATES DEPARTMENT OF LABOR, BUREAU OF LABOR STATISTICS (US) [11265201] 1694, **1536**

NEWS BEACON (FAIR LAWN, N.J.) (US/8750-3913) [11407118] **5814**

NEWS BEAT (MEDUCTIC, N.B.) See SABIAN NEWS BEAT CATALOG **4151**

NEWS / BECKMAN CENTER FOR THE HISTORY OF CHEMISTRY (US/1052-0414) [19246909] **987**

NEWS BRIEF - ENVIRONMENTAL LAW CENTRE (EDMONTON) (CN/1188-2565) [26245350] **3115**

NEWS BRIEFS : A PUBLICATION OF THE LOUISIANA STATE BAR ASSOCIATION (US) [10245120] **3017**

NEWS / BRITISH COLUMBIA MEDICAL ASSOCIATION (CN/0715-5379) [09538875] **3621**

NEWS BULLETIN (JA/0449-5314) [01794883] **4699**

NEWS BULLETIN - ANIMAL DEFENCE LEAGUE OF CANADA (CN/0044-829X) [02305951] **226**

NEWS BULLETIN - ARKANSAS BAR ASSOCIATION (US/0198-702X) [05929700] **3017**

NEWS BULLETIN (AUSTIN, TEX.) (US/0096-9117) [01765940] **4228**

NEWS BULLETIN - BRAZILIAN-AMERICAN CHAMBER OF COMMERCE (US/0300-7464) [01422787] **1638**

NEWS BULLETIN (DETROIT) (US/0094-8071) [01786633] **2292**

NEWS BULLETIN - DEVELOPMENT OFFICE, CARLETON UNIVERSITY (CN/0319-3284) [02442304] **1837**

NEWS BULLETIN / FLORIDA COLLEGE (US/8750-751X) [01382755] **1093**

NEWS BULLETIN - INTERNATIONAL UNION OF FOOD & ALLIED WORKERS' ASSOCIATIONS (SZ) [05285042] 2351, **1694**

NEWS BULLETIN / MICHIGAN BUSINESS EDUCATION ASSOCIATION (US/0026-2048) [01605444] 1768, **699**

NEWS BULLETIN / NATIONAL COUNCIL OF TEACHERS OF MATHEMATICS (US/0277-1365) [07506502] **3524**

NEWS BULLETIN OF THE AUSTRALIAN DENTAL ASSOCIATION (AT/0810-7440) [I08107440] **1331**

NEWS BULLETIN - SASKATCHEWAN RAIL COMMITTEE (CN/0708-028X) [04879779] **5433**

NEWS BULLETIN - SCHOOL LIBRARY ASSOCIATION OF VICTORIA (AT) [I03109224] 1768, **3234**

NEWS BULLETIN - SPECIAL LIBRARIES ASSOCIATION, BOSTON CHAPTER (US) [02465143] **3234**

NEWS BULLETIN (SYDNEY, AUSTRALIA) (AT) [16884170] 987, **1093**

NEWS BULLETIN / THAILAND. KRASUANG KANTANGPRATHET. KROM SARANITHET See THAILAND FOREIGN AFFAIRS NEWSLETTER / INFORMATION DEPARTMENT, MINISTRY OF FOREIGN AFFAIRS **4498**

● NEWS BULLETIN / THE MUSICAL BOX SOCIETY INTERNATIONAL (US/1071-0191) [28523637] **4140**

NEWS BUREAU CONTACTS *CEASED.* (US/1054-3791) [21312309] **1135**

NEWS - BUREAU OF LABOR STATISTICS (US) [03665341] 1694, **1537**

NEWS BURLINGTON (CN/0317-9885) [02248294] **5790**

NEWS (CALIFORNIA ASSOCIATION OF COMMUNITY COLLEGES) (US) [08970022] **1837**

NEWS / CALIFORNIA ASSOCIATION OF HOSPITALS AND HEALTH SYSTEMS (US) [15345805] **3789**

NEWS CANADA (TORONTO) (CN/0823-9118) [11847677] **2541**

NEWS / CANADIAN CENTRE FOR STUDIES IN PUBLISHING (CN/1183-4609) [24690905] **4817**

NEWS (CANADIAN SOCIETY OF CINEMATOGRAPHERS) (CN/0820-3431) [16656409] **4075**

NEWS CAST - AMERICAN IRIS SOCIETY. REGION 4 (US/0401-913X) [04990626] **2425**

NEWS CHRONICLE (PAWLING, N.Y.), THE (US/0747-2188) [10635483] **5719**

NEWS-CHRONICLE (SHIPPENSBURG, PA.) (US) [12850887] **5738**

NEWS CIRCLE, THE (US/0193-1814) [05161023] **2269**

NEWS-CITIZEN (VANDERGRIFT, PA.) (US) [15158715] **5738**

NEWS (CLAREMONT GRADUATE SCHOOL) (US/8750-2216) [11135204] **1093**

NEWS

NEWS (CLAY CITY, IND.) (US) [13400370] **5666**

NEWS-COMMERCIAL, THE (US) [15004332] **5701**

NEWS / CONSERVATION EDUCATION ASSOCIATION (US) [21696099] **2200**

NEWS / CONSUMER ACTION LEAGUE (CN/0711-7248) [08854798] **1298**

NEWS - CONSUMER FEDERATION OF AMERICA (US/0193-4635) [05259517] **1298**

NEWS CORPORATION (CN/1187-3493) [25313822] **1118**

●NEWS-DEMOCRAT & LEADER (US/1066-8071) [26925067] **5682**

NEWS-DEMOCRAT (CARROLLTON, KY.) (US) [13189562] **5682**

NEWS-DEMOCRAT (RUSSELLVILLE, KY.) See NEWS-DEMOCRAT & LEADER **5682**

NEWS-DEMOCRAT (RUSSELLVILLE, KY.) (US) [13997682] **5682**

NEWS-DIGEST (AMITE, LA.) (US) [16993018] **5684**

NEWS DIGEST / CHINESE INFORMATION AND CULTURE CENTER (US) [24155247] **2660**

NEWS DIGEST INTERNATIONAL (AT) [06345455] **4530, 2670**

NEWS DIGEST - INTERNATIONAL INSTITUTE OF MUNICIPAL CLERKS (US/0145-2290) [02711105] **4669**

NEWS DIGEST - ITA CEASED. (US/0146-4647) [02957498] **5133**

NEWS DIGEST / NICHCY (US) [23706298] **4391**

●NEWS DIMENSIONS (US/1064-3699) [26269607] **5647**

NEWS-DISPATCH (MICHIGAN CITY, IND.) (US/1047-6016) [11377778] **5666**

NEWS. EMPLOYMENT COST INDEX / UNITED STATES DEPARTMENT OF LABOR, BUREAU OF LABOR STATISTICS (US) [08732259] 1694, **1537**

NEWS-ENTERPRISE ELIZABETHTOWN, KY.) (US) [13904943] **5682**

NEWS-EXAMINER, THE (US) [13168790] **5657**

NEWS EXTRA (CN/0835-9989) [17408433] **2541**

NEWS, FACTS, ACTIONS (US) **909**

NEWS (FARMERSBURG, IND.) (US) [14814421] **5666**

NEWS - FEDERAL HOME LOAN BANK BOARD (US) [03470896] **801**

NEWS / FEDERAL-PROVINCIAL ENVIRONMENTAL ASSESSMENT REVIEW PANEL, HALIFAX-DARTMOUTH METROLITAN WASTEWATER MANAGEMENT SYSTEM (CN/1187-3663) [25127777] **2237**

NEWS - FEMINIST PARTY OF CANADA (CN/0226-1944) [06299057] **5562**

NEWS - FLORIDA ASSOCIATION OF SOIL AND WATER CONSERVATION DISTRICT SUPERVISORS (US/0744-3366) [08197767] **2200**

●NEWS FOR ENTREPRENEURIAL MOTHERS (US/1064-6973) [26458454] **5562, 699**

NEWS FOR INVESTORS (US/1053-5470) [03790655] **909**

NEWS FOR KIDS (US/1058-8795) [24418154] **1067**

●NEWS FOR NETWORK USERS (US/1065-0652) [26496638] **1243**

NEWS FOR SENIORS (CN/0710-958X) [08418999] **5180**

NEWS FOR SOUTH CAROLINA LIBRARIES (US/0146-1842) [01696372] **3234**

"NEWS" FOR THE CANADIAN RABBIT BREEDER CEASED. (CN/0545-8269) [02083541] **216**

NEWS FOR YOU (SYRACUSE, N.Y.) (US/0884-3910) [12428477] **5719**

NEWS (FREDERICK, MD.) (US) [09625223] **5686**

NEWS FROM ABMAC (US/0196-3856) [05790027] **3621**

NEWS FROM, ACUSNY (US) [23728946] **1837**

NEWS FROM C.U.N.Y. LIBRARIES (US/0747-6035) [10762209] **3234**

NEWS FROM CANADA-JAPAN SOCIETY OF VANCOUVER (CN/0382-8417) [02813724] **5234**

NEWS FROM CHRISTIE'S (US) [06537460] **360**

NEWS FROM DBDH (DK/0904-9681) [I09049681] **2607**

NEWS FROM DRAFTING WILLS AND TUST AREEMENTS (US/0733-4184) [08582382] **3118**

NEWS FROM DUN & BRADSTREET, INC. BUSINESS ECONOMICS DIVISION. WEEKLY FAILURES (US/0273-1622) [07028092] **1508**

NEWS FROM ICELAND (IC) [05730543] **2520**

NEWS FROM ICTP / INTERNATIONAL CENTRE FOR THEORETICAL PHYSICS (IT) [20283623] **4413**

NEWS FROM INDIAN COUNTRY : THE JOURNAL (US) [18515137] **2269**

NEWS FROM ISDS (FR/0257-0009) [10394824] **3234**

NEWS FROM ISRAEL (II) [04531808] **2507**

NEWS FROM ITALY (IT) [19604184] **2490**

NEWS FROM MITI (JA) [11718894] **847**

NEWS FROM NATIVE CALIFORNIA (US/1040-5437) [15705268] **2749**

NEWS FROM OECD / ORGANISATION FOR ECONOMIC CO-OPERATION AND DEVELOPMENT CEASED. (FR) [03896110] **1508**

NEWS FROM RILA (US/0891-3498) [09573701] **360**

NEWS FROM ROHDE & SCHWARZ (GW/0028-9108) [09720674] **934**

NEWS FROM THE CANADIAN MUSICAL HERITAGE SOCIETY (CN/1181-6023) [23598376] **4140**

NEWS FROM THE CENTRE - INSTITUTE FOR NONPROFIT ORGANIZATIONS (CN/0225-0446) [06054070] **5298**

NEWS FROM THE FOUNDATION / FOUNDATION FOR THE IMPROVEMENT OF LIVING AND WORKING CONDITIONS (IE/0258-1965) [24225503] **1694**

NEWS FROM THE HARVARD UNIVERSITY ART MUSEUMS See HARVARD UNIVERSITY ART MUSEUMS REVIEW **4088**

NEWS FROM THE HILL (WASHINGTON) (US/0270-0662) [06337938] **3102**

NEWS FROM THE LIBRARY OF CONGRESS (US/0731-3527) [08141069] **3234**

NEWS FROM THE NORTHWEST (US/0747-8739) [10796774] **2462**

●NEWS FROM THE OC CORRAL (CN/1194-823X) [29396138] **112**

NEWS FROM THE OCEANOGRAPHER OF THE NAVY (US/1056-7348) [23828708] **4181**

NEWS FROM THE PHILADELPHIA ZOO (US) [04795553] **5592**

NEWS FROM THE RARE BOOK ROOM (CN/0085-4166) [02322375] **421**

NEWS FROM UKRAINE (UN) [01715805] **5811**

NEWS FROM WITHIN (IS) **2770**

NEWS FROM WORKERS' COMPENSATION (CN/1185-0264) [23659240] **1694**

NEWS FROM XINHUA NEWS AGENCY, CHINA. WEEKLY ISSUE CEASED. (UK/0142-6567) [10195748] **2507**

NEWS-GAZETTE (CHAMPAIGN, ILL.) (US/1042-3354) [16535031] **5661**

NEWS-GAZETTE (SAINT CLOUD, FLA.) (US/8750-5029) [11479506] **5650**

NEWS-GRAM - CHRISTIAN BUSINESS MEN OF CANADA (CN/0710-5770) [08777584] **4981**

NEWS GRAPHIC PILOT See OZAUKEE COUNTY NEWS GRAPHIC **5770**

NEWS GUARD (US) **5733**

NEWS: HEALTH ACTION INTERNATIONAL, HAI (MY) **4793**

NEWS - HEALTHCARE INFORMATION AND MANAGEMENT SYSTEMS SOCIETY (US/1066-9078) [24019195] **3790**

NEWS HERALD (EAGLE BEND, MINN.), THE (US/8750-4693) [11459619] **5697**

NEWS-HERALD (FRANKLIN, PA) (US) [13454036] **5738**

NEWS-HERALD (MORGANTON, N.C.), THE (US/8750-3980) [11378014] **5724**

NEWS HERALD (SARALAND, ALA.), THE CEASED. (US/0747-4512) [10880497] **5627**

NEWS-HERALD, THE (US) [17989546] **5729**

NEWS - HOSPITAL ASSOCIATION OF NEW YORK STATE (US/0018-5574) [02478536] **3790**

NEWS IBM (US) **1288**

NEWS IN BRIEF (TORONTO) (CN/0706-554X) [04589243] **1508**

NEWS IN ENGINEERING (US/0028-9205) [02160976] **1989**

NEWS IN PHYSIOLOGICAL SCIENCES (US/0886-1714) [12848725] **584**

●NEWS INC (US) **1118**

NEWS INDIA (NEW YORK) (US/0199-901X) [06284593] **2269**

●NEWS INDIA-TIMES (US/1071-0248) [28535752] **2269**

NEWS (INDIANA BASKETBALL HALL OF FAME) See INDIANA BASKETBALL HISTORY : A PUBLICATION OF THE INDIANA BASKETBALL HALL OF FAME **4900**

NEWS / INDIANA HISTORICAL SOCIETY (US/1047-708X) [13453576] **2749**

NEWS - INTERMEDIATE TEACHERS ASSOCIATION (CN/0225-9354) [06141431] **1867**

NEWS - INTERNATIONAL ASSOCIATION OF PERSONNEL IN EMPLOYMENT SECURITY (US/0020-6008) [13013484] **1694**

NEWS (INTERNATIONAL FRIENDSHIP LEAGUE OF THE GDR) (GW) [19371584] **2700**

NEWS / INTERNATIONAL SOCIETY FOR ROCK MECHANICS (PO/0539-0281) [03546951] **1389**

●NEWS- INTERNET SOCIETY (PRINT ED.) (US/1060-7803) [25060449] **1243**

NEWS-ITEM (COMBINED ED.) (US) [14088698] **5738**

NEWS / JAPAN GLASS ARTCRAFTS ASSOCIATION (JA) [11386595] **2592**

NEWS JOURNAL (US) [30500395] **5682**

NEWS JOURNAL (US) [24841952] **5682**

●NEWS JOURNAL / INTERNATIONAL SOCIETY FOR ROCK MECHANICS (PO) [30495408] **1389**

NEWS JOURNAL (MANSFIELD, OHIO) (US) [12717053] **5729**

NEWS JOURNAL - SOCIETY FOR COMMERCIAL ARCHEOLOGY (U.S.) (US/0735-1399) [07046159] 276, **304**

NEWS JOURNAL (WILMINGTON, DEL.), THE (US/1042-4121) [16073699] **5647**

NEWS, (LAREDO, TEX.), THE (US/0747-1750) [10637257] **5752**

NEWS LEADER (US) [14089777] **5764**

NEWS-LEADER (US/0163-4011) [04377055] **5650**

NEWS-LEADER (SPRINGFIELD, MO.) (US/0893-3448) [15564106] **5704**

NEWS LEADER, THE (US) [19679781] **5654**

NEWS LETTER - BAR ASSOCIATION OF SRI LANKA (CE) [02506458] **3017**

NEWS LETTER - CUMBRIA FAMILY HISTORY SOCIETY (UK/0140-1912) [I01401912] **2462**

NEWS LETTER / FLUE-CURED TOBACCO COOPERATIVE STABILIZATION CORPORATION (US) [09940075] **5373**

NEWS LETTER FROM THE INSTITUTE OF EARLY AMERICAN HISTORY & CULTURE, A (US/0020-2843) [02325674] **2749**

NEWS LETTER - INDIA (REPUBLIC). DEPT. OF SOCIAL WELFARE, THE (II) [05535544] **5298**

NEWS LETTER - LIBRARIANS' CHRISTIAN FELLOWSHIP OF AUSTRALIA (AT/0810-042X) [I0810042X] **3234**

NEWS LETTER / MATHEMATICAL ASSOCIATION (UK/0465-3696) [06097116] **3524**

NEWS LETTER - MCGILL UNIVERSITY COMPUTING CENTRE (CN/0380-478X) [02056250] 1160, **1197**

NEWS LETTER / MONTANA GEOLOGICAL SOCIETY (US) [15314066] **1389**

NEWS LETTER / NATIONAL REHABILITATION ASSOCIATION See NRA NEWSLETTER (ALEXANDRIA, VA.) **4381**

NEWS-LETTER - NATIONAL SOCIETY OF UNITED STATES DAUGHTERS OF 1812 (US/0271-7522) [01645207] 2749, **5234**

NEWS-LETTER OF THE AMERICAN ANTIQUARIAN SOCIETY (US/0569-2229) [01479297] **4831**

NEWS LETTER OF THE ASTRONOMICAL SOCIETY OF NEW YORK (US/0148-9992) [03407554] **397**

NEWS LETTER OF THE PARKE SOCIETY (US/0148-3994) [03301147] **2462**

NEWS-LETTER OF THE SOCIETY FOR THE STUDY OF SOUTHERN LITERATURE, THE (US/0197-8071) [06071935] **3416**

NEWS LETTER OF THE SOCIETY OF ARCHIVISTS (UK/0142-2278) [I01422278] **2482**

NEWS LETTER OF THE ST. ANDREW'S SOCIETY OF TORONTO (CN/0822-2401) [10513501] **5234**

NEWS LETTER / POPULATION CENTRE BANGALORE (II) [05905619] 4555, **590**

NEWS LETTER / PRESERVATION LEAGUE OF NEW YORK STATE (US/0882-7478) [04055150] **304**

NEWS — Alphabetical Title Index

NEWS LETTER / THE UNIVERSITY OF VIRGINIA (US/0042-0271) [01775976] **4669**

NEWS LIBRARY NEWS (US/1047-417X) [15685905] **3234**

NEWS - LIBRARY OF CONGRESS. NATIONAL LIBRARY SERVICE FOR THE BLIND AND PHYSICALLY HANDICAPPED (US/1046-1663) [04518845] **4391**

NEWS MAGAZINE - HAMILTON LAW ASSOCIATION *See* HAMILTON LAWYER **2976**

NEWS (MAPLE RIDGE) (CN/0227-2598) [08071412] **5790**

NEWS MEDIA & THE LAW, THE (US/0149-0737) [03562814] 1118, **3017**

●NEWS MEDIA YELLOW BOOK (US/1071-8931) [28761903] 1118, **1927**

NEWS MEDIA YELLOW BOOK OF WASHINGTON AND NEW YORK *See* NEWS MEDIA YELLOW BOOK **1927**

NEWS MEDIA YELLOW BOOK OF WASHINGTON AND NEW YORK, THE (US/1043-2620) [19366700] **1118**

NEWS MESSENGER (US) [21981195] **5708**

NEWS MESSENGER (MARSHALL, TEX.) (US/1053-5705) [22581915] **5752**

NEWS-MESSENGER, THE (US) [16898636] **5729**

NEWS MESSENGER, THE (US/0164-9086) [04232934] **5759**

NEWS / METROPOLITAN TORONTO REFERENCE LIBRARY (CN/0842-9707) [19491185] **3234**

NEWS MONITORING SERVICE (US/0277-5263) [03018682] **2749**

NEWS / MONTANA STATE LIBRARY (US) [10418939] **3234**

NEWS - MUSEUM PROFESSIONALS GROUP (UK/0266-0946) [I02660946] **4094**

NEWS 'N' NOTES - INDUSTRIAL EDUCATION COUNCIL OF THE ALBERTA TEACHERS' ASSOCIATION (CN/0709-0528) [05585034] **1867**

NEWS - NATIONAL CAMPAIGN FOR THE ARTS (UK/0957-9044) [I09579044] **326**

NEWS (NATIONAL LIBRARY OF MEDICINE (US)) (US/0027-965X) [03439741] 3621, **3234**

NEWS / NATIONAL SCIENCE FOUNDATION (US) [08026526] **5133**

NEWS (NEW RICHMOND, WIS.) (US) [13224107] **5769**

NEWS - NEW YORK STATE PUBLIC EMPLOYMENT RELATIONS BOARD (US/0732-1988) [04352326] **1694**

NEWS/NORTH (CN/0828-1521) [07298645] **5790**

NEWS NOTES & DEADLINES (US) **2922**

NEWS NOTES & QUOTES (US) [10992636] **1093**

NEWS NOTES - MARYKNOLL JUSTICE AND PEACE OFFICE (US/1064-1556) [24002622] **4530**

NEWS NOTES - NEWARK MUSEUM (US/0028-9256) [02600475] **4094**

NEWS OF DELAWARE COUNTY (UPPER DARBY, PA. : MARPLE-NEWTOWN--SPRINGFIELD ED.) (US) [18951398] **5738**

NEWS OF HYMNODY (UK/0263-2306) [08985616] **4981**

NEWS OF LITURGY (UK) [09312807] **4981**

NEWS OF MUSLIMS IN EUROPE *CEASED.* (UK/0143-9774) [08407984] **5044**

NEWS OF NEW YORK (US/0028-9264) [03547516] **3621**

NEWS OF NORWAY (US/0028-9272) [01760321] **2700**

NEWS OF ORANGE COUNTY, THE (US/1071-1716) [27102282] **5724**

NEWS OF THE EARTH (US/1052-2239) [22218689] **2178**

NEWS OF THE HIGHLANDS, THE (US) [12290588] **5719**

NEWS OF THE LEPIDOPTERISTS' SOCIETY (US/0091-1348) [03774720] **5592**

NEWS OF THE WORLD, THE (UK) [16294849] **5812**

NEWS OF THE WORLD'S CHILDREN (UNITED STATES COMMITTEE FOR UNICEF) (US/0028-9299) [05785449] **5298**

NEWS ON INDONESIA (US/0545-8617) [04534595] **4530**

NEWS - ONTARIO COUNCIL OF RABBIT CLUBS (CN/0703-783X) [03519968] **5234**

NEWS - ONTARIO FEDERATION OF INDEPENDENT SCHOOLS (CN/1187-5437) [25882767] **1768**

NEWS - ONTARIO. MINISTRY OF COMMUNITY AND SOCIAL SERVICES (CN/1183-644X) [24296650] **5298**

NEWS - ONTARIO PUBLIC SCHOOL TEACHERS' FEDERATION (1989) (CN/0846-4715) [20677358] **1768**

NEWS - OREGON HISTORICAL SOCIETY (US/0474-4535) [01794472] **2749**

NEWS / OXFAM AMERICA (US) [16520703] **5298**

NEWS / PAN AMERICAN DEVELOPMENT FOUNDATION (US/8755-3848) [07323571] **1619**

NEWS PHOTOGRAPHER (US/0199-2422) [02251750] 2922, **4372**

NEWS-PILOT (US/0747-4180) [10828335] **5637**

NEWS-PRESS (GLENDALE, CALIF.) *See* GLENDALE NEWS-PRESS (1993) **5635**

NEWS PREVIEWS (US/0095-2680) [04292301] **4817**

NEWS. PRODUCTIVITY AND COSTS (US/0738-2650) [09278060] **1619**

NEWS PROGRESS (SULLIVAN, ILL.) (US/0744-141X) [08042519] **5661**

NEWS QUARTERLY OF THE MCDONOUGH COUNTY GENEALOGICAL SOCIETY (US/8756-6923) [11617836] **2462**

●NEWS / RADIOSUISSE SERVICES (UK) [25621538] **1197**

NEWS. REAL EARNINGS IN ... / UNITED STATES DEPARTMENT OF LABOR, BUREAU OF LABOR STATISTICS (US) [09749804] **1694**

NEWS-RECORD (GILLETTE, WYO.), THE (US/0739-4926) [09765227] **5772**

NEWS-RECORD OF MAPLEWOOD AND SOUTH ORANGE (US) [19581188] **5711**

NEWS REGISTER (US) **5733**

NEWS RELEASE - CALIFORNAIA. ADMINISTRATIVE OFFICE OF THE COURTS (US) [07023944] **3142**

NEWS RELEASE FROM CONGRESSMAN AL BALDUS (US) [05519303] **4484**

NEWS RELEASE FROM THE CHESS PRESS SYNDICATE (US/0149-9394) [03581141] **4864**

NEWS-REPORT (BICKNELL, IND.) (US/1060-6165) [25052476] **5666**

NEWS REPORT (NATIONAL RESEARCH COUNCIL (US)) (US/0027-8432) [02513757] **5133**

NEWS-REPORTER (US) [19935345] **5644**

NEWS REPORTER, THE (US) [11966287] **5724**

NEWS-REPORTER (WASHINGTON, GA.) (US) [12611143] **5654**

NEWS-REVIEW (INYOKERN, CALIF.), THE (US/0893-9004) [15711029] **5637**

NEWS REVIEW (MATTITUCK, NEW YORK) (US) **5719**

NEWS REVIEW (RIVERHEAD, N.Y.) (US) [11421657] **5719**

NEWS REVIEW (SUMNER, WASH.) *CEASED.* (US) [17336762] **5761**

NEWS (ROBLIN) (CN/0229-7752) [08302846] **5790**

NEWS - SCOTTISH COUNCIL ON DISABILITY *See* DISABILITY NEWS **4387**

NEWS-SENTINEL (FORT WAYNE, IND.) (US) [08807796] **5666**

NEWS / SOCIETY OF ARCHITECTURAL HISTORIANS, SOUTHERN CALIFORNIA CHAPTER (US/1062-6301) [15743072] **304**

NEWS : SOUTH BAY COOPERATIVE LIBRARY SYSTEM *See* SEARCH (SANTA CLARA, CALIF.) **3248**

NEWS, SOUTHERN AFRICA (CN/0709-6119) [05696313] **5790**

NEWS SPREADER, THE (CN/0229-7728) [08099479] **112**

NEWS-SUN (FAIRMOUNT, IND.) (US) [15145640] **5666**

NEWS-SUN (KENDALLVILLE, IND.) (US/8750-0876) [10961365] **5666**

NEWS-SUN (NEWPORT, PA.), THE (US/0889-3810) [13447381] **5738**

NEWS-SUN (SEBRING, FLA.), THE (US/1074-8342) [29858590] **5650**

NEWS TALK (US/0733-6586) [20747548] 5318, **1927**

NEWS (TELL CITY, IND.) (US/0887-0837) [13079489] **5666**

NEWS, THE (US) [21015378] **5697**

NEWS, THE (US) [09472648] **5627**

NEWS, THE (US) [16677909] **5752**

NEWS, THE (US) **1837**

NEWS, THE (US) [08818005] **5661**

NEWS / THEATRE ONTARIO (CN/0821-4476) [09551442] **5366**

NEWS-TIMES (DANBURY, CONN.), THE (US/1044-4106) [08505328] **5646**

NEWS TIMES (NEWPORT, OR.) (US/0888-2010) [13506772] **5733**

NEWS TRANSCRIPT (US/0191-5908) [04921973] **5711**

●NEWS TRIBUNE, THE (US) [28950096] **5761**

NEWS TRIBUNE (WOODBRIDGE, N.J.) (US/1069-2681) [15538314] **5711**

NEWS / UNITED STATES DEPARTMENT OF LABOR, OFFICE OF INFORMATION (US) [01588528] **1694**

NEWS UPDATE / CANADIAN AIR TRAFFIC CONTROL, ASSOCIATION (CN/0713-536X) [08955973] **30**

NEWS, VIEWS AND REVIEWS - ARCHITECTURAL INSTITUTE OF BRITISH COLUMBIA (CN/0715-4100) [09157095] **304**

NEWS-VIRGINIAN, THE (US/8750-7862) [11779672] **5759**

NEWS - WATER RESOURCES RESEARCH INSTITUTE OF THE UNIVERSITY OF NORTH CAROLINA (US/0549-799X) [05279630] **5536**

NEWS WAVE (CN/0715-3341) [09106604] **326**

NEWS WEEKLY, THE (US/0747-136X) [10569986] **2490**

NEWS / WESTERN RESERVE HISTORICAL SOCIETY (US/0882-3154) [11781205] **2749**

NEWSART (TORONTO) (CN/0703-8704) [03781975] **360**

NEWSBANK ELECTRONIC INFORMATION SYSTEM *See* NEWSBANK REFERENCE SERVICE COMPUTER FILE **1197**

NEWSBANK ELECTRONIC INFORMATION SYSTEM [COMPUTER FILE] (US) [21680575] **1197**

NEWSBANK : HEALTH (US) [05584395] **4793**

●NEWSBANK REFERENCE SERVICE COMPUTER FILE (US) [25705545] **1197**

NEWSBEAT (AT/030-794X) **5298**

NEWSBOARD (MONTREAL, QUEBEC) (CN/0711-0480) [08330361] **2403**

NEWSBOY (US/0028-9396) [06328283] 434, **3416**

NEWSBREAK (AT) **3170**

NEWSBREAK / NATIONAL CONFERENCE ON SOVIET JEWRY (US) [21887232] **2269**

NEWSBRIEF / AMERICAN CONSERVATORY OF MUSIC (US/0735-7079) [08622076] **4140**

NEWSBRIEF : EMPLOYMENT, OPPORTUNITY, EMPOWERMENT (US) [24624135] **4392**

NEWSBRIEF - UNITED SOCIETY FOR THE PROPAGATION OF THE GOSPEL (UK/0958-2770) [I09582770] **4981**

NEWSBYTES : NEWS NETWORK *CEASED.* (US) **1243**

NEWSCALL NEWSLETTER, THE (CN/0225-1248) [06136420] **2749**

NEWSCAP (CN/0821-736X) [10446161] **1867**

NEWSCURRENTS (MADISON, WIS.) (US/8756-3940) [11570345] 1768, **5211**

NEWSDATA (AT) **2309**

NEWSDAY INDEX TO THE SUFFOLK EDITION (US) [07423226] **2490**

NEWSDAY. NASSAU EDITION (US/0278-5587) [05371847] **5719**

NEWSDAY (NEW YORK ED.) (US/0889-793X) [10862536] **5719**

NEWSEARCH (US) [14189775] **3621**

NEWSETTE - PHILIPPINE INSTITUTE OF CERTIFIED PUBLIC ACCOUNTANTS (PH) [01799148] **749**

NEWSFACES IN HIGH TECHNOLOGY (US/0899-1235) [17996665] **5133**

NEWSFILE (TORONTO) (CN/0711-1762) [08882634] **5790**

NEWSFLASH GREEN EUROPE / EUROPEAN COMMUNITY (BE) [11270883] **112**

NEWSFLASH / NEW BRUNSWICK TEACHERS' ASSOCIATION (CN/0715-5484) [09340456] **1768**

NEWSFRONT GREEK SHIPPING INTELLIGENCE (GR) **5453**

NEWSHEET - COUNCIL FOR ENVIRONMENTAL EDUCATION (UK/0960-9199) [I09609199] **2178**

NEWSINDEX FOR SMALL BUSINESS ENTREPRENEURS, THE (US/1056-0289) [23446927] **699**

NEWSLEAF - ONTARIO GENEALOGICAL SOCIETY (CN/0380-1616) [01761293] **2462**

NEWSLETTER (IS) [17816585] 2269, **4484**

Alphabetical Title Index — NEWSLETTER

●NEWSLETTER : A PUBLICATION OF THE ALBERTA TEACHERS' ASSOCIATION, ENGLISH AS A SECOND LANGUAGE COUNCIL (CN/1189-4881) [26714732] **1901**

NEWSLETTER / ACADEMY OF CANADIAN WRITERS (CN/0712-9955) [08858376] **3416**

NEWSLETTER - ADVISORY COUNCIL ON HISTORIC PRESERVATION *See* REPORT - ADVISORY COUNCIL ON HISTORIC PRESERVATION **2757**

NEWSLETTER - AFRICAN-AMERICAN FAMILY HISTORY ASSOCIATION (US/0893-4290) [06246443] 2269, **2463**

NEWSLETTER (AFRO-AMERICAN HISTORICAL AND GENEALOGICAL SOCIETY (WASHINGTON, D.C.) : 1983) (US/0882-8474) [11974299] 2269, **2749**

NEWSLETTER / ALBERTA ASSOCIATION OF COLLEGE LIBRARIANS (CN/0829-4321) [13263528] **3234**

NEWSLETTER / ALBERTA HERITAGE FOUNDATION FOR MEDICAL RESEARCH (CN/0715-2396) [09332203] **3621**

NEWSLETTER - ALBERTA HOME AND SCHOOL COUNCILS' ASSOCIATION (CN/1193-6541) [27202857] **1768**

NEWSLETTER - ALBERTA SURFACE RIGHTS FEDERATION (CN/0823-8561) [11431394] **112**

NEWSLETTER - ALBERTA TEACHERS' ASSOCIATION (CN/0316-599X) [02247612] **1867**

NEWSLETTER - ALBERTA TEACHERS' ASSOCIATION. RELIGIOUS AND MORAL EDUCATION COUNCIL (CN/1193-8722) [27898407] 1768, **4981**

NEWSLETTER - AMBULANCE & MEDICAL SERVICES ASSOCIATION OF AMERICA (US/0192-6055) [04989107] **3725**

NEWSLETTER (AMERICAN ACADEMY OF PSYCHIATRY AND THE LAW) (US/0896-5633) [09069105] 3017, **3931**

NEWSLETTER / AMERICAN AEROBICS ASSOCIATION (US/8755-8742) [11425136] **2600**

NEWSLETTER - AMERICAN ASSOCIATION FOR THE ADVANCEMENT OF SLAVIC STUDIES (US/0883-9549) [02257244] **2700**

NEWSLETTER / AMERICAN ASSOCIATION OF BIBLE COLLEGES (US/0736-2595) [09075386] **4981**

NEWSLETTER / AMERICAN ASSOCIATION OF BOTANICAL GARDENS AND ARBORETA (US/0569-2423) [07244344] 2425, **519**

NEWSLETTER / AMERICAN ASSOCIATION OF PASTORAL COUNSELORS (US/1065-383X) [26611109] **4981**

NEWSLETTER (AMERICAN ASSOCIATION OF SWINE PRACTITIONERS) *See* SWINE HEALTH AND PRODUCTION **222**

NEWSLETTER - AMERICAN ASSOCIATION OF TISSUE BANKS (US/0270-2673) [06383587] **3621**

NEWSLETTER - AMERICAN COUNCIL OF LEARNED SOCIETIES (US/1041-5963) [16744303] **5234**

NEWSLETTER / AMERICAN FEDERATION FOR CLINICAL RESEARCH (US/1052-7982) [19924609] **3621**

NEWSLETTER - AMERICAN HISTORICAL SOCIETY OF GERMANS FROM RUSSIA (US) [02251886] **2463**

NEWSLETTER - AMERICAN MUSICAL INSTRUMENT SOCIETY (US/0160-2365) [01795398] **4140**

NEWSLETTER - AMERICAN PLANNING ASSOCIATION, TEXAS CHAPTER (US) [05332608] **2829**

NEWSLETTER (AMERICAN PSYCHOLOGICAL ASSOCIATION. DIVISION OF HUMANISTIC PSYCHOLOGY) *See* HUMANISTIC PSYCHOLOGIST, THE **4589**

NEWSLETTER. AMERICAN RECORDER SOCIETY (US) [08252048] **4140**

NEWSLETTER - AMERICAN RESEARCH CENTER IN EGYPT (US/0402-0731) [04904846] 2660, **276**

NEWSLETTER - AMERICAN SCHOOLS OF ORIENTAL RESEARCH (US/0361-6029) [04660377] 276, **1768**

NEWSLETTER - AMERICAN SHORE AND BEACH PRESERVATION ASSOCIATION (US/0517-4856) [04567010] **2200**

NEWSLETTER - AMERICAN SOCIETY OF BREWING CHEMISTS (US/0149-7308) [02444763] **987**

NEWSLETTER - AMERICAN SOCIETY OF INDEXERS (US/0733-3048) [03703230] **3234**

NEWSLETTER / AMERICAN SOCIETY OF INTERNATIONAL LAW (US/1049-7803) [18377098] **3133**

NEWSLETTER - AMERICAN THEOLOGICAL LIBRARY ASSOCIATION (US/0003-1399) [01480909] 4981, **3235**

NEWSLETTER & DIGEST OF SELECTED OPINIONS OF STATE ATTORNEYS GENERAL (US/0094-226X) [01786102] **3142**

NEWSLETTER & GALLERY GUIDE / NATIONAL PALACE MUSEUM (CH/1011-9086) [23065405] **4094**

NEWSLETTER AND INTERIM REPORT / ROYAL BANK OF CANADA (CN/0710-5924) [08854803] **801**

NEWSLETTER AND PROCEEDINGS OF THE S.E.H.A (US/0036-1275) [02429652] **276**

NEWSLETTER - APPALACHIAN CENTER, BEREA COLLEGE (US) [05772134] **1093**

NEWSLETTER / APPLIED SCIENCE TECHNOLOGISTS AND TECHNICIANS OF BRITISH COLUMBIA (CN/0834-1788) [16206106] **5133**

NEWSLETTER / ARMSTRONG LABORATORY HUMAN RESOURCES DIRECTORATE, HUMAN SYSTEMS DIVISION (AFSC) (US) [24123230] **4052**

NEWSLETTER / ASIAN/PACIFIC AMERICAN LIBRARIANS ASSOCIATION (US/1040-8517) [18429211] **3235**

NEWSLETTER / ASSOCIATION FOR CANADIAN THEATRE RESEARCH (CN/1193-7564) [26328074] **5366**

NEWSLETTER - ASSOCIATION FOR CHINESE MUSIC RESEARCH (US/1071-0639) [28484510] **4140**

NEWSLETTER (ASSOCIATION FOR ISRAEL STUDIES) *See* ISRAEL STUDIES BULLETIN **2768**

NEWSLETTER - ASSOCIATION FOR NATIVE DEVELOPMENT IN THE PERFORMING AND VISUAL ARTS (CN/0316-8409) [02247215] **326**

NEWSLETTER - ASSOCIATION FOR THE ADVANCEMENT OF BALTIC STUDIES, INC (US/0162-976X) [04271263] **5211**

NEWSLETTER - ASSOCIATION FOR WOMEN IN MATHEMATICS (US) [04363176] **5562**

NEWSLETTER - ASSOCIATION OF AMERICAN LAW SCHOOLS. SECTION ON WOMEN IN LEGAL EDUCATION (US/0732-2771) [03918478] 5562, **3017**

NEWSLETTER (ASSOCIATION OF ANCIENT HISTORIANS) (CN/0710-7331) [08415782] **1078**

NEWSLETTER - ASSOCIATION OF BRITISH COLUMBIA DRAMA EDUCATORS (CN/0708-9597) [05258164] **5366**

NEWSLETTER - ASSOCIATION OF FAMILY AND CONCILIATION COURTS. CALIFORNIA CHAPTER, THE (US/0747-8038) [11025878] **2889**

NEWSLETTER - ASSOCIATION OF LAW LIBRARIES OF UPSTATE NEW YORK (US/0197-4815) [03304929] 3017, **3235**

NEWSLETTER. ASSOCIATION OF PACIFIC SYSTEMATISTS (US/1017-5679) [15809493] **519**

NEWSLETTER - ASSOCIATION OF SYSTEMATICS COLLECTIONS (US/0147-7889) [03197829] 467, **4094**

NEWSLETTER / ATLANTIC CANADA INSTITUTE (CN/0713-4479) [09113420] **2541**

NEWSLETTER / ATWATER INSTITUTE (CN/1185-1821) [24257197] **1118**

NEWSLETTER - AUGUST DERLETH SOCIETY (US/0272-9911) [06963190] **3416**

NEWSLETTER / AUSTIN FAMILIES ASSOCIATION OF AMERICA (US/1060-3263) [24929949] **2463**

NEWSLETTER / AUSTRALIA-JAPAN RESEARCH CENTRE (AT) [16751947] **5133**

NEWSLETTER - AUSTRALIAN AND NEW ZEALAND SOCIETY OF NUCLEAR MEDICINE (AT/0159-8376) [I01598376] **3848**

NEWSLETTER - AUSTRALIAN ANTHROPOLOGICAL SOCIETY (AT/0727-3134) [I07273134] **242**

NEWSLETTER - AUSTRALIAN ASSOCIATION OF FILM AND VIDEO LIBRARIES (AT/0728-3717) [I07283717] 1118, **3235**

NEWSLETTER - AUSTRALIAN COAL ASSOCIATION (AT/0813-1767) [I08131767] **2147**

NEWSLETTER - AUSTRALIAN COMPARATIVE AND INTERNATIONAL EDUCATION SOCIETY (AT/0812-0803) [I08120803] **1768**

NEWSLETTER / AUSTRALIAN LAW LIBRARIANS' GROUP (AT/0311-5984) [06028923] 3017, **3235**

NEWSLETTER / AUSTRALIAN MAP CIRCLE (AT/0811-9511) [10685480] **2570**

NEWSLETTER - AUSTRALIAN PHOTOGRAMMETRIC AND REMOTE SENSING SOCIETY (AT/0816-0376) [I08160376] **1358**

NEWSLETTER - AUTOMATED OFFICE CO (US/0749-8608) [11190821] **4212**

NEWSLETTER / B.C.A.I. CENTRE (CN/0715-4526) [09166942] **216**

NEWSLETTER / B.C. ALLIANCE CONCERNED WITH EARLY PREGNANCY AND PARENTHOOD (CN/1184-1478) [23598658] 590, **5298**

NEWSLETTER - BEATRIX POTTER SOCIETY (UK/0260-3780) [I02603780] 5234, **3416**

NEWSLETTER - BILL PRANKARD EVANGELISTIC ASSOCIATION (CN/0823-9606) [11559774] **4981**

NEWSLETTER BIOCHEMICAL AND HEALTH RESEARCH (BE) 4793, **491**

NEWSLETTER / BLAIR COUNTY GENEALOGICAL SOCIETY (US/1056-6953) [17560869] **2463**

NEWSLETTER (BLUE MOUNTAIN CENTER OF MEDITATION) *See* LITTLE LAMP, THE **4974**

NEWSLETTER - BLUE MOUNTAINS BRUCE TRAIL CLUB (CN/0225-7735) [06299471] **4875**

NEWSLETTER - BLUEGRASS CLUB OF NEW YORK (US/0098-3632) [02241050] **4140**

NEWSLETTER - BOOSEY AND HAWKES INC (US/0006-7598) [01536818] **4140**

NEWSLETTER (BRITISH ARACHNOLOGICAL SOCIETY) (UK) [11229717] **5592**

NEWSLETTER / BRITISH COLUMBIA CHORAL FEDERATION (CN/0822-8175) [10522268] **4140**

NEWSLETTER - BRITISH COLUMBIA COUNCIL FOR THE FAMILY (CN/0706-9022) [04589240] **2284**

NEWSLETTER / BRITISH COLUMBIA GENEALOGICAL SOCIETY (CN/0229-527X) [08307988] **2463**

NEWSLETTER / BRITISH COLUMBIA SOCIAL STUDIES TEACHERS' ASSOCIATION OF THE BRITISH COLUMBIA TEACHERS' FEDERATION (CN/0843-0764) [20026935] 5211, **1901**

NEWSLETTER - BRITISH INSTITUTE OF INTERNATIONAL AND COMPARATIVE LAW (UK/0308-2482) [02244693] **3133**

NEWSLETTER - BRITISH LIBRARY. SCIENCE REFERENCE AND INFORMATION SERVICE (UK/0951-4635) [I09514635] **5133**

NEWSLETTER - BRITISH SCIENCE FICTION ASSOCIATION (UK/0307-3335) [I03073335] **3417**

NEWSLETTER - BRITISH SOCIETY FOR PLANT GROWTH REGULATION (UK/0963-7001) [I09637001] **519**

NEWSLETTER - BUCKS COUNTY GENEALOGICAL SOCIETY (US/1047-2770) [10395756] **2463**

NEWSLETTER (BUDGET AND PROGRAM (FIRM)) (US) [06026644] **4739**

NEWSLETTER - BUFFALO AND ERIE COUNTY HISTORICAL SOCIETY (US/0521-5722) [04255273] **2749**

NEWSLETTER - BULGARIAN STUDIES ASSOCIATION (US/0193-8649) [05250714] **2624**

NEWSLETTER - BUREAU OF LABORATORIES (US) [06584156] **2237**

NEWSLETTER - BYRON SOCIETY (US/0196-8998) [04272806] **5234**

NEWSLETTER (CALDWELL COUNTY GENEALOGICAL SOCIETY) *See* CALDWELL COUNTY GENEALOGICAL SOCIETY, INC **2441**

NEWSLETTER - CALIFORNIA ACADEMY OF SCIENCES *See* ACADEMY NEWSLETTER, THE **5079**

NEWSLETTER/CALIFORNIA CONFEDERATION OF THE ARTS *See* CALIFORNIA ARTS ADVOCATE **317**

NEWSLETTER / CALIFORNIA COUNCIL FOR INTERNATIONAL TRADE (US/0738-9485) [09708217] **847**

NEWSLETTER / CALIFORNIA GENEALOGICAL ASSOCIATION (US/8756-694X) [11603149] **2463**

NEWSLETTER (CALIFORNIA GENEALOGICAL SOCIETY) *See* CGS NEWS - CALIFORNIA GENEALOGICAL SOCIETY **2442**

NEWSLETTER / CALIFORNIA NATIVE PLANT SOCIETY, BRISTLECONE CHAPTER (US) [15809708] **519**

NEWSLETTER - CAMPUS MINISTRY WOMEN (ORGANIZATION) *CEASED.* (US/0276-9565) [04691620] **5562**

NEWSLETTER - CANADA JAPAN TRADE COUNCIL (CN/0045-4214) [01803660] **1638**

NEWSLETTER / CANADIAN ASSOCIATION FOR GRADUATE EDUCATION IN LIBRARY, ARCHIVAL, AND INFORMATION STUDIES (CN/0845-5376) [20244378] 3235, **1837**

NEWSLETTER Alphabetical Title Index

NEWSLETTER / CANADIAN ASSOCIATION OF MUSIC LIBRARIES (CN/0383-1299) [10684096] 4141, **3235**

NEWSLETTER / CANADIAN ASSOCIATION OF RHODES SCHOLARS (CN/0821-039X) [09670514] **1837**

NEWSLETTER - CANADIAN ASSOCIATION OF SLAVISTS (CN/0381-6133) [02304201] **2520**

NEWSLETTER - CANADIAN ASSOCIATION OF SPORT SCIENCES. NATIONAL PHYSICAL FITNESS APPRAISAL CERTIFICATION AND ACCREDITATION PROGRAM (CN/1193-4263) [I11934263] **1857**

NEWSLETTER - CANADIAN ASSOCIATION ON GERONTOLOGY (CN/0712-676X) [10330425] **5180**

NEWSLETTER - CANADIAN ATHLETIC THERAPISTS ASSOCIATION (CN/0822-7578) [10386191] **3955**

NEWSLETTER (CANADIAN BAND ASSOCIATION. ONTARIO CHAPTER) (CN/0833-9503) [15372889] **4141**

NEWSLETTER (CANADIAN BOOKBINDERS AND BOOK ARTISTS GUILD) (CN/0822-9538) [10680982] **4831**

NEWSLETTER - CANADIAN CONSERVATION INSTITUTE (1987) See CCI NEWSLETTER OTTAWA **2189**

NEWSLETTER - CANADIAN EDUCATION ASSOCIATION (CN/0008-3445) [02335596] **1867**

NEWSLETTER - CANADIAN GEOTHERMAL RESOURCES ASSOCIATION (CN/0705-1891) [04129428] **1389**

NEWSLETTER - CANADIAN INSTITUTE OF UKRAINIAN STUDIES (CN/0702-8474) [03418001] **2700**

NEWSLETTER (CANADIAN MAGAZINE PUBLISHERS ASSOCIATION) (CN/1184-7379) [24266828] **4817**

NEWSLETTER - CANADIAN MEDICAL AND BIOLOGICAL ENGINEERING SOCIETY (CN/0384-1820) [03284767] **3695**

NEWSLETTER (CANADIAN MODERN PENTATHLON ASSOCIATION) (CN/0823-7948) [10845172] **4908**

NEWSLETTER - CANADIAN MUSEUM OF FLIGHT AND TRANSPORTATION (1990) (CN/1184-065X) [23598433] **30**

NEWSLETTER / CANADIAN OWNERS & PILOTS ASSOCIATION (CN/0826-1997) [11108188] **30**

NEWSLETTER - CANADIAN PHYSIOTHERAPY ASSOCIATION. SPORTS PHYSIOTHERAPY DIVISION (CN/0824-2917) [10216675] **3955**

NEWSLETTER - CANADIAN RESEARCH INSTITUTE FOR THE ADVANCEMENT OF WOMEN (CN/0229-7256) [08205579] **5562**

NEWSLETTER - CANADIAN SCIENCE WRITER'S ASSOCIATION (CN/0703-217X) [03681029] **2922**

NEWSLETTER / CANADIAN SOCIETY OF AGRICULTURAL ENGINEERING (CN/0714-3044) [09201160] **160**

NEWSLETTER - CANADIAN SOCIETY OF ENVIRONMENTAL BIOLOGISTS (CN/0318-5133) [03436117] **2200**

NEWSLETTER - CANADIAN SOCIETY OF MICROBIOLOGISTS / BULLETIN DE NOUVELLES - SOCIETET CANADIENNE DES MICROBIOLOGISTES (CN/0316-4934) [02624512] **568**

NEWSLETTER / CANADIAN TELEBOOK AGENCY (CN/0825-7752) [11777620] **4817**

NEWSLETTER - CANADIAN WAR MUSEUM. FRIENDS OF THE CANADIAN WAR MUSEUM (CN/1181-9413) [24256496] **4052**

NEWSLETTER - CANADIANS FOR A DEMOCRATIC WORKPLACE (CN/0703-5861) [03951219] 944, **1694**

NEWSLETTER / CAPITAL DISTRICT GENEALOGICAL SOCIETY (US) [11476168] **2463**

NEWSLETTER - CARIBBEAN ASSOCIATION OF NOVA SCOTIA (CN/0703-959X) [04040058] **2749**

NEWSLETTER - CASSETTE INFORMATION SERVICES (US/0095-1366) [01795477] **1901**

NEWSLETTER - CATALOG OF LANDSCAPE RECORDS IN THE UNITED STATES (PROJECT) (US/1046-2627) [17912324] **2425**

NEWSLETTER - CCLM See CCLM NEWSLETTER **3373**

NEWSLETTER - CENTER FOR HOLOCAUST STUDIES (BROOKLYN, NEW YORK, N.Y.) (US/0737-8092) [03946217] 5051, **2700**

NEWSLETTER - CENTER FOR MIGRATION STUDIES (U.S.) (US/8756-4467) [11558385] **1920**

NEWSLETTER - CENTER FOR REFORMATION RESEARCH (US/0362-563X) [02192930] **4981**

NEWSLETTER / CENTER FOR SOUTH ASIA STUDIES, UNIVERSITY OF CALIFORNIA AT BERKELEY (US) [23170997] **2660**

NEWSLETTER - CENTRAL AMERICAN REFUGEE CENTER, CARECEN (US) [25325332] **1920**

NEWSLETTER - CENTRAL ARCHIVES FOR THE HISTORY OF THE JEWISH PEOPLE (IS/0377-1784) [01796483] 5051, **2482**

NEWSLETTER / CENTRE FOR EDITING EARLY CANADIAN TEXTS (CN/0713-3960) [09033876] **3417**

NEWSLETTER - CENTRE FOR HEALTH ECONOMICS (UK/0950-2424) [I09502424] **4793**

NEWSLETTER - CHANGE (CN/0821-6657) [09747719] **3235**

NEWSLETTER - CHARLES RENNIE MACKINTOSH SOCIETY (UK/0141-559X) [I0141559X] **304**

NEWSLETTER (CHINESE AMERICAN LIBRARIANS ASSOCIATION) (US/0736-8887) [09074642] **3235**

NEWSLETTER - CINEMA ORGAN SOCIETY See CINEMA ORGAN SOCIETY : NEWSLETTER **5230**

NEWSLETTER / CLERMONT COUNTY GENEALOGICAL SOCIETY (US/0749-0631) [10545595] **2463**

NEWSLETTER - COACH HOUSE PRESS (CN/0827-3146) [11847668] **2922**

NEWSLETTER - COLCHESTER HISTORICAL SOCIETY (CN/0821-2430) [09511064] **2749**

NEWSLETTER - COLLEGE MUSIC SOCIETY (US) [04124444] **4141**

NEWSLETTER - COLORADO RIVER ASSOCIATION (US/0588-5035) [03229298] **4876**

NEWSLETTER - COLUMBIA UNIVERSITY. CENTER FOR SOCIAL POLICY AND PRACTICE IN THE WORKPLACE SUSPENDED. (US/0892-631X) [15247136] **1695**

NEWSLETTER / COMMITTEE ON SOCIALIST STUDIES (CN/0712-5275) [09137719] **4544**

NEWSLETTER - COMMON SHORES (US/0883-1726) [12182985] **4842**

NEWSLETTER (COMMONWEALTH SCIENCE COUNCIL (GREAT BRITAIN). EARTH SCIENCES PROGRAMME) (UK/0588-7739) [08138721] **1358**

NEWSLETTER - COMMUNICATION EFFECTIVENESS CENTRE (CN/0707-3062) [08010251] **1118**

NEWSLETTER - COMPARATIVE AND INTERNATIONAL EDUCATION SOCIETY OF CANADA (1975) (CN/0705-4084) [03960162] **1768**

NEWSLETTER : CONCERT RECORDINGS (US) [01795408] 5318, **4141**

NEWSLETTER / CONFERENCE GROUP ON ITALIAN POLITICS & SOCIETY (US/0896-9825) [17358185] **4530**

NEWSLETTER (CONFERENCE GROUP ON ITALIAN POLITICS AND SOCIETY) See BIANNUAL NEWSLETTER OF THE CONFERENCE GROUP ON ITALIAN POLITICS & SOCIETY, THE **4516**

NEWSLETTER - CONSORTIUM OF RHODE ISLAND ACADEMIC AND RESEARCH LIBRARIES (US/0882-6846) [11673552] **3235**

NEWSLETTER / CORNELL UNIVERSITY LIBRARIES, FLOWER VETERINARY LIBRARY (US) [11024595] 5517, **3235**

NEWSLETTER / COUNCIL OF NOVA SCOTIA ARCHIVES (CN/0829-7142) [13277114] **2482**

NEWSLETTER - COURT PRACTICE INSTITUTE (US/0098-9843) [02242007] **3142**

NEWSLETTER - COWAN CLAN UNITED (US/0090-6093) [01785351] **2463**

NEWSLETTER (CRIMINAL LAWYERS' ASSOCIATION (TORONTO, ONT.)) (CN/0715-5980) [09631071] **3108**

NEWSLETTER - CROSS-CULTURAL COMMUNICATION CENTRE (CN/0828-6965) [12577627] **2269**

NEWSLETTER - CUBA HISTORICAL SOCIETY, THE (US/0197-9027) [04572775] **2749**

NEWSLETTER (CYPRUS POPULAR BANK) (CY/0254-3214) [11625256] **801**

NEWSLETTER - DALHOUSIE UNIVERSITY. SCHOOL OF LIBRARY AND INFORMATION STUDIES (CN/0840-3902) [19450761] **3235**

●NEWSLETTER - DANISH CENTRE FOR TECHNICAL AIDS FOR REHABILITATION AND EDUCATION (DK) [I09081755] **1882**

NEWSLETTER / DECORATIVE ARTS SOCIETY 1890-1940 (UK) [09100589] **374**

NEWSLETTER - DEPARTMENT OF ABORIGINAL AFFAIRS, WESTERN AUSTRALIA (AT) [02577231] **242**

NEWSLETTER - DEPARTMENT OF POTTERY TECHNOLOGY, UNIVERSITY OF LEIDEN (NE/0168-7913) [15294677] **276**

NEWSLETTER DESIGN (US) **4817**

NEWSLETTER - DEVELOPMENTAL DISABILITIES SPECIALTY SECTION, AMERICAN OCCUPATIONAL THERAPY ASSOCIATION See DEVELOPMENTAL DISABILITIES SPECIAL INTEREST SECTION NEWSLETTER **1877**

NEWSLETTER - DISASTER OPERATIONS OFFICE, STATE OF MISSOURI (US/0364-0337) [02602037] **1073**

NEWSLETTER - DIXON GALLERY AND GARDENS (US) [05670594] 360, **4094**

NEWSLETTER / DUBUQUE COUNTY-KEY CITY GENEALOGICAL SOCIETY (US/1072-0359) [21867926] **2463**

NEWSLETTER - EARLY CHILDHOOD EDUCATION COUNCIL (CN/0316-2079) [02199090] **1768**

NEWSLETTER - EARTH SCIENCES HISTORY GROUP (AT/0815-7235) [I08157235] **1358**

NEWSLETTER - EARTHQUAKE ENGINEERING RESEARCH INSTITUTE (US/0270-8337) [04199961] **1409**

NEWSLETTER, EAST ASIAN ART & ARCHAEOLOGY (US/8755-4593) [06477897] 276, **360**

NEWSLETTER (ENABLEMENT INFORMATION SERVICE (BOSTON, MASS.)) CEASED. (US) [09845028] **4981**

NEWSLETTER / EQUINE RESEARCH CENTRE AT GUELPH (CN/0835-5509) [20001090] **2801**

NEWSLETTER - EUBIOS ETHICS INSTITUTE (NZ/1170-5485) [I11705485] **2252**

NEWSLETTER - EXECUTIVE COMMITTEE, LEAGUE OF CANADIAN POETS (CN/0319-6658) [02585425] **3467**

NEWSLETTER - FAIRFAX GENEALOGICAL SOCIETY (FAIRFAX COUNTY, VA.) (US/0895-2078) [13989962] **2463**

NEWSLETTER / FAMILY HISTORY SOCIETY OF ARIZONA (US) [11467247] **2463**

NEWSLETTER - FEDERAL STATISTICS USERS' CONFERENCE (US/0014-9225) [01250712] **5334**

NEWSLETTER / FEDERATION OF CATHOLIC PARENT-TEACHER ASSOCIATIONS OF ONTARIO (CN/0227-6291) [07966348] 5033, **1768**

NEWSLETTER - FEDERATION OF ONTARIO MEMORIAL SOCIETIES (CN/0711-3838) [08651944] **2407**

NEWSLETTER / FEDERATION OF SCHOOLS OF ACCOUNTANCY (US/0885-565X) [07754218] **749**

NEWSLETTER - FEDERATION OF UGANDA EMPLOYERS, COMMERCE & INDUSTRY (UG) [04512961] 1695, **1619**

NEWSLETTER - FIGURE SKATING COACHES OF CANADA (CN/0826-2969) [11278709] **4908**

NEWSLETTER - FILM STUDIES ASSOCIATION OF CANADA (CN/0227-5015) [08071643] **4075**

NEWSLETTER - FINGER LAKES LIBRARY SYSTEM (US/0195-4016) [05461892] **3235**

NEWSLETTER - FLIGHT SAFETY FOUNDATION (US/0428-5735) [17857111] **30**

NEWSLETTER - FLORIDA ARTHRITIS FOUNDATION (US) [01397515] **3806**

NEWSLETTER - FLORIDA FRIENDS OF BLUEGRASS SOCIETY (US/0160-5119) [03688458] **4141**

NEWSLETTER - FLORIDA GENEALOGICAL SOCIETY (US/0739-6007) [09788881] **2463**

NEWSLETTER FOR AMERICAN-GERMAN CULTURAL STUDIES IN THE SOUTHEAST (US) [09816100] **5252**

NEWSLETTER FOR BEEKEEPERS IN TROPICAL & SUBTROPICAL COUNTRIES (UK) [21019033] **112**

NEWSLETTER FOR DENTISTS (US/1044-3142) [19728669] **1331**

●NEWSLETTER FOR INTERNATIONAL COLLABORATION (JA/0919-8822) [29535336] **112**

NEWSLETTER FOR INVENTORS, A (US/0270-2401) [06389582] **5133**

●NEWSLETTER FOR PEOPLE WITH LACTOSE INTOLERANCE AND MILK ALLERGY (US) **3675**

NEWSLETTER FOR RSEEA CEASED. (US/8756-8942) [11695281] **112**

NEWSLETTER FOR TARGUMIC & COGNATE STUDIES (CN/0704-5905) [03304682] **3306**

NEWSLETTER FOR THE ROCKY MOUNT HISTORICAL ASSOCIATION (US) [07683208] **2749**

6730

Alphabetical Title Index — NEWSLETTER

NEWSLETTER FOR UGARITIC STUDIES (CN/0702-8245) [11764693] **3417**

NEWSLETTER / FREMONT-CUSTER HISTORICAL SOCIETY (US/0882-3774) [11833243] **2749**

NEWSLETTER - FRIENDS OF MICRONESIA (US/0095-1234) [01794634] **2670**

NEWSLETTER (FRIENDS OF THE OTTAWA PUBLIC LIBRARY) (CN/0822-658X) [11050424] **3235**

NEWSLETTER FROM C.A.R.E.E.'S CHRISTIAN-MARXIST ENCOUNTER TASK GROUP (US/0732-9253) [08484647] **4981**

● NEWSLETTER FROM DICK B. ON THE SPIRITUAL ROOTS OF ALCOHOLICS ANONYMOUS, A (US/1068-302X) [27636338] **4981**

NEWSLETTER FROM THE COMMISSION FOR SCIENTIFIC RESEARCH IN GREENLAND (DK/0106-1372) [06228029] **5133**

NEWSLETTER - FRONTENAC HISTORIC FOUNDATION (CN/0381-0119) [05789477] 2749, **304**

NEWSLETTER - GARDEN HISTORY SOCIETY (1981) (UK/0269-4123) [07540605] **2425**

NEWSLETTER - GENEALOGICAL SOCIETY OF NEW JERSEY (US) [06705950] **2463**

NEWSLETTER (GENEALOGICAL SOCIETY OF ORIGINAL MUSCOGEE COUNTY) (US/0742-9258) [08788972] **2463**

NEWSLETTER - GEOGRAPHY TEACHERS' ASSOCIATION OF VICTORIA *See* INTERACTION MELBOURNE **1897**

NEWSLETTER - GEOLOGICAL SOCIETY OF AUSTRALIA INC. SPECIALIST GROUP ON SOLID - EARTH GEOPHYSICS (AT/1030-0457) [I10300457] **1409**

NEWSLETTER - GERONTOLOGY SPECIALTY SECTION, AMERICAN OCCUPATIONAL THERAPY ASSOCIATION *See* GERONTOLOGY SPECIAL INTEREST SECTION NEWSLETTER **3752**

NEWSLETTER - GLASGOW & WEST OF SCOTLAND FAMILY HISTORY SOCIETY (UK/0141-8009) [I01418009] **2463**

NEWSLETTER - GLASS ART *See* JOURNAL / GLASS ART SOCIETY **2591**

NEWSLETTER (GOLDEN RODS & REELS, VICTORIA, B.C.) (CN/0828-7236) [12227620] **2309**

NEWSLETTER, GRAVURE ENVIRONMENTAL (US/0271-1699) [06541542] **4567**

NEWSLETTER - GUIDANCE AND COUNSELLING ASSOCIATION (CN/0315-2995) [02247465] **1882**

NEWSLETTER - HALIFAX DISTRICT SCHOOL BOARD. LIBRARY DEPT. (1989) (CN/1189-9999) [30673768] **3235**

NEWSLETTER / HARVARD WOMEN'S LAW ASSOCIATION (US) [23196010] 5562, **3017**

NEWSLETTER / HEALTH AND PHYSICAL EDUCATION PROJECT (UK) [16082748] **1857**

NEWSLETTER - HERITAGE ST. CATHARINES (CN/0821-0373) [09670616] **2749**

NEWSLETTER (HISTORICAL SOCIETY OF OTTAWA) (CN/0711-3803) [08680997] **2749**

NEWSLETTER (HISTORICAL SOCIETY OF SOUTH AUSTRALIA) (AT) [16856386] **2670**

NEWSLETTER / HISTORY OF SCIENCE SOCIETY (US/0739-4934) [04625125] **5133**

NEWSLETTER (HOOD COUNTY GENEALOGICAL SOCIETY) (US) **2463**

NEWSLETTER / HULL FAMILY ASSOCIATION, THE (US) [25388415] **2463**

NEWSLETTER - HUMAN RIGHTS COMMISSION OF BRITISH COLUMBIA (CN/0226-2770) [06300222] **4511**

NEWSLETTER (HUMANE SOCIETY OF OTTAWA-CARLETON) (CN/0712-2950) [08828170] **5298**

NEWSLETTER (HUMANISTIC MATHEMATICS NETWORK) *See* HUMANISTIC MATHEMATICS NETWORK JOURNAL **3508**

NEWSLETTER - HUNTSVILLE ASSOCIATION OF FOLK MUSICIANS (US/0091-9764) [01788761] **4141**

NEWSLETTER - IAMSLIC (US/0193-9254) [05269471] **1453**

NEWSLETTER - IATEFL (UK/0257-6554) [I02576554] **3306**

NEWSLETTER - IEA HEAT PUMP CENTER (GW/0724-7028) [I07247028] **2607**

NEWSLETTER / IEEE PROFESSIONAL COMMUNICATION SOCIETY (US/1043-433X) [19467518] **2073**

NEWSLETTER - IFLA. SECTION OF BIOLOGICAL AND MEDICAL SCIENCES LIBRARIES (US/0250-4294) [06035499] 467, 3621, **3235**

NEWSLETTER - ILLINOIS STATE BAR ASSOCIATION (US) [01784890] 4511, **3017**

NEWSLETTER IMMOBILIARE (IT) **2829**

NEWSLETTER / INDIANA COVERED BRIDGE SOCIETY (US) [09037183] **2749**

NEWSLETTER - INFANT FEEDING ACTION COALITION (CN/1194-6180) [28474112] **5298**

NEWSLETTER (INFORMATION AND PRIVACY COMMISSIONER/ONTARIO) *See* IRC PERSPECTIVES **4658**

NEWSLETTER / INNISFIL HISTORICAL SOCIETY (CN/0713-8806) [09106473] **2749**

NEWSLETTER - INSTITUTE FOR STUDIES IN AMERICAN MUSIC (US/0145-8396) [02723610] **4141**

NEWSLETTER - INSTITUTE OF BREWING, AUSTRALIA AND NEW ZEALAND SECTION (AT/0816-0694) [I08160694] **2370**

NEWSLETTER (INSTITUTE OF MEDICAL AND VETERINARY SCIENCE (S. AUST.). LABORATORY ANIMAL CENTER) *See* IMVS NEWSLETTER / PREPARED BY THE STAFF OF THE INSTITUTE OF MEDICAL AND VETERINARY SCIENCE **5511**

NEWSLETTER - INSTITUTE OF MEDICINE (US/0363-4671) [02413264] **3621**

NEWSLETTER / INSTITUTE OF VICTORIA LIBRARIANS (CN/0827-2743) [20365740] **3235**

NEWSLETTER - INTER-SOCIETY COLOR COUNCIL (US/0300-7588) [05305499] **5133**

NEWSLETTER - INTERNATIONAL ASSOCIATION FOR CEREAL CHEMISTRY (AU/0254-5837) [I02545837] **2351**

NEWSLETTER - INTERNATIONAL ASSOCIATION FOR SOCIAL SCIENCE SERVICE AND TECHNOLOGY *See* IASSIST QUARTERLY **3258**

NEWSLETTER / INTERNATIONAL ASSOCIATION OF SCHOOL LIBRARIANSHIP (US) [06155269] **3235**

NEWSLETTER (INTERNATIONAL BOARD FOR PLANT GENETIC RESOURCES. REGIONAL COMMITTEE FOR SOUTHEAST ASIA) (TH) [12334719] 550, **519**

NEWSLETTER - INTERNATIONAL BOARD ON BOOKS FOR YOUNG PEOPLE. CANADIAN SECTION (1980) (CN/0831-9197) [16054157] **1067**

NEWSLETTER - INTERNATIONAL BOARD ON BOOKS FOR YOUNG PEOPLE. CANADIAN SECTION (1980) (CN/0831-9197) [16056642] **1067**

NEWSLETTER - INTERNATIONAL CONGRESS ON HIGH SPEED PHOTOGRAPHY AND PHOTONICS (US/0272-7994) [06937946] **4372**

NEWSLETTER (INTERNATIONAL OMBUDSMAN INSTITUTE) (CN/0229-2181) [07865644] **3017**

NEWSLETTER - INTERNATIONAL ORGANIZATION OF PLANT BIOSYSTEMATISTS (SZ/0254-8844) [I02548844] **519**

NEWSLETTER - INTERNATIONAL PRISONERS AID ASSOCIATION (US/0195-7252) [05633945] **3170**

NEWSLETTER / INTERNATIONAL UNION FOR THE SCIENTIFIC STUDY OF POPULATION (BE/0771-2022) [12939246] **4555**

NEWSLETTER - INTERNATIONAL UNIVERSITY (INDEPENDENCE, MO.) (US/0748-9684) [11055530] **1837**

NEWSLETTER - INUIT CULTURAL INSTITUTE (CN/0709-7794) [05765440] **2749**

NEWSLETTER - IOWA ARCHEOLOGICAL SOCIETY (US/0578-655X) [02243127] 2624, **276**

NEWSLETTER - IRISH MUSEUMS ASSOCIATION (IE/0332-284X) [I0332284X] **4094**

NEWSLETTER / JOHNSTON COUNTY GENEALOGICAL SOCIETY (US/0737-4321) [09342436] **2463**

NEWSLETTER - KANSAS ANTHROPOLOGICAL ASSOCIATION (1989) (US/1069-0360) [24457787] **242**

NEWSLETTER / KANSAS FOLKLORE SOCIETY (US) [01784006] **2323**

NEWSLETTER / KEMPTVILLE & DISTRICT HISTORICAL SOCIETY (CN/1180-081X) [24257021] **2749**

NEWSLETTER / KENT ARCHAEOLOGICAL SOCIETY (UK) [12332680] **276**

NEWSLETTER - KITCHENER WATERLOO REGIONAL FOLK ARTS MULTICULTURAL CENTRE (CN/0713-6285) [08923970] **2749**

NEWSLETTER. LABOUR RELATIONS. CONSTRUCTION ASSOCIATION OF MONTREAL AND THE PROVINCE OF QUEBEC (CN/0317-0993) [02247815] **1695**

NEWSLETTER - LAKE GEORGE PARK COMMISSION (US) [05005758] **2200**

NEWSLETTER - LAND MANAGEMENT INFORMATION CENTER (US) [05038079] **4669**

NEWSLETTER - LATIN AMERICAN FREE TRADE ASSOCIATION (UY) [02694262] **847**

NEWSLETTER - LAW SOCIETY OF ALBERTA (CN/0715-3465) [05932357] **3017**

NEWSLETTER - LEAGUE OF OREGON CITIES (1980) (US/0731-1435) [06657897] **4669**

NEWSLETTER - LEARN (CN/0821-2228) [09581893] **1768**

NEWSLETTER - LEARNING RESOURCES COUNCIL OF THE ALBERTA TEACHERS' ASSOCIATION (CN/0380-8491) [02585057] **1867**

NEWSLETTER - LEARNING STYLES NETWORK (NATIONAL ASSOCIATION OF SECONDARY SCHOOL PRINCIPALS) (US/0745-5450) [09768714] **1901**

NEWSLETTER / LETHBRIDGE HISTORICAL SOCIETY (CN/0838-7249) [18241962] **2749**

NEWSLETTER - LIBRARY ASSOCIATION OF AUSTRALIA. NORTHERN TERRITORY BRANCH (AT/0157-2229) [I01572229] **3235**

NEWSLETTER (LINCOLN-LANCASTER COUNTY GENEALOGICAL SOCIETY) (US/0892-6182) [15248505] **2463**

NEWSLETTER - LITTLE BIG HORN ASSOCIATES (US/0459-5866) [02244447] **2749**

NEWSLETTER / LONDON AND MIDDLESEX COUNTY HISTORICAL SOCIETY (CN/0824-5614) [10768262] **2749**

NEWSLETTER - LONDON (ONT.). PLANNING DIVISION (CN/1188-1429) [25652242] **2829**

NEWSLETTER - LONG POINT BIRD OBSERVATORY (CN/0317-9575) [02248292] **5618**

NEWSLETTER - MACRO SYSTEMS. INSTITUTE FOR RESOURCE DEVELOPMENT. DEMOGRAPHIC AND HEALTH SURVEYS (US/1049-2364) [21182055] **4793**

NEWSLETTER / MAINE HISTORICAL SOCIETY (US/0882-4223) [11749020] **2749**

NEWSLETTER - MANITOBA ASSOCIATION FOR EDUCATIONAL DATA SYSTEMS (CN/0821-3674) [09448580] **1224**

NEWSLETTER - MANITOBA ASSOCIATION OF SCHOOL TRUSTEES (CN/0024-7928) [02058515] **1867**

NEWSLETTER / MANITOBA LIBRARY TRUSTEES ASSOCIATION (CN/0823-1184) [09925363] **3235**

NEWSLETTER - MANITOBA UNDERWATER COUNCIL (CN/0383-7742) [03232863] **4908**

NEWSLETTER / MAP ONLINE USERS GROUP **SUSPENDED.** (US/0749-338X) [10667944] 1275, **3235**

NEWSLETTER MARC. USERS GROUP (UK/0144-7599) [I01447599] **3235**

NEWSLETTER (MARIGOLD LIBRARY SYSTEM) (CN/0713-2727) [09033910] **3235**

NEWSLETTER / MARKETING SCIENCE INSTITUTE (US/0733-5768) [06391523] **934**

NEWSLETTER - MARYLAND DEPARTMENT OF STATE PLANNING (US/0147-9334) [03249164] **2829**

NEWSLETTER - MASSACHUSETTS BAY DISTRICT, UNITARIAN UNIVERSALIST CHURCHES (US/0364-667X) [02071755] **4981**

NEWSLETTER - MASSACHUSETTS STATE LABOR COUNCIL (US) [05518285] **1695**

NEWSLETTER (MATHEMATICAL ASSOCIATION) (UK) [20465329] **3524**

NEWSLETTER / MCGILL UNIVERSITY GRADUATE SCHOOL OF LIBRARY AND INFORMATION STUDIES (CN/0843-0217) [20443573] 3235, **1837**

NEWSLETTER - MEDICAL RESEARCH COUNCIL (OTTAWA) (CN/0047-6560) [02607529] **3621**

NEWSLETTER - MEMORIAL SOCIETY ASSOCIATION OF CANADA (CN/0701-1377) [03436206] **2407**

NEWSLETTER (MEMORIAL UNIVERSITY OF NEWFOUNDLAND. MARITIME HISTORY GROUP) (CN/0820-3911) [16636682] **5453**

NEWSLETTER - MEN'S AWARENESS NETWORK (US) [02360980] **3931**

6731

NEWSLETTER — Alphabetical Title Index

NEWSLETTER - MENTAL HEALTH SPECIALTY SECTION, AMERICAN OCCUPATIONAL THERAPY ASSOCIATION *See* MENTAL HEALTH SPECIAL INTEREST SECTION NEWSLETTER **4790**

NEWSLETTER - MICHIGAN STATE UNIVERSITY, LATIN AMERICAN STUDIES CENTER (US) [05319121] **2750**

NEWSLETTER - MID-AMERICA ASSOCIATION OF LAW LIBRARIES (US) [03439472] 3017, **3235**

NEWSLETTER - MINERALOGICAL ASSOCIATION OF CANADA (CN/0076-8936) [02247923] **1443**

NEWSLETTER - MINISTRY OF HEALTH (VICTORIA) (CN/0226-2789) [06300203] **4793**

NEWSLETTER - MISSIONS ADVANCED RESEARCH AND COMMUNICATIONS CENTER (US/0740-6460) [01604465] **4982**

NEWSLETTER - MISSISSIPPI ARCHAEOLOGICAL ASSOCIATION (1983) (US/1052-9101) [11181806] **276**

NEWSLETTER / MONMOUTH COUNTY HISTORICAL ASSOCIATION (US/0740-8781) [10029242] **2750**

NEWSLETTER - MONROE COUNTY HISTORICAL SOCIETY (WIS.) (US/1075-248X) [29980898] **2750**

NEWSLETTER - MONTREAL JOINT HOSPITAL INSTITUTE (CN/0229-8759) [08439971] **5298**

NEWSLETTER / MONTREAL POETS' INFORMATION EXCHANGE (CN/0712-6239) [09336335] **3467**

NEWSLETTER (MUSEUM ETHNOGRAPHERS' GROUP (GREAT BRITAIN)) *See* JOURNAL OF MUSEUM ETHNOGRAPHY / MUSEUM ETHNOGRAPHERS' GROUP **239**

NEWSLETTER - MUSIC OCLC USERS GROUP (US/0161-1704) [03873235] **4141**

NEWSLETTER / MUSICOLOGICAL SOCIETY OF AUSTRALIA (AT/0155-0543) [04244850] **4141**

NEWSLETTER (MUSKIES, INC.) *See* MUSKIE : THE OFFICIAL PUBLICATION OF MUSKIES, INC **4875**

NEWSLETTER - NAFSA: ASSOCIATION OF INTERNATIONAL EDUCATORS (WASHINGTON, D.C.) (US/1067-4780) [25491668] **1768**

NEWSLETTER / NATIONAL ALOPECIA AREATA FOUNDATION, NAAF (US/0894-1769) [15875602] **3715**

NEWSLETTER - NATIONAL ASSOCIATION FOR THE VISUAL ARTS (AT/1032-9617) [I10329617] **326**

NEWSLETTER - NATIONAL ASSOCIATION OF FRIENDSHIP CENTRES (CN/0821-6509) [09816140] **5298**

NEWSLETTER (NATIONAL ASSOCIATION OF PRIVATE PSYCHIATRIC HOSPITALS) (US/0027-8637) [02264597] 3931, **3790**

NEWSLETTER - NATIONAL ASSOCIATION OF SOCIAL WORKERS. WASHINGTON STATE CHAPTER (US/0745-3531) [09094240] **5299**

NEWSLETTER - NATIONAL BOARD OF OCCUPATIONAL SAFETY AND HEALTH (SW/0348-7598) [04029596] **4794**

NEWSLETTER / NATIONAL CARTOGRAPHIC INFORMATION CENTER *CEASED.* (US/0364-7064) [02325765] **2582**

NEWSLETTER - NATIONAL CENTER FOR THE STUDY OF COLLECTIVE BARGAINING IN HIGHER EDUCATION AND THE PROFESSIONS (U.S.) (US/0737-9285) [07433886] 944, **1837**

NEWSLETTER (NATIONAL CONTRACT MANAGEMENT ASSOCIATION (U.S.)) *See* CONTRACT MANAGEMENT **2956**

NEWSLETTER - NATIONAL COUNCIL FOR INTERNATIONAL VISITORS (US/0196-9420) [05908963] **2911**

NEWSLETTER - NATIONAL COUNCIL FOR THERAPY AND REHABILITATION THROUGH HORTICULTURE (U.S.) (US/0739-1609) [04393665] **2425**

NEWSLETTER (NATIONAL COUNCIL OF WOMEN OF CANADA) (CN/0712-3035) [08867847] **5562**

NEWSLETTER / NATIONAL EARLY AMERICAN GLASS CLUB (US) [09100544] **2592**

NEWSLETTER - NATIONAL FARMERS UNION (CN/0316-3369) [02040800] **112**

NEWSLETTER - NATIONAL HEAD INJURY FOUNDATION *See* NATIONAL HEAD INJURY FOUNDATION'S TBI CHALLENGE!, THE **3619**

NEWSLETTER (NATIONAL HEAD INJURY FOUNDATION (U.S.)) (US) [13723881] **3621**

NEWSLETTER - NATIONAL LEGAL AID RESEARCH CENTRE (CN/0715-4186) [09159541] **3180**

NEWSLETTER - NATIONAL OPINION RESEARCH CENTER (US/0077-5266) [03905575] **5252**

NEWSLETTER / NATIONAL SURVIVAL INSTITUTE (CN/0715-3368) [09234449] **2219**

NEWSLETTER - NATIONAL TECHNICAL ASSOCIATION (US/0276-2471) [04153847] **5133**

NEWSLETTER - NATIONAL WEATHER ASSOCIATION (US/0271-1044) [04254201] **1432**

NEWSLETTER / NATIVE ART STUDIES ASSOCIATION OF CANADA (CN/0831-2885) [16320091] **2269**

NEWSLETTER /NCAB *See* NCA/TCS NEWSLETTER **539**

NEWSLETTER - NEPAL NATURE CONSERVATION SOCIETY (NP) [02246796] **2200**

NEWSLETTER (NETTAI NOGYO KENKYU SENTA) *See* NEWSLETTER FOR INTERNATIONAL COLLABORATION **112**

NEWSLETTER / NEW HAMPSHIRE SOCIETY OF GENEALOGISTS (US/8755-173X) [11199378] **2463**

NEWSLETTER (NEW JERSEY. BUREAU OF FIRE SAFETY) *See* NEW JERSEY FIRE FOCUS : THE OFFICIAL NEWSLETTER OF THE NJ BUREAU OF FIRE SAFETY **2292**

NEWSLETTER - NEW MEXICO LIBRARY ASSOCIATION (US/0893-2956) [02272402] **3235**

NEWSLETTER - NEW YORK BOTANICAL GARDEN (US/0550-6565) [01760028] **519**

NEWSLETTER - NEW ZEALAND. NATURE CONSERVATION COUNCIL (NZ/0111-686X) [01785783] **2200**

NEWSLETTER NEWSLETTER, THE (US/0885-6966) [12719234] 4982, **2922**

NEWSLETTER / NIAGARA CHILDREN'S SERVICES COMMITTEE (CN/0229-2742) [08713523] **5299**

NEWSLETTER - NORTH AMERICAN SOCIETY FOR SPORT HISTORY (US) [04340136] **4908**

NEWSLETTER / NORTH AMERICAN SOCIETY OF OCEANIC HISTORY (US/1065-2329) [04877024] **4181**

NEWSLETTER / NORTHWESTERN SOCIETY OF INTESTINAL RESEARCH (CN/0715-3236) [09128292] **3800**

NEWSLETTER - NOTTINGHAMSHIRE LOCAL HISTORY COUNCIL *See* NOTTINGHAMSHIRE HISTORIAN, THE **2701**

NEWSLETTER - NOVA SCOTIA BIRD SOCIETY (CN/0383-9567) [02482101] **5592**

NEWSLETTER (NOVA SCOTIA DESIGNER CRAFTS COUNCIL) *See* NOVA SCOTIA CRAFT NEWS / NSDCC **374**

NEWSLETTER / NOVA SCOTIA LIBRARY ASSOCIATION (CN/1182-0209) [22367037] **3235**

NEWSLETTER / NOVA SCOTIA SCHOOL BOARDS ASSOCIATION (CN/0702-9292) [08003271] **1867**

NEWSLETTER - OECD NUCLEAR ENERGY AGENCY (FR) [03154793] **2156**

NEWSLETTER OF BALUCHISTAN STUDIES (IT) [15675210] **2660**

NEWSLETTER OF LABORATORY SPECTROSCOPY FOR PLANETARY SCIENCES (US) [06354302] **397**

NEWSLETTER OF SWEDISH BUILDING RESEARCH (SW) [04068222] 2829, **622**

NEWSLETTER OF THE A.A.P.S.C (US/0093-0237) [01789812] 3931, **3907**

NEWSLETTER OF THE AFRO-AMERICAN RELIGIOUS HISTORY GROUP OF THE AMERICAN ACADEMY OF RELIGION (US/0889-6178) [04821541] 2269, 4982, **2750**

NEWSLETTER OF THE ALBERTA FAMILY HISTORIES SOCIETY (CN/0820-8379) [09528038] **2463**

NEWSLETTER OF THE AMERICAN ASSOCIATION OF AUSTRALIAN LITERARY STUDIES (US/0894-7945) [16240548] **3349**

NEWSLETTER OF THE AMERICAN COMMITTEE TO ADVANCE THE STUDY OF PETROGLYPHS AND PICTOGRAPHS (US/0278-2871) [07764442] **242**

NEWSLETTER OF THE AMERICAN DIALECT SOCIETY (US/0002-8193) [01479773] **3306**

NEWSLETTER OF THE AMERICAN HANDEL SOCIETY (US/0888-8701) [13745793] **4141**

NEWSLETTER OF THE AMERICAN INSTITUTE OF STRESS, THE (US/1047-2517) [20667642] **3621**

NEWSLETTER OF THE ASSOCIATION FOR STUDY OF AMERICAN INDIAN LITERATURES *See* STUDIES IN AMERICAN INDIAN LITERATURE **3441**

NEWSLETTER OF THE ASSOCIATION OF OFFICIAL SEED ANALYSTS, THE (US/0004-5764) [07904760] **112**

NEWSLETTER OF THE AUSTRALIAN ASSOCIATION FOR MARITIME HISTORY (AT/0158-5312) [10499126] **4181**

NEWSLETTER OF THE AUSTRALIAN ROBOT ASSOCIATION (AT/0726-3716) [I07263716] **1220**

NEWSLETTER OF THE C A F (CN/0700-9798) [03403102] **5252**

NEWSLETTER OF THE CENTER FOR PROCESS STUDIES (US/0360-618X) [01906431] **4982**

NEWSLETTER OF THE CHICAGO GENEALOGICAL SOCIETY (US/0193-8770) [04025633] **2463**

NEWSLETTER OF THE CPA/SCP SECTION ON WOMEN & PSYCHOLOGY (CN/0831-9510) [15246879] **4605**

NEWSLETTER OF THE ERNST KRENEK ARCHIVE (US/1053-9948) [22294164] **4141**

NEWSLETTER OF THE EUROPEAN ASSOCIATION FOR JAPANESE STUDIES *See* BULLETIN OF THE EUROPEAN ASSOCIATION FOR JAPANESE STUDIES **2502**

NEWSLETTER OF THE FOOD, DRUG, AND COSMETIC LAW SECTION *See* FOOD, DRUG, COSMETIC, AND MEDICAL DEVICE LAW DIGEST **2971**

NEWSLETTER OF THE GANANOQUE HISTORICAL SOCIETY (CN/0831-9871) [15299503] **2750**

NEWSLETTER OF THE GARDEN CONSERVANCY, THE (US/1065-2108) [25142412] **2425**

NEWSLETTER OF THE GYPSY LORE SOCIETY (US/1070-4604) [26536852] **2323**

NEWSLETTER OF THE GYPSY LORE SOCIETY, NORTH AMERICAN CHAPTER *See* NEWSLETTER OF THE GYPSY LORE SOCIETY **2323**

NEWSLETTER OF THE HAWK MIGRATION ASSOCIATION OF NORTH AMERICA, THE (US/0278-7806) [04797400] **5592**

NEWSLETTER OF THE INTERNATIONAL ACADEMY FOR THE STUDY OF TOURISM (SP/1012-8042) [19817216] **5486**

NEWSLETTER OF THE INTERNATIONAL DAIRY FEDERATION (BE) **197**

NEWSLETTER OF THE JEWISH LAW ASSOCIATION (UK/0952-8997) [18804817] **5051**

NEWSLETTER OF THE KINGS COUNTY HISTORICAL AND ARCHIVAL SOCIETY, INC (CN/0824-1732) [11856715] **2750**

NEWSLETTER OF THE LAMBERT-LAMBERTH ASSOCIATION (US/0090-5704) [01785019] **2463**

NEWSLETTER OF THE LAW SOCIETY OF THE AUSTRALIAN CAPITAL TERRITORY *See* GAZETTE - LAW SOCIETY OF THE AUSTRALIAN CAPITAL TERRITORY **2973**

NEWSLETTER OF THE MIDWEST CHINESE STUDENT & ALUMNI SERVICES (US/0544-070X) [09366029] **1102**

NEWSLETTER OF THE MUSIC CRITICS ASSOCIATION, INC (US/0198-8921) [06238895] **4141**

NEWSLETTER OF THE NEBRASKA VETERINARY TECHNICIAN ASSOCIATION (US) **5517**

NEWSLETTER OF THE NEW YORK STATE COUNCIL FOR THE SOCIAL STUDIES, THE (US) [09733720] 1768, **5211**

NEWSLETTER OF THE NEWTH/NUTH FAMILY HISTORY SOCIETY (UK) [09170743] **2463**

NEWSLETTER OF THE NORTH CAROLINA FOLKLORE SOCIETY (US/0888-6121) [13675817] **2323**

NEWSLETTER OF THE NORTH CENTRAL ILLINOIS GENEALOGICAL SOCIETY *See* NORTH CENTRAL ILLINOIS GENEALOGICAL SOCIETY **2464**

NEWSLETTER OF THE NORTH SUBURBAN GENEALOGICAL SOCIETY (US/0743-1341) [10503628] **2463**

NEWSLETTER OF THE SOCIETY FOR ENVIRONMENTAL THERAPY (UK/0264-5807) [15199850] **2178**

NEWSLETTER OF THE SOCIETY OF CLINICAL PSYCHIATRISTS *See* BRITISH JOURNAL OF CLINICAL AND SOCIAL PSYCHIATRY **3922**

NEWSLETTER OF THE SOUTHWEST VIRGINIA COPENHAVER FAMILY (US/0883-2099) [11855763] **2463**

NEWSLETTER OF THE SPECIALIST GROUP IN TECTONICS & STRUCTURAL GEOLOGY (AT/1035-3593) [10772555] **1389**

NEWSLETTER OF THE SSIS (US/0145-7861) [02775944] **2660**

NEWSLETTER OF THE TEXTILE MUSEUM ASSOCIATION OF SOUTHERN CALIFORNIA (US) **5354**

NEWSLETTER OF THE TILES AND ARCHITECTURAL CERAMICS SOCIETY (UK) **304**

Alphabetical Title Index — NEWSLETTER

NEWSLETTER OF THE YELLOWHEAD REGIONAL LIBRARY (CN/0708-1979) [04955170] **3235**

NEWSLETTER ON DENGUE, YELLOW FEVER, AND AEDES AEGYPTI IN THE AMERICAS (US/0378-6781) [04326236] **3621**

NEWSLETTER ON EDUCATION AND TRAINING PROGRAMMES FOR INFORMATION PERSONNEL (NE) [14269143] 1837, **3236**

NEWSLETTER ON INTELLECTUAL FREEDOM (US/0028-9485) [02636322] **3236**

NEWSLETTER ON NEWSLETTERS, THE (US/0028-9507) [02416557] **2922**

NEWSLETTER ON SERIALS PRICING ISSUES (US/1046-3410) [20386539] **3236**

NEWSLETTER ON SURFACE ROUGHNESS (SW) **3485**

NEWSLETTER ON THE OIL EMBARGO AGAINST SOUTH AFRICA *CEASED.* (NE/0169-3956) [12634320] **4266**

NEWSLETTER / ONTARIO ASSOCIATION OF LIBRARY TECHNICIANS (CN/0229-2645) [08302760] **3236**

NEWSLETTER - ONTARIO CAMPUS CULTURE ASSOCIATION (CN/0380-2795) [02585132] **386**

NEWSLETTER / ONTARIO COMMITTEE ON THE STATUS OF WOMEN *SUSPENDED.* (CN/0227-6879) [08010248] **5562**

NEWSLETTER - ONTARIO CULTURAL OLYMPIC PROGRAM (CN/0700-9860) [03291487] **326**

NEWSLETTER / ONTARIO FORESTRY ASSOCIATION (CN/0834-2008) [16081634] **2389**

NEWSLETTER - ONTARIO GENEALOGICAL SOCIETY, KINGSTON BRANCH *See* KINGSTON RELATIONS **2457**

NEWSLETTER - ONTARIO MINISTRY OF AGRICULTURE AND FOOD (CN/0228-202X) [06777781] 2351, **112**

NEWSLETTER (OPEN DOOR SOCIETY OF OTTAWA) (CN/0712-3132) [08890899] **5299**

NEWSLETTER - OPERA LYRA OTTAWA (CN/1187-0362) [25066866] 4141, **386**

NEWSLETTER / OPERA ORCHESTRA OF NEW YORK (US/0736-6876) [09174909] **4141**

NEWSLETTER - OPTOMETRIC HISTORICAL SOCIETY (US) [01785711] **4216**

NEWSLETTER - ORAL HISTORY ASSOCIATION (US/0474-3253) [01115351] **2624**

NEWSLETTER (OREGON HISTORICAL SOCIETY) *See* NEWS - OREGON HISTORICAL SOCIETY **2749**

NEWSLETTER - ORGANIC GROWERS CO-OPERATIVE (CN/0317-0527) [02247636] **112**

NEWSLETTER - OTTAWA WOMEN'S CENTRE (CN/0382-8271) [02757926] **5562**

NEWSLETTER - PACIFIC STUDIES INSTITUTE (GU) [06060436] **2670**

NEWSLETTER / PASTORAL DEVELOPMENT NETWORK (UK) [20117681] **2911**

NEWSLETTER - PENNSYLVANIA ACADEMY OF SCIENCE (US/0160-4228) [02719376] **5133**

NEWSLETTER - PENNSYLVANIA STATE UNIVERSITY. ENVIRONMENTAL RESOURCES RESEARCH INSTITUTE (US/1041-701X) [15372809] **2237**

NEWSLETTER - PEOPLE'S MEDICAL SOCIETY (U.S.) (US/0736-4873) [09142643] **3621**

NEWSLETTER - PHARMACEUTICAL MANUFACTURERS ASSOCIATION (US/0196-7061) [01761653] **4318**

NEWSLETTER - PITTSBURGH REGIONAL LIBRARY CENTER, INC (US/0196-6707) [06023569] **3236**

NEWSLETTER - PLANETARY ASSOCIATION FOR CLEAN ENERGY (CN/0708-918X) [05385222] 2237, **1951**

NEWSLETTER (POMPEIIANA, INC.) *See* POMPEIIANA NEWSLETTER **3311**

NEWSLETTER - PRAIRIE RELIGIOUS LIBRARY ASSOCIATION (CN/0225-5758) [08003158] **4982**

NEWSLETTER (PRESIDENT'S COUNCIL ON PHYSICAL FITNESS AND SPORTS (U.S.)) (US/0364-8079) [02582125] 4908, **2600**

NEWSLETTER / PRINCE EDWARD ISLAND MUSEUM AND HERITAGE FOUNDATION (CN/0823-8324) [11634775] **4094**

NEWSLETTER : PROFESSIONAL SECRETARIES INTERNATIONAL (US) **4207**

NEWSLETTER - PROVINCIAL COUNCIL OF WOMEN OF BRITISH COLUMBIA (CN/0707-0195) [04631872] **5562**

NEWSLETTER - REMOTE SENSING ASSOCIATION OF AUSTRALASIA (AT/1039-2017) [10392017] **1358**

NEWSLETTER/ REMOTE SENSING SOCIETY (UK) 2570, **1358**

NEWSLETTER (RENTON HISTORICAL SOCIETY) *See* NEWSLETTER / RENTON HISTORICAL SOCIETY AND MUSEUM **4094**

NEWSLETTER / RENTON HISTORICAL SOCIETY AND MUSEUM (US/1064-2730) [26243020] **4094**

NEWSLETTER (RESEARCH CENTRE FOR ISLAMIC HISTORY, ART, AND CULTURE) (TU) [14991347] 2851, **326**

NEWSLETTER / ROSE FAMILY ASSOCIATION (US/0747-6728) [10761107] **2464**

NEWSLETTER / ROSS COUNTY GENEALOGICAL SOCIETY (US/0740-4395) [09925689] **2464**

NEWSLETTER (ROUND TABLE OF NATIONAL CENTRES FOR LIBRARY SERVICES) (NE) [11810844] **3236**

NEWSLETTER (ROYAL CANADIAN COLLEGE OF ORGANISTS) (CN/0829-4291) [15492633] **4141**

NEWSLETTER / ROYAL COMMISSION ON THE HISTORICAL MONUMENTS OF ENGLAND (UK/0957-0241) [25742893] **2700**

NEWSLETTER (ROYAL SCHOOL OF CHURCH MUSIC (WARREN, CONN.) (US/0748-0148) [10840933] **4141**

NEWSLETTER (S.U.C.C.E.S.S.) (CN/0823-7999) [11046638] **5299**

NEWSLETTER. SAFETY. CONSTRUCTION ASSOCIATION OF MONTREAL AND THE PROVINCE OF QUEBEC (CN/0317-5804) [02441636] **622**

NEWSLETTER - SALT CITY SONG MINERS TRADITIONAL FOLK MUSIC CLUB OF CENTRAL NEW YORK (US/0191-1791) [04764686] **4141**

NEWSLETTER - SASKATCHEWAN ARCHAEOLOGICAL SOCIETY (CN/0227-7514) [06563194] **276**

NEWSLETTER - SASKATCHEWAN HUMAN RIGHTS COMMISSION *See* SASK RIGHTS **4512**

NEWSLETTER / SCARBOROUGH HISTORICAL SOCIETY (CN/0822-8353) [10517618] 2750, **5234**

NEWSLETTER - SCHOOL OF MEDICAL EDUCATION, UNIVERSITY OF NEW SOUTH WALES (AT/0816-8059) [17301558] 1882, **3621**

NEWSLETTER - SCOTTISH CIVIC TRUST (UK/0969-1200) [l09691200] **2700**

NEWSLETTER (SCRIPPS INSTITUTION OF OCEANOGRAPHY ASSOCIATES) *See* EXPLORATIONS (LA JOLLA, CALIF.) **1449**

NEWSLETTER - SEARL NATIONAL SPACE RESEARCH CONSORTIUM, UNITED KINGDOM DIVISION (US/0147-3417) [03145616] **30**

NEWSLETTER - SIBERIAN HUSKY CLUB OF AMERICA (US/0583-1776) [01792798] **4287**

NEWSLETTER - SOCIAL SCIENCE COMPUTING LABORATORY (CN/0714-6647) [09602925] 1197, **5211**

NEWSLETTER-SOCIAL WELFARE HISTORY GROUP (US/0560-3870) [04329783] **5299**

NEWSLETTER / SOCIETY FOR ARMENIAN STUDIES (US/0740-5510) [09972874] **2660**

NEWSLETTER - SOCIETY FOR HISTORIANS OF AMERICAN FOREIGN RELATIONS (US/0740-6169) [02434611] **4530**

NEWSLETTER - SOCIETY FOR INDUSTRIAL ARCHAEOLOGY (US) [04154634] **276**

NEWSLETTER - SOCIETY FOR THE PRESERVATION OF LONG ISLAND ANTIQUITIES (US/0583-9181) [02063221] **251**

NEWSLETTER - SOCIETY FOR THE STUDY OF MIDWESTERN LITERATURE (U.S.) (US/0085-6304) [02003400] **3417**

NEWSLETTER / SOCIETY OF ARCHITECTURAL HISTORIANS OF GREAT BRITAIN (UK) [09106421] **304**

NEWSLETTER - SOCIETY OF IRISH PLANT PATHOLOGISTS (IE/0332-3285) [l03323285] **520**

NEWSLETTER / SOCIETY OF THE SEVEN SAGES (CN/0701-9890) [09201210] **3417**

NEWSLETTER (SOUTH AND MESO-AMERICAN INDIAN INFORMATION CENTER : 1990) *See* ABYA YALA NEWS **2253**

NEWSLETTER - SOUTH AND MESO-AMERICAN INDIAN INFORMATION CENTER (1990) (US/1056-5876) [23825291] **2269**

NEWSLETTER - SOUTH AUSTRALIAN ADVISORY COMMITTEE ON LIBRARY SERVICES TO THE DISABLED (AT/0810-0926) [l08100926] 4392, **3236**

NEWSLETTER / SOUTH AUSTRALIAN ASSOCIATION OF STATE SCHOOLS (AT) **1867**

NEWSLETTER - SOUTH BEND AREA GENEALOGICAL SOCIETY (US/1069-9317) [28201419] 2464, **4555**

NEWSLETTER - SOUTH CAROLINA STATE ETHICS COMMISSION (US) [06553426] **2252**

NEWSLETTER - SOUTH-EAST ASIA LIBRARY GROUP (UK/0308-4035) [05802739] **3236**

NEWSLETTER - SOUTHEASTERN WISCONSIN REGIONAL PLANNING COMMISSION (US/0584-4266) [01955718] **2829**

NEWSLETTER (SOUTHWESTERN ANTHROPOLOGICAL ASSOCIATION) (US) [09841856] **242**

NEWSLETTER - SPECIAL EDUCATION ASSOCIATION (CN/0381-8144) [02940961] **1882**

NEWSLETTER - SPECIAL EDUCATION COUNCIL OF THE ALBERTA TEACHERS' ASSOCIATION (CN/0315-3509) [02230450] **1882**

NEWSLETTER (SPECIAL PROGRAMME FOR RESEARCH AND TRAINING IN TROPICAL DISEASES) *See* TDR NEWS **3987**

NEWSLETTER (SPINAL CORD SOCIETY (U.S.)) (US/8750-0728) [10960049] **3843**

NEWSLETTER / STANISLAUS COUNTY GENEALOGICAL SOCIETY (US/0882-9527) [11857271] **2464**

NEWSLETTER-STATE, COURT, AND COUNTY LAW LIBRARIES SECTION (US/0197-2707) [05978811] 3017, **3236**

NEWSLETTER - STATE LIBRARY OF TASMANIA 1986 (AT/0819-1816) [l08191816] **3236**

NEWSLETTER - STATISTICAL SOCIETY OF AUSTRALIA (AT/0314-6820) [l03146820] **5334**

NEWSLETTER - STUDY GROUP ON EIGHTEENTH-CENTURY RUSSIA (UK/0306-8455) [01796073] **2700**

NEWSLETTER / SUFFOLK COUNTY ARCHAEOLOGICAL ASSOCIATION (US) [08465375] **276**

NEWSLETTER - SUZUKI TALENT EDUCATION ASSOCIATION OF AUSTRALIA (VICTORIA) (AT/0726-2183) [07262183] **4141**

NEWSLETTER - TASK FORCE ON WOMEN'S ISSUES (CN/0715-4283) [09336393] **5563**

NEWSLETTER - TENNESSEE ANTHROPOLOGICAL ASSOCIATION (US/0196-0377) [02364881] **242**

NEWSLETTER / TENNESSEE CITIZENS FOR WILDERNESS PLANNING (US/0890-8842) [13802827] **2200**

NEWSLETTER - TEXAS UNITED COMMUNITY SERVICES (US) [05041893] **5299**

NEWSLETTER / THE AMERICAN BRAHMS SOCIETY (US/8756-8357) [10576557] **4141**

NEWSLETTER / THE AMERICAN INSTITUTE OF WINE & FOOD (US) [17628724] **2351**

NEWSLETTER - THE ASSOCIATION FOR THE ANTHROPOLOGICAL STUDY OF PLAY (US/0887-140X) [06670195] **4853**

NEWSLETTER / THE AUSTRALIAN FEDERATION FOR THE WELFARE OF ANIMALS (AT) [25196136] 5592, **5517**

NEWSLETTER / THE CALGARY INSTITUTE FOR THE HUMANITIES (CN/0715-433X) [09149672] **2851**

NEWSLETTER / THE COSTUME SOCIETY (UK) [10055483] **5366**

NEWSLETTER / THE CROW WING COUNTY HISTORICAL SOCIETY (US/0895-0822) [12871866] **2750**

NEWSLETTER - THE DONIZETTI SOCIETY (UK) [04860100] **5234**

NEWSLETTER - THE INNUIT GALLERY OF ESKIMO ART (CN/0228-3484) [07313919] **360**

NEWSLETTER - THE INTERNATIONAL COUNCIL ON THE FUTURE OF THE UNIVERSITY (US/0362-9015) [02153358] **1837**

NEWSLETTER - THE JOHN MACMURRAY SOCIETY (CN/0705-1611) [03963491] **5234**

NEWSLETTER - THE NATURE CONSERVANCY (U.S.). IOWA CHAPTER (US) [06265680] **2200**

NEWSLETTER - THE SOCIETY OF ARCHITECTURAL HISTORIANS (US/0049-1195) [01765904] **304**

NEWSLETTER — Alphabetical Title Index

NEWSLETTER - THE UNIVERSITY OF TENNESSEE COMPUTING CENTER (US) [06567340] **1197**

NEWSLETTER - THE WILDLIFE CLUBS OF KENYA ASSOCIATION *CEASED.* (KE) [02246858] **5593**

NEWSLETTER / THIRD WORLD LIBRARIES INTEREST GROUP (CN/0840-769X) [19486539] **3236**

NEWSLETTER TO MEMBERS OF THE TEXAS BAPTIST HISTORICAL SOCIETY (US) [09278634] **2624**

NEWSLETTER / TORONTO OCCUPATIONAL HEALTH RESOURCE COMMITTEE (CN/0822-028X) [09666939] **2865**

NEWSLETTER - TOURISM INDUSTRY ASSOCIATION OF CANADA (1990) *See* TOURISM TODAY OTTAWA **5493**

NEWSLETTER / TRAVELING EXHIBITION INFORMATION SERVICE (US/0733-463X) [07709978] **360**

NEWSLETTER TRENDS (CN/1185-5088) [25313900] **4817**

NEWSLETTER / TRI-STATE HORSEMEN'S ASSOCIATION (US) [08562315] **2801**

NEWSLETTER (TURKISH STUDIES ASSOCIATION) *See* TURKISH STUDIES ASSOCIATION BULLETIN **3355**

NEWSLETTER / U.N.B. TEMPERANCE UNION (CN/0708-3599) [08295056] **5299**

NEWSLETTER - UK ONLINE USER GROUP (UK/0957-8544) [I09578544] **1275**

NEWSLETTER / UNITED NATIVE FRIENDSHIP CENTRE (CN/0823-6275) [09816358] **2750**

NEWSLETTER (UNITED STATES BOARD ON BOOKS FOR YOUNG PEOPLE) (US) [12929596] **4831**

NEWSLETTER - UNITED STATES. NAVY. SUPPLY CORPS (US/0360-716X) [02244047] **4181**

NEWSLETTER - UNIVERSITY OF ALBERTA, WESTERN CANADIANA PUBLICATIONS PROJECT (CN/0704-7495) [03791182] **421**

NEWSLETTER (UNIVERSITY OF MASSACHUSETTS AT AMHERST. WATER RESOURCES RESEARCH CENTER) (US) [09798509] **5536**

NEWSLETTER - UNIVERSITY OF SOUTHERN CALIFORNIA. ARMENIAN MUSICAL STUDIES (US/0732-8966) [08449569] **4141**

NEWSLETTER (UNIVERSITY OF TORONTO. FACULTY OF SOCIAL WORK. ALUMNI ASSOCIATION) (CN/0711-723X) [08655382] **5252**

NEWSLETTER-UNIVERSITY OF WASHINGTON *CEASED.* (US/0744-8821) [08623211] **1197**

NEWSLETTER - UPPER CANADA RAILWAY SOCIETY (1980) (CN/0845-8847) [20776805] **5433**

NEWSLETTER/UTAH GENEALOGICAL ASSOCIATION (US) [02254333] **2464**

NEWSLETTER - VANCOUVER HISTORICAL SOCIETY (1980) (CN/0823-0161) [09801051] **2750**

NEWSLETTER - VANCOUVER ISLAND REGIONAL LIBRARY (CN/0380-1691) [02443333] **3236**

NEWSLETTER - VERMONT INSTITUTE OF NATURAL SCIENCE (US) [05861589] **5133**

NEWSLETTER / VIETNAMESE ASSOCIATION, TORONTO (CN/0712-1288) [08724041] **2269**

NEWSLETTER / VIRGINIA BEACH GENEALOGICAL SOCIETY (US/1044-5897) [19837303] **2464**

NEWSLETTER - VIRGINIA STATE BAR. YOUNGER MEMBERS CONFERENCE (US/0094-2251) [01791374] **3017**

NEWSLETTER - VISUAL ARTS & CRAFTS COMMUNICATION COUNCIL OF ALBERTA (CN/0704-0296) [03797333] **374**

NEWSLETTER / W.H. AUDEN SOCIETY (UK) [19074444] **3467**

NEWSLETTER - WATERLOO POTTERS' WORKSHOP (CN/0708-1952) [05018238] **374**

NEWSLETTER - WAYNE STATE UNIVERSITY LIBRARIES (US/0146-6348) [02981587] **3236**

NEWSLETTER / WEST COAST ENVIRONMENTAL LAW RESEARCH FOUNDATION (CN/0715-4275) [09201090] **3115**

NEWSLETTER - WESTERN ASSOCIATION FOR ART CONSERVATION (US/1052-0066) [21315424] 4094, **326**

NEWSLETTER - WESTERN PENNSYLVANIA BLUEGRASS COMMITTEE (US) [02246833] **4141**

NEWSLETTER - WESTMORLAND HISTORICAL SOCIETY (CN/0382-0831) [02275093] **2750**

NEWSLETTER / WHITMAN COUNTY GENEALOGICAL SOCIETY (US/0887-6959) [11700418] **2464**

NEWSLETTER - WILLEM MENGELBERG SOCIETY (US/1051-0788) [07499709] **4141**

NEWSLETTER / WISCONSIN LABOR HISTORY SOCIETY (US/0731-3373) [08094732] **1695**

NEWSLETTER / WISCONSIN STATE GENEALOGICAL SOCIETY (US) [07527191] **2464**

NEWSLETTER - WOMEN HERITAGE AND MUSEUMS (UK/0968-6266) [I09686266] **4094**

NEWSLETTER - WOMEN'S CAUCUS-RELIGIOUS STUDIES (US/0362-4676) [02171985] **4982**

NEWSLETTER - WOMEN'S EQUAL RIGHTS ASSOCIATION (CN/0711-4478) [08773972] **5563**

NEWSLETTER - WOMEN'S INTER-CHURCH COUNCIL OF CANADA (CN/0822-2061) [11084991] **4982**

NEWSLETTER - WORLD FEDERATION FOR MENTAL HEALTH (CN/0319-6992) [05654853] **3931**

NEWSLETTER-WRITERS GUILD OF AMERICA, WEST (US/0043-9533) [04955565] **3417**

NEWSLETTER - WRITERS' UNION OF CANADA (CN/0382-831X) [03199477] **3417**

NEWSLETTER (YORK UNIVERSITY (TORONTO, ONT.). INSTITUTE FOR SOCIAL RESEARCH) (CN/0834-1729) [16074508] **5211**

NEWSLETTERS IN PRINT (US/0899-0425) [17977723] **4817**

NEWSLETTERS ON STRATIGRAPHY (NE/0078-0421) [01760323] 4228, **1389**

NEWSLETTERS ON THE BLACK EXPERIENCE, COMPUTER USE, FEMINISM, LAW, MEDICINE, TEACHING *See* APA NEWSLETTERS ON THE BLACK EXPERIENCE, COMPUTER USE, FEMINISM, LAW, MEDICINE, TEACHING **4341**

NEWSLETTERS ON THE BLACK EXPERIENCE, COMPUTER USE, FEMINISM, LAW, MEDICINE, TEACHING : A PUBLICATION OF THE AMERICAN PHILOSOPHICAL ASSOCIATION (US) [25169048] **4353**

NEWSLETTERS / UNESCO, MAJOR REGIONAL PROJECT, GEOLOGY FOR DEVELOPMENT (FR) [10189363] **1389**

NEWSLIB BRISBANE (AT/0312-5270) [I03125270] **3236**

NEWSLINE (US) [11942821] **2750**

NEWSLINE / AMERICAN ASSEMBLY OF COLLEGIATE SCHOOLS OF BUSINESS (US/0360-697X) [25394601] 1837, **699**

NEWSLINE / AMERICAN MEDICAL ASSOCIATION AUXILIARY, INC (US/1057-6371) [24083138] **3621**

NEWSLINE (ASSOCIATED BUILDERS & CONTRACTORS (U.S.)) *See* ABC TODAY **597**

NEWSLINE - (COLUMBIA UNIVERSITY. GRADUATE SCHOOL OF ARCHITECTURE PLANNING AND PRESERVATION) (US/1052-5831) [22334414] **304**

NEWSLINE - MANITOBA LIBRARY ASSOCIATION (CN/0227-6569) [08205437] **3236**

NEWSLINE - NATIONAL RURAL ELECTRIC WOMEN'S ASSOCIATION (U.S.) (US/0744-7531) [08521474] **2073**

NEWSLINE (SPRINGFIELD, VA.) (US/1045-3350) [06662936] **5133**

NEWSLINE - TRAVEL INDUSTRY ASSOCIATION OF AMERICA (US/0749-985X) [09169804] **5486**

NEWSLINE - UNIVERSITY OF WINDSOR (CN/0709-4132) [06166598] **1837**

NEWSLINE (WASHINGTON) (US/0148-8511) [03375781] **5388**

NEWSLINK (US) [21390811] **4606**

NEWSMAGAZINE - CENTRE FOR WOMEN. HUMBER COLLEGE OF APPLIED ARTS AND TECHNOLOGY. CENTRE FOR CONTINUOUS LEARNING (CN/0316-5094) [02247828] 5563, **1838**

NEWSMAKERS (DETROIT, MICH.) (US/0899-0417) [17977680] **434**

NEWSNET ACTION LETTER (US/0888-8698) [10456116] **3236**

●NEWSNET (STANFORD, CALIF.) (US/1074-3057) [28894543] **2700**

NEWSNOTES - CENTER FOR LAW AND EDUCATION (U.S.) (US/0276-203X) [05432675] 1768, **3017**

NEWSOURCES (HALIFAX) (CN/1183-1170) [23598330] **1805**

NEWSPACKET (ORILLIA) (CN/0384-1642) [02545148] **3417**

NEWSPAPER ABSTRACTS (US/1056-1684) [23467864] **2464**

NEWSPAPER ABSTRACTS (US) **5814**

NEWSPAPER ABSTRACTS ONDISC (US/1064-993X) [26449314] **5814**

●NEWSPAPER ADVERTISING SOURCE (US/1071-4529) [28642207] **763**

NEWSPAPER & PERIODICAL ABSTRACTS [ONLINE DATABASE] (US) **5814**

NEWSPAPER FINANCIAL EXECUTIVE JOURNAL (US/0889-4590) [13305435] 4817, **2922**

NEWSPAPER FOCUS (UK/0957-9125) [I09579125] **5812**

NEWSPAPER FUND ADVISER UPDATE (US) **5711**

NEWSPAPER GEOG. LIST - CARLETON UNIVERSITY (CN/0823-132X) [10763775] **5790**

NEWSPAPER GUILD *See* NEWSPAPER GUILD, AFL-CIO, CLC CONSTITUTION, THE **1695**

NEWSPAPER GUILD, AFL-CIO, CLC CONSTITUTION, THE (US/0270-2223) [06350541] **1695**

NEWSPAPER GUILD. CONVENTION *See* PROCEEDINGS, ANNUAL CONVENTION - NEWSPAPER GUILD. CONVENTION **1703**

NEWSPAPER INVESTOR (US/1042-4326) [19071519] **909**

NEWSPAPER OF CARDIOLOGY (US) **3708**

NEWSPAPER OF THE CANADIAN WORKERS' ASSOCIATION (CN/0225-3100) [06054152] **1695**

NEWSPAPER RATES AND DATA (US/0038-9544) [06273353] **763**

NEWSPAPER RESEARCH JOURNAL (US/0739-5329) [06887314] **4817**

NEWSPAPER TECHNIQUES (DARMSTADT, GERMANY) (GW) [07424573] **4817**

NEWSPAPER (TORONTO) (CN/0227-7409) [06689212] **5790**

NEWSPAPERS AND PERIODICALS CURRENTLY RECEIVED BY THE LIBRARY OF PARLIAMENT INCLUDING THE READING ROOM OF THE HOUSE OF COMMONS (CN/0708-1596) [05072012] **4699**

NEWSPAPERS & TECHNOLOGY (US/1052-5572) [22301719] **5644**

NEWSPAPERS CAREER DIRECTORY (US/0889-8499) [14091640] **2922**

NEWSPAPERS IN MICROFORM (ANN ARBOR, MICH. *See* SERIALS & NEWSPAPERS IN MICROFORM **424**

NEWSPAPERS IN MICROFORM: FOREIGN COUNTRIES *CEASED.* (US/0192-1231) [04868776] **5647**

●NEWSPAPERS ONLINE (US/1065-8947) [25771501] **1927**

NEWSPAPERS RECEIVED CURRENTLY IN THE LIBRARY OF CONGRESS (US/0093-6464) [07093410] **5647**

NEWSPEACE (UK/0048-0304) [03170067] **4982**

NEWSRAIL (AT/0310-7477) [19676396] **5433**

NEWSREAL (US/0730-224X) [07968988] **4817**

NEWSREPORT - STUDENT PRESS SERVICE *See* SPS NEWSREPORT **2924**

NEWSROOM DIRECTORY & GUIDE TO THE ILLINOIS ENVIRONMENTAL PROTECTION AGENCY (US) [06107993] 2237, **4669**

NEWSTIME (LONDON, ENGLAND) *CEASED.* (UK) [08567770] 5813, **4817**

NEWSTIME - PUBLIC SERVICE ALLIANCE OF CANADA. NATIONAL COMPONENT (CN/1184-9797) [24690750] **4669**

NEWSTODAY (CN/0227-2202) [06958603] **1867**

NEWSVIEWS / CANADIAN JEWELLERS INSTITUTE (CN/0824-2194) [10052126] **2915**

NEWSWATCH (LAGOS) (NR/0189-8892) [12681315] **2499**

NEWSWEEK (INTERNATIONAL, ATLANTIC EDITION) (UK/0163-7053) [04447924] **2490**

NEWSWEEK (INTERNATIONAL, PACIFIC EDITION) (US/0163-7061) [04447810] **2490**

NEWSWEEK ON CAMPUS *CEASED.* (US/0741-8981) [10199285] **1838**

NEWSWEEK (SHIVELY, KY.) *See* SOUTHWEST NEWSWEEK, THE **2546**

NEWSWEEK (SHIVELY, KY.) *See* SOUTHWEST NEWSWEEK, THE **5682**

NEWSWEEK (SHIVELY, KY.) (US) [13715039] **5682**

NEWSWEEK (U.S. ED.) (US/0028-9604) [01760328] **2490**

NEWSWEEKLY (US) [20481819] **5689**

NEWSWIRE (US/0270-9783) [02658982] **2923**

NEWTON COUNTY ENTERPRISE (US) [14879991] **5666**

NEWTON-EVANS RESEARCH COMPANY'S MARKET TRENDS DIGEST FOR THE COMPUTER, COMMUNICATIONS, AND CONTROLS INDUSTRIES (US/0891-1037) [14629162] **1197**

NEWTON GRAPHIC, THE (US/0739-3849) [09729501] **5689**

NEWTON KANSAN (NEWTON, KAN. : 1952) (US) [11586510] **5677**

NEWTON RECORD, THE (US) [10366433] **5701**

NEWTON TAB, THE (US/0745-2047) [08924270] **5689**

NEWYORK WOMAN *CEASED.* (US/0888-9775) [13765170] **5563**

NEWZINDEX (NZ/0111-0608) [I01110608] **699, 732**

NEXIS (US) **699, 732**

NEXTWORLD (SAN FRANCISCO, CALIF.) *CEASED.* (US/1061-6616) [24526987] **1197**

NEXUS (US) [03381510] **3417**

NEXUS (US) [07040550] **1838**

NEXUS (AURORA, COLO.) (US) [09358159] **3236**

NEXUS (HAMILTON, ONT.) (CN/0711-5342) [08499634] **242**

NEXUS II (CN/0838-6498) [18115989] **5563**

NEXUS (NEWARK, N.J.) (US/0277-237X) [02385466] **763**

NEXUS NEWSLETTER (CN/1186-950X) [25313784] **1768**

NEXUS NEWSLETTER / MOVEMENT FOR CANADIAN LITERACY (CN/1186-950X) [25313782] **1768**

NEXUS (WILMINGTON) (US/0197-8519) [06122336] **3170**

NEYAGAWA-SHI (JAPAN) *See* NEYAGAWA-SHI TOKEISHO **5334**

NEYAGAWA-SHI TOKEISHO (JA) [01797813] **5334**

NEZAVISIMAIA GAZETA (RU) [24498172] **5809**

●NEZAVISIMAIA MOLDOVA : ORGAN PARLAMENTA I PRAVITELSTVA RESPUBLIKI MOLDOVA (MV) [24925581] **5806**

NEZAVISIMAYA GAZETA. FRENCH EDITION (FR) **5801**

NFAIS NEWSLETTER (US/0090-0893) [02584453] **3236**

●NFAIS YEARBOOK OF THE INFORMATION INDUSTRY, THE (US/1062-7952) [25744676] **3236**

NFEC DIRECTORY OF ENVIRONMENTAL INFORMATION SOURCES (US/0090-4864) [01169461] **2219**

NFF UPDATE (US/0882-6536) [11987320] **4484**

NFI BLUE BOOK (US/1067-4454) [11721486] **2309**

NFI MAGAZINE : NEDERLANDS FILM INSTITUUT *CEASED.* (NE) **4075**

NFL SUPERPRO (US/1060-3514) [24496308] **4864**

NFM-THEMAREEKS AMSTERDAM (NE/0926-3411) [I09263411] **4075**

NFO REPORTER, THE (US/1055-2634) [01758952] **112**

NFPA BUYERS' GUIDE *See* NFPA JOURNAL. BUYERS' GUIDE : FIRE PROTECTION AND FIRE SERVICE REFERENCE DIRECTORY **2292**

NFPA HANDBOOK OF THE NATIONAL ELECTRICAL CODE (US) [04398218] **2073**

NFPA INSPECTION MANUAL (US) 2292, **2865**

NFPA JOURNAL (US/1054-8793) [23004557] **2292**

●NFPA JOURNAL. BUYERS' GUIDE : FIRE PROTECTION AND FIRE SERVICE REFERENCE DIRECTORY (US) [25363270] **2292**

NFPC NEWS NOTES / NATIONAL FEDERATION OF PRIESTS' COUNCILS (US/0738-3886) [08611768] **4982**

NFT HIGHLIGHTS (US) [12427106] **2389**

NG. NIEUWSBLAD GEZONDHEIDSZORG *CEASED.* (NE/0922-744X) [I0922744X] **3621**

NGAM : CAHIERS DU DEPARTEMENT DE LITTERATURE AFRICAINE COMPAREE, UNIVERSITE DE YAOUNDE (CM) [04064307] **3417**

NGAN-HANG QUOC-GIA VIET-NAM *See* KINH-TE TAP-SAN **1571**

NGAN PHNG (US/1054-0466) [22730573] **3417**

NGAO (TZ) [01792054] **2889**

NGC NEWS *CEASED.* (DK) **4266**

NGHIEN CU KINH TE (VM) [01795774] **1508**

NGHIEN CUU LICH SU (VM/0866-7497) [02241021] **2660**

NGI'S GAS PRICE INDEX (US) **4266**

NGOMA (EDITION FRANCAISE) (CN/0712-2837) [08794447] **1883**

NGOMA (ENGLISH EDITION) (CN/0712-2829) [08790885] **1883**

NGON NG (VM) [04738821] **3306**

NGOUI VIET DAILY NEWS. ENGLISH SECTION (US/1056-5124) [14258091] **5637**

NGUYET SAN MINH DUC (VM) [02244284] **5234**

●NGV NEWS (US/1065-3422) [26577102] **4266**

NHAC VIET (US/1063-1909) [21530871] **4141**

NHAN BAN (FR/0153-3762) [I01533762] **5801**

NHEA/NEA EDUCATOR (US/0276-9123) [04791303] **1768**

NHIC NEWSLETTER *CEASED.* (US/1180-5838) **3621**

NHK LABORATORIES NOTE (JA/0027-657X) [I0027657X] **5133**

NHRC REPORT (US/0161-1607) [03851596] **3621**

NHSC HEALTH CARE PRACTITIONERS (US) [04939627] **3725**

NHSF NEWS / NATIONAL HISPANIC SCHOLARSHIP FUND (US) [24557056] **2269**

NIA JOURNAL (NR/0189-1162) [I01891162] **305**

NIAAA-RUCAS ALCOHOLISM TREATMENT SERIES (US/0147-0515) [04121445] **1347**

NIAGARA ANGLICAN, THE (CN/0703-5888) [03951067] **5065**

NIAGARA BRUCE TRAIL CLUB *See* NIAGARA BRUCE TRAIL CLUB **4876**

NIAGARA BRUCE TRAIL CLUB (CN/C706-7429) [05018220] **4876**

NIAGARA BUSINESS DIRECTORY (CN/0336-768X) [17742832] **699**

NIAGARA CHILDREN'S SERVICES COMMITTEE *See* NEWSLETTER / NIAGARA CHILDREN'S SERVICES COMMITTEE **5299**

NIAGARA FALLS REVIEW (CN/0839-1572) [18921977] **5790**

NIAGARA GAZETTE (US) [10905911] **5719**

NIAGARA GUILD OF CRAFTS (CN/0703-6825) [03452891] **374**

NIAGARA INSTITUTE *See* PERSPECTIVES / THE NIAGARA INSTITUTE **5212**

NIAGARA INSTITUTE *See* AGENDA / THE NIAGARA INSTITUTE **859**

NIAGARA JOURNAL, THE (US/0749-7253) [11167067] **5769**

NIAGARA - WHEATFIELD TRIBUNE (US) **5719**

NIAGARA'S HISTORICAL MUSEUMS ... DIRECTORY (CN/1182-6649) [23231536] **2750**

NIAGARA'S SEASONS (CN/0714-4202) [09050372] **5486**

NIAID CATALOG OF TISSUE TYPING ANTISERA (US/0148-8562) [03388428] **568**

NIAID MANUAL OF TISSUE TYPING TECHNIQUES (US/0147-7277) [05929684] **3675**

NIAS REPORT (DK) [27536264] **2660**

NIBBLE (US/0734-3795) [08181109] **1280**

NIBBLES, ELS *See* EASTERN EXPRESS (OMAHA, NEB.) **3208**

NICARAGUA *See* DECRETOS-LEYES Y LEYES DE LA REPUBLICA DE NICARAGUA **2959**

NICARAGUA ECONOMIC REPORT (US) [24170294] **1508**

NICARAGUA. OFICINA EJECUTIVA DE ENCUESTAS Y CENSOS *See* TURISMO, ENCUESTA **5498**

NICARAGUA THROUGH OUR EYES *CEASED.* (NQ) [13563474] **2750**

NICARAGUA UPDATE (US) [11286807] **2750**

NICARAGUA (WASHINGTON, D.C. 1982) (US/8755-4968) [09734857] **2750**

NICARAUAC : REVISTA BIMESTRAL DEL MINISTERIO DE CULTURA *CEASED.* (NQ) [06912250] **5252**

NICE HISTORIQUE (FR/1141-1791) [06311075] **2700**

NICE MATIN (FR) **5801**

NICHD ANNUAL REPORT (US/0741-4684) [09103539] **3907**

NICHE (BALTIMORE, MD.) (US/1064-0347) [19657189] **955**

NICHI-BEI JOSEI JANARU (US/0898-8900) [17942574] **5563**

NICHI BEI TIMES (US/0739-2443) [04601742] **5637**

NICHI-FUTSU BIJUTSU GAKKAI KAIHO (JA) [10889813] 360, **276**

NICHIDAI IGAKU ZASSHI (JA/0029-0424) [09787071] **3622**

NICHIJOGO SHINDAN / ASAHI SHINBUNSHA YOGO KANJI HEN (JA) [10781252] **3306**

NICHOLAS CHRONICLE, THE (US) [13148739] **5764**

NICHOLLS STATE UNIVERSITY *See* PROFESSIONAL PAPERS SERIES (BIOLOGY) **470**

NICHOLS SCHOOL (BUFFALO, N.Y.) *See* ALUMNI DIRECTORY - NICHOLS SCHOOL (BUFFALO, N.Y.) **1099**

NICHTKONVENTIONELLE LITERATUR LINGUISTIK : INHALTSVERZEICHNIS DER NEUERWERBUNGEN (GW) [04444205] **3336**

NICKEL TOPICS (1966) (US/0730-7764) [04900747] **4013**

NICKEL (TORONTO) (CN/0829-8351) [15999677] **4013**

NICKLE'S CANADIAN ENERGY INDEX (CN/0835-1996) [16887074] **1951**

NICKLE'S DAILY OIL BULLETIN (CN/0709-681X) [I0709681X] **4266**

NICKLE'S OIL AND GAS STATISTICS QUARTERLY (CN/1184-1761) [23599117] **4284**

NICM ASSOCIATES NEWSLETTER (US) [03578567] **4982**

NICOLA VALLEY HISTORICAL QUARTERLY (CN/0708-8132) [06132618] **2750**

NICOLAUS. STUDI STORICI (IT/1121-323X) [11121323X] **2624**

NIDA AL-ISLAM (UA) [05199092] **5044**

NIDA RESEARCH MONOGRAPH (US/1046-9516) [18275944] **1347**

NIDI RAPPORT (NE/0922-7210) [I09227210] **4555**

NIE INFORMATION SERVICE (US/1049-1872) [21171507] **4817**

NIE NOTES (US/0743-8362) [10681597] **1901**

NIE WARSZAWA (PL/0867-2237) [I08672237] **4484**

NIEDERDEUTSCHE BEITRAEGE ZUR KUNSTGESCHICHTE (GW/0078-0537) [02661605] **360**

NIEDERDEUTSCHES WORT (GW/0078-0545) [04474735] **3306**

NIEDERLANDE : ENERGIEWIRTSCHAFT (GW) [04521498] **1951**

NIEDERLANDE, LANDWIRTSCHAFT / BUNDESSTELLE FUR AUSSENHANDELSINFORMATION (GW) [08913505] **112**

NIEDERLANDE: WIRTSCHAFT IN ZAHLEN UND WIRTSCHAFTSDOKUMENTATION (GW) [06267147] **1575**

NIEDERLANDE : WIRTSCHAFTLICHE ENTWICKLUNG UND PROGNOSE (GW) [06285409] **1575**

NIEDEROSTERREICHISCHE LANDES-LANDWIRTSCHAFTSKAMMER *See* LAGEBERICHT DER NIEDEROSTERREICHISCHEN LAND- UND FORSTWIRTSCHAFT **103**

NIEDEROSTERREICHISCHE SOZIALHILFE UND JUGENDWOHLFAHRTSPFLEGE (AU) [03665309] **5299**

NIEDERSACHSEN IN ZAHLEN (GW) [05372312] **5334**

NIEDERSACHSISCHE DENKMALPFLEGE (GW/0545-9370) [04652614] **360**

NIEDERSACHSISCHES ARZTEBLATT (GW/0028-9795) [04566200] **3622**

NIEDERSACHSISCHES JAHRBUCH FUER LANDESGESCHICHTE (GW/0078-0561) [11977649] **2624**

NIEDERSACHSISCHES LANDESVERWALTUNGSAMT *See* INDUSTRIE **1611**

NIEDERSACHSISCHES LANDESVERWALTUNGSAMT *See* STRASSENVERKEHRSUNFAELLE **5445**

NIEDERSACHSISCHES LANDESVERWALTUNGSAMT *See* BERGBAU UND VERARBEITENDES GEWERBE **2135**

NIEDERSACHSISCHES LANDESVERWALTUNGSAMT *See* VERZEICHNIS DER BERUFSBILDENDEN SCHULEN **1917**

NIEDERSACHSISCHES LANDESVERWALTUNGSAMT *See* ARBEITSKRAFTEERHEBUNG IN DER LANDWIRTSCHAFT **1651**

NIEDERSACHSISCHES — Alphabetical Title Index

NIEDERSACHSISCHES LANDESVERWALTUNGSAMT See VERZEICHNIS DER ALLGEMEINBILDENDEN SCHULEN **1798**

NIEDERSACHSISCHES LANDESVERWALTUNGSAMT See SCHULDEN DES LANDES, DER GEMEINDEN, SAMTGEMEINDEN UND LANDKREISE **4747**

NIEDERSACHSISCHES LANDESVERWALTUNGSAMT See AUSLANDER **5322**

NIEDERSACHSISCHES ZAHNARZTEBLATT (GW/0173-6868) [05392051] **1331**

NIEDERSAECHSISCHE WIRTSCHAFT (GW) [06698864] **1575**

NIEDERSAECHSISCHES WOERTERBUCH (GW) **1927**

NIELSEN MARKETING TRENDS (ENGLISH ED.) (US/1040-6948) [18504612] **934**

NIELSEN NEWSCAST, THE (US/0468-1835) [01760344] **1135**

NIELSEN REPORT ON TELEVISION / NIELSEN MEDIA RESEARCH (US) [05395472] **1135**

NIEMAN REPORTS (US/0028-9817) [01607410] **2923**

NIEN CHING JEN CEASED. (HK) [01797561] 1067, **2507**

NIEN GIAM VIET-NAM, MONTREAL (CN/0712-5054) [09157042] **2750**

NIEPODLEGOSC (US/0272-0280) [02265105] **2700**

NIEREN- UND HOCKDRUCKKRANKHEITEN (GW/0300-5224) [02556607] **3622**

NIETZSCHE BRIEFWECHSEL (GW) **4353**

NIETZSCHE-STUDIEN (GW/0342-1422) [01776111] **4353**

NIETZSCHE WERKE (GW) **4353**

NIEUW KERKELIJK HANDBOEK See VAN ALPHEN'S NIEUW KERKELIJK HANDBOEK **5068**

NIEUW NEUF (BE) 2902, **305**

NIEUW WERELDTIJDSCHRIFT : NWT (BE/0773-3577) [11613010] **2520**

NIEUWE DRENTSE VOLKSALMANAK (NE) [04652741] **2700**

NIEUWE DROGIST (NE/0927-0574) [I09270574] 405, **4318**

NIEUWE MAAND, DE (BE) **5211**

NIEUWE REVU (NE) **2284**

NIEUWE STEM (NE/0169-6777) [04542609] **2520**

NIEUWE TAALGIDS (NE/0028-9922) [01760349] **3306**

NIEUWE VERENIGING VAN AANNEMERS GROOTBEDRIJF See NIVAG CONTOUR **622**

NIEUWE WEST-INDISCHE GIDS (NE/0028-9930) [01760350] 2851, **5211**

NIEUWE WISKRANT (NE) **3524**

NIEUWSBLAD TRANSPORT (NE) **5388**

NIEUWSBRIEF - LIGA VOOR MENSENRECHTEN (BE/0772-5183) [I07725183] **3017**

NIEUWSBRIEF MILIEUTECHNOLOGIE (NE/0924-4301) [I09244301] **2178**

NIEUWSBRIEF / NEDERLANDS FOTOARCHIEF (NE/0927-8311) [I09278311] **4372**

NIEUWSBRIEF PZ (NE) **4212**

NIEUWSTRIBUNE (NE) **1118**

NIF NEWSLETTER (FI) [01787118] **2323**

NIF REPORT (US/1045-666X) [20181789] **2660**

NIF WEEKLY (II) [08084776] **909**

NIGER (NG/0550-6891) [01794476] **2642**

NIGER (FR) [01795564] **1575**

NIGER. MINISTERE DES AFFAIRES ETRANGERES ET DE LA COOPERATION See LISTE DES MEMBRES DES CORPS DIPLOMATIQUE ET CONSULAIRE ET DES ORGANISATIONS INTERNATIONALES **4528**

NIGER. MINISTERE DU DEVELOPPEMENT ET DE LA COOPERATION. DIRECTION DE LA STATISTIQUE See BULLETIN DE STATISTIQUE - REPUBLIQUE DU NIGER, MINISTERE DU DEVELOPPEMENT ET DE LA COOPERATION, DIRECTION DE LA STATISTIQUE **5324**

NIGER. MINISTERE DU PLAN ET DE LA PLANIFICATION REGIONALE See PROGRAMME DES INVESTISSEMENTS DE L'ETAT ... ET BUDGET D'INVESTISSEMENT ... **4742**

NIGER (NIGERIA). MINISTRY OF INFORMATION See NIGER STATE BUDGET SPEECH **4669**

NIGER. SERVICE DE LA STATISTIQUE. BULLETIN TRIMESTRIEL DE STATISTIQUE See BULLETIN DE STATISTIQUE - REPUBLIQUE DU NIGER, MINISTERE DU DEVELOPPEMENT ET DE LA COOPERATION, DIRECTION DE LA STATISTIQUE **5324**

NIGER STATE BUDGET SPEECH (NR) [06955881] **4669**

NIGER STATE (NIGERIA) See GAZETTE - NIGER STATE OF NIGERIA **2973**

NIGER STATE (NIGERIA) See ESTIMATES OF THE MILITARY GOVERNMENT OF NIGER STATE OF NIGERIA / NIGER STATE OF NIGERIA **4646**

NIGER STATE (NIGERIA) See ESTIMATES OF THE GOVERNMENT OF NIGER STATE OF NIGERIA **4646**

NIGER STATE (NIGERIA). ESTIMATES OF THE MILITARY GOVERNMENT OF NIGER STATE OF NIGERIA See ESTIMATES OF THE GOVERNMENT OF NIGER STATE OF NIGERIA **4646**

NIGER, WIRTSCHAFTSDATEN UND WIRTSCHAFTSDOKUMENTATION / BUNDESSTELLE FUR AUSSENHANDELSINFORMATION (GW) [08917938] **1575**

NIGERBIBLIOS (NR/0331-0000) [03092120] **3236**

NIGERIA See GUIDELINES FOR THE ROLLING PLAN **4730**

NIGERIA See NATIONAL ROLLING PLAN **4738**

NIGERIA See APPROVED REVENUE, RECURRENT AND CAPITAL ESTIMATES (NIGERIA) **4711**

NIGERIA COMPANY HANDBOOK AND GUIDE TO OPERATING BUSINESS IN NIGERIA (NR) [20116334] **909**

NIGERIA. DEPT. OF AGRICULTURAL RESEARCH See APPROVED RESEARCH PROGRAMME - FEDERAL DEPARTMENT OF AGRICULTURAL RESEARCH **62**

NIGERIA. DEPT. OF PETROLEUM RESOURCES. MONTHLY PETROLEUM INFORMATION See MONTHLY PETROLEUM INFORMATION **4265**

NIGERIA, EASTERN. MINISTRY OF ECONOMIC DEVELOPMENT AND RECONSTRUCTION. STATISTICS DIVISION See ECONOMIC INDICATORS; EAST-CENTRAL STATE - (NIGERIA) **1557**

NIGERIA : ENERGIEWIRTSCHAFT (GW) [05064469] **1951**

NIGERIA. FEDERAL OFFICE OF STATISTICS See ANNUAL ABSTRACT OF STATISTICS - NIGERIA. FEDERAL OFFICE OF STATISTICS **5321**

NIGERIA FORESTRY INFORMATION BULLETIN (NR/0331-0353) [01784862] **2389**

NIGERIA HOMENEWS (UK) **2500**

NIGERIA. MINISTRY OF FINANCE AND ECONOMIC PLANNING. ECONOMIC PLANNING DIVISION See RETAIL MARKET PRICES OF SOME FOOD ITEMS IN PLATEAU STATE, SELECTED FROM SOME LOCAL GOVERNMENT IN THE STATE **2356**

NIGERIA. NATIONAL UNIVERSITIES COMMISSION See BULLETIN OF THE NATIONAL UNIVERSITIES COMMISSION **1813**

NIGERIA ... OFFICIAL HANDBOOK (NR) [13141194] **2500**

NIGERIA. PRINTING DIVISION See OFFICE DIRECTORY : LAGOS AREA **4670**

NIGERIA. SECURITIES AND EXCHANGE COMMISSION See REPORT AND ACCOUNTS FOR THE YEAR ENDED 31ST DECEMBER ... / THE SECURITIES AND EXCHANGE COMMISSION (NIGERIA) **912**

NIGERIA YEAR BOOK (NR/0078-0685) [01141891] **2500**

NIGERIAN ACCOUNTANT, THE (NR/0048-0371) [11942569] **749**

NIGERIAN BAR JOURNAL (NR) [01760357] **3017**

NIGERIAN BOOKS IN PRINT (NR) [06181889] **4831**

NIGERIAN BUSINESS DIGEST (NR/0048-038X) [05317428] **699**

NIGERIAN CHRISTIAN, THE (NR/0029-005X) [02195239] **4982**

NIGERIAN CONSTITUTIONAL LAW REPORTS (NR) [08795609] **3093**

NIGERIAN CURRENT LAW REVIEW : THE JOURNAL OF THE NIGERIAN INSTITUTE OF ADVANCED LEGAL STUDIES (NR/0189-207X) [09431921] **3017**

NIGERIAN ECONOMIC SOCIETY See PROCEEDINGS OF THE ANNUAL CONFERENCE OF THE NIGERIAN ECONOMIC SOCIETY **1513**

NIGERIAN ENTERPRISE (NR) [10554353] **847**

NIGERIAN FIELD (UK/0029-0076) [02277360] **4169**

NIGERIAN FRONTLINE NEWS (US/1040-1598) [18336107] **1118**

NIGERIAN JOURNAL OF ECONOMIC AND SOCIAL STUDIES, THE (NR/0029-0092) [02449123] 5211, **1508**

NIGERIAN JOURNAL OF ENTOMOLOGY (NR/0331-0094) [02242843] **5593**

NIGERIAN JOURNAL OF FORESTRY (NR/0374-9584) [02254451] **2389**

NIGERIAN JOURNAL OF GUIDANCE AND COUNSELLING, THE (NR/0794-0831) [16017953] **4606**

NIGERIAN JOURNAL OF INDUSTRIAL RELATIONS (NR/0794-8883) [18761586] **1619**

NIGERIAN JOURNAL OF INTERNATIONAL AFFAIRS (NR/0331-3646) [02244034] **4530**

NIGERIAN JOURNAL OF MEDICAL SCIENCES (NR/0331-4316) [05538434] **3622**

NIGERIAN JOURNAL OF MICROBIOLOGY (NR/0794-1293) [25625895] **568**

NIGERIAN JOURNAL OF NUTRITIONAL SCIENCES (NR/0189-0913) [09770910] **4195**

NIGERIAN JOURNAL OF PAEDIATRICS (NR/0302-4660) [07700698] **3907**

NIGERIAN JOURNAL OF PALMS AND OIL SEEDS (NR/0795-8692) [24421686] **112**

NIGERIAN JOURNAL OF PHARMACEUTICAL SCIENCES (NR/0189-322X) [16390732] **4318**

NIGERIAN JOURNAL OF PHARMACY (NR/0331-670X) [10808773] **4318**

NIGERIAN JOURNAL OF PHYSIOLOGICAL SCIENCES : OFFICIAL PUBLICATION OF THE PHYSIOLOGICAL SOCIETY OF NIGERIA (NR/0794-859X) [18713763] **584**

NIGERIAN JOURNAL OF POLICY AND STRATEGY (NR/0189-5923) [17257942] **4484**

NIGERIAN JOURNAL OF PUBLIC AFFAIRS, THE (NR) [02265117] **4669**

NIGERIAN JOURNAL OF SCIENCE (NR/0029-0114) [02449124] **5134**

NIGERIAN JOURNAL OF THEOLOGY, THE (NR) [14090896] **4982**

NIGERIAN LAW JOURNAL, THE (NR/0078-0774) [01606690] **3017**

NIGERIAN LIBRARIES (NR/0029-0122) [01695540] **3236**

NIGERIAN LIBRARY AND INFORMATION SCIENCE REVIEW (NR/0189-4412) [10804729] **3236**

NIGERIAN MEDICAL JOURNAL (NR/0300-1652) [05109426] **3622**

NIGERIAN MEDICAL PRACTITIONER, THE (LB/0189-0964) [10502449] **3986**

NIGERIAN MUSIC AWARDS See NIGERIAN MUSIC AWARDS ANNUAL, THE **4141**

NIGERIAN MUSIC AWARDS ANNUAL, THE (NR) [23829496] **4141**

NIGERIAN NATIONAL PETROLEUM CORPORATION. ECONOMIC RESEARCH AND INTELLIGENCE DEPT See MONTHLY PETROLEUM INFORMATION **4265**

NIGERIAN NEWS, THE (US/0749-5145) [10619504] **2500**

NIGERIAN NURSE (NR) [02254267] **3862**

NIGERIAN PETROLEUM NEWS (NR/0189-7233) [01897233] **4266**

NIGERIAN PORTS AUTHORITY. MANAGEMENT SERVICES DIVISION See BI-LINGUAL MAGAZINE **5447**

NIGERIAN STAGE, THE (NR/1115-201X) [23225751] **5366**

NIGERIAN YELLOW PAGES : AN A TO Z TRADE DIRECTORY (NR/0331-0973) [07647778] **847**

NIGHT CRY (US) [12690681] **3417**

NIGHT LIGHT, THE (US/0888-9368) [13752018] **4606**

●NIGHT SONGS (US/1068-4468) [27674031] **3459**

NIGHTINGALE (OTTAWA) (CN/0849-2646) [23238181] **3622**

NIGHTINGALE REPORT (CN) 1135, **4075**

NIGHTMARES ON ELM STREET (US/1056-3660) [23671826] **4864**

NIGHTMOVES (CN/0824-6718) [11085116] **4141**

NIGHTOUT (CN/0384-5842) [03248502] 4853, **4141**

NIGHTWINDS (CN/0715-5549) [09538829] **3417**

NIGOG +, LE (CN/0820-8255) [09766474] **4818**

NIGRIZIA (IT/0029-0173) [05291026] **4982**

NIH ADVISORY COMMITTEES (US) [17570217] **4794**

NIH ALMANAC (US/8756-601X) [04158997] 5299, **4794**

NIH DATA BOOK (US/8755-4674) [08836241] 4794, **3622**

NIH HEALTHLINE : CONSUMER HEALTH INFORMATION FROM THE NATIONAL INSTITUTES OF HEALTH (US) [25111433] **4794**

NIH NEWS & FEATURES / NATIONAL INSTITUTES OF HEALTH (US) [28580560] **3622**

NIH PUBLICATION (US/0737-6863) [09430062] **4794**

NIH PUBLICATIONS LIST (US/0027-6650) [02070912] **4810**

NIH RECORD, THE (US/1057-5871) [02251258] **4794**

NIH REPOSITORY OF HUMAN AND MOUSE DNA PROBES AND LIBRARIES / AMERICAN TYPE CULTURE COLLECTION (US) [20741064] **467**

NIHILISTIC REVIEW, THE (US/1055-842X) [23359274] **3417**

NIHON BENTOSU KENKYUKAI *See* NIHON BENTOSU KENKYUKAI SHI **4169**

NIHON BENTOSU KENKYUKAI SHI (JA) [09213126] **4169**

NIHON BUKKYO GAKKAI *See* NIPPON BUKKYO GAKKAI NEMPO **5021**

NIHON BUKKYO SHIGAKU / NIHON BUKKYO SHIGAKUKAI (JA/0385-5805) [09167213] **5021**

NIHON BUNGAKU (JA) [01799743] **3417**

NIHON CHINETSU GAKKAI SHI (JA/0388-6735) [10153453] **1416**

NIHON CHIZU SENTA *See* CHIZU SENTA NYUSU **2581**

NIHON CHOGAKKAI SHI (JA) [15477049] **5618**

NIHON CHUTO GAKKAI NENPO (JA) [16197904] **2660**

NIHON DAIGAKU. GEIJUTSU GAKUBU *See* NIHON DAIGAKU GEIJUTSUGAKUBU KIYO: SOSAKUHEN **326**

NIHON DAIGAKU. GEIJUTSU GAKUBU *See* NIHON DAIGAKU GEIJUTSUGAKUBU KIYO **326**

NIHON DAIGAKU GEIJUTSUGAKUBU KIYO (JA) [03060750] **326**

NIHON DAIGAKU GEIJUTSUGAKUBU KIYO: SOSAKUHEN (JA) [05235810] **326**

NIHON DAIGAKU. IGAKUBU *See* NIHON UNIVERSITY JOURNAL OF MEDICINE, THE **3622**

NIHON DAIGAKU KOGAKUBU KIYO. BUNRUI A (JA/0285-6174) [10382898] **1989**

NIHON DAIGAKU KOGAKUBU KIYO. BUNRUI B, IPPAN KYOIKU HEN (JA/0285-6182) [10801887] **1989**

NIHON DAIGAKU KOGAKUBU KIYO. DAI 1-SHU, KOGAKU HEN *See* NIHON DAIGAKU KOGAKUBU KIYO. BUNRUI A **1989**

NIHON DAIGAKU NOJUIGAKUBU GAKUJUTSU KENKYU HOKOKU (JA/0078-0839) [01590176] 5517, **113**

NIHON DAIGAKU RIKO GAKUBU IPPAN KYOIKU KYOSHITSU IHO (JA/0286-7370) [12359077] **1838**

NIHON DAIGAKU, TOKYO. NOJUIGAKUBU *See* NIHON DAIGAKU NOJUIGAKUBU GAKUJUTSU KENKYU HOKOKU **113**

NIHON DENSHI ZAIRYO GIJUTSU KYOKAI KAIHO (JA/0285-3833) [10439208] **2074**

NIHON DENSHIN DENWA KOSHA. MUSASHINO DENKI TSUSHIN KENKYUJO *See* NEMPO: NIHON DENSHIN DENWA KOSHA DENKI TSUSHIN KENKYUJO **2073**

NIHON DOBUTSUEN SUIZOKUKAN NENPO (JA) [08713555] **5593**

NIHON DOJO HIRYOGAKU ZASSHI (JA/0029-0610) [03611961] **179**

NIHON EIGA SHINARIO SENSHU (JA) [10344282] **3417**

NIHON EIYO SHOKURYO GAKKAI SHI (JA/0287-3516) [09492059] **4195**

NIHON FUDOSAN KENKYUJO *See* ZENKOKU SHIGAICHI KAKAKU SHISU **4848**

NIHON FUDOSAN KENKYUJO *See* TAHATA KAKAKU OYOBI KOSAKURYO SHIRABE **139**

NIHON FUKUGO ZAIRYO GAKKAI SHI (JA/0385-2563) [04203471] **2107**

NIHON FUKUSHI NENKAN (JA) [03660337] **5299**

NIHON GAKUHO / HENSHUSHA, OSAKA DAIGAKU BUNGAKUBU NIHONGAKU KENKYUSHITSU (JA) [08831972] **2660**

NIHON GAKUJUTSU KAIGI *See* REPORT - GEOLOGICAL SURVEY OF JAPAN **1394**

NIHON GAKUSHIIN *See* PROCEEDINGS OF THE JAPAN ACADEMY. SERIES A: MATHEMATICAL SCIENCES **3528**

NIHON GAKUSHIIN *See* PROCEEDINGS OF THE JAPAN ACADEMY. SERIES B: PHYSICAL AND BIOLOGICAL SCIENCES **469**

NIHON GAN CHIRYO GAKKAI SHI (JA/0021-4671) [04128720] **3821**

NIHON GANESKI, KOBUTSH, KOSHOGAKKAI *See* SHI - NIHON GANSEKI, KOBUTSU, KOSHOGAKKAI. JOURNAL OF THE JAPANESE ASSOCIATION OF MINERALOGISTS, PETROLOGISTS AND ECONOMIC GEOLOGISTS **1360**

NIHON GARASU KOGEI KYOKAI *See* NEWS / JAPAN GLASS ARTCRAFTS ASSOCIATION **2592**

NIHON GASU KYOKAI *See* GAS UTILITY INDUSTRY IN JAPAN **4258**

NIHON GASU KYOKAISHI (JA/0029-0211) [09490228] **4266**

NIHON GASU TABIN GAKKAI SHI (JA/0387-4168) [10172296] **2123**

NIHON GEIJUTSUIN *See* NIHON GEIJUTSUIN YORAN **326**

NIHON GEIJUTSUIN YORAN (JA) [01797164] **326**

NIHON GEKA GAKKAI *See* NIHON GEKA GAKKAI ZASSHI **3970**

NIHON GEKA GAKKAI ZASSHI (JA/0301-4894) [01351243] **3970**

NIHON GENSHIRYOKU GAKKAI *See* NIHON GENSHIRYOKU GAKKAISHI **1951**

NIHON GENSHIRYOKU GAKKAISHI (JA/0004-7120) [05979212] **1951**

NIHON GENSHIRYOKU KINKYUJO *See* GENKEN KENKYU SEIKA SHOROK SHU **2155**

NIHON GIJUTSUSHIKAI *See* LIST OF MEMBERS - THE ASSOCIATION OF JAPANESE CONSULTING ENGINEERS **2027**

NIHON GINKO GAIKOKU-KYOKU *See* BALANCE OF PAYMENTS MONTHLY **773**

NIHON GINKO. TOKEIKYOKU *See* KEIZAI TOKEI GEPPO. ECONOMIC STATISTICS MONTHLY **1535**

NIHON HADI KYOKAI KAIHO. BULLETIN OF THE THOMAS HARDY SOCIETY OF JAPAN (JA) [06568479] **3417**

NIHON HAKUSHIROKU (JA) [01790076] **421**

NIHON HAKUYO KIKAN GAKKAI *See* NIHON HAKUYO KIKAN GAKKAI SHI. JOURNAL OF THE MARINE ENGINEERING SOCIETY IN JAPAN **1989**

NIHON HAKUYO KIKAN GAKKAI SHI. JOURNAL OF THE MARINE ENGINEERING SOCIETY IN JAPAN (JA) [04830150] 4181, **1989**

NIHON HOIGAKU ZASSHI (JA/0047-1887) [10462928] **3622**

NIHON HYOJUN SANGYO BUNRUI; GOJUON SAKUIN HYO (JA/0303-6065) [01796946] **5334**

NIHON IGAKU HOSHASEN GAKKAI *See* NIHON IGAKU HOSHASEN GAKKAI ZASSHI **3944**

NIHON IGAKU HOSHASEN GAKKAI ZASSHI (JA/0048-0428) [05670611] **3944**

NIHON IKUEIKAI *See* NIHON IKUEIKAI **1867**

NIHON IKUEIKAI (JA) [01799688] **1867**

NIHON ISHIKAI *See* NIPPON ISHIKAI ZASSHI. JOURNAL OF THE JAPAN MEDICAL ASSOCIATION **3622**

NIHON ISHINKIN GAKKAI ZASSHI (JA/0916-4804) [I09164804] **576**

NIHON IYO MASU SUPEKUTORU GAKKAI KOENSHU (JA/0916-085X) [I0916085X] **3622**

NIHON JIKI KYOMEI IGAKKAI ZASSHI (JA/0914-9457) [I09149457] **3695**

NIHON JOKUNSHA MEIKAN (JA) [02239358] **2464**

NIHON JOMIN BUNKA KIYO (JA) [01797094] **2660**

NIHON JOSHI DAIGAKU KIYO. BUNGAKUBU (JA/0288-3031) [12141883] **2507**

NIHON JOZO KYOKAI SHI (JA) [18309137] **987**

NIHON JUI CHIKUSAN DAIGAKU KENKYU HOKOKU (JA/0373-8361) [10555988] **5517**

NIHON KAGAKU RYOHO GAKKAI *See* NIHON KAGAKU RYOHO GAKKAI SOKAI SHOROKUSHU **3622**

NIHON KAGAKU RYOHO GAKKAI SOKAI SHOROKUSHU (JA) [02244833] **3622**

NIHON KAGAKU SORAN *See* KAGAKU GIJUTSU BUNKEN SOKUHO. KAGAKU. KAGAKU KOGYO HEN : KOKUNAI-HEN **2005**

NIHON KAIHATSU GINKO *See* GYOMU HOKOKUSHO - NIHON KAIHATSU GINKO **790**

NIHON KAIHATSU GINKO. CHOSABU *See* CHOSA **657**

NIHON KAIKO SHI SHI (JA) [06713855] **3467**

NIHON KAIKU SUISAN KENKYUJO KENKYU (JA/0021-4620) [01983343] **2309**

NIHON KAIKU SUISAN KENKYUJO, NIIGATA *See* NIHON KAIKU SUISAN KENKYUJO KENKYU **2309**

NIHON KAIMEN IGAKKAI ZASSHI (JA/0288-8262) [10379365] **467**

NIHON KAIYO GAKKAI *See* JOURNAL OF THE OCEANOLOGICAL SOCIETY OF KOREA **1450**

NIHON KAIYO GAKKAI *See* NIPPON KAIYO GAKKAI MEIBO **1453**

NIHON KAIYO GAKKAI. JOURNAL OF THE OCEANOGRAPHICAL SOCIETY OF JAPAN *See* JOURNAL OF OCEANOGRAPHY **1450**

NIHON KAKIN GAKKAISHI (JA/0029-0254) [05463636] **216**

NIHON KANGO KYOKAI *See* KAIIN JITTAI CHOSA **3860**

NIHON KANGO KYOKAI *See* NIHON KANGO KYOKAI CHOSA KENKYU HOKOKU **3862**

NIHON KANGO KYOKAI CHOSA KENKYU HOKOKU (JA/0911-0844) [04627392] **3862**

NIHON KANKYO EISEI SENTA SHOHO (JA/0389-0805) [10379334] **2178**

NIHON KANZEI KYOKAI *See* YUSHUTSU TOKEI HIMMOKU HYO. / EXPORT STATISTICAL SCHEDULE: JAPAN **735**

NIHON KANZEI KYOKAI *See* YUNYU TOKEI HIMMOKU HYO **735**

NIHON KANZEI KYOKAI *See* YUSHUTSUNYU TOKEI HIMMOKU HYO **858**

NIHON KASAI GAKKAI RONBUNSHU (JA/0546-0794) [08260221] **1989**

NIHON KASEI GAKKAISHI (JA/0913-5227) [16244655] **2792**

NIHON KAZE KOGAKKAI SHI (JA) [10190167] **1989**

NIHON KEIEI SHINDAN GAKKAI NENPO (JA) [09898411] **699**

NIHON KEISEI GEKA GAKKAI KAISHI (JA/0389-4703) [19584506] **3970**

NIHON KEIZAI KENKYU (JA) [01799683] **1508**

NIHON KEIZAI KENKYU SENTA *See* GOKANEN KEIZAI YOSOKU **1564**

NIHON KEIZAI KENKYU SENTA *See* QUARTERLY FORECAST OF JAPAN'S ECONOMY **1594**

NIHON KEIZAI KENKYU SENTA. JAPAN'S ECONOMY *See* QUARTERLY FORECAST OF JAPAN'S ECONOMY **1594**

NIHON KEIZAI NI TSUYOKUNARU HON / AKIYAMA TETSU HEN (JA) [08855826] **1508**

NIHON KEIZAI NO GENKYO (JA) [07212864] **1575**

NIHON KEIZAI O CHUSHIN TO SURU KOKUSAI HIKAKU TOKEI (JA) [10331354] **1575**

NIHON KENCHIKU GAKKAI KEIKAKUKEI RONBUN HOKOKUSHU (JA/0910-8017) [13660645] **622**

NIHON KENCHIKU GAKKAI KOZOKEI RONBUN HOKOKUSHU (JA/0910-8025) [16781226] **2027**

NIHON KESSHO GAKKAI SHI (JA/0369-4585) [09756179] **1033**

NIHON KESSHO SEICHO GAKKAI SHI (JA/0385-6275) [10379408] **1033**

NIHON KIKAI GAKKAI *See* NIHON KIKAI GAKKAI RONBUNSHU. A **2123**

NIHON KIKAI GAKKAI *See* NIHON KIKAI GAKKAI RONBUNSHU. C **2123**

NIHON KIKAI GAKKAI RONBUNSHU. A (JA/0387-5008) [05261416] **2123**

NIHON KIKAI GAKKAI RONBUNSHU. B (JA/0387-5016) [05261466] **2093**

NIHON KIKAI GAKKAI RONBUNSHU. C (JA/0387-5024) [05759171] **2123**

NIHON KIKAI KOGYO RENGOKAI *See* NIKKIREN KAIYO SHIRYO INDEKKUSU **2093**

NIHON KIKAI KOGYO RENGOKAI *See* ENGINEERING INDUSTRY IN JAPAN **1973**

NIHON KIKAIGAKKAI *See* NIHON KIKAI GAKKAI RONBUNSHU. B **2093**

NIHON KINGAKKAI *See* NIPPON KINGAKKAI KAIHO **520**

NIHON KINGAKKAI KAIHO *See* MYCOSCIENCE **518**

NIHON KINZOKU GAKKAI *See* NIPPON KINZOKU GAKKAISHI **4013**

NIHON — Alphabetical Title Index

NIHON KINZOKU GAKKAI KAIHO (JA/0369-4747) [10075242] **4013**

NIHON KISHO GAKKAI *See* JOURNAL OF THE METEOROLOGICAL SOCIETY OF JAPAN **1427**

NIHON KOGYO DAIGAKU KENKYU HOKOKU (JA/0389-2514) [10463365] **5134**

NIHON KOGYO SEIHIN SORAN (JA) [09003172] **847**

NIHON KOKAI GAKKAI RONBUNSHU (JA/0388-7405) [16781055] **4181**

NIHON KOKOGAKU NEMPO (JA) [01797098] **276**

NIHON KOKU GAKKAI *See* TRANSACTIONS OF THE JAPAN SOCIETY FOR AERONAUTICAL AND SPACE SCIENCES **38**

NIHON KOKUSAI IRYODAN. TONAN AJIA IRYO JOHO SENTA. COMMITTEE ON HEALTH STATISTICS *See* SEAMIC HEALTH STATISTICS **4562**

NIHON KOKUSEI ZUE (JA) [01209008] **2660**

NIHON KOKUYU TETSUDO. FACTS AND FIGURES *See* BUSINESS REPORT **5430**

NIHON KOKUYU TETSUDO. FACTS AND FIGURES *See* ANNUAL REPORT / WEST JAPAN RAILWAY COMPANY **5429**

NIHON KOKUYU TETSUDO. FACTS AND FIGURES *See* ANNUAL REPORT **5429**

NIHON KONTAKUTO RENZU GAKKAI KAISHI (JA/0374-9851) [I03749851] **3877**

NIHON KOSEIBUTSU GAKKAI *See* TRANSACTIONS AND PROCEEDINGS OF THE PALAEONTOLOGICAL SOCIETY OF JAPAN **4231**

NIHON KOSHOHIN KAGAKUKAI SHI (JA) [09856948] **1027**

NIHON KYOBU GEKA GAKKAI ZASSHI (JA/0369-4739) [01778290] **3970**

NIHON KYOBU RINSHO (JA/0385-3667) [08260099] **3800**

NIHON KYOBU SHIKKAN GAKKAI ZASSHI (JA/0301-1542) [10110174] **3800**

NIHON KYOIKU GYOSEI GAKKAI NEMPO (JA) [08381330] **1867**

NIHON KYOIKU KOGAKU ZASSHI (JA) [09285677] **5134**

NIHON KYOIKU NENKAN (GYOSEI, KABUSHIKI KAISHA) (JA) [08369513] **1768**

NIHON KYOIKUHO GAKKAI *See* NIHON KYOIKUHO GAKKAI NEMPO **3017**

NIHON KYOIKUHO GAKKAI NEMPO (JA) [01796919] **1768, 3017**

NIHON KYOSANTO KOKUSAI MONDAI JUYO ROMBUN SHU (JA) [03040524] **4544**

NIHON KYOSHOKUIN KUMIAI *See* NIKKYOSO NO TATAKAI **1769**

NIHON MASUKOMI SORAN (JA) [01797314] **1118**

NIHON MOKUZAI GAKKAI *See* MOKUZAI GAKKAISHI **2403**

NIHON NAIBUNPI GAKKAI ZASSHI (JA/0029-0661) [10938387] **467**

NIHON NAIKA GAKKAI ZASSHI (JA/0021-5384) [06439754] **3800**

NIHON NO DENSHI KEISANKI (JA) [10221166] **1197**

NIHON NO HAKUBUTSUKAN SORAN (JA) [01790291] **4094**

NIHON NO HAKUSHO / NIHON JOHO KYOIKU KENKYUKAI HEN (JA) [08982587] **1576**

NIHON NO JIDO ENGEKI (JA) [10528197] **1067, 5367**

NIHON NO KAGAKUSHA / NIHON KAGAKUSHA KAIGI HENSHU (JA) [11668913] **5134**

NIHON NO KEIEISHA. 1-BU, ZEN JOJO KAISHA, SHACHO NO KEIEI SENRYAKU TO JINBUTSUZO (JA) [09857021] **1508**

NIHON NO KYOIKU SHIGAKU : KYOIKUSHI GAKKAI KIYO / KYOIKUSHI GAKKAI HENSHU IINKAI HEN (JA) [11463464] **1769**

NIHON NO MINKEN KYOIKU (JA) [01797162] **1769**

NIHON NO PURANTO YUSHUTSU SENRYAKU (JA) [02556760] **847**

NIHON NO ROSHI KANKEI (JA) [01790074] **1695**

NIHON NO SHINGAKU / NIHON KIRISUTOKYO GAKKAI HEN (JA) [09583781] **4982**

NIHON NO TEIRYU (JA/0288-4623) [10436917] **2660**

NIHON NO YURYO KAISHA HACHIJUHASSHA (JA) [05759731] **801**

NIHON NO YUSHU EIGA (JA) [02243435] **4075**

NIHON NOGAKU TOSHOKAN KYOGIKAI *See* NIHON NOGAKU TOSHOKAN KYOGIKAI KAIHO **113**

NIHON NOGAKU TOSHOKAN KYOGIKAI KAIHO (JA) [02246434] **3237, 113**

NIHON NOGYO KISHOGAKKAI *See* NOGYO KISHO **1432**

NIHON ONGAKU BUNKEN YOSHI MOKUROKU (JA) [01790310] **4141**

NIHON ONSEIGAKKAI *See* ONSEIGAKKAI KAIHO **3308**

NIHON OYO DOBUTSU KONCHU GAKKAISHI (JA/0021-4914) [04524421] **5612**

NIHON OYO JIKI GAKKAISHI (JA/0285-0192) [09572193] **4444**

NIHON PR NENKAN (JA) [10220941] **763**

NIHON PURANKUTON GAKKAI HO (JA) [05069018] **556**

NIHON PURASUCHIKKUSU SHINPO (JA/0029-0351) [I00290351] **4457**

NIHON RAIGAKKAI ZASSHI (JA/0386-3980) [04840784] **3622**

NIHON RAISENSHINGU NENKAN (JA) [11732710] **1306**

NIHON REITO KYOKAI RONBUNSHU (JA/0910-0040) [12071967] **2607**

NIHON REKISHI (JA/0386-9164) [01760369] **2660**

NIHON REOROJI GAKKAI SHI (JA/0387-1533) [09234976] **5234**

NIHON RINGAKKAI SHI (JA/0021-485X) [03780577] **2389**

NIHON RINGAKKAT *See* NIHON RINGAKKAI SHI **2389**

NIHON RINSHO (JA/0047-1852) [09802595] **3622**

NIHON RINSHO KAGAKKAI. NENKAI *See* NIHON RINSHO KAGAKKAI NENKAI KIROKU **987**

NIHON RINSHO KAGAKKAI NENKAI KIROKU (JA/0288-7878) [28213344] **987**

NIHON RINSHO SEIRI GAKKAI ZASSHI (JA/0286-7052) [I02867052] **584**

NIHON ROBOTTO GAKKAI. ROBOTTO SHINPOJUMU YOKOSHU / ROBOTICS SOCIETY OF JAPAN. PREPRINTS OF ROBOTICS SYMPOSIUM (JA) [I09187375] **1989**

NIHON RODO KEBNKYU ZASSHI (JA/0916-3808) [21730083] **1695**

NIHON RODO KYOKAI JIGYO NENJI HOKOKU (JA) [03212088] **1695**

NIHON RONEN IGAKKAI *See* NIHON RONEN IGAKKAI ZASSHI **3754**

NIHON RONEN IGAKKAI ZASSHI (JA/0300-9173) [04184811] **3754**

NIHON SAIKINGAKU ZASSHI (JA/0021-4930) [02274141] **467**

NIHON SAKKYOKUKA KYOGIKAI *See* CATALOG OF PUBLICATIONS - THE JAPAN FEDERATION OF COMPOSERS **4108**

NIHON SAKUMOTSU GAKKAI *See* NIHON SAKUMOTSU GAKKAI KIJI **179**

NIHON SAKUMOTSU GAKKAI KIJI (JA/0011-1848) [03783245] **179**

NIHON SAKUMOTSU GAKKAI KYUSHU SHIBUKAIHO (JA/0285-3507) [I02853507] **179**

NIHON SAKUMOTSU GAKKAI TOHOKU SHIBU KAIHO (JA/0911-7067) [I09117067] **179**

NIHON SANKA FUJINKA GAKKAI KANTO RENGO CHIHO BUKAI KAIHO (JA/0285-8096) [27467035] **3765**

NIHON SEISHI RENGOKAI *See* PULP & PAPER STATISTICS **4240**

NIHON SEISHOGAKU KENKYUJO *See* ANNUAL OF THE JAPANESE BIBLICAL INSTITUTE **5014**

NIHON SEITAI GAKKAI SHI (JA/0021-5007) [09709910] **2219**

NIHON SEMABI KOSHA. GENRYO HOMBU *See* KOKUNAISAN HATABAKO KAISETSUSHO **5373**

NIHON SEMBAI KOSHA *See* SEMBAI TOKEI NEMPO **1626**

NIHON SEMBAI KOSHA *See* NIHON SEMBAI KOSHA KIKO YORAN **1620**

NIHON SEMBAI KOSHA. CHUBU SHISHA *See* JIGYO TOKEI **1613**

NIHON SEMBAI KOSHA. CHUO KENKYUJO *See* KENKYU HOKOKU.--NIHON SEMBAI KOSHA CHUO KENKYUJO **5373**

NIHON SEMBAI KOSHA KIKO YORAN (JA) [03216604] **1620**

NIHON SEMBAI KOSHA. SEISAN HOMBU *See* SHISHA CHIHOKYOKU TABAKO KOSAKU SHIKEH SEISEKI **5373**

NIHON SEMBAI KOSHA. SEISAN HOMBU. CHIHOKYOKU TABAKO KOSAKU SHIKEN SEISEKI *See* SHISHA CHIHOKYOKU TABAKO SHIKEH SEISEKI **5373**

NIHON SEMPAKU MUSEN DENSHINKYOKU KYOKUMEIROKU (JA) [06792868] **1135**

NIHON SENCHU KENKYUKAI *See* NIHON SENCHU KENKYUKAI SHI **5593**

NIHON SENCHU KENKYUKAI SHI (JA) [03236997] **5593**

NIHON SENI KIKAI GAKKAI *See* JOURNAL OF THE TEXTILE MACHINERY SOCIETY OF JAPAN **5353**

NIHON SENI KIKAI GAKKAI *See* SENI KIKAI GAKKAI SHI **5355**

NIHON SENSHU KYOKAI *See* SENKYO KAIUM NEMPO **5456**

NIHON SERAMIKKUSU KYOKAI GAKUJUTSU RONBUNSHI (JA/0914-5400) [20160639] **2592**

NIHON SETCHAKU GAKKAI SHI (JA/0916-4812) [24772360] **1027**

NIHON SHAKAITO (1945-) *See* SEISAKU SHIRYO **4685**

NIHON SHASHIN GAKKAISHI (JA/0369-5662) [09534026] **4372**

NIHON SHIKA DAIGAKU KIYO. IPPAN KYOIKU KEI (JA/0385-1605) [10447849] **1331**

NIHON SHINSEIJI GAKKAI ZASSHI (JA/0029-0386) [I00290386] **3765**

NIHON SHISHUBYO GAKKAI KAISHI (JA/0385-0110) [09980410] **1331**

NIHON SHIYO KYOKUSHU / NIHON SHIJIN RENMEI HEN (JA) [10180511] **4141**

NIHON SHOKAKIBYO GAKKAI ZASSHI (JA/0446-6586) [09733651] **3800**

NIHON SHOKUBUTSU BYORI GAKKAI, TOKYO *See* NIPPON SHOKUBUTSU BYORI GAKKAI **520**

NIHON SHOKUHIN KOGYO GAKKAI SHI (JA/0029-0394) [03762461] **2351**

NIHON SHOKUHIN TEION HOZO GAKKAISHI (JA/0914-7675) [I09147675] **2351**

NIHON SHONIKA GAKKAI ZASSHI (JA/0001-6543) [10463135] **3907**

NIHON SHOSEN SEMPUKU TOKEI (JA) [01797136] **4181**

NIHON SHOTEN KUMIAI RENGOKAI *See* NISSHOREN ZENKOKU SHOTEN MEIBO **4831**

NIHON SHUPPANJIN SOKAN (JA) [02859735] **4818**

NIHON SOCHI GAKKAI *See* NIHON SOCHI GAKKAI SHI **203**

NIHON SOCHI GAKKAI SHI (JA/0447-5933) [05069015] **203**

NIHON SOKUCHI GAKKAI *See* SOKUCHI GAKKAISHI **2576**

NIHON SONGAI HOKEN KYOKAI *See* FACT BOOK, NON-LIFE INSURANCE IN JAPAN **2879**

NIHON SUGAKKAI *See* PUBLICATIONS OF THE MATHEMATICAL SOCIETY OF JAPAN **3529**

NIHON SUGAKKAI *See* JOURNAL OF THE MATHEMATICAL SOCIETY OF JAPAN **3515**

NIHON SUISAN GAKKAI *See* NIHON SUISAN GAKKAI SHI **2309**

NIHON SUISAN GAKKAI SHI (JA/0021-5392) [01772390] **556, 2309**

NIHON TANTEI MEIKAN (JA) [06361260] **3170**

NIHON TEITAION KENKYUKAI KAISHI (JA) [19584522] **3622**

NIHON TEMMON GAKKAI *See* PUBLICATIONS OF THE ASTRONOMICAL SOCIETY OF JAPAN **398**

NIHON TO BURAJIRU (JA) [03530543] **2750**

NIHON TODO KYOKAI *See* NIHON RODO KYOKAI JIGYO NENJI HOKOKU **1695**

NIHON TOKEI GAKKAISHI (TOKYO. 1970) (JA/0389-5602) [08676183] **5334**

NIHON TOKEI GEPPO (JA) [02265132] **5334**

NIHON TOKEI NENKAN (JA/0389-9004) [01142088] **5334**

NIHON UNIVERSITY JOURNAL OF MEDICINE, THE (JA/0546-0352) [01778780] **3622**

NIHON UNIVERSITY SCHOOL OF DENTISTRY *See* JOURNAL OF NIHON UNIVERSITY SCHOOL OF DENTISTRY **1327**

NIHON YAKURIGAKU ZASSHI (JA/0015-5691) [11008524] **4318**

NIHON YOTON GAKKAISHI (JA/0913-882X) [I09138382X] **5593**

NIHON YUSHUTSUNYU GINKO *See* GYOMU HOKOKUSHO - NIHON YUSHUTSUNYU GINKO **790**

NIHON YUSHUTSUNYU GINKO, TOKYO. KAIGAI TOSHI KENKYIJO *See* KAIGAI TOSHI KENKYUJO HO **905**

NIHON ZAIRYO GAKKAI. FUSHOKU BOSHOKU BUMON IINKAI *See* FUSHOKU BOSHOKU BUMON IINKAI KENKYU SHUKAI SHIRYO **2102**

NIHON ZAIRYO GAKKAI. FUSHOKU BOSHOKU BUMON IINKAI See FUSHOKU BOSHOKU BUMON IINKAI SHIRYO **2102**

NIHON ZENKOKU SHOSHI / HENSHU, KOKURITSU KOKKAI TOSHOKAN SHUSHU SEIRIBU (JA/0389-4002) [09652670] **421**

NIHON ZOSEN GAKKAI RONBUNSHU (JA/0514-8499) [08829656] **4181**

NIHON ZOSEN GAKKAISHI (JA/0386-1597) [13036109] **5453**

NIHONGAKU (JA) [11069951] **2660**

NIHONGO JANARU (JA/0912-5361) [15498401] **3306**

NIHONGO KYOIKU (JA/0389-4037) [09319579] **3306**

NIHONGO-NO-TOSHO (CN/0710-5304) [09543120] **4831**

NIHONGO TO NIHONGO KYÔIKU (JA) [02917168] **3306**

NIHONGOGAKU (JA) [10445468] **3306**

NIIGATA DAIGAKU. CHOKOSO TAIKKIKO KANSOKUJO See BULLETIN OF THE NIIGATA AIRGLOW OBSERVATORY **1421**

NIIGATA DAIGAKU KEIZAIGAKU NENPO (JA) [05848882] **1576**

NIIGATA DAIGAKU KOGAKUBU KENKYU HOKOKU (JA/0374-4345) [10444462] **1989**

NIIGATA DAIGAKU. KYOIKU GAKUBU See NIIGATA DAIGAKU KYOIKUGAKUBU KIYO: SHIZEN KAGAKU HEN **5134**

NIIGATA DAIGAKU KYOIKUGAKUBU KIYO: SHIZEN KAGAKU HEN (JA) [01790144] **5134**

NIIGATA DAIGAKU. KYOIKUGAKUBU. NIIGATA DAIGAKU KYOIKUGAKUBU KIYO See NIIGATA DAIGAKU KYOIKUGAKUBU KIYO: SHIZEN KAGAKU HEN **5134**

NIIGATA DAIGAKU. NOGAKUBU See NIIGATA DAIGAKU NOGAKUBU KENKYU HOKOKU **113**

NIIGATA DAIGAKU NOGAKUBU ENSHURIN HOKOKU (JA/0549-4818) [10383061] **2389**

NIIGATA DAIGAKU NOGAKUBU KENKYU HOKOKU (JA/0385-8634) [03903198] **113**

NIIGATA DAIGAKU NOGAKUBU KIYO. MEMOIRS OF THE FACULTY OF AGRICULTURE, NIIGATA UNIVERSITY (JA/0549-4826) [02858528] **113**

NIIGATA DAIGAKU. RIGAKUBU See SCIENCE REPORTS OF NIIGATA UNIVERSITY. SERIES D (BIOLOGY) **472**

NIIGATA DAIGAKU. RIGAKUBU. CHISHITSU KOBUTSUGAKU KYOSHITSU See NIIGATA DAIGAKU RIGAKUBU CHISHITSU KOBUTSUGAKU KYOSHITSU KENKYU HOKOUKU **1389**

NIIGATA DAIGAKU RIGAKUBU CHISHITSU KOBUTSUGAKU KYOSHITSU KENKYU HOKOUKU (JA) [04139600] **1389**

NIIGATA DAIGAKU. SEIKATSU CHIIKI SAIGAI KENKYU SENTA See KENKYU NEMPO - NIIGATA DAIGAKU SEKISETSU CHIIKI SAIGAI KENKYU SENTA **1385**

NIIGATA IGAKKAI ZASSHI (JA/0029-0440) [10376969] **3622**

NIIGATA-KEN NOGYO SHIKENJO See NIIGATA-KEN NOGYO SHIKENJO KENKYU HOKOKU **113**

NIIGATA-KEN NOGYO SHIKENJO KENKYU HOKOKU (JA/0549-4869) [05064828] **113**

NIIGATA-KEN SUISAN SHIKENJO See NIIGATA-KEN SUISAN SHIKENJO NEMPO **2309**

NIIGATA-KEN SUISAN SHIKENJO NEMPO (JA/0303-0245) [01797143] **2309**

NIIGATA RIKAGAKU : THE JOURNAL OF PHYSICS AND CHEMISTRY OF NIIGATA (JA) [10379013] 987, **4413**

NIIGATA YAKKA DAIGAKU KENKYU HOKOKU (JA/0285-3663) [09572225] **4318**

NIIHAMA KOGYO KOTO SENMON GAKKO KIYO. RIKOGAKU HEN (JA/0286-2743) [10442875] 1989, **5134**

●NIJ PROGRAM PLAN / NATIONAL INSTITUTE OF JUSTICE (US) [28233401] **3170**

NIKE (GW) [14148398] **360**

NIKEPHOROS : ZEITSCHRIFT FUER SPORT & KULTUR IM ALTERTUM (GW/0934-8913) [20606423] **4908**

NIKITSKII BOTANICHESKII SAD (IALTA, UKRAINE) See BIULLETEN GOSUDARSTVENNOGO NIKITSKOGO BOTANICHESKOGO SADA **502**

NIKKA TAIMUSU (CN/0226-2002) [06183780] **5790**

NIKKAKYO GEPPO (JA/0029-0483) [10448278] **987**

NIKKAN KOKUBO KEIZAI TSUSHIN. THE KOKUBO KEIZAI TSUSHIN (JA) [03910228] **4052**

NIKKEI ANNUAL FOREIGN CORPORATION REPORTS (JA) [07335018] **801**

NIKKEI BAITO (JA/0289-6508) [I02896508] **1197**

NIKKEI BAITO: NIKKEI BYTE (JA/0289-6508) [20537615] **1270**

NIKKEI : BIMONTHLY FORUM FOR IDEAS AND NEWS FROM NIHON KEIZAI SHIMBUN, INC (JA) [19347959] **2507**

NIKKEI BUSINESS (JA) **699**

NIKKEI COMMUNICATION (JA) **1118**

NIKKEI DESIGN (JA) **305**

NIKKEI EREKUTORONIKUSU. NIKKEI ELECTRONICS (JA) [05530170] **2074**

NIKKEI KINYU SHINBUN (JA) **801**

NIKKEI KONPYUTA (JA/0285-4619) [11482353] **1238**

NIKKEI MEKANIKARU (JA/0386-3638) [I03863638] **2107**

NIKKEI MICRODEVICES (JA) **5134**

NIKKEI OFFICE (JA) **944**

NIKKEI PAIONIYA AYUMI NO ATO (US) [09345670] **2750**

NIKKEI PASOKON (JA) [10536098] **1238**

NIKKEI SANGYO SHIMBUN (JA) [10250941] **5805**

NIKKEI SATELLITE EDITION (JA) **5805**

NIKKEI TRENDY (JA) **1620**

NIKKEI VOICE (CN/0844-5869) [19960694] **2750**

NIKKEI WEEKLY (JA) [23898553] 4484, **1638**

NIKKIREN KAIYO SHIRYO INDEKKUSU (JA) [02245417] **2093**

NIKKYOSO NO TATAKAI (JA) [01797148] **1769**

NIKON WORLD (US) [02265134] **4372**

NIKUBUTA RYUTSU KOZO CHOSA HOKOKU (JA) [10356145] **1620**

NILES LIFE, THE (US/0194-8628) [05062554] **5661**

NILES SPECTATOR (US/0744-5393) [08338809] **5661**

NILITE NEWS (CN/0319-2792) [02442237] **3237**

NILSON REPORT, THE (US) **801**

●NIMA/NELSON DIRECTORY OF MINORITY AND WOMAN-OWNED INVESTMENT MANAGERS (US/1062-0907) [25522462] **910**

NIMBUS TWO (CN/0710-2658) [08267941] **3417**

NIMHANS JOURNAL (II) [09746560] 3843, **3931**

NIMLO MODEL ORDINANCE SERVICE (US) [01771636] **4669**

NIMLO RESEARCH REPORT / NATIONAL INSTITUTE OF MUNICIPAL LAW OFFICERS (US) [04655336] **3170**

NIMLO'S CONGRESSIONAL NEWS (US) [13646780] **4669**

NIMMER ON COPYRIGHT (US) [01624054] **1306**

NIMROD : A MAGYAR VADASZOK ORSZAGOS SZOEVETSEGENEK LAPJA (HU/0549-494X) [01188677] **4876**

NIMROD (TULSA) (US/0029-053X) [02608409] **3417**

NIN. NEDELJNE INFORMATIVNE NOVINE (YU/0027-6685) [04741434] **2520**

NINA LYTTON'S OPEN SYSTEMS ADVISOR (US/1043-9854) [19645418] **1238**

NINCDS MUSCULAR DYSTROPHY AND THE NEUROMUSCULAR DISORDERS RESEARCH PROGRAM See NINCDS NEUROMUSCULAR DISORDERS RESEARCH PROGRAM, THE **3843**

NINCDS NEUROMUSCULAR DISORDERS RESEARCH PROGRAM, THE (US) [04445857] **3843**

NINCDS RESEARCH PROGRAM. EPILEPSY, THE (US) [06549660] **3843**

NINCDS RESEARCH PROGRAM. MULTIPLE SCLEROSIS, THE (US/0888-8035) [06550025] **3843**

NINCDS RESEARCH PROGRAM. MUSCULAR DYSTROPHY AND OTHER NEUROMUSCULAR DISORDERS, THE (US) [06549796] **3843**

NINE (SEATTLE, WASH.) (US/1050-513X) [21507118] **1135**

NINETEEN (UK) **1067**

NINETEEN (FR/0757-1984) [I07571984] **1067**

NINETEENTH CENTURY (US/0097-5184) [01799009] **360**

NINETEENTH CENTURY CONTEXTS (US/0890-5495) [14267357] 2851, **3417**

NINETEENTH-CENTURY FRENCH STUDIES (US/0146-7891) [01061280] **3349**

NINETEENTH-CENTURY LITERATURE (US/0891-9356) [13799808] **3417**

NINETEENTH-CENTURY LITERATURE CRITICISM (US/0732-1864) [07959285] **3349**

NINETEENTH CENTURY PROSE (US/1052-0406) [19677030] **3417**

NINETEENTH CENTURY STUDIES (II) [01790493] **3417**

NINETEENTH-CENTURY STUDIES (ANN ARBOR, MICH.) (US/1056-425X) [23715072] **3417**

NINETEENTH-CENTURY STUDIES (CHARLESTON, S.C.) (US/0893-7931) [15646330] **3417**

NINETEENTH CENTURY : THE MAGAZINE OF THE VICTORIAN SOCIETY IN AMERICA (US) **360**

NINETEENTH CENTURY THEATRE (US/0893-3766) [15499348] **5367**

NINETY (FR) [28696503] **381**

NING-HSIA HUA PAO (CC) [11654182] **2660**

NING-HSIA SHE HUI KO HSUEH (CH) [10607096] **5234**

NING-HSIA TA HSUEH HSUEH PAO. SHE HUI KO HSUEH PAN (CC) [09302615] **2507**

NINGAS (US/0164-6966) [04417290] **2270**

NINGEN KOGAKU (JA/0549-4974) [I05494974] **2123**

NINGEN KYOIKU (JA) [04440605] **1901**

NINGEN TO KANKYO (JA/0286-438X) [10379180] **2178**

NINGXIA NONG-LIN KE-JI (CH/1002-204X) [I1002204X] 2389, **113**

NINMEN KANKEI HOREISHU / HENSHU NIHON JINJI GYOSEI KENKYUJO (JA) [08875275] **4704**

NINNAU : THE NORTH AMERICAN WELSH NEWSLETTER (US/0890-0485) [09502322] 2750, **2270**

NINS. NEW ISSUES IN NEUROSCIENCES *CEASED.* (US/1012-9871) [I10129871] **3843**

NINTENDO (AT) **4864**

NINTENDO POWER (US/1041-9551) [18893582] **4864**

NINTH DISTRICT DENTAL SOCIETY OF THE STATE OF NEW YORK See BULLETIN OF THE NINTH DISTRICT DENTAL SOCIETY **1318**

NIO-KRONIEK (AMSTERDAM) See INZET AMSTERDAM **2910**

NIOSH CERTIFIED EQUIPMENT LIST AS OF ... (US/0883-7457) [10306765] **2866**

NIOSH CURRENT INTELLIGENCE BULLETIN (US/0893-4940) [04822752] **2866**

NIOSH REPORT ON OCCUPATIONAL SAFETY AND HEALTH (US/0742-7603) [10407308] **2866**

NIP (CINCINNATI, OHIO. 1993) (US/1074-0791) [29602757] **2491**

NIP MAGAZINE See NIP (CINCINNATI, OHIO. 1993) **2491**

NIPH ANNALS *SUSPENDED.* (NO/0332-5652) [04558323] **4794**

NIPISSING VOYAGEUR (CN/1180-1883) [24265603] **2464**

NIPPON BUKKYO GAKKAI NEMPO (JA) [06567064] **5021**

NIPPON BUTSURI GAKKAI See JOURNAL OF THE PHYSICAL SOCIETY OF JAPAN **4410**

NIPPON BUTSURIGAKKAI SHI (JA/0029-0181) [04854595] **4413**

NIPPON BYOINKAI ZASSHI (JA/0385-9363) [02050453] **3790**

NIPPON DAICHO KOMONBYO GAKKAI ZASSHI (JA/0047-1801) [01125085] **3622**

NIPPON EISEIGAKU ZASSHI (JA/0021-5082) [05666269] **4794**

NIPPON FUNIN GAKKAI ZASSHI (JA/0029-0629) [07023286] **3765**

NIPPON GAKUSHIIN KIYO (JA/0388-0036) [I03880036] **1769**

NIPPON GANKA GAKKAI See NIPPON GANKA GAKKAI ZASSHI **3877**

NIPPON GANKA GAKKAI ZASSHI (JA/0029-0203) [01378498] **3877**

NIPPON GOMU KYOKAISHI (JA/0029-022X) [I0029022X] **5076**

NIPPON HIFUKA GAKKAI ZASSHI (JA/0021-499X) [01892031] **3722**

NIPPON HINYO-KIBYO GAKKAI ZASSHI See NIPPON HINYOKIKA GAKKAI ZASSHI **3992**

NIPPON HINYOKIKA GAKKAI ZASSHI (JA/0021-5287) [01641116] **3992**

NIPPON IKA DAIGAKU ZASSHI (JA/0048-0444) [08516085] **3622**

NIPPON INSATSU GAKKAISHI (JA/0914-3319) [I09143319] **4567**

NIPPON ISHIKAI ZASSHI. JOURNAL OF THE JAPAN MEDICAL ASSOCIATION (JA/0021-4493) [09884688] **3622**

NIPPON JIBI INKOKA GAKKAI KAIHO (JA/0030-6622) [01640356] **3889**

NIPPON JUISHI KAI *See* NIPPON JUISHIKAI ZASSHI **5517**

NIPPON JUISHIKAI ZASSHI (JA/0446-6454) [01696818] **5517**

NIPPON KAGAKUKAI *See* NIPPON KAGAKUKAI (1972) **987**

NIPPON KAGAKUKAI *See* BULLETIN OF THE CHEMICAL SOCIETY OF JAPAN **963**

NIPPON KAGAKUKAI (1972) (JA/0369-4577) [01716882] **987**

NIPPON KAISUI GAKKAI-SHI (JA/0369-4550) [I03694550] **5536**

NIPPON KAIYO GAKKAI MEIBO (JA) [03084859] **1453**

NIPPON KINGAKKAI KAIHO (JA/0029-0289) [04178736] **520**

NIPPON KINZOKU GAKKAISHI (JA/0021-4876) [02253196] **4013**

NIPPON KOKAN KABUSHIKI KAISHA *See* NIPPON KOKAN TECHNICAL REPORT. OVERSEAS **4013**

NIPPON KOKAN TECHNICAL REPORT. OVERSEAS (JA/0546-1731) [06398463] **4013**

NIPPON KOKU GEKA GAKKAI ZASSHI (JA) [07700872] **3970**

NIPPON KOKUKA GAKKAI ZASSHI (JA/0029-0297) [03523076] **1331**

NIPPON KOSHU EISEI ZASSHI (JA/0546-1766) [08978945] **4794**

NIPPON KYOSEI SHIKA GAKKAI ZASSHI. JOURNAL OF JAPAN ORTHODONTIC SOCIETY (JA) [07640695] **1331**

NIPPON NANDEMO JIKKETSU (JA) [06601981] **2660**

NIPPON NETTAI IGAKKAI ZASSHI (JA/0304-2146) [01140394] **3986**

NIPPON NOGEI KAGAKU KAISHI (JA/0002-1407) [01760400] **987**, **113**

NIPPON ONSEN KIKO BUTSURI IGAKKAI ZASSHI (JA/0029-0343) [I00290343] **3622**

NIPPON SANKA FUJINKA GAKKAI *See* NIPPON SANKA FUJINKA GAKKAI ZASSHI **3766**

NIPPON SANKA FUJINKA GAKKAI ZASSHI (JA/0300-9165) [05381620] **3766**

NIPPON SANSHI-GAKU ZASSHI (JA/0037-2455) [06112818] **5593**

NIPPON SEIKEIGEKAGAKKAI ZASSHI (JA/0021-5325) [06439996] **3883**

NIPPON SEIRIGAKU ZASSHI (JA/0031-9341) [05178138] **584**

NIPPON SHIKA HYORON. THE NIPPON DENTAL REVIEW (JA) [07648082] **1331**

NIPPON SHIKA IGAKKAI KAIHO (JA/0387-4346) [05851919] **1331**

NIPPON SHIKA ISHIKAI ZASSHI (JA/0047-1763) [06439606] **1331**

NIPPON SHIKA MASUI GAKKAI *See* NIPPON SHIKA MASUI GAKKAI ZASSHI **1331**

NIPPON SHIKA MASUI GAKKAI ZASSHI (JA/0301-0899) [01353615] **1331**

NIPPON SHOKUBUTSU BYORI GAKKAI (JA/0031-9473) [01715242] **520**

NIPPON STEEL NEWS (JA/0048-0352) [01466502] 1620, **4013**

NIPPON STEEL TECHNICAL REPORT (JA) [05864615] **4013**

NIPPON TEKKO KYOKAI *See* TRANSACTIONS OF THE IRON AND STEEL INSTITUTE OF JAPAN **4022**

NIPPON YAKUGAKKAI *See* YAKUGAKU ZASSHI **4333**

NIPPON YAKUZAISHIKAI ZASSHI (JA/0369-674X) [09770350] **4318**

NIR NEWS (UK/0960-3360) [I09603360] **4413**

NIR. NORDISKT IMMATERIELLT RATTSSKYDD (SW/0027-6723) [I00276723] **1306**

NIRA NEWS (JA) **5211**

NIRA REPORT (JA) [07111814] **1576**

NIRA SOGO KINKYU KAIHATSU KIKO ... NENJI HOKOKUSHO (JA) [02980140] **5211**

NIRANTARA (II) [11768795] **3417**

NIRMALYA : SRI JAGANNATHA MISANA MUKHAPATRA (II) [09797827] **5041**

NIRSA DIRECTORY (NATIONAL INTRAMURAL RECRETIONAL SPORTS ASSOCIATION) *See* RECREATIONAL SPORTS DIRECTORY **4914**

NIRSA JOURNAL (US) [09415593] 4853, **4908**

NIS SCIENTIFIC JOURNAL (II/0970-7557) [I09707557] **4908**

NISHI NIHON HIFUKA (JA/0386-9784) [09531457] **3722**

NISHI NIHON HINYOKIKA (JA/0029-0726) [I00290726] **3992**

NISQUALLY VALLEY NEWS, THE (US) [18338016] **5761**

NISSAT NEWSLETTER (II/0970-0188) [I09700188] **5134**

NISSEI BYOIN IGAKU ZASSHI (JA/0301-2581) [01353640] **3622**

NISSEKI REBYU (JA/0285-5275) [10421376] **5134**

NISSHIN SEIKO GIHO (JA/0387-2327) [10447948] **4013**

NISSHOREN ZENKOKU SHOTEN MEIBO (JA) [01797345] **4831**

NISSSEI BYOIN *See* NISSEI BYOIN IGAKU ZASSHI **3622**

NIST BUILDING SCIENCE SERIES (US/1049-7579) [21310094] **622**

NIST CALIBRATION SERVICES USERS GUIDE. FEE SCHEDULE (US) [19904263] **4031**

NIST JOURNAL (PH) [17785850] **5134**

NIST SPECIAL PUBLICATION (US/1048-776X) [18972013] **4413**

NIST TECHNICAL NOTE (US/1054-013X) [19210773] **4031**

NIST UPDATE (US) [19565342] **4032**

NISTRU : [ORGAN AL UNIUNII SKRIITORILOR DIN RSS MOLDOVENIASKE] (MV) [08099143] **3417**

NISTRUL *See* NISTRU : [ORGAN AL UNIUNII SKRIITORILOR DIN RSS MOLDOVENIASKE] **3417**

NITCHU KANKEI (JA) [10592847] **2660**

NITCHU KEIZAI KYOKAI *See* NITCHU KEIZAI KYOKAI KAIHO **847**

NITCHU KEIZAI KYOKAI KAIHO (JA) [05204891] **847**

NITCHU-NISSO BOEKI HANNEMPO (JA) [04824880] **847**

●NITE-WRITER'S LITERARY ARTS JOURNAL (US/1062-1423) [25532033] **3417**

NITEROI (BL) [01787670] **2750**

NITRIC OXIDE (UK/1351-525X) 491, **3622**

NITROGEN (UK/0029-0777) [02449131] **987**

NITROGEN FIXING TREE RESEARCH REPORTS : A PUBLICATION OF THE NITROGEN FIXING TREE ASSOCIATION (NFTA) (TH) [09883725] 113, **2389**

NITTANY GROTTO NEWS (US/0732-5398) [08376809] **1358**

NITTEN *See* TANSHOKUBAN NITTEN SHOSHU **382**

NITTEN *See* NITTEN SAKUHIN SHU **360**

NITTEN SAKUHIN SHU (JA) [11607515] **360**

NIUGINI CAVER (PP/0310-3773) [05213078] **1409**

NIVA : ORHAN HALOUNAHA PRALENNIA BELARUSKAHA HRAMADSKA-KULTURNAHA TAVARYSTVA (PL/0546-1960) [12568709] **2270**

NIVAG CONTOUR (NE/0376-6802) [02473969] **622**

NIVE-PUBLICATIE (NE) [02246979] **880**

NIWATORI NO KENKYU; THE NIWATORI-NO-KENKYU (JA) [05085227] **217**

NIXON NEWS, THE (US) [14634646] **5752**

NIXON WEEKLY NEWS *See* NIXON NEWS, THE **5752**

NIYOJANA (NP) [02239631] **590**

NJ AUDUBON (US/0886-6619) [04232675] **2200**

NJ VOTER (US/1073-2268) [29355930] **4669**

NJCM BULLETIN / NEDERLANDS JURISTEN COMITE VOOR DE MENSENRECHTEN (NE) [08252882] **4511**

NJEA REVIEW (US/0027-6758) [01716522] **1769**

NJPC BULLETIN (US/0161-5513) [03947213] **3862**

NJW-COR COMPUTERREPORT : DER NEUEN JURISTISCHEN WOCHENSCHRIFT : INFORMATIONSMANAGEMENT AND BUROORGANISATION IN DER JUSTISCHEN PRAXIS (GW/0934-8778) [19060853] 1197, **3017**

NJW-RECHTSPRECHUNGS-REPORT, ZIVILRECHT (GW/0179-4043) [13476994] **3090**

NKK TECHNICAL REVIEW (JA/0915-0544) [I09150544] **5134**

NLA GATEWAYS (AT) **3237**

NLADA CORNERSTONE (US/0739-9111) [06507977] **3180**

NLGI SPOKESMAN (US/0027-6782) [02166003] **2123**

NLM TECHNICAL BULLETIN, THE (US/0146-3055) [03261123] 3622, **3237**

NLR: NATIONAL LIBRARY REPORTER (US/0095-053X) [01796244] **3237**

NLRB ADVICE MEMORANDUM REPORTER (US/0194-8784) [03598187] **3152**

NMB BANKBLAD (NE) **801**

NMFS FISHERIES MARKET NEWS REPORT (US/1060-3654) [24151877] **2309**

NML TECHNICAL JOURNAL (II/0027-6839) [02621206] **4013**

NMM WEEKLY (US/0270-255X) [06389708] **4842**

NMR IN BIOMEDICINE (UK/0952-3480) [19558856] **3622**

NMRA BULLETIN (US/0027-9722) [05715753] **5433**

NN&Q. NEWS, NOTES, AND QUOTES (US/0028-923X) [04090767] **1769**

NO-CHIKUSANGYOYO KOTEI SHISAN HYOKA HYOJUN (JA) [06073420] 217, **749**

NO-DIG INTERNATIONAL (UK/0960-4405) [25180139] **2027**

NO. ... IN A SERIES OF LOCAL HISTORY MONOGRAPHS (UK) [12166437] **2624**

●NO LIMITS WORLD (IT/1121-6379) [I11216379] 4908, **4876**

NO-LOAD FUND INVESTOR, THE (US/0736-6256) [06903485] **910**

NO SHINKEI GEKA (JA/0301-2603) [01350682] **3843**

NO-TILL FARMER (US/0091-9993) [03015492] **179**

NO TO SHINKEI (JA/0006-8969) [01607521] **3844**

NOA NEWSLETTER (US/0749-9345) [09397793] **4141**

NOAA DATA REPORT ERL GLERL (US/0733-4044) [07229212] **1416**

NOAA DATA REPORT MESA (US/0360-2842) [02172340] **2219**

NOAA PROFESSIONAL PAPER (US/0360-6066) [02172460] **1453**

NOAA TECHNICAL REPORT NWS (US/0739-4292) [04291172] **1432**

NOAA'S OFFICE OF UNDERSEA RESEARCH ... REPORT (US/0741-1782) [10083470] **1453**

NOAH (IS/0792-0318) [20496644] **3418**

NOAH'S ARK (US/0892-4945) [10143039] 5051, **1067**

NOBEL LECTURES OF PHYSIOLOGY OR MEDICINE *CEASED*. (NE) **3622**

NOBEL SYMPOSIA (SW/0346-8313) [02084629] **5134**

NOBELSTIFTELSEN *See* PRIX NOBEL, LES **2852**

NOBELSTIFTELSEN *See* ARSREDOVISNING / NOBELSTIFTELSEN **3144**

NOBLE OFFICIAL CATALOG OF BUREAU PRECANCELS, THE (US) [05701379] **2786**

NOBLES COUNTY REVIEW (US) [01760407] **5697**

NOBLESVILLE DAILY LEDGER (US) [13858926] **5666**

NOBO (HARLEM HEIGHTS, N.Y.) (US/1056-683X) [23829788] **2270**

NOBODY QUARTERLY, THE (US/1062-4171) [25614883] **3418**

NOBU (JA) [02441244] **2902**

NOCALL NEWSLETTER / NORTHERN CALIFORNIA ASSOCIATION OF LAW LIBRARIES (US) [07352087] 3017, **3237**

NOCONA NEWS, THE (US) [14634654] **5753**

NOCTES ROMANAE (SZ/0078-0936) [01760408] **4353**

NOCTILUCA (CN/0384-5176) [02546896] **3418**

●NOCTILUCA (NORWOOD, MASS.) (US/1061-0480) [25170640] **3467**

NOD & CONVERSION (DK) [24993852] **4053**

NODA SANGYO KAGAKU KENKYUJO *See* REPORT OF THE NODA INSTITUTE FOR SCIENTIFIC RESEARCH **493**

NODAK PHARMACIST (US) [02253504] **4318**

NODE, THE (US/0882-8075) [11984857] **5211**

NODONG KYONGJE RIBYU (KO) [10149637] **1695**

NOESIS (BUCHAREST, ROMANIA) (RM) [07364684] **5134**

NOETIC SCIENCES BULLETIN (US/0897-1013) [17275173] **4606**

NOETIC SCIENCES REVIEW (US/0897-1005) [17203781] **4606**

NOEUD (CN/0227-0021) [08078675] **5033**

NOEUD (CHARLESBOURG) (CN/1188-4444) [25883322] **2389**

NOGET OM SOCIALE FORHOLD, ADMINISTRATION OG POLITISKE INSTITUTIONER (DK) [11347377] **5299**

NOGYO DOBOKU GAKKAI See NOGYO DOBOKU GAKKAI RONBUNSHU **179**

NOGYO DOBOKU GAKKAI RONBUNSHU (JA/0387-2335) [11313903] **179**

NOGYO DOBOKU SHIKENJO GIHO. A: TOCHI KAIRYO See NOGYO DOBOKU SHIKENJO GIHO. LI, NOCHI SEIBI **113**

NOGYO DOBOKU SHIKENJO GIHO. C: ZOKO (JA) [03134651] 2028, **113**

NOGYO DOBOKU SHIKENJO GIHO. HE, SUIKO (JA/0287-0029) [11823278] 1989, **113**

NOGYO DOBOKU SHIKENJO GIHO. LI, NOCHI SEIBI (JA/0287-0029) [12042926] **113**

NOGYO DOBOKU SHIKENJO GIHO. WM, SUIRI (JA/0287-0029) [10250433] **113**

NOGYO DOBOKU SHIKENJO, HIRATSUKA, JAPAN See NOGYO DOBOKU SHIKENJO GIHO. C: ZOKO **113**

NOGYO GIJUTSU KENKYUJO HOKOKU. C: BYORI KONCHU (JA/0077-4847) [03338966] **2425**

NOGYO GIJUTSU KENKYUJO HOKOKU. H: KEIEI TOCHI RIYO (JA/0077-4863) [03213745] **113**

NOGYO GIJUTSU KENKYUJO HOKOKU. RENZOKU B: DOJO HIRYO (JA/0077-4839) [03415745] **113**

NOGYO HAKUSHO (JA) [01799675] **113**

NOGYO KANKYO GIJUTSU KENKYUJO HOKOKU (JA/0911-9450) [13862641] **113**

NOGYO KANKYO GIJUTSU KENKYUJO NENPO (JA/0910-2000) [12705430] **520**

NOGYO KANSOKU (JA) [05589698] **113**

NOGYO KEIEI KENKYU SEIKA SHUHO / NOGYO KEIEI KENKYU SEIKA KANKO IINKAI HEN (JA) [08794517] **113**

NOGYO KENKYU SENTA KENKYU HOKOKU (JA/0289-3207) [21201197] **113**

NOGYO KIKAI GAKKAI See NOGYO KIKAI GAKKAISHI **160**

NOGYO KIKAI GAKKAI KYUSHU SHIBUSHI (JA/0917-9720) [I09179720] **113**

NOGYO KIKAI GAKKAISHI (JA/0285-2543) [03762748] **160**

NOGYO KIKAIKA KENKYUSHO HOKOKU (JA/0387-8139) [09170486] **160**

NOGYO KISHO (JA/0021-8588) [03762359] 113, **1432**

NOGYO OYOBI ENGEI (JA/0369-5247) [01590086] 2425, **113**

NOGYO ROPPO (JA) [02243911] 113, **3017**

NOGYO SEIBUTSU SHIGEN KENKYUJO KENKYU HOKOKU (JA/0911-6575) [16818237] **179**

NOGYO SHISETSU (JA/0388-8517) [I03888517] **113**

NOGYO SHOTOKU TOKEI (JA) [01790120] **113**

NOGYO SOGO KENKYU (JA/0387-3242) [03798981] **113**

NOGYO TO KEIZAI (JA) [05235051] **113**

NOGYOSHA DAIGAKKO (JAPAN) See NOGYOSHA DAIGAKKO NEMPO **113**

NOGYOSHA DAIGAKKO NEMPO (JA) [02954148] **113**

●NOI (RU) [26100114] **5051**

NOI DONNE (IT) [05938752] **5252**

NOI E L'AMBIENTE (IT) **2219**

NOI POLIZIA (IT) **3170**

NOI VIGILI *CEASED.* (IT) **1073**

NOIR D'ENCRE (CN/1183-1138) [24256748] **360**

NOISE & VIBRATION IN INDUSTRY: NVI (UK/0950-8163) [17588656] **1620**

NOISE & VIBRATION WORLDWIDE (UK/0957-4565) [21242173] **2178**

NOISE-CON PROCEEDINGS (US/0736-2935) [01037024] **2178**

NOISE CONTROL ENGINEERING JOURNAL (US/0736-2501) [08974064] **2178**

NOISE NEWS (US/0146-4809) [02250737] **2179**

●NOISE/NEWS INTERNATIONAL (US/1021-643X) [27920843] **2028**

NOISE (PARIS, FRANCE) (FR/0765-121X) [13620646] **360**

NOISE POLLUTION PUBLICATIONS ABSTRACTS (US/0733-172X) [07832481] **2179**

NOISE REGULATION REPORT (US/1043-5565) [18617585] **2179**

NOK LAPJA (HU) [06402421] **5563**

NOKA KEIZAI CHOSA HOKOKU (JA) [05663182] **113**

NOKA SHIKIN DOTAI TOKEI (JA) [01797047] **113**

NOKA SHUGYO DOKO CHOSA HOKOKUSHO (JA) [05672390] **114**

NOKO SHIRYO TOKEI NEMPO (JA) [05593557] **203**

NOKO TO ENGEI (JA) [09954256] 2425, **114**

NOKTA (TU) [10805922] **2491**

NOLO NEWS (US/0890-2208) [09496424] 1298, **3017**

NOLOAD FUND X (US/0194-0104) [05297723] **910**

NOLPE NOTES (US/0047-8997) [01759314] 1769, **3017**

NOLSLETTER (US/0270-8884) [06498885] **3180**

NOMA (NR/0331-6742) [06001305] **114**

NOMAD NEWS (US/0149-6301) [03511133] **5421**

NOMAD (WILLOWDALE) (CN/0705-3940) [03956600] **5486**

NOMADIC PEOPLES (CN/0822-7942) [09704736] **2270**

NOME NUGGET (NOME, ALASKA: 1938) (US/0745-9106) [02720350] **5629**

NOMEN NUDUM (AT/0159-818X) [08002259] 4228, **1390**

NOMENCLATOR ZOOLOGICUS (UK/0078-0952) [01716374] **5593**

NOMENCLATURE DE LA TECHNIQUE DES METAUX (FR) **4013**

NOMENCLATURE DES BUREAUX TELEGRAPHIQUES OUVERTS AU SERVICE INTERNATIONAL (SZ) [12354129] **1161**

NOMENCLATURE DES VOIES DE TELECOMMUNICATION UTILISEES POUR LA TRANSMISSION DES TELEGRAMMES. LIST OF TELECOMMUNICATION CHANNELS USED FOR THE TRANSMISSION OF TELEGRAMS. NOMENCLATOR DE LA VIAS DE TELECOMUNICACION EMPLEADAS PARA LA TRANSMISION DEL TELEGRAMAS (SZ/0252-1792) [03324514] **1161**

NOMIKO VEMA (GR) [11082496] **3018**

NOMIKON VEMA See NOMIKO VEMA **3018**

NOMINA (UK/0141-6340) [04999241] **3306**

NOMINAL LIST OF PRACTISING LIBRARIANS IN NIGERIA (NR) [06109646] **3237**

NOMISMATIKA KHRONIKA (GR) [01792074] **2782**

NOMMO: AFRICAN STUDENT NEWSMAGAZINE AT UCLA (US) [15254085] **2270**

NOMOS (FORTALEZA, BRAZIL) (BL) [08264422] **3018**

NOMOS (ROME, ITALY) (IT) [20140862] **3018**

NON-CASH BENEFITS SIC SURVEY (US) [10411328] 2889, **1695**

NON-CREDIT LEARNING NEWS (US/0886-0165) [12788586] **1801**

NON-DESTRUCTIVE TESTING - AUSTRALIA (AT/0157-6461) [03469298] **1989**

NON DESTRUCTIVE TESTING JOURNAL, JAPAN: NDTJ, THE (JA) [10256319] **2107**

NON-FERROUS METAL DATA (US/0360-9553) [02245137] **4013**

NON-FERROUS METAL WORKS OF THE WORLD (UK/0078-0987) [01781145] **4013**

NON-FOODS MERCHANDISING (US/0029-103X) [05142557] **2351**

NON-FUEL MINERAL INDUSTRY / CANADA DEPARTMENT OF ENERGY, THE (CN) [09434425] **1951**

NON-LINEAR WORLD (US/0942-5608) **3524**

NON-METAL MINES (CN/0226-4609) [07870773] 1443, **1363**

NON-METALLIC MINERAL PRODUCTS INDUSTRIES (OTTAWA) (CN/0835-0167) [16891513] **1443**

NON-METALLIC MINERAL PRODUCTS INDUSTRIES (OTTAWA) (CN/0835-0167) [16891473] **1443**

NON-PROFIT LEGAL & TAX LETTER (US/1066-1018) [24316990] 5299, **4739**

NON-PROFIT ORGANIZATION TAX LETTER (US/0550-8401) [06029207] **5299**

NON-PROFIT REPORT See PHILANTHROPY MONTHLY, THE **4338**

NON-PROFIT TAX LETTER (US) **4739**

NON-SPORT MARKETPLACE (US/1061-7175) [25417656] **2775**

NON-TILLAGE CROP PRODUCTION IN NORTHERN NEW SOUTH WALES: PROCEEDINGS OF THE PROJECT TEAM MEETING (AT) [16462087] **179**

NON-WAGE PROVISIONS IN SASKATCHEWAN COLLECTIVE AGREEMENTS (CN/0830-0763) [15602345] **1695**

NONALIGNED THIRD WORLD ANNUAL (US/0273-0499) [04674428] **1576**

NONCELLO, IL (IT/0029-1080) [07231311] 2700, **326**

NONCITRUS FRUITS & NUTS. MID-YEAR SUPPLEMENT (US/1057-7912) [04168708] **114**

NONCITRUS FRUITS AND NUTS. SUMMARY (US/1060-2666) [13221472] **114**

NONDESTRUCTIVE TESTING AND EVALUATION (US/1058-9759) [21278151] **2123**

NONDESTRUCTIVE TESTING MONOGRAPHS AND TRACTS (US/0730-7152) [08046838] **1989**

NONFERROUS METALS ALERT (US) [25521475] **4014**

NONG-LIN XUE BAO (CH/0550-3744) [02255838] 2389, **114**

NONGCHON MULKA CHONGNAM (KO) [10509577] 114, **155**

NONGCHON SAENGHWAL KWAHAK (KO) [23434991] **5134**

NONGCUN KEXUE (CC) **5134**

NONGNIM NONJIP (KO) [04782002] 2389, **114**

NONGOCHON KAEBAL (KO) [04473472] **5252**

NONGOP KIBAN CHOSONG SAOP TONGGYE YONBO (KO) [06872342] 114, **155**

NONGOP KIGYE YONGAM (KO) [11201974] **160**

NONGOP KWAHAK YONGU (KO) [25374468] **114**

NONGSA SIHOM YONGU NONMUNJIP (KO) [14372905] 576, **114**

NONGSA SIHOM YON'GU NONMUNJIP. CHANGMUL POHO P'YON (KO/1013-9389) [I10139389] **114**

NONGSA SIHOM YONGU NONMUNJIP. CHANGMULPYON (KO) [14779717] **114**

NONGSA SIHOM YON'GU NONMUNJIP. CHON-T'UKCHAK P'YON (KO/1013-9397) [I10139397] 179, **114**

NONGSA SIHOM YON'GU NONMUNJIP. CH'UKSAN P'YON (KO/1013-9400) [I10139400] **5517**

NONGSA SIHOM YON'GU NONMUNJIP. KACH'UK UISAENG P'YON (KO/1013-9419) [I10139419] **5517**

NONGSA SIHOM YON'GU NONMUNJIP. NONG KIGYE-NONGGYONG-CHAMOP-NONG RI-KYUNI P'YON (KO/1013-9427) [I10139427] **114**

NONGSA SIHOM YON'GU NONMUNJIP. SAENGMYONG KONGHAK P'YON (KO/1013-9435) [I10139435] **3695**

NONGSA SIHOM YONGU NONMUNJIP. SIKHWAN, KYUNI, NONGGAPYON (KO) [14780066] **114**

NONGSA SIHOM YON'GU NONMUNJIP. SUDO P'YON (KO/1013-9443) [I10139443] 2351, **114**

NONGSA SIHOM YON'GU NONMUNJIP. T'OYANG PIRYO P'YON (KO/1013-9370) [I10139370] **2425**

NONGSA SIHOM YON'GU NONMUNJIP. WONYE P'YON (KO/1010-562X) [I1010562X] **2426**

NONGSA SIHOM YONGU POGO. CHUKSAN, KAWI (KO) [07843808] **114**

NONGSA SIHOM Y'ONGU POGO. NOGKI, NOGKA, NOGKY'UNG (KO) [07843828] **114**

NONGSA SIHOM YONGU POGO. NONGKONG, NONGCHON KYUNGYON, JAMUP (KO) [12247516] 114, **160**

NONGSA SIHOM YONGU POGO. WONYE (KO) [12247547] **2426**

NONGYE JIXIE XUEBAO (CH/1000-1298) [I10001298] **160**

NONLINEAR ANALYSIS (UK/0362-546X) [03463117] **3524**

NONLINEAR DIFFERENTIAL EQUATIONS AND APPLICATIONS (US/1021-9722) **3524**

NONLINEAR DIGEST *CEASED.* (GW/0942-5594) **3524**

NONLINEAR DYNAMICS (NE/0924-090X) [23103684] **1989**

NONLINEAR OPTICS *See* MOLECULAR CRYSTALS AND LIQUID CRYSTALS SCIENCE AND TECHNOLOGY SECTION B, NONLINEAR OPTICS **4438**

NONLINEAR OPTICS *See* MOLECULAR CRYSTALS AND LIQUID CRYSTALS SCIENCE AND TECHNOLOGY: SECTION A, MOLECULAR CRYSTALS AND LIQUID CRYSTALS **1032**

NONLINEAR OPTICS *See* MOLECULAR CRYSTALS AND LIQUID CRYSTALS SCIENCE AND TECHNOLOGY SECTION D, DISPLAY AND IMAGING **4438**

NONLINEAR SCIENCE TODAY (US/0938-9008) [22379158] **5134**

NONLINEAR TOPICS IN THE MATHEMATICAL SCIENCES (NE/0925-6660) [I09256660] **3524**

NONLINEAR VIBRATION PROBLEMS (PL/0044-1597) [04948339] **4413**

NONLINEARITY (BRISTOL) (UK/0951-7715) [17623398] **3524**

NONMUNJIP. CHAYON KWAHAKPYON (KO) [13385807] **4169**

NONMUNJIP (CHEJU TAEHAK) *See* NONMUNJIP. CHAYON KWAHAKPYON **4169**

NONMUNJIP (HALLIM TAEHAK) (KO) [10024317] **1838**

NONMUNJIP (TONGNAE YOJA CHONMUN TAEHAK) (KO) [10377952] **2507**

●NONPROFIT ALMANAC (US/1060-7889) [25101664] **5299**

NONPROFIT AND VOLUNTARY SECTOR QUARTERLY (US/0899-7640) [18212349] **5299**

NONPROFIT COMPUTER SOURCEBOOK (US/1049-9210) [21354197] **1238**

NONPROFIT COUNSEL, THE (US/0742-3497) [10309275] **4338**

●NONPROFIT FINANCIAL ADVISOR (US/1074-6331) [29799570] **801**

NONPROFIT INSIGHTS (US/1056-4594) [23719141] **4739**

NONPROFIT MANAGEMENT & LEADERSHIP (US/1048-6682) [21014533] **880**

●NONPROFIT MANAGEMENT DIGEST (US/1074-2654) [29633262] **880**

NONPROFIT MANAGEMENT STRATEGIES (US/1051-9602) [22160163] **5299**

NONPROFIT MARKETING REPORT (US/1064-4911) [26294931] **934**

NONPROFIT REPORT (BOSTON, MASS.), THE (US/1056-5094) [23728252] **749**

NONPROFIT TIMES, THE (US/0896-5048) [15675270] **880**

NONPROFIT WORLD (US) [13400501] **5299**

●NONRENEWABLE RESOURCES (US/0961-1444) [26570647] 1508, **2201**

NONRUBBER FOOTWEAR: ANNUAL SURVEY OF PRODUCERS AND IMPORTERS (US/0196-4712) [05622073] 1086, **847**

NONRUBBER FOOTWEAR : U.S. PRODUCTION, IMPORTS FOR CONSUMPTION, APPARENT U.S. CONSUMPTION, EMPLOYMENT, WHOLESALE PRICE INDEX, AND CONSUMER PRICE INDEX (US/0198-8417) [06217466] **1086**

NONVIOLENCE TODAY (AT/1031-6434) [I10316434] **4484**

NONVIOLENT ACTIVIST, THE (US/8755-7428) [11451391] **3133**

NONWOVENS ABSTRACTS (UK/9036-1234) [22283150] 5354, **5360**

NONWOVENS INDUSTRY (US/0163-4429) [03865914] 5354, **1620**

NONWOVENS INDUSTRY EXECUTIVE REPORT (US) **5354**

NONWOVENS MARKETS (US) **5354**

NONWOVENS MARKETS AND FIBER STRUCTURES REPORT (US/1053-9832) [20506574] **5354**

NONWOVENS WORLD *See* NEW NONWOVENS WORLD, THE **5354**

NOORDBRABANTS HISTORISCH JAARBOEK (NE) [13533650] **2624**

NOORTEKALENDER (ER) [19651098] **1927**

NOPA DEALER OPERATING RESULTS (US/1049-3743) [07648577] **4212**

NOPA INDUSTRY REPORT (US/0746-5467) [10125289] **4212**

NOPA MANUFACTURER SELLING COSTS SURVEY (US/0741-3238) [08500425] **4212**

NOPA OFFICE MARKET UPDATE (US/1060-3522) [24944133] **4212**

NOPA UPDATE (US) **4212**

NOR KIANK (US/0194-0074) [05289766] **5637**

NOR OR (US) [08770155] **5637**

NOR SEROUNT (CN/0703-4512) [03382027] **4982**

NORA: NORDIC JOURNAL OF WOMEN'S STUDIES (NO/0803-8740) [28566695] **5563**

NORAGRIC OCCASIONAL PAPERS. SERIES C : DEVELOPMENT AND ENVIRONMENT (NO/0802-0957) [I08020957] **114**

NORBA-ARTE (SP/0213-2214) [15279580] **360**

NORBA. REVISTA DE GEOGRAFIA (SP/0213-3709) [15279320] **2570**

NORBA. REVISTA DE HISTORIA (SP/0213-375X) [15313336] **2624**

NORBORNE DEMOCRAT-LEADER (US) [13515706] **5704**

NORC REPORTER, THE (US/0893-5998) [15600301] **5252**

NORD E SUD (IT/0029-1188) [02146271] **2700**

NORD-EST PLUS (CN/1187-4953) [25313865] **5790**

NORD GENEALOGIE (FR) [06300873] **2464**

NORD (HEARST) (CN/0382-8883) [03202131] **5790**

NORD NYTT (DK) [06307275] **2323**

NORD-OSTSEE-KANAL JAHRESBERICHT (GW) [11625817] **5453**

●NORD OUEST (SAINT-BASILE) (CN/1188-1321) [25883049] **326**

NORD REVY : TIDSSKRIFT FOR REGIONAL UDVIKLING, NAERINGSLIV, MILJOE (NO/0802-8818) [23024309] **2829**

NORD-SUD AKTUELL (GW/0933-1743) [20782600] **4530**

NORD SUD EXPORT (FR/0244-4623) [02444623] **847**

NORD SUD MAGAZINE *CEASED.* (BE) [18124982] **1576**

NORDELBINGEN (GW/0078-1037) [01760430] **360**

NORDELBISCHE EVANGELISCH-LUTHERISCHE KIRCHE. SYNOD *See* BERICHT UBER DIE VERHANDLUNGEN DER ORDENTLICHEN SYNODE DE NORDELBISCHEN EV.-LUTH. KIRCHE **5056**

NORDEN (NEW YORK, N.Y.) (US/0895-2612) [09473030] **5719**

NORDEN NEWS (US/0890-3727) [01760431] **5577**

NORDEN; NORD-NORGES LANDBRUKSTIDSSKRIFT (NO) [09954356] 2389, 2426, **114**

NORDENS JARNVAGAR (SW) [01791296] **5433**

NORDESTE, CONJUNTURA INDUSTRIAL (BL/0101-2177) [04784055] **1620**

NORDESTE ECONOMICO (BL) [10708501] **1576**

NORDESTE EM NUMEROS (BL) [04994854] **5334**

NORDEUROPA STUDIEN (GW) [04221408] **2700**

NORDFRIESISCHES JAHRBUCH (GW/0078-1045) [01785049] **2700**

NORDFRIESLAND CHRONIK (GW) [01786566] **2700**

NORDHARZER JAHRBUCH (GW) **2624**

NORDIA (FI/0356-1437) [11741146] **2570**

NORDIC (US/0163-5905) [04283290] **4908**

NORDIC HYDROLOGY (DK/0029-1277) [01760433] **1416**

NORDIC INSTITUTE OF FOLKLORE *See* NIF NEWSLETTER **2323**

NORDIC JOURNAL OF BOTANY (DK/0107-055X) [07429089] **520**

NORDIC JOURNAL OF FRESHWATER RESEARCH (SW/1100-4096) [20383882] **2309**

NORDIC JOURNAL OF INTERNATIONAL LAW (NE/0902-7351) [14921933] **3133**

NORDIC JOURNAL OF LINGUISTICS (NO/0332-5865) [04409340] **3306**

NORDIC JOURNAL OF PSYCHIATRY (NO/0803-9488) [I08039488] **3931**

NORDIC JOURNAL OF PSYCHIATRY. SUPPLEMENT (NO/0803-9496) [I08039496] **3932**

NORDIC JOURNAL OF SOVIET AND EAST EUROPEAN STUDIES *CEASED.* (SW/0281-8353) [11546612] **2700**

NORDIC PULP & PAPER (FI/0784-5073) [I07845073] **4235**

NORDIC PULP & PAPER RESEARCH JOURNAL (SW/0283-2631) [14755741] **4235**

NORDIC ROAD & TRANSPORT RESEARCH (SW/1101-5179) [I11015179] **5442**

NORDIC SKIING COMPETITION GUIDE (US/0277-7452) [07687753] **4908**

NORDIC SOUNDS (DK/0108-2914) [I01082914] **5318**

NORDIC SOUNDS / NORDIC COUNCIL OF MINISTERS/NOMUS, THE SECRETARIAT FOR NORDIC CULTURAL COOPERATION (DK) [09460947] **4141**

NORDIC THEATRE STUDIES (DK/0904-6380) [20408769] **5367**

NORDIC WEST (US/0749-601X) [11148827] **4908**

NORDICA (DK/0109-3967) [12040096] **3418**

NORDICOM REVIEW OF NORDIC MASS COMMUNICATION RESEARCH, THE (SW/0349-6244) [07633161] **1118**

NORDISK ADMINISTRATIVT TIDSSKRIFT (DK/0029-1285) [01760435] **4669**

NORDISK ALKOHOL TIDSKRIFT (FI/0782-9671) [24768812] **1347**

NORDISK ARBEIDSMARKEDSUTVALG *See* ARBEIDSMARKED OG ARBEIDSMARKEDSPOLITIKK I NORDEN. TYOMARKKINAT JA TYOMARKKINAPOLITIIKKA **1651**

NORDISK ARKITEKTURFORSKNING (SW/1102-5824) [I11025824] **305**

NORDISK CELLULOSA (SW/0281-6733) [16656851] **4235**

NORDISK DOMSSAMLING (NO/0029-1315) [I00291315] **3018**

NORDISK FORSAKRINGSTIDSKRIFT (SW/0029-1358) [01639966] **2889**

NORDISK FORUM (NO) [05897251] **2520**

NORDISK HANDELSKALENDER, SKANDINAVIASK ADRESSEBOG (DK/0549-6233) [02251327] **699**

NORDISK JARNBANETIDSKRIFT (SW) [06462032] **5433**

NORDISK JORDBRUGSFORSKNING (NO/0048-0495) [04051266] **114**

NORDISK JUDAISTIK / SCANDINAVIAN JEWISH STUDIES (SW/0348-1646) [11546256] **5051**

NORDISK LANTBRUNSEKONOMISK TIDSKRIFT *See* NORDISKT LANTBRUK **114**

NORDISK MEDICIN (SW/0029-1420) [01115290] **3622**

NORDISK MEDICINHISTORISK AARSBOK (SW/0303-6480) [01132589] **3623**

NORDISK MEJERIINDUSTRI (SW) [02252689] **197**

NORDISK NUMISMATISK ARSSKRIFT. SCANDINAVIAN NUMISMATIC JOURNAL (SW/0078-107X) [01680839] **2782**

NORDISK PEDAGOGIK (DK/0901-8050) [I09018050] **1769**

NORDISK POSTTIDSKRIFT (SW) [06456606] **1146**

NORDISK PSYKIATRISK TIDSSKRIFT *See* NORDIC JOURNAL OF PSYCHIATRY **3931**

NORDISK PSYKIATRISK TIDSSKRIFT. SUPPLEMENT (OSLO) *See* NORDIC JOURNAL OF PSYCHIATRY. SUPPLEMENT **3932**

NORDISK PSYKOLOGI (DK/0029-1463) [01760444] **4606**

NORDISK SEXOLOGI (DK/0108-271X) [27428206] 5188, **4606**

NORDISK SOSIALT ARBEID (NO/0333-1342) [09798534] **5299**

NORDISK ST-FORUM (NO/0801-7220) [16349806] **5211**

NORDISK TIDSKRIFT FOR BETEENDETERAPI (SW/0345-1402) [02328145] **4606**

NORDISK TIDSKRIFT FOR BOK-OCH BIBLIOTEKSVASEN (SW/0029-148X) [01760450] **3237**

NORDISK TIDSSKRIFT FOR DOVUNDERVISNINGEN (SW/0029-1471) [03179311] 4392, **1883**

NORDISK TIDSSKRIFT FOR INTERNATIONAL RET. PUBLIKATIONSSERIE (DK) [06364465] **3133**

NORDISK TIDSSKRIFT FOR KRIMINALVIDENSKAB (DK/0029-1528) [01760454] **3170**

NORDISK TIDSSKRIFT FOR LOGOPEDI OG FONIATRI. SCANDINAVIAN JOURNAL OF LOGOPEDICS AND PHONIATRICS (DK/0105-1539) [05082169] **3889**

NORDISK TIDSSKRIFT FOR SPECIALPAEDAGOGIK (NO/0048-0509) [10820085] **1883**

NORDISK TIDSSKRIFT FOR STRAEFFERET *See* NORDISK TIDSSKRIFT FOR KRIMINALVIDENSKAB **3170**

NORDISKA AFRIKAINSTITUTET *See* RESEARCH REPORT **5215**

NORDISKT LANTBRUK (SW) [06437973] **114**

NORDISKT NAMNFORSKARREGISTER (SW) [02240943] **3306**

NORDLYD (NO/0332-7531) [06505036] **3306**

NORDRHEIN-WESTFALEN. FINANZMINISTER. MITTEILUNGSBLATT (GW) **4739**

NORDSTJERNAN (1991) (US/1059-7670) [24728237] **5719**

NOR'EASTER (NARRAGANSETT) (US) **467**

NORELCO REPORTER (US/0029-1625) [01645498] **5134**

NOREX INFORMATION PARIS-LA DEFENSE (FR/0224-3016) [I02243016] **1197**

NORFOLK ANCESTOR : JOURNAL OF THE NORFOLK & NORWICH GENEALOGICAL SOCIETY, THE (UK/0140-5403) [07234230] **2464**

NORFOLK ARCHAEOLOGY (UK/0142-7962) [11258524] **276**

NORFOLK ARCHAEOLOGY, OR, MISCELLANEOUS TRACTS RELATING TO THE ANTIQUITIES OF THE COUNTY OF NORFOLK *See* NORFOLK ARCHAEOLOGY **276**

NORFOLK DAILY NEWS (US) **5707**

NORFOLK GAZETTE, THE (CN/0704-0245) [03889985] **5790**

NORFOLK GENEALOGY (UK) [08083829] **2464**

NORFOLK ISLAND *See* ANNUAL REPORT ON THE TERRITORY OF NORFOLK ISLAND **4629**

NORFOLK SOUTHERN CORPORATION *See* ANNUAL REPORT / NORFOLK SOUTHERN **5429**

NORGES APOTEKERFORENINGS TIDSSKRIFT (NO/0029-1668) [10116493] **4318**

NORGES AUTOMOBIL-FORDUND *See* MED BIL I EUROPA **2697**

NORGES BANK *See* SKRIFTSERIE **811**

NORGES BANK *See* ECONOMIC BULLETIN **1482**

NORGES GEOGRAFISKE OPPMALING *See* KARTKATALOG / NORGES GEOGRAFISKE OPPMALING **2580**

NORGES GEOGRAFISKE OPPMALING *See* ARSBERETNING / NORGES GEOGRAFISKE OPPMALING **2555**

NORGES GEOLOGISKE UNDERSKELSE *See* ARBOK - NORGES GEOLOGISKE UNDERSKELSE **1366**

NORGES. GEOLOGISKE UNDERSKELSE *See* ARSMELDING - NORGES GEOLOGISKE UNDERSKELSE **1366**

NORGES GEOTEKNISKE INSTITUTT *See* PUBLIKASJON - NORGES GEOTEKNISKE INSTITUTT **1392**

NORGES KOMMUNEKALENDER (NO) [03501732] **1576**

NORGES LANDBRUKSHGSKOLE. INSTITUTT FOR DRIFTSLAERE OG LANDBRUKSKONOMI. MELDING *See* MELDING / NORGES LANDBRUKSHGSKOLE, INSTITUTT FOR LANDBRUKSKONOMI **107**

NORGES SAMARBEID MED UTVIKLINGSLANDENE (NO) [02472125] **1576**

NORGES SJKARTVERK *See* KATALOG OVER NORSKE SJKART OG NAUTISKE PUBLIKASJONER **4185**

NORGES VETERINRHGSKOLE *See* ARSMELDING - NORGES VETERINRHGSKOLE **5504**

NORIN GYOGYO JOHO (JA) [02998427] **2309**

NORIN GYOGYO KINYU KOKO *See* GYOMU TOKEI NEMPO - NORIN GYOGYO KINYU KOKO **790**

NORIN GYOGYO KINYU KOKO *See* AGRICULTURE, FORESTRY, AND FISHERIES FINANCE CORPORATION : REPORT **53**

NORIN KENKYU KEISAN SENTA (JAPAN). NORIN KENKYU KEISAN SENTA HOKOKU. A *See* NORIN SUISAN KENKYU KEISAN SENTA HOKOKU. A / BULLETIN OF THE COMPUTING CENTER FOR RESEARCH IN AGRICULTURE, FORESTRY, AND FISHERY. SERIES A **114**

NORIN SUISAN KANKEI SHIKEN KENKYU YORAN (JA) [01797313] **114**

NORIN SUISAN KENKYU KEISAN SENTA HOKOKU. A / BULLETIN OF THE COMPUTING CENTER FOR RESEARCH IN AGRICULTURE, FORESTRY, AND FISHERY. SERIES A (JA/0388-8436) [10611767] **114**

NORIN SUISAN KENKYU KEISAN SENTA HOKOKU. B (JA/0389-3103) [11026309] **114**

NORIN SUISAN TOKEI SHIHYO (JA) [01797057] **114**

NORIN-SUISANGYO NI KANSURU CHIIKI BUNSEKISHO SORAN (JA) [05758518] **155**

NORIN-SUISANGYO SEISAN SHISU (JA) [07039058] **2389**

NORIN SUISANSHO DOBUTSU IYAKUHIN KENSAJO (JAPAN) *See* DOBUTSU IYAKUHIN KENSAJO NEMPO **5509**

NORIN SUISANSHO HOKURIKU NOGYO SHIKENJO *See* HOKURIKU NOGYO SHIKENJO HOKOKU **93**

NORIN SUISANSHO KACHIKU EISEI SHIKENJO *See* NORIN SUISANSHO KACHIKU EISEI SHIKENJO NEMPO **5517**

NORIN SUISANSHO KACHIKU EISEI SHIKENJO KENKYU HOKOKU (JA/0388-2403) [10384636] **5517**

NORIN SUISANSHO KACHIKU EISEI SHIKENJO NEMPO (JA) [05691000] **5517**

NORIN SUISANSHO KOHO (JA) [09962561] **114**

NORIN SUISANSHO NOGYO KANKYO GIJUTSU KENKYUJO (JAPAN) *See* NOGYO KANKYO GIJUTSU KENKYUJO NENPO **520**

NORIN SUISANSHO TOKEIHYO (JA) [05769490] **114**

NORINSHO DOBUTSU IYAKUHIN KENSAJO NEMPO *See* DOBUTSU IYAKUHIN KENSAJO NEMPO **5509**

NORINSHO KACHIKU EISEI SHIKENJO (JAPAN) *See* NORINSHO KACHIKU EISEI SHIKENJO NEMPO **5517**

NORINSHO KACHIKU EISEI SHIKENJO NEMPO (JA) [02628859] **5517**

NORINSHO KAJU SHIKENJO (JAPAN) *See* KAJU SHIKENJO NYUSU **2422**

NORINSHO KANTO RINBOKU IKUSHUJO *See* NEMPO - NORINSHO KANTO RINBOKU IKUSHUJO **2425**

NORINSHO NEMPO (JA) [01790244] **114**

NORINSHO NOGYO GIJUTSU KENKYUJO (JAPAN) *See* NOGYO GIJUTSU KENKYUJO HOKOKU. C : BYORI KONCHU **2425**

NORINSHO NOGYO GIJUTSU KENKYUJO (JAPAN) *See* NOGYO GIJUTSU KENKYUJO HOKOKU. H : KEIEI TOCHI RIYO **113**

NORINSHO NOGYO GIJUTSU KENKYUJO (JAPAN) *See* NOGYO GIJUTSU KENKYUJO HOKOKU. RENZOKU B: DOJO HIRYO **113**

NORINSHO NOYAKU KENSAJO *See* NOYAKU KENSAJO HOKOKU **115**

NORINSHO SANSHI SHIKENJO (JAPAN) *See* SANSHI SHIKENJO NEMPO **5597**

NORINSHO SATOKIBIGEN GENSHU NOJO *See* GYOMU HOKOKU - NORINSHO SATOKIBIGEN GENSHU NOJO **173**

NORINSHO YOKOHAMA SHOKUBUTSU BOIKIJO *See* SHOKUBUTSU BOEKIJO CHOSA KENKYU HOKOKU **2431**

NORM EVANS' SEAHAWK REPORT (US/0197-8349) [06154325] **4908**

NORMA CUBANA (CU) [07055461] **114**, **155**

NORMAL (NEW YORK, N.Y.) *CEASED.* (US/0892-5836) [15232639] **326**

NORMALE UND PATHOLOGISCHE ANATOMIE (GW/0303-2418) [01777581] **3679**

NORMALISATIE MAGAZINE *See* NORMALISATIE-NIEUWS (DELFT) **4032**

NORMALISATIE MAGAZINE (NE/0921-8211) [I09218211] **4032**

●NORMALISATIE-NIEUWS (DELFT) (NE/0929-2985) [I09292985] **4032**

NORMALSATIE (NE) **880**, **699**

NORMAN COUNTY INDEX (US) [01760468] **5697**

NORMAN MACKENZIE ART GALLERY *See* MACKENZIE OUTREACH **357**

NORMAN PATERSON SCHOOL OF INTERNATIONAL AFFAIRS *See* BIBLIOGRAPHY SERIES - NORMAN PATERSON SCHOOL OF INTERNATIONAL AFFAIRS (CARLETON UNIVERSITY) **4501**

NORMAN TRANSCRIPT (NORMAN, OKLA.) (US) [13763878] **5732**

NORMANDIE (FR) [03489358] **5421**, **4908**

NORMAS LEGALES (PE) [07032076] **3018**

NORMAT (NO/0801-3500) [05182282] **3524**

NORMATIVA GENERALE (IT) **1508**

NORMATIVA SUL SERVIZIO FARMACEUTICO (IT) **4318**

NORMATIVA TECNICA (IT) **5134**

NORME (CN) [05257056] **622**

NORME DI COMPORTAMENTO IN MATERIA TRIBUTARIA (IT) **1508**

NORMELEC (FR) **5134**

NORMENSTELLE LUFTFAHRT *See* LUFTFAHRT-NORMEN-VERZEICHNIS **28**

NORNA-RAPPORTER (SW/0346-6728) [05319558] **3306**

NOROIL (NO/0332-544X) [05399212] **4266**

NOROIL CONTACTS (UK/0964-4636) [I09644636] **4266**

NOROIS (FR/0029-182X) [01760469] **2570**

NORRIDGE HARWOOD HEIGHTS NEWS (US/1054-7932) [22971662] **5661**

NORRIDGE NEWS (US/0885-7814) [12715694] **5661**

NORRONE TEKSTER (NO) **2482**

NORSEMAN (NO/0029-1846) [06403914] **2520**

NORSK ANTHROPOLOGISK TIDSSKRIFT (NO/0802-7285) **242**

NORSK ARTILLERI TIDSSKRIFT (NO) **4053**

NORSK BOKFORTEGNELSE (NO/0029-1870) [01760675] **3418**, **5807**

NORSK BOKFORTEGNELSE. MUSIKKTRYKK. THE NORWEGIAN NATIONAL BIBLIOGRAPHY / UTARBEIDET VED NORSK MUSIKKSAMLING, UNIVERSITETSBIBLIOTEKET I OSLO (NO/0800-9805) [13302433] **4142**

NORSK FARMACEUTISK TIDSSKRIFT (DK/0029-1935) [02265169] **4318**

NORSK FILOSOFISK TIDSSKRIFT (NO/0029-1943) [I00291943] **4353**

NORSK GEOGRAFISK TIDSSKRIFT (NO/0029-1951) [01715904] **2571**

NORSK GEOLOGISK TIDSSKRIFT (NO/0029-196X) [01760475] **1390**

NORSK HAGETIDEND (NO/0029-1986) [04051285] **520**, **2426**

NORSK IDRETT (NO/0029-1994) [I00291994] **4908**

NORSK INSTITUTT FOR VANNFORSKNING (NO/0333-3280) [01799913] **5536**

NORSK KONOMISK TIDSSKRIFT (NO) [18161172] **1508**

NORSK LANDBRUK (NO) [03776158] **114**

NORSK LANDBRUKSFORSKING (NO/0801-5333) [16785331] **115**

NORSK LANDBRUKSFORSKING. SUPPLEMENT (NO/0802-0914) [16786117] **115**

NORSK LINGVISTISK TIDSSKRIFT : NLT (NO/0800-3076) [11962611] **3306**

NORSK LITTERR ARBOK (NO/0078-1266) [01792617] **3418**

NORSK MILITRT TIDSSKRIFT (NO/0029-2028) [10419737] **4053**

NORSK MUSIKERBLAD (NO/0029-2044) [04296470] **4142**

NORSK MUSIKKGRANSKNING; MEDDELELSER FRA NORSK SAMFUND FOR MUSIKKGRANSKNING, NORSK MUSIKKSAMLINGS VENNER. ARBOK (NO) [01760480] **4142**

NORSK MUSIKKTIDSSKRIFT (NO/0332-5482) [09436305] **1769**, **4142**

NORSK OLJEREVY (NO/0332-5490) [I03325490] **4266**

NORSK PEDAGOGISK TIDSSKRIFT (NO) [06497513] **1769**

NORSK PETROLEUMSFORENING *See* YEAR BOOK FOR NORWEGIAN PETROLEUM SOCIETY **4283**

NORSK POLARINSTITUTT *See* SKRIFTER - NORSK POLARINSTITUTT **5158**

NORSK POLARINSTITUTT *See* MEDDELELSER / NORSK PALARINSTITUTT **5127**

NORSK SKOGBRUK (NO/0029-2087) [03791176] **2389**

NORSK SLEKTSHISTORISK TIDSSKRIFT (NO/0029-2141) [01760485] **2464**

NORSK SPRAKNEMND. SKRIFTER *See* SKRIFTER - NORSK SPRAKRAD **3321**

NORSK SPRAKRAD *See* SKRIFTER - NORSK SPRAKRAD **3321**

NORSK STATSVITENSKAPELIG TIDSSKRIFT (NO/0801-1745) [15188476] **4484**

NORSK TEKSTILTIDENDE (NO/0029-2168) [04051291] **5354**

NORSK — Alphabetical Title Index

NORSK TEOLOGISK TIDSSKRIFT (NO/0029-2176) [01696485] **4982**

NORSK TIDENDE FOR DET INDUSTRIELLE RETTSVERN. DEL I: PATENTER (NO/0029-2206) [06895705] **1306**

NORSK TIDSSKRIFT FOR MISJON (NO/0029-2214) [01773485] **4982**

NORSK TIDSSKRIFT FOR SJOVESEN (NO/0029-2222) [06313619] **4181**

NORSK UKEBLAD (NO/0029-2257) [01760487] **5807**

NORSK UTENRIKSPOLITISK ARBOK (NO) [05730583] **4530**

●NORSK VEG-OG VEGTRAFIKKPLAN (NO) [22582465] **5442**

NORSK VETERINARTIDSSKRIFT (NO) [l00292273] **5517**

NORSK VETERINRTIDSSKIRFT 1970 (NO/0332-5741) [l03325741] **5517**

NORSKE ADVOKATFORENING *See* RETTENS GANG **3039**

NORSKE BANKFORENING *See* ANNUAL REPORT / THE NORWEGIAN BANKERS' ASSOCIATION **772**

NORSKE CREDIT BANK *See* ANNUAL REPORT / DEN NORSKE CREDITBANK **771**

NORSKE HANDELSKAMMER I LONDON *See* YEAR BOOK **821**

NORSKE LAEGEFORENING *See* TIDSSKRIFT FOR DEN NORSKE LAEGEFORENING; TIDSSKRIFT FOR PRAKTISK MEDISIN. THE JOURNAL OF THE NORWEGIAN MEDICAL ASSOCIATION **3645**

NORSKE VERITAS (ORGANIZATION) *See* ANNUAL REPORT / DET NORSKE VERITAS **5447**

NORSKLREREN (NO/0332-7264) [l03327264] 3418, **3306**

NORTE (MEXICO, D.F.) (MX/0188-2848) [01100583] **3467**

NORTE (MICROFICHE), EL (MX) [04650473] **5806**

NORTE SUR (US/1058-7683) [24383049] **2571**

NORTH (DK/0105-1512) [03235695] **360**

NORTH AFRICA SERIES (US/0066-0981) [01787013] **2642**

NORTH AMERICA INDIANS. CD-ROM (US) **2750**

NORTH AMERICAN AIRCRAFT & AEROSPACE MUSEUM GUIDE (US) [22980500] **30**

NORTH AMERICAN BED & BREAKFAST REGISTRY, THE (US/1059-0730) [24476273] **2808**

NORTH AMERICAN BIRD BANDER (US/0363-8979) [02394576] **5618**

NORTH AMERICAN COPIER & COPYBOARD GUIDE (US/0889-9819) [17724517] **4567**

NORTH AMERICAN CULTURE (US/0882-1968) [11791319] **5253**

NORTH AMERICAN DIRECTORY & REFERENCE GUIDE OF ASIAN INDIAN BUSINESSES AND INDEPENDENT PROFESSIONAL PRACTITIONERS ALONG WITH COMMUNITY REFERENCE GUIDE & TRAVEL INFORMATION (US/0883-3583) [12095682] **699**

NORTH AMERICAN DIRECTORY OF CONTRACT MANUFACTURERS IN ELECTRONICS (US/1052-0716) [22171767] **2074**

NORTH AMERICAN DIRECTORY OF EXOTIC ANIMAL & BIRD OWNERS (US) [23197686] **4287**

NORTH AMERICAN DIRECTORY OF MONTESSORI SCHOOLS (US/0193-9874) [03689939] **1901**

NORTH AMERICAN ELECTRIC RELIABILITY COUNCIL *See* ANNUAL REPORT / NORTH AMERICAN ELECTRIC RELIABILITY COUNCIL **2035**

NORTH AMERICAN ELECTRONIC TYPEWRITER GUIDE *CEASED.* (US/0889-9827) [14217877] **4213**

NORTH AMERICAN ENERGY REVIEW, THE (US/0275-3898) [07109692] **1951**

NORTH AMERICAN FALCONERS' ASSOCIATION *See* JOURNAL OF THE NORTH AMERICAN FALCONERS' ASSOCIATION, THE **4874**

●NORTH AMERICAN FARM EQUIPMENT JOURNAL (US) [30641154] **160**

NORTH AMERICAN FAUNA (US/0078-1304) [01444066] **5593**

NORTH AMERICAN FISHERMAN (US/1043-2450) [19359935] **2309**

NORTH AMERICAN FLORA (US/0078-1312) [01760506] **520**

NORTH AMERICAN GLADIOLUS COUNCIL *See* BULLETIN - NORTH AMERICAN GLADIOLUS COUNCIL **505**

NORTH AMERICAN GUIDE TO NUDE RECREATION (US) [22169466] **5486**

NORTH AMERICAN HUMAN RIGHTS DIRECTORY *CEASED.* (US/0270-2282) [06364280] **4511**

NORTH AMERICAN HUNTER (US/0194-4320) [04647268] **4876**

NORTH AMERICAN HUNTING DIRECTORY (US) **4876**

●NORTH AMERICAN JOURNAL OF ECONOMICS AND FINANCE (US/1062-9408) [25812115] 801, **1508**

NORTH AMERICAN JOURNAL OF FISHERIES MANAGEMENT (US/0275-5947) [07164440] **2309**

NORTH AMERICAN LAKE MANAGEMENT SOCIETY *See* MEMBERSHIP DIRECTORY / NORTH AMERICAN LAKE MANAGEMENT SOCIETY **1505**

NORTH AMERICAN LIBRARY EDUCATION DIRECTORY AND STATISTICS (US/0090-0605) [03902066] 3237, **3259**

NORTH AMERICAN LICENSING INDUSTRY BUYERS GUIDE (UK) [25390277] **934**

NORTH AMERICAN LICENSING TRIBUNE (UK) **1306**

NORTH AMERICAN MULTINATIONAL BANKING (US/0883-4628) [08420224] **801**

NORTH AMERICAN MULTINATIONAL BANKING/FOREIGN EXCHANGE SERVICES (US) [10330842] **801**

NORTH AMERICAN NEW PRODUCT REPORT, THE (US/0899-0158) [17972596] **3485**

●NORTH AMERICAN OUTLOOK (US/1071-5584) [28678792] **4739**

NORTH AMERICAN RADIO-TV STATION GUIDE (US/0078-1347) [02640373] **1135**

NORTH AMERICAN REPORT ON FREE TRADE (US) **847**

NORTH AMERICAN RETAIL FURRIERS DIRECTORY (US/0740-9117) [10048333] **3185**

NORTH AMERICAN REVIEW OF ECONOMICS AND FINANCE *See* NORTH AMERICAN JOURNAL OF ECONOMICS AND FINANCE **1508**

NORTH AMERICAN REVIEW, THE (US/0029-2397) [04604572] **3349**

NORTH AMERICAN SIMMENTAL *See* SIMMENTAL SHIELD **221**

NORTH AMERICAN SOCIETY FOR SPORT HISTORY *See* NEWSLETTER - NORTH AMERICAN SOCIETY FOR SPORT HISTORY **4908**

NORTH AMERICAN SOCIETY OF OCEANIC HISTORY *See* NEWSLETTER / NORTH AMERICAN SOCIETY OF OCEANIC HISTORY **4181**

NORTH AMERICAN SOCIETY OF OCEANIC HISTORY *See* PROCEEDINGS OF THE NORTH AMERICAN SOCIETY FOR OCEANIC HISTORY **4182**

NORTH AMERICAN STEEL MARKET OUTLOOK (US/1062-0702) [25485511] **4014**

NORTH AMERICAN TRADE GUIDE (US) **847**

NORTH AMERICAN VEXILLOLOGICAL ASSOCIATION *See* NAVA NEWS / NORTH AMERICAN VEXILLOLOGICAL ASSOCIATION **2623**

NORTH AMERICAN WHITETAIL (US/0746-6250) [10197463] **4876**

NORTH AMERICAN WOLF SOCIETY *See* JOURNAL OF THE NORTH AMERICAN WOLF SOCIETY **5589**

NORTH & CENTRAL AMERICAN DIRECTORY (US/0734-1741) [08457017] **4142**

NORTH ATLANTIC TREATY ORGANIZATION *See* NATO HANDBOOK, THE **3133**

NORTH ATLANTIC TREATY ORGANIZATION. ADVISORY GROUP FOR AEROSPACE RESEARCH AND DEVELOPMENT *See* AGARD CONFERENCE PROCEEDINGS **6**

NORTH ATLANTIC TREATY ORGANIZATION. ADVISORY GROUP FOR AEROSPACE RESEARCH AND DEVELOPMENT *See* AGARD HIGHLIGHTS **6**

NORTH ATLANTIC TREATY ORGANIZATION. ADVISORY GROUP FOR AEROSPACE RESEARCH AND DEVELOPMENT *See* AGARD LECTURE SERIES **6**

NORTH ATLANTIC TREATY ORGANIZATION. EXPERT PANEL ON AIR POLLUTION MODELING *See* PROCEEDINGS OF THE MEETING OF THE EXPERT PANEL ON AIR POLLUTION MODELING **2239**

NORTH ATLANTIC TREATY ORGANIZATION. SCIENTIFIC AFFAIRS DIVISION *See* NATO CONFERENCE SERIES. I. ECOLOGY **2219**

NORTH BALTIMORE NEWS, THE (US) [10009374] **5729**

NORTH BATTLEFORD NEWS OPTIMIST (CN) **5790**

NORTH BEACH BEACON *See* GRAYS HARBOR BEACON **5761**

NORTH BENGAL UNIVERSITY REVIEW (II) [08622211] **1838**

NORTH BORNEO *See* COLONY OF NORTH BORNEO ANNUAL REPORT **1552**

NORTH BRABANT (NETHERLANDS) *See* BEGROTING DER INKOMSTEN EN UITGAVEN VAN DE PROVINCIE NOORD-BRABANT **4713**

NORTH CADDO COUNTY NEWS, THE (US/8750-3719) [11349180] **5732**

NORTH CAROLINA (US) [21422766] 4669, **699**

NORTH CAROLINA ADMINISTRATIVE CODE. LIST OF RULES AFFECTED / STATE OF NORTH CAROLINA, DEPARTMENT OF JUSTICE (US) [07817014] **4669**

NORTH CAROLINA AGRICULTURAL CHEMICALS MANUAL (US/0091-7508) [05437589] **115**

NORTH CAROLINA AGRICULTURAL STATISTICS (US/0091-3693) [04781104] **115**

NORTH CAROLINA ANNUAL PROGRAM PLAN AMENDMENT (US) [06240425] 4392, **1883**

NORTH CAROLINA ARCHITECTURE (US/1045-3253) [16665781] **305**

NORTH CAROLINA ASSOCIATION OF EDUCATORS *See* NCAE NEWS BULLETIN **1867**

NORTH CAROLINA ATTORNEY GENERAL REPORTS (US/0364-362X) [02640733] **3142**

NORTH CAROLINA BAR ASSOCIATION *See* BAR NOTES **2940**

NORTH CAROLINA BEACON (US/1064-4830) [26295902] **5724**

NORTH CAROLINA BOATING ACCIDENT STATISTICS (US/0148-8090) [03375231] **597**

NORTH CAROLINA CENTRAL LAW JOURNAL (US/0549-7434) [01760556] **3018**

NORTH CAROLINA CHRISTIAN ADVOCATE (US/0029-2435) [04112540] **5724**

NORTH CAROLINA COUNCIL OF WOMEN'S ORGANIZATIONS *See* NORTH CAROLINA COUNCIL OF WOMEN'S ORGANIZATIONS ANNUAL DIRECTORY **5234**

NORTH CAROLINA COUNCIL OF WOMEN'S ORGANIZATIONS ANNUAL DIRECTORY (US) [05419093] 5563, **5234**

NORTH CAROLINA. COURT OF APPEALS *See* NORTH CAROLINA COURT OF APPEALS REPORTS **3018**

NORTH CAROLINA COURT OF APPEALS REPORTS (US/0549-7450) [01681248] **3018**

NORTH CAROLINA. CRIMINAL JUSTICE TRAINING AND STANDARDS COUNCIL *See* ANNUAL REPORT - CRIMINAL JUSTICE TRAINING AND STANDARDS COUNCIL **3157**

NORTH CAROLINA DATA FILE (US/0095-4284) [01783868] **1576**

NORTH CAROLINA DENTAL GAZETTE (US/0091-164X) [02265190] **1331**

NORTH CAROLINA. DEPT. OF COMMUNITY COLLEGES *See* ANNUAL STATISTICAL REPORT / NORTH CAROLINA DEPARTMENT OF COMMUNITY COLLEGES **1809**

NORTH CAROLINA. DEPT. OF HUMAN RESOURCES *See* NORTH CAROLINA STATE PLAN FOR ALCOHOL AND DRUG ABUSE **1347**

NORTH CAROLINA. DEPT. OF HUMAN RESOURCES. DIVISION OF FACILITY SERVICES *See* STATE MEDICAL FACILITIES PLAN (RALEIGH, N.C.) **4804**

NORTH CAROLINA. DEPT. OF HUMAN RESOURCES. TITLE XX BRANCH *See* FINAL TITLE XX COMPREHENSIVE ANNUAL SERVICES PLAN FOR NORTH CAROLINA **5285**

NORTH CAROLINA. DEPT. OF JUSTICE *See* NORTH CAROLINA ATTORNEY GENERAL REPORTS **3142**

NORTH CAROLINA. DEPT. OF NATURAL RESOURCES AND COMMUNITY DEVELOPMENT *See* CIVIL WORKS WATER RESOURCES DEVELOPMENT PROGRAM **5532**

NORTH CAROLINA. DEPT. OF PUBLIC EDUCATION *See* CURRENT EXPENSE DISBURSEMENTS BY SOURCE OF FUNDS **1862**

NORTH CAROLINA. DEPT. OF PUBLIC INSTRUCTION. DIVISION OF RESEARCH *See* REPORT OF STUDENT PERFORMANCE **1778**

NORTH CAROLINA. DEPT. OF PUBLIC INSTRUCTION. DIVISION OF SCIENCE *See* NORTH CAROLINA SCIENCE TEACHER PROFILE / DIVISION OF SCIENCE, NORTH CAROLINA DEPARTMENT OF PUBLIC INSTRUCTION **1867**

NORTH CAROLINA. DEPT. OF SOCIAL SERVICES See BIENNIAL REPORT - NORTH CAROLINA. STATE DEPARTMENT OF SOCIAL SERVICES OF THE DEPARTMENT OF HUMAN RESOURCES **5274**

NORTH CAROLINA. DEPT. OF TRANSPORTATION See BIENNIAL REPORT - NORTH CAROLINA DEPARTMENT OF TRANSPORTATION **5377**

NORTH CAROLINA DIRECTORY OF LICENSED AUCTIONEERS, APPRENTICE AUCTIONEERS, AND AUCTION FIRMS (US) [07519658] **699**

NORTH CAROLINA. DIVISION FOR EXCEPTIONAL CHILDREN See NORTH CAROLINA ANNUAL PROGRAM PLAN AMENDMENT **1883**

NORTH CAROLINA. DIVISION OF HEALTH SERVICES. OFFICE OF LOCAL ADMINISTRATION See NORTH CAROLINA LOCAL HEALTH DEPARTMENTS : BUDGETARY, ECONOMIC, AND OTHER PERTINENT DATA **4794**

NORTH CAROLINA. DIVISION OF HIGHWAYS. PLANNING AND RESEARCH BRANCH See HIGHWAY TRAFFIC STATISTICS **5401**

NORTH CAROLINA. DIVISION OF HIGHWAYS. PLANNING AND RESEARCH BRANCH See NORTH CAROLINA MUNICIPAL EXPENDITURES FROM STATE STREET-AID ALLOCATIONS **5442**

NORTH CAROLINA. DIVISION OF SOCIAL SERVICES See SOCIAL SERVICES PERSONNEL IN NORTH CAROLINA COUNTIES **5309**

NORTH CAROLINA. DIVISION OF STATE BUDGET See GOVERNOR'S STATE OF THE STATE MESSAGE AND BUDGET SUMMARY **4729**

NORTH CAROLINA. DIVISION OF STATE BUDGET See BUDGET - STATE OF NORTH CAROLINA, THE **4715**

NORTH CAROLINA. DIVISION OF STATE BUDGET AND MANAGEMENT. RESEARCH AND PLANNING SERVICES See NORTH CAROLINA POPULATION PROJECTIONS **4555**

NORTH CAROLINA. DIVISION OF YOUTH SERVICES See BIENNIAL REPORT / STATE OF NORTH CAROLINA, DEPARTMENT OF HUMAN RESOURCES, DIVISION OF YOUTH SERVICES **3158**

NORTH CAROLINA. DRUG COMMISSION See STATISTICAL DATA **1350**

NORTH CAROLINA. DRUG COMMISSION See NORTH CAROLINA STATE PLAN FOR DRUG ABUSE PREVENTION FUNCTIONS, THE **1347**

NORTH CAROLINA ECONOMIC ANNUAL REVIEW (US/0732-9326) [07862226] **1576**

NORTH CAROLINA EDUCATION (US/0029-2451) [02449155] **1769**

NORTH CAROLINA EDUCATION DIRECTORY (US/0278-4971) [01696480] **1769**

NORTH CAROLINA EMPLOYMENT LAW LETTER (US/1054-6359) [22923768] **3152**

NORTH CAROLINA ENGINEER (US) [06375248] **1989**

NORTH CAROLINA ENGLISH TEACHER (US/0887-5596) [07336926] **1901**

NORTH CAROLINA FACTS (DALLAS, TEX.) (US/0895-8106) [16809755] **2541**

NORTH CAROLINA FARM BUREAU NEWS (US/0744-9593) [08682881] **115**

NORTH CAROLINA FARM INCOME (US) [21313497] **115**

NORTH CAROLINA FERTILIZER TONNAGE REPORT (US) [08875336] **179**

NORTH CAROLINA FERTILIZER TONNAGE REPORT, MIXED FERTILIZER BY GRADES AND BY COUNTIES See NORTH CAROLINA FERTILIZER TONNAGE REPORT **179**

NORTH CAROLINA FLOWER GROWERS' BULLETIN (US) [16937511] **2426**

NORTH CAROLINA FOLKLORE JOURNAL (US/0090-5844) [01779188] **2323**

NORTH CAROLINA GAME & FISH (US/0897-8816) [17648064] **4876**

NORTH CAROLINA GENEALOGICAL SOCIETY See NORTH CAROLINA GENEALOGICAL SOCIETY JOURNAL, THE **2464**

NORTH CAROLINA GENEALOGICAL SOCIETY JOURNAL, THE (US/0360-1056) [02244842] **2464**

NORTH CAROLINA. GENERAL ASSEMBLY See INDEX OF LEGISLATION **2981**

●NORTH CAROLINA GEOGRAPHER, THE (US/1065-2973) [26566774] **2571**

NORTH CAROLINA. GEOLOGICAL SURVEY SECTION See BULLETIN - NORTH CAROLINA, DEPARTMENT OF NATURAL RESOURCES AND COMMUNITY DEVELOPMENT, DIVISION OF LAND RESOURCES, GEOLOGICAL SURVEY SECTION **1370**

●NORTH CAROLINA HEALTH CARE IN PERSPECTIVE (US/1065-4348) [26606002] **4794**

NORTH CAROLINA HISTORICAL REVIEW, THE (US/0029-2494) [01760560] **2750**

NORTH CAROLINA. HUMAN RELATIONS COMMISSION See ANNUAL REPORT - NORTH CAROLINA HUMAN RELATIONS COMMISSION **5191**

NORTH CAROLINA HUMANITIES (US) **2851**

NORTH CAROLINA IN PERSPECTIVE (US/1065-5611) [25374618] **5334**

NORTH CAROLINA INDEPENDENT, THE (US/0737-8254) [09461031] **5724**

NORTH CAROLINA INFORMATION AND FACT BOOK, THE (US/0193-547X) [04786862] **2750**

NORTH CAROLINA INSIGHT (US) [09729191] **4669**

NORTH CAROLINA. INTANGIBLES TAX SECTION See DISTRIBUTION REPORT OF INTANGIBLE PERSONAL PROPERTY TAX COLLECTIONS AND SPECIAL ALLOCATIONS **4720**

NORTH CAROLINA INTEGRATED TOBACCO PEST MANAGEMENT ... ANNUAL REPORT (US) [05307532] **5373**

NORTH CAROLINA JOURNAL OF INTERNATIONAL LAW AND COMMERCIAL REGULATION (US/0743-1759) [04643761] **3133**

NORTH CAROLINA LABOR FORCE ESTIMATES BY COUNTY, AREA, AND STATE See NORTH CAROLINA LABOR FORCE ESTIMATES BY COUNTY, DEFINED MULTI-COUNTY LABOR AREAS, STATE MULTI-COUNTY PLANNING REGIONS **1695**

NORTH CAROLINA LABOR FORCE ESTIMATES BY COUNTY, DEFINED MULTI-COUNTY LABOR AREAS, STATE MULTI-COUNTY PLANNING REGIONS (US/0147-0531) [03086562] **1695**

NORTH CAROLINA. LABOR MARKET INFORMATION DIVISION See EMPLOYMENT SECURITY LOCAL OFFICE OPERATIONS ANNUAL **1667**

NORTH CAROLINA LAW MONITOR, THE *CEASED.* (US/0883-7783) [11965167] **3018**

NORTH CAROLINA LAW REVIEW (US/0029-2524) [01760563] **3018**

NORTH CAROLINA LAWYERS WEEKLY (US/1041-1747) [17792467] **3018**

NORTH CAROLINA LIBRARIES (US/0029-2540) [01760564] **3237**

●NORTH CAROLINA LITERARY REVIEW (US/1063-0724) [25850956] **3418**

NORTH CAROLINA LOCAL HEALTH DEPARTMENTS : BUDGETARY, ECONOMIC, AND OTHER PERTINENT DATA (US/0098-5783) [02241258] **4794**

NORTH CAROLINA. MANPOWER COUNCIL See BIENNIAL REPORT - NORTH CAROLINA MANPOWER COUNCIL **1655**

NORTH CAROLINA MANUAL (US) [01760536] **4699**

NORTH CAROLINA MANUFACTURING FIRMS ... DIRECTORY See DIRECTORY OF NORTH CAROLINA MANUFACTURING FIRMS **667**

NORTH CAROLINA MEDICAL JOURNAL (WINSTON-SALEM) (US/0029-2559) [01605759] **3916**

NORTH CAROLINA MEDICAL SOCIETY See TRANSACTIONS - NORTH CAROLINA MEDICAL SOCIETY **3647**

NORTH CAROLINA. MIGRANT EDUCATION SECTION See MIGRANT EDUCATION: STATE EVALUATION REPORT **1764**

NORTH CAROLINA MINORITY BUSINESS DIRECTORY (US/0148-0839) [03265139] **699**

NORTH CAROLINA MUNICIPAL EXPENDITURES FROM STATE STREET-AID ALLOCATIONS (US/0361-9532) [02441333] **5442**

NORTH CAROLINA. MUSEUM OF ART, RALEIGH See BULLETIN - NORTH CAROLINA MUSEUM OF ART **4086**

●NORTH CAROLINA NATURALIST (US/1070-468X) [28384716] **4169**

NORTH CAROLINA NEWS MEDIA DIRECTORY (US) **1118**

NORTH CAROLINA. OFFICE OF STATE PERSONNEL See SALARY PLAN, STATE OF NORTH CAROLINA **4684**

NORTH CAROLINA PLUMBING-HEATING-COOLING FORUM (US/0739-3830) [09724139] **2607**

NORTH CAROLINA. POLICE INFORMATION NETWORK See STATE OF NORTH CAROLINA UNIFORM CRIME REPORT **3083**

NORTH CAROLINA POPULATION PROJECTIONS (US) [04610349] **4555**

NORTH CAROLINA QUERIES (US/0897-7755) [17624231] **2464**

NORTH CAROLINA. RECREATION COMMISSION See BIENNIAL REPORT OF THE NORTH CAROLINA RECREATION COMMISSION **4849**

NORTH CAROLINA. RECREATION DIVISION See COUNTY RECREATION & PARK SERVICES STUDY (NORTH CAROLINA) **4706**

NORTH CAROLINA. RECREATION DIVISION See MUNICIPAL RECREATION & PARK SERVICES STUDY **4707**

NORTH CAROLINA RECREATIONAL AND PARK REVIEW (US/0164-4254) [04721847] **4853**

NORTH CAROLINA REGISTER, THE (US) [13686205] **3018**

NORTH CAROLINA RESEARCHER, THE (US/0048-0665) [04112556] **3018**

NORTH CAROLINA RULES OF COURT. FEDERAL (US/1058-255X) [24207627] **3018**

NORTH CAROLINA RULES OF COURT. STATE (US/1058-2568) [24222765] **3018**

NORTH CAROLINA RULES OF COURT, WITH AMENDMENTS RECEIVED TO ... (US/0732-281X) [06950834] **3142**

NORTH CAROLINA SCIENCE TEACHER PROFILE / DIVISION OF SCIENCE, NORTH CAROLINA DEPARTMENT OF PUBLIC INSTRUCTION (US) [10886752] **1867**

NORTH CAROLINA. SECRETARY OF STATE See NORTH CAROLINA MANUAL **4699**

NORTH CAROLINA STATE BAR NEWSLETTER, THE (US/1047-5524) [09013011] **3018**

NORTH CAROLINA STATE BAR QUARTERLY (US/0164-6850) [03921860] **3018**

NORTH CAROLINA STATE PLAN FOR ALCOHOL AND DRUG ABUSE (US/0193-9424) [05243072] **1347**

NORTH CAROLINA STATE PLAN FOR DRUG ABUSE PREVENTION FUNCTIONS See NORTH CAROLINA STATE PLAN FOR DRUG ABUSE PREVENTION FUNCTIONS, THE **1347**

NORTH CAROLINA STATE PLAN FOR DRUG ABUSE PREVENTION FUNCTIONS, THE (US/0197-1050) [05952214] **1347**

NORTH CAROLINA STATE UNIVERSITY AT RALEIGH. SCHOOL OF FOREST RESOURCES See TECHNICAL REPORT - SCHOOL OF FOREST RESOURCES. NORTH CAROLINA STATE UNIVERSITY **2396**

NORTH CAROLINA STUDIES IN THE ROMANCE LANGUAGES AND LITERATURES (US/0885-6001) [01781817] **3306**

NORTH CAROLINA. UNIVERSITY. LIBRARY. HANES FOUNDATION FOR THE STUDY OF THE ORIGIN AND DEVELOPMENT OF THE BOOK See PUBLICATIONS **4148**

NORTH CAROLINA ZIP+4 STATE DIRECTORY (US) [11526392] **1146**

NORTH CAROLINIANA SOCIETY See ANNUAL REPORTS OF THE NORTH CAROLINIANA SOCIETY, INC. AND THE NORTH CAROLINA COLLECTION **2721**

NORTH CASTLE NEWS (US/8750-4537) [11487016] **5719**

NORTH CENTRAL ASSOCIATION OF COLLEGES AND SCHOOLS (U.S.). COMMISSION ON INSTITUTIONS OF HIGHER EDUCATION See BRIEFING **1812**

NORTH CENTRAL ASSOCIATION TODAY See NCA TODAY **1837**

NORTH CENTRAL CAMPING See CAMPBOOK. NORTH CENTRAL **4870**

NORTH CENTRAL FOREST EXPERIMENT STATION (ST. PAUL, MINN.) See FOREST STATISTICS FOR IOWA **2399**

NORTH CENTRAL ILLINOIS GENEALOGICAL SOCIETY (US/0743-961X) [10707212] **2464**

NORTH CENTRAL NEW MEXICO SALARY SURVEY (US/0196-416X) [05802691] **1695**

NORTH CENTRAL NORTH DAKOTA GENEALOGICAL RECORD (US/0736-5667) [08147331] **2464**

NORTH CENTRAL REGIONAL LIBRARY SYSTEM (ONT.) See RAPPORT - NORTH CENTRAL REGIONAL LIBRARY SYSTEM (NEWSLETTER) **3244**

NORTH CENTRAL SALES GUIDE TO HIGH-TECH COMPANIES (US/1040-0540) [18304515] **5134**

NORTH CENTRAL STATE, NIGERIA. MILITARY GOVERNOR'S OFFICE See BUDGET SPEECH OF HIS EXCELLENCY THE MILITARY GOVERNOR **4715**

NORTH — Alphabetical Title Index

NORTH CENTRAL WEED SCIENCE SOCIETY (U.S.) *See* PROCEEDINGS / NORTH CENTRAL WEED SCIENCE SOCIETY **2429**

NORTH CENTRAL WOMEN'S STUDIES NEWSLETTER (US) [08691897] **5563**

NORTH CHESHIRE FAMILY HISTORIAN 1975 (UK/0306-9206) [I03069206] **2464**

NORTH COUNTRY ANVIL (US) [03595919] **2541**

NORTH COUNTRY FARM NEWS (US) [06071300] **115**

NORTH COUNTRY GAZETTE (US/0745-628X) [09328143] **5719**

NORTH COUNTRYMAN, THE (US) [10871205] **5719**

NORTH COUNTY BLADE-CITIZEN, THE (US/1059-5694) [24640663] **5637**

NORTH COUNTY LIVING (US/0164-3665) [04634236] **2541**

NORTH CREEK NEWS ENTERPRISE, THE (US/8750-9245) [11935710] **5719**

NORTH DAKOTA *See* AGENCY BUDGET DETAIL **4708**

NORTH DAKOTA ACADEMIC LIBRARY STATISTICS (US/0094-5455) [01794872] **3237**, **3259**

NORTH DAKOTA ACADEMY OF SCIENCE *See* PROCEEDINGS OF THE NORTH DAKOTA ACADEMY OF SCIENCE **5141**

NORTH DAKOTA ACCIDENT FACTS (US/0095-7712) [01798569] **5442**

NORTH DAKOTA. ADJUTANT GENERAL'S DEPT *See* BIENNIAL REPORT - ADJUTANT GENERAL'S DEPARTMENT, STATE OF NORTH DAKOTA **4037**

NORTH DAKOTA. ADJUTANT GENERAL'S OFFICE. REPORT *See* BIENNIAL REPORT - ADJUTANT GENERAL'S DEPARTMENT, STATE OF NORTH DAKOTA **4037**

NORTH DAKOTA. AGRICULTURAL EXPERIMENT STATION, FARGO. MIP INTERDISCIPLINARY RESEARCH TEAM *See* ANNUAL REPORT ON MARKETING, IRRIGATION, PRODUCTION **163**

NORTH DAKOTA AGRICULTURAL STATISTICS (FARGO, N.D.) (US/0737-1624) [08008202] **115**, **155**

NORTH DAKOTA AND SOUTH DAKOTA LEGAL DIRECTORY, THE (US/0748-2752) [09499629] **3018**

NORTH DAKOTA ARCHAEOLOGICAL ASSOCIATION NEWSLETTER (US) [09237429] **276**

NORTH DAKOTA CASE NAMES CITATOR (US) **3018**

NORTH DAKOTA. COMBINED LAW ENFORCEMENT COUNCIL *See* NORTH DAKOTA COMPREHENSIVE CRIMINAL JUSTICE PLAN **3170**

NORTH DAKOTA COMPREHENSIVE CRIMINAL JUSTICE PLAN (US/0098-0498) [01799233] **3170**

NORTH DAKOTA COMPREHENSIVE LAW ENFORCEMENT PLAN *See* NORTH DAKOTA COMPREHENSIVE CRIMINAL JUSTICE PLAN **3170**

NORTH DAKOTA COUNCIL ON THE ARTS AND HUMANITIES *See* BIENNIAL REPORT / NORTH DAKOTA COUNCIL ON THE ARTS **316**

NORTH DAKOTA COUNCIL ON THE ARTS AND HUMANITIES. BIENNIAL REPORT *See* BIENNIAL REPORT / NORTH DAKOTA COUNCIL ON THE ARTS **316**

NORTH DAKOTA CROP & LIVESTOCK STATISTICS *See* NORTH DAKOTA AGRICULTURAL STATISTICS (FARGO, N.D.) **155**

NORTH DAKOTA. DEPT. OF BANKING AND FINANCIAL INSTITUTIONS *See* REPORT TO THE STATE BANKING BOARD, STATE CREDIT UNION BOARD, AND TO THE GOVERNOR **808**

NORTH DAKOTA. DEPT. OF HUMAN SERVICES *See* BIENNIAL REPORT / NORTH DAKOTA, DEPT. OF HUMAN SERVICES **5274**

NORTH DAKOTA. DEPT. OF PUBLIC INSTRUCTION *See* NORTH DAKOTA EDUCATIONAL FACTS **1769**

NORTH DAKOTA. DEPT. OF PUBLIC INSTRUCTION *See* AMENDED ANNUAL PROGRAM PLAN, PART B, EDUCATION OF THE HANDICAPPED ACT AS AMENDED BY PUBLIC LAW 94-142 **1874**

NORTH DAKOTA. DIVISION OF ALCOHOLISM AND DRUG ABUSE *See* NORTH DAKOTA STATE PLAN FOR ALCOHOL, DRUG ABUSE PREVENTION, TREATMENT, AND REHABILITATION PROGRAMS **1347**

NORTH DAKOTA. DIVISION OF HEALTH FACILITIES *See* PATIENT ORIGIN DATA FOR NORTH DAKOTA HOSPITALS AND NURSING HOMES **3790**

NORTH DAKOTA. EDUCATION FACT FINDING COMMISSION *See* ANNUAL REPORT / EDUCATION FACT FINDING COMMISSION, STATE OF NORTH DAKOTA, THE **1725**

NORTH DAKOTA EDUCATIONAL FACTS (US/0148-7485) [03357572] **1769**

NORTH DAKOTA FARM REPORTER (US/0196-9897) [01980702] **115**

NORTH DAKOTA FARM RESEARCH (US/0097-5338) [01760621] **115**

NORTH DAKOTA. GEOLOGICAL SURVEY *See* REPORT OF INVESTIGATION - NORTH DAKOTA GEOLOGICAL SURVEY **1394**

●NORTH DAKOTA HEALTH CARE IN PERSPECTIVE (US/1065-4356) [26606033] **4794**

NORTH DAKOTA HIGHWAY SAFETY IMPROVEMENT PROGRAM, ANNUAL REPORT (US/0361-8099) [02247123] **4794**, **5442**

NORTH DAKOTA HIGHWAY SAFETY PLAN (US) [10101583] **5442**

NORTH DAKOTA HISTORY (US/0029-2710) [06781857] **2750**

NORTH DAKOTA HORIZONS (US) [01760622] **2750**

NORTH DAKOTA IN PERSPECTIVE (LAWRENCE, KAN.) (US/1065-562X) [26660759] **5334**

NORTH DAKOTA INDUSTRIAL COMMISSION HEARING NOTICES AND ORDERS (US) 1620, **4266**

NORTH DAKOTA INSECTS PUBLICATION (US) [05385654] **5612**

NORTH DAKOTA JUDICIAL MASTER PROGRAM, THE (US/0148-9445) [03392906] **3142**

NORTH DAKOTA JUDICIAL NEWS (US/0362-1812) [02441129] **3018**

NORTH DAKOTA. JUDICIAL PLANNING COMMITTEE *See* NORTH DAKOTA JUDICIAL MASTER PROGRAM, THE **3142**

NORTH DAKOTA LAW REVIEW (US/0029-2745) [01760623] **3018**

NORTH DAKOTA LEAGUE OF CITIES *See* BULLETIN - NORTH DAKOTA LEAGUE OF CITIES **4634**

NORTH DAKOTA. LEGISLATIVE ASSEMBLY. LEGISLATIVE COUNCIL *See* LEGISLATIVE ASSEMBLY REPORT ON APPROPRIATIONS AND ESTIMATED REVENUES **4736**

NORTH DAKOTA MUSIC EDUCATOR (US/0029-2753) [01588536] **4142**

NORTH DAKOTA OUTDOORS (US/0029-2761) [01760628] **4876**

NORTH DAKOTA PEACE OFFICER (US/0744-5148) [03243749] **3170**

NORTH DAKOTA QUARTERLY, THE (US/0029-277X) [01606908] **2541**

NORTH DAKOTA R E C MAGAZINE (US) [01645887] 1298, **1542**

NORTH DAKOTA. SOCIAL SERVICE BOARD *See* STATISTICS : CALENDAR YEAR REVIEW **5267**

NORTH DAKOTA. STATE BOARD FOR VOCATIONAL EDUCATION *See* STATE PLAN FOR VOCATIONAL EDUCATION IN NORTH DAKOTA / STATE BOARD FOR VOCATIONAL EDUCATION **1916**

NORTH DAKOTA. STATE BOARD OF PHARMACY *See* ANNUAL REPORT - NORTH DAKOTA STATE BOARD OF PHARMACY **4291**

NORTH DAKOTA. STATE BOARD OF REGISTRATION FOR PROFESSIONAL ENGINEERS AND LAND SURVEYORS *See* ROSTER OF REGISTERED PROFESSIONAL ENGINEERS AND LAND SURVEYORS : ANNUAL REPORT **2030**

NORTH DAKOTA STATE COLLEGE OF SCIENCE *See* ALUMNI DIRECTORY **1097**

NORTH DAKOTA. STATE DEPT. OF HEALTH *See* STATE PLAN FOR HOSPITAL AND MEDICAL FACILITIES CONSTRUCTION **3792**

NORTH DAKOTA. STATE DEPT. OF HEALTH *See* NORTH DAKOTA STATE PLAN FOR DEVELOPMENTAL DISABILITIES SERVICES AND FACILITIES CONSTRUCTION **5299**

NORTH DAKOTA. STATE HIGHWAY COMMISSION. REPORT *See* BIENNIAL REPORT - NORTH DAKOTA STATE HIGHWAY DEPARTMENT **5439**

NORTH DAKOTA. STATE HIGHWAY DEPT *See* BIENNIAL REPORT - NORTH DAKOTA STATE HIGHWAY DEPARTMENT **5439**

NORTH DAKOTA. STATE LABORATORIES DEPT *See* BIENNIAL REPORT OF THE STATE LABORATORIES AND CONSUMER AFFAIRS DEPARTMENT **4632**

NORTH DAKOTA. STATE LIBRARY COMMISSION *See* NORTH DAKOTA ACADEMIC LIBRARY STATISTICS **3259**

NORTH DAKOTA. STATE LIBRARY COMMISSION *See* NORTH DAKOTA STATE PLAN FOR LIBRARY DEVELOPMENT **3237**

NORTH DAKOTA STATE PLAN FOR ALCOHOL, DRUG ABUSE PREVENTION, TREATMENT, AND REHABILITATION PROGRAMS (US) [05965587] **1347**

NORTH DAKOTA STATE PLAN FOR DEVELOPMENTAL DISABILITIES SERVICES AND FACILITIES CONSTRUCTION (US/0091-1070) [01786264] **5299**

NORTH DAKOTA STATE PLAN FOR LIBRARY DEVELOPMENT (US/0160-0095) [03576569] **3237**

NORTH DAKOTA STATE PLAN FOR VOCATIONAL EDUCATION *See* STATE PLAN FOR VOCATIONAL EDUCATION IN NORTH DAKOTA / STATE BOARD FOR VOCATIONAL EDUCATION **1916**

NORTH DAKOTA STATE UNIVERSITY. COOPERATIVE EXTENSION SERVICE *See* AGRICULTURAL SITUATION AND OUTLOOK **52**

NORTH DAKOTA. STATE UNIVERSITY OF AGRICULTURE AND APPLIED SCIENCE, FARGO. DEPT. OF AGRICULTURAL EDUCATION *See* NORTH DAKOTA VOCATIONAL AGRICULTURE FARM BUSINESS MANAGEMENT EDUCATION **115**

NORTH DAKOTA STATE UNIVERSITY. WATER RESOURCES RESEARCH INSTITUTE *See* RESEARCH REPORT WI **5539**

NORTH DAKOTA. STATE WATER CONSERVATION COMMISSION *See* BIENNIAL REPORT - NORTH DAKOTA. STATE WATER CONSERVATION COMMISSION **5531**

NORTH DAKOTA. TAX DEPT *See* BIENNIAL REPORT FROM THE OFFICE OF STATE TAX COMMISSIONER ... TO THE GOVERNOR AND THE OFFICE OF MANAGEMENT AND BUDGET, STATE OF NORTH DAKOTA **4713**

NORTH DAKOTA. TRAFFIC ENGINEERING DIVISION *See* NORTH DAKOTA HIGHWAY SAFETY IMPROVEMENT PROGRAM, ANNUAL REPORT **5442**

NORTH DAKOTA. TRAFFIC ENGINEERING DIVISION *See* NORTH DAKOTA ACCIDENT FACTS **5442**

NORTH DAKOTA TRAFFIC REPORT (US/0549-852X) [02639095] **5442**

NORTH DAKOTA. TRANSPORTATION SERVICES DIVISION *See* NORTH DAKOTA TRAFFIC REPORT **5442**

NORTH DAKOTA VEHICULAR CRASH FACTS (US) [19461659] **4794**, **5442**

NORTH DAKOTA VOCATIONAL AGRICULTURE FARM BUSINESS MANAGEMENT EDUCATION (US/0097-7853) [01798700] **115**

NORTH DAKOTA WELFARE STATISTICS, CALENDAR YEAR REVIEW *See* STATISTICS : CALENDAR YEAR REVIEW **5267**

NORTH DAKOTA WHEAT VARIETIES (US) [02252649] **179**

NORTH-DEBAT (DK/0105-984X) [I0105984X] **360**

NORTH DELTA SENTINEL (CN/0316-0203) [02247300] **5790**

NORTH EAST COAST INSTITUTION OF ENGINEERS AND SHIPBUILDERS, NEWCASTLE-UPON-TYNE *See* TRANSACTIONS - NORTH EAST COAST INSTITUTION OF ENGINEERS AND SHIPBUILDERS **1999**

NORTH-EAST INDIA COUNCIL FOR SOCIAL SCIENCE RESEARCH *See* JOURNAL OF THE NORTH-EAST INDIA COUNCIL FOR SOCIAL SCIENCE RESEARCH, THE **5207**

NORTH EAST OUT DOORS (US/0199-8463) [06212672] **4876**

NORTH-EAST QUARTERLY (II) [09107467] **2660**

NORTH-EAST REGION COMMUNITY BOOSTER, THE (CN/0703-9034) [03979852] **5790**

NORTH EASTERN AFFAIRS (II/0301-6404) [02239377] **2660**

NORTH EASTERN COUNCIL (INDIA) *See* JOURNAL OF THE NORTH EASTERN COUNCIL **1570**

NORTH EASTERN LINGUISTIC SOCIETY *See* PROCEEDINGS OF NELS **3312**

NORTH EUROPEAN FOOD AND DAIRY JOURNAL (DK/0903-9759) [17368764] **2351**

NORTH FORCE MAGAZINE (US) [24512807] **699**

NORTH FRONTENAC NEWS (CN/0700-950X) [03291455] **5790**

NORTH GEORGIA JOURNAL (US/8756-9256) [11742399] **2750**

NORTH GEORGIA NEWS, THE (US) [19346950] **5654**

NORTH HILLS NEWS RECORD (US/8750-5916) [11586665] **5738**

NORTH-HOLLAND LINGUISTIC SERIES (US) [13877971] **3306**

Alphabetical Title Index — NORTHEAST

NORTH-HOLLAND MATHEMATICAL LIBRARY (NE/0924-6509) [05861953] 3524, **3237**

NORTH-HOLLAND MATHEMATICS STUDIES (NE/0304-0208) [01695416] **3524**

NORTH HOLLAND (NETHERLANDS) *See* BEGROTING. TOELICHTING **4713**

NORTH HOLLAND (NETHERLANDS). BEGROTING: MEMORIE VAN TOELICHTING *See* BEGROTING. TOELICHTING **4713**

NORTH-HOLLAND SERIES IN APPLIED MATHEMATICS AND MECHANICS (NE/0167-5931) [13877775] **2123**

NORTH-HOLLAND SERIES IN STATISTICS AND PROBABILITY (NE/0168-1974) [09379092] **3524**

NORTH HOLLAND SERIES IN SYSTEM SCIENCE AND ENGINEERING (US/0885-5110) [08489267] **5134**

NORTH INDIA CHURCHMAN, THE (II) [01716949] **4982**

NORTH-INFORMATION (DK/0105-2624) [I01052624] **360**

NORTH INTERLAKE ECHO (CN/1182-6126) [23242458] **5791**

NORTH IOWA TIMES (1867) (US) [10958768] **5672**

NORTH IRISH ROOTS (UK/0264-9217) [I02649217] **2464**

NORTH JACKSON PROGRESS (US/0164-9108) [04232976] **5627**

NORTH JEFFERSON NEWS, THE (US) [14120606] **5627**

●NORTH JERSEY COMPUTERUSER (US/1064-0444) [26199587] **1197**

NORTH JERSEY HERALD & NEWS, THE (US/0895-8807) [16816434] **5711**

NORTH JERSEY HIGHLANDER, THE (US/0029-2850) [07718442] **2750**

NORTH JERSEY PROSPECTOR, THE (US/0745-8908) [09541285] **5711**

NORTH JERSEY SUBURBANITE, THE (US/0191-4936) [04936126] **5711**

NORTH KAWARTHA TIMES (CN/0823-7387) [10398410] **5791**

NORTH KOREA QUARTERLY (GW/0340-014X) [02244138] **4484**

NORTH KOREA SEEN FROM ABROAD (KO) [03693217] **2660**

NORTH LAKE TAHOE BONANZA (US/0192-3129) [05055103] **5708**

NORTH LANCE (CN/0821-2376) [09506585] **5791**

NORTH LIGHT (US/0749-6400) [11166925] **360**

NORTH LOUISIANA GENEALOGICAL SOCIETY JOURNAL (US) [10660584] **2464**

NORTH MERIDIAN OBSERVER (US) [18371106] **5666**

NORTH MIDDLESEX FAMILY HISTORY SOCIETY *See* NORTH MIDDLESEX FAMILY HISTORY SOCIETY GENEALOGICAL DIRECTORY, THE **2464**

NORTH MIDDLESEX FAMILY HISTORY SOCIETY GENEALOGICAL DIRECTORY, THE (UK) [12240577] **2464**

NORTH MUNSTER ANTIQUARIAN JOURNAL (IE/0332-0820) [I03320820] **1078**

NORTH OAHU PLANET (US) [23247032] **5656**

NORTH OF 60. MINES AND MINERALS ACTIVITIES (CN/0590-580X) [01795141] **2147**

NORTH PEACE PICTORIAL (CN/0700-3420) [03264595] **2541**

NORTH PLATTE TELEGRAPH *See* TELEGRAPH (NORTH PLATTE, NEB.) **5707**

NORTH QUEENSLAND NATURALIST (AT/0078-1630) [06243159] **4169**

NORTH RHINE-WESTPHALIA (GERMANY). GEOLOGISCHES LANDESAMT *See* TATIGKEITSBERICHT - GEOLOGISCHES LANDESAMT NORDRHEIN-WESTFALIA **1399**

NORTH RHINE-WESTPHALIA (GERMANY). KULTUSMINISTERIUM *See* GEMEINSAMES AMTSBLATT DES KULTUSMINISTERIUMS UND DES MINISTERIUMS FUR WISSENSCHAFT UND FORSCHUNG DES LANDES NORDRHEIN-WESTFALEN **1748**

NORTH RHINE-WESTPHALIA (GERMANY). LANDESAMT FUR DATENVERARBEITUNG UND STATISTIK *See* INDUSTRIE IN NORDRHEIN-WESTFALEN, DIE **5328**

NORTH RHINE-WESTPHALIA (GERMANY). LANDESAMT FUR DATENVERARBEITUNG UND STATISTIK *See* GESUNDHEITSWESEN IN NORDRHEIN-WESTFALEN, DAS **4810**

NORTH RHINE-WESTPHALIA (GERMANY). LANDESAMT FUR DATENVERARBEITUNG UND STATISTIK *See* STRASSEN, BRUCKEN UND PARKEINRICHTUNGEN **4689**

NORTH RHINE-WESTPHALIA (GERMANY). LANDESAMT FUR DATENVERARBEITUNG UND STATISTIK *See* ARBEITSKOSTEN IM HANDEL SOWIE IM BANK- UND VERSICHERUNGSGEWERBE, DIE **1651**

NORTH RHINE-WESTPHALIA (GERMANY). LANDESAMT FUR DATENVERARBEITUNG UND STATISTIK *See* LANDWIRTSCHAFT IN NORDRHEIN-WESTFALEN, DIE **104**

NORTH RHINE-WESTPHALIA (GERMANY). LANDESAMT FUR DATENVERARBEITUNG UND STATISTIK *See* BEVOLKERUNG IN NORDRHEIN-WESTFALEN, DIE **4561**

NORTH RHINE-WESTPHALIA (GERMANY). LANDESAMT FUR DATENVERARBEITUNG UND STATISTIK *See* REGIONALISIERTE SCHULERPROGNOSEN **1796**

NORTH RHINE-WESTPHALIA (GERMANY). LANDESAMT FUR DATENVERARBEITUNG UND STATISTIK *See* BAUWIRTSCHAFT UND BAUTATIGKEIT IN NORDRHEIN-WESTFALEN **5323**

NORTH RHINE-WESTPHALIA (GERMANY). LANDESAMT FUR DATENVERARBEITUNG UND STATISTIK *See* WOHNGELD IN NORDRHEIN-WESTFALEN **2841**

NORTH RHINE-WESTPHALIA (GERMANY). LANDESAMT FUR DATENVERARBEITUNG UND STATISTIK *See* BILDUNGSWESEN IN NORDRHEIN-WESTFALEN, DAS **1728**

NORTH RHINE-WESTPHALIA (GERMANY). MINISTERIUM FUER WIRTSCHAFT, MITTELSTAND UND VERKEHR *See* FORSCHUNGSBERICHTE DES LANDES NORDRHEIN-WESTFALEN **5105**

NORTH RHINE-WESTPHALIA. KULTUSMINISTERIUM. AMTSBLATT *See* GEMEINSAMES AMTSBLATT DES KULTUSMINISTERIUMS UND DES MINISTERIUMS FUR WISSENSCHAFT UND FORSCHUNG DES LANDES NORDRHEIN-WESTFALEN **1748**

NORTH RHINE-WESTPHALIA. LANDESAMT FUR DATENVERARBEITUNG UND STATISTIK *See* AUSSENHANDEL NORDRHEIN-WESTFALENS : AUS- UND EIN-FUHR. VORLAEUFIGE ERGEBNISSE, DER **824**

NORTH RHINE-WESTPHALIA. LANDESAMT FUR DATENVERARBEITUNG UND STATISTIK *See* AUSSENHANDEL NORDRHEIN-WESTFALENS, DER **726**

NORTH RHINE-WESTPHALIA. LANDESAMT FUR DATENVERARBEITUNG UND STATISTIK *See* EINFUHR NORDRHEIN-WESTFALENS, DIE **832**

NORTH RHINE-WESTPHALIA. LANDESAMT FUR DATENVERARBEITUNG UND STATISTIK *See* KREISSTANDARDZAHLEN **5330**

NORTH RHINE-WESTPHALIA. STATISTISCHES LANDESAMT. AUSFUHR NORDRHEIN-WESTFALENS IM JAHR *See* AUSFUHR NORDRHEIN-WESTFALENS, DIE **824**

NORTH SAN ANTONIO TIMES, THE (US) [16844544] **5753**

NORTH SCOTT PRESS, THE (US) [18757181] **5672**

NORTH SEA MONITOR (NE/0168-1753) [I01681753] **5453**

NORTH SEA OIL & GAS DIRECTORY (UK) [09098981] **4266**

NORTH SEA RIG REPORT (UK) [I09590986] **4266**

NORTH SEA SERVICE (UK) **4266**

NORTH SEA SERVICE MONTHLY REPORT *See* NORTH SEA SERVICE **4266**

NORTH SEA SEVICE (UK) **4266**

NORTH SEA VALUATION SERVICE (UK) **4266**

NORTH SHORE (US/0164-5366) [04562960] **2541**

NORTH SHORE (MINEOLA, N.Y.) (US) [08622690] **2541**

NORTH SHORE NEWS (CN/0712-5348) [09137859] **5791**

NORTH SHORE SENTINEL (CN/0715-5786) [09403323] **5791**

NORTH SHORE : SUNDAY (US) [28658080] **5689**

NORTH SHORE TIMES (STE-THERESE) (CN/0701-0761) [03406400] **5791**

NORTH SIDE NEWS (US) [08797799] **5657**

NORTH SIDE TOPICS, BROAD RIPPLE-GLENDALE, THE (US) [23199605] **5666**

NORTH SOUTH (US/1058-3416) [24119006] **4484**

●NORTH-SOUTH ISSUES (US) [26540079] **2751**

NORTH / SOUTH ISSUES : BIBLIOGRAPHY OF THEORETICAL AND CURRENT EVENT ANALYSIS (FR) **421**

NORTH-SOUTH NEWS *See* REVIEW - NORTH-SOUTH INSTITUTE (OTTAWA) **1625**

NORTH SOUTH TRADER'S CIVIL WAR (US/1053-0010) [20978045] **2624**

NORTH STAR (US/0092-2021) [01789281] **4142**

NORTH STAR BAPTIST (US/0744-0278) [06459103] **4982**

NORTH STONE REVIEW, THE (US/1046-9389) [01714178] **3418**

NORTH SUBURBAN PRESS (US/0892-1792) [15144254] **5697**

NORTH SURBURBAN PRESS *See* LITTLE CANADA PRESS **5696**

NORTH SURBURBAN PRESS *See* VADNAIS HEIGHTS PRESS **5699**

NORTH SURBURBAN PRESS *See* SHOREVIEW PRESS **5698**

NORTH TEXAS DAILY, THE (US) [17435854] **5753**

NORTH TEXAS TRAIL TRACERS (US/0893-2948) [15171951] **2464**

NORTH THOMPSON JOURNAL (CN/0823-7425) [10451255] **2541**

NORTH VERNON PLAIN DEALER, THE (US) [11912443] **5666**

NORTH VERNON SUN (US) [11171199] **5666**

NORTH WEST COURANT (CN/0838-4967) [19579712] **3185**

NORTH WEST EUROPE COMPANY REPORT (UK) **4266**

NORTH WEST EUROPE SERVICE (UK) **4266**

NORTH WEST EUROPE SERVICE (UK) **4266**

NORTH-WESTERN EUROPEAN LANGUAGE EVOLUTION (DK/0108-8416) [10547447] **3306**

NORTH-WESTERN EUROPEAN LANGUAGE EVOLUTION. SUPPLEMENT (DK/0900-8675) [15147493] **3306**

NORTH-WESTERN STATE SCHOOL DIRECTORY (NR) [03488092] **1769**

NORTH WIND (UK/0265-7295) [18594011] **3418**

NORTH WIND (VANCOUVER) (CN/0316-6953) [02247788] **5299**

NORTH WOODS CALL, THE (US/0029-2958) [03462983] 2201, **4876**

NORTH YORK CONSUMER, THE (CN/0225-2082) [06156757] **5791**

NORTH YORK NEWS (1970?) (CN/0841-2707) [20109304] **5791**

NORTH YORK (ONT.) *See* LIVING IN NORTH YORK **2568**

NORTH YORK (ONT.) *See* INFO / NORTH YORK **4656**

NORTH YORK PUBLIC LIBRARY ONT.). URBAN AFFAIRS SECTION *See* CENTRAL LIBRARY SELECTED ACQUISITIONS RELATING TO URBAN AFFAIRS **413**

NORTHAMPTON COUNTY REPORTER, THE (US) [01716859] **3018**

NORTHAMPTONSHIRE PAST & PRESENT (UK) [01607585] **2700**

NORTHBOUND (EAGLE RIVER, WIS.) (US/1070-812X) [20181413] **2201**

NORTHBROOK LIFE (US/0191-6300) [05011315] **5661**

NORTHBROOK NEWS/VOICE (US/0745-9777) [09650256] **5661**

NORTHBROOK STAR (US/0744-9550) [08672182] **5661**

NORTHEAST (US/0549-8880) [02420107] **3418**

NORTHEAST AFRICAN STUDIES (US/0740-9133) [05899077] **2500**

NORTHEAST ALABAMA SETTLERS (US/0742-583X) [05845079] **2464**

NORTHEAST & MIDWEST MINING DIRECTORY (US/1060-8036) [25067315] **2147**

●NORTHEAST ANTHROPOLOGY (US/1068-9982) [27876398] **242**

NORTHEAST EQUINE JOURNAL (US) **2801**

NORTHEAST FISH AND WILDLIFE CONFERENCE *See* TRANSACTIONS - NORTHEAST FISH & WILDLIFE CONFERENCE **2315**

NORTHEAST FOLKLORE (US/0078-1681) [02182916] **2323**

NORTHEAST GEORGIAN (US) [19550403] **5654**

NORTHEAST GULF SCIENCE (US/0148-9836) [03398258] 556, **1453**

NORTHEAST

Alphabetical Title Index

NORTHEAST HISTORICAL ARCHAEOLOGY (US/0048-0738) [03531764] **2751**

NORTHEAST IMPROVER, THE (US/0145-9112) [01524666] **197**

NORTHEAST INDIAN QUARTERLY *See* AKWE:KON JOURNAL **2717**

NORTHEAST JOURNAL OF BUSINESS & ECONOMICS, THE (US/8755-5123) [11036462] 699, **1508**

●NORTHEAST JOURNAL OF TRANSPORTATION, THE (US/1061-8090) [25471486] **5388**

NORTHEAST MARYLAND WASTE DISPOSAL AUTHORITY *See* ANNUAL REPORT AND AUDITED FINANCIAL STATEMENTS / NORTHEAST MARYLAND WASTE DISPOSAL AUTHORITY **2224**

NORTHEAST MISSISSIPPI DAILY JOURNAL (US/0744-5431) [08338968] **5701**

NORTHEAST MISSISSIPPI HISTORICAL & GENEALOGICAL SOCIETY QUARTERLY, THE (US/1060-5568) [07495851] **2464**

NORTHEAST MONITORING PROGRAM ... ANNUAL REPORT (US/0748-9110) [09865426] 1453, **2237**

NORTHEAST OHIO LEGAL SERVICES *See* NOLSLETTER **3180**

NORTHEAST OIL AND GAS WORLD (US/1070-4469) [28226476] **4267**

NORTHEAST OIL WORLD (US/0884-4771) [12364050] **4267**

NORTHEAST PENNSYLVANIA BUSINESS JOURNAL (US) [17392128] **699**

NORTHEAST PETROLEUM DIRECTORY (US) **4267**

NORTHEAST POWER REPORT (US/1049-0736) [20991643] **2074**

NORTHEAST REAL ESTATE NEWS (US/1047-8833) [20805276] **4842**

NORTHEAST RECYCLING COUNCIL NEWS (US) **2237**

NORTHEAST REPORTER (US) [16458249] **5666**

NORTHEAST RIDING (US/0746-7893) [10290855] **4082**

NORTHEAST SUN (US/0738-971X) [09498604] **1951**

NORTHEAST TIMES (PHILADELPHIA, PA. : 1971) (US) [12603305] **5738**

NORTHEAST WILDLIFE (US) [28856396] **2201**

NORTHEASTER (US) [08647893] **5697**

NORTHEASTERN CAMPING *See* CAMPBOOK. NORTHEASTERN **4870**

NORTHEASTERN FOREST EXPERIMENT STATION (RADNOR, PA.) *See* REPORT - NORTHEASTERN FOREST EXPERIMENT STATION (BROOMALL, PA.) (1977/78) **2392**

NORTHEASTERN GEOLOGY (US/0194-1453) [05324931] **1390**

NORTHEASTERN JOURNAL OF AGRICULTURAL AND RESOURCE ECONOMICS (US/0899-367X) [11878420] **115**

NORTHEASTERN NEVADA HISTORICAL SOCIETY *See* QUARTERLY - NORTHEASTERN NEVADA HISTORICAL SOCIETY **2756**

NORTHEASTERN NEWS, THE (US/0029-3032) [04123463] **1093**

NORTHEASTERN RESOURCES COMMITTEE *See* MINUTES OF THE MEETING - NORTHEASTERN RESOURCES COMMITTEE **2198**

NORTHEASTERN STATES *See* NORTHEASTERN TOUR BOOK **5486**

NORTHEASTERN TOUR BOOK (US/0468-6853) [01793860] **5486**

NORTHEASTERN WEED SCIENCE SOCIETY (U.S.). MEETING *See* PROCEEDINGS OF THE ... ANNUAL MEETING OF THE NORTHEASTERN WEED SCIENCE SOCIETY **2180**

NORTHERN ALBERTA FARMER (FORT SASKATCHEWAN) (CN/0715-4674) [09166954] **115**

NORTHERN AQUACULTURE (CN/1183-2428) [23121868] **2309**

NORTHERN ARCHITECT (UK/0305-0173) [04935773] **305**

NORTHERN BREED, THE (CN/0703-8364) [03520250] **2751**

NORTHERN BUSINESS AND ECONOMIC REVIEW *CEASED.* (US/0732-1899) [08320265] **1593**

●NORTHERN BUSINESS INFORMATION'S TELECOM PERSPECTIVES (US/1078-523X) [31113557] **1161**

NORTHERN CALIFORNIA BUSINESS DIRECTORY (NEWPORT BEACH, CALIF.) (US/1052-8822) [22409061] **699**

NORTHERN CALIFORNIA COURT RULES (US) **3142**

NORTHERN CALIFORNIA HOME & GARDEN *CEASED.* (US/0898-1191) [17739479] **2902**

NORTHERN CALIFORNIA HORSEMAN'S DIRECTORY *See* CALIFORNIA/NEVADA HORSEMAN'S DIRECTORY **2797**

NORTHERN CALIFORNIA JEWISH BULLETIN (US/0745-0664) [08810011] **5051**

●NORTHERN CALIFORNIA LEGAL RESOURCE MANUAL (US/1056-2508) [23600156] **3018**

NORTHERN CALIFORNIA MEDICINE (US) **3623**

NORTHERN CALIFORNIA MONTHLY (US/0897-8298) [17636429] **2541**

NORTHERN CALIFORNIA SUN (US/8755-8866) [11006249] **1951**

NORTHERN CATHOLIC HISTORY (UK/0307-4455) [03200539] 2700, **5033**

NORTHERN CERAMIC SOCIETY *See* JOURNAL - NORTHERN CERAMIC SOCIETY **2591**

NORTHERN COLORADO BUSINESS INFORMATION FACTBOOK (US) [04023205] **700**

NORTHERN COLORADO BUSINESS REVIEW (US) [04271577] **700**

NORTHERN COLORADO COMPENSATION SURVEY (US) [11706753] **1695**

NORTHERN CURLING REVIEW (CN/0829-3856) [19043757] **4908**

NORTHERN DECISIONS *CEASED.* (CN/0715-7983) [10858469] **3115**

NORTHERN ENGINEER, THE *SUSPENDED.* (US/0029-3083) [02265207] **1989**

NORTHERN FOREST EXPERIMENT STATION *See* U. S. FOREST SERVICE RESEARCH NOTE NOR **2397**

NORTHERN HISTORY (UK/0078-172X) [01760664] **2624**

NORTHERN ILLINOIS UNIVERSITY LAW REVIEW (US/0734-1490) [07341361] **3018**

NORTHERN INDIANA HEALTH SYSTEMS AGENCY *See* ANNUAL REPORT - NORTHERN INDIANA HEALTH SYSTEMS AGENCY **4766**

NORTHERN INDIANA HEALTH SYSTEMS AGENCY *See* ANNUAL IMPLEMENTATION PLAN FOR NORTHERN INDIANA, AN **4765**

NORTHERN IRELAND (UK) [02436142] **2808**

NORTHERN IRELAND ANNUAL ABSTRACT OF STATISTICS (IE/0267-6044) [11065460] **5335**

NORTHERN IRELAND. DEPT. OF EDUCATION *See* SUMMARY OF EDUCATION AND LIBRARY BOARDS' ACCOUNTS TOGETHER WITH THE REPORT OF THE COMPTROLLER AND AUDITOR GENERAL **1872**

NORTHERN IRELAND. DEPT. OF FINANCE *See* STATEMENT OF SUMS REQUIRED ON ACCOUNT **4750**

NORTHERN IRELAND. DEPT. OF FINANCE *See* FINANCIAL STATEMENT - DEPARTMENT OF FINANCE (NORTHERN IRELAND) **4725**

NORTHERN IRELAND. DEPT. OF FINANCE *See* PUBLIC INCOME & EXPENDITURE **4743**

NORTHERN IRELAND. DEPT. OF HEALTH AND SOCIAL SERVICES *See* SUMMARY OF HEALTH AND PERSONAL SOCIAL SERVICES ACCOUNTS **4804**

NORTHERN IRELAND. DEPT. OF HEALTH AND SOCIAL SERVICES. SUMMARY OF HEALTH SERVICES ACCOUNTS *See* SUMMARY OF HEALTH AND PERSONAL SOCIAL SERVICES ACCOUNTS **4804**

NORTHERN IRELAND. DEPT. OF THE ENVIRONMENT *See* DISTRICT COUNCILS SUMMARY OF STATEMENTS OF ACCOUNTS - (NORTHERN IRELAND) **4720**

NORTHERN IRELAND. DEPT. OF THE ENVIRONMENT *See* ANNUAL REPORT - DEPARTMENT OF THE ENVIRONMENT (NORTHERN IRELAND) **2160**

NORTHERN IRELAND. EASTERN HEALTH AND SOCIAL SERVICES BOARD *See* ANNUAL REPORT / EASTERN HEALTH AND SOCIAL SERVICES BOARD, NORTHERN IRELAND **4765**

NORTHERN IRELAND ELECTRICITY SERVICE *See* ANNUAL REPORT AND ACCOUNTS - NORTHERN IRELAND ELECTRICITY SERVICE **2035**

NORTHERN IRELAND HOUSING EXECUTIVE *See* ACCOUNTS OF THE NORTHERN IRELAND HOUSING EXECUTIVE **2813**

NORTHERN IRELAND LAW REPORTS, THE (IE) [04995933] **3018**

NORTHERN IRELAND LEGAL QUARTERLY, THE (IE/0029-3105) [01760668] **3018**

NORTHERN IRELAND. MINISTRY OF FINANCE. FINANCIAL STATEMENT *See* FINANCIAL STATEMENT - DEPARTMENT OF FINANCE (NORTHERN IRELAND) **4725**

NORTHERN IRELAND. MINISTRY OF FINANCE. PUBLIC INCOME AND EXPENDITURE, NORTHERN IRELAND *See* PUBLIC INCOME & EXPENDITURE **4743**

NORTHERN IRELAND. NATURE RESERVES COMMITTEE *See* REPORT OF THE NATURE RESERVES COMMITTEE **2203**

NORTHERN IRELAND. STANDING ADVISORY COMMISSION ON HUMAN RIGHTS *See* REPORT OF THE STANDING ADVISORY COMMISSION ON HUMAN RIGHTS **4512**

NORTHERN IRELAND. TRAINING COUNCIL *See* NORTHERN IRELAND TRAINING COUNCIL REPORT **1695**

NORTHERN IRELAND TRAINING COUNCIL REPORT (UK) [04156422] **1695**

NORTHERN JOURNAL OF APPLIED FORESTRY (US/0742-6348) [10394971] **2389**

NORTHERN JOURNAL, THE (CN/0715-514X) [09318305] **5791**

NORTHERN KENTUCKY LAW REVIEW (US/0198-8549) [02986901] **3018**

NORTHERN LIFE (SUDBURY) (CN/0700-527X) [03400004] **5791**

NORTHERN LIGHTS (US) [12147526] **2541**

NORTHERN LIGHTS (CHELMSFORD) (CN/0822-0808) [12204289] **3467**

NORTHERN LOGGER AND TIMBER PROCESSOR, THE (US/0029-3156) [03236807] **2403**

NORTHERN MARIANA ISLANDS REPORTS : CASES ARGUED AND DETERMINED IN THE SUPREME COURT OF THE COMMONWEALTH OF THE NORTHERN MARIANA ISLANDS (NW) [24037683] **3019**

●NORTHERN MARINER : JOURNAL OF THE CANADIAN NAUTICAL RESEARCH SOCIETY LE MARIN DU NORD : REVUE DE SOCIETE CANADIENNE POUR LA RECHERCHE NAUTIQUE, THE (CN/1183-112X) [23830597] **4181**

NORTHERN MICHIGAN NEWS (US/0194-3014) [05431370] **5693**

NORTHERN MINER MAGAZINE, THE *CEASED.* (CN/0830-9396) [15157807] **2147**

NORTHERN MINER, THE (CN/0029-3164) [02084190] **2147**

NORTHERN MOSAIC (THUNDER BAY) *SUSPENDED.* (CN/0384-0840) [03233228] **5791**

NORTHERN MOSAIC (LLOYDMINSTER) (CN/0824-3484) [10335046] **326**

NORTHERN NECK OF VIRGINIA HISTORICAL MAGAZINE (US/0549-9186) [04308825] **2751**

NORTHERN NEW ENGLAND LEGAL DIRECTORY, MAINE, NEW HAMPSHIRE, AND VERMONT, THE (US/0194-0015) [04845041] **3019**

NORTHERN NEW ENGLAND REVIEW (US/0190-3012) [02606456] **3418**

NORTHERN NUT GROWERS ASSOCIATION *See* ANNUAL REPORT OF THE NORTHERN NUT GROWERS ASSOCIATION **61**

NORTHERN OHIO LIVE (US/0271-5147) [06631805] **2541**

NORTHERN ONTARIO BUSINESS (CN/0710-2755) [08260440] **700**

NORTHERN ONTARIO CATALOG (CN/1181-1358) [24256979] **3237**

NORTHERN ONTARIO CONSTRUCTION & RESOURCE INDUSTRIES DIRECTORY, PURCHASING GUIDE (CN/0229-1983) [09355019] **622**

NORTHERN PEN (CN/0229-0391) [08046044] **5791**

NORTHERN PERSPECTIVE (AT/0314-989X) 3467, **3418**

NORTHERN PERSPECTIVES (CN/0380-5522) [02084553] 2219, **2201**

NORTHERN PIONEER, THE (CN/0383-1221) [02862234] **5791**

NORTHERN POLITICS REVIEW (CN/0823-9576) [11703546] **4502**

NORTHERN RAVEN, THE (US/0277-0997) [03804764] **4169**

NORTHERN RESEARCH AND EDUCATION AT YUKON COLLEGE (CN/1183-0875) [24368274] **2751**

NORTHERN REVIEW, THE (US/0894-3362) [15998764] **326**

NORTHERN REVIEW (WHITEHORSE) (CN) [18921204] 5211, **326**

NORTHERN SCOTLAND (UK/0306-5278) [01796510] **2700**

NORTHERN SOCIAL SCIENCE REVIEW (US/0196-1063) [05720697] **5211**

NORTHERN STAR (LAKE VILLAGE, IND.) (US) [14866962] **5666**

Alphabetical Title Index — NORTHWESTERN

NORTHERN STATE COLLEGE *See* FINANCIAL REPORT - NORTHERN STATE COLLEGE **1824**

NORTHERN STATE TEACHERS' COLLEGE, ABERDEEN, S.D. FINANCIAL REPORT *See* FINANCIAL REPORT - NORTHERN STATE COLLEGE **1824**

NORTHERN STATES POWER COMPANY. ENGINEERING VICE PRESIDENTIAL STAFF DEPT *See* ENVIRONMENTAL MONITORING AND ECOLOGICAL STUDIES PROGRAM **2168**

NORTHERN SUN (US) [17063858] **4053**

NORTHERN TERRITORY. DEPT. OF PRIMARY INDUSTRY AND FISHERIES *See* ANNUAL REPORT - NORTHERN TERRITORY. DEPARTMENT OF PRIMARY INDUSTRY AND FISHERIES **2294**

●NORTHERN TERRITORY IN FOCUS (AT/1037-1176) [26343512] **2670**

NORTHERN TERRITORY LEGISLATION (AT) **3019**

NORTHERN TERRITORY PARENT (AT/0811-7195) [I08117195] **1867**

NORTHERN TERRITORY STATISTICAL SUMMARY *See* NORTHERN TERRITORY IN FOCUS **2670**

NORTHERN TIMES (WHITEHORSE) (CN/0227-2512) [06958549] **5791**

NORTHERN VICTORIA FRUITGROWER (AT) [03726643] **179**

NORTHERN VIRGINIA MAGAZINE (US/1050-6063) [21550742] **2541**

NORTHERN VIRGINIA MARKETING DIRECTORY (US/1058-5494) [22902695] **934**

NORTHERN VIRGINIA SUN (US/1065-1632) [26521489] **5759**

NORTHERN VIRGINIAN *SUSPENDED.* (US/0164-6710) [04428344] **2541**

NORTHERN VOICE (CN/1183-5869) [24690798] **2201**

NORTHERN WOMAN JOURNAL (CN/0824-4081) [10441071] **5563**

NORTHERN WYOMING DAILY NEWS, THE (US) [22425750] **5772**

NORTHERN YUKON NATIONAL PARK (CN/1186-799X) [24571282] **4707**

NORTHERN YUKON NATIONAL PARK (CN/1186-799X) [24571283] **4707**

NORTHERNHER (YELLOWKNIFE) (CN/1181-7496) [23469504] **5563**

NORTHERNTIER LEGAL JOURNAL (US/0735-5505) [08674334] **3019**

NORTHFIELD NEWS, THE (US/1053-542X) [10155250] **5697**

NORTHGLENN-THORNTON SENTINEL (US) **5644**

NORTHLAND QUARTERLY, THE (US/0899-708X) [18185919] **3418**

NORTHLAND TODAY MAGAZINE (US/0707-3364) [04635261] **5486**

NORTHLIGHT (TEMPE, ARIZ.) *SUSPENDED.* (US/0277-8076) [04960386] **4372**

NORTHLINE (CN/0714-475X) [09166849] **1838**

NORTHPOINT (CN/0380-0881) [02085985] **5134**

NORTHPORT JOURNAL (US) [10906437] **5719**

NORTHROP FRYE NEWSLETTER (US/1058-062X) [19695164] **4353**

NORTHROP UNIV. LAW J. AEROSP., BUS. TAX *CEASED.* (US/0887-4301) [13223658] **3019**

NORTHSHORE CITIZEN (1990) (US/1057-3771) [21575492] **5761**

NORTHSIDE NEIGHBOR, THE (US/0192-0731) [04997717] **5654**

NORTHSIDE SUN, THE (US) [15491268] **5701**

NORTHSTAR NEWS & ANALYSIS *CEASED.* (US/1051-0249) [21766552] **2270**

NORTHUMBERLAND NEWS *CEASED.* (CN/0228-0531) [06958971] **5791**

●NORTHUMBERLAND PUBLISHERS' WEEKENDER (CN/1186-5601) [26497762] **5791**

NORTHUMBRIANA (UK) [06499699] **2520**

NORTHVILLE RECORD (NORTHVILLE, MICH. : 1871) (US/1050-2467) [12253302] **5693**

NORTHWARD JOURNAL *CEASED.* (CN/0706-0955) [05528418] **360**

NORTHWEST ALABAMIAN (HALEYVILLE, ALA.) (US) [15390334] **5627**

NORTHWEST ANTHROPOLOGICAL RESEARCH NOTES (US/0029-3296) [02859332] **242**

NORTHWEST ARKANSAS TIMES (FAYETTEVILLE, AR.) (US/1066-3355) [18117496] **5632**

NORTHWEST ARTS *CEASED.* (US/0744-4680) [04976676] **326**

NORTHWEST ASSOCIATION OF SCHOOLS AND COLLEGES. MEETING *See* PROCEEDINGS & DIRECTORY / NORTHWEST ASSOCIATION OF SCHOOLS AND COLLEGES **1842**

NORTHWEST ATLANTIC FISHERIES ORGANIZATION *See* ANNUAL REPORT / NORTHWEST ATLANTIC FISHERIES ORGANIZATION **2294**

NORTHWEST ATLANTIC FISHERIES ORGANIZATION. SCIENTIFIC COUNCIL *See* SCIENTIFIC COUNCIL REPORTS **2312**

NORTHWEST BAPTIST WITNESS (US/0745-2195) [08924525] **5065**

NORTHWEST BERRY PROCESSING REPORT (US) **115**

NORTHWEST BOAT TRAVEL (US/0192-1169) [05019858] **5486**, **594**

NORTHWEST CANADA ECHOES *See* ECHOES (MEDICINE HAT) **4955**

NORTHWEST CHESS (US/0146-6941) [02996952] **4864**

NORTHWEST COLLEGE *See* ALUMNI DIRECTORY / NORTHWEST COLLEGE **1099**

●NORTHWEST COLORADO OFFICIAL TRAVEL GUIDE (US/1062-1415) [25532056] **5486**

NORTHWEST CORPORATION ANNUAL REPORT (US) [13714697] **801**

NORTHWEST DENTISTRY (US/0029-2915) [01624056] **1331**

NORTHWEST DISCOVERY (US/0272-1570) [06738848] **4169**

NORTHWEST ENERGY NEWS (US/0885-5870) [08363281] **2201**

NORTHWEST ENVIRONMENTAL JOURNAL *See* ILLAHEE (SEATTLE, WASH.) **2173**

NORTHWEST ENVIRONMENTAL JOURNAL, THE (US/0749-7962) [11193852] **2179**

NORTHWEST ETHNIC NEWS (US/0894-3109) [12570451] **2270**

NORTHWEST EUROPE UPSTREAM PETROLEUM DATABASE (UK) **4267**

NORTHWEST EVANGELICAL BAPTIST JOURNAL (CN/1180-5323) [25796335] **5065**

NORTHWEST EXPERIENCE, THE (US/0197-3665) [06007986] **1576**

NORTHWEST EXPLORER (SIOUX LOOKOUT) *CEASED.* (CN/0712-5089) [09128378] **5791**

NORTHWEST EXPLORER (YELLOWKNIFE) (CN/0820-6724) [09925389] **2541**

NORTHWEST FARM EQUIPMENT JOURNAL (US/0029-3350) [07405925] **160**

NORTHWEST FLORIDA DAILY NEWS (US/0898-168X) [17737533] **5650**

NORTHWEST FOLKLORE (US/0029-3369) [01715794] **2323**

NORTHWEST GEOLOGY *CEASED.* (US/0096-7769) [01375771] **1390**

NORTHWEST GEORGIA HISTORICAL & GENEALOGICAL QUARTERLY (US/0887-588X) [08721737] **2464**

NORTHWEST GRAPE GROWER AND WINEMAKER (US) [11763847] **2370**

NORTHWEST HISTORICAL SERIES (US/0078-1789) [01995241] **2751**

NORTHWEST INDIAN NEWS (US/0146-1877) [02868613] **2270**

NORTHWEST LABOR PRESS (US/0894-444X) [15712350] **5733**

●NORTHWEST LITERARY FORUM (US/1062-3353) [25587345] **3349**

NORTHWEST LIVING *CEASED.* (US/0888-5346) [13663036] **2541**

NORTHWEST MISSOURI GENEALOGY SOCIETY JOURNAL (US/0741-8248) [10189854] **2464**

NORTHWEST (NEW YORK, N.Y.) (US/0898-2031) [17742557] **2571**

NORTHWEST OHIO QUARTERLY (US/0029-3407) [01760706] **2751**

NORTHWEST OIL REPORT (US/0739-0262) [09701244] **4267**

NORTHWEST PALATE, THE (US/0892-8363) [15272824] **2351**

NORTHWEST PARKS & WILDLIFE (US/1060-4812) [24944949] **4169**

NORTHWEST PASSAGES HISTORICAL NEWSLETTER (US/0885-7628) [12714650] **2751**

NORTHWEST PLAYER (US/0737-5530) [09002354] **4908**

NORTHWEST PORTFOLIO *CEASED.* (US/1040-1784) [18338517] **2571**

NORTHWEST POWER PLANNING COUNCIL (U.S.) *See* UPDATE! / NORTHWEST POWER PLANNING COUNCIL **1959**

NORTHWEST PUBLIC POWER BULLETIN (US/1055-6761) [02860500] **1951**

NORTHWEST QUILL *See* MIDTOWN NEWS **5732**

●NORTHWEST REGIONAL FORECAST OF POWER LOADS AND RESOURCES FOR ... / COMPILED BY PACIFIC NORTHWEST UTILITIES CONFERENCE COMMITTEE, SYSTEM PLANNING OFFICE (US) [09664345] **1951**

NORTHWEST RELOCATION NEWS *See* SMALL TOWN OBSERVER, THE **2835**

NORTHWEST REVIEW (EUGENE, OR.) (US/0029-3423) [01760710] **3349**

NORTHWEST REVIEW OF BOOKS, THE (US/0886-5256) [12835707] **4831**

NORTHWEST RUNNER (US/0883-7945) [12212835] **4908**

NORTHWEST SAILBOARD (US) **594**

NORTHWEST SAILBOARD (US/1063-8164) [16350735] **4908**

NORTHWEST SAILBOARD'S GORGE GUIDE *See* GORGE GUIDE **4850**

NORTHWEST SALES GUIDE TO HIGH-TECH COMPANIES (US/1040-0516) [18304447] **5134**

NORTHWEST SCIENCE (US/0029-344X) [01681012] **5134**

NORTHWEST-SIGNAL (US) [16702048] **5729**

NORTHWEST STAR (US/0739-0955) [09817685] **5686**

NORTHWEST TECHNOCRAT, THE (US/0029-3474) [05424852] **1593**

NORTHWEST TERRITORIES *See* NORTHWEST TERRITORIES GAZETTE; PART II **4670**

NORTHWEST TERRITORIES *See* ANNUAL REPORT OF THE GOVERNMENT OF THE NORTHWEST TERRITORIES **4628**

NORTHWEST TERRITORIES *See* NORTHWEST TERRITORIES GAZETTE. PART 1 **4670**

NORTHWEST TERRITORIES. COMMISSIONER *See* ANNUAL REPORT OF THE COMMISSIONER OF THE NORTHWEST TERRITORIES **4628**

NORTHWEST TERRITORIES. FINANCIAL MANAGEMENT SECRETARIAT *See* MAIN ESTIMATES - FINANCIAL MANAGEMENT SECRETARIAT (YELLOWKNIFE. 1987) **4663**

NORTHWEST TERRITORIES GAZETTE. PART 1 (CN/0225-5898) [06132942] **4670**

NORTHWEST TERRITORIES GAZETTE; PART II (CN/0713-2123) [06167251] **4670**

NORTHWEST TERRITORIES. LEGISLATIVE ASSEMBLY *See* HANSARD : OFFICIAL REPORT / LEGISLATIVE ASSEMBLY OF THE NORTHWEST TERRITORIES **4654**

NORTHWEST TERRITORIES REPORTS (CN/0824-3433) [10517692] **3019**

NORTHWEST TERRITORIES REPORTS (CN/0824-3433) [11278820] **3019**

NORTHWEST TERRITORIES TEACHER'S ASSOCIATION *See* HANDBOOK FOR MEMBERS OF THE NORTHWEST TERRITORIES TEACHERS' ASSOCIATION, A **1895**

NORTHWEST TERRITORIES. TERRITORIAL HOSPITAL INSURANCE SERVICES *See* ANNUAL REPORT - TERRITORIAL HOSPITAL INSURANCE SERVICES AND MEDICARE **2874**

NORTHWEST TRAIL TRACER (US/0740-4999) [09612496] **2464**

NORTHWEST TRAVEL (US/1059-9681) [23261825] **5486**

NORTHWEST WOMEN (US) [18957558] **5563**

NORTHWEST WOMEN IN BUSINESS *See* NORTHWEST WOMEN **5563**

NORTHWESTERN CAMPING *See* CAMPBOOK. NORTHWESTERN **4870**

NORTHWESTERN CAMPING & TRAILERING; INCLUDING LOCATION MAPS (US) [01791930] **4853**

NORTHWESTERN DENTAL RESEARCH (US/1062-0311) [20979166] **1331**

NORTHWESTERN FINANCIAL REVIEW (US/1042-1254) [18943479] **801**

NORTHWESTERN JEWELER, THE (US/0029-3490) [01760724] **2915**

NORTHWESTERN JOURNAL OF INTERNATIONAL LAW & BUSINESS (US/0196-3228) [05072661] **3102**

NORTHWESTERN LINDQUIST-ENDICOTT REPORT, THE *CEASED.* (US/1051-3000) [17537630] **4207**

NORTHWESTERN — Alphabetical Title Index

NORTHWESTERN LUTHERAN (MILWAUKEE, WIS.), THE (US/0029-3512) [01760726] **5065**

NORTHWESTERN MINDANAO RESEARCH JOURNAL (PH/0115-2009) [02244728] **2660**

NORTHWESTERN NATURALIST : A JOURNAL OF VERTEBRATE BIOLOGY (US/1051-1733) [20730986] 467, 5618, **4169**

NORTHWESTERN REGIONAL LIBRARY SYSTEM (ONT.) See TALKING BOOKS CATALOGUE SUPPLEMENT **4832**

NORTHWESTERN REGIONAL LIBRARY SYSTEM (ONT.) See TAPES BY MAIL CATALOGUE **4160**

NORTHWESTERN REPORTER CASE NAMES CITATOR (US) **3019**

NORTHWESTERN SPORTSMAN (US/0164-3134) [04612537] **4908**

NORTHWESTERN STATE UNIVERSITY OF LOUISIANA See ALUMNI DIRECTORY / NORTHWESTERN **1099**

NORTHWESTERN STATES See NORTHWESTERN TOUR BOOK **5486**

NORTHWESTERN TOUR BOOK (US/0094-078X) [01793694] 5421, **5486**

NORTHWESTERN UNIVERSITY LAW REVIEW (US/0029-3571) [01607632] **3019**

NORTHWESTERNER (LARKSPUR, CALIF.) (US/0894-0800) [15748835] **5433**

NORTHWOODS PRESS (US) [22583196] **5697**

NORTON BANKRUPTCY LAW AND PRACTICE (US) [09507845] **3088**

NORTON DAILY TELEGRAM (NORTON, KAN. : 1928) (US) [12356183] **5678**

NORTON NOTES (US/1049-1821) [21170434] **2284**

NORVEG (NO/0029-3601) [01760743] **242**

NORWALK REFLECTOR (NORWALK, OHIO : DAILY) (US/0745-4023) [09134639] **5729**

NORWALK WEEKLY TRADER (US/0191-9091) [04952008] **2541**

NORWAY See NATIONAL BUDGET, THE **4738**

NORWAY (NO) [05003986] **848**

NORWAY CURRENT, THE (US/1071-2607) [28601277] **5693**

NORWAY. DEPARTEMENTET FOR INDUSTRI OG HANDVERK See LISTE OVER GODKJENTE ENTREPRENRER **1616**

NORWAY. DIREKTORATET FOR ARBEIDSTILSYNET See RAPPORT OM VIRKSOMHETEN **2868**

NORWAY. DIREKTORATET FOR UTVIKLINGSHJELP See NORGES SAMARBEID MED UTVIKLINGSLANDENE **1576**

NORWAY. DIREKTORATET FOR UTVIKLINGSHJELP See NORWAY'S ASSISTANCE TO DEVELOPING COUNTRIES **1576**

NORWAY. FINANS- OG TOLLDEPARTEMENTET See REVISED NATIONAL BUDGET / ROYAL NORWEGIAN MINISTRY OF FINANCE, THE **4747**

NORWAY. FINANS- OG TOLLDEPARTEMENTET See FINAL BUDGET PROPOSAL / ROYAL NORWEGIAN MINISTRY OF FINANCE **4724**

NORWAY. FISKERIDIREKTORATET See FISKERIDIREKTORATETS SKRIFTER. SERIE HAVUNDERSKELSER **2304**

NORWAY. FORSIKRINGSRADET See FORSIKRINGSSELSKAPER **2881**

NORWAY. LANDBRUKSDEPARTEMENTET See LANDBRUKSDIREKTRENS ARSMELDING **104**

NORWAY. LUFTFARTSVERKET See ARSRAPPORT **12**

NORWAY. OLJEDIREKTORATET See ARSBERETNING - OLJEDIREKTORATET **2134**

NORWAY. STATISTISK SENTRALBYRA See STATISTISK ARBOK **5343**

NORWAY. STATISTISK SENTRALBYRA See FYLKESTINGSVALGET. COUNTY COUNCIL ELECTIONS **4698**

NORWAY. STATISTISK SENTRALBYRA See SKATTESTATISTIKK: KOMMUNER OG HANDELSDISTRIKTER **4748**

NORWAY. STATISTISK SENTRALBYRA See KOMMUNEVALGET **4698**

NORWAY. STATISTISK SENTRALBYRA See LNNSSTATISTIKK FOR ANSATTE I VAREHANDEL **1536**

NORWAY. STATISTISK SENTRALBYRA See UNDERVISNINGSSTATISTIKK : AVSLUTTET UTDANNING **1798**

NORWAY. STATISTISK SENTRALBYRA See STATISTISK MANEDSHEFTE **5344**

NORWAY. STATISTISK SENTRALBYRA See STATISTISK ARBOG FOR NORGE (MICROFICHE) **5343**

NORWAY. STATISTISK SENTRALBYRA See DOEDSARSAKER. HOVEDTABELLER **4561**

NORWAY. STATISTISK SENTRALBYRA See UTDANNINGSSTATISTIKK : VAKSENOPPLRING **1802**

NORWAY. STATISTISK SENTRALBYRA See MANEDSSTATISTIKK OVER UTENRIKSHANDELEN **1536**

NORWAY. STATISTISK SENTRALBYRA See STRUKTURTALL FOR KOMMUNENES KONOMI **4701**

NORWAY. STATISTISK SENTRALBYRA See UTDANNINGSSTATISTIKK : OVERSIKT **1798**

NORWAY. STATISTISK SENTRALBYRA See UTDANNINGSSTATISTIKK : GRUNNSKOLER **1806**

NORWAY. STORTINGET See STORTINGET I NAVN OG TALL **4689**

NORWAY. TELEDIREKTORATET See TELEGRAMADRESSEBOK FOR NORGE **1166**

NORWAY. TELEGRAFSTYRET. TELEGRAMADRESSEBOK FOR NORGE See TELEGRAMADRESSEBOK FOR NORGE **1166**

NORWAY TIMES (US/0891-6322) [10802915] **5719**

NORWAY'S ASSISTANCE TO DEVELOPING COUNTRIES (NO) [02631366] **1576**

NORWEGEN : ENERGIEWIRTSCHAFT (GW) [04969973] **1951**

NORWEGEN, WIRTSCHAFT IN ZAHLEN UND WIRTSCHAFTSDOKUMENTATION / BUNDESSTELLE FUER AUSSENHANDELSINFORMATION (GW) [11563073] **1508**

NORWEGIAN-AMERICAN HISTORICAL ASSOCIATION See AUTHOR SERIES **2722**

NORWEGIAN - AMERICAN HISTORICAL ASSOCIATION See TOPICAL STUDIES **2763**

NORWEGIAN-AMERICAN STUDIES (US/0078-1983) [01760811] **2751**

NORWEGIAN ARCHAEOLOGICAL REVIEW (NO/0029-3652) [01645936] **276**

NORWEGIAN JOURNAL OF AGRICULTURAL SCIENCES (NO/0801-5341) [17396444] **115**

NORWEGIAN JOURNAL OF AGRICULTURAL SCIENCES. SUPPLEMENT (NO) [20029230] **115**

NORWEGIAN OFFSHORE INDEX (NO/0377-1806) [02246051] **4267**

NORWEGIAN TRACKS (US) [03633870] **1920**

NOR'WESTING (US/0739-747X) [09804531] **594**

NORWICH BULLETIN (US) [08766538] **5646**

NORWICH NEWSLETTER See IFR NEWS **2344**

NORWOOD REGISTER (CN) **5791**

NORWOOD YOUNG AMERICA TIMES (US) [22612867] **5689**

NOS (UK) [24314900] **2270**

NOS ECOLES (OTTAWA) (CN/0229-110X) [08773938] 1769, **5033**

NOS JEUNES (ENGLISH EDITION) (CN/0315-1948) [02604522] **1769**

NOS LUTTES (1981) (CN/0711-1304) [08489222] **1695**

NOS LUTTES EXPRESS (CN/0227-4906) [07802289] **1695**

NOS OISEAUX (SZ/0029-3725) [05205447] **4169**

NOS SOURCES (CN/0227-0404) [08185787] **2464**

NOSA MUNJE SARYE YONGUJIP (KO) [01797434] **3152**

NOSA TERRA, A (SP/0213-3105) [15716586] 5486, **5269**

NOSAGYO KENKYU (JA/0389-1763) [03891763] **2426**

NOSELEUTIKE (GR) [20106730] **3862**

NOSOKOMEIAKA HRONIKA (GR/0369-5700) [11364404] **3623**

NOSON KEIKAKU GAKKAISHI (JA/0912-9731) [I09129731] **2829**

NOSOTRAS (NQ) [28290170] **5563**

NOSP-MIKRO (NO/0357-1955) [I03571955] **421**

NOSSIDE : QUADERNI DI SCRITTURA FEMMINILE (IT) [23236908] **3418**

NOSSO MINISTERIO DO REINO PARA O CANADA (CN/0823-2598) [10052066] **5065**

NOSTALGIA ILLUSTRATED (US/0149-9327) [03574250] **2541**

NOSTALGIA NEWSLETTER (US/0300-6794) [01376126] **2541**

NOSTOC MAGAZINE (US) [08850943] **3467**

NOSTRADAMUS. EDITION QUEBECOISE (CN/0380-4127) [02851744] **4242**

NOSTRUM (UK) **4794**

NOTA BENE (PARIS, FRANCE) (FR/0249-6275) [09123446] **3418**

NOTA LEPIDOPTEROLOGICA (GW/0342-7536) [05224172] **467**

NOTABLE CANADIAN CHILDREN'S BOOKS. SUPPLEMENT (CN/0715-2612) [09452769] **3237**

NOTABLE READING PROJECTS (US/0098-1125) [01798708] **1901**

NOTAE PRAEHISTORICAE : INFORMATIEBLAD UITGEGEVEN DOOR DE N F W O CONTACTGROEP, PREHISTOIRE (BE) [21922694] **276**

NOTARZT, DER (GW/0177-2309) [12922940] **3725**

NOTAS DE ALGEBRA Y ANALISIS (AG/0078-2009) [02511110] **3524**

NOTAS DE FISICA (BL) [05870399] **4413**

NOTAS DE GEOMETRIA Y TOPOLOGIA / INMABB - CONICET **SUSPENDED.** (AG/0325-8963) [07414950] **3524**

NOTAS DE LA SOCIEDAD MATEMATICA DE CHILE (CL) [08273069] **3524**

NOTAS DE MATEMATICA DISCRETA (AG/0326-1336) [11129260] **3524**

NOTAS DE POBLACION (CL/0303-1829) [01792265] **4555**

●NOTAS EJECUTIVAS SOBRE MEDIO AMBIENTE Y DESARROLLO: BOLETIN INFORMATIVO PREPARADO CONJUNTAMENTE POR LA DIVISION DE MEDIO AMBIENTE Y ASENTAMIENTOS HUMANOS Y LOS SERVICIOS DE INFORMACION DE LA COMISION ECONOMICA PARA AMERICA LATINA Y EL CARIBE, CEPAL (CL) [25821637] **1508**

NOTAS SOBRE LA ECONOMIA Y EL DESARROLLO / CEPAL, COMISION ECONOMICA PARA AMERICA LATINA Y EL CARIBE (CL/0257-2168) [11592210] **1508**

NOTAS TECNICAS - FACULTAD DE AGRONOMIA (MONTEVIDEO) (UY/0797-0323) [19125863] **115**

NOTAS TRIMESTRALES DEL COMITE DE IGLESIAS (PY) [18242948] **4511**

NOTAS Y NOTICIAS LINGUISTICAS (BO) [09841881] **3306**

NOTATION (ENGLISH EDITION) (CN/0712-2772) [08808144] **386**

NOTATKI ORNITOLOGICZNE (PL/0550-0842) [01462302] **5618**

NOTATKI POCKIE (PL) [06454873] **2700**

NOTE ANNUELLE DE STATISTIQUE - DIRECTION DE LA STATISTIQUE ET DE LA COMPTABILITE NATIONALE (CM) [02441403] **5335**

NOTE DE CONJONCTURE DE L'I.N.S.E.E (FR/0766-6268) [11882101] **1576**

NOTE DE CONJONCTURE INTERNATIONALE (FR) [22495630] **1638**

NOTE DE RECHERCHE - INSTITUT DE RECHERCHE EN EXPLORATION MINERALE (CN/0227-3543) [06688746] **1443**

NOTE DE SERVICE - ASSOCIATION CANADIENNE DES PROFESSEURS D'UNIVERSITE (CN/0384-9260) [05842307] **1838**

NOTE DI MATEMATICA (IT) [11334979] **3524**

NOTE D'INFORMATION / ASSOCIATION DES BIBLIOTHECAIRES FRANCAIS (FR/0180-4278) [07103989] **3237**

NOTE D'INFORMATION ECONOMIQUE - COMITE PROFESSIONNEL DU PETROLE (FR/1156-2560) [I11562560] **4267**

NOTE D'INFORMATION SUR LA CONSTRUCTION (CN/0701-5224) [03418408] **622**

NOTE D'INFORMATION TECHNIQUE - CENTRE SCIENTIFIQUE ET TECHNIQUE DE LA CONSTRUCTION (FR/0379-6264) [11010072] **622**

NOTE ECONOMICHE - MONTE DEI PASCHI DI SIENA (IT/0391-8289) [10764676] **1593**

NOTE FINANCIERE ANNUELLE / BANQUE DE FRANCE, SECRETARIAT REGIONAL, REGION ALSACE (FR/0292-2290) [12085101] **801**

NOTE FINANCIERE ANNUELLE. ILE-DE-FRANCE (FR/0181-1010) [19057365] **801**

NOTE FINANCIERE ANNUELLE. MIDI-PYRENEES (FR/0247-4069) [19057262] **801**

Alphabetical Title Index — NOTICIERO

NOTE HEBDOMADAIRE - CHAMBRE DE COMMERCE ET D'INDUSTRIE DE LA REPUBLIQUE POPULAIRE DE BENIN (DM) [02580061] **1620**

NOTE ON THE PROCEEDINGS / COMMITTEE ON WORK ON PLANTATIONS (SZ/0535-1219) [06328053] 115, **1695**

NOTE PAD (US) [22205254] **3525**

NOTE, RECENSIONI, NOTIZIE (IT) [19866979] **3418**

NOTE - SERVICE DE LA RECHERCHE FORESTIERE (CN/0712-0680) [09021596] **2390**

NOTE TECHNIQUE DU CENTRE DE RECHERCHES AGRONOMIQUE DE L'ETAT (BE/0771-0607) [08725930] **115**

NOTE TECHNIQUE - LE FONDS DE RECHERCHES FORESTIERES DE L'UNIVERSITE LAVAL (CN) [03985522] **2390**

NOTE TO CAPCO (CN/0849-2212) [23243118] **4245**

NOTE TRIMESTRIELLE DE CONJONCTURE / STATEC, LUXEMBOURG (LU) [06770204] **1508**

NOTEBOOK FOR THE MAYA HIEROGLYPHIC WRITING WORKSHOP AT TEXAS (US) [08134489] **276**

NOTEBOOK OF EMPIRICAL PETROLOGY (US/0362-0050) [01476551] **1459**

NOTEBOOK (WASHINGTON RESEARCH COUNCIL) (US) [15123365] **4739**

NOTEBOOKS FOR STUDY AND RESEARCH - INTERNATIONAL INSTITUTE FOR RESEARCH AND EDUCATION (FR/0298-7902) [I02987902] 2624, **4484**

NOTES AFRICAINES (SG/0029-3954) [01760822] **2642**

NOTES AND ABSTRACTS IN AMERICAN AND INTERNATIONAL EDUCATION (US/0029-3962) [01781433] **1796**

NOTES AND DOCUMENTS - UNITED NATIONS, CENTRE AGAINST APARTHEID (US/0251-7787) [I02517787] **4511**

NOTES & FURPHIES (AT) [07217249] **3418**

NOTES AND MISCELLANY SYDNEY (AT/0155-4255) [I01554255] **1769**

NOTES AND NEWS / DURHAM EAST SOIL & CROP IMPROVEMENT ASSOCIATION (CN/0712-6522) [09432722] **179**

NOTES AND QUERIES (UK/0029-3970) [02623018] **3306**

NOTES & QUERIES FOR SOMERSET AND DORSET (UK/0029-3989) [01760827] **2700**

NOTES AND RECORDS OF THE ROYAL SOCIETY OF LONDON (UK/0035-9149) [01586875] **5134**

NOTES (ASSOCIATION OF GOVERNING BOARDS OF UNIVERSITIES AND COLLEGES : 1982) *See* TRUSTEESHIP (WASHINGTON, D.C.) **1851**

NOTES BIBLIOGRAPHIQUES (FR/0468-8678) [I04688678] **3418**

NOTES BIBLIOGRAPHIQUES CARAIBES (GP/0180-4103) [05179489] **421**

NOTES BLEUES *See* NOTES BLEUES DE BERCY / MINISTERE DE L'ECONOMIE ET DES FINANCES, MINISTERE DU BUDGET, LES **4739**

●NOTES BLEUES DE BERCY / MINISTERE DE L'ECONOMIE ET DES FINANCES, MINISTERE DU BUDGET, LES (FR) [27695401] **4739**

NOTES BLEUES (QUARTERLY) *See* NOTES BLEUES DE BERCY / MINISTERE DE L'ECONOMIE ET DES FINANCES, MINISTERE DU BUDGET, LES **4739**

NOTES - CANADIAN ASSOCIATION OF YOUTH ORCHESTRAS (CN/0830-8411) [13512705] **4142**

NOTES - CANADIAN FEDERATION OF STUDENTS, ONTARIO (CN/0827-2514) [11734788] **1838**

NOTES / COUR DE JUSTICE DES COMMUNANTES EUROPEENES, DIRECTION RECHERCHE, DOCUMENTATION ET BIBLIOTHEQUE (LU) [20075826] **3019**

NOTES DE CONJONCTURE (FRANCE. DIRECTION DEPARTEMENTALE DE L'AGRICULTURE DE LA REUNION. SERVICE DE STATISTIQUE AGRICOLE) (FR/0335-4024) [09460921] **115**

NOTES DE RECHERCHE (UNIVERSITE DE MONTREAL. FACULTE DE L'AMENAGEMENT) (CN/0226-9988) [08422632] **2829**

NOTES DE RECHERCHE (UNIVERSITY OF OTTAWA. DEPT. OF POLITICAL SCIENCE) (CN/0713-8199) [08996162] **4484**

NOTES DE RECHERCHES - GEOGRAPHIE. UNIVERSITE D'OTTAWA (CN/0824-295X) [10195239] **2571**

NOTES D'INFORMATION ECONOMIQUE (FR) **1508**

NOTES D'INFORMATION ET STATISTIQUES (FR/0005-559X) [02495269] **5335**

NOTES DU CENTRE D'ETUDES DU TOURISME, LES (CN/0229-2718) [08010322] **5486**

NOTES DU LABORATOIRE DE PALEONTOLOGIE DE L'UNIVERSITE DE GENEVA (SZ/0253-3251) [05919624] **4228**

NOTES ET DOCUMENTS - DEPARTEMENT DE GEOGRAPHIE. UNIVERSITE DE MONTREAL (CN/0710-1767) [11543839] **2571**

NOTES ET DOCUMENTS D'OCEANOGRAPHIE (NN) [12981520] **2309**

NOTES ET DOCUMENTS (INSTITUT INTERNATIONAL JACQUES MARITAIN) (IT) [07488223] **4354**

NOTES ET ETUDES DOCUMENTAIRES (FR/0029-4004) [09563599] **2520**

NOTES ET MEMOIRES - COMPAGNIE FRANCAISE DES PETROLES (FR/0588-8700) [03407372] **1390**

NOTES FROM EASTMAN (US) [05387879] **4142**

NOTES FROM MOTHER EARTH'S CENTRE (CN/1187-8304) [25796537] **326**

NOTES FROM NIAGARA (CN/0229-2750) [08651761] **2465**

NOTES FROM SURVIVAL INTERNATIONAL U.S.A (US) [18689698] **4511**

NOTES FROM UNDERGROUND *SUSPENDED.* (US/0550-0974) [03384576] **5388**

NOTES - NEW YORK (N.Y.) DEPT. OF RECORDS AND INFORMATION SERVICES (US/0731-2385) [08143041] **4670**

NOTES - NEW YORK PALEONTOLOGICAL SOCIETY (US) [01792561] **4228**

NOTES : NEWSLETTER OF THE ASSOCIATION OF GOVERNING BOARDS OF UNIVERSITIES AND COLLEGES *CEASED.* (US/0738-3460) [08840265] **1838**

NOTES ON AMERICA'S FOLK ART ENVIRONMENTS (US) 2323, **360**

NOTES ON ANTHROPOLOGY AND INTERCULTURAL COMMUNITY WORK *SUSPENDED.* (US/1044-0410) [16414349] **242**

NOTES ON COMPUTING (1987) (US/1049-9865) [21344242] **1261**

NOTES ON CONTEMPORARY LITERATURE (US/0029-4047) [01641404] **3349**

NOTES ON FOREIGN TRADE (GR) [02441250] **848**

NOTES ON FOREIGN TRADE AND MAIN ECONOMIC DATA (GR) [04601810] **848**

NOTES ON HIGHER EDUCATION *CEASED.* (AT/0310-5695) [I03105695] **1838**

NOTES ON LINGUISTICS (US/0736-0673) [04215839] **3306**

NOTES ON LITERACY (US/0737-6707) [09429214] **3307**

NOTES ON MATHEMATICS AND ITS APPLICATIONS (US/0888-6113) [13676027] **3525**

NOTES ON MISSISSIPPI WRITERS *CEASED.* (US/0029-4071) [03930520] **3418**

NOTES ON MODERN IRISH LITERATURE (US/1045-6619) [20185297] **3418**

NOTES ON NUMERICAL FLUID MECHANICS (GW) [05274541] **4429**

NOTES ON NURSING SCIENCE (US/0896-8047) [17290884] **3862**

NOTES ON PURE MATHEMATICS (AT/0818-304X) [06872089] **3525**

NOTES ON SCRIPTURE IN USE (US/0737-2876) [09336741] **5018**

NOTES ON SELECTED ACQUISITIONS (US/0572-8312) [03234154] **3237**

NOTES ON TEACHING ENGLISH (US/0163-7088) [04423835] 1901, **3307**

NOTES ON THE SCIENCE OF BUILDING *CEASED.* (AT/0300-371X) [01422439] **623**

NOTES ON TIN *SUSPENDED.* (UK/0535-3378) [01753742] **4014**

NOTES ON TRANSLATION (US/0734-0788) [03116127] **5018**

NOTES ON UNIONS (CN/0316-0386) [02624589] **1695**

NOTES ON VIRGINIA (US/0163-1632) [04297380] 2751, **305**

NOTES (PHILADELPHIA, PA.) (US/0027-4380) [01605994] 3237, **4142**

NOTES PLUS (US/0738-8624) [09659966] 3307, **1901**

NOTES. SUPPLEMENT FOR MEMBERS (US) [04919065] 3237, **4142**

NOTES VERTES ECONOMIQUE. SERIE INFORMATIONS RAPIDES (FR/0291-8897) [I02918897] **1508**

NOTES VERTES ECONOMIQUES. SERIE CONJONCTURE (FR/0291-8900) [I02918900] **1508**

NOTFALL-MEDIZIN (ERLANGEN) (GW/0341-2903) [01953412] **3725**

NOTFALLVORSORGE UND ZIVILE VERTEIDIGUNG (GW/0938-7390) [22609765] **1073**

NOTICE D'INFORMATION A L'USAGE DES AGENTS DE LA COOPERATION : REPUBLIQUE DU SENEGAL (FR) [04424768] **2642**

NOTICE OF DECISION ON PUBLIC INTEREST REPRESENTATIONS (CN/1184-0587) [23247407] **848**

NOTICE PAPER / SENATE & HOUSE OF REPRESENTATIVES (AT) **4670**

NOTICE TO IMPORTERS (CN/0225-414X) [06047585] **848**

NOTICE TO MARINERS (US/0092-1262) [04507973] **4181**

●NOTICE TO MARINERS (ANNUAL EDITION 1976) (US/0700-1789) [31425692] **4181**

NOTICE TO MEMBERS. FUTURES MEMORANDUM (TORONTO STOCK EXCHANGE) (CN/0710-5088) [08507419] **910**

NOTICE TO MEMBERS. OPTIONS MEMORANDUM (TORONTO STOCK EXCHANGE) (CN/0710-5096) [08507423] **910**

NOTICE TO MEMBERS - TORONTO STOCK EXCHANGE (CN/0710-507X) [08507407] **910**

NOTICE TO MEMBERS - TRANS CANADA OPTIONS INC (CN/0710-5746) [08854813] **801**

NOTICES OF THE AMERICAN MATHEMATICAL SOCIETY (US/0002-9920) [01480366] **3525**

NOTICES TO AIRMEN (US/1057-9621) [04276638] **30**

NOTICIA GEOMORFOLOGICA (BL/0029-4128) [02300274] **2571**

NOTICIARIO ARQUEOLOGICO HISPANICO (SPAIN. SUBDIRECCION GENERAL DE ARQUEOLOGIA) (SP) [07598741] **2076**

NOTICIARIO DE HISTORIA AGRARIA (SP/1132-1261) [24993858] **115**

NOTICIAS ALIADAS (PE) [06207083] **2512**

NOTICIAS - COUNCIL FOR INTER-AMERICAN COOPERATION *See* NOTICIAS - NATIONAL FOREIGN TRADE COUNCIL **848**

NOTICIAS CULTURALES (CK/0020-370X) [02265252] **2851**

NOTICIAS DE GALAPAGOS (BE) [03700486] **2201**

NOTICIAS DE IDEA *See* REVISTA IDEA / INSTITUTO PARA EL DESARROLLO DE EMPRESARIOS EN LA ARGENTINA **1582**

NOTICIAS DE LA CONSTRUCCION (SP) **623**

NOTICIAS DE LA REPUBLICA DE CHINA (CH) [06738630] **2507**

●NOTICIAS DE OCR / OFFICINA DE DERECHOS CIVILES (US) [25689776] **4511**

NOTICIAS DEL MUNDO (US/0888-143X) [12561199] **5719**

NOTICIAS DEL PUERTO DE MONTEREY (US/0886-7151) [05424117] 2624, **326**

NOTICIAS (HISPANIC NATIONAL BAR ASSOCIATION) (US) [20238526] **3019**

NOTICIAS INDIGENISTAS DE AMERICA (MX) [08072098] 242, **2270**

NOTICIAS MEDICAS (SP) **3623**

NOTICIAS - NATIONAL FOREIGN TRADE COUNCIL *CEASED.* (US/0747-0878) [04059679] **848**

NOTICIAS : ORGANO OFICIAL DEL SINDICATO MEDICO DEL URUGUAY (UY) [26147574] **3623**

NOTICIAS - SANTA BARBARA HISTORICAL SOCIETY (US/0581-5916) [01914739] **2751**

NOTICIECC (US/0887-3674) [12489442] **1769**

NOTICIERO ALFONSI (US/1044-8853) [09776084] **2701**

NOTICIERO DE LA AMBAC (MX) [01780769] **3237**

NOTICIERO - SOCIEDAD ARGENTINA DE INVESTIGACION OPERATIVA (AG/0325-5298) [I03255298] **1989**

NOTICIERO TECNICO SOBRE INCENDIOS (CK/0120-5722) [I01205722] **2292**

NOTIFIABLE — Alphabetical Title Index

NOTIFIABLE OFFENCES RECORDED BY THE POLICE (UK) **3171**

NOTIFICATIONS / HCRS INFORMATION EXCHANGE (US/0736-1394) [08783060] 4853, **2201**

● NOTIONS, POTIONS (US/1059-566X) [24633250] **3418**

NOTISES (EVANSTON, ILL.) (US/1057-1019) [12182086] **3237**

NOTISUR (AG) [16520732] **1695**

NOTISUR (ALBUQUERQUE, N.M.) (US/1060-4189) [24990710] **4530**

NOTITIAE (VC/0029-4306) [01586528] **5033**

NOTIZIARIO : AITN, IL (IT) **3623**

NOTIZIARIO ASSICURATIVO (IT) **2889**

NOTIZIARIO ASSINDUSTRIA GENOVA (IT) **2889**

NOTIZIARIO CHIMICO E FARMACEUTICO (IT/0550-1156) [04051316] **988**

NOTIZIARIO CHIRURGICO (IT/0392-3584) [07192832] **3970**

NOTIZIARIO COMMERCIALE (IT) [09862632] **848**

NOTIZIARIO DEL CENTRO DI DOCUMENTAZIONE (IT/0392-4270) [I03924270] **421**

NOTIZIARIO DEL CONSIGLIO REGIONALE DELLA LIGURIA (IT) [01799464] **3019**

NOTIZIARIO DEL LAVORO E PREVIDENZA (IT/0394-3623) [I03943623] **1695**

NOTIZIARIO DELL'ECOLOGIA, IL (IT) [15366889] **2219**

NOTIZIARIO DI AMNESTY INTERNATIONAL (IT) **4511**

NOTIZIARIO DI GIURISPRUDENZA DEL LAVORO (IT/0392-4335) [I03924335] **3019**

NOTIZIARIO ELETTRICO (IT) **2074**

NOTIZIARIO ENEA. SICUREZZA E PROTEZIONE (IT) **1695**

NOTIZIARIO GENERALE SEZIONE AMBIENTE (IT) **2219**

NOTIZIARIO GIURIDICO REGIONALE (IT) [01790051] 4670, **3019**

NOTIZIARIO IAP (IT) **3019**

NOTIZIARIO ISTAT. SERIE 1 : ATTIVITA PRODUTTIVA. FOGLLIO 14 : STATISTICA DEL COMMERCIO CON L'ESTERO *CEASED.* (IT) [02981544] **5335**

NOTIZIARIO ISTAT. SERIE 2: STATISTICHE DELL'ATTIVITA PRODUTTIVA *CEASED.* (IT) **5335**

NOTIZIARIO ISTAT. SERIE 3 : POPOLAZIONE. FOGLIO 31 : ANDAMENTO DEMOGRAFICO *CEASED.* (IT) [04304936] **5335**

NOTIZIARIO ISTAT. SERIE 4: ARGOMENTI VARI *CEASED.* (IT) **5335**

NOTIZIARIO - ISTITUTO GIAPPONESE DI CULTURA (IT) [06691466] **2507**

NOTIZIARIO ISTITUTO STORICO IN CUNEO E PROVINCIA *See* PRESENTE E LA STORIA, IL **2626**

NOTIZIARIO LEGISLATIVO DEGLI UFFICI FISCALI E AMMINISTRATIVI DELLO STATO (IT) **3019**

NOTIZIARIO / SOCIETA ITALIANA DE BIOCHIMICA CLINICA (IT/0392-7091) [09951676] **988**

NOTIZIARIO STATISTICO - ANFIA (IT) [03250785] **5401**

NOTIZIARIO STATISTICO INAIL (IT) **5335**

NOTIZIARIO SULLE MALATTIE DELLE PIANTE (IT/0468-9291) [01760831] **520**

NOTIZIARIO TECNICO TESSILE (IT) **5373**

NOTIZIARIO TELECOMUNICAZIONI INTERNAZIONALI (IT) **1161**

NOTIZIARIO TESSILE ABBIGLIAMENTO (IT) 1086, **5354**

NOTIZIARIO - UNIVERSITA DEGLI STUDI DI TRIESTE (IT) [06396377] **1838**

NOTIZIE AIRI (IT) **5134**

NOTIZIE DA PALAZZO ALBANI (IT/0391-4364) [02365595] **360**

NOTIZIE DEGLI SCAVI DI ANTICHITA / ACCADEMIA NAZIONALE DEI LINCEI (IT) [09069234] **276**

NOTIZIE DELLA SCUOLA (IT) **1867**

NOTIZIE E DOCUMENTI (IT/0392-7032) [I03927032] **4484**

NOTIZIE INTERNATIONALI: BOLLETTINO BIMESTRALE DELLA FIOM-CGIL (IT) **1695**

NOTIZIE STATISTICHE / ISTITUTO NAZIONALE DELLA PREVIDENZA SOCIALE (IT) [04919653] **5299**

NOTNAIA LETOPIS (RU) [07818864] **4142**

NOTORNIS (NZ/0029-4470) [01585717] **5619**

NOTORNIS / ORNITHOLOGICAL SOCIETY OF NEW ZEALAND (NZ) [09339977] **5619**

NOTORU DAMU SEISHIN JOSHI DAIGAKU *See* NOTORU DAMU SEISHIN JOSHI DAIGAKU KIYO : BUNKAGAKU HEN **5253**

NOTORU DAMU SEISHIN JOSHI DAIGAKU KIYO : BUNKAGAKU HEN (JA) [05058870] **5253**

NOTORU DAMU SEISHIN JOSJI DAIGAKU *See* NOTORU DAMU SEISHIN JOSJI DAIGAKU KIYO : GAIKOKUGO GAIKOKU BUNGAKU HEN **3307**

NOTORU DAMU SEISHIN JOSJI DAIGAKU KIYO : GAIKOKUGO GAIKOKU BUNGAKU HEN (JA) [04546241] **3307**

NOTRE DAME CONFERENCES IN MEDIEVAL STUDIES (US) **2701**

NOTRE-DAME DU CAP (CN/0700-6500) [02759342] **5033**

NOTRE-DAME DU LIBAN (FR) [19257272] **2851**

NOTRE DAME ESTATE PLANNING INSTITUTE *See* ANNUAL NOTRE DAME ESTATE PLANNING INSTITUTE **3117**

NOTRE DAME JOURNAL OF FORMAL LOGIC (US/0029-4527) [01760836] **4354**

NOTRE DAME JOURNAL OF LAW, ETHICS & PUBLIC POLICY (US/0883-3648) [11701704] 2252, **3019**

NOTRE DAME LAW REVIEW, THE (US/0745-3515) [09060517] **3019**

NOTRE DAME MAGAZINE (US/0161-987X) [04078199] **1838**

NOTRE DAME MATHEMATICAL LECTURES (US/0885-5862) [01645136] **3525**

NOTRE DAME STUDIES IN AMERICAN CATHOLICISM (US) [05362271] **5033**

NOTRE DAME STUDIES IN LAW AND CONTEMPORARY ISSUES (US/0894-0657) [11976827] **3019**

NOTRE DAME TECHNICAL REVIEW, THE (US/0029-4543) [04123615] **5134**

NOTRE ECONOMIE (CN/0711-8287) [09631207] **1508**

NOTRE HISTOIRE (FR) **2701**

NOTRE HOPITAL (CN/0704-8815) [04039531] **3790**

NOTRE PAIN QUOTIDIEN (CAP-DE-LA-MADELEINE, QUEBEC) (CN/0820-7526) [09519484] **4982**

NOTRE SEMAINE COMMUNAUTAIRE (CN/0384-0530) [03235757] **4982**

NOTRE TEMPS PARIS. 1968 (FR/0029-456X) [I0029456X] **2851**

NOTRES (CN/0029-4578) [02458012] **5033**

NOTTAWASAGA/SUNNIDALE NEWS, THE (CN/0710-1740) [08324050] **5791**

NOTTINGHAM, ENG. UNIVERSITY. DEPT. OF MINING ENGINEERING *See* MINING DEPARTMENT MAGAZINE **2145**

NOTTINGHAM FRENCH STUDIES (UK/0029-4586) [01242039] **3418**

NOTTINGHAM MEDIEVAL STUDIES (UK/0078-2122) [01713742] 3418, **2624**

NOTTINGHAM QUARTERLY (UK) [06784966] **2701**

NOTTINGHAMSHIRE FAMILY HISTORY SOCIETY : JOURNAL (UK/0141-3821) [07893723] **2465**

NOTTINGHAMSHIRE HISTORIAN, THE (UK) [04196520] **2701**

NOTULAE NATURAE OF THE ACADEMY NATURAL SCIENCES OF PHILADELPHIA (US/0029-4608) [01460715] **5134**

NOTULAE ODONATOLOGICAE (NE/0166-6584) [04101222] **467**

NOUAKCHOTT-INFORMATION (MU) [03506235] **2642**

NOUKOGUDE EESTI TERVISHOID. ZDRAVOOKHRNENIE SOVETSKOI ESTONII (ER) [06471573] **3623**

NOUL CINEMA (RM) [22578067] **4075**

NOUS (FR) **5253**

NOUS (BLOOMINGTON) (US/0029-4624) [01760840] **4354**

NOUS DEUX COLLECTION (FR/1158-5803) [11585803] **2520**

NOUS JOURNAL (CN/0318-2835) [02442824] 1067, **3418**

NOUS LES ENSEIGNANTS DE L'ONTARIO (CN/0225-1078) [05842213] **1867**

NOUS TOUTES (CN/0821-0381) [09666896] **5299**

NOUS VOULONS LIRE PESSAC (FR/0153-9027) [01539027] 1067, **3349**

NOUTATI IN STIINTE ALE NATURII SI IN PEDAGOGIE (RM) [05182926] **1838**

NOUVA UMANITA (IT) [08613517] **2851**

NOUVEAU (US/0731-9592) [08255787] **623**

NOUVEAU BIOLOGISTE, LE (FR/0181-3684) [I01813684] **467**

NOUVEAU-BRUNSWICK. ASSEMBLEE LEGISLATIVE. COMITE SPECIAL DE LA CONSTITUTION *See* TRANSCRIPT OF SELECT COMMITTEE ON THE CONSTITUTION (FRENCH EDITION) **4691**

NOUVEAU CARABIN (CN/0704-0156) [03887343] **1838**

NOUVEAU CODE DE PROCEDURE CIVILE ET CODE DE PROCEDURE CIVILE (FR) [02802523] **3090**

NOUVEAU COMMERCE, LE (FR/0550-1326) [04685976] **848**

NOUVEAU COSMOS-EXPRESS, LE (CN/0319-4345) [02583135] **30**

NOUVEAU DEHOVE, LE (FR) **5211**

NOUVEAU DETECTIVE, LE (FR/0753-4000) [I07534000] **3171**

NOUVEAU DIALOGUE (CN/0317-1442) [02442032] **4354**

NOUVEAU DIALOGUE EN BREF (CN/0849-1593) [23237043] **3862**

NOUVEAU DICTIONNAIRE DES BIOGRAPHIES FRANCAISES ET ETRANGERES / PUBLIE SOUS LA DIRECTION DE DOMINIQUE LABARRE DE RAILLICOURT ... (FR) [05236335] **434**

NOUVEAU DIRE, LE (FR) [02558988] **1620**

NOUVEAU JOURNAL DE CHARPENTE MENUISERIE PARQUETS (FR/0029-4675) [I00294675] **623**

NOUVEAU JOURNAL DE ST-MICHEL, LE (CN/0712-2489) [08794386] **5791**

NOUVEAU PARAQUAD (CN/0848-8770) [21344732] **4392**

NOUVEAU POUVOIR JUDICIAIRE, LE (FR) [02243098] **3142**

NOUVEAU RECUEIL COMPLET DES FABLIAUX (NE) **3418**

NOUVEAUTES (BELLES LETTRES (FIRM)) (FR) [14204550] **421**

NOUVEAUTES DE LA BIBLIOTHEQUE ADMINISTRATIVE *CEASED.* (CN/0833-0050) [17556359] 3237, **4670**

NOUVEAUTES TECHNIQUES MARITIMES (FR) [06338734] **4181**

NOUVEAUX CAHIERS D'ALLEMAND (FR/0758-170X) [12441294] **3418**

NOUVEAUX CAHIERS, LES (FR/0550-1350) [02617931] 2660, **5051**

NOUVEAUX CAHIERS MARIALS (FR/0297-7486) [I02977486] **4982**

NOUVEL AFRIQUE ASIE, LE (FR/1141-9946) [21881087] 1638, **4484**

NOUVEL AGRICULTEUR, LE (FR) [14581738] **115**

NOUVEL ECONOMISTE, LE (FR) [02441402] **1576**

NOUVEL EDUCATEUR CANNES, LE (FR/0991-9708) [I09919708] **1769**

NOUVEL ESSOR MARCELLE MALLET (CN/0823-6240) [10420789] 2624, **4982**

NOUVEL-EST (CN/0821-7378) [10634720] **5791**

NOUVEL OBSERVATEUR ENTERPRISES ET TELECOMMUNICATIONS (FR) **1161**

NOUVEL OBSERVATEUR (PARIS), LE (FR/0029-4713) [02642682] **2520**

NOUVEL OFFICIEL DE L'AMEUBLEMENT (FR) **2906**

NOUVELLE ACROPOLE (MONTREAL) (CN/1183-3637) [24266237] **4354**

NOUVELLE ALTERNATIVE, LA (FR/0764-7565) [15748473] **4511**

NOUVELLE (BEAUMONT) (CN/0827-2085) [11559868] **5791**

NOUVELLE CLIO (PARIS, FRANCE) (FR) [01995181] **2701**

NOUVELLE DU HAUT ST-FRANCOIS (CN/0701-113X) [03402940] **2541**

NOUVELLE ECOLE (FR/0048-0967) [02418634] **5253**

NOUVELLE FEMME (MONTREAL, QUEBEC) (CN/0824-0671) [11825404] **5563**

NOUVELLE GAZETTE DE LA TRANSFUSION : BULLETIN D'INFORMATION DE L'ADTS, LA (FR/0293-9495) [17382790] 539, **3623**

NOUVELLE LITTERATURE ET IDEOLOGIE (CN/0703-8011) [06562703] **3418**

NOUVELLE REPUBLIQUE DE BORDEAUX ET DU SUD-OUEST, LA (FR) [20608857] **5801**

NOUVELLE REVUE D'AERONAUTIQUE ET D'ASTRONAUTIQUE (FR/1247-5793) **30**

NOUVELLE REVUE DE MEDECINE DE TOULOUSE *CEASED.* (FR/0246-0122) [12365423] **3623**

NOUVELLE REVUE DE PARIS (MONACO) (MC) [12778254] **3418**

NOUVELLE REVUE DE PSYCHANALYSE *CEASED.* (FR/0223-565X) [02611928] **4606**

NOUVELLE REVUE D'ENTOMOLOGIE (FR/0374-9797) [01714788] **5612**

NOUVELLE REVUE D'ETHNOPSYCHIATRIE (FR/0762-6819) [12897295] **242**

NOUVELLE REVUE D'ONOMASTIQUE (FR/0755-7752) [12375236] **421**

NOUVELLE REVUE DU CAIRE, LA (UA) [02611884] **2642**

NOUVELLE REVUE DU SON, DES IDEES, DES NOUVEAUTES, TOUS LES PRIX, LA (FR) [03383247] **5318**

NOUVELLE REVUE DU SON PARIS, LA (FR/0397-3190) [l03973190] **2491**

NOUVELLE REVUE DU XVIE SIECLE (FR/0294-1414) [11724353] **3418**

NOUVELLE REVUE FRANCAISE D'HEMATOLOGIE (GW/0029-4810) [05306238] **3773**

NOUVELLE REVUE FRANCAISE (PARIS, FRANCE : 1959) (FR/0029-4802) [04576887] **3418**

NOUVELLE REVUE INTERNATIONALE; PROBLEMES DE LA PAIX ET DU SOCIALISME, LA (FR/0048-0975) [04715732] **4544**

NOUVELLE REVUE PEDAGOGIQUE (FR/0029-4837) [02418641] **1769**

NOUVELLE REVUE THEOLOGIQUE (BE/0029-4845) [01589620] **4982**

NOUVELLE TOUR DE FEU, LA (FR/0294-4030) [08904920] **3467**

NOUVELLES ACQUISITIONS - UNIVERSITE DE MONTREAL, BIBLIOTHEQUE DE MEDECINE VETERINAIRE (CN/0705-6370) [04097814] **3237**

NOUVELLES ARCHIVES HOSPITALIERES (FR/0029-4853) [05654908] **3790**

NOUVELLES - ASSOCIATION DES BIBLIOTHEQUES DE L'ONTARIO. GUILDE DES SERVICES EN FRANCAIS (CN/0822-7527) [10386363] **3237**

NOUVELLES - ASSOCIATION DES PROFESSEURS DE FRANCAIS DES UNIVERSITES ET COLLEGES CANADIENS (CN/0821-4549) [17364941] 3418, **3307**

NOUVELLES - ASTED (CN/0316-0963) [02307051] **3237**

NOUVELLES ATLANTIQUES (BE) [04952516] **4484**

NOUVELLES (CANADA. DIVISION DU TRANSPORT DES MARCHANDISES DANGEREUSES) (CN/0710-0922) [08091160] **2866**

NOUVELLES CARTESIENNES (NE) [07056274] **4354**

NOUVELLES (CENTRALE DE L'ENSEIGNEMENT DU QUEBEC) (CN/0710-5568) [08693691] 1769, **1695**

NOUVELLES - CICIAMS (BE/0378-2735) [02833081] 5299, **5033**

NOUVELLES / CONSEIL DES MONUMENTS ET SITES DU QUEBEC (CN/0226-1278) [08070920] **2751**

NOUVELLES CSN (CN/0712-8789) [08811708] **1695**

NOUVELLES DE CAMMAC MONTREAL (CN/0828-6035) [12093207] **4142**

NOUVELLES DE LA BIBLIOTHEQUE CENTRALE DE PRET. REGION DU SAGUENAY-LAC-SAINT-JEAN (CN/0316-0432) [02441932] **3237**

NOUVELLES DE LA DDIPE, LES (CN/0229-8244) [08192972] **1901**

NOUVELLES DE LA F M O Q (ENGLISH EDITION) (CN/0318-0549) [03261337] **3623**

NOUVELLES DE LA FIPESO, LES (FR/1016-7048) [10167048] **1769**

NOUVELLES DE LA PETITE ENTREPRISE (CN/0708-6148) [06467588] **700**

NOUVELLES DE L'A.Q.T (CN/0826-2799) [11046647] **4413**

NOUVELLES DE LA REPUBLIQUE DES LETTRES (NAPLES, ITALY) (IT/0392-2332) [07842003] **3307**

NOUVELLES DE LA SCIENCE ET DES TECHNOLOGIES (BE/0771-7369) [24262748] **5135**

NOUVELLES DE L'ACADEMIE / ACADEMIE DES SCIENCES, LES (FR/0246-1226) [10861698] **5135**

NOUVELLES DE L'ESTAMPE (FR/0029-4888) [04811391] **4567**

NOUVELLES DE PARIS (FR) **2520**

NOUVELLES DERMATOLOGIQUES, LES (FR/0752-5370) [l07525370] **3722**

NOUVELLES DES PETITS FRERES (CN/0382-7992) [02743016] **5299**

NOUVELLES DES SWINGERS (CN/0226-5958) [06472174] **5188**

NOUVELLES D'ICITTE (CN/0715-7541) [09606642] **2751**

NOUVELLES D'OGILVIE (CN/0822-8434) [11734680] **1620**

NOUVELLES D'ORLEANS, LES (FR/0293-6186) [l02936186] **2520**

NOUVELLES D'OUTREMENT (CN/0227-8472) [06958881] **5791**

NOUVELLES DU BUREAU NATIONAL (CN/1185-202X) [24257312] **5486**

NOUVELLES DU CAMEROUN (US) [04518959] **2642**

NOUVELLES DU LIVRE ANCIEN (FR/0335-752X) [05337976] **4831**

NOUVELLES DU PATRIMOINE (BE/0773-9796) [l07739796] **305**

NOUVELLES ESTHETIQUES (AMERICAN ED.), LES (FR/1043-9641) [19636925] **405**

NOUVELLES ESTHETIQUES (FRENCH ED.), LES (FR) **405**

NOUVELLES ESTHETIQUES (ITALIAN ED.), LES (FR) **405**

NOUVELLES ET DOCUMENTS - LA PROVINCE CANADIENNE DES PERES DE SAINTE-CROIX (CN/0707-7211) [04747050] **4982**

NOUVELLES FEUILLES FAMILIALES (BE) **2284**

NOUVELLES FISCALES DU QUEBEC (CN/0706-4624) [04631508] **4739**

NOUVELLES FISCALES (PARIS), LES (FR/0399-1636) [l03991636] **801**

NOUVELLES GRAPHIQUES (BE/0029-4926) [l00294926] **381**

NOUVELLES HYDRO, PROJETS D'EQUIPEMENT EN BASSE-COTE-NORD (CN/0846-0795) [23659518] **2093**

NOUVELLES INSTRUCTIONS POUR L'ENSEIGNEMENT DES LETTRES DANS LE SECOND CYCLE DU SECOND DEGRE / CENTRE REGIONAL DE DOCUMENTATION PEDAGOGIQUE DE PARIS, LES (FR) [10092990] **3307**

NOUVELLES / LA FEDERATION DES SOCIETES D'HISTOIRE DU QUEBEC (CN/0829-2612) [13192073] **2751**

NOUVELLES, LES (US/0270-174X) [06340644] **1306**

NOUVELLES NORD-SUD *See* REVUE : UN BULLETIN DE L'INSTITUT NORD-SUD **1625**

NOUVELLES NUCLEAIRES, LES (FR) **4448**

NOUVELLES - ONTARIO. MINISTERE DES SERVICES SOCIAUX ET COMMUNAUTAIRES (CN/1183-6458) [25607944] **5299**

NOUVELLES PRATIQUES SOCIALES (CN/0843-4468) [19730334] **5299**

NOUVELLES QUESTIONS FEMINISTES (FR/0248-4951) [07668830] **5563**

NOUVELLES. RELATIONS OUVRIERES. ASSOCIATION DE LA CONSTRUCTION DE MONTREAL ET DU QUEBEC (CN/0317-0977) [02247811] 623, **1695**

NOUVELLES. SECURITE. ASSOCIATION DE LA CONSTRUCTION DE MONTREAL ET DU QUEBEC (CN/0384-7470) [03348855] **623**

NOUVELLES - UNION INTERNATIONALE DES LSYNDICATS DES TRAVAILLEURS DU COMMERCE (XR) [04115939] **1695**

NOUVELLES UNIVERSITAIRES EUROPEENNES (BE) [04712219] **1838**

NOUVELLES UNIVERSITAIRES (MONTREAL) (CN/0709-8006) [06245512] 1838, **1695**

NOUVEUX OUVRAGES DE REFERENCE, LISTE ANNUELLE / BIBLIOTHEQUE NATIONALE, DEPARTMENT DES LIVRES IMPRIMES, SALLE DES CATALOGUES ET DES BIBLIOGRAPHIES (FR/0240-866X) [08260959] **421**

NOVA (PO) [03031475] **326**

NOVA ACTA LEOPOLDINA (GW/0369-5034) [05060554] **5135**

NOVA (BROOKFIELD, WIS.) (US/1047-2398) [20645129] **5033**

NOVA BULGARSKA MUZIKA / SUIUZ NA BULGARSKITE KOMPOZITORI (BU) [07134855] **4142**

NOVA ET VETERA (FRIBOURG) (SZ/0029-5027) [02449185] **4982**

NOVA HEDWIGIA (GW/0029-5035) [01760858] **520**

NOVA HRVATSKA *CEASED.* (UK/0143-3563) [07563841] **2660**

●NOVA JOURNAL OF ALGEBRA AND GEOMETRY (US/1060-9881) [25147839] **3525**

NOVA LAW REVIEW (US/1049-0248) [15205255] **3019**

NOVA MATICA (YU/0353-8052) [22968415] **3349**

NOVA (MIDDLETON) (CN/0316-019X) [02247298] **5791**

NOVA MYSL (XR/0322-905X) [02665548] **4184**

NOVA POESIA BRASILEIRA, A (BL) [10983365] **3467**

NOVA PROIZVODNJA (XV/0029-5051) [06454798] **5135**

NOVA QUARTERLY (US/1041-6900) [16828101] **1093**

NOVA RENASCENCA (PO) [08020562] **2851**

NOVA SCOTIA *See* ROYAL GAZETTE **3045**

NOVA SCOTIA AGRICULTURAL COLLEGE *See* ALUMNI DIRECTORY / NOVA SCOTIA AGRICULTURAL COLLEGE **1099**

NOVA SCOTIA BIRD SOCIETY *See* NEWSLETTER - NOVA SCOTIA BIRD SOCIETY **5592**

NOVA SCOTIA BIRDS (CN) [11901092] **5593**

NOVA SCOTIA BUSINESS JOURNAL (CN/0820-2737) [16440227] **700**

NOVA SCOTIA CHRISTMAS TREE JOURNAL (CN/0832-8293) [17835353] **2390**

NOVA SCOTIA. COMMUNITY PLANNING DIVISION *See* PLANNING GUIDELINE SERIES **2831**

●NOVA SCOTIA CRAFT NEWS / NSDCC (CN/1193-011X) [26715151] **374**

NOVA SCOTIA DEPARTMENT OF COMMUNITY SERVICES, THE (CN/0844-7535) [20189167] **4670**

NOVA SCOTIA. DEPT. OF AGRICULTURE AND MARKETING *See* ANNUAL REPORT OF THE DEPARTMENT OF AGRICULTURE AND MARKETING (HALIFAX) **61**

NOVA SCOTIA. DEPT. OF AGRICULTURE AND MARKETING *See* CO-OPERATIVE ASSOCIATIONS IN NOVA SCOTIA **1541**

NOVA SCOTIA. DEPT. OF CONSUMER AFFAIRS *See* ANNUAL REPORT - NOVA SCOTIA DEPARTMENT OF CONSUMER AFFAIRS **1293**

NOVA SCOTIA. DEPT. OF FINANCE *See* ESTIMATES OF THE GOVERNMENT OF NOVA SCOTIA **4722**

NOVA SCOTIA. DEPT. OF FISHERIES *See* ANNUAL REPORT OF DEPARTMENT OF FISHERIES (HALIFAX) **2295**

NOVA SCOTIA. DEPT. OF MUNICIPAL AFFAIRS *See* ANNUAL REPORT OF MUNICIPAL STATISTICS **4696**

NOVA SCOTIA. DEPT. OF SOCIAL SERVICES *See* ANNUAL REPORT - DEPARTMENT OF SOCIAL SERVICES (HALIFAX) **5272**

NOVA SCOTIA DIRECTORY OF MANUFACTURERS (CN/0381-4912) [02624797] **3485**

NOVA SCOTIA. ENVIRONMENTAL CONTROL COUNCIL *See* ANNUAL REPORT - ENVIRONMENTAL CONTROL COUNCIL **3109**

NOVA SCOTIA FARM COMPUTING NEWS, THE (CN/1182-8986) [23264704] **1197**

NOVA SCOTIA GENEALOGIST, THE (CN/0714-3672) [11746051] **2465**

NOVA SCOTIA HISTORICAL REVIEW (CN/0227-4752) [07579113] **2751**

NOVA SCOTIA HOSTELLER (CN/0707-087X) [04635145] 5486, **2808**

NOVA SCOTIA. HOUSE OF ASSEMBLY *See* DEBATES AND PROCEEDINGS - NOVA SCOTIA HOUSE OF ASSEMBLY **4641**

NOVA SCOTIA. HOUSE OF ASSEMBLY. STANDING COMMITTEE ON PUBLIC ACCOUNTS. STEERING COMMITTEE *See* REPORT OF THE STEERING COMMITTEE TO THE STANDING COMMMITTEE ON PUBLIC ACCOUNTS **4746**

NOVA SCOTIA LAW NEWS (CN/0316-6325) [02247654] **3019**

NOVA SCOTIA LIBERAL, THE (CN/0703-1793) [05789481] **4484**

NOVA SCOTIA LIBRARY ASSOCIATION *See* INFORMATION FOR MEMBERS / NOVA SCOTIA LIBRARY ASSOCIATION **3215**

NOVA SCOTIA MEDICAL JOURNAL, THE (CN/0838-2638) [18318002] **3623**

NOVA SCOTIA MUSEUM *See* MUSEUMNEWS (HALIFAX) **4093**

NOVA SCOTIA. PAY EQUITY COMMISSION *See* PAY EQUITY NEWSLETTER / NOVA SCOTIA PAY EQUITY COMMISSION, THE **1701**

NOVA SCOTIA PICTORIAL COUNTRY INNS, BED & BREAKFAST AND MUCH MORE (CN/1184-0390) [23302801] **2808**

NOVA SCOTIA PROVINCIAL HEALTH COUNCIL *See* ANNUAL REPORT FOR THE FISCAL YEAR ENDING ... / NOVA SCOTIA PROVINCIAL HEALTH COUNCIL **4765**

NOVA SCOTIA READING SPECIALISTS ASSOCIATION *See* NSRSA. NOVA SCOTIA READING SPECIALISTS ASSOCIATION **1769**

NOVA SCOTIA REAL PROPERTY PRACTICE MANUAL (CN) 4842, **3019**

NOVA SCOTIA REPORTS (FREDERICTON) (CN/0048-0983) [09099862] **3019**

NOVA SCOTIA SCHOOL LIBRARY ASSOCIATION *See* NSSLA BULLETIN **3237**

NOVA SCOTIA SCHOOL TELEVISION. ELEMENTARY (CN/0713-648X) [08920434] **1769**

NOVA SCOTIA TEACHERS UNION. LANGUAGE TEACHERS ASSOCIATION. CONFERENCE *See* LTA CONFERENCE **3300**

NOVA SCOTIA TEACHERS UNION. PRIMARY ELEMENTARY TEACHERS ASSOCIATION. CONFERENCE *See* CONFERENCE REPORT - PRIMARY ELEMENTARY TEACHERS ASSOCIATION **1862**

NOVA SCOTIA. TUBERCULOSIS CONTROL SERVICES *See* ANNUAL REPORT - TUBERCULOSIS CONTROL SERVICES, NOVA SCOTIA **3948**

NOVA SCOTIA WORKER, THE (CN/0228-717X) [08330440] **1695**

NOVA SCOTIAN INSTITUTE OF SCIENCE *See* PROCEEDINGS OF THE NOVA SCOTIAN INSTITUTE OF SCIENCE **5141**

NOVA TRGOVINA (YU/0469-0281) [02665579] **848**

NOVAIA INOSTRANNAIA LITERATURA PO OBSHCHESTVENNYM NAUKAM: EKONOMIKA (RU/0134-2835) [02978474] **1593**

NOVAIA INOSTRANNAIA LITERATURA PO OBSHCHESTVENNYM NAUKAM: FILOSOFIIA I SOTSIOLOGIIA (RU) [02981187] **4354**

NOVAIA INOSTRANNAIA LITERATURA PO OBSHCHESTVENNYM NAUKAM: GOSUDARSTVO I PRAVO (RU) [03408143] **3019**

NOVAIA INOSTRANNAIA LITERATURA PO OBSHCHESTVENNYM NAUKAM: IAZYKOZNANIE (RU) [02727266] **3307**

NOVAIA INOSTRANNAIA LITERATURA PO OBSHCHESTVENNYM NAUKAM: ISTORIIA, ARKHEOLOGIIA, ETNOGRAFIIA (RU) [02724524] **276**

NOVAIA INOSTRANNAIA LITERATURA PO OBSHCHESTVENNYM NAUKAM: LITERATUROVEDENIE (RU) [03158302] **3418**

NOVAIA INOSTRANNAIA LITERATURA PO OBSHCHESTVENNYM NAUKAM: NAUKOVEDENIE (RU) [02835700] **5135**

NOVAIA INOSTRANNNAIA LITERATURA PO OBSHCHESTVENNYM NAUKAM. LITERATUROVEDENIE *See* NOVAIA LITERATURA PO SOTSIALNYM I GUMANITARNYM NAUKAM. LITERATUROVEDENIE / ROSSIISKAIA AKADEMIIA NAUK, INSTITUT NAUCHNOI INFORMATSII PO OBSHCHESTVENNYM NAUKAM **3419**

NOVAIA LITERATURA PO OBSHCHESTVENNYM NAUKAM. ISTORIIA, ARKHEOLOGIIA, ETNOGRAFIIA *See* NOVAIA OTECHESTVENNAIA LITERATURA PO OBSHCHESTVENNYM NAUKAM. ISTORIIA, ARKHEOLOGIIA, ETNOGRAFIIA / ROSSIISKAIA AKADEMIIA NAUK, INSTITUT NAUCHNOI INFORMATSII PO OBSHCHESTVENNYM NAUKAM **2624**

● NOVAIA LITERATURA PO SOTSIALNYM I GUMANITARNYM NAUKAM. EKONOMIKA / ROSSIISKAIA AKADEMIIA NAUK, INSTITUT NAUCHNOI INFORMATSII PO OBSHCHESTVENNYM NAUKAM (RU) [30314537] **1508**

● NOVAIA LITERATURA PO SOTSIALNYM I GUMANITARNYM NAUKAM. GOSUDARSTVO I PRAVO / ROSSIISKAIA AKADEMIIA NAUK, INSTITUT NAUCHNOI INFORMATSII PO OBSHCHESTVENNYM NAUKAM (RU) [30337146] 3019, **4484**

● NOVAIA LITERATURA PO SOTSIALNYM I GUMANITARNYM NAUKAM. ISTORIIA, ARKHEOLOGIIA, ETNOLOGIIA / ROSSIISKAIA AKADEMIIA NAUK, INSTITUT NAUCHNOI INFORMATSII PO OBSHCHESTVENNYM NAUKAM (RU) [30491949] **276**

● NOVAIA LITERATURA PO SOTSIALNYM I GUMANITARNYM NAUKAM. LITERATUROVEDENIE / ROSSIISKAIA AKADEMIIA NAUK, INSTITUT NAUCHNOI INFORMATSII PO OBSHCHESTVENNYM NAUKAM (RU) [30454282] **3419**

● NOVAIA OTECHESTVENNAIA I INOSTRANNAIA LITERATURA PO OBSHCHESTVENNYM NAUKAM. AFRIKA. BLIZHNII I SREDNII VOSTOK / ROSSIISKAIA AKADEMIIA NAUK, INSTITUT NAUCHNOI INFORMATSII PO OBSHCHESTVENNYM NAUKAM (RU) [29780556] **3419**

● NOVAIA OTECHESTVENNAIA I INOSTRANNAIA LITERATURA PO OBSHCHESTVENNYM NAUKAM. IUZHNAIA I IUGO-VOSTOCHNAIA AZIIA, DALNYI VOSTOK / ROSSIISKAIA AKADEMIIA NAUK, INSTITUT NAUCHNOI INFORMATSII PO OBSHCHESTVENNYM NAUKAM (RU) [29741575] **2660**

NOVAIA OTECHESTVENNAIA I INOSTRANNAIA LITERATURA PO OBSHCHESTVENNYM NAUKAM. RELIGIOVEDENIE / ROSSIISKAIA AKADEMIIA NAUK, INSTITUT NAUCHNOI INFORMATSII PO OBSHCHESTVENNYM NAUKAM (RU/0134-2932) [29788823] 4354, **4982**

NOVAIA OTECHESTVENNAIA INOSTRANNA (RU) 2701, **2465**

NOVAIA OTECHESTVENNAIA LITERATURA PO OBSHCHESTVENNYM NAUKAM. EKONOMIKA (RU) [28083473] **1508**

NOVAIA OTECHESTVENNAIA LITERATURA PO OBSHCHESTVENNYM NAUKAM. FILOSOFIIA I SOTSIOLOGIIA / ROSSIISKAIA AKADEMIIA NAUK, INSTITUT NAUCHNOI INFORMATSII PO OBSHCHESTVENNYM NAUKAM (RU) [28625934] 5253, **4354**

NOVAIA OTECHESTVENNAIA LITERATURA PO OBSHCHESTVENNYM NAUKAM. GOSUDARSTVO I PRAVO (RU) [28084861] **3019**

NOVAIA OTECHESTVENNAIA LITERATURA PO OBSHCHESTVENNYM NAUKAM. IAZYKOZNANIE / ROSSIISKAIA AKADEMIIA NAUK, INSTITUT NAUCHNOI INFORMATSII PO OBSHCHESTVENNYM NAUKAM (RU) [29767571] **3307**

NOVAIA OTECHESTVENNAIA LITERATURA PO OBSHCHESTVENNYM NAUKAM. ISTORIIA, ARKHEOLOGIIA, ETNOGRAFIIA *See* NOVAIA LITERATURA PO SOTSIALNYM I GUMANITARNYM NAUKAM. ISTORIIA, ARKHEOLOGIIA, ETNOLOGIIA / ROSSIISKAIA AKADEMIIA NAUK, INSTITUT NAUCHNOI INFORMATSII PO OBSHCHESTVENNYM NAUKAM **276**

NOVAIA OTECHESTVENNAIA LITERATURA PO OBSHCHESTVENNYM NAUKAM. ISTORIIA, ARKHEOLOGIIA, ETNOGRAFIIA / ROSSIISKAIA AKADEMIIA NAUK, INSTITUT NAUCHNOI INFORMATSII PO OBSHCHESTVENNYM NAUKAM (RU) [29741782] 277, **2624**

NOVAIA OTECHESTVENNAIA LITERATURA PO OBSHCHESTVENNYM NAUKAM. LITERATUROVEDENIE *See* NOVAIA LITERATURA PO SOTSIALNYM I GUMANITARNYM NAUKAM. LITERATUROVEDENIE / ROSSIISKAIA AKADEMIIA NAUK, INSTITUT NAUCHNOI INFORMATSII PO OBSHCHESTVENNYM NAUKAM **3419**

NOVAIA OTECHESTVENNAIA LITERATURA PO OBSHCHESTVENNYM NAUKAM. LITERATUROVEDENIE / ROSSIISKAIA AKADEMIIA NAUK, INSTITUT NAUCHNOI INFORMATSII PO OBSHCHESTVENNYM NAUKAM (RU) [28644387] **3459**

NOVAIA OTECHESTVENNAIA LITERATURA PO OBSHCHESTVENNYM NAUKAM. NAUKOVEDENIE / ROSSIISKAIA AKADEMIIA NAUK, INSTITUT NAUCHNOI INFORMATSII PO OBSHCHESTVENNYM NAUKAM (RU/0134-2754) [29741651] **5135**

NOVAIA SOVETSKAIA I INOSTRANNAIA LITERATURA PO BIBLIOTEKOVEDENIIU I BIBLIOGRAFII (RU) [02506433] **3237**

NOVAIA SOVETSKAIA I INOSTRANNAIA LITERATURA PO ISKUSSTVU: OBSHCHIE VOPROSY ISKUSSTVA, ESTETIKA (RU) [02652288] **360**

NOVAIA SOVETSKAIA I INOSTRANNAIA LITERATURA PO ISKUSSTVU: TANETS, TSIRK, ESTRADA (RU) [02999072] **386**

NOVAIA SOVETSKAIA I INOSTRANNAIA LITERATURA PO KULTURA I ISKUSSTVU: MUZYKA (RU) [03386930] **4142**

NOVAIA SOVETSKAIA I INOSTRANNAIA LITERATURA PO KULTURE I ISKUSSTVU: KULTURNO-PROSVETITELNAIA RABOTA I NARODNOE TVORCHESTVO (RU) [02880124] **5211**

NOVAIA SOVETSKAIA I INOSTRANNAIA LITERATURA PO KULTURE I ISKUSSTVU : OBSHCHIE PROBLEMY KULTURY I KULTURNOGO STROITELSTVA (RU) [02477781] **3419**

NOVAIA SOVETSKAIA I INOSTRANNAIA LITERATURA PO OBSHCHESTVENNYM NAUKAM: GERMANSKAIA DEMOKRATICHESKAIA RESPUBLIKA (RU) [03031017] **2701**

NOVAIA SOVETSKAIA I INOSTRANNAIA LITERATURA PO OBSHCHESTVENNYM NAUKAM. BLIZHNII I SREDNII VOSTOK, AFRIKA *See* NOVAIA OTECHESTVENNAIA I INOSTRANNAIA LITERATURA PO OBSHCHESTVENNYM NAUKAM. AFRIKA. BLIZHNII I SREDNII VOSTOK / ROSSIISKAIA AKADEMIIA NAUK, INSTITUT NAUCHNOI INFORMATSII PO OBSHCHESTVENNYM NAUKAM **3419**

NOVAIA SOVETSKAIA I INOSTRANNAIA LITERATURA PO OBSHCHESTVENNYM NAUKAM. BOLGRAIIA (RU) [22917882] **421**

NOVAIA SOVETSKAIA I INOSTRANNAIA LITERATURA PO OBSHCHESTVENNYM NAUKAM: CHEKHOSLOVATSKAIA SOTSIALISTICHESKAIA RESPUBLIKA (RU) [03067086] **2701**

NOVAIA SOVETSKAIA I INOSTRANNAIA LITERATURA PO OBSHCHESTVENNYM NAUKAM. IUZHNAIA I IUGO-VOSTOCHNAIA AZIIA, DALNYI VOSTOK *See* NOVAIA OTECHESTVENNAIA I INOSTRANNAIA LITERATURA PO OBSHCHESTVENNYM NAUKAM. IUZHNAIA I IUGO-VOSTOCHNAIA AZIIA, DALNYI VOSTOK / ROSSIISKAIA AKADEMIIA NAUK, INSTITUT NAUCHNOI INFORMATSII PO OBSHCHESTVENNYM NAUKAM **2660**

NOVAIA SOVETSKAIA I INOSTRANNAIA LITERATURA PO OBSHCHESTVENNYM NAUKAM. POLSKAIA NARODNAIA RESPUBLIKA (RU/0134-2924) [03074768] **2701**

NOVAIA SOVETSKAIA I INOSTRANNAIA LITERATURA PO OBSHCHESTVENNYM NAUKAM. PROBLEMY ATEIZMA I RELIGII *See* NOVAIA OTECHESTVENNAIA I INOSTRANNAIA LITERATURA PO OBSHCHESTVENNYM NAUKAM. RELIGIOVEDENIE / ROSSIISKAIA AKADEMIIA NAUK, INSTITUT NAUCHNOI INFORMATSII PO OBSHCHESTVENNYM NAUKAM **4982**

NOVAIA SOVETSKAIA I INOSTRANNAIA LITERATURA PO OBSHCHESTVENNYM NAUKAM. RUMYNIIA (RU/0202-2540) [22947428] **421**

NOVAIA SOVETSKAIA I INOSTRANNAIA LITERATURA PO OBSHCHESTVENNYM NAUKAM. STRANY AZII I AFRIKI. OBSHCHIE PROBLEMY (RU) [02999130] **2660**

NOVAIA SOVETSKAIA LITERATURA PO KULTURE I ISKUSSTVU: MUZEEVEDENIE I OKHRANA PAMIATNIKOV (RU) [02608758] **4094**

NOVAIA SOVETSKAIA LITERATURA PO OBSHCHESTVENNYM NAUKAM (RU) [23228829] 5211, **3419**

NOVAIA SOVETSKAIA LITERATURA PO OBSHCHESTVENNYM NAUKAM: EKONOMIKA (RU) [02976032] 1576, **3419**

NOVAIA SOVETSKAIA LITERATURA PO OBSHCHESTVENNYM NAUKAM. FILOSOFSKIE NAUKI *See* NOVAIA OTECHESTVENNAIA LITERATURA PO OBSHCHESTVENNYM NAUKAM. FILOSOFIIA I SOTSIOLOGIIA / ROSSIISKAIA AKADEMIIA NAUK, INSTITUT NAUCHNOI INFORMATSII PO OBSHCHESTVENNYM NAUKAM **4354**

NOVAIA SOVETSKAIA LITERATURA PO OBSHCHESTVENNYM NAUKAM: GOSUDARSTVO I PRAVO *See* NOVAIA OTECHESTVENNAIA LITERATURA PO OBSHCHESTVENNYM NAUKAM. GOSUDARSTVO I PRAVO **3019**

NOVAIA SOVETSKAIA LITERATURA PO OBSHCHESTVENNYM NAUKAM. IAZYKOZNANIE *See* NOVAIA OTECHESTVENNAIA LITERATURA PO OBSHCHESTVENNYM NAUKAM. IAZYKOZNANIE / ROSSIISKAIA AKADEMIIA NAUK, INSTITUT NAUCHNOI INFORMATSII PO OBSHCHESTVENNYM NAUKAM **3307**

NOVAIA SOVETSKAIA LITERATURA PO OBSHCHESTVENNYM NAUKAM. LITERATUROVEDENIE *See* NOVAIA OTECHESTVENNAIA LITERATURA PO OBSHCHESTVENNYM NAUKAM. LITERATUROVEDENIE / ROSSIISKAIA AKADEMIIA NAUK, INSTITUT NAUCHNOI INFORMATSII PO OBSHCHESTVENNYM NAUKAM **3459**

NOVAIA SOVETSKAIA LITERATURA PO OBSHCHESTVENNYM NAUKAM. NAUKOVEDENIE *See* NOVAIA OTECHESTVENNAIA LITERATURA PO OBSHCHESTVENNYM NAUKAM. NAUKOVEDENIE / ROSSIISKAIA AKADEMIIA NAUK, INSTITUT NAUCHNOI INFORMATSII PO OBSHCHESTVENNYM NAUKAM **5135**

NOVAJA I NOVEJSAKA ISTORIJA (MOSKVA) (RU/0130-3864) [01760876] **2624**

NOVALIS (SZ) [24166106] **2520**

NOVAMAQUINA 2000 *SUSPENDED*. (SP/0210-0118) [I02100118] **2123**

NOVARA (IT) [06589818] **1508**

NOVARA, ITALY (PROVINCE). CAMERA DI COMMERCIO, INDUSTRIA, ARTIGIANATO E AGRICOLTURA *See* NOVARA **1508**

NOVARIEN (IT) [07054533] **5033**

NOVAS TABELAS DO IMPOSTO DE RENDA PARA ... ASSALARIADOS E NAO-ASSALARIADOS (BL) [11833272] **3020**

NOVASCOPE (US/0892-5003) [15274325] **2491**

NOVATEUR, LE (CN/0825-0596) [11559810] **1620**

NOVATO ADVANCE (US) [26780170] **5638**

NOVEDADES; REVISTA LITERARIA Y DE INFORMACION GRAFICA (MX) [07107250] **2541**

NOVEL (US/0029-5132) [01760877] **3349**

NOVEL & SHORT STORY WRITER'S MARKET (US/0897-9812) [17682410] 4818, **3419**

NOVELA POLICIACA (SP) **3020**

NOVELLEREGISTER (DK/0106-035X) [08241524] **3459**

NOVENYTERMELES (HU/0546-8191) [05378220] 520, **179**

NOVENYVEDELEM (HU/0133-0829) [02309305] **520**

NOVESE, IL (IT) **5804**

NOVI DNI (CN/0048-1017) [01760880] **2270**

NOVI LIST (CI/0350-4301) [I03504301] **5799**

NOVI MATAJUR (IT) [02241598] **2701**

NOVI SKRIZALI (CN/1186-2017) [10189933] **4982**

NOVI VJESNIK (CI) [25813668] **5799**

NOVIJ SLAH (CN/0029-5310) [16975098] **5791**

NOVINKY HUDEBNI LITERATURY (XR) [02561393] **4142**

NOVINKY LITERATURY : EKONOMIE (XR) [02692946] **1508**

NOVINKY LITERATURY. POLITIKA (XR) [08378409] **5211**

NOVINKY LITERATURY : PSYCHOLOGIE (XR) [01795208] **4622**

NOVITATES ARTHROPODAE (US/0278-3274) [04975570] **5593**

NOVITATES BOTANICAE UNIVERSITATIS CAROLINAE (XR/0862-5158) [I08625158] **520**

NOVO DIABETES CARE PROFILE (US/1054-9412) [23026734] **3732**

NOVO MUNDO (TORONTO) (CN/0822-8035) [10440740] **5791**

NOVOE RUSSKOE SLOVO (US/0730-8949) [02265277] **5719**

NOVOE SLOVO (BERLIN, GERMANY) (GW) [21021260] **5802**

NOVOE V RUSSKOI LEKSIKE : SLOVARNYE MATERIALY / AKADEMIIA NAUK SSSR, INSTITUT RUSSKOGO IAZYKA (RU) [08063134] 1927, **3307**

NOVOE V TEKHNIKE I TEKHNOLOGII PROIZVODSTVA FANERY, DREVESNOSTRUZHECHYNKH PLIT I DREVESNOSLOISTYKH PLASTIKOV (RU) [05119003] **2403**

NOVOE V ZARUBEZHNOI LINGVISTIKE *CEASED.* (RU) [04993751] **3307**

NOVOE V ZHIZNI, NAUKE. KULTURA I RELIGIIA *See* KULTURA I RELIGIIA **4972**

NOVOE V ZHIZNI, NAUKE, TEKHNIKE. SERIIA ISKUSSTVO *See* MIR ISKUSSTV **325**

NOVOE VIEMIA (MOSCOW, R.S.F.S.R.) (RU/0137-0723) [08118914] **4530**

NOVOE VREMIA (RU/0137-0723) [04741135] **4530**

NOVON (SAINT LOUIS, MO.) (US/1055-3177) [23138710] **520**

NOVOS ESTUDOS CEBRAP (BL/0101-3300) [08793654] 1509, 4354, **4485**

NOVOS POETAS DO CEARA; ANTOLOGIA, OS (BL) [01783421] **3467**

NOVOSTI LITERATURY I DOKUMENTATSII. SERIIA: OBUCHENIE I KOMMUNISTICHESKOE VOSPITANIE V VYSSHIKH I SREDNIKH SPETSIALNYKH UCHEBNYKH ZAVEDENIIAKH (RU) [04263478] **1796**

NOVOSTI LITERATURY I DOKUMENTATSII. SERIIA: UPRAVLENIE, EKONOMIKA I PROGNOZIROVANIE VYSSHEGO I SREDNEGO SPETSIALNOGO OBRAZOVANIIA (RU) [04263685] **1796**

NOVOSTI LITERATURY I DOKUMENTATSII. SERIIA: VYSSHEE I SREDNEE SPETSIALNOE OBRAZOVANIE ZA RUBEZHOM (RU) [04219996] **1796**

NOVOSTI NAUCHNOI LITERATURY: TEATR *See* TEATR **5369**

NOVOSTI TEKHNICHESKOI LITERATURY. RAZDEL A. SERIIA IX: INZHENERNYE IZYSKANIIA V STROITELSTVE. STROITELSTVO I ARKHITEKTURA (RU) [02359250] **2028**

NOVOSTI TEKHNICHESKOI LITERATURY. RAZDEL A. SERIIA XI: TRANSPORTNOE STROITELSTVO. STROITELSTVO I ARKHITEKTURA (RU) [02359323] **2028**

NOVOSTI TEKHNICHESKOI LITERATURY. RAZDEL PROEKTIROVANIE I STROITELSTVO. STROITELSTVO I ARKHITEKTURA (RU) [04222325] **633**

NOVOSTI TEKHNICHESKOI LITERATURY. RAZDEL SERIIA III: RAIONNAIA PLANIROVKA I GRADOSTROITELSTVO. STROITELSTVO I ARKHITEKTURA (RU) [02399190] **305**

NOVOSTI TEKHNICHESKOI LITERATURY. STROITELSTVO I ARKHITEKTURA. RAZDEL A. SERIIA VIII: STROITELNYE KONSTRUKTSII, STROITELNAIA FIZIKA (RU) [02468132] **623**

NOVOSTI TEKHNICHESKOI LITERATURY. STROITELSTVO I ARKHITEKTURA. RAZDEL SERIIA V: SELSKO-KHOZIAISTVENNYE KOMPLEKSY, PREDPRIIATIIA, ZDANIIA I SOORUZHENIIA (RU) [02476953] **623**

NOVOSTI TEKHNICHESKOI LITERATURY. STROITELSTVO I ARKHITEKTURA. RAZDEL SERIIA VI. ORGANIZATSIIA, MEKHANIZATSIIA I PROIZVODSTVO STROITELNO-MONTAZHNYKH RABOT (RU) [02505839] **623**

NOVOSTI TEKHNICHESKOI LITERATURY. STROITELSTVO I ARKHITEKTURA. RAZDEL SERIIA VII. STROITELNYE MATERIALY I IZDELIIA, KHARAKTERISTIKA I PRIMENENIE (RJ) [02505995] **2028**

NOVOSTI TEKHNICHESKOI LITERATURY. STROITELSTVO I ARKHITEKTURA. RAZDEL SERIIA X: SANITARNAIA TEKHNIKA, INZHENERNOE OBORUDOVANIE ZDANII (RU) [02503287] **2237**

NOVOSTI TEKHNICHESKOI LITERATURY. STROITELSTVO I ARKHITEKTURA. RAZDEL SERIIA XII: VODOKHOZIAISTVENNOE STROITELSTVO (RU) [02485987] **2093**

NOVOSTI V TSELULOZNO-KHARTIENATA PROMISHLENOST / MINISTERSTVO NA GORITE I GORSKATA PROMISHLENOST, DSO, "TSELULOZA I KHARTIIA"-NIITSKH (BU/0204-9562) [11232102] **4235**

NOVOTO V TEORIIATA I SOTSIALNATA PRAKTIKA. DURZHAVA I PRAVO (BU) [19937717] **3020**

NOVUM GEBRAUCHSGRAPHIK (GW/C302-9794) [01794141] **381**

NOVUM TESTAMENTUM (NE/0048-1009) [01760885] **5018**

NOVY DIKOBRAZ (CS) [21506143] **4864**

NOVY ORIENT (XR/0029-5302) [04693016] **2660**

NOVY SLOVAK (XO/1210-2059) [I12102059] **5810**

NOVYE DANNYE O MINERALAKH / AKADEMIIA NAUK SSSR, MINERALOGICHESKIEĬ MUZEI IM. A.E. FERSMANA (RU/0203-5626) [10417297] **1443**

●NOVYE KNIGI (RU) [25958356] **421**

NOVYE KNIGI SSSR *See* NOVYE KNIGI **421**

NOVYE KNIGI ZA RUBEZHOM: SERIIA A. MATEMATIKA, MEKHANIKA, ASTRONOMIIA, FIZIKA, GEOFIZIKA, KHIMIIA, GEOLOGIIA (RU) [06498527] **5135**

NOVYE KNIGI ZA RUBEZHOM: SERIIA B. TEKHNIKA (RU) [06498534] **5135**

NOVYE KNIGI ZA RUBEZHOM: SERIIA V. BIOLOGIIA, MEDITSINA, SELSKOE KHOZIAISTVO (RU) [06498516] **467**

NOVYE TOVARY (RU) [06498570] **848**

NOVYI GORIZONT (LV) [25614509] **3419**

●NOVYIA KNIHI BELARUSI (BW) [26336239] **421**

NOVYIA KNIHI BSSR *See* NOVYIA KNIHI BELARUSI **421**

NOVYJ MIR (RU/0130-7673) [01696763] **3349**

NOVYJ ZURNAL (US/0029-5337) [02449193] **2851**

NOW AND THEN (DOWNSVIEW) (CN/0229-690X) [08205493] **3020**

NOW AND THEN (JOHNSON CITY, TENN.) (US/0896-2693) [11710993] **2751**

NOW AND THEN (MUNCY) (US/0029-5361) [01760888] **2751**

NOW DIG THIS (UK) **4142**

NOW L.A. / OFFICIAL PUBLICATION OF THE LOS ANGELES CHAPTER, NATIONAL ORGANIZATION FOR WOMEN (NOW) (US/0741-9627) [09737642] **5563**

NOW-NYS ACTION REPORT (US/8750-7005) [11686953] **5563**

NOW (RIVERVIEW) (CN/0229-5296) [08311758] **386**

NOW (TORONTO. 1981) (CN/0712-1326) [08651772] 386, **4853**

NOWA SZKOLA (PL) [06498496] **1769**

NOWA WIES (PL) [06514410] **2520**

NOWE DROGI *CEASED.* (PL/0029-5388) [02265307] **5211**

NOWE KSIAZKI (PL) [01760890] **421**

●NOWE PODKARPACIE (PL) [28571023] **5808**

NOWE PRAWO *CEASED.* (PL) [01760891] **2520**

NOWINY (PL/0137-9534) [20860544] **5808**

NOWINY JELENIOGORSKIE (PL/0208-6883) [I02086883] **2520**

NOWOCZESNY BIZNESMEN (CN/1189-010X) [24860493] **700**

NOWOSCI TORUN (PL/0137-9259) [01379259] **5808**

NOWOTWORY (PL/0029-540X) [06307108] **3821**

NOWY TYDZIEN (PL) [24185500] **5808**

NOYAKU KENSAJO HOKOKU (JA/0369-4658) [03955395] **115**

NOYAU, LE (CN/0226-8124) [06316391] **115**

NPGA REPORTS (US/1040-0354) [18297264] **4267**

NPGUO CHOSA HOKOKUSHO (JA) [06226727] **115**

NPIRS NEWS / NATIONAL PESTICIDE INFORMATION RETRIEVAL SYSTEM (US) [10220344] **4246**

NPL NEWS (UK/0143-1536) [I01431536] **4413**

NPRA FOREIGN TRADE STATISTICS ON SELECTED PETROCHEMICALS (US) **4267**

NPTA MANAGEMENT NEWS (US/0739-2214) [09719825] 880, **4235**

NRA. NAVAL RESERVE ASSOCIATION NEWS (US/0162-2129) [04145240] **4181**

NRA NEWSLETTER (ALEXANDRIA, VA.) (US/0279-5507) [07093026] **4381**

NRA TOURNAMENT NEWS (US) **4908**

NRAO NEWSLETTER (US/0894-5985) [10048287] **397**

NRBA RADIONEWTECH (US/0736-4237) [09124739] **1135**

NRBA SALES AND PROMOTION NEWS (US/0277-0245) [07484660] **1135**

NRC CALENDAR, THE (US/1071-2267) [28577102] 1951, **3020**

NRC FM RADIO LOG *See* FM RADIO LOG **1111**

NRC HANDELSBLAD (NE) **5806**

NRC SOLAR INFORMATION SERIES (CN/0711-270X) [06077115] **1951**

NRC TELEPHONE DIRECTORY (US/1056-9081) [22271388] **4670**

NRC TLD DIRECT RADIATION MONITORING NETWORK (US/0883-3311) [08934210] **4438**

●NRCCSA NEWS / NATIONAL RESOURCE CENTER ON CHILD SEXUAL ABUSE OF THE NATIONAL CENTER ON CHILD ABUSE AND NEGLECT (US) [26018305] **5299**

NRCP DIRECTORY (PH/0116-6107) [09235298] **5135**

NRCP RESEARCH BULLETIN (PH) [02176782] **5135**

NRCSA PROGRAM DIRECTORY. EUROPE (US/0278-3789) [07788775] **1769**

NRDC NEWSLINE (US) [09865150] **3115**

NRDC WORLD ENVIRONMENT ALERT (US/0196-2493) [05785756] **2201**

NRECA--APPA LEGAL REPORTING SERVICE (US/0362-8833) [02379203] 4761, **3020**

●NREL SCIENCE & TECHNOLOGY IN REVIEW (US) [25615412] **1951**

NRI QUARTERLY ECONOMIC REVIEW / NOMURA RESEARCH INSTITUTE (JA) [23730148] **1509**

NRI QUARTERLY ECONOMIC REVIEW (TOKYO, JAPAN : 1989) *See* QUARTERLY ECONOMIC REVIEW **1579**

NRI SPECIAL PUBLICATION (PP) [21284476] **5135**

NRIM CREEP DATA SHEET (JA) [10343941] **4014**

NRL MEMORANDUM REPORT (US/0502-3378) [08143251] **4181**

NRL REPORT (US) [07354002] **4181**

NRMA AD/PRO (US/0748-8327) [11013958] **763**

NRPB REPORT (UK) [20493530] **3944**

NRRI QUARTERLY BULLETIN (US/8756-632X) [11613519] 4761, **4699**

NRTA BULLETIN (US/1044-1107) [19686039] 1769, **5180**

NS Alphabetical Title Index

NS TRAILS (CN/1184-9754) [24266868] **2751**

NSA MAGAZINE (US/0098-5570) [02241658] **1838**

NSAA NEWS (US/1042-6256) [19090927] **4908**

NSBA NEWS MICROFORM (US) [14437070] **3020**

NSCA JOURNAL (US/1073-2721) [28201416] **1857**

NSCA MEMBERS' HANDBOOK (UK/0140-6787) [05426034] **2179**

NSCLC WASHINGTON WEEKLY (US/0277-7460) [05039648] **5180**, **3020**

NSDA SALES SURVEY OF THE SOFT DRINK INDUSTRY (US) [03407097] **2370**

NSDB-UP RESEARCH HIGHLIGHTS (PH) [07529478] **5135**

NSEA VOICE (US/0891-9011) [10527574] **1769**

NSF FOOD SERVICE EQUIPMENT STANDARDS (US) [04750747] **2351**

NSF GRANT POLICY MANUAL (US) [03458908] **5135**

NSFRE JOURNAL (US/0196-3295) [05781411] **5299**

NSFRE NEWS (US/0890-2828) [14193109] **763**

NSG TECHNICAL REPORT (JA/0289-6672) [I02896672] **2592**

NSGA BUYING GUIDE (US) [05041348] **4908**

NSGA RETAIL FOCUS (US/1045-2087) [19119623] **4908**

NSI ADVISORY (US/1060-4731) [25002189] **4670**

NSIAA NEWS (CN/0712-6298) [09336554] **5135**

NSM REPORT (US/0279-2893) [06046246] **934**

NSMEA NOTES (CN/0821-3283) [09543121] **4142**

NSOA BULLETIN (US/0146-9975) [03061784] **1769**, **4142**

NSPA WASHINGTON REPORTER, THE (US/0469-3922) [07108036] **749**

NSPE PEI INDUSTRY FORUM *See* INDUSTRY ENGINEER **1978**

NSPI NEWSLETTER (US/0744-9976) [08699764] **4853**

NSRSA. NOVA SCOTIA READING SPECIALISTS ASSOCIATION (CN/0709-6569) [05534301] **1769**

NSS BULLETIN, THE (US/0146-9517) [02087737] **1359**

NSS NEWS (US/0027-7010) [02850592] **1359**

NSSLA BULLETIN (CN/0707-2457) [04653826] **3237**

NSTA BI-WEEKLY NEWSLETTER (US) **5388**

NSTA REPORT / NATIONAL SCIENCE TEACHERS ASSOCIATION (US) [11360749] **5135**, **1901**

NSTZ : NEUE ZEITSCHRIFT FUER STRAFRECHT (GW) [09126413] **3108**

NSUKKA LIBRARY NOTES (NR/0331-1481) [09573102] **3237**

NSV REPORT (US) [14254416] **5253**

NSW AGRICULTURE TODAY (AT) **115**

NSW DAIRYMEN'S DIGEST (AT) [09927727] **197**

NSW FARMER AND GRAZIER *See* NSW AGRICULTURE TODAY **115**

NSW JOURNAL OF SPECIAL EDUCATION (AT/0814-0960) [I08140960] **1883**

NSWMA REPORTS FOR THE WASTE MANAGEMENT INDUSTRY / NATIONAL SOLID WASTES MANAGEMENT ASSOCIATION (US) [04768872] **2237**

NT. NEWS ON TESTS (US/0271-8472) [04894792] **1769**

NT, TECNICA & TECNOLOGIA / AMMA (IT) [20028381] **2123**

NTA FORUM : PERSPECTIVES, IDEAS AND NEWS FROM THE NATIONAL TAX ASSOCIATION (US) [24888271] **4739**

NTA-TIA BOOKSHELF (US/0091-0783) [01786096] **4739**

NTDPMA BUYERS GUIDE, THE (US/0275-3340) [05080128] **2123**, **951**

NTDRA DEALER NEWS (US/0027-7045) [04108930] **5076**

NTDRA MEMBERGRAM (US/0744-5679) [08372636] **5076**

NTDRA TIRE DEALERS SURVEY (US/0077-5886) [01783418] **5076**

NTH MAN (US/1047-7462) [20233942] **4864**

NTI. NOUVELLES TECHNOLOGIES DE L'INFORMATION (FR/0992-3020) [I09923020] **5135**

NTIA REPORT (US/0271-9703) [06692687] **1161**

NTIAC NEWSLETTER (US/0730-8086) [08081405] **1989**

NTIS ALERT. AGRICULTURE & FOOD (US) **2351**, **115**

NTIS ALERT. ASTRONOMY & ASTROPHYSICS (US) **397**

NTIS ALERT. BIOMEDICAL TECHNOLOGY & HUMAN FACTORS ENGINEERING (US) **3695**

NTIS ALERT. BUILDING INDUSTRY TECHNOLOGY (US/0163-1500) **623**

● NTIS ALERT. BUSINESS & ECONOMICS (US/1074-1674) [25601747] **1509**, **700**

NTIS ALERT. CIVIL ENGINEERING (US) **2028**

NTIS ALERT. COMBUSTION, ENGINES & PROPELLANTS (US) **2123**

NTIS ALERT. COMMUNICATION (US) **1118**

NTIS ALERT. COMPUTERS, CONTROL & INFORMATION THEORY (US) **1197**

NTIS ALERT. DETECTION & COUNTERMEASURES (US) **2074**

NTIS ALERT. ELECTROTECHNOLOGY (US) **2074**

NTIS ALERT. ENERGY (US) **1951**

NTIS ALERT. ENVIRONMENTAL POLLUTION & CONTROL (US) **2237**

NTIS ALERT. FOREIGN TECHNOLOGY **CEASED.** (US) **5135**

NTIS ALERT. GOVERNMENT INVENTIONS FOR LICENSING (US) **1306**

● NTIS ALERT. HEALTH CARE / PREPARED BY THE NATIONAL TECHNICAL INFORMATION SERVICE, U.S. DEPARTMENT OF COMMERCE, TECHNOLOGY ADMINISTRATION (US) [25172019] **3790**, **4794**

NTIS ALERT. LIBRARY & INFORMATION SCIENCES (US) **3237**

NTIS ALERT. MANUFACTURING TECHNOLOGY (US) **1197**, **3485**

NTIS ALERT. MATERIALS SCIENCES (US) **2107**

NTIS ALERT. MATHEMATICAL SCIENCES (US) **3525**

● NTIS ALERT. MEDICINE & BIOLOGY (US) [25255960] **467**, **3623**

NTIS ALERT. NAVIGATION, GUIDANCE & CONTROL (US) **4181**

NTIS ALERT. OCEAN TECHNOLOGY & ENGINEERING (US) **1453**

NTIS ALERT. ORDNANCE (US) **4053**

NTIS ALERT. PHOTOGRAPHY & RECORDING DEVICES (US) **5318**, **4372**

NTIS ALERT. PROBLEM-SOLVING INFORMATION FOR STATE & LOCAL GOVERNMENTS (US) [25184687] **4670**

● NTIS ALERT. REGIONAL & URBAN PLANNING & TECHNOLOGY (US/1071-9466) [26287151] **2829**

NTIS ALERT. SPACE TECHNOLOGY (US) **30**

NTIS ALERT. TRANSPORTATION (US) **5388**

NTIS ALERT. URBAN & REGIONAL TECHNOLOGY & DEVELOPMENT (US) [25518261] **2829**

NTIS BIBLIOGRAPHIC DATABASE (US/1064-0479) [19615164] **5135**, **5175**

NTIS (DUBLIN, OHIO) (US/0897-3474) [18672693] **421**

NTIS TITLE INDEX ON MICROFICHE (US/0731-3004) [06128193] **5135**

NTM (SZ/0036-6978) [01758962] **5135**

NTSB REPORTER (US/0745-9874) [09658343] **5388**

NTT NEWSLETTER (US) **1161**

NTT R & D (JA/0915-2326) [21027355] **1161**

NTT REVIEW (JA/0915-2334) [20155315] **1161**

NTT SHISETSU (JA) **1161**

NTT TOPICS *See* NTT NEWSLETTER **1161**

NTZ : NACHRICTENTECHNISCHE ZEITSCHRIFT (GW/0027-707X) [07263817] **1161**

NU SCIENCE (SA) [03402855] **4413**

NUA-AOIS (IE) [19651243] **3419**

NUA : INTERNATIONAL JOURNAL OF NEPHROLOGY, UROLOGY, ANDROLOGY (IT/0392-4629) [07764297] **3992**

NUAN LIU (CH) [09454913] **2661**

NUC. AUDIOVISUAL MATERIALS (US/0734-7669) [08829434] **4080**

NUC. BOOKS (US/0734-7650) [08829353] **3237**

NUC. CARTOGRAPHIC MATERIALS (US/0734-7634) [08808363] **2571**

NUC COMPACT : COMPACT NEWS IN NUCLEAR MEDICINE **CEASED.** (GW/0344-3752) [11287627] **3848**

NUC URBAN EXCHANGE (US/0888-5303) [13651832] **2829**

NUCLEAR CANADA YEARBOOK (CN/0383-8536) [03248241] **2156**, **1951**

NUCLEAR DATA NEWSLETTER (AU/0257-6376) [02576376] **1951**

NUCLEAR DATA SHEETS (NEW YORK) (US/0090-3752) [01784955] **4448**

NUCLEAR ENERGY (1978) (UK/0140-4067) [03850224] **1951**

NUCLEAR ENERGY DATA / OECD (FR) [20079368] **1952**

NUCLEAR ENGINEER, THE (UK/0262-5091) [06907212] **2156**

NUCLEAR ENGINEERING AND DESIGN (NE/0029-5493) [06033981] **2156**

NUCLEAR ENGINEERING ENROLLMENTS AND DEGREES (US/8755-9145) [04710478] **2156**

NUCLEAR ENGINEERING INTERNATIONAL (UK/0029-5507) [01760899] **2157**

NUCLEAR ESPANA (SP/0212-1891) [14777005] **5253**

NUCLEAR EUROPE WORLDSCAN (SZ/1016-5975) [21488823] **2157**

NUCLEAR FUEL CYCLE **CEASED.** (US/0735-2506) [08485143] **1952**

NUCLEAR FUSION (AU/0029-5515) [01760900] **4448**

NUCLEAR GEOPHYSICS (UK/0886-0130) [28484408] **1409**

NUCLEAR INDEX, THE (US) [12222323] **1952**

NUCLEAR INDEX, THE (US/0271-0706) [06527036] **4449**

NUCLEAR INDIA (II/0029-5523) [05342118] **2157**

NUCLEAR INDUSTRY, THE (US/0564-9099) [01799485] **2157**

NUCLEAR INSTRUMENTS & METHODS IN PHYSICS RESEARCH. SECTION A, ACCELERATORS, SPECTROMETERS, DETECTORS AND ASSOCIATED EQUIPMENT (NE/0168-9002) [10511074] **4449**

NUCLEAR INSTRUMENTS & METHODS IN PHYSICS RESEARCH. SECTION B, BEAM INTERACTIONS WITH MATERIALS AND ATOMS (NE/0168-583X) [10511347] **4449**

NUCLEAR LAW BULLETIN (FR/0304-341X) [01717075] **3020**

NUCLEAR LAW BULLETIN (FR/0304-3428) [11977724] **1952**, **3020**

NUCLEAR LICENSING REPORTS (US/0893-3774) [15499308] **4449**, **2157**

NUCLEAR MAGNETIC RESONANCE (UK/0305-9804) [01640278] **4444**

NUCLEAR MAGNETIC RESONANCE SPECTROMETRY ABSTRACTS (UK/0048-1033) [02251499] **4445**

NUCLEAR MEDICINE (GW/0029-5566) [11205304] **3848**

● NUCLEAR MEDICINE AND BIOLOGY (UK) [27891947] **3848**

NUCLEAR MEDICINE ANNUAL (US/0272-0108) [06576425] **3848**

NUCLEAR MEDICINE COMMUNICATIONS (UK/0143-3636) [07611841] **3848**

NUCLEAR MEDICINE IN CANCER DIAGNOSIS AND MANAGEMENT (US) [03458557] **3821**, **3848**

NUCLEAR MEDICINE LITERATURE UPDATING AND INDEXING SERVICE, THE **CEASED.** (US/0888-742X) [13721190] **4670**

NUCLEAR MEDICINE (NEW YORK, N.Y.) (US/0896-0607) [16897331] **3623**

NUCLEAR-MEDIZIN. SUPPLEMENTUM (GW/0550-3175) [03436368] **3848**

NUCLEAR MONITOR, THE (US/0889-3411) [12930963] **1952**, **4449**

NUCLEAR NEWS (HINSDALE) (US/0029-5574) [02550791] **2157**

NUCLEAR NOTES (TORONTO) (CN/0713-0597) [08720548] **2157**

NUCLEAR PHYSICS. A (NE/0375-9474) [01760903] **4449**

NUCLEAR PHYSICS NEWS (US/1061-9127) [25451604] **4449**

NUCLEAR PHYSICS. SECTION B, PROCEEDINGS SUPPLEMENT (NE/0920-5632) [17555513] **4449**

NUCLEAR PLANT JOURNAL (US/0892-2055) [15117927] **2866**, **1952**

NUCLEAR PLANT MAINTENANCE NEWSLETTER (US/1054-9447) [23028757] **2157**

NUCLEAR POWER PLANT OPERATING EXPERIENCE ... ANNUAL REPORT (US/0198-6465) [04724725] **2157**

NUCLEAR REACTOR SAFETY (US/0735-2492) [08900939] **2157**

Alphabetical Title Index

NUCLEAR REACTORS AND TECHNOLOGY CEASED. (US/0896-5153) [17197475] **2157**

NUCLEAR REGULATION REPORTS (US/0360-7690) [02244781] 1952, **3115**

NUCLEAR REGULATORY COMMISSION ISSUANCES (US/0147-2909) [02274907] **1952**

NUCLEAR REGULATORY COMMISSION ISSUANCES : OPINIONS AND DECISIONS OF THE NUCLEAR REGULATORY COMMISSION WITH SELECTED ORDERS (US) [08247375] 1952, **4670**

NUCLEAR SAFETY (US/0029-5604) [01760906] **2157**

NUCLEAR SAFETY & CLEANUP REPORT (US/1066-016X) [26829163] **2237**

NUCLEAR SCIENCE ABSTRACTS OF POLAND (PL) [04206448] **4449**

NUCLEAR SCIENCE AND ENGINEERING (US/0029-5639) [01760907] 4449, **2157**

NUCLEAR SCIENCE AND TECHNIQUES (CC/1001-8042) [l10018042] **4449**

NUCLEAR SCIENCE APPLICATIONS (SZ/0191-1686) [09341239] **4449**

NUCLEAR SCIENCE APPLICATIONS CEASED. (SZ/0191-1686) [04814042] **4449**

NUCLEAR SCIENCE INFORMATION OF JAPAN (JA/0029-5620) [02449204] **4449**

NUCLEAR SCIENCE RESEARCH CONFERENCE SERIES (US/0250-4375) [06156013] **4449**

NUCLEAR SCIENCE SERIES, REPORT (US) [01759368] **2157**

NUCLEAR SECTOR FOCUS (CN/0838-3871) [19317743] 2157, **1952**

NUCLEAR SPECTRUM CEASED. (AT/0815-0249) [12350618] **2157**

NUCLEAR STANDARDS NEWS (US/0029-5655) **2157**

NUCLEAR TECHNOLOGY (US/0029-5450) [01798226] **2157**

NUCLEAR TIMES (NEW YORK, N.Y.) CEASED. (US/0734-5836) [08771147] 4530, **4485**

NUCLEAR WASTE MANAGEMENT PROGRAM SUMMARY DOCUMENT (US/0196-772X) [04966149] **2237**

NUCLEAR WASTE NEWS (SILVER SPRING, MD.) (US/0276-2897) [07188677] **2237**

NUCLEARES (BOGOTA) (CK/0120-7067) [15469816] **1952**

NUCLEARFUEL (US/0149-3574) [03475657] **2157**

●NUCLEIC ACIDS ABSTRACTS (1994) (US/1070-2466) [28310015] 491, **478**

NUCLEIC ACIDS AND MOLECULAR BIOLOGY (GW/0933-1891) [16677261] **491**

NUCLEIC ACIDS AND PROTEIN SYNTHESIS (NE/0005-2787) [04970118] 496, **491**

NUCLEIC ACIDS RESEARCH (UK/0305-1048) [01791693] **491**

NUCLEIC ACIDS SYMPOSIUM SERIES (UK/0261-3166) [06724047] **491**

NUCLEON (XR/0302-8542) [25331402] **2157**

NUCLEONICS WEEK (US/0048-105X) [01910195] 4449, **1952**

NUCLEOSIDES & NUCLEOTIDES (US/0732-8311) [08441044] **491**

NUCLEOTECNICA (CL/0716-0054) [14642214] 4449, **2157**

NUCLEUS (CALCUTTA) (II/0029-568X) [01681113] 539, **550**

NUCLEUS (CAMBRIDGE, MASS.) (US/0888-5729) [09888356] **4053**

NUCLEUS (CAMBRIDGE), THE (US/0362-0026) [02166160] **988**

NUCLEUS (KARACHI) (PK/0029-5698) [06375430] **1952**

NUCOS [MICROFORM] : NATIONAL UNION CATALOGUE OF SERIALS HELD IN AUSTRALIAN LIBRARIES (AT/0812-9258) [12184478] **3237**

NUDE & NATURAL (US/1070-9835) [20053758] **2491**

NUDE PACIFIC TRAVEL GUIDE (US/1053-0746) [22454184] **5486**

NUDIS VERBIS (US/0147-3573) [03146016] **3142**

NUDIST PARK GUIDE See NORTH AMERICAN GUIDE TO NUDE RECREATION **5486**

NUDISTES DU QUEBEC (CN/0702-8504) [03439415] **4794**

NUESTRA ARQUITECTURA (AG/0029-5701) [02861628] **305**

NUESTRA BANDERA : REVISTA TEORICA Y POLITICA DEL PARTIDO COMUNISTA DE ESPANA (SP) [09780982] **4530**

NUESTRA CABANA (SP/0210-5659) [l02105659] **217**

NUESTRA CIUDAD (AG) [08177948] **326**

NUESTRA HISTORIA (AG/0029-571X) [02617160] **2552**

NUESTRA PARROQUIA (US) **4982**

NUESTRAS RAICES (QUARTERLY) (US/1045-2427) [20037092] 2270, **2465**

NUESTRO (US/0147-3247) [03140175] **2270**

NUESTRO MINISTERIO DEL REINO PARA EL CANADA (CN/0823-258X) [10036679] **5065**

NUESTRO TIEMPO (SP/0029-5795) [05368060] **2851**

NUEVA ANTROPOLOGIA (MX) [02306014] **242**

NUEVA BANDERA, LA (US) **2751**

NUEVA BIOMETRICA (SP) **3623**

NUEVA CIENCIA (VE) [02580433] **1509**

NUEVA ELECTRONICA (SP) **2074**

NUEVA ENFERMERIA (SP/0210-8275) [07643488] **3862**

NUEVA FRONTERA (CK) [03182654] **2552**

NUEVA FRONTERA. DOCUMENTOS (CK) [04012562] **1576**

NUEVA GEOGRAFIA DE PUERTO RICO (SP) **2571**

NUEVA INTERNACIONAL (US/1056-8921) [23888026] **4485**

NUEVA LINEA (HAVANA, CUBA) SUSPENDED. (CU) [10641374] **2465**

NUEVA LUZ (US/0887-5855) [13313213] **4372**

NUEVA NARRATIVA HISPANOAMERICANA (US/0048-1084) [02265325] **3419**

NUEVA POLITICA (VE) [03625055] **4485**

NUEVA REVISTA COLOMBIANA DE FOLCLOR (CK/0120-8195) [17642054] **2323**

NUEVA REVISTA DE FILOLOGIA HISPANICA (MX/0185-0121) [01760914] **3307**

NUEVA SOCIEDAD (VE/0251-3552) [02242639] **2751**

NUEVAMERICA (AG/0325-6960) [15482625] **1769**

NUEVO ESTILO (SP) [l02121662] **360**

NUEVO LUNES, EL (SP/1133-9535) [l11339535] 5253, **1509**

NUEVO TEXTO CRITICO (US/1048-6380) [17457138] **3419**

●NUEXCO REVIEW (US/1074-8695) [29876022] **2157**

NUEZ (NEW YORK, N.Y.), LA (US/0898-1140) [17720006] **3419**

NUFUSBILIM DERGISI. THE TURKISH JOURNAL OF POPULATION STUDIES (TU/0259-6334) [20187514] **4555**

NUGGET (SAN FRANCISCO, CALIF.), THE (US/1059-9711) [22393391] **2465**

NUGGETS (YREKA) (US/0194-3464) [05391384] **2323**

NUIT BLANCHE (CN/0823-2490) [10082585] **3419**

NUIT DES TEMPS (FR/0550-3604) [03183504] **360**

NUKEM MARKET REPORT ON THE NUCLEAR FUEL CYCLE (GW) **2158**

NUKLEARE ENTSORGUNG (GW/0723-0893) [09298693] **1952**

NUKLEARMEDIZINER, DER (GW/0723-7065) [11176241] **3848**

NUKLEONIKA (PL/0029-5922) [05697578] **2158**

NUMAZU KOGYO KOTO SENMON GAKKO KENKYU HOKOKU (JA/0286-2794) [10382370] **5135**

NUMBER OF ADMINISTRATORS AND SUPERVISORS, CLASSROOM TEACHERS, AND SPECIAL SERVICES PERSONNEL EMPLOYED IN EACH NEW JERSEY PUBLIC SCHOOL DISTRICT BY COUNTY (US/0097-7861) [01799123] **1867**

NUMBER OF FARMS AND LAND IN FARMS / IOWA CROP AND LIVESTOCK REPORTING SERVICE (US) [05955864] **115**

NUMBER OF FARMS, EMPLOYMENT, MACHINERY, IRRIGATION AND FERTILISER USAGE, TASMANIA See NUMBER OF RURAL ESTABLISHMENTS, IRRIGATION AND FERTILISER USAGE, TASMANIA / AUSTRALIAN BUREAU OF STATISTICS **116**

NUMBER OF RURAL ESTABLISHMENTS, IRRIGATION AND FERTILISER USAGE, TASMANIA / AUSTRALIAN BUREAU OF STATISTICS (AT/0157-065X) [07600938] **116**

NUMBER ONE (US) [07253331] **3419**

NUMBER THEORY (GW/0720-2563) [09224570] **3525**

NUMBERS NEWS, THE (US/0732-1597) [07757812] **4555**

NUMEN (INTERNATIONAL ASSOCIATION FOR THE HISTORY OF RELIGIONS) (NE/0029-5973) [01760916] **4982**

NUMERICA (MX) [03377590] **1576**

NUMERICAL ALGORITHMS (NE/1017-1398) [24440982] **3525**

NUMERICAL ANALYSIS (UK/0720-258X) [03775591] **3525**

NUMERICAL FUNCTIONAL ANALYSIS AND OPTIMIZATION (US/0163-0563) [04291358] **3525**

NUMERICAL HEAT TRANSFER. PART A, APPLICATIONS (US/1040-7782) [18524715] 2123, **4432**

NUMERICAL HEAT TRANSFER. PART B, FUNDAMENTALS (US/1040-7790) [18524840] 2123, **4432**

●NUMERICAL LINEAR ALGEBRA WITH APPLICATIONS (UK/1070-5325) [28398684] **3525**

NUMERICAL LISTING OF SUPRAPHON LP RECORDS / SUPRAPHON (US) [09098269] 5318, **4142**

NUMERICAL METHODS FOR PARTIAL DIFFERENTIAL EQUATIONS (US/0749-159X) [11079861] **3525**

NUMERICAL METHODS IN FRACTURE MECHANICS : PROCEEDINGS OF THE ... INTERNATIONAL CONFERENCE (UK) [24666451] **3525**

NUMERICAL METHODS IN THERMAL PROBLEMS : PROCEEDINGS OF THE FIRST INTERNATIONAL CONFERENCE (UK) [08268513] **1989**

NUMERICAL SOLUTION OF PARTIAL DIFFERENTIAL EQUATIONS (US/0362-3017) [01767052] **3525**

NUMERICAL WEATHER PREDICTION ACTIVITIES (US/0565-8136) [01348180] **1432**

NUMERISCHE ERGEBNISSE UND MAGNETOGRAMME WINGST / DEUTSCHES HYDROGRAPHISCHES INSTITUT (GW) [10656664] **4445**

NUMERISCHE MATHEMATIK (GW/0029-599X) [01760917] **3525**

NUMERISCHES VERZEICHNIS DER POSTLEITZAHLEN See NUMERISCHES VERZEICHNIS DER POSTLEITZAHLEN IM VERWALTUNGSBEREICH DER DEUTSCHEN BUNDESPOST GEGLIEDERT NACH LEITEINHEITEN / [HERAUSGEGEBEN VOM BUNDESMINISTERIUM FUER DAS POST- UND FERNMELDEWESEN] **1146**

NUMERISCHES VERZEICHNIS DER POSTLEITZAHLEN IM VERWALTUNGSBEREICH DER DEUTSCHEN BUNDESPOST GEGLIEDERT NACH LEITEINHEITEN / [HERAUSGEGEBEN VOM BUNDESMINISTERIUM FUER DAS POST- UND FERNMELDEWESEN] (GW) [08210974] **1146**

NUMERO ESTADISTICO (AG) [10923355] **203**

NUMERO (MONTREAL) (CN/0822-644X) [11046633] **326**

NUMISMA (MADRID) (SP/0029-6015) [06342751] **2782**

NUMISMATIC AUCTION / CHARLTON AUCTIONS (CN/0822-4900) [10007926] **2782**

NUMISMATIC CHRONICLE (UK/0078-2696) [06780403] **2782**

NUMISMATIC CIRCULAR, THE (UK) [03039900] **2782**

NUMISMATIC LITERATURE (US/0029-6031) [01760920] 2782, **2779**

NUMISMATIC NEWS (KRAUSE PUBLICATIONS : 1977) (US/0029-604X) [01713671] **2782**

NUMISMATIC NEWS WEEKLY See NUMISMATIC NEWS (KRAUSE PUBLICATIONS : 1977) **2782**

NUMISMATIC NOTES AND MONOGRAPHS (NEW YORK) (US/0078-2718) [01639451] **2782**

NUMISMATIC SOCIETY OF INDIA See JOURNAL OF THE NUMISMATIC SOCIETY OF INDIA, THE **2781**

NUMISMATIC STUDIES (US/0517-404X) [01760922] **2782**

NUMISMATICA E ANTICHITA (SZ) [05746661] **251**

NUMISMATICA, LA (IT) **2782**

NUMISMATICKE LISTY (XR) [13179672] **2782**

NUMISMATICKY SBORNIK (XR/0546-9414) [01695107] **2782**

NUMISMATIQUE ET CHANGE REVIGNY-SUR-ORNAIN (FR/0335-1971) [l03351971] **2782**

NUMISMATISCHE ZEITSCHRIFT (AU/0250-7838) [02627177] **2782**

NUMISMATISCHES NACHRICHTENBLATT (GW) [06457092] **2782**

NUMISMATIST: FOR COLLECTORS OF COINS, MEDALS, TOKENS AND PAPER MONEY, THE (US/0029-6090) [04900608] **2782**

NUMISMATIST, THE (US/0029-6090) [01713845] **2782**

NUMIZMATICKE VIJESTI / HRVATSKO NUMIZMATICKO DRUSTVO (CI/0546-9422) [11712363] **2782**

NUMIZMATIKA I EPIGRAFIKA / AKADEMIIA NAUK SSSR, INSTITUT ARKHEOLOGII (RU/0130-7754) [06408801] 277, **2782**

NUMIZMATIKA I SFRAGISTIKA / AKADEMIIA NAUK UKRAINSKOI SSR, INSTITUT ARKHEOLOGII (UN/0550-371X) [01606929] **2782**

NUMIZMATIKAI KOZLONY (HU) [03234103] **2782**

NUMMUS. 2. SERIE (PO) [05217451] **2782**

NUNATSIAQ NEWS (CN/0702-7915) [03409689] **5791**

NUNC PRO TUNC (US/1056-487X) [23724975] **3020**

NUNCIUS (IT) [15586319] **5135**

NUNG KUNG SHANG PU TUNG CHI PIAO (US) [04815593] **5335**

NUNG MIN WEN HSUEH (CC) [11571690] **3419**

NUNG TSUN KUNG TSO TUNG HSUN (CC) [11605493] **116**

NUNG TSUN WEN I (CH) [09212888] **326**

NUNG YEH CHI HSIEH (CH) [09631101] **160**

NUNG YEH CHI HSIEH HSUEH PAO (CC) [09958998] **160**

NUNG YEH CHI HSIEH I PAO See NUNG YEH CHI HSIEH HSUEH PAO **160**

NUNG YEH CHING CHI (CH/0546-9600) [05302425] **116**

NUNG YEH CHING CHI (SHEN-YANG SHIH, CHINA) (CH) [10578317] **116**

NUNG YEH CHING YING KUAN LI (CC) [11901533] **116**

NUNG YEH HUAN CHING PAO HU (CC/1000-0267) [11632081] 116, **2237**

NUNS' ISLAND JOURNAL (CN/0227-2121) [06958567] **5791**

NUNTIA *CEASED.* (VC) [09237479] **5033**

NUOVA AGENDA DEI COMUNI (IT) **4670**

NUOVA ANTOLOGIA (IT/0029-6147) [04903122] **2491**

NUOVA BOLLETTINO DI FARMACOLOGIA CLINICA (IT) **4318**

NUOVA CIVILTA DELLE MACCHINE (IT) [12017900] **4354**

NUOVA CLINICA OTORINOLARINGOIATRICA, LA (IT/0392-1433) [07256670] **3890**

NUOVA COLLEZIONE DI TESTI UMANISTICI INEDITI ORARI (IT) [01760925] **2851**

NUOVA CORRENTE (IT/0029-6155) [02620964] **4354**

NUOVA ECOLOGIA, LA (IT) **2219**

NUOVA ELETTRAUTO (IT) **2074**

NUOVA ELETTRONICA (IT) **2074**

NUOVA EUROPA, LA (IT) **4983**

NUOVA FINESTRA (IT) [09720660] **634**

NUOVA GIURISPRUDENZA CIVILE COMMENTATA, LA (IT) [14264895] **3090**

NUOVA PAIDEIA (IT) **1868**

NUOVA PROSA (IT) [19093373] **3419**

NUOVA RASSEGNA DI LEGISLAZIONE DOTTRINA E GIURISPRUDENZA (IT/0392-7059) [I03927059] **3020**

NUOVA RIVISTA DI NEUROLOGIA (IT) [25728525] **3844**

NUOVA RIVISTA MUSICALE ITALIANA (IT/0029-6228) [01760926] **4142**

NUOVA RIVISTA STORICA (IT/0029-6236) [01695297] **2624**

NUOVA RIVISTA TRIBUTARIA (IT) **749**

NUOVA SARDEGNA, LA (IT) **5804**

NUOVA SCIENZA (IT) **5135**

NUOVA SECONDARIA (IT) **1868**

NUOVA TARIFFA DOGNALE INTEGRATA (IT) **848**

NUOVA VENEZIA (IT) **5804**

NUOVA VICENZA *CEASED.* (IT) **5804**

NUOVE LEGGI CIVILI COMMENTATE (IT/0391-3740) [I03913740] **3020**

NUOVI ANNALI DELLA SCUOLA SPECIALE PER ARCHIVISTI E BIBLIOTECARI (IT) [17939726] **2482**

NUOVI ARGOMENTI (IT/0029-6295) [01586140] **2520**

NUOVI QUADERNI DEL MERIDIONE *SUSPENDED.* (IT/0550-3841) [08867144] **2520**

NUOVI STUDI FANESI (IT) [19406410] **2491**

●NUOVI STUDI LIVORNESI / ASSOCIAZIONI DI STORIA, LETTERE E ARTI LIVORNESI (IT) [30210698] **2851**

NUOVI STUDI POLITICI (IT) [01786817] **4485**

NUOVI STUDI STORICI (IT/0391-8475) [20900904] **2624**

NUOVO ALBERO A ELICA (IT) **1067**

NUOVO AREOPAGO, IL (IT/0394-8846) [I03948846] **4983**

NUOVO CANTIERE, IL (IT) [22999050] **623**

NUOVO CIMENTO DELLA SOCIETA ITALIANA DI FISICA. SEZIONE B (IT/0369-4100) [04324775] 397, **4413**

NUOVO CIMENTO DELLA SOCIETA ITALIANA DI FISICA [SEZIONE] C, IL (IT/0390-5551) [04241600] **4413**

NUOVO CIMENTO DELLA SOCIETA ITALIANA DI FISICA, [SEZIONE] D (IT/0392-6737) [08724239] 1056, **4449**

NUOVO CIMENTO DELLA SOCIETA ITALIANA DI FIZICA. SEZIONE A (IT/0369-4097) [04324732] **4449**

NUOVO CORRIERE FILATELICO, IL (IT) [02649524] **2786**

NUOVO GOVERNO LOCALE, IL (IT/0393-8212) [15692089] **4670**

NUOVO LABORATORIO ODONTOTECNICO, IL (IT/0394-1388) [I03941388] **1331**

NUOVO MEZZOGIORNO (IT/0029-6376) [06332821] 4485, **1509**

NUOVO MONDO (EDMONTON) (CN/0821-6525) [09770573] **5791**

NUOVO OSSERVATORE, IL (IT) **1509**

NUOVO PAESE (AT/0311-6166) [I03116166] **2701**

NUOVO PROGRESSO VETERINARIO *See* PROGRESSO VETERINARIO : ORGANO UFFICIALE DELLA FEDERAZIONE NAZIONALE ORDINI VETERINARI ITALIANI **5519**

NUOVO PROGRESSO VETERINARIO : ORGANO DELL' ASSOCIAZIONE NAZ. VETERINARI ITALIANI, IL (IT) [09443763] **5517**

NUOVO SAGGIATORE : BOLLETTINO DELLA SOCIETA ITALIANA DI FISICA, IL (IT) [12292529] **4413**

NUOVO TARIFFARIO DOGANALE *See* TARIFFARIO DOGANALE TARIC **1523**

NUR-I HAYAT (II) [02245589] **5044**

NURADEEN (US/8756-4637) [11564902] **5044**

NUREG/CR (UNITED STATES. NUCLEAR REGULATORY COMMISSION) (US/0278-1670) [04681088] 4450, **2158**

NURNBERGER FORSCHUNGEN (GW/0078-2653) [02631455] **2701**

NURNBERGER FORSCHUNGSBERICHTE (GW) [14178451] **5135**

NURSCENE (CN/0382-8476) [03193450] **3862**

NURSE AIDE VIP (US) **3754**

NURSE ANESTHESIA *CEASED.* (US/0897-7437) [17613807] 3862, **3683**

NURSE AUTHOR & EDITOR (US/1054-2353) [22785930] **3862**

NURSE EDUCATION TODAY (UK/0260-6917) [09461926] **3862**

NURSE EDUCATOR (US/0363-3624) [02456539] **3863**

NURSE PRACTITIONER FORUM (US/1045-5485) [20148926] **3863**

NURSE PRACTITIONER, THE (US/0361-1817) [02010430] **3863**

NURSE SEARCH (US/0893-4738) [16001809] **3863**

NURSE, THE PATIENT & THE LAW, THE (US/0196-6790) [05848371] 3863, **3020**

NURSE TO NURSE (CN/0849-3383) [23231298] **3863**

NURSE TRAINING (US/0364-0698) [02582129] **3863**

NURSEREVIEW : A CLINICAL UPDATE SYSTEM (US) [18336046] **3863**

NURSERY BUSINESS GROWER (US/1050-6217) [21215657] **2426**

●NURSERY CROP PRODUCTION GUIDE FOR COMMERCIAL GROWERS (CN/1181-9820) [24860162] **180**

NURSERY DIGEST *See* SOUTHERN NURSERY DIGEST **2431**

NURSERY, GREENHOUSE VEGETABLE & ORNAMENTAL PRODUCTION GUIDE FOR COMMERCIAL GROWERS *See* NURSERY CROP PRODUCTION GUIDE FOR COMMERCIAL GROWERS **180**

NURSERY MANAGER (US) [11575443] **2426**

NURSERY RETAILER (US) [24914990] **2435**

NURSERY TEACHER *See* TWOS AND THREES TEACHER **1908**

NURSERY TEACHER GUIDE (SPRINGFIELD, MO.) (US/1059-3241) [24565351] 1901, **4983**

NURSERY TEACHER GUIDE (SPRINGFIELD, MO.) *See* PRESCHOOL TEACHER GUIDE **4987**

NURSERY TEACHERS' GUIDE (CHURCH OF GOD OF PROPHECY ED.) (US/0746-2417) [09882005] **1901**

NURSERY TRADER (UK) **2906**

NURSERY WORLD (UK/0029-6422) [I00296422] **2284**

NURSES' DRUG ALERT (US/0191-2291) [03454563] **3863**

●NURSES' DRUG GUIDE (US/1062-9092) [25805753] **3863**

NURSING (US/0360-4039) [01300106] **3863**

NURSING ABSTRACTS (US/0195-3354) [04928034] 3863, **3661**

NURSING ADMINISTRATION QUARTERLY (US/0363-9568) [02757991] **3863**

NURSING & ALLIED HEALTH CINAHL CAMBRIDGE. CD-ROM (US) 3863, **3661**

NURSING & ALLIED HEALTH (CINAHL)-CD [COMPUTER FILE] (US) [24636511] 3863, **3661**

NURSING & ALLIED HEALTH (CINAHL) ... SUBJECT HEADING LIST (US/0888-0530) [13475310] 3238, **3863**

NURSING & HEALTH CARE (US/0276-5284) [07041499] **3863**

NURSING AND HEALTH CARE (SHERMAN OAKS, CALIF.) (US/0740-3992) [09940143] **3863**

NURSING AND HEALTH SCIENCE EDUCATION REVIEW (AT/1033-6273) **3863**

NURSING AND PALLIATIVE CARE *See* PROGRESS IN PALLIATIVE CARE **3867**

NURSING ASSISTANT : OFFICIAL PUBLICATION OF THE AMERICAN ASSOCIATION OF NURSING ASSISTANTS (US/0892-7669) [10641311] **3863**

NURSING BC (CN/1185-3638) [23657442] **3863**

NURSING BIBLIOGRAPHY (UK/0300-9947) [04684290] **421**

NURSING BUSINESS NEWS *CEASED.* (US/0885-7091) [12709550] 3863, **700**

NURSING CAREER DIRECTORY (US/0192-2394) [04874029] 4207, **3863**

NURSING CLINICS OF NORTH AMERICA, THE (US/0029-6465) [01587777] **3863**

NURSING DATA REVIEW (US/0894-3656) [13513078] 1838, **3863**

NURSING DATASOURCE : A RESEARCH REPORT (US) [22445878] 1838, **3864**

●NURSING DEPARTMENT COMPENSATION REPORT (US/1066-6184) [27016154] **3864**

NURSING DIAGNOSIS (US/1046-7459) [20502150] **3864**

NURSING DIAGNOSIS NEWSLETTER (US/0890-7188) [08575348] **3864**

NURSING DIMENSIONS EDUCATION SERIES (US/0731-5961) [07819433] **3864**

NURSING ... DRUG HANDBOOK (US/0273-320X) [07046728] 4318, **3864**

NURSING ECONOMIC$ (US/0746-1739) [09819144] **3864**

NURSING. EDICION ESPANOLA (SP/0212-5382) [I02125382] **3864**

NURSING EDUCATION VIDEO NEWSLETTER (US) [24150465] **3864**

NURSING EDUCATORS MICROWORLD (US/0893-1356) [15360084] **3864**

●NURSING ETHICS (UK/0969-7330) **3864**

NURSING EXAMINATION REVIEW BOOK (US) [01760934] **3864**

NURSING EXECUTIVE (HOSPITAL ED.) *CEASED.* (US/8756-7598) [11656764] **3864**

NURSING FORUM (HILLSDALE) (US/0029-6473) [01760935] **3864**

●NURSING HISTORY REVIEW (US/1062-8061) [25749144] **3864**

NURSING HOME MEDICINE (US/1070-1370) [28281704] 3754, **3790**

NURSING HOME PRACTITIONER (US) 3790, **5299**

NURSING HOME SALARY & BENEFITS REPORT (US/0275-1070) [05935044] **3790**

Alphabetical Title Index — NY

NURSING HOMES (1991) (US/1061-4753) [25147010] 5180, **3790**

NURSING HOMES IN WASHINGTON STATE (US/0278-7059) [07858404] **3790**

NURSING HOMES (TORONTO) (CN/0712-1342) [08559440] **3790**

NURSING ... I.V. DRUG HANDBOOK (US/1040-2373) [18354583] **3864**

NURSING INQUIRY (AT/1320-7881) **3864**

NURSING JOB GUIDE (US) [10833383] **3864**

NURSING JOB NEWS See NURSINGWORLD JOURNAL **3866**

NURSING JOURNAL OF INDIA (II/0029-6503) [01772303] **3864**

NURSING JOURNALS INDEX, THE (US/0738-8292) [09635534] **3864**

NURSING MANAGEMENT (US/0744-6314) [07831317] 880, **3864**

NURSING MATTERS (US/0272-9512) [06987892] **3864**

NURSING MIRROR INCORPORATING MIDWIVES JOURNAL & QUEENS NURSING JOURNAL (UK) [07474058] **3864**

NURSING MONTREAL (CN/0710-6157) [05261415] **3864**

●NURSING NEW ZEALAND (NZ/1172-1979) [28179563] **3864**

NURSING OPPORTUNITIES (US) [02255112] **3865**

NURSING OUTLOOK (US/0029-6554) [01716274] **3865**

NURSING (OXFORD) (UK/0142-0372) [06950714] **3865**

NURSING PRACTICE (CN/0828-4660) [11888306] **3865**

NURSING PRAXIS IN NEW ZEALAND INC (NZ/0112-7438) [26562757] **3865**

NURSING PROGRAMS AND ENTRANCE REQUIREMENTS AT CANADIAN UNIVERSITIES (CN/0229-7345) [08378937] **3865**

NURSING QUALITY CONNECTION (US/1055-6818) [23274135] **3865**

NURSING QUEBEC (CN/0381-6419) [03304128] **3865**

NURSING RECRUITMENT & RETENTION (US/1051-4341) [21959243] **3865**

NURSING RESEARCH ABSTRACTS (UK/0141-3899) [05729162] **3865**

NURSING RESEARCH (BOSTON) (US/0098-0358) [01357036] **3865**

NURSING RESEARCH (NEW YORK) (US/0029-6562) [01760937] **3865**

NURSING RSA (SA/0258-1647) [15552478] **3865**

NURSING SCAN IN ADMINISTRATION (US/1056-3091) [21364111] **3865**

NURSING SCAN IN RESEARCH (US/0897-5647) [17554309] **3865**

NURSING SCIENCE QUARTERLY (US/0894-3184) [15993336] **3865**

NURSING SPECTRUM (US) **3865**

●NURSING STAFF DEVELOPMENT INSIDER (US/1057-8323) [24124340] **3865**

NURSING STANDARD (UK/0029-6570) [22305931] **3865**

NURSING STUDIES INDEX (US) [02253719] **3865**

NURSING SUBJECT HEADINGS (US) [01609307] **3865, 3238**

NURSING THE ELDERLY See ELDERLY CARE **3855**

NURSING THE ELDERLY : IN HOSPITAL, HOMES AND THE COMMUNITY (UK/0956-8115) [20225379] **3865**

NURSING TIMES (1987) (UK/0954-7762) [18067723] **3865**

NURSING TIMES [MICROFORM] : NT (US) [18660544] **3865**

NURSINGCONNECTIONS (WASHINGTON, D.C.) (US/0895-2809) [16786171] **3866**

NURSINGWORLD DIGEST See NURSINGWORLD JOURNAL **3866**

NURSINGWORLD JOURNAL (US/0745-8630) [09526623] **3866**

NURTURING SUSPENDED. (CN/0713-3898) [09523792] **2284**

NUS ECONOMIC JOURNAL, THE (SI) [24317044] **1509**

NUSA, LINGUISTIC STUDIES IN INDONESIAN AND LANGUAGES IN INDONESIA (IO) [04420234] **3307**

NUSANTARA (MY) [01784309] **5211**

NUSAS NEWSLETTER (SA) [01788520] **1838**

NUT EDUCATION REVIEW (UK/0951-7855) [15814367] **1769**

NUT GROWER (US/0745-3469) [01760941] **180**

NUT KERNEL, THE (US/0738-596X) [05795797] **2426**

NUTCRACKER, THE (CN/0384-1499) [03258635] **4544**

NUTHING SACRED (US/1061-9771) [25497919] **3419**

NUTIDA MUSIK (SW/0029-6597) [02127918] **4142**

NUTIRDATE (AT) **4195, 2600**

NUTMEG (US/0364-7781) [02653871] **1838**

NUTRI-TOPICS (CONSUMER) (US/1053-8887) [22684725] **4195**

NUTRI-TOPICS / FOOD AND NUTRITION INFORMATION CENTER, NATIONAL AGRICULTURAL LIBRARY (US/1053-8895) [22684781] **4195**

NUTRI-TOPICS (HEALTH PROFESSIONAL/RESEARCHER) (US/1053-8879) [22684645] **4195**

NUTRICIA SYMPOSIUM (US/0167-4587) [08086400] 988, **467**

NUTRICION CLINICA DIETETICA HOSPITALARIA (SP/0211-6057) [09051797] **4195**

NUTRICION HOSPITALARIA (SP/0212-1611) [22887298] **4195**

NUTRIENT REQUIREMENTS OF DOMESTIC ANIMALS (US/0160-6948) [03734919] **5517**

NUTRIGUIDE (CN/0701-1997) [03409669] **4195**

NUTRIPLAN (CN/0225-1272) [06958835] **2792**

NUTRISYON (PH/0115-4516) [06239311] **4195**

NUTRITION ABSTRACTS AND REVIEWS. SERIES A: HUMAN & EXPERIMENTAL (UK/0309-1295) [03392112] 4195, **4201**

NUTRITION ABSTRACTS AND REVIEWS. SERIES B. LIVESTOCK FEEDS AND FEEDING (UK/0309-135X) [02847839] 203, **155**

NUTRITION ACTION HEALTH LETTER (US/0885-7792) [12715775] **4195**

NUTRITION AND CANCER (US/0163-5581) [04415504] 3821, **4195**

NUTRITION AND CLINICAL NUTRITION (US/0360-7259) [01917192] **4195**

NUTRITION & DIETARY CONSULTANT, THE (US/8750-8370) [11848355] **4195**

NUTRITION AND FOOD SAFETY (SZ) **4195**

NUTRITION & FOOD SCIENCE (UK/0034-6659) [26489277] **4195**

NUTRITION & FOOD SCIENCE (UK/0034-6659) [01604672] **4195**

NUTRITION AND HEALTH (BERKHAMSTED) (UK/0260-1060) [08790842] **4195**

NUTRITION AND HEALTH (NEW YORK) CEASED. (US/0270-658X) [06436388] **4195**

●NUTRITION & MENTAL HEALTH (CN/1199-7699) [31095644] 4794, **4195**

NUTRITION AND THE BRAIN (US/0149-2667) [03263126] 3844, **4196**

NUTRITION & THE M.D (US/0732-0167) [07886419] **4196**

NUTRITION (BURBANK, LOS ANGELES COUNTY, CALIF.) (US/0899-9007) [17651592] **4196**

NUTRITION CENTER OF THE PHILIPPINES See REPORT OF THE NUTRITION CENTER OF THE PHILIPPINES **4198**

NUTRITION CLINICS (US/0888-3483) [13562641] **4196**

NUTRITION CLINIQUE ET METABOLISME (FR/0985-0562) [21591724] **4196**

NUTRITION FORUM (PHILADELPHIA, PA.) (US/0748-8165) [11010946] **4196**

NUTRITION FUNDING REPORT, THE (US/0892-1474) [15097190] **4196**

NUTRITION HEALTH REVIEW (US/0164-7202) [04403738] **4196**

NUTRITION IN CLINICAL PRACTICE (US/0884-5336) [12406345] **4196**

NUTRITION LEGISLATION AND REGULATORY NEWS (US) **4196**

NUTRITION LEGISLATION NEWS (US/8756-6060) [11635703] 4196, **3020**

NUTRITION, METABOLISM, AND CARDIOVASCULAR DISEASES : NMCD (GW/0939-4753) [24317923] **3708**

NUTRITION NEWS (RIVERSIDE, CALIF.) (US/8756-5919) [11605343] **4196**

NUTRITION NEWS (ROSEMONT) (US/0369-6464) [01760945] **4196**

NUTRITION NEWSLETTER (US) [05455287] **4196**

NUTRITION NEWSLINE CEASED. (US/0898-1604) [17734814] **4196**

NUTRITION NOTES (US) [02416648] **4196**

NUTRITION NOW (US/0892-6042) [15265638] **4196**

NUTRITION POST (CN) **4196**

NUTRITION QUARTERLY (CN/0710-166X) [08336352] **4196**

NUTRITION REPORT, THE (US/0740-8684) [10047501] **4196**

NUTRITION RESEARCH (US/0097-0166) [01420279] **4196**

NUTRITION RESEARCH (NEW YORK, N.Y.) (US/0271-5317) [06669348] **4196**

NUTRITION RESEARCH NEWSLETTER (US/0736-0037) [09047356] 4197, **4201**

NUTRITION RESEARCH REVIEWS (UK/0954-4224) [18998070] **4197**

NUTRITION REVIEWS (US/0029-6643) [01586326] **4197**

NUTRITION SAVVY (US/0889-7034) [14039612] **4197**

NUTRITION SOCIETY See PROCEEDINGS OF THE NUTRITION SOCIETY **4197**

NUTRITION SOCIETY OF AUSTRALIA. CONFERENCE See PROCEEDINGS OF THE NUTRITION SOCIETY OF AUSTRALIA **4198**

NUTRITION SOCIETY OF INDIA See PROCEEDINGS OF THE NUTRITION SOCIETY OF INDIA **4198**

NUTRITION SOCIETY OF NEW ZEALAND See PROCEEDINGS OF THE NUTRITION SOCIETY OF NEW ZEALAND **4198**

NUTRITION (SPRINGFIELD, IL) (US) [07465118] **4197**

NUTRITION TODAY (ANNAPOLIS) (US/0029-666X) [01451261] **4197**

NUTRITION UPDATE (NEW YORK, N.Y.) (US/0735-4762) [08936958] **4197**

NUTRITION UPDATE (SAN CLEMENTE, CALIF.) (US/0892-6204) [15244283] 4201, **3623**

NUTRITION WEEK (US/0736-0096) [09069677] **4197**

NUTRITIONAL BIOCHEMICALS (US) [06097868] **4197**

NUTRITIONAL PERSPECTIVES (US/0160-3922) [03674298] **4197**

NUTS & VOLTS MAGAZINE (US/1065-2035) [26528932] **4413**

NUTSHELL NEWS (US/0164-3290) [02250513] 2775, **374**

NUTSHELL (SNOWMASS VILLAGE, COLO.) (US/0740-7971) [10008954] **944**

NUTSHELL, THE (US) [05230835] **2426**

NUTZFAHRZEUG, DAS (GW) [06395170] **5388**

NUTZUNGSARTEN DER BODENFLACHEN (GW) [11135074] **1509**

NUUSBRIEF (SA/0039-4807) [08773697] **5234**

NUUSBRIEF - AFRIKAANS-DUITSE KULTUURUNIE (SA) [03279483] **2642**

NUWE VOERTUIE GEREGISTREER / REPUBLIEK VAN SUID-AFRIKA, SENTRALE STATISTIEKDIENS (SA) [11907783] **5421**

NUYTSIA (AT/0085-4417) [02449217] **520**

NV; NEUE VERPACKUNG (GW/0341-0390) [01788839] **4220**

NVB. NOISE & VIBRATION BULLETIN (UK/0144-7785) [04555309] **2179**

NVS NIEUWS (NE) **4794**

NWFN NEWSJOURNAL : A WOMEN'S FITNESS RESOURCE (US/1056-120X) [23469661] 5563, **2600**

NWSA DIRECTORY OF WOMEN'S STUDIES PROGRAMS, WOMEN'S CENTERS, AND WOMEN'S RESEARCH CENTERS : A PUBLICATION OF THE NATIONAL WOMEN'S STUDIES ASSOCIATION (US) [23200053] **5563**

NWSA JOURNAL (US/1040-0656) [18305154] **5563**

NWSS NEWS (US) **3307**

NWT DATA BOOK SUSPENDED. (CN/0711-6330) [08489296] **2571**

NWT HELP DIRECTORY (CN/0846-0701) [23659084] **5299**

NY See CITY JOURNAL (NEW YORK, N.Y.), THE **4468**

NY CARLSBERG GLYPTOTEK See MEDDELELSER FRA NY CARLSBERG GLYPTOTEK **358**

●NY FOOD LETTER, THE (US/1065-7967) [26738898] **2351**

NY I SVERIGE (SW) [04447190] **2701**

NY LITTERATUR OM KVINNOR : EN BIBLIOGRAFI / GOTEBORGS UNIVERSITETSBIBLIOTEK, KVINNOHISTORISKA SAMLINGARNA (SW/0348-7962) [07354719] **5572**

NY-PENN NEWS (US) [09726156] **4794**

NY POLITIK (DK/0029-6759) [05266421] **2520**

NY SCHOOL BOARDS (US/1055-1395) [23055569] **1868**

NYA ANTIK & AUKTION (SW/0346-9212) [09100600] **251**

NYAC NEWS (US/0275-5114) [05797373] **4670**

NYADARSA PAMJIKARANA BULETINA (II/0258-0853) [04733699] **5335**

NYALA / NATIONAL FAUNA PRESERVATION SOCIETY OF MALAWI (MW) [08382604] **2201**

NYAME AKUMA (CN/0713-5815) [05986575] **277**

NYCAP NEWS (US/1070-7336) [24183695] **2179**

NYE BGER (BIBLIOTEKSCENTRALEN (DENMARK) (DK/0907-1717) [21011147] **421**

NYE BONYTT (NO/0029-6783) [01760954] **2520**

NYEA ADVOCATE (US/0161-7982) [04024754] **1769**

NYEIBAN NUIHAG HOI JI (KO/0254-5985) [04885376] **3623**

NYELVTUDOMANYI KOEZLEMENYEK (HU/0029-6791) [01760955] **3307**

NYENGU BOGO - NYENNAM DAIHAGGYO GONNEB GISUR NYENGUSO (KO/0250-3395) [10578123] **5135**

NYENGU BOGO - RIMMOG NYUGJON NYENGUSO (KO/0073-9294) [10535353] **520, 2390**

NYIREGYHAZI JOSA ANDRAS MUZEUM EVKONYVE, A (HU/0547-0196) [24997249] **2323**

NYJD BULLETIN (US) [22287029] **1331**

NYLA BULLETIN (US/0027-7134) [01643547] **3238**

NYLON HIGHWAY (US/1071-2615) [28601355] **4876, 1409**

NYMPHAEA (RM/0253-4649) [02244310] **4169, 1359**

NYPIRG AGENDA (US/1044-3134) [19750782] **1298**

NYQUIST REPORT ON FUNDING FOR COMMUNITY, JUNIOR, AND TECHNICAL COLLEGES (US/1070-8871) [28482155] **1838**

NYS. NYDANSKE STUDIER & ALMEN KOMMUNIKATIONSTEORI (DK/0106-8040) [06885611] **1118, 3307**

NYSAC COUNTY DIRECTORY (US) [06947115] **4670**

NYSE WEEKLY STOCK BUYS (US/1060-6629) [25046018] **910**

NYSLAA NETWORK CONNECTION / NEW YORK STATE LIBRARY ASSISTANTS' ASSOCIATION (US) [23290557] **3238**

NYSSBITS *CEASED.* (US) [10014247] **1868**

NYT FRA ISLAND (DK) [04710529] **2701**

NYT FRA MILJSTYRELSENS REFERENCELABORAFORIUM (DK/0105-791X) [11714025] **1018**

NYT OM ARBEJDSMILJ SKANDINAVIEN I SKANDINAVIEN (DK/0901-6473) [09016473] **1696**

NYTT - FORSKNINGSSTIFTELSEN SKOGSARBETEN (SW/0347-5883) [09959190] **2390**

NYTT FRA NORGE (NO) [22461080] **5807**

NYTT NORSK TIDSSKRIFT (NO/0800-336X) [11925835] **4485**

NYUGATI MAGYARSAG (CALGARY) (CN/0715-5840) [09379112] **2751**

NZ ART AUCTION RECORDS (NZ) [01793623] **360**

NZ BUSINESS (NZ/0113-4957) [I01134957] **700**

NZ. NEUE ZEITSCHRIFT FUER MUSIK (1979) (GW/0170-8791) [04754773] **4142**

NZCTU DIRECTORY (NZ) [24186291] **848**

NZNU NEWS *See* NURSING NEW ZEALAND **3864**

NZOI OCEANOGRAPHIC FIELD REPORT (NZ/0110-5205) [09939916] **1453**

NZTD DOMESTIC RESEARCH SERIES (NZ/1170-5469) [I11705469] **5486**

NZTD ECONOMIC RESEARCH SERIES (NZ) [24692167] **5486**

NZTD REGIONAL RESEARCH SERIES (NZ/1170-831X) [I11170831X] **5486**

NZTP OVERSEAS MARKET RESEARCH SERIES (NZ/0112-9724) [I01129724] **5486**

O A C E T T NEWSLETTER (CN/0318-5338) [02442089] **1989**

O AGRONOMICO (BL) [03499791] **116**

O & A MARKETING NEWS (US/0192-009X) [05086077] **934, 5421**

O ARQUEOLOGO PORTUGUES (PO) [01725200] **277**

O-BLEK (STOCKBRIDGE, MASS.) *CEASED.* (US/0896-3053) [16997122] **3419**

O.C.C.G.E. INFORMATIONS / OCCGE, SECRETARIAT GENERAL (UV/0253-3901) [10679051] **3715, 3736**

O.C.G.S. NEWSLETTER / OLMSTED COUNTY GENEALOGY SOCIETY (US) [26889437] **2465**

O C P, ON CONTINUING PRACTICE (CN/0315-1042) [02010312] **4318**

O C S NOUVELLES (CN/0381-8632) [02604068] **1118**

O COMERCIO E A INDUSTRIA AUTOMOVEL EM PORTUGAL (PO) [20122280] **1576**

O ELLEN AGGELIAPHOROS (CN/0229-7892) [08315698] **5791**

O EMPREITEIRO (BL) [02531659] **1989**

O.F.I. OCCASIONAL PAPERS (UK/0269-5790) [17169633] **2390**

+-O I.E. PLUS MOINS ZERO *CEASED.* (BE) [05660553] **360**

O + I.E. UND P, OLHYDRAULIK UND PNEUMATIK (GW/0341-2660) [03833952] **2093**

O.N.E. NEWSLETTER (CN/0229-1428) [09145927] **4197**

O PLUS E (JA/0911-5943) [I09115943] **1118**

O PODER (BL) [02241174] **2751**

O R G A NEWS (CN/0383-9028) [03245012] **5421, 4267**

O R G A NEWSLINE (CN/0228-0469) [06860138] **5422**

O.R.L.-DIPS (SP/0210-7309) [08025869] **3890**

● O.R. PRODUCT DIRECTORY / ASSOCIATION OF OPERATING ROOM NURSES (US) [30627061] **3970**

O.R.S.T.O.M. (AGENCY : FRANCE) *See* CAHIERS O.R.S.T.O.M. SERIE PEDOLOGIE **1352**

O.R.S.T.O.M. (AGENCY : FRANCE) *See* EDITIONS / ORSTOM **415**

O.S.B.E.R. OIL SPILL BULLETIN AND ENVIRONMENTAL REVIEW (UK/0959-9134) [I09599134] **2238**

O.S.E.A. NEWSLETTER (CN/0832-5618) [18047138] **360**

O SOLO (BL/0584-0821) [02586064] **180**

OA JOHO (JA) [10357935] **4213**

OA KANREN SHINBUN KIJI SORAN (JA) [12190566] **1118**

OAA NEWS (US) [18838621] **3877**

OAC NEWSLETTER *See* VIEWPOINT (COLUMBUS) **332**

OAG AIR CARGO GUIDE (US/0191-152X) [04798890] **5388**

OAG BUSINESS TRAVEL PLANNER (NORTH AMERICAN ED.) (US/1053-0002) [22257680] **2808**

OAG CRUISE AND SHIPLINE GUIDE (US/1061-799X) [24184822] **5453**

OAG DESKTOP FLIGHT GUIDE (NORTH AMERICAN ED.) (US/1057-0918) [23472818] **5486**

OAG DESKTOP FLIGHT GUIDE (WORLDWIDE ED.) (US/1057-0454) [23598811] **5486**

OAG EUROPE & MIDDLE EAST POCKET FLIGHT GUIDE *See* OAG POCKET FLIGHT GUIDE (EUROPE & MIDDLE EAST ED.) **5486**

OAG FLIGHT PLANNER EUROPE, MIDDLE EAST & AFRICA (UK) **30, 5486**

OAG FLIGHTDISK (EUROPEAN ED.) (US) **5486**

OAG FLIGHTDISK (NORTH AMERICAN ED.) (US) **5486**

OAG FLIGHTDISK PREMIUM WORLDWIDE EDITION (UK) **30, 5486**

OAG FLIGHTDISK (WORLDWIDE ED.) (US) **5486**

OAG OFFICIAL TRAVELER FLIGHT GUIDE (US) **5486**

● OAG OFFICIAL TRAVELER. TRAVEL GUIDE (US/1073-0338) [26151584] **5486, 2808**

OAG PACIFIC AREA POCKET FLIGHT GUIDE (US/0745-5275) [09263112] **5486**

OAG POCKET FLIGHT GUIDE (EUROPE & MIDDLE EAST ED.) (US/8750-0310) [10940331] **5486**

OAG POCKET FLIGHT GUIDE (LATIN AMERICAN/CARIBBEAN ED.) (US) **5486**

OAG POCKET FLIGHT GUIDE (NORTH AMERICAN EDITION) (US/0743-8249) [10674232] **5486**

OAG POCKET FLIGHT GUIDE (WORLDWIDE ED.) (US/1067-8158) [27019108] **5487**

OAG TRAVEL DISC [CD ROM] (UK) **30, 5487**

● OAG TRAVEL PLANNER (EUROPEAN ED.) (US/1075-1548) [25287678] **2808**

OAG TRAVEL PLANNER. (EUROPEAN EDITION) (US/0894-1718) **5487**

OAG TRAVEL PLANNER, HOTEL & MOTEL REDBOOK (EUROPEAN ED.) *See* OAG TRAVEL PLANNER (EUROPEAN ED.) **2808**

OAG TRAVEL PLANNER, HOTEL & MOTEL REDBOOK (PACIFIC ASIA ED.) *See* OAG TRAVEL PLANNER (PACIFIC ASIA ED.) **5487**

● OAG TRAVEL PLANNER (PACIFIC ASIA ED.) (US/1069-2150) [25287610] **2808, 5487**

OAG WAG FARES SUPPLEMENT (UK) **30, 5487**

OAG WORLD AIRWAYS GUIDE (UK) **30, 5487**

OAG WORLDWIDE CRUISE & SHIPLINE GUIDE (US/0097-8779) [03161731] **5487**

OAH COUNCIL OF CHAIRS NEWSLETTER (US/1071-5622) [25652522] **2751**

OAH NEWSLETTER (US/1059-1125) [07981472] **2751**

OAHA NEWS BULETIN (CN) **3623**

OAHU (US/1042-8054) [19226817] **5487**

OAHU UPDATE, THE (US/1042-8038) [19226444] **5487**

OAK BAY STAR (CN/0380-4542) [02443251] **5791**

OAK BROOK PRESS *See* PRESS (ELMHURST, ILL. : OAK BROOK ED.) **5661**

OAK CREEK PICTORIAL (OAK CREEK, WIS. : 1982) (US) [12919871] **5769**

OAK LAKE TOWN AND COUNTRY NEWS (CN/0702-763X) [03409574] **5791**

OAK LEAVES (US) [08807353] **5661**

OAK LEAVES (BAY CITY, TEX.) (US/0740-8013) [10004215] **2465**

OAK RIDGE ASSOCIATED UNIVERSITIES *See* ANNUAL REPORT / OAK RIDGE ASSOCIATED UNIVERSITIES **4446**

OAK RIDGE ASSOCIATED UNIVERSITIES. INSTITUTE FOR ENERGY ANALYSIS *See* INSTITUTE FOR ENERGY ANALYSIS NEWS **1947**

OAK RIDGE NATIONAL LABORATORY *See* REVIEW / OAK RIDGE NATIONAL LABORATORY **4451**

OAK RIDGE NATIONAL LABORATORY. CHEMICAL TECHNOLOGY DIVISION *See* TRANSURANIUM PROCESSING PLANT SEMIANNUAL REPORT OF PRODUCTION, STATUS, AND PLANS **1959**

OAK RIDGE NATIONAL LABORATORY. INDUSTRIAL SAFETY AND APPLIED HEALTH PHYSICS DIVISION *See* INDUSTRIAL SAFETY AND APPLIED HEALTH PHYSICS ANNUAL REPORT FOR ... **2863**

OAK RIDGE NATIONAL LABORATORY. INSTRUMENTATION AND CONTROLS DIVISION *See* INSTRUMENTATION AND CONTROLS DIVISION ANNUAL PROGRESS REPORT **1947**

OAK RIDGE NATIONAL LABORATORY. MATHEMATICS AND STATISTICS RESEARCH DEPT *See* MATHEMATICS AND STATISTICS RESEARCH DEPARTMENT PROGRESS REPORT **3542**

OAK RIDGE NATIONAL LABORATORY. METALS AND CERAMICS DIVISION *See* METALS AND CERAMICS DIVISION ANNUAL PROGRESS REPORT **4011**

OAK RIDGER, THE (US/0890-6009) [13377175] **5746**

OAK SQUARE (US/0894-7899) [16267728] **3419**

OAKDALE LEADER (US) [20380592] **5638**

OAKES ACORNS (US/0897-7771) [15471566] **2465**

OAKLAND (US/0192-5946) [05117716] **2541**

OAKLAND BUSINESS MONTHLY *CEASED.* (US/8750-0981) [10983000] **700**

OAKLAND CITY JOURNAL (US) [11379058] **5666**

OAKLAND POST (US) [10546299] **5638**

OAKLAND PRESS (US) **5693**

OAKLAND TRIBUNE (OAKLAND, CALIF. 1991) (US/1068-5936) [23907014] **5638**

OAKLAND UNIVERSITY *See* OAKLAND UNIVERSITY ... ALUMNI DIRECTORY **1102**

OAKLAND UNIVERSITY ... ALUMNI DIRECTORY (US) [24298510] **1102**

OAKLEY GRAPHIC, THE (US) [11718271] **5678**

OAKS GAZETTE *See* OJAI AND VALLEY NEWS, THE **5638**

OALA NEWS (CN/0847-3080) [24256536] **2426**

OAMARU LICENSING TRUST (N.Z.) *See* REPORT OF THE OAMARU LICENSING TRUST FOR THE YEAR ENDED **4681**

●O&P BUSINESS NEWS (US/1060-3220) [24925808] **3623, 700**

OAPSE/AFSCME ADVOCATE (US/0893-5106) [15547831] **1696, 1868**

OARDC RESEARCH BULLETIN (US) [21490516] **116**

OARDC RESEARCH CIRCULAR (US) [25196915] **116**

OAS CECON TRADE NEWS (US/0250-6203) [07049178] **848**

OASIS : BIMESTRALE DI NATURA ECOLOGIA FOTOGRAFIA (IT) [12932611] **4169**

OATES, BOB. PROLOG *See* PROLOG (LOS ANGELES) **4913**

OAU ECHO (ET) [09936863] **2500**

OAU IN A MONTH (SA) [10223190] **2500**

OAXACA CULTURAL: SU MUSICA (MX) [05000903] **4142**

OAZ, OSTERREICHISCHE APOTHEKER-ZEITUNG (AU/0253-5238) [04428831] **4318**

OB/GYN ANNALS **CEASED.** (US/1069-8787) [28177238] **3766**

OB/GYN CLINICAL ALERT (US/0743-8354) [10681512] **3766**

OB. GYN. NEWS (US/0029-7437) [06473317] **3766**

OB-GYN OBSERVER (US/0029-7445) [02251902] **3766**

●OB/GYN RESIDENT, THE (US/1058-1677) [24235912] **3766**

OB/GYN ROUNDS (US/1055-5595) [23235991] **3766**

OB/GYN TRENDS AT MOUNT SINAI SCHOOL OF MEDICINE (US/0883-492X) [12153279] **3766**

OBAYASHI REPOTO (JA/0389-3693) [I03893693] **5135**

OBCHOD VE SVETE (XR) [01785029] **848**

OBELEZJA (YU) [01791698] **2520**

OBER INCOME LETTER (US/0882-6323) [11925108] **910**

OBERBAYERISCHES ARCHIV (GW/0342-1686) [02898523] **2701**

●OBERFLACEHEN WERKSTOFFE / SURFACES MATERIAUX (SZ) [29437170] **2107**

OBERFLACHE (GW/0029-7488) [03698820] **4014**

OBERFLACHE - SURFACE (SZ/0048-1270) [08988965] **4224, 4014**

OBERFLAECHE *See* OBERFLACEHEN WERKSTOFFE / SURFACES MATERIAUX **2107**

OBERISUKU (JA) [01790316] **3419**

OBERLIN HERALD (OBERLIN, KAN. : 1951) (US) [10884823] **5678**

OBERLIN REVIEW, THE (US/0029-7526) [04123706] **1093**

OBERON (JA/0288-6065) [I02886065] **3419**

OBEROSTERREICHISCHE HEIMATBLATTER (AU/0029-7550) [06466187] **2701**

OBERPFALZ, DIE (GW/0342-9873) [I03429873] **2701**

OBERRHEINISCHE STUDIEN KARLSRUHE (GW/0930-522X) [I0930522X] **2701**

OBERRHEINISCHER GEOLOGISCHER VEREIN *See* JAHRESBERICHTE UND MITTEILUNGEN DES OBERRHEINISCHEN GEOLOGISCHEN VEREINES **1384**

OBERSTEIRISCHE RUNDSCHAU (AU) [12129628] **5778**

OBERVOLTA : WIRTSCHAFTSDATEN UND WIRTSCHAFTSDOKUMENTATION (GW) [06229716] **1576**

OBESITY & HEALTH (US/1044-1522) [19694960] **4794, 4197**

●OBESITY RESEARCH (US/1071-7323) [27927462] **3623**

OBESITY SURGERY (UK/0960-8923) [23835796] **3970**

OBF, OF THE PEOPLE, BY THE PEOPLE, FOR THE PEOPLE (US/0360-1781) [02244183] **4485**

OBG DIAGNOSIS (US/0738-3029) [09587484] **3766**

OBG MANAGEMENT (US/1044-307X) [19744910] **3766**

OBIETTIVI E DOCUMENTI VETERINARI (IT/0392-1913) [I03921913] **5517**

OBIETTIVO MODA (IT) **1086**

OBIHIRO CHIKUSAN DAIGAKU *See* OBIHIRO CHIKUSAN DAIGAKU GAKUJUTSU KENKYU HOKOKU DAI-1-BU **116**

OBIHIRO CHIKUSAN DAIGAKU GAKUJUTSU KENKYU HOKOKU DAI-1-BU (JA/0470-925X) [02016928] **5517, 116**

OBION ORIGINS (US) [13134646] **2465**

OBIRIN DAIGAKU. TANKI DAIGAKU *See* OBIRIN RON SHU : IPPAN KYOIKU HEN **2851**

OBIRIN RON SHU : IPPAN KYOIKU HEN (JA) [02245172] **2851**

OBITER DICTA (1963) **CEASED.** (CN/0029-7585) [02551066] **3020**

OBJECT MAGAZINE (US/1055-3614) [23158504] **1288**

OBJECT-ORIENTED STRATEGIES (US/1059-4108) [24586056] **880**

OBJECT-ORIENTED SYSTEMS (UK/0969-9767) 1280, **1248**

OBJECTIF - A.L.P.A (CN/0712-6107) [09336537] **4372**

OBJECTIF AFRIQUE DU SUD (SZ) [19224030] **5211**

OBJECTIF EUROPE STRASBOURG (FR/0221-0703) [I02210703] **2520**

OBJECTIF PREVENTION (MONTREAL) (CN/0705-0577) [03900133] **4794**

OBJECTIFS DANS LE DOMAINE DES AFFAIRES SOCIALES ET DE LA FAMILLE, LES (CN) [01789811] **5300**

OBJECTION (CN/0711-7639) [08898761] **3020**

OBJECTIVE : JUSTICE (US/0029-7593) [03511485] **4511**

OBJECTIVE TESTING FOR PROFESSIONAL PILOTS LICENCES (UK) **30**

OBJECTOR (SAN FRANCISCO, CALIF.) (US/0279-103X) [07534019] **3183**

OBJEKTIV HELLERUP (DK/0107-6329) [I01076329] **4372**

OBJETS ET MONDES **SUSPENDED.** (FR/0029-7615) [02265352] **4169**

OBLIGATION, L' (CN/0227-1540) [06562797] **2751**

OBOE, FAGOTT (GW/0933-4556) [I09334556] **4142**

OBOE, KLARINETTE, FAGOTT (GW) [19837353] **4142**

OBOGASHCHENIE RUD CHERNYKH METALLOV (RU) [01795138] **2147**

OBRA (MONTREAL) (CN/0821-2686) [09448395] **4983**

OBRA SINDICAL EDUCACION Y DESCANSO, BARCELONA *See* AGENDA - OBRA SINDICAL EDUCACION Y DESCANSO, BARCELONA **2672**

OBRABOTKA SIMVOLNOI INFORMATSII (RU) [01791830] **3307**

OBRAS (MX) [02661661] **623**

OBRAS PUBLICAS *See* SOP **1627**

OBRAZOTVORCHE MYSTETSTVO (UN) [06551789] **326**

OBRERO REBELDE, EL (US/0194-1593) [05356710] **1696**

OBREROS EN MARCHA (US) [04459697] **1696**

OBROBKA PLASTYCZNA (PL/0472-4313) [06609487] **4014**

OBSCA I SRAVNITELNA PATOLOGIJA (BU/0324-1998) [03022156] **3896**

OBSCENITY LAW BULLETIN (US/0195-1696) [02810102] **3020**

OBSERVADOR (BUENOS AIRES, ARGENTINA), EL (AG) [11041459] **2552**

OBSERVADOR ECONOMICO, EL (UY) [26251622] **1509**

OBSERVATEUR DE L'OCDE, L' (FR/0304-3398) [04110819] **1509**

OBSERVATEUR ORTHODOXE, L' (CN/0824-653X) [10857617] **4983**

OBSERVATEUR (TORONTO) (CN/1185-6351) [25066487] **5791**

OBSERVATIONS (CARY, N.C.) (US/1057-2902) [24001072] **1288**

OBSERVATIONS CLIMATOLOGIQUES (BE/0524-7810) [03000391] **1433**

OBSERVATIONS ET DIAGNOSTICS ECONOMIQUES (FR/0751-6614) [12075223] **1509**

OBSERVATIONS ET DIAGNOSTICS ECONOMIQUES. LETTRE DE L'OFCE (FR) [18150064] **1509**

OBSERVATIONS FROM THE TREADMILL (US/0048-1335) [03036757] **4606**

OBSERVATIONS (OTTAWA) (CN/1180-2863) [23247943] **2571**

OBSERVATOIRE DE GENEVE *See* PUBLICATIONS DE L'OBSERVATOIRE DE GENEVE. SERIE B **398**

OBSERVATORIO ASTRONOMICO DE MADRID *See* MEMORIA / OBSERVATORIO ASTRONOMICO NACIONAL **397**

OBSERVATORIO ASTRONOMICO DE MADRID *See* BOLETIN ASTRONOMICO DEL OBSERVATORIO DE MADRID **393**

OBSERVATORIO ASTRONOMICO DE QUITO *See* BOLETIN ASTRONOMICO. SERIE B **393**

OBSERVATORIO ASTRONOMICO MUNICIPAL DE ROSARIO *See* BOLETIN - OBSERVATORIO ASTRONOMICO MUNICIPAL DE ROSARIO **393**

OBSERVATORY, THE (UK/0029-7704) [04953657] **397**

OBSERVER (DACCA, BANGLADESH) *See* BANGLADESH OBSERVER, THE **5778**

OBSERVER (DE WITT, IOWA. NATIONAL ED.) (US/0886-8808) [13030928] **5672**

OBSERVER-DISPATCH (UTICA ED.), THE (US/0890-0329) [10886202] **5719**

OBSERVER ECCENTRIC (US) **5693**

OBSERVER (HERNDON, VA.), THE (US/1063-8466) [26147783] **5759**

OBSERVER (LONDON) (UK/0029-7712) [05653614] **5813**

OBSERVER (NEW YORK, N.Y. : 1985) (US/0886-4306) [12886011] **3020**

OBSERVER (NORTHPORT, N.Y.) (US) [10906819] **5719**

OBSERVER-PATRIOT, THE **CEASED.** (US) [26687387] **5646**

OBSERVER (PHILADELPHIA (PA.)) (US) [07626758] **2541**

OBSERVER (PHILADELPHIA, PA.) (US/0279-9529) [07329651] **3623**

OBSERVER : PRBO IN PRINT : QUARTERLY JOURNAL OF THE POINT REYES BIRD OBSERVATORY (US) [21173957] **5619**

OBSERVER-REPORTER (US/0891-0693) [02265357] **5738**

OBSERVER (RIO RANCHO, N.M.), THE (US/1049-7374) [21310212] **5712**

OBSERVER (ROCKFORD), THE (US/0029-7739) [04123749] **5033**

OBSERVER, THE (US) [15118313] **5666**

OBSERVER, THE (US) [17500248] **5684**

OBSERVER, THE (US) [25060643] **5646**

OBSERVER, THE (US) [25993166] **5741**

OBSERVER'S HANDBOOK, THE (CN/0080-4193) [02624615] **397**

OBSHCHESTVENNAIA MYSL ZA RUBEZHOM. KNIZHNOE OBOZRENTE (RU) [22513116] **5211**

OBSHCHESTVENNOE PITANIE (RU) [06585274] **5072**

OBSHCHESTVENNYE NAUKI I SOVREMENNOST : ONS (RU/0869-0499) [24013139] **4544, 5211**

OBSHCHESTVENNYE NAUKI V ROSSII. SERIIA 2, EKONOMIKA *See* SOTSIALNYE I GUMANITARNYE NAUKI. SERIIA 2, EKONOMIKA : OTECHESTVENNAIA I ZARUBEZHNAIA LITERATURA / ROSSIISKAIA AKADEMIIA NAUK, INSTITUT NAUCHNOI INFORMATSII PO OBSHCHESTVENNYM NAUKAM **1521**

OBSHCHESTVENNYE NAUKI V ROSSII. SERIIA 2, EKONOMIKA / ROSSIISKAIA AKADEMIIA NAUK, INSTITUT NAUCHNOI INFORMATSII PO OBSHCHESTVENNYM NAUKAM (RU) [28545202] **1509**

OBSHCHESTVENNYE NAUKI V ROSSII. SERIIA 3, FILOSOFIIA *See* SOTSIALNYE I GUMANITARNYE NAUKI. SERIIA 3, FILOSOFSKIE NAUKI : OTECHESTVENNAIA I ZARUBEZHNAIA LITERATURA / ROSSIISKAIA AKADEMIIA NAUK, INSTITUT NAUCHNOI INFORMATSII PO OBSHCHESTVENNYM NAUKAM **4361**

OBSHCHESTVENNYE NAUKI V ROSSII. SERIIA 3, FILOSOFIIA / ROSSIISKAIA AKADEMIIA NAUK, INSTITUT NAUCHNOI INFORMATSII PO OBSHCHESTVENNYM NAUKAM (RU) [27996980] **4354**

OBSHCHESTVENNYE NAUKI V ROSSII. SERIIA 4, GOSUDARSTVO I PRAVO *See* SOTSIALNYE I GUMANITARNYE NAUKI. SERIIA 4, GOSUDARSTVO I PRAVO. ZARUBEZHNAIA LITERATURA / ROSSIISKAIA AKADEMIIA NAUK, INSTITUT NAUCHNOI INFORMATSII PO OBSHCHESTVENNYM NAUKAM **3056**

OBSHCHESTVENNYE NAUKI V ROSSII. SERIIA 4, GOSUDARSTVO I PRAVO *See* SOTSIALNYE I GUMANITARNYE NAUKI. SERIIA 4, GOSUDARSTVO I PRAVO. OTECHESTVENNAIA LITERATURA / ROSSIISKAIA AKADEMIIA NAUK, INSTITUT NAUCHNOI INFORMATSII PO OBSHCHESTVENNYM NAUKAM **3056**

OBSHCHESTVENNYE — Alphabetical Title Index

OBSHCHESTVENNYE NAUKI V ROSSII. SERIIA 4, GOSUDARSTVO I PRAVO / ROSSIISKAIA AKADEMIIA NAUK, INSTITUT NAUCHNOI INFORMATSII PO OBSHCHESTVENNYM NAUKAM (RU) [28004614] 4485, **3020**

OBSHCHESTVENNYE NAUKI V ROSSII. SERIIA 5, ISTORIIA See SOTSIALNYE I GUMANITARNYE NAUKI. SERIIA 5, ISTORIIA. OTECHESTVENNAIA LITERATURA / ROSSIISKAIA AKADEMIIA NAUK, INSTITUT NAUCHNOI INFORMATSII PO OBSHCHESTVENNYM NAUKAM **2630**

OBSHCHESTVENNYE NAUKI V ROSSII. SERIIA 5, ISTORIIA / ROSSIISKAIA AKADEMIIA NAUK, INSTITUT NAUCHNOI INFORMATSII PO OBSHCHESTVENNYM NAUKAM (RU) [28004707] **2624**

OBSHCHESTVENNYE NAUKI V ROSSII. SERIIA 6, IAZYKOZNANIE See SOTSIALNYE I GUMANITARNYE NAUKI. SERIIA 6, IAZYKOZNANIE. OTECHESTVENNAIA LITERATURA / ROSSIISKAIA AKADEMIIA NAUK, INSTITUT NAUCHNOI INFORMATSII PO OBSHCHESTVENNYM NAUKAM **3322**

OBSHCHESTVENNYE NAUKI V ROSSII. SERIIA 6, I AZYKOZNANIE / ROSSIISKAIA AKADEMIIA NAUK, INSTITUT NAUCHNOI INFORMATSII PO OBSHCHESTVENNYM NAUKAM (RU) [27994823] **3307**

OBSHCHESTVENNYE NAUKI V ROSSII. SERIIA 7, LITERATUROVEDENIE / ROSSIISKAIA AKADEMIIA NAUK, INSTITUT NAUCHNOI INFORMATSII PO OBSHCHESTVENNYM NAUKAM (RU) [28004537] **3419**

OBSHCHESTVENNYE NAUKI V SSSR. SERIIA 1 : PROBLEMY NAUCHNOGO KOMMUNIZMA **CEASED**. (RU/0202-2036) [02336751] **5211**

OBSHCHESTVENNYE NAUKI V SSSR. SERIIA 2 : EKONOMIKA See OBSHCHESTVENNYE NAUKI V ROSSII. SERIIA 2, EKONOMIKA / ROSSIISKAIA AKADEMIIA NAUK, INSTITUT NAUCHNOI INFORMATSII PO OBSHCHESTVENNYM NAUKAM **1509**

OBSHCHESTVENNYE NAUKI V SSSR. SERIIA 3, FILOSOFSKIE NAUKI See OBSHCHESTVENNYE NAUKI V ROSSII. SERIIA 3, FILOSOFIIA / ROSSIISKAIA AKADEMIIA NAUK, INSTITUT NAUCHNOI INFORMATSII PO OBSHCHESTVENNYM NAUKAM **4354**

OBSHCHESTVENNYE NAUKI V SSSR. SERIIA 4, GOSUDARSTVO I PRAVO See OBSHCHESTVENNYE NAUKI V ROSSII. SERIIA 4, GOSUDARSTVO I PRAVO / ROSSIISKAIA AKADEMIIA NAUK, INSTITUT NAUCHNOI INFORMATSII PO OBSHCHESTVENNYM NAUKAM **3020**

OBSHCHESTVENNYE NAUKI V SSSR. SERIIA 5, ISTORIIA See OBSHCHESTVENNYE NAUKI V ROSSII. SERIIA 5, ISTORIIA / ROSSIISKAIA AKADEMIIA NAUK, INSTITUT NAUCHNOI INFORMATSII PO OBSHCHESTVENNYM NAUKAM **2624**

OBSHCHESTVENNYE NAUKI V SSSR. SERIIA 6, I AZYKOZNANIE See OBSHCHESTVENNYE NAUKI V ROSSII. SERIIA 6, IAZYKOZNANIE / ROSSIISKAIA AKADEMIIA NAUK, INSTITUT NAUCHNOI INFORMATSII PO OBSHCHESTVENNYM NAUKAM **3307**

OBSHCHESTVENNYE NAUKI V SSSR. SERIIA 7, LITERATUROVEDENIE See OBSHCHESTVENNYE NAUKI V ROSSII. SERIIA 7, LITERATUROVEDENIE / ROSSIISKAIA AKADEMIIA NAUK, INSTITUT NAUCHNOI INFORMATSII PO OBSHCHESTVENNYM NAUKAM **3419**

OBSHCHESTVENNYE NAUKI V TADZHIKISTANE; UKAZATEL LITERATURY (TA) [02243482] **5227**

OBSHCHESTVENNYE NAUKI ZA RUBEZHOM. SERIIA 2 : EKONOMIKA (RU) [02162599] 4544, **1509**

OBSHCHESTVENNYE NAUKI ZA RUBEZHOM. SERIIA 2, EKONOMIKA OBSHCHESTVENNYE NAUKI See SOTSIALNYE I GUMANITARNYE NAUKI. SERIIA 2, EKONOMIKA : OTECHESTVENNAIA I ZARUBEZHNAIA LITERATURA / ROSSIISKAIA AKADEMIIA NAUK, INSTITUT NAUCHNOI INFORMATSII PO OBSHCHESTVENNYM NAUKAM **1521**

OBSHCHESTVENNYE NAUKI ZA RUBEZHOM. SERIIA 3, FILOSOFIIA See SOTSIALNYE I GUMANITARNYE NAUKI. SERIIA 3, FILOSOFSKIE NAUKI : OTECHENNAIA I ZARUBEZHNAIA LITERATURA / ROSSIISKAIA AKADEMIIA NAUK, INSTITUT NAUCHNOI INFORMATSII PO OBSHCHESTVENNYM NAUKAM **4361**

OBSHCHESTVENNYE NAUKI ZA RUBEZHOM. SERIIA 4: GOSUDARSTVO I PRAVO (RU) [02335710] **3020**

OBSHCHESTVENNYE NAUKI ZA RUBEZHOM. SERIIA 5: ISTORIIA (RU) [02171323] **2624**

OBSHCHESTVENNYE NAUKI ZA RUBEZHOM. SERIIA 6: IAZYKOZNANIE (RU) [02162581] **3307**

OBSHCHESTVENNYE NAUKI ZA RUBEZHOM. SERIIA 7: LITERATUROVEDENIE (RU/0202-2117) [02160634] **3419**

OBSHCHESTVENNYE NAUKI ZA RUBEZHOM. SERIIA 8: NAUKOVEDENIE (RU) [02176469] **5135**

OBSHCHESTVENNYE NAUKI ZA RUBEZHOM. SERIIA 9 : VOSTOKOVEDENIE I AFRIKANISTIKA (RU) [02853277] **2661**

●OBSHCHESTVO I EKONOMIKA (RU/0207-3676) [27359450] **1576**

OBSHCHIE PROBLEMY KULTURY I KULTURNOGO STROITELSTVA: NAUCHNYI REFERATIVNYI SBORNIK (RU) [05345469] **327**

OBSHTESTVO I PRAVO (BU/0204-8523) [06868872] **3020**

OBSIDIAN II (US/0888-4412) [13573529] **3419**

OBST UND GARTEN (GW/0029-7798) [05371582] **2426**

OBSTBAU (GW) [02476998] **116**

OBSTBAUVERSUCHSRING DES ALTEN LANDES, JORK See MITTEILUNGEN DES OBSTBAUVERSUCHSRINGES DES ALTEN LANDES **2424**

OBSTERNTE. REIHE 3.4 / HERAUSGEBER, STATISTISCHES BUNDESMAST, WIESBADEN (GW) [08412553] **116**

OBSTETRIC ANESTHESIA DIGEST (US/0275-665X) [07192944] 3766, **3683**

OBSTETRICA ET GYNECOLOGICA (OULU) (FI/0358-4844) [04771213] **3766**

OBSTETRICAL & GYNECOLOGICAL SURVEY (US/0029-7828) [01760994] **3766**

OBSTETRICIA Y GINECOLOGIA LATINO-AMERICANAS (AG/0029-7836) [01607985] **3766**

OBSTETRICS AND GYNAECOLOGY (OTTAWA) (CN/0824-7404) [11559829] **3766**

OBSTETRICS AND GYNECOLOGY CLINICS OF NORTH AMERICA (US/0889-8545) [14091825] **3766**

OBSTETRICS AND GYNECOLOGY (NEW YORK. 1953) (US/0029-7844) [01643950] **3766**

OBSTETRICS & GYNECOLOGY (NEW YORK. 1970) (US/0078-298X) [01785299] **3766**

OBSTETRICS & GYNECOLOGY REVIEW (US/1060-507X) [24548787] **3766**

OBZOR (BU/0029-7852) [02265360] 360, **3419**

OBZORJE PACIFIKA (CN/0048-1343) [03258512] **2751**

OBZORNAIA INFORMATSIIA: BIBLIOTEKOVEDENIE I BIBLIOGRAFOVEDENIE (RU) [05350383] **3238**

OBZORNAIA INFORMATSIIA: RESTAVRATSIIA, ISSLEDOVANIE I KHRANENIE MUZEINYKH KHUDOZHESTVENNYKH TSENNOSTEI (RU) [05350453] 360, **4094**

OBZORNAIA INFORMATSIIA. RESTAVRATSIIA PAMIATNIKOV ISTORII I KULTURY / MINISTERSTVO KULTURY SSSR, GOSUDARSTVENNAIA ORDENA LENINA BIBLIOTEKA SSSR IMENI V.I. LENINA (RU/0234-6540) [24162908] **327**

OBZORNIK ZA MATEMATIKO IN FIZIKO (XV/0473-7466) [06002590] 4413, **3525**

OCALA STAR-BANNER (US/0163-3201) [04349584] **5650**

OCAW REPORTER (US/8756-1727) [11406456] **1696**

OCB (BL) [09990884] **1543**

OCCASIONAL BIBLIOGRAPHICAL PAPERS (US) [03234550] **421**

OCCASIONAL BULLETIN / PACIFIC & ASIAN AMERICAN CENTER FOR THEOLOGY & STRATEGIES (US) [08539811] **4053**

OCCASIONAL ESSAYS (CR) [04678417] **4983**

OCCASIONAL MISCELLANY OF THE LIBRARY COMPANY OF PHILADELPHIA (US/0734-3698) [07368657] **3238**

OCCASIONAL - NOVA SCOTIA MUSEUM (CN/0704-5824) [02249966] **4094**

OCCASIONAL PAPER (US) [19959420] **4530**

OCCASIONAL PAPER (UK) [28301640] **3623**

OCCASIONAL PAPER (AUSTRALIAN BUREAU OF AGRICULTURAL AND RESOURCE ECONOMICS) See ABARE RESEARCH REPORT **42**

OCCASIONAL PAPER - AUSTRALIAN GEOSCIENCE INFORMATION ASSOCIATION (AT/0816-6234) [I08166234] **1359**

OCCASIONAL PAPER - BOSTON UNIVERSITY. CENTER FOR ARCHAEOLOGICAL STUDIES (US/0748-7339) [10992742] **277**

OCCASIONAL PAPER / BUREAU OF AGRICULTURAL ECONOMICS, CANBERRA (AT) [03684130] **116**

OCCASIONAL PAPER - BUREAU OF TRANSPORT AND COMMUNICATIONS ECONOMICS (AT/1032-0539) [I10320539] **1509**

OCCASIONAL PAPER - CANADIAN WILDLIFE SERVICE (CN/0576-6370) [02248737] **2201**

OCCASIONAL PAPER - CENTRE FOR ENVIRONMENTAL STUDIES, UNIVERSITY OF TASMANIA (AT/1034-1412) [I10341412] **2179**

OCCASIONAL PAPER (COMMITTEE FOR ECONOMIC DEVELOPMENT OF AUSTRALIA) (AT) [12192583] **1576**

OCCASIONAL PAPER - COUNCIL ON ECONOMIC PRIORITIES (US/0271-0528) [06550692] **1509**

OCCASIONAL PAPER - DEPARTMENT OF EDUCATION, UNIVERSITY OF SYDNEY (AT/0156-708X) [I0156708X] **1769**

OCCASIONAL PAPER - DEPT. OF GEOGRAPHY, UNIVERSITY OF GUYANA (GY) [01515806] **2571**

OCCASIONAL PAPER - ECONOMICS PROGRAM (II) [04061905] 116, **1509**

OCCASIONAL PAPER - FACULTY OF ENVIRONMENTAL STUDIES. UNIVERSITY OF WATERLOO (CN/0317-8641) [02248362] **2179**

OCCASIONAL PAPER (FAMILY POLICY STUDIES CENTRE (GREAT BRITAIN)) (UK) [12310219] **2284**

OCCASIONAL PAPER - FREEDOM FORUM MEDIA STUDIES CENTER (US/1062-6166) [25291609] **2923**

OCCASIONAL PAPER - GRADUATE CENTER FOR LATIN AMERICAN STUDIES (VANDERBILT UNIVERSITY) (US/0083-5234) [01468410] **2751**

OCCASIONAL PAPER (GREAT BRITAIN. FORESTRY COMMISSION) (UK) [11679518] **2390**

OCCASIONAL PAPER / INDIANA CENTER ON GLOBAL CHANGE AND WORLD PEACE (US) [24521003] **4530**

OCCASIONAL PAPER (INSTITUTE FOR EUROPEAN DEFENCE & STRATEGIC STUDIES (LONDON, ENGLAND)) (UK) [12690661] **4530**

OCCASIONAL PAPER / INTERNATIONAL MONETARY FUND (US/0251-6365) [07563709] **801**

OCCASIONAL PAPER (INTERNATIONAL OMBUDSMAN INSTITUTE) (CN/0711-6349) [08499763] **4670**

OCCASIONAL PAPER - JOHANNESBURG. UNIVERSITY OF THE WITWATERSRAND. DEPT. OF GEOGRAPHY AND ENVIRONMENTAL STUDIES (SA) [05324322] **2179**

OCCASIONAL PAPER - MAXWELL GRADUATE SCHOOL OF CITIZENSHIP AND PUBLIC AFFAIRS. METROPOLITAN STUDIES PROGRAM (US/0732-507X) [03104514] **4670**

OCCASIONAL PAPER - MISSOURI ACADEMY OF SCIENCE (US/0148-0944) [03267603] **5135**

OCCASIONAL PAPER / NEW ZEALAND INSTITUTE OF INTERNATIONAL AFFAIRS (NZ/0113-1044) [18796245] 4530, **4485**

OCCASIONAL PAPER - PORIM (MY/0127-2209) [09523629] **1027**

OCCASIONAL PAPER - PROGRAM IN URBAN AND REGIONAL STUDIES (US) [04455896] **2829**

OCCASIONAL PAPER - RESERVE BANK OF AUSTRALIA (AT/0080-178X) [01908643] 801, **732**

OCCASIONAL PAPER SERIES - FISHERIES AND WILDLIFE DIVISION, MINISTRY FOR CONSERVATION (AT/0810-5766) [20042330] **2201**

OCCASIONAL PAPER / SOCIETY OF ANTIQUARIES OF LONDON (UK/0953-7155) [12791995] **2701**

OCCASIONAL PAPER (SOUTH PACIFIC SMALLHOLDER PROJECT) (AT) [16653578] **116**

OCCASIONAL PAPER - SOUTH PACIFIC SMALLHOLDER PROJECT, UNIVERSITY OF NEW ENGLAND (AT/0814-7973) [I08147973] 700, **1509**

OCCASIONAL PAPER (TRANSNATIONAL CORPORATIONS RESEARCH PROJECT (UNIVERSITY OF SYDNEY)) (AT) [17190678] **700**

OCCASIONAL PAPER (UNIVERSITY OF BRITISH COLUMBIA. CENTRE FOR TRANSPORTATION STUDIES) (CN/0712-1067) [08507497] **5388**

OCCASIONAL PAPER (UNIVERSITY OF CALIFORNIA, LOS ANGELES. AFRICAN STUDIES CENTER) **CEASED**. (US/0068-6190) [01779389] **2642**

OCCASIONAL PAPER (UNIVERSITY OF COLORADO, BOULDER. INSTITUTE OF ARCTIC AND ALPINE RESEARCH) (US/0069-6145) [02533928] **5136**

OCCASIONAL PAPER / UNIVERSITY OF KEELE, DEPARTMENT OF GEOGRAPHY (UK) [22096796] **2571**

OCCASIONAL PAPER - UNIVERSITY OF SYDNEY, AUSTRALIAN LANGUAGE RESEARCH CENTRE (AT/0042-0093) [04325019] **3307**

OCCASIONAL PAPER / WESTERN ASSOCIATION OF MAP LIBRARIES (US/0278-3835) [06586774] **2582**

OCCASIONAL PAPER / WYE COLLEGE, UNIVERSITY OF LONDON, DEPARTMENT OF AGRICULTURE, HORTICULTURE AND THE ENVIRONMENT (UK/0957-0985) [24606543] 2179, 2426, **116**

OCCASIONAL PAPERS (UK) **4983**

OCCASIONAL PAPERS (SA/0065-387X) [03313669] **2851**

OCCASIONAL PAPERS (US) [01554125] **3020**

OCCASIONAL PAPERS - APPLIED LINGUISTICS ASSOCIATION OF AUSTRALIA (AT/0314-3937) [06449869] **3307**

OCCASIONAL PAPERS - ART LIBRARIES SOCIETY OF NORTH AMERICA (US/0730-7160) [08045788] 327, **3238**

OCCASIONAL PAPERS - BOWDOIN COLLEGE. MUSEUM OF ART (US/0893-0589) [08532101] 360, **4094**

OCCASIONAL PAPERS - CHICAGO. UNIVERSITY. INDUSTRIAL RELATIONS CENTER (US/0529-0937) [03078855] **1696**

OCCASIONAL PAPERS - DEPARTMENT OF HISTORY, ARKANSAS TECH UNIVERSITY (US) [06954790] **2624**

OCCASIONAL PAPERS - DEPARTMENT OF POLITICAL SCIENCE. CARLETON UNIVERSITY (CN/0229-7000) [07970442] **4485**

OCCASIONAL PAPERS - DEPT. OF ENGLISH LOCAL HISTORY, LEICESTER UNIVERSITY (UK/0078-303X) [01755749] **2701**

OCCASIONAL PAPERS - DUGDALE SOCIETY (UK) [01698481] **5234**

OCCASIONAL PAPERS - FREER GALLERY OF ART (US/0071-9382) [02353707] **360**

OCCASIONAL PAPERS FROM THE MUSEUM OF VICTORIA (AT/0814-1819) [12007302] **4169**

OCCASIONAL PAPERS (GROUP OF THIRTY) (US/0278-1468) [07718864] **1638**

OCCASIONAL PAPERS IN ANTHROPOLOGY (US/0078-3005) [01781149] **242**

OCCASIONAL PAPERS IN ARCHAEOLOGY *CEASED.* (US/0473-7482) [02638869] **277**

OCCASIONAL PAPERS IN ENTOMOLOGY (US/0362-2622) [02288422] **5612**

OCCASIONAL PAPERS IN ETHNIC AND IMMIGRATION STUDIES (CN/0828-1513) [06823874] 1920, **2270**

OCCASIONAL PAPERS IN INTERCULTURAL LEARNING (US/8756-9078) [11732409] **1769**

OCCASIONAL PAPERS IN LANGUAGE, LITERATURE AND LINGUISTICS. SERIES A (US/0889-6356) [05343183] 3419, **3307**

OCCASIONAL PAPERS - NATIONAL HORTICULTURAL RESEARCH INSTITUTE (NR/0795-4123) [I07954123] **2426**

OCCASIONAL PAPERS / NATIONAL INSTITUTE OF ECONOMIC AND SOCIAL RESEARCH (UK/0077-4928) [01759266] 5211, **1509**

OCCASIONAL PAPERS - NEVADA STATE MUSEUM (US/0077-7919) [05754799] **4094**

OCCASIONAL PAPERS / NUFFIELD PROVINCIAL HOSPITALS TRUST (UK) [20423383] **3623**

OCCASIONAL PAPERS OF THE BRITISH COLUMBIA PROVINCIAL MUSEUM (CN/0068-1636) [03192986] **4169**

OCCASIONAL PAPERS OF THE CALIFORNIA ACADEMY OF SCIENCES (US/0068-5461) [01359099] **5136**

OCCASIONAL PAPERS OF THE IDAHO MUSEUM OF NATURAL HISTORY (US/0196-7703) [05876199] 4169, **4094**

OCCASIONAL PAPERS OF THE IDAHO STATE UNIVERSITY MUSEUM *See* OCCASIONAL PAPERS OF THE IDAHO MUSEUM OF NATURAL HISTORY **4094**

OCCASIONAL PAPERS OF THE INSTITUTION OF MINING AND METALLURGY (UK) [09185107] 4014, **2147**

OCCASIONAL PAPERS OF THE MUSEUM OF NATURAL HISTORY (LAWRENCE) (US/0091-7958) [01755000] **4169**

OCCASIONAL PAPERS OF THE MUSEUM OF NATURAL SCIENCE (US/1050-4842) [20663722] **5593**

OCCASIONAL PAPERS OF THE MUSEUM OF ZOOLOGY, UNIVERSITY OF MICHIGAN (US/0076-8413) [01757337] 4170, **5593**

OCCASIONAL PAPERS OF THE WESTERN FOUNDATION OF VERTEBRATE ZOOLOGY (US/0511-7542) [01326458] **5593**

OCCASIONAL PAPERS ON ANTIQUITIES (US/8756-047X) [11464054] 360, **251**

OCCASIONAL PAPERS ON COMMUNITY DEVELOPMENT - EAST AFRICAN LITERATURE BUREAU (TZ) [01783160] **2829**

OCCASIONAL PAPERS ON LINGUISTICS (US/0885-5773) [06342558] **3307**

OCCASIONAL PAPERS ON MOLLUSKS (US/0073-0807) [01837849] **5593**

OCCASIONAL PAPERS ON PUBLIC MANAGEMENT (FR) 1509, **880**

OCCASIONAL PAPERS ON RELIGION IN EASTERN EUROPE (US/0731-5465) [07917563] **4983**

OCCASIONAL PAPERS ON RELIGION IN EASTERN EUROPE *See* RELIGION IN EASTERN EUROPE **4991**

OCCASIONAL PAPERS ON TECHNOLOGY (UK/0306-7343) [01761636] **4094**

OCCASIONAL PAPERS ON THE NEAR EAST *CEASED.* (US/0732-6475) [08416148] 277, **2661**

OCCASIONAL PAPERS / REPRINTS SERIES IN CONTEMPORARY ASIAN STUDIES (US/0730-0107) [05515768] **2661**

OCCASIONAL PAPERS / SCANDINAVIAN INSTITUTE OF ASIAN STUDIES (UK/0266-206X) [20041942] **2661**

OCCASIONAL PAPERS SERIES - DEPARTMENT OF GEOGRAPHY, UNIVERSITY OF GLASGOW (UK/0264-3499) [02643499] **2571**

OCCASIONAL PAPERS. SOUTH ASIA SERIES (US/0076-812X) [01779178] **2661**

OCCASIONAL PAPERS - SWENSON SWEDISH IMMIGRATION RESEARCH CENTER (US/1056-6120) [23747565] **1920**

OCCASIONAL PAPERS - THE MUSEUM, TEXAS TECH UNIVERSITY (US/0149-175X) [01772711] **4094**

OCCASIONAL PAPERS - UNITED METHODIST BOARD OF HIGHER EDUCATION AND MINISTRY (US/0273-0960) [04625199] 4983, **1838**

OCCASIONAL PAPERS - UNIVERSITY OF ARKANSAS MUSEUM (US/0148-0960) [03267497] **4094**

OCCASIONAL PAPERS / UNIVERSITY OF ESSEX, DEPARTMENT OF LANGUAGE AND LINGUISTICS (UK) [16725144] **3307**

OCCASIONAL PAPERS - UNIVERSITY OF ILLINOIS (URBANA-CHAMPAIGN CAMPUS). GRADUATE SCHOOL OF LIBRARY AND INFORMATION SCIENCE (US/0276-1769) [07320017] **3238**

OCCASIONAL PAPERS (UNIVERSITY OF NEW MEXICO. MUSEUM OF SOUTHWESTERN BIOLOGY) (US/0749-2421) [10515117] 467, 5593, **2219**

OCCASIONAL PAPERS - VIRGINIA LIBRARY ASSOCIATION (US/0195-6329) [05526980] **3238**

OCCASIONAL PAPERS / WORLD FOOD PROGRAMME (IT) [18611597] **2351**

OCCASIONAL PUBLICATION (US) [03201100] **3238**

OCCASIONAL PUBLICATION - BOREAL INSTITUTE FOR NORTHERN STUDIES (CN/0068-0303) [03455908] **2751**

OCCASIONAL PUBLICATION / FRESHWATER BIOLOGICAL ASSOCIATION (UK) [03536430] **467**

OCCASIONAL PUBLICATION / INSTITUTE OF AFRICAN STUDIES, UNIVERSITY OF IBADAN (NR/0536-2326) [10794616] **1093**

OCCASIONAL PUBLICATION - NARRAGANSETT MARINE LABORATORY (US/0556-8560) [01161926] **1453**

OCCASIONAL PUBLICATION (UNIVERSITY OF LONDON. INSTITUTE OF ARCHAEOLOGY) (UK) [07786494] **277**

OCCASIONAL PUBLICATIONS IN CLASSICAL STUDIES *SUSPENDED.* (US/0275-2158) [04935187] **1078**

OCCASIONAL PUBLICATIONS IN NORTHEASTERN ANTHROPOLOGY (US/0276-8607) [07267853] 277, **242**

OCCASIONAL PUBLICATIONS OF THE DEPARTMENT OF GEOGRAPHY (URBANA) (US/0271-0366) [02110846] **2571**

OCCASIONAL PUBLICATIONS SERIES / ANGLO-NORMAN TEXT SOCIETY (UK) [12151348] **2624**

OCCASIONAL REPORT - LAW SOCIETY OF UPPER CANADA (CN/0383-9656) [03284772] **3020**

OCCASIONAL RESEARCH PAPER (BRIGHAM YOUNG UNIVERSITY. SCHOOL OF LIBRARY AND INFORMATION SCIENCES) *CEASED.* (US/0148-2068) [03280235] **3238**

OCCASIONAL RESEARCH PAPERS - DEPARTMENT OF RELIGIOUS STUDIES AND PHILOSOPHY, MAKERERE UNIVERSITY (SA) [02441334] 4354, **4983**

OCCASIONAL REVIEW (SAN JOSE, CALIF.), THE (US/0885-5919) [08064383] 3349, **3467**

OCCASIONAL REVIEW, THE (US/0097-8221) [01799173] **2541**

OCCASIONAL SERIES - HISTORIC SOCIETY OF LANCASHIRE AND CHESHIRE (UK) [04928113] **2701**

OCCASIONAL STUDENT PAPER (UNIVERSITY OF BRITISH COLUMBIA. CENTRE FOR TRANSPORTATION STUDIES) (CN/0229-9704) [08099373] **5388**

OCCASIONAL STUDIES OF THE ECONOMIC COMMISSION FOR EUROPE (SZ) **1638**

OCCASIONAL SYMPOSIUM (UK/0572-7022) [02505541] **5517**

OCCULT OBSERVER, THE (UK/0969-1375) [I09691375] **4242**

OCCULTATION NEWSLETTER (US/0737-6766) [09425209] **398**

●OCCUPATIONAL AND ENVIRONMENTAL MEDICINE (UK/1351-0711) [29750123] 3623, **2866**

OCCUPATIONAL AND ENVIRONMENTAL MEDICINE REPORT, THE (US/0894-2811) [15973635] **5300**

OCCUPATIONAL BRIEFS / CGP (US/1064-7333) [05514156] **4207**

OCCUPATIONAL COMPENSATION SURVEY--PAY AND BENEFITS. AUSTIN, TX / U.S. DEPARTMENT OF LABOR, BUREAU OF LABOR STATISTICS (US) [25970000] **1696**

OCCUPATIONAL COMPENSATION SURVEY--PAY AND BENEFITS. BOSTON *See* OCCUPATIONAL COMPENSATION SURVEY--PAY ONLY. BOSTON, MASSACHUSETTS, METROPOLITAN AREA / U.S. DEPARTMENT OF LABOR, BUREAU OF LABOR STATISTICS **1697**

●OCCUPATIONAL COMPENSATION SURVEY--PAY AND BENEFITS. BRUNSWICK, GA / U.S. DEPARTMENT OF LABOR, BUREAU OF LABOR STATISTICS (US) [27466736] **1696**

●OCCUPATIONAL COMPENSATION SURVEY--PAY AND BENEFITS. CHARLESTON, SC / U.S. DEPARTMENT OF LABOR, BUREAU OF LABOR STATISTICS (US) [26702930] **1696**

●OCCUPATIONAL COMPENSATION SURVEY--PAY AND BENEFITS. CINCINNATI, OHIO-KENTUCKY-INDIANA, METROPOLITAN AREA / U.S. DEPARTMENT OF LABOR, BUREAU OF LABOR STATISTICS (US) [27213932] 1509, **1696**

●OCCUPATIONAL COMPENSATION SURVEY--PAY AND BENEFITS. CLARKSVILLE-HOPKINSVILLE, TN-KY / U.S. DEPARTMENT OF LABOR, BUREAU OF LABOR STATISTICS (US) [26703073] **1696**

OCCUPATIONAL COMPENSATION SURVEY--PAY AND BENEFITS. DALLAS, TEXAS, METROPOLITAN AREA / U.S. DEPARTMENT OF LABOR, BUREAU OF LABOR STATISTICS (US/1068-4611) [26522007] 1509, **1696**

●OCCUPATIONAL COMPENSATION SURVEY--PAY AND BENEFITS. FLORENCE, SC / U.S. DEPARTMENT OF LABOR, BUREAU OF LABOR STATISTICS (US) [26726043] **1696**

●OCCUPATIONAL COMPENSATION SURVEY--PAY AND BENEFITS. FRESNO, CA / U.S. DEPARTMENT OF LABOR, BUREAU OF LABOR STATISTICS (US) [26725845] **1696**

●OCCUPATIONAL COMPENSATION SURVEY--PAY AND BENEFITS. GARY-HAMMOND, INDIANA, METROPOLITAN AREA (US/1068-4581) [26997899] **1696**

●OCCUPATIONAL COMPENSATION SURVEY--PAY AND BENEFITS. GREENSBORO-WINSTON SALEM-HIGH POINT, NC / U.S. DEPARTMENT OF LABOR, BUREAU OF LABOR STATISTICS (US) [26702145] **1696**

OCCUPATIONAL

Alphabetical Title Index

●OCCUPATIONAL COMPENSATION SURVEY--PAY AND BENEFITS. HUNTSVILLE, ALABAMA, METROPOLITAN AREA / U.S. DEPARTMENT OF LABOR, BUREAU OF LABOR STATISTICS (US) [26960759] **1696**

●OCCUPATIONAL COMPENSATION SURVEY--PAY AND BENEFITS. JACKSON, MISSISSIPPI, METROPOLITAN AREA / U.S. DEPARTMENT OF LABOR, BUREAU OF LABOR STATISTICS (US) [26994628] **1696**

OCCUPATIONAL COMPENSATION SURVEY--PAY AND BENEFITS. LOS ANGELES-LONG BEACH, CALIFORNIA, METROPOLITAN AREA (US) [26952759] **1696**

●OCCUPATIONAL COMPENSATION SURVEY--PAY AND BENEFITS. MELBOURNE-TITUSVILLE-PALM BAY, FL / U.S. DEPARTMENT OF LABOR, BUREAU OF LABOR STATISTICS (US) [28360999] **1696**

●OCCUPATIONAL COMPENSATION SURVEY--PAY AND BENEFITS. MONTGOMERY, AL / U.S. DEPARTMENT OF LABOR, BUREAU OF LABOR STATISTICS (US) [26703183] **1696**

●OCCUPATIONAL COMPENSATION SURVEY--PAY AND BENEFITS. SALINAS-SEASIDE-MONTEREY, CA / U.S. DEPARTMENT OF LABOR, BUREAU OF LABOR STATISTICS (US) [26295247] **1696**

●OCCUPATIONAL COMPENSATION SURVEY--PAY AND BENEFITS. SELMA, AL / U.S. DEPARTMENT OF LABOR, BUREAU OF LABOR STATISTICS (US) [27466699] **1696**

●OCCUPATIONAL COMPENSATION SURVEY--PAY AND BENEFITS. SOUTH BEND-MISHAWAKA, INDIANA, METROPOLITAN AREA / U.S. DEPARTMENT OF LABOR, BUREAU OF LABOR STATISTICS (US) [28100944] **1697**

●OCCUPATIONAL COMPENSATION SURVEY--PAY AND BENEFITS. ST. LOUIS, MISSOURI-ILLINOIS, METROPOLITAN AREA / U.S. DEPARTMENT OF LABOR, BUREAU OF LABOR STATISTICS (US) [26994444] 5335, **1697**

●OCCUPATIONAL COMPENSATION SURVEY--PAY AND BENEFITS. TOLEDO, OH / U.S. DEPARTMENT OF LABOR, BUREAU OF LABOR STATISTICS (US) [26727828] **1697**

●OCCUPATIONAL COMPENSATION SURVEY--PAY AND BENEFITS. TUCSON-DOUGLAS, AZ / U.S. DEPARTMENT OF LABOR, BUREAU OF LABOR STATISTICS (US) [26295331] **1697**

●OCCUPATIONAL COMPENSATION SURVEY--PAY AND BENEFITS. VALLEJO-FAIRFIELD-NAPA, CA / U.S. DEPARTMENT OF LABOR, BUREAU OF LABOR STATISTICS (US) [26387921] **1697**

●OCCUPATIONAL COMPENSATION SURVEY--PAY AND BENEFITS. VERMONT / U.S. DEPARTMENT OF LABOR, BUREAU OF LABOR STATISTICS (US) [28227762] **1697**

●OCCUPATIONAL COMPENSATION SURVEY--PAY AND BENEFITS. WASHINGTON, D.C.-MARYLAND-VIRGINIA, METROPOLITAN AREA / U.S. DEPARTMENT OF LABOR, BUREAU OF LABOR STATISTICS (US) [27091075] **1697**

●OCCUPATIONAL COMPENSATION SURVEY--PAY AND BENEFITS. WICHITA, KS / U.S. DEPARTMENT OF LABOR, BUREAU OF LABOR STATISTICS (US) [26703297] **1697**

●OCCUPATIONAL COMPENSATION SURVEY--PAY ONLY. ARKANSAS--FORESTRY / U.S. DEPARTMENT OF LABOR, BUREAU OF LABOR STATISTICS (US) [26726792] **1697**

●OCCUPATIONAL COMPENSATION SURVEY--PAY ONLY. ATLANTA, GEORGIA, METROPOLITAN AREA / U.S. DEPARTMENT OF LABOR, BUREAU OF LABOR STATISTICS (US) [27723063] **1697**

●OCCUPATIONAL COMPENSATION SURVEY--PAY ONLY. AUSTIN, TX / U.S. DEPARTMENT OF LABOR, BUREAU OF LABOR STATISTICS (US) [29681854] **1697**

●OCCUPATIONAL COMPENSATION SURVEY--PAY ONLY. BELL COUNTY, TX--FAST FOOD RESTAURANTS / U.S. DEPARTMENT OF LABOR, BUREAU OF LABOR STATISTICS (US) [28271685] 2351, **1697**

OCCUPATIONAL COMPENSATION SURVEY--PAY ONLY. BILLINGS, MONTANA, METROPOLITAN AREA / U.S. DEPARTMENT OF LABOR, BUREAU OF LABOR STATISTICS (US) [26034479] **1697**

●OCCUPATIONAL COMPENSATION SURVEY--PAY ONLY. BOSTON, MASSACHUSETTS, METROPOLITAN AREA / U.S. DEPARTMENT OF LABOR, BUREAU OF LABOR STATISTICS (US) [27555729] **1697**

OCCUPATIONAL COMPENSATION SURVEY--PAY ONLY. CHEYENNE, WY / U.S. DEPARTMENT OF LABOR, BUREAU OF LABOR STATISTICS (US) [27002305] **1697**

OCCUPATIONAL COMPENSATION SURVEY--PAY ONLY. DAYTON-SPRINGFIELD, OHIO, METROPOLITAN AREA / U.S. DEPARTMENT OF LABOR, BUREAU OF LABOR STATISTICS (US) [28768245] **1697**

OCCUPATIONAL COMPENSATION SURVEY--PAY ONLY. DUVAL COUNTY, FL--FAST FOOD RESTAURANTS / U.S. DEPARTMENT OF LABOR, BUREAU OF LABOR STATISTICS (US) [28350227] **1697**

OCCUPATIONAL COMPENSATION SURVEY--PAY ONLY. ESCAMBIA COUNTY, FL--FAST FOOD RESTAURANTS / U.S. DEPARTMENT OF LABOR, BUREAU OF LABOR STATISTICS (US) [28386727] 2351, **1697**

●OCCUPATIONAL COMPENSATION SURVEY--PAY ONLY. HARDIN COUNTY, KY--FAST FOOD RESTAURANTS / U.S. DEPARTMENT OF LABOR, BUREAU OF LABOR STATISTICS (US) [28386833] **1697**

●OCCUPATIONAL COMPENSATION SURVEY--PAY ONLY. HARRISON COUNTY, MS--FAST FOOD RESTAURANTS / U.S. DEPARTMENT OF LABOR, BUREAU OF LABOR STATISTICS (US) [28386889] **1697**

●OCCUPATIONAL COMPENSATION SURVEY--PAY ONLY. ISLAND COUNTY, WA--FAST FOOD RESTAURANTS / U.S. DEPARTMENT OF LABOR, BUREAU OF LABOR STATISTICS (US) [28389841] **1698**

●OCCUPATIONAL COMPENSATION SURVEY--PAY ONLY. KANSAS CITY, MISSOURI-KANSAS, METROPOLITAN AREA / U.S. DEPARTMENT OF LABOR, BUREAU OF LABOR STATISTICS (US) [27690689] **1698**

●OCCUPATIONAL COMPENSATION SURVEY--PAY ONLY. LAKE COUNTY, IL--FAST FOOD RESTAURANTS / U.S. DEPARTMENT OF LABOR, BUREAU OF LABOR STATISTICS (US) [28350301] 2351, **1698**

●OCCUPATIONAL COMPENSATION SURVEY--PAY ONLY. LAUDERDALE COUNTY, MS--FAST FOOD RESTAURANTS / U.S. DEPARTMENT OF LABOR, BUREAU OF LABOR STATISTICS (US) [28386918] **1698**

●OCCUPATIONAL COMPENSATION SURVEY--PAY ONLY. LEAVENWORTH, KS--FAST FOOD RESTAURANTS / U.S. DEPARTMENT OF LABOR, BUREAU OF LABOR STATISTICS (US) [28288139] **1698**

●OCCUPATIONAL COMPENSATION SURVEY--PAY ONLY. MINNEAPOLIS-ST. PAUL, MINNESOTA-WISCONSIN, METROPOLITAN AREA / U.S. DEPARTMENT OF LABOR, BUREAU OF LABOR STATISTICS (US) [27370882] **1698**

●OCCUPATIONAL COMPENSATION SURVEY--PAY ONLY. MISSISSIPPI--FORESTRY / U.S. DEPARTMENT OF LABOR, BUREAU OF LABOR STATISTICS (US) [26726677] **1698**

●OCCUPATIONAL COMPENSATION SURVEY--PAY ONLY. MONTGOMERY COUNTY, MD--FAST FOOD RESTAURANTS / U.S. DEPARTMENT OF LABOR, BUREAU OF LABOR STATISTICS (US) [28392349] **1698**

●OCCUPATIONAL COMPENSATION SURVEY--PAY ONLY. NEW YORK, NEW YORK, METROPOLITAN AREA (US) [27902052] **4014**

●OCCUPATIONAL COMPENSATION SURVEY--PAY ONLY. NORFOLK, VA--FAST FOOD RESTAURANTS / U.S. DEPARTMENT OF LABOR, BUREAU OF LABOR STATISTICS (US) [28485488] **1698**

OCCUPATIONAL COMPENSATION SURVEY--PAY ONLY. NORTHERN NEW YORK / U.S. DEPARTMENT OF LABOR, BUREAU OF LABOR STATISTICS (US) [29527439] **1698**

●OCCUPATIONAL COMPENSATION SURVEY--PAY ONLY. OAKLAND, CALIFORNIA, METROPOLITAN AREA / U.S. DEPARTMENT OF LABOR, BUREAU OF LABOR STATISTICS (US) [27365921] **1698**

●OCCUPATIONAL COMPENSATION SURVEY-- PAY ONLY. PORTSMOUTH-CHILLICOTHE-GALLIPOLIS, OH / U.S. DEPARTMENT OF LABOR, BUREAU OF LABOR STATISTICS (US) [28396193] **1698**

●OCCUPATIONAL COMPENSATION SURVEY--PAY ONLY. PROVIDENCE, RI / U.S. DEPARTMENT OF LABOR, BUREAU OF LABOR STATISTICS (US) [26703836] **1698**

●OCCUPATIONAL COMPENSATION SURVEY--PAY ONLY. PUERTO RICO / U.S. DEPARTMENT OF LABOR, BUREAU OF LABOR STATISTICS (US) [29839454] **1698**

●OCCUPATIONAL COMPENSATION SURVEY--PAY ONLY. SACRAMENTO, CALIFORNIA, METROPOLITAN AREA (US) [27901977] **1698**

●OCCUPATIONAL COMPENSATION SURVEY--PAY ONLY. SALT LAKE CITY-OGDEN, UTAH, METROPOLITAN AREA / U.S. DEPARTMENT OF LABOR, BUREAU OF LABOR STATISTICS (US) [27180325] **1698**

●OCCUPATIONAL COMPENSATION SURVEY--PAY ONLY. SAN FRANCISCO, CALIFORNIA, METROPOLITAN AREA / U.S. DEPARTMENT OF LABOR, BUREAU OF LABOR STATISTICS (US) [27175294] **1698**

OCCUPATIONAL COMPENSATION SURVEY--PAY ONLY. SAN JOSE, CALIFORNIA, METROPOLITAN AREA (US) [28298954] **1698**

OCCUPATIONAL COMPENSATION SURVEY--PAY ONLY. SPRINGFIELD, IL / U.S. DEPARTMENT OF LABOR, BUREAU OF LABOR STATISTICS (US) [25969193] **1698**

●OCCUPATIONAL COMPENSATION SURVEY--PAY ONLY. TOPEKA, KS / U.S. DEPARTMENT OF LABOR, BUREAU OF LABOR STATISTICS (US) [26703386] **1698**

OCCUPATIONAL COMPENSATION SURVEY--PAY ONLY. UPPER PENINSULA, MI / U.S. DEPARTMENT OF LABOR, BUREAU OF LABOR STATISTICS (US) [27097429] **1698**

●OCCUPATIONAL COMPENSATION SURVEY--PAY ONLY. WASHINGTON, DC--FAST FOOD RESTAURANTS / U.S. DEPARTMENT OF LABOR, BUREAU OF LABOR STATISTICS (US) [28392464] 2351, **1699**

OCCUPATIONAL COMPENSATION SURVEY--PAY ONLY. WORCESTER, MASSACHUSETTS, METROPOLITAN AREA / U.S. DEPARTMENT OF LABOR, BUREAU OF LABOR STATISTICS (US) [25993705] **1699**

OCCUPATIONAL DEVELOPMENTS MAGAZINE (US/0271-5589) [05526768] **4207**

OCCUPATIONAL EARNINGS AND WAGE TRENDS IN METROPOLITAN AREAS (US) [04758798] **1699**

OCCUPATIONAL EDUCATION (US/0360-5434) [02441064] **1914**

OCCUPATIONAL EDUCATION FORUM (US/0890-8427) [07646473] **1914**

●OCCUPATIONAL EMPLOYMENT AND OPENINGS, NEW YORK STATE (US) [25699733] **4207**

OCCUPATIONAL EMPLOYMENT TRENDS IN THE STATE OF OREGON (US) [07630449] **1699**

OCCUPATIONAL HAZARDS (US/0029-7909) [02390044] **2866**

OCCUPATIONAL HEALTH (UK/0029-7917) [04253507] 3866, **2866**

OCCUPATIONAL HEALTH & SAFETY (US/0362-4064) [02214952] **2866**

OCCUPATIONAL HEALTH & SAFETY CANADA (CN) **2866**

OCCUPATIONAL HEALTH AND SAFETY DIRECTORY (AT) **2866**

OCCUPATIONAL HEALTH AND SAFETY HEALTH FACILITIES REPORT (US) **2866**

OCCUPATIONAL HEALTH AND SAFETY LAW (CN/0706-5019) [04433108] 2866, **3020**

OCCUPATIONAL HEALTH AND SAFETY LETTER (US/0196-058X) [01760999] **2866**

OCCUPATIONAL HEALTH & SAFETY MAGAZINE (CN/0846-9229) [22632529] **2866**

OCCUPATIONAL HEALTH & SAFETY NEWS DIGEST (US/0896-3835) [12340143] **2866**

OCCUPATIONAL HEALTH FOUNDATION, INSTITUTE OF OCCUPATIONAL HEALTH (FI/0250-6602) [04566758] **2866**

OCCUPATIONAL HEALTH MAGAZINE (AT/1032-0989) [I10320989] **2866**

OCCUPATIONAL HEALTH MANAGEMENT *CEASED.* (US) **2866**

OCCUPATIONAL HEALTH NEWSLETTER (AT) **2866**

OCCUPATIONAL HEALTH REVIEW (LONDON) (UK/0951-4600) [16358401] **2866**

●OCCUPATIONAL HYGIENE (US/1061-0251) [25161113] **2866**

OCCUPATIONAL INJURIES AND ILLNESSES IN CONNECTICUT (US) [04109766] **2866**

OCCUPATIONAL INJURIES AND ILLNESSES IN MAINE (US/0198-7771) [06206121] **2866**

OCCUPATIONAL INJURIES AND ILLNESSES IN ... SUMMARY (US) [07898649] **2867**

OCCUPATIONAL INJURIES AND ILLNESSES IN THE UNITED STATES BY INDUSTRY (US/0162-010X) [04072093] **2867**

OCCUPATIONAL INJURIES AND ILLNESSES. IOWA (US) [05435404] **2867**

Alphabetical Title Index — OCHRONA

OCCUPATIONAL INJURIES AND ILLNESSES. SUMMARY (WASHINGTON) (US/0272-0957) [06217348] **2867**

OCCUPATIONAL MEDICAL DIGEST, THE (US) [21124502] **3623**

●OCCUPATIONAL MEDICINE (UK/0962-7480) [25655070] **3623**

OCCUPATIONAL MEDICINE (PHILADELPHIA, PA.) (US/0885-114X) [12566522] **2867**

OCCUPATIONAL NEEDS. WESTERN NEW YORK REGION (US) [22198134] **1699**

OCCUPATIONAL OUTLOOK AND DEVELOPMENT (US) [06240111] **4207**

OCCUPATIONAL OUTLOOK FOR VOCATIONAL AND TECHNICAL JOBS IN TENNESSEE, THE (US) [21022421] **1699**

OCCUPATIONAL OUTLOOK HANDBOOK (US/0082-9072) [01773253] **4207**

OCCUPATIONAL OUTLOOK QUARTERLY (US/0199-4786) [02725385] **1699**

OCCUPATIONAL OUTLOOK ... WESTERN NEW YORK REGION OF NEW YORK STATE : ALLEGANY COUNTY, CATTARAUGUS COUNTY, CHAUTAUQUA COUNTY, ERIE COUNTY, NIAGARA COUNTY (US) [26641244] **4207**

OCCUPATIONAL PATTERNS OF SELECTED NONMANUFACTURING INDUSTRIES IN UTAH (US) [06133533] **4207**

OCCUPATIONAL PENSIONS (UK/0952-231X) [I0952231X] **2889**

OCCUPATIONAL PENSIONS LAW REPORTS (UK/0967-8115) [I09678115] **3152**

OCCUPATIONAL PREFERENCES OF HIGH SCHOOL SENIORS IN TEN COUNTIES IN IDAHO, THE (US) [08321808] **4207**

OCCUPATIONAL PROFILES (US) **1699**

OCCUPATIONAL PROFILES OF OREGON'S MANUFACTURING INDUSTRIES (US/0147-1333) [03124759] 3485, **1699**

OCCUPATIONAL PROFILES OF SELECTED NON-MANUFACTURING INDUSTRIES IN OREGON (US/0148-2890) [03289254] **4207**

OCCUPATIONAL PROGRAMS IN CALIFORNIA PUBLIC COMMUNITY COLLEGES (US/0731-8650) [05922619] 1838, **4207**

OCCUPATIONAL PROJECTIONS (US) **1699**

OCCUPATIONAL PROJECTIONS AND TRAINING DATA *CEASED.* (US/0273-382X) [05133145] **4207**

OCCUPATIONAL SAFETY AND HEALTH ABSTRACTS (SZ/0029-7984) [01761004] **2867**

OCCUPATIONAL SAFETY & HEALTH (BIRMINGHAM) (UK/0143-5353) [02449230] **2867**

OCCUPATIONAL SAFETY AND HEALTH LAW (US/0737-1268) [05630282] 2867, **3020**

OCCUPATIONAL SAFETY AND HEALTH (NEW YORK) (US/0146-3632) [02900935] **2867**

OCCUPATIONAL SAFETY & HEALTH REPORTER (US/0095-3237) [01796421] **2867**

OCCUPATIONAL SAFETY AND HEALTH SERIES (SZ/0078-3129) [05397239] **2867**

OCCUPATIONAL SAFETY AND HEALTH TRAINING GRANTS (US/0161-9446) [04047164] **2867**

OCCUPATIONAL SAFETY AND HEALTH. VOLUME 1. GENERAL INDUSTRY STANDARDS (US) [02784547] **2867**

OCCUPATIONAL SAFETY AND HEALTH. VOLUME 3. CONSTRUCTION STANDARDS (US) [02787543] **2867**

OCCUPATIONAL SAFETY AND HEALTH. VOLUME 4. OTHER REGULATIONS AND PROCEDURES (US) [02788019] **2867**

OCCUPATIONAL SAFETY AND HEALTH. VOLUME 5. FIELD OPERATIONS MANUAL (US) [02788110] **2867**

OCCUPATIONAL STARTING WAGES IN THE STATE OF UTAH AND UTAH PLANNING DISTRICTS (US) [08433122] **4207**

OCCUPATIONAL SUPPLY AND DEMAND (US) [05870748] **4207**

OCCUPATIONAL THERAPY IN HEALTH CARE (US/0738-0577) [09500767] **1883**

OCCUPATIONAL THERAPY IN MENTAL HEALTH (US/0164-212X) [04618110] 3932, **2867**

OCCUPATIONAL THERAPY INDEX : CURRENT AWARENESS TOPICS SERVICE (UK/0950-6675) [17515989] **1883**

●OCCUPATIONAL THERAPY INTERNATIONAL (UK/0966-7903) **4381**

OCCUPATIONAL THERAPY JOURNAL OF RESEARCH (US/0276-1599) [07317028] **1883**

OCCUPATIONAL THERAPY PRACTICE *CEASED.* (US/1044-3207) [19751555] **1883**

OCCUPATIONAL TRAINING IN WASHINGTON STATE IN VOCATIONAL-TECHNICAL INSTITUTES, COMMUNITY COLLEGES, PRIVATE SCHOOLS AND COLLEGES, AND APPRENTICESHIP PROGRAMS (US) [06688028] **1915**

OCCUPATIONAL WAGE SURVEY. DAYTONA BEACH, FLORIDA *See* AREA WAGE SURVEY. DAYTONA BEACH, FLORIDA, METROPOLITAN AREA **1652**

OCCUPATIONAL WAGE SURVEY. FRESNO, CALIFORNIA *See* AREA WAGE SURVEY. FRESNO, CALIFORNIA, METROPOLITAN AREA **1652**

OCCUPATIONAL WAGE SURVEY. MUSKOGEE AREA (US) [10568999] **1699**

OCCUPATIONAL WAGE SURVEY : OKLAHOMA CITY METROPOLITAN AREA (US) [06262104] **1699**

OCCUPATIONAL WAGE SURVEY. SACRAMENTO, CALIFORNIA *See* AREA WAGE SURVEY. SACRAMENTO, CALIFORNIA, METROPOLITAN AREA **1653**

OCCUPATIONAL WAGE SURVEY. SHAWNEE, OKLAHOMA (US) [08585001] **1699**

OCCUPATIONAL WAGE SURVEY. TULSA METROPOLITAN AREA (US) [10548505] **1699**

OCCUPATIONS IN THE LABOR MARKET (US) [24091499] **1699**

OCCUPATIONS OF FEDERAL WHITE-COLLAR AND BLUE-COLLAR WORKERS (US/0739-1404) [09560734] **4207**

OCCURRENCE (US/0146-9118) [03058208] **3467**

OCEAN AGE (JA) [06593561] **1453**

OCEAN AIR INTERACTIONS (US/0743-0876) [10502565] **1359**

OCEAN AND COASTAL LAW JOURNAL (US) **3182**

OCEAN AND COASTAL LAW MEMO (US/1052-6730) [20620070] **3182**

●OCEAN & COASTAL MANAGEMENT (UK/0964-5691) [25502871] **1453**

OCEAN & SHORELINE MANAGEMENT *See* OCEAN & COASTAL MANAGEMENT **1453**

OCEAN CHALLENGE *CEASED.* (UK) [22656059] **1453**

OCEAN CONSTRUCTION LOCATOR *See* OFFSHORE FIELD DEVELOPMENT INTERNATIONAL **1620**

OCEAN COUNTY OBSERVER (US/0746-5416) [10124598] **5711**

OCEAN COUNTY REVIEW (US/1053-4555) [11674328] **5711**

OCEAN DEVELOPMENT AND INTERNATIONAL LAW (US/0090-8320) [05503028] **3182**

OCEAN DRILLING PROGRAM *See* PROCEEDINGS OF THE OCEAN DRILLING PROGRAM. PART A, INITIAL REPORT **1391**

OCEAN ENGINEERING (US/0029-8018) [01642028] **2093**

OCEAN ENGINEERING (US) [08703131] **1989**

OCEAN ENGINEERING INFORMATION CENTRE *See* OEIC INFORMATION BULLETIN **1454**

OCEAN ENGINEERING INFORMATION SERIES (US/0078-3137) [01641801] **2094**

OCEAN INDUSTRY *CEASED.* (US/0029-8026) [01761005] **4267**

OCEAN LEADER *See* SEAFOOD LEADER **2313**

OCEAN MODELLING (UK/1013-9281) [10932235] **1453**

OCEAN NAVIGATOR (US/0886-0149) [12789142] 4181, **1453**

OCEAN OIL WEEKLY REPORT (US) [03229692] **4267**

OCEAN PHYSICS AND ENGINEERING *CEASED.* (US/0890-5460) [14261463] **1453**

OCEAN REALM (US/0738-9833) [09650227] **1453**

OCEAN RESOURCES (CN/0823-2903) [10436259] **1453**

OCEAN RESOURCES ENGINEERING (US/0146-9126) [03058009] **2094**

OCEAN SCIENCE NEWS (US/0029-8069) [05455731] **1453**

●OCEAN SEA DIVERS WORLDWIDE DIVING DIRECTORY (US) [26733474] **4908**

OCEAN SPORTS INTERNATIONAL (US/0899-2622) [18047324] **4908**

OCEAN SPRINGS RECORD (US) [16103091] **5701**

OCEAN STATE BUSINESS (US/0741-9929) [10265660] **700**

OCEAN TECHNOLOGY & ENGINEERING / NTIS *See* NTIS ALERT. OCEAN TECHNOLOGY & ENGINEERING **1453**

OCEAN THERMAL ENERGY CONVERSION REPORT TO CONGRESS (US) [10847265] 1454, **1952**

OCEAN VOICE (UK/0261-6777) [08592297] **4181**

OCEAN WORLD (US/0164-632X) [03889668] **1454**

OCEAN YEARBOOK (US/0191-8575) [04659410] **1454**

OCEANIA (AT/0029-8077) [01761006] **2670**

OCEANIA MONOGRAPHS, THE (AT/1030-6412) [08783076] **242**

OCEANIC ABSTRACTS (BETHESDA, MD.) (US/0748-1489) [10879915] 556, 1454, **1363**

OCEANIC LINGUISTICS (US/0029-8115) [01585594] **3307**

OCEANIC LINGUISTICS. SPECIAL PUBLICATION (US/0078-3188) [03801639] **3308**

OCEANIS : SERIE DE DOCUMENTS OCEANOGRAPHIQUES (FR/0182-0745) [08334467] **1454**

OCEANOGRAPHIC DATA EXCHANGE (US/0278-8748) [01427301] **1454**

●OCEANOGRAPHIC LITERATURE REVIEW (UK/0967-0653) [27447767] 1454, **1363**

OCEANOGRAPHIC MONTHLY SUMMARY (US/0277-6197) [07254297] **1454**

OCEANOGRAPHIC REPORT (WASHINGTON) (US/0082-9625) [01127919] **1454**

OCEANOGRAPHICAL MAGAZINE (JA/0369-707X) [07041914] **1454**

OCEANOGRAPHICAL STATION LIST (AT/0069-7362) [01154070] **1454**

OCEANOGRAPHIE. NOTES ET DOCUMENTS (FP/0755-3412) [26234783] **1454**

OCEANOGRAPHY AND MARINE BIOLOGY (UK/0078-3218) [01099384] 556, **1454**

OCEANOGRAPHY (WASHINGTON, D.C.) (US/1042-8275) [18927903] **1454**

OCEANOLOGIA (PL/0078-3234) [02739677] **1454**

OCEANOLOGICA ACTA (FR/0399-1784) [04217243] **1454**

OCEANOLOGY (WASHINGTON. 1965) (US/0001-4370) [01761011] **1454**

OCEANOLOGY (WASHINGTON. 1966) *CEASED.* (US/0029-8158) [03271528] **1454**

OCEANOS (PO) [21194132] **2701**

OCEANS (FR) [06416060] **4908**

OCEANS POLICY STUDY SERIES (US/8755-0474) [11324507] **3182**

OCEANUS (WOODS HOLE) (US/0029-8182) [01761014] **1454**

OCERKI FIZIKO-HIMICESKOJ PETROLOGII (RU/0320-6386) [10265785] 1459, **1443**

OCHANOMIZU IGAKU ZASSHI (JA/0472-4674) [10376961] **3623**

OCHANOMIZU JOSHI DAIGAKU JIMBUN KAGAKU KIYO (JA/0472-4682) [05875236] **327**

OCHANOMIZU JOSHI DAIGAKU, TOKYO *See* OCHANOMIZU JOSHI DAIGAKU JIMBUN KAGAKU KIYO **327**

OCHERK (RU) [07615895] **3419**

OCHERKI ISTORII RUSSKOI ETNOGRAFII, FOLKLORISTIKI I ANTROPOLOGII (RU) [04627290] **242**

OCHEYEDAN PRESS-THE MELVIN NEWS, THE (US) [15204134] **5672**

OCHISTKA VODNOGO I VOZDUSHNOGO BASSEINOV NA PREDORIIATIIAKH CHERNOI METALLURGII (RU) [02246348] **4014**

OCHRANA ROSTLIN (XR) [23722761] 2201, **520**

OCHRONA POWIETRZA (PL/0137-3714) [I01373714] **5136**

OCHRONA PRACY (PL/0029-8220) [09498216] **2867**

OCHRONA PRZED KOROZJA (PL/0473-7733) [06539478] **2028**

OCHRONA PRZYRODY (PL/0078-3250) [01387906] **4170**

OCHRONA SRODOWISKA; PROGNOZOWANIE I PLANOWANIE ROZWOJU NAUKI I TECHNIKI. KONFERENCJA NAUKOWA, WROCLAW, 4-6 II 1971 (PL) [20893024] **5335**

OCHRONA SRODOWISKA - RACHUNEK STRAT I KORZYSCI SPOLECZNYCH (PL) [18170175] **5335**

OCHRONA SRODOWISKA: REFLEKSJE PRAWNE, EKONOMICZNE I SOCIOLOGICZNE (PL) [07170704] **5335**

OCHRONA ZABYTKOW (PL/0029-8247) [02691085] **2701**

OCHRONO ROSLIN (PL/0029-8239) [09960611] **116**

OCHS JOURNAL : PUBLICATION OF THE ORANGE COUNTY HISTORICAL SOCIETY (US) [20550264] **2751**

OCIC NEWSLETTER See CINE & MEDIA **1106**

OCIDENTE (PO) [01644566] **2520**

OCJP NEWSLINE : OFFICE OF CRIMINAL JUSTICE PLANNING QUARTERLY NEWSLETTER *SUSPENDED.* (US) [25146968] **3171**

OCLA-LINK (CN/0842-4136) [19465175] 3021, **3238**

OCLAE (CU/0029-6961) [02674592] **1770**

OCLC See OCLC ANNUAL REPORT **3238**

OCLC/AMIGOS COLLECTION ANALYSIS CD (US/1044-4858) [19804880] **3238**

OCLC ANNUAL REPORT (US/1044-3800) [15601580] **3238**

●OCLC CJK350 NEWSLETTER (US/1054-268X) [22829770] **3238**

OCLC MICRO (US/8756-5196) [11584468] 1270, **3238**

OCLC NEWSLETTER (US/0163-898X) [02418671] **3238**

●OCLC SELECTED TITLES (US/1060-6033) [25043803] **3238**

●OCLC SYSTEMS AND SERVICES (US/1065-075X) [26498687] **3238**

OCMW FOCUS (BE) **2829**

●O'CONNOR REPORT (SEATTLE, WASH.) (US/1064-265X) [26238587] **4794**

OCONOMOWOC ENTERPRISE, THE (US) [13297691] **5769**

OCONTO COUNTY TIMES-HERALD (US) [13072572] **5769**

OCR REPORT / OFFICE FOR CIVIL RIGHTS (US) [25689652] **4511**

OCROTIREA NATURII SI A MEDIULUI INCONJURATOR (RM/0253-1879) [06312278] **4170**

OCSM NEWSLETTER (CN/0823-8162) [11607586] **4142**

OCTAGONIAN See OCTAGONIAN OF SIGMA ALPHA MU, THE **1093**

OCTAGONIAN OF SIGMA ALPHA MU, THE (US/0744-6969) [08515284] **1093**

OCTANE (CN/0835-1740) [16860499] **4267**

OCTANE WEEK (US/1072-8740) **4267**

OCTAVO (LONDON, ENGLAND) (UK) [15123372] 381, **4567**

OCTO-GRAPHE (CN/0836-690X) [17743306] **1868**

OCTOBER (CAMBRIDGE, MASS.) (US/0162-2870) [02576782] **327**

OCTOBER (MONTREAL) (CN/0226-112X) [08720594] **4544**

OCTOBRE (MONTREAL) (CN/0226-1138) [08720586] **4544**

OCTRA (GABON) See BILAN / OCTRA, LE **5429**

OCULAR REVIEW (US/0748-2892) [10952017] **3971**

OCULAR SURGERY NEWS (US/8750-3085) [11219949] **3971**

OCULAR SURGERY NEWS INTERNATIONAL EDITION (US/1047-9120) [20810596] 3877, **3971**

OCULAR THERAPEUTICS AND MANAGEMENT (US/1050-0650) [21395483] **3623**

OCULI (NE/0923-0033) [17190656] **360**

OCULUS (NE) **4216**

OCULUS (NEW YORK, N. Y.) (US/0885-5927) [10493833] **305**

OCUPACION Y DESOCUPACION, SECTORES URBANOS DE LAS REGIONES IV A X, EXCEPTO EL GRAN SANTIAGO (CL) [05285715] **1699**

ODA SUGGESTED FEE GUIDE FOR GENERAL PRACTITIONERS (CN/0826-6905) [11847696] **1331**

ODAN NEWSLETTER (US/1059-3144) [24563074] **5033**

ODCA INFORMA (VE) [25003021] **4983**

ODELJENJE ISTORIJSKIH NAUKA / SRPSKA AKADEMIJA NAUKA I UMETNOSTI (YU) [22538543] **2624**

O'DELL MEMORIAL MONOGRAPH (UK) [01761019] **2571**

ODENSE UNIVERSITET See ETUDES ROMANES (ODENSE) **3280**

ODENSE UNIVERSITET See STUDIES IN LITERATURE (ODENSE) **3442**

ODENSE UNIVERSITET See STUDIES IN LINGUISTICS **3326**

ODENSE UNIVERSITET See STUDIES IN HISTORY AND SOCIAL SCIENCES **2631**

ODENSE UNIVERSITET See ODENSE UNIVERSITY STUDIES IN ENGLISH **3308**

ODENSE UNIVERSITET See CLASSICAL STUDIES (ODENSE) **1076**

ODENSE UNIVERSITY STUDIES IN ENGLISH (DK/0078-3293) [02664400] **3308**

ODENSE UNIVERSITY STUDIES IN PSYCHIATRY AND MEDICAL PSYCHOLOGY (DK/0105-0621) [01856443] **3932**

ODENSE UNIVERSITY STUDIES IN SCANDINAVIAN LANGUAGES AND LITERATURES (DK) [01785326] 3419, **3308**

ODESSA AMERICAN, THE (US) [12443550] **5753**

ODESSA RECORD, THE (US/1062-2934) [10818116] **5761**

ODI/IIMI IRRIGATION MANAGEMENT NETWORK PAPER (UK) [20124899] **180**

ODI INDEX TO DEVELOPMENT LITERATURE (UK/0954-190X) [I0954190X] **3419**

ODINI (MW) [14221388] **4983**

ODL SOURCE (US/0193-3086) [04270237] **3238**

ODONATOLOGICA (NE/0375-0183) [03062720] **467**

ODONTO-STOMATOLOGIE TROPICALE (FR/0251-172X) [07764375] **1331**

ODONTOLOGISKA FOERENINGEN TIDSKRIFT (SW) [06371503] **1331**

ODONTOLOGO (PANAMA), EL (PN/0472-5158) [02087598] **1331**

ODONTOSTOMATOLOGIA E IMPLANTOPROTESI (MILAN, ITALY : 1989) (IT) [20818196] **1331**

ODONTOSTOMATOLOGIKE PROODOS (GR/0029-8506) [11308797] **1331**

ODP RESTAURO (IT) **374**

ODRA (PL/0472-5182) [06552142] **2520**

ODRODZENIE I REFORMACJA W POLSCE (PL/0029-8514) [02690104] **2701**

ODTU GELISME DERGISI (TU/1010-9935) [08706834] **2911**

ODTU : GELISME DERGISI (TU) [04184331] 4670, **1509**

ODU *SUSPENDED.* (NR/0029-8522) [01761025] **2642**

ODUMA (NR/0331-1422) [02635350] **327**

ODVETVOVA A OBOROVA INFORMACNI STREDISKA A SPECIALIZOVANE INFORMACNI INSTITUCE V CSSR (XR) [07949176] **1838**

O'DWYER (J.R.) COMPANY See O'DWYER'S DIRECTORY OF CORPORATE COMMUNICATIONS **763**

O'DWYER'S DIRECTORY OF CORPORATE COMMUNICATIONS (US/0149-1091) [03100876] **763**

O'DWYER'S DIRECTORY OF PUBLIC RELATIONS EXECUTIVES (US/0191-0051) [04781780] **763**

O'DWYER'S DIRECTORY OF PUBLIC RELATIONS FIRMS (US/0078-3374) [01472234] **763**

O'DWYER'S FARA REPORT (US/1055-3304) [23156477] 3021, **700**

O'DWYER'S FARA REPORT See O'DWYER'S WASHINGTON REPORT **700**

O'DWYER'S PR MARKET PLACE NEWSLETTER (US) **763**

O'DWYER'S PR SERVICES REPORT (US/1043-2957) [19378561] **763**

●O'DWYER'S WASHINGTON REPORT (US) 3021, **700**

ODYSSEE (MONTREAL) (CN/0229-8023) [09313008] **5300**

ODYSSEUS (FLUSHING, N.Y.) (US/0883-3664) [12055946] **5487**

ODYSSEY. A JOURNAL OF THE CENTRAL CALIFORNIA COUNCIL OF DIVING CLUBS (US) **5234**

ODYSSEY (PETERBOROUGH, N.H.) (US/0163-0946) [04298081] 1067, **398**

ODYSSEY (TORONTO. 1991) (CN/1183-2029) [24266324] **3467**

ODZ. POLAND. POLITECHNIKA See ELEKTRYKA **2052**

ODZKIE TOWARZYSTWO NAUKOWE. KOMISJA JEZYKOWA See ROZPRAWY KOMISJI JEZYKOWEJ. ODZKIE TOWARZYSTWO NAUKOWE **3318**

OE REPORT (UK/0309-2097) [I03092097] **5354**

OE REPORTS (US/1048-6879) [17453354] **4438**

OEA FOCUS (US/0743-7986) [08917864] **1770**

OE&M. OFFICE EQUIPMENT & METHODS (1979) (CN/0709-5228) [05585726] **4213**

OEBALIA (IT/0392-6613) [02802763] 1454, **556**

OECD See BL BLANKET ORDER **1464**

OECD COUNTRY REPORT (FR) **1509**

OECD DEVELOPMENT COOPERATION REVIEW (FR) **2911**

OECD. ECONOMIC OUTLOOK (FR/0474-5574) [01963467] **1509**

OECD ECONOMIC OUTLOOK. HISTORICAL STATISTICS (FR) [08678315] **1576**

OECD ECONOMIC STUDIES (FR/0255-0822) [10401210] **1576**

OECD ECONOMIC SURVEYS (FR/0376-6438) [10157875] **1509**

OECD ECONOMIC SURVEYS : AUSTRALIA (FR) [01787196] **1576**

OECD ECONOMIC SURVEYS : AUSTRIA (FR/0474-5124) [01107784] **1509**

OECD ECONOMIC SURVEYS: BELGIUM-LUXEMBOURG (FR) [03512104] **1510**

OECD ECONOMIC SURVEYS: CANADA (FR/0474-5140) [01147690] **1510**

OECD ECONOMIC SURVEYS. CZECH AND SLOVAK FEDERAL REPUBLIC See OECD ECONOMIC SURVEYS. THE CZECH AND SLOVAK REPUBLICS / CENTRE FOR CO-OPERATION WITH THE ECONOMIES IN TRANSITION **1577**

OECD ECONOMIC SURVEYS: DENMARK (FR/0474-5159) [01151398] **1510**

OECD ECONOMIC SURVEYS : FINLAND (FR) [03301050] **1576**

OECD ECONOMIC SURVEYS : FRANCE (FR/03377334] **1576**

OECD ECONOMIC SURVEYS: GERMANY (FR/02649956) **1510**

OECD ECONOMIC SURVEYS: GREECE (FR) [02635452] **1510**

OECD ECONOMIC SURVEYS. HUNGARY : CENTRE FOR CO-OPERATION WITH EUROPEAN ECONOMIES IN TRANSITION (FR) [24610515] **1510**

OECD ECONOMIC SURVEYS: ICELAND (FR/0474-5191) [01161433] **1510**

OECD ECONOMIC SURVEYS : IRELAND (FR) [03300956] **1576**

OECD ECONOMIC SURVEYS: ITALY (FR) [03300983] **1576**

OECD ECONOMIC SURVEYS: JAPAN (FR) [07002179] **1510**

OECD ECONOMIC SURVEYS : NETHERLANDS (FR) [03318594] **1576**

OECD ECONOMIC SURVEYS: NEW ZEALAND (FR) [01962352] **1510**

OECD ECONOMIC SURVEYS: NORWAY (FR) [01275912] **1510**

●OECD ECONOMIC SURVEYS: POLAND (FR/0376-6438) [26187079] **1510**

OECD ECONOMIC SURVEYS : PORTUGAL (FR) [03300958] **1576**

OECD ECONOMIC SURVEYS: SPAIN (FR) [02635427] **1510**

OECD ECONOMIC SURVEYS: SWEDEN (FR/02589179] **1510**

OECD ECONOMIC SURVEYS: SWITZERLAND (FR) [01098319] **1510**

OECD ECONOMIC SURVEYS. THE CZECH AND SLOVAK REPUBLICS / CENTRE FOR CO-OPERATION WITH THE ECONOMIES IN TRANSITION (FR) [30061854] **1577**

OECD ECONOMIC SURVEYS : TURKEY (FR) [03294864] **1577**

OECD ECONOMIC SURVEYS : UNITED KINGDOM (FR) [03283643] **1577**

OECD ECONOMIC SURVEYS : UNITED STATES (FR/0474-5329) [03294863] **1577**

OECD FINANCIAL STATISTICS. METHODOLOGICAL SUPPLEMENT / STATISTIQUES FINANCIERES DE L'OCDE. SUPPLEMENT METHODOLOGIQUE (FR/0304-3371) [08523788] **1510**

OECD FINANCIAL STATISTICS. MONTHLY SUPPLEMENT: INTEREST RATES. STATISTIQUES FINANCIERES DE L'OCDE. SUPPLEMENT MENSUEL: TAUX D'INTERET (FR) [04116600] 802, **732**

OECD FINANCIAL STATISTICS. PART 2, FINANCIAL ACCOUNTS OF OECD COUNTRIES. ITALY (FR/0304-3371) [23197564] **802**

OECD FINANCIAL STATISTICS. PART 3, NON-FINANCIAL ENTERPRISES FINANCIAL STATEMENTS (FR) [08134190] **732**

OECD FINANCIAL STATISTICS. PT. 2, FINANCIAL ACCOUNTS OF OECD COUNTRIES (FR) [21277417] **802**

OECD NUCLEAR ENERGY AGENCY *See* URANIUM RESOURCES, PRODUCTION, AND DEMAND : A JOINT REPORT / BY THE EUROPEAN NUCLEAR ENERGY AGENCY AND THE INTERNATIONAL ATOMIC ENERGY AGENCY **1630**

OECD NUCLEAR ENERGY AGENCY *See* NEWSLETTER - OECD NUCLEAR ENERGY AGENCY **2156**

OECD OBSERVER (FR/0029-7054) [01964492] **1510**

OECOLOGIA (GW/0029-8549) [01353676] **2219**

OECOLOGIA AQUATICA (SP/0210-9352) [04431063] **2219**

OECS LAW REPORTS, THE (BB) [25909032] **3021**

OECUMENE : INTERNATIONAL BIBLIOGRAPHY 1975- INDEXED BY COMPUTER ; BIBLIOGRAPHIE INTERNATIONALE 1975- ETABLIE PAR ORDINATEUR (FR/0079-9300) [04082281] **421**

OECUMENISME (EDITION FRANCAISE) (CN/0383-4301) [02391213] **4983**

OEF NEWS *See* CONTACT - ONTARIO EQUESTRIAN FEDERATION **2798**

OEFFENTLICHE BIBLIOTHEKEN IN BADEN-WUERTTEMBERG / HERAUSGEGEBEN VON DEN STAATLICHEN BUECHEREISTELLEN FREIBURG ... [ET AL.] (GW) [07801619] **3238**

OEGUGO KYOYUK (KO) [10853396] **1901**

OEGUK KWAHAK KISUL TONGBO. NONGOP (KO) [08265430] **116**

OEGUK KWAHAK KISUL TONGBO. SUUI CHUKSAN (KO) [10287755] **5517**

OEGUK MUNHAK (KO) [11077393] **3419**

OEGUK MUNHWA YONGU (KO) [08336868] **3308**

OEHWAN UNHAENG WOLBO (KO) [07940908] 802, **1638**

OEIC INFORMATION BULLETIN (CN/0226-7683) [07817319] 1989, **1454**

OEIL DE FEU (CN/0702-8024) [03409695] **5300**

OEIL, L' (SZ) **5136**

OEIL LAUSANNE, L' (SZ/0029-862X) [I0029862X] **327**

OEIL NU (CN/1181-9405) [23237817] **327**

OEIL OUVERT (CN/0821-7033) [09818985] **5300**

OEIL REVUE D'ART (FR) **360**

OEKO TEST (GW) 2179, **1298**

OEKV INFORMATIONEN (AU) [06311531] **1952**

OEKWA HAKHOE CHI (KO) [05282009] **3971**

OEM DESIGN (UK/0306-0381) [03581379] **3485**

●OEM INDUSTRY (US/1072-2580) [28911428] **3485**

OEM INTEGRATOR, THE (US/1048-8928) [21074440] 1243, **3485**

●OEM MAGAZINE (US/1071-8990) [28627405] 1289, **1248**

OEM OFF-HIGHWAY (US/1048-3039) [20915247] 1620, **3485**

OEP : OFFICE EQUIPMENT & PRODUCTS (JA/0387-5245) [10864946] **4213**

OERI BULLETIN (US/1054-9919) [23041978] **1770**

OESTERBOTTEN (FI/0357-9956) [09603190] **2701**

OESTERREICH IN GESCHICHTE UND LITERATUR MIT GEOGRAPHIE (AU/1013-9966) [02577837] 3419, 2571, **2701**

OESTERREICHISCHE AKADEMIE DER WISSENSCHAFTEN *See* TAATIGKEITSBERICHT DER OESTERREICHISCHEN AKADEMIE DER WISSENSCHAFTEN **5161**

OESTERREICHISCHE BIBLIOGRAPHIE. REIHE A (AU) [16470193] **421**

OESTERREICHISCHE BIBLIOGRAPHIE. REIHE B, VERZEICHNIS DER OSTERREICHISCHEN HOCHSCHULSCHRIFTEN (AU) [18329591] 1838, **1796**

OESTERREICHISCHE GLASER-ZEITUNG (AU/0029-9162) [05162367] **2592**

OESTERREICHISCHE MILITAERISCHE ZEITSCHRIFT (AU/0048-1440) [02626243] **4053**

OESTERREICHISCHE WASSERWIRTSCHAFT (AU/0029-9588) [03795104] **2094**

OESTERREICHISCHE ZEITSCHRIFT FUER KUNST UND DENKMALPFLEGE (AU/0029-9626) [05063070] 4094, **361**

OESTERREICHISCHE ZEITSCHRIFT FUER VOLKSKUNDE (AU/0029-9669) [08606013] **2323**

OESTERREICHISCHES JAHRBUCH (AU) [02265401] **2520**

OESTERREICHISCHES PATENBLATT (AU/0253-5327) [10517933] **1306**

OESTERREICHS WEIDWERK : ILLUSTRIERTE MONATSHEFTE FUER JAGD, FISCHEREI UND NATURSCHUTZ MIT DEN OFFIZIELLEN NACHRICHTEN OESTERREICHISCHER LANDESJAGDVERBAENDE (AU) [22284863] **4876**

OESTERRIECHISCHE BIBLIOGRAPHIE. SONDERHEFT - PRAKTISCHE MUSIK (AUSWAHL) (AU) [02660450] **4142**

OEUVRES COMPLETES DE DIDEROT (FR) **3419**

OEUVRES COMPLETES OF JULES MICHELOT (FR) **2701**

OEUVRES DE DESCARTES *CEASED.* (FR) **3525**

OEUVRES ET CRITIQUES (FR/0338-1900) [04201009] **3349**

OF A LIKE MIND (US/0892-5984) [15265546] 5563, **4186**

OF CABBAGES AND KINGS (US/0000-1376) [23124378] 3419, **1067**

OF COMPOUND INTEREST (CN/0710-5975) [08854809] **1067**

OF CONSUMING INTEREST (ARLINGTON, VA.) (US/0030-0047) [02250514] **1298**

OF COUNSEL (NEW YORK, N.Y.) (US/0730-3815) [08000327] 880, **3021**

OF SEA AND SHORE (US/0030-0055) [03918395] **5593**

OF SUBSTANCE (US/0743-3085) [10548599] **3021**

OFA FOOD BASKET (CN/0229-7191) [08364196] **180**

OFALLON COUNTY JOURNAL (US) **5704**

OFARI'S BI-MONTHLY (US/1068-5987) [17727792] 2270, **4485**

OFCOR, COMPARATIVE STUDY (NE/0923-4195) [19591456] **116**

OFCOR DISCUSSION PAPER (NE/1019-6544) [10196544] **116**

OFDA ANNUAL REPORT / OFFICE OF U.S. FOREIGN DISASTER ASSISTANCE, AGENCY FOR INTERNATIONAL DEVELOPMENT (US) [17597906] **2911**

OFEQ (TEL-AVIV) (IS/0302-8119) [01792810] **1577**

OFF DUTY (GW) **4853**

OFF-HOLLYWOOD REPORT *See* FILMMAKER (LOS ANGELES, CALIF.) **4071**

OFF-HOLLYWOOD REPORT, THE (US/1045-1706) [19992561] **4075**

OFF-LEAD (US/0094-0186 #y 0094-0816) [01399208] **4287**

OFF LICENCE NEWS (UK/0043-5775) [I00435775] **2370**

OFF. MAN., STATE MO (US/0196-4739) [08316697] **4670**

OFF OUR BACKS (US/0030-0071) [01038241] **5563**

OFF-PRICE NEWS OF ..., THE (US/0748-917X) [11017644] **956**

OFF-PRICE NEWS. THE BOOK ON OUTLET & OFF-PRICE LEASING, THE (US/0748-9153) [11017992] **956**

OFF ROAD AND 4 WHEEL DRIVE (UK/0953-203X) [I0953203X] **5422**

OFF ROAD CYCLING (US) [01785709] **4082**

OFF-ROAD (LOS ANGELES) (US/0363-1745) [02431034] **5422**

OFF ROAD MUNCHEN (GW/0172-4185) [I01724185] **5388**

OFF-ROAD VEHICLES AND ADVENTURE *See* OFF-ROAD (LOS ANGELES) **5422**

OFF THE RECORD (TORONTO. 1990) (CN/1182-0055) [22367226] **2482**

OFF THE SHELF (HUMBLE, TEX.) *CEASED.* (US/1059-3993) [23458677] 1067, **3420**

OFF THE SHELF (TORONTO) (CN/1184-8367) [24368414] **3238**

OFFA (GW/0078-3714) [02661001] **2520**

OFFALY RESOURCES FOR ENVIRONMENTAL STUDIES / COUNTY OFFALY VOCATIONAL EDUCATION COMMITTEE (IE/0332-4397) [07664260] **2238**

OFFARM (SP/0212-047X) [I0212047X] **4318**

OFFARM: REVISTA DE LA OFICINA DE FARMACIA (SP) **4318**

OFFENDERS ADMITTED TO ADULT CORRECTIONAL INSTITUTIONS (MADISON) (US/0093-321X) [01791747] **3171**

OFFENDERS RELEASED FROM ADULT CORRECTIONAL INSTITUTIONS (MADISON) (US/0092-9956) [01791954] **3171**

OFFENDERS RELEASED FROM DIVISION OF CORRECTIONS ADULT INSTITUTIONS IN . *See* OFFENDERS RELEASED FROM ADULT CORRECTIONAL INSTITUTIONS (MADISON) **3171**

OFFENDERS RESIDENT IN WISCONSIN JUVENILE CORRECTIONAL INSTITUTIONS ON .. WITH FIVE-YEAR TRENDS FOR ... (MADISON, WIS. : 1979) *See* RESIDENTS IN WISCONSIN JUVENILE CORRECTIONAL INSTITUTIONS (1979) **3175**

OFFENE SYSTEME (GW/0941-1968) **1197**

OFFENE TOR, DAS (GW) [02325678] 5367, **4142**

OFFENSIV LINKS (AU) [03476958] **4544**

OFFENSIVES COMMUNAUTAIRES ET CULTURELLES (CN/0228-7935) [07805636] **1699**

OFFENTLICHE ABFALLBESEITIGUNG (GW) [10549141] **2238**

OFFENTLICHE DIENST, DER (AU) [05858387] **1699**

OFFENTLICHE GESUNDHEITSWESEN *See* GESUNDHEITSWESEN, DAS **4776**

OFFENTLICHE SEKTOR, DER (AU) [02537885] **4739**

OFFENTLICHE VERWALTUNG, DIE (GW/0029-859X) [04075142] **3021**

OFFERINGS FOR ... (US) [12246198] **2426**

OFFICAL INTERMODAL GUIDE : DIRECTORY OF INTERMODAL SERVICES, FACILITIES AND PERSONNEL, THE (US) [10906525] **5388**

OFFICE *See* MANAGING OFFICE TECHNOLOGY **878**

OFFICE & BRANCH MANAGER'S BULLETIN (US/1065-7185) [26704856] **880**

OFFICE & INFORMATION MANAGEMENT INTERNATIONAL : JOURNAL OF THE INSTITUTE OF ADMINISTRATIVE MANAGEMENT (UK) [21717597] **880**

OFFICE AUTOMATION (US/0472-6049) [05253080] 880, **4213**

OFFICE AUTOMATION (IT) **4213**

OFFICE AUTOMATION CONFERENCE DIGEST *CEASED.* (US/0272-4855) [06832028] **4213**

OFFICE AUTOMATION NEWS : THE PUBLICATION OF THE OFFICE AUTOMATION SOCIETY INTERNATIONAL (US/0882-0198) [11763978] **4213**

OFFICE AUTOMATION REPORT, THE *SUSPENDED.* (US/0886-6767) [11668482] **4213**

OFFICE BELGE DU COMMERCE EXTERIEUR *See* COMMERCE EXTERIEUR DE L'UNION ECONOMIQUE BELGO-LUXEMBOURGEOISE, LE **828**

OFFICE BUYER (UK) **4207**

OFFICE COMPUTING REPORT (US/1057-8889) [24123866] 4213, **1197**

OFFICE CONNECTIONS (CN/0824-4073) [10440790] **4213**

OFFICE DE LA CONSTRUCTION DU QUEBEC *See* BULLETIN - OFFICE DE LA CONSTRUCTION DU QUEBEC **4635**

OFFICE DE LA CONSTRUCTION DU QUEBEC *See* ANALYSE DE L'INDUSTRIE DE LA CONSTRUCTION AU QUEBEC **598**

OFFICE DE LA SECURITE DU REVENU DES CHASSEURS ET PIEGEURS CRIS (QUEBEC) *See* RAPPORT ANNUEL / OFFICE DE LA SECURITE DU REVENU DES CHASSEURS ET PIEGEURS CRIS **5303**

●OFFICE DEALER (UK) **4207**

OFFICE DES COMMUNICATIONS SOCIALES *See* O C S NOUVELLES **1118**

OFFICE

OFFICE DES PRIX DU BATIMENT. TOUS CORPS D'ETAT (FR/0294-0787) [I02940787] **1511**

OFFICE DIRECTORY - DEPT. OF ESTABLISHMENT & TRAINING (SQ) [03466850] **4670**

OFFICE DIRECTORY : LAGOS AREA (NR) [02956773] **4670**

OFFICE DU CREDIT AGRICOLE DU QUEBEC *See* RAPPORT DE L'OFFICE DU CREDIT AGRICOLE DU QUEBEC CONCERNANT L'ADMINISTRATION DE LA LOI SUR LE CREDIT FORESTIER **806**

OFFICE EQUIPMENT (US/1056-859X) [23881579] **700**

OFFICE EQUIPMENT AND SUPPLIES MARKET IN CANADA, THE (CN/0705-5153) [04589993] **4213**

OFFICE EQUIPMENT EXPORTER (US) **5453**

OFFICE EQUIPMENT INDEX *CEASED.* (UK/0305-635X) [I0305635X] **4213**

OFFICE EQUIPMENT NEWS (UK/0110-1072) **3485**

OFFICE EQUIPMENT NEWS (UK/0030-0187) [22413435] **4213**

OFFICE FURNITURE (IT/1120-2386) [I11202386] **4213**

OFFICE GUIDE (US/0273-964X) [05899168] **700**

OFFICE GUIDE TO ORLANDO (US/0733-1266) [08534934] **4213**

OFFICE HEALTH AND SAFETY (UK) 700, **4794**

OFFICE HOURS (US) **700**

OFFICE INTERNATIONAL DE LA VIGNE ET DU VIN *See* BULLETIN DE L'OIV **69**

OFFICE LAYOUT (IT) **4213**

●OFFICE LEASING DIRECTORY (CN/1189-5993) [27165352] **4842**

OFFICE LEVEL REPORT ON FLORIDA BANK DEPOSITS *See* BRANCH DEPOSIT REPORT OF FLORIDA BANK AND THRIFT INSTITUTIONS **780**

OFFICE LEVEL REPORT ON FLORIDA BANK DEPOSITS / FLORIDA BANKERS ASSOCIATION (US) [10944362] **802**

OFFICE MAGAZINE WILMINGTON, KENT *CEASED.* (UK/0269-3046) [I02693046] **4213**

OFFICE MANAGEMENT (US/0737-8122) [09461626] **700**

OFFICE-MANAGEMENT (BADEN-BADEN) (GW/0722-2572) [08609322] **880**

OFFICE NURSE, THE (US/0893-6595) [15609905] **3866**

OFFICE OF AIR AND WATER PROGRAMS PUBLICATION (US) [01795469] **2179**

OFFICE OF COMPREHENSIVE PLANNING. FAIRFAX CO., VA *See* CAPITAL IMPROVEMENT PROGRAM (FAIRFAX) **4636**

OFFICE OF ELECTRICITY REGULATION ANNUAL REPORT (UK) **2074**

OFFICE OF ENVIRONMENT STATEMENT OF PROGRAMS (US) [04167533] **2179**

OFFICE OF HEALTH ECONOMICS (LONDON, ENGLAND) *See* OHE INFORMATION SHEET **4794**

OFFICE OF HEALTH TECHNOLOGY ASSESSMENT REPORTS / NATIONAL CENTER FOR HEALTH SERVICES RESEARCH AND HEALTH CARE TECHNOLOGY ASSESSMENT (US) [14941769] **5136**

OFFICE OF INSPECTOR GENERAL SEMIANNUAL REPORT TO CONGRESS / UNITED STATES DEPARTMENT OF AGRICULTURE, OFFICE OF INSPECTOR GENERAL (US) [22865313] **115**

OFFICE OF INSTRUCTIONAL TECHNOLOGY NEWSLETTER (US/0747-0649) [10519351] **5136**

OFFICE OF OKLAHOMA STATE BOARD OF PHARMACY *See* ANNUAL REPORT / OFFICE OF OKLAHOMA STATE BOARD OF PHARMACY **4291**

OFFICE OF RESEARCH PROGRAMS LIST OF SELECTED PUBLICATIONS & RESEARCH PROJECTS IN PROGRESS (US/0148-7213) [03354876] **3171**

OFFICE OF THE PRESIDENT DECISIONS ON LABOR ISSUES, WITH DOCTRINAL SUMMARIES AND NOTES (PH) [06510808] **3152**

OFFICE OF THE STATE ARCHEOLOGIST REPORTS (US/0272-1856) [01155585] **277**

OFFICE POLICY SURVEY, TWIN CITY AREA (US/0734-7421) [08790872] **1699**

OFFICE PROCEDURES *CEASED.* (US/0885-1131) [12566480] **3738**

OFFICE PRODUCTS ANALYST, THE (US/0197-4602) [06032272] **4213**

OFFICE PRODUCTS DEALER (WHEATON) (US/0199-1329) [05589504] **4213**

OFFICE PRODUCTS GOLD BOOK (CN/1184-0536) [23236474] **4213**

OFFICE PRODUCTS, MASTER CATALOG & BUYING GUIDE (US/0163-9935) [01786046] **4213**

OFFICE PRODUCTS NEWS (DARLINGHURST) (AT/1034-6686) [25207369] **4213**

OFFICE PROFESSIONAL, THE (US/0739-3156) [09718861] **1118**

OFFICE SECRETARY (UK/0951-6824) [I09516824] **4207**

OFFICE SKILLS PROGRAM (US) **700**

OFFICE SKILLS WORKSHOP *CEASED.* (US) [04270940] **700**

OFFICE (STAMFORD. 1936), THE (US/0030-0128) [04901738] **4213**

OFFICE SUPERVISOR'S DEVELOPMENT PROGRAM (US) **880**

OFFICE SUPERVISOR'S UPDATE PROGRAM (US) **880**

OFFICE SUPPLIES BUSINESS MAGAZINE, THE (CN/1184-0528) [23236517] **4213**

OFFICE SYSTEMS ERGONOMICS REPORT *CEASED.* (US/0749-3932) [10189285] **1989**

OFFICE SYSTEMS (GEORGETOWN, CONN.) (US/8750-3441) [11202805] **4213**

OFFICE SYSTEMS RESEARCH JOURNAL (US/0737-8998) [09503789] **700**

OFFICE, TECHNOLOGY AND PEOPLE *See* INFORMATION TECHNOLOGY & PEOPLE (WEST LINN, OR.) **870**

OFFICE TECHNOLOGY MANAGEMENT *CEASED.* (US/0733-5164) [08605981] **4213**

OFFICE TECHNOLOGY MANAGEMENT (GARDEN CITY, N.Y.) *CEASED.* (US/1061-4656) [24583774] **880**

OFFICE TOPICS (US/0746-5122) [08489904] **944**

OFFICE TRADE NEWS (UK/0269-2430) [I02692430] **700**

OFFICE WORLD NEWS (US/0164-5951) [04523516] **4213**

OFFICEMATION PRODUCT REPORTS (US/0733-2564) [08118748] **4213**

Alphabetical Title Index

OFFICER AND WARRANT OFFICER DIRECTORY (US/0732-7587) [08401553] **4053**

OFFICER REVIEW (US/0736-7317) [06354110] **4053**

OFFICER, THE (US/0030-0268) [02804911] **4053**

OFFICERS / ALBERTA SOCIETY OF ARTISTS (CN/0228-9474) [07817246] **361**

OFFICERS, COMMITTEES, CONSTITUTION AND BY-LAWS, MEMBERS / GROLIER CLUB (US/0362-8019) [06800340] **5234**

OFFICERS, COMMITTEES, CONSTITUTION AND BY-LAWS, MEMBERS, REPORTS OF OFFICERS AND COMMITTEES (US/0362-8019) [01590378] **5234**

OFFICERS MANAGER'S LETTER (US/0745-9602) [09627353] **880**

OFFICERS OF PENNSYLVANIA AGRICULTURAL ORGANIZATIONS (US/0160-2594) [03642740] **116**

OFFICERS' REPORT & DAILY CONVENTION PROCEEDINGS - HOTEL AND RESTAURANT EMPLOYEES AND BARTENDERS INTERNATIONAL UNION (US) [04736774] **5072**

OFFICERSFORBUNDSBLADET (SW) [06469867] **4053**

OFFICIAL A.A.U. BASKETBALL HANDBOOK (US/0090-4414) [01785246] **4908**

OFFICIAL AAU CODE AND DIRECTORY (US) [07503257] **4908**

OFFICIAL AAU KARATE RULES *See* USA KARATE FEDERATION RULES & REGULATIONS **4928**

OFFICIAL AAU PHYSIQUE HANDBOOK : OFFICIAL RULES (US/0148-3560) [03298309] **2600**

OFFICIAL AAU SYNCHRONIZED SWIMMING HANDBOOK (US) [01795594] **4908**

OFFICIAL AAU TAE KWON DO RULES (US/0198-7941) [05717003] **2600**

OFFICIAL AAU TRACK AND FIELD HANDBOOK (US/0361-347X) [02168980] **4908**

OFFICIAL AAU TRAMPOLINE AND TUMBLING HANDBOOK (US/0361-2899) [02156009] **4909**

OFFICIAL ABSTRACT OF VOTES, GENERAL ELECTION (US/0363-2938) [02438240] **4485**

OFFICIAL ABSTRACT OF VOTES : PRIMARY ELECTION (US/0360-4373) [02243971] **4485**

OFFICIAL AIRLINE GUIDES, INC. OAG NORTH AMERICAN POCKET FLIGHT GUIDE *See* OAG POCKET FLIGHT GUIDE (NORTH AMERICAN EDITION) **5486**

●OFFICIAL AMERICAN BOARD OF MEDICAL SPECIALTIES (ABMS) DIRECTORY OF BOARD CERTIFIED ANESTHESIOLOGISTS, THE (US/0000-1546) [29761384] 3916, **3683**

OFFICIAL AMERICAN BOARD OF MEDICAL SPECIALTIES (ABMS) DIRECTORY OF BOARD CERTIFIED MEDICAL SPECIALISTS *See* OFFICIAL AMERICAN BOARD OF MEDICAL SPECIALTIES (ABMS) DIRECTORY OF BOARD CERTIFIED MEDICAL SPECIALISTS, THE **3623**

●OFFICIAL AMERICAN BOARD OF MEDICAL SPECIALTIES (ABMS) DIRECTORY OF BOARD CERTIFIED MEDICAL SPECIALISTS, THE (US/0000-1406) [29464146] 3916, **3623**

OFFICIAL AMERICAN BOARD OF MEDICAL SPECIALTIES (ABMS) DIRECTORY OF BOARD CERTIFIED MEDICAL SPECIALISTS, THE (US/0000-1406) [26294008] 3916, **3623**

●OFFICIAL AMERICAN BOARD OF MEDICAL SPECIALTIES (ABMS) DIRECTORY OF BOARD CERTIFIED NUCLEAR MEDICINE SPECIALISTS, THE (US/0000-1457) [27081516] 3916, **3849**

●OFFICIAL AMERICAN BOARD OF MEDICAL SPECIALTIES (ABMS) DIRECTORY OF BOARD CERTIFIED ORTHOPAEDIC SURGEONS, THE (US/0000-1597) [29761604] **3883**

●OFFICIAL AMERICAN BOARD OF MEDICAL SPECIALTIES (ABMS) DIRECTORY OF BOARD CERTIFIED OTOLARYNGOLOGISTS, THE (US/0000-1600) [29761641] 3916, **3890**

●OFFICIAL AMERICAN BOARD OF MEDICAL SPECIALTIES (ABMS) DIRECTORY OF BOARD CERTIFIED PEDIATRICIANS, THE (US/0000-1627) [29762069] **3907**

●OFFICIAL AMERICAN BOARD OF MEDICAL SPECIALTIES (ABMS) DIRECTORY OF BOARD CERTIFIED SURGEONS, THE (US/0000-1678) [29762296] 3916, **3971**

●OFFICIAL AMERICAN BOARD OF MEDICAL SPECIALTIES (ABMS) DIRECTORY OF BOARD CERTIFIED THORACIC SURGEONS, THE (US/0000-1481) [27081666] 3916, **3971**

OFFICIAL AND INDUSTRIAL LEASING DIRECTORY (WINNIPEG, MAN.) *See* OFFICE LEASING DIRECTORY **4842**

OFFICIAL ARMY NATIONAL GUARD REGISTER (US/0193-6557) [02564195] **4053**

OFFICIAL ARROW STREET GUIDE OF OTTAWA AND DISTRICT *SUSPENDED.* (CN/0316-8077) [02247239] **5487**

OFFICIAL BASEBALL GUIDE (US/0078-3838) [02420953] **4909**

OFFICIAL BASEBALL REGISTER (US/0162-542X) [02418704] 4909, **4856**

OFFICIAL BASEBALL RULES (US/0078-3846) [04173637] **4909**

OFFICIAL BASKETBALL RULES FOR MEN AND WOMEN (CN/0473-8853) [09336525] **4909**

OFFICIAL BLACKBOOK PRICE GUIDE OF UNITED STATES COINS, THE (US/0193-9610) [04740050] **2782**

OFFICIAL BLACKBOOK PRICE GUIDE OF UNITED STATES PAPER MONEY *See* OFFICIAL BLACKBOOK PRICE GUIDE OF UNITED STATES PAPER MONEY, THE **2782**

OFFICIAL BLACKBOOK PRICE GUIDE OF UNITED STATES PAPER MONEY, THE (US/0195-3540) [05425619] **2782**

OFFICIAL BLACKBOOK PRICE GUIDE OF UNITED STATES POSTAGE STAMPS, THE (US/0195-3559) [05425578] **2786**

OFFICIAL BOARD MARKETS (US/0030-0284) [02335657] **4235**

OFFICIAL BRAND LAWS (LINCOLN) (US/0093-0229) [01791450] **3021**

OFFICIAL BULLETIN OF THE THEATRICAL STAGE EMPLOYEES AND MOVING PICTURE MACHINE OPERATORS OF THE UNITED STATES AND CANADA (US/0020-5885) [02262485] 4075, **5367**

OFFICIAL BULLETIN / RECREATION ASSOCIATION OF NOVA SCOTIA (CN/0711-7760) [08701039] **4853**

OFFICIAL BULLETIN. SERIES A / INTERNATIONAL LABOUR OFFICE (SZ/0378-5882) [02335631] **3152**

OFFICIAL BULLETIN. SERIES B / INTERNATIONAL LABOUR OFFICE (SZ/0378-5890) [02335643] **1699**

OFFICIAL CALIFORNIA APARTMENT JOURNAL (US/0191-6335) [04947779] **2829**

OFFICIAL CANDIDATES PAMPHLET (US/0091-0090) [01784610] 4670, **4485**

OFFICIAL

OFFICIAL CATHOLIC DIRECTORY, THE (US/0078-3854) [01587620] **5013**

OFFICIAL CHINESE CUSTOMS GUIDE / GENERAL OFFICE OF THE CUSTOMS GENERAL ADMINISTRATION OF THE PEOPLE'S REPUBLIC OF CHINA, THE (HK) [15351025] **4670**

OFFICIAL CITY GUIDE (US/1055-1778) [23098987] **5487**

OFFICIAL CODE/DIRECTORY / AMATEUR ATHLETIC UNION OF THE UNITED STATES, INC (US) [24226326] **4909**

OFFICIAL CODE OF GEORGIA ANNOTATED. ADVANCE INFORMATION SERVICE (US/0747-6965) [09287041] **3021**

OFFICIAL COLLECTORS JOURNAL / BY THE HOUSE OF COLLECTIBLES, INC, THE ***CEASED.*** (US) [10691013] **2775**

OFFICIAL COMPILATION OF THE CODES, RULES AND REGULATIONS OF THE STATE OF NEW YORK (US) [01714679] **3021**

OFFICIAL COMPILATION RULES AND REGULATIONS OF THE STATE OF GEORGIA (US) **4670**

OFFICIAL COMPILATION RULES AND REGULATIONS OF THE STATE OF TENNESSEE; CONTAINING ALL OF THE RULES APPROVED FOR PRINTING BY THE SECRETARY OF STATE, DULY COMPILED, ARRANGED AND NUMBERED AS REQUIRED BY LAW (US) [03472648] **4670**

OFFICIAL COMPREHENSIVE DEVELOPMENT PLAN (US/0360-1463) [02243499] **2830**

●OFFICIAL COMPUTER USER'S TRAVEL COMPANION (ASIAN ED.) (US/1065-9560) [26815478] **1197**

●OFFICIAL COMPUTER USER'S TRAVEL COMPANION (EUROPEAN ED.) (US/1065-9579) [26815493] **1197**

●OFFICIAL COMPUTER USER'S TRAVEL COMPANION (NORTH AMERICAN ED.) (US/1065-9536) [26814015] **1197**

OFFICIAL CONGRESSIONAL DIRECTORY (US/0160-9890) [01239877] **4670**

●OFFICIAL CRUISE GUIDE (US/1065-2450) [26537782] **5487**

OFFICIAL DAILY BULLETIN - VANCOUVER STOCK EXCHANGE (CN/0384-9465) [03291390] **910**

OFFICIAL DECISIONS, OPINIONS AND RELATED MATTERS OF THE PUBLIC EMPLOYMENT RELATIONS BOARD OF THE STATE OF NEW YORK (US/0279-1005) [07522552] **3021**

OFFICIAL DETECTIVE (US/0894-1211) [15806569] **5074**

OFFICIAL DIRECTORY (US) [01792177] **3171**

OFFICIAL DIRECTORY - NEW JERSEY STATE BAR ASSOCIATION (US) [04821645] **3021**

OFFICIAL DIRECTORY OF CANADIAN MUSEUMS AND RELATED INSTITUTIONS, THE (CN/0829-0474) [11232530] **4094**

OFFICIAL DIRECTORY OF COMMERCIAL TRAFFIC EXECUTIVES, WITH AN APPENDIX OF TRANSPORTATION COMMISSIONS AND ORGANIZATIONS *See* OFFICIAL DIRECTORY OF INDUSTRIAL AND COMMERCIAL TRAFFIC EXECUTIVES, THE **5388**

OFFICIAL DIRECTORY OF DATA PROCESSING, COMPUTER USERS EASTERN USA (US/0276-6442) [07370004] **1261**

OFFICIAL DIRECTORY OF DATA PROCESSING, COMPUTER USERS SOUTHERN USA (US/0276-6434) [06232469] **1261**

OFFICIAL DIRECTORY OF DATA PROCESSING, COMPUTER USERS WESTERN USA (US/0278-5889) [07844892] **1261**

OFFICIAL DIRECTORY OF DATA PROCESSING, EDP SYSTEM USERS MIDWESTERN USA (US/0276-6450) [07195032] **1261**

OFFICIAL DIRECTORY OF INDUSTRIAL AND COMMERCIAL TRAFFIC EXECUTIVES, THE (US/0192-2629) [03178319] **5388**

OFFICIAL DIRECTORY OF NEW JERSEY LIBRARIES AND MEDIA CENTERS (US/0748-2469) [10769584] **3238**

OFFICIAL DIRECTORY OF REGISTERED DOCTORS OF MEDICINE *See* OFFICIAL DIRECTORY OF REGISTERED DOCTORS OF MEDICINE, MEDICAL CORPORATIONS AND DOCTORS OF CHIROPODY-PODIATRY **3916**

OFFICIAL DIRECTORY OF REGISTERED DOCTORS OF MEDICINE, MEDICAL CORPORATIONS AND DOCTORS OF CHIROPODY-PODIATRY (US/0148-3579) [03297902] **3916**

OFFICIAL DIRECTORY OF REGISTERED NURSES AND LICENSED PRACTICAL NURSES (US/0360-2850) [02243529] **3866**

OFFICIAL DIRECTORY OF REGISTERED PROFESSIONAL NURSES AND LICENSED PRACTICAL NURSES HOLDING LICENSES PERMITTING PRACTICE IN THE STATE OF NEVADA *See* OFFICIAL DIRECTORY OF REGISTERED NURSES AND LICENSED PRACTICAL NURSES **3866**

OFFICIAL DIRECTORY TO U.S. FLEA MARKETS / FROM THE EDITORS OF THE HOUSE OF COLLECTIBLES, THE (US) [16142575] **251**

OFFICIAL DIRECTORY / U.S. ARMY CORPS OF ENGINEERS (US/0278-6559) [07848372] **4053**

OFFICIAL DIRECTORY - VIRGINIA BANKERS ASSOCIATION (US/0160-5267) [03688500] **802**

OFFICIAL DIVING RULES AND REGULATIONS OF UNITED STATES DIVING, INC (US) [08311401] **4909**

OFFICIAL DU CYCLE ET DU MOTORCYCLE *See* OFFICIEL DU CYCLE ET DE LA MOTO PARIS, L' **4082**

OFFICIAL ENCYCLOPEDIA OF ANTIQUES AND COLLECTIBLES, THE (US/0743-8729) [10681944] **252**

OFFICIAL EXPORT GUIDE (US/0278-6389) [07844674] **848**

OFFICIAL FAX DIRECTORY (CANADIAN ED.) ***CEASED.*** (CN/0838-6811) [18241653] **1161**

OFFICIAL FIELD HOCKEY RULES FOR SCHOOL GIRLS (US/0362-3270) [02279876] **4909**

OFFICIAL FINANCIAL STATEMENT (US) [08077120] **5388**

OFFICIAL GAZETTE (GW/0041-8021) **1306**

OFFICIAL GAZETTE - EAST CENTRAL STATE OF NIGERIA (NR) [03477585] **3021**

OFFICIAL GAZETTE OF THE UNITED STATES PATENT AND TRADEMARK OFFICE. PATENTS (US/0098-1133) [02240595] **1306**

OFFICIAL GAZETTE OF THE UNITED STATES PATENT AND TRADEMARK OFFICE. TRADEMARKS (US/0360-5132) [02240594] **1307**

OFFICIAL GRE/CGS DIRECTORY OF GRADUATE PROGRAMS, THE (US) [24932694] **1838**

OFFICIAL GUIDE & RECORD BOOK / THE NATIONAL HOCKEY LEAGUE (CN/0828-6647) [12227581] **4909**

OFFICIAL GUIDE FOR GMAT REVIEW *See* GMAT REVIEW **1825**

OFFICIAL GUIDE FOR GMAT REVIEW / PREPARED FOR THE GRADUATE MANAGEMENT ADMISSION COUNCIL BY EDUCATIONAL TESTING SERVICE, THE (US) [14988670] 700, **1838**

OFFICIAL GUIDE FOR THE TRANSPORTATION OF HAZARDOUS MATERIALS, THE (US/1054-9277) [22932576] **2238**

OFFICIAL GUIDE, HOTELS AND RESTAURANTS IN GREAT BRITAIN AND IRELAND, THE (UK) [07997484] 5072, **2808**

OFFICIAL GUIDE, OUTDOOR POWER EQUIPMENT (US/0735-6676) [08941851] **160**

OFFICIAL GUIDE - TIME FINANCE ADJUSTERS (FIRM) (US/0732-2798) [08245125] **802**

OFFICIAL GUIDE TO AIRLINE CAREERS ***CEASED.*** (US) [04440269] **4207**

OFFICIAL GUIDE TO AMERICAN HISTORIC INNS, THE (US/1043-1195) [19318771] 5487, **2808**

OFFICIAL GUIDE TO BUYING & SELLING ANTIQUES AND COLLECTIBLES, THE ***CEASED.*** (US/0743-8702) [10200677] 2775, **252**

OFFICIAL GUIDE TO COIN COLLECTING, THE ***CEASED.*** (US/0747-5683) [07901675] **2782**

OFFICIAL GUIDE TO FLIGHT ATTENDANT CAREERS (US/8755-044X) [10287796] **4207**

OFFICIAL GUIDE TO FOOD SERVICE AND HOSPITALITY MANAGEMENT CAREERS, THE (US/8755-0431) [10625018] 5072, **4207**

OFFICIAL GUIDE TO GMAT / PREPARED FOR THE GRADUATE MANAGEMENT ADMISSION COUNCIL BY EDUCATIONAL TESTING SERVICE, THE (US) [09035992] **1838**

●OFFICIAL GUIDE TO THE AMERICAN MARKETPLACE, THE (US) [26065570] **934**

OFFICIAL GUIDE TO THE HOTELS-RESTAURANTS, COUNTRY HOTELS & INNS OF FRANCE, THE (FR) [18530622] **2808**

OFFICIAL GUIDE TO TRAVEL AGENT & TRAVEL CAREERS, THE (US/8755-0458) [07420394] 5487, **4207**

OFFICIAL GUIDE TO U.S. LAW SCHOOLS, THE (US/0886-3342) [12873821] 3021, **1838**

OFFICIAL GUIDE, TRACTORS AND FARM EQUIPMENT (US/0162-6809) [02753861] **160**

OFFICIAL HANDBOOK / INTERNATIONAL AMATEUR ATHLETIC FEDERATION (UK) [05238037] **4909**

OFFICIAL HANDBOOK OF THE AAU CODE (US/0091-3405) [01786786] **4909**

OFFICIAL HELICOPTER BLUE BOOK. RECIPROCATING ENGINE HELICOPTERS (US/1056-7755) [23846235] **31**

OFFICIAL HELICOPTER BLUE BOOK, THE (US/0890-7498) [14632033] **30**

OFFICIAL HELICOPTER BLUE BOOK. TURBINE ENGINE HELICOPTERS (US/1056-7763) [23847771] **31**

OFFICIAL HELLENIC YEAR BOOK (1984) (CN/0823-8596) [11579897] **2752**

OFFICIAL HERD RECORDING STATISTICS (AT) [04278538] 197, **155**

OFFICIAL HIGH SCHOOL BASEBALL RULES (US/0736-7821) [09201243] **4909**

OFFICIAL HIGH SCHOOL BOYS GYMNASTICS RULES (US/0740-9532) [09294335] **4909**

OFFICIAL HIGH SCHOOL FOOTBALL RULES (US/0747-9808) [10470599] **4909**

OFFICIAL HIGH SCHOOL ICE HOCKEY RULES (US/0735-651X) [08941777] **4909**

OFFICIAL HIGH SCHOOL SPIRIT RULES BOOK (US) [22379518] **4909**

OFFICIAL HOLIDAYS TO BE OBSERVED BY FEDERAL RESERVE OFFICES DURING THE YEAR ... (US) [03458850] **802**

OFFICIAL HOTEL AND RESORT GUIDE (US) [07690883] **2808**

OFFICIAL HOTEL & RESORT GUIDE'S CRUISE GUIDE *See* OFFICIAL CRUISE GUIDE **5487**

OFFICIAL HOTEL GUIDE (US/1056-1862) [23373272] **2808**

OFFICIAL IDENTIFICATION AND PRICE GUIDE TO AMERICAN FOLK ART, THE ***CEASED.*** (US) [18956049] **374**

OFFICIAL IDENTIFICATION AND PRICE GUIDE TO ANTIQUE & MODERN DOLLS, THE (US/1046-7289) [19882702] **252**

OFFICIAL ... IDENTIFICATION AND PRICE GUIDE TO ANTIQUES AND COLLECTIBLES, THE (US/1050-6144) [20537707] **252**

OFFICIAL IDENTIFICATION AND PRICE GUIDE TO POSTCARDS, THE (US/1059-0056) [23349631] **2775**

OFFICIAL IDENTIFICATION AND PRICE GUIDE TO POTTERY & PORCELAIN, THE (US/1054-5972) [20707962] **374**

OFFICIAL IDENTIFICATION GUIDE TO EARLY AMERICAN FURNITURE, THE ***CEASED.*** (US/8755-609X) [11339501] **2906**

OFFICIAL IDENTIFICATION GUIDE TO GLASSWARE, THE ***CEASED.*** (US/8755-5530) [11324517] **2592**

OFFICIAL IDENTIFICATION GUIDE TO GUNMARKS, THE ***CEASED.*** (US) [11948309] **2775**

OFFICIAL IDENTIFICATION GUIDE TO VICTORIAN FURNITURE, THE ***CEASED.*** (US/8755-5522) [11325637] **2906**

OFFICIAL INTERMODAL EQUIPMENT REGISTER, THE (US/0190-6690) [04745802] **5388**

OFFICIAL INTERNATIONAL BUSINESS DIRECTORY OF THE SPANISH SPEAKING WORLD (US/0735-5513) [08695551] **700**

OFFICIAL INVESTORS GUIDE, BUYING, SELLING GOLD COINS, THE ***CEASED.*** (US/0747-8682) [08208256] **910**

OFFICIAL INVESTORS GUIDE, BUYING, SELLING SILVER COINS, THE ***CEASED.*** (US/0747-8526) [08675486] 2782, **910**

OFFICIAL INVESTORS GUIDE, BUYING, SELLING SILVER DOLLARS, THE ***CEASED.*** (US/0747-8674) [08207802] 2783, **910**

OFFICIAL IOWA MANUFACTURERS DIRECTORY (US/1056-6872) [22522310] **3485**

OFFICIAL IPLOCA DIRECTORY (US) [23376045] **4267**

OFFICIAL JOURNAL - ILLINOIS POLICE ASSOCIATION (US/0019-2171) [04074315] **3171**

OFFICIAL JOURNAL OF THE EUROPEAN COMMUNITIES: DEBATES OF THE EUROPEAN PARLIAMENT (LU/0378-5041) [02111540] **4670**

OFFICIAL JOURNAL OF THE EUROPEAN COMMUNITIES : INFORMATION AND NOTICES (LU/0378-6986) [01785436] **3133**

OFFICIAL — Alphabetical Title Index

OFFICIAL JOURNAL OF THE EUROPEAN COMMUNITIES : LEGISLATION (LU/0378-6978) [01785437] **3021**

OFFICIAL JOURNAL OF THE INSTITUTE OF LABOUR RELATIONS, UNIVERSITY OF SOUTH AFRICA (SA/0379-8410) [04326767] **1699**

OFFICIAL JOURNAL OF THE PROCEEDINGS OF THE SENATE AND HOUSE OF REPRESENTATIVES OF THE STATE OF LOUISIANA AND THE LEGISLATIVE CALENDAR (US/0362-3556) [02324958] **4485**

OFFICIAL JOURNAL (PATENTS) (UK/0030-0330) [06459457] **1307**

OFFICIAL (LOS ANGELES) (US/0192-5784) [05032502] **2607**

OFFICIAL LOS ANGELES LAKERS YEARBOOK, THE (US) [25751965] **4909**

● OFFICIAL MAJOR LEAGUE BASEBALL ROOKIE LEAGUE MAGAZINE FOR KIDS (US/1061-9178) [25488930] **4909**

OFFICIAL MAJOR LEAGUE BASEBALL STAT BOOK, THE (US/1054-4038) [22877127] **4909**

OFFICIAL MANITOBA SHIP-BY-TRUCK DIRECTORY (1983) (CN/0713-8776) [09547367] **5388**

OFFICIAL MEETING FACILITIES GUIDE (US/0094-5242) [01794162] **2808**

OFFICIAL MEETING FACILITIES GUIDE, EUROPE (US/1054-3309) [22830820] **2808**

● OFFICIAL MEETING FACILITIES GUIDE, NORTH AMERICA (US/1070-4515) [25692168] **2808**

OFFICIAL METHODS OF ANALYSIS OF THE ASSOCIATION OF OFFICIAL ANALYTICAL CHEMISTS (US/0066-961X) [02438068] **1018**

OFFICIAL MICHIGAN (US/0471-1688) [06172784] **5693**

OFFICIAL MINUTES: MEETING OF THE STATE BOARD OF EDUCATION (US) [02245119] **1868**

OFFICIAL MOTOR CARRIER DIRECTORY (US/0472-6243) [02914602] **5388**

OFFICIAL MUSEUM DIRECTORY, THE (US/0090-6700) [01264511] **4094**

OFFICIAL MUSEUM PRODUCTS AND SERVICES DIRECTORY, THE (US/0276-637X) [07374299] **4094**

OFFICIAL MUSIC & RECORD DIRECTORY (US/0162-3540) [04147626] **4143**

OFFICIAL NASCAR YEARBOOK AND PRESS GUIDE, THE (US/0891-4648) [14877759] **4909**

OFFICIAL NATIONAL COLLEGIATE ATHLETIC ASSOCIATION BASKETBALL RULES & INTERPRETATIONS, THE (US/0163-2817) [04330148] **4909**

OFFICIAL NATIONAL COLLEGIATE ATHLETIC ASSOCIATION BASKETBALL STATISTICIANS' MANUAL, THE (US) [08303648] **4909**, **4856**

OFFICIAL NATIONAL COLLEGIATE ATHLETIC ASSOCIATION FOOTBALL STATISTICIANS' MANUAL, THE (US) [05984667] **4909**

OFFICIAL NATIONAL FEDERATION BASKETBALL RULE BOOK (US/0270-8280) [06120513] **4909**

OFFICIAL NATIONAL FOOTBALL LEAGUE GUIDE (US/0091-0821) [01786176] **4909**

OFFICIAL ... NATIONAL FOOTBALL LEAGUE RECORD & FACT BOOK (US/0883-4199) [11110341] **4909**

OFFICIAL NBA GUIDE (US) [07958530] **4909**

● OFFICIAL ... NCAA BASKETBALL (US/1063-1089) [24857446] **4909**

OFFICIAL ... NCAA FOOTBALL / NATIONAL COLLEGIATE ATHLETIC ASSOCIATION (US) [24359356] **4910**

OFFICIAL NEW YORK STATE EDUCATION DEPARTMENT REPORTS (US/1058-5567) [24333787] **1770**

OFFICIAL NEWS AND INFORMATION - INTERNATIONAL DAIRY FEDERATION (BE) [03357102] **197**

OFFICIAL NEWSLETTER - WESTERN AUSTRALIAN EGG MARKETING BOARD (AT) [04954154] 217, **934**

OFFICIAL OFFICE MACHINES & BUSINESS EQUIPMENT USED PRICES GUIDE BLUE BOOK, THE (US/1070-938X) [28511155] **4214**

OFFICIAL OPENING AND CLOSING HOURS OF THE BOARD OF GOVERNORS AND FEDERAL RESERVE BANKS, ALSO HOLIDAYS *See* OFFICIAL HOLIDAYS TO BE OBSERVED BY FEDERAL RESERVE OFFICES DURING THE YEAR ... **802**

OFFICIAL OPINIONS FROM THE SUPREME JUDICIAL COURT OF MASSACHUSETTS EDITION (US/0896-1077) [11495290] **3021**

OFFICIAL OVERSTREET COMIC BOOK PRICE GUIDE, THE (US/0891-8872) [15023972] **4864**

OFFICIAL PENCIL PUZZLES & WORD GAMES (US/0278-9884) [07941206] **4864**

OFFICIAL PGA TOUR BOOK (US/1042-8798) [08278465] **4910**

OFFICIAL PGA TOUR MEDIA GUIDE *See* OFFICIAL PGA TOUR BOOK **4910**

OFFICIAL PLAYING RULES FOR THE CANADIAN FOOTBALL LEAGUE, THE (CN/0316-151X) [02248088] **4910**

OFFICIAL POLICY RESOLUTIONS ADOPTED AT THE ANNUAL CONFERENCE OF MAYORS (US/1066-9574) [21179737] **4671**

OFFICIAL PRICE GUIDE, PAPERBACKS, THE (US) [23334157] **4831**

OFFICIAL PRICE GUIDE TO AMERICAN SILVER AND SILVER PLATE, THE (US/0743-9784) [07049807] **4014**

OFFICIAL PRICE GUIDE TO ANTIQUE & MODERN FIREARMS, THE (US/0743-9776) [07367513] **4053**

OFFICIAL PRICE GUIDE TO ANTIQUE CLOCKS, THE (US/0743-9571) [09560942] 252, **2916**

OFFICIAL PRICE GUIDE TO ANTIQUE JEWELRY, THE (US/0742-5805) [08181894] **2915**

OFFICIAL PRICE GUIDE TO BASEBALL CARDS (1984), THE (US/0748-3317) [10135617] **2775**

● OFFICIAL ... PRICE GUIDE TO BASKETBALL CARDS, THE (US/1062-6980) [24852305] **2775**

● OFFICIAL PRICE GUIDE TO BEER CANS (1993), THE (US/1069-8426) [28620128] **2775**

OFFICIAL PRICE GUIDE TO BEER CANS AND COLLECTIBLES *See* OFFICIAL PRICE GUIDE TO BEER CANS (1993), THE **2775**

OFFICIAL PRICE GUIDE TO BEER CANS & COLLECTIBLES, THE (US/0884-0237) [12225859] **2775**

OFFICIAL PRICE GUIDE TO BOTTLES, OLD & NEW, THE (US/0747-8747) [08059798] **2776**

OFFICIAL PRICE GUIDE TO COLLECTIBLE CAMERAS, THE (US/0882-2999) [11741406] **2776**

OFFICIAL PRICE GUIDE TO COLLECTIBLE RECORDS, THE (US/8756-4955) [10557125] **4143**

OFFICIAL PRICE GUIDE TO COLLECTIBLE TOYS, THE (US/0743-8680) [10081147] **2584**

OFFICIAL PRICE GUIDE TO COLLECTIBLES OF THE THIRD REICH, THE *CEASED.* (US/0748-8726) [11005702] **4053**

OFFICIAL PRICE GUIDE TO COLLECTOR CARS, THE (US/8756-1654) [08778572] 5422, **2776**

OFFICIAL PRICE GUIDE TO COLLECTOR GUNS, THE *CEASED.* (US/0747-7589) [10215168] **2776**

OFFICIAL PRICE GUIDE TO COLLECTOR HANDGUNS, THE (US/0747-7570) [09973057] **2776**

OFFICIAL PRICE GUIDE TO COLLECTOR KNIVES, THE (US/0747-5357) [07949426] **2776**

OFFICIAL PRICE GUIDE TO COLLECTOR PLATES, THE (US/0743-8710) [09469702] **2776**

OFFICIAL PRICE GUIDE TO COLLECTOR PRINTS, THE (US/0747-8178) [07432439] 361, **2776**

OFFICIAL PRICE GUIDE TO COMIC BOOKS & COLLECTIBLES, THE (US/0748-5840) [10774233] **2776**

OFFICIAL PRICE GUIDE TO FOOTBALL CARDS (1984), THE (US/0748-1365) [10412073] **2776**

OFFICIAL PRICE GUIDE TO GLASSWARE, THE (US/0743-8699) [10509160] **2592**

OFFICIAL PRICE GUIDE TO HOCKEY AND BASKETBALL CARDS (US/1062-7227) [20499409] 4910, **2776**

OFFICIAL PRICE GUIDE TO HOCKEY CARDS (US) [24674600] 4910, **2776**

OFFICIAL PRICE GUIDE TO HUMMEL FIGURINES & PLATES, THE (US/0748-5522) [06925234] 2592, **2776**

OFFICIAL PRICE GUIDE TO KITCHEN COLLECTIBLES, THE (US/0743-8672) [09974033] 2812, **2776**

OFFICIAL PRICE GUIDE TO MILITARY COLLECTIBLES, THE (US/0747-5691) [07934930] 4053, **2776**

OFFICIAL PRICE GUIDE TO MINT ERRORS AND VARIETIES, THE *CEASED.* (US/0748-2108) [10889528] **2783**

OFFICIAL PRICE GUIDE TO MUSIC COLLECTIBLES (ORLANDO, FLA. : 1984), THE (US/0748-111X) [10500502] **4143**

OFFICIAL PRICE GUIDE TO OLD BOOKS & AUTOGRAPHS, THE (US/0747-5047) [07901520] 4831, **2776**

OFFICIAL PRICE GUIDE TO ORIENTAL COLLECTIBLES, THE (US/0747-5365) [09973973] 252, **2776**

OFFICIAL PRICE GUIDE TO PAPER COLLECTIBLES, THE *SUSPENDED.* (US/0747-5373) [07901570] **2776**

OFFICIAL PRICE GUIDE TO PAPERBACKS & MAGAZINES, THE (US/0743-9792) [09262861] 4818, **2776**

OFFICIAL PRICE GUIDE TO POCKET KNIVES, THE *CEASED.* (US/0748-1152) [09973880] **4014**

OFFICIAL PRICE GUIDE TO POTTERY & PORCELAIN, THE (US/0747-5705) [09388315] **2592**

OFFICIAL PRICE GUIDE TO RADIO, TV & MOVIE MEMORABILIA, THE (US/0748-7606) [10982873] 4075, **1135**

OFFICIAL PRICE GUIDE TO RECORDS, THE (US/0747-7392) [09468666] **4143**

OFFICIAL PRICE GUIDE TO ROYAL DOULTON, THE (US/0748-0121) [08309709] **2592**

OFFICIAL PRICE GUIDE TO SCIENCE FICTION & FANTASY COLLECTIBLES, THE (US/8755-2787) [11193943] **2776**

OFFICIAL PRICE GUIDE TO SCOUTING COLLECTIBLES, THE (US/0747-5055) [09262660] 2776, **5234**

OFFICIAL PRICE GUIDE TO SPORTS COLLECTIBLES, THE (US/0748-1160) [09973824] **4910**

OFFICIAL PRICE GUIDE TO TOYS, THE (US/0747-5756) [09588470] **2584**

OFFICIAL PRICE GUIDE TO WICKER, THE (US/0743-8737) [09238788] **2906**

OFFICIAL PROCEEDINGS, ANNUAL MEETING - AMERICAN ASSOCIATION OF FEED MICROSCOPISTS (US/0569-2628) [02229111] **116**

OFFICIAL PROCEEDINGS - INTERNATIONAL WATER CONFERENCE (US/0739-4977) [08125404] **5536**

OFFICIAL PRODUCTION RECORDS OF PURE BRED REGISTERED DAIRY COWS IN NEW SOUTH WALES (AT) [02953934] **217**

OFFICIAL PROPERTY MANAGEMENT DIRECTORY (METROPOLITAN WASHINGTON), THE (US/1057-9486) [24017956] **4842**

OFFICIAL PUBLICATION - ASSOCIATION OF AMERICAN FEED CONTROL OFFICIALS (US) [01514551] **203**

OFFICIAL PUBLICATION - ASSOCIATION OF AMERICAN PESTICIDE CONTROL OFFICIALS, INC (US) [04043307] **4246**

OFFICIAL PUBLICATION - ASSOCIATION OF AMERICAN PLANT FOOD CONTROL OFFICIALS (US/0094-8764) [01796529] **116**

OFFICIAL RAILWAY EQUIPMENT REGISTER, THE (US/0030-0373) [04123821] **5433**

OFFICIAL RAILWAY GUIDE (FREIGHT SERVICE ED.), THE (US/1069-1715) [27942230] **5433**

OFFICIAL RAILWAY GUIDE (NORTH AMERICAN FREIGHT SERVICE ED.) *See* OFFICIAL RAILWAY GUIDE (FREIGHT SERVICE ED.), THE **5433**

OFFICIAL RAILWAY GUIDE (NORTH AMERICAN FREIGHT SERVICE EDITION) (US/0190-6704) [04745773] **5433**

OFFICIAL RAILWAY GUIDE. NORTH AMERICAN PASSENGER TRAVEL EDITION *See* OFFICIAL RAILWAY GUIDE. NORTH AMERICAN TRAVEL EDITION. UNITED STATES, CANADA AND MEXICO, THE **5433**

OFFICIAL RAILWAY GUIDE. NORTH AMERICAN TRAVEL EDITION. UNITED STATES, CANADA AND MEXICO, THE (US/0273-9658) [07048740] **5433**

OFFICIAL READ-EASY BASKETBALL RULES OF THE NATIONAL COLLEGIATE ATHLETIC ASSOCIATION (US) [03901105] **4910**

OFFICIAL RECORD OF PROCEEDINGS / HONG KONG URBAN COUNCIL (HK) [09424922] **4671**

OFFICIAL RECORDS - ECONOMIC AND SOCIAL COUNCIL (US/0082-8092) [01172097] **4530**

OFFICIAL RECORDS. SUPPLEMENT FOR ... / UNITED NATIONS, SECURITY COUNCIL (US) [09604461] **4530**

OFFICIAL REGISTER - AMERICAN SOCIETY OF CIVIL ENGINEERS (US/0402-1142) [01480783] **2028**

OFFICIAL REGULATIONS AND PLAYING RULES. LITTLE LEAGUE, SENIOR LEAGUE, BIG LEAGUE SOFTBALL (US) [11856170] **4910**

OFFICIAL REPORT - ASSOCIATION OF CLASSROOM TEACHERS (US/0090-4651) [01785071] **1868**

OFFICIAL REPORT / GENERAL ASSEMBLY (US) [08320136] **2351**

OFFICIAL REPORT OF DEBATES - COUNCIL OF EUROPE, PARLIAMENTARY ASSEMBLY (FR/0252-0664) [02243034] **4671**

Alphabetical Title Index — OHIO

OFFICIAL REPORT OF DEBATES / COUNCIL OF EUROPE, STANDING CONFERENCE OF LOCAL AND REGIONAL AUTHORITIES OF EUROPE (FR/0252-0540) [12791205] **4671**

OFFICIAL REPORT OF DEBATES (HANSARD) - ONTARIO. LEGISLATIVE ASSEMBLY. SELECT COMMITTEE ON ONTARIO IN CONFEDERATION (CN/1183-3580) [23659442] **4485**

OFFICIAL REPORT OF DEBATES OF THE LEGISLATIVE ASSEMBLY (CN) [02249636] **3021**

OFFICIAL REPORT OF THE ... CONGRESS (US) [09584207] **5065**

OFFICIAL REPORTS OF THE PARLIAMENTARY DEBATES (HANSARD) (AT) [02418470] **4671**

OFFICIAL REPORTS OF THE SUPREME COURT (US/0364-0973) [02532452] **3021**

OFFICIAL RETURNS OF THE GENERAL ELECTION *See* OFFICIAL RETURNS OF THE PRIMARY AND GENERAL ELECTIONS / STATE OF WEST VIRGINIA **4699**

OFFICIAL RETURNS OF THE PRIMARY AND GENERAL ELECTIONS / STATE OF WEST VIRGINIA (US) [08541815] **4699**

OFFICIAL RETURNS OF THE PRIMARY ELECTION *See* OFFICIAL RETURNS OF THE PRIMARY AND GENERAL ELECTIONS / STATE OF WEST VIRGINIA **4699**

OFFICIAL RETURNS ... PRIMARY ELECTION (US) [18851772] **4485**

OFFICIAL RULES FOR COMPETITIVE SWIMMING (US/0091-3413) [01786785] **4910**

OFFICIAL RULES FOR PROFESSIONAL FOOTBALL (US/0196-7827) [05885312] **4910**

OFFICIAL RULES OF THE UNITED STATES VOLLEYBALL ASSOCIATION *See* OFFICIAL ... UNITED STATES VOLLEYBALL RULES **4910**

OFFICIAL RULES / RINGETTE CANADA (CN/0711-0537) [08486100] **4910**

OFFICIAL SOFTWARE FOR GMAT REVIEW [COMPUTER FILE], THE (US) [25163069] **700**

OFFICIAL SOUTH AFRICAN MUNICIPAL YEARBOOK (SA) [01716346] **4671**

OFFICIAL SOUTH AFRICAN TRADE UNIONS DIRECTORY AND INDUSTRIAL RELATIONS HANDBOOK (SA) [21887281] **1699**

OFFICIAL SOUTHERN CALIFORNIA PORTS MARITIME DIRECTORY AND GUIDE (US/0094-8454) [01795437] **5453**

OFFICIAL SOUVENIR PROGRAM OF SPOLETO FESTIVAL U.S.A, THE (US/0147-5991) [03199781] **386**

OFFICIAL STANDARD NAMES GAZETTEER (US) [02565596] **2571**

●OFFICIAL STAR TREK FAN CLUB OF CANADA (CN/1192-7445) [28166170] **5234**

OFFICIAL STEAMSHIP GUIDE INTERNATIONAL (US/0030-0381) [01761070] **5487**

OFFICIAL STEAMSHIP SERVICE DIRECTORY, THE (US/0734-1016) [08675659] **5453**

●OFFICIAL STRIP JOINT GUIDE : THE O.S.J.G, THE (US/1065-8327) [26756852] **3996**

OFFICIAL SUMMARY OF SECURITY TRANSACTIONS AND HOLDINGS (US/0364-2267) [01590127] **4739**

OFFICIAL TRAVELLER'S GUIDE TO CANADA, THE (CN/1186-7949) [24623438] **5487**

OFFICIAL TRUCK CAMPER TRADE-IN GUIDE *See* TRUCK CAMPER TRADE-IN GUIDE **5398**

OFFICIAL UNITED STATES TENNIS ASSOCIATION TENNIS YEARBOOK (US) [20413085] **4910**

OFFICIAL UNITED STATES TENNIS ASSOCIATION YEARBOOK AND TENNIS GUIDE WITH THE OFFICIAL RULES, THE (US/0196-5425) [03860698] **4910**

OFFICIAL UNITED STATES TENNIS TOURNAMENT DIRECTORY (US/0145-7977) [03175109] **4910**

OFFICIAL ... UNITED STATES VOLLEYBALL RULES (US) [09228545] **4910**

OFFICIAL USFL GUIDE AND REGISTER (US/0742-4299) [10355266] **4910**

OFFICIAL USSR MINISTRY OF HEALTH DIRECTORY OF HEALTH RESOURCES, THE (US/1056-3369) [23669568] **4794**

OFFICIAL VIDEO DIRECTORY & BUYER'S GUIDE, THE (US/0890-782X) [14439679] **5318**

OFFICIAL VOLLEYBALL RULES FOR GIRLS AND WOMEN (US) [02365069] **4910**

OFFICIAL VOTERS PAMPHLET (US) [27152580] **4485**

OFFICIAL WATER POLO RULES (US) [07967978] **4910**

OFFICIAL WISCONSIN AUTOMOBILE VALUATION GUIDE (US/0736-7988) [04284552] **5422**

OFFICIAL YEAR BOOK (KE) [01791924] **910**

OFFICIAL YEAR BOOK - MALAYSIA (MY/0076-3373) [01588552] **2507**

OFFICIALS OF FLORIDA MUNICIPALITIES / FLORIDA LEAGUE OF CITIES (US) [01410804] **4671**

OFFICIEL DE LA DROGUERIE, ET SON COMPLEMENT "PLASTIQUES", L' (FR) [06416092] **4457**

OFFICIEL DE LA FOURRURE 1960, L' (FR/1162-5724) [11625724] **3185**

OFFICIEL DE LA PUBLICITE AU QUEBEC, L' (CN/0228-0213) [07822595] **763**

OFFICIEL DE L'AUTOMOBILE, L' *CEASED.* (FR/0030-0454) [I00300454] **5422**

OFFICIEL DES COMITES D'ENTERPRISE ET SERVICES SOCIAUX, L' (FR) [05620117] **5300**

OFFICIEL DES CONGRES ET DU TOURISME D'AFFAIRES, L' (FR/0755-1460) [I07551460] **700**

OFFICIEL DES DERMATOLOGISTES ET VENEREOLOGISTES, L' (FR/0996-553X) [21744736] **3722**

OFFICIEL DES MATHEMATIQUES CIRCULAIRE D'INFORMATION (FR) **3525**

OFFICIEL DES TEXTILES (FR) **5355**

OFFICIEL DES TRANSPORTS PARIS, L' (FR/1156-3133) [I11563133] **5388**

●OFFICIEL DU CYCLE ET DE LA MOTO PARIS, L' (FR/1240-8751) [I12408751] **4082**

OFFICIEL DU CYCLE ET DU MOTOCYCLE, L' (FR/0751-994X) [I0751994X] **4082**

OFFICIEL DU PRET A PORTER, L' (FR) [10002017] **1086**

OFFICIEL FORTEGNELSE OVER DANSKE SKIBE MED KENDINGSSIGNALER / UDGIVIT AF HANDELSMINISTERIET (DK) [06950931] **5453**

OFFICIER DE RESERVE *See* ARMEE ET DEFENSE **4036**

OFFRAMP (US) [18467194] **305**

OFFSET-TECHNIK (GW/0178-1197) [I01781197] **4567**

OFFSETPRAXIS (GW/0030-0594) [I00300594] 4567, **4372**

OFFSHORE BUSINESS (UK/0956-6732) [I09566732] **2094**

OFFSHORE CENTRES REPORT (UK/0952-7125) [I09527125] **4267**

OFFSHORE (CONROE, TEX.) (US/0030-0608) [03507076] **4267**

OFFSHORE DRILLING MONTHLY *See* OIL SERVICES & DRILLING MONTHLY **4270**

OFFSHORE DRILLING MONTHLY (US/0895-3023) [15566698] **4267**

OFFSHORE ENGINEER (UK/0305-876X) [02246079] **2094**

●OFFSHORE ENGINEERING INFORMATION BULLETIN (UK/0961-8163) [I09618163] **3238**

OFFSHORE FIELD DEVELOPMENT INTERNATIONAL (US/1058-5869) [24335710] **1620**

OFFSHORE GEODETIC ARCHIVE (UK) **2094**

OFFSHORE INDUSTRIAL DIRECTORY (CN/0712-0745) [08406215] **4267**

OFFSHORE INSTALLATIONS : GUIDANCE ON DESIGN, CONSTRUCTION AND CERTIFICATION (UK) **4267**

OFFSHORE INSTALLATIONS : GUIDANCE ON LIFE SAVING APPLIANCE (UK) **2094**

OFFSHORE INTELEX DRILLING WORLDWIDE (UK) **4267**

OFFSHORE INTERNATIONAL NEWSLETTER, THE (US/1058-5842) [24334689] **4267**

OFFSHORE INVESTMENT (UK/0954-0628) [17899182] **910**

OFFSHORE LICENCE REPORT (UK) 3021, **4267**

OFFSHORE RESEARCH FOCUS (UK/0309-4189) [I03094189] **4267**

OFFSHORE RESOURCES *CEASED.* (CN/0820-0858) [10027690] **4267**

OFFSHORE RIG LOCATION REPORT, THE (US/0733-0928) [02142467] **4267**

OFFSHORE RIG LOCATION RIG REPORT *See* OFFSHORE RIG LOCATOR **4267**

OFFSHORE RIG LOCATOR (US) **4267**

OFFSHORE RIG NEWSLETTER, THE (US/0147-1481) [02134976] **4267**

OFFSHORE SCIENTIFIC & TECHNICAL PUBLICATIONS (US) [13978254] **2094**

OFFSHORE SERVICE VESSEL REGISTER / COMPILED AND PUBLISHED BY H. CLARKSON & COMPANY LIMITED, THE (UK/0309-040X) [05114386] **5453**

OFFSHORE SERVICE VESSELS. A GUIDE TO THE AMERICAN FLEET (US/0887-6827) [13313585] **5453**

OFFSHORE SERVICE VESSELS. A GUIDE TO THE FOREIGN FLEET (US/0734-9386) [08828183] **4267**

OFFSHORE TAX PLANNING REVIEW (UK) [I09611363] **4739**

●OFFSHORE TECHNOLOGY (TULSA, OKLA.) (US/1067-103X) [27134230] **4267**

OFFSHORE TECHNOLOGY YEARBOOK (US/0094-9124) [01790853] **4268**

OFFSHORE TUGS. A GUIDE TO THE AMERICAN FLEET (US/0887-6835) [10785472] **4268**

OFFSHORE (WEST NEWTON) (US/0274-9394) [06714531] **594**

OFFSHORE WORLDWIDE (US/1056-8263) [23887754] **4853**

OFFSPRING (US/0472-6340) [04874779] **1805**

OFICINA (BL) [01787885] **5422**

OFICINA DE LIVROS: NOVIDADES CATALOGADAS NA FONTE (BL) [02245952] **421**

●OFICINA, LA (US) **951**

OFIOLITI (IT/0391-2612) [03972987] **1443**

OFSAA BULLETIN (CN/1185-135X) [24257137] **4910**

OFTALMOLOG (DK/0108-5344) [I01085344] 3877, **3624**

OFTALMOLOGIA (RM) [24245918] **3877**

OFTALMOLOGIA. REVISTA D'OR (SP) **3877**

OFTALMOLOGICESKIJ ZURNAL (KIEV) (UN/0030-0675) [01778307] **3877**

OFTALMOLOGIJA (BU/0374-2105) [07539344] **3877**

OGAM (FR/0030-0691) [01696845] **2701**

OGBOMOSO JOURNAL OF THEOLOGY (NR/1115-232X) [15745658] **4983**

OGDEN'S REVISED CALIFORNIA REAL PROPERTY LAW (US) [09753924] **3021**

OGEMAW COUNTY HERALD (US) **5693**

OGGI (IT/0030-0705) [02449257] **2491**

OGGI 7 (US/1059-4760) [24603294] **5711**

OGGI CANADA (CN/0712-4929) [09313021] **5791**

OGGI E DOMANI (IT) [01799370] **2520**

OGGIDOMANI ANZIANI : TRIMESTRALE DELLA FEDERAZIONE NAZIONALE PENSIONATI-CISL (IT) [26280664] **1699**

OGLE COUNTY LIFE, ROCK VALLEY SHOPPER, THE (US/1045-3059) [20067374] **5661**

OGLE GENEALOGIST : A PUBLICATION OF THE OGLE/OGLES FAMILY ASSOCIATION, THE (US) [07324021] **2465**

OGNEUPORY (RU/0369-7290) [02449258] **4014**

OGNI (SALZBURG, AUSTRIA) (AU) [20154767] **5778**

OGONEK (RU/0131-0097) [01761076] **2520**

OGRODNICTWO (PL/0239-9326) [01477277] **2426**

OGUN STATE (NIGERIA). HIGH COURT *See* SELECTED JUDGEMENTS OF THE OGUN STATE HIGH COURT / OGUN STATE OF NIGERIA **3047**

OH BOY *See* MY GUY **2490**

OH BOY MONTHLY (UK) **2491**

OH CALCUTTA (II/0377-7596) [01784152] **2507**

OH! IDAHO (US/1051-2373) [19935103] **2541**

OH! ZONE *CEASED.* (US/1054-8718) [23001880] **2179**

OHA LAW JOURNAL (US) [22841159] **5300**

OH&S CANADA (CN/0827-4576) [16636730] **2867**

OH&S SURVIVAL KIT (CN) **2867**

OHE BRIEFING (UK/0305-6031) [I03056031] **4794**

OHE INFORMATION SHEET (UK) [04898136] 1511, **4794**

OHIO *See* BALDWIN'S OHIO REVISED CODE, WITH RULES OF PRACTICE, ANNOTATED **2939**

OHIO — Alphabetical Title Index

OHIO *See* OHIO MOTOR VEHICLE LAWS **3021**

OHIO *See* BALDWIN'S OHIO TAX LAW AND RULES **2939**

OHIO *See* PAGE'S OHIO REVISED CODE, ANNOTATED, CONTAINING THE TEXT OF THE OFFICIAL OHIO REVISED CODE, EFFECTIVE OCT. 1, 1953 CURRENT MATERIAL **3024**

OHIO *See* OHIO PROBATE CODE, ANNOTATED **3022**

OHIO *See* OHIO CIVIL PRACTICE, PROCEDURE, AND FORMS **3090**

OHIO (US/0279-3504) [07781106] **2541**

OHIO AFL-CIO *See* WORKERS' COMPENSATION MANUAL FOR UNION REPRESENTATIVES **3155**

OHIO. AGRICULTURAL RESEARCH AND DEVELOPMENT CENTER *See* REGIONAL RESEARCH REPORT - OHIO AGRICULTURAL RESEARCH AND DEVELOPMENT CENTER **125**

OHIO AGRICULTURAL RESEARCH AND DEVELOPMENT CENTER *See* OARDC RESEARCH CIRCULAR **116**

OHIO AGRICULTURAL RESEARCH AND DEVELOPMENT CENTER *See* SPECIAL CIRCULAR - OHIO AGRICULTURAL RESEARCH AND DEVELOPMENT CENTER **136**

OHIO AGRICULTURAL STATISTICS SERVICE. OHIO AGRICULTURAL STATISTICS AND OHIO DEPARTMENT OF AGRICULTURE ANNUAL REPORT *See* ANNUAL REPORT AND AGRICULTURAL STATISTICS / STATE OF OHIO DEPARTMENT OF AGRICULTURE **60**

OHIO ALMANAC (US/0473-9760) [05153738] **2541**

OHIO APPELLATE DECISIONS INDEX. CRIMINAL CASES (US/0748-5891) [08653795] **3108**

OHIO ARCHAEOLOGIST (US/0048-153X) [02265415] **277**

OHIO ARCHIVIST (1987), THE (US/1047-5400) [16940460] **3239**

OHIO ARTS COUNCIL *See* OHIO ARTS COUNCIL BIENNIAL REPORT **327**

OHIO ARTS COUNCIL. ANNUAL REPORT *See* OHIO ARTS COUNCIL BIENNIAL REPORT **327**

OHIO ARTS COUNCIL BIENNIAL REPORT (US/0731-3284) [07578734] **327**

OHIO. ATTORNEY GENERAL'S OFFICE *See* OPINIONS OF THE ATTORNEY GENERAL OF OHIO **3142**

OHIO. AUDITOR OF STATE *See* ANNUAL REPORT - AUDITOR OF STATE **4710**

OHIO. AUDITOR OF STATE *See* OHIO SCHOOLS - OHIO. AUDITOR OF STATE **1868**

OHIO. AUDITOR OF STATE *See* OHIO LIBRARIES **3239**

OHIO BANKER, THE (US/0030-0802) [02449259] **802**

OHIO BAR REPORTS (US/0742-9266) [09233179] **3021**

OHIO BEEF CATTLE RESEARCH & INDUSTRY REPORT (US/1068-0195) [25465091] **217**

OHIO BEER BOOK (US) **2370**

OHIO BEVERAGE JOURNAL (US/0740-1361) [09938540] **2370**

OHIO BIOLOGICAL SURVEY *See* INFORMATIVE CIRCULAR - OHIO BIOLOGICAL SURVEY **458**

OHIO BIOLOGICAL SURVEY *See* BIOLOGICAL NOTES (COLUMBUS) **445**

OHIO. BOARD OF REGENTS *See* OHIO INSTRUCTIONAL GRANTS ANNUAL REPORT **1838**

OHIO. BOARD OF TAX APPEALS *See* BOARD OF TAX APPEALS DECISIONS **4713**

OHIO. BUREAU OF BUSINESS RESEARCH *See* OHIO INVENTORY OF BUSINESS AND INDUSTRIAL CHANGE **700**

OHIO. BUREAU OF WORKMEN'S COMPENSATION. REPORT *See* ANNUAL REPORT / OHIO INDUSTRIAL COMMISSION [AND] OHIO BUREAU OF WORKERS' COMPENSATION **1649**

OHIO CHESS BULLETIN (US/0885-6583) [10140302] **4864**

OHIO CHRISTIAN NEWS (US/0030-0845) [09008865] **4983**

OHIO CHRONICLE, THE (US) 4392, **1093**

OHIO CIVIL LIBERTIES (US/0274-5615) [02416956] **4511**

OHIO CIVIL PRACTICE, PROCEDURE, AND FORMS (US) [01761098] **3090**

OHIO COLLEGE ASSOCIATION *See* TRANSACTIONS AND DIRECTORY **1850**

OHIO CONGRESS OF PARENTS & TEACHERS *See* OHIO PARENTS AND TEACHERS ASSOCIATION NEWS **1770**

OHIO COUNCIL ON FAMILY RELATIONS *See* PROCEEDINGS, ANNUAL CONVENTION - OHIO COUNCIL ON FAMILY RELATIONS **2285**

OHIO COUNTY NEWS (RISING SUN, IND.) (US) [11743978] **5666**

OHIO. COURTS *See* OHIO OFFICIAL REPORTS **3021**

OHIO COURTS ... SUMMARY (US) [01681108] **3082**

OHIO CPA JOURNAL, THE (US/0749-8284) [07218771] **749**

OHIO CROP AND WEATHER (US/0735-6811) [08120491] **116**

OHIO CUES (US) **2752**

OHIO DENTAL JOURNAL, THE (US/0030-087X) [07290150] **1331**

OHIO. DEPARTMENT OF NATURAL RESOURCES. DIVISION OF WATER *See* INFORMATION CIRCULAR - STATE OF OHIO, DEPARTMENT OF NATURAL RESOURCES, DIVISION OF WATER **5534**

OHIO. DEPT. OF ADMINISTRATIVE SERVICES *See* ANNUAL FINANCIAL REPORT OF THE DIRECTOR OF ADMINISTRATIVE SERVICES **4709**

OHIO. DEPT. OF AGRICULTURE *See* ANNUAL REPORT AND AGRICULTURAL STATISTICS / STATE OF OHIO DEPARTMENT OF AGRICULTURE **60**

OHIO. DEPT. OF ECONOMIC AND COMMUNITY DEVELOPMENT *See* OHIO POPULATION ESTIMATES **4555**

OHIO. DEPT. OF ECONOMIC AND COMMUNITY DEVELOPMENT *See* WATER AND SEWER PROGRAMS FOR OHIO **5542**

OHIO. DEPT. OF EDUCATION. DIVISION OF FEDERAL ASSISTANCE *See* EDUCATIONAL OPPORTUNITIES THROUGH FEDERAL ASSISTANCE PROGRAMS - (OHIO) **1742**

OHIO. DEPT. OF HEALTH. REPORT OF VITAL STATISTICS *See* REPORT OF VITAL STATISTICS FOR OHIO **4811**

OHIO. DEPT. OF INDUSTRIAL AND ECONOMIC DEVELOPMENT *See* STATISTICAL ABSTRACT OF OHIO **5339**

OHIO. DEPT. OF MENTAL HEALTH *See* ANNUAL REPORT / DEPARTMENT OF MENTAL HEALTH **4765**

OHIO. DEPT. OF MENTAL HEALTH AND MENTAL RETARDATION. BUREAU OF STATISTICS *See* MONTHLY STATISTICAL SUMMARY REPORT - STATE OF OHIO, DEPARTMENT OF MENTAL HEALTH AND MENTAL RETARDATION, DIVISION OF BUSINESS ADMINISTRATION, BUREAU OF STATISTICS **4810**

OHIO. DEPT. OF TAXATION *See* ANNUAL REPORT OF THE OHIO DEPARTMENT OF TAXATION **4710**

OHIO. DEPT. OF TAXATION *See* DISTRIBUTION OF MOTOR VEHICLE REGISTRATION FEES AND FUEL TAXES TO OHIO CITIES **5413**

OHIO. DEPT. OF TAXATION *See* VEHICLE REGISTRATION AND MOTOR FUEL TAXES, AMOUNTS DISTRIBUTED TO LOCAL GOVERNMENTS, BY COUNTY **4693**

OHIO. DEPT. OF TAXATION *See* STATE LOCAL GOVERNMENT FUND, AMOUNTS DISTRIBUTED TO COUNTIES AND BASIS FOR DISTRIBUTION, BY COUNTY **4749**

OHIO. DEPT. OF TAXATION *See* VALUE OF PUBLIC UTILITY REAL AND PERSONAL PROPERTY BY COUNTY **4693**

OHIO. DEPT. OF TAXATION *See* STATE LOCAL GOVERNMENT FUND, AMOUNTS DISTRIBUTED DIRECTLY TO MUNICIPALITIES LEVYING INCOME TAXES AND BASIS FOR DISTRIBUTION, BY MUNICIPALITY **4749**

OHIO. DEPT. OF TRANSPORTATION *See* STATUS OF OHIO'S CAPITAL AND OPERATING NEEDS FOR PUBLIC TRANSPORTATION, THE **5393**

OHIO DISTRICT COURT REVIEW (US/0274-7294) [06115970] **3021**

OHIO. DIVISION OF GEOLOGICAL SURVEY *See* MISCELLANEOUS REPORT - STATE OF OHIO, DEPARTMENT OF NATURAL RESOURCES, DIVISION OF GEOLOGICAL SURVEY **1388**

OHIO. DIVISION OF GEOLOGICAL SURVEY *See* GUIDEBOOK - STATE OF OHIO, DEPARTMENT OF NATURAL RESOURCES, DIVISION OF GEOLOGICAL SURVEY **1382**

OHIO. DIVISION OF GEOLOGICAL SURVEY *See* REPORT OF INVESTIGATIONS - STATE OF OHIO, DEPARTMENT OF NATURAL RESOURCES, DIVISION OF GEOLOGICAL SURVEY **1394**

OHIO. DIVISION OF GEOLOGICAL SURVEY *See* BULLETIN - OHIO. DIVISION OF GEOLOGICAL SURVEY **1370**

OHIO. DIVISION OF GEOLOGICAL SURVEY *See* BULLETIN - OHIO. DIVISION OF GEOLOGICAL SURVEY **1370**

OHIO. DIVISION OF SAFETY AND HYGIENE *See* ANNUAL REPORT / THE DIVISION OF SAFETY AND HYGIENE, BUREAU OF WORKERS' COMPENSATION **2859**

OHIO. DIVISION OF SAVINGS AND LOAN ASSOCIATIONS AND SAVINGS BANKS *See* ANNUAL REPORT / DIVISION, SAVINGS AND LOAN ASSOCIATIONS AND SAVINGS BANKS **771**

OHIO. DIVISION OF VITAL STATISTICS *See* BIRTHS AND DEATHS BY JURISDICTION OF RESIDENCE. MARRIAGES AND DIVORCES BY COUNTY **5323**

OHIO. DIVISION OF VITAL STATISTICS *See* REPORT OF VITAL STATISTICS FOR OHIO **4811**

OHIO DOCUMENTS (US/0147-2542) [02421024] **4671**

OHIO EDUCATION ASSOCIATION *See* RESEARCH BULLETIN - OHIO EDUCATION ASSOCIATION **1779**

OHIO EMPLOYMENT LAW LETTER (US/1046-9206) [20584320] **3153**

OHIO EMPLOYMENT PRACTICES LAW MONTHLY *CEASED.* (US/1060-7781) [25060608] **3153**

OHIO ENGINEER, THE (US/0194-9276) [01911385] **1989**

● OHIO ENVIRONMENTAL MONTHLY (US/1063-9594) [26208336] **3115**

OHIO EPA *See* ANNUAL REPORT / OHIO ENVIRONMENTAL PROTECTION AGENCY **2161**

OHIO FACTS (DALLAS, TEX.) (US/1040-4872) [18230642] **2541**

OHIO FARMER COUNTY LINE RURAL DIRECTORY : CRAWFORD COUNTY, THE (US/0149-2934) [03454278] **2752**

OHIO FARMER COUNTY LINE RURAL DIRECTORY : HURON COUNTY, THE (US/0148-981X) [03403807] **2752**

OHIO FARMER, THE (US/0030-0896) [01761133] **116**

OHIO FISH AND WILDLIFE REPORT (US/0085-4468) [01690747] **2201**

OHIO FISHERMAN (US/0889-2407) [13826354] **4876**

OHIO FLORISTS' ASSOCIATION *See* BULLETIN - OHIO FLORISTS' ASSOCIATION **2434**

OHIO FLORISTS ASSOCIATION FLOWER GROWERS HOTLINE (US) 2426, **2435**

OHIO FOLKLORE (US/0733-4737) [08570688] **2323**

OHIO FRUIT JOURNAL (US) [05955667] **180**

OHIO GAME & FISH (US/0897-9170) [17664608] **4876**

OHIO GENEALOGICAL HELPER, THE (US/0362-0743) [02441479] **2465**

OHIO GENEALOGICAL SOCIETY NEWSLETTER, THE (US/1052-858X) [16994467] **2465**

OHIO. GENERAL ASSEMBLY. LEGISLATIVE SERVICE COMMISSION *See* SUMMARY OF ENACTMENTS **3061**

OHIO GEOLOGY NEWSLETTER (US/1045-4756) [09411211] **1390**

OHIO GOLFER MAGAZINE (US/0743-6874) [10639463] **4910**

OHIO GRANGER (US/0749-4009) [10732200] **116**

OHIO GRAPHIC (US) [17559275] **5729**

● OHIO HEALTH CARE IN PERSPECTIVE (US/1065-4364) [26606063] **4794**

OHIO HIGH SCHOOL ATHLETE, THE (US/1064-0908) [02428137] 1857, **4910**

OHIO HISTORY (US/0030-0934) [04912349] **2752**

OHIO HOLSTEIN NEWS (US/0199-7580) [06130744] **197**

OHIO IN PERSPECTIVE (US/1065-5638) [25086242] **5335**

OHIO INDUSTRY ENVIRONMENTAL ADVISOR (US) **2179**

OHIO INSTRUCTIONAL GRANTS ANNUAL REPORT (US/0145-8183) [02793641] **1838**

OHIO INVENTORY OF BUSINESS AND INDUSTRIAL CHANGE (US/0362-9716) [02386923] **700**

OHIO JOURNAL OF SCIENCE, THE (US/0030-0950) [04309463] **5136**

OHIO JOURNAL OF THE ENGLISH LANGUAGE ARTS (US) [23075719] **3420**

OHIO LAWYER (COLUMBUS, OHIO : 1987) (US) [15037665] **3021**

OHIO. LEGISLATIVE BUDGET COMMITTEE *See* ANNUAL REPORT - STATE OF OHIO, LEGISLATIVE BUDGET OFFICE OF THE LEGISLATIVE SERVICE COMMISSION, LEGISLATIVE BUDGET COMMITTEE **4710**

OHIO. LEGISLATIVE SERVICE COMMISSION *See* DIGEST OF ENACTMENTS, GENERAL ASSEMBLY **2961**

OHIO. LEGISLATIVE SERVICE COMMISSION. LEGISLATION *See* SUMMARY OF ENACTMENTS **3061**

OHIO LEPIDOPTERIST (US/0884-5956) [09739976] 5612, **5593**

OHIO LIBRARIES *CEASED.* (US/0360-8069) [02245032] **3239**

OHIO LIBRARIES (COLUMBUS, OHIO. 1988) (US/1046-4336) [17717818] **3239**

OHIO MANUFACTURERS DIRECTORY (US/0737-7495) [09035632] **3485**

OHIO MEDIA SPECTRUM (US/0192-6942) [03092591] **3239**

OHIO MEDICINE (US/0892-2454) [15131679] **3624**

OHIO MONITOR MAGAZINE *See* BWC NEWS **1657**

OHIO MONTHLY RECORD (US/0163-0008) [02810092] **3021**

OHIO MOTOR VEHICLE LAWS (US) [04426155] 5389, **3021**

OHIO MOTORIST (US/0030-0985) [04127296] **5422**

OHIO MOTORISTS ASSOCIATION (US) **5389**

OHIO NEWS MEDIA DIRECTORY (US) [06245110] **1119**

OHIO NEWS (WOOSTER, OHIO) (US/0899-4862) [10379992] **197**

OHIO NORTHERN UNIVERSITY LAW REVIEW (US/0094-534X) [01794338] **3021**

OHIO NURSES' REVIEW (US/0030-0993) [05236235] **3866**

OHIO NURSING HOME COMMISSION *See* REPORT OF THE OHIO NURSING HOME COMMISSION TO THE GOVERNOR AND OHIO GENERAL ASSEMBLY **3792**

OHIO. OFFICE OF MANPOWER DEVELOPMENT *See* ANNUAL REPORT **1648**

OHIO. OFFICE OF THE GOVERNOR *See* BUDGET IN BRIEF **4714**

OHIO OFFICIAL REPORTS (US) [01645469] **3021**

OHIO OFFICIAL REPORTS (CINCINNATI, OHIO) *See* REPORTS OF MISCELLANEOUS CASES ARGUED AND DETERMINED IN THE COURTS OF OHIO: OTHER THAN THE SUPREME COURT AND THE COURTS OF APPEALS OF OHIO **3039**

OHIO PARENTS AND TEACHERS ASSOCIATION NEWS (US/0199-0918) [05582965] **1770**

OHIO POLICE CHIEF, THE (US/0164-8357) [04315091] **3171**

OHIO POPULATION ESTIMATES (US/0149-1520) [03440435] **4555**

OHIO PROBATE CODE, ANNOTATED (US) [06333675] **3022**

OHIO PUBLIC EMPLOYEE REPORTER (US) [10892968] **1699**

OHIO QUERIES (US/0897-7747) [17623831] **2465**

OHIO RACEWALKER (US) **4910**

OHIO READING TEACHER (US/0030-1035) [02427838] 1902, **3308**

OHIO RECORDS & PIONEER FAMILIES/CROSSROADS OF OUR NATION (US) **2465**

OHIO REGIONAL ART DIRECTORY, THE (US/0736-9824) [09278843] **381**

OHIO REGISTER OF MANUFACTURERS (US/0884-173X) [11809091] **3485**

OHIO REPORT (COLUMBUS, OHIO) (US/1063-990X) [08887137] **4671**

OHIO REPUBLICAN NEWS (US/0164-6524) [02427821] **4485**

OHIO RESTAURANT HOTLINE (US/1060-6114) [22486555] **5072**

OHIO RESTAURANT JOURNAL (US/0746-5270) [10117131] **5072**

OHIO REVIEW (ATHENS), THE (US/0360-1013) [01302780] **3420**

OHIO RUNNER, THE (US/0279-9634) [07391105] 2600, **4910**

OHIO SCHOOLS - OHIO. AUDITOR OF STATE (US/0361-3356) [02246147] **1868**

OHIO SCHOOLS - OHIO EDUCATION ASSOCIATION (US/0030-1086) [06370950] **1868**

OHIO SLAVIC & EAST EUROPEAN NEWSLETTER (US/1048-6615) [21014193] **2701**

OHIO SOURCEBOOK *See* OHIO'S OFFICIAL SOURCEBOOK **381**

OHIO SPEECH JOURNAL, THE (US/0078-4052) [01761155] **1119**

●OHIO SPORTS ALMANAC (US/1061-8368) [25472867] **4910**

OHIO STATE BAR ASSOCIATION REPORT (1981) (US/0744-8376) [08078842] **3022**

OHIO STATE JOURNAL ON DISPUTE RESOLUTION (US/1046-4344) [13019638] **3022**

OHIO STATE LAW JOURNAL (US/0048-1572) [01586808] **3022**

OHIO STATE MANUFACTURERS GUIDE, THE *CEASED.* (US/0275-1887) [07098252] **3485**

OHIO. STATE PARKING COMMISSION *See* ANNUAL REPORT / STATE OF OHIO, STATE PARKING COMMISSION **5403**

OHIO. STATE PERSONNEL BOARD OF REVIEW *See* SPBR REVIEW **4705**

OHIO STATE UNIVERSITY. CENTER FOR VOCATIONAL AND TECHNICAL EDUCATION *See* VT RESEARCH SERIES **1917**

OHIO STATE UNIVERSITY. DEPT. OF LINGUISTICS *See* WORKING PAPERS IN LINGUISTICS (COLUMBUS, OHIO) **3333**

OHIO STATEWIDE COMPREHENSIVE OUTDOOR RECREATION PLAN. ACTION PROGRAM (US) [08232596] **4853**

OHIO. SUPREME COURT *See* REPORTS OF CASES ARGUED AND DETERMINED IN THE SUPREME COURT OF OHIO **3038**

OHIO TAVERN NEWS (US/0030-1183) [04123862] 2808, **5072**

OHIO TAX REVIEW (US/1071-4243) [15379169] **4274**

OHIO TEAMSTER, THE (US/0199-7734) [06097030] **1700**

OHIO THOROUGHBRED, THE (US) [01155858] **2801**

OHIO UNDERWRITER (US) [18925787] **2889**

●OHIO UST CLAIMS DIGEST (US/1062-3817) [25609373] **3022**

OHIO VALLEY CAVER (US/0730-8531) [07747352] **1409**

OHIO VALLEY PHILOSOPHY OF EDUCATION SOCIETY *See* PHILOSOPHICAL STUDIES IN EDUCATION **4356**

OHIO VALLEY RETAILER (US/0192-2467) [05025303] **934**

OHIO WESLEYAN MAGAZINE, THE (US/0030-1221) [04123876] **1093**

OHIO WOODLANDS (US) [03679673] 2201, **2390**

OHIO WRITER (US/0896-5730) [17210559] **2923**

OHIOANA QUARTERLY (US/0030-1248) [02435009] 327, **3420**

OHIONET *See* ANNUAL REPORT OF OHIONET **3190**

OHIONET *See* OHIONETWORK **2541**

OHIONETWORK (US/0163-7819) [04553865] **2541**

●OHIO'S OFFICIAL SOURCEBOOK (US/1067-5957) [27006099] **381**

OHIOSCAPES NEWSLETTER (US) **2830**

OHITURA (SP/0211-5905) [I02115905] **242**

OHLA NEWSLINE (CN/0843-5901) [19936500] 3790, **3239**

OHM (JA/0386-5576) [10451768] **2074**

OHS BULLETIN (CN/0714-6736) [08595037] **2541**

OHU DAIGAKU SHIGAKUSHI (JA/0916-2313) [I09162313] **1331**

OIBF INFO (AU/1019-1801) [I10191801] **1620**

OIDEAS (IE) [06481065] **1770**

OIEC BIMESTRIEL BULLETIN (BE/0770-1683) [10940639] **1883**

OIGA (PE/0030-1280) [02265443] **2552**

OIKONOMIKA APOTELESMATA ETOUS ... / VASILEION TES HELLADOS, HIDRYMA KOINONIKON ASPHALISEON, DIOIKESIS, OIKON. HYPERESIAI, D/NSIS LOGISTERIOU (GR) [20334248] **1700**

OIKOS (DK/0030-1299) [01643453] **2220**

OIKOS : RIVISTA QUADRIMESTRALE PER UNA ECOLOGIA DELLE IDEE *SUSPENDED.* (IT) [23670476] **2220**

OIKUMENE (HU) [03265642] **2625**

OIL & ENERGY TRENDS (UK/0950-1045) [05810311] 1952, **4268**

OIL & ENERGY TRENDS ANNUAL STATISTICAL REVIEW (UK/0953-1033) [I09531033] **4284**

OIL & ENERGY TRENDS. STATISTICS REVIEW *See* OIL & ENERGY TRENDS ANNUAL STATISTICAL REVIEW **4284**

OIL & GAS AUSTRALIA (AT/0727-6842) [I07276842] **4268**

OIL AND GAS DEVELOPMENTS IN PENNSYLVANIA (US) [04966960] **4268**

OIL & GAS DIRECTORY (HOUSTON, TEX. 1970) (US) [02361845] **4268**

OIL & GAS EXPLORATION JOURNAL (CALGARY, ALTA.) (CN/0833-9422) [15367825] **4268**

OIL AND GAS FEDERAL INCOME TAX MANUAL (US/0474-0076) [01150769] **4268**

OIL AND GAS FIELD CODE MASTER LIST (US/0738-9809) [09210138] **4268**

OIL AND GAS FIELD STUDIES (US/0161-0961) [03383573] **4268**

OIL & GAS FINANCE & ACCOUNTANCY (UK/0902-3752) 4268, **749**

OIL & GAS FINANCE AND ACCOUNTING (UK/0962-3752) [I09623752] 4268, **749**

OIL AND GAS GAZETTE (AT/1038-1317) [I10381317] **4268**

OIL AND GAS INFORMATION (FR) [20347771] **4268**

OIL & GAS INTERESTS NEWSLETTER (US/1073-0265) [22652678] **4268**

OIL & GAS INVESTOR (US/0744-5881) [08119074] 910, **4268**

OIL & GAS JOURNAL (US/0030-1388) [02390105] **4268**

OIL AND GAS LAW (US) [01769896] 4268, **3022**

OIL & GAS NEWS YEARBOOK (SI/0217-6602) [23183863] **4268**

OIL AND GAS NOTICE AND FORMS (US) **4268**

OIL & GAS (OXFORD, OXFORDSHIRE) (UK/0263-5070) [09165809] 4268, **3022**

OIL & GAS PRODUCING INDUSTRY IN YOUR STATE, THE (US) [11434966] **4268**

OIL AND GAS PRODUCTION IN KANSAS (US/0273-3811) [03702401] **4268**

OIL AND GAS PRODUCTION REPORT (CN/0702-8202) [03979690] **4268**

OIL AND GAS PRODUCTION REPORT. NORTHERN ROCKIES (US/0270-5400) [06429967] **4268**

OIL AND GAS PRODUCTION REPORT. SOUTHERN ROCKIES (US/0270-5419) [06428857] **4268**

OIL AND GAS PRODUCTION REPORT [MICROFORM] / NORTH DAKOTA STATE INDUSTRIAL COMMISSION (US) [24524383] **4268**

OIL & GAS REPORT (NORTH VANCOUVER, B.C.) (CN/0831-4799) [14954627] **4268**

OIL & GAS REPORT (TALLAHASSEE, FLA.) (US/0735-7583) [01410773] **4269**

OIL AND GAS REPORT (UNIVERSITY OF ALA.) (US/0364-2984) [02276550] **4269**

OIL AND GAS REPORTER (US/0472-7630) [01606606] **4269**

OIL & GAS RESERVE DISCLOSURES (US/0894-5322) [11625922] **4269**

●OIL & GAS RUSSIA & POST SOVIET REPUBLICS. HYDROCARBONS BRIEF (UK/0967-537X) [I0967537X] **4269**

OIL & GAS STOCKS HANDBOOK / STANDARD & POOR'S CORPORATION *CEASED.* (US/0736-8372) [09085008] 4269, **910**

OIL & GAS TAX ALERT / THE RESEARCH INSTITUTE OF AMERICA (US/0731-4620) [08198488] 1952, **4739**

OIL & GAS TAX QUARTERLY (US/0030-1396) [01761165] **4269**

OIL AND GAS TAXES *See* OIL & GAS TAXES NATURAL RESOURCES **4269**

OIL & GAS TAXES NATURAL RESOURCES (US) [11563321] **4269**

OIL & GAS TECHNOLOGY (US/8750-4804) [11486872] **4269**

OIL AND GAS (URBANA, ILL.) (US/0747-5306) [06206554] **4269**

OIL & NATURAL GAS PRODUCING INDUSTRY IN YOUR STATE, THE (US) **4269**

OIL CITY NEWS LETTER (UK) **4269**

OIL DAILY, THE (US/0030-1434) [01776121] **4269**

OIL DAILY'S LUBRICANTS WORLD, THE (US/1066-3002) [24852464] **4269**

OIL DIRECTORY OF LOUISIANA AND PRODUCTION SURVEY (US) [07828247] **4269**

OIL DIRECTORY OF TEXAS (US/0471-3893) [02363608] **4269**

OIL/ENERGY STATISTICS BULLETIN AND CANADIAN OIL REPORTS (US/0276-5977) [07387332] 1952, **1963**

OIL EXPRESS (US/0195-0576) [05238152] **4269**

OIL

OIL GAS (GW/0342-5622) [03333053] **4269**

OIL, GAS & PETROCHEM EQUIPMENT (US/0030-1353) [02619162] **4269**

OIL, GAS, MARINE DIRECTORY OF THE GULF SOUTH/ATLANTIC COAST (US/0162-5675) [04174667] **4269**

OIL IN CALIFORNIA (US/0279-6325) [07130535] **4269**

OIL IN THE ROCKIES (US/0276-5985) [07387368] **4269**

OIL INDUSTRY COMPARATIVE APPRAISALS I *See* HEROLD'S COMPARATIVE APPRAISAL REPORTS **4259**

OIL INDUSTRY COMPARATIVE APPRAISALS II *See* HEROLD'S COMPARATIVE APPRAISAL REPORTS **4259**

OIL INDUSTRY COMPARATIVE APPRAISALS III *See* HEROLD'S COMPARATIVE APPRAISAL REPORTS **4259**

OIL INDUSTRY IN YOUR STATE *See* OIL PRODUCING INDUSTRY IN YOUR STATE, THE **4270**

OIL INDUSTRY NEWS (US/0743-6289) [10625422] **4269**

OIL INDUSTRY OUTLOOK (US/1051-6565) [15293173] **4269**

OIL, LIFESTREAM OF PROGRESS (US/0030-1310) [02265448] **4269**

OIL MARKET REPORT (FR) [23657447] **4269**

OIL MARKET TRENDS (UK) **4269**

OIL MARKET UPDATE (CN/1184-1664) [23263676] **4269**

OIL MILL GAZETTEER (US/0030-1442) [04123894] **2015**

OIL PACKER INTERNATIONAL (UK/0957-655X) [I0957655X] **4269, 4220**

OIL PATCH MAGAZINE (CN/0838-6366) [18242167] **4269**

OIL PIPE LINE TRANSPORT (ANNUAL ED.) (CN/0410-5591) [01606157] **4270**

OIL PIPE LINE TRANSPORT (MONTHLY ED.) (CN/0380-4615) [02443664] **4270**

OIL PRICE DATABOOK (US/0193-4171) [05178803] **4270**

OIL PRICE INFORMATION SERVICE (US/0279-7801) [07244686] **4270**

OIL PRODUCING INDUSTRY IN YOUR STATE, THE (US/0191-0396) [01199976] **4270**

OIL PRODUCTION LEDGER (US) **4270**

OIL REPORT MEDITERRANEAN (IE) **4270**

OIL SCOUTS DIRECTORY (US/0742-7263) [09592171] **4270**

OIL SERVICES & DRILLING MONTHLY (US) **4270**

OIL SHALE SYMPOSIUM PROCEEDINGS (US/0271-0315) [05515210] **4270**

OIL SPILL INTELLIGENCE REPORT (US/0195-3524) [04604874] **4270**

OIL SPILL U.S. LAW REPORT (US/1055-9175) [23379165] **3022**

OIL TAXATION ACTS (UK) **4739, 4270**

OIL TECHNOLOGISTS' ASSOCIATION OF INDIA *See* JOURNAL OF THE OIL TECHNOLOGISTS' ASSOCIATION OF INDIA, THE **4262**

OIL WORLD ANNUAL (GW) [16961823] **1511, 116**

OIL WORLD STATISTICS (UK/0306-770X) [01796509] **4270, 4284**

OILFIELD REVIEW / SCHLUMBERGER (US/0923-1730) [20117908] **4270**

OILGAS (SP) **4270**

OILMAN. NEWSLETTER (UK/0263-1024) [I02631024] **4270**

OILS AND FATS (CN/0527-5911) [02443616] **180**

OILS & FATS INTERNATIONAL (UK/0267-8853) [13337840] **1620**

OILS & FATS INTERNATIONAL (UK/0267-8852) **1620**

OILS AND OILSEEDS JOURNAL (II/0369-769X) [09542725] **1044**

OILS, FATS AND OILSEEDS. FINLAND : SUMMARY OF TRADE (UK) [20649933] **1620**

OILSEEDS (UK/0265-0002) [12187220] **116**

●OILSEEDS & INDUSTRIAL CROPS (UK) [30791330] **116**

OILSEEDS - SITUATION AND OUTLOOK (AT) [03683259] **116**

●OILSEEDS, WORLD MARKETS AND TRADE / UNITED STATES DEPARTMENT OF AGRICULTURE, FOREIGN AGRICULTURE SERVICE (US) [29824683] **1620**

OILWEEK (CN/0030-1515) [01713730] **4270**

OILWEEK PULSE (CN/1185-3794) [23591839] **4270**

OISEAU ET LA REVUE FRANCAISE D'ORNITHOLOGIE *CEASED.* (FR/0030-1531) [01761168] **5619**

OIT INFORMACIONES (SZ) [06136643] **1700**

OITA, JAPAN (PREFECTURE) KANKYO HOKENBU *See* KANKYO HOZEN NO GENKYO TO TAISAKU **2235**

OITA-KEN KOGAI EISEI SENTA *See* OITA-KEN KOGAI EISEI SENTA NENPO **2238**

OITA-KEN KOGAI EISEI SENTA NENPO (JA) [08724142] **2238**

OJAI *See* OJAI AND VALLEY NEWS, THE **5638**

OJAI AND VALLEY NEWS, THE (US) [29510094] **5638**

OJAI VALLEY NEWS *See* OJAI AND VALLEY NEWS, THE **5638**

OJANCANO (CHAPEL HILL, N.C.) (US/0899-983X) [18282929] **3420**

OJC THE OHIO JEWISH CHRONICLE, THE (US) [25023102] **5051, 5729**

OJCD (NE) **3022**

OJIBWAY-CREE RESOURCE CENTRE *See* OJIBWAY CREE RESOURCE CENTRE CATALOGUE **2270**

OJIBWAY CREE RESOURCE CENTRE CATALOGUE (CN/0821-5979) [09688382] **2270**

OJIBWE TIMES, THE (US/0897-4977) [17527056] **5697**

OJINDEX (NE) **421**

OK AGE TENDRE (FR/0021-566X) **1067**

OK PODIUM (FR) **1770**

OKAJIMAS FOLIA ANATOMICA JAPONICA (JA/0030-154X) [01777667] **3679**

OKAMI : JOURNAL DE LA SOCIETE D'HISTOIRE D'OKA (CN/0835-5770) [24039271] **2752**

OKANAGAN HISTORY (CN/0830-0739) [14954760] **2752**

OKANAGAN LIFE (KELOWNA. 1988) (CN/0840-5492) [19461970] **2541**

OKANAGAN LIFE PROGRESS (CN/0849-0872) [22154552] **701**

OKANAGAN SEASONS (CN/0823-8243) [11360479] **2542**

OKAPI (FR/0751-6002) [I07516002] **5593**

OKARCHE CHIEFTAIN, THE (US/8750-393X) [11407274] **5732**

OKAY AMERICA (US/1056-1595) [23478441] **2542**

OKAYAMA DAIGAKA NOGAKUBU GAKUJUTSU HOKUKU (JA/0474-0254) [01641845] **116**

OKAYAMA DAIGAKU. NOGAKUBU *See* OKAYAMA DAIGAKA NOGAKUBU GAKUJUTSU HOKUKU **116**

OKAYAMA RIKA DAIGAKU KIYO. A, SHIZEN KAGAKU (JA/0285-7685) [10386048] **5136**

OKC ACTION (US/1043-4259) [19330631] **2542**

OKEANOLOGIJA (RU/0030-1574) [04966792] **1454**

●O'KEEFE'S GUIDE. MID-ATLANTIC REGIONAL DIRECTORY (US/1064-1793) [26235730] **5300**

O'KEEFE'S THE LAWS OF WEIGHTS & MEASURES (UK) **4032**

OKHA (NR) [11209750] **2625**

OKHRANA PRIRODNYKH VOD URALA (RU) [01791543] **5537**

OKHRANA TRUDA I SOTSIALNOE STRAKHOVANIE (RU/0131-2618) [05583452] **5300, 2867**

OKI TECHNICAL REVIEW (JA/0912-5566) [I09125566] **5136**

OKIKA O HAWAII, NA (US/0099-8745) [02144850] **2426**

OKIKE (NR/0331-0566) [02251757] **3420**

OKIKE EDUCATIONAL SUPPLEMENT (NR) [08342316] **3420**

OKINAWA HOGAKU (JA) [04480787] **3022**

OKINAWA KEIZAI TOKEI NEMPO (JA) [03146507] **1577**

OKINAWA-KEN (JAPAN). KIKAKU CHOSEIBU *See* OKINAWA-KEN NO KEIZAI GAIKYO **1577**

OKINAWA-KEN NO KEIZAI GAIKYO (JA) [03178903] **1577**

OKINAWA-KEN TOKEI NENKAN (JA) [01790309] **5335**

OKINAWA-KEN TOKEISHO (JA) [01797173] **116**

OKINAWA KENRITSU HAKUBUTSUKAN *See* OKINAWA KENRITSU HAKUBUTSUKAN NEMPO **4094**

OKINAWA KENRITSU HAKUBUTSUKAN *See* OKINAWA KENRITSU HAKUBUTSUKAN DAYORI **4094**

OKINAWA KENRITSU HAKUBUTSUKAN DAYORI (JA) [04793550] **4094**

OKINAWA KENRITSU HAKUBUTSUKAN NEMPO (JA) [02881366] **4094**

OKINAWA KOKUSAI DAIGAKU BUNGAKUBU KIYO: EIBUNGAKKA-HEN (JA) [05885316] **3308**

OKINAWA KOKUSAI DAIGAKU BUNGAKUBU KIYO : SHAKAIGAKKA-HEN (JA) [02998414] **5211**

OKINAWA KOKUSAI DAIGAKU. EIBUNGAKKA *See* OKINAWA KOKUSAI DAIGAKU BUNGAKUBU KIYO: EIBUNGAKKA-HEN **3308**

OKINAWA KOKUSAI DAIGAKU. KYOYOBU *See* OKINAWA KOKUSAI DAIGAKU KYOYOBU KIYO **1770**

OKINAWA KOKUSAI DAIGAKU KYOYOBU KIYO (JA) [02959210] **1770**

OKINAWA KOKUSAT DAIGAKU. BUNGAKUBU. SHAKAIGAKKA *See* OKINAWA KOKUSAI DAIGAKU BUNGAKUBU KIYO : SHAKAIGAKKA-HEN **5211**

OKINAWA MINWA NO KAI *See* OKINAWA MINWA NO KAI KAIHO **2323**

OKINAWA MINWA NO KAI KAIHO (JA) [03013680] **2323**

OKINAWA NO SHINKO KAIHATSU (JA) [02639254] **2830**

OKINAWA NOGYO SENSASU HOKOKUSHO (JA) [05579472] **117**

OKINAWA NORIN SUISAN TOKEI NEMPO (JA) [02246949] **117**

OKINAWA (PREFECTURE). TOKEIKA *See* OKINAWA NOGYO SENSASU HOKOKUSHO **117**

OKINAWA TOSHOKAN KYOKAI *See* OKINAWA TOSHOKAN KYOKAI SHI **3239**

OKINAWA TOSHOKAN KYOKAI SHI (JA) [01797343] **3239**

OKINAWA YUSEI KANRI JIMUSHO TOKEI NEMPO (JA) [04223485] **1146**

OKKI (NE) **1067**

OKLAHOMA ACADEMY OF SCIENCE *See* PROCEEDINGS OF THE OKLAHOMA ACADEMY OF SCIENCE **5141**

OKLAHOMA. AERONAUTICS COMMISSION *See* ANNUAL REPORT / OKLAHOMA. AERONAUTICS COMMISSION **11**

OKLAHOMA AERONAUTICS COMMISSION *See* ACTIVITY REPORT / OKLAHOMA AERONAUTICS COMMISSION **3**

OKLAHOMA AERONAUTICS COMMISSION. ANNUAL REPORT *See* ACTIVITY REPORT / OKLAHOMA AERONAUTICS COMMISSION **3**

OKLAHOMA AGRICULTURAL EXPERIMENT STATION *See* BULLETIN B - OKLAHOMA STATE UNIVERSITY. AGRICULTURAL EXPERIMENT STATION **68**

OKLAHOMA AGRICULTURAL STATISTICS (US) [03474460] **117, 155**

OKLAHOMA AIRPORT DIRECTORY *See* DIRECTORY OF OKLAHOMA AIRPORTS **18**

OKLAHOMA. ALCOHOLIC BEVERAGE CONTROL BOARD *See* ANNUAL REPORT OF THE OKLAHOMA ALCOHOLIC BEVERAGE CONTROL BOARD **1341**

●OKLAHOMA ALMANAC (US) [28048151] **1927**

OKLAHOMA ANNUAL PLANNING REPORT (US) [06319885] **1700**

OKLAHOMA ANTHROPOLOGICAL SOCIETY *See* BULLETIN OF THE OKLAHOMA ANTHROPOLOGICAL SOCIETY **233**

OKLAHOMA. ATTORNEY GENERAL'S OFFICE *See* DIGEST OF OPINIONS OF THE ATTORNEY GENERAL **3140**

OKLAHOMA BANKER (US/0030-1647) [04123925] **802**

OKLAHOMA BAPTIST CHRONICLE, THE (US/0889-745X) [04227988] **4983**

OKLAHOMA BAR ASSOCIATION (1939-) HANDBOOK - OKLAHOMA BAR ASSOCIATION **2976**

OKLAHOMA BAR JOURNAL, THE (US/0030-1655) [01761196] **3022**

OKLAHOMA. BOARD OF NURSE REGISTRATION AND NURSING EDUCATION *See* ANNUAL REPORT - BOARD OF NURSE REGISTRATION AND NURSING EDUCATION **3851**

OKLAHOMA. BOARD OF PHARMACY. REPORT *See* ANNUAL REPORT / OFFICE OF OKLAHOMA STATE BOARD OF PHARMACY **4291**

OKLAHOMA BUSINESS (US/0192-9593) [03525453] **701**

OKLAHOMA BUSINESS BULLETIN (US/0030-1671) [01775400] **701**

OKLAHOMA

OKLAHOMA CITY UNIVERSITY See OKLAHOMA CITY UNIVERSITY LAW REVIEW **3022**

OKLAHOMA CITY UNIVERSITY LAW REVIEW (US/0364-9458) [02693896] **3022**

OKLAHOMA CONSTITUTION, THE (US/0890-1007) [04810721] **4671**

OKLAHOMA COURT RULES AND PROCEDURE. FEDERAL (US/1065-9587) [21122464] **3022**

OKLAHOMA COWMAN (US/0030-1698) [04098066] **217**

OKLAHOMA DAILY, THE (US/0030-171X) [04098163] **5732**

OKLAHOMA DECISIONS REPORTED IN PACIFIC REPORTER, SECOND SERIES (US/0747-2986) [10686360] **3022**

OKLAHOMA DENTAL ASSOCIATION See OKLAHOMA DENTAL ASSOCIATION JOURNAL **1331**

OKLAHOMA DENTAL ASSOCIATION JOURNAL (US/0164-9442) [04248446] **1331**

OKLAHOMA. DEPARTMENT OF COMMISSIONERS OF THE LAND OFFICE See ANNUAL REPORT - DEPARTMENT OF COMMISSIONERS OF THE LAND OFFICE (OKLAHOMA CITY) **4627**

OKLAHOMA. DEPT. OF ECONOMIC AND COMMUNITY AFFAIRS See ANNUAL REPORT - STATE OF OKLAHOMA, DEPARTMENT OF ECONOMIC AND COMMUNITY AFFAIRS **1546**

OKLAHOMA. DEPT. OF HUMAN SERVICES See ANNUAL REPORT - OKLAHOMA. DEPT. OF HUMAN SERVICES **5272**

OKLAHOMA. DEPT. OF LIBRARIES See ODL SOURCE **3238**

OKLAHOMA. DEPT. OF LIBRARIES See ANNUAL REPORT OF OKLAHOMA LIBRARIES / COMPILED BY THE OKLAHOMA DEPARTMENT OF LIBRARIES **3191**

OKLAHOMA. DEPT. OF LIBRARIES See LONG-RANGE PROGRAM ... UPDATE & EXTENSION AND ANNUAL PROGRAM / OKLAHOMA DEPARTMENT OF LIBRARIES **3229**

OKLAHOMA. DEPT. OF LIBRARIES. PUBLIC INFORMATION OFFICE See ANNUAL REPORT, OKLAHOMA PUBLIC LIBRARIES IN COMMUNITIES AND STATE LIBRARIES / PREPARED BY THE DEPT. OF LIBRARIES, PUBLIC INFORMATION OFFICE **3191**

OKLAHOMA. DEPT. OF MENTAL HEALTH See STATE PLAN FOR COMPREHENSIVE MENTAL HEALTH SERVICES : ANNUAL REVIEW AND PROGRESS REPORTS FOR THE STATE OF OKLAHOMA **4804**

OKLAHOMA. DEPT. OF MENTAL HEALTH. DIVISION ON ALCOHOLISM See ALCOHOL TECHNICAL REPORTS **1339**

OKLAHOMA. DEPT. OF MINES See REPORT FOR CALENDAR YEAR ... / CHIEF MINE INSPECTOR, DEPARTMENT OF MINES **2149**

OKLAHOMA. DEPT. OF MINES. ANNUAL REPORT See REPORT FOR CALENDAR YEAR ... / CHIEF MINE INSPECTOR, DEPARTMENT OF MINES **2149**

OKLAHOMA. DEPT. OF PUBLIC SAFETY. SERVICES & RECORDS DIVISION See OKLAHOMA TRAFFIC ACCIDENT FACTS **5442**

OKLAHOMA DIRECTORY OF MANUFACTURERS AND PROCESSORS (US/1051-919X) [21390475] **1620**

OKLAHOMA EAGLE, THE (US/0745-385X) [09114180] **5732**

OKLAHOMA ECONOMIC OUTLOOK (US/0734-404X) [08086130] **1511**

OKLAHOMA. EDUCATION COUNCIL See BIENNIAL REPORT - OKLAHOMA EDUCATION COUNCIL **1727**

OKLAHOMA EDUCATIONAL TELEVISION AUTHORITY See ANNUAL REPORT - OKLAHOMA EDUCATIONAL TELEVISION AUTHORITY **1888**

● OKLAHOMA EMPLOYMENT LAW LETTER (US/1066-1123) [26860596] **3022**

OKLAHOMA EMPLOYMENT SECURITY COMMISSION. RESEARCH AND PLANNING DIVISION See OKLAHOMA ANNUAL PLANNING REPORT **1700**

OKLAHOMA. EMPLOYMENT SECURITY COMMISSION. RESEARCH AND PLANNING DIVISION See OCCUPATIONAL WAGE SURVEY : OKLAHOMA CITY METROPOLITAN AREA **1699**

OKLAHOMA. EMPLOYMENT SECURITY COMMISSION. RESEARCH AND PLANNING DIVISION See OKLAHOMA RURAL MANPOWER REPORT **1700**

OKLAHOMA FARM STATISTICS (US/0279-7712) [07252151] 117, **155**

OKLAHOMA FARMER-STOCKMAN, THE (US/0145-9392) [02807103] **117**

OKLAHOMA GAZETTE (US) **2542**

OKLAHOMA GENEALOGICAL SOCIETY QUARTERLY (US/0474-0742) [07321118] **2465**

OKLAHOMA GEOLOGY NOTES (US/0030-1736) [02390078] 2147, **1443**

OKLAHOMA GOVERNMENT PUBLICATIONS (US) [07208376] **4485**

OKLAHOMA. GOVERNOR See STATE OF OKLAHOMA EXECUTIVE BUDGET **4749**

OKLAHOMA. GOVERNOR. BUDGET See STATE OF OKLAHOMA EXECUTIVE BUDGET **4749**

● OKLAHOMA HEALTH CARE IN PERSPECTIVE (US/1065-4372) [26606100] **4794**

OKLAHOMA HEALTH PLANNING COMMISSION See AFFIRMATIVE ACTION PLAN / OKLAHOMA HEALTH PLANNING COMMISSION **4763**

OKLAHOMA HEALTH STATISTICS (US/0098-5651) [02241347] 4794, **4810**

OKLAHOMA HIGHWAY SAFETY OFFICE See REPORT TO THE PEOPLE **5443**

OKLAHOMA HOME & LIFE STYLE CEASED. (US/0895-1586) [15464440] **2542**

OKLAHOMA IN PERSPECTIVE (US/1065-5646) [26660924] **5335**

OKLAHOMA. INDIAN AFFAIRS COMMISSION See BIENNIAL REPORT - OKLAHOMA INDIAN AFFAIRS COMMISSION **2256**

OKLAHOMA JAYCEES See SOONER JAYCEE **5236**

OKLAHOMA JOURNAL OF FORENSIC MEDICINE (US/0363-2679) [02456568] **3742**

OKLAHOMA LAW REVIEW (US/0030-1752) [01715371] **3022**

OKLAHOMA LEGAL DIRECTORY, THE (US) [03723101] **3022**

OKLAHOMA LEGISLATIVE DIRECTORY (US) [09117368] **4671**

OKLAHOMA LIBRARIAN (US/0030-1760) [01761199] **3239**

● OKLAHOMA LIVING (US/1064-8968) [26148447] **2542**

● OKLAHOMA MANUFACTURERS REGISTER (US/1059-4523) [24595514] 3486, **1620**

OKLAHOMA NATIONAL STOCK YARDS CO See COMPARATIVE RECEIPTS AND SHIPMENTS OF LIVE STOCK FOR MONTHS ENDING ... / OKLAHOMA NATIONAL STOCK YARDS CO **209**

OKLAHOMA NURSE, THE (US/0030-1787) [04098263] **3866**

OKLAHOMA OBSERVER, THE (US/0030-1795) [04098289] **4485**

OKLAHOMA OCCUPATIONAL EMPLOYMENT STATISTICS (US/0147-8052) [03231244] 1700, **1537**

OKLAHOMA. OFFICE OF COMMUNITY AFFAIRS AND PLANNING See ANNUAL REPORT - THE STATE OF OKLAHOMA, OFFICE OF COMMUNITY AFFAIRS AND PLANNING **4629**

OKLAHOMA. OFFICE OF THE AUDITOR AND INSPECTOR See ANNUAL REPORT, FISCAL YEAR ENDED JUNE 30 ... / STATE OF OKLAHOMA, STATE AUDITOR AND INSPECTOR **4710**

OKLAHOMA OIL REPORTER, THE (US/0745-2268) [07770029] **4270**

OKLAHOMA. PLANT INDUSTRY DIVISION See SUMMARY INSPECTION REPORT OF OFFICIAL SAMPLES ON SEED, FEED, FERTILIZER & AG-LIME **203**

OKLAHOMA POLICE PENSION & RETIREMENT BOARD See ANNUAL REPORT / OKLAHOMA POLICE PENSION & RETIREMENT BOARD **3157**

● OKLAHOMA POLITICS (US/1065-0695) [26496981] **4485**

OKLAHOMA. PUBLIC EMPLOYEES RETIREMENT SYSTEM See ANNUAL REPORT - OKLAHOMA PUBLIC EMPLOYEES RETIREMENT SYSTEM **4629**

OKLAHOMA. PUBLIC HEALTH STATISTICS DIVISION See OKLAHOMA HEALTH STATISTICS **4810**

OKLAHOMA READER, THE (US/0030-1833) [04167908] 1902, **3308**

OKLAHOMA REALTOR (US/0745-5046) [09242329] **4842**

OKLAHOMA REGISTER, THE (US/0741-8612) [10187453] **3022**

OKLAHOMA RETAILER (US/0030-1841) [05143163] **956**

OKLAHOMA RURAL MANPOWER REPORT (US/0090-8037) [01786047] 117, **1700**

OKLAHOMA RURAL NEWS (US/0048-1610) [04098333] **117**

OKLAHOMA SERIES, THE (US/0271-6941) [05651825] **2752**

OKLAHOMA. STATE BOARD OF EXAMINERS OF PSYCHOLOGISTS See ANNUAL REPORT - OKLAHOMA. STATE BOARD OF EXAMINERS OF PSYCHOLOGISTS **4574**

OKLAHOMA STATE BOARD OF PUBLIC ACCOUNTANCY See DIRECTORY OF CERTIFIED PUBLIC ACCOUNTANTS AND PUBLIC ACCOUNTANTS OF OKLAHOMA **743**

OKLAHOMA. STATE BOARD OF VOCATIONAL AND TECHNICAL EDUCATION See ACCOUNTABILITY REPORT, AND ... STATE PLAN FOR THE ADMINISTRATION OF VOCATIONAL EDUCATION IN THE STATE OF OKLAHOMA **1909**

OKLAHOMA. STATE BOARD OF VOCATIONAL AND TECHNICAL EDUCATION See OKLAHOMA STATE MINI-PLAN FOR THE ADMINISTRATION OF VOCATIONAL EDUCATION UNDER THE VOCATIONAL EDUCATION AMENDMENTS OF 1968 **1915**

OKLAHOMA. STATE DEPT. OF EDUCATION See ANNUAL REPORT OF INDIAN EDUCATION IN EASTERN OKLAHOMA **1725**

OKLAHOMA. STATE DEPT. OF EDUCATION See ANNUAL PROGRAM PLAN AMENDMENT FOR PART B OF THE EDUCATION OF THE HANDICAPPED ACT AS AMENDED BY PUBLIC LAW 94-142 **1875**

OKLAHOMA. STATE DEPT. OF EDUCATION See SUPERINTENDENT'S NEWSLETTER **1873**

OKLAHOMA. STATE DEPT. OF EDUCATION. STATE-FEDERAL PROGRAMS DIVISION See FINANCIAL REPORT - DIVISION OF FEDERAL PROGRAMS **1864**

OKLAHOMA. STATE DEPT. OF HEALTH. PUBLIC HEALTH STATISTICS, STATE OF OKLAHOMA See OKLAHOMA HEALTH STATISTICS **4810**

OKLAHOMA. STATE DEPT. OF VOCATIONAL AND TECHNICAL EDUCATION See DESCRIPTIVE REPORT OF PROGRAM ACTIVITIES FOR VOCATIONAL EDUCATION (OKLAHOMA CITY) **1912**

OKLAHOMA. STATE DEPT. OF VOCATIONAL AND TECHNICAL EDUCATION. EDUCATIONAL EQUITY DIVISION See ANNUAL STATUS REPORT ON FEMALE AND MALE STUDENTS AND EMPLOYEES IN VOCATIONAL EDUCATION (OKLAHOMA) **1910**

OKLAHOMA. STATE ELECTION BOARD See ELECTION RESULTS AND STATISTICS / STATE OF OKLAHOMA **4502**

OKLAHOMA. STATE EMPLOYMENT SERVICE See HANDBOOK OF EMPLOYMENT SECURITY PROGRAM STATISTICS **1533**

OKLAHOMA STATE FIRE COMMISSION. COMMISSION ON FIRE PROTECTION, PERSONNEL STANDARDS, AND EDUCATION See ANNUAL REPORT OF THE COMMISSION ON FIRE PROTECTION, PERSONNEL STANDARDS, AND EDUCATION **2288**

OKLAHOMA STATE MINI-PLAN FOR THE ADMINISTRATION OF VOCATIONAL EDUCATION UNDER THE VOCATIONAL EDUCATION AMENDMENTS OF 1968 (US/0362-5966) [02303109] **1915**

OKLAHOMA STATE REGENTS FOR HIGHER EDUCATION See COMPLIANCE WITH TITLE VI OF THE CIVIL RIGHTS ACT: ANNUAL REPORT **1818**

OKLAHOMA. STATE REGENTS FOR HIGHER EDUCATION See BIENNIAL REPORT - OKLAHOMA STATE REGENTS FOR HIGHER EDUCATION **1811**

OKLAHOMA. STATE TREASURER See BALANCE SHEET - STATE TREASURER OF THE STATE OF OKLAHOMA **4712**

OKLAHOMA. STATE WATER QUALITY LABORATORY See ANNUAL REPORT, PUBLIC WATER SUPPLIES FOR THE STATE OF OKLAHOMA, NORTHWEST DISTRICT **2224**

OKLAHOMA TAX COMMISSION See STATE PAYMENTS TO LOCAL GOVERNMENT **4749**

OKLAHOMA TAX COMMISSION See STATE AND MUNICIPAL SALES AND USE TAX COLLECTION REPORTS **4749**

OKLAHOMA. TAX COMMISSION See BRIEF OUTLINE OF THE OKLAHOMA REVENUE SYSTEM, A **4713**

OKLAHOMA TAX COMMISSION See STATE SALES TAX COLLECTIONS REPORT **4749**

OKLAHOMA TAX COMMISSION. OKLAHOMA SALES TAX INCLUDING OPERATIONS OF THE USE TAX. STATISTICAL REPORT See STATE SALES TAX COLLECTIONS REPORT **4749**

OKLAHOMA — Alphabetical Title Index

OKLAHOMA TODAY (US/0030-1892) [02864131] 5269, **2752**

OKLAHOMA TODAY (US/0030-1892) [08226253] **2542**

OKLAHOMA. TOURISM AND RECREATION DEPT *See* ANNUAL REPORT - OKLAHOMA TOURISM AND RECREATION DEPARTMENT **5500**

OKLAHOMA TRAFFIC ACCIDENT FACTS (US) [06811995] **5442**

OKLAHOMA TRIENNIAL STATE HEALTH PLAN (US/0740-7343) [09978101] **4794**

OKLAHOMA UNION FARMER, THE (US/0030-1620) [04098346] **117**

OKLAHOMA UTILITIES DIRECTORY (US) [05724604] **4761**

OKLAHOMA VETERINARIAN, THE *CEASED.* (US/0474-0785) [01714528] **5517**

OKLAHOMA WATER RESOURCES BOARD *See* ANNUAL REPORT - OKLAHOMA WATER RESOURCES BOARD **5529**

OKLAHOMA WOMEN'S FRONT PAGE NEWS (US/1071-1643) [24325010] **5563**

OKLAHOMA'S WATER QUALITY STANDARDS (US/8756-8322) [11618476] **2238**

OKLEE HERALD (US) [01761204] **5697**

OKMULGEE COUNTY GENEALOGICAL SOCIETY NEWSLETTER (US) **2465**

OKOLICE (PL/0239-6874) [I02396874] **3420**

OKOLOGIE DER VOGEL (GW/0173-0711) [10005135] **5593**

OKOLONA MESSENGER (US) [16103582] **5701**

OKONOMI OG POLITIK (DK/0030-1906) [01715272] **1577**

OKONOMISK RAPPORT (NO/0332-5555) [13134842] **701**

OKONOMISK UTSYN *See* KONOMISKE ANALYSER **1502**

OKUGAI RODOSHA SHOKUSHUBETSU CHINGIN CHOSA HOKOKU (JA) [01799720] **1700**

OKUMENISCHE RUNDSCHAU (GW/0029-8654) [01696668] **4983**

OKUMENISCHER TASCHENBUCHKOMMENTAR ZUM NEUEN TESTAMENT (GW) **4983**

OKURASHO KOKUSAI KINYUKYOKU NEMPO (JA) [03865614] **910**

OLAC NEWSLETTER (US) [12073695] **3239**

OLAJ, SZAPPAN, KOZMETIKA (HU/0472-8602) [06646959] **117**

OLAM HADASH (US/0472-8637) [04098533] **2625**

OLAM HO-OMANUT (IS) [06381518] **361**

OLAMENU (US/0030-2139) [04098546] 5051, **1805**

OLATHE DAILY NEWS, THE (US/0886-9871) [12982228] **5678**

OLD AGE SECURITY, GUARANTEED INCOME SUPPLEMENT, SPOUSE'S ALLOWANCE (CN/0712-3388) [08871419] 5300, **2889**

OLD BOTTLE MAGAZINE *CEASED.* (US/0030-1965) [01775481] 277, **252**

OLD CAR VALUE GUIDE *CEASED.* (US/0475-1876) [06111204] 2776, **5422**

OLD CARS (US/0048-1637) [03774621] 2776, **5422**

OLD CARS PRICE GUIDE (US/0194-6404) [04903196] **5422**

OLD COLONY MEMORIAL (US) [22299017] **5689**

OLD DOMINION GARDENER (US/0274-6956) [05521810] **2426**

OLD DOMINION UNIVERSITY *See* FINANCIAL REPORT / OLD DOMINION UNIVERSITY **1824**

OLD DUTCH POST STAR (US) [22829826] **5719**

OLD EDINBURGH CLUB *See* BOOK OF THE OLD EDINBURGH CLUB, THE **5229**

OLD ENGLISH NEWSLETTER (US/0030-1973) [02428532] 1902, **3420**

OLD ENGLISH NEWSLETTER. SUBSIDIA (US/0739-8549) [05951140] 3308, **3420**

OLD FARMER'S ALMANAC. SPECIAL CANADIAN EDITION, THE (US/0276-3060) [07339267] **1927**

OLD FARMER'S ALMANAC, THE (US/0078-4516) [23009604] **1927**

OLD FARMER'S ALMANACK, THE (US) [01776933] **2542**

OLD FASHIONED PATCHWORK (US) **374**

OLD FORT NEWS (US/0196-7045) [01761210] **2752**

OLD HICKORY REVIEW (US/0890-0450) [05590417] **3420**

OLD-HOUSE JOURNAL *See* PERIOD HOUSE & ITS GARDEN **2902**

OLD-HOUSE JOURNAL CATALOG *See* OLD-HOUSE JOURNAL RESTORATION DIRECTORY **305**

OLD-HOUSE JOURNAL CATALOG, THE (US/0271-7220) [05804163] **623**

●OLD-HOUSE JOURNAL RESTORATION DIRECTORY (US) **305**

OLD-HOUSE JOURNAL, THE (US/0094-0178) [01393566] **623**

●OLD-HOUSE JOURNAL'S HISTORIC HOUSE PLANS, THE (US/1071-0868) [28542498] **305**

OLD LADY OF THREADNEEDLE STREET, THE (UK) [06457045] **2520**

OLD LAWRENCE REMINISCENCES (US/1044-1905) [19704874] **2465**

OLD LYONS RECORDER, THE (US) [20602970] **5644**

OLD MILL NEWS (US/0276-3338) [04828943] 203, **305**

OLD NEWS IS GOOD NEWS ANTIQUES GAZETTE, THE (US/1045-8182) [20256230] **252**

OLD NEWS (MARIETTA, PA.) (US/1047-3068) [20664413] **2625**

OLD NORTHWEST, THE *CEASED.* (US/0360-5531) [02244729] **2752**

OLD OREGON (US/8755-9536) [06450477] **1094**

●OLD OTOHATCHER DISTRICT REPORTER (US/1061-6985) [25405887] **2465**

OLD PRINT SHOP (NEW YORK, N.Y.) *See* OLD PRINT SHOP PORTFOLIO, THE **4567**

OLD PRINT SHOP PORTFOLIO, THE (US/0891-7604) [01586527] 381, **4567**

OLD SOUTH LEAFLETS (US) [01604943] **2752**

OLD SPARTANBURG DISTRICT GENEALOGY *CEASED.* (US/0887-6231) [13302696] **2465**

OLD STURBRIDGE VISITOR (US/0744-3781) [08227851] **4094**

OLD TESTAMENT ABSTRACTS (US/0364-8591) [03789752] 5018, **5013**

OLD TESTAMENT ESSAYS (SA/1010-9919) [09951949] **5018**

OLD TIME COUNTRY *CEASED.* (US/1044-1042) [18035921] **4143**

OLD-TIME CROCHET (US/1050-9518) [20705165] **374**

OLD-TIME HERALD (US/1040-3582) [18390108] **4143**

OLD TIMER (US/0147-2089) [03118183] **2752**

OLD TOY SOLDIER (US/1064-4164) [26280967] **2585**

OLD TRAILS (US/0148-575X) [03335333] **2752**

OLD WATER-COLOUR SOCIETY (LONDON, ENGLAND). CLUB *See* ANNUAL VOLUME / THE OLD WATER-COLOUR SOCIETY'S CLUB **337**

OLD WEST (US/0030-2058) [02052815] **2752**

OLD WEST RIDING (UK/0268-6554) [13740338] **2625**

OLD WESTMORELAND (US) [07790834] **2465**

OLD WORLD ARCHAEOLOGY NEWSLETTER (US/0732-1635) [06909410] **277**

OLDE MACHINERY MART (AT/1031-4555) [I10314555] **2123**

OLDE TIMES (US/0883-6442) [12183371] **2752**

OLDENBURGISCHE FAMILIENKUNDE (GW) [05025999] **2465**

OLDER AMERICAN (BOSTON, MASS.), THE (US/0738-9639) [09696993] **3754**

●OLDER AMERICANS INFORMATION DIRECTORY (US/1072-477X) [28959552] **5180**

OLDER CAR / TRUCK RED BOOK (US/1071-5452) [28659913] **5422**

OLDER NEBRASKAN'S VOICE, THE (US) [06281375] **5181**

OLDER TRUCK BLUE BOOK, THE (US/1041-9756) [18895467] **5422**

OLDHAM ERA (LAGRANGE, KY.) (US) [16272309] **5682**

●OLDIE (LONDON) (UK/0965-2507) [I09652507] **2520**

●OLDTIMERS (AUGUSTA, GA.) (US/1061-9763) [25497810] **4143**

●OLE. OPTO & LASER EUROPE (UK/0966-9809) [I09669809] **4438**

OLEAGINEUX (FR/0030-2082) [01645387] 1027, **117**

OLEO (SP) [09962818] **1044**

OLEODINAMICA PNEUMATICA LUBRIFICAZIONE (IT/0391-8645) [I03918645] **5136**

OLEOSCOPE PARIS (FR/1153-4664) [I11534664] **117**

OLIFANT (US/0381-9132) [02588057] **3420**

OLIMPIISKAIA PANORAMA : [ORGAN OLIMPIISKOGO KOMITETA SSSR] (RU) [08264575] **4910**

OLIPHANT WASHINGTON SERVICE (US/0733-0200) [08509573] **1952**

OLIPHANT WASHINGTON SERVICE. DIGEST AND CALENDAR OF ACTIVITIES OF THE...CONGRESS ... SESSION OF POSSIBLE INTEREST (US/0733-0227) [08509518] **4270**

OLIPHANT WASHINGTON SERVICE. ENERGY SUMMARY (US/0733-0219) [08509471] **1952**

OLIVAE (MADRID, SPAIN : ENGLISH EDITION) (SP/0255-9994) [13143016] **2352**

OLIVE HILL TIMES (OLIVE HILL, KY.) (US) [14402566] **5682**

OLIVIA TIMES-JOURNAL (US) [01761227] **5697**

OLJYPOSTI (FI) [02459329] **4270**

●OLLANTAY THEATER MAGAZINE (US/1065-805X) [26740921] **5367**

OLLON CHUNGJAE (KO) [09054847] **3022**

OLLON HAKPO (KO) [08302545] **3308**

OLLON SAHOE MUNHWA (KO) [25187435] **1119**

OLMSTE(A)D'S GENEALOGY RECORDED (US/0162-0800) [04102333] **2465**

OLNEY DAILY MAIL (US) [13344059] **5661**

OLNEY ENTERPRISE, THE (US) [14229040] **5753**

OLNEY TIMES (US) [12661073] **5738**

O'LOCHLAINNS PERSONAL JOURNAL OF IRISH FAMILIES (US/1056-0378) [23452576] **2465**

OLOMOUC, MORAVIA. PALACKEHO UNIVERSITA. FILOSOFICKA FAKULTA *See* ACTA UNIVERSITATIS PALACKIANAE OLOMUCENSIS. FACULTAS PHILOSOPHICA. HISTORICA **2672**

OLOMOUC, MORAVIA. PALACKEJP UNIVERSITA. FILOSOFICKA FAKULTA *See* PHILOSOPHICA, AESTHETICA **4355**

OLOMOUCKO-LUBLINSKY RUSISTICKY SBORNIK (XR) [20215757] **3420**

OLS NEWS : THE INDEPENDENT VOICE OF OPEN LEARNING (UK/0169-9729) **1770**

OLSCHWANGER JOURNAL (US/0882-1933) [10515141] 5051, **2465**

OLSEN'S AGRIBUSINESS REPORT (US/0197-9361) [06163249] 701, **117**

OLSEN'S BIOTECHNOLOGY REPORT *CEASED.* (US/0889-616X) [13997544] **3695**

OLSEN'S FISHERMAN'S NAUTICAL ALMANACK, CONTAINING TIDE TABLES AND DIRECTORY OF BRITISH FISHING VESSELS (UK) [06027474] **5453**

●OLSON'S BOOK OF LIBRARY CLIP ART (US/1061-4060) [25301918] **361**

OLSZTYNSKIE STUDIA DEMOGRAFICZNE (PL) [01787492] **1593**

OLTON ENTERPRISE (OLTON, TEX. : 1926) (US) [14556047] **5753**

OLTRE IL PONTE (IT) [11912817] **1700**

OLWELT. OIL WORLD (GW) [06746165] **4270**

●OLYMPIA & YORK BANKRUPTCY NEWS (US/1062-9777) [25830615] **802**

OLYMPIAN (NEW YORK, N.Y.), THE (US/0094-9787) [01795885] **4910**

OLYMPIAN (OLYMPIA, WASH.) (US/0746-7575) [10253415] **5761**

OLYMPIAN (SAN FRANCISCO) (US/0030-2163) [04098562] **4910**

OLYMPIC ENCYCLOPEDIA (SZ) [12774763] **4910**

OLYMPIC PANORAMA *SUSPENDED.* (RU) [10160828] **4910**

OLYMPIC REVIEW (SZ/0377-192X) [02244777] **4910**

OLYMPISCHE FORSCHUNGEN (GW/0474-1242) [01680928] **2851**

OLYMPISCHES FEUER (GW/0471-5640) [I04715640] **4910**

OLYMPRESS 1976 (CN/0316-6384) [02248000] **4910**

OM GYMNASIET STUDENTERKURSUS OG HF (DK/0109-9485) [19481365] **1770**

OM LANGSBRUGETS KULTURPLANTER OF DERTIL HRENDE FRAVL *See* TIDSSKRIFT FOR PLANTEAVL **189**

Alphabetical Title Index — ONDE

OM REVIEW (US/1071-3956) [28058114] **880**

OMAHA STAR, THE (US) [09536912] **5707**

OMAHA WORLD-HERALD (OMAHA, NB : 1954 : SUNRISE ED.) (US) [01585533] **5707**

O'MAHONY JOURNAL, THE (IE) [12600473] **2465**

O'MAHONY RECORDS SOCIETY *See* O'MAHONY JOURNAL, THE **2465**

OMAK-OKANOGAN COUNTY CHRONICLE, THE (US/1064-2617) [17319982] **5761**

OMALY SY ANIO (MG) [03737048] **2642**

OMAN: ENERGIEWIRTSCHAFT (GW) [05063948] **1952**

OMBUDSMAN OFFICE PROFILES / INTERNATIONAL OMBUDSMAN OFFICE PROFILES (CN/0714-6132) [09096461] **3022**

OMBUDSMEN AND SMALL BUSINESS SERVICES NEWS (US) [05716072] **701**

OMCA RESOURCE GUIDE (CN/1187-4198) [25589998] **1620**

OMEGA 3 NEWS (US) **4794**

OMEGA (FARMINGDALE) (US/0030-2228) [01761236] **4606**

OMEGA GENERATION. BIBLIOGRAFIA ECONOMICA (IT) **1511**

OMEGA (OXFORD) (UK/0305-0483) [01785334] **880**

OMELLETTE, L' (CN/0712-3345) [08867758] **5791**

OMH. OFFICES MUNICIPAUX D'HABITATION (CN/0228-8494) [08419037] **2830**

OMIKK HIRADO (HU/0230-6514) [I02306514] **3239**

OMINECA ADVERTISER, THE (CN/0708-000X) [04747174] **5791**

OMLADINSKE : LIST SAVEZA SOCIJALISTICKE OMLADINE SRBIJE (YU) [08899331] **2284**

OMLADINSKE NOVINE *See* OMLADINSKE : LIST SAVEZA SOCIJALISTICKE OMLADINE SRBIJE **2284**

OMNI (CN/0831-6465) [14878088] **3624**

OMNI (NEW YORK, N.Y.) (US/0149-8711) [03568173] **2542**

OMNI ONLINE DATABASE DIRECTORY (US/0895-187X) [11910905] 1275, **3239**

OMNI : OPTICAL MEDIA NEWS AND INFORMATION (UK) [23984143] **1277**

OMNIA MEDICA ET THERAPEUTICA. ARCHIVIO (IT/0390-6825) [02901396] **3624**

OMNIA : REVISTA DE LA COORDINACION GENERAL DE ESTUDIOS DE POSGRADO (MX) [22379916] **1838**

OMNIBUS (LONDON) (UK/0261-507X) [09287753] **1770**

●OMNIFORCE (BROOKLYN, NEW YORK, N.Y.) (US/1062-2594) [25561802] **4864**

OMNIPRATICIEN (SCARBOROUGH) (CN/1195-0242) [28745187] **3624**

OMRO HERALD, THE (US/8755-3961) [11292025] **5769**

OMS INTERNATIONAL *See* OMS OUTREACH **4983**

OMS OUTREACH (US/0274-9459) [06767190] **4983**

OMUN YONGU (KO) [01797424] **3308**

OMVARDAREN (SW/0280-4123) [11374120] **3866**

ON & OFF ROAD MAINTENANCE AND FUEL COST INDEX (US/0749-5692) [11124227] **5422**

●ON BALANCE (DENVER, COLO.) (US/1062-7049) [25701987] **4606**

ON BALANCE (VANCOUVER) (CN/0840-612X) [19292507] 4671, **1119**

ON BEYOND WAR (US/0887-9567) [13432758] **4485**

ON CAMPUS (SASKATOON) (CN/0711-3617) [08770630] **1839**

ON CAMPUS (WASHINGTON, D.C.) (US/1064-1971) [07961161] **1839**

ON CAMPUS WITH WOMEN (US/0734-0141) [02376679] **5563**

ON CARL (US/1042-2706) [18991844] **3239**

ON CASSETTE (NEW YORK, N.Y.: 1989) *See* WORDS ON CASSETTE **427**

●ON COURSE (SPRINGFIELD, MO.) (US/1061-0952) [25181722] 1067, **4983**

ON COURT (CN/0824-6629) [10857597] **4911**

ON CUE (US/1041-6234) [18025199] **1770**

ON-DEMAND VIDEO *See* PHILLIPS BUSINESS INFORMATION'S INTERACTIVE VIDEO NEWS **4372**

ON DISENO (SP) **2902**

ON DIT (AT/0030-2333) [02889470] **5777**

ON FILM (NZ/0112-2789) [14152176] **4075**

ON FILM (SANTA BARBARA) *SUSPENDED.* (US/0161-1585) [03861406] **4075**

ON-FLIGHT ORIGIN AND DESTINATION / ORIGINE ET DESTINATION PAR VOL (CN) [04895780] **31**

ON GUARD (US) **701**

ON GUARD (CLEVELAND, TENN.) (US/0738-758X) [02250522] **4983**

ON GUARD (NEW YORK, N.Y.) (US/1064-007X) [18216902] **4053**

ON HER MAJESTY'S SERVICE (CN/0384-5265) [03227437] **4485**

ON KEY (US/0734-0281) [08672750] **4143**

ON-LINE (DURHAM, N.H.) (US/0731-8367) [08252283] 1270, **1243**

ON LINE (GAINESVILLE, FLA.) (US/0748-2345) [10908219] **117**

ON LINE/ON WARD (CN/0827-4932) [13119051] **1275**

ON-LINE REVIEW (UK/0309-314X) [02998180] **1275**

ON-LINE SYSTEMS *See* PRODUCTION NEWS **1622**

ON LOCATION *CEASED.* (US/0149-7014) [03758217] 1135, **4075**

ON LOCATION, THE NATIONAL FILM & VIDEOTAPE PRODUCTION DIRECTORY *CEASED.* (US/0740-1159) [04408536] **4075**

ON ONE WHEEL (US/0893-4606) [15547016] **429**

ON OUR BACKS (US/0890-2224) [14191920] **2795**

ON OUR WAY (PRINCE ALBERT) (CN/1180-5765) [23686609] **3420**

ON! (PETERBOROUGH, N.H.) *CEASED.* (US/1052-438X) [22293624] **1197**

●ON POINTE (US/1060-3972) [24987586] **1314**

●ON PRODUCTION AND POST-PRODUCTION (US/1067-6120) [25544538] **4075**

ON Q (MILWAUKEE, WIS.) (US/1053-1580) [22465666] **944**

ON RECORD (TORONTO) (CN/0821-7882) [09951430] **5300**

ON SCENE (US/0093-2124) [01792065] **4181**

ON SCENE (CALGARY) (CN/1183-1049) [23598343] **3725**

ON-SHORE WEEKLY (UK) **2147**

ON SHORE WEEKLY (UK) **4270**

ON-SITE (EDMONTON) (CN/0702-5459) [06858279] **2830**

ON-SITE INSIGHTS (US) **5537**

ON SITE (WASHINGTON, D.C.) (US/0098-7727) [02239509] **623**

ON S'PARLE (CN/0382-8220) [02813999] **4853**

ON-STAGE STUDIES (US/0749-1549) [05015614] **5367**

ON STAGE (WASHINGTON) (US/0163-2132) [04320565] **386**

ON TAP (ENGLISH ED.) (US/0832-2562) [16220946] **2370**

●ON TAP (MORGANTOWN, W.VA.) (US/1061-9291) [25494742] 5537, **5300**

ON TARGET (CANADIAN EDITION) (CN/0380-5980) [02092561] **4485**

ON TARGET (TRENTON, N.J.) (US/0734-5550) [08839962] **1868**

ON TARGET WEEKLY (CN/0822-5729) [10092678] **5487**

ON THE AIR MAGAZINE (US/1057-9893) [21243328] **1135**

ON THE ARIZONA SET (US) **386**

ON THE BEAM (US/0740-218X) [09889022] **4392**

ON THE DECK (US/0030-235X) [08166286] 31, **117**

ON THE ISSUES (US/0895-6014) [12962040] **5563**

ON THE LEVEL ASHFIELD (AT/1036-8124) [I10368124] 5188, **2600**

ON THE LINE (COLLEGE, PARK MD.) (US/0190-2571) [03545939] **3171**

ON THE LINE MAGAZINE (US/0147-4693) [03175884] 381, **4485**

●ON THE LOOSE IN EASTERN EUROPE / WRITTEN BY BERKELEY STUDENTS IN COOPERATION WITH THE ASSOCIATED STUDENTS OF THE UNIVERSITY OF CALIFORNIA (US) [27019910] **5487**

●ON THE LOOSE IN MEXICO / WRITTEN BY BERKELEY STUDENTS IN COOPERATION WITH THE ASSOCIATED STUDENTS OF THE UNIVERSITY OF CALIFORNIA (US) [27019902] **5487**

●ON THE LOOSE IN THE PACIFIC NORTHWEST & ALASKA / WRITTEN BY BERKELEY STUDENTS IN COOPERATION WITH THE ASSOCIATED STUDENTS OF THE UNIVERSITY OF CALIFORNIA (US) [27023166] **5487**

ON THE MOVE (BUFFALO, N.Y.) (US) [07133020] **5389**

ON THE MOVE (SASKATOON) (CN/1180-7563) [22135142] **1857**

ON THE RECORDS (AT/1030-9837) [I10309837] **3022**

ON THE RISK (US/0885-4416) [12645462] **2889**

ON THE ROAD (BROOKLYN, NEW YORK, N.Y.) (US/1044-4327) [19784820] **3239**

ON THE RUN (CN/0229-088X) [08143797] **4911**

ON THE SAFE SIDE (US) **701**

ON THE STATE OF THE PUBLIC HEALTH (1963) (UK/0072-6087) [01784967] **4795**

ON THE STRATEGY OF INDUSTRIALIZATION IN DEVELOPING COUNTRIES AND THE EXPERIENCES IN THE ECONOMIC AND SOCIAL DEVELOPMENT IN SOCIALIST COUNTRIES (GW) [06911725] **1620**

ON TRACK (CN/0708-6008) [05071972] **31**

ON TRACK (HARLINGEN, TEX.) (US/1054-836X) [22980819] **4911**

ON TRACK (SANTA ANA, CALIF.) (US/0279-2737) [07715308] 5422, **4911**

ON WATCH (WASHINGTON) (US/0149-6557) [03521040] **3183**

ON WORKERS COMPENSATION (US) **1700**

ON YOUR OWN, A DIRECTORY FOR WOMEN (CN/0827-8717) [12030673] 5563, **5300**

ON YOUR OWN, A DIRECTORY FOR YOUNG MEN (CN/0827-8725) [11895317] 3996, **5300**

ON-YOUR-OWN GUIDE TO ASIA, THE (US/0162-5950) [04178900] **5487**

ONALASKA COMMUNITY LIFE (US/1053-6906) [21092492] **5769**

ONATRIO RECYCLING RESOURCEBOOK (CN) **2238**

ONAWA DEMOCRAT (ONAWA, IOWA : 1967) (US/0899-6520) [17204183] **5672**

ONAWA SENTINEL (US) [13991421] **5672**

ONAWAY OUTLOOK (US) **5693**

ONCE UPON A TIME (ARLINGTON, TEX.) (US/0882-9071) [11886063] **2786**

ONCE UPON A TIME (ST. PAUL, MINN.) (US/1071-2526) [28596855] **1067**

ONCODISC (PHILADELPHIA, PA.) (US/0897-5639) [17554205] **3821**

ONCOGENE (UK/0950-9232) [15797680] **3821**

ONCOGENE RESEARCH *CEASED.* (US/0890-6467) [14294205] **3821**

ONCOGENES (UK/0950-0561) [21982514] **550**

ONCOGENES AND GROWTH FACTORS ABSTRACTS (US/1043-8963) [19596355] 3821, **3661**

ONCOLOGIA (BARCELONA) (SP/0378-4835) [03226584] **3821**

ONCOLOGIA GINECOLOGICA (IT) [18581896] **3766**

ONCOLOGIA PORTO (PO/0871-5718) [I08715718] **3821**

●ONCOLOGIST'S POCKET GUIDE, THE (US/1070-0900) [28276667] **3821**

ONCOLOGY (SZ/0030-2414) [01605579] **3821**

ONCOLOGY DATA BASE FOCUS (US/0891-8147) [12028985] **3822**

ONCOLOGY ISSUES (US/1046-3356) [18932853] 3790, **3822**

ONCOLOGY JOURNAL / ALLEGHENY GENERAL HOSPITAL (US) [22123638] **3822**

ONCOLOGY NURSING FORUM (US/0190-535X) [04661240] 3822, **3866**

ONCOLOGY REPORTS (GR/1021-335X) [29502443] **3822**

●ONCOLOGY RESEARCH (US/0965-0407) [24773354] **3822**

ONCOLOGY TIMES (US/0276-2234) [06405119] **3822**

ONCOLOGY UPDATE (US/0883-4903) [12144019] **3822**

ONCOLOGY (WILLISTON PARK, N.Y.) (US/0890-9091) [14450212] **3822**

ONDA TV (IT) **2520**

ONDE ELECTRIQUE (FR/0030-2430) [01761251] 1135, **2074**

ONDE FORTALEZA (BL) [02413210] **701**

ONDE METRIQUE ET DECIMETRIQUE (BE) **4032**

ONDERHOUD INTERIEUR (NE) **2902**

ONDERHOUD WATERGANGEN / CENTRAAL BUREAU VOOR DE STATISTIEK, AFDELING NATUURLIJK MILIEU (NE/0168-5295) [10909210] **2094**

ONDERNEMEN (BE/0772-3326) [I07723326] **5065**

ONDERNEMING (NE) [06718133] **880**

ONDERNEMING, DE (BE/0777-6349) [I07776349] **2607**

ONDERSTEPOORT JOURNAL OF VETERINARY RESEARCH, THE (SA/0030-2465) [01761252] **5517**

ONDERWIJS EN GEZONDHEIDSZORG (NE) **1883**

ONDERWIJS EN MEDIA (NE) [06470255] **1902**

ONDERWIJSLITERATUUR (NE/0167-6644) [09834488] 1770, **1796**

ONDERWIJSVERSLAG (NE) [02441140] **1770**

ONDERZOEK HUISHOUDENS MET EENMALIGE UITKERING / CENTRAAL BUREAU VOOR DE STATISTIEK, HOOFDAFDELING STATISTIEKEN VAN INKOMEN EN CONSUMPTIE (NE/0168-454X) [11392770] **5335**

ONDERZOEK NAAR VAKANTIES EN UITGAAN, DAG- EN VERBLIJFSRECREATIE / CENTRAAL BUREAU VOOR DE STATISTIEK, HOOFDAFDELING SOCIAAL-CULTURELE STATISTIEKEN (NE) [10340447] **1700**

ONE ACCORD (US) [01640074] **4983**

ONE AND TWO FAMILY DWELLING CODE; UNDER THE NATIONALLY RECOGNIZED MODEL CODES (US) [06239139] **623**

ONE CHURCH (US/0030-2503) [01981426] **5039**

ONE DIRECTORY OF CHIROPRACTIC *See* NATIONAL DIRECTORY OF CHIROPRACTIC, THE **3806**

ONE IN CHRIST (UK/0030-252X) [01761256] **4983**

ONE IN TEN (US/0258-610X) [I0258610X] **1067**

ONE MEADWAY (US/1055-5609) [23235955] **3349**

ONE ON ONE (ALBANY, N.Y.) (US/0733-639X) [08615551] **3022**

ONE PEACEFUL WORLD (US) 4197, **2220**

ONE-PERSON LIBRARY, THE (US/0748-8831) [11026249] **3239**

ONE SHOW - ONE CLUB FOR ART & COPY (NEW YORK, N.Y.), THE (SZ/0273-2033) [07706747] **763**

ONE SKY REPORT (CN/0713-7753) [09025968] **1638**

ONE TO ONE (US/0739-5442) [09768613] **1135**

ONE TO ONE (UPPER DARBY, PA.) (US/1061-4796) [25321907] 1067, **5018**

ONE, TWO, THREE, FOUR *SUSPENDED.* (US/0889-0536) [13806863] **4143**

ONE VOICE (US) [05811036] **5627**

●ONE WOMAN'S OPINION (US/1066-2960) [26915926] **5563**

ONE WORLD (EDMONTON) *CEASED.* (CN/0475-0209) [02092586] **1770**

ONE WORLD (GENEVA) (SZ/0303-125X) [01781731] **4983**

O'NEIL DATABASE (US/0749-3401) [10513036] **802**

ONESTEP FORWARD (CN/1180-9183) [22185535] **4207**

ONGAKU GAKKAI *See* ONGAKUGAKU. JOURNAL OF THE JAPANESE MUSICOLOGICAL SOCIETY **4143**

ONGAKU GEIJUTSU (JA/0030-2600) [01761260] **4143**

ONGAKUGAKU. JOURNAL OF THE JAPANESE MUSICOLOGICAL SOCIETY (JA) [08608310] **4143**

ONGC BULLETIN (II) [08175080] **4270**

ONGOING ACTIVITIES IN EUROPEAN STANDARDS (BE) **4032**

ONGOING CURRENT BIBLIOGRAPHY OF PLASTIC AND RECONSTRUCTIVE SURGERY (1980) (US/0733-4060) [07910634] **3661**

ONI BOROLIS ZA SCHASTE NARODNOE (RU) [08804681] **4544**

ONICLASSEUR, ELEMENTS DU DROIT DE L'IMMIGRATION (FR) [19300460] **1920**

ONION (CN/0380-285X) [02585068] **361**

ONION CREEK FREE PRESS (US) [04311439] **5753**

ONION WORLD (US/0892-578X) [15233865] **2426**

ONISEP COMMUNIQUE (FR) **4207**

ONKO SOSHI (JA) [09856678] **5234**

ONKOLOGIE (SZ/0378-584X) [04226874] **3822**

ONKOLOGIJA (KIEV) (UN/0369-7436) [01229068] **3822**

ONKOLOGISCHE KLINIK (GW/0936-1502) [23835103] **3822**

ONKOLOGISCHES JOURNAL / INFORMATIONSDIENST, BEHRINGWERKE AG (GW/0932-2760) [19262032] **3822**

ONLINE ACCESS (US/0898-2015) [16522046] 1275, **1248**

ONLINE & CD NOTES (UK/0144-025X) **3239**

●ONLINE & CDROM REVIEW : THE INTERNATIONAL JOURNAL OF ONLINE & OPTICAL INFORMATION SYSTEMS (UK) [27743281] 1277, **1275**

ONLINE BIBLIOGRAPHIC DATABASES *SUSPENDED.* (UK) [07579912] 1197, **3239**

ONLINE BUSINESS INFORMATION (UK/0267-9515) [19540610] **701**

ONLINE BUSINESS SOURCEBOOK (UK/0953-5055) [20639387] 701, **1275**

ONLINE/CD-ROM BUSINESS SOURCEBOOK (UK) 701, **1275**

ONLINE/CD-ROM ... CONFERENCE PROCEEDINGS *CEASED.* (US) [22884671] **1275**

ONLINE (COLOGNE, GERMANY : 1982) (GW) [10067685] **1197**

ONLINE COMMUNICATIONS (US/0887-6215) [13302496] **1197**

ONLINE CURRENTS (AT/0816-956X) [I0816956X] **3239**

ONLINE DATABASE SEARCH SERVICES DIRECTORY *CEASED.* (US/0741-0077) [10062770] 1254, **3239**

●ONLINE FILES (UK/0967-6090) [I09676090] **1275**

ONLINE HELIDATA (UK/0951-9904) [I09519904] **31**

ONLINE HOTLINE NEWS SERVICE (US/1040-6646) [18492782] **1197**

●ONLINE JOURNAL OF CURRENT CLINICAL TRIALS, THE (US/1059-2725) [24529831] **3624**

ONLINE REVIEW: THE INTERNATIONAL JOURNAL OF ONLINE INFORMATION SYSTEMS (US) [09537277] **1275**

ONLINE TODAY (US/0891-4672) [11541538] 1275, **3239**

ONLINE (WATERLOO, ONT.) *See* PHOENIX (WATERLOO) **3468**

ONLINE (WESTON, CONN.) (US/0146-5422) [02860390] **1275**

ONLINE WITH ADULT AND CONTINUING EDUCATORS (US/0899-7934) [16386952] **1801**

●ONLY FOR KIDS MINI MAG (US/1066-2952) [26915785] **1067**

ONLY THE BEST (US/1053-4326) [14067068] 1902, **1224**

ONO (KO) [04561192] **3308**

ONO (CHUNGNAM TAEHAKKYO. PUSOL ONO HULLYONWON) (KO) [10083589] **3308**

ONOHAK (KO) [04426789] **3308**

ONOMA (BE/0078-463X) [01645764] **3308**

ONOMASTICA CANADIANA (CN/0078-4656) [02240808] 2571, **3308**

ONOMASTICA JUGOSLAVICA (CI/0475-0934) [01799294] 2571, **3308**

ONOMASTICA (WROCAW) (PL/0078-4648) [01761262] **2571**

ONOMASTICKY ZPRAVODAJ CSAV (XR) [11440179] **3308**

ONOMATA : REVUE ONOMASTIQUE (GR) **3308**

ONONDAGA COUNTY PUBLIC LIBRARY *See* ANNUAL REPORT / ONONDAGA COUNTY PUBLIC LIBRARY **3191**

ONONDAGA VALLEY NEWS (US/0745-4848) [09227676] **5719**

ONOWAY TRIBUNE (CN/0823-7131) [10224866] **5791**

ONS AMSTERDAM (NE/0166-1809) [06470236] **2701**

ONS ERFDEEL (BE/0030-2651) [04736754] **327**

ONS GEESTEIJK ERF (BE/0774-2827) [02671327] **4983**

ONS NEWS (US/0890-5215) [14254616] **3866**

●ONS NURSING SCAN IN ONCOLOGY (US/1062-5720) [25669014] **3866**

ONSAT (US/0747-4059) [10810538] **1136**

ONSEI NO KENKYU. THE STUDY OF SOUNDS (JA/0474-1528) [02265482] **4453**

ONSEIGAKKAI KAIHO (JA/0911-0402) [01761264] **3308**

ONSEN KOGAKKAI SHI (JA/0369-7665) [10461992] **2147**

ONSHORE WELL RESULTS SERVICE (UK) **4270**

ONT. SHEEP NEWS (CN/0844-5303) [19936286] 5517, **217**

ONTARIO *See* ONTARIO CORPORATION AND INCOME TAX LEGISLATION INCLUDING MINING TAXES AND SMALL BUSINESS DEVELOPMENT CORPORATIONS **701**

ONTARIO *See* ONTARIO PLANNING ACT **3023**

ONTARIO *See* ONTARIO GAZETTE, THE **3022**

ONTARIO *See* ONTARIO SECURITIES LEGISLATION **701**

ONTARIO *See* GUIDE DES ORGANISMES, CONSEILS ET COMMISSIONS DU GOUVERNEMENT DE L'ONTARIO **4653**

ONTARIO *See* GUIDE, AGENCIES, BOARDS & COMMISSIONS, GOVERNMENT OF ONTARIO, A **4653**

ONTARIO *See* FREEDOM OF INFORMATION AND PROTECTION OF INDIVIDUAL PRIVACY. DIRECTORY OF GENERAL RECORDS **4650**

ONTARIO *See* ONTARIO BUSINESS CORPORATIONS ACT WITH REGULATIONS (CCH CANADIAN) **3102**

ONTARIO. ADDICTION RESEARCH FOUNDATION *See* PRODUCT CATALOGUE - ONTARIO. ADDICTION RESEARCH FOUNDATION **422**

ONTARIO ADVISORY COUNCIL ON MULTICULTURALISM AND CITIZENSHIP *See* ANNUAL REPORT / ONTARIO ADVISORY COUNCIL ON MULTICULTURALISM AND CITIZENSHIP **2720**

ONTARIO ADVISORY COUNCIL ON SENIOR CITIZENS *See* ANNUAL REPORT - ONTARIO ADVISORY COUNCIL ON SENIOR CITIZENS **5178**

ONTARIO AGRICULTURAL COLLEGE. DEPT. OF LAND RESOURCE SCIENCE *See* ANNUAL REPORT - LAND RESOURCE SCIENCE. UNIVERSITY OF GUELPH **163**

ONTARIO AGRICULTURAL COLLEGE. SCHOOL OF ENGINEERING *See* TECHNICAL REPORT - UNIVERSITY OF GUELPH, SCHOOL OF ENGINEERING **1998**

ONTARIO AMATEUR FOOTBALL ASSOCIATION *See* DIRECTORY / ONTARIO AMATEUR FOOTBALL ASSOCIATION **4892**

ONTARIO AMATEUR WRESTLING ASSOCIATION *See* ONTARIO AMATEUR WRESTLING ASSOCIATION RESULTS BOOK **4911**

ONTARIO AMATEUR WRESTLING ASSOCIATION RESULTS BOOK (CN/0822-6806) [10440995] **4911**

ONTARIO AND QUEBEC SALES TAX WITH RELATED TAXES *See* QUEBEC SALES TAX WITH RELATED TAXES **4743**

ONTARIO ANNOTATED FAMILY LAW SERVICE (BOUND EDITION) (CN/0824-4669) [10615558] **3122**

ONTARIO ANNUAL PRACTICE (1973) (CN/0318-3556) [02441728] **3142**

ONTARIO APPEAL CASES (BOUND CUMULATION) (CN/0827-3308) [10971723] **3022**

ONTARIO ARCHAEOLOGICAL SOCIETY *See* ONTARIO ARCHAEOLOGICAL SOCIETY INDEX TO PUBLICATIONS, THE **277**

ONTARIO ARCHAEOLOGICAL SOCIETY INDEX TO PUBLICATIONS, THE (CN) [25064697] **277**

ONTARIO ARCHAEOLOGY (CN/0078-4672) [02530555] **277**

ONTARIO ARENAS ASSOCIATION *See* ONTARIO RECREATION FACILITIES ASSOCIATION **4853**

ONTARIO. ASSEMBLEE LEGISLATIVE. COMITE PERMANENT DES FINANCES ET DES AFFAIRES ECONOMIQUES *See* CONSULTATIONS PREBUDGETAIRES/ COMITE PERMANENT DES FINANCES ET DES AFFAIRES ECONOMIQUES **4719**

ONTARIO ASSOCIATION FOR GEOGRAPHIC AND ENVIRONMENTAL EDUCATION *See* MONOGRAPH / ONTARIO ASSOCIATION GEOGRAPHIC ENVIRONMENTAL EDUCATION, THE **2569**

ONTARIO ASSOCIATION OF ARCHERS. EASTERN ZONE *See* EASTERN ZONE NEWSLETTER - ONTARIO ASSOCIATION OF ARCHERS **4893**

ONTARIO ASSOCIATION OF CERTIFIED ENGINEERING TECHNICIANS AND TECHNOLOGISTS *See* O A C E T T NEWSLETTER **1989**

ONTARIO ASSOCIATION OF CHILDREN'S AID SOCIETIES *See* JOURNAL - ONTARIO ASSOCIATION OF CHILDREN'S AID SOCIETIES **5293**

ONTARIO ASSOCIATION OF SPEECH-LANGUAGE PATHOLOGISTS AND AUDIOLOGISTS *See* MEMBERSHIP DIRECTORY / OSLA **3889**

ONTARIO BIRD BANDING (CN/0475-025X) [02401149] **5619**

ONTARIO BIRDS (CN/0822-3890) [12266681] **5619**

ONTARIO BLUEWATER VISITOR GUIDE (CN/1184-969X) [24690840] **5487**

ONTARIO BRANCH NEWS (CN/0710-345X) [08185714] **4795**

ONTARIO BUDGET (CN/0381-2332) [11722130] **4739**

ONTARIO BUSINESS *CEASED.* (CN/0227-1397) [06516317] **701**

ONTARIO BUSINESS CORPORATIONS ACT WITH REGULATIONS (CCH CANADIAN) (CN/0316-6481) [02247660] **3102**

ONTARIO CAMPUS CULTURE ASSOCIATION *See* NEWSLETTER - ONTARIO CAMPUS CULTURE ASSOCIATION **386**

ONTARIO/CANADA ACCOMMODATIONS (CN/0707-8102) [09476067] **2808**

ONTARIO/CANADA CAMPING (CN) [04087569] **5487**

ONTARIO CHESS NEWS (CN/0712-2195) [08882685] **4864**

ONTARIO COLLEGE NEWSLETTER (CN/0714-444X) [09050404] **1094**

ONTARIO COLLEGE OF PHARMACY *See* O C P, ON CONTINUING PRACTICE **4318**

ONTARIO. COLLEGE RELATIONS COMMISSION *See* ANNUAL REPORT / COLLEGE RELATIONS COMMISSION **1809**

ONTARIO. COMMISSION DE REVISION DE L'AIDE SOCIALE *See* BULLETIN - ONTARIO. SOCIAL ASSISTANCE REVIEW BOARD **5275**

ONTARIO CONSERVATION NEWS (CN/0383-6479) [02918284] 2238, **2201**

ONTARIO CORN PRODUCER (CN/0008-7297) [13917827] **117**

ONTARIO CORPORATION AND INCOME TAX LEGISLATION INCLUDING MINING TAXES AND SMALL BUSINESS DEVELOPMENT CORPORATIONS (CN/0225-1795) [06132326] **701**

ONTARIO. CORPORATIONS TAX BRANCH *See* INFORMATION BULLETIN - CORPORATIONS TAX BRANCH **4732**

ONTARIO COUNCIL BULLETIN (CN/0380-8831) [02141324] **4671**

ONTARIO. COUNCIL FOR FRANCO-ONTARIAN AFFAIRS *See* BULLETIN - CONSEIL DES AFFAIRES FRANCO-ONTARIENNES **4634**

ONTARIO COUNCIL OF RABBIT CLUBS *See* NEWS - ONTARIO COUNCIL OF RABBIT CLUBS **5234**

ONTARIO COUNCIL OF UNIVERSITY LIBRARIES *See* DIRECTORY OF O.C.U.L. LIBRARIES **3207**

ONTARIO CRAFT (CN/0229-1320) [08099349] **374**

ONTARIO CRICKET "PITCH" (CN/1183-4072) [25066422] **4911**

ONTARIO DEMOCRAT, THE (CN/0827-2247) [11802953] **4485**

ONTARIO DENTAL ASSOCIATION *See* ODA SUGGESTED FEE GUIDE FOR GENERAL PRACTITIONERS **1331**

ONTARIO DENTIST (CN/0300-5275) [02092759] **1332**

ONTARIO. DEPARTMENT OF MINES AND NORTHERN AFFAIRS *See* FEDERAL-ONTARIO AEROMAGNETIC SURVEY MAPS **1375**

ONTARIO. DEPT. OF AGRICULTURE AND FOOD. FARM ECONOMICS, COOPERATIVES AND STATISTICS BRANCH. FRUIT AND VEGETABLE PRODUCTION IN ONTARIO, ANNUAL SUMMARY *See* SEASONAL FRUIT & VEGETABLE REPORT (ANNUAL SUMMARY) **2431**

ONTARIO. DIVISION OF FORESTS *See* FOREST RESEARCH INFORMATION PAPER **2381**

ONTARIO. EDUCATION ADMINISTRATION DIVISION. NORTHWESTERN ONTARIO REGIONAL OFFICE *See* DIRECTORY - NORTHWESTERN ONTARIO REGION, MINISTRY OF EDUCATION **1735**

ONTARIO EDUCATION REVIEW (TORONTO. 1982) (CN/0822-6601) [10339536] **1839**

ONTARIO ELECTRICAL CONTRACTOR, THE (CN/0711-3501) [08770485] **2074**

ONTARIO ELEMENTARY AND SECONDARY SCHOOL ENROLMENT PROJECTIONS *CEASED.* (CN/0709-4795) [10634648] **1770**

ONTARIO ENERGY REVIEW (CN/0226-9392) [08407195] **1952**

ONTARIO ENGLISH CATHOLIC TEACHERS' ASSOCIATION *See* REPORTER - ONTARIO ENGLISH CATHOLIC TEACHERS' ASSOCIATION **1903**

ONTARIO. ENVIRONMENTAL APPROVALS BRANCH *See* E A UPDATE SUMMARY **2164**

●ONTARIO ENVIRONMENTAL LEGISLATION (CN/1195-163X) [29533963] **3115**

ONTARIO FAMILY LAW REPORTER (CN/0835-636X) [16570634] **3122**

ONTARIO FARMER (WESTERN ED.) (CN/0831-3865) [14954723] **117**

ONTARIO FEDERATION OF AGRICULTURE *See* MEMBERS' DIGEST - ONTARIO FEDERATION OF AGRICULTURE **107**

ONTARIO FEDERATION OF LABOUR *See* CONSTITUTION - ONTARIO FEDERATION OF LABOUR **1661**

ONTARIO FEDERATION OF LABOUR *See* STEWARDS' LEGISLATIVE HANDBOOK **3154**

ONTARIO FENCER (CN/0228-9075) [08064020] **4911**

ONTARIO FIELD BIOLOGIST, THE *CEASED.* (CN/0078-4834) [01345965] 2201, **467**

ONTARIO FINANCES (CN/0383-5863) [03265033] **4739**

●ONTARIO FISCAL OUTLOOK (CN/1188-2867) [26290746] **4739**

ONTARIO. FISH AND WILDLIFE BRANCH *See* RESOURCE MANAGEMENT REPORT **2204**

ONTARIO FISHERMAN (CN/0822-8736) [10620427] **2309**

ONTARIO FOLKDANCER (CN/0384-5052) [02545611] 2323, **1314**

ONTARIO. FONDATION DE LA RECHERCHE SUR LA TOXICOMANIE *See* CATALOGUE DES PRODUITS EN FRANCAIS **412**

ONTARIO GAZETTE, THE (CN/0030-2937) [02937766] **3022**

ONTARIO GENEALOGICAL SOCIETY *See* DIRECTORY OF SURNAMES - ONTARIO GENEALOGICAL SOCIETY **2445**

ONTARIO GENEALOGICAL SOCIETY *See* NEWSLEAF - ONTARIO GENEALOGICAL SOCIETY **2462**

ONTARIO GENEALOGICAL SOCIETY. LEEDS & GRENVILLE BRANCH *See* NEWS & VIEWS - ONTARIO GENEALOGICAL SOCIETY, LEEDS & GRENVILLE BRANCH **2462**

ONTARIO GENEALOGICAL SOCIETY. QUINTE BRANCH *See* MEMBERSHIP LIST / THE QUINTE BRANCH, O.G.S **2460**

ONTARIO GENEALOGICAL SOCIETY. SEMINAR *See* SEMINAR ANNUAL - ONTARIO GENEALOGICAL SOCIETY **2472**

ONTARIO GENEALOGICAL SOCIETY WATERLOO-WELLINGTON BRANCH *See* BRANCH NOTES / WATERLOO-WELLINGTON BRANCH, ONTARIO GENEALOGICAL SOCIETY **2439**

ONTARIO GEOGRAPHY (CN/0078-4850) [01761294] **2571**

ONTARIO GEOLOGICAL SURVEY *See* PUBLICATIONS PRICE LIST / ONTARIO GEOLOGICAL SURVEY AND MINERAL RESOURCES BRANCH **1392**

ONTARIO GEOLOGICAL SURVEY. GEOSCIENCE DATA CENTRE *See* GENERAL INDEX TO PUBLISHED REPORTS, MINERAL RESOURCES GROUP **2139**

ONTARIO GEOLOGICAL SURVEY MISCELLANEOUS PAPER (CN/0704-2752) [03992260] **1390**

ONTARIO GOLF NEWS (CN/0710-2801) [08332587] **4911**

ONTARIO GOVERNMENT PUBLICATIONS ANNUAL CATALOGUE ... (CN/0227-2628) [07627626] **421**

ONTARIO GOVERNMENT PUBLICATIONS MONTHLY CHECKLIST (CN/0316-1617) [02248383] **4671**

ONTARIO GRADUATE SCHOLARSHIP PROGRAM (CN/0225-2260) [06047962] **1839**

ONTARIO GRAPE GROWER, THE (CN/0380-6057) [02093063] 2370, **2426**

ONTARIO HERITAGE FOUNDATION *See* ANNUAL REPORT--ONTARIO HERITAGE FOUNDATION **2721**

ONTARIO HIGHWAY BRIDGE DESIGN CODE / ONTARIO MINISTRY OF TRANSPORTATION AND COMMUNICATIONS, HIGHWAY ENGINEERING DIVISION (CN) [11708853] **2028**

ONTARIO. HIGHWAY TRANSPORT BOARD *See* ANNUAL REPORT OF THE ONTARIO HIGHWAY TRANSPORT BOARD **5376**

ONTARIO. HISTORICAL PLANNING AND RESEARCH BRANCH. RESEARCH REPORT *See* ARCHAEOLOGICAL RESEARCH REPORT (TORONTO) **257**

ONTARIO HISTORY (CN/0030-2953) [01761296] **2752**

ONTARIO HOSPITALS DIRECTORY (CN/0826-6808) [11712017] **3790**

ONTARIO. HOSPITALS DIVISION. ANNUAL REPORT OF THE HOSPITALS DIVISION, DEPARTMENT OF HEALTH UPON THE ONTARIO MENTAL HOSPITALS AND MENTAL HEALTH SERVICES OF THE PROVINCE OF ONTARIO *See* ANNUAL REPORT OF THE MENTAL HEALTH DIVISION OF THE DEPARTMENT OF HEALTH OF THE PROVINCE OF ONTARIO **4766**

ONTARIO HOTEL AND MOTEL ASSOCIATION *See* MEMBERSHIP DIRECTORY & BUYERS' GUIDE / ONTARIO HOTEL AND MOTEL ASSOCIATION **2807**

ONTARIO HUMAN RIGHTS COMMISSION *See* ANNUAL REPORT OF THE ONTARIO HUMAN RIGHTS COMMISSION **4504**

ONTARIO HYDRO *See* ANNUAL REPORT / ONTARIO HYDRO **2035**

ONTARIO HYDRO *See* ONTARIO HYDRO STATISTICAL YEARBOOK (1973) **4699**

ONTARIO HYDRO STATISTICAL YEARBOOK (1973) (CN/0382-2834) [01791407] 4761, **4699**

ONTARIO INSTITUTE FOR STUDIES IN EDUCATION *See* CURRICULUM SERIES **1892**

ONTARIO INSTITUTE FOR STUDIES IN EDUCATION *See* SYMPOSIUM SERIES **1786**

ONTARIO INSURANCE COMMISSION *See* ANNUAL REPORT - ONTARIO INSURANCE COMMISSION **2873**

ONTARIO JOINT FICTION RESERVE *See* MANUAL & DIRECTORY - ONTARIO JOINT FICTION RESERVE **3229**

ONTARIO JUDO NEWSLETTER (CN/0834-2105) [16221299] **4911**

ONTARIO LABOUR *CEASED.* (CN/0707-5022) [04219744] **1700**

●ONTARIO LABOUR AND EMPLOYMENT LEGISLATION (CN/1195-0196) [30801199] **3153**

ONTARIO LABOUR RELATIONS BOARD *See* ANNUAL REPORT / ONTARIO LABOUR RELATIONS BOARD **3144**

ONTARIO LAND SURVEYOR, THE (CN/0316-2001) [01721221] **2028**

●ONTARIO LANDLORD AND TENANT LEGISLATION (CN/1195-3136) [29592998] **3022**

ONTARIO. LANDS AND WATERS POLICY BRANCH *See* CONSERVATION AUTHORITY DIRECTORY **2190**

ONTARIO LAWYER'S PHONE BOOK, THE (CN/0845-4825) [19931685] **3023**

ONTARIO. LEGISLATIVE ASSEMBLY *See* PROCEEDINGS AT THE OPENING OF THE LEGISLATIVE ASSEMBLY OF THE PROVINCE OF ONTARIO **4675**

ONTARIO. LEGISLATIVE ASSEMBLY. SELECT COMMITTEE ON ONTARIO IN CONFEDERATION *See* OFFICIAL REPORT OF DEBATES (HANSARD) - ONTARIO. LEGISLATIVE ASSEMBLY. SELECT COMMITTEE ON ONTARIO IN CONFEDERATION **4485**

ONTARIO. LEGISLATIVE ASSEMBLY. STANDING COMMITTEE ON REGULATIONS AND OTHER STATUTORY INSTRUMENTS *See* LEGISLATURE OF ONTARIO DEBATES. OFFICIAL REPORT (HANSARD). STANDING COMMITTEE ON REGULATIONS AND OTHER STATUTORY INSTRUMENTS **3002**

ONTARIO. LEGISLATIVE ASSEMBLY. STANDING COMMITTEE ON RESOURCES DEVELOPMENT *See* HANSARD OFFICIAL REPORT OF DEBATES / LEGISLATIVE ASSEMBLY OF ONTARIO, STANDING COMMITTEE ON RESOURCES DEVELOPMENT **4654**

ONTARIO. LEGISLATIVE ASSEMBLY. STANDING COMMITTEE ON SOCIAL DEVELOPMENT *See* HANSARD, OFFICIAL REPORT OF DEBATES / LEGISLATIVE ASSEMBLY OF ONTARIO, STANDING COMMITTEE ON SOCIAL DEVELOPMENT **4654**

ONTARIO. LEGISLATIVE ASSEMBLY. STANDING COMMITTEE ON THE OMBUDSMAN *See* HANSARD OFFICIAL REPORT OF DEBATES **4654**

ONTARIO LIBRARY SERVICE ESCARPMENT *See* ONTARIO LIBRARY SERVICE ESCARPMENT : DIRECTORY **3239**

ONTARIO LIBRARY SERVICE ESCARPMENT : DIRECTORY (CN/0820-537X) [16728269] **3239**

ONTARIO — Alphabetical Title Index

ONTARIO LIBRARY SERVICE, NIPIGON *See* TALKING BOOKS (THUNDER BAY) **4833**

ONTARIO LIBRARY SERVICE, NORTH *See* NORTHERN ONTARIO CATALOG **3237**

ONTARIO LIBRARY SERVICE, NORTH *See* MAILBOX LIBRARY SERVICE **3229**

ONTARIO LIBRARY SERVICE, RIDEAU *See* DIRECTORY / ONTARIO LIBRARY SERVICE, RIDEAU **3208**

ONTARIO LUPUS ASSOCIATION *See* ONTARIO LUPUS ASSOCIATION NEWSLETTER (1985) **3806**

ONTARIO LUPUS ASSOCIATION NEWSLETTER (1985) (CN/0827-7389) [14878149] **3806**

ONTARIO MANUFACTURING & DIVERSIFICATION OPPORTUNITIES *See* MANUFACTURING + MARKETING OPPORTUNITIES; BULLETIN **3484**

ONTARIO MATHEMATICS GAZETTE (CN/0030-3011) [02572692] **1770**, **3525**

ONTARIO MEDICAL REVIEW (CN/0030-302X) [02093170] **3624**

ONTARIO MEDICAL TECHNOLOGIST / ONTARIO SOCIETY OF MEDICAL TECHNOLOGISTS (CN/0228-877X) [07888606] **3624**

ONTARIO MEDICINE (CN/0712-6689) [09547384] **3916**

●ONTARIO MENNONITE HISTORY (CN/1192-5515) [29970244] **4983**

ONTARIO. MENTAL HEALTH DIVISION *See* ANNUAL REPORT OF THE MENTAL HEALTH DIVISION OF THE DEPARTMENT OF HEALTH OF THE PROVINCE OF ONTARIO **4766**

ONTARIO MILK PRODUCER (CN/0030-3038) [01641803] **197**

ONTARIO. MINISTERE DES SERVICES SOCIAUX ET COMMUNAUTAIRES *See* NOUVELLES - ONTARIO. MINISTERE DES SERVICES SOCIAUX ET COMMUNAUTAIRES **5299**

ONTARIO. MINISTRY OF AGRICULTURE AND FOOD *See* NEWSLETTER - ONTARIO MINISTRY OF AGRICULTURE AND FOOD **112**

ONTARIO. MINISTRY OF AGRICULTURE AND FOOD. ECONOMICS BRANCH *See* SEASONAL FRUIT AND VEGETABLE REPORT **133**

ONTARIO. MINISTRY OF AGRICULTURE AND FOOD. ECONOMICS BRANCH *See* SEASONAL FRUIT & VEGETABLE REPORT (ANNUAL SUMMARY) **2431**

ONTARIO. MINISTRY OF AGRICULTURE AND FOOD. NEWSLETTER *See* AGRICULTURAL NEWSLETTER (SUDBURY) **50**

ONTARIO. MINISTRY OF AGRICULTURE AND FOOD STATISTICS SECTION *See* AGRICULTURAL STATISTICS FOR ONTARIO **150**

ONTARIO. MINISTRY OF CITIZENSHIP *See* ANNUAL REPORT / MINISTRY OF CITIZENSHIP **4627**

ONTARIO. MINISTRY OF COLLEGES AND UNIVERSITIES *See* NATIVE STUDIES IN COLLEGES AND UNIVERSITIES **2268**

ONTARIO. MINISTRY OF COLLEGES AND UNIVERSITIES *See* REPORT OF THE MINISTRY OF COLLEGES AND UNIVERSITIES **1844**

ONTARIO. MINISTRY OF COLLEGES AND UNIVERSITIES *See* ONTARIO GRADUATE SCHOLARSHIP PROGRAM **1839**

ONTARIO. MINISTRY OF COMMUNITY AND SOCIAL SERVICES *See* NEWS - ONTARIO. MINISTRY OF COMMUNITY AND SOCIAL SERVICES **5298**

ONTARIO. MINISTRY OF CULTURE AND COMMNICATIONS *See* ANNUAL REPORT - MINISTRY OF CULTURE AND COMMUNICATIONS (TORONTO) **1149**

ONTARIO. MINISTRY OF EDUCATION *See* RAPPORT DU MINISTRE DE L'EDUCATION (TORONTO) **1776**

ONTARIO. MINISTRY OF EDUCATION *See* EDUCATION FUNDING MODEL, THE **1739**

ONTARIO. MINISTRY OF ENERGY *See* MEDIUM-TERM PLANNING GUIDELINES **1950**

ONTARIO. MINISTRY OF GOVERNMENT SERVICES *See* ANNUAL REPORT - MINISTRY OF GOVERNMENT SERVICES **4627**

ONTARIO. MINISTRY OF HOUSING *See* ANNUAL REPORT - MINISTRY OF HOUSING (TORONTO. 1986) **2814**

ONTARIO. MINISTRY OF INDUSTRY AND TOURISM *See* ONTARIO/CANADA CAMPING **5487**

ONTARIO. MINISTRY OF LABOUR. RESEARCH BRANCH *See* WAGES, HOURS OF WORK AND OVERTIME PAY PROVISIONS IN SELECTED INDUSTRIES. ONTARIO **1717**

ONTARIO. MINISTRY OF MUNICIPAL AFFAIRS *See* ANNUAL REPORT **4626**

ONTARIO. MINISTRY OF NATURAL RESOURCES *See* FOREST RESEARCH REPORT **2381**

ONTARIO. MINISTRY OF NATURAL RESOURCES *See* SUMMARY OF THE HUNTING REGULATIONS (TORONTO) **4879**

ONTARIO. MINISTRY OF NATURAL RESOURCES *See* STATISTICS - ONTARIO MINISTRY OF NATURAL RESOURCES **2185**

ONTARIO. MINISTRY OF THE ATTORNEY GENERAL *See* ANNUAL REPORT - MINISTRY OF THE ATTORNEY GENERAL (TORONTO) **3139**

ONTARIO. MINISTRY OF THE ENVIRONMENT. RESEARCH AND TECHNOLOGY BRANCH *See* REPORT ON ENVIRONMENTAL RESEARCH, TECHNOLOGY DEVELOPMENT AND AWARENESS ACTIVITIES **2181**

ONTARIO. MINISTRY OF TOURISM AND RECREATION *See* ANNUAL REPORT - MINISTRY OF TOURISM AND RECREATION (TORONTO) **5461**

ONTARIO. MINISTRY OF TRANSPORTATION *See* INSIDE ROUTES **5384**

ONTARIO. MINISTRY OF TRANSPORTATION *See* ANNUAL REPORT / ONTARIO, MINISTRY OF TRANSPORTATION **5376**

ONTARIO. MINISTRY OF TREASURY AND ECONOMICS *See* ONTARIO BUDGET **4739**

ONTARIO. MINISTRY OF TREASURY, ECONOMICS AND INTERGOVERNMENTAL AFFAIRS. LOCAL GOVERNMENT ORGANIZATION BRANCH *See* STATUS REPORT - COUNTY RESTRUCTURING STUDIES PROGRAM **4688**

ONTARIO. MINISTRY OF TREASURY, ECONOMICS AND INTERGOVERNMENTAL AFFAIRS. MUNICIPAL PLANNING & DEVELOPMENT BRANCH *See* ONTARIO POPULATION STATISTICS **4562**

ONTARIO MOTOR COACH ASSOCIATION *See* OMCA RESOURCE GUIDE **1620**

ONTARIO MUNICIPAL ACT (CN/1195-0188) [29533958] **3023**

ONTARIO. MUNICIPAL BOARD *See* ONTARIO MUNICIPAL BOARD REPORTS **3023**

ONTARIO MUNICIPAL BOARD REPORTS (CN/0318-7527) [02442928] **3023**

●ONTARIO MUSEUM ANNUAL (CN/1188-9578) [27165351] **4095**

ONTARIO MUSEUM ASSOCIATION *See* ONTARIO MUSEUM ANNUAL **4095**

ONTARIO NEST RECORDS SCHEME (CN/0228-0787) [07295276] **5593**

ONTARIO NEWS BULLETIN / WCTU (CN/0229-4540) [08323946] **4983**

ONTARIO. NORTHWESTERN ONTARIO FOREST TECHNOLOGY DEVELOPMENT UNIT *See* WORKPLAN (TORONTO) **2210**

ONTARIO NUMISMATIST, THE (CN/0048-1815) [02093197] **2783**

ONTARIO NURSING HOME JOURNAL *CEASED.* (CN/0829-6340) [13770196] **3790**

ONTARIO NURSING HOMES (CN/0712-9971) [08808265] **3790**

ONTARIO. OFFICE OF THE OMBUDSMAN *See* ANNUAL REPORT - OMBUDSMAN. ONTARIO (1984) **4629**

ONTARIO OUT OF DOORS (CN/0707-3178) [04635225] **4876**

ONTARIO OUTDOOR GUIDE & CALENDAR (CN/0827-2352) [11734409] **4876**

ONTARIO OUTDOORSMAN (CN/0823-6453) [09951396] **4876**

ONTARIO PETROLEUM INSTITUTE. CONFERENCE *See* ANNUAL CONFERENCE / THE ONTARIO PETROLEUM INSTITUTE **4249**

ONTARIO PIPELINE (CN/0380-1624) [02093634] **5537**

●ONTARIO PLANNING ACT (CN/1195-017X) [30013243] **3023**

ONTARIO POPULATION STATISTICS (CN) [01791845] **4562**

ONTARIO. PROGRAMME D'EDUCATION SCOLAIRE SUR LES PECHES *See* BULLETIN DU PROGRAMME D'EDUCATION SCOLAIRE SUR LES PECHES **4870**

ONTARIO PSYCHOLOGICAL ASSOCIATION *See* DIRECTORY - ONTARIO PSYCHOLOGICAL ASSOCIATION **4585**

ONTARIO PSYCHOLOGIST, THE (CN/0030-3054) [01042296] **4606**

ONTARIO PUBLIC SCHOOL MEN TEACHERS' FEDERATION *See* NEWSTODAY **1867**

ONTARIO PUBLIC SCHOOL TEACHERS' FEDERATION *See* HANDBOOK : CONSTITUTION, DIRECTORY, BYLAWS, POLICIES, BUDGET, LEGISLATION / ONTARIO PUBLIC SCHOOL FEDERATION **1864**

ONTARIO PUBLIC SECTOR (CN/0841-0798) [I08410798] **4671**

ONTARIO RACING COMMISSION *See* RULES OF STANDARDBRED RACING **2802**

ONTARIO RACING COMMISSION *See* RULES OF THOROUGHBRED RACING **2802**

●ONTARIO REAL ESTATE LEGISLATION (CN/1195-3152) [29970381] **3023**

ONTARIO RECREATION FACILITIES ASSOCIATION (CN) **4853**

ONTARIO RECYCLING UPDATE (CN/0823-6143) [09859909] **2238**

ONTARIO REPORTS (1963) (CN/0030-3089) [01714025] **3023**

ONTARIO RETAIL GASOLINE AND AUTOMOTIVE SERVICE ASSOCIATION *See* O R G A NEWS **4267**

ONTARIO RETAIL GASOLINE AND AUTOMOTIVE SERVICE ASSOCIATION *See* O R G A NEWSLINE **5422**

ONTARIO REVIEW (WINDSOR, ONT.) (CN/0316-4055) [02240867] **3420**

ONTARIO SCHOOL COUNSELLORS' ASSOCIATION *See* ONTARIO SCHOOL COUNSELLORS' ASSOCIATION REVIEW **1770**

ONTARIO SCHOOL COUNSELLORS' ASSOCIATION *See* BYLAWS & DIRECTORY / ONTARIO SCHOOL COUNSELLORS' ASSOCIATION **1861**

ONTARIO SCHOOL COUNSELLORS' ASSOCIATION REVIEW (CN/0315-8535) [02093806] **1770**

ONTARIO SECURITIES LEGISLATION (CN/0316-6031) [02247598] **701**

ONTARIO SHARE AND DEPOSIT INSURANCE CORPORATION *See* ANNUAL REPORT / ONTARIO SHARE AND DEPOSIT INSURANCE CORPORATION **2873**

●ONTARIO SMALL CLAIMS COURT PRACTICE (CN/1191-159X) [25882864] **3023**

ONTARIO SNOWMOBILER (CN/0383-7009) [02547364] **4911**

ONTARIO SOCIAL ACTION NEWSLETTER, THE (CN/1187-0389) [25066266] **5300**

ONTARIO. SOCIAL ASSISTANCE REVIEW BOARD *See* BULLETIN - ONTARIO. SOCIAL ASSISTANCE REVIEW BOARD **4635**

ONTARIO. SOCIAL ASSISTANCE REVIEW BOARD *See* SUMMARIES OF DECISIONS / SOCIAL ASSISTANCE REVIEW BOARD **5312**

ONTARIO SPECTRUM (CN/0227-4175) [07822683] **1839**

ONTARIO SPORTSCENE (CN/0225-5782) [06141457] **4911**

ONTARIO. TASK FORCE HYDRO *See* REPORT - TASK FORCE HYDRO **4682**

ONTARIO. TAXATION AND FISCAL POLICY BRANCH *See* ONTARIO FINANCES **4739**

ONTARIO TEACHERS' FEDERATION *See* ONTARIO TEACHERS' FEDERATION SUBMISSION TO THE CABINET, THE **1770**

ONTARIO TEACHERS' FEDERATION SUBMISSION TO THE CABINET, THE (CN/0225-7645) [06461332] **1770**

ONTARIO TECHNOLOGIST, THE (CN/0380-1969) [02095414] **5136**

ONTARIO TRAFFIC SAFETY (CN/0702-8040) [03680770] **5442**

ONTARIO TREE IMPROVEMENT AND FOREST BIOMASS INSTITUTE *See* FOREST RESEARCH (TORONTO) **2381**

ONTARIO VACATION FARM ASSOCIATION *See* ONTARIO VACATION FARMS **5487**

ONTARIO VACATION FARMS (CN/0712-1636) [08651919] **5487**

ONTARIO VETERINARY ASSOCIATION. DIRECTORY *See* DIRECTORY / COLLEGE OF VETERINARIANS OF ONTARIO. [DISKETTE] **5509**

ONTARIO WAGE DEVELOPMENTS, COLLECTIVE BARGAINING SETTLEMENTS (CN/0848-7049) [23455469] **1700**

ONTARIO WASTE MANAGEMENT CORPORATION *See* OWMC EXCHANGE, THE **2238**

ONTARIO. WATER RESOURCES BRANCH *See* WATER WELL RECORDS FOR ONTARIO **5548**

ONTARIO WATER SKIER, THE (CN/0226-5702) [06562785] **4911**

ONTARIO. WOMEN'S BUREAU *See* WOMEN IN THE LABOUR FORCE **5570**

ONTARIO. WORKERS' COMPENSATION APPEALS TRIBUNAL *See* WCAT IN FOCUS **3073**

ONTARIO WRESTLER (CN/0226-1561) [06295862] **4911**

ONTARIO. YOUTH FISHERIES EDUCATION PROGRAM *See* YOUTH FISHERIES EDUCATION PROGRAM : [NEWSLETTER] **2316**

●ONTARIO'S ACCESS AND PRIVACY LEGISLATION, AN ANNOTATION (CN/1189-3419) [25796750] **3023**

ONTHEBUS (LOS ANGELES, CALIF.) (US/1043-884X) [19595753] **3420**

ONTOGENEZ (RU/0475-1450) [05298605] **467**

ONTONAGON HERALD (US) **5693**

ONU CRONICA MENSUAL (US/0472-3724) [06272466] **2911, 4530**

ONUL UI CHAEK (KO) [11063075] **2661**

ONUL UI HANGUK (JA) [08134051] **2661**

ONUL UI HANGUK (SEOUL, KOREA : 1983) (KO) [09534600] **2507**

ONZE *See* ONZE MONDIAL **5253**

ONZE LUCHTMACHT (NE) [06470283] **31**

ONZE MONDIAL (FR) **5253**

ONZE TAAL (AMSTERDAM, NETHERLANDS) (NE) [09040257] **3308**

ONZE VOGELS (NE) [06463920] **5619**

OOGST *CEASED*. (NE/0923-0769) [22175154] **180**

OOMPHALOSKEPSIS (CN/0229-6047) [08036509] **2542**

OOP KISUL (KO) [08224139] **2310**

OOPS MESSENGER (US/1055-6400) [22538101] **1280**

OOPS REPORT, THE (UK/0953-5349) [I09535349] **1280**

OOQ, OCCUPATIONAL OUTLOOK QUARTERLY (US/0029-7968) [01715748] **4207**

OOR (NE) [11097747] **4143**

OP CIT (IT/0030-3305) [04317121] **305, 361**

OP. CIT. : BOLETIN DEL CENTRO DE INVESTIGACIONES HISTORICAS (PR) [14038774] **2625**

OP. CIT. (MEXICO CITY, MEXICO) (MX) [08339654] **4143**

●OP-ED (BELLINGHAM, WASH.) (US/1061-9046) [25487671] **2542**

OP-JOURNAL (GW/0178-1715) [I01781715] **3624**

OP PAD (DEN HAAG) (NE/0168-3845) [I01683845] **4876, 5487**

OPA PRATIQUE (FR/0983-8201) [I09838201] 3950, **3890**

●OPAC DIRECTORY (US/1066-1425) [26870131] **1198**

OPADY ATMOSFERYCZNE (PL) [04402162] **1433**

OPAL, THE *CEASED*. (CN/0030-3062) [02096092] **5367**

OPASQUIA TIMES (CN/0707-5448) [04746850] **5791**

OPAVA, CZECHOSLOVAK REPUBLIC. SLEZSKE MUZEUM *See* CASOPIS SLEZSKEHO MUZEA. SERIE C. DENDROLOGIE **506**

OPCAO (PO) [03111644] **434**

OPCS MONITOR. ADOPTIONS (UK) [05063860] **4555**

OPCS MONITOR. BIRTHS AND DEATHS (UK) [05065376] **4555**

OPCS MONITOR. BIRTHS BY BIRTH PLACE OF PARENT (UK) [05065418] **4555**

OPCS MONITOR. CENSUS MONITORS (UK/0144-5537) [08986317] **4555**

OPCS MONITOR. CONGENITAL MALFORMATIONS (UK) [05065470] **4555**

OPCS MONITOR. DEATHS BY CAUSE (UK) [05065540] **4555**

OPCS MONITOR. DEATHS FROM ACCIDENTS *CEASED*. (UK) [08618543] **4555**

OPCS MONITOR. INFANT AND PERINATAL MORTALITY (UK) [05065600] **4555**

OPCS MONITOR. INFECTIOUS DISEASES (UK) [08618548] **4555**

OPCS MONITOR. LEGAL ABORTIONS / OFFICE OF POPULATION CENSUS & SURVEYS (UK/0953-3362) [05065651] **4555**

OPCS MONITOR. MID-YEAR ESTIMATES OF THE POPULATION OF NEW COMMONWEALTH AND PAKISTANI ETHNIC ORIGIN (UK) [05065700] **4555**

OPCS MONITOR. POPULATION PROJECTIONS (UK) [08618557] **4555**

OPCS MONITOR. REGISTRAR GENERAL'S WEEKLY RETURN FOR ENGLAND AND WALES (UK) [08618562] **4555**

OPD *CEASED*. (US) [27988685] **4214**

OPD CHEMICAL BUYERS DIRECTORY (US/0276-539X) [04740196] **1027**

OPD RESTAURO : QUADERNI DELL OPIFICIO DELLE PIETRE DURE E LABORATORI DI RESTAURO DI FIRENZE / MINISTERO PER I BENI CULTURALI E AMBIENTALI, OPIFICIO DELLE PIETRE DURE E LABORATORIO DI RESTAURO DI FIRENZE (IT) [16160584] **361**

OPEC BULLETIN (AU/0474-6279) [05304804] **4270**

OPEC FUND FOR INTERNATIONAL DEVELOPMENT *See* ANNUAL REPORT / THE OPEC FUND **2907**

OPEC FUND NEWSLETTER (AU) [09993644] **1511**

OPEC MEMBER COUNTRY PROFILES (AU) [10092042] **1620**

OPEC REVIEW (US/0277-0180) [05203697] **4270**

OPELIKA AUBURN NEWS (US/1044-7539) [11712983] **5627**

OPEN (NE/0030-3372) [01761308] **3239**

OPEN CHANNEL (US) **1198**

●OPEN COMPUTING (US/1078-2370) [30861496] **1264**

OPEN DEUR - MINISTERIE VAN NEDERLANDSE KULTUUR (BE/0030-3399) [I00303399] **327**

OPEN DOOR (BRITISH COLUMBIA LIBRARY TRUSTEES ASSOCIATION) (CN/0709-8634) [08010254] **3239**

OPEN DOOR (LEXINGTON, KY.), THE (US/0732-6319) [08398985] **1102**

OPEN DOOR (RALEIGH) (US/0030-3410) [01681074] **1839**

OPEN DOORS (NEW YORK) (US/0078-5172) [01773892] **1796**

OPEN DOORS (SANTA ANA, CALIF.) (US/8756-5234) [08879846] **4983**

OPEN EARTH *CEASED*. (UK/0141-3619) [04616101] **1359**

OPEN ECONOMIES REVIEW (NE/0923-7992) [22223619] **1511**

OPEN ENTRIES (US/0739-6848) [09792034] **1915**

OPEN-FILE REPORT (ATLANTA, GA.) (US/0277-948X) [07382812] **1390**

OPEN-FILE REPORT - BUREAU OF MINES (US) [01918812] **2147**

OPEN FILE REPORT MICROFORM / U.S. GEOLOGICAL SURVEY (US/0196-1497) [07496646] **1390**

OPEN FILE REPORT (SOCORRO, N.M.) (US/0731-5066) [06396530] **2147**

OPEN HANDS (US/0888-8833) [13739097] **4983, 2795**

OPEN HOUSE (US) 305, **2902**

OPEN HOUSE INTERNATIONAL (NE/0168-2601) [10416572] **305**

●OPEN INFORMATION SYSTEMS (US/1068-5553) [26327920] **1248**

OPEN INTEREST (CN/0707-0926) [04631874] **910**

●OPEN INTEREST/ THE TORONTO STOCK EXCHANGE (CN) [25540695] **910**

OPEN LEARNING (UK/0268-0513) [13247203] **1801**

OPEN LETTER GEELONG (AT/1035-4727) [I10354727] **1883**

OPEN LETTER (TORONTO) (CN/0048-1939) [02096108] **3420**

OPEN MIND (COLOMBO, SRI LANKA) (CE) [19367716] **2507**

OPEN MINDS (US/1043-3880) [19484130] **4606**

OPEN READING (US) [03388140] **3420**

OPEN SEASON GUIDE (US/1046-8013) [20538872] **2889**

OPEN SPACE (OPEN SPACES SOCIETY, GREAT BRITAIN) (UK) [09055558] **2201**

OPEN SQUARES, THE (US/0891-3447) [11990634] **1314**

OPEN SYSTEMS COMMUNICATION (US/0741-2851) [10144314] 1248, **1243**

OPEN SYSTEMS DATA TRANSFER (US/0741-286X) [10135478] 1248, **1243**

●OPEN SYSTEMS PRODUCTS DIRECTORY (US/1069-0409) [27695783] **1198**

OPEN SYSTEMS REPORT (US/1052-701X) [22354515] 1248, **1243**

OPEN SYSTEMS (SUTTON, SURREY, ENGLAND) *CEASED*. (UK/0960-9911) [22619886] **1243**

●OPEN SYSTEMS TODAY (US/1061-0839) [25178011] **1248**

OPEN SYSTEMS TODAY (US) [25495400] **1198**

OPEN UNIVERSITY *See* POSTGRADUATE PROSPECTUS AND STUDENT HANDBOOK **1842**

OPEN UNIVERSITY *See* BA DEGREE HANDBOOK **1811**

OPEN UNIVERSITY *See* GUIDE FOR APPLICANTS FOR UNDERGRADUATE COURSES **1826**

OPEN UNIVERSITY *See* COURSES HANDBOOK - THE OPEN UNIVERSITY **1818**

OPEN WHEEL (US/0279-0254) [07444880] **4911**

OPEN WINDOWS (US/0162-4296) [04165909] **4983**

OPEN WORD (GY) [22410298] **5802**

OPENBAAR BESTUUR (NE) **4671**

OPENBAAR KUNSTBEZIT IN VLAANDEREN (BE) 305, **327**

OPENBAAR VERVOER (NE/0030-3461) [06469134] **5389**

OPENING (AT/0156-9600) [I01569600] **1770**

OPENING EDUCATION FOR CHILDREN AND YOUTH *See* JOURNAL OF CHILDREN AND YOUTH **1756**

OPENING NIGHT ON BROADWAY (US) **5367**

OPENINGS : JOB OPPORTUNITIES FOR SCHOLARS OF RELIGION (US) [13107658] **4208**

OPENMIND (LONDON. 1983) (UK/0265-511X) [11252126] **4795**

OPER (GW) [03133348] **4143**

OPER HEUTE (GW) [06001705] **4143**

OPER UND BALLETT IM FILM (AU) [03765654] 4075, **4143**

OPER UND KONZERT (MUNCHEN) (GW/0030-3518) [06469136] **4143**

OPERA AMERICA NEWSLINE (US/1062-7243) [25006921] 4143, **386**

OPERA ANNUAL U.S (US/0899-3645) [18077659] **4143**

OPERA AUSTRALIA (AT) [15710668] **4143**

OPERA BOTANICA (DK/0078-5237) [01644224] **520**

OPERA BOTANICA BELGICA (BE/0775-9592) [I07759592] **520**

OPERA BOTANICA SEZIONE A (IT) [02391232] **520**

OPERA CANADA (CN/0030-3577) [06534367] **4143**

OPERA COMPANION, THE *CEASED*. (US/0889-9398) [09287861] **4143**

OPERA CORCONTICA (XR/0474-2559) [04152748] **4170**

OPERA FANATIC (US/0891-3757) [14815944] **4143**

OPERA INTERNATIONAL (FR) [06682721] **4143**

OPERA JOURNAL, THE (US/0030-3585) [01761319] **4143**

OPERA (LONDON) (UK/0030-3526) [02574662] **4143**

OPERA MILANO. 1987, L' (IT/1121-4112) [I11214112] **4143**

OPERA MONTHLY (US/0897-6554) [17577755] 386, **4143**

OPERA-MUSICAL THEATER (US/8756-856X) [04799307] **4143**

OPERA NEWS (US/0030-3607) [01590631] **4143**

OPERA NOW (UK/0958-501X) [22220823] **4144**

OPERA QUARTERLY, THE (US/0736-0053) [09068655] **4144**

OPERA REVIEW (US/0146-6062) [03408706] **4144**

OPERA SCENE (US) **4144**

OPERA SCENE (DURHAM, N.C.) (US/1056-6791) [23829629] 4144, **386**

OPERA SCHEDULES *See* WORLD OPERA SCHEDULE **4159**

OPERATEUR ECONOMIQUE (MONTHLY) *CEASED*. (NG) [19231105] **1577**

OPERATING & TRAFFIC STATISTICS *See* ANALYSIS OF CLASS 1 RAILROADS **5400**

OPERATING BUDGET AS ADOPTED BY THE METROPOLITAN COUNCIL ON ... (CN) [12018172] **4739**

OPERATING BUDGET REQUEST FOR THE ILLINOIS PUBLIC COMMUNITY COLLEGE SYSTEM (US) [07537537] **1839**

OPERATING BUDGET - TEXAS. STATE PURCHASING AND GENERAL SERVICES COMMISSION (US/0732-0493) [07940322] **4671**

OPERATING COSTS OF TRUCKS IN CANADA (CN/0831-8212) [11773522] **5389**

OPERATING EXPERIENCE WITH NUCLEAR POWER STATIONS IN MEMBER STATES (AU) [02441256] **2158**

OPERATING FINANCE REPORT FOR ILLINOIS PUBLIC COMMUNITY COLLEGES *CEASED*. (US/0361-9060) [02246662] **1839**

OPERATING — Alphabetical Title Index

OPERATING FINANCIAL DATA FOR ILLINOIS PUBLIC JUNIOR COLLEGES (US/0093-4208) [01792525] **1839**

OPERATING INSTITUTIONS OF HIGHER EDUCATION IN PENNSYLVANIA LEGALLY AUTHORIZED TO GRANT DEGREES (US) [08834658] **1839**

OPERATING INSTRUCTIONS HANDBOOK FOR LABOR CERTIFICATION PROGRAM FOR IMMIGRANT WORKERS. CHAPTER 1 (US) [04178427] **1700**

OPERATING PERFORMANCE REPORT FOR THE PHCP WHOLESALE/DISTRIBUTION INDUSTRY. PVF DISTRIBUTING INDUSTRY (US/1045-6198) [12727582] **2607**

OPERATING PLAN - STATE LIBRARY OF OHIO (US/0097-823X) [02427898] **3239**

OPERATING RATIOS OF SECOND DISTRICT MEMBER BANKS (US/0091-2565) [01786661] **802**

OPERATING REPORT, NEW YORK STATE COMPTROLLER : THE TAXPAYERS' WATCHDOG (US) [09747819] **4739**

OPERATING RESULTS. MEN'S RETAIL CLOTHING STORES (CN/0829-7401) [05931622] 1086, **1088**

OPERATING RESULTS. RETAIL DRUG STORES (CN/0829-741X) [04747253] 4318, **4334**

OPERATING RESULTS. RETAIL FLORISTS (CN/0833-2274) [19729511] **2435**

OPERATING RESULTS. RETAIL JEWELLERY STORES (CN/0833-2282) [11966585] **2915**

OPERATING REVENUE AND EXPENSE STATISTICS CLASS A AND B PRIVATE GAS UTILITIES IN WISCONSIN (US/0098-3225) [02239805] 4761, **4699**

OPERATING ROOM PRODUCT DIRECTORY See O.R. PRODUCT DIRECTORY / ASSOCIATION OF OPERATING ROOM NURSES **3970**

OPERATING ROOM PRODUCT DIRECTORY : ORPD / ASSOCIATION OF OPERATING ROOM NURSES, INC (US) [20544882] **3624**

OPERATING ROOM RISK MANAGEMENT (US) **3624**

OPERATING SECTION PROCEEDINGS (US/0362-4994) [02293181] **4271**

OPERATING SURVEY OF CANADIAN RETAILING (CN/0824-6769) [09929038] **956**

OPERATING SYSTEMS REVIEW (US/0163-5980) [01460456] **1248**

OPERATING YEAR ANNUAL REPORT (IT) [19765379] **5422**

OPERATION AND EFFECT OF THE DOMESTIC INTERNATIONAL SALES CORPORATION LEGISLATION ... ANNUAL REPORT, THE (US/0740-3488) [04161502] **848**

OPERATION AND EFFECTS OF THE GENERALIZED SYSTEM OF PREFERENCES (US) [08527338] **848**

OPERATION LIBERTE (CN/0706-9294) [04518981] **4511**

OPERATIONAL COSTINGS FOR TRANSPORT MANAGEMENT (UK) 881, **5389**

OPERATIONAL GEOGRAPHER, THE *CEASED.* (CN/0822-4838) [10216654] **2571**

OPERATIONAL HYDROLOGY REPORT (SZ/0379-1335) [01791337] **1417**

● OPERATIONAL REVIEW ... FARM DEBT REVIEW BOARDS (CN/1189-7627) [30097707] **117**

OPERATIONS & PRODUCTION MANAGEMENT ABSTRACTS (UK) 2099, **2006**

OPERATIONS BUDGET / STATE OF UTAH (US) [08968890] **4739**

OPERATIONS FORESTIERES ET DE SCIERIE (CN/0030-3631) [02096135] **2390**

OPERATIONS FORUM (US/0887-2104) [11117140] **2238**

OPERATIONS INSTRUCTIONS, REGULATIONS, AND INTERPRETATIONS (US) [03715192] **1920**

OPERATIONS MANAGEMENT REVIEW (US/0734-1458) [08686970] **881**

OPERATIONS MANUAL OF THE NATIONAL ASSOCIATION OF REALTORS (US/0147-1929) [03113900] **4842**

OPERATIONS OF BANK PEMBANGUNAN INDONESIA (IO) [02242604] **802**

OPERATIONS REPORT - STATE CORPORATION COMMISSION, DIVISION OF AERONAUTICS (US/0147-7730) [03224964] **31**

OPERATIONS REPORT / VIRGINIA DEPARTMENT OF AVIATION (US) [08212867] **31**

OPERATIONS RESEARCH (US/0030-364X) [02394608] **3525**

OPERATIONS RESEARCH LETTERS (NE/0167-6377) [08254896] **5136**

OPERATIONS RESEARCH/MANAGEMENT SCIENCE (US/0030-3658) [01761326] 1198, **1209**

OPERATIONS RESEARCH/MANAGEMENT SCIENCE YEARBOOK (US/0473-0496) [02265496] **881**

OPERATIONS RESEARCH SOCIETY OF AMERICA See PUBLICATIONS IN OPERATIONS RESEARCH **5235**

OPERATIVE DENTISTRY (US/0361-7734) [02111976] **1332**

OPERATIVE DENTISTRY. SUPPLEMENT (US/0163-3473) [04336644] **1332**

OPERATIVE (NEW YORK, N.Y.) (US/0737-2183) [09330082] **2542**

OPERATIVE ORTHOPADIE UND TRAUMATOLOGIE (GW/0934-6694) [I09346694] **3883**

OPERATIVE ORTHOPAEDICS UPDATES (US/1056-7097) [23823967] **3883**

OPERATIVE TECHNIQUES IN ORTHOPAEDICS (US/1048-6666) [21015588] **3883**

OPERATIVE TECHNIQUES IN OTOLARYNGOLOGY--HEAD AND NECK SURGERY (US/1043-1810) [19336708] **3890**

● OPERATIVE TECHNIQUES IN PLASTIC AND RECONSTRUCTIVE SURGERY (US/1071-0949) [28551955] **3971**

● OPERATIVE TECHNIQUES IN SPORTS MEDICINE (US/1060-1872) [24890394] **3955**

OPERATOR THEORY, ADVANCES AND APPLICATIONS (SZ) [06908827] **3526**

OPERATORE SANITARIO, L' (IT/0392-5153) [07792012] **3624**

OPERE D'ARTE CONTEMPORANEA : CATALOGHI E LISTINI (IT) **327**

OPERNHAUS ZURICH See JAHRBUCH **4124**

OPERNWELT (GW/0030-3690) [01645860] **4144**

OPETTAJIEN PALVELUSSUHTEEN EHDOT (FI) [18974068] **1902**

OPFLOW (US/0149-8029) [03562132] **5537**

OPHEA JOURNAL (CN/0840-822X) [19491474] **1857**

OPHELIA (DK/0078-5326) [01624094] 2220, **556**

OPHTALMOLOGIE E71 (FR) **3877**

OPHTALMOLOGIE (PARIS) (FR/0989-3105) [19022610] **3877**

OPHTHALMIC & PHYSIOLOGICAL OPTICS (UK/0275-5408) [07159339] **4216**

OPHTHALMIC DRUG FACTS (US/1043-1780) [19335022] **3877**

OPHTHALMIC GENETICS (NE) **550**

OPHTHALMIC LITERATURE (UK/0030-3720) [01714243] **3877**

OPHTHALMIC OBSERVER (US/0743-6378) [10625130] **3877**

OPHTHALMIC PAEDIATRICS AND GENETICS (NE/0167-6784) [08501674] 3907, **550**

OPHTHALMIC PLASTIC AND RECONSTRUCTIVE SURGERY (US/0740-9303) [10038007] 3971, **3877**

OPHTHALMIC PRACTICE (CN/0832-9869) [16888276] **3877**

OPHTHALMIC RESEARCH (SZ/0030-3747) [01761331] **3877**

OPHTHALMIC REVIEWS (US) **3877**

OPHTHALMIC STAFF REPORT (US) **3877**

OPHTHALMIC SURGERY (US/0022-023X) [01761334] 3877, **3971**

● OPHTHALMOLOGE : ZEITSCHRIFT DER DEUTSCHEN OPHTHALMOLOGISCHEN GESELLSCHAFT, DER (GW/0941-293X) [25596144] **3877**

● OPHTHALMOLOGIA CROATICA (CI/0353-9881) [26850513] **3877**

OPHTHALMOLOGICA (BASEL) (SZ/0030-3755) [01716836] **3877**

OPHTHALMOLOGICA ET OTO-RHINO-LARYNGOLOGICA (OULU) (FI/0358-4852) [04879989] 3890, **3877**

OPHTHALMOLOGICAL SOCIETY OF EGYPT See BULLETIN **3873**

OPHTHALMOLOGISCHE NACHRICHTEN (GW/0943-898X) **3877**

OPHTHALMOLOGY ALERT *CEASED.* (US/1047-0808) [20601793] **3877**

OPHTHALMOLOGY DIGEST (1979) (US/0048-1955) [05984165] **3878**

OPHTHALMOLOGY (GLENDALE, CALIF.) (US/0271-1281) [03438028] **3878**

OPHTHALMOLOGY MANAGEMENT (US/0746-1070) [09765100] **3878**

OPHTHALMOLOGY REPORT (US/1044-1557) [19697649] **3878**

OPHTHALMOLOGY RESIDENT, THE *CEASED.* (US/1067-2346) [27166142] **3878**

OPHTHALMOLOGY (ROCHESTER, MINN.) (US/0161-6420) [03661682] **3878**

OPHTHALMOLOGY. SOURCEBOOK AND REFERENCE GUIDE / THE AMERICAN ACADEMY OF OPHTHALMOLOGY (US) [22487686] **3878**

OPHTHALMOLOGY TIMES (US/0193-032X) [05109953] **3878**

OPHTHALMOLOGY WORLD NEWS (US/1077-8292) **3878**

OPINIAO, A (PO) [02242782] **2520**

OPINION (II) [01645897] **4485**

OPINION (US) [04762007] **3023**

OPINION (UK) [02243847] 1700, **4704**

OPINION DE BAGDAD, L' (IQ) [03219825] **4485**

OPINION JEUNESSE (BE) **1770**

OPINION, LA (AG) [03012544] **1298**

OPINION; LITERARY QUARTERLY (II) [02245780] **3420**

OPINION (LOS ANGELES, CALIF.), LA (US/0276-590X) [06401875] **5638**

OPINION / STATE OF NEW MEXICO, OFFICE OF THE ATTORNEY GENERAL, DEPARTMENT OF JUSTICE (US) [09514115] **3142**

OPINION-TRIBUNE, THE (US/0746-4398) [10048742] **5672**

OPINIONS (CN/0822-1014) [10344013] **4671**

OPINIONS OF THE ATTORNEY GENERAL OF CALIFORNIA (US) [01552361] **3142**

OPINIONS OF THE ATTORNEY GENERAL OF KENTUCKY (US/0748-9080) [04309749] **3142**

OPINIONS OF THE ATTORNEY GENERAL OF KENTUCKY FOR THE PERIOD JANUARY 1, 1968- JOHN B. BRECKINRIDGE, ATTORNEY GENERAL, 1968-1972 (US) [01755075] **3142**

OPINIONS OF THE ATTORNEY GENERAL OF OHIO (US/0748-6170) [01761081] **3142**

OPINIONS OF THE ATTORNEY GENERAL OF THE STATE OF OREGON (US) [06345366] **3142**

OPINIONS OF THE ATTORNEY GENERAL OF THE STATE OF WISCONSIN (US) [01645750] **3142**

OPINIONS OF THE COMPTROLLER RELATING TO MUNICIPAL GOVERNMENT See OPINIONS OF THE NEW YORK STATE COMPTROLLER **3023**

OPINIONS OF THE NEW YORK STATE COMPTROLLER (US/0743-7668) [08029886] **3023**

OPINIONS ON REVIEW FOR THE YEAR ... / STATE OF MICHIGAN, DEPARTMENT OF LABOR, WORKERS' COMPENSATION APPEAL BOARD AND APPELLATE COMMISSION (US) [11750196] **3153**

OPINIONS (PHILATELIC FOUNDATION (NEW YORK, N.Y.)) (US/8755-3562) [11311455] **2786**

OPLEIDING & ONTWIKKELING (NE/0922-0895) [I09220895] 701, **1770**

OPM NEWS (LONDON, ENGLAND) (UK) [11203283] **3624**

OPOLE OPOLE (PL/0137-8546) [I01378546] **2520**

OPOLSKI ROCZNIK MUZEALNY (PL/0474-2885) [06570629] 4095, **2701**

OPORTO, PORTUGAL. UNIVERSIDADE. INSTITUTO DE ZOOLOGIA See ANAIS DA FACULDADE DE CIENCIAS **5082**

OPP NEWS, THE (US) [12046671] **5627**

OPPELN. WYZSZA SZKOA PEDAGOGICZNA See FILOLOGIA POLSKA **3388**

OPPIKOULUT (FI) [05467575] **1770**

OPPILAITOSLUETTELO (FI) [02244093] **1770**

OPPORTUNITIES (US) [02255847] **4208**

OPPORTUNITIES ABROAD FOR EDUCATORS, FULBRIGHT TEACHER EXCHANGE PROGRAM (US) [12293164] **1902**

OPPORTUNITIES ABROAD FOR TEACHERS (US/0078-5458) [06821037] **1902**

OPPORTUNITIES FOR GRADUATES (SA) [02667259] **4208**

OPPORTUNITIES FOR MATRICULANTS AND SCHOOL LEAVERS (SA) [03823601] **4208**

Alphabetical Title Index — ORA

OPPORTUNITIES IN AGRICULTURE, DEVELOPMENT & BIOLOGICALLY RELATED ARTS & SCIENCES (UK) 5136, **117**

OPPORTUNITIES IN IOWA'S AREA SCHOOLS (US/0093-3465) [01789295] **1839**

OPPORTUNITIES (SCARBOROUGH) (CN/0711-7159) [08581314] **1700**

OPPORTUNITY (CHICAGO, ILL. : 1983) (US/0741-3750) [09745660] **701**

OPPORTUNITY EVALUATION NEWSLETTER (US/1055-3924) [23161520] **881**

OPPORTUNITY NOCS (US/0897-6031) [17564153] **881**

OPPORTUNITY STILL KNOCKS : FREEDOM'S LIVING PROOF OF THE OPPORTUNITIES IN OUR AMERICAN WAY OF LIFE / HORATIO ALGER AWARDS COMMITTEE OF THE AMERICAN SCHOOLS AND COLLEGES ASSOCIATION (US) [01480713] **2752**

OPPORTUNITY VALLEY NEWS (US) [16820892] **5753**

OPPORTUNITY (WINNIPEG) (CN/0383-0098) [02242495] **1577**

OPREDELITEL RASTENII SREDNEI AZII (UZ) [09965131] **520**

OPSEARCH (II/0030-3887) [01911495] 3526, **881**

OPSEU NEWS (CN/0229-8104) [08302831] **1700**

OPSIS KALOPSIS (SW/0283-653X) [10283653X] **3420**

OPSTINE U SR SRBIJI (CI) [02243385] **5335**

OPT, THE MAGAZINE ON PEOPLE AND THINGS (US/0095-5868) [02239912] **5211**

OPTICA APPLICATA (PL/0078-5466) [06570632] **4438**

OPTICA PURA Y APLICADA (SP/0030-3917) [06102642] **4439**

OPTICAL AND QUANTUM ELECTRONICS (UK/0306-8919) [01782144] **4439**

OPTICAL COMPUTING & PROCESSING (UK/0954-2264) [24446486] **1277**

OPTICAL DEVICES & FIBERS (JA) [08541224] **1161**

OPTICAL DISC IN LIBRARIES : USES & TRENDS (US) [22265819] **3239**

OPTICAL ENGINEERING (US/0091-3286) [01785642] **4439**

OPTICAL ENGINEERING (NEW YORK, N.Y.) (US/0892-354X) [12496814] 4439, **1989**

●OPTICAL FIBER TECHNOLOGY (US/1068-5200) [27695213] **4439**

OPTICAL FIBRES (UK) **4439**

OPTICAL INDUSTRY & SYSTEMS ENCYCLOPEDIA & DICTIONARY, THE (US/0191-0639) [04770598] **4439**

OPTICAL INFORMATION PROCESSING (US/0162-7643) [04212799] **4439**

●OPTICAL MATERIALS (NE/0925-3467) [25926480] **4439**

OPTICAL MATERIALS AND ENGINEERING NEWS (US) **4439**

●OPTICAL MEMORY & NEURAL NETWORKS (US/1060-992X) [25148146] **1215**

OPTICAL MEMORY NEWS (US/0741-5869) [10176780] **1277**

OPTICAL MEMORY REPORT, THE (US/8755-1195) [11258139] 1620, **1277**

●OPTICAL PRACTITIONER (UK) [27724085] **3878**

OPTICAL PRISM (CN/0824-3441) [10335052] **4216**

OPTICAL PROPERTIES OF SOLIDS (US) [10698093] **1056**

OPTICAL PUBLISHING DIRECTORY See CD-ROM FINDER : THE WORLD OF CD-ROM PRODUCTS FOR INFORMATION SEEKERS **3257**

OPTICAL PUBLISHING DIRECTORY, THE (US/0896-9841) [15815136] **4818**

OPTICAL REVIEW (JA) **4439**

OPTICAL SCIENCES CENTER NEWSLETTER (US/0066-7609) [02003480] **4216**

OPTICAL SOCIETY OF AMERICA See JOURNAL OF THE OPTICAL SOCIETY OF AMERICA **4437**

OPTICAL WORLD (UK) [08881844] **3878**

OPTICHESKII ZHURNAL (RU) [27821542] **4439**

OPTICIAN, THE (UK/0030-3968) [09025230] **4216**

OPTICS AND LASER TECHNOLOGY (UK/0030-3992) [04952296] **4439**

OPTICS AND LASERS IN ENGINEERING (UK/0143-8166) [07368359] 1989, **4439**

OPTICS AND PHOTONICS NEWS (US/1047-6938) [20744879] **4439**

OPTICS AND SPECTROSCOPY (US/0030-400X) [01761346] **4439**

OPTICS COMMUNICATIONS (NE/0030-4018) [01761347] **4439**

OPTICS INDEX (PRINT) (US/1071-8842) [09130751] **4439**

OPTICS LETTERS (US/0146-9592) [03058079] **4439**

OPTIK (STUTTGART) (GW/0030-4026) [01761348] **4440**

OPTIK; ZEITSCHRIFT FUER LICHT- UND ELEKTRONENOPTIK (GW) [04010591] **4440**

OPTIKA ATMOSFERY See OPTIKA ATMOSFERY I OKEANA **4440**

OPTIKA ATMOSFERY. ENGLISH. ATMOSPHERIC OPTICS See ATMOSPHERIC AND OCEANIC OPTICS **1420**

●OPTIKA ATMOSFERY I OKEANA (RU) [26770634] **4440**

OPTIKA I SPEKTROSKOPIJA (RU/0030-4034) [04715424] **4440**

OPTIMA FARMA (NE/0920-2110) **4318**

OPTIMA (MONTREAL) (CN/1181-9790) [23296041] **374**

OPTIMAL CONTROL APPLICATIONS & METHODS (UK/0143-2087) [05468409] **1220**

OPTIMIST (ABILENE), THE (US/0030-4069) [04109361] **1094**

OPTIMIST HOTLINE (US/0744-9755) [08690436] **5234**

OPTIMIST INTERNATIONAL See OPTIMIST MAGAZINE, THE **5234**

OPTIMIST INTERNATIONAL See OPTIMIST HOTLINE **5234**

OPTIMIST MAGAZINE, THE (US/0744-4672) [01639155] **5234**

OPTIMIZACIJA (RU/0134-3998) [07031647] **3526**

OPTIMIZATION (US) [04326423] **3526**

OPTIMIZATION METHODS AND SOFTWARE (UK/1055-6788) [23272531] **1198**

OPTIMIZATION TECHNIQUES; PROCEEDINGS OF THE IFIP CONFERENCE ON OPTIMIZATION TECHNIQUES (GW) [07408101] **3526**

OPTIMST, THE (CN/0384-5230) [03230436] **5563**

OPTIMUM (OTTAWA) (CN/0475-1906) [03232602] **701**

OPTION ADVISOR /INCLS/ SPECIAL BULLETIN (US) **910**

OPTION/BIO PARIS (FR/0992-5945) [l09925945] **467**

OPTION FINANCE ED. FRANCAISE (FR/0989-1900) [l09891900] **802**

OPTION GRAND AIR (CN/1183-4889) [24623512] **4876**

OPTION (LOS ANGELES, CALIF.) (US/0882-178X) [11793776] **4144**

OPTION PAIX (CN/0823-9703) [11559807] **4530**

OPTION QUALITE (FR/0755-6225) [l07556225] **1620**

OPTION SERRE (CN/0838-1674) [18603892] **2426**

OPTIONS (AU) [05301003] **1248**

OPTIONS CARRIERES (CN/0835-3921) [18800344] **4208**

OPTIONS - CENTRALE DE L'ENSEIGNEMENT DU QUEBEC (CN/1183-3092) [24266793] **2752**

OPTIONS IN LEARNING (US) **1883**

OPTIONS MEDITERRANEENNES. SERIE A : SEMINAIRES MEDITERRANEENS (FR/1016-121X) [23965344] **117**

OPTIONS MEDITERRANEENNES. SERIE B : ETUDES ET RECHERCHES (FR/1016-1228) [23965198] **117**

OPTIONS MONTREUIL (FR/1154-5658) [11545658] **1511**

OPTIONS SERDANG (MY/0127-8436) [l01278436] **117**

OPTIONS (WAYNE, N.J.) (US/0362-2770) [02208475] 5051, **2270**

OPTIQUE FRANCAISE ET L'OPTICIEN LUNETIER, L' (FR) [15368292] **4216**

OPTISCHE IN FOTOTECHNISCHE INDUSTRIE, KLOKKEN- EN UURWERKINDUSTRIE / CENTRAAL BUREAU VOOR DE STATISTIEK, HOOFDAFDELING STATISTIEKEN VAN INDUSTRIE EN BOUWNIJVERHEID (NE/0925-0182) [11883991] **2916**

OPTIV (MCLEAN, VA.) CEASED. (US/1066-9493) [25485777] **1198**

OPTO ELECTRONIQUE (FR/0247-4808) [10988652] **2074**

OPTO MAGAZINE (BE) **3878**

OPTO PRESSE (CN/0227-0730) [08308056] **4216**

OPTOELECTRONICS DISCONTINUED DEVICES CEASED. (US/0732-4235) [08079084] **2074**

OPTOELECTRONICS, INSTRUMENTATION, AND DATA PROCESSING (US/8756-6990) [12437594] 1261, **4440**

OPTOELECTRONICS (TOKYO) (JA/0912-5434) [16397879] **2074**

OPTOELEKTRONIKA I POLUPROVODNIKOVAA TEHNIKA (UN/1011-6559) [09592368] **2074**

OPTOELEKTRONISCHE BAUELEMENTE (GW) [02480870] **2074**

OPTOLASER MILANO CEASED. (IT/1120-8724) [l11208724] **2074**

●OPTOMETRIC BUSINESS STRATEGIST (US/1062-6395) [25688724] 701, **3878**

OPTOMETRIC ECONOMICS (US/1052-7346) [22363834] **4216**

OPTOMETRIC EDUCATION (US/0098-6917) [25120947] **4216**

OPTOMETRIC HISTORICAL SOCIETY See NEWSLETTER - OPTOMETRIC HISTORICAL SOCIETY **4216**

OPTOMETRIC MANAGEMENT (US/0030-4085) [03454683] **4216**

OPTOMETRIC WORLD (US/0030-4107) [04098602] **4216**

OPTOMETRIE (GW/0030-4123) [20361530] **4216**

OPTOMETRISTE (CN/0708-3173) [05720089] **4216**

OPTOMETRY AND VISION SCIENCE (US/1040-5488) [18446899] **4217**

OPTOMETRY (CHICAGO, ILL.) (US/1050-4451) [21492162] **4217**

OPTOMETRY CLINICS : THE OFFICIAL PUBLICATION OF THE PRENTICE SOCIETY (US/1050-6918) [21574275] **4217**

OPTOMETRY TIMES (US/0890-7080) [12195908] **4217**

OPTOMETRY TODAY (II) [09212444] **4217**

OPTOMETRY TODAY (LONDON) (UK/0268-5485) [12605097] **4217**

OPUKHOLI OPORNO-DVIGATELNOGO APPARATA (RU) [06038575] **3822**

OPUNTIA (CALGARY) (CN/1183-2703) [24256743] **3420**

OPUS (CHATSWORTH, CALIF.) See SCHWANN OPUS **5318**

OPUS (COPENHAGEN, DENMARK) (DK/0107-2919) [09656726] **4144**

OPUS INCERTUM (US/0882-7087) [11935877] **305**

OPUS INTERNATIONAL (FR/0048-2056) [08222978] **327**

OPUS (LONDON, ONT.) (CN/0700-5318) [03406082] **4144**

OPUS MUSICUM (XR/0231-7362) [04940049] **4144**

OPUS (ST. JOHN'S) (CN/0225-6355) [06034857] **4144**

OPUSCULA ARCHAEOLOGICA (ZAGREB, CROATIA) (CI/0473-0992) [06313739] **277**

OPUSCULA ATHENIENSIA (SW/0078-5520) [02449313] **1078**

OPUSCULA MEDICA CEASED. (SW/0030-414X) [01624496] **3624**

OPUSCULA MUSEALIA (PL/0239-9989) [16187266] **4095**

OPUSCULA ROMANA (SW/0471-7309) [02637784] **1078**

OPUSCULA ZOOLOGICA FLUMINENSIA (SZ/1010-5220) [17285305] **5612**

OPUSCULA ZOOLOGICA - INSTITUTUM ZOOSYSTEMATICUM UNIVERSITATIS BUDAPESTINENSIS (HU/0473-1034) [03800953] **5593**

OPUSCULUM (FI/0358-5581) [08793005] **3239**

OPUTORONIKUSU (JA/0286-9659) [10423406] **4440**

OPVOEDING & KULTUUR (SA) [04321010] **1770**

OPZIJ (NE) **5563**

OR BLANC (CN/0383-1949) [03209797] **5791**

OR INSIGHT (UK/0953-5543) [l09535543] **1770**

OR MANAGER (US/8756-8047) [11664418] 3971, **3866**

OR/MS TODAY (US) [05304709] **5136**

●OR REPORTS (US/1065-8173) [26751535] **3971**

OR-SPEKTRUM (GW/0171-6468) [07366154] **5136**

ORA DI RELIGIONE, L' (IT/1121-1563) [l11211563] **4983**

ORA, L' (IT) 5804

ORACION DE LAS HORAS (SP) 4984

ORACLE MAGAZINE (US/1065-3171) [26571837] 1198

ORACLE NEWS *CEASED.* (US/1052-3367) [22252740] 1198

●ORACLE POETRY (US/1056-5035) [23725817] 3467

ORACLE (SANTA ANA, CALIF.), THE (US/0746-8822) [10410710] 4606

ORACLE STORY (US/1056-5027) [23725805] 3420

ORACLE, THE (US) 1094

ORACLE, THE (II) [06796805] 2661

ORACLE, THE (US) [01696634] 5697

ORAFO ITALIANO (IT/0471-7376) [I04717376] 2915

ORAFO VALENZANO, L' *See* VALENZA GIOIELLI 2915

ORAITA (IS) [07709967] 5051

ORAL AND MAXILLOFACIAL SURGERY CLINICS OF NORTH AMERICA (US/1042-3699) [19027378] 3971

ORAL AND MAXILLOFACIAL SURGERY DIRECTORY OF THE WORLD (US/0147-1449) [03114455] 1332, 3971

●ORAL DISEASES (UK) 3624

ORAL ENGLISH (US/0147-9962) [01773332] 3308

ORAL HEALTH (CN/0030-4204) [01731584] 1332

ORAL HISTORY ASSOCIATION *See* NEWSLETTER - ORAL HISTORY ASSOCIATION 2624

ORAL HISTORY ASSOCIATION OF AUSTRALIA JOURNAL (AT/0158-7366) [I01587366] 2670

ORAL HISTORY (COLCHESTER) (UK/0143-0955) [03812547] 5253, 2625

ORAL HISTORY IN NEW ZEALAND (NZ/0113-5376) [19117912] 2670

ORAL HISTORY INDEX *CEASED.* (US/1047-3467) [20667665] 2625

ORAL HISTORY (PORT MORESBY, PAPUA NEW GUINEA) (PP/0310-2556) [04128019] 2625

ORAL HISTORY REVIEW, THE (US/0094-0798) [01793844] 2625

ORAL MICROBIOLOGY AND IMMUNOLOGY (DK/0902-0055) [15172006] 1332

ORAL-PROPHYLAXE / HERAUSGEBER, VEREIN FUER ZAHNHYGIENE E.V (GW/0724-4991) [10641503] 1332

ORAL RADIOLOGY (JA/0911-6028) [18305123] 3944, 1332

ORAL SURGERY DIRECTORY OF THE WORLD *See* ORAL AND MAXILLOFACIAL SURGERY DIRECTORY OF THE WORLD 3971

ORAL SURGERY, ORAL MEDICINE, ORAL PATHOLOGY (US/0030-4220) [01761358] 3971, 1332

●ORAL SURGERY, ORAL MEDICINE, ORAL PATHOLOGY, ORAL RADIOLOGY, AND ENDODONTICS (US) 1332

ORAL TRADITION (US/0883-5365) [12183158] 2323

ORALL NEWSLETTER (US/1048-2199) [06081323] 3023, 3239

ORALRAMA! (US) 5188

ORANA (AT/0045-6705) [07379030] 1067, 3239

ORANGE COAST (US/0279-0483) [07479329] 2542

ORANGE COUNTY APARTMENT NEWS (US/0747-3435) [10755730] 2830

ORANGE COUNTY BUSINESS AND INDUSTRIAL DIRECTORY (US) [04080725] 701

●ORANGE COUNTY BUSINESS DIRECTORY (US/1059-7077) [24681123] 701

ORANGE COUNTY BUSINESS FIRST (US) 701

ORANGE COUNTY BUSINESS JOURNAL (NEWPORT BEACH, CALIF.) (US/1051-7480) [08162031] 701

ORANGE COUNTY BUSINESS TO BUSINESS *CEASED.* (US/0733-9534) [08692242] 1511, 701

ORANGE COUNTY BUSINESSWEEK (US/0892-6107) [15265416] 701

ORANGE COUNTY CALIFORNIA GENEALOGICAL SOCIETY *See* QUARTERLY - ORANGE COUNTY CALIFORNIA GENEALOGICAL SOCIETY 2469

ORANGE COUNTY GENEALOGICAL SOCIETY (US/0736-0185) [06405068] 2465

ORANGE COUNTY JEWISH HERITAGE (US/0030-4298) [04098622] 5638

ORANGE COUNTY LAWYER (US/0897-5698) [17554922] 3023

ORANGE COUNTY MEDICAL ASSOCIATION *See* BULLETIN OF THE OCMA, THE 3560

ORANGE COUNTY, NEW YORK, CEMETERIES SERIES (US) [03910183] 2465

ORANGE COUNTY NEWS (US/0192-0421) [05094221] 5638

ORANGE COUNTY POST (US) [17395198] 5720

ORANGE COUNTY REGISTER, THE (US/0886-4934) [12199155] 5638

ORANGE COUNTY REPORTER (SANTA ANA, CALIF.) (US/1060-2585) [23283620] 3023

ORANGE COVE NEWS (US) [26780155] 5638

ORANGE LEADER (ORANGE, TEX.) (US/0885-8047) [11615684] 5753

ORANGE REVIEW, THE (US) [16658482] 5759

ORANGE UTILIZATION, PRICES & YIELD (US) [09965206] 1620

ORANGEVILLE CITIZEN, THE (CN/0319-180X) [02442230] 5792

ORANJE VRYSTAAT EN NOORD-KAAPSE GIDS ORANGE FREE STATE AND NORTHERN CAPE DIRECTORY (SA/0378-9292) [11582921] 2500

ORATOR (OTTAWA) (CN/1181-9219) [24368128] 5033

ORATORI DEL GIORNO, GLI (IT/0393-4012) [I03934012] 3023

ORATORII, GLI (IT) 4144

ORATORY, THE *CEASED.* (CN/0384-1871) [02541729] 4984

ORB (HARVARD), THE (US/0361-5472) [01950782] 4984

ORBEN'S COMEDY FILLERS (US/0048-2099) [03369456] 4864

ORBIS ACADEMICUS (GW/0474-330X) [02630478] 3239

ORBIS ANTIQUUS (GW/0078-5555) [02637813] 1078

ORBIS BIBLICUS ET ORIENTALIS (SZ) [02635180] 4984

ORBIS; BULLETIN INTERNATIONAL DE DOCUMENTATION LINGUISTIQUE (BE/0030-4379) [01761362] 3308

ORBIS GEOGRAPHICUS. ADRESSAR GEOGRAPHIQUE DU MONDE. WORLD DIRECTORY OF GEOGRAPHY. GEOGRAPHISCHES WELTADRESSBUCH *CEASED.* (GW/0030-4395) [01761363] 2571

ORBIS LITTERARUM (DK/0105-7510) [01589833] 3420

ORBIS MUSICAE (IS/0303-3937) [01039910] 4144

ORBIS (PHILADELPHIA) (US/0030-4387) [01761361] 4053, 4485

ORBIS (YOULGREAVE, DERBYSHIRE) (UK/0030-4425) [04048464] 3467

ORBIT (AMSTERDAM) (NE/0167-6830) [08836266] 3971, 3878

ORBIT (GAYA, INDIA) (II) [09221428] 3420

ORBIT (NEW YORK) *CEASED.* (US/0474-3326) [02704827] 3420

ORBIT (TORONTO) (CN/0030-4433) [01779208] 1902

ORBIT VIDEO *CEASED.* (US/1042-1149) [18944872] 4075

ORBITAL (IE) [06463033] 988

ORBUS (US/0890-6432) [14361691] 701

ORC REPORT (CN/0826-3019) [11085124] 4876

ORCAMENTO DA DESPESA PARA ... 1, CLASSIFICACAO ORGANICA, FUNCIONAL E ECONOMICA / REPUBLICA PORTUGUESA, MINISTERIO DA HABITACAO, OBRAS PUBLICAS E TRANSPORTES, DEPARTAMENTO DOS TRANSPORTES (PO) [11416945] 5389

ORCAMENTO DA DESPESA PARA ... / MINISTERIO DA EDUCACAO E CIENCIA (PO) [07816619] 1770

ORCAMENTO DA UNIAO. PROJETO DE LEI / SECRETARIA DE PLANEJAMENTO DA PRESIDENCIA DA REPUBLICA, SECRETARIA DE ORCAMENTO E FINANCAS (BL) [09963936] 4739

ORCAMENTO DO ESTADO (BL) [11128141] 4739

ORCAMENTO EMPRESAS (BL) [08917704] 4671

ORCAMENTO GERAL PARA O ANO ECONOMICO DE ... / REPUBLICA PORTUGESA, GOVERNO DE MACAU, SERVICOS DE FINANCAS (MH) [09711844] 4739

ORCAMENTO MONETARIO PARA ... (BL) [07108469] 802

ORCAMENTO PROGRAMA DE ... / GOVERNO DO ESTADO DE SAO PAULO, SECRETARIA DE ECONOMIA E PLANEJAMENTO (BL) [05864155] 4739

ORCAMENTO-PROGRAMA ... E ORCAMENTO PLURIANUAL DE INVESTIMENTOS / GOVERNO DO ESTADO DE PERNAMBUCO, SECRETARIA DE PLANEJAMENTO, COORDENADORIA DE ORCAMENTO (BL) [06495866] 4739

ORCHADIAN, THE (AT/0474-3342) [05285487] 2426

ORCHARD (KELOWNA) (CN/1180-2251) [23238084] 2352, 117

ORCHARDIST OF NEW ZEALAND, THE (NZ/0110-6260) [05298891] 180

ORCHESTER, DAS (GW/0030-4468) [03657688] 4144

ORCHESTRA CANADA (CN/0380-1799) [02098468] 4144

ORCHESTRA RESOURCE GUIDE (CN/0824-3654) [10365069] 4144

ORCHID ADVOCATE, THE (US/0097-9546) [01799237] 2426

ORCHID DIGEST, THE (US/0199-9559) [01774027] 2426

ORCHID MONOGRAPHS (NE) [14696167] 2426

ORCHID REVIEW (UK/0030-4476) [01605832] 2436

ORCHIDEE, DIE (GW/0473-1425) [05225883] 2426

ORCHIDEEN (NE) [16469715] 2094

ORCRIST (US/0474-3369) [04835925] 3420

ORD & BILD (SW/0030-4492) [01761364] 3349

ORDEM, A (BL) [05345915] 5033

ORDENANZAS LABORALES PARA LA INDUSTRIA Y COMERCIO : SEGURIDAD E HIGIENE EN EL TRABAJO, PLAN NACIONAL Y ORDENANZA GENERAL (SP) [03249216] 2867

ORDER (DORDRECHT) (NE/0167-8094) [11027742] 3526

ORDER OF AGROLOGISTS OF QUEBEC *See* REPERTOIRE DES MEMBRES / ORDRE DES AGRONOMES DU QUEBEC 125

ORDER OF ARCHITECTS OF QUEBEC *See* TABLEAU DES MEMBRES - ORDRE DES ARCHITECTES DU QUEBEC 309

ORDER OF ENGINEERS OF QUEBEC *See* PLAN (MONTREAL) 1990

ORDER OF ST. JOHN. PRIORY OF CANADA *See* ROLL OF THE ORDER - THE PRIORY OF CANADA 3175

ORDER PAPER AND NOTICE PAPER (CN/0848-2659) [20337343] 4671

ORDER / UNITED STATES OF AMERICA, FEDERAL ENERGY REGULATORY COMMISSION (US) [04507561] 1952

ORDERS IN COUNCIL (OTTAWA) (CN/0227-3268) [06688667] 3023

ORDERS OF DAY. MINUTES OF PROCEEDINGS - COUNCIL OF EUROPE. PARLIAMENT ASSEMBLY (FR/0377-1962) [02242266] 4671

ORDINAIRE DU PSYCHANALYSTE, L' (FR/0395-000X) [02156392] 4606

ORDINAIRE MEXIQUE, AMERIQUE CENTRALE, L' (FR) [19557876] 2512

ORDINANCE LAW ANNOTATIONS (US) [04237729] 3023

ORDINANCES (JA) [01765425] 3023

ORDINANCES OF HONG KONG (HK) [01752243] 4671

ORDINARY MEETING OF SHAREHOLDERS - BANQUE INTERNATIONALE POUR L'AFRIQUE OCCIDENTALE (FR) [05063186] 802

ORDINATEUR INDIVIDUEL, L' (FR) 1198

ORDINE PUBBLICO : ORGANO D'INFORMAZIONE PER LE FORZE DI POLIZIA (IT) [27076057] 3171

ORDNANCE (ABERDEEN PROVING GROUND, MD.) *CEASED.* (US/0895-822X) [16817935] 4053

ORDNANCE & MUNITIONS FORECAST (US) 4053

ORDO (GW/0048-2129) [01761366] 1511

ORDO (1977) (CN/0708-711X) [05586171] 5033

ORDO POLITICUS (GW) [01414365] 4486

ORDONNANCE. DOSSIER (CN/0710-6130) [08767234] 4318

ORDONNANCE (MONTREAL) (CN/0710-6122) [08767244] 4318

ORDRE DES AGRONOMES DU QUEBEC *See* REPERTOIRES DES MEMBRES 125

Alphabetical Title Index — OREGON

ORDRE DES COMPTABLES AGREES DU QUEBEC. COMITE DE TERMINOLOGIE FRANCAISE *See* TERMINOLOGIE COMPTABLE **752**

ORDRE DES DENTISTES DU QUEBEC *See* ANNUAIRE DENTAIRE / ORDRE DES DENTISTES DU QUEBEC **1316**

ORDRE DES INGENIEURS FORESTIERS DU QUEBEC *See* REPERTOIRE DES MEMBRES - ORDRE DES INGENIEURS FORESTIERS DU QUEBEC **2392**

ORDRE DES PODIATRES DU QUEBEC *See* RAPPORT ANNUEL - L'ORDRE DES PODIATRES DU QUEBEC **3918**

ORDRE HOSPITALIER (CN/0226-9996) [08099315] **4984**

ORDRE HOSPITALIER DE ST-JEAN DE DIEU *See* ORDRE HOSPITALIER **4984**

ORDRES DES COMPTABLES AGREES DU CANADA ET DES BERMUDES *See* ANNALES DE L'EXAMEN FINAL UNIFORME / ORDRES DES COMPTABLES AGREES DU CANADA ET DES BERMUDES **738**

ORE 12 (IT) **5804**

ORE GEOLOGY REVIEWS (NE/0169-1368) [13845976] **1390**

OREGON *See* SPECIAL LAWS ENACTED BY THE REGULAR SESSION OF THE LEGISLATIVE ASSEMBLY, THE **3058**

OREGON *See* SUMMARY OF ELECTION LAWS ENACTED BY THE LEGISLATIVE ASSEMBLY - OREGON **3061**

OREGON ACADEMY OF SCIENCE *See* PROCEEDINGS OF THE OREGON ACADEMY OF SCIENCE **5141**

OREGON. ADVISORY COMMITTEE TO THE STATE LAND BOARD *See* BIENNIAL REPORT, OREGON'S SUBMERGED AND SUBMERSIBLE LANDS **4632**

OREGON AGRI-FACTS (US/0279-0874) [07518800] **117**

OREGON AGRICULTURE *See* OREGON FARM BUREAU NEWS **117**

OREGON AGRICULTURE & FISHERIES STATISTICS (US) [18029245] **2310**, **117**

OREGON ARTS COMMISSION *See* OREGON ARTS COMMISSION: ANNUAL REPORT **327**

OREGON ARTS COMMISSION: ANNUAL REPORT (US) [03315032] **327**

OREGON BARS (US/0733-2475) [08545898] **3023**

OREGON BARTLETT PEAR COMMISSION *See* SEASON SUMMARY - OREGON BARTLETT PEAR COMMISSION **2431**

OREGON BIRDS (US/0890-2313) [14231475] **5593**

OREGON BLUE BOOK (US/0196-4577) [01250670] **4671**

OREGON BOARD OF EDUCATION *See* BIENNIAL REPORT - OREGON BOARD OF EDUCATION **1727**

OREGON. BOARD ON POLICE STANDARDS AND TRAINING. RESEARCH AND MANAGEMENT SERVICES *See* ANNUAL PERSONNEL AND BUDGET STUDY OF OREGON LAW ENFORCEMENT AGENCIES **3156**

OREGON BUSINESS (US/0279-8190) [07193801] **701**

OREGON COAST (US/0744-8317) [08585315] **5487**

OREGON CONIFER (US/0164-5536) [04535029] **2390**

OREGON COUNTRY LIBRARY (US) [08612012] **3239**

OREGON. DEPT. OF EDUCATION *See* VOCATIONAL EDUCATION IN OREGON **1917**

OREGON. DEPT. OF EDUCATION *See* STATE PLAN FOR THE ADMINISTRATION OF VOCATIONAL EDUCATION UNDER THE VOCATIONAL EDUCATION AMENDMENTS OF 1968, AND PART F OF THE HIGHER EDUCATION ACT OF 1965 (SALEM) **1916**

OREGON. DEPT. OF EDUCATION *See* RACIAL AND ETHNIC SURVEY **2271**

OREGON. DEPT. OF EDUCATION *See* ANNUAL PROGRAM PLAN TITLE IV ESEA **1725**

OREGON. DEPT. OF EDUCATION *See* STATE PLAN FOR TITLE IV OF THE ELEMENTARY AND SECONDARY EDUCATION ACT AS AMENDED, EDUCATIONAL IMPROVEMENT, RESOURCES, AND SUPPORT **1872**

OREGON. DEPT. OF FISH AND WILDLIFE *See* STATEWIDE COMPREHENSIVE PLAN FOR FISH AND WILDLIFE ON THE NATIONAL FORESTS IN THE STATE OF OREGON, A **2206**

OREGON. DEPT. OF FORESTRY *See* FOREST INSECT AND DISEASE CONDITIONS IN THE PACIFIC NORTHWEST **2380**

OREGON. DEPT. OF JUSTICE *See* OPINIONS OF THE ATTORNEY GENERAL OF THE STATE OF OREGON **3142**

OREGON. DEPT. OF REVENUE *See* COUNTY ASSESSMENT STATUS REPORT (SALEM) **4719**

OREGON. DEPT. OF REVENUE. RESEARCH AND SPECIAL SERVICES DIVISION *See* OREGON PROPERTY TAX STATISTICS **4699**

OREGON. DEPT. OF REVENUE. RESEARCH AND SPECIAL SERVICES DIVISION *See* PERSONAL INCOME TAX IN OREGON, THE **4740**

OREGON. DEPT. OF TRANSPORTATION. OFFICE OF DIRECTOR *See* ANNUAL REPORT - OFFICE OF DIRECTOR. OREGON DEPARTMENT OF TRANSPORTATION **5376**

OREGON. DEPT. OF TREASURY *See* ANNUAL REPORT OF THE STATE TREASURER FOR THE PERIOD JANUARY 1 ... TO DECEMBER 31 ... / DEPARTMENT OF TREASURY **4710**

OREGON DIRECTORY OF AMERICAN INDIAN RESOURCES (US/0733-477X) [07840319] **2270**

OREGON ECONOMIC AND REVENUE FORECAST (US) [08756883] **4739**

OREGON EDUCATION (US/0030-4689) [02265516] **1770**

OREGON. EDUCATIONAL COORDINATING COUNCIL *See* FACILITIES INVENTORY OF INSTITUTIONS OF HIGHER EDUCATION IN OREGON **1823**

OREGON. EDUCATIONAL COORDINATING COUNCIL *See* POST HIGH SCHOOL PLANS SURVEY **1841**

OREGON. ELECTIONS DIVISION *See* OFFICIAL ABSTRACT OF VOTES, GENERAL ELECTION **4485**

OREGON. ELECTIONS DIVISION *See* OFFICIAL ABSTRACT OF VOTES : PRIMARY ELECTION **4485**

OREGON. ELECTIONS DIVISION *See* SUMMARY REPORT OF CAMPAIGN CONTRIBUTIONS AND EXPENDITURES, PRIMARY ELECTION **4497**

OREGON. EMPLOYMENT DIVISION *See* ANNUAL REPORT - EMPLOYMENT DIVISION **1649**

OREGON. EMPLOYMENT DIVISION. RESEARCH AND STATISTICS SECTION *See* OCCUPATIONAL PROFILES OF OREGON'S MANUFACTURING INDUSTRIES **1699**

OREGON. EMPLOYMENT DIVISION. RESEARCH AND STATISTICS SECTION *See* OCCUPATIONAL PROFILES OF SELECTED NON-MANUFACTURING INDUSTRIES IN OREGON **4207**

OREGON. EMPLOYMENT DIVISION. RESEARCH AND STATISTICS SECTION *See* FINANCING THE OREGON UNEMPLOYMENT INSURANCE PROGRAM **1532**

OREGON. EXECUTIVE DEPT. PERSONNEL DIVISION OPERATIONS AND DEVELOPMENT UNIT *See* REPRESENTABLE COMPENSATION PLAN - OREGON. EXECUTIVE DEPT. PERSONNEL DIVISION. OPERATIONS AND DEVELOPMENT UNIT **4683**

OREGON FARM BUREAU NEWS (US/0162-5179) [04169930] **117**

OREGON FARMER-STOCKMAN *See* PACIFIC FARMER-STOCKMAN **118**

OREGON. FISH COMMISSION *See* EDUCATIONAL BULLETIN - FISH COMMISSION OF OREGON **2300**

OREGON FOCUS (PORTLAND, OR.) (US/0896-6672) [16847950] **1136**

OREGON GEOLOGY (US/0164-3304) [04614953] **1390**

OREGON. GOVERNOR'S STEERING COMMITTEE FOR MANAGEMENT SELECTION AND DEVELOPMENT *See* MANAGEMENT SELECTION AND DEVELOPMENT, ANNUAL STATUS REPORT **4664**

OREGON GRANGE BULLETIN (US/0030-4697) [04098627] **117**

OREGON. HAZELNUT MARKETING BOARD *See* ANNUAL REPORT / HAZELNUT MARKETING BOARD **163**

●OREGON HEALTH CARE IN PERSPECTIVE (US/1065-4380) [26606121] **4795**

OREGON HEALTH FORUM (US/1056-6767) [23829151] **4795**

OREGON HISTORICAL QUARTERLY (US/0030-4727) [01714620] **2752**

OREGON HISTORICAL SOCIETY *See* OREGON HISTORICAL QUARTERLY **2752**

OREGON HISTORICAL SOCIETY *See* NEWS - OREGON HISTORICAL SOCIETY **2749**

OREGON HISTORY (US) **2752**

OREGON HORTICULTURAL SOCIETY. MEETING *See* ANNUAL REPORT ... ANNUAL MEETING / OREGON HORTICULTURAL SOCIETY **2409**

OREGON IN PERSPECTIVE (US/1065-5654) [26660993] **5335**

OREGON INDIVIDUAL INCOME TAX: PUBLICATION 17 1/2/OREGON DEPARTMENT OF REVENUE (US) [08316671] **4739**

OREGON. INTERGOVERNMENTAL RELATIONS DIVISION *See* HANDBOOK OF STATE PROGRAMS FOR LOCAL GOVERNMENTS **4654**

OREGON. INTERIM COMMITTEE ON EDUCATION *See* REPORT OF THE LEGISLATIVE INTERIM COMMITTEE ON EDUCATION (SALEM) **1778**

OREGON INTERNATIONAL TRADE DIRECTORY (US/0731-9096) [07699575] **848**

OREGON LABOR MARKET INFORMATION DIRECTORY (US/0732-6084) [07668779] **1700**

OREGON. LAW ENFORCEMENT COUNCIL *See* OREGON'S COMPREHENSIVE CRIMINAL JUSTICE PLAN **3171**

OREGON LAW REVIEW (US/0196-2043) [01761423] **3023**

OREGON LEGISLATION (US/0148-379X) [03257160] **3023**

OREGON. LEGISLATIVE ASSEMBLY. LEGISLATIVE COUNSEL COMMITTEE *See* FINAL TABLES AND INDEX TO LEGISLATIVE MEASURES **2970**

OREGON. LEGISLATIVE ASSEMBLY. LEGISLATIVE COUNSEL COMMITTEE *See* DIGEST OF OREGON LAWS **2961**

OREGON LIBRARY NEWS (US/0030-4735) [02265517] **3239**

OREGON MATHEMATICS TEACHER, THE (US/0891-9089) [11412634] **1839**, **3526**

OREGON. MOTOR VEHICLES DIVISION *See* ACCIDENT AND VIOLATION ANALYSIS FOR LICENSED OREGON DRIVERS **5438**

OREGON. MOTOR VEHICLES DIVISION *See* OREGON TRAFFIC ACCIDENTS. FOCUS ON MOTORCYCLES **5442**

OREGON MUSIC EDUCATOR (US) [08630738] **4144**

OREGON. NATIONAL GUARD *See* COMMUNITY ACTIVITIES (SALEM) **4039**

OREGON NURSE (US/0030-4751) [04810319] **3866**

OREGON. OFFICE OF SUPERINTENDENT OF PUBLIC INSTRUCTION *See* OREGON SCHOOL DIRECTORY **1770**

OREGON OPTOMETRY (US/0274-6549) [06492593] **4217**

OREGON PERSONAL INCOME TAX ANNUAL STATISTICS (US) [14254458] **4740**, **4699**

OREGON PHARMACIST (US/0473-2456) [04979303] **4318**

OREGON PROPERTY TAX STATISTICS (US/0145-4269) [02734493] **4740**, **4699**

OREGON. PUBLIC UTILITY COMMISSIONER *See* RAILROAD ACCIDENTS IN OREGON **5401**

OREGON PUBLISHER (US/0745-6379) [01779209] **4818**

OREGON RATIO AND ASSESSMENT ROLL DATA FOR LOCALLY ASSESSED PROPERTY (US) [07851095] **4740**

OREGON RULES OF COURT. FEDERAL (US) [21001734] **3023**

OREGON RULES OF COURT. STATE (US) [21001853] **3023**

OREGON SALMON AND STEELHEAD SPORT CATCH STATISTICS (US/0731-3306) [07622546] **2310**, **2317**

OREGON SCHOOL COMMUNITY COLLEGE DIRECTORY (US/0090-5623) [01785510] **1839**

OREGON SCHOOL DIRECTORY (US/0078-5679) [01761383] **1770**

OREGON SCHOOL STUDY COUNCIL *See* OSSC BULLETIN **1771**

OREGON SCHOOL STUDY COUNCIL. BULLETIN *See* OSSC BULLETIN **1771**

OREGON. SOLID WASTE DIVISION *See* ANNUAL REPORT - OREGON. SOLID WASTE DIVISION **2224**

OREGON STATE BAR *See* ANNUAL REPORTS - OREGON STATE BAR **2935**

OREGON STATE BAR *See* MEMBERSHIP DIRECTORY - OREGON STATE BAR **3009**

OREGON STATE BAR BULLETIN, THE (US/0030-4816) [01585579] **3023**

OREGON STATE BAR. COMMITTEE ON CONTINUING LEGAL EDUCATION *See* PRACTICAL SKILLS COURSE **3030**

OREGON STATE BAR. COMMITTEE ON CONTINUING LEGAL EDUCATION *See* OREGON LEGISLATION **3023**

... OREGON STATE BAR ECONOMIC SURVEY, THE (US/0734-0966) [08665144] **3023**

OREGON Alphabetical Title Index

OREGON. STATE BOARD OF ENGINEERING EXAMINERS See REGISTRY OF ENGINEERS AND LAND SURVEYORS AND REPORT OF THE STATE BOARD OF ENGINEERING EXAMINERS OF OREGON **1993**

OREGON STATE BOARD OF RADIOLOGIC TECHNOLOGY See DIRECTORY OF LICENSEES - OREGON STATE BOARD OF RADIOLOGIC TECHNOLOGY **3941**

OREGON. STATE COMMUNITY SERVICES PROGRAM See SOCIAL ACCOUNTING FOR OREGON : SOCIO-ECONOMIC INDICATORS **1584**

OREGON. STATE COUNCIL ON DEVELOPMENTAL DISABILITIES See STATE OF OREGON COMPREHENSIVE DEVELOPMENTAL DISABILITIES PLAN **4394**

OREGON STATE MONOGRAPHS. STUDIES IN EDUCATION AND GUIDANCE (US/0078-5792) [13695509] **1770**

OREGON. STATE PARKS AND RECREATION DIVISION See PROGRESS REPORT - OREGON STATE PARKS AND RECREATION DIVISION **4707**

OREGON. STATE UNIVERSITY. CORVALLIS. AIR RESOURCES CENTER See AIR RESEARCH SUMMARY **2223**

OREGON STATE UNIVERSITY. DEPARTMENT OF OCEANOGRAPHY See TECHNICAL REPORT - DEPARTMENT OF OCEANOGRAPHY. SCHOOL OF SCIENCE. OREGON STATE UNIVERSITY **1457**

OREGON STATE UNIVERSITY. ENGINEERING EXPERIMENT STATION See CIRCULAR - ENGINEERING EXPERIMENT STATION, OREGON STATE UNIVERSITY **1968**

OREGON STATE UNIVERSITY. EXTENSION SERVICE See FS **89**

OREGON STATE UNIVERSITY. FOREST RESEARCH LABORATORY. RESEARCH NOTE - SCHOOL OF FORESTRY, FOREST RESEARCH LABORATORY, OREGON STATE UNIVERSITY See RESEARCH CONTRIBUTION **2392**

OREGON STATE UNIVERSITY. FOREST RESEARCH LABORATORY. RESEARCH PAPER - FOREST RESEARCH LABORATORY, OREGON STATE UNIVERSITY See RESEARCH CONTRIBUTION **2392**

OREGON TEACHERS OF ENGLISH TO SPEAKERS OF OTHER LANGUAGES See ORTESOL JOURNAL, THE **3308**

OREGON TRAFFIC ACCIDENTS. FOCUS ON MOTORCYCLES (US) [06254191] 4082, **5442**

OREGON TRAFFIC ACCIDENTS ... SUMMARY / OREGON DEPARTMENT PF TRANSPORTATION, MOTOR VEHICLES DIVISION (US) [17331886] **5422**

OREGON TRAFFIC SAFETY COMMISSION See HIGHWAY SAFETY PLAN / OTSC **5441**

OREGON TRANSPORTATION COMMISSION See OREGON TRANSPORTATION COMMISSION POLICIES **5389**

OREGON TRANSPORTATION COMMISSION POLICIES (US/0148-9704) [03400347] **5389**

OREGON VITAL STATISTICS REPORT FOR CALENDAR YEAR (US) [14910118] **4810**

OREGON. VOCATIONAL REHABILITATION DIVISION See ANNUAL REPORT / OREGON VOCATIONAL REHABILITATION DIVISION **1649**

OREGON. VOCATIONAL REHABILITATION DIVISION. BI-ANNUAL REPORT See ANNUAL REPORT / OREGON VOCATIONAL REHABILITATION DIVISION **1649**

OREGON WHEAT (US/0897-5051) [17758394] **1620**

OREGON WILDLIFE (US/0094-7113) [01794353] **2201**

OREGON. WILDLIFE COMMISSION See OREGON WILDLIFE COMMISSION FINANCIAL STATEMENT **4876**

OREGON WILDLIFE COMMISSION FINANCIAL STATEMENT (US/0362-8264) [02354079] **4876**

OREGON. WILDLIFE COMMISSION. RESEARCH DIVISION See FISHERY RESEARCH REPORT **2303**

OREGONIAN (PORTLAND, OR. 1937), THE (US/8750-1317) [09278915] **5734**

OREGON'S AGRICULTURAL PROGRESS **SUSPENDED.** (US/0474-4721) [01761428] **117**

OREGON'S COMPREHENSIVE CRIMINAL JUSTICE PLAN (US/0361-7254) [02247027] **3171**

OREM-GENEVA TIMES (US) [13015748] **5757**

ORFF ECHO, THE (US/0095-2613) [01796279] 1770, **4144**

ORFORDVILLE JOURNAL AND FOOTVILLE NEWS (US) [12925573] **5769**

ORGAMATIK (SZ) **5136**

ORGAN (ABBOTSFORD) (CN/0703-1254) [03645251] **3420**

ORGAN (BOURNEMOUTH) (UK/0030-4883) [01640101] **4144**

ORGAN HANDBOOK (US/0882-2085) [09932446] **4144**

ORGAN HISTORICAL SOCIETY. NATIONAL CONVENTION See ORGAN HANDBOOK **4144**

ORGAN MOUNTAIN TRAILBLAZER (US/0899-1960) [18028300] **2752**

ORGAN (WINNIPEG) (CN/0703-1246) [03589193] **3420**

ORGAN YEARBOOK, THE (NE/0920-3192) [01785030] **4144**

ORGANA AUSTRIACA (AU) [02851973] **4144**

ORGANI DI TRASMISSIONE (IT) [01785505] **2123**

ORGANIC AND ORGANOMETALLIC CRYSTAL STRUCTURES; BIBLIOGRAPHY (NE) [02246630] 1044, **1033**

ORGANIC CHEMISTRY OF DRUG SYNTHESIS, THE (US/8755-383X) [11293757] **1044**

ORGANIC CHEMISTRY SERIES (PERGAMON PRESS) (UK) [09332300] **1044**

ORGANIC COMPOUNDS : REACTIONS AND METHODS (US/0092-6094) [01784393] **1045**

ORGANIC FARMER (MONTPELIER, VT.) **CEASED.** (US/1063-6803) [22607431] **117**

ORGANIC FARMING INDEX (UK/0952-8962) [20448112] **117**

ORGANIC FOOD MATTERS; THE JOURNAL OF SUSTAINABLE AGRICULTURE **CEASED.** (US) [20742329] **117**

ORGANIC GARDENING (1988) (US/0897-3792) [17469633] **2426**

ORGANIC GEOCHEMISTRY (UK/0146-6380) [03637170] **1390**

ORGANIC GROWERS CO-OPERATIVE See NEWSLETTER - ORGANIC GROWERS CO-OPERATIVE **112**

ORGANIC MASS SPECTROMETRY (UK/0030-493X) [01587414] 1045, **1018**

ORGANIC PHOTOCHEMISTRY (NEW YORK) (US/0078-6152) [01761432] **1045**

ORGANIC PREPARATIONS AND PROCEDURES INTERNATIONAL (US/0030-4948) [02210394] 1770, **1045**

ORGANIC REACTION MECHANISMS (UK/0474-4772) [00928204] **1045**

ORGANIC REACTIONS (US) [04761515] **1056**

ORGANIC REACTIONS (US/0078-6179) [01259595] **1045**

ORGANIC REACTIVITY (ER/0131-8314) [01761433] **1045**

ORGANIC SEMINAR ABSTRACTS (US/0445-3611) [02253007] **1045**

ORGANIC SYNTHESES (US/0078-6209) [01644392] **1045**

ORGANIC SYNTHESES. COLLECTIVE VOLUME (US/0078-6217) [01761434] **1045**

ORGANIC SYNTHESES VIA METAL CARBONYLS (US) [01320904] **1045**

ORGANIC SYNTHESIS (US/1047-773X) [20682501] **1045**

ORGANIC WHOLESALE MARKET REPORT / OMNIS, ORGANIC MARKET NEWS AND INFORMATION SERVICE (US) [13031220] **117**

ORGANISATION DE COOPERATION ET DE DEVELOPPEMENT ECONOMIQUES See ETUDES ECONOMIQUES DE L'O C D E: CANADA **1489**

ORGANISATION DE L'ENSEIGNEMENT EN FRANCE, L' (FR) [02403878] **1868**

ORGANISATION FOR ECONOMIC CO-OPERATION AND DEVELOPMENT See OECD ECONOMIC SURVEYS : FINLAND **1576**

ORGANISATION FOR ECONOMIC CO-OPERATION AND DEVELOPMENT See OECD ECONOMIC SURVEYS: NEW ZEALAND **1510**

ORGANISATION FOR ECONOMIC CO-OPERATION AND DEVELOPMENT See INDUSTRIAL PRODUCTION. PRODUCTION INDUSTRIELLE **1567**

ORGANISATION FOR ECONOMIC CO-OPERATION AND DEVELOPMENT See OECD ECONOMIC SURVEYS: CANADA **1510**

ORGANISATION FOR ECONOMIC CO-OPERATION AND DEVELOPMENT See OECD ECONOMIC SURVEYS : FRANCE **1576**

ORGANISATION FOR ECONOMIC CO-OPERATION AND DEVELOPMENT See PULP AND PAPER **4237**

ORGANISATION FOR ECONOMIC CO-OPERATION AND DEVELOPMENT See ENERGY CONSERVATION IN THE INTERNATIONAL ENERGY AGENCY; REVIEW **1939**

ORGANISATION FOR ECONOMIC CO-OPERATION AND DEVELOPMENT See INDUSTRIE DE LA CHAUSSURE ET DES CUIRS ET PEAUX BRUTS ET TANNES DANS LES PAYS DE L'OCDE; STATISTIQUES. THE FOOTWEAR, RAW HIDES AND SKINS AND LEATHER INDUSTRY IN OECD COUNTRIES; STATISTICS, L' **3184**

ORGANISATION FOR ECONOMIC CO-OPERATION AND DEVELOPMENT See REVIEW OF FISHERIES IN OECD MEMBER COUNTRIES **2311**

ORGANISATION FOR ECONOMIC CO-OPERATION AND DEVELOPMENT See OECD ECONOMIC SURVEYS: ITALY **1576**

ORGANISATION FOR ECONOMIC CO-OPERATION AND DEVELOPMENT See OECD ECONOMIC SURVEYS **1509**

ORGANISATION FOR ECONOMIC CO-OPERATION AND DEVELOPMENT See OECD ECONOMIC SURVEYS : UNITED STATES **1577**

ORGANISATION FOR ECONOMIC CO-OPERATION AND DEVELOPMENT See OECD ECONOMIC SURVEYS : AUSTRALIA **1576**

ORGANISATION FOR ECONOMIC CO-OPERATION AND DEVELOPMENT See OECD ECONOMIC SURVEYS: DENMARK **1510**

ORGANISATION FOR ECONOMIC CO-OPERATION AND DEVELOPMENT See OECD ECONOMIC SURVEYS: ICELAND **1510**

ORGANISATION FOR ECONOMIC CO-OPERATION AND DEVELOPMENT See INDICATORS OF INDUSTRIAL ACTIVITY **1609**

ORGANISATION FOR ECONOMIC CO-OPERATION AND DEVELOPMENT See OECD OBSERVER **1510**

ORGANISATION FOR ECONOMIC CO-OPERATION AND DEVELOPMENT See OECD ECONOMIC SURVEYS: SPAIN **1510**

ORGANISATION FOR ECONOMIC CO-OPERATION AND DEVELOPMENT See OECD. ECONOMIC OUTLOOK **1509**

ORGANISATION FOR ECONOMIC CO-OPERATION AND DEVELOPMENT See OECD ECONOMIC SURVEYS : UNITED KINGDOM **1577**

ORGANISATION FOR ECONOMIC CO-OPERATION AND DEVELOPMENT See MAIN ECONOMIC INDICATORS **1573**

ORGANISATION FOR ECONOMIC CO-OPERATION AND DEVELOPMENT See OECD ECONOMIC SURVEYS: NORWAY **1510**

ORGANISATION FOR ECONOMIC CO-OPERATION AND DEVELOPMENT See STATISTIQUES DE RECETTES PUBLIQUES DES PAYS MEMBRES DE L'OCDE: UNE CLASSIFICATION NORMALISEE **4700**

ORGANISATION FOR ECONOMIC CO-OPERATION AND DEVELOPMENT See OECD ECONOMIC SURVEYS: GREECE **1510**

ORGANISATION FOR ECONOMIC CO-OPERATION AND DEVELOPMENT See OECD ECONOMIC SURVEYS: SWEDEN **1510**

ORGANISATION FOR ECONOMIC CO-OPERATION AND DEVELOPMENT See OECD ECONOMIC SURVEYS: AUSTRIA **1509**

ORGANISATION FOR ECONOMIC CO-OPERATION AND DEVELOPMENT See OECD ECONOMIC SURVEYS : IRELAND **1576**

ORGANISATION FOR ECONOMIC CO-OPERATION AND DEVELOPMENT See OECD ECONOMIC SURVEYS : NETHERLANDS **1576**

ORGANISATION FOR ECONOMIC CO-OPERATION AND DEVELOPMENT See NEWS FROM OECD / ORGANISATION FOR ECONOMIC CO-OPERATION AND DEVELOPMENT **1508**

ORGANISATION FOR ECONOMIC CO-OPERATION AND DEVELOPMENT See OECD ECONOMIC SURVEYS: BELGIUM-LUXEMBOURG **1510**

ORGANISATION FOR ECONOMIC CO-OPERATION AND DEVELOPMENT See OECD ECONOMIC SURVEYS: GERMANY **1510**

ORGANISATION FOR ECONOMIC CO-OPERATION AND DEVELOPMENT See OECD ECONOMIC SURVEYS : TURKEY **1577**

ORGANISATION FOR ECONOMIC CO-OPERATION AND DEVELOPMENT See OECD ECONOMIC SURVEYS : PORTUGAL **1576**

ORGANISATION FOR ECONOMIC CO-OPERATION AND DEVELOPMENT. COMMITTEE ON TOURISM See TOURISM POLICY AND INTERNATIONAL TOURISM IN OECD MEMBER COUNTRIES **5493**

ORIENTALIA

ORGANISATION FOR ECONOMIC CO-OPERATION AND DEVELOPMENT. DEVELOPMENT ASSISTANCE COMMITTEE *See* DEVELOPMENT CO-OPERATION EFFORTS AND POLICIES OF THE MEMBERS OF THE DEVELOPMENT ASSISTANCE COMMITTEE; REVIEW **2908**

ORGANISATION FOR ECONOMIC CO-OPERATION AND DEVELOPMENT. DEVELOPMENT ASSISTANCE COMMITTEE *See* GEOGRAPHICAL DISTRIBUTION OF FINANCIAL FLOWS TO LESS DEVELOPED COUNTRIES (COMMITMENTS) **2909**

ORGANISATION FOR ECONOMIC CO-OPERATION AND DEVELOPMENT. DEVELOPMENT CENTRE *See* LATEST INFORMATION ON NATIONAL ACCOUNTS OF DEVELOPING COUNTRIES. INFORMATIONS RECENTES SUR LES COMPTES NATIONAUX DES PAYS EN DEVELOPPEMENT **1502**

ORGANISATION FOR ECONOMIC CO-OPERATION AND DEVELOPMENT. SECRETARIAT *See* PROGRAMME OF WORK AND BUDGET **1579**

ORGANISATION POPULAIRE (CN/0381-1522) [03230473] **5300**

ORGANISATION UNIVERSITAIRE INTERAMERICAINE *See* INTERAMERICA (ED. FRANCAISE) **1830**

ORGANISATIONS AND PEOPLE - SUCCESSFUL DEVELOPMENT (UK/1350-6269) 1770, **881**

ORGANISCHE CHEMIE IN EINZELDARSTELLUNGEN (GW/0078-6225) [08694975] **1045**

ORGANISER (II) [05350712] 4486, **5253**

ORGANISME REGIONAL DE DEVELOPPEMENT DU CENTRE-NORD *See* PROJET DE BUDGET - ORGANISME REGIONAL DE DEVELOPPEMENT DU CENTRE-NORD **1579**

ORGANISME REGIONAL DE DEVELOPPEMENT DU CENTRE-NORD *See* PROGRAMME D'ACTIVITES - ORGANISME REGIONAL DE DEVELOPPEMENT DU CENTRE-NORD **1579**

ORGANIST'S COMPANION, THE (US/0749-3533) [05809200] **4144**

ORGANISTS' REVIEW (UK/0048-2161) [05998636] **4144**

ORGANIZACIJA IN KADRI (YU/0350-1531) [05638730] **881**

ORGANIZACIJA POSLOVANJA (YU) [01795628] **944**

ORGANIZACIJA RADA (YU/0471-9506) [I04719506] **1700**

ORGANIZACIJA SAMOUPRAVLJANJA OUR (YU) [02620755] **1620**

ORGANIZACIJE I ZAJEDNICE / SOCIJALISTICKA FEDERATIVNA REPUBLIKA JUGOSLAVIJA, SAVEZNI ZAVOD ZA STATISTIKU (YU) [09176997] **1620**

ORGANIZACIJE IN SKUPNOSTI V GOSPODARSTVU IN NEGOSPODARSTVU V SR SLOVENIJI / ZAVOD SR SLOVENIJE ZA STATISTIKO (XV) [07560223] **701**

ORGANIZACION LABOR *See* ORGANIZACION LABOR **3023**

ORGANIZACION LABOR (PY) [04372250] **3023**

ORGANIZACJA I ZARZADZANIE (PL) [04479758] **1620**

ORGANIZAJCA, METODY, TECHNIKA (PL) [06586430] **701**

ORGANIZATION (UK) [I13505084] **881**

ORGANIZATION CHART MANUAL / STATE OF CALIFORNIA, DEPARTMENT OF MOTOR VEHICLES (US) [08938070] **5422**

ORGANIZATION DEVELOPMENT JOURNAL (US/0889-6402) [11084516] **881**

ORGANIZATION : FEDERAL INSURANCE ADMINISTRATION (US) [03781491] **2889**

ORGANIZATION FOR ECONOMIC CO-OPERATION AND DEVELOPMENT *See* OECD FINANCIAL STATISTICS. MONTHLY SUPPLEMENT: INTEREST RATES. STATISTIQUES FINANCIERES DE L'OCDE. SUPPLEMENT MENSUEL: TAUX D'INTERET **732**

ORGANIZATION FOR ECONOMIC COOPERATION AND DEVELOPMENT *See* AGRICULTURAL POLICY REPORTS (SERIES) **51**

ORGANIZATION FOR ECONOMIC COOPERATION AND DEVELOPMENT *See* STATISTICS OF FOREIGN TRADE. STATISTIQUES DU COMMERCE EXTERIER. SERIES B. TRADE BY COMMODITIES: COUNTRY SUMMARIES. ECHANGES PAR PRODUITS: RESUME PAR PAYS **733**

ORGANIZATION FOR ECONOMIC COOPERATION AND DEVELOPMENT *See* INDUSTRIE SIDERURGIQUE. IRON AND STEEL INDUSTRY, L' **4004**

ORGANIZATION FOR ECONOMIC COOPERATION AND DEVELOPMENT *See* REVIEWS OF NATIONAL POLICIES FOR EDUCATION **1780**

ORGANIZATION FOR ECONOMIC COOPERATION AND DEVELOPMENT. ECONOMIC AND DEVELOPMENT REVIEW COMMITTEE *See* BLEU **1548**

ORGANIZATION FOR ECONOMIC COOPERATION AND DEVELOPMENT. LIBRARY *See* BIBLIOGRAPHIE SPECIALE ANALYTIQUE **3257**

ORGANIZATION OF AMERICAN HISTORIANS. MEETING *See* PROGRAM OF THE ANNUAL MEETING - ORGANIZATION OF AMERICAN HISTORIANS **2755**

ORGANIZATION OF AMERICAN STATES *See* DIRECTORY / ORGANIZATION OF AMERICAN STATES **4644**

ORGANIZATION OF AMERICAN STATES. BOARD OF EXTERNAL AUDITORS *See* AUDIT OF ACCOUNTS AND FINANCIAL STATEMENTS ; REPORT TO THE GENERAL ASSEMBLY OF THE ORGANIZATION OF AMERICAN STATES BY THE BOARD OF EXTERNAL AUDITORS **739**

ORGANIZATION OF AMERICAN STATES. CAPITAL MARKETS DEVELOPMENT PROGRAM *See* INFORMATIVE BULLETIN - CAPITAL MARKETS DEVELOPMENT PROGRAM **901**

ORGANIZATION OF AMERICAN STATES. DEPT. OF PUBLICATIONS AND CONFERENCES *See* PUBLICACIONES Y CONFERENCIAS : INFORME TRIMESTRAL - DEPARTAMENTO DE PUBLICACIONES Y CONFERENCIAS **3134**

ORGANIZATION OF AMERICAN STATES. DEVELOPMENT FINANCING PROGRAM *See* FINANCIAMIENTO DEL DESARROLLO **4726**

ORGANIZATION OF AMERICAN STATES. GENERAL SECRETARIAT *See* CHIEFS OF STATE AND CABINET MINISTERS OF THE AMERICAN REPUBLICS **4637**

ORGANIZATION OF AMERICAN STATES. GENERAL SECRETARIAT *See* CATALOG OF PUBLICATIONS - OAS. CATALOGO DE PUBLICACIONES - OEA **412**

ORGANIZATION OF AMERICAN STATES. PERMANENT COUNCIL *See* SUMMARY OF THE DECISIONS TAKEN AT THE MEETINGS AND TEXTS OF THE RESOLUTIONS APPROVED **3136**

ORGANIZATION OF AMERICAN STATES. SECRETARY GENERAL *See* ANNUAL REPORT OF THE SECRETARY GENERAL TO THE GENERAL ASSEMBLY **3123**

ORGANIZATION OF THE GOVERNMENT OF ALBERTA (CN/0226-286X) [07727679] **4671**

ORGANIZATION OF TROPICAL AMERICAN NEMATOLOGISTS *See* OTAN NEWSLETTER **5593**

ORGANIZATION: OFFICE OF THE ASSISTANT SECRETARY FOR POLICY DEVELOPMENT AND RESEARCH (US) [03791895] **2830**

ORGANIZATION SCIENCE (US/1047-7039) [20750087] **881**

ORGANIZATION STUDIES (GW/0170-8406) [06172557] **5211**

ORGANIZATION TRENDS (US/0882-5769) [11885743] 5234, **4338**

ORGANIZATIONAL BEHAVIOR AND HUMAN DECISION PROCESSES (US/0749-5978) [11148651] **4606**

ORGANIZATIONAL BEHAVIOR TEACHING REVIEW *See* JOURNAL OF MANAGEMENT EDUCATION : A PUBLICATION OF THE ORGANIZATIONAL BEHAVIOR TEACHING SOCIETY **1757**

ORGANIZATIONAL DYNAMICS (US/0090-2616) [01784891] **881**

ORGANIZATIONAL LEADERSHIP OF HUMAN RESOURCES. THE KNOWLEDGE AND THE SKILLS (US) **881**

ORGANIZATIONS EXEMPT FROM LIMITED SALES AND USE TAX (US/0739-1374) [09650459] **4740**

ORGANIZATIONS OF STATE GOVERNMENT OFFICIALS DIRECTORY (US/1069-5168) [27959328] **4671**

ORGANIZATSIIA SISTEMATICHESKIKH I PREDMETNYKH KATALOGOV NAUCHNYKH BIBLIOTEK (RU) [04259871] **3240**

ORGANIZATSIIA UPRAVLENIIA (RU) [02239320] **881**

ORGANIZER MAILING, THE (US/1063-9233) [26183585] **4671**

ORGANIZER : NEWSLETTER OF THE NATIONAL ALLIANCE AGAINST RACIST AND POLITICAL REPRESSION, THE (US) [11258975] **4511**

ORGANIZER (SAN FRANCISCO, CALIF.), THE (US/1059-2369) [23762099] **5638**

ORGANIZER (WASHINGTON, D.C.) (US/0885-6036) [08537752] **5253**

ORGANIZING CORPORATE AND OTHER ENTERPRISES (US) [01772099] **701**

ORGANIZZAZIONE SANITARIA (IT/0394-283X) [I0394283X] **3790**

ORGANO, L' (IT) [06458603] **4144**

ORGANO OFICIAL DE LA JUNTA CIVICO-MILITAR CUBANA (US/0272-4650) [05640252] **2752**

ORGANOMETALLIC CHEMISTRY IN THE USSR *CEASED*. (UK/0955-8586) [24363244] **1045**

ORGANOMETALLIC CHEMISTRY (LONDON. 1972) (UK/0301-0074) [01783654] **1045**

ORGANOMETALLIC COMPOUNDS (UK/0030-5138) [04031677] **1045**

ORGANOMETALLICS (US/0276-7333) [07411854] **1045**

ORGANON (PL/0078-6500) [03022050] **5136**

ORGANOPHOSPHORUS CHEMISTRY (UK/0306-0713) [01639401] **1045**

ORGASME (CN/0712-6018) [09313077] **5188**

ORGEL (AMERSFOORT, NETHERLANDS) (NE) [10794557] **4144**

ORGLET (DK) [01789067] **4145**

ORGONOMIC FUNCTIONALISM (RANGELEY, ME.) (US/1054-075X) [22752751] **3932**

ORGUE (PARIS), L' (FR/0030-5170) [03246638] **4145**

ORIENS (NE/0078-6527) [01761497] **2661**

ORIENS ANTIQUUS (IT/0030-5189) [01761498] **2661**

ORIENS CHRISTIANUS (GW/0340-6407) [01642167] **5039**

ORIENS EXTREMUS (GW/0030-5197) [01589734] **3420**

ORIENT (JA) [02337850] 2661, **277**

ORIENT (DEUTSCHES ORIENT-INSTITUT) (GW/0030-5227) [02679292] **2661**

ORIENT (MONTREAL) (CN/0472-0490) [02530580] **4984**

ORIENT, THE (II) [02441060] **2661**

ORIENTAL ART (UK/0030-5278) [01761503] **361**

ORIENTAL CERAMIC SOCIETY *See* TRANSACTIONS OF THE ORIENTAL CERAMIC SOCIETY **2595**

ORIENTAL CERAMIC SOCIETY OF HONG KONG *See* BULLETIN OF THE ORIENTAL CERAMIC SOCIETY OF HONG KONG, THE **2586**

ORIENTAL GEOGRAPHER (BG/0030-5308) [01761506] **2571**

ORIENTAL INSECTS (US/0030-5316) [01761507] **5612**

ORIENTAL INSECTS MONOGRAPH (US) [08658261] **5612**

ORIENTAL INSTITUTE COMMUNICATIONS (US/0146-678X) [01644165] **3308**

ORIENTAL INSTITUTE PUBLICATIONS (US/0069-3367) [01554130] **277**

ORIENTAL INSTITUTE RESEARCH ARCHIVES ACQUISITIONS LIST (US) [25724958] **2625**

ORIENTAL INSTITUTE (VADODARA, INDIA) *See* JOURNAL OF THE ORIENTAL INSTITUTE, M.S. UNIVERSITY OF BARODA **2505**

ORIENTAL JOURNAL OF CHEMISTRY (II/0970-020X) [13258895] **988**

ORIENTAL MONOGRAPH SERIES (AT/0474-6546) [02676882] **2661**

ORIENTAL PUBLICATIONS (UK/0068-6891) [01552612] **2661**

ORIENTAL RUG REVIEW (US/1044-4807) [08771903] **2902**

ORIENTAL SOCIETY OF AUSTRALIA *See* JOURNAL OF THE ORIENTAL SOCIETY OF AUSTRALIA, THE **2656**

ORIENTAL STUDIES (US/0474-6589) [02675488] **2661**

ORIENTAL STUDIES IN THE USSR (RU/0235-6740) [19474563] **2661**

ORIENTAL STUDIES IN THE USSR SERIES / USSR ACADEMY OF SCIENCES, INSTITUTE OF ORIENTAL STUDIES (RU) [20344790] **2661**

ORIENTALIA CHRISTIANA ANALECTA (IT) [01604105] **5039**

ORIENTALIA CHRISTIANA PERIODICA (IT/0030-5375) [01588715] **5039**

ORIENTALIA; COMMENTARI PERIODICI DE REBUS ORIENTIS ANTIQUI (IT/0030-5367) [01773339] **2661**

ORIENTALIA GANDENSIA (BE/0474-6627) [04969372] 1079, **3308**

ORIENTALIA
Alphabetical Title Index

ORIENTALIA GOTHOBURGENSIA (SW/0085-4522) [02673566] 3420, **3308**

ORIENTALIA LOVANIENSIA ANALECTA (BE) [05543532] **2661**

ORIENTALIA LOVANIENSIA PERIODICA (BE/0085-4522) [01761511] 2661, **3308**

ORIENTALIA RHENO-TRAIECTINA (NE) [02673637] **2661**

ORIENTALIA SUECANA (SW/0078-6578) [02449337] **2661**

ORIENTALISTISCHE LITERATURZEITUNG (GW) [08743326] **3308**

ORIENTAMENTI DELLA GIURISPRUDENZA DEL LAVORO (IT) **3023**

ORIENTAMENTI PEDAGOGICI (IT/0030-5391) [01588251] **1770**

ORIENTATION A LA GESTION FINANCIERE (CN) [03980291] **802**

ORIENTATION (MONTREAL. 1986) (CN/0833-0530) [16687629] **1700**

ORIENTATION-NOUVELLES (CN/0228-1457) [06859855] **1770**

ORIENTATION SCOLAIRE ET PROFESSIONNELLE (FR/0249-6739) [I02496739] **1839**

ORIENTATIONS ET POLITIQUES DE L'U P A (CN/0382-7852) [02802153] **117**

ORIENTATIONS (HONG KONG) (HK/0030-5448) [01774029] **2661**

●ORIENTATIONS STRATEGIQUES DES ARCHIVES NATIONALES DU CANADA (CN/0844-7594) [20019480] **2482**

ORIENTATIONS STRATEGIQUES DES ARCHIVES PUBLIQUES DU CANADA *See* ORIENTATIONS STRATEGIQUES DES ARCHIVES NATIONALES DU CANADA **2482**

ORIENTATIONS (TORONTO) (CN/0710-2151) [09145740] **1839**

●ORIENTATIONS TRIENNALES ET PLAN ANNUEL / GOUVERNEMENT DU QUEBEC, CONSEIL DU STATUT DE LA FEMME (CN/0845-0382) [20316559] **5212**

ORIENTE AGROPECUARIO (VE) [05014293] **117**

ORIENTE CRISTIANO (IT) [20006375] **4984**

ORIENTE MODERNO (IT/0030-5472) [01695076] **2661**

ORIENTE-OCCIDENTE / INSTITUTO LATINOAMERICANO DE INVESTIGACIONES COMPARADAS SOBRE ORIENTE Y OCCIDENTE (ILICOD), UNIVERSIDAD DEL SALVADOR Y CONICET (AG/0325-8823) [09861789] **4984**

ORIENTEERING CANADA (CN/0227-6658) [08071782] **4911**

ORIENTEERING NORTH AMERICA (US/0886-1080) [12829515] **4911**

ORIENTEERING WORLD (SW/1015-4965) **4911**

ORIENTEERING WORLD : ORIENTIERUNGSLAUF AUS ALLER WELT (SW/1015-4965) [28733688] **4911**

ORIENTIERUNG (ZURICH) (SZ/0030-5502) [05225551] **4984**

ORIENTIERUNGEN ZUR WIRTSCHAFTS- UND GESELLSCHAFTSPOLITIK (GW/0724-5246) [I07245246] **5212**

ORIENTO (JA) [03618444] **2661**

ORIGIN-DESTINATION SURVEY OF AIRLINE PASSENGER TRAFFIC - DOMESTIC (US) [05058426] **31**

ORIGIN OF KENTUCKY COLLEGE AND UNIVERSITY ENROLLMENTS (US) [03173492] 1839, **1796**

ORIGIN TO DESTINATION. SHIPMENTS OF WESTERN LUMBER BY STATE AND MODE OF TRANSPORTATION (US/0732-0981) [08311871] **2403**

ORIGINAL BRITISH THEATRE DIRECTORY, THE (UK) [17642565] **5367**

●ORIGINAL GREAT SMOKY MOUNTAIN SAMPLER, THE (US/1061-4265) [25305940] **5487**

●ORIGINAL ... HIGHWAY 17 ALMANAC & GAZETTEER, THE (US/1054-4585) [22893999] **1927**

ORIGINAL HOME PLANS *CEASED.* (US/0899-4390) [18096782] **305**

ORIGINAL NEW ENGLAND GUIDE, THE (US/0734-4066) [07715309] **5487**

ORIGINAL NEWS PEPPER, THE (US/1071-233X) [22869339] **3907**

ORIGINAL NINJA, THE *CEASED.* (US/0896-9337) [17338133] **4864**

ORIGINAL RECIPES (US/1044-4637) [19793862] **2792**

ORIGINAL STATISTICS, ENGLAND AND WALES. SUPPLEMENTARY TABLES. VOL. 2, PROCEEDINGS IN THE CROWN COURT (UK) [08299403] 3171, **3082**

ORIGINAL WNC BUSINESS JOURNAL, THE (US/1065-027X) [26486371] **701**

ORIGINI (REGGIO EMILIA, ITALY) (IT) [17212207] **361**

ORIGINS BIBLICAL CREATION SOCIETY (UK/0953-2773) [I09532773] **4984**

ORIGINS (CHICAGO, ILL. 1984) (US/0890-8133) [12205009] **5018**

ORIGINS (GA.) (US) **2465**

ORIGINS (GRAND RAPIDS, MICH.) (US/0889-0501) [11646019] **2752**

ORIGINS (LOMA LINDA) (US/0093-7495) [01792930] 5018, **5136**

ORIGINS OF BEHAVIOR, THE (US/0094-6206) [01020186] **4606**

ORIGINS OF LIFE AND EVOLUTION OF THE BIOSPHERE (NE/0169-6149) [11807392] 491, **467**

ORIGINS RESEARCH (US/0748-9919) [11046746] **4354**

ORIGINS (WASHINGTON) (US/0093-609X) [01792456] **5033**

ORIJIN SHOSETSU JIDAI (JA) [03180486] **3420**

ORILLIA SUN (CN/0823-6763) [10051979] **5792**

ORILLIA TODAY [MICROFORM] (CN/1186-4893) [25796340] **5792**

ORINI SAE NONGMIN (KO) [11258003] **2507**

ORIOLE (ATLANTA), THE (US/0030-5553) [01761518] **5593**

ORION (IT) **4486**

ORION (SZ/0030-557X) [11149577] **398**

ORION COMPUTER PRICE WATCH (US/1056-8573) [23881726] **1245**

ORION JOHANNESBURG (SA/0259-191X) [I0259191X] **1989**

ORION MARKETING TRADE-IN GUIDE (US/0192-7302) [05053231] **934**

ORION (NEW YORK, N.Y.) (US/1058-3130) [24200839] **4170**

ORISSA, INDIA. IRRIGATION AND POWER DEPT *See* PERFORMANCE BUDGET - ORISSA, INDIA. IRRIGATION AND POWER DEPT **2094**

ORITA (NR/0030-5596) [02430085] **4984**

ORIZONT (RM/0030-560X) [06643936] **3420**

ORKESTER JOURNALEN (SW/0030-5642) [01773288] 5318, **4145**

ORL-HEAD AND NECK NURSING (US/1064-3842) [25786565] **3890**

ORL; JOURNAL FOR OTO-RHINO-LARYNGOLOGY AND ITS BORDERLANDS (SZ/0301-1569) [01638880] **3890**

ORLANDO BUSINESS JOURNAL (US/8750-8656) [11874103] **702**

ORLANDO MAGAZINE (US/0279-1323) [07568118] **2542**

ORLANDO SENTINEL, THE (US/0744-6055) [08377285] **5650**

ORLANDO SPECTATOR, THE (US/1070-860X) [28480800] **5650**

ORNAMENT COLLECTOR, THE (US/0895-9730) [16877535] **2776**

ORNAMENT (LOS ANGELES, CALIF.) (US/0148-3897) [03526104] 1086, **2915**

ORNAMENTAL CROPS, NATIONAL MARKET TRENDS / UNITED STATES DEPARTMENT OF AGRICULTURE, AGRICULTURAL MARKETING SERVICE, FRUIT AND VEGETABLE MARKET NEWS SERVICE (US) **180**

ORNAMENTAL HORTICULTURE (UK/0305-4934) [03817515] 2426, **2434**

ORNAMENTAL/MISCELLANEOUS METAL FABRICATOR (US/0191-5940) [04968202] **4014**

ORNAMENTALS NORTHWEST (1981) *SUSPENDED.* (US/0030-4778) [20127197] **2426**

ORNIS FENNICA (FI/0030-5685) [01761527] **5619**

ORNIS SCANDINAVICA *See* JOURNAL OF AVIAN BIOLOGY **5618**

ORNIS SCANDINAVICA (NO/0030-5693) [01605883] **5619**

ORNIS SVECICA (SW) [25637220] **5619**

ORNITHOLOGICAL MONOGRAPHS (US/0078-6594) [01424194] **5619**

ORNITHOLOGICAL NEWSLETTER (US/0274-564X) [06406079] **5619**

ORNITHOLOGICAL REPORT FOR - YORKSHIRE NATURALISTS' UNION (UK) [09665314] **5619**

ORNITHOLOGICAL SOCIETY OF THE MIDDLE EAST *See* BULLETIN - ORNITHOLOGICAL SOCIETY OF THE MIDDLE EAST **5616**

ORNITHOLOGISCHE BEOBACHTER (SZ/0030-5707) [03705001] **5619**

ORNITHOLOGISCHE GESELLSCHAFT IN BAYERN, MUNICH *See* ANZEIGER DER ORNITHOLOGISCHEN GESELLSCHAFT IN BAYERN **5614**

ORNITHOLOGISCHE GESELLSCHAFT IN BAYERN, MUNICH *See* VERHANDLUNGEN DER ORNITHOLOGISCHEN GESELLSCHAFT IN BAYERN **5620**

ORNITHOLOGISCHE MITTEILUNGEN (GW/0030-5723) [02401151] **5619**

ORNITHOLOGISCHE VERHANDLUNGEN / HERAUSGEGEBEN VON DER ORNITHOLOGISCHEN GESELLSCHAFT IN BAYERN V (GW) [24051269] **5619**

ORNITHOLOGISCHER ANZEIGER / HERAUSGEGEBEN VON DER ORNITHOLOGISCHEN GESELLSCHAFT IN BAYERN E.V (GW/0940-3256) [24884540] **5619**

ORNITOLOGIIA (RU/0474-7313) [01449187] **5593**

ORO MADRE (US/0730-3475) [07994722] **3421**

ORO VALLEY TERRITORIAL *CEASED.* (US/0888-3963) [13266234] **5630**

ORO VALLEY VOICE (US/8750-1260) [11005581] **5630**

ORO-VESPRA INDEPENDENT [MICROFORM] (CN/1186-4265) [25313871] **5792**

ORODHA MAALUM YA BEI / JAMHURI YA MUUNGANO WA TANZANIA, TUME YA BEI YA TAIFA (TZ) [10992099] **1594**

OROLOGI (IT) **2916**

OROMOCTO POST, THE (CN/0710-5460) [08713629] **5792**

ORPHEUS BERLIN (GW/0932-6111) [I09326111] **4145**

ORPHEUS : RIVISTA DI UMANITA CLASSICA E CRISTIANA (IT/0030-5790) [04812373] **1079**

ORPHIC LUTE (US/0030-5804) [03390568] **3467**

ORQUIDEA (MEXICO. 1971) (MX/0300-3701) [05225864] **520**

ORQUIDEOLOGIA (CK/0120-1433) [05331779] **2427**

ORS NOTE (US) [15188542] **5300**

ORSA JOURNAL ON COMPUTING (US/0899-1499) [18006127] **1198**

ORSTOM ACTUALITES (FR/0758-833X) [19227514] **5136**

ORSZAG VILAG *CEASED.* (HU) [06641324] **2520**

ORSZAGOS ERDESZETI EGYESULET *See* ERDO, AZ **2379**

ORSZAGOS SZECHENYI KONYVTAR *See* MIKROFILMEK CIMJEGYZEKE. MODERN NYOMTATVANYOK / ORSZAGOS SZECHENYI KONYVTAR **3231**

ORTA DERECELI OKULLAR OKUL ICI SPOR FAALIYETLERI (TU) [18678515] 1902, **4911**

ORTA DOGU TEKNIK UNIVERSITESI (ANKARA, TURKEY). MIMARLK FAKULTESI *See* M.E.T.U. JOURNAL OF THE FACULTY OF ARCHITECTURE **303**

ORTE (SZ) [03494259] **3421**

ORTESOL JOURNAL, THE (US/0192-401X) [05034965] **3308**

ORTHO GRAPHE, L' *See* ORTHOGRAPHE PLUS **1770**

ORTHODONTIC DIRECTORY OF THE WORLD (US) [03834262] **1332**

ORTHODONTIC REVIEW (US/0895-5034) [16668045] **1332**

ORTHODONTIE FRANCAISE, L' (FR/0078-6608) [07541469] **1332**

ORTHODOX CATHOLIC VOICE, THE (US) [09974065] **5039**

ORTHODOX CHURCH IN AMERICA *See* YEARBOOK AND CHURCH DIRECTORY OF THE ORTHODOX CHURCH IN AMERICA **5040**

ORTHODOX CHURCH, THE (US/0048-2269) [02669144] **5039**

ORTHODOX HERALD, THE (US/0744-1495) [01605382] **5039**

ORTHODOX LIFE (US/0030-5820) [01641539] **5040**

ORTHODOX MONITOR, THE (US) [11717725] **4984**

ORTHODOX OBSERVER (US/0731-2547) [07050370] **4984**

ORTHODOX THOUGHT AND LIFE : A JOURNAL DEVOTED TO POPULAR ORTHODOX ENLIGHTENMENT AND EASTERN CHRISTIAN SPIRITUALITY (US/0737-738X) [15189492] **4984**

ORTHODOX TRADITION (US/0742-4019) [10332224] **4984**

ORTHODOX WORD, THE (US/0030-5839) [01779213] **5040**

ORTHODOXIE HEUTE (GW/0931-0347) **5040**

●ORTHOGRAPHE PLUS (CN/1191-5099) [26715121] **1770**

ORTHOPADISCHE PRAXIS (GW/0030-588X) [00972547] **3883**

ORTHOPAEDIC KNOWLEDGE UPDATE ... HOME STUDY SYLLABUS (US/0892-7685) [10112085] **3883**

ORTHOPAEDIC NETWORK NEWS (US/1059-311X) [24562854] **3883**

●ORTHOPAEDIC PHYSICAL THERAPY CLINICS OF NORTH AMERICA (US/1059-1516) [24486704] **3883, 4381**

ORTHOPAEDIC PRODUCT NEWS (UK/0954-4755) [I09544755] **3883**

ORTHOPAEDIC RESEARCH SOCIETY *See* TRANSACTIONS OF THE ANNUAL MEETING OF THE ORTHOPAEDIC RESEARCH SOCIETY **3885**

ORTHOPAEDIC REVIEW (US/0094-6591) [01026757] **3883**

ORTHOPAEDIC TRANSACTIONS (US/0162-9379) [03486915] **3884**

ORTHOPAEDICS (GLENDALE, CALIF.) (US/0271-132X) [05730587] **3884**

●ORTHOPAEDICS INTERNATIONAL EDITION (US) **3884**

ORTHOPAEDIE-TECHNIK (GW/0340-5591) [I03405591] **3884**

ORTHOPEDIC CLINICS OF NORTH AMERICA, THE (US/0030-5898) [01761532] **3884**

ORTHOPEDIC NURSING / NATIONAL ASSOCIATION OF ORTHOPEDIC NURSES (US/0744-6020) [08424301] **3866, 3884**

ORTHOPEDIC PRODUCT NEWS *CEASED.* (US/1042-704X) [19111156] **3884**

ORTHOPEDIC RESIDENT, THE *CEASED.* (US/1056-4543) [23717469] **3884**

ORTHOPEDIC SURGEON'S COMPENDIUM OF DRUG THERAPY, THE (US/0276-4350) [07361288] **3884**

ORTHOPEDIC SURGEONS' LEGAL LETTER (US/0741-7470) [09089119] **3742**

ORTHOPEDIC SURGERY (NE/0014-4371) [01568596] **3971, 3661**

ORTHOPEDICS (THOROFARE) (US/0147-7447) [04389249] **3884**

ORTHOPEDICS TODAY (US/0279-5647) [07096845] **3884**

ORTHOPEDIE TRAUMATOLOGIE : EUROPEAN JOURNAL OF ORTHOPAEDIC SURGERY & TRAUMATOLOGY : ORGANE OFFICIEL DE LA SOCIETE D'ORTHOPEDIE ET DE TRAUMATOLOGIE DE L'EST DE LA FRANCE (SOTEST) ET DU GROUPE D'ETUDE POUR LA CHIRURGIE OSSEUSE (GECO) (FR/0940-3264) [25545427] **3884**

ORTHOVISIES (NE/0167-4439) [07480135] **1883**

ORTNAMNSSALLSKAPET I UPPSALA (SWEDEN) *See* ORTNAMNSSALLSKAPETS I UPPSALA ARSSKRIFT **3308**

ORTNAMNSSALLSKAPETS I UPPSALA ARSSKRIFT (SW/0473-4351) [01779214] **3308**

ORTODONCIA ESPANOLA (SP) **1332**

ORTODOXIA (RM) [04870169] **5040**

ORTONVILLE INDEPENDENT (US) [01761534] **5697**

ORTOPEDIA E TRAUMATOLOGIA OGGI (IT/0392-1417) [12185633] **3884**

ORTOPEDIJA, TRAVMATOLOGIJA I PROTEZIROVANIE (RU/0030-5987) [01604426] **3884**

ORTSVERZEICHNIS II, VERZEICHNIS DER ORTE IM BEREICH DER DEUTSCHEN POSTVERWALTUNGEN (GW) [03353738] **1146**

ORTUNG UND NAVIGATION (GW/0474-7550) [I04747550] **4181**

ORVOSI HETILAP (HU/0030-6002) [05587292] **3624**

ORVOSI KONYVTAROS, AZ (HU/0030-6010) [02265557] **3240**

ORVOSKEPZES (BUDAPEST) (HU/0030-6037) [06644735] **3624**

ORVOSTORTENETI KOZLEMENYEK (HU/0010-3551) [01041937] **3624, 2625**

ORYX (UK/0030-6053) [01715279] **2201**

ORYZA (II/0474-7615) [05298955] **180**

ORZECZNICTWO GOSPODARCZE (PL) [26558150] **3102**

ORZECZNICTWO SADU NAJWYZSZEGO. IZBA CYWILNA I ADMINISTRACYJNA ORAZ IZBA PRACY I UBEZPIECZEN SPOECZNYCH (PL/0209-2182) [01762531] **5300**

OS/2 DEVELOPER (US/1073-0729) [29305946] **1198**

●OS/2 MAGAZINE (US/1073-1547) [29347258] **1198**

●OS/2 MONTHLY (US/1068-6835) [27750699] **1198**

●OS2 PROFESSIONAL (US/1069-6814) [28135131] **1289**

OSAGE COUNTY CHRONICLE (BURLINGAME, KAN. : 1983) (US/1040-6077) [12185797] **5678**

OSAHRC REPORTS (US/0094-7776) [01795353] **2867, 3023**

OSAKA CITY MEDICAL JOURNAL (JA/0030-6096) [01644166] **3624**

OSAKA DAIGAKU IGAKU ZASSHI (JA/0030-6169) [01761539] **3624**

OSAKA DAIGAKU (JAPAN). SANGYO KAGAKU KENKYUJO *See* MEMOIRS OF THE INSTITUTE OF SCIENTIFIC AND INDUSTRIAL RESEARCH, OSAKA UNIVERSITY **5128**

OSAKA DAIGAKU. KEIZAI GAKUBU *See* OSAKA DAIGAKU KEIZAIGAKU **1594**

OSAKA DAIGAKU KEIZAIGAKU (JA) [06895041] **1594**

OSAKA DAIGAKU. KOGAKUBU *See* TECHNOLOGY REPORTS OF THE OSAKA UNIVERSITY **1998**

OSAKA DAIGAKU. KYOYOBU *See* SCIENCE REPORTS - OSAKA UNIVERSITY. COLLEGE OF GENERAL EDUCATION **1858**

OSAKA DAIGAKU. NINGEN-KAGAKUBU *See* OSAKA DAIGAKU NINGEN-KAGAKUBU KIYO **243**

OSAKA DAIGAKU NINGEN-KAGAKUBU KIYO (JA) [02325244] **1770, 243**

OSAKA DAIGAKU. YOSETSU KOGAKU KENKYUJO *See* TRANSACTIONS OF JWRI **4022**

OSAKA DENKI TSUSHIN DAIGAKU KENKYU RONSHU. JINBUN SHAKAI KAGAKU HEN (JA) [10809651] **1839**

OSAKA DENKI TSUSHIN DAIGAKU KENKYU RONSHU. SHIZEN KAGAKU HEN (JA/0386-4987) [10814293] **5136**

OSAKA ECONOMIC PAPERS *See* OSAKA DAIGAKU KEIZAIGAKU **1594**

OSAKA-FU KAGAKU KYOIKU SENTA *See* KENKYU HOKOKU SHUROKU **1760**

OSAKA-FU- KOJO BENRAN (JA) [03689014] **702**

OSAKA FURITSU DAIGAKU *See* BULLETIN OF THE UNIVERSITY OF OSAKA PREFECTURE. SERIES B: AGRICULTURE AND BIOLOGY **70**

OSAKA FURITSU DAIGAKU, SAKAI, JAPAN *See* BULLETIN OF UNIVERSITY OF OSAKA PREFECTURE. SERIES A : ENGINEERING AND NATURAL SCIENCES **1967**

OSAKA FURITSU KOGYO GIJUTSU KENKYUJO *See* GYOMU NEMPO - OSAKA FURITSU KOGYO GIJUTSU KENKYUJO **5108**

OSAKA FURITSU NAKANOSHIMA TOSHOKAN *See* OSAKA FURITSU NAKANOSHIMA TOSHOKAN ZOKA TOSHO MOKUROKU **3240**

OSAKA FURITSU NAKANOSHIMA TOSHOKAN *See* OSAKA FURITSU NAKANOSHIMA TOSHOKAN KIYO **3240**

OSAKA FURITSU NAKANOSHIMA TOSHOKAN KIYO (JA) [02245030] **3240**

OSAKA FURITSU NAKANOSHIMA TOSHOKAN ZOKA TOSHO MOKUROKU (JA) [02245031] **3240**

OSAKA FURITSU YUHIGAOKA TOSHOKAN *See* OSAKA FURITSU YUHIGAOKA TOSHOKAN ZOKA TOSHO MOKUROKU **3240**

OSAKA FURITSU YUHIGAOKA TOSHOKAN ZOKA TOSHO MOKUROKU (JA) [02245029] **3240**

OSAKA JOURNAL OF MATHEMATICS (JA/0030-6126) [01761542] **3526**

OSAKA KANKU FUKEN KISHO KENKYUKAI *See* OSAKA KANKU FUKEN KISHO KENKYUKAI SHI **1433**

OSAKA KANKU FUKEN KISHO KENKYUKAI SHI (JA) [02244468] **1433**

OSAKA KOGYO GIJUTSU SHIKENJO *See* OSAKA KOGYO GIJUTSU SHIKENJO, KIHO **5136**

OSAKA KOGYO GIJUTSU SHIKENJO *See* YORAN - KOGYO GIJUTSUIN OSAKA KOGYO GIJUTSU SHIKENJO **996**

OSAKA KOGYO GIJUTSU SHIKENJO *See* OSAKA KOGYO GIJUTSU SHIKENJO NEMPO **988**

OSAKA KOGYO GIJUTSU SHIKENJO *See* OSAKA KOGYO GIJUTSU SHIKENJO HOKOKU **1989**

OSAKA KOGYO GIJUTSU SHIKENJO HOKOKU (JA/0472-1438) [05192236] **1989**

OSAKA KOGYO GIJUTSU SHIKENJO, KIHO (JA/0472-142X) [04552778] **5136**

OSAKA KOGYO GIJUTSU SHIKENJO NEMPO (JA) [01799681] **988**

OSAKA NO REKISHI / OSAKA SHISHI HENSANJO (JA) [07529161] **2661**

OSAKA-SHI IGAKKAI ZASSHI (JA/0386-4103) [09802529] **3790**

OSAKA SHIKA DAIGAKU *See* JOURNAL OF OSAKA DENTAL UNIVERSITY **1327**

OSAKA SHIRITSU DAIGAKU. KOGAKUBU *See* MEMOIRS OF THE FACULTY OF ENGINEERING, OSAKA CITY UNIVERSITY **1987**

OSAKA SHIRITSU KANKYO KAGAKY KENKYUJO HOKOKU. CHOSA KENKYU NEMPO (JA/0285-5801) [09572101] 2179, **4795**

OSAKA SHIRITSU SHIZEN KAGAKU HAKUBUTSUKAN *See* SHIZENSHI KENKYU. / OCCASIONAL PAPERS FROM THE OSAKA MUSEUM OF NATURAL HISTORY **4172**

OSAKA SHOIN JOSHI DAIGAKU GAKUJUTSU KENKYUKAI *See* OSAKA SHOIN JOSHI DAIGAKU RON SHU **1839**

OSAKA SHOIN JOSHI DAIGAKU RON SHU (JA) [02243581] **1839**

OSAKA ZEIKAN (JA) [02244643] **4740**

OSAMAYOR : GRADUATE STUDENT MAGAZINE / DEPT. OF HISPANIC L & L, UNIVERSITY OF PITTSBURGH (US) [21966096] **3308**

OSAP ANNOUNCEMENT, SUMMARY AND ANALYSIS (CN/0823-8804) [11449426] **1839**

OSAP PREVENTION PIPELINE *See* CSAP PREVENTION PIPELINE / CENTER FOR SUBSTANCE ABUSE PREVENTION, THE **1342**

OSAP PREVENTION PIPELINE / OFFICE FOR SUBSTANCE ABUSE PREVENTION, THE (US) [25667321] **1347**

OSAP TECHNICAL REPORT / [OFFICE OF SUBSTANCE ABUSE PREVENTION] (US) [23155985] **1347**

OSAR/OSALL (SA) [06746057] **3023, 3240**

OSAWATOMIE (US/0097-8906) [01799503] **4544**

OSAWATOMIE GRAPHIC-NEWS, THE (US) [08802620] **5678**

OSBORNE COMPANY *See* ANNUAL CATALOGUE OF ART CALENDARS ... **336**

OSBORNE COUNTY FARMER (OSBORNE, KAN. : 1958) (US/1040-9033) [12268310] **5678**

OSC BULLETIN (CN/0226-9325) [08598160] **910**

OSCA REPORTS (1990) (CN/1193-9524) [28061945] **1868**

OSCAR ISRAELOWITZ'S GUIDE TO JEWISH NEW YORK CITY *CEASED.* (US) [18902482] **5269**

OSCAR ISRAELOWITZ'S GUIDE TO THE LOWER EAST SIDE (US) [16704428] **2542**

OSCAR MUSICA (IT) [12310449] **4145**

OSCAR : OTTAWA SOUTH COMMUNITY ASSOCIATION REVIEW (CN/0715-5476) [09804059] **5792**

OSCEOLA COUNTY GAZETTE-TRIBUNE, THE (US) [14987205] **5672**

OSCEOLA SENTINEL-TRIBUNE (US/0745-6247) [09314117] **5672**

OSCEOLA SUN (OSCEOLA, WIS.) (US) [13119741] **5769**

OSCEOLA (TALLAHASSEE, FLA.), THE (US/0747-0991) [10546049] **4911**

OSD, OS MAP ADDITIONS LIST (UK) [19409629] **2571**

OSEANOLOGI DI INDONESIA (IO) [02245666] **556**

OSEBNI DOHODKI ZA DOLOCENE POKLICE / ZAVOD SR SLOVENIJE ZA STATISTIKO (XV) [07934552] **1577**

OSEILLEUR, L' (CN/0228-2119) [07313893] **2752**

OSERS NEWS IN PRINT (US/0888-5508) [13660940] **5300**

OSGOOD JOURNAL, THE (US) [11379103] **5666**

OSGOODE HALL LAW JOURNAL (CN) [02349900] **3023**

OSGOODE HALL LAW JOURNAL (1960) (CN/0030-6185) [01761550] **3023**

OSGOODE HALL OBITER DICTA *See* OBITER DICTA (1963) **3020**

OSHA 1910 COMPLIANCE MANUAL (US) **2867**

OSHA 1926 COMPLIANCE MANUAL (US) **2867**

OSHA CD-ROM (US/1065-9277) [25363814] **2867**

OSHA COMPLIANCE ADVISOR (US/0896-9949) [17360977] **2867**

OSHA PUBLICATIONS & TRAINING MATERIAL (US) [05763134] **2868**

OSHA TRAINING BULLETIN FOR SUPERVISORS (US/0896-9957) [17360963] **2868**

OSHA WEEK (US/1057-1485) [23957383] **2868**

OSHANEWS (US/0740-1418) [05976998] **2868**

OSHAWA THIS WEEKEND (CN/0229-7744) [08324000] **5792**

OSHKAABEWIS — Alphabetical Title Index

OSHKAABEWIS NATIVE JOURNAL (US/1053-0193) [22435298] **3421**

OSHKOSH ADVANCE-TITAN (US/0300-676X) [01372701] **5769**

OSHKOSH NORTHWESTERN (OSHKOSH, WIS. : 1979 : DAILY) (US) [15247465] **5769**

OSI PRODUCT & EQUIPMENT NEWS (US/0898-0489) [17697181] **1198**

OSIA NEWS (US/0886-182X) [12850557] **2491**

OSIAGNIECIA NAUKOWO-BADAWCZE POLITECHNIKI GDANSKIEJ W ... ROKU / POLITECHNIKA GDANSKA (PL) [08265242] **5136**

OSINETTER NEWSLETTER, THE (US/0888-6997) [13696224] **1198**

OSIRIS (BRUGES) (US/0369-7827) [01761551] **5135**

OSIRIS (SCHENECTADY, N.Y.) (US/0095-019X) [02449359] **3467**

OSJECKI ZBORNIK (CI/0473-4882) [06472672] **4095**

OSKALOOSA HERALD (OSKALOOSA, IOWA : 1977) (US/0898-2066) [15866829] **5672**

OSKALOOSA INDEPENDENT, THE (US) [11821333] **5678**

OSLA. ONTARIO ASSOCIATION OF SPEECH-LANGUAGE PATHOLOGISTS AND AUDIOLOGISTS (CN/0836-4362) [17235668] **3896**

OSLENYTANI VITAK (HU) [09609133] **4228**

OSLER LIBRARY NEWSLETTER (CN/0085-4557) [02265564] **3624**

OSLO. UNIVERSITET. BOTANISK HAVE *See* INDEX SEMINUM **2420**

OSMANIA JOURNAL OF ENGLISH STUDIES (II/0474-8107) [01761558] **3421**

OSMANIA PAPERS IN LINGUISTICS (II/0970-0277) [02245634] **3308**

OSMANIA UNIVERSITY, HYDERABAD, INDIA. CENTRE OF EXPLORATION GEOPHYSICS *See* C. E. G. BULLETIN **2136**

OSMANL ARASTRMALAR (TU) [07969253] **2661**

OSMOSE (MONTREAL) (CN/0829-5131) [13448544] **3866**

OSNABRUCKER LAND HEIMAT-JAHRBUCH (GW) [04219415] **2701**

OSNABRUCKER MITTEILUNGEN (GW/0474-8158) [02671480] **327**

OSNOVANIIA, FUNDAMENTY I MEKHANIKA GRUNTOV (RU) [06586325] **2028**

OSNOVNE I SREDNJE SKOLE (YU) [01785882] 1771, **1796**

OSNOVNE IN SREDNJE SOLE (XV) [06969213] **1771**

OSNOVNE SOLE PO KRAJEVNIH SKUPNOSTIH (XV) [06875586] **1771**

OSNOVNI UCILISTA VO SRM SPORED GRADSKO-SELSKO PODRACJE (YU) [06907945] 1771, **1796**

OSNOVY BALKANSKOGO IAZYKOZNANIIA (RU) [23984053] **3309**

OSON (KO) [09201199] 594, **2310**

OSPEDALE (IT/0030-6231) [I00306231] **3790**

OSPEDALE MAGGIORE (IT/0369-7843) [01778322] **3790**

OSPEDALE PSICHIATRICO (IT/0048-2285) [10596064] **3932**

OSPEDALI DELLA VITA, GLI (IT) **3790**

OSPEDALI D'ITALIA-CHIRURGIA (IT/0030-6266) [01778323] **3971**

OSPEDALI ITALIANI-PEDIATRIA (E SPECIALITA CHIRURGICHE) (IT/0020-6274) [I00306274] **3907**

OSPEDALITA PRIVATA (IT) **3790**

OSPREY (CN/0710-4847) [08674376] **4170**

OSSA *CEASED.* (SW/0345-8865) [02177827] **3624**

OSSC BULLETIN (US/0095-6694) [02153848] **1771**

OSSC REPORT (US/0733-2548) [08437963] **1771**

OSSERVATORE ROMANO, L' (VC/0030-6312) [01604708] **5813**

OSSERVATORE SANITARIO (IT) **3790**

OSSERVATORIO ASTRONOMICO DI BRERA *See* OSSERVAZIONI METEOROLOGICHE **1433**

OSSERVATORIO DELLE ARTI / ACCADEMIA CARRARA *SUSPENDED.* (IT) [19415618] **361**

OSSERVATORIO FINANZIARIO REGIONALE / ISTITUTO DI STUDI SULLE REGIONI - C.N.R (IT) [10490721] **4740**

OSSERVATORIO ISFOL (IT) [20333699] **5137**

OSSERVATORIO SUL MERCATO IMMOBILIARE (IT) **4842**

OSSERVATORIO SUL MERCATO ORTOFRUTTICOLO (IT) **180**

OSSERVAZIONI METEOROLOGICHE (IT) [20059574] **1433**

OSSIAN BEE, THE (US) [15203245] **5672**

OSSIAN JOURNAL, THE (US) [13871409] **5666**

OSSIPEE VALLEY TIMES (US/1049-2399) [21182724] **5708**

OST-DOKUMENTATION BILDUNGS- UND WISSENSCHAFTSPOLITIK (AU) [24530041] **4486**

OSTBAIRISCHE GRENZMARKEN (GW/0078-6845) [02682585] **327**

OSTEO (FR) **4795**

● OSTEOARTHRITIS AND CARTILAGE (UK/1063-4584) [26040908] **3806**

OSTEOLOGIE (SZ/1019-1291) **3800**

OSTEOPATHIC ANNALS *CEASED.* (US/0092-9336) [03252165] **3624**

OSTEOPATHIC PHYSICIAN'S COMPENDIUM OF DRUG THERAPY, THE (US/0272-7064) [06880333] **4318**

OSTEOPATHIE *See* OSTEO **4795**

OSTEOPATHIE : THERAPIES MANUELLES (FR/0753-6019) [I1167380X] **4795**

OSTEOPOROSIS INTERNATIONAL : A JOURNAL ESTABLISHED AS RESULT OF COOPERATION BETWEEN THE EUROPEAN FOUNDATION FOR OSTEOPOROSIS AND THE NATIONAL OSTEOPOROSIS FOUNDATION OF THE USA (UK/0937-941X) [22815329] **3806**

OSTEOPOROSIS UPDATE (US/0894-3311) [15998069] **3624**

OSTERREICH IN AMERIKANISCHE SICHT (US/0882-3006) [11804591] **3421**

OSTERREICHISCHDS SCHULENVERZEICHNIS. MHS (AU) [21883398] **1915**

OSTERREICHISCHE AKADEMIE DER WISSENSCHAFTEN *See* ALMANACH - OSTERREICHISCHE AKADEMIE DER WISSENSCHAFTEN **2513**

OSTERREICHISCHE AMTSVORMUND, DER (AU) [05272946] **3122**

OSTERREICHISCHE ARBEITSGEMEINSCHAFT FUR NEUROPATHOLOGIE. JAHRESTAGUNG *See* AKTUELLE PROBLEME DER NEUROPATHOLOGIE **3892**

OSTERREICHISCHE ARZTEZEITUNG (AU/0029-8786) [I00298786] **3624**

OSTERREICHISCHE BAUZEITUNG (AU/0029-8891) [01789869] **623**

OSTERREICHISCHE BEITRAGE ZU METEOROLOGIE UND GEOPHYSIK (AU/1016-6254) [10166254] 1409, **1433**

OSTERREICHISCHE BETRIEBSWIRT *See* JOURNAL FUER BETRIEBWIRTSCHAFT **1613**

OSTERREICHISCHE BIBLIOGRAPHIE. REIHE C, NEUERE AUSLANDISCHE AUSTRIACA. AUSWAHLBIBLIOGRAPHIE / BEARBEITET UND HERAUSGEGEBEN VON DER OSTERREICHISCHEN NATIONALBIBLIOTHEK (AU) [25962043] **421**

OSTERREICHISCHE BOLSCHEWIKI-LENINISTEN *See* BULLETIN DER BOLSCHEWIKI-LENINISTEN **4540**

OSTERREICHISCHE CHEMIE-ZEITSCHRIFT (AU/03142885] **988**

OSTERREICHISCHE DENTISTENZEITSCHRIFT *See* OSTERREICHISCHE ZAHNARZTE ZEITUNG : OZZ **1332**

OSTERREICHISCHE FORSTZEITUNG (1987) (AU) [16162860] **2390**

OSTERREICHISCHE GALERIE *See* MITTEILUNGEN DER OSTERREICHISCHEN GALERIE **358**

OSTERREICHISCHE GEOGRAPHISCHE GESELLSCHAFT *See* MITTEILUNGEN DER OSTERREICHISCHEN GEOGRAPHISCHEN GESELLSCHAFT **2569**

OSTERREICHISCHE GEOLOGISCHE GESELLSCHAFT *See* MITTEILUNGEN DER OSTERREICHISCHEN GEOLOGISCHEN GESELLSCHAFT **1388**

OSTERREICHISCHE GESELLSCHAFT FUER FAMILIENPLANUNG. WISSENSCHAFTLICHE TAGUNG *See* FAMILIENPLANUNG / WISSENSCHAFTLICHE TAGUNG DER OSTERREICHISCHEN GESELLSCHAFT FUER FAMILIENPLANUNG **588**

OSTERREICHISCHE GESELLSCHAFT FUR MUSIKWISSENSCHAFT *See* MITTEILUNGEN DER OSTERREICHISCHEN GESELLSCHAFT FUER MUSIKWISSENSCHAFT **4131**

OSTERREICHISCHE GESELLSCHAFT FUR RAUMFORSCHUNG UND RAUMPLANUNG *See* BERICHTE ZUR RAUMFORSCHUNG UND RAUMPLANUNG **2816**

OSTERREICHISCHE HISTORISCHE BIBLIOGRAPHIE (AU/0067-236X) [00986645] **2636**

OSTERREICHISCHE HOCHSCHULSTATISTIK (AU/0067-2343) [01814922] **1839**

OSTERREICHISCHE JURISTEN-ZEITUNG (AU/0029-9251) [01641202] **3024**

OSTERREICHISCHE KERAMISCHE RUNDSCHAU (AU/0472-5522) [03920966] **2593**

OSTERREICHISCHE LANDERBANK *See* LANDERBANK ECONOMIC BULLETIN **1502**

OSTERREICHISCHE LANDESBERICHTE ZUM INTERNATIONALEN KONGRESS FUER DAS RECHT DER ARBEIT UND DER SOZIALEN SICHERHEIT (AU) [02239447] **3153**

OSTERREICHISCHE MILCHWIRTSCHAFT (AU) [09423860] **197**

OSTERREICHISCHE MONATSHEFTE (AU/0029-9308) [02128055] **2701**

OSTERREICHISCHE OSTHEFTE (AU/0029-9375) [01761039] **2701**

OSTERREICHISCHE RINDERZUCHT. CATTLE BREEDING IN AUSTRIA. L'ALLEVAMENTO BOVINO IN AUSTRIA, DIE (AU) [04903658] **217**

OSTERREICHISCHE SOZIALVERSICHERUNG, DIE (AU) [01795329] 2889, **5300**

OSTERREICHISCHE TEXTILE-ZEITUNG (AU) [04051697] **5355**

OSTERREICHISCHE VOLKSKUNDLICHE BIBLIOGRAPHIE (AU) [06134795] **2325**

OSTERREICHISCHE ZAHNARZTE ZEITUNG : OZZ (AU) **1332**

OSTERREICHISCHE ZAHNTECHNIKER HANDWERK : OFFIZIELLES ORGAN DER BUNDESINNUNG DER ZAHNTECHNIKER, DAS (AU) [25545703] **1332**

OSTERREICHISCHE ZEITSCHRIFT FUER POLITIKWISSENSCHAFT (AU/0378-5149) [01115296] **4486**

OSTERREICHISCHE ZEITSCHRIFT FUER STATISTIK UND INFORMATIK (AU/1015-0811) [I10150811] **2352**

OSTERREICHISCHE ZEITSCHRIFT FUER STATISTIK UND INFORMATIK (AU) [13567906] **5212**

OSTERREICHISCHE ZEITSCHRIFT FUER VERMESSUNGSWESEN UND PHOTOGRAMMETRIE (GW) [05530202] **2571**

OSTERREICHISCHE ZEITSCHRIFT FUR VERMESSUNGSWESEN *See* OSTERREICHISCHE ZEITSCHRIFT FUER VERMESSUNGSWESEN UND PHOTOGRAMMETRIE **2571**

OSTERREICHISCHE ZOLL UND STEUER NACHRICHTEN (AU) [07828699] **4740**

OSTERREICHISCHER ENERGIEKONSUMENTEN-VERBAND *See* OEKV INFORMATIONEN **1952**

OSTERREICHISCHER FRISEUR (AU) **405**

OSTERREICHISCHER MARKENANZEIGER (AU) **1307**

OSTERREICHISCHER RAIFFEISENVERBAND *See* BERICHT / OSTERREICHISCHER RAIFFEISENVERBAND **778**

OSTERREICHISCHES ANWALTSBLATT (AU) [03259341] **3024**

OSTERREICHISCHES ARCHAOLOGISCHES INSTITUT *See* JAHRESHEFTE DES OSTERREICHISCHEN ARCHAOLOGISCHEN INSTITUTES IN WIEN **271**

OSTERREICHISCHES ARCHIV FUER KIRCHENRECHT (AU/0029-9820) [02627203] **4984**

OSTERREICHISCHES FORSCHUNGSINSTITUT FUR SPARKASSENWESEN. SCHRIFTENREIHE *See* VIERTELJAHRES-SCHRIFTENREIHE - OSTERREICHISCHES FORSCHUNGSINSTITUT FUR SPARKASSENWESEN **815**

OSTERREICHISCHES FORSCHUNGSZENTRUM SEIBERSDORF *See* JAHRESBERICHT / OSTERREICHISCHES FORSCHUNGSZENTRUM SEIBERSDORF **4448**

OSTERREICHISCHES INSTITUT FUER WIRTSCHAFTSFORSCHUNG See MONATSBERICHTE - OESTERREICHISCHES INSTITUT FUER WIRTSCHAFTSFORSCHUNG **1505**

OSTERREICHISCHES JAHRBUCH FUER EXLIBRIS UND GEBRAUCHSGRAPHIK (AU/0078-3633) [03732194] **361**

OSTERREICHISCHES JAHRBUCH FUER INTERNATIONALE POLITIK (AU/1015-616X) [13585151] **4530**

OSTERREICHISCHES JOURNAL FUER SPORTMEDIZIN (AU) [06600351] **3955**

OSTERREICHISCHES RECHT DER WIRTSCHAFT (AU) [10880786] **3024**

OSTERREICHISCHES STATISTISCHES ZENTRALAMT See WOHNUNGEN, DIE **2839**

OSTERREICHISCHES STATISTISCHES ZENTRALAMT See UMWELTDATEN **2245**

OSTERREICHISCHES STATISTISCHES ZENTRALAMT See SACHGUETERERZEUGUNG SCHNELLBERICHT **3487**

OSTERREICHISCHES STATISTISCHES ZENTRALAMT See GROSS- UND EINZELHANDELSSTATISTIK **838**

OSTERREICHISCHES STATISTISCHES ZENTRALAMT See OSTERREICHISCHE HOCHSCHULSTATISTIK **1839**

OSTERREICHISCHES STATISTISCHES ZENTRALAMT See RINDERRASSENERHEBUNG **156**

OSTERREICHISCHES STATISTISCHES ZENTRALAMT See INDUSTRIESTATISTIK **1534**

OSTERREICHISCHES STATISTISCHES ZENTRALAMT See STATISTISCHE NACHRICHTEN - OSTERREICHISCHES STATISTISCHES ZENTRALAMT **5343**

OSTERREICHISCHES STATISTISCHES ZENTRALAMT See GEMEINDEUBERSICHT **4553**

OSTERREICHISCHES STATISTISCHES ZENTRALAMT See ERHEBUNG DER LAND- UND FORSTWIRTSCHAFTLICHEN ARBEITSKRAFTE **1532**

OSTERREICHISCHES STATISTISCHES ZENTRALAMT See STATISTISCHES HANDBUCH FUER DIE REPUBLIK OESTERREICH **5343**

OSTERREICHS FISCHEREI (AU/0029-9987) [01761053] **2310**

OSTEUROPA-INSTITUT MUNCHEN See JAHRESBERICHT - OSTEUROPA-INSTITUT **5205**

OSTEUROPA-RECHT (GW/0030-6444) [01761568] **3024**

OSTEUROPA (STUTTGART) (GW/0030-6428) [01586529] **4486**

OSTEUROPA UND DER INTERNATIONALE KOMMUNISMUS (GW) [13714251] **4544**

OSTEUROPA WIRTSCHAFT (GW/0030-6460) [01761569] **1511**

OSTEUROPASTUDIEN DER HOCHSCHULEN DES LANDES HESSEN. REIHE I, GIESSENER ABHANDLUNGEN ZUR AGRAR- UND WIRTSCHAFTSFORSCHUNG DES EUROPAISCHEN OSTENS (GW/0078-6888) [02044544] **118**

OSTINFORMATION (GW) [01783937] **1577**

OSTKIRCHLICHE STUDIEN (GW/0030-6487) [01761572] **5040**

OSTOMY QUARTERLY (US/0030-6517) [02252961] **3971**

OSTOMY/WOUND MANAGEMENT (US/0889-5899) [14088884] **3624**

OSTRACODOLOGIST See CYPRIS **4226**

OSTREICULTEUR FRANCAIS, L' (FR/0297-4932) [I02974932] **2310**

OSTRICH NEWS (US/1067-7712) [21002388] **217**

●OSTRICH NEWS RATITE DIRECTORY, THE (US/1068-5774) [27705560] 118, **5517**

OSTRICH. SUPPLEMENT, THE (SA) [05313520] **5593**

OSTRICH, THE (SA/0030-6525) [01643047] **5619**

OSTRUCAVANJE RADNIKA U RADNIM ORGANIZACIJAMA (YU) [01789036] 1700, **1537**

OSU QUEST (US/0279-0025) [06751157] 5137, **1839**

OSVOENIE KOSMICHESKOGO PROSTRANSTVA V SSSR (RU) [02441178] **31**

OSWEGO COUNTY HISTORICAL SOCIETY See JOURNAL - OSWEGO COUNTY HISTORICAL SOCIETY **2743**

OSZK HIRADO (HU/0324-2064) [I03242064] **3240**

OT WEEK (US/0893-1712) [15372378] 3624, **1883**

OTA VIEWPOINT (CN/0824-2224) [10061806] **5389**

OTAGO DAILY TIMES, THE (NZ) [18399729] **5807**

OTAGO LAW REVIEW (NZ/0078-6918) [01792082] **3024**

OTAGO UNIVERSITY STUDIES IN PREHISTORIC ANTHROPOLOGY See UNIVERSITY OF OTAGO STUDIES IN PREHISTORIC ANTHROPOLOGY **247**

OTAN NEWSLETTER (US/0886-6864) [05712803] **5593**

OTAR (NE) [06705917] **2028**

OTBOR I OBRABOTKA INFORMATSII / AKADEMIIA NAUK UKRAINSKOI SSR, FIZIKO-MEKANICHESKII INSTITUT IM. G.V. KARPENKO (UN) [18664425] **3486**

OTC CHART MANUAL (US) [08464361] **910**

OTC HANDBOOK *CEASED.* (US/0733-026X) [07948831] **910**

OTC NEWS & MARKET REPORT (UK/0956-2559) [I09562559] **4318**

OTCHIZNA (PL) [02265577] **2520**

OTECHESTVEN VESTNIK (BU) [22375146] **5779**

●OTECHESTVENNAIA GEOLOGIIA (RU) [28105114] **1390**

●OTECHESTVENNAIA ISTORIIA (RU) [26265290] 2702, **2466**

OTHER CLARE (IE/0332-088X) [I0332088X] 277, **2702**

OTHER DAIRY BREEDS WITH IMPROVED CONTEMPORARY COMPARISONS (UK) [06520788] **197**

OTHER FRONT, THE (IS) **2770**

OTHER ISRAEL : NEWSLETTER OF THE ISRAELI COUNCIL FOR ISRAELI-PALESTINIAN PEACE, THE (IS/0792-4615) [10859606] **2270**

OTHER MANUFACTUREING INDUSTRIES (CN/0835-0191) [18652129] **3486**

OTHER MISCELLANEOUS MANUFACTURING INDUSTRIES (CN/0384-398X) [05257523] 3486, **3490**

OTHER SIDE OF MEXICO, THE (MX) [18157133] **4486**

OTHER SIDE OF THE BOAT (US) **4984**

OTHER SIDE (SAVANNAH), THE (US/0145-7675) [02250527] **4984**

OTHER VOICES (HIGHLAND PARK, ILL.) (US/8756-4696) [11566862] **3421**

OTIS RUSH (AT/0819-7288) [I08197288] **327**

OTKRYTIIA, IZOBRETENIIA See IZOBRETENIIA : OFITSIALNYI PATENTNYI BIULLETEN **1305**

OTO REVIEW (US/0197-0674) [05917440] **3890**

OTO-RHINO-LARYNGOLOGIA NOVA (SZ/1014-8221) [24245943] **3890**

OTO-RINO-LARINGOLOGIIA (BU/0473-5609) [07600076] **3890**

OTOLARYNGOLOGIA POLSKA (PL/0030-6657) [06286324] **3890**

OTOLARYNGOLOGIC CLINICS OF NORTH AMERICA, THE (US/0030-6665) [01761675] **3890**

OTOLARYNGOLOGY (JA) **3890**

OTOLARYNGOLOGY AND HEAD AND NECK SURGERY (US/0194-5998) [07236111] **3971**

OTOLARYNGOLOGY, AUDIOLOGY : AN ILLUSTRATED DESK DIARY (CN/1057-3704) [24020363] **3890**

OTOLARYNGOLOGY--HEAD AND NECK SURGERY. SOUND RECORDING (US) [07793489] **3890**

●OTOLARYNGOLOGY JOURNAL CLUB JOURNAL, THE (US/1070-8049) [28471616] **3890**

●OTOLOGY-NEUROTOLOGY (NEW YORK, N.Y.) (US/1077-1123) [30698591] **3624**

OTOMESHON (JA/0473-5587) [I04735587] **2124**

OTORHINOLARYNGOLOGIE, STOMATOLOGIE, PATHOLOGIE, CERVICOFACIALE, E72 (FR) **3625**

OTORINOLARINGOLOGIA (IT/0392-6621) [07831875] **3890**

OTORINOLARINGOLOGIA PEDIATRICA, L' (IT/1120-3455) [I11203455] **3890**

OTOT (IS) [04688203] **763**

OTRO DERECHO, EL (CK) [21266056] **3024**

OTTAGONO (IT/0391-7487) [13563760] 2902, **305**

OTTAGONO (IT/0391-7487) [04088181] 305, 2099, **2902**

OTTAGONO (IT/0391-7487) [27024739] **3486**

OTTAGONO. ENGLISH. OTTAGONO See OTTAGONO **3486**

OTTAR (NO/0030-6703) [01125961] **4170**

OTTAWA ARCHAEOLOGIST, THE (CN/0702-7974) [03412299] **277**

OTTAWA BANDING GROUP (CN/0827-2298) [11575663] **5619**

OTTAWA BRANCH NEWS - ONTARIO GENEALOGICAL SOCIETY (CN/0708-5583) [06244521] **2466**

OTTAWA BUSINESS MAGAZINE (CN/0849-1836) [22934652] **702**

OTTAWA BUSINESS QUARTERLY (CN/1193-1485) [I11931485] **702**

OTTAWA-CARLETON HEADLINER (CN/1183-4374) [25127451] **118**

OTTAWA CITIZEN. MICROFORM, THE (CN/0839-3222) [18299588] **5792**

OTTAWA CITIZEN SKI GUIDE, THE (CN/0846-1074) [24368673] **4911**

OTTAWA CITY DIRECTORY (TORONTO, ONT.) (CN) [10310569] **2571**

OTTAWA CO-OPERATIVE DIRECTORY (CN/0228-8656) [08028113] **1543**

OTTAWA COUNTY EXPONENT, THE (US) [11914717] **5729**

OTTAWA GREENS NEWSLETTER (CN/0826-1113) [10862180] **4486**

OTTAWA HERALD, THE (US) [11284417] **5678**

OTTAWA-HULL, CANADA'S CAPITAL (CN/0849-2093) [23237184] **5487**

OTTAWA-HULL GASTRONOMIC (CN/0714-8232) [09071320] **5072**

OTTAWA, HULL (NEPEAN) (CN/0822-8086) [10517753] **2572**

OTTAWA-HULL (OTTAWA, ONT.) (CN/0826-2527) [11100362] **386**

OTTAWA-HULL : THE KEY (CN/0705-2820) [04129483] **2572**

●OTTAWA JEWISH BULLETIN (1993) (CN/1196-1929) [29533996] **2270**

OTTAWA JEWISH BULLETIN & REVIEW (CN/0319-1303) [02442109] **2270**

OTTAWA JOURNAL (INDEX) (CN/0226-1081) [06272608] **2542**

OTTAWA LAW REVIEW (CN/0048-2331) [01645540] **3024**

OTTAWA LETTER (CN/0702-8210) [03417919] **4671**

OTTAWA MOSAIC, THE (CN/0828-8690) [12816373] **5253**

OTTAWA NEWSLETTER (CN/0700-995X) [03291500] **5300**

OTTAWA ON THE RECORD (CN/0828-5713) [11919015] **4486**

OTTAWA PUBLIC LIBRARY See PERIODICALS - OTTAWA PUBLIC LIBRARY (1991) **3240**

OTTAWA QUARTERLY (CN/0713-8091) [09029892] **1620**

OTTAWA R & D REPORT (CN/0380-6251) [02097736] **5137**

OTTAWA REPORTER, THE (CN/0715-3325) [09149665] **5792**

OTTAWA SUN, THE (CN/0843-2570) [19898585] **5792**

●OTTAWA VALLEY OFFICIAL TRAVEL GUIDE (CN/1191-2650) [26497701] **5487**

OTTAWA VALLEY PEOPLE'S YELLOW PAGES (CN/0383-6967) [03235800] **2572**

OTTAWA VALLEY ... TRAVEL GUIDE See OTTAWA VALLEY OFFICIAL TRAVEL GUIDE **5487**

OTTAWA WOMEN'S CENTRE See NEWSLETTER - OTTAWA WOMEN'S CENTRE **5562**

OTTAWA'S SENIOR EXECUTIVES GUIDE See CANADIAN FEDERAL GOVERNMENT HANDBOOK **4636**

OTTERWISE (PORTLAND, ME.) *CEASED.* (US/1052-8415) [22404319] **1067**

OTTO NOVECENTO (IT) **3421**

OTTO RANK ASSOCIATION See JOURNAL OF THE OTTO RANK ASSOCIATION **4602**

OTTUMWA COURIER (US/0886-4209) [12884181] **5672**

OUA/DATA'S ... GUIDE TO CORPORATE & FOUNDATION GIVING IN VERMONT (US/0884-996X) [11942387] **4338**

OUA/DATA'S ... GUIDE TO CORPORATE GIVING IN MAINE (US/0883-2730) [11942481] **4338**

OUA/DATA'S ... GUIDE TO CORPORATE GIVING IN RHODE ISLAND (US) [11942589] **4338**

OUACHITA CITIZEN, THE (US/0746-7478) [10239747] **5684**

OUACHITA COUNTY HISTORICAL QUARTERLY (US) [04601039] **2752**

OUD HOLLAND (NE/0030-672X) [01761581] **361**

OUDERS VAN NU (NE) 1067, **2284**

OUDTESTAMENTISCHE Alphabetical Title Index

OUDTESTAMENTISCHE STUDIEN (NE/0169-7226) [01777062] **5018**

OUEST AFRICAIN, L' (SG) [01787692] **2642**

OUEST FRANCE (FR) **5801**

OUEST MEDICAL PARIS (FR/0048-2366) [I00482366] **3625**

OUI (US/0090-2047) [01784788] **2491**

OUI ALBUM (US/0146-4183) [02943449] **4372**

OUR ANIMALS (US/0030-6789) [15347317] **2252**

OUR BABY. BURDA (AT) **1086**

OUR DIOCESE (GRAND FALLS) (CN/0823-7069) [10339458] **5033**

OUR DOGS MANCHESTER (UK/0955-9469) [I09559469] **4287**

OUR EARTH (US) 2179, 2572, **1928**

OUR FAMILY (BATTLEFORD) (CN/0030-6843) [01641119] 2284, **4984**

OUR FAMILY HERITAGE (US/0091-6447) [01787640] **2466**

OUR FAMILY LEGACY (US/0731-325X) [08139039] **2466**

OUR FOURFOOTED FRIENDS (US/0030-6851) [04101043] **4287**

OUR GENERATION (MONTREAL) (CN/0030-686X) [01773344] **4544**

OUR GIFTED CHILDREN (US/1055-1336) [23091914] **1883**

OUR HERITAGE (US) [15188549] **2466**

OUR HERITAGE (US) [05659643] **2752**

OUR HERITAGE (WILLS POINT, TEX.) (US/0733-4559) [07495897] **2466**

OUR KID'S MAGAZINE (US) [10526916] **1067**

OUR KINGDOM MINISTRY. FOR CANADA (CN/0823-2547) [10052162] **4984**

OUR LADY'S DIGEST *CEASED.* (US/0030-6886) [01774032] **4984**

OUR LAND (US) [20029301] **2201**

OUR LIBRARY PRESENTS ... (US) [08099655] **3240**

OUR LITTLE YELLOW BOOK (CN/0822-8256) [10451445] **2902**

OUR LIVING OCEANS : THE ... ANNUAL REPORT ON THE STATUS OF U.S. LIVING MARINE RESOURCES (US) [25301390] 2310, **556**

OUR MEN (US/1055-1522) [23094945] **3996**

OUR MISSION FIELDS *See* ROYAL SERVICE **5067**

OUR NAME'S THE GAME (US/0738-8306) [07855125] **2466**

OUR OWN (US) **2795**

OUR REGION *CEASED.* (US/0892-192X) [15124259] **2830**

OUR RIGHT TO KNOW (US/0886-9049) [13043175] **4486**

OUR SCHOOLS (CN/0384-6636) [02653746] **1771**

OUR SCHOOLS (OTTAWA) (CN/0229-1096) [08773942] 1771, **5033**

OUR SCHOOLS, OUR SELVES (CN/0840-7339) [19568884] **1771**

● OUR SCHOOLS USA (US/1063-9845) [26184753] **1771**

OUR SOUTHERN HOME *See* SUMTER COUNTY JOURNAL **5628**

OUR SUNDAY VISITOR (US/0030-6967) [01640481] **5034**

OUR SUNDAY VISITOR'S CATHOLIC HERITAGE (US/1057-929X) [24169741] **5034**

OUR TIMES *CEASED.* (US/0891-9208) [14921811] **3932**

OUR TIMES (TORONTO) (CN/0822-6377) [10676927] **1700**

OUR TOWN (US/0194-1712) [05357027] **5769**

OUR VOICE (US) [05634849] 2889, **1700**

OUR VOICE (NEW YORK, N.Y. 1990) (US/1064-0207) [23709277] **3890**

OUR WORLD (DAYTONA BEACH, FLA.) (US/1044-6699) [19864041] 2795, **5487**

OUR WRITE MIND (US/1055-4130) [23167813] **3421**

OUR ... YEAR / REGIONAL PLANNING COUNCIL (US) [11377404] **2830**

OURAY COUNTY PLAINDEALER (US) [11326274] **5644**

OURS (MINNEAPOLIS, MINN.) *See* ADOPTIVE FAMILIES **5270**

OURS (MINNEAPOLIS, MINN.) (US/0899-9333) [18277370] 2284, **5300**

OUSLEY NEWSLETTER (US/0733-6381) [08488112] **2466**

● OUT & ABOUT (NEW HAVEN, CONN.) (US/1066-7776) [27045973] **2795**

OUT AUCKLAND (NZ/0110-4454) [I01104454] **2795**

OUT HEALTH (US/0278-5811) [07844995] 5188, **4795**

OUT IN VIDEO (US/1056-103X) [23466701] **387**

OUT/LOOK (SAN FRANCISCO, CALIF.) *CEASED.* (US/0896-7733) [17286887] **2795**

● OUT (NEW YORK, N.Y.) (US/1062-7928) [25743067] **2795**

OUT OF DOORS (PIERRE, S.D.) (US/0883-6809) [12193041] 2220, **4876**

OUT SOCIALISM (US/0738-3436) [09553595] **4544**

OUT WEST (SACRAMENTO, CALIF.) (US/0899-1413) [18005524] 2542, **5488**

OUTAOUAIS FORESTIER (CN/1182-7696) [23237053] **2390**

OUTAOUAIS GENEALOGIQUE (CN/0707-8137) [10326390] **2466**

● OUTBOARD BOAT BLUE BOOK (US/1070-3500) [25274401] **594**

OUTBOARD BOAT TRADE-IN GUIDE BLUE BOOK *See* OUTBOARD BOAT BLUE BOOK **594**

OUTBOUND (WILLOWDALE) (CN/0843-1566) [20113975] **31**

OUTCOMES MEASUREMENT AND MANAGEMENT (US) **3625**

OUTCROP (DENVER, COLO.) (US/0888-5184) [10181853] **1390**

OUTDOOR (UK) **4876**

OUTDOOR ALBERTA (CN/0827-2964) [11825380] **4876**

OUTDOOR AMERICA (1971) (US/0021-3314) [03057275] **4170**

OUTDOOR & TRAVEL PHOTOGRAPHY *CEASED.* (US/1058-7756) [24369916] **4372**

OUTDOOR ATLANTIC (CN/0228-0604) [06757801] **4876**

OUTDOOR BUYERS GUIDE *See* BUYERS GUIDE TO OUTDOOR ADVERTISING, THE **756**

OUTDOOR CALIFORNIA (US/0030-7025) [01761595] **4876**

OUTDOOR CANADA (CN/0315-0542) [02097766] **4876**

OUTDOOR COMMUNICATOR : THE OFFICIAL JOURNAL OF THE NEW YORK STATE OUTDOOR EDUCATION ASSOCIATION, THE (US) [09006556] 1771, **4876**

OUTDOOR CREST (1975) (CN/0700-9909) [03403148] **4876**

OUTDOOR DELAWARE (GW/1068-3240) [26462552] **2201**

OUTDOOR EDGE (CN/1186-8023) [25313698] **4876**

OUTDOOR GUIDE (US/0048-2420) [02866001] **4876**

OUTDOOR HIGHLIGHTS (US/0279-8700) [06614450] **4876**

● OUTDOOR ILLINOIS (SPRINGFIELD, ILL.) (US/1072-7175) [29189971] **4877**

OUTDOOR INDIANA (US/0030-7068) [01781561] 4877, **4707**

OUTDOOR JOURNAL *CEASED.* (US/0890-7196) [02430208] **4877**

OUTDOOR LIFE DEER HUNTER'S YEARBOOK (US/0734-2918) [08718186] **4877**

OUTDOOR LIFE (NEW YORK, N.Y.) (US/0030-7076) [01761598] **4877**

OUTDOOR NETWORK NEWSLETTER, THE (US/1050-7485) [21583513] **1771**

OUTDOOR NEWS (OKLAHOMA CITY, OKLA.) (US/0279-9065) [07349944] **2201**

OUTDOOR OKLAHOMA (US/0030-7106) [01640769] 2201, **4877**

OUTDOOR PHOTOGRAPHER (US/0890-5304) [14255205] **4372**

OUTDOOR PRESS, THE (US/0739-0602) [09679038] **4877**

OUTDOOR RAILROADER (US/1057-0268) [23915388] **5433**

OUTDOOR RECREATION IN GEORGIA (US/0148-401X) [03301857] **4877**

OUTDOOR RECREATION IN ILLINOIS ... ACTION PROGRAM (US) [07711106] **4853**

OUTDOOR RETAILER (US/0279-8107) [07267334] **956**

OUTDOOR SPORTS & RECREATION (US/0892-8355) [15267335] 4911, **4877**

OUTDOOR SPORTSMAN (POINT PLEASANT) (US/0272-9342) [06956152] **4877**

OUTDOOR WOMAN (US/1048-8871) [21062146] 5564, **4877**

OUTDOOR WRITERS ASSOCIATION OF AMERICA *See* DIRECTORY - OUTDOOR WRITERS ASSOCIATION OF AMERICA **2919**

OUTDOORD HIGHLIGHTS *See* OUTDOOR ILLINOIS (SPRINGFIELD, ILL.) **4877**

OUTDOORS ILLUSTRATED *CEASED.* (UK/0962-1016) [I09621016] **4877**

OUTDOORS TODAY (US/0199-3666) [05815590] **4877**

OUTDOORS UNLIMITED (US/0030-7181) [06777104] **3421**

OUTDOORS WEST (US) [05261465] 2201, **4877**

OUTER BANKS CURRENT (US/8750-0418) [10945482] **5724**

OUTER CONTINENTAL SHELF OIL AND GAS INFORMATION PROGRAM (U.S.) *See* GULF OF MEXICO UPDATE : OUTER CONTINENTAL SHELF OIL & GAS ACTIVITIES **2090**

OUTER CONTINENTAL SHELF OIL AND GAS LEASING AND PRODUCTION PROGRAM (U.S.) *See* ANNUAL REPORT / OUTER CONTINENTAL SHELF OIL AND GAS LEASING AND PRODUCTION PROGRAM **4250**

OUTER-ISLAND PRICES OF WHOLESALE FRESH FRUITS AND VEGETABLES (US/0160-4589) [03678464] **180**

OUTERBRIDGE (US/0739-4969) [03390967] **3421**

OUTFRONT (OTTAWA) (CN/0821-6258) [10105557] **4392**

OUTLAW BIKER MAGAZINE (US/0885-2030) **4082**

OUTLAW BIKER TATTOO REVUE (US/1047-1499) [20613671] **5269**

OUTLAW BIKER TATTOO REVUE SPECIALS (US/1056-8131) [23887733] **5269**

OUTLINE OF ACTIVITIES - GOVERNMENT OF MAHARASHTRA (II) [02240228] **4672**

OUTLINE OF JAPANESE TAXES, AN (JA) [01782760] **4740**

OUTLINE OF PATENT OFFICE INTERFERENCE PRACTICE *See* OUTLINE OF PTO PATENT INTERFERENCE PRACTICE **1307**

OUTLINE OF POSTGRADUATE PROGRAMMES / UNIVERSITY OF ZAMBIA (ZA) [08580400] **1839**

OUTLINE OF PTO PATENT INTERFERENCE PRACTICE (US/0160-5623) [03695488] **1307**

OUTLINE OF RCRA CERCLA (US) **3115**

OUTLOOK (US) [05463625] **1094**

OUTLOOK (US) [06517475] **763**

OUTLOOK (UK) **2572**

OUTLOOK - CANADIAN JEWISH OUTLOOK SOCIETY (CN/0834-0242) [13342371] **5051**

OUTLOOK CONCENTRATED PHOSPHATES (UK) 1511, **1045**

OUTLOOK - EDMONTON ART GALLERY (CN/1184-2288) [24337623] **361**

OUTLOOK / EDUCATIONAL COMMISSION FOR FOREIGN MEDICAL GRADUATES (US/0737-4429) [09428324] 1839, **3625**

OUTLOOK FOR COLLECTIVE BARGAINING IN NEW ENGLAND IN ... / U.S. DEPARTMENT OF LABOR, BUREAU OF LABOR STATISTICS, NEW ENGLAND REGIONAL OFFICE, THE (US) [06436795] **1700**

● OUTLOOK FOR FARM COMMODITY PROGRAM SPENDING, THE (US) [21615947] **5647**

OUTLOOK FOR SUMMER TRAVEL (US/0748-0830) [10880893] **5488**

OUTLOOK FOR THE MEDIA (US/0737-8858) [09481578] **3309**

OUTLOOK FOR TRAVEL AND TOURISM (US/0737-8815) [09248015] **5488**

OUTLOOK FOR U.S. AGRICULTURAL EXPORTS (1982) (US/0739-8891) [09330726] **118**

OUTLOOK (GRAND RAPIDS, MICH.), THE (US/8750-5754) [04275756] **5065**

OUTLOOK (LETHBRIDGE) (CN/0382-4780) [03079352] **3171**

OUTLOOK (LINCOLN, NEB.) (US/0887-977X) [13433103] **4984**

● OUTLOOK NEW CHURCH. GENERAL CONFERENCE (UK/0969-1049) [I09691049] **4984**

OUTLOOK (NEW YORK, N.Y. 1937), THE (US/0030-7246) [01642664] **910**

OUTLOOK ON AGRICULTURE (UK/0030-7270) [01761604] **118**

OUTLOOK ON AT&T *CEASED.* (US/0885-6176) [12681655] **1161**

OUTLOOK ON IBM (US/0742-9916) [10481269] **1238**

OUTLOOK ON SCIENCE POLICY (UK/0165-0262) [05805482] **5137**

OUTLOOK ON THE SWEDISH ECONOMY (SW) [06156431] **1577**

OUTLOOK (OTHELLO, WASH.), THE (US/1056-8328) [16993162] **5761**

Alphabetical Title Index — OXFORD

OUTLOOK / OUTLOOK SASK CANADA (CN) **2752**

OUTLOOK (OVIEDO, FLA.) *See* SEMINOLE OUTLOOK **5651**

OUTLOOK (PALO ALTO) (US/0273-835X) [06878240] **749**

OUTLOOK (SANTA MONICA, CALIF.), THE (US/0898-5375) [15064250] **5638**

OUTLOOK (SEATTLE, WASH. : 1983) (US/0737-3732) [09360452] **590**

OUTLOOK SULPHUR (UK) 1511, **1037**

●OUTLOOK, THE REVENUE PICTURE FOR ... (US) [24663441] **1594**

OUTLOOK (VANCOUVER) (CN/0700-4176) [02753613] **5234**

OUTLOOK (WAKE FOREST, N.C.) *See* SOUTHEASTERN OUTLOOK **4998**

OUTLOOK (WASHINGTON, D.C. : 1988) (US/0898-5766) [17855527] **623**

OUTLOOK (WASHINGTON, D.C. 1989) (US/1044-5706) [19110171] 1839, **5564**

OUTPATIENT SURGERY *CEASED.* (US/0885-1166) [12567901] **3971**

OUTPOST EXCHANGE (US/0748-3394) [11013823] 4197, **1298**

OUTPOSTS POETRY QUARTERLY (UK) [08973851] **3467**

OUTPUT (SZ/0303-8351) [05748628] **1261**

OUTPUT MODE (US/0193-7391) [05256471] **4818**

OUTPUT OESTERREICH (AU) [02412741] **702**

OUTPUT (RICHMOND HILL) (CN/1184-9770) [24690794] **1224**

OUTREACH (CHICAGO) (US/0270-207X) [06323297] **3725**

OUTREACH (STILLWATER, OKLA.) (US/0744-6934) [08515570] **1094**

●OUTREACH (WASHINGTON, D.C 1992) (US/1063-1798) [25910971] 5564, **702**

OUTREMER (PARIS, FRANCE : 1982) *SUSPENDED.* (FR/0014-2816) [09554021] 1511, **2500**

OUTREMONT (QUEBEC) *See* BULLETIN MUNICIPAL / OUTREMONT **4634**

OUTRIDER (INDOOROOPILLY, QLD.) (AT/0813-5886) [16897423] **3421**

OUTRIDER / WYOMING STATE LIBRARY, THE (US/0030-7319) [02251763] **3240**

OUTSIDE (1980) (US/0278-1433) [06050977] **4877**

●OUTSIDE KIDS (US/1069-420X) [28036658] **1067**

OUTSIDE PLANT (US/0747-8763) [10795314] **1119**

OUTSIDES (LONDON, ENGLAND) (UK) [12147882] **5212**

OUTSTANDING EDUCATORS IN AMERICA (US/0093-4259) [01784488] **1771**

OUTSTANDING ELEMENTARY TEACHERS OF AMERICA (US/0090-4082) [01783684] **1805**

OUTSTANDING INVESTOR DIGEST (US/0891-463X) [14957982] **910**

OUTSTANDING LEADERS IN ELEMENTARY AND SECONDARY EDUCATION (US/0147-2151) [03122949] **1771**

OUTSTANDING YOUNG WOMEN OF AMERICA (US) [01597856] 434, **5564**

●OUTSTATE BUSINESS (US/1064-3621) [26272095] **702**

OUTUKUMPU NEWS (FI) [02256448] 702, **4014**

OUTWARD BOUND (US/0749-4459) [11129123] **4877**

OUVROIR (SAINTE-MARIE-DE-BEAUCE) (CN/1181-9286) [23242550] **4984**

OVALTA / ASSOCIATION TOURISTIQUE REGIONALE DE L'ABITIBI-TEMISCAMINGUE (CN/0714-3877) [09050432] **1620**

OVATION REPORT ON COST EFFECTIVE PRODUCTS, THE (US/1056-3172) [23659798] **3625**

OVER-55 FINANCIAL MANAGEMENT LETTER (US/0886-9782) [13053447] 1511, **802**

OVER HERE : REVIEWS IN AMERICAN STUDIES (UK) [15693712] **2752**

OVER-THE-COUNTER 1000 YELLOW BOOK *See* NASDAQ YELLOW BOOK **696**

OVER-THE-COUNTER AND REGIONAL EXCHANGE STOCK REPORTS (US) [01640607] **910**

OVER-THE-COUNTER SPECIAL SITUATIONS SERVICE *See* VALUE LINE OTC SPECIAL SITUATIONS SERVICE, THE **918**

OVER THE EDGE *CEASED.* (US/1077-3703) [30791522] **4877**

OVER THE SPILLWAY *See* DIGESTER, OVER THE SPILLWAY, THE **2227**

OVER THE YEARS (US) [01761608] **2625**

OVERALL PROGRAM DESIGN FOR COMPREHENSIVE METROPOLITAN PLANNING AND DECISION MAKING (US) [01786820] **2830**

OVERALL REAL PROPERTY TAXES (US) [20909967] **4740**

OVERHEIDSMANAGEMENT : VAKBLAD VOOR FINANCIEN AUTOMATISERING EN PERSONEEL 7 ORGANISATIE (NE/0928-8503) 749, 802, **4672**

OVERIJSSELSE HISTORISCHE BIJDRAGEN : VERSLAGEN EN MEDEDELINGEN VAN DE VEREENIGING TOT BEOEFENING VAN OVERIJSSELSCH REGT EN GESCHIEDENIS (NE/0165-6465) [09459693] **2702**

OVERLAND (AT/0030-7416) [01713792] 3421, **2511**

OVERLAND JOURNAL (US/0738-1093) [09521950] **2752**

OVERLAND PARK SUN, THE (US) [11946652] **5678**

OVERLANDER (AT/0156-0832) [01560832] **4853**

OVERSEAS ARRIVALS AND DEPARTURES, AUSTRALIA (AT) [06043686] 5389, **5401**

OVERSEAS ASSIGNMENT DIRECTORY SERVICE (US/0735-231X) [03786690] **5488**

OVERSEAS BROADCASTERS CIRCUIT (UK/0958-6857) [I09586857] **1136**

●OVERSEAS BUILDER (US/1062-6921) [25697356] **623**

OVERSEAS BUSINESS *CEASED.* (US/1048-0722) [20845809] **702**

OVERSEAS BUSINESS REPORTS *CEASED.* (US/0082-9846) [01792851] **848**

OVERSEAS COMMON CARRIER SECTION 214 APPLICATIONS ACCEPTED FOR FILING (US) [03457299] **1161**

OVERSEAS DEVELOPMENT (UK) [05377024] **2911**

OVERSEAS DEVELOPMENT COUNCIL *See* ANNUAL REPORT - OVERSEAS DEVELOPMENT COUNCIL **1598**

OVERSEAS EMPLOYMENT NEWSLETTER (CN/1183-3203) [19470035] **4208**

OVERSEAS EMPLOYMENT OPPORTUNITIES FOR EDUCATORS (US) [06713893] 1902, **1700**

OVERSEAS FOOD LEGISLATION MANUAL (UK) 3024, **2352**

OVERSEAS JOB-PERSONALQUARTER (US/0743-0892) [10502681] **1700**

OVERSEAS JOBS EXPRESS (UK/0966-7660) [I09667660] **4208**

OVERSEAS LIVING *SUSPENDED.* (US/0882-8938) [12001664] **2542**

OVERSEAS NEWSPAPERS AND PERIODICALS GUIDE BOOK (UK) [18658056] **5813**

OVERSEAS OUTLOOK (US/0161-1828) [03856813] **4392**

OVERSEAS POSTS (NZ/0114-6971) [I01146971] **4672**

OVERSEAS PRESS CLUB OF AMERICA *See* MEMBERSHIP DIRECTORY AND AMERICAN CORRESPONDENTS OVERSEAS **2922**

OVERSEAS TRADE FIJI (FJ) [08320032] **848**

OVERSEAS TRADE STATISTICS OF THE UNITED KINGDOM (UK/0436-3574) [01640689] **732**

OVERSEAS TRADE (WELLINGTON, N.Z.) (NZ) [20411455] **848**

OVERSEAS TRADING (AT) [04918912] **848**

OVERSEAS TRANSACTIONS / BUSINESS STATISTICS OFFICE (UK) [08142355] **910**

OVERSEAS UNIVERSITIES (UK) [01792863] **1839**

OVERSIGT OVER FINANSLOVFORSLAGET FOR ... BILAG (DK) [10004090] **4740**

OVERSIGT OVER RAPPORTER M.M. VEDRRENDE VANDKRAFTUNDERSGELSEL I GRNLAND PR. 30 JUNI (DK/0107-4997) [19483596] **1417**

OVERSIGT OVER VEJBUDGETTERNE (DK) [19463281] **5442**

OVERTONES (US) [06456976] **4145**

OVERTONES (LINCOLN, NEB.) *See* N-COMPASS (LINCOLN, NEB.) **3232**

OVERTONES (LINCOLN, NEB.) (US/0884-920X) [09887148] **3240**

OVERTURE (LOS ANGELES) (US/0030-7556) [04101270] **4145**

OVERVIEW (US/0030-7564) [02866103] **5034**

OVERVIEW (CN) [20617307] **5335**

OVERVIEW - FARMERS HOME ADMINISTRATION (US/0271-7654) [06272290] **118**

OVERVIEW OF BLOOD (US/0093-9404) [01796253] **3773**

OVERVIEW OF LEGISLATION IN THE SESSION OF THE ILLNOIS GENERAL ASSEMBLY, AN (US) [03718143] **3024**

OVERVIEW / STATE OF WASHINGTON, DEPARTMENT OF SOCIAL & HEALTH SERVICES, AN (US) [10268143] **4795**

OVERVIEW (TORONTO) (CN/0700-3617) [03348831] **4486**

OVERVIEW (UNIVERSITY OF ALBERTA. COMPUTING SERVICES) (CN/0824-5894) [10845233] **1261**

OVERWEIGHT VEHICLES- PENALTIES & PERMITS : REPORT TO CONGRESS FROM THE SECRETARY OF TRANSPORTATION (US) [10181241] **5389**

OVID GAZETTE, THE (US/0745-8398) [09497098] **5720**

OVO MAGAZINE (1978) *CEASED.* (CN/0704-9153) [03983901] **4372**

OVOCHIVNYTSTVO I BASHTANNYTSTVO (UN/0131-0062) [04816014] **180**

OVOSHCHEBODSTVO I BAKHCHEVODSTVO (UN) [26885419] **520**

OVOSHTARSTVO, GRADINARSTVO I KONSERVNA PROMISHLENOST (BL/0205-1710) [25678964] 2352, 2427, **180**

OVR BULLETIN BOARD *See* VRA BULLETIN BOARD **4694**

OVTA NEWS (CN/1184-8944) [24368385] **5488**

OVTSEVODSTVO (UN) [09967595] **217**

OVTSEVODSTVO (RU/0030-7572) [09808702] **217**

OWEN SOUND LIFE (CN/0704-0237) [03797404] **5792**

OWEN SOUND SUN TIMES (CN) **5792**

OWEN WISTER REVIEW (US/1069-2215) [10902198] 327, **1094**

OWEN'S AFRICA BUSINESS DIRECTORY (UK/0953-6132) [18630654] **702**

OWENSVILLE STAR-ECHO *See* STAR-ECHO, THE **5667**

OWENSVILLE STAR-ECHO (OWENSVILLE IND. : 1991) *See* SOUTH GIBSON STAR-TIMES **5667**

OWINGS MILLS TIMES (US/1041-0880) [18654593] **5686**

OWITT NEWS (CN/1185-2542) [24368003] **5564**

OWL CREEK JOURNAL, THE (US/1044-6486) [19860764] **3421**

OWL (DON MILLS) (CN/0382-6627) [02801944] **1067**

OWL OF MINERVA, THE (US/0030-7580) [02052944] **4354**

OWMC EXCHANGE, THE (CN/0715-0237) [10685389] **2238**

OWNER AND MANAGER (US/0882-6242) [11905498] **881**

OWNER BUILDER MAGAZINE (AT/0728-7275) [I07287275] 2201, **623**

OWNER BUILT HOME PLANS (US) **305**

OWNERS & OFFICERS OF PRIVATE COMPANIES (US/1056-3326) [23665032] **702**

OWNERS AT WORK (US/1046-5049) [20433908] **1543**

OWNERSHIP STRUCTURE OF PRINCIPAL PETROLEUM COMPANIES IN CANADA (CN/0842-2982) [19451186] **4271**

OWOCE, WARZYWA, KWIATY (PL) [04051850] **2427**

OWOSSO ARGUS-PRESS, THE (US) [09802802] **5693**

OWYHEE AVALANCHE (HOMEDALE, IDAHO : 1985) (US/8750-6823) [11672005] **5657**

OWYHEE OUTPOST (US/0889-6380) [09624788] **2753**

OXBRIDGE DIRECTORY OF NEWSLETTERS (US/0163-7010) [04442592] **2923**

OXFORD (UK/0030-7645) [01604503] **1094**

OXFORD AGRARIAN STUDIES (UK/0264-5491) [01773345] **118**

OXFORD ART JOURNAL (UK/0142-6540) [04893476] **361**

OXFORD BIOLOGY READERS *See* CAROLINA BIOLOGY READERS **450**

OXFORD BULLETIN OF ECONOMICS AND STATISTICS (UK/0305-9049) [01071103] **1577**

OXFORD CHEMISTRY SERIES (UK) [09967709] **988**

OXFORD

OXFORD EAGLE (US) [16108132] **5701**

OXFORD ECONOMIC PAPERS (UK/0030-7653) [01589736] **1594**

OXFORD ENERGY FORUM (UK/0959-7727) [I09597727] **1952**

OXFORD ENGINEERING SCIENCE SERIES (UK/0953-3222) [15306132] **1990**

OXFORD FORESTRY MEMOIRS *CEASED.* (UK) [01761640] **2390**

OXFORD GERMAN STUDIES (UK/0078-7191) [01640444] **3421**

OXFORD GERMAN STUDIES : BOOK SUPPLEMENT (UK/0141-8149) [06670543] **2702**

OXFORD HISTORY OF ENGLAND, THE (UK) [08648348] **2702**

OXFORD HISTORY OF ENGLISH ART (UK) [13776636] **361**

OXFORD HISTORY OF ENGLISH LITERATURE, THE (UK) [08438294] **3421**

OXFORD HISTORY OF MODERN EUROPE (UK) **2702**

OXFORD ILLUSTRATED ENCYCLOPAEDIA *CEASED.* (UK) [21146529] **1928**

OXFORD JOURNAL OF ARCHAEOLOGY (UK/0262-5253) [08673843] **277**

OXFORD JOURNAL OF LEGAL STUDIES (UK/0143-6503) [07636038] **3024**

OXFORD LITERARY REVIEW, THE (UK/0305-1498) [05116754] **3349**

OXFORD MAGAZINE (UK/0268-1137) [16274350] **1102**

OXFORD MEDICAL SCHOOL GAZETTE (UK/0030-7661) [06538413] **3625**

OXFORD MEDIEVAL TEXTS (UK/0474-974X) [05581121] **2702**

OXFORD MODERN LANGUAGES AND LITERATURE MONOGRAPHS (UK) **3421, 3309**

OXFORD MONOGRAPHS ON BIOGEOGRAPHY (UK/0958-6601) [13622231] **468**

OXFORD MONOGRAPHS ON MEDICAL GENETICS (UK) [13080098] **550, 3625**

OXFORD PHYSICS SERIES (UK) [06427860] **4413**

OXFORD POETRY (OXFORD, OXFORDSHIRE) (UK) [10813103] **3467**

OXFORD REVIEW OF ECONOMIC POLICY (UK/0266-903X) [12168802] **1511**

OXFORD REVIEW OF EDUCATION (UK/0305-4985) [02122838] **1771**

OXFORD REVIEWS OF REPRODUCTIVE BIOLOGY (UK/0260-0854) [06321542] **584**

OXFORD SLAVONIC PAPERS (UK/0078-7256) [01644774] **3309, 2702, 3336**

OXFORD STUDIES IN ANCIENT PHILOSOPHY (UK/0265-7651) [10455317] **4354**

OXFORD STUDIES IN COMPARATIVE EDUCATION (UK/0961-2149) **1771**

OXFORD STUDIES IN THE HISTORY OF ART AND ARCHITECTURE (UK) [01781352] **305, 361**

OXFORD SURVEYS IN EVOLUTIONARY BIOLOGY (UK/0265-072X) [12015365] **468**

OXFORD SURVEYS OF PLANT MOLECULAR AND CELL BIOLOGY (UK/0264-861X) [11242341] **584**

OXFORD TODAY (UK/0954-1306) [19255384] **2521**

OXFORD. UNIVERSITY. EXPLORATION CLUB *See* BULLETIN - OXFORD UNIVERSITY EXPLORATION CLUB **2557**

OXFORDSHIRE FAMILY HISTORIAN, THE (UK) [03230967] **2466**

OXFORDSHIRE FAMILY HISTORY SOCIETY *See* DIRECTORY OF MEMBERS' RESEARCH. SUPPLEMENT / OXFORDSHIRE FAMILY HISTORY SOCIETY **2445**

OXFORDSHIRE RECORD SOCIETY *See* OXFORDSHIRE RECORD SOCIETY; [ANNUAL REPORT] **2702**

OXFORDSHIRE RECORD SOCIETY; [ANNUAL REPORT] (UK) [06469934] **2702**

OXIDATION COMMUNICATIONS (BU/0209-4541) [06336734] **1045**

OXIDATION OF METALS (US/0030-770X) [01110546] **1037, 4014**

OXONIENSIA (UK) [01761645] **305, 277**

OXY-FUEL NEWS (US/1072-8759) **4271**

OXY TODAY *CEASED.* (US) [08786912] **4271**

OXYGEN RADICALS (UK/0950-057X) [I0950057X] **491**

OXYGEN (SAN FRANCISCO, CALIF.) (US/1056-2613) [23606560] **3349**

OXYMAG : JOURNAL D'INFORMATION PROFESSIONNELLE DES INFIRMIERS ANESTHESISTES (FR/0990-1310) [20626829] **3683**

OXYRHYNCHUS PAPYRI, THE (UK/0306-9222) [02265599] **3421**

OXYTOCIN AND VASOPRESSIN (UK/1351-5330) **3732**

OYE! (NEW YORK, N.Y.) *CEASED.* (US/1055-1190) [23086076] **1902**

OYEZ MAGAZINE *See* OYEZ REVIEW **1094**

OYEZ REVIEW (US) [03393734] **3024, 1094**

OYO BUTSURI (JA/0369-8009) [09510770] **4413**

OYO, NIGERIA (STATE). PUBLIC SERVICE COMMISSION *See* REPORT OF THE PUBLIC SERVICE COMMISSION **4705**

OYO STATE (NIGERIA) *See* OYO STATE OF NIGERIA GAZETTE **3024**

OYO STATE OF NIGERIA GAZETTE (NR) [04824914] **3024**

OYO STATE OF NIGERIA STATISTICAL HANDBOOK (NR) [19028917] **5335**

OYO STATE YEAR BOOK AND WHO'S WHO (NR) [08585470] **434, 2642**

OYO YAKURI (JA/0300-8533) [01350654] **3983, 4319**

OZ ARTS MAGAZINE (AT/1037-1311) [I10371311] **327**

OZ COLLECTOR, THE (US/0886-8697) [13056862] **3421**

OZ (MANHATTAN, KAN.) (US/0888-7802) [07985211] **305**

OZARK HAPPENINGS NEWSLETTER (US/1053-2765) [13337843] **2466**

OZARK MOUNTAIN COUNTRY REVIEW *See* BRANSON'S COUNTRY REVIEW **4105**

OZARK PERIODICAL INDEX (US/0275-9713) [06026840] **2753, 2636**

OZARK SOCIETY JOURNAL *CEASED.* (US/0743-9032) [09486313] **2753**

OZARK VISITOR (US/0890-2690) [14203977] **5704**

OZAR'KIN / OZARKS GENEALOGICAL SOCIETY (US) [07092822] **2466**

OZARKS MOUNTAINEER, THE (US/0030-7769) [03773430] **2753**

OZARKSWATCH (SPRINGFIELD, MO.) (US/1044-8500) [18936590] **2542**

OZAUKEE COUNTY GUIDE (GRAFTON, WIS.) (US) [12063672] **5769**

OZAUKEE COUNTY NEWS GRAPHIC (US/1056-9006) [23890732] **5770**

OZAUKEE PRESS (PORT WASHINGTON, WIS. : 1969) (US/0749-7164) [11167262] **5770**

OZE. OSTERREICHISCHE ZEITSCHRIFT FUER ELEKTRIZITATSWIRTSCHAFT *CEASED.* (AU/0029-9618) [04213929] **2074**

OZIANA (US) [20102796] **3421**

OZONA STOCKMAN, THE (US) [13698535] **5753**

OZONE CHEMISTRY AND TECHNOLOGY (US) [01847164] **2015**

OZONE DATA FOR THE WORLD (CN/0030-7777) [01787548] **1433**

OZONE NEWS (US/1065-5905) [26778953] **5212**

OZONE : SCIENCE & ENGINEERING (US/0191-9512) [04965176] **1037**

OZONEWS IN JAPAN (JA/0917-8260) [I09178260] **2179**

OZS, OSTERREICHISCHE ZEITSCHRIFT FUER SOZIOLOGIE (AU/1011-0070) [03376023] **5253**

OZW, OESTERREICHISCHE ZEITSCHRIFT FUER WIRTSCHAFTSRECHT (AU/0379-4407) [02776480] **3102**

P.A.A. AFFAIRS (US/0300-6816) [01423574] **4555**

P.A.G.E. JOURNAL (CN/1184-2644) [24265583] **4530**

P.A.G.E. NEWS (CN/1184-0676) [23231614] **1771**

P. A. L., PREVENT, AVOID LOSSES (CN/0707-2228) [04754923] **3171**

P-A-M BULLETIN (US/1063-9136) [20403328] **4413, 3526**

P & S / THE COLLEGE OF PHYSICIANS AND SURGEONS OF COLUMBIA UNIVERSITY (US/0743-507X) [10412819] **3625**

P.B.X. SYSTEMS GUIDE (US/0092-8828) [01784493] **2074**

P.C.C (FR/0396-0064) [I03960064] **4235**

P C DISC (SP) **1198**

P.C. NETWORK ADVISOR (UK) **1243**

P D B, PROFESSIONAL DEVELOPMENT BULLETIN (CN/0384-0972) [02517711] **1771**

P. D. DIGEST (CN/0709-0188) [05529167] **1796**

P-D NEWS (US/0478-9997) [06924771] **944**

P.E.I. LABOUR MARK. BULL (CN/0826-9475) [10860460] **1700**

P.E.N. NEW POETRY (UK) [13771965] **3421**

P/E NEWS INDEX GUIDE AND KEYWORD LIST / AMERICAN PETROLEUM INSTITUTE (US) [14286162] **4271**

P. E. O. RECORD (US/0746-5130) [01587219] **5235**

P+ : EUROPEAN PARTICIPATION MONITOR (IE/1017-6713) [26173121] **881**

P F C REPORT, I (TH) **2310**

P FORM (US/1067-2222) [27164635] **361**

P.H.M. - REVUE HORTICOLE (FR) [01377599] **2427**

P I B C NEWS (CN/0048-4326) [02103978] **2830**

P.I.P.E.R., PENSIONS & INVESTMENT'S PERFORMANCE EVALUATION REPORT (US/0164-176X) [04579414] **910**

P I Q PRODUITS POUR L'INDUSTRIE QUEBECOISE (CN/0701-1687) [03409786] **3486**

P-IM : PROFESSIONAL IMAGING (NE) **4567**

P.J.R. PRAXIS JURIDIQUE ET RELIGION (FR/0758-802X) [11824408] **3024, 4984**

P M E : REVUE DE LA PETITE ET MOYENNE ENTREPRISE (CN/0705-0674) [03956578] **702**

P/M LITERATURE REFERENCE GUIDE (US/0097-7241) [02382706] **4014**

P. M. PETER MOOSLEITNERS INTERESSANTES MAGAZIN (GW/0176-4152) [I01764152] **2491**

P/M TECHNOLOGY NEWSLETTER (US/0734-4805) [08686099] **4014**

P-NOTES / FID, FEDERATION INTERNATIONALE DE DOCUMENTATION (NE/0378-7656) [07533685] **3240**

P-O-P TIMES (US/1040-8169) [18543168] **763**

P.O.V. : A NEWSLETTER FOR MANITOBA ACTORS (CN/1180-5137) [23243200] **4075, 5367**

P/PM TECHNOLOGY (US/0899-1804) [18022558] **1620**

P / PURDUE UNIVERSITY, COOPERATIVE EXTENSION SERVICE (US/1040-2365) [13697157] **217**

P. R. D. SERIES (SA) [01783961] **2147**

P.S.A. PEUGEOT-CITROEN *See* P.S.A. PEUGEOT-CITROEN. RAPPORT **1620**

P.S.A. PEUGEOT-CITROEN. RAPPORT (FR) [04428195] **1620**

P S A REPORTER (AT) **4672**

● P.S.I. GUIDE, PREFIX/SUFFIX IDENTIFICATION FOR BEARINGS (US/1065-8491) [26777731] **3309**

P.S. POST-SCRIPTUM (CN/0228-3492) [09075926] **2542**

P S R MONITOR (US) **4486, 3625**

P SERIES - COMMITTEE FOR ECONOMIC DEVELOPMENT OF AUSTRALIA (AT) [03635493] **1511**

P. T. T. I. STUDIES (SZ/1015-6844) [01791343] **1146**

P.T.T. INFORMATIONS *See* PTT INFO **1120**

P.U.R. ANALYSIS OF INVESTOR-OWNED ELECTRIC AND GAS UTILITIES, THE (US/0733-4915) [08596813] **4761**

P5. PERSONAL PARTICIPATION IN PURSUIT OF PHYSICAL PROFICIENCY (CN/0713-4207) [08996016] **2600**

PA. JAYCEES FUTURE (US/0744-8392) [08593776] **5235**

PA. PRODUKTIONSAUTOMATISIERUNG (GW/0941-7680) [I09417680] **1621**

PA SHIH NIEN TAI SAN WEN HSUAN / PA SHIH NIEN TAI SAN WEN HSUAN PIEN CHI TSU HSUAN PIEN (CC) [11529866] **3421, 3309**

PA TIMES (US/1041-6323) [16725131] **4672**

PA. TOWNSHIP NEWS (US/0162-5160) [04169507] **4672**

PAA FLUKT (NO) **1920**

PAABS REVISTA *CEASED.* (US/0090-7855) [01785327] **584, 491**

PAAC NOTES (CHICAGO, ILL.) (US/1059-7913) [20122851] **3715**

PAACNOTES *See* JOURNAL OF THE PHYSICIANS ASSOCIATION FOR AIDS CARE **3674**

Alphabetical Title Index — PACIFIC

PAAR SAMMUKEST EESTI KIRJANDUSE UURIMISE TEED (ER/0552-7155) [02691932] 2323, **3421**

PAC-FINDER SYSTEM 34/36 SOFTWARE DIRECTORY (US/0741-4978) [10175965] **1289**

PAC-NEWS *CEASED.* (US/0743-1430) [10177095] **3240**

PACE BUYER'S GUIDES. CAR FACTS (US/1056-1889) [23526696] **5422**

PACE BUYER'S GUIDES. DOMESTIC & FOREIGN TRUCK & VAN PRICES NEW & USED (US/1050-7272) [21582234] **5389**

PACE BUYER'S GUIDES. DOMESTIC & FOREIGN TRUCK, VAN, 4X4 PRICES, NEW & USED (US/1064-4628) [26279325] **5422**

PACE BUYER'S GUIDES. FOREIGN AND JAPANESE CAR PRICES, NEW & USED *See* PACE BUYER'S GUIDES. NEW & USED IMPORT CAR PRICES **5422**

PACE BUYER'S GUIDES. FOREIGN AND JAPANESE CAR PRICES, NEW & USED (US/1065-6707) [26646956] **5422**

PACE BUYER'S GUIDES. FOREIGN CAR PRICES NEW & USED (US/1050-5423) [21509711] **5422**

PACE BUYER'S GUIDES. NEW & USED IMPORT CAR PRICES *CEASED.* (US/1069-3238) [27991197] **5422**

PACE BUYER'S GUIDES. NEW CAR PRICES (US/1049-8583) [21307785] **5422**

PACE BUYER'S GUIDES. TRUCK AND VAN PRICES (US) **5422**

PACE BUYER'S GUIDES. TRUCK FACTS (US/1056-1870) [23526657] **5422**

PACE BUYER'S GUIDES. USED CAR PRICES (US/1050-5415) [21509534] **5422**

PACE ENVIRONMENTAL LAW REVIEW (US/0738-6206) [09632561] **3115**

PACE (HUNTINGTON, IND.) (US/1048-4523) [03957129] 1771, **4984**

●PACE INTERNATIONAL LAW REVIEW (US) [30384741] **3133**

PACE LAW REVIEW (US/0272-2410) [06796884] **3024**

PACE PETROLEUM COKE QUARTERLY (US) **4271**

PACE. PROCESS AND CHEMICAL ENGINEERING (AT/0156-949X) [07213711] **1027**

PACE SYNTHETIC FUELS REPORT (US/0737-1926) [09296925] **1952**

PACE YEARBOOK OF INTERNATIONAL LAW (US/1052-3448) [19984780] **3133**

PACEMAKER UPDATE INTERNATIONAL (UK) **2801**

PACER (QUINLAN, TEX.), THE *CEASED.* (US/0748-3872) [10062440] **2542**

PACER (WINNIPEG, MAN.) (CN/0229-3463) [08770672] **4911**

●PACHACAMAC : REVISTA DEL MUSEO DE LA NACION (PE) [28627519] **4095**

PACIFECON SURVEY OF DEVELOPMENT ACTIVITY IN NEW ZEALAND (AT/1031-5969) [10315969] **2911**

PACIFIC AFFAIRS (CN/0030-851X) [01761665] **4486**

PACIFIC AND ASIAN JOURNAL OF ENERGY (II/0970-3888) [19471828] **1952**

PACIFIC ANTHROPOLOGICAL RECORDS *CEASED.* (US/0078-740X) [01716363] 277, **243**

PACIFIC AREA DESTINATION HANDBOOK (US/0363-4817) [02478546] **5488**

PACIFIC AREA TRAVEL ASSOCIATION *See* PATA ANNUAL STATISTICAL REPORT **5488**

PACIFIC AREA TRAVEL ASSOCIATION *See* PACIFIC AREA DESTINATION HANDBOOK **5488**

PACIFIC ARTS (US) [23006784] **327**

●PACIFIC ASIAN BUSINESS REVIEW (US/1061-8619) [25481802] **702**

PACIFIC ASIAN STUDIES (GU) [04008362] **2670**

PACIFIC AUTOMOTIVE NEWS (US/0744-8155) [08582144] **5422**

●PACIFIC BASIN/ASEAN BUSINESS (US/1064-9832) [26495156] **702**

PACIFIC BASIN ECONOMIC OUTLOOK (US/8755-0911) [11188566] **1577**

PACIFIC BASIN ECONOMIC UPDATE (US/8755-6006) [11338287] **1577**

●PACIFIC-BASIN FINANCE JOURNAL (NE/0927-538X) [28369372] **802**

PACIFIC BASIN QUARTERLY (US/0191-3387) [04865709] **1577**

PACIFIC BEACH LIGHT *CEASED.* (US/0895-3457) [16571728] **5638**

PACIFIC BOATING ALMANAC. NORTHERN CALIFORNIA & NEVADA (US/0193-3515) [03307044] **595**

PACIFIC BOATING ALMANAC. PACIFIC NORTHWEST & ALASKA (US/0899-9368) [15667654] **595**

PACIFIC BOATING ALMANAC. SOUTHERN CALIFORNIA, ARIZONA & BAJA (US/0193-3507) [03307150] **595**

PACIFIC BUILDER & ENGINEER (US/0030-8544) [05065205] **2028**

PACIFIC BULLETIN (US) [12097626] **4053**

PACIFIC BUSINESS NEWS (US/0030-8552) [06598784] **5656**

PACIFIC CITIZEN, THE (US/0030-8579) [01774036] **5638**

PACIFIC COAST AQUACULTURE (CN) **2310**

PACIFIC COAST ARCHAEOLOGICAL SOCIETY *See* PACIFIC COAST ARCHAEOLOGICAL SOCIETY QUARTERLY **277**

PACIFIC COAST ARCHAEOLOGICAL SOCIETY QUARTERLY (US/0552-7252) [04683531] **277**

PACIFIC COAST BOWHUNTER *See* WESTERN BOWHUNTER **4880**

PACIFIC COAST DIRECTORY OF TRANSPORTATION *See* COAST MARINE & TRANSPORTATION DIRECTORY **5379**

PACIFIC COAST ENTOMOLOGICAL SOCIETY *See* MEMOIRS OF THE PACIFIC COAST ENTOMOLOGICAL SOCIETY **5591**

PACIFIC COAST JOURNAL (US/0894-4458) [11826167] **2801**

●PACIFIC COAST JOURNAL (CAMPBELL, CALIF.) (US/1065-1594) [26515892] **3421**

PACIFIC COAST LEGAL DIRECTORY *See* CALIFORNIA LEGAL DIRECTORY, THE **2946**

PACIFIC COAST NURSERYMAN & GARDEN SUPPLY DEALER (US/0192-7159) [04905239] **2427**

PACIFIC COAST OBSTETRICAL AND GYNECOLOGICAL SOCIETY *See* TRANSACTIONS OF THE PACIFIC COAST OBSTETRICAL AND GYNECOLOGICAL SOCIETY **3769**

PACIFIC COAST OIL DIRECTORY (US) [12872666] **4271**

PACIFIC COAST PETROLEUM DIRECTORY (US) **4271**

PACIFIC COAST PHILOLOGY (US/0078-7469) [02449380] **3421**

PACIFIC COAST STUDIO DIRECTORY (US/0731-2059) [07938827] **4075**

PACIFIC COMPUTER WEEKLY (AT/0817-6213) [08176213] **1198**

●PACIFIC CONSERVATION BIOLOGY (AT/1038-2097) **2201**

PACIFIC DAILY NEWS (GU/0196-2485) [05785524] **5802**

PACIFIC DISCOVERY (US/0030-8641) [01761670] 4170, **5137**

PACIFIC ECONOMIC BULLETIN (AT/0817-8038) [17539840] **1511**

PACIFIC ECONOMIC COOPERATION (US/0898-7904) [15297171] **1511**

●PACIFIC FARMER (US/1071-6548) [28493293] **118**

PACIFIC FARMER-STOCKMAN (US/1062-256X) [25490081] **118**

PACIFIC FISHERIES REVIEW (US/0892-9076) [15329328] **2310**

PACIFIC FISHING (US/0195-6515) [05585808] **2310**

PACIFIC FLYER AVIATION NEWS (US) **31**

PACIFIC FLYWAY WATERFOWL REPORT (US/0740-6940) [06021920] **5593**

PACIFIC FOCUS (KO) [13844566] **2661**

PACIFIC FOOD & DRINK NEWS *CEASED.* (CN/1182-5790) [23238083] **2352**

PACIFIC FORESTRY CENTRE *See* REPORTS AND PUBLICATIONS - PACIFIC FORESTRY CENTRE **2392**

PACIFIC FRIEND (JA) [01791952] **2661**

PACIFIC FRUIT NEWS (US/0030-8668) [04101567] **2352**

PACIFIC GILLNETTER (CN/1195-3365) [29593061] **2310**

PACIFIC GROVE, PEBBLE BEACH TRIBUNE (US/0746-8423) [10319162] **5638**

PACIFIC HALIBUT FISHERY REGULATIONS (US) [02008815] **2310**

PACIFIC HISTORICAL REVIEW (US/0030-8684) [01645286] **2753**

PACIFIC HORTICULTURE (US/0163-7843) [02356913] **2427**

PACIFIC INFORMATION SERVICE ON STREET-DRUGS (US/0148-5733) [03337948] **4319**

PACIFIC ISLANDS EDUCATION (NZ) [01785715] **1771**

PACIFIC ISLANDS MONTHLY (AT/0030-8722) [01606263] **2670**

PACIFIC ISLANDS MONTHLY LOCAL CLIMATOLOGICAL DATA. MICROFORM (US) [10858420] **1433**

PACIFIC ISLANDS STUDIES AND NOTES (US/0085-459X) [02687421] **2670**

PACIFIC ISLANDS (TRUST TERRITORY). CONGRESS OF MICRONESIA. JOINT COMMITTEE ON PROGRAM AND BUDGET PLANNING *See* TRUST TERRITORY BUDGET PLAN **4757**

PACIFIC ISLANDS (TRUST TERRITORY). CONGRESS OF MICRONESIA. LIBRARY *See* CONGRESS OF MICRONESIA BIBLIOGRAPHY **4697**

PACIFIC ISLANDS YEAR BOOK (FJ) [01087005] **2511**

PACIFIC JOURNAL OF MATHEMATICS (US/0030-8730) [01761678] **3526**

PACIFIC JOURNAL OF ORIENTAL MEDICINE, THE (US/8756-0321) [11455235] **3625**

PACIFIC JOURNAL OF THEOLOGY, THE (FJ/0552-7414) [01586402] **4984**

PACIFIC LAW JOURNAL (US/0030-8757) [01761679] **3024**

PACIFIC LINGUISTICS. SERIES A (AT) [15124861] **3309**

PACIFIC LINGUISTICS. SERIES A, OCCASIONAL PAPERS *See* PACIFIC LINGUISTICS. SERIES A **3309**

PACIFIC LINGUISTICS. SERIES B: MONOGRAPHS (AT/0078-754X) [01761681] **3309**

PACIFIC LINGUISTICS. SERIES C: BOOKS (AT/0078-7558) [01590261] **3309**

PACIFIC LINGUISTICS. SERIES D: SPECIAL PUBLICATIONS (AT/0078-7566) [07031484] **3309**

PACIFIC MAGAZINE (HONOLULU, HAWAII) (US/0744-1754) [08085509] **2511**

PACIFIC M&A REPORTER *See* ASIAN M&A AND INVESTMENT DATABASE **891**

PACIFIC MARINE FISHERIES COMMISSION *See* BULLETIN / PACIFIC MARINE FISHERIES COMMISSION **2298**

PACIFIC MARINE SCIENCE REPORT (CN/0713-2565) [01794034] **1455**

PACIFIC MARITIME MAGAZINE (US/0741-7586) [10219131] **5453**

PACIFIC MOTORSPORT (CN/0319-2113) [02442110] **4911**

PACIFIC MOUNTAIN QUARTERLY (US/0738-1867) [09545780] **2830**

PACIFIC MUSIC (CN/0846-3530) [25066815] **4145**

PACIFIC NEWS BULLETIN (AT/0818-1624) [08181624] **2511**

PACIFIC NEWS SERVICE (US/0194-5084) [04782016] **2491**

PACIFIC NORTHWEST (US/0199-6363) [06046595] **2542**

PACIFIC NORTHWEST EXECUTIVE (US/1043-5212) [12359360] **702**

PACIFIC NORTHWEST FORUM, THE (US) [04217756] **2753**

PACIFIC NORTHWEST INSECT CONTROL HANDBOOK *SUSPENDED.* (US) [04316074] **4246**

PACIFIC NORTHWEST LIBRARY ASSOCIATION *See* PNLA QUARTERLY **3241**

PACIFIC NORTHWEST PLANT DISEASE CONTROL HANDBOOK *SUSPENDED.* (US) [04413012] **2427**

PACIFIC NORTHWEST QUARTERLY (US/0030-8803) [02392232] **2753**

PACIFIC NORTHWEST REGION ENVIRONMENTAL QUALITY PROFILE / UNITED STATES ENVIRONMENTAL PROTECTION AGENCY, REGION 10 (US) [07119247] **2238**

PACIFIC NORTHWEST TRADE DIRECTORY (US) [10995194] **848**

PACIFIC NORTHWEST WEED CONTROL HANDBOOK *SUSPENDED.* (US/0899-3041) [12380538] **2427**

PACIFIC NORTHWESTERNER, THE (US/0030-882X) [02869192] **2753**

PACIFIC OIL AND GAS WORLD (US/1071-9628) [28814502] **4271**

PACIFIC OIL WORLD (US/0008-1329) [02240068] **4271**

PACIFIC PERSPECTIVE *CEASED.* (FJ/0377-2543) [01798084] **2670**

PACIFIC PHILOSOPHICAL QUARTERLY (UK/0279-0750) [06272734] **4354**

PACIFIC PRINTERS PILOT (US/0552-7511) [05121907] **4567**

PACIFIC PROGRESS (CN/0821-4484) [09562910] **1839**

PACIFIC PUBLICATIONS (FIRM) See PAPUA NEW GUINEA HANDBOOK **2670**

PACIFIC QUARTER HORSE ASSOCIATION See QUARTER HORSE OF THE PACIFIC COAST, THE **2801**

PACIFIC RAIL NEWS (US/8750-8486) [11861259] **5433**

PACIFIC REPORT (RED HILL) (AT/1031-6981) [I10316981] 4486, **702**

PACIFIC RESEARCH : A PERIODICAL OF THE PEACE RESEARCH CENTRE, AUSTRALIAN NATIONAL UNIVERSITY (AT/1031-9379) [19096518] **4530**

PACIFIC RESEARCH MONOGRAPH (AT/0155-9060) [08235382] **2670**

PACIFIC RESEARCH TITLES (US) **5212**

PACIFIC REVIEW (OXFORD, ENGLAND) (UK/0951-2748) [18300850] **4486**

PACIFIC REVIEW (SAN BERNARDINO, CALIF.) (US/1043-5050) [10121704] **2542**

PACIFIC REVIEW (SAN DIEGO, CALIF.) (US/0739-8360) [09834503] **3421**

PACIFIC RIM ENTREPRENEUR. ASIAN MARKET UPDATE (US/1054-8068) [22974851] **848**

●PACIFIC RIM TELECOMMUNICATIONS (US) **1161**

PACIFIC SCIENCE (US/0030-8870) [01605384] **5137**

PACIFIC SCIENCE ASSOCIATION See INFORMATION BULLETIN - PACIFIC SCIENCE ASSOCIATION **5113**

PACIFIC SEABIRD GROUP See BULLETIN / PACIFIC SEABIRD GROUP **5616**

PACIFIC SHIPPER (US/0030-8900) [04101608] **5453**

PACIFIC SHIPPER'S TRANSPORTATION SERVICES DIRECTORY : TSD (US) [27464110] **5453**

PACIFIC STARS AND STRIPES (JA) [06548540] **5805**

PACIFIC STUDIES (US/0275-3596) [04093926] **2670**

PACIFIC STUDIES INSTITUTE See NEWSLETTER - PACIFIC STUDIES INSTITUTE **2670**

PACIFIC SUN (US/0048-2641) [04101631] **5638**

PACIFIC TELECOMMUNICATIONS See PACIFIC TELECOMMUNICATIONS REVIEW **1119**

PACIFIC TELECOMMUNICATIONS REVIEW (US/1066-3894) [I10663894] **1119**

PACIFIC THEOLOGICAL REVIEW **SUSPENDED.** (US/0360-1897) [01820744] **4984**

PACIFIC TRAFFIC **CEASED.** (US/0030-8943) [05190154] **5442**

PACIFIC TRIBUNE (VANCOUVER, B.C.) (CN) [10049113] **5792**

PACIFIC TRIBUNE (VANCOUVER, B.C.) See TRIBUNE, THE **5796**

PACIFIC TROPICAL BOTANICAL GARDEN See MEMOIR - PACIFIC TROPICAL BOTANICAL GARDEN **517**

PACIFIC UNION RECORDER (US/0744-6381) [08462621] **4984**

PACIFIC UPDATE **CEASED.** (UK) [23883058] **702**

PACIFIC VIEWPOINT (NZ/0030-8978) [01587837] 5253, **1577**

PACIFIC VOCATIONAL INSTITUTE See AUDIO VISUAL CATALOGUE - PACIFIC VOCATIONAL INSTITUTE **1888**

PACIFIC WORLD (NZ/0113-0846) [18453890] **2201**

PACIFIC YACHTING (CN/0030-8986) [02098195] **595**

PACIFICA (GU) [10766829] **5802**

PACIFICA : AUSTRALIAN THEOLOGICAL STUDIES (AT) [19882768] **4984**

PACIFICAN (US/0030-8994) [04101655] **1094**

PACIFIST, THE **CEASED.** (UK/0048-265X) [04481791] **4530**

PACING AND CLINICAL ELECTROPHYSIOLOGY (US/0147-8389) [03578626] **3708**

PACK & PADDLE (US/1059-4493) [24595186] **4911**

PACK & PRINT (SA) [08400047] 4567, **4220**

PACK INFO NEWSLETTER (US) **4220**

PACK-O-FUN (US/0030-901X) [01761698] **1067**

PACK OF APPLES AND APPLE PRODUCTS (CN/1180-5986) [25112471] **2352**

PACK OF CANNED TOMATOES AND TOMATO PRODUCTS (CN/1180-5943) [25066218] **2352**

PACK OF PROCESSED ASPARAGUS (CN/1180-5900) [24640341] **2352**

PACK OF PROCESSED BEANS, GREEN AND WAX (CN/1180-5951) [25066233] **2352**

PACK OF PROCESSED CARROTS (CN/1180-596X) [25066238] **2352**

PACK OF PROCESSED CORN (CN/1180-5935) [25066228] **2352**

PACK OF PROCESSED PEAS (CN/1180-5927) [25066212] **2352**

PACK OF SELECTED PROCESSED FRUITS (EXCL. APPLES) (CN/1180-5919) [25589782] **2352**

PACK OF SELECTED PROCESSED FRUITS (EXCL. APPLES) (CN/1180-5919) [25589784] **2352**

PACK OF SELECTED PROCESSED VEGETABLES (CN/1180-5978) [25112318] **2352**

PACKAGE PLAN FOR FOTONOVELAS / CHILDRENS PACKAGE SPANISH LANGUAGE POPULAR FICTION (US) 1067, **3421**

PACKAGE PRINTING AND CONVERTING (US/0895-1608) [16406150] 4567, **4220**

PACKAGE TRAVEL (US/1052-682X) [22349742] **4220**

PACKAGE X (US/0160-9912) [02252866] **4740**

PACKAGED FLUID MILK SALES IN FEDERAL MILK ORDER MARKETS (US/0148-3951) [03302181] **197**

PACKAGED SOFTWARE REPORTS / MIC (US/0747-9573) [09819145] 702, 1274, **1289**

PACKAGING (UK/0030-9060) [02449391] **4220**

PACKAGING (AT) **4220**

PACKAGING ABSTRACTS See PIRA PACKAGING ABSTRACTS **4221**

PACKAGING AND CONVERTING TECHNOLOGY (US) **4220**

PACKAGING (BOSTON, MASS.) (US/0746-3820) [09980789] **4220**

PACKAGING DESIGN **CEASED.** (US/0030-9109) [01695123] **4220**

PACKAGING DESIGN IN JAPAN (JA) [13145838] 2099, **4220**

PACKAGING DIGEST (CHICAGO, ILL.) (US/0030-9117) [02449392] **4220**

PACKAGING ENCYCLOPEDIA & TECHNICAL DIRECTORY (US) [22352569] **4220**

PACKAGING INDIA (II/0030-9125) [02768261] **4220**

PACKAGING INDUSTRY DIRECTORY (UK/0269-9834) [I02699834] **4220**

PACKAGING JAPAN (JA/0288-3864) [17463721] **4220**

PACKAGING MARKETPLACE **SUSPENDED.** (US) [05205449] **4220**

PACKAGING NEWS (AT) **4220**

PACKAGING NEWS (LONDON) (UK/0030-9133) [09700614] **4220**

PACKAGING OF HEALTHCARE DEVICES AND PRODUCTS (US) 934, **3625**

●PACKAGING PRODUCTIVITY (US/1061-2300) [25218993] **4221**

PACKAGING SCIENCE AND TECHNOLOGY ABSTRACTS (GW/0722-3218) [I07223218] **5175**

PACKAGING STRATEGIES (US/8755-6189) [11383969] **4221**

●PACKAGING TECHNOLOGY & ENGINEERING (US/1067-411X) [27205981] **4221**

PACKAGING TECHNOLOGY AND SCIENCE (UK/0894-3214) [16014555] **4221**

PACKAGING TODAY LONDON (UK/0268-0920) [I02680920] **4221**

PACKAGING TRENDS : JAPAN (JA) **4221**

PACKAGING WEEK (UK/0267-6117) [13827640] **4221**

PACKARD CORMORANT, THE (US/0362-9368) [02381013] **5422**

PACKER RED BOOK See RED BOOK (CHICAGO), THE **849**

PACKER, THE (US/0030-9168) [04233151] **2352**

PACKERS AND STOCKYARDS RESUME (US) [01590206] **217**

PACKER'S PRODUCE AVAILABILITY AND MERCHANDISING GUIDE, THE (US/0147-6378) [02211603] **118**

PACKET (JACKSON, MISS. : 1985) (US) [14407569] **3240**

PACKUNG & TRANSPORT (GW/0724-8490) [10498181] 4221, **5389**

PACS & LOBBIES (US/0886-6457) [10902238] **4511**

PACT; A PANORAMA OF INDUSTRY, AGRICULTURE, COMMERCE & TRADE (II) [01784131] **1772**

PACT : REVUE DU GROUPE EUROPEEN D'ETUDES POUR LES TECHNIQUES PHYSIQUES, CHIMIQUES ET MATHEMATIQUES APPLIQUEES A L'ARCHEOLOGIE (FR/0257-8727) [03803845] **277**

PADABALI (BG) [08756265] **3467**

PADAGOGIK UND SCHULALLTAG (GW) [25257978] **1771**

PADAGOGIK (WEINHEIM AN DER BERGSTRASSE, GERMANY) (GW/0043-3446) [18487231] **1771**

PADAGOGISCHES ZENTRUM, BERLIN. INFORMATIONSSTELLE GESAMTSCHULEN See GESAMTSCHUL-INFORMATIONEN **1748**

PADANG, INDONESIA. INSTITUT KEGURUAN DAN ILMU PENDIDIKAN See BULETIN IKIP PADANG **1729**

PADANIA (IT) [18152607] **1700**

PADDLE POWER **SUSPENDED.** (AT/0818-0210) [I08180210] **4877**

PADDLER (CN/0835-0310) [16390647] **595**

PADDLER (FALLBROOK, CALIF.) (US/1058-5710) [24335468] 4911, **4877**

PADERBORNER GEOGRAPHISCHE STUDIEN (GW/0935-9621) [I09359621] **2572**

PADF IN ACTION (US) [05887061] **2911**

PADIATRIE UND GRENZGEBIETE (GW/0030-932X) [06401702] **3907**

PADIATRIE UND PADOLOGIE (AU/0030-9338) [01714179] **3907**

PADIATRIE UND PADOLOGIE. SUPPLEMENTUM (AU/0300-9556) [01778331] **3907**

PADIATRISCHE PRAXIS (GW/0030-9346) [06401762] **3907**

PADOMJU LATVIJAS SIEVIETE (LV) [06607648] **2521**

PADOVA E IL SUO TERRITORIO (IT) [17948825] **2702**

PADRES' TRAIL (US/0030-9222) [04101719] **4985**

PADUA. MUSEO CIVICO See BOLLETTINO DEL MUSEO CIVICO DI PADOVA ... **4085**

PADUA MUSEO CIVICO BOLLETTINO (IT) **4095**

PADUA. UNIVERSITA. SEMINARIO MATEMATICO See RENDICONTI - SEMINARIO MATEMATICO DELLA UNIVERSITA DI PADOVA **3531**

PADUCAH GASEOUS DIFFUSION PLANT See ENVIRONMENTAL MONITORING REPORT, UNITED STATES DEPARTMENT OF ENERGY, PADUCAH GASEOUS DIFFUSION PLANT **1943**

PADUCAH POST, THE (US) [13698558] **5753**

PADUCAH SUN (1978), THE (US/1050-0030) [08804709] **5682**

PADUK (KO) [11355607] **4864**

PADUK YONGAM (KO) [12173342] **4864**

PADUSA (IT/0393-0149) [18502758] 243, **277**

PADVERKEERBOTSINGS / SENTRALE STATISTIEKDIENS (SA) [18396041] **5442**

PAE - MITTEILUNGEN (GW) **1771**

PAEDAGOGICA BELGICA ACADEMICA **CEASED.** (BE/0079-0370) [06405951] **1839**

PAEDAGOGICA HISTORICA (BE/0030-9230) [01641215] **1771**

PAEDAGOGISCHE ARBEITSSTELLE FUER ERWACHSENENBILDUNG SCHRIFTEN (GW) **1771**

PAEDAGOGISCHE STUDIEN (NE/0165-0645) [02430861] **1771**

PAEDAGOGISCHE WELT (GW) [05222738] **1771**

PAEDIATRIC ANAESTHESIA (FR/1155-5645) [25786411] **3907**

PAEDIATRIC AND PERINATAL EPIDEMIOLOGY (UK/0269-5022) [15994243] 3907, **3736**

PAEDIATRIC CARDIOLOGY (UK/0261-7021) [07545715] 3709, **3907**

PAEDIATRIC NURSING (UK) [22445450] 3907, **3866**

PAEDIATRICA INDONESIANA (IO/0030-9311) [05038074] **3907**

PAEDIATRISCHE FORTBILDUNGSKURSE FUER DIE PRAXIS **CEASED.** (SZ/0078-7795) [02265623] **3907**

PAEDOVITA (US/0737-5131) [09408804] **5300**

PAEKKWANG (KO) [09578662] **2507**

PAESAGGIO URBANO (IT/1120-3544) **2830**

PAESE DELLE DONNE, IL (IT) **5564**

PAFAI JOURNAL (II/0255-7177) [10386958] **1027**

Alphabetical Title Index — PAKISTAN

PAFAMS UPDATE (US/8756-2650) [12348009] 1839, **3625**

PAFT ADVOCATE / PAFT, PENNSYLVANIA FEDERATION OF TEACHERS (US) [21187433] 1700, **1902**

●PAGAN MUSE & WORLD REPORT (US/1068-2473) [27480815] **4186**

PAGANS FOR PEACE (CN/0838-1550) [20781724] **4242**

PAGE (CHICAGO, ILL.), THE (US/1056-6023) [21547729] 1234, **1263**

PAGE NEWS AND COURIER (US) [14979218] **5759**

PAGE ON THE LAW OF WILLS, INCLUDING PROBATE, WILL CONTESTS, EVIDENCE, TAXATION, CONFLICTS, ESTATE PLANNING FORMS, AND STATUTES RELATING TO WILLS (US) [01772130] **3118**

PAGE PEDIGREE (US/0897-7763) [15745626] **2466**

PAGEANTRY (ALTAMONTE SPRINGS, FLA.) (US/1075-3133) [25271675] **2542**

PAGEANTRY MAGAZINE (US) **2542**

PAGELAND PROGRESSIVE JOURNAL, THE (US/1063-8415) [26183087] **5743**

PAGEMAKER IN-DEPTH (US/1052-6560) [22343736] **1289**

●PAGEMAKER IN-DEPTH (1992) (US/1064-6736) [26371827] **1198**

PAGEMAKER IN-DEPTH (MACINTOSH ED.) See PAGEMAKER IN-DEPTH (1992) **1198**

PAGEMAKER IN-DEPTH (WINDOWS ED.) (US/1054-8173) [22994398] **1198**

PAGEMAKER IN-DEPTH (WINDOWS ED.) See PAGEMAKER IN-DEPTH (1992) **1198**

PAGES (CHICAGO, ILL.) (US/0883-6752) [12183718] **2923**

PAGES DE L'EVENEMENT, LES (FR/0152-0741) [I01520741] **2491**

PAGES JAUNES DE L'INDUSTRIE, LES See BOTTIN DE L'INDUSTRIE DE LA MUSIQUE AU QUEBEC **4104**

PAGES (NORTHEAST ED.) (US/0742-4981) [10307158] 31, **5488**

PAGE'S OHIO REVISED CODE, ANNOTATED, CONTAINING THE TEXT OF THE OFFICIAL OHIO REVISED CODE, EFFECTIVE OCT. 1, 1953 CURRENT MATERIAL (US) [01588382] **3024**

PAGIDEX (CN/0823-7492) [10386249] 405, **4319**

PAGINAS (CENTRO DE ESTUDIOS Y PUBLICACIONES) (PE) [04993262] **4985**

PAGINAS DE CONTENIDO: CIENCIAS DE LA INFORMACION (CR) [06452280] **3240**

PAGINE DI PSICOMOTRICITA (IT) **3625**

PAGINE GIOVANI (IT) **1067**

PAHA NEWSLETTER (US/0739-9766) [08891881] **2270**

PAHANG. JABATAN PERTANIAN NEGERI See LAPURAN TAHUNAN - JABATAN PERTANIAN NEGERI PAHANG **104**

PAHLAWAN DALAM KENANGAN (MY) [01790714] **4053**

PAHODOC CEASED. (US/0254-3419) [05734572] **4795**

PAI BOLETIN INFORMATIVO (US/0251-4729) [07525068] **4795**

PAI KO CHIH SHIH (CC) [05143471] **1928**

PAID MY DUES (US/0097-8035) [01799171] **4145**

PAIDEIA (IT/0030-9435) [02699345] **421**

PAIDEIA (BUFFALO) CEASED. (US/0190-1176) [01713573] **4354**

PAIDEUMA (ORONO) (US/0090-5674) [01785546] 3349, **434**

PAIDEUMA (WIESBADEN) (GW/0078-7809) [01761716] **243**

PAIDIKA (NE/0167-5907) [23236718] 5188, **2796**

PAIMAN (PK) [02239397] **2507**

PAIN (AMSTERDAM) (NE/0304-3959) [02962157] **3896**

PAIN AND HEADACHE (SZ/0255-3910) [11472276] **3844**

PAIN AND PAIN RELIEF See PROGRESS IN PALLIATIVE CARE **3867**

PAIN CLINIC, THE (NE/0169-1112) [13926159] **3625**

PAIN DIGEST (US/0938-9016) [22379201] **3625**

PAIN MANAGEMENT UPDATE (US/1056-294X) [23657107] **3625**

●PAIN MEDICINE JOURNAL CLUB JOURNAL (US) **3625**

PAIN RESEARCH AND CLINICAL MANAGEMENT (NE/0921-3287) [18974486] **3625**

●PAIN REVIEWS (UK/0968-1302) **3625**

PAIN. SUPPLEMENT (AMSTERDAM) (NE/0167-6482) [07754741] **3625**

PAINE, WEBBER, MITCHELL, HUTCHINS. CONFERENCE See OUTLOOK FOR THE MEDIA **3309**

PAINJANA CEASED. (II) [02246614] **2507**

PAINT & COATINGS INDUSTRY (US/0884-3848) [12408576] **4224**

PAINT & INK INTERNATIONAL (UK/0953-9891) [24176280] **4224**

PAINT & RESIN (UK/0261-5746) [07589539] **4224**

PAINT CHECK (US/1059-6313) [24649998] **4853**

PAINT HORSE JOURNAL (1979) (US/0164-5706) [04554801] **2801**

PAINT RED BOOK (US/0090-5402) [01785509] **4224**

PAINT TITLES (UK/0144-4425) [I01444425] **4226**

PAINTBALL (BURBANK, LOS ANGELES COUNTY, CALIF.) CEASED. (US/1043-4771) [19498293] 4911, **4864**

●PAINTBOX (LOS ANGELES, CALIF.) (US/1064-7589) [26391567] **1067**

PAINTBRUSH (LARAMIE) (US/0094-1964) [01794144] **3467**

PAINTED BRIDE QUARTERLY, THE (US/0362-7969) [02339039] **3467**

PAINTED HILLS REVIEW (US/1053-9247) [22692828] **3421**

PAINTER CLAN, THE (US) [09310868] **2466**

PAINTERS & ALLIED TRADES DISTRICT COUNCIL 9 SPOTLITE NEWS (US/0734-4317) [05734967] **1700**

PAINTINDIA (II/0556-4409) [01640543] 4567, **4224**

PAINTINDIA. ANNUAL (II/0030-9540) [06507673] 4567, **4224**

PAINTING & DECORATING JOURNAL See PROFESSIONAL PAINTER & DECORATOR **4225**

PAINTING & DECORATING JOURNAL See PAINTING & DECORATING (LONDON, ENGLAND) **4224**

PAINTING & DECORATING (LONDON, ENGLAND) (UK/0956-9227) [14230700] **4224**

PAINTING & WALLCOVERING CONTRACTOR (US/0735-9713) [09039417] 2902, **4224**

PAINTING ANNUAL (US/0737-4291) [08718807] **361**

PAINTSVILLE HERALD, THE (US) [13153861] **5682**

PAIPU (JA) [02413725] **2507**

PAIS & [I.E. E] FILHOS (BL) [06536241] **2284**

PAIS, EL (SP) [03665750] **5810**

PAIS INTERNATIONAL (US/1064-4660) [26395126] 5212, **1511**

PAIS INTERNATIONAL IN PRINT (US/1051-4015) [22135592] 5212, 4672, **5227**

PAIS (MADRID, SPAIN : 1976). ANUARIO (SP) [09455888] **2625**

PAIS (MADRID, SPAIN : EDICION INTERNACIONAL) (SP) [09913410] **5810**

PAIS ON CD-ROM [COMPUTER FILE] (US) [22355516] 5212, 4672, **5227**

●PAIS (PEABODY, MASS.) (US/1072-0103) [28834387] 5212, 4672, **5227**

PAIS VASCO (SPAIN) See EUSKAL HERRIKO AGINTARITZAREN ALDIZKARIA / BOLETIN OFICIAL DEL PAIS VASCO **2968**

PAIX D'URGENCE (CN/0826-2764) [11084986] **4530**

PAK POST : A PUBLICATION OF THE PAKISTAN POST OFFICE (PK) [24346923] **1146**

PAKISTAN ACADEMY OF SCIENCES See PROCEEDINGS OF THE PAKISTAN ACADEMY OF SCIENCES **5141**

PAKISTAN ACCOUNTANT, THE (PK) [01639873] **749**

PAKISTAN ADMINISTRATION : A JOURNAL OF THE PAKISTAN ADMINISTRATIVE STAFF COLLEGE (PK) [07804580] **1868**

PAKISTAN AFFAIRS (US/0030-963X) [01681318] **2661**

PAKISTAN AGRICULTURE (PK/0253-2883) [05841522] **118**

PAKISTAN & GULF ECONOMIST (PK) [08714999] **702**

PAKISTAN ARCHAEOLOGY (PK/0078-7868) [01761742] **277**

PAKISTAN BAR COUNCIL See JOURNAL / PAKISTAN BAR COUNCIL **2990**

PAKISTAN -- BASIC FACTS (PK/0078-7892) [01761737] **4740**

PAKISTAN BOOK OF CRICKET (PK) [03728632] **4911**

●PAKISTAN (BOULDER, COLO.) (US/1061-6101) [25380502] **2507**

PAKISTAN BUDGETS (PK) [17015312] **1511**

PAKISTAN BUSINESS & SHOPPING GUIDE (PK/0250-4340) [09521039] 956, **702**

PAKISTAN. CENTRAL BOARD OF REVENUE See FEDERAL TAXES ADMINISTRATION REPORT **4649**

PAKISTAN. CENTRAL STATISTICAL OFFICE See MONTHLY FOREIGN TRADE STATISTICS OF PAKISTAN **1536**

PAKISTAN CHEMIST AND DRUGGIST (PK/0030-9680) [01761744] **4319**

PAKISTAN COOPERATIVE REVIEW (PK) [04328952] **1543**

PAKISTAN COTTONS, THE (PK) [01695394] **180**

PAKISTAN DEVELOPMENT REVIEW (PK/0030-9729) [01589037] **1511**

PAKISTAN DIRECTORY OF TRADE AND INDUSTRY (PK) [03322458] **848**

PAKISTAN. ECONOMIC ADVISER'S WING See ECONOMY SURVEY **1487**

PAKISTAN. ECONOMIC ADVISOR'S WING See PAKISTAN BUDGETS **1511**

PAKISTAN ECONOMIC AND SOCIAL REVIEW (PK/1011-002X) [01084619] **1577**

PAKISTAN : ENERGIEWIRTSCHAFT (GW) [05667200] **1952**

PAKISTAN EXPORTS (PK/0030-977X) [01774046] **848**

PAKISTAN EXPORTS (KARACHI, PAKISTAN : 1982) (PK) [11483771] **848**

PAKISTAN. FINANCE DIVISION See EXPLANATORY MEMORANDUM ON THE BUDGET (ISLAMABAD) **4723**

PAKISTAN HISTORICAL SOCIETY See JOURNAL OF THE PAKISTAN HISTORICAL SOCIETY **2656**

PAKISTAN HORIZON (PK/0030-980X) [01713821] **2770**

PAKISTAN HOTEL & RESTAURANT GUIDE (PK/0250-4359) [12277433] 5072, **2808**

PAKISTAN HOTEL AND TRAVEL REVIEW (PK) [05229464] 5488, **2808**

PAKISTAN HOTEL GUIDE (PK/0552-8968) [01800373] **2808**

PAKISTAN HOTELS & TOURISM (PK) [03658449] 5488, **2808**

PAKISTAN INSURANCE SURVEY & WHO'S WHO (PK) [02658593] **434**

PAKISTAN INSURANCE YEAR BOOK, THE (PK) [01774051] **2889**

PAKISTAN JOURNAL OF AGRICULTURAL RESEARCH (PK/0251-0480) [08294363] **118**

PAKISTAN JOURNAL OF AGRICULTURAL SOCIAL SCIENCES : BI-ANNUAL JOURNAL OF PAKISTAN AGRICULTURAL RESEARCH COUNCIL, ISLAMABAD (PK) [17992789] **118**

PAKISTAN JOURNAL OF AGRICULTURE, AGRICULTURAL ENGINEERING & VETERINARY SCIENCES (PK/1015-3055) [13771806] 5517, **118**

PAKISTAN JOURNAL OF AMERICAN STUDIES (PK) [10611007] **2753**

PAKISTAN JOURNAL OF APPLIED ECONOMICS (PK/0254-9204) [09003433] **1511**

PAKISTAN JOURNAL OF BIOCHEMISTRY (PK/0300-8185) [01730016] **491**

PAKISTAN JOURNAL OF BOTANY (PK/0556-3321) [01604340] **520**

●PAKISTAN JOURNAL OF CLINICAL PSYCHOLOGY (PK/1019-438X) [28893013] **4606**

PAKISTAN JOURNAL OF COMMUNITY MEDICINE : THE OFFICIAL JOURNAL OF THE PUBLIC HEALTH ASSOCIATION OF PAKISTAN, THE (PK) [19170084] **4795**

PAKISTAN JOURNAL OF FORESTRY, THE (PK/0030-9818) [01587482] **2390**

PAKISTAN JOURNAL OF HISTORY AND CULTURE (PK) [07783924] **2770**

PAKISTAN JOURNAL OF HYDROCARBON RESEARCH (PK/1017-0626) [I10170626] **1045**

PAKISTAN JOURNAL OF LOCAL GOVERNMENT (PK) [02256225] **4672**

PAKISTAN JOURNAL OF NEMATOLOGY : AN OFFICIAL PUBLICATION OF PAKISTAN SOCIETY OF NEMATOLOGISTS (PK) [09656104] **5593**

PAKISTAN JOURNAL OF OTOLARYNGOLOGY (PK/0257-4985) [12813169] **3890**

PAKISTAN — Alphabetical Title Index

PAKISTAN JOURNAL OF PHARMACEUTICAL SCIENCES (PK/1011-601X) [22473014] **4319**

PAKISTAN JOURNAL OF PHARMACY (PK/0030-9850) [01761755] **4319**

PAKISTAN JOURNAL OF PSYCHOLOGICAL RESEARCH : PJPR (PK) [15686961] **4606**

PAKISTAN JOURNAL OF PSYCHOLOGY (PK/0030-9869) [01781913] **4606**

PAKISTAN JOURNAL OF SCIENCE (PK/0030-9877) [01638920] **5137**

PAKISTAN JOURNAL OF SCIENTIFIC AND INDUSTRIAL RESEARCH (PK/0030-9885) [01761756] **5137**

PAKISTAN JOURNAL OF SCIENTIFIC RESEARCH (PK/0552-9050) [01761757] **5137**

PAKISTAN JOURNAL OF SOCIAL SCIENCES (PK) [11195611] **5212**

PAKISTAN JOURNAL OF STATISTICS (PK) [14174022] **5335**

PAKISTAN JOURNAL OF ZOOLOGY (PK/0030-9923) [01761759] **5593**

PAKISTAN LABOUR GAZETTE (PK/0552-9069) [01640110] **3153**

PAKISTAN LAW JOURNAL (PK) [02945566] **3024**

PAKISTAN LIBRARY BULLETIN (PK/0030-9966) [02265636] **3240**

PAKISTAN MANAGEMENT REVIEW (PK) [01774053] **881**

PAKISTAN. MINISTRY OF RAILWAYS *See* ANNUAL BUDGET STATEMENT OF PAKISTAN RAILWAYS **5429**

PAKISTAN PEDIATRIC JOURNAL (PK) [01761764] **3907**

PAKISTAN PICTORIAL (PK/0377-2586) [01776138] **2770**

PAKISTAN POPULATION REVIEW (PK) [24359300] **4556**

PAKISTAN. RAILWAY BOARD *See* RAILWAY BUDGET : IMPROVEMENT FUND WORKS PROGRAMME, THE **5435**

PAKISTAN. RAILWAY BOARD *See* SUPPLEMENTARY BUDGET STATEMENT OF PAKISTAN RAILWAYS **5437**

PAKISTAN. RAILWAY BOARD *See* RAILWAY BUDGET IN BRIEF, THE **5435**

PAKISTAN. RAILWAY BOARD *See* RAILWAY BUDGET : DEMANDS FOR GRANTS FOR THE PAKISTAN RAILWAYS, THE **5435**

PAKISTAN. RAILWAY BOARD *See* EXPLANATORY MEMORANDUM AND STATISTICAL SUPPLEMENT, PAKISTAN RAILWAY BUDGET **5400**

PAKISTAN SEAFOOD DIGEST (PK/1010-3562) [16700251] **2352**

PAKISTAN. STATISTICAL DIVISION *See* REVIEW OF FOREIGN TRADE **850**

PAKISTAN STATISTICAL YEARBOOK (PK/0078-8023) [01084417] **5335**

PAKISTAN. SUPREME COURT *See* PAKISTAN SUPREME COURT REPORTS, THE **3024**

PAKISTAN SUPREME COURT CASES (PK) [11017940] **3024**

PAKISTAN SUPREME COURT REPORTS, THE (PK) [01761738] **3024**

PAKISTAN SURVEY *See* DAKSHINESIA **2650**

PAKISTAN SYSTEMATICS (PK) [03937217] **520**

PAKISTAN TIMES (PK) [12575002] **5807**

PAKISTAN TIMES MICROFORM (PK) [01781444] **5807**

PAKISTAN TRADE DIRECTORY (PK) [11588801] **848**

PAKISTAN VETERINARIAN : A PUBLICATION OF PAKISTAN VETERINARY MEDICAL ASSOCIATION, THE (PK) [22474781] **5517**

PAKISTAN VETERINARY JOURNAL (PK/0253-8318) [09086773] 217, **5518**

PAKISTAN, WIRTSCHAFTLICHE ENTWICKLUNG (GW) [01798763] **1577**

PAKISTAN, WIRTSCHAFTSDATEN UND WIRTSCHAFTSDOKUMENTATION / BUNDESSTELLE FUER AUSSENHANDELSINFORMATION (GW) [11218353] **1577**

PAKISTAN YEAR BOOK (PK/0552-9263) [02703114] **2507**

PAKISTANI ADAB (PK) [02240266] **3421**

PAKISTAN'S BALANCE OF PAYMENTS (PK/0078-852X) [01774139] **802**

PAKIZAH INTIRNASHINAL (CN/0711-4222) [08555892] 2270, **5564**

PAKKAUS (FI/0031-0131) [I00310131] **702**

PAKSHIKA RUDRAVANI (II) [02246616] **2507**

PAL, PACKAGING AND LABELING. FEDERAL LEGISLATIVE AND REGULATORY SUPPLEMENT (US/0145-434X) [02722193] **4221**

PALABRA (SP) **4985**

PALABRA, LA *SUSPENDED.* (US/0277-1535) [05880579] **3421**

PALABRA Y EL HOMBRE, LA (MX/0185-5727) [02713706] **2851**

PALABRE, LA (CN/0701-0230) [03402803] **1543**

PALACHUV HLASATEL (CN/0317-7033) [08648107] **5792**

PALACIO, EL (US/0031-0158) [01641774] **2753**

PALAEO ICHTHYOLOGICA (GW/0724-6331) [10077946] **4228**

PALAEOBOTANIST (LUCKNOW) (II/0031-0174) [01605086] **521**

PALAEOBULGARICA. STAROBULGARISTIKA (BU) [04350874] **2702**

●PALAEOCLIMATES (US/1063-7176) [26123605] **4228**

PALAEOECOLOGY OF AFRICA AND THE SURROUNDING ISLANDS (NE/0168-6208) [05348681] **4228**

PALAEOGEOGRAPHY, PALAEOCLIMATOLOGY, PALAEOECOLOGY (NE/0031-0182) [01761774] 1390, **4228**

PALAEOHISTORIA (HAARLEM) (NE/0552-9344) [02707548] **277**

PALAEONTOGRAPHIA ITALICA (IT/0373-0972) [01761775] **1390**

PALAEONTOGRAPHICA. ABTEILUNG A : PALAOZOOLOGIE, STRATIGRAPHIE (GW/0375-0442) [01776140] **4229**

PALAEONTOGRAPHICA. ABTEILUNG B : PALAOPHYTOLOGIE (GW/0375-0299) [02509436] **4229**

PALAEONTOGRAPHICA AMERICANA (US/0078-8546) [01696623] **4229**

PALAEONTOGRAPHICA CANADIANA (CN/0821-7556) [11580428] **4229**

PALAEONTOGRAPHICAL SOCIETY (GREAT BRITAIN) *See* PALAEONTOGRAPHICAL SOCIETY MONOGRAPHS **4229**

PALAEONTOGRAPHICAL SOCIETY MONOGRAPHS (UK/0376-2734) [02184684] **4229**

PALAEONTOLOGIA AFRICANA (SA/0078-8554) [01697140] **4229**

PALAEONTOLOGIA CATHAYANA (CC) [10812476] **1390**

PALAEONTOLOGIA INDICA (II/0379-5225) [01099303] **4229**

PALAEONTOLOGIA JUGOSLAVICA (CI/0552-9352) [02190804] **4229**

PALAEONTOLOGIA POLONICA (PL/0078-8562) [02449412] **4229**

PALAEONTOLOGICAL ASSOCIATION FIELD GUIDES TO FOSSILS (UK) [11152806] **4229**

PALAEONTOLOGICAL SOCIETY OF INDIA *See* JOURNAL OF THE PALAEONTOLOGICAL SOCIETY OF INDIA **4227**

PALAEONTOLOGY (UK/0031-0239) [01761779] **4229**

PALAEONTOLOGY NEWSLETTER (UK/0954-9900) [19452045] **4229**

PALAEOVERTEBRATA (FR/0031-0247) [05351892] **4229**

PALAESTRA (MACOMB, ILL.) (US/8756-5811) [11409079] 4911, **4392**

PALAESTRA ... UNTERSUCHUNGEN UND TEXTE AUS DER DEUTSCHEN UND ENGLISCHEN PHILOLOGIE (GW) [06219183] **3309**

PALAIOS (US/0883-1351) [12094230] 1443, **4229**

PALAIS DE LA DECOUVERIE (PARIS, FRANCE) *See* REVUE DU PALAIS DE LA DECOUVERTE **5148**

PALAN, LE (CN/0705-0879) [04255971] **4985**

PALANTE (CU/0552-9395) [02687461] **3421**

PALAONTOLOGISCHE ZEITSCHRIFT (GW/0031-0220) [01761778] **4229**

●PALATE AND SPIRIT (US/1061-7701) [25455575] **2352**

PALATE PLEASERS (US/0893-0244) [15314211] **2352**

PALATINE IMMIGRANT, THE (US/0884-5735) [06185727] **2466**

PALATINE PATTER (US/8755-6014) [06190326] **2466**

PALATKA DAILY NEWS (US/0163-5050) [04402148] **5650**

PALAUY DULCET ANTONIO MANUAL DEL LIBRERO HISPANO AMERICANO (UK) **4818**

PALAWIJI NEWS (IO/0215-2711) [19576403] **118**

PALCHON UL WIHAN TOJON (KO) [10203964] **1577**

PALEOBIOLOGY (US/0094-8373) [02241064] 468, **4229**

PALEOBIOS (US/0031-0298) [03918136] **4229**

PALEOCEANOGRAPHY (US/0883-8305) [12224892] **1455**

PALEOCLIMAS (BL/0100-5472) [02414756] **4229**

PALEONTOLOGIA MEXICANA (MX/0543-7652) [01716608] **4229**

PALEONTOLOGICAL JOURNAL (US/0031-0301) [01639478] **4229**

PALEONTOLOGICESKIJ ZURNAL (RU/0031-031X) [05174067] **4230**

PALEONTOLOGY AND GEOLOGY OF THE BADWATER CREEK AREA, CENTRAL WYOMING (US) [05242062] 1390, **4230**

PALEOPATHOLOGY NEWSLETTER (US/0148-4737) [03303159] 243, **278**

PALEORIENT (FR/0153-9345) [02552402] **2770**

PALERMO. UNIVERSITA. INSTITUTO DI AGRONOMIA GENERALE E COLTIVAZIONI ERBACEE *See* QUADERNI DI AGRONOMIA **123**

PALESTINE (BEIRUT) (LE/0377-2616) [02244700] **4531**

PALESTINE EXPLORATION QUARTERLY (UK/0031-0328) [07199833] **278**

PALESTINE FOCUS *CEASED.* (US/0883-8577) [12257122] **2625**

PALESTINE HERALD-PRESS (US/1053-5748) [14980924] **5753**

PALESTINE HUMAN RIGHTS BULLETIN (US/0737-5549) [08609071] **4511**

PALESTINE-ISRAEL BULLETIN (US/0160-984X) [03805212] **4511**

PALESTINE (NEW YORK. 1976) *CEASED.* (US/0191-7900) [03408891] **4531**

PALESTINE PERSPECTIVES (US/0163-3716) [04351048] **4531**

PALESTINE REFUGEES TODAY (US/0031-0336) [01714577] 4531, **5300**

PALESTINE YEARBOOK OF INTERNATIONAL LAW, THE (CY) [12660783] **3133**

PALESTINIAN STATISTICAL ABSTRACT / PALESTINE LIBERATION ORGANIZATION, PALESTINE NATIONAL FUND, CENTRAL BUREAU OF STATISTICS (SY) [07995959] **5335**

PALESTINSKII SBORNIK (RU/0131-2642) [01761786] **2770**

PALESTRA DEL CLERO (IT) [05822702] **4985**

PALETTE TALK (US/0276-1971) [04275821] **361**

PALETTEN (SW/0031-0352) [01761787] **361**

PALI PARAGU BWE YA PUGGO MYA I HTEIRUPPATTI MYA (BR) [02719018] **5021**

PALI TAKKATHO BAHO AHPWE *See* PALI PARAGU BWE YA PUGGO MYA I HTEIRUPPATTI MYA **5021**

PALIMPSEST (IOWA CITY), THE (US/0031-0360) [01761788] **2753**

PALINET NEWS (US/0278-9469) [02520631] **3240**

PALISADE POST (CN/0826-9971) [13448889] **278**

PALISADE TRIBUNE & VALLEY REPORT, THE (US) [23130706] **5644**

PALISADES INTERSTATE PARK COMMISSION *See* ANNUAL REPORT ... NEW YORK, NEW JERSEY / PALISADES INTERSTATE PARK COMMISSION **4628**

PALKKATILASTO (FI) [02241838] **1700**

PALLADIAN STUDIES IN AMERICA (US/0741-7543) [10236968] **305**

PALLADIO (IT/0031-0379) [01761790] **305**

PALLADIUM-ITEM (US) [09295187] **5666**

PALLADIUM-TIMES, THE (US) [10972624] **5720**

PALLAS (NE) [05189918] **4053**

PALLAS (TOULOUSE, FRANCE) (FR/0031-0387) [02242244] **3309**

PALLAVOLO (IT/0390-3133) [I03903133] **4911**

PALLET & CASE (UK) 1621, **3486**

PALLET ENTERPRISE (US/1065-3651) [25810387] **2403**

PALLETIZER *See* MODERN MATERIALS HANDLING **3484**

PALLIATIVE CARE INDEX (UK/0961-4591) [I09614591] **3625**

PALLIATIVE MEDICINE (UK/0269-2163) [15697947] **3625**

PALLISER PAGES (CN/0824-152X) [11807914] **3240**

Alphabetical Title Index — PANORAMA

PALM BEACH BOOKS OF FACTS & FIRSTS, THE (US/1042-637X) [19098698] **1928**

PALM BEACH LIFE (US/0031-0417) [04101731] **2542**

PALM BEACH POST, THE (US) [11319156] **5650**

PALM BEACH REVIEW (US/0884-8785) [12487885] **3024**

PALM BEACH REVIEW AND BUSINESS RECORD *See* PALM BEACH REVIEW **3024**

PALM JOURNAL (US) [22304064] **521**

PALM SPRINGS DESERT SUN (US) [11319579] **5638**

PALM SPRINGS LIFE (US/0031-0425) [04101748] **2542**

PALMARES - ALL CANADA POETRY CONTESTS (CN/0822-1561) [10840832] **3467**

PALMARES LA QUEBECOISE (CN/0319-8421) [02442956] **4145**

PALMAS DE GRAN CANARIA: AGENDA, LAS (SP) [02240533] **2702**

PALMER RUSTLER, THE (US) [14201416] **5753**

PALMER'S IN COMPANY (UK/0961-8295) [I09618295] **3024**

PALMETTO AVIATION (US/0737-657X) [06361331] **31**

PALMETTO BANKER (US/0164-5773) [04139164] **802**

PALMETTO (ORLANDO, FLA.), THE (US/0276-4164) [07368434] **2427**

PALMETTO STAR NEWS (US/0199-0861) [05581561] **5235**

PALMOIL STATISTICAL HANDBOOK (MY) [08971838] 118, **155**

PALMOIL UPDATE (MY/0127-0605) [09626930] **1621**

PALMYONG TUKHO (KO) [09051220] **1307**

PALMYRA ENTERPRISE (US/8755-0539) [11248403] **5770**

PALO ALTO (CALIF.). CITY MANAGER *See* TWO YEAR BUDGET/ CITY OF PALO ALTO **4757**

PALO ALTO WEEKLY (US/0199-1159) [05624488] **5638**

PALOMINO HORSES (US/0031-045X) [02250739] **2801**

PALOS VERDES REVIEW *SUSPENDED.* (US/0745-2462) [08972287] **2542**

PALOS VERDES SOCIAL REVIEW *See* PALOS VERDES REVIEW **2542**

PALYNOLOGY (US/0191-6122) [03503321] **1390**

PALYNOS (US/0256-1670) [11361692] 4230, **521**

PAMATKY A PRIRODA (XR/0139-9853) [02608976] **2702**

PAMATKY ARCHAEOLOGICKE A MISTOPISNE *See* PAMATKY ARCHEOLOGICKE **278**

PAMATKY ARCHEOLOGICKE (XR/0031-0506) [08796185] **278**

PAMIATNIKI KULTURY. NOVYE OTKRYTIIA (RU) [02244063] **327**

PAMIATNIKI OTECHESTVA : ALMANAKH VSEROSSIISKOGO OBSHCHESTVA OKHRANY PAMIATNIKOV ISTORII I KULTURY (RU) [07701626] **327**

PAMIATNIKI TURKMENISTANA (TK/0131-2677) [01795413] **2702**

PAMIETNIK LITERACKI (PL/0031-0514) [01761800] **3421**

PAMIETNIK LITERACKI (ZWIAZEK PISARZY POLSKICH NA OBCZYZNIE) (UK) [08857737] **3421**

PAMIETNIK SOWIANSKI (PL/0078-866X) [01775036] **3309**

PAMIETNIK TEATRALNY (PL/0031-0522) [02265651] **3421**

PAMIETNIKARSTWO POLSKIE (PL/0137-3234) [02243608] **434**

PAMPA NEWS (PAMPA, TEX. : 1976)- (US) [15212692] **5753**

PAMPHLET - DEPARTMENT OF EMPLOYMENT AND SOCIAL SERVICES (BALTIMORE) (US/0092-8720) [01787266] **5300**

PAMPHLET - MAINE DEPARTMENT OF INLAND FISHERIES AND GAME, INFORMATION AND EDUCATION DIVISION (US/0460-6590) [01510834] **2201**

PAMPHLET - OFFICE OF PERSONNEL MANAGEMENT (US/0197-6885) [06068804] **4704**

PAMPHLET SERIES - INTERNATIONAL MONETARY FUND (US/0538-8759) [07557680] **1511**

PAMPHLET SERIES / ORAL HISTORY ASSOCIATION (US) [12821903] **2625**

PAMPHLET SERIES - UNIVERSITY OF CALIFORNIA, LOS ANGELES. CHICANO STUDIES CENTER (US) [06590387] **2270**

PAMPHLET - U.S. DEPARTMENT OF LABOR, EMPLOYMENT STANDARDS ADMINISTRATION, WOMEN'S BUREAU (US/0500-490X) [02686040] 5564, **1700**

PAMPHLETS (UK) [01755839] **3240**

PAMTECO TRACINGS (US/1047-3173) [20661179] **2466**

PAN (MX) [09973852] **2352**

PAN AFRICAN BOOK WORLD (NR) [08713783] **4818**

PAN AFRICAN INSTITUTE FOR DEVELOPMENT *See* RAPPORT D'ACTIVITES / INSTITUT PANAFRICAIN POUR LE DEVELOPPEMENT **1623**

PAN AFRICAN INSTITUTE FOR DEVELOPMENT. REGION AFRIQUE CENTRALE FRANCOPHONE. CENTRE DE DOCUMENTATION *See* BULLETIN BIBLIOGRAPHIQUE ANNUEL **411**

PAN-AFRICAN SOCIAL SCIENCE REVIEW (NR/8755-7436) [11389835] **5212**

PAN AM CLIPPER *CEASED.* (US/0278-1263) [05876484] **31**

PAN-AMERICAN ASSOCIATION OF BIOCHEMICAL SOCIETIES *See* PAABS REVISTA **491**

PAN AMERICAN DEVELOPMENT FOUNDATION *See* PADF IN ACTION **2911**

PAN AMERICAN FEDERATION OF ENGINEERING SOCIETIES *See* REVISTA UPADI **1994**

PAN AMERICAN FOOT AND MOUTH DISEASE CENTER *See* BOLETIN DEL CENTRO PANAMERICANO DE FIEBRE AFTOSA **3558**

PAN AMERICAN HEALTH ORGANIZATION *See* PROPOSED PROGRAM AND BUDGET ESTIMATES - PAN AMERICAN HEALTH ORGANIZATION **4797**

PAN AMERICAN INSTITUTE OF GEOGRAPHY AND HISTORY. COMMISSION ON GEOPHYSICS *See* BOLETIN **1402**

PAN AMERICAN SANITARY BUREAU *See* BULLETIN OF THE PAN AMERICAN HEALTH ORGANIZATION **4769**

PAN AMERICAN SANITARY BUREAU *See* BOLETIN DE LA OFICINA SANITARIA PANAMERICANA **4769**

PAN AMERICAN SANITARY BUREAU *See* ANNUAL REPORT OF THE DIRECTOR - PAN AMERICAN SANITARY BUREAU. BUREAU **3712**

PAN AMERICAN YEARBOOK, THE (US) [02184445] **5488**

PAN DEL MUERTO (CN/1183-8337) [25796579] **3421**

PAN-EROTIC REVIEW (US/0896-2898) [16990201] **5188**

PAN HUA I SHU (CC) [11248879] **381**

PAN (OFFENBURG) (GW/0720-423X) [09158636] **361**

PAN (OFFENBURG, GERMANY) *See* PAN SPEZIAL **361**

PAN-PACIFIC ENTOMOLOGIST, THE (US/0031-0603) [01761823] **5612**

PAN PIPES (US/0889-7581) [07953861] **4145**

PAN SPEZIAL *CEASED.* (GW) [25996631] **361**

PAN YUEH TAN (CC) [07220433] **2507**

PAN Z WAMI (US/0274-9009) [06686336] **4985**

PANACHE (US/0031-062X) [02241119] **3422**

PANADERIA NOTICIAS (SP) **2352**

PANAMA. ARCHIVO NACIONAL *See* BOLETIN INFORMATIVO DEL ARCHIVO NACIONAL DE PANAMA **2724**

PANAMA CANAL COMPANY *See* ANNUAL REPORT - PANAMA CANAL COMPANY, CANAL ZONE GOVERNMENT **4629**

PANAMA CANAL REVIEW, THE (PN/0031-0646) [01774059] **5454**

PANAMA CANAL SPILLWAY, THE (PN/0364-8044) [02582102] **5454**

PANAMA (CITY). UNIVERSIDAD. FACULTAD DE ADMINISTRACION PUBLICA Y COMERCIO *See* REVISTA FACULTAD DE ADMINISTRACION PUBLICA Y COMERCIO **4683**

PANAMA. DIRECCION DE ESTADISTICA Y CENSO *See* ESTADISTICA PANAMENA. SITUACION ECONOMICA, SECCION 331 : ANUARIO DE COMERCIO EXTERIOR **728**

PANAMA. DIRECCION DE ESTADISTICA Y CENSO *See* ESTADISTICA PANAMENA; BOLETIN SEMANAL **5327**

PANAMA. DIRECCION DE ESTADISTICA Y CENSO *See* ESTADISTICA PANAMENA. SERIE H.2 : INFORMACION AGROPECUARIA, PRECIOS PAGADOS POR EL PRODUCTOR AGROPECUARIO **153**

PANAMA. DIRECCION DE ESTADISTICA Y CENSO *See* ESTADISTICA PANAMENA. SERIE K : ANUARIO DE COMERCIO EXTERIOR **833**

PANAMA EN CIFRAS / DIRECCION DE ESTADISTICA Y CENSO (PN) [02255460] **5335**

PANAMA : WIRTSCHAFTLICHE ENTWICKLUNG (GW) [02519631] **1577**

PANAMA, WIRTSCHAFTSDATEN / BUNDESSTELLE FUER AUSSENHANDELSINFORMATION (GW) [08982528] **1511**

PANAMAX BULK CARRIERS (UK/0955-632X) [20321743] **848**

PANCAYATA DARPANA (NP) [01790476] **4672**

PANCREAS (US/0885-3177) [12616452] **3800**

PANCREATIC AND SALIVARY SECRETION (UK/0142-825X) [I0142825X] **3732**

PANDORA (US/0733-1207) [08515065] **5564**

PANDORA (DENVER, COLO.) (US/0275-519X) [06350834] **3422**

PANDORA TIMES (US) [16896767] **5729**

P&T (LAWRENCEVILLE, N.J.) (US/1052-1372) [22095729] **3625**

PANDUAN AKHBAR DAN MEDIA. PRESS AND MEDIA GUIDE (MY) [03279486] **2923**

PANEL BUILDING (UK/0965-4712) [I09654712] **305**

PANEL DISCUSSION SERIES (US/0739-1978) [09700922] **3024**

PANEL PROCEEDINGS SERIES - INTERNATIONAL ATOMIC ENERGY AGENCY (AU/0074-1876) [01775286] 2158, **1952**

PANEL RESOURCE PAPER (US/0739-2346) [09706402] **1902**

PANEL STUDY OF INCOME DYNAMICS (US/1060-4952) [24919390] **1511**

PANEL STUDY OF INCOME DYNAMICS: PROCEDURES AND TAPE CODES, A (US) [03103084] **4740**

PANEL WORLD (US/1048-826X) [21052766] **2403**

PANELLENIA EKTHESE VIVLIOU : KATALOGOS (GR) [20270555] **4831**

PANELLENION HEMEROLOGION TOU ETOUS (TU) [20256278] **3422**

PANGEA : BULLETIN D'INFORMATION SUR LA COOPERATION GEOLOGIQUE INTERNATIONALE / CENTRE INTERNATIONAL POUR LA FORMATION ET LES ECHANGES GEOLOGIQUES (FR/0760-1751) [10676116] **1390**

PANGGONG (KO) [04905240] **2625**

PANGON (KO) [08000263] **3309**

PANGSONG PYOLLAM (KO) [10281916] **1136**

PANGSONG YONGU (KO) [08957242] **1136**

PANHANDLE HERALD, THE (US/8756-2464) [11492494] **5753**

PANHANDLE-PLAINS HISTORICAL REVIEW (US/0148-7795) [01761837] **2753**

PANHANDLE PRESS (CHESTER, W. VA.) (US) [12818339] **5764**

PANHANDLER, THE (US/0738-8705) [07806138] **3467**

PANHELLENICALLY SPEAKING ... THE RUSHEE'S HANDBOOK (US) [01330084] **5235**

PANIM LE-KHAN ULE-KHAN (IS) [18664510] **4486**

PANINFORMATIC *See* INFORMATIC USERS **1188**

PANJAB AFFAIRS (CN/0228-8230) [08036633] **2662**

PANJAB UNIVERSITY *See* RESEARCH BULLETIN. SCIENCE SECTION **5146**

PANJAB UNIVERSITY RESEARCH BULLETIN. ARTS (II) [17960082] **327**

PANJAB. URDU (CN/0701-0508) [03436093] **2753**

PANJABI ESHEEA TAEEMZ (MARCH, 1975) (CN/0715-4801) [09336465] **5792**

PANJI MASYARAKAT (IO/0377-2632) [01796365] **2662**

PANMINERVA MEDICA (IT/0031-0808) [01696532] **3625**

PANOLA STORY, THE (US/0730-1693) [04457936] **2466**

PANOLA WATCHMAN (CARTHAGE, TEX. : 1873) (US) [14072179] **5753**

PANOLIAN (BATESVILLE, MISS. : 1914) (US) [14512203] **5701**

PANOPTICON (BE) [07939989] **3171**

●PANORAMA (AG) [27123123] **2552**

PANORAMA — Alphabetical Title Index

PANORAMA (IT/0553-1098) [04843182] **2521**

PANORAMA (BE) **203**

PANORAMA (XR) [05913078] **4076**

PANORAMA (AT/0314-2531) [03999405] **1771**

PANORAMA (BL) [02243207] **2753**

PANORAMA (UK) **4221**

PANORAMA (NE/0031-0867) [06535173] **5488**

PANORAMA ACTUAL DEL MEDICAMENTO (SP) **3625**

PANORAMA AFRICAIN (SG/0377-2640) [01793715] **2642**

PANORAMA CENTROAMERICANO. SERIE TEMAS Y DOCUMENTOS DE DEBATE (GT) [17763291] **4486**

PANORAMA CONTITERO (SP) **2352**

PANORAMA DA ECONOMIA BRASILEIRA (BL) [09504630] **1577**

PANORAMA DE LA ECONOMIA (AG) [02727417] **1577**

PANORAMA DE LA ECONOMIA ESPANOLA (SP) [01788999] **1577**

PANORAMA DIFESA (IT/0394-3429) [I03943429] **4053**

PANORAMA DU MEDECIN (FR) **3625**

PANORAMA ECONOMICO DE COSTA RICA / MINISTERIO DE PLANIFICACION NACIONAL Y POLITICA ECONOMICA, DIRECCION DE POLITICA ECONOMICA Y SOCIAL (CR) [27415040] **1511**

PANORAMA ECONOMICO LATINOAMERICANO (HAVANA, CUBA : 1977) (CU) [05819720] **1511**

PANORAMA ENGLISH ED (SP/1130-9865) [I11309865] **4095**

PANORAMA ESTATISTICO DO SETOR BANCARIO (BL) [01795325] 802, **732**

PANORAMA FLORICOLO (IT/1120-2068) [I11202068] **521**

PANORAMA / GEORGIA CONSERVANCY (US) [18094852] **2202**

PANORAMA (HOUSTON, TEX.) (US/0885-6311) [08510348] **749**

PANORAMA (HULL) (CN/0705-9213) [04130127] **387**

PANORAMA ISKUSSTV (RU) [05638974] **327**

PANORAMA LESZCZYNSKA (PL/0138-0907) [I01380907] **2521**

PANORAMA (LEVALLOIS) (FR/0299-4690) [I02994690] **956**

PANORAMA MINERO (AG) [03484514] **2147**

PANORAMA MODA & ABBIGLIAMENTO (IT) **2491**

PANORAMA MUSIQUES (FR) [07525780] **4145**

PANORAMA - NORANDA (ED. FRANCAISE) (CN/0824-4871) [10681032] **1621**

PANORAMA - NORANDA (ENGLISH ED.) (CN/0225-6592) [10681029] **2147**

PANORAMA OF EC INDUSTRY (LU) [19060217] **1621**

●PANORAMA OF EU INDUSTRY (LU) [30743027] **1621**

PANORAMA PANADERO (SP/0212-6524) [I02126524] **2352**

PANORAMA PARIS. 1986 (FR/0299-6898) [I02996898] **5034**

PANORAMA (PARIS, FRANCE) (FR) [11975708] **5212**

PANORAMA POLSKA *CEASED*. (PL) [04381033] **2702**

PANORAMA : REVIST MUJORE E MINISTRISE SE BUJGESISE (AA) [27985363] **118**

PANOS-TUOTOS (FI/0784-9656) [19549798] **1577**

PANOSCOPE (UK/0951-8819) [16679525] **1511**

PANSTWO I PRAWO (PL/0031-0980) [02265693] **3024**

PANSTWOWE WYDAWNICTWO NAUKOWE *See* DYSPONENDA PUBLIKACJI **415**

PANTA-RHEI (IO) [04377298] **3024**

PANTAGRAPH (BLOOMINGTON, ILL.) (US) [16418931] **5661**

PANTHEIST VISION (US/0742-5368) [10370996] **4354**

PANTHEON *CEASED*. (GR) **327**

PANTNAGAR JOURNAL OF RESEARCH (II/0377-9386) [02768196] **5137**

PANTOC : PUBLICACIONES ANTROPOLOGICAS DE OCCIDENTE (MX) [08137866] **2753**

PANTOGRAPH OF POSTAL STATIONERY, THE (US/0893-9055) [08680667] **2786**

PAO HSUEH (CH) [01761844] **2923**

PAO KAO WEN HSUEH HSUAN KAN (CC) [11434215] **3422**

PAOLI NEWS, THE (US) [12181980] **5666**

PAOLI REPUBLICAN, THE (US) [12182297] **5666**

PAPANICOLAOU CANCER RESEARCH INSTITUTE *See* DIRECTOR'S REPORT - PAPANICOLAOU CANCER RESEARCH INSTITUTE AT MIAMI FLORIDA **3816**

PAPEIS AVULSOS DE ZOOLOGIA (SAO PAULO) (BL/0031-1049) [01792929] **5594**

PAPEL, O (BL/0031-1057) [02241754] **4235**

PAPELES DE ECONOMIA ESPANOLA (SP/0210-9107) [08692806] **1577**

PAPER AGE (US/0031-1081) [02449423] **4235**

PAPER - AMERICAN SOCIETY OF AGRICULTURAL ENGINEERS (US/0149-9890) [02490239] 118, **1990**

PAPER AND ALLIED PRODUCTS (OTTAWA) (CN/0835-0094) [17718183] **4235**

PAPER & BOARD ABSTRACTS (UK/0307-0778) [09391752] 4235, **4240**

●PAPER AND FOREST PRODUCTS / SALOMON BROTHERS (US) [27246945] **2390**

PAPER & PACKAGING ANALYST (UK/0959-9266) [22214722] 4235, **4221**

PAPER & TWINE JOURNAL (US/0031-1103) [05025356] **4235**

PAPER ASIA (SI) [20669394] **4235**

PAPER ASIA NEWS : THE ASIAN PULP & PAPER NEWSLETTER (SI/0958-0824) **4235**

PAPER BAG INSTITUTE, NEW YORK *See* STATISTICAL REVIEW (NEW YORK) **4222**

PAPER BOOK OF THE DELTA THETA PHI LAW FRATERNITY, INTERNATIONAL (US) [18438208] **3024**

PAPER BUYERS' ENCYCLOPEDIA : FINE PAPER DIRECTORY AND SAMPLE BOOK, THE (US) [22927173] **4235**

PAPER CLIPP (US/0886-8212) [12998833] **4235**

PAPER COLLECTORS' MARKETPLACE : PCM (US) [12779778] **4831**

PAPER CONSERVATION NEWS (US/0092-5497) [01789887] **3240**

PAPER CONSERVATION NEWS (LONDON) (UK/0140-1033) [07719858] **4235**

PAPER CONSERVATOR (UK/0309-4227) [03806912] **4235**

PAPER - CORROSION (US) [04988817] **2015**

PAPER EUROPE (UK/0955-7806) [I09557806] **4236**

PAPER EUROPEAN DATA BOOK (UK/0950-4478) [I09504478] **4236**

PAPER FACTS & FIGURES (UK) [15712564] **4236**

PAPER, FILM AND FOIL CONVERTER (US/0031-1138) [01761848] 4221, **4236**

PAPER FOCUS (UK/0950-3420) [I09503420] **4236**

PAPER - GEOLOGICAL SURVEY OF CANADA (CN/0068-7650) [02603689] **1390**

PAPER INDUSTRY (MONTGOMERY, ALA.) (US/1048-8251) [21052516] **4236**

PAPER (INTERNATIONAL ORGANIZATION FOR THE ELIMINATION OF ALL FORMS OF RACIAL DISCRIMINATION) (UK/0259-2878) [14185795] **4511**

PAPER (LONDON) (UK/0306-8234) [01780672] **4236**

PAPER MARKET DIGEST (UK) **4236**

PAPER MONEY (US/0031-1162) [04075167] **2783**

PAPER (NEW YORK, N.Y.) (US/0892-3809) [15177012] 2491, **327**

PAPER - PACIFIC GROUP FOR POLICY ALTERNATIVES (CN/0824-1341) [11807720] **5300**

PAPER, PAPERBOARD & WOOD PULP (US/0884-6545) [10196586] 4236, **4240**

PAPER PILE QUARTERLY (US/1049-6572) [21270804] 4240, **4236**

PAPER RECYCLER (US/1072-1223) [26926496] **2238**

PAPER. SERIES B (GW) [22877565] **3309**

PAPER. SERIES C (GW) [22787312] **3309**

PAPER. SOUTHERN AFRICA (SA/0254-3494) [I02543494] **4236**

PAPER SUMMARIES - AMERICAN SOCIETY FOR NONDESTRUCTIVE TESTING (US/0272-4723) [06878314] 4413, **1990**

PAPER TECHNOLOGY (1989) (UK/0958-6024) [19657927] **4236**

PAPERASSE (CN/0712-2977) [08790929] **5792**

PAPERBACKS BY MAIL (CN/0822-5818) [10156903] **4831**

PAPERBOARD PACKAGING (US/0031-1227) [01640761] **4221**

PAPERBOARD PACKAGING'S INTERNATIONAL CONTAINER DIRECTORY (US/0741-4129) [10128819] **4221**

PAPERBOARD PACKAGING'S OFFICIAL CONTAINER DIRECTORY (US/0198-8867) [06239313] **4221**

PAPERBOUND BOOKS FOR YOUNG PEOPLE *CEASED*. (US/0198-6414) [05133343] **1072**

PAPERBOUND BOOKS IN PRINT (US/0031-1235) [03404649] **4822**

PAPERCAST (FR/0299-9781) [I02999781] **4236**

PAPERI JA PUU (FI/0031-1243) [01761854] **4236**

PAPERNEWS *See* PAPER FACTS & FIGURES **4236**

PAPERPLATES (TORONTO) (CN/1183-3742) [24265783] **2542**

PAPERPRINTPACK INDIA (II/0048-2862) [I00482862] **4236**

PAPERS (AT) 1067, **3422**

PAPERS - AMERICAN SOCIETY OF MECHANICAL ENGINEERS (US/0402-1215) [01777402] **2124**

PAPERS AND DISCUSSIONS (TI/0570-5274) [02600451] **4271**

PAPERS AND DISCUSSIONS - ASSOCIATION OF MINE MANAGERS OF SOUTH AFRICA (SA) [01518436] **2147**

PAPERS AND MONOGRAPHS - AMERICAN ACADEMY IN ROME (IT/0065-681X) [01894803] **305**

PAPERS AND ORDER PAPERS PRESENTED : OFFICIAL REPORT / PARLIAMENT OF THE COOK ISLANDS (CW) [21577099] **4486**

PAPERS AND PROCEEDINGS, IDAHO STATE TAX INSTITUTE (US) [04737862] **4740**

PAPERS AND PROCEEDINGS OF APPLIED GEOGRAPHY CONFERENCES (US/0747-5160) [10366886] **2572**

PAPERS AND PROCEEDINGS OF THE ROYAL SOCIETY OF TASMANIA (AT/0080-4703) [01331538] **5137**

PAPERS AND PROCEEDINGS - TASMANIAN HISTORICAL RESEARCH ASSOCIATION (AT/0039-9809) [03685354] **2670**

PAPERS AND RECORDS - THUNDER BAY HISTORICAL MUSEUM SOCIETY (CN/0703-7058) [03129220] 2753, **4095**

PAPERS AND STUDIES IN CONTRASTIVE LINGUISTICS (PL/0137-2459) [01781053] **3309**

PAPERS DE TURISME (SP/0214-8021) [I02148021] **5488**

PAPERS DELIVERED AT THE ANNUAL CONFERENCE ON THE CARIBBEAN (US) [01389393] **2753**

PAPERS - FLORIDA STATE UNIVERSITY, TALLAHASSEE. OCEANOGRAPHIC INSTITUTE (US) [01327501] 557, **1455**

PAPERS FROM THE ANNUAL CONFERENCE (US/0566-330X) [01542497] **2427**

PAPERS FROM THE ... ANNUAL CONGRESS / CANADIAN ETHNOLOGY SOCIETY (CN) [08727272] **243**

PAPERS GIVEN AT THE ... ANNUAL CONFERENCE ON EDITORIAL PROBLEMS, UNIVERSITY OF TORONTO (CN/0891-1908) [14867665] **3422**

PAPERS IN AGRICULTURAL AND FOOD ECONOMICS NORTHERN IRELAND (UK/0956-5280) [I09565280] 1511, **118**

PAPERS IN ANTHROPOLOGY (MUSEUM OF NEW MEXICO) (US/0581-6165) [01142044] **243**

PAPERS IN APPLIED LINGUISTICS--MICHIGAN (US/0895-7894) [13807589] **3309**

PAPERS IN AUSTRALIAN LINGUISTICS (AT/0078-9062) [03836130] **3309**

PAPERS IN AUSTRONESIAN LINGUISTICS (AT) [26970735] **3309**

PAPERS IN CANADIAN ECONOMIC DEVELOPMENT (CN/0833-1871) [19411390] **2830**

PAPERS IN COMPARATIVE STUDIES (US/0736-9123) [08891720] **2851**

PAPERS IN EDUCATION AND DEVELOPMENT (TZ) [04994027] **1771**

PAPERS IN FOREST POLICY (US) [22650607] **2390**

PAPERS IN INTERNATIONAL STUDIES : LATIN AMERICAN SERIES (US/0149-4880) [03524824] **2753**

PAPERS IN LINGUISTICS OF MELANESIA (AT/0078-9127) [07406135] **3309**

PAPERS IN MANITOBA ARCHAEOLOGY. FINAL REPORT (CN/0706-0475) [02769628] **278**

PAPERS IN MANITOBA ARCHAEOLOGY. POPULAR SERIES (CN/0706-0505) [02831413] **278**

PAPERS IN MANITOBA ARCHAEOLOGY. PRELIMINARY REPORT (CN/0706-0491) [02769635] **278**

PAPERS IN METEOROLOGY AND GEOPHYSICS (JA/0031-126X) [01761858] 1409, **1433**

PAPERS IN PHILIPPINE LINGUISTICS (AT/0078-9143) [02729734] **3309**

PAPERS IN PIDGIN AND CREOLE LINGUISTICS (AT/0811-0026) [05111210] **3309**

PAPERS IN REGIONAL SCIENCE : THE JOURNAL OF THE REGIONAL SCIENCE ASSOCIATION INTERNATIONAL (US/1056-8190) [23721873] **2830**

PAPERS IN ROMANCE *SUSPENDED*. (US/0195-7260) [05637468] 3422, **3309**

PAPERS IN SLAVIC PHILOLOGY (US/0161-8822) [03954773] **3309**

PAPERS IN SOUTH EAST ASIAN LINGUISTICS (AT/0078-9178) [02729680] **3309**

PAPERS IN THE SOCIAL SCIENCES (US/0732-1082) [08317245] **5212**

PAPERS - KROEBER ANTHROPOLOGICAL SOCIETY (US/0023-4869) [01782656] **243**

PAPERS OF DWIGHT DAVID EISENHOWER (US) **4486**

PAPERS OF FREDERICK LAW OLMSTEAD (US) **4486**

PAPERS OF GEORGE CATLETT MARSHALL (US) **4486**

PAPERS OF LEVERETT SALTONSTOLL, THE (US/0743-2097) [10585133] **2625**

●PAPERS OF ROBERT TREAT PAINE, THE (US/1059-1079) [24483492] **3422**

PAPERS OF SHIP RESEARCH INSTITUTE (JA/0563-7546) [06182620] **4181**

PAPERS OF THE ... ALGONQUIAN CONFERENCE (CN) [11194820] **3309**

PAPERS OF THE ... ANNUAL CONFERENCE OF THE TEXTILE INSTITUTE (UK) [11223063] **5355**

PAPERS OF THE ... ANNUAL MEETING OF THE SEMINAR ON THE ACQUISITION OF LATIN AMERICAN LIBRARY MATERIALS (US) [11154195] **3240**

PAPERS OF THE ARCHAEOLOGICAL SOCIETY OF NEW MEXICO (US/0587-1719) [03353699] **278**

PAPERS OF THE AUSTRALASIAN TRANSPORT RESEARCH FORUM (AT) [28478412] **5389**

PAPERS OF THE BIBLIOGRAPHICAL SOCIETY OF AMERICA, THE (US/0006-128X) [05898924] **422**

PAPERS OF THE BIBLIOGRAPHICAL SOCIETY OF CANADA (CN/0067-6896) [02441825] **422**

PAPERS OF THE BRITISH SCHOOL AT ROME (UK/0068-2462) [01537364] **278**

PAPERS OF THE CANADIAN SOCIETY OF CHURCH HISTORY (CN/0226-3564) [06562690] **4985**

PAPERS OF THE EAST-WEST POPULATION INSTITUTE (US/0732-0531) [06685602] **4556**

PAPERS OF THE JAPANESE STUDIES CENTRE (AT/0725-0177) [11018114] **2662**

PAPERS OF THE LEEDS INTERNATIONAL LATIN SEMINAR (UK) [23227523] **1079**

PAPERS OF THE NEW WORLD ARCHAEOLOGICAL FOUNDATION (US/0077-8915) [01142787] **278**

PAPERS OF THE PEABODY MUSEUM OF ARCHAEOLOGY AND ETHNOLOGY, HARVARD UNIVERSITY (US/0079-0303) [01159187] **278**

PAPERS OF THOMAS A. EDISON (US) **4486**

PAPERS ON BUSINESS ADMINISTRATION (IT) [02241284] **881**

PAPERS ON FRENCH SEVENTEENTH CENTURY LITERATURE (GW/0343-0758) [03806111] **3422**

PAPERS ON LANGUAGE & LITERATURE (US/0031-1294) [02449428] **3422**

PAPERS ON PALEONTOLOGY (US/0148-3838) [01942098] **4230**

PAPERS ON PLANNING AND DESIGN (CN/0225-2724) [06156599] **2830**

PAPERS PRESENTED AND ORDER PAPERS *See* PAPERS AND ORDER PAPERS PRESENTED : OFFICIAL REPORT / PARLIAMENT OF THE COOK ISLANDS **4486**

PAPERS PRESENTED AND ORDER PAPERS - COOK ISLANDS. LEGISLATIVE ASSEMBLY (CW) [05244869] **4486**

PAPERS PRESENTED AT THE ALLERTON PARK INSTITUTE (US/0536-4604) [03296655] **3240**

PAPERS PRESENTED AT THE ... ANNUAL CONFERENCE / RURAL ELECTRIC POWER CONFERENCE (US/0734-7464) [03854772] **2074**

PAPERS PRESENTED AT THE ANNUAL CONVENTION (CN/0083-8799) [01203740] 5537, **2238**

PAPERS PRESENTED AT THE ANNUAL MEETING OF THE AFRICAN STUDIES ASSOCIATION (US) [01797962] **2500**

PAPERS PRESENTED AT THE ... INDUSTRIAL MINERALS INTERNATIONAL CONGRESS (UK/0959-9983) [21822651] **4014**

PAPERS PRESENTED AT THE INTERNATIONAL SYMPOSIUM OF JET CUTTING TECHNOLOGY (UK) **2074**

PAPERS PRESENTED AT THE MEETING (US/0569-3802) [01781859] **1045**

PAPERS PRESENTED AT THE MID-WINTER MEETING OF THE ALBERTA BRANCH OF THE CANADIAN BAR ASSOCIATION *CEASED*. (CN/0715-4534) [09204490] **3024**

PAPERS PRESENTED AT THE PICA CONFERENCE (US/0736-7805) [07683945] **2074**

PAPERS PRESENTED AT THE SHORT COURSE IN PAINT TECHNOLOGY (US) [01333904] 1839, **2015**

PAPERS PRESENTED AT THE ... TECHNICAL CONFERENCE ON OCEANOGRAPHIC CARTOGRAPHY (US/0254-5799) [10984601] 2583, **1455**

PAPERS PRESENTED TO THE ... ANNUAL TECHNICAL CONFERENCE / CANADIAN MARITIME INDUSTRIES ASSOCIATION (CN) [17747228] **5454**

PAPERS PRINTED FOR MID-YEAR EXAMINATIONS. SECTION 2. MATHEMATICS, SCIENCES (US) [03692301] **3526**

PAPERS - QUEENSLAND. UNIVERSITY, BRISBANE. DEPT. OF ENTOMOLOGY (AT/0079-8916) [01434903] **5594**

PAPERS READ AT THE MEETING OF GRAND DRAGONS, KNIGHTS OF THE KU KLUX KLAN (US) [04098165] **5235**

PAPERS READ BEFORE THE SOCIETY (UK) [01567950] **3422**

PAPERS: REVISTA DE SOCIOLOGIA (SP) [04449217] **5253**

PAPERS / THE CARLYLE SOCIETY (UK) [20917503] **3422**

PAPERS (UNIVERSITY OF QUEENSLAND. DEPT. OF GEOLOGY) (AT/0079-8932) [01763297] **1390**

PAPERS USED AT THE ANNUAL EXAMINATIONS IN LAW HELD AT HARVARD UNIVERSITY (US) [01713534] **3024**

PAPERS VICTORIA PARK (AT/1034-9243) [I10349243] 3422, **1067**

PAPERS - WEST TENNESSEE HISTORICAL SOCIETY (US/0361-6215) [01769643] **2753**

PAPERTREE LETTER (US/1180-9175) [22185541] 2390, **4236**

PAPERWORK AND RED TAPE (US/0196-5786) [05356301] **4672**

PAPERWORK SIMPLIFICATION (US) [06601496] **881**

PAPERWORKER, THE (US/0363-6437) [02531644] **1700**

PAPETERIE, LA (FR/0031-1308) [03875478] **4236**

PAPETIER DE FRANCE, LE (FR) [06542176] **4236**

PAPETIER (QUEBEC) (CN/0048-2889) [02098793] **4236**

PAPETIERES DU QUEBEC, LES (CN/0847-2645) [23242560] **4236**

PAPIER & DRUCK (AU) [16313486] 4567, **4236**

PAPIER AUS OSETERREICH (AU/1011-0186) [11809268] **4236**

PAPIER, CARTON ET CELLULOSE (FR/0031-1367) [09490242] **4236**

PAPIER, DAS (GW/0031-1340) [01780675] **4236**

PAPIER UND DRUCK *CEASED*. (GW/0031-1375) [01761861] 4567, **4237**

PAPIER UND KUNSTSTOFF VERARBEITER (GW/0048-2897) **4237**

PAPIER- UND ZELLSTOFF-DIENST (GW/0171-1458) [I01711458] **4237**

PAPIERE ZUR LINGUISTIK (GW) [05511610] **3309**

PAPIERE ZUR TEXTLINGUISTIK (GW/0341-3195) [02715185] **3309**

PAPIERMACHER, DER (GW) **4237**

PAPILLION TIMES (US/0883-1394) [10585509] **5707**

PAPILLOMAVIRUS REPORT (UK/0957-4190) [22154072] **3626**

PAPINEAU'S GUIDE TO BALI (SI) [07781030] **5488**

PAPINEAU'S GUIDE TO BALI, ISLAND PARADISE *See* PAPINEAU'S GUIDE TO BALI **5488**

PAPINEAU'S GUIDE TO JAKARTA (SI/0377-2659) [01795813] **5488**

PAPINEAU'S GUIDE TO SINGAPORE (SI/0129-8682) [07321828] **5488**

PAPINEAU'S GUIDE TO SRI LANKA (SI/0129-9743) [08839397] **5488**

PAPINEAU'S GUIDE TO THAILAND (SI/0129-8534) [07317739] **5488**

PAPIR A CELUL'OZA : P + C (XR) [11487657] **4237**

PAPIRI (IT) [01642959] **278**

PAPIRIPAR (HU/0031-1448) [09467354] **4237**

●PAPIROS DEL SIGLO VEINTE (AG) [28279256] **3422**

PAPPUS (CN/0710-0469) [07728895] **521**

PAPRIPARI ES NYOMDAIPARI SZAKIRODALMI TAJEKOZTATO (HU/0231-0740) [I0231 0740] 4567, **4237**

PAPSTE UND PAPSTTUM (GW) [06705060] **5034**

PAPUA AND NEW GUINEA JOURNAL OF EDUCATION *See* PAPUA NEW GUINEA JOURNAL OF EDUCATION **1771**

PAPUA AND NEW GUINEA LAW REPORTS *See* PAPUA NEW GUINEA LAW REPORTS **3024**

PAPUA-NEUGUINEA, WIRTSCHAFTSDATEN UND WIRTSCHAFTSDOKUMENTATION / BUNDESSTELLE FUER AUSSENHANDELSINFORMATION (GW) [11455162] **1578**

PAPUA NEW GUINEA *See* GOVERNMENT GAZETTE **4475**

PAPUA NEW GUINEA. AUDITOR-GENERAL'S OFFICE *See* REPORT OF THE AUDITOR GENERAL ON THE PUBLIC ACCOUNTS ... / PAPUA NEW GUINEA **4745**

PAPUA NEW GUINEA. BUREAU OF STATISTICS *See* SUMMARY OF NEW MOTOR VEHICLES REGISTERED **5426**

PAPUA NEW GUINEA. BUREAU OF STATISTICS *See* CATALOGUE OF STATISTICAL INFORMATION ON PAPUA NEW GUINEA **5325**

PAPUA NEW GUINEA. BUREAU OF STATISTICS *See* REGISTERED MOTOR VEHICLES **5424**

PAPUA NEW GUINEA. BUREAU OF STATISTICS *See* SURVEY OF RETAIL SALES AND SELECTED SERVICES **958**

PAPUA NEW GUINEA. BUREAU OF STATISTICS *See* STATISTICS FROM RELIGIOUS ORGANIZATIONS **5013**

PAPUA NEW GUINEA. BUREAU OF STATISTICS *See* WORKERS' COMPENSATION STATISTICS **1540**

PAPUA NEW GUINEA HANDBOOK (AT) [02653383] **2670**

PAPUA NEW GUINEA JOURNAL OF EDUCATION (PP/0031-1472) [04072307] **1771**

PAPUA NEW GUINEA LAW REPORTS (AT/0085-4689) [05722892] **3024**

PAPUA NEW GUINEA MEDICAL JOURNAL (PP/0031-1480) [10429051] **3626**

PAPUA NEW GUINEA NATIONAL BIBLIOGRAPHY (PP/0252-8347) [07626120] **422**

PAPUA NEW GUINEA POST COURIER SELECTIVE INDEX (PP) [07267567] **1146**

PAPUA-NEW GUINEA (TER.) DEPT. OF PUBLIC HEALTH *See* ANNUAL REPORT - DEPARTMENT OF PUBLIC HEALTH **4765**

PAPUA NEW GUINES. BUREAU OF STATISTICS *See* CAPITAL EXPENDITURE BY PRIVATE BUSINESSES (PAPUA NEW GUINEA) **894**

PAPYROLOGICA BRUXELLENSIA (BE/0078-9402) [02003960] **3422**

PAPYROLOGICA COLONIENSIA (GW/0078-9410) [03454770] **2702**

PAPYROLOGICA LUGDUNO-BATAVA (NE) [01761863] **278**

PAPYROLOGISCHE TEXTE UND ABHANDLUNGEN (GW) [02002017] **4985**

PAPYRUS BODMER (SZ) [07017315] 4985, **3422**

PAQ

Alphabetical Title Index

PAQ REVIEW : THE INDEPENDENT MAGAZINE FOR COMPAQ COMPUTER USERS (US) [18671990] **1198**

PAR-DELA LE RIDEAU (CN/0711-0758) [08458562] **2753**

PAR EXCELLANCE MAGAZINE (US/0886-4527) [12890223] **4911**

PAR. PUBLIC ADMINISTRATION REVIEW POPULATION (US/0033-3352) [01623952] **4672**

PAR SI PAR LA (CN/0712-290X) [08808173] **4145**

PARA (BRAZIL : STATE) *See* EMENTARO DA LEGISLACAO ESTADUAL **2965**

PARA (BRAZIL : STATE). SECRETARIA DE ESTADO DE ADMINISTRACAO *See* RELATORIO DE ATIVIDADES - SECRETARIA DE ESTADO DE ADMINISTRACAO **4679**

PARA FISCAL : ORGAO OFICIAL DA ASSOCIACAO DOS FISCAIS DE TRIBUTOS ESTADUAIS DO PARA (BL) [10200546] **3024**

PARA-LEGAL UPDATE **SUSPENDED.** (US/0146-2954) [02917441] **3025**

PARABANCARIA **CEASED.** (IT) **802**

PARABLES, ETC (US/0744-2017) [08105275] **4985**

PARABOLA (AT) **3526**

PARABOLA (MT. KISCO) (AT/0362-1596) [02210234] **4985**, **2323**

PARABOLE (CN/0709-0056) [05258091] **5018**

PARACHUTE (CN/0318-7020) [02851563] **361**

PARACHUTE PAGES (US) **4911**

PARACHUTIST (WASHINGTON) (US/0031-1588) [04101788] **4911**

PARACLETE (SPRINGFIELD, MO.) (US/0190-4639) [04720379] **5065**

PARADE (US) [01772138] **2542**

PARADE SAUVAGE. BULLETIN (FR/0767-7138) [12954876] **3422**

PARADES AND PAGEANTRY (CN) **4145**

PARADIGM SHIFT : PATRICIA SEYBOLD'S GUIDE TO THE INFORMATION REVOLUTION **CEASED.** (US/1054-3929) [22877147] **1198**

PARADIGMA (IT) [03567198] **3422**

PARADIGMI (IT) [13770824] **4354**

PARADOX DEVELOPER'S JOURNAL (US/1051-9696) [22160217] **1289**

PARADOX INFORMANT (US/1058-7071) [24361829] **1280**

PARADOX USER'S JOURNAL (US/0889-2911) [13502969] **1289**

● PARADOXIST MOVEMENT, THE (US/1055-761X) [23293244] **4354**

PARAGLIDE (US/0745-9688) [06601155] **4053**

PARAGLIDE (FORT BRAGG, N.C.) (US/0891-7965) [10774290] **5724**

PARAGONE (IT/0031-1650) [05017254] **327**

PARAGONE. LETTERATURA (IT) [02265710] **1079**

PARAGRAPH (MODERN CRITICAL THEORY GROUP) (UK/0264-8334) [12130734] **3309**

PARAGRAPH POOLE (UK/0953-8577) [09538577] **2851**

PARAGRAPH (STRATFORD) (CN/1182-543X) [23237170] **3422**

PARAGRAPHIC (CN/0048-2935) [02099125] 4392, **1883**

PARAGUAY ECONOMICO : PUBLICACION MENSUAL DEL BANCO PARAGUAYO DE DATOS (PY) [05692032] **1511**

PARAGUAY : ENERGIEWIRTSCHAFT (GW) [05064286] **1952**

PARAGUAY NOTICIAS (PY) [23122304] **2753**

PARAGUAY WIRTSCHAFTLICHE ENTWICKLUNG / BUNDESSTELLE FUER AUSSENHANDELSINFORMATION (GW) [08725010] **1578**

PARAIBA (BRAZIL : STATE). SECRETARIA DOS TRANSPORTES E OBRAS *See* RELATORIO DE ATIVIDADES / GOVERNO DO ESTADO DA PARAIBA, SECRETARIA DOS TRANSPORTES E OBRAS **5391**

PARALEGAL, THE **SUSPENDED.** (US/0739-3601) [09719551] **3025**

● PARALLEL ALGORITHMS AND APPLICATIONS (US/1063-7192) [26123823] **1248**

PARALLEL COMPUTING (NE/0167-8191) [11197165] **1248**

PARALLEL PROCESSING LETTERS (SI/0129-6264) [25207655] **1280**

PARALLELES (UNIVERSITE DE GENEVE. ECOLE DE TRADUCTION ET D'INTERPRETATION) (SZ) [08829652] **3310**

PARALLELI ROZZANO **CEASED.** (IT/1121-5542) [I11215542] **3349**

PARALLELOGRAM INTERNATIONAL (UK/0953-7252) [21571111] **1198**

PARALLELOGRAMME (VANCOUVER) (CN/0703-8712) [03781968] **361**

PARAMAGNITNYI REZONANS (RU/0370-0704) [05621895] **4445**

PARAMETERS (CARLISLE, PA.) (US/0031-1723) [01039883] **4053**

PARAMETRO (IT/0031-1731) [04910132] **2830**

PARAMETRO; MENSILE INTERNATIONALE DI ARCHITETTURA & URBANISTICA (IT) [05011186] **305**

PARANA (BRAZIL : STATE). COORDENACAO DA ADMINISTRACAO FINANCEIRA DO ESTADO *See* BALANCO GERAL / GOVERNO PARANA, SECRETARIA DE ESTADO DAS FINANCAS, COORDENACAO DA ADMINISTRACAO FINANCEIRA DO ESTADO **4712**

PARANA (BRAZIL : STATE). COORDENADORIA DE ORCAMENTO E PROGRAMACO *See* FONTES DE FINANCIAMENTO PARA O SETOR PUBLICO ESTADUAL **4727**

PARANA, BRAZIL (STATE). MINISTERIO PUBLICO *See* MP **3012**

PARANA INFORMACOES (BL) [01791506] **1578**

PARAPARA (VE) [21920628] **3422**

PARAPET, THE (CN/0384-0417) [02505167] **4053**

PARAPLEGIA (UK/0031-1758) [01761869] **4392**

PARAPLEGIA NEWS (US/0031-1766) [03615923] **4392**

PARAPSYCHOLOGICAL ASSOCIATION *See* RESEARCH IN PARAPSYCHOLOGY **4243**

PARAPSYCHOLOGICAL JOURNAL OF SOUTH AFRICA (SA) **4242**

PARAPSYCHOLOGICAL MONOGRAPHS (US/0078-9437) [01761870] **4242**

PARAPSYCHOLOGY IN THE USSR (US/0748-0156) [10834091] **4242**

● PARAPSYCHOLOGY, NEW AGE, AND THE OCCULT (US/1065-3031) [26566691] 4186, **4242**

PARAPSYCHOLOGY (OTTAWA) (CN/0227-6119) [08036698] **4242**

PARAPSYCHOLOGY REVIEW **CEASED.** (US/0031-1804) [01761872] **4242**

PARASCOPE (US/0738-1247) [08031330] **3142**

PARASITE IMMUNOLOGY (UK/0141-9838) [05337508] **3675**

● PARASITE : JOURNAL DE LA SOCIETE FRANCAISE DE PARASITOLOGIE (FR/1252-607X) [30395671] **468**

PARASITIC DISEASES (US/0730-9562) [08090317] **568**

PARASITICA (BE/0031-1812) [01761873] **521**

PARASITOLOGIA AL DIA : REVISTA DE LA SOCIEDAD CHILENA DE PARASITOLOGIA (CL/0716-0720) [11810814] **3626**

PARASITOLOGIA HUNGARICA (HU/0303-688X) [01075715] **468**

PARASITOLOGY (UK/0964-7570) 492, **3626**

PARASITOLOGY (UK/0031-1820) [01714177] **492**

PARASITOLOGY RESEARCH (1987) (GW/0932-0113) [15110644] **468**

PARASITOLOGY TODAY (REFERENCE ED.) (UK/0169-4707) [13876797] **468**

PARASSITOLOGIA (IT/0048-2951) [06622450] **468**

PARATERETES : PERIODIKE EKDOSE LOGOU KAI TECHNES, O (GR/1012-0211) [27204714] 361, **3422**

PARATRACKS / CANADIAN PARAPLEGIC ASSOCIATION-MANITOBA DIVISION (CN/0832-0543) [15180917] **4392**

PARATUS (SA) [02705871] **4053**

PARAVISIE (NE) **4242**

PARAVOICE (CN/0228-9938) [08028301] **4911**

PARAZITOLOGICHESKII SBORNIK (RU) [05583292] **468**

PARAZITOLOGIJA (RU/0031-1847) [06609121] **468**

PARC DES VEHICULES UTILITAIRES IMMATRICULES *See* FICHIER CENTRAL DES AUTOMOBILES, PARC ET IMMATRICULATIONS / MINISTERE DES TRANSPORTS, DIRECTION DES AFFAIRES ECONOMIQUES, FINANCIERES ET ADMINISTRATIVES, DEPARTEMENT DES STATISTIQUES DES TRANSPORTS **5415**

PARC ET IMMATRICULATIONS DES VEHICULES UTILITAIRES / MINISTERE DES TRANSPORTS, DEPARTEMENT DES STATISTIQUES DES TRANSPORTS (FR) [09250335] **5423**

● PARC NATIONAL DES ILES-DE-LA-BAIE-GEORGIENNE, PLAN DE GESTION (CN/1191-4726) [26758063] **4707**

● PARC NATIONAL DES ILES-DU-SAINT-LAURENT, PLAN DE GESTION (CN/1191-470X) [26758056] **4707**

PARCHEMIN, LE (BE) [05224253] 434, **2466**

PARCOURS, LE (CN/0383-8927) [03303865] **1883**

PARCS DEPARTEMENTAUX DE L'EQUIPEMENT, LES (FR) [11017827] **2202**

PARCS PARIS. 1987 (FR/0982-6246) [I09826246] **2202**

PARDES, HA- (US) [02241514] **5051**

● PARDIS (WEST ORANGE, N.J.) (US/1062-8428) [25769228] **2270**

PARENT (AT/0156-5044) [I01565044] **1771**

PARENT & CHILD **CEASED.** (US/1041-178X) [18675932] **2284**

PARENT AND CITIZEN (AT/0726-7126) [I07267126] **1771**

PARENT AND PRESCHOOLER : PP (US/0887-0365) [13067483] **1771**

PARENT CARE (BETHANY, OKLA.) (US/1058-5583) [24329441] **2284**

PARENT CARE / YOUR CHILD CARE NEWS-LINE (CN/1195-1893) **2284**

PARENT COOPERATIVE PRESCHOOLS INTERNATIONAL *See* DIRECTORY - PARENT COOPERATIVE PRESCHOOLS INTERNATIONAL **1803**

PARENT WORKSHOP, THE (US/1060-0027) [24843336] **2284**

PARENTAL GUIDANCE (US) **4985**, **2284**

PARENTALK (RICHMOND HILL) (CN/1183-6393) [25423211] **2284**

PARENTERAL DRUG ASSOCIATION *See* TECHNICAL MONOGRAPH - PARENTERAL DRUG ASSOCIATION, INC **4330**

PARENTGUIDE NEWS (US/0896-1468) [16926316] **2284**

PARENTING FOR PEACE AND JUSTICE NETWORK : [NEWSLETTER] (US/0890-3859) [14221497] **5300**

PARENTING (SAN FRANCISCO, CALIF.) (US/0890-247X) [14179299] **2284**

PARENTING STUDIES **SUSPENDED.** (US/0737-5123) [09405072] **2284**

● PARENTLIFE (NASHVILLE, TENN.) (US/1074-326X) [29682149] 1805, **2284**

PARENTS (UK) **2284**

PARENTS & CHILDREN MAGAZINE *See* AUSTRALIA'S PARENTS : THE PRACTICAL PARENTING MAGAZINE **2277**

PARENTS AND CHILDREN TOGETHER **CEASED.** (US/1050-7108) [21577537] **2284**

PARENTS & TEENAGERS (US/0897-8697) [17645779] **2284**

PARENTS' CHOICE (US/0161-8164) [06866094] **2284**

PARENTS D'AUJOURD'HUI (CN/0705-713X) [04249770] **2284**

PARENTS DE COEUR **CEASED.** (CN/1191-1727) [25883034] **5300**

PARENTS DE COEUR (CN/1191-1727) [25883030] **2284**

PARENT'S DIGEST (CHILLIWACK) (CN/0835-5754) [18242181] **2284**

PARENTS' GUIDE TO CHILDREN'S ENTERTAINMENT **CEASED.** (US/1059-9207) [24809679] 2284, **1136**

PARENTS' GUIDE TO CHILDREN'S VIDEO (SANTA MONICA, CALIF.) *See* PARENTS' GUIDE TO CHILDREN'S ENTERTAINMENT **1136**

PARENTS (LONDON) (UK/0260-7514) [I02607514] **2284**

PARENTS MAKE THE DIFFERENCE! (US/1046-0446) [20314468] **2285**

PARENTS (PARIS), LES (FR/0553-2159) [07158214] **2285**

PARENTS' PRESS (US/0889-8863) [14114466] **2285**

PARENTS REPORT / THE INTERNATIONAL SCHOLARSHIP FOUNDATION (CN/1183-8779) [25796414] **1839**

PARENT'S SAY (AT/0818-8114) [I08188114] **1772**

PARENTS SHOPPING GUIDE (AT/1030-1968) [I10301968] **2285**

● PARENTWISE (UK) **4985**

PARERGON (AT/0313-6221) [01785479] 3422, **1079**

PARFUMERIE, DIE (AU) [04064016] **405**

PARFUMERIE UND KOSMETIK (GW/0031-1952) [04064044] **405**

PARFUMS, COSMETIQUES, AROMES (FR/0337-3029) [01354682] **405**

PARIS AND ENVIRONS : HOTELS AND RESTAURANTS (FR) [04733730] 5072, **2808**

PARIS CAPITALE... - PMR ED. FRANCAISE (FR/1166-2344) [11662344] **2521**

PARIS. ECOLE PRATIQUE DES HAUTES-ETUDES. CENTRE D'ETUDES ECONOMIQUES *See* ETUDES ET MEMOIRES **5469**

PARIS. ECOLE PRATIQUE DES HAUTES ETUDES. SECTION DES SCIENCES ECONOMIQUES ET SOCIALES *See* INDUSTRIE ET ARTISANAT **1611**

PARIS ET ILE-DE-FRANCE / PUBLIES PAR LA FEDERATION DES SOCIETES ET ARCHEOLOGIQUES DE PARIS ET DE L'ILE DE FRANCE (FR/0428-1551) [05863174] **2702**

PARIS (FRANCE). PREFECTURE DE POLICE. LABORATOIRE CENTRA_ *See* POLLUTION ATMOSPHERIQUE ET NUISANCES / PREFECTURE DE POLICE, LABORATOIRE CENTRAL **2238**

PARIS. INSTITUT TECHNIQUE DU BATIMENT ET DES TRAVAUX PUBLICS *See* ANNALES DE L'INSTITUT TECHNIQUE DU BATIMENT ET DES TRAVAUX PUBLICS **598**

PARIS-MATCH (FR/0031-2029) [01761906] **2521**

PARIS-MATCH 1976 (FR/0397-1635) [I03971635] **2521**

PARIS / MICHELIN (FR) [10817081] **5488**

PARIS NEWS, THE (US/8756-2081) [11487318] **5753**

PARIS PASSION : THE MAGAZINE OF THE FRENCH CAPITAL (FR) [19676276] **2521**

PARIS-PEKIN (FR) [07881446] **2662**

PARIS POST-INTELLIGENCER, THE (US/0893-3669) [15512535] **5746**

PARIS PROJET (FR) [03853191] **2830**

PARIS REVIEW, THE (US/0031-2037) [01641889] **3422**

PARIS REVIEW, THE (US/04972631) **3422**

PARIS SUCCESS (BE) **1086**

PARIS. UNIVERSITE. INSTITUT D'ETHNOLOGIE *See* TRAVAUX ET MEMOIRES DE L'INSTITUT D'ETHNOLOGIE **5225**

PARIS. UNIVERSITE. INSTITUT D'ETUDES SLAVES *See* COLLECTION DE GRAMMAIRES **3274**

PARIS. UNIVERSITE. INSTITUT D'ETUDES SLAVES *See* TRAVAUX **2713**

PARIS. UNIVERSITE. INSTITUT D'ETUDES SLAVES *See* BIBLIOTHEQUE RUSSE **3269**

PARIS. UNIVERSITE. INSTITUT D'ETUDES SLAVES *See* DOCUMENTS PEDAGOGIQUES **3277**

PARISH COMMUNICATION (US/0279-7828) [07525177] **4985**

PARISH PAPER, THE (US) [01781054] **4985**

PARISH TEACHER (US/0738-7962) [04122992] **4985**

PARISIEN (FR) **2491**

PARISTHITI (NP) [08620530] **2662**

PARITY (US/0278-0224) [07702267] **5564, 1701**

PARK & GROUNDS MANAGEMENT (US/1057-204X) [23025895] **4707**

PARK & RECREATION OPPORTUNITIES JOB BULLETIN *See* NATIONAL JOB BULLETIN **4206**

PARK CITIES NEWS, THE (US) [16751850] **5753**

PARK CITY DAILY NEWS (US) [14217238] **5682**

PARK CITY MAIN STREET MAP (US/1046-9540) [20571865] **2583**

PARK FALLS HERALD, THE (US) [13119456] **5770**

PARK RECORD (1964), THE (US/0745-9483) [09614042] **5757**

PARK RIDGE ADVOCATE (US/0744-5385) [08338858] **5661**

PARK RIDGE EDITION OF THE TIMES HERALD (US/0895-013X) [16401826] **5661**

PARK SCIENCE (US/0735-9462) [08558042] **2202**

PARK WORLD (UK) **3486**

PARKE COUNTY SENTINEL (US/1044-7822) [13105234] **5666**

PARKE SOCIETY *See* NEWS LETTER OF THE PARKE SOCIETY **2462**

PARKER DIRECTORY OF CALIFORNIA ATTORNEYS (US/0196-6138) [05854394] **3025**

PARKER PAPERS (US/0898-5456) [15794510] **2466**

PARKER'S BUSINESS STATUTES AND SECURITIES RULES OF TEXAS (US/0749-0607) [11050615] **3102**

PARKER'S GAZETTE *CEASED.* (US/0890-6939) [14399205] **2753**

PARKERSBURG SENTINEL (PARKESBURG, W.VA. : 1893) (US) [13415989] **5764**

PARKERSBURGH NEWS (1916) (US/8750-3956) [11377809] **5764**

PARKETT (GW/0256-0917) [12226189] **361**

PARKI NARODOWE (PL/0867-6550) [I08676550] **2220**

PARKING REVIEW (UK/0962-3566) [I09623566] **5442**

PARKING SECURITY REPORT (US/1052-9985) [22435378] **4795**

PARKING TECHNOLOGY (US/1055-890X) [23364557] **5389**

PARKING (WASHINGTON, D.C.) (US/0031-2193) [03041176] **5423**

PARKING WORLD *See* PARKING (WASHINGTON, D.C.) **5423**

PARKINSON NETWORK (CN/0824-7315) [11543834] **3626**

PARKINSONISM AND RELATED DISORDERS (UK/1353-8020) **3626**

PARKLAND REGIONAL LIBRARY NEWSLETTER (CN/0820-2931) [16458841] **3240**

PARKLAWN COMPUTER CENTER (U.S.) *See* ANNUAL REPORT - PARKLAWN COMPUTER CENTER **4766**

PARKS AND GROUNDS (SA) [05811580] **2427**

PARKS AND. GROUNDS (SA/0258-2457) [I02582457] **4707**

PARKS & RECREATION (ARLINGTON, VA.) (US/0031-2215) [01761919] **4707**

PARKS & RECREATION AUCKLAND (NZ/0114-8087) [I01148087] **4707**

PARKS & SPORTS GROUNDS (UK/0031-224X) [I0031224X] **4877, 5488**

PARKS CANADA RESEARCH BULLETIN *See* RESEARCH BULLETIN (CANADA PARKS) **2757**

PARKS, GOLF COURSES & SPORTS GROUNDS (1975) (UK/0954-3880) [I09543880] **4707**

PARKS NEWBURY (UK/0960-233X) [I0960233X] **2202**

PARKWATCH (AT) **2202**

PARLAMENT, DAS (GW/0553-3139) [05349672] **4486**

PARLAMENTO (ROME, ITALY) (IT) [09176124] **4486**

PARLANCE (II) [05261801] **2662**

PARLANDO (HU/0133-2767) [03278101] **4145**

PARLEMENT EN KIEZER: JAARBOEK (NE) [01792710] **4486**

PARLEMENTS ET FRANCOPHONIE (FR/0258-4751) [I02584751] **4486**

PARLIAMENT OF WESTERN AUSTRALIA DIGEST, THE (AT/0312-6862) [02240030] **3025**

PARLIAMENTARIAN (UK/0031-2282) [06385202] **4672**

PARLIAMENTARY AFFAIRS (UK/0031-2290) [01761923] **4672**

PARLIAMENTARY ALERT (CN/0821-5154) [09606643] **4672**

PARLIAMENTARY AND EUROPEAN COMMUNITY NEWS BULLETIN (UK) **4672**

PARLIAMENTARY DEBATES (HANSARD). HOUSE OF COMMONS OFFICIAL REPORT (UK/0309-8826) [08962771] **4672**

PARLIAMENTARY DEBATES (HANSARD). HOUSE OF LORDS OFFICIAL REPORT, THE (UK/0309-8834) [08353752] **4672**

PARLIAMENTARY DEBATES (HANSARD), THE SENATE (FJ) [02244071] **4672**

PARLIAMENTARY DEBATES. HOUSE OF REPRESENTATIVES (NZ) [04826506] **4672**

PARLIAMENTARY DEBATES, HOUSE OF REPRESENTATIVES, WEEKLY HANSARD (AT/0519-6124) [01518750] **4672**

PARLIAMENTARY DEBATES, SENATE, WEEKLY HANSARD (AT/0519-6140) [03392781] **4672**

PARLIAMENTARY DEBATES SYDNEY (AT/0155-6290) [I01556290] **4672**

● PARLIAMENTARY DIRECTORY (OTTAWA. 1992) (CN/1188-8652) [26714642] **4672**

PARLIAMENTARY GOVERNMENT (CN/0709-4582) [05842296] **4672, 4486**

PARLIAMENTARY HISTORY : A YEARBOOK (UK/0264-2824) [09608691] **4672**

PARLIAMENTARY JOURNAL (US/0048-2994) [02265732] **4486**

● PARLIAMENTARY WEEKLY QUARTERLY REPORT, THE (CN/1188-2387) [26714850] **4487**

PARLIAMENTS, ESTATES & REPRESENTATION (UK/0260-6755) [08349211] **4487**

PARLONS AFFAIRES, BEAUCE-ETCHEMINS (CN/1186-1274) [24267120] **702**

PARLONS AFFAIRES DANS LES LAURENTIDES (CN/1184-1117) [23598504] **702**

PARLONS PEDAGOGIE (CN/0712-9947) [08828190] **1839**

PARLONS PLEIN AIR, CHASSE, PECHE (CN/1191-4335) [26497741] **4877**

PARLONS RAISON (1983) (CN/0821-3003) [11081693] **3422**

PARMA NELL'ARTE (IT/0391-7622) [02677254] **327**

PARMA REVIEW, THE (US) [19024855] **5657**

PARNASS (AU) [21064346] **327**

PARNASSO (FI/0031-2320) [01680732] **3422**

PARNASSOS (GR/0048-301X) [04948356] 1079, **3310**

PARNASSUS : POETRY IN REVIEW (US/0048-3028) [02142037] 3349, **3467**

PARODIANA (AG/0325-9684) [07645573] **521**

PARODONTOLOGIE : DIE ZEITSCHRIFT FUER DIE PRAXIS (GW/0937-1532) [24466709] **1332**

PAROIKIAKA NEA (CN/0700-947X) [03403077] **5792**

PAROLA DEL PASSATO, LA (IT/0031-2355) [01761929] 3310, **1079**

PAROLA DEL POPOLO, LA (US) [02243512] **4544**

PAROLA LETTERARIA, LA (IT) [08251783] **3422**

PAROLE DE L'ORIENT (LE) [02150383] **4985**

PAROLE IN THE UNITED STATES (US) [04675551] **3171**

● PAROLECHIAVE (IT) [28702000] **4544**

PAROLES ET MUSIQUE MENSUEL *SUSPENDED.* (FR/0247-0357) [I02470357] **4145**

PAROLES GELEES : UCLA FRENCH STUDIES (US) [12875923] **3422**

PAROPAKARI (II) [02239296] **5041**

PAROVOZNIK (RU) [12365047] **5433**

PARPU, JONNI GISUR (KO/0253-3200) [05256841] **4237**

PARQUES Y JARDINES (SP/0213-4489) [02099236] **4707**

PARROTT TALK (US/0093-9811) [01792351] **2466**

PARSIANA (II) [01774581] **3422**

PARSONS ADVOCATE (US/0747-3303) [10742733] **5746**

PARSONS, BRINCKERHOFF, QUADE & DOUGLAS *See* ELIZABETH RIVER TUNNEL SYSTEM, NORFOLK, VIRGINIA, CONSULTING ENGINEERS ... ANNUAL REPORT **2088**

PARSONS NEWS, THE (US) [12234132] **5678**

PARSONS SUN (PARSONS, KAN. : 1929) (US) [12276956] **5678**

PART B NEWS (US/0893-8121) [15646146] **2889**

PART DE L'IL, LA (BE/0773-9532) [I07739532] 4354, **361**

PARTAGE (MONTREAL) (CN/0824-1821) [11868918] **5018**

PARTECIPARE : RIVISTA DI STUDI CORPORATIVI (IT) [26919053] **702**

PARTENAIRE (SAINT-HUBERT) (CN/0841-7997) [19257273] 2285, **5564**

PARTENAIRES PARIS. 1985 (FR/0992-390X) [I0992390X] **702**

PARTIAL DIFFERENTIAL EQUATIONS (GW/0720-261X) [09449170] **3526**

PARTIALLY ORDERED SYSTEMS (US) **5137**

PARTICIPATION IN ADULT EDUCATION (US/0736-4792) [08938104] **1802**

PARTICIPATION IN ADULT EDUCATION, FINAL REPORT *See* PARTICIPATION IN ADULT EDUCATION **1802**

PARTICIPATION (OTTAWA) (CN/0709-6941) [09023850] **4487**

PARTICLE ACCELERATORS (US/0031-2460) [01714376] **4413**

PARTICLE — Alphabetical Title Index

PARTICLE & PARTICLE SYSTEMS CHARACTERIZATION (GW/0934-0866) [18009683] 4413, **988**

PARTICLE WORLD (UK/1043-6790) [19526987] **4450**

PARTICLE WORLD COMMUNICATIONS : THE INTERNATIONAL JOURNAL OF SUBNUCLEAR PHYSICS (UK) **4450**

PARTICLEBOARD AND MEDIUM DENSITY FIBERBOARD (US) [03057155] **848**

PARTICLEBOARD, WAFERBOARD, AND FIBREBOARD (CN/1180-5099) [22160005] **2403**

PARTICULATE SCIENCE AND TECHNOLOGY (US/0272-6351) [06887061] **2015**

PARTICULIER IMMOBILIER PARIS. 1986, LE (FR/0992-6054) [I09926054] **2285**

PARTICULIER, LE (FR/0031-2495) [04044700] **2285**

PARTICULIER PRATIQUE PARIS, LE (FR/0995-6840) [I09956840] **2285**

PARTIE PRENANTE (FR/0294-0531) [I02940531] 4985, **1772**

PARTIINAIA ZHIZN (UZ) [06605813] **4487**

PARTING GIFTS (US/1043-3325) [19104419] **3467**

PARTISAN REVIEW (1936) (US/0031-2525) [05661185] 3422, **4544**

PARTLOW PERSPECTIVE (US) [05809086] **1883**

PARTNERS (CALGARY) (CN/1187-8320) [25796539] **4271**

PARTNERS IN PHARMACEUTICAL CARE (US/1061-6322) [25381513] **4319**

PARTNERS IN PRINT (CN/1195-4981) **881**

PARTNERS IN RESEARCH FOR DEVELOPMENT (AT/1031-1009) [19238731] **118**

PARTNERS (KANATA) (CN/1185-1953) [24257324] **5137**

PARTNER'S REPORT (US/0892-4805) [15207529] 881, **3025**

PARTNER'S REPORT (NEW YORK, N.Y. 1989) (US/1043-7428) [19543827] **881**

PARTNERS TASK FORCE FOR GAY AND LESBIAN COUPLES (US) **5188**

PARTNERSHIP (ATLANTA, GA.) (US) [08556160] 118, **702**

PARTNERSHIP FEDERAL AND STATE INCOME TAX REPORTING (US/1052-8806) [22407200] **4740**

PARTNERSHIP (SACRAMENTO, CALIF.) *See* EMPLOYMENT AND TRAINING PARTNERSHIP : A PUBLICATION OF THE STATE JOB TRAINING COORDINATING COUNCIL, THE **1913**

PARTNERSHIP TAXATION (US) [11275443] **3090**

PARTNERSHIPS (US/0749-4696) [11128419] **1621**

PARTNERSHIPS IN EDUCATION JOURNAL (US/1042-6590) [19103906] **1772**

● PARTS BUSINESS (US/1072-5598) [29009520] **5423**

PARTY & PAPER RETAILER (US/0899-6008) [18149278] **956**

PARTY LIFE (II/0377-2667) [01797686] **4544**

PARTY LINE / THE MEDIA NEWSLETTER (US) **1119**

PARTY SOURCE (US/1060-6726) [25151789] **2585**

● PARTY TIMES (US/1064-8224) [26409558] **2352**

PARVA LEX (IT) **1868**

PARYATANA : PARYATANA SAMBANDHI PATRIKA (NP) [25701989] **5488**

PARYAVARAN ABSTRACTS (II) [12950367] **2238**

PAS (EVANSTON, ILL.) (US/1053-1319) [22459279] **2642**

PAS GRAPHIC, THE (CN/0229-4702) [08023776] **5792**

PAS MEMO (US/1040-7340) [04422092] **2830**

PAS RESEARCH PAPER SERIES (US/1018-5089) [24336100] **802**

PASAA (TH/0125-2488) [03341400] **3310**

PASADENA CITIZEN (1990) (US/1050-3773) [21473452] **5753**

PASADENA HERITAGE (US/0889-5864) [12005424] **2753**

PASADENA JOURNAL OF BUSINESS *CEASED.* (US/0743-6610) [10634930] **702**

PASADENA STAR-NEWS (US/1069-2827) [13056995] **5638**

PASAULIO LIETUVIU KATALIKU ZINYNAS (US) [03296188] **5034**

PASCAL. 65, PSYCHOLOGIE, PSYCHOPATHOLOGIE, PSYCHIATRIE (FR) [24933388] 3932, **4606**

PASCAL. 68, GENETIQUE HUMAINE (FR/1146-5549) [24731977] **550**

PASCAL. 75, CARDIOLOGIE ET APPAREIL CIRCULATOIRE (FR/1146-559X) [24731948] **3709**

PASCAL. 205, SCIENCES DE L'INFORMATION, DOCUMENTATION (FR) [24866266] **3240**

PASCAL. 215, BIOTECHNOLOGIES (FR/1146-5034) [24732010] **3695**

PASCAL & MODULA2 (US/0748-4127) [10615076] **1280**

PASCAL. E 18, CHROMATOGRAPHIE (FR/1146-5344) [I11465344] **988**

PASCAL. E 27, METHODES DE FORMATION ET TRAITEMENT DES IMAGES (FR/1146-5360) [I11465360] 4440, **4426**

PASCAL. E 48, ENVIRONNEMENT COSMIQUE TERRESTRE, ASTRONOMIE ET GEOLOGIE EXTRATERRESTRE (FR/1146-545X) [I1146545X] 1390, **398**

PASCAL. E 57, BIOLOGIE MARINE *CEASED.* (FR/1146-5476) [I11465476] 5594, **468**

PASCAL. E 58, GENETIQUE (FR/1146-5484) [I11465484] **550**

PASCAL. E 61, MICROBIOLOGIE (FR/1146-5492) [I11465492] **468**

PASCAL. E 62, IMMUNOLOGIE (FR/1146-5506) [I11465506] **3675**

PASCAL. E 63, TOXICOLOGIE (FR/1146-5514) [I11465514] **3983**

PASCAL. E 74, PNEUMOLOGIE (FR/1146-5581) [I11465581] **3950**

PASCAL. E 76, GASTROENTEROLOGIE, FOIE, PANCREAS, ABDOMEN (FR/1146-5603) [I11465603] **3747**

PASCAL. E 77, NEPHROLOGIE, VOIES URINAIRES (FR/1146-5611) [I11465611] **3992**

PASCAL. E 78, NEUROLOGIE (FR/1146-562X) [I1146562X] **3844**

PASCAL. E 83, ANESTHESIE ET REANIMATION (FR/1146-5670) [I11465670] **3844**

PASCAL. E 89, CANCER (FR/1146-5697) [I11465697] **3822**

PASCAL. E29, SEMICONDUCTEURS, MATERIAUX ET COMPOSANTS *CEASED.* (FR/1146-5387) [23848440] **2074**

PASCAL. E34, ROBOTICS, CONTROL THEORY AND INDUSTRIAL PROCESSES AUTOMATION (FR/1146-5425) [22932509] **1215**

PASCAL EXPLORE E11, PHYSIQUE ATOMIQUE ET MOLECULAIRE PLASMAS *See* PHYSIQUE, ATOMIQUE ET MOLECULAIRE PLASMAS **4450**

PASCAL EXPLORE E13, STRUCTURE DES LIQUIDES ET DES SOLIDES CRISTALLOGRAPHIE *See* STRUCTURE DES LIQUIDES ET DES SOLIDES CRISTALLOGRAPHIE, E13 **1033**

PASCAL EXPLORE. E30 : MICROSCOPIE ET DIFFRACTION ELECTRONIQUE *See* MICROSCOPIE ELECTRONIQUE ET DIFFRACTION ELECTRONIQUE. E30 **5128**

PASCAL EXPLORE. E32: METROLOGIE ET APPAREILLAGE EN PHYSIQUE ET PHYSICOCHIMIE *See* METROLOGIE ET APPAREILLAGE EN PHYSIQUE ET PHYSICOCHIMIE. E32 **1056**

PASCAL EXPLORE. E33: INFORMATIQUE *See* INFORMATIQUE. E33 **1189**

PASCAL EXPLORE. E64: ENDOCRINOLOGIE HUMAINE ET EXPERIMENTALE ENDOCRINOPATHIES *See* ENDOCRINOLOGIE HUMAINE ET EXPERIMENTALE ENDOCRINOPATHIES. E64 **3729**

PASCAL EXPLORE : E71, OPHTALMOLOGIE *See* OPHTALMOLOGIE E71 **3877**

PASCAL EXPLORE. E72, OTORHINOLARYNGOLOGIE, STOMATOLOGIE, PATHOLOGIE CERVICOFACIALE (FR/0761-2192) [19484329] **3890**

PASCAL EXPLORE E73, DERMATOLOGIE MALADIES SEXUELLEMENT TRANSMISSIBLES *See* DERMATOLOGIE MALADIES SEXUELLEMENT TRANSMISSIBLES. E73 **3719**

PASCAL EXPLORE. E74, PNEUMOLOGIE (FR/0761-2214) [19484572] **3950**

PASCAL EXPLORE. E79, PATHOLOGIE ET PHYSIOLOGIE OSTEOARTICULAIRES (FR/0761-2265) [18319959] **3884**

PASCAL EXPLORE. E80 : HEMATOLOGIE *See* HEMATOLOGIE. E80 **488**

PASCAL EXPLORE. E81: MALADIES METABOLIQUES *See* MALADIES METABOLIQUES. E81 **3606**

PASCAL EXPLORE. E82, GYNECOLOGIE, OBSTETRIQUE, ANDROLOGIE (FR/0761-229X) [17725733] **3766**

PASCAL EXPLORE. E83, ANESTHESIE ET REANIMATION (FR/0761-2303) [18320965] **3683**

PASCAL EXPLORE. E84, GENIE BIOMEDICALE, INFORMATIQUE BIOMEDICALE (FR/0761-2311) [17725753] **3695**

PASCAL. F 10, MECANIQUE, ACOUSTIQUE ET TRANSFERT DE CHALEUR (FR/1146-5107) [I11465107] 4432, **4453**

PASCAL. F 17, CHIMIE GENERALE MINERALE ET ORGANIQUE (FR/1146-5123) [I11465123] **988**

PASCAL. F 25, TRANSPORTS TERRESTRES ET MARITIMES *CEASED.* (FR/1146-5166) [I11465166] **5389**

PASCAL. F 40, MINERALOGIE, GEOCHIMIE, GEOLOGIE EXTRATERRESTRE (FR/1146-5174) [I11465174] **1359**

PASCAL. F 41, GISEMENTS METALLIQUES ET NON METALLIQUES (FR/1146-5182) [I11465182] **4014**

PASCAL. F 46, HYDROLOGIE, GEOLOGIE DE L'INGENIEUR, FORMATIONS SUPERFICIELLES (FR/1146-5239) [I11465239] 1390, **1417**

PASCAL. F 47, PALEONTOLOGIE (FR/1146-5247) [I11465247] **4230**

PASCAL. F 52, BIOCHIMIE, BIOPHYSIQUE MOLECULAIRE, BIOLOGIE MOLECULAIRE ET CELLULAIRE (FR/1146-5255) [I11465255] 496, **492**

PASCAL. F 54, REPRODUCTION DES VERTEBRES, EMBRYOLOGIE DES VERTEBRES ET DES INVERTEBRES (FR/1146-5271) [I11465271] **5594**

PASCAL. F 70, PHARMACOLOGIE, TRAITEMENTS MEDICAMENTEUX (FR/1146-5301) [I11465301] **4319**

PASCAL FOLIO. F16, CHIMIE ANALYTIQUE, MINERALE ET ORGANIQUE (FR/0761-1749) [14233331] 1037, 1045, **1018**

PASCAL FOLIO. F23: GENIE CHIMIQUE INDUSTRIE CHIMIQUE ET PARACHIMIQUE *See* GENIE CHIMIQUE INDUSTRIES CHIMIQUE ET PARACHIMIQUE. F23 **976**

PASCAL FOLIO, F24. POLYMERS PEINTURES BOIS *See* POLYMERES PEINTURES BOIS, F24 **4225**

PASCAL FOLIO. F41, GISEMENTS METALLIQUES ET NON METALLIQUES, ECONOMIE MINIERE (FR/0761-182X) [11748852] 1390, **2147**

PASCAL FOLIO. F42, ROCHES CRISTALLINES *See* ROCHES CRISTALLINES. F42 **1033**

PASCAL FOLIO F43 : ROCHES SEDIMENTAIRES GEOLOGIE MARINE *See* ROCHES SEDIMENTAIRES GEOLOGIE MARINE, F43 **1395**

PASCAL FOLIO. F44: STRATIGRAPHIE GEOLOGIE REGIONALE GEOLOGIE GENERALE *See* STRATIGRAPHIE GEOLOGIE REGIONALE GEOLOGIE GENERALE. F44 **2576**

PASCAL FOLIO. F45. TECTONIQUE, GEOPHYSIQUE INTERNE *See* TECTONIQUE, GEOPHYSIQUE INTERNE F45 **1205**

PASCAL FOLIO. F52, BIOCHIMIE, BIOPHYSIQUE MOLECULAIRE, BIOLOGIE MOLECULAIRE ET CELLULAIRE (FR/0761-1897) [14705259] **468**

PASCAL FOLIO. F53, ANATOMIE ET PHYSIOLOGIE DES VERTEBRES (FR/0761-1900) [11314244] **3679**

PASCAL FOLIO. F55, BIOLOGIE VEGETALE (FR/0761-1927) [11643306] **468**

PASCAL FOLIO. F70, PHARMACOLOGIE, TRAITEMENTS MEDICAMENTEUX (FR/0761-1943) [13992604] **4319**

PASCAL FOLIO / GENIE CHIMIQUE INDUSTRIE. CHIMIQUE ET PARACHIMIQUE (FR) **1027**

PASCAL. T 260, ZOOLOGIE FONDAMENTALE ET APPLIQUEE DES INVERTEBRES (FR/1146-5077) [I11465077] **5594**

PASCAL. T 295, BATIMENT TRAVAUX PUBLICS (FR/1146-5093) [I11465093] 623, **2006**

PASCAL THEMA. T230: ENERGIE *See* ENERGIE. T230 **1938**

PASCAL THEMA. T280: SCIENCES AGRONOMIQUES. PRODUCTIONS VEGETALES *See* SCIENCES AGRONOMIQUES. PRODUCTIONS VEGETALES. T280 **185**

PASCAL. VOL. 4, TERRE, OCEAN, ESPACE (FR/1146-5018) [22503185] 1359, **1363**

PASEANTE, EL (SP) [14763923] **361**

Alphabetical Title Index — PATHWAYS

PASICRISIE BELGE. RECUEIL GENERAL DE LA JURISPRUDENCE DES COURS ET TRIBUNAUX (BE/0031-2614) [01761943] **3025**

PASINOMIE : COLLECTION COMPLETE DES LOIS, ARRETES ET REGLEMENTS GENERAUX... (BE) [03819534] **3025**

PASO ROBLES COUNTRY NEWS, THE (US/0195-0134) [05213199] **5638**

PASOS SAN JOSE (CR/1016-9857) [I10169857] **4985**

PASQUE PETALS (US/0031-2649) [01761944] **3467**

PASQUIN, LE (CN/0710-5185) [08811542] **2466**

PASS CHRISTIAN REVIEW, THE (US/1060-9083) [25105246] **2543**

PASS IN REVIEW (US) [16275347] 4053, **4831**

PASS PROMOTER, THE (CN/0380-4135) [02443137] **5792**

PASSAGES (EVANSTON, ILL.) (US/1056-6783) [23829462] **2851**

PASSAGES NORTH (US/0278-0828) [07701869] 381, **3422**

PASSAGES TO FREEDOM See BEST OF KERVIN FONDREN, THE **3460**

PASSAGES (WASHINGTON, D.C.) (US/1071-3158) [28605687] **590**

PASSAIC COUNTY DENTAL SOCIETY NEWSLETTER (US) **1332**

PASSAIC REVIEW (US/0731-4663) [08201309] **3349**

PASSANT, EN (CN/0822-5672) [10809785] **4864**

PASSATO E PRESENTE (IT) [02679250] **4544**

PASSATO E PRESENTE (FLORENCE, ITALY) (IT/0392-4815) [10026924] **2625**

PASSE-SPORTS (CN/0820-070X) [09379219] **4911**

PASSENGER AND IMMIGRATION LISTS BIBLIOGRAPHY, 1538-1900 (US) **2466**

PASSENGER AND IMMIGRATION LISTS INDEX. SUPPLEMENT (US/0736-8267) [09228872] **2466**

PASSENGER BUS AND URBAN TRANSIT STATISTICS (CN/0383-5766) [02872202] **5389**

PASSENGER BUS AND URBAN TRANSIT STATISTICS (MONTHLY ED.) (CN/0829-1756) [14938535] **5389**

PASSENGER PIGEON, THE (US/0031-2703) [01696622] **5619**

PASSENGER SERVICES CONFERENCE RESOLUTIONS MANUAL / IATA (CN/0256-3282) [10613181] **31**

PASSENGER TIMETABLE : GREAT BRITAIN INTER-CITY, LOCAL AND SUBURBAN SERVICES, IRISH, CHANNEL ISLAND, COASTAL SERVICES (UK) [05881054] **5433**

PASSENGER TIMETABLE : INTERNATIONAL, INTER-CITY, SEALINK, SEASPEED SERVICES, GREAT BRITAIN-CONTINENT OF EUROPE (UK) [05802775] **5433**

PASSENGER TRAIN ANNUAL (US/1042-7937) [04915231] **5433**

PASSENGER TRAIN JOURNAL (US/0160-6913) [03711843] **5433**

PASSENGER TRANSPORT (US/0364-345X) [01761945] **5389**

PASSEPORT (CN/0228-2631) [06859939] **5488**

PASSEPORT GASTRONOMIQUE. MONTREAL ET ALENTOURS (CN/0226-7292) [06511798] **5072**

PASSEPORT GASTRONOMIQUE. QUEBEC ET ALENTOURS (CN/0710-040X) [12199476] **5072**

PASSERELLE, LA (FR/0031-2711) [02707582] **3422**

PASSING SHOW (NEW YORK, N.Y.) (US/1061-8112) [03662519] **5367**

PASSING TONES (CN/0712-5062) [09106532] **4145**

PASSION MAGAZINE (JA) **2507**

PASSION MENS (JA) **3996**

PASSKAZY O'MUZYKE (RU) [01797980] **4145**

PASSPORT (CHICAGO) (US/0031-272X) [03616530] **5488**

PASSPORT OFFICE WORKLOADS AND ACCOMPLISHMENTS (US/0362-8469) [02362592] **4673**

PASSPORT TO LEGAL UNDERSTANDING (US/0737-7630) [09287643] **3025**

PASSPORT TO WORLD BAND RADIO (US/0897-0157) [17359982] 1161, **1136**

PASSWORD (EL PASO) (US/0031-2738) [03199090] **2753**

PAST & PRESENT (UK/0031-2746) [01713839] **2625**

PAST & PRESENT (WATERLOO) (CN/0702-7125) [03409499] 1772, **2852**

PAST, PRESENT & FUTURE (US/0895-0857) [09263728] **2543**

PASTA JOURNAL (US/8750-9393) [11946013] **2352**

PASTAHHH See POSITIVELY PASTA! **2353**

PASTFINDER (US/0888-9163) [13754416] **2466**

PASTFINDER (SAINT JOSEPH, MICH.) (US/0091-6897) [01787899] **2466**

PASTICCERIA INTERNAZIONALE (IT/0392-4718) [09113392] **2352**

PASTIMES (ARMDALE) (CN/0229-6993) [07970434] **252**

PASTORAL BULLETIN, THE (TR) **4985**

PASTORAL CARE IN EDUCATION (UK/0264-3944) [17606020] **1772**

PASTORAL DEVELOPMENT NETWORK (OVERSEAS DEVELOPMENT INSTITUTE) See NEWSLETTER / PASTORAL DEVELOPMENT NETWORK **2911**

PASTORAL HORIZONS CEASED. (AT) **5034**

PASTORAL LIFE (US/0031-2762) [01641624] **4985**

PASTORAL MUSIC (US/0363-6569) [02560837] **4145**

PASTORAL MUSIC NOTEBOOK (US/0145-6636) [03578411] **4145**

PASTORAL POPULAR (CL) [02707563] **4985**

PASTORAL PSYCHOLOGY (US/0031-2789) [01761948] 4985, **4607**

PASTORAL SCIENCES (CN/0713-3383) [09340458] **4985**

PASTORAL SHARING (HK) **4985**

PASTORAL TIMES (AT) [11620515] **5777**

PASTORALE-QUEBEC (CN/0383-2236) [02393209] **5034**

PASTORALE SCOLAIRE (QUEBEC) (CN/0227-1095) [06515764] **4985**

PASTORALTHEOLOGIE (GW/0031-2827) [07264842] **4985**

PASTOR'S BULLETIN (CN/0226-5001) [06299502] **4985**

PASTOR'S STORY FILE, THE (US/0882-3545) [11823658] **4985**

●PASTOR'S TAX & MONEY (US/1061-978X) [25497990] **4985**

PASTOS (SP/0210-1270) [I02101270] **118**

PASTOS Y FORRAJES (CU/0258-5987) [I02585987] **118**

PASTOS Y FORRAJES; BOLETIN DE LA CAMPANA NACIONAL DE PASTOS (CK) [07521127] **118**

PASTRYCOOKS AND BAKERS NEWS MONTHLY (AT/0818-6561) [08186561] **2353**

PASTURAS TROPICALES (CK/1012-7410) [18422124] **118**

PASU PALANA PRAGATI (II) [02240254] **217**

PATA ANNUAL STATISTICAL REPORT (US) [06468907] **5488**

PATA TRAVEL NEWS See TRAVEL NEWS AMERICAS **5496**

PATALOGO. CINEMA + TELEVISIONE + VIDEO, IL (IT) [19549443] 4372, **4076**

PATCHWORK (UK) **2776**

PATENT (SW) [03765774] **1307**

●PATENT ABSTRACTS. AGRICULTURALS (US/1065-0482) [26530084] 118, **1307**

●PATENT ABSTRACTS. CHEMICAL PRODUCTS (US/1065-0474) [26530048] 1028, **1307**

●PATENT ABSTRACTS. ENVIRONMENT, TRANSPORT & STORAGE (US/1066-2103) [26891281] **1307**

●PATENT ABSTRACTS. PETROLEUM & SPECIALTY PRODUCTS (US/1065-0466) [26530011] 4271, **1307**

●PATENT ABSTRACTS. PETROLEUM PROCESSES (US/1065-0458) [26529957] 4271, **1307**

●PATENT ABSTRACTS. PETROLEUM SUBSTITUTES (US/1065-044X) [26529893] 4271, **1307**

●PATENT ABSTRACTS. POLYMERS (US/1065-2167) [26529936] 988, **1307**

PATENT AND TRADEMARK FORMS (US) [01754095] **1307**

PATENT AND TRADEMARK OFFICE NOTICES (US) [07486587] **1307**

PATENT ANTITRUST (US/0272-8621) [04701519] 3102, **1307**

●PATENT APPLICATIONS HANDBOOK / BY STEPHEN A. BECKER (US) [26556526] **1307**

PATENT COOPERATION TREATY AND REGULATIONS (SZ) **1307**

PATENT DIGEST (US) 2812, **1307**

●PATENT INDEX (US/1065-0423) [26065806] **4271**

PATENT INTELLIGENCE AND TECHNOLOGY REPORT (US/1071-2631) [10193756] **1307**

PATENT JOURNAL, INCLUDING TRADE MARKS DESIGNS AND COPYRIGHT IN CINEMATOGRAPH FILMS (SA/0031-286X) [12219421] **1307**

PATENT LAW ANNUAL (US) [08298374] 3025, **1307**

PATENT LAW HANDBOOK (US/0192-8198) [04605449] **1307**

PATENT NEWSLETTER. LASERS/ELECTRO-OPTICS, THE CEASED. (US/0742-275X) [10304559] **1307**

PATENT OFFICE EXAMINATION REVIEW COURSE (US/0147-6173) [03208429] **3025**

PATENT OFFICE JOURNAL (NZ) [02449094] **1307**

PATENT OFFICE RECORD, THE (CN/0008-4670) [01552979] **1307**

PATENT OFFICE RULES AND PRACTICES (US) [01771472] 3025, **1307**

PATENT, TRADEMARK, AND COPYRIGHT LAWS (US/0741-1219) [10094578] **1307**

PATENT WORLD (UK/0950-2513) [15617497] **1307**

PATENTBLATT (GW/0031-2894) [I00312894] **1307**

PATENTE DI GUIDA, LA (IT/1120-4176) [I11204176] **5389**

PATENTIMAGES (NEW HAVEN, CONN.) (US/1064-2692) [26243545] **1307**

PATENTNI GLASNIK (YU/0031-2908) [06608189] **1308**

PATENTS ALPHABETICAL SUBJECT INDEX See PATENT INDEX **4271**

PATENTS & LICENSING (JA/0388-7081) [12489671] **1308**

PATENTS (HADLEY, N.Y.), THE (US/0882-5912) [11900144] **2466**

PATENTS THROUGHOUT THE WORLD / BY WM. WALLACE WHITE AND BYFLEET G. RAVENSCROFT (US) [16511498] **1308**

PATH FINDER (VANCOUVER) (CN/0707-8617) [05258071] **3626**

PATHFINDER (CALGARY) (CN/0227-2881) [06635183] **4877**

PATHFINDER (DALLAS, TEX.) (US/1057-5731) [24071322] **2906**

PATHOBIOLOGY (BASEL) (SZ/1015-2008) [21357241] 539, **3896**

PATHOLINGUISTICA (GW/0173-301X) [04677858] 4392, **3891**

PATHOLOGE, DER (GW/0172-8113) [06596853] **3896**

PATHOLOGICA (IT/0031-2983) [01681013] **3896**

PATHOLOGIE ET BIOLOGIE (PARIS) (FR/0369-8114) [01334632] 468, **3896**

PATHOLOGIE ET PHYSIOLOGIE OSTEOARTICULAIRES (FR) **3897**

PATHOLOGY (AT/0031-3025) [01761961] **3897**

PATHOLOGY ANNUAL (US/0079-0184) [01640370] **3897**

●PATHOLOGY INTERNATIONAL (AT/1320-5463) [29788956] **3897**

PATHOLOGY PATTERNS (US/1050-9194) [19610766] **3897**

●PATHOLOGY (PHILADELPHIA, PA.) (US/1041-3480) [18729559] **3897**

PATHOLOGY, RESEARCH AND PRACTICE (GW/0344-0338) [04124817] **3897**

PATHOPHYSIOLOGY (NE/0928-4680) **584**

PATHOS. MONOGRAFIAS DE PATOLOGIA MEDICA (SP) **3709**

PATHWAY OF TRUTH (US) **5065**

PATHWAY TO GOD (II) [01784214] **4985**

PATHWAYS & PASSAGES (US/0887-8919) [13439518] **2467**

PATHWAYS (CHESTNUT HILL, MASS.) (US/0899-9252) [14275748] **4673**

PATHWAYS FOR YOUNG ADULTS. STUDENT (US/1040-1822) [18339529] **4985**

PATHWAYS FOR YOUNG ADULTS. TEACHER (US/1040-1830) [18339543] **4985**

PATHWAYS (FREDERICTON) (CN/0710-7773) [08737562] **1883**

PATHWAYS (HAMILTON) (CN/0840-8114) [20284790] **2179**

PATHWAYS — Alphabetical Title Index

PATHWAYS (MAYNARDVILLE, TENN.) (US/8755-4747) [09811112] **2753**

PATHWAYS TO OUTDOOR COMMUNICATION : OFFICIAL PUBLICATION OF THE NEW YORK STATE OUTDOOR EDUCATION ASSOCIATION (US) [24581956] **2179**

PATIENT ACCOUNTS (US/0195-7775) [05689217] 749, **3790**

PATIENT CARE (US/0031-305X) [01781641] **3738**

PATIENT CARE FLOW CHART MANUAL (US/0270-1553) [06327122] **3738**

PATIENT CARE LAW (US/0730-5524) [08014336] 3866, **3025**

PATIENT CARE NEDERLAND (BE/0770-4224) [I07704224] **3626**

PATIENT CARE PUBLICATIONS, INC. SPECIAL PUBLICATIONS GROUP *See* PATIENT CARE FLOW CHART MANUAL **3738**

PATIENT CARE REVIEW (US/0147-3913) [03146875] **3790**

PATIENT EDUCATION NEWSLETTER (US/0278-8209) [07997054] 1772, **4795**

PATIENT MANAGEMENT (NZ/0110-4578) [03304670] 881, **3626**

PATIENT MANAGEMENT (SEAFORTH) (NZ/0314-660X) [09495667] **3626**

PATIENT OF THE MONTH PROGRAM (CN/1188-0236) **3626**

PATIENT ORIGIN DATA FOR NORTH DAKOTA HOSPITALS AND NURSING HOMES (US/0147-0957) [03110439] **3790**

●PATIENT OUTCOMES (US/1069-6520) [28130330] **3790**

PATIENT UPDATE *SUSPENDED*. (CN/0847-8090) [20658936] **3790**

PATIENTORIENTIERTE ALLGEMEINMEDIZIN (GW/0177-8161) [10547088] **3626**

PATIENTS RIGHTS IN CALIFORNIA *See* PATIENTS RIGHTS REPORTER **3025**

PATIENTS RIGHTS REPORTER (US) **3025**

PATIO (FR) [11331953] **4607**

PATISSERIE BOULANGERIE NEUILLY-SUR-SEINE (FR/0998-4933) [I09984933] **2353**

PATMA-BANASIRAKAN HANDES (AI/0130-6812) [02183660] **3310**

PATMOS (SP) **4985**

PATNA UNIVERSITY JOURNAL (II) [01644573] **1839**

PATOLOGIA (SP) **3897**

PATOLOGIA E CLINICA OSTETRICA E GINECOLOGICA *CEASED*. (IT/0304-0313) [01060476] **3766**

PATOLOGIA POLSKA (PL/0031-3114) [06523000] **3897**

PATOLOGICESKAJA FIZIOLOGIJA I EKSPERIMENTALNAJA TERAPIJA (RU/0031-2991) [01681126] **584**

PATON WELDING JOURNAL, THE (UK/0957-798X) [I0957798X] **4027**

PATRE (FR) [09978057] **217**

PATRICIA NEWS BULLETIN (CN/0316-5418) [02247546] **4053**

PATRICIA SEYBOLD'S OFFICE COMPUTING REPORT (US/0894-9921) [16393462] 1261, **1292**

PATRICIAN, THE (CN/0316-4942) [02247342] **4053**

PATRIDES (TORONTO) (CN/0824-359X) [10392055] 1920, **2270**

PATRIMOINE TRIFLUVIEN (CN/1187-2713) [25423704] **2830**

●PATRIOMONIO CULTURAL (UY) [29043112] **2852**

PATRIOT (RU) [27246545] **5809**

PATRIOT (BU) [06619257] **4053**

PATRIOT (HARRISBURG, PA. : DAILY) (US/1041-4029) [12961063] **5738**

PATRIOT LEDGER (CITY EDITION), THE (US) [22448116] **5689**

PATRIOT LEDGER (SOUTH EDITION), THE (US) [22448062] **5689**

PATRIOT LEDGER (SUBURBAN EDITION), THE (US) [22448164] **5689**

PATRIOT REVIEW, THE (US/1056-4314) [23711215] **1094**

PATRIS (VANCOUVER) (CN/0715-5913) [09631054] **5792**

PATRISTIC AND BYZANTINE REVIEW, THE (US/0737-738X) [08838760] 2702, **4985**

PATRISTICA ET MEDIAEVALIA (AG/0325-2280) [04235921] **4354**

PATRISTICS (US/0360-652X) [01895187] **4985**

PATRISTISCHE TEXTE UND STUDIEN (GW/0553-4003) [02000346] **4985**

PATROLOGIA ORIENTALIS (BE) [01716246] **2662**

PATRONS PICK TORONTO'S FAVOURITE RESTAURANTS (CN/1185-2151) [24368429] **5072**

PATTERN RECOGNITION (UK/0031-3203) [01761969] **1215**

PATTERN RECOGNITION AND IMAGE ANALYSIS (US/1054-6618) [22937645] 1252, **3526**

PATTERN RECOGNITION LETTERS (NE/0167-8655) [09363661] **1234**

PATTERNS *See* STONE COUNTRY **3472**

PATTERNS OF PREJUDICE (UK/0031-322X) [01604898] **2270**

PATTERSON'S AMERICAN EDUCATION (US/0079-0230) [01247732] **1772**

PATTERSON'S ELEMENTARY EDUCATION (US/1044-1417) [19279086] **1772**

PATTERSON'S SCHOOLS CLASSIFIED (US/0553-4054) [02256584] **1839**

PATTON (TOMS RIVER, N.J.) (US/1052-3278) [22247474] **2467**

PATTON UTILITY NEWS *See* TEXAS PUBLIC UTILITY NEWS **4762**

PATTON'S ... FANTASY BASEBALL PRICE GUIDE (US/1046-7963) [19582181] **2776**

PAUL DE HAEN, INC *See* DE HAEN NEW PRODUCT SURVEY **4299**

PAUL EDWARDS' TRAVEL CONFIDENTIAL (US/1056-0025) [23443359] **5488**

●PAUL KAGAN'S BOX OFFICE CHAMPIONS. ACTORS/ACTRESSES (US/1064-7236) [26381329] 4076, **387**

●PAUL KAGAN'S BOX OFFICE CHAMPIONS. DIRECTORS (US/1063-2573) [25947039] **4076**

●PAUL KAGAN'S BOX OFFICE CHAMPIONS. PRODUCERS (US/1064-7228) [26381279] 4076, **387**

●PAUL KAGAN'S BOX OFFICE CHAMPIONS. SCREENWRITERS (US/1064-7244) [26381313] 4076, **387**

PAUL KAGAN'S RECORD OF TV STATION DEALS (US/1055-3789) [23110691] **1136**

●PAUL MCCARTNEY MAGAZINE (US/1057-039X) [23915834] **4145**

PAUL VALERY (FR) [02244313] **3422**

PAULDING COUNTY PROGRESS (US) [16896749] **5729**

PAULDING NEIGHBOR, THE (US/0192-0685) [04997636] **5654**

PAULLINA TIMES-SUTHERLAND COURIER (PAULLINA ED.) (US) [16279921] **5672**

PAUL'S RECORD MAGAZINE (US/0360-2109) [02244181] 5318, **4145**

PAULY'S REALENCYCLOPADIE (GW) **252**

PAUNCH (US/0031-3262) [02509477] **3422**

PAURNAMASI (II) [10465767] **4354**

PAUTA (MX) [11807176] **4145**

PAVIA. UNIVERSITA. ISTITUTO BOTANICO E LABORATORIO CRITTOGAMICO *See* ATTI - PAVIA. UNIVERSITA. ISTITUTO BOTANICO E LABORATORIO CRITTOGAMICO **500**

PAVING FORUM (US) [01761973] **2028**

PAVO (II/0031-3297) [01761975] **5619**

PAW PRINTS *CEASED*. (US/0163-562X) [04412153] **1067**

PAWLEYS ISLAND PERSPECTIVE, THE (US/0276-0851) [07310411] **3350**

PAWN REVIEW, THE *CEASED*. (US/0162-0061) [03398480] **3422**

PAWN TO INFINITY (CN/0847-0561) [23243214] **3462**

PAWNEE REPUBLICAN (US) [10562631] **5707**

PAX (UK) [01586025] **2521**

PAX (US) [10590263] **5253**

PAX CHRISTI USA (US/0897-9545) [16137823] **4985**

PAX REGIS (CN/0031-3335) [02653651] **4985**

PAY & BENEFITS BULLETIN (UK/0143-8328) [I01438328] **944**

PAY AND BENEFITS SOURCEBOOK (UK) **2889**

PAY EQUITY GUIDE (CN/0838-0058) [19298623] **702**

PAY EQUITY NEWSLETTER / NOVA SCOTIA PAY EQUITY COMMISSION, THE (CN/1180-4890) [23659236] **1701**

PAY LESS TAX LEGALLY (US/0191-9660) [04927804] **4740**

PAY SCALES OF SCHOOL TEACHERS IN INDIA (II) [05544104] **1868**

PAY STRUCTURE OF THE FEDERAL CIVIL SERVICE (US/0161-2964) [12441797] 4673, **1701**

PAY TV NEWSLETTER, THE (US/0146-0072) [02828077] **1136**

PAYAM-I IMAM (US) [10106876] 2702, **2662**

PAYING FOR COLLEGE (US) **1839**

●PAYING LESS FOR COLLEGE (US/1062-3205) [25586043] **1839**

PAYK-I NAJAT / JABHAH-I NAJAT-I IRAN (DK) [11960896] **2770**

PAYMENT SYSTEMS WORLDWIDE (US/1051-7359) [21314361] **802**

PAYPERVIEWS (HARTSDALE, N.Y.) (US/0896-1840) [16942639] **1136**

PAYPHONE EXCHANGE (US/0890-6785) [14366149] 1161, **702**

PAYROLL ACCOUNTING (US/0277-5840) [07582047] **749**

●PAYROLL CURRENTLY (US/1065-6529) [26666508] **4740**

PAYROLL EXCHANGE (US/0194-6196) [04890284] **1701**

PAYROLL GUIDE (US) [05627842] **1701**

PAYROLL HANDBOOK (UK) **749**

PAYROLL MANAGER'S LETTER (US/0895-7975) [12765830] **1512**

PAYROLL MANAGER'S REVIEW (UK) **944**

PAYROLL PRACTITIONER'S MONTHLY (US/1047-6571) [19523386] **1701**

PAYROLL RECORDS AND ACCOUNTING *See* PAYROLL ACCOUNTING **749**

PAYS BAS-NORMAND, LE (FR/0031-3386) [I00313386] **2702**

PAYS D'ALBE, LE (FR/1169-2421) [I11692421] **2702**

PAYS D'ALSACE (FR/0245-8411) [10179638] 278, **2702**

PAYS D'AUGE LISIEUX. 1951, LE (FR/1149-3305) [I11493305] **2521**

PAYS DE BOURGOGNE (FR/0475-9516) [08417441] **362**

PAYS DE DINAN, LE (FR) [11546703] 5269, **327**

PAYS D'EUROPE OCCIDENTALE EN ..., LES (FR) [09914158] **2702**

PAYS GAUMAIS, LE (BE/0776-3689) [I07763689] 2702, **278**

PAYS LORRAIN, LE (FR/0031-3394) [02718679] 278, **2702**

PAYS SEDANAIS, LE (FR/0338-4659) [I03384659] **2702**

PAYSAGE ACTUALITES (FR/0395-2916) [07546565] **2427**

PAYSANS (FR/0479-7353) [09978420] **119**

●PAYTECH (NEW YORK, N.Y.) (US/1063-9047) [26175302] **749**

PAZ & JUSTICIA (UY) [13495072] **4511**

PAZIFISCHE RUNDSCHAU (CN/0048-3095) [09499005] **5792**

PB - U.S. CLEARINGHOUSE FOR FEDERAL SCIENTIFIC AND TECHNICAL INFORMATION (US) [02311420] **5137**

PBA BRIEF (US) [03806693] **3025**

●PBC AUTO GUIDE (US/1059-2083) [24499142] **5423**

●PBC BUSINESS GUIDE (US/1059-2075) [24499203] **702**

●PBC COMPREHENSIVE HEALTH BRIEFS (US/1059-2067) [24499174] **4795**

●PBC CREDIT BRIEFS (US/1059-2059) [24499224] **802**

●PBC EMPLOYMENT BRIEFS (US/1059-2040) [24499244] **4208**

PBC FEDERAL TAX GUIDE (US/1059-2032) [24499289] **4740**

●PBC GOVERNMENT PROGRAMS NEWSLETTER (US/1059-2024) [24499318] **4673**

●PBC HOUSING BRIEFS (US/1059-2016) [24499349] **2830**

●PBC IMMIGRATION BRIEFS (US/1059-2008) [24499368] **1920**

●PBC SCIENCE BRIEFS (US/1059-1990) [24499381] **5137**

●PBC SENIOR NEWSLETTER (US/1059-1982) [24506890] **702**

●PBC TAX BRIEFS (US/1059-1974) [24499393] **4740**

●PBC TRAVEL NEWSLETTER (US/1059-1966) [24506902] **702**

PBI EXCHANGE (US/1041-3243) [18354511] **5300**

PBO-BLAD / SOCIAAL-ECONOMISCHE RAAD (NE) [15099525] **1578**

PC ABSTRACTS (US/0743-2534) [10538862] **1270**

PC ACCOUNTING *CEASED*. (US) [19831510] 1198, **749**

PC ACTIVE (NE/0925-5745) [I09255745] **1270**

PC ACTUAL (SP/1130-9954) [I11309954] **1198**

Alphabetical Title Index — PEACEWORK

PC ADVISOR CEASED. (US/1054-867X) [23010313] **1198**

PC AI (US/0894-0711) [15617485] 1270, **1215**

PC BUSINESS INFO (NE) **1198**

PC BUSINESS SOFTWARE (UK/0954-2833) [18209523] 702, 1289, **1270**

PC BUSINESS WORLD (UK/0266-8483) [I02668483] **1245**

PC BUYERS GUIDE CEASED. (US/8756-2634) [10786855] 1289, **1270**

PC CAD DIGEST (US/0895-5069) [16661406] **1198**

PC COMPANION CEASED. (US/0886-0181) [12788525] **1198**

PC COMPUTER MAINTENANCE ANNUAL (US/1045-5701) [19863807] **1270**

PC/COMPUTING (NEW YORK, N.Y.) (US/0899-1847) [18025521] **1270**

PC DEALER (UK/0950-5474) [I09505474] **1238**

PC DIGEST RATINGS REPORT (US/1042-3575) [19018708] **1270**

PC DISK QUARTERLY SUSPENDED. (US/0897-8913) [17656515] **1198**

PC FAST FACTS (US/1045-7240) [20215299] **1270**

●PC GAMER (US/1351-3540) [I13513540] 1198, **4864**

PC GAMES (PETERBOROUGH, N.H.) (US/1042-2943) [19002947] **4864**

●PC GRAPHICS & VIDEO (US/1077-5862) [29994484] **1234**

PC GUIDE USA. CD-ROM (US) **1198**

PC HOME JOURNAL CEASED. (US) **1270**

PC LAN (UK) **1270**

PC LAPTOP COMPUTERS MAGAZINE (US/1043-1314) [19320065] **1270**

PC LETTER (US) **1198**

PC LIFE (US/0890-4863) [17273870] **1198**

PC-MAGAZIN (GW/0177-0977) [I01770977] **1199**

PC MAGAZINE (US/0888-8507) [15128481] **1270**

PC MAGAZINE (UK/0953-7708) [23231301] **1271**

PC MAGAZINE (IT) **1271**

PC MAGAZINE. CHINESE EDITION (CH) **1271**

PC MAGAZINE EN ESPANOL (US/1069-9953) [28210102] **1199**

PC MAGAZINE (NEW YORK, N.Y.) (US/0888-8507) [13566002] **1271**

PC MAGAZINE (NEW YORK, N.Y.) (US/0888-8507) [17196472] **1271**

PC MAGAZINE. PORTUGUESE EDITION (PO) **1271**

PC MANAGER'S LETTER (US/1069-9228) [28201624] 1261, **881**

PC MICRO MAGAZINE (BE) **1271**

PC-NETZE (GW/0936-4315) [I09364315] **1199**

PC NOVICE (US/1052-1186) [21984867] **1271**

PC, PERSONAL COMMUNICATIONS SHOW DAILY (US/0363-1885) [02431446] **2074**

PC PERSONAL COMPUTER See BUSINESS COMPUTING **1172**

PC PLUS (NE) **1271**

PC PLUS (UK) [17555432] 1289, **1271**

PC-PRAXIS 1989 (GW/0940-6743) [I09406743] **1199**

●PC PRESENTATIONS, PRODUCTIONS (US/1065-9099) [26790653] **1271**

PC PROFESSIONALE (IT/1121-3337) [I11213337] **1199**

PC PUBLISHING (US/0896-8209) [16877578] 1199, **4818**

PC PUBLISHING AND PRESENTATIONS CEASED. (US/1056-540X) [23734950] **1263**

PC QUOTES (US) [12018830] **1271**

PC REF CEASED. (US/0891-9127) [15029977] 1289, **1271**

PC REPORT (US) [18168871] **1271**

PC RETAILING (US/0746-6773) [10213852] **1245**

PC/SFA ... SNACK FOOD MANAGEMENT REPORT (US/0734-6530) [08774541] **2353**

PC-SIG MAGAZINE (US/1042-0681) [17280474] 1271, **1289**

●PC SOFTDIR (US/1069-0913) [27129216] **1289**

PC SOURCES CEASED. (US/1052-6579) [22343771] **1199**

PC STREET PRICE INDEX, THE (US) **1245**

PC STREET PRICE INDEX, THE (US/1071-2259) [28576999] **1248**

PC SUPPORT ADVISOR (SYDNEY) (AT/1031-3966) [I10313966] **1271**

PC TECHNIQUES (US/1053-6205) [22135036] 1271, **1289**

PC TELEMART SOFTWARE DIRECTORY (US) [10926994] **1199**

PC TODAY (US/1040-6484) [18484062] **1271**

PC TODAY MACCLESFIELD (UK/0960-0124) [I09600124] **1199**

PC USER (LONDON, ENGLAND) (UK/0263-5720) [12414428] **1271**

●PC VISION (US/1065-8645) [26782584] **1271**

PC WEEK (IT) **1199**

PC WEEK (AUSTRALIAN EDITION) (AT/1030-6137) **1199**

PC WEEK (U.S. ED.) (US/0740-1604) [09905674] **1271**

PC WEEK (UK ED.) (UK/0269-3011) [14929421] **1271**

PC-WELT (GW/0175-0496) [I01750496] **1199**

PC WORLD (US/0737-8939) [09468047] 1239, 1245, **1271**

PC WORLD (SP) **1199**

●PC WORLD (US) [27198203] **1271**

PC WORLD ITALIA (IT/1120-8066) [I11208066] **1271**

PC WORLD MADRID (SP/0213-1307) [I02131307] **1271**

PC WORLD MAGAZINE (IT) **1199**

PC WORLD NORGE 1987 (NO/0801-5236) [I08015236] **1271**

PC YEAR BOOK (UK/0954-6286) [I09546286] **1245**

PC YOUTH TODAY (CN/0820-6260) [09519547] **4487**

PCA MESSENGER, THE CEASED. (US/0191-4162) [04897547] **4986**

PCARRD MONITOR, THE (PH/0116-3140) [10094896] **119**

PCB IN WATER : A BIBLIOGRAPHY (US) [04740429] **5549**

PCB MAGAZINE (IT) **5137**

PCEC. PRIVATE CAREER EDUCATION COUNCIL (CN/0705-3126) [03827621] **4208**

PCGAMES SUSPENDED. (US/0897-893X) [17656225] **1230**

PCH. PETROLEUM CONCESSION HANDBOOK (US/0275-6129) [06859687] **4271**

PCH. PHYSICOCHEMICAL HYDRODYNAMICS (UK/0191-9059) [04964902] **1056**

PCHELOVODSTVO (RU/0369-8629) [01643852] **119**

PCI JOURNAL (US/0887-9672) [12789822] **2028**

PCI REVIEW / PRESS COUNCIL OF INDIA (II) [07869726] **1119**

●PCIA JOURNAL (US/1075-7821) [30094247] **1161**

PCIM EUROPE (GW) **1990**

PCM (US/0747-0460) [10501798] **1271**

PCM LE PONT (FR/0986-1793) [I09861793] 2028, **5442**

PCN NEWS (US/1051-3833) [21941855] **1119**

PCNA MONTHLY / PALESTINE CONGRESS OF NORTH AMERICA (US) [12562384] **2270**

PCNETTER NEWSLETTER, THE (US/0893-8075) [15650566] **1199**

PCR INFORMATION See ECHOES **4955**

PCR INFORMATION : REPORTS AND BACKGROUND PAPERS (SZ) [09364212] **5253**

PCR METHODS AND APPLICATIONS (US/1054-9803) [23041597] **1045**

PCR / PRODUCTION AND CASTING REPORT (UK/0142-632X) **1621**

PCS (ALEXANDRIA, VA.) (US) [24426206] **1119**

PCS NEWS (US/1070-6607) [28448923] **1119**

PCS, THE REGULATORY CHALLENGE (US/1065-111X) [26508961] **1119**

PCSO BULLETIN (US/0191-7951) [04896992] **1332**

PCSS POLICY MONOGRAPH SERIES (PH) [14256321] **2852**

PCT APPLICANT'S GUIDE (SZ) [16144920] **1308**

PCT GAZETTE (SZ) [05325438] **1308**

PCT, PEST CONTROL TECHNOLOGY See PEST CONTROL TECHNOLOGY **4246**

PCTE NEWSLETTER (FR) **1199**

PCU JOURNAL OF EDUCATIONAL RESEARCH See GRADUATE SCHOOL RESEARCH JOURNAL : A PUBLICATION OF GRADUATE SCHOOL OF BUSINESS ADMINISTRATION AND GRADUATE SCHOOL OF EDUCATION **1826**

PCWORLD (HK) **1271**

PDA JOURNAL OF PHARMACEUTICAL SCIENCE AND TECHNOLOGY (US) [31066421] **4319**

PDQ CEASED. (US/0194-2530) [05365795] **4567**

PDR FAMILY GUIDE TO PRESCRIPTION DRUGS (US) **4319**

●PDR GUIDE TO DRUG INTERACTIONS, SIDE EFFECTS, INDICATIONS, (US) [27345788] **4319**

●PDR LIBRARY ON CD ROM WITH THE MERCK MANUAL (US/1068-6924) [27774951] **4319**

PDR, RESEARCH AND TECHNOLOGY PROGRAM (US) [03194244] **2830**

PDRC CURRENTS See CHINA CURRENTS : A PHILIPPINE QUARTERLY ON CHINA CONCERNS **2648**

PDS UPDATE (US/0892-6980) [15307329] **4319**

PE See P-NOTES / FID, FEDERATION INTERNATIONALE DE DOCUMENTATION **3240**

PE DRILLING ENGINEERING See SPE DRILLING AND COMPLETIONS **4278**

PE. PLAST EUROPE (GW/0941-3596) [I09413596] **4457**

PEA RIVER TRAILS (US/8756-4181) [11535840] **2467**

PEABODY ESSAYS IN MUSIC HISTORY (US/1042-4350) [13826640] **4145**

PEABODY ESSEX MUSEUM COLLECTIONS (US/1074-0457) [29401924] 4095, **2753**

PEABODY JOURNAL OF EDUCATION (US/0161-956X) [04013686] **1772**

PEACE AND CHANGE (US/0149-0508) [01116490] **4531**

PEACE AND CONFLICT REPORT (SA) **4531**

PEACE & DEMOCRACY NEWS (US/0749-5900) [11148759] **4531**

PEACE AND ENVIRONMENT NEWS (CN/1181-9391) [24265481] **2179**

PEACE AND FREEDOM (US/0015-9093) [02255123] 4487, **5564**

PEACE & SECURITY CEASED. (CN/0831-1846) [15205040] **4531**

PEACE AND THE SCIENCES (AU) [06158329] **4531**

PEACE AND TRUTH (UK) [06464403] **4986**

PEACE ARCH NEWS WEEKENDER, THE (CN/0821-5251) [09606645] **5792**

PEACE CORPS TIMES (US/0884-9196) [04116037] **2911**

PEACE COURIER (FI/0031-594X) [00989525] **4531**

PEACE MAGAZINE (CN/0826-9521) [13448481] **4531**

PEACE NEWS FOR NONVIOLENT REVOLUTION (UK) [25783664] **4487**

PEACE NEWSLETTER (SYRACUSE, N.Y.) (US/0735-4134) [07912614] **4531**

PEACE OFFICER (WARREN, MICH.) (US/0031-3556) [04104561] **3171**

PEACE REPORTER (US/1049-0779) [21122409] 4487, **1772**

PEACE RESEARCH (CN/0008-4697) [00887456] **4531**

PEACE RESEARCH ABSTRACTS. CD-ROM (CN) **4531**

PEACE RESEARCH ABSTRACTS JOURNAL (US/0031-3599) [01605735] 4531, **4502**

PEACE RESEARCH IN JAPAN (JA) [03874171] **4531**

PEACE RESEARCH REVIEWS (CN/0553-4283) [01641606] **4487**

PEACE REVIEW (PALO ALTO, CALIF.) (US/1040-2659) [18362800] **4531**

PEACE RIVER, ALASKA HIGHWAY TOUR AND VACATION GUIDE (CN/1186-6101) [24368246] **5488**

PEACE RIVER NEWSLETTER (CN/0848-6786) [23455450] **119**

PEACEKEEPING & INTERNATIONAL RELATIONS (CN/1187-3485) [23475336] **4531**

PEACEMAKER (PH/0116-5747) [I01165747] **2270**

PEACEMAKER, THE (US/0031-3602) [03884462] **4487**

PEACEMAKERS (US/0895-9714) [16878709] **4487**

PEACEWORK (CAMBRIDGE, MASS.) (US/0748-0725) [10064983] **4487**

PEACH

PEACH TIMES (US/0031-3610) [02430221] **2427**

PEAK DISTRICT MINES HISTORICAL SOCIETY *See* BULLETIN OF THE PEAK DISTRICT MINES HISTORICAL SOCIETY **2135**

PEAK PERFORMANCE (UK/0962-0184) [I09620184] **4853**

PEAK PERFORMANCE SELLING (US/1043-4364) [19467439] **881**

PEAK RUNNING PERFORMANCE (US) 1857, **4911**

PEAKE STUDIES (SZ/1013-1191) [19252824] **3422**

PEANUT FARMER, THE (US/0031-3653) [04171474] **180**

PEANUT GROWER, THE (US/1042-9379) [19254119] **180**

PEANUT INDUSTRY GUIDE (US/0740-2562) [09888119] 2353, **119**

PEANUT JOURNAL AND NUT WORLD *CEASED.* (US/0031-3661) [02430160] **2353**

PEANUT MARKETING SUMMARY CROP (US/0273-4923) [07051434] **180**

PEANUT REPORT (US) **180**

PEANUT RESEARCH (US/0479-7558) [02403611] **180**

PEANUT SCIENCE (US/0095-3679) [01795327] **180**

PEANUT STOCKS AND PROCESSING (US/0499-0579) [01780470] **180**

PEARL PRESS, THE (US/0747-1904) [10633291] **5701**

PEARLAND JOURNAL, THE (US) [16907906] **5753**

PEAR'S CYCLOPAEDIA (UK) **1928**

PEASANT STUDIES *SUSPENDED.* (US/0149-1547) [02180135] **5212**

PEAT ABSTRACTS (IE) [01791327] **2147**

PEAT, MARWICK, MITCHELL & CO *See* PRINCIPLES AND PRESENTATION : BANKING **803**

PEAT, MARWICK, MITCHELL & CO *See* PRINCIPLES AND PRESENTATION : SAVINGS AND LOAN **750**

PEAT NEWS (CN/0706-1307) [05528005] **119**

PEB EXCHANGE (INT/1018-9327) [I10189327] **1772**

PEBBLE (CRETE) *CEASED.* (US/0031-3696) [01608028] **3423**

PECAN MARKETING SUMMARY ... CROP FOR THE STATES OF ALABAMA, FLORIDA, GEORGIA, LOUISIANA, NEW MEXICO, NORTH CAROLINA, OKLAHOMA, SOUTH CAROLINA, TEXAS / FEDERAL-STATE MARKET NEWS SERVICE (US) [07779827] **181**

●PECAN SOUTH (US) [26495374] **119**

PECAN SOUTH INCLUDING PECAN QUARTERLY (US/8750-5797) [11509801] **181**

PECHE ET LES POISSONS PARIS, LA (FR/0031-3718) [I00313718] **2310**

PECHE MARITIME (PARIS, FRANCE) (FR/0031-3726) [09490318] **5454**

PECHEUR ET CHASSEUR QUEBECOIS (CN/0703-9107) [03979856] **4912**

PECOS FREE PRESS AND ENTERPRISE (US) [15370192] **5753**

PECOS TRAILS *SUSPENDED.* (US/0736-6442) [08417998] **2467**

PECU REVIEW, THE (CN/0225-9753) [08415816] **1512**

PECUNIA. BRUXELLES, DE (BE/1015-6283) [I10156283] **881**

PED FORUM (US/1046-2082) [17575569] **4704**

PEDAGOGIA E VITA (IT/0031-3777) [I00313777] **1067**

PEDAGOGIA MEDICA *CEASED.* (IT/1120-8627) [I11208627] **3626**

PEDAGOGIA PARA EL ADIESTRAMIENTO (MX) [02242025] **944**

PEDAGOGIC REPORTER, THE (US/0031-3793) [04940525] 2270, **1772**

PEDAGOGICHESKIE PROBLEMY FORMIROVANIIA POZNAVATELNYKH INTERESOV UCHASHCHIKHSIA (RU) [05764176] **4607**

PEDAGOGICKA FAKULTA V BANSKEJ BYSTRICI *See* CUDZIE JAZYKY **3276**

PEDAGOGICKA FAKULTA V PLZNI *See* SBORNIK. UMENI **4152**

PEDAGOGICKY BIBLIOGRAFICKY SPRAVODAJ. SERIA B : ZAHRANICNE PERIODIKA (XO) [06622599] **1796**

PEDAGOGIE COLLEGIALE (CN/0835-8974) [18116672] **1840**

PEDAGOGIEKJOERNAAL (SA/0256-520X) [10626025] **1772**

PEDAGOGIES BRUXELLES (BE/0778-0893) [I07780893] **1772**

PEDAGOGIKA (XR/0031-3815) [02196288] **1772**

PEDAGOGIKA (BU) [24135297] **1772**

●PEDAGOGIKA (RU) [26144800] **1772**

PEDAGOGIQUES (CN/0383-0802) [02813922] **1840**

PEDAGOGISCHE BIJDRAGEN (BE) **1772**

PEDAGOSKA STVARNOST (YU) [06623695] **1772**

PEDALPOINT (US/0272-9199) [06966228] **4145**

PEDIATRE, LE (FR/0397-9180) [I03979180] **1772**

●PEDIATRIA / ASOCIATIA MEDICALA ROMANA, SOCIETATEA ROMANA DE PEDIATRIE (RM/1220-580X) [30548690] **3907**

PEDIATRIA (LIMA, PERU) (PE/1012-8964) [10546433] **3907**

PEDIATRIA MEDICA E CHIRURGICA, LA (IT/0391-5387) [07259701] 3971, **3907**

PEDIATRIA MODERNA (BL/0031-3920) [I00313920] **3907**

PEDIATRIA (NAPOLI) (IT/0031-3890) [01716444] **3907**

PEDIATRIA OGGI MEDICA E CHIRURGICA (IT/0391-898X) [12185499] 3971, **3907**

PEDIATRIA POLSKA (PL/0031-3939) [06285477] **3907**

PEDIATRIA (SANTIAGO) (CL/0375-9563) [01779235] **3907**

PEDIATRIA (SAO PAULO) *SUSPENDED.* (BL/0101-3858) [07627742] **3907**

PEDIATRIC AIDS AND HIV INFECTION (US/1045-5418) [22352248] 3908, **3675**

PEDIATRIC ALERT *CEASED.* (IT) **3908**

PEDIATRIC ALERT (US/0160-0184) [03600868] **3908**

PEDIATRIC ALLERGY AND IMMUNOLOGY : OFFICIAL PUBLICATION OF THE EUROPEAN SOCIETY OF PEDIATRIC ALLERGY AND IMMUNOLOGY (DK/0905-6157) [23835706] **3675**

PEDIATRIC ANAESTHESIA (FR) 3908, **3684**

PEDIATRIC AND ADOLESCENT ENDOCRINOLOGY (SZ/0304-4254) [02969057] 3732, **3908**

PEDIATRIC AND ADOLESCENT MEDICINE (SZ/1017-5989) [23243611] **3908**

PEDIATRIC ANNALS (US/0090-4481) [01772141] **3908**

PEDIATRIC ASTHMA, ALLERGY & IMMUNOLOGY (US/0883-1874) [12072879] 3675, **3908**

PEDIATRIC CARDIOLOGY (US/0172-0643) [05108352] 3709, **3908**

PEDIATRIC CLINICS OF INDIA (II/0048-3133) [08786970] **3908**

PEDIATRIC CLINICS OF NORTH AMERICA, THE (US/0031-3955) [01643666] **3908**

PEDIATRIC CONFERENCES FROM THE BABIES' HOSPITAL UNIT, UNITED HOSPITALS OF NEWARK, NEW JERSEY *See* PEDIATRIC CONFERENCES FROM THE CHILDREN'S HOSPITAL OF NEWARK **3908**

PEDIATRIC CONFERENCES FROM THE CHILDREN'S HOSPITAL OF NEWARK (US/0097-5982) [01289547] **3908**

PEDIATRIC DENTAL JOURNAL : INTERNATIONAL JOURNAL OF JAPANESE SOCIETY OF PEDIATRIC DENTISTRY (JA/0917-2394) [25588525] **1332**

PEDIATRIC DENTISTRY (US/0164-1263) [04586450] **1332**

PEDIATRIC DENTISTRY TODAY (US/1046-2791) [20376421] 3908, **1332**

PEDIATRIC DERMATOLOGY (US/0736-8046) [09229112] 3722, **3908**

PEDIATRIC EMERGENCY & CRITICAL CARE (US/1059-0870) [24477875] **3908**

PEDIATRIC EMERGENCY CARE (US/0749-5161) [11136192] 3908, **3725**

PEDIATRIC EXERCISE SCIENCE (US/0899-8493) [18237253] **3908**

PEDIATRIC HABILITATION (US/0731-5902) [07480432] **3908**

PEDIATRIC HEMATOLOGY AND ONCOLOGY (US/0888-0018) [13451091] 3908, 3822, **3773**

PEDIATRIC INFECTIOUS DISEASE JOURNAL, THE (US/0891-3668) [14710189] 3715, **3908**

PEDIATRIC LENGTH OF STAY BY DIAGNOSIS AND OPERATION, UNITED STATES (US/0891-1223) [09426478] **3908**

PEDIATRIC MANAGEMENT *SUSPENDED.* (US/1051-3272) [21929594] **3908**

PEDIATRIC MENTAL HEALTH (US/0278-4998) [07828657] **3909**

PEDIATRIC NEPHROLOGY (US/0097-5257) [02239429] 3992, **3909**

PEDIATRIC NEPHROLOGY (BERLIN, WEST) (GW/0931-041X) [15991488] 3992, **3909**

PEDIATRIC NETWORK (US/0742-1605) [10293209] **3909**

PEDIATRIC NEUROLOGY (US/0887-8994) [11930271] 3844, **3909**

PEDIATRIC NEUROSURGERY (SZ/1016-2291) [24861594] 3844, **3909**

PEDIATRIC NEWS (US/0031-398X) [06354117] **3909**

PEDIATRIC NOTES (US/0738-8691) [05997489] **3909**

PEDIATRIC NURSING (US/0097-9805) [01799580] 3909, **3866**

PEDIATRIC NURSING [MICROFORM] (US/0097-9805) [13778981] 3909, **3866**

PEDIATRIC OPTOMETRY & VISION THERAPY *CEASED.* (US/1055-2359) [23123769] **4217**

PEDIATRIC PATHOLOGY (US/0277-0938) [07496568] 3909, **3897**

PEDIATRIC PATHOLOGY *See* PEDIATRIC PATHOLOGY AND LABORATORY MEDICINE **3897**

●PEDIATRIC PATHOLOGY AND LABORATORY MEDICINE (UK/1077-1042) [30697806] **3897**

PEDIATRIC PHYSICAL THERAPY (US/0898-5669) [17850316] 4381, **3909**

●PEDIATRIC PRIMARY CARE (US/1071-5711) [28679041] **3909**

PEDIATRIC PULMONOLOGY (US/8755-6863) [11383709] **3909**

PEDIATRIC PULMONOLOGY. SUPPLEMENT (US/1054-187X) [19033623] 3950, **3909**

PEDIATRIC RADIOLOGY (GW/0301-0449) [01696630] 3909, **3944**

PEDIATRIC REPORT'S CHILD HEALTH NEWSLETTER *CEASED.* (US/1065-1284) [22992907] **3909**

PEDIATRIC RESEARCH (US/0031-3998) [01761994] **3909**

PEDIATRIC REVIEWS AND COMMUNICATION (SZ/0882-9225) [12009144] **3909**

●PEDIATRIC ROUNDS (US/1062-8789) [25778329] **3909**

PEDIATRIC SOCIAL WORK (US/0195-5926) [05509640] **5300**

PEDIATRIC SURGERY INTERNATIONAL (GW/0179-0358) [12967030] 3971, **3909**

PEDIATRIC THERAPEUTICS & TOXICOLOGY *See* PEDIATRIC PRIMARY CARE **3909**

PEDIATRIC THERAPEUTICS AND TOXICOLOGY (US/0893-6218) [15604940] **3909**

PEDIATRIC THERAPY (US) [07548490] **3910**

PEDIATRIC WORLD (US/0479-785X) [02254896] **3910**

PEDIATRICIAN *CEASED.* (SZ/0300-1245) [12891409] **3910**

PEDIATRICS DIGEST (1979) (US/0198-6341) [06167168] **3910**

PEDIATRICS. EDICION ESPANOLA (SP/0210-5721) [I02105721] **3910**

PEDIATRICS EDIZIONE ITALIANA (IT/1120-7507) [I11207507] **3910**

PEDIATRICS (EVANSTON) (US/0031-4005) [01761995] **3910**

PEDIATRICS FOR PARENTS (US/0730-6725) [08044514] 2285, **3910**

PEDIATRICS (GLENDALE, CALIF.) (US/0271-1346) [03438682] **3910**

PEDIATRICS IN REVIEW (US/0191-9601) [04967866] **3910**

PEDIATRICS (NEW YORK, N.Y.) (US/0079-0400) [01785302] **3910**

PEDIATRIE (FR/0031-4021) [01606642] **3910**

PEDIATRIE (BUCHAREST, ROMANIA) *See* PEDIATRIA / ASOCIATIA MEDICALA ROMANA, SOCIETATEA ROMANA DE PEDIATRIE **3907**

PEDIATRIE (LYONS, FRANCE : 1948) *See* ARCHIVES DE PEDIATRIE : ORGANE OFFICIEL DE LA SOCIETE FRANCAISE DE PEDIATRIE **3900**

PEDIATRIE PRATIQUE PARIS (FR/0993-9717) [I09939717] **3910**

PEDIATRIE / UNIUNEA SOCIETATILOR DE STIINTE MEDICALE DIN ROMANIA (RM/1220-580X) [24146657] **3910**

PEDIATRIJA (RU/0031-403X) [05115092] **3910**

PEDIATRIJA (SOFIA) (BU/0479-7876) [01385454] **3910**

PEDIATRIK CERRAHI DERGISI (TU/1016-5142) [I10165142] 3971, **3910**

PEDIGREE POINTERS / STEVENS POINT AREA GENEALOGICAL SOCIETY (US/0749-6192) [11139462] **2467**

PEDIGREE SEARCHERS (US) **2467**

PEDMED (SA/1017-1711) [I10171711] **3626**

PEDOBIOLOGIA (GW/0031-4056) [01761997] **181**

PEDOLOGIE (BE/0079-0419) [02403571] **181**

PEDOMAN PELAKSANAAN PENGADAAN DALAM NEGERI (IO) [02970837] **203**

PEDOSPHERE (CC) [24998618] **181**

PEDRALBES (SP) [09242760] **2702**

PEE DEE REGIONAL HEALTH SYSTEMS AGENCY, INC *See* DRAFT HEALTH SYSTEMS PLAN FOR SOUTH CAROLINA HEALTH SERVICE AREA II **4774**

PEEK (65) (US/0739-0653) [09711372] 1289, **1264**

PEEKE REPORT / METRO WASHINGTON DC EDITION / (MONDAY ONLY, BY MAIL) (US) **5686**

PEEL FARM NEWS (CN/0226-6520) [06477587] **119**

PEEL LABOUR (CN/1185-0175) [23598293] **1701**

PEEL MULTICULTURAL SCENE (CN/0715-5328) [09336451] **2270**

PEEL SENIORS REGIONAL NEWS (CN/0319-0196) [02442155] **5181**

PEELINGS II : THE MAGAZINE OF APPLE SOFTWARE EVALUATION (US/0744-2475) [08134797] 1265, 1289, **1271**

PEER ANNUAL REPORT AND CUMULATIVE SUMMARIES OF REPORTS ISSUED THROUGH ... (US) [07785871] **4673**

PEER FACILITATOR QUARTERLY (US/0741-2282) [10112363] **1772**

PEER MORDEKHAI (US) [01796275] **5051**

PEGASUS (UK/0031-4080) [10513755] **4053**

PEGASUS (NORWALK, CONN.) (US/1045-7836) [20230327] **3423**

PEGAZ (FR) **4271**

PEGBAR (CN/0828-9247) [12846991] **381**

PEGBOARD (MENLO PARK, CALIF.) (US/0892-5763) [15234029] **1230**

PEGG. ASSOCIATION OF PROFESSIONAL ENGINEERS, GEOLOGISTS AND GEOPHYSICISTS OF ALBERTA (MONTHLY ED.) (CN/0823-1745) [09951484] 1359, **1990**

PEGG, THE (CN/0030-7912) [02102932] 1391, **1990**

PEGO YA MOHLAKISI-MOGOLO KA DITSHUPAMOLATO TSA MMUSO WA LEBOWA LE YA DITSHUPAMOLATO TSA DIPUSWANA TIKOLOGONG MO NGWAGATSHELETENG (SA) [05701102] **4740**

PEI-CHING CHI CHUN (PEKING, CHINA) *See* BEI-JING ZHI CHUN **4465**

PEI-CHING KO CHI TA HSUEH HSUEH PAO (CH/1001-053X) [25187897] **4014**

PEI-CHING KUNG YUN SHIH LIAO / PEI-CHING SHIH TSUNG KUNG HUI KUNG JEN TUNG SHIH YEN CHIU TSU PIEN (CH) [09146545] **1701**

PEI-CHING LIN YEH TA HSUEH HSUEH PAO (CC/1000-1522) [24231741] **2390**

PEI-CHING NUNG YEH TA HSUEH HSUEH PAO *See* BEIJING NONGYE DAXUE XUEBAO **65**

PEI-CHING SHIH FAN HSUEH YUAN HSUEH PAO (CC) [21110290] **1772**

PEI-CHING SHIH FAN TA HSUEH HSUEH PAO : SHE HUI KO HSUEH PAN. BEIJING SHIFAN DAXUE XUEBAO (CC) [05350473] **5212**

PEI-CHING TA HSUEH HSUEH PAO: CHE HSUEH SHE HUI KO HSUEH PAN (CC) [01797480] **5212**

PEI-CHING TZU JAN PO WU KUAN YEN CHIU PAO KAO (CC) [08697842] **4170**

PEI-CHING WEN HSUEH (CC) [08391491] **3423**

PEI FANG WEN HSUEH (CC) [06818123] **3423**

PEI LEI HSUEH PAO (CH) [09808405] **5594**

PEIN KURINIKKU (JA/0388-4171) [I03884171] **3626**

PEINTURES CAHIERS THEORIQUES (FR) **362**

PEKIN DAILY TIMES (US/0745-7863) [09459989] **5661**

PEKIN INFORMATION (CC) [15194002] **4487**

PELANCAR (MY) [03519513] **1543**

PELANGI TOOWOOMBA (AT/0815-6816) [I08156816] 3310, **5212**

PELERIN D'ARES, LE (FR/0182-7634) [19796723] **3310**

PELERIN MAGAZINE (FR/0764-4663) [I07644663] 2491, **4986**

PELHAM HERALD (CN/0834-7042) [16374722] **5792**

PELHAM JOURNAL, THE (US/1060-3646) [21544095] **5654**

PELICAN GUIDE TO THE BAHAMAS (US/0740-5529) [09965179] **5488**

PELICAN HISTORY OF ART, THE (UK/0553-4755) [02013234] **362**

PELICAN NEWS (US/0031-4161) [04104591] **3866**

PELICAN RAPIDS PRESS (US) [01762004] **5698**

●PELIT 1992 (FI/1235-1199) [I12351199] **1272**

PELITA BPKS (IO/0126-3692) [03338205] 2285, **5300**

●PELIZZA'S POSITIVE PRINCIPLES FOR BETTER LIVING (US/1070-6674) [28448191] **4607**

PELLICCE MODA (IT) 1086, **3185**

PELLISSIPPIAN (CLINTON, TENN.) (US/0736-5594) [07720214] **2467**

PELOPONNESIAKA (GR/0553-478X) [01604070] **2702**

PELOUBET'S SELECT NOTES ON THE INTERNATIONAL BIBLE LESSONS FOR CHRISTIAN LIVING. UNIFORM SERIES (US) [04322057] **5018**

PELUQUERIAS (SP) **405**

PELVIC SURGEON, THE (US/0198-5000) [06186284] **3971**

PEM NEWS *SUSPENDED.* (UK/0265-9743) [I02659743] **4319**

PEM : PLANT ENGINEERING AND MAINTENANCE (CN/0710-362X) [08534517] 3486, **2124**

PEMBERITAAN PENELITIAN TANAMAN INDUSTRI (IO/0216-9657) [09634266] 181, **119**

PEMBIMBING PEMBACA (IO) [02484459] **3240**

PEMBIMBING PEMBATJA *See* PEMBIMBING PEMBACA **3240**

PEMBINA NEW ERA (US) [01762006] **5726**

PEMBROKE MAGAZINE, THE (US/0097-496X) [01377947] **3423**

PEMBROKE REPORTER (US/0746-6056) [10143196] **5689**

PEMERIKSA (IO) [07184570] **4740**

PEMMICAN JOURNAL, THE (CN/0710-3670) [08499616] **2753**

PEN AND INK (CN/0833-9414) [15876403] **362**

PEN-BASED COMPUTING (US/1054-4011) [22876977] **1248**

●PEN COMPUTER REPORT (US/1062-6344) [25686803] **1199**

PEN INTERNATIONAL (UK) [08850279] **3423**

PEN PRIMARY ENGLISH NOTES (AT) **1902**

PEN-VISTA. BILINGUAL EDITION (CN/0705-3908) [03900282] **3171**

PEN WOMAN (1944), THE (US/0031-4242) [02251767] **5564**

PEN WORLD (US/1045-1188) [19992791] 362, **2776**

PENANT (FR/0336-1551) [01967141] **3025**

PENASEE GLOBE (US/0895-8580) [16836602] **5693**

PENCA (IO) [02244884] **2507**

PENDER POST (US) [28598394] **5724**

PENDIDIKAN NON FORMIL DKI JAKARTA (IO) [10355367] **1772**

PENDLETON TIMES (PENDLETON, IND.) (US) [13363755] **5764**

PENDUDUK CINA JAWA-MADURA : HASIL REGISTRASI PENDUDUK (IO) [03803936] **4556**

PENDUDUK JAWA-BARAT, HASIL REGISTRASI PENDUDUK (IO) [01790745] **5335**

PENDUDUK JAWA TENGAH, HASIL REGISTRASI *See* PENDUDUK JAWA TENGAH, HASIL REGISTRASI PENDUDUK **5335**

PENDUDUK JAWA TENGAH, HASIL REGISTRASI PENDUDUK (IO) [09835154] **5335**

PENDUDUK SUMATERA UTARA (IO) [02439056] **5335**

PENDULUM (KINGSTON) (CN/0704-481X) [05840899] **3171**

PENELITIAN MASALAH KESEJAHTERAAN SOSIAL ANAK PROPINSI JAWA BARAT (IO) [09679772] **5300**

PENELOPE (LISBON, PORTUGAL) (PO/0871-7486) [20654958] **2625**

PENFIELD POST-REPUBLICAN (US/0746-1747) [08684709] **5720**

PENGER OG KREDITT (NO) [01791284] **802**

PENGUIN ACCOMMODATION GUIDE (AT) **5488**

PENGUIN GUIDE TO ENGLAND & WALES *See* BERLITZ TRAVELLER'S GUIDE TO ENGLAND & WALES, THE **5462**

PENGUIN GUIDE TO FRANCE *See* BERLITZ TRAVELLER'S GUIDE TO FRANCE, THE **5462**

PENGUIN GUIDE TO GREECE, THE (US/1043-4607) [19481607] **5488**

PENGUIN GUIDE TO IRELAND *See* BERLITZ TRAVELLER'S GUIDE TO IRELAND, THE **5463**

PENGUIN GUIDE TO ITALY *See* BERLITZ TRAVELLER'S GUIDE TO ROME AND NORTHERN ITALY, THE **5463**

PENGUIN GUIDE TO ITALY *See* BERLITZ TRAVELLER'S GUIDE TO ROME AND SOUTHERN ITALY, THE **5463**

PENGUIN GUIDE TO LONDON (NEW YORK, N.Y.) *See* BERLITZ TRAVELLER'S GUIDE TO LONDON, THE **5463**

PENGUIN GUIDE TO MEXICO *See* BERLITZ TRAVELER'S GUIDE TO MEXICO, THE **5462**

PENGUIN GUIDE TO NEW YORK CITY *See* BERLITZ TRAVELLER'S GUIDE TO NEW YORK CITY, THE **5463**

PENGUIN GUIDE TO NEW YORK CITY, THE (US/0898-8072) [17913264] **5488**

PENGUIN GUIDE TO PORTUGAL, THE (US/1043-4585) [19481512] **5488**

PENGUIN GUIDE TO SAN FRANCISCO & NORTHERN CALIFORNIA *See* BERLITZ TRAVELLER'S GUIDE TO SAN FRANCISCO & NORTHERN CALIFORNIA, THE **5463**

PENGUIN GUIDE TO SPAIN, THE (US/1043-4593) [19481552] **5488**

PENGUIN GUIDE TO THE CARIBBEAN *See* BERLITZ TRAVELLER'S GUIDE TO THE CARIBBEAN, THE **5463**

●PENGUIN GUIDE TO TURKEY (US/1049-1465) [21140503] **5488**

PENINJAU (IO) [02240310] **4986**

PENINJAU SEJARAH (MY/0553-4968) [11643647] **1902**

PENINSULA DAILY NEWS (US/1050-7000) [17023385] **5761**

PENINSULA GATEWAY, THE (US/1066-2065) [17331527] **5761**

PENINSULA HERITAGE (US/0895-8165) [16534210] **5034**

PENINSULA MAGAZINE (US/0162-1327) [04103687] **2543**

PENINSULA POETS (US/0031-4307) [03398960] **3468**

PENINSULA (REDWOOD CITY, CALIF.) *CEASED.* (US/0888-4846) [13609783] **2543**

PENINSULA (SAN MATEO), LA (US/0197-2197) [04874028] **2754**

PENINSULE (FR/0249-3047) [09614504] **2662**

PENITENTES, LOS (MY) [05243934] **5300**

PENJERDEL CORPORATION *See* PENJERDEL LOCATION & MARKET GUIDE OF THE DELAWARE VALLEY, THE **1578**

PENJERDEL LOCATION & MARKET GUIDE OF THE DELAWARE VALLEY, THE (US/0147-5886) [03196738] **1578**

PENN AR BED BREST (FR/0553-4992) [I05534992] **468**

PENN DENTAL JOURNAL, THE (US/0031-4331) [01714743] **1332**

PENN JERSEY BAPTIST (US/0195-1815) [05338947] **5065**

PENN PALS (US/8756-811X) [11661857] **2467**

PENN SOUNDS (US/1046-0292) [20311217] **4145**

PENN STATE HORTICULTURAL REVIEWS (US) [07294532] **2427**

PENNINGTON CENTER NUTRITION SERIES (US/1063-8822) [24944542] **4197**

PENNINGTON COUNTY NEWS (US/0897-3873) [17480950] **5744**

PENNSBORO NEWS, THE (US) [13201870] **5764**

PENNSTATE AGRICULTURE (US/0889-5929) [11452107] **119**

●PENNSTATE SPORTS MEDICINE NEWSLETTER (US/1064-2188) [26234174] **3955**

●PENNSYLVANIA ABSTRACT / PREPARED BY THE PENNSYLVANIA STATE DATA CENTER (US) [26631591] **5335**

PENNSYLVANIA ACADEMY OF SCIENCE *See* NEWSLETTER - PENNSYLVANIA ACADEMY OF SCIENCE **5133**

PENNSYLVANIA — Alphabetical Title Index

PENNSYLVANIA. AGRICULTURAL EXPERIMENT STATION. DEPT. OF AGRICULTURAL EDUCATION. TEACHER EDUCATION RESEARCH SERIES *See* TEACHER EDUCATION RESEARCH SERIES (PENNSYLVANIA STATE UNIVERSITY. DEPT. OF AGRICULTURAL AND EXTENSION EDUCATION) **1906**

PENNSYLVANIA ANGLER (US/0031-434X) [01607101] **2310**

PENNSYLVANIA ARCHAEOLOGIST (US/0031-4358) [04139084] **278**

PENNSYLVANIA ARCHITECT (US/1062-8649) [20737294] **305**

PENNSYLVANIA ART EDUCATOR, THE (US/1059-3829) [24601713] **362**, **1772**

PENNSYLVANIA ASSOCIATIONS CODE AND RELATED MATERIALS (US) [25491970] **3102**

PENNSYLVANIA BAR ASSOCIATION *See* PBA BRIEF **3025**

PENNSYLVANIA BAR ASSOCIATION *See* PENNSYLVANIA BAR ASSOCIATION QUARTERLY **3025**

PENNSYLVANIA BAR ASSOCIATION LAWYERS DIRECTORY (US/8755-0342) [08526025] **3025**

PENNSYLVANIA BAR ASSOCIATION QUARTERLY (US/0196-2051) [01589423] **3025**

PENNSYLVANIA BEACON, THE (US/0745-2586) [09009472] **5738**

PENNSYLVANIA BULLETIN (HARRISBURG) (US/0162-2137) [01762056] **3025**

PENNSYLVANIA. BUREAU OF CORRECTION *See* BUREAU OF CORRECTION ANNUAL REPORT **3159**

PENNSYLVANIA. BUREAU OF EDUCATIONAL STATISTICS. CALCULATOR *See* CALCULATOR **1730**

PENNSYLVANIA. BUREAU OF FORESTRY *See* ANNUAL REPORT - PENNSYLVANIA. BUREAU OF FORESTRY **2375**

PENNSYLVANIA. BUREAU OF OCCUPATIONAL INJURY AND DISEASE COMPENSATION. DATA INPUT SECTION *See* PENNSYLVANIA WORK INJURIES **2868**

PENNSYLVANIA. BUREAU OF PLANT INDUSTRY *See* SEED ANALYSIS REPORT **2431**

PENNSYLVANIA. BUREAU OF TOPOGRAPHIC AND GEOLOGIC SURVEY *See* OIL AND GAS DEVELOPMENTS IN PENNSYLVANIA **4268**

PENNSYLVANIA. BUREAU OF TOPOGRAPHIC AND GEOLOGIC SURVEY *See* SPECIAL BULLETIN - PENNSYLVANIA. BUREAU OF TOPOGRAPHIC AND GEOLOGIC SURVEY **1397**

PENNSYLVANIA. BUREAU OF TOPOGRAPHIC AND GEOLOGIC SURVEY *See* INFORMATION CIRCULAR - PENNSYLVANIA. BUREAU OF TOPOGRAPHIC AND GEOLOGIC SURVEY **1382**

PENNSYLVANIA. BUREAU OF VOCATIONAL EDUCATION *See* ANNUAL DESCRIPTIVE REPORT: VOCATIONAL TECHNICAL EDUCATION IN PENNSYLVANIA **1910**

PENNSYLVANIA. BUREAU OF VOCATIONAL, TECHNICAL AND CONTINUING EDUCATION *See* PENNSYLVANIA STATE PLAN FOR THE ADMINISTRATION OF VOCATIONAL-TECHNICAL EDUCATION PROGRAMS, A **1915**

PENNSYLVANIA BUSINESS AND TECHNOLOGY (US/1065-0261) [25032430] **5137**

●PENNSYLVANIA BUSINESS MAGAZINE (US/1060-5436) [25032516] **702**

PENNSYLVANIA BUSINESS SURVEY *CEASED.* (US/0031-4382) [02449476] **702**

PENNSYLVANIA CHIEFS OF POLICE ASSOCIATION *See* PENNSYLVANIA CHIEFS OF POLICE ASSOCIATION BULLETIN **3171**

PENNSYLVANIA CHIEFS OF POLICE ASSOCIATION BULLETIN (US/0031-4404) [04104664] **3171**

PENNSYLVANIA. CHILDREN'S TRUST FUND *See* CHILDREN'S TRUST FUND OF PENNSYLVANIA ANNUAL REPORT, THE **5279**

PENNSYLVANIA. CITIZENS' ADVISORY COUNCIL *See* ANNUAL REPORT - CITIZENS ADVISORY COUNCIL (HARRISBURG) **2160**

PENNSYLVANIA CIVIL APPELLATE REPORTER *CEASED.* (US/1062-1822) [25537082] **3090**

●PENNSYLVANIA COMMERCIAL REAL ESTATE (US/1059-6526) [24656676] **4842**

PENNSYLVANIA. COMMONWEALTH CHILD DEVELOPMENT COMMITTEE *See* CHILD DEVELOPMENT STATE PLAN (PENNSYLVANIA) **5278**

PENNSYLVANIA. COMMONWEALTH COURT *See* COMMONWEALTH COURT REPORTS **2953**

PENNSYLVANIA CONTRACTOR (US/0031-4412) [05131372] **2607**

PENNSYLVANIA. COUNCIL FOR SEXUAL MINORITIES *See* REPORT OF PENNSYLVANIA COUNCIL FOR SEXUAL MINORITIES **4559**

PENNSYLVANIA COUNCIL ON THE ARTS. INTERAGENCY CRAFTS COMMITTEE *See* FINE CRAFTS IN PENNSYLVANIA : A SIGHTSEERS AND SHOPPERS GUIDE **373**

PENNSYLVANIA COUNTY DATA BOOK (US) [09295084] **5335**

PENNSYLVANIA CPA JOURNAL (US/0746-1062) [09673525] **749**

PENNSYLVANIA CRIME COMMISSION *See* REPORT - PENNSYLVANIA CRIME COMMISSION **3174**

PENNSYLVANIA CROP REPORTING SERVICE *See* PENNSYLVANIA FARM FUEL SURVEY **119**

PENNSYLVANIA CROP REPORTING SERVICE *See* PENNSYLVANIA ORCHARD AND VINEYARD SURVEY **2427**

PENNSYLVANIA DAIRY FARMSHINE (US/0195-1971) [05350873] **197**

PENNSYLVANIA DENTAL JOURNAL (US/0031-4439) [01644801] **1332**

PENNSYLVANIA. DEPT. OF COMMERCE. BUREAU OF STATISTICS, RESEARCH AND PLANNING *See* EXPORT BY PENNSYLVANIA MANUFACTURERS **834**

PENNSYLVANIA. DEPT. OF COMMUNITY AFFAIRS. INFORMATION SERVICES CENTER *See* TAX COLLECTORS MANUAL **4752**

PENNSYLVANIA. DEPT. OF EDUCATION *See* PENNSYLVANIA STATE PLAN VOCATIONAL-TECHNICAL EDUCATION PROGRAMS **1915**

PENNSYLVANIA. DEPT. OF EDUCATION *See* SPECIAL EDUCATION PROGRAMS/SERVICES **1885**

PENNSYLVANIA. DEPT. OF EDUCATION *See* ANNUAL DATA PLAN / PENNSYLVANIA DEPARTMENT OF EDUCATION **1724**

PENNSYLVANIA. DEPT. OF EDUCATION *See* DROPOUT RATE BY SCHOOL DISTRICT **1794**

PENNSYLVANIA. DEPT. OF PUBLIC WELFARE *See* INCOME MAINTENANCE BULLETIN / COMMONWEALTH OF PENNSYLVANIA, DEPARTMENT OF PUBLIC WELFARE **5289**

PENNSYLVANIA. DEPT. OF REVENUE *See* PENNSYLVANIA TAX COMPENDIUM **4740**

PENNSYLVANIA DEVELOPMENTAL DISABILITIES PLANNING COUNCIL *See* STATE PLAN FOR DEVELOPMENTAL DISABILITIES (HARRISBURG, PA.) **4688**

PENNSYLVANIA DIRECTORY OF MANUFACTURERS (HOHOKUS, N.J.) (US/0733-5237) [06897856] **3486**

PENNSYLVANIA. DIVISION OF EDUCATION STATISTICS *See* ACT 511 TAXES **1859**

PENNSYLVANIA. DIVISION OF EDUCATION STATISTICS *See* RATIO **1776**

PENNSYLVANIA. DIVISION OF EDUCATION STATISTICS *See* STATISTICAL REPORT SERIES - DIVISION OF EDUCATIONAL STATISTICS **1797**

PENNSYLVANIA. DIVISION OF EDUCATION STATISTICS *See* CALCULATOR **1730**

PENNSYLVANIA. DIVISION OF FOREST PEST MANAGEMENT *See* ANNUAL REPORT OF OPERATIONS AND FOREST PEST CONDITIONS **2375**

PENNSYLVANIA EDUCATION (US/0031-4455) [01779236] **1772**

PENNSYLVANIA EDUCATION & EMPLOYMENT WEEKLY (US/1056-1013) [23466597] **1701**, **1772**

PENNSYLVANIA EDUCATION DIRECTORY (US/0738-3983) [03594259] **1772**

PENNSYLVANIA EDUCATION LAW REPORT (US/0893-9691) [15717027] **1772**, **3025**

PENNSYLVANIA EMPLOYMENT LAW LETTER (US/1052-4363) [22293234] **3153**

PENNSYLVANIA ENERGY (US) [17811489] **1952**

●PENNSYLVANIA ENVIRONMENTAL COMPLIANCE UPDATE (US/1072-9143) [29236666] **3115**

PENNSYLVANIA ENVIRONMENTAL LAW LETTER (US/1046-6568) [20478112] **3115**

PENNSYLVANIA ETHNIC STUDIES NEWSLETTER (US/8755-8416) [01939322] **2270**

PENNSYLVANIA EXPORTERS : A DIRECTORY OF PENNSYLVANIA MANUFACTURERS WITH EXPORT SALES (US) [14174069] **848**

PENNSYLVANIA FACTS (US/0894-3850) [16057215] **2754**, **2543**

PENNSYLVANIA FARM FUEL SURVEY (US) [05794460] **119**

PENNSYLVANIA FARMER (US/0031-4471) [02449487] **119**

PENNSYLVANIA FISH COMMISSION *See* BOAT PENNSYLVANIA **592**

●PENNSYLVANIA FISHERMAN (US/1057-8331) [24124371] **4877**

PENNSYLVANIA FLOWER GROWERS *See* BULLETIN - PENNSYLVANIA FLOWER GROWERS **2435**

PENNSYLVANIA FOLKLIFE (US/0031-4498) [02430169] **2323**, **2754**

PENNSYLVANIA FORESTS (US/0031-4501) [01714748] **2390**

PENNSYLVANIA FRUIT NEWS (US) [05224246] **181**

PENNSYLVANIA GAME & FISH (US/0897-8808) [17648006] **4877**

PENNSYLVANIA. GAME COMMISSION *See* RESEARCH BULLETIN - PENNSYLVANIA GAME COMMISSION **2203**

PENNSYLVANIA GAME NEWS (US/0031-451X) [01605080] **4877**

PENNSYLVANIA GENEALOGICAL MAGAZINE, THE (US/0882-3685) [06405053] **2467**

PENNSYLVANIA. GENERAL ASSEMBLY. LEGISLATIVE BUDGET AND FINANCE COMMITTEE *See* ANNUAL REPORT TO THE GENERAL ASSEMBLY / LEGISLATIVE BUDGET AND FINANCE COMMITTEE **4710**

PENNSYLVANIA. GENERAL ASSEMBLY. LEGISLATIVE BUDGET AND FINANCE COMMITTEE *See* ANNUAL REPORT OF THE LEGISLATIVE BUDGET AND FINANCE COMMITTEE FOR THE REGULAR SESSION OF THE GENERAL ASSEMBLY OF THE COMMONWEALTH OF PENNSYLVANIA **4710**

PENNSYLVANIA. GENERAL ASSEMBLY. LEGISLATIVE BUDGET AND FINANCE COMMITTEE *See* STATISTICAL DIGEST - LEGISLATIVE BUDGET AND FINANCE COMMITTEE **4699**

PENNSYLVANIA. GENERAL ASSEMBLY. SPECIAL JOINT COMMITTEE TO REVIEW RETIREMENT COST-OF-LIVING SUPPLEMENTS AND FUNDING SOURCES *See* REPORT / SPECIAL JOINT COMMITTEE OF THE GENERAL ASSEMBLY TO REVIEW RETIREMENT COST-OF-LIVING SUPPLEMENTS AND FUNDING SOURCES **4682**

PENNSYLVANIA GEOGRAPHER, THE (US/0553-5980) [02360329] **2572**

PENNSYLVANIA GEOLOGY (US/0048-3214) [00826203] **1391**

PENNSYLVANIA GOLDEN GUERNSEY NEWS (US/0164-6222) [04485068] **197**

●PENNSYLVANIA GOLFER MAGAZINE (US/1060-5460) [25032841] **4912**

PENNSYLVANIA. GOVERNOR'S COUNCIL ON DRUG AND ALCOHOL ABUSE *See* ANNUAL REPORT - GOVERNOR'S COUNCIL ON DRUG AND ALCOHOL ABUSE **1341**

●PENNSYLVANIA HEALTH CARE IN PERSPECTIVE (US/1065-4399) [26606150] **4795**

PENNSYLVANIA HERITAGE (1974) (US/0270-7500) [02449495] **2754**

PENNSYLVANIA HIGH SCHOOL ATHLETIC YEARBOOK (US/0734-0230) [08659298] **4912**

PENNSYLVANIA HIGH-TECH DIRECTORY *See* PENNSYLVANIA TECHNOLOGY DIRECTORY **5137**

PENNSYLVANIA. HISTORICAL AND MUSEUM COMMISSION *See* ANTHROPOLOGICAL SERIES / PENNSYLVANIA. HISTORICAL AND MUSEUM COMMISSION **229**

PENNSYLVANIA HISTORICAL BIBLIOGRAPHY (US/0273-3412) [07039848] **422**

PENNSYLVANIA HISTORY (US/0031-4528) [01762058] **2754**

PENNSYLVANIA HOSPITALS (US/0744-5636) [08353345] **3790**

PENNSYLVANIA IN PERSPECTIVE (US/1065-5662) [26661088] **5336**

PENNSYLVANIA INDUSTRY ENVIRONMENTAL ADVISOR (US) **2179**

PENNSYLVANIA JOURNAL OF HEALTH, PHYSICAL EDUCATION, RECREATION, DANCE (US/0279-0033) [07426460] **1314**, **4853**, **1902**

PENNSYLVANIA JURY VERDICT REVIEW AND ANALYSIS (US/8750-8052) [09089266] **3090**

PENNSYLVANIA JUVENILE COURT DISPOSITIONS (US/0092-3605) [01789484] **3025**, **3082**

PENNSYLVANIA LAW ENFORCEMENT JOURNAL (US/0161-9136) [04052980] **3171**

PENNSYLVANIA LAW FINDER (US/0741-5540) [09664771] **3025**

PENNSYLVANIA LAW JOURNAL (1992) (US/1065-0962) [26177072] **3025**

PENNSYLVANIA LAW JOURNAL (PHILADELPHIA, PA. : 1977) *See* PENNSYLVANIA LAW JOURNAL-REPORTER **3025**

PENNSYLVANIA LAW JOURNAL-REPORTER (US/0279-8166) [07319937] **3025**

●PENNSYLVANIA LAWN, AND GARDEN MAGAZINE (US/1060-5398) [25032245] **2427**

PENNSYLVANIA LAWYER, THE (US/0193-4821) [04911475] **3025**

PENNSYLVANIA LIBRARY ASSOCIATION *See* PLA BULLETIN **3241**

PENNSYLVANIA MAGAZINE (CAMP HILL, PA.) (US/0744-4230) [08253945] 2543, **5488**

PENNSYLVANIA MAGAZINE OF HISTORY AND BIOGRAPHY, THE (US/0031-4587) [01762062] 2636, **2754**

PENNSYLVANIA MANUFACTURING CONFECTIONERS' ASSOCIATION *See* PROCEEDINGS OF THE PRODUCTION CONFERENCE **2354**

PENNSYLVANIA MASS TRANSIT STATISTICAL REPORT (US) [09493374] **5401**

PENNSYLVANIA MEDICINE (US/0031-4595) [01762064] **3626**

PENNSYLVANIA MENNONITE HERITAGE (US/0148-4036) [03620499] 2754, **2467**

PENNSYLVANIA MESSAGE (US/0031-4609) [04105127] **4392**

PENNSYLVANIA MINUTEMAN, THE (US/1051-3450) [13737759] **5235**

PENNSYLVANIA MONTHLY LOCAL CLIMATOLOGICAL DATA. MICROFORM (US) [10857379] **1433**

PENNSYLVANIA MUNICIPAL AUTHORITIES DIRECTORY *See* DIRECTORY OF MUNICIPAL AUTHORITIES IN PENNSYLVANIA **4644**

PENNSYLVANIA MUSIC EDUCATORS ASSOCIATION *See* PMEA NEWS **4146**

PENNSYLVANIA NATURALIST, THE (US/0164-7822) [04351816] **4170**

PENNSYLVANIA NURSE, THE (US/0031-4617) [02449507] **3866**

PENNSYLVANIA. OFFICE OF THE AUDITOR GENERAL *See* FISCAL REPORT FOR THE FISCAL PERIOD ENDED JUNE 30 ... / COMMONWEALTH OF PENNSYLVANIA, OFFICE OF THE AUDITOR GENERAL **4726**

PENNSYLVANIA ORCHARD AND VINEYARD SURVEY (US/0090-0737) [01784682] 181, **2427**

●PENNSYLVANIA PERSONAL INJURY REPORTER (US/1067-2400) [27166050] **3025**

PENNSYLVANIA PHARMACIST (US/0031-4633) [02449512] **4319**

PENNSYLVANIA POLICE CRIMINAL LAW BULLETIN, THE (US/0098-7174) [02240913] **3171**

PENNSYLVANIA POLITICAL REPORT *See* PENNSYLVANIA REPORT **4673**

PENNSYLVANIA PUBLIC EMPLOYEE REPORTER (US) [04636060] **1701**

PENNSYLVANIA QUERIES (US/1044-6915) [17928004] **2467**

●PENNSYLVANIA REAL ESTATE (US/1059-6534) [24656709] **4842**

PENNSYLVANIA RECREATION & PARKS (US/0742-793X) [10442509] **4707**

PENNSYLVANIA REPORT (US) [15116627] **4673**

PENNSYLVANIA REPORTER (US/0745-8037) [05825551] **3025**

PENNSYLVANIA RESEARCHER, THE *CEASED.* (US/0048-3249) [04105255] **3025**

PENNSYLVANIA REVIEW (PITTSBURGH, PA.), THE (US/8756-5668) [11630540] 3350, **3423**

PENNSYLVANIA RULES OF COURT. FEDERAL (US/1047-5087) [18302872] **3142**

PENNSYLVANIA SCHOOL LAWS & RULES ANNOTATED (US) [22647468] 1772, **3025**

PENNSYLVANIA SCHOOL STUDY COUNCIL. OFFICE OF MANAGEMENT INFORMATION *See* ANNUAL FINANCIAL ANALYSIS FOR PENNSYLVANIA SCHOOLS **1860**

PENNSYLVANIA SPEECH COMMUNICATION ANNUAL, THE (US/0889-5570) [05393272] **1119**

PENNSYLVANIA SPORTSMAN, THE (US/0274-6336) [06493651] 4912, **4877**

PENNSYLVANIA. STATE CENTER FOR HEALTH STATISTICS AND RESEARCH *See* STATISTICAL NEWS **4811**

PENNSYLVANIA. STATE HORSE RACING COMMISSION *See* ANNUAL REPORT, HORSE RACING, HARNESS RACING **2797**

PENNSYLVANIA STATE PARKS / PENNSYLVANIA DEPARTMENT OF ENVIRONMENTAL RESOURCES, BUREAU OF STATE PARKS, ENVIRONMENTAL EDUCATION AND INTERPRETIVE SECTION (US) [22940122] **4707**

PENNSYLVANIA STATE PLAN, DEVELOPMENTAL DISABILITIES SERVICES AND FACILITIES CONSTRUCTION ACT OF 1970 *See* STATE PLAN FOR DEVELOPMENTAL DISABILITIES (HARRISBURG, PA.) **4688**

PENNSYLVANIA STATE PLAN FOR THE ADMINISTRATION OF VOCATIONAL-TECHNICAL EDUCATION PROGRAMS, A (US/0091-5114) [01786972] **1915**

PENNSYLVANIA STATE PLAN VOCATIONAL-TECHNICAL EDUCATION PROGRAMS (US) [06473438] **1915**

PENNSYLVANIA. STATE POLICE. BUREAU OF RESEARCH AND DEVELOPMENT *See* UNIFORM CRIME REPORTS, COMMONWEALTH OF PENNSYLVANIA **3084**

PENNSYLVANIA STATE UNIVERSITY. AGRICULTURAL EXPERIMENT STATION *See* BULLETIN - PENNSYLVANIA STATE UNIVERSITY, COLLEGE OF AGRICULTURE, AGRICULTURAL EXPERIMENT STATION **70**

PENNSYLVANIA STATE UNIVERSITY. COLLEGE OF EARTH AND MINERAL SCIENCE *See* DIRECTORY OF ALUMNI / PENNSYLVANIA STATE UNIVERSITY, COLLEGE OF EARTH AND MINERAL SCIENCES **1101**

PENNSYLVANIA STATE UNIVERSITY. COLLEGE OF EARTH AND MINERAL SCIENCES *See* ALUMNI DIRECTORY / PENNSTATE COLLEGE OF EARTH AND MINERAL SCIENCES **1099**

PENNSYLVANIA STATE UNIVERSITY. COLLEGE OF SCIENCE *See* COLLEGE OF SCIENCE ALUMNI DIRECTORY, THE PENNSYLVANIA STATE UNIVERSITY **1101**

PENNSYLVANIA STATE UNIVERSITY. INSTITUTE OF RESEARCH ON LAND AND WATER RESOURCES *See* RESEARCH PUBLICATION **2203**

PENNSYLVANIA STATISTICAL ABSTRACT *See* PENNSYLVANIA ABSTRACT / PREPARED BY THE PENNSYLVANIA STATE DATA CENTER **5335**

PENNSYLVANIA STOCKMAN AND FARMER *See* PENNSYLVANIA FARMER **119**

PENNSYLVANIA TAX COMPENDIUM (US) [10599932] **4740**

PENNSYLVANIA TAX HANDBOOK (US) [11229833] 4740, **3025**

●PENNSYLVANIA TECHNOLOGY DIRECTORY (US) [24594527] **5137**

PENNSYLVANIA TOWNSHIP NEWS *See* PA. TOWNSHIP NEWS **4672**

PENNSYLVANIA TRANSPORTATION INSTITUTE *See* STATUS REPORT - PENNSYLVANIA TRANSPORTATION INSTITUTE **5444**

PENNSYLVANIA TRIAL LAWYERS ASSOCIATION. PERSONAL INJURY REPORTER *See* PENNSYLVANIA PERSONAL INJURY REPORTER **3025**

PENNSYLVANIA. UNIVERSITY. BOARD OF TRUSTEES *See* MINUTES OF THE TRUSTEES OF THE COLLEGE, ACADEMY AND CHARITABLE SCHOOLS, UNIVERSITY OF PENNSYLVANIA **1866**

PENNSYLVANIA WORK INJURIES (US/0148-821X) [03372616] **2868**

PENNSYLVANIA WORKERS' COMPENSATION LAW REPORTER (US/0899-9104) [18260126] **3153**

PENNSYLVANIA ZIP+4 STATE DIRECTORY (US) [11530637] **1146**

PENNSYLVANIAN (US/0031-4714) [01774063] **4673**

PENNSYLVANIA'S INSURED UNEMPLOYED (US/0553-5115) [06159342] **1701**

PENNSYLVANIA'S LABOR FORCE (US) [17812007] **1701**

PENNY MINING STOCK REPORT (US/0743-8508) [10685667] 4014, **910**

PENNY PRESS, THE (CN/0700-9127) [03304158] **4864**

PENNY SAVER (LANCASTER), THE (US/0192-8406) [05103621] **5738**

PENNY STOCK HANDBOOK (US/0090-9327) [01786114] **910**

PENNY STOCK INSIGHT (US/1041-6544) [18820879] **910**

PENNYSAVER SHOPPING GUIDE (US/0279-4209) [07833375] **1298**

●PENOLOGICAL INFORMATION BULLETIN / COUNCIL OF EUROPE (FR/0254-5225) [30382452] **3171**

PENORRA : REVISTA TRIMESTRAL DE POESIA, LA (SP) **3468**

PENS, PENCILS, AND MARKING DEVICES (US/0739-8271) [09607819] **1621**

PENSACOLA HISTORY ILLUSTRATED (US) [10315292] **2754**

PENSACOLA JUNIOR COLLEGE DEPARTMENT OF ENGLISH *See* HALF TONES TO JUBILEE **3463**

PENSACOLA NEWS JOURNAL (US) [16281143] **5650**

●PENSAMIENTO CENTROAMERICANO (CR) [26584091] **2512**

PENSAMIENTO ECONOMICO (AG) [02390950] **848**

PENSAMIENTO IBEROAMERICANO (SP/0212-0208) [08790796] **1512**

PENSAMIENTO (MADRID) (SP/0031-4749) [01585663] **4354**

PENSAMIENTO PROPIO : BOLETIN DE INFORMACION Y ANALISIS (NQ) [09957496] **1512**

PENSAMIENTOS (US) [06186248] **4607**

PENSE PROGRESS (CN/0715-5735) [09502227] **5792**

PENSEE (FR/0031-4773) [01644633] **2521**

PENSEE CATHOLIQUE, LA (FR/0031-4781) [05934171] 4354, **5034**

PENSEE DE BAGOT (CN/0826-2276) [10852415] **5792**

PENSEE (PORTLAND) (US/0098-776X) [02241221] **5137**

PENSIERO ECONOMICO MODERNO (IT) **1594**

PENSIERO MAZZINIANO, IL (IT) [20716764] **4487**

PENSIERO POLITICO, IL (IT/0031-4846) [02788399] **4487**

PENSIOEN BULLETIN (NE) **802**

PENSION AND PROFIT SHARING PLANS FOR SMALL & MEDIUM SIZE BUSINESS (US/0742-7085) [10416260] **703**

PENSION BENEFIT GUARANTY CORPORATION *See* ANALYSIS OF SINGLE EMPLOYER DEFINED BENEFIT PLAN TERMINATIONS **1643**

PENSION BENEFIT GUARANTY CORPORATION *See* ACTUARIAL TABLES EFFECTIVE FOR TERMINATIONS **2872**

●PENSION BENEFITS (US/1063-2476) [25937120] 1701, **911**

PENSION BOARDS (US/0360-9782) [02245159] **5065**

PENSION COMMISSION OF ONTARIO BULLETIN, THE (CN/1180-1565) [23258640] **4740**

PENSION DIGEST (US) **703**

PENSION FUND DIRECTORY (US/0731-5619) [07499825] 1701, **911**

PENSION FUND LITIGATION REPORTER (US/1052-9640) [20922449] **3025**

PENSION FUNDS AND THEIR ADVISERS (UK/0140-6647) [07927301] **911**

PENSION HANDBOOK (US/1042-9433) [18145517] 1701, **3026**

●PENSION PLAN ADMINISTRATOR (US) [30373799] **911**

PENSION PLAN COVERAGE IN CANADA (CN/0835-8583) [24861030] 1701, **1537**

PENSION PLANS IN CANADA *See* PENSION PLANS IN CANADA : STATISTICAL HIGHLIGHTS AND KEY TABLES **1537**

PENSION PLANS IN CANADA : STATISTICAL HIGHLIGHTS AND KEY TABLES (CN) 1701, **1537**

PENSION PLANS IN QUEBEC (CN/0225-4530) [06512662] **1701**

●PENSION, PROFIT-SHARING, WELFARE, AND OTHER COMPENSATION PLANS (US/1071-0477) [26877379] **3153**

PENSION TAX REPORTS (CN/1183-1634) [23295956] **4740**

PENSION WORLD (US/0098-1753) [02240868] **1701**

PENSIONATO D'ITALIA *See* LIBERETA **5294**

PENSIONERS VOICE (SYDNEY) (AT/1035-3615) [110353615] **2889**

PENSIONS & INVESTMENT AGE. EDITORIAL INDEX (US/0275-0333) [07074167] **911**

PENSIONS & INVESTMENTS *See* P.I.P.E.R., PENSIONS & INVESTMENT'S PERFORMANCE EVALUATION REPORT **910**

PENSIONS & INVESTMENTS (1990) (US/1050-4974) [20977506] **911**

PENSIONS — Alphabetical Title Index

PENSIONS DIRECTORY **SUSPENDED.** (US) [05197316] 1701, **911**

PENSIONS LAW REPORTS (UK) 911, 1701, **1347**

PENSIONS MANAGEMENT (UK) **2889**

PENSIONS MANAGEMENT (US) [16935785] **944**

PENSIONS TODAY (UK) **2889**

PENSIONS WORLD (UK/0307-191X) [I0307191X] **2889**

PENSIONSVERSICHERUNGSANSTALT DER ANGESTELLTEN *See* BERICHT - PENSIONSVERSICHERUNGSANSTALT DER ANGESTELLTEN **1655**

PENTAGRAM PAPERS (UK/0309-2135) [I03092135] **305**

PENTECOSTAL EVANGEL (US/0031-4897) [01680876] **5066**

PENTECOSTAL FREE-WILL BAPTIST MESSENGER (US/0745-2330) [03778638] **5066**

PENTECOSTAL MESSENGER, THE (US/0031-4919) [04075014] **5066**

PENTECOSTAL MINISTER, THE **CEASED.** (US/0279-7038) [07222851] **4986**

PENTECOSTAL TESTIMONY, THE (CN/0031-4927) [02612778] **4986**

PENTHOUSE FORUM (1988) (US/1043-0210) [19252232] **3996**

PENTHOUSE HOT TALK (US/0898-1086) [17719870] **3996**

PENTHOUSE LETTERS (US/0883-8798) [12253630] **3996**

PENTHOUSE (NEW YORK) (US/0090-2020) [01784790] **3996**

PENTHOUSE PHOTO WORLD (US/0363-003X) [02404617] **4372**

PENTHOUSE VARIATIONS (US/0274-5143) [06370682] **3996**

PENTJA *See* PENCA **2507**

PENTON'S CONTROLS & SYSTEMS (US/1061-0235) [25148748] 1990, **3486**

PENUNTUN WISATA (IO) [02245650] **2662**

PENVISION NEWS (US/1055-2596) [23129378] **1621**

PENYATA TAHUNAN BAHAGIAN PARIT DAN TALIAIR, KEMENTERIAN PERTANIAN MALAYSIA BAGI TAHUN ... (MY) [09640046] **2094**

PENYATA TAHUNAN - SURUHANJAYA PERKHIDMATAN AWAM NEGERI PERAK (MY) [03789268] **4673**

PENYELIDIK (IO) [01790755] **5212**

PENYULUH LANDREFORM & AGRARIA (IO) [02245136] 1512, **119**

PENYULUH SOSIAL (IO) [02436355] **5301**

PENYULUH SOSIAL REMAJA (IO) [02239656] **2507**

PENZUGY ES SZAMVITEL *See* PENZUGYI SZEMLE **749**

PENZUGYI SZEMLE (HU) [03727643] **749**

●PEOPLE AND EDUCATION (US/1063-7877) [26139378] **1772**

PEOPLE & ENERGY (US/0163-6952) [04444623] **1952**

PEOPLE & PERSPECTIVES (CN/0381-7075) [03412291] **881**

PEOPLE AND PRACTICE (CN) 2285, **2792**

PEOPLE AND PROJECTS (RH) [02735386] **5253**

●PEOPLE & THE PLANET / IPPF, UNFPA, IUCN (UK/0968-1655) [25968974] 2220, **4556**

PEOPLE, ANIMALS, ENVIRONMENT *See* INTERACTIONS / DELTA SOCIETY **4286**

PEOPLE (AUSTRALIAN EDITION) (AT) **2511**

PEOPLE (CHICAGO. 1974) (US/0093-7673) [01792449] **2543**

PEOPLE DYNAMICS (SA/1019-6196) [29607002] **944**

PEOPLE (ENGLISH ED.) **CEASED.** (UK/0301-5645) [01792302] **590**

●PEOPLE FOR A NEW SYSTEM (US) [27052182] **4544**

PEOPLE FOR THE AMERICAN WAY *See* QUARTERLY REPORT / PEOPLE FOR THE AMERICAN WAY **4512**

PEOPLE IN POLITICS (SA) **4487**

PEOPLE IN POWER (UK) **4531**

PEOPLE IN THE NEWS (US/1062-2713) [25565165] **434**

PEOPLE OF ACTION (CN/1189-0347) [25351907] **2179**

PEOPLE OF DESTINY (US/1050-8597) [19367314] **4986**

PEOPLE OF GOD/ SERVING THE MULTI-CULTURED PEOPLE OF THE ARCHDIOCESE OF SANTA FE (US) **5034**

PEOPLE OF NEPAL : A RESEARCH AND DIGESTIVE QUARTERLY JOURNAL OF NEPAL SOCIOLOGY (NP) [25755086] **5253**

PEOPLE (PALO ALTO. 1979), THE **SUSPENDED.** (US/0199-350X) [05809590] **4544**

PEOPLE POWER (US/0148-0030) [03262871] **1298**

●PEOPLE, PROPERTY, PROSPECTS (US/1058-5664) [24329931] **1512**

PEOPLE (RALEIGH) (US/0145-2932) [02720837] **5301**

PEOPLE (RENO) (US/0146-6593) [02996370] **4795**

PEOPLE SEARCHING NEWS (US/1047-6598) [16151757] **5301**

PEOPLE (ST. PAUL) (US/0094-8462) [01794074] **5301**

PEOPLE, THE (SE) [06499809] **2642**

●PEOPLE TRENDS (US/1065-0253) [26485568] **881**

PEOPLE (VANCOUVER) (CN/1181-9626) [24280594] **1512**

PEOPLE WITH SPECIAL NEEDS **CEASED.** (US/0731-566X) [08215055] **1883**

PEOPLES' APPALACHIA (US/0079-0737) [01788397] **1578**

PEOPLE'S CLASSIFIEDS, THE (CN/0822-9163) [10676880] **848**

PEOPLE'S CULTURE (KANSAS CITY, KAN.) (US/1071-7250) [24928158] **4544**

PEOPLE'S DAILY GRAPHIC *See* DAILY GRAPHIC **5802**

PEOPLE'S DEMOCRACY (II) [01774582] **4545**

PEOPLE'S FOLK DANCE DIRECTORY (US/0160-5550) [03690200] **1314**

PEOPLE'S FOREST, THE (CN/0317-1388) [02247795] **2390**

PEOPLE'S KOREA, THE (JA/0031-5036) [01588136] **5805**

PEOPLE'S REPUBLIC OF CHINA BIOGRAPHICAL APPEARANCES (US/0145-7586) [02806027] **4673**

PEOPLE'S REPUBLIC OF CHINA YEAR-BOOK (CC) [10612022] **2662**

PEOPLES SECTOR (II) [01784180] 4673, **703**

PEOPLE'S VOICE (ROME, ITALY) (UK) [13273241] **4487**

PEOPLE'S WEEKLY WORLD (US) [22607888] **2491**

PEOPLE'S WEEKLY WORLD [MICROFORM] (US) [23379341] **5720**

PEOPLE'S WORLD (BERKELEY) (US/0031-5044) [01608328] **5638**

PEOPLE'S YELLOW PAGES OF AMERICA (US/0097-255X) [01790807] **5301**

PEOPLING OF THE BRITISH PERIPHERIES IN THE EIGHTEENTH CENTURY, THE (AT) [21359087] **2625**

PEP (MAMARONECK, N.Y.) (US/0031-5060) [10677646] **4864**

PEPPERDINE LAW REVIEW (US/0092-430X) [01789808] **3026**

PEPTIDE AND PROTEIN REVIEWS **CEASED.** (US/0731-1753) [08129876] **492**

PEPTIDE CHEMISTRY : PROCEEDINGS OF THE ... SYMPOSIUM OF PEPTIDE CHEMISTRY (JA/0388-3698) [10386384] **988**

PEPTIDE HORMONE RECEPTORS (UK/0268-1552) [02681552] **492**

PEPTIDE INFORMATION / PEPTIDE INSTITUTE, PROTEIN RESEARCH FOUNDATION (JA/0385-8847) [08982703] **1046**

PEPTIDE RESEARCH (US/1040-5704) [18182228] **1046**

PEPTIDE SCIENCES (US/1069-2630) [27965837] **988**

PEPTIDES (NEW YORK, N.Y. : 1980) (US/0196-9781) [05926089] 3747, **492**

PEPTIDES. SUPPLEMENTS (US) **988**

PEQUOD (US/0149-0516) [02746565] **3423**

PER LA FILOSOFIA (IT) [15514165] **4354**

PER LEERLING BESCHIKBAAR GESTELDE BEDRAGEN VOOR HET LAGER ONDERWIJS **CEASED.** (NE) [01796615] **1772**

PERABA (IO) [01795474] **5034**

PERADARSTVO (YU/0031-6792) [I00316792] **119**

PERAK. SURUHANJAYA PERKHIDMATAN AWAM *See* PENYATA TAHUNAN - SURUHANJAYA PERKHIDMATAN AWAM NEGERI PERAK **4673**

PERAKLIT, HA- (IS) [05760166] **3026**

PERANGKAAN PERTANIAN SARAWAK (MY) [07106737] 119, **155**

PERANGKAAN TAHUNAN PERIKANAN (MY/0126-8856) [01795570] 2310, **2317**

PERATURAN DAERAH DAERAH ISTIMEWA YOGYAKARTA (IO) [02310744] **3026**

PERCENTAGE OF LINE ITEMS OF GENERAL FUND BUDGETS FOR USD'S (US) [04572245] **1868**

PERCEPTION & PSYCHOPHYSICS (US/0031-5117) [01762090] **4607**

PERCEPTION (LONDON) (UK/0301-0066) [01788163] 3626, **4607**

PERCEPTION (OTTAWA) (CN/0704-5263) [03369282] **5301**

PERCEPTIONS (MILLBURN, N.J.) (US) [09244484] **1883**

PERCEPTIONS (TOLEDO, OH.) (US/1070-0358) [28239728] **3423**

PERCEPTUAL AND MOTOR SKILLS (US/0031-5125) [04704366] **4607**

PERCUSSION NEWS / P.A.S. PERCUSSIVE ARTS SOCIETY, (US) [15097236] **4145**

PERCUSSIONER INTERNATIONAL AUDIO MAGAZINE (US/0743-8621) [10690826] **5318**

PERCUSSIVE NOTES (US/0553-6502) [01762096] **4145**

PERDESI PANJAB (CN/0708-9503) [05257159] **5792**

PERE MARIE-CLEMENT STAUB, A., SON EXEMPLE, SA PAROLE, SON OEUVRE (CN/1187-5429) [25423756] **5034**

PERE MARQUETTE LECTURE IN THEOLOGY, THE (US) [22154984] **4986**

PEREGRINE FUND NEWSLETTER, THE (US) [02250532] **2202**

PEREGRINE FUND (U.S.) *See* PEREGRINE FUND NEWSLETTER, THE **2202**

PEREMENNYE ZVEZDY (RU/0373-7683) [04284409] **398**

PEREMENNYE ZVEZDY. PRILOZHENIE (RU) [07058278] **398**

PERENNIAL PLANTS (US) **2427**

PERES DE SAINTE-CROIX. PROVINCE CANADIENNE *See* LISTE DES RELIGIEUX ET CATALOGUE DES MAISONS ET OEUVRES / CONGREGATION DE SAINTE-CROIX, SOCIETE DES PERES, LA PROVINCE CANADIENNE **4974**

PERES DE SAINTE-CROIX. PROVINCE CANADIENNE *See* NOUVELLES ET DOCUMENTS - LA PROVINCE CANADIENNE DES PERES DE SAINTE-CROIX **4982**

PERESTROIKA ANNUAL **CEASED.** (UK/0958-3939) [19538665] 4545, **4487**

PERETS (UN) [06622830] **3350**

PERFECT LAWYER, THE (US/1049-3964) [21216688] 3026, **1292**

PERFECT VISION, THE (US/0895-4143) [16644742] 5318, **1136**

PERFICIT (SP) [02744238] **3310**

PERFIL (BL) [01788416] **4673**

PERFIL DO ESTADO DA BAHIA : ESTATISTICAS SELECIONADAS / GOVERNO DO ESTADO DA BAHIA, SECRETARIA DO PLANEJAMENTO, CIENCIA E TECNOLOGIA, CENTRO DE ESTATISTICA E INFORMACOES, CEI (BL/0103-7641) [25012192] **2202**

PERFIL DO MARANHAO (BL) [09064463] **2552**

PERFIL LABORAL : REVISTA DE LA DIRECCION DEL TRABAJO Y PREVISION SOCIAL DEL ESTADO DE BAJA CALIFORNIA (MX) [24182910] **1701**

PERFIL MUNICIPAL (BL) [07379084] **5336**

PERFILES EDUCATIVOS (MX) [05712274] **1840**

PERFORATIONS (CN/0715-9862) [10008043] **4076**

PERFORM (UK) [10632899] **4145**

PERFORMANCE (US/0006-1883) [01783886] **387**

PERFORMANCE (US) [02842807] **4221**

PERFORMANCE & INSTRUCTION (1985) (US/0884-1985) [12308960] **1773**

PERFORMANCE APPRAISALS : THE LATEST LEGAL NIGHTMARE (US) [20001754] **944**

PERFORMANCE AUDIT (US) [02455947] **4740**

PERFORMANCE BIKES (UK/0268-4942) [I02684942] **5389**

PERFORMANCE BUDGET (II) [06445181] **119**

PERFORMANCE BUDGET - DEPARTMENT OF EDUCATION (II) [06528317] **1773**

PERFORMANCE BUDGET - DEPARTMENT OF FISHERIES (II) [07492590] **2310**

PERFORMANCE BUDGET - DEPARTMENT OF WOMAN AND CHILD WELFARE (II) [07714919] **5301**

PERFORMANCE BUDGET: IRRIGATION AND POWER DEPARTMENT (II) [01797707] **4740**

PERFORMANCE BUDGET OF AGRICULTURE, FORESTS, AND CO-OPERATION DEPARTMENT. AGRICULTURE (II) [06282151] **119**

PERFORMANCE BUDGET OF AGRICULTURE, FORESTS, AND CO-OPERATION DEPARTMENT. CO-OPERATION (II) [06274946] **1543**

PERFORMANCE BUDGET OF AGRICULTURE, FORESTS, AND CO-OPERATION DEPARTMENT. FOREST (II) [06274941] **119**

PERFORMANCE BUDGET OF HEALTH AND FAMILY WELFARE DEPARTMENT (II) [06495053] **4795**

PERFORMANCE BUDGET OF PORTS AND FISHERIES DEPARTMENT (FISHERIES) (II) [09661064] 2310, **4740**

PERFORMANCE BUDGET OF REVENUE DEPARTMENT - GUJARAT, INDIA (STATE) (II) [06452216] **4740**

PERFORMANCE BUDGET ON ANIMAL HUSBANDRY & VETERINARY (II) [05002381] 119, **5518**

PERFORMANCE BUDGET - ORISSA, INDIA. IRRIGATION AND POWER DEPT (II) [03800636] **2094**

PERFORMANCE BUDGET - WEST BENGAL STATE ELECTRICITY BOARD (II) [06045038] **4673**

PERFORMANCE CAR (UK/0265-6183) [11201781] **5423**

PERFORMANCE CHEMICALS (UK) [15011008] **1028**

PERFORMANCE COMPARISON, CANADIAN POOLED PENSION FUNDS (CN/0228-3212) [06960437] 2890, **1701**

PERFORMANCE EVALUATION (NE/0166-5316) [07325531] **1261**

PERFORMANCE EVALUATION REVIEW (US/0163-5999) [03824171] **1289**

PERFORMANCE (FORT WORTH, TEX.) (US/0882-9314) [05295748] 4145, **387**

PERFORMANCE IMPROVEMENT QUARTERLY (US/0898-5952) [17858576] **703**

PERFORMANCE MANAGEMENT MAGAZINE (US/0734-029X) [08672801] **882**

PERFORMANCE MATERIALS (US/0888-3467) [13561907] **1621**

PERFORMANCE MATERIALS TECHNOLOGY *CEASED.* (UK) **1028**

PERFORMANCE MATERIALS TECHNOLOGY *CEASED.* (UK) **2107**

PERFORMANCE (MONTREAL, QUEBEC) (CN/0710-2895) [08854730] **945**

●PERFORMANCE MUSCLECARS (US) [30928991] **5423**

PERFORMANCE NEWSPAPER *See* PERFORMANCE (FORT WORTH, TEX.) **387**

PERFORMANCE OF PERSERO COMMERCIAL BANKS IN INDONESIA, THE (IO) **802**

PERFORMANCE (OTTAWA) (CN/0832-1213) [15299318] **1146**

PERFORMANCE PRACTICE REVIEW (US/1044-1638) [18712767] **4145**

PERFORMANCE RANKING GUIDE *CEASED.* (UK) **802**

PERFORMANCE REPORT & DIRECTORY OF MONEY MARKET FUNDS *See* MONEY MARKET FUND SURVEY'S COMPLETE DIRECTORY OF MONEY MARKET FUNDS **907**

PERFORMANCE REPORT - MINISTRY OF POSTS & TELECOMMUNICATIONS (CE) [06492198] **1161**

PERFORMANCE REPORT - MINISTRY OF PUBLIC ADMINISTRATION AND HOME AFFAIRS (CE) [06451053] **4673**

PERFORMANCE REPORT TO THE LEGISLATURE- LEGISLATIVE BUDGET BOARD (US/0360-9405) [02242580] **4673**

PERFORMANCE REVIEW (II) [22871883] **4740**

PERFORMANCE REVIEW (RESTON, VA.), THE (US/0882-3480) [11807950] **1199**

PERFORMANCE STREET CAR (AT) **5423**

PERFORMANCE (TORONTO) (CN/0229-7965) [08364072] **387**

PERFORMANCE (VANIER) (CN/0832-8196) [16457859] 2600, **4912**

PERFORMANCES MARSEILLE (FR/0996-5882) [l09965882] **1773**

PERFORMER / PROGRAM MAGAZINE *See* TRAVELOGUE MAGAZINE **5497**

PERFORMER (TORONTO) (CN/1193-3968) [27019148] **1314**

PERFORMING ARTS & ENTERTAINMENT IN CANADA (CN/1185-3433) [23978985] **387**

PERFORMING ARTS BIOGRAPHY MASTER INDEX (US) [08402696] **387**

PERFORMING ARTS COUNCIL, O.F.S *See* SUKOVS-NUUS **388**

PERFORMING ARTS FORUM (US/0739-1161) [08058415] **387**

●PERFORMING ARTS HEALTH NEWS (US/1065-6642) [26668139] **4795**

PERFORMING ARTS (HOUSTON) (US/0192-4192) [05065970] **387**

PERFORMING ARTS IDEABOOKS (US/0730-9031) [08093924] **387**

PERFORMING ARTS JOURNAL (US/0735-8393) [03946138] **387**

PERFORMING ARTS (LOS ANGELES EDITION) *CEASED.* (US/0031-5222) [03404641] **387**

PERFORMING ARTS (NEWSBANK, INC.) (US) [11578394] **387**

PERFORMING ARTS RESOURCES (US/0360-3814) [02242981] **387**

PERFORMING ARTS (SINGAPORE) (SI/0217-4820) [11553738] **387**

PERFORMING ARTS / STATISTICS CANADA, EDUCATION, CULTURE AND TOURISM DIVISION (CN/0838-4452) [19545597] 387, **334**

●PERFORMING ARTS STUDIES (US/1068-8153) [27820271] **387**

PERFORMING WOMAN, THE (US/0191-1554) [04790575] 5564, **4145**

PERFUMER & FLAVORIST (US/0272-2666) [06751162] **1028**

PERFUMERY & ESSENTIAL OIL RECORD. YEAR BOOK, THE (UK) [20919969] **405**

PERFUSION (UK/0267-6591) [13390594] **3709**

PERFUSION : DURCHBLUTUNGSSTORUNGEN UND ARTERIOSKLEROSE IN KLINIK UND PRAXIS (GW/0935-0020) [24466686] **3626**

PERFUSION LIFE (US/0747-3079) [10701553] **3773**

PERGAMENISCHE FORSCHUNGEN (GW/0418-968X) [05763458] **2572**

PERHAM ENTERPRISE-BULLETIN (US) [01695207] **5698**

PERHEET (FI) [10160903] **2285**

PERHILITAN (MY) [11690524] 4170, **5594**

PERIFERIA (SP) **305**

PERINATAL CARE (US/0160-3701) [03672009] **3766**

PERINATAL DEATHS, AUSTRALIA (AT) [11982407] 4556, **4562**

PERINATAL PRACTICE (UK/0893-6293) [11328571] **3766**

PERINATAL PRESS (US/0160-7219) [03736352] **3766**

PERINATALMEDIZIN : OFFIZIELLES MITTEILUNGSBLATT DER DEUTSCHEN GESELLSCHAFT FUER PERINATALE MEDIZIN (GW/0936-7160) [24625975] **3767**

PERINATOLOGIA CLINICA (SP) [07372903] **3767**

PERIO REPORTS (US/1055-0712) [23068004] **1332**

PERIOD HOME (UK/0261-3204) [07720327] **305**

PERIOD HOME RENOVATOR BUYER'S GUIDE (AT/1036-3181) [I10363181] **2907**

PERIOD HOME RENOVATORS GUIDE *See* PERIOD HOME RENOVATOR BUYER'S GUIDE **2907**

PERIOD HOUSE & ITS GARDEN (UK/0966-1530) [l09661530] **2902**

PERIOD LIVING (UK/0958-1987) [I09581987] **2902**

PERIOD PIECE & PAPERBACK *See* VIGIL **3451**

PERIODIC JOURNAL OF BIBLIOGRAPHY, THE (US/1058-4056) [24227764] **422**

PERIODICA (MX/0185-1004) [10353130] 5137, **5175**

PERIODICA DE RE CANONICA (IT) [25404839] **4986**

PERIODICA ISLAMICA : AN INTERNATIONAL CONTENTS JOURNAL (MY/0128-3715) [24368761] **5044**

PERIODICA MATHEMATICA HUNGARICA (HU/0031-5303) [01762107] **3526**

PERIODICA MUSICA *CEASED.* (CN/0822-7594) [09947491] **4145**

PERIODICA POLYTECHNICA. CHEMICAL ENGINEERING. HIMIJA (HU/0324-5853) [01586431] **2015**

PERIODICA POLYTECHNICA. CIVIL ENGINEERING *CEASED.* (HU/0553-6626) [l05536626] **2028**

PERIODICA POLYTECHNICA: ELECTRICAL ENGINEERING. ELEKTROTECHNIK (HU/0031-532X) [01909517] **2075**

PERIODICA POLYTECHNICA : MECHANICAL ENGINEERING. MASHINOSTROENIE (HU/0324-6051) [02765297] **2124**

PERIODICA POLYTECHNICA : TRANSPORTATION ENGINEERING. TRANSPORT (HU/0303-7800) [02287153] **5389**

PERIODICAL (COUNCIL ON AMERICA'S MILITARY PAST) (US) [08801176] **4053**

PERIODICAL GUIDE FOR COMPUTERISTS *SUSPENDED.* (US/0147-3077) [03136985] **1261**

PERIODICAL HOLDINGS / HELEN K. MUSSALLEM LIBRARY, CANADIAN NURSES ASSOCIATION (CN/0710-2437) [08496660] **3866**

PERIODICAL PUBLISHING (CN/0847-1231) [23247490] **4818**

PERIODICAL SOURCE INDEX (FORT WAYNE, IND.) (US/1065-9056) [15689202] **2467**

PERIODICAL SUBSCRIPTION PLAN B (INCLUDES REPORT, STATE COURT JOURNAL, SURVEY OF JUDICIAL SALARIES, AND ANNUAL REPORT) (US) [11474921] **3026**

PERIODICAL TITLE ABBREVIATIONS (US/0737-7843) [03226184] **3240**

PERIODICAL WRITERS ASSOCIATION OF CANADA *See* DIRECTORY OF MEMBERS - PERIODICAL WRITERS ASSOCIATION OF CANADA **2919**

PERIODICALS *See* ALGONQUIN PERIODICALS, UNION LISTING / ALGONQUIN RESOURCE CENTRE, STUDENT SERVICES DIVISION **3189**

PERIODICALS AND NEWSPAPERS IN THE COLLECTIONS OF THE LIBRARY OF PARLIAMENT (CN/0702-0260) [04520968] **3259**

PERIODICALS AND SOURCES (US/0272-3654) [05973065] **422**

PERIODICALS CURRENTLY RECEIVED *CEASED.* (US) [05346134] **2006**

PERIODICALS DIGEST, DENTISTRY *CEASED.* (US/0272-8850) [06970097] **1333**

●PERIODICALS IN PRINT, AUSTRALIA, NEW ZEALAND & PAPUA NEW GUINEA (AT/1030-2476) [30791735] **422**

PERIODICALS IN SOUTH AFRICAN LIBRARIES : EXPLANATORY NOTES AND LIST OF CONTRIBUTING LIBRARIES (SA) [04841369] **422**

PERIODICALS / OTTAWA PUBLIC LIBRARY (CN/1187-225X) [25313994] **3240**

PERIODICALS - OTTAWA PUBLIC LIBRARY (1991) (CN/1187-225X) [25313992] **3240**

PERIODICALS PUBLISHING RECORD (CN/0701-7936) [04129894] **422**

PERIODICALS RECEIVED IN THE UNECA LIBRARY (ET) [01484433] **422**

PERIODICALS SCANNED AND ABSTRACTED. LIFE SCIENCES COLLECTION (US/0891-3889) [11239026] 5137, **5175**

PERIODICITE (CN/0712-3019) [08867828] **4673**

PERIODICO DI MINERALOGIA (IT/0369-8963) [06618475] **1443**

PERIODICOS Y REVISTAS ESPANOLAS E HISPANOAMERICANAS (SP) **4818**

PERIODICUM BIOLOGORUM (CI/0031-5362) [02244759] **468**

PERIODIEK WOORDENBOEK VAN ADMINISTRATIEVE EN GERECHTELIJKE BESLISSINGEN (NE) [06267294] **3026**

PERIODIEKE RAPPORTAGE - LANDBOUW-ECONOMISCH INSTITUUT (NE/0921-7169) [l09217169] **1512**

PERIODIQUES - BIBLIOTHEQUE. CEGEP DE MAISONNEUVE (CN/0228-6599) [07805538] **422**

PERIODONTAL CASE REPORTS *See* PERIODONTAL CLINICAL INVESTIGATIONS : OFFICIAL PUBLICATION OF THE NORTHEASTERN SOCIETY OF PERIODONTISTS **1333**

●PERIODONTAL CLINICAL INVESTIGATIONS : OFFICIAL PUBLICATION OF THE NORTHEASTERN SOCIETY OF PERIODONTISTS (US/1065-2418) [26022833] **1333**

●PERIODONTAL INSIGHTS (CN/1195-2008) [30097594] **1333**

PERIODONTICS FOR GPS (US/1057-445X) [24038389] **1333**

PERIODONTOLOGY (AT) **1333**

●PERIODONTOLOGY 2000 (DK/0906-6713) [28479411] **1333**

PERIOPERATIVE — Alphabetical Title Index

●PERIOPERATIVE OPTIONS AND OPPORTUNITIES (US/1070-8979) [28490385] **3626**

●PERIPHERALS HANDBOOK (US/1063-1496) [25105509] **1272**

PERIPHERALS REVIEW *See* COMPUTER PERIPHERALS REVIEW **1264**

PERIPHERY LISMORE (AT/1034-0580) [I10340580] **374**

PERIPLO (SP) [05766165] **4170**

PERISCOPE (OXFORD) (US/0191-0302) [04761511] **3153**

PERISCOPE. SPHERES (FR/0298-9018) [I02989018] **5137**

PERISHABLES HANDLING (US) [05218437] **2353**

PERISTIL (ZAGREB) (CI/0553-6707) [02768638] 305, **362**

PERITIA (IE/0332-1592) [09271498] **2702**

PERITONEAL DIALYSIS INTERNATIONAL (US/0896-8608) [17309238] **3800**

PERJUANGAN (SI) [03783511] **1701**

PERKEMBANGAN BULANAN HARGA ECERAN BAHAN MAKANAN POKOK & BAHAN PENTING LIANNYA DI IBUKOTA PROPINSI INDONESIA (IO) [05106094] **1594**

PERKEMBANGAN PROYEK BIPIK (IO) [03603222] **1621**

PERKIN-ELMER ANALYTICAL NEWS (UK/0309-2690) [03562180] **5137**

PERKIN TRANSACTIONS 1 (UK/0300-922X) [01033975] **1046**

PERKIN TRANSACTIONS. 2 (UK/0300-9580) [01064266] **1046**

PERKINS JOURNAL (US/0730-2142) [07866781] **4986**

PERKINS PRESS (US/0898-1574) [17730241] **2467**

PERKUMPULAN KELUARGA BERENCANA INDONESIA *See* IPPA-NEWSLETTER **589**

PERLIN 1980 (FR/0244-9811) [I02449811] **1067**

PERLITE (US) [03057783] 1443, 2147, **2006**

PERLY'S BLUEMAP ATLAS, METROPOLITAN TORONTO AND VICINITY (CN/0820-8174) [09457208] **2572**

PERMACULTURE ACTIVIST, THE (US/0897-7348) [17606076] **119**

PERMACULTURE INTERNATIONAL JOURNAL (AT/1037-8480) [I10378480] **119**

PERMAFROST (US/0740-7890) [04174858] **3350**

PERMAFROST AND PERIGLACIAL PROCESSES (UK/1045-6740) [20213362] **1391**

PERMANENCE/DURABILITY OF THE BOOK (US/0553-6774) [02719652] **4831**

PERMANENCY REPORT / CWL/PERMANENT FAMILIES FOR CHILDREN *CEASED.* (US) [10424188] **5301**

PERMANENT COLLECTION ILLUSTRATED CHECKLIST (US/0748-559X) [10956511] **362**

PERMANENT FUND DIVIDENDS. COMMUNITY PROFILE / STATE OF ALASKA, DEPARTMENT OF REVENUE (US) [09780074] **4740**

PERMANENT HEALTH INSURANCE : THE CITY FINANCIAL REVIEW (UK) **2890**

PERMANENT REVOLUTION (LONDON, ENGLAND : 1983) *CEASED.* (UK/0264-2778) [12018080] 4545, **1701**

PERMIAN HISTORICAL ANNUAL (US/0553-6901) [04873940] **2754**

PERMIS ACCORDES AUX COMPAGNIES ETRANGERES (CN/0226-7403) [05781730] **4740**

PERMSKII POLITEKHNICHESKII INSTITUT *See* MEZHVUZOVSKII SBORNIK NAUCHNYKH TRUDOV / PERMSKII POLITEKHNICHESKII INSTITUT **5128**

PERMUTED MEDICAL SUBJECT HEADINGS (US/1045-2338) [03467406] 3626, **3240**

PERNAMBUCO (BRAZIL). COORDENADORIA DE ORCAMENTO *See* ORCAMENTO-PROGRAMA ... E ORCAMENTO PLURIANUAL DE INVESTIMENTOS / GOVERNO DO ESTADO DE PERNAMBUCO, SECRETARIA DE PLANEJAMENTO, COORDENADORIA DE ORCAMENTO **4739**

PERNAMBUCO (BRAZIL). DEPARTAMENTO DE ESTRADAS DE RODAGEM *See* DER-PE RELATORIO / GOVERNO DO ESTADO DE PERNAMBUCO, SECRETARIA DOS TRANSPORTES, ENERGIA E COMUNICACOES, DEPARTAMENTO DE ESTRADAS DE RODAGEM **5439**

PERNAMBUCO, BRAZIL DEPARTAMENTO DE ESTRADAS DE RODAGEM *See* REVISTA DO DER PERNAMBUCO **5443**

PERNAMBUCO (BRAZIL). DIRETORIA GERAL DAS FINANCAS. FINANCAS *See* DESEMPENHO DAS FINANCAS PUBLICAS DE PERNAMBUCO **4720**

PERNAMBUCO (BRAZIL). PROCURADORIA FISCAL DO ESTADO *See* REVISTA DA PROCURADORIA FISCAL **4747**

PERNAMBUCO, BRAZIL (STATE). ASSESSORIA DE COMUNICACAO FAZENDARIA *See* ASSESSOR, O **4711**

PERNAMBUCO, BRAZIL (STATE). DEPARTAMENTO DE ESTRADAS DE RODAGEM. NOTICIAS *See* REVISTA DO DER PERNAMBUCO **5443**

PERNAMBUCO, BRAZIL (STATE). SECRETARIA DE INDUSTRIA E COMERCIO *See* PERNAMBUCO INDUSTRIAL, SUDENE : PROJETOS APROVADOS **1578**

PERNAMBUCO, BRAZIL (STATE). SECRETARIA DO SANEAMENTO, HABITACAO E OBRAS *See* BOLETIM TECNICO DA SECRETARIA DO SANEAMENTO, HABITACAO E OBRAS **2225**

PERNAMBUCO, BRAZIL (STATE). UNIVERSIDADE FEDERAL. INSTITUTO DE ANTIBIOTICOS *See* REVISTA DO INSTITUTO DE ANTIBIOTICOS **4328**

PERNAMBUCO, BRAZIL (STATE). UNIVERSIDADE FEDERAL. INSTITUTO DE BIOCIENCIAS *See* MEMORIAS DO INSTITUTO DE BIOCIENCIAS (RECIFE) **464**

PERNAMBUCO INDUSTRIAL, SUDENE : PROJETOS APROVADOS (BL) [02298139] **1578**

PERONISMO Y SOCIALISMO (AG) [02239818] **2754**

PERQUIMANS COUNTY HISTORICAL SOCIETY *See* YEAR BOOK - PERQUIMANS COUNTY HISTORICAL SOCIETY **2766**

PERRIS PROGRESS, THE (US) [27823328] **5638**

PERRY CHIEF (PERRY, IOWA : 1983) (US/0746-7222) [10248979] **5672**

PERRY COUNTY TIMES, THE (US) [13348625] **5738**

PERRY DAILY JOURNAL, THE (US/0746-7559) [10253534] **5732**

PERRY HERALD (1912) (US/1065-1128) [13998480] **5720**

PERRY NEWS-HERALD (US/0747-0967) [10545720] **5650**

PERRY TIMES (PERRY, GA.) *See* HOUSTON TIMES-JOURNAL **5654**

PERRYMAN REPORT, THE (US/1047-8280) [18129983] **1512**

PERRY'S ENVIRONMENT AND THE LAW DIGEST (US/1048-4647) [20954726] **3115**

PERRYSBURG MESSENGER-JOURNAL (US/1064-2021) [10009367] **5730**

PERRYTON HERALD, THE (US) [14257041] **5753**

PERS (NE) **4567**

PERS/ALRA INFORMATION BULLETIN (US) [16505183] 4673, **882**

PERS INDONESIA (IO) [03127424] **2923**

PERSATUAN BIOKIMIA MALAYSIA. CONFERENCE *See* PROCEEDINGS OF THE MALAYSIAN BIOCHEMICAL SOCIETY CONFERENCE **492**

PERSATUAN GURU REPUBLIK INDONESIA. PENGURUS BESAR *See* LAPORAN KERJA PENGURUS BESAR PERSATUAN GURU REPUBLIK INDONESIA **1761**

PERSATUAN KELAB-KELAB BELIA MALAYSIA *See* LAPURAN TAHUNAN - PERSATUAN KELAB-KELAB BELIA MALAYSIA **2282**

PERSATUAN MAHASIWA INDONESIA DI AMERIKA SERIKAT. NEW YORK CHAPTER *See* MIMBAR PERMIAS. ENGLISH EDITION **1764**

PERSATUAN PELAYARAN NIAGA INDONESIA *See* ALMANAK INSA **5447**

PERSEA (US) [06498375] **3423**

PERSECUTION OF HUMAN RIGHTS MONITORS *CEASED.* (US/1057-0624) [19542737] **4511**

PERSEKUTUAN PEKILAND-PEKILANG MALAYSIA *See* DIRECTORY - PERSEKUTUAN PEKILAND-PEKILANG MALAYSIA **3478**

PERSI COMPONENT UNIT FINANCIAL REPORT FOR THE FISCAL YEAR ENDED ... (US) [25808046] 4740, **4704**

PERSIAN GULF UPDATE (US) [24652928] **2754**

PERSICA (NE/0079-0893) [01762113] **2662**

PERSIMMON HILL (US/0093-707X) [01793011] **2754**

PERSISTENCE OF VISION (US) [12043117] **4076**

PERSISTENT PAIN: MODERN METHODS OF TREATMENT (UK) [05071392] **3626**

PERSON-CENTERED REVIEW *CEASED.* (US/0883-2293) [12093967] **4607**

PERSONA Y DERECHO (SP/0211-4526) [02256687] **3090**

PERSONAL ADVANTAGE/FINANCIAL (US/1044-503X) [19817651] **703**

PERSONAL AND DEPARTMENTAL COMPUTING CORPORATE PLANNER (US) **1248**

PERSONAL AND MEDICAL INJURIES LAW LETTER (UK) **3026**

PERSONAL BEST (US) **2600**

PERSONAL COMPOSITION REPORT, THE (US) [13201480] **4567**

PERSONAL COMPUTER (IT) 1265, **1289**

PERSONAL COMPUTER AGE (US/0737-2906) [09120672] **1272**

PERSONAL COMPUTER MAGAZINE (LONDON) (UK/0957-2279) [25218739] **1272**

PERSONAL COMPUTER OUTLOOK (US) **1199**

PERSONAL COMPUTER REPORT (MINEOLA, N.Y.) (US/0894-3532) [16044540] **1199**

PERSONAL COMPUTER WORLD (UK/0142-0232) [05300162] 703, **1272**

PERSONAL COMPUTERS MAGAZINE (NE) **1272**

PERSONAL COMPUTING INDUSTRY REPORT (US/0275-6900) [07231625] **1272**

●PERSONAL DEVICES REPORT (US) **1161**

PERSONAL ENGINEERING & INSTRUMENTATION NEWS (US/0748-0016) [10855123] 1272, **1230**

PERSONAL FINANCE (ARLINGTON, VA.) (US/0164-7768) [04334755] **803**

PERSONAL FINANCE, AUSTRALIA (AT/0816-6048) [I08166048] 803, **732**

PERSONAL FINANCIAL MANAGEMENT (UK) 803, **749**

PERSONAL FINANCIAL PLANNING (BOSTON, MASS.) (US/1044-4343) [19763664] **803**

PERSONAL GROWTH AND BEHAVIOR (US/0732-0779) [08225010] **4607**

●PERSONAL HEALTH REPORTER (US/1061-4125) [25301681] **4795**

PERSONAL IDENTIFICATION NEWS (US/0883-5608) [12184326] 703, **1227**

PERSONAL IM OEFFENTLICHEN DIENST (GW) [10514448] **4699**

PERSONAL INCOME BY MAJOR SOURCE AND EARNINGS BY MAJOR INDUSTRY, COUNTIES [COMPUTER FILE] (US) [19866385] **1512**

PERSONAL INCOME FOR UNITED STATES, NEW JERSEY, AND COUNTIES (US) [06522432] **1578**

PERSONAL INCOME IN AREAS AND COUNTIES OF NEW YORK STATE (US) [04608503] **1512**

PERSONAL INCOME TAX IN OREGON, THE (US/0091-5661) [01787735] **4740**

PERSONAL INCOME TAX. INCOME TAX RETURNS BY COUNTY / OHIO DEPARTMENT OF TAXATION (US) [08941516] **4740**

PERSONAL INCOME TAX. INCOME TAX RETURNS BY INCOME CLASS / OHIO DEPARTMENT OF TAXATION (US) [08941487] **4740**

PERSONAL INJURIES AND QUANTUM REPORTS (UK/0965-7991) [I09657991] **1701**

PERSONAL INJURY DEFENSE REPORTER (US/1045-9677) [12573609] **3090**

PERSONAL INJURY LAW AND MEDICAL REVIEW (UK/1351-3850) **3026**

PERSONAL INJURY LAW DEFENSE BULLETIN : A NEWSLETTER FOR DEFENSE COUNSEL, INSURANCE AND CORPORATE CLAIMS MANAGEMENT, THE (US) [17725881] 2890, **3102**

PERSONAL INJURY NEWSLETTER (US/1047-8566) [01570287] **3026**

PERSONAL INJURY RESEARCHER, THE (US/0048-3435) [04105336] **3026**

PERSONAL INJURY REVIEW (US) [17022110] **3026**

●PERSONAL INJURY VERDICT REVIEWS (US/1067-2427) [27191904] **3026**

PERSONAL INJURY VERDICT REVIEWS. COMMERCIAL & INDUSTRIAL PRODUCTS *See* PERSONAL INJURY VERDICT REVIEWS **3026**

PERSONAL INJURY VERDICT REVIEWS. CONSUMER PRODUCTS *See* PERSONAL INJURY VERDICT REVIEWS **3026**

Alphabetical Title Index — PERSONNEL

PERSONAL INJURY VERDICT REVIEWS. FOOD, LODGING, SPORTS & ENTERTAINMENT FACILITIES See PERSONAL INJURY VERDICT REVIEWS **3026**

PERSONAL INJURY VERDICT REVIEWS. MEDIA AND GOVERNMENT (US/0749-6567) [11093754] **3026**

PERSONAL INJURY VERDICT REVIEWS. PERSONAL LIABILITY See PERSONAL INJURY VERDICT REVIEWS **3026**

PERSONAL INJURY VERDICT REVIEWS. PHYSICIAN & HOSPITAL NEGLIGENCE (US/8755-5220) [11355766] **3026**

PERSONAL INJURY VERDICT REVIEWS. PROFESSIONAL NEGLIGENCE See PERSONAL INJURY VERDICT REVIEWS **3026**

PERSONAL INJURY VERDICT REVIEWS. PUBLIC & PRIVATE PASSENGER SERVICES See PERSONAL INJURY VERDICT REVIEWS **3026**

PERSONAL INJURY VERDICT REVIEWS. RETAILING, BANKING, AND OTHER SERVICE ESTABLISHMENTS (US/0749-6583) [11093711] **3026**

PERSONAL INJURY VERDICT REVIEWS. TRANSPORTATION PRODUCTS See PERSONAL INJURY VERDICT REVIEWS **3026**

PERSONAL INJURY VERDICT REVIEWS. TRUCKING, RAILROAD & MARINE LINES (US/0749-6591) [11093570] **3026**

PERSONAL INJURY VERDICT REVIEWS. UTILITIES, CONSTRUCTION & INDUSTRY See PERSONAL INJURY VERDICT REVIEWS **3026**

PERSONAL INJURY VERDICT REVIEWS. VEHICULAR NEGLIGENCE See PERSONAL INJURY VERDICT REVIEWS **3026**

PERSONAL INJURY VERDICT SURVEY. ALABAMA EDITION (US/8755-6413) [11431802] **3026**

PERSONAL INJURY VERDICT SURVEY. ALASKA EDITION (US/8755-6618) [11432865] **3026**

PERSONAL INJURY VERDICT SURVEY. ARIZONA EDITION (US/8755-6774) [11433880] **3026**

PERSONAL INJURY VERDICT SURVEY. ARKANSAS EDITION (US/8755-6782) [11433922] **3026**

PERSONAL INJURY VERDICT SURVEY. CALIFORNIA EDITION (US/8755-6790) [11433951] **3026**

PERSONAL INJURY VERDICT SURVEY. COLORADO EDITION (US/8755-6731) [11433667] **3026**

PERSONAL INJURY VERDICT SURVEY. CONNECTICUT EDITION (US/8755-6596) [11432807] **3026**

PERSONAL INJURY VERDICT SURVEY. DELAWARE EDITION (US/8755-6529) [11432291] **3026**

PERSONAL INJURY VERDICT SURVEY. FLORIDA EDITION (US/8755-6723) [11433650] **3026**

PERSONAL INJURY VERDICT SURVEY. GEORGIA EDITION (US/8755-6758) [11433765] **3026**

PERSONAL INJURY VERDICT SURVEY. HAWAII EDITION (US/8755-674X) [11433707] **3027**

PERSONAL INJURY VERDICT SURVEY. IDAHO EDITION (US/8755-6693) [11433570] **3027**

PERSONAL INJURY VERDICT SURVEY. ILLINOIS EDITION (US/8755-6685) [11433548] **3027**

PERSONAL INJURY VERDICT SURVEY. INDIANA EDITION (US/8755-6715) [11433626] **3027**

PERSONAL INJURY VERDICT SURVEY. IOWA EDITION (US/8755-6669) [11433527] **3027**

PERSONAL INJURY VERDICT SURVEY. KANSAS EDITION (US/8755-6677) [11433539] **3027**

PERSONAL INJURY VERDICT SURVEY. KENTUCKY EDITION (US/8755-6707) [11433599] **3027**

PERSONAL INJURY VERDICT SURVEY. LOUISIANA EDITION (US/8755-6820) [11434033] **3027**

PERSONAL INJURY VERDICT SURVEY. MAINE EDITION (US/8755-6545) [11432453] **3027**

PERSONAL INJURY VERDICT SURVEY. MARYLAND EDITION (US/8755-6537) [11432327] **3027**

PERSONAL INJURY VERDICT SURVEY MASSACHUSETTS EDITION (US/8755-2809) [I87552809] **3027**

PERSONAL INJURY VERDICT SURVEY. MICHIGAN EDITION (US/8755-6499) [11432206] **3027**

PERSONAL INJURY VERDICT SURVEY MINNESOTA EDITION (US/8755-6502) [I87556502] **3027**

PERSONAL INJURY VERDICT SURVEY. MISSISSIPPI EDITION (US/8755-6480) [11432162] **3027**

PERSONAL INJURY VERDICT SURVEY. MISSOURI EDITION (US/8755-6472) [11432064] **3027**

PERSONAL INJURY VERDICT SURVEY. MONTANA EDITION (US/8755-6464) [11432010] **3027**

PERSONAL INJURY VERDICT SURVEY. NEBRASKA EDITION (US/8755-6642) [11432965] **3027**

PERSONAL INJURY VERDICT SURVEY NEVADA EDITION (US/8755-6588) [I87556588] **3027**

PERSONAL INJURY VERDICT SURVEY. NEW HAMPSHIRE EDITION (US/8755-6391) [11361976] **3027**

PERSONAL INJURY VERDICT SURVEY NEW JERSEY EDITION (US/8755-2825) [I87552825] **3027**

PERSONAL INJURY VERDICT SURVEY. NEW MEXICO EDITION (US/8755-6375) [11434194] **3027**

PERSONAL INJURY VERDICT SURVEY. NEW YORK EDITION (US/8755-6383) [11434052] **3027**

PERSONAL INJURY VERDICT SURVEY. NORTH CAROLINA EDITION (US/8755-6359) [11434095] **3028**

PERSONAL INJURY VERDICT SURVEY. NORTH DAKOTA EDITION (US/8755-6812) [11434008] **3028**

PERSONAL INJURY VERDICT SURVEY. OHIO EDITION (US/8755-6367) [11434140] **3028**

PERSONAL INJURY VERDICT SURVEY. OKLAHOMA EDITION (US/8755-6405) [11362208] **3028**

PERSONAL INJURY VERDICT SURVEY. OREGON EDITION (US/8755-6766) [11433814] **3028**

PERSONAL INJURY VERDICT SURVEY. PENNSYLVANIA EDITION (US/8755-6804) [11433975] **3028**

PERSONAL INJURY VERDICT SURVEY RHODE ISLAND (US/8755-2817) [I87552817] **3028**

PERSONAL INJURY VERDICT SURVEY. SOUTH CAROLINA EDITION (US/8755-6448) [11431923] **3028**

PERSONAL INJURY VERDICT SURVEY. SOUTH DAKOTA EDITION (US/8755-6456) [11431982] **3028**

PERSONAL INJURY VERDICT SURVEY. TENNESSEE EDITION (US/8755-643X) [11431873] **3028**

PERSONAL INJURY VERDICT SURVEY. TEXAS EDITION (US/8755-6421) [11431835] **3028**

PERSONAL INJURY VERDICT SURVEY. UTAH EDITION (US/8755-6650) [11433313] **3028**

PERSONAL INJURY VERDICT SURVEY. VERMONT EDITION (US/8755-6626) [11432899] **3028**

PERSONAL INJURY VERDICT SURVEY. VIRGINIA EDITION (US/8755-657X) [11432704] **3028**

PERSONAL INJURY VERDICT SURVEY. WASHINGTON, D.C. EDITION (US/8755-6510) [11432389] **3028**

PERSONAL INJURY VERDICT SURVEY. WASHINGTON EDITION (US/8755-6553) [11432529] **3028**

PERSONAL INJURY VERDICT SURVEY. WEST VIRGINIA EDITION (US/8755-6561) [11432670] **3028**

PERSONAL INJURY VERDICT SURVEY. WISCONSIN EDITION (US/8755-660X) [11432836] **3028**

PERSONAL INJURY VERDICT SURVEY. WYOMING EDITION (US/8755-6634) [11432926] **3028**

PERSONAL INVESTING NEWS *CEASED*. (US/1042-3087) [18159076] **911**

PERSONAL INVESTING (WOODLAND HILLS, CALIF.) (US/0738-4017) [09600028] **911**

PERSONAL INVESTMENT (AT) [10167151] **911**

PERSONAL LIABILITY DIGEST (US/0149-6131) [03528788] **3028**

●PERSONAL MEDICAL ADVISOR (US/1065-0687) [26496848] **3626**

PERSONAL; MENSCH UND ARBEIT IM BETRIEB (GW) [05592252] **945, 1701**

PERSONAL (MUNCHEN) (GW/0031-5605) [05845303] **945**

PERSONAL PROPERTY SECURITY ACT (CN/0821-5510) [09046972] **3028**

PERSONAL PUBLISHING See BUSINESS PUBLISHING (CAROL STREAM, ILL.) **4812**

PERSONAL RELATIONSHIPS (UK/1350-4126) **2285**

PERSONAL REPORT FOR THE PROFESSIONAL SECRETARY (US/0893-2549) [15472216] **4208**

●PERSONAL REPORT. PRACTICE DEVELOPMENT AND WEALTH ACCUMULATION FOR THE PERIODONTIST, THE (US/1069-269X) [27966488] **911, 1333**

PERSONAL REPORT. PRACTICE MANAGEMENT AND FINANCIAL PLANNING FOR THE PERIODONTIST See PERSONAL REPORT. PRACTICE DEVELOPMENT AND WEALTH ACCUMULATION FOR THE PERIODONTIST, THE **1333**

PERSONAL ROBOTICS MAGAZINE (US/0748-9315) [11036620] **1215**

PERSONAL ROBOTICS NEWS (US/0737-8505) [09462075] **1215**

PERSONAL ROMANCES (US/0031-5613) [04105376] **5074**

PERSONAL SELLING POWER (US/0738-8594) [08349600] **934**

PERSONAL SOCIAL SERVICES STATISTICS, ESTIMATES (UK) [06508489] 5301, **5266**

PERSONAL TAX & FINANCIAL PLANNING GUIDE (US/0743-3921) [10527554] **4740**

PERSONAL TAXATION ABROAD (US) **4741**

PERSONALFEUHRUNG (GW/0723-3868) [07233868] **945**

PERSONALHISTORISK TIDSSKRIFT (DK/0300-3655) [01586068] **2467**

PERSONALIST FORUM, THE (US/0889-065X) [12288990] **4355**

PERSONALITIES CARIBBEAN (JM/0553-7150) [01762116] **434**

PERSONALITIES OF AMERICA (US) [09032756] **434**

PERSONALITIES OF THE SOUTH (US) [01624306] **434**

PERSONALITY AND INDIVIDUAL DIFFERENCES (UK/0191-8869) [04965018] **4607**

PERSONALITY & SOCIAL PSYCHOLOGY BULLETIN (US/0146-1672) [02878896] **4607**

PERSONALITY ASSESSMENT SYSTEM FOUNDATION JOURNAL (US/0740-4379) [09930309] **4607**

PERSONALITY, PSYCHOPATHOLOGY, AND PSYCHOTHERAPY (US/0888-9740) [12876336] **4607**

PERSONALITY STUDY AND GROUP BEHAVIOUR (II) [08407011] **4607**

PERSONALRAT, DER (GW/0175-9299) [12699756] **4704**

PERSONALSITUATIONEN (SW) [06212021] **1701, 3626**

PERSONATION AND PSYCHOTHERAPY (AU/0253-5254) [05187448] **3932**

PERSONBESKATNINGEN I INDKOMSTARET. See SKATTER OG AFGIFTER **4748**

PERSONEEL STATUUT : ORGAN VAN DE NEDERLANDSE VERENIGING VAN AMBTENAREN VAN DE BURGERLIJKE STAND (NEVABS), HET (NE) [10785610] **3028**

PERSONEELSBELEID (NE/0031-5656) [I00315656] **945**

PERSONELE IMKOMENSVERDELING, REGIONALE GEGEVENS / CENTRAAL BUREAU VOOR DE STATISTIED, HOOFDAFDELING STATISTIEKEN VAN INKOMEN EN CONSUMPTIE, DE (NE) [10339759] **1578**

PERSONELE INKOMENSVERDELING ... WERKENDE GEHUWDE VROUWEN / CENTRAAL BUREAU VOOR DE STATISTIEK, HOOFDAFDELING STATISTIEKEN VAN INKOMEN EN CONSUMPTIE, DE (NE) [09509395] **1512**

PERSONELE VERMOGENSVERDELING ... REGIONALE GEGEVENS / CENTRAAL BUREAU VOOR DE STATISTIEK, HOOFDAFDELING STATISTIEKEN VAN INKOMEN EN CONSUMPTIE, DE (NE) [09461644] **4741**

PERSONEN-COMPASS (AU) [06526987] **703**

PERSONHISTORISK TIDSKRIFT (SW/0031-5699) [01762119] **2467, 434**

PERSONNEL ADVISORY BULLETIN (US/0164-5811) [04511788] **945**

PERSONNEL ALERT (MAYWOOD, N.J.), THE (US/1044-2189) [19730357] **945**

PERSONNEL ASSISTANT (US) **945**

●PERSONNEL ASSISTANT'S HANDBOOK (UK/1351-0614) [I13510614] **945**

PERSONNEL CONSULTANT *SUSPENDED*. (US/0161-2425) [03880568] **945**

PERSONNEL COUNTS AND SALARIES OF TEXAS PUBLIC ELEMENTARY AND SECONDARY SCHOOL DISTRICTS (US) [08099433] **1868**

PERSONNEL ECCLESIASTIQUE / ARCHDIOCESE DE KINSHASA (CG) [11721700] **5034**

●PERSONNEL EXECUTIVES CONTACTBOOK (US/1068-4751) [27688862] **945**

PERSONNEL FORUM (US/0146-597X) [02990290] **945**

PERSONNEL GUIDE TO CANADA'S TRAVEL INDUSTRY (CN/0048-3451) [I00483451] **5488**

PERSONNEL IN PRACTICE (UK) **945**

PERSONNEL JOURNAL (US/0031-5745) [01605910] **945**

PERSONNEL LAW UPDATE (US) [15875624] **3153**

PERSONNEL LICENSING; INTERNATIONAL STANDARDS AND RECOMMENDED PRACTICES. ANNEX TO THE CONVENTION ON INTERNATIONAL CIVIL AVIATION (CN) [01608239] **31**

PERSONNEL LITERATURE (US/0031-5753) [04792386] **4704**

PERSONNEL MANAGEMENT (US/0149-2675) [02518413] **945**

PERSONNEL MANAGEMENT ABSTRACTS (US/0031-577X) [01762125] **945, 732**

PERSONNEL MANAGEMENT IN STATE AND LOCAL GOVERNMENTS / OFFICE OF PERSONNEL MANAGEMENT (US) [06618096] **945**

PERSONNEL MANAGEMENT (LONDON. 1969) (UK/0031-5761) [01782151] **945**

●PERSONNEL MANAGEMENT PLUS (UK) [28909813] **945**

PERSONNEL MANAGEMENT PROGRAM (US) **945**

PERSONNEL MANAGEMENT REFORM (US) [06417143] **945**

PERSONNEL MANAGEMENT SERIES (WASHINGTON) (US/0498-935X) [01459090] **4704**

PERSONNEL MANAGEMENT TRAINING CENTER COURSE CATALOGUE (US) [03319790] **4704**

PERSONNEL NEWS (US) [07943667] **4704**

PERSONNEL (OTTAWA) (CN/0715-5514) [09498960] **4673**

PERSONNEL POLICY BRIEFS (US/1040-4252) [15227543] **945**

PERSONNEL POLICY MANUAL (US) **945**

PERSONNEL POSTSCRIPT (US/0886-2125) [12849900] **3626**

PERSONNEL PRACTICE IDEAS (US/0896-985X) [17360169] **945**

PERSONNEL PSYCHOLOGY (US/0031-5826) [01263860] **945, 4607**

PERSONNEL REPORT (US/0095-0394) [01796227] **945**

PERSONNEL RESEARCH AND DEVELOPMENT CENTER OF THE U. S. CIVIL SERVICE COMMISSION, THE (US/0148-6977) [03354440] **4704**

PERSONNEL REVIEW (UK/0048-3486) [04717907] **945**

PERSONNEL TODAY (II) [14982158] **882**

PERSONNEL + TRAINING ABSTRACTS (UK/0305-067X) [06838520] **946, 732**

PERSONNEL TRAINING AND EDUCATION (UK/0960-1619) [21613791] **3241**

PERSONNEL TRAINING BULLETIN. [AUDIO CASSETTE] (UK) **946**

PERSONNES C.L.E.F *CEASED*. (CN/0824-1902) [11807713] **3028**

PERSONS ENROLLED FOR MEDICARE (US/0730-7950) [07762126] **3626, 2890**

PERSONS NOT IN THE LABOUR FORCE (AT) [05185811] **1701, 1537**

PERSOON EN GEMEENSCHAP (BE/0031-5842) [I00315842] **1773**

PERSOONIA (NE/0031-5850) [01762127] **576**

PERSOONIA. SUPPLEMENT (NE) [05905090] **576**

PERSPECTA (US/0079-0958) [01588272] **305**

PERSPECTIVA (PE) [02739923] **1578**

PERSPECTIVA DO SAL, A (BL) [03613717] **1621**

PERSPECTIVA ESCOLAR (SP) [04078384] **1773**

PERSPECTIVA MUNDIAL (US/0164-3169) [03143037] **1701**

PERSPECTIVA SOCIAL (SP) [01789470] **5253**

PERSPECTIVA (SOUTH HADLEY, MASS.) (US/1059-0536) [24323972] **1773, 3310**

PERSPECTIVA TEOLOGICA (BL/0102-4469) [05053747] **4986**

PERSPECTIVAS DE DIALOGO (UY) [02266000] **5034**

PERSPECTIVAS DEL SISTEMA FINANCIERO (SP) [29696453] **1578**

PERSPECTIVAS EN PSICOLOGIA (CK/0120-3878) [11407195] **4607**

PERSPECTIVAS INTERNACIONALES EN PLANIFICACION FAMILIAR (US/0190-3195) [04690378] **2285**

PERSPECTIVAS : REVISTA TRIMESTRAL DE EDUCACION (SP/0304-3053) [14176048] **1119, 1773**

PERSPECTIVAS / UNIVERSIDADE ESTADUAL PAULISTA (BL/0101-3459) [11664557] **5212**

PERSPECTIVE (ALBANY, N.Y. 1983) (US/0743-6475) [10620300] **3029**

PERSPECTIVE (AUSTIN, TEX.) (US/0898-8420) [17930612] **1512**

PERSPECTIVE (BOSTON, MASS. 1990) (US/1071-4154) [23262886] **4531**

PERSPECTIVE (COLUMBUS, OHIO) (US/0745-3027) [04903989] **5235**

PERSPECTIVE (EDMONTON) (CN/0316-5388) [02247482] **4673**

PERSPECTIVE, EN (CN/1189-3516) [25796567] **1578**

PERSPECTIVE (FRANKFORT, KY.) *See* WORKFORCE (WASHINGTON, D.C.) **1719**

PERSPECTIVE (LUBBOCK) (US/0197-2545) [05758784] **2830**

PERSPECTIVE (MADISON, WIS.) (US/0888-9732) [13778206] **3029**

PERSPECTIVE (MINNESOTA. DEPT. OF CORRECTIONS) (US) [08300480] **3171**

PERSPECTIVE (MUNCHEN) (GW) [05695110] **5034**

PERSPECTIVE / NATIONAL COUNCIL FOR GEOGRAPHIC EDUCATION (US) [02253435] **2572**

PERSPECTIVE OF PHYSICS (UK/0260-4280) [03961001] **4413**

PERSPECTIVE ON AGING (US/0096-2740) [01193050] **3754**

PERSPECTIVE ON BOND INSURANCE (US) [24470044] **911**

●PERSPECTIVE ON HEALTH CARE FINANCE (US) [26776733] **911**

●PERSPECTIVE REGIONALE DE DEVELOPPEMENT DE LA MAIN-D'OEUVRE POUR L'ANNEE (CN/1186-7620) [24402135] **4673**

●PERSPECTIVE : TEACHING LEGAL RESEARCH AND WRITING (US) [26717771] **3029**

PERSPECTIVE (TORONTO. 1967) (CN/0384-8922) [02701386] **4986**

PERSPECTIVE (TRENTON) (US/0091-2875) [01786928] **1773**

PERSPECTIVES (US) **4673**

PERSPECTIVES (US/1049-636X) [21268419] **4208**

PERSPECTIVES (FR) **2911**

PERSPECTIVES '93 (US) **5336**

PERSPECTIVES : A JOURNAL OF REFORMED THOUGHT (US) [13922000] **4986**

PERSPECTIVES AGRICOLES (FR/0399-8533) [10303593] **119**

●PERSPECTIVES / ALBERTA ASSOCIATION OF REGISTERED OCCUPATIONAL THERAPISTS (CN/1193-1248) [26714709] **3932**

PERSPECTIVES - AMERICAN BAR ASSOCIATION. COMMISSION ON WOMEN IN THE PROFESSION (US/1062-1083) [24677168] **5564, 3029**

PERSPECTIVES - AMERICAN PROBATION AND PAROLE ASSOCIATION (US/0821-1507) [05982728] **3171**

PERSPECTIVES / AMERICAN PRODUCTIVITY & QUALITY CENTER (US) [19907239] **1512**

PERSPECTIVES (ARLINGTON, VA.) (US/0743-0388) [03600594] **5212, 4673**

●PERSPECTIVES BUDGETAIRES DE L'ONTARIO (CN/1188-2875) [26290740] **4741**

PERSPECTIVES CANADA (ENGLISH EDITION) (CN/0710-4669) [04843043] **5253**

PERSPECTIVES - CENTER FOR HEALTH ADMINISTRATION STUDIES, UNIVERSITY OF CHICAGO (US/0094-4483) [00994237] **4795**

PERSPECTIVES CLIMATIQUES (CN) [06132922] **1433**

●PERSPECTIVES / COMMISSAIRE A L'INFORMATION ET A LA PROTECTION DE LA VIE PRIVEE/ONTARIO (CN/1188-3006) [26290924] **4673**

PERSPECTIVES DOCUMENTAIRES EN EDUCATION (FR) [22409355] **1773**

PERSPECTIVES ECONOMIQUES DE LA PROFESSION DU BATIMENT DANS LA REGION NORD (NORD-PAS-DE-CALAIS) (FR) [05791389] **623**

PERSPECTIVES ECONOMIQUES (TORONTO) (CN/0831-3571) [14938247] **1512**

PERSPECTIVES ET REALITES (FR) [03268280] **4673**

PERSPECTIVES - GERONTOLOGICAL NURSING ASSOCIATION (CN/0831-7445) [11762723] **3754, 3866**

PERSPECTIVES GLOBALES DES LA HEPATITIS (US/1061-6047) [25378123] **3715**

PERSPECTIVES (GRAND RAPIDS, MICH.) (US/0888-5281) [13651430] **4986**

●PERSPECTIVES IN APPLIED NUTRITION (US/1070-6224) [28441374] **4197**

PERSPECTIVES IN ASTHMA (UK/0738-4688) [09495707] **3950**

PERSPECTIVES IN BIOLOGY AND MEDICINE (US/0031-5982) [01762134] **3626, 468**

PERSPECTIVES IN BIOMECHANICS (SZ/0272-6327) [06887355] **3626**

PERSPECTIVES IN CARDIOLOGY (CN/0828-6396) [13191881] **3709**

PERSPECTIVES IN CLINICAL MEDICINE (US/1049-3247) [21206996] **3626**

PERSPECTIVES IN COLON AND RECTAL SURGERY (US/0894-8054) [16259365] **3971**

PERSPECTIVES IN COMPUTING (BOSTON, MASS.) (US) [15157773] **1199**

PERSPECTIVES IN COVENANT EDUCATION (US/1070-8944) [17789131] **1773**

PERSPECTIVES IN DRUG DISCOVERY & DESIGN (NE) **4319**

PERSPECTIVES IN E.N.T.-IMMUNOLOGY (IT/1120-2556) [I11202556] **3675**

PERSPECTIVES IN EDUCATION AND DEAFNESS (US/1051-6204) [20943056] **1883, 4392**

PERSPECTIVES IN EDUCATION (BARODA) (II/0970-1575) [12642412] **1773**

PERSPECTIVES IN EDUCATION (JOHANNESBURG, SOUTH AFRICA) (SA/0258-2236) [20485287] **1773**

PERSPECTIVES IN ENERGY (UK/0961-1347) [I09611347] **1953**

PERSPECTIVES IN ENGINEERING (US) **1990**

PERSPECTIVES IN ETHOLOGY (US/0738-4394) [03567901] **5518**

PERSPECTIVES IN GENERAL SURGERY (US/1045-3741) [20082738] **3971**

PERSPECTIVES IN HEALTHCARE RISK MANAGEMENT *See* JOURNAL OF HEALTHCARE RISK MANAGEMENT : THE JOURNAL OF THE AMERICAN SOCIETY FOR HEALTHCARE RISK MANAGEMENT **873**

PERSPECTIVES IN HYPERTENSION SERIES (US/0898-6770) [17193986] **3626**

PERSPECTIVES IN INFORMATION MANAGEMENT *CEASED*. (UK/0960-6513) [21269433] **3241**

PERSPECTIVES IN LAW & PSYCHOLOGY (US/0160-4422) [03666194] **4607, 3029**

PERSPECTIVES IN LONG-TERM CARE (US/0018-4195) [02250741] **3626**

PERSPECTIVES IN MATHEMATICAL LOGIC (GW/0344-4325) [08460605] **3526**

PERSPECTIVES IN MEXICAN AMERICAN STUDIES (US/0889-8448) [14086720] **2625**

PERSPECTIVES IN NEUROENDOCRINE RESEARCH (US/0361-0225) [01984416] **3732**

PERSPECTIVES IN NEUROLOGICAL SURGERY (US/1045-3733) [20082690] **3844, 3971**

PERSPECTIVES IN NURSING (US/0894-1076) [10117531] **3866**

PERSPECTIVES IN ORTHOPAEDIC SURGERY *CEASED*. (US/1045-375X) [20082775] **3884, 3972**

PERSPECTIVES IN PEDIATRIC PATHOLOGY (SZ/0091-2921) [01783669] **3910**

PERSPECTIVES IN PERSONALITY (UK/1057-8994) [12637094] **4607**

PERSPECTIVES IN PLASTIC SURGERY (US/0892-3957) [15182166] **3972**

PERSPECTIVES IN PSYCHIATRIC CARE (US/0031-5990) [01762139] **3932, 3866**

PERSPECTIVES IN PSYCHIATRY (UK) [24625188] **3932**

PERSPECTIVES IN PSYCHOLOGICAL RESEARCHES (II/0971-1562) [I09711562] **4607**

PERSPECTIVES IN PSYCHOTHERAPY (US/0735-4037) [08917741] **4607**

PERSPECTIVES IN RELIGIOUS STUDIES (US/0093-531X) [01378270] **4986**

Alphabetical Title Index — PESTICIDE

PERSPECTIVES IN SOCIAL WORK *CEASED.* (US/0079-1040) [06257882] **5253**

PERSPECTIVES IN VASCULAR SURGERY (US/0894-8046) [16259397] **3972**

PERSPECTIVES - INSTITUT D'ASSURANCE DU CANADA (CN/0843-0985) [20114067] **2890**

PERSPECTIVES : INTERNATIONAL INSTITUTE FOR ENVIRONMENT & DEVELOPMENT (UK) **2179**

PERSPECTIVES (MANHATTAN, KAN.) (US/8756-7679) [11652774] **1840**

PERSPECTIVES MEDIEVALES (FR/0338-2338) [06911310] **3423**

PERSPECTIVES OF NEW MUSIC (US/0031-6016) [01762140] 4146, **1240**

PERSPECTIVES ON ACADEMIC GAMING & SIMULATION (UK) [04732538] **1902**

PERSPECTIVES ON ADDICTIONS NURSING (US/1057-1639) [23964259] **3867**

PERSPECTIVES ON BIOINORGANIC CHEMISTRY (UK/1062-239X) [24292815] 492, **1037**

PERSPECTIVES ON CATS (US) [10381093] **5518**

PERSPECTIVES ON DEATH AND DYING SERIES (US/0733-6217) [06574902] **4355**

●PERSPECTIVES ON DEVELOPMENTAL NEUROBIOLOGY (US/1064-0517) [26208083] **468**

PERSPECTIVES ON FILM (US/0196-3007) [05777866] **4076**

PERSPECTIVES ON HUMAN EVOLUTION (US/0090-0745) [02730391] **243**

PERSPECTIVES ON LABOUR AND INCOME (CN/0840-8750) [20141599] 1701, **1537**

PERSPECTIVES ON LOCAL PUBLIC FINANCE AND PUBLIC POLICY (US/0740-0624) [09584242] **4741**

PERSPECTIVES ON MARKETING MANAGEMENT (UK/1051-1806) [21885281] **934**

PERSPECTIVES ON MUTUAL FUND ACTIVITY (US) **911**

PERSPECTIVES ON POLITICAL SCIENCE (US/1045-7097) [20190409] **4487**

PERSPECTIVES ON PREVENTION *CEASED.* (US/0889-8413) [14086602] **3626**

●PERSPECTIVES ON SCIENCE (US/1063-6145) [26085129] **5137**

PERSPECTIVES ON SCIENCE AND CHRISTIAN FAITH (US/0892-2675) [15139894] 5137, **4986**

PERSPECTIVES ON SOCIAL PROBLEMS (US/1047-0905) [19958051] **5253**

PERSPECTIVES ON SOUTHERN AFRICA (US) [02733969] **4487**

PERSPECTIVES ON STAFFING & SCHEDULING (US/0890-4421) [14233775] 946, **3790**

PERSPECTIVES ON TECHNOLOGY (US/0893-2123) [15467225] **882**

PERSPECTIVES ON THE HISTORY OF ECONOMIC THOUGHT (UK) [19723661] **1594**

PERSPECTIVES ON THE MEDICAL TRANSCRIPTION PROFESSION (US/1066-3533) [26936814] **3626**

PERSPECTIVES ON WRITING AND SPEECH : RESEARCH, INSTRUCTION, AND CURRICULUM DEVELOPMENT (US/0192-2017) [04964582] **3310**

PERSPECTIVES - ONTARIO WORKERS' COMPENSATION INSTITUTE (CN/1185-7099) [25313974] **1701**

PERSPECTIVES PHARMACEUTIQUES (CN/0841-6109) [18903386] **4319**

PERSPECTIVES PSYCHIATRIQUES PARIS (FR/0031-6032) [I00316032] **3932**

PERSPECTIVES (RENSSELAER, IND.) (US/0890-9792) [08783673] **1840**

PERSPECTIVES (RIDGEFIELD, CONN.) (US/0745-3485) [09094051] **1990**

PERSPECTIVES ROSEMONT / COLLEGE DE ROSEMONT (CN/1183-6482) [25589823] **1840**

PERSPECTIVES (SASKATOON) (CN/0316-3334) [02103003] 1773, **5212**

PERSPECTIVES - ST. BONIFACE GENERAL HOSPITAL (CN/1187-5011) [25652345] **3790**

PERSPECTIVES - ST. BONIFACE GENERAL HOSPITAL (CN/1187-5011) [25652343] **3791**

PERSPECTIVES STATISTIQUES (QUEBEC) (CN/0712-8223) [09503748] 2890, **5301**

PERSPECTIVES, STUDIES IN TRANSLATOLOGY (DK) [28519644] **3310**

PERSPECTIVES SYDNEY (AT/0155-2821) [I01552821] **1773**

PERSPECTIVES / THE NIAGARA INSTITUTE (CN/0711-4931) [08693589] **5212**

PERSPECTIVES (TOLEDO, OHIO) *SUSPENDED.* (US/0883-6086) [12171361] 1773, **3350**

PERSPECTIVES (TORONTO) (CN/0318-3238) [02441713] **1512**

PERSPECTIVES - UNESCO (INT/0304-3045) [I03043045] **1773**

PERSPECTIVES (WASHINGTON, D.C. 1984) (US/0743-7021) [10643565] **2754**

PERSPEKTIEF (NE/0167-9104) [13527182] **4372**

PERSPEKTIVA (RU) [15130249] **3423**

PERSPEKTIVA ANGKATAN LAUT (IO) [03731898] **4181**

PERSPEKTIVANALYSEN / OLJEDIREKTORATET (NO) [11746758] **4271**

PERSPEKTIVEN DER FORSCHUNG UND IHRER FORDERUNG / DFG, DEUTSCHE FORSCHUNGSGEMEINSCHAFT (GW/0933-1271) [18029061] **5138**

PERSPEKTIVEN DER PHILOSOPHIE (NE/0171-1288) [03465145] **4355**

PERSPEKTIVEN (VIENNA, AUSTRIA) (AU) [18392961] **623**

PERSPEKTIVY (RU/0131-2278) [22619271] **4545**

PERSPEKTYWY (PL/0031-6059) [04265734] **2521**

PERSPICACITE (CN/0381-7318) [03210026] **1840**

PERSUASIONS. OCCASIONAL PAPERS (VICTORIA) (CN/0835-9628) [11104848] **3423**

PERSUASIONS (VICTORIA) (CN/0821-0314) [09938427] **3423**

PERTAMINA (ORGANIZATION) *See* PERTAMINA, PETUNJUK TELEPON **1161**

PERTAMINA (ORGANIZATION) *See* BULLETIN PERTAMINA **4252**

PERTAMINA, PETUNJUK TELEPON (IO) [02240814] **1161**

PERTANIAN (IO) [09062627] **119**

PERTANIKA (MY/0126-6128) [04431960] 5518, **119**

●PERTANIKA JOURNAL OF TROPICAL AGRICULTURAL SCIENCE (MY) [30449008] **119**

PERTH COUNTY PROFILES (CN/0828-9735) [13207860] **2467**

PERTINENT LEGISLATION AFFECTING NURSES : PLAN (US/1060-4243) [24992881] **3867**

PERU. ARCHIVO GENERAL DE LA NACION *See* REVISTA DEL ARCHIVO GENERAL DE LA NACION (LIMA) **2483**

PERU. ARCHIVO GENERAL DE LA NACION *See* CATALOGO DEL ARCHIVO GENERAL DE LA NACION **2481**

PERU BANKING PORTFOLIO (PE) [10049454] **803**

PERU, CARTA MINERA (PE) [09564872] **5807**

PERU, CRONOLOGIA POLITICA (PE) [02649590] **4487**

PERU DAILY TRIBUNE (PERU, IND. : 1980) (US) [15296474] **5666**

PERU, DIRECTORIO DE EXPORTADORES (PE) [06506811] **848**

PERU ECONOMICO (PE) [04609685] **1578**

PERU EXPORTA (PE) [01789561] **849**

PERU EXPORTA (ASOCIACION DE EXPORTADORES DEL PERU) *See* PERU, DIRECTORIO DE EXPORTADORES **848**

PERU, GUIA DE HOTELES Y TURISMO (PE) [17367646] **2808**

PERU INFORMA (PE) [04473651] **1578**

PERU. MINISTERIO DE ALIMENTACION. DIRECCION GENERAL DE INFORMATICA Y ESTADISTICA *See* ESTADISTICA - MINISTERIO DE ALIMENTACION DIRECCION GENERAL DE INFORMATICA Y ESTADISTICA **153**

PERU. MUSEO NACIONAL *See* REVISTA DEL MUSEO NACIONAL (LIMA) **244**

PERU. SERVICIO DE INFORMACION DE MERCADEO AGROPECUARIO *See* MOVIMIENTO DE PRODUCTOS AGRICOLAS ALIMENTICIOS INGRESADOS A LIMA METROPOLITANA **110**

PERU. SERVICIO ESPECIAL DE SALUD PUBLICA *See* INFORME ANUAL DE ACTIVIDADES - SERVICIO ESPECIAL DE SALUD PUBLICA **4784**

PERU SOLIDARITY FORUM (PE) [26790110] **4511**

PERU. SUPERINTENDENCIA DE BANCA Y SEGUROS *See* BOLETIN ESTADISTICO **779**

PERU: WIRTSCHAFTSDATEN UND WIRTSCHAFTSDOKUMENTATION (GW) [06257889] **1578**

PERUGIA. UNIVERSITA. FACOLTA DI AGRARIA *See* ANNALI DELLA FACOLTA DI AGRARIA UNIVERSITA PERUGIA **59**

PERUGIA. UNIVERSITA. ISTITUTO DI FILOLOGIA LATINA *See* MATERIALI E CONTRIBUTI PER LA STORIA DELLA NARRATIVA GRECO-LATINA **3301**

PERUSKOULUT (FI) [03228313] **1773**

PERUVIAN QUARTERLY REPORT (PE) [08881155] **1578**

PERUVIAN TIMES (US) [01794601] **1578**

PERVOPOKHODNIK (US) [02243643] **2702**

PESA JOURNAL (AT/0729-4069) [18462105] **4271**

PESC RECORD (US/0275-9306) [03794753] **2075**

PESCARE (IT) **2310**

PESCE, IL (IT) **2310**

PESHTIGO TIMES (PESHTIGO, WIS. : 1949) (US) [13245773] **5770**

PESQUISA AGROPECUARIA BRASILEIRA (BL/0100-204X) [04901659] **119**

PESQUISA BRASILEIRA DO DISCO (BL) [02441262] 4146, **5318**

PESQUISA E PLANEJAMENTO ECONOMICO (RIO DE JANEIRO) (BL/0100-0551) [01791152] **1512**

PESQUISA EM ANDAMENTO - CENTRO NACIONAL DE PESQUISA DE UVA E VINHO (BL/0102-9738) [I01029738] **2370**

PESQUISA EM ANDAMENTO - EMPAER (BL/0101-9651) [I01019651] **119**

PESQUISA MUNICIPAL / FUNDACAO SISTEMA ESTADUAL DE ANALISE DE DADOS, SEADE (BL/0101-8612) [08053974] **2830**

PESQUISA NACIONAL DO SUCESSO (BL) [03216646] 5318, **4146**

PESQUISA OPERACIONAL (BL/0101-7438) [21275906] **5138**

PESQUISA VETERINARIA BRASILEIRA (BL/0100-736X) [07525292] **5518**

PESQUISAS. ANTROPOLOGIA (BL/0553-8467) [02449583] **243**

PESQUISAS. BOTANICA (BL/0373-840X) [I0373840X] **521**

PESQUISAS. HISTORIA (BL/0101-9619) [02449584] **2625**

PESQUISAS - INSTITUTO DE GEOCIENCIAS. UNIVERSIDADE FEDERAL DO RIO GRANDE DU SUL (BL/0100-5375) [04898761] **1391**

PEST ADVISORY LEAFLET (NL/1017-6276) [I1017-6276] **4246**

PEST-BANK [COMPUTER FILE] (US) [22467369] 119, **4246**

PEST CONTROL (US/0031-6121) [01716238] **4246**

PEST CONTROL CANADA (CN/0833-9090) [15299039] **4246**

PEST CONTROL LETTER (US) [05730426] **4246**

PEST CONTROL TECHNOLOGY (US/0730-7608) [08057728] **4246**

PEST LEAFLET (VICTORIA) (CN/0715-0830) [07803329] 2390, **4246**

PEST MANAGEMENT (US/0744-6357) [08460809] **4246**

PEST MANAGEMENT & CROP DEVELOPMENT BULLETIN (US/1056-3431) [21434232] **181**

PEST MANAGEMENT PAPERS *CEASED.* (CN/0703-7643) [02918718] **2238**

PEST MANAGEMENT REPORT ... (CN/0710-7935) [09276624] **4246**

PEST MEGYEI KONYVTAROS (HU/0209-6145) [I02096145] **3241**

PEST MEGYEI ORVOS-GYOGYSZERESZ NAPOK TUDOMANYOS KOZLEMENYEI (HU/0139-4215) [06971570] **3627**

PEST RESISTANCE MANAGEMENT (US) **4246**

PESTALK (AT) **4246**

PESTDOC (UK) 3983, 4246, **4248**

PESTICIDE ANALYTICAL MANUAL (US) [02256625] **4246**

PESTICIDE & TOXIC CHEMICAL NEWS (US/0146-0501) [02765072] **4246**

PESTICIDE BIOCHEMISTRY AND PHYSIOLOGY (US/0048-3575) [01762155] **4246**

PESTICIDE CHEMICAL NEWS GUIDE (US) **4246**

PESTICIDE MANUAL (UK) **4246**

PESTICIDE

PESTICIDE MANUAL, THE (UK) 4246, **119**

PESTICIDE OUTLOOK (UK/0956-1250) [22409904] **4246**

PESTICIDE-PCB IN FOODS PROGRAM (US/0361-4522) [02169893] **4246**

PESTICIDE SCIENCE (UK/0031-613X) [01762159] **4246**

PESTICIDE USAGE SURVEY REPORT (UK) [09979918] **4247**

PESTICIDES See PESTICIDES ANNUAL **4247**

PESTICIDES AND YOU (US/0896-7253) [11771639] **4247**

PESTICIDES ANNUAL (II) [02339899] **4247**

PESTICIDES-CIPAC METHODS AND PROCEEDINGS SERIES : COLLABORATIVE INTERNATIONAL PESTICIDES ANALYTICAL COUNCIL PUBLICATIONS (UK/0258-7602) [10587084] **4247**

PESTICIDES IN THE ENVIRONMENT (US) [01954445] **4247**

PESTICIDES NEWS (UK/0967-6597) [I09676597] **2179**

PESTICIDES : REFERENCE BOOK. 500 PESTICIDES APPROVED UNDER THE CONTROL OF PESTICIDES REGULATIONS (UK) **4247**

PESTICIDES REGISTER, THE (UK/0955-7458) [I09557458] **4247**

PESTICIDES REVIEW (AT) [03687612] **4247**

PESTICIDES (SACRAMENTO) (US/0092-6752) [04287980] **4247**

PESTICIDES TRUST AFFILIATION (UK) **4247**

PESTICIDRESTER I DANSKE LEVNEDSMIDLER (DK/0108-2086) [10102309] **4247**

PESTOLOGY (BOMBAY) (II/0970-3012) [07259074] **4247**

PET AGE (US/0098-5406) [02240661] **4287**

PET ANIMAL HEALTH LETTER, THE (US/0731-468X) [08197903] **4287, 5518**

PET BUSINESS (US/0191-4766) [04935502] **4287**

PET CARE REPORT (US/1047-3815) [20709033] **4287**

PET DEALER (US/0553-8572) [04105536] **4287**

PET DEALER ANNUAL GUIDE (US/0553-8572) **4287**

PET FOCUS (US/1046-2112) [20362924] **4287**

PET LOVERS' GAZETTE (US/0742-9746) [10494297] **4287**

PET VETERINARIAN CEASED. (US/1050-7418) [21546349] **5518**

PETA JOURNAL (CN/1183-4544) [24570893] **1773**

PETA NEWS (US/0899-9708) [16282008] **226**

PETAWAWA NATIONAL FORESTRY INSTITUTE See REALISATIONS RECENTES A PETAWAWA **2392**

PETAWAWA POST (CN/0712-9173) [08781450] **4054**

PETER BERLIN REPORT ON SHRINKAGE CONTROL (EXECUTIVE ED.), THE (US/0890-250X) [14204412] **1621**

PETER BERLIN REPORT ON SHRINKAGE CONTROL (STORE MANAGERS ED.), THE (US/0890-2496) [14204689] **1621**

PETER DAG INVESTMENT LETTER, THE (US/0196-9323) [05917867] **911**

PETER PAUL, INC See PETER PAUL, INC. ANNUAL REPORT **703**

PETER PAUL, INC. ANNUAL REPORT (US) [02723819] **703**

PETER WILLCOCKS SOCIETY See JOURNAL - THE PETER WILLCOCKS SOCIETY **2456**

PETERA STUCKAS LATVIJAS VALSTS UNIVERSITATE. EKONOMISKAS INFORMACIJAS MEHANIZETAS APSTRADES ORGANIZACIJAS KATEDRA See EKONOMISKAS INFORMACIJAS APSTRADES MEHANIZACIJA **743**

PETERA STUCKAS LATVIJAS VALSTS UNIVERSITATE. EKONOMISKAS KIBERNETIKAS KATEDRA See TEORETICHESKIE VOPROSY AVTOMATIZIROVANNYKH SISTEM UPRAVLENIIA **1205**

PETERA STUCKAS LATVIJAS VALSTS UNIVERSITATE. SKAITLOSANAS CENTRS See RASCETY ATOMNYH I JADERNYH KONSTANT **4450**

PETERA STUCKAS LATVIJAS VALSTS VALSTS UNIVERSITATE. VISPAREJAS VESTURES KATEDRA See PILSETU VESTURES PROBLEMAS **2830**

PETERA STUCKAS LAVIJAS VALSTS UNIVERSITATE. FIZIKAS GEOGRAFIJAS KATEDRA See VOPROSY FIZICHESKOI GEOGRAFII LATVIISKOI SSR **2579**

PETERBOROUGH EXAMINER (CN) **5792**

PETERBOROUGH EXAMINER (DAILY ED.) (CN/0839-0878) [19251956] **5792**

PETERBOROUGH TRANSCRIPT, THE (US) [11087173] **5708**

PETERMANNS GEOGRAPHISCHE MITTEILUNGEN (GW/0031-6229) [06340888] **2572**

PETERNAKAN DAN UNGGAS (IO) [03285311] **217**

PETERS NOTES (US/0364-5487) [02608368] **4146**

PETERSEN'S 4 WHEEL & OFF-ROAD (US/0162-3214) [04149539] **4912**

●PETERSEN'S ... ANNUAL TURKEY HUNTING (US/1059-1753) [24496647] **4877**

●PETERSEN'S AUTOTRONICS (US/1073-4724) [29411318] **5318**

PETERSEN'S BIG BOOK OF AUTO REPAIR (US/0730-3580) [04583630] **5423**

PETERSEN'S BOWHUNTING (US/1049-9768) [21365990] **4877**

●PETERSEN'S ... COLLEGE BASKETBALL (US/1059-5805) [24639295] **4912**

PETERSEN'S ... COLLEGE FOOTBALL (US/0276-2129) [06957765] **4912**

PETERSEN'S COMPLETE BOOK OF PLYMOUTH, DODGE, CHRYSLER (US/0092-4512) [01784451] **5423**

PETERSEN'S FISHING CEASED. (US/1041-4703) [18774366] **4912**

●PETERSEN'S GOLFING (US/1073-4716) [29411396] **4912**

PETERSEN'S HOW TO TUNE YOUR CAR (US/0271-3527) [06599021] **5423**

PETERSEN'S HUNTING (US/0146-4671) [02957193] **4912**

PETERSEN'S HUNTING ANNUAL (US/0095-5124) [01790825] **4912, 4877**

PETERSEN'S KIT CAR (US/0883-5705) [11741663] **5423**

PETERSEN'S MUSCLECAR RESTORATION & PERFORMANCE (US/1068-1892) [27464552] **5423**

PETERSEN'S PHOTOGRAPHIC (US/0199-4913) [05937411] **4372**

PETERSEN'S PREVIEW ... COLLEGE FOOTBALL (US/1059-2571) [24520270] **4912**

PETERSEN'S PREVIEW ... PRO FOOTBALL (US/1059-1680) [18597872] **4912**

PETERSEN'S PRO BASEBALL (US/0148-3153) [03295698] **4912**

PETERSEN'S ROD & CUSTOM (US/1045-120X) [20005170] **4912, 5423**

PETERSEN'S WHEELS AFIELD (US) [06534777] **5423**

PETERSON CABLE ADDRESS DIRECTORY See PETERSON DIRECTORY **1161**

PETERSON DIRECTORY (US/0882-8296) [11893147] **803, 1161**

PETERSON REPORT - CONSTRUCTION CEASED. (AT) **623**

PETERSON'S ANNUAL GUIDES/GRADUATE STUDY (US/0163-6111) [14473684] **1840**

PETERSON'S ANNUAL GUIDES TO GRADUATE STUDY. BOOK 1, PETERSON'S GUIDE TO GRADUATE AND PROFESSIONAL PROGRAMS (US/0894-9344) [16319040] **1840**

PETERSON'S ANNUAL GUIDES TO GRADUATE STUDY. BOOK 3, PETERSON'S GUIDE TO GRADUATE PROGRAMS IN THE BIOLOGICAL AND AGRICULTURAL SCIENCES (US/0894-9360) [16319263] **1840**

PETERSON'S ANNUAL GUIDES TO GRADUATE STUDY. BOOK 4, PETERSON'S GUIDE TO GRADUATE PROGRAMS IN THE PHYSICAL SCIENCES AND MATHEMATICS (US/0894-9379) [16319329] **1840**

PETERSON'S COLLEGE MONEY HANDBOOK (US/0894-9395) [16320103] **1840**

PETERSON'S COLLEGE SELECTION SERVICE. FOUR-YEAR COLLEGES (US/0884-8416) [12488319] **1840**

PETERSON'S COLLEGE SELECTION SERVICE. TWO-YEAR COLLEGES (US/0884-2299) [12322428] **1840**

PETERSON'S COMPETITIVE COLLEGES (US/0887-0152) [11832597] **1840**

PETERSON'S FINANCIAL AID SERVICE (US/0884-4119) [12412387] **1840**

PETERSON'S GRADLINE [COMPUTER FILE] (US) [22297597] **1840**

PETERSON'S GRANTS FOR GRADUATE STUDENTS See PETERSON'S GRANTS FOR GRADUATE STUDY **1840**

●PETERSON'S GRANTS FOR GRADUATE STUDY (US/1058-6377) [24345215] **1840**

●PETERSON'S GRANTS FOR POST-DOCTORAL STUDY (US/1058-9287) [24433920] **1840**

PETERSON'S GUIDE TO COLLEGE ADMISSIONS (US) [07563285] **1840**

PETERSON'S GUIDE TO COLLEGES IN NEW ENGLAND (US/0742-4973) [10354176] **1840**

PETERSON'S GUIDE TO COLLEGES IN NEW YORK (US/0742-4965) [10354156] **1840**

PETERSON'S GUIDE TO COLLEGES IN THE MIDDLE ATLANTIC STATES (US/0742-4957) [10354121] **1841**

PETERSON'S GUIDE TO COLLEGES IN THE MIDWEST (US/0742-4949) [10354093] **1841**

●PETERSON'S GUIDE TO COLLEGES IN THE SOUTH (US/1069-0085) [27927412] **1841**

PETERSON'S GUIDE TO COLLEGES IN THE SOUTHEAST (US/0882-309X) [11809498] **1841**

PETERSON'S GUIDE TO COLLEGES IN THE SOUTHWEST (US/0882-3103) [11809287] **1841**

PETERSON'S GUIDE TO COLLEGES IN THE WEST (US/0888-8159) [13724583] **1841**

PETERSON'S GUIDE TO FOUR-YEAR COLLEGES (US/0894-9336) [16316336] **1841**

PETERSON'S GUIDE TO GRADUATE PROGRAMS IN BUSINESS, EDUCATION, HEALTH, AND LAW (US/0897-6023) [17562025] **4208**

PETERSON'S GUIDE TO GRADUATE PROGRAMS IN ENGINEERING AND APPLIED SCIENCES (US/0894-9387) [16319404] **1841**

PETERSON'S GUIDE TO GRADUATE PROGRAMS IN THE HUMANITIES AND SOCIAL SCIENCES (US/0894-9352) [16319155] **1841**

PETERSON'S GUIDE TO GRADUATE PROGRAMS IN THE HUMANITIES AND SOCIAL SCIENCES See PETERSON'S GUIDE TO GRADUATE PROGRAMS IN THE HUMANITIES, ARTS, AND SOCIAL SCIENCES **1841**

●PETERSON'S GUIDE TO GRADUATE PROGRAMS IN THE HUMANITIES, ARTS, AND SOCIAL SCIENCES (US) [29457657] **1841**

PETERSON'S GUIDE TO INDEPENDENT SECONDARY SCHOOLS (US/0894-9409) [16320259] **1773**

●PETERSON'S GUIDE TO NURSING PROGRAMS (US/1073-7820) [29533645] **3867**

●PETERSON'S GUIDE TO PRIVATE SECONDARY SCHOOLS (US/1066-5366) [26988116] **1773**

PETERSON'S GUIDE TO TWO-YEAR COLLEGES (US/0894-9328) [16316263] **1841**

●PETERSON'S GUIDE TO VOCATIONAL AND TECHNICAL SCHOOLS. EAST (US/1069-1367) [27943745] **1915**

●PETERSON'S GUIDE TO VOCATIONAL AND TECHNICAL SCHOOLS. WEST (US/1069-1375) [27943831] **1915**

PETERSON'S JOB OPPORTUNITIES FOR BUSINESS AND LIBERAL ARTS GRADUATES (US/1048-3411) [20921364] **703**

PETERSON'S JOB OPPORTUNITIES FOR ENGINEERING, SCIENCE, AND COMPUTER GRADUATES (US/1048-342X) [20921405] **4208**

●PETERSON'S JOB OPPORTUNITIES IN BUSINESS (US/1070-6615) [28444968] **4208**

●PETERSON'S JOB OPPORTUNITIES IN ENGINEERING AND TECHNOLOGY (US/1071-068X) [28539350] **4208**

●PETERSON'S JOB OPPORTUNITIES IN HEALTH CARE (US/1071-0671) [28539335] **4208**

●PETERSON'S JOB OPPORTUNITIES IN THE ENVIRONMENT (US/1071-183X) [28564066] **4208**

PETERSON'S REGISTER OF HIGHER EDUCATION (US/1046-2406) [20367287] **1841**

PETERSON'S ROD & CUSTOM See ROD & CUSTOM (1990) **5424**

●PETERSON'S SPORTS SCHOLARSHIPS AND COLLEGE ATHLETIC PROGRAMS (US/1069-1383) [27943863] **1841**

●PETERSON'S STUDY ABROAD (US/1069-6504) [28130277] **1773**

PETERSON'S SUMMER OPPORTUNITIES FOR KIDS AND TEENAGERS (US/0894-9417) [16320341] **4853**

PETFISH MONTHLY See PRACTICAL FISHKEEPING **2310**

PETFOOD INDUSTRY (US/0031-6245) [03435994] **4287**

PETIT A PETIT (CN/0712-8576) [09358880] **5301**

PETIT ALMANACH DES LETTRES, LE (CN/0700-9194) [03412318] **3423**

PETIT COURRIER DE BAR-SUR-SEINE, LE (FR) [20335304] **5801**

PETIT GUIDE STATISTIQUE DE LA LORRAINE (FR) [02897287] **5336**

PETIT INTELLECTUEL, LE (CN/0709-3497) [06017256] **4864**

PETIT JOURNAL DES GRANDES EXPOSITIONS, LE (FR) [04782858] **362**

PETIT JOURNAL DU BRASSEUR (BE/0031-6253) [04064159] **2370**

PETIT LAROUSSE ILLUSTRE (FR) [06024995] **1928**

PETIT LEBEY ... DES BISTROTS PARISIENS, LE (FR) [17065437] **5072**

PETIT MEUNIER (FR) **5801**

PETIT PERROQUET, LE (FR) [02878701] **5454**

PETIT PROMENEUR, LE (CN/0225-2066) [06054095] **5792**

PETIT RAPPORTEUR DE STONEHAM, TEWKESBURY ET ST-ADOLPHE, LE (CN/0710-085X) [08415756] **4673**

PETITE CAISSE (CN/0712-2705) [08867736] **5792**

PETITE NATION, LA (CN/0228-9954) [08071322] **5792**

PETITS PROPOS CULINAIRES (UK/0142-4857) [07288545] 2353, **4197**

PETOFI IRODALMI MUZEUM (BUDAPEST, HUNGARY) *See* PETOFI IRODALMI MUZEUM EVKONYVE, A **3423**

PETOFI IRODALMI MUZEUM EVKONYVE, A (HU/0524-8906) [03019311] **3423**

PETOROTEKKU (JA/0386-2763) [10465407] **4271**

PETOSKEY NEWS REVIEW (US) **5693**

PETRA (GW/0031-630X) [I0031630X] 2792, **5564**

PETRI NET NEWSLETTER (GW/0931-1084) [I09311084] **1199**

PETROBRAS INTERNACIONAL *See* RELATORIO DE ATIVIDADES - PETROBRAS INTERNACIONAL **1624**

PETROBRAS NEWS (BL/0103-5266) [04966292] **4271**

PETROCHEMICAL NEWS (US/0031-6342) [04013328] 1046, **4271**

PETROCHEMICAL REPORT (US) **4271**

PETROCHEMICALS & REFINING (SI) **4271**

PETROCHIMICA CHIMICA ORGANICA: SERVIZI DOCUMONT (IT) **4271**

PETROCOMPANIES (UK) **1953**

PETROCULTURE JOURNAL (US) [09965761] **1459**

PETROFAX (AT) 1953, **4271**

PETROGLYPH (US) [21360797] 3423, **4170**

PETROGRAM (TALLAHASSEE, FLA.) (US/1060-5258) [25019443] **4271**

PETROLE. ELEMENTS STATISTIQUES (1968) (FR/0069-6552) [01213139] **4271**

PETROLE ET ENTERPRISE (FR/0755-7981) [10035327] **4271**

PETROLE ET GAZ EN AFRIQUE (FR) **4272**

PETROLE ET LE GAZ ARABES (FR/0150-6463) **4272**

PETROLE ET TECHNIQUES (FR/0152-5425) [03527066] **4272**

PETROLEO BRASILEIRO, S.A. SERVICO DE PESSOAL *See* RECURSOS HUMANOS **706**

PETROLEO BRASILEIRO, S.A. SERVICO JURIDICO. BIBLIOTECA *See* BOLETIM DA BIBLIOTECA **2942**

PETROLEO, EL (MX) [02242705] **4272**

PETROLEO INTERNACIONAL (US/0093-7851) [01792925] **4272**

PETROLEO Y OTROS DATOS ESTADISTICOS (VE/0083-5390) [01209277] **4272**

PETROLEO Y PETROQUIMICA INTERNACIONAL *See* PETROLEO INTERNACIONAL **4272**

PETROLEOS MEXICANOS *See* INFORME DE LABORES **4260**

PETROLEOS MEXICANOS *See* MEMORIA DE LABORES / PETROLEOS MEXICANOS **4264**

PETROLEOS MEXICANOS *See* MEMORIA DE LABORES - PETROLEOS MEXICANOS **4264**

PETROLEOS MEXICANOS *See* PETROLEO, EL **4272**

PETROLEUM (VE) **4272**

PETROLEUM ABSTRACTS INFORMATION SYSTEM DESCRIPTOR FREQUENCY LIST *See* DESCRIPTOR FREQUENCY LIST **3205**

PETROLEUM ABSTRACTS (TULSA, OKLA.) (US/0031-6423) [02266028] 4272, **4284**

PETROLEUM ACCOUNTING AND FINANCIAL MANAGEMENT JOURNAL (US) [19764155] **4272**

PETROLEUM ACTIVITY REPORT (US/0360-974X) [04560808] **4272**

PETROLEUM & NATURAL GAS INDUSTRY OF INDONESIA (IO) [01796136] **4272**

PETROLEUM & TBA MARKETER *See* PETROLEUM MARKETER (NEW HAVEN) **4273**

PETROLEUM ARGUS FUNDAMENTALS MONTHLY (UK) **4272**

PETROLEUM ASIA JOURNAL (II/0970-3098) [05997185] **4272**

PETROLEUM/C-STORE PRODUCTS (US/0899-6369) [18176435] **4272**

PETROLEUM CHEMISTRY (UK/0965-5441) [25514342] **4272**

PETROLEUM ECONOMIST (ENGLISH EDITION) (UK/0306-395X) [02240358] **4272**

PETROLEUM/ENERGY BUSINESS NEWS INDEX (US/0098-7743) [02242224] **4272**

PETROLEUM ENGINEER INTERNATIONAL (US/0164-8322) [02449594] **4272**

PETROLEUM EQUIPMENT *See* PETROLEUM/C-STORE PRODUCTS **4272**

PETROLEUM EXPLORATION, DEVELOPMENT, AND PRODUCTION IN INDIANA DURING ... (US) [24245061] **4272**

PETROLEUM EXPLORATION IN NEW ZEALAND NEWS (NZ/0113-0501) [I01130501] **4272**

PETROLEUM EXPLORATION MAP (US/0277-6650) [07608549] **4272**

PETROLEUM FEEDSTOCKS IN ... (US/0743-5274) [10586958] 1621, **4272**

PETROLEUM FINANCE WEEK (US/1077-5285) [30826047] **4272**

PETROLEUM FRONTIERS (US/0740-1817) [09888951] **4272**

PETROLEUM GAZETTE (MELBOURNE) (AT/0048-3591) [08787010] **4272**

PETROLEUM GEOLOGY (US/0553-8882) [01762171] **4272**

●PETROLEUM GEOSCIENCE (UK/1354-0793) 1391, **4272**

PETROLEUM INDEPENDENT (US/0747-2528) [02378976] **4272**

PETROLEUM INDUSTRY PROFILES (US/1064-1807) [26234512] **4273**

PETROLEUM INFORMATION CORPORATION *See* RESUME (DENVER) **4277**

PETROLEUM INFORMATION INTERNATIONAL *CEASED*. (US/0730-7632) [08069579] **4273**

PETROLEUM INFORMATION SERVICE (PP/1021-3600) [I10213600] **4273**

PETROLEUM INFORMATION'S NATIONAL EXPLORATION DAILY (US/0899-7543) [09765199] **4273**

PETROLEUM INFORMATION'S NATIONAL WILDCAT MONTHLY (US/0744-8007) [08037153] **4273**

PETROLEUM INTELLIGENCE WEEKLY (US/0480-2160) [01794440] **4273**

PETROLEUM LEGISLATION (FIRM : NEW YORK, N.Y.) *See* ASIA & AUSTRALASIA. BASIC OIL LAWS AND CONCESSION CONTRACTS, ORIGINAL TEXTS. SUPPLEMENT (PHOTOCOPY) **4251**

PETROLEUM LEGISLATION, NEW YORK *See* EUROPE : BASIC OIL LAWS AND CONCESSION CONTRACTS. ORIGINAL TEXTS. SUPPLELMENT **2967**

PETROLEUM MANAGEMENT (HOUSTON, TEX.) (US/0884-4550) [12377521] **4273**

PETROLEUM MARKET DATA (US) [05037860] **4273**

PETROLEUM MARKET INTELLIGENCE (US/1047-630X) [15807722] **4273**

PETROLEUM MARKETER (NEW HAVEN) (US/0362-7799) [02337878] **4273**

PETROLEUM MARKETER'S HANDBOOK *See* BLOOMBERG ENERGY HANDBOOK **1934**

PETROLEUM MARKETERS' HANDBOOK (US/0747-5721) [08020914] **4273**

PETROLEUM MARKETING ANNUAL / ENERGY INFORMATION ADMINISTRATION, OFFICE OF OIL AND GAS, U.S. DEPARTMENT OF ENERGY (US) [15233107] **4273**

PETROLEUM MARKETING MONTHLY (US/0741-9643) [09583990] 4273, **934**

PETROLEUM MONITOR FAX SERVICE (NO) **4273**

PETROLEUM NEWS *CEASED*. (SI/0253-0775) [05065491] **4273**

PETROLEUM NEWSLETTER, THE (AT/0312-9837) [03529595] **4273**

PETROLEUM OUTLOOK (US/0031-6490) [05350357] **4273**

PETROLEUM POLITICS (US/1050-866X) [21550264] **4273**

PETROLEUM PROCESSING IN CANADA (CN/0821-8544) [09719537] **4273**

PETROLEUM REFINING AND PETROCHEMICALS (US) [03726109] **4273**

PETROLEUM REVIEW (LONDON. 1978) (UK/0020-3076) [02240076] **4273**

PETROLEUM SERVICES ANNUAL PETROLEUM REVIEW *CEASED*. (UK) **4273**

PETROLEUM SERVICES WEEKLY SCOUTING SERVICE - OFF SHORE (UK) **4273**

PETROLEUM SERVICES WEEKLY SERVICE (UK) **4273**

PETROLEUM SERVICES WEEKLY SERVICE ONSHORE REPORT (UK) **4273**

PETROLEUM SOFTWARE DIRECTORY (US) [12181793] 1289, **4273**

PETROLEUM SOFTWARE SOURCEBOOK FOR PERSONAL COMPUTERS (US) [18840659] 1289, **4274**

PETROLEUM SUBSTITUTES (US) [03720093] 4274, **4284**

PETROLEUM SUPPLY ANNUAL / ENERGY INFORMATION ADMINISTRATION, OFFICE OF OIL AND GAS, U.S. DEPARTMENT OF ENERGY (US) [08771430] **4274**

PETROLEUM SUPPLY MONTHLY (US/0733-0553) [08517121] **4274**

PETROLEUM TAXATION, PETROLEUM LEGISLATION REPORT (US/0733-6241) [06859725] **4274**

PETROLEUM TERMINAL ENCYCLOPEDIA (US/0897-2001) [17430781] **4274**

PETROLEUM TIMES, A BUSINESS REVIEW (UK) [19804856] **4274**

PETROLEUM TODAY (US/0031-6555) [01586848] **4274**

PETROLIA-ENNISKILLEN GAZETTE, THE (CN/0229-7701) [08205520] **5792**

PETROLIERE INTERNATIONAL (MILANO) (IT/0391-9919) [02243196] **4274**

PETROLOGIE (FR/0336-1837) [03286257] **1459**

●PETROLOGY (US/0869-5911) [28211891] **1459**

PETROMIN (SINGAPORE) (SI/0129-1122) [09934733] **4274**

PETROMONEY *See* PETROLEUM FINANCE WEEK **4272**

PETROMONEY REPORT *See* MIDEAST MARKETS **846**

PETROSTRATEGIES ENGLISH ED (FR/0298-6027) [02986027] **1953**

PETROSTRATEGIES (FRENCH EDITION) (FR/0298-9507) **4274**

●PETROSYSTEMS WORLD (US/1073-6425) [29504641] 1289, 4274, **1265**

PETS MAGAZINE (1985) (CN/0831-2621) [14878482] **4287**

PETTIT REPORT ON THE POLITICS OF SAN FRANCISCO, THE (US/0270-5516) [06515267] **4487**

PETUNJUK KELURAHAN WILAYAH JAKARTA BARAT (IO) [05252092] **5336**

PETUNJUK KELURAHAN WILAYAH JAKARTA PUSAT (IO) [05256351] **5336**

PETUNJUK KELURAHAN WILAYAH JAKARTA SELATAN (IO) [05537870] **5336**

PETUNJUK KELURAHAN WILAYAH JAKARTA TIMUR (IO) [05539691] **5336**

PETUNJUK KELURAHAN WILAYAH JAKARTA UTARA (IO) [05593376] **5336**

PETUNJUK-PETUNJUK BURUH (MY/0127-1253) [19060583] **1701**

PETUNJUK TENTANG PERGURUAN TINGGI DI INDONESIA (IO) [04387907] **1841**

PEULOT STATISTIYOT HADASHOT *See* PEULOT U-FIRSUMIM STATISTIYIM HADASHIM BE-YISRAEL **5336**

PEULOT U-FIRSUMIM STATISTIYIM HADASHIM BE-YISRAEL (IS) [02550494] **5336**

PEUPLE BRETON, LE (FR/0245-9507) [I02459507] **2271**

PEUPLE/COURRIER DE LA COTE-DU-SUD (CN/0713-679X) [08916531] **5792**

PEUPLE DE LA CHAUDIERE (CN/0228-703X) [07818117] **5792**

PEUPLE, LE (FR) [05898304] **1701**

PEUPLE Alphabetical Title Index

PEUPLE (ST-AGAPIT) (CN/0228-5703) [08003187] **5792**

PEUPLE-TRIBUNE (CN/0383-7572) [03248103] **5792**

PEUPLES *CEASED.* (UK/0306-8331) [I03068331] **590**

PEUPLES & LIBERATIONS BRUXELLES (BE/1370-0081) [I13700081] **4487**

PEUPLES & LIBERATIONS (BRUXELLES) *See* ANTIPODES BRUXELLES **4464**

PEUPLES DU MONDE (FR/0555-9952) [04267102] **4986**

PEUPLES MEDITERRANEENS (FR/0399-1253) [04105794] **2702**

PEUPLES (MONTREAL) (CN/0822-1723) [11245834] **2271**

PEX (AT/0310-4184) [I03104184] 2147, **4274**

PEZ Y LA SERPIENTE, EL (NQ/0031-6652) [01695471] 3423, **327**

PFA NEWSLETTER (US) 327, **4372**

PFALZER HEIMAT (GW/0031-6679) [02723096] **2702**

PF&M ANALYSES (US) **2890**

PFEIFFER'S OFFICIAL FREQUENT FLYER GUIDE (US/0898-6371) [17863255] **5389**

PFERDEHEILKUNDE (GW/0177-7726) [13294243] **5518**

PFLANZENARZT, DER (AU/0031-6733) [05250025] **521**

PFLANZENSCHUTZ (SZ) [09980293] **521**

PFLANZENSCHUTZ NACHRICHTEN (GW/0079-1342) [03792428] **181**

PFLANZENSCHUTZ-NACHRICHTEN BAYER (ENGLISH ED.) (GW/0170-0405) [20303359] **2427**

PFLANZENSCHUTZMITTEL-VERZEICHNIS. TEIL 1: ACKERBAU, WIESEN UND WEIDEN, HOPFENBAU, SONDERKULTUREN, NICHTKULTURLAND, GEWASSER (GW) [05733963] **4247**

PFLANZENSCHUTZMITTEL-VERZEICHNIS. TEIL 2: GEMUSEBAU, OBSTBAU, ZIERPFLANZENBAU (GW) [05733944] 2427, **4247**

PFLANZENSCHUTZMITTEL-VERZEICHNIS. TEIL 6: ANERKANNTE PFLANZENSCHUTZ- UND VORRATSSCHUTZGERATE (GW) [05733884] **160**

PFLANZENSOZIOLOGIE; EINE REIHE VEGETATIONSKUNDLICHER GEBIETSMONOGRAPHIEN (GW) [01715489] 521, **2427**

PFLANZLICHE ERZEUGUNG (LU/0378-3588) [18265340] **181**

PFLEGE (SZ) [19584671] **3867**

●PFLEGE AKTUELL / DBFK, DEUTSCHER BERUFSVERBAND FUER PFLEGEBERUFE (GW/0944-8918) [30402730] **3867**

PFLEGEN AMBULANT (GW/0937-0277) [09370277] **3627**

PFLUGERS ARCHIV (GW/0031-6768) [01762182] **584**

PFLUGERVILLE PRESS, THE (US/1056-5167) [23734354] **5753**

PGA MAGAZINE (1989) (US/1044-1204) [19688997] **4912**

PGRC/E-ILCA GERMPLASM NEWSLETTER (ET/1013-0314) [09886494] **521**

PH, POLICY HOLDER INSURANCE JOURNAL (UK/0032-2679) [05887318] **2890**

PHAENOMENOLOGICA (NE/0079-1350) [01605552] **4355**

PHALANX (ALEXANDRIA) (US/0195-1920) [05345238] 4054, **2107**

PHALARIS : NUOVA SERIE DEL GIORNALE BIMESTRALE DI ARCHITETTURA DELLA FONDAZIONE A. MASIERI *CEASED.* (IT) [23198974] **306**

PHALGU : PHALGU SAHITYA SAMSADARA MUKHAPATRA (II) [11790281] **3423**

PHANOMENOLOGISCHE FORSCHUNGEN. PHENOMENOLOGICAL STUDIES. RECHERCHES PHENOMENOLOGIQUES (GW) [05745967] **4355**

PHANTASMAGORIA (UNIVERSITY HEIGHTS) (US/0197-680X) [06076793] **2491**

PHANTASTIC PHINDS FOR PHYS. ED (US/1056-6603) [23885171] **1857**

PHARE (ROUYN) (CN/0713-5734) [08967826] **2754**

PHARES ET SIGNAUX DE BRUME *See* FEUX ET SIGNAUX DE BRUME **4176**

PHARM-AID (CHATHAM, N.J.) (US/1043-5905) [19507026] **4319**

PHARMA BUSINESS (UK) **4319**

PHARMA DIALOG (GW/0172-0104) [04754390] **4319**

PHARMA-FLASH (SZ/0378-7958) [I03787958] **4319**

PHARMA INTERNATIONAL (TRI-LINGUAL EDITION) (SZ/0301-1348) [10982671] **4319**

PHARMA JAPAN (JA/0285-4937) 703, **4319**

PHARMA KEFTIKON DELTION (GR) **4319**

PHARMA-MARKETING-JOURNAL (GW/0721-5665) [I07215665] 934, **1512**

PHARMA MIX (IT) **4319**

PHARMA SELECTA (NE/0169-6882) [01696882] 988, **4319**

PHARMA TECHNOLOGIE JOURNAL (GW/0931-9700) [14938977] **4319**

PHARMACA (CI/0031-6857) [10991770] **4319**

PHARMACEASED (UK) **4319**

PHARMACEUTICA ACTA HELVETIAE (SZ/0031-6865) [01696992] **4319**

PHARMACEUTICAL & BIOTECH DAILY (US/1074-8636) [29871183] **4320**

PHARMACEUTICAL AND COSMETIC EQUIPMENT *See* PHARMACEUTICAL PROCESSING **4321**

PHARMACEUTICAL & COSMETIC REVIEW (SA/1015-4760) [25206745] **4320**

PHARMACEUTICAL AND PHARMACOLOGICAL LETTERS (GW/0939-9488) [26850717] **4320**

PHARMACEUTICAL BUSINESS NEWS (UK/0956-0661) [24327493] 703, **4320**

PHARMACEUTICAL CHEMISTRY JOURNAL (US/0091-150X) [01786340] 1046, **4320**

PHARMACEUTICAL CODEX, THE (UK) [06340306] **4320**

PHARMACEUTICAL COMPANY PROFILES (UK) **4320**

PHARMACEUTICAL DAILY (US/1071-5096) [28657498] 4320, **3695**

PHARMACEUTICAL ENGINEERING (US/0273-8139) [06952902] **4320**

PHARMACEUTICAL EXECUTIVE (US/0279-6570) [07151354] **4320**

PHARMACEUTICAL HISTORIAN (UK/0079-1393) [07531447] **4320**

PHARMACEUTICAL INDUSTRY WEEKLY (US/1078-2885) [4320]

PHARMACEUTICAL JOURNAL (1933) (UK/0031-6873) [07100767] **4320**

PHARMACEUTICAL JOURNAL OF KENYA (KE/0378-228X) [02726694] **4320**

PHARMACEUTICAL LITIGATION REPORTER (US/0887-7815) [13368498] 4320, **3029**

PHARMACEUTICAL MANUFACTURERS ASSOCIATION *See* NEWSLETTER - PHARMACEUTICAL MANUFACTURERS ASSOCIATION **4318**

PHARMACEUTICAL MANUFACTURING (US/0747-3796) [10788676] **4320**

PHARMACEUTICAL MANUFACTURING REVIEW (UK/0955-3894) [24179087] 4320, **3486**

PHARMACEUTICAL MARKETING (UK) [I09693963] 934, **4320**

PHARMACEUTICAL MEDICINE (BASINGSTOKE) (UK/0265-0673) [11806597] **4320**

PHARMACEUTICAL NEWS CAPSULE (SPECIAL ED.) (US/1040-0931) [13053167] **4320**

PHARMACEUTICAL NEWS CAPSULE, THE (US/0891-2793) [11188518] **4320**

PHARMACEUTICAL NEWS INDEX (US/0362-4439) [02223449] 4320, **4334**

PHARMACEUTICAL PACKAGING *See* HEALTHCARE PACKAGING **4219**

PHARMACEUTICAL PERSPECTIVES (US) **4320**

PHARMACEUTICAL PHYSICIAN (UK/0960-6548) [I09606548] **4320**

PHARMACEUTICAL POLICY AND PRACTICE (UK) **4320**

PHARMACEUTICAL PREPARATIONS, EXCEPT BIOLOGICALS (US/0732-8419) [03820473] **4320**

PHARMACEUTICAL PROCESSING (US/1049-9156) [21356628] **4321**

PHARMACEUTICAL PRODUCTION TECHSOURCE (US/0891-9461) [13160955] 1621, **4321**

PHARMACEUTICAL RESEARCH (US/0724-8741) [09679417] **4321**

PHARMACEUTICAL SCIENCE COMMUNICATIONS (UK/1351-6337) **4321**

PHARMACEUTICAL STRTEGIC ALLIANCE (US) **4321**

PHARMACEUTICAL TECHNOLOGY (US/0147-8087) [03230945] **4321**

PHARMACEUTICAL TECHNOLOGY INTERNATIONAL (US/0164-6826) [19538460] **4321**

PHARMACEUTICAL TIMES (UK) **4321**

PHARMACEUTICALS & BIOLOGICALS (SZ) 468, **4321**

PHARMACEUTIQUES PARIS (FR/1240-0866) [I12400866] **4321**

PHARMACEUTISCH WEEKBLAD (NE/0031-6911) [10700705] **4321**

PHARMACEUTISCH WEEKBLAD. SCIENTIFIC EDITION (NE/0167-6555) [05538576] **4321**

PHARMACIE HOSPITALIERE FRANCAISE, LA (FR/0369-9579) [11339756] **3791**

PHARMACIE MONDIALE (FR) [04596790] **4321**

PHARMACIE RURALE PARIS (FR/0994-4370) [I09944370] **4321**

PHARMACIEN DE FRANCE (FR/0031-6938) [I00316938] **4321**

PHARMACIEN HOPITAL, LE (FR) **4321**

PHARMACIEN HOSPITALIER, LE (FR/0768-9179) [I07689179] **4321**

PHARMACIEN, LE (CN/0031-692X) [02717801] **4321**

PHARMACIST NEWS (CN) **4321**

PHARMACOCHEMISTRY LIBRARY (NE/0165-7208) [03895276] 988, **4321**

●PHARMACOECONOMICS (NZ/1170-7690) [25169261] **4321**

●PHARMACOEPIDEMIOLOGY AND DRUG SAFETY (UK/1053-8569) [22683758] **4321**

PHARMACOGENETICS (UK/0960-314X) [25209701] 550, **4321**

PHARMACOGNOSY TITLES *CEASED.* (US) [01607472] **4321**

PHARMACOKINETICS *CEASED.* (GW/0233-237X) [12658536] 3627, **4321**

PHARMACOLOGICA ET PHYSIOLOGICA (OULU) (FI/0358-4828) [04880023] 585, **4322**

PHARMACOLOGICAL RESEARCH (UK/1043-6618) [19409285] **4322**

PHARMACOLOGICAL REVIEWS (US/0031-6997) [00824083] **4322**

PHARMACOLOGICAL TREATMENT OF THE CLIMACTERIC SYNDROME (IT) **4322**

PHARMACOLOGIE PRATIQUE (CN/0316-7526) [02247904] **4322**

PHARMACOLOGIST, THE (US/0031-7004) [01491186] **4322**

PHARMACOLOGY (SZ/0031-7012) [01597962] **4322**

PHARMACOLOGY AND THE SKIN (SZ/1011-291X) [18320095] 4322, **3722**

PHARMACOLOGY & THERAPEUTICS (OXFORD) (UK/0163-7258) [04981366] **4322**

PHARMACOLOGY & TOXICOLOGY (DK/0901-9928) [15172115] 3983, **4322**

PHARMACOLOGY & TOXICOLOGY. SUPPLEMENT (DK/0901-9936) [15666557] 3983, **4322**

PHARMACOLOGY, BIOCHEMISTRY AND BEHAVIOR (US/0091-3057) [01787728] 4608, **4322**

PHARMACOLOGY BIOCHEMISTRY & BEHAVIOR. SUPPLEMENT (US) [03574286] 492, 4608, **4322**

●PHARMACOLOGY COMMUNICATIONS (SZ/1060-4456) [25027891] **4322**

PHARMACOLOGY IN NURSING (US/0737-8882) [07800151] 4322, **3867**

PHARMACOLOGY RESEARCH ASSOCIATE PROGRAM OF THE NATIONAL INSTITUTE OF GENERAL MEDICAL SCIENCES, NATIONAL INSTITUTES OF HEALTH (US) [05770209] **4322**

●PHARMACOLOGY, TOXICOLOGY & THERAPEUTICS (US/1063-8946) [26173724] 3983, **4322**

PHARMACOPEIAL FORUM (US/0363-4655) [02411116] **4322**

PHARMACOPSYCHIATRY (GW/0176-3679) [10555814] 3932, **4323**

PHARMACOPSYCHIATRY SUPPLEMENT (GW/0936-9589) [I09369589] 3932, **4323**

PHARMACOPSYCHOECOLOGIA VARANASI (II/0970-3926) [I09703926] 4323, **4608**

●PHARMACORESOURCES : WORLD PHARMACOECONOMIC NEWS, VIEWS, AND PRACTICAL APPLICATION (NZ/1172-8299) **4323**

PHARMACOS CHANDIGARH (II/0369-951X) [I0369951X] **4323**

PHARMACOTHERAPY (US/0277-0008) [07491625] **4323**

PHARMACTUEL (CN/0834-065X) [15731901] **4323**

PHARMACY & THERAPEUTICS FORUM (US/0195-542X) [05513861] **4323**

Alphabetical Title Index — PHILIPPINE

PHARMACY BUSINESS (US/1060-4537) [24692434] 882, **4323**

●PHARMACY CADENCE (US/1064-797X) [26393994] **4323**

PHARMACY HEALTH-LINE (US/0739-9596) [09899132] **4323**

PHARMACY LAW DIGEST (US/0149-1717) [03453510] **4323, 3029**

PHARMACY LAWS UPDATE SERVICE (US) **4323**

PHARMACY NEWS AND REVIEW (US/8750-4790) [11486783] **4323**

PHARMACY PRACTICE (MISSISSAUGA) (CN/0829-2809) [12873913] **4323**

PHARMACY PRACTICE NEWS (US/0886-988X) [13136320] **4323**

PHARMACY SCHOOL ADMISSION REQUIREMENTS (US/0149-1113) [03429640] **4323**

PHARMACY STUDENT, THE (US/0279-5272) [07087642] **4323**

PHARMACY TIMES (US/0003-0627) [01762198] **4323**

●PHARMACY TODAY (US/1077-2839) [30756321] **4323**

PHARMACY TODAY LONDON (UK/0968-042X) [I0968042X] **4323**

PHARMACY TODAY (WASHINGTON, D.C.) (US/1042-0991) [18941134] **4323**

PHARMACY TRADE (AT) **4323**

PHARMACY UPDATE (UK/0267-7334) [13405558] **4323**

PHARMACY WEST (US/0191-6394) [03928627] **4323**

PHARMACY WORLD (NR/0189-7705) [I01897705] **4323**

●PHARMACY WORLD & SCIENCE : PWS (NE/0928-1231) [27661771] **4324**

PHARMAKLINIK *See* CIENCIA PHARMACEUTICA **4296**

PHARMAKLINIK (MADRID) (SP/1011-4386) [25545341] **4324**

PHARMAKOTHERAPIE *SUSPENDED*. (GW/0344-7154) [06697778] **4324**

PHARMAKRITIK INTERNATIONAL (UK/0959-3853) [I09593853] **4324**

PHARMALERT (BALTIMORE, MD.) (US/0278-6850) [07810948] **4324**

PHARMAPROJECTS (UK) [09695235] **4324**

PHARMASCOPE (US) [06371177] **4324**

PHARMASOURCES (US/0730-1278) [07955840] **4324**

PHARMASTRUCTURES IN PRINT (UK) **4324**

PHARMATHERAPEUTICA *SUSPENDED.* (UK/0308-051X) [02145498] **4324**

PHARMATIMES BOMBAY (II/0031-6849) [I00316849] **4324**

PHARMAZEUTISCHE INDUSTRIE, DIE (GW/0031-711X) [04415878] **4324**

PHARMAZEUTISCHE RUNDSCHAU (GW/0031-7128) [06572315] **4324**

PHARMAZEUTISCHE VERFAHRENSTECHNIK HEUTE *CEASED.* (GW/0173-1890) [07891578] **4324**

PHARMAZEUTISCHE ZEITUNG (GW/0031-7136) [04064211] **4324**

PHARMAZIE, DIE (GW/0031-7144) [01779245] **4324**

PHARMAZIE HEUTE (GW/0369-979X) [04613022] **4324**

PHARMAZIE IN UNSERER ZEIT (GW/0048-3664) [09874816] **4324**

PHARMCHEM NEWSLETTER, THE (US/0146-3128) [02904585] **4324**

PHARMEUROPA ED. FRANCAISE (INT/1013-5294) [I10135294] **4324**

PHARMINDEX *CEASED.* (US/0031-7152) [01608032] **4324**

PHARMSTUDENT (II/0379-556X) [11481816] **4324**

PHAROS (UK/0048-3672) [20915597] **5269**

PHAROS OF ALPHA OMEGA ALPHA-HONOR MEDICAL SOCIETY, THE (US/0031-7179) [02266050] **3627**

PHAROS-TRIBUNE, THE (US) [15864244] **5666**

PHASE (SP) [03943287] **5034**

PHASE AND CYCLE (US/1056-4888) [23725035] **3468**

PHASE DIAGRAMS FOR CERAMISTS (ANNUAL) *See* PHASE EQUILIBRIA DIAGRAMS (ANNUAL) **2593**

PHASE DIAGRAMS FOR CERAMISTS (FINAL COMPILATION) *See* PHASE EQUILIBRIA DIAGRAMS (FINAL COMPILATION) **2593**

PHASE EQUILIBRIA DIAGRAMS (ANNUAL) *CEASED.* (US/1065-5034) [26667142] **2593**

●PHASE EQUILIBRIA DIAGRAMS (FINAL COMPILATION) (US/1065-500X) [26667126] **2593**

PHASE III PROFILES (US/1056-5671) [23740047] **4324**

PHASE TRANSITIONS (US/0141-1594) [05689238] **4414**

PHASE TRANSITIONS AND CRITICAL PHENOMENA (UK/1062-7901) [08055783] 3526, **4414**

PHASIS (BL) [05638285] **3310**

PHAT : PRESENTATION HOUSE ARTS TABLOID (CN/0711-7515) [08537557] 387, **381**

PHAT-TRIEN XA-HOI (VM) [01786250] **5253**

●PHC PROFIT REPORT (US/1071-2372) [28577081] **2607**

PHELON'S DISCOUNT & JOBBING TRADE (US) [23459798] **956**

PHELON'S RESIDENT BUYERS AND MERCHANDISE BROKERS OF DEPARTMENT STORE MERCHANDISE, READY TO WEAR, MILLINERY *See* SHELDON'S RETAIL DIRECTORY OF THE UNITED STATES AND CANADA AND PHELON'S RESIDENT BUYERS AND MERCHANDISE BROKERS **957**

PHELONS WOMENS APPAREL & ACCESSORY SHOPS (US) **5564**

PHELON'S WOMEN'S APPAREL SHOPS (US/0737-3430) [09170781] 956, **1086**

PHELPS COUNTY GENEALOGICAL SOCIETY QUARTERLY (US/0884-2140) [12169829] **2467**

PHENIX (FR/0300-3639) [01422585] **4864**

PHENIX CITIZEN (1973) (US) [12258825] **5627**

PHENIX (ST-FULGENCE) (CN/0318-9317) [02441911] **5792**

PHENOMENA (TORONTO) (CN/0701-4945) [03453114] **4242**

PHENOMENOLOGICAL INQUIRY (US/0885-3886) [12629414] 2852, **4355**

PHENOMENOLOGY AND PEDAGOGY *CEASED.* (CN/0820-9189) [09986007] 1773, **4355**

PHENOMENOLOGY & SOCIAL SCIENCE NEWSLETTER (US) **5212**

PHI BETA DELTA INTERNATIONAL REVIEW (US) [22806405] **1773**

PHI DELTA CHI FRATERNITY *See* COMMUNICATOR OF PHI DELTA CHI FRATERNITY, THE **5230**

PHI DELTA KAPPAN (US/0031-7217) [01762202] **1773**

PHI KAPPA PHI *See* PHI KAPPA PHI NEWSLETTER **5235**

PHI KAPPA PHI NEWSLETTER (US/0093-5328) [01903005] **5235**

PHI : PLANNING FOR HEALTH ISSUES (US) [08648092] **4795**

PHI THETA PAPERS *CEASED.* (US/0553-9536) [08037178] **1094**

PHI ZERO *CEASED.* (CN/0318-4412) [02442003] **4355**

PHI ZETA. ZETA CHAPTER *See* ANNUAL PHI ZETA RESEARCH DAY OF THE ZETA CHAPTER **5503**

PHILA-PRESSE (CN/0319-4094) [02443241] **2786**

PHILADELPHIA ARCHITECT (US/1071-1651) [20369065] **306**

PHILADELPHIA ASSOCIATION FOR PSYCHOANALYSIS *See* JOURNAL OF THE PHILADELPHIA ASSOCIATION FOR PSYCHOANALYSIS **3930**

●PHILADELPHIA BAR REPORTER (US/0145-3491) [27482492] **3029**

PHILADELPHIA BUSINESS JOURNAL (US/0744-3587) [08223613] **703**

PHILADELPHIA CITY PAPER (US/0733-6349) [08638319] **5738**

PHILADELPHIA DAILY NEWS (PHILADELPHIA, PA. : 1925) (US) [12904443] **5738**

PHILADELPHIA FOLKSONG SOCIETY NEWSLETTER (US) **4146**

PHILADELPHIA GAY NEWS (US) [12715464] **5738**

PHILADELPHIA HOME VIEWER, THE (US/0745-0540) [08770574] **2543**

PHILADELPHIA INQUIRER (1969), THE (US/0885-6613) [08733259] **5738**

PHILADELPHIA MAGAZINE (1967) (US/0031-7233) [07134788] **2543**

PHILADELPHIA MEDICINE (US/0031-7306) [01589326] 4324, **3627**

PHILADELPHIA NATIONAL BANK *See* COMMENTS **783**

PHILADELPHIA NEW OBSERVER, THE (US/0890-8435) [14552816] **5738**

PHILADELPHIA PAPERS, THE (US/1041-9039) [18885150] **4531**

PHILADELPHIA TRIBUNE (1884) (US/0746-956X) [02266077] **5738**

PHILADELPHIA YEARLY MEETING NEWS *See* PYM NEWS: A PUBLICATION OF THE RELIGIOUS SOCIETY OF FRIENDS **4988**

PHILANTHROPIC DIGEST (US/0480-2853) [02449621] **4338**

PHILANTHROPIC TRENDS DIGEST, THE (US/1065-1659) [22770443] **4338**

PHILANTHROPIST, THE (CN/0316-3849) [02103497] **4338**

PHILANTHROPY MONTHLY, THE (US/1071-6661) [04989670] **4338**

PHILANTHROPY. THE QUARTERLY NEWSLETTER OF THE AUSTRALIAN ASSOCIATION OF PHILANTHROPY (AT) **4338**

PHILATELIC AUCTION / CHARLTON AUCTIONS (CN/0822-4919) [10007932] **2786**

PHILATELIC AUCTION - TOREX (CN/0822-496X) [10007957] **2786**

PHILATELIC BULLETIN (AT) [03696850] **2786**

PHILATELIC CHIT CHAT FROM CHARLIE (US) **2786**

PHILATELIC EXPORTER, THE (UK/0031-7381) [10464932] **1146**

PHILATELIC JOURNALIST, THE *CEASED.* (US/0048-3710) [02826356] **2786**

PHILATELIC LITERATURE REVIEW (US/0270-1707) [06350979] **2786**

PHILATELIC OBSERVER (US/0273-5598) [07079372] **2786**

PHILATELIC REVIEW (UK) [07695560] **2786**

●PHILATELIC SHOPPER, THE (US) [26734244] **2786**

PHILATELIE AU QUEBEC (CN/0381-7547) [14181439] **2786**

PHILATELIST AND PJGB, THE (UK/0260-6739) [07419666] **2786**

PHILATELY FROM AUSTRALIA (AT) [06510140] **2786**

PHILHARMONISCHES ORCHESTER DER STADT DORTMUND *See* KONZERTE / PHILHARMONISCHES ORCHESTER DER STADT DORTMUND **4128**

PHILIGRAM (1980) (CN/0711-5350) [08559392] **2075**

PHILIPPINE ABSTRACTS (PH/0031-7438) [05218442] **422**

PHILIPPINE AGRICULTURIST, THE (PH/0031-7454) [08418329] **119**

PHILIPPINE ALMANAC & HANDBOOK OF FACTS (PH) [01783717] **2507**

PHILIPPINE ARCHITECTURE, ENGINEERING, & CONSTRUCTION RECORD (PH/0031-7470) [02719522] 1990, **306**

PHILIPPINE BRIEFINGS (PH) [03076419] **5253**

PHILIPPINE BUSINESS REVIEW (PH/0115-1746) [04023260] **703**

PHILIPPINE-CANADIAN TRADE GUIDE (CN/0703-1998) [05257039] **849**

PHILIPPINE CASE LAW (PH) [07768921] **3029**

PHILIPPINE COCONUT AUTHORITY. AGRICULTURAL RESEARCH DEPT *See* ANNUAL REPORT - AGRICULTURAL RESEARCH DEPARTMENT, PHILIPPINE COCONUT AUTHORITY **60**

PHILIPPINE COMMISSION ON AUDIT JOURNAL *See* COMMISSION ON AUDIT JOURNAL **4718**

PHILIPPINE CONSTRUCTION DIRECTORY (PH) [08895704] **623**

PHILIPPINE DEVELOPMENT (PH/0115-0073) [03250064] **1578**

PHILIPPINE DEVELOPMENT REPORT (PH) [05344081] **1578**

PHILIPPINE DIRECTORY OF FINANCIAL INSTITUTIONS (PH) [08014793] **803**

PHILIPPINE ECONOMIC INDICATORS *CEASED.* (PH) [03363079] **1578**

PHILIPPINE ECONOMIC JOURNAL, THE (PH/0031-7500) [05004457] **1512**

PHILIPPINE EDUCATIONAL FORUM, THE (PH) [06510165] **1773**

PHILIPPINE ENTOMOLOGIST (PH/0369-9536) [01716812] **5594**

PHILIPPINE FARMERS' JOURNAL (PH/0115-0928) [05224211] **120**

PHILIPPINE FOOD BALANCE SERIES (PH) [04242555] **2353**

PHILIPPINE FORESTRY STATISTICS (PH) [07808940] 2390, **2399**

PHILIPPINE GEOGRAPHICAL JOURNAL (PH/0031-7551) [01589153] **2572**

PHILIPPINE HUMAN RIGHTS UPDATE (PH) [13421437] **4511**

PHILIPPINE INQUIRER (PH/0116-0443) [01160443] **5807**

PHILIPPINE — Alphabetical Title Index

PHILIPPINE INSTITUTE OF ACCOUNTANTS. NEWSETTE *See* NEWSETTE - PHILIPPINE INSTITUTE OF CERTIFIED PUBLIC ACCOUNTANTS **749**

PHILIPPINE INSTITUTE OF CERTIFIED PUBLIC ACCOUNTANTS *See* NEWSETTE - PHILIPPINE INSTITUTE OF CERTIFIED PUBLIC ACCOUNTANTS **749**

PHILIPPINE JOURNAL OF ANIMAL INDUSTRY, THE (PH/0048-3761) [01762241] **217**

PHILIPPINE JOURNAL OF BIOTECHNOLOGY (PH/0117-0503) [I01170503] **3695**

PHILIPPINE JOURNAL OF CARDIOLOGY (PH/0115-1029) [06047046] **3709**

PHILIPPINE JOURNAL OF COCONUT STUDIES, THE (PH/0115-6500) [03041044] 2353, **181**

PHILIPPINE JOURNAL OF COUNSELING PSYCHOLOGY (PH) **4608**

PHILIPPINE JOURNAL OF CROP SCIENCE, THE (PH/0115-2025) [03271029] **181**

PHILIPPINE JOURNAL OF EDUCATION, THE (PH/0031-7624) [02726046] **1773**

PHILIPPINE JOURNAL OF FISHERIES, THE (PH/0048-377X) [05218453] **2310**

PHILIPPINE JOURNAL OF FOOD SCIENCE AND TECHNOLOGY (PH) [06755283] **2353**

PHILIPPINE JOURNAL OF INTERNAL MEDICINE (PH/0556-0071) [I05560071] **3800**

PHILIPPINE JOURNAL OF LABOR AND INDUSTRIAL RELATIONS (PH) [20568494] **1701**

PHILIPPINE JOURNAL OF LINGUISTICS (PH/0048-3796) [01791000] **3310**

PHILIPPINE JOURNAL OF MICROBIOLOGY AND INFECTIOUS DISEASES, THE (PH/0115-0324) [12444637] 3715, **568**

PHILIPPINE JOURNAL OF NURSING, THE (PH/0048-3818) [04841184] **3867**

PHILIPPINE JOURNAL OF NUTRITION (PH/0031-7640) [02584587] **4197**

PHILIPPINE JOURNAL OF OPHTHALMOLOGY (PH/0031-7659) [06865198] **3878**

PHILIPPINE JOURNAL OF PSYCHOLOGY (PH/0115-3153) [03567568] **4608**

PHILIPPINE JOURNAL OF PUBLIC ADMINISTRATION (PH/0031-7675) [01762245] **4673**

PHILIPPINE JOURNAL OF SCIENCE, THE (PH/0031-7683) [01588263] **5138**

PHILIPPINE JOURNAL OF VETERINARY MEDICINE (PH/0031-7705) [01762246] **5518**

PHILIPPINE JOURNAL OF VOLCANOLOGY *SUSPENDED.* (PH) [12934721] **1409**

PHILIPPINE JOURNAL OF WEED SCIENCE (PH) [05395257] **181**

PHILIPPINE LABOR REPORTS : DECISIONS AND RULINGS OF SUPREME COURT, NATIONAL LABOR RELATIONS COMMISSION, BUREAU OF LABOR RELATIONS, AND OTHER LABOR AGENCIES (PH) [07954804] **3153**

PHILIPPINE LABOR REVIEW (PH/0115-2629) [04183565] **1701**

PHILIPPINE LAW AND JURISPRUDENCE (PH) [04950509] **3029**

PHILIPPINE LAW GAZETTE (PH/0115-2483) [03339026] **3142**

PHILIPPINE LAW JOURNAL (PH/0031-7721) [01762247] **3029**

PHILIPPINE LAW REPORT, THE (PH) [03864086] **3029**

PHILIPPINE LETTER, THE (US/0379-2870) [04602980] 1512, **703**

PHILIPPINE LUMBERMAN, THE (PH/0024-7316) [01624166] **2403**

PHILIPPINE MINING & ENGINEERING JOURNAL (PH/0048-3842) [02884278] **1443**

PHILIPPINE NEWS (US) [13459632] **5638**

PHILIPPINE NEWS & FEATURES (PH/0116-5038) [I01165038] **2662**

PHILIPPINE NEWS BULLETIN (CN/0712-5550) [09223184] **2662**

PHILIPPINE OVERSEAS EMPLOYMENT ANNUAL-DIRECTORY (PH) [11535887] **1702**

PHILIPPINE PHYTOPATHOLOGY (PH/0115-0804) [01624346] **521**

PHILIPPINE POPULATION JOURNAL (PH/0116-7960) [14350558] **590**

PHILIPPINE QUARTERLY OF CULTURE AND SOCIETY (PH/0115-0243) [02161552] 243, **5253**

PHILIPPINE REVIEW OF BUSINESS AND ECONOMICS *See* PHILIPPINE REVIEW OF ECONOMICS & BUSINESS, THE **1512**

PHILIPPINE REVIEW OF BUSINESS AND ECONOMICS, THE (PH/0031-7780) [02266088] 1512, **703**

PHILIPPINE REVIEW OF ECONOMICS & BUSINESS, THE (PH/0115-9011) [12194364] 703, **1512**

PHILIPPINE SCIENCE & TECHNOLOGY ABSTRACTS (PH/0115-8724) [21109556] 5138, **5175**

PHILIPPINE SCIENTIST, THE (PH/0079-1466) [02766615] 521, 5594, **557**

PHILIPPINE SEAS (PH/0115-9003) [10985468] **3182**

PHILIPPINE SOCIAL SCIENCE COUNCIL *See* PSSC SOCIAL SCIENCE INFORMATION **5214**

PHILIPPINE SOCIAL SCIENCES REVIEW (PH) [19256756] **5212**

PHILIPPINE SOCIOLOGICAL REVIEW (PH/0031-7810) [01643833] **5253**

PHILIPPINE STATISTICAL YEARBOOK (PH) [03975849] 1537, **703**

PHILIPPINE STATISTICIAN, THE (PH/0031-7829) [04293032] **5336**

PHILIPPINE STUDIES (PH/0031-7837) [01643944] 5212, **2625**

PHILIPPINE SUGAR COMMISSION QUARTERLY (PH) [11555084] **181**

PHILIPPINE SUPREME COURT REPORTS ANNOTATED / COMPILED, ANNOTATED AND EDITED BY THE EDITORIAL STAFF OF THE CENTRAL LAWBOOK PUBLISHING CO., INC (PH) [12292619] **3029**

PHILIPPINE TECHNICAL INFORMATION SHEETS (PH) **5138**

PHILIPPINE TECHNOLOGY JOURNAL (PH/0116-7294) [19610051] **5138**

PHILIPPINE TIMES, THE (US/0147-9555) [03254016] **2662**

PHILIPPINE WITNESS (US) [14348112] **4511**

PHILIPPINE WOMEN'S UNIVERSITY FORUM (PH) [20857872] **1773**

PHILIPPINE YEARBOOK (PH) [03581002] **5336**

PHILIPPINE YEARBOOK OF INTERNATIONAL LAW, THE (PH/0115-8805) [01776180] **3133**

PHILIPPINEN : ENERGIEWIRTSCHAFT (GW) [05064269] **1953**

PHILIPPINEN, WIRTSCHAFTLICHE ENTWICKLUNG / BUNDESSTELLE FUR AUSSENHANDELSINFORMATION (GW) [07681576] **1578**

PHILIPPINEN, WIRTSCHAFTSDATEN UND WIRTSCHAFTSDOKUMENTATION / BUNDESSTELLE FUR AUSSENHANDELSINFORMATION (GW) [09399632] **1578**

PHILIPPINES *See* VITAL LEGAL DOCUMENTS IN THE NEW PEOPLE'S GOVERNMENT **3072**

PHILIPPINES *See* COMPILATION OF PRESIDENTIAL DECREES - (PHILIPPINES) **2954**

PHILIPPINES. ARMED FORCES *See* AFP ANNUAL REPORT **4033**

PHILIPPINES. BUREAU OF AGRICULTURAL ECONOMICS *See* BAECON BI-MONTHLY REPORTER **64**

PHILIPPINES. BUREAU OF AGRICULTURAL ECONOMICS. ECONOMICS *See* PRICES RECEIVED BY FARMERS **121**

PHILIPPINES. BUREAU OF ENERGY UTILIZATION *See* QUARTERLY REVIEW / BUREAU OF ENERGY UTILIZATION **1954**

PHILIPPINES BUSINESS DIRECTORY (PH) [07356073] **703**

PHILIPPINES. CIVIL SERVICE COMMISSION *See* CIVIL SERVICE REPORTER (QUEZON CITY) **4702**

PHILIPPINES. DEPT. OF NATURAL RESOURCES *See* DNR PERFORMANCE REPORT **2191**

PHILIPPINES. DEPT. OF TRADE AND INDUSTRY *See* ANNUAL REPORT / DEPARTMENT OF TRADE AND INDUSTRY **822**

PHILIPPINES INFORMATION PARIS (FR/0994-6993) [I09946993] **4511**

PHILIPPINES JOURNAL OF OPERATIONS RESEARCH (PH) **1990**

PHILIPPINES. NATIONAL ECONOMIC AND DEVELOPMENT AUTHORITY *See* PHILIPPINE ECONOMIC INDICATORS **1578**

PHILIPPINES. NATIONAL ECONOMIC AND DEVELOPMENT AUTHORITY *See* NATIONAL INCOME ACCOUNTS, THE **1575**

PHILIPPINES. NATIONAL STATISTICS OFFICE *See* VITAL STATISTICS REPORT **5346**

PHILIPPINES. SECURITIES AND EXCHANGE COMMISSION *See* ANNUAL REPORT - SECURITIES AND EXCHANGE COMMISSION **891**

PHILIPPINES. SECURITIES AND EXCHANGE COMMISSION *See* SEC QUARTERLY BULLETIN, THE **3047**

PHILIPPINES. SUPREME COURT *See* PHILIPPINE CASE LAW **3029**

PHILIPPINES TODAY (PH) [01786085] **2507**

PHILIPPINES TODAY (WASHINGTON, D.C. : 1983) (US) [10005130] **5647**

PHILIPPINES UPDATE (US) [14348490] **4511**

PHILIPPINES WATER RESOURCES ABSTRACTS (PH) [02994905] **5537**

PHILIPPINIANA SACRA (PH/0554-0577) [02735076] 4355, **2625**

● PHILIP'S GEOGRAPHICAL DIGEST (UK) [25541877] **2572**

PHILIPS JOURNAL OF RESEARCH (NE/0165-5817) [04055725] 5138, **2075**

PHILIPS TECHNISCH TIJDSCHRIFT *CEASED.* (NE) [06742241] **5138**

PHILIPS' TECHNISCHE RUNDSCHAU (NE) [06541406] **2075**

PHILIPS WELDING REPORTER (NE) [04996691] **4027**

PHILIPSBURG MAIL, THE (US) [09388893] **5706**

● PHILLIPS BUSINESS INFORMATION'S COMMUNICATIONS STANDARDS NEWS (US/1077-4696) [30808332] 1248, **1243**

● PHILLIPS BUSINESS INFORMATION'S INTERACTIVE VIDEO NEWS (US/1076-4526) [30487298] **4372**

PHILLIPS COUNTY HISTORICAL REVIEW (US/1046-4204) [20316311] **2754**

PHILLIPS COUNTY NEWS (MALTA, MONT. : 1928) (US) [12996494] **5706**

PHILLIPS COUNTY REVIEW (PHILLIPSBURG, KAN. : 1945) (US) [12388017] **5678**

PHILLIPS INTERNATIONAL PAPER DIRECTORY (UK/0954-8521) [19243481] **4237**

PHILLIPS INTERNATIONAL PULP & PAPER DIRECTORY (UK) **4237**

PHILLIPS PAPER TRADE DIRECTORY *See* PHILLIPS INTERNATIONAL PULP & PAPER DIRECTORY **4237**

PHILLIPS PUBLISHING'S ... TELEPHONE INDUSTRY DIRECTORY (US) [19283402] **1161**

PHILLIPS SHIELD (US/0161-2697) [03880619] **4274**

PHILLIPS UNIVERSITY (ENID, OKLA.). GRADUATE SEMINARY *See* SEMINARY NEWS (ENID, OKLA.) **4996**

PHILLIPS UNIVERSITY, ENID, OKLAHOMA. GRADUATE SEMINARY. PHILLIPS SEMINARY NEWS *See* SEMINARY NEWS (ENID, OKLA.) **4996**

PHILLYSPORT (PHILADELPHIA, PA.) *CEASED.* (US/0898-2503) [17761511] **2543**

PHILOBIBLON (GW/0031-7969) [01762265] 2776, **362**

PHILOCRITIQUE (CN/0820-7313) [09457079] **4355**

PHILOLOGICAL MONOGRAPHS (US/0079-1628) [01480550] **3310**

PHILOLOGICAL PAPERS (1947) (US/0363-3470) [02417134] **3310**

PHILOLOGICAL QUARTERLY (US/0031-7977) [01762267] **3310**

PHILOLOGICAL SOCIETY (GREAT BRITAIN) *See* TRANSACTIONS OF THE PHILOLOGICAL SOCIETY **3329**

PHILOLOGICAL SOCIETY, LONDON *See* PUBLICATIONS OF THE PHILOLOGICAL SOCIETY **3313**

PHILOLOGIE ET LINGUISTIQUE ROMANES *See* LINGUISTIQUE ET SCIENCES HUMAINES **3299**

PHILOLOGIKE KYPROS / TOU HELLENIKOU PNEUMATIKOU HOMILOU KYPROU (CY) [09650341] **3310**

PHILOLOGISCHE STUDIEN UND QUELLEN (GW/0554-0674) [02762891] **3310**

PHILOLOGOS (GR) **1079**

PHILOLOGUS (GW/0031-7985) [01166994] **3310**

PHILOMEL (PHILADELPHIA, PA.) (US/1052-4878) [09343352] **3423**

PHILOSOPHER (MONTREAL, QUEBEC) (CN/0827-1887) [14937882] **4355**

PHILOSOPHER, THE (UK) [05455998] **4355**

PHILOSOPHER'S INDEX (US/0031-7993) [04187784] 4355, **4365**

PHILOSOPHES MEDIEVAUX (BE/0079-1679) [02745533] **4355**

PHILOSOPHIA (DK) [08183926] **4355**

PHILOSOPHIA (FR) [08528693] **4355**

Alphabetical Title Index — PHOTO

PHILOSOPHIA ANTIQUA
(NE/0079-1687) [02002024] **4355**

PHILOSOPHIA MATHEMATICA
(US/0031-8019) [01604214] **3526**

PHILOSOPHIA NATURALIS
(GW/0031-8027) [01496341] **4355**

PHILOSOPHIA PERENNIS (SZ)
[20466048] **4355**

PHILOSOPHIA (RAMAT GAN)
(IS/0048-3893) [01038914] **4355**

PHILOSOPHIA REFORMATA
(NE/0031-8035) [04441406] **4355**

PHILOSOPHIC EXCHANGE
(US/0193-5046) [01781976] **4355**

PHILOSOPHICA (II) [05205248] **4355**

PHILOSOPHICA (BE/0379-8402)
[04546726] **4355**

PHILOSOPHICA, AESTHETICA
(XR/0474-1021) [01607428] **4355**

PHILOSOPHICAL AND SOCIAL
ASPECTS OF SCIENCE AND
TECHNOLOGY SERIES / USSR
ACADEMY OF SCIENCES, THE
SCIENTIFIC COUNCIL FOR
PHILOSOPHICAL AND SOCIAL
ASPECTS OF SCIENCE AND
TECHNOLOGY (RU) [16965807] **5138**

PHILOSOPHICAL BOOKS
(UK/0031-8051) [01762276] **4355**

PHILOSOPHICAL CURRENTS (NE)
[01781058] **4355**

PHILOSOPHICAL FORUM, THE
(US/0031-806X) [01787155] **4355**

PHILOSOPHICAL INQUIRIES
(US/1054-2884) [22833905] **4355**

PHILOSOPHICAL INQUIRY
(GR/1105-235X) [05143336] **4355**

PHILOSOPHICAL INVESTIGATIONS
(US/0190-0536) [04163437] **4355**

PHILOSOPHICAL MAGAZINE. A,
PHYSICS OF CONDENSED MATTER,
DEFECTS AND MECHANICAL
PROPERTIES (UK/0141-8610)
[03761053] **4414**

PHILOSOPHICAL MAGAZINE. B,
PHYSICS OF CONDENSED MATTER,
STRUCTURAL, ELECTRONIC,
OPTICAL, AND MAGNETIC
PROPERTIES (UK/0958-6644)
[15674497] **4414**

PHILOSOPHICAL MAGAZINE LETTERS
(UK/0950-0839) [15131625] **4414**

PHILOSOPHICAL PAPERS
(GRAHAMSTOWN) (SA/0556-8641)
[02541791] **4356**

PHILOSOPHICAL PSYCHOLOGY
(UK/0951-5089) [18260761] 4356, **4608**

PHILOSOPHICAL QUARTERLY, THE
(UK/0031-8094) [01465673] **4356**

PHILOSOPHICAL REVIEW, THE
(US/0031-8108) [01695555] **4356**

PHILOSOPHICAL SOCIETY (FOURAH
BAY COLLEGE) See JOURNAL OF THE
PHILOSOPHICAL SOCIETY **4351**

PHILOSOPHICAL SPECULATIONS IN
SCIENCE FICTION & FANTASY
(US/0276-0886) [07310473] **3423**

PHILOSOPHICAL STUDIES
(NE/0031-8116) [01490601] **4356**

PHILOSOPHICAL STUDIES (DUBLIN,
IRELAND) *CEASED.* (IE/0554-0739)
[01762282] **4356**

PHILOSOPHICAL STUDIES IN
EDUCATION (US/0160-7561)
[03759193] 1773, **4356**

PHILOSOPHICAL STUDIES SERIES
(NE) [15626473] **4356**

PHILOSOPHICAL TOPICS
(US/0276-2080) [07322398] **4356**

PHILOSOPHICAL TRANSACTIONS.
BIOLOGICAL SCIENCES
(UK/0080-4622) [22541245] **468**

PHILOSOPHICAL TRANSACTIONS OF
THE ROYAL SOCIETY OF LONDON.
SERIES B; BIOLOGICAL SCIENCES
(UK/0962-8436) [01403239] **468**

PHILOSOPHICAL TRANSACTIONS -
ROYAL SOCIETY OF LONDON.
PHYSICAL SCIENCES AND
ENGINEERING (UK/0962-8428)
[22204120] 1990, **4414**

PHILOSOPHIE (PARIS, FRANCE : 1984)
(FR/0294-1805) [11096874] **4356**

PHILOSOPHIE POLITIQUE PARIS. 1991
(FR/1162-325X) [I1162325X] **4487**

PHILOSOPHIQUES (CN/0316-2923)
[02746864] **4356**

PHILOSOPHISCHE ABHANDLUNGEN
(GW/0175-6508) [02755740] **4355**

PHILOSOPHISCHE RUNDSCHAU
(GW/0031-8159) [01465678] **4356**

PHILOSOPHISCHE RUNDSCHAU.
BEIHEFT (GW/0554-0828) [04479446]
4356

PHILOSOPHISCHER
LITERATURANZEIGER
(GW/0031-8175) [02266100] **4356**

PHILOSOPHISCHES JAHRBUCH
(FREIBURG) (GW/0031-8183)
[01716029] **4356**

PHILOSOPHY (UK) [04936007] **4356**

PHILOSOPHY AND COMPUTING
CEASED. (US) 1199, **4356**

PHILOSOPHY AND LITERATURE
(US/0190-0013) [02715857] 3423, **4356**

PHILOSOPHY AND MEDICINE
(NE/0376-7418) [02395327] 3627, **4356**

PHILOSOPHY AND
PHENOMENOLOGICAL RESEARCH
(US/0031-8205) [01496324] **4356**

PHILOSOPHY & PUBLIC AFFAIRS
(US/0048-3915) [01586988] **5212**

PHILOSOPHY & RHETORIC
(US/0031-8213) [01715085] **4357**

PHILOSOPHY AND SOCIAL ACTION
(II/0377-2772) [02245593] **5253**

PHILOSOPHY & SOCIAL CRITICISM
(US/0191-4537) [04098836] 2252, **4357**

PHILOSOPHY EAST & WEST
(US/0031-8221) [01485347] **4357**

PHILOSOPHY IN CONTEXT
SUSPENDED. (US/0742-2733)
[02738239] **4357**

PHILOSOPHY IN SCIENCE
(US/0277-2434) [07530206] 5175, **5138**

PHILOSOPHY (LONDON)
(UK/0031-8191) [01762289] **4357**

PHILOSOPHY OF EDUCATION
(EDWARDSVILLE, ILL.) (US/8756-6575)
[09655209] **1902**

PHILOSOPHY OF EDUCATION
SOCIETY (U.S.). MEETING See
PHILOSOPHY OF EDUCATION
(EDWARDSVILLE, ILL.) **1902**

PHILOSOPHY OF MUSIC EDUCATION
NEWSLETTER See PHILOSOPHY OF
MUSIC EDUCATION REVIEW **4146**

● PHILOSOPHY OF MUSIC EDUCATION
REVIEW (US/1063-5734) [26068047]
1773, **4146**

PHILOSOPHY OF RELIGION AND
THEOLOGY : PROCEEDINGS
(US/0149-4376) [03487873] **4986**

PHILOSOPHY OF SCIENCE
ASSOCIATION See PSA (EAST
LANSING, MICH.) **5143**

PHILOSOPHY OF SCIENCE
ASSOCIATION See PHILOSOPHY OF
SCIENCE ASSOCIATION
NEWSLETTER **5138**

PHILOSOPHY OF SCIENCE
ASSOCIATION NEWSLETTER
CEASED. (US/0163-0881) [04298783]
5138

PHILOSOPHY OF SCIENCE (EAST
LANSING) (US/0031-8248) [01606760]
5138

PHILOSOPHY OF THE SOCIAL
SCIENCES (US/0048-3931) [01587778]
5212

PHILOSOPHY, PSYCHIATRY, &
PSYCHOLOGY (US) 3932, 4608, **4357**

PHILOSOPHY, THEOLOGY
(US/0890-2461) [14228352] 4986, **4357**

PHILOSOPHY TODAY (CELINA)
(US/0031-8256) [01762294] **4357**

PHILSOM/S : PERIODICAL HOLDINGS
IN THE LIBRARY OF THE SCHOOL OF
MEDICINE BY SUBJECT (US)
[01788271] 3627, **3241**

PHLEBOLOGIE (FR/0031-8280)
[05256032] **3709**

PHLEBOLOGIE STUTTGART
(GW/0939-978X) [I0939978X] **3709**

PHLEBOLOGIE UND PROKTOLOGIE
(GW/0340-305X) [09809562] **3800**

PHLEBOLOGY / VENOUS FORUM OF
THE ROYAL SOCIETY OF MEDICINE
(UK/0268-3555) [22304962] **3800**

PHLI ENVIRONMENTAL LIFE LETTER,
THE (US/1056-7399) [23841315] **2179**

PHLS MICROBIOLOGY DIGEST
(UK/0265-3400) [11154536] **568**

PHNG ONG (VM) [01786249] **2662**

PHOBLACHT, AN (IE) **5803**

PHOEBE (ONEONTA, N.Y.)
(US/1045-0904) [20041898] 3468, **5564**

PHOEBUS (US/0193-8061) [04378581]
362

PHOENICS JOURNAL OF
COMPUTATIONAL FLUID DYNAMICS &
ITS APPLICATIONS, THE (UK)
[I09698248] **1289**

PHOENIX (US) **3423**

PHOENIX (NE) [01789914] **278**

PHOENIX (KO) [05515853] 3423, **3310**

PHOENIX (1989) (US/1045-1773)
[19807440] **2543**

PHOENIX AND VICINITY POPULAR
STREET ATLAS, INCLUDING
MARICOPA COUNTY (CENSUS TRACT
EDITION) (US/0733-7574) [08653889]
2572

PHOENIX GAZETTE (US) [02251533]
5630

PHOENIX HOME/GARDEN
(US/0270-9341) [06542756] 2792, **2902**

PHOENIX (MINNEAPOLIS, MINN.), THE
(US/0893-4509) [15580934] **4608**

PHOENIX (OTTAWA. 1983)
(CN/0822-2460) [10611264] **1543**

PHOENIX REVIEW (AT/0819-3606)
[17285093] **3423**

PHOENIX RISING (TORONTO, ONT.)
CEASED. (CN/0710-1457) [09086718]
4511, **3932**

PHOENIX (STANFORD, CALIF.)
(US/0195-8593) [05233488] **243**

PHOENIX (TORONTO) (CN/0031-8299)
[01762296] **1079**

PHOENIX : VOICE OF THE SCRAP
RECYCLING INDUSTRY (US)
[20939607] **2238**

● PHOENIX (WATERLOO)
(CN/1191-8632) [27649107] **3468**

PHOLEOS (US/0733-8864) [08160468]
1409

PHONAI. LAUTBIBLIOTHEK DER
EUROPAEISCHEN SPRACHEN UND
MUNDARTEN. DEUTSCHE REIHE
(SZ/0554-0992) [01645341] **3310**

PHONE LINK : THE OFFICIAL
NEWSLETTER OF KIDS HELP PHONE
(CN/1181-6910) [23598287] **5301**

PHONE TES PROODOU (GR)
[02241408] **5138**

PHONEDISC CALIFORNIA. CD-ROM
CEASED. (US) **1161**

PHONEDISC EASTERN EDITION.
CD-ROM (US) **1161**

PHONEDISC USA RESIDENTIAL
(EASTERN & WESTERN EDITIONS)
(US) **1161**

PHONEDISC USA WESTERN EDITION.
CD-ROM (US) **1161**

PHONEDISC WESTERN EDITION.
CD-ROM See PHONEDISC USA
RESIDENTIAL (EASTERN & WESTERN
EDITIONS) **1161**

PHONEFICHE, COMMUNITY
CROSS-REFERENCE GUIDE
(US/1053-7279) [22611262] **1119**

PHONETICA (SZ/0031-8388) [01642569]
3310

PHONETICIAN, THE (US/0741-6164)
[10190695] **3310**

PHONO (AU) [06527043] 4146, **5318**

PHONO PRESS (GW) [02307172] 4146,
5318

PHONOGRAPHIC BULLETIN
(UK/0253-004X) [01789068] **5318**

PHONOLOG LIST-O-TAPES (US)
[06521035] **4146**

PHONOLOG REPORTER (US)
[05013894] **4146**

PHONOLOG REPORTS (US/0279-6562)
[07137496] **4146**

PHONOLOGY (UK/0952-6757)
[18432463] **3310**

PHOROLOGIKE ENEMEROSIS (GR)
[10813849] **4741**

PHOROLOGIKE EPITHEORESIS (GR)
[01792893] **4741**

PHOSPHOLIPIDS (UK/0264-9624)
[I02649624] **492**

PHOSPHORE PARIS (FR/0249-8138)
[I02498138] **1068**

PHOSPHORUS AND POTASSIUM
(UK/0031-8426) [02449646] **988**

PHOSPHORUS, SULFUR, AND
SILICON AND THE RELATED
ELEMENTS (US/1042-6507)
[19099238] **1037**

PHOT ARGUS EDITION GENERALE
(FR/0151-7848) [I01517848] **4372**

PHOTO & VIDEO RETAILER
(AT/1036-384X) [I1036384X] **4372**

PHOTO ANSWERS (UK/0956-8719)
[20284668] **4372**

PHOTO BUSINESS (US/0890-8753)
[14442033] **4372**

PHOTO COMMERCE EXPRESS
(CN/0380-6766) [02578650] **849**

PHOTO COMMUNIQUE (CN/0708-5435)
[05258179] **4373**

PHOTO CRAFT NEWS (US/0194-1348)
[05320959] **4373**

PHOTO/DESIGN *CEASED.*
(US/0888-5680) [13140999] **4373**

PHOTO DISTRICT NEWS (EASTERN
ED.) (US/1045-8158) [20254856] 882,
4373

PHOTO DISTRICT NEWS
(MIDWESTERN ED.) (US/1048-0161)
[20841363] 882, **4373**

PHOTO DISTRICT NEWS (SOUTHERN
ED.) (US/1048-0153) [20841207] 882,
4373

PHOTO DISTRICT NEWS. (WESTERN
ED.) (US/1048-0145) [20840851] 882,
4373

PHOTO ELECTRONIC IMAGING
(US/1060-4936) [24851932] **4373**

PHOTO - FORUM *CEASED.* (AT)
[05012783] **4373**

PHOTO — Alphabetical Title Index

PHOTO INFORMATION ALMANAC **CEASED.** (US/0093-1365) [01791034] **4373**

PHOTO INTERNATIONAL TOKYO. 1969 (JA/0289-0143) [I02890143] **4373**

PHOTO INTERPRETATION (FR/0031-8523) [01762300] **4373**

PHOTO ITALIA **CEASED.** (IT) **4373**

PHOTO JEUNESSE (FR) **4373**

PHOTO-LAB-INDEX (US/0884-9528) [02225791] **4373**

PHOTO LAB MANAGEMENT (US/0164-4769) [04750398] **4378, 4373**

PHOTO LIFE (CN/0700-3021) [03248520] **4373**

PHOTO MARKETING (US/0031-8531) [07793142] **4373**

PHOTO OPPORTUNITY (US/0899-4587) [18098617] **4373, 882**

PHOTO PARIS (FR/0399-8568) [I03998568] **4373**

PHOTO PIPELINE (CN/0826-5712) [12069376] **4373**

PHOTO PORTFOLIO ANNUAL (SZ) [11160829] **4373**

PHOTO RESOURCES (US/0736-671X) [09181237] **4373**

PHOTO REVIEW, THE (US/0363-6488) [12870977] **4373**

PHOTO ROSTER (US/0190-5449) [04719015] **4842**

PHOTO SELECTION (1991) (CN/1187-1725) [25127456] **4373**

PHOTO STAR (US/0191-7935) [04938932] **5730**

PHOTO TECHNIQUE (UK) [I13514121] **4374**

PHOTO TECHNIQUE INTERNATIONAL (GW) [10790691] **4374**

PHOTO TECHNIQUE (LONDON, ENGLAND) **CEASED.** (UK) [09696261] **4374**

PHOTOCHEMICAL AND PHOTOBIOLOGICAL REVIEWS (US/0363-499X) [02430557] **469**

PHOTOCHEMISTRY AND PHOTOBIOLOGY (UK/0031-8655) [01762302] **1056**

PHOTOCHEMISTRY (LONDON) (UK/0556-3860) [01715129] **1056**

PHOTODERMATOLOGY, PHOTOIMMUNOLOGY & PHOTOMEDICINE (DK/0905-4383) [21920498] **3675, 3722**

PHOTOFINISHING NEWS LETTER (US/0889-2393) [13827234] **4374**

PHOTOGENIES (FR) [11292107] **4374**

PHOTOGRAMMETRIC ENGINEERING AND REMOTE SENSING (US/0099-1112) [02241518] **4374, 1990**

PHOTOGRAMMETRIC JOURNAL OF FINLAND (FI) [04266064] **4374**

PHOTOGRAMMETRIC RECORD, THE (UK/0031-868X) [01762307] **2028, 2572**

PHOTOGRAPH COLLECTOR, THE (US/0271-0838) [06546552] **4374**

PHOTOGRAPH COLLECTORS' RESOURCE DIRECTORY / THE PHOTOGRAPHIC ARTS CENTER, THE (US) [10214220] **4374**

PHOTOGRAPHE, LE (FR/0369-9560) [05243830] **4324**

PHOTOGRAPHER, THE **CEASED.** (UK/0031-8698) [06691739] **4374**

PHOTOGRAPHER (VANCOUVER) (CN/0701-1326) [02660666] **4374**

PHOTOGRAPHER'S ALMANAC, THE (US) [09133550] **4374**

PHOTOGRAPHER'S FORUM (US/0194-5467) [04815062] **4374**

PHOTOGRAPHER'S MARKET (US/0147-247X) [03469714] **4374**

PHOTOGRAPHIC ART MARKET (US/1053-7031) [09612305] **4374**

●PHOTOGRAPHIC BUYERS GUIDE (US/1066-0704) [26833617] **4374**

PHOTOGRAPHIC CANADIANA (CN/0704-0024) [05018235] **4374**

PHOTOGRAPHIC INSIGHT **CEASED.** (US/0898-7572) [17896370] **4374**

PHOTOGRAPHIC JOURNAL (1956) (UK/0031-8736) [05813487] **4374**

PHOTOGRAPHIC PROCESSING (US/0031-8744) [07201985] **4374**

PHOTOGRAPHIC TECHNIQUES IN SCIENTIFIC RESEARCH (UK/0302-4210) [01783656] **4374**

PHOTOGRAPHIC TECHNOLOGY USSR (US/0092-4709) [01789679] **4374**

PHOTOGRAPHIC TRADE NEWS *See* PHOTOGRAPHIC TRADE NEWS MASTER BUYING GUIDE **4374**

PHOTOGRAPHIC TRADE NEWS MASTER BUYING GUIDE (US) [04456176] **4374**

PHOTOGRAPHICA (US) [19696378] **4374**

PHOTOGRAPHIE (SZ) [03397542] **4374**

PHOTOGRAPHIES MAGAZINE (FR/0988-7679) [21509151] **4374**

PHOTOGRAPHS (NEW YORK, N.Y. : 1982) (US/0740-4158) [08260310] **4374**

PHOTOGRAPHY ANNUAL **CEASED.** (US/0079-1849) [01325878] **4374**

PHOTOGRAPHY IN NEW YORK (US/1040-0346) [18296944] **4374**

PHOTOGRAPHY INDEX (US/0193-2810) [05160969] **4374**

PHOTOGRAPHY (LONDON, ENGLAND : 1986) **SUSPENDED.** (UK/0950-2009) [14950966] **4374**

PHOTOGRAPHY MARKET PLACE **SUSPENDED.** (US/0095-439X) [02240317] **4374**

PHOTOGRAPHY YEAR BOOK (UK) [03814763] **4375**

PHOTOHISTORICA (BE) [06597824] **4375**

PHOTO*LETTER (US) [10981479] **4375**

PHOTOLETTER, THE (US/0190-1400) [06757850] **4375**

PHOTOMAG (VILLE LEMOYNE) (CN/0226-7411) [06515142] **4375**

PHOTONICS AND OPTOELECTRONICS (US/1067-5345) [27261344] **2075, 4440**

PHOTONICS DIRECTORY, THE (US/1044-1425) [19560145] **4440**

PHOTONICS EUROPEAN DIRECTORY (US/1056-9324) [23845971] **3486**

PHOTONICS SPECTRA (PITTSFIELD, MASS. 1982) (US/0731-1230) [08099271] **4440**

PHOTONIRVACHAK (DEHRA DUN) (II/0255-660X) [03500587] **1391**

PHOTOPLAY COMBINED WITH MOVIE MIRROR *See* MOVIE MIRROR **4075**

PHOTOPRO (TITUSVILLE, FLA.) (US/1049-8974) [21344988] **4375**

PHOTORESEARCHER / EUROPEAN SOCIETY FOR THE HISTORY OF PHOTOGRAPHY (UK/0958-2606) [23029393] **4375**

PHOTOSCOOP / PICTORIAL MAGAZINE (BE) **4375**

PHOTOSYNTHESIS BIBLIOGRAPHY (NE) [01459625] **478**

PHOTOSYNTHESIS RESEARCH (NE/0166-8595) [06802818] **521**

PHOTOSYNTHETICA (NE/0300-3604) [01762312] **521, 2220, 492**

PHOTOVIDEO (CN/0834-227X) [16220893] **4076, 4375**

PHOTOVISION (SP/0211-7029) [08546079] **4375**

PHOTOVOLTAIC INSIDER'S REPORT (US/0731-4671) [08197467] **2075, 1953**

PHOTOVOLTAICS TECHNIQUE **CEASED.** (CN/0824-3794) [10634828] **4414**

PHP INTANASHONARU (JA) [02382757] **2507**

PHRONEMA (AT/0819-4920) [I08194920] **4986, 1094**

PHRONESIS (NE/0031-8868) [04359643] **4357**

PHRONESIS (HEIDELBERG, GERMANY) (NE/0031-8868) [20059403] **4357**

PHRONESIS. REVISTA DE NEUROLOGIA, NEUROCIRUGIA Y PSIQUIATRIA (SP) [01778353] **4608, 3844**

PHS GRANTS POLICY MEMORANDUM (US) [03454344] **5686**

PHS SUPPLY SERVICE CENTER (U.S.) *See* MEDICAL SUPPLY CATALOG / U.S. PUBLIC HEALTH SERVICE **3611**

PHSC JOURNAL (CN/0714-8305) [09106492] **1146**

PHTHIOTIKA CHRONIKA (GR) [20571728] **1079**

PHU NU DIEN DAN (VM) [02243162] **5564**

PHUKET MARINE BIOLOGICAL CENTER (TH/0858-1088) [04719159] **557**

PHYCOLOGIA (OXFORD) (UK/0031-8884) [01642231] **521**

PHYCOLOGICAL RESEARCH (AT/1322-0829) **469**

PHYCOLOGICAL STUDIES (US/0554-1174) [01781827] **469**

PHYKOS (II/0554-1182) [01762317] **521**

PHYLLIS SCHLAFLY REPORT, THE (US/0556-0152) [04105633] **4487**

PHYLON (1960) (US/0031-8906) [01642817] **5213**

PHYS 13 NEWS (CN/0710-0140) [08308060] **4414**

●PHYS ED JOURNAL OF SPORTS MEDICINE, THE (US/1062-9297) [25812071] **3955**

PHYSICA A (NE/0378-4371) [02156672] **4414**

PHYSICA B. CONDENSED MATTER (NE/0921-4526) [18484113] **4414**

PHYSICA C. SUPERCONDUCTIVITY (NE/0921-4534) [17642006] **4414**

PHYSICA. D (NE/0167-2789) [06510433] **4414**

PHYSICA MEDICA (IT/1120-1797) [I11201797] **3627**

PHYSICA SCRIPTA (SW/0031-8949) [01089110] **4414**

PHYSICA STATUS SOLIDI. A: APPLIED RESEARCH (GW/0031-8965) [01639590] **4414**

PHYSICA STATUS SOLIDI. B : BASIC RESEARCH (GW/0370-1972) [01762323] **4415**

PHYSICAL ACOUSTICS (US/0893-388X) [02251734] **4453**

PHYSICAL & OCCUPATIONAL THERAPY IN GERIATRICS (US/0270-3181) [06389623] **3754, 4381**

PHYSICAL & OCCUPATIONAL THERAPY IN PEDIATRICS (US/0194-2638) [05365306] **3910, 4381**

PHYSICAL CHEMISTRY OF FAST REACTIONS (US/0144-963X) [06135755] **1056**

PHYSICAL CONDITION REPORT OF COMMERCIAL DRIVERS INVOLVED IN ACCIDENTS (US/0090-2896) [01786492] **4795, 5389**

PHYSICAL DISABILITIES SPECIAL INTEREST SECTION NEWSLETTER (US/0279-411X) [07841477] **4392, 1883**

PHYSICAL EDUCATION DIGEST (CN/0843-2635) [20285218] **4912**

PHYSICAL EDUCATION GOLD BOOK **CEASED.** (US/0733-7272) [08641718] **1857**

PHYSICAL EDUCATION INDEX (CAPE GIRARDEAU) (US/0191-9202) [04014045] **1857, 1796**

PHYSICAL EDUCATION REVIEW (UK/0140-7708) [04951980] **1857**

PHYSICAL EDUCATOR, THE (US/0031-8981) [01762326] **1857**

PHYSICAL FACILITIES AT INSTITUTIONS OF HIGHER EDUCATION IN WEST VIRGINIA (US/0093-884X) [01793261] **1841**

PHYSICAL FITNESS/SPORTS MEDICINE **CEASED.** (US/0163-2582) [03622655] **3955, 2600**

PHYSICAL GEOGRAPHY (US/0272-3646) [06607694] **2572**

PHYSICAL MEDICINE AND REHABILITATION (US/0888-7357) [13713015] **3884**

PHYSICAL MEDICINE AND REHABILITATION CLINICS OF NORTH AMERICA (US/1047-9651) [20832177] **4381, 4392**

PHYSICAL METHODS IN ORGANIC CHEMISTRY (US) [01590159] **1046**

●PHYSICAL OCEANOGRAPHY (NE) [28101202] **1455**

PHYSICAL PROTECTION OF NUCLEAR FACILITIES, QUARTERLY PROGRESS REPORT / SANDIA LABORATORIES ; PREPARED FOR DIVISION OF SAFEGUARDS, FUEL CYCLE AND ENVIRONMENTAL RESEARCH, OFFICE OF NUCLEAR REGULATORY RESEARCH, U.S. NUCLEAR REGULATORY COMMISSION (US) [08329262] **2158**

PHYSICAL RESEARCH REPORT (US/0095-6686) [01798193] **2028**

PHYSICAL REVIEW. A (US/1050-2947) [21266025] **4415**

PHYSICAL REVIEW ABSTRACTS (US/0048-4024) [01762329] **4415**

PHYSICAL REVIEW AND PHYSICAL REVIEW LETTERS INDEX (US/0094-0003) [03811892] **4415**

PHYSICAL REVIEW. A[15], STATISTICAL PHYSICS, PLASMAS, FLUIDS, AND RELATED INTERDISCIPLINARY TOPICS (US) [20978116] **4415**

PHYSICAL REVIEW B : CONDENSED MATTER (US/0163-1829) [04206245] **4415**

PHYSICAL REVIEW C : NUCLEAR PHYSICS (US/0556-2813) [01639677] **4450**

PHYSICAL REVIEW. D (US) [24181870] **4450**

PHYSICAL REVIEW D : PARTICLES AND FIELDS (US/0556-2821) [01762331] **4415**

PHYSICAL REVIEW. D[15], PARTICLES, FIELDS, GRAVITATION, AND COSMOLOGY (US) [24290285] **4450**

●PHYSICAL REVIEW E. STATISTICAL PHYSICS, PLASMAS, FLUIDS, AND RELATED INTERDISCIPLINARY TOPICS (US/1063-651X) [26103502] **4415**

PHYSICAL REVIEW LETTERS (US/0031-9007) [01715834] **4415**

PHYSICAL SCIENCES ON FILE (US) [17650507] **5138**

PHYSICAL TECHNIQUES IN MEDICINE (UK/0162-2528) [04116901] **4415, 3695**

PHYSICAL THERAPY (US/0031-9023) [01762333] **4381**

●PHYSICAL THERAPY FORUM (KING OF PRUSSIA, PA. 1994) (US/1075-4342) [30054940] **4381**

PHYSICAL THERAPY FORUM (MIDDLE ATLANTIC ED.) (US/8750-2119) [11108245] **4381**

PHYSICAL THERAPY FORUM (MIDDLE ATLANTIC ED.) *See* PHYSICAL THERAPY FORUM (KING OF PRUSSIA, PA. 1994) **4381**

PHYSICAL THERAPY FORUM (MIDWEST/SOUTHERN ED.) *See* PHYSICAL THERAPY FORUM (KING OF PRUSSIA, PA. 1994) **4381**

PHYSICAL THERAPY FORUM (NORTHEAST ED.) *See* PHYSICAL THERAPY FORUM (KING OF PRUSSIA, PA. 1994) **4381**

PHYSICAL THERAPY FORUM (WESTERN ED.) *See* PHYSICAL THERAPY FORUM (KING OF PRUSSIA, PA. 1994) **4381**

PHYSICAL THERAPY PRACTICE *CEASED.* (US/1054-8513) [22994167] **4381**

●PHYSICAL THERAPY REIMBURSEMENT NEWS (US/1073-9483) [29569122] **4381**

PHYSICAL THERAPY TODAY (US/1042-2579) [18980930] **4381**

PHYSICIAN (US) **4986, 3916**

PHYSICIAN AND SPORTSMEDICINE, THE (US/0091-3847) [01787159] **3955**

PHYSICIAN ASSISTANT (1983) (US/8750-7544) [09265622] **3627**

PHYSICIAN ASSISTANT NEWSLETTER OF ETHICS (US) [29537047] **3627, 2252**

●PHYSICIAN COMPENSATION AND PRODUCTION SURVEY (US/1064-4563) [26287976] **3627**

PHYSICIAN EAST (US/0192-2963) [04744008] **3627**

PHYSICIAN EXECUTIVE (US/0898-2759) [13191440] **3916**

PHYSICIAN EXECUTIVE REVIEW (US) **3916**

PHYSICIAN MANAGER (US/1055-1603) [23096642] **3791**

PHYSICIAN MANPOWER IN OREGON DATA BOOK (US/0148-5490) [03323640] **3916**

PHYSICIAN MARKETPLACE UPDATE *CEASED.* (US/1051-2632) [21224724] **3627**

PHYSICIAN REFERRAL UPDATE (US) **3627**

●PHYSICIAN SALARY SURVEY REPORT, HOSPITAL-BASED AND GROUP PRACTICE (US) [25756029] **3916**

PHYSICIAN'S ADVISORY, THE (US) **3916**

PHYSICIANS & COMPUTERS (US/0891-8163) [12617214] **1261**

PHYSICIANS' CURRENT PROCEDURAL TERMINOLOGY (US/0276-8283) [07432280] **3627, 1928**

PHYSICIANS' DESK REFERENCE (COMPACT DISK ED.) (US/1046-2694) [20371510] **4324**

PHYSICIANS' DESK REFERENCE DRUG INTERACTIONS & SIDE EFFECTS INDEX (US) [23189521] **4324**

PHYSICIANS' DESK REFERENCE FOR NONPRESCRIPTION DRUGS (US/1044-1395) [06261197] **4324**

PHYSICIANS' DESK REFERENCE FOR OPHTHALMOLOGY (US/0091-6803) [04608789] **3878**

PHYSICIANS' DESK REFERENCE FOR RADIOLOGY AND NUCLEAR MEDICINE (US) [05297546] **3849, 3944**

PHYSICIANS' DESK REFERENCE (PRINT ED.) (US/0093-4461) [01311259] **4325**

PHYSICIANS DESK REFERENCE : SUPPLEMENT (US) **4325**

PHYSICIANS DRG NEWSLETTER *CEASED.* (US/0748-8211) [11012763] **5301**

PHYSICIAN'S DRG WORKING GUIDEBOOK, THE (US) [16076978] **3916**

PHYSICIANS' DRUG ALERT *See* PRIMARY CARE MEDICINE DRUG ALERTS **4325**

PHYSICIANS FEE GUIDE / AS COMPILED BY HEALTHCARE CONSULTANTS, INC (US) [22701535] **3916, 3791**

PHYSICIANS FINANCIAL NEWS (US/8750-9407) [11945916] **3627, 803**

PHYSICIANS' GENERIX *See* PHYSICIANS' GENRX **4325**

●PHYSICIANS' GENRX (US) [27472267] **4325**

PHYSICIAN'S GUIDE FOR TRAVEL & MEDICAL CONVENTION PLANNING (CN/1188-1771) [25652381] **5488, 3791**

PHYSICIAN'S GUIDE TO MONEY MANAGEMENT (US/0883-4911) [12144071] **803**

●PHYSICIANS' GUIDE TO RARE DISEASES (US/1053-9727) [22713459] **3627**

PHYSICIAN'S HANDBOOK (US/0079-192X) [01762336] **3627**

PHYSICIAN'S MANAGEMENT (US/0031-9066) [02251535] **3627**

PHYSICIAN'S MANAGEMENT MANUAL (CN) **3916**

PHYSICIAN'S MANAGEMENT MANUALS *CEASED.* (CN/0705-6311) [03935266] **3916**

PHYSICIAN'S MARKETING & MANAGEMENT (US/1042-2625) [18979040] **3627**

PHYSICIANS MEDICARE AUTHORITY (US) **3627**

●PHYSICIAN'S MEDLINE PLUS (US/1065-6545) [26666819] **3241, 3627, 3661**

PHYSICIAN'S NEWSLETTER (1990) (CN/0848-676X) [23455427] **3916**

PHYSICIAN'S NEWSLETTER - SASKATCHEWAN. SASKATCHEWAN HEALTH (CN/1187-5062) [25352043] **3627**

PHYSICIAN'S PAYMENT UPDATE (US/1055-629X) [23244523] **882, 3627**

PHYSICIAN'S RELATIONS ADVISOR (US) **3627**

PHYSICIAN'S RELATIONS UPDATE (US) **3916**

PHYSICIAN'S RESOURCE MANUAL ON OSTEOPOROSIS (UK) [17844879] **3806**

PHYSICIAN'S SPORTSLIFE (US/0883-4938) [12153366] **2600**

PHYSICIANS' TRAVEL & MEETING GUIDE (US/0745-4554) [09181368] **5488**

PHYSICIAN'S WEEKLY (US/1047-3793) [18891729] **3627**

PHYSICIAN'S WORLD (US/0091-200X) [01786498] **3916**

PHYSICS ABSTRACTS (UK/0036-8091) [01762338] **4415, 4427**

PHYSICS ABSTRACTS. AUTHOR INDEX (UK) [07294773] **4415**

PHYSICS ABSTRACTS. SUBJECT INDEX (UK) [07294719] **4415**

PHYSICS AND CHEMISTRY IN SPACE (GW/0079-1938) [01643242] **988, 4415**

PHYSICS AND CHEMISTRY OF GLASSES (UK/0031-9090) [01762340] **2593**

PHYSICS AND CHEMISTRY OF LIQUIDS (US/0031-9104) [01310250] **1056**

PHYSICS AND CHEMISTRY OF MATERIALS WITH LAYERED STRUCTURES (NE/0378-1917) [02314199] **988, 4415**

PHYSICS AND CHEMISTRY OF MINERALS (GW/0342-1791) [03339258] **1443**

PHYSICS AND CHEMISTRY OF THE EARTH (UK/0079-1946) [01281118] **1359**

PHYSICS AND DEVELOPMENT / INTERNATIONAL ATOMIC ENERGY AGENCY AND UNITED NATIONS EDUCATIONAL, SCIENTIFIC, AND CULTURAL ORGANIZATION, INTERNATIONAL CENTRE FOR THEORETICAL PHYSICS (IT) [18432678] **4415**

PHYSICS BRIEFS (UK/0170-7434) [04689432] **4415, 4427**

●PHYSICS-DOKLADY (US/1063-7753) [26141755] **4415**

PHYSICS EDUCATION (UK/0031-9120) [01762342] **4415**

PHYSICS EDUCATION (MADRAS) (II/0970-5953) [25797207] **4415, 1841**

PHYSICS ESSAYS (CN/0836-1398) [18581649] **4415**

PHYSICS IN CANADA (CN/0031-9147) [02110541] **4415**

PHYSICS IN MEDICINE & BIOLOGY (UK/0031-9155) [01762343] **469, 479**

PHYSICS LETTERS : PART A (NE/0375-9601) [02449671] **4416**

PHYSICS LETTERS : PART B (NE/0370-2693) [02449672] **4450**

PHYSICS MANPOWER, EDUCATION AND EMPLOYMENT STUDIES (US/0569-5716) [01791408] **4416, 4427**

PHYSICS NEWS (BOMBAY) (II) [02279919] **4416**

●PHYSICS OF ATOMIC NUCLEI (US/1063-7788) [26139790] **4450**

●PHYSICS OF FLUIDS (1994) (US/1070-6631) [28447185] **4416**

PHYSICS OF FLUIDS. A, FLUID DYNAMICS (US/0899-8213) [18233939] **4416**

PHYSICS OF FLUIDS. A, FLUID DYNAMICS *See* PHYSICS OF FLUIDS (1994) **4416**

PHYSICS OF FLUIDS. B, PLASMA PHYSICS *See* PHYSICS OF PLASMAS **4416**

PHYSICS OF FLUIDS. B, PLASMA PHYSICS (US/0899-8221) [18233933] **4416**

PHYSICS OF HIGH ENERGY DENSITY (RU/1061-7582) [25442494] **4416**

PHYSICS OF METALS (US/0275-9144) [07250491] **4014**

PHYSICS OF METALS AND METALLOGRAPHY, THE *CEASED.* (UK/0031-918X) [01645143] **4014**

PHYSICS OF METALS AND METALLOGRAPHY, THE (RU) **4015**

●PHYSICS OF PARTICLES AND NUCLEI (US/1063-7796) [26139714] **4450**

●PHYSICS OF PLASMAS (US/1070-664X) [28447471] **4416**

PHYSICS OF THE EARTH AND PLANETARY INTERIORS (NE/0031-9201) [00878793] **1391**

PHYSICS OF THE SOLID STATE (US/1063-7834) [26137046] **4416**

PHYSICS REPORTS (NE/0370-1573) [01313698] **4416**

PHYSICS REVIEW DEDDINGTON (UK/0959-8472) [I09598472] **4416**

PHYSICS TEACHER, THE (US/0031-921X) [01715336] **4416, 1902**

PHYSICS TODAY (US/0031-9228) [01605044] **4416**

●PHYSICS, USPEKHI (US/1063-7869) [26136230] **4416**

PHYSICS WORLD (UK/0953-8585) [18665522] **4416**

PHYSIFAX (US) [06607671] **3627**

PHYSIK DATEN (GW/0344-8401) [04291689] **4416**

PHYSIK IN UNSERER ZEIT (GW/0031-9252) [04064235] **4416**

PHYSIK UND DIDAKTIK (GW/0340-8515) [I03408515] **4417, 1902**

PHYSIKALISCHE BLATTER (GW/0031-9279) [06445472] **4417**

PHYSIKALISCHE EIGENSCHAFTEN VON BODEN DER SCHWEIZ / PROFESSUR FUR BODENPHYSIK ETH, ZURICH (SZ) [08790893] **181**

PHYSIKALISCHE MEDIZIN (GW/0940-6689) [26890949] **4381**

PHYSIKALISCHE MEDIZIN, REHABILITATIONSMEDIZIN, KURORTMEDIZIN (GW/0940-6689) [I09406689] **3627**

PHYSIOLOGIA PLANTARUM (DK/0031-9317) [01762354] **585, 521**

PHYSIOLOGIC AND PHARMACOLOGIC BASES OF DRUG THERAPY (US/0736-4326) [08559481] **585, 4325**

PHYSIOLOGICAL AND MOLECULAR PLANT PATHOLOGY (UK/0885-5765) [12680272] **521**

PHYSIOLOGICAL CHEMISTRY AND PHYSICS AND MEDICAL NMR (US/0748-6642) [10169370] **496, 469**

PHYSIOLOGICAL ENTOMOLOGY (UK/0307-6962) [02132356] **5612**

●PHYSIOLOGICAL MEASUREMENT (UK/0967-3334) [27890544] **4417, 3695**

PHYSIOLOGICAL PHARMACOLOGY : A COMPREHENSIVE TREATISE (US) [02251833] **585, 4325**

PHYSIOLOGICAL RESEARCH / ACADEMIA SCIENTIARUM BOHEMOSLOVACA (XR) [24169523] **585**

PHYSIOLOGICAL REVIEWS (US/0031-9333) [01762360] **585**

PHYSIOLOGICAL SOCIETY *See* MONOGRAPHS OF THE PHYSIOLOGICAL SOCIETY **584**

PHYSIOLOGICAL SOCIETY OF PHILADELPHIA *See* MONOGRAPHS OF THE PHYSIOLOGICAL SOCIETY OF PHILADELPHIA **584**

PHYSIOLOGICAL ZOOLOGY (US/0031-935X) [01587071] **5594**

PHYSIOLOGIST, THE (US/0031-9376) [01762362] **585**

PHYSIOLOGY & BEHAVIOR (US/0031-9384) [01714854] **585**

PHYSIOLOGY AND ECOLOGY JAPAN (JA/0370-9612) [09600729] **469, 2220**

PHYSIOLOGY AND PATHOPHYSIOLOGY OF THE SKIN, THE (UK/0141-2841) [03880410] **585**

PHYSIOLOGY CANADA (1983) (CN/0822-9058) [10181371] **585**

PHYSIOQUEBEC (CN/0708-1006) [04955109] **4381**

PHYSIOTHERAPY (UK/0031-9406) [01762364] **4382**

PHYSIOTHERAPY — Alphabetical Title Index

PHYSIOTHERAPY CANADA (CN/0300-0508) [02940706] **3627**

PHYSIOTHERAPY IN SPORT (UK/0954-0741) [l09540741] **3955**

PHYSIOTHERAPY INDEX : CURRENT AWARENESS TOPICS SERVICES (UK/0950-6659) [17588576] **4382**

PHYSIOTHERAPY THEORY AND PRACTICE (UK/0959-3985) [22472719] **4382**

PHYSIQUE, ATOMIQUE ET MOLECULAIRE PLASMAS (FR) **4450**

PHYSIQUE, CHIMIE. LEXIQUE (FR/0154-0300) [07087760] **3241**

PHYSIS (FIRENZE) (IT/0031-9414) [06616104] **5138**

PHYSIS. SECCIONES A, B Y C (AG/0326-1441) [04890748] 521, **5594**

PHYTA MONOGRAPH (II) [15264850] **521**

PHYTIATRIE-PHYTOPHARMACIE *CEASED.* (FR/0031-8876) [04064265] **521**

PHYTOCHEMICAL ANALYSIS (UK/0958-0344) [23673004] 492, **522**

PHYTOCHEMICAL BULLETIN (US/0898-3437) [11452457] **522**

PHYTOCHEMICAL SOCIETY OF EUROPE See ANNUAL PROCEEDINGS OF THE PHYTOCHEMICAL SOCIETY OF EUROPE **480**

PHYTOCHEMISTRY (OXFORD) (UK/0031-9422) [01762365] **522**

PHYTOCOENOLOGIA (GW/0340-269X) [02436369] **522**

PHYTOLOGIA (US/0031-9430) [01590036] 2220, **522**

PHYTOLOGIA MEMOIRS (US) [07072970] **522**

PHYTOMA (FR/0370-2723) [01762366] **522**

PHYTOMA LA DEFENSE DES VEGETAUX (FR) **522**

PHYTOMA, LA DEFENSE DES VEGETAUX (FR/1164-6993) [l11646993] **120**

PHYTOMEDICINE (GW/0944-7113) **3627**

PHYTOMORPHOLOGY (II/0031-9449) [01604856] **522**

PHYTON (BUENOS AIRES) (AG/0031-9457) [01762368] **522**

PHYTON (HORN) (AU/0079-2047) [01762367] **522**

PHYTOPARASITICA (IS/0334-2123) [02387054] 120, **522**

PHYTOPATHOLOGIA MEDITERRANEA (IT/0031-9465) [01762369] **522**

PHYTOPATHOLOGICAL PAPERS (UK/0069-7141) [01564466] **522**

PHYTOPATHOLOGY (US/0031-949X) [01762372] **522**

PHYTOPHAGA (II) [18056686] **5612**

PHYTOPHAGA (IT/0393-8131) [103938131] **5612**

PHYTOPHTHORA NEWSLETTER (UK/0748-6693) [05023438] **523**

PHYTOPHYLACTICA *CEASED.* (SA/0370-1263) [01762373] **523**

PHYTOPROTECTION (CN/0031-9511) [01762374] **181**

PI HA-ATON. MUSAF (IS) [05242134] **5213**

PI KAPPA DELTA *See* FORENSIC OF PI KAPPA DELTA, THE **1111**

PI KAPPA PHI *See* STAR AND LAMP OF PI KAPPA PHI, THE **1095**

PI MU EPSILON *See* PI MU EPSILON JOURNAL **3526**

PI MU EPSILON JOURNAL (US/0031-952X) [01762376] **3526**

PI QUALITY (US) **1199**

PIACT PAPERS (US/0197-6699) [06074430] **590**

PIACT PRODUCT NEWS (US/0198-7445) [06214025] **590**

PIANO *CEASED.* (IT) [04139208] **2830**

●PIANO & KEYBOARD (US/1067-3881) [27194480] **4146**

PIANO & ORGAN (US) **4146**

PIANO AND ORGAN PURCHASER'S GUIDE *See* PURCHASER'S GUIDE TO THE MUSIC INDUSTRIES, THE **4148**

PIANO GUILD NOTES (US/0031-9546) [01004537] **4146**

PIANO-JAHRBUCH (GW/0173-8607) [06705195] **4146**

PIANO JOURNAL / EUROPEAN PIANO TEACHERS ASSOCIATION (UK/0267-7253) [07683283] **4146**

●PIANO (PORT TOWNSEND, WASH.) (US/1066-1530) [26876576] **4146**

PIANO QUARTERLY *See* PIANO & KEYBOARD **4146**

PIANO QUARTERLY, THE (US/0031-9554) [04631597] **4146**

PIANO STYLIST & JAZZ WORKSHOP *See* KEYBOARD CLASSICS & PIANO STYLIST **4127**

PIANO STYLIST & JAZZ WORKSHOP, THE (US/1041-2492) [18694718] **4146**

PIANO TECHNICIAN'S JOURNAL (US/0031-9562) [02434398] **4146**

PIAO CHUN HUA (CH) [11451873] **4032**

PIAO CHUN HUA TUNG HSUN / BIAOZHUNHUA TONGXUN (CC) [09578938] **4032**

PIATT COUNTY HISTORICAL AND GENEALOGICAL SOCIETY, THE (US/8755-7029) [11365905] **2467**

PIAZZA (SZ) [20085308] **1920**

PIB/LNA. MAGAZINE TOTALS, CLASS TOTALS (US) [17469242] **763**

PIB MAGAZINE ADVERTISING ANALYSIS. ADVERTISING PAGE INDEX (US/0749-0992) [11104428] **763**

PIB MAGAZINE ADVERTISING ANALYSIS. CURRENT QUARTER BRAND-MAGAZINE DETAIL (US/0741-3254) [10107804] **763**

PIBROCH, THE (US) [06765263] **2754**

PIB'S BUSINESS & INCENTIVES (US/1056-5442) [23736256] **703**

PIC (DOYLESTOWN, PA.) (US/0739-5302) [09763052] **1883**

PIC NEWSLETTER (FJ) [10012130] **3241**

PIC : PEOPLE IN CAMERA (UK/0956-2281) [l09562281] **4375**

PICA (CN/0225-7114) [06299269] 2220, **4170**

PICAYUNE ITEM, THE (US) [16258441] **5701**

PICCOLA IMPRESA (IT) [29813655] **703**

PICCOLA RASSEGNA IL MODELLARIO (IT) **2491**

PICCOLE NOTE *See* NOTE, RECENSIONI, NOTIZIE **3418**

PICCOLO AZIONISTA (IT) **882**

PICCOLO DI ALESSANDRIA, IL (IT) **1333**

PICENUM SERAPHICUM (IT) [02245701] **5034**

PICKENS COUNTY HERALD (US/0893-0767) [15344667] **5627**

PICKER ART GALLERY JOURNAL / THE PICKER ART GALLERY, COLGATE UNIVERSITY, THE (US) [19608531] 4095, **362**

PICKER GALLERY *See* PICKER ART GALLERY JOURNAL / THE PICKER ART GALLERY, COLGATE UNIVERSITY, THE **362**

PICKERINGTON TIMES-SUN, THE (US/0746-9101) [10382930] **5730**

●PICKING THE "RIGHT" BIBLE STUDY PROGRAM (US/1061-1010) [25180761] **5018**

PICKUP (UK) **1773**

PICKUP, VAN & 4WD ROAD TEST ANNUAL AND BUYERS' GUIDE (US) [05090262] 5423, **951**

PICKUPS 'N PANELS IN PRINT (US/0747-1041) [10547201] **5389**

PICKWORLD IRVINE, CALIF (US/1066-2154) [l10662154] **1199**

PICM PROFESION. INVESTIGACION Y CLINICA MEDICA (SP) **3627**

PICSOU MAGAZINE (FR/0767-807X) [I0767807X] **1068**

PICTON, LE (FR/0151-6086) [I01516086] **2702**

PICTORIAL GAZETTE, THE (US) [25575488] **5646**

PICTORIAL NEW VAUTIER MAGAZINE (BE) **4375**

PICTORIAL PRICE GUIDE TO AMERICAN ANTIQUES AND OBJECTS MADE FOR THE AMERICAN MARKET / BY DOROTHY HAMMOND (US) [11863807] **252**

PICTURE ATLAS OF THE WORLD (US) 2572, **1928**

PICTURE FRAMING MAGAZINE (US/1052-9977) [22435331] 374, **2776**

PICTURE HOUSE (UK/0263-7553) [I02637553] **4076**

PICTURE PERFECT (US/1045-0629) **4375**

PICTURE (SANTA FE SPRINGS, CALIF.) (US/0732-1511) [08140552] **4375**

PICTURE SHOW ANNUAL (UK) [02432026] **4076**

PIE, PUBLICATIONS INDEXED FOR ENGINEERING (US/0085-4581) [01978892] **1990**

PIECES OF EIGHT (US) [20068974] **803**

●PIECEWORK (LOVELAND, COLO.) (US/1067-2249) [27163936] 5185, **374**

PIED PIPER (AT/0813-7846) [I08137846] 3423, **1068**

PIEDMONT HERALD (PIEDMONT, W. VA.) (US) [13047419] **5764**

PIEDMONT JOURNAL-INDEPENDENT, THE (US/0890-6017) [18957493] **5627**

PIEDMONT LIBRARIES ACQUISITIONS INFORMATION NETWORK *See* PLAIN TALK **3241**

PIEDMONT LITERARY REVIEW *CEASED.* (US/0275-357X) [07119003] **3423**

PIEDRA BOCONA, LA (NQ) [27748696] 1578, **2830**

PIEGAN STORYTELLER, THE (US/0195-5799) [03370212] **2754**

PIEL (SP) **3185**

PIELGRZYM POLSKI (PL) [07341735] **5066**

PIEMONTE TUTTOVACANZA (IT) **5489**

PIEMONTEUROPA (IT) **2491**

PIERCE COUNTY : A LABOR MARKET INFORMATION REPORT OF THE RESEARCH AND ANALYSIS BRANCH, WASHINGTON STATE EMPLOYMENT SECURITY DEPARTMENT / PREPARED IN COOPERATION WITH THE EMPLOYMENT AND TRAINING ADMINISTRATION, U.S. DEPARTMENT OF LABOR (US) [11858098] **1702**

PIERCE COUNTY BUSINESS EXAMINER (US) [18435670] 703, **5761**

PIERCE COUNTY HERALD (ELLSWORTH, WIS.) (US/8755-3244) [11285276] **5770**

PIERCE COUNTY HERALD (PUYALLUP, WASH.) (US/0192-1401) [05019614] **5761**

PIERCE COUNTY POPULAR STREET ATLAS (CENSUS TRACT ED.) (US/0733-7663) [08655752] **2572**

PIERCE COUNTY TRIBUNE, THE (US) [01608357] **5726**

PIERCE PIANO ATLAS (US/0733-429X) [06228692] **4146**

PIERRE-BRILLANT (CN/0711-4753) [08659271] **5793**

PIERRE-FORT - PIERRE GENEALOGICAL SOCIETY, THE (US/0737-7975) [09445548] 434, **2467**

PIERRE JEAN JOUVE (FR/0294-0086) [09930541] **3423**

PIERRES VIVANTES (CN/0226-3572) [06512301] **5034**

PIG FARMER *See* PORK JOURNAL **218**

PIG FARMER, THE (AT/0031-9740) [02580650] **217**

PIG FARMING (UK/0031-9759) [02387033] **217**

PIG INTERNATIONAL (EUROPE, ASIA, AFRICA, LATIN AMERICA AND OCEANIA EDITION (US/0191-8834) [04970445] **217**

PIG IRON (US/0362-5214) [02289915] **3423**

●PIG JOURNAL, THE (UK/1352-9749) [I13529749] **5518**

PIG MANAGEMENT SCHEME RESULTS (UK) [03962995] **217**

PIG NEWS AND INFORMATION (UK/0143-9014) [06732050] 217, **155**

PIG PAPER, THE (US/0710-3034) [08415753] **4146**

PIG STATISTICS, NUMBER AND WEIGHT OF PIGS SLAUGHTERED AT BACON FACTORIES (IE/0791-3044) [l07913044] **120**

PIG SURVEY (IE/0791-3095) **217**

PIG VETERINARY JOURNAL (UK/0956-0939) [20108092] **5518**

PIGE KEJI (CC/0253-3642) [08691018] **3185**

PIGMENT & RESIN TECHNOLOGY (UK/0369-9420) [01762392] **4225**

PIGMENT CELL (SZ/0301-0139) [01775043] **539**

PIGS (NE/0168-9533) [11716485] **217**

PIK. PRAXIS DER INFORMATIONSVERARBEITUNG UND KOMMUNIKATION (GW/0930-5157) [l09305157] **1199**

PIKA NI YAKARETE, HIBAKU TAIKENKI (JA) [11465745] **2662**

PIKA NOZNA (PL/0137-4710) [I01374710] **4912**

PIKE & FISCHER RADIO REGULATION / BOARD OF EDITORS : HENRY G. FISCHER ... [ET AL.] (US) [09927795] **1162**

PIKE & FISCHER SHIPPING REGULATION (US) **5454**

PIKE COUNTY DISPATCH (MILFORD, PA.) (US) [15061250] **5738**

PIKE FEE DIRECTORY (US) **1136**

PIKE REGISTER (US) [16145663] **5666**

PIKES PEAK JOURNAL, THE (US) [22539683] **5644**

PIKESTAFF FORUM, THE (US/0192-8716) [05103685] **2543**

PILGRIM JOURNAL, THE (US/0885-4947) [12655194] **5235**

PILGRIMAGE (US/0361-0802) [01607016] **4608**

PILIPINAS (US/0889-5244) [11102944] **2662**

PILKINGTON GLASS AGE NEWS (UK) [09022492] **2593**

PILLAR, THE (US) [02252692] **3171**

PILLSBURY FAST AND HEALTHY MAGAZINE (US/1059-8073) [24773158] **2353, 4197**

PILOT (BOSTON, MASS.), THE (US/0744-933X) [05796345] **31**

PILOT (CLAYGATE) (UK/0300-1695) [01784796] **31**

PILOT INDEPENDENT (US) [20770189] **5698**

PILOT (MONTREAL) (CN/0380-6618) [02103533] **31**

PILOT NEWS (US/0193-211X) [05166105] **31**

PILOT STUDIES APPROVED FOR STATE AID IN PUBLIC SCHOOL SYSTEMS IN VIRGINIA (US/0079-2071) [03315128] **1902**

PILOT STUDIES FOR STATE AID IN PUBLIC SCHOOL DIVISIONS IN VIRGINIA (US) [08854747] **1868**

PILOT UND FLUGZEUG (GW) [10055657] **31**

PILOTE *CEASED.* (FR) [01605296] **5389**

PILOTING, SEAMANSHIP, AND SMALL BOAT HANDLING / CHARLES F. CHAPMAN ; WITH REVISIONS BY ELBERT S. MALONEY ... [ET AL.] (US) [03389272] **4181**

PILOTS AUDIO UPDATE (US) **31**

PILOTS GUIDE TO CALIFORNIA AIRPORTS (US) **31**

PILSETU VESTURES PROBLEMAS (LV) [02468131] **2702, 2830**

PIMA CATALOG (US/0739-2133) [09662593] **4237**

PIMA COUNTY EMPLOYER WAGE SURVEY (US/0145-9155) [02811499] **1702**

PIMA MAGAZINE (US/1046-4352) [17350292] **4237**

PIMIENTA *CEASED.* (US/0146-2075) [02872729] **3996**

PIMLICO PROUDLY PRESENTS ... RUNNING, PREAKNESS *See* PREAKNESS, THE **2801**

PIMPA MILANO (IT/1122-1305) [I11221305] **327**

PIMS (HK) **3627**

PIMS MEDIA DIRECTORY (UK/0261-5169) [I02615169] **763**

PIMS MONTHLY PETROLEUM REPORT *See* MONTHLY ENERGY REVIEW **1950**

PIN UPS (CN/0382-9286) [02862174] **4375**

PINARDIERE (CN/0713-4169) [08898833] **2467**

PINCKNEY DISTRICT CHAPTER QUARTERLY (US/1062-7782) [25739946] **2467**

PINCKNEY POST AND WHITMORE LAKER, THE (US/0192-7906) [05079318] **5693**

PINE BLUFF COMMERCIAL (US) [09526643] **5632**

PINE CITY PIONEER (US/0892-2012) [01762401] **5698**

PINE COUNTY COURIER (US) [01762402] **5698**

PINE LOG, THE (US) [16664434] **5753**

PINE RIVER JOURNAL (US) [01762408] **5698**

PINE TREE FLYER (US/0743-4448) [10577493] **5434**

PINEAL RESEARCH REVIEWS *CEASED.* (US/0738-4955) [09608144] **585**

PINELAND HOSPITAL AND TRAINING CENTER *See* ANNUAL REPORT - PINELAND HOSPITAL & TRAINING CENTER **3776**

PINELLAS COUNTY REVIEW (US/0746-746X) [10239901] **4843, 803**

PINELLAS PARK NEWS (US/0745-5631) [09287180] **5650**

PINES & NEEDLES (US) [02457759] **2390**

PINEVILLE SUN (US) [24798563] **5682**

PING CHOU WEN HUA (CC) [11001298] **1928**

PING CHU CHUAN TUNG CHU MU HSUAN / LIAO-NING SHENG WEN HUA CHU CHU MU KUNG TSO SHIH PIEN (CC) [08197420] **3310**

PING CHUAN TUNG TU (CC/1000-0240) [09510137] **1391**

PING PANG SHIH CHIEH (CC) [10719271] **4912**

PINHOLE JOURNAL (US/0885-1476) [12568489] **4375**

PINK & BLUE DIRECTORY, THE (CN/1185-9504) [25423436] **2285, 5564**

●PINK BOOK (MOUNTAIN VIEW, CALIF.), THE (US/1065-5867) [26639761] **5185**

●PINK SHEET ON THE LEFT (1993), THE (US/1070-0285) [27952500] **4487**

PINK SHEET ON THE NEW LEFT (US) [01762411] **4487**

PINKERTON EYE ON TRAVEL (US) **5489**

●PINKERTON WORLD STATUS MAP (US) [25641618] **5489**

PINT NIEUWS (NE/1380-6084) [I13806084] **2370**

PINTER REVIEW, THE (US/0895-9706) [16878624] **3423**

PINTU GERBANG : MAJALAH BULANAN DIREKTORAT JENDRAL IMIGRASI (IO) [11163300] **1920**

PINTURA : AMERICAN ROCK ART RESEARCH ASSOCIATION NEWSLETTER, LA (US/0748-4577) [10177661] **362**

PINTURAS Y ACABADOS INDUSTRIALES (SP/0031-9953) [06601505] **4225**

PIONEER, ALL-ALASKA WEEKLY, THE *CEASED.* (US/0747-3729) [10788790] **5629**

PIONEER AMERICA SOCIETY *See* TRANSACTIONS - PIONEER AMERICA SOCIETY **2763**

PIONEER (BEMIDJI, MINN.), THE (US/0899-1812) [18033610] **5698**

PIONEER (BIG RAPIDS, MICH.), THE (US/8750-5533) [11501900] **5693**

PIONEER BRANCHES (US) **2467**

PIONEER (CHETWYND) (CN/0228-0523) [06758211] **5793**

PIONEER CHRISTIAN MONTHLY (CN/0846-5320) [20787390] **4986**

PIONEER (COCHRANE) (CN/0710-5428) [08655370] **5793**

PIONEER HERALD, THE (US/0892-1261) [11987830] **5672**

PIONEER HERITAGE SERIES, THE (US/0079-2098) [05269951] **2754**

PIONEER (LAWRENCE, KAN.), THE (US/0739-4101) [09719185] **2467**

PIONEER (MEMPHIS, TENN.) (US/0893-5254) [15562512] **4986**

PIONEER NEWS (SHEPHERDSVILLE, KY.), THE (US/0746-8806) [10401644] **5682**

PIONEER PATHFINDER (US/0736-8208) [04164125] **2467**

PIONEER RECORD (US/1043-0458) [10074741] **2467**

PIONEER-REPUBLICAN OF IOWA COUNTY, THE (US) [12213278] **5672**

PIONEER, THE (US) [20715688] **5638**

PIONEER TIMES (US/0739-6155) [06190376] **2467**

PIONEER WAGON, THE (US/0735-309X) [08913574] **2467**

PIONER (RU) [01585591] **1068**

PIONERIIA (UN) [06630083] **2521**

PIONERO (CU) [04537931] **2467**

PIONERSKAIA PRAVDA (RU) [06634080] **1068**

PIONERSKII MUZYKALNYI KLUB (RU) [06618649] **4146**

PIONNIER (SILLERY) (CN/1191-1069) [25882668] **2467**

PIONYRSKA STAFETA (XR) [07293659] **5235**

PIP COLLEGE "HELPS" NEWSLETTER (US/0732-5258) [08392151] **1883**

PIPE BAND (UK) [01773294] **4146**

PIPE LINE INDUSTRY (HOUSTON, TEX.) (US/0032-0145) [01762417] **2124**

PIPELINE (UK) **4274**

PIPELINE ACCIDENT REPORTS. BRIEF FORMAT / NATIONAL TRANSPORTATION SAFETY BOARD (US) [04202843] **2868**

PIPELINE & GAS JOURNAL (US/0032-0188) [01717037] **4274**

PIPELINE & UTILITIES CONSTRUCTION (US/0896-1069) [12845994] **4761, 2124**

PIPELINE AUTHORITY *See* REPORT - PIPELINE AUTHORITY **4682**

PIPELINE (CAMPBELL, MO.) (US) [14643725] **2468**

PIPELINE DIGEST (US/0197-1506) [05969713] **4274**

PIPELINE ENGINEERING : PRESENTED AT THE ... ANNUAL ENERGY-SOURCES TECHNOLOGY CONFERENCE AND EXHIBITION / SPONSORED BY THE PETROLEUM DIVISION, ASME (US) [25394164] **4274**

PIPELINE INTELLIGENCE REPORT (US) **4274**

PIPELINE SAFETY ADVISORY BULLETIN (US) [05523292] **4274**

PIPELINE (ST. PAUL, MINN.) (US/1055-9051) [23365049] **1119**

PIPELINE (ST. PAUL, MINN.) (US/1055-9051) [23365173] **1119**

PIPELINES ABSTRACTS : BHRA ABSTRACTS JOURNAL (UK/0265-3990) [19113040] **2124**

PIPES & PIPELINES INTERNATIONAL (1965) (UK/0032-020X) [02449686] **2238, 4274**

PIPES OF PAN *See* INSCAPE (PASADENA) **3396**

PIPESTONE COUNTY STAR (US) [20859658] **5698**

PIPING AND PROCESS MACHINERY (JA) **2124**

PIPUL / PEOPLE (KO) [26429578] **5253**

PIQUA DAILY CALL (PIQUA, OHIO : 1927) (US) [17420156] **5730**

PIQUALITY (US/1058-8787) [24418125] **1199**

●PIQUE (NEW YORK, N.Y.) (US/1061-2505) [25237219] **4375**

PIRA (ASSOCIATION) *See* PIRA PACKAGING ABSTRACTS **4221**

PIRA PACKAGING ABSTRACTS (UK) [02246737] **4221**

PIRACY, COUNTERFEITING AND INFRINGEMENT REPORT (US) **1308, 3029**

PIRINEOS (SP/0373-2568) [01955856] **2220**

PIROGUE (ISSY-LES-MOULINEAUX, FRANCE) (FR/0048-4229) [19250308] **2521**

PIRSIG ON MINNESOTA PLEADING (US) [01777284] **3029**

PISA NONJIP (KO) [04870364] **1841**

PISATEL I ZHIZN / LITERATURNYI INSTITUT IMENI A. M. GORKOGO SOIUZA PISATELEI SSSR (RU/0554-2065) [01590089] **3423**

PISCATAQUIS OBSERVER, THE (US) [09242907] **5646**

PISCES (CN/0825-7914) [11868945] **2310**

PISCEVAJA PROMYSLENNOST (KIEV. 1977) (UN/0136-9172) [03110862] **2353**

PISCICULTEUR DE FRANCE (FR/0335-2811) [I03352811] **2310**

PISCICULTURE FRANCAISE (FR) **2310**

PISCICULTURE FRANCAISE D'EAU VIVE ET D'ETANG SAUMATRE ET MARINE, LA (FR/0295-317X) [I0295317X] **2310, 469**

PISCINAS (SP/0210-6868) [I02106868] **623**

PISCINE OGGI (IT/0390-3230) [I03903230] **4912**

PISCINES, SPAS MAGAZINE (FR/0295-5725) [I02955725] **623, 306**

PISHCHEVAIA PROMYSHLENNOST (RU/0235-2486) [20737990] **2353**

PISMA V ASTRONOMICESKIJ ZURNAL (RU/0320-0108) [02245144] **398**

PISMA V ZHURNAL EKSPERIMENTALNOI I TEORETICHESKOI FIZIKI (RU/0370-274X) [05472018] **4417**

PISMA V ZURNAL TEHNICESKOJ FIZIKI (RU/0320-0116) [05119492] **4417**

PIST PROTTA (DK/0107-6442) [I01076442] **3468**

PISTES CAMEROUNAISES (CM) [03257637] **2642**

PISTONS INSIDER : OFFICIAL MAGAZINE OF THE DETROIT PISTONS (US) [22584465] **4912**

PISUM GENETICS (AT) **550**

PISUM NEWSLETTER *See* PISUM GENETICS **550**

PISUM NEWSLETTER, THE (US) [05281429] **550**

PIT & QUARRY (US/0032-0293) [01762429] **2147**

PIT & QUARRY DIRECTORY OF THE U.S. NONMETALLIC MINING INDUSTRIES (US/0732-4898) [08360419] **2148**

PIT & QUARRY HANDBOOK AND BUYERS GUIDE FOR THE NONMETALLIC MINERALS INDUSTRIES (US/0146-1893) [02869214] **2148**

PITA JOURNAL (CN/0848-8460) [21340765] **1805**

PITCH-IN NEWS (CN/0847-9607) [20781781] **2202**

PITCH PIPE, THE (US/0882-214X) [06597486] **4146**

PITIRRE, EL *CEASED.* (PR) [21050461] **5808**

PITMAN MONOGRAPHS AND SURVEYS IN PURE AND APPLIED MATHEMATICS (UK/0269-3666) [15304816] **3526**

PITMAN RESEARCH NOTES IN MATHEMATICS SERIES (UK/0269-3674) [15012038] **3526**

PITT MAGAZINE (US) [15307582] **1102**

PITT NEWS, THE (US) [07198568] **5738**

PITT RIVERS MUSEUM *See* OCCASIONAL PAPERS ON TECHNOLOGY **4094**

PITTIERIA (VE) [02449687] **2390**

PITTMAN-ROBERTSON BULLETIN (HARTFORD) (US) [01510712] **2310**

PITTMAN-ROBERTSON GAME MANAGEMENT TECHNICAL SERIES (US/0270-739X) [05269973] **2202**

PITTSBURG POSTDISPATCH, THE (US/0746-7389) [10248445] **5638**

PITTSBURGH BUSINESS TIMES-JOURNAL (US/0883-7910) [11950728] **703**

PITTSBURGH CITY PAPER (US/1066-0062) [I10660062] **2543**

PITTSBURGH CLUB DIRECTORY (US) [23387038] **5235**

PITTSBURGH HISTORY (US/1069-4706) [19376227] **2754**

PITTSBURGH LEGAL JOURNAL (US/0032-0331) [01762437] **3029**

PITTSBURGH MUSICIAN (US) [02266180] **4146**

PITTSBURGH POST-GAZETTE (PITTSBURGH, PA. 1978) (US/1068-624X) [10846671] **5738**

PITTSBURGH PRESS, THE (US) [02266185] **5738**

PITTSBURGH QUARTERLY : A MAGAZINE FOR CREATIVE FICTION, POETRY & NONFICTION, THE (US/1054-6340) [22923597] **3423**

PITTSBURGH REGIONAL LIBRARY CENTER *See* NEWSLETTER - PITTSBURGH REGIONAL LIBRARY CENTER, INC **3236**

PITTSBURGH SERIES IN PHILOSOPHY AND HISTORY OF SCIENCE (US) [10446139] **5138**

PITTSBURGH UNDERGRADUATE REVIEW, THE (US/0734-3140) [07490253] **2852**

PITTURE E VERNICI (IT/0048-4245) [12118193] **3486**

PIU BELLA (IT/1120-4451) [I11204451] **5564**

PIVOT (STATE COLLEGE, PA.) (US/0554-2324) [02253371] **3468**

PIXEL (IT/0392-8217) [I03928217] **1234**

PIXEL : LE MAGAZINE DES NOUVELLES IMAGES (FR) **1199**

PIXEL (TORONTO) *CEASED.* (CN/0835-8095) [18926093] **1234**

PIXEL VISION (FR) [27359948] **1234**

PIXEL (WATSONVILLE, CALIF.) *SUSPENDED.* (US/1049-8052) [21134979] 5138, **1234**

PIZZA AND PASTA (US) **2353**

PIZZA TODAY (US/0743-3115) [10548528] **2353**

PJG (MIAMI, FLA.) (US/1043-0083) [19287392] 5619, **2427**

PKA AKTUELL (GW/0944-7032) **4325**

PKV PUBLIK (GW/0176-3261) [01763261] **2890**

PL, PETROLEUM LEGISLATION (US) [02869123] **4274**

PLA BULLETIN (US/0197-9299) [03637992] **3241**

PLACAR (BL) [06457030] **4912**

PLACE IN THE COUNTRY, A (US/0279-9278) [07364967] **2830**

PLACE (INDIANA) (US/0094-3452) [01794203] **5489**

PLACE-NAME-INDEX [COMPUTER FILE] (US) [22289629] **2572**

PLACEMENT BULLETIN - ASSOCIATION OF AMERICAN LAW SCHOOLS (US) [03462326] **3029**

PLACEMENT NEWS *SUSPENDED.* (US) [06846529] **4208**

PLACENTA (EASTBOURNE) (UK/0143-4004) [05312765] **539**

●PLACER HERALD, THE (US) [29211207] **5638**

PLACER ROCKLIN HERALD *See* PLACER HERALD, THE **5638**

PLACES (CAMBRIDGE, MASS.) (US/0731-0455) [08097845] **306**

PLACES OF INTEREST (US/0731-096X) [07963465] **2796**

PLACES TO PRACTICE (INTERNAL MEDICINE/CARDIOLOGY ED.) (US/1055-9086) [23366099] 3709, **3800**

PLACOTEUX (CN/0708-207X) [08072147] **2543**

PLAFSEP. PROCESSING (LIBRARIES)--ANECDOTES, FACETIAE, SATIRE, ETC.--PERIODICALS (US/0149-6417) [03519865] **3241**

PLAGES (FR) **4853**

PLAGUE WATCH (US/1060-2542) [24923756] **5213**

PLAIN DEALER (CLEVELAND, OHIO : 1961) (US) [07742580] **5730**

PLAIN DEALER (FREDERICTON) (CN/0701-0877) [03402728] **5793**

PLAIN RAPPER, THE *CEASED.* (US/0032-0412) [01590132] 1347, **5301**

PLAIN TALK (US/0148-4141) [03313700] **3241**

PLAIN TEXTS SERIES / ANGLO-NORMAN TEXT SOCIETY (UK) [11200462] **3423**

PLAIN TRUTH (PASADENA, CALIF.), THE (US/0032-0420) [01762445] **4986**

PLAINDEALER (WICHITA, KAN. 1919), THE (US/0898-4360) [12624678] **5678**

PLAINFIELD MESSENGER (PLAINFIELD, IND. : 1984) (US) [14763825] **5666**

PLAINS ANTHROPOLOGIST (US/0032-0447) [01640279] 2754, **2271**

PLAINS POETRY JOURNAL (US/0730-6172) [08037308] **3468**

PLAINS REPORTER (US) [19484578] **5726**

PLAINS TALK (US/0554-2375) [01605600] **2754**

PLAINSMAN (AUBURN, ALA.) *See* AUBURN PLAINSMAN, THE **5625**

PLAINSMAN-CLARION, THE (US) [14211063] **5672**

PLAINSONG AND MEDIAEVAL MUSIC SOCIETY (GREAT BRITAIN) *See* PLAINSONG AND MEDIEVAL MUSIC **4146**

●PLAINSONG AND MEDIEVAL MUSIC (UK/0961-1371) [26226266] **4146**

PLAINSONG (BOWLING GREEN, KY.) (US/0275-0074) [07068969] **3468**

PLAINSONGS (US) **3423**

PLAINSWOMAN *SUSPENDED.* (US/0148-902X) [03400725] **5564**

PLAINVIEW DAILY HERALD (PLAINVIEW, TEX. : 1956) (US) [14762569] **5753**

PLAINVILLE TIMES (PLAINVILLE, KAN. : 1904) (US) [12487523] **5678**

PLAINWELL-THE UNION ENTERPRISE (US) **5720**

PLAISANCIERS (CN/0820-5086) [16687590] **595**

PLAISIR DES JEUX (MONTREAL) (CN/1186-2289) [24368361] **4864**

PLAMUK (BU/0032-0528) [02160426] **3424**

PLAN AND PRINT (US/0032-0595) [04849087] 4567, **1234**

●PLAN - BRITISH COLUMBIA. RESOURCE MANAGEMENT BRANCH (CN/1187-3264) [25127864] 4673, **1359**

PLAN CANADA (CN/0032-0544) [02103577] **2830**

PLAN CANADA NEWS (CN/0700-9011) [03304167] **5301**

PLAN DE ACTIVIDADES - CENTRO DE INVESTIGACIONES EDUCATIVAS (AG) [06314530] **1774**

PLAN DE EMPRESA *CEASED.* (SP) [15038473] **5389**

PLAN DE LA CAISSE DES DEPOTS, LE (FR) [14686019] **4741**

●PLAN D'ENTREPRISE DE CANMET (CN/1187-6255) [25883166] **1443**

PLAN EAST AFRICA (KE) [01786090] **2830**

PLAN ECONOMICO (NQ) [19946585] **1578**

PLAN FINANCIER - COMMISSION DE L'ENSEIGNEMENT SUPERIEUR DES PROVINCES MARITIMES (CN) [03959806] **803**

PLAN FOR DEPARTMENT ON AGING (US) [09504735] **3754**

PLAN FOR ILLINOIS DEPARTMENT OF REHABILITATION SERVICES (US) [08161752] **4673**

PLAN FOR THE ADMINISTRATION OF VOCATIONAL EDUCATION, A (US) [12096332] **1915**

PLAN (MONTREAL) (CN/0032-0536) [09602982] **1990**

PLAN OG ARBEID (NO/0032-0609) [05786874] **1702**

●PLAN REGIONAL DE DEVELOPPEMENT DE LA MAIN-D'OEUVRE, REGION DE LANAUDIERE (CN/1193-4018) [26923781] **1702**

PLAN REGIONAL DE DEVELOPPEMENT DE LA MAIN-D'OEUVRE, REGIONS LAURENTIDES ET LANAUDIERE *See* PLAN REGIONAL DE DEVELOPPEMENT DE LA MAIN-D'OEUVRE, REGION DE LANAUDIERE **1702**

PLAN SPONSOR (US) **911**

PLAN TRIENNAL DE DEVELOPPEMENT / UNIVERSITE DU QUEBEC A CHICOUTIMI (CN/0822-5451) [10082763] **1841**

PLANATAS PULSS (LV) [03714205] **4531**

PLANCHE MAGAZINE (FR/0242-6986) [I02426986] **4912**

●PLANEACION & DESARROLLO (CK) [26440818] **1578**

PLANEAMENTO (LISBOA) (PO/0870-3043) [06135859] **1512**

PLANECON ENERGY REPORT (US) **1953**

PLANECON REPORT (US/0895-3317) [13680303] **1638**

PLANECON REVIEW & OUTLOOK 1578, **4531**

PLANECON TRADE & FINANCE REVIEWS (US) 1578, **849**

PLANEJAMENTO AGORA (BL) [14644480] **590**

PLANEJAMENTO E POLITICAS PUBLICAS (BL/0103-4138) [22144396] **4673**

PLANERA BYGGA BO (SW/1100-0678) [21130567] 624, **2830**

PLANET THREE (US/1050-3536) [21469470] 1068, **5213**

PLANET TODAY (CN/1183-6040) [24623776] **2179**

PLANETARIAN, THE (US/0090-3213) [01785011] **398**

PLANETARY AND SPACE SCIENCE (UK/0032-0633) [01762457] **398**

PLANETARY ASSOCIATION FOR CLEAN ENERGY *See* NEWSLETTER - PLANETARY ASSOCIATION FOR CLEAN ENERGY **1951**

PLANETARY CITIZEN : HONORING THE EARTH, HUMANITY, AND THE SACRED IN ALL LIFE *CEASED.* (US/1056-8522) [23880448] **4357**

PLANETARY ENCOUNTER (US/0882-5408) [11881892] **398**

PLANETARY REPORT, THE (US/0736-3680) [07546430] 31, **398**

PLANEWS (SI/0129-2838) [08365945] **2830**

PLANIROVANIE, TSENOOBRAZOVANIE I KHOZRASCHET V UGOLNOI PROMYSHLENNOSTI (RU) [05875685] **2148**

PLANNED AIR POLLUTION RESEARCH / STATE OF CALIFORNIA, AIR RESOURCES BOARD (US) [25909733] **2238**

PLANNED GIFTS COUNSELOR, THE (US/0891-4443) [14779388] **882**

PLANNED GIVING TODAY (US/1052-4770) [22294534] **4338**

PLANNED INNOVATION (UK/0141-2175) [06660847] **882**

●PLANNED PARENTHOOD CHALLENGES / INTERNATIONAL PLANNED PARENTHOOD FEDERATION (UK) [29422600] 590, **2285**

PLANNED PARENTHOOD NEWFOUNDLAND/LABRADOR (CN/0836-6233) [17631345] **590**

PLANNED PARENTHOOD OF TORONTO (CN/0710-6343) [08439978] **590**

PLANNED SAVINGS (UK/0032-0668) [I00320668] **803**

PLANNER (LONDON) *CEASED.* (UK/0309-1384) [02505244] **2830**

PLANNER, THE (US/0895-3570) [16576433] **803**

PLANNING (UK) **4673**

PLANNING (SA) [22190863] **306**

PLANNING & CHANGING (US/0032-0684) [01762462] **1774**

PLANNING & DEVELOPMENT (US) **2831**

PLANNING & DEVELOPMENT NEWS (US) [19111314] **2831**

PLANNING AND DEVELOPMENT STATISTICS ... ACTUALS / CIPFA, STATISTICAL INFORMATION SERVICE (UK/0260-8642) [07718253] 4741, **4699**

PLANNING AND DEVELOPMENT STATISTICS. ESTIMATES (UK) [05055829] 2831, **2840**

PLANNING & PUBLIC POLICY (US) [02254284] **4673**

PLANNING AND RESEARCH PROGRAM (US) [07438797] **5389**

Alphabetical Title Index

PLANNING AND RESOURCE DEVELOPMENT SERIES (US/0556-3968) [01170784] **2202**

PLANNING AND ZONING : A LAW BULLETIN PUBLISHED BY THE INSTITUTE OF GOVERNMENT, THE UNIVERSITY OF NORTH CAROLINA AT CHAPEL HILL (US) [23107952] **2831**

PLANNING & ZONING NEWS (US/0738-114X) [09491466] 3029, **2831**

PLANNING APPEAL DECISIONS (ANDOVER, ENGLAND) (UK/0268-3644) [18563304] **2831**

PLANNING BULLETIN (UK/0495-9728) [02082727] **2831**

PLANNING (CHICAGO, ILL. 1969) (US/0001-2610) [01762461] **2831**

PLANNING COMMISSIONERS JOURNAL (US/1058-5605) [24329893] **2831**

PLANNING ENVIRONMENT INTERNATIONAL *See* INTERIM GUIDE FOR ENVIRONMENTAL ASSESSMENT **2825**

PLANNING FOR HIGHER EDUCATION (US/0736-0983) [01697297] **1841**

PLANNING FOR THE DEVELOPMENTALLY DISABLED (US) [03512021] **5301**

PLANNING GUIDE ESEA IV, PART B: LIBRARIES AND LEARNING RESOURCES (US/0148-0413) [03262035] **1868**

PLANNING GUIDELINE SERIES (CN/0228-2410) [03216507] **2831**

PLANNING HISTORY (UK/0959-5805) [I09595805] **2702**

PLANNING HISTORY PRESENT (US/1071-1953) [17812504] **2831**

PLANNING IN NORTHEASTERN ILLINOIS (US/0048-4318) [05002567] **2831**

PLANNING INFORMATION FOR VOCATIONAL EDUCATION (US) [07860168] **1915**

PLANNING INFORMATION FOR VOCATIONAL EDUCATION : STATE OF IOWA / IOWA DEPARTMENT OF JOB SERVICE, RESEARCH AND ANALYSIS DEPARTMENT, LABOR MARKET INFORMATION UNIT (US) [06260029] 1702, **1915**

PLANNING INSTITUTE OF BRITISH COLUMBIA *See* P I B C NEWS **2830**

●PLANNING JOB CHOICES (US) [28865919] **4208**

●PLANNING JOB CHOICES (TWO-YEAR COLLEGE ED.) (US) [28923143] **4208**

PLANNING LEGISLATION IN NEW YORK STATE (US/0091-4053) [01786610] 2831, **3029**

PLANNING NEWS (ALBANY, N.Y.) (US/0885-6737) [04623796] **2831**

PLANNING NEWS SOUTH MELBOURNE (AT/0313-3796) [I03133796] **2831**

PLANNING OUTLOOK *See* JOURNAL OF ENVIRONMENTAL PLANNING AND MANAGEMENT **2826**

PLANNING PERSPECTIVES : PP (UK/0266-5433) [13879953] **2831**

PLANNING PRACTICE + RESEARCH (UK/0269-7459) [I02697459] **2831**

PLANNING QUARTERLY (NEW ZEALAND PLANNING INSTITUTE) (NZ) [08821960] **2831**

PLANNING REPORT - MINNESOTA HIGHER EDUCATION COORDINATING BOARD (US/0149-0540) [03419230] **1841**

PLANNING REVIEW (US/0094-064X) [01784496] **882**

PLANNING, ZONING, AND DEVELOPMENT LAWS (US) [11008807] 2831, **3029**

PLANNUNG UND ANALYSE (GW) **934**

PLANO ANUAL DE TRABALO - SUDAP (BL) [06457161] **120**

PLANO DE ACAO - BANCO DE DESENVOLVIMENTO DE MINAS GERAIS (BL) [03603281] **803**

PLANO DE OBJETIVOS: PIPMO - RJ (BL) [02511608] **1774**

PLANO ESTADUAL DE EDUCACAO (BL) [04690542] **1774**

PLANO ESTADUAL PARA APLICACAO DE CREDITO RURAL NO RIO GRANDE DO NORTE (BL) [02241960] **803**

PLANO OPERATIVO ANUAL - BANCO DE DESENVOLVIMENTO DE MINAS GERAIS (BL) [06025497] **803**

PLANO OPERATIVO ANUAL / GOVERNO DO ESTADO DE SERGIPE, SECRETARIA DO PLANEJAMENTO (BL) [08264947] **4741**

PLANO RODOVIARIO ESTADUAL (BL) [02468378] **5442**

PLANO STAR COURIER (1986) (US/0895-4305) [16653327] **5753**

PLANODION (GR/1105-2473) [25235425] **3424**

PLANS (CN/0380-6723) [02104002] **2831**

PLANS DE DEVELOPPEMENT DES PAYS D'AFRIQUE NOIRE, LES (FR) [04207465] **1578**

PLANS DE MAISONS DU QUEBEC (CN/0826-4392) [11355539] **624**

PLANT AND CELL PHYSIOLOGY (JA/0032-0781) [01762468] **523**

PLANT AND EQUIPMENT EXPENDITURES AND PLANS (US/1064-0614) [22615198] **1621**

PLANT AND EQUIPMENT EXPENDITURES: UNPUBLISHED DATA (US) **1537**

PLANT & GARDEN (CN) **2427**

PLANT & INDUSTRIAL ENGINEER'S DIGEST *See* ENGINEER'S DIGEST (WILLOW GROVE) **1974**

PLANT AND SOIL (NE/0032-079X) [01586439] 523, **181**

PLANT & WORKS ENGINEERING (UK) **1990**

PLANT BIBLIOGRAPHY (US/0886-683X) [03909243] **2427**

PLANT BIOLOGY (US/0894-4563) [14066929] **523**

PLANT BIOLOGY SERIES (US) [15105789] **469**

PLANT BIOTECHNOLOGY (UK) [23592755] 3695, **523**

PLANT BIOTECHNOLOGY (UK/0260-5902) [24523869] 3696, **523**

PLANT BREEDING (GW/0179-9541) [14182926] 120, **523**

PLANT BREEDING ABSTRACTS (UK/0032-0803) [01713749] 120, **155**

PLANT BREEDING REVIEWS (US/0730-2207) [07967643] 523, **2427**

PLANT, CELL AND ENVIRONMENT (UK/0140-7791) [03994800] **523**

PLANT CELL INCOMPATABILITY NEWSLETTER (US) [12773056] **523**

PLANT CELL REPORTS (GW/0721-7714) [08037527] **539**

PLANT CELL, THE (US/1040-4651) [18424872] 523, **539**

PLANT CELL, TISSUE AND ORGAN CULTURE (NE/0167-6857) [07984574] 539, **523**

PLANT CONSERVATION (US) **2427**

PLANT DISEASE (US/0191-2917) [04844576] **181**

PLANT DISEASE RESEARCH (II/0970-4914) [I09704914] **523**

PLANT DOCTOR. CD-ROM (US) **2427**

PLANT ENGINEERING (US/0032-082X) [01587601] 882, **1990**

PLANT ENGINEERING & TECHNOLOGY, PET (JA) [01798754] **1990**

PLANT FOODS FOR HUMAN NUTRITION (DORDRECHT) (NE/0921-9668) [16945201] **4197**

PLANT GENETIC RESOURCES ABSTRACTS (UK/0966-0100) [I09660100] 523, **479**

PLANT GENETIC RESOURCES NEWSLETTER (IT/0048-4334) [06158455] **120**

PLANT GENETICS AND BREEDING REVIEW (II) [20255367] **523**

PLANT GROWTH REGULATION (NE/0167-6903) [08743345] **523**

PLANT GROWTH REGULATOR ABSTRACTS (UK/0305-9154) [02037511] 120, **155**

PLANT GROWTH REGULATOR SOCIETY OF AMERICA. MEETING *See* PROCEEDINGS OF THE PLANT GROWTH REGULATOR SOCIETY OF AMERICA **525**

PLANT HEALTH GUIDE (US) **2427**

PLANT INVENTORY (US/0361-9974) [04358481] **2427**

PLANT JOURNAL : FOR CELL AND MOLECULAR BIOLOGY, THE (UK/0960-7412) [24508149] **523**

PLANT MATERIAL DESCRIPTION (II) [16819902] **182**

PLANT MOLECULAR BIOLOGY (NE/0167-4412) [08122145] 523, **550**

PLANT MOLECULAR BIOLOGY REPORTER (US/0735-9640) [09039650] **523**

PLANT/OPERATIONS PROGRESS (US/0278-4513) [07821763] **2015**

PLANT PATHOLOGY (UK/0032-0862) [01588811] **524**

PLANT PATHOLOGY CIRCULAR (US/0032-0870) [01374268] **524**

PLANT PEST NEWSLETTER (US) **524**

PLANT PHYSIOLOGY AND BIOCHEMISTRY (FR/0981-9428) [15699322] 492, **524**

PLANT PHYSIOLOGY (BETHESDA) (US/0032-0889) [01642351] **524**

PLANT PHYSIOLOGY BIOCHEMISTRY (II/0254-3591) [09378445] **524**

PLANT PHYSIOLOGY COMMUNICATIONS (CC) [09648575] **585**

PLANT PROTECTION (YU) [01781253] **524**

PLANT PROTECTION ABSTRACTS *SUSPENDED.* (IS/0032-0897) [05251671] **4247**

PLANT PROTECTION AND QUARANTINE PROGRAMS (US/0097-8787) [01798720] 4247, **2427**

PLANT PROTECTION BULLETIN (II/0378-0449) [01752785] **524**

PLANT PROTECTION QUARTERLY (AT/0815-2195) [12617904] **120**

PLANT RESEARCH AND DEVELOPMENT (GW/0340-2843) [03048499] **524**

PLANT SCIENCE BULLETIN (US/0032-0919) [01606449] **524**

PLANT SCIENCE (LIMERICK) (IE/0168-9452) [12148556] **524**

PLANT SERVICES (US/0199-8013) [06164507] **2124**

PLANT SOURCE LIST (EDMONTON, ALTA. : 1989) *See* MEMBERSHIP DIRECTORY, PLANT SOURCE LIST **2424**

PLANT SPECIES BIOLOGY (JA/0913-557X) [15686244] **524**

PLANT SYSTEMATICS AND EVOLUTION (AU/0378-2697) [02243542] **524**

PLANT SYSTEMS & EQUIPMENT (US/0744-3900) [08243908] **3486**

PLANT, TECHNOLOGY & SAFETY MANAGEMENT SERIES (US) [21282783] **2868**

PLANT TISSUE CULTURE (BG/1018-8029) [I10188029] **524**

PLANT VARIETIES & SEEDS (UK/0952-3863) [19226674] 120, **2427**

PLANT VARIETIES JOURNAL (AT/1030-9748) [18854002] **2428**

PLANT VARIETY PROTECTION OFFICE OFFICIAL JOURNAL (US/0740-6002) [06165338] **2428**

PLANT (WILLOWDALE) (CN/0845-4213) [19061207] **882**

PLANTA (GW/0032-0935) [03386633] **524**

PLANTA MEDICA (GW/0032-0943) [01762474] 525, **4325**

PLANTA MEDICA. SUPPLEMENT (GW) [01672954] 525, **4325**

PLANTBESKERMINGSNUUS (SA/1010-1640) [14175860] **525**

PLANTE-A-TOUT (CN/0823-6984) [10092674] **2428**

PLANTENBEURS, DE (NE) **2428**

PLANTER, THE (MY/0126-575X) [03005852] **120**

PLANTER'S BULLETIN (RUBBER RESEARCH INSTITUTE OF MALAYSIA) (MY/0032-096X) [02046058] **5076**

PLANTERS' CHRONICLE, THE (II/0032-0978) [09542742] **2353**

PLANTERS JOURNAL AND AGRICULTURIST, THE (II/0032-0986) [09983493] **120**

PLANTES DE MONTAGNE / BULLETIN DE LA SOCIETE DES AMATEURS DE JARDINS ALPINS (FR/0476-9813) [05966254] **2428**

PLANTES MEDICINALES ET PHYTOTHERAPIE *CEASED.* (FR/0032-0994) [04064345] 4325, **525**

PLANTFINDER (PEMBROKE PINES, FLA.) (US/1071-3670) [15522770] **2428**

PLANTI NEWS (MY/0127-306X) [I0127306X] **2428**

PLANTING MANUAL (MY) [01755299] **2428**

PLANTING TO HARVEST; ANNUAL CROP WEATHER SUMMARY (US/0163-4976) [02309158] **182**

PLANTLINE (AT/0726-4623) [I07264623] **3486**

PLANTS ALIVE (US/0146-3659) [01188559] **2428**

PLANTS & GARDENS (US/0362-5850) [01762475] **2428**

PLANTS AND GARDENS *See* BROOKLYN BOTANIC GARDEN 21ST CENTURY GARDENING SERIES **2410**

PLANTS & GARDENS NEWS / BROOKLYN BOTANIC GARDEN (US) [13717839] **2428**

●PLANTS & PEOPLE : SOCIETY FOR ECONOMIC BOTANY NEWSLETTER (US) [28312564] **525**

PLANTS FOR TOXICITY ASSESSMENT (US/1058-1189) [24225374] **4325**

●PLANT'S REVIEW OF BOOKS (US/1064-4741) [26294153] **4831**

PLANTS — Alphabetical Title Index

PLANTS, SITES & PARKS (US/0191-2933) [04848686] **703**

PLANTSMAN *See* NEW PLANTSMAN, THE **2425**

PLANTSMAN, THE (UK/0143-0106) [06293737] **2428**

PLANUNGSSTUDIEN (GW) [02998873] **703**

PLASIR DE LA MAISON (FR) **2812**

PLASMA CHEMISTRY AND PLASMA PROCESSING (US/0272-4324) [06842269] 988, **2015**

PLASMA DEVICES AND OPERATIONS (US/1051-9998) [22164468] **5138**

PLASMA NEWS REPORT (US/0892-6352) [15243537] **1028**

PLASMA PHYSICS AND CONTROLLED FUSION (UK/0741-3335) [10127017] **4450**

PLASMA PHYSICS AND CONTROLLED NUCLEAR FUSION RESEARCH (AU/0589-1469) [04916775] **4417**

●PLASMA PHYSICS REPORTS (US/1063-780X) [26139430] **4417**

PLASMA SOURCES SCIENCE AND TECHNOLOGY (UK/0963-0252) **4417**

PLASMAPHERESIS (US/0894-6779) [16180684] **3627**

●PLASMAS AND POLYMERS : AN INTERNATIONAL JOURNAL (US) **4417**

PLASMID (US/0147-619X) [03510004] **550**

●PLAST EUROPE : PE : KUNSTSTOFFE (GW/0941-3596) [29946222] **4457**

PLAST RIVISTA DELLE MATERIE PLASTICHE (IT) **4457**

PLASTE UND KAUTSCHUK (GW/0048-4350) [02449734] **4457**

PLASTER JACKET, THE *CEASED.* (US/0554-288X) [03295729] **4230**

PLASTERING INDUSTRIES *See* WALLS & CEILINGS **631**

PLASTFORUM SCANDINAVIA (SW/0347-8262) [l03478262] **4457**

PLASTIC AND RECONSTRUCTIVE BREAST SURGERY (US) [18554242] **3972**

PLASTIC AND RECONSTRUCTIVE SURGERY (1963) (US/0032-1052) [01697142] **3972**

PLASTIC CANVAS! MAGAZINE (US/1045-1854) [20041431] **374**

PLASTIC CANVAS WORLD (US/1072-6373) [29147223] **5185**

PLASTIC FIGURE AND PLAYSET COLLECTOR (US) 2776, **2585**

PLASTIC NEWS INTERNATIONAL (AT) **2107**

PLASTIC RAP (US/0899-7519) [18204268] **4457**

PLASTIC SURGERY (NE/0014-438X) [01568597] **3972**

PLASTIC SURGERY NEWS (ARLINGTON HEIGHTS, ILL.) (US/1043-4119) [19451865] **3972**

PLASTIC SURGERY OUTLOOK (US/0892-3965) [15182264] **3972**

PLASTIC SURGICAL NURSING (US/0741-5206) [09866226] 3972, **3867**

PLASTIC WASTE STRATEGIES (US/1046-3046) [20376335] 2238, **4221**

PLASTICHESKIE MASSY (RU/0554-2901) [02449737] **4457**

PLASTICO MODERNO (BL/0102-1931) [l01021931] **4457**

PLASTICOS & I.E. E BORRACHA (BL) [01789936] 5077, **4457**

PLASTICOS UNIVERSALES (SP/0303-4011) [02572428] **4457**

PLASTICS AGE (JA/0551-0503) [10465437] **4457**

PLASTICS & ENVIRONMENT (US/1051-0567) [21793384] **4457**

PLASTICS AND RUBBER INTERNATIONAL (UK/0309-4561) [03234639] 5077, **4457**

PLASTICS AND RUBBER: MATERIALS AND APPLICATIONS (UK/0307-9414) [02537680] **5077**

PLASTICS & RUBBER WEEKLY (UK/0032-1168) [06079791] 5077, **4457**

PLASTICS BRIEF/ DESIGN AND MATERIALS NEWSLETTER (US/1041-0821) [18647849] **4457**

PLASTICS BRIEF/ EXTRUSION AND BLOW MOLDING NEWSLETTER (US/1041-0813) [18647771] **4457**

PLASTICS BRIEF/ REINFORCED PLASTICS NEWSLETTER (US/1041-0805) [18647578] **4457**

PLASTICS BRIEF/ THERMOPLASTIC MARKETING NEWSLETTER (US/1041-083X) [18647615] **4457**

PLASTICS BULLETIN (BE) **4457**

PLASTICS BUSINESS (CN/0229-0413) [08046104] **4457**

PLASTICS BUSINESS NEWS (US/0734-1784) [08690517] **4458**

PLASTICS CANVAS CORNER (US/1045-3806) [20082896] 374, **4458**

PLASTICS COMPOUNDING (US/0148-9119) [03524801] **4458**

PLASTICS DESIGN FORUM (US/0362-9376) [02381377] **4458**

●PLASTICS DIGEST (US/1069-4358) [27134566] **4458**

PLASTICS ENGINEERING (US/0091-9578) [02245015] **4458**

PLASTICS ENGINEERING (NEW YORK, N.Y.) (US/1040-2527) [08091966] **1990**

PLASTICS FOCUS (US/0554-2952) [12335074] **4458**

PLASTICS IN BUILDING CONSTRUCTION (US/0147-2429) [03128946] 4458, **624**

PLASTICS IN CONSTRUCTION (CN/0381-9620) [03245022] 4458, **624**

PLASTICS INDUSTRY DIRECTORY, THE (UK) [20228309] **4458**

PLASTICS INDUSTRY EUROPE (UK/0268-8247) [l02688247] **4458**

PLASTICS INDUSTRY NEWS (JA/0032-1206) [l00321206] **4458**

PLASTICS INDUSTRY NEWS (DENVER, COLO.) (US/0886-9022) [13043393] **4458**

PLASTICS MACHINERY & EQUIPMENT (US/0149-4899) [03496688] **4458**

PLASTICS MANUFACTURING CAPABILITIES IN MISSISSIPPI (US/0099-0450) [02506390] **4458**

PLASTICS MANUFACTURING HANDBOOK AND BUYERS' GUIDE (NEW YORK, N.Y. : 1980/81) (US) [08327205] **4458**

PLASTICS MATERIALS. ADHESIVES (US/1041-2050) [18676255] **1056**

PLASTICS MATERIALS. ADHESIVES, SEALANTS, AND PRIMERS (US) [24394381] 4458, **1056**

PLASTICS MATERIALS. PLASTICS (US/1045-0769) [19834922] **4458**

PLASTICS NEWS (AKRON, OHIO) (US/1042-802X) [19219607] **4458**

PLASTICS PROCESSING & MACHINERY : TRENDS IN END-USE CONVERTING (US) **4458**

PLASTICS RECYCLING AS A FUTURE BUSINESS OPPORTUNITY : PROCEEDINGS, TECHNOLOGY EXCHANGE PROGRAM (US/1046-2201) [20124578] **4458**

PLASTICS, RUBBER AND COMPOSITES PROCESSING AND APPLICATIONS (UK/0959-8111) [23276579] 2107, 5077, **4458**

PLASTICS SOUTHERN AFRICA (SA/0032-2660) [10737190] **2107**

PLASTICS TECHNOLOGY (US/0032-1257) [01645089] **4458**

PLASTICS WEEK (NEW YORK, N.Y.) (US/1044-9663) [19961053] **4458**

PLASTICS WORLD (US/0032-1273) [01639876] **4458**

PLASTICSBRIEF. INJECTION MOLDING NEWSLETTER (US/1041-0791) [18633420] **4459**

PLASTICULTURE (FR) [01944734] 120, **4459**

PLASTIQUES MODERNES ELASTOMERES (FR/0032-1303) [02449759] 5077, **4459**

PLASTIZINE (CN/0715-5719) [09379010] **381**

PLASTVERARBEITER, DER (GW/0032-1338) [06547632] **4459**

PLATE WORLD *CEASED.* (US/0195-5780) [05464719] 374, **2593**

PLATEAU ELECTRIC NEWS (US/8750-8591) [11869094] **2075**

PLATEAU (FLAGSTAFF, AZ : 1939) (US/0032-1346) [02530033] **2543**

PLATEAUX (FR) **387**

PLATELETS (UK/0953-7104) [25526070] **3773**

PLATELETS SHEFFIELD (UK/0142-8268) [l01428268] **3773**

PLATFORM (NE) **120**

PLATING AND SURFACE FINISHING (US/0360-3164) [02243585] **4225**

PLATINUM-GROUP METALS IN ... (US) [03078031] 4015, 2148, **4026**

PLATINUM METALS REVIEW (UK/0032-1400) [01762481] **4015**

PLATON (GR/1105-073X) [04935040] **1079**

PLATOU (R.S.) A/S *See* PLATOU REPORT, THE **5454**

PLATOU REPORT, THE (NO) [01789642] **5454**

PLATTE COUNTY GAZETTE (1988), THE (US/0899-5737) [18142888] **5704**

PLATTE COUNTY, MISSOURI, HISTORICAL & GENEALOGICAL SOCIETY BULLETIN (US) [12002032] **2468**

PLATTE COUNTY RECORD-TIMES, THE (US) [25125198] **5772**

PLATTE VALLEY REVIEW (US/0092-4318) [01789608] **2543**

PLATTELANDS POST ('S-GRAVENHAGE. 1988) (NE/0922-2197) [l09222197] **120**

PLATTEVILLE JOURNAL (PLATTEVILLE, WIS. : 1966) (US) [13078549] **5770**

●PLATT'S METALS WEEK (US/1076-3937) [28454290] **4015**

PLATT'S OIL MARKETING BULLETIN (US/0277-0415) [07485253] 4274, **934**

PLATT'S OIL PRICE HANDBOOK AND OILMANAC (US/0160-4457) [01099360] **4274**

PLATT'S OILGRAM NEWS (US/0163-1284) [04298876] **4274**

PLATT'S OILGRAM NEWS SERVICE *See* PLATT'S OILGRAM NEWS **4274**

PLATT'S OILGRAM PRICE REPORT (US/0163-1292) [04298839] **4275**

PLATT'S OILGRAM PRICE SERVICE *See* PLATT'S OILGRAM PRICE REPORT **4275**

PLATTSBURGH STUDIES IN THE HUMANITIES (US/1061-6012) [25377362] **2852**

PLATTSMOUTH EVENING JOURNAL (US) [13412993] **5707**

PLAY & CULTURE *CEASED.* (US/0894-4253) [16074330] **5213**

PLAY AND PARENTING CONNECTIONS (CN/0835-4014) [16856376] 2585, **3241**

●PLAY (GAINESVILLE, FLA.) (US/1062-6956) [25698037] 1068, **4864**

PLAY INDEX (US/0554-3037) [01717025] **5367**

PLAY IT SAFE (US/0882-8768) [12001832] **703**

PLAY METER *See* PLAY METER MAGAZINE **4864**

PLAY METER MAGAZINE (US/1048-8243) [21052261] 4146, **4864**

PLAY SOURCE (US) **5367**

PLAY THE RED (US/0277-1098) [07511201] **3468**

PLAYBACK AND FAST FORWARD (II) [15515703] **703**

PLAYBACK LONDON (UK/0952-2360) [l09522360] **3241**

PLAYBACK (TORONTO) (CN/0836-2114) [16798773] 4076, **1136**

PLAYBILL (US/0551-0678) [02298132] **5367**

PLAYBOAR MAGAZINE (CN/0710-0361) [08332699] **4287**

PLAYBOARD (CN/0048-4415) [02600835] 4146, **387**

PLAYBOY COLLECTORS GUIDE & PRICE LIST, THE (CN/0228-7226) [09250161] **3996**

PLAYBOY INDEX, THE (US) [04969396] 2491, **3996**

●PLAYBOY PRESENTS INTERNATIONAL PLAYMATES (US/1062-2284) [25540869] **3996**

●PLAYBOY'S BEAUTY QUEENS (US/1063-9608) [26204839] **3996**

●PLAYBOY'S CALENDER GIRLS (US/1063-9616) [26204879] **3996**

●PLAYBOY'S CAREER GIRLS (US/1061-9070) [25487755] **3996**

●PLAYBOY'S GIRLS OF THE WORLD (US/1061-9089) [25487810] **3996**

●PLAYBOY'S TWINS (US/1066-5110) [26970974] **3996**

PLAYER (ATLANTIC CITY, N.J.), THE (US/1047-5303) [20715410] **4865**

PLAYERS (US/0149-466X) [03487858] **3996**

PLAYGIRL (US/0032-1494) [03455031] **5564**

PLAYGROUND DAILY NEWS (MICROFICHE) (US) [04328431] **5650**

PLAYGUY (US/0733-5695) [08620543] **3996**

PLAYING-CARD WORLD (UK/0966-4033) [l09664033] 2776, **4865**

PLAYING FOR K.E.E.P.S. (TEEN ED.) (US/1058-2495) [24242306] **1774**

PLAYING FOR K.E.E.P.S. (TOTS ED.) (US/1058-2320) [24242273] **1774**

PLAYING RULES (US/0361-3976) [02246536] **4912**

PLAYS AND PLAYERS (UK/0032-1559) [02243805] **5367**

PLAYS & PLAYWRIGHTS (US) [13341654] 5367, **3424**

PLAYS (BOSTON) (US/0032-1540) [01605120] 1068, **5367**

PLAYS BY WOMEN (UK) **5367**

PLAYS IN PROCESS **CEASED.** (US/0736-0711) [09069132] 3424, **5367**

PLAYS INTERNATIONAL (UK/0268-2028) [13473187] **5367**

PLAYTHINGS (US/0032-1567) [01639353] **2585**

PLAYWRIGHT'S COMPANION, THE (US/0887-1507) [13179624] **5367**

PLAZA (CAMBRIDGE, MASS.) **CEASED.** (US/0885-6680) [04699386] **3424**

PLAZA MAYOR (PE) [09634890] **2831**

PLC INSIDER'S NEWSLETTER **See** CONTROLS DIGEST **1181**

PLC INSIDER'S NEWSLETTER, THE (US/1040-9718) [18597417] 1289, **1265**

PLD NEWSLETTER (AT/0815-841X) [I0815841X] **3241**

PLEA. PUBLIC LEGAL EDUCATION ASSOCIATION OF SASKATCHEWAN (CN/0715-4224) [09201147] **3029**

PLEADER, THE (US/0196-6782) [05848738] **3029**

PLEADINGS OF THE INTERNATIONAL COURT OF JUSTICE SERIES (NE) **3133**

PLEASANT GROVE REVIEW (US/8755-9072) [11449898] **5757**

PLEASANTON EXPRESS, THE (US) [13661715] **5753**

PLEASANTS COUNTY LEADER (US) [12141490] **5764**

PLEASURE BOATING (US/0191-7366) [04947107] 5489, **595**

PLEASURE BOATING FL **See** CARIBBEAN SPORTS TRAVEL QUARTERLY **592**

PLEASURE HUNT MAGAZINE (US/0883-2382) [12095245] **5489**

PLEASURE QUEST (US) **5188**

PLEASURE TRAVEL MARKETS: THE HIGHLIGHTS REPORTS (US) **5489**

PLEIN AIR (MONTREAL, QUEBEC) **See** GEO PLEIN-AIR **4896**

PLEIN CADRE (CN/0227-115X) [06635045] **4375**

PLEIN DROIT : LA REVUE DE GISTI (FR/0987-3260) [18485188] 1921, **1702**

PLEIN-JOUR SUR CHARLEVOIX (CN/0317-0683) [02247849] **5793**

PLEIN-JOUR SUR LA MANICOUAGAN, LE (CN/1184-972X) [24690826] **5793**

PLEIN MONDE, EN (CN/0319-4078) [02442996] **4986**

PLEIN SOLEIL (MONTREAL) (CN/0384-7810) [03406310] **3732**

PLEINE FORME / SOCIETE CANADIENNE DU CANCER (CN/0714-735X) [09336432] **3822**

PLEINE MARGE (FR/0295-1630) [12875648] 3424, **362**

PLEINS FEUX SUR LE TAXI (CN/0701-1725) [03409748] **5389**

● PLENTY GOOD ROOM (US/1069-2479) [27964946] **4986**

PLENTYWOOD HERALD (US) [14082396] **5706**

PLENUM PRESS HANDBOOKS OF HIGH-TEMPERATURE MATERIALS (US/0079-2357) [05060473] 2107, **4015**

PLERUS (PR/0048-4466) [03595929] 703, **1512**

PLESSE-ARCHIV (GW) [04926375] **2702**

PLEXUS (OAKLAND, CALIF.) (US/0274-5526) [06399842] **5564**

PLI KNOW HOW (UK) [01785202] **5138**

PLI NEWS (US/0479-0219) [04546014] **3029**

PLIMOTH PLANTATION JOURNAL : THE NEWSLETTER OF PLIMOTH PLANTATION (US/0894-7589) [12012608] **2754**

PLL NEWSLETTER (US) [13457863] 3029, **3241**

PLON (PL) [04064374] **2521**

PLONGEE (CN/0228-3530) [07298630] **4912**

PLOT (IT) [25357294] **3424**

PLOT POITIERS (FR/0397-7471) [03977471] **3527**

PLOUGH, THE (US/0740-9125) [10338094] **4986**

PLOUGHSHARES (US/0048-4474) [02256746] 328, **3424**

PLOUGHSHARES MONITOR (CN/0703-1866) [03681038] **4532**

PLOVDIV, BULGARIA. VISSH SELSKOSTOPANSKI INSTITUT **See** NAUCHNI TRUDOVE - VISSH SELSKOSTOPANSKI INSTITUT "VASIL KOLAROV" PLOVDIV **111**

PLOW, THE (US/0032-1613) [08520193] **2625**

PLOWMAN (BROOKLIN) (CN/0840-707X) [19461361] **3468**

PLS LISTING. HYDROELECTRIC PLANTS, TRANSMISSION LINES AND SUBSTATIONS OPERATED BY THE BUREAU OF RECLAMATION **See** PLS LISTING. POWER FACILITIES OPERATED BY THE BUREAU OF RECLAMATION **2075**

PLS LISTING. POWER FACILITIES OPERATED BY THE BUREAU OF RECLAMATION (US/0271-7166) [01193306] **2075**

PLUG IN (CN/0704-0628) [04433041] **3241**

PLUIMVEEHOUDERIJ, DE (NE) [04064395] **217**

PLUM CREEK ALMANAC (US/0898-5197) [10892619] **2468**

PLUMAS COUNTY, CALIF. DEPT. OF AGRICULTURE **See** PLUMAS-SIERRA COUNTIES CROP REPORT **182**

PLUMAS-SIERRA COUNTIES CROP REPORT (US) [01337324] **182**

PLUMB LINE (ONEONTA, ALA.), THE (US/1059-2881) [24536043] **4986**

PLUMBING (UK/0032-1656) **2607**

PLUMBING & MECHANICAL (US/8750-6041) [11585136] **2607**

PLUMBING AND MECHANICAL CONNECTION (AT/1034-3075) [I10343075] **2607**

PLUMBING BUSINESS (US) **2607**

PLUMBING ENGINEER (US/0192-1711) [05120960] **2607**

PLUMBING FIXTURES (US/0145-4951) [02541417] **2607**

PLUMBING, HEATING, AIR CONDITIONING WHOLESALER **See** WHOLESALER (ELMHURST), THE **2609**

PLUMBING-HEATING-COOLING CATALOG : PHC (US/0278-5722) [07786112] **2607**

PLUMBING, HEATING, PIPING (US/1055-3231) [23150236] **2607**

PLUMBLINE (US/0741-1421) [06111196] **1841**

PLUNKETT DEVELOPMENT SERIES (UK/0143-8484) [10193497] **1543**

PLURAL **CEASED.** (MX/0185-4925) [01326271] **328**

PLURAL (BL) [05863965] **4487**

PLURAL SOCIETIES **CEASED.** (NE/0048-4482) [01559838] **5213**

PLURILINGUA (BE) **3310**

PLUS: A MATHEMATICAL MAGAZINE (UK) **3527**

PLUS (BAIERSBRONN) (GW) **1086**

PLUS (LONGVIEW, TEX.) (US/8750-3964) [11377873] **5753**

PLUS-MOINS-ZERO. REVUE D ART COMTEMPORAIN (BE) **328**

PLUS (PAWLING, N.Y.) (US/0747-217X) [10635625] **4986**

PLYMOUTH BULLETIN (US/0032-1737) [04108374] **5423**

PLYMOUTH POSTNEWS (US) [22000470] **5698**

PLYN (XR/0032-1761) [11591051] **4275**

PLZENSKY LEKARSKY SBORNIK (XR/0551-1038) [01778358] **3628**

PM ENVIRONMENTAL NEWSLETTER **See** ENVIRONMENT BUSINESS **2165**

PM NET WORK, THE (US/1040-8754) [18795791] **882**

PM PLUS (UK) [22575940] **946**

PM. PRAXIS DER MATHEMATIK (GW/0032-7042) [04602463] **3527**

PM REPORT (GW) **4325**

PMA NEWSLETTER (US) **4325**

PMA SALARY SURVEY / PERSONNEL MANAGEMENT ASSOCIATION OF GREATER KANSAS CITY (US) [11724351] **1702**

PMA STATISTICAL FACTBOOK (US) [13377757] 4334, **4325**

PMBR, PHYSICIANS'S MEDICAL BOOK REFERENCE (US/0093-2248) [01791840] **3628**

PMC. PRACTICE OF MINISTRY IN CANADA (CN/0825-0391) [11278687] **4986**

PMD, PHARMACEUTICAL MARKETERS DIRECTORY (US/0149-0885) [03422003] **4325**

PME (LAVAL) (CN/0828-8089) [18596000] **703**

PMEA NEWS (US/0030-8102) [03873794] 1774, **4146**

PMI. POWDER METALLURGY INTERNATIONAL **CEASED.** (GW/0048-5012) [01641876] **4015**

PMLA PAPER (US) **3311**

PMS ACCESS (US) 3767, **5564**

PMS AKTUELL (SZ) [20511602] **3932**

PMTF (RU/0044-4626) [05294305] **4417**

PN. PRACTICAL NURSING CAREER **SUSPENDED.** (US/0145-8981) [02766780] 1841, **3867**

PN REVIEW (MANCHESTER, GREATER MANCHESTER : 1979) (UK/0144-7076) [06000393] **3350**

PNC REVIEW (JA) [12798021] **4450**

PNCC STUDIES (US/0734-4570) [08745903] **4987**

PNEU MICHELIN (FIRM) **See** PROVENCE **5489**

PNEU MICHELIN (FIRM) **See** PARIS AND ENVIRONS : HOTELS AND RESTAURANTS **2808**

PNEU MICHELIN (FIRM) **See** ESPANA, PORTUGAL **5469**

PNEU MICHELIN (FIRM) **See** HOLLANDE **2691**

PNEU MICHELIN (FIRM) **See** ITALIE **5481**

PNEU MICHELIN (FIRM) **See** ROME **5490**

PNEU MICHELIN (FIRM) **See** ALPES : SAVOIE, DAUPHINE **2672**

PNEU MICHELIN (FIRM) **See** CORSE **5467**

PNEU MICHELIN (FIRM) **See** MAROC **5484**

PNEU MICHELIN (FIRM) **See** CHATEAUX DE LA LOIRE **5466**

PNEU MICHELIN (FIRM) **See** COTE DE L'ATLANTIQUE **2684**

PNEUMA (SPRINGFIELD) (US/0272-0965) [05198011] **5066**

PNEUMATIKE KYPROS (CY/0554-3363) [01795053] **3424**

PNEUMATIQUE, LE **See** COMMUNICATION PNEU **1107**

PNEUMATIQUE PARIS, LE (FR/0296-9386) [I02969386] 5423, **5077**

PNEUMOLOGIE (GW/0934-8387) [19492754] **3950**

PNEUMONOLOGIA I ALERGOLOGIA POLSKA : ORGAN POLSKIEGO TOWARZYSTWA FTYZJOPNEUMONOLOGICZNEGO, POLSKIEGO TOWARZYSTWA ALERGOLOGICZNEGO, I INSTYTUT U GRUZLICY I CHOROB PUC (PL) [27639056] **3950**

PNEUMONOLOGIA POLSKA (PL/0376-4761) [02112046] **3950**

PNEVMOLOGIIA I FTIZIATRIIA (BU/0324-1491) [02901500] **3950**

PNLA QUARTERLY (US/0030-8188) [01761655] **3241**

PNPA PRESS (US/0030-8196) [02509534] **4818**

PNPA PRESS BULLETIN **See** PNPA PRESS **4818**

PNW COAST LUMBER PRICE INDEX (US/0735-066X) [08860272] **2403**

POA (1985) (US/0882-9624) [12046424] **2801**

● POBEREZE (PHILADELPHIA, PA.) (US/1057-932X) [24224034] 3424, **2271**

POBRZEZE (PL) [01787076] **2521**

POCAHONTAS RECORD-DEMOCRAT (US) [16626839] **5672**

POCAHONTAS STAR HERALD (US) [19684357] **5632**

POCAHONTAS TIMES (US/0738-8373) [09694614] **5764**

POCH (SZ) [01788273] **4545**

POCHVENNYI INSTITUT IMENI V. V. DOKUCHAEVA **See** BIULLETEN POCHVENNOGO INSTITUTA IMENI V. V. DOKUCHAEVA **165**

POCHVOVEDENIE (RU/0032-180X) [01590336] **182**

POCHVOVEDENIE I AAGROKHIMIIA / BELORUSSKII NAUCHNO-ISSLEDOVATELSKII INSTITUT POCHVOVEDENIIA I AGROKHIMII (RU) [08122206] **182**

POCKET BOOK OF HEALTH STATISTICS (II) [05108907] **4810**

POCKET BOOK OF LABOUR STATISTICS (NEW DELHI, INDIA) (II) [09934734] 1702, **1537**

POCKET BOOK OF PRO FOOTBALL, THE (US/0148-8007) [03372228] **4912**

POCKET BOOK OF PUNJAB LABOUR STATISTICS (II) [01784161] **1537**

POCKET DIRECTORY OF THE CALIFORNIA LEGISLATURE (US/0163-3333) [03943633] **4673**

POCKET GUIDE FOR THE MOVIES ON VIDEO (US/0896-6680) [17242994] **4076**

POCKET GUIDE TO EUROPEAN INDIVIDUAL TAXES (US) [06670767] **4741**

POCKET LIST OF RAILROAD OFFICIALS (INTERNATIONAL ED.), THE (US/1044-4688) [19789932] **5434**

POCKET LIST OF RAILROAD OFFICIALS, THE (US/0032-1826) [03473014] **5434**

POCKET — Alphabetical Title Index

POCKET PAGES (US/1050-0790) [21385099] **2776**

POCKET PDR [COMPUTER FILE] (US/1055-0178) [23055764] **3628**

POCKET PRICE GUIDE (US/0742-4442) [10329358] **2812**

POCKET PRO GOLF MAGAZINE (CN/0821-2023) [09448355] **4912**

POCKET YEAR BOOK, AUSTRALIA (AT) [06101108] **1928**

POCKET YEAR BOOK OF NEW SOUTH WALES, AUSTRALIA, THE **CEASED.** (AT/0159-9321) [07507262] **1928**

POCKET YEAR BOOK OF SOUTH AUSTRALIA (AT) [05633871] **1928**

POCKETAX QUEBECOIS (CN/0821-4697) [09562931] **4741**

POCKETBOOK OF PEDIATRIC ANTIMICROBIAL THERAPY (US/8755-5476) [11477548] 3910, **4325**

POCKETBOOK OF PHILIPPINE STATISTICS (PH) [08014897] **5336**

POCKETBOOK OF STATISTICS: JAMAICA (JM) [06468928] **1537**

POCKETS (US/0278-565X) [07827728] 4987, **1068**

POCS TECHNICAL PAPER (US) [09098065] **1391**

POCZNIK KOMISJI HISTORYCZNOLITERACKIEJ (PL/0079-3302) [02857562] **3424**

PODIATRIC PRODUCTS (US/0890-3972) [14222367] **3918**

PODIATRY MANAGEMENT (US/0744-3528) [08208008] **3918**

PODIATRY TRACTS (US/0894-6116) [17886855] **3918**

PODIUM (GW) [02754948] **3424**

PODIUM (ASSOCIATION) See PODIUM **3424**

PODIUM (CHICAGO, ILL.), THE **CEASED.** (US/0886-1897) [05175969] **4146**

PODIUM : LE MAGAZINE (FR) **1774**

PODIUMKUNSTEN (NE/0924-2937) [21726359] **387**

PODKARPACIE See NOWE PODKARPACIE **5808**

PODO SAJIN YONGAM NEWS PHOTOGRAPHY ANNUAL (KO) [07448150] **4375**

PODSTAWY GOSPODARKI W SRODOWISKU MORSKIM / POLSKA AKADEMIIA NAUK, KOMITET BADAN MORZA (PL/0208-8274) [11294715] **1455**

PODVIG (PERIODICAL) (RU) [08426362] **3424**

POE MESSENGER, THE (US/0276-3737) [05022706] **3424**

POE STUDIES (US/0090-5224) [01785571] 3350, **434**

POEM (US/0032-1885) [00824187] **3468**

●POEM FINDER ON DISC (US/1063-1666) [25936312] **3468**

POEM I TANTSUEM (RU) [08498622] **4146**

POEMES INEDITS (CN/0048-4520) [02103141] **3468**

POEMONDE (FR) [06430199] **3468**

POESIA (BL) [04237038] **3468**

POESIA (VE) [01240214] **3468**

POESIA DE VENEZUELA (VE/0032-1893) [02266285] **3468**

POESIA (MADRID, SPAIN) (SP) [05506363] **3468**

POESIE (BASEL, SWITZERLAND) (SZ/0378-0643) [18912379] **3424**

POESIE; LA POESIE FRANCAISE DE BELGIQUE (FR/0048-4555) [02253331] **3468**

POESIE (PARIS, FRANCE : 1984) (FR/0752-272X) [11092496] 362, **3468**

POESIE PRESENTE (FR/0048-4563) [02234706] **3468**

POESIEALBUM (GW) [03768128] **3468**

POET (II/0032-194X) [05686599] **3468**

POET AND CRITIC (AMES, IOWA) (US/0032-1958) [01586492] **3468**

POET LORE (US/0032-1966) [01606293] **3468**

POET PEU A PEU, THE (US/0190-6682) [04765348] **3468**

POET (SHREVEPORT, LA.), THE (US/0748-4062) [10937920] **3468**

POETCRIT MARANDA (II/0970-2830) [09702830] **3468**

POETI A GRADARA (IT) [02239439] **3468**

POETIC JUSTICE : CONTEMPORARY AMERICAN POETRY (US) **3468**

POETIC LICENCE (CALGARY) (CN/0708-9562) [05257150] **3468**

POETICA (JA) [06454373] **3468**

POETICA (MUNCHEN) (NE/0303-4178) [01762507] 3311, **3424**

POETICA; ZEITSCHRIFT FUER SPRACH- UND LITERATURWISSENSCHAFT (GW) [10902934] **3468**

POETICS (US/1043-0814) [19300678] **3468**

POETICS (AMSTERDAM) (NE/0304-422X) [00834054] **3468**

POETICS JOURNAL **SUSPENDED.** (US/0731-5236) [08209024] **3350**

POETICS TODAY (US/0333-5372) [06301422] **3424**

POETIQUE (FR/0032-2024) [01640759] **3469**

POETRY & AUDIENCE (UK/0032-2040) [03407697] **3469**

POETRY AUSTRALIA (AT/0032-2059) [02148844] **3469**

POETRY BOOK SOCIETY See POETRY BOOK SOCIETY BULLETIN **3469**

POETRY BOOK SOCIETY BULLETIN (UK/0551-1690) [07052766] **3469**

POETRY CANADA REVIEW (CN/0709-3373) [07802431] **3350**

POETRY (CHICAGO) (US/0032-2032) [01762510] **3469**

POETRY CRITICISM (US/1052-4851) [22401447] **3469**

POETRY DIMENSION ANNUAL (US) [03714686] **3469**

POETRY DURHAM (UK) [09922325] **3469**

POETRY EAST (US/0197-4009) [06017129] **3469**

POETRY FLASH (US/0737-4747) [08998510] **3469**

POETRY FROM OXFORD (UK/0477-0943) [20397834] **3469**

●POETRY IN PENNSYLVANIA (US/1062-9386) [25812212] **3469**

POETRY INDEX ANNUAL (US/0736-3966) [09079341] **3469**

POETRY IRELAND REVIEW, THE (IE/0332-2998) [10101456] **3469**

POETRY/LA **SUSPENDED.** (US/0275-1739) [07077703] **3469**

POETRY MAG, A (US/0730-8868) [08077646] **3469**

POETRY MAILING LIST, THE (US) [08146361] **3469**

POETRY MARKETS FOR CANADIANS (CN/0843-2287) [17735594] **3469**

POETRY MONASH (AT/0314-6855) [06712878] **3469**

POETRY MONTREAL (CN/0822-9937) [10862193] **3469**

POETRY 'N' PROSE (CN/0821-5790) [09658251] **3469**

POETRY NEWSLETTER (US) [03410937] **3469**

POETRY NIPPON (JA/0032-2105) [03410948] **3469**

POETRY NORTHWEST (US/0032-2113) [01762518] **3469**

POETRY: PEOPLE (US) [03407654] **3469**

POETRY PILOT (US/0554-3983) [02755905] **3469**

POETRY PROJECT See POETRY PROJECT NEWSLETTER, THE **3469**

●POETRY PROJECT NEWSLETTER, THE (US) [26381234] **3469**

POETRY REVIEW (LONDON) (UK/0032-2156) [01642610] **3350**

POETRY TORONTO **CEASED.** (CN/0381-6591) [09635027] **3469**

POETRY WALES (UK/0032-2202) [02756034] **3469**

POETS AND AUTHORS (US/0149-9831) [03587028] **3424**

POETS & WRITERS (US/0891-6136) [14929081] **3470**

POETS AT WORK (US) **3470**

●POET'S GUILD (US/1065-836X) [26757202] **3470**

POET'S HANDBOOK (US) [19837285] **3470**

POET'S MARKET (US/0883-5470) [12173767] **3470**

POETS ON (US/0146-3136) [02821950] **3470**

POET'S VOICE (BATH, SOMERSETSHIRE), THE (UK) [10384734] **3470**

POEZIJA (KIIV) (UN/0130-8483) [02152590] **3470**

POEZJA **CEASED.** (PL/0032-2237) [01762525] **3470**

●POF NEWSLETTER (US/1064-1068) [26207215] 1162, **4440**

POGGENDORFFS BIOGRAPHISCH LITERARISCHES HANDWOERTERBUCH DER EXAKTEN NATURWISSENSCHAFTEN (GW) **3424**

POGON SAHOE NONJIP (KO) [23190947] 5301, **4556**

POGON YONGAM (KO) [12124634] 5301, **4795**

POHANG SANGUI (KO) [10270030] **820**

POHOM HAKHOE CHI (KO) [08534920] **2890**

POHOM TONGGYE YONBO (KO) [08094262] 2890, **2897**

POHOM TONGGYE YON'GAM (KO) [05624843] 2890, **2897**

POINT (ALEXANDRIA) (CN/0228-9199) [08070865] **5793**

POINT (BATHURST) (CN/0227-2288) [07295011] **5793**

POINT COMMUN, LE (FR/0710-2364) [08330357] **5793**

POINT DE REPERE (MONTREAL) (CN/0822-8833) [10712735] **422**

POINT DE VUE IMAGES DU MONDE (FR) **120**

POINT DE VUE (SENNETERRE) (CN/0229-3277) [08010239] **5793**

POINT D'INTERROGATION (CHICOUTIMI) (CN/0710-6491) [08770561] **1702**

POINT D'INTERROGATION ?. ENGLISH SECTION (CN/0710-6521) [08680899] **1702**

POINT D'INTERROGATION (MONTREAL) (CN/0226-7950) [08680893] **1702**

POINT (DOLBEAU) (CN/0382-6309) [02851640] **5793**

POINT ECONOMIQUE DE L'AUVERGNE, LE (FR) [06257676] 5336, **5253**

POINT (LASALLE) (CN/0319-5805) [02442268] **5793**

POINT, LE (FR) [05872439] **3350**

●POINT LINE POLY. HOST (US/1062-5674) [25667805] **1990**

●POINT LINE POLY. PC (US/1061-3838) [25278685] **1199**

POINT (MONTREAL) (CN/0316-7852) [02247961] **849**

POINT OF BEGINNING- POB (US/0739-3865) [09316540] **2028**

POINT OF CONTACT (US) **2543**

POINT OF REFERENCE (US/0094-4998) [01793906] **2625**

POINT OF VIEW (II) [01784072] **2572**

POINT OF VIEW (US/1062-7456) [25725416] **4487**

POINT OF VIEW (US) [03916015] **3108**

POINT OF VIEW (CLEVELAND) (US/0032-2318) [03698711] **4674**

POINT OF VIEW (SOMERVILLE) (US/0098-4345) [01446651] **3867**

POINT PLEASANT REGISTER (DAILY : 1942) (US) [13083410] **5764**

POINT, SECTEUR DES GRAINS (ED. DE L'EST) (CN/0848-7189) [23658995] **203**

POINT, SECTEUR DES GRAINS (ED. DE L'OUEST) (CN/0848-7197) [23658992] **203**

POINT SERIES (PP/0253-2913) [12339091] **4987**

POINT SPREAD PLAYBOOK (US/0273-3420) [07038054] **4912**

POINT SUR LES PROJETS DU SAINT-MAURICE, LE (CN/1189-0355) [25352016] **2220**

POINT THEOLOGIQUE, LE (FR) [06406097] **4987**

POINT VETERINAIRE, LE (FR/0335-4997) [04185727] **5518**

POINTE DE L'EGLISE HISTORICAL AND GENEALOGICAL SOCIETY : [NEWSLETTER] See LA POINTE, A **2457**

POINTER, THE (US/0032-2350) [02449770] **1774**

POINTER, THE (US/0554-4246) [01589855] 4392, **1883**

POINTS A POINTS (CN/0823-7697) [10522294] **5185**

POINTS DE VENTE PARIS (FR/0150-1844) [01501844] **934**

POINTS EAST (US/1063-6269) [13959598] **5052**

POINTS ET CONTREPOINTS (FR/0032-2369) [04608542] **3470**

POISONED PEN, THE **CEASED.** (US) [08710124] **3350**

POJISTNY OBZOR (XR) [06783511] **2890**

POJUNG SABO (KO) [10254415] **2890**

POKETTO NORIN SUISAN TOKEI (JA) [08648178] **120**

POKROKY MATEMATYKY, FYSIKY A ASTRONOMIE (XR/0032-2423) [02166225] **5138**

POL ADVISOR (US) **3628**

POLA (IO) [01797891] **306**

POLAND *See* MONITOR POLSKI : DZIENNIK URZEDOWY RZECZYPOSPOLITEJ POLSKIEJ **3011**

● POLAND BUSINESS REPORT (US/1063-679X) [26147133] **703**

POLAND. GLOWNY URZAD STATYSTYCZNY *See* BIULETYN STATYSTYCZNY **5323**

POLAND. GOWNY KOMITET KULTURY FIZYCZNEJ I SPORTU *See* DZIENNIK URZEDOWY GOWNEGO KOMITETU KULTURY FIZYCZNEJ I SPORTU **2596**

POLAND. GOWNY URZAD STATYSTYCZNY *See* ROCZNIK STATYSTYCZNY FINANSOW **4747**

POLAND. GOWNY URZAD STATYSTYCZNY *See* ROCZNIK STATYSTYCZNY **5337**

POLAND. GOWNY URZAD STATYSTYCZNY *See* UBEZPIECZENIA MAJATKOWE I OSOBOWE **2895**

POLAND. GOWNY URZAD STATYSTYCZNY *See* ROCZNIK STATYSTYKI MIEDZYNARODOWEJ **5338**

POLAND. GOWNY URZAD STATYSTYCZNY *See* ROCZNIK STATYSTYCZNY SZKOLNICTWA **1781**

POLAND. GOWNY URZAD STATYSTYCZNY *See* CZYNNI ZAWODOWO W GOSPODARCE NARODOWEJ **1662**

POLAND. GOWNY URZAD STATYSTYCZNY *See* BUDZETY GOSPODARSTW DOMOWYCH **1465**

POLAND. GOWNY URZAD STATYSTYCZNY *See* ROCZNIK STATYSTYCZNY GOSPODARKI MORSKIEJ **4182**

POLAND. GOWNY URZAD STATYSTYCZNY *See* ROCZNIK STATYSTYCZNY ROLNICTWA I GOSPODARKI ZYWNOSCIOWEJ **130**

POLAND. GOWNY URZAD STATYSTYCZNY *See* RUCH ZATRUDNIONYCH W GOSPODARCE USPOECZNIONEJ **1709**

POLAND. GOWNY URZAD STATYSTYCZNY *See* ROCZNIK STATYSTYCZNY BUDOWNICTWA **1582**

POLAND. GOWNY URZAD STATYSTYCZNY *See* KULTURA FIZYCZNA **1857**

POLAND. GOWNY URZAD STATYSTYCZNY *See* WYNIKI SPISU ROLNICZEGO **147**

POLAND. GOWNY URZAD STATYSTYCZNY. ROCZNIK STATYSTYCZNY FINANSOW (DLC) 75219175 *See* ROCZNIKI STATYSTYCZNE. FINANSE / GOWNY URZAD STATYSTYCZNY **810**

POLAND. GOWNY URZAD STATYSTYCZNY. ROCZNIK STATYSTYCZNY SZKOLNICTWA *See* ROCZNIKI STATYSTYCZNE. SZKOLNICTWO / GOWNY URZAD STATYSTYCZNY **1781**

POLAND LEADER (US/0883-6523) [12178062] **5730**

POLAND. MINISTERSTWO KOMUNIKACJI *See* DZIENNIK TARYF I ZARZADEN KOLEJOWYCH. WYDAWNICTWO MINISTERSTWA KOMUNIKACJI **5431**

POLAND. MINISTERSTWO OSWIATY I WYCHOWANIA *See* DZIENNIK URZEDOWY MINISTERSTWA OSWIATY I WYCHOWANIA **1862**

POLAND. MINISTERSTWO PRACY, PAC I SPRAW SOCJALNYCH *See* DZIENNIK URZEDOWY MINISTERSTWA PRACY, PAC I SPRAW SOCJALNYCH **3146**

POLAND. MINISTERSTWO ROLNICTWA, LESNICTWA I GOSPODARKI ZYWNOSCIOWEJ *See* DZIENNIK URZEDOWY MINISTERSTWA ROLNICTWA, LESNICTWA I GOSPODARKI ZYWNOSCIOWEJ **80**

POLAND. SAD NAJWYZSZY *See* ORZECZNICTWO SADU NAJWYZSZEGO. IZBA CYWILNA I ADMINISTRACYJNA ORAZ IZBA PRACY I UBEZPIECZEN SPOECZNYCH **5300**

POLAND. URZAD PATENTOWY *See* BIULETYN - POLAND. URZAD PATENTOWY **1301**

POLAR (FR) [23994421] **3424**

POLAR AND GLACIOLOGICAL ABSTRACTS (UK/0957-5073) [21213633] **2572**

POLAR BIOLOGY (GW/0722-4060) [08839597] 525, **5594**

POLAR GEOGRAPHY AND GEOLOGY (US/0273-8457) [06509386] **1391**

POLAR LIBRARIES BULLETIN (US/1049-7765) [21309017] **3241**

POLAR RECORD, THE (UK/0032-2474) [01762535] **5138**

POLAR RESEARCH (NO) [09085655] 469, **1359**

POLAR TIMES, THE (US/0032-2482) [01762537] **2572**

POLARFORSCHUNG (GW/0032-2490) [01716758] **5138**

POLEMIC (AT) [26556578] **3029**

POLEMICA *CEASED.* (CR) [13546323] **5213**

POLEN : VOLKSWIRTSCHAFTSPLAN UND BUDGETDATEN (GW) [04440908] **1578**

POLESTAR (UK) **1774**

POLEVYE ISSLEDOVANIIA INSTITUTA ETNOGRAFII (RU) [02246849] **243**

● POLEZNYE MODELI, PROMYSHLENNYE OBRAZTSY : OFITSIALNYI BIULLETEN KOMITETA ROSSIISKOI FEDERATSII PO PATENTAM I TOVARNYM ZNAKAM (RU) [30480146] **1308**

POLIBEA (SP) [24034598] **1884**

POLICE AND CONSTABULARY ALMANAC (UK/0477-2008) [I04772008] **3171**

POLICE AND LAW ENFORCEMENT (US/0092-8933) [01781063] **3171**

POLICE AND SECURITY NEWS (US/1070-8111) [28473572] **3171**

POLICE BADGE, THE (US/0147-8877) [04287522] **3171**

POLICE CALL, FIRE EMERGENCY RADIO DIRECTORY (US/0098-177X) [02240705] **1136**

POLICE CAREER DIGEST (US/8756-355X) [18922733] **3171**

POLICE (CARLSBAD, CALIF.) (US/0893-8989) [15702554] **3171**

POLICE CHIEF, THE (US/0032-2571) [05037558] **3171**

POLICE CHRONICLE, THE (US/0747-2579) [04298077] **3172**

POLICE COLLECTORS NEWS (US/1071-1724) [21281615] **3172**

● POLICE COMPUTER REVIEW (US/1061-1509) [25191810] 1265, 3172, **1289**

POLICE FORCE STATISTICS (UK) [01792887] 3172, **3082**

POLICE GOVERNOR (CN/1185-0361) [23599067] **3172**

POLICE JOURNAL (CHICHESTER) (UK/0032-258X) [01762542] **3172**

POLICE LABOR MONTHLY (US/0749-5595) [09367814] 1702, **3172**

POLICE LAW JOURNAL (US/0892-6573) [15265291] **3172**

POLICE LIABILITY REVIEW (US/1046-6835) [20494173] **3172**

POLICE LIFE (AT) **3172**

POLICE LIFE ANNUAL *See* POLICE LIFE (ANNUAL) **3172**

POLICE LIFE (ANNUAL) (SI) [08084572] **3172**

POLICE MARKSMAN, THE (US/0164-8365) [04315114] **3172**

POLICE MISCONDUCT AND CIVIL RIGHTS LAW REPORT (US/0738-0623) [09504217] 3172, **4511**

POLICE OFFICER GRIEVANCES BULLETIN (US/0887-8285) [13393000] **3172**

● POLICE OFFICERS JOURNAL, THE (US/1062-5216) [25647183] 3172, **1702**

POLICE REQUIREMENT SUPPORT UNIT BULLETIN (UK) **3172**

POLICE REVIEW (LONDON) (UK/0309-1414) [06557882] **3172**

POLICE SCIENCE ABSTRACTS *See* CRIMINOLOGY, PENOLOGY AND POLICE SCIENCE ABSTRACTS **3080**

POLICE STATISTICS ACTUALS (UK) [05593398] 3172, **3082**

POLICE STATISTICS (CHARTERED INSTITUTE OF PUBLIC FINANCE AND ACCOUNTANCY. STATISTICAL INFORMATION SERVICE) (UK) [09568271] 3172, **3082**

POLICE STUDIES (US/0141-2949) [03834971] **3172**

POLICE SURGEON, THE (UK/0308-0242) [16530633] **3742**

POLICE WORLD (UK) [06134918] **3172**

POLICIES AND METHODOLOGIES. DATA PROCESSING SECURITY AND CONTROL (US/0736-6817) [09181845] **1261**

POLICIES IN REVIEW (US/1045-9936) [19209578] **2890**

POLICING (UK/0267-0739) [12621233] **3172**

POLICING AND SOCIETY (SZ/1043-9463) [19617340] **3172**

POLICING POLICY *CEASED.* (UK/0967-1773) **3172**

POLICLINICO, SEZIONE CHIRURGICA (IT/0032-2636) [I00322636] **3972**

POLICLINICO; SEZIONE CHIRURGICA (IT) [01762544] **3628**

POLICLINICO, SEZIONE MEDICA (IT/0048-4717) [I00484717] **3628**

POLICLINICO; SEZIONE PRACTICA (IT) [01643716] **3972**

POLICY ANALYSES IN INTERNATIONAL ECONOMICS (US/0733-1738) [08575344] **1639**

POLICY ANALYSIS (PH/0115-1746) **703**

POLICY ANALYSIS (CATO INSTITUTE) (US/1069-8124) [09653357] **4487**

POLICY AND POLITICS (UK/0305-5736) [02266303] **4487**

POLICY AND PROCEDURES HANDBOOK (US/0197-2596) [05970751] **3029**

POLICY AND PROCEDURES MANUAL FOR GUIDANCE OF FEDERAL AGENCIES. TITLE 4. CLAIMS (US) [04508151] **4674**

POLICY AND RESEARCH REPORT (US/0741-8485) [05694939] **5213**

POLICY & RESEARCH SERIES (US/1013-3429) [18760243] **803**

POLICY BRIEF / WASHINGTON RESEARCH COUNCIL (US) [24572211] **4674**

POLICY BULLETIN - THE NATURE CONSERVANCY (US/0470-3855) [01348202] **2202**

POLICY (CENTRE FOR INDEPENDENT STUDIES (N.S.W.)) (AT/1032-6634) [21469292] **4487**

● POLICY COUNSEL (US) [26110025] **4674**

POLICY FORUM / UNIVERSITY OF ILLINOIS AT URBANA-CHAMPAIGN, INSTITUTE OF GOVERNMENT AND PUBLIC AFFAIRS (US) [18096736] **4674**

POLICY GUIDE OF THE AMERICAN CIVIL LIBERTIES UNION (US/0275-3170) [05091906] **4511**

POLICY-HOLDER *See* PH, POLICY HOLDER INSURANCE JOURNAL **2890**

POLICY IMPACT ANALYSIS (UK/0967-7836) **120**

POLICY NOTES (US/8755-9412) [11451982] **4488**

POLICY OPTIONS (CN/0226-5893) [06515582] **4488**

POLICY, ORGANIZATION AND RULES - GIRL GUIDES OF CANADA (CN/0316-8158) [03348808] **5235**

POLICY PAPERS (HU) [22418661] **4532**

POLICY PAPERS IN HUMAN RESOURCES AND INDUSTRIAL RELATIONS *CEASED.* (US/0073-9421) [02758685] **1702**

POLICY PAPERS IN INTERNATIONAL AFFAIRS (US/0731-6321) [05361178] **4532**

POLICY POSITIONS (US/0160-7456) [03623591] **4674**

POLICY POSITIONS. WINTER MEETING SUPPLEMENT (US/0160-7456) [07701641] **4674**

POLICY PUBLISHERS AND ASSOCIATIONS DIRECTORY *CEASED.* (US/0272-0671) [05956490] 4818, **5213**

POLICY RESEARCH PROJECT REPORT (US/0196-0369) [02337132] **4674**

POLICY RESEARCH WORKING PAPERS (US) [25212960] 803, **1512**

POLICY RESOLUTIONS ADOPTED BY THE CONSTITUTIONAL CONVENTION (US/0587-4971) [01479849] **1702**

POLICY REVIEW (WASHINGTON) (US/0146-5945) [03665154] **5213**

POLICY SCIENCES (NE/0032-2687) [01316133] **4488**

POLICY STATISTICS SERVICE *CEASED.* (US/0163-8920) [04523195] 2890, **2897**

POLICY STUDIES (UK/0144-2872) [07904658] **4488**

POLICY STUDIES DIRECTORY, THE *CEASED.* (US/0362-6016) [02357925] **5213**

POLICY STUDIES JOURNAL (US/0190-292X) [01316083] 4674, **4488**

● POLICY STUDIES PAPERS (US/1061-1843) [25218410] **1702**

POLICY STUDIES REVIEW (US/0278-4416) [07714805] 4674, **4488**

POLIFONIA ARAGONESA (SP) [17169831] **4146**

POLIGRAFIA (RM/0032-2695) [06550917] **4567**

POLIGRAFICESKAJA PROMYSLENNOST. OBZORNAJA INFORMACIJA (RU/0134-9147) [11065330] **4567**

POLIGRAFICHESKAIA — Alphabetical Title Index

POLIGRAFICHESKAIA PROMYSHLENNOST. BIBLIOGRAFICHESKAIA INFORMATSIIA: NOVOSTI TEKHNICHESKOI LITERATURY (RU) [02240806] **4567**

POLIGRAFICO ITALIANO, IL (IT) [06534059] **4567**

POLIGRAFIKA (PL/0373-9864) [10677732] **4567**

POLIISIN JA TULLIN TIETON TULLEET RIKOKSET, PAIHTYNEENA SAILOON OTETUT JA PYSAKOINTIVIRHEET (FI) [03492726] **3172**

POLIISIN TIETOON TULLUT RIKOLLISUUS (FI/0355-2160) [05166875] 3172, **3082**

POLIMERI (ZAGREB) (CI/0351-1871) [10048471] **4459**

POLIMERIM VE-HOMARIM PLASTIYIM (IS/0370-2561) [01784368] **4459**

POLIMERY (PL/0032-2725) [04064410] **1037**

POLIMERY V MELIORACII I VODNOM HOZJAJSTVE (LV/0130-8246) [02244056] 5537, **2094**

POLIMERY W MEDYCYNIE (PL/0370-0747) [01562132] **3628**

POLIN *CEASED.* (UK/0268-1056) [15070027] **5052**

POLIO NETWORK NEWS (US) [20351374] **3628**

POLIOMYELITIS SURVEILLANCE (1978) (US/0734-6611) [07961064] **4795**

POLIPLASTI E PLASTICI RINFORZATI (IT/0032-2768) [09573968] **4459**

POLIS (BOLOGNA, ITALY) (IT) [17787844] **5253**

POLIS (BOSTON, MASS.) (US/0738-6400) [07486700] **3470**

POLIS : POLITICHESKIE ISSLEDOVANIIA / AKADEMIIA NAUK SSSR (RU) [24012970] **4488**

POLISH AFFAIRS (LONDON, ENGLAND : 1974) *CEASED.* (UK) [04993656] **4488**

POLISH AGRICULTURE (FR/0992-4426) [17742475] **120**

POLISH AMERICAN JOURNAL (1985 : NATIONAL ED.) (US) [11864142] **5720**

POLISH AMERICAN STUDIES (CHICAGO, ILL.) (US/0032-2806) [01762549] **2754**

POLISH AMERICAN WORLD (US) [12961462] **5720**

POLISH-ANGLOSAXON STUDIES / UNIWERSYTET IM. ADAMA MICKIEWICZA W POZNANIU (PL/0860-5882) [18114029] **2271**

POLISH ANIMATED FILMS CATALOGUE (PL) [03632694] **4076**

POLISH ART STUDIES (PL/0208-7243) [06654851] **328**

POLISH CANADIAN SCHOLARS, SCIENTISTS, WRITERS & ARTISTS (CN/0383-9958) [03230528] **328**

POLISH DIGEST & EASTERN EUROPEAN AFFAIRS (US) [25019393] **2271**

POLISH DOCUMENTARY AND EDUCATIONAL FILMS (PL) [04969115] **4076**

POLISH ECOLOGICAL BIBLIOGRAPHY (PL/0032-2830) [01236959] **2185**

POLISH ECOLOGICAL STUDIES (PL/0324-8763) [02244945] **2220**

POLISH ENGINEERING (1970) (PL/0374-4078) [01785613] **1990**

POLISH FAIR MAGAZINE (PL) [05000748] **703**

POLISH FAMILY TREE SURNAMES (US/0271-2644) [03364795] **2468**

POLISH FEATURE FILMS (PL) [07261034] **4076**

POLISH FOREIGN TRADE (PL) [01681367] **849**

POLISH GENEALOGICAL SOCIETY NEWSLETTER (US/0735-9349) [08467778] **2468**

POLISH HERITAGE (US/0735-9209) [08395521] **2754**

POLISH JOURNAL OF APPLIED CHEMISTRY (PL) [25636086] **2015**

POLISH JOURNAL OF CHEMISTRY (PL/0137-5083) [03875870] **988**

● POLISH JOURNAL OF FOOD AND NUTRITION SCIENCES / POLISH ACADEMY OF SCIENCES (PL/1230-0322) [26099863] **2353**

POLISH JOURNAL OF OCCUPATIONAL MEDICINE AND ENVIRONMENTAL HEALTH (PL/0867-8383) [26926957] **3628**

● POLISH JOURNAL OF PATHOLOGY : OFFICIAL JOURNAL OF THE POLISH SOCIETY OF PATHOLOGISTS (PL) [31021470] **3897**

● POLISH JOURNAL OF PHARMACOLOGY (PL) [28711812] **4325**

POLISH JOURNAL OF PHARMACOLOGY AND PHARMACY (PL/0301-0244) [01586290] **4325**

POLISH JOURNAL OF SOIL SCIENCE (PL/0079-2985) [01586014] **182**

POLISH MUSEUM OF AMERICA QUARTERLY, THE *SUSPENDED.* (US/0149-9653) [03585717] **4095**

POLISH MUSIC *SUSPENDED.* (PL/0032-2946) [02434320] **4146**

POLISH POLAR RESEARCH (PL/0138-0338) [08357127] **5138**

POLISH POLITICAL SCIENCE / POLISH ASSOCIATION OF POLITICAL SCIENCE (PL/0208-7375) [09525589] **4488**

POLISH POPULATION REVIEW / POLISH DEMOGRAPHIC SOCIETY [AND] CENTRAL STATISTICAL OFFICE (PL/0867-7905) [26272209] **4556**

POLISH PSYCHOLOGICAL BULLETIN (PL/0079-2993) [01642832] **4608**

POLISH REVIEW (NEW YORK. 1956), THE (US/0032-2970) [01762556] 2852, **5213**

POLISH SOCIOLOGICAL BULLETIN, THE (PL/0032-2997) [01653997] **5253**

POLISH SOCIOLOGICAL REVIEW (PL) **5253**

POLISH SOCIOLOGY OF LAW NEWSLETTER, THE (PL) [07039564] 5254, **3029**

POLISH STUDIES PROGRAM MONOGRAPHS (US) [20184799] **2852**

POLISH TECHNICAL AND ECONOMIC ABSTRACTS (PL/0032-3004) [02265362] 5138, **1512**

POLISH TECHNICAL REVIEW (PL/0032-3012) [06615378] **5138**

POLISH WESTERN AFFAIRS (PL/0032-3039) [01606392] **4488**

POLISH WESTERN ASSOCIATION OF AMERICA *See* QUARTERLY **2704**

POLISH YEARBOOK OF INTERNATIONAL LAW, THE (PL/0554-498X) [01784633] **3134**

POLITECHNIKA ODZKA *See* SKAD OSOBOWY W ROKU AKADEMICKIM ... / POLITECHNIKA ODZKA **5158**

POLITECHNIKA POANANSKA *See* INFORMATOR I SKAD OSOBOWY NA ROK AKADEMICKI ... / POLITECHNIKA POZNANSKA **1978**

POLITECHNIKA WROCAWSKA. INSTYTUT ARCHITEKTURY I URBANISTYKI *See* SERIA KONFERENCJE **308**

POLITECHNIKA WROCAWSKA. INSTYTUT CYBERNETYKI TECHNICZNEJ *See* SERIA MONOGRAFIE - POLITECHNIKA WROCAWSKA, INSTYTUT CYBERNETYKI TECHNICZNEJ **2128**

POLITECHNIKA WROCAWSKA. INSTYTUT GORNICTWA *See* PRACE NAUKOWE INSTYTUTU GORNICTWA POLITECHNIKI WROCAWSKIEJ. MONOGRAFIE **2148**

POLITECHNIKA WROCAWSKA. INSTYTUT MATEMATYKI *See* SERIA STUDIA I MATERIAY - POLITECHNIKA WROCAWSKA, INSTYTUT MATEMATYKI **3534**

POLITECHNIKA WROCAWSKA. INSTYTUT MATEMATYKI *See* PRACE NAUKOWE INSTYTUTU MATEMATYKI POLITECHNIKI WROCAWSKIEJ **3527**

POLITECHNIKA WROCAWSKA. INSTYTUT MATEMATYKI *See* SERIA MONOGRAFIE - POLITECHNIKA WROCAWSKA, INSTYTUT MATEMATYKI **3534**

POLITECHNIKA WROCAWSKA. INSTYTUT MATERIAOZNAWSTWA I MECHANIKI TECHNICZNEJ *See* KONFERENCJE **2027**

POLITECNICO DI MILANO. DIPARTIMENTO DI INGEGNERIA STRUTTURALE *See* SUMMARIES OF PUBLICATIONS / DIPARTIMENTO DI INGEGNERIA STRUTTURALE, POLITECNICO DI MILANO **2032**

POLITECNICO MILANO. 1988 *CEASED.* (IT/1120-8902) [I11208902] **306**

POLITEIA (VE) [02787002] **4488**

POLITICA (DK/0105-0710) [05866266] **4488**

POLITICA (BL) [03019701] **4488**

POLITICA AGRARIA (IT) [04993473] **120**

POLITICA DEL DIRITTO (IT/0032-3063) [23076934] **4488**

POLITICA DEL TURISMO (IT) **5489**

POLITICA E ESTRATEGIA (BL/0102-2636) [12432871] **4532**

POLITICA ECONOMICA (IT) [13913565] **1512**

POLITICA ED ECONOMIA (ROME, ITALY : 1970) (IT/0551-326X) [02787133] **1512**

POLITICA EXTERIOR (SP/0213-6856) [23162495] **4532**

● POLITICA EXTERNA (BL) [27153439] **4532**

POLITICA HERMETICA (FR) [18453776] 4488, **4987**

POLITICA INTERNACIONAL CARACAS (VE/0798-1147) [I07981147] **4488**

POLITICA INTERNAZIONALE (IT) [04745649] **1578**

POLITICA (SPERLING & KUPFER EDITORI) (IT) [20184811] **4488**

POLITICA (UNIVERSIDAD DE CHILE. INSTITUTO DE CIENCIA POLITICA) (CL) [09487642] **4488**

POLITICA Y ECONOMIA (AG) [01789340] **1578**

POLITICA Y SOCIEDAD (MADRID, SPAIN) (SP/0210-7872) [20081499] **5213**

POLITICAL ACTION COMMENTARY (US) **3350**

POLITICAL AFFAIRS (US/0032-3128) [06371312] **4488**

POLITICAL ALERTS (CN/0712-4295) [08584584] **4488**

POLITICAL ANALYSIS (US/1047-1987) [20621181] **4488**

POLITICAL AND ECONOMIC CONDITIONS IN SOUTHERN AFRICA (US/1056-5280) [23730143] **1578**

POLITICAL AND SOCIAL CHANGE MONOGRAPH (AT/0727-5994) [12173288] **4488**

POLITICAL ANIMAL (1993), THE (US/1070-1753) [28304668] **4488**

POLITICAL ARCHIVES OF RUSSIA (US/1069-093X) [25938634] 4674, **4545**

POLITICAL BEHAVIOR (US/0190-9320) [04769287] 5254, **4488**

POLITICAL CHANGE (II) [07037841] **4489**

POLITICAL CHRONICLE, THE (US/1042-3885) [19031748] **4489**

● POLITICAL COMMUNICATION (US/1058-4609) [24298351] 1119, **4489**

POLITICAL COMMUNICATION AND PERSUASION *See* POLITICAL COMMUNICATION **4489**

POLITICAL CORRECTION (US/1056-6740) [23844779] **4489**

POLITICAL DIGEST (NR) [10246285] **4489**

● POLITICAL ECONOMY JOURNAL OF INDIA : A QUARTERLY JOURNAL OF THE CENTRE FOR INDIAN DEVELOPMENT STUDIES (II/0971-2097) [26906785] 4489, **1512**

POLITICAL EDUCATION COMMITTEE NATIONAL NEWSLETTER *See* AMERICAN IRISH NEWSLETTER, THE **2609**

● POLITICAL FINANCE LOBBY REPORTER (US/0270-353X) [06390870] **4489**

POLITICAL FOCUS / NATIONAL ASSOCIATION OF ARAB AMERICANS (US) [12061703] **2271**

● POLITICAL GEOGRAPHY (UK/0962-6298) [25104907] 4489, **2572**

POLITICAL GEOGRAPHY QUARTERLY *See* POLITICAL GEOGRAPHY **2572**

POLITICAL HANDBOOK OF THE WORLD (1975) (US/0193-175X) [01550268] **4489**

POLITICAL HISTORY OF RUSSIA (US) 2662, **4545**

POLITICAL INQUIRY (US/0092-9735) [01791020] **4489**

POLITICAL ISSUES IN NURSING (UK/0883-4504) [12141727] **3867**

POLITICAL PIX *CEASED.* (US/0895-4712) [16651998] 381, 4489, **2923**

POLITICAL PORTRAITS (UK) **434**

POLITICAL POWER AND SOCIAL THEORY (US/0198-8719) [06154599] 5254, **4489**

POLITICAL PSYCHOLOGY (US/0162-895X) [04251478] **4608**

POLITICAL PULSE (US/8756-9248) [11742294] **4489**

POLITICAL PULSE'S EDUCATION BEAT (US/1058-4226) [24301563] **1774**

POLITICAL QUARTERLY (LONDON. 1930) (UK/0032-3179) [01762568] **4489**

POLITICAL QUOTATIONS : A COLLECTION OF NOTABLE SAYINGS ON POLITICS FROM ANTIQUITY THROUGH 1988 (US) [19718584] 3424, **4489**

POLITICAL REPORT *See* ROTHENBERG POLITICAL REPORT **4495**

● POLITICAL RESEARCH QUARTERLY (US/1065-9129) [26790930] **4489**

POLITICAL RESOURCE DIRECTORY (NATIONAL ED.) (US/0898-4271) [17405841] **4489**

POLITICAL RISK DATABASE *CEASED.* (US/0890-4928) [16047751] **4489**

POLITICAL RISK SERVICES LETTER (US/0887-7629) [12770275] **1512**

Alphabetical Title Index

POLSKI

... POLITICAL RISK YEARBOOK. MIDDLE EAST & NORTH AFRICA, THE (US/0897-8530) [17645720] **4489**

... POLITICAL RISK YEARBOOK. NORTH & CENTRAL AMERICA, THE (US/0897-8557) [17644888] **4489**

... POLITICAL RISK YEARBOOK. SOUTH AMERICA, THE (US/0897-8549) [17645615] **4489**

... POLITICAL RISK YEARBOOK. SUB-SAHARAN AFRICA, THE (US/0889-2725) [13824919] **4489**

POLITICAL RISK YEARBOOK. VOL. 5, ASIA & THE PACIFIC (US/0897-8565) [24235901] **4489**

POLITICAL RISK YEARBOOK. VOL. 6, EUROPE. COUNTRIES OF THE EUROPEAN COMMUNITY (US/1053-8771) [22683990] **4532**

POLITICAL RISK YEARBOOK. VOL 7, EUROPE. OUTSIDE THE EUROPEAN COMMUNITY (US/1053-878X) [22684010] **4490**

POLITICAL SCIENCE (US) [05113823] **4490**

POLITICAL SCIENCE (NZ/0032-3187) [01762570] **4490**

POLITICAL SCIENCE ABSTRACTS. ANNUAL SUPPLEMENT (US/0731-8022) [08042061] **4490**

POLITICAL SCIENCE AND RELATED DISCIPLINES / INTERNATIONAL CURRENT AWARENESS SERVICES ***CEASED.*** (UK/0960-1538) [23888196] **4490**

POLITICAL SCIENCE QUARTERLY (US/0032-3195) [01604215] **4490**

POLITICAL SCIENCE REVIEW (II/0554-5196) [01589571] **4490**

POLITICAL SCIENCE REVIEWER, THE (US/0091-3715) [01786931] **4490**

POLITICAL SCIENCE TEACHER (US) [18905021] **4490**, **1774**

POLITICAL SCIENCE UTILIZATION DIRECTORY, THE ***CEASED.*** (US/0362-4765) [02309653] **4490**

POLITICAL SCIENTIST (II/0032-3209) [01681166] **4490**

POLITICAL STUDIES (UK/0032-3217) [01641383] **4490**

POLITICAL THEORY (US/0090-5917) [01785573] **4490**

POLITICAL WARFARE ***CEASED.*** (US/1056-3334) [23666895] **4054**, **4532**

●POLITICAL WOMAN (WHITE PLAINS, N.Y.) (US/1069-6652) [28130357] **5564**, **4490**

POLITICHE DEL LAVORO ***CEASED.*** (IT) [16265978] **4490**

POLITICHE SOCIALI E SERVIZI / CENTRO DI DOCUMENTAZIONE SUI SERVIZI SOCIALI GIOVANNI MARIA CORNAGGIA MEDICI (IT) [19647521] **5301**

POLITICHESKAIA ORGANIZATSIIA OBSHCHESTVA I UPRAVLENIE PRI SOTSIALIZME (RU/0202-2273) [11835025] **4490**

POLITICHESKI IZSLEDVANIIA (BU/0861-4830) [25864406] **4490**

POLITICKA MISAO (CI/0032-3241) [05626736] **4490**

POLITICO; RIVISTA ITALIANA DI SCIENZE POLITICHE, IL (IT/0032-325x) [02169078] **4490**

POLITICS & MARKETS (US/0749-4416) [10829507] **4490**

POLITICS AND POLICY ***CEASED.*** (US/0743-1082) [10510033] **4490**

POLITICS & SOCIETY (US/0032-3292) [01315994] **4490**, **5213**

POLITICS AND SOCIETY IN GERMANY, AUSTRIA, AND SWITZERLAND (UK/0954-6030) [23715916] **5254**

POLITICS AND THE INDIVIDUAL (GW/0939-6071) [I09396071] **4490**

POLITICS AND THE LIFE SCIENCES (US/0730-9384) [08123994] **4490**

POLITICS (BATON ROUGE) (US/0194-3669) [05373662] **4491**

POLITICS BRIEFING (UK) [18514533] **4491**

POLITICS IN MINNESOTA (US) [11778775] **4491**

POLITICS (MANCHESTER (GREATER MANCHESTER)) (UK/0263-3957) [10903269] **4491**

POLITICS REVIEW (UK/0959-8480) [28572195] **4491**

POLITICS TODAY (UK) [02754874] **4491**

POLITICS TODAY (SANTA BARBARA) (US/0160-4929) [03694883] **4491**

POLITIE-ALMANAK (NE) [06558068] **3172**

POLITIE MAGAZINE (NE/0925-0980) [I09250980] **3172**

POLITIEK MEMO (NE) [04071789] **4674**

POLITIIKKA (FI/0032-3365) [06337865] **4491**

POLITIK UND KULTUR (GW) [02468746] **4491**

POLITIKA (LI) [23059495] **4545**

POLITIKA EKONOMIE (XR/0032-3233) [02769304] **1512**

POLITIKA THEMATA (GR) [18887985] **2703**

POLITIKEN (DK) **5799**

POLITIKON (SA/0258-9346) [02244809] **4491**

POLITIKWISSENSCHAFTLICHE PAPERBACKS (GW) [17248098] **4491**

POLITINFORMATOR I AGITATOR (BW) [01791876] **4674**

POLITIQUE AFRICAINE (PARIS, FRANCE : 1981) (FR/0244-7827) [07641388] **4491**

POLITIQUE DE LA SCIENCE (SZ) [15540338] **5138**

POLITIQUE ET ENVIRONNEMENT / GROUPE D'ETUDES ET DE RECHERCHES SUR LES POLITIQUES ENVIRONNEMENTALES (CN/1183-7993) [24690532] **4491**

POLITIQUE ETRANGERE DE LA FRANCE, LA (FR/0532-4092) [02397625] **4491**

POLITIQUE INDUSTRIELLE (FR/0766-6047) [I07666047] 4491, **1621**

POLITIQUE INTERNATIONALE (FR/0221-2781) [04893725] **4532**

POLITIQUE : REVUE INTERNATIONALE DES IDEES, DES INSTITUTIONS ET DE LA VIE POLITIQUE (FR) [09546168] **4491**

POLITIQUES DE POPULATION (BE) [15131734] **4556**

POLITIQUES ET MANAGEMENT PUBLIC (FR/0758-1726) [I07581726] 882, **4491**

POLITISCHE BILDUNG (STUTTGART, GERMANY) (GW/0554-5455) [09210813] **4491**

POLITISCHE MEINUNG, DIE (GW/0032-3446) [01589215] **5213**

POLITISCHE STUDIEN (GW/0032-3462) [02004041] **4491**

POLITISCHER BERICHT DES ZENTRALEN KOMITEES DES KOMMUNISTISCHEN BUNDES WESTDEUTSCHLAND AN DIE ORDENTLICHE DELEGIERTENKONFERENZ (GW) [02579328] **2703**

POLITISCHES JAHRBUCH DER CHRISTLICH - DEMOKRATISCHEN UNION DEUTSCHLANDS (GW/0578-0225) [03135454] **4491**

POLITIX (FR/0295-2319) [21893150] **4491**

POLITY (US/0032-3497) [01762581] **4491**

POLITYKA (PL/0032-3500) [06547308] **4491**

POLITYKA I CHAS : ZHURNAL T SK KOMPARTII UKRAINY (UN/0868-8273) [24119580] **4545**

POLIZEI, TECHNIK, VERKEHR *See* POLIZEI, VERKEHR + TECHNIK **3172**

POLIZEI, VERKEHR + TECHNIK (GW) [10381613] **3172**

POLIZIA MODERNA (IT) [06534458] **3172**

POLJOPRIVREDA I SUMARSTVO (YU/0554-5579) [08251970] **120**

POLJOPRIVREDNA ZNANSTVENA SMOTRA (YU/0370-0291) [06741972] **120**

POLK COUNTY ELEGANCE (US/0745-3191) [09067856] **2543**

POLK COUNTY ENTERPRISE (US) [14524654] **5753**

●POLK FINANCIAL INSTITUTIONS DIRECTORY (US) [28399781] **803**

POLKA NEWS, THE (US/0273-6454) [06780491] 4146, **1314**

POLK'S ALBANY (ALBANY COUNTY, N.Y.) CITY DIRECTORY (US) [06111898] **2572**

POLK'S BANK DIRECTORY (INTERNATIONAL ED.) (US/1058-0603) [14125916] **803**

POLK'S BANK DIRECTORY (NORTH AMERICAN ED.) (US/1058-0611) [14764317] **803**

POLK'S BANK DIRECTORY (NORTH AMERICAN ED.) *See* POLK FINANCIAL INSTITUTIONS DIRECTORY **803**

POLK'S MINNEAPOLIS SUBURBAN CITY DIRECTORY (US) [01762592] **2572**

POLK'S ROCHESTER SUBURBAN (MONROE COUNTY, N.Y.) DIRECTORY (US) [06211110] **2572**

POLK'S SAGUENAY DIRECTORY (CN/0316-0556) [02247493] **2572**

POLLED HEREFORD WORLD (1965) (US/0162-7953) [04223267] **217**

POLLING REPORT, THE (US/0887-171X) [13136836] **5254**

●POLLOCK POTPOURRI (US/1062-7855) [25740087] **2468**

POLLSTAR (FRESNO, CALIF.) (US/1067-6945) [18872113] **4146**

POLLUSTOP (FR/0300-3574) [01785819] **2238**

POLLUTING INCIDENTS IN AND AROUND U.S. WATERS (US/0092-0320) [01787140] 5537, **2238**

POLLUTING SPILLS IN U.S. WATERS *See* POLLUTING INCIDENTS IN AND AROUND U.S. WATERS **2238**

POLLUTION ABSTRACTS. ANNUAL INDEX (US/0191-1724) [04810114] **2185**

POLLUTION ABSTRACTS WITH INDEXES (US/0032-3624) [01762599] 2238, **2185**

POLLUTION ATMOSPHERIQUE ET NUISANCES / PREFECTURE DE POLICE, LABORATOIRE CENTRAL (FR) [25588602] **2238**

POLLUTION ATMOSPHERIQUE (PARIS, FRANCE) (FR/0032-3632) [12297980] **2238**

POLLUTION (BOCA RATON) (US/0273-253X) [01153243] **2238**

POLLUTION CONTROL (US) **2238**

POLLUTION CONTROL JOURNAL (US/0095-6074) [01798112] **2238**

POLLUTION DE L'EAU DE L'AIR ET DU SOL DECHETS BRUIT, E36 (FR) 2180, **2238**

POLLUTION ENGINEERING (US/0032-3640) [01642767] **2238**

POLLUTION ENGINEERING AND TECHNOLOGY (US/0148-4435) [03338242] **2238**

POLLUTION EQUIPMENT NEWS (US/0032-3659) [02449780] **2239**

POLLUTION PREVENTION (UK) **2239**

POLLUTION PREVENTION ADVISOR (US/1056-4586) [23719098] **2239**

POLLUTION PREVENTION LONDON (UK/0965-5948) [I09655948] **2239**

POLLUTION PREVENTION REVIEW (US/1053-4253) [22529186] **2239**

POLLUTION RESEARCH (II/0257-8050) [10296022] **2239**

POLLUTION TECHNOLOGY REVIEW ***CEASED.*** (US/0090-516X) [01605002] **2239**

POLNOHOSPODARSKA VEDA. SERIA A, POLNOHOSPODARSTVO (XO) [11869114] **120**

POLNOHOSPODARSTVO (XO/0551-3677) [03792556] **120**

POLO (GAITHERSBURG, MD.) (US/0146-4574) [02942329] 2801, **4912**

POLOISTE, LE (CN/0226-5443) [06299592] **4912**

POLONICA (PL) [02245059] **3311**

POLONISTYKA (PL) [04075225] **3311**

POLONUS PHILATELIC SOCIETY *See* BULLETIN OF THE POLONUS PHILATELIC SOCIETY **2784**

POLP ASIST [COMPUTER FILE] (US) [24675059] **1308**

POLSK KULTUR (NO) [11172555] **2703**

POLSKA 2000 / KOMITET BADAN I PROGNOZ "POLSKA 2000" POLSKIEJ AKADEMII NAUK (PL/0079-3620) [05026860] **2703**

POLSKA AKADEMIA NAUK. CENTRUM MEDYCYNY DOSWIADCZALNEJ I KLINICZNEJ *See* REPORT OF SCIENTIFIC ACTIVITIES **3633**

POLSKA AKADEMIA NAUK. INSTYTUT MASZYN PRZEPYWOWYCH *See* PRACE INSTYTUTU MASZYN PRZEPYWOWYCH **2125**

POLSKA BIBLIOGRAFIA NAUK KOSCIELNYCH (PL/0303-2272) [05690703] **4987**

POLSKA BIBLIOGRAFIA PARAZYTOLOGICZNA (PL) [02243349] **5594**

POLSKA BIBLIOGRAFIA PRAWNICZA / POLSKA AKADEMIA NAUK, INSTYTUT PANSTWA I PRAWA (PL/0551-3855) [09632363] **3082**

POLSKA, DANE STATYSTYCZNE (PL/0860-6811) [18275947] **5336**

POLSKA SZTUKA LUDOWA (PL/0032-3721) [02148488] **362**

POLSKA ZBROJNA (PL) [22656693] **5808**

POLSKI INSTYTUT SPRAW MIEDZYNARODOWYCH *See* ACTIVITY OF THE POLISH INSTITUTE OF INTERNATIONAL AFFAIRS **4461**

POLSKI, LAS (PL) [04089366] **2390**

POLSKI PRZEGLAD CHIRURGICZNY (PL/0032-373X) [01778366] **3972**

POLSKI PRZEGLAD RADIOLOGII (PL/0860-1089) [10661007] 3944, **3849**

POLSKI TYGODNIK LEKARSKI (1960) (PL/0032-3756) [07640119] **3628**

POLSKI — Alphabetical Title Index

POLSKI ZWIAZEK KROTKOFALOWCOW See BIULETYN - POLSKI ZWIAZEK KROTKOFALOWCOW **2036**

POLSKIE ARCHIWUM HYDROBIOLOGII (PL/0032-3764) [03979098] **557**

POLSKIE ARCHIWUM MEDYCYNY WEWNETRZNEJ (PL/0032-3772) [06523174] **3800**

POLSKIE ARCHIWUM WETERYNARYJNE See ARCHIVUM VETERINARIUM POLONICUM / POLISH ACADEMY OF SCIENCES, COMMITTEE OF VETERINARY SCIENCES **5504**

POLSKIE KSIAZKI (TORONTO) (CN/0710-5290) [09448365] **4831**

POLSKIE PISMO ENTOMOLOGICZNE (PL/0032-3780) [01641554] **5612**

POLSKIE TOWARZYSTWO BOTANICZNE See ACTA SOCIETATIS BOTANICORUM POLONIAE **497**

POLSKIE TOWARZYSTWO MATEMATYCZNE See ANNALES SOCIETATIS MATHEMATICAE POLONAE. COMMENTATIONES MATHEMATICAE **3493**

POLSKIE TOWARZYSTWO MATEMATYCZNE See ROCZNIKI POLSKOGO TOWARZYSTWA MATEMATYCZNEGO, SERIA 3: MATEMATYKA STOSOWANA **3532**

POLSKIE TOWARZYSTWO MATEMATYCZNE See ROCZNIKI POLSKOGO TOWARZYSTWA MATEMATYCZNEGO, SERIA 2. WIADOMOSCI MATEMATYCZNE **3532**

POLSO, IL (IT/0392-9264) [I03929264] **3628**

POLTOX [COMPUTER FILE] (US) [22298904] **3983, 2239**

POLUPROVODNIKOVAIA ELEKTRONIKA V TEKHNIKE SVIAZI (RU) [05069027] **2075**

POLYCOM (NR) [07631720] **2511**

POLYCYCLIC AROMATIC COMPOUNDS (US/1040-6638) [18492443] **988**

POLYDOXY (US/0146-888X) [03058836] **5052**

POLYGON (SZ) [25361157] **2521**

POLYGRAPH, DER (GW/0032-3845) [06547428] 1119, **4567**

POLYGRAPH LAW REPORTER (US/0196-1179) [05398290] **3029**

POLYGRAPH (LINTHICUM HEIGHTS) (US/0197-7024) [04603695] **3172**

POLYHEDRON (UK/0277-5387) [07590197] **1037**

POLYLINGUA (HOUGHTON, MICH.) (US/1045-6716) [20214048] **3311**

POLYMER BLENDS, ALLOYS, AND INTERPENETRATING POLYMER NETWORKS ABSTRACTS (US/0893-6684) [15615497] **988**

POLYMER BULLETIN (BERLIN, WEST) (GW/0170-0839) [04622523] **1056**

POLYMER COMPOSITES (US/0272-8397) [06932010] **4459**

POLYMER CONTENTS (UK/0883-153X) [12195004] 4459, 5077, **4461**

POLYMER DEGRADATION AND STABILITY (UK/0141-3910) [04996062] 4459, **988**

POLYMER ENGINEERING AND SCIENCE (US/0032-3888) [01587960] **988**

●POLYMER GELS AND NETWORKS (UK/0966-7822) [28286718] 1046, **2015**

POLYMER (GUILFORD) (UK/0032-3861) [02228301] **1046**

POLYMER INTERNATIONAL (UK/0959-8103) [22840502] **4459**

POLYMER JOURNAL (JA/0032-3896) [01589439] **1046**

POLYMER MONOGRAPHS (NEW YORK, N.Y. : 1981) (US/0275-5777) [07164856] **1046**

POLYMER NETWORKS & BLENDS (CN/1181-9510) [24265994] **1046**

POLYMER NEWS (US/0032-3918) [02266354] **4459**

POLYMER-PLASTICS TECHNOLOGY AND ENGINEERING (SOFTCOVER ED.) (US/0360-2559) [01915296] **2015**

POLYMER PREPRINTS, AMERICAN CHEMICAL SOCIETY, DIVISION OF POLYMER CHEMISTRY (US/0032-3934) [I00323934] **989**

POLYMER PREPRINTS: JAPAN (JA) **989**

POLYMER PROCESS ENGINEERING See POLYMER-PLASTICS TECHNOLOGY AND ENGINEERING (SOFTCOVER ED.) **2015**

POLYMER PROCESSING AND RHEOLOGY (US) **4459**

●POLYMER REACTION ENGINEERING (US/1054-3414) [22851226] **1990**

POLYMER RECYCLING (UK/0969-5990) **1028**

POLYMER SCIENCE (RU/0965-545X) [25636234] **989**

●POLYMER SCIENCE. SERIES B (RU) [28282604] **989**

POLYMER TESTING (UK/0142-9418) [07144177] 5077, **4459**

POLYMER YEARBOOK (SZ/0738-1743) [09535237] **1046**

POLYMERES PEINTURES BOIS, F24 (FR) **4225**

POLYMERIC MATERIALS SCIENCE AND ENGINEERING (US/0743-0515) [09843285] **4459**

POLYMERS & POLYMER COMPOSITES (UK/0967-3911) [28101872] 1991, **4459**

POLYMERS & RUBBER ASIA (UK/0268-9812) [02689812] **4459**

POLYMERS CERAMICS AND COMPOSITES ALERT (UK) **4459**

POLYMERS FOR ADVANCED TECHNOLOGIES (UK/1042-7147) [19116214] **1028**

POLYMERS IN BIOLOGY AND MEDICINE (US/0272-6335) [06125962] 3628, **469**

POLYMERS PAINT COLOUR YEAR BOOK (UK/0078-7817) [01794202] 4459, **4225**

POLYMETRIC REPORT (N.Y.S.E. ED.) (CN/0711-7965) [11100271] **873**

POLYMETRIC REPORT (T.S.E. ED.) (CN/0822-6970) [10199197] **911**

POLYNESIAN SOCIETY (N.Z.) See JOURNAL OF THE POLYNESIAN SOCIETY **3292**

POLYNUCLEAR AROMATIC HYDROCARBONS (US/0191-2232) [04810785] **3822**

POLYPEPTIDES SHEFFIELD (UK/0143-4225) [I01434225] 492, **3628**

POLYPHONY (TORONTO) (CN/0704-7002) [04079708] **2754**

POLYSCOPE, COMPUTER, ELECTRONICS, COMMUNICATION (SZ) **2075**

POLYSCOPE (MONTREAL) (CN/0710-3522) [08327362] **1094**

POLYSCOPE (SAINT-LEONARD D'ASTON, QUEBEC) (CN/0228-7099) [07802261] **1774**

POLYTECHNIC ENGINEER, THE (US/0032-406X) [03623211] **1991**

POLYTECHNISCH TIJDSCHRIFT (NE) **2028**

POLYTECHNISCH TIJDSCHRIFT. ELEKTRONICA ELEKTROTECHNIEK (1990) (NE/0925-5672) [26075555] **2075**

POLYTECHNISCH TIJDSCHRIFT. WERKTUIGBOUW (NE/0032-4108) [02943795] **2124**

POLYTECHNISCHE BILDUNG UND ERZIEHUNG (SZ) [06405081] **1915**

POLYTECHNISCHE TIJDSCHRIFT (NE) **5139**

POLYTHEMATICAL COLLECTED REPORTS OF THE MEDICAL FACULTY OF THE PALACKY UNIVERSITY (XR/0301-2549) [01445832] **3628**

POMERANIAN REGISTRY, THE (US/1058-3637) [24278373] **4287**

POMERANIAN REVIEW (US/0744-8546) [08602583] **4287**

POMIARY, AUTOMATYKA, KONTROLA (PL/0032-4140) [06635761] **1221**

POMJOE PUNSOK (SEOUL, KOREA : 1983) (KO) [11429904] **3082**

POMME D'API (FR/0182-6220) [I01826220] **2852**

POMME DE TERRE FRANCAISE, LA (FR/0032-4159) [04064433] **182**

POMMERSCHEN LEUTE, DIE (US/0747-6558) [10760857] 2703, **2468**

POMMU YONGU (KO) [11477808] **3029**

POMNYUN (KO) [05194237] **5021**

POMONA COLLEGE TODAY (US/1042-0827) [18934470] **1841**

POMONA : NORTH AMERICAN FRUIT EXPLORERS' QUARTERLY (US/0748-6510) [07673819] 2776, **2428**

POMONA TODAY See POMONA COLLEGE TODAY **1841**

POMORANIA ANTIQUA (PL/0556-0691) [02781312] **4230**

POMOST (US/0884-0172) [12203339] **2703**

POMPA (US) **3350**

POMPANO LEDGER (US) **5650**

POMPEIIANA NEWSLETTER (US/0892-5941) [15250306] 3336, **3311**

POMYCZEK (PL/0137-8511) [I01378511] **1068**

PONCA CITY NEWS, THE (US) [13723460] **5732**

PONCHATOULA TIMES, THE (US) [20882084] **5684**

PONDERING KENTUCKY (US) **2543**

●PONIECKI NEWSLETTER/INFORMATOR (US/1062-824X) [25760810] **2923**

PONS INFORMATIU (SP) **1347**

PONT, LE (CN/0227-2296) [07294998] **5793**

PONTE (FIRENZE), IL (IT/0032-423X) [01641093] **3350**

PONTE (WILLOWDALE) (CN/0316-7232) [02441584] **5254**

PONTIAC; CHASSIS SHOP MANUAL (US/0149-9637) [02165948] **5423**

PONTIAC-OAKLAND COUNTY LEGAL NEWS (US/0739-0203) [09701723] **3029**

PONTIAC SHOP MANUAL SUPPLEMENT (CN/0700-3447) [03278907] **5423**

PONTICA (RM) [02434482] **278**

PONTIFICAL INSTITUTE OF MEDIAEVAL STUDIES See PONTIFICAL INSTITUTE OF MEDIAEVAL STUDIES. STUDIES AND TEXTS **2703**

PONTIFICAL INSTITUTE OF MEDIAEVAL STUDIES. STUDIES AND TEXTS (CN/0082-5328) [01767636] **2703**

PONTIFICIA UNIVERSIDAD JAVERIANA. FACULTAD DE FILOSOFIA Y LETRAS See UNIVERSITAS HUMANISTICA **1851**

PONTOTOC COUNTY QUARTERLY, OKLAHOMA (US) [15214004] **2468**

PONTOTOC PROGRESS, THE (US) [14996573] **5701**

PONY (UK) [01672990] **2801**

●PONY EXPRESS (GAINESVILLE, FLA.) (US/1065-285X) [26572011] **4170**

PONY JOURNAL See JOURNAL OF THE AMERICAN SHETLAND PONY CLUB **2800**

PONY JOURNAL, THE (US/0199-5537) [04943069] **2801**

POODLE REVIEW, THE (US/0477-5449) [05192320] **4287**

POODLE VARIETY (US/0882-2816) [11982059] **4287**

POOL & BILLIARD MAGAZINE (US/1049-2852) [21193717] **4912**

POOL & SPA MARKETING (CN/0711-2998) [08486207] **934**

POOL & SPA MARKETING. SUPPLEMENT (CN/0711-3005) [08465788] **934**

POOL & SPA NEWS (US/0194-5351) [04799774] **703**

POOL & SPA NEWS DIRECTORY ISSUE (US) [06181247] **4853**

POOL NEWS DIRECTORY See POOL & SPA NEWS DIRECTORY ISSUE **4853**

POOL PLAYER'S NATIONAL POCKET BILLIARDS DIRECTORY, THE (US/1053-7236) [22616757] **4865**

POOLEY'S FLIGHT GUIDE, UNITED KINGDOM AND IRELAND / COMPILED WITH THE ASSISTANCE OF THE CIVIL AVIATION AUTHORITY (UK) [07964505] **31**

POOP SHEET, THE (US/0195-0037) [05188869] **4912**

POOR JOE'S CALIFORNIA ALMANACK (US) [04138159] **2543**

POOR JOE'S COLORADO ALMANACK (US) [04138117] **2543**

POOR JOE'S INDIANA ALMANACK (US/0160-8193) [03758276] **2543**

POOR JOE'S MISSOURI ALMANACK (US) [03916258] **2543**

POOR JOE'S NORTH CAROLINA ALMANACK (US) [04138141] **2543**

POOR JOE'S OHIO STATE ALMANACK (US/0160-8185) [03758404] **2543**

POOR JOE'S PENNSYLVANIA FARM ALMANACK (US/0362-8523) [02362639] **2543**

POOR JOE'S WASHINGTON ALMANACK (US/0160-8207) [03758475] **2543**

POOR KONRAD (US/0741-1588) [09028544] **4987**

POOR RICHARD'S RECORD (US/0361-9419) [02359934] **1841**

POOR'S ANNUAL DIVIDEND RECORD See ANNUAL DIVIDEND RECORD / STANDARD AND POOR'S CORPORATION **890**

POP DIRECTORY (US/0556-5189) [01789916] **4147**

POP MUSIC SURVEY (US) **4147**

POP ROCK (CN/0713-8121) [09026009] **4147**

POPCHO (KO) [08516117] **3029**

POPCORN / IOWA CROP AND LIVESTOCK REPORTING SERVICE (US) [06230828] **182**

POPE COUNTY HISTORICAL ASSOCIATION QUARTERLY (US) [04600585] 2468, **2754**

Alphabetical Title Index — POPULATION

POPE COUNTY TRIBUNE (US) [01762646] **5698**

POPE FAMILY REGISTER, THE (US/0360-9421) [02244960] **2468**

POPE SPEAKS, THE (US/0032-4353) [01762647] **5034**

POPE TEACHES, THE (UK) [07215083] **5034**

POPHAK (KO) [20838972] **3029**

POPHAM FAMILY NEWSLETTER (US/0882-8687) [12011058] **2468**

POPI (FR/0299-3147) [I02993147] **1068**

POPIS SUMSKOG FONDA ... GODINE / SOCIJALISTICKA REPUBLIKA SRBIJA, REPUBLICKI ZAVOD ZA STATISTIKU (CI) [11424136] **2390**

POPLINE (US) [05332304] **4556**

●POPOL-NA (NQ) [28174847] **4674**

POPOLA CINIO, EL (CC) [05720653] **2662**

POPOLI (IT/0394-4247) [I03944247] **2521**

POPSI (UK/0958-5702) [I09585702] **422**

POPULACNI ZPRAVY (XR/0231-55‑3) [05291940] **4556**

POPULAR ARCHAEOLOGY (US/0300-774X) [01359689] **278**

POPULAR ARCHAEOLOGY. TECHNICAL PUBLICATION (US) [07427074] **278**

POPULAR BRIDGE MONTHLY *See* INTERNATIONAL POPULAR BRIDGE MONTHLY **4851**

POPULAR CERAMICS (US/0032-4477) [02253333] **2593**

POPULAR COMMUNICATIONS (US/0733-3315) [08575421] **1119**

●POPULAR COMMUNICATIONS COMMUNICATIONS GUIDE (US/1059-2164) [24513801] **1119**

POPULAR COMMUNICATIONS SUMMER COMMUNICATIONS GUIDE *CEASED*. (US/1062-8843) [25784289] **1119**

POPULAR CRAFTS (UK/0144-2937) [06699063] **374**

POPULAR CRAFTS PROJECTS (UK) **374**

POPULAR CROSSWORDS (NEW YORK, N.Y.) (US/0194-6749) [04941488] **4865**

POPULAR CULTURE ASSOCIATION NEWSLETTER : PCAN (US) [12789045] **2754**

●POPULAR CULTURE IN LIBRARIES (US/1053-8747) [22683574] **3241**

POPULAR CYCLING *CEASED*. (US/0146-2652) [02902715] **429**

POPULAR ELECTRONICS (1989) (US/1042-170X) [18964412] **2075**

POPULAR FLYING (UK/0032-4493) [01762656] **31**

POPULAR GARDENING INDOORS (US/0147-4723) [02829684] **2428**

POPULAR GOVERNMENT (US/0032-4515) [01762658] 4674, **4491**

POPULAR HI-FI (TEDDINGTON, MIDDLESEX) *See* NEW HI-FI SOUND **5318**

POPULAR HISTORIA (SW/1102-0822) [I11020822] **2703**

POPULAR HOT RODDING (US/0032-4523) [02251539] **5423**

POPULAR MECHANICS DO-IT-YOURSELF YEARBOOK (US/0360-2273) [02244320] **5423**

POPULAR MECHANICS (NEW YORK. 1959) (US/0032-4558) [03643271] **5139**

POPULAR MINING (US/8756-6257) [11630393] **2148**

POPULAR MUSIC : AN ANNOTATED INDEX OF AMERICAN POPULAR SONGS (US/0886-442X) [11357881] **4147**

POPULAR MUSIC AND SOCIETY (US/0300-7766) [01762660] **4147**

POPULAR MUSIC (CAMBRIDGE UNIVERSITY PRESS) (UK/0261-1430) [08513124] **4147**

POPULAR MUSIC MAGAZINE (US/0198-8158) [05934825] **4147**

POPULAR MUSIC NEWS (US/0092-4741) [01784630] **4147**

POPULAR MUSIC PERIODICALS INDEX (LONDON, ENGLAND) (UK) [18850332] **4147**

POPULAR PATCHWORK (UK) **375**

POPULAR PERIODICAL INDEX *CEASED*. (US/0092-9727) [01791628] **422**

POPULAR PHOTOGRAPHY (1955) (US/0032-4582) [01762661] **4375**

POPULAR PHOTOGRAPHY'S INVITATION TO PHOTOGRAPHY *CEASED*. (US/0075-0301) [01783197] **4375**

POPULAR PHOTOGRAPHY'S SLR PHOTOGRAPHY (UK/0747-8798) [10743188] **4375**

POPULAR PLASTICS & PACKAGING (II) [24091649] **4459**

POPULAR PSYCHOLOGY (SHERMAN OAKS) (US/0091-5157) [01787639] **4608**

POPULAR SCIENCE (NEW YORK, N.Y.) (US/0161-7370) [04015531] **5139**

POPULAR SCIENCE SERIES (US/0360-0297) [01308636] **5139**

POPULAR SERIES (CARSON CITY, NEV.) (US/0077-7927) [02851150] **4095**

POPULAR SPORTS FACE-OFF (US/0092-5969) [01789976] **4912**

POPULAR SPORTS. SOCCER ILLUSTRATED (US/0195-9476) [05694171] **4912**

POPULAR STATISTICS (US/1041-3782) [12100295] **3527**

POPULAR TALISMAN BULLETIN (US/0032-4655) [03471287] **3350**

POPULAR WOODWORKING (US/0884-8823) [12486652] **2403**

POPULASI (IO/0853-0262) [23724248] **4556**

POPULATION (FR/0032-4663) [01762663] **4556**

POPULATION ANALYSIS OF THE ILLINOIS ADULT PRISON SYSTEM (US/0093-5603) [01784618] **3172**

POPULATION & DEVELOPMENT (US/0897-3849) [17488848] **4556**

POPULATION AND DEVELOPMENT REVIEW (US/0098-7921) [01613929] 5213, **4556**

POPULATION AND EMPLOYMENT WORKING PAPER (SZ) [06629276] 1702, **4556**

POPULATION AND ENVIRONMENT (US/0199-0039) [05511021] 590, 4608, **4556**

POPULATION AND LABOUR FORCE PROJECTIONS / CENTRAL STATISTICS OFFICE (IE/0790-9969) [18587011] 1702, **4556**

POPULATION AND LABOUR RESEARCH NEWS : A REPORT ON RESEARCH AND RELATED POLICY ACTIVITIES IN THE ILO'S POPULATION LABOUR POLICIES PROGRAMME (US) [15598685] **4556**

POPULATION AND LAND USE BULLETIN *CEASED*. (US) [16141049] **2831**

POPULATION AND VITAL STATISTICS REPORT (NEW YORK, N.Y.) (US) [01606673] **4562**

POPULATION ASSOCIATION OF AMERICA *See* P.A.A. AFFAIRS **4555**

POPULATION (BOCA RATON) (US/0273-2548) [01167304] **4556**

POPULATION BULLETIN (US/0032-468X) [01644995] **4556**

POPULATION BULLETIN OF THE UNITED NATIONS (US/0251-7604) [05655827] **4556**

POPULATION COUNCIL *See* ANNUAL REPORT / THE POPULATION COUNCIL **4549**

POPULATION COUNCIL (NEW YORK, N.Y.) *See* ALUMNI DIRECTORY - POPULATION COUNCIL **1099**

POPULATION EDUCATION IN ASIA AND THE PACIFIC NEWSLETTER (TH) [09055652] **4557**

POPULATION EDUCATION IN ASIA AND THE PACIFIC NEWSLETTER AND FORUM (TH) [19082072] **4557**

POPULATION EDUCATION INTERCHANGE (US) [14104868] **4557**

POPULATION EDUCATION PROGRAMME SERVICE (TH) [10649464] **4557**

POPULATION ESTIMATE AND HOUSING INVENTORY FOR THE CITY OF LOS ANGELES AS OF OCTOBER 1 ... (LOS ANGELES (CALIF.)) (US) [11119161] 4557, **2831**

POPULATION ESTIMATES AND ... PER CAPITA INCOME ESTIMATES FOR COUNTIES, INCORPORATED PLACES, AND MINOR CIVIL DIVISIONS. OHIO / U.S. DEPARTMENT OF COMMERCE, BUREAU OF THE CENSUS (US) [11562819] **4557**

POPULATION ESTIMATES AND ... PER CAPITA INCOME ESTIMATES FOR COUNTIES, INCORPORATED PLACES, AND SELECTED MINOR CIVIL DIVISIONS. INDIANA / U.S. DEPARTMENT OF COMMERCE, BUREAU OF THE CENSUS (US) [11635196] **4557**

POPULATION ESTIMATES FOR NEW JERSEY (TRENTON, N.J. : 1981) (US) [10858663] **4557**

POPULATION ESTIMATES FOR OREGON (US) [21171707] **4557**

POPULATION ET FAMILLE *SUSPENDED*. (BE/0523-1159) [03134557] **4557**

POPULATION ET SANTE TROPICALES (FR/0758-6868) [I07586868] **3986**

POPULATION ET SOCIETES (FR/0184-7783) [03866844] **4557**

POPULATION GEOGRAPHY : A JOURNAL OF THE ASSOCIATION OF POPULATION GEOGRAPHERS OF INDIA (II) [12351696] **4557**

POPULATION IN LOCAL GOVERNMENT AREAS *See* ESTIMATED RESIDENT POPULATION IN LOCAL GOVERNMENT AREAS / AUSTRALIAN BUREAU OF STATISTICS, SOUTH AUSTRALIAN OFFICE **4562**

POPULATION INDEX (US/0032-4701) [06232525] 4557, **4562**

POPULATION MOBILITY IN HAWAII (US/0094-0348) [01793841] **4557**

POPULATION MOVEMENT (US) [01784007] **3173**

POPULATION NEWSLETTER (US/0048-4849) [01696861] **4557**

POPULATION : PERSPECTIVE (US/0091-5610) [01783720] **4557**

POPULATION PROFILE OF THE UNITED STATES (US) [08620294] **4557**

POPULATION PROJECTIONS AREA (UK/0950-7582) [03388318] **4557**

POPULATION PROJECTIONS BY MINOR CIVIL DIVISIONS, SEX, AGE GROUP, AND COUNTY (US) [10945545] **4557**

POPULATION REFERENCE BUREAU *See* PRB REPORT **4559**

POPULATION REFERENCE BUREAU *See* WORLD POPULATION DATA SHEET OF THE POPULATION REFERENCE BUREAU, INC **4561**

POPULATION REPORT. SERIES I, PERIODIC ABSTINENCE (ENGLISH ED.) *CEASED*. (US/0097-9090) [01038205] 590, **4557**

POPULATION REPORTS (BALTIMORE, MD.) (US/0887-0241) [03511761] **4557**

POPULATION REPORTS. SERIES A, ORAL CONTRACEPTIVES (ENGLISH ED.) (US/0097-9074) [01038140] 590, **4557**

POPULATION REPORTS. SERIES B, INTRAUTERINE DEVICES (ENGLISH ED.) (US/0092-9344) [02255469] 590, **4557**

POPULATION REPORTS. SERIES C, FEMALE STERILIZATION (ENGLISH ED.) (US/0891-0030) [07755031] 590, **4557**

POPULATION REPORTS. SERIES D, MALE STERILIZATION (ENGLISH ED.) (US/0891-0049) [10550228] 590, **4558**

POPULATION REPORTS. SERIES E, LAW AND POLICY (ENGLISH ED.) (US/0097-9082) [01038167] 590, **4558**

POPULATION REPORTS. SERIES H, BARRIER METHODS (ENGLISH ED.) (US/0093-4496) [02255473] 590, **4558**

POPULATION REPORTS. SERIES J, FAMILY PLANNING PROGRAMS (ENGLISH ED.) (US/0091-925X) [02256733] 590, **4558**

POPULATION REPORTS. SERIES K, INJECTABLES AND IMPLANTS (ENGLISH ED.) (US/0097-9104) [01360440] 590, **4558**

POPULATION REPORTS. SERIES L, ISSUES IN WORLD HEALTH (ENGLISH ED.) (US/0197-5838) [04938451] **4558**

POPULATION REPORTS. SERIES M, SPECIAL TOPICS (ENGLISH ED.) (US/0733-9135) [07699545] 590, **4558**

POPULATION REPRINTS (CN/0317-3100) [02442889] **4558**

POPULATION RESEARCH *CEASED*. (CC) [15648787] **4558**

POPULATION RESEARCH ABSTRACT (II/0971-1996) [I09711996] **4558**

POPULATION RESEARCH AND POLICY REVIEW (NE/0167-5923) [08537674] 4491, **4558**

POPULATION REVIEW (US/0032-471X) [00809274] **4558**

POPULATION SCIENCES : JOURNAL OF INTERNATIONAL ISLAMIC CENTER FOR POPULATION STUDIES AND RESEARCH, AL-AZHAR UNIVERSITY, CAIRO (UA) [11978416] 590, **4558**

POPULATION STATISTICS. CD-ROM (US) **4558**

POPULATION STUDIES (UK/0032-4728) [01711968] **4558**

POPULATION STUDIES (II) [01784192] **4558**

POPULATION STUDIES (US) [27923370] **4558**

POPULATION STUDIES (STRASBOURG, FRANCE) (FR) [03977597] **4558**

POPULATION STUDIES - UNITED NATIONS (US/0082-805X) [01768037] **4558**

POPULATION STUDIES (UNIVERSITY OF FLORIDA. POPULATION PROGRAM) *See* FLORIDA POPULATION STUDIES **4553**

POPULATION TIMES, THE (BG) [09104952] **590**

POPULATION TODAY (US/0749-2448) [10377361] **4558**

6837

POPULATION — Alphabetical Title Index

POPULATION TRENDS (UK/0307-4463) [02246338] **4562**

POPULATION TRENDS AND PUBLIC POLICY (US/0736-7716) [09221697] **4559**

POPULATION - UNITED NATIONS FUND FOR POPULATION ACTIVITIES *CEASED.* (US/0251-8996) [05848867] **4559**

POPULI (ENG. EDITION) *See* POPULI / UNITED NATIONS POPULATION FUND **4559**

POPULI (ENGLISH ED.) (US/0251-6861) [02457027] **4559**

● POPULI / UNITED NATIONS POPULATION FUND (US) [26495663] **4559**

POPYURA SAIENSU (JA) [10378368] **5139**

POR EL RESCATE DEMOCRATICO DE LA REVOLUCION NICARAGUENSE / MOVIMIENTO DEMOCRATICO NICARAGUENSE (CR) [08885159] **2754**

POR ESTO (MX) [10249514] **4545**, **1702**

POR QUE (SAO PAULO, BRAZIL) (BL) [10791095] **2521**

PORAC LAW ENFORCEMENT NEWS (US/0744-1983) [08101355] **3173**

PORADNIK BIBLIOTEKARZA (PL/0032-4752) [02266369] **3241**

PORADNIK GOSPODARSKI (PL) [04064468] **120**

PORADNIK JEZYKOWY (PL/0551-5343) [02266370] **3311**

PORADNIK PLANTATORA (PL) [02659613] **182**

PORANTIM (BL) [10453460] **2271**

PORC EXPRESS (CN/1182-851X) [23236433] **217**

PORC MAGAZINE (FR) **217**

PORC QUEBEC (CN/1182-1000) [22716234] **217**

PORCELAIN ARTIST (US/0888-0336) [13449838] **2593**

PORCH (US/0163-3872) [03289125] **3470**

PORCS (CN/0481-2468) [03219477] **217**

PORCUPINE PRESS (CN/1182-9044) [23238189] **5793**

PORIM BULLETIN (MY/0127-0249) [09368529] **2353**

PORIM TECHNOLOGY (MY/0127-0257) [09227397] **120**

PORK (US/0745-3787) [09114009] **217**

PORK 92 (US) **218**

PORK CITY PRESS (US) **5650**

PORK INDUSTRY GAZETTE (NZ/0302-4563) [09986489] **218**

PORK JOURNAL (AT/1032-3759) [29897765] **218**

PORK MONEY II (US) **218**

POROCILO O RAZISKOVANJU PALEOLITA, NEOLITA IN ENEOLITA V SLOVENIJI / UNIVERZA V LJUBLJANI, ARHEOLOSKI ODDELEK FILOZOSKE FAKULTETE (XV) [09098220] **278**

POROSHKOVAIA METALLURGIIA (US/0038-5735) [09558776] **4015**

POROSHKOVAIA METALLURGIIA (KIEV, UKRAINE). ENGLISH. SOVIET POWDER METALLURGY AND METAL CERAMICS *See* POWDER METALLURGY AND METAL CERAMICS **4015**

POROSHKOVAIA METALLURGIIA / TALLINSKII POLITEKHNICHESKII INSTITUT (ER) [08578355] **4015**

POROSHKOVAJA METALLURGIJA (KIEV) (UN/0032-4795) [06777962] **4015**

PORPHYRE (FR) **3350**

PORRIMER (SENUR) (KO/0379-153X) [08500067] **1028**

PORSCHE PANORAMA (US/0147-3565) [03150649] **5423**

PORT ALBERNI DIRECTORY (BUSINESS EDITION) (CN/0318-2940) [02441850] **2573**

PORT AUTHORITY OF NEW YORK AND NEW JERSEY *See* FOREIGN TRADE : THE PORT OF NEW YORK AND NEW JERSEY **836**

PORT AUTONOME DE PARIS *See* BILAN/PERSPECTIVES **5447**

PORT AUTONOME DE PARIS *See* TRAFIC **5457**

PORT BUSTAMANTE ... HANDBOOK (JM) [09298018] **5454**

PORT CHALLENGER (US/0745-1776) [08900459] **218**

PORT CONSTRUCTION AND OCEAN TECHNOLOGY (UK/0264-8733) [14178707] **624**

PORT D'ANVERS *See* JAARBOEK VAN DE HAVEN VAN ANTWERPEN. ANNUAIRE DU PORT D'ANVERS. ANTWERP PORT ANNUAL **5450**

PORT DE LA POINTE DES GALETS, STATISTIQUES PORTUAIRES (RE) [19260655] **120**

PORT DEVELOPMENT INTERNATIONAL (UK/0267-4823) [15321862] **5454**

PORT DOVER MAPLE LEAF (CN/0834-7166) [16390854] **5793**

PORT ENGINEERING MANAGEMENT (UK/0965-8203) [I09658203] **624**

PORT FOLIO, PORT OF CHITTAGONG (BG) [07039865] **5454**

PORT GIBSON REVEILLE (PORT GIBSON, MISS.: 1890) (US) [14874994] **5701**

PORT HOLE (SCARBOROUGH) (CN/0830-8705) [15483036] **595**

PORT HURON TIMES HERALD (US) [09803143] **5693**

PORT ISABEL SOUTH PADRE ISLAND PRESS (US) [13363610] **5753**

PORT JEFFERSON RECORD (1969) (US/0893-4304) [11088818] **5720**

PORT LAVACA WAVE, THE (US/1062-1199) [14767555] **5753**

PORT OF BALTIMORE HANDBOOK (US/0465-1146) [09986130] **5454**

PORT OF BOSTON HANDBOOK (US/0149-208X) [03451084] **5454**

PORT OF DETROIT WORLD HANDBOOK (US/0160-5526) [03698234] **5454**

PORT OF HALIFAX (HALIFAX-DARTMOUTH PORT COMMISSION) (CN/0834-0862) [15716583] **5454**

PORT OF HELSINKI HANDBOOK (FI/0359-7431) [10339960] **5454**

PORT OF HOUSTON (US/1064-7686) [20126207] **5389**

PORT OF HOUSTON FOREIGN TRADE (US/0438-623X) [04111084] **849**

PORT OF KINGSTON HANDBOOK (JM) [03225905] **5454**

PORT OF LONDON (UK/0030-8064) [02244666] **5454**

PORT OF LONDON AUTHORITY *See* HANDBOOK OF TIDE TABLES, PARTICULARS OF DOCKS, &C **4177**

PORT OF NEW ORLEANS ANNUAL DIRECTORY (US/0085-5030) [02435166] **5454**

PORT OF NEW ORLEANS RECORD (US/1046-9265) [19409770] **849**

PORT OF SPAIN, TRINIDAD AND TOBAGO. PUBLIC HEALTH DEPT *See* ADMINISTRATION REPORT - PORT OF SPAIN, TRINIDAD AND TOBAGO. PUBLIC HEALTH DEPT **4763**

PORT OF TOKYO (JA) [05352119] **5454**

PORT OF TOLEDO NEWS (US/0032-4868) [02563948] **4181**

PORT OF TORONTO NEWS (CN/0477-6410) [02105488] **5454**

PORT ORCHARD INDEPENDENT (US) [17297781] **5762**

PORT STATISTICS *CEASED.* (UK/0263-9149) [09180949] **5401**

PORT STATISTICS FOR THE FOREIGN TRADE OF THE UNITED KINGDOM (UK) [05718486] **849**, **732**

PORT TOWNSEND JEFFERSON COUNTY LEADER, THE (US/1050-1460) [18770100] **5762**

PORTABLE 100 (1986) (US/0888-0131) [15700514] **1199**

PORTABLE COMPANION, THE (US/0732-7501) [08425011] **1272**

PORTABLE COMPUTER (US/0738-1220) [09507164] **1272**

● PORTABLE MBA EXECUTIVE SERVICE, THE (US/1064-6337) [26345543] **704**

PORTABLE OFFICE. BUYER'S GUIDE ... (US/1054-7576) [22974033] **4214**

PORTABLE OFFICE (PETERBOROUGH, N.H.) (US/1054-2736) [22718670] **1272**

PORTABLE OFFICE, THE *CEASED.* (US/0898-8935) [17943007] **1119**

PORTABLE PAPER, THE *CEASED.* (US/0886-9138) [13033513] **1199**

PORTAGE DISPATCH (PORTAGE, PA. : 1948) (US) [15159615] **5738**

PORTAGE LAKES HERALD, THE (US/0746-6021) [10142382] **5730**

PORTAGE (RIVIERE-DU-LOUP) (CN/0228-6262) [08003203] **5793**

PORTAL (NANAIMO) (CN/1183-5214) [25066721] **3424**

PORTALES NEWS-TRIBUNE (US) [16936093] **5712**

PORTALS OF PRAYER (US/0032-4884) [01762675] **5018**

PORTAVOZ (CK) [25226377] **4512**

PORTAVOZ (BO) [25781844] **1136**

PORTAVOZ PICHONIANO (AG) [23997760] **3932**, **4608**

PORTE A PORTE (CN/0823-3403) [10638765] **1543**

PORTE & CANCELLI (IT/1120-2637) [I11202637] **1621**

PORTE-VOIX, LE (CN/0225-3593) [06511847] **5301**

PORTER, WRIGHT, MORRIS & ARTHUR'S OHIO ENVIRONMENTAL LAW LETTER (US/1052-4355) [22293189] **3115**

PORTER'S GUIDE TO CONGRESSIONAL ROLL CALL VOTES. HOUSE (US/0748-2310) [10908151] **4674**

PORTER'S GUIDE TO CONGRESSIONAL ROLL CALL VOTES. SENATE (US/0748-2329) [10906730] **4491**

PORTEURS DE LUMIERE (CN/1188-5300) [26497582] **4608**

PORTFOLIO (US) [03416674] **849**

PORTFOLIO (HAMILTON) (CN/0707-2481) [04634840] **5454**

PORTFOLIO ILLUSTRATORI *See* PORTFOLIO ILLUSTRATORI E FOTOGRAFI **4375**

PORTFOLIO ILLUSTRATORI E FOTOGRAFI *SUSPENDED.* (IT) **4375**

PORTFOLIO LETTER (US) **911**

PORTFOLIO MAGAZINE EDINBURGH (UK/0960-3913) [I09603913] **4375**

PORTFOLIO (NEW YORK. 1979) (US/0163-092X) [05108197] **362**

PORTFOLIO OF TRACKWORK PLANS (US) **5434**

PORTFOLIO OF TRACKWORK PLANS. SUPPLEMENT (US) **5434**

PORTFOLIO (ZEPHYRHILLS, FLA.) (US/1053-3869) [22521764] **4375**

● PORTHOLE (DEERFIELD BEACH, FLA.) (US/1070-9479) [28520907] **5489**

PORTICUS (US/8755-2035) [04540711] **362**

PORTLAND ART ASSOCIATION. (OR.) *See* BULLETIN - PORTLAND ART ASSOCIATION (OR.) **345**

PORTLAND CEMENT ASSOCIATION *See* DESIGN AND CONTROL OF CONCRETE MIXTURES **612**

PORTLAND FAMILY CALENDAR (US/0890-3840) [14226547] **2543**

PORTLAND MONTHLY (US/0887-5340) [13292223] **2573**

PORTLAND OBSERVER (US) [09286929] **5734**

PORTLAND, OR. UNIVERSITY *See* UNIVERSITY OF PORTLAND REVIEW **2548**

PORTLAND PHYSICIAN SCRIBE, THE (US/8756-646X) [09516728] **3628**

PORTLAND PRESS HERALD, THE (US) [09341113] **5685**

PORTLAND REV. (1981) (US/0885-7121) [08679157] **3424**

PORTO DI SAVONA (IT) [06608542] **5454**

PORTOLAN / WASHINGTON MAP SOCIETY, THE (US) [11954104] **2573**

PORTOS E NAVIOS (BL/0101-5664) [06537616] **4181**

PORTRAIT DE LA FISCALITE DES PARTICULIERS AU QUEBEC, STATISTIQUES / REDIGE PAR LE MINISTERE DU REVENU DU QUEBEC (CN/0837-9831) [18457319] **3029**

PORTRAITS (NEW YORK, N.Y.) (US/1062-9661) [25820741] **4375**

PORTS AND DREDGING (NE/0166-5766) [11452885] **5454**

PORTS AND DREDGING & OIL REPORT *See* PORTS AND DREDGING **5454**

PORTS AND HARBORS (JA/0554-7555) [07012964] **5454**

PORTS ANNUAL. CANADIAN PORTS EDITION (CN/0225-5456) [05712267] **5454**

PORTS / ASSOCIATED BRITISH PORTS (UK/0262-1630) [10820473] **5454**

PORTS DESIGNATED IN APPLICATION OF THE INTERNATIONAL HEALTH REGULATIONS (SZ) [02245813] **5454**

PORTSMOUTH DAILY TIMES (1984), THE (US/8750-6963) [14207760] **5730**

PORTSMOUTH HERALD, THE (US/0746-6218) [10164166] **5709**

PORTUGAL *See* DIARIO DA REPUBLICA **2960**

PORTUGAL. ADMINISTRACAO GERAL DO PORTO DE LISBOA *See* GUIA - ADMINISTRACAO-GERAL DO PORTO DE LISBOA **5449**

PORTUGAL. AQUIVO HISTORICO MILITAR *See* BOLETIM DO ARQUIVO HISTORICO MILITAR **4038**

Alphabetical Title Index — POSTEPY

PORTUGAL, AZOREN UND MADEIRA : WIRTSCHAFT IN ZAHLEN UND WIRTSCHAFTSDOKUMENTATION (GW) [06260095] **1578**

PORTUGAL. COMISSAO NACIONAL DO AMBIENTE *See* RELATORIO DE ACTIVIDADES **1580**

PORTUGAL. DEPARTAMENTO DOS TRANSPORTES *See* ORCAMENTO DA DESPESA PARA ... 1, CLASSIFICACAO ORGANICA, FUNCIONAL E ECONOMICA / REPUBLICA PORTUGUESA, MINISTERIO DA HABITACAO, OBRAS PUBLICAS E TRANSPORTES, DEPARTAMENTO DOS TRANSPORTES **5389**

PORTUGAL : ENERGIEWIRTSCHAFT (GW) [04221116] **1953**

PORTUGAL EXPORTER (PO) [01213657] **849**

PORTUGAL, FORSCHUNGSPOLITIK UND FORSCHUNGSPRAXIS / BUNDESSTELLE FUER AUSSENHANDELSINFORMATION (GW) [11455217] **5139**

PORTUGAL. INSTITUTO NACIONAL DE ESTATISTICA. SERVICOS CENTRAIS *See* BOLETIM TRIMESTRAL DAS ESTATISTICAS DA AGRICULTURA E DA PESCA : CONTINENTE E ILHAS ADJACENTES **151**

PORTUGAL. INSTITUTO NACIONAL DE ESTATISTICA. SERVICOS CENTRAIS *See* BOLETIM MENSAL DAS ESTATISTICAS DA AGRICULTURA E DA PESCA **67**

PORTUGAL. INSTITUTO NACIONAL DE ESTATISTICA. SERVICOS CENTRAIS *See* STATISTIQUES DU BATIMENT ET DE L'HABITATION : CONTINENT, AZORES ET MADERE **1539**

PORTUGAL. INSTITUTO NACIONAL DE ESTATISTICA. SERVICOS CENTRAIS *See* STATISTIQUES DE LA JUSTICE : CONTINENT ET ILES ADJACENTES **3083**

PORTUGAL. MINISTERIO DA EDUCACAO E CIENCIA *See* ORCAMENTO DA DESPESA PARA ... / MINISTERIO DA EDUCACAO E CIENCIA **1770**

PORTUGAL. MINISTERIO DO EXERCITO *See* DESENVOLVIMENTO DO ORCAMENTO DA DESPESA FIXADA PARA O ANO ECONOMICO **4042**

PORTUGAL. MINISTERIO DO TRABALHO. SERVICO DE INFORMACAO CIENTIFICA E TECNICA *See* BOLETIM DO TRABALHO E EMPREGO. 2A I.E. SEGUNDA SERIE **3144**

PORTUGAL. SERVICO DE ADMINISTRACAO MILITAR *See* REVISTA TRIMESTRAL - SERVICO DE ADMINISTRACAO MILITAR **4055**

PORTUGAL, WIRTSCHAFTLICHE ENTWICKLUNG (GW) [01798759] **1578**

PORTUGALIAE ACTA BIOLOGICA. SERIE A. MORFOLOGIA, FISIOLOGIA, GENETICA E BIOLOGIA GERAL (PO/0032-5147) [05197237] **585**

PORTUGALIAE MATHEMATICA (PO/0032-5155) [01762700] **3527**

PORTUGALIAE PHYSICA (PO/0048-4903) [05935977] **4417**

PORTUGIESISCHE FORSCHUNGEN (PL) [01431249] **5254**

PORTUGIESISCHE FORSCHUNGEN DER GORRESGESELLSCHAFT. ERSTE REIHE, AUFSATZE (GW/0079-421X) [01762702] **2703**

PORTUGUESE AMERICAN, THE (US/8750-2143) [11108418] **2271**

PORTUGUESE STUDIES (UK/0267-5315) [12331260] 3311, **2625**

PORTUGUESE STUDIES REVIEW (US/1057-1515) [23958782] **2703**

PORTUGUESE TIMES (NEW BEDFORD, MASS.) (US/0746-3928) [10013097] **5689**

PORTUS (OTTAWA) *CEASED.* (CN/0832-8587) [14705348] **5454**

PORZELLAN + GLAS : P + G / ORGAN DES BUNDESVERBANDES DES GLAS-, PORZELLAN- UND KERAMIK-EINZELHANDELS *CEASED.* (GW) [08971332] 2907, **2593**

POS NEWS (US) **803**

POSEBNA IZDANJA INSTITUTA ZA ZASTITU BILJA (YU/0408-9952) [05050940] **525**

POSEBNI IZDANIJA - MATEMATICKI FAKULTET NA UNIVERZITETOT "KIRIL I METODIJ", SKOPJE (XN/0352-3853) [I03523853] **3527**

POSEIDON (SZ) [06639155] **4912**

POSEV (GW/0032-5201) [01639964] **4491**

POSEY COUNTY NEWS & THE TIMES (US) [22699812] **5666**

POSIBLE (SP) [02561823] **2703**

POSIDONIA NEWSLETTER (FR/0758-8623) [I07588623] **1455**

POSIE I.E. POESIE (FR/0152-0032) [04289353] **3470**

● POSISJON (NO) **2573**

POSITIF (FR/0048-4911) [03943070] **4076**

POSITION CLASSIFICATION, PAY, AND EMPLOYEE BENEFITS (US) [04406753] **1702**

POSITION-CLASSIFICATION STANDARDS FOR WHITE COLLAR POSITIONS UNDER THE GENERAL SCHEDULE (US) [02784242] **4674**

POSITIONS DES THESES (FR/0755-2076) [I07552076] 2482, **1841**

● POSITIONS (DURHAM, N.C.) (US/1067-9847) [27402923] **243**

POSITIONS LUTHERIENNES (FR/0032-5228) [01777736] **5066**

POSITIVE ALTERNATIVES (US/1065-0075) [24292851] **1513**

POSITIVE APPROACH, A (US/0891-8791) [15049499] **4392**

POSITIVE ATTITUDE POSTERS (US) [09152496] **946**

POSITIVE HEALTH (UK/0958-5737) [I09585737] **1146**

POSITIVE IMPACT (US) [26736199] **704**

POSITIVE INK (US/1040-0494) [18304355] **1774**

● POSITIVE LIVING (US) [26191417] 3675, 3715, **4795**

POSITIVE (LONDON, ONT.) (CN/0229-9712) [08091455] 362, **3241**

POSITIVE TEACHING (UK) **1902**

● POSITIVELY FOR KIDS (US/1065-1969) [26522651] **2285**

POSITIVELY PASTA! (US/1070-9320) [28514362] **2353**

POSLOVNI DNEVNIK - TANJUG (YU) [02960192] **1579**

POSLOVNI VODIC SR SRBIJE SA REGISTROM ORGANIZACIJA OSTALIH REPUBLIKA (YU) [09823318] **2703**

POSOL *CEASED.* (CN/0701-0192) [03412098] **5034**

POSSIBLES (CN/0703-7139) [03680943] 328, **5213**

POST ALLOCATION OF FUNDS AND TRAINING ACTIVITY SUMMARY (US/0147-8060) [03231165] **3173**

POST AND COURIER, THE (US/1061-5105) [24558607] **5743**

POST CARD COLLECTORS' BULLETIN *CEASED.* (US/0740-1728) [09877386] **2776**

POST (CARLE PLACE, N.Y.) (US/0891-5628) [14970499] **1162**

POST CRESCENT (APPLETON, WIS.) (US) [15602487] **5770**

POST DISPATCH, THE (US) [14257393] **5753**

POST FALLS TRIBUNE (US) [18734622] **5657**

POST FOOTBALL GUIDE (UK) [01785324] **4912**

POST-GAZETTE (BOSTON, MASS.) (US/0888-0107) [09529221] **5689**

POST HARVEST SCIENCE AND TECHNOLOGY RESEARCH (US/0739-4284) [09674485] **120**

POST HIGH SCHOOL PLANS SURVEY (US/0362-7977) [02339795] **1841**

POST, KENYA (KE/0253-5963) [03353211] **5139**

POST MAGAZINE (UK) [14994744] **2890**

POST-MARKETING SURVEILLANCE (NE/0269-2333) [17727707] **935**

POST-MEDIEVAL ARCHAEOLOGY (UK/0079-4236) [02834163] **278**

POST (MIDDLEBURG, PA. 1976), THE (US/1043-4291) [14444566] **5738**

POST MORTEM ESTATE PLANNING (US/0734-4406) [04767253] **3118**

POST NEWS (UK) 956, **2075**

POST OFFICE GUIDE (SQ) [03728605] **1146**

POST OFFICES IN THE UNITED KINGDOM (UK) [04771167] **1146**

POST-POLIO DIRECTORY (US/1051-6492) [21363719] **3628**

POST-POLITISCHE INFORMATION (GW/0938-555X) [I0938555X] **4491**

POST-REGISTER, THE (US) [12292787] **5657**

POST ROCK (US/0149-3744) [03136513] **4795**

POST SCRIPT (JACKSONVILLE, FLA.) (US/0277-9897) [07673970] **4076**

POST SCRIPTS / COMMISSION ON PEACE OFFICER STANDARDS AND TRAINING (US) [09156928] **3173**

POST SCRIPTS (INDIANAPOLIS) *CEASED.* (US/0162-3060) [04150506] **4865**

POST-SEARCH LIGHT, THE (US) [21366654] **5654**

POST-SECONDARY ENROLMENT STATISTICS (CN/0823-2164) [10235977] 1842, **1796**

● POST-SOVIET AFFAIRS (US/1060-586X) [25038402] 4491, **1513**

● POST-SOVIET GEOGRAPHY (US/1060-5851) [25038320] **2573**

POST-SOVIET PROSPECTS (US) [27341479] **4491**

POST-SOVIET WEAPONS COMPLEX MONITOR (US) **4054**

POST-STANDARD, THE (US) [06341619] **5720**

POST-STAR (GLENS FALLS, N.Y. : 1974) (US/0897-0505) [11480882] **5720**

POST-SUMMER ELECTRIC POWER SURVEY (US/0190-5597) [04719216] **1953**

POST-, TELEFON- UND TELEGRAFEN-AMTSBLATT. FEUILLE OFFICIELLE DES POSTES, TELEPHONES ET TELEGRAPHES. FOGLIO UFFICIALE DELLE POSTE, DEI TELEFONI E DEI TELEGRAFI (SZ) [06870401] **1162**

POST-TELEGRAPH (PRINCETON, MO.) (US) [21456173] **5704**

POST, THE (US) [26947497] **5646**

POST-TRIBUNE (GARY, IND.) (US/8750-3492) [02266386] **5666**

POST UND SPORT (GW/0343-4168) [I03434168] **4913**

POSTA (HU) [07320455] **1146**

POSTA (LAKE OSWEGO, OR.), LA (US/0885-7385) [12713437] **2786**

POSTAGE STAMP PRICES OF THE UNITED STATES, UNITED NATIONS, AND CANADA AND PROVINCES (US/0272-5363) [06781999] **2786**

POSTAL BULLETIN (US/0364-863X) [02642814] **1146**

POSTAL CONTRACTING MANUAL (US) [02784652] **1146**

POSTAL GUIDE / LE GUIDE DES POSTES (CN) **1146**

POSTAL HISTORY ANNUAL, THE (UK) [08863615] **1146**

POSTAL HISTORY JOURNAL (US/0032-5341) [05037365] **1146**

POSTAL LAWS AND REGULATIONS OF THE UNITED STATES OF AMERICA *CEASED.* (US) [07444858] 1146, **3030**

POSTAL LEADER / UNITED STATES POSTAL SERVICE, THE (US) [26593302] **1146**

POSTAL LIFE (US/0032-5368) [01762710] **1146**

POSTAL OPERATIONS MANUAL (US) [05166371] **1146**

POSTAL RECORD, THE (US/0032-5376) [01762712] **1146**

POSTAL SERVICE MANUAL (US) [02784700] **1146**

POSTAL STATIONERY (US/0554-8373) [01786623] **2786**

POSTAL SUPERVISOR, THE (US/0032-5384) [04108949] **1146**

POSTAL, TELEGRAPH AND TELEPHONE WORKERS' INTERNATIONAL *See* P. T. T. I. STUDIES **1146**

POSTAL WATCH (US/1052-3944) [22283096] **1147**

POSTAL WORLD (US) [04274664] **1147**

POSTCARD CLASSICS (US/0897-4020) [17493758] **375**

POSTCARD COLLECTOR (US/0746-6102) [10161034] **2777**

POSTCENSAL ANNUAL ESTIMATES OF POPULATION BY MARITAL STATUS, AGE, SEX AND COMPONENTS OF GROWTH FOR CANADA, PROVINCES AND TERRITORIES (CN/0827-9624) [14178368] 4559, **4562**

POSTDOCTORAL RESEARCH ASSOCIATESHIPS : OPPORTUNITIES FOR RESEARCH AT THE U.S. DEPARTMENT OF COMMERCE, NATIONAL BUREAU OF STANDARDS ... IN ASSOCIATION WITH THE NATIONAL RESEARCH COUNCIL ... (US) [05282558] **849**

POSTDOCTORAL RESEARCH FELLOWSHIP OPPORTUNITIES / NATIONAL INSTITUTES OF HEALTH (US) [28408099] **3628**

POSTE E TELECOMUNICAZIONI NELLO SVILUPPO DELLA SOCIETA (IT/0390-5942) [I03905942] 1162, **1147**

POSTECRAN (CN/1188-195X) [25883059] **387**

POSTEPY ASTRONAUTYKI (PL/0373-5982) [06645284] **398**

POSTEPY ASTRONOMII (PL/0032-5414) [01921719] **398**

POSTEPY BIOCHEMII (PL/0032-5422) [04064502] **492**

POSTEPY BIOLOGII KOMORKI (PL/0324-833X) [01796514] **539**

POSTEPY — Alphabetical Title Index

POSTEPY CYBERNETYKI (PL/0137-3595) [08092920] **1221**

POSTEPY FIZYKI (PL/0032-5430) [06218658] **4417**

POSTEPY HIGIENY I MEDYCYNY DOSWIADCZALNEJ (PL/0032-5449) [07498216] **4795**

POSTEPY MIKROBIOLOGII (PL/0079-4252) [04064525] **568**

POSTEPY NAUK ROLNICZYCH (PL/0032-5457) [03792716] **120**

POSTEPY REHABILITACJI / AKADEMIA WYCHOWANIA FIZYCZNEGO (PL/0860-6161) [28078822] **4382**

POSTGESCHICHTE (SZ) [07677786] **2786**

POSTGRADUATE DOCTOR. AFRICA (UK/0142-7946) [06952750] **3628**

POSTGRADUATE DOCTOR. CARIBBEAN (UK/0267-0275) [17301531] **3628**

POSTGRADUATE DOCTOR. MIDDLE EAST EDITION (UK/0140-7724) [06972706] **3628**

POSTGRADUATE EDUCATION FOR GENERAL PRACTICE (UK/0959-4299) [26671970] **3738**

POSTGRADUATE INSTITUTE OF MEDICAL EDUCATION AND RESEARCH, CHANDIGARH *See* BULLETIN OF POSTGRADUATE INSTITUTE OF MEDICAL EDUCATION AND RESEARCH, CHANDIGARH **3560**

POSTGRADUATE MEDICAL JOURNAL (UK/0032-5473) [01762715] **3628**

POSTGRADUATE MEDICAL JOURNAL. SUPPLEMENT (UK/0370-0593) [05185007] **3628**

POSTGRADUATE MEDICINE (US/0032-5481) [01762716] **3628**

POSTGRADUATE OBSTETRICS & GYNECOLOGY (US/0194-3898) [05382735] **3767**

POSTGRADUATE PROSPECTUS AND STUDENT HANDBOOK (UK) [02470748] **1842**

POSTGRADUATE PROSPECTUS / POST GRADUATE SCHOOL, AHMADU BELLO UNIVERSITY (NR) [09788303] **1842**

POSTGRADUATE RADIOLOGY (US/0273-0278) [06999165] **3944**

POSTGRADUATE STUDENTSHIPS IN THE SOCIAL SCIENCES *See* SSRC STUDENTSHIP HANDBOOK. POSTGRADUATE STUDENTSHIPS IN THE SOCIAL SCIENCES **5223**

POSTHARVEST BIOLOGY AND TECHNOLOGY (NE/0925-5214) [24464669] **182**

POSTHARVEST NEWS AND INFORMATION (UK/0957-7505) [24152276] **120, 155**

POSTHORN, THE (US/0551-6897) [02909233] **2786**

POSTHYPE (US/0743-6025) [10644161] **2491**

POSTILLA (US/0079-4295) [01674648] **4170**

POSTILLA BOHEMICA (GW) [04829265] **3311, 3424**

POSTILLON DE CHAMPLAIN (CN/0229-320X) [08454652] **5793**

POSTMASTERS' ADVOCATE (US/0032-5511) [04108971] **1147**

POSTMASTERS GAZETTE (US/0032-552X) [04108992] **1147**

POSTMODERN CULTURE (US/1053-1920) [22471982] **2852**

POSTMODERN STUDIES (NE/0923-0483) [I09230483] **3424**

POSTPRAXIS, DIE (GW/0554-842X) [06547347] **1147**

POSTS AND TELECOMMUNICATIONS CORPORATION (ZIMBABWE) *See* ANNUAL REPORT / POSTS AND TELECOMMUNICATIONS CORPORATION **1149**

POSTSCRIPT LANGUAGE JOURNAL *See* POSTSCRIPT REVIEW **1281**

POSTSCRIPT REVIEW **SUSPENDED.** (US) **1281**

●POSTSECONDARY EDUCATION OPPORTUNITY (US/1068-9818) [27871396] **1842**

POSTSECONDARY SCHOOL INFORMATION (US) [06971205] **1915**

POSTVILLE HERALD (US) [14927782] **5672**

POT-HOOKS & HANGERS (US/0091-7230) [01787983] **3470**

POTASH REVIEW (SZ/0032-5546) [04604661] **182**

POTATO ABSTRACTS (UK/0308-7344) [02942459] **182, 156**

POTATO-BREEDING PROGRAM, USDA, THE (US) [03998616] **182**

●POTATO BUSINESS WORLD (UK/0968-7661) [27750633] **120, 2353**

POTATO COUNTRY (US/0886-4780) [12895120] **182**

POTATO EYES (US/1041-9926) [18882248] **3424**

POTATO GROWER (AT/0815-6514) [02631129] **182**

POTATO GROWER OF IDAHO (US/0146-499X) [02949816] **182**

●POTATO GROWER : POTATO GROWER OF IDAHO MAGAZINE (US) [28948328] **120, 182**

POTATO GROWERS ASSOCIATION OF CALIFORNIA *See* POTATO REFERENCE YEARBOOK **182**

POTATO REFERENCE YEARBOOK (US) [02575856] **182**

POTATO RESEARCH (NE/0014-3065) [08631860] **182**

POTATO REVIEW (UK/0961-7655) [I09617655] **182**

POTATO STATISTICAL YEARBOOK (US/0739-0238) [09701311] **182, 156**

POTATOES (UK) [08832966] **121**

POTATOES AND SWEETPOTATOES (US/0499-0587) [02679600] **182**

POTATOES IN FOOD SYSTEMS RESEARCH SERIES (PE) [12880866] **2353**

POTATOES / NATIONAL AGRICULTURAL STATISTICS SERVICE, UNITED STATES DEPARTMENT OF AGRICULTURE, AGRICULTURAL STATISTICS BOARD (US) [20696683] **2428**

POTATOES (NEW YORK CROP REPORTING SERVICE) (US) [09547844] **182**

POTBOILER (RICHMOND) (CN/0228-3344) [07805825] **3424**

POTENCIA (SP/0032-5600) [I00325600] **624**

●POTENTIAL ANALYSIS : AN INTERNATIONAL JOURNAL DEVOTED TO THE INTERACTIONS BETWEEN POTENTIAL THEORY, PROBABILITY THEORY, GEOMETRY AND FUNCTIONAL ANALYSIS (US/0926-2601) [26680442] **3527**

POTENTIAL LABOR SUPPLY, ARKANSAS (US) [07979529] **1702**

POTENTIALS IN MARKETING (US/0032-5619) [01762725] **935**

POTENTIALS MART (US) [12575297] **763**

POTERE LOCALE, IL (IT) [15146064] **4674**

POTOMAC ALMANAC (US/0194-2182) [05363687] **5687**

POTOMAC APPALACHIAN (MAY 1972) (US/0098-8154) [00989530] **4877**

POTOMAC APPALACHIAN TRAIL CLUB *See* POTOMAC APPALACHIAN (MAY 1972) **4877**

POTOMAC BASIN REPORTER (US) [02401126] **5537**

POTOMAC (CHICAGO) (US/0149-0893) [03137428] **4545**

POTOMAC CHILDREN (US/0883-9905) [12277544] **1068**

POTOMAC LAW REVIEW (US/0192-9801) [04942989] **3030**

POTPOURRI (US) [06362669] **1842**

POTPOURRI PARTY-LINE *See* FLORA-LINE, THE **2435**

POTRAVINARSKE VEDY (XR) [25568956] **2353**

POTREBITELSKAIA KOOPERATSIIA KAZAKHSTANA (KZ/0130-2507) [24329560] **1543**

POTREBITELSKAIA KOOPERATSIIA : PK (RU/0234-8098) [25669332] **1298**

POTSDAMER FORSCHUNGEN. REIHE A (GW/0138-4198) [05637887] **1774**

POTTER (NZ/0113-583X) [I0113583X] **2593**

POTTER AND MONROES TAX PLANNING WITH PRECEDENTS (UK) **4741**

POTTER COUNTY HISTORICAL SOCIETY QUARTERLY BULLETIN (US/0895-0865) [16686417] **2625**

POTTER LEADER-ENTERPRISE (US/0895-6839) [16729019] **5738**

POTTERSFIELD PORTFOLIO, THE **CEASED.** (CN/0226-0840) [06264690] **3424**

POTTERY IN AUSTRALIA (AT/0048-4954) [06597481] **2593**

POTTERY SOUTHWEST (US/0738-8020) [08047616] **278, 2593**

POTTSBORO PRESS (US/0747-4253) [10842313] **5753**

POTTSVILLE REPUBLICAN (POTTSVILLE, PA. : 1942) (US) [12851117] **5738**

POUGHKEEPSIE JOURNAL (POUGHKEEPSIE, N.Y. : 1960) (US) [11526830] **5720**

POULTRY ABSTRACTS (UK/0306-1582) [01950919] **218, 156**

POULTRY ADVISER (II/0970-1958) [01732109] **218**

●POULTRY AND AVIAN BIOLOGY REVIEWS (UK) **469, 218**

POULTRY AND EGG MARKET NEWS REVIEW (US/0279-9871) [07415602] **218**

POULTRY AND EGG MARKETING (US/0032-5716) [04109026] **218**

POULTRY BOOKLET (UK) [05161585] **218**

POULTRY FORUM : OFFICIAL POULTRY JOURNAL OF THE NATIONAL FARMERS' UNION (UK) [07481825] **218**

POULTRY INTERNATIONAL (US/0032-5767) [05060604] **218**

POULTRY / IOWA CROP AND LIVESTOCK REPORTING SERVICE (US) [06260086] **218**

POULTRY JOURNAL 1987 **CEASED.** (UK/0954-7185) [09547185] **218**

POULTRY MARKET NEWS REPORT (CHICAGO, ILL.) (US/0744-298X) [08166647] **218**

POULTRY MARKET REPORT (CN/0381-3649) [02760411] **218**

POULTRY MARKET REVIEW (CN) [09700871] **218**

POULTRY MARKET STATISTICS (US/0565-1980) [02971543] **218, 156**

POULTRY PRESS (US/0032-5783) [04109343] **218**

POULTRY PROCESSING (US/0898-4565) [17819371] **2353**

POULTRY SCIENCE (US/0032-5791) [01643522] **218**

POULTRY SCIENCE REVIEWS (UK/0964-6604) [26876350] **218**

POULTRY SCIENCE SYMPOSIUM (UK/0306-7610) [06675030] **218**

POULTRY SCIENCE SYMPOSIUM SERIES (UK/0966-7318) **218**

POULTRY SLAUGHTER (US/0364-2682) [02552111] **218**

POULTRY TIMES (NATIONAL ED.) (US/0885-3371) [12609153] **218**

POULTRY TODAY & TOMORROW (II/0971-0752) [25396749] **218**

POULTRY WORLD (UK/0032-5813) [01714007] **219**

POUMONS (CN/0318-9236) [02442106] **3951**

POUR (FR/0245-9442) [15586296] **5254**

POUR EN SAVOIR PLUS SUR LE TIERS MONDE ET L'ETAT DU MONDE EN **CEASED.** (FR) [19379924] **2491**

POUR LA DANSE, CHAUSSONS ET PETITS RATS **CEASED.** (FR/0183-3189) [12652563] **387**

POUR LA SCIENCE (FR/0153-4092) [07055072] **5139**

POUR LA SUITE DES JEUX (CN/0824-4170) [10441309] **4913**

POUR MIEUX ENTREPRENDRE (CN/1183-188X) [24256512] **704**

POUR MIEUX ENTREPRENDRE : A PUBLICATION OF THE COMMITTEE ON SMALL BUSINESS (CN/1183-1898) [24256513] **704**

POURQUOI **CEASED.** (FR) **4853**

POURQUOI CHANTER? (CN/0705-8780) [04249990] **4147**

POUVOIRS (FR/0152-0768) [04243362] **4532**

●POUVOIRS PUBLICS AU QUEBEC (CN/1183-482X) [25066751] **4674**

POVERKHNOST (US/0734-1520) [08682187] **989, 4417**

POVERTY (UK/0032-5856) [06367354] **5301**

POVERTY AND DEVELOPMENT (NE/0926-1524) [I09261524] **2911**

●POVERTY AND SOCIAL POLICY PAPER (US/1014-9783) [25735186] **5301**

POVERTY IN TEXAS (US/0097-7950) [02246602] **5254**

POVERTY LAW REPORT (US) [01780294] **3180**

POVERTY LINES AUSTRALIA (AT/0814-5105) [08145105] **5213**

POVOADOS DO ESTADO DA BAHIA (BL) [01795927] **2831**

POVOLZHSKII KRAI (RU) [02240798] **2703**

POVUNGNITUK (CN/0700-4249) [03279398] **2271**

POWDER (US/0145-4471) [02737854] **4913**

POWDER AND BULK ENGINEERING (US/0897-6627) [17758791] **1991**

POWDER/BULK SOLIDS (US/8750-6653) [11646096] **4221**

POWDER COATING (US/1055-0259) [23062972] **1991**

POWDER COATING CONFERENCE (US/0092-0479) [01784514] **4015**

POWDER COATINGS *CEASED.* (US/0163-4542) [04380548] **4225**

POWDER COATINGS BULLETIN (UK/0140-8445) [10495275] **4225**

POWDER DIFFRACTION (US/0885-7156) [12709942] 1991, **4015**

POWDER DIFFRACTION FILE (US) [01480760] **1037**

POWDER DIFFRACTION FILE ALPHABETICAL INDEX : INORGANIC COMPOUNDS (US) [04810529] **1037**

POWDER DIFFRACTION FILE ALPHABETICAL INDEX. INORGANIC PHASES (US/8756-0127) [07929139] **1037**

POWDER DIFFRACTION FILE ORGANIC PHASES SEARCH MANUAL. HANAWALT, ALPHABETICAL, FORMULAE (US/0736-0851) [07929130] **1046**

POWDER DIFFRACTION FILE SEARCH MANUAL ALPHABETICAL LISTING : INORGANIC COMPOUNDS *See* POWDER DIFFRACTION FILE ALPHABETICAL INDEX : INORGANIC COMPOUNDS **1037**

POWDER DIFFRACTION FILE SEARCH MANUAL (FINK METHOD) : INORGANIC (US/0092-1300) [01788955] **1018**

POWDER DIFFRACTION FILE SEARCH MANUAL, HANAWALT METHOD: INORGANIC (US/0092-1319) [01788954] **1037**

POWDER DIFFRACTION FILE SEARCH MANUAL : ORGANIC (US/0092-0576) [01788984] **1046**

POWDER HANDLING & PROCESSING (GW/0934-7348) [22947493] **2148**

POWDER METALLURGY (UK/0032-5899) [01762739] **4015**

●POWDER METALLURGY AND METAL CERAMICS (US/1068-1302) [27448299] **4015**

POWDER METALLURGY CONFERENCE & EXHIBITION *See* ADVANCES IN POWDER METALLURGY & PARTICULATE MATERIALS **3997**

POWDER METALLURGY SCIENCE & TECHNOLOGY (US/0048-5020) [02449816] **4015**

POWDER METALLURGY SCIENCE AND TECHNOLOGY (II/0971-0728) [I09710728] **4015**

POWDER SPRINGS NEIGHBOR (US/0191-5525) [05005155] **5654**

POWDER TECHNOLOGY (SZ/0032-5910) [01762740] **2016**

POWDERHOUND SKI MAGAZINE'S NEW ZEALAND SKI GUIDE (AT/0818-1128) [I08181128] **4913**

POWELL ALERT, THE (US/0198-9936) [06287128] 803, **1299**

POWELL GOLD INDUSTRY GUIDE AND INTERNATIONAL MINING ANALYST, THE (US/0146-7204) [03008281] **2148**

POWELL MONETARY ANALYST *See* POWELL GOLD INDUSTRY GUIDE AND INTERNATIONAL MINING ANALYST, THE **2148**

POWELL MONETARY ANALYST, THE (US/0146-7190) [03008330] **1513**

POWELL PATHS (US/0739-2478) [09690651] **2468**

POWELL TRIBUNE, THE (US/0740-1078) [09868344] **5772**

POWER (US/0032-5929) [05763548] **1953**

POWER AND ELITES (US/0743-9253) [10719006] **5213**

POWER AND MOTORYACHT (US/0886-4411) [12887935] **595**

POWER & SAIL *See* MOTOR BOAT AND YACHTING **594**

POWER & WORKS ENGINEERING (1974) (UK/0307-0697) [02241178] **1991**

POWER BOAT AND SKI (SA/1018-1385) [10181385] **595**

POWER BOATING CANADA (CN/0838-0872) [18314831] **595**

POWER COUNTY PRESS, THE (US) [08802832] **5657**

POWER DELIVERY PRODUCT NEWS (US/1071-2445) [28595407] 2075, **1953**

POWER DIRECTORY (US/0271-2652) [06568357] **2075**

POWER ENGINEER (BOMBAY) (II/0032-5953) [01209291] **2124**

POWER ENGINEERING (BARRINGTON, ILL.) (US/0032-5961) [06371149] 2075, **2124**

●POWER ENGINEERING INTERNATIONAL (US/1069-4994) [28097306] **2075**

POWER ENGINEERING JOURNAL (UK/0950-3366) [15244928] **2075**

POWER ENGINEERING (NEW YORK) (US/0160-5216) [02247112] **2124**

POWER ENGINEERING (RUSSIAN ACADEMY OF SCIENCES) (US) **2124**

POWER ENGINEERING (USSR ACADEMY OF SCIENCES) *See* POWER ENGINEERING (RUSSIAN ACADEMY OF SCIENCES) **2124**

POWER EQUIPMENT AUSTRALASIA (AT/0817-6043) [I08176043] **2124**

●POWER EQUIPMENT TRADE (US/1063-0414) [25715920] **634**

POWER EUROPE (UK) **2075**

POWER FARMING MAGAZINE (AT/0311-1911) [09941717] **160**

POWER IN ASIA, THE ASIAN ELECTRICITY MARKET (UK) [21573786] **2075**

POWER INTERNATIONAL (UK/0950-1487) [13532025] **2124**

POWER LINE (WASHINGTON, D.C.), THE *SUSPENDED.* (US/0738-5676) [04075250] 1299, **1953**

POWER MARKETS WEEK (US) **2075**

POWER MEDIA SELECTS (US/1045-9545) [20293031] **1119**

POWER PACK *CEASED.* (US/0894-041X) [11143652] **1068**

POWER PLAY (US/0739-8018) [09806395] **1199**

POWER PRODUCTS BUSINESS (US/1056-4063) 704, **2124**

POWER PROTECTION (CN/0477-8626) [02247420] **1991**

POWER REACTOR CONFERENCE PROCEEDINGS (US) [01304553] **2158**

POWER REACTOR EVENTS *SUSPENDED.* (US/0741-1359) [06316122] **2158**

POWER REPORT ON AUTOMOTIVE MARKETING, THE (US/1042-9581) [18006073] 935, **5423**

●POWER SMART ANNUAL REPORT (CN/1192-2354) [28166565] **1953**

POWER SOURCE (US) [27320386] **1953**

POWER SUPPLY POSITION IN THE COUNTRY (II) [07011671] **2075**

POWER TECHNOLOGY NEWS (US/0748-8505) [11019083] **1991**

POWER TOOLS (US) **2812**

POWER TRANSISTORS AND POWER HYBRID CIRCUITS (US/0093-0296) [01791529] **2075**

POWER TRANSMISSION DESIGN (US/0032-6070) [01762748] **2124**

POWER TRANSMISSION DESIGN ... GUIDE TO PT PRODUCTS (US/1070-1702) [25524388] **2124**

POWER USER *CEASED.* (US/1064-8801) [26446772] **1199**

POWERBOAT REPORTS (US/1040-3663) [18394114] **595**

POWERBOAT (VAN NUYS, CALIF.) (US/0032-6089) [03977304] 4913, **595**

POWERCONVERSION & INTELLIGENT MOTION (US/0885-0259) [12541442] **1991**

POWERLIFTING USA (US/0199-8536) [06215165] 2600, **4913**

POWERSOURCE (US) [30843449] **1199**

POWERSYSTEM (US) **5423**

POWERTECHNICS MAGAZINE (US/0882-7419) [11960655] **4417**

POWESHIEK COUNTY SEARCHER (US) [12855577] **2468**

POWOKI OCHRONNE (PL/0137-3846) [05512336] **1991**

POWTECH; PROCEEDINGS OF THE INTERNATIONAL POWDER TECHNOLOGY AND BULK SOLIDS CONFERENCE (UK) [04954318] **5139**

POWWOW TRAILS (US/0048-5055) [04525414] **2754**

POWYS NOTES (US/1058-7691) [13431553] **3350**

POWYS REVIEW, THE (UK/0309-1619) [04143835] **3350**

POYNETTE PRESS, THE (US) [12744393] **5770**

POZARNI OCHRANA (XR) [06745030] **2292**

POZEMNI STAVBY (XR/0477-8685) [06744567] **624**

POZHARNOE DELO (RU) [06744390] **2292**

POZITSIIA (RU) [23476847] **5809**

POZNAJ SWIAT (PL/0032-6143) [05626720] **2573**

POZNAJ SWOJ KRAJ (PL) [06645167] **2703**

POZNAN STUDIES IN THE PHILOSOPHY OF THE SCIENCES AND THE HUMANITIES (NE/0303-8157) [04934992] **4357**

POZNANSKIE TOWARZYSTWO PRZYJACIO NAUK. KOMISJA BIOLOGICZNA *See* BULLETIN DE LA SOCIETE DES AMIS DES SCIENCES ET DES LETTRES DE POZNAN. SERIE D. SCIENCES BIOLOGIQUES **449**

POZNANSKIE TOWARZYSTWO PRZYJACIO NAUK. KOMISJA JEZYKOZNAWCZA *See* PRACE KOMISJI JEZYKOZNAWCZEJ **3311**

POZNANSKIE TOWARZYSTWO PRZYJACIO NAUK. KOMISJA NAUK ROLNICZYCH *See* PRACE KOMISJI NAUK ROLNICZYCH I KOMISJI NAUK LESNYCH **121**

PP; POLICIA PORTUGUESA (PO) [01785986] **3173**

●PPC ACCOUNTING AND AUDITING UPDATE, THE (US/1065-3643) [26593774] **749**

PPF SURVEY (US/0361-7467) [02369587] **946**

PPG INDUSTRIES FOUNDATION *See* PPG INDUSTRIES FOUNDATION : REPORT **5301**

PPG INDUSTRIES FOUNDATION : REPORT (US/0278-9108) [07870503] **5301**

PPG SHAREHOLDER NEWS (US) [05150559] **911**

PPI NEWSWIRE SERVICE *See* PPI THIS WEEK **4237**

PPI THIS WEEK (BE) **4237**

PPM. PET PRODUCT MARKETING (UK/0262-5849) [I02625849] 935, **4287**

PPMP. PSYCHOTHERAPIE, PSYCHOSOMATIK, MEDIZINISCHE PSYCHOLOGIE (GW/0937-2032) [I09372032] **4608**

PPO LETTER, THE (US/1054-2396) [22786722] **2890**

PPS-REPORT *CEASED.* (GW/0930-8490) [I09308490] **1621**

PPT EXPRESS (US/1068-8897) [27841585] **5301**

PPURI (US/0886-5507) [07996602] **2507**

PR ACTIVITY REPORT (US/0892-9343) [15296714] **3241**

PR & V : PR EN VOORLICHTING (NE) **763**

PR CASEBOOK (US/0275-3677) [06802541] **763**

PR-MAGAZIN (GW/0342-8702) [I03428702] **763**

PR NEWS (US) [26369731] **763**

PR. PHARMACEUTICAL REPRESENTATIVE (US/0161-8415) [04038216] **4325**

PR PLANNER (UK) **763**

PR REPORTER (EXETER, N.H.) (US/0048-2609) [02176680] **764**

PR - TEXAS AGRICULTURAL EXPERIMENT STATION (US/1058-1138) [11100435] **121**

PR WEEK (UK) [22039557] **764**

PR WEEK (UK/0267-6087) [I02676087] **764**

PR WORLD (UK/0951-7693) [I09517693] **764**

PRABHA, DIVALI ANKA (II) [01783604] **2507**

PRABUDDHA BHARATA (II/0032-6178) [01774404] **5041**

PRACA I ZABEZPIECZENIE SPOECZNE (PL/0032-6186) [06308840] **1621**

PRACA KSIEGARSKA *See* PRZEGLED KSIEGARSKI I WYDAWNICZY **4831**

PRACE (PL/0543-1905) [02601640] **1702**

PRACE ARCHEOLOGICZNE (PL/0083-4300) [02464714] **278**

PRACE BIAOSTOCKIEGO TOWARZYSTWA NAUKOWEGO (PL/0067-6470) [02404754] 2482, **1842**

PRACE GEOGRAFICZNE (PL/0083-4343) [02263296] **2573**

PRACE GEOGRAFICZNE - POLSKA AKADEMIA NAUK (PL/0373-6547) [02436802] **2573**

PRACE I MATERIALY ETNOGRAFICZNE. TRAVAUX ET MATERIAUX ETHNOGRAPHIQUES (PO) [05686907] **243**

PRACE I MATERIAY MUZEUM ARCHEOLOGICZNEGO I ETNOGRAFICZNEGO W LODZI. SERIA ARCHEOLOGICZNA (PL/0458-1520) [02992185] **278**

PRACE I MATERIAY ZOOTECHNICZNE / INSTYTUT GENETYKE I HODOWLI ZWIERZAT POLSKIEJ AKADEMII NAUK (PL/0137-1649) [14581498] **5594**

PRACE I STUDIA GEOGRAFICZNE / UNIWERSYTET WARSZAWSKI, WYDZIA GEOGRAFII I STUDIOW REGIONALNYCH (PL) [07360710] **2573**

PRACE INSTYTUT TECHNOLOGII DREWNA (PL/0032-6240) [07198983] **2403**

PRACE INSTYTUTU BADAWCZEGO LESNICTWA (PL) [20910946] **2390**

PRACE — Alphabetical Title Index

PRACE INSTYTUTU ELEKTROENERGETYKI I STEROWANIA UKADOW POLITECHNIKI SLASKIEJ (PL) [04447238] **2075**

PRACE INSTYTUTU GEOLOGICZNEGO (PL/0208-645X) [05771158] **1391**

PRACE INSTYTUTU JEZYKA POLSKIEGO (PL) [10548682] **3311**

PRACE INSTYTUTU MASZYN PRZEPYWOWYCH (PL/0079-3205) [05182456] **2125**

PRACE INSTYTUTU METALURGII ZELAZA IM, ST. STASZICA (PL/0137-9941) [04657556] **4015**

PRACE INSTYTUTU METEOROLOGII I GOSPODARKI WODNEJ (PL/0137-1347) [02242014] **1433**

PRACE INSTYTUTU ODLEWNICTWA (PL/0450-8955) [11447035] **4015**

PRACE INSTYTUTU SADOWNICTWA I KWIACIARSTWA W SKIERNIEWICACH *See* PRACE INSTYTUTU SADOWNICTWA I KWIACIARSTWA W SKIERNIEWICACH. SERIA B, ROSLINY OZDOBNE **2428**

PRACE INSTYTUTU SADOWNICTWA I KWIACIARSTWA W SKIERNIEWICACH. SERIA B, ROSLINY OZDOBNE (PL/0324-8437) [09770967] **2428**

PRACE INSTYTUTU TECHNIKI BUDOWLANEJ (PL/0138-0796) [04728341] **624, 2028**

PRACE INSTYTUTU TECHNOLOGII ELEKTRONOWEJ CEMI (PL/0138-0915) [I01380915] **2075**

PRACE IPI PAN / ICS PAS REPORTS (PL) [03791153] **3527, 1200**

PRACE JEZYKOZNAWCZE (PL) [05793948] **3311**

PRACE KOMISJI HISTORII SZTUKI. POZNANSKIE TOWARZYSTWO PRZYJACIO NAUK (PL/0079-466X) [I0079466X] **2626**

PRACE KOMISJI JEZYKOZNAWCZEJ (PL/0079-4678) [02801011] **3311**

PRACE KOMISJI JEZYKOZNAWSTWA / POLSKA AKADEMIA NAUK--ODDZIA W KRAKOWIE (PL/0079-3310) [02922976] **3311**

PRACE KOMISJI NAUK ROLNICZYCH I KOMISJI NAUK LESNYCH (PL/0079-4708) [01799585] **121**

PRACE - KRAKOW. AKADEMIA GORNICZO-HUTNICZA. INSTYTUT PODSTAW BUDOWY MASZYN (PL) [05418148] **4015, 2148**

PRACE MATEMATYCZNE (PL/0239-7978) [06400281] **3527**

PRACE NAUKOWE INSTYTUT OCHRONY ROSLIN (PL/0554-8004) [01642146] **4247**

PRACE NAUKOWE INSTYTUTU BUDOWNICTWA POLITECHNIKI WROCAWSKIEJ. SERIA KONFERENCJE (PL) [04980469] **624**

PRACE NAUKOWE INSTYTUTU GORNICTWA POLITECHNIKI WROCAWSKIEJ. MONOGRAFIE (PL/0324-9689) [05637439] **2148**

PRACE NAUKOWE INSTYTUTU MATEMATYKI POLITECHNIKI WROCAWSKIEJ (PL) [03265451] 2125, **3527**

PRACE NAUKOWE INSTYTUTU METROLOGII ELEKTRYCZNEJ POLITECHNIKI WROCAWSKIEJ. SERIA MONOGRAFIE (PL) [03422564] **2075**

PRACE NAUKOWE - POLITECHNIKA WARSZAWSKA. MECHANIKA (PL/0137-2335) [05419053] **2125**

PRACE OSRODKA BADAWCZO-ROZWOJOWEGO PRZETWORNIKOW OBRAZU (PL/0208-9092) [08237048] **5139**

PRACE POLONISTYCZNE (PL/0079-4791) [01762750] **3424**

PRACE. SERIA A (PL/0521-9310) [03020718] **2852**

PRACE. SERIA B (PL) [03020783] **1991**

PRACE VURH VODNANY (XR) [05359765] **2310**

PRACE VYZKUMNEHO USTAVU GEOLOGICKEHO INZENYRSTVI (XR/0139-763X) [02832419] **4275**

PRACE VYZKUMNEHO USTAVU LESNIHO HOSPODARSTVI A MYSLIVOSTI (XR/0139-5807) [01639809] **2390**

PRACE Z NAUK SPOECZNYCH (PL/0208-5437) [02316493] **5213**

PRACE ZOOLOGICZNE (PL) [05793901] **5594**

PRACETA (II) [01800222] **2507**

PRACHEACHON (CB) **5779**

PRACHYA PRATIBHA (II) [01586846] **2662**

PRACI BHASA-VIJNAN (CALCUTTA) (II/0970-9940) [02256120] **3311**

PRACINA NEPALA : [PURATATTVA VIBHAGAKO MUKHAPATRA] (NP) [08809243] **278**

PRACOVNI LEKARSTVI (XR/0032-6291) [06526603] **3628**

PRACTICA ODONTOLOGICA (MX/0185-5905) [15085382] **1333**

PRACTICAL ACCOUNTANT, THE (US/0032-6321) [01431100] **749**

PRACTICAL ALLERGY & IMMUNOLOGY (CN/0831-0998) [15276431] **3675**

PRACTICAL APPROACH TO PATENTS, TRADEMARKS AND COPYRIGHTS, A (SZ/0142-5927) [04814033] **1308**

PRACTICAL AQUACULTURE & LAKE MANAGEMENT *CEASED.* (US/1057-218X) [19273315] **2310**

PRACTICAL ASPECTS OF DIABETES MANAGEMENT *CEASED.* (US/0897-2931) [17448071] **3732**

PRACTICAL BOAT OWNER (UK/0032-6348) [06593920] **595**

PRACTICAL CARDIOLOGY *CEASED.* (US/0361-3372) [02246375] **3709**

PRACTICAL CLINICAL GUIDES (US) [22893141] **3628**

PRACTICAL COMMUNICATIONS (US/0891-8910) [15046971] **1347**

PRACTICAL DIABETES (UK/0266-447X) [12813241] **3732**

PRACTICAL DIABETOLOGY (US/0730-3491) [07993146] **3732**

PRACTICAL ELECTRONICS (UK/0032-6372) [16783831] **2075**

PRACTICAL ENDODONTICS (US/1056-7933) [23853812] **1333**

PRACTICAL ENGLISH TEACHING *CEASED.* (UK/0260-4752) [I02604752] **1902**

●PRACTICAL ENVIRONMENTAL REGULATION (US/1056-1102) [23467024] **2180**

PRACTICAL FARM IDEAS QUARTERLY (UK/0968-0136) [I09680136] **160**

PRACTICAL FISHKEEPING (UK) [06756542] **4287, 2310**

PRACTICAL FOOD HYGIENE (UK) **2353**

PRACTICAL FORESTRY (US/1044-2200) [19730719] **2390**

PRACTICAL GARDENING (UK/0032-6399) [I00326399] **2428**

PRACTICAL GASTROENTEROLOGY (US/0277-4208) [07531149] **3747**

PRACTICAL GUIDE TO PLANNED GIVING (US) [22441335] **4338**

PRACTICAL GUIDE TO THE BANKRUPTCY REFORM ACT (US) **3088**

PRACTICAL GUIDES FOR SUCCESSFUL DENTISTRY / PREPARED BY THE AUSTRALIAN DENTAL STANDARDS LABORATORY FOR THE AUSTRALIAN DENTAL ASSOCIATION (AT/0729-1345) [09912850] **1333**

PRACTICAL HOMEOWNER *CEASED.* (US/1042-4601) [16532796] **624**

PRACTICAL HORSEMAN (US/0090-8762) [05728288] **2801**

PRACTICAL HYDROPONICS (AT/1037-5457) [I10375457] **525, 2428**

PRACTICAL LABOR LAW: COURSE MANUAL (US/0195-3656) [05387846] **3153**

PRACTICAL LAW FOR COMPANIES (UK) **3030**

PRACTICAL LAWYER, THE (US/0032-6429) [01762759] **3030**

PRACTICAL LAWYER'S LAW OFFICE MANAGEMENT MANUAL, THE (US/0092-248X) [01788427] **882, 3030**

PRACTICAL LITIGATOR, THE (US/1047-6261) [20765675] **3030**

PRACTICAL MACHINERY MANAGEMENT FOR PROCESS PLANTS (US) [13513336] **3486**

PRACTICAL METHODS IN CLINICAL IMMUNOLOGY SERIES (UK/0262-8783) [06972735] **3675**

PRACTICAL METHODS IN ELECTRON MICROSCOPY *CEASED.* (NE) [01773295] **573**

PRACTICAL OPTOMETRY (CN/1181-6058) [23598289] **4217**

●PRACTICAL PC (UK/0965-6219) [I09656219] **1200**

PRACTICAL PEDIATRICS (US) [08258681] **3910**

PRACTICAL PERIODONTICS AND AESTHETIC DENTISTRY (US/1042-2722) [18992655] **1333**

PRACTICAL PHOTOGRAPHY (UK) [11890336] **4375**

PRACTICAL PREMISES SECURITY (UK) **5177**

PRACTICAL REAL ESTATE LAWYER, THE (US/8756-0372) [11452510] **4843, 3030**

PRACTICAL REVIEWS IN ANESTHESIOLOGY (US/0896-5315) [10846974] **3684**

PRACTICAL REVIEWS IN CANCER MANAGEMENT (US/0896-5307) [07411350] **3822**

PRACTICAL REVIEWS IN CARDIOLOGY (US/0896-5463) [17208536] **3709**

PRACTICAL REVIEWS IN DERMATOLOGY (US/1046-7076) [20496682] **3722**

PRACTICAL REVIEWS IN EMERGENCY MEDICINE (US/0896-5382) [17207272] **3725**

PRACTICAL REVIEWS IN FAMILY PRACTICE (US/0896-5412) [17207948] **3738**

PRACTICAL REVIEWS IN GASTROENTEROLOGY (US/0896-5439) [17208209] **3747**

PRACTICAL REVIEWS IN GENERAL SURGERY (US) **3972**

PRACTICAL REVIEWS IN INTERNAL MEDICINE (1984) (US/0896-5323) [11684877] **3800**

PRACTICAL REVIEWS IN NUCLEAR MEDICINE (US/0896-5331) [07411285] **3849**

PRACTICAL REVIEWS IN OB/GYN (US/0896-5390) [17207451] **3767**

PRACTICAL REVIEWS IN ORAL MAXILLOFACIAL SURGERY (US/0896-5447) [17208298] **3972**

PRACTICAL REVIEWS IN ORTHODONTICS (US/1046-7106) [20496738] **1333**

PRACTICAL REVIEWS IN PATHOLOGY (US/0896-534X) [08563835] **3897**

PRACTICAL REVIEWS IN PEDIATRIC DENTISTRY (US/1051-0265) [21925336] **1333**

PRACTICAL REVIEWS IN PEDIATRICS (US/0896-5455) [17208425] **3910**

PRACTICAL REVIEWS IN PSYCHIATRY (BIRMINGHAM, ALA.) (US/0896-5358) [14339382] **3932**

PRACTICAL REVIEWS IN RADIOLOGY (US/0896-5374) [17207229] **3944**

PRACTICAL REVIEWS IN SURGERY (US/0896-5404) [17207528] **3972**

PRACTICAL REVIEWS IN UROLOGY (US/0896-5420) [17208024] **3992**

PRACTICAL RISK MANAGEMENT (US) [06037556] **2890**

PRACTICAL SAILOR, THE (US/0161-8059) [04024473] **595**

PRACTICAL SKILLS COURSE (US) [05961931] **3030**

PRACTICAL SPECTROSCOPY (US/0148-9054) [03398939] **1018**

PRACTICAL SUPERVISION (US/0742-7859) [10438273] **882**

PRACTICAL SURVIVAL (US/1058-2274) [24241781] **4877**

PRACTICAL TAX GUIDE FOR THE HORSE OWNER, A (US/0741-4595) [10151611] **2801**

PRACTICAL TAX LAWYER, THE (US/0890-4898) [14055760] **4741, 3030**

PRACTICAL TAX PLANNING AND PRECEDENTS (UK) **3030, 4741**

PRACTICAL WARGAMER (UK/0953-0592) [I09530592] **2777**

PRACTICAL WILL DRAFTING (US/0192-3889) [04365275] **3118**

PRACTICAL WINERY/VINEYARD (US/1057-2694) [16940628] **2370**

PRACTICAL WIRELESS (UK/1041-0857) [14513282] **1136**

PRACTICAL WOOD WORKING (UK/0032-6488) [02251541] **634**

PRACTICE BIRMINGHAM (UK/0950-3153) [I09503153] **5301**

PRACTICE BUILDER, THE (US/0883-3036) [12113971] **704**

PRACTICE : ISSUED TO THE MEMBERS OF THE ROYAL INSTITUTE OF BRITISH ARCHITECTS BY THE PRACTICE DEPARTMENT (UK) [13660624] **306**

PRACTICE LIFE *CEASED.* (US/0742-1435) [10292885] **882, 3629**

●PRACTICE MANAGEMENT AND MARKETING NEWS IN PEDIATRIC DENTISTRY (US/1064-1203) [26209074] **1333**

PRACTICE MARKETING (UK/0961-8333) [I09618333] **935**

PRACTICE (NEW YORK, N.Y.) (US/0742-9940) [10466371] **4545**

PRACTICE NURSE (UK/0953-6612) [I09536612] **3867**

PRACTICE NURSING (UK/0964-9271) [I09649271] **3867**

PRACTICE PERSONNEL BULLETIN *CEASED.* (US/0888-9066) [13769596] 3629, **946**

●PRACTICE UNDER THE CALIFORNIA FAMILY CODE : DISSOLUTION, LEGAL SEPARATION, NULLITY (US) [29902747] **3122**

PRACTICE UNDER THE CALIFORNIA FAMILY LAW ACT *See* PRACTICE UNDER THE CALIFORNIA FAMILY CODE : DISSOLUTION, LEGAL SEPARATION, NULLITY **3122**

●PRACTICES (CINCINNATI, OHIO) (US/1059-7239) [24688622] **306**

PRACTICIENS ET 3 EME AGE (FR/0182-1377) [01821377] **3629**

PRACTICING ANTHROPOLOGY (US/0888-4552) [05040497] **243**

PRACTICING ARCHITECT (US/0888-3424) [09992699] **306**

PRACTICING CPA, THE (US/0885-6931) [10592629] **750**

PRACTICING FAMILY LAWYER, THE (US/0148-9763) [03402293] **3122**

PRACTICING TO TAKE THE GRE GENERAL TEST (US) [20087557] **1774**

PRACTISING ADMINISTRATOR, THE (AT/0157-3357) [I01573357] **1868**

PRACTISING LAW INSTITUTE *See* PLI NEWS **3029**

PRACTISING LAW INSTITUTE *See* EQUIPMENT LEASING **2967**

PRACTISING LAW INSTITUTE *See* LITIGATION COURSE HANDBOOK SERIES **3003**

PRACTISING LAW INSTITUTE *See* REAL ESTATE CLOSINGS **4844**

PRACTISING LAW INSTITUTE *See* PATENT OFFICE EXAMINATION REVIEW COURSE **3025**

PRACTISING LAW INSTITUTE *See* REAL ESTATE LAW AND PRACTICE COURSE HANDBOOK SERIES **3034**

PRACTISING MANAGER (AT/0159-1193) [14589267] **882**

PRACTITIONER EDIZIONE ITALIANA *SUSPENDED.* (IT/0391-7282) [I03917282] **3629**

PRACTITIONER (RESTON), THE (US/0192-6160) [01240240] **1868**

PRACTITIONER, THE (UK/0032-6518) [01762763] **3738**

●PRACTITIONERS 1120S DESKBOOK (US/1061-2084) [25255504] **1513**

●PRACTITIONERS 5500 DESKBOOK (US/1064-7724) [26393961] **3030**

PRACTITIONERS' CHILD LAW BULLETIN (UK/0961-0804) [I09610804] **3030**

PRACTITIONERS GUIDE TO SUCCESSFUL TAX PRACTICE (US/1056-9928) [23917247] **4741**

●PRACTITIONER'S INCOME TAX ACT, THE (CN/1193-1701) [26714829] **4741**

PRADALGE (UK/0556-1094) [02435653] **3424**

PRADHIKRTA : GURU NANAKA DEVA YUNIVARSITI KE HINDI VIBHAGA KI SODHA PATRIKA (II) [11775316] **3311**

PRADIPA (GW) [19946418] **1774**

PRAEGER MONOGRAPHS IN INFECTIOUS DISEASE (US/0892-1857) [09897636] 3715, **4795**

●PRAEGER SERIES IN CRIMINOLOGY AND CRIME CONTROL POLICY (US/1060-3212) [24925783] **3173**

●PRAEGER SERIES IN PRESIDENTIAL STUDIES (US/1062-0931) [25523601] **4492**

●PRAEGER SERIES IN TRANSFORMATIONAL POLITICS AND POLITICAL SCIENCE (US/1061-5261) [25343657] **4492**

PRAEGER SPECIAL STUDIES IN INTERNATIONAL BUSINESS, FINANCE, AND TRADE (US/0160-4333) [03685604] **704**

PRAEHISTORISCHE ZEITSCHRIFT (GW/0079-4848) [01762765] **243**

PRAEVENTION UND REHABILITATION (GW/0937-552X) [I0937552X] **3629**

PRAGMATICS & BEYOND COMPANION SERIES (NE/0920-3079) [12588008] **3311**

PRAGMATICS & BEYOND NEW SERIES (NE/0922-842X) [I0922842X] **3311**

●PRAGMATICS & COGNITION (NE/0929-0907) [28093764] 1200, **3311**

PRAGMATICS. MICROFICHE (UK/0309-8141) [04146214] **3311**

PRAGMATICS : QUARTERLY PUBLICATION OF THE INTERNATIONAL PRAGMATICS ASSOCIATION (BE/1018-2101) [24202578] **3311**

PRAGUE BULLETIN OF MATHEMATICAL LINGUISTICS, THE (XR/0032-6585) [02608651] **3311**

●PRAGUE ECONOMIC PAPERS (XR/1210-0455) [27255728] **1513**

PRAGUE. HYDROMETEOROLOGICKY USTAV *See* VYROCNI ZPRAVA HYDROMETEOROLOGICKEHO USTAVU **1418**

PRAGUE. NARODNI MUUZEUM *See* SBORNIK. RADA C: LITERARNI HISTORIE **3433**

PRAGUE POST (XR) [27141839] **5799**

PRAGUE STUDIES IN ENGLISH (XR) [09505833] **3424**

PRAGUE STUDIES IN MATHEMATICAL LINGUISTICS (US/0079-4856) [01762773] **3527**

PRAGUE. UNIVERSITA KARLOVA LEKARSKA FAKULTA V HDADCI KRALOVE *See* SBORNIK VEDECKYCH PRACI LEKARSKE FAKULTY KARLOVY UNIVERSITY V HRADCI KRALOVE **3638**

PRAGUE. UNIVERSITA KAROLVA *See* ACTA. HISTORIA UNIVERSITATIS CAROLINAE PRAGENSIS **1807**

PRAGUE. VYSOKA SKOLA ZEMEDELSKA. FAKULTA AGRONOMICKA *See* SBORNIK VYSOKE SKOLY ZEMEDELSKE V PRAZE, FAKULTA AGRONOMICKA. RADA C: ZEMEDELSKE MELIORACE, ZEMEDELSKE STAVBY **132**

PRAHA-MOSKVA (XR) [06653204] **4532**

PRAHISTORISCHE BRONZEFUNDE (GW) [02767659] **278**

PRAHISTORISCHE BRONZEFUNDE. ABTEILUNG VII (GW) [14364316] **2626**

PRAHISTORISCHE BRONZEFUNDE. ABTEILUNG XX (GW) [14363966] **2626**

PRAHISTORISCHE FORSCHUNGEN / HERAUSGEGEBEN VON DER ANTHROPOLOGISCHEN GESELLSCHAFT IN WIEN (AU/0032-6534) [01762764] **243**

PRAIRIE ARTS (CN/0821-4891) [09590452] **328**

PRAIRIE (CANYON, TEX.) (US) [15021840] **5753**

PRAIRIE FARMER (US/0032-6615) [08568624] **121**

PRAIRIE FIRE (WINNIPEG) (CN/0821-1124) [09801056] **3424**

PRAIRIE FORUM (CN/0317-6282) [03406033] 2180, **2754**

PRAIRIE GARDEN (CN/0315-6850) [02248153] **2428**

PRAIRIE GLEANER, THE (US/0032-6623) [08997193] **2468**

PRAIRIE HARVESTER (CN/0383-7653) [10814004] **4987**

PRAIRIE-HOTELIER *CEASED.* (CN/1180-999X) [22367186] **2809**

PRAIRIE JOURNAL OF CANADIAN LITERATURE, THE (CN/0827-2921) [11825369] **3424**

PRAIRIE LANDSCAPE MAGAZINE (CN/0820-6848) [09519503] **2428**

PRAIRIE LORE (US/0032-6631) [02251543] **2755**

PRAIRIE MESSENGER (CN/0032-664X) [02587655] **5793**

PRAIRIE NATURALIST, THE (US/0091-0376) [01785564] **4170**

PRAIRIE PROGRESS NEWSLETTER (CN/1188-2255) [11882255] **1513**

PRAIRIE ROOTS (US/0197-3037) [05974294] **2468**

PRAIRIE ROSE, THE (US/0032-6666) [02252962] **3867**

PRAIRIE SCHOONER (US/0032-6682) [01762775] **3424**

PRAIRIE SOUNDS (CN/0822-7500) [10386220] **4147**

PRAIRIE STATE PATRIOT (US/0196-3481) [05791977] **2755**

PRAIRIE STATER (US/0195-2854) [19032702] **2543**

PRAIRIE SUN (US/0162-8976) [04253128] **5661**

PRAIRIE WEED (CN/0229-6632) [08071394] 3091, **525**

PRAIRIE WOMAN (CN/0229-5059) [08071932] **5564**

PRAIRIELAND PIONEER (US/0892-6131) [11525328] **2468**

PRAJNALOKA (NAGPUR, INDIA) (II) [08426867] **4357**

PRAJNAN (II/0032-6690) [01641743] **803**

PRAKAMPANA (NP) [02246619] **3425**

PRAKLIT, HA- (IS) [01762776] **5052**

PRAKRUTI (II) [02429468] **5139**

PRAKTIESE TEOLOGIE IN S.A (SA/1010-8017) [110108017] **4987**

PRAKTIJKBLAD VOOR MEDEZEGGENSCHAP (NE/0921-2442) [I09212442] **946**

PRAKTIJKMANAGEMENT (NE/0169-1910) [01691910] 882, **4325**

PRAKTIKA TES EN ATHENAIS ARCHAIOLOGIKES HETAIREIAS (GR/1105-0969) [08447726] **278**

PRAKTISCH MANAGEMENT (BE/0772-6856) [I07726856] **882**

PRAKTISCHE KIEFERORTHOPAEDIE *See* KIEFERORTHOPAEDIE : DIE ZEITSCHRIFT FUER DIE PRAXIS **1329**

PRAKTISCHE LANDTECHNIK (AU) **121**

PRAKTISCHE METALLOGRAPHIE (GW/0032-678X) [01606019] **4015**

PRAKTISCHE SCHADLINGSBEKAMPFER, DER (GW/0032-6801) [03793284] **182**

PRAKTISCHE THEOLOGIE (NE) [02199247] **4987**

PRAKTISCHE TIERARZT (GW/0032-681X) [01714635] **5518**

PRAMANA (II/0304-4289) [01797824] **4417**

PRAMIERUNG VON FLURBEREINIGUNGEN (GW) [02998462] **121**

PRANA (NE/0165-4373) [I01654373] **2852**

PRANCING HORSE, THE (US/0363-5678) [02466091] **5235**

PRANGANA (NP) [02239609] **3425**

PRANIKEE : JOURNAL OF ZOOLOGICAL SOCIETY OF ORISSA (II) [10946564] **5594**

PRAPARATOR (GW/0032-6542) [05843414] **4170**

PRAPFALLS (CN/0712-9726) [08977484] **3241**

PRASA POLSKA (PL) [06655147] **2923**

PRASADA (CALCUTTA, INDIA) (II) [10643809] **3425**

PRASARA (II) [02240193] **1802**

PRASHASNIKA (II) [02245588] **4674**

PRASSI E TEORIA *CEASED.* (IT) [02377606] **5235**

PRASTUTIPARBA (II) [10513299] **3425**

PRATFALL : THE "WAY OUT WEST" PERIODICAL TRIBUTE TO STAN AND OLLIE (US) [08165129] **4076**

PRATIBHA INDIA (II) [08756639] 328, **1842**

PRATICA AMMINISTRATIVA (IT) **750**

PRATICA AZIENDALE (IT) [07322910] **704**

PRATICA PSICOMOTORIA (IT) **3629**

PRATICA SOCIALE *SUSPENDED.* (IT) **5213**

PRATICA SOCIALE *SUSPENDED.* (IT) **4608**

PRATIQUE DU SOUDAGE, LA (BE) [01795832] **4027**

PRATIQUE LONDON (UK/0269-1396) [I02691396] 1147, **3715**

PRATIQUE MEDICALE & CHIRURGICALE DE L'ANIMAL DE COMPAGNIE (FR/0758-1882) [09778853] **5518**

PRATIQUE MEDICALE, LA *CEASED.* (FR/0750-6155) [08984385] **3629**

PRATIQUE PRIVEE, LA (CN/0225-0993) [06635197] **306**

PRATIQUE VETERINAIRE EQUINE (FR/0395-8639) [03950740] 2801, **5518**

PRATIQUES (FR/0338-2389) [06478426] **3311**

PRATIQUES CORPORELLES (FR/0292-9651) [16529986] 4608, **3844**

PRATIQUES DE FORMATION SAINT-DENIS (FR/0292-2215) [I02922215] **1802**

PRATO STORIA E ARTE (IT/0032-6925) [07767037] **362**

PRATT CITY COMMUNITY NEWSLETTER *See* PRATT CITY COMMUNITY NEWSPAPER **5628**

●PRATT CITY COMMUNITY NEWSPAPER (US/1061-1908) [25216384] **5628**

PRATT INSTITUTE CREATIVE ARTS THERAPY REVIEW (US/0196-8459) [05913814] 328, **3932**

PRATT JOURNAL OF ARCHITECTURE *CEASED.* (US/0883-7279) [12223821] **306**

PRATT TRIBUNE (PRATT, KAN. : 1964) (US/1048-3675) [12212962] **5678**

PRATT'S GUIDE TO VENTURE CAPITAL SOURCES (US/0884-1616) [11310738] **911**

PRATTVILLE PROGRESS (PRATTVILLE, ALA.), THE (US/1044-0380) [17799786] **5628**

PRAVDA (RU) [01762779] **5809**

PRAVDA (XO) [24803948] **5810**

PRAVDA NA VIKEND (XO) [01787316] **2521**

PRAVDA (PRAGUE, CZECHOSLAVAKIA) (XO) [09976368] **5810**

PRAVDA UKRAINY : ORGAN TSENTRALNOGO KOMITETA KOMMUNISTICHESKOI PARTII UKRAINY, VERKHOVNOGO SOVETA I SOVETA MINISTROV UKRAINSKOI SSR (UN) [09987978] **5811**

PRAVDA VOSTOKA (UZ) [06635579] **2703**

PRAVENTION (GW/0170-2602) [05083356] **4795**

PRAVITELSTVENNYI VESTNIK (MOSCOW, R.S.F.S.R.) (RU) [19093116] **2703**

PRAVNA MISAO (BN) [06656131] **3030**

PRAVNE SVESKE (YU) [06657383] 5301, **2890**

PRAVNEHISTORICKE STUDIE (XR/0079-4929) [01715627] **2703**

●PRAVNI PRAXE (XR/1210-0900) [28004801] **3030**

PRAVNIK (PRAGUE, CZECHOSLOVAKIA) (XR) [09555089] **3030**

PRAVNY OBZOR : CASOPIS USTAVU STATU A PRAVA SLOVENKEJ AKADEMIE VIED (XO) [11126481] **3030**

PRAVO A ZAKONNOST *See* PRAVNI PRAXE **3030**

PRAVO A ZALONNOST (CS) [23753300] **3030**

PRAVOSLAVLJE (YU) [06655455] **5040**

PRAVOSLAVNAIA RUS (US/0032-7018) [01780299] **4987**

PRAVOSLAVNAJA ZIZN (US/0032-6992) [01762780] **5040**

PRAVOSLAVNOE OBOZRENIE (CN/0225-0292) [06131694] **5040**

PRAWO I ZYCIE : ORGAN ZRZESZENIA PRAWNIKOW POLSKICH (PL) [06661265] **3030**

PRAWO PRZEDSIEBIORCY (PL/1230-2856) [I12302856] **3030**

PRAXIOLOGY (PL/0138-0311) [09124474] **5254**

PRAXIS (BL) [06612501] **4796**

PRAXIS DARLING HEIGHTS (AT/0726-6847) [I07266847] **1902**

PRAXIS DER ANASTHESIOLOGIE UND INTENSIVMEDIZIN (GW/0932-9196) [19523324] **3972**

PRAXIS DER KINDERPSYCHOLOGIE UND KINDERPSYCHIATRIE (GW/0032-7034) [02266417] 3932, **4608**

PRAXIS DER KINDERPSYCHOLOGIE UND KINDERPSYCHIATRIE BEIHEFT (GW) [05845298] **4608**

PRAXIS DER KLINISCHEN VERHALTENSMEDIZIN UND REHABILITATION (GW/0933-842X) [24625873] **3932**

PRAXIS DER NATURWISSENSCHAFTEN BIOLOGIE (GW/0177-8382) [I01778382] **469**

PRAXIS DER NATURWISSENSCHAFTEN CHEMIE (GW/0177-9516) [I01779516] **989**

PRAXIS DER NATURWISSENSCHAFTEN PHYSIK (GW/0177-8374) [I01778374] **4417**

PRAXIS DER PSYCHOMOTORIK (GW/0170-060X) [04558347] **1884**

PRAXIS DER PSYCHOTHERAPIE UND PSYCHOSOMATIK (GW/0171-791X) [05244263] **4608**

PRAXIS DEUTSCH (GW/0341-5279) [I03415279] 1902, **3311**

PRAXIS GRUNDSCHULE (GW/0170-3722) [I01703722] **1094**

PRAXIS (ITHACA) (US/0161-0414) [03233791] **930**

PRAXIS : JOURNAL OF POLITICAL SCIENCE (PH/0116-709X) **4492**

PRAXIS KURIER, KONGRESS-SYNOPSE AKTUELL : PK (GW/0176-4616) [10104513] **3629**

PRAXIS MEDICI REUMATIZAM *See* REUMATIZAM **3806**

PRAXIS MEDIZINISCHER DOKUMENTATION / DEUTSCHER VERBAND MEDIZINISCHER DOKUMENTARE E.V (GW/0722-477X) [11602779] 1200, **3629**

PRAXIS VETERINARIA (CI/0350-4441) [10983891] **5518**

PRAXISMAGAZIN (GW/0941-1046) **3629**

PRAY TOGETHER INSTRUCTIONS FOR LECTORS AND COMMENTATORS (US) **4987**

PRAY TOGETHER MISSALETTE (US) **4567**

PRAYASA (NP) [01790550] **3425**

PRAYER GROUP DIRECTORY (US/0747-5748) [10192799] **5034**

PRAYERS FOR WORSHIP (US/0274-600X) [06433809] **4987**

PRAYING (KANSAS CITY, MO.) (US/0895-4968) [11603195] **5034**

PRAZSKE STREDISKO STATNI PAMATKOVE PECE A OCHRANY PRIRODY *See* STALETA PRAHA **309**

PRB REPORT (US/0146-7646) [02380307] **4559**

PRC NEWSLETTER (US/8755-3902) [10874819] **4375**

PRC OFFICIAL ACTIVITIES AND MONTHLY BIBLIOGRAPHY *See* CHINA MONTHLY DATA / INSTITUTE OF ASIAN AFFAIRS **4468**

PRC OFFICIAL ACTIVITIES AND MONTHLY BIBLIOGRAPHY / INSTITUTE OF ASIAN AFFAIRS (GW) [04782772] 4492, **4502**

PRD. PUBLIZISTIKWISSENSCHAFTLICHER REFERATE-DIENST (GW) [06571609] **422**

PRE- AND PERI-NATAL PSYCHOLOGY JOURNAL (US/0883-3095) [12118151] 5254, **3767**

PRE-LAW JOURNAL (US/0741-1162) [10084620] **3030**

PRE-PARENT ADVISER (US/1047-384X) [20707293] **2285**

PRE- (PRAIRIE VILLAGE, KAN.) (US/1042-0304) [18910590] **4818**

PRE/TEXT (US/0731-0714) [07291716] 1119, **3311**

PREACHER'S MAGAZINE, THE (US/0162-3982) [01717007] **4987**

PREACHER'S PERIODICAL, THE (US/0744-8562) [08602187] **4987**

PREACHER'S QUARTERLY *See* WORSHIP AND PREACHING **5010**

PREACHING (JACKSONVILLE, FLA.) (US/0882-7036) [11936171] **4987**

PREAKNESS, THE (US/0195-6272) [05048721] **2801**

PREAUTHORIZATION OF PLANNING ACTIVITIES OF THE BUREAU OF RECLAMATION, THE CORPS OF ENGINEERS, AND THE SOIL CONSERVATION SERVICE (US/0565-0631) [02620716] **5537**

PRECAMBRIAN RESEARCH (NE/0301-9268) [01792859] **1391**

PRECANCEL FORUM (US/0273-5415) [06582657] **1147**

PRECEDENTS FOR THE CONVEYANCER (UK) [01604905] **3030**

PRECEPTA MEDICA (FR/0983-5075) [19078405] **3629**

PRECEPTOR (US) **4987**

PRECEPTROL (US/0743-6505) [10686747] **568**

PRECIO$ AGROPECUARIOS (AG/0326-1565) [10919718] **121**

PRECIOS DE PRODUCTOS E INSUMOS AGROPECUARIOS (UY) [05163462] **121**

PRECIOUS FIBERS *CEASED.* (US/0886-4268) [12888240] **5355**

PRECIOUS METALS (BROOKLYN, N.Y.) (US/0730-1901) [07964088] **4015**

PRECIOUS METALS BULLETIN (SA) **4015**

PRECIOUS METALS DIGEST (US/0740-4069) [09935525] **911**

PRECIOUS METALS MONTHLY REVIEW (US/0735-4770) [08948171] **4015**

PRECIOUS METALS (TORONTO, ONT.) (CN/8756-0917) [11501220] **4015**

PRECIOUSTONE NEWSLETTER *See* GEMSTONE PRICE REPORT **2914**

PRECIPITATION ON THE MUSKINGUM RIVER WATERSHED, OHIO, BY 30 MINUTE PERIODS (US) [05270582] 1417, **1433**

PRECIS ANALYTIQUE DES TRAVAUX DE L'ACADEMIE DES SCIENCES, BELLES-LETTRES ET ARTS DE ROUEN (FR/1154-7707) [01636550] 328, **2852**

PRECIS DE CONCORDANCE DE LA CONVENTION COLLECTIVE C.S.D.-F.A.S. ... EN VIGUEUR DANS LES CENTRES D'ACCEUIL MEMBRES DE L'ASSOCIATION DES CENTRES D'ACCEUIL DU QUEBEC (CN/1186-1371) [24280001] **1702**

PRECIS DE CONCORDANCE DE LA CONVENTION COLLECTIVE F.P.S.S.S.(C.E.Q.) ... EN VIGUEUR DANS LES CENTRES D'ACCUEIL MEMBRES DE L'ASSOCIATION DES CENTRES D'ACCEUIL DU QUEBEC (CN/1186-1355) [24280002] **1702**

PRECIS DE CONCORDANCE DE LA CONVENTION COLLECTIVE U.Q.I.I. ... EN VIGUEUR DANS LES CENTRES D'ACCUEIL MEMBRES DE L'ASSOCIATION DES CENTRES D'ACCEUIL DU QUEBEC (CN/1186-1363) [24280003] **803**

PRECIS (DENVILLE, N.J.) (US/0739-4489) [06681679] **2075**

PRECIS (NEW YORK, N.Y.) *CEASED.* (US/0887-8781) [07386733] **306**

PRECISELY (US/0163-4631) [04389188] **3425**

PRECISION ENGINEERING (US/0141-6359) [05626686] **2125**

PRECISION MACHINERY. INCORPORATING LIFE SUPPORT TECHNOLOGY (US/1045-4160) [19257699] **3696**

PRECISION SHOOTING (US/0048-5144) [06970376] **4877**

PRECISION TOOLMAKER (UK/0264-4703) [13902011] **2125**

PRECO MEDIO DE GENEROS ALIMENTICIOS DE SALVADOR (BL) [01795684] **1621**

PRECOS MINIMOS: NORTE-NORDESTE *See* PRECOS MINIMOS: REGIOES CENTRO-OESTE, SUDESTE E SUL **121**

PRECOS MINIMOS: REGIOES CENTRO-OESTE, SUDESTE E SUL (BL) [16315147] **121**

PRECOS RECEBIDOS PELOS AGRICULTORES (BL) [01790912] **121**

PREDI-BRIEFS (CLEVELAND) (US/0551-9276) [04256431] **1621**

PREDI-BRIEFS : FERTILIZER & AG CHEMICALS *CEASED.* (US) [03105021] **121**

PREDI-BRIEFS : ORGANIC CHEMICALS *CEASED.* (US) [03095431] **1046**

PREDI-BRIEFS : TEXTILES & FIBERS *CEASED.* (US) [03104986] **5355**

PREDICAMENT, THE (US/0199-0705) [05575413] **4913**

PREDICASTS' BASEBOOK (US/0738-9906) [01050860] **1513**

PREDICASTS F & S INDEX EUROPE (US/0270-4536) [06442041] **704**

PREDICASTS F & S INDEX EUROPE ANNUAL (US/0277-9684) [06843567] **1579**

PREDICASTS F & S INDEX INTERNATIONAL (US/0270-4528) [06522648] 704, **732**

PREDICASTS F & S INDEX OF CORPORATE CHANGE (US/0744-2785) [08167045] **1621**

PREDICASTS F & S INDEX UNITED STATES (US/0270-4544) [06441873] **704**

PREDICASTS F & S INDEX UNITED STATES (ANNUAL EDITION) *See* F&S INDEX UNITED STATES ANNUAL **675**

PREDICASTS F&S INDEX. INTERNATIONAL ANNUAL (US/0277-9692) [06719293] **1621**

PREDICASTS F&S INDEX. UNITED STATES ANNUAL EDITION (US/0277-9676) [06551505] **422**

PREDICASTS FORECASTS (US/0278-0135) [06661104] 1579, **1537**

PREDICASTS, INC *See* SOURCE DIRECTORY OF PREDICASTS, INC, THE **425**

PREDICASTS, INC. WORLD PRODUCT CASTS *See* WORLDCASTS. PRODUCT **1632**

PREDICASTS, INC. WORLD REGIONAL CASTS *See* WORLDCASTS. REGIONAL **1632**

PREDICTIONS & PRESCRIPTIONS *CEASED.* (US/1062-5178) [25645526] **882**

PREDICTIONS / JOJO SAVARD (CN/0846-068X) [24256431] **390**

PREDNASKY ... LETHNEHO SEMINARA SLOVENSKEHO JAZYKA A KULTURY (XO) [19906887] **3311**

PREDSKOLSKA VYCHOVA (XO) [06637388] **1805**

PREFABBRICAZIONE, LA *CEASED.* (IT/0032-7255) [06601529] **624**

PREFACE (SASKATOON. 1990) (CN/1184-1125) [23226778] **3241**

PREFERRED SHARE QUARTERLY (CN/1184-7409) [24266829] **911**

PREFERRED SHARES & WARRANTS (CN/0829-383X) [13369117] **911**

●PREFERRED STOCK (DENVER, COLO.) (US/1065-7762) [26733928] **2543**

PREFERRED STOCK HANDBOOK (US/0735-4819) [08921680] **911**

PREFERRED TRAVELLER (US/0893-4746) [15537727] **5489**

PREGLED NA MAGISTERSKI TRUDOVI ODBRANETI NA UNIVERZITETITE VO SR MAKEDONIJA VO PERIODOT ... / NARODNA I UNIVERAITETSKA BIBLIOTEKA KLIMENT OHRIDSKI--SKOPJE, REFERALEN CENTAR (YU/0352-9444) [19011494] **1842**

PREGLED PREDAVANJA (BN) [04796384] **1842**

PREGLED SUDSKE PRAKSE (CI) [01787010] **3030**

PREGON DE LA TFP (AG) [09103977] **4987**

PREGONERO (WASHINGTON, D.C.), EL (US/8750-9326) [11929587] **5647**

●PREHISTOIRE ANTHROPOLOGIE MEDITERRANEENNES (FR/1167-492X) [27261687] **243**

PREHISTOIRE ARIEGEOISE : BULLETIN DE LA SOCIETE PREHISTORIQUE DE L'ARIEGE (FR/0245-9523) [08569535] **1409**

PREHISTORIC SOCIETY (LONDON, ENGLAND) *See* PROCEEDINGS OF THE PREHISTORIC SOCIETY **243**

PREHL'AD LESNICKEJ, DREVARSKEJ, CELULOZOVEJ A PAPIERENSKEJ LITERATURY (XO/0032-7328) [04551596] **4237**

PREHLED LESNICKE A MYSLIVECKE LITERATURY (XR) [06635593] **2390**

PREHOSPITAL AND DISASTER MEDICINE (US/1049-023X) [20761085] 5301, **3629**

PREHOSPITAL CARE REPORTS *CEASED.* (US/1063-3332) [25980855] **3725**

PREHRAMBENO-TEHNOLOSKA I BIOTEHNOLOSKA REVIJA (YU/0352-9193) [15026048] 3696, **2353**

PREISE, LOEHNE, WIRTSCHAFTSRECHNUNGEN (GW) [17257322] 1513, **1537**

PREISE. REIHE 3, PREISINDEX FUER DEN WARENEINGANG DES PRODUZIERENDEN GEWERBES / STATISTISCHES BUNDESAMT (GW) [24508385] **1594**

PREISE. REIHE 8 : PREISE UND PREISINDIZES FUER DIE EIN UND AUSFUHR (GW) [05304330] **1594**

PREISE. REISE 6 : INDEX DER GROSSHANDELSVERKAUFSPREISE (GW) [04970630] **1594**

PREISTORIA ALPINA (IT) [04388911] **278**

PRELAW ADVISER'S KIT (US/0747-878X) [08253925] **3030**

PRELIMINARY DETERMINATION OF EPICENTERS (WEEKLY) (US) [09986424] **4674**

PRELIMINARY REPORT AND FORECAST OF SOLAR GEOPHYSICAL DATA (US) [06452679] **1409**

PRELIMINARY REPORT ON U.S. PRODUCTION OF SYNTHETIC ORGANIC CHEMICALS / UNITED STATES INTERNATIONAL TRADE COMMISSION (US) [02641504] **1028**

PRELIMINARY STATEMENT OF CANADIAN INTERNATIONAL TRADE (CN/0828-1998) [19328113] **849**

PRELO : REVISTA DA IMPRENSA NACIONAL/CASA DA MOEDA *SUSPENDED.* (PO/0871-0430) [12391040] **3425**

PRELUDE (CALGARY) (CN/0381-890X) [02604139] **4147**

PRELUDIUM (NE) [06644012] **4147**

PREMI INTERNACIONAL DIBUIX JOAN MIRO. CATALEG (SP) [01783820] **362**

PREMI INTERNACIONAL DIBUIX JOAN MIRO. SECRETARIAT *See* PREMI INTERNACIONAL DIBUIX JOAN MIRO. CATALEG **362**

PREMIER HOG PRODUCER (US/8750-5673) [11521354] **219**

PREMIER HOTELS OF GREAT BRITAIN (UK) [12753212] **2809**

PREMIERA KATOWICE (PL/0867-2288) [08672288] **4076**

PREMIERE, EN (CN/0701-077X) [03406409] **4076**

PREMIERE (MISSISSAUGA) (CN/0831-9782) [15299255] **4076**

PREMIERE (NEW YORK, N.Y. 1987) (US/0894-9263) [16388050] **4076**

PREMIERE PARIS (FR/0399-3698) [03993698] **4853**

PREMIERS PRIX ... DES CONCOURS MEMBRES DE LA FEDERATION, LES (SZ) [25847764] **4147**

PREMIOS CLARIN Y LARRA / CIENCIAS DE LA INFORMACION (SP) [20940507] **3425**

PREMISES & FACILITIES MANAGEMENT (UK/0965-4739) [09654739] **4214**

PREMISES LIABILITY REPORT (US/1055-730X) [23283443] **3030**

PREMIUM BUYERS' GUIDE *See* INCENTIVE (NEW YORK) **955**

PREMIUM CHANNELS TV BLUEPRINT (US/1040-5534) [18449778] **1136**

PREMIUM, INCENTIVE, & TRAVEL BUYERS (US) [13640261] **732**

PREMIUM INCENTIVE BUSINESS (US) [01780301] **704**

PREMONITIONS ARRETON (UK/0968-6185) [09686185] **3425**

PRENATAL DIAGNOSIS (UK/0197-3851) [06017178] **3767**

PRENONS NOTRE MUSIQUE EN MAIN! (CN/0228-0868) [06958858] **4147**

PRENSA ECONOMICA (AG) [03792920] **1513**

PRENSA, LA (AG) [02953588] **5777**

PRENSA LITERARIA, LA (NQ) [06164774] 3425, **328**

PRENSA MEDICA ARGENTINA (AG/0032-745X) [01762788] **3629**

PRENSA (ORLANDO, FLA.), LA (US/0888-756X) [13726830] **5650**

PRENSA (SAN ANTONIO, TEX. : WEEKLY) (US) [11362458] **5753**

PRENSA SAN DIEGO, LA (US/0738-9183) [09701921] **2271**

PRENTICE-HALL 1040 HANDBOOK *CEASED.* (US/0191-233X) [04752238] **4741**

PRENTICE-HALL ACCOUNTING FACULTY DIRECTORY (US/0277-6618) [06674515] **750**

PRENTICE HALL CREATIVE SECRETARY'S LETTER, THE (US/1059-633X) [18728553] **4208**

PRENTICE-HALL, INC *See* PRENTICE-HALL 1040 HANDBOOK **4741**

PRENTICE-HALL, INC *See* SUBCHAPTER S ELECTION FOR "SMALL BUSINESS CORPORATIONS.", THE **714**

PRENTICE-HALL, INC *See* STATE AND LOCAL TAXES; REPORT BULLETIN **4749**

PRENTICE-HALL, INC. FEDERAL CONTROL OF BANKING *See* CONTROL OF BANKING **3086**

PRENTICE-HALL, INCORPORATED *See* SALES TAXES **751**

PRENTICE-HALL, INCORPORATED *See* TAX IDEAS **4753**

PRENTICE HALL'S FEDERAL TAXATION. COMPREHENSIVE VOLUME (US/1050-0170) [21378306] **4741**

PRENTICE HALL'S FEDERAL TAXATION. COMPREHENSIVE VOLUME (COMPLIMENTARY INSTRUCTOR'S COPY) (US/1050-0162) [21377758] **4741**

PRENTICE HALL'S FEDERAL TAXATION. CORPORATIONS, PARTNERSHIPS, ESTATES, AND TRUSTS (US/0898-2635) [17765740] **4741**

PRENTICE HALL'S FEDERAL TAXATION. CORPORATIONS, PARTNERSHIPS, ESTATES, AND TRUSTS (ANNOTATED INSTRUCTOR'S ED.) (US/1049-8435) [21321948] **4741**

PRENTICE HALL'S FEDERAL TAXATION. INDIVIDUALS (US/0898-2627) [17765203] **4741**

PRENTICE HALL'S FEDERAL TAXATION. INDIVIDUALS (ANNOTATED INSTRUCTOR'S ED.) (US/1049-8044) [21313891] **4741**

PRENTISS HEADLIGHT, THE (US/0742-8316) [10448969] **5701**

PREODOLENIE (RU) [27139492] **4392**

PREP POWER POLL (US) **4913**

PREP SCHOOL (UK/0963-8601) [I09638601] **1774**

PREPAID HEALTHCARE ASSEMBLY DIRECTORY : ... REPORT BASED ON ... DATA / MEDICAL GROUP MANAGEMENT ASSOCIATION (US/1061-0219) [25157350] **3791**

PREPARATION OF ANNUAL DISCLOSURE DOCUMENTS (US/0276-6094) [06064638] **3030**

PREPARATION OF ANNUAL DOCUMENTS DISCLOSURE *See* PREPARATION OF ANNUAL DISCLOSURE DOCUMENTS **3030**

PREPARATIVE BIOCHEMISTRY (US/0032-7484) [01589130] **492**

PREPARATIVE CHROMATOGRAPHY (US/0890-9075) [14449944] **989**

PREPARATIVE INORGANIC REACTIONS (US/0079-4988) [01639195] **1037**

PREPARED FOODS (US/0747-2536) [10665942] **2353**

PREPARING A TOXIC TORT CASE FOR TRIAL (US/1062-1687) [23666824] **3030**

PREPARING FOR THE FUTURE : ESA'S TECHNOLOGY PROGRAMME QUARTERLY (NE/1018-8657) [24780986] **31**

PREPARING PERSONAL INJURY CASES FOR TRIAL (US/0882-9748) [09059308] **3030**

PREPARING YOUR CORPORATE TAX RETURNS (CN/0713-8946) [09113442] **4741**

PREPARING YOUR INCOME TAX RETURNS : CANADA AND PROVINCES (CN/0588-6589) [02248196] **4741**

PREPARONS L'AVENIR *CEASED.* (FR/0556-137X) [I0556137X] **5139**

PREPODAVANIE INOSTRANNYKH IAZYKOV (RU) [05123520] 1902, **3311**

PREPODAVANIE ISTORII V SHKOLE (RU/0132-0696) [01762805] 1902, **2626**

PREPRESS BULLETIN, THE (US/8750-2224) [11135827] 381, **5034**

PREPRESS COMPUTING MAGAZINE (NE/0928-6500) [I09286500] **1263**

PREPRESS MAGAZINE *See* PREPRESS COMPUTING MAGAZINE **1263**

PREPRINT / AKADEMIIA NAUK SSSR, INSTITUT OBSHCHEI FIZIKI (RU) [20619121] **4417**

PREPRINT EXTENDED ABSTRACT - AMERICAN CHEMICAL SOCIETY. DIVISION OF ENVIRONMENTAL CHEMISTRY (US/0740-0667) [09859877] **989**

PREPRINT (FIZICHESKII INSTITUT IMENI P.N. LEBEDEVA) (RU) [20520182] **4417**

PREPRINT FROM THE BUREAU OF MINES MINERALS YEARBOOK (US) [02704715] 1443, **2148**

PREPRINT (INSTITUT ANALITICHESKOGO PRIBOROSTROENIIA (AKADEMIIA NAUK SSSR) (RU) [20511320] **5139**

PREPRINT (INSTITUT FIZIKI METALLOV (AKADEMIIA NAUK SSSR) (RU) [20900421] **4417**

PREPRINT (INSTITUT GEOLOGII I GEOFIZIKI (AKADEMIIA NAUK SSSR)) (RU) [20520220] 1409, **1391**

PREPRINT (MURMANSKII MORSKOI. BIOLOGICHESKII INSTITUT) (RU) [20900422] **469**

PREPRINT SERIES - DESERT RESEARCH INSTITUTE (US/0548-3662) [01415039] **1433**

PREPRINT SERIES OF THE DEPARTMENT OF MATHEMATICS / UNIVERZA V LJUBLJANI, INSTITUT ZA MATEMATIKO, FIZIKO IN MEHANIKO, OFFELEK ZA MATEMATIKO (XV) [08521235] **3527**

PREPRINTS A / TECHNICAL SECTION, CANADIAN PULP AND PAPER ASSOCIATION (CN/0822-5206) [10335031] **4237**

PREPRINTS - AMERICAN CHEMICAL SOCIETY. DIVISION OF PETROLEUM CHEMISTRY (US/0569-3799) [01846159] 4275, **1028**

PREPRINTS B / TECHNICAL SECTION, CANADIAN PULP AND PAPER ASSOCIATION (CN/0822-5214) [10335010] **4237**

PREPRINTS / CONFERENCE ON SEVERE LOCAL STORMS (US/0190-9193) [04408182] **1433**

PREPRINTS IN PARTICLES AND FIELDS *CEASED.* (US) [06225469] **5139**

PREPRINTS OF PAPERS OF THE SAE TRANSACTIONS (US) [06366603] **1991**

PREPRINTS OF PAPERS PRESENTED - AMERICAN CHEMICAL SOCIETY. DIVISION OF FUEL CHEMISTRY (US/0569-3772) [06342167] 4275, **989**

PREPRINTS OF PAPERS PRESENTED AT THE AES CONVENTIONS (US) [09942469] **5318**

PREPRINTS OF THE SOCIETY OF MINING ENGINEERS OF THE AIME ANNUAL MEETING (US) **2148**

PREREFUNDED BOND SERVICE (US/0737-9595) [09485563] **803**

PRESBYTERIAN CHURCH IN AMERICA *See* PCA MESSENGER, THE **4986**

PRESBYTERIAN CHURCH IN CANADA. GENERAL ASSEMBLY *See* ACTS AND PROCEEDINGS OF THE GENERAL ASSEMBLY OF THE PRESBYTERIAN CHURCH IN CANADA **5054**

PRESBYTERIAN CHURCH OF NEW ZEALAND. GENERAL ASSEMBLY *See* YEAR BOOK AND PROCEEDINGS OF THE GENERAL ASSEMBLY - PRESBYTERIAN CHURCH OF NEW ZEALAND **5069**

PRESBYTERIAN HERALD : THE RECORD OF THE PRESBYTERIAN CHURCH IN IRELAND, THE (IE/0032-7530) [05785759] **5066**

PRESBYTERIAN HISTORY (CN/0827-9713) [13207651] **4987**

PRESBYTERIAN KEY, THE (US/0361-2724) [01762812] **5066**

PRESBYTERIAN LAYMAN, THE (US/0555-0572) [01908220] **5066**

PRESBYTERIAN OUTLOOK (RICHMOND, VA.) (US/0032-7565) [01776660] **5066**

PRESBYTERIAN RECORD (MONTREAL) (CN/0032-7573) [02600733] **5066**

PRESBYTERIAN SURVEY (US/0032-759X) [02740097] **5066**

PRESBYTERION (US/0193-6212) [02254159] **5066**

●PRESCHOOL CHILDREN'S CHURCH TEACHER GUIDE (US/1059-339X) [24568309] **4987**

PRESCHOOL / KINDERGARTEN PAPERS *CEASED.* (US) **1805**

PRESCHOOL PERSPECTIVES *CEASED.* (US/0748-4054) [10937990] **1805**

●PRESCHOOL TEACHER GUIDE (US/1072-1460) [28872412] **4987**

PRESCHOOLERS AT CHURCH AND HOME (US/1048-5260) [20967734] **4987**

PRESCOLAIRE (CN/0712-9963) [08818719] **1805**

PRESCOTT — Alphabetical Title Index

PRESCOTT EVENING COURIER (US) [15262241] **5630**

PRESCOTT JOURNAL (PRESCOTT, WIS. : 1930) (US) [13034602] **5770**

PRESCOTT TRIBUNE *See* PRESCOTT JOURNAL (PRESCOTT, WIS. : 1930) **5770**

PRESCOTT'S WEEKLY (US/0194-9748) [05166368] **5630**

PRESCRIBER (UK/0959-6682) **3629**

PRESCRIBERS' JOURNAL (UK/0032-7611) [11853714] **4325**

PRESCRIBING REFERENCE FOR OBSTETRICIANS & GYNECOLOGISTS (US/1051-4171) [21956912] **3767**

PRESCRIPTION DRUG NEWS (US/0882-8628) [12009323] **4325**

PRESCRIPTION DRUGS (US/8756-8950) [06159541] **4325**

PRESCRIPTION PHARMACEUTICALS AND BIOTECHNOLOGY (US/1068-5324) 803, **4325**

PRESCRIPTION PRODUCTS GUIDE (AT/0818-4445) [16564719] **4325**

PRESCRIPTIONS (SAINTE-FOY, QUEBEC) *See* CORONER (SAINTE-FOY) **4772**

PRESENCA FILOSOFICA (BL) [01799494] **4357**

PRESENCE AFRICAINE (PARIS, FRANCE : 1967) *SUSPENDED.* (FR/0032-7638) [04140088] **2271**

● PRESENCE (CAMBRIDGE, MASS.) (US/1054-7460) [22964204] 1221, **1216**

PRESENCE DE L'ENSEIGNEMENT AGRICOLE PRIVE (FR/0339-0055) [I03390055] 1774, **121**

PRESENCE FRANCOPHONE (CN/0048-5195) [02106502] **3425**

● PRESENCE (MONTREAL. 1992) (CN/1188-5580) [26714681] **4987**

PRESENCIA (ES) [18578152] **4674**

PRESENCIA (BO) [02266429] **5779**

PRESENCIA ECUMENICA : BOLETIN INFORMATIVO DE ACCION ECUMENICA (VE) [17276994] **4987**

PRESENT BAMBERG (GW/0032-7697) [I00327697] 362, 2585, **375**

PRESENT (MATANE) (CN/0712-2640) [08867623] **5793**

PRESENT PARIS (FR/0750-3253) [I07503253] **2627**

PRESENT TRUTH AND HERALD OF CHRIST'S EPIPHANY, THE (US/0032-7700) [04109090] **4987**

PRESENT TRUTH OF THE APOKALYPSIS, THE (US/0745-192X) [08924375] **4987**

PRESENTATION FONCTIONNELLE DU BUDGET DE L'ETAT (FR) [01798203] **4741**

PRESENTATION PRODUCTS *See* PRESENTATIONS **946**

PRESENTATION PRODUCTS MAGAZINE (US/1041-9780) [18894433] **704**

PRESENTATION - SOCIETE ROYALE DU CANADA (CN/0317-0179) [02247641] **5235**

PRESENTATION TO THE PREMIER AND PROVINCIAL CABINET (CN/0228-2488) [06966015] **1579**

PRESENTATIONS (US) [08741628] **1991**

PRESENTATIONS (US) [28951352] **946**

PRESENTE E LA STORIA, IL (IT/1121-7499) [I11217499] **2626**

PRESENTFUTURES REPORT, THE (US/1055-2405) [23124717] **1621**

● PRESENTING AND COMMISSIONING (US) [25300310] **328**

PRESENTING THE SEASON (US) 4339, **5235**

PRESENZA PASTORALE (IT/0032-7727) [I00327727] **5034**

PRESERVATION BRIEFS (US/0885-7016) [04176720] **2755**

PRESERVATION LAW REPORTER (US/0882-715X) [08312620] 4843, **3030**

PRESERVATION PERSPECTIVE (US) [08741599] **2755**

PRESERVATION PROGRESS (CHARLESTON) (US/0478-1392) [05329781] 2202, **306**

PRESERVATION REPORT (US) [04726671] **2755**

PRESERVATION TECH NOTES (US/0741-9023) [10232538] **306**

PRESIDENCE DE LA REPUBLIQUE (FR/0759-2744) [I07592744] **4674**

PRESIDENT (NEW YORK), THE (US/0552-007X) [03386235] **882**

PRESIDENTE PRUDENTE. FACULDADE DE FILOSOFIA, CIENCIAS E LETRAS. DEPARTAMENTO DE EDUCACAO *See* BOLETIM - PRESIDENTE PRUDENTE. FACULDADE DE FILOSOFIA, CIENCIAS E LETRAS. DEPARTMENTO DE EDUCACAO **1728**

PRESIDENTIAL ADDRESS / CHAMBER OF MINES OF SOUTH AFRICA (SA) [24462955] **2148**

PRESIDENTIAL ADDRESS OF THE AUSTRALIAN ACADEMY OF TECHNOLOGICAL SCIENCES *CEASED.* (AT/0314-9935) [I03149935] **5139**

PRESIDENTIAL STUDIES QUARTERLY (US/0360-4918) [02242880] **4674**

● PRESIDENTS & PRIME MINISTERS (US/1060-5088) [25014925] **4492**

PRESIDENT'S COMMISSION ON WHITE HOUSE FELLOWSHIPS (U.S.) *See* WHITE HOUSE FELLOWSHIPS, THE **4705**

PRESIDENT'S ... ENVIRONMENT AND CONSERVATION CHALLENGE AWARDS, THE (US) [25748821] **2202**

PRESIDENTS : IT ALL STARTED WITH GEORGE (US) **4674**

PRESIDENT'S NATIONAL URBAN POLICY REPORT, THE (US/0163-8602) [04344420] **2831**

PRESIDENTS REPORT - COLONIAL WILLIAMSBURG FOUNDATION, THE (US/0270-3467) [01564126] **5235**

PRESIDENT'S REPORT - FLORIDA. ATLANTIC UNIVERSITY, BOCA RATON (US/0532-9329) [01380516] **1842**

PRESIDENT'S TEAM *SUSPENDED.* (US) **4674**

PRESLIA (XR/0032-7786) [01762820] **525**

PRESQUE ISLE COUNTY ADVANCE (US) **5693**

PRESS ADVERTISER (PONTIAC), THE (US/0192-6519) [05082823] **5693**

PRESS AND ADVERTISERS YEAR BOOK (II) [07063224] **764**

PRESS AND JOURNAL, THE (US) [12877018] **5739**

PRESS AND STANDARD (WALTERBORO, S.C.) (US) [13090281] **5743**

PRESS & SUN-BULLETIN (US/0886-8816) [12636926] **5720**

PRESS AND THE PEOPLE : THE ... ANNUAL REPORT OF THE GENERAL COUNCIL OF THE PRESS, THE *CEASED.* (UK/0435-2459) [02468631] **2923**

PRESS ARGUS-COURIER (US/0885-9086) [12758564] **5632**

PRESS (ATLANTIC CITY, N.J. : 1971) (US) [13786878] **5711**

PRESS COMMUNIQUE (FR) [19781559] **4512**

PRESS COUNCIL *See* PRESS AND THE PEOPLE : THE ... ANNUAL REPORT OF THE GENERAL COUNCIL OF THE PRESS, THE **2923**

PRESS DEMOCRAT (SANTA ROSA, CALIF.) (US/0747-220X) [10635334] **5638**

PRESS-DISPATCH, THE (US) [14234095] **5666**

PRESS (ELMHURST, ILL. : OAK BROOK ED.) (US/1043-3236) [19380216] **5661**

PRESS-ENTERPRISE (BLOOMSBURG, PA.) (US/0746-0724) [09668910] **5739**

PRESS-ENTERPRISE (RIVERSIDE, CALIF.) (US/0746-4258) [10036595] **5638**

PRESS FOR CONVERSION (CN/1183-8892) [24860206] **4054**

PRESS HANDBOOK (US) [04152286] **121**

PRESS INDEPENDENT (CN/1182-9931) [22719668] **2543**

PRESS-INDEX BIDANG ILMU-ILMU SOSIAL DAN KEMANUSIAAN (IO) [07661317] **5803**

PRESS (LITTLETON, COLO.) (US/1052-6587) [22341598] **1086**

PRESS MAGAZINE *See* PRESS (LITTLETON, COLO.) **1086**

PRESS MAGAZINE, THE (US/0744-3161) [08186395] **1086**

PRESS-NEWS, THE (US) [17899803] **5730**

PRESS, RADIO AND TV GUIDE : AUSTRALIA, NEW ZEALAND AND THE PACIFIC ISLANDS (AT) [01643120] 1119, **1125**

PRESS RELEASE - INTERNATIONAL WHEAT COUNCIL (UK) [05285152] **203**

PRESS REPORT, THE *CEASED.* (US/1040-1342) [18332909] **3629**

PRESS-REPUBLICAN (US/1041-4754) [17350193] **5720**

PRESS REVIEW (TORONTO) (CN/0706-9286) [04518982] **2923**

PRESS-SENTINEL, THE (US) [20378829] **5654**

PRESS-STAR (NEW LONDON, WIS. : 1979) (US) [13276925] **5770**

PRESS-TELEGRAM (US) [11172461] **5638**

PRESS, THE (US) [01479078] **5698**

PRESS WOMAN, THE (US/0032-7824) [02254352] 5564, **2923**

PRESSDOK [COMPUTER FILE] (HU) [23132733] **422**

PRESSE (BE/0478-1546) **2923**

PRESSE DER SOWJETUNION, DIE (SZ) [06759168] **2923**

PRESSE, DIE (AU/0032-7832) [05176542] **5778**

PRESSE DU CAMEROUN *See* CAMEROON TRIBUNE **5779**

PRESSE FRANCAISE, DIFFUSION PAR ABONNEMENTS (FR) [19551255] **422**

PRESSE HANDBUCH / VERBAND OSTERREICHISCHER ZEITUNGSHERAUSGEBER UND ZEITUNGSVERLEGER (AU) [12264110] **4567**

PRESSE-INFORMATION / DEUTSCHE VERKEHRSWACHT (GW) [08516121] **2923**

PRESSE-INFORMATIONEN (GW) [01798123] **2703**

PRESSE-LIBRE (CN/0711-2963) [08503286] **2543**

PRESSE MEDICALE (1983), LA (FR/0755-4982) [09262901] **3629**

PRESSE (MONTREAL) (CN) **5793**

PRESSE PAPIERS (IT) **1774**

PRESSE THERMALE ET CLIMATIQUE (FR/0032-7875) [09490069] **1433**

PRESSE UND SPRACHE (GW/0935-8064) [I09358064] **2923**

PRESSENS ARBOG / UDGIVET AF DANSK PRESSEHISTORISK SELSKAB (DK) [01645509] **2923**

PRESSESCHAU OSTWIRTSCHAFT (AU) [06663384] 704, **1639**

PRESSESEMINAR DER BFA : REFERATE / HERAUSGEBER, BUNDESVERSICHERUNGSANSTALT FUER ANGESTELLTE, DEZERNAT FUER PRESSE UND OFFENTLICHKEITSARBEIT (GW) [19496602] **2521**

PRESSTIME (US/0194-3243) [05395189] **4818**

PRESSURE *CEASED.* (US/0274-9556) [06728290] **2094**

PRESSURE (BETHESDA, MD.) (US/0889-0242) [11922752] **3629**

PRESSURIZED WATER REACTORS; BIBLIOGRAPHY (PL) [01790878] **422**

PRESTACAO DE CONTAS (BL) [04953489] **4741**

PRESTACAO DE CONTAS DA GESTACAO DO EXERCICIO DE ... (BL) [09868230] **4741**

PRESTACAO DE CONTAS DO GOVERNO DO ESTADO *See* PRESTACAO DE CONTAS **4741**

PRESTEL DIRECTORY, THE (UK/0266-0288) [10589487] **1162**

PRESTIGE BEAUTE (CN/0704-7908) [03797423] **405**

PRESTO (CN/0318-9325) [02441935] **4913**

PRESTON COUNTY NEWS, THE (US) [13181898] **5764**

PRESTON PIPE REPORT (US) **4016**

PRESUPUESTO - IGLESIA EVANGELICA ESPANOLA (SP) [02242903] **4987**

PRESUPUESTO PRO PROGRAMA - INSTITUTO AUTONOMO ADMINISTRACION DE FERROCARRILES DEL ESTADO, DIVISION DE PRESUPUESTO (VE) [04814141] **5434**

PRESUPUESTO Y GASTO PUBLICO (SP/0210-5977) [17449093] **4741**

PRESUPUESTO Y LA ECONOMIA ESPANOLA, EL (SP) [02242802] **1579**

PRESUPUESTOS PROVINCIALES Y PRESUPUESTO NACIONAL DISTRIBUIDO FOR PROVINCIAS (AG) [01787226] **4741**

PRETEXTE (MONTREAL) (CN/0226-367X) [06512068] **3425**

PRETEXTES (TROIS-RIVIERES) (CN/0711-4966) [08700932] **3425**

PRETEXTS (SA/1015-549X) [23602509] **3350**

PRETIRES, CONFERENCE TECHNOLOGIQUE ESTIVALE (CN/0707-8951) [04879662] **4237**

PRETORIA ORIENTAL SERIES (NE/0555-0912) [02001923] **2662**

PRETRE ET PASTEUR (CN/0383-8307) [05897547] **4987**

PRETRES DIOCESAINS (FR) **5034**

PRETRIAL REPORTER, THE (US/0193-4015) [03686604] **3173**

Alphabetical Title Index

PRIMARY

PREUSSENLAND : MITTEILUNGEN DER HISTORISCHEN KOMMISSION FUR OST- UND WESTPREUSSISCHE LANDESFORSCHUNG (GW/0032-7972) [05038102] **2703**

PREUVES (MONTREAL) (CN/0714-850X) [09086812] **405**

PREVENIR LES RISQUES DU METIER (FR) **2868**

PREVENIR MARSEILLE (FR/0247-2406) [I02472406] **5489**

PREVENIR (MONTREAL) (CN/0315-1557) [02106130] **2521**

PREVENIR (QUEBEC) (CN/0700-5075) [03400077] **2403**

PREVENT (UK/0300-2659) [01784883] **3629**

PREVENT BLINDNESS NEWS (US) [05086373] **4392**

PREVENTIE (NE) **2292**

●PREVENTING INJURY (US/1056-9588) [23904005] **2868**

PREVENTING SCHOOL FAILURE (US/1045-988X) [20306182] **1884**

PREVENTING SEXUAL ABUSE *CEASED.* (US/0886-6694) [12956107] **5301**

PREVENTION AU CANADA, LA (CN/0317-5987) [02441774] **4796**

PREVENTION (EMMAUS) (US/0032-8006) [01641993] **4796**

PREVENTION IN HUMAN SERVICES (US/0270-3114) [06389761] **4810**

PREVENTION NETWORK *CEASED.* (CN/0849-6854) [21345020] **1348**

PREVENTION PIPELINE *See* OSAP PREVENTION PIPELINE / OFFICE FOR SUBSTANCE ABUSE PREVENTION, THE **1347**

PREVENTION PREVIEW (CN/0711-1681) [08854762] **4796**

PREVENTION ROUTIERE INTERNATIONALE : [PUBLICATION TRIMESTRIELLE DE LA PRI], LA (FR) [09529656] **5442**

PREVENTION SANTE (FR/0247-6800) [I02476800] **4796**

PREVENTION UPDATE NEWSLETTER (US/0882-5513) [11885054] **5301**

PREVENTION'S LOSE WEIGHT GUIDEBOOK (US/1060-9385) [25118626] **2600**

PREVENTION'S MEDICAL HEALING YEARBOOK / WRITTEN BY THE STAFF OF RODALE PRESS (US) [23132724] **2600**

●PREVENTION'S QUICK AND HEALTHY LOW-FAT COOKING (US/1064-7503) [26388048] **2792, 2601, 2353**

PREVENTIQUE (FR/0766-5687) [12546432] **2868**

PREVENTIVE LAW REPORTER (US/0734-1660) [08783707] **3030**

PREVENTIVE MEDICINE (1972) (US/0091-7435) [01605081] **4796, 3629**

PREVENTIVE MEDICINE NEWSLETTER *See* ACPM NEWS **3544**

PREVENTIVE PEDIATRICS *CEASED.* (UK) [18713797] **3910**

PREVENTIVE VETERINARY MEDICINE (NE/0167-5877) [08756139] **5518**

PREVENZIONE & ASSISTENZA DENTALE (IT) [13406466] **1333**

PREVENZIONE OGGI (IT/1120-2971) [I11202971] **3629**

PREVIDENCIA, A (BL) [04154899] **2890**

PREVIDENCIA SOCIAL, URBANA E RURAL (BL) [09578826] **5301**

PREVIEW *CEASED.* (US/0899-9821) [18282825] **3241**

PREVIEW (US/0892-2896) [09444343] **362**

PREVIEW - CANADIAN CONSTRUCTION ASSOCIATION (CN/1186-9100) [25313796] **624**

PREVIEW (NORTHBROOK, ILL.) *CEASED.* (US/0738-0690) [09512985] **704**

PREVIEW OF THE INSTITUTO NACIONAL DE HIDROCARBUROS ANNUAL REPORT FOR ... (SP) [12166140] 2016, **4674**

PREVIEW OF UNITED STATES SUPREME COURT CASES (US/0363-0048) [01780302] **3031**

PREVIEW (RICHARDSON, TEX.) (US/0892-6468) [15304933] **387**

PREVIEW (WASHINGTON) (US/0194-3847) [05368458] **4076**

PREVIEWS GUIDE TO THE WORLD'S FINE REAL ESTATE *CEASED.* (US) [04606896] **4843**

PREVIEWS INCORPORATED *See* PREVIEWS GUIDE TO THE WORLD'S FINE REAL ESTATE **4843**

PREVIEWS OF HEAT AND MASS TRANSFER (US/0094-9477) [01795529] **4432**

PREVISIONE DEI BILANCI BANCARI (IT) **803**

PREVISIONI DELL ECONOMIA ITALIANA (IT) **1513**

PREVISIONS BUDGETAIRES DES MUNICIPALITES (CN) [20957281] **4741**

PREVISIONS BUDGETAIRES POUR L'EXERCICE (CG) [01787966] **1842**

PREVISOES IONOSFERICAS MUF (BL) [05814306] **1433**

PREVOYANCE (CN/0710-0671) [08690456] 5423, **4796**

PREVOYANCE : PUBLICATION DE L'OFFICE D'ASSURANCE ACCIDENTS DU TRAVAIL, MALADIE, ET MATERNITE (HT) [08334299] **2868**

PREVUE (READING, PA.) (US/1045-1234) [18076799] **1119**

PREZZARIO MATERIALI OPERE EDILI PROVINCIA GENOVA (IT) **2028**

PREZZI AGRICOLI (IT) **121**

PREZZI INFORMATIVI DELL EDILIZIA MATERIALI ED OPERE COMPIUTE : IMPIANTI TECNICI (IT) **624**

PREZZI INFORMATIVI DELL EDILIZIA MATERIALI ED OPERE COMPIUTE : NUOVE COSTRUZIONI (IT) **624**

PREZZI INFORMATIVI DELL EDILIZIA MATERIALI ED OPERE COMPIUTE : OPERE DI URBANIZ E INFRASTRUTTURE (IT) **2028**

PREZZI INFORMATIVI DELL EDILIZIA MATERIALI ED OPERE COMPIUTE : RECUPERO RISTRUT E MAUTEZIONE (IT) **2028**

PREZZI INFORMATIVI DELLE OPERE EDILI IN MILANO (IT) **2028**

PREZZI INFORMATIVI MATERIALI DA COSTRUZIONE E OPERE EDILI : REGGIO EMILIA (IT) **2028**

PREZZI INFORMATIVI OPERE EDILI DI MANUTENZIONE (IT) **2029**

PREZZI INFORMATIVI OPERE EDILI DI VICENZA (IT) **2029**

PREZZIARIO DELLE OPERE EDILI DI BRESCIA E PROVINCIA (IT) **2029**

PREZZIARIO OPERE EDILI PROVINCIA VERONA (IT) **624**

PRI REPORT (US) [12592815] **946**

PRI REVIEW. INTERNATIONAL ROAD SAFETY (LU) 5442, **4796**

PRIAMURE MOE (RU) [01791544] **3425**

PRIBOROSTROENIE (MINSK) (BW/0203-2805) [06429163] **3486**

PRIBORY I SISTEMY UPRAVLENIJA (RU/0032-8154) [09858616] **1248**

PRIBORY I TEHNIKA EKSPERIMENTA (RU/0032-8162) [01980393] **5139**

PRICE AND ORDER FORM FOR SCIENCE INSTRUCTIONAL MATERIALS *See* PRICE LIST AND ORDER FORM FOR SCIENCE INSTRUCTIONAL MATERIALS **1868**

PRICE FAMILY OF AMERICA *See* PRICES OF AMERICA, THE **2468**

PRICE GUIDE TO ANTIQUE AND CLASSIC CAMERAS (US) [12849349] **4375**

PRICE INDEX NUMBERS FOR CURRENT COST ACCOUNTING (UK) [02926398] **1594**

PRICE INDEX OF OPERATING COSTS FOR RENT STABILIZED APARTMENT HOUSES IN NEW YORK CITY (US/0362-9724) [02382086] **1702**

PRICE LIST AND ORDER FORM FOR ENGLISH INSTRUCTIONAL MATERIALS (US) [20001626] 3311, **1902**

PRICE LIST AND ORDER FORM FOR SCIENCE INSTRUCTIONAL MATERIALS (US) [22636553] **1868**

PRICE LIST / BARWAL DAHLA FARM (US) [12047983] **2428**

PRICE LIST / ENVIRONMENTAL SEED PRODUCERS, INC (US) [12219803] **2428**

PRICE MOMENTUM CHARTS AND REPORT / QUANTITATIVE ANALYSIS SERVICE (US/0748-9102) [11009206] **911**

PRICE TRENDS (US/0148-3765) [03288737] **2593**

PRICE, WATERHOUSE AND COMPANY *See* SURVEY OF ACCOUNTING AND REPORTING PRACTICES OF REAL ESTATE DEVELOPERS, A **4847**

PRICE WATERHOUSE INVESTOR'S TAX ADVISER (POCKET BOOKS), THE (US/1056-7690) [22858480] **4741**

PRICED CATALOGUE OF STAMPS OF FOREIGN COUNTRIES (US) [08210386] **2786**

PRICES AND EARNINGS AROUND THE GLOBE (SZ) [06701373] **1579**

PRICES OF AGRICULTURAL PRODUCTS AND SELECTED INPUTS IN EUROPE AND NORTH AMERICA (US) [02243927] 1639, **121**

PRICES OF AMERICA, THE (US/0740-2805) [08597323] **2468**

PRICES RECEIVED BY FARMERS (PH) [02243101] **121**

PRICES RECEIVED BY FARMERS. MINNESOTA-WISCONSIN MANUFACTURING GRADE MILK PRICE SERIES AND FINAL TWO-STATE ESTIMATES FOR . *See* PRICES RECEIVED. MINNESOTA-WISCONSIN MANUFACTURING GRADE MILK /UNITED STATES DEPARTMENT OF AGRICULTURE, STATISTICAL REPORTING SERVICE, CROP REPORTING BOARD **121**

PRICES RECEIVED. MINNESOTA-WISCONSIN MANUFACTURING GRADE MILK /UNITED STATES DEPARTMENT OF AGRICULTURE, STATISTICAL REPORTING SERVICE, CROP REPORTING BOARD (US) [13660613] 2353, **121**

PRICING ADVISOR, THE (US/0748-4755) [10959088] 704, **1513**

PRICING STRATEGY (US/0889-9894) [17724331] **803**

PRICING STRATEGY AND PRACTICE (UK) 935, **951**

PRIDE INSTITUTE JOURNAL OF LONG TERM HOME HEALTH CARE (US/0743-5088) [10218735] **4796**

PRIER (FR) **4987**

PRIEST RIVER TIMES (US/0740-3348) [09935282] **5657**

PRIEST, THE (US/0032-8200) [01762840] **5034**

PRIESTHOOD AND BROTHERHOOD (US/0161-0090) [03798432] **4987**

PRIESTS & PEOPLE (UK/0952-6390) [16137506] **5034**

PRIF REPORTS (GW) [19876669] **4532**

PRIF REPORTS IN ENGLISH *See* PRIF REPORTS **4532**

PRIHODKI IN ODHODKI ORGANIZACIJ ZDRUZENEGA DELA NEPROIZVODNIH DEJAVNOSTI (XV) [10706081] **1621**

PRIKLADNAA MATEMATIKA (RU/0134-6350) [I01346350] **3527**

PRIKLADNAIA GEOFIZIKA (RU/0371-3970) [02306359] **1443**

PRIKLADNAIA IADERNAIA SPEKTROSKOPIIA (RU/0370-2715) [10866957] **4440**

PRIKLADNAIA INFORMATIKA (RU) [08256148] **1261**

PRIKLADNAIA MATEMATIKA I MEKHANIKA (RU) [04536929] **3527**

PRIKLADNAIA MEKHANIKA (RU) [02520696] **2125**

PRIKLADNAJA BIOHIMIJA I MIKROBIOLOGIJA (RU/0555-1099) [03333031] 568, **492**

PRIKLADNAJA MATEMATIKA I MEHANIKA (RU/0032-8235) [01762842] 3527, **2125**

PRIKLADNAJA MEHANIKA (KIEV) (UN/0032-8243) [01762843] **2125**

PRIKLADNYE PROBLEMY PROCHNOSTI I PLASTICHNOSTI (RU) [05663321] **2107**

PRILOZI I GRAA (CI/0449-5527) [02219349] **3311**

PRILOZI PROUCAVANJU JEZIKA (YU/0555-1137) [02790337] **3311**

PRILOZI ZA KNJIZEVNOST, JEZIK, ISTORIJU I FOLKLOR (YU/0350-6673) [05690863] **3311**

PRILOZI ZA ORIJENTALNU FILOLOGIJU (BN/0555-1153) [04994036] **1079**

PRIMA BALLERINA *CEASED.* (US/1046-6460) [20477721] **1314**

PRIMA COMUNICAZIONE (IT/0390-3311) [I03903311] **1119**

PRIMAL INSTITUTE *See* PRIMAL INSTITUTE NEWSLETTER, THE **4608**

PRIMAL INSTITUTE NEWSLETTER, THE (US/0164-5056) [04579908] **4608**

PRIMARILY NURSING (US/0739-4446) [09736256] **3867**

PRIMARY AND GENERAL ELECTION RETURNS - LOUISIANA (US) [07062462] **4674**

PRIMARY CARDIOLOGY (US/0363-5104) [02471352] **3709**

PRIMARY CARE (US/0095-4543) [01784481] **3738**

PRIMARY CARE & CANCER (US/0743-8176) [10686356] 3738, **3822**

PRIMARY CARE CASE MANAGEMENT NEWSLETTER (US/0887-2414) [11629365] **3738**

PRIMARY CARE EMERGENCY DECISIONS *CEASED.* (US/8756-5390) [11589307] **3738**

PRIMARY CARE FOCUS (US/0732-1260) [08049616] **3738**

●PRIMARY CARE LETTER (US) [29630914] **3629**

PRIMARY CARE MANAGEMENT (UK/0969-4978) [29369241] **3739**

PRIMARY — Alphabetical Title Index

- PRIMARY CARE MEDICINE DRUG ALERTS (US/1061-0359) [25161937] **4325**
- PRIMARY CARE NEWSLETTER (US/1071-2496) [28597223] **3629, 5301**
- PRIMARY CARE PSYCHIATRY (UK/1355-2570) **3932**

PRIMARY CARE REPORTS *CEASED*. (US/1040-2497) [18279139] **3629**

- PRIMARY CARE UPDATE FOR OB/GYNS (US/1068-607X) [27720256] **3767**
- PRIMARY CHILDREN'S CHURCH TEACHER GUIDE (US/1059-3403) [24568337] **4987**

PRIMARY COLOR 'N' DO STORIES *See* PRIMARY KID-CRAFTS **1068**

PRIMARY COPPER INDUSTRY OF ARIZONA IN ... / ARIZONA DEPT. OF MINERAL RESOURCES, THE (US) [08039360] **2148**

PRIMARY DIABETOLOGY (US/0895-0660) [16438569] **3732**

PRIMARY EDUCATION AUSTRALIA *CEASED*. (AT/0048-5284) **1805**

PRIMARY FOREST INDUSTRY OF WEST VIRGINIA, THE (US/0160-2284) [03632865] **2391**

PRIMARY GEOGRAPHER (UK/0956-277X) [10956277X] **2573**

PRIMARY HEALTH CARE MANAGEMENT (UK/0960-250X) [I0960250X] **3739**

PRIMARY IRON AND STEEL (CN/0380-7851) [02588322] **4016**

PRIMARY-JUNIOR KID-CRAFTS (IS/0270-6288) [06476086] **1068**

PRIMARY KID-CRAFTS (US/0270-6318) [06481278] **1068**

PRIMARY LIFE (UK/0962-8789) [26639590] **1902**

PRIMARY MATHEMATICS (UK/0032-8294) [01796749] **3527**

PRIMARY METAL INDUSTRIES (1985) (CN/0835-0116) [17237759] **4016**

PRIMARY ONE (US/0273-5148) [07061920] **5019**

- PRIMARY ONE STUDENT GUIDE (US/1059-3276) [24567978] **5066**

PRIMARY PLANNER (CN/0848-7839) [23238188] **1805**

PRIMARY PREVENTION OF PSYCHOPATHOLOGY (US/0161-8776) [04031033] **3932**

PRIMARY SCHOOL MANAGER (UK/0967-3865) **1868**

PRIMARY SCIENCE BULLETIN CANBERRA (AT/0155-4395) [I01554395] **5139, 1902**

PRIMARY SCIENCE REVIEW (UK/0269-2465) [I02692465] **1902, 5139**

- PRIMARY SEARCH (US/1065-2485) [26537704] **1774, 1796**

PRIMARY SENSORY NEURON (NE/0929-9637) **5139**

PRIMARY SOURCE (JACKSON, MISS.) (US/0741-6563) [08241397] **2482**

PRIMARY SOURCES AND ORIGINAL WORKS (US/1042-8216) [19225167] **2482, 3241**

PRIMARY TEACHER (US/0277-9188) [07703213] **1902**

- PRIMARY TEACHER GUIDE (US/1059-3268) [24565432] **5066**

PRIMARY TEACHING AND MICROS *See* JUNIOR EDUCATION **1759**

PRIMARY TEACHING STUDIES (UK/0268-2176) [I02682176] **1902**

PRIMARY TEXTILE INDUSTRIES (CN/0835-0043) [18121095] **5355**

PRIMARY TREASURE (US/0032-8316) [04109119] **1068**

PRIMARY TWO *See* PRIMARY TWO STUDENT GUIDE **5066**

- PRIMARY TWO STUDENT GUIDE (US/1059-3284) [24567996] **5066**
- PRIMARY VOICES K-6 (US/1068-073X) [27426291] **3311, 1805**

PRIMATE CONSERVATION (US/0898-6207) [12294229] **2202**

PRIMATE EYE (UK/0305-8417) [I03058417] **5594**

PRIMATE NEWS (US/0032-8324) [01589553] **5518**

PRIMATE REPORT (GW/0343-3528) [06837762] **5594**

PRIMATES (JA/0032-8332) [01762845] **5594**

PRIMAVERA (CHICAGO) (US/0364-7609) [02618649] **3425**

PRIME AREAS (CN/0032-8359) [02107692] **1902**

PRIME CONTRACT AWARDS BY REGION AND STATE (US) [09059024] **4054**

PRIME CONTRACT AWARDS BY SERVICE CATEGORY AND FEDERAL SUPPLY CLASSIFICATION (US) [09058909] **4054**

PRIME CONTRACT AWARDS BY STATE (US/1058-0301) [02576761] **4674**

PRIME CONTRACT AWARDS IN LABOR SURPLUS AREAS *CEASED*. (US/1058-014X) [07853230] **4054**

PRIME CONTRACT AWARDS OVER $25,000 OUTSIDE THE UNITED STATES (US) [10467887] **4054**

PRIME NUMBER (AT/0816-9349) [I08169349] **3527**

PRIME RATE UPDATE SERVICE (US/1047-112X) [20608975] **803**

PRIME REAL ESTATE (US) **4843**

PRIME SOURCE MINI REFERENCE DIRECTORY. MOST WANTED NAMES AND ADDRESSES OF : CHAIN STORES AND DEPARTMENT STORES (US/0742-4183) [10335362] **956**

PRIME SOURCE MINI REFERENCE DIRECTORY. MOST WANTED NAMES AND ADDRESSES OF--FOREIGN CONSULATE [I.E. CONSULATES] IN U.S.A (US/0742-4191) [10331837] **4532**

PRIME SOURCE MINI REFERENCE DIRECTORY. MOST WANTED NAMES AND ADDRESSES OF : IMPORTER REGISTER (US/0742-4175) [10333501] **704**

PRIME SOURCE MINI REFERENCE DIRECTORY. MOST WANTED NAMES AND ADDRESSES OF : MAIL ORDER COMPANIES (US/0742-4124) [10335018] **704**

PRIME SOURCE MINI REFERENCE DIRECTORY. MOST WANTED NAMES AND ADDRESSES OF : MAILING LIST COMPANIES (US/0742-4132) [10369539] **704**

PRIME SOURCE MINI REFERENCE DIRECTORY. MOST WANTED NAMES AND ADDRESSES OF : MANUFACTURERS' REPRESENTATIVES (US/0742-4140) [10369461] **704**

PRIME SOURCE MINI REFERENCE DIRECTORY. MOST WANTED NAMES AND ADDRESSES OF : VENTURE CAPITAL COMPANY (US/0742-4159) [10335299] **704**

PRIME TIME MAGAZINE (CN/0824-5479) [10669142] **5181**

PRIME TIME (NEW YORK) (US/0194-2611) [05365968] **5181**

PRIME TIMES (MADISON) (US/0195-5934) [05513859] **5181**

PRIMEIRA INSTANCIA (BL) [02239996] **3031**

PRIMER ACTO (SP/0032-8367) [00825181] **5367**

PRIMER OF LABOR RELATIONS (US/0272-0574) [01639822] **1702**

PRIMER SERIES FOR HEALTH CARE PROFESSIONALS (US) [17383216] **3791, 3031**

PRIMERJALNA KNJIZEVNOST (XV/0351-1189) [24252996] **3425**

PRIMERNYE TEMATIKA I PLANY TEORETICHESKIKH SEMINAROV (RU) [02246635] **4545**

PRIMETIME / PARENTAL RESOURCES FOR INVOLVEMENT IN MIGRANT EDUCATION PROJECT (US) [23751333] **5301, 1774**

PRIMITIVE BAPTIST YEARBOOK (US/0092-4415) [01789898] **5066**

PRIMO MAGGIO (IT) [02441185] **1702**

PRIMROSES (US/0162-6671) [04031194] **525, 2428**

PRIMUS (TERRE HAUTE, IND.) (US/1051-1970) [21889576] **3527**

PRINCE ALBERT SUN (CN/0714-8534) [09088974] **5793**

PRINCE EDWARD ISLAND *See* ROYAL GAZETTE. PRINCE EDWARD ISLAND **2544**

PRINCE EDWARD ISLAND. DEPT. OF COMMUNITY AND CULTURAL AFFAIRS *See* ANNUAL REPORT OF THE PRINCE EDWARD ISLAND DEPARTMENT OF COMMUNITY AND CULTURAL AFFAIRS **4628**

PRINCE EDWARD ISLAND. DEPT. OF HEALTH AND SOCIAL SERVICES *See* ANNUAL REPORT - DEPARTMENT OF HEALTH AND SOCIAL SERVICES (CHARLOTTETOWN) **4765**

PRINCE EDWARD ISLAND. DEPT. OF THE ENVIRONMENT *See* ANNUAL REPORT - PRINCE EDWARD ISLAND. DEPT. OF THE ENVIRONMENT (1989) **2187**

PRINCE EDWARD ISLAND. ENVIRONMENTAL CONTROL COMMISSION *See* ANNUAL REPORT - PRINCE EDWARD ISLAND. ENVIRONMENTAL CONTROL COMMISSION **2161**

PRINCE EDWARD ISLAND HERITAGE FOUNDATION *See* REPORT OF THE PRINCE EDWARD ISLAND HERITAGE FOUNDATION **2757**

PRINCE EDWARD ISLAND HOUSING CORPORATION *See* ANNUAL REPORT / PRINCE EDWARD ISLAND HOUSING CORPORATION **2815**

PRINCE EDWARD ISLAND. LEGISLATIVE ASSEMBLY *See* JOURNAL OF THE LEGISLATIVE ASSEMBLY OF THE PROVINCE OF PRINCE EDWARD ISLAND **4659**

PRINCE EDWARD ISLAND LENDING AUTHORITY *See* ANNUAL REPORT / PRINCE EDWARD ISLAND LENDING AUTHORITY **772**

PRINCE EDWARD ISLAND MUNICIPAL DIRECTORY (CN/1187-3000) [24470505] **4674**

PRINCE EDWARD ISLAND. OFFICE OF THE AUDITOR GENERAL *See* REPORT OF THE AUDITOR GENERAL OF PRINCE EDWARD ISLAND TO THE LEGISLATIVE ASSEMBLY **4745**

PRINCE EDWARD ISLAND SOIL & CROP IMPROVEMENT ASSOCIATION *See* COMPETITIONS, SUMMARIES, PROJECTS, TRIALS **75**

- PRINCE GEORGE CITY DIRECTORY (BUSINESS ED.) (CN/1191-923X) [27725099] **2573**

PRINCE GEORGE DIRECTORY *See* PRINCE GEORGE CITY DIRECTORY (BUSINESS ED.) **2573**

PRINCE GEORGE'S COMMUNITY COLLEGE *See* STUDENT HANDBOOK - PRINCE GEORGE'S COMMUNITY COLLEGE **1849**

PRINCE GEORGE'S COUNTY GENEALOGICAL SOCIETY BULLETIN (US/1052-1380) [05822415] **2468**

PRINCE GEORGE'S JOURNAL, THE (US/0162-2099) [04122626] **5759**

PRINCE RUPERT DAILY NEWS (CN) **5793**

PRINCE WILLIAM NEWSLETTER (US/0890-829X) [14404432] **2428, 624**

PRINCETON ALUMNI WEEKLY (US/0149-9270) [02436114] **1102**

PRINCETON DAILY CLARION (PRINCETON, IND. : 1960) (US) [12257355] **5666**

PRINCETON HISTORY (US/0276-2730) [04993631] **2755**

PRINCETON LEADER *See* TIMES-LEADER, THE **5682**

PRINCETON LEADER, THE (US) [14136993] **5682**

PRINCETON MAGAZINE (PRINCETON, N.J. : 1982) (US/0744-7515) [08521940] **1094**

PRINCETON MATHEMATICAL SERIES (US/0079-5194) [01762854] **3527**

PRINCETON MONOGRAPHS IN ART AND ARCHEOLOGY (US/0079-5208) [01604589] **278, 362**

PRINCETON PACKET, THE (US/0746-178X) [09832958] **5711**

- PRINCETON PAPERS IN NEAR EASTERN STUDIES (US/1065-9382) [26797905] **2662**

PRINCETON RECOLLECTOR *CEASED*. (US/0196-1136) [05016964] **2755**

PRINCETON SEMINARY BULLETIN, THE (US/0032-8413) [01762855] **4987**

PRINCETON STUDIES IN INTERNATIONAL FINANCE (US/0081-8070) [01762856] **1639**

PRINCETON STUDIES IN MATHEMATICAL ECONOMICS (US/0079-5240) [01762857] **1513**

PRINCETON STUDIES IN MUSIC (US/0079-5259) [01762858] **4147**

PRINCETON THEOLOGICAL SEMINARY *See* PRINCETON SEMINARY BULLETIN, THE **4987**

PRINCETON TIMES (PRINCETON, W.VA. : WEEKLY) (US) [13041590] **5764**

PRINCETON TIMES-REPUBLIC (US/8755-397X) [11292073] **5770**

PRINCETON UNIVERSITY. ART MUSEUM *See* RECORD OF THE ART MUSEUM, PRINCETON UNIVERSITY **4095**

PRINCETON UNIVERSITY. INDUSTRIAL RELATIONS SECTION *See* SELECTED REFERENCES - INDUSTRIAL RELATIONS SECTION, PRINCETON UNIVERSITY **1538**

PRINCETON UNIVERSITY. INTERNATIONAL FINANCE SECTION *See* SPECIAL PAPERS IN INTERNATIONAL ECONOMICS **1640**

PRINCETON UNIVERSITY LIBRARY CHRONICLE, THE (US/0032-8456) [01695247] **5213, 2852**

PRINCETON WEEKLY BULLETIN (US) **1842**

PRINCIPAL AGRICULTURAL COMMODITIES, TASMANIA / AUSTRALIAN BUREAU OF STATISTICS (AT/0157-0641) [08320092] **849, 121**

PRINCIPAL (ARLINGTON, VA.) (US/0271-6062) [06681687] **1868**

PRINCIPAL (EAST LANSING) (US/0199-6371) [04553678] **1868, 1805**

Alphabetical Title Index — PRIVATE

PRINCIPAL INTERNATIONAL BUSINESSES (US/0097-6288) [01799241] **704**

PRINCIPAL ISSUE (CN/0711-0103) [08261146] **1868**

PRINCIPAL MATTERS (AT) **1868**

PRINCIPAL USES OF LEAD AND ZINC (UK) **4016**

PRINCIPAL USES OF LEAD AND ZINC (UK) [09374208] **4016**

PRINCIPALES ENTREPRISES IVOIRIENNES : TRAVAUX PUBLICS, GENIE-CIVIL, BATIMENT ET ACTIVITES CONNEXES (IV) [01796714] **1621**

PRINCIPALES EXPORTATIONS (CM) [02243481] **849**

PRINCIPALES INDUSTRIES INSTALLEES EN COTE D'IVOIRE (IV) [02416675] **1579**

PRINCIPALES INDUSTRIES IVOIRIENNES *See* PRINCIPALES INDUSTRIES INSTALLEES EN COTE D'IVOIRE **1579**

PRINCIPALES PROCEDURES DE FINANCEMENT DES BESOINS DES ENTREPRISES ET DES MENAGES (FR) [20513638] **803**

PRINCIPALES PRODUCTIONS VEGETABLES / ROYAUME DU MAROC, MINISTERE DE L'AGRICULTURE ET DE LA REFORME AGRAIRE, SECRETARIAT GENERAL, DIVISION DES AFFAIRES ECONOMIQUES (MR) [07885218] **1622**

PRINCIPAL'S REPORT (NEW YORK, N.Y.) (US/1044-4998) [19817889] **882**

PRINCIPAL'S REPORT TO COUNCIL - UNIVERSITY OF RHODESIA (RH) [03942457] **1842**

PRINCIPAUX FAITS ECONOMIQUES DANS LE DOMAINE INTERNATIONAL (BE) [04147807] **1579**

PRINCIPAUX RESULTATS SCIENTIFIQUES ET TECHNIQUES (FR) [25483294] **1391**

PRINCIPE DE VIANA (SP/0032-8472) [02266459] **2703**

PRINCIPES (US/0032-8480) [02279971] **525**

PRINCIPI CONTABILI (IT) **750**

PRINCIPI REVISIONE (IT) **750**

PRINCIPLES & PRACTICE OF INFECTIOUS DISEASE (UK) **3715**

PRINCIPLES AND PRESENTATION : BANKING (US/0195-6264) [03829239] **803**

PRINCIPLES AND PRESENTATION. MINING (US/0278-0739) [04261584] **2148**

PRINCIPLES AND PRESENTATION. RETAILING (US/0278-6486) [03963871] **956**

PRINCIPLES AND PRESENTATION : SAVINGS AND LOAN (US/0194-0600) [04164571] **750**

PRINCIPLES AND TECHNIQUES OF HUMAN RESEARCH AND THERAPEUTICS (US/0094-9264) [01071486] **4325**

PRINCIPLES OF CIVIL SERVICE LAW / BY ROBERT G. VAUGHN ; UNDER THE SPONSORSHIP OF THE NATIONAL CIVIL SERVICE LEAGUE (US) [09485326] **3031**

PRINCIPLES OF CLINICAL ELECTROCARDIOGRAPHY (US/0894-2285) [04795132] **3709**

PRINCIPLES OF COMPUTER SCIENCE SERIES (US/0888-2096) [13519402] **1200**

PRING MARKET REVIEW (US/0892-189X) [15124393] **804**

PRINSBURG NEWS (US/8750-0E98) [10961521] **5698**

PRINT ACTION (CN/0380-2752) [02105987] **4567**

PRINT : AMERICA'S REGIONAL DESIGN ANNUAL (US) **381**

PRINT & GRAPHICS (US/0273-9550) [07042700] 381, **4568**

PRINT BUSINESS REGISTER (US) **4568**

PRINT BUYER (1982) (UK/0264-5424) [09846335] **4568**

PRINT BUYING (UK) [16682283] **4568**

PRINT COLLECTOR'S NEWSLETTER, THE (US/0032-8537) [01696653] **381**

PRINT EDUCATION MAGAZINE (US) [03143098] **4568**

PRINT-EQUIP NEWS (US/0048-5314) [04936976] **381**

PRINT MEDIA PRODUCTION DATA (US/0555-1633) [01642538] **764**

● PRINT MEDIA PRODUCTION SOURCE (US/1071-4545) [28642352] **764**

PRINT (NEW YORK) (US/0032-8510) [01762867] 764, **381**

● PRINT PRICE INDEX (US/1058-2339) [24242378] **381**

PRINT PRODUCTION DIRECTORY (AT/1033-6885) [I10336885] **4568**

PRINT PUBLISHING FOR THE SCHOOL MARKET (US/1058-4749) [24303923] 1774, **4818**

PRINT QUARTERLY (UK/0265-8305) [10635032] **4568**

PRINTED CIRCUIT DESIGN (US) **2075**

PRINTED CIRCUIT EXCHANGE *See* PRINTED CIRCUIT FABRICATION **2075**

PRINTED CIRCUIT FABRICATION (US/0274-8096) [06598287] **2075**

PRINTERS BUYER'S GUIDE AND HANDBOOK (US/0890-7234) [14171954] 1248, **1265**

PRINTERS HOT LINE (US/0192-6314) [05069490] **4568**

PRINTER'S NEWS (WELLINGTON) (NZ/0048-5330) [06637216] **4568**

PRINTERS YEARBOOK : THE COMPREHENSIVE GUIDE TO THE PRINTING INDUSTRY (UK) [09079575] **4568**

PRINTING ABSTRACTS (UK/0031-109X) [02449861] 4568, **4570**

PRINTING & CONVERTING MATTERS (UK) **4568**

PRINTING AND GRAPHIC ARTS BUYERS : PGAB (US/0741-1979) [10108839] 381, **4568**

PRINTING BUSINESS REPORT (US) **4568**

PRINTING HISTORICAL SOCIETY *See* JOURNAL OF THE PRINTING HISTORICAL SOCIETY **3292**

PRINTING HISTORY (US/0192-9275) [05086720] **4568**

PRINTING IMPRESSIONS (US/0032-860X) [01762876] 4818, **4568**

PRINTING INDUSTRIES (UK/0307-7195) [01795584] **4568**

PRINTING JOURNAL (US/0191-8273) [04975238] **4568**

PRINTING MANAGER (US) **4568**

PRINTING, PUBLISHING AND ALLIED INDUSTRIES (CN/0575-9412) [02762970] 4818, **4568**

PRINTING SALES INDEX *See* PRINTING BUSINESS REPORT **4568**

PRINTING SOURCE (CN/1188-3030) [25589841] **4568**

PRINTING TRADES DIRECTORY (UK) [04244642] **4568**

PRINTING WORLD (UK/0032-8715) [04584003] **4568**

PRINTINGNEWS. EAST (US/1046-8595) [20548677] **4568**

PRINTINGNEWS. MIDWEST (US/1048-6860) [21001136] **4568**

PRINTING'S PC QUARTERLY (US) [11488710] **4568**

PRINTOUT (NEWTONVILLE, MASS.) (US/0738-6613) [09637602] 1200, **4569**

PRINTOUT (SAINT CLOUD, MINN.) (US/0273-8201) [06954452] **1239**

PRINTS (ALTON) *SUSPENDED.* (US/0274-5097) [05277980] **4569**

● PRINTWEAR & PROMOTION (UK/0967-2486) [I09672486] **4569**

PRINTWEAR MAGAZINE (US/0898-3313) [17795604] **5355**

PRINTWEEK (UK) **4569**

PRINTWORLD DIRECTORY OF CONTEMPORARY PRINTS AND PRICES (US/0734-2721) [08433858] 4569, **381**

PRIONS EN EGLISE (EDITION DOMINICALE) (CN/0383-8277) [02592624] **4988**

PRIORDA (BU/0032-8731) [06114671] **5139**

PRIORITIES (US) [19699171] **2601**

PRIORITIES FOR RESEARCH, EXTENSION, AND HIGHER EDUCATION : A REPORT TO THE SECRETARY OF AGRICULTURE (US/0749-1328) [10755225] **121**

PRIORITIES (VANCOUVER) (CN/0700-6543) [02804361] **5564**

PRIORITY HEALTH PROBLEMS OF MICHIGAN (US) [06319125] **4796**

PRIORITY ISSUES IN MENTAL HEALTH : A BOOK SERIES PUBLISHED UNDER THE AUSPICES OF THE WORLD FEDERATION FOR MENTAL HEALTH *CEASED.* (NE/0168-1796) [07935915] **4796**

PRIRODI RANIH USJEVA I VOCA / SOCIJALISTICKA REPUBLIKA HRVATSKA, REPUBLICKI ZAVOD ZA STATISTIKU (CI) [09873299] **182**

PRIRODNI VEDY (XR/0139-6544) [06933138] **5139**

PRIRODNYE RESURSY VOLZHSKO-KAMSKOGO KRAIA: ZHIVOTNYI MIR (RU) [20145930] **5594**

PRIRODNYE USLOVIIA ZAPADNOI SIBIRI (RU) [05472563] **1391**

PRIRODOVEDNE PRACE USTAVU AKADEMIE VED CESKE REPUBLIKY V BRNE (XR) [30366414] 5594, **4170**

PRIRODOVEDNE PRACE USTAVU CESKOSLOVENSKE AKADEMIE VED V BRNE (XR/0032-8758) [01553765] **5594**

PRIS OCH KONKURRENS *See* KONKURRENS/ UITGAVEN AV STATENS PRIS- OCH KONKURRENSVERK I SAMARBETE MED NARINGSFRIHETSOMBUDSMANNEN OCH MARKNADSDOMSTOLEN **1502**

PRISCILLA PAPERS (US/0898-753X) [17893554] **4988**

PRISM (II) [06595102] **2662**

PRISM (US) **2890**

PRISM INTERNATIONAL (CN/0032-8790) [01762881] **3425**

PRISM (NAIROBI, KENYA) (KE) [12111553] **5044**

● PRISM (NEW YORK, N.Y., 1993) (US/1068-476X) [27688789] **3867**

PRISM (OTTAWA) (CN/0317-2341) [02248009] **5301**

PRISM (SAINT PAUL, MINN.) (US/0887-5049) [13262931] **4988**

PRISMA *CEASED.* (GE) [06972284] **2491**

PRISMA (IO) [02441184] 5213, **1513**

PRISMA (JAKARTA, INDONESIA) (IO/0301-6269) [01792724] **2662**

PRISMA LATINOAMERICANO (CU) [05864522] **4532**

PRISMA (SASKATOON) (CN/0380-8815) [02585016] **3311**

PRISME (MONTREAL) (CN/0383-1833) [03202317] **4865**

PRISME (QUEBEC. 1964) (CN/0713-5521) [08902995] **5793**

PRISMET (NO/0032-8447) [01776662] 1903, **4988**

PRISON AND INMATE POPULATION FORECAST, STATE OF WASHINGTON *See* INMATE POPULATION FORECAST UPDATE, STATE OF WASHINGTON **3166**

PRISON DECISIONS (US/0270-2703) [03742713] **3173**

PRISON INFORMATION BULLETIN *See* PENOLOGICAL INFORMATION BULLETIN / COUNCIL OF EUROPE **3171**

PRISON JOURNAL (PHILADELPHIA, PA.), THE (US/0032-8855) [01762885] **3173**

PRISON LAW & ADVOCACY (US/0739-7577) [07028003] **3173**

PRISON LAW MONITOR (US/0161-9632) [04171754] **3173**

● PRISON LIFE (US/1065-0709) [26498531] **3173**

PRISON REPORT (UK/0953-4377) [I09534377] **3108**

PRISON SERVICE JOURNAL (UK/0300-3558) [01452049] **3173**

PRISONERS IN STATE AND FEDERAL INSTITUTION ON ... (US) [21911224] **3173**

PRISPEVKI ZA NOVEJSO ZGODOVINO (XV) [17984898] 4545, **1702**

PRITEL LIDU : CASOPIS SLEZSKE CIRKVE EVANGELICKE (XR) [07287312] **4988**

PRIVACY ACT ISSUANCES ... COMPILATION (US/0190-8146) [03084918] **3031**

● PRIVACY & AMERICAN BUSINESS (US/1070-0536) [28239905] **704**

PRIVACY EN REGISTRATIE (NE) **4512**

PRIVACY JOURNAL (US/0145-7659) [02251780] **1227**

PRIVACY TIMES (US/1063-7222) [10898251] **3031**

PRIVATE ACTS OF THE STATE OF TENNESSEE PASSED BY THE GENERAL ASSEMBLY (US/0196-4224) [05068273] **4674**

PRIVATE AND PUBLIC INVESTMENT IN CANADA. INTENTIONS (CN/0823-065X) [12755912] **911**

PRIVATE AND PUBLIC INVESTMENT IN CANADA. REVISED INTENTIONS (CN/0823-0668) [15168072] **911**

PRIVATE ASSET MANAGEMENT (US) **911**

PRIVATE BANKER INTERNATIONAL (IE/0953-7031) [21364145] **804**

PRIVATE CABLE (US/0745-8711) [09526195] **1136**

● PRIVATE CABLE INVESTOR (US/1068-4514) [27673681] **1136**

PRIVATE CAREER EDUCATION COUNCIL *See* PCEC. PRIVATE CAREER EDUCATION COUNCIL **4208**

PRIVATE CARRIER (US/0032-8871) [01785290] **5389**

PRIVATE CLIENT BUSINESS (UK) **3031**

PRIVATE CLUBS (US/0887-8420) [13429507] **5235**

PRIVATE COMPANY SECRETARY'S MANUAL (UK) [20415142] 704, **4208**

PRIVATE DEVELOPMENT CORPORATION OF THE PHILIPPINES *See* MONTHLY ECONOMIC LETTER - PRIVATE DEVELOPMENT CORPORATION OF THE PHILIPPINES **799**

PRIVATE EDUCATION LAW REPORT (US/0890-121X) [14181485] 1868, **3031**

PRIVATE EQUITY ANALYST, THE (US/1057-526X) [24048424] **911**

PRIVATE EYE (UK/0032-888X) [01762890] **3350**

PRIVATE EYE WEEKLY (US) **2543**

●PRIVATE FLEET DIRECTORY, THE (US/1061-4761) [25259689] **5390**

PRIVATE INDEPENDENT SCHOOLS (US/0079-5399) [01482898] **1774**

PRIVATE INVESTMENTS ABROAD. PROBLEMS AND SOLUTIONS IN INTERNATIONAL BUSINESS (US) [23266073] 911, **1639**

PRIVATE INVESTMENTS AND INTERNATIONAL TRANSACTIONS IN ASIAN AND SOUTH PACIFIC COUNTRIES (US) [02386708] **912**

PRIVATE LABEL (EXECUTIVE EDITION) (US/0897-4845) [17524536] **882**

PRIVATE LABEL (GENERAL ED.) (US/0190-9851) [04782057] **882**

PRIVATE LABEL PRODUCT NEWS (US/0892-6727) [15236836] **3486**

PRIVATE LIBRARY (UK/0032-8898) [05167875] **3241**

PRIVATE PASSENGER AUTOMOBILE INSURANCE (US) [09209832] 5423, **2890**

PRIVATE PILOT (NEW YORK, N.Y.) (US/0032-8901) [02449870] **31**

PRIVATE PLACEMENT LETTER (US) **912**

PRIVATE PLACEMENT LETTER (US) **804**

PRIVATE PLACEMENT REPORTER (US) **704**

PRIVATE PLACEMENTS *See* PRIVATE PLACEMENT LETTER **804**

PRIVATE POST, THE (UK) [04852148] **2787**

●PRIVATE POWER EXECUTIVE (US/1075-0592) [28311438] **1953**

PRIVATE PRACTICE *CEASED.* (US/0032-891X) [01588403] **3629**

PRIVATE PRESS BOOKS (UK) [04823830] 4569, **4831**

PRIVATE PSYCHIATRIC HOSPITALS (US/0162-9913) [04261420] 3932, **3791**

PRIVATE RADIO RULES (US) **1136**

PRIVATE REAL ESTATE LIMITED PARTNERSHIPS (US/0271-0897) [04289909] **4843**

PRIVATE SCHOOL MONITOR (US/1071-1457) [12176219] **1774**

PRIVATE SCHOOLS OF THE UNITED STATES (US/0885-1603) [12568854] **1774**

PRIVATE SECURITY CASE LAW REPORTER (US/0738-6958) [09670710] **3031**

PRIVATE VARNISH (US/1047-9473) [13661995] **5434**

PRIVATISATION INTERNATIONAL (UK/0961-4206) [I09614206] **1639**

PRIVATISATION REPORT (AT/1036-9988) [I10369988] **4675**

PRIVATIZATION REPORT, THE (US/0890-815X) [14403317] **1622**

PRIVE (NE) **2285**

PRIVE, LE (CN/0701-9009) [04039947] **1774**

PRIVILEGED TRAVELER, THE *CEASED.* (US/0887-4131) [13258878] **5489**

PRIX DE REVIENT DES LOGEMENTS NEUFS EN ... / MINISTERE DE L'URBANISME ET DU LOGEMENT, DIRECTION DES AFFAIRES ECONOMIQUES ET INTERNATIONALES, LE (FR) [11055664] **2831**

PRIX DES ENERGIES (FR) **1953**

PRIX, INDICES DES PRIX ET COUT DE LA VIE A LOME (TG) [01787870] **1513**

PRIX INFORMATION (ALGER) (AE/0303-1799) [01793376] **1594**

PRIX NOBEL, LES (SW/0546-8175) [01644058] **2852**

PRIZE COLLEGE STORIES *CEASED.* (US/0079-5445) [03731933] **3425**

PRIZE STORIES (US/0079-5453) [03534721] **3425**

PRIZE-WINNING ART (US) [08464173] **362**

PRIZE-WINNING PAINTINGS (US) [10253642] **362**

PRIZMA (BN/0353-6386) [24079713] **3312**

PRO-ACTION (US/1044-3886) [19766207] **3242**

PRO ADMINISTRATOR (US/1050-2297) [21426800] **882**

PRO BASKETBALL (US/0360-2125) [02239710] **4913**

PRO BIKE NEWS (US/1064-2765) [09006262] **429**

PRO CALIMA : PERIODISCHE PUBLIKATION DER VEREINIGUNG PRO CALIMA (SZ) [12895841] **278**

PRO-CHOICE NEWS (CN/0836-7221) [17636431] **590**

●PRO/E, THE MAGAZINE (US/1069-6113) [28119162] **1200**

●PRO ECCLESIA (NORTHFIELD, MINN.) (US/1063-8512) [26175322] **4988**

PRO FILE: THE OFFICIAL DIRECTORY OF THE AMERICAN INSTITUTE OF ARCHITECTS (US/0190-8766) [09505081] **306**

PRO FOOTBALL GUIDE (US/0732-1902) [10599792] **4913**

PRO FOOTBALL ILLUSTRATED (US/1054-0156) [07617687] **4913**

PRO FOOTBALL TODAY (US/1059-4833) [24639582] **4913**

PRO FOOTBALL WEEKLY (US/0032-9053) [04109133] **4913**

PRO (FORT ATKINSON, WIS.) (US/1041-5610) [18800523] **2428**

PRO-FUND NOTES (US/1059-0048) [24458656] **5301**

PRO JUVENTUTE (SZ/1012-7895) [I10127895] **1068**

PRO-LIFE NEWS (CN/0715-4356) [09223214] 4512, **3767**

PRO METAL (GW) [06598086] **4016**

PRO-MOTION (US/0739-9340) [09836739] 5072, **935**

PRO MOTION NEWSLETTER (US/0316-4985) [09453931] **1857**

PRO MUNDI VITA STUDIES *CEASED.* (BE/1012-4543) [17849573] **5034**

PRO MUSICA MAGAZINE (US/0363-5244) [02413173] **4147**

PRO MUSICA SANA (US/0361-9559) [02441430] 4076, **4147**

PRO-NAT (SA) [06107551] **2500**

PRO NE NATA : PRN (US/1044-4025) [19523393] **3867**

PRO PHARMACOPOEA (IT) **4325**

PRO PRINCIPAL (US/1042-0487) [18922592] **1868**

PRO REGE (US/0276-4830) [04409405] 4988, **1842**

PRO REVIEW, THE (US/0748-9099) [11027692] **4375**

PRO SE (US/0093-8858) [01792675] 5564, **3031**

PRO SOUND NEWS (EUROPEAN ED.) (UK/0269-4735) [15181744] **5318**

PRO SOUND NEWS (INTERNATIONAL ED.) (US/0164-6338) [23281054] **5318**

PRO SOUND NEWS (U.S. ED.) (US/0164-6338) [04443743] **5318**

PRO SOUND NEWS. US ED *See* PRO SOUND NEWS (INTERNATIONAL ED.) **5318**

PRO VETERINARIO ENGLISH ED (BE/0777-8309) [I07778309] **5518**

PRO WRESTLING ILLUSTRATED (US/1043-7576) [17835707] **4913**

PROA *SUSPENDED.* (CK/0032-9150) [05320653] **306**

PROBABILISTIC ENGINEERING MECHANICS (UK/0266-8920) [13223289] **2125**

PROBABILITY AND MATHEMATICAL STATISTICS (PL/0208-4147) [08889711] 3527, **3542**

PROBABILITY AND MATHEMATICAL STATISTICS (NEW YORK, N.Y.) (US/0079-5607) [01639839] **3527**

PROBABILITY AND STOCHASTIC PROCESSES (GW/0720-2628) [09449853] **3527**

PROBABILITY IN THE ENGINEERING AND INFORMATIONAL SCIENCES (US/0269-9648) [15354091] **1991**

PROBABILITY, PURE AND APPLIED (US) [11679606] **3527**

PROBABILITY THEORY AND RELATED FIELDS (GW/0178-8051) [12576209] 5336, **3527**

PROBABLE LEVELS OF R&D EXPENDITURES IN ... (US) [06349077] **5139**

PROBATE AND PROPERTY (CHICAGO, ILL. : 1987) (US/0164-0372) [14914005] 4843, **3118**

PROBATE COUNSEL, THE (US) [04275824] **3031**

PROBATE LAW JOURNAL (US/0737-3112) [09171659] **3031**

PROBATE LAWYER, THE (US/0094-999X) [01795997] **3031**

PROBATE PRACTICE REPORTER (US/1044-7423) [19227892] **3118**

PROBATE REPORTER (US/0362-4773) [02362683] **3031**

PROBATION ADMINISTRATIVE MANAGEMENT SYSTEM / JUVENILE PROBATION MANAGEMENT INFORMATION SYSTEM (US) [09379279] **3173**

PROBATION AND PAROLE DIRECTORY (COLLEGE PARK, MD.) (US/0732-0965) [08134438] **3173**

PROBATION AND PAROLE LAW REPORTS (US/0276-6965) [06051336] **3173**

PROBATION & PAROLE STATISTICS (REGINA) (CN/0317-3828) [01793114] 3173, **3082**

PROBATION JOURNAL (UK) [02250541] 5301, **3173**

PROBATION SERVICE STATISTICS ... ACTUALS *See* PROBATION SERVICE STATISTICS ... ESTIMATES AND ... ACTUALS **3082**

PROBATION SERVICE STATISTICS ... ESTIMATES (UK/0264-6544) [10053161] 3173, **3082**

●PROBATION SERVICE STATISTICS ... ESTIMATES AND ... ACTUALS (UK) [31034061] 3173, **3082**

PROBATION STATISTICS, ENGLAND AND WALES / HOME OFFICE (UK/0265-573X) [12390812] 3173, **3082**

PROBE (US/1062-4155) [25615271] **5139**

PROBE (CN/0834-1494) [15484347] **1333**

PROBE (BELTSVILLE, MD.) (US/1057-2600) [23990757] 550, **525**

PROBE (CHICAGO, ILL.) (US) [03942586] 5564, **4988**

PROBE DIRECTORY OF FOREIGN DIRECT INVESTMENT IN THE UNITED STATES (US/0094-3134) [01794261] **912**

PROBE (LONDON) (CN/0380-7916) [02113024] **2239**

PROBE (LONDON. 1954) (UK/0032-9185) [02834131] **1333**

PROBE (MELBOURNE) (AT/0310-4044) [I03104044] **1774**

PROBE TELECOMMUNICATIONS JOURNAL *CEASED.* (US/0195-9174) [03962708] **1162**

PROBIN HITAISHI (BG/1012-9197) [10547237] **3754**

PROBLEM ASSET REPORTER (US/1071-4960) [28652110] **804**

PROBLEM BEHAVIOR MANAGEMENT (US/0731-2326) [08140394] **4608**

PROBLEM DE AGROFITOTEHNIE TEORETICA SI APLICATA (RM/0254-7279) [08286919] **121**

PROBLEM OBSERVER (UK) **4865**

PROBLEM-SOLVING INFORMATION FOR STATE & LOCAL GOVERNMENTS *See* NTIS ALERT. PROBLEM-SOLVING INFORMATION FOR STATE & LOCAL GOVERNMENTS **4670**

PROBLEMAS BARCELONA (SP/0032-9223) [I00329223] **4865**

PROBLEMAS DE ORGANIZACION DE LA CIENCIA (CU) [02243883] **5139**

PROBLEMAS DEL DESARROLLO (MX/0301-7036) [02266475] 1579, **1639**

PROBLEMATA SEMIOTICA (SP) [17238528] **3312**

PROBLEMATIQUE (DOWNSVIEW) (CN/1181-7488) [24690943] **4492**

PROBLEME DE GENETICA TEORETICA SI APLICATA (RM) [05307670] **121**

PROBLEME DE INFORMARE SI DOCUMENTARE (RM/0032-924X) [03198970] **3242**

PROBLEME DE LINGUISTICA GENERALA (RM) [02803347] **3312**

PROBLEME DE PROTECTIA PLANTELOR (RM/0254-2293) [09382849] 121, **4247**

PROBLEME DER KUSTENFORSCHUNG IM SUDLICHEN NORDSEEGEBIET (GW/0343-7965) [03639567] **2573**

PROBLEME EKONOMIKE (AA) [02564149] **1579**

PROBLEMES AUDIOVISUELS (FR/0249-3756) [09414500] **1136**

PROBLEMES D'AMERIQUE LATINE (FR/0765-1333) [04129101] **2512**

PROBLEMES ECONOMIQUES (FR/0032-9304) [02782492] **1579**

PROBLEMES POLITIQUES ET SOCIAUX (FR/0015-9743) [02820564] **5213**

Alphabetical Title Index — PROCEEDINGS

PROBLEMI ATTUALI DI SCIENZA E DI CULTURA (IT/0369-8408) [02587719] **5139**

PROBLEMI DEL SOCIALISMO (IT/0552-1807) [05002779] **4545**

PROBLEMI DEL TERRITORIO (IT) [20386115] **2832**

PROBLEMI DELLA AMMINISTRAZIONE PUBBLICA (IT) **4675**

PROBLEMI DELLA PEDAGOGIA, I (IT) [05874488] **1774**

PROBLEMI DELL'INFORMAZIONE (IT) [03825199] **764**

PROBLEMI DI BIOETICA (IT) **469**

PROBLEMI DI CIVILTA (IT) [06640330] **5213**

PROBLEMI DI GESTIONE (IT) **704**

PROBLEMI DI GESTIONE DELL IMPRESA (IT) **882**

PROBLEMI DI SESSUALITA E FECONDITA UMANA (IT) **5188**

PROBLEMI NA GEOGRAFIIATA (BU/0204-7209) [02243164] **2573**

PROBLEMI NA HIGIENATA (BU/0323-9179) [03012976] **4796**

PROBLEMI NA HRANENETO (BU/0205-003X) [06374683] **4197**

PROBLEMI NA IZKUSTVOTO (BU) [02266479] **328**

PROBLEMI NA METEOROLOGIATA I HIDROLOGIATA (BU/0205-2741) [I02052741] **1417**

PROBLEMI NA NUKLEARNATA MEDITSINA, RADIOBIOLOGIIATA I RADIATSIONNATA KHIGIENA / MEDITSINSKA AKADEMIIA (BU) [27723877] **3944**

PROBLEMI NA ONKOLOGIIATA (BU/0323-9209) [01208374] **3822**

PROBLEMI NA TEKHNICHESKATA KIBERNETIKA *See* PROBLEMI NA TEKHNICHESKATA KIBERNETIKA I ROBOTIKATA **1252**

PROBLEMI NA TEKHNICHESKATA KIBERNETIKA I ROBOTIKATA (BU/0204-9848) [08356850] **1252**

PROBLEMIST, THE (UK/0032-9398) [04115731] **4865**

PROBLEMISTA (PL) **4865**

PROBLEMS AND PROGRESS IN MEDICAL CARE; ESSAYS ON CURRENT RESEARCH (UK) [09506444] **3629**

PROBLEMS IN ANESTHESIA *CEASED.* (US/0889-4698) [13899257] **3684**

PROBLEMS IN CRITICAL CARE *CEASED.* (US/0889-4701) [13899277] **3629**

PROBLEMS IN GENERAL SURGERY *CEASED.* (US/0739-8328) [09814563] **3972**

PROBLEMS IN OPTOMETRY *CEASED.* (US/1043-6278) [19499214] **4217**

PROBLEMS IN PLASTIC AND RECONSTRUCTIVE SURGERY *CEASED.* (US/1050-0197) [21370660] **3972**

PROBLEMS IN RADIOLOGY (US) **3944**

PROBLEMS IN RESPIRATORY CARE *CEASED.* (US/0897-9677) [17680141] **3951**

PROBLEMS IN TEXTILE GEOGRAPHY / INTERNATIONAL STANDING WORKING GROUP ON TEXTILE GEOGRAPHY (PL/0860-7427) [19408420] **5355**

PROBLEMS IN THE BEHAVIOURAL SCIENCES (UK) [20386229] **4603**

PROBLEMS IN UROLOGY *CEASED.* (US/0889-471X) [13899309] **3992**

PROBLEMS IN VETERINARY MEDICINE *CEASED.* (US/1041-0228) [18611787] **5518**

PROBLEMS OF COMMUNISM (UK) [06217559] **4545**

PROBLEMS OF COMMUNISM (WASHINGTON, D.C.) *CEASED.* (US/0032-941X) [01762908] **4545**

PROBLEMS OF CULTURE / COMMITTEE FOR CULTURE, RESEARCH INSTITUTE FOR CULTURE AT THE COMMITTEE FOR CULTURE, AND THE BULGARIAN ACADEMY OF SCIENCES (BU/0204-8620) [09843964] **5254**

●PROBLEMS OF ECONOMIC TRANSITION (US/1061-1991) [25215924] **1513**

PROBLEMS OF ECONOMICS (US/0032-9436) [01642678] **1513**

PROBLEMS OF INFECTIOUS AND PARASITIC DISEASES (BU/0204-9155) [04442813] **3715**

PROBLEMS OF INFORMATION TRANSMISSION (US/0032-9460) [02449873] **2076**

PROBLEMS OF NATIONAL LIBERATION (II) [02278607] **4545**

PROBLEMS OF POST-COMMUNISM (US/1075-8216) [30211310] **4545**

PROBLEMS OF THE SCIENCE OF SCIENCE (PL) [01949799] **5139**

PROBLEMS OF UNITED STATES ECONOMIC DEVELOPMENT (US/0588-7194) [01713498] **1513**

PROBLEMY (PL/0032-9487) [I00329487] **5140**

PROBLEMY ALKOHOLIZMU 1976 (PL/0032-9495) [I00329495] **1348**

PROBLEMY AMERIKANISTKI (RU) [05454840] **2755**

PROBLEMY ANALITICESKOJ HIMII (RU/0370-2677) [10607057] **1018**

PROBLEMY ARKTIKI I ANTARKTIKI (RU/0555-2648) [03215808] **4170**

PROBLEMY BIONIKI (UN/0555-2656) [06676205] **1991**

PROBLEMY DALNEGO VOSTOKA (RU) [01681596] **2662**

PROBLEMY DAL'NEGO VOSTOKA (US) [06565139] **4532**

PROBLEMY DIALEKTIKI (RU) [05158311] **4357**

PROBLEMY EKONOMICHESKOGO I NAUCHNO-TEKHNICHESKOGO SOTRUDNICHESTVA STRAN-CHLENOV SEV / MEZHDUNARODNYI INSTITUT EKONOMICHESKIKH PROBLEM MIROVOI SOTSIALISTICHESKOI SISTEMY [I] MEZHDUNARODNYI TSENTR NAUCHNOI I TEKHNICHESKOI INFORMATSII (RU) [10727983] **1579**

PROBLEMY EKONOMICZNE (PL/0079-578X) [02782608] **1513**

PROBLEMY ENDOKRINOLOGII (RU/0375-9660) [05255989] **3732**

PROBLEMY FIZIKI ATMOSFERY (RU/0552-2056) [05294265] 1433, **4417**

PROBLEMY GIDROGEOLOGII I INZHENERNOGO GRUNTOVEDENIIA (RU) [04164642] **1417**

PROBLEMY INDUSTRIALNOI PSIKHOLOGII (RU) [05331626] 4608, **704**

PROBLEMY ISTORII KRITIKI I POETIKI REALIZMA (RU) [05458638] **3425**

PROBLEMY IZUCHENIIA INOSTRANNYKH IAZYKOV V ZAOCHNOI I VECHERNEI VYSSHEI SHKOLE (RU) [06875397] **3312**

PROBLEMY JADERNOJ FIZIKI I KOSMICESKIH LUCHEJ (RU/0131-3142) [02676373] **4450**

PROBLEMY JAKOSCI (PL) [06645618] **1622**

PROBLEMY KINETIKI I KATALIZA (RU/0370-0305) [10874544] **4417**

PROBLEMY KONTROLIA I ZASHCHITA ATMOSFERY OT ZAGRIAZNENIIA (UN) [06402262] **2239**

PROBLEMY KOSMICESKOJ BIOLOGII (RU/0555-2788) [03289606] **469**

PROBLEMY KRIOBIOLOGII (UN) [24593478] **469**

PROBLEMY KRISTALLOKHIMII / AKADEMIIA NAUK SSSR, NAUCHNYI SOVET PO KHIMICHESKOI KINETIKE I STROENIIU, ORDENA LENINA INSTITUT OBSHCHEI I NEORGANICHESKOI KHIMII IM. N.S. KURNAKOVA (RU) [12318740] **1033**

PROBLEMY MASHINOSTROENIIA I NADEZHNOSTI MASHIN / AKADEMIIA NAUK SSSR (RU/0235-7119) [21379786] **2125**

PROBLEMY MASINOSTROENIJA (UN/0131-2928) [02246151] **2125**

PROBLEMY MATEMATICESKOJ FIZIKI (RU/0555-2818) [05874486] **4417**

PROBLEMY MATEMATICHESKOGO ANALIZA (RU) [01696529] **3527**

PROBLEMY MEDYCYNY WIEKU ROZWOJOWEGO (PL/0303-2264) [01399262] **3629**

PROBLEMY METALLURGICESKOGO PROIZVODSTVA (UN/0235-4233) [I02354233] **4016**

PROBLEMY METODA I ZHANRA (RU/0134-8876) [05005028] **3425**

PROBLEMY MIROVOGO REVOLIUTSIONNOGO PROTSESSA / AKADEMIIA OBSHCHESTVENNYKH NAUK PRI TSK KPSS (RU) [08828493] **4545**

PROBLEMY MUZYKALNOI NAUKI (RU) [01788221] **4147**

PROBLEMY OBOGASHCHENIIA TVERDYKH GOEIUCHIKH ISKOPAEMYKH (RU) [01784570] **2148**

PROBLEMY OSVOENIIA PUSTYN (US/0278-4750) [07622078] **2202**

PROBLEMY OSVOENIIA PUSTYN (TK/0032-9428) [06563896] 2220, **121**

PROBLEMY PARTIINOGO I GOSUDARSTVENNOGO STROITELSTVA / AKADEMIIA OBSHCHESTVENNYKH NAUK PRI TSK KPSS (RU) [08265994] **4492**

PROBLEMY PEREDACI INFORMACII (RU/0555-2923) [05696571] **5140**

PROBLEMY PRAWA KARNEGO (PL) [03128366] **3108**

PROBLEMY PRAWA PRZEWOZOWEGO / WNIWERSYTET SLASKI (PL) [07388336] 5390, **3031**

PROBLEMY PRAWNE HANDLU ZAGRANICZNEGO (PL) [07228170] 849, **3134**

PROBLEMY PROCNOSTI (KIEV) (UN/0556-171X) [09859225] **1991**

PROBLEMY PROJEKTOWE (PL/0239-2089) [12058217] **4016**

PROBLEMY RAZVITIIA ZARUBEZHNOGO ISKUSSTVA (RU) [06699775] **362**

PROBLEMY REGIONALNOGO DEMOGRAFICHESKOGO PROGNOZIROVANIIA V SISTEME NARODNOKHOZIAISTVENNOGO PLANIROVANIIA / GOSPLAN TADZHIKSKOI SSR, NAUCHNO-ISSLEDOVATELSKII INSTITUT EKONOMIKI I EKONOMIKO-MATEMATICHESKIKH METODOV PLANIROVANIIA S VYCHISLITELNYM TSENTROM (RU) [07910563] **4559**

PROBLEMY RODZINY (PL/0552-2234) [I05522234] **2285**

PROBLEMY ROZWOJU BUDOWNICTWA / INSTYTUT ORGANIZACJI MECHANIZACJI BUDOWNICTWA (PL) [25779016] **624**

PROBLEMY SEVERA / AKADEMIIA NAUK SSSR, SIBIRSKOE OTDELENIE, GOSUDARSTVENNAIA PUBLICHNAIA NAUCHNO-TEKHNICHESKAIA BIBLIOTEKA (RU/0134-3963) [02241968] **422**

PROBLEMY SOTSIALISTICHESKOI ZAKONNOSTI (UN) [05341914] **3153**

●PROBLEMY SOTSIALNOI GIGIENY I ISTORIIA MEDITSINY / NII SOTSIALNOI GIGIENY, EKONOMIKI I UPRAVLENIIA ZDRAVOOKHRANENIEM IM N.A. SEMASHKO RAMN, AO ASSOTSIATSIIA 'MEDITSINSKAIA LITERATURA.' (RU/0869-866X) [30423266] **4796**

PROBLEMY SOVETSKOI LITERATURY, METOD, ZHANR, KHARAKTER (RU) [06600124] **3425**

PROBLEMY SOVREMENNOI KHIMII KOORDINATSIONYKH SOEDINENII (RU) [04686436] **1056**

PROBLEMY SOVREMENNOJ ANALITICESKOJ KHIMII (RU/0136-8079) [12099665] **1018**

PROBLEMY SPECIALNOJ ELEKTROMETALLURGII (UN/0131-1611) [02999575] **4016**

PROBLEMY STOMATOLOGII (TASKENT) (RU/0302-6930) [01334551] **1333**

PROBLEMY SZKOLNICTWA I NAUK MEDYCZNYCH (PL/0137-4982) [03737361] **3629**

PROBLEMY TECHNIKI W MEDYCYNIE (PL/0370-2219) [11446985] **3629**

PROBLEMY TEORII GRAVITATSII I ELEMENTARNYKH CHASTITS (RU/0370-2189) [09648866] **4450**

PROBLEMY TEORII I PRAKTIKI UPRAVLENIIA (RU/0257-9928) [12128819] **882**

PROBLEMY TUBERKULEZA (RU/0032-9533) [01716338] **3951**

PROBLEMY TURYSTYKI (PL/0138-0478) [I01380478] **5489**

PROBLEMY VOSTOCHNOI EVROPY (US/0739-7119) [08583530] **4492**

PROBLEMY ZHURNALISTIKI (RU/0321-3501) [05281445] **2923**

PROBLEMY ZIMOVEDENIIA (RU) [01796713] **1433**

PROBLEMY ZOOLOGII (RU) [03930988] **5595**

PROBUS (NE/0921-4771) [20336418] **3312**

PROC. - BRIGHTON CROP PROT. CONF., PESTS DIS (UK/0955-1514) [22839994] 4247, **182**

PROCEEDINGS - CALIFORNIA WEED CONFERENCE *See* CALIFORNIA WEED SCIENCE SOCIETY PROCEEDINGS **2411**

PROCEDURAL SKILLS AND OFFICE TECHNOLOGY BULLETIN (US/1065-1489) [26515746] **3791**

PROCEDURE DI AMMINISTRAZIONE DEL PERSONALE (IT) **946**

PROCEDURE REVISIONE FISCALE ADEMPIMENTI SOSTITUTO IMPOSTA (IT) **750**

PROCEDURE REVISIONE FISCALE IMPOSTA VALORE AGGIUNTO (IT) 4741, **3031**

PROCEDURE REVISIONE FISCALE REDDITO IMPRESA (IT) **4741**

PROCEEDINGS / A & WMA ANNUAL MEETING (US/1052-6102) [21247221] **2180**

PROCEEDINGS, A&WMA ANNUAL MEETING (US/0193-9688) [22215588] **2239**

PROCEEDINGS — Alphabetical Title Index

PROCEEDINGS - ABRASIVE ENGINEERING SOCIETY (U.S.). CONFERENCE/EXHIBITION (US/0734-9629) [06296946] **4016**

PROCEEDINGS / ACM IEEE DESIGN AUTOMATION CONFERENCE *CEASED.* (US/0738-100X) [09508687] **1234**

PROCEEDINGS ACM SIGUCCS USER SERVICES CONFERENCE (US) **1200**

PROCEEDINGS (AKADEMYAH HA-LEUMIT HA-YISREELIT LE-MADAIM) (IS/0578-9230) [01754002] **2852**

PROCEEDINGS - ALLERTON CONFERENCE ON COMMUNICATION, CONTROL AND COMPUTING (US/0732-6181) [03704794] **2076**

PROCEEDINGS - AMERICAN BAR ASSOCIATION. SECTION OF INSURANCE, NEGLIGENCE AND COMPENSATION LAW (US) [01479512] **2890, 3031**

PROCEEDINGS / AMERICAN LAW INSTITUTE (US/0065-9045) [02186274] **3031**

PROCEEDINGS - AMERICAN MERCHANT MARINE AND MARITIME INDUSTRY CONFERENCE (US/1053-3494) [18124014] **5454**

PROCEEDINGS / AMERICAN SOCIETY FOR CONSERVATION ARCHAEOLOGY (US) [04937740] **279**

PROCEEDINGS - AMERICAN SOCIETY FOR THE ADVANCEMENT ANESTHESIA IN DENTISTRY (US/0164-1700) [04567304] **1333, 3684**

PROCEEDINGS AND ABSTRACTS, AMERICAN INSTITUTE FOR DECISION SCIENCES, ANNUAL MEETING, WESTERN REGIONAL CONFERENCE (US) [03104749] **4608**

PROCEEDINGS AND ADDRESSES OF THE AMERICAN PHILOSOPHICAL ASSOCIATION (US/0065-972X) [01480553] **4357**

PROCEEDINGS & DIRECTORY / NORTHWEST ASSOCIATION OF SCHOOLS AND COLLEGES (US) [25806882] **1842**

PROCEEDINGS AND MINUTES, ANNUAL MEETING OF THE AGRICULTURAL RESEARCH INSTITUTE (US/0148-2572) [03284142] **121**

PROCEEDINGS AND PAPERS OF THE ANNUAL CONFERENCE OF THE CALIFORNIA MOSQUITO AND VECTOR CONTROL ASSOCIATION (US/0160-6751) [03474590] **2239**

PROCEEDINGS AND PAPERS OF THE GEORGIA ASSOCIATION OF HISTORIANS, THE (US/0275-3863) [07142549] **2626**

PROCEEDINGS AND REPORTS - FLORIDA STATE UNIVERSITY, CENTER FOR YUGOSLAV-AMERICAN STUDIES, RESEARCH AND EXCHANGES *CEASED.* (US/0196-9730) [02500532] **2703**

PROCEEDINGS AND REPORTS OF MEETINGS (SP) [06054424] **2310**

PROCEEDINGS AND TRANSACTIONS OF THE ALL-INDIA ORIENTAL CONFERENCE (II) [01663564] **3312**

PROCEEDINGS; ANNUAL AAZPA CONFERENCE (US/0090-4473) [01785229] **5595**

PROCEEDINGS ... ANNUAL CONFERENCE / AGRONOMY SOCIETY OF NEW ZEALAND (NZ/0110-6589) [08178327] **121**

PROCEEDINGS : ANNUAL CONFERENCE - ASSOCIATION OF COLLEGE AND UNIVERSITY AUDITORS (US) [01794537] **750**

PROCEEDINGS. ANNUAL CONFERENCE - CANADIAN ACADEMIC ACCOUNTING ASSOCIATION (CN/0711-3730) [10220727] **750**

PROCEEDINGS. ANNUAL CONFERENCE - CANADIAN ASSOCIATION OF ADMINISTRATIVE SCIENCES (CN/0318-5036) [02746291] **882**

PROCEEDINGS, ANNUAL CONFERENCE - NATIONAL CENTER FOR THE STUDY OF COLLECTIVE BARGAINING IN HIGHER EDUCATION AND THE PROFESSIONS (U.S.) CONFERENCE (US/0742-3667) [08478741] **1842**

PROCEEDINGS, ANNUAL CONFERENCE OF GUIDANCE PERSONNEL IN OCCUPATIONAL EDUCATION (US/0277-6332) [04991843] **1915**

PROCEEDINGS ... ANNUAL CONFERENCE OF THE AMERICAN COUNCIL ON CONSUMER INTERESTS (US/0275-1356) [03727187] **1299**

PROCEEDINGS ... ANNUAL CONFERENCE OF THE TROPICAL AND SUBTROPICAL FISHERIES TECHNOLOGICAL SOCIETY OF THE AMERICAS (US/1045-7127) [18719396] **2310**

PROCEEDINGS - ANNUAL CONTRACTOR'S CONFERENCE OF THE ARTIFICIAL KIDNEY PROGRAM OF THE NATIONAL INSTITUTE OF ARTHRITIS, METABOLISM, AND DIGESTIVE DISEASES (US/0147-5258) [03187993] **3800**

PROCEEDINGS / ANNUAL CONVENTION AND REGULATORY SYMPOSIUM, NATIONAL ASSOCIATION OF REGULATORY UTILITY COMMISSIONERS (US) [06727337] **4675**

PROCEEDINGS, ANNUAL CONVENTION - GAS PROCESSORS ASSOCIATION (US/0096-8870) [01796087] **4275**

PROCEEDINGS ... ANNUAL CONVENTION ... / ILLINOIS STATE FEDERATION OF LABOR (US) [05420345] **1702**

PROCEEDINGS, ANNUAL CONVENTION - NEW BRUNSWICK FEDERATION OF LABOUR (CN/0225-9060) [06183722] **1702**

PROCEEDINGS, ANNUAL CONVENTION - NEWSPAPER GUILD. CONVENTION (US/0741-7950) [04075081] **1703**

PROCEEDINGS, ANNUAL CONVENTION - OHIO COUNCIL ON FAMILY RELATIONS (US/0273-334X) [07015102] **2285**

● PROCEEDINGS ... ANNUAL GENERAL MEETING (US/1070-6488) [27567165] **5077**

PROCEEDINGS, ANNUAL GOVERNOR'S CONFERENCE ON THE HANDICAPPED (US/0436-2438) [07339084] **4392**

PROCEEDINGS ... ANNUAL GROUP HEALTH INSTITUTE / GROUP HEALTH ASSOCIATION OF AMERICA (US) [07493272] **4796**

PROCEEDINGS. ANNUAL MEAT SCIENCE INSTITUTE (US/0090-5631) [05351860] **2353**

PROCEEDINGS / ANNUAL MEETING. ASSOCIATION FOR APPLIED PSYCHOPHYSIOLOGY (US) [21616431] **4608**

PROCEEDINGS, ANNUAL MEETING ELECTRON MICROSCOPY OF AMERICA *See* MICROSCOPY SOCIETY OF AMERICA PROCEEDINGS **573**

PROCEEDINGS, ... ANNUAL MEETING, ELECTRON MICROSCOPY SOCIETY OF AMERICA (US/0424-8201) [01567744] **573**

PROCEEDINGS, ANNUAL MEETING, INSTITUTE OF NUCLEAR MATERIALS MANAGEMENT (US) [06283729] **2158**

PROCEEDINGS, ANNUAL MEETING - NEW JERSEY MOSQUITO CONTROL ASSOCIATION, INC (US/0198-7267) [03959571] **2239**

PROCEEDINGS, ... ANNUAL MEETING OF THE AMERICAN WOOD-PRESERVERS' ASSOCIATION (US/0066-1198) [07790813] **2403**

PROCEEDINGS, ANNUAL MEETING OF THE AMERICAN WOOD-PRESERVERS' ASSOCIATION (US/0066-1198) [01480985] **2403**

PROCEEDINGS ... ANNUAL MEETING OF THE CANADIAN TRANSPORTATION RESEARCH FORUM (CN/1183-2770) [28166221] **5390**

PROCEEDINGS, ANNUAL MEETING OF THE UNITED STATES ANIMAL HEALTH ASSOCIATION (US/0082-8750) [01768729] **5519**

PROCEEDINGS ANNUAL MEETING / SOCIETY OF AMERICAN FORESTERS, NORTHERN CALIFORNIA SECTION (US/0489-555X) [08076046] **2391**

PROCEEDINGS, ANNUAL MEETING - WASHINGTON STATE HORTICULTURAL ASSOCIATION (US/0149-6905) [01624214] **2428**

PROCEEDINGS - ANNUAL PITTSBURGH COAL CONFERENCE (US/1075-7961) [30262794] **1953**

PROCEEDINGS ... ANNUAL PITTSBURGH COAL CONFERENCE (US/1075-8313) [17164255] **1953**

PROCEEDINGS ... ANNUAL RELIABILITY AND MAINTAINABILITY SYMPOSIUM (US/0149-144X) [03451180] **4221**

● PROCEEDINGS / ANNUAL SIMULATION SYMPOSIUM (US) [26203207] **1282**

PROCEEDINGS. ANNUAL SYMPOSIUM. INCREMENTAL MOTION CONTROL SYSTEMS AND DEVICES (US/0092-1661) [03436726] **2076**

PROCEEDINGS - ANNUAL SYMPOSIUM ON INSTRUMENTATION FOR THE PROCESS INDUSTRIES (US/0096-7963) [05192312] **3486**

PROCEEDINGS, ANNUAL TECHNICAL MEETING - INSTITUTE OF ENVIRONMENTAL SCIENCES (US/0361-2007) [02039081] **5140**

PROCEEDINGS / ... ANNUAL THIRD WORLD CONFERENCE (US/0885-2316) [12603524] **5213, 1639**

PROCEEDINGS / ... ANNUAL WORKSHOP ON INTERACTIVE COMPUTING, CAD/CAM, ELECTRICAL ENGINEERING EDUCATION (US) [09623554] **1200, 1991**

PROCEEDINGS - ASSOCIATION OF EUROPEAN PAEDIATRIC CARDIOLOGISTS (FR) [05723145] **3709, 3910**

PROCEEDINGS - ASSOCIATION OF INDIAN UNIVERSITIES (II) [02981570] **1774**

PROCEEDINGS - ASTRONOMICAL SOCIETY OF AUSTRALIA (AT/0066-9997) [02241427] **398**

PROCEEDINGS AT THE OPENING OF THE LEGISLATIVE ASSEMBLY OF THE PROVINCE OF ONTARIO (CN/1184-2849) [23659480] **4675**

PROCEEDINGS AWWA ANNUAL CONFERENCE (US/0360-814X) [02158028] **5537, 4761**

PROCEEDINGS - AWWA WATER QUALITY TECHNOLOGY CONFERENCE (US/0164-0755) [04571384] **5537**

PROCEEDINGS - BELGIAN CONGRESS OF ANESTHESIOLOGY (BE/0772-1404) [06953115] **3972**

PROCEEDINGS / BELTWIDE COTTON CONFERENCES (US/1059-2644) [23980054] **182**

PROCEEDINGS - BIENNIAL CORNELL ELECTRICAL ENGINEERING CONFERENCE (US/0161-3219) [03898436] **2076**

PROCEEDINGS. BIOLOGICAL SCIENCES / THE ROYAL SOCIETY (UK/0962-8452) [26606430] **469**

PROCEEDINGS - BIRD CONTROL SEMINAR *SUSPENDED.* (US/0067-8945) [01043855] **5619**

PROCEEDINGS - CALIFORNIA WEED CONFERENCE (US/0097-1731) [02241094] **2428**

PROCEEDINGS - CANADIAN CONFERENCE ON COAL (CN/0824-8605) [I08248605] **1443**

PROCEEDINGS (CANADIAN FEDERATION OF BIOLOGICAL SOCIETIES : 1982) (CN) [08893238] **469**

PROCEEDINGS - CANADIAN INSTITUTE OF ACTUARIES (CN/0229-0995) [09925304] **2890**

PROCEEDINGS - CANADIAN LABOUR CONGRESS, CONSTITUTIONAL CONVENTION (CN/0225-0403) [06183304] **1703**

PROCEEDINGS - CANADIAN SOCIETY FOR CIVIL ENGINEERING (CN/0226-2053) [06272349] **2029**

PROCEEDINGS - CANADIAN SYMPOSIUM ON REMOTE SENSING (CN/0713-7060) [03177790] **31**

PROCEEDINGS / CARNAHAN CONFERENCE ON SECURITY TECHNOLOGY (US/0884-5409) [11138592] **3173**

PROCEEDINGS / COINAGE OF THE AMERICAS CONFERENCE (US/8756-6265) [11633297] **2783**

PROCEEDINGS / COLLOQUIUM ON THE LAW OF OUTER SPACE (US/0069-5831) [01564096] **32, 3031**

PROCEEDINGS - COMMITTEE ON COMPUTER TECHNOLOGY (US/0091-5122) [01783744] **2029, 5442**

PROCEEDINGS - COMMONWEALTH MINING AND METALLURGICAL CONGRESS (UK/0700-5741) [02961630] **4016, 2148**

PROCEEDINGS / CONFERENCE OF CONSULTING ACTUARIES, THE (US) [27646427] **2890**

PROCEEDINGS / CONFERENCE ON ARTIFICIAL INTELLIGENCE APPLICATIONS (US/1043-0989) [16671019] **1216**

PROCEEDINGS / CONFERENCE ON COMPACT TRANSFORMATION GROUPS (GW) [01783708] **3527**

PROCEEDINGS - CONFERENCE ON FEDERAL INFORMATION RESOURCES (US) [01784044] **3242**

PROCEEDINGS ... CONFERENCE ON GROUND CONTROL IN MINING (US) [10014817] **2148**

PROCEEDINGS / CONFERENCE ON LOCAL COMPUTER NETWORKS (US) [17022071] **1243**

PROCEEDINGS / CONGRESS OF THE INTERNATIONAL ACADEMY OF FORENSIC AND SOCIAL MEDICINE (BE) [11774622] **3742**

PROCEEDINGS - CONSORTIUM ON REVOLUTIONARY EUROPE (US/0093-2574) [01784392] **2703**

PROCEEDINGS, CONSTITUTIONAL CONVENTION OF THE INDUSTRIAL UNION DEPARTMENT, AFL-CIO (US/0569-4612) [08702658] **1703**

PROCEEDINGS - CONVENTION, CANADIAN UNION OF PUBLIC EMPLOYEES (CN/0380-7770) [03230359] **1703**

PROCEEDINGS - CORNELL NUTRITION CONFERENCE FOR FEED MANUFACTURERS (US) [01565118] **203**

PROCEEDINGS - CORPORATE AVIATION SAFETY SEMINAR (US/0736-4709) [09151905] **32**

PROCEEDINGS

PROCEEDINGS - COUNTY JUDGES' AND COMMISSIONERS' CONFERENCE (US/0590-0123) [01565338] **4675**

PROCEEDINGS / CVPR, IEEE COMPUTER SOCIETY CONFERENCE ON COMPUTER VISION AND PATTERN RECOGNITION (US/1063-6919) [09981093] **1200**

PROCEEDINGS - DEVON ARCHAEOLOGICAL SOCIETY (UK/0305-5795) [I03055795] **279**

PROCEEDINGS, DIRECTORY AND HANDBOOK OF THE NATIONAL ASSOCIATION OF ACADEMIES OF SCIENCE, THE (US/0739-361X) [09719308] **5140**

PROCEEDINGS - DISTILLERS FEED CONFERENCE (1980) (US/0742-5546) [09740686] **2353**

PROCEEDINGS - DISTILLERS FEED RESEARCH COUNCIL CONFERENCE (US) [01566784] **121**

PROCEEDINGS - DORSET NATURAL HISTORY AND ARCHAEOLOGICAL SOCIETY (UK/0070-7112) [01566909] **279, 4170**

PROCEEDINGS / ELECTRIC FURNACE CONFERENCE (US/0096-0128) [01567701] **4016**

PROCEEDINGS - ELECTROCHEMICAL SOCIETY (US/0161-6374) [03983334] **1034**

PROCEEDINGS / ELECTRONIC COMPONENTS & TECHNOLOGY CONFERENCE (US/0569-5503) [22232989] **2076**

PROCEEDINGS / ELECTRONICS TEST AND MEASUREMENT CONFERENCE (US/0734-659X) [08767727] **2076**

PROCEEDINGS - ENDOCRINE SOCIETY OF AUSTRALIA (AT/0312-4738) [01240554] **3732**

PROCEEDINGS / EUROPEAN CONFERENCE ON DESIGN AUTOMATION AND THE EUROPEAN EVENT IN ASIC DESIGN (US/1066-1409) [26868632] **1221**

PROCEEDINGS / EUROPEAN CONFERENCE ON SOIL MECHANICS AND FOUNDATION ENGINEERING (MX/0254-4679) [09813356] **2125**

PROCEEDINGS / EXECUTIVES' CONFERENCE, INSTITUTE OF PAPER SCIENCE AND TECHNOLOGY (US) [23873391] **4237**

PROCEEDINGS / FALL JOINT COMPUTER CONFERENCE ; SPONSORED BY ACM AND COMPUTER SOCIETY OF THE IEEE (US) [15309980] **1200**

PROCEEDINGS - FERTILISER SOCIETY (UK/0369-9277) [01359737] **182**

PROCEEDINGS - FIRE SERVICE EXTENSION SCHOOL, WEST VIRGINIA UNIVERSITY (US) [01372626] **2029**

PROCEEDINGS - FLORIDA CORRECTIONAL EDUCATION ASSOCIATION (US/0430-7615) [01384475] **3173**

PROCEEDINGS - FRONTIERS IN EDUCATION CONFERENCE (US/0190-5848) [02723744] **1991**

PROCEEDINGS / FRONTIERS OF POWER CONFERENCE (US/0730-7985) [08060137] **1953**

PROCEEDINGS - GEOSCIENCE INFORMATION SOCIETY (US/0072-1409) [01751107] **1359**

PROCEEDINGS - GOVERNOR'S CONFERENCE ON STATE, COUNTY, AND MUNICIPAL RELATIONS (US) [01448959] **4675**

PROCEEDINGS - GOVERNOR'S WORKSHOP FOR COMMUNITY COLLEGE TRUSTEES (US) [05197985] **1842**

PROCEEDINGS - GRAPHICS INTERFACE (CN/0713-5424) [10220186] **1243**

PROCEEDINGS - HARDWOOD SYMPOSIUM OF THE HARDWOOD RESEARCH COUNCIL (US/0193-8495) [03972249] **2403**

●PROCEEDINGS / IAPR INTERNATIONAL CONFERENCE ON PATTERN RECOGNITION (US) [26971504] **4440**

PROCEEDINGS ICDSC : INTERNATIONAL CONFERENCE ON DIGITAL SATELLITE COMMUNICATIONS *CEASED.* (GW) **32**

PROCEEDINGS - IEEE COMPUTER SOCIETY SYMPOSIUM ON RESEARCH IN SECURITY AND PRIVACY (US/1063-7109) [21999651] **1227**

PROCEEDINGS / IEEE IECON (US) [09604541] **2076**

PROCEEDINGS / IEEE INFOCOM (US/0743-166X) [08704142] **1162, 1200**

PROCEEDINGS / IEEE INTERNATIONAL CONFERENCE ON COMPUTER DESIGN : VLSI IN COMPUTERS SPONSORED BY IEEE COMPUTER SOCIETY AND IEEE CIRCUITS AND SYSTEMS SOCIETY TECHNICAL COMMITTEES (US) [10354080] **1200**

PROCEEDINGS / IEEE INTERNATIONAL CONFERENCE ON ROBOTICS AND AUTOMATION (US/1050-4729) [20178691] 1991, **1221**

PROCEEDINGS / IEEE ... ULTRASONICS SYMPOSIUM (US/1051-0117) [14185238] **2076**

PROCEEDINGS - IIE INTEGRATED SYSTEMS CONFERENCE (US/1069-367X) [21707868] **2099**

PROCEEDINGS ... ILLINOIS SPECIALTY GROWERS ASSOCIATION CONVENTION AND TRANSACTIONS OF THE ILLINOIS STATE HORTICULTURAL SOCIETY FOR THE YEAR *See* TRANSACTIONS OF THE ILLINOIS STATE HORTICULTURAL SOCIETY FOR THE YEAR **2432**

PROCEEDINGS IN PRINT (US/0032-9568) [01586717] **41**

PROCEEDINGS IN THE MUNICIPAL COURTS (US/0550-6387) [01759833] **3082**

PROCEEDINGS / INDIANA ACADEMY OF THE SOCIAL SCIENCES (US/0537-3247) [02586217] **5213**

PROCEEDINGS / INDO-PACIFIC FISHERY COMMISSION (TH/0258-4190) [07160011] **2310**

PROCEEDINGS - INDUSTRIAL WASTE CONFERENCE (US) [04532213] **1028**

PROCEEDINGS / INSTITUT TEKNOLOGI BANDUNG (IO/0522-2133) [02356034] **5140**

PROCEEDINGS / INSTITUTE OF ENVIRONMENTAL SCIENCES (US/0090-0729) [03466127] 2180, **1991**

PROCEEDINGS - INSTITUTE OF FOOD SCIENCE AND TECHNOLOGY (U.K.) (UK/0144-1493) [01132519] 1028, **2353**

PROCEEDINGS - INSTITUTE OF REFRIGERATION (UK/0073-9677) [I00739677] **2607**

PROCEEDINGS - INSTITUTION OF CIVIL ENGINEERS. PART 1, DESIGN AND CONSTRUCTION *See* PROCEEDINGS OF THE INSTITUTION OF CIVIL ENGINEERS. CIVIL ENGINEERING **2029**

PROCEEDINGS - INSTITUTION OF CIVIL ENGINEERS. PART 1, DESIGN AND CONSTRUCTION *See* PROCEEDINGS OF THE INSTITUTION OF CIVIL ENGINEERS. MUNICIPAL ENGINEER **2029**

PROCEEDINGS - INSTITUTION OF CIVIL ENGINEERS. PART 1, DESIGN AND CONSTRUCTION *See* PROCEEDINGS OF THE INSTITUTION OF CIVIL ENGINEERS, TRANSPORT **2029**

PROCEEDINGS - INSTITUTION OF CIVIL ENGINEERS. PART 1, DESIGN AND CONSTRUCTION *See* PROCEEDINGS OF THE INSTITUTION OF CIVIL ENGINEERS. WATER, MARITIME AND ENERGY **2094**

PROCEEDINGS - INSTITUTION OF CIVIL ENGINEERS. PART 2, RESEARCH AND THEORY *See* PROCEEDINGS OF THE INSTITUTION OF CIVIL ENGINEERS. CIVIL ENGINEERING **2029**

PROCEEDINGS - INSTITUTION OF CIVIL ENGINEERS. PART 2, RESEARCH AND THEORY *See* PROCEEDINGS OF THE INSTITUTION OF CIVIL ENGINEERS. MUNICIPAL ENGINEER **2029**

PROCEEDINGS - INSTITUTION OF CIVIL ENGINEERS. PART 2, RESEARCH AND THEORY *See* PROCEEDINGS OF THE INSTITUTION OF CIVIL ENGINEERS, TRANSPORT **2029**

PROCEEDINGS - INSTITUTION OF CIVIL ENGINEERS. PART 2, RESEARCH AND THEORY *See* PROCEEDINGS OF THE INSTITUTION OF CIVIL ENGINEERS. WATER, MARITIME AND ENERGY **2094**

PROCEEDINGS / INTERNATIONAL CEMENT SEMINAR (US/0277-8211) [07080662] **5140**

PROCEEDINGS - INTERNATIONAL COMPUTER SOFTWARE & APPLICATIONS CONFERENCE (US/0730-3157) [03644029] 1230, **1289**

PROCEEDINGS - INTERNATIONAL CONFERENCE ON COMPUTER LANGUAGES (US/1074-8970) [19133268] **1200**

PROCEEDINGS / INTERNATIONAL CONFERENCE ON COMPUTERS AND APPLICATIONS (US) [10941968] **1200**

PROCEEDINGS / INTERNATIONAL CONFERENCE ON DATA ENGINEERING (US/1063-6382) [19762049] 306, **1254**

PROCEEDINGS - INTERNATIONAL CONFERENCE ON INSTRUMENTATION FOR HIGH-ENERGY PHYSICS (IT) [04200993] **4450**

PROCEEDINGS - INTERNATIONAL CONFERENCE ON LARGE HIGH VOLTAGE ELECTRIC SYSTEMS (CIGRE) (FR/1016-2437) [02754361] **2076**

PROCEEDINGS - INTERNATIONAL CONFERENCE ON SOFTWARE ENGINEERING (US/0270-5257) [02723707] 1230, **1289**

PROCEEDINGS - INTERNATIONAL CONFERENCE ON THE PEACEFUL USES OF ATOMIC ENERGY (US) [05011712] **1953**

PROCEEDINGS - INTERNATIONAL CONGRESS OF NEURO-PSYCHOPHARMACOLOGY (NE/0069-5769) [03192285] 4325, **3844**

PROCEEDINGS - INTERNATIONAL CONGRESS ON CATALYSIS (NE) [04698058] **989**

PROCEEDINGS - INTERNATIONAL POWER SOURCES SYMPOSIUM (UK) [02056066] 1953, **2076**

PROCEEDINGS / INTERNATIONAL SYMPOSIUM ON DISEASES IN ZOO ANIMALS *See* ERKRANKUNGEN DER ZOOTIERE : VERHANDLUNGSBERICHT DES INTERNATIONALEN SYMPOSIUMS UEBER DIE ERKRANKUNGEN DER ZOOTIERE **5509**

PROCEEDINGS - INTERNATIONAL SYMPOSIUM ON MULTIPLE-VALUED LOGIC (US/0195-623X) [02668964] **1230**

PROCEEDINGS - INTERNATIONAL SYMPOSIUM ON SUBSCRIBER LOOPS AND SERVICES (US/1012-0343) [I10120343] **2076**

PROCEEDINGS - INTERNATIONAL SYMPOSIUM ON URBAN HYDROLOGY, HYDRAULICS, AND SEDIMENT CONTROL (1981) (US/0732-2607) [08334628] **2094**

PROCEEDINGS - INTERNATIONAL TELEMETERING CONFERENCE (US/0884-5123) [05986151] **2076**

PROCEEDINGS, INTERNATIONAL WATER CONFERENCE, ENGINEERS SOCIETY OF WESTERN PENNSYLVANIA (US/0099-409X) [I0099409X] **2094**

PROCEEDINGS / INTERNATIONAL ZURICH SEMINAR ON DIGITAL COMMUNICATIONS (SZ/1015-8057) [02455215] 1119, **1200**

PROCEEDINGS / INTERNEPCON ELECTRONIC PACKAGING CONFERENCE (UK) [19330874] **4221**

PROCEEDINGS - IRONMAKING CONFERENCE (US/0099-6874) [01643619] **4016**

PROCEEDINGS - ISLE OF MAN NATURAL HISTORY AND ANTIQUARIAN SOCIETY (UK) [02166086] **4170**

PROCEEDINGS (JAPAN SOCIETY (LONDON, ENGLAND)) (UK) [15680299] **5235**

PROCEEDINGS - JOINT SPE/DOE SYMPOSIUM ON ENHANCED OIL RECOVERY (US/0278-3711) [07308563] **4275**

PROCEEDINGS - LIGHTWOOD RESEARCH CONFERENCE (US/0198-0130) [06177489] **2403**

PROCEEDINGS / LIVESTOCK CONSERVATION INSTITUTE (US) [19918998] **219**

PROCEEDINGS - MARYLAND NUTRITION CONFERENCE FOR FEED MANUFACTURERS (US/0542-8386) [01756763] **121**

PROCEEDINGS. MATHEMATICAL AND PHYSICAL SCIENCES / THE ROYAL SOCIETY (UK/0962-8444) [22221422] 989, 4417, **3527**

PROCEEDINGS. MATHEMATICAL AND PHYSICAL SCIENCES / THE ROYAL SOCIETY (UK/0962-8444) [26606303] **4417**

PROCEEDINGS - NATIONAL ADVISORY BOARD FOR WILD FREE-ROAMING HORSES & BURROS (US) [04062318] **2801**

PROCEEDINGS - NATIONAL CONFERENCE OF THE AUSTRALIAN SOCIETY FOR OPERATIONS RESEARCH (AT/0312-1933) [I03121933] **1991**

PROCEEDINGS - NATIONAL ONLINE MEETING (US/0739-1471) [07626119] **1275**

PROCEEDINGS - NATIONAL PEACH COUNCIL (US/0092-2633) [02745174] **2353**

PROCEEDINGS - NATIONAL RELAY CONFERENCE (US/0077-5401) [04178782] **2076**

PROCEEDINGS / NATIONAL SYMPOSIUM ON MINING, HYDROLOGY, SEDIMENTOLOGY AND RECLAMATION (US/1046-3887) [20379014] **1417**

PROCEEDINGS - NEW ENGLAND-ST. LAWRENCE VALLEY GEOGRAPHICAL SOCIETY (US/0160-3159) [01116521] **2573**

PROCEEDINGS, NOBCCHE (US/0896-2367) [16966794] **989**

PROCEEDINGS Alphabetical Title Index

PROCEEDINGS - NORTH AMERICAN MOTOR VEHICLE EMISSIONS CONTROL CONFERENCE (US/0278-5986) [07743783] **2239**

PROCEEDINGS / NORTH CENTRAL WEED SCIENCE SOCIETY (US) [22199068] **2429**

PROCEEDINGS - NORTHEAST WATER RESOURCE RESEARCH DIRECTORS' MEETING (US) [03095405] **2094**

PROCEEDINGS - NORTHEASTERN FOREST TREE IMPROVEMENT CONFERENCE (US/0549-8929) [01587585] **2391**

PROCEEDINGS - NOTRE DAME INSTITUTE ON CHARITABLE GIVING, FOUNDATIONS, AND TRUSTS (US) [03429791] **4339**

PROCEEDINGS OF A CONFERENCE ON BANK STRUCTURE AND COMPETITION (US/0084-9146) [03931230] **804**

PROCEEDINGS OF ALUMINUM EXTRUSION TECHNOLOGICAL SEMINAR (US) [17064233] **4016**

PROCEEDINGS OF AMERICAN PEANUT RESEARCH AND EDUCATION SOCIETY, INC (US/0197-8748) [06139738] **183**

PROCEEDINGS OF ... ANNUAL CONFERENCE / HAWAIIAN SUGAR TECHNOLOGISTS (US) [29643723] **183**

PROCEEDINGS OF ... ANNUAL MEETING - AMERICAN ASSOCIATION OF VETERINARY LABORATORY DIAGNOSTICIANS *CEASED.* (US/0098-3543) [02240321] **5519**

PROCEEDINGS OF ANNUAL WASHINGTON POTATO CONFERENCE AND TRADE FAIR (US) [03299468] **183**

PROCEEDINGS OF FLICC FORUMS ON FEDERAL INFORMATION POLICIES (US/1061-7485) [25425866] **4675**

PROCEEDINGS OF GOLD AND MONEY SESSION AND GOLD TECHNICAL SESSION (US/0197-5013) [06036159] **2783**

PROCEEDINGS OF HYDROLOGY SYMPOSIUM *CEASED.* (CN/0073-4225) [01752440] **1417**

PROCEEDINGS OF INNOVATION CANADA INC (CN/0711-0235) [08378892] **704**

PROCEEDINGS OF INTERNATIONAL CONFERENCE ON NUMERICAL ANALYSIS OF SEMICONDUCTOR DEVICES INTEG CIR : NASECODE (IE) **2076**

PROCEEDINGS OF INTERNATIONAL SYMPOSIUM OF SPACE TECHNOLOGY & SCIENCE (JA) **32**

PROCEEDINGS OF INTERNATIONAL WIRE AND CABLE SYMPOSIUM (US/0091-7702) [01786017] **2076**

PROCEEDINGS OF JAPANESE SOCIETY OF SUGAR BEET TECHNOLOGISTS (JA/0912-1048) [22649592] **183**

PROCEEDINGS OF JAPANESE SYMPOSIUM ON PLASMA CHEMISTRY (JA/0915-1699) [l09151699] 3773, **989**

PROCEEDINGS OF KIT MATHEMATICS WORKSHOP / KOREA INSTITUTE OF TECHNOLOGY, MATHEMATICS RESEARCH CENTER (KO) [22367645] **3528**

PROCEEDINGS OF LUNAR AND PLANETARY SCIENCE (US) [24034625] **398**

PROCEEDINGS OF METAL BULLETIN'S INTERNATIONAL FERRO-ALLOYS CONFERENCE (UK) [05538393] **4016**

PROCEEDINGS OF ... NATIONAL CONVENTION OF THE AMERICAN LEGION (US) [23806130] **4054**

PROCEEDINGS OF NATIONAL WASTE PROCESSING CONFERENCE (1976) (US/0145-4781) [02739004] **2239**

PROCEEDINGS OF NELS (US/0883-5500) [11124471] **3312**

PROCEEDINGS OF NEW YORK UNIVERSITY ... ANNUAL INSTITUTE ON FEDERAL TAXATION (US) [06744975] **4741**

PROCEEDINGS OF NEW YORK UNIVERSITY ANNUAL NATIONAL CONFERENCE ON LABOR (US/0193-3418) [03824399] **3153**

PROCEEDINGS OF ... PAKISTAN CONGRESS OF ZOOLOGY (PK) [18690363] **5595**

PROCEEDINGS OF PARASITOLOGY (PK/1018-2500) [l10182500] **568**

PROCEEDINGS OF POWERCON *CEASED.* (US/0192-494X) [05016587] **2076**

PROCEEDINGS OF SPIE--THE INTERNATIONAL SOCIETY FOR OPTICAL ENGINEERING (US/0277-786X) [07633702] **1991**

PROCEEDINGS OF SUMMER INSTITUTE ON PARTICLE PHYSICS (US/0146-1273) [02858460] **4418**

PROCEEDINGS OF SYMPOSIA IN PURE MATHEMATICS (US/0082-0717) [01767041] **3528**

PROCEEDINGS OF SYMPOSIUM - DESERT TORTOISE COUNCIL (US/0191-3875) [03006455] **5595**

PROCEEDINGS OF SYMPOSIUM ... OF THE ASSOCIATION OF BRITISH WILD ANIMAL KEEPERS (UK/0308-4167) [05786573] **2202**

PROCEEDINGS OF ... SYNTHETIC PIPELINE GAS SYMPOSIUM (US/0146-6267) [01624471] **4275**

PROCEEDINGS OF THE ACADEMY OF NATURAL SCIENCES OF PHILADELPHIA (US/0097-3157) [01382862] **4170**

PROCEEDINGS OF THE ACADEMY OF POLITICAL SCIENCE (US) [01460720] **4492**

PROCEEDINGS OF THE ACADEMY OF POLITICAL SCIENCE *SUSPENDED.* (US/0065-0684) [14908024] **4492**

PROCEEDINGS OF THE ACADEMY OF RELIGION AND PSYCHICAL RESEARCH ... ANNUAL ACADEMIC CONFERENCE (US) [12857911] **4242**

PROCEEDINGS OF THE ACADEMY OF SCIENCES OF THE USSR. APPLIED PHYSICS SECTIONS (US) [01478809] **4418**

PROCEEDINGS OF THE ACADIAN ENTOMOLOGICAL SOCIETY *See* PROCEEDINGS OF THE ... ANNUAL MEETING / ACADIAN ENTOMOLOGICAL SOCIETY **5595**

PROCEEDINGS OF THE AEDS CONVENTION (US) [02239428] **1868**

PROCEEDINGS OF THE AESF ANNUAL TECHNICAL CONFERENCE, THE (US/1075-7988) [18130151] **2076**

PROCEEDINGS OF THE ALL-INDIA CONGRESS OF ZOOLOGY (II/0569-0242) [05812962] **5595**

PROCEEDINGS OF THE ALUMINIUM EXTRUSION TECHNOLOGICAL SEMINAR (US) **4016**

PROCEEDINGS OF THE AMERICAN ACADEMY AND INSTITUTE OF ARTS AND LETTERS (US/0145-8493) [03454094] 3425, **328**

● PROCEEDINGS OF THE AMERICAN ACADEMY OF ARTS AND LETTERS (US) [30834763] **328**

PROCEEDINGS OF THE AMERICAN ACADEMY OF CARDIOVASCULAR PERFUSION, THE (US/0894-1084) [12075687] **3709**

PROCEEDINGS OF THE AMERICAN ANTIQUARIAN SOCIETY (US/0044-751X) [01479298] **2755**

PROCEEDINGS OF THE AMERICAN CATHOLIC PHILOSOPHICAL ASSOCIATION (US/0065-7638) [06029215] 5034, **4357**

PROCEEDINGS OF THE AMERICAN CONTROL CONFERENCE (US/0743-1619) [08789320] **1991**

PROCEEDINGS OF THE AMERICAN COUNTRY LIFE CONFERENCE *See* PROCEEDINGS OF THE CONFERENCE OF THE AMERICAN COUNTRY LIFE ASSOCIATION, INC **5254**

PROCEEDINGS OF THE AMERICAN ETHNOLOGICAL SOCIETY (US/0731-4108) [01479824] **243**

PROCEEDINGS OF THE AMERICAN MATHEMATICAL SOCIETY (US/0002-9939) [01480367] **3528**

PROCEEDINGS OF THE AMERICAN PHILOSOPHICAL SOCIETY (US/0003-049X) [01480557] **4357**

PROCEEDINGS OF THE AMERICAN POWER CONFERENCE (US/0097-2126) [02641323] **2125**

PROCEEDINGS OF THE AMERICAN RAILWAY ENGINEERING ASSOCIATION (US) [14137354] **5434**

PROCEEDINGS OF THE AMERICAN SOCIETY FOR COMPOSITES ... TECHNICAL CONFERENCE (US) [21175583] **1991**

PROCEEDINGS OF THE ANNUAL AAMI/FDA CONFERENCE ON MEDICAL DEVICE REGULATION (US/0146-146X) [02833265] **3696**

PROCEEDINGS OF THE ... ANNUAL ACM SYMPOSIUM ON THEORY OF COMPUTING (US/0737-8017) [08523599] **1200**

PROCEEDINGS OF THE ANNUAL AIR TRAFFIC CONTROL ASSOCIATION FALL CONFERENCE (US/0192-8740) [04356453] **32**

PROCEEDINGS OF THE ... ANNUAL APPALACHIAN UNDERGROUND CORROSION SHORT COURSE (US/0066-538X) [02313248] 2107, **2016**

PROCEEDINGS OF THE ANNUAL ASSEMBLY MEETING (US/0145-9589) [02844177] **32**

PROCEEDINGS OF THE ... ANNUAL BANGLADESH SCIENCE CONFERENCE (BG) [07808471] **5140**

PROCEEDINGS OF THE ... ANNUAL BRITISH ROBOT ASSOCIATION CONFERENCE (UK) [17456442] **1216**

PROCEEDINGS OF THE...ANNUAL BUSINESS FORECASTING CONFERENCE HELD AT UCLA. VOLUME II, THE UCLA BUSINESS FORECAST FOR CALIFORNIA *See* UCLA BUSINESS FORECAST FOR CALIFORNIA, THE **1525**

PROCEEDINGS OF THE ANNUAL COCCIDIOIDOMYCOSIS STUDY GROUP MEETING (US/0191-1856) [04761790] **3630**

PROCEEDINGS OF THE ANNUAL COMPUTER PERSONNEL RESEARCH CONFERENCE (US/0069-8148) [01799506] 1281, **1239**

PROCEEDINGS OF THE ANNUAL CONFERENCE (UK/0582-303X) [02972933] **3242**

PROCEEDINGS OF THE ANNUAL CONFERENCE - AMERICAN SOCIETY OF UNIVERSITY COMPOSERS (US/0066-0701) [01788925] **4147**

PROCEEDINGS OF THE ... ANNUAL CONFERENCE AND COURSE ON LITERACY (US) [25970801] **1774**

PROCEEDINGS OF THE ... ANNUAL CONFERENCE AND EXPOSITION OF THE NATIONAL COMPUTER GRAPHICS ASSOCIATION, INC (US/0732-8028) [08434098] **1234**

PROCEEDINGS OF THE ... ANNUAL CONFERENCE / ASSOCIATION FOR POPULATION/FAMILY PLANNING LIBRARIES AND INFORMATION CENTERS INTERNATIONAL (US/1054-2531) [05586480] **2285**

PROCEEDINGS OF THE ANNUAL CONFERENCE - CANADIAN COUNCIL ON INTERNATIONAL LAW (CN/0317-9087) [02441650] **3134**

PROCEEDINGS OF THE ANNUAL CONFERENCE : ESOMAR (UK) [01782731] **5336**

PROCEEDINGS OF THE ANNUAL CONFERENCE FOR MUNICIPAL CLERKS (US/0573-2913) [06352318] **4675**

PROCEEDINGS OF THE ... ANNUAL CONFERENCE / INSTITUT DE READAPTATION DE MONTREAL (CN/0824-0493) [11607451] **4392**

PROCEEDINGS OF THE ... ANNUAL CONFERENCE / NORTH AMERICAN LAKE MANAGEMENT SOCIETY *See* LAKE AND RESERVOIR MANAGEMENT **2235**

PROCEEDINGS OF THE ANNUAL CONFERENCE OF CANADIAN TECHNICAL ASPHALT ASSOCIATION (CN/0712-2470) [08790791] **2029**

PROCEEDINGS OF THE ... ANNUAL CONFERENCE OF THE ASSOCIATION FOR BUSINESS SIMULATION AND EXPERIENTIAL LEARNING (US/0278-2375) [08699694] **704**

PROCEEDINGS OF THE ... ANNUAL CONFERENCE OF THE ASSOCIATION OF COLLEGE UNIONS - INTERNATIONAL (US/0147-1120) [02292888] **1842**

PROCEEDINGS OF THE ANNUAL CONFERENCE OF THE FORESTRY ASSOCIATION OF NIGERIA (NR) [05211307] **2391**

PROCEEDINGS OF THE ... ANNUAL CONFERENCE OF THE HOSPITAL MANAGEMENT SYSTEMS SOCIETY (US/0193-0486) [05108951] 882, **3791**

PROCEEDINGS OF THE ANNUAL CONFERENCE OF THE LAW OF THE SEA INSTITUTE (US/0557-8620) [02953108] **3182**

PROCEEDINGS OF THE ... ANNUAL CONFERENCE OF THE NATIONAL ASSOCIATION OF CHURCH BUSINESS ADMINISTRATORS *See* ANNUAL CONFERENCE / NATIONAL ASSOCIATION OF CHURCH BUSINESS ADMINISTRATORS **4935**

PROCEEDINGS OF THE ANNUAL CONFERENCE OF THE NIGERIAN ECONOMIC SOCIETY (NR/0331-0361) [01793955] **1513**

PROCEEDINGS OF THE ... ANNUAL CONFERENCE OF THE REMOTE SENSING SOCIETY (UK) [10553863] **1359**

PROCEEDINGS OF THE ANNUAL CONFERENCE OF THE WESTERN COLLEGE READING ASSOCIATION (US) [02784414] **1842**

PROCEEDINGS OF THE ... ANNUAL CONFERENCE ON TAXATION HELD UNDER THE AUSPICES OF THE NATIONAL TAX ASSOCIATION-TAX INSTITUTE OF AMERICA (US/1066-8608) [u1781473] **4742**

PROCEEDINGS OF THE ANNUAL CONFERENCE ON WATER FOR TEXAS (US/0495-2340) [01204724] **5537**

PROCEEDINGS OF THE ... ANNUAL CONFERENCE SOUTHEASTERN ASSOCIATION OF FISH AND WILDLIFE AGENCIES (US/0276-7929) [03989697] 2310, **4913**

PROCEEDINGS OF THE ... ANNUAL CONFERENCES (US) [08808162] 2252, **4675**

PROCEEDINGS

PROCEEDINGS OF THE ANNUAL CONGRESS OF THE SOUTH AFRICAN SUGAR TECHNOLOGISTS' ASSOCIATION (SA/0373-045X) [02501017] **2353**

PROCEEDINGS OF THE ANNUAL CONVENTION (US/0069-1267) [01553581] **4988**

PROCEEDINGS OF THE ANNUAL CONVENTION - AMERICAN ASSOCIATION OF BOVINE PRACTITIONERS. CONVENTION (US/0743-0450) [03236888] **5519**

PROCEEDINGS OF THE ANNUAL CONVENTION - AMERICAN RAILWAY ENGINEERING ASSOCIATION (US/0096-0268) [01480650] **5434**

PROCEEDINGS ... OF THE ANNUAL CONVENTION / AUTOMOTIVE ENGINE REBUILDERS ASSOCIATION (U.S.) (US) [08842099] **5423**

PROCEEDINGS OF THE ANNUAL CONVENTION - CANON LAW SOCIETY OF AMERICA (US/0277-9889) [01640045] **5034**

PROCEEDINGS OF THE ANNUAL CONVENTION - CHRISTIAN ASSOCIATION FOR PSYCHOLOGICAL STUDIES (US/0092-072X) [01789064] 4609, **4988**

PROCEEDINGS OF THE ... ANNUAL CONVENTION, INCLUDING THE ... ANNUAL CONVENTION OF THE WESTERN CANADA SECTION, AMERICAN WATER WORKS ASSOCIATION, AND THE ... ANNUAL CONVENTION OF THE WESTERN CANADA POLLUTION CONTROL ASSOCIATION, WATER POLLUTION CONTROL FEDERATION (CN/0833-5192) [14766935] 2239, **5537**

PROCEEDINGS OF THE ANNUAL CONVENTION - INDONESIAN PETROLEUM ASSOCIATION (IO/0126-1126) [01268264] **4275**

PROCEEDINGS OF THE ANNUAL CONVENTION OF THE AMERICAN ASSOCIATION OF BOVINE PRACTITIONERS *See* AMERICAN ASSOCIATION OF BOVINE PRACTITIONERS. CONFERENCE. AMERICAN ASSOCIATION OF BOVINE PRACTITIONERS CONFERENCE: [PROCEEDINGS] **205**

PROCEEDINGS OF THE ANNUAL CONVENTION OF THE AMERICAN ASSOCIATION OF EQUINE PRACTITIONERS (US/0065-7182) [01479373] 5519, **2801**

PROCEEDINGS OF THE ... ANNUAL CONVENTION OF THE AMERICAN RAILWAY BRIDGE AND BUILDING ASSOCIATION (US) [01480647] **2029**

PROCEEDINGS OF THE ANNUAL CONVENTION OF THE DAUGHTERS OF THE REPUBLIC OF TEXAS (US/0162-0053) [03236681] **2755**

PROCEEDINGS OF THE ANNUAL CONVENTION OF THE NATIONAL ASSOCIATION OF SYNAGOGUE ADMINISTRATORS (US/0145-4366) [02740731] **5052**

PROCEEDINGS OF THE ANNUAL CONVENTION OF THE NATIONAL COLLEGIATE ATHLETIC ASSOCIATION (1967) (US/0077-3808) [05932745] **4913**

PROCEEDINGS OF THE ANNUAL CONVENTION OF THE SUGAR TECHNOLOGISTS' ASSOCIATION OF INDIA (II/0370-2057) [02578875] **121**

PROCEEDINGS OF THE ... ANNUAL CONVENTION OF THE WIRE ASSOCIATION INTERNATIONAL, INC (US/0731-4191) [08349850] **4016**

PROCEEDINGS OF THE ... ANNUAL DREDGING SEMINAR (US/0748-7533) [10983585] **2094**

PROCEEDINGS OF THE ANNUAL EASTERN SNOW CONFERENCE (US/0424-1932) [01780855] **1359**

PROCEEDINGS OF THE ... ANNUAL FINANCIAL MANAGEMENT CONFERENCE, THE (US/0740-3453) [03127939] 4742, **4675**

PROCEEDINGS OF THE ANNUAL FREQUENCY CONTROL SYMPOSIUM *See* PROCEEDINGS OF THE IEEE INTERNATIONAL FREQUENCY CONTROL SYMPOSIUM **4418**

PROCEEDINGS OF THE ANNUAL GOVERNOR'S WORKSHOP ON INTERGOVERNMENTAL RELATIONS AND REGIONAL PLANNING (SAN ANTONIO) (US/0092-8445) [01789695] **2832**

PROCEEDINGS OF THE ANNUAL GULF AND CARIBBEAN FISHERIES INSTITUTE AND THE ANNUAL INTERNATIONAL GAME FISH RESEARCH CONFERENCE (US/0361-2953) [02044542] **2310**

PROCEEDINGS OF THE ANNUAL HEALTH CARE INFORMATION AND MANAGEMENT SYSTEMS CONFERENCE (US/1048-8987) [21069997] **3791**

PROCEEDINGS OF THE ANNUAL INSTITUTE - EASTERN MINERAL LAW FOUNDATION (U.S.). ANNUAL INSTITUTE (US/0733-6098) [07143160] 4275, **3031**

PROCEEDINGS OF THE ... ANNUAL INSTITUTE OF OIL AND GAS LAW AND TAXATION (US/0895-1578) [06712182] 4275, **3031**

PROCEEDINGS OF THE ... ANNUAL INSTITUTE ON COAL MINING HEALTH, SAFETY AND RESEARCH (US) [07433813] **2868**

PROCEEDINGS OF THE ANNUAL INSTITUTE ON SECURITIES LAWS AND REGULATIONS (US/0161-4002) [03889649] **3031**

PROCEEDINGS OF THE ... ANNUAL INSTITUTE ON STATE AND LOCAL TAXATION AND CONFERENCE ON PROPERTY TAXATION (US) [10763009] **4742**

PROCEEDINGS OF THE ANNUAL INSTITUTE - ROCKY MOUNTAIN MINERAL LAW INSTITUTE (US/0886-747X) [01764464] **3115**

PROCEEDINGS OF THE ANNUAL INTERNATIONAL CONFERENCE OF THE IEEE ENGINEERING IN MEDICINE AND BIOLOGY SOCIETY (US) [18956110] **3696**

PROCEEDINGS OF THE ... ANNUAL IOWA STATE REGULATORY CONFERENCE (US) [19993314] **4761**

PROCEEDINGS OF THE ANNUAL JOINT MEETING OF THE PUBLIC ADVISORY COMMITTEE ON THE ENVIRONMENT AND THE ENVIRONMENT COUNCIL OF ALBERTA (CN) [13176185] **2239**

PROCEEDINGS OF THE ANNUAL MEETING (US/0070-1076) [02070354] **1842**

PROCEEDINGS OF THE ANNUAL MEETING (US) [03456998] **4325**

PROCEEDINGS OF THE ... ANNUAL MEETING / ACADIAN ENTOMOLOGICAL SOCIETY (CN/0822-5915) [10440761] **5595**

PROCEEDINGS OF THE ... ANNUAL MEETING / AMERICAN SOCIETY OF BAKERY ENGINEERS (US/0066-0582) [01480776] **2354**

PROCEEDINGS OF THE ANNUAL MEETING - AMERICAN SOCIETY OF INTERNATIONAL LAW (US/0272-5037) [05898329] **3134**

PROCEEDINGS OF THE ANNUAL MEETING AND REGIONAL MEETING - AMERICAN ASSOCIATION OF RAILROAD SUPERINTENDENTS (US/0276-7724) [05731505] **5434**

PROCEEDINGS OF THE ANNUAL MEETING / ARKANSAS STATE HORTICULTURAL SOCIETY (US/0749-4327) [10052497] 121, **2429**

PROCEEDINGS OF THE ANNUAL MEETING - CANADIAN PEST MANAGEMENT SOCIETY (CN/0227-7980) [06703300] **4247**

PROCEEDINGS OF THE ANNUAL MEETING - FERTILIZER INDUSTRY ROUND TABLE (US/0071-4607) [01327768] **183**

PROCEEDINGS OF THE ANNUAL MEETING - FLORIDA GROUP CHILD CARE ASSOCIATION (US) [01306316] **5301**

PROCEEDINGS OF THE ANNUAL MEETING - FLORIDA STATE BEEKEEPERS ASSOCIATION (US) [01359780] **122**

PROCEEDINGS OF THE ANNUAL MEETING - INDUSTRIAL RELATIONS RESEARCH ASSOCIATION (1978) (US/0277-7347) [05272920] **1703**

PROCEEDINGS OF THE ... ANNUAL MEETING / INTERNATIONAL OMEGA ASSOCIATION (US/0278-9396) [07920318] 32, **4181**

PROCEEDINGS OF THE ANNUAL MEETING - NATIONAL ACADEMY OF ARBITRATORS. MEETING (US/0148-4176) [01639575] **2868**

PROCEEDINGS OF THE ANNUAL MEETING - NATIONAL ASSOCIATION OF SCHOOLS OF MUSIC (US/0190-6615) [28126808] 1903, **4147**

PROCEEDINGS OF THE ANNUAL MEETING - NATIONAL COUNCIL FOR AGRICULTURAL EDUCATION (TZ) [04068202] **122**

PROCEEDINGS OF THE ANNUAL MEETING OF THE BERKELEY LINGUISTICS SOCIETY (US/0363-2946) [02451782] **3312**

PROCEEDINGS OF THE ANNUAL MEETING OF THE CANADIAN HYDROMETALLURGISTS (CN/0318-417X) [02441978] **4016**

PROCEEDINGS OF THE ANNUAL MEETING OF THE CANADIAN MINERAL PROCESSORS (CN/0590-5850) [01553190] **4016**

PROCEEDINGS OF THE ANNUAL MEETING OF THE CANADIAN PUBLIC HEALTH ASSOCIATION (CN/0319-2644) [02443156] **4796**

PROCEEDINGS OF THE ANNUAL MEETING OF THE DECISION SCIENCES INSTITUTE (US/0898-9567) [15179044] **882**

PROCEEDINGS OF THE ANNUAL MEETING OF THE ENTOMOLOGICAL SOCIETY OF ALBERTA (CN/0071-0709) [02943183] **5612**

PROCEEDINGS OF THE ANNUAL MEETING OF THE FLORIDA STATE HORTICULTURAL SOCIETY (US/0886-7283) [05756119] **2429**

PROCEEDINGS OF THE ... ANNUAL MEETING OF THE LIFE INSURERS CONFERENCE (US/0075-9414) [10969377] **2890**

PROCEEDINGS OF THE ... ANNUAL MEETING OF THE NATIONAL COUNCIL ON RADIATION PROTECTION AND MEASUREMENTS (US/0195-7740) [05665781] 4796, **3944**

PROCEEDINGS OF THE ... ANNUAL MEETING OF THE NORTHEASTERN WEED SCIENCE SOCIETY (US/0078-1703) [04402495] **2180**

PROCEEDINGS OF THE ... ANNUAL MEETING OF THE SOCIETY OF PROSPECTIVE MEDICINE (US/0276-1483) [07337546] **3630**

PROCEEDINGS OF THE ANNUAL MEETING OF THE WESTERN SOCIETY FOR FRENCH HISTORY (US/0099-0329) [02242512] **2703**

PROCEEDINGS OF THE ANNUAL MEETING - SOUTHWESTERN PHILOSOPHY OF EDUCATION SOCIETY (US/0584-5041) [05379563] **1774**

PROCEEDINGS OF THE ... ANNUAL MEETING / UNIFORM LAW CONFERENCE OF CANADA (CN/0318-4900) [09701197] **3031**

PROCEEDINGS OF THE ANNUAL MEETING, WESTERN WASHINGTON HORTICULTURAL ASSOCIATION (US/0160-1156) [02784217] **2429**

PROCEEDINGS OF THE ANNUAL MISSOURI RIVER BASIN GOVERNORS' CONFERENCE (US/0160-5518) [03696320] **5537**

PROCEEDINGS OF THE ANNUAL NACD CONVENTION (US/0748-7576) [10978654] **2202**

PROCEEDINGS OF THE ANNUAL NEW MEXICO WATER CONFERENCE (US/0161-4924) [03940144] **5537**

PROCEEDINGS OF THE ANNUAL NORTH AMERICAN POWER SYMPOSIUM (US/0895-4097) [16634282] **2076**

PROCEEDINGS OF THE ANNUAL NORTHEASTERN FOREST INSECT WORK CONFERENCE (US/0160-2950) [03107595] 2391, **2239**

PROCEEDINGS OF THE ANNUAL NORTHWEST WOOD PRODUCTS CLINIC (US/0078-1797) [01760715] **2403**

PROCEEDINGS OF THE ANNUAL PACIFIC ISLANDS STUDIES CONFERENCE, UNIVERSITY OF HAWAII, THE (US/0272-3441) [06778424] **2670**

PROCEEDINGS OF THE ANNUAL RECIPROCAL MEAT CONFERENCE OF THE AMERICAN MEAT SCIENCE ASSOCIATION (US/0198-8999) [06239696] **219**

PROCEEDINGS OF THE ... ANNUAL ROAD SCHOOL (US) [01605334] **2029**

PROCEEDINGS OF THE ANNUAL ROCKY MOUNTAIN BIOENGINEERING SYMPOSIUM (US/0148-1002) [03267310] 1991, **469**

PROCEEDINGS OF THE ANNUAL SEMINAR OF THE CALIFORNIA COMMUNITY HEALTH INSTITUTE (US/0162-0657) [04071918] **4796**

PROCEEDINGS OF THE ANNUAL SOUTHEASTERN SYMPOSIUM ON SYSTEM THEORY (US/0094-2898) [04109338] **1200**

PROCEEDINGS OF THE ANNUAL SOUTHWESTERN PETROLEUM SHORT COURSE (US/0361-5987) [02093344] 1991, **4275**

PROCEEDINGS OF THE ANNUAL STUDENT SYMPOSIUM ON MARINE AFFAIRS (US/0270-1480) [05663080] **557**

PROCEEDINGS OF THE ... ANNUAL SYMPOSIUM ON ENGINEERING GEOLOGY & GEOTECHNICAL ENGINEERING (US) [22201289] **1391**

PROCEEDINGS OF THE ANNUAL SYMPOSIUM ON REDUCTION OF COSTS IN HAND-OPERATED GLASS PLANTS (US/0362-2991) [02665173] **2593**

PROCEEDINGS OF THE ANNUAL SYMPOSIUM, SAFE ASSOCIATION (US/0743-846X) [06301135] **32**

PROCEEDINGS OF THE ANNUAL TALL TIMBER FIRE ECOLOGY CONFERENCE (US) [09385334] 2292, **2391**

PROCEEDINGS OF THE ANNUAL TECHNICAL CONFERENCE (US/0737-5921) [09397090] **3486**

PROCEEDINGS OF THE ANNUAL TECHNICAL SYMPOSIUM - WILD GOOSE ASSOCIATION. TECHNICAL SYMPOSIUM (US/0883-542X) [11855459] **2202**

PROCEEDINGS OF THE ... ANNUAL TRI-SERVICE CONFERENCE ON THE BIOLOGICAL EFFECTS OF MICROWAVE RADIATION (US) [04970416] 469, **4440**

PROCEEDINGS — Alphabetical Title Index

PROCEEDINGS OF THE ... ANNUAL UNIVERSITY OF GUELPH NUTRITION CONFERENCE FOR FEED MANUFACTURERS (CN) [09728123] **203**

PROCEEDINGS OF THE ANNUAL VETERINARY MEDICAL FORUM (US/0894-7708) [13867987] 3800, **5519**

PROCEEDINGS OF THE ARAB SCHOOL ON SCIENCE AND TECHNOLOGY *CEASED.* (US/0730-7845) [08057514] **5140**

PROCEEDINGS OF THE ARISTOTELIAN SOCIETY (UK/0066-7374) [01591972] **4358**

PROCEEDINGS OF THE ARKANSAS ACADEMY OF SCIENCE (US/0097-4374) [01514142] **5140**

PROCEEDINGS OF THE ASIS ANNUAL MEETING (US/0044-7870) [03601238] **3242**

PROCEEDINGS OF THE ASIS MID-YEAR MEETING (US) [04099301] **3242**

PROCEEDINGS OF THE ... ASSEMBLY OF THE INTERNATIONAL RUBBER STUDY GROUP (UK) [08758172] **5077**

PROCEEDINGS OF THE ASSOCIATION FOR CONTINUING HIGHER EDUCATION (US) [04031489] **1842**

●PROCEEDINGS OF THE ASSOCIATION FOR EDUCATION IN JOURNALISM AND MASS COMMUNICATION SOUTHEAST COLLOQUIUM (US/1064-5403) [26326176] **2923**

PROCEEDINGS OF THE ASSOCIATIONS OF ORTHODOX JEWISH SCIENTISTS (US/0571-6489) [03382670] **5052**

PROCEEDINGS OF THE ... AUSTRALIA-NEW ZEALAND CONFERENCE ON SOIL MECHANICS AND FOUNDATION ENGINEERING (NZ/0067-1525) [02257986] **183**

PROCEEDINGS OF THE AUSTRALIAN ASSOCIATION OF GERONTOLOGY (AT/0311-9297) [01000054] **3754**

PROCEEDINGS OF THE AUSTRALIAN CERAMIC CONFERENCE (AT/0155-9796) [01785621] **2593**

PROCEEDINGS OF THE AUSTRALIAN CONFERENCE ON ELECTROCHEMISTRY (UK/0067-1827) [04930532] **1035**

PROCEEDINGS OF THE AUSTRALIAN PHYSIOLOGICAL AND PHARMACOLOGICAL SOCIETY (AT/0067-2084) [05837421] 4326, **585**

PROCEEDINGS OF THE AUSTRALIAN SOCIETY FOR BIOCHEMISTRY AND MOLECULAR BIOLOGY : ABSTRACTS OF PAPERS PRESENTED AT THE ... ANNUAL CONFERENCE OF THE SOCIETY HELD ... (AT) [25066462] **492**

PROCEEDINGS OF THE AUSTRALIAN SOCIETY OF ANIMAL PRODUCTION (AT/0067-2149) [01518865] **219**

PROCEEDINGS OF THE BAIL ... CONFERENCE (IE/0332-3226) [12172544] **5140**

PROCEEDINGS OF THE ... BIENNIAL CONFERENCE OF THE CANADIAN SOCIETY FOR COMPUTATIONAL STUDIES OF INTELLIGENCE (CN/0710-0825) [08311672] **1216**

PROCEEDINGS OF THE ... BIENNIAL CONVENTION OF THE INTERNATIONAL LONGSHOREMEN'S AND WAREHOUSEMEN'S UNION (US) [05638376] **1703**

PROCEEDINGS OF THE BIOLOGICAL SOCIETY OF WASHINGTON (US/0006-324X) [01536434] **469**

PROCEEDINGS OF THE BOSTON AREA COLLOQUIUM IN ANCIENT PHILOSOPHY (US) **4358**

PROCEEDINGS OF THE BRITISH ACADEMY (UK/0068-1202) [01772818] **1774**

PROCEEDINGS OF THE BRITISH MASONRY SOCIETY (UK/0950-9615) [17275878] **624**

PROCEEDINGS OF THE BRITISH SOCIETY FOR THE STUDY OF PROSTHETIC DENTISTRY (UK) **1333**

PROCEEDINGS OF THE BUSINESS AND ECONOMIC STATISTICS SECTION (US/0066-0736) [01169353] **1537**

PROCEEDINGS OF THE BUSINESS LAW SECTION ANNUAL MEETING (US/1060-4081) [24165092] **3102**

PROCEEDINGS OF THE CAJAL CLUB (US/0092-6930) [01789127] 469, **3680**

PROCEEDINGS OF THE CALIFORNIA ACADEMY OF SCIENCES, 4TH SERIES (US/0068-547X) [01289190] **5140**

PROCEEDINGS OF THE CALIFORNIA CONFERENCE ON RUBBER-TOUGHENED PLASTICS (US/0271-9312) [06705183] 5077, **4459**

PROCEEDINGS OF THE CAMBRIDGE ANTIQUARIAN SOCIETY (UK/0309-3603) [01552625] 1079, **2626**

PROCEEDINGS OF THE CAMBRIDGE COLLOQUIUM ON MYCENAEAN STUDIES (UK) [06866287] **2626**

PROCEEDINGS OF THE CAMBRIDGE PHILOLOGICAL SOCIETY (UK/0068-6735) [01552639] **3312**

PROCEEDINGS OF THE CAMBRIDGE PHILOLOGICAL SOCIETY. SUPPLEMENT (UK/0068-6743) [03106028] **3312**

PROCEEDINGS OF THE CANADIAN AGRICULTURAL OUTLOOK CONFERENCE (CN/0704-2426) [06534383] **122**

PROCEEDINGS OF THE CANADIAN ASSOCIATION FOR LABORATORY ANIMAL SCIENCE (CN/0708-7624) [05840859] **5519**

PROCEEDINGS OF THE CANADIAN SOCIETY FOR HORTICULTURAL SCIENCE (CN/0315-6877) [02443081] **2429**

PROCEEDINGS OF THE CASUALTY ACTUARIAL SOCIETY (US/0893-2980) [06165871] **2890**

PROCEEDINGS OF THE CENTER FOR JEWISH-CHRISTIAN LEARNING (US/0887-4913) [13256356] 5052, **4988**

PROCEEDINGS OF THE ... CHEMISTS' CONFERENCE (UK) [04116238] **1018**

PROCEEDINGS OF THE CLASSICAL ASSOCIATION (UK) [04937066] **3312**

PROCEEDINGS OF THE CLINICAL DIALYSIS AND TRANSPLANT FORUM (US/0094-6044) [01014065] **3992**

PROCEEDINGS OF THE COLLEGE OF NATURAL SCIENCES. SECTION I, MATHEMATICS *See* JANYEN GWAHAG DAIHAG NONMUNJIB **5117**

PROCEEDINGS OF THE CONFERENCE - ASSOCIATION FOR COMPUTATIONAL LINGUISTICS. MEETING (US/0736-587X) [09121073] **3312**

PROCEEDINGS OF THE ... CONFERENCE / INTERNATIONAL COAL TESTING CONFERENCE (US/0740-5162) [09960369] **1028**

PROCEEDINGS OF THE CONFERENCE OF THE AMERICAN ACADEMY OF ADVERTISING (1985) (US/0883-2404) [12096045] **764**

PROCEEDINGS OF THE CONFERENCE OF THE AMERICAN COUNTRY LIFE ASSOCIATION, INC (US/0271-4558) [05769646] **5254**

PROCEEDINGS OF THE ... CONFERENCE OF THE AUSTRALIAN SOCIETY OF SUGAR CANE TECHNOLOGISTS (AT/0726-0822) [08198818] **183**

PROCEEDINGS OF THE ... CONFERENCE OF THE INTERNATIONAL ORGANIZATION OF CITRUS VIROLOGISTS (US/0074-7203) [03402000] **183**

PROCEEDINGS OF THE CONFERENCE ON ASSISTANCE TO LOCAL GOVERNMENT (US) [04404175] **4742**

PROCEEDINGS OF THE ... CONFERENCE ON COORDINATION CHEMISTRY (XO) [15323280] **1056**

PROCEEDINGS OF THE CONFERENCE ON EXPLOSIVES AND BLASTING TECHNIQUES (US/0732-619X) [04279802] **1991**

●PROCEEDINGS OF THE ... CONFERENCE ON MEDIEVALISM (US/0899-3106) [18063655] **2703**

PROCEEDINGS OF THE CONFERENCE ON PROBABILITY THEORY (RM) [01793507] **3528**

PROCEEDINGS OF THE CONFERENCE ON PUBLIC RELATIONS IN PUBLIC UNDERTAKINGS (II/0300-3698) [01784285] **764**

PROCEEDINGS OF THE CONFERENCE ON REMOTE SYSTEMS TECHNOLOGY (US/0069-8644) [02552708] **5140**

PROCEEDINGS OF THE CONFERENCE - SOCIETY FOR THE ADVANCEMENT OF FOOD SERVICE RESEARCH (US/0081-1483) [02500985] **2354**

PROCEEDINGS OF THE CONGRESS - EUROPEAN BREWERY CONVENTION (NE/0071-2531) [01568413] **2370**

PROCEEDINGS OF THE CONGRESS - INTERNATIONAL SOCIETY OF SUGARCANE TECHNOLOGISTS *See* PROCEEDINGS OF THE INTERNATIONAL SOCIETY OF SUGARCANE TECHNOLOGISTS **183**

PROCEEDINGS OF THE CONGRESS OF THE INTERNATIONAL INSTITUTE OF PUBLIC FINANCE (US/0195-8917) [05701105] **4742**

PROCEEDINGS OF THE ... CONSTITUTIONAL CONVENTION OF THE AFL-CIO (US/0569-4515) [06996927] **1703**

PROCEEDINGS OF THE CONSTITUTIONAL CONVENTION OF THE AFL-CIO (US/0569-4515) [02201214] **1703**

PROCEEDINGS OF THE CONSTITUTIONAL CONVENTION OF THE UNITED STEEL WORKERS OF AMERICA (US) [01498323] **1703**

PROCEEDINGS OF THE ... CONTINENTAL CONGRESS OF THE NATIONAL SOCIETY OF THE DAUGHTERS OF THE AMERICAN REVOLUTION (US) [05243125] **2755**

PROCEEDINGS OF THE ... CONVENTION (UK/0143-0610) [08808242] **3425**

PROCEEDINGS OF THE CONVENTION - INSTITUTE OF BREWING AUSTRALIAN AND NEW ZEALAND SECTION (AT/0367-6897) [I03676897] **2370**

PROCEEDINGS OF THE CONVENTION - INTERNATIONAL ASSOCIATION OF FISH AND WILDLIFE AGENCIES (US/0161-3332) [03905764] **2202**

PROCEEDINGS OF THE COURT OF JUSTICE AND OF THE COURT OF FIRST INSTANCE OF THE EUROPEAN COMMUNITIES (LU) [23056649] **3031**

PROCEEDINGS OF THE DESERT FISHES COUNCIL (US) [08191423] **2310**

PROCEEDINGS OF THE DIGITAL EQUIPMENT COMPUTER USERS SOCIETY *SUSPENDED.* (US/0095-2095) [03740391] **1200**

PROCEEDINGS OF THE DREDGING SEMINAR *See* PROCEEDINGS OF THE ... ANNUAL DREDGING SEMINAR **2094**

PROCEEDINGS OF THE EASTER SCHOOL IN AGRICULTURAL SCIENCE, UNIVERSITY OF NOTTINGHAM (UK/0078-2092) [02252235] **122**

PROCEEDINGS OF THE ... EASTERN STATES CONFERENCE ON LINGUISTICS (US/1048-1656) [15045637] **3312**

PROCEEDINGS OF THE EDINBURGH MATHEMATICAL SOCIETY (UK/0013-0915) [01567485] **3528**

●PROCEEDINGS OF THE ELECTRICAL ELECTRONICS INSULATION CONFERENCE & ELECTRICAL MANUFACTURING & COIL WINDING (US/1071-6270) [28695702] **2076**

PROCEEDINGS OF THE ... ENTOMOLOGICAL CONGRESS - ENTOMOLOGICAL SOCIETY OF SOUTHERN AFRICA (SA/1010-2566) [07885873] **5613**

PROCEEDINGS OF THE ENTOMOLOGICAL SOCIETY OF MANITOBA (CN/0315-2146) [01568020] **5613**

PROCEEDINGS OF THE ENTOMOLOGICAL SOCIETY OF ONTARIO (CN/0071-0768) [02247922] **5595**

PROCEEDINGS OF THE ENTOMOLOGICAL SOCIETY OF WASHINGTON (US/0013-8797) [01568029] **5595**

PROCEEDINGS OF THE ERDA SEMIANNUAL PHOTOVOLTAIC ADVANCED MATERIALS PROGRAM (US) [04092696] **1953**

PROCEEDINGS OF THE ... EUROPEAN CONFERENCE ON MIXING (UK/0144-8846) [05659625] **2016**

PROCEEDINGS OF THE EUROPEAN ELECTRO-OPTICS MARKETS AND TECHNOLOGY CONFERENCE (UK) [04245911] **2076**

PROCEEDINGS OF THE EUROPEAN PROSTHODONTIC ASSOCIATION, THE (UK/0258-6185) [I02586185] **3630**

PROCEEDINGS OF THE EUROPEAN PROSTHODONTIC ASSOCIATION, THE (UK) **1333**

PROCEEDINGS OF THE FACULTY OF ENGINEERING OF TOKAI UNIVERSITY (JA) [03426617] **1991**

PROCEEDINGS OF THE FACULTY OF SCIENCE OF TOKAI UNIVERSITY (JA/0563-6795) [01586826] **5140**

PROCEEDINGS OF THE ... FID CONGRESS (UK) [08420398] **3242**

●PROCEEDINGS OF THE FIRST BIANNUAL INTERNATIONAL CONFERENCE ON ADVANCES IN MANAGEMENT (US/1059-356X) [24572346] 946, **883**

PROCEEDINGS OF THE FLORIDA TURF-GRASS MANAGEMENT CONFERENCE (US) [01313268] **2429**

PROCEEDINGS OF THE FLUID POWER SYMPOSIUM (UK) **2094**

PROCEEDINGS OF THE ... FORAGE AND GRASSLAND CONFERENCE (US/0886-6899) [05175982] **122**

PROCEEDINGS OF THE FORUM SESSIONS / FORUM ON FUNDAMENTAL SURGICAL PROBLEMS (US) [01317487] **3972**

PROCEEDINGS OF THE FOUNDATION FOR ORTHODONTIC RESEARCH *CEASED.* (US) [05114240] **1333**

PROCEEDINGS OF THE FULL BOARD MEETING - ISCU AB (FR/0303-1136) [00931379] **5140**

PROCEEDINGS OF THE ... GENERAL SYNOD, OFFICIAL REPORT / ANGLICAN CHURCH OF AUSTRALIA (AT) [09603505] **4988**

PROCEEDINGS OF THE GEOLOGISTS' ASSOCIATION (UK/0016-7878) [01570717] **1391**

PROCEEDINGS OF THE GOVERNMENT STATISTICS SECTION / AMERICAN STATISTICAL ASSOCIATION (US) [22658845] **4492**

PROCEEDINGS OF THE GREAT PLAINS AGRICULTURAL COUNCIL (US/0434-5835) [01751558] **122**

PROCEEDINGS OF THE GREENWOOD GENETIC CENTER (US/0733-124X) [08508688] **550**

PROCEEDINGS OF THE GULF AND CARIBBEAN FISHERIES INSTITUTE (US) [01771835] **2310**

PROCEEDINGS OF THE HAMPSHIRE FIELD CLUB AND ARCHAEOLOGICAL SOCIETY (UK/0142-8950) [06821521] **279**

PROCEEDINGS OF THE HAWAIIAN ENTOMOLOGICAL SOCIETY (US/0073-134X) [01751891] **5613**

PROCEEDINGS OF THE HEALTH POLICY FORUM (US/0195-976X) [05672629] **4796**

PROCEEDINGS OF THE HEAT TRANSFER AND FLUID MECHANICS INSTITUTE (US/0097-059X) [01259048] **2125**

PROCEEDINGS OF THE HUGUENOT SOCIETY OF GREAT BRITAIN AND IRELAND (UK) [17247823] **5066**

●PROCEEDINGS OF THE HUMAN FACTORS AND ERGONOMICS SOCIETY ... ANNUAL MEETING (US/1071-1813) [28563946] **2125**

PROCEEDINGS OF THE HUMAN FACTORS SOCIETY ANNUAL MEETING (US/0163-5182) [04353174] **2125**

PROCEEDINGS OF THE ... HYDRAULICS CONFERENCE / IOWA INSTITUTE OF HYDRAULIC RESEARCH (US) [04923155] **2094**

PROCEEDINGS OF THE ICMR SEMINAR (JA/0914-4404) [26926886] **3630**

PROCEEDINGS OF THE IEEE (US/0018-9219) [01753228] **2076**

PROCEEDINGS OF THE ... IEEE/ASME JOINT RAILROAD CONFERENCE (US) [25023976] 1992, **5434**

PROCEEDINGS OF THE ... IEEE CONFERENCE ON DECISION & CONTROL (US/0743-1546) [10549092] **2077**

PROCEEDINGS OF THE ... IEEE FREQUENCY CONTROL SYMPOSIUM (US/1068-7491) [27789679] **4418**

PROCEEDINGS OF THE IEEE INTERNATIONAL FREQUENCY CONTROL SYMPOSIUM (US) [29560689] **4418**

PROCEEDINGS OF THE IFAC WORLD CONGRESS (GW) [01784936] **2125**

PROCEEDINGS OF THE ILLINOIS MOSQUITO AND VECTOR CONTROL ASSOCIATION (US/1049-0221) [21111182] **5613**

PROCEEDINGS OF THE INDIAN ACADEMY OF SCIENCE. EARTH AND PLANETARY SCIENCES (II/0253-4126) [06748467] **1359**

PROCEEDINGS OF THE INDIAN ACADEMY OF SCIENCES. ANIMAL SCIENCES (II/0253-4118) [06748642] **5595**

PROCEEDINGS OF THE INDIAN ACADEMY OF SCIENCES. CHEMICAL SCIENCES (II/0253-4134) [06748714] **989**

PROCEEDINGS OF THE INDIAN ACADEMY OF SCIENCES. MATHEMATICAL SCIENCES (II/0253-4142) [06748514] **3528**

PROCEEDINGS OF THE INDIAN ACADEMY OF SCIENCES. PLANT SCIENCES (II/0253-410X) [06748593] **525**

PROCEEDINGS OF THE INDIAN NATIONAL SCIENCE ACADEMY. PART A, PHYSICAL SCIENCES (II/0370-0046) [01790558] **5140**

PROCEEDINGS OF THE INDIAN NATIONAL SCIENCE ACADEMY. PART B, BIOLOGICAL SCIENCES (II/0073-6600) [01640663] **469**

PROCEEDINGS OF THE INDIAN SCIENCE CONGRESS (II/0373-0786) [01752977] **5140**

PROCEEDINGS OF THE INDIAN SOCIETY OF THEORETICAL AND APPLIED MECHANICS (II/0589-3143) [03808049] **2125**

PROCEEDINGS OF THE INDIANA ACADEMY OF SCIENCE (US/0073-6767) [01258916] **5140**

PROCEEDINGS OF THE INDUSTRIAL COMPUTING CONFERENCE (US/1058-8655) [24413021] **1200**

PROCEEDINGS OF THE INDUSTRIAL WASTE, ADVANCED WATER AND SOLID WASTE CONFERENCE (US/0163-2345) [04300601] **2239**

PROCEEDINGS OF THE INDUSTRIAL WASTE CONFERENCE (US/0073-7682) [02067351] **2239**

PROCEEDINGS OF THE INSTITUTE IN TECHNICAL AND INDUSTRIAL COMMUNICATIONS (US) [01251409] **1119**

PROCEEDINGS OF THE INSTITUTE OF ACOUSTICS (UK/0309-8117) [I03098117] **4453**

PROCEEDINGS OF THE INSTITUTE OF NAVIGATION ANNUAL MEETING (US) **4181**

PROCEEDINGS OF THE INSTITUTE OF PETROLEUM (UK/0950-8708) [11223531] **4275**

PROCEEDINGS OF THE INSTITUTE ON PLANNING, ZONING, AND EMINENT DOMAIN (US/0730-3009) [01753261] 2832, **3031**

●PROCEEDINGS OF THE INSTITUTION OF CIVIL ENGINEERS. CIVIL ENGINEERING (UK/0965-089X) [25243631] **2029**

PROCEEDINGS OF THE INSTITUTION OF CIVIL ENGINEERS. GEOTECHNICAL ENGINEERING (UK) **1992**

●PROCEEDINGS OF THE INSTITUTION OF CIVIL ENGINEERS. MUNICIPAL ENGINEER (UK/0965-0903) [25920573] **2029**

●PROCEEDINGS OF THE INSTITUTION OF CIVIL ENGINEERS. STRUCTURES AND BUILDINGS (UK/0965-0911) [25479470] **2029**

●PROCEEDINGS OF THE INSTITUTION OF CIVIL ENGINEERS. TRANSPORT (UK/0965-092X) [25479485] 5390, **2029**

●PROCEEDINGS OF THE INSTITUTION OF CIVIL ENGINEERS. WATER, MARITIME AND ENERGY (UK/0965-0946) [25920500] 5537, **2094**

PROCEEDINGS OF THE INSTITUTION OF ELECTRICAL ENGINEERS (UK/0020-3270) [01606670] **2077**

PROCEEDINGS OF THE INSTITUTION OF MECHANICAL ENGINEERS (UK/0020-3483) [05123060] **2125**

PROCEEDINGS OF THE INSTITUTION OF MECHANICAL ENGINEERS. PART A, JOURNAL OF POWER AND ENERGY (UK/0957-6509) [21531945] **2126**

PROCEEDINGS OF THE INSTITUTION OF MECHANICAL ENGINEERS. PART B, JOURNAL OF ENGINEERING MANUFACTURE (UK/0954-4054) [19502289] **2126**

PROCEEDINGS OF THE INSTITUTION OF MECHANICAL ENGINEERS. PART C, JOURNAL OF MECHANICAL ENGINEERING SCIENCE (UK/0954-4062) [19502272] **2126**

PROCEEDINGS OF THE INSTITUTION OF MECHANICAL ENGINEERS. PART D, JOURNAL OF AUTOMOBILE ENGINEERING (UK/0954-4070) [19686979] **2126**

PROCEEDINGS OF THE INSTITUTION OF MECHANICAL ENGINEERS. PART E, JOURNAL OF PROCESS MECHANICAL ENGINEERING (UK/0954-4089) [19905122] **2126**

PROCEEDINGS OF THE INSTITUTION OF MECHANICAL ENGINEERS. PART F, JOURNAL OF RAIL AND RAPID TRANSIT (UK/0954-4097) [19786779] 5390, **2126**

PROCEEDINGS OF THE INSTITUTION OF MECHANICAL ENGINEERS. PART G, JOURNAL OF AEROSPACE ENGINEERING (UK/0954-4100) [19966973] 2126, **32**

PROCEEDINGS OF THE INSTITUTION OF MECHANICAL ENGINEERS. PART H, JOURNAL OF ENGINEERING IN MEDICINE (UK/0954-4119) [19502231] **3696**

PROCEEDINGS OF THE INSTITUTION OF MECHANICAL ENGINEERS. PART I, JOURNAL OF SYSTEMS & CONTROL ENGINEERING (UK/0959-6518) [23684443] **2126**

●PROCEEDINGS OF THE INSTITUTION OF MECHANICAL ENGINEERS. PART J, JOURNAL OF ENGINEERING TRIBOLOGY (UK/1350-6501) [29876485] **2126**

PROCEEDINGS OF THE INTERAGENCY WORKSHOP (US) [06874430] **3173**

PROCEEDINGS OF THE INTERAMERICAN SOCIETY FOR TROPICAL HORTICULTURE (CR) [20807570] 122, **2429**

PROCEEDINGS OF THE INTERNATIONAL AIR CARGO FORUM (US/1043-4712) [19465702] 32, **5390**

PROCEEDINGS OF THE INTERNATIONAL AND ASSOCIATION RAILWAY OPERATING OFFICERS INC (US) **5434**

PROCEEDINGS OF THE INTERNATIONAL BIOMETRIC CONFERENCE (RM/0379-1718) [03244964] **469**

PROCEEDINGS OF THE INTERNATIONAL CENTRE FOR HEAT AND MASS TRANSFER *CEASED.* (US/0272-880X) [06970394] **4418**

PROCEEDINGS OF THE INTERNATIONAL CONFERENCE / ... COASTAL ENGINEERING CONFERENCE (US/0893-8717) [13514443] **2029**

PROCEEDINGS OF THE INTERNATIONAL CONFERENCE ON BASEMENT TECTONICS (US/0270-5427) [06248278] **1391**

PROCEEDINGS OF THE INTERNATIONAL CONFERENCE ON DISTRIBUTED COMPUTING SYSTEMS (US/1063-6927) [24267263] **1243**

PROCEEDINGS OF THE INTERNATIONAL CONFERENCE ON FIRE SAFETY (US/0193-306X) [05163255] 4796, **2292**

PROCEEDINGS OF THE INTERNATIONAL CONFERENCE ON FLUIDIZED BED COMBUSTION (US/0197-453X) [06035168] **4418**

PROCEEDINGS OF THE ... INTERNATIONAL CONFERENCE ON INFORMATION SYSTEMS / SPONSORED BY RESEARCH AND EDUCATION IN INFORMATION SYSTEMS, THE SOCIETY FOR MANAGEMENT INFORMATION SYSTEMS IN COOPERATION WITH SPECIAL INTEREST GROUP ON BUSINESS DATA PROCESSING, ASSOCIATION FOR COMPUTING MACHINERY AND COLLEGE ON INFORMATION SYSTEMS, THE INSTITUTE OF MANAGEMENT SCIENCES (US) [08216539] **1200**

PROCEEDINGS OF THE INTERNATIONAL CONFERENCE ON LASERS (US/0190-4132) [04392950] 4418, **5140**

PROCEEDINGS OF THE ... INTERNATIONAL CONFERENCE ON OFFSHORE MECHANICS AND ARCTIC ENGINEERING / ORGANIZED BY OMAE CONFERENCE COMMITTEE AND ASME OFFSHORE MECHANICS AND ARCTIC ENGINEERING DIVISION (US) [17742672] **2094**

PROCEEDINGS OF THE INTERNATIONAL CONFERENCE ON PARALLEL PROCESSING (US/0190-3918) [03909777] **1261**

PROCEEDINGS OF THE ... INTERNATIONAL CONFERENCE ON SOCIAL WELFARE (US) [01607269] **5301**

PROCEEDINGS OF THE INTERNATIONAL CONFERENCE ON THERMAL INSULATION (US/0734-7499) [07809008] **1992**

PROCEEDINGS OF THE ... INTERNATIONAL CONGRESS OF REFRIGERATION (GW) [08353324] **2607**

PROCEEDINGS OF THE INTERNATIONAL CONGRESS ON ANIMAL REPRODUCTION & ARTIFICIAL INSEMINATION (NE) **5519**

PROCEEDINGS OF THE INTERNATIONAL CONGRESS ON CATALYSIS (NE) [01641019] **1028**

PROCEEDINGS OF THE INTERNATIONAL CONGRESS ON EXPERIMENTAL MECHANICS (US/1046-672X) [11929960] **1992**

PROCEEDINGS OF THE INTERNATIONAL CONGRESS ON HIGH SPEED PHOTOGRAPHY AND PHOTONICS (US/1018-9181) [05671260] **4375**

PROCEEDINGS OF THE INTERNATIONAL CONGRESS ON MEDICAL RECORDS (UK/0534-9354) [04703556] **3630**

PROCEEDINGS OF THE INTERNATIONAL CONGRESS ON METALLIC CORROSION (US/0074-4123) [02255049] 2107, **2016**

PROCEEDINGS OF THE ... INTERNATIONAL CONGRESS ON RHEOLOGY (US) [02149549] **4418**

PROCEEDINGS OF THE ... INTERNATIONAL CRYOGENIC ENGINEERING CONFERENCE (UK/0308-5422) [07824286] **1992**

PROCEEDINGS OF THE INTERNATIONAL GAS RESEARCH CONFERENCE (US/0736-5721) [09236923] **4275**

PROCEEDINGS OF THE INTERNATIONAL GRASSLAND CONGRESS (JA) **122**

PROCEEDINGS OF THE INTERNATIONAL INSTRUMENTATION SYMPOSIUM (US/0277-7576) [02751623] **32**

PROCEEDINGS OF THE ... INTERNATIONAL MATADOR CONFERENCE (UK) [18546303] 2521, **4913**

PROCEEDINGS OF THE ... INTERNATIONAL MEETING OF THE INSTITUTE OF MANAGEMENT SCIENCES (UK) [10719460] **883**

PROCEEDINGS — Alphabetical Title Index

PROCEEDINGS OF THE INTERNATIONAL MICROELECTRONICS CONFERENCE (JA) [09941537] **2077**

PROCEEDINGS OF THE ... INTERNATIONAL MODAL ANALYSIS CONFERENCE & EXHIBIT (US/1046-6770) [12688884] **1992**

PROCEEDINGS OF THE INTERNATIONAL ORNITHOLOGICAL CONGRESS (AT/0074-7211) [01640865] **5595**

PROCEEDINGS OF THE INTERNATIONAL PEACE RESEARCH ASSOCIATION *CEASED.* (NE) [02253700] **4532**

PROCEEDINGS OF THE ... INTERNATIONAL PHYSICOCHEMICAL HYDRODYNAMICS CONFERENCE (UK) [07661937] **1056**

PROCEEDINGS OF THE INTERNATIONAL PYROTECHNICS SEMINAR (UK/0270-1898) [06352951] **989**

PROCEEDINGS OF THE INTERNATIONAL SCHOOL OF HYDROCARBON MEASUREMENT (US/0145-7594) [02779125] **989**

PROCEEDINGS OF THE INTERNATIONAL SCHOOL OF PHYSICS "ENRICO FERMI" (NE/0074-784X) [01587090] **4418**

PROCEEDINGS OF THE INTERNATIONAL SOCIETY OF SUGARCANE TECHNOLOGISTS (US/0096-7580) [01394133] **183**

PROCEEDINGS OF THE INTERNATIONAL SYMPOSIUM ON COMPUTER AIDED SEISMIC ANALYSIS AND DISCRIMINATION (US/0732-0175) [07911459] 1224, **5140**

PROCEEDINGS OF THE ... INTERNATIONAL SYMPOSIUM ON CONTROLLED RELEASE OF BIOACTIVE MATERIALS (US) [16057833] **989**

PROCEEDINGS OF THE ... INTERNATIONAL SYMPOSIUM ON MICROELECTRONICS (US) [17611007] **2077**

●PROCEEDINGS OF THE INTERNATIONAL SYMPOSIUM ON REMOTE SENSING AND GLOBAL ENVIRONMENTAL CHANGE (US/1068-9281) [27859553] **1409**

PROCEEDINGS OF THE INTERNATIONAL SYMPOSIUM ON REMOTE SENSING OF ENVIRONMENT *See* PROCEEDINGS OF THE INTERNATIONAL SYMPOSIUM ON REMOTE SENSING AND GLOBAL ENVIRONMENTAL CHANGE **1409**

PROCEEDINGS OF THE INTERNATIONAL TECHNICAL CONFERENCE ON SLURRY TRANSPORTATION (US/0739-5825) [05361238] **2094**

PROCEEDINGS OF THE INTERNATIONAL WORKSHOP ON GROSS PROPERTIES OF NUCLEI AND NUCLEAR EXCITATIONS (GW/0720-8715) [09587740] **4450**

PROCEEDINGS OF THE ... INTERSOCIETY ENERGY CONVERSION ENGINEERING CONFERENCE (US/0146-955X) [07080594] 1992, **1953**

PROCEEDINGS OF THE ... IPI-CONGRESS (SZ) [10873102] **1028**

PROCEEDINGS OF THE IRISH BIBLICAL ASSOCIATION (IE/0332-4427) [08583839] **5019**

PROCEEDINGS OF THE JAPAN ACADEMY. SERIES A: MATHEMATICAL SCIENCES (JA/0386-2194) [03403745] **3528**

PROCEEDINGS OF THE JAPAN ACADEMY. SERIES B: PHYSICAL AND BIOLOGICAL SCIENCES (JA/0386-2208) [03403778] 4418, **469**

PROCEEDINGS OF THE JAPAN CONGRESS ON MATERIALS RESEARCH (JA/0368-3141) [07592903] 2016, **1992**

PROCEEDINGS OF THE JOHNS HOPKINS WORKSHOP ON CURRENT PROBLEMS IN PARTICLE THEORY (US/0275-617X) [07181561] **4418**

PROCEEDINGS OF THE KONINKLIJKE NEDERLANDSE AKADEMIE VAN WETENSCHAPPEN (1990) (NE/0924-8323) [21722084] **5140**

PROCEEDINGS OF THE LAURANCE REID GAS CONDITIONING CONFERENCE (US/0887-6746) [13318731] **4275**

PROCEEDINGS OF THE LEBEDEV PHYSICS INSTITUTE OF THE ACADEMY OF SCIENCES OF RUSSIA (US/0896-8462) [17255092] **4418**

PROCEEDINGS OF THE LEEDS PHILOSOPHICAL AND LITERARY SOCIETY, LITERARY AND HISTORICAL SECTION (UK/0024-0281) [02308462] 2852, **5235**

PROCEEDINGS OF THE LEEDS PHILOSOPHICAL AND LITERARY SOCIETY. SCIENTIFIC SECTION (UK/0369-9986) [01606217] **2852**

PROCEEDINGS OF THE LEHIGH COUNTY HISTORICAL SOCIETY (US/0273-2912) [01755740] **2755**

PROCEEDINGS OF THE LINGUISTIC CIRCLE OF MANITOBA AND NORTH DAKOTA (CN/0075-9597) [02247446] **3312**

PROCEEDINGS OF THE LINNEAN SOCIETY OF NEW SOUTH WALES (AT/0370-047X) [01755950] **4170**

PROCEEDINGS OF THE LONDON MATHEMATICAL SOCIETY (UK/0024-6115) [01606055] **3528**

PROCEEDINGS OF THE LOUISIANA ACADEMY OF SCIENCES, THE (US/0096-9192) [01756222] **5141**

PROCEEDINGS OF THE MALAYSIAN BIOCHEMICAL SOCIETY CONFERENCE (MY/0126-9208) [11285887] **492**

PROCEEDINGS OF THE MARINE SAFETY COUNCIL (US/0364-0981) [02520397] **4182**

PROCEEDINGS OF THE MASSACHUSETTS HISTORICAL SOCIETY (US/0076-4981) [01695300] **2755**

PROCEEDINGS OF THE MATHEMATICAL AND PHYSICAL SOCIETY OF EGYPT (UA) [02179585] 4418, **3528**

●PROCEEDINGS OF THE ... MEETING / ASSOCIATION OF RESEARCH LIBRARIES (US/1075-0886) [29933536] **3242**

PROCEEDINGS OF THE MEETING. - FEDERAL RESERVE RELATIONS COMMITTEE (US) [01313247] **804**

PROCEEDINGS OF THE ... MEETING OF THE AGRICULTURAL CREDIT BOARD (II/0377-2861) [02405946] **804**

PROCEEDINGS OF THE MEETING OF THE EXPERT PANEL ON AIR POLLUTION MODELING (BE/0377-7669) [01790874] **2239**

PROCEEDINGS OF THE ... MEETING OF THE FRENCH COLONIAL HISTORICAL SOCIETY (US/0362-7055) [02319935] **2703**

PROCEEDINGS OF THE ... MEETING OF THE INTERNATIONAL RUBBER STUDY GROUP (UK) [08968710] **5077**

PROCEEDINGS OF THE MEETING ON CARDIOVASCULAR EPIDEMIOLOGY AND BIOSTATISTICS TRAINING PROGRAMS (US) [06698041] 3736, **3709**

PROCEEDINGS OF THE MICHIANA AREA HISTORIANS (US/0886-733X) [02428436] **2626**

PROCEEDINGS OF THE MICROSCOPICAL SOCIETY OF CANADA (CN/0381-1751) [03248159] **573**

PROCEEDINGS OF THE ... MIDWEST SYMPOSIUM ON CIRCUITS AND SYSTEMS (US) [21538015] **2077**

PROCEEDINGS OF THE MINERAL WASTE UTILIZATION SYMPOSIUM (US/0160-0206) [01781909] **1444**

PROCEEDINGS OF THE MONTANA ACADEMY OF SCIENCES (US/0096-9206) [01268558] **5141**

PROCEEDINGS OF THE MUMPS USERS' GROUP MEETING (US/0276-699X) [07399099] **1200**

PROCEEDINGS OF THE MUSKEG RESEARCH CONFERENCE (CN/0541-4393) [01078697] **2573**

PROCEEDINGS OF THE NATIONAL ACADEMY OF SCIENCE OF THE UNITED STATES OF AMERICA (US/0027-8424) [01607201] **5141**

PROCEEDINGS OF THE NATIONAL ACADEMY OF SCIENCES, INDIA. SECTION A : PHYSICAL SCIENCES (II/0369-8203) [01759019] 398, 989, **4418**

PROCEEDINGS OF THE NATIONAL ACADEMY OF SCIENCES, INDIA. SECTION B : BIOLOGICAL SCIENCES (II/0369-8211) [01759020] **5141**

PROCEEDINGS OF THE ... NATIONAL AGRICULTURAL PLASTICS CONGRESS (US/1073-1768) [11957236] 122, **4459**

PROCEEDINGS OF THE NATIONAL ASSOCIATION OF ANIMAL BREEDERS (US/0077-3255) **219**

PROCEEDINGS OF THE NATIONAL ASSOCIATION OF INSURANCE COMMISSIONERS (US/0363-0358) [01606231] **2890**

PROCEEDINGS OF THE NATIONAL CONFERENCE OF SOUTH AFRICAN SURVEYORS (SA) [02240620] **2029**

PROCEEDINGS OF THE ... NATIONAL CONFERENCE OF THE AUSTRALIAN MUSIC THERAPY ASSOCIATION HELD IN ..., THE (AT/0314-528X) [20225068] **4147**

PROCEEDINGS OF THE NATIONAL CONFERENCE ON BUSINESS ETHICS (US) [04093833] **704**

PROCEEDINGS OF THE NATIONAL CONFERENCE ON COMPLETE WATER REUSE (US) [05725115] **5537**

PROCEEDINGS OF THE NATIONAL CONFERENCE ON FLUID POWER (US/0160-8428) [04686517] **2095**

PROCEEDINGS OF THE NATIONAL CONFERENCE ON OUTDOOR RECREATION RESEARCH (US) [01073613] **4877**

PROCEEDINGS OF THE NATIONAL CONFERENCE ON PUBLIC GAMING (US/0093-7878) [01793057] **3173**

PROCEEDINGS OF THE NATIONAL GROUND WATER QUALITY SYMPOSIUM *CEASED.* (US/0886-9235) [02191085] **5537**

PROCEEDINGS OF THE NATIONAL INSTITUTE FOR PETROLEUM LANDMEN (US/0547-7441) [01095899] **4275**

PROCEEDINGS OF THE NATIONAL OCEAN SURVEY HYDROGRAPHIC SURVEY CONFERENCE, ... ANNUAL MEETING (US/0276-4849) [07355881] **4182**

PROCEEDINGS OF THE ... NATIONAL OUTDOOR ACTION CONFERENCE ON AQUIFER RESTORATION, GROUND WATER MONITORING, AND GEOPHYSICAL METHODS / SPONSORS, THE ASSOCIATION OF GROUND WATER SCIENTISTS AND ENGINEERS (DIVISION OF NWWA) & U.S. EPA-EMSL (US) [17382923] **5537**

PROCEEDINGS OF THE ... NATIONAL PASSIVE SOLAR CONFERENCE (US) [13771520] **1953**

PROCEEDINGS OF THE NATIONAL SCIENCE COUNCIL, REPUBLIC OF CHINA. PART A, PHYSICAL SCIENCE AND ENGINEERING (CH/0255-6588) [11710654] **5141**

PROCEEDINGS OF THE NATIONAL SCIENCE COUNCIL, REPUBLIC OF CHINA. PART B, LIFE SCIENCES (CH/0255-6596) [11475356] **3630**

PROCEEDINGS OF THE NATIONAL SEMINAR ON YEAR-ROUND EDUCATION (US/0095-2451) [01794253] **1869**

PROCEEDINGS OF THE NATIONAL TECHNICAL MEETING / INSTITUTE OF NAVIGATION (US) **4182**

PROCEEDINGS OF THE NATIONAL TECHNICAL MEETING / THE INSTITUTE OF NAVIGATION (US) [11874343] **4182**

PROCEEDINGS OF THE NEW ENGLAND RAILROAD CLUB (US) [02449029] **5434**

PROCEEDINGS OF THE NEW SOUTH WALES SOCIETY FOR COMPUTERS AND THE LAW (AT/0813-8230) [08138230] 1200, **3031**

PROCEEDINGS OF THE NEW ZEALAND GEOGRAPHY CONFERENCE (NZ/1170-5698) [01606909] **2573**

PROCEEDINGS OF THE NEW ZEALAND GRASSLAND ASSOCIATION (NZ/0369-3902) [01624041] **122**

PROCEEDINGS OF THE NEW ZEALAND INSTITUTE OF ARGRICULTURAL SCIENCE & THE NEW ZEALAND SOCIETY HORTICULTURAL SCIENCE ANNUAL CONVENTION (NZ/1172-2827) [11722827] **122**

●PROCEEDINGS OF THE NEW ZEALAND PLANT PROTECTION CONFERENCE (NZ/1172-0719) [27398019] 4247, **525**

PROCEEDINGS OF THE NEW ZEALAND SOCIETY OF ANIMAL PRODUCTION (NZ/0370-2731) [01760291] **219**

PROCEEDINGS OF THE NEW ZEALAND WEED AND PEST CONTROL CONFERENCE *See* PROCEEDINGS OF THE NEW ZEALAND PLANT PROTECTION CONFERENCE **525**

PROCEEDINGS OF THE NIPR SYMPOSIUM ON ANTARCTIC GEOSCIENCES (JA/0914-2029) [17980695] **1391**

PROCEEDINGS OF THE NIPR SYMPOSIUM ON ANTARCTIC METEORITES (JA/0914-5621) [19080901] **398**

PROCEEDINGS OF THE NIPR SYMPOSIUM ON POLAR BIOLOGY (JA/0914-563X) [18605179] **557**

PROCEEDINGS OF THE NIPR SYMPOSIUM ON POLAR METEOROLOGY AND GLACIOLOGY (JA/0914-2037) [18032159] **1433**

PROCEEDINGS OF THE NIPR SYMPOSIUM ON UPPER ATMOSPHERE PHYSICS (JA) [18733180] **4445**

PROCEEDINGS OF THE NORTH AMERICAN SOCIETY FOR OCEANIC HISTORY (US/0198-7194) [05230606] **4182**

PROCEEDINGS OF THE NORTH DAKOTA ACADEMY OF SCIENCE (US/0096-9214) [01727617] **5141**

PROCEEDINGS OF THE NORTH OF ENGLAND SOILS DISCUSSION GROUP (UK/0263-9335) [03332986] **183**

PROCEEDINGS OF THE NORTHERN LIBRARIES COLLOQUY (CN/0702-0147) [02537669] **3242**

Alphabetical Title Index — PROCEEDINGS

PROCEEDINGS OF THE NOVA SCOTIAN INSTITUTE OF SCIENCE (CN/0078-2521) [01362991] **5141**

PROCEEDINGS OF THE NUTRITION SOCIETY (UK/0029-6651) [01760948] **4197**

PROCEEDINGS OF THE NUTRITION SOCIETY OF AUSTRALIA (AT/0314-1004) [04815902] **4198**

PROCEEDINGS OF THE NUTRITION SOCIETY OF INDIA (II/0253-7567) [06455259] **4198**

PROCEEDINGS OF THE NUTRITION SOCIETY OF NEW ZEALAND (NZ/0110-4187) [07432314] **4198**

PROCEEDINGS OF THE OCEAN DRILLING PROGRAM. PART A, INITIAL REPORT (US/0884-5883) [12406767] **1391**

PROCEEDINGS OF THE OKLAHOMA ACADEMY OF SCIENCE (US/0078-4303) [01761193] **5141**

PROCEEDINGS OF THE OREGON ACADEMY OF SCIENCE (US/0370-1093) [04552291] **5141**

PROCEEDINGS OF THE PAKISTAN ACADEMY OF SCIENCES (PK/0377-2969) [01790645] **5141**

PROCEEDINGS OF THE ... PAVING AND TRANSPORTATION CONFERENCE ... (US) [09335831] **2029**

PROCEEDINGS OF THE PEORIA ACADEMY OF SCIENCE (US/0079-0745) [03918254] **4170**

PROCEEDINGS OF THE PLANT GROWTH REGULATOR SOCIETY OF AMERICA (US/0731-1664) [08124467] **525**

PROCEEDINGS OF THE PLANT GROWTH REGULATOR WORKING GROUP (US/0149-7685) [03544533] **2429**

PROCEEDINGS OF THE PMR CONFERENCE (US/0272-8710) [04553500] 3425, **1079**

PROCEEDINGS OF THE PREHISTORIC SOCIETY (UK/0079-497X) [05904850] **243**

PROCEEDINGS OF THE PRODUCTION CONFERENCE (US) [05655528] **2354**

PROCEEDINGS OF THE PUBLIC LIBRARIES BOARD STAFF CONFERENCE AND SEMINAR (UG) [02678912] **3242**

PROCEEDINGS OF THE RED DEER SURGICAL SOCIETY (CN/0711-4915) [08651914] **3972**

PROCEEDINGS OF THE ... REPRESENTATIVE ASSEMBLY / NATIONAL EDUCATION ASSOCIATION OF THE UNITED STATES (US) [06248210] **1869**

PROCEEDINGS OF THE RESEARCH INSTITUTE OF ATMOSPHERICS, NAGOYA UNIVERSITY (JA/0077-264X) [06107394] **1433**

PROCEEDINGS OF THE RESIDENTIAL CONFERENCE OF THE AUSTRALIAN INSTITUTE OF CRIMINOLOGY (AT) [01796091] **3173**

PROCEEDINGS OF THE ROBERT A. WELCH FOUNDATION CONFERENCES ON CHEMICAL RESEARCH (US/0557-1588) [01681090] **989**

PROCEEDINGS OF THE ROCHESTER ACADEMY OF SCIENCE (US/0096-4166) [01379666] **5141**

PROCEEDINGS OF THE ROCKBRIDGE HISTORICAL SOCIETY (US/0080-3383) [01904762] **2755**

PROCEEDINGS OF THE ROYAL INSTITUTION OF GREAT BRITAIN (UK/0035-8959) [10622343] **5141**

PROCEEDINGS OF THE ROYAL IRISH ACADEMY (IE) [07806551] **3425**

PROCEEDINGS OF THE ROYAL IRISH ACADEMY. SECTION A. MATHEMATICAL AND PHYSICAL SCIENCES (IE/0035-8975) [05188355] 5141, **3528**

PROCEEDINGS OF THE ROYAL IRISH ACADEMY. SECTION B. BIOLOGICAL, GEOLOGICAL AND CHEMICAL SCIENCE (IE/0035-8983) [06260923] **470**

PROCEEDINGS OF THE ROYAL IRISH ACADEMY. SECTION C. ARCHAEOLOGY, CELTIC STUDIES, HISTORY, LINGUISTICS AND LITERATURE (IE/0035-8991) [05185340] **279**

PROCEEDINGS OF THE ROYAL NETHERLANDS ACADEMY OF ARTS AND SCIENCES: BIOLOGICAL, CHEMICAL, GEOLOGICAL, PHYSICAL AND MEDICAL SCIENCES (NE/0924-8328) **5141**

PROCEEDINGS OF THE ROYAL SOCIETY OF CANADA. DELIBERATIONS DE LA SOCIETE ROYALE DU CANADA (CN) [07186415] **5235**

PROCEEDINGS OF THE ROYAL SOCIETY OF EDINBURGH. SECTION A. MATHEMATICA (UK/0308-2105) [02914891] **3528**

PROCEEDINGS OF THE ROYAL SOCIETY OF EDINBURGH. SECTION B, BIOLOGICAL SCIENCES *CEASED.* (UK/0269-7270) [04545910] 4170, **470**

PROCEEDINGS OF THE ROYAL SOCIETY OF NEW ZEALAND *SUSPENDED.* (NZ/0557-4161) [01696234] **5141**

PROCEEDINGS OF THE ROYAL SOCIETY OF QUEENSLAND (AT/0080-469X) [01639402] **5141**

PROCEEDINGS OF THE ROYAL SOCIETY OF VICTORIA (AT/0035-9211) [01764622] **5141**

PROCEEDINGS OF THE SAN DIEGO BIOMEDICAL SYMPOSIUM (US/0095-5876) [01798076] **3696**

PROCEEDINGS OF THE SAN DIEGO SOCIETY OF NATURAL HISTORY (US/1059-8707) [22535368] **4170**

● PROCEEDINGS OF THE SCHOOL OF SCIENCE OF TOKAI UNIVERSITY (JA/0563-6759) [28235671] **5142**

PROCEEDINGS OF THE SECTION ON QUALITY AND PRODUCTIVITY (US) **5336**

PROCEEDINGS OF THE SECTION ON STATISTICAL EDUCATION - AMERICAN STATISTICAL ASSOCIATION. SECTION ON STATISTICAL EDUCATION (US/0733-1282) [06506521] **5336**

PROCEEDINGS OF THE SECTION ON STATISTICAL GRAPHICS (US/1048-5635) [16881414] **5336**

PROCEEDINGS OF THE SECTION ON STATISTICS AND THE ENVIRONMENT / AMERICAN STATISTICAL ASSOCIATION (US) [26649187] **2180**

PROCEEDINGS OF THE SECTION ON SURVEY RESEARCH METHODS (US/0733-5830) [05456475] **3542**

PROCEEDINGS OF THE SEMINAR FOR ARABIAN STUDIES (UK) [01784569] **2662**

PROCEEDINGS OF THE ... SEMINAR OF CATASTROPHISM AND ANCIENT HISTORY (US/0890-5592) [10971910] **2626**

PROCEEDINGS OF THE SEMINAR OF THE CONFERENCE OF INSURANCE LEGISLATORS (US/0160-4163) [03662113] **2890**

PROCEEDINGS OF THE SOCIAL STATISTICS SECTION (WASHINGTON) (US/C066-0752) [02050847] **5336**

PROCEEDINGS OF THE SOCIETY FOR CALIFORNIA ARCHAEOLOGY (US/0897-0947) [17396569] **279**

PROCEEDINGS OF THE SOCIETY FOR EXPERIMENTAL BIOLOGY AND MEDICINE (US/0037-9727) [01765882] 470, **3630**

PROCEEDINGS OF THE SOCIETY FOR EXPERIMENTAL MECHANICS (US/1046-6789) [12093287] **4429**

PROCEEDINGS, OF THE SOCIETY FOR EXPERIMENTAL STRESS ANALYSIS (US/0036-1313) [02052827] **2126**

PROCEEDINGS OF THE SOCIETY FOR INFORMATION DISPLAY *See* JOURNAL OF THE SOCIETY FOR INFORMATION DISPLAY **3221**

PROCEEDINGS OF THE SOCIETY FOR PSYCHICAL RESEARCH (UK/0081-1475) [01765888] **4609**

PROCEEDINGS OF THE SOCIETY OF ANTIQUARIES OF SCOTLAND (UK/0081-1564) [01589079] 2626, **279**

● PROCEEDINGS OF THE SOCIETY OF MAGNETIC RESONANCE IN MEDICINE (US/1065-9889) [26823906] 3630, **4445**

PROCEEDINGS OF THE SOUTH ATLANTIC PHILOSOPHY OF EDUCATION SOCIETY (US) **1774**

PROCEEDINGS OF THE SOUTH CAROLINA HISTORICAL ASSOCIATION, THE (US/0361-6207) [01969179] **2755**

PROCEEDINGS OF THE SOUTH DAKOTA ACADEMY OF SCIENCE (US/0096-378X) [01766143] **5142**

PROCEEDINGS OF THE SOUTHEAST ASIA PETROLEUM EXPLORATION SOCIETY (SI) [17504578] **4275**

PROCEEDINGS OF THE SOUTHERN PASTURE AND FORAGE CROP IMPROVEMENT CONFERENCE (US/0193-6425) [02638744] **183**

PROCEEDINGS OF THE SPECIAL COMMITTEE OF THE SENATE ON A NORTHERN GAS PIPELINE (CN/0707-8994) [04879962] **4275**

PROCEEDINGS OF THE SPECIAL COMMITTEE OF THE SENATE ON NATIONAL DEFENCE (CN/0840-1705) [11816241] **4054**

PROCEEDINGS OF THE SPECIAL COMMITTEE OF THE SENATE ON SCIENCE POLICY (CN) [03819774] **5142**

PROCEEDINGS OF THE SPECIAL COMMITTEE OF THE SENATE ON THE NORTHERN PIPELINE (CN/0707-9001) [04879974] **4275**

PROCEEDINGS OF THE SPECIAL CONVENTION OF THE NATIONAL COLLEGIATE ATHLETIC ASSOCIATION (US/0094-4459) [01793207] **4913**

PROCEEDINGS OF THE SPECIAL SENATE COMMITTEE ON RETIREMENT AGE POLICIES (CN/0708-1421) [04879951] **1703**

PROCEEDINGS OF THE SPI ANNUAL TECHNICAL/MARKETING CONFERENCE (US/0740-8897) [10059069] **989**

PROCEEDINGS OF THE ... SPRING MEETING (INDUSTRIAL RELATIONS RESEARCH ASSOCIATION : 1979) (US/0733-0898) [07913533] 946, **1703**

PROCEEDINGS OF THE STANDING SENATE COMMITTEE ON AGRICULTURE AND FORESTRY (CN/0842-3008) [15260843] **122**

PROCEEDINGS OF THE STANDING SENATE COMMITTEE ON BANKING, TRADE AND COMMERCE (CN/0829-7460) [02442344] 804, **849**

PROCEEDINGS OF THE STANDING SENATE COMMITTEE ON FISHERIES (CN/0842-2990) [15022624] **2311**

PROCEEDINGS OF THE STANDING SENATE COMMITTEE ON FOREIGN AFFAIRS (CN/0576-3819) [02442346] **4532**

PROCEEDINGS OF THE STANDING SENATE COMMITTEE ON LEGAL AND CONSTITUTIONAL AFFAIRS (CN/0576-3835) [04232808] **3093**

PROCEEDINGS OF THE STANDING SENATE COMMITTEE ON NATIONAL FINANCE (CN/0576-3851) [02248535] **4675**

● PROCEEDINGS OF THE STANDING SENATE COMMITTEE ON PRIVILEGES, STANDING RULES AND ORDERS (CN/1193-5251) [26655362] **4675**

PROCEEDINGS OF THE STANDING SENATE COMMITTEE ON TRANSPORT AND COMMUNICATIONS (CN/1189-2005) [02442340] 5390, **1119**

PROCEEDINGS OF THE STATISTICAL COMPUTING SECTION (US/0149-9963) [03054461] **3528**

PROCEEDINGS OF THE ... STEELMAKING CONFERENCE (US/0895-9900) [15615218] **4016**

PROCEEDINGS OF THE SUBCOMMITTEE ON CHILDHOOD EXPERIENCES AS CAUSES OF CRIMINAL BEHAVIOUR (CN/0707-9044) [03564962] **3173**

PROCEEDINGS OF THE SUBCOMMITTEE ON NATIONAL DEFENCE (CN) [08101923] **4054**

PROCEEDINGS OF THE SUBCOMMITTEE ON OFF-TRACK BETTING (CN/0708-4978) [05257827] **2801**

● PROCEEDINGS OF THE SUBCOMMITTEE ON SECURITY AND NATIONAL DEFENCE (CN/1193-1612) [26758026] **4054**

● PROCEEDINGS OF THE SUBCOMMITTEE ON SECURITY AND NATIONAL DEFENCE (FRENCH EDITION) (CN/1193-1612) [26758030] **4054**

PROCEEDINGS OF THE SUFFOLK INSTITUTE OF ARCHAEOLOGY AND HISTORY (UK/0262-6004) [03962215] 2626, **279**

PROCEEDINGS OF THE ... SUGAR PROCESSING RESEARCH CONFERENCE (US/0730-6490) [08030322] **989**

PROCEEDINGS OF THE SUMMER COMPUTER SIMULATION CONFERENCE (US/0094-7474) [01790859] **1283**

PROCEEDINGS OF THE ... SYMPOSIUM ON ENGINEERING ASPECTS OF MAGNETOHYDRODYNAMICS (US) [22982458] **1992**

PROCEEDINGS OF THE ... SYMPOSIUM ON THE GEOLOGY OF THE BAHAMAS (BF) [19412450] **1391**

PROCEEDINGS OF THE ... SYMPOSIUM ON THERMOPHYSICAL PROPERTIES *CEASED.* (US/0082-0989) [04534935] **1056**

PROCEEDINGS OF THE TEACHERS GUILD OF NEW SOUTH WALES (AT) [I03138682] **1774**

PROCEEDINGS OF THE TECHNICAL CONFERENCE ON ARTIFICIAL INSEMINATION AND REPRODUCTION (US/0190-4531) [01641087] **219**

PROCEEDINGS OF THE TECHNICAL PROGRAM - INTERNATIONAL MICROELECTRONICS CONFERENCE (US/0163-917X) [04341835] **2077**

PROCEEDINGS OF THE TECHNICAL PROGRAM - NATIONAL NOISE AND VIBRATION CONTROL CONFERENCE (US/0149-3019) [03422359] **2239**

PROCEEDINGS OF THE TECHNOLOGICAL CONFERENCE (II) [03565367] **5355**

● PROCEEDINGS OF THE THEMATIC CONFERENCE ON REMOTE SENSING FOR MARINE AND COASTAL ENVIRONMENTS (US/1066-3711) [26926246] **2180**

PROCEEDINGS — Alphabetical Title Index

PROCEEDINGS OF THE ... TIHANY SYMPOSIUM ON RADIATION CHEMISTRY (HU/0134-126X) [07498915] **989**

PROCEEDINGS OF THE TOPOLOGY CONFERENCE, THE (US/0196-3880) [05794526] **3528**

PROCEEDINGS OF THE ... TRIENNIAL ASSEMBLY (... MEETING) OF THE CANADIAN COUNCIL OF CHURCHES, THE (CN/0227-4337) [07822726] **4988**

PROCEEDINGS OF THE TRIENNIAL CONFERENCE (NE/0071-2507) [01568412] **183**

PROCEEDINGS OF THE ... U.S. NATIONAL CONGRESS OF APPLIED MECHANICS (US) [01768762] **2126**

PROCEEDINGS OF THE U.S. PUBLIC HEALTH SERVICE COOPERATIVE STUDIES (RENAL DISEASE AND HYPERTENSION) (US) [11732226] **3992**, **3709**

PROCEEDINGS OF THE UNITARIAN UNIVERSALIST HISTORICAL SOCIETY, THE (US/0731-4078) [07764268] **5066**

PROCEEDINGS OF THE UNIVERSITY OF NEWCASTLE-UPON-TYNE PHILOSOPHICAL SOCIETY (UK/0078-0251) [04911796] **4358**

PROCEEDINGS OF THE UNIVERSITY OF OTAGO MEDICAL SCHOOL (NZ/0301-6331) [01567096] **3630**

PROCEEDINGS OF THE VIRGIL SOCIETY (UK/0083-629X) [01587570] **5235**

PROCEEDINGS OF THE WASHINGTON STATE ENTOMOLOGICAL SOCIETY (US/0043-0773) [01663476] **5613**

PROCEEDINGS OF THE ... WASHINGTON STATE UNIVERSITY INTERNATIONAL PARTICLEBOARD/COMPOSITE MATERIALS SYMPOSIUM (US) [15604152] **2404**

PROCEEDINGS OF THE WATER-BORNE AND HIGHER-SOLIDS COATINGS SYMPOSIUM (US/0164-0402) [04562309] **4459**

PROCEEDINGS OF THE ... WEST INDIES AGRICULTURAL ECONOMICS CONFERENCE (TR) [03818632] **122**

PROCEEDINGS OF THE WEST VIRGINIA ACADEMY OF SCIENCE (US/0096-4263) [01647000] **5142**

PROCEEDINGS OF THE WESTERN ASSOCIATION OF FISH AND WILDLIFE AGENCIES AND THE WESTERN DIVISION AMERICAN FISHERIES ASSOCIATION (US/0198-6600) [04067283] **2202**

PROCEEDINGS OF THE WESTERN FOUNDATION OF VERTEBRATE ZOOLOGY (US/0511-7550) [01424534] **5595**

PROCEEDINGS OF THE WESTERN PHARMACOLOGY SOCIETY (US/0083-8969) [01778435] **3983**, **4326**

PROCEEDINGS OF THE WESTERN SNOW CONFERENCE (US/0161-0589) [01769762] **1359**

PROCEEDINGS OF THE WESTERN SOCIETY OF WEED SCIENCE (US/0091-4487) [01794297] **2429**, **183**

PROCEEDINGS OF THE WORKSHOP OF THE CANADIAN AGRICULTURAL ECONOMICS SOCIETY (CN/0707-4808) [04635194] **122**

PROCEEDINGS OF THE WORLD BANK ANNUAL CONFERENCE ON DEVELOPMENT ECONOMICS (US/1014-7268) [20942966] **1513**

PROCEEDINGS OF THE WORLD CONGRESS (NE/0084-1641) [01588921] **3630**

PROCEEDINGS OF THE ... WORLD CONGRESS OF THE INTERNATIONAL WATER SUPPLY ASSOCIATION (UK) [15227241] **5537**

PROCEEDINGS OF THE YORKSHIRE GEOLOGICAL SOCIETY (UK/0044-0604) [01587861] **1391**

PROCEEDINGS OF THE ZOOLOGICAL SOCIETY (II/0373-5893) [07633782] **5595**

PROCEEDINGS OF THIS SOCIETY'S SEMINAR - SHEEP & BEEF CATTLE SOCIETY OF THE NEW ZEALAND VETERINARY ASSOCIATION (NZ/0114-4553) [01144553] **219**

PROCEEDINGS - OFFSHORE TECHNOLOGY CONFERENCE (US/0160-3663) [03672922] **2095**

PROCEEDINGS - PACIFIC CHEMICAL ENGINEERING CONGRESS (US/0197-727X) [06475846] **2016**

PROCEEDINGS, PAPERS AND SUMMARIES OF DISCUSSIONS AT THE ... CONFERENCE (UK) [01782419] **3242**

PROCEEDINGS - PHILIP MORRIS SCIENCE SYMPOSIUM (US/0093-450X) [04752155] **989**, **5142**

PROCEEDINGS PLP. PRODUCT LIABILITY PREVENTION CONVENTION (US/0162-2919) [04138584] **4221**

PROCEEDINGS PLP. PRODUCT LIABILITY PREVENTION SEMINAR (US/0162-279X) [04110234] **4221**

PROCEEDINGS - PUBLIC LAW SECTION OF THE STATE BAR OF CALIFORNIA (US) [06880232] **3031**

PROCEEDINGS (QUEEN'S UNIVERSITY (KINGSTON, ONT.). CENTRE FOR RESOURCE STUDIES) (CN/0711-6039) [08499841] **1444**, **2148**

PROCEEDINGS - REFINING DEPARTMENT *CEASED.* (US/0364-4030) [03815249] **4275**

PROCEEDINGS, REGION 6 CONFERENCE (US/0272-4677) [06878092] **2077**

PROCEEDINGS - REGIONAL CONFERENCE FOR AFRICA (AO) [01908207] **183**

PROCEEDINGS - RELIABILITY PHYSICS SYMPOSIUM (US/0080-0821) [01908071] **2077**

PROCEEDINGS / RESEARCH AND DEVELOPMENT SESSION (INDIA) (II) [11681347] **2095**

PROCEEDINGS - ROAD BUILDERS CLINIC (US/0080-3278) [01590201] **1992**

PROCEEDINGS - ROCKY MOUNTAIN SYMPOSIUM ON MICROCOMPUTERS: SYSTEMS, SOFTWARE, ARCHITECTURE (US/0278-291X) [04334715] **1272**

PROCEEDINGS - ROYAL MICROSCOPICAL SOCIETY (UK/0035-9017) [01764600] **573**

PROCEEDINGS - SEMINAR ON THE ANALYSIS OF SECURITY PRICES (US) [03259833] **912**

PROCEEDINGS - SEMINAR/WORKSHOP ON PLANNING, DESIGN AND IMPLEMENTATION OF BICYCLE AND PEDESTRIAN FACILITIES (US) [05165764] **429**

PROCEEDINGS / SHIP TECHNOLOGY AND RESEARCH (STAR) SYMPOSIUM *SUSPENDED.* (US) [06469488] **4182**

PROCEEDINGS / SOCIETY OF AMERICAN FORESTERS. NORTHERN CALIFORNIA SECTION *See* PROCEEDINGS ANNUAL MEETING / SOCIETY OF AMERICAN FORESTERS, NORTHERN CALIFORNIA SECTION **2391**

PROCEEDINGS - SOCIETY OF AUTOMOTIVE ENGINEERS (US/8756-8470) [11667882] **1992**

PROCEEDINGS - SOUTHEASTERN ASSOCIATION OF STATE HIGHWAY AND TRANSPORTATION OFFICIALS (U.S.). MEETING (US/0735-0805) [08038388] **5390**

PROCEEDINGS / SOUTHERN AND SOUTHWESTERN RAILWAY ASSOCIATION (US) [07506353] **5434**

PROCEEDINGS - SOUTHERN ASSOCIATION OF COLLEGES AND SCHOOLS; THE SOUTHERN ASSOCIATION NEWSLETTER (US/0038-3813) [05859489] **1842**

PROCEEDINGS - SOUTHERN MARKETING ASSOCIATION (US) [05105669] **935**

PROCEEDINGS, SOUTHERN WEED SCIENCE SOCIETY (US/0362-4463) [01426258] **2429**

PROCEEDINGS / SPACE CONGRESS (US/0584-6099) [08399943] **32**

PROCEEDINGS - SPORT B. C., ANNUAL GENERAL MEETING (CN/0709-7069) [06020826] **4913**

PROCEEDINGS - STATEN ISLAND INSTITUTE OF ARTS AND SCIENCES *SUSPENDED.* (US/0039-0240) [06497985] **328**

PROCEEDINGS / STC, SOCIETY FOR TECHNICAL COMMUNICATION ANNUAL CONFERENCE (US) [29433790] **5142**

PROCEEDINGS / SYMPOSIUM AND EXHIBITION ON THE ART OF GLASSBLOWING (US/0743-409X) [10539293] **2593**

PROCEEDINGS--SYMPOSIUM OF THE WORLD ASSOCIATION OF VETERINARY HYGIENISTS (NE/0510-8004) [05153657] **5519**

PROCEEDINGS, SYMPOSIUM ON ADVANCED MANUFACTURING (US) **3486**

PROCEEDINGS / SYMPOSIUM ON COMPUTER ARITHMETIC (US/1063-6889) [07840711] **1200**, **3528**

PROCEEDINGS - SYMPOSIUM ON INSTRUMENTATION FOR THE PROCESS INDUSTRIES (TEXAS A & M UNIVERSITY) (US/0738-3231) [06662623] **1028**

PROCEEDINGS / SYMPOSIUM ON LOGIC IN COMPUTER SCIENCE (US/1043-6871) [14153294] **1200**

PROCEEDINGS - SYMPOSIUM ON MACHINE PROCESSING OF REMOTELY SENSED DATA (US) [03595383] **1261**

PROCEEDINGS - SYMPOSIUM ON NONLINEAR ESTIMATION THEORY AND ITS APPLICATIONS (US) [01783905] **3528**

PROCEEDINGS - TAGA (US/0082-2299) [04826488] **381**

PROCEEDINGS - TALL TIMBERS CONFERENCE ON ECOLOGICAL ANIMAL CONTROL BY HABITAT MANAGEMENT (US/0564-7207) [01443263] **2220**, **4247**

PROCEEDINGS / TALL TIMBERS FIRE ECOLOGY CONFERENCE (US) [25715832] **2220**

PROCEEDINGS / THE ... ANNUAL IEEE INTERNATIONAL ASIC CONFERENCE AND EXHIBIT (US/1063-0988) [25848540] **2077**

PROCEEDINGS / THE ANNUAL SYMPOSIUM ON COMPUTER APPLICATIONS IN MEDICAL CARE (US) [21128398] **1200**, **3630**

PROCEEDINGS - THE AUSTRALIAN ACADEMY OF THE HUMANITIES (AT/0067-1592) [03229390] **2852**

PROCEEDINGS / THE INSTITUTE FOR BRIQUETTING AND AGGLOMERATION (US) [15608745] **2016**

PROCEEDINGS, THE ... INTERNATIONAL SYMPOSIA (KO) [09869653] **5142**

PROCEEDINGS - THE RADIO CLUB OF AMERICA, INC (US/0033-779X) [06399086] **1120**

PROCEEDINGS / THE SOIL AND CROP SCIENCE SOCIETY OF FLORIDA (US/0096-4522) [01489546] **183**

PROCEEDINGS - UNITED STATES. BUREAU OF THE CENSUS (US/1059-7328) [12279381] **5336**

PROCEEDINGS - UNITED STATES NAVAL INSTITUTE (US/0041-798X) [02496995] **4182**

PROCEEDINGS - UNIVERSITY/GOVERNMENT/INDUSTRY MICROELECTRONICS SYMPOSIUM (US/0749-6877) [09950735] **2077**

PROCEEDINGS - UNIVERSITY OF BRISTOL SPELAEOLOGICAL SOCIETY (UK/0373-7527) [05348817] **279**, **1409**

PROCEEDINGS - USA-JAPAN COMPUTER CONFERENCE *CEASED.* (US) [04785854] **1200**

PROCEEDINGS - VERTEBRATE PEST CONFERENCE (US/0507-6773) [04317360] **4247**

PROCEEDINGS, VERY LARGE DATA BASES (US/0730-9317) [08103070] **1254**

PROCEEDINGS - WESTERN HEMISPHERE NUTRITION CONGRESS *CEASED.* (US/0163-6847) [02488796] **4198**

PROCEEDINGS / WESTERN SECTION, AMERICAN SOCIETY OF ANIMAL SCIENCE (US) [12016558] **219**

PROCEEDINGS / WESTERN SECTION, AMERICAN SOCIETY OF ANIMAL SCIENCE AND WESTERN BRANCH, CANADIAN SOCIETY OF ANIMAL SCIENCE (US) [21728992] **5519**

PROCEEDINGS - WILDERNESS CONFERENCE (US/0511-9456) [01326270] **4171**

PROCEEDINGS - WINTER SIMULATION CONFERENCE (US/0891-7736) [14986340] **1283**

PROCEEDINGS - WORLD MAGNESIUM CONFERENCE (US/0161-5769) [15299409] **4016**

PROCEEDINGS - WORLD ORCHID CONFERENCE (US/0510-9221) [01723622] **2429**

PROCEEDINGS / WORLD PETROLEUM CONGRESS (UK/0084-2176) [01770183] **4275**

PROCEEDINGS [OF THE CONFERENCE] (AT/0572-1431) [01518863] **5442**

PROCES ARNHEM (NE/0165-0076) [01650076] **3173**

PROCES CAHIERS D'ANALYSE POLITIQUE ET JURIDIQUE (FR) **3032**

PROCES-VERBAL - CONGRES DU TRAVAIL DU CANADA, ASSEMBLEE STATUTAIRE (CN/0225-0411) [06180598] **1703**

PROCES-VERBAL DE LA REUNION DU ... / MINISTERE DE LA SANTE ET DE LA SECURITE SOCIALE, COMMISSION DES COMPTES DE LA SECURITE SOCIALE (FR) [07808341] **5302**

PROCES-VERBAL DU CONGRES DE LA CSN (1978) (CN/0225-655X) [06141408] **1703**

PROCES-VERBAL DU CONGRES GENERAL ANNUEL - SOCIETE SAINT-JEAN-BAPTISTE DE QUEBEC (CN/0384-7357) [03264610] **5235**

PROCES-VERBAUX - INTERNATIONAL ASSOCIATION FOR THE PHYSICAL SCIENCES OF THE OCEAN (US/0254-2005) [04200032] **1455**

PROCESO (MX) [03210750] **2543**

PROCESO DE DATOS (SP/0210-122X) [l0210122X] **1261**

PROCESOS (EC) [25754849] **3032**

PROCESS (CN) [02249703] **3032**

●PROCESS ANALYTICAL CHEMISTRY SOURCE BOOK (US/1063-0708) [25850861] **1018**

Alphabetical Title Index — PRODUCTIVITY

PROCESS AND CHEMICAL ENGINEERING (UK/0960-5045) [23167220] 2016, **2006**

PROCESS & PLANT ENGINEERING (II) [13058104] 1028, **2016**

PROCESS, ARCHITECTURE (JA/0386-037X) [04049049] **306**

PROCESS BIOCHEMISTRY (UK) [24165108] 3696, **2016**

PROCESS CESSON-SEVIGNE (FR/0998-6650) [I09986650] **197**

PROCESS CONTROL & QUALITY (US/0924-3089) [23665521] **2016**

PROCESS ENGINEERING (AT/0159-3935) [09603136] **1992**

PROCESS ENGINEERING (UK/0370-1859) [02065189] **2016**

PROCESS ENGINEERING INDEX (UK/0264-7176) [I02647176] **2016**

PROCESS EQUIPMENT GUIDE (CN) [02443236] **989**

PROCESS EQUIPMENT NEWS (UK) **3486**

●PROCESS HEATING (US/1077-5870) [30839798] **4432**

PROCESS INDUSTRIES CANADA **CEASED.** (CN/0826-7243) [11514140] **2016**

PROCESS MAGAZINE : LE MENSUEL DES TECHNIQUES LAITIERES ET ALIMENTAIRES (FR) 198, **2354**

PROCESS PLANT CONSTRUCTION ESTIMATING STANDARDS: THE RICHARDSON RAPID SYSTEM (US) [01749682] **624**

PROCESS SAFETY AND ENVIRONMENTAL PROTECTION (UK/0957-5820) [21768585] **2180**

●PROCESS SAFETY PROGRESS (US/1066-8527) [27061056] **1028**

PROCESS STUDIES (US/0360-6503) [01776663] **4358**

PROCESS TECHNOLOGY CONFERENCE PROCEEDINGS / SPONSORED BY THE PROCESS TECHNOLOGY DIVISION OF THE IRON AND STEEL SOCIETY, INC (US) [18596146] **5142**

PROCESS TECHNOLOGY PROCEEDINGS (NE) [15104006] **1200**

PROCESS (WASHINGTON, D.C.) **CEASED.** (US/1053-1556) [22465201] **2354**

PROCESSED & PACKAGED FOOD DIGEST (UK) **2354**

PROCESSED FISHERY PRODUCTS, ANNUAL SUMMARY (US/0148-5296) [03259889] **2311**

PROCESSED WORLD (US/0735-9381) [08273812] 4545, **3425**

PROCESSING (UK/0305-439X) [02242332] **2016**

PROCESSING (CHICAGO ILL.) (US/0896-8659) [17308274] **1028**

PROCESSING OF ADVANCED MATERIALS (UK/0960-3158) [I09603158] **5142**

PROCHE-ORIENT CHRETIEN (IS/0032-9622) [01606732] **5040**

PROCHE-ORIENT, ETUDES ECONOMIQUES (LE/0254-9379) [09618827] **1513**

PROCHE-ORIENT, ETUDES JURIDIQUES (LE/0032-9649) [01624457] **3032**

PROCLAIM (NASHVILLE) (US/0162-4326) [01645602] **4988**

PROCOF MEDICAL (FR/0762-4476) [10707281] **3630**

PROCOMM ENTERPRISES MAGAZINE **CEASED.** (US/0896-7229) [17279736] **1162**

PROCTOR (AT) **3032**

PROCTOR JOURNAL, THE (US) [21095811] **5698**

PROCURADORES (SP) [02723098] **3032**

PROCUREMENT (UK) [01791604] **951**

PROCUREMENT ETHICS DESKTOP REFERENCE (US) [24880524] 2252, **4675**

PROCUREMENT POLICIES AND PROCEDURES (US) [04781658] **2832**

PROCUREMENT WEEKLY (UK/0306-1922) [I03061922] **704**

PRODEI (SP/0079-5836) [04706824] **3486**

PRODOTTO CHIMICO **See** PRODOTTO CHIMICO & AEROSOL SELEZIONE **989**

PRODOTTO CHIMICO & AEROSOL SELEZIONE **SUSPENDED.** (IT/0032-9673) [11520406] **989**

PRODUCAO AGRICOLA (BL) [02241863] **122**

PRODUCAO DA EXTRACAO VEGETAL E DA SILVICULTURA (BL) [22194182] **2391**

PRODUCAO DE CALCADOS NO RIO GRANDE DO SUL **See** CENSO DO CALCADO RS / ASSOCIACAO COMERCIAL E INDUSTRIAL DE NOVO HAMBURGO **1082**

PRODUCAO DE CANA-DE-ACUCAR ALAGOAS; INFORME SAFRA/ASPLANA (BL) [07191007] **183**

PRODUCCION ANIMAL. GLOSSARIUM (LU) [19059308] **5519**

PRODUCCION OVINA / SECRETARIADO URUGUAYO DE LA LANA (UY) [19914114] **5595**

PRODUCCION Y DISTRIBUCION (US/1048-1877) [20863414] **705**

PRODUCE BUSINESS (US/0886-5663) [12932207] **2354**

PRODUCE NEWS (US/0032-969X) [04109334] **2354**

PRODUCER (PORT WASHINGTON, N.Y.) (US/1067-439X) [27212565] **1162**

PRODUCER PRICE INDEXES (EXPANDED VERSION) (US/0882-5270) [11962976] 1703, **1622**

PRODUCER PRICE INDEXES / U.S. DEPARTMENT OF LABOR, BUREAU OF LABOR STATISTICS (US) [04507849] **912**

PRODUCER PRICE INDICES. MM22 (UK) **1594**

●PRODUCER REPORT (US/1068-5391) [27697271] **4147**

PRODUCER'S MASTERGUIDE, THE (US/0732-6653) [08412817] 4076, **1136**

PRODUCERS QUARTERLY (US/1053-6450) [22601333] **1162**

PRODUCT ALERT (US/0740-3801) [09947876] **2354**

PRODUCT & PROCESS INNOVATION (US/1058-546X) [23611800] 5142, **2099**

PRODUCT CATALOGUE - ONTARIO. ADDICTION RESEARCH FOUNDATION (CN/1181-8646) [23455422] **422**

PRODUCT DATA INTERNATIONAL (US/1050-7043) [21574565] **5142**

PRODUCT DESIGN AND VALUE ENGINEERING (CN/0555-3105) [02603564] **1992**

PRODUCT DEVELOPMENT DIRECTORY (US/1064-8526) [20051826] **3630**

PRODUCT DIRECTORY OF THE REFRACTORIES INDUSTRY IN THE UNITED STATES **See** DIRECTORY OF THE REFRACTORIES INDUSTRY **1024**

PRODUCT FINISHING (LONDON) (UK/0032-9762) [02449880] **4016**

PRODUCT LIABILITY INTERNATIONAL (UK) [04747591] **3032**

PRODUCT LIABILITY TRENDS **CEASED.** (US/0164-9574) [03406161] **3032**

PRODUCT LIABILITY UPDATE (US/0192-5075) [05015338] **3032**

PRODUCT PROFILES NUTRIENT UPDATE (US) **4198**

PRODUCT PROMOTION (US) [05387653] 2354, **1622**

PRODUCT SAFETY & LIABILITY REPORTER (US/0092-7732) [01788141] **4796**

PRODUCT SAFETY & THE LAW (US/0094-5463) [01794556] 4796, **3032**

PRODUCT SAFETY LETTER (US/0098-7530) [01591289] **1299**

PRODUCT SAFETY NEWS (US) **2868**

PRODUCT SAFETY UP TO DATE (US/0091-8954) [01788390] **4796**

PRODUCT SAFETY WATCHDOG SERVICE. ALERT BULLETIN **See** REGULATORY WATCHDOG SERVICE. ALERT BULLETIN **4679**

PRODUCT SOS (US/1064-850X) [12761305] **3630**

PRODUCT TESTING WITH CONSUMERS FOR RESEARCH GUIDANCE (US/1064-8534) [26434759] **1622**

PRODUCTEUR D'AMIANTE, LE (CN/0478-4049) [02107744] **624**

PRODUCTEUR DE LAIT QUEBECOIS, LE (CN/0228-1686) [07805592] **198**

PRODUCTEUR DE PORC QUEBECOIS (CN/0229-7876) [08790868] **219**

PRODUCTEUR LAITIER (BEDFORD. 1990) (CN/1187-662X) [26066683] **198**

PRODUCTEUR PLUS, LE (CN/1183-9929) [25423675] **122**

PRODUCTIA VEGETALA : HORTICULTURA **CEASED.** (RM) [02253125] **2429**

PRODUCTION (US/0032-9819) [02437595] **2126**

PRODUCTION AND ACTIVITY REPORT (US) **4275**

PRODUCTION AND CONSUMPTION OF FERTILISERS; ANNUAL REVIEW (II/0430-3288) [02995805] **122**

PRODUCTION AND DISPOSITION OF TOBACCO PRODUCTS (CN/0708-336X) [04040294] **5373**

PRODUCTION & INDUSTRIAL EQUIPMENT DIGEST (UK) **3486**

PRODUCTION AND INVENTORIES OF PROCESS CHEESE AND INSTANT MILK POWDER (CN/0705-551X) [04250140] **198**

PRODUCTION AND INVENTORY MANAGEMENT JOURNAL (US/0897-8336) [17600824] 1622, **883**

PRODUCTION AND MARKETING EGGS, CHICKENS AND TURKEYS, CALIFORNIA (US) [04307668] **219**

●PRODUCTION AND OPERATIONS MANAGEMENT (US/1059-1478) [24486745] **883**

PRODUCTION AND SHIPMENTS OF BLOW-MOULDED PLASTIC BOTTLES (CN/0713-9098) [09528144] **4460**

PRODUCTION AND SHIPMENTS OF STEEL PIPE AND TUBING (CN/0835-5797) [18420244] **4016**

PRODUCTION AND STOCKS OF EGGS AND POULTRY **See** PRODUCTION OF EGGS **219**

PRODUCTION AND STOCKS OF EGGS AND POULTRY (CN/0708-4897) [05374443] **219**

PRODUCTION AND STOCKS OF TEA, COFFEE, AND COCOA (CN/0709-2768) [05589697] **2370**

PRODUCTION BULLETIN (KONEDOBU, PAPUA NEW GUINEA) **See** RURAL INDUSTRIES (KONEDOBU, PAPUA NEW GUINEA) **1625**

PRODUCTION CREDIT ASSOCIATIONS, OPERATING STATISTICS (US/0272-9768) [06968354] 804, **732**

PRODUCTION DE LA BRANCHE EXPLOITATION FORESTIERE ET PRODUCTION DES BRANCHES SCIERIE ET CARBONISATION EN FORET **See** BRANCHES EXPLOITATION FORESTIERE, CARBONISATION EN FORET ET SCIERIE : RESULTATS STATISTIQUES **2376**

PRODUCTION EMPLOYEES COST SURVEY (US/0277-4119) [07546980] 4569, **1703**

PRODUCTION ENGINEERING : RESEARCH AND DEVELOPMENTS IN GERMANY (GW) **1992**

PRODUCTION IMPROVEMENT PROGRAM (US) **1622**

PRODUCTION JOURNAL (UK/0032-9878) [10757596] **4818**

PRODUCTION MACHINERY **CEASED.** (AT) **1622**

PRODUCTION NEWS (US/0195-1904) [05345287] **1622**

PRODUCTION NOTES (US) **328**

●PRODUCTION OF EGGS (CN) [31354448] **219**

PRODUCTION OF MILK AND MILK PRODUCTS (IE/0791-3036) [I07913036] **198**

PRODUCTION OF POULTRY AND EGGS (CN/0068-7189) [01552754] **219**

PRODUCTION OF SELECTED BISCUITS (CN/0227-1761) [08496155] **2354**

PRODUCTION PLANNING & CONTROL (UK/0953-7287) [22930139] **1622**

PRODUCTION, PRICES, EMPLOYMENT, AND TRADE IN NORTHWEST FOREST INDUSTRIES (US/0364-1252) [02186486] 2404, **1622**

PRODUCTION RESEARCH REPORT - UNITED STATES DEPARTMENT OF AGRICULTURE (US/0082-979X) [01590533] **122**

PRODUCTION RESOURCE, THE (US/1054-9099) [23011481] **1622**

PRODUCTION, SALES, AND STOCKS OF MAJOR APPLIANCES (CN/0825-1339) [11491462] 1622, **2812**

PRODUCTION, SHIPMENTS, AND STOCKS ON HAND OF SAWMILLS EAST OF THE ROCKIES (CN/0380-464X) [05930385] **2404**

PRODUCTION, SHIPMENTS AND STOCKS ON HAND OF SAWMILLS IN BRITISH COLUMBIA (CN/0318-7942) [02443526] **1622**

PRODUCTION SUPERVISOR'S BULLETIN (US) 883, **1622**

PRODUCTIONS ANIMALES (PARIS, 1988) (FR/0990-0632) [26392834] 219, **5519**

PRODUCTIQUE AFFAIRES PARIS (FR/1240-3946) [I12403946] 1221, **1216**

PRODUCTIVE AGING NEWS (US/0887-3798) [13201812] **5302**

PRODUCTIVITY (II) [01774409] **1622**

PRODUCTIVITY AND COST OF EMPLOYMENT. LOCAL SERVICE CARRIERS (US) [04157630] 32, **1703**

PRODUCTIVITY AND PRODUCTION BULLETIN (UK) [07679339] 2148, **1622**

PRODUCTIVITY AND TRAINING REPORT / GATF (US) [10550743] **381**

PRODUCTIVITY — Alphabetical Title Index

PRODUCTIVITY MANAGEMENT (US) **705**

PRODUCTIVITY MEASURES FOR SELECTED INDUSTRIES AND GOVERNMENT SERVICES / U.S. DEPARTMENT OF LABOR, BUREAU OF LABOR STATISTICS (US) [17827206] **1703**

PRODUCTIVITY NEWS (II) [06608547] **705**

PRODUCTIVITY PLUS *See* QUALITY AND PRODUCTIVITY PLUS **706**

PRODUCTIVITY REPORT FOR ALL PRODUCERS BY STATE, COUNTY, & TYPE MINING (US/0735-8172) [09048055] **2148**

PRODUCTIVITY RESEARCH PROGRAM FOR FY ..., THE (US) [08574822] **946**

PRODUCTIVITY SOFTWARE (US/1040-1482) [18335589] **1289**

PRODUCTIVITY (STAMFORD, CONN.) (US/0275-8040) [07228496] 3486, **883**

PRODUCTIVITY VIEWS (US/0891-7167) [15002401] **883**

PRODUCTO (CARACAS, VENEZUELA) (VE) [10734264] **764**

PRODUCTORES DE HORTALIZAS (US) **122**

PRODUCTOS DEL MAR (SP) **122**

PRODUCTS FINISHING (US/0032-9940) [01762921] **3486**

PRODUCTS FINISHING DIRECTORY (US/0478-4251) [05636729] **4016**

PRODUCTS LIABILITY AND TRANSPORTATION LEGAL DIRECTORY (US/0272-1767) [06753081] 5390, **3032**

PRODUCTS LIABILITY REPORTS (US/0162-122X) [01564336] **3032**

PRODUCTS SHIPPED BY CANADIAN MANUFACTURERS (CN/0575-9455) [03776924] **3486**

PRODUITS D'EXPLOITATION FORESTIERE ET DE SCIERIE, ET PRINCIPAUX PRODUITS DERIVES (FR) [04841503] **2404**

PRODUITS FRAIS LEVALLOIS-PERRET (FR/1167-539X) [I1167539X] **2354**

PRODUKSI BUAH-BUAHAN DI JAWA (IO) [21245522] **122**

PRODUKSI PERIKANAN LAUT YANG DIJUAL DI PELELANGAN/TEMPAT PENDARATAN IKAN DI JAWA-MADURA (IO) [03278516] **2311**

PRODUKSI TANAMAN BAHAN MAKANAN DI INDONESIA (IO) [03290568] **183**

PRODUKTHAFTUNG AKTUELL : PH (AU) [18674595] **3032**

PRODUKTIESTATISTIEKEN. BIERBROUWERIJEN EN MOUTERIJEN (NE) [01792583] **2370**

PRODUKTIESTATISTIEKEN : BROOD-, BESCHUIT-, BANKET-, KOEKEN BISCUITFABRIEKEN (W.O. BROOD- EN BANKETBAKKERIJEN) (NE/0168-5813) [02439040] **2354**

PRODUKTIESTATISTIEKEN, RIJWIEL- EN MOTORRIJWIELINDUSTRIE *See* CBS RIJWIEL- EN MOTORRIJWIELINDUSTRIE / CENTRAAL BUREAU VOOR DE STATISTIEK, HOOFDAFDELING STATISTIEKEN VAN INDUSTRIE EN BOUWNIJVERHEID **428**

PRODUKTIESTATISTIEKEN: SUIKERINDUSTRIE *See* SUIKERINDUSTRIE, ZETMEEL- EN ZETMEELDERIVATENINDUSTRIE **1628**

PRODUKTION 1978 (GW/0344-6166) [I03446166] **1622**

PRODUKTPROGRAM, STATSFORETAGSGRUPPEN (SW) [02242213] **1622**

PRODUKTSCHAP VOOR LANDBOUWZAAIZADEN *See* JAARVERSLAG - PRODUKTSCHAP VOOR LANDBOUWZAAIZADEN **98**

PRODURRE PER ABITARE (IT) [05227832] **2907**

PRODUTTIVITA (IT/0032-9991) [06616376] **5142**

PRODUZIERENDES GEWERBE (HAMBURG, GERMANY) (GW/0723-7774) [10640335] **1622**

PRODUZIERENDES GEWERBE. REIHE 4.1.1 : BESCHAFTIGUNG, UMSATZ UND ENERGIEVERSORGUNG DER UNTERNEHMEN UND BETRIEBE IM BERGBAU UND IM VERARBEITENDEN GEWERBE (GW) [06049942] 1953, **1703**

PRODUZIERENDES GEWERBE. REIHE 4.2.3., KONZENTRATIONSSTATISTISCHE DATEN FUER DEN BERGBAU UND DAS VERARBEITENDE GEWERBE SOWIE DAS BAUGEWERBE / HERAUSGEBER, STATISTISCHES BUNDESAMT WIESBADEN (GW) [17685475] **1444**

PRODUZIERENDES GEWERBE. REIHE 3.2, STRUKTUR DER PRODUKTION IM PRODUZIERENDEN GEWERBE / HERAUSGEBER, STATISTISCHES BUNDESAMT WIESBADEN (GW) [16926691] **1622**

PRODUZIERENDES GEWERBE. REIHE 6.1, BESCHAFTIGUNG, UMSATZ, INVESTITIONEN UND KOSTENSTRUKTUR DER UNTERNEHMEN IN DER ENERGIE UND WASSERVERSORGUNG / HERAUSGEBER STATISTISCHES BUNDESAMT (GW) [12842793] **2126**

PRODUZIERENDES GEWERBE. REIHE 6.3: KOSTENSTRUKTUR DER UNTERNEHMEN IN DER ENERGIE- UND WASSERVERSORGUNG *SUSPENDED.* (GW) [06299748] **2126**

PRODUZIONE ANIMALE (IT/0033-0000) [02456626] **5519**

PRODUZIONE E COMMERCIO : PRODOTTI AGRICOLO-ALIMENTARI E FLORICOLI (IT) [02613665] **122**

PROEDUCATION (US/8756-5188) [11439160] **1774**

PROEFSTATION VOOR DE AKKERBOUW EN DE GROENTETEELT IN DE VOLLEGROND *See* PUBLIKATIE - PROEFSTATION VOOR DE AKKERBOUW EN DE GROENTETEELT IN DER VOLLEGROND **123**

PROEFSTATION VOOR DE RUNDVEENOUDERIJ *See* PUBLIKATIE - PROEFSTATION VOOR DE RUNDVEEBOUDERIJ **219**

PROFANE (CN/0227-4523) [08045920] **243**

PROFESION MEDICA (SP) **3630**

PROFESIONES Y EMPRESAS (SP/1130-765X) [I1130765X] **1703**

PROFESSION (US/0740-6959) [06395160] **3312**

PROFESSION COMPTABLE, LA (FR/0766-9208) [I07669208] **750**

PROFESSION POLITIQUE PARIS (FR/0992-5163) [I09925163] **4492**

PROFESSIONAL, ADMINISTRATIVE, TECHNICAL AND CLERICAL PAY IN NEW YORK (US/0362-9953) [02367429] **1703**

PROFESSIONAL ADMINISTRATOR, THE *See* JOURNAL OF CORPORATE MANAGEMENT, THE **3101**

PROFESSIONAL AGENT, THE (US/0148-8899) [03383560] **2890**

●PROFESSIONAL AND OCCUPATIONAL LICENSING DIRECTORY (US/1070-3322) [28318383] **4208**

PROFESSIONAL AND SERVICE DIRECTORY, METRO TORONTO (CN/0821-2619) [09387159] **1622**

PROFESSIONAL APARTMENT MANAGEMENT (US/0891-2599) [14695452] **4843**

PROFESSIONAL AUDIO BUYERS REFERENCE GUIDE (US/0747-752X) [10807069] **5318**

PROFESSIONAL BOATBUILDER MAGAZINE (US/1043-2035) [19339077] **595**

●PROFESSIONAL BUILDER (1993) (US/1072-0561) [28639718] **624**

PROFESSIONAL BUILDER & REMODELER (US/1053-6353) [22497090] **624**

PROFESSIONAL CALENDAR (UK/0953-7279) [I09537279] **3242**

PROFESSIONAL CARE OF MOTHER AND CHILD (UK/0964-4156) [24785083] **3767**

PROFESSIONAL CAREERS SOURCEBOOK (US/1045-9863) [20306171] **4208**

PROFESSIONAL CARWASHING (US/0191-6823) [04936941] **935**

PROFESSIONAL CARWASHING & DETAILING (US) **5423**

PROFESSIONAL CLEANING JOURNAL (US/1043-4232) [19461193] **1703**

PROFESSIONAL COMMUNICATOR, THE (US/0891-1207) [12958943] 5564, **1120**

PROFESSIONAL COMPUTING *CEASED.* (US/0742-1036) [10262401] **1272**

PROFESSIONAL COMPUTING (PRAHRAN, VICTORIA, AUSTRALIA) *CEASED.* (AT) [12966509] **1201**

PROFESSIONAL CORPORATION OF PHYSICIANS OF QUEBEC *See* BULLETIN - PROFESSIONAL CORPORATION OF PHYSICIANS OF QUEBEC **3561**

PROFESSIONAL COUNSELOR (US) [29964119] **4609**

PROFESSIONAL COUNSELOR MAGAZINE *See* PROFESSIONAL COUNSELOR **4609**

PROFESSIONAL DESIGN SUPPLEMENT (US/0148-6632) [03337760] **624**

PROFESSIONAL DIRECTORY / THE AMERICAN INSTITUTE OF CHEMISTS (US/0084-6376) [08890450] **990**

PROFESSIONAL DOCUMENT RETRIEVAL *SUSPENDED.* (US/8755-0253) [11246187] **3242**

PROFESSIONAL EDITION OF J.K. LASSER'S YOUR INCOME TAX, THE (US) [07109361] **4742**

PROFESSIONAL EDUCATOR, THE (US/0196-786X) [05901507] **1903**

PROFESSIONAL ELECTRONICS / THE OFFICIAL JOURNAL OF NESDA AND ISCET (US) [09291387] 883, **2077**

PROFESSIONAL EMPLOYEES IN STATE GOVERNMENT (US/0744-6721) [08490668] **4675**

PROFESSIONAL ENGINEERING (UK/0953-6639) [17972759] **2127**

PROFESSIONAL ENGINEERS AND LAND SURVEYORS REPORT / STATE BOARD OF REGISTRATION FOR PROFESSIONAL ENGINEERS AND LAND SURVEYORS (US) [11453243] **2029**

PROFESSIONAL ENGINEERS REPORT *See* PROFESSIONAL ENGINEERS AND LAND SURVEYORS REPORT / STATE BOARD OF REGISTRATION FOR PROFESSIONAL ENGINEERS AND LAND SURVEYORS **2029**

●PROFESSIONAL ETHICS (GAINESVILLE, FLA.) (US/1063-6579) [26103927] 705, **2252**

PROFESSIONAL FLORAL DESIGNER, THE (US/0889-9924) [16702274] **2436**

PROFESSIONAL FUNDRAISING (UK) **4339**

PROFESSIONAL GENEALOGISTS OF ARKANSAS *See* PROFESSIONAL GENEALOGISTS OF ARKANSAS NEWSLETTER **2468**

PROFESSIONAL GENEALOGISTS OF ARKANSAS NEWSLETTER (US/1040-4430) [18420048] **2468**

PROFESSIONAL GEOGRAPHER, THE (US/0033-0124) [06442093] **2573**

PROFESSIONAL GOLFERS' ASSOCIATION OF AMERICA. TOURNAMENT PLAYERS DIVISION *See* TOUR BOOK, THE **4926**

PROFESSIONAL HORTICULTURE *See* HORTICULTURIST/ INSTITUTE OF HORTICULTURE, THE **2419**

PROFESSIONAL HOTEL & RESTAURANT INTERIORS (UK/0959-2687) [I09592687] 2809, 5072, **2902**

PROFESSIONAL INCOME OF ENGINEERS (1981) (US/0735-7850) [08621062] **1992**

PROFESSIONAL INSURANCE AGENTS OF NEW YORK (US/0883-8240) [12230778] **2890**

PROFESSIONAL INVESTOR (UK/0958-2541) [20787339] **912**

PROFESSIONAL INVESTOR, THE (US/0889-0897) [12297773] **912**

PROFESSIONAL KARATE (US/0098-0706) [01799459] 2601, **4913**

PROFESSIONAL LANDSCAPER (UK) **2429**

PROFESSIONAL LAWYER : PL / SPECIAL COORDINATING COMMITTEE ON PROFESSIONALISM, AMERICAN BAR ASSOCIATION CENTER FOR PROFESSIONAL RESPONSIBILITY, THE (US/1042-5675) [19084640] 2252, **3032**

PROFESSIONAL LIABILITY (US/0275-0503) [07077449] 3916, **3032**

PROFESSIONAL LIABILITY NEWSLETTER (US/0555-3385) [02256691] 3630, **2890**

PROFESSIONAL LIABILITY REPORTER (US/0145-3505) [02728438] **3032**

PROFESSIONAL LICENSING REPORT (US/1043-2051) [18700508] **4208**

●PROFESSIONAL MANAGER (UK) [27089165] **883**

PROFESSIONAL MANAGER'S DIGEST, THE (CN/0710-4804) [08680805] **883**

PROFESSIONAL MANAGING (US) **883**

PROFESSIONAL MARKETING REPORT *CEASED.* (US/0160-0362) [03620794] **935**

PROFESSIONAL MEDICAL ASSISTANT, THE (US/0033-0140) [02449886] **3630**

PROFESSIONAL MEETING MANAGEMENT (US) **764**

PROFESSIONAL MODEL NEWSLETTER (US/1058-1081) [24221255] **2777**

PROFESSIONAL MONITOR / MICHIGAN ASSOCIATION OF THE PROFESSIONS, THE (US/0744-7817) [08551095] **3032**

PROFESSIONAL MUSICIAN (DOWNSVIEW) (CN/0829-8998) [14473448] **4147**

PROFESSIONAL NEGLIGENCE (UK/0267-078X) [11940045] **3032**

PROFESSIONAL NEGLIGENCE LAW REPORTER (US/1051-3744) [21954428] **3032**

PROFESSIONAL NEWS (AT/0818-206X) [I0818206X] **1805**

●PROFESSIONAL NURSE. DRUG UPDATE (UK) [26501812] 3867, **4326**

Alphabetical Title Index — PROGETTARE

PROFESSIONAL NURSE (LONDON, ENGLAND) (UK/0266-8130) [14933637] **3867**

PROFESSIONAL OFFICE DESIGN (US/0882-6781) [12166802] **2902**

PROFESSIONAL PAINTER & DECORATOR (UK) 2903, **4225**

PROFESSIONAL PAPER - INDIANA STATE UNIVERSITY. DEPT. OF GEOGRAPHY AND GEOLOGY (US/0885-775X) [01425970] 1392, **2573**

PROFESSIONAL PAPERS (SAUDI ARABIA. DEPUTY MINISTRY FOR MINERAL RESOURCES) (SU/1012-8786) [09460112] **1392**

PROFESSIONAL PAPERS SERIES (BIOLOGY) (US) [04533140] **470**

PROFESSIONAL PERSONNEL CHARACTERISTICS (US/0360-0785) [02240389] **1842**

PROFESSIONAL PHOTOGRAPHER (UK/0019-784X) [06340329] **4375**

PROFESSIONAL PHOTOGRAPHER (1964), THE (US/0033-0167) [01696300] **4375**

PROFESSIONAL PHOTOGRAPHY (AT) **4376**

PROFESSIONAL PILOT (US/0191-6238) [04912880] **32**

PROFESSIONAL PRINTER (UK/0308-4205) [01785565] **4569**

PROFESSIONAL PRODUCTION (GW/0932-0393) [l09320393] **4076**

PROFESSIONAL PSYCHOLOGY, RESEARCH AND PRACTICE (US/0735-7028) [08996897] **4609**

●PROFESSIONAL PUBLISHING UPDATE (US/1066-0674) [26833364] **4818**

PROFESSIONAL PULIZIE *CEASED.* (IT/1120-8368) [I11208368] **2127**

PROFESSIONAL QUILTER MAGAZINE, THE (US/0891-5237) [14876929] **5185**

PROFESSIONAL READING GUIDE FOR EDUCATIONAL ADMINISTRATORS (AT) **1869**

PROFESSIONAL REAL ESTATE REPORTS (US/0749-8012) [11198866] **4843**

PROFESSIONAL REGULATION NEWS (US/0741-4749) [10137140] **3916**

PROFESSIONAL RENOVATION (CN/1182-0470) [22254438] **2903**

●PROFESSIONAL REPORT : A PUBLICATION OF THE SOCIETY OF INDUSTRIAL AND OFFICE REALTORS (US/1067-4764) [27246985] **4843**

PROFESSIONAL REPORT - ALASKA. DIVISION OF GEOLOGICAL AND GEOPHYSICAL SURVEYS (US/0737-6022) [09180096] 1409, **1392**

PROFESSIONAL REPORT (BOSTON, MASS.) (US/0889-3438) [13324141] **1201**

PROFESSIONAL REPORT OF INDUSTRIAL AND OFFICE REAL ESTATE *See* PROFESSIONAL REPORT : A PUBLICATION OF THE SOCIETY OF INDUSTRIAL AND OFFICE REALTORS **4843**

PROFESSIONAL RESPONSIBILITY (US/0362-8531) [02361837] **3032**

PROFESSIONAL ROOFING (US/0896-5552) [17202780] **624**

PROFESSIONAL SAFETY (US/0099-0027) [02240108] **2868**

PROFESSIONAL SCHOLAR *CEASED.* (US/1064-7961) [26393973] **2852**

PROFESSIONAL SCHOOLS FACTSHEETS (CN/0709-2482) [05842445] 4208, **1842**

PROFESSIONAL SECRETARY'S DEVELOPMENT PROGRAM (US) **4208**

PROFESSIONAL SELF-EVALUATION AND CONTINUING EDUCATION PROGRAM (US/0093-8580) [00932481] **3944**

PROFESSIONAL SELLING (US) **956**

PROFESSIONAL SELLING : FINANCIAL SERVICES EDITION (US) **956**

PROFESSIONAL SELLING SERVICE (US) **956**

PROFESSIONAL SERVICE FIRM'S REPORT ON CONTROLLING BENEFITS & DEFERRED COMPENSATION *See* IOMA'S REPORT ON CONTROLLING BENEFITS COSTS FOR LAW, DESIGN, CPA, AND OTHER PROFESSIONAL SERVICE FIRMS **872**

PROFESSIONAL SERVICES MANAGEMENT JOURNAL (US/0732-2119) [04718503] **883**

PROFESSIONAL SKATER, THE (US/8750-9369) [11945057] **4913**

PROFESSIONAL SKIER, THE (US/1065-1314) [26513646] **4913**

PROFESSIONAL SOUND (DURANGO, COLO. : 1989) (US/1044-4793) [19729752] **4453**

PROFESSIONAL SOUND (TORONTO) (CN/1186-1797) [24368172] **4453**

PROFESSIONAL STAINED GLASS (US/0885-1808) [12573904] **2593**

PROFESSIONAL STANDARDS REVIEW ORGANIZATIONS (US/0196-0407) [05655057] **4796**

PROFESSIONAL SURVEYOR (US/0278-1425) [07717896] **2029**

PROFESSIONAL TELEPHONE SELLING (US) **935**

PROFESSIONAL TRANSLATOR & INTERPRETER *CEASED.* (UK/0995-616X) **3312**

PROFESSIONAL UPDATE (UK/0969-434X) **3630**

PROFESSIONAL UPHOLSTERER, THE *CEASED.* (US/0882-1518) [11790721] **2903**

●PROFESSIONAL VCR REPAIR TRAINING MANUAL AND BUSINESS PLAN, THE (US/1064-2668) [26241320] 705, **2812**

PROFESSIONAL VIDEO INTERNATIONAL YEARBOOK (UK/0261-1910) [11054208] **1136**

PROFESSIONAL WOMEN AND MINORITIES (US/0190-1796) [04651039] **5564**

PROFESSIONALITA (IT) **1775**

PROFESSIONALS (US/0744-3471) [08205231] **3725**

PROFESSIONALS AND THEIR ADDICTIONS (US/1046-7785) [20511585] **4796**

PROFESSIONAL'S GUIDE TO PATIENT DRUG FACTS (US) **4326**

PROFESSIONALS IN CHEMISTRY *CEASED.* (US/0732-460X) [02746114] **990**

PROFESSIONAL'S TIRE HANDBOOK, THE (US/0161-7214) [03996821] **5423**

PROFESSIONE, ARCHITETTO (IT) [17631709] **306**

PROFESSIONEL GOLFERS' ASSOCIATION OF AMERICA *See* OFFICIAL PGA TOUR BOOK **4910**

PROFESSIONI INFERMIERISTICHE (IT/0033-0205) [I00330205] **3867**

PROFESSIONS EDUCATION RESEARCHER QUARTERLY : PERQ (US/1052-7060) [22361905] **1775**

PROFESSOR BUSINESS : A TEACHING PRIMER FOR FACULTY, THE (US) **1903**

PROFESSOR DIVINSKY'S SELECT RESTAURANT GUIDE (CN/0704-6561) [04256228] **5072**

PROFESSOR DR. F. DE VRIES LECTURES (NE/0552-2668) [02767906] **5142**

PROFESSOR IN THE CLASSROOM (US) **1903**

PROFI MUNSTER (GW/0937-1583) [l09371583] **122**

PROFIEL VAN BEROEPSONDERWIJS EN VOLWASSENENEDUCATIE (NE/0927-4898) [I09274898] **1775**

PROFIL (LONGUEUIL) (CN/0715-7975) [09670443] **849**

PROFIL MAHASISWA UNIVERSITAS KATOLIK INDONESIA ATMA JAYA (IO) [03603087] **1842**

PROFIL MAHASISWA UNIVERSITAS KATOLIK PARAHYANGAN (IO) [07043387] **1842**

PROFIL : SOZIALDEMOKRATISCHE ZEITSCHRIFT FUR POLITIK, WIRTSCHAFT UND KULTUR (SZ/0555-3482) [05669311] **4545**

PROFIL (TROIS-RIVIERES) (CN/0836-1576) [20001760] **4796**

PROFIL (VIENNA, AUSTRIA : 1979) (AU) [10950755] **2521**

PROFILE (US/1053-9840) [09056975] 1842, **1869**

PROFILE (LOS ANGELES, CALIF. 1974) (US/0095-151X) [01796288] **4913**

PROFILE (NORFOLK, VA.) (US/0145-112X) [02663194] **4054**

PROFILE OF ECONOMIC REGION 1 (US) [09122304] **1703**

PROFILE OF ECONOMIC REGION 2 (US) [09122243] **1703**

PROFILE OF ECONOMIC REGION 3 (US) [09122139] **1703**

PROFILE OF ECONOMIC REGION 4 (US) [09122080] **1703**

PROFILE OF ECONOMIC REGION 5 (US) [09121981] **1703**

PROFILE OF ECONOMIC REGION 6 / PREPARED BY OCCUPATIONAL INFORMATION UNIT (US) [09121860] **1704**

PROFILE OF ECONOMIC REGION 7 (US) [09121827] **1704**

PROFILE OF ECONOMIC REGION 8 (US) [09121400] **1704**

PROFILE OF ECONOMIC REGION 9 (US) [09121332] **1704**

PROFILE OF ECONOMIC REGION 10 (US) [09121144] **1704**

PROFILE OF ECONOMIC REGION 11 (US) [09121036] **1704**

PROFILE OF ECONOMIC REGION 12 (US) [09120985] **1704**

PROFILE OF ECONOMIC REGION 13 (US) [09117486] **1704**

PROFILE OF ECONOMIC REGION 14 (US) [09117408] **1704**

PROFILE OF ENVIRONMENTAL QUALITY. REGION 8: COLORADO, MONTANA, NORTH DAKOTA, SOUTH DAKOTA, UTAH, WYOMING (US/0193-1652) [05120774] **2239**

PROFILE OF REAL ESTATE FIRMS (US/0742-5074) [10344445] **4843**

PROFILE OF STATE-CHARTERED BANKING, A (US/0734-6638) [03100568] **804**

PROFILE (OMAHA) (US/0162-5241) [04098569] **705**

●PROFILE (SOUTH PORTLAND, ME.) (US/1071-3808) [28626448] **705**

PROFILE SURVEY - ASSOCIATION OF COLLEGE, UNIVERSITY AND COMMUNITY ART ADMINISTRATORS (US/0736-9360) [04427976] **328**

PROFILE SURVEY - ASSOCIATION OF PERFORMING ARTS PRESENTERS (US) **387**

PROFILE, THE (US) [04849426] **279**

PROFILES (US/1047-2568) [12648427] **1775**

PROFILES IN HEALTHCARE MARKETING (US/1040-7480) [17425930] 4796, **935**

PROFILES IN HOSPITAL PHARMACY (US) **4326**

PROFILES IN PRACTICAL EDUCATION (CN) [05850074] **1775**

●PROFILES INTERNATIONAL (US/1058-3068) [24258289] **2543**

PROFILES OF GENIUS SERIES (IE/0332-3218) [12414532] **5142**

PROFILES OF KENTUCKY PUBLIC SCHOOLS (US) [01783481] **1775**

PROFILES OF MISSOURI PUBLIC SCHOOLS (US) [07935180] **1775**

PROFILES OF REGULATORY COMPLIANCE (US/0884-9110) [12533571] **5302**

PROFILES OF SCHEDULED AIR CARRIER OPERATIONS BY STAGE LENGTH (US) [02243209] **32**

PROFILES OF SCHEDULED AIR CARRIER PASSENGER TRAFFIC, TOP 100 U.S. AIRPORTS (US/0360-0041) [02242272] **32**

PROFILES, PATHWAYS, AND DREAMS (US/1047-8329) [20790373] 990, **434**

PROFILES (SOLANA BEACH, CALIF.) *CEASED.* (US/8755-464X) [11314031] **1272**

PROFILO DEI DIALETTI ITALIANI (IT) [06507872] **3312**

PROFILS (FR) **5336**

PROFILS DE L'ECONOMIE NORD-PAS-DE-CALAIS (FR) [06288533] **1513**

PROFILS D'ENTREPRISES QUEBECOISES (CN/0229-348X) [07865707] **705**

●PROFIT (ARMONK, N.Y.) (US/1061-9194) [25491187] **705**

PROFIT-BUILDING STRATEGIES FOR BUSINESS OWNERS *CEASED.* (US/0889-9967) [14136181] 705, **804**

PROFIT MANAGEMENT (US/1054-1225) [22754433] **883**

PROFIT (TORONTO) (CN/1183-1324) [24368420] **705**

PROFITABILITY REPORT (US) **912**

PROFITABLE CRAFT MERCHANDISING (US/0147-5304) [03190549] **375**

PROFITABLE LAWYER, THE (US/0743-5401) [10598892] **3032**

PROFITABLE MACHINE KNITTING : THE PRACTICAL AND SENSIBLE GUIDE TO EARNING MONEY WITH YOUR KNITTING MACHINE (UK) [19641810] **5185**

PROFITMAKER, THE (US/0748-8335) [11014036] **849**

PROFITRAVEL (GW) [22131916] 5489, **705**

PROFITS / FEDERAL BUSINESS DEVELOPMENT BANK (CN/0711-0316) [08541296] **804**

PROFODCIL BULLETIN (II) [05298924] 849, **2354**

PROFOTO (SA/0033-0329) [I00330329] **4376**

●PROFSOIUZY (RU/0132-1196) [27703223] **1704**

PROGENITOR (AT/0725-914X) [I0725914X] **2468**

PROGETTARE (IT) **5142**

PROGETTISTA, IL (IT) **5142**

PROGETTO : BIMESTRALE DELLA CISL DI POLITICA DEL LAVORO (IT) [10131109] **1704**

PROGETTO CARE ITALIA (IT/0393-8018) [I03938018] **4796**

PROGETTO IMPRESA : REVISTA DI FINANZA E COMMERCIO ESTERO (IT) **705**

PROGETTO UFFICIO **SUSPENDED.** (IT) **4214**

PROGNOSE ZUM LEHRERBEDARF IN BAYERN (GW) [06821174] **1869**

PROGNOSEBERICHT ZUR VERKEHRSENTWICKLUNG (GW) [19406445] **5390**

PROGNOSIS (XR) [25198875] **5799**

PROGNOSTICO AGRICOLA (BL) [20549089] **122**

PROGNOZIROVANIE RAZVITIIA BIBLIOTECHNOGO DELA V SSSR (RU) [05656356] **3242**

PROGRAM ADMINISTRATION REVIEW OF THE SOCIAL SECURITY DISABILITY INSURANCE AND THE SUPPLEMENTAL SECURITY INCOME VOCATIONAL REHABILITATION PROGRAMS (US/0194-3871) [05259285] 2891, 5302, **1704**

PROGRAM - AMERICAN DAIRY SCIENCE ASSOCIATION. MEETING (US/0886-702X) [04309124] **198**

PROGRAM AND ABSTRACTS / INTERSCIENCE CONFERENCE ON ANTIMICROBIAL AGENTS AND CHEMOTHERAPY (US/0733-6373) [02255368] **568**

PROGRAM AND ABSTRACTS OF PAPERS - INTERNATIONAL ASSOCIATION FOR DENTAL RESEARCH (US/0534-669X) [01208916] **1333**

PROGRAM AND ABSTRACTS OF THE CANADIAN PALEONTOLOGY CONFERENCE ... AND PANDER SOCIETY MEETING (CN/1183-028X) [25589889] 1392, 1444, **4230**

PROGRAM & FINANCIAL PLAN - TEXAS. REHABILITATION COMMISSION (US) [05979278] **1704**

PROGRAM & LEGISLATIVE ACTION BULLETIN (US) 5564, **4492**

PROGRAM AND PROJECT ACCOMPLISHMENTS (NEW ORLEANS) (US/0093-8106) [01792492] **2239**

PROGRAM AND RESOURCE DIGEST, THE (US/0197-8187) [05355548] **4675**

PROGRAM (ASLIB) (UK/0033-0337) [01606739] **3242**

PROGRAM BUDGET REQUEST - EDUCATIONAL COMMUNICATIONS BOARD (US/0145-9899) [02825395] **1842**

PROGRAM BUDGET STATEMENT (US/0192-9747) [05090651] **4796**

PROGRAM - CANADIAN LIBRARY ASSOCIATION, CONFERENCE (CN/0381-1476) [03285072] **3242**

PROGRAM CATALOGUE (US) [01787567] **362**

PROGRAM / CHICAGO SYMPHONY ORCHESTRA (US) [01554191] **4147**

PROGRAM-CURRICULUM PLANS (US/0147-3336) [03144526] **5066**

PROGRAM DIRECTORY - ARKANSAS DEPARTMENT OF PLANNING (US/0360-2869) [02243725] **4675**

PROGRAM DIRECTORY / MASSACHUSETTS DEPARTMENT OF EDUCATION (US/0898-8633) [16133847] **1775**

PROGRAM EVALUATION IN THE HEALTH FIELDS (US/0731-8073) [05753376] **4796**

PROGRAM FOR THE INTRODUCTION AND ADAPTATION OF CONTRACEPTIVE TECHNOLOGY See PIACT PAPERS **590**

PROGRAM FOR THE INTRODUCTION AND ADAPTATION OF CONTRACEPTIVE TECHNOLOGY See PIACT PRODUCT NEWS **590**

PROGRAM GUIDE (MARYLAND CENTER FOR PUBLIC BROADCASTING) See MARYLAND PUBLIC TV **1134**

PROGRAM GUIDE - SOUTH DAKOTA PUBLIC TELEVISION (US/0161-9845) [04080741] **1136**

PROGRAM HIGHLIGHTS (US/0278-5374) [07770373] **3630**

PROGRAM INFORMATION NOTICE See ANNUAL PROGRAM INFORMATION NOTICE **1932**

PROGRAM INFORMATION SERIES REPORT (US/0091-0511) [01785766] **5302**

PROGRAM KEGIATAN - KANTOR WILAYAH DEPARTEMEN P DAN K DKI JAKARTA (IO) [05428926] **1775**

PROGRAM KELUARGA BERENCANA NASIONAL DALAM GRAFIK DAN GAMBAR (IO) [14689523] **590**

PROGRAM LONDON. 1987 (UK/0952-8865) [I09528865] **1248**

PROGRAM MANAGER (US/0199-7114) [06114885] **883**

PROGRAM MANAGERS NEWSLETTER See PROGRAM MANAGER **883**

PROGRAM MATERIALS FOR SEMINAR FOR GEORGIA DISTRICT ATTORNEYS (US/0092-5977) [05377973] **3108**

PROGRAM; NEWS OF COMPUTERS IN LIBRARIES (UK/0033-0337) [02033693] 1201, **3242**

PROGRAM NOTES - ASSOCIATION OF UNIVERSITY PROGRAMS IN HEALTH ADMINISTRATION (US/0098-1559) [01388161] **3791**

PROGRAM NOW (UK/0953-9344) [I09539344] **1281**

PROGRAM OF PLENARY SESSIONS AND ADVANCE ABSTRACTS OF SHORT COMMUNICATIONS (DK/0906-9666) [I09069666] 3732, **3661**

PROGRAM OF RESEARCH (AT) [10014786] **2391**

PROGRAM OF STUDIES - NEWFOUNDLAND. DIVISION OF PROGRAM DEVELOPMENT (CN/1186-8295) [24623981] **1903**

PROGRAM OF THE ANNUAL MEETING - ORGANIZATION OF AMERICAN HISTORIANS (US/0197-9884) [12359023] **2755**

PROGRAM ON ENVIRONMENT AND BEHAVIOR MONOGRAPH (US/0737-5425) [08943577] **5213**

PROGRAM OVERVIEW - WASTEWATER TECHNOLOGY CENTRE, CANADA (CN/0849-3650) [23248060] 5537, **2240**

PROGRAM PERFORMANCE MEASUREMENT (CN) [07767258] **4742**

PROGRAM PLAN - UNITED STATES. FOOD SAFETY AND INSPECTION SERVICE (US/0735-2395) [08869473] **4198**

PROGRAM PLANS. NURSING BASIC SERIES (US/0734-1431) [08699630] **3867**

PROGRAM/ PROCEEDINGS / AMERICAN SOCIETY OF CLINICAL ONCOLOGY (US) [21958981] **3822**

PROGRAM REPORT - ATOMIC INDUSTRIAL FORUM (US) [02974227] **1953**

PROGRAM REPORT - INTERNATIONAL RICE RESEARCH INSTITUTE (PH/0117-0880) [I01170880] **183**

PROGRAM REPORT / NATIONAL HEART, LUNG, AND BLOOD INSTITUTE, DIVISION OF LUNG DISEASES (US/0192-9305) [04844615] **3951**

PROGRAM REPORT (NATIONAL SCIENCE FOUNDATION (US)) (US/0195-6132) [03170635] **5142**

PROGRAM REPORT OF THE UNITED STATES TRAVEL AND TOURISM ADMINISTRATION (US) [10855206] **5489**

PROGRAM REQUIREMENTS MEMORANDA FOR FISCAL YEAR ... : MUNICIPAL WASTEWATER TREATMENT WORKS CONSTRUCTION GRANTS PROGRAM / UNITED STATES ENVIRONMENTAL PROTECTION AGENCY, OFFICE OF WATER PROGRAMS OPERATIONS (US) [04276134] 5537, **2240**

PROGRAM STATEMENTS / WESTERN AUSTRALIA (AT) [24258232] **4742**

PROGRAM STATISTICS - MICHIGAN DEPARTMENT OF SOCIAL SERVICES (US/0093-7835) [01792427] 5302, **5266**

PROGRAM STATUS REPORT ... TO THE GOVERNOR AND LEGISLATURE / STATE OF FLORIDA, HOSPITAL COST CONTAINMENT BOARD (US) [08575633] **3791**

PROGRAM TRENDS FOR BUSINESS AND INDUSTRY (US) **705**

PROGRAM UPDATE ... AS OF DECEMBER 31 ... / CLEAN COAL TECHNOLOGY DEMONSTRATION PROGRAM (US) [23666581] 2148, **1444**

PROGRAMA (PO) [05537554] **5367**

PROGRAMA DE ESTUDIOS CONJUNTOS SOBRE INTEGRACION ECONOMICA LATINOAMERICANA See ENSAYOS ECIEL **1488**

PROGRAMA NACIONAL DE MAIZ PALOMERO / DGEA (MX) [08973715] **1622**

PROGRAMA NACIONAL DE PESQUISA AGROPECUARIA : PRONAPA / EMBRAPA, EMPRESA BRASILEIRA DE PESQUISA AGROPECUARIA (BL) [02244163] **122**

PROGRAMA SIEMBRA-EXPORTACION DE AJO / DGEA (MX) [08925240] **122**

PROGRAMA SIEMBRA-EXPORTACION DE BERENJENA / DGEA (MX) [08924541] **1622**

PROGRAMA SIEMBRA-EXPORTACION DE CALABACITA / DGEA (MX) [08925327] **122**

PROGRAMA SIEMBRA-EXPORTACION DE CEBOLLA (MX) [08933197] **122**

PROGRAMA SIEMBRA-EXPORTACION DE CHILE BELL / DGEA (MX) [08964629] **2354**

PROGRAMA SIEMBRA-EXPORTACION DE FRESA / DGEA (MX) [08964482] **2354**

PROGRAMA SIEMBRA-EXPORTACION DE GARBANZO / DGEA (MX) [09965841] **1622**

PROGRAMA SIEMBRA-EXPORTACION DE MELON / DGEA (SP) [09960267] **1622**

PROGRAMA SIEMBRA-EXPORTACION DE PEPINO / DGEA (MX) [08966371] **2354**

PROGRAMA SIEMBRA-EXPORTACION DE PIMIENTA GORDA / DGEA (MX) [08969099] **2354**

PROGRAMA SIEMBRA-EXPORTACION DE SANDIA / DGEA (MX) [08977605] **2354**

PROGRAMA SIEMBRA-EXPORTACION DE TOMATE / DGEA (MX) [08924579] **2354**

PROGRAMACAO DA REGIAO NORDESTE (BL) [04485916] **122**

PROGRAMI IZDANJA IZDAVACKIH ORGANIZACIJA UDRUZENOG RADA ZA ... GODINU / UDRUZENJE IZDAVAĈCA I KNJIZARA JUGOSLAVIJE (YU) [07326719] **422**

PROGRAMM-BUDGET (GW/0175-8438) [11821871] **4742**

PROGRAMMA DRASEOS HYPERESIAS POLITIKES AEROPORIAS (GR) [01798156] **32**

PROGRAMMA DRASTERIOTETOS (GR) [01792348] **5254**

●PROGRAMMABLE LOGIC, NEWS & VIEWS (US/1064-1394) [26211696] **1239**

PROGRAMMAZIONE IN SARDEGNA, LA (IT) [01787660] **1579**

PROGRAMME ANNUEL DES DEPENSES DANS LE NORD (CN/0382-2494) [03191388] **4742**

PROGRAMME BUDGET (UK) [01791250] **4742**

PROGRAMME D'ACTIVITE - B.D.I (IV) [02241266] **1622**

PROGRAMME D'ACTIVITES - ORGANISME REGIONAL DE DEVELOPPEMENT DU CENTRE-NORD (UV) [05160105] **1579**

PROGRAMME D'ACTIVITES SODENKAM (CM) [07079733] **804**

PROGRAMME D'AIDE ... DU MINISTERE DES AFFAIRES CULTURELLES AIDE AUX ARTISTES PROFESSIONNELS (CN/1187-0621) [25079385] **328**

PROGRAMME D'ASSOCIE / INSTITUT D'ASSURANCE DU CANADA (CN/0820-0777) [09519532] **2891**

●PROGRAMME DE BOURSES DES GOUVERNEMENTS ETRANGERS / ADMINISTRE PAR LE CONSEIL INTERNATIONAL D'ETUDES CANADIENNES (CN/1191-3282) [26290299] **4675**

PROGRAMME DE LOISIR (CN/0712-8088) [08724143] **387**

PROGRAMME DE PERFECTIONNEMENT, PERFECTIONNEMENT COLLECTIF (CN/1185-2453) [24571326] **1775**

PROGRAMME DE PERFECTIONNEMENT, PERFECTIONNEMENT COLLECTIF POUR LE PERSONNEL DES SERVICES DE L'EDUCATION DES ADULTES (CN/1185-2437) [24571328] **1802**

PROGRAMME DE PREVENTION CONTRE LA GRELE DE L'ASSOCIATION NATIONALE D'ETUDE ET DE LUTTE CONTRE LES FLEAUX ATMOSPHERIQUES (FR/0373-7349) [17210140] **1433**

PROGRAMME DE RECHERCHE - INSTITUT DE RECHERCHE DES TRANSPORTS (IV) [03024800] **5390**

PROGRAMME DES ACTIVITES CULTURELLES ET SPORTIVES (CN/0828-5705) [12168366] **4913**

PROGRAMME DES COURS / UNIVERSITE LIBRE DE BRUXELLES (BE) [19097911] **1094**

PROGRAMME DES INVESTISSEMENTS DE L'ETAT ... ET BUDGET D'INVESTISSEMENT ... (NG) [19994420] **4742**

PROGRAMME DU ... EXERCICE - CHAMBRE DE COMMERCE DU DISTRICT DE MONTREAL (CN/0705-7334) [09313010] **821**

PROGRAMME F.I.A.C (CN/0820-6120) [09581983] **2891**

PROGRAMME OF ACTION / WORLD PEACE COUNCIL (FR) [07782401] **4532**

PROGRAMME OF WORK (IE) [19379866] **1704**

PROGRAMME OF WORK AND BUDGET (FR/0377-2993) [02244725] **1579**

PROGRAMME POUR LES AUTOCHTONES, NOUVELLES, LE (CN/1185-9954) [25590158] **4675**

PROGRAMME, PROCEEDINGS / CANADIAN FEDERATION OF BIOLOGICAL SOCIETIES (CN/0845-5066) [20505344] 492, **585**

●PROGRAMME PROFILES (NZ/1171-2031) [27697866] 849, **1513**

PROGRAMME REVIEW AND FINANCIAL STATEMENTS (UK) [03618895] **590**

PROGRAMME SOUVENIR. FESTIVAL DU VOYAGEUR, ST. BONIFACE, MANITOBA (CN/0229-2572) [08071815] **4853**

PROGRAMME TRIENNAL DES ACTIVITES DU BUREAU DE DEVELOPPEMENT INDUSTRIEL (FI) [02241267] **1622**

PROGRAMME WITH ABSTRACTS - CANADIAN METEOROLOGICAL AND OCEANOGRAPHIC SOCIETY (CN/0842-0408) [21400828] 1433, **1455**

PROGRAMMERS INFORMATION NETWORK (US) **4707**

●PROGRAMMER'S PROVANTAGE COMPUTER PRODUCTS BUYER'S GUIDE (US/1076-9714) [30658526] 1272, **1281**

PROGRAMMERS ROM. CD-ROM (US) 1272, **1281**

●PROGRAMMES DE SUBVENTIONS ET DE BOURSES DE CARRIERE DU CONSEIL QUEBECOIS DE LA RECHERCHE SOCIALE (CN/1191-7431) [27477011] **5214**

PROGRAMMES ET ENGAGEMENTS ELECTORAUX (FR) [06262185] **4492**

PROGRAMMES - SOCIETE QUEBECOISE DE SPELEOLOGIE (CN/0711-6187) [08920491] **1409**

PROGRAMMING AND COMPUTER SOFTWARE (US/0361-7688) [02286986] 1289, **1281**

PROGRAMMIROVANIE (RU/0132-3474) [03318418] 1289, **1281**

PROGRAMS & ACCOMPLISHMENTS (US) [02240107] **1433**

PROGRAMS AND PLANS / ENVIRONMENTAL RESEARCH LABORATORIES (US/0149-6034) [03506167] **5142**

PROGRAMS AND PROGRESS (US/0363-0625) [02404081] **5302**

PROGRAMS AND SCHOOLS (US/0197-2804) [05120111] **1915**

PROGRAMS AT WORK / BRITISH COLUMBIA FORESTRY ASSOCIATION (CN/1185-9806) [25423679] **2391**

PROGRAMS PROVIDING SERVICES TO BATTERED WOMEN (US/0272-4448) [06808254] **5302**

PROGRAMS REGULATIONS - INSTITUTE OF CANADIAN BANKERS (CN/0821-607X) [09743213] **804**

[PROGRAMS] / ST. LOUIS SYMPHONY ORCHESTRA (US) [08339181] **4160**

PROGRES AGRICOLE ET VITICOLE, LE (FR/0369-8173) [04063976] **122**

PROGRES DU NORD, AHUNTSIC (CN/0822-563X) [10061761] **5793**

PROGRES EN ANDROLOGIE (FR) [20350965] **3630**

PROGRES EN HEMATOLOGIE (FR/0246-0149) [09034093] **3773**

PROGRES EN NEONATOLOGIE / JOURNEES NATIONALES DE NEONATOLOGIE (SZ/0251-5601) [17800689] **3911**

PROGRES EN UROLOGIE : JOURNAL DE L'ASSOCIATION FRANCAISE D'UROLOGIE ET DE LA SOCIETE FRANCAISE D'UROLOGIE (FR) [28357833] **3992**

PROGRES FORESTIER, LE (CN/0705-4130) [03980078] **2391**

PROGRES, LE (FR) [12156998] **5801**

PROGRES REALISE EN SIGNALISATION MARITIME DURANT L'ANNEE ... / ASSOCIATION INTERNATIONALE DE SIGNALISATION MARITIME (FR) [19736236] **5454**

PROGRES TECHNIQUE, LE (FR/0397-8060) [03234906] **5142**

PROGRESO (MEXICO) (MX/0555-3768) [01793102] **2543**

PROGRESOS DE OBSTETRICIA Y GINECOLOGIA (SP/0304-5013) [I03045013] **3767**

PROGRESOS EN DIAGNOSTICO PRENATAL (SP/1130-0523) [I11300523] **3767**

PROGRESOS EN LAS ENFERMEDADES CARDIOVASCULARES (SP) **3709**

PROGRESOS EN PSICOARMACOLOGIA (SP/0211-8351) [08539532] **4326**

PROGRESS AGAINST CANCER (TORONTO) (CN/0319-3071) [02442275] **3822**

PROGRESS AND CHALLENGE, WASTE-TO-ENERGY PROJECTS (US/8756-4866) [11501912] **2240**

PROGRESS AND TOPICS IN CYTOGENETICS (US/0733-9003) [08677704] **539**

PROGRESS (CAVE CITY, KY. 1988), THE (US/1055-9531) [18035974] **5682**

PROGRESS (CLEARFIELD, PA. : 1946) (US) [12136125] **5739**

PROGRESS-EXAMINER, THE (US) [12180325] **5666**

PROGRESS IN AEROSPACE SCIENCES (UK/0376-0421) [05174954] **32**

PROGRESS IN AIDS PATHOLOGY (US/1042-363X) [19028281] 3897, **4796**

PROGRESS IN AIR POLLUTION CONTROL (US/0098-0463) [01799323] **2240**

PROGRESS IN ANESTHESIOLOGY (US/0099-1546) [01672976] **3684**

PROGRESS IN ANESTHESIOLOGY (SAN ANTONIO, TEX.) (US/0891-5784) [14913934] **3684**

PROGRESS IN APPLIED MICROCIRCULATION (ENGLISH ED.) (SZ/1017-8686) [09624187] **3630**

PROGRESS IN ASTRONAUTICS AND AERONAUTICS (US/0079-6050) [07586114] **32**

PROGRESS IN BASIC AND CLINICAL PHARMACOLOGY (SZ/1011-0267) [18265617] **4326**

PROGRESS IN BATTERIES & SOLAR CELLS (US/0198-7259) [05123510] **2077**

PROGRESS IN BEHAVIOR MODIFICATION (US/0099-037X) [02243256] **4609**

PROGRESS IN BEHAVIORAL STUDIES *CEASED.* (US/0891-0111) [14524057] **4609**

PROGRESS IN BIOCHEMICAL PHARMACOLOGY (US/0079-6085) [01762940] **4326**

●PROGRESS IN BIOCHEMISTRY AND BIOTECHNOLOGY (US) 3696, **492**

PROGRESS IN BIOMEDICAL ENGINEERING (NE/0920-5438) [11009140] **3696**

PROGRESS IN BIOPHYSICS AND MOLECULAR BIOLOGY (US/0079-6107) [01715038] 492, **496**

PROGRESS IN BIOTECHNOLOGY (NE/0921-0423) [13045866] **492**

PROGRESS IN BOTANY (GW/0340-4773) [03281005] **525**

PROGRESS IN BRAIN RESEARCH (NE/0079-6123) [01587158] **3844**

PROGRESS IN CANCER RESEARCH AND THERAPY (US/0145-3726) [02720642] **3822**

PROGRESS IN CARDIOLOGY (PHILADELPHIA, PA. : 1988) (US) [17793818] **3709**

PROGRESS IN CARDIOVASCULAR DISEASES (US/0033-0620) [01624043] **3709**

PROGRESS IN CARDIOVASCULAR NURSING (US/0889-7204) [14039202] 3867, **3709**

PROGRESS IN CLINICAL AND BIOLOGICAL RESEARCH (US/0361-7742) [02111943] **470**

PROGRESS IN CLINICAL BIOCHEMISTRY AND MEDICINE (GW/0177-8757) [11009237] 3630, **492**

PROGRESS IN CLINICAL MEDICINE (UK) [10549345] **3630**

PROGRESS IN CLINICAL NEUROPHYSIOLOGY *CEASED.* (SZ/0378-4045) [03593733] 585, **3844**

PROGRESS IN CLINICAL PHARMACOLOGY (GW/0721-4049) [07853726] **4326**

PROGRESS IN CLINICAL PHARMACY (NE/0167-5028) [08448214] **4326**

PROGRESS IN CLINICAL RHEUMATOLOGY (US/0742-745X) [10426570] **3806**

PROGRESS IN COLLOID & POLYMER SCIENCE (GW/0340-255X) [01372269] **1056**

PROGRESS IN COMMUNICATION (US/0148-5342) [03315588] **4392**

PROGRESS IN COMMUNICATION SCIENCES (US/0163-5689) [04415468] **1120**

PROGRESS IN COMPUTER SCIENCE (US/0743-1597) [08513347] **1201**

PROGRESS IN CONTEMPORARY CARTOGRAPHY (UK/0275-8768) [06808267] **2583**

PROGRESS IN CRYSTAL GROWTH AND CHARACTERIZATION OF MATERIALS (UK/0960-8974) [22522482] **1033**

PROGRESS IN DRUG RESEARCH (SZ/0071-786X) [01778215] **4326**

PROGRESS IN ELECTROMAGNETICS RESEARCH (US/1043-626X) [19499147] **4445**

PROGRESS IN ENDOCRINE RESEARCH AND THERAPY (US/0890-7048) [11374657] **3732**

PROGRESS IN ENERGY AND COMBUSTION SCIENCE (UK/0360-1285) [01830378] 2127, **1954**

●PROGRESS IN EXPERIMENTAL PERSONALITY AND PSYCHOPATHOLOGY RESEARCH (US/1056-7151) [23820247] **3932**

PROGRESS IN EXPERIMENTAL PERSONALITY RESEARCH *See* PROGRESS IN EXPERIMENTAL PERSONALITY AND PSYCHOPATHOLOGY RESEARCH **3932**

PROGRESS IN EXPERIMENTAL TUMOR RESEARCH (SZ/0079-6263) [01695607] **3822**

PROGRESS IN EXTRACTIVE METALLURGY (US/0091-6145) [01799902] **4016**

PROGRESS IN FILTRATION AND SEPARATION (NE/0167-6938) [06193157] **1028**

PROGRESS IN FOOD & NUTRITION SCIENCE (UK/0306-0632) [02245759] **4198**

PROGRESS IN GASTROENTEROLOGY *CEASED.* (US/0079-6271) [01777683] **3747**

PROGRESS IN GROWTH FACTOR RESEARCH (US/0955-2235) [17962661] **990**

PROGRESS IN HAZARDOUS CHEMICALS HANDLING AND DISPOSAL (US/0090-5860) [01785251] 1028, **2240**

PROGRESS IN HEMOSTASIS AND THROMBOSIS (US/0362-6350) [01586215] **3773**

PROGRESS IN HETEROCYCLIC CHEMISTRY (UK) [20508116] **990**

PROGRESS IN HISTOCHEMISTRY AND CYTOCHEMISTRY (GW/0079-6336) [01590508] **540**

PROGRESS IN HPLC (NE/0920-9832) [13831190] **990**

PROGRESS IN HUMAN GEOGRAPHY (UK/0309-1325) [03682235] **2573**

PROGRESS IN IMMUNOLOGY (NE) [02256129] **3676**

PROGRESS IN IMPROVING PROGRAM AND BUDGET INFORMATION FOR CONGRESSIONAL USE (US/0194-2824) [05348376] **4742**

PROGRESS IN INDUSTRIAL MICROBIOLOGY (AMSTERDAM, NETHERLANDS) (UK/0079-6352) [01762953] **568**

PROGRESS IN INORGANIC CHEMISTRY (US/0079-6379) [01645674] **1037**

PROGRESS IN INTER-GROUP AND RACE RELATIONS (SA) [06825974] **5254**

PROGRESS IN LIPID RESEARCH (UK/0163-7827) [04427076] **1046**

●PROGRESS IN LIVER DISEASES (PHILADELPHIA, PA.) (US/1060-913X) [25107533] **3800**

PROGRESS IN LOW TEMPERATURE PHYSICS (NE/0079-6417) [01644081] **4418**

PROGRESS IN MACROCYCLIC CHEMISTRY (US/0195-4237) [04871011] **1046**

PROGRESS IN MATERIALS SCIENCE (UK/0079-6425) [01624195] **2107**

PROGRESS IN MATHEMATICS (BOSTON, MASS.) (US/0743-1643) [06073963] **3528**

PROGRESS IN MEDICAL AND ENVIRONMENTAL PHYSICS (UK/0265-9697) [09769845] **4418**

PROGRESS IN MEDICAL RADIATION PHYSICS (US/0730-2339) [07980907] **3944**

PROGRESS IN MEDICAL VIROLOGY (US/0079-645X) [01762957] **569**

PROGRESS IN MEDICINAL CHEMISTRY (NE/0079-6468) [01762958] 4326, **990**

PROGRESS IN MIGRAINE RESEARCH (UK/0262-6330) [08794813] **3844**

PROGRESS IN MOLECULAR AND SUBCELLULAR BIOLOGY (US/0079-6484) [01640631] **470**

PROGRESS IN MUTATION RESEARCH (US/0731-2849) [07935993] **551**

PROGRESS IN NATURAL SCIENCE : COMMUNICATION OF STATE KEY LABORATORIES OF CHINA (CC/1002-0071) [24841119] **5142**

PROGRESS IN NEURAL NETWORKS (US/1055-713X) [23274030] **1244**

PROGRESS — Alphabetical Title Index

PROGRESS IN NEURO-PSYCHOPHARMACOLOGY & BIOLOGICAL PSYCHIATRY (UK/0278-5846) [07845411] 3932, **4326**

PROGRESS IN NEUROBIOLOGY (UK/0301-0082) [01785429] 470, **3844**

PROGRESS IN NEUROENDOCRINIMMUNOLOGY *CEASED.* (US/1045-2001) [20053050] **3732**

PROGRESS IN NEUROLOGICAL SURGERY (SZ) [01624451] **3972**

PROGRESS IN NEUROPATHOLOGY (US/0099-9016) [01777301] **3844**

PROGRESS IN NONLINEAR DIFFERENTIAL EQUATIONS AND THEIR APPLICATIONS (SZ) [21550184] **3528**

PROGRESS IN NUCLEAR ENERGY (NEW SERIES) (UK/0149-1970) [06883174] **2158**

PROGRESS IN NUCLEAR MAGNETIC RESONANCE SPECTROSCOPY (UK/0079-6565) [01427374] **4450**

PROGRESS IN NUCLEIC ACID RESEARCH AND MOLECULAR BIOLOGY (US/0079-6603) [00981428] **470**

PROGRESS IN OBSTETRICS AND GYNAECOLOGY (UK/0261-0140) [07643773] **3767**

PROGRESS IN OCEANOGRAPHY (UK/0079-6611) [01161747] 557, **1455**

PROGRESS IN OPTICS (NE/0079-6638) [01762966] **4440**

PROGRESS IN ORGANIC COATINGS (SZ/0300-9440) [01585841] **4225**

●PROGRESS IN PALLIATIVE CARE (UK/0969-9260) [30471746] **3867**

PROGRESS IN PAPER RECYCLING (US/1061-1452) [24851399] 2240, **4237**

PROGRESS IN PARTICLE AND NUCLEAR PHYSICS (UK/0146-6410) [04259037] **4450**

●PROGRESS IN PEDIATRIC CARDIOLOGY (US/1058-9813) [24450735] 3911, **3709**

PROGRESS IN PEDIATRIC HEMATOLOGY/ONCOLOGY (US/0146-1540) [02833433] 3911, 3822, **3773**

PROGRESS IN PEDIATRIC SURGERY (GW/0079-6654) [01775050] 3972, **3911**

PROGRESS IN PESTICIDE BIOCHEMISTRY AND TOXICOLOGY (UK/0887-6142) [09962416] **4247**

PROGRESS IN PHARMACOLOGY AND CLINICAL PHARMACOLOGY (GW/0934-9545) [19484202] **4326**

●PROGRESS IN PHOTOVOLTAICS (UK/1062-7995) [25744745] **2077**

PROGRESS IN PHYCOLOGICAL RESEARCH (UK/0167-8574) [08891431] **525**

PROGRESS IN PHYSICAL GEOGRAPHY (UK/0309-1333) [03672747] 2180, **2573**

PROGRESS IN PHYSICAL ORGANIC CHEMISTRY (US/0079-6662) [01695425] **1046**

PROGRESS IN PLANNING (UK/0305-9006) [01049759] **2832**

PROGRESS IN POLYMER SCIENCE (UK/0079-6700) [00928213] **1047**

PROGRESS IN POLYMER SCIENCE, JAPAN (JA/0286-2999) [01320885] **1047**

PROGRESS IN PROBABILITY (US/1050-6977) [21187666] **3542**

PROGRESS IN PROBABILITY AND STATISTICS *See* PROGRESS IN PROBABILITY **3542**

PROGRESS IN PROTEIN-LIPID INTERACTIONS (NE/0168-9614) [12606867] **990**

PROGRESS IN PSYCHOBIOLOGY AND PHYSIOLOGICAL PSYCHOLOGY (US/0363-0951) [02220806] 4609, **585**

PROGRESS IN PUBLIC EDUCATION ABOUT CANCER (SZ) [20698353] **3822**

PROGRESS IN QUANTUM ELECTRONICS (UK/0079-6727) [01190536] **2077**

PROGRESS IN REACTION KINETICS (US/0079-6743) [01762973] **1057**

PROGRESS IN REPRODUCTIVE BIOLOGY AND MEDICINE (SZ/0254-105X) [10409405] 3732, **470**

PROGRESS IN RESEARCH IN EMPHYSEMA AND CHRONIC BRONCHITIS *See* PROGRESS IN RESPIRATION RESEARCH **3951**

PROGRESS IN RESOURCE MANAGEMENT AND ENVIRONMENTAL PLANNING (UK/0271-7395) [06258064] **2240**

PROGRESS IN RESPIRATION RESEARCH (SZ/0079-6751) [01606744] **3951**

●PROGRESS IN RETINAL AND EYE RESEARCH (UK/1350-9462) [29972326] **3878**

PROGRESS IN RETINAL RESEARCH (UK/0278-4327) [07827887] 4217, **585**

PROGRESS IN RUBBER AND PLASTICS TECHNOLOGY (UK/0266-7320) [12629337] 4460, **5077**

PROGRESS IN RURAL POLICY AND PLANNING (UK/0956-4187) [24242566] **2832**

PROGRESS IN SCIENTIFIC COMPUTING (US/0885-7733) [10543011] **1201**

PROGRESS IN SELF PSYCHOLOGY (US/0893-5483) [12999725] **4609**

PROGRESS IN SOLID STATE CHEMISTRY (UK/0079-6786) [01585626] **1057**

PROGRESS IN STROKE RESEARCH (UK/0144-865X) [05884646] **3709**

PROGRESS IN SURFACE SCIENCE (UK/0079-6816) [00958121] **1057**

PROGRESS IN SURGERY (SZ/0079-6824) [01762977] **3972**

PROGRESS IN SURGICAL PATHOLOGY (US/0271-2350) [06566258] **3972**

PROGRESS IN TECHNOLOGY (US/0583-936X) [01587039] **5142**

PROGRESS IN TECHNOLOGY SERIES (US) [08101228] **5423**

PROGRESS IN THE ASTRONAUTICAL SCIENCES (NE/0555-4306) [01762978] **32**

PROGRESS IN THE IMPLEMENTATION OF MOTOR VEHICLE EMISSION STANDARDS (US/0098-7069) [02242251] **2240**

PROGRESS IN THE PSYCHOLOGY OF LANGUAGE *CEASED.* (UK/0268-7364) [13211322] **3312**

PROGRESS IN THEORETICAL ORGANIC CHEMISTRY (NE/0165-2362) [10549561] **1057**

PROGRESS IN TOURISM, RECREATION, AND HOSPITALITY MANAGEMENT (UK/0952-5424) [20451688] 2809, **5489**

PROGRESS IN TRANSFUSION MEDICINE (UK/0268-2613) [13858417] **3773**

PROGRESS IN UNDERWATER SCIENCE (UK) [04527901] **1455**

PROGRESS IN UROLOGY : JOURNAL OF THE FRENCH UROLOGICAL ASSOCIATION AND OF THE FRENCH SOCIETY OF UROLOGY (FR) [25281074] **3992**

PROGRESS IN VETERINARY & COMPARATIVE OPHTHALMOLOGY (US/1061-5768) [23912963] **5519**

PROGRESS IN VETERINARY NEUROLOGY (US/1061-575X) [21458459] **5519**

PROGRESS-INDEX, THE (US) [14046626] **5759**

PROGRESS (MUSCLE SHOALS, ALA.) (US/0730-7322) [07514672] **123**

PROGRESS NOTES - CANADIAN WILDLIFE SERVICE (CN/0069-0023) [02248968] **470**

PROGRESS OF DIGESTIVE ENDOSCOPY (JA) [02521222] **3630**

PROGRESS OF EDUCATION IN THE UNITED STATES OF AMERICA (US/0191-8540) [02705317] **1775**

PROGRESS OF EDUCATION, THE (II/0033-0663) [05371630] **1775**

PROGRESS OF MATHEMATICS (II/0555-4330) [01762981] **3528**

PROGRESS OF PHYSICS (US/0033-0671) [01799601] **4418**

PROGRESS OF THE COLOMBO PLAN (CE/0588-4241) [01564119] **2911**

PROGRESS OF THEORETICAL PHYSICS (JA/0033-068X) [01762983] **4429**

PROGRESS OF THEORETICAL PHYSICS. SUPPLEMENT (JA/0375-9687) [02449902] **4418**

PROGRESS REPORT (IE) [01788179] **5142**

PROGRESS REPORT (HK) [09791352] **4675**

PROGRESS REPORT - AMERICAN PHYSICAL THERAPY ASSOCIATION (US/0162-3907) [04162931] **4382**

PROGRESS REPORT - ARKANSAS NATURAL HERITAGE COMMISSION (US) [06202708] **4171**

PROGRESS REPORT / ASIAN VEGETABLE RESEARCH AND DEVELOPMENT CENTER (CH/0258-3089) [20512913] **123**

PROGRESS REPORT - COAST INSTITUTE OF TECHNOLOGY (KE) [03897959] **5142**

PROGRESS REPORT - EAR RESEARCH INSTITUTE *CEASED.* (US/0197-3657) [05984282] **3891**

PROGRESS REPORT - F.I.A.B (NE/0377-7693) [01794381] **3242**

PROGRESS REPORT / GLOBAL PROGRAMME ON AIDS (SZ) [20051042] **3676**

PROGRESS REPORT - HEALTH AND SAFETY RESEARCH DIVISION (US/0731-7050) [05873080] **4797**

PROGRESS REPORT - IDAHO. AGRICULTURAL EXPERIMENT STATION (US/0886-7038) [04251677] **123**

PROGRESS REPORT - INSTITUTE OF HYDRODYNAMICS AND HYDRAULIC ENGINEERING (LYNGBY) (DK/0301-7176) [04763597] **2095**

PROGRESS REPORT - INTERNATIONAL INSTITUTE OF SEISMOLOGY AND EARTHQUAKE ENGINEERING (JA) [03216126] **1409**

PROGRESS REPORT - MAINE LAW ENFORCEMENT PLANNING AND ASSISTANCE AGENCY (US/0090-6107) [01785243] **3173**

PROGRESS REPORT - MICHIGAN DEPARTMENT OF SOCIAL SERVICES. OFFICE OF YOUTH SERVICES (US/0091-2883) [01785788] **5302**

PROGRESS REPORT OF CONSERVATION ACTIVITIES (US) [05636354] **2202**

PROGRESS REPORT OF THE MONTANA STATE WATER PLAN (US) [01791091] **2095**

PROGRESS REPORT ON PESTICIDES AND RELATED ACTIVITIES (US/0565-243X) [02687913] **4247**

PROGRESS REPORT ON TRIP ENDS GENERATION RESEARCH COUNTS (SAN FRANCISCO) (US/0092-6159) [02343279] **5390**

PROGRESS REPORT - OREGON STATE PARKS AND RECREATION DIVISION (US/0473-2014) [01332157] **4707**

PROGRESS REPORT PELITA P.K3A (IO) [03431731] **5302**

PROGRESS REPORT - SOCIETE D'ENERGIE DE LA BAIE JAMES (CN/0713-4916) [06570371] 5537, **705**

PROGRESS REPORT - SOUTHEAST SOUTH DAKOTA EXPERIMENT FARM (US) [06782116] **123**

PROGRESS REPORT SUMMARIES - ASIAN VEGETABLE RESEARCH AND DEVELOPMENT CENTER (CH/0258-3097) [20513203] **183**

PROGRESS REPORT. THE MINORITY BUSINESS ENTERPRISE PROGRAM (US/0091-4630) [01786738] **705**

PROGRESS REPORT / THE UNITED STATES-JAPAN COOPERATIVE CANCER RESEARCH PROGRAM (US/0278-5382) [04750211] **3822**

PROGRESS REPORT TO THE GOVERNOR'S HIGHWAY SAFETY OFFICE (US/0149-6328) [03511093] **5390**

PROGRESS REPORT / UNIVERSITY OF JAMMU (II) [12224657] **1842**

PROGRESS REPORTS IN ETHNOMUSICOLOGY (US) [11717556] **4147**

PROGRESS REPORTS (WELDING RESEARCH COUNCIL (US)) (US/0743-1651) [04017021] **4027**

PROGRESS (SEATTLE, WASH.), THE (US/0739-6023) [09781172] **5034**

PROGRESS TIMES (US/0890-2666) [14203960] **5753**

PROGRESS (WELLS, NEV.) (US/0747-0029) [10461426] **5734**

PROGRESSI CLINICI. CHIRUGIA (IT/0393-764X) [19884455] **3972**

PROGRESSI CLINICI. MEDICINA (IT) [19485022] **3630**

PROGRESSI IN PATOLOGIA CARDIOVASCOLARE (IT/0033-0701) **3709**

PROGRESSIO (IT) **3350**

PROGRESSIONS : A TECHNICAL JOURNAL FOR DEVELOPERS IN PROGRESS (US) **1201**

PROGRESSIVE ARCHITECTURE (US/0033-0752) [04967033] **306**

PROGRESSIVE FARMER (US/0033-0760) [05350924] **123**

PROGRESSIVE FARMER FOR FLORIDA, THE (US) [01193906] **123**

PROGRESSIVE FARMING (ISLAMABAD, PAKISTAN) (PK) [07721100] **123**

PROGRESSIVE FISH-CULTURIST, THE (US/0033-0779) [01762990] **2311**

PROGRESSIVE GROCER EXECUTIVE REPORT *CEASED.* (US/8755-0571) [11246892] **2354**

PROGRESSIVE GROCER, THE (US/0033-0787) [01606348] **2354**

PROGRESSIVE GROCER'S DIRECTORY OF CONVENIENCE STORES (US/1046-5332) [19135846] **956**

PROGRESSIVE GROCER'S ... DIRECTORY OF MASS MERCHANDISERS (US/0890-7986) [14392711] **956**

PROGRESSIVE GROCER'S ... MARKET SCOPE (US) [17743663] **2354**

PROGRESSIVE GROCER'S MARKETING GUIDEBOOK (US/0079-6921) [03442088] 2354, **935**

PROGRESSIVE HORTICULTURE (II/0970-3020) [05157093] **2429**

PROGRESSIVE LIBRARIAN (US/1052-5726) [22328319] **3242**

PROGRESSIVE (MADISON), THE (US/0033-0736) [01762985] **4532**

PROGRESSIVE PERIODICALS DIRECTORY (US/1054-1985) [20404285] **4822**

PROGRESSIVE PLATTER (US/0738-8861) [09700977] **4147**

PROGRESSIVE RAILROADING (US/0033-0817) [04175009] **5434**

PROGRESSIVE RENTALS (US/8750-6106) [11589883] **705**

PROGRESSIVE REVIEW (WASHINGTON, D.C.), THE (US/0889-2202) [12411431] **4675**

PROGRESSIVE WOMAN *CEASED.* (US/0033-0833) [01775403] **5564**

PROGRESSIVE WORLD (US) [04115984] **4988**

PROGRESSO FOTOGRAFICO, EL (SP) [04302300] **4376**

PROGRESSO MEDICO (ROMA) (IT/0370-1514) [06284770] **3972**

●PROGRESSO VETERINARIO : ORGANO UFFICIALE DELLA FEDERAZIONE NAZIONALE ORDINI VETERINARI ITALIANI (IT) [28004495] **5519**

PROGRESSOR-TIMES (US) [09129426] **5730**

PROHEMIO (IO) [04432344] **3312**

PROHIBIDO (UY) [23904522] **1136**

PROINE, HE (US/0749-3126) [08035506] **5720**

PROIZVODSTVO CHUGUNA / MINISTERSTVO VYSSHEGO I SREDNEGO SPETSIALNOGO OBRAZOVANIIA RSFSR, MAGNITOGORSKII GORNO-METALLURGICHESKII INSTITUT IM. G.I. NOSOVA (RU) [11060574] **4016**

PROIZVODSTVO OGNEUPOROV (RU/0132-5183) [09406157] **4017**

PROIZVODSTVO SPECIALNYH OGNEUPOROV (RU/0321-4966) [03026823] **4017**

PROIZVODSTVO STALI V KISLORODNO-KONVERTORNYH I MARTENOVSKIH CEHAH (RU/0201-873X) [10861166] **4017**

PROIZVODSTVO TEKHNICHESKOGO I STROITELNOGO STEKLA / GOSUDARSTVENNYI NAUCHNO-ISSLEDOVATELSKII INSTITUT STEKLA, SARATOVSKII FILIAL (RU) [08014238] **2593**

PROJECT (FR) **5214**

●PROJECT AND TRADE FINANCE (UK) [28082624] **804**

PROJECT APPRAISAL (UK/0268-8867) [16265132] **912**

PROJECT BREED DIRECTORY (US/1045-2044) [20039837] 5519, **2252**

PROJECT CONCERN INTERNATIONAL ... ANNUAL REPORT (US/0749-3789) [11086643] **2911**

PROJECT CONCERN INTERNATIONAL (ORGANIZATION) *See* PROJECT CONCERN INTERNATIONAL ... ANNUAL REPORT **2911**

PROJECT CONCERN'S ANNUAL REPORT *See* PROJECT CONCERN INTERNATIONAL ... ANNUAL REPORT **2911**

PROJECT FINANCE *See* PROJECT FINANCE INTERNATIONAL **804**

PROJECT FINANCE. ASIA BRIEFING *See* PROJECT FINANCE INTERNATIONAL **804**

PROJECT FINANCE EUROPE *See* PROJECT FINANCE INTERNATIONAL **804**

PROJECT FINANCE INTERNATIONAL (UK/0967-5914) [l09675914] **804**

PROJECT FINANCE MONTHLY, THE (US/1071-4324) [22424619] **804**

PROJECT FINANCING (UK) **804**

PROJECT HEAD START (U.S.) *See* HEAD START NEWSLETTER **5287**

PROJECT INFORMATION EXCHANGE (SELECTED DOCUMENTS) (CN/0708-5710) [05533716] **5302**

PROJECT INFORMATION REPORT (KE) [10241953] **2832**

PROJECT LOOK-LISTEN-THINK-RESPOND ANNUAL REPORT (US) **1120**

PROJECT MAGAZINE (CN/0828-9239) [12846984] **1992**

PROJECT MANAGEMENT JOURNAL (US/8756-9728) [10677350] **883**

PROJECT MANAGER TODAY (UK/0957-1853) **883**

PROJECT MODEL *See* ANNUAL REPORT - PROJECT MODEL **1910**

PROJECT MONOGRAPH (INSTITUTE FOR URBAN DESIGN (U.S.)) (US) [12338414] **2832**

PROJECT NORTH JOURNAL (CN/0829-1489) [12711857] 4492, **2271**

PROJECT OUTCOMES REPORTING (US/0271-4698) [05784141] **1775**

PROJECT: PROGRESS NEWSLETTER (CN/0702-8032) [03409710] **3242**

PROJECT REFERENCE FILE (US/0364-2925) [02275637] **624**

PROJECT REPORT (UNIVERSITY OF ALBERTA. DEPT. OF RURAL ECONOMY) (CN) [19905974] **123**

PROJECT SKYWATER BIENNIAL REPORT (US/0565-0682) [01259557] **5537**

PROJECT SKYWATER; BIENNIAL REPORT (US/0146-8979) [03049814] **1433**

PROJECT SKYWATER FISCAL YEAR ... REPORT / ATMOSPHERIC RESOURCES RESEARCH PROGRAM (US) [05983540] **1433**

PROJECT STATEMENT DAN PEDOMAN PELAKSANAAN D.I.K. & D.I.P (IO) [02439122] **5302**

PROJECT SUMMARIES - NATIONAL SCIENCE FOUNDATION (U.S.). DIVISION OF SCIENCE RESOURCES STUDIES (US/0748-2701) [09400172] **5142**

PROJECT SUMMARIES OF THE CENTER FOR BUILDING TECHNOLOGY, NATIONAL BUREAU OF STANDARDS (US/0360-5051) [03176785] **624**

PROJECTED PULP AND PAPER MILLS IN THE WORLD (IT) [06078035] **4237**

PROJECTIONS OF EDUCATION STATISTICS TO ... (US) [07724707] 1775, **1796**

PROJECTIONS OF THE POPULATION OF THE UNITED STATES ... (ADVANCE REPORT) (US) [09901856] **4559**

PROJECTIONS OF THE POPULATION OF VOTING AGE FOR STATES / U.S. DEPARTMENT OF COMMERCE, BUREAU OF THE CENSUS (US) [08742783] **4559**

PROJECTIONS OF THE POPULATIONS OF AUSTRALIA, STATES AND TERRITORIES (AT/0816-3391) [23114680] **4559**

PROJECTS & DEVELOPMENT INDIA LTD *See* ANNUAL REPORT - PROJECTS & DEVELOPMENT INDIA LTD **1598**

PROJECTS AND PEOPLE *See* PEOPLE AND PROJECTS **5253**

PROJECTS IN METAL (US/0897-070X) [17390139] **4017**

PROJECTS IN PROGRESS (COLUMBUS, OHIO) (US/0735-9365) [05236264] **1915**

PROJECTS, PRODUCTS, AND SERVICES OF THE NATIONAL CENTER FOR EDUCATIONAL STATISTICS (US/0092-6620) [01799558] 1775, **1796**

PROJECTS RECOMMENDED FOR DEAUTHORIZATION, ANNUAL REPORT (US/0361-2651) [02246281] **2095**

PROJECTS REVIEW (LONDON, ENGLAND) (UK/0265-4644) [08876375] **306**

PROJEKT (PL/0033-0957) [02829558] **362**

PROJEKTDOKUMENTATION HOCHSCHULPLANUNG (GW) [02471578] **1842**

PROJET (FR/0033-0884) [02883960] 5302, **1639**

PROJET BIO-ALIMENTAIRE (CN/0849-2352) [22928317] **123**

PROJET DE BUDGET DE PROGRAMMES (BL) [05624424] **4054**

PROJET DE BUDGET - ORGANISME REGIONAL DE DEVELOPPEMENT DU CENTRE-NORD (UV) [05002461] **1579**

PROJET EDUCATIF (SAINT-JEROME) (CN/0821-7629) [10082511] **1842**

PROJETO (BL/0101-1766) [01786548] 633, **306**

PROJETO DE LEI ORCAMENTARIA ANUAL - COORDENACAO DO SISTEMA DE ORCAMENTO (BL) [03226650] **804**

PROKLA (GW/0342-8176) [02660583] **1594**

PROLACTIN SHEFFIELD (UK/0142-8276) [l01428276] **3732**

PROLETARIAN PATH (II) [02245570] **4545**

PROLETARIAN REVOLUTION (MONTREAL) (CN/0229-0685) [08770580] **4545**

PROLOG (LOS ANGELES) (US/0095-3946) [01796582] **4913**

PROLOGO (MADRID, SPAIN) (SP) [20383091] **4831**

PROLOGUE (WASHINGTON) (US/0033-1031) [01762998] 2755, **2482**

PROMADATA, PROMOTION, MARKETING & ADVERTISING DATA (SA) [07321601] **764**

PROMECANICA BARCELONA (SP/0214-3135) [l02143135] **2127**

PROMED (AU) **3630**

PROMENADE (MONTREAL) (CN/0382-7542) [03230392] **388**

PROMENY (CZECHOSLOVAK SOCIETY OF ARTS AND SCIENCES IN AMERICA) (US/0033-1058) [01762999] **2852**

PROMET I VEZE / SOCIJALISTICKA REPUBLIKA HRVATSKA, REPUBLICKI ZAVOD ZA STATISTIKU (CI) [09879657] **5390**

PROMET TURISTA U PRIMORSKIM OPCINAMA / SOCIJALISTICKA REPUBLIKA HRVATSKA, REPUBLICKI ZAVOD ZA STATISTIKU (FR) [11702204] **5489**

PROMETEI (RU/0555-4608) [06686856] **434**

PROMETEO (MILAN, ITALY) (IT) [10471983] **5214**

PROMETHEUS (AT/0810-9028) [11544335] **3242**

PROMETHEUS (IT) [04352610] **3425**

PROMETHEUS (WASHINGTON, D.C.) (US/0048-5535) [01577996] **1775**

PROMIN (AU) [20347100] **5778**

PROMISE (REGINA) (CN/0826-533X) [11245863] **5066**

PROMO (DANBURY, CONN.) (US/1047-1707) [19714902] **935**

PROMO NEWS (US/1046-8447) [20609445] **935**

PROMOBIL (GW) 5489, **5423**

PROMOBIL SPEZIAL (GW) **5489**

PROMOCLIM A (FR/0249-6526) [09921621] **2607**

PROMOFLUID (FR) **764**

PROMOSAFE (NEDERLANDSE ED.) (BE/0771-2839) [02722297] **2868**

PROMOTEC. AGGIORNAMENTO ELETTRICO (IT/1121-371X) [l1121371X] **2077**

PROMOTEUR ZAIROIS : BULLETIN D'INFORMATION ECONOMIQUE DU CENTRE DE COMMERCE INTERNATIONAL DU ZAIRE, LE (CG) [09789397] **849**

PROMOTING COMMUNITY HEALTH (US/0161-6471) [03319762] **3630**

●PROMOTION AND EDUCATION (FR/0751-7149) [29716367] 1903, **4797**

●PROMOTION DE LA SANTE AU CANADA (CN/1195-6755) [31354438] **2240**

PROMOTION DE LA SANTE (OTTAWA) (CN/0833-7608) [17314666] **2240**

PROMOTION (TORONTO) (CN/0701-0702) [03436247] **764**

PROMOTIONAL ACTIVITIES IN THE LEAD AND ZINC INDUSTRIES (UK) **4017**

PROMOTIONS & INCENTIVES (UK/0266-7991) [11642245] **883**

PROMOZIONE (IT) **764**

PROMT / PREDICASTS OVERVIEW OF MARKETS AND TECHNOLOGY (US/0161-8032) [04038295] 1622, **1537**

PROMYSHLENNYE OBRAZTSY, TOVARNYE ZNAKI *See* POLEZNYE MODELI, PROMYSHLENNYE OBRAZTSY : OFITSIALNYI BIULLETEN KOMITETA ROSSIISKOI FEDERATSII PO PATENTAM I TOVARNYM ZNAKAM **1308**

PROMYSHLENNYE OBRAZTSY, TOVARNYE ZNAKI : OFITSIALNYI BIULLETEN GOSUDARSTVENNOGO KOMITETA SSSR PO DELAM IZOBRETENII I OTKRYTII (RU/0208-2888) [09840773] **1308**

PROMYSHLENNYI TRANSPORT (RU/0131-5560) [02241227] 5434, **3487**

PROMYSLENNAJA ENERGETIKA (RU/0033-1155) [06686039] **2077**

PROMYSLENNAJA TEPLOTEHNIKA (UN/0204-3602) [07396167] **2127**

PROMYSLENNOE STROITELSTVO I INZENERNYE SOORUZENIJA (UN/0033-1198) [10983483] **624**

PRONTUARIO CONTRIBUTI PIROLA (IT) [13832374] **4742**

PRONTUARIO COSTO VITA (IT) **705**

PROOF : MAANBLAD VOOR DESKTOP PUBLISHING EN GRAFISCHE TOEPASSINGEN (NE) **1263**

PROOFS (TULSA) (US/0033-1236) [02266541] **1333**

PROOFTEXTS (US/0272-9601) [06979338] **3425**

PROP. 65 NEWS (US/0895-5042) [16667997] **3115**

PROPAGANDA (NEW HYDE PARK, N.Y.) (US/0737-0776) [09274382] **4147**

PROPAGANDA   Alphabetical Title Index

PROPAGANDA REVIEW (US/1047-0239) [18702787] **764**

PROPANE CANADA (CN/0033-1260) [01904735] **4275**

PROPELLANTS, EXPLOSIVES, PYROTECHNICS (GW/0721-3115) [08537472] **1028**

PROPELLER (EAST DETROIT) (US/0194-6218) [04889791] **4913**

PROPERTIES (US/0033-1287) [06793853] **4843**

PROPERTIES OF RADIOACTIVE WASTES AND WASTE CONTAINERS, PROGRESS REPORT / NUCLEAR WASTE MANAGEMENT RESEARCH GROUP, DEPARTMENT OF NUCLEAR ENERGY, BROOKHAVEN NATIONAL LABORATORY (US) [08496273] **2240**

PROPERTIES OF RADIOACTIVE WASTES AND WASTE CONTAINERS, STATUS REPORT / NUCLEAR WASTE MANAGEMENT DIVISION, DEPARTMENT OF NUCLEAR ENERGY, BROOKHAVEN NATIONAL LABORATORY (US) [09513379] **2158**

PROPERTY AND CASUALTY INSURANCE (CN/1187-645X) [25590032] **2891**

PROPERTY AND CASUALTY INSURANCE (CN/1187-645X) [25590035] **2891**

PROPERTY-CASUALTY INDUSTRY REPORTS (US) **1622**

PROPERTY/CASUALTY INSURANCE FACTS (US/1050-4710) [20815969] **2891**

PROPERTY DATA UPDATE **CEASED.** (US/0888-6903) [13691928] **4418**

PROPERTY DISPOSITION HANDBOOK (US) [04484534] **2832**

PROPERTY DISPOSITION HANDBOOK; ONE TO FOUR FAMILY PROPERTIES (US) [02927386] **2832**

PROPERTY FINANCE (UK/0955-8658) **4843, 804**

PROPERTY HIGHLIGHTS (US) [04288048] **4675**

PROPERTY INVESTOR (AT) **4843, 912**

PROPERTY LAW BULLETIN (UK) [07064635] **3032**

PROPERTY MANAGEMENT. (LONDON) (UK/0263-7472) [I02637472] **4843**

PROPERTY MANAGEMENT MONTHLY (US/1054-3848) [22874520] **4843**

PROPERTY MARKET REPORT ... / MINISTRY OF FINANCE MALAYSIA, KUALA LUMPUR (MY) [09234673] **4843**

PROPERTY OUTLOOK (MY) [10609033] **4843**

PROPERTY, PLANNING, AND COMPENSATION REPORTS (UK) [13536112] **2832, 3032**

PROPERTY REVIEW (HK) [06713890] **4843**

PROPERTY REVIEW OXFORD (UK/0966-8225) [I09668225] **4843**

PROPERTY TAX DATA, NEW JERSEY TAXING DISTRICTS, TAX RATES, TAX LEVIES, ASSESSMENT RATIOS (US) [01795450] **4742**

PROPERTY TAX JOURNAL (US/0731-0285) [08098216] **4843, 4742**

PROPERTY TAX RATES, ASSESSMENT RATIOS AND TAX LEVIES, NEW JERSEY TAXING DISTRICTS See PROPERTY TAX DATA, NEW JERSEY TAXING DISTRICTS, TAX RATES, TAX LEVIES, ASSESSMENT RATIOS **4742**

PROPERTY TAX REPORT (US/0744-6926) [08515633] **4742**

PROPERTY TAX STATISTICAL REPORT FROM THE OFFICE OF STATE TAX COMMISSIONER ... ON ... PROPERTY TAXES LEVIED AND PROPERTY VALUATION (US) [10157518] **4742, 4699**

PROPERTY TAX STATISTICS (US) [20610369] **4742**

PROPERTY TAXES (US) **4742**

PROPERTY VALUATION REPORT (US) [05928213] **4742**

PROPHETIC VOICES (NOVATO, CALIF.) (US/0734-3027) [08721656] **4358, 3425**

PROPHETIC WITNESS See YOUR TOMORROW **5011**

PROPHYLAXIS AND PREVENTION IN GYNAECOLOGIC ONCOLOGY NEW TRENDS (IT) **3767**

PROPLINER AVIATION MAGAZINE (UK) **32**

PROPOS, A (FR) [22290292] **705**

PROPOS DE CUISINE (CN/0821-1264) [09977334] **624**

PROPOS PEDAGOGIQUES (CN/0227-0927) [08099439] **1775**

PROPOS (QUEBEC), A (CN/1186-2432) [24368226] **5254**

PROPOSED BIENNIAL BUDGET PRESENTED BY GOVERNOR TO LEGISLATURE (US) [03283388] **4742**

PROPOSED BUDGET / ADOPTED BY THE STATE BOARD OF EDUCATION (US) [06479405] **1869**

PROPOSED BUDGET FOR THE MARYLAND-NATIONAL CAPITAL PARK AND PLANNING COMMISSION. MONTGOMERY COUNTY PROGRAMS, A (US) [10796892] **4742, 4707**

PROPOSED COMPREHENSIVE ANNUAL SERVICE PROGRAM PLAN FOR THE STATE OF HAWAII (US/0148-317X) [03285585] **5302**

PROPOSED COMPREHENSIVE ANNUAL SERVICES PLAN (INDIANAPOLIS) (US/0147-6157) [06732816] **5302**

PROPOSED COMPREHENSIVE ANNUAL SERVICES PROGRAM PLAN (US) [06879849] **5302**

PROPOSED COMPREHENSIVE ANNUAL SERVICES PROGRAM PLAN (US) [04917749] **5302**

PROPOSED COMPREHENSIVE ANNUAL SERVICES PROGRAM PLAN (US) [05668083] **5302**

PROPOSED COMPREHENSIVE ANNUAL SOCIAL SERVICES PLAN (US) [03079709] **5302**

PROPOSED COMPREHENSIVE ANNUAL SOCIAL SERVICES PROGRAM PLAN FOR THE STATE OF WASHINGTON (US) [05111735] **5302**

PROPOSED CONNECTICUT STATE PLAN ON AGING (US/0160-2101) [03623633] **5302**

PROPOSED FISCAL YEAR ... PROGRAM. FINAL ENVIRONMENTAL IMPACT STATEMENT / BONNEVILLE POWER ADMINISTRATION (US) [08691057] **2240**

PROPOSED LEGISLATIVE PROGRAM - DEPARTMENT OF THE INTERIOR (MY) [01220337] **3032**

PROPOSED MICHIGAN ANNUAL SOCIAL SERVICES PLAN (US/0362-7446) [02315462] **5302**

PROPOSED MICHIGAN ANNUAL TITLE XX SERVICES PLAN (US) [07040279] **5302**

PROPOSED PROGRAM AND BUDGET ESTIMATES - PAN AMERICAN HEALTH ORGANIZATION (US/1012-9685) [05886753] **4797**

PROPOSED RULES AND FINAL RULES ADOPTED (US) **4276**

PROPOSED, STATE OF CALIFORNIA, ANNUAL STATEWIDE SOCIAL SERVICES PLAN (US/0149-5097) [03487902] **5302**

PROPOSED, STATE OF CALIFORNIA, COMPREHENSIVE ANNUAL SERVICES PROGRAM PLAN See PROPOSED, STATE OF CALIFORNIA, ANNUAL STATEWIDE SOCIAL SERVICES PLAN **5302**

PROPOSED TITLE XX COMPREHENSIVE SERVICES PROGRAM PLAN (US) [07989414] **5302**

PROPOSED TITLE XX SOCIAL SERVICES: COMPREHENSIVE ANNUAL SERVICES PROGRAM PLAN FOR THE STATE OF TEXAS (US) [05174910] **5302**

●PROPOSITION TARIFAIRE (CN/1187-9947) [26621257] **1513**

●PROPOSITO : REVISTA DE LITERATURA, ARTE Y CINE, A (PR) [26622875] **3425, 328**

PROPOSTA (BL) [03318948] **1775**

PROPOSTE E DISEGNI LEGGE (IT) **3032**

PROPRIETARY SCHOOL DIRECTORY (US/0145-4609) [02737753] **1775**

PROPRIETATIBUS LITTERARUM. SERIES DIDACTICA, DE (NE) [04541102] **3425**

PROPRIETATIBUS LITTERARUM. SERIES MAIOR, DE (NE/0070-3060) [01697728] **3425**

PROPRIETATIBUS LITTERARUM. SERIES PRACTICA, DE (NE/0070-3087) [01697712] **3425**

PROPRIETE INDUSTRIELLE BULLETIN DOCUMENTAIRE (FR) **1623**

PROPRIETE INDUSTRIELLE, LE (SZ) [06591011] **1308**

PROPUESTA Y CONTROL (AG) [03397559] **1579**

PROPYLENE ANNUAL (US/0095-4128) [01796758] **1047**

PRORODEO SPORTS NEWS (US/0161-5815) [03832409] **4913**

PROSCENIO (IT) [15495638] **5367**

PROSCENIUM CHAPBOOKS, THE (US) [05684856] **3425**

PROSCOP MEDIA (FR) [03351118] **1120**

PROSE STUDIES (UK/0144-0357) [06701851] **3425**

PROSECUTOR, THE (US/0027-6383) [05095734] **3108**

PROSECUTORS' BULLETIN, THE (US/0098-8774) [02240846] **3108**

PROSECUTORS' NOTES (SW) [10254741] **3108**

PROSIT (US/0147-5274) [03190577] **375**

PROSOPOPEES : PUBLICATION ERRATIQUE DE L'ACADEMIE DE MUSEOLOGIE EVOCATOIRE (FR) **4095**

PROSPECT (NE) [18392953] **2832**

PROSPECT ADELAIDE (AT/0814-7094) [I08147094] **1802**

PROSPECT (AFRICAN EXPLOSIVES AND CHEMICAL INDUSTRIES) (SA/0033-1481) [08178227] **3487**

PROSPECT EDINBURGH. 1978 (UK/0143-8883) [I01438883] **306**

PROSPECT PERTH (AT/1033-5196) [I10335196] **2148**

PROSPECT RESEARCHER'S GUIDE TO BIOGRAPHICAL COLLECTIONS (US) **705**

PROSPECT UNION EDUCATIONAL EXCHANGE, CAMBRIDGE, MASS. EDUCATIONAL OPPORTUNITIES OF GREATER BOSTON, DAY AND EVENING COURSES FOR WORKING MEN AND WOMEN. CATALOGUE See EDUCATIONAL OPPORTUNITIES OF GREATER BOSTON **1800**

PROSPECT (VANCOUVER) (CN/0843-6819) [20493913] **4017, 2148**

PROSPECTING IN AREAS OF GLACIATED TERRAIN (UK/0141-3376) [03828148] **2148**

PROSPECTIVE ET SANTE (FR/0152-2108) [08853616] **3543**

PROSPECTIVE (MONTREAL. 1984) (CN/0823-8138) [11607563] **2891**

PROSPECTIVE PAYMENT SURVIVAL See HOSPITAL'S MEDICARE POLICY & PAYMENT REPORT, THE **3786**

PROSPECTIVE PLANTINGS / IOWA CROP AND LIVESTOCK REPORTING SERVICE (US) [06260047] **183**

PROSPECTIVE REIMBURSEMENT SYSTEM BASED ON PATIENT CASE-MIX FOR NEW JERSEY HOSPITALS, A (US/0737-5913) [06059321] **3791**

PROSPECTOR : EXPLORATION AND INVESTMENT BULLETIN, THE (CN/1181-6414) [23242630] **2149**

PROSPECTOR (LAS VEGAS, NV) (US) [11837775] **2468**

PROSPECTS FOR AUTOMOBILE INSURANCE UNDERWRITING RESULTS (US) [10369837] **2891**

PROSPECTS (NEW YORK) (US/0361-2333) [02033274] **2755**

PROSPECTS OF IRAQ BIOLOGY (IQ) [02779198] **470**

PROSPECTS (PARIS) (FR/0033-1538) [01785563] **1775**

PROSPECTUS (US/1055-7407) [23284879] **4217**

PROSPECTUS AND HANDBOOK - UNIVERSITY OF MELBOURNE (AT/1038-0124) [I10380124] **1843**

PROSPECTUS - CO-OPERATIVE COLLEGE, MOSHI (TZ) [03489114] **1843**

PROSPECTUS - CONCORDES (CN/0822-5141) [10179268] **4913**

PROSPECTUS - THE INSTITUTE OF FINANCE MANAGEMENT (TZ) [03076751] **804, 883**

PROSPEK (IO/0853-0785) [22607637] **1513**

PROSPETTI COSTO ORARIO DELLA MAMODOPERA : ASSISTAL (IT) **1704**

PROSPETTIVA (IT/0394-0802) [03570552] **279, 362**

PROSPETTIVE ASSISTENZIALI (IT) **5302**

PROSPETTIVE D'ARTE (IT/0393-0165) [I03930165] **328**

PROSPETTIVE DELL ECONOMIA (IT) [23480168] **1579**

PROSPETTIVE DELL'INDUSTRIA ITALIANA, LE (IT) [03941038] **1513**

PROSPETTIVE IN PEDIATRIA (IT/0301-3642) [10129308] **3911**

PROSPETTIVE LIBRI (IT) [09009836] **2626**

PROSPETTIVE PSICOANALITICHE NEL LAVORO ISTITUZIONALE (IT) [18713575] **4609**

PROSPETTIVE SETTANTA (IT) [06298452] **2508**

PROSPETTIVE SOCIALI E SANITARIE (IT/0393-9510) [I03939510] **1704**

PROSPEZIONI ARCHEOLOGICHE QUADERNI / FONDAZIONE. CARLO M. LERICI (IT) [25120181] **279**

Alphabetical Title Index — PRUFROCK

PROSPICE (UK/0308-2776) [03423790] **3426**

PROSSER RECORD-BULLETIN (US) [16991498] **5762**

PROSTAGLANDIN PERSPECTIVES (UK/0267-1336) [16182192] **3631**

PROSTAGLANDINS (US/0090-6980) [00827203] **585**

PROSTAGLANDINS & THERAPEUTICS (US/0162-9352) [04248492] **3631**

PROSTAGLANDINS-BIOLOGY (UK/0142-8284) [20878725] **3732**

PROSTAGLANDINS, LEUKOTRIENES, AND CANCER (US/0924-1914) [12336061] **3823**

PROSTAGLANDINS, LEUKOTRIENES, AND ESSENTIAL FATTY ACIDS (UK/0952-3278) [17466156] **3631**

PROSTATE. SUPPLEMENT, THE (US/1050-5881) [21142207] **3992**

PROSTATE, THE (US/0270-4137) [06411628] **3800**

PROSTHETICS AND ORTHOTICS INTERNATIONAL (DK/0309-3646) [03486810] 3884, **4392**

PROSTOR (KZ) [09244585] **3350**

PROSTOVOLJNE DEJAVNOSTI UCENCEV OSNOVNIH IN SREDNJIH SOL V SOLSKEM LETU / ZAVOD SR SLOVENIJE ZA STATISTIKO (XV) [07935805] **1775**

PROSVETA ENLIGHTENMENT (US) [09509957] **2891**

PROSVETENA ZENA (XN) [0668630-] **5564**

PROTEASES & INHIBITORS (UK/0950-0588) [I09500588] **470**

PROTEC (IT/1120-1681) [I11201681] **2220**

PROTECT (US) **2180**

PROTECT (GREAT BARRINGTON) (US/0093-2256) [01791355] **625**

PROTECTA-PROTEZIONE CIVILE ECOLOGIA AMBIENTE (IT) **2220**

PROTECTING CHILDREN (US/0893-4231) [10580773] **5302**

PROTECTING THE CORPORATE OFFICER AND DIRECTOR FROM LIABILITY (US/0192-5547) [04975424] **3102**

PROTECTION DE L'ENVIRONNEMENT SUISSE (SZ) **2220**

PROTECTION OF ASSETS BULLETIN (US/0740-137X) [09938792] **804**

PROTECTION OF ASSETS MANUAL (US) **804**

PROTECTION OF ASSETS MANUAL TESTING PROGRAM (US) **804**

PROTECTION OF METALS (US/0033-1732) [02449913] **4017**

PROTECTION OFFICER NEWS (US/1057-087X) [22185805] **3173**

PROTECTION REPORT R8 (US/1061-7825) [20379394] **2391**

PROTECTIVE COATINGS ON METALS (US/0079-7030) [01022750] **4017**

PROTECTOR (SZ/0256-4319) [I02564319] **3174**

PROTEE (CN/0300-3523) [01422520] 3426, **3312**

PROTEGEZ-VOUS (CN/0701-8517) [02249770] **1299**

PROTEIN ABNORMALITIES *CEASED*. (US/0736-4547) [08683530] **586**

PROTEIN ENGINEERING (UK/0269-2139) [15234798] **492**

PROTEIN EXPRESSION AND PURIFICATION (US/1046-5928) [20461371] **551**

●PROTEIN PROFILE (UK/1070-3667) [28355454] **470**

●PROTEIN SCIENCE : A PUBLICATION OF THE PROTEIN SOCIETY (US/0961-8368) [25450084] 496, **493**

PROTEIN SEQUENCES & DATA ANALYSIS *CEASED*. (GW/0931-9506) [16973948] **470**

PROTEINS (US/0887-3585) [13196210] **470**

PROTEINS, POST-TRANSLATIONAL PROCESSING (UK/0952-0406) [I09520406] **470**

PROTESTANT EPISCOPAL CHURCH IN THE U.S.A. COMMITTEE ON TRUST FUNDS *See* TRUST FUNDS **5068**

PROTESTANT REFORMED THEOLOGICAL JOURNAL (US/1070-8138) [04163696] **4988**

PROTESTANTESIMO (IT/0033-1767) [02165935] **5066**

PROTEUS (ALEXANDRIA, VA.) (US/0090-2071) [01784793] **328**

PROTEUS (SHIPPENSBURG, PA.) (US/0889-6348) [11640737] **3426**

PROTEXTILE (CN/0825-8031) [12150499] **5355**

PROTEZIONE CIVILE E SOCIETA OGGI (IT) **1073**

PROTEZIONE CIVILE ITALIANA, LA (IT) **1073**

PROTOCOL DIGEST *CEASED*. (US/1071-2194) [28593331] 4675, **4054**

PROTOCOL OF THE COLLOQUY OF THE CENTER FOR HERMENEUTICAL STUDIES IN HELLENISTIC AND MODERN CULTURE (US/0098-0900) [01380540] 2852, **1079**

PROTOKOLL (GW/0522-9138) [02755081] **849**

PROTOKOLL - DEUTSCHER BUNDESTAG (GW) [03752427] **4492**

PROTON NMR COLLECTION. CUMULATIVE CHEMICAL CLASS INDEX (US) [06134837] 4445, **4450**

PROTOPLASMA (AU/0033-183X) [02456897] **540**

PROTOPLASMA. SUPPLEMENTUM (AU/0934-8727) [20450326] **5595**

PROTOTYPE MODELER *CEASED*. (US/0734-1482) [08697305] **2777**

PROTOZOENFAUNA (GW/0932-142X) [20281297] **470**

PROTOZOOLOGICAL ABSTRACTS (UK/0309-1287) [03133036] 5595, **5604**

PROTOZOOLOGIJA (RU/0136-7439) [04304297] **569**

PROUD (US/0048-5632) [05422111] **3174**

PROUST RESEARCH ASSOCIATION *See* PROUST RESEARCH ASSOCIATION NEWSLETTER **3350**

PROUST RESEARCH ASSOCIATION NEWSLETTER (US/0048-5659) [02881829] **3350**

PROUT PRESS (WASHINGTON, D.C.) (US/1045-7585) [20230378] **5647**

PROVENANCE (US/0739-4241) [09729332] **2483**

PROVENANCE (LONDON) (CN/0826-1164) [10852436] **4095**

PROVENCAL, LE (FR) [12602362] **5801**

PROVENCE (FR) [05951792] **5489**

PROVENCE-COTE D'AZUR (HACHETTE (FIRM)) (FR) [18955225] 5489, **2573**

PROVENCE GENEALOGIQUE PORT-DE-BOUC (FR/0337-6591) [I03376591] **2468**

PROVENCE HISTORIQUE; REVUE TRIMESTRIELLE (FR/0033-1856) [01623610] **2703**

PROVENCE MEDICALE (FR) **3631**

PROVENCE / MICHELIN (UK) [06180939] **5489**

PROVERBIUM (COLUMBUS, OHIO) (US/0743-782X) [10675104] **2323**

PROVIDENCE BUSINESS NEWS (US/0887-8226) [13388522] **5741**

PROVIDENCE DES PAUVRES, MERE GAMELIN, LA (CN/0705-0917) [04039659] **5066**

PROVIDENCE JOURNAL, THE (US) [09440205] **5741**

PROVIDENCE OF THE POOR, MOTHER EMILIE GAMELIN (CN/0705-0925) [04039642] **4988**

●PROVIDENCE (PROVIDENCE, R.I.) (US/1063-7974) [26139911] **2626**

PROVIDENCE VISITOR (1984), THE (US/8750-5452) [11486189] 5034, **5741**

PROVIDER (VANCOUVER) *CEASED*. (CN/1183-045X) [24860376] **2285**

PROVIDER (WASHINGTON, D.C.) (US/0888-0352) [13354801] **5302**

PROVINCE (CN/0839-3311) [18450141] **5793**

PROVINCE OF BRITISH COLUMBIA BUDGET (CN/0229-5253) [09021668] **4742**

PROVINCE OF NOVA SCOTIA, CANADA, THE (CN/0226-0425) [06273433] **1513**

PROVINCE OF QUEBEC CHAMBER OF COMMERCE *See* REPERTOIRE / LA CHAMBRE DE COMMERCE DE LA PROVINCE DE QUEBEC **821**

PROVINCETOWN ADVOCATE (US) [09525013] **5690**

PROVINCIA CREMONA (IT) **5804**

PROVINCIA GRANDA (IT) **5804**

PROVINCIA PAVESE (IT) **2491**

PROVINCIAL AND MUNICIPAL FINANCES (CN/0317-946X) [02244558] **4742**

PROVINCIAL BUILDING & CONSTRUCTION TRADES COUNCIL OF ONTARIO (CN/0714-3206) [09089000] **625**

PROVINCIAL COUNCIL OF WOMEN OF BRITISH COLUMBIA *See* NEWSLETTER - PROVINCIAL COUNCIL OF WOMEN OF BRITISH COLUMBIA **5562**

PROVINCIAL ECONOMIC ACCOUNTS (CN/0706-3083) [16386295] **4742**

PROVINCIAL FILM LIBRARY RESOURCE CATALOGUE (CN/0823-3306) [11558245] **3242**

PROVINCIAL FINANCIAL ASSISTANCE TO MUNICIPALITIES, BOARDS AND COMMISSIONS (CN/0383-5855) [10252400] **4742**

PROVINCIAL GEOLOGISTS JOURNAL (CN/0825-7159) [11209505] **1392**

PROVINCIAL GOVERNMENT ENTERPRISE FINANCE (CN/0575-9463) [02242696] **4675**

PROVINCIAL GROSS DOMESTIC PRODUCT BY INDUSTRY (CN/0712-8762) [08700415] **4742**

PROVINCIAL JUDGES JOURNAL (CN/0709-5139) [05585587] **3142**

PROVINCIAL MEMBERS OF PARLIAMENT (METRO) (CN/0711-3943) [08499648] **4675**

PROVINCIAL NEWSJOURNAL - INFANT DEVELOPMENT PROGRAMMES OF B.C (CN/0824-9946) [11543844] **5302**

PROVINCIAL OUTLOOK. ECONOMIC FORECAST (CN/0827-5785) [16636786] **1579**

PROVINCIAL OUTLOOK. EXECUTIVE SUMMARY (CN/0832-3542) [15051206] **1513**

PROVINCIAL REPORT - CANADIAN FORESTRY ASSOCIATION OF BRITISH COLUMBIA (CN/0828-6256) [12064733] **2391**

PROVING GROUND : ENVIRONMENTAL RESEARCH & TECHNOLOGY DEVELOPMENT, THE (CN/1188-0368) [25352071] 2180, **5142**

PROVINS ET SA REGION : BULLETIN DE LA SOCIETE D'HISTOIRE ET D'ARCHEOLOGIE DE PROVINS (FR/0399-0508) [09989987] **279**

PROVINSIALE OUDITEUR SE VERSLAG VOOR DIE MIDDELEREKENINGS EN DIE FINANSIEREKENINGS, DIE (SA) [02413761] **4742**

PROVISIONAL POPULATION ESTIMATES FOR NEW JERSEY *See* POPULATION ESTIMATES FOR NEW JERSEY (TRENTON, N.J. : 1981) **4557**

PROVISIONAL VERBATIM RECORD, PLENARY MEETING (FR) [05733491] **5142**

PROVISIONS OF CALIFORNIA COLLECTIVE BARGAINING AGREEMENTS (US) [05363819] **1704**

PROVISO STAR-SENTINEL (US/0195-251X) [05424202] **5661**

PROVOKING THOUGHTS *CEASED*. (US/1044-6893) [19869723] **4609**

PROVOQUE (LONGUEUIL) (CN/1183-7500) [24570897] **219**

PROXY STATEMENTS (US) **3102**

PROYECCION (GRANADA) (SP/0478-6378) [08074751] **4988**

PROYECCIONES AGROPECUARIAS / MINISTERIO DE AGRICULTURA (CK) [05314690] **123**

PROYECTO 2000 *SUSPENDED*. (SP/0213-6171) [I02136171] **2127**

PROYECTO DE PRESUPUESTO. SECTOR CENTRAL (CK) [07700152] **3032**

PROYECTOS QUIMICOS (SP) **1028**

PROYEK BIPIK (INDONESIA) *See* PERKEMBANGAN PROYEK BIPIK **1621**

PROYEK PENGEMBANGAN INFORMASI PENDIDIKAN *See* STATISTIK PENDIDIKAN SMA SELURUH INDONESIA **1798**

PROYEK PENGEMBANGAN INFORMASI PENDIDIKAN *See* TABEL AKHIR STATISTIK PENDIDIKAN SLTP/SLTA SMP SELURUH INDONESIA **1798**

PROYEK PENGEMBANGAN INFORMASI PENDIDIKAN *See* STATISTIK PENDIDIKAN ST SELURUH INDONESIA **1916**

PROZAH (IS) [05724638] 328, **3426**

PROZESSRECHTLICHE ABHANDLUNGEN (GW) [01763029] **3032**

PRS JOURNAL (US/0030-8250) [02600697] 4988, **4358**

PRS NEWS (UK/0309-0019) [17970629] **5235**

PRS YEARBOOK (UK/0309-0884) [18690940] **4147**

PRSA DIRECTORY / PUBLIC RELATIONS SOCIETY OF AMERICA (US) [07781945] **764**

PRUDENT SPECULATOR, THE (US/0743-0809) [10509676] **912**

PRUDENTIA (NZ) [02186721] **3426**

PRUDENTIA IURIS (AG/0326-2774) [08881971] **3032**

PRUDHOE BAY JOURNAL (US/0743-8303) [10681120] **5629**

PRUFROCK JOURNAL, THE (US/1047-1855) [20620771] 1068, **1884**

PRUMYSLOVE VLASTNICTVI / VYDAVA FEDERALNI URAD PRO VYNALEZY (XR/0862-8726) [26122713] **1308**

PRUSSIA. OBERVERWALTUNGSGERICHT **See** ENTSCHEIDUNGEN DES PREUSSISCHEN OBERVERWALTUNGSGERICHTS. HRSG. VON JEBENS ... UND VON MEYEREN **2966**

PRVI STATISTICNI PODATKI ZA LETO ... (Z OCENO) IN SPREMLJANJE RESOLUCIJE O POLITIKI IZVAJANJA DRUZBENEGA PLANA SR SLOVENIJE V LETU ... / ZAVOD SR SLOVENIJE ZA STATISTIKO (XV) [12186904] **5336**

PRYOR REPORT, THE (US/0742-9770) [10481522] 883, **4209**

PRZEDMIOTOWY KATALOG SKADOWY (PL) [01789665] **422**

PRZEGLAD ANTROPOLOGICZNY (PL/0033-2003) [02266559] **243**

PRZEGLAD ARCHEOLOGICZNY (PL/0079-7138) [02827259] **279**

PRZEGLAD BIBLIOGRAFICZNY PISMIENNICTWA EKONOMICZNEGO (PL/0032-8138) [02822041] **1537**

PRZEGLAD BIBLIOTECZNY (PL/0033-202X) [01763032] **3242**

PRZEGLAD BUDOWLANY (PL/0033-2038) [I00332038] **625**

PRZEGLAD DERMATOLOGICZNY (PL/0033-2526) [06285349] **3722**

PRZEGLAD ELEKTROTECHNICZNY (PL/0033-2097) [06651718] **2077**

PRZEGLAD EPIDEMIOLOGICZNY (PL/0033-2100) [01310087] 3715, **3736**

PRZEGLAD GEODEZYJNY (PL) [07844343] **2029**

PRZEGLAD GEOFIZYCZNY (PL/0033-2135) [03215774] **1433**

PRZEGLAD GEOGRAFICZNY (PL/0033-2143) [01645121] **2573**

PRZEGLAD GEOLOGICZNY (PL/0033-2151) [05174041] **1392**

PRZEGLAD GORNICZY (PL/0033-216X) [02449915] **2149**

PRZEGLAD HISTORYCZNY (PL/0033-2186) [02155018] **2703**

PRZEGLAD HODOWLANY (PL/0137-4214) [10026098] **219**

PRZEGLAD HUMANISTYCZNY (PL/0033-2194) [01681404] **2852**

PRZEGLAD INFORMACJI O AFRYCE / CENTRALNY INSTYTUT INFORMACJI NAUKOWO-TECHNICZNEJ I EKONOMICZNEJ (PL) [02906440] **422**

PRZEGLAD INFORMACJI O NAUKOZNAWSTWIE (PL) [06613828] **5142**

PRZEGLAD INFORMACYJNO-DOKUMENTACYJNY. SERIA: HYDROLOGIA I OCEANOLOGIA (PL) [04584704] 1455, **1417**

PRZEGLAD KATOLICKI (PL/0239-7471) [15864038] **5034**

PRZEGLAD KOLEJOWY ELEKTROTECHNICZNY (PL) [06628045] **5434**

PRZEGLAD KOLEJOWY MECHANICZNY (PL/0033-2224) [06628022] **5434**

PRZEGLAD KOLEJOWY PRZEWOZOWY (PL) [06628006] **5434**

PRZEGLAD KOMUNIKACYJNY (PL) [06627937] **5390**

PRZEGLAD KONINSKI (PL/0138-0893) [I01380893] **2521**

PRZEGLAD LEKARSKI (PL/0033-2240) [09522902] **3631**

PRZEGLAD MECHANICZNY (PL/0033-2259) [06633709] **2127**

PRZEGLAD MLECZARSKI (PL/0478-6599) [04064662] **198**

PRZEGLAD MORSKI (PL) [06634428] **4182**

PRZEGLAD (NACZELA ORGANIZACJA TECHNICZNA (POLAND)) (PL/0137-8783) [09866038] **1704**

PRZEGLAD NARODOWY (PL/0867-3772) [I08673772] **2521**

PRZEGLAD OC (PL) [01791161] **1073**

PRZEGLAD ODLEWNICTWA (PL/0033-2275) [06629638] **4017**

PRZEGLAD ORIENTALISTYCZNY (PL/0033-2283) [02152507] **3426**

PRZEGLAD PAPIERNICZY (PL/0033-2291) [07809566] **4237**

PRZEGLAD PIEKARSKI I CUKIERNICZY (PL) [02111507] **2354**

PRZEGLAD PISMIENNICTWA ZAGADNIEN INFORMACJI (PL) [08716748] **3242**

PRZEGLAD PODATKOWY (PL/0867-7514) [I08677514] **4742**

PRZEGLAD POWSZECHNY (PO) [11471162] **4988**

PRZEGLAD PSYCHOLOGICZNY (PL/0048-5675) [06629793] **4609**

PRZEGLAD RELIGIOZNAWCZY (PL) [26888770] **4988**

PRZEGLAD RUSYCYSTYCZNY (PL) [04771032] **3312**

PRZEGLAD SKORZANY (PL/0370-1743) [06633251] **3185**

PRZEGLAD SOCJOLOGICZNY (PL/0033-2356) [03044260] **5254**

PRZEGLAD SPAWALNICTWA (PL/0033-2364) [10687278] **5142**

PRZEGLAD SPORTOWY (PL/0137-9267) [I01379267] **4913**

PRZEGLAD STATYSTYCZNY (PL/0033-2372) [02824967] **5336**

PRZEGLAD STOSUNKOW MIEDZYNARODOWYCH (PL) [03400664] **4532**

PRZEGLAD TECHNICZNY (PL/0033-2380) [10757434] **5143**

PRZEGLAD TELEKOMUNIKACYJNY (PL) [06635119] **1162**

PRZEGLAD TYGODNIOWY (PL/0209-0023) [16399013] **2521**

PRZEGLAD USTAWODAWSTWA GOSPODARCZEGO (PL/0137-5490) [10739423] **3102**

PRZEGLAD WOKIENNICZY; MIESIECZNIK NAUKOWO-TECHNICZNY (PL/0033-2410) [09598772] **5355**

PRZEGLAD ZACHODNI (PL/0033-2437) [02152344] **2703**

PRZEGLAD ZACHODNIOPOMORSKI / INSTYTUT ZACHODNIOPOMORSKI (PL/0552-4245) [05702250] **2703**

PRZEGLAD ZBOZOWO-MYNARSKI (PL/0033-2461) [04064721] **203**

PRZEGLAD ZOOLOGICZNY (PL/0033-247X) [04892788] **5595**

PRZEGLAD ZWIAZKOWY (PL) [06613072] **1704**

PRZEGLED KSIEGARSKI I WYDAWNICZY (PL) [01789251] **4831**

PRZEKROJ (PL) [06477408] **2521**

PRZELAND HISTORYCZNO-OSIATOWY (PL/0033-2178) [02319591] **1775**

PRZELAND POLONIJNY (PL) [03217866] **2271**

PRZEMYS CHEMICZNY (PL/0033-2496) [01763034] **2016**

PRZEMYS DROBNY I USUGI (PL) [06127790] **1513**

PRZEMYS DRZEWNY (PL/0373-9856) [04064785] **635**

PRZEMYS FERMENTACYJNY I OWOCOWO-WARZYWNY (PL/0137-2645) [05873487] **1028**

PRZEMYS ROLNY I SPOZYWCZY (PL) [06755255] **2354**

PRZEMYS SPOZYWCZY (PL/0033-250X) [09558867] **2354**

PRZEMYSOWY INSTYTUT AUTOMATYKI I POMIAROW **See** BIULETYN PRZEMYSKOWEGO INSTYTUTE AUTOMATYKI I POMIAROW **2111**

PRZESZOSC DEMOGRAFICZNA POLSKI (PL/0079-7189) [01763035] **2271**

PRZEWALSKI HORSE (NE/0167-7926) [05061884] **2801**

PRZEWODNIK BIBLIOGRAFICZNY (PL/0033-2518) [01605421] **422**

PRZEWODNIK KATOLICKI (PL) [06615240] **5034**

PRZYJACIEL PRZY PRACY (PL) [06623009] **2868**

PRZYJACIOKA (PL) [06645867] **5564**

PRZYRODA POLSKA (PL/0552-430X) [06645628] **4171**

PS (CN/0825-0197) [11084996] **1843**

PS. PERIODIEK VOOR SOCIALE VERZEKERNIG, SOCIALE VOORZIENIENGEN EN ARBEIDSRECHT (NE/0165-0734) [I01650734] **2891**

PS, POLITICAL SCIENCE & POLITICS (US/1049-0965) [19491865] **4492**

PS, POSTSECONDARY EDUCATION IN NEW YORK STATE (US/0193-4902) [04935621] **1775**

PS (WASHINGTON, D.C.) (US/0475-2953) [04507968] **4054**

PSA CONTRACTS BULLETIN (UK/0955-1204) [I09551204] **1513**

PSA (EAST LANSING, MICH.) (US/0270-8647) [01783962] 4358, **5143**

PSA JOURNAL (US/0030-8277) [01604221] **4376**

PSA NEWS (SI/0217-4715) [10980015] **849**

PSALLITE (AG/0033-2542) [01788831] **4147**

PSBA BULLETIN (US/0162-3559) [02449917] **1869**

PSE ECONOMIC ANALYST : A JOURNAL OF THE PUNJAB SCHOOL OF ECONOMICS (II) [07936202] **1514**

PSE OUTDOOR ADVENTURES BOWHUNTING ANNUAL (US/0198-9154) [06243043] 4913, **4878**

PSEUDEPIGRAPHA VETERIS TESTAMENTI GRAECE (NE) [01607566] **5019**

PSG NEWSLETTER (US/0031-9627) [07051672] **4147**

PSI CHI **See** PSI CHI NEWSLETTER **4609**

PSI CHI NEWSLETTER (US/0033-2569) [03725933] 5235, **4609**

PSI FORCE (US/0899-7888) [18217177] **4865**

PSI-INFO / PUBLIC SERVICES INTERNATIONAL (FR) [23721975] 1704, **4704**

PSI-M (US/0197-2138) [05982503] **4242**

PSI NEWS & VIEWS (UK/0306-4026) [02239978] **1704**

PSI RESEARCH (US/0749-2898) [09661125] **4242**

PSI RESEARCH RESULTS (UK) **4492**

PSICHIATRIA DELL'INFANZIA E DELL-ADOLESCENZA (IT/0393-361X) [11662195] **4609**

PSICHIATRIA E PSICOTERAPIA ANALITICA (IT/0393-9774) [I03939774] **3932**

PSICHIATRIA E TERRITORIO (IT) **3932**

PSICHIATRIA GENERALE E DELL'ETA EVOLUTIVA (IT/0555-5299) [I05555299] **3932**

PSICO : REVISTA SEMESTRAL DO INSTITUTO DE PSICOLOGIA DA PUC RIO GRANDE DO SUL, BRASIL (BL) [23657381] **4609**

PSICOACTIVA : REVISTA CIENTIFICA DEL CENTRO DE INFORMACION Y EDUCACION PARA LA PREVENCION DEL ABUSO DE DROGAS (PE) [18999710] 3631, **1348**

PSICOANALISI CONTRO (IT/0393-6902) [I03936902] 4609, **3932**

PSICOBIETTIVO ROMA (IT/0392-2952) [I03922952] **4609**

PSICODEIA (SP/0377-8320) [02480923] **4609**

PSICOLOGIA (BL/0101-6016) [07570807] **4609**

PSICOLOGIA CONTEMPORANEA (IT/0390-346X) [I0390346X] **4609**

PSICOLOGIA E LAVORO (IT) [01787669] **1704**

PSICOLOGIA E SCUOLA (IT/0392-680X) [I0392680X] **1884**

PSICOLOGIA ITALIANA **CEASED.** (FI) [09987632] **4609**

● PSICOLOGIA, PSICOPATOLOGIA & PSICOSOMATICA DELLA DONNA (US) 5564, **4609**

PSICOLOGIA SOCIALE (IT/0394-7904) [I03947904] **4609**

PSICOLOGIA. TEORIA E PESQUISA (BL/0102-3772) [I01023772] **4609**

PSICOLOGICA (SP/0211-2159) [I02112159] **4609**

PSICOPATOLOGIA (SP/0211-5549) [26147136] **3932**

PSICOSI (US) **4609**

PSICOTERAPIA E SCIENZE UMANE (IT) [18128403] **3932**

PSICOTHEMA OVIEDO (SP/0214-9915) [I02149915] **4609**

PSIHIJATRIJA DANAS (YU/0350-2538) [04226314] **3932**

PSIHOLOGICESKIJ ZURNAL (RU/0205-9592) [06505303] **4609**

PSIKHOLOGIIA (BU) [01799466] **4609**

PSIQUIS (SP/0210-8348) [09421936] **3933**

PSITTACOSIS SURVEILLANCE (US/0195-573X) [05452417] **4797**

PSLG. PUBLIC SERVICE & LOCAL GOVERNMENT (UK/0144-4212) [08308313] 5302, **4675**

PSP : PFLANZENSCHUTZ-PRAXIS (GW/0723-0311) [09700824] **525**

PSR QUARTERLY : A JOURNAL OF MEDICINE AND GLOBAL SURVIVAL **See** MEDICINE AND GLOBAL SOCIETY **3613**

PSR QUARTERLY (BALTIMORE, MD.), THE (US/1051-2438) [21898126] **3631**

PSSC SOCIAL SCIENCE INFORMATION (PH) [02747596] **5214**

PSYCHANALYSE A L'UNIVERSITE **CEASED.** (FR/0338-2397) [03977428] **4609**

PSYCHANALYSTES **CEASED.** (FR/0242-9616) [I02429616] **3933**

PSYCHE (GW/0033-2623) [02171054] **4609**

PSYCHE (CAMBRIDGE, MASS.) (US/0033-2615) [02449921] **5595**

PSYCHIATRIA DANUBINA (CI/0353-5053) [I03535053] **3933**

PSYCHIATRIA ET NEUROLOGIA JAPONICA (JA/0033-2658) [07092730] 3844, 3933

PSYCHIATRIA FENNICA (IT/0079-7227) [02266571] 3933

PSYCHIATRIA POLSKA (PL/0033-2674) [06410743] 3933

PSYCHIATRIC ABSTRACTS AND COMMENT **CEASED**. (US/1042-041X) [18912600] 3933

PSYCHIATRIC ANNALS (US/0048-5713) [01642929] 3933

PSYCHIATRIC BULLETIN OF THE ROYAL COLLEGE OF PSYCHIATRISTS (UK/0955-6036) [19079191] 3933

PSYCHIATRIC CLINICS OF NORTH AMERICA, THE (US/0193-953X) [04049021] 3933

PSYCHIATRIC FORUM, THE (US/0033-2690) [02056506] 3933

PSYCHIATRIC GENETICS (UK/0955-8829) [23835780] 3933, 551

PSYCHIATRIC HOSPITAL, THE **CEASED**. (US/0885-7717) [09359621] 3933, 3791

PSYCHIATRIC LENGTH OF STAY BY DIAGNOSIS, UNITED STATES (US/0898-0543) [17700543] 3933, 3791

PSYCHIATRIC LENGTH OF STAY BY DIAGNOSIS, UNITED STATES, NORTH CENTRAL REGION (US/0898-249X) [17761878] 3791

PSYCHIATRIC LENGTH OF STAY BY DIAGNOSIS, UNITED STATES, NORTHEASTERN REGION (US/0898-0527) [17700624] 3933, 3791

PSYCHIATRIC LENGTH OF STAY BY DIAGNOSIS, UNITED STATES, SOUTHERN REGION (US/0898-0519) [17700778] 3933, 3791

PSYCHIATRIC LENGTH OF STAY BY DIAGNOSIS. UNITED STATES, WESTERN REGION (US/0898-0535) [17700680] 3791

PSYCHIATRIC MEDICINE UPDATE (US/0163-1721) [04307046] 3933

PSYCHIATRIC NEWS (US/0033-2704) [02266577] 3933

PSYCHIATRIC OUTPATIENT PROGRAM (US/0091-0422) [01785639] 3933

PSYCHIATRIC QUARTERLY (US/0033-2720) [01715671] 3933

PSYCHIATRIC RESIDENT **CEASED**. (US/1058-1693) [24235928] 3933

PSYCHIATRIC TIMES, THE (US/0893-2905) [15495949] 3933

PSYCHIATRIE DE L'ENFANT, LA (FR/0079-726X) [01763043] 3933

PSYCHIATRIE EN VERPLEGING (BE) 3867, 3933

PSYCHIATRIE : ENCYCLOPEDIE MEDICO CHIRURGICALE (FR) 3933

PSYCHIATRIE MAGAZINE ROYAN (FR/1147-7970) [I11477970] 3933

PSYCHIATRIE, NEUROLOGIE UND MEDIZINISCHE PSYCHOLOGIE. BEIHEFTE (GW) [07607833] 3844, 3934

PSYCHIATRIE, RECHERCHE ET INTERVENTION EN SANTE MENTALE DE L'ENFANT : P.R.I.S.M.E (CN/1180-5501) [23237410] 3934

PSYCHIATRISCHE PRAXIS (GW/0303-4259) [00944842] 3934

PSYCHIATRIST'S CLINICAL UPDATE (US/1050-6489) [21567883] 3934

PSYCHIATRIST'S COMPENDIUM OF DRUG THERAPY, THE (US/0276-4393) [07360980] 3934

PSYCHIATRY (US) [12422679] 3934

PSYCHIATRY AND THE HUMANITIES (US/0363-8952) [02551436] 3934

PSYCHIATRY DIGEST (1979) (US/0278-4602) [05577158] 3934

PSYCHIATRY DRUG ALERTS (US/0894-4873) [16115582] 3934

PSYCHIATRY (GLENDALE, CALIF.) (US/0271-1311) [03442238] 3934

PSYCHIATRY IN PRACTICE (UK/0262-5377) [08853714] 3934

PSYCHIATRY MALPRACTICE PROTECTOR **CEASED**. (US/1062-3523) [25585845] 3032, 3934

PSYCHIATRY (NORWALK, CONN.) (US/0897-6317) [17576903] 3934

PSYCHIATRY RESEARCH (IE/0165-1781) [05636342] 3934

PSYCHIATRY RESEARCH : NEUROIMAGING SECTION (IE/0925-4927) 3934

PSYCHIATRY (WASHINGTON, D.C.) (US/0033-2747) [01763044] 3934

PSYCHIC ALMANAC, THE (US/1051-6581) [22036627] 4242

PSYCHIC NEWS (UK/0033-2801) 4610

PSYCHIC OBSERVER **SUSPENDED**. (US/0048-573X) [02250544] 4242

PSYCHIC (SAN FRANCISCO) (US/0033-2798) [01716634] 4242

PSYCHO-LINGUA (II/0377-3132) [01790527] 3312

● PSYCHO-ONCOLOGY (CHICHESTER, ENGLAND) (UK/1057-9249) [24222735] 3823

PSYCHO PHARMAKO THERAPIE (GW/0944-6877) 4610, 4326

PSYCHOANALYSE (BE/0772-9219) [18540495] 4610

● PSYCHOANALYSE: KLINIK UND KULTURKRITIK (GW/0941-4428) [25786733] 4610

PSYCHOANALYSIS AND CONTEMPORARY THOUGHT (US/0161-5289) [03946816] 4610

PSYCHOANALYSIS AND PSYCHOTHERAPY (US/1057-5723) [20496624] 3934

PSYCHOANALYST : A MONOGRAPH OF THE WESTCHESTER CENTER FOR THE STUDY OF PSYCHOANALYSIS AND PSYCHOTHERAPY AND THE PSYCHOANALYTIC ASSOCIATION OF THE WESTCHESTER CENTER, THE (US/1062-6069) [25605318] 4610

● PSYCHOANALYTIC ABSTRACTS (US/1066-9884) [27117223] 4610, 4622

PSYCHOANALYTIC BOOKS (US/1044-2103) [19729514] 4610

PSYCHOANALYTIC DIALOGUES (US/1048-1885) [20863332] 4610

PSYCHOANALYTIC INQUIRY (US/0735-1690) [07968797] 3934

PSYCHOANALYTIC INQUIRY BOOK SERIES (US/0899-9244) [09763921] 3934

PSYCHOANALYTIC PERSPECTIVES ON ART : PPA **CEASED**. (US/0896-7938) [12919918] 362

PSYCHOANALYTIC PSYCHOLOGY (US/0736-9735) [09277498] 4610

PSYCHOANALYTIC PSYCHOTHERAPY (UK/0266-8734) [20104035] 4610, 3934

PSYCHOANALYTIC QUARTERLY, THE (US/0033-2828) [01763047] 4610

PSYCHOANALYTIC REVIEW (1963) (US/0033-2836) [01624251] 4610

PSYCHOANALYTIC STUDY OF SOCIETY (US/0079-7294) [01585993] 3934, 5214

PSYCHOANALYTIC STUDY OF THE CHILD, THE (US/0079-7308) [01307929] 4610

PSYCHOBIOLOGY AND PSYCHOPATHOLOGY (US/0278-1719) [07628230] 4610

PSYCHOBIOLOGY (AUSTIN, TEX.) (US/0889-6313) [13979047] 4610

PSYCHODRAMA AND GROUP PSYCHOTHERAPY MONOGRAPHS (US) [01763051] 3934

● PSYCHODYNAMIC COUNSELLING (UK/1353-3339) 4610

PSYCHOEDUCATIONAL JOURNAL FOR THE TREATMENT OF CHILDREN (US/0147-6009) [03198967] 1884

PSYCHOHISTORY REVIEW, THE (US/0363-891X) [02548869] 4610, 2626

PSYCHOLOGIA (JA/0033-2852) [01348709] 4610

PSYCHOLOGIA A PATOPSYCHOLOGIA DIETATA (XO) [05464400] 4610, 3934

PSYCHOLOGIA UNIVERSALIS (GW/0555-5582) [09510751] 4610

PSYCHOLOGIA WYCHOWAWCZA (PL/0033-2860) [02308213] 1903

PSYCHOLOGICA BELGICA (BE/0033-2879) [05118891] 4610

PSYCHOLOGICAL ABSTRACTS (US/0033-2887) [01763052] 4610, 4623

PSYCHOLOGICAL ASSESSMENT (US/1040-3590) [18390376] 4610

PSYCHOLOGICAL BULLETIN (US/0033-2909) [01681351] 4610

PSYCHOLOGICAL INQUIRY (US/1047-840X) [20792906] 4611

PSYCHOLOGICAL ISSUES (US/0048-5748) [01763054] 4611

PSYCHOLOGICAL MEDICINE (UK/0033-2917) [01588231] 4611

PSYCHOLOGICAL MEDICINE. MONOGRAPH SUPPLEMENT (UK/0264-1801) [08831190] 3631, 4611

PSYCHOLOGICAL PERSPECTIVES (US/0033-2925) [01907432] 4611

PSYCHOLOGICAL RECORD, THE (US/0033-2933) [01353882] 4611

PSYCHOLOGICAL REPORTS (US/0033-2941) [01318827] 4611

PSYCHOLOGICAL RESEARCH (GW/0340-0727) [01069731] 4611

PSYCHOLOGICAL RESEARCH BULLETIN **CEASED**. (SW/0555-5620) [03462993] 4611

PSYCHOLOGICAL REVIEW (US/0033-295X) [01318836] 4611

PSYCHOLOGICAL SCIENCE (US/0956-7976) [20652877] 4611

PSYCHOLOGICAL STUDIES (II/0033-2968) [02813919] 4611

PSYCHOLOGICAL TEST BULLETIN **CEASED**. (AT/1031-7511) [I10317511] 4611

PSYCHOLOGIE & EDUCATION (FR) [22602616] 4611

PSYCHOLOGIE & MAATSCHAPPIJ (NE) [10591673] 4612

● PSYCHOLOGIE CLINIQUE EG PROJECTIVE (FR) 4612

PSYCHOLOGIE FRANCAISE (FR/0033-2984) [01763058] 4612

PSYCHOLOGIE FUER DIE PRAXIS : ORGAN DER GESELLSCHAFT FUER PSYCHOLOGIE DER DEUTSCHEN DEMOKRATISCHEN REPUBLIK (GW/0233-0202) [10784857] 4612

PSYCHOLOGIE IN ERZIEHUNG UND UNTERRICHT (GW/0342-183X) [01791925] 1903

PSYCHOLOGIE-INFORMATION / GESELLSCHAFT FUER PSYCHOLOGIE DER DEUTSCHEN DEMOKRAITISCHEN REPUBLIK (AU) [10217921] 4612

PSYCHOLOGIE LISSE (NE/0167-6598) [I01676598] 4612

PSYCHOLOGIE MEDICALE (FR/0048-5756) [01420498] 4612

PSYCHOLOGIE PREVENTIVE (CN/0714-3494) [09084888] 4612

PSYCHOLOGIE QUEBEC (CN/0824-1724) [12064656] 4612

PSYCHOLOGIE V EKONOMICKE PRAXI (XR/0033-300X) [06650912] 705

PSYCHOLOGIES (FR) [09847173] 4612

PSYCHOLOGISCH GESEHEN (GW) [05845293] 4612

PSYCHOLOGISCHE BEITRAEGE (GW/0033-3018) [02001918] 4612

PSYCHOLOGISCHE PRAXIS (SZ/0079-7413) [03577977] 4612

PSYCHOLOGISCHE RUNDSCHAU (GW/0033-3042) [01763060] 4612

PSYCHOLOGISCHER INDEX / HERAUSGEBER ZENTRALSTELLE FUER PSYCHOLOGISCHE INFORMATION UND DOKUMENTATION AN DER UNIVERSITAET TRIER (GW) [10077040] 4612

PSYCHOLOGISCHES KOLLOQUIUM (GW/0555-5701) [04765520] 4612

PSYCHOLOGIST, THE (UK/0952-8229) [17369312] 4612

PSYCHOLOGISTS REGISTERED IN ONTARIO (CN/0713-5750) [09000607] 4612

PSYCHOLOGUE QUEBECOIS, LE (CN/0318-1707) [02441772] 4612

PSYCHOLOGY AND AGING (US/0882-7974) [11982277] 3754, 4612

PSYCHOLOGY AND DEVELOPING SOCIETIES (II/0971-3336) [20379807] 4612

PSYCHOLOGY & HEALTH (SZ/0887-0446) [13068409] 4612, 4797

PSYCHOLOGY & MARKETING (US/0742-6046) [10384095] 935

PSYCHOLOGY & SOCIAL THEORY (US/0277-2469) [07529062] 5254, 4612

PSYCHOLOGY AND SOCIOLOGY OF SPORT (US/0885-7423) [12712886] 5254, 4612

● PSYCHOLOGY, CRIME & LAW (UK/1068-316X) [27644820] 3091, 4612

PSYCHOLOGY (GUILFORD) (US/0272-3794) [06644321] 4612

PSYCHOLOGY IN THE SCHOOLS (US/0033-3085) [01763062] 1775, 4612

PSYCHOLOGY (MENTOR) (US/0095-1145) [02239686] 4613

PSYCHOLOGY OF ADDICTIVE BEHAVIORS (US/0893-164X) [15430950] 4613

PSYCHOLOGY OF LEARNING AND MOTIVATION, THE (US/0079-7421) [01638923] 4613

PSYCHOLOGY OF MUSIC (UK/0305-7356) [01792229] 4613, 4147

PSYCHOLOGY OF WOMEN QUARTERLY (UK/0361-6843) [02529664] 5565

● PSYCHOLOGY, PUBLIC POLICY, AND LAW (US/1076-8971) [30635125] 3032, 4613

PSYCHOLOGY (SAVANNAH) (US/0033-3077) [01715840] 4613

PSYCHOLOGY SURVEY **CEASED**. (UK) [04532707] 4613

● PSYCHOLOGY TODAY (US/0033-3107) [25065736] 4613

PSYCHOLOGY TODAY (US/0033-3107) [01081160] 4613

PSYCHOLOOG (NE/0033-3115) [I00333115] 4613

PSYCHOLOY — Alphabetical Title Index

●PSYCHOLOY REVIEW (UK/1354-1129) **4613**

PSYCHOMED (GW/0935-2937) [24844803] **4613**

PSYCHOMETRIKA (US/0033-3123) [01763064] **4613**

PSYCHOMOTRICITE, LA *CEASED.* (FR/0151-5845) [04847010] **4613**

PSYCHOMUSICOLOGY (US/0275-3987) [07123224] **4147**

PSYCHONEPHROLOGY *CEASED.* (US/0731-5899) [07723996] **3992**

PSYCHONEUROENDOCRINOLOGY (UK/0306-4530) [01343872] **3732**

●PSYCHONOMIC BULLETIN & REVIEW (US/1069-9384) [28204902] **4613**

PSYCHONOMIC SOCIETY *See* BULLETIN OF THE PSYCHONOMIC SOCIETY **4579**

PSYCHONOMIC SOCIETY *See* PSYCHONOMIC BULLETIN & REVIEW **4613**

PSYCHOPATHOLOGIA (IT/0394-7912) [I03947912] **4613**

PSYCHOPATHOLOGY (SZ/0254-4962) [10322077] **3934**

PSYCHOPHARMACOLOGIA (GW/0033-3158) [03826971] **4613, 4326**

PSYCHOPHARMACOLOGY (AMSTERDAM) *CEASED.* (NE/0167-9198) [09478744] **4613, 4326**

PSYCHOPHARMACOLOGY BULLETIN (US/0048-5764) [01643323] **4326, 4613**

PSYCHOPHARMACOLOGY (NEW YORK) (US/0161-0139) [02902335] **4613, 4326**

PSYCHOPHARMACOLOGY SERIES (GW/0931-6795) [15285945] **4613, 4326**

PSYCHOPHARMACOLOGY UPDATE (US/1068-5308) [27697409] **4326**

PSYCHOPHYSIOLOGY (US/0048-5772) [01642717] **4613, 586**

PSYCHOSCOPE (US) **4613**

PSYCHOSOCIAL REHABILITATION JOURNAL (US/0147-5622) [03197246] **3934**

PSYCHOSOMATIC MEDICINE (US/0033-3174) [01763069] **3935, 3631**

PSYCHOSOMATIC MEDICINE : PROCEEDINGS OF THE ... INTERNATIONAL CONGRESS OF THE ACADEMY OF PSYCHOSOMATIC MEDICINE (NE) [08429554] **4613, 3631**

PSYCHOSOMATICS (WASHINGTON, D.C.) (US/0033-3182) [01763070] **3631**

PSYCHOSOZIAL (GW/0171-3434) [07517009] **4613**

PSYCHOSOZIALER STRESS UND KORONARE HERZKRANKHEIT (GW) [09567649] **3709**

PSYCHOTHERAPEUT, DER (GW) **4613**

PSYCHOTHERAPIE FORUM (AU) **4614**

PSYCHOTHERAPIE, PSYCHOSOMATIK, MEDIZINISCHE PSYCHOLOGIE (GW/0173-7937) [06211330] **4614**

PSYCHOTHERAPIES (GENEVA, SWITZERLAND) (SZ/0251-737X) [17301526] **3935**

PSYCHOTHERAPY AND PSYCHOSOMATICS (SZ/0033-3190) [01763071] **4614, 3935**

PSYCHOTHERAPY FINANCES (US/0163-1543) [04306950] **4614**

PSYCHOTHERAPY IN PRIVATE PRACTICE (US/0731-7158) [08235783] **4614**

PSYCHOTHERAPY LETTER, THE (US/1062-9475) [25814394] **3935, 4614**

PSYCHOTHERAPY PATIENT, THE (US/0738-6176) [09632176] **4614, 3935**

PSYCHOTHERAPY RESEARCH (US/1050-3307) [21464424] **4614**

PSYCHOTHERAPY RESEARCH REVIEW SERIES (US/0732-7986) [08448904] **3631**

PSYCHOTHERAPY TODAY (US/1047-9848) [20836265] **4614**

●PSYCHOTRAIN (FAYETTEVILLE, ARK.) (US/1064-363X) [26272927] **3426**

PSYCHOTRONIK (AU/0379-7449) [04571354] **4242**

PSYCHOTROPES (MONTREAL) *CEASED.* (CN/0715-9684) [10008035] **1348**

PSYCHOTROPICS (RENO, NEV.) (US/0895-5727) [16707548] **3986**

PSYCHWARE SOURCEBOOK (US/1042-4717) [17543769] **4614, 1775**

PSYCINFO (US) **4614, 4623**

PSYCLIT DATABASE (US) [19613770] **4614, 4623**

PSYCSCAN: APPLIED EXPERIMENTAL AND ENGINEERING PSYCHOLOGY (US/0891-0685) [14560894] **4614, 4623**

PSYCSCAN. APPLIED PSYCHOLOGY (US/0271-7506) [06683480] **4614, 4623**

●PSYCSCAN: BEHAVIOR ANALYSIS (US) **4614**

PSYCSCAN. CLINICAL PSYCHOLOGY (US/0197-1484) [05969775] **4614, 4623**

PSYCSCAN. DEVELOPMENTAL PSYCHOLOGY (US/0197-1492) [05979518] **4614, 4623**

PSYCSCAN. LD/MR (US/0730-1928) [07966847] **4614, 4623**

●PSYCSCAN. NEUROPSYCHOLOGY (US/1058-6660) [24351633] **4614, 3844, 4623**

PSYCSCAN: PSYCHOANALYSIS (US/0889-5236) [13913212] **4614, 4623**

PSYKE & LOGOS (DK/0107-1211) [I01071211] **4614**

PSYKOLOGIA (FI/0355-1067) [01290314] **4614**

PSYKOLOGISK PDAGOGISK RADGIVNING (DK/0906-219X) [I0906219X] **4614**

PSYKOLOGISK SKRIFTSERIE AARHUS (DK/0900-8527) [18532314] **4614**

PSZCZELARSTWO (PL/0478-7080) [04064875] **5595**

PSZICHOLOGIA: AZ MTA PSZICHOLOGIAI INTEZETENEK FOLYOIRATA (HU/0230-0508) [10288893] **4614**

PSZICHOLOGIAI TANULMANYOK (HU) [05038120] **4614**

●PT (ALEXANDRIA, VA.) (US/1065-5077) [26621572] **4382**

PT : CIVIELE TECHNIEK *See* CIVIELE TECHNIEK **1968**

PT DISTRIBUTOR, THE (US/1045-3962) [20103714] **2127**

PT. ELEKTROTECHNIEK ELEKTRONICA (NE/0032-4086) [09071394] **2077**

PT. PROCESTECHNIEK (NE/0032-4094) [09071348] **5143, 1992**

PTA BULLETIN (US/0883-2579) [06616747] **1869**

PTA HANDBOOK, THE (US/0361-266X) [02153975] **1775**

PTA HEUTE (GW/0302-167X) [01110677] **4326**

PTA IN DER APOTHEKE (GW/0722-1029) [08964669] **4326**

PTA TODAY (US/0195-2781) [05460470] **1775**

PTC NEWSLETTER (US/0736-8232) [07913633] **1308**

PTERIDINES *CEASED.* (GW/0933-4807) [18083986] **5143**

PTERIDOLOGIA (US/0749-7741) [05217632] **525**

PTERIDOLOGIST (UK/0266-1640) [11272044] **525**

PTI JOURNAL (US) **5390**

PTIT FOCUS (TH/0857-7749) [I08577749] **4276**

P'TIT ROBERT, LE (CN/0823-6135) [09938466] **5302**

PTITSEVODSTVO (RU/0033-3239) [05381666] **219**

PTJ. PASSENGER TRAIN JOURNAL *See* PASSENGER TRAIN JOURNAL **5433**

PTN (MELVILLE, N.Y.) (US/1053-8968) [20126265] **4376**

PTR. PHYTOTHERAPY RESEARCH (UK/0951-418X) [17419275] **525**

PTRC PROCEEDINGS (UK) **5390**

PTS NEWSLETTER DATABASE [ONLINE DATABASE] (US) **705, 732**

PTS ONLINE NEWS (US) [16973709] **3242**

PTSD RESEARCH QUARTERLY (US/1050-1835) [21420167] **3631**

PTT-GESCHAFTSBERICHT UND FINANZRECHNUNG / PTT (SZ) [20159480] **1147**

PTT INFO *CEASED.* (FR/0247-7114) [11416707] **1120**

PTT : REVUE (XR/0322-8207) [I03228207] **1120**

PTT-ZEITSCHRIFT (SZ) [06538259] **1147**

PU SHIH HSING HSIANG (HK) [02660090] **4242**

PUB. - INSTITUT CANADIEN DE TOLE D'ACIER EN BATIMENT (CN/0826-4538) [11240735] **2029**

PUB NEWSLETTER (BE) **764, 4818**

PUBBLICA AMMINISTRAZIONE OGGI (IT/0394-8412) [I03948412] **4675**

PUBBLICAZIONI CERES (IT) **1514**

PUBBLICAZIONI DEL CENTRO STATISTICA AZIENDALE (IT) **5336**

PUBBLICAZIONI DELL'UNIVERSITA CATTOLICA DEL SACRO CUORE (IT/0300-1792) [05189997] **422**

PUBBLICAZIONI DELL'UNIVERSITA CATTOLICA DEL SACRO CUORE. CONTRIBUTI, SERIE III. SCIENZE FILOSOFICHE *CEASED.* (IT/0076-8677) [02558454] **4358**

PUBBLICAZIONI - FERRARA. CIVICO MUSEO DE STORIA NATURALE (IT/0428-2396) [03288411] **4171**

PUBBLICAZIONI UFFICIO STUDI BNL (IT) **804**

PUBBLICITA DOMANI (IT) **764**

PUBBLICITA IN ITALIA *SUSPENDED.* (US) [02230212] **764**

PUBBLICITA ITALIA (IT) [27065864] **935, 764**

PUBBLICITA ITALIA TODAY (IT) **2491**

PUBBLICITA SUCCESSO (IT) **764**

PUBBLICO IMPIEGO LOCALE (IT) **4675**

PUBFAX *CEASED.* (US/8756-4084) [11558251] **4818**

PUBL HERPETOL (US/0161-5009) [03957412] **5595**

PUBLI 10 (FR/0751-5464) [I07515464] **764**

PUBLI-CABLE, INC *See* CABLE HANDBOOK **1129**

PUBLI-NORMES (CN/0712-8193) [08923986] **764**

PUBLIC-ACCESS COMPUTER SYSTEMS NEWS (US/1050-6004) [21547573] **1201**

PUBLIC-ACCESS COMPUTER SYSTEMS REVIEW (ELECTRONIC ED.), THE (US/1048-6542) [20987125] **1201**

PUBLIC-ACCESS COMPUTER SYSTEMS REVIEW, THE (US/1063-164X) [25907292] **3243**

●PUBLIC ACCOUNTING PRACTICE MANUAL (US) [24873986] **750**

PUBLIC ACCOUNTING REPORT (US/0161-309X) [03899354] **750**

PUBLIC ACCOUNTS: ALBERTA (CN/0317-4999) [01798958] **4743**

PUBLIC ACCOUNTS (REGINA) (CN/0706-2710) [02249954] **4743**

PUBLIC ADMINISTRATION AND DEVELOPMENT (UK/0271-2075) [06578188] **4675**

PUBLIC ADMINISTRATION AND PUBLIC POLICY (US) [05780113] **4676**

PUBLIC ADMINISTRATION (LONDON) (UK/0033-3298) [02266601] **4704**

PUBLIC ADMINISTRATION QUARTERLY (US/0734-9149) [08828546] **4676**

PUBLIC ADMINISTRATION TIMES (US/0149-8797) [03578845] **4676**

PUBLIC ADMINISTRATION UPDATE (US/0148-4168) [03321299] **4676**

PUBLIC ADMINISTRATOR AND THE COURTS, THE (US/0735-4703) [08920422] **3032, 4676**

PUBLIC ADVISORY COMMITTEES, AUTHORITY, STRUCTURE, FUNCTIONS, MEMBERS (US/0147-4251) [03170071] **4797**

PUBLIC AFFAIRS COMMENT (US/0033-3395) [01763079] **4676**

PUBLIC AFFAIRS QUARTERLY (US/0887-0373) [13067377] **4676**

PUBLIC AFFAIRS REPORT (US/0033-3417) [01763081] **4676**

PUBLIC AFFAIRS SERIES (MORGANTOWN) (US/0511-6635) [01184078] **1623**

PUBLIC AFFAIRS (VERMILLION) (US/0555-5914) [01763078] **4676**

●PUBLIC AND ACCESS SERVICES QUARTERLY (US/1056-4942) [23725478] **3243**

PUBLIC AND INDEPENDENT SCHOOLS BOOK (UK) [22928768] **1775**

PUBLIC AND LOCAL ACTS OF THE LEGISLATURE OF THE STATE OF MICHIGAN (US/0893-2573) [01757300] **3032**

PUBLIC AND PRIVATE ELEMENTARY AND SECONDARY EDUCATION STATISTICS / NATIONAL CENTER FOR EDUCATION STATISTICS (US) [25609955] **1775**

PUBLIC AND SPECIAL ACTS (US/0360-7704) [02243933] **3032**

PUBLIC ARCHIVES CANADA *See* ARCHIVES CANADA MICROFICHES **2479**

PUBLIC ARCHIVES CANADA *See* ACCESSIONS - PUBLIC ARCHIVES CANADA **406**

PUBLIC ARCHIVES OF CANADA *See* REGISTER OF POST-GRADUATE DISSERTATIONS IN PROGRESS IN HISTORY AND RELATED SUBJECTS **2627**

PUBLIC ARCHIVES OF NOVA SCOTIA *See* ANNUAL REPORT OF THE BOARD OF TRUSTEES FOR THE YEAR - PUBLIC ARCHIVES OF NOVA SCOTIA **2479**

●PUBLIC ART ISSUES (US/1062-5089) [25643491] **362**

PUBLIC

PUBLIC ART REVIEW (US/1040-211X) [18352903] 306, **362**

PUBLIC ASSISTANCE FOR MINNESOTA INDIANS (US/0090-7138) [01785248] 5303, **2271**

PUBLIC ASSISTANCE FUNDING REPORT *See* CHILDREN & YOUTH FUNDING REPORT **5278**

PUBLIC ASSISTANCE FUNDING REPORT (US/1069-1340) [27944338] **5303**

PUBLIC ASSISTANCE RECIPIENT AND EXPENDITURE STUDY (US) [06132765] **5303**

PUBLIC ASSISTANCE REPORT (SILVER SPRING, MD.) *See* PUBLIC ASSISTANCE FUNDING REPORT **5303**

PUBLIC ASSISTANCE REPORT (SILVER SPRING, MD.) (US/1056-7100) [23820084] **5303**

PUBLIC AUTHORITIES DIRECTORY (UK) [06493489] **4676**

PUBLIC BODIES / MANAGEMENT AND PERSONNEL OFFICE (UK) [09898042] **4676**

PUBLIC BROADCASTING NEWS *See* WJCT MAGAZINE **1143**

PUBLIC BROADCASTING REPORT, THE (US/0193-3663) [04959753] **1136**

PUBLIC BUDGETING & FINANCE (US/0275-1100) [07086258] 1514, **4743**

PUBLIC BUDGETING AND FINANCIAL MANAGEMENT (US/1042-4741) [19062335] **4743**

PUBLIC CHOICE (NE/0048-5829) [03208518] 4492, **1514**

PUBLIC CITIZEN (US/0738-5927) [08597432] **1299**

PUBLIC CLEANSING SERVICE IN TOKYO (JA) [05350255] **4676**

PUBLIC COMMON SCHOOL ENROLLMENT FORECASTS FOR ... BIENNIUM BUDGET, STATE OF WASHINGTON *See* PUBLIC SCHOOLS, K-12 AND HANDICAPPED ENROLLMENT FORECASTS ... BIENNIAL BUDGET **1884**

PUBLIC COMMUNICATION AND BEHAVIOR (US/0887-932X) [13505945] 5254, **1120**

PUBLIC COMMUNICATIONS MAGAZINE (US/1041-6943) [18825567] **1120**

PUBLIC CONTRACT LAW JOURNAL (US/0033-3441) [01589985] **3033**

PUBLIC CONTRACT NEWSLETTER (US/0569-3314) [01587850] **3033**

PUBLIC CONTRIBUTIONS ACT ... ANNUAL REPORT ..., THE (CN/0381-4327) [09399247] **5303**

PUBLIC CULTURE (US/0899-2363) [18040687] **328**

PUBLIC DEFENDERS' WORKSHOP *See* ANNUAL PUBLIC DEFENDERS' WORKSHOP **3105**

PUBLIC DOCUMENTS (BATON ROUGE, LA.) (US/0099-2410) [09171688] **4699**

PUBLIC DOCUMENTS OF LOUISIANA (BATON ROUGE, LA : 1981) (US) [10660748] **4676**

●PUBLIC DOMAIN REPORT (US/1070-2555) [28309559] **328**

PUBLIC EDUCATION DIRECTORY (US/0160-8126) [03663365] **1775**

PUBLIC EDUCATION FINANCES (US) [22883555] **1775**

PUBLIC EDUCATION IN MICHIGAN; BACKGROUND PAPER (US) [03146638] **1775**

PUBLIC EDUCATION SERIES (US/0272-2658) [04582503] **5595**

PUBLIC EMPLOYEE BENEFIT PLANS (US) [26655902] 2891, **4705**

PUBLIC EMPLOYEE MAGAZINE, THE (US/1062-5992) [25680481] **4705**

PUBLIC EMPLOYEE PRESS (NEW YORK) (US/0033-345X) [02496206] 4676, **1704**

PUBLIC EMPLOYEE RELATIONS COUNSELLOR (US/0197-0232) [05929340] **3153**

PUBLIC EMPLOYEE RELATIONS LIBRARY (US) [01763087] **4705**

PUBLIC EMPLOYEE REPORTER FOR THE STATE OF CALIFORNIA (US) **1704**

PUBLIC EMPLOYEE TERMINATIONS LAW BULLETIN (US) [22683489] 3033, **1704**

PUBLIC EMPLOYEE, THE (SI) [05329583] **4705**

PUBLIC EMPLOYEES CONFERENCE PROCEEDINGS (US/0273-3439) [07039786] 4676, **1704**

PUBLIC EMPLOYEES RETIREMENT ASSOCIATION OF NEW MEXICO *See* ANNUAL REPORT - PUBLIC EMPLOYEES' RETIREMENT ASSOCIATION OF NEW MEXICO **1649**

PUBLIC EMPLOYEES RETIREMENT SYSTEM OF OHIO *See* ANNUAL FINANCIAL REPORT FOR THE CALENDAR YEAR ENDED DECEMBER 31 ... - PUBLIC EMPLOYEES RETIREMENT SYSTEM OF OHIO **4626**

PUBLIC EMPLOYMENT (1965) (US/0196-4437) [01190847] **4676**

PUBLIC EMPLOYMENT PERSPECTIVE. PENNSYLVANIA (US/0195-0770) [05259126] **1704**

PUBLIC EMPLOYMENT RECRUITER BULLETIN : PERB (US/0892-5933) [15220360] **1704**

PUBLIC EMPLOYMENT RELATIONS REPORTER (US) [05239055] **1704**

PUBLIC ENTERPRISE / INTERNATIONAL CENTER FOR PUBLIC ENTERPRISES IN DEVELOPING COUNTRIES (YU/0351-3564) [08027935] 1639, **2911**

PUBLIC EXECUTIVE PROJECT BULLETIN (US/0730-1863) [05238718] **4676**

PUBLIC FAX DIRECTORY, THE (US/1042-9336) [19244918] **1162**

PUBLIC FINANCE (NE/0033-3476) [01696524] **4743**

PUBLIC FINANCE (AT) [04801147] **4743**

PUBLIC FINANCE AND ACCOUNTANCY (UK/0305-9014) [01232474] 750, **4743**

PUBLIC FINANCE FOUNDATION (GREAT BRITAIN) *See* ANNUAL REPORT / PUBLIC FINANCE FOUNDATION **4710**

PUBLIC FINANCE: GOVERNMENT AUTHORITIES (AT) [03460908] **4743**

PUBLIC FINANCE (LONDON, ENGLAND) (UK) [29045925] **4743**

PUBLIC FINANCE QUARTERLY (US/0048-5853) [01785152] **4743**

PUBLIC FULL-TIME PROFESSIONAL STAFF AVERAGE SALARIES FOR THE ... SCHOOL YEAR BY LOCAL ADMINISTRATIVE UNIT / STATE OF MAINE (US) [04698565] **1869**

PUBLIC FUND DIGEST (US/0736-7848) [09198409] **4743**

PUBLIC GAMING INTERNATIONAL (US/1042-1912) [16749647] **4743**

PUBLIC GAMING NEWSLETTER *CEASED.* (US/0196-2558) [05786327] **4865**

PUBLIC GARDEN, THE (US/0885-3894) [12629321] **2429**

PUBLIC GENERAL ACTS AND GENERAL SYNOD MEASURES, THE (UK) [16723887] 3033, **4676**

PUBLIC HEALTH (SZ) **4797**

PUBLIC HEALTH COMMENTS (US/0895-8157) [16814544] **4797**

PUBLIC HEALTH (LONDON) (UK/0033-3506) [01338322] **4797**

PUBLIC HEALTH MACROVIEW (US/1060-7714) [18485621] **4797**

PUBLIC HEALTH NEWS (UK) **4797**

PUBLIC HEALTH NURSING (BOSTON, MASS.) (US/0737-1209) [09311215] **3867**

PUBLIC HEALTH REPORTS (1974) (US/0033-3549) [06343820] **4797**

PUBLIC HEALTH REPORTS (1974) (US/0033-3549) [01799423] **4797**

PUBLIC HEALTH REVIEWS (IS/0301-0422) [02715873] **4797**

PUBLIC HEALTH STATISTICS (NEW ORLEANS) (US/0148-5555) [04595825] **4811**

PUBLIC HEALTH UPDATE (WASHINGTON, D.C.) (US/1060-7706) [25059745] **4797**

PUBLIC HISTORIAN, THE (US/0272-3433) [04617561] **2626**

PUBLIC HOLIDAYS IN 154 INDEPENDENT COUNTRIES (US) [03722856] **5269**

PUBLIC HOUSING DEVELOPMENT HANDBOOK (US) [03113874] **2832**

PUBLIC INCOME & EXPENDITURE (UK) [07217303] **4743**

PUBLIC INFORMATION CIRCULAR - GEOLOGICAL SURVEY OF WYOMING (US/0160-3655) [03672801] **1392**

PUBLIC INFORMATION CIRCULAR - IOWA GEOLOGICAL SURVEY (US/0375-6653) [02251015] **1392**

PUBLIC INNOVATION ABROAD (US/0887-4468) [13230866] **2832**

PUBLIC INTEREST LAW REVIEW, THE (US/1058-384X) [23923262] **3033**

PUBLIC INTEREST, THE (US/0033-3557) [01642714] **5214**

PUBLIC INTERNATIONAL LAW (GW/0340-7349) [03127540] **3134**

PUBLIC JUSTICE REPORT (US/0742-5325) [06898218] 4492, **4676**

PUBLIC LAND AND RESOURCES LAW DIGEST, THE (US/0148-6489) [02052022] **3115**

PUBLIC LAND LAW REVIEW, THE (US/0732-0264) [07047125] 2202, **3033**

PUBLIC LANDS NEWS (US/0270-8094) [02322114] **2202**

PUBLIC LAW (US/0033-3565) [01004517] **3033**

PUBLIC LAW REVIEW (AT/1034-3024) [22836565] **3033**

PUBLIC LAWS (US) [02602882] **3033**

PUBLIC LAWS OF THE STATE OF RHODE ISLAND AND PROVIDENCE PLANTATIONS PASSED AT THE GENERAL ASSEMBLY (US) [01764285] **3033**

PUBLIC LEDGER, THE (UK) [18680192] **5813**

PUBLIC LEGAL EDUCATION AND INFORMATION SERVICE OF NEW BRUNSWICK *See* ACTIVITY REPORT - PUBLIC LEGAL EDUCATION AND INFORMATION SERVICE OF NEW BRUNSWICK **4623**

PUBLIC LETTER (MISSISSAUGA) (CN/0715-5646) [09428189] **2543**

PUBLIC LIBRARIES (US/0163-5506) [03889688] **3243**

PUBLIC LIBRARIES IN QUEENSLAND, STATISTICAL BULLETIN (AT) [03508965] 3243, **3259**

PUBLIC LIBRARY CATALOG (US) [03365006] **3243**

PUBLIC LIBRARY EXPENDITURE IN SCOTLAND (UK) [09715132] **3243**

PUBLIC LIBRARY JOURNAL (UK/0268-893X) [14402974] **3243**

PUBLIC LIBRARY PROGRAM GUIDELINES (US/0195-6922) [05129072] **3243**

PUBLIC LIBRARY QUARTERLY (NEW YORK, N.Y.) (US/0161-6846) [03992852] **3243**

PUBLIC LIBRARY SERVICES NEWSLETTER (CN/0706-7798) [05026499] **3243**

PUBLIC LIBRARY STATISTICS ... ESTIMATES (UK/0307-0522) [08973688] 3243, **3259**

PUBLIC LIBRARY WATCH (US/1051-0931) [21822534] **3243**

●PUBLIC MANAGER (POTOMAC, MD.), THE (US/1061-7639) [25453575] **4676**

PUBLIC MONEY & MANAGEMENT (UK/0954-0962) [18268471] **4743**

PUBLIC NETWORK EUROPE (UK/0963-5084) [109635084] **1514**

PUBLIC NOTICE - FEDERAL COMMUNICATIONS COMMISSION. CABLE TELEVISION AUTHORIZATION ACTIONS (US) [03454241] **1136**

PUBLIC NOTICE - FEDERAL COMMUNICATIONS COMMISSION. CABLE TELEVISION CERTIFICATE OF COMPLIANCE ACTIONS (US) [03454362] **1136**

PUBLIC NOTICE - FEDERAL COMMUNICATIONS COMMISSION. DOMESTIC PUBLIC LAND MOBILE RADIO SERVICE (US) [03457337] **1136**

PUBLIC NOTICE - FEDERAL COMMUNICATIONS COMMISSION. EXPERIMENTAL ACTIONS (US) [03457362] **1120**

PUBLIC NOTICE - FEDERAL COMMUNICATIONS COMMISSION. SAFETY AND SPECIAL ACTIONS (US) [03457418] **1120**

PUBLIC OPINION AND BROADCASTING STANDARDS / BROADCASTING STANDARDS COUNCIL (UK/0960-3999) [23735943] **1136**

PUBLIC OPINION (CHAMBERSBURG, PA. : 1974 : DAILY) (US) [16963120] **5739**

PUBLIC OPINION QUARTERLY (US/0033-362X) [01639357] **5254**

PUBLIC PAPERS OF THE PRESIDENTS OF THE UNITED STATES (US/0079-7626) [01198154] **4676**

PUBLIC PARKING AUTHORITY OF PITTSBURGH (PA.) *See* FINANCIAL STATEMENTS AND SUPPLEMENTAL SCHEDULES FOR THE YEARS ENDED SEPTEMBER 30 ... AND INDEPENDENT AUDITOR'S REPORT **5415**

PUBLIC PERSONNEL ASSOCIATION. PERSONNEL REPORT *See* PERSONNEL REPORT **945**

PUBLIC PERSONNEL MANAGEMENT (US/0091-0260) [01786406] **946**

PUBLIC PERSPECTIVE, THE (US/1050-5067) [21403951] **5336**

PUBLIC POLICY AND ADMINISTRATION (UK) [14917294] **4676**

PUBLIC POLICY AND AGING REPORT, THE (US/1055-3037) [17799311] **5181**

PUBLIC POLICY STUDIES (GREENWICH, CT.) *CEASED.* (US) [13848418] **4677**

PUBLIC POLICY STUDIES IN THE SOUTH (US) [02381004] **5214**

PUBLIC POWER (US/0033-3654) [01763106] **4762**

PUBLIC POWER WEEKLY (US/0747-3613) [10775370] **4762**

PUBLIC — Alphabetical Title Index

PUBLIC PROCUREMENT LAW REVIEW (UK/0963-8245) [25923857] **3033**

PUBLIC PRODUCTIVITY & MANAGEMENT REVIEW (US/1044-8039) [19909534] **4705**

PUBLIC PROGRAMS NEWSLETTER (US/0890-0655) [14160771] **2323**

PUBLIC PULSE, THE (US/1053-9751) [01763107] **5214**

PUBLIC RADIO PROGRAMMING FISCAL YEAR ... / PREPARED FOR CPB BY NATIONAL PUBLIC RADIO'S OFFICE OF AUDIENCE RESEARCH AND PROGRAM EVALUATION (US) [18355060] **1136**

PUBLIC RELATIONS (UK) [02669989] **764**

PUBLIC RELATIONS ALMANAC FOR EDUCATORS, THE (US/0273-3757) [07034055] **764**

PUBLIC RELATIONS CAREER DIRECTORY (US/0882-8288) [12004169] **764**

PUBLIC RELATIONS (HARLOW, ENGLAND) See INSTITUTE OF PUBLIC RELATIONS JOURNAL, THE **760**

PUBLIC RELATIONS JOURNAL OF INDIA (II/0033-3689) [02245628] **764**

PUBLIC RELATIONS JOURNAL. PRSA REGISTER ISSUE (US) [13141421] **765**

PUBLIC RELATIONS JOURNAL, THE (US/0033-3670) [02230151] **764**

PUBLIC RELATIONS NEWS See PR NEWS **763**

PUBLIC RELATIONS QUARTERLY (US/0033-3700) [05534599] **765**

PUBLIC RELATIONS RESEARCH ANNUAL See JOURNAL OF PUBLIC RELATIONS RESEARCH **761**

PUBLIC RELATIONS REVIEW (RIVERDALE, N.Y.) (US/0363-8111) [02549647] **765**

PUBLIC RELATIONS SOCIETY OF AMERICA See PUBLIC RELATIONS JOURNAL. PRSA REGISTER ISSUE **765**

PUBLIC RELATIONS SOCIETY OF AMERICA See PRSA DIRECTORY / PUBLIC RELATIONS SOCIETY OF AMERICA **764**

●PUBLIC RELATIONS TACTICS (US) **765**

PUBLIC RELATIONS YEAR BOOK (UK/0262-9534) [I02629534] **765**

PUBLIC RELATIONS YEAR BOOK (UK) **765**

PUBLIC RESEARCH REPORT (SW) [19618973] **4182, 306**

PUBLIC REVENUES FROM ALCOHOL BEVERAGES (US/0148-0863) [03261202] **2370**

PUBLIC RISK (US/0891-7183) [15011774] **1514**

PUBLIC ROADS (US/0033-3735) [01586080] **2029, 5442**

●PUBLIC SAFETY ON-LINE (US/1072-9321) [29241923] **1162**

PUBLIC SCHOOL ENROLLMENT (US) [04909597] **1775**

PUBLIC SCHOOL ENROLLMENT AND STAFF, NEW YORK STATE (US/0197-2901) [04327928] **1776**

PUBLIC SCHOOL FINANCE PROGRAMS OF THE UNITED STATES AND CANADA (US) [19069378] **1776**

PUBLIC SCHOOL PROFESSIONAL PERSONNEL REPORT, NEW YORK STATE (US) [04332503] **1869**

PUBLIC SCHOOL REPORT (TOPEKA, KAN. : 1978) (US) [04286172] **1776**

●PUBLIC SCHOOLS, K-12 AND HANDICAPPED ENROLLMENT FORECASTS ... BIENNIAL BUDGET (US) [26890876] **1884**

PUBLIC SCHOOLS. PROFESSIONAL PERSONNEL (US) [25564401] **1869**

PUBLIC SCIENCE NEWSLETTER CEASED. (US/0091-1720) [02241313] **5143**

PUBLIC SECTOR ACCOUNTS OF LIBERIA (LB/0377-3167) [01798401] **4743**

PUBLIC SECTOR DEBT, AUSTRALIA (AT/1031-7112) [I10317112] **4743, 4699**

PUBLIC SECTOR EMPLOYMENT AND REMUNERATION / STATISTICS CANADA, PUBLIC INSTITUTIONS DIVISION, EMPLOYMENT SECTION (CN/1188-0619) [26139429] **4705**

PUBLIC SECTOR HEALTH CARE RISK MANAGEMENT (US/0270-8973) [06511060] **3791**

●PUBLIC SECTOR JOB BULLETIN (US/1072-3773) [28922206] **4209**

PUBLIC SECTOR LABOR RELATIONS (US/0734-726X) [04701581] **3153**

PUBLIC SECTOR MANAGEMENT (TORONTO) (CN/1183-1081) [24368455] **4705**

●PUBLIC SECTOR QUALITY REPORT (US/1067-4489) [27231377] **732**

PUBLIC SECTOR, THE (CN/0700-2092) [04755201] **4677**

PUBLIC SECTOR (WELLINGTON) (NZ/0110-5191) [05161035] **4677**

PUBLIC SERVANT. DIE STAATSAMPTENAAR, THE (SA/0033-376X) [05318505] **4677**

PUBLIC SERVICE ACTION (UK) **5235**

PUBLIC SERVICE ALLIANCE OF CANADA. GRIEVANCE AND ADJUDICATION SECTION See GRIEVANCE AND ADJUDICATION SECTION REPORTS / PUBLIC SERVICE ALLIANCE OF CANADA **2975**

PUBLIC SERVICE COMMISION OF CANADA. ADVISORY COMMITTEE TO THE PRIME MINISTER ON THE BUSINESS/GOVERNMENT EXECUTIVE EXCHANGE PROGRAM See REPORT ON THE ADVISORY COMMITTEE TO THE PRIME MINISTER ON THE BUSINESS/GOVERNMENT EXECUTIVE EXCHANGE PROGRAM **707**

PUBLIC SERVICE COMMISSION OF CANADA See BULLETIN - PUBLIC SERVICE COMMISSION OF CANADA **4635**

PUBLIC SERVICE COMMISSION OF CANADA See DIRECTIONS - PUBLIC SERVICE COMMISSION OF CANADA **4643**

PUBLIC SERVICE COMMISSION OF WESTERN AUSTRALIA See ANNUAL REPORT / PUBLIC SERVICE COMMISSION OF WESTERN AUSTRALIA **4701**

PUBLIC SERVICE COMMISSION OF WISCONSIN. ACCOUNTS AND FINANCE DIVISION See OPERATING REVENUE AND EXPENSE STATISTICS CLASS A AND B PRIVATE GAS UTILITIES IN WISCONSIN **4699**

PUBLIC SERVICE COMMISSION OF WISCONSIN. ACCOUNTS AND FINANCE DIVISION See TELEPHONE STATISTICS : SELECTED FINANCIAL DATA FOR WISCONSIN TELEPHONE COMPANIES **1125**

PUBLIC SERVICE MANAGEMENT PENSION PLAN, ANNUAL REPORT (CN/0842-7259) [19990115] **4677**

PUBLIC SERVICE STAFF RELATIONS BOARD DECISIONS (CN/0822-1790) [09470337] **3033**

PUBLIC SERVICES INTERNATIONAL See PSI NEWS & VIEWS **1704**

PUBLIC STAMP AUCTION (CN/0714-8941) [09113399] **2787**

PUBLIC TECHNOLOGY (US/0882-1445) [11794518] **5143**

PUBLIC TECHNOLOGY NEWS See PUBLIC TECHNOLOGY **5143**

PUBLIC (TORONTO) (CN/0845-4450) [19904244] **2852, 328**

PUBLIC TRANSIT REPORT (US/0148-4087) [03320953] **5390**

PUBLIC TRANSPORT INTERNATIONAL (BE/1016-796X) [22167353] **5390**

●PUBLIC UNDERSTANDING OF SCIENCE (UK/0963-6625) [25512020] **5143**

PUBLIC USE OF THE NATIONAL PARKS SYSTEMS (WASHINGTON) (US/0093-3074) [01788940] **2202**

PUBLIC UTILITIES ACT 1951 (BB) [01785561] **4677**

PUBLIC UTILITIES AND TRANSPORTATION NEWSLETTER (US/0147-359X) [03145894] **5390, 4677**

PUBLIC UTILITIES BOARD FOR THE PROVINCE OF ALBERTA See ANNUAL REPORT - ALBERTA PUBLIC UTILITIES BOARD **4626**

PUBLIC UTILITIES FORTNIGHTLY (US/0033-3808) [01639840] **4762**

PUBLIC UTILITIES LAW ANTHOLOGY (US/0095-5086) [01790855] **4762, 3033**

PUBLIC UTILITIES REPORTS (US/0196-7843) [01763113] **4762**

PUBLIC UTILITIES REPORTS ADVANCE SHEETS (US) **4762**

PUBLIC UTILITIES REPORTS UTILITY WEEKLY (US) 1162, **4762**

PUBLIC WAREHOUSING (CN/0704-5387) [03980255] **705**

PUBLIC WATER SUPPLY REPORT (US) [10148795] **5537**

PUBLIC WELFARE ACTIVITIES IN ARIZONA (US/0360-6600) [01738375] **5303**

PUBLIC WELFARE DIRECTORY, THE (US/0163-8297) [01238190] **5303**

PUBLIC WELFARE STATISTICS See PUBLIC WELFARE ACTIVITIES IN ARIZONA **5303**

PUBLIC WELFARE (WASHINGTON) (US/0033-3816) [01763115] **5303**

PUBLIC WORKS (US/0033-3840) [01606878] **4677, 1992**

PUBLIC WORKS FINANCING (US) **4743**

PUBLIC WORKS (LONDON, ONT.) CEASED. (CN/0827-5556) [12356852] **3350**

PUBLIC WORKS NEWS (US/0146-5473) [02960935] **4677**

PUBLIC WORKS PRO-VIEWS (US/0882-7230) [11991502] **883**

PUBLIC WORKS PROGRESS (US/0148-5814) [03337758] **4677**

PUBLICACAO ACIESP (BL/0100-7092) [08382680] **5143**

PUBLICACAO DO INSTITUTO DE PESQUISAS DA MARINHA (BL/0524-3130) [01127972] **470**

PUBLICACAO IPEN (BL/0101-3084) [09051075] **4418**

PUBLICACAO. SERIE 2-M. RELATORIO DOS SERVICOS EXECUTADOS (AG) [01897335] **2095**

PUBLICACION (AG) [01537618] **3631**

PUBLICACION (AG) [01941604] **1417**

PUBLICACION ESR (AG) [01787959] **123**

PUBLICACION - INSTITUTO ANTARTICO ARGENTINO (AG) [08091630] **2574**

PUBLICACION MISCELANEA / ESTACION EXPERIMENTAL AGRO-INDUSTRIAL OBISPO COLOMBRES (AG) [08500827] **123**

PUBLICACION QUINCENAL See CONFEDERACION DE CAMARAS INDUSTRIALES **1552**

PUBLICACION TECNICA (ESTACION EXPERIMENTAL REGIONAL AGROPECUARIAANGUIL) (AG/0325-2132) [13288911] **123**

PUBLICACION - VENEZUELA. UNIVERSIDAD CENTRAL. CONSEJO DE DESARROLLO CIENTIFICO Y HUMANISTICO (VE/0506-6034) [01486924] **2852**

PUBLICACIONES (CL/0577-8468) [01554276] **1514**

PUBLICACIONES (CL/0577-8298) [03020630] **5595**

PUBLICACIONES (SP) [02533530] **4148**

PUBLICACIONES (SP) [02855801] **5537, 1417**

PUBLICACIONES - CHILE. UNIVERSIDAD, SANTIAGO. SEMINARIO DE DERECHO PUBLICO (CL/0577-8573) [03115920] **3033**

PUBLICACIONES DE LA FUNDACION UNIVERSITARIA ESPANOLA. BIBLIOTECA DE HISPANISMO (SP) [06286168] **423**

PUBLICACIONES DEL DEPARTAMENTO DE MATEMATICAS UNIVERSIDAD DE EXTREMADURA (SP) [28188206] **3528**

PUBLICACIONES DEL INSTITUTO CARO Y CUERVO. SERIE BIBLIOGRAFICA (CK) [08784495] **3312, 3336**

PUBLICACIONES DEL MUSEO MUNICIPAL DE CIENCIAS NATURALES LORENZO SCAGLIA (GT) [05810268] **4095**

PUBLICACIONES DEL SEMINARIO MATEMATICO GARCIA DE GALDEANO (SP) [19890660] **3528**

PUBLICACIONES DIETETICAS ALTER (SP) **4198**

PUBLICACIONES EDITADAS EN ESPANOL See LIBROS EN ESPANOL ... TITULOS **4830**

PUBLICACIONES EN CIENCIAS AGRICOLAS (SP/0577-8425) [03105580] **123**

PUBLICACIONES ESPECIALES - INSTITUTO ESPANOL DE OCEANOGRAFIA (SP/0214-7378) [I02147378] **1455**

PUBLICACIONES - FUNDACION VITORIA Y SUAREZ (AG/0429-8829) [01391327] **5235**

PUBLICACIONES - INSTITUTO DE FISIOGRAFIA Y GEOLOGIA (AG/0041-8684) [06844406] **1392**

PUBLICACIONES OFICIALES (SP/0213-5760) [I02135760] **4677**

PUBLICACIONES - QUITO. UNIVERSIDAD CENTRAL DEL ECUADOR (EC) [01437535] **3134**

PUBLICACIONES. SERIE BIBLIOGRAFICA (CK/0073-991X) [01564106] **423**

PUBLICACIONES. SERIE : SEMINARIOS (VE/0506-6115) [01487868] **1869**

PUBLICACIONES. SERIES MINOR (CK/0073-9928) [01564107] **3426, 3312**

PUBLICACIONES Y CONFERENCIAS : INFORME TRIMESTRAL - DEPARTAMENTO DE PUBLICACIONES Y CONFERENCIAS (US) [02246770] **3134**

PUBLICACIONS MATEMATIQUES / DEPARTAMENT DE MATEMATIQUES, UNIVERSITAT AUTONOMA DE BARCELONA (SP/0214-1493) [18121192] **3529**

PUBLICACOES DO MUSEU E LABORATORIO MINERALOGICO E GEOLOGICO DA UNIVERSIDADE DE COIMBRA (PO) [21963323] **1444, 1392**

Alphabetical Title Index — PUBLICATIONS

●PUBLICAR EN ANTROPOLOGIA Y CIENCIAS SOCIALES (AG/0327-6627) [28290237] **243**

PUBLICATION - AGRICULTURE CANADA (ENGLISH ED.) (CN/0828-2870) [06230833] **123**

PUBLICATION / ALASKA GEOLOGICAL SOCIETY (US/0749-9671) [10008780] **1392**

PUBLICATION - AMERICAN ACADEMY AND INSTITUTE OF ARTS AND LETTERS (US/0275-505X) [05787169] **328**

PUBLICATION - AMERICAN FEDERATION OF LABOR AND CONGRESS OF INDUSTRIAL ORGANIZATIONS (US/0569-4523) [01479851] **1704**

PUBLICATION - AMERICAN INSTITUTE OF THE HISTORY OF PHARMACY (US/0270-0611) [06301581] **4327**

PUBLICATION - ARIZONA STATE UNIVERSITY. CENTER FOR METEORITE STUDIES (US/0570-9652) [05090233] **398**

PUBLICATION - ARKANSAS WATER RESOURCES RESEARCH CENTER (US/0889-6224) [01884850] **5537**

PUBLICATION B / CENTRE INTERNATIONAL DE RECERCHES SUR LE BILINGUISME (CN/0704-7037) [02229230] **3312**

PUBLICATION B. CENTRE INTERNATIONAL DE RECHERCHES SUR LE BILINGUISME (CN/0704-7037) [08440033] **3312**

PUBLICATION BULLETIN (NETHERLANDS. CENTRAAL PLANBUREAU) (NE) [18251723] **1514**

PUBLICATION - CALIFORNIA STATE WATER RESOURCES CONTROL BOARD (US/0096-1728) [01370349] **5537**

PUBLICATION - CANADIAN FORESTRY SERVICE (CN/0300-5844) [02762338] **2391**

PUBLICATION CATALOG OF THE U.S. DEPARTMENT OF HEALTH AND HUMAN SERVICES (US/0278-0143) [07207516] **5303**

PUBLICATION - CENTRAL BOARD OF IRRIGATION AND POWER (II/0379-3494) [I03793494] **123**

PUBLICATION - CENTRE DE RECHERCHES D'HISTOIRE ANCIENNE (FR/0069-178X) (04770980] **2626**

PUBLICATION - COASTAL PLAINS CENTER FOR MARINE DEVELOPMENT SERVICES (US/0886-9227) [04974784] **1455**

PUBLICATION - CORNELL UNIVERSITY WATER RESOURCES AND MARINE SCIENCES CENTER (US) [01186888] **5538**

PUBLICATION - DAKAR. UNIVERSITE. CENTRE DE HAUTES ETUDES AFRO-IBERO-AMERICAINES (SG/0418-2898) [01559249] **1843**

PUBLICATION DE L'OBSERVATOIRE ASTRONOMIQUE DE STRASBOURG. SERIE ASTRONOMIE ET SCIENCES HUMAINES (FR/0989-6228) [21172114] **398**

PUBLICATION DESIGN ANNUAL (US/0885-6370) [09348497] **4818, 381**

PUBLICATION / DIVISION OF AGRICULTURE AND NATURAL RESOURCES, UNIVERSITY OF CALIFORNIA (US) [16401971] **123**

PUBLICATION E (US) [09701126] **5595**

PUBLICATION - ENVIRONMENT PROTECTION AUTHORITY OF VICTORIA (AT/0159-8430) [I01598430] **2180**

PUBLICATION / EUROPEAN ASSOCIATION FOR ANIMAL PRODUCTION (UK/0071-2477) [02252238] **219**

PUBLICATION (FIJI METEOROLOGICAL SERVICE) (FJ) [11183365] **1433**

PUBLICATION - FLORIDA WATER RESOURCES RESEARCH CENTER (US/0071-6200) [01421973] **5538**

PUBLICATION - FORT BURGWIN RESEARCH CENTER (US/0071-7754) [01377140] **5143**

PUBLICATION / GULLANE LOCAL HISTORY SOCIETY (UK) [19496248] **2626**

PUBLICATION - HISTORICAL SOCIETY OF WASHINGTON COUNTY, VIRGINIA *CEASED.* (US/0092-0851) [01788538] **2755**

PUBLICATION (ILLINOIS. GENERAL ASSEMBLY. LEGISLATIVE COUNCIL) (US) [01752597] **4677**

PUBLICATION INDEX - COLLEGE OF ARTS & SCIENCES, UNIVERSITY OF FLORIDA (US/0147-605X) [03208255] **1843**

PUBLICATION - INTERNATIONAL UNION OF GEOLOGICAL SCIENCES (CN/0254-2897) [06805109] **1392**

PUBLICATION IWR (US) [05538320] **5538**

PUBLICATION - MIDDLE TENNESSEE SECTION, TENNESSEE STATE PLANNING OFFICE (US) [02246385] **2832**

PUBLICATION NOTE / U.S. DEPARTMENT OF HEALTH AND HUMAN SERVICES, PUBLIC HEALTH SERVICE, OFFICE OF HEALTH RESEARCH, STATISTICS, AND TECHNOLOGY, NATIONAL CENTER FOR HEALTH STATISTICS (US) [04877820] **4677**

PUBLICATION OCCASIONNELLE - CENTRE INTERNATIONAL POUR LA FORMATION ET LES ECHANGES GEOLOGIQUES (FR/0769-0541) [I07690541] **1392**

PUBLICATION OF TECHNICAL PAPERS AND PROCEEDINGS OF THE ANNUAL MEETING OF SUGAR INDUSTRY TECHNOLOGISTS, INC (US/0099-9032) [02289823] **2354**

PUBLICATION OF THE ADOLESCENT PREGNANCY PREVENTION CLEARINGHOUSE *See* CDF'S CHILD, YOUTH, AND FAMILY FUTURES CLEARINGHOUSE **5276**

PUBLICATION OF THE AMERICAN DIALECT SOCIETY (US/0002-8207) [01479774] **3312**

PUBLICATION OF THE HANNAH INSTITUTE FOR THE HISTORY OF MEDICINE (CN/0704-0148) [04571401] **3631**

PUBLICATION OF THE KRESS LIBRARY OF BUSINESS AND ECONOMICS *CEASED.* (US/0073-0777) [01590561] **1514, 705**

PUBLICATION / OREGON STATE UNIVERSITY, SEA GRANT COLLEGE PROGRAM (US/0360-8972) [03176749] **1455**

PUBLICATION PROFILES (CN) [21271578] **765**

PUBLICATION - SASKATCHEWAN ADVISORY COUNCIL ON THE STATUS OF WOMEN (CN/0380-8297) [04432920] **5565**

PUBLICATION SERIES. BIBLIOGRAPHIC SERIES (UNIVERSITY OF TORONTO. FACULTY OF SOCIAL WORK) (CN/0710-0310) [08562661] **1796**

PUBLICATION SERIES. MONOGRAPH SERIES (UNIVERSITY OF TORONTO. FACULTY OF SOCIAL WORK) (CN/0710-0329) [08562653] **5303**

PUBLICATION SERIES / NETHERLANDS INSTITUTE FOR SEA RESEARCH (NE/0166-106X) [03861173] **1455, 557**

PUBLICATION SERIES - TRANSPORT GROUP. DEPARTMENT OF CIVIL ENGINEERING. UNIVERSITY OF WATERLOO (CN/0316-5922) [02247633] **5793**

PUBLICATION SERIES. WORKING PAPERS ON SOCIAL WELFARE IN CANADA (CN/0710-0299) [08562666] **5303**

PUBLICATION SP (US/0193-2527) [05148759] **625**

PUBLICATION - STATE OF CALIFORNIA RECREATION COMMISSION (US) [01166637] **4853**

PUBLICATION - THE SCOTTISH AGRICULTURAL COLLEGES (UK/0308-5708) [03968088] **123**

PUBLICATION / UNIVERSITE DE MONTREAL, CENTRE DE RECHERCHE SUR LES TRANSPORTS (CN/0709-9851) [07799516] **5390**

PUBLICATION (UNIVERSITY OF ALASKA (SYSTEM). COOPERATIVE EXTENSION SERVICE) (US) [10030384] **1543**

PUBLICATION (UNIVERSITY OF GUELPH. UNIVERSITY SCHOOL OF RURAL PLANNING AND DEVELOPMENT) (CN/0826-0273) [10805631] **2832**

PUBLICATION (UNIVERSITY OF TORONTO. DEPT. OF CIVIL ENGINEERING) (CN/0316-7968) [02247996] **2029**

PUBLICATION (UNIVERSITY OF WESTERN AUSTRALIA. DEPT. OF GEOLOGY) (AT/0156-9287) [08126274] **1392**

PUBLICATION - VETERINARY CONTINUING EDUCATION, MASSEY UNIVERSITY (NZ/0112-9643) [20540559] **5519**

PUBLICATION - WATER RESOURCES RESEARCH CENTER, UNIVERSITY OF MASSACHUSETTS AT AMHERST (US/0542-9315) [01711393] **5538**

PUBLICATIONES DEL DEPARTAMENTO DE ZOOLOGIA / UNIVERSIDAD DE BARCELONA, FACULTAD DE BIOLOGIA (SP/0210-4814) [05138630] **5595**

PUBLICATIONES MATHEMATICAL (DEBRECEN) (HU/0033-3883) [01566010] **3529**

PUBLICATIONS ADVICE (AT/0156-4722) [I01564722] **423**

PUBLICATIONS. AFRICAN SERIES (US) [02146630] **2642**

PUBLICATIONS AND FINAL REPORTS ON CONTRACTS AND GRANTS (US) [08900979] **2240**

PUBLICATIONS AND PATENTS OF THE EASTERN UTILIZATION RESEARCH AND DEVELOPMENT DIVISION (US/0098-566X) [02240812] **123**

PUBLICATIONS AND PATENTS - UNITED STATES. AGRICULTURAL RESEARCH SERVICE. EASTERN REGIONAL RESEARCH CENTER (1981) (US/0740-2848) [09563416] **1308**

PUBLICATIONS AND RULES FILED *See* PUBLICATIONS FILED WITH THE STATE RECORDS CENTER FOR THE YEAR ... **4677**

PUBLICATIONS AND STAFF REPORTS LISTING - OFFICE OF CONGRESSIONAL AND PUBLIC AFFAIRS, FEDERAL ENERGY REGULATORY COMMISSION (US) [06594148] **1954**

PUBLICATIONS - ASBL CENTRE D'HISTOIRE ET D'ART DE LA THUDINIE (BE) [02694580] **3426, 2626**

PUBLICATIONS / AUGUSTAN REPRINT SOCIETY (US/0885-7954) [01518624] **2704, 3426**

PUBLICATIONS CATALOG (US) [08266832] **5390**

PUBLICATIONS CATALOG - AMERICAN HOSPITAL ASSOCIATION (US/0569-5090) [01691470] **3791**

PUBLICATIONS CATALOG, LOG 1 (US) [23761475] **4677**

PUBLICATIONS CATALOGUE - ATOMIC ENERGY CONTROL BOARD (CN/0711-9917) [08741080] **1954**

PUBLICATIONS CATALOGUE / INSTITUTE FOR RESEARCH IN CONSTRUCTION (CN/1185-9628) [25883156] **625**

PUBLICATIONS CATALOGUE - INSTITUTE FOR RESEARCH IN CONSTRUCTION (OTTAWA) (CN/1185-9628) [25883160] **633**

PUBLICATIONS: CLASSICAL STUDIES (US/0068-6344) [01552459] **1079**

PUBLICATIONS - COMMITTEE ON TAXATION, RESOURCES AND ECONOMIC DEVELOPMENT (US/0590-6598) [03307906] **4743**

PUBLICATIONS / COUNCIL OF EUROPE (FR/0252-0524) [20820958] **4532**

PUBLICATIONS - DAKAR. UNIVERSITE. SECTION DE LANGUES ET LITTERATURES (SG/0418-2960) [01561434] **3426, 3312**

PUBLICATIONS DE LA COUR EUROPEENNE DES DROITS DE L'HOMME SERIE A, ARRETS ET DECISIONS (FR) [08950304] **3134**

PUBLICATIONS DE LA COUR EUROPEENNE DES DROITS DE L'HOMME SERIE B, MEMOIRES (FR) [01568436] **4512**

PUBLICATIONS DE LA SOCIETE HISTORIQUE ET ARCHEOLOGIQUE DANS LE LIMBOURG (NE/0167-6652) [03979530] **306**

PUBLICATIONS DE LA SORBONNE. HISTOIRE ANCIENNE ET MEDIEVALE (FR/0290-4500) [12381894] **2626**

PUBLICATIONS DE LA SORBONNE. SERIE FRANCE XIXE-XXE SIECLES (FR) [13106983] **2704**

PUBLICATIONS DE L'INSTITUT DE MATHEMATIQUE DE L'UNIVERSITE DE STRASBOURG (FR/0992-647X) [I0992647X] **3529**

PUBLICATIONS DE L'INSTITUT DE RECHERCHE MATHEMATIQUES DE RENNES (FR/0997-5489) [I09975489] **3529**

PUBLICATIONS DE L'INSTITUT DE STATISTIQUE DE L'UNIVERSITE DE PARIS (FR/0553-2930) [01590153] **5336**

PUBLICATIONS DE L'INSTITUT D'ETUDES MEDIEVALES *SUSPENDED.* (CN/0384-8825) [02483788] **2626**

PUBLICATIONS DE L'INSTITUT D'ETUDES MEDIEVALES D'OTTAWA *See* PUBLICATIONS DE L'INSTITUT D'ETUDES MEDIEVALES **2626**

PUBLICATIONS DE L'INSTITUT MATHEMATIQUE (BELGRADE) (YU/0350-1302) [02059023] **3529**

PUBLICATIONS DE L'INSTITUT UNIVERSITAIRE DE HAUTES ETUDES INTERNATIONALES (SZ) [01570594] **1843**

PUBLICATIONS DE L'OBSERVATOIRE ASTRONOMIQUE DE BEOGRAD (YU/0373-3742) [03266324] **398**

PUBLICATIONS DE L'OBSERVATOIRE DE GENEVE. SERIE B (SW) [04368218] **398**

PUBLICATIONS DE L'U.E.R. MATHEMATIQUES PURES ET APPLIQUEES / IRMA, UNIVERSITE DES SCIENCES ET TECHNIQUES (FR) [07449133] **3529**

PUBLICATIONS DE L'UNIVERSITE DE DIJON (FR) [01668261] **1843**

PUBLICATIONS DU BUREAU DE LA STATISTIQUE DU QUEBEC, LES (CN/1186-2262) [24296701] **423**

PUBLICATIONS — Alphabetical Title Index

PUBLICATIONS DU CENTRE DE RECHERCHES EN MATHEMATIQUES PURES. SERIE I (FR/0259-4897) [04022324] **3529**

PUBLICATIONS DU CENTRE D'ETUDES DE LA MUSIQUE FRANCAISE AUX XVIIIE & XIXE SIECLES (FR) [10233245] **4148**

PUBLICATIONS DU DEPARTEMENT DE MATHEMATIQUES (FI/0076-1656) [08076578] **3529**

PUBLICATIONS ECONOMETRIQUES (FR/0339-7041) [23074632] **3529**

PUBLICATIONS - EDINBURGH. ROYAL OBSERVATORY (UK) [06325811] **398**

PUBLICATIONS EN SERIES RECUES REGULIEREMENT PAR LA SALLE DES CATALOGUES / SALLE DES CATALOGUES ET DES BIBLIOGRAPHIES (FR) [08261018] **423**

PUBLICATIONS - ENGLISH PLACE-NAME SOCIETY (UK/0071-0636) [01986092] **2574**

PUBLICATIONS FILED WITH THE STATE RECORDS CENTER FOR THE YEAR ... (US) [08831544] **4677**

PUBLICATIONS. GEOGRAPHIC MONOGRAPH SERIES (US/0073-6953) [02152585] **2574**

PUBLICATIONS - GEORGIA. UNIVERSITY. INSTITUTE OF COMMUNITY AND AREA DEVELOPMENT (US/0072-1298) [01448228] **2832**

PUBLICATIONS / GYPSY LORE SOCIETY, NORTH AMERICAN CHAPTER (US/8756-7245) [08232011] 243, **2323**

PUBLICATIONS - HAWAII INSTITUTE OF GEOPHYSICS (US) [07980418] **1409**

PUBLICATIONS IN ANTHROPOLOGY AND HISTORY *CEASED.* (US/0897-8352) [03492400] 2626, **243**

PUBLICATIONS IN ARCHAEOLOGY (COLUMBIA, MO.) (US/8755-5743) [11384175] **279**

PUBLICATIONS IN ARCHAEOLOGY (OTTAWA) (CN/0712-4260) [02248854] **279**

PUBLICATIONS IN CLIMATOLOGY (US/0160-9599) [01553661] **1433**

PUBLICATIONS IN CONDUCT AND COMMUNICATION (US/0556-2678) [02725945] **1094**

PUBLICATIONS IN ENGINEERING : PIE : PUBLICATIONS ABSTRACTED AND INDEXED IN THE ... ENGINEERING INFORMATION DATABASES (US) [27833134] **1992**

PUBLICATIONS IN FOOD MICROBIOLOGY (US/1058-0352) [24202693] 2354, **569**

PUBLICATIONS IN INDIANA MEDICAL HISTORY (US/0743-6017) [10643657] **3631**

PUBLICATIONS IN INDUSTRIAL RELATIONS (US) [01836528] **1704**

PUBLICATIONS IN MEDIEVAL SCIENCE (US) [01716269] **2704**

PUBLICATIONS IN OPERATIONS RESEARCH (US) [01761327] **5235**

PUBLICATIONS IN OPERATIONS RESEARCH SERIES (US/0885-7881) [08134165] **1201**

PUBLICATIONS IN PRINT (WASHINGTON, D.C.) (US/1059-6801) [24293988] **5035**

PUBLICATIONS INDEX / NATIONAL HEALTH STATISTICS CENTRE (NZ) [15987490] **4811**

PUBLICATIONS INDEX / THE AUSTRALASIAN INSTITUTE OF MINING AND METALLURGY ; PRODUCED BY AUSTRALIAN MINERAL FOUNDATION (AT) [17409323] **2149**

PUBLICATIONS - INDUSTRIAL RELATIONS RESEARCH ASSOCIATION (SP) [01623767] 946, **1704**

PUBLICATIONS ISSUED - AUSTRALIAN BUREAU OF STATISTICS (AT/1031-0673) [I10310673] **423**

PUBLICATIONS LIST (COMMONWEALTH AGRICULTURAL BUREAUX) *See* JOURNAL SUBSCRIPTION PRICE LIST / COMMONWEALTH AGRICULTURAL BUREAUX **101**

PUBLICATIONS LIST - MANITOBA. DEPARTMENT OF NATURAL RESOURCES (CN/0713-6986) [08964052] **2202**

PUBLICATIONS, LIST OF MEMBERS AND RULES / SELDEN SOCIETY (UK) [01772427] **3033**

PUBLICATIONS / LONDON RECORD SOCIETY (UK/0085-2848) [01589092] **2704**

PUBLICATIONS MATHEMATIQUES DE LA FACULTE DES SCIENCES DE BESANCON ANALYSE NON LINEAIRE (FR/0995-4325) [I09954325] **3529**

PUBLICATIONS MATHEMATIQUES DE LA FACULTE DES SCIENCES DE BESANCON. THEORIE DES NOMBRES (FR/0768-9284) [07689284] **3529**

PUBLICATIONS MATHEMATIQUES DE L'UNIVERSITE PARIS VII (FR) [13543216] **3529**

PUBLICATIONS MATHEMATIQUES DE L'UNIVERSITE PIERRE ET MARIE CURIE (FR) [06561941] **3529**

PUBLICATIONS MATHEMATIQUES. INSTITUT DES HAUTES ETUDES SCIENTIFIQUES (FR/0073-8301) [01638929] **3529**

PUBLICATIONS. (MONOGRAPH SERIES) (UK/0576-9515) [01553575] **5035**

PUBLICATIONS - NATIONAL ENVIRONMENTAL RESEARCH CENTER (US) [01784000] **2180**

PUBLICATIONS - NEW MEXICO. UNIVERSITY. DIVISION OF GOVERNMENT RESEARCH (US) [04083612] **1843**

[PUBLICATIONS] / NORTHAMPTON COUNTY HISTORICAL AND GENEALOGICAL SOCIETY (US) [04214352] **2478**

PUBLICATIONS: OCCASIONAL PAPERS (US) [06854724] **1843**

PUBLICATIONS OF THE AMERICAN FOLKLIFE CENTER (US/0741-7896) [07686770] **2323**

PUBLICATIONS OF THE AMERICAN FOLKLORE SOCIETY (US) [06966645] **2323**

PUBLICATIONS OF THE ARKANSAS PHILOLOGICAL ASSOCIATION (US/0160-3124) [03655768] **3312**

PUBLICATIONS OF THE ASTRONOMICAL SOCIETY OF JAPAN (JA/0004-6264) [01518489] **398**

PUBLICATIONS OF THE ASTRONOMICAL SOCIETY OF THE PACIFIC (US/0004-6280) [01518491] **398**

PUBLICATIONS OF THE AUSTRALIAN BUREAU OF STATISTICS (AT/0312-4819) [02241855] **5336**

PUBLICATIONS OF THE BEDFORDSHIRE HISTORICAL RECORD SOCIETY (UK/0067-4826) [01519314] **2704**

PUBLICATIONS OF THE COLONIAL SOCIETY OF MASSACHUSETTS (US) [01564125] **2755**

PUBLICATIONS OF THE CONSORTIUM FOR COMPARATIVE LEGISLATIVE STUDIES *CEASED.* (US) [04434020] **3033**

PUBLICATIONS OF THE DEPARTMENT OF ASTRONOMY OF THE UNIVERSITY OF CAPE TOWN (SA) [08295715] **399**

PUBLICATIONS OF THE DUGDALE SOCIETY (UK) [01589353] **3426**

PUBLICATIONS OF THE ENGLISH GOETHE SOCIETY (UK/0959-3683) [01567951] 434, **3426**

PUBLICATIONS OF THE EUROPEAN COMMUNITIES. CATALOGUE (LU) [06796717] **1579**

PUBLICATIONS OF THE FACULTY (US/0419-8069) [01699226] **1869**

PUBLICATIONS OF THE FOOD AND RESOURCE ECONOMICS DEPARTMENT, UNIVERSITY OF FLORIDA (US/0149-4481) [03493183] **123**

PUBLICATIONS OF THE GENERAL SOCIETY OF COLONIAL WARS (US/0882-2336) [11256518] **5235**

PUBLICATIONS OF THE HARLEIAN SOCIETY. NEW SERIES, THE (UK) [I13515438] **2468**

PUBLICATIONS OF THE INSTITUTE OF GEOPHYSICS (PL/0208-8525) [05687647] **1409**

PUBLICATIONS OF THE INSTITUTE OF GEOPHYSICS. D (PL/0138-0125) [04221536] **1409**

PUBLICATIONS OF THE INSTITUTE OF GEOPHYSICS. G (PL/0208-8061) [04221548] **1409**

PUBLICATIONS OF THE INSTITUTE OF GOVERNMENT. CUMULATIVE SUPPLEMENT (US/0147-7641) [03224805] **4699**

PUBLICATIONS OF THE INSTITUTE OF HISTORY, GENERAL HISTORY, UNIVERSITY OF TURKU, FINLAND (FI) [06884886] **2626**

PUBLICATIONS OF THE INSTITUTE OF SOCIAL STUDIES. PAPERBACK SERIES (NE) [02057045] **5214**

PUBLICATIONS OF THE INTERNATIONAL BUREAU OF FISCAL DOCUMENTATION (NE/0074-2112) [01753424] **750**

PUBLICATIONS OF THE INTERNATIONAL MARITIME ORGANIZATION (UK) [18770049] 5454, **4182**

PUBLICATIONS OF THE LEANDER MCCORMICK OBSERVATORY OF THE UNIVERSITY OF VIRGINIA (US/0160-2519) [03335272] **399**

PUBLICATIONS OF THE LINCOLN RECORD SOCIETY, THE (UK/0267-2634) [01586643] **2704**

PUBLICATIONS OF THE LOUISIANA GEOLOGICAL SURVEY (US/1046-0551) [03300554] **1392**

PUBLICATIONS OF THE MATHEMATICAL SOCIETY OF JAPAN (US/0549-4540) [06345598] **3529**

PUBLICATIONS OF THE MCMASTER UNIVERSITY ASSOCIATION FOR 18TH CENTURY STUDIES (CN/0700-6896) [01775870] **2626**

PUBLICATIONS OF THE MISSOURI PHILOLOGICAL ASSOCIATION (US/0194-035X) [05282130] **3313**

PUBLICATIONS OF THE MODERN LANGUAGE ASSOCIATION OF AMERICA (US/0030-8129) [06070439] 3350, **3313**

PUBLICATIONS OF THE NATIONAL ASTRONOMICAL OBSERVATORY OF JAPAN (JA/0915-3640) [20504224] **399**

PUBLICATIONS OF THE NATIONAL GEODETIC SURVEY (US/0747-6698) [10768845] **399**

PUBLICATIONS OF THE NATIONAL INSTITUTE OF JUSTICE. SUPPLEMENT (US) [08540137] **4677**

PUBLICATIONS OF THE NATIONAL INSTITUTE OF MENTAL HEALTH (US) [06416557] **4797**

PUBLICATIONS OF THE NATIONAL RESEARCH COUNCIL OF CANADA (CN/0077-5584) [04792644] **5143**

PUBLICATIONS OF THE NEBRASKA STATE HISTORICAL SOCIETY (US/0191-037X) [04781365] **2755**

PUBLICATIONS OF THE NUTTALL ORNITHOLOGICAL CLUB (US/0550-4082) [01760950] **5619**

PUBLICATIONS OF THE PHILOLOGICAL SOCIETY (UK) [01643914] 1079, **3313**

PUBLICATIONS OF THE PIPE ROLL SOCIETY, THE (UK) [01713908] **5235**

PUBLICATIONS OF THE RAMANUJAN INSTITUTE (II) [01780334] **3529**

PUBLICATIONS OF THE RESEARCH INSTITUTE FOR MATHEMATICAL SCIENCES. SERIES A (JA/0034-5318) [07915540] **3529**

PUBLICATIONS OF THE SELDEN SOCIETY, THE (UK) [01765351] **3033**

PUBLICATIONS OF THE SETO MARINE BIOLOGICAL LABORATORY. SPECIAL PUBLICATION SERIES (JA/0389-6609) [09149724] **557**

PUBLICATIONS OF THE STATE OF ILLINOIS (US) [01752608] **4677**

PUBLICATIONS OF THE TECHNICAL UNIVERSITY FOR HEAVY INDUSTRY. SERIES B: METALLURGY (HU/0324-4679) [02841723] **4017**

PUBLICATIONS OF THE TEXAS FOLK-LORE SOCIETY (US/0082-3023) [01767350] **2324**

PUBLICATIONS OF THE THORESBY SOCIETY (UK/0082-4232) [01607698] **5235**

PUBLICATIONS OF THE UNITED STATES NAVAL OBSERVATORY (US/0083-2448) [01713904] **1433**

PUBLICATIONS OF THE UNIVERSITY OF KUOPIO. COMMUNITY HEALTH. SERIES ORIGINAL REPORTS (FI/0357-3346) [06596883] 3736, **4797**

PUBLICATIONS OF THE UNIVERSITY OF SOUTH AFRICA (SA) [03302924] **423**

PUBLICATIONS OF THE US GEOLOGICAL SURVEY. CD-ROM (US) **1359**

PUBLICATIONS OF THE WATER AND ENVIRONMENT RESEARCH INSTITUTE (FI/0783-9472) [20039721] **1417**

PUBLICATIONS OF THE WEST VIRGINIA GEOLOGICAL SURVEY (US/0360-1625) [02396747] 5538, **1392**

PUBLICATIONS ON ASIA (US) [01674605] **2662**

PUBLICATIONS ON OCEAN DEVELOPMENTAL PUBLISHING COMPANY B.V (NE) [20558607] **1455**

PUBLICATIONS ON RUSSIA AND EASTERN EUROPE (US/0079-7790) [01716151] **4492**

PUBLICATIONS PRICE LIST / ONTARIO GEOLOGICAL SURVEY AND MINERAL RESOURCES BRANCH (CN/0714-0053) [09021773] **1392**

PUBLICATIONS REPORT - NATIONAL CENTER FOR HEALTH SERVICES RESEARCH AND DEVELOPMENT (US/0098-812X) [02242105] **4811**

PUBLICATIONS RESOURCE MANUAL (SPRINGFIELD) (US/0094-2987) [01794040] **3243**

PUBLICATIONS REVIEW, INNOVATION & MANAGEMENT (UK) [09367382] **705**

PUBLICATIONS ROMANES ET FRANCAISES (SZ/0079-7812) [06976303] **3426**

PUBLICATIONS (SCOTTISH TEXT SOCIETY) (UK) [01765293] **3426**

PUBLICATIONS SERIES (JOINT CENTRE ON MODERN EAST ASIA) (CN/0713-7982) [08996135] **2662**

PUBLICATIONS - SMALL BUSINESS ADMINISTRATION (US) [03022499] **705**

PUBLICATIONS - SOCIETE DES TEXTES FRANCAIS MODERNES (FR) [05658325] **3313**

PUBLICATIONS STATISTIQUES DES ADMINISTRATIONS (FR) [02353204] **5336**

PUBLICATIONS / SURREY RECORD SOCIETY (UK) [03110246] **2468**

[PUBLICATIONS] / SUSSEX RECORD SOCIETY (UK) [01766879] **2634**

PUBLICATIONS / TECHNICAL RESEARCH CENTRE OF FINLAND (FI/0358-5069) [08756954] **5143**

PUBLICATIONS TECHNIQUES DES CHARBONNAGES DE FRANCE (FR/0766-7159) [10756288] **2149**

●PUBLICATIONS (TOPOR & ASSOCIATES) (US/1063-1771) [25909908] **1843**

PUBLICATIONS - UNIVERSITY OF CHICAGO. CENTER FOR MIDDLE EASTERN STUDIES (US/0069-3324) [01554113] **2770**

PUBLICATIONS - UNIVERSITY OF TEXAS, BUREAU OF ECONOMIC GEOLOGY (US/0082-3341) [01767333] **1392**

PUBLICATIONS UPDATE / THE WORLD BANK (US) [15667725] **804**

PUBLICATIONS - VIRGINIA MUSEUM OF FINE ARTS, RICHMOND (US) [01556042] 362, **4095**

PUBLICITAIRE (MONTREAL) *CEASED.* (CN/0229-9720) [08469751] **765**

●PUBLICITY AND MEDIA RESOURCES FOR BOOK PUBLISHERS (US/1063-1739) [25909760] **4818**

●PUBLICITY DIRECTORY FOR THE DESIGN, ENGINEERING, AND BUILDING INDUSTRIES, THE (US/1064-4733) [26294096] 307, 1992, **625**

PUBLICITY RECORD *See* MEDIA NEWS KEYS **1117**

PUBLICOTEC (SP/0377-2624) [01792324] **765**

PUBLICS (MONTREAL) (CN/1184-8782) [24368399] **765**

PUBLICUS (BASEL, SWITZERLAND) (SZ) [11387162] **4677**

PUBLIKACIJE ELEKTROTEHNICKOG FAKULTETA. SERIJA MATEMATIKA (YU/0353-8893) [24861146] **3529**

PUBLIKACIJE ELEKTROTEHNICKOG FAKULTETA. UNIVERZITET U BEOGRADU. SERIJA ELEKTROENERGETIKA (SZ/0351-4749) [02475092] **2077**

PUBLIKACIJE. SERIJA : ELEKTRONIKA, TELEKOMUNIKACIJE, AUTOMATIKA (YU/0409-0179) [03177857] 1162, **2077**

PUBLIKASJON - NORGES GEOTEKNISKE INSTITUTT (NO/0078-1193) [03832454] 1409, **1392**

PUBLIKATIE 1 / LANDBOUW-ECONOMISCH INSTITUUT, STAFAFDELING (NE) [07984601] **123**

PUBLIKATIE 2 / LANDBOUW-ECONOMISCH INSTITUUT, AFDELING STRUCTUURONDERZOEK (NE) [03270991] **123**

PUBLIKATIE - INSTITUUT VOOR BEWARING EN VERWERKING VAN LANDBOUWPRODUKTEN (NE) [04305566] **2355**

PUBLIKATIE - INSTITUUT VOOR MECHANISATIE, ARBEID EN GEBOUWEN (NE/0169-2143) [02676891] **123**

PUBLIKATIE - PROEFSTATION VOOR DE AKKERBOUW EN DE GROENTETEELT IN DER VOLLEGROND (NE) [06155590] **123**

PUBLIKATIE - PROEFSTATION VOOR DE RUNDVEEBOUDERIJ (NE) [02979036] **219**

PUBLIKATIE / PROEFSTATION VOOR DE RUNDVEEHOUDERIJ, SCHAPENHOUDERIJ EN PAARDENHOUDERIJ (NE) [10201488] **219**

PUBLIKATIE / SOCIAAL-ECONOMISCHE RAAD (NE) [10664549] **1514**

PUBLIKATIES VAN DE GEZONDHEIDSORGANISATIE T. N. O. SERIE A : ALGEMENE ONDERWERPEN (IO/0165-7259) [03918364] **3631**

PUBLIKATION / CHALMERS TEKNISKA HOGSKOLA, GOTEBORG, INSTITUTIONEN FOR VATTENFORSORJNINGS- OCH AVLOPPSTEKNIK (SW/0280-4026) [09983548] **2240**

PUBLIKATION - INSTITUT FOR SOCIAL MEDICIN, KBENHAVNS UNIVERSITET (DK/0105-4139) [02904539] **3631**

PUBLIKATION - SUNDHEDSMINISTERIET. LEVNEDSMIDDELSTYRELSEN (DK/0903-9783) [l09039783] **2355**

PUBLIKATIONEN (EIDGENOSSISCHE TECHNISCHE HOCHSCHULE ZURICH. INSTITUT FUR ORTS-, REGIONAL- UND LANDESPLANUNG) (SZ) [13044765] **5143**

PUBLIKATIONEN ZU WISSENSCHAFTLICHEN FILMEN. SEKTION BIOLOGIE (GW) [05591689] **470**

PUBLIKATIONEN ZU WISSENSCHAFTLICHEN FILMEN, SEKTION TECHNISCHE WISSENSCHAFTEN, NATURWISSENSCHAFTEN (GW/0073-8433) [02243877] **5143**

PUBLIQUE ARTE. CD-ROM (US) **381**

PUBLISH! (SAN FRANCISCO, CALIF.) (US/0897-6007) [14951562] **1263**

PUBLISHED (US/0882-7400) [11965267] **3426**

PUBLISHED BY CSD (UK/0308-0803) [02242746] **4705**

PUBLISHED SEARCH BIBLIOGRAPHIES FROM THE NTIS BIBLIOGRAPHIC DATA BASE. AGRICULTURE AND FOOD / U.S. DEPARTMENT OF COMMERCE, NATIONAL TECHNICAL INFORMATION SERVICE (US) [08434369] 123, 2355, **156**

PUBLISHED SEARCH BIBLIOGRAPHIES FROM THE NTIS BIBLIOGRAPHIC DATA BASE. BUSINESS AND MANAGEMENT / U.S. DEPARTMENT OF COMMERCE, NATIONAL TECHNICAL INFORMATION SERVICE (US) [08434572] 705, **732**

PUBLISHED SEARCH BIBLIOGRAPHIES FROM THE NTIS BIBLIOGRAPHIC DATA BASE. COMMUNICATION AND ELECTROTECHNOLOGY / U.S. DEPARTMENT OF COMMERCE, NATIONAL TECHNICAL INFORMATION SERVICE (US) [08434399] 1120, 2078, **1125**

PUBLISHED SEARCH BIBLIOGRAPHIES FROM THE NTIS BIBLIOGRAPHIC DATA BASE. ENERGY / U.S. DEPARTMENT OF COMMERCE, NATIONAL TECHNICAL INFORMATION SERVICE (US) [08434482] 1954, **1963**

PUBLISHED SEARCH BIBLIOGRAPHIES FROM THE NTIS BIBLIOGRAPHIC DATA BASE. HEALTH AND MEDICINE / U.S. DEPARTMENT OF COMMERCE, NATIONAL TECHNICAL INFORMATION SERVICE (US) [08681633] 3631, **3661**

PUBLISHED SEARCH CATALOG (US) [15174341] **5176**

PUBLISHED SEARCH MASTER CATALOG / U.S. DEPARTMENT OF COMMERCE, NATIONAL TECHNICAL INFORMATION SERVICE (US) [19927445] 5143, **1125**

PUBLISHER (HODDESDON, ENGLAND) (UK/0269-3003) [14947594] **4818**

PUBLISHER (OTTAWA) *CEASED.* (CN/0380-8025) [02125575] **4818**

PUBLISHERS' AUXILIARY (US/0048-5942) [01763123] 2923, **4818**

PUBLISHERS' CATALOGS ANNUAL *CEASED.* (US/0735-665X) [05957455] **4818**

PUBLISHERS DIRECTORY (US/0742-0501) [10259501] **4818**

PUBLISHERS, DISTRIBUTORS, & WHOLESALERS OF THE UNITED STATES (US/0000-0671) [08008367] **4822**

PUBLISHERS IDEA EXCHANGE (US/0741-5966) [10191231] **4818**

PUBLISHERS' INTERNATIONAL ISBN DIRECTORY / INTERNATIONAL ISBN AGENCY, BERLIN (GW) [20350746] **4822**

PUBLISHER'S MONTHLY (II) [01774412] **4818**

PUBLISHER'S MULTINATIONAL DIRECT (US/0887-316X) [13181040] **4818**

PUBLISHERS REPORTS (UK/0953-7899) [09537899] **4819**

PUBLISHERS' TRADE LIST ANNUAL, THE (US/0079-7855) [05759360] **4822**

PUBLISHERS WEEKLY (US/0000-0019) [02489456] **4831**

PUBLISHING & DISTRIBUTION FAX-SPEED NEWS FROM AMERICA : PDN (US/0898-7076) [17885914] **4819**

PUBLISHING & PRODUCTION EXECUTIVE (US/1048-3055) [20919440] 1263, **4819**

PUBLISHING BIBLIOGRAPHY LIBRARIES AND ARCHIVES IN RUSSIA AND EASTERN EUROPE (GW) **3259**

PUBLISHING EDUCATION NEWSLETTER (US/0190-048X) [04625759] **4819**

PUBLISHING, ENTERTAINMENT, ADVERTISING AND ALLIED FIELDS LAW QUARTERLY (US/0555-6392) [01695133] **3033**

PUBLISHING HISTORY (UK/0309-2445) [03864287] **4819**

PUBLISHING NEWS (UK) **4819**

PUBLISHING NEWS (STAMFORD, CT.) *See* FOLIO'S PUBLISHING NEWS **4815**

PUBLISHING NOTES (US/0894-282X) [15973215] **4819**

PUBLISHING RESEARCH QUARTERLY (US/0741-6148) [22684485] **4819**

●PUBLISHING TECHNOLOGY REVIEW (UK/1351-0177) **4819**

PUBLISHING TRENDS & TRENDSETTERS (US/1061-6780) [24094721] **4819**

PUBLISISTIK (NE/0555-6406) [03018521] **3313**

PUBLIUS (US/0048-5950) [01999955] **4492**

PUBLIZISTIK (GW/0033-4006) [01643660] **2923**

PUBLIZISTIK-HISTORISCHE BEITRAGE (GW) [07013714] **2626**

PUC BULLETIN (US/0896-5927) [16925890] **4762**

PUCE A L'ORIELLE (MONTREAL) *CEASED.* (CN/0824-068X) [11816226] **1776**

PUCK (CHARLEVILLE-MEZIERES) (FR/0993-0701) [21214842] **2777**

PUCK STOPS HERE!, THE (US/1063-1518) [25911152] **4913**

PUCKERBRUSH REVIEW (US/0890-3433) [10990654] **3350**

PUCL BULLETIN (II) [09251253] **4512**

PUDDING MAGAZINE (US/0196-5913) [05849718] **3470**

PUEBLO CHIEFTAIN (US) [22408216] **5644**

PUEBLOS DEL TERCER MUNDO (SP) [10111175] **2911**

PUEBLOS INDIGENAS Y EDUCACION (EC) [18000985] **1776**

PUENTE (LUND, SWEDEN) (SW) [20293079] **4545**

PUERTO AUTONOMO DE BARCELONA *See* ANUARIO DEL PUERTO AUTONOMO DE BARCELONA **5447**

PUERTO DEL SOL (US/0738-517X) [02635700] **3426**

PUERTO RICO *See* LAWS OF PUERTO RICO ANNOTATED **2997**

PUERTO RICO. BUREAU OF BANKS AND FINANCIAL INSTITUTIONS *See* COMPARATIVE FINANCIAL CONDITION OF COMMERCIAL BANKS IN PUERTO RICO **783**

PUERTO RICO. BUREAU OF EMPLOYMENT SECURITY. RESEARCH SECTION *See* MANPOWER TRAINING NEEDS, PUERTO RICO **1689**

PUERTO RICO. BUREAU OF LABOR STATISTICS *See* EMPLEO, HORAS Y SALARIOS EN LOS ESTABLECIMIENTOS MANUFACTUREROS PROMOVIDOD POR LA ADMINISTRACION DE FOMENTO ECONOMICO O LA COMPANIA DE FOMENTO INDUSTRIAL DE PUERTO RICO **1664**

PUERTO RICO. BUREAU OF LABOR STATISTICS *See* EMPLEO, HORAS Y SALARIOS EN LAS INDUSTRIAS MANUFACTURERAS DE PUERTO RICO. EMPLOYMENT, HOURS AND EARNINGS IN THE MANUFACTURING INDUSTRIES IN PUERTO RICO **1664**

PUERTO RICO BUSINESS REVIEW (US/0270-126X) [04521381] **705**

PUERTO RICO. DEPT. OF FINANCE *See* INFORME ANUAL DEL TESORERO DE PUERTO RICO **4732**

PUERTO RICO. DEPT. OF THE TREASURY *See* ECONOMY AND FINANCES, PUERTO RICO **1487**

PUERTO RICO. DEPT. OF THE TREASURY. OFFICE OF ECONOMIC AND FINANCIAL RESEARCH. REPORT ON FINANCES AND ECONOMY *See* ECONOMY AND FINANCES, PUERTO RICO **1487**

PUERTO RICO DEVELOPMENT COMPANY. ANNUAL REPORT *See* ANNUAL REPORT / PUERTO RICO INDUSTRIAL DEVELOPMENT COMPANY **891**

PUERTO RICO. DIVISION OF ORAL HEALTH *See* INFORME ANUAL; SERVICIOS ODONTOLOGICOS **1325**

PUERTO RICO ECONOMIC INDICATORS / GOVERNMENT DEVELOPMENT BANK FOR PUERTO RICO (PR) [14047970] **1579**

PUERTO RICO HEALTH SCIENCES JOURNAL (PR/0738-0658) [09424146] **3631**

PUERTO RICO INDUSTRIAL DEVELOPMENT COMPANY *See* ANNUAL REPORT / PUERTO RICO INDUSTRIAL DEVELOPMENT COMPANY **891**

PUERTO RICO. INSULAR POLICE *See* INFORME ANUAL - ESTADO LIBRE ASOCIADO DE PUERTO RICO, POLICIA DE PUERTO RICO **3166**

PUERTO

PUERTO RICO LIBRE! (US/0033-4030) [01387848] **4492**

PUERTO RICO LIVING (US/0033-4049) [06534014] **2544**

PUERTO RICO MUNICIPAL FINANCE AGENCY *See* ANNUAL REPORT AND AUDITED FINANCIAL STATEMENTS AS OF ... **4709**

PUERTO RICO. OFFICE OF COURT ADMINISTRATION *See* INFORME ANUAL DEL DIRECTOR ADMINISTRATIVO DE LOS TRIBUNALES **2982**

PUERTO RICO OFFICIAL INDUSTRIAL DIRECTORY (PR/0090-3612) [01784964] **1623, 3487**

PUERTO RICO. PLANNING BOARD *See* EXTERNAL TRADE STATISTICS (SAN JUAN) **728**

PUERTO RICO. PUBLIC SERVICE COMMISSION *See* ANNUAL REPORT OF THE PUBLIC SERVICE COMMISSION TO THE HONORABLE GOVERNOR OF PUERTO RICO **4629**

PUERTO RICO. PUBLIC SERVICE COMMISSION *See* INFORME ANUAL - ESTADO LIBRE ASOCIADO DE PUERTO RICO, COMISION DE SERVICIO PUBLICO **4656**

PUERTO RICO. SUPREME COURT *See* JURISPRUDENCIA DEL TRIBUNAL SUPREMO DE PUERTO RICO **2991**

PUERTO RICO. SUPREME COURT *See* DECISIONES DEL TRIBUNAL SUPREMO DE PUERTO RICO [COMPUTER FILE] **2959**

PUERTO RICO. SUPREME COURT *See* DECISIONES DE PUERTO RICO **2959**

PUERTO RICO TAXES (US/0735-7893) [08996703] **4743**

PUERTO RICO. UNIVERSITY. FACULTY OF HUMANITIES *See* CUADERNOS DE LA FACULTAD DE HUMANIDADES **2845**

PUERTO RICO. UNIVERSITY. SOCIAL SCIENCE RESEARCH CENTER *See* REPORT **5215**

PUERTO RICO (WASHINGTON. 1976) (US/0147-5908) [03196810] **1579**

PUERTO RICO. WATER RESOURCES AUTHORITY *See* SPECIAL REPORT - WATER RESOURCES AUTHORITY, A **5539**

PUERTOS ESPANOLES (SP) [01785051] **5454**

PUGET SOUND BUSINESS JOURNAL (US/8750-7757) [11683053] **705**

PUGET SOUND COMPUTER USER (US/0886-8174) [12999009] **1201**

PUGET SOUND UPDATE : ... ANNUAL REPORT OF THE PUGET SOUND AMBIENT MONITORING PROGRAM (US) [22257980] **2180, 5538**

PUGLIA (IT) **5805**

PUGSLEY, JOHN A *See* JOHN A. PUGSLEY'S COMMON SENSE VIEWPOINT **904**

PUHELINYRITYSTEN TILINPAATOSTILASTO (FI/0788-3080) [23012887] **1162**

PUISSANCE (BE) **5214**

PUKHAN INMYONG SAJON (KO) [10747098] **2662**

PUKPANG CHONOL (KO) [25531744] **4545**

PULA (BS/0256-2316) [04902760] **4533**

PULASKI CITIZEN (PULASKI, TENN. : 1866) (US) [12351972] **5746**

PULASKI COUNTY JOURNAL (US) [11070367] **5666**

PULASKI NEWS (US) [12654818] **5770**

PULCE (IT) **1514**

PULGWANG (KO) [11339354] **5021**

PULGYO MUNHWA (KO) [01797423] **5022**

PULGYO (SEOUL, KOREA) (KO) [10048502] **5022**

PULITZER PRIZES, THE (US/0896-2197) [16961420] **3426**

PULIZIA INDUSTRIALE E SANIFICAZIONE (IT) **2868**

PULLAENTU KONSOL SUCHUL (KO) [08053993] **625**

PULLER, THE (US/8750-4219) [03457915] **160**

PULLMAN HERALD (US) [17408151] **5762**

PULMONARY PHARMACOLOGY (EDINBURGH) (UK/0952-0600) [18785609] **3951**

PULMONARY PHARMACOLOGY SHEFFIELD (UK/0954-3333) [I09543333] **4327**

PULP & PAPER (US/0033-4081) [02480521] **4237**

PULP AND PAPER (FR/0335-377X) [02600859] **4237**

PULP & PAPER BULLETIN (US/0197-1069) [05952159] **4237**

PULP & PAPER BUYERS GUIDE (US) [06464787] **4238**

PULP & PAPER CANADA ANNUAL AND DIRECTORY (CN/0709-2563) [05863804] **4238**

PULP & PAPER CANADA GRADE DIRECTORY (CN/1181-6562) [23598189] **4238**

PULP AND PAPER CAPACITIES (IT) [03497035] **4238**

PULP & PAPER FORECASTER (US/0898-6886) [17883223] **4238**

PULP AND PAPER FOUNDATION *See* ANNUAL REPORT - PULP AND PAPER FOUNDATION (1988) **4232**

PULP & PAPER INTERNATIONAL (US/0033-409X) [01763160] **4238**

PULP & PAPER INTERNATIONAL THIS WEEK (BE) **4238**

PULP & PAPER JOURNAL (CN/0713-5807) [08199500] **4238**

PULP AND PAPER MAGAZINE *See* EUROPEAN PAPERMAKER **4233**

PULP & PAPER PROJECT REPORT (US/0748-1608) [10909431] **4238**

PULP & PAPER PROJECT REVIEW MONTHLY (FI) **4238**

PULP AND PAPER RESEARCH INSTITUTE OF CANADA *See* ANNUAL REPORT - PULP AND PAPER RESEARCH INSTITUTE OF CANADA **4232**

PULP AND PAPER RESEARCH INSTITUTE OF CANADA. REPORT *See* ANNUAL REPORT - PULP AND PAPER RESEARCH INSTITUTE OF CANADA **4232**

PULP & PAPER REVIEW (US/0161-7079) [03990383] **4238**

PULP & PAPER STATISTICS (JA) [01796428] **4238, 4240**

PULP & PAPER WEEK (US/0738-0917) [09516495] **4238**

PULP VOICES, OR, SCIENCE FICTION VOICES (US/0747-7600) [10773954] **3426**

PULPIT DIGEST (1978) (US/0160-838X) [03780269] **4988**

PULPIT RESOURCE (US/0195-1548) [04445167] **4988**

PULPWOOD AND WOOD RESIDUE STATISTICS (CN/0575-9536) [01552758] **4238, 2404**

PULPWOOD HIGHLIGHTS (US/0748-142X) [06206761] **4238**

PULPWOOD PRODUCTION IN THE LAKE STATES BY COUNTY (US) [10266427] **4238**

PULPWOOD PRODUCTION IN THE NORTH CENTRAL REGION BY COUNTY (US) [02365253] **4238**

PUL'S (RU/0236-0268) [22617090] **1068**

PULS (LONDON, ENGLAND) (UK/0143-5531) [08206780] **3426**

PULSE (1984) (US/0747-8631) [10841181] **4988**

PULSE BEATS ALCOHOL & DRUG ABUSE (US) **1348**

PULSE BUYERS GUIDE (SA) **2078**

PULSE CROP NEWS (CN/0846-3204) [25066640] **183**

PULSE (KLOOF) (SA/0256-6028) [10833663] **2078**

PULSE LONDON. 1959 (UK/0048-6000) [I00486000] **3631**

PULSE OF RADIO *See* RADIO INK **1137**

PULSE (PICO RIVERA) (US/0555-6953) [01695322] **5519**

PULSE (SALT LAKE CITY, UTAH) (US/1056-3008) [23610008] **5565**

PULSE (WHEATON, ILL. : 1984) *See* WORLD PULSE **5010**

PULSE (YANKEE GROUP) (US/0749-4920) [11092656] **1239**

PULSO DEL PERIODISMO (US/1051-8126) [22107191] **2923**

PULVERTAFT PAPERS (UK/0261-118X) [10357792] **2468**

PUMJIL KWALLI HAKHOE CHI (KO) [08557141] **4221**

PUMP & PRESS (CN/0318-9260) [02942591] **2370**

PUMPS AND COMPRESSORS (US/0276-2544) [03092501] **2127**

PUMPS AND OTHER FLUIDS MACHINERY ABSTRACTS (UK/0302-2870) [01793150] **2127**

●PUMPS AND SYSTEMS (US/1065-108X) [26508498] **2127**

PUNCH DIGEST FOR CANADIAN DOCTORS *See* STITCHES : THE JOURNAL OF MEDICAL HUMOUR **3643**

PUNCH IN INTERNATIONAL TRAVEL & ENTERTAINMENT MAGAZINE (US/1053-3842) [22521866] **5489**

PUNCH (LONDON) *CEASED.* (UK/0033-4278) [01714437] **3426**

PUNCTURE (SAN FRANCISCO, CALIF.) (US/1047-4528) [20697237] **4148**

PUNDIT (CN/0712-1318) [08655379] **3426**

PUNIME MATEMATIKE (YU/0352-5759) [I03525759] **3529**

PUNISHER (NEW YORK, N.Y. 1987), THE (US/1040-5372) [16519383] **4865**

PUNISHER WAR JOURNAL, THE (US/1044-4610) [19078575] **4865**

PUNJAB AGRICULTURAL UNIVERSITY *See* JOURNAL OF RESEARCH, PUNJAB AGRICULTURAL UNIVERSITY **100**

PUNJAB, HARYANA & DELHI CHAMBER OF COMMERCE AND INDUSTRY *See* DIRECTORY OF MEMBERS - PUNJAB HARYANA & DELHI CHAMBER OF COMMERCE AND INDUSTRY **819**

PUNJAB HORTICULTURAL JOURNAL, THE (II/0033-4324) [01588462] **2429**

PUNJAB (INDIA) *See* DETAILED ESTIMATES OF REVENUE OF THE PUNJAB GOVERNMENT FOR THE YEAR ... **4720**

PUNJAB (INDIA) *See* ANNUAL FINANCIAL STATEMENT AND EXPLANATORY MEMORANDUM ON THE BUDGET OF THE PUNJAB GOVERNMENT **4709**

PUNJAB (INDIA). FINANCE DEPT *See* NEW EXPENDITURE FOR THE YEAR **4738**

PUNJAB (INDIA). LABOUR DEPT *See* POCKET BOOK OF PUNJAB LABOUR STATISTICS **1537**

PUNJAB, INDIA (STATE). ECONOMIC AND STATISTICAL ORGANISATION *See* ECONOMICS OF AGRICULTURAL PRODUCTION AND FARM MANAGEMENT IN PUNJAB **81**

PUNJAB, INDIA (STATE). LEGISLATURE. LEGISLATIVE ASSEMBLY. PUBLIC ACCOUNTS COMMITTEE *See* REPORT ON THE APPROPRIATION ACCOUNTS OF THE GOVERNMENT OF PUNJAB AND THE REPORTS OF THE COMPTROLLER AND AUDITOR GENERAL OF INDIA **4746**

PUNJAB JOURNAL OF ENGLISH STUDIES : PJES (II) [16103068] **3313**

PUNJAB MEDICAL JOURNAL (II/0033-4340) [01607650] **3631**

PUNJAB NATIONAL BANK. DIRECTORS' REPORT AND STATEMENT OF ACCOUNTS *See* ANNUAL REPORT - PUNJAB NATIONAL BANK **772**

PUNJAB NATIONAL BANK, LTD *See* ANNUAL REPORT - PUNJAB NATIONAL BANK **772**

PUNJAB UNIVERSITY JOURNAL OF ZOOLOGY (PK/1016-1597) [17947117] **5596**

PUNSOK HWAHAK (KN/0555-781X) [08798428] **1018**

PUNTA, EN (SP) [03647992] **1120**

PUNTO (VE) [04483244] **307**

PUNTO CRITICO (MX) [03346225] **4492, 1514**

PUNTO DE VISTA (AG/0326-3061) [05305817] **2552**

PUNTO, IL (IT) **5565**

PUNTO Y HORA DE EUSKAL HERRIA (GW) [10089688] **2704**

PUNTOS (US/1040-8061) [18202466] **5214**

PUNTOS CARDINALES (US/0895-9498) [16859483] **4988**

PUPIL SERVICES (US) [04915504] **1903**

PUPIL TRANSPORTATION NEWS (US/0730-5443) [08039463] **5390**

PUPIL TRANSPORTATION STATISTICS, ILLINOIS PUBLIC SCHOOLS (US/0092-4644) [01800117] **1776, 5390, 1796**

PUPILS IN SOUTH CAROLINA SCHOOLS (US) [07547897] **1776**

PUPPET CENTRE TRUST *See* ANIMATIONS **5361**

PUPPET MASTER, THE (UK) [10757702] **4865**

PUPPETRY JOURNAL, THE (US/0033-443X) [01713940] **5367**

PUR EXECUTIVE INFORMATION SERVICE *See* PUBLIC UTILITIES REPORTS UTILITY WEEKLY **4762**

PUR EXECUTIVE INFORMATION SERVICE *See* PUR LETTER **4762**

PUR LETTER (US) **4762**

PURABHILEKH-PURATATVA : JOURNAL OF THE DIRECTORATE OF ARCHIVES, ARCHAEOLOGY AND MUSEUM, PANAJI-GOA (II) [11870629] **2662, 279**

PURANAM (II) [01696126] **3426**

PURASUCHIKKUSU (JA/0555-7887) [I05557887] **4460**

Alphabetical Title Index — QATAR

PURATATTVA (II) [01781072] **2662**

PURATATTVA NEW DELHI (II/0970-2105) [I09702105] **279**

PURBA (IO/0127-1857) [09179381] **2662**

PURCELL REGISTER, THE (US) [13764414] **5732**

PURCHASER'S GUIDE TO THE MUSIC INDUSTRIES, THE (US) [07865525] **4148**

PURCHASER'S LEGAL ADVISER (US/0898-994X) [11535450] **951**

PURCHASING (1936) (US/0033-4448) [03133058] **951**

PURCHASING & SUPPLY MANAGEMENT / INSTITUTE OF PURCHASING AND SUPPLY (UK/0309-7242) [03950363] 883, **951**

PURCHASING EXECUTIVE'S BULLETIN (US) **951**

PURCHASING JOURNAL See PROCUREMENT **951**

PURCHASING MANAGEMENT (CN/0841-615X) [19032302] **951**

PURCHASING MANAGERS REPORT ON BUSINESS (US/0270-5621) [06438477] **1623**

PURCHASING PERFORMANCE BENCHMARKS FOR THE CARBON STEEL INDUSTRY / CAPS, CENTER FOR ADVANCED PURCHASING STUDIES (US/1060-054X) [24855503] **4017**

●PURCHASING PERFORMANCE BENCHMARKS FOR THE NONFERROUS METALS INDUSTRY (US/1062-5860) [25677766] **951**

●PURCHASING PERFORMANCE BENCHMARKS FOR THE PAPER INDUSTRY (US/1061-3757) [25277459] **4238**

PURCHASING PERFORMANCE BENCHMARKS FOR THE U.S. AEROSPACE/DEFENSE CONTRACTING INDUSTRY / CAPS, CENTER FOR ADVANCED PURCHASING STUDIES (US/1058-434X) [24296651] **951**

●PURCHASING PERFORMANCE BENCHMARKS FOR THE U.S. APPLIANCE INDUSTRY (US/1062-2063) [25538324] **951**

PURCHASING PERFORMANCE BENCHMARKS FOR THE U.S. COMPUTER AND TELECOMMUNICATIONS EQUIPMENT INDUSTRY (US/1056-750X) [23835672] 1162, 1239, **951**

●PURCHASING PERFORMANCE BENCHMARKS FOR THE U.S. CONSTRUCTION/ENGINEERING INDUSTRY (US/1060-6009) [25043450] **625**

PURCHASING PERFORMANCE BENCHMARKS FOR THE U.S. FOOD MANUFACTURING INDUSTRY (US/1057-7351) [24111211] 2355, **951**

PURCHASING PERFORMANCE BENCHMARKS FOR THE U.S. TRANSPORTATION INDUSTRY / CAPS, CENTER FOR ADVANCED PURCHASING STUDIES (US/1058-1251) [24238863] **5390**

PURCHASING POINTERS See SMART BUYING **951**

PURCHASING PREFERENCE SURVEY : MATERIALS HANDLING EQUIPMENT (CN/0317-6363) [03258607] **951**

PURCHASING PREFERENCE SURVEY : OFFICE EQUIPMENT AND SUPPLIES (CN/0317-6339) [03245135] 4214, **951**

PURCHASING PREFERENCE SURVEY : TRAFFIC/TRANSPORTATION (CN/0317-6347) [03245137] 5390, **951**

PURCHASOR, NEW YORK STATE (US/0191-9237) [05013428] **951**

PURDUE ALUMNUS, THE (US/0033-4502) [04109270] **1102**

PURDUE EXPONENT, THE (US) [06638028] **5666**

PURDUE UNIVERSITY. COOPERATIVE EXTENSION SERVICE See HO **2418**

PURDUE UNIVERSITY. COOPERATIVE EXTENSION SERVICE See PUBLICATION E **5595**

PURDUE UNIVERSITY, LAFAYETTE, IND See FINANCIAL REPORT - PURDUE UNIVERSITY **1824**

PURDUE UNIVERSITY MONOGRAPHS IN ROMANCE LANGUAGES (NE/0165-8743) [08248481] 3426, **3313**

PURDUE UNIVERSITY. WATER RESOURCES RESEARCH CENTER See FISCAL YEAR PROGRAM REPORT / WATER RESOURCES RESEARCH CENTER, PURDUE UNIVERSITY **5533**

PURE AND APPLIED CHEMISTRY (UK/0033-4545) [01763191] **990**

PURE AND APPLIED GEOPHYSICS (SZ/0033-4553) [01792046] **1409**

PURE AND APPLIED MATHEMATICS (US/0079-8177) [02253630] **3529**

PURE AND APPLIED MATHEMATICS (NEW YORK. 1949) (US/0079-8169) [01763193] **3529**

PURE AND APPLIED MATHEMATIKA SCIENCES (II) [05694004] **3529**

PURE AND APPLIED OPTICS: JOURNAL OF THE EUROPEAN OPTICAL SOCIETY PART A (UK/0963-9659) **4440**

PURE AND APPLIED PHYSICS CEASED. (US/0079-8193) [02480560] **4418**

PURE BEAUTE, LA (CN/0226-9449) [08079113] **2544**

PURE-BRED DOGS, AMERICAN KENNEL GAZETTE (US/0033-4561) [01680833] **4287**

PURE CHEMICALS DAIICHI (JA/0285-192X) [I0285192X] **990**

PUREBRED PICTURE, THE (US/8750-1880) [11096791] **219**

PURETINGU TO KOTINGU (JA/0287-7414) [I02877414] **1028**

PURINTO KAIRO GAKKAI DENJI TOKUSEI KENKYU BUKAI KOKAI KENKYUKAI RONBUNSHU (JA/0917-5555) [I09175555] **2078**

PURNAMA RAYA (MY) [02240305] **2832**

PURNAWIRAWAN (JAKARTA) (IO/0303-5190) [01790697] **2662**

PURO CUENTO (BOGOTA, COLOMBIA) (CK) [09140997] **1028**

PURPA LINES (US/0886-7178) [12930959] 4762, **1954**

PURPA LINES See POWER SOURCE **1953**

PURPAN (FR/0395-8655) [I03958655] **123**

PURPOSE AND METHODS IN FISHERIES STATISTICS : DOCUMENT (IO/0426-7680) [01215862] 2311, **2317**

PURRRRR! (US/0731-0366) [08098014] **4287**

PURSUIT (COLUMBIA) SUSPENDED. (US/0033-4685) [01763197] 5143, **4243**

PURSUITS (US/1047-3912) [20707009] **434**

PURTI RESEARCH SUMMARIES (US/1047-8272) [20808089] **4762**

PURVADESH (UK/0144-946X) [07821041] **2662**

PUSAN SUSAN TAEHAK YON'GU POGO (KO) [05184049] **5143**

PUSAT DOKUMENTASI ILMIAH NASIONAL See DAFTAR TAMBAHAN KOLEKSI MIKROFIS **2650**

PUSAT DOKUMENTASI ILMIAH NASIONAL See LAPORAN TAHUNAN PUSAT DOKUMENTASI ILMIAH NASIONAL **396**

PUSAT DOKUMENTASI ILMIAH NASIONAL (INDONESIA) See ANNUAL REPORT - INDONESIAN NATIONAL SCIENTIFIC DOCUMENTATION CENTER **5084**

PUSAT METEOROLOGI DAN GEOFISIKA See CLIMATOLOGICAL DATA FOR JAKARTA OBSERVATORY **1422**

PUSAT METEOROLOGI DAN GEOFISIKA. DATA-DATA IKLIM DI INDONESIA See DATA-DATA IKLIM DI INDONESIA **1425**

PUSAT PENELITIAN ATMA JAYA See ANNUAL REPORT / PUSAT PENELITIAN UNIVERSITAS KATOLIK INDONESIA ATMA JAYA **1725**

PUSAT PENELITIAN ATMA JAYA See REPORT ON THE CENTRE'S ACTIVITIES - PUSAT PENELITIAN ATMA JAYA **1581**

PUSAT PENELITIAN ATMA JAYA See PROFIL MAHASISWA UNIVERSITAS KATOLIK INDONESIA ATMA JAYA **1842**

PUSAT PENELITIAN DAN PENGEMBANGAN GEOLOGI See LAPORAN TAHUNAN PUSAT PENELITIAN DAN PENGEMBANGAN GEOLOGI **1386**

PUSAT RISET DIRGANTARA (INDONESIA) See BERITA PUSAT RISET DIRGANTARA, LAPAN **14**

PUSH! (NEW YORK, N.Y.) (US/1054-3686) [22865005] **382**

PUSH, THE SUSPENDED. (AT) [21366718] **2671**

PUSHCART PRIZE, THE (US/0149-7863) [02743381] **3426**

PUSPANIAGA (MY) [02840995] **1579**

PUT I SAOBRACAJ (KO) [06635473] **2029**

PUT ON THE BRAKES! BULLETIN / OSAP (US) [25843363] **1843**

PUTEOLI, STUDI DI STORIA ANTICA (IT) [05699428] **2704**

PUTESHESTVIE V SSSR (RU) **5489**

PUTI POVYSHENIIA UROZHAINOSTI POLEVYKH KULTUR / BELOUSSKII NAUCHNO-ISSLEDOVATELSKII INSTITUT ZEMLEDELIIA (RU) [10038099] **183**

PUTNAM COUNTY COURIER (CARMEL, N.Y. : 1852) (US/0890-1147) [09988383] **5646**

PUTNAM COUNTY SENTINEL (OTTAWA, OHIO : 1865) (US) [11696438] **5730**

PUTNAM COUNTY VIDETTE (US) [16897447] **5730**

●PUTNAM COURIER-TRADER, THE (US) [28388800] **5646**

PUTNAM DEMOCRAT (WINFIELD, W. VA.) (US) [14903027] **5764**

PUTNAM TRADER (CARMEL, N.Y.) See PUTNAM COURIER-TRADER, THE **5646**

PUTTING OUT : A PUBLISHING RESOURCE GUIDE FOR LESBIAN & GAY WRITERS (US/1054-6804) [22937277] 2796, 2923, **3426**

PUXICO PRESS (US) [20175707] **5704**

●PUZZLER (MINNETONKA, MINN.), THE (US/1062-1164) [25527394] **4865**

PV NEWS (US/0739-4829) [09743360] **1954**

PVP - AMERICAN SOCIETY OF MECHANICAL ENGINEERS. PRESSURE VESSELS AND PIPING DIVISION (US/0277-027X) [07483260] **2127**

PW PERSONEELSMANAGEMENT (NE) **705**

PWA COALITION NEWSLINE See PWA NEWSLINE **3715**

PWA NEWSLINE (US/1069-3637) [29751155] **3715**

PWACONTACT (CN/0822-4706) [20366899] **1928**

PXE AWARENESS (US/1044-5854) [19836347] **3631**

PYM NEWS: A PUBLICATION OF THE RELIGIOUS SOCIETY OF FRIENDS (US/1055-839X) [23353142] **4988**

PYNCHON NOTES (US/0278-1891) [07317180] **3426**

PYOLGON'GON (KO) [05059512] **2508**

PYONGHWA TONGIL YOMWON (KO) [11180251] **2662**

PYONJIBIN HYOPHOE PO (KO) [09273393] **2923**

●PYRAMID (BURKE, VA.) (US/1065-3619) [26593500] **804**

PYRAMID (MOUNT PLEASANT, UTAH) (US) [12680634] **5757**

PYRENAE (SP/0079-8215) [01429781] **279**

PYRENEES LOURDES. 1950 (FR/0033-474X) [I0033474X] **2574**

PYRETHRUM POST (KE/0048-6043) [01763201] 990, **470**

PYROTECHNICA (US/0272-6521) [06895641] **1028**

PYTHIAN INTERNATIONAL (US/0199-0144) [05515184] **5235**

PYTTERSEN'S NEDERLANDSE ALMANAK (NE) [06657807] **2521**

PZ WISSENSCHAFT : PHARMAZEUTISCHE ZEITUNG, WISSENSCHAFTSAUSGABE (GW/0935-5901) [25200031] **4327**

Q.A.G.T. NEWSLETTER (CN/0822-6911) [10451550] **2574**

Q.A.S.A. BULLETIN (CN/0316-4888) [02247337] **1869**

Q-DEX (LISLE, ILL.) (US/1071-2623) [28601425] **3033**

Q (LONDON) (UK/0955-4955) [21893115] **4148**

Q-PRAXIS (GW/0947-0077) **1623**

Q-PROBES ANATOMIC PATHOLOGY MODULE. 3 Q-PROBES (US) **3897**

Q-PROBES CLINICAL PATHOLOGY MODULE. 6 Q-PROBES (US) **3897**

Q.T.C. TODAY (CN/0828-5780) [11895355] **4989**

Q T DIRECTORY (IT) **5489**

QA REVIEW CEASED. (US/1047-4773) [20505294] **4797**

QADAYA AL-ASR (YE) [12115991] **2662**

QADAYA ARABIYAH (LE) [01797940] **2770**

QADMONIOT (IS/0033-4839) [03062695] **279**

QAFILAT AL-ZAYT (SU) [05248412] **2770**

QAIMAT AL-INTAJ AL-FIKRI AL-QATARI LI-AM / DAWLAT QATAR, WIZARAT AL-TARBIYAH WA-AL-TALIM, DAR AL-KUTUB AL-QATARIYAH (KO) [09710810] **423**

QATAR : ENERGIEWIRTSCHAFT (GW) [06528320] **1954**

QATAR. PROTOCOL DEPT See LIST OF DIPLOMATIC CORPS - QATAR. PROTOCOL DEPT **3132**

QATAR UNIVERSITY SCIENCE BULLETIN (QA/0255-6677) [10462652] **5143**

QATAR

QATAR: WIRTSCHAFTLICHE ENTWICKLUNG (GW) [05699807] **1579**

QATAR : WIRTSCHAFTSDATEN UND WIRTSCHAFTSDOKUMENTATION (QA) [05955419] **1579**

QATAR YEAR BOOK *See* YEAR BOOK (QATAR. WIZARAT AL-ILAM) **2668**

QAUMI AVAZ (IS) [08849449] **2508**

QAUMI RAJ (SI) [02240242] **3426**

QAZAQ SSR GHYLYM AKADEMIIASYNYNG KHABARLARY (KZ/0002-3175) [09534220] **1392**

QC (FOREST HILLS, N.Y.) (US/0276-7120) [07414500] **2544**

QCPE BULLETIN (US/0889-7514) [07963600] **1057**

QDP REPORTS (US/0730-6377) [08030785] **705**

QED STATE-BY-STATE SCHOOL GUIDE. NEW YORK (US) [23742798] **1776**

QED STATE-BY-STATE SCHOOL GUIDE [MASSACHUSETTS] (US/1062-1342) [23258655] **1776**

QEDEM MONOGRAPHS OF THE INSTITUTE OF ARCHAEOLOGY (IS) [06406115] **279**

QI (FAIRFAX, VA.) (US/1056-4004) [23712614] **2601**

QI/TQM (US) **3631**

QIGONG (SAN FRANCISCO, CALIF.) (US/1050-2173) [21424940] **4913**

QIGONG YU KEXUE (CC/1000-0895) [11434342] **2601**

QINGBAO KEXUE (CC/1000-8489) [07254259] **3243**

QINGHUA XUEBAO (CH/0577-9170) [01554381] **2770**

QIRAAT SIYASIYAH (US/1061-5636) [25276435] **4492**

QIT ACCOUNTING RESEARCH JOURNAL (AT) **750**

QIYYUM (II/0303-139X) [01790779] **2180**

● QJM : MONTHLY JOURNAL OF THE ASSOCIATION OF PHYSICIANS (UK) [30841057] **3631**

QRB. QUALITY REVIEW BULLETIN (US/0097-5990) [01297544] **3791**

QRC ADVISOR (US/0747-7384) [10790673] **3791**

● QRM (WASHINGTON, D.C.) (US/1060-8931) [25100934] **4148**

QRQ (IS/0302-6248) [01784365] **4843**

QRZ DX (US/0744-8554) [08602223] **1162**

QST (US/0033-4812) [01623841] **1136**

QST CANADA *CEASED.* (CN/0840-6170) [19491024] **1992**

QTGO. QUADERNI DI TECNICA E GESTIONE OSPEDALIERA *CEASED.* (IT/1120-7906) [I11207906] **3791**

QUAD CITY DAILY REPORTER *See* QUAD CITY REPORTER, THE **705**

QUAD-CITY HERALD (US) [17319763] **5762**

● QUAD CITY REPORTER, THE (US/1064-2986) [25130141] **705**

QUAD-CITY TIMES (US) [08811373] **5672**

QUAD COMMUNITY PRESS (US/0892-1806) [15144197] **5698**

QUAD (PAISLEY) (CN/0706-8808) [04448749] **4054**

● QUAD REPORT, THE (US/1072-3129) [28902874] **2202**

QUADERN CAPS (SP/0213-4462) [I02134462] **3632**

Alphabetical Title Index

QUADERNI ANALITICI / ISTITUTO NAZIONALE PER LO STUDIO DELLA CONGIUNTURA (IT) [28471574] **2491**

QUADERNI BIANCHI *CEASED.* (IT) [07567911] **4677**

QUADERNI CALABRESI : QUADERNI DEL MEZZOGIORNO E DELLE ISOLE (IT) **2521**

QUADERNI / CENTRO DI RICERCHE INFORMATICHE PER I BENI CULTURALI (IT) [26002420] **2483**, **3243**

QUADERNI CERIS (IT) **5143**

QUADERNI COSTITUZIONALI (IT) [08899321] **3093**

QUADERNI CRITICI DE L'ALBERO (IT) [08781456] **3350**

QUADERNI D'ARCHEOLOGIA REGGIANA / SOCIETA REGGIANA D'ARCHEOLOGIA (IT) [11620120] **279**

QUADERNI DEI DIALOGHI DI ARCHEOLOGIA (IT) [17670974] **279**

QUADERNI DEL CENTRO FAMIGLIA (IT) **2285**

QUADERNI DEL CIRCOLO ROSSELLI (IT) [11446080] **2704**

QUADERNI DEL DIPARTIMENTO DI LINGUE E LETTERATURE STRANIERE MODERNE (IT) [23099326] 3313, **3426**

QUADERNI DEL DIRITTO DEL LAVORO (IT) **3033**

QUADERNI DEL MUSEO DI STORIA NATURALE DI LIVORNO (1982) (IT) [10222414] **4171**

QUADERNI DELL ISTITUTO DI STORIA DELL ARTE MEDIEVALE E MODERNA, FACOLTA DI LETTERE E FILOSOFIA, UNIVERSITA DI MESSINA (IT/0391-3813) [04261553] **362**

QUADERNI DELLA BASSA MODENESE / GRUPPO STUDI BASSA MODENESE (IT) [20288282] **3350**

QUADERNI DELLA BRIANZA, I (IT) [06985620] **2704**

QUADERNI DELLA CIVICA STAZIONE IDROBIOLOGICA DI MILANO (IT) [01798090] **471**

QUADERNI DELLA FONDAZIONE S. CARLO (IT) [18279925] **4989**

QUADERNI DELLA NUTRIZIONE (IT/0033-488X) [01763203] **4198**

QUADERNI DELLA RASSEGNA DEGLI ARCHIVI DI STATO (IT/0579-1316) [02720626] **2483**

QUADERNI DELLA RIVISTA DI POLITICA AGRARIA (IT) [05325063] **123**

QUADERNI DELLA RIVISTA ITALIANA DI MUSICOLOGIA / A CURA DELLA SOCIETA ITALIANA DI MUSICOLOGIA (IT/0394-4395) [09494632] **4148**

QUADERNI DELL'ACCADEMIA CHIGIANA (IT/0065-0714) [05806602] **4148**

QUADERNI DELL'ARCHIVIO DIOCESANO DI MOLFETTA-RUVO-GIOVINAZZO TERLIZZI (IT) [19651227] **4989**

QUADERNI DELL'ISTITUTO DI ARCHEOLOGIA E STORIA ANTICA / LIBERA UNIVERSITA ABRUZZESE DEGLI STUDI "G. D'ANNUNZIO", CHIETI (IT/0393-6821) [08863428] 2704, **279**

QUADERNI DELL'ISTITUTO DI STORIA DELL'ARCHITETTURA (IT/0485-4152) [01931129] **307**

QUADERNI DELL'UNIONE MATEMATICA ITALIANA (IT) [05958254] **3529**

QUADERNI DI AGRONOMIA (IT) [05386944] **123**

QUADERNI DI ARCHEOLOGIA DELLA LIBIA (IT/0079-8258) [02807400] 362, **279**

QUADERNI DI AZIONE SOCIALE (IT/0033-4901) [05912808] **1704**

QUADERNI DI BRERA (MILANO, 1974-) (IT) [02801215] **362**

QUADERNI DI CINEMA (IT/0393-8379) [09451962] **4076**

QUADERNI DI CLINICA OSTETRICA E GINECOLOGICA (IT/0033-491X) [09585530] **3767**

QUADERNI DI COMUNICAZIONE AUDIOVISIVA E NUOVE TECNOLOGIE *See* MULTIMEDIA **1117**

QUADERNI DI CONTRACCEZIONE, FERTILITA, SESSUALITA (IT/0391-9935) [05904846] **5188**

QUADERNI DI CULTURA FRANCESE (IT/0481-097X) [01432524] **5254**

QUADERNI DI CURE PALLIATIVE (IT) **3632**

QUADERNI DI DIRITTO DEL LAVORO E RELAZIONI INDUSTRIALI (IT) **3033**

QUADERNI DI DIRITTO E POLITICA ECCLESIASTICA (IT) [15722536] **4989**

QUADERNI DI DIRITTO URBANISTICO (IT) **2832**

QUADERNI DI DOCUMENTAZIONE DELLA CINETECA NAZIONALE (IT) [08454928] **4076**

QUADERNI DI ECONOMIA DEL LAVORO (IT/0390-105X) [I0390105X] **1704**

QUADERNI DI FILOLOGIA GERMANICA DELLA FACOLTA DI LETTERE E FILOSOFIA DELL'UNIVERSITA DI BOLOGNA (IT) [07344941] **3313**

QUADERNI DI INFORMATICA *CEASED.* (IT) **1201**

QUADERNI DI LETTERATURE IBERICHE E IBEROAMERICANE (IT) [12294373] **3426**

QUADERNI DI LINGUE E LETTERATURE STRANIERE / UNIVERSITA DEGLI STUDI DI PALERMO, FACOLTA DI MAGISTERO, ISTITUTO DI LINGUE E LETTERATURE STRANIERE (IT) [10092748] **3313**

QUADERNI DI LINGUE E LETTERATURE / UNIVERSIT·A DEGLI STUDI DI PADOVA, FACOLTA DI ECONOMIA E COMMERCIO, ISTITUTO DI LINGUE E LETTERATURE STRANIERE DI VERONA (IT) [07499899] 3313, **3426**

QUADERNI DI MEDICINA E CHIRURGIA : QMC (IT/0393-5930) [18526362] **3973**

QUADERNI DI NEUROPATOLOGIA (IT) **3844**

QUADERNI DI OCCIDENTALE (IT) [19338882] **2626**

QUADERNI DI PALAZZO VENEZIA (IT) [09075085] **362**

QUADERNI DI PSICOTERAPIA INFANTILE (IT) **3911**

QUADERNI DI RADIOLOGIA (IT/0048-6086) [01778223] **3944**

QUADERNI DI RICERCA E DOCUMENTAZIONE (IT) **1514**

QUADERNI DI RICERCA (SOCIETA AGRICOLA E FORESTALE) (IT) [15147070] **2391**

QUADERNI DI SANITA PUBBLICA (IT/0393-9529) [I03939529] **4797**

QUADERNI DI SCHEDE UMANISTICHE (IT) [27552991] 3313, **3426**

QUADERNI DI SCIENZA POLITICA (IT) **4492**

QUADERNI DI SCIENZE ANTROPOLOGICHE (IT/0393-1099) [I03931099] **243**

QUADERNI DI SEMANTICA (IT/0393-1226) [07703290] **3313**

QUADERNI DI SOCIOLOGIA (IT/0033-4952) [01320626] **5254**

QUADERNI DI STORIA (IT) [03464043] 1079, **2626**

QUADERNI DI STORIA ANTICA E DI EPIGRAFIA (IT) [04101536] **2626**

QUADERNI DI STORIA DELL'ECONOMIA POLITICA *CEASED.* (IT) [12074998] **4492**

QUADERNI DI STORIA URBANA E RURALE (IT) [19377904] **2626**

QUADERNI DI STUDI ARABI (IT) [18140061] **2662**

QUADERNI DI TERZO MONDO (IT/0391-7312) [I03917312] **4492**

QUADERNI DI URBANISTICA E INFORMAZIONI (IT/0394-0926) [25175025] **2832**

QUADERNI D'ITALIANISTICA (CN/0226-8043) [06688379] **3426**

QUADERNI EMILIANI (IT/1120-9232) [06826441] **2832**

QUADERNI EUROPEI (IT) **3350**

QUADERNI FIORENTINI (IT/0392-1867) [I03921867] **3350**

QUADERNI FIORENTINI PER LA STORIA DEL PENSIERO GIURIDICO MODERNO (IT) [01791676] **3033**

QUADERNI / FONDAZIONE GIANGIACOMO FELTRINELLI (IT) [09355060] **5214**

QUADERNI GIURIDICI DELL IMPRESA *CEASED.* (IT) **883**

QUADERNI IBERO-AMERICANI (IT/0033-4960) [01198564] **3350**

QUADERNI INTERNAZIONALI DI STORIA DELLA MEDICINA E DELLA SANITA (IT) [28551925] **5143**

QUADERNI ISRIL (IT) **1705**

QUADERNI - ISTITUTO DI RICERCA SULLE ACQUE (IT/0390-6329) [05130615] **5538**

QUADERNI ITALIANI DI PSICHIATRIA (IT) [13805251] **3935**

QUADERNI MARCHIGIANI DI MEDICINA *SUSPENDED.* (IT/0392-9620) [19261988] **3632**

QUADERNI MEDIEVALI (IT) [03792886] **2704**

QUADERNI MONOTEMATICI DI DIRITTO TRIBUTARIO (IT) **3033**

QUADERNI PATAVINI DI LINGUISTICA (IT/0393-24865) [08256647] **3313**

QUADERNI PER LA SCUOLA CATTOLICA (IT) [24203029] **5035**

QUADERNI PER LA STORIA DELL'UNIVERSITA DI PADOVA (IT/0078-7760) [05108955] **1843**

QUADERNI PER LA STORIA DI CASTELBOLOGNESE (IT) [18251742] **2626**

QUADERNI PIGNONE (IT/0393-3245) [02266670] **2108**

QUADERNI SARDI (IT) [19946447] **2626**

QUADERNI SARDI DI ECONOMIA (IT/0391-8394) [08608926] **1579**

QUADERNI SARDI DI ECONOMIA PODPORUJICI JEDMPTA STATU TEXAS (US/0745-8800) [08608721] **2755**

QUADERNI SICILIANI (IT) [02243200] **2704**

QUADERNI STORICI (IT/0301-6307) [04356418] **2704**

QUADERNI URBINATI DI CULTURA CLASSICA (IT/0033-4987) [02807459] **1079**

QUADERNI UTINENSI (IT/0392-873X) [13706597] 2704, **3427**

QUADERNI VENETI (IT/0394-2694) [13551440] **3427**

QUADERNI VIVALDIANI (IT) [07113105] **4148**

QUADERNO (IT) [05377899] **307**

QUADERNO MONTESSORI (IT) **1884**

QUADERNS D'ALLIBERAMENT (SP/0210-7554) [10093069] 5214, **4493**

QUADERNS D'ARQUEOLOGIA I HISTORIA DE LA CIUTAT / AJUNTAMENT DE BARCELONA, MUSEU D'HISTORIA DE LA CIUTAT, SEMINARI D'INVESTIGACIO "A. DURAN I SANPERE." (SP/0211-478X) [17789389] 2704, **279**

QUADERNS D'ARQUITECTURA I URBANISME (SP/0211-9595) [08272678] **307**

QUADERNS D'ARQUITECTURA I URBANISME (SP) [08300216] 2832, **307**

QUADERNS D'ARQUITECTURA I URBANISME. EXTRA (SP) [08300169] 2832, **307**

QUADERNS DE L'INSTITUT CATALA D'ANTROPOLOGIA (SP/0211-5557) [15530441] **243**

QUADERNS D'HISTORIA TARRACONENSE (SP) [06992859] **2704**

QUADRANGLE (NEW YORK, N.Y.) (JS) [12604248] **1094**

QUADRANGLE REPORT (US/0589-3720) [01375210] **1392**

QUADRANT (AT/0033-5002) [01433031] **2511**

QUADRANT (NEW YORK) *SUSPENDED.* (US/0033-5010) [03422017] **4614**

QUADRANTE (IT) [06662000] **4054**

QUADRENNIAL REPORT TO THE PRESIDENT ON THE ADEQUACY OF SPECIAL PAY FOR PHYSICIANS AND DENTISTS IN THE DEPARTMENT OF VETERANS AFFAIRS (US) [20697097] 1333, **3916**

QUADRENNIAL REVIEW OF MILITARY COMPENSATION (US/0882-6935) [11004934] **4054**

QUADRIMESTRE *CEASED.* (IT) [18567841] **3091**

QUADROS DE DETALHAMENTO DAS DESPESAS / GOVERNO DO ESTADO DO RIO DE JANEIRO (BL) [24987434] **4743**

QUAERE (MINNEAPOLIS) (US/0362-3564) [01716677] **3033**

QUAERENDO (NE/0014-9527) [01643642] **4831**

QUAESTIONES DISPUTATAE (GW/0481-1216) [01447508] **4989**

QUAESTIONES MATHEMATICAE : JOURNAL OF THE SOUTH AFRICAN MATHEMATICAL SOCIETY : TYDSKRIF VAN DIE SUID-AFRIKAANSE WISKUNDEVERENIGING (SA/0379-9468) [03956764] **3529**

QUAESTIONSA OECONOMICAE (GW) [01763209] **1514**

QUAI VOLTAIRE, REVUE LITTERAIRE (FR) [23979852] **3427**

QUAIL UNLIMITED MAGAZINE (US/0746-2638) [09898326] **5619**

●QUAKE (NEW YORK, N.Y.) (US/1070-969X) [28521860] **1068**

QUAKER COMMITTEE ON JAILS & JUSTICE (1981) (CN/0824-6521) [11100284] **3174**

QUAKER CONCERN (CN/0229-1916) [07869985] 2271, 4512, **5066**

QUAKER HISTORY (US/0033-5053) [01776671] 2755, **4989**

QUAKER LIFE (US/0033-5061) [01643814] **4989**

QUAKER : MONATSHEFTE DER DEUTSCHEN FREUNDE, DER (GW) [07147991] **4989**

QUAKER MONTHLY (UK/0033-507X) [02282431] **4989**

QUAKER QUERIES (US/0899-1332) [15213873] **2468**

QUAKER RELIGIOUS THOUGHT (US/0033-5088) [01640075] **5066**

QUAKER SERVICE BULLETIN / AMERICAN FRIENDS SERVICE COMMITTEE (US/0033-510X) [01780326] **5254**

QUAKER YEOMEN, THE (US/0737-8246) [09460929] **2468**

QUALE IMPRESA (IT/0391-6146) [I03916146] **1514**

QUALESOCIETA (IT) [02242721] **2521**

QUALIFICATION STANDARDS FOR WHITE COLLAR POSITIONS UNDER THE GENERAL SCHEDULE (US) [02784961] **4677**

QUALIFIED PLAN UPDATE (US/1062-7480) [25724571] **912**

QUALIFIED REMODELER (US/0098-9207) [02242569] **625**

QUALIS (US/0735-6854) [08963886] **4819**

QUALITA (IT) [29643050] **849**

QUALITA PARIS (FR/1163-2283) [I11632283] **2852**

QUALITATIVE HEALTH RESEARCH (US/1049-7323) [21286673] **4797**

QUALITATIVE RESEARCH METHODS (US/0888-5397) [13651718] **5214**

QUALITATIVE SOCIOLOGY (US/0162-0436) [03764203] **5254**

QUALITE (DOLLARD-DES-ORMEAUX) (CN/0226-3432) [06757663] **883**

QUALITE EN MOUVEMENT PARIS LA DEFENSE (FR/1162-1982) [I11621982] **4032**

QUALITE SANTE PARIS *SUSPENDED.* (FR/0997-9638) [I09979638] **3632**

QUALITE TOTALE (CN) **883**

QUALITIQUE PARIS (FR/0767-9432) [I07679432] **2852**

QUALITY ABSTRACTS (US/1071-1945) [28566669] **883**

QUALITY & PRODUCTIVITY IMPROVEMENT NEWSLETTER, THE *SUSPENDED.* (US/0884-4038) [12365945] **1623**

QUALITY AND PRODUCTIVITY MANAGEMENT (US/0895-2272) [16517594] **883**

●QUALITY & PRODUCTIVITY ONE HUNDRED NEWSLETTER (US/1062-9440) [25813377] 1623, **705**

QUALITY AND PRODUCTIVITY PLUS (US/1042-072X) [18929025] **706**

QUALITY & QUANTITY (NE/0033-5177) [01643815] 5227, **3529**

QUALITY AND RELIABILITY (US) [19400654] **1992**

QUALITY AND RELIABILITY ASSURANCE (US/0147-4995) [03180682] **883**

QUALITY AND RELIABILITY ENGINEERING INTERNATIONAL (UK/0748-8017) [11011245] **1992**

QUALITY ASSURANCE ABSTRACTS *CEASED.* (UK/0269-297X) [I0269297X] **5303**

QUALITY ASSURANCE AND UTILIZATION REVIEW *See* AMERICAN JOURNAL OF MEDICAL QUALITY **3776**

QUALITY ASSURANCE AND UTILIZATION REVIEW : OFFICIAL JOURNAL OF THE AMERICAN COLLEGE OF UTILIZATION REVIEW PHYSICIANS (US/0885-713X) [12715265] **3632**

QUALITY ASSURANCE BULLETIN (US/1040-0664) [18305814] **883**

QUALITY ASSURANCE IN EDUCATION (UK/0968-4883) **1869**

QUALITY ASSURANCE IN HEALTH CARE (UK/1040-6166) [18471458] **4797**

QUALITY ASSURANCE IN HEALTH CARE *See* INTERNATIONAL JOURNAL FOR QUALITY IN HEALTH CARE : JOURNAL OF THE INTERNATIONAL SOCIETY FOR QUALITY IN HEALTH CARE **3588**

QUALITY ASSURANCE (SAN DIEGO, CALIF.) (US/1052-9411) [22415381] **5143**

QUALITY AUSTRALIA (AT/0813-0272) [I08130272] **883**

QUALITY BANNER POSTER (US) **706**

QUALITY BRIEFING (US/1059-3918) [24581982] 884, **1623**

QUALITY BRIEFING *See* CONFERENCE BOARD'S MEMBERSHIP UPDATE, THE **864**

QUALITY BY DESIGN (US/0893-360X) [15514568] **625**

QUALITY CARE ADVOCATE (US/0892-6174) [14372550] **5303**

QUALITY CITIES (US/0892-4171) [15188519] **4677**

QUALITY CONTROL AND APPLIED STATISTICS (US/0033-5207) [01696635] 5143, **5176**

QUALITY CONTROL AND APPLIED STATISTICS YEARBOOK (US/0480-9068) [01714498] **1992**

QUALITY CONTROL AND RELIABILITY *See* QUALITY AND RELIABILITY ASSURANCE **883**

QUALITY CONTROL REPORTS (US/0163-2418) [01715286] 4327, **3487**

QUALITY CONTROL SCANNER, THE (US/0739-6732) [09796231] **4569**

QUALITY CONTROL : STATES' CORRECTIVE ACTION ACTIVITIES (US/0361-2643) [02246164] **5303**

QUALITY CRAFTS MARKET, THE (US/0277-349X) [04709379] **375**

QUALITY CROSSWORD PUZZLES (US/0480-676X) [05529945] **4865**

QUALITY DIGEST (US/1049-8699) [17469778] 946, **1705**

QUALITY ENGINEERING (US/0898-2112) [17743171] **1992**

QUALITY EXECUTIVE, THE (US/1044-0941) [19683181] **884**

QUALITY FORUM (LONDON) (UK/0959-3268) [21548884] **4032**

QUALITY HEALTHCARE & OUTCOMES (US/1058-6415) [24345611] **3632**

●QUALITY IN HEALTH CARE : QHC (UK/0963-8172) [26501582] **3632**

QUALITY IN HEALTHCARE MANAGEMENT (US) 4797, **3632**

QUALITY IN PRACTICE : A BULLETIN FROM THE ROYAL COLLEGE OF GENERAL PRACTITIONERS (UK) [12184777] **3739**

QUALITY INTELLIGENCE INTERNATIONAL (UK) **1201**

QUALITY LETTER FOR HEALTHCARE LEADERS, THE (US/1047-5311) [20719200] **3791**

QUALITY LIVING *CEASED.* (US/0892-1415) [15096390] **2491**

●QUALITY MANAGEMENT IN HEALTH CARE (US/1063-8628) [26178154] 3791, **884**

●QUALITY MANAGEMENT JOURNAL, THE (US/1068-6967) [27758215] **946**

QUALITY MANAGEMENT UPDATE (US) 3792, **3632**

QUALITY OBSERVER, THE (US/1057-9583) [24171283] **884**

●QUALITY OF LIFE (US/1064-7988) [26394021] **3867**

●QUALITY OF LIFE RESEARCH (UK/0962-9343) [26585855] **4392**

QUALITY OF MARKETS MONTHLY FACT SHEET (UK) [24099721] **1514**

QUALITY OF MARKETS QUARTERLY (UK/0953-3133) [17249217] **912**

QUALITY OF MARKETS QUARTERLY REVIEW (UK) [26595127] **804**

QUALITY OUTCOMES DRIVEN EDUCATION (US) **1776**

QUALITY POSTINGS (US) **706**

QUALITY PROGRESS (US/0033-524X) [01587356] 3487, **1993**

QUALITY PUBLICATION (US/0464-8005) [01640272] **2355**

QUALITY QUIPS (US/1058-0417) [24185933] **884**

QUALITY RESOURCE MONITOR *CEASED.* (US/1040-0079) [17588566] **3632**

QUALITY ROCK READER (US/0360-4071) [02244544] **4148**

●QUALITY SERVICE UPDATE (US/1063-2654) [25958200] **884**

QUALITY TECHNOLOGY HANDBOOK (UK/0266-3104) [06109690] **5143**

QUALITY TRAVEL (IT) **5489**

QUALITY WHEAT FROM THE PACIFIC NORTHWEST--USA (US) [05161549] **183**

QUALITY (WHEATON) (US/0360-9936) [02245118] **884**

●QUALITY WORLD. TECHNICAL SUPPLEMENT (UK) [30456928] **4032**

QUANAH TRIBUNE-CHIEF (US) [14266797] **5753**

QUAND DIEU PARLE AUX HOMMES (FR/0292-5451) [I02925451] **4989**

QUANTA (PITTSBURGH, PA.) (US/1053-8496) [22652866] **3427**

QUANTITATIVE APPLICATIONS IN THE SOCIAL SCIENCES (US/0149-192X) [03573686] **5214**

QUANTITATIVE AUSWERTUNG VON DUNNSCHICHT CHROMATOGRAMMEN *CEASED.* (GW) **5143**

QUANTITATIVE EVALUATION OF CALIFORNIA VOCATIONAL EDUCATION PROGRAMS, A (US) [08325066] **1915**

QUANTITATIVE LINGUISTICS (GW/0179-3616) [05856470] 3530, **3313**

QUANTITATIVE STRUCTURE-ACTIVITY RELATIONSHIPS (GW/0931-8771) [14268674] 990, **4327**

QUANTUM (US) [25879422] **3427**

QUANTUM AND SEMICLASSICAL OPTICS: JOURNAL OF THE EUROPEAN OPTICAL SOCIETY - B (UK) **4418**

●QUANTUM ELECTRONICS (NEW YORK, N.Y. 1993) (US/1063-7818) [26668986] **2078**

QUANTUM LEAP (US/1056-3679) [23671724] **4865**

QUANTUM LONDON (UK/0961-1452) [I09611452] **3033**

QUANTUM MEDICINE (US) [19278375] **3632**

QUANTUM OPTICS *See* JOURNAL OF THE EUROPEAN OPTICAL SOCIETY, PART B, QUANTUM OPTICS **4437**

QUANTUM PHYSICS AND ITS APPLICATIONS (US/0481-1275) [01433128] **4418**

QUANTUM (WASHINGTON, D.C.) (US/1048-8820) [20922619] 4419, **3530**

QUANTUS
Alphabetical Title Index

QUANTUS, COMPENDIUM OF DIRECTORS (US/0733-6438) [08612796] **884**

QUARBER MERKUR (GW) [12660717] **3427**

QUARDERNI DI MERCEOLOGIA *See* RIVISTA DI MERCEOLOGIA **1625**

QUARKXPRESS IN-DEPTH *CEASED.* (US/1048-8863) [21070094] **1289**

QUARRIES AND SAND PITS (CN/0226-4617) [08744870] 1444, **1363**

QUARRY (KINGSTON) (CN/0033-5266) [01763212] **3427**

QUARRY MANAGEMENT (UK/0950-9526) [10561058] **2149**

QUARRY WEST (US/0736-4628) [03006702] **3427**

QUART DE ROND (CN/0709-0692) [05385208] **625**

QUARTAR (GW/0375-7471) [05947506] **1392**

QUARTER CIRCLE (CN/0228-0612) [06757936] **2801**

QUARTER HORSE JOURNAL (1953), THE (US/0164-6656) [04424468] **2801**

QUARTER HORSE OF THE PACIFIC COAST, THE (US/0093-8238) [05527637] **2801**

QUARTER HORSE REFERENCE (US/0090-435X) [01785199] **2802**

QUARTER NOTES (TORONTO) (CN/0711-0170) [09336597] **4148**

QUARTER RACING RECORD, THE *SUSPENDED.* (US/0091-7516) [04057548] **2802**

QUARTER RACING WORLD *See* SPEEDHORSE (MONTHLY), THE **2802**

QUARTER RUNNING HORSE CHART BOOK, THE *CEASED.* (US/0888-0859) [05015363] **2802**

QUARTERLY ABSTRACTS (DENRYOKU CHUO KENKYUJO (TOKYO, JAPAN)) (JA) [08416305] **2078**

QUARTERLY AGRICULTURAL STATISTICAL BULLETIN (ZA) [02243472] 5336, **156**

QUARTERLY AIRCRAFT OPERATING COSTS AND STATISTICS (US) 5336, **32**

QUARTERLY / ALLIANCE AGAINST FRAUD IN TELEMARKETING, COORDINATED BY THE NATIONAL CONSUMERS' LEAGUE (US/1055-4491) [23184827] **3174**

QUARTERLY - ASSOCIATION OF PROFESSIONAL GENEALOGISTS (U.S.) (US/1056-6732) [24035536] **2468**

QUARTERLY BALANCE OF PAYMENTS - BANGLADESH BANK. STATISTICS DEPT (BG) [03054104] **804**

QUARTERLY BANK AND SAVINGS & LOAN RATING SERVICE (US/1051-8010) [20610880] **804**

QUARTERLY BENCHMARKS (US/8756-4599) [11567111] **4614**

QUARTERLY BIBLIOGRAPHY OF MAJOR TROPICAL DISEASES (US/0192-6640) [05071266] **3986**

QUARTERLY BIBLIOGRAPHY ON CULTURAL DIFFERENCES, A (US/0481-1356) [05753098] **2276**

QUARTERLY / BOULDER GENEALOGICAL SOCIETY (US/0735-6730) [08212760] **2469**

QUARTERLY BULLETIN (AT) [01789517] **5390**

QUARTERLY BULLETIN - ARCHEOLOGICAL SOCIETY OF VIRGINIA (US/0003-8202) [02444919] **280**

QUARTERLY BULLETIN - ASHTABULA COUNTY HISTORICAL SOCIETY (US/0895-1152) [09455711] **2755**

QUARTERLY BULLETIN / BANK OF JAMAICA (JM) [05506541] **805**

QUARTERLY BULLETIN - BANK OF THAILAND (TH/0125-605X) [07855222] **805**

QUARTERLY BULLETIN - BANK VAN DE NEDERLANDSE ANTILLEN (CENTRAL BANK) (NA) [05539020] **805**

QUARTERLY BULLETIN (CALIFORNIA. STATE BOARD OF ACCOUNTANCY) *See* BULLETIN / STATE BOARD OF ACCOUNTANCY **740**

QUARTERLY BULLETIN - CENTRAL BANK OF IRELAND (IE) [02999187] **805**

QUARTERLY BULLETIN / DE NEDERLANDSCHE BANK N.V (NE/0167-3998) [09908235] **805**

QUARTERLY BULLETIN - DEPARTMENT OF REGIONAL PLANNING, COUNTY OF LOS ANGELES, CALIFORNIA (US/0363-5775) [02498381] **2832**

QUARTERLY BULLETIN OF COCOA STATISTICS / BULLETIN TRIMESTRIEL DE STATISTIQUES DU CACAO (UK/0308-4469) [01983729] 2355, **2362**

QUARTERLY BULLETIN OF CONSTRUCTION STATISTICS (BF) [03686375] **633**

QUARTERLY BULLETIN OF THE ALPINE GARDEN SOCIETY (UK/0002-6476) [10249996] **2429**

QUARTERLY BULLETIN OF THE AMERICAN ASSOCIATION OF TEACHERS OF ESPERANTO (US/0002-7499) [05932366] 1903, **3313**

QUARTERLY BULLETIN OF THE COMPUTER SOCIETY OF THE IEEE TECHNICAL COMMITTEE ON DATA ENGINEERING (US/1053-1238) [18755705] **1254**

QUARTERLY BULLETIN OF THE INTERNATIONAL ASSOCIATION OF AGRICULTURAL INFORMATION SPECIALISTS (NE) [23378925] 3243, **124**

QUARTERLY BULLETIN OF THE NORTH AMERICAN LILY SOCIETY, INC (US) [12018668] **2429**

QUARTERLY BULLETIN OF THE SOUTH AFRICAN LIBRARY (SA/0038-2418) [01949768] 2642, **3243**

QUARTERLY BULLETIN / ROSWELL MUSEUM AND ART CENTER (US/0557-3645) [06880005] **4095**

QUARTERLY BULLETIN - SOUTH AFRICAN RESERVE BANK (SA/0038-2620) [01792278] **805**

QUARTERLY BULLETIN - UNITED STATES. BUREAU OF ALCOHOL, TOBACCO AND FIREARMS (US/1057-9958) [10057599] **4677**

QUARTERLY BUSINESS FAILURES (US) [15361686] **3088**

QUARTERLY BUSINESS REVIEW (US/0362-5435) [02297724] **706**

QUARTERLY BUSINESS SURVEY REPORT (HK) [13189738] 706, **732**

QUARTERLY BYTE, THE (US/1052-5521) [22212279] **4843**

QUARTERLY - CANADIAN CAT ASSOCIATION (CN/0828-4865) [12064696] **4287**

QUARTERLY - CANADIAN GOAT SOCIETY (CN/0708-9570) [05362433] **220**

QUARTERLY CARGO REVIEW (US) [03458028] **32**

QUARTERLY / CENTRAL GEORGIA GENEALOGICAL SOCIETY, INC (US/0738-8209) [09628038] **2469**

QUARTERLY / CHRISTIAN LEGAL SOCIETY (US/0736-0142) [09012690] 4989, **3033**

QUARTERLY COAL REPORT (WASHINGTON, D.C.) (US/0736-4598) [08911051] **1954**

QUARTERLY COMMODITY STATISTICS - LEMBAGA PEMASARAN PERTANIAN PERSEKUTUAN (MY) [01784328] **1537**

QUARTERLY COMPLETION REPORT (US/1045-4020) [12210977] **4276**

QUARTERLY CONSENSUS FORECAST OF KEY ECONOMIC INDICATORS (US/0888-787X) [13748598] **1579**

QUARTERLY COUNTRY RISK REPORTS (HK) **1514**

●QUARTERLY DEC JOURNAL *SUSPENDED.* (US/1063-1216) [25866755] **706**

QUARTERLY DEMOGRAPHIC STATISTICS (CN/0835-4057) [17598878] 4559, **4562**

QUARTERLY DIGEST OF STATISTICS (MM) [05587703] **5337**

QUARTERLY DIGEST OF STATISTICS (ACCRA, GHANA : 1981) (GH) [11632998] **1579**

QUARTERLY DIGEST OF STATISTICS (ZIMBABWE. CENTRAL STATISTICAL OFFICE) (RH) [10840314] **5337**

QUARTERLY DIGEST OF UNPUBLISHED DECISIONS OF THE COMPTROLLER GENERAL OF THE UNITED STATES : CONTRACTS (US/0499-499X) [01642032] 750, **4677**

QUARTERLY DOMESTIC & GLOBAL FORECASTS OF KEY ECONOMIC INDICATORS (US/0888-787X) **1514**

QUARTERLY DRY BULK MARKET REPORT (UK/0265-0029) [I02650029] **849**

QUARTERLY / DUTCH FAMILY HERITAGE SOCIETY (US/1056-8875) [23853928] **2469**

QUARTERLY ECONOMIC AND FINANCIAL REVIEW / BANK OF GUYANA, RESEARCH DEPT (GY) [23093923] **805**

QUARTERLY ECONOMIC AND STATISTICAL REVIEW / RESERVE BANK OF ZIMBABWE (RH) [08738207] 1514, **1537**

QUARTERLY ECONOMIC BULLETIN (UK) [15648706] **1514**

QUARTERLY ECONOMIC BULLETIN - CENTRAL BANK OF TRINIDAD AND TOBAGO (TR) [04282134] **1579**

QUARTERLY ECONOMIC COMMENTARY (IE/0376-7191) [05087201] **1514**

QUARTERLY ECONOMIC COMMENTARY (GLASGOW) (UK/0306-7866) [03601443] **1579**

QUARTERLY ECONOMIC REPORT (US) [06553556] **4743**

QUARTERLY ECONOMIC REPORT (TR/0041-3046) [02096486] **1514**

●QUARTERLY ECONOMIC REVIEW (JA) [28261738] **1579**

QUARTERLY ECONOMIC REVIEW (HANGUK UNHAENG) (KO) [01800991] **1580**

●QUARTERLY ECONOMIC REVIEW / THE CENTRAL BANK OF THE BAHAMAS (BF) [27000757] **805**

QUARTERLY ECONOMIC REVIEW / UGANDA COMMERCIAL BANK (UG) [09834203] **1580**

QUARTERLY ENERGY BALANCE (FR) **1954**

QUARTERLY ESTIMATES OF GROSS DOMESTIC PRODUCT (HK) [27439882] **706**

QUARTERLY ESTIMATES OF TRUSTEED PENSION FUNDS (CN/0700-205X) [03300681] **1705**

QUARTERLY EXECUTIVE TREND REPORT (US/0737-5956) [09397009] **1348**

QUARTERLY FINANCIAL AND STATISTICAL REVIEW - BANK OF ZAMBIA (ZA) [07532206] **805**

QUARTERLY FINANCIAL REPORT FOR MANUFACTURING, MINING AND TRADE CORPORATIONS (US/0098-681X) [02241693] **1623**

QUARTERLY FINANCIAL STATISTICS FOR ENTERPRISES (CN/1180-3169) [24831799] 706, **732**

QUARTERLY FORECAST OF JAPAN'S ECONOMY (JA/0910-075X) [06176547] **1594**

QUARTERLY GEOLOGICAL NOTES - GEOLOGICAL SURVEY OF SOUTH AUSTRALIA (AT/0584-3219) [01766075] **1392**

QUARTERLY GUIDE TO THE ECONOMY / PREPARED BY RAL MERCHANT BANK LIMITED (RH) [21766127] **1514**

QUARTERLY IMMIGRATION BULLETIN (CN) [01774872] **1921**

QUARTERLY INDEX ISLAMICUS (UK/0308-7395) [03415908] 5044, **5013**

QUARTERLY INDEX TO CURRENT CONTENTS. LIFE SCIENCES (US/0196-5530) [05848362] **3632**

QUARTERLY INDEX TO CURRENT PROGRAMS *See* CONFERENCE PAPERS QUARTERLY INDEX **414**

QUARTERLY INDEX TO PERIODICAL LITERATURE, EASTERN AND SOUTHERN AFRICA (KE/1018-1555) [24433891] **3427**

QUARTERLY INJURY & ILLNESS INCIDENCE REPORT (US/0195-9344) [05740429] **2868**

QUARTERLY INTERNATIONAL MIGRATION AND TOURIST STATISTICS / ZIMBABWE (RH) [27457969] 5489, **5500**

QUARTERLY - INTERNATIONAL PLASTIC MODELERS' SOCIETY. UNITED STATES BRANCH (US/0744-7493) [08529345] **4460**

QUARTERLY / INTERNATIONAL SOCIETY OF BARRISTERS (US/0020-8752) [02262634] **3033**

QUARTERLY JOURNAL - AGRICULTURAL DEVELOPMENT AND ADVISORY SERVICE, POULTRY SECTION. ABSTRACTS SECTION (UK) [05461678] **220**

QUARTERLY JOURNAL - CANADIAN GENERAL STANDARDS BOARD (CN/0713-1674) [08977719] **4677**

QUARTERLY JOURNAL - FLORIDA AGRICULTURAL AND MECHANICAL UNIVERSITY, TALLAHASSEE, THE (US) [01325570] **1843**

QUARTERLY JOURNAL - JOHN HOWARD SOCIETY OF QUEBEC (CN/0703-5675) [03951107] **3174**

QUARTERLY JOURNAL OF ADMINISTRATION, THE (NR/0001-8333) [05297328] **1869**

QUARTERLY JOURNAL OF BUSINESS AND ECONOMICS (US/0747-5535) [10761886] 1514, **706**

QUARTERLY JOURNAL OF ECONOMICS, THE (US/0033-5533) [01763227] **1514**

QUARTERLY JOURNAL OF ENGINEERING GEOLOGY, THE (UK/0481-2085) [01763229] 1392, **2029**

QUARTERLY JOURNAL OF EXPERIMENTAL PSYCHOLOGY. A, HUMAN EXPERIMENTAL PSYCHOLOGY, THE (UK/0272-4987) [06855549] **4614**

QUARTERLY JOURNAL OF EXPERIMENTAL PSYCHOLOGY. B, COMPARATIVE AND PHYSIOLOGICAL PSYCHOLOGY, THE (UK/0272-4995) [06855602] **4614**

QUARTERLY JOURNAL OF FORESTRY (UK/0033-5568) [01763231] **2391**

QUARTERLY

QUARTERLY JOURNAL OF IDEOLOGY (US/0738-9752) [04388173] 4493, **5254**

QUARTERLY JOURNAL OF MATHEMATICS (UK/0033-5606) [01643667] **3530**

QUARTERLY JOURNAL OF MECHANICS AND APPLIED MATHEMATICS, THE (UK/0033-5614) [01334524] 3530, **2127**

QUARTERLY JOURNAL OF MEDICINE *See* QJM : MONTHLY JOURNAL OF THE ASSOCIATION OF PHYSICIANS **3631**

QUARTERLY JOURNAL OF MEDICINE, THE (UK/0033-5622) [01763235] **3632**

QUARTERLY JOURNAL OF MUSIC TEACHING AND LEARNING, THE (US/1066-0437) [25971718] **4148**

QUARTERLY JOURNAL OF RLA (II) [03261236] **3243**

QUARTERLY JOURNAL OF SPEECH, THE (US/0033-5630) [01763239] **1120**

QUARTERLY JOURNAL OF SURGICAL SCIENCES (II/0033-5657) [01763242] **3973**

QUARTERLY JOURNAL OF TECHNICAL PAPERS *SUSPENDED.* (UK/0269-1183) [14073834] **4276**

QUARTERLY JOURNAL OF THE ALL-INDIA INSTITUTE OF LOCAL SELF-GOVERNMENT, BOMBAY (II) [25800512] **4677**

QUARTERLY JOURNAL OF THE EXPERIMENTAL FOREST OF NATIONAL TAIWAN UNIVERSITY (CH/0255-6014) [22649479] **2391**

QUARTERLY JOURNAL OF THE MYTHIC SOCIETY (BANGALORE), THE (II) [02500179] **4989**

QUARTERLY JOURNAL OF THE ROYAL ASTRONOMICAL SOCIETY, THE (UK/0035-8738) [01641523] **399**

QUARTERLY JOURNAL OF THE ROYAL METEOROLOGICAL SOCIETY (UK/0035-9009) [06271813] **1434**

QUARTERLY JOURNAL / OFFICE OF THE COMPTROLLER OF THE CURRENCY (US/0738-2146) [09360403] **805**

QUARTERLY LABOUR FORCE STATISTICS (FR/0255-3627) [09553359] **1537**

QUARTERLY LAW NOTES AND ALUMNI NEWS (US) [03021601] 1102, **3033**

QUARTERLY LITERATURE REPORTS : POLYMERS (UK/0032-3977) [01792030] **1047**

QUARTERLY LITERATURE REPORTS : SURFACE ACTIVITY (UK) [01792031] **1029**

QUARTERLY MAGAZINE / MUSIC TEACHERS' ASSOCIATION OF NEW SOUTH WALES (AT/0155-5367) [14288428] **4148**

QUARTERLY MAGAZINE - MUSIC TEACHERS' ASSOCIATION OF NEW SOUTH WALES (AT/0810-7211) [I08107211] 1903, **4148**

QUARTERLY - MIAMI MALACOLOGICAL SOCIETY (US/0090-323X) [01784926] **5596**

QUARTERLY MINERAL STATISTICS (AT) [20339926] **2149**

QUARTERLY MLS STATISTICAL SURVEY (CN/0839-640X) [19098958] **4843**

QUARTERLY MODEL OUTLOOK (PHILADELPHIA, PA. : 1982) (US) [10885575] **1594**

QUARTERLY MUG *See* MUMPS COMPUTING **1196**

QUARTERLY - MUSEUM OF THE FUR TRADE (US/0027-4135) [03022453] 4095, **2756**

QUARTERLY NATIONAL ACCOUNTS--ESA / COMPTES NATIONAUX TRIMESTRIELS--SEC / EUROSTAT (LU/0258-2066) [16479902] **1580**

QUARTERLY NATIONAL ACCOUNTS (PARIS, FRANCE : 1983) (FR/0257-7801) [09774174] **1514**

QUARTERLY - NATIONAL BOOK CENTRE BANGLADESH (II) [03519638] **4831**

QUARTERLY (NEW YORK, N.Y. : 1987) (US/0893-3103) [15501074] **3427**

QUARTERLY NEWS JOURNAL OF THE CROSBY ARBORETUM, A (US/0741-9635) [10006688] **5235**

QUARTERLY NEWS-LETTER - BOOK CLUB OF CALIFORNIA (US/0006-7202) [01536741] **4831**

QUARTERLY NEWSLETTER / CANADIAN FORESTRY ASSOCIATION OF BRITISH COLUMBIA (CN/0710-0566) [08315830] **2391**

QUARTERLY NEWSLETTER (FAO REGIONAL OFFICE FOR ASIAN AND THE PACIFIC. ASIA AND PACIFIC PLANT PROTECTION COMMISSION) (TH) [12320802] **124**

QUARTERLY NEWSLETTER / FOOD DISTRIBUTION RESEARCH SOCIETY, INC (US) [03185203] **2355**

QUARTERLY NEWSLETTER - INTERNATIONAL COMMISSION ON OCCUPATIONAL HEALTH (SZ/0258-0748) [I02580748] **2868**

QUARTERLY NEWSLETTER OF THE LABORATORY OF COMPARATIVE HUMAN COGNITION, THE (US/0278-4351) [04725397] **4615**

QUARTERLY NEWSLETTER - STANDING COMMITTEE ON ENVIRONMENTAL LAW (US) [02343916] **3115**

QUARTERLY NEWSLETTER - TEA RESEARCH FOUNDATION OF CENTRAL AFRICA (MW) [02694181] **183**

QUARTERLY NEWSLETTER - WOMEN'S THEOLOGICAL CENTER (BOSTON, MASS.) (US/1062-6565) [25425885] 5565, **4989**

QUARTERLY - NORTHEASTERN NEVADA HISTORICAL SOCIETY (US/0160-9602) [03787140] **2756**

QUARTERLY NOTES / GEOLOGICAL SURVEY OF NEW SOUTH WALES (AT/0155-3410) [03525672] **1392**

QUARTERLY OCCUPATIONAL SUPPLY/DEMAND OUTLOOK (US) [08616424] **1705**

QUARTERLY OF APPLIED MATHEMATICS (US/0033-569X) [01763246] **3530**

QUARTERLY OF CANADIAN STUDIES FOR THE SECONDARY SCHOOL, THE (CN/0317-2139) [02125647] **1776**

QUARTERLY OF THE CULTURAL TRIANGLE (CE) [12095301] **280**

QUARTERLY OF THE NATIONAL ASSOCIATION AND CENTER FOR OUTLAW AND LAWMAN HISTORY (LARAMIE, WYO.) *See* QUARTERLY OF THE NATIONAL ASSOCIATION FOR OUTLAW AND LAWMAN HISTORY, INC **2756**

QUARTERLY OF THE NATIONAL ASSOCIATION FOR OUTLAW AND LAWMAN HISTORY, INC (US/1071-4189) [28639295] **2756**

QUARTERLY OF THE NATIONAL WRITING PROJECT AND THE CENTER FOR THE STUDY OF WRITING, THE (US/0896-3592) [17031947] **1776**

QUARTERLY OIL COMPANY PERFORMANCE *CEASED.* (US/0888-7799) [13748265] **4276**

QUARTERLY OIL STATISTICS AND ENERGY BALANCES (FR) [19272595] **1963**

QUARTERLY - OLDE MECKLENBURG GENEALOGICAL SOCIETY (N.C.) (US/0895-4755) [14175910] **2469**

QUARTERLY / OLYMPIA GENEALOGICAL SOCIETY (US) [08838956] **2469**

QUARTERLY - ORANGE COUNTY CALIFORNIA GENEALOGICAL SOCIETY (US/0030-4263) [04178143] 434, **2469**

QUARTERLY / OREGON GENEALOGICAL SOCIETY (US/0738-1891) [09517737] **2469**

QUARTERLY OUTLOOK FOR MAJOR FINANCIAL MARKETS (CN/1186-0022) [24265911] **805**

QUARTERLY PERFORMANCE REPORT (UK) **805**

QUARTERLY - PHI LAMBDA KAPPA MEDICAL FRATERNITY (US/0739-2079) [09496221] **3917**

QUARTERLY - PLANT GROWTH REGULATOR SOCIETY OF AMERICA (US/1042-3524) [19017708] **2429**

QUARTERLY PREDICTIONS (NZ/0033-5711) [11569912] **1580**

QUARTERLY PRINTING INDUSTRY BUSINESS INDICATOR REPORT (US) [10613954] **4569**

QUARTERLY PROGRESS REPORT ON BLOWDOWN HEAT TRANSFER SEPARATE-EFFECTS PROGRAM FOR ... / ENGINEERING TECHNOLOGY DIVISION (US) [09513686] **4432**

QUARTERLY REPORT / BANCO POPULAR DE PUERTO RICO (PR) [07877879] **805**

QUARTERLY REPORT. ENERGY INFORMATION REPORT BY CONGRESS ... REQUIRED BY PUBLIC LAW 93-319, AMENDED BY PUBLIC LAW 94-163 *See* MONTHLY ENERGY REVIEW **1950**

QUARTERLY REPORT FOR THE QUARTER ENDED ... / GAMING CONTROL BOARD (US) [10734993] **3174**

QUARTERLY REPORT / INSURERS ADVISORY ORGANIZATION OF CANADA / IAO (CN) **2891**

QUARTERLY REPORT (MERCER ISLAND, WASH.), THE (US/0882-8679) [12011180] **706**

QUARTERLY REPORT - MIT SEA GRANT PROGRAM (US/0273-1355) [07030590] **5143**

QUARTERLY REPORT / NEBRASKA DEPARTMENT OF SOCIAL SERVICES (US) [18214781] **5303**

QUARTERLY REPORT OF FOREIGN AND DOMESTIC DEVELOPMENTS AFFECTING ENERGY (US) [04765860] **1954**

QUARTERLY REPORT OF MANUFACTURE AND SALES OF SNUFF, SMOKING, AND CHEWING TOBACCO *See* TOBACCO STOCKS **917**

QUARTERLY REPORT OF SELECTED RESEARCH PROJECTS (US) [19558306] **124**

QUARTERLY REPORT OF THE ATTORNEY GENERAL OF ALABAMA (US) [01478888] **3142**

QUARTERLY REPORT OF THE INTER-AMERICAN TROPICAL TUNA COMMISSION, THE (US/1048-6259) [14516673] **2311**

QUARTERLY REPORT ON ENERGY RELATED SOFTWARE IN CALGARY (CN) 1954, **1289**

QUARTERLY REPORT ON ENERGY SUPPLY-DEMAND IN CANADA (CN/0702-0465) [04448878] **1954**

QUARTERLY REPORT ON MONEY FUND EXPENSE RATIOS (US/0897-2044) [17430656] **805**

QUARTERLY REPORT ON THE OPERATION AND BUSINESS OF THE ELECTRICITY POOL IN ENGLAND AND WALES (UK) **2078**

QUARTERLY REPORT ON THE STATUS OF THE STEEL INDUSTRY : REPORT TO THE COMMITTEE ON WAYS AND MEANS ON INVESTIGATION NO. 332-226 UNDER SECTION 332 OF THE TARIFF ACT OF 1930 (US) [23260992] **4017**

QUARTERLY REPORT / PEOPLE FOR THE AMERICAN WAY (US) [10226389] **4512**

QUARTERLY REPORT - STATE GAMING CONTROL BOARD (US/0195-4709) [05459856] 4865, **4677**

QUARTERLY REPORT. SUN COMPANY (US) **4276**

QUARTERLY REPORTS - RAILWAY TECHNICAL RESEARCH INSTITUTE (JA/0033-9008) [03127232] 2030, **5434**

QUARTERLY REVIEW / BUREAU OF ENERGY UTILIZATION (PH) [09397221] **1954**

QUARTERLY REVIEW (CENTRAL BANK OF BELIZE. RESEARCH DEPT.) (BH) [09807321] **805**

QUARTERLY REVIEW - CENTRAL BANK OF MALTA. RESEARCH DIVISION (MM) [07600556] **805**

QUARTERLY REVIEW / CENTRAL BANK OF SOLOMON ISLANDS (SA) [23723500] **805**

QUARTERLY REVIEW (CENTRAL BANK OF THE BAHAMAS) *See* QUARTERLY ECONOMIC REVIEW / THE CENTRAL BANK OF THE BAHAMAS **805**

QUARTERLY REVIEW (CENTRAL BANK OF THE BAHAMAS) *See* QUARTERLY STATISTICAL DIGEST / THE CENTRAL BANK OF THE BAHAMAS **806**

QUARTERLY REVIEW - CIPEC *CEASED.* (FR/1015-0064) [02537918] **1623**

QUARTERLY REVIEW - FEDERAL RESERVE BANK OF MINNEAPOLIS (US/0271-5287) [03389378] 1514, **805**

QUARTERLY REVIEW - FEDERAL RESERVE BANK OF NEW YORK (US/0147-6580) [02737435] **805**

QUARTERLY REVIEW / KOREA EXCHANGE BANK (KO) [25068048] **805**

QUARTERLY REVIEW (MAGYAR NEMZETI BANK) *See* MONTHLY REPORT / NATIONAL BANK OF HUNGARY **800**

QUARTERLY REVIEW / NATIONAL WESTMINSTER BANK (UK/0028-0399) [02566793] **1514**

QUARTERLY REVIEW OF BIOLOGY, THE (US/0033-5770) [01715101] **471**

QUARTERLY REVIEW OF COMMISSION PROCEEDINGS *See* NCPC QUARTERLY **2829**

QUARTERLY REVIEW OF DRILLING STATISTICS FOR THE UNITED STATES (US/0033-5789) [02255870] 4276, **4284**

QUARTERLY REVIEW OF ECONOMICS AND BUSINESS *See* QUARTERLY REVIEW OF ECONOMICS AND FINANCE, THE **1515**

●QUARTERLY REVIEW OF ECONOMICS AND FINANCE, THE (US/1062-9769) [25810487] 706, **1515**

QUARTERLY REVIEW OF FILM AND VIDEO (SZ/1050-9208) [19693646] **4076**

QUARTERLY REVIEW OF HISTORICAL STUDIES, THE (II/0033-5800) [01774418] **2627**

QUARTERLY REVIEW OF LITERATURE. POETRY SERIES (US) [24156718] **3470**

QUARTERLY
Alphabetical Title Index

QUARTERLY REVIEW OF METHANE FROM COAL SEAMS TECHNOLOGY (US/8756-9655) [11740438] 1954, **1392**

QUARTERLY REVIEW OF THE EASTERN NORTH CAROLINA GENEALOGICAL SOCIETY, THE **CEASED.** (US/0739-8840) [05812998] **2469**

QUARTERLY REVIEW OF WINES (US/0740-1248) [09885420] **2370**

QUARTERLY REVIEW ON DOUBLESPEAK (US/0735-5920) [07516558] 3313, **1120**

QUARTERLY REVIEW / RESERVE BANK OF FIJI (FJ) [12766997] **805**

QUARTERLY REVIEW - SKANDINAVISKA ENSKILDA BANKEN **CEASED.** (SW/0347-3139) [01786985] **1580**

QUARTERLY REVIEW / SVERIGES RIKSBANK (SW/0346-6583) [07501653] **805**

QUARTERLY REVIEW / THE CENTRAL BANK OF THE BAHAMAS (MM) [02409956] **805**

QUARTERLY REVIEW - UNITED METHODIST BOARD OF HIGHER EDUCATION AND MINISTRY (U.S.) (US/0270-9287) [06520386] **5066**

QUARTERLY REVIEWS OF BIOPHYSICS (UK/0033-5835) [01586799] **496**

QUARTERLY / ROYAL CANADIAN MOUNTED POLICE, THE (CN/0824-9415) [10192411] **3174**

QUARTERLY / SAN BERNARDINO COUNTY MUSEUM ASSOCIATION (US/0195-864X) [01916499] **4095**

QUARTERLY SHIPMENTS OF HOUSEHOLD FURNITURE PRODUCTS (CN/1180-5897) [24280186] **2907**

QUARTERLY SHIPMENTS OF OFFICE FURNITURE PRODUCTS (CN/0701-7898) [02442399] **4214**

QUARTERLY - ST. LAWRENCE COUNTY HISTORICAL ASSOCIATION, THE (US/0558-1931) [02456902] **2756**

QUARTERLY - ST. LOUIS GENEALOGICAL SOCIETY (US/0036-2956) [04905525] **2469**

QUARTERLY STATEMENTS OF FINANCIAL OPERATIONS ENDING ... (CN/0849-3596) [23247974] **4743**

QUARTERLY STATISTICAL BULLETIN OF THE HOSIERY INDUSTRY See HOSIERY STATISTICS / NAHM **5351**

●QUARTERLY STATISTICAL DIGEST / THE CENTRAL BANK OF THE BAHAMAS (BF) [27000910] **806**

QUARTERLY STATISTICAL REPORT - EDISON ELECTRIC INSTITUTE. STATISTICAL DEPT (US/0749-9183) [09309776] 4762, **4699**

QUARTERLY STATISTICS - DE NEDERLANDSCHE BANK N.V (NE) [01799454] 1515, **1537**

QUARTERLY STEEL COMMENT (CN/1186-9275) [24623764] **4017**

QUARTERLY SUMMARY / NATIONAL AUSTRALIA BANK (AT/1031-332X) [18012906] **806**

QUARTERLY SUMMARY OF FEDERAL, STATE, AND LOCAL TAX REVENUE (US/1057-9699) [21481445] **4743**

QUARTERLY SUMMARY OF TITLE XX SERVICES AND EXPENDITURES IN NORTH CAROLINA / DEPARTMENT OF HUMAN RESOURCES, DIVISION OF PLANS AND OPERATIONS (US) [07143707] **5303**

QUARTERLY SUMMARY - UNITED STATES. SOUTHEAST ENVIRONMENTAL RESEARCH LABORATORY, ATHENS, GA (US) [02717483] **2180**

QUARTERLY SUPPLEMENT, DIRECTORY OF PUBLIC HIGH-TECH CORPORATIONS (US) [12957154] **5143**

QUARTERLY SUPPLEMENT TO THE ... ANNUAL DEPARTMENT OF DEFENSE BIBLIOGRAPHY OF LOGISTICS STUDIES AND RELATED DOCUMENTS / DEFENSE LOGISTICS STUDIES INFORMATION EXCHANGE (US) [11104046] **4054**

QUARTERLY SURVEY OF ADVERTISING EXPENDITURE (UK/0951-7766) [I09517766] **765**

QUARTERLY SURVEY OF JAPANESE FINANCE & INDUSTRY (JA) [02241819] **806**

QUARTERLY SURVEY OF THE MEXICAN ECONOMY (MX) [06860536] **1515**

QUARTERLY / THE ALLERGY AND ENVIRONMENTAL HEALTH ASSOCIATION (CN/0849-3138) [23238135] **3676**

QUARTERLY - THE MUSEUM OF THE FUR TRADE (US/0027-4135) [01758873] **3185**

QUARTERLY TRACKING SYSTEM, ENERGY USING AND CONSERVATION EQUIPMENT IN HOMES (US) [04864245] **1954**

QUARTERLY TRAVEL REPORT / REPUBLIC OF TRINIDAD AND TOBAGO, CENTRAL STATISTICAL OFFICE (TR) [10037067] 5489, **5500**

QUARTERLY UPDATE (UK) [24573015] **849**

QUARTERLY UPDATE (NATIONAL AUDIOVISUAL CENTER) (US) [06507469] **4076**

QUARTERLY WEST (US/0194-4231) [03350193] **3427**

●QUARTERLY / WORLD AFFAIRS CANADA, THE (CN/1188-6870) [26714943] **4533**

●QUARTERLY / WORLD AFFAIRS CANADA, THE (CN/1188-6870) [26714945] **4533**

QUARTERLY YEKATIT (ET) [19011283] **2508**

QUARTERMASTER PROFESSIONAL BULLETIN (US/0896-9795) [17350817] **4545**

QUARTIER LATIN (MONTREAL. 1976) (CN/0382-8530) [02802396] **1843**

QUARTZ CRYSTAL (US) [04446290] 2149, **2006**

QUARTZ DEVICES DIRECTORY (US) **3487**

QUATERNAIRE : BULLETIN DE L'ASSOCIATION FRANCAISE POUR L'ETUDE DU QUATERNAIRE : INTERNATIONAL JOURNAL OF THE FRENCH QUATERNARY ASSOCIATION (FR/1142-2904) [22575089] 4230, **1393**

QUATERNARY AUSTRALASIA (AT/0811-0433) [11386132] **1393**

QUATERNARY INTERNATIONAL (UK/1040-6182) [18471518] **1393**

QUATERNARY NEWSLETTER (UK/0143-2826) [I01432826] **1393**

QUATERNARY OF SOUTH AMERICA AND ANTARCTIC PENINSULA (NE) [10691408] **2756**

QUATERNARY RESEARCH (US/0033-5894) [01332293] **1393**

QUATERNARY SCIENCE REVIEWS (UK/0277-3791) [07580090] **1393**

QUATERNARY STUDIES IN POLAND / POLISH ACADEMY OF SCIENCES, BRANCH OFFICE IN POZNAN, COMMITTEE OF QUATERNARY RESEARCH (PL/0137-9798) [08077627] **1393**

QUA'TOQTI (US/0739-0122) [06168880] **5630**

QUATRE FLEUVES, LES **SUSPENDED.** (FR) [05885454] **5035**

QUATRE SAISONS DU JARDINAGE, LES (FR/0242-4959) [02424959] **2429**

QUATRE-TEMPS (CN/0820-5515) [16850585] 2429, **525**

QUATRE-TEMPS (MONTREAL) (CN/0820-5515) [16210634] **526**

●QUATRE VENTS (OTTAWA) (CN/1183-8949) [28395978] **884**

QUATTRO ZAMPE (IT/0394-5898) [I03945898] **5519**

QUATTRORUOTINE ROZZANO (IT/1121-5550) [I11215550] **2777**

QUAYLE QUARTERLY, THE **CEASED.** (US/1049-5452) [21135365] **4677**

QUE CHOISIR ? PARIS (FR/0033-5932) [I00335932] **1299**

QUE FAZER? (NE) [02241711] **4545**

QUE ME (FR) **1776**

●QUE PASA PANAMA! NEWSLETTER (US/1064-9026) [26458732] **2756**

QUE PASA SAN ANTONIO (US) **5489**

QUE PASA (TEANECK, N.J.) **CEASED.** (US/0899-2576) [18045626] **2491**

QUE TAL! (NEW YORK, N.Y.) (US/0033-5940) [04109278] **3313**

QUE VOUS EN SEMBLE? (BD) [07333443] **243**

QUEBEC A VOTRE PORTEE, LE (CN/0836-0014) [19712402] **2756**

QUEBEC ASSOCIATION FOR CHILDREN WITH LEARNING DISABILITIES. LIBRARY See SUPPLEMENT (MONTREAL) **1885**

QUEBEC ASSOCIATION FOR THE MENTALLY RETARDED See ANNUAL BRIEF SUBMITTED BY THE QUEBEC ASSOCIATION FOR THE MENTALLY RETARDED TO THE GOVERNMENT OF QUEBEC **5271**

QUEBEC ASSOCIATION OF SCHOOL ADMINISTRATORS See Q.A.S.A. BULLETIN **1869**

QUEBEC ASSOCIATION OF SCHOOL ADMINISTRATORS See DIRECTORY OF MEMBERS - QUEBEC ASSOCIATION OF SCHOOL ADMINISTRATORS **1862**

QUEBEC AU BOUT DES DOIGTS (CN/0381-6443) [02606794] **4865**

QUEBEC BOOKS (US/0739-070X) [09679110] **4831**

QUEBEC BUREAU OF STATISTICS See STATISTIQUES DE LA PRODUCTION MINERALE **1398**

QUEBEC CAMPING ASSOCIATION See ANNUAIRE - ASSOCIATION DES CAMPS DU QUEBEC **4869**

QUEBEC CANADA (MONTREAL) (CN/0709-5643) [05696424] **4493**

QUEBEC-CANADA (MOVEMENT) See QUEBEC CANADA (MONTREAL) **4493**

QUEBEC CHRONICLE-TELEGRAPH (CN) **5793**

QUEBEC CONSTRUCTION (ED. MENSUELLE) (CN/0829-5263) [14879399] **625**

QUEBEC DEPOSIT AND INVESTMENT FUND See ANNUAL REPORT - CAISSE DE DEPOT ET PLACEMENT DU QUEBEC **770**

QUEBEC DIMANCHE (CN/0820-7216) [09582040] **5793**

QUEBEC EN REVUE(S) (CN/0711-5598) [09809025] **328**

QUEBEC ETUDIANT (STE-FOY) (CN/0705-3096) [03827585] **1843**

QUEBEC FILM INDUSTRY HANDBOOK (CN/0225-316X) [06035185] **4076**

QUEBEC FRANCAIS (CN/0316-2052) [08718996] **3427**

QUEBEC FRANCE (CN/0840-8785) [20008187] **5214**

QUEBEC FURNITURE MANUFACTURERS' ASSOCIATION See JOURNAL / Q.F.M.A. **2906**

QUEBEC G (CN/0824-0965) [11762379] **2796**

QUEBEC INTER (CN/0225-9745) [08354871] **4533**

QUEBEC LIBRARY ASSOCIATION See BULLETIN A B Q **3197**

QUEBEC MARINE FISHERIES, MONTHLY LANDING STATISTICS BY SPECIES (CN/1187-7693) [25796671] **2311**

QUEBEC NATURE (CN/0381-1123) [03412025] **4878**

QUEBEC PENSION BOARD See ANNUAL REPORT - QUEBEC PENSION BOARD **1649**

QUEBEC PHARMACIE (CN/0048-6280) [02126182] **4327**

QUEBEC PHARMACIE (MONTREAL, 1981) (CN/0826-9874) [19044273] **4327**

QUEBEC (PROVINCE) See LOIS DU QUEBEC **3004**

QUEBEC (PROVINCE) See LOIS DU TRAVAIL **3004**

QUEBEC (PROVINCE) See CODE DU TRAVAIL DU QUEBEC ET REGLEMENTS **1659**

QUEBEC (PROVINCE) See CODE DE PROCEDURE CIVILE DU QUEBEC, L.R.Q. C-25, ET LOIS ET REGLEMENTS CONNEXES **2951**

QUEBEC (PROVINCE) See GAZETTE OFFICIELLE DU QUEBEC, PARTIE 2; LOIS ET REGLEMENTS **2973**

QUEBEC (PROVINCE) See CODE MUNICIPAL FD DU QUEBEC **4638**

QUEBEC (PROVINCE) See GAZETTE OFFICIELLE DU QUEBEC. PARTIE 1. AVIS JURIDIQUE **2533**

QUEBEC (PROVINCE) See CODE DE PROCEDURE CIVILE (EDITIONS THEMIS) **2951**

QUEBEC (PROVINCE) See QUEBEC SALES TAX WITH RELATED TAXES **4743**

QUEBEC (PROVINCE). ASSEMBLEE LEGISLATIVE See DEBATS DE L'ASSEMBLEE LEGISLATIVE DU QUEBEC **4642**

QUEBEC (PROVINCE) ASSEMBLEE NATIONALE See JOURNAL DES DEBATS (QUEBEC) **4478**

QUEBEC (PROVINCE). ASSEMBLEE NATIONALE See REPERTOIRE LEGISLATIF DE L'ASSEMBLEE DU QUEBEC **3037**

QUEBEC (PROVINCE). ASSEMBLEE NATIONALE See JOURNAL DES DEBATS. INDEX **2986**

QUEBEC (PROVINCE). ASSEMBLEE NATIONALE. COMMISSION D'ETUDE DES QUESTIONS AFFERENTES A L'ACCESSION DU QUEBEC A LA SOUVERAINETE See JOURNAL DES DEBATS - QUEBEC (PROVINCE). ASSEMBLEE NATIONALE. COMMISSION D'ETUDE DES QUESTIONS AFFERENTES A L'ACCESSION DU QUEBEC A LA SOUVERAINETE **4658**

QUEBEC (PROVINCE). ASSEMBLEE NATIONALE. COMMISSION D'ETUDE SUR TOUTE OFFRE D'UN NOUVEAU PARTENARIAT DE NATURE CONSTITUTIONNELLE See JOURNAL DES DEBATS - QUEBEC (PROVINCE). ASSEMBLEE NATIONALE. COMMISSION D'ETUDE SUR TOUTE OFFRE D'UN NOUVEAU PARTENARIAT DE NATURE CONSTITUTIONELLE **4658**

QUEBECOIS

QUEBEC (PROVINCE). ASSEMBLEE NATIONALE. COMMISSION PARLEMENTAIRE SUR L'AVENIR POLITIQUE ET CONSTITUTIONNEL DU QUEBEC *See* JOURNAL DES DEBATS - QUEBEC (PROVINCE). ASSEMBLEE NATIONALE. COMMISSION PARLEMENTAIRE SUR L'AVENIR POLITIQUE ET CONSTITUTIONNEL DU QUEBEC **4658**

QUEBEC (PROVINCE). BUREAU D'AUDIENCES PUBLIQUES SUR L'ENVIRONNEMENT *See* RAPPORT ANNUEL / BUREAU D'AUDIENCES PUBLIQUES SUR L'ENVIRONNEMENT **1580**

QUEBEC (PROVINCE). BUREAU DE LA STATISTIQUE. DIRECTION DE LA PRODUCTION STATISTIQUE *See* FRUITS (QUEBEC) **1607**

QUEBEC (PROVINCE) BUREAU DE LA STATISTIQUE. SERVICE DU TRAVAIL ET DE LA MAIN-D'OEUVRE *See* ENQUETE SUR L'EMPLOI ET LA REMUNERATION **1667**

QUEBEC (PROVINCE) BUREAU OF STATISTICS *See* PORCS **217**

QUEBEC (PROVINCE). CENTRALE DES BIBLIOTHEQUES *See* BIBLIO-JEUNES; NIVEAUX PRESCOLAIRE ET ELEMENTAIRE: SUPPLEMENT **408**

QUEBEC (PROVINCE). CENTRE DE RECHERCHE ET DE STATISTIQUES SUR LE MARCHE DU TRAVAIL *See* JURISPRUDENCE EN DROIT DU TRAVAIL. DECISIONS DES COMMISSAIRES DU TRAVAIL **3150**

QUEBEC (PROVINCE). CINEMATHEQUE *See* CATALOGUE DES DOCUMENTS AUDIOVISUELS **4065**

QUEBEC (PROVINCE). COMITE DE DEONTOLOGIE POLICIERE *See* RAPPORT ANNUEL - QUEBEC (PROVINCE). COMITE DE DEONTOLOGIE POLICIERE **4678**

QUEBEC (PROVINCE). COMITE DES INVENTAIRES AERIENS DU GROS GIBIER *See* RAPPORT DES INVENTAIRES AERIENS DU GROS GIBIER **5596**

QUEBEC (PROVINCE). COMMISSION DE FORMATION PROFESSIONNELLE DE LA MAIN-D'OEUVRE. REGION DE QUEBEC, CHAUDIERE-APPALACHES ET NORD DU QUEBEC *See* PERSPECTIVE REGIONALE DE DEVELOPPEMENT DE LA MAIN-D'OEUVRE POUR L'ANNEE **4673**

QUEBEC (PROVINCE). COMMISSION DE TOPONYMIE *See* REPERTOIRE TOPONYMIQUE DU QUEBEC (1988) **2574**

QUEBEC (PROVINCE). COMMISSION DE TOPONYMIE. SERVICE DE L'ANIMATION ET DE LA DIFFUSION *See* TOPONYME, LE **2577**

QUEBEC (PROVINCE). COMMISSION DES AFFAIRES SOCIALES *See* DECISIONS DE LA COMMISSION DES AFFAIRES SOCIALES **4642**

QUEBEC (PROVINCE). COMMISSION DES TRANSPORTS *See* RAPPORT ANNUEL - COMMISSION DES TRANSPORTS DU QUEBEC **5390**

QUEBEC (PROVINCE) COMMISSION DES VALEURS MOBILIERES *See* BULLETIN DE STATISTIQUES - COMMISSION DES VALEURS MOBILIERES DU QUEBEC **893**

QUEBEC (PROVINCE). COMMISSION QUEBECOISE DES LIBERATIONS CONDITIONNELLES *See* RAPPORT ANNUEL - COMMISSION QUEBECOISE DES LIBERATIONS CONDITIONNELLES **5303**

QUEBEC (PROVINCE). CONSEIL CONSULTATIF DE L'ENVIRONNEMENT *See* RAPPORT ANNUEL / CONSEIL CONSULTATIF DE L'ENVIRONNEMENT **4678**

QUEBEC (PROVINCE). CONSEIL CONSULTATIF DU TRAVAIL ET DE LA MAIN-D'OEUVRE *See* LISTE ANNOTEE D'ARBITRES DE GRIEFS **1688**

QUEBEC (PROVINCE). CONSEIL DE LA FAMILLE *See* RAPPORT ANNUEL / CONSEIL DE LA FAMILLE **2285**

QUEBEC (PROVINCE). CONSEIL DE LA LANGUE FRANCAISE *See* RAPPORT ANNUEL - CONSEIL DE LA LANGUE FRANCAISE **3314**

QUEBEC (PROVINCE). CONSEIL DE LA PROTECTION DU CONSOMMATEUR *See* RAPPORT ANNUEL - CONSEIL DE LA PROTECTION DU CONSOMMATEUR **1299**

QUEBEC (PROVINCE). CONSEIL DES UNIVERSITES *See* BULLETIN D'INFORMATION - CONSEIL DES UNIVERSITES (SAINTE-FOY) **1812**

QUEBEC (PROVINCE). CONSEIL DU STATUT DE LA FEMME *See* ORIENTATIONS TRIENNALES ET PLAN ANNUEL / GOUVERNEMENT DU QUEBEC, CONSEIL DU STATUT DE LA FEMME **5212**

QUEBEC (PROVINCE). CONSEIL DU TRESOR *See* BUDGET: ESTIMATES (QUEBEC) **4714**

QUEBEC (PROVINCE). CONSEIL DU TRESOR *See* BUDGET. ADDITIONAL INFORMATION : ESTIMATES **4714**

QUEBEC (PROVINCE). CURATELLE PUBLIQUE *See* RAPPORT ANNUEL DU CURATEUR PUBLIC (1977) **4798**

QUEBEC (PROVINCE). DEPT. OF AGRICULTURE AND COLONIZATION *See* MERITE AGRICOLE ET MERITE DU DEFRICHEUR **108**

QUEBEC (PROVINCE). DEPT. OF FINANCE *See* FINANCIAL STATEMENTS OF QUEBEC GOVERNMENT ENTERPRISES **4726**

QUEBEC (PROVINCE). DEPT. OF FINANCE *See* HIGHLIGHTS : BUDGET SPEECH AND ESTIMATES **1493**

QUEBEC (PROVINCE). DEPT. OF INDUSTRY AND COMMERCE. COMMUNICATIONS DIVISION *See* CATALOGUE DES PUBLICATIONS - MINISTERE DE L'INDUSTRIE ET DU COMMERCE, DIRECTION DES COMMUNICATIONS **826**

QUEBEC (PROVINCE). DEPT. OF JUSTICE *See* RAPPORT ANNUEL - MINISTERE DE LA JUSTICE **3034**

QUEBEC (PROVINCE). DEPT. OF NATURAL RESOURCES *See* REPERTOIRE DES PUBLICATIONS **2203**

QUEBEC (PROVINCE). DEPT. OF NATURAL RESOURCES *See* RAPPORT ANNUEL - QUEBEC (PROVINCE). DEPT. OF NATURAL RESOURCES **2203**

QUEBEC (PROVINCE). DIRECTION DE LA RECHERCHE GEOLOGIQUE *See* RAPPORTS D'ACTIVITE / DIRECTION DE LA RECHERCHE GEOLOGIQUE **1393**

QUEBEC (PROVINCE). DIRECTION GENERALE DE L'EDITION GOUVERNEMENTALE. BIBLIOTHEQUE ADMINISTRATIVE *See* RAPPORT D'ACTIVITES - LA BIBLIOTHEQUE ADMINISTRATIVE **3243**

QUEBEC (PROVINCE). DIRECTION GENERALE DE L'ENERGIE *See* RAPPORT ANNUEL - ENERGIE QUEBEC **1954**

QUEBEC (PROVINCE). DIRECTION GENERALE DES ASSURANCES *See* RAPPORT ANNUEL DU SURINTENDANT DES ASSURANCES (QUEBEC. 1977) **2891**

QUEBEC (PROVINCE). ELECTRICITY AND GAS BOARD *See* RAPPORT ANNUEL - REGIE DE L'ELECTRICITE ET DU GAZ **4678**

QUEBEC (PROVINCE). GREFFE DES TRIBUNAUX D'ARBITRAGE DU SECTEUR DE L'EDUCATION *See* RECUEIL DES SENTENCES DE L'EDUCATION **1869**

QUEBEC (PROVINCE). INSTITUT NATIONAL DE PRODUCTIVITE *See* RAPPORT ANNUEL / INSTITUT NATIONAL DE PRODUCTIVITE **4678**

QUEBEC (PROVINCE). MINISTERE DE LA FONCTION PUBLIQUE. GREFFE DU TRIBUNAL D'ARBITRAGE *See* SENTENCES ARBITRALES DE LA FONCTION PUBLIQUE **1710**

QUEBEC (PROVINCE). MINISTERE DE L'AGRICULTURE, DES PECHERIES ET DE L'ALIMENTATION *See* RAPPORT ANNUEL / MINISTERE DE L'AGRICULTURE, DES PECHERIES ET DE LA'ALIMENTATION **4678**

QUEBEC (PROVINCE). MINISTERE DE L'AGRICULTURE, DES PECHERIES ET DE L'ALIMENTATION *See* RAPPORT ANNUEL. MERITE AGRICOLE **124**

QUEBEC (PROVINCE). MINISTERE DE L'AGRICULTURE, DES PECHERIES ET DE L'ALIMENTATION. SOUS-MINISTERIAT DES AFFAIRES ECONOMIQUES *See* CARREFOUR BIO-ALIMENTAIRE **2330**

QUEBEC (PROVINCE). MINISTERE DE L'ENERGIE ET DES RESSOURCES *See* DOCUMENTATION DU MINISTERE DE L'ENERGIE ET DES RESSOURCES, REPERTOIRE **1555**

QUEBEC (PROVINCE). MINISTERE DE L'ENERGIE ET DES RESSOURCES *See* RAPPORT ANNUEL - MINISTERE DE L'ENERGIE ET DES RESSOURCES (QUEBEC) **2203**

QUEBEC (PROVINCE). MINISTERE DE L'ENERGIE ET DES RESSOURCES. CENTRE DE DOCUMENTATION ET DE RENSEIGNEMENTS *See* INFOR-MER. MINES **2004**

QUEBEC (PROVINCE). MINISTERE DES AFFAIRES CULTURELLES *See* REPERTOIRE TELEPHONIQUE - QUEBEC (PROVINCE). MINISTERE DES AFFAIRES CULTURELLES **4680**

QUEBEC (PROVINCE). MINISTERE DES AFFAIRES SOCIALES *See* CENTRES HOSPITALIERS. GUIDE BUDGETAIRE **3778**

QUEBEC (PROVINCE). MINISTERE DES COMMUNICATIONS. BIBLIOTHEQUE ADMINISTRATIVE *See* LISTE BIMESTRIELLE DES PUBLICATIONS DU GOUVERNEMENT DU QUEBEC **4698**

QUEBEC (PROVINCE). MINISTERE DES COMMUNICATIONS. BIBLIOTHEQUE ADMINISTRATIVE *See* NOUVEAUTES DE LA BIBLIOTHEQUE ADMINISTRATIVE **4670**

QUEBEC (PROVINCE). MINISTERE DES FINANCES *See* BUDGET. BUDGET SPEECH AND ADDITIONAL INFORMATION **4714**

QUEBEC (PROVINCE). MINISTERE DES FINANCES *See* GOUVERNEMENT DU QUEBEC : PUBLIC ACCOUNTS **4728**

QUEBEC (PROVINCE). MINISTERE DES FINANCES *See* BUDGET. RENSEIGNEMENTS SUPPLEMENTAIRES : REFORME DE LA FISCALITE MUNICIPALE **4715**

QUEBEC (PROVINCE). MINISTERE DES FINANCES *See* BUDGET. DISCOURS SUR LE BUDGET ET RENSEIGNEMENTS SUPPLEMENTAIRES **4714**

QUEBEC (PROVINCE) MINISTERE DES FINANCES. DIRECTION DES COMMUNICATIONS *See* BUDGET. COMMUNIQUES (QUEBEC) **4634**

QUEBEC (PROVINCE). MINISTERE DES FINANCES. DIRECTION GENERALE DES ETUDES ECONOMIQUES ET FISCALES *See* BUDGET. RENSEIGNEMENTS SUPPLEMENTAIRES : IMPOTS **4715**

QUEBEC (PROVINCE). NATIONAL ASSEMBLY *See* JOURNAL DES DEBATS : COMMISSIONS PARLEMENTAIRES **4478**

QUEBEC (PROVINCE) NATIONAL ASSEMBLY. STANDING COMMISSION ON REFORM OF THE ELECTORAL DISTRICTS *See* REPORT OF THE STANDING COMMISSION ON REFORM OF THE ELECTORAL DISTRICTS **4681**

QUEBEC (PROVINCE) OFFICE DE LA CONSTRUCTION *See* RAPPORT D'ACTIVITES - OFFICE DE LA CONSTRUCTION DU QUEBEC **4678**

QUEBEC (PROVINCE). OFFICE DES PROFESSIONS *See* RAPPORT D'ACTIVITES - OFFICE DES PROFESSIONS DU QUEBEC **4678**

QUEBEC (PROVINCE). PROGRAMME D'AIDE A LA RECHERCHE SUR L'ENSEIGNEMENT ET L'APPRENTISSAGE *See* REPERTOIRE DES PROJETS DE RECHERCHE DU PAREA **1844**

QUEBEC (PROVINCE). PROTECTEUR DU CITOYEN *See* CHRONIQUES DU PROTECTEUR DU CITOYEN **4637**

QUEBEC (PROVINCE). ROADS DEPT *See* ROUTES QUEBECOISES, LES **5444**

QUEBEC (PROVINCE) SECTION DES TAUX DE LOCATION *See* REPERTOIRE DES TAUX DE LOCATION **2833**

QUEBEC (PROVINCE). SERVICE DE RECHERCHE EN DEFENSE DES CULTURES *See* RAPPORT ANNUEL - SERVICE DE RECHERCHE EN DEFENSE DES CULTURES **4678**

QUEBEC (PROVINCE). SERVICE DES ASSURANCES *See* ANNUAL REPORT OF THE SUPERINTENDENT OF INSURANCE (QUEBEC. 1977) **2873**

QUEBEC (PROVINCE). SERVICE DES ASSURANCES *See* RAPPORT ANNUEL - SERVICE DES ASSURANCES **2891**

QUEBEC (PROVINCE). SERVICE QUALITE DES EAUX *See* ANNUAIRE. QUALITE DES EAUX **5529**

QUEBEC (PROVINCE). TREASURY BOARD *See* ESTIMATES, HIGHLIGHTS - TREASURY BOARD **4721**

QUEBEC ROCK (CN/0226-7187) [06511878] **4148**

QUEBEC SALES TAX WITH RELATED TAXES (CN) [05687869] **4743**

QUEBEC SCEPTIQUE (CN/0843-865X) [22135480] **4243**

QUEBEC SCIENCE (CN/0021-6127) [02126218] **5143**

QUEBEC SOCCER (CN/0228-6351) [08071737] **4914**

QUEBEC SPECTRUM (CN/0227-3438) [06272758] **1843**

QUEBEC STUDIES (US/0737-3759) [09360295] **2756**

QUEBEC SUD-OUEST (CN/0707-7572) [04784126] **5793**

QUEBEC TECHNOLOGIE (CN/0711-5288) [08651778] **5144**

QUEBEC-URSS INFORMATION (CN/0822-9902) [11085153] **2704**

QUEBEC VERT (CN/0705-6923) [04098078] **2202**

QUEBEC VOYAGES (CN/0225-0454) [06132056] **5489**

QUEBEC YACHTIING, VOILE & MOTEUR (CN/0833-918X) [15465535] **595**

QUEBECENSIA (CN/0226-210X) [06515606] **2756**

QUEBECER, THE (CN/0824-2348) [10082578] **4493**

QUEBECOIS DU COMTE DE VANIER, LE (CN/0703-4784) [03564464] **4493**

QUEBECOIS　　　Alphabetical Title Index

QUEBECOIS LIBRE D'OUTREMONT, LE (CN/0710-5797) [08713688] **5793**

QUEBECOIS VAUDREUIL-SOULANGES, LE (CN/0823-6321) [10450948] **4493**

QUEBECOISEAUX (MONTREAL) (CN/0843-9656) [20977407] **5619**

QUEBRA-MAR (BL) [07220343] **5454**

QUEEN See HARPERS & QUEEN **5558**

QUEEN CHARLOTTE ISLANDS OBSERVER (CN) **5793**

QUEEN CITY HERITAGE (US/0746-3472) [09870324] **2756**

QUEEN OF PEACE WILDERNESS GAZETTE (US) **4989**

QUEEN STREET MAGAZINE (CN/0380-2000) [02443354] **328**

QUEENS BAR BULLETIN (US/0048-6302) [01643361] **3033**

QUEENS COLLEGE (CHARLOTTE, N.C.) See ALUMNAE DIRECTORY - QUEENS COLLEGE (CHARLOTTE, N.C.) **1096**

QUEENS COLLEGE LAW JOURNAL (US/0730-9724) [06012816] **3033**

QUEENS COLLEGE (NEW YORK, N.Y.) See ALUMNI DIRECTORY - QUEENS COLLEGE (NEW YORK, N.Y.) **1099**

QUEENS COLLEGE STUDIES IN LIBRARIANSHIP (US/0146-8677) [03639029] **3243**

QUEENS COUNTY DENTAL SOCIETY (N.Y.). INSTITUTE FOR CONTINUING DENTAL EDUCATION See BULLETIN OF THE INSTITUTE FOR CONTINUING DENTAL EDUCATION OF THE QUEENS COUNTY DENTAL SOCIETY **1318**

QUEEN'S GAZETTE (CN/0319-2725) [02442203] **1843**

QUEEN'S LAW JOURNAL (CN/0316-778X) [01639522] **3033**

QUEEN'S PAPERS IN INDUSTRIAL RELATIONS (CN/0838-6609) [16167449] **1705**

QUEEN'S PAPERS IN PURE AND APPLIED MATHEMATICS (CN/0079-8797) [01763283] **3530**

QUEEN'S PARK DIRECTORY (CN/1193-0721) [26245447] **4699**

QUEENS PARK UPDATE (CN) **4677**

QUEEN'S QUARTERLY (CN/0033-6041) [01763284] **2852, 5214**

QUEEN'S UNIVERSITY (BELFAST, NORTHERN IRELAND) See QUEEN'S UNIVERSITY PAPERS IN SOCIAL ANTHROPOLOGY, THE **243**

QUEEN'S UNIVERSITY (KINGSTON, ONT.) See QUEEN'S PAPERS IN PURE AND APPLIED MATHEMATICS **3530**

QUEEN'S UNIVERSITY (KINGSTON, ONT.). CENTRE FOR RESOURCE STUDIES See ANNUAL REPORT FOR THE PERIOD ... / QUEEN'S UNIVERSITY, CENTRE FOR RESOURCE STUDIES **2186**

QUEEN'S UNIVERSITY (KINGSTON, ONT.). CENTRE FOR RESOURCE STUDIES See C R S PERSPECTIVES **2136**

QUEEN'S UNIVERSITY, KINGSTON, ONT. INSTITUTE FOR ECONOMIC RESEARCH See DISCUSSION PAPER - INSTITUTE FOR ECONOMIC RESEARCH. QUEEN'S UNIVERSITY. KINGSTON, ONTARIO **1480**

QUEEN'S UNIVERSITY PAPERS IN SOCIAL ANTHROPOLOGY, THE (IE) [04026868] **243**

QUEENSLAND See ESTIMATES OF THE PROBABLE WAYS AND MEANS AND EXPENDITURE OF THE GOVERNMENT OF QUEENSLAND **4722**

QUEENSLAND ACCOMMODATION AND CARAVANNING DIRECTORY (AT) [03011412] **5489**

QUEENSLAND ARCHAEOLOGICAL RESEARCH (AT/0814-3021) [13809412] **280**

QUEENSLAND. AUDITOR-GENERAL'S DEPT See AUDITOR-GENERAL'S REPORT TO THE LEGISLATIVE ASSEMBLY ON HIS AUDIT OF THE TREASURER'S ANNUAL STATEMENT FOR THE FINANCIAL YEAR ENDED 30TH JUNE ..., THE **4712**

QUEENSLAND. AUDITOR-GENERAL'S DEPT. AUDITOR-GENERAL'S ANNUAL REPORT UPON THE TREASURER'S ANNUAL STATEMENT See AUDITOR-GENERAL'S REPORT TO THE LEGISLATIVE ASSEMBLY ON HIS AUDIT OF THE TREASURER'S ANNUAL STATEMENT FOR THE FINANCIAL YEAR ENDED 30TH JUNE ..., THE **4712**

QUEENSLAND BOTANY BULLETIN (AT) [09805841] **526**

QUEENSLAND. COMMISSIONER OF LAND TAX See ANNUAL REPORT OF THE COMMISSIONER OF LAND TAX ON THE OPERATION OF THE ACTS DURING THE YEAR ... / QUEENSLAND **4628**

QUEENSLAND. COMPTROLLER-GENERAL OF PRISONS See ANNUAL REPORT **3157**

QUEENSLAND COUNTRY LIFE (AT/0033-6084) [10049644] **124**

QUEENSLAND CULTURAL ORGANISATIONS AND MAJOR NATIONAL AND INTERSTATE ORGANISATIONS (AT) [17751289] **328**

QUEENSLAND DAIRY FARMER (AU) **198**

QUEENSLAND DAIRYFARMER, THE (AT) [10049813] **198**

QUEENSLAND DEPARTMENT OF FORESTRY See FORESTRY, ANNUAL REPORT **2381**

QUEENSLAND. DEPARTMENT OF THE CO-ORDINATOR GENERAL OF PUBLIC WORKS See REPORT OF THE CO-ORDINATOR-GENERAL OF PUBLIC WORKS, QUEENSLAND **4681**

QUEENSLAND. DEPT. OF CHILDREN'S SERVICES See REPORT OF THE DIRECTOR - DEPARTMENT OF CHILDREN'S SERVICES **5305**

QUEENSLAND. DEPT. OF COMMERCIAL AND INDUSTRIAL DEVELOPMENT See ANNUAL REPORT **3475**

QUEENSLAND. DEPT. OF COMMUNITY SERVICES See ANNUAL REPORT / DEPARTMENT OF COMMUNITY SERVICES **5272**

QUEENSLAND. DEPT. OF COMMUNITY SERVICES See ANNUAL REPORT OF THE UNDER SECRETARY, DEPARTMENT OF COMMUNITY SERVICES **5272**

QUEENSLAND. DEPT. OF EMPLOYMENT, VOCATIONAL EDUCATION, TRAINING, AND INDUSTRIAL RELATIONS See ANNUAL REPORT / DEPT. OF EMPLOYMENT, VOCATIONAL EDUCATION, TRAINING, AND INDUSTRIAL RELATIONS **1649**

QUEENSLAND. DEPT. OF FORESTRY. DIVISION OF TECHNICAL SERVICES See REPORT OF RESEARCH ACTIVITIES - DIVISION OF TECHNICAL SERVICES, QUEENSLAND DEPARTMENT OF FORESTRY **2392**

QUEENSLAND. DEPT. OF FORESTRY. DIVISION OF TECHNICAL SERVICES. REPORT OF RESEARCH ACTIVITIES - DIVISION OF TECHNICAL SERVICES, QUEENSLAND DEPARTMENT OF FORESTRY See RESEARCH REPORT / DIVISION OF TECHNICAL SERVICES (RESEARCH AND UTILIZATION), QUEENSLAND DEPARTMENT OF FORESTRY **2393**

QUEENSLAND. DEPT. OF INDUSTRY DEVELOPMENT See ANNUAL REPORT **4626**

QUEENSLAND. DEPT. OF JUSTICE See ANNUAL REPORT / DEPARTMENT OF JUSTICE, QUEENSLAND GOVERNMENT **2934**

QUEENSLAND. DEPT. OF PRIMARY INDUSTRIES See ANNUAL REPORT - DEPARTMENT OF PRIMARY INDUSTRIES, QUEENSLAND **60**

QUEENSLAND. DIVISION OF PLANT INDUSTRY See BULLETIN **2411**

QUEENSLAND FAMILY HISTORIAN : JOURNAL OF THE QUEENSLAND FAMILY HISTORY SOCIETY, INC (AT/0811-3394) [13727039] **2469**

QUEENSLAND FAMILY HISTORY SOCIETY See QUEENSLAND FAMILY HISTORIAN : JOURNAL OF THE QUEENSLAND FAMILY HISTORY SOCIETY, INC **2469**

QUEENSLAND FOREST SERVICE See ANNUAL REPORT / QUEENSLAND FOREST SERVICE **2375**

QUEENSLAND FRUIT AND VEGETABLE NEWS (AT/0033-6122) [10049977] **184, 2429**

QUEENSLAND GEOGRAPHICAL JOURNAL. NEW SERIES (AT/0155-400X) [03765321] **2574**

QUEENSLAND GOVERNMENT DIRECTORY (AT/0313-3656) [I03133656] **4677**

QUEENSLAND GOVERNMENT INDUSTRIAL GAZETTE, THE (AT/0155-9362) [18048063] **3153**

QUEENSLAND GOVERNMENT MINING JOURNAL (AT/0033-6149) [02450005] 1393, **2149**

QUEENSLAND GRAINGROWER, THE (AT) [03732950] **203**

QUEENSLAND. INDUSTRIAL GAZETTE See QUEENSLAND GOVERNMENT INDUSTRIAL GAZETTE, THE **3153**

QUEENSLAND. LAND COURT See QUEENSLAND LAND COURT REPORTS **3034**

QUEENSLAND LAND COURT REPORTS (AT) [02380341] **3034**

QUEENSLAND LAW REPORTER (AT/0726-0784) [07260784] **3034**

QUEENSLAND LAW SOCIETY See QUEENSLAND LAW SOCIETY JOURNAL, THE **3034**

QUEENSLAND LAW SOCIETY JOURNAL, THE (AT/0313-4253) [05247581] **3034**

QUEENSLAND LAWYER, THE (AT/0312-1658) [02441130] **3034**

QUEENSLAND MASTER BUILDER (AT/0048-6361) [100486361] **625**

QUEENSLAND MUSEUM, BRISBANE See MEMOIRS OF THE QUEENSLAND MUSEUM **4167**

QUEENSLAND NATURALIST (AT/0079-8843) [01763304] **4171**

QUEENSLAND NURSE, THE (AT/0815-936X) [11117986] **3867**

QUEENSLAND PLANNING LAW REPORTS (AT/0727-095X) [I0727095X] **3034**

QUEENSLAND POCKET YEAR BOOK, THE (AT) [06654990] **1928**

QUEENSLAND. PREMIER'S DEPT See ANNUAL REPORT / THE PREMIER'S DEPARTMENT **4629**

QUEENSLAND PROPERTY REPORT (AT) **4843**

QUEENSLAND. PUBLIC TRUST OFFICE See ANNUAL REPORT OF THE PUBLIC TRUSTEE OF QUEENSLAND FOR THE FINANCIAL YEAR ENDED 30TH JUNE **4710**

QUEENSLAND RAILWAYS See ANNUAL REPORT FOR YEAR ENDED 30 JUNE ... / QUEENSLAND RAILWAYS **5429**

QUEENSLAND RAILWAYS See ANNUAL REPORT FOR YEAR ENDED 30 JUNE ... / QUEENSLAND RAILWAYS **5429**

QUEENSLAND REPORTS (AT) [01763305] **3034**

QUEENSLAND SCIENCE TEACHER (AT) **5144, 1903**

QUEENSLAND STUDIES IN GERMAN LANGUAGE AND LITERATURE (AT/0818-3279) [01434584] **3313**

QUEENSLAND TEACHERS JOURNAL (AT/0033-6238) [I00336238] **1903**

QUEENSLAND TEACHERS PROFESSIONAL MAGAZINE (AT/0813-8206) [I08138206] **1903**

QUEENSLAND TOURIST & TRAVEL CORPORATION See ANNUAL REPORT OF THE QUEENSLAND TOURIST & TRAVEL CORPORATION **5461**

QUEENSLAND. UNIVERSITY, BRISBANE See CALENDAR OF THE UNIVERSITY OF QUEENSLAND **1813**

QUEENSLAND. UNIVERSITY, BRISBANE. DEPT. OF CIVIL ENGINEERING See BULLETIN - QUEENSLAND. UNIVERSITY, BRISBANE. DEPT. OF CIVIL ENGINEERING **2019**

QUEENSLAND. UNIVERSITY, BRISBANE. DEPT. OF ENTOMOLOGY See PAPERS - QUEENSLAND. UNIVERSITY, BRISBANE. DEPT. OF ENTOMOLOGY **5594**

QUEENSLAND WRITER (AT/0819-9752) [I08199752] **3427**

QUEENSLAND YEAR BOOK (AT/0085-5359) [07030160] **1928**

QUEENSWEEK (US/0747-086X) [10545468] **5720**

QUEHACER NACIONAL (AG) [09651703] **4493**

QUEHACER : REVISTA BIMESTRAL DEL CENTRO DE ESTUDIOS Y PROMOCION DEL DESARROLLO-DESCO (PE) [07448636] **4677**

● QUEKETT JOURNAL OF MICROSCOPY, THE (UK/0969-3823) [28095707] **573**

QUEL CORPS? (FR/0337-6338) [I03376338] **1776**

QUELLE (KOLN) (GW/0033-6246) [02828549] **1705**

QUELLEN UND BEITRAEGE ZUR GESCHICHTE DER STADT STADTLOHN (GW) [19739189] **2704**

QUELLEN UND DARSTELLUNGEN ZUR ZEITGESCHICHTE (GW/0481-3545) [01763308] **2627**

QUELLEN UND FORSCHUNGEN AUS ITALIENISCHEN ARCHIVEN UND BIBLIOTHEKEN (GW/0079-9068) [01763309] **2627**

QUELLEN UND FORSCHUNGEN ZUR AGRARGESCHICHTE (GW/0481-3553) [01442648] **124**

QUELLEN UND FORSCHUNGEN ZUR GESCHICHTE DER STADT MUNSTER (GW/0930-9292) [05110524] **2704**

QUELLEN UND FORSCHUNGEN ZUR REFORMATIONSGESCHICHTE (GW) [01714406] **4989**

QUELLEN UND FORSCHUNGEN ZUR SPRACH- UND KULTURGESCHICHTE DER GERMANISCHEN VOLKER (GW/0481-3596) [01641098] **3313**

QUELLEN UND STUDIEN ZUR GESCHICHTE DES OSTLICHEN EUROPA (GW) [01763313] **2704**

QUELLEN UND STUDIEN ZUR GESCHICHTE OSTEUROPAS (GW/0079-9114) [02853801] **2704**

QUELLEN UND STUDIEN ZUR PHILOSOPHIE (GW) [01763315] **4358**

Alphabetical Title Index — R

QUELLEN UND STUDIEN ZUR VERFASSUNGSGESCHICHTE DES DEUTSCHEN REICHES IN MITTELALTER UND NEUZEIT, HRSG. VON KARL ZEUMER (GW) [01763316] **2704**

QUELLEN ZUR GESCHICHTE OBEROESTERREICHS (AU) [25612994] **2704**

QUELLEN ZUR THEATERGESCHICHTE (AU/0259-0786) [03054406] **5367**

QUELLENKATALOGE ZUR MUSIKGESCHICHTE (GW/0079-905X) [04216956] **4148**

QUELLENSCHRIFTEN ZUR WESTDEUTSCHEN VOR- UND FRUHGESCHICHTE (GW) [08796146] **2627**

QUENTIN CAMERON'S OIL & GAS BULLETIN (AT) **4276**

QUERCUS (SP/0212-0054) [I02120054] **2180**

QUERY (US) **1249**

QUESNEL CARIBOO OBSERVER (CN/1195-5023) [29735982] **5793**

QUEST (II/0018-7437) [01763319] **3350**

QUEST : FOR A POSITIVE LIFESTYLE (US/1064-4059) [18240193] **2796**

●QUEST (GRAND RAPIDS, MICH.) (US/1065-7738) [26732869] **32**

QUEST INFORMATION (AT) **2149**

QUEST (LUSAKA, ZAMBIA) (ZA/1011-226X) [17351648] **4358**

QUEST: MANHATTAN PROPERTIES & COUNTRY ESTATES (UK) **4843**

QUEST (NATIONAL ASSOCIATION FOR PHYSICAL EDUCATION IN HIGHER EDUCATION) (US/0033-6297) [01763320] **1857, 3955**

QUEST (REDONDO BEACH) (US/0149-6670) [03520623] **5144**

QUEST STAR (US/0277-5360) [07586626] **3427**

QUEST (WASHINGTON, D.C. 1991) (US/1059-4566) [24594785] **4171**

QUEST (WHEATON, ILL.), THE (US/1040-533X) [18441178] **4358**

QUEST WHO'S WHO (US/0148-9844) [03400465] **434**

QUESTAO SOCIAL NO BRASIL, A (BL) [10164058] **5214**

QUESTE ISTITUZIONI (IT) [17900895] **5214**

QUESTIIO (SP/0210-8054) [I02108054] **1993**

QUESTION DE SPIRITUALITE, TRADITION, LITTERATURES (FR) [05947551] **4243**

QUESTION-MARK (US) [05372938] **3174**

QUESTIONE AGRARIA : QA, LA (IT) [11092518] **124**

QUESTIONE CRIMINALE, LA (IT) [02661833] **3174**

QUESTIONE GIUSTIZIA (IT) [09467628] **3108**

QUESTIONS ACTUELLES DU SOCIALISME (YU/0033-6351) [06683048] **4545**

QUESTIONS AND ANSWERS IN GENERAL TOPOLOGY (JA) [12000853] **2574**

QUESTIONS (BIRMINGHAM) (UK/0954-920X) [I0954920X] **5144, 1903**

QUESTIONS DE CULTURE (CN/0229-6829) [11679748] **5214**

QUESTIONS D'ODONTO-STOMATOLOGIE, LES (FR/0750-2524) [I07502524] **1334**

QUESTIONS ET REPONSES (BE) [01792567] **4678**

QUESTIONS LITURGIQUES (BE) [06152314] **4989**

QUEUEING SYSTEMS (NE/0257-0130) [15962294] **1993**

QUI FAIT QUOI (CN/0828-6140) [12045258] **388**

QUI PARLE (US/1041-8385) [18898222] **2852**

QUI TOURING (IT/0042-546X) [I0042546X] **5489**

QUI-VIVE INTERNATIONAL (FR/0297-2638) [14292793] **3313**

QUICK (AT) **1224**

QUICK & EASY CRAFTS (US/1048-3659) [20928044] **5185**

QUICK & EASY CROCHET (US/0885-0631) [12566178] **5185**

QUICK & EASY PLASTIC CANVAS (US/1048-5341) [20968891] **375**

QUICK & EASY QUILTING (US/1045-5965) [20154893] **5185**

QUICK ANSWER, THE (US/1052-3820) [22271324] **1255**

QUICK BIBLIOGRAPHY SERIES - NATIONAL AGRICULTURAL LIBRARY (US/1052-5378) [02627977] **124**

QUICK DIRECTORY (US) **912**

QUICK FOOT (US/0194-9055) [05092122] **4376**

QUICK FROZEN FOODS ANNUAL PROCESSORS' DIRECTORY AND BUYERS' GUIDE (US/0890-5517) [13915564] **2355**

QUICK FROZEN FOODS INTERNATIONAL (US/0033-6416) [02250745] **2355**

QUICK 'N EASY COOKIN' (US/0893-2247) [15433808] **2792**

●QUICK N EASY COUNTRY COOKIN (US/1075-7384) [30135812] **2792**

QUICK PRINTING (US/0191-4588) [04901842] **4569**

QUICK REFERENCE GUIDE TO SCHOOL DROPOUTS (US/1055-3428) [23157425] **1776**

QUICK RESPONSE NEWS See JUST-IN-TIME & QUICK RESPONSE NEWS **843**

●QUICK TRIPS TRAVEL LETTER (US/1064-0339) [26202518] **5489**

QUICKBORN (GW) [03674363] **3313**

QUICKBORN, VEREINIGUNG VON FREUNDEN DER NIEDERDEUTSCHEN SPRACHE UND LITERATUR IN HAMBURG. MITTEILUNGEN See QUICKBORN **3313**

QUICKSERVICE OPERATIONS MANAGEMENT See RESTAURANT EXECUTIVE **5072**

QUICKTIME FORUM See CONVERGE (SUNNYVALE, CALIF.) **1109**

QUICKTIME FORUM, THE (US/1062-9009) [25799328] **1120**

QUID? (FR/0532-6656) [02822208] **1928**

QUIEN ES QUIEN EN LA PAZ (BO) [23290274] **434**

QUIEN VENDE EN ESPANA LOS PRODUCTOS EXTRANJEROS (SZ) [01788402] **849**

QUIET REVOLUTION (JACKSON, MISS.) (US) [09724356] **4989**

QUILL AND SCROLL (IOWA CITY) (US/0033-6505) [01715061] **2923**

QUILL (CHICAGO), THE (US/0033-6475) [01763332] **2923**

QUILL OF ALPHA XI DELTA, THE (US) **5235**

QUILL, QUEENSLAND INTER-LIBRARY LIAISON (AT) [02275661] **3243**

QUILT DIGEST, THE CEASED. (US/0740-4093) [09763519] **5185**

QUILT (NEW YORK, N.Y.) (US/1059-0684) [24469603] **375**

QUILT WORLD (US/0149-8045) [03552353] **5185**

QUILTER'S NEWSLETTER MAGAZINE (US/0274-712X) [06533923] **5185**

QUILTER'S TREASURY CEASED. (US/1072-9259) **5185**

●QUILTESSENCE (THIEF RIVER FALLS, MINN.) (US/1064-7325) [26385293] **5185**

QUILTING AND RELATED NEEDLEWORK (US/0190-0935) [04626601] **5185**

QUILTING TODAY (US/1040-4457) [18419680] **5185**

QUILTMAKER (WHEATRIDGE, COLO.) (US/1047-1634) [16060968] **5185**

QUIMERA (BARCELONA, SPAIN) (SP/0211-3325) [07916884] **3351**

QUIMICA 2000 (SP/0213-4152) [I02134152] **990**

QUIMICA ANALITICA SALAMANCA (SP/0212-0569) [I02120569] **1018**

QUIMICA & DERIVADOS (BL) [06792251] **2016**

QUIMICA E INDUSTRIA (MADRID) (SP/0033-6521) [01443649] **1029**

QUIMICA HOY (SP/0213-7828) [05781539] **990**

QUIMICA NOVA (BL/0100-4042) [09051990] **990**

QUINCAILLERIE, MATERIAUX (CN/0318-8531) [06249305] **625**

QUINCY COLLEGE BULLETIN (US/0033-6556) [04420916] **1094**

QUINCY HERALD-WHIG, THE (US/0746-6358) [10117886] **5661**

QUINCY SUN, THE (US) [22400827] **5690**

QUINCY VALLEY POST-REGISTER, THE (US) [17197064] **5762**

QUINLAN PRIVATE TRUCK LAW REPORT, THE (US/0736-2846) [09089215] **5423, 3034**

QUINOLONES BULLETIN : REPORTS ON GYRASE INHIBITORS (GW/0176-912X) [19961279] **3632**

QUINOLONEWS INTERNATIONAL CEASED. (FR) **2671**

QUINQUENNIAL REVIEW (CN/0845-4025) [20135217] **2832**

QUINQUEREME CEASED. (UK/0140-3397) [05348722] **3313**

QUINTESSENCE (SP) **2852**

●QUINTESSENCE (CHICAGO, ILL.) (US/1076-2833) [30446053] **3983, 2180, 3661**

QUINTESSENCE INTERNATIONAL (IT) **1334**

QUINTESSENCE INTERNATIONAL (BERLIN : 1985) (GW) [11707007] **1334**

QUINTESSENCE OF DENTAL TECHNOLOGY : QDT (US) [24626261] **1334**

QUINTESSENZ BIBLIOTHEK. ASTHMA UND ALLERGIE (GW) [24914324] **3676**

QUINTESSENZ DER ZAHNTECHNIK, DIE (GW/0340-4641) [01891274] **1334**

QUINTESSENZ JOURNAL (GW/0033-6599) [04116789] **1334**

QUINTESSENZA, LA CEASED. (IT/0390-6841) [02904834] **1334**

QUINTO LINGO SUSPENDED. (US/0033-6602) [01589228] **3313**

QUILL, QUEENSLAND INTER-LIBRARY LIAISON (AT) [02275661] **3243**

QUINZAINE LITTERAIRE, LA (FR/0048-6493) [01763335] **3427**

QUIPU (MX/0185-5093) [10901545] **5144**

QUIRAMA (CK) [01795300] **2552**

QUIRES (CN/0826-4996) [11355521] **4148**

QUIRK'S MARKETING RESEARCH REVIEW (US/0893-7451) [15636081] **765**

QUITO. UNIVERSIDAD CENTRAL DEL ECUADOR See PUBLICACIONES - QUITO. UNIVERSIDAD CENTRAL DEL ECUADOR **3134**

QUITO. UNIVERSIDAD CENTRAL. FACULTAD DE JURISPRUDENCIA Y CIENCIAS SOCIALES See F.J., REVISTA DE LA FACULTAD DE JURISPRUDENCIA Y CIENCIAS SOCIALES **2968**

QUMRAN CHRONICLE (PL/0867-8715) [I08678715] **5019**

QUO VADIS ELEKTRONIKA (XR) [10125848] **2078**

QUOI DE 9 (CN/0228-6238) [08063840] **5303**

QUOI DE NEUF? / OMPAC, ORGANISATION MONTREALAISE DES PERSONNES ATTEINTES DE CANCER (CN/1187-5658) [25423795] **5303**

QUOI DE NEUF? (STE-FOY) (CN/0822-7292) [12150522] **1776**

QUOI DE N'OEUF (CN/0821-6924) [09796254] **220**

QUONDAM ET FUTURUS (BIRMINGHAM, ALA.) (US/8755-3627) [23893550] **3351**

QUORUM (OTTAWA) (CN/0225-5014) [06167122] **2544**

QUORUM REPORT (US/0882-3456) [11808012] **4678**

QUOTE (ATLANTA, GA.) (US/0273-6705) [01606958] **3427**

"QUOTE UNQUOTE" (CN/0229-978X) [08296982] **1094**

QUOTES & ANECDOTES (US) **2491**

QUOTIDIANO DI LECCE, IL (IT) **5805**

QUOTIDIEN DE PARIS (FR) **5801**

QUOTIDIEN DE STATISTIQUE CANADA (CN/0380-6103) [15168118] **4699**

QUOTIDIEN DES TELECOMS, LE (FR) **1162**

QUOTIDIEN DU MEDECIN (FR/0336-0067) [I03360067] **5801**

QUOTIDIEN DU PHARMACIEN, LE (FR/0764-5104) [I07645104] **4327**

QUOTIDIEN JURIDIQUE (FR) **3034**

●QURANIC GUIDANCE (US/1064-0770) [26208862] **5044**

●QWL NEWS & ABSTRACTS / WORK RESEARCH UNIT (UK) [25806778] **946**

QZ. QUALITAT UND ZUVERLASSIGKEIT (GW/0720-1214) [I07201214] **1623**

R A C V S OUT AND ABOUT (AT) **5489**

R A C V'S ATTRACTIONS AUSTRALIA (AT) **5489**

R A I F. RESEAU D'ACTION ET D'INFORMATION POUR LES FEMMES (CN/0705-3762) [03900422] **2285, 5565**

R.A.P.H.A.T. REGROUPEMENT DES ASSOCIATIONS DE PERSONNES HANDICAPEES DE L'ABITIBI-TEMISCAMINGUE (CN/0822-9279) [10680953] **4392, 5303**

R AND B MAGAZINE (US) [01788341] **4148**

R & D ACTIVITIES IN STATE GOVERNMENT AGENCIES (US/0565-8284) [01269781] **5144**

R — Alphabetical Title Index

R & D CONTRACTS, GRANTS FOR TRAINING, CONSTRUCTION, AND MEDICAL LIBRARIES (US) [22448658] **5144**

R & D CONTRACTS MONTHLY (US/0033-6793) [00932511] **5144**

R & D MANAGEMENT (UK/0033-6807) [01853518] **5144**

R & D MONOGRAPH (US/0148-8023) [02412100] **1705**

R AND D OUTLOOK (CN/0836-1371) [18183649] **1623**

R & R (LOS ANGELES, CALIF.) (US/1076-6502) [30056759] **1137**

●R & R MILITARY RETIREE: RETIREMENT & RELOCATION MILITARY RETIREE (US/1055-2081) [23121640] **4054**

R & S REPORT (HONOLULU) (US/0093-3481) [01789607] **5337**

●R.B (US) [30687615] 1515, **124**

R.C.M. MAGAZINE (UK/0033-684X) [04450659] **4148**

R.C.M. RADIO COMMANDE MAGAZINE (FR/0290-9693) [I02909693] **1120**

R/C MODEL BOATS & RACING (US/1062-757X) [25775257] **4914**

R/C RACE BOATS See R/C MODEL BOATS & RACING **4914**

R.E.P. (OVERLAND PARK, KAN.) CEASED. (US/1058-9678) [22261249] **5318**

R.E.P.P.: RESERVE EXECUTIVE PRACTICE POINTS / FIRST NATIONS RESOURCE COUNCIL (CN/0846-3093) [25066632] **2271**

R.E.S. NEWS EXCHANGE See REC NEWS EXCHANGE **4989**

R. E. TODAY (UK) 1776, **4989**

R.F. DESIGN (US/0163-321X) [04349886] **1993**

R.F.M., REVUE FRANCAISE DE MECANIQUE (FR/0373-6601) [05188572] **2127**

R.G.S. REVUE GENERALE DE SECURITE (FR/0242-6277) [I02426277] **2868**

R.H.M. ASSOCIATES, INC See R.H.M. SURVEY OF WARRANTS, OPTIONS & LOW-PRICE STOCKS, THE **912**

R.H.M. CONVERTIBLE SURVEY, THE CEASED. (US) [06296895] **912**

R.H.M. SURVEY OF WARRANTS, OPTIONS & LOW-PRICE STOCKS, THE CEASED. (US/0196-6901) [02920432] **912**

●R.H. MACY & CO. BANKRUPTCY NEWS (US/1061-317X) [25249967] **806**

R.I.A. (PARIS, 1977) (FR/0035-4244) [04209085] **2355**

R. I. BULLETIN (US/0146-1222) [02871802] **2923**

R.L. POLK & CO See ANNUAL NATIONAL VEHICLE POPULATION PROFILE : IMPORT CARS **5403**

R.L. POLK & CO See ANNUAL NATIONAL VEHICLE POPULATION PROFILE : LIGHT TRUCKS **5403**

R L S, REGIONAL LANGUAGE STUDIES ... NEWFOUNDLAND (CN/0079-9335) [02578359] **3313**

R N D REVUE NOTRE DAME (CN/0035-3795) [02627560] **5035**

R.P. INTERNACIONAL DE RELACIONES PUBLICAS (SP/0211-3333) [I02113333] **765**

R P M WEEKLY (CN/0033-7064) [02126390] **4148**

R.P.N.A.M. UPDATE (CN/0822-4048) [09774720] 3935, **3867**

R.R. DONNELLEY AND SONS COMPANY. FINANCIAL PRINTING DIVISION See DONNELLEY SEC HANDBOOK **3099**

R.R.I.M. PLANTING MANUAL (MY) [07804242] **184**

R - RAND CORPORATION (US/0192-3692) [01606260] **5144**

R.S.A. POSTAGE STAMP CATALOGUE (SA) [01786726] **2787**

R T S. REVISTA DE TREBALL SOCIAL (SP/0212-7210) [I02127210] **5254**

R.T.V.A (FR/0483-786X) [10050337] **5519**

R.U.S.I. AND BRASSEY'S DEFENCE YEARBOOK (UK) [06633579] **4054**

R.U.S.I. AND BRASSEY'S DEFENCE YEARBOOK (UK/0097-4803) [02041153] **4054**

R8-RG / USDA, FOREST SERVICE, SOUTHERN REGION (US) [26875845] **2391**

RAADGEVENDE INTERPARLEMENTAIRE BENELUSRAAD : VERSLAG (BE) [11205762] **4678**

RAADSADVIEZEN / RAAD VOOR DE KUNST (NE/0927-9806) [I09279806] **328**

RAAKPUNT (MAARSSEN) (NE/0166-4298) [I01664298] 3935, **2285**

●RABBINICS TODAY (US/1066-0585) [I10660585] **5052**

RABBIT BRAIN RESEARCH (NE) [01585517] **5596**

RABBIT TRACKS (US) **2469**

RABELS ZEITSCHRIFT FUER AUSLANDISCHES UND INTERNATIONALES PRIVATRECHT (GW/0033-7250) [07683469] **3134**

RABIDA (SP) [14903774] **3427**

RABINDRABHARATI JOURNAL (II) [01784091] **2508**

RABOCHAIA TRIBUNA (RU) [21056914] **5809**

RABOCHII KLASS I SOTSIALNYI PROGRESS (RU) [28606517] 4545, **1705**

RABOTNITSA (RU) [04426812] **1705**

RAC CAMPING & CARAVANNING GUIDE - EUROPE (UK) **5489**

RAC NEWSLETTER (US/0163-9838) [04550296] 1993, **2006**

RAC, REFRIGERATION AND AIR CONDITIONING (UK) [04772097] **2607**

RACAR (CN/0315-9906) [02247889] **362**

RACCOLTA ATTI NORMATIVI (IT) **3034**

RACCOLTA NORMATIVA REGIONE TOSCANA (IT) **4678**

RACCOLTA SISTEMATICA DI GIURISPRUDENZA COMMENTATA (IT) [01763354] **3034**

RACCOLTA UFFICIALE DECRETI See RACCOLTA ATTI NORMATIVI **3034**

RACCOLTA UFFICIALE DELLE SENTENZE E ORDINANZE (IT) [01716054] **3034**

RACCOLTA VINCIANA (IT) [04426927] 2627, **363**

RACCOON CEASED. (US/0148-0162) [03256345] **3470**

RACE & CLASS (UK/0306-3968) [02240562] **2271**

RACE RELATIONS & INDUSTRY (US/0033-7315) [02920155] **946**

RACE RELATIONS NEWS (SA) [20149380] **5254**

RACE RELATIONS SURVEY / SOUTH AFRICAN INSTITUTE OF RACE RELATIONS (SA) [12849939] **4493**

RACECAR ENGINEERING (UK/0961-1096) [25517455] 1993, **5423**

RACEFORM UP-TO-DATE FORM BOOK (UK) [06182879] 4914, **2802**

RACEFORM UP-TO-DATE FORM BOOK. NATIONAL HUNT EDITION (UK) [10689972] **2802**

RACER (TORONTO) (CN/0380-7762) [02126667] **4914**

●RACER (TUSTIN, CALIF.) (US/1066-6060) [26150714] **4914**

RACER WEST, THE (CN/0834-311X) [16390696] **4914**

RACETRACK (AT) **4914**

RACIAL AND ETHNIC REPORT : PUPIL ENROLLMENT (US) [07397365] 2271, **1776**

RACIAL AND ETHNIC SURVEY (US/0090-1059) [01784655] **2271**

RACIAL, ETHNIC, AND SEX ENROLLMENT DATA FROM INSTITUTIONS OF HIGHER EDUCATION (US/0192-9879) [04430492] 2271, **1843**

RACIAL/ETHNIC DISTRIBUTION OF STAFF AND STUDENTS IN CALIFORNIA PUBLIC SCHOOLS (US) [08041047] **1776**

RACINE LABOR (US) **1705**

RACING, FARM, CORPORATE, AND STABLE NAMES (US/0733-6500) [08615980] **2802**

RACING FOR KIDS (US/1056-7623) [23846188] **1068**

RACING GREYHOUNDS (US/1042-9174) [19257588] 4914, **4865**

RACING PIGEON BULLETIN (US/0146-8383) [02382005] **4914**

RACING PIGEON PICTORIAL (UK/0033-7404) [02391572] **4914**

RACING PIGEON, THE (UK/0033-7390) [02278668] **4914**

RACING STAR WEEKLY (US/0033-7439) [03903159] **2802**

RACIOS DE GESTAO (PO) [07076111] **806**

RACKETT (CN/0229-9844) [08360284] **4148**

RACKHAM JOURNAL OF THE ARTS AND HUMANITIES, THE (US/0731-4817) [07067622] **2852**

RACKING REVIEW, THE (US/0744-6829) [08496320] **2802**

RACONTE (CN/0713-3928) [09021804] **5423**

RACONTEUR (US/1050-9402) [21709659] **2627**

RACONTEUR (BATON ROUGE, LA. ANNUAL ED.), LE (US/0893-4525) [12985848] 2483, **2469**

RACONTEUR (TIMMINS) (CN/0712-2810) [08818747] **5793**

RACQUET (NEW YORK, N.Y. : 1985) (US/0883-8429) [12232533] **4914**

RACQUETBALL CANADA (1981) (CN/0229-7396) [08028196] **4914**

●RACZ' FINANCIAL DIRECTORY (US/1065-724X) [26708825] **806**

RAD (BL) [01795123] **1515**

RAD DISPANZERA ZA PLUCNE BOLESTI I TUBERKULOZU (YU/0351-4331) [06126470] **3632**

RAD HARLOW (UK/0264-6412) [I02646412] **3944**

RAD HRVATSKE AKADEMIJE ZNANOSTI I UMJETNOSTI (CI) [26798727] **1094**

RAD (NEW YORK), DAS (US/0033-7455) [04048986] 1903, **3313**

RAD! : REVIEW AND DISCUSSION OF ROCK & ROLL CULTURE (US) **4148**

RAD VOJVOANSKIH MUZEJA (YU/0550-2209) [01913382] **4095**

RADAR AND ELECTRONICS See I.P.R.E. REVIEW, THE **2056**

RADAR BULLETIN (UK/0954-237X) [I0954237X] **4393**

RADAR FORECAST (US) **4054**

RADDLE MOON (CN/0826-5909) [11422249] **3427**

RADEX RUNDSCHAU (AU/0370-3657) [01911408] **4445**

RADIANCE (OAKLAND, CALIF.) (US/0889-9495) [14104912] 4797, **405**

RADIANSKA UKRAINA (UN) [04579601] **2704**

RADIANSKA ZHINKA See ZHINKA **5572**

RADIANSKE PRAVO (UN/0485-8573) [05471010] **3034**

RADIATION AND ENVIRONMENTAL BIOPHYSICS (GW/0301-634X) [01793951] **496**

RADIATION CURING BUYER'S GUIDE (US/0197-8039) [06115030] **3944**

RADIATION EFFECTS AND DEFECTS IN SOLIDS (US/1042-0150) [18904315] **1057**

RADIATION EFFECTS BULLETIN (US/0888-448X) [13578211] **990**

RADIATION EMBRITTLEMENT (US/1040-3078) [18372154] **4440**

RADIATION MEASUREMENTS (UK/1350-4487) **4440**

RADIATION MEDICINE (JA/0288-2043) [10585646] **3944**

●RADIATION ONCOLOGY INVESTIGATIONS (US/1065-7541) [26716443] **3823**

●RADIATION PHYSICS AND CHEMISTRY (UK/0969-806X) [27781815] 990, **4419**

RADIATION PHYSICS, BIOPHYSICS AND RADIATION BIOLOGY (US) [04680083] 496, **4440**

RADIATION PROTECTION ACTIVITIES (US/0161-7796) [04007985] **2240**

RADIATION PROTECTION DOSIMETRY (UK/0144-8420) [07781851] **4440**

RADIATION PROTECTION IN AUSTRALIA (AT/0729-7963) [I07297963] 3944, **4798**

RADIATION PROTECTION MANAGEMENT (US/0740-0640) [09865244] 2158, **2868**

RADIATION RESEARCH (US/0033-7587) [01763361] **4441**

●RADIATION THERAPIST: THE JOURNAL OF THE RADIATION ONCOLOGY SCIENCES (US) [25786550] **3944**

RADIATSIONNAIA BEZOPASNOST I ZASHCHITA AES (RU/0137-0057) [02974643] **2158**

●RADIATSIONNAIA BIOLOGIIA, RADIOECOLOGIIA / ROSSIISKAIA AKADEMIIA NAUK (RU) [29254243] **4441**

RADICAL AMERICA (US/0033-7617) [00827296] 1705, **4493**

RADICAL HISTORIANS NEWSLETTER (US/0730-1812) [05130822] **2627**

RADICAL HISTORY REVIEW (US/0163-6545) [03140092] **4545**

RADICAL PHILOSOPHY (UK/0300-211X) [01784782] **4358**

RADICAL TEACHER (CAMBRIDGE) (US/0191-4847) [03948551] **1776**

RADIKAL (RU) [24185068] **5809**

RADIO (RU/0033-765X) [06923955] **1137**

Alphabetical Title Index — RADMARKT

●RADIO ADVERTISING SOURCE (US/1071-4707) [28643783] **1137**, **765**

RADIO AGE (AUGUSTA, GA.) (US/0892-6360) [15243592] **1137**

RADIO AMATEUR CALLBOOK. INTERNATIONAL LISTINGS, EXCLUSIVE OF NORTH AMERICA & HAWAII (US/0892-8002) [12883777] **1137**

RADIO AMATEUR CALLBOOK MAGAZINE : UNITED STATES LISTINGS (US/0033-7706) [02872223] **1137**

RADIO AMATEUR CALLBOOK. NORTH AMERICAN LISTINGS, INCLUDING HAWAII & US POSSESSIONS (US) [12883800] **1137**

RADIO AMATEUR DU QUEBEC (CN/0848-8452) [21320879] **1137**

RADIO & ELECTRONICS CONSTRUCTOR (UK) [01788196] **2078**

RADIO & MUSIC (UK) **4148**

RADIO & RECORDS (US/0277-4860) [06225739] **1137**

RADIO & RECORDS *See* R & R (LOS ANGELES, CALIF.) **1137**

RADIO AND TELEVISION BROADCASTING (CN/0575-9560) [02443766] **1137**

RADIO AND TELEVISION BROADCASTING STATIONS (AT/0812-2016) [20155806] **1137**

RADIO & TELEVISION CAREER DIRECTORY (US/1062-0737) [24168711] **1137**

RADIO AND TELEVISION SERVICING (UK/0307-3165) [01800171] **2078**

RADIO ATIVITE INC (CN/0822-7926) [10615594] **4148**

RADIO BUSINESS REPORT (US/0741-8469) [10222195] **1137**

RADIO CANADA INTERNATIONAL *See* RCI NEWSLETTER **1138**

RADIO CANADA INTERNATIONAL *See* BULLETIN DE RCI **1128**

RADIO-CHICAGO **SUSPENDED.** (US/1044-9647) [19961277] **1137**

RADIO CLUB OF AMERICA *See* PROCEEDINGS - THE RADIO CLUB OF AMERICA, INC **1120**

RADIO COLLEZIONE COMPLETA : ENCYCLOPEDIE MEDIE CHIRURGICALE (IT) **3973**

RADIO COMMON CARRIER RULES (US) **1137**

RADIO COMMUNICATION (UK/0033-7803) [02246100] **1162**, **2078**

RADIO COMMUNICATIONS REPORT (US/0744-0618) [08002255] **1137**

RADIO CONSTRUCTOR *See* RADIO & ELECTRONICS CONSTRUCTOR **2078**

RADIO CONTACTS **CEASED.** (US/0146-6852) [03008441] **1137**

RADIO CONTROL ACTION SERIES (US/1054-2256) **2777**

RADIO CONTROL BOAT MODELER (US/1043-8009) [19568742] **2777**, **375**

RADIO CONTROL BOAT MODELLER (UK/0268-5248) [02685248] **2777**

RADIO CONTROL BUYERS GUIDE (US/0098-9215) [02242582] **2777**

RADIO CONTROL CAR ACTION (US/0886-1609) [12847662] **2777**

RADIO CONTROL MODEL CARS (UK/0953-0576) **2777**

●RADIO CONTROL MODEL CARS (1992) (US/1061-7213) [25418137] **2777**

RADIO CONTROL MODEL CARS AND TRUCKS (US/1061-7205) [25418029] **2777**

RADIO CONTROL MODEL WORLD (UK) **1120**

RADIO CONTROL MODELS & ELECTRONICS (UK/0033-7838) [06544162] **2777**

RADIO CONTROL MODELS & ELECTRONICS : RCM AND E (UK/0269-8307) [22394150] **2777**

RADIO CONTROL PRODUCTS DIRECTORY (US/0090-9157) [01785467] **375**

RADIO CONTROL SCALE AIRCRAFT (UK) [28013566] **2777**

RADIO CORPORATION OF AMERICA *See* TECHNICAL NOTES - RCA **1140**

RADIO-ELECTRONICS (US/0033-7862) [04855440] **1137**, **2078**

RADIO ELEKTRONIK SCHAU (AU) [13959769] **2078**

RADIO-, FERNSEH-, PHONO-PRAXIS (GW) [07045481] **2078**

RADIO, FERNSEHEN, ELEKTRONIK (GW/0033-7900) [13168092] **1137**

RADIO FINANCIAL REPORT / NAB (US/1041-5017) [11878361] **1137**

RADIO FREQUENCY PLAN (US/0148-0715) [03133972] **1137**

RADIO FUN (US/1055-887X) [23363928] **1137**

RADIO GUIDE (MADISON) (US/0199-6606) [04349756] **1137**

RADIO I TELEWIZJA (PL) **388**

RADIO IN THE UNITED STATES (US/0740-2341) [09940412] **1137**

●RADIO INK (US/1064-587X) [26340370] **1137**

RADIO LOCAL MARKETS SOURCE (US/1071-4669) [28643658] **1137**, **765**

RADIO MODELLER (UK/0144-0713) [06699041] **2777**

RADIO (MONTREAL) (CN/0709-552X) [05534331] **1137**

RADIO NACIONAL DE ESPANA (SP) **2521**

RADIO NAVIGATIONAL AIDS : ATLANTIC AND MEDITERRANEAN AREA (US/0363-5597) [02479717] **4182**

RADIO NEW YORK : LISTENER'S GUIDE TO RADIO PROGRAMMING IN THE GREATER NEW YORK AREA (US/1053-1068) [22455141] **1137**

RADIO OCH TELEVISION *See* ELEKTRONIK VARLDEN **2052**

RADIO ONLY *See* RADIO : THE MONTHLY MANAGEMENT TOOL **1137**

RADIO PC REPORT (US/0742-5783) [10367219] **1137**

RADIO PROMOTION BULLETIN (US/1044-985X) [19987087] **765**, **1120**

RADIO REGULARS (US/1061-6705) [25395144] **1137**

RADIO RSA, JOHANNESBURG *See* RSA CALLING **2643**

RADIO SCIENCE (US/0048-6604) [01763372] **1409**

RADIO TECHNICAL COMMISSION FOR AERONAUTICS (U.S.) *See* PROCEEDINGS OF THE ANNUAL ASSEMBLY MEETING **32**

RADIO TECHNOLOGY INTERNATIONAL (UK/0963-0678) [09630678] **5144**, **1137**

RADIO : THE MONTHLY MANAGEMENT TOOL (US) [25170124] **1137**

RADIO TIMES (UK/0033-8060) [01763373] **1137**

RADIO TODAY (US) [01607286] **1137**

RADIO/TV HIGHLIGHTS (US/0883-640X) [12178911] **1137**

RADIO WORLD (FALLS CHURCH, VA.) (US/0274-8541) [06653533] **1138**

RADIO Y TELEVISION **CEASED.** (US/0033-8133) [05166118] **1138**

RADIOACTIVE EXCHANGE, THE (US/0891-3013) [08703529] **2240**

RADIOACTIVE MATERIALS RELEASED FROM NUCLEAR POWER PLANTS ... ANNUAL REPORT (US) [04706689] **2240**

●RADIOACTIVE WASTE MANAGEMENT AND ENVIRONMENTAL RESTORATION (UK/1065-609X) [26648615] **2240**

RADIOACTIVE WASTE MANAGEMENT AND THE NUCLEAR FUEL CYCLE (SZ/0739-5876) [09052909] **2240**

RADIOACTIVE WASTE MANAGEMENT (CHUR, SWITZERLAND : 1981) (SZ/0275-7273) [07227687] **2240**

RADIOACTIVE WASTE MANAGEMENT HANDBOOK (US/0898-8161) [17924386] **2240**

RADIOACTIVE WASTE MANAGEMENT (OAK RIDGE, TENN.) (US/0275-3707) [07144381] **2240**

RADIOACTIVITY & RADIOCHEMISTRY (US/1045-845X) [20270597] **1029**

RADIOAKTIIVISUUSHAVAINTOJA (FI/0071-5220) [01793225] **1434**

RADIOBIOLOGIA. RADIOTHERAPIA **CEASED.** (GW/0033-8184) [02266742] **3945**

RADIOBIOLOGIIA (RU/0033-8192) [02384176] **3945**

RADIOCARBON (US/0033-8222) [02244603] **1393**

●RADIOCHEMISTRY (NEW YORK, N.Y.) (US/1066-3622) [26923191] **990**

RADIOCHIMICA ACTA (US/0033-8230) [01696976] **1057**

RADIOCOMM IN CANADA *See* RADIOCOMM MAGAZINE **1138**

●RADIOCOMM MAGAZINE (CN/1196-0809) [28745107] **1138**

RADIOCOMMUNICATIONS MAGAZINE (FR/0986-2900) [I09862900] **1162**

RADIOELEKTRONIKA I ELEKTROSVIAZ (RU/0321-222X) [04980459] **1162**

RADIOGRAPHER (AT/0033-8273) [10441946] **3632**

RADIOGRAPHICS (US/0271-5333) [06611251] **3945**

RADIOGRAPHY TODAY (UK/0954-8211) [18617323] **4441**

RADIOHIMIJA (RU/0033-8311) [01906250] **3945**

RADIOISOTOPES (JA/0033-8303) [01853173] **5144**

RADIOISOTOPY (XR/0322-8657) [11577842] **4419**

RADIOLIT (GW) **3945**

RADIOLOGE, DER (GW/0033-832X) [01763375] **3945**

RADIOLOGIA DIAGNOSTICA **CEASED.** (GW/0033-8354) [01715759] **3945**

RADIOLOGIA IUGOSLAVICA (XV/0485-893X) [10967584] **3945**

RADIOLOGIA MADRID (SP/0033-8338) [I00338338] **3945**

RADIOLOGIA MEDICA (IT/0033-8362) [01763377] **3945**

RADIOLOGIC CLINICS OF NORTH AMERICA, THE (US/0033-8389) [01763378] **3945**

RADIOLOGIC TECHNOLOGY (US/0033-8397) [01646035] **3945**

RADIOLOGICA (OULU) (FI/0358-4887) [04813721] **3945**

RADIOLOGICAL HEALTH BULLETIN (US/0888-8086) [09885342] **3945**

RADIOLOGICAL INSPECTION REPORTS (US/1054-8815) [23004540] **2240**

RADIOLOGICAL PROTECTION BULLETIN (UK/0308-4272) [I03084272] **4419**

RADIOLOGICAL QUALITY OF THE ENVIRONMENT (US/0363-9819) [02521595] **2240**

RADIOLOGIE **CEASED.** (GW/0720-3322) [07235618] **3945**

●RADIOLOGIST (BALTIMORE, MD.), THE (US/1069-1286) [27952027] **3945**

RADIOLOGY (US) **3945**

RADIOLOGY (US/0033-8419) [01763380] **3945**

RADIOLOGY & IMAGING LETTER (US/0741-160X) [10094611] **3945**, **3849**

RADIOLOGY ECONOMIC STRATEGIES (US) **3946**

RADIOLOGY MANAGEMENT (US/0198-7097) [06167199] **3946**

RADIOLOGY OUTLOOK (US/0896-8748) [17310444] **3946**

RADIOLOGY RESIDENT, THE **CEASED.** (US/1063-8563) [26150150] **3946**

RADIOLOGY TODAY (US/0893-1054) [15259654] **3946**

RADIOLOGY. [MICROFICHE] (US) **3946**

RADIONAVIGATION JOURNAL (US/0161-3715) [03902353] **4182**

RADIOPHARMACY AND RADIOPHARMACOLOGY YEARBOOK (US/0748-6111) [10979838] **4327**, **3849**

RADIOPHYSICS AND QUANTUM ELECTRONICS (US/0033-8443) [02241240] **4441**

RADIOPROTECTION (FR/0033-8451) [06752813] **4798**

RADIOSATROFIZIKAS OBSERVATORIJA (LATVIJAS PSR ZIMANTU AKADEMIJA) *See* ISSLEDOVANIE SOLNTSA I KRASNYKH ZVEZD **396**

RADIOSCAN MAGAZINE (SPANISH ED.) (US/1050-3641) [21473522] **1120**

RADIOSCHAU *See* RADIO ELEKTRONIK SCHAU **2078**

RADIOSCIENTIST AND INFORMATION BULLETIN *See* RADIOSCIENTIST BULLETIN **1410**

●RADIOSCIENTIST BULLETIN (BE) **1410**

RADIOSPEKTROSKOPIIA (RU/0131-8098) [04940295] **4441**

RADIOTEHNIKA (HARKOV) (UN/0485-8972) [11032775] **1138**

RADIOTEHNIKA (MOSKVA) (RU/0033-8486) [01908546] **1138**

RADIOTEKHNIKA I ELEKTRONIKA (RU/0033-8494) [01713885] **2078**

RADIOTEKHNIKA I ELEKTRONIKA. ENGLISH. SOVIET JOURNAL OF COMMUNICATIONS TECHNOLOGY & ELECTRONICS *See* JOURNAL OF COMMUNICATIONS TECHNOLOGY & ELECTRONICS **2068**

RADIOTHERAPY AND ONCOLOGY (NE/0167-8140) [10321932] **3946**, **3823**

RADIOWEEK (US/1054-9048) [19174731] **1138**

RADIUS (MENDOCINO, CALIF.) (US/0886-7771) [12998691] **328**

RADIUS (STUTTGART, GERMANY) **CEASED.** (GW/0033-8532) [05226475] **4989**

RADIX (BERKELEY, CALIF.) (US/0275-0147) [04800301] **4989**

RADMARKT (GW) **4082**

RADNE Alphabetical Title Index

RADNE ORGANIZACIJE VANPRIVREDNIH DELATNOSTI (YU) [01795718] **5337**

RADNEWS TEDDINGTON (UK/0966-9698) [I09669698] **4225**

RADNICI I CIST LICNI DOHODAK PO OPSTINAMA U SRBIH / REPUBLICKI ZAVOD ZA STATISTIKU SRBIH (BN) [08399435] 1515, **1537**

RADNICI PREMA STEPENU STRUONOG OBRAZOVANJA / SOCIJALISTICKA REPUBLIKA SRBIJA, REPUBLICKI ZAVOD ZA STATISTIKU (CI) [11302683] **1705**

RADNICI U DRUSTVENOM SEKTORU, VANPRIVREDA, PREMA POPISU RADNIKA SA STANJEM ... GODINE / SOCIJALISTICKA REPUBLIKA SRBIJA, REPUBLICKI ZAVOD ZA STATISTIKU (YU) [24448315] **4545**

RADON DIRECTORY, THE (US/1049-6963) [21277397] **1029**

RADON NEWS DIGEST (US/0896-7180) [17281305] **2241**

RADON RESEARCH PROGRAM *See* ENVIRONMENTAL RADON PROGRAM, SUMMARIES OF RESEARCH IN FY ... / ENVIRONMENTAL SCIENCES DIVISION, OFFICE OF HEALTH AND ENVIRONMENTAL RESEARCH [AND] OFFICE OF ENERGY RESEARCH, DEPARTMENT OF ENERGY **1943**

●RADONEZH, VEK XX (RU) [26448709] **3427**

RADOVI MATEMATICKI / AKADEMIJA NAUKA I UMJETNOSTI BOSNE I HERCEGOVINE (BN/0352-6100) [12634960] **3530**

RADOVI MEDICINSKOG FAKULTETA U ZAGREBU *See* CROATIAN MEDICAL JOURNAL **3569**

RADOVI ODJELJENJE DRUSTVENIH NAUKA (BN/0350-0039) [06347589] **1843**

RADOVI POLJOPRIVREDNOG FAKULTETA UNIVERZITETA U SARAJEVU (BN) [18213297] **124**

RADOVI. RAZDIO FILOZOFIJE, PSIHOLOGIJE, SOCIOLOGIJE I PEDAGOGIJE / SVEUCILISTE U SPLITU, FILOZOFSKI FAKULTET--ZADAR (YU/0352-6798) [15722188] 4615, **4358**

RADOVI STAROSLAVENSKOG ZAVODA (CI) [22037441] **3313**

RADOVI SUMARSKOG FAKULTETA I INSTITUTA ZA SUMARSTVO U SARAJEVU (BN/0581-748X) [04673278] **2391**

RADOVI - SVEUCILISTE U SPLITU, FILOZOFSKI FAKULTET, RAZDIO FILOLOS-KIH ZNANOSTI (CI/0350-3623) [09545373] **4358**

RADOVI ZAVODA JUGOSLAVENSKE AKADEMIJE ZNANOSTI I UMJETNOSTI U ZADRU (CI/0351-6709) [08325298] **2704**

RADOVI ZAVODA ZA SLAVENSKU FILOLOGIJU (CI/0514-5090) [01474328] **3314**

RADSRAPPORT (SW) [10866935] **4171**

RADTECH REPORT (US/1056-0793) [23456979] **4419**

RADUGA (ER/0234-8179) [23921446] **2521**

RADUGA (UN/0033-8591) [01908783] **3427**

●RADWASTE MAGAZINE (US/1070-9541) [28521391] **2241**

RADWASTE NEWS *CEASED.* (US/0737-6960) [09433751] 2220, **2241**

RAFI COMMUNIQUE / RURAL ADVANCEMENT FUND INTERNATIONAL (US) [20604503] 3696, **124**

RAFIDAN (JA/0285-4406) [22526203] **2770**

RAFIKI (CN/0706-6937) [05018575] **2911**

RAFT (CLEVELAND, OHIO) (US/0891-0545) [14552310] **3314**

RAFU SHIMPO (US) [12939028] **5638**

RAG MAG (GOODHUE, MINN.) (US/0742-2768) [03040157] **3427**

RAG, REVISTA ADMINISTRATIVA DO GRANDE RIO (BL) [04424811] **4493**

RAG: THE ALL MUSIC MAGAZINE (US) **4148**

RAG TIMES (US/0090-4570) [01785386] **4148**

RAGAN REPORT, THE (US/0197-6060) [06069407] 1120, **706**

RAGAZZI (IT) **1776**

RAGGUAGLIO LIBRARIO, IL (IT/0033-8648) [02864603] 3427, **423**

RAGIONAMENTI SUI FATTI E LE IMMAGINI DELLA STORIA (IT) [24477683] **2627**

RAGIONI CRITICHE, LE (IT/0391-4283) [01786295] **329**

RAGIUSAN. RASSEGNA GIURIDICA DELLA SANITA (IT/1120-1762) [I11201762] 4798, **3034**

RAGTIMER, THE (CN/0033-8672) [02129059] **4148**

RAH-I ZINDAGI (US/0278-9957) [07970905] **2508**

RAHAVARD : NASHRIYAH-I ANJUMAN-I DUSTDARAN-I FARHANG-I FARSI (US/0742-8014) [09651535] **2662**

RAHNAMAY-I MAJALLAH'HA-YI IRAN (IR/0378-7443) [I03787443] **423**

RAHOITUSMARKKINATILASTOA (FI) [02243045] **806**

RAHWAY NEWS-RECORD (US) [12413085] **5711**

RAIBURARIANZU FORAMU (JA/0289-5420) [11680201] **3243**

RAICES : JUDAISMO CONTEMPORANEO (AG) [25495784] 2271, **5052**

RAICES (MADRID, SPAIN) (SP/0212-6753) [16403075] **2271**

RAID (AACHEN, GERMANY) *See* AL-RAID / YUSDIRUHA AL-MARKAZ AL-ISLAMI FI AKHIN (MASJID BILAL) WA-ITTIHAD AL-TALABAH AL-MUSLIMIN FI URUBBA **5041**

RAID (JAMIYAT AL-MUALLIMIN AL-KUWAYTIYAH) (KU) [09710697] **2508**

RAID (LUCKNOW, INDIA) (II) [10939736] **5044**

RAID : RADIO AMATEUR IDAHO DIRECTORY (US) [17748673] **1120**

RAIDA / INSTITUTE FOR WOMEN'S STUDIES IN THE ARAB WORLD, BEIRUT UNIVERSITY COLLEGE (LE) [07622460] **5565**

RAIL CARRIER SERVICE. INCLUDES SUPPLEMENTS (US) 849, **5390**

RAIL CLASSICS & RAILWAY QUARTERLY (US/0743-9075) [10685626] **5434**

RAIL ENGINEERING INTERNATIONAL (1981) (UK/0141-4615) [09675046] **5434**

RAIL HOBBYIST (US/0738-1778) [09537057] **5434**

RAIL IN CANADA (CN/0843-4530) [21531570] **5434**

RAIL INTERNATIONAL (BE/0020-8442) [01424231] **5434**

RAIL MART, THE (US/1070-7751) [28468815] **5434**

RAIL PARIS, LE (FR/0989-8220) [I09898220] **5434**

RAIL PASSENGER STATISTICS IN THE NORTHEAST CORRIDOR (US/0091-9667) [01788058] **5435**

RAIL SYNDICALISTE, LE (FR/0150-1313) [06576348] **5435**

RAIL TRANSIT DIRECTORY (US/0360-5272) [02244521] **5435**

RAIL TRANSPORT (II) [21699947] **5435**

RAILFAN & RAILROAD (US/0163-7266) [04455820] **5435**

RAILNEWS (UK) **5435**

RAILPACE NEWSMAGAZINE (US/0745-5267) [09263281] **5435**

RAILPOWER (UK/0262-8805) [I02628805] **5435**

RAILROAD ACCIDENT INVESTIGATION REPORTS (US/0160-1261) [03617571] **5435**

RAILROAD ACCIDENT REPORT. BRIEF FORMAT (US/0148-0200) [03256670] 4798, **5435**

RAILROAD ACCIDENTS IN OREGON (US/0093-2140) [01791172] **5401**

RAILROAD CAR JOURNAL (US/0091-5572) [01787663] **5435**

RAILROAD COMMISSION OF TEXAS. OIL AND GAS DIVISION *See* ANNUAL PRODUCTION BY ACTIVE FIELDS, OIL AND GAS DIVISION **4250**

RAILROAD COMMISSION OF TEXAS. OIL AND GAS DIVISION. ENGINEERING RESEARCH AND INSPECTION *See* SURVEY OF SECONDARY AND ENHANCED RECOVERY OPERATIONS IN TEXAS, A **4280**

RAILROAD FACTS (WASHINGTON, D.C.) (US/0742-1850) [10043784] **5435**

RAILROAD HISTORY (US/0090-7847) [01785797] **5435**

RAILROAD MODEL CRAFTSMAN (US/0033-877X) [05848357] 2585, **2777**

●RAILROAD RETIREMENT AND UNEMPLOYMENT INSURANCE SYSTEMS HANDBOOK (US) [25699438] 5435, **2891**

RAILROAD REVENUES, EXPENSES, AND INCOME: CLASS I RAILROADS IN THE UNITED STATES (US) [01715255] **5435**

RAILROAD STATION HISTORICAL SOCIETY *See* BULLETIN - RAILROAD STATION HISTORICAL SOCIETY, THE **5430**

RAILROAD TEN-YEAR TRENDS (US/1041-4746) [11473040] **5435**

RAILROADER (RH) **5435**

RAILROADIANA EXPRESS, THE (US/0199-3445) [05803267] 5435, **2777**

RAILS (WELLINGTON) (NZ/0110-6155) [I01106155] **5435**

RAILSBACK LINES (US/8756-9132) [11683876] **2469**

RAILWATCH (UK/0267-5943) [I02675943] **5435**

RAILWAY AGE (BRISTOL) (US/0033-8826) [01586268] **5435**

RAILWAY & LOCOMOTIVE HISTORICAL SOCIETY *See* ANNUAL REPORT - THE RAILWAY & LOCOMOTIVE HISTORICAL SOCIETY, INC **5429**

RAILWAY AND LOCOMOTIVE HISTORICAL SOCIETY. SOUTHERN CALIFORNIA CHAPTER *See* CHAPTER AND RAIL NEWS AS VIEWED FROM THE OBSERVATION PLATFORM **5430**

RAILWAY BUDGET : DEMANDS FOR GRANTS FOR THE PAKISTAN RAILWAYS, THE (PK) [03249579] **5435**

RAILWAY BUDGET : IMPROVEMENT FUND WORKS PROGRAMME, THE (PK) [03256891] **5435**

RAILWAY BUDGET IN BRIEF, THE (PK) [03265165] **5435**

RAILWAY CARLOADINGS (MONTHLY ED.) (CN/0380-6308) [02871974] **5435**

RAILWAY CARMEN'S JOURNAL (US/0033-8850) [01763396] **5435**

RAILWAY FREIGHT TRAFFIC (OTTAWA. QUARTERLY EDITION) (CN/0317-3437) [01798312] **5435**

RAILWAY GAZETTE INTERNATIONAL (UK/0373-5346) [02246087] **5436**

RAILWAY HISTORY MONOGRAPH, THE (US/0093-8505) [01786322] **5436**

RAILWAY JOURNAL *See* BMWE JOURNAL **1655**

RAILWAY LINE CLEARANCES (US/0190-6763) [04748250] **5436**

RAILWAY MAGAZINE (LONDON) (UK/0033-8923) [02254878] **5436**

RAILWAY MODELLER (UK/0033-8931) [I00338931] **2777**

RAILWAY OPERATING STATISTICS (MONTHLY ED.) (CN/0380-5964) [02871898] **5436**

RAILWAY PASSENGER CAR ANNUAL (US/0094-2278) [01794134] **5436**

RAILWAY TRANSPORT (CN) [01796658] **5436**

RAILWAY WORLD ANNUAL (UK/0082-5891) [07318019] **5436**

RAILWAY WORLD, THE (US) [07865790] **5436**

RAILWAYMEN'S UNION OF MALAYA *See* BIENNIAL REPORT AND STATEMENT OF ACCOUNTS - RAILWAYMEN'S UNION OF MALAYA **1655**

RAILWAYS (SA/0254-2218) [04691205] **5436**

●RAILWAYS AFRICA (SA) [27943495] **5436**

RAILWAYS OF AUSTRALIA NETWORK *See* NETWORK (MELBOURNE (VIC.) **5433**

RAIN FOREST (PORT ALBERNI, B.C.) (CN/0712-7871) [08777577] **3427**

RAINBOW HERALD, THE (US/0748-7312) [10992998] **4989**

RAINBOW NEWS *CEASED.* (US/0892-337X) [15155604] **1201**

RAINBOW (PROSPECT, KY.) (US/0746-4797) [10063325] 1235, **1272**

RAINCOAST (CN/0708-9961) [05359782] **1068**

RAINCOAST CHRONICLES *SUSPENDED.* (CN/0315-2804) [02604332] **2756**

RAINER FOUNDATION *See* ANNUAL REPORT AND ACCOUNTS / THE RAINER FOUNDATION **3157**

RAINEY TIMES (US/0734-2055) [08038473] **2469**

RAINFALL REPORT (RH/0085-5693) [09710386] **1434**

RAINFOREST ACTION NETWORK ALERT & WORLD RAINFOREST REPORT (US) 2220, **2180**

RAINMAKER'S REVIEW, THE (US) **3034**

RAINS COUNTY LEADER (US) [14201380] **5753**

RAIRO. INFORMATIQUE THEORIQUE ET APPLICATIONS (FR/0988-3754) [13661266] **1261**

RAIRO. MATHEMATICAL MODELLING AND NUMERICAL ANALYSIS (FR/0764-583X) [12351558] **3530**

RAIRO : RECHERCHE OPERATIONNELLE (FR/0399-0559) [03260689] **5144**

RAISE THE STAKES (US/0278-7016) [07864341] **2491**

RAISED DOT COMPUTING NEWSLETTER *CEASED.* (US/0890-0019) [14223958] **1201**

RAISING ARIZONA KIDS (US/1051-4295) [21958552] **2285**

RAISING KIDS *CEASED.* (US/0895-3740) [16577197] **2285**

RAISON PRESENTE (FR/0033-9075) [01866381] 2852, **4358**

RAIVAAJA (FITCHBURG, MASS.) (US/1059-4779) [13677702] **5690**

RAJAH (US) **3351**

RAJANI PUBLICATIONS U.S.A., INC (US/1057-6835) [24101656] **329**

RAJASTHAN BOARD JOURNAL OF EDUCATION. RAJASTHANA BORDA SIKSHANA PATRIKA, THE (II/0033-9083) [05936317] **1776**

RAJASTHAN ECONOMIC JOURNAL (II) [04614510] **1515**

RAJASTHAN, INDIA *See* RULES COMPENDIUM UNDER CENTRAL ACTS **3045**

RAJASTHAN, INDIA. HOUSING BOARD *See* ANNUAL STATEMENT OF ACCOUNTS - HOUSING BOARD. RAJASTHAN, INDIA **2815**

RAJASTHAN JOURNAL OF ENGLISH STUDIES, THE (II/0377-3310) [02243464] **3314**

RAJASTHAN LAW WEEKLY, THE (II/0377-7723) [02239581] **3034**

RAJASTHAN MEDICAL JOURNAL, THE (II/0485-9561) [09352571] **3632**

RAJASTHAN STATE CURRENT STATUTES (II) [10444066] **3034**

RAJASTHAN UNIVERSITY STUDIES IN ENGLISH (II/0448-1690) [02529865] **3427**

RAJASTHANA KE AJANE BRAJABHASHA SAHITYAKARA DARAPANA (II) [24204810] **3427**

RAJASTHANNI SABADA KOSA (II) [02919863] **3314**

RAJPUT (PK) [02239641] **2662**

RAKAM (IT/0033-9113) [I00339113] **5565**

RAKE REGISTER, THE (US) [16830129] **5672**

RAKENNUSKUSTANNUSINDEKSI, PIENTALON RAKENNUSKUSTANNUSINDEKSI JA MAATALOUDEN TUOTANTORAKENNUKSEN RAKENNUSKUSTANNUSINDEKSI (FI) [10223033] **625**

RAKENNUSTEKNIIKKA (FI/0033-913X) [02450044] **625**

RAKENNUSTEN LAMMITUSENERGIAN KAYTTO (FI) [19055906] **625**

RAKENNUSTUOTANTO (FI) [04360942] **625**

RAKENTAJAIN KALENTERI / SUOMEN RAKENNUSMESTARILIITTO (FI/0355-550X) [09818997] **625**

RAKENTAMINEN (FI) [20142563] 3487, **625**

RAKTARGAZDALKODAS *See* ANYAGGAZDALKODAS ES RAKTARGAZDALKODAS **1598**

RAKUNO KAGAKU, SHOKUHIN NO KENKYU (JA/0385-0218) [07228112] 2355, **198**

RALLS COUNTY HERALD-ENTERPRISE, THE (US/8750-7625) [11735902] **5704**

RALLY (MELBOURNE) *CEASED.* (AT/0300-3515) [01424337] **5303**

RALLY REGULATIONS (WILLOWDALE) (CN/0381-9493) [02604385] **4914**

RALLYE (US/0363-7697) [02534837] **4914**

RALLYE : REGLEMENTS (CN/0822-529X) [10061659] **4914**

RAM (GR) **3351**

RAM DIGEST, THE (US/0147-9059) [03245769] 625, 4843, **2832**

RAM PAGE, THE (US) [16158110] **5753**

RAM RESEARCH BANKCARD UPDATE (US/1040-8959) [18572559] **806**

RAM RESEARCH'S CARDTRAK (US/1053-9719) [22712874] 806, **1299**

RAM UPDATE (US/1059-7204) [24687143] **5072**

RAMA ANNUAL (CN/0710-2674) [08260690] **912**

RAMAKRISHNA MISSION, INDIA. INSTITUTE OF CULTURE *See* BULLETIN OF THE RAMAKRISHNA MISSION INSTITUTE OF CULTURE **2843**

RAMBLING ON (AT) **4914**

RAMBUNCTIOUS REVIEW (US/0889-1664) [13843748] **3427**

RAMDIL SOCIAL SCIENCE RESOURCE GUIDES (US/1054-6871) [22938746] **5214**

RAMON MAGSAYSAY AWARDS, THE (PH) [08395266] **5235**

RAMON Y CAJAL. REVISTA MEDICA DEL HOSPITAL RAMON Y CAJAL (SP) **3792**

RAMPIKE (TORONTO) (CN/0711-7647) [16458427] 329, **3427**

RAM'S HORN (HANOVER, N.H.), THE (US/0272-2747) [06828353] 1776, **3314**

RAM'S HORN (SCOTSBURN) (CN/0827-4053) [12178024] **124**

RAMSES : RAPPORT ANNUEL SUR LE SYSTEME ECONOMIQUE ET LES STRATEGIES (FR) [07534445] **1580**

RAMSEY COUNTY HISTORY (US/0485-9758) [01763426] **2756**

RAMSEY COUNTY REVIEW (US) [01607591] **5698**

RAMURI (RM) [07385757] **2521**

RAMUS (AT/0048-671X) [01781448] 3351, **1079**

RANCH & COAST *CEASED.* (US/0164-8780) [04286670] **5489**

RANCH MAGAZINE, THE (US/0145-8515) [02791343] **220**

RANCHER. SAN JOAQUIN COUNTY EDITION *See* RANCHER. SOUTHERN SAN JOAQUIN VALLEY EDITION **124**

RANCHER. SOUTHERN SAN JOAQUIN VALLEY EDITION (US/0090-0281) [05737088] **124**

RANCHI UNIVERSITY MATHEMATICAL JOURNAL (II/0079-9602) [09034498] **3530**

RANCHLAND NEWS (US/0745-4279) [09146472] **2544**

RANCHO MIRAGE POST (US/0884-6170) [12401487] **5638**

RAND CORPORATION *See* R - RAND CORPORATION **5144**

RAND CORPORATION *See* SELECTED RAND ABSTRACTS **424**

RAND JOURNAL OF ECONOMICS, THE (US/0741-6261) [10187004] **1594**

RAND MCNALLY AND COMPANY *See* STANDARD HIGHWAY MILEAGE GUIDE **1929**

RAND MCNALLY AND COMPANY *See* ROAD ATLAS : UNITED STATES, CANADA, AND MEXICO **1929**

RAND MCNALLY AND COMPANY *See* RAND MCNALLY ROAD ATLAS & TRIP PLANNER **5490**

RAND MCNALLY AND COMPANY *See* RAND MCNALLY ... COMMERCIAL ATLAS & MARKETING GUIDE **1928**

RAND MCNALLY AND COMPANY *See* VACATION & TRAVEL GUIDE **5498**

RAND MCNALLY AND COMPANY *See* INTERNATIONAL ATLAS. [EDITORS: RUSSELL L. VOISIN AND OTHERS] **1926**

RAND MCNALLY BUSINESS TRAVELER'S ROAD ATLAS (US) **5489**

RAND MCNALLY CAMPGROUND & TRAILER PARK GUIDE, EASTERN (US/0733-8309) [08372835] **4708**

RAND MCNALLY ... COMMERCIAL ATLAS & MARKETING GUIDE (US) [14644752] **1928**

RAND MCNALLY COSMOPOLITAN WORLD ATLAS (US) **1928**

RAND MCNALLY EASTERN CAMPGROUNDS & TRAILER PARKS *See* RAND MCNALLY CAMPGROUND & TRAILER PARK GUIDE, EASTERN **4708**

RAND MCNALLY INTERSTATE ROAD ATLAS (US) [01152171] **1928**

RAND MCNALLY ROAD ATLAS & TRIP PLANNER (US/1075-1688) [23097743] **5490**

RAND MCNALLY ROAD ATLAS & VACATION GUIDE (US) **5490**

RAND MCNALLY ROAD ATLAS OF EUROPE (US) **5490**

RAND MCNALLY WORLD FACTS & MAPS (US/1057-9834) [20685196] **1928**

RAND MCNALLY ZIP CODE FINDER (US) 1928, **1147**

RAND PAPER SERIES (US/0092-2803) [01789205] **5144**

RAND RESEARCH REVIEW (US/0740-9281) [03270176] **1515**

RANDALLSTOWN NEWS (US/0883-7104) [12197500] **5687**

RANDAX EDUCATION GUIDE *See* RANDAX EDUCATION GUIDE TO COLLEGES SEEKING STUDENTS **1843**

RANDAX EDUCATION GUIDE TO COLLEGES SEEKING STUDENTS (US) [10570203] **1843**

R&D - ALBERTA RESEARCH COUNCIL (CN/0830-1093) [I08301093] **5144**

R&D EVALUATION NEWSLETTER (FR) **706**

R&D FOCUS (UK) **4327**

● R&D INNOVATOR (US/1061-1894) [25216435] **5144**

R&D RATIOS & BUDGETS (US) [19087505] **1623**

R&D REVIEW (JACKSON, MISS.) (US/0735-0872) [08832110] **5144**

RANDOL BUYER'S GUIDE (US/1057-4921) [22037036] **2149**

RANDOL MINING DIRECTORY (US/1054-027X) [22162162] **2149**

RANDOLPH LEADER, THE (US) [09237931] **5628**

RANDOLPH-MACON WOMAN'S COLLEGE *See* ALUMNAE DIRECTORY / RANDOLPH-MACON WOMAN'S COLLEGE **1096**

RANDOLPH REPORTER, THE (US/0191-703X) [04926569] **5711**

● RANDOM & COMPUTATIONAL DYNAMICS (US/1061-835X) [25472898] **2127**

RANDOM HARVEST WEEKLY (US/8750-0930) [10969450] **5720**

RANDOM LENGTHS BUYERS' & SELLERS' GUIDE (US/0891-7833) [15000777] **2404**

RANDOM LENGTHS (EUGENE, OR.) (US/0483-9420) [01763436] **2404**

RANDOM LENGTHS EXPORT (US/1052-942X) [13192106] **2404**

RANDOM LENGTHS (SAN PEDRO, CALIF.) (US/0891-8627) [15028135] **5638**

RANDOM LENGTHS YARDSTICK (US/1055-0895) [23070791] **2391**

RANDOM LENGTHS YEARBOOK (1985) (US/1045-2796) [15810487] **2404**

RANDOM OPERATORS AND STOCHASTIC EQUATIONS (NE/0926-6364) **1244**

● RANDOM REALITIES (US/1065-8343) [26756974] **3427**

RANDOM STRUCTURES AND ALGORITHMS (US/1042-9832) [19275021] **3530**

RANGA CAKALLASA (II) [02240225] **2526**

RANGAREKHA : ODISA LALITA KALA EKADEMI MUKHAPATRA (II) [11351177] **363**

RANGE (NE/0033-9199) [01913519] **1162**

RANGE AND PASTURE (US) [02044297] **124**

RANGE HISTORY (US) [03458048] **2627**

RANGE MANAGEMENT NEWSLETTER (AT/0812-4930) [08124930] **124**

RANGE SCIENCE SERIES (DENVER) (US/0190-5511) [01472841] **5144**

RANGE SCIENCE SERIES (FORT COLLINS, COLO.) (US/0277-9404) [02902601] **124**

RANGEFINDER (SANTA MONICA), THE (US/0033-9202) [00830999] **4376**

RANGELAND JOURNAL, THE (AT/1036-9872) [24340706] 124, **2391**

RANGEL'S REPORTS (US/0882-312X) [11821515] **2627**

RANGER (US) **4708**

RANGER RICK (US/0738-6656) [09542474] 4171, **1068**

RANGER RICK (OTTAWA) (CN/0828-8739) [13297662] **4171**

RANGER RICK'S NATURESCOPE (US) [12706802] 5596, **4171**

RANGER, THE (US/0192-8171) [05093955] **5762**

RANGIFER (NO/0333-256X) [I0333256X] 5519, **5596**

RANJIT (CN/0715-3910) [09223175] **5793**

RANKIN COUNTY NEWS (US) [14816182] **5701**

RANKING OF THE STATES (US) **1776**

RANKING THE BANKS / AMERICAN BANKER (US/1057-8854) [24139018] **806**

RANKINGS OF THE COUNTIES AND SCHOOL DISTRICTS OF SOUTH CAROLINA (US) [04222235] **1776**

RANKINGS OF THE STATES (US/0077-4332) [03170450] **1776**

RANLIAO HUAXUE XUEBAO (CC/0253-2409) [08384529] 1954, **990**

RANOK (UN) [04865811] **2521**

RANSOM COUNTY GAZETTE AND ENTERPRISE *See* RANSOM COUNTY GAZETTE, THE **5726**

RANSOM COUNTY GAZETTE AND ENTERPRISE, THE (US) [20077896] **5726**

RANSOM COUNTY GAZETTE, THE (US) [29391981] **5726**

RAP MASTERS (US/1056-4705) [23716577] **4148**

RAPA BULLETIN (TH/1011-6435) [I10116435] **2508**

RAPA PUBLICATION (KO/1014-191X) [I1014191X] **2662**

RAPATRIES — Alphabetical Title Index

RAPATRIES : BILAN ANNUEL DU SECRETARIAT D'ETAT AUPRES DU PREMIER MINISTRE CHARGE DES RAPATRIES (FR) [09812224] **5303**

RAPHAEL'S ASTRONOMICAL EPHEMERIS OF THE PLANETS' PLACES (UK) [05368722] **399**

RAPID CITY DAILY JOURNAL *See* RAPID CITY JOURNAL, THE **5744**

RAPID CITY JOURNAL, THE (US) [02250546] **5744**

RAPID COMMUNICATIONS (NE) [09096921] **5596**

RAPID COMMUNICATIONS IN MASS SPECTROMETRY (UK/0951-4198) [16180039] **1018**

RAPID COMMUNICATIONS (SUPPLEMENTS) (NE) [09496717] **5596**

●RAPID PROTOTYPING JOURNAL (UK/1355-2546) **1201**

RAPID PROTOTYPING REPORT (US/1059-6399) [24652440] **1201**

RAPID REPORTS. AGRICULTURE, FORESTRY, AND FISHERIES / EUROSTAT (LU/1017-5776) [23374185] **124**

RAPID REPORTS. ECONOMY AND FINANCE / EUROSTAT (LU) [19918837] **4743**

RAPID REPORTS. ENERGY AND INDUSTRY / EUROSTAT (LU) [20002262] **1954**

RAPID REPORTS. POPULATION AND SOCIAL CONDITIONS / EUROSTAT (LU) [20500613] **4559**

RAPID REPORTS. REGIONS / EUROSTAT (LU) [19023714] **4559**

RAPORT - INSTYTUT FIZYKI I TECHNIKI JADROWEJ AGH (PL/0302-9034) [02682359] **4450**

RAPORT O STANIE, ZAGROZENIU I OCHRONIE SRODOWISKA ... (PL/0209-3871) [24105585] **2180**

RAPORT O WYBRANYCH PROBLEMACH GOSPODARKI SWIATOWEJ / INSTYTUT FINANSOW (PL) [24435314] **1580**

RAPORTA ZOMU KONAKONI NOMUTARELI-NTONI KOMBINGA ZOYIVARO YONDANGO ZETUROPOVETA ZAKAVANGO NEYI YEPANGERO LYORUDI *See* RAPORTA ZOMUKONAKONI NOMUTARELI-NTONI KOMBINGA ZOYIVARO YEPANGERO LYAKAVANGO KUMWE NEZI ZOMAPANGERO GORUDI MOSIRONGO ZOMUMVHO **4743**

RAPORTA ZOMUKONAKONI NOMUTARELI-NTONI KOMBINGA ZOYIVARO YEPANGERO LYAKAVANGO KUMWE NEZI ZOMAPANGERO GORUDI MOSIRONGO ZOMUMVHO (SA) [02243274] **4743**

●RAPPAGES (BEVERLY HILLS, CALIF.) (US/1063-1283) [25762971] **4148**

RAPPEL (MONTREAL) (CN/0710-5789) [08774059] **4878**

RAPPORT (BE) [01791099] **2149**

RAPPORT ADMINISTRATIF - INSTITUT NATIONAL GENEVOIS (SZ) [01799596] **2521**

RAPPORT ANNUEL - AGENCE DE PROMOTION DES INVESTISSEMENTS (TI) [02461276] **1623**

RAPPORT ANNUEL AU PRESIDENT DE LA REPUBLIQUE ET AU PARLEMENT / COMMISSION DE LA SECURITE DES CONSOMMATEURS (FR/0767-4538) [16642609] **849**

RAPPORT ANNUEL - BANQUE NATIONALE POUR LE COMMERCE (MG) [05141815] **806**

RAPPORT ANNUEL : BANQUE NATIONALE SUISSE (SZ) **806**

RAPPORT ANNUEL / BUREAU D'AUDIENCES PUBLIQUES SUR L'ENVIRONNEMENT (CN/0711-5571) [09766476] **1580**

RAPPORT ANNUEL / BUREAU DE LA PROTECTION CIVILE DU QUEBEC (CN/0714-7805) [09767877] **4054**

RAPPORT ANNUEL / BUREAU INTERNATIONAL DE L'HEURE (FR/0068-4236) [05057308] **399**

RAPPORT ANNUEL - CAISSE CENTRALE DE COOPERATION ECONOMIQUE (FR) [04810931] **2911**

RAPPORT ANNUEL / CANADIAN NATIONAL (CN) [09553657] **1120, 5390**

RAPPORT ANNUEL / CEI (SZ) [08361973] **2078**

RAPPORT ANNUEL - CENTRE DE RECHERCHE INDUSTRIELLE DU QUEBEC (CN/0706-2508) [04252350] **1623**

RAPPORT ANNUEL / CENTRE NATIONAL D'ETUDES SPATIALES (FR) [22742660] **32**

RAPPORT ANNUEL - CENTRE TECHNIQUE FORESTIER TROPICAL DU CAMEROUN (CM) [01786035] **2391**

RAPPORT ANNUEL - CHAMBRE DE COMMERCE, D'INDUSTRIE ET DES MINES DU CAMEROUN (CM) [02376857] 1580, **821**

RAPPORT ANNUEL - COMITE DE CONCERTATION ET DE CONTROLE DU PETROLE (BE) [06992203] **4276**

RAPPORT ANNUEL / COMMISSION DE PROTECTION DU TERRITOIRE AGRICOLE DU QUEBEC (CN/0712-4600) [09697474] **2203**

RAPPORT ANNUEL - COMMISSION DES SERVICES JURIDIQUES (CN/0703-0762) [09242901] **3034**

RAPPORT ANNUEL - COMMISSION DES TRANSPORTS DU QUEBEC (CN/0702-0996) [06337319] **5390**

RAPPORT ANNUEL / COMMISSION MUNICIPALE DU QUEBEC (CN/0229-8139) [08081462] **4678**

RAPPORT ANNUEL - COMMISSION QUEBECOISE DES LIBERATIONS CONDITIONNELLES (CN/0228-8435) [06240417] **5303**

RAPPORT ANNUEL / CONSEIL CONSULTATIF DE L'ENVIRONNEMENT (CN/0837-7138) [17863647] **4678**

RAPPORT ANNUEL / CONSEIL DE LA FAMILLE (CN/0847-3587) [21098370] **2285**

RAPPORT ANNUEL - CONSEIL DE LA LANGUE FRANCAISE (CN/0229-9259) [05922860] **3314**

RAPPORT ANNUEL - CONSEIL DE LA PROTECTION DU CONSOMMATEUR (CN/0319-8774) [06235038] **1299**

RAPPORT ANNUEL - CONSEIL NATIONAL DU CREDIT (FR) [03054996] **4744**

RAPPORT ANNUEL - CONSEIL REGIONAL DE LA SANTE ET DES SERVICES SOCIAUX DE L'OUTAOUAIS (CN/0837-5496) [19506054] **4798**

RAPPORT ANNUEL - CONSEIL REGIONAL DE LA SANTE ET DES SERVICES SOCIAUX DE QUEBEC (CN/0710-2305) [06236943] **5303**

RAPPORT ANNUEL / CONSEIL SUPERIEUR DES CLASSES MOYENNES (BE) [11451216] **4678**

RAPPORT ANNUEL - CORPORATION DES BIBLIOTHECAIRES PROFESSIONNELS DU QUEBEC (CN/0226-8019) [07966589] **3243**

RAPPORT ANNUEL / CORPORATION PROFESSIONNELLE DES COMPTABLES EN ADMINISTRATION INDUSTRIELLE DU QUEBEC (CN/0824-2976) [09673827] **750**

RAPPORT ANNUEL DE LA BANQUE DE KINSHASA (CG) [03880639] **806**

RAPPORT ANNUEL DE LA BANQUE DE LA REPUBLIQUE DU BURUNDI (BD) [02337574] **806**

RAPPORT ANNUEL DE LA BANQUE NATIONALE DE BELGIQUE (BE) **806**

RAPPORT ANNUEL DE LA CAISSE NATIONALE DES AUTOROUTES (FR) [04304425] **5442**

RAPPORT ANNUEL DE LA DATAR, LE (FR) [11526157] **4678**

RAPPORT ANNUEL DE LA DIRECTION DE L'INDUSTRIE / REPUBLIQUE DU SENEGAL, MINISTERE DU DEVELOPPEMENT INDUSTRIEL ET L'ARTISANAT, DIRECTION DE L'INDUSTRIE (SG) [11951718] **1623**

RAPPORT ANNUEL DE L'INSTITUTE MONETAIRE LUXEMBOURGEOIS POUR L'ANNEE ... / ANNUAL REPORT OF THE IML FOR THE YEAR ... INSTITUT MONETAIRE LUXEMBOURGEOIS (LU) [26751084] **806**

RAPPORT ANNUEL DES ACTIVITES (ASSOCIATION TOURISTIQUE REGIONALE RICHELIEU RIVE-SUD) (CN/0229-2858) [07857999] **1623**

RAPPORT ANNUEL / DIRECTION DEPARTEMENTALE DES AFFAIRES SANITAIRES ET SOCIALES (RE) [09469978] **4798**

RAPPORT ANNUEL DU CONSEIL D'ADMINISTRATION - FONDS MONETAIRE INTERNATIONAL *CEASED.* (US/0250-7501) [04702908] **1515**

RAPPORT ANNUEL DU CONSEIL D'ADMINISTRATION SUR L'ACTIVITE DE LA CAISSE NATIONALE DES AUTOROUTES EN ... (FR) [07333901] **5443**

RAPPORT ANNUEL DU CURATEUR PUBLIC (1977) (CN/0824-8567) [06208287] **4798**

RAPPORT ANNUEL DU DEPARTEMENT DE GEOLOGIE ET DE MINERALOGIE DU MUSEE ROYAL DE L'AFRIQUE CENTRALE (BE/0378-0953) [01587537] **1393**

RAPPORT ANNUEL DU SERVICE HYDROGRAPHIQUE ET OCEANOGRAPHIQUE DE LA MARINE (FR/0989-5876) [12826523] **1455**

RAPPORT ANNUEL DU SURINTENDANT DES ASSURANCES (QUEBEC. 1977) *CEASED.* (CN/0225-3208) [08327967] **2891**

RAPPORT ANNUEL - ENERGIE QUEBEC (CN) [05872405] **1954**

RAPPORT ANNUEL / FONDS FCAR, FONDS POUR LA FORMATION DE CHERCHEURS ET L'AIDE A LA RECHERCHE (CN/0837-645X) [19861209] **5144**

RAPPORT ANNUEL - GENERALE DES CARRIERES ET DES MINES (CG) [06293641] **1623**

RAPPORT ANNUEL - GROUPE INTERMINISTERIEL D'EVALUATION DE L'ENVIRONNEMENT (FR) [03074914] **2241**

RAPPORT ANNUEL / INSTITUT DE POLICE DU QUEBEC (CN/1188-1968) [25652433] **3174**

RAPPORT ANNUEL - INSTITUT FONDAMENTAL D'AFRIQUE NOIRE (SG) [02240823] **2642**

RAPPORT ANNUEL / INSTITUT NATIONAL DE PRODUCTIVITE (CN/0229-8538) [08124439] **4678**

RAPPORT ANNUEL / INSTITUT NATIONAL DE RECHERCHE SCIENTIFIQUE (I.N.R.S.) (RW) [19011366] **5144**

RAPPORT ANNUEL / INSTITUT NATIONAL POUR L'ETUDE ET LA RECHERCHE AGRONOMIQUE (CG) [01785821] **124**

RAPPORT ANNUEL / LA CORPORATION PROFESSIONNELLE DES PHYSIOTHERAPEUTES DU QUEBEC (CN/0227-7611) [08309279] **4382**

RAPPORT ANNUEL - L'ORDRE DES PODIATRES DU QUEBEC (CN) [03080941] **3918**

RAPPORT ANNUEL. MERITE AGRICOLE (CN/0701-6557) [09779152] **124**

RAPPORT ANNUEL - MINISTERE DE LA JUSTICE (CN) [05842620] **3034**

RAPPORT ANNUEL - MINISTERE DE LA SANTE PUBLIQUE (RW) [06930453] **4798**

RAPPORT ANNUEL / MINISTERE DE L'AGRICULTURE, DES PECHERIES ET DE LA'ALIMENTATION (CN/0715-6219) [09779976] **4678**

RAPPORT ANNUEL - MINISTERE DE L'ENERGIE ET DES RESSOURCES (QUEBEC) (CN/0228-9113) [07701857] **2203**

RAPPORT ANNUEL - MUSEE NATIONAL DES SCIENCES ET DE LA TECHNOLOGIE (OTTAWA) (CN/1187-3736) [25796650] **5144**

RAPPORT ANNUEL / OFFICE DE LA SECURITE DU REVENU DES CHASSEURS ET PIEGEURS CRIS (CN/0715-7770) [08244665] 2891, **5303**

RAPPORT ANNUEL / OFFICE NATIONAL DES FORETS (FR/0984-5453) [17685380] **2391**

RAPPORT ANNUEL - OFFICE NATIONAL DES PORTS DU CAMEROUN (CM) [03589325] **5455**

RAPPORT ANNUEL - ONSS (BE) [02380299] **5303**

RAPPORT ANNUEL - QUEBEC (PROVINCE). COMITE DE DEONTOLOGIE POLICIERE (CN/1183-868X) [25352040] **4678**

RAPPORT ANNUEL - QUEBEC (PROVINCE). DEPT. OF NATURAL RESOURCES (CN) [01784954] **2203**

RAPPORT ANNUEL - REGIE DE L'ASSURANCE-DEPOTS DU QUEBEC (CN/0701-5666) [05929695] **806**

RAPPORT ANNUEL - REGIE DE L'ELECTRICITE ET DU GAZ (CN/0711-7132) [09091440] **4678**

RAPPORT ANNUEL ... / REGIE DES ENTREPRISES DE CONSTRUCTION DU QUEBEC (CN/0229-8643) [08391857] **625**

RAPPORT ANNUEL / REGIE DES LOTERIES DU QUEBEC (CN/1187-0893) [25855141] **4678**

RAPPORT ANNUEL / REGIE DES PERMIS D'ALCOOL DU QUEBEC (CN/0710-376X) [10395428] **4678**

RAPPORT ANNUEL - REGIE DES RENTES DU QUEBEC (CN/0380-4585) [05842965] 5303, **2891**

RAPPORT ANNUEL, REGIME DES ALLOCATIONS FAMILIALES DU QUEBEC (CN/0380-5387) [06180221] **5303**

RAPPORT ANNUEL - SERVICE DE RECHERCHE EN DEFENSE DES CULTURES (CN/0713-4711) [08878490] **4678**

RAPPORT ANNUEL - SERVICE DES ASSURANCES (CN) [04899102] **2891**

RAPPORT ANNUEL - SOCIETE DE DEVELOPPEMENT INDUSTRIEL DU QUEBEC (CN) [06132594] **806**

RAPPORT ANNUEL - SOCIETE DES ALCOOLS DU QUEBEC (1986?) (CN/0845-924X) [20983555] **4678**

RAPPORT ANNUEL / SOCIETE QUEBECOISE D'INFORMATION JURIDIQUE (CN/0710-6394) [08124584] **3243**

Alphabetical Title Index — RAPPORT

RAPPORT ANNUEL - SOCIETE QUEBECOISE D'INITIATIVES AGRO-ALIMENTAIRES (CN/0708-6059) [06184710] **124**

RAPPORT ANNUEL SUR L'ASSURANCE-VIEILLESSE, SURVIVANTS ET INVALIDITE FEDERALE ET SUR LE REGIME DES ALLOCATIONS EN FAVEUR DES MILITAIRES ET DES PERSONNES ASTREINTES A SERVIR DANS L'ORGANISATION DE LA PROTECTION CIVILE (SZ) [02240740] **5303**

RAPPORT ANNUEL SUR L'ENERGIE: RECHERCHE, DEVELOPPEMENT ET DEMONSTRATION (FR) [06990474] **1954**

RAPPORT ANNUEL SUR L'EVALUATION DE LA POLITIQUE NATIONALE DE RECHERCHE ET DE DEVELOPPEMENT TECHNOLOGIQUE (FR) [20436835] **1623**

RAPPORT ANNUEL - UNION POUR LA COORDINATION DE LA PRODUCTION ET DU TRANSPORT DE L'ELECTRICITE (GW) [01793967] **2078**

RAPPORT AU COMITE INTERNATIONAL DES POIDS ET MESURES (FR) [03024662] **4032**

RAPPORT AU PRESIDENT DE LA REPUBLIQUE (FR) [03594051] **4744**

RAPPORT AU PRESIDENT DE LA REPUBLIQUE (FR) [01799031] **806**

RAPPORT AU PRESIDENT DE LA REPUBLIQUE DU CONSEIL DES IMPOTS (FR) **4744**

RAPPORT AU PRESIDENT DE LA REPUBLIQUE ET AU PARLEMENT (FR/0767-4538) [22829125] **4493**

RAPPORT AUX PARENTS *See* INFO-PARENTS **2281**

RAPPORT BIPM (FR/0026-1394) [10458102] **1434**

RAPPORT BISANNUEL D'ACTIVITE - LABORATOIRE ASSOCIE AU C.N.R.S NO 132 ETUDES GEOLOGIQUES OUEST-AFRICAINES (FR) [06968098] **1393**

RAPPORT CANADIEN A L'INDUSTRIE SUR LES SCIENCES HALIEUTIQUES ET AQUATIQUES (CN/0704-3708) [08828300] **2311**

RAPPORT - CHR. MICHELSENS INSTITUTT, AVDELING FOR SAMFUNNSVITENSKAP OG UTVIKLING (NO/0803-0030) [08030030] **5214**

RAPPORT / CITIZEN ADVOCACY, OTTAWA-CARLETON (CN/1180-503X) [24266821] **5303**

RAPPORT - COMMISSION BANCAIRE (FR) [13273711] **806**

RAPPORT (COMMISSION DE CONTROLE DE L'ENERGIE *See* RESEARCH REPORT / ATOMIC ENERGY CONTROL BOARD **1955**

RAPPORT - CONSEIL DE DIRECTION DU FONDS DE DEVELOPPEMENT ECONOMIQUE ET SOCIAL (FR) [03074965] **4744**

RAPPORT D'ACTIVITE (FR) [09780906] **1162**

RAPPORT D'ACTIVITE - BANQUE CENTRALE DES ETATS DE L'AFRIQUE CENTRALE (FR) [02241896] **806**

RAPPORT D'ACTIVITE / BUREAU NATIONAL DE METROLOGIE (FRANCE) (FR/0750-7313) [09705833] **4032**

RAPPORT D'ACTIVITE - CENTRE D'ETUDES DES SYSTEMES D'INFORMACION DES ADMINISTRATIONS (FRANCE) (FR) [10572895] **3243**

RAPPORT D'ACTIVITE / CENTRE DE CREATION INDUSTRIELLE (FR) [07118185] **3487**

RAPPORT D'ACTIVITE - CENTRE NATIONAL DE DOCUMENTATION SCIENTIFIQUE ET TECHNIQUE (BE/0069-1968) [03054415] **5144**

RAPPORT D'ACTIVITE / CHAMBRE DE COMMERCE ET D'INDUSTRIE DE POINTE-A-PITRE (GP) [24170282] **821**

RAPPORT D'ACTIVITE / CHARBONNAGES DE FRANCE (FR) [09975598] **2149**

RAPPORT D'ACTIVITE ... DE L'INSTITUT PANAFRICAIN POUR LE DEVELOPPEMENT *See* RAPPORT D'ACTIVITES / INSTITUT PANAFRICAIN POUR LE DEVELOPPEMENT **1623**

RAPPORT D'ACTIVITE / DIVISION TECHNIQUE GENERALE (FR) [10237943] **2078**

RAPPORT D'ACTIVITE - ELECTRICITE DE FRANCE, DIRECTION DES AFFAIRES EXTERIEURES ET DE LA COOPERATION (FR) [04308844] **2078**

RAPPORT D'ACTIVITE - ELECTRICITE DE FRANCE, DIRECTION DES ETUDES ET RECHERCHES (FR) [04404073] **2078**

RAPPORT D'ACTIVITE - INSTITUT AFRICAIN POUR LE DEVELOPPEMENT ECONOMIQUE ET SOCIAL (IV) [02243197] **1515**

RAPPORT D'ACTIVITE - INSTITUT AFRICAIN POUR LE DEVELOPPEMENT ECONOMIQUE ET SOCIAL - FORMATION (IV) [04199113] **1776**

RAPPORT D'ACTIVITE - INSTITUT DE RECHERCHES TECHNOLOGIQUES (GO) [05071387] **5144**

RAPPORT D'ACTIVITE - INSTITUT D'EMISSION DES DEPARTEMENTS D'OUTRE-MER (FR/0534-0713) [06826010] **1580**

RAPPORT D'ACTIVITE - INSTITUT D'HYGIENE ET D'EPIDEMIOLOGIE (BE) [04286619] **4798**

RAPPORT D'ACTIVITE / INSTITUT NATIONAL DES SCIENCES DE L'UNIVERS (FR) [16403362] **1410**, **399**

RAPPORT D'ACTIVITE - INSTITUT UNIVERSITAIRE D'ETUDES DU DEVELOPPEMENT (SZ) [07426698] **1623**

RAPPORT D'ACTIVITE / MINISTERE DE LA SANTE, MINISTERE DU TRAVAIL, INSERM, SERVICE CENTRAL DE PROTECTION CONTRE LES RAYONNEMENTS IONISANTS (FR/0245-3827) [17382872] **4441**

RAPPORT D'ACTIVITE - MINISTERE DE L'EQUIPEMENT (FR) [02537997] **5254**

RAPPORT D'ACTIVITE / NATIONAL SHIPPERS COUNCIL OF CAMEROON (CM) [11688488] **5455**

RAPPORT D'ACTIVITE - SERVICE PROVINCIAL DE STATISTIQUE DU CENTRE-SUD (CM) [03595904] **5337**

RAPPORT D'ACTIVITE - SURETE DU QUEBEC (CN/0831-6473) [06860993] **3174**

RAPPORT D'ACTIVITE / UNION SYNDICALE SUISSE (SZ) [16845343] **1705**

RAPPORT D'ACTIVITES / CENTRE QUEBECOIS DE COORDINATION SUR LE SIDA (CN/1189-3087) [25590190] **3676**, **3715**, **4798**

RAPPORT D'ACTIVITES DE L'INSTITUT DE PHONETIQUE (BE) [05958089] **3314**

RAPPORT D'ACTIVITES DU ... / ORGANISATION DE L'UNITE AFRICAINE, CENTRE D'ETUDES LINGUISTIQUES ET HISTORIQUES PAR TRADITION ORALE (NG) [12224263] **3314**

RAPPORT D'ACTIVITES / INSTITUT PANAFRICAIN POUR LE DEVELOPPEMENT (SA) [11499604] **1623**

RAPPORT D'ACTIVITES - LA BIBLIOTHEQUE ADMINISTRATIVE (CN) [02242943] **3243**

RAPPORT D'ACTIVITES / LE BUREAU DE LA STATISTIQUE DU QUEBEC (CN/1185-5460) [24986845] **5337**

RAPPORT D'ACTIVITES - OFFICE DE LA CONSTRUCTION DU QUEBEC (CN/0226-3084) [06618149] **4678**

RAPPORT D'ACTIVITES - OFFICE DES PROFESSIONS DU QUEBEC (CN/0703-0770) [02240624] **4678**

RAPPORT D'ACTIVITES - REPUBLIQUE DE COTE D'IVOIRE, BUREAU DE DEVELOPPEMENT INDUSTRIEL (IV) [02240750] **1623**

RAPPORT D'ACTIVITES - REPUBLIQUE UNIE DU CAMEROUN, SERVICE PROVINCIAL STATISTIQUE DU NORD CAMEROUN (CX) [01798328] **5337**

RAPPORT D'ACTIVITES - SOCIETE D'AMENAGEMENT ET D'EXPLOITATION DES TERRES DU DELTA (SG) [05234403] **124**

RAPPORT D'ACTIVITES - SOCIETE DEVELOPPEMENT DU CACAO (CM) [09351394] **1623**

RAPPORT D'ACTIVITES SUR LES RECHERCHES A L'ENSTA (FR) [05426615] **5144**

RAPPORT D'ACTIVITIE - CAISSE NATIONALE DE L'ASSURANCE MALADIE DES TRAVAILLEURS SALARIES (FR) [05132574] **2891**, **1705**

RAPPORT D'ACTIVITIE / CENTRE REGIONAL D'ENERGIE SOLAIRE (ML) [19018584] **2127**

RAPPORT D'ACTIVITIES - SERVICE DE L'HABITATION ET DE L'URBANISME. VILLE DE MONTREAL (CN/0317-7742) [02248157] **4678**

RAPPORT DE GESTION ET COMPTE FINANCIER DES PTT / PTT (SZ) [20329115] **1147**

RAPPORT DE LA DIRECTION DES RECHERCHES SUR LA CONSOMMATION (CN) [02872086] **1515**

RAPPORT DE L'OFFICE DU CREDIT AGRICOLE DU QUEBEC CONCERNANT L'ADMINISTRATION DE LA LOI SUR LE CREDIT FORESTIER (CN/0711-1835) [06098567] **806**

RAPPORT DE PRESENTATION ET EXPOSE DES MOTIFS DE LA DECISION MODIFICATIVE ... / REPUBLIQUE FRANCAISE, DEPARTEMENT DE LA MARTINIQUE. CONSEIL GENERAL (MQ) [19071569] **4744**

RAPPORT DE RECHERCHE - ECOLE DES HAUTES ETUDES COMMERCIALES (MONTREAL) (CN/0709-986X) [10852334] **1515**, **706**

RAPPORT DE RECHERCHE LPC (FR/0222-8394) [07408530] **2030**

RAPPORT DE RECHERCHE (UNIVERSITE LAVAL. DEPARTEMENT D'INFORMATIQUE) (CN) [09809062] **1262**

RAPPORT DE SYNTHESE (CHAMBRE FRANCAISE DE COMMERCE ET D'INDUSTRIE EN ALGERIE) (AE) [08758969] **3102**

RAPPORT DES ACTIVITES DU BUREAU DE NUTRITION (HT) [06128069] **4198**

RAPPORT DES INVENTAIRES AERIENS DU GROS GIBIER (CN) [06259782] **5596**

RAPPORT DU ... CONGRES DE L'INSTITUT CANADIEN DE RECHERCHE EN RELATIONS INDUSTRIELLES (CN) [06621871] **1705**

RAPPORT DU CONSEIL D'ADMINISTRATION A L'ASSEMBLEE GENERALE ORDINAIRE DES ACTIONNAIRES (SZ) [04803924] **806**

RAPPORT DU CONSEIL D'ADMINISTRATION, BILAN, RESOLUTIONS DE L'ASSEMBLEE GENERALE ORDINAIRE / UNION SENEGALAISE DE BANQUE POUR LE COMMERCE ET L'INDUSTRIE (SG) [11413509] **1515**

RAPPORT DU CONSEIL D'ADMINISTRATION - CREDIT LYONNAIS (FR) [05243674] **806**

RAPPORT DU CONSEIL D'ADMINISTRATION SUR LES OPERATIONS DE L'EXERCICE ... / SOCIETE NATIONALE DU LOGEMENT (BE) [19061621] **1705**

RAPPORT DU CONSEIL NATIONAL DU CREDIT (FR) **806**

RAPPORT DU MINISTRE DE L'EDUCATION (TORONTO) (CN/0706-6333) [06191606] **1776**

RAPPORT DU PRESIDENT GENERAL - SYNDICAT DES FONCTIONNAIRES PROVINCIAUX DU QUEBEC (CN/0848-8061) [21103248] **1705**

RAPPORT DU SERVICE DE LA BIBLIOTHEQUE DE L'UNIVERSITE DU QUEBEC A CHICOUTIMI (CN/0822-4986) [10057407] **3243**

RAPPORT DU VERIFICATEUR GENERAL DU CANADA A LA CHAMBRE DES COMMUNES (1979) (CN/0821-8129) [09471682] **4678**

RAPPORT ECONOMIQUE ANNUEL - CHAD. MINISTERE DU COMMERCE ET DE L'INDUSTRIE (CD) [01785820] **1580**

RAPPORT ET RESOLUTIONS DU CONSEIL D'ADMINISTRATION, RAPPORT DES COMMISSAIRES AUX COMPTES (FR) [04308273] **806**

RAPPORT ET TRAVAUX - GROUPE DE RECHERCHE SUR LA SOCIETE MONTREALAISE AU 19E SIECLE (CN/0225-6959) [06264568] **2756**

RAPPORT - FORINTEK CANADA CORP., LABORATOIRE DE L'EST (CN/0824-2089) [10220672] **2391**

RAPPORT GENERAL D'ACTIVITE - LABORATOIRE CENTRAL DES PONTS ET CHAUSSEES (FR) [01785556] **2030**

RAPPORT GENERAL D'ACTIVITE / MINISTERE DE L'AGRICULTURE, DIRECTION DE LA QUALITE (FR) [07784408] **4678**

RAPPORT GENERAL / MINISTERE DE L'EDUCATION NATIONALE (FR) [20863853] **1869**

RAPPORT GENERAL SUR LA SECURITE SOCIALE (BE) [05542293] **5304**

RAPPORT - GRONLANDS GEOLOGISKE UNDERSOGELSE (DK/0418-6559) [01566170] **1393**

RAPPORT / INSTITUUT VOOR BODEMVRUCHTBAARHEID (NE/0434-6793) [03276573] **184**

RAPPORT - INSTITUUT VOOR VEEVOEDINGSONDERZOEK (NE/0922-3282) [08016232] **124**, **220**

RAPPORT ... INSUFFISANCE RENALE AU CANADA (CN/1184-0161) [23598149] **3992**

RAPPORT / JONKOPINGS LANS MUSEUM (SW/0349-7887) [12258516] **243**

RAPPORT (LOS ANGELES, CALIF.) (US/1061-6861) [25071085] **3427**, **388**

RAPPORT MANUSCRIT CANADIEN DES SCIENCES HALIETIQUES ET AQUATIQUES (CN/0706-6589) [08598096] **5538**

RAPPORT NATIONAL DE CONJONCTURE SCIENTIFIQUE : CHIMIE (FR) [02686321] **990**

RAPPORT NATIONAL DE CONJONCTURE SCIENTIFIQUE: INFORMATIQUE ET MOYENS DE CALCUL POLYVALENTS (FR) [03081049] **1201**

RAPPORT Alphabetical Title Index

RAPPORT NATIONAL DE CONJONCTURE SCIENTIFIQUE : MATHEMATIQUES PURES ET METHODOLOGIE MATHEMATIQUE (FR) [03116600] **3530**

RAPPORT NATIONAL DE CONJONCTURE SCIENTIFIQUE : PHYSIQUE (FR) [02743119] **4419**

RAPPORT NATIONAL DE CONJONCTURE SCIENTIFIQUE : RAPPORT DE SYNTHESE (FR) [02724339] **5145**

RAPPORT NATIONAL DE CONJONCTURE SCIENTIFIQUE : SCIENCES DE LA VIE (FR) [02724663] **471**

RAPPORT NATIONAL DE CONJONCTURE SCIENTIFIQUE : SCIENCES DE L'HOMME (FR) [02715473] **5254**

RAPPORT NATIONAL DE LA CONJONCTURE SCIENTIFIQUE : SCIENCES DE LA TERRE ET DE L'ESPACE (FR) [02743165] **1359**

RAPPORT - NORTH CENTRAL REGIONAL LIBRARY SYSTEM (NEWSLETTER) (CN/0715-5867) [09511072] **3244**

RAPPORT OM KONTROLLEN MED KONSUMMLKPRODUKTER FOR ARET (DK/0107-8666) [19753322] **198**

RAPPORT OM VIRKSOMHETEN (NO) [18500794] **2868**

RAPPORT / PROEFSTATION VOOR DE RUNDVEEHOUDERIJ, SCHAPENHOUDERIJ EN PAARDENHOUDERIJ (NE) [10233798] **220**

RAPPORT PROVISOIRE SUR LES ACTIVITES DU SECTEUR (IV) [02240376] **2149**

RAPPORT SCIENTIFIQUE - INSTITUT FRANCAIS D'OCEANIE, CENTRE D'OCEANOGRAPHIE (NL) [01215119] **1455**

RAPPORT SCIENTIFIQUE - INSTITUT FRANCAIS D'OCEANIE, SECTION OCEANOGRAPHIE (NL/0078-2149) [01215110] **1455**

RAPPORT - SECTION D'EXPERIMENTATION DE BOBO-DIOULASSO, INSTITUT DE RECHERCHES DU COTON ET DES TEXTILES EXOTIQUES (FR) [03402825] **2429**

RAPPORT - STATENS JORDBRUGS KONOMISKE INSTITUT (DK/0108-7398) [I01087398] **124**

RAPPORT / STATENS JORDBRUGSKONOMISK INSTITUT (DK/0108-7401) [17801638] **124**

RAPPORT STATISTIQUE - COMITE NATIONAL DE LA POMME DE TERRE (FR) [02686099] **2355**

RAPPORT STATISTIQUE SUR LES ACCIDENTS DE LA ROUTE EN ... / CONFERENCE EUROPEENNE DES MINISTRES DES TRANSPORTS (FR) [13040430] **5401**

RAPPORT SUR LA CULTURE DU RIZ PLUVIAL AU SENEGAL ORIENTAL (SG) [03236433] **124**

RAPPORT SUR LA SITUATION ECONOMIQUE ET PERSPECTIVES D'AVENIR DE LA CIRCONSCRIPTION *See* SITUATION ECONOMIQUE ET PERSPECTIVES D'AVENIR **1584**

RAPPORT SUR LE COMMERCE EXTERIEUR DES PRODUITS DE LA PECHE EN ... (FR) [11740599] **2311**

RAPPORT SUR LE DEVELOPPEMENT DANS LE MONDE (US/0271-1710) [06561848] **806**

RAPPORT SUR LES ACTIVITES - CHAMBRE REGIONALE DE COMMERCE ET D'INDUSTRIE D'ALSACE (FR) [01784878] **821**

RAPPORT SUR LES COMPTES DE LA NATION (FR) [00942597] **1580**

RAPPORT SUR LES FEMMES (CN/0824-3883) [10420557] **5214**

RAPPORT SUR LES PROJETS / LA SOCIETE CANADIENNE DE LA CROIX-ROUGE (CN/1180-0178) [22473461] **5304**

RAPPORT SUR L'INDUSTRIE FORESTIERE (CN/0824-3832) [10392509] **2391**

RAPPORT (SVENSKA BIBLIOTEKARIESAMFUNDET) (SW/0280-719X) [19863404] **3244**

RAPPORT / SVERIGES LANTBRUKSUNIVERSITE. INSTITUTIONEN FOR TRADGARDSVETENSKAP (SW/0348-4157) [07104981] **2429**

RAPPORT - SVERIGES LANTBRUKSUNIVERSITET, INSTITUTION FOR VIRKESLARA (SW/0348-4599) [05959918] **2391**

RAPPORT - SVERIGES LANTBRUKSUNIVERSITET, INSTITUTIONEN FOR BYGGNADSTEKNIK (SW/0348-0259) [06792844] **124**

RAPPORT / SVERIGES LANTBRUKSUNIVERSITET, INSTITUTIONEN FOR EKOLOGI OCH MILJOVARD (SW/0348-422X) [21551976] 2220, **2391**

RAPPORT (SVERIGES LANTBRUKSUNIVERSITET. INSTITUTIONEN FOR EKONOMI) (SW/0284-3153) [19551365] **124**

RAPPORT - SVERIGES LANTBRUKSUNIVERSITET, INSTITUTIONEN FOR EKONOMI OCH STATISTIK. REPORT - DEPARTMENT OF ECONOMICS AND STATISTICS (SW/0347-982X) [04757247] 1515, **1537**

RAPPORT - SVERIGES LANTBRUKSUNIVERSITET, INSTITUTIONEN FOR HUSDJURS UTFODRING OCH VARD (SW/0347-9838) [10476370] **5519**

RAPPORT (SVERIGES LANTBRUKSUNIVERSITET. INSTITUTIONEN FOR HUSDJURSHYGIEN) (SW/0283-0698) [18461016] **5519**

RAPPORT / SVERIGES LANTBRUKSUNIVERSITET. INSTITUTIONEN FOR MIKROBIOLOGI (SW/0348-4041) [08960475] 569, **124**

RAPPORT - SVERIGES LANTBRUKSUNIVERSITET. INSTITUTIONEN FOR SKOGLIG GENETIK OCH VAXTFYSIOLOGI. REPORT - SWEDISH UNIVERSITY OF AGRICULTURAL SCIENCES, DEPARTMENT OF FOREST GENETICS AND PLANT PHYSIOLOGY (SW/0348-7954) [05973767] 526, 551, **2392**

RAPPORT (SVERIGES LANTBRUKSUNIVERSITET. INSTITUTIONEN FOR SKOGSPRODUKTION) (SW/0348-7636) [08101573] **2392**

RAPPORT TECHNIQUE (UNIVERSITE LAVAL. DEPARTEMENT D'INFORMATIQUE) (CN) [09929538] **5145**

RAPPORT (TORONTO. 1981) *CEASED.* (CN/0229-740X) [08205505] **1515**

RAPPORTER FRA GEOLOGISK INSTITUTT (NO/0332-5113) [07532815] **1393**

RAPPORTER FRAN JORDEBEARBETNINGSAVDELNINGEN, SVERIGES LANTBRUKSUNIVERSITET (SW/0348-0976) [06046568] **184**

RAPPORTER OCH MEDDELANDEN - SVERIGES GEOLOGISKA UNDERSOKNING (SW/0349-2176) [06218319] **1393**

RAPPORTER OCH NOTISER - LUNDS UNIVERSITETS NATURGEOGRAFISKA INSTITUTION (SW/0348-3339) [I03483339] **2574**

RAPPORTER OCH UPPSATSER - SVERIGES LANTBRUKSUNIVERSITET INSTITUTIONEN FOR SKOGSGENETIK (SW/0348-565X) [05859731] **2392**

RAPPORTI CER (IT) **1515**

RAPPORTI E STUDI / ISTITUTO VENETO DI SCIENZE, LETTERE ED ARTI, COMMISSIONE DI STUDIO DEI PROVVEDIMENTI PER LA CONSERVAZIONE E DIFESA DELLA LAGUNA E DELLA CITTA DI VENEZIA (IT) [20340907] **2095**

RAPPORTI ISTISAN (IT/0391-1675) [15367565] **3632**

RAPPORTO CONGIUNTURA (IT) **1515**

RAPPORTO CSC / CONFINDUSTRIA, CENTRO STUDI (IT) [16652738] **1623**

RAPPORTO DI ATTIVITA / ISTITUTO DI RICERCA SULLE ACQUE (IT) [09903684] **5538**

RAPPORTO IRS SUL MERCATO AZIONARIO (IT) **821**

RAPPORTO SULLA INDUSTRIA COTONIERA ITALIANA (IT) [03530336] **1623**

RAPPORTO SULLA INDUSTRIA COTONIERA LINIERA / ASSOCIAZIONE COTONIERA LINIERA E DELLE FIBRE AFFINI (IT) [27402709] **5355**

RAPPORTO SULLA SITUAZIONE SOCIALE DEL PAESE (IT) [02245674] **5254**

RAPPORTS ANNUELS - BANQUE NATIONALE POUR LE DEVELOPPEMENT INDUSTRIEL (FR) [05141635] **806**

RAPPORTS D'ACTIVITE / DIRECTION DE LA RECHERCHE GEOLOGIQUE (CN/0837-757X) [20213908] **1393**

RAPPORTS DE CONSTRUCTION SOUTHAM (CN/0822-5028) [10061665] **625**

RAPPORTS DE LA SECTION DES GRIEFS ET DE L'ARBITRAGE (CN/0822-7829) [11283947] **3034**

RAPPORTS DES COMMISSIONS DE TRAVAIL (SZ) [02757447] **1993**

RAPPORTS D'ESSAI DE TRACTEUR (FR) **161**

RAPPORTS ET PROCES-VERBAUX DES REUNIONS COMMISSION INTERNATIONALE POUR L'EXPLORATION SCIENTIFIQUE DE LA MER MEDITERRANEE (MC/0373-434X) [03385645] **1455**

RAPPORTS HET FRANSE BOEK (NE) [06007219] **3427**

RAPPORTS SCIENTIFIQUE ET TECHNIQUES DE L'IFREMER (FR/0761-3970) [15677046] **1455**

RAPRA ABSTRACTS (UK/0033-6750) [02450045] 5077, **5078**

RAPRA NEWS (UK/0140-041X) [07076607] **5077**

RAPRA REVIEW REPORTS (US/0889-3144) [13844281] **2108**

RAPS : FACHZEITSCHRIFT FUER OL- UND EIWEISSPFLANZEN (GW/0724-4606) [12035697] **125**

RAPTOR REPORT (US/1048-8030) [07565056] 226, 2203, **5620**

RARE AMERICANA (US/0098-485X) [02240666] **423**

RARE BOOKS AND MANUSCRIPTS LIBRARIANSHIP (US/0884-450X) [12368635] **3244**

RARE BOOKS NEWSLETTER (UK) [21109633] **4832**

RARE BOOKS : TRENDS, COLLECTIONS, SOURCES *CEASED.* (US) [10813052] 4832, **2777**

RARE COIN REVIEW (US/0095-263X) [01796469] **2783**

RARE COINS & MEDALS (US) [05635920] **2783**

RARE EARTH BULLETIN (UK/0307-8531) [01791111] **5145**

RARE FRUIT COUNCIL OF AUSTRALIA INC. NEWSLETTER (AT/0726-1470) [I07261470] **2430**

RARITAN (US/0275-1607) [07087821] 3427, **3351**

RAS NEWSLETTER (US/0094-7709) [01795026] **423**

RAS; ROHR, ARMATUR, SANITAR, HEIZUNG (GW/0033-6769) [07241053] **2608**

RASAYANA SAMIKSHA (II/0379-7635) [02954551] **990**

RASCETY ATOMNYH I JADERNYH KONSTANT (LV/0302-8453) [05692551] **4450**

RASCHET PROSTRANSTVENNYKH KONSTRUKTSII; SBORNIK STATEI (RU) [20871688] **2127**

RASD UPDATE (US/0198-8344) [06237253] **3244**

RASEN (GW/0341-9789) [06434950] **2430**

RASHTRABHASHA SANDESA : HINDI SAHITYA SAMMELANA KA MUKHAPATRA (II) [10452808] **3314**

RASHTRIYA PANCAYATA NIYAMAVALI (NP) [02239628] **4678**

RASHUT HA-NEMALIM BE-YISRAEL *See* SUMMARY AND OBJECTIVES **5457**

RASILIMALI *SUSPENDED.* (TZ) [02239709] **1580**

RASMI (KATHMANDU, NEPAL) (NP) [11985640] **3314**

RASPISANIE DVIZHENIIA RECHNYKH PASSAZHIRSKIKH SUDOV OSNOVNYKH TRANSPORTNYKH LINII NA NAVIGATSIIU (RU) [01791249] **5390**

RASPODELA STANOVA I KREDITA ZA STANOVE U ... GODINI / SOCIJALISTICKA REPUBLIKA SRBIJA, REPUBLICK ZAVOD ZA STATISTIKU (YU) [08340908] **2832**

RASPOZNAVANIE OBRAZOV (LV) [02241930] **2078**

RASPRAVE ZAVODA ZA HRVATSKI JEZIK (CI) [27190006] **3314**

RASPROSTRANENIE PECHATI (RU) [06125695] **2923**

RASSEGNA SOVIETICA (IT/0033-9857) [08651790] **329**

RASSEGNA ALIMENTARE (IT) **2370**

RASSEGNA AMMINISTRATIVA DELLA SANITA (IT) **4798**

RASSEGNA AMMINISTRATIVA DELLA SCUOLA (IT/0393-4586) [I03934586] **1869**

RASSEGNA (BOLOGNA) (IT/0393-0203) [08037716] **307**

RASSEGNA CHIMICA (IT/0033-9334) [04071234] **990**

RASSEGNA CONGIUNTURALE / CONFINDUSTRIA, CENTRO STUDI *CEASED.* (IT) [14963691] 1623, **1537**

RASSEGNA D'ARTE (IT) [01786822] **363**

RASSEGNA DEGLI ARCHIVI DI STATO (IT/0392-1522) [09116571] **2483**

RASSEGNA DEI BENI CULTURALI *CEASED.* (IT) 280, **252**

RASSEGNA DEL BITUME (IT) **4276**

RASSEGNA DEL CENTRO DI CULTURA E STORIA AMALFITANA (IT) [18540503] **329**

RASSEGNA DELL AVVOCATURA DELLO STATO (IT) **3034**

RASSEGNA DELL ECONOMIA LUCANA (IT) [06652610] **1515**

RASSEGNA DELL IMBALLAGGIO E CONFEZIONAMENTO (IT) **4221**

Alphabetical Title Index

RASSEGNA DELL' ISTRUZIONE SECONDARIA (IT/0033-9466) [I00339466] **1776**

RASSEGNA DELLA LETTERATURA SUI CICLI ECONOMICI / ISTITUTO NAZIONALE PER LO STUDIO DELLA CONGIUNTURA (IT/0033-944X) [06686968] **1594**

RASSEGNA DELLA LETTURATURA ITALIANA, LA (IT/0033-9423) [05025780] **1079**

RASSEGNA DELLA STAMPA (IT) **2924**

RASSEGNA DELLE LOCAZIONI E DEL CONDOMINIO (IT) **4843**

RASSEGNA DI ARCHITETTURA E URBANISTICA (IT/0392-8608) [08616046] **307**

RASSEGNA DI CULTURA E VITA SCOLASTICA (IT) [11049351] **5214**

RASSEGNA DI DERMATOLOGIA E SIFILOGRAFIA (IT/0033-9490) [10709967] **3722**

RASSEGNA DI DIRITTO CIVILE (IT/0393-182X) [I0393182X] **3091**

RASSEGNA DI DIRITTO E TECN CA DELLA ALIMENTAZIONE (IT/0392-7113) [I03927113] **2355**

RASSEGNA DI DIRITTO LEGISLAZIONE E MEDICINA LEGALE VETERINARIA (IT/0300-3485) [01425224] **5519**

RASSEGNA DI DIRITTO PUBBLICO (IT/0033-9512) [01605046] **3034**

RASSEGNA DI FISCO E FINANZA *CEASED.* (IT) **1515**

RASSEGNA DI LETTERATURA TOMISTICA (IT/0557-6857) [01776676] 4358, **3427**

RASSEGNA DI MEDICINA DEI LAVORATORI (IT) **3632**

RASSEGNA DI MEDICINA INTERNA (IT) [18418566] **3801**

RASSEGNA DI MEDICINA SPERIMENTALE (IT/0033-9555) [09558876] **586**

RASSEGNA DI PEDAGOGIA (IT) [03522761] **1776**

RASSEGNA DI PENSIONISTICA (IT/1120-2831) [I11202831] **5304**

RASSEGNA DI PSICOLOGIA : QUADRIMESTRALE DEI DIPARTIMENTI DI PSICOLOGIA E DI PSICOLOGIA DI SVILUPPO E SOCIALIZZAZIONE DELL'UNIVERSITA "LA SAPIENZA" DI ROMA (IT) [13380368] **4615**

RASSEGNA DI PSICOTERAPIE, IPNOSI : ORGANO UFFICIALE QUADRIMESTRALE DELLA F.I.S.P.I.R. (FEDERAZIONE ITALIANA STUDIO PSICOTERAPIE, IPNOSI E STATI DI RILASSAMENTO) (IT) [19261945] **2858**

RASSEGNA DI SERVIZIO SOCIALE (IT/0033-9601) **4798**

RASSEGNA DI SERVIZIO SOCIALE (IT/0033-9601) [I00339601] **5304**

RASSEGNA DI STATISTICHE DEL LAVORO *CEASED.* (IT/0033-961X) [05530811] 1705, **1537**

RASSEGNA DI STUDI E NOTIZIE. RACCOLTA DELLE STAMPE A. BERTARELLI. RACCOLTA DI ARTE APPLICATA. MUSEO DEGLI STRUMENTI MUSICALI (IT/0394-4808) [I03944808] **329**

RASSEGNA DI STUDI ETIOPICI (IT) [02266763] **2642**

RASSEGNA DI STUDI PSICHIATRICI (IT/0033-9636) [07579862] **3935**

RASSEGNA DI STUDI TURISTICI *SUSPENDED.* (IT/0392-7164) [03927164] **5490**

RASSEGNA DI TEOLOGIA (IT/0033-9644) [09209957] **4969**

RASSEGNA DI UROLOGIA E NEFROLOGIA (IT/0033-992X) [I0033992X] **3992**

RASSEGNA ECONOMICA (IT/0390-010X) [06085209] **1515**

RASSEGNA ECONOMICA DELLA PROVINCIA DI SONDRIO (IT) [06648106] **1580**

RASSEGNA ECONOMICA: SIENA (IT) [06527120] **1580**

RASSEGNA ECONOMICA: TERNI (IT) [07112617] **1515**

RASSEGNA FORENSE (IT) [06726310] **3034**

RASSEGNA GALLARATESE DI STORIA E D'ARTE (IT) [01794892] **2704**

RASSEGNA GIURIDICA DELL ENERGIA ELETTRICA (IT) **3034**

RASSEGNA GRAFICA (IT) **4569**

RASSEGNA IBERISTICA (IT/0392-4777) [06360455] **3428**

RASSEGNA INTERNAZIONALE DI CLINICA E TERAPIA (IT/0033-9695) [01586934] **3632**

RASSEGNA ISTITUZIONALE REGIONE LOMBARDIA (IT) **4678**

RASSEGNA ITALIANA DI CHIRURGIA PEDIATRICA (IT/0390-0495) [03625044] **3973**

RASSEGNA ITALIANA DI CRIMINOLOGIA : ORGANO UFFICIALE DELLA SOCIETA ITALIANA DI CRIMINOLOGIA : BULLETIN DU CENTRE INTERNATIONAL DE CRIMINOLOGIE CLINIQUE (IT) [27062047] **3174**

RASSEGNA ITALIANA DI LINGUISTICA APPLICATA (IT/0033-9725) [01869237] **3314**

RASSEGNA ITALIANA DI SOCIOLOGIA (IT/0079-9734) [01605285] **5255**

RASSEGNA MEDICA SARDA (IT/0033-9776) [01778824] **3632**

RASSEGNA MENSILE DELLE IMPOSTE (IT) **750**

RASSEGNA MENSILE DI ISRAEL, LA (IT/0033-9792) [01855686] **5052**

RASSEGNA MUSICALE CURCI (IT/0033-9806) [02266766] **4148**

RASSEGNA PARLAMENTARE (IT/0486-0373) [05530817] **3093**

RASSEGNA PENITENZIARIA E CRIMINOLOGICA (IT) [06902862] **3174**

RASSEGNA PETROLIFERA (IT/0390-587X) [I0390587X] **4276**

RASSEGNA POSTELEGRAFONICA (IT) **1147**

RASSEGNA SINDACALE (IT/0033-9849) [06681720] **1705**

RASSEGNA STAMPA ACRI (IT) **4819**

RASSEGNA STAMPA HANDICAP (IT) **5304**

RASSEGNA STORICA DEL RISORGIMENTO (IT/0033-9873) [01608137] **2704**

RASSEGNA STORICA TOSCANA (IT/0033-9881) [01855566] **2704**

RASSEGNA TAR (IT) **4678**

RASSEGNA TRIBUTARIA : RT (IT) [10842078] **4744**

RASSEMBLEMENT DES CITOYENS DE MONTREAL *See* JOURNAL DU R C M, LE **4478**

RASSKAZ (RU) [07490609] **3428**

RASTENIEVDNI NAUKI *SUSPENDED.* (BU/0568-465X) [02385333] **2430**

RASTER (NE/0033-9938) [04523659] **3428**

RASTITELNYE RESURSY (RU/0033-9946) [02578995] **526**

RASY I NARODY (RU) [01780335] **4512**

RAT EN MUIS (NE/0481-8024) [02477100] **2241**

RAT NEWS LETTER (US/0309-1848) [03803933] **5519**

RATARSTVO, VOCARSTVO I VINOGRADARSTVO (YU) [01798775] **125**

RATE REVIEW TOPICS (US/0190-5139) [04677517] **3632**

RATE SUPPORT GRANT STATISTICS / SOCIETY OF COUNTY TREASURERS (UK/0142-5137) [07120829] 4744, **4699**

RATE%GRAM (US/0887-7408) [13338577] **1515**

RATEKO (SW/0033-9962) [I00339962] **1120**

RATEL (UK/0305-1218) [07600481] **5596**

RATEN AMERIKA KENKYU NENPO (JA/0286-1127) [08964852] **2756**

RATES OF CHANGE IN ECONOMIC DATA FOR TEN INDUSTRIAL COUNTRIES (US/0430-1994) [02383508] **806**

RATHBUN, RATHBONE, RATHBURN FAMILY HISTORIAN (US/0737-7711) [07087698] **2469**

RATING AND INCOME TAX *See* RATING AND VALUATION REPORTER **3034**

RATING AND VALUATION REPORTER (UK) [01763459] 4744, **3034**

RATING APPEALS (UK) [01789515] 4843, **3034**

RATINGS BOOK, THE (US/0742-0684) [10255437] 1272, **1292**

RATIO (US) [06593496] **1776**

RATIO JURIS (UK/0952-1917) [17503201] **3034**

RATIO (OXFORD) (UK/0034-0006) [01497450] **4358**

RATIONALITY AND SOCIETY (US/1043-4631) [19467922] **5214**

RATIONELL REINIGEN (GW/0173-9220) [I01739220] **625**

RATIONELLE BURO *See* RATIONELLES BURO + I.E. UND EDV **706**

RATIONELLES BURO + I.E. UND EDV (GW) [01791104] **706**

RATIOS OF CALIFORNIA PUBLIC SCHOOL NONTEACHING EMPLOYEES TO CLASSROOM TEACHERS (US/0271-2393) [05977840] **1869**

RATON RANGE (1985) (US/0896-1093) [12331582] **5713**

RATP SAVOIR FAIRE PARIS (FR/1168-3392) [I11683392] **5390**

RAUCH GUIDE TO THE U.S. PAINT INDUSTRY, THE (US/8755-0261) [11246247] **4225**

RAUMFORSCHUNG UND RAUMORDNUNG (GW/0034-0111) [01855554] **33**

RAUMORDNUNGSBERICHT ... DER BUNDESREGIERUNG (GW) [25746011] **5304**

RAUMPLANUNG, INFORMATIONSHEFTE / EJPD, BUNDESAMT FUR RAUMPLANUNG (SZ) [09222173] **2832**

RAVALLI REPUBLIC (US) [14222444] **5706**

RAVE REVIEW, THE (US/0732-6742) [08417682] **3185**

●RAVEN PRESS SERIES ON MOLECULAR AND CELLULAR BIOLOGY (US) [25532023] **540**

RAVEN, THE (US/0034-0146) [01608116] **5596**

RAVEN (TRENTON, N.J.) (US/1071-0043) [28530082] 2853, 2627, **5214**

RAVENSWOOD NEWS, THE (US) [12889775] **5764**

RAVI (PK) [01608162] **3428**

RAVITSEMIS- JA MAJOITUSLIIKKEIDEN TYONTEKIJOIDEN JA TOIMIHENKILOIDEN PALKAT. LONERNA FOR ARBETSTAGARE OCH FUNKTIONARER INOM FORPLAGNADS- OCH HARBARGERINGSRORELSER (FI) [05788817] **1705**

RAW MATERIALS REPORT (SW/0349-6287) [07989808] **2203**

RAW STEEL PRODUCTION IN 11 PRODUCING DISTRICTS (US) **4017**

RAW VISION (UK/0955-1182) [19906087] **363**

RAWLINSON'S AUSTRALIAN CONSTRUCTION HANDBOOK (AT/0810-8064) [I08108064] **625**

RAWLINSONS NEW ZEALAND CONSTRUCTION HANDBOOK (NZ) **625**

RAY (JO) [21480183] **5805**

RAY PALMER'S FORUM *See* SEARCH MAGAZINE (AMHERST) **35**

RAYDAN (YE) [06860724] **2662**

RAYNE ACADIAN TRIBUNE (US) [04219661] **5684**

RAYNE INDEPENDENT, THE (US/0746-7567) [10253454] **5684**

RAYON JEUNESSE (CN/0841-758X) [18810305] **1068**

RAYON (SAINTE-AGATHE-DES-MONTS) (CN/0715-8912) [09692493] **3244**

RAYONNEMENTS IONISANTS (FR/0397-9210) [I03979210] **4441**

RAYS (IT/0390-7740) [03578685] **3946**

RAYS FROM THE ROSE CROSS (US/0744-432X) [05592632] **4243**

RAYTOWN DISPATCH (US) [21894862] **5704**

RAZA, LA (US/0034-0219) [01763464] **2271**

RAZA LAW JOURNAL, LA (US/8755-8815) [09982196] 2271, **3034**

RAZISKAVE IN STUDIJE - KMETIJSKI INSTITUT SLOVENIJE (XV/0352-5686) [04527053] **125**

RAZKOPKI I PROUCHVANIIA. FOUILLES ET RECHERCHES (BU) [04879841] **280**

RAZON MESTIZA, LA (US) [02381261] **5565**

RAZON Y FE (SP/0034-0235) [01763465] **2853**

RAZONES (MEXICO CITY, MEXICO) (MX) [07186090] **4533**

RAZORUZHENIE, VELENIE VREMENI (RU) [11581770] **3134**

RAZVEDKA I OKHRANA NEDR (RU/0034-026X) [09933086] **2149**

RAZVITIE LICHNOSTI V USLOVIIAKH SOTSIALIZMA (RU) [05769379] 4545, **4615**

RAZVITIE SOTSIALNOI SFERY V SSSR (RU) [18707414] **4545**

RAZVOJ (CI/0352-4728) [14955285] 1639, **2911**

RAZVOJ, DEVELOPMENT INTERNATIONAL (CI/0352-8553) [18028998] **1639**

RB (II/0377-8460) [02990004] **625**

RB ELEKTRONICA MAGAZINE (NE) **2078**

RBBS-PC IN A BOX. CD-ROM (US) 1272, **1289**

RBC — Alphabetical Title Index

RBC. REVISIONES SOBRE BIOLOGIA CELULAR (SP/0213-7119) [13115547] **540**

RBM. PSIQUIATRIA (BL) [12033443] **3935**

RBM. REVISTA BRASILEIRA DE MANDIOCA (BL/0101-563X) [10037987] **125**

RBM. REVUE EUROPEENNE DE BIOTECHNOLOGIE MEDICALE (FR/0222-0776) [I02220776] **5145**

RBMS NEWSLETTER (US/0743-1481) [10528634] **4832**

RBRVS STEP BY STEP (US) **2891**

RC AND D RELEASE *CEASED*. (US/0092-9638) [01788701] 2292, **2392**

RC MODELER (1969) (US/0033-6866) [01786398] 33, **2777**

RCA CORPORATION. SOLID STATE DIVISION *See* POWER TRANSISTORS AND POWER HYBRID CIRCUITS **2075**

RCA CORPORATION. SOLID STATE DIVISION *See* C.O.S.-M.O.S. DIGITAL INTEGRATED CIRCUITS **2037**

RCA CORPORATION. SOLID STATE DIVISION *See* LINEAR INTEGRATED CIRCUITS AND MOS DEVICES **2071**

RCA CORPORATION. SOLID STATE DIVISION *See* THYRISTORS, RECTIFIERS, AND DIACS **2084**

RCAR OPTIONS (US) [18409723] **590**

RCC KOUDE & LUCHTBEHANDELING (NE) **2608**

●RCD. ROCK COMPACT DISC MAGAZINE (UK/0965-190X) [I0965190X] **4148**

RCDA (NEW YORK, N.Y.) (US/1061-656X) [24857617] 4545, **4989**

RCDA. RELIGION IN COMMUNIST DOMINATED AREAS (US/0034-3978) [01201299] 4989, **4546**

RCGS NEWSLETTER (US/1057-185X) [23294885] **2469**

RCI NEWSLETTER (CN/1182-4581) [23248116] **1138**

RCO UPDATE (CN) **2241**

RCOG DIPLOMATE, THE (UK/1351-8402) **3767**

RCRA LAND DISPOSAL RESTRICTIONS : A GUIDE TO COMPLIANCE / COMPILED AND PUBLISHED BY MCCOY AND ASSOCIATES, THE (US) [26469918] **2180**

RCRA REGULATIONS AND KEYWORD INDEX (US) [17500245] **2180**

RCUH ANNUAL REPORT (US/0273-2211) [07009562] **5145**

RDE. RECHT DER ELEKTRIZITATSWIRTSCHAFT (GW/0936-5893) [I09365893] 3034, 2078, **1954**

RDH (US/0279-7720) [07252307] **1334**

RDI MONOGRAPHS ON FOREIGN AID AND DEVELOPMENT (US/0748-0644) [10873969] **4533**

RDS *SUSPENDED*. (IT/0035-5240) [I00355240] **1869**

RE ARTS & LETTERS : REAL (US/1054-5212) [19680999] 3428, **329**

RE/MAX INTER (CN/0712-5976) [09606637] **4843**

RE METALLICA, DE (PE/1010-0962) [11244402] 2149, **4017**

RE-NEW (PORT HOPE) (CN/0845-5341) [19962559] **2832**

RE NEWS DIGEST *CEASED*. (US/0895-5700) [16704725] **1954**

RE. REGIONE EUROPA *SUSPENDED*. (IT/1120-754X) [I1120754X] **1639**

RE. REVISTA DE EDIFICACION (SP/0213-8948) [I02138948] **307**

●RE SUPEKKU (JA) [26140537] **329**

RE-VIEW (NEW YORK) *SUSPENDED*. (US/0161-5114) [06741657] **363**

REA REPORT, THE (US/1057-090X) [23936447] **1515**

REABILITIROVAN POSMERTNO (RU) [20153739] **4493**

REACH (CN/0841-9507) [19276883] **4393**

REACH TH' PEOPLE (CN/0825-7507) [11734407] **5367**

REACH (VANCOUVER) *CEASED*. (CN/0712-5364) [09145949] **3632**

REACHING THE MANITOBA MARKET (CN/0706-8085) [04433070] **765**

REACHOUT (US) **4989**

●REACTION! (UK/1353-1190) **990**

REACTION KINETICS AND CATALYSIS LETTERS (HU/0304-4122) [03263990] **1057**

REACTIONS (AT/0157-7271) [06634261] 1348, **3632**

REACTIONS (UK) **2891**

REACTIONS (AUCKLAND) *See* REACTIONS WEEKLY **4327**

REACTIONS (LONDON) (UK/0953-5640) [09386493] **2891**

REACTIONS WEEKLY (NZ/0114-9954) [28493176] **4327**

REACTIVE AND FUNCTIONAL POLYMERS (NE) **1047**

REACTIVE POLYMERS (NE/0923-1137) [19582017] **1047**

REACTIVITY AND STRUCTURE (US/0341-2377) [02163900] **1047**

REACTOR SAFETY RESEARCH PROGRAMS, QUARTERLY PROGRESS REPORT (BROOKHAVEN NATIONAL LABORATORY, DEPT. OF NUCLEAR ENERGY) *See* WATER REACTOR SAFETY RESEARCH DIVISION QUARTERLY PROGRESS REPORT / DEPARTMENT OF NUCLEAR ENERGY, BROOKHAVEN NATIONAL LABORATORY **2159**

READ, AMERICA! (US/0891-4214) [14765903] **1776**

●READ-EASY BASKETBALL RULES (US/1074-6242) [29000268] **4914**

READ-EASY FOOTBALL RULES (US) [22171849] **4914**

READ-EASY MEN'S AND WOMEN'S BASKETBALL RULES (US/1070-079X) [22498808] **4914**

READ (MIDDLETOWN) (US/0034-0359) [03905702] **1903**

READ 'N DO STORIES (US/0190-2679) [04680559] **1777**

READ ON (RH) [15625493] **1777**

READ (UKARUMPA, PAPUA NEW GUINEA) (PP) [08645000] **1884**

READAPTATION PARIS (FR/0484-0305) [I04840305] **5145**

READER (US) [17542939] **5661**

READER (HOUGHTON, MICH.) (US/0742-9681) [09614909] **1777**

READER (SAN DIEGO, CALIF.) (US) [08193122] **5638**

READER SERVICES LAW LIBRARIAN (US) [07745910] **3244**

READER (VANCOUVER) (CN/0827-4940) [13529793] **4832**

●READERLY/WRITERLY TEXTS (US/1066-3630) [26923188] **3351**

READER'S ADVISER, THE (US/0094-5943) [06058886] **3459**

READERS ADVISORY SERVICE : SELECTED TOPICAL BOOKLISTS *SUSPENDED*. (US/0094-8098) [01795349] **423**

READER'S CHOICE (TORONTO) (CN/0712-4376) [08932797] **3428**

READER'S DIGEST BASIA ED (HK/0034-0383) [I00340383] **2271**

READER'S DIGEST (CANADIAN EDITION) (CN/0034-0413) [02075921] **2544**

READER'S DIGEST CONDENSED BOOKS (US) [00964181] **2491**

READERS DIGEST. FINNISH EDITION (FI) **2491**

READERS' DIGEST (KOREAN EDITION) (KO) **2491**

READER'S DIGEST. LARGE-TYPE EDITION (US/0163-6405) [04453816] **2491**

READER'S DIGEST SOUTH AFRICAN ED (SA/0034-0456) [I00340456] **2500**

READER'S DIGEST, THE (US/0034-0375) [01763471] **2491**

READERS' GUIDE ABSTRACTS. CD-ROM (US/0899-1553) **2497**

READERS' GUIDE ABSTRACTS (MICROFORM) (US/0886-0092) [12789350] **423**

READER'S GUIDE ABSTRACTS (PRINT ED. : SEMIANNUAL) *See* READERS' GUIDE ABSTRACTS (SCHOOL AND PUBLIC LIBRARY ED.) **3259**

READERS' GUIDE ABSTRACTS (SCHOOL AND PUBLIC LIBRARY ED.) (US/1058-1219) [24222337] 3244, **3259**

READERS' GUIDE ABSTRACTS SCHOOL AND PUBLIC LIBRARY EDITION *See* READERS' GUIDE ABSTRACTS SELECT EDITION **2497**

READERS' GUIDE ABSTRACTS SELECT EDITION (US) 2492, **2497**

READERS' GUIDE TO PERIODICAL LITERATURE (US/0034-0464) [01763473] 3428, **2497**

READERS PAYE : PII HANDBOOK (UK) 3034, **4744**

READING ACHIEVEMENT TEST REPORT (US/0099-0744) [02242182] **1903**

READING AND LITERATURE : GENERAL INFORMATION YEARBOOK (US/0097-5214) [01795648] **1903**

READING & WRITING (NE/0922-4777) [20068809] **3314**

●READING & WRITING QUARTERLY (UK/1057-3569) [24020427] **1884**

READING AROUND SERIES (AT/0812-1710) [I08121710] **1777**

READING-BERKS AUTO CLUB MAGAZINE (US/0744-7043) [08515833] **5423**

READING CLINIC, THE *CEASED*. (US/0146-1176) [02860452] **1777**

READING EAGLE (US) [12609554] **5739**

READING EDGE (CROWNSVILLE, MD.), THE (US/1040-3558) [18390625] 3428, **3244**

READING EDUCATION *SUSPENDED*. (AT/0312-9543) [I03129543] **1777**

READING, ENG. UNIVERSITY. DEPT. OF AGRICULTURE AND HORTICULTURE *See* GUIDE TO THE DEPARTMENT, UNIVERSITY FARMS AND EXPERIMENTAL STATIONS WITH A SUMMARY OF RESEARCH **91**

READING HORIZONS (US/0034-0502) [01763478] 1903, **3314**

READING IMPROVEMENT (US/0034-0510) [02244315] 1903, **3314**

READING IN A FOREIGN LANGUAGE (UK/0264-2425) [09607541] 1903, **3314**

READING INSTRUCTION JOURNAL, THE (US/0275-441X) [07142886] **1843**

READING MANITOBA (CN/0228-9652) [07817553] 3314, **1903**

READING MEDIEVAL STUDIES : ANNUAL PROCEEDINGS OF THE GRADUATE CENTRE FOR MEDIEVAL STUDIES IN THE UNIVERSITY OF READING (UK) [11956752] **2704**

READING PLUS (NEW YORK, N.Y.) (US/0882-6196) [11902545] **3428**

READING PROFESSOR (US) **1903**

READING PSYCHOLOGY (UK/0270-2711) [05874107] 1903, **4615**

READING RAINBOW GAZETTE *CEASED*. (US/0894-6140) [16151668] **5720**

READING RESEARCH AND INSTRUCTION (US/0886-0246) [12702956] 1903, **3314**

READING RESEARCH QUARTERLY (US/0034-0553) [01763481] 1903, **3314**

READING STYLES NEWSLETTER (US) 3314, **1777**

READING (SUNDERLAND) (UK/0034-0472) [01770913] 3314, **1903**

READING TEACHER, THE (US/0034-0561) [01681346] 1903, **3314**

READING TIME (AT/0155-218X) [I0155218X] **3428**

READING TIMES (READING, PA. : 1923) (US) [12574969] **5739**

READING TODAY : A BIMONTHLY NEWSPAPER OF THE INTERNATIONAL READING ASSOCIATION (US) [12406912] **1777**

READINGS - AMERICAN ORTHOPSYCHIATRIC ASSOCIATION (US/0886-3784) [12923727] **3935**

READINGS AND PERSPECTIVES IN MEDICINE *CEASED*. (US/0737-0822) [08248479] **3632**

READINGS IN BEHAVIOR MODIFICATION (US) [06008370] **4615**

READINGS IN EARLY CHILDHOOD EDUCATION (US) [13486442] **1805**

READINGS IN EDUCATIONAL PSYCHOLOGY : CONTEMPORARY PERSPECTIVES (US/0363-5953) [02511442] **1884**

READINGS IN GULF COAST GEOLOGY (US/0735-1216) [07378726] **1393**

READINGS IN INTRODUCTORY MACROECONOMICS (US/1056-1781) [16918857] **1515**

READINGS IN MANAGEMENT : ANNUAL EDITIONS (US/0195-4784) [05434629] **884**

READINGS IN MORAL THEOLOGY (US) [11881890] **4989**

READINGS IN PERSONAL GROWTH AND ADJUSTMENT (US/0198-912X) [06094046] **4615**

READINGS IN SOUTHERN FINANCE (US/0430-1862) [01350593] **806**

READINGS IN SPANISH-ENGLISH CONTRASTIVE LINGUISTICS (PR) [01784464] **3314**

READINGS ON EQUAL EDUCATION (US/0270-1448) [06350622] **1884**

●READMORE REPORTER, THE (US/1060-5673) [25037700] 3244, **3632**

READY FOR ENGLISH (IT) **1777**

READY, SET, GO! DESIGNSTUDIO IN-DEPTH *See* READY, SET, GO! IN-DEPTH (1992) **4569**

●READY, SET, GO! IN-DEPTH (1992) (US/1064-7120) [26378709] **4569**

READYWEAR. INTERNATIONAL TRADE INFORMATION SERVICE FOR CLOTHING MANUFACTURERS (GW) [07139295] 1087, **5355**

REAGENT CHEMICALS : AMERICAN CHEMICAL SOCIETY SPECIFICATIONS (US) [06849271] **990**

REAKCIONNAJA SPOSOBNOST I MEHANIZMY REAKCIJ ORGANICESKIH SOEDINENIJ (RU/0320-2909) [02520231] **1057**

REAL ACADEMIA DE CIENCIAS EXACTAS, FISICAS Y NATURALES DE MADRID *See* REVISTA DE LA REAL ACADEMIA DE CIENCIAS EXACTAS, FISICAS Y NATURALES DE MADRID **5148**

REAL ACADEMIA DE CIENCIAS Y ARTES DE BARCELONA *See* MEMORIAS **5209**

REAL ACADEMIA DE LA HISTORIA (SPAIN) *See* BOLETIN DE LA REAL ACADEMIA DE LA HISTORIA (MADRID) **2611**

REAL ACADEMIA ESPANOLA *See* DICCIONARIO HISTORICO DE LA LENGUA ESPANOLA **3277**

REAL ACADEMIA ESPANOLA *See* BOLETIN DE LA REAL ACADEMIA ESPANOLA **3269**

REAL ANALYSIS (GW/0720-2601) [09450117] **3530**

REAL ANALYSIS EXCHANGE (US/0147-1937) [03113834] **3530**

REAL (BERLIN, WEST) (GW/0723-0338) [09051548] **3428**

REAL ESTATE ACCOUNTING & TAXATION *CEASED.* (US/0897-0262) [13519599] **4843**

REAL ESTATE AGENCY LAW QUARTERLY (US) **4843**

REAL ESTATE ANALYSIS AND PLANNING SERVICE (US/0882-9144) [11940737] **4843**

REAL ESTATE ANALYST, THE (US) [01632639] **4843**

REAL ESTATE AND CONSTRUCTION REPORT (US/0147-9946) [03251673] 625, **4843**

REAL ESTATE AND PUBLIC UTILITY PROPERTY TAXES (US/0732-0701) [07442058] 4744, **4843**

REAL ESTATE & THE LAW (US/0270-7683) [06467643] 3034, **4843**

REAL ESTATE ASSESSMENT/SALES RATIO STUDY (US/0095-3032) [01796399] 4744, **4843**

REAL ESTATE BOARD REPORT, THE (US/0276-4792) [07368840] **4843**

REAL ESTATE BULLETIN (SACRAMENTO, CALIF.) (US/0734-7839) [07988427] **4844**

REAL ESTATE BUSINESS (US/0744-642X) [08467449] **4844**

REAL ESTATE CAPITAL MARKETS REPORT (US/1064-1491) [26226049] **1515**

REAL ESTATE CENTER JOURNAL (US/0893-3332) [15378565] **4844**

REAL ESTATE CLOSINGS (US/0148-2718) [03280701] **4844**

REAL ESTATE COMPUTER REVIEW (US/0742-5600) [10365487] 1201, **4844**

REAL ESTATE COORDINATOR. SUPPLEMENT (US) [14051362] **4844**

REAL ESTATE: DEBTORS' AND CREDITOR'S RIGHTS (US/0734-9653) [08828606] **806**

REAL ESTATE DEVELOPMENT ANNUAL, THE (CN/0319-1087) [02443235] **4844**

REAL ESTATE DEVELOPMENT (OTTAWA) (CN/1187-6468) [25590041] **4844**

REAL ESTATE DIGEST, THE (US/0882-8733) [12001317] **4844**

REAL ESTATE DIRECTORY OF MANHATTAN (US/0098-8936) [02242142] **4844**

REAL ESTATE DIRECTORY OF THE BOROUGH OF MANHATTAN *See* REAL ESTATE DIRECTORY OF MANHATTAN **4844**

REAL ESTATE EDUCATION AND RESEARCH SPECIAL ACCOUNT / DEPARTMENT OF COMMERCE, DIVISION OF REAL ESTATE (US) [11096372] **4844**

REAL ESTATE/ENVIRONMENTAL LIABILITY NEWS (US/1046-9966) [20581544] **4844**

REAL ESTATE FINANCE (US/0748-318X) [10755820] **4844**

REAL ESTATE FINANCE JOURNAL, THE (US/0898-0209) [12398653] 912, **4844**

REAL ESTATE FINANCE TODAY (US/0742-0021) [10239955] **4844**

REAL ESTATE FINANCING REPORT (US/0735-0678) [08871694] 4744, **4844**

REAL ESTATE FINANCING UPDATE *CEASED.* (US/0891-9852) [11365538] **4844**

REAL ESTATE FORUM (US/0034-0707) [04947085] **4844**

REAL ESTATE INSIDER (US/0034-0715) [03400822] **4844**

REAL ESTATE INVESTING LETTER (US) [04376608] 912, **4844**

REAL ESTATE ISSUES (US/0146-0595) [02851239] **4844**

REAL ESTATE JOURNAL, THE (CN/0832-0780) [15999750] **4844**

REAL ESTATE LAW AND PRACTICE COURSE HANDBOOK SERIES (US/0548-7366) [05061589] 4844, **3034**

REAL ESTATE LAW BRIEF CASE (US/0034-0758) [03907297] **4844**

REAL ESTATE LAW JOURNAL (US/0048-6868) [01789231] 4844, **3034**

REAL ESTATE LAW REPORT (US/0162-752X) [03292376] 4844, **3035**

REAL ESTATE LEASING REPORT (US/0748-3163) [10941610] **4844**

REAL ESTATE LICENSE LAW AND RULES AND REGULATIONS (US) [06068885] 4844, **3035**

REAL ESTATE NEWS (BALTIMORE) (US/0273-6667) [06804239] **4844**

REAL ESTATE NEWS (TORONTO) (CN/0225-2783) [06141465] **4844**

REAL ESTATE NEWSLINE (US/0749-8640) [11190139] **4844**

REAL ESTATE NEWSLINE (KNOXVILLE, TENN.) (US/1054-0458) [22771270] **4844**

REAL ESTATE OUTLOOK MARKET TRENDS AND INSIGHTS (US) **4845**

REAL ESTATE PROFESSIONAL, THE (US/0744-4516) [08274132] **4845**

REAL ESTATE PROFILES (US) **4845**

REAL ESTATE RECORD AND BUILDER'S GUIDE (1941) (US/0034-0774) [03907353] **4845**

REAL ESTATE REPORT (REAL ESTATE RESEARCH CORPORATION) (US) [09457754] **4845**

REAL ESTATE REPORT (STORR, CONN.) (US/0079-9890) [03475126] **4845**

REAL ESTATE RESEARCH COUNCIL OF SOUTHERN CALIFORNIA *See* REAL ESTATE AND CONSTRUCTION REPORT **4843**

REAL ESTATE REVIEW (BOSTON, MASS.) (US/0034-0790) [01696567] **4845**

REAL ESTATE REVIEW'S WHO'S WHO IN REAL ESTATE (US/0737-3600) [09337443] 4845, **434**

REAL ESTATE SALES/CLOSINGS LAW BULLETIN (US/8755-8262) [11451593] **4845**

REAL ESTATE SECURITIES & CAPITAL MARKETS *SUSPENDED.* (US/1052-4622) [22237848] **4845**

REAL ESTATE SECURITIES AND SYNDICATION INSTITUTE *See* RESSI REVIEW **4846**

REAL ESTATE SECURITIES LETTER (US/0275-1127) [07088155] **4845**

REAL ESTATE SYNDICATION ALERT *CEASED.* (US/8750-510X) [10541154] **4845**

REAL ESTATE SYNDICATIONS (US/1048-7492) [08518843] **4845**

REAL ESTATE SYNDICATOR *See* REAL ESTATE SECURITIES & CAPITAL MARKETS **4845**

REAL ESTATE SYNDICATOR, THE (US/8756-8411) [11666946] **4845**

REAL ESTATE TAX DIGEST (ALBANY, N.Y.), THE (US/8756-3835) [06833448] 4744, **4845**

REAL ESTATE TAX IDEAS (US/0162-7538) [04220725] **4845**

REAL ESTATE TODAY (US/0034-0804) [01050484] **4845**

REAL ESTATE TRENDS IN METROPOLITAN VANCOUVER (CN/0085-5405) [02441922] **4845**

REAL ESTATE VENTURE ANALYSIS (US/0092-3672) [05214385] **4845**

● REAL ESTATE WORKOUTS & ASSET MANAGEMENT (US/1063-4290) [26025250] **4845**

REAL ESTATE WORKOUTS AND BANKRUPTCIES (US) [11688755] 4845, **806**

REAL ETATE MARKET IN NEW ZEALAND, THE (NZ) [06440329] **4845**

REAL LIFE MAGAZINE (US/0739-196X) [08576392] **363**

REAL PEOPLE (US/1040-9335) [18580260] **2544**

● REAL PEOPLE, REAL JOBS (US/1062-385X) [25603048] **1705**

REAL POTTERY *CEASED.* (UK) [16847177] **2593**

● REAL PROPERTY ASSESSMENT. YEAR ONE (CN/1187-7200) [25652168] **4845**

REAL PROPERTY (GARDENA) (US/0198-893X) [06240286] 4845, **3035**

REAL PROPERTY LAW, REAL PROPERTY ACTIONS AND PROCEEDINGS LAW, AND RELATED MISCELLANEOUS STATUTES, AS AMENDED (US) [06059044] **3035**

REAL PROPERTY LAW REPORTER (US/0898-1698) [05118897] **3035**

REAL PROPERTY LAW SECTION NEWSLETTER (US/0147-135X) [03131280] 3091, **4845**

REAL PROPERTY, PROBATE AND TRUST JOURNAL (US/0034-0855) [01713959] **3118**

REAL PROPERTY REPORT (US) [23932834] **4678**

REAL PROPERTY REPORTS (CN/0703-4687) [03564353] **3035**

REAL PROPERTY SECTION NEWS (US) [01794564] 4845, **3035**

● REAL TIME GRAPHICS (US/1064-5004) [26346325] **1235**

● REAL-TIME IMAGING (UK/1077-2014) [30720172] **1201**

REAL-TIME INTERFACE (US/1059-552X) [24636666] **1201**

REAL TIME MAGAZINE (BE/1018-0303) [I10180303] **1221**

REAL-TIME SIGNAL PROCESSING (US/8755-3619) [10054936] **2078**

REAL-TIME SYSTEMS (US/0922-6443) [20501906] **1201**

REAL TRENDS (US/1071-1805) [26188100] **4845**

REAL WEST *CEASED.* (US/0034-0898) [02275381] **2756**

REALE ACCADEMIA NAZIONALE DEI LINCEI. NOTIZIE DEGLI SCABI DI ANTICHITA *See* NOTIZIE DEGLI SCAVI DI ANTICHITA / ACCADEMIA NAZIONALE DEI LINCEI **276**

REALES SITIOS (SP/0486-0993) [02850364] **363**

REALISATIONS RECENTES A PETAWAWA *CEASED.* (CN/0824-8826) [10862374] **2392**

REALITAS (SP) [01799150] **4358**

REALITE (QUEBEC) (CN/0384-6016) [03303889] **4243**

REALITES DE LA FOI. DIGEST (SZ/0254-301X) [I0254301X] **4989**

REALITES INDUSTRIELLES (FR) [21494234] **2149**

REALITES THERAPEUTIQUES EN DERMATO-VENEROLOGIE (FR/1155-2492) [I11552492] **3722**

REALITES (TUNIS, TUNISIA) (TI) [09460824] **2642**

REALITY DUBLIN (IE/0034-0960) [I00340960] **5035**

REALITY (HOUSTON, TEX.) (US/1041-8199) [18854318] **1334**

REALITY NOW (HOUSTON, TEX.) (US/1041-8253) [18854407] **1334**

REALKREDITRADET *See* BERETNING OG REGNSKAB - REALKREDITRADET **778**

REALLEXIKON DER ASSYRIOLOGIE UND VORDERASIATISCHEN ARCHEOLOGIE (GW) 1993, **280**

REALLEXIKON ZUR BYZANTINISCHEN KUNST (GW) [01763492] **1079**

REALLEXIKON ZUR DEUTSCHEN KUNSTGESCHICHTE (GW) 1993, **329**

REALSCAN. BROWARD COUNTY (US/1053-8917) [22685051] **4845**

REALSCAN. DADE COUNTY (US/1053-8925) [22695618] **4845**

REALSCAN. PALM BEACH COUNTY [COMPUTER FILE] : REAL ESTATE MARKET INFORMATION SYSTEMS (US/1056-8344) [23872304] **4845**

REALTA (IT) **884**

REALTOR (LANSING, MICH.) (US/0886-8794) [13031005] **4845**

REALTOR NEWS (US/0279-6309) [07132442] **4846**

REALTY (IT) **4846**

REALTY (US/0481-9004) [03969999] **4846**

REALTY AND BUILDING (US/0034-1045) [04734279] 625, **4846**

REALTY BLUEBOOK (US/0090-399X) [01783696] **4846**

REALTY PARTNERSHIP IN DEFAULT, THE (US) [24878066] **4846**

REALTY. RELOCATION. REVIEW (US/0270-7721) [06507443] **4846**

REALTY STOCK REVIEW (US) [07232123] **4846**

REANIMATION D'URGENCES (FR) **3725**

REANIMATION ET MEDECINE D'URGENCE *CEASED.* (FR/0246-1234) [05966008] **3725**

REANIMATION, SOINS INTENSIFS, MEDECINE D'URGENCE (FR/0765-5290) [I07655290] **3632**

REAPER; NEW ZEALAND'S EVANGELICAL MONTHLY (NZ/0034-107X) [01644463] **4989**

REAPPRAISALS, CANADIAN WRITERS (CN) [11989044] **3428**

REASON (US/0048-6906) [01795184] **5214**

REASON PAPERS (US/0363-1893) [02430120] **5215**

REB. REVISTA ECLESIASTICA BRASILEIRA (BL/0101-8434) [01697166] **5035**

REBE UND WEIN WEINSBERG (GW/0034-1118) [I00341118] **2370**

REBECCA WINTERS GENEALOGICAL SOCIETY *See* TRAIL SEEKERS **2475**

REBEL (US/0486-1140) [05347605] **4238, 1705**

REBEL YOUTH *CEASED.* (CN/0824-0574) [14259710] **5255**

REBIS CHAPBOOK SERIES, THE (US/0147-0396) [03153699] **3470**

REBOOTING (PITTSBURGH, PA.) (US/1057-0225) [23921087] **1993**

REBORN ARMENIA *CEASED.* (AI) [22378997] **2521**

REBUS (PL/0239-8796) [I02398796] **4865**

REBUS, DE (SA/0250-0329) [10101235] **3035**

REC NEWS EXCHANGE (US) **4989**

REC NEWSLETTER, THE (US/0899-014X) [17972563] 1209, **3530**

RECAL *See* RECAL CURRENT AWARENESS **3244**

RECAL CURRENT AWARENESS (UK) **3244**

RECALL (UK/0034-1150) [02600842] **1903**

RECALL/REGULATORY ANALYSIS (US/0890-8451) [14554141] **3035**

RECAPITULATIF MENSUEL DES SIGNALEMENTS D'ORIGINE CEDOCAR (FR) [03989031] **5145**

●RECAREERING NEWSLETTER (US/1068-199X) [27469423] **4209**

RECEIPTS AND SHIPMENTS OF LIVESTOCK FOR THE YEAR (US) [01554110] **220**

RECEIVABLES OUTSTANDING AT FINANCE COMPANIES / BOARD OF GOVERNORS OF THE FEDERAL RESERVE SYSTEM (US) [11878299] **807**

RECEIVABLES REPORT, THE (US/1060-0418) [23991534] 3792, **807**

RECEIVING TUBE MANUAL (US) [06354436] **2078**

RECENT ACHIEVEMENTS IN RESTORATIVE NEUROLOGY (SZ) [12269217] **3844**

RECENT ACTIVITIES - HASTINGS CENTER (US/0360-9006) [02239523] **2253**

RECENT ADDITIONS / MUNICIPAL REFERENCE LIBRARY, CITY OF CHICAGO (US/0300-7081) [01350978] **3244**

RECENT ADDITIONS TO BAKER LIBRARY (US/0735-2336) [05536606] **3244**

●RECENT ADVANCES IN ACTIVE CONTROL OF SOUND AND VIBRATION (US) 1120, **2078**

RECENT ADVANCES IN ANAESTHESIA AND ANALGESIA (UK/0309-2305) [02490230] **3684**

RECENT ADVANCES IN ANIMAL NUTRITION (UK/0269-5642) [08371148] **5520**

RECENT ADVANCES IN CARDIAC ARRHYTHMIAS (UK/0951-807X) [10776213] **3709**

RECENT ADVANCES IN CARDIOLOGY (UK) [04574451] **3710**

RECENT ADVANCES IN CLINICAL BIOCHEMISTRY *CEASED.* (UK/0143-6767) [03820375] **493**

RECENT ADVANCES IN CLINICAL NEUROLOGY (UK/0307-7403) [01731136] **3844**

RECENT ADVANCES IN CLINICAL NUCLEAR MEDICINE (UK/0308-2458) [01812538] **3849**

RECENT ADVANCES IN CLINICAL NUTRITION (UK/0260-8170) [07858640] **4198**

RECENT ADVANCES IN CLINICAL PHARMACOLOGY AND TOXICOLOGY (UK/0957-5545) [19503592] **4327**

RECENT ADVANCES IN CLINICAL THERAPEUTICS (US/0730-8019) [07972676] **3632**

RECENT ADVANCES IN CLINICAL VIROLOGY *CEASED.* (UK/0143-6775) [03365892] 569, **3632**

RECENT ADVANCES IN COMMUNITY MEDICINE (UK/0144-1256) [04674955] **4798**

RECENT ADVANCES IN CROSSLINKING & CURING (UK/0144-6266) [I01446266] **4225**

RECENT ADVANCES IN DERMATOLOGY (UK/0309-2747) [02481002] **3722**

RECENT ADVANCES IN DIABETES *CEASED.* (UK/0264-7397) [09741178] **3733**

RECENT ADVANCES IN ENDOCRINOLOGY AND METABOLISM (UK/0140-9123) [03559684] **3733**

RECENT ADVANCES IN EPILEPSY (UK/0264-7400) [09741199] **3844**

RECENT ADVANCES IN GASTROENTEROLOGY (UK/0141-5581) [05327495] **3747**

RECENT ADVANCES IN GERIATRIC MEDICINE *CEASED.* (UK/0144-0519) [04213236] **3754**

RECENT ADVANCES IN HAEMATOLOGY (UK/0143-697X) [05306550] **3773**

RECENT ADVANCES IN HEPATOLOGY (UK/0264-7532) [09715287] **3801**

RECENT ADVANCES IN HISTOPATHOLOGY (UK/0143-6953) [05182001] **540**

RECENT ADVANCES IN INFECTION *CEASED.* (UK/0144-1078) [04682008] **3715**

RECENT ADVANCES IN MEDICINE (EDINBURGH) (UK/0143-6791) [05843863] **3633**

RECENT ADVANCES IN NEUROPATHOLOGY (UK/0144-0535) [04682058] **3844**

RECENT ADVANCES IN NUMERICAL METHODS IN FLUIDS / EDITED BY TAYLOR AND K. MORGAN (UK) [07127654] **4429**

RECENT ADVANCES IN NURSING *CEASED.* (UK/0144-6592) [07073965] **3868**

RECENT ADVANCES IN OBSTETRICS AND GYNAECOLOGY (UK/0143-6848) [03990218] **3767**

RECENT ADVANCES IN OCCUPATIONAL HEALTH *CEASED.* (UK/0261-1449) [07643791] **3633**

RECENT ADVANCES IN OPHTHALMOLOGY (UK/0309-2437) [02376907] **3878**

RECENT ADVANCES IN ORTHOPAEDICS (UK/0308-4914) [01901241] **3884**

RECENT ADVANCES IN OTOLARYNGOLOGY (UK/0143-6813) [04540145] **3891**

RECENT ADVANCES IN PAEDIATRIC SURGERY (UK/0308-4906) [01901253] **3911**

RECENT ADVANCES IN PAEDIATRICS (UK/0309-0140) [02758398] **3911**

RECENT ADVANCES IN PERINATAL MEDICINE (UK/0264-2417) [10359610] **3767**

RECENT ADVANCES IN PHYTOCHEMISTRY (US/0079-9920) [01763499] **526**

RECENT ADVANCES IN PLASTIC SURGERY (UK/0309-2674) [02311370] **3973**

RECENT ADVANCES IN RADIOLOGY AND MEDICAL IMAGING (UK/0143-6961) [04656598] **3946**

RECENT ADVANCES IN RENAL MEDICINE *CEASED.* (UK/0264-3081) [09263260] **3992**

RECENT ADVANCES IN RESPIRATORY MEDICINE (UK/0308-6623) [02353867] **3951**

RECENT ADVANCES IN RHEUMATOLOGY (UK/0309-2283) [02415799] **3806**

RECENT ADVANCES IN SEXUALLY TRANSMITTED DISEASES AND AIDS (UK) [24144732] **3715**

RECENT ADVANCES IN SURGERY (UK/0143-8395) [05280488] **3973**

RECENT ADVANCES IN TROPICAL MEDICINE (UK/0266-3775) [11652625] **3986**

RECENT ADVANCES IN ULTRASOUND IN BIOMEDICINE (US/0148-2319) [03594683] **3633**

RECENT ADVANCES IN UROLOGY/ANDROLOGY (UK/0261-8788) [07832295] **3992**

RECENT AMERICAN HISTORY (US/0899-2371) [18041093] **2756**

RECENT AND RECOMMENDED MEDICAL BOOKS (CN/0228-0655) [06757924] **3633**

RECENT AWARDS IN ENGINEERING (US/0736-7090) [08884620] **1993**

RECENT BOOKS IN MEXICO (MX/0486-1205) [01644056] 3351, **3244**

RECENT DEVELOPMENTS IN ALCOHOLISM (US/0738-422X) [09483824] **1348**

RECENT DEVELOPMENTS IN THE CHEMISTRY OF NATURAL CARBON COMPOUNDS (HU/0079-9947) [02409385] **1047**

RECENT DEVELOPMENTS OF NEUROBIOLOGY IN HUNGARY (HU/0079-9955) [02266788] 3733, **3844**

RECENT ETHICS OPINIONS (US/0276-055X) [03935714] **2253**

RECENT LAWS OF NEPAL (NP) [20852047] **3035**

RECENT PROGRESS IN HORMONE RESEARCH (US/0079-9963) [01763501] **3733**

RECENT PUBLICATION OF RANGE RESEARCH (US) [08370537] **125**

RECENT PUBLICATIONS IN NATURAL HISTORY (US/0738-0925) [09502741] **4174**

RECENT PUBLICATIONS OF THE PACIFIC NORTHWEST RESEARCH STATION (US) [14230080] **2392**

RECENT PUBLICATIONS (SOUTHERN FOREST EXPERIMENT STATION (NEW ORLEANS, LA.)) (US) [09306291] **2392**

RECENT REPORTS (INTERMOUNTAIN RESEARCH STATION (OGDEN, UTAH)) (US) [12629759] **2392**

RECENT RESEARCH RESULTS / U.S. DEPARTMENT OF HOUSING AND URBAN DEVELOPMENT, OFFICE OF POLICY DEVELOPMENT AND RESEARCH (US) [06659702] **2832**

RECENT RESEARCHES IN AMERICAN MUSIC (US/0147-0078) [03081690] **4148**

RECENT RESEARCHES IN ECOLOGY, ENVIRONMENT, AND POLLUTION (II) [20187646] **2220**

RECENT RESEARCHES IN GEOLOGY (II) [04335744] **1393**

RECENT RESEARCHES IN THE MUSIC OF THE BAROQUE ERA (US/0484-0828) [01643860] **4148**

RECENT RESEARCHES IN THE MUSIC OF THE CLASSICAL ERA (US/0147-0086) [03393903] **4148**

RECENT RESEARCHES IN THE MUSIC OF THE MIDDLE AGES AND EARLY RENAISSANCE (US/0362-3572) [02326516] **4149**

RECENT RESEARCHES IN THE MUSIC OF THE NINETEENTH AND EARLY TWENTIETH CENTURIES (US/0193-5364) [05229420] **4149**

RECENT RESEARCHES IN THE MUSIC OF THE RENAISSANCE (US/0486-123X) [01763503] **4149**

RECENT RESULTS IN CANCER RESEARCH (GW/0080-0015) [01018105] **3823**

RECENT SOCIAL AND ECONOMIC TRENDS (US) [02961918] **1515**

RECENT TITLES IN LAW FOR THE SUBJECT SPECIALIST. AGRICULTURE, ANIMAL, AND FOOD LAW (US/0899-0662) [17986462] 125, **3035**

RECENT TITLES IN LAW FOR THE SUBJECT SPECIALIST. COMMUNICATION LAW (US/0899-0883) [17992886] 1120, **3035**

RECENT TITLES IN LAW FOR THE SUBJECT SPECIALIST. CONSTITUTIONAL LAW, HUMAN RIGHTS, AND CITIZENSHIP (US/0899-0875) [17992821] **3093**

RECENT TITLES IN LAW FOR THE SUBJECT SPECIALIST. CONTRACT LEASE, AND SALES LAW (US/0899-0867) [17992746] **3035**

RECENT TITLES IN LAW FOR THE SUBJECT SPECIALIST. COPYRIGHT AND ENTERTAINMENT LAW (US/0899-0859) [17992674] 1308, **3035**

RECENT TITLES IN LAW FOR THE SUBJECT SPECIALIST. CRIMINAL LAW, PROCEDURE AND CRIMINOLOGY (US/0899-0840) [17992583] **3108**

RECENT TITLES IN LAW FOR THE SUBJECT SPECIALIST. ENTERPRISE ORGANIZATION (US/0899-0824) [17992428] **3035**

RECENT TITLES IN LAW FOR THE SUBJECT SPECIALIST. EVIDENCE, PRATICE, AND PROCEDURE (US/0899-0816) [17992343] **3035**

RECENT TITLES IN LAW FOR THE SUBJECT SPECIALIST. FAMILY LAW AND SOCIAL WELFARE (US/0899-0808) [17991914] **3122**

RECENT TITLES IN LAW FOR THE SUBJECT SPECIALIST. LABOR AND EMPLOYMENT (US/0899-0794) [17991842] **3153**

RECENT TITLES IN LAW FOR THE SUBJECT SPECIALIST. MEDICINE AND HEALTH LAW (US/0899-0778) [17987080] 3633, **3035**

RECENT TITLES IN LAW FOR THE SUBJECT SPECIALIST. MILITARY AND SECURITY LAW (US/0899-076X) [17986996] **3183**

RECENT TITLES IN LAW FOR THE SUBJECT SPECIALIST. MUNICIPAL AND ADMINISTRATIVE LAW, AND POLITICS (US) [19786619] **3035**

RECENT TITLES IN LAW FOR THE SUBJECT SPECIALIST. PROPERTY (REAL AND CHATTEL), AND CONSTRUCTION LAW (US/0899-0697) [17986587] **3035**

Alphabetical Title Index — RECOMMENDATIONS

RECENT TITLES IN LAW FOR THE SUBJECT SPECIALIST. RESOURCE, ENVIRONMENTAL, AND ENERGY LAW (US/0899-0689) [17986548] **3116**

RECENT TITLES IN LAW FOR THE SUBJECT SPECIALIST. TAXATION AND ESTATE PLANNING (US/0899-0670) [17986498] **4744**

RECENT TITLES IN LAW FOR THE SUBJECT SPECIALIST. TECHNOLOGY AND DESIGN PROTECTION (US/0899-0751) [17986958] **3035**

RECENT TITLES IN LAW FOR THE SUBJECT SPECIALIST. TORTS, LIABILITY, AND INDEMNITY (US/0899-0743) [17986866] **3035**

RECENT TITLES IN LAW FOR THE SUBJECT SPECIALIST. TRADE REGULATION AND ECONOMICS (US/0899-0735) [17986823] **3035**

RECENT TITLES IN LAW FOR THE SUBJECT SPECIALIST. TRANSPORTATION AND MARITIME LAW (US/0899-0727) [17986769] **3182**

RECENT TITLES IN LAW FOR THE SUBJET SPECIALIST. BANKING, FINANCE (INCLUDING SECURITIES), AND INVESTMENT (US/0899-0891) [17993608] **3088**

RECENTI PROGRESSI IN MEDICINA (IT/0034-1193) [03307320] **3801**

RECEPTOR BIOCHEMISTRY AND METHODOLOGY (US/0888-7500) [10577206] **471**

RECEPTOR (CLIFTON, N.J. JOURNAL) (US/1052-8040) [22390814] **493**

●RECEPTORS AND CHANNELS (US/1060-6823) [25052428] **990**

RECEPTORS AND LIGANDS IN INTERCELLULAR COMMUNICATION (US/0742-4108) [09262635] **540**

RECERQUES (SP/0210-380X) [05930328] **1580**

RECETTES ET LES DEPENSES DES EXPLOITATIONS AGRICOLES EN ... / REPUBLIQUE FRANCAISE, MINISTERE DE L'AGRICULTURE, DIRECTION GENERALE DE L'ADMINISTRATION ET DU FINANCEMENT, SERVICE CENTRAL DES ENQUETES ET ETUDES STATISTIQUES, LES (FR) [12205859] **125**

RECEUIL DES LOIS ET DE LA LEGISLATION FINANCIERE (FR) **4678**

RECHARGER (RIVERSIDE, CALIF.) (US/1053-7503) [22622103] **2241**

RECHENSCHAFTSBERICHT DES PRASIDENTEN / FU BERLIN (GW) [07935642] **1843**

RECHENSCHAFTSBERICHT DES REDTORS DER UNIVERSITAT BREMEN (GW) [11778753] **1843**

RECHENTECHNIK DATENVERARBEITUNG *CEASED.* (GW/0300-3450) [01420218] **1262**

RECHERCHE AEROSPATIALE (FR/0034-1223) [01855656] **33**

RECHERCHE AEROSPATIALE (TECHNICAL TRANSLATION) (FR/0244-9056) [08015667] **33**

RECHERCHE DEVELOPPEMENT AU QUEBEC, LA (CN/1187-1768) [24691002] **5145**

RECHERCHE-DEVELOPPEMENT POUR LES FORMATEURS DES SECTEURS TECHNIQUE ET PROFESSIONNEL (CN/1187-0273) [24986850] **1777**

RECHERCHE EN DANSE, LA (FR/0752-5729) [11278708] **1314**

RECHERCHE EN EDUCATION MUSICALE AU QUEBEC (CN/0844-5923) [20444499] 4149, **1777**

RECHERCHE EN MATIERE D'ECONOMIE DES TRANSPORTS (FR/0304-3320) [01977859] 5390, **1515**

RECHERCHE EN SOINS INFIRMIERS (FR/0297-2964) [02972964] **3868**

RECHERCHE ET APPLICATIONS EN MARKETING (FR/0767-3701) [07673701] **935**

RECHERCHE ET ARCHITECTURE (FR/0373-4285) [01796056] **307**

RECHERCHE ET DEVELOPPEMENT DANS LES ENTREPRISES (FR) [20348850] **1623**

RECHERCHE ET FORMATION PARIS. 1987 (FR/0988-1824) [09881824] **1843**

RECHERCHE ET INDUSTRIE (FR/0767-0273) [07670273] 1623, **5145**

RECHERCHE ET SANTE (FR) **4798**

RECHERCHE (PARIS. 1970) (FR/0029-5671) [01715785] **5145**

RECHERCHE PHOTOGRAPHIQUE, LA (FR) [17641090] **4376**

RECHERCHE SOCIALE (FR/0034-124X) [02266791] **5255**

RECHERCHE SUR LES GRANDES CIVILISATIONS. SYNTHESE *See* SYNTHESE (EDITIONS RECHERCHE SUR LES CIVILISATIONS) **2712**

RECHERCHE TECHNOLOGIE 1985 (FR/0765-0779) [07650779] **1623**

RECHERCHE TECHNOLOGIE (1985) *See* ENSEIGNEMENT SUPERIEUR & RECHERCHE PARIS **1605**

RECHERCHES ACTUELLES - INSTITUT CATHOLIQUE DE PARIS (FR) [03180290] **5035**

RECHERCHES AMERINDIENNES AU QUEBEC (CN/0318-4137) [02442005] **2756**

RECHERCHES AMERINDIENNES AU QUEBEC (CN/0318-4137) [11285222] **243**

RECHERCHES ANGLAISES ET NORD-AMERICAINES : RANAM (FR) [19056510] **3428**

RECHERCHES AUGUSTINIENNES (FR/0484-0887) [01774074] **4989**

RECHERCHES CROISEES ARAGON/ELSA TRIOLET / GROUPE DE RECHERCHES EN LINGUISTIQUE ET SEMIOTIQUE (GRELIS), BESANCON [ET] FONDS ELSA TRIOLET-ARAGON DU CNRS, PARIS (FR) [20367693] **3314**

RECHERCHES DE SCIENCE RELIGIEUSE (FR/0034-1258) [01763505] **4989**

RECHERCHES DE THEOLOGIE ANCIENNE ET MEDIEVALE (BE/0034-1266) [01763506] **4989**

RECHERCHES ECONOMIQUES DE LOUVAIN (BE/0770-4518) [02266792] **1515**

RECHERCHES EN DIDACTIQUE DES MATHEMATIQUES REVUE (FR/0246-9367) [02469367] **3530**

RECHERCHES EN LINGUISTIQUE ETRANGERE (FR) [03688931] **3315**

RECHERCHES EN MATHEMATIQUES APPLIQUEES (FR) **3530**

RECHERCHES ET TRAVAUX - UNIVERSITE DE GRENOBLE (FR) [03949655] **1843**

RECHERCHES FEMINISTES (CN/0838-4479) [18595902] **5565**

RECHERCHES GERMANIQUES (FR/0399-1989) [01763508] **2853**

RECHERCHES HAITIENNES (HT) [06258271] **2756**

RECHERCHES, HANDICAPS ET VIE CHRETIENNE (FR/1156-833X) [1156833X] 4990, **5304**

RECHERCHES INSTITUTIONNELLES (FR) [07098832] **2521**

RECHERCHES INTERNATIONALES : CAHIERS DE L'INSTITUT DE RECHERCHES MARXISTES (FR) [08011858] **4546**

RECHERCHES REGIONALES: COTE D'AZUR ET CONTREES LIMITROPHES (FR/0996-3634) [06671298] **2704**

RECHERCHES SOCIOGRAPHIQUES (CN/0034-1282) [01763510] **5255**

RECHERCHES SOCIOLOGIQUES (BE/0303-9625) [01786038] **5215**

RECHERCHES SUR DIDEROT ET SUR L'ENCYCLOPEDIE (FR/0769-0886) [15566106] **3428**

RECHERCHES SUR L'HISTOIRE DES INSTITUTIONS ET DU DROIT (RM) [04053942] **3134**

RECHERCHES SUR L'IMAGINAIRE (FR/0765-1155) [07651155] **3428**

RECHERCHES SUR TOURS (FR) [11507132] **2704**

RECHNOI TRANSPORT (RU) [04879736] **5455**

RECHNUNGSABSCHLUSS DES LANDES VORARLBERG (AU) [07612112] **4744**

RECHT & PSYCHIATRIE (GW/0724-2247) [07242247] **3935**

RECHT (BERN, SWITZERLAND) (SZ) [10110989] **3035**

RECHT DER ARBEIT / [HERAUSGEBER OSTERREICHISCHER ARBEITERKAMMERTAG], DAS (AU) [09222007] **3153**

RECHT DER DATENVERARBEITUNG : RDV (GW/0178-8930) [15159248] **1227**

RECHT DER ELEKTRIZITATSWIRTSCHAFT (GW/0171-712X) [06805550] 3035, **1954**

RECHT DER INTERNATIONALEN WIRTSCHAFT (GW/0340-7926) [02588525] **3035**

RECHT DER JUGEND *See* RECHT DER JUGEND UND DES BILDUNGSWESEN **3035**

RECHT DER JUGEND UND DES BILDUNGSWESEN (GW/0034-1312) [09444466] 1777, **3035**

RECHT DER SCHULE (AU) [06870422] 1777, **3036**

RECHT DER WIRTSCHAFT, DAS (GW) [03226412] **3102**

RECHT DER WOHNUNGSWIRTSCHAFT (GW) [10583643] **3036**

RECHT EN KRITIEK (NE) [02242391] **3036**

RECHT IM AMT, DAS (GW) [07045773] **3093**

RECHT IN OST UND WEST (GW/0486-1485) [01763515] **3036**

RECHT UND GESELLSCHAFT (MUNCHEN) (GW/0341-7050) [01795514] **3036**

RECHT UND MEDIZIN (GW/0172-116X) [05854131] **3742**

RECHT UND POLITIK (GW/0344-7871) [03447871] 4678, **3036**

RECHT UND SCHADEN (GW/0343-9771) [08005450] 2891, **3036**

RECHT UND STEUERN IM GAS- UND WASSERFACH : R+S / HERAUSGEGEBEN VOM BUNDESVERBAND DER DEUTSCHEN GAS- UND WASSERWIRTSCHAFT E.V (GW) [20104925] **4276**

RECHT ZOLL UND VERFAHREN (GW) **3134**

RECHTS- UND STAATSWISSENSCHAFTEN (AU/0080-0163) [01716122] **4493**

RECHTSARCHIV DER WIRTSCHAFT *See* RECHT DER WIRTSCHAFT, DAS **3102**

RECHTSBIBLIOGRAPHIE (SZ) [08602392] **3082**

RECHTSGELEERD MAGAZIN THEMIS (NE) [01623892] **3036**

RECHTSHISTORISCHES JOURNAL (GW/0723-1180) [10305265] **3036**

RECHTSKUNDIG WEEKBLAD (BE) [11715474] **3036**

RECHTSMEDIZIN BERLIN (GW/0937-9819) [109379819] **3742**

RECHTSPRAAK VAN DE WEEK (NE) **3036**

RECHTSPRAAK VREEMDELINGENRECHT / [NEDERLANDS CENTRUM BUITENLANDERS] (NE) [08116209] **3036**

RECHTSPRECHUNG FRANKFURT (GW/0931-6183) [109316183] **3036**

RECHTSPRECHUNG IN STRAFSACHEN (SZ) [02246761] **3108**

RECHTSPRECHUNG ZUM WIEDERGUTMACHUNGSRECHT (GW) [01645129] **3036**

RECHTSPRECHUNGSKARTEI GEWERBLICHER RECHTSSCHUTZ (GW) **3036**

RECHTSRHEINISCHES KOLN (GW/0179-2938) [03713678] **2704**

RECHTSTHEORIE (GW/0034-1398) [02588437] **3036**

●RECIPE DIGEST (US) **2355**

RECIPE SOURCES NEWSLETTER (US) **2792**

RECIPIENTS OF LOCAL SERVICE AIR CARRIERS' UNIT COSTS (US) [02707541] **33**

RECIPROCAL MEAT CONFERENCE OF THE AMERICAN MEAT SCIENCE ASSOCIATION *See* PROCEEDINGS OF THE ANNUAL RECIPROCAL MEAT CONFERENCE OF THE AMERICAN MEAT SCIENCE ASSOCIATION **219**

RECIPROCAL MEAT CONFERENCE. REPORT OF PROCEEDINGS *See* PROCEEDINGS OF THE ANNUAL RECIPROCAL MEAT CONFERENCE OF THE AMERICAN MEAT SCIENCE ASSOCIATION **219**

RECLAMATION REVIEW *SUSPENDED.* (UK/0160-788X) [03765302] **125**

RECOGNITION & IDENTIFICATION INDUSTRY BLUE BOOK (US) [15492365] **3487**

RECOLLETS (AUGUSTINIAN). PROVINCIA DE SAN JOSE *See* BOLETIN DE LA PROVINCIA DE SAN JOSE DE LA ORDEN DE AGUSTINOS RECOLETOS **4939**

RECOMBINANT DNA *CEASED.* (UK/0261-4979) [02614979] **551**

RECOMBINANT DNA MATERIALS LISTING (US) **551**

RECOMBINANT DNA RESEARCH (US/0148-480X) [03295593] **551**

RECOMBINANT DNA TECHNICAL BULLETIN *CEASED.* (US/0196-0229) [03559885] **3696**

RECOMBINANT DNA, VECTORS & HOSTS (US/0743-6521) [10686812] **569**

RECOMMEND FLORIDA (US/0034-1452) [05065332] **5490**

RECOMMENDATIONS (FR) [07851889] **1777**

RECOMMENDATIONS AND REPORTS / ADMINISTRATIVE CONFERENCE OF THE UNITED STATES (US/0882-9217) [08187894] **4678**

RECOMMENDATIONS AND RESOLUTIONS / COUNCIL OF EUROPE, COMMITTEE OF MINISTERS (FR) [09201458] **3036**

RECOMMENDATIONS FOR LEGISLATIVE CONSIDERATION ON PUBLIC EDUCATION IN TEXAS (US) [06672364] 1777, **3036**

RECOMMENDATIONS — Alphabetical Title Index

RECOMMENDATIONS / INTERNATIONAL CONFERENCE ON EDUCATION (FR) [08046060] **1777**

RECOMMENDATIONS OF THE WEST VIRGINIA BOARD OF EDUCATION FOR LEGISLATIVE ACTION (US) [08755431] 1777, **3036**

●RECOMMENDATIONS ON TOURISM STATISTICS (SP) 5490, **5500**

RECOMMENDED COUNTY INNS (US/1047-4668) [19997883] **2809**

RECOMMENDED REFERENCE BOOKS FOR SMALL AND MEDIUM-SIZED LIBRARIES AND MEDIA CENTERS (US/0277-5948) [07610929] **1928**

RECOMMENDED RULES FOR CARE OF POWER BOILERS (US/0272-3506) [04128128] **2127**

RECOMMENDED RULES FOR THE CARE AND OPERATION OF HEATING BOILERS (US) [04128034] **2127**

RECOMMENDED SALARIES AND BENEFITS FOR CAREER SERVICE EMPLOYEES (US/0146-9916) [03092636] **4678**

RECOMMENDED VIDEOS FOR SCHOOLS (US/1061-0499) [25170942] 1777, **1138**

RECONCILIATION QUARTERLY (NEW MALDEN, SURREY) (UK/0034-1479) [03169972] 1777, **4990**

RECONQUISTA *CEASED.* (SP/0484-1379) [I04841379] **4054**

RECONSTRUCTION (CAMBRIDGE, MASS.) (US/1049-1392) [21140808] **2271**

RECONSTRUCTION SURGERY AND TRAUMATOLOGY (SZ/0080-0260) [01640213] **3973**

RECONSTRUCTIONIST (US/0034-1495) [01586770] **5052**

RECONSTRUCTIVE SURGERY (US) [20489482] **3973**

RECORD-A-REF. SUPPLEMENT; COMMERCIAL RECORD REFERENCE (US/0362-7683) [02067723] **1928**

RECORD-ADVANCE AND SEA CLIFF NEWS *See* RECORD PILOT **5720**

RECORD ADVERTISER (US/0199-0438) [05533520] **5739**

RECORD-ARGUS (GREENVILLE, PA. : 1985) (US) [15074984] **5739**

●RECORD BOOK / CANADIAN HOCKEY LEAGUE (CN/1191-3975) [26497595] **4914**

RECORD CITIZEN *See* RECORD ENTERPRISE (PLYMOUTH, N.H.), THE **5709**

RECORD (COATESVILLE, PA.) (US) [14978998] **5739**

RECORD COLLECTOR (UK) **4149**

RECORD COLLECTOR, THE (UK/0034-155X) [02626621] **4149**

RECORD COLLECTORS JOURNAL, THE (US/0099-0817) [02243294] **5318**

RECORD COLLECTOR'S MONTHLY (US/8755-6154) [11384031] 4149, **2777**

RECORD-COURIER (US) [09416752] **5730**

RECORD-COURIER (GARDNERVILLE, NEV.) (US/8755-4631) [11314282] **5708**

RECORD-COURIER (JOHNSON CITY, TEX. : 1981) (US) [14509515] **5753**

RECORD DELTA, THE (US) [13291758] **5764**

RECORD EDUCATIONAL LEADERSHIP (US) **1869**

RECORD ENTERPRISE (PLYMOUTH, N.H.), THE (US/1070-745X) [28405919] **5709**

RECORD - GARLAND COUNTY HISTORICAL SOCIETY, THE (US/0163-6820) [02365090] **2756**

RECORD-GAZETTE (US/0747-1521) [10579989] **5638**

RECORD - GEOLOGICAL SURVEY OF WESTERN AUSTRALIA (AT/0728-2311) [I07282311] **1393**

RECORD (GRAFTON, N.D.) (US/0747-1181) [10554622] **5726**

RECORD (GRAFTON, N.D.) *See* WALSH COUNTY RECORD (1992), THE **5726**

RECORD (HACKENSACK, N.J.) (US) [10806291] **5711**

RECORD HERALD (US) [13048395] **5739**

RECORD-HERALD AND INDIANOLA TRIBUNE, THE (US/0895-3287) [16013053] **5672**

RECORD HORSEMAN *See* HORSE SHEETS **2799**

RECORD HOUSES AND APARTMENTS OF THE YEAR (US) [05282592] 307, **2903**

RECORD - I.E.E.E. SYMPOSIUM ON COMPUTER SOFTWARE RELIABILITY (US/0091-469X) [01787096] **1281**

RECORD IN EDUCATIONAL ADMINISTRATION AND SUPERVISION (US/0739-0580) [08348321] **1869**

RECORD INTERIORS (US/0277-6219) [07378543] **2903**

RECORD-JOURNAL (US) [26296463] **5646**

RECORD KEEPING BOOK FOR COSHH (UK) **750**

RECORD (LOUISVILLE, KY.), THE (US/0746-8474) [10319347] **5682**

RECORD (MEMPHIS, TN) (US) [07710433] **5746**

RECORD / NEW ZEALAND GEOLOGICAL SURVEY (NZ/0112-465X) [11908265] **1393**

RECORD (NORWOOD) (US/0196-402X) [02251370] **1993**

RECORD OF CONFERENCE PAPERS - PETROLEUM AND CHEMICAL INDUSTRY CONFERENCE (US/0090-3507) [01785020] **2016**

RECORD OF NEW ISSUES (CN/0832-0748) [12413118] **912**

RECORD OF PROCEEDINGS *See* PROCEEDINGS / ANNUAL SIMULATION SYMPOSIUM **1282**

RECORD OF PROCEEDINGS - GENERAL COUNCIL. UNITED CHURCH OF CANADA (CN/0082-7878) [02248154] **5066**

RECORD OF PUBLICATIONS / INTERNATIONAL INSTITUTE OF TROPICAL AGRICULTURE (NR) [10987196] **156**

RECORD OF RESEARCH (KE) [17216448] **125**

RECORD OF THE AMERICAN BUREAU OF SHIPPING (US) [03704778] **5455**

RECORD OF THE ART MUSEUM, PRINCETON UNIVERSITY (US/0032-843X) [01640386] 363, **4095**

RECORD OF THE ASSOCIATION OF THE BAR OF THE CITY OF NEW YORK, THE (US/0004-5837) [02250650] **3036**

RECORD OF WILLS : SURROGATES COURT. STATEN ISLAND, NEW YORK (US/1055-2863) **2469**

RECORD-OUTLOOK, THE (US/0747-2161) [10635516] **5739**

RECORD PILOT (US) [23129766] **5720**

RECORD - POSITION LOCATION AND NAVIGATION SYMPOSIUM (US) [05112941] **2078**

RECORD (RENOVO, PA.) (US) [12159164] **5739**

RECORD RESEARCH (US/0034-1592) [04554179] **4149**

RECORD ROUNDUP (NORTH CAMBRIDGE, MASS.) (US/1071-4170) [15170513] 5318, **4149**

RECORD SEARCHLIGHT (US) [20396150] **5638**

RECORD SERIES / YORKSHIRE ARCHAEOLOGICAL SOCIETY (UK) [08162835] **280**

RECORD SOCIETY FOR THE PUBLICATION OF ORIGINAL DOCUMENTS RELATING TO LANCASHIRE AND CHESHIRE : PUBLICATIONS (UK) [04770942] **2704**

RECORD - SOCIETY OF ACTUARIES. MEETING (US/0730-2983) [04449258] **2891**

RECORD (SOMERVILLE, MASS.) (US/1054-1675) [22774885] 3917, **4512**

RECORD STOCKMAN, THE (US/0034-1614) [03883389] **220**

RECORD SYDNEY (AT/0310-4729) [I03104729] **2483**

RECORD - TENNESSEE DEPARTMENT OF HUMAN SERVICES, THE (US/0360-4608) [02244155] **5304**

RECORD (TORONTO) (CN/0712-8290) [08730550] **4149**

RECORD (TROY, N.Y.) (US/1053-8976) [17567490] **5720**

RECORD WARBURTON (AT/0819-5633) [I08195633] **4990**

RECORD (WASHINGTON, D.C. : 1975) (US/0145-8566) [02791090] **3036**

RECORD WORLD (US/0034-1622) [03664749] **5318**

RECORDER *CEASED.* (CN/0832-0322) [15128289] **2149**

RECORDER (AT/0155-8722) [05369837] **1705**

RECORDER (AMSTERDAM, N.Y.) (US/0739-2540) [09720919] **5720**

RECORDER (GREENFIELD, MASS.) (US) [13663298] **5690**

RECORDER HERALD (US) [13172183] **5657**

RECORDER MAGAZINE, THE *CEASED.* (UK/0306-4409) [21586535] **4149**

RECORDER (MONTEREY, VA.) (US/0888-9473) [13777572] **5759**

RECORDER (NEW YORK, N.Y. 1985), THE (US/0885-7741) [12769999] **2627**

RECORDER REVIEW (US/0361-5855) [02247036] **5318**

RECORDER (SAN FRANCISCO, CALIF.) (US) 3036, **5639**

RECORDER, THE (US/0362-6121) [04509714] **3036**

RECORDER, THE (UK) [10869982] **4149**

RECORDER (TORONTO) *CEASED.* (CN/0704-7231) [03956440] **4149**

RECORDER WEVELGEM (BE/0776-3093) [I07763093] 1012, **990**

RECORDING FOR THE BLIND *See* CATALOG OF TAPE RECORDED BOOKS / RECORDINGS FOR THE BLIND **4385**

RECORDING INDUSTRY INDEX (US/0276-6078) [06801101] **5318**

●RECORDING : THE MAGAZINE FOR THE RECORDING MUSICIAN (US) [31020245] **5318**

RECORDS & RETRIEVAL REPORT, THE (US/8756-0089) [11447877] **884**

RECORDS MANAGEMENT BULLETIN (UK) **884**

RECORDS MANAGEMENT JOURNAL (LONDON, ENGLAND) (UK) [20478201] **3244**

RECORDS MANAGEMENT QUARTERLY (1986) (US/1050-2343) [13500939] **884**

RECORDS - NATIONAL MUSEUM OF NEW ZEALAND (NZ/0110-943X) [03476275] **4095**

RECORDS OF BUCKINGHAMSHIRE, OR, PAPERS AND NOTES ON THE HISTORY, ANTIQUITIES, AND ARCHITECTURE OF THE COUNTY, TOGETHER WITH THE PROCEEDINGS OF THE ARCHITECTURAL AND ARCHAEOLOGICAL SOCIETY FOR THE COUNTY OF BUCKINGHAM (UK) [01780066] 280, **307**

RECORDS OF CIVILIZATION, SOURCES AND STUDIES (US/0080-0287) [01763536] **2627**

RECORDS OF EARLY ENGLISH DRAMA (CN/0700-9283) [03350219] 2853, **5367**

RECORDS OF EXOTICS (US/0364-7153) [02652625] 4878, **4914**

RECORDS OF HUNTINGDONSHIRE (UK/0034-1738) [06164249] **2705**

RECORDS OF NEW JERSEY BIRDS (US) [09823862] **5620**

RECORDS OF NEW JERSEY BIRDS / NEW JERSEY AUDUBON SOCIETY (US) [09872609] **5620**

RECORDS OF SELECTED PLAYERS (US/0363-8766) [02546526] **4914**

RECORDS OF THE ACADEMY (US/0065-6844) [01926674] **329**

RECORDS OF THE AMERICAN CATHOLIC HISTORICAL SOCIETY OF PHILADELPHIA (US/0002-7790) [01479632] **5035**

RECORDS OF THE AUCKLAND INSTITUTE AND MUSEUM (NZ/0067-0464) [02445118] **5145**

RECORDS OF THE AUSTRALIAN MUSEUM (AT/0067-1975) [01385608] 244, **5596**

RECORDS OF THE AUSTRALIAN MUSEUM. SUPPLEMENT (AT/0812-7387) [10252295] 244, **5596**

RECORDS OF THE BOTANICAL SURVEY OF INDIA (II/0375-0728) [02255355] **526**

RECORDS OF THE GENERAL CONFERENCE OF THE UNITED NATIONS EDUCATIONAL, SCIENTIFIC AND CULTURAL ORGANIZATION (FR) [01491462] **5235**

RECORDS OF THE GEOLOGICAL SURVEY OF INDIA (II/0370-5226) [01752790] **1393**

RECORDS OF THE GEOLOGICAL SURVEY OF NEW SOUTH WALES (AT/0370-5242) [01641113] **1393**

RECORDS OF THE GEOLOGICAL SURVEY OF PAKISTAN (PK/0078-8163) [01321399] **1393**

RECORDS OF THE SOUTH AUSTRALIAN MUSEUM (AT/0376-2750) [02489475] **4095**

RECORDS OF THE WESTERN AUSTRALIAN MUSEUM (AT/0312-3162) [02242195] **4171**

RECORDS OF THE ZOOLOGICAL SURVEY OF INDIA (II/0375-1511) [01776039] **5596**

RECORDS OF THE ZOOLOGICAL SURVEY OF INDIA. MISCELLANEOUS PUBLICATION. OCCASIONAL PAPER (II/0970-0714) [03526491] **5596**

RECORDS OF VERMONT BIRDS (US/0197-3169) [05121904] **5620**

RECORDS OF WILLS, SURROGATES COURT, STATEN ISLAND, NEW YORK (RICHMOND COUNTY) (US/1055-2863) [23133481] **3036**

RECOUP (CN/0709-6402) [05694722] **2241**

Alphabetical Title Index — RED

RECOUP'S MATERIALS RECYCLING MARKETS (CN/0884-4526) [12620960] **2241**

RECOVERING LITERATURE (US/0300-6425) [01330063] **3351**

RECOVERING (SAN FRANCISCO, CALIF.) (US/0896-2391) [16976229] **1348**

RECOVERY NOW (US/1043-3163) [19403802] **3633**

RECOVERY TODAY (US/1061-7191) [25418616] **5304**

RECREACTION (VANIER) **CEASED.** (CN/0710-6025) [08099323] **4708**

RECREATIE EN TOERISME (NE/0165-4179) [I01654179] 4853, **5490**

RECREATION AND OUTDOOR LIFE DIRECTORY **CEASED.** (US) [05347753] 4878, **4853**

RECREATION AND PARK EDUCATION CURRICULUM CATALOG (US/0148-2882) [01781738] **4708**

RECREATION AND PARK YEARBOOK (US) [01165893] **4853**

RECREATION AND PARKS LAW REPORTER (US/0743-5649) [10607496] 4708, **3036**

RECREATION BRITISH COLUMBIA (1985) (CN/0830-1913) [14955483] **4853**

RECREATION CANADA (CN/0031-2231) [02130935] **4853**

RECREATION CANADA (FRENCH EDITION) (CN/0031-2231) [02129680] **4853**

RECREATION EXCHANGE (AT) **4853**

RECREATION EXECUTIVE REPORT (US/0890-2194) [10642449] **4853**

RECREATION MELTON MOWBRAY (UK/0961-2580) [I09612580] **4854**

RECREATION PRACTITIONERS BULLETIN (CN/0824-7323) [11283979] **4854**

RECREATION QUEBEC (CN/0847-432X) [21348468] **4865**

RECREATION RESOURCES (US/1046-316X) [20365732] **4854**

RECREATION STATISTICS (US/0362-7837) [02329813] **4856**

RECREATION VEHICLE FINANCING (US/0733-530X) [08594953] 5423, **4744**

RECREATION VEHICLE MARKETING REPORT (US) **5423**

RECREATIONAL FLYER, THE (CN/0845-8391) [20278681] **33**

RECREATIONAL SPORTS DIRECTORY (US) [12212054] 1843, **4914**

RECREATIONAL VEHICLE BLUE BOOK (US/0733-4745) [08574777] **5391**

RECREATIONAL VEHICLE LIFE (1984) **CEASED.** (CN/0833-9791) [15492954] **4854**

RECRUIT & RETAIN (US/0278-2766) [07760435] **3868**

RECRUITER JOURNAL (US/0747-573X) [10617976] **4054**

RECRUITING & SUPERVISION TODAY (CN/1187-9378) [26497740] **946**

RECRUITING TRENDS (US/0034-1827) [06731403] **706**

RECRUITING TRENDS (EAST LANSING) (US/0163-5611) [04401649] **1705**

RECRUITMENT AND DEVELOPMENT REPORT (UK/0959-146X) [I0959146X] **946**

RECRUITMENT AND RETENTION IN HIGHER EDUCATION (US/0891-012X) [14523985] **1843**

RECRUITMENT & RETENTION REPORT (US/1044-0666) [19675755] **3868**

●RECRUITMENT, RETENTION, & RESTRUCTURING REPORT (US/1044-0666) [30610861] **3868**

RECRUITMENT SELECTION AND RETENTION (UK) **946**

RECRUITMENT SOLUTION, THE (US/1058-2118) [24188105] **765**

RECSAM ANNUAL REPORT (MY/0377-3450) [01797868] **5145**

RECSAM (ORGANIZATION) See RECSAM ANNUAL REPORT **5145**

RECTANGLE, THE (US/0888-4757) [05338569] **3428**

RECUEIL ANNUEL DES PAGES JURIDIQUES DE LA VIE OUVRIERE (FR) **3036**

RECUEIL DALLOZ See RECUEIL DALLOZ SIREY DE DOCTRINE, DE JURISPRUDENCE ET DE LEGISLATION **3036**

RECUEIL DALLOZ SIREY (FR) [02588319] **3036**

RECUEIL DALLOZ SIREY DE DOCTRINE, DE JURISPRUDENCE ET DE LEGISLATION (FR/0034-1835) [01763547] **3036**

RECUEIL DE DROIT DE LA FAMILLE (CN/0832-8927) [16736311] **3122**

RECUEIL DE DROIT FISCAL QUEBECOIS (CN/0704-2035) [06966088] **3036**

RECUEIL DE DROIT IMMOBILIER (CN/0832-8943) [16736316] **3036**

RECUEIL DE LA JURISPRUDENCE DE LA COUR (LU) [05425167] **3036**

RECUEIL DE L'ASSOCIATION DES AMIS DU VIEUX HAVRE (FR/1149-767X) [I1149767X] **2705**

RECUEIL DE MEDECINE VETERINAIRE (FR/0034-1843) [05979665] **5520**

RECUEIL DE MEMOIRES ET TRAVAUX PUBLIE PAR LE SOCIETE D'HISTOIRE DU DROIT ET DES INSTITUTIONS DES ANCIENS PAYS DE DROIT ECRIT (FR/0583-8282) [01952650] **3036**

RECUEIL DES ACTES ADMINISTRATIFS - ARDENNES, PREFECTURE (FR/0298-6957) [I02986957] **4678**

RECUEIL DES ACTES ADMINISTRATIFS DE LA PREFECTURE DE LA REUNION (FR/0753-0759) [10654061] **3093**

●RECUEIL DES ACTES ADMINISTRATIFS DE LA PREFECTURE DES ARDENNES ET DES SERVICES DECONCENTRES DE L'ETAT (FR/1252-5367) [I12525367] **4678**

RECUEIL DES ACTES ADMINISTRATIFS DU DEPARTEMENT DES ARDENNES (FR/0298-6965) [I02986965] **4678**

RECUEIL DES ARRETS, AVIS CONSULTATIFS ET ORDONNANCES / COUR INTERNATIONALE DE JUSTICE (NE) [07700049] **3134**

RECUEIL DES BREVETS D'INVENTION (BE/0034-1851) [04038915] **1308**

RECUEIL DES COURS - ACADEMIE DE DROIT INTERNATIONAL (NE/0169-5436) [01680848] **3134**

RECUEIL DES DECISIONS / COMITES D'APPEL DE LA FONCTION PUBLIQUE (CN/1180-3533) [23259464] **4679**

RECUEIL DES DECISIONS DU CONSEIL D'ETAT, STATUANT AU CONTENTIEUX ET DU TRIBUNAL DES CONFLITS ET DES JUGEMENTS DES TRIBUNAUX ADMINISTRATIFS (FR) [01442552] **4679**

RECUEIL DES FILMS (MONTREAL) (CN/0085-543X) [02441950] **4076**

RECUEIL DES HISTORIENS DE LA FRANCE. DOCUMENTS FINANCIERS (FR/0515-1864) [01460647] **2705**

RECUEIL DES HISTORIENS DE LA FRANCE. OBITUAIRES (FR/0080-0325) [01460648] 2705, **434**

RECUEIL DES HISTORIENS DE LA FRANCE. POUILLES (FR) [01460649] **5035**

RECUEIL DES LOIS, DECRETS, ET ARRETES / ROYAUME DE BELGIQUE (BE) [09047166] **3134**

RECUEIL DES MEMBRES - LA FEDERATION DE L'AGRICULTURE DE L'ONTARIO **CEASED.** (CN/0225-0977) [06021258] **125**

RECUEIL DES OBSERVATIONS EN SURFACE / DIRECTION DU SERVICE DE L'AVIATION CIVILE EN POLYNESIE FRANCAISE, SERVICE DE LA METEOROLOGIE (FP) [19406105] **1434**

RECUEIL DES SENTENCES DE L'EDUCATION (CN/0704-7630) [06506919] **1869**

RECUEIL DES TRAVAUX (SZ) [01772322] **329**

RECUEIL DES TRAVAUX CHIMIQUES DES PAYS-BAS (1920) (NE/0165-0513) [06899170] **991**

RECUEIL D'EVALUATIONS DES OUVRAGES COURANTS DU BATIMENT (FR/0246-9561) [02469561] **625**

RECUEIL EN MATIERE DE PROTECTION DU TERRITOIRE AGRICOLE (CN/1183-0271) [23455417] **3037**

RECUEIL EN RESPONSABILITE ET ASSURANCE (CN/0832-8935) [16744950] **3037**

RECUEIL FISCAL. COURS D'IMPOT (CN/0712-6573) [09340475] **750**

RECUEIL FISCAL. PROBLEMES ET SOLUTIONS (CN/0712-6565) [09340470] **4744**

RECUEIL LINGUISTIQUE DE BRATISLAVA (XO) [01763555] **3315**

RECUEIL OFFICIEL DES LOIS FEDERALES (SZ) [18182217] **3037**

RECUEIL PERIODIQUE DES JURIS-CLASSEURS : DROIT CIVIL (FR) [02244817] **3091**

RECUEIL STATISTIQUE DU POITOU-CHARENTES (FR) [03263610] **5337**

RECUEIL STATISTIQUES (FR) **5337**

RECUEILS DE JURISPRUDENCE DU QUEBEC. COUR PROVINCIALE, COUR DES SESSIONS DE LA PAIX, COUR DE BIEN-ETRE SOCIAL See RECUEILS DE JURISPRUDENCE DU QUEBEC. COUR PROVINCIALE, COUR DES SESSIONS DE LA PAIX, TRIBUNAL DE LA JEUNESSE **3037**

RECUEILS DE JURISPRUDENCE DU QUEBEC. COUR PROVINCIALE, COUR DES SESSIONS DE LA PAIX, TRIBUNAL DE LA JEUNESSE (CN/0830-0402) [11511066] **3037**

RECUEILS DE LA SOCIETE JEAN BODIN POUR L'HISTOIRE COMPARATIVE DES INSTITUTIONS (BE) [01777553] **5215**

RECUPERARE. EDILIZIA DESIGN IMPIANTI (IT/0392-4599) [I03924599] **307**

RECURRING BIBLIOGRAPHY OF HYPERTENSION **CEASED.** (US/0090-1326) [01778830] **3710**

RECURSIVE REASONING REPORTS (US/1053-427X) [22529325] **2271**

RECURSOS HUMANOS (BL) [02242192] **706**

RECURSOS HUMANOS (BL) [02242749] **3917**

RECUSANT HISTORY (UK/0034-1932) [01624181] **2705**

RECYCLAGE RECUPERATION PARIS (FR/1156-962X) [I1156962X] **2220**

RECYCLED PAPER NEWS (US/1051-9831) [22162131] 4238, **2241**

RECYCLING (GW/0174-1446) [I01741446] **2180**

RECYCLING CANADA (CN/1183-8809) [25423714] **2241**

RECYCLING LEAD AND ZINC: THE CHALLENGE OF THE 1990'S (UK) **4017**

RECYCLING OF METALLIFEROUS MATERIALS (UK) [22966608] **4017**

RECYCLING RELATED NEWSLETTERS, PUBLICATIONS, PERIODICALS, ETC. : AN UPDATING REFERENCE (US/1053-0525) [22440799] 1299, **2180**

●RECYCLING SOURCEBOOK (US/1064-4938) [26319519] **2241**

●RECYCLING TODAY (US) [27120317] **2241**

RECYCLING TODAY (MUNICIPAL (POST-CONSUMER) MARKET ED.) See RECYCLING TODAY **2241**

RECYCLING TODAY (MUNICIPAL (POST-CONSUMER) MARKET ED.) (US/1051-0109) [21766331] **2241**

RECYCLING TODAY (SCRAP PROCESSING MARKET ED.) (US/1051-1091) [21864164] **2241**

RECYCLING TODAY (SCRAP PROCESSING MARKET ED.) See RECYCLING TODAY **2241**

RECYCLING UPDATE (US/0736-1890) [09091468] 2241, **2220**

RECYCLING UPDATE-TELEMARKETING SCRIPT PRESENTATIONS EDITION (US) **2241**

RED ALERT (UK) 1515, **706**

RED APPLE BULLETIN (US) [20497450] **5657**

RED BASS (US/0883-0126) [11672283] **329**

RED BAY NEWS (RED BAY, ALA. : 1963) (US) [13740375] **5628**

RED BLUFF TEHAMA COUNTY DAILY NEWS (US) [27847225] **5639**

●RED BOOK (US) [27743656] **4327**

RED BOOK (CHICAGO), THE (US/0190-6070) [02391590] 184, **849**

RED BOOK CONSTRUCTION REGISTER (US/0148-0014) [03262929] **625**

RED BOOK DIRECTORY OF MAJOR BAKERIES (US) [08687315] **935**

RED BOOK DRUG TOPICS UPDATE See RED BOOK UPDATE **4327**

RED BOOK. NUMERICAL PHONE INDEX OF GREATER MONTREAL (CN/0381-7229) [03202329] **1928**

RED BOOK OF HOUSING MANUFACTURERS, THE (US/0149-7642) [02580263] **625**

RED BOOK OF OPHTHALMOLOGY, THE (US/0146-4582) [02941604] **3878**

RED BOOK UPDATE (US) **4327**

RED BOOK (WORTHINGTON) (US/0198-9162) [05761260] **2407**

RED CEDAR REVIEW (US/0034-1967) [01643536] **3428**

RED CLOUD COUNTRY (US/0300-6344) [01329873] **2271**

RED CONTABLE AGRARIA NACIONAL / MINISTERIO DE AGRICULTURA, SECRETARIA GENERAL TECNICA (SP) [06952229] **125**

RED CROSS. GERMANY (DEMOCRATIC REPUBLIC) DEUTSCHES ROTES KREUZ See DEUTSCHES ROTES KREUZ DER DEUTSCHEN DEMOKRATISCHEN REPUBLIK **5282**

RED CROSS. GERMANY (FEDERAL REPUBLIC). DEUTSCHES ROTES KREUZ *See* JAHRBUCH - DEUTSCHES ROTES KREUZ **5291**

RED CROSS, RED CRESCENT : THE INTERNATIONAL MAGAZINE OF THE LEAGUE OF RED CROSS AND RED CRESCENT SOCIETIES (SZ) [18077914] **5304**

RED CROSS TODAY / BRITISH COLUMBIA-YUKON DIVISION (CN/0711-4044) [08499613] **5304**

RED DATA BOOK (SZ) [01731821] **226**

RED DEER, ALBERTA, CITY DIRECTORY *See* RED DEER CITY DIRECTORY (1992) **2574**

●RED DEER CITY DIRECTORY (1992) (CN/1191-9302) [27809652] **2574**

RED DEER SURGICAL SOCIETY *See* PROCEEDINGS OF THE RED DEER SURGICAL SOCIETY **3972**

RED FOX REVIEW *CEASED*. (US/0742-454X) [02844188] **3428**

RED MENACE (CN/0711-2270) [08649581] **4546**

RED NOTEBOOK. COMMUNICATING WITH HEARING PEOPLE, THE (US) **4393**

RED RIVER COMMUNITY COLLEGE. LEARNING RESOURCES CENTRE *See* 16 MM FILM CATALOGUE - RED RIVER COMMUNITY COLLEGE, LEARNING RESOURCES CENTRE **4062**

RED RIVER VALLEY HERITAGE PRESS, THE (US/0739-1838) [03259486] **2756**

RED RIVER VALLEY HISTORICAL REVIEW (US/0362-6415) [02314256] **2756**

RED RIVER VALLEY POTATO GROWER *See* VALLEY POTATO GROWER **143**

RED ROCK NEWS *See* SEDONA RED ROCK NEWS **5630**

RED TAPE (AT) **5304**

RED TAPE (DETROIT, MICH.) (US/0735-7427) [08278996] **3244**

RED THE NET. HOTLINE, LA (US/1043-223X) [18502400] **1777**

RED THE NET, LA (US/0274-8657) [18502383] **1777**

RED TIDE NEWSLETTER (IE/0791-248X) [I0791248X] **1455**

RED WING REPUBLICAN EAGLE (US) [10115138] **5698**

REDACCION (AG) [02240021] **3351**

●REDACTEUR (MONTREAL) (CN/1188-2670) [25796361] **626**

REDAI HAIYANG (CC/1000-3053) [09880299] **1455**

REDBOOK (US/0034-2106) [05434081] **5565**

●REDBOOK (CHAGRIN FALLS, OHIO), THE (US/1073-273X) [29378416] **2407**

REDBOOK MAGAZINE *See* REDBOOK **5565**

REDBOOK / TAA, TEXAS APARTMENT ASSOCIATION (US/0731-0153) [08073166] **2832**

REDCLIFF REVIEW (CN/0701-0079) [03279428] **5793**

REDDING PILOT, THE (US) [26991634] **5646**

REDDITCH & DISTRICT BUSINESS DIRECTORY *See* COMMERCE BUSINESS DIRECTORIES REDDITCH ED **658**

●REDE NACIONAL FEMINISTA DE SAUDE E DIREITOS REPRODUTIVOS : BOLETIM (BL) [28290254] 5565, **590**

REDEGRELSE FOR SITUATIONEN VEDRØRENDE ALKOHOL- OG NARKOTIKAMISBRUGET (DK) [19508804] **1348**

REDEMPTION DIGEST AND CORPORATE ACTIONS (US/1056-506X) [23726141] **807**

REDEN-BERATER, DER (GW/0932-1543) [I09321543] **1120**

REDFEARN'S WILLS AND ADMINISTRATION OF ESTATES IN FLORIDA (US) **3119**

REDFEARN'S WILLS AND ADMINISTRATION OF ESTATES IN GEORGIA (US) **3037**

REDFIELD JOURNAL-OBSERVER *See* REDFIELD PRESS, THE **5744**

REDFIELD PRESS, THE (US) [13554449] **5744**

REDI REALTY REPORT (US/1051-0737) [21571000] 626, **4846**

REDIA (IT/0370-4327) [01763597] **5613**

REDIRECTIONS (KIRKLAND, WASH.) (US/1046-4549) [20407532] **884**

REDLAND GUIDE TO THE RECOMMENDATIONS, REGULATIONS AND STATUTORY AND ADVISORY BODIES OF THE CONSTRUCTION INDUSTRY (UK) [20292076] **626**

REDLANDS, CALIF. UNIVERSITY. FOREIGN POLICY RESEARCH ASSOCIATION *See* JOURNAL OF THE FOREIGN POLICY RESEARCH ASSOCIATION OF THE UNIVERSITY OF REDLANDS **4527**

REDNECK REVIEW OF LITERATURE, THE (US/0887-5715) [13323908] **3428**

REDOUBT (AT/1030-4932) [18634091] **3428**

●REDOX REPORT (UK/1351-0002) **3633**

REDS REPORT (US/1057-9540) [19903974] **4914**

REDSTART, THE (US/0034-2165) [02144431] **5596**

REDUCCIONS (SP) [07556846] **3470**

REDUNDANCY IN NEW ZEALAND (NZ/0110-1943) [02240752] **1705**

REDWOOD CITY ALMANAC (US/0195-0533) [05233809] **5639**

REDWOOD FALLS REDWOOD GAZETTE (US) [01695195] **5698**

REDWOOD NEWS (US) [10062002] 307, **2404**

REDWOOD RESEARCHER (US/0890-2968) [08235415] **2469**

REED-DUNN'S BUSINESS REVIEW (US/0730-6563) [08030351] **706**

REEDE (ER) [22785689] **329**

REEDER'S ECONOMIC DIGEST (US/0890-9954) [14576869] **1515**

REEDLEY EXPONENT, THE (US) [27297866] **5639**

REED'S COMMERCIAL SALVAGE PRACTICE (UK) [17768794] **5455**

REEDUCATION ORTHOPHONIQUE (FR/0034-222X) [I0034222X] **3315**

REEDUCATION POSTURALE GLOBALE (FR/0294-0922) [I02940922] **3806**

REEF MISES A JOUR (FR) **2777**

REEL DIRECTORY, THE (US/8755-786X) [11323708] **4077**

REEL WEST DIGEST (CN/0821-7947) [09929571] **4077**

REENBOU (CN/0225-2104) [06272783] **3470**

REESE RIVER REVEILLE (AUSTIN, NEV. : 1950) *CEASED*. (US) [10686808] **5708**

REEVES JOURNAL (US/0048-7066) [05120838] **2608**

REFA NACHRICHTEN (GW/0033-6874) [06637732] **946**

REFER (UK/0144-2384) [08092822] **3244**

REFERATEBLATT ZUR RAUMENTWICKLUNG (GW/0341-2512) [03866830] **4679**

REFERATEORGAN MESSEN MECHANISCHER GROSSEN (GW/0722-0057) [I07220057] **1993**

REFERATEORGAN SCHWEISSEN UND VERWANDTE VERFAHREN (GW/0340-4749) [I03404749] **4027**

REFERATI I SAOPSTENJA - NAUCNI SASTANAK SLAVISTA U VUKOVE DANE (YU) [02244815] **3315**

REFERATIVA DE EDUCACION : RE (CU/0138-7871) [19986499] **1777**

●REFERATIVNYI ZHURNAL. 04, 04D, BIOLOGIIA. FIZIKO-KHIMICHESKAIA BIOLOGIIA / VSESOIUZNYI INSTITUT NAUCHNOI I TEKHNICHESKOI INFORMATSII (RU/0869-4095) [26253021] 496, **493**

REFERATIVNYI ZHURNAL. 08, GEOLOGIIA (RU) [11898124] **1394**

REFERATIVNYI ZHURNAL. 13, MATEMATIKA (RU) [21010496] **3530**

REFERATIVNYI ZHURNAL. 26, FIZIKO-KHIMICHESKAIA BIOLOGIIA *See* REFERATIVNYI ZHURNAL. 04, 04D, BIOLOGIIA. FIZIKO-KHIMICHESKAIA BIOLOGIIA / VSESOIUZNYI INSTITUT NAUCHNOI I TEKHNICHESKOI INFORMATSII **493**

REFERATIVNYI ZHURNAL. 29, SVIAZ (RU) [19217949] **1162**

REFERATIVNYI ZHURNAL: BIOFIZIKA (RU) [02503431] **496**

REFERATIVNYI ZHURNAL. BIOLOGICHESKAIA KHIMIIA (RU) [01763604] 991, **471**

REFERATIVNYI ZHURNAL: ELEKTRONIKA (RU) [06651427] **2078**

REFERATIVNYI ZHURNAL. ELEKTROTEKHNIKA / GOSUDARSTVENNYI KOMITET SSSR PO NAUKE I TEKHNIKE, AKADEMIIA NAUK SSSR, VSESOIUZNYI INSTITUT NAUCHNOI I TEKHNICHESKOI INFORMATSII (RU/0203-5189) [08671352] **2079**

REFERATIVNYI ZHURNAL: ELEKTROTEKHNIKA I ENERGETIKA (RU/0034-2327) [05060073] **2079**

REFERATIVNYI ZHURNAL. ENERGETIKA / GOSUDARSTVENNYI KOMITET SSSR PO NAUKE I TEKHNIKE, AKADEMIIA NAUK SSSR, VSESOIUZNYI INSTITUT NAUCHNOI I TEKHNICHESKOI INFORMATSII (RU/0203-5308) [08671370] **2079**

REFERATIVNYI ZHURNAL FARMAKOLOGIYA OBSHCHAYA FARMAKOLOGIYA NERVNOI SISTEMY (RU/0134-580X) 4327, **471**

REFERATIVNYI ZHURNAL. FIZIKA (RU/0034-2343) [01763607] **4419**

REFERATIVNYI ZHURNAL. GEOGRAFIIA. D, BIOGEOGRAFIIA (RU) [19748839] 2574, **471**

REFERATIVNYI ZHURNAL: ISSLEDOVANIE KOSMICHESKOGO PROSTRANSTVA (RU) [07003884] **399**

REFERATIVNYI ZHURNAL. KARTOFEL' I OVOSHCHI *CEASED*. (RU) [10560026] **184**

REFERATIVNYI ZHURNAL: KHIMICHESKOE, NEFTEPERERABATYVAIUSHCHEE I POLIMERNOE MASHINOSTROENIE (RU) [04162527] **1029**

REFERATIVNYI ZHURNAL. KHIMIIA / AKADEMIIA NAUK SSSR, INSTITUT NAUCHNOI INFORMATSII (RU/0202-6325) [01763611] **991**

REFERATIVNYI ZHURNAL. LESOVODSTVO I AGROLESOMELIORATSIIA / MINISTERSTVO SELSKOGO KHOZIAISTVA SSSR (RU) [10064830] **2392**

REFERATIVNYI ZHURNAL : METALLURGIIA (RU/0034-2491) [07003172] **4017**

REFERATIVNYI ZHURNAL. METROLOGIIA I IZMERITELNAIA TEKHNIKA (RU/0034-2505) [08727375] **4032**

REFERATIVNYI ZHURNAL. MOLOCHNOE I MIASNOE SKOTOVODSTVO / MINISTERSTVO SELSKOGO KHOZIAISTVA SSSR (RU) [10066914] **220**

REFERATIVNYI ZHURNAL. N.51, ASTRONOMIIA (RU/0486-2236) [06128462] **399**

REFERATIVNYI ZHURNAL : OBSHCHIE VOPROSY PATOLOGII (RU/0131-1301) [01950699] **3897**

REFERATIVNYI ZHURNAL: ORGANIZATSIIA I BEZOPASNOST DOROZHNOGO DVIZHENIIA (RU) [02500654] 5443, **5401**

REFERATIVNYI ZHURNAL: PCHELOVODSTVO, SHELKOVODSTVO (RU/0132-358X) [06898699] **125**

REFERATIVNYI ZHURNAL: PROMYSHLENNYI TRANSPORT (RU) [07223760] **5391**

REFERATIVNYI ZHURNAL: RADIOTEKHNIKA (RU) [07262440] **1120**

REFERATIVNYI ZHURNAL. SERIIA 2, ZEMLEDELIE.-- (RU/0134-2878) [08354860] **125**

REFERATIVNYI ZHURNAL: ZEMLEPOLZOVANIE, ZEMLEUSTROISTVO, OKHRANA POCHV (RU) [02884336] **184**

REFERATIVNYJ ZURNAL - VSESOJUZNYJ INSTITUT NAUCNOJ I TEHNICESKOJ INFORMACII. 53. IMMUNOLOGIJA. ALLERGOLOGIJA (RU/0202-9030) [06074510] **3676**

REFERATIVNYJ ZURNAL - VSESOJUZNYJ INSTITUT NAUCNOJ I TEHNICESKOJ INFORMACII. 66, KORROZIJA I ZASCITA OT KORROZII (RU/0131-3533) [07619720] **4017**

REFERATIVNYJ ZURNAL - VSESOJUZNYJ INSTITUT NAUCNOJ I TEHNICESKOJ INFORMACII. 70. RADIACIONNAJA BIOLOGIJA (RU/0131-355X) [02503493] **471**

REFERATIVNYJ ZURNAL - VSESOJUZNYJ INSTITUT NAUCNOJ I TEHNICESKOJ INFORMACII. BIOLOGIJA (RU/0034-2300) [01763605] **479**

REFERATIVNYJ ZURNAL - VSESOJUZNYJ INSTITUT NAUCNOJ I TEHNICESKOJ INFORMACII, GEOGRAFIJA (RU/0034-2378) [01763609] **2574**

REFERATIVNYJ ZURNAL - VSESOJUZNYJ INSTITUT NAUCNOJ I TEHNICESKOJ INFORMACII. TEHNOLOGIJA MASINOSTROENIJA (RU/0034-2599) [07005266] **2127**

REFERATIVNYJ ZURNAL - VSESOUZNYJ INSTITUT NAUCNOJ I TEHNICESKOJ INFORMACII. 77, FARMAKOLOGIA INSTITUT NAUCNOJ SISTEM, HIMIOTERAPEVTICESKIE SREDSTVA (RU/0202-5132) [I02025132] **471**

REFERATIVNYJ ZURNAL - VSESOUZNYJ INSTITUT NAUCNOJ I TEHNICESKOJ INFORMACII. MEHANIKA (RU/0034-2483) [11652828] **2127**

REFEREE (ARLINGTON, VA.), THE (US/0896-7695) [17286858] **1018**

REFEREE (FRANKSVILLE, WIS.) (US/0733-1436) [04829802] **4914**

Alphabetical Title Index — REFUAH

REFERENCE AID, CHIEFS OF STATE, AND CABINET MEMBERS OF FOREIGN GOVERNMENTS (US) [03458727] **4493**

REFERENCE AND RESEARCH BOOK NEWS (US/0887-3763) [13197618] **3244**

REFERENCE BOOK & BUYERS GUIDE / ICHCA, INTERNATIONAL CARGO HANDLING CO-ORDINATION ASSOCIATION (UK/0266-3996) [10764779] **849**

REFERENCE BOOK & LIST OF MEMBERS / THE INCORPORATED ASSOCIATION OF ARCHITECTS & SURVEYORS (UK) [07936695] **307**

REFERENCE BOOK FOR WORLD TRADERS (US) [04320468] **849**

REFERENCE BOOK OF CORPORATE MANAGEMENTS (US/0735-6498) [06477648] **935**, **884**

REFERENCE BOOK OF MARINE INSURANCE CLAUSES (UK) [06546333] **2891**

REFERENCE BOOK REVIEW INDEX **CEASED.** (US) [08124855] 1928, **1930**

REFERENCE BOOK REVIEW, THE (US/0272-1988) [02998377] **1928**

REFERENCE BOOKS BULLETIN (US/8755-0962) [11247254] **3244**

REFERENCE (COMMUNAUTE URBAINE DE MONTREAL. OFFICE DE L'EXPANSION ECONOMIQUE) (CN/0712-4236) [08581291] **1515**

REFERENCE (COMMUNAUTE URBAINE DE MONTREAL. OFFICE D'EXPANSION ECONOMIQUE. ENGLISH EDITION) (CN/0712-4244) [08581286] **1516**

REFERENCE - COMPUTING SERVICES. UNIVERSITY OF ALBERTA (CN/0822-997X) [11046588] 1281, **1262**

REFERENCE DATA FOR ENGINEERS : RADIO, ELECTRONICS, COMPUTER, AND COMMUNICATIONS (US/1066-2731) [12389215] **2079**

REFERENCE DATA REPORT (US/0146-2172) [02881911] **5145**

REFERENCE DATA SERIES (AU) [09843417] **4450**

REFERENCE DESK : QUARTERLY JOURNAL OF THE ENCYCLOPEDISTS: INTERNATIONAL ENCYCLOPEDIA SOCIETY (US/1055-4777) [23189636] **1928**

REFERENCE GUIDE TO ADDICTION COUNSELING (US) 1348, **4615**

REFERENCE GUIDE TO COUNSELING CHILDREN AND ADOLESCENTS (US) **4615**

REFERENCE GUIDE TO ENGLISH LITERATURE (US) **3428**

REFERENCE GUIDE TO HANDBOOKS AND ANNUALS (US) [07256411] **1928**

●REFERENCE GUIDE TO HOMEBUILDING ARTICLES (US) [25298153] **307**

REFERENCE GUIDE TO HOMEBUILDING ARTICLES (US) [25727111] 626, **307**

REFERENCE GUIDE TO MANAGING ADDICTION PROGRAMS **CEASED.** (US) 1348, **4615**

REFERENCE GUIDES TO ARCHIVAL AND MANUSCRIPT SOURCES IN WORLD HISTORY (US/1054-9110) [23011510] **2627**

●REFERENCE GUIDES TO NATIONAL LEGAL SYSTEMS (US/1059-9134) [24888468] **3142**

REFERENCE INFORMATION PAPER (US/0147-0817) [03094877] **2483**

REFERENCE INFORMATION PAPERS **See** REFERENCE INFORMATION PAPER **2483**

REFERENCE LIBRARIAN, THE (US/0276-3877) [07374895] **3244**

REFERENCE LIST OF HEALTH SCIENCE RESEARCH IN CANADA (CN/0704-3899) [04394028] **3633**

REFERENCE POINT (US/0889-2113) [06159059] **2355**

REFERENCE POINT. CUMULATIVE INDEX : FOOD INDUSTRY ABSTRACTS (US/0889-2113) [08703650] **2355**

REFERENCE POINTS **CEASED.** (US/1048-5384) [20969179] **3244**

REFERENCE REPORT : A PUBLICATION OF EDUCATIONAL MATERIALS DISTRIBUTORS **CEASED.** (US/0735-1534) [08872513] **1903**

REFERENCE REVIEWS (UK/0950-4125) [17489670] **1928**

REFERENCE (SAINT LOUIS, MO.) (US/0897-103X) [17407710] **3951**

REFERENCE SERIES (CN) [03196961] **3244**

REFERENCE SERIES - EXTERNAL AFFAIRS CANADA (CN/0228-3808) [05843098] **4679**

REFERENCE SERIES. HEMATOLOGY (CN/0824-6882) [11073596] **3773**

REFERENCE SERIES. MICROBIOLOGY (CN/0826-421X) [11197211] **569**

REFERENCE SERVICES BIBLIOGRAPHIES (AT) [02365123] **3259**

REFERENCE SERVICES REVIEW (US/0090-7324) [01785811] **1928**

REFERENCE SHELF, THE (US) [01642339] **1120**

REFERENCE SOURCE (US) [15177135], **2355**

REFERENCE SOURCES FOR THE SOCIAL SCIENCES AND HUMANITIES (US/0730-3335) [07986952] **5215**

REFERENCE TABLES - CANADIAN PULP AND PAPER ASSOCIATION (CN/0317-0934) [02247713] **4238**

REFERENCE TABLES. DRUG ARRESTS AND DISPOSITIONS (SACRAMENTO) (US/0093-383X) [01792289] **3174**

REFERENCE / TEXAS A & M UNIVERSITY, DEPARTMENT OF OCEANOGRAPHY (US/0735-5939) [01209135] **1455**

REFERENCE UPDATE BASIC EDITION [COMPUTER FILE] (US) 3633, **3661**

REFERENCE UPDATE CLINICAL EDITION [COMPUTER FILE] (US) 3801, **3661**

REFERENCE UPDATE DELUXE EDITION [COMPUTER FILE] (US) 3633, **3661**

REFERENCECLIPPER **CEASED.** (US/0894-3117) [15989588] **1201**

REFERENCES DE LA DISTRIBUTION (FR) **1516**

REFERENCES DE LA POSTE PARIS (FR/0983-1924) [I09831924] **1147**

REFERENCES DESIGN MALAKOFF (FR/0996-5912) [I09965912] **375**

REFERENCES TO CONTEMPORARY PAPERS ON ACOUSTICS (US/0163-0970) [04203697] **4453**

REFERRALS OF CHILDREN TO REPORTERS AND CHILDREN'S HEARINGS (UK) **5304**

REFINED PETROLEUM AND COAL PRODUCTS INDUSTRIES (CN/0835-0175) [18005136] **4276**

REFINED PETROLEUM PRODUCTS (MONTHLY ED.) (CN/0380-8629) [02588205] **4276**

REFINED PETROLEUM PRODUCTS. VOLUME 2. CONSUMPTION OF PETROLEUM PRODUCTS (CN/0575-9587) [02585928] **4276**

REFINING & GAS PROCESSING INDUSTRY : WORLDWIDE (US/1062-5658) [25013001] **4276**

REFINING THE CAREER EDUCATION CONCEPT (US) [06351644] 4209, **1915**

REFINISHING MATERIALS GUIDE: DOMESTIC AND IMPORTED (US) **5424**

REFLECTION (NE/0922-4238) [18735555] **4990**

REFLECTION (NEW HAVEN) (US/0362-0611) [01971276] **4990**

REFLECTIONS (AT/0156-7799) [I01567799] 1777, **3530**

REFLECTIONS (CHAMPAIGN, ILL.) (US/0739-9448) [09846351] **307**

REFLECTIONS (CORPUS CHRISTI, TEX.) (US/0732-488X) [05867882] **2469**

REFLECTIONS (INDIANAPOLIS, IND.) (US/0885-8144) [05065657] 5236, **3868**

REFLECTIONS (LONDON, ONT.) (CN/0824-5517) [10676912] **1843**

REFLECTIONS (LOS ANGELES) (US/0272-1368) [06772227] **3725**

REFLECTIONS (NORTH BATTLEFORD. 1976) (CN/0384-0697) [03245090] **3244**

REFLECTIONS (OKLAHOMA CITY) (US/0098-9223) [02242560] **3801**

REFLECTIONS ON CANADIAN LITERACY : RCL **SUSPENDED.** (CN/1180-1239) [22193016] 1903, **1884**

REFLECTIONS ON HIGHER EDUCATION (UK/0954-2396) [24161035] **1843**

REFLECTIONS ON REALITY (US/1055-1581) [23096306] **4990**

REFLECTIONS ON SPACE (US/0883-5837) [10326360] **33**

REFLECTIONS (ORILLIA) (CN/1184-6305) [24266592] **3428**

REFLECTIONS (TAZEWELL, TENN.) (US/1071-0515) [19087384] **2756**

REFLECTIONS ... : THE WANDERER REVIEW OF LITERATURE, CULTURE, THE ARTS (US) [11381429] **4990**

REFLECTOR (1983), THE (US/0893-3286) [09867061] **5701**

REFLECTOR (AMARILLO, TEX.), THE (US/0484-2685) [07627518] **2469**

REFLECTOR DEN BOSCH (NE/0927-2704) [I09272704] 2705, **5255**

REFLECTOR (UNIVERSITY PARK, MD.), THE (US/0739-7356) [08353806] **3315**

REFLET (CN/0227-4558) [07802217] **5391**

REFLET D'AMOS, LE (CN/0707-5529) [04746855] **5793**

REFLET DE MON MILIEU (CN/0229-3560) [08078744] **5793**

REFLET DE TADOUSSAC (CN/0821-1728) [09770517] **2544**

REFLET (EMBRUN, ONT.) (CN/0833-8116) [15141228] **2544**

REFLET (HULL) (CN/1181-8565) [25314184] **1777**

REFLET TEMISCAMIEN, LE (CN/1186-2025) [24267046] **5793**

REFLETS DE LA PHILATELIE AU QUEBEC (CN/0383-1132) [03202236] **2787**

REFLETS DE L'ECONOMIE FRANC-COMTOISE (FR/0395-904X) [06288455] **1516**

REFLETS DU NORD (CN/1181-7372) [23236380] **2756**

REFLETS ET PERSPECTIVES DE LA VIE ECONOMIQUE (BE/0034-2971) [02822152] **1639**

REFLEX (SEATTLE, WASH.) (US/1054-3465) [15465127] **329**

REFLEXION (MONTREAL) (CN/0710-3638) [08794518] **1094**

REFLEXIONES (SANTA FE, N.M.) (US/1040-0265) [18299834] **5490**

REFORM (AT) [02588348] **3037**

REFORM (UK/0306-7262) [06060672] **5067**

REFORM JUDAISM (US/0482-0819) [03994936] **5052**

REFORMA **See** REFORMA NEWSLETTER **3244**

REFORMA AGRARIA (BL/0102-1184) [01795839] **125**

REFORMA ECONOMICA HOY (US/1058-7632) [24368065] **1516**

REFORMA NEWSLETTER (US/0891-8880) [05712711] **3244**

REFORMATION AND REVIVAL (US) **4990**

●REFORMATION & REVIVAL JOURNAL (US/1071-7277) [26139270] **4990**

REFORMATION REVIEW, THE **SUSPENDED.** (US/0034-303X) [01763620] **5019**

REFORMATION TODAY (UK/0034-3048) [06342965] **4990**

REFORMATIONSGESCHICHTLICHE STUDIEN UND TEXTE (GW/0080-0473) [01763621] **5035**

REFORMATUSOK LAPJA (HU) [07436354] **5067**

REFORMED LITURGY AND MUSIC (US/0362-0476) [08834524] 4149, **4990**

REFORMED PERSPECTIVE (CN/0714-8208) [09088986] **4990**

REFORMED REVIEW (HOLLAND, MICH.) (US/0034-3064) [01604531] **4990**

REFORMED THEOLOGICAL REVIEW, THE (AT/0034-3072) [01776679] **4990**

REFORMED WORLD (SZ/0034-3056) [01763623] **4990**

REFORMED WORSHIP (US/0890-8583) [14407647] **4990**

REFORMER (EDMONTON) (CN/0842-3148) [19298795] **4493**

REFORMING THE HEALTH CARE SYSTEM : STATE PROFILES / SUSAN OEHME RAETZMAN (US) [24149470] **4798**

REFRACTIVE & CORNEAL SURGERY (US/1042-962X) [19215323] **3878**

REFRACTORIES (BUREAU OF THE CENSUS) **CEASED.** (US/0161-0406) [02541413] **4441**

REFRACTORIES (NEW YORK) (US/0034-3102) [02131402] **4017**

REFRACTORY GIRL (AT/0310-4168) [04304441] **5565**

REFRACTORY MATERIALS (US/0080-049X) [01716874] **2149**

REFRESHER COURSES IN ANESTHESIOLOGY (US/0363-471X) [02411440] **3684**

REFRIGERATED & FROZEN FOODS (US/1061-6152) [25380339] **2355**

REFRIGERATED TRANSPORTER (US/0034-3129) [08899345] **5391**

REFRIGERATION (US) [01763626] **2608**

REFRIGERATION AND AIR CONDITIONING (CROYDON, ENGLAND : 1988) (UK) [18727530] **2608**

REFRIGERATION AND AIR CONDITIONING YEAR BOOK (UK) [19918044] **2608**

REFRIGERATION SERVICE & CONTRACTING (US) [23250989] **2608**

REFUAH VETERINARITH **See** ISRAEL JOURNAL OF VETERINARY MEDICINE **5512**

REFUGE (TORONTO. ENGLISH EDITION) (CN/0229-5113) [08507280] **5304**

REFUGEE ABSTRACTS *See* REFUGEE SURVEY QUARTERLY **1921**

REFUGEE ABSTRACTS : A PUBLICATION OF THE INTERNATIONAL REFUGEE INTEGRATION RESOURCE CENTRE (SZ/0253-1445) [09491528] **1921**

REFUGEE COMMUNITY NEWS (UK/0957-7858) [I09577858] **1921**

REFUGEE ISSUES (UK/0951-113X) [I0951113X] **1921**

REFUGEE REPORTS (US/0884-3554) [06640524] **1921**

REFUGEE RESETTLEMENT PROGRAM (US/0735-8334) [08978057] **5304**

●REFUGEE SURVEY QUARTERLY (SZ) [30697301] **1921**

REFUGEE UPDATE ENGLISH ED (CN/0251-6500) [I02516500] **4512**

REFUGEES & HUMAN RIGHTS NEWSLETTER (US/0195-5276) [05619614] **1921**

REFUGEES - UNITED NATIONS HIGH COMMISSIONER FOR REFUGEES (SZ/0252-791X) [10530451] **1921**

REFUND EXPRESS (US/0896-7350) [17283705] **2492**

REFUNDING MAKES CENTS (US) **2492**

REFUNDING UPDATE (US/0736-1688) [09091828] **1299**

REFUNDLE BUNDLE (US/0194-0139) [05297813] **1299**

REFUSE HAULING WAGE SURVEY, RIVERSIDE-SAN BERNARDINO-ONTARIO, CALIF. / U.S. DEPARTMENT OF LABOR, BUREAU OF LABOR STATISTICS (US) [09399057] **1705**

REFUSE NEWS (US) **2241**

REGAN REPORT ON HOSPITAL LAW, THE (US/0034-317X) [02312761] 3792, **3037**

REGAN REPORT ON MEDICAL LAW (US/0034-3188) [03372374] 3633, **3037**

REGAN REPORT ON NURSING LAW, THE (US/0034-3196) [01278817] **3868**

REGARD NOUVEAU (CN/0823-6631) [09951405] **5793**

REGARD SUR LA BIBLIOTHEQUE DU COLLEGE DE L'ASSOMPTION (CN/0822-6983) [10620216] **3244**

REGARDIE'S *CEASED.* (US/0279-5965) [07107829] 706, **4846**

REGARDS (CENTRE COMMUNAUTAIRE LAIC JUIF, BRUSSELS, BELGIUM) (BE) [07134023] **2705**

REGARDS SUR ISRAEL (MONTREAL) (CN/0384-9120) [02719328] **4493**

REGARDS SUR L'ACTUALITE (FR/0337-7091) [02240077] **4679**

REGARDS SUR L'ILE-DE-FRANCE / INSTITUT NATIONAL DE LA STATISTIQUE ET DES ETUDES ECONOMIQUES, DIRECTION REGIONALE DE PARIS (FR) [18633923] **1516**

REGATE INTERNATIONAL PARIS. (1987) (FR/0989-6961) [I09896961] **595**

REGATTA (UK) 595, **4914**

REGELSAMLING FOR STTEARET ... (DK) [09960119] **1903**

REGELUNGS TECHNIK (GW) [04574397] **1221**

REGELUNGSTECHNIK (DUSSELDORF, GERMANY) (GW/0340-3955) [10595400] **2127**

REGENERATION *CEASED.* (US/8756-3002) [11541731] **125**

REGENSBURGER BEITRAEGE ZUR DEUTSCHEN SPRACH- UND LITERATURWISSENSCHAFT: REIHE B, UNTERSUCHUNGEN (GW/0170-8872) [02846230] **3428**

REGENSBURGER MATHEMATISCHE SCHRIFTEN (GW/0179-9746) [I01799746] **3530**

REGENSBURGER TRICHTER, DER (GW/0930-4967) [I09304967] **3530**

REGENT PARK COMMUNITY NEWS (CN/0704-7053) [03797346] **5793**

REGENT PARK T.O.! (CN/1185-1872) [24257154] **5793**

REGENT UNIVERSITY LAW REVIEW (US/1056-3962) [23703674] **3037**

REGENTS ... PROGRESS REPORT ON THE REGENTS STATEWIDE PLAN FOR THE DEVELOPMENT OF POSTSECONDARY EDUCATION IN NEW YORK STATE, THE (US) [23455434] **1843**

●REGENTS ... STATEWIDE PLAN FOR HIGHER EDUCATION IN NEW YORK STATE, THE (US) [27355061] **1843**

REGERINGENS BERATTELSE TILL RIKSDAGEN OM UTVECKLINGSSAMARBETET (FI/0782-7881) [19770792] 2911, **1516**

REGESZETI DOLGOZATOK (HU/0521-4785) [I05214785] **280**

REGFILE-SYSTEM (US) **2180**

REGFILE SYSTEM SERVICE FOR WMD (US) **2180**

REGGAE REPORT (US/1065-3023) [20512160] **4149**

REGGAE YEARBOOK (US) **4149**

REGGEBOGE, DER (US/0034-3269) [01855408] **2756**

REGIE AUTONOME DES TRANSPORTS PARISIENS. DIRECTION DES ETUDES GENERALES *See* BULLETIN DE DOCUMENTATION ET D'INFORMATION - DIRECTION DES ETUDES GENERALES **5430**

REGIE DE L'ASSURANCE-DEPOTS DU QUEBEC *See* RAPPORT ANNUEL - REGIE DE L'ASSURANCE-DEPOTS DU QUEBEC **806**

REGIE DES ENTREPRISES DE CONSTRUCTION DU QUEBEC *See* RAPPORT ANNUEL ... / REGIE DES ENTREPRISES DE CONSTRUCTION DU QUEBEC **625**

REGIE DES LOTERIES DU QUEBEC *See* RAPPORT ANNUEL / REGIE DES LOTERIES DU QUEBEC **4678**

REGIE DES PERMIS D'ALCOOL DU QUEBEC *See* RAPPORT ANNUEL / REGIE DES PERMIS D'ALCOOL DU QUEBEC **4678**

REGIE DES RENTES DU QUEBEC *See* RAPPORT ANNUEL, REGIME DES ALLOCATIONS FAMILIALES DU QUEBEC **5303**

REGIE DES RENTES DU QUEBEC *See* RAPPORT ANNUEL - REGIE DES RENTES DU QUEBEC **2891**

REGIME DELLE IMPORTAZIONI, ESPORTAZIONI E NORME VALUTARIE (IT/1120-6535) [11206535] **1639**

REGIME DISCIPLINAIRE DES AGENTS DES ETABLISSEMENTS SANITAIRES ET SOCIAUX PUBLICS (FR) **4798**

REGINA (CN/0315-212X) [02443115] **2544**

REGINA - CITY OF REGINA (CN/0821-7769) [09951362] **2756**

REGINA FRIENDSHIP CENTRE *See* REGINA FRIENDSHIP CENTRE NEWSLETTER **5304**

REGINA FRIENDSHIP CENTRE NEWSLETTER (CN/0317-5782) [02248255] **5304**

REGINA MAGAZINE (CN/0704-6685) [03979917] **5490**

REGINA. ROSS INDUSTRIAL PARK (CN/0710-1821) [08205754] **2833**

REGINA THIS MONTH (CN/0713-5777) [09029863] **2574**

REGIO (IT) **1516**

REGIO MAGAZIN (GW) **2492**

REGION 1 SUBMISSION TO THE GOVERNMENT OF PRINCE EDWARD ISLAND (CN/0822-4250) [09816148] **125**

REGION EXPORTA, LA (SP) [02349635] **849**

REGION II REPORT (US) [03457194] **2203**

REGION TOMORROW, THE (US) [24401546] **2833**

REGION (WASHINGTON, D.C.), THE (US/0732-586X) [07340846] 4679, **2833**

●REGIONAL AIR INTERNATIONAL (US/1070-065X) [28261567] **33**

REGIONAL AIRLINE DIRECTORY, THE (US) [25721962] **33**

REGIONAL ANESTHESIA (US/0146-521X) [02973140] **3684**

REGIONAL AVIATION WEEKLY (US/1044-9450) [15034542] **33**

REGIONAL BIBLIOGRAPHY SERIES (AT) **1410**

REGIONAL BUSINESS REVIEW (US/8755-1977) [10626237] **849**

REGIONAL CABLE REPORT, THE *CEASED.* (US) [17375603] **1162**

REGIONAL CALENDAR (US) **1087**

REGIONAL CANCER TREATMENT *CEASED.* (GW/0935-0411) [18883784] **3823**

REGIONAL CATALOGUE OF EARTHQUAKES (UK/0034-334X) [01868041] **1410**

REGIONAL CENTRE FOR BOOK PROMOTION IN AFRICA *See* BULLETIN OF INFORMATION - REGIONAL CENTRE FOR BOOK PROMOTION IN AFRICA **4827**

REGIONAL COLLEGE OF EDUCATION, MYSORE *See* RESEARCH REPORTS IN EDUCATION **1904**

REGIONAL CONFERENCE SERIES IN MATHEMATICS (US/0160-7642) [01606611] **3530**

REGIONAL COTTON VARIETY TESTS (US/0193-9513) [05294123] **184**

REGIONAL DE DRUMMONDVILLE (CN/0711-4834) [08569926] **5793**

REGIONAL DELIGHT (NO/0802-1473) [20937234] **3661**

REGIONAL DEVELOPER (AT) [05987257] **2833**

REGIONAL DEVELOPMENT COMMUNICATOR (PH) [10413327] **1623**

REGIONAL DEVELOPMENT DIALOGUE (JA/0250-6505) [06963121] **2833**

REGIONAL DEVELOPMENT JOURNAL, THE (AT) [16732357] **2833**

REGIONAL DEVELOPMENT NEWS (NZ) [09637327] **2833**

REGIONAL DIRECTORY - CAPITAL AREA PLANNING COUNCIL (US/0740-4611) [07782115] **4679**

REGIONAL DIRECTORY OF MINORITY & WOMEN-OWNED BUSINESS FIRMS (CENTRAL ED.) (US/1047-7799) [20780157] **706**

REGIONAL DIRECTORY OF MINORITY AND WOMEN-OWNED BUSINESS FIRMS (EASTERN ED.) (US/1047-7802) [20780488] **706**

REGIONAL DIRECTORY OF MINORITY & WOMEN-OWNED BUSINESS FIRMS. (WESTERN EDITION) (US/0886-3946) [12921615] 5565, **706**

REGIONAL ECHO, THE (CN/0319-1656) [02442226] **5793**

REGIONAL ECONOMIC CO-OPERATION SERIES *CEASED.* (US/0082-8122) [01580504] **1516**

REGIONAL ECONOMIC PROJECTIONS SERIES (US/0090-9262) [01785323] **1516**

REGIONAL ECONOMIES AND MARKETS (US/0896-2537) [14953116] **1516**

●REGIONAL ECONOMIST, THE (US) [27372235] **807**

REGIONAL EDUCATIONAL BUILDING INSTITUTE FOR AFRICA *See* LETTRE **1761**

REGIONAL FIRMS' RETAIL SALES MANAGEMENT REPORT (US) **935**

REGIONAL FURNITURE (UK/0953-0800) [I09530800] 635, **252**

REGIONAL IMMUNOLOGY *CEASED.* (US/0896-0623) [16898492] **3676**

REGIONAL INDUSTRIAL BUYING GUIDE (US) [17244159] **1623**

REGIONAL INDUSTRIAL BUYING GUIDE BY STANDARD INDUSTRIAL CLASSIFICATION CODE. UPSTATE NEW YORK (US/1059-9924) [24788228] **1623**

REGIONAL INDUSTRIAL BUYING GUIDE. CAPITAL CITIES (US/1042-5489) [17004254] 951, **1624**

REGIONAL INDUSTRIAL BUYING GUIDE. GREATER ALLEGHENY (US/1042-5497) [16932109] 951, **1624**

REGIONAL INDUSTRIAL BUYING GUIDE. GREATER DELAWARE VALLEY (US/1042-5500) [16828778] 951, **1624**

REGIONAL INDUSTRIAL BUYING GUIDE. GREATER NEW YORK (US/1042-5519) [17742602] 951, **1624**

REGIONAL INDUSTRIAL BUYING GUIDE. NORTH CENTRAL TRI-STATE (US/1042-5527) [17622373] 951, **1624**

REGIONAL INDUSTRIAL BUYING GUIDE. NORTHERN OHIO (US/1042-5551) [16652227] 951, **1624**

REGIONAL INDUSTRIAL BUYING GUIDE. OHIO VALLEY (US/1042-556X) [16903134] **1624**

REGIONAL INDUSTRIAL BUYING GUIDE. UPSTATE NEW YORK (US/1058-2088) [22757922] 1624, **2128**

REGIONAL INDUSTRIAL BUYING GUIDE. WESTERN NEW ENGLAND (US/1042-5586) [17687732] 951, **1624**

REGIONAL INFORMATION SERVICE (US/0734-2942) [08710968] **1580**

REGIONAL INFORMATION SERVICE. NORTH CENTRAL REGION (US/0734-2985) [08710878] **1580**

REGIONAL INFORMATION SERVICE. NORTHEAST REGION (US/0734-2977) [08710906] **1580**

REGIONAL INFORMATION SERVICE. SOUTHERN REGION (US/0734-2950) [08710934] **1580**

REGIONAL INFORMATION SERVICE. WESTERN REGION (US/0734-2969) [08710922] **1580**

REGIONAL INSTITUTE OF HIGHER EDUCATION AND DEVELOPMENT *See* BULLETIN - REGIONAL INSTITUTE OF HIGHER EDUCATION AND DEVELOPMENT **1813**

REGIONAL JOURNAL OF SOCIAL ISSUES (AT/0158-7102) [08342757] **5255**

REGIONAL (KENORA) (CN/0827-2611) [11734725] **2544**

REGIONAL LABOR MARKET REVIEW. ATLANTIC COASTAL REGION (US) [11544304] **1705**

REGIONAL LABOR MARKET REVIEW. SOUTHERN NEW JERSEY REGION (US) [11795764] **1705**

Alphabetical Title Index — REGISTRY

REGIONAL NEWS (CAYUGA) (CN/0704-0261) [03956479] **5794**

REGIONAL NEWS (LA CROSSE, IND.) (US) [16000324] **5666**

REGIONAL NEWSPAPER, THE (CN/0712-1083) [08651996] **5794**

REGIONAL NIAGARA INDUSTRIAL DIRECTORY (CN/0826-5046) [11245804] **1624**

REGIONAL OCCUPATIONAL CENTERS AND PROGRAMS *CEASED.* (US/0361-8102) [02247138] **1915**

REGIONAL OUTLOOK, SOUTHEAST ASIA (SI/0218-3056) [26114066] **2663**

REGIONAL PAPERS - NATIONAL INSTITUTE OF ECONOMIC AND SOCIAL RESEARCH (UK) [02530031] **1516**

REGIONAL PLAN NEWS (US/0034-3374) [01908716] 2833, **4679**

REGIONAL PLANNING COUNCIL (MD.) *See* OUR ... YEAR / REGIONAL PLANNING COUNCIL **2830**

REGIONAL POLITICS & POLICY (UK) [24331331] **4493**

REGIONAL PROFILES (US/0362-3713) [02290575] **5255**

REGIONAL REFLECTIONS (CN/0715-5050) [09336492] **4679**

REGIONAL REPORT ON TOP MANAGEMENT COMPENSATION (US/1056-9561) [23882519] 1705, **884**

REGIONAL RESEARCH REPORT - OHIO AGRICULTURAL RESEARCH AND DEVELOPMENT CENTER (US) [03985263] **125**

REGIONAL REVIEW (BOSTON, MASS.) (US/1062-1865) [22746138] **807**

REGIONAL REVIEW NEWSLETTER (CN/0824-6556) [10862203] **2833**

REGIONAL SCIENCE AND URBAN ECONOMICS (NE/0166-0462) [01334639] 1516, **2833**

REGIONAL SCIENCE AND URBAN ECONOMICS [MICROFORM] (US/0166-0462) [23020576] **2833**

REGIONAL SCIENCE PERSPECTIVES (US/0097-1197) [01763634] **1516**

REGIONAL SCIENCE RESEARCH INSTITUTE *See* MONOGRAPH SERIES - REGIONAL SCIENCE RESEARCH INSTITUTE **1506**

REGIONAL SCIENCE RESEARCH INSTITUTE *See* BIBLIOGRAPHY SERIES - REGIONAL SCIENCE RESEARCH INSTITUTE **1530**

REGIONAL SCIENCE RESEARCH INSTITUTE *See* RSRI ABSTRACTS **2834**

REGIONAL SCIENCE RESEARCH INSTITUTE *See* RSRI DISCUSSION PAPER SERIES **5149**

REGIONAL SERVICES OUTLOOK (US/8755-2779) [11218249] **1580**

REGIONAL STUDIES (UK/0034-3404) [01763635] **5215**

REGIONAL STUDIES (INSTITUTE OF REGIONAL STUDIES (ISLAMABAD, PAKISTAN)) (PK/0254-7988) [11411693] **2833**

REGIONAL SURVEYS OF THE WORLD (UK) **1929**

REGIONAL TELEGRAPH, THE (CN/0317-5847) [02248256] **5794**

REGIONAL THEATRE DIRECTORY (US/1041-9411) [11937012] **5367**

REGIONAL TOPICS (US/0361-0691) [01908532] **2833**

REGIONAL TOURISM MONITOR (AT) [16934398] **5490**

REGIONAL TRENDS / CENTRAL STATISTICAL OFFICE (UK) [07446429] **5337**

REGIONALE WEST (US/1040-1377) [18333114] **307**

REGIONALISIERTE SCHULERPROGNOSEN (GW) [06072105] 1777, **1796**

REGIONALNAIA I GENETICHESKAIA MINERALOGIIA (UN) [05140531] **1444**

REGIONALSTRUKTUR BADEN-WURTTEMBERG: GEMEINDEN (GW) [06805787] **5337**

REGIONE E GOVERNO LOCALE (IT/0393-7437) [I03937437] **4679**

REGIONER. FLLESSKABETS KONOMISKE BISTAND TIL INVESTERINGER / REGIONEN. FINANZBEITRAEGE DER GEMEINSCHAFT FUER INVESTITIONEN / REGIONS. THE COMMUNITY'S FINANCIAL PARTICIPATION IN INVESTMENTS (LU) [15323708] **912**

REGIONI / I.S.G.R.E., ISTITUTO DI STUDI GIURIDICI REGIONALI, LE (IT) [01796140] **4493**

REGIONI IN CIFRE, LE (IT) [03603546] **5337**

REGION'S AGENDA, THE (US/0034-3420) [01855506] 1516, **2833**

REGISTAR JUGOSLOVENSKE PRIVREDE (YU) [02676643] **1580**

REGISTER AND FIRM INDEX / THE ALBERTA ASSOCIATION OF ARCHITECTS (CN/1182-6606) [23231545] **307**

REGISTER AND MANUAL - STAGE OF CONNECTICUT (US/0270-6245) [06464114] **4679**

REGISTER CITIZEN (US/0746-8180) [10310442] **5646**

REGISTER (CORPUS CHRISTI, TEX.) *See* REFLECTIONS (CORPUS CHRISTI, TEX.) **2469**

REGISTER-GUARD, THE (US/0739-8557) [09836354] **5734**

REGISTER HERALD (MILLBROOK, N.Y.) (US) [11151367] **5720**

REGISTER (KANSAS CITY, MO.), THE (US/0899-3572) [18082734] **220**

REGISTER (MONTREAL, 1980) (CN/0226-7586) [06515043] **2627**

REGISTER-NEWS (BORDENTOWN, N.J.) (US) [12533214] **5711**

REGISTER / NORTH CAROLINA STATE BOARD OF CERTIFIED PUBLIC ACCOUNTANT EXAMINERS (US) [03865754] **750**

REGISTER (OELWEIN, IOWA) *See* DAILY REGISTER (OELWEIN, IOWA) **5669**

REGISTER OF AMERICAN YACHTS (US/1045-0416) [19980276] **595**

REGISTER OF AUSTRALIAN MINING (AT) [06237115] **2149**

REGISTER OF CANADIAN HONOURS, THE (CN/1185-4235) [24623667] **2469**

REGISTER OF CANADIAN HONOURS, THE (CN/1185-4235) [24623668] **2469**

REGISTER OF CERTIFIED PUBLIC ACCOUNTANTS AND PUBLIC ACCOUNTANTS REGISTERED TO PRACTICE IN CONNECTICUT (US) [05430948] **750**

REGISTER OF CERTIFIED PUBLIC ACCOUNTANTS AND RULES AND REGULATIONS *See* ANNUAL REGISTER, CERTIFIED PUBLIC ACCOUNTANTS **738**

REGISTER OF COMMISSIONED AND WARRANT OFFICERS OF THE UNITED STATES NAVY AND MARINE CORPS (US) [01777246] **4182**

REGISTER OF COMMISSIONED AND WARRANTED OFFICERS OF THE COAST GUARD RESERVE *See* REGISTER OF RESERVE OFFICERS **4182**

REGISTER OF COMMONWEALTH STATISTICAL COLLECTIONS (AT/0818-3856) [26522688] **423**

REGISTER OF EDUCATIONAL RESEARCH IN THE UNITED KINGDOM (UK) [05257214] **1777**

REGISTER OF FORMER CADETS. SUPPLEMENT (US/0743-1449) [10539394] **4055**

REGISTER OF GRADUATES AND FORMER CADETS OF THE UNITED STATES MILITARY ACADEMY (US/0090-2357) [01643305] **4055**

REGISTER OF INDEXERS (US/0149-4694) [03005207] **3244**

REGISTER OF MEMBERS - FACULTY OF BUILDING (UK) [01784732] **626**

REGISTER OF NATIONAL CERTIFIED COUNSELORS (US/0886-277X) [12878109] **5304**

● REGISTER OF NORTH AMERICAN HOSPITALS (US/1062-7340) [25719789] **3792**

REGISTER OF OFFICERS - COAST GUARD (US/0364-8753) [02671762] **4182**

REGISTER OF OFFSHORE UNITS, SUBMERSIBLES & DIVING SYSTEMS (UK) [03779932] **5455**

REGISTER OF POST-GRADUATE DISSERTATIONS IN PROGRESS IN HISTORY AND RELATED SUBJECTS (CN/0068-8088) [02593639] **2627**

REGISTER OF REPORTING LABOR ORGANIZATIONS (US/0565-9310) [03357980] **1705**

REGISTER OF RESERVE OFFICERS (US/0147-8982) [03137427] **4182**

REGISTER OF RETIREMENT BENEFIT PLANS REPORTED UNDER THE WELFARE AND PENSION PLANS DISCLOSURE ACT (US/0091-357X) [01786763] 2891, **1705**

REGISTER OF SHIPS (LLOYD'S REGISTER OF SHIPPING) (UK/0141-4909) [05576993] **5455**

REGISTER OF THE AMERICAN SADDLEBRED HORSE ASSOCIATION (INCORPORATED), THE (US/0736-0134) [08264831] **2802**

REGISTER OF THE KENTUCKY HISTORICAL SOCIETY, THE (US/0023-0243) [02263214] **2756**

REGISTER OF THE SPENCER MUSEUM OF ART, THE (US/0733-866X) [05062886] 363, **4095**

REGISTER OF VALVES (UK) 626, 2868, **4276**

REGISTER OP DE STAATSCOURANT EN HET STAATSBLAD (NE) [18858643] **423**

REGISTER OVER GALLANDE SFS-FORFATTNINGAR (SW) [01794992] **3244**

REGISTER PLANNED EMERGENCY PRODUCERS (US/0094-1905) [04055242] **4055**

REGISTER (SHREWSBURY, N.J.), THE (US/0884-4704) [12383583] **5711**

REGISTER / SOUTH DAKOTA, LEGISLATIVE RESEARCH COUNCIL (US) [31048296] **3037**

REGISTER STAR (US/0747-2374) [10649538] **5720**

REGISTER VAN SIELKUNDLIGES EN PSIGOTEGNICI VIR DIE REPUBLIEK VAN SUID-AFRIKA (SA) [08037058] **4615**

REGISTER - WASHINGTON STATE BOARD OF ACCOUNTANCY (US) [03804778] **750**

REGISTERED HOLSTEIN TYPE-PRODUCTION SIRE SUMMARIES (US) [22163630] **220**

REGISTERED MOTOR VEHICLES (PP) [01795334] **5424**

REGISTERED NURSE (TORONTO) (CN/0840-8831) [19743434] **3868**

REGISTERED PHYSICIANS IN THE STATE OF NEVADA (US) [08732273] **3917**

REGISTERED PRIVATE VOCATIONAL SCHOOLS (CN/0822-0956) [11640017] **1915**

REGISTERED PROFESSIONAL SANITARIANS ... ROSTER (US) [11905183] **2241**

REGISTERED REPRESENTATIVE, THE (US/0193-1865) [05162086] **912**

REGISTERED TRADE UNIONS IN SOUTH AFRICA (SA/0377-3485) [02241058] **1705**

REGISTERS AND DIRECTORY - ROYAL COLLEGE OF VETERINARY SURGEONS (UK/0305-6643) [03225003] **5520**

REGISTR PERIODICHESKIKH IZDANII STRAN-CHLENOV MTSNTI. CHAST I: NUMERATSIONNYI RIAD (RU) [04280131] **423**

REGISTR PERIODICHESKIKH IZDANII STRAN-CHLENOV MTSNTI. CHAST II: VSPOMOGATELNYE UKAZATELI (RU) [04215030] **2924**

REGISTRANTS, LOBBYISTS (US) [09652491] **4679**

REGISTRATION OF BIRTHS & DEATHS ACT. ANNUAL REPORT (II/0376-5288) [04050645] **4559**

REGISTRE-ANNUAIRE - MENSA CANADA (CN/0714-4261) [08774082] **5236**

REGISTRE CANADIEN DES INSUFFISANCES ET DES TRANSPLANTATIONS D'ORGANES *See* RAPPORT ... INSUFFISANCE RENALE AU CANADA **3992**

● REGISTRE CANADIEN DES PROPRIETES PATRIMONIALES, ... RAPPORT ANNUEL, LE (CN/1188-9551) [26289984] **4679**

REGISTRE DE L'ISDS ED. SUR BANDE MAGNETIQUE (FR/0256-8888) [I02568888] **3244**

REGISTRE DE L'ISDS (ED. SUR MICROFICHE) (FR/0257-2222) [05968529] 4832, **4819**

REGISTRERADE FORDON EFTER FABRIKAT DEN ... (SW) [10292792] **5424**

REGISTROVAIA KNIGA MORSKIKH SUDOV SSSR / REGISTR SOIUZA SSR REGISTER BOOK OF SEA-GOING SHIPS OF THE USSR / REGISTER OF SHIPPING OF THE USSR (RU) [08006303] **5455**

REGISTRY HANDBOOK. COMMON NAMES. MICROFORM (US) [06550548] **991**

REGISTRY HANDBOOK: NUMBER SECTION. SUPPLEMENT (US) [03269152] **991**

REGISTRY OF CHARITABLE ORGANIZATIONS (US) [05713971] **5304**

REGISTRY OF ENGINEERS AND LAND SURVEYORS AND REPORT OF THE STATE BOARD OF ENGINEERING EXAMINERS OF OREGON (US/0363-7034) [02534499] **1993**

REGISTRY OF MEMBERS - CLINICAL SOCIOLOGY ASSOCIATION (US/0733-0251) [08490890] **5255**

REGISTRY OF THE AMERICAN BOARD FOR CERTIFICATION IN ORTHOTICS AND PROSTHETICS, INC (US/0164-0526) [04552342] **3884**

REGISTRY OF TOXIC EFFECTS OF CHEMICAL SUBSTANCES [MICROFORM] (US/0361-2546) [04508155] 2868, **3983**

REGISTRY OF WOMEN IN RELIGIOUS STUDIES, A *SUSPENDED.* (US/0887-8331) [08158445] 5565, **4990**

REGLAMENTACION — Alphabetical Title Index

REGLAMENTACION DEL SECTOR LABORAL (SP) [03815517] **3153**

REGLEMENT OFFICIEL DE JEU POUR LA LIGUE CANADIENNE DE FOOTBALL (CN/0316-1536) [02248090] **4914**

REGLEMENTATION GENERALE, REGLES ET REGLEMENTS / FONDS MONETAIRE INTERNATIONAL *CEASED.* (US/0250-7315) [07585444] **1516**

REGLEMENTATION POUR LE TRANSPORT DES MARCHANDISES DANGEREUSES (CN/0256-3231) [12740303] **2180**

REGLEMENTS - A S T E D (CN/0384-5095) [03248001] **3245**

REGLEMENTS OFFICIELS / ASSOCIATION CANADIENNE D'ATHLETISME (CN/0710-4391) [08458452] **4914**

REGLEMENTS RELATIFS AUX PROGRAMMES - INSTITUT DES BANQUIERS CANADIENS (CN/0821-6088) [09743204] **807**

●REGLES BUDGETAIRES DU MINISTRE DES TRANSPORTS CONCERNANT LE TRANSPORT DES ELEVES (CN/1193-3836) [26888876] **4744**

●REGLES BUDGETAIRES POUR L'ANNEE SCOLAIRE ..., COMMISSION SCOLAIRE DU LITTORAL (CN) [26889193] **4744**, **1777**

●REGLES BUDGETAIRES POUR L'ANNEE SCOLAIRE ..., COMMISSION SCOLAIRE KATIVIK (CN) [26889202] **4744**, **1777**

●REGLES BUDGETAIRES POUR L'ANNEE SCOLAIRE ..., ECOLE DES NASKAPIS (CN) [26889214] **4744**, **1777**

REGLES DE CATALOGAGE ANGLO-AMERICAINE. VERSION FRANCAISE. BULLETIN (CN/0318-8000) [02443101] **3245**

REGLES DE L'ART HAUTE ET BASSE TENSION (FR) **2079**

REGLES DU JEU CANADIENNES POUR LE FOOTBALL AVEC PLAQUE (CN/1187-1865) [25423602] **4914**

REGMI RESEARCH SERIES (NP) [01642163] **2663**

REGNO, IL (IT/0034-3498) [03601347] **5035**

REGNSKABSRESULTATER FRA DANSKE LANDBRUG (DK) [04205818] **1516**, **125**

REGNUM VEGETABLE (GW/0080-0694) [01763640] **526**

REGROUPEMENT DES INFIRMIERES ET INFIRMIERS DU QUEBEC *See* SPECIAL NEGO **1711**

REGULAE BENEDICTI STUDIA (GW) [02058992] **4990**

REGULAR MEETING - BOARD OF MISSISSIPPI LEVEE COMMISSIONERS (US/0544-4462) [02776822] **4679**

●REGULATED CHEMICALS DIRECTORY (US/1058-1707) [24235938] **991**

REGULATED ELECTRIC STUDY (JEFFERSON CITY) (US/0093-0741) [01791935] **4679**

REGULATED RIVERS (UK/0886-9375) [13041400] **1359**

REGULATION OF INSURANCE (UK) **2891**

REGULATION UPDATE & OPERATING AUTHORITY BULLETIN *CEASED.* (CN/0849-2921) [23231193] **5391**

REGULATIONS AND SYLLABUSES : BUSINESS EDUCATION SINGLE SUBJECT AND GROUP CERTIFICATE EXAMINATIONS (UG) [02246926] **1777**, **706**

REGULATIONS IN THE AREAS OF TRANSPORT, LABELLING, CLASSIFICATION AND STORAGE, AFFECTING THE RECYCLING OF LEAD (UK) **2180**, **4017**

REGULATIONS / INTERNATIONAL SKATING UNION (SZ) [11975687] **4914**

REGULATIONS OF HONG KONG / INCLUDING PROCLAMATIONS, ORDERS IN COUNCIL, ETC. FOR THE YEAR ..., THE (HK) [01643829] **4679**

REGULATIONS OF THE CIVIL AERONAUTICS BOARD (US) [02782324] **33**

REGULATORY AFFAIRS (US/1043-2752) [19367661] **3792**

REGULATORY AFFAIRS BULLETIN (UK/0950-3374) [I09503374] **4327**

REGULATORY AFFAIRS JOURNAL (UK/0960-7889) [I09607889] **4327**, **3633**

●REGULATORY AFFAIRS JOURNAL (DEVICES), THE (UK) **4327**, **3633**

REGULATORY ALERT (US/0147-9091) [03245705] **3037**

REGULATORY ANALYST. MEDICAL WASTE (US/1065-1063) [26508462] **2241**, **3633**

REGULATORY AND TECHNICAL REPORTS (ABSTRACT INDEX JOURNAL) (US) [24252005] **2158**

REGULATORY COMPLIANCE UPDATE (US/1055-4122) [23167784] **2180**

REGULATORY COMPLIANCE WATCH (US/1064-4342) [26184907] **807**

REGULATORY EYE (US/0193-4686) [05211066] **4679**

REGULATORY FOCUS *CEASED.* (US) [10620730] **5145**

REGULATORY GUIDE / U.S. NUCLEAR REGULATORY COMMISSION, OFFICE OF STANDARDS DEVELOPMENT (US) [05542780] **2158**, **2868**

REGULATORY MONTHLY MINUTES (US) **4679**

REGULATORY PEPTIDES (NE/0167-0115) [06819454] **1047**

REGULATORY REPORTER (US/0194-0376) [05269771] **3116**

●REGULATORY TIMES, THE (CN/1193-1442) [25765121] **1954**

REGULATORY TOXICOLOGY AND PHARMACOLOGY (US/0273-2300) [07033938] **3983**, **4327**

REGULATORY UPDATE (PHILADELPHIA, PA.) (US/1065-1896) [26522635] **3037**

REGULATORY WATCHDOG SERVICE. ALERT BULLETIN (US/0275-0902) [07088827] **4679**

●REHAB & COMMUNITY CARE MANAGEMENT (CN/1192-2508) [28558047] **3633**

REHAB BRIEF (US/0732-2623) [08333936] **1884**

REHAB MANAGEMENT (US/0899-6237) [18161312] **4382**

REHAB PURCHASING GUIDE (US) [09216343] **951**

REHABILITACION (MADRID) (SP/0048-7120) [04206784] **4382**

REHABILITASIE IN SUID-AFRIKA (SA/0034-3501) [00990128] **3633**

REHABILITATION & HEALTHCARE MARKETING *CEASED.* (US) **5304**, **935**

REHABILITATION COUNSELING BULLETIN (US/0034-3552) [03128510] **1884**

REHABILITATION DIGEST (CN/0048-7139) [02131585] **4393**

REHABILITATION EDUCATION (ELMSFORD, N.Y.) (US/0889-7018) [14039568] **1884**

REHABILITATION GAZETTE (US/0361-4166) [02067312] **4393**

REHABILITATION INDEX / THE BRITISH LIBRARY, MEDICAL INFORMATION SERVICE (UK/0955-0984) [24148905] **4382**

REHABILITATION INSTITUTE OF MONTREAL. MEETING *See* PROCEEDINGS OF THE ... ANNUAL CONFERENCE / INSTITUT DE READAPTATION DE MONTREAL **4392**

REHABILITATION NURSING (US/0278-4807) [07154385] **3868**

REHABILITATION NURSING CONCEPTS & PRACTICE (US) **3868**

●REHABILITATION NURSING RESEARCH (US/1070-5767) [28399087] **4382**, **3868**

REHABILITATION PSYCHOLOGY (US/0090-5550) [01640879] **4382**, **4615**

REHABILITATION PUBLICATION (US/0065-9983) [04258673] **4327**

REHABILITATION R&D PROGRESS REPORTS (US/0882-7753) [11224158] **4382**

REHABILITATION (STUTTGART) (GW/0034-3536) [01587370] **3633**

REHABILITATION TECHNOLOGY (CN/1183-7454) [24690677] **3696**

REHABILITATION TECHNOLOGY (CN/1183-7454) [24690687] **3696**

REHABILITATION TODAY (US/1054-2280) [22787017] **3792**

REHABILITATION WORLD *CEASED.* (US/0360-0726) [02243972] **4393**

REHOVOT (IS) [02744649] **5145**

REI CRETARIAE ROMANAE FAUTORES *See* REI CRETARIAE ROMANAE FAUTORUM ACTA **2593**

REI CRETARIAE ROMANAE FAUTORUM ACTA (SZ/0484-3401) [02851963] **2593**

REI CRETARIAE ROMANAE FAUTORUM UBIQUE CONSISTENTIUM ACTA *See* REI CRETARIAE ROMANAE FAUTORUM ACTA **2593**

REICHENBACHIA / STAATLICHES MUSEUM FUER TIERKUNDE IN DRESDEN (GW/0070-7279) [02404786] **5613**

REICHSGETZBLATT *See* BUNDESGESETZBLATT **2945**

REICHSMINISTERIALBLATT : ZENTRALBLATT FUER DAS DEUTSCHE REICH / HERAUSSEGEBEN IM REICHSMINISTERIUM DES INNERN (GW) [09166747] **2705**

REIDEL TEXTS IN THE MATHEMATICAL SCIENCES (NE/0921-9315) [25188073] **3530**

●REID'S ADMINISTRATIVE LAW (CN/1196-5266) [28579059] **3037**

REID'S ADMINISTRATIVE LAW LETTER (CN/1183-708X) [25066650] **3037**

REID'S DIGEST OF ADMINISTRATIVE LAW *See* REID'S ADMINISTRATIVE LAW **3037**

REIDSVILLE REVIEW, THE (US) [13277377] **5724**

REIGN OF THE SACRED HEART (US/0048-7155) [03909136] **5035**

REIGOS Y DRENAJES XXI (SP/0213-3660) [19964874] **2095**

REIHE DER SCHRIFTEN - FREIES DEUTSCHES HOCHSTIFT (GW/0344-6786) [01380763] **3428**

REIHE GERMANISTISCHE LINGUISTIK (GW) [12093406] **3315**

REIHE INFORMATIK (GW/0941-9780) [I09419780] **1201**

REIHE SIEGEN (GW) [06037217] **3428**

REIMBURSEMENT ADVISOR (US/0884-2795) [12359137] **3792**

REIMBURSEMENT UPDATE SALT LAKE CITY, UTAH (US/1064-1548) [I10641548] **706**

REINARDUS : YEARBOOK OF THE INTERNATIONAL REYNARD SOCIETY (NE/0925-4757) [18276063] **3428**

REINBECK COURIER (US) [16083806] **5672**

REINE UND ANGEWANDTE METALLKUNDE IN EINZELDARSTELLUNGEN (GW/0080-0791) [01763650] **1993**

REINFORCED PLASTICS (LONDON) (UK/0034-3617) [02253236] **4460**

REINIGER + WASCHER (GW/0034-3625) [03647910] **5355**

REINRAUMTECHNIK *CEASED.* (GW/0931-9190) [I09319190] **5145**

REINSURANCE (UK/0048-7171) [04754825] **2891**

REINSURANCE DIGEST (US) [18719660] **2891**

REINSURANCE DIRECTORY (US/0747-5276) [10735389] **2891**

REINSURANCE LAW (UK) **2891**, **3037**

REINSURANCE LAW REPORTS (UK/0961-7264) [I09617264] **2891**, **3037**

REINSURANCE MARKET REPORT (UK/0266-8653) [I02668653] **2891**

REINSURANCE REPORTER (US/0034-3641) [15596588] **2891**

REINWARDTIA (IO/0034-365X) [01643277] **526**

REIS [COMPUTER FILE] : REGIONAL ECONOMIC INFORMATION SYSTEM (US) [24674014] **1516**

REISEVERKEHR DER SCHWEIZER IM AUSLAND (SZ) [03307039] **2574**

●REIT HANDBOOK : COMPLETE GUIDE TO THE REAL ESTATE INVESTMENT TRUST INDUSTRY (US) [28396390] **4846**

REIT HANDBOOK OF MEMBER TRUSTS (US) [01789802] **4846**, **912**

REIT SOURCEBOOK (US) [23152248] **4846**

REITEN UND FAHREN *CEASED.* (GW/0720-5104) **4914**

REITO (JA/0034-3714) [09733657] **2608**

REJASTHAN LIBRARY ASSOCIATION *See* QUARTERLY JOURNAL OF RLA **3243**

REJOICE! (UNIVERSITY, MISS.) *CEASED.* (US/1044-1034) [19687552] **4149**

REKAMAN PERISTIWA ... (IO) [09929762] **1516**, **5255**

REKAMAN SEJARAH (IO) [12099310] **4533**

REKINDLE (US/0193-7359) [05255487] **2292**

REKISHI HYORON (JA/0386-8907) [01763655] **2627**

REKISHI KORON (JA) [03082028] **2663**

REKISHI TO BUNKA (JA) [02245272] **2627**

REKISHIGAKU KENKYU (JA/0386-9237) [01696434] **2663**

REKISTERIIN MERKITYT UUDET MOOTTORIAJONEUVOT (FI) [02242850] **5424**

REKREAKSIE (NE/0166-2651) [I01662651] **4878**, **4854**

REKURIESHON KENKYU (JA) [09428587] **4854**

RELACAO DAS INDUSTRIAS COM MAIS DE 20 I.E. VINTE EMPREGADOS NO ESTADO DO RIO GRANDE DO SUL (BL) [02176663] **1580**

RELACAO DE AUTORIDADES - ASSESSORIA DE RELACOES PUBLICAS (BL) [02244465] **4679**

RELACION DE INGENIEROS DE CAMINOS, CANALES Y PUERTOS (SP) [01785494] **1993**

RELACION DE LOS INGENIEROS DE CAMINOS, CANALES Y PUERTOS (SP) [02242038] 626, **2030**

RELACIONES (AG) [07019253] **244**

RELACIONES / COLEGIO DE MICHOACAN (MX/0185-3929) [07077589] **2756**

RELACIONES DE LA SOCIEDAD ARGENTINA DE ANTROPOLOGIA (AG) [01696307] **244**

RELACIONES INTERNACIONALES (MX/0185-0814) [03689346] **4533**

RELACIONES LABORALES (SP/0213-0556) [I02130556] **1706**

RELACIONES MEXICO-ESTADOS UNIDOS, BIBLIOGRAFIA ANUAL (MX) [10253803] **4502**

RELAIS LOISIR (CN/0848-7413) [23598734] **388**

●RELATIONAL DATABASE JOURNAL (US/1074-6404) [28444393] **1255**

RELATIONAL JOURNAL *See* IT SPECTRUM **5117**

RELATIONS BETWEEN THE PEOPLE'S REPUBLIC OF CHINA AND I. FEDERAL REPUBLIC OF GERMAN, II. GERMAN DEMOCRATIC REPUBLIC IN ... AS SEEN BY XINHUA NEWS AGENCY : A DOCUMENTATION, THE (GW) [13873616] **4533**

RELATIONS ECOLES PROFESSIONS (FR/1143-354X) [1143354X] **1843**

RELATIONS INDUSTRIELLES / INDUSTRIAL RELATIONS (CN/0034-379X) [02131677] **1706**

RELATIONS INTERNATIONALES (FR/0335-2013) [03850733] **4533**

RELATIONS INTERNATIONALES ET STRATEGIQUES (FR/1157-5417) [24488499] **4533**

RELATIONS (MONTREAL) (CN/0034-3781) [01770924] **5035**

RELATIONS PUBLIQUES INFORMATIONS (FR/0034-3811) **765**

RELATIVE VALUE ANALYSIS (US/0162-0584) [04078182] **912**

RELATIVE VALUES FOR PHYSICIANS (US) **3917**

RELATIVELY SEEKING (US/0747-5624) [10735677] **2469**

RELATIVELY SPEAKING (EDMONTON) (CN/0701-8878) [04879800] **2469**

RELATORIO (BL) [18707010] **5145**

RELATORIO ANNUAL - SERVICO SOCIAL DO COMERCIO, ADMINISTRACAO REGIONAL NO ESTADO DO PARA (BL) [03339049] **5304**

RELATORIO ANUAL (BL) [05584038] **4451**

RELATORIO ANUAL (BL) [01792986] **807**

RELATORIO ANUAL (BL) [01786939] **5304**

RELATORIO ANUAL - ASSOCIACAO BRASILEIRA DA INDUSTRIA FARMACEUTICA (BL) [06457057] **4327**

RELATORIO ANUAL - BANERJ (BL) [06903040] **807**

RELATORIO ANUAL - COMISSAO NACIONAL DE ENERGIA NUCLEAR (BL) [05059004] **2158**

RELATORIO ANUAL DA DIRETORIA - ASSOCIACAO BRASILEIRA PARA O DESENVOLVIMENTO DAS INDUSTRIAS DE BASE (BL) [03197071] **1624**

RELATORIO ANUAL DA DIRETORIA - CETESB (BL) [03265475] **2241**

RELATORIO ANUAL DE ATIVIDADES (BL) [25590310] **5304**

RELATORIO ANUAL DE ATIVIDADES REFERENTE AO EXERCICIO DE . *See* RELATORIO ANUAL DE ATIVIDADES **5304**

RELATORIO ANUAL DE ATIVIDADES REFERENTE AO EXERCICIO DE ... / SERVICO SOCIAL DA INDUSTRIA, DEPARTAMENTO REGIONAL DO RIO GRANDE DO NORTE (BL) [08006526] **1706**

RELATORIO ANUAL DE ATIVIDADES REFERENTE AO EXERCICIO DE ... / SESI, DEPARTAMENTO REGIONAL DO ESTADO DO RIO DE JANEIRO (BL) [11028717] **1706**

RELATORIO ANUAL DE PESQUISA. HORTICULTURA / EMPRESA DE PESQUISA AGROPECUARIA DO CEARA (BL) [09403377] **2430**

RELATORIO ANUAL / INDI (BL) [26844656] **1624**

RELATORIO ANUAL / IRB (BL) [02697582] **2891**

RELATORIO ANUAL / MINISTERIO DA INDUSTRIA E DO COMERCIO, CONSELHO DE DESENVOLVIMENTO INDUSTRIAL, SECRETARIA EXECUTIVA (BL/0102-2504) [08969309] **4679**

RELATORIO ANUAL / SERVICO SOCIAL DO COMERCIO, ADMINISTRACAO NACIONAL (BL) [11701951] **5304**

RELATORIO ANUAL / SERVICO SOCIAL DO COMERCIO, ADMINISTRACAO REGIONAL DE MATO GROSSO (BL) [11039279] **1706**

RELATORIO ANUAL - SOCIEDADE BRASILEIRA DE CULTURA JAPONESA (BL) [04341184] **2756**

RELATORIO - BANERJ *See* RELATORIO ANUAL - BANERJ **807**

RELATORIO CELPE (BL) [03929996] **1624**

RELATORIO - CENAFOR (BL) [03076734] **1915**

RELATORIO - CEPISA (BL) [02241574] **2079**

RELATORIO - CONSELHO DE NAO-FERROSOS E DE SIDERURGIA (BL) [03921529] 4017, **1624**

RELATORIO - CONSELHO NACIONAL DE DESPORTOS (BL) [05591383] **4914**

RELATORIO DA ADMINISTRACAO - TELEBRAS (BL) [04844712] **1162**

RELATORIO DA DIRETORIA (BL) [02471448] **1624**

RELATORIO DA DIRETORIA - CORSAN (BL) [02239865] **2241**

RELATORIO DA DIRETORIA EXECUTIVA - COMPANHIA DE DENSENVOLVIMENTO DE DISTRITOS INDUSTRIAIS DO MARANHAO (BL) [03523166] **1580**

RELATORIO DA DIRETORIA / SAMRIG (BL) [11325756] **1624**

RELATORIO DA GESTAO / CONSELHO DE REITORES DAS UNIVERSIDADES BRASILEIRAS (BL) [17197726] **1843**

RELATORIO DA GESTAO DA DIRETORIA DO INSTITUTO DOS ADVOGADOS DO RIO GRANDE DO SUL (BL) [01799524] **3037**

RELATORIO DA PRESIDENCIA (BL) [01787601] **4419**

RELATORIO DA PRESIDENCIA REFERENTE AOS TRABALHOS DA ... / SENADO FEDERAL (BL) [07710763] **4679**

RELATORIO DAS ATIVIDADES ADMINISTRATIVAS (BL) [01787600] **4419**

RELATORIO DAS ATIVIDADES ADMINISTRATIVAS DA INSPETORIA-GERAL DE FINANCAS DO MINISTERIO DA FAZENDA (BL) [03107509] **4744**

RELATORIO DAS ATIVIDADES DA COMPANHIA DE HABITACAO DO ESTADO DE SANTA CATARINA (BL) [02441376] **2833**

RELATORIO DAS ATIVIDADES DE ... E PROGRAMACAO PARA ... (BL) [09934272] **4276**

RELATORIO DAS ATIVIDADES DO EXERCICIO DE ... (BL) [10293445] **849**

RELATORIO DAS ATIVIDADES - EMPRESA BRASILEIRA DE PLANEJAMENTO DE TRANSPORTES (BL) [04138266] **5391**

RELATORIO DE ACTIVIDADES (BL) [01791987] **1580**

RELATORIO DE ATIVADADES - SECRETARIA DE INFRA-ESTRUTURA REGIONAL E URBANA (BL) [07150991] **1624**

RELATORIO DE ATIVIDADES - BANCO DE DESENVOLVIMENTO DO CEARA (BL) [01789622] **807**

RELATORIO DE ATIVIDADES / BANCO DO ESTADO DO ACRE, S.A (BL) [11591070] **807**

RELATORIO DE ATIVIDADES / CONSELHO DE REITORES DAS UNIVERSIDADES BRASILEIRAS (BL) [26883160] **1844**

RELATORIO DE ATIVIDADES - FINANCIADORA DE ESTUDOS E PROJETOS (BL) [02302109] **807**

RELATORIO DE ATIVIDADES - FUNDACAO EDUCACIONAL PADRE LANDELL DE MOURA (BL) [05930424] **1777**

RELATORIO DE ATIVIDADES - FUNDACAO PARA O LIVRO DO CEGO NO BRASIL (BL) [06821557] **5304**

RELATORIO DE ATIVIDADES / GOVERNO DO ESTADO DA PARAIBA, SECRETARIA DOS TRANSPORTES E OBRAS (BL) [11951960] **5391**

RELATORIO DE ATIVIDADES - PETROBRAS INTERNACIONAL (BL) [03703856] **1624**

RELATORIO DE ATIVIDADES - SECRETARIA DE ADMINISTRACAO DO ESTADO DO ESPIRITO SANTO (BL) [02241903] **4679**

RELATORIO DE ATIVIDADES - SECRETARIA DE ESTADO DE ADMINISTRACAO (BL) [03306185] **4679**

RELATORIO DE ATIVIDADES - SECRETARIA DE TECNOLOGIA INDUSTRIAL (BL) [04544061] **5145**

RELATORIO DE ATIVIDADES - SERVICO SOCIAL DO COMERCIO, ADMINISTRACAO REGIONAL NO ESTADO DE GOIAS (BL) [02441354] **5304**

RELATORIO DE GESTAO / COMPANHIA DE SANEAMENTO DE MINAS GERAIS (BL) [28444652] **2241**

RELATORIO - DEPARTAMENTO REGIONAL DO MARANHAO, SENAI (BL) [03718686] **375**

RELATORIO - DIRECCAO PROVINCIAL DOS SERVICOS DE SAUDE E ASSISTENCIA (MZ/0254-0282) [04725749] **4798**

RELATORIO - EMPRESA DE TURISMO DA BAHIA (BL) [01792485] **5490**

RELATORIO ESTATISTICO (BL) [08438743] **4238**

RELATORIO ESTATISTICO DE INFORMACOES ECONOMICO-TRIBUTARIAS / GOVERNO DO ESTADO DE MINAS GERAIS, SECRETARIA DE ESTADO DA FAZENDA, DIRECTORIA DA RECEITA ESTADUAL, CENTRO DE INFORMACOES ECONOMICO-FISCAIS (BL) [09911785] 4744, **4699**

RELATORIO ESTATISTICO (SALVADOR, BRAZIL) (BL) [10790986] 3174, **3082**

RELATORIO ESTATISTICO - SERVICO DE ESTATISTICA POLICIAL E CRIMINAL (BL) [04258194] 3174, **3082**

RELATORIO - FUNDACAO PARA O LIVRO DO CEGO NO BRASIL *See* RELATORIO DE ATIVIDADES - FUNDACAO PARA O LIVRO DO CEGO NO BRASIL **5304**

RELATORIO - FUNDACAO ZOOBOTANICA DO RIO GRANDE DO SUL (BL) [02244916] **4171**

RELATORIO GERAL / SENAC, ADMINISTRACAO REGIONAL EM SERGIPE (BL) [11409070] **706**

RELATORIO / SENAI RS (BL) [09503890] **1706**

RELATORIO - SERVICO NACIONAL DE APRENDIZAGEM INDUSTRIAL, DEPARTAMENTO REGIONAL DO AMAZONAS (BL) [02999503] **1706**

RELATORIO - SERVICO NACIONAL DE APRENDIZAGEM INDUSTRIAL, DEPARTAMENTO REGIONAL DO PARANA (BL) [02241936] **1706**

RELATORIO SETORIAL, GOVERNO DO ESTADO DE SAO PAULO (BL) [06821301] **5304**

RELATORIO SINTETICO SOBRE O PROGRAMA DE IRRIGACAO DO NORDESTE (BL) [05144601] 184, **2095**

RELATORIO TECNICO ANUAL DE ... / COMISSAO NACIONAL DE ENERGIA NUCLEAR, INSTITUTO DE ENGENHARIA NUCLEAR (AG) [10345201] **2158**

RELATORIO TECNICO ANUAL DO CENTRO DE TECHNOLOGIA AGRICOLA E ALIMENTAR (BL) [09176132] **125**

RELATORIOS E COMUNICOES - INSTITUTO DE INVESTIGACAO CIENTIFICA DE ANGOLA (AO/0003-343X) [05693943] **5145**

RELAX (BANNOCKBURN, ILL.) (US/1058-4811) [11987549] 3633, **5490**

RELAY MINIATURE AND SUBMINIATURE D.A.T.A. BOOK (US/0095-0815) [01795815] **2079**

RELAZIONE DEL CONSIGLIO DIRETTIVO ALLA ASSEMBLEA GENERALE DEI SOCI (IT) [05367211] **1624**

RELAZIONE DELLA CORTE DEI CONTI AL PARLAMENTO SULLA GESTIONE FINANZIARIA DEGLI ENTI SOTTOPOSTI A CONTROLLO IN APPLICAZIONE DELLA LEGGE 21 MARZO 1958, N. 259 (IT) [10583201] 4798, **3037**

RELAZIONE GENERALE SULLA SITUAZIONE ECONOMICA DEL PAESE (IT/0075-1995) [02736778] **1516**

RELAZIONE PROVVISORIA DEL CONSIGLIO DIRETTIVO PER L'ANNO (IT) [08190866] **3134**

RELAZIONE SULLA SITUAZIONE ECONOMICA DELLA CALABRIA NEL / CENTRO DI STUDI E DI RICERCHE ECONOMICO-SOCIALI DELLA CALABRIA (IT) [21022095] **1516**

RELAZIONE SULL'ATTIVITA SVOLTA NEL ... (IT) [21022385] **1516**

RELAZIONI E BILANCIO / INA, ISTITUTO NAZIONALE DELLE ASSICURAZIONI (IT) [08414641] **2891**

RELAZIONI INTERNAZIONALI (IT/0034-3846) [04598414] **4533**

RELC JOURNAL (SI/0033-6882) [01906527] **3315**

RELEASE (AT/0157-3470) [I01573470] **3174**

RELEASE 1.0 (US/1047-935X) [12132222] 1289, **1239**

RELEASE (CALGARY) (CN/0229-9437) [08099380] **329**

RELEASE PRINT (US/0890-5231) [14256475] **4077**

RELEASE (VANCOUVER) (CN/1182-3976) [23242625] **4149**

RELEASES FROM JUVENILE INSTITUTIONS (1979) (US/0277-7282) [07518916] **3174**

RELEASING HORMONES (UK/0142-8314) [I01428314] **3733**

RELEVANT RESEARCH FOR SCHOOL DECISIONS / ERS *CEASED.* (US) [24233741] **1777**

RELEVE DES INSCRIPTIONS (CN/0827-8156) [13348667] 1844, **1796**

RELEVE DES NOUVEAUX INSCRITS (CN/0826-0974) [10805548] **1844**

RELEVE, LA (RW) [02661792] **2642**

RELIABILITY ANALYSIS CENTER (U.S.) *See* RAC NEWSLETTER **2006**

RELIABILITY ASSESSMENT (US/0898-3933) [16929212] 4762, **2079**

RELIABILITY ENGINEERING & SYSTEM SAFETY (UK/0951-8320) [17600845] 2868, **1993**

RELIABILITY PHYSICS (US/0735-0791) [03766693] **2079**

RELIABILITY REVIEW (MILWAUKEE, WIS.) (US/0277-9633) [07667827] **1993**

RELIA+IBLE (US) [17164226] **4846**

RELICS (US/0034-3897) **2757**

RELIEF BODEN PALAOKLIMA (GW) [07989783] **1359**

RELIEF (MONTREAL) (CN/1181-8824) [23599107] **3792**

RELIGIAO E SOCIEDADE *SUSPENDED.* (BL/0100-8587) [03850226] **4990**

RELIGII MIRA (RU) [09353696] **4990**

RELIGIOLOGIQUES (MONTREAL) (CN/1180-0135) [23236420] **4990**

RELIGION AND AMERICAN CULTURE (US/1052-1151) [22190505] **4990**

RELIGION & DEMOCRACY (US) [12634159] 4493, **4990**

RELIGION AND LIFE LETTERS (US/0730-2363) [07971942] **4990**

RELIGION & LITERATURE (US/0888-3769) [10673651] 3428, **4990**

RELIGION & PUBLIC EDUCATION (US/1056-7224) [11151171] 4990, **1777**

RELIGION AND REASON (NE/0080-0848) [02907272] **4990**

RELIGION AND SOCIETY (BANGALORE, INDIA) (II/0034-3951) [07616639] **4991**

RELIGION AND SOCIETY REPORT (II/0578-0039) [02947326] **4991**

RELIGION & SOCIETY REPORT, THE (US/0742-6984) [10415931] **4991**

RELIGION AND SOCIETY (THE HAGUE) (GW) [09004709] **4991**

RELIGION AND THE SOCIAL ORDER (US/1061-5210) [24476972] **4991**

RELIGION (BOCA RATON) (US/0273-2556) [05163047] **4991**

RELIGION IN COMMUNIST LANDS *See* RELIGION, STATE & SOCIETY : THE KESTON JOURNAL **4991**

●RELIGION IN EASTERN EUROPE (US/1069-4781) [27841722] **4991**

RELIGION IN MALAWI (MW) [17490773] **4991**

RELIGION IN USSR (RU) [20695604] **4991**

RELIGION INDEX ONE. PERIODICALS (US/0149-8428) [03568980] 4991, **5013**

RELIGION INDEX TWO : MULTI-AUTHOR WORKS (US/0149-8436) [03569016] **4991**

RELIGION INDEXES. THESAURUS (US/0730-6350) [07987053] **3245**

RELIGION INDEXES [COMPUTER FILE] (US) [22294366] **5013**

RELIGION (LONDON. 1971) (UK/0048-721X) [01763658] **4991**

●RELIGION, STATE & SOCIETY : THE KESTON JOURNAL (UK/0963-7494) [25837096] 4546, **4991**

RELIGION TEACHER'S JOURNAL (US/0034-401X) [01696878] **4991**

RELIGION WATCH (US/0886-2141) [12862638] **4991**

RELIGION, WISSENSCHAFT, KULTUR (AT) **4991**

RELIGION Y ESCUELA (SP) 1777, **4991**

RELIGIONE E SCUOLA (IT) 1777, **4991**

RELIGIONEN DER MENSCHHEIT, DIE (GW/0486-3585) [02847810] **4991**

RELIGIONI E SOCIETA (FLORENCE, ITALY) (IT) [15648828] **4991**

RELIGIONSGESCHICHTLICHE VERSUCHE UND VORARBEITEN (GW) [01049765] 1079, **4991**

RELIGIONSVIDENSKABELIGT TIDSSKRIFT (DK/0108-1993) [09953939] **4991**

RELIGIOUS AND THEOLOGICAL ABSTRACTS (US/0034-4044) [01607912] 4991, **5013**

RELIGIOUS BOOKS IN PRINT (UK/0305-960X) [11221879] **4991**

RELIGIOUS BROADCASTING (US/0034-4079) [03448651] 4991, **1138**

RELIGIOUS COALITION FOR ABORTION RIGHTS NEWSLETTER (US) [26898875] 4991, **590**

RELIGIOUS EDUCATION (US/0034-4087) [01604941] **4991**

RELIGIOUS EDUCATION JOURNAL OF AUSTRALIA (AT/0815-3094) [I08153094] 4992, **1777**

RELIGIOUS FREEDOM REPORTER (US/0275-3529) [07118891] 4992, **3093**

RELIGIOUS FUNDING MONITOR *CEASED.* (US/0896-8187) [17294895] **4992**

RELIGIOUS HERALD, THE (US/0738-7318) [07295863] **4992**

RELIGIOUS HUMANISM (US/0034-4095) [01590577] **4992**

RELIGIOUS LEADERS OF AMERICA (DETROIT, MICH.) (US/1057-2961) [24004139] **4992**

RELIGIOUS LIFE (CHICAGO, ILL.) (US/0279-0459) [07479127] **4992**

RELIGIOUS LIFE REVIEW (IE) [07817481] **4992**

RELIGIOUS PERSPECTIVES (US/0486-3658) [06427871] **4992**

RELIGIOUS SOCIALISM (US/0278-7784) [04799567] **4992**

RELIGIOUS STUDIES AND THEOLOGY (CN/0829-2922) [11811652] **4992**

RELIGIOUS STUDIES IN THE USSR SERIES / USSR ACADEMY OF SCIENCES (RU) [16920616] **4992**

RELIGIOUS STUDIES NEWS (US/0885-0372) [12541650] **4992**

RELIGIOUS STUDIES REVIEW (US/0319-485X) [01682754] **4992**

RELIGIOUS TRADITIONS (AT/0156-1650) [04699861] **4992**

RELIX (US/0146-3489) [02909516] **4149**

RELOCALISER : LA LETRE DE LA MOBILITE-DEMOSCOOP (FR) **946**

RELOCATABLE BUSINESS (US/1070-8081) [28473333] **706**

●RELOCATION COMPASS (US/1069-5923) [28122837] **884**

RELOCATION FACT BOOK (US) 706, **4846**

RELOCATION HANDBOOK (UK/0967-0424) [I09670424] **4846**

RELOCATION / REALTY UPDATE (US) [29593392] 4846, **946**

RELOCATION REPORT, THE (US/0275-7613) [07231543] **4846**

RELOCATION TRENDS SURVEY (US) [08138871] **706**

REMAINS TO BE FOUND (US/0738-5889) [06383969] **2469**

REMARK *CEASED.* (US/0742-8162) [10462519] **1201**

REMARQUES ARABO-AFRICAINES *SUSPENDED.* (BE) [04327543] **2642**

REMEDIAL AND SPECIAL EDUCATION (US/0741-9325) [10233624] **1884**

REMEDIATION (NEW YORK, N.Y.) (US/1051-5658) [21990540] **2180**

REMEDIATION REVIEW : A JOURNAL OF HAZARDOUS WASTE MANAGEMENT / NEW YORK STATE DEPARTMENT OF ENVIRONMENTAL CONSERVATION (US) [18852528] **2241**

REMEDIES (US/0098-7999) [02242380] **3037**

REMEMBER THAT SONG (US/0889-8790) [14137654] **4149**

REMEMBERING YESTERDAY (US) **5181**

REMINDER (US) [29583777] **5646**

REMINDER LIST OF ELIGIBLE ACHIEVEMENTS *See* WRITING AWARDS : REMINDER LIST OF ELIGIBLE RELEASES **4080**

REMINDER. ZONE ONE. BRANDON, GROVELAND, ATLAS AND HADLEY TOWNSHIPS, THE (US/0194-245X) [05350140] **5693**

REMINERALIZE THE EARTH (US/1066-4106) [26947936] **184**

REMINGTON PRESS (REMINGTON, IND.) (US) [14994689] **5666**

●REMINGTON REPORT, THE (US/1070-3411) [28322750] **706**

●REMINISCE EXTRA (US/1069-8957) [28193635] **2544**

REMINISCE (GREENDALE, WIS.) (US/1057-2368) [23981832] **2544**

REMISIS (FR/0766-6500) [I07666500] **1921**

REMITTANCE AND DOCUMENT PROCESSING TODAY (US/1050-9186) [18201061] **5145**

REMNANTS (UK/0269-9656) [I02699656] **2705**

●REMODEL NOW (US/1060-3735) [24947637] **2903**

REMODELING CONTRACTOR *CEASED.* (US/0034-4249) [04358207] **626**

REMODELING ... COSTBOOK / BNI, BUILDING NEWS (US/1060-5797) [25002418] **626**

REMODELING IDEAS (US/0731-7409) [03507125] **626**

REMODELING (WASHINGTON, D.C.) (US/0885-8039) [12732797] **626**

REMONSTRANTS WEEKBLAD : RW (NE) [07301673] **4992**

REMOTE COMPUTING DIRECTORY (US/0098-0722) [01799557] **1239**

REMOTE SENSING: AN OPERATIONAL TECHNOLOGY FOR THE MINING AND PETROLEUM INDUSTRIES (UK) **4276**

REMOTE SENSING IN CANADA (CN) [03980484] **5145**

REMOTE SENSING NEWSLETTER IN ANTHROPOLOGY AND ARCHAEOLOGY (US/0894-5217) [16122478] **4419**

REMOTE SENSING OF EARTH RESOURCES (ALBUQUERQUE, N.M.), THE *CEASED.* (US/1055-9922) [23441396] 2203, **4419**

REMOTE SENSING OF ENVIRONMENT (US/0034-4257) [01331772] **1410**

REMOTE SENSING QUARTERLY LITERATURE REVIEW (US/0882-2409) [11737780] **2574**

REMOTE SENSING REVIEWS (SZ/0275-7257) [07228211] **1993**

REMOTE SENSING SOCIETY *See* PROCEEDINGS OF THE ... ANNUAL CONFERENCE OF THE REMOTE SENSING SOCIETY **1359**

REMOTELY PILOTED MAGAZINE (US/0163-643X) [04418737] **33**

REMSEN BELL-ENTERPRISE (US) [16969703] **5672**

REMUNERATION IN EUROPE REPORT (UK) 1706, **884**

REN WU (CC) 3428, **434**

RENACIMIENTO (RIO PIEDRAS, P.R.) (PR) [10278145] **3428**

RENAISSANCE AND BAROQUE (US/0897-7836) [17624573] **2627**

RENAISSANCE AND MODERN STUDIES (UK/0486-3720) [01763684] **2853**

RENAISSANCE AND REFORMATION (CN/0034-429X) [04249697] 3428, **2705**

RENAISSANCE AND REFORMATION (CN/0034-429X) [01642154] **2705**

RENAISSANCE AND RENASCENCES IN WESTERN LITERATURE (US/0193-9815) [05293821] **3428**

RENAISSANCE (ARDMORE, PA.) (US/1072-3625) [28919743] **2271**

RENAISSANCE BULLETIN, THE (JA/0388-0796) [03910704] **3428**

RENAISSANCE (CHICOUTIMI) (CN/1182-9478) [23296013] **2601**

RENAISSANCE DRAMA (US/0486-3739) [01589388] **5367**

RENAISSANCE DU VIEUX METZ, LA (FR/1158-2626) [I11582626] **329**

RENAISSANCE MONOGRAPHS (JA) [13775709] **329**

RENAISSANCE PAPERS (US/0584-4207) [06409210] **3428**

RENAISSANCE QUARTERLY (US/0034-4338) [05372932] 2627, **3428**

RENAISSANCE STUDIES (UK/0269-1213) [16402936] **2705**

RENAISSANCE TOO MAGAZINE (US/0742-9908) [10479389] **2544**

RENAISSANCE UNIVERSAL JOURNAL (US/0712-4767) [02247068] **4533**

RENAL EDUCATOR (AT/0816-990X) [I0816990X] **3992**

RENAL FAILURE (US/0886-022X) [12788863] **3992**

RENAL FAMILY *CEASED.* (CN/0714-8879) [09088963] **3993**

RENAL FAMILY (ED. FRANCAISE) (CN/0820-7283) [09543118] **3993**

RENAL PHYSIOLOGY (UK/0300-3434) [01448610] **3993**

Alphabetical Index — REPERTOIRE

RENAL PHYSIOLOGY AND BIOCHEMISTRY (SZ/1011-6524) [19116586] **3993**

RENAL TRANSPLANTATION AND DIALYSIS (UK/0142-8357) [I01428357] **3633**

RENALIFE : THE QUARTERLY JOURNAL OF THE NATIONAL ASSOCIATION OF PATIENTS ON HEMODIALYSIS AND TRANSPLANTATION (US) [14076646] **3633**

RENASCENCE (US) [04723619] **4149, 3428**

RENASCENCE. ESSAYS ON VALUES IN LITERATURE (US/0034-4346) [01763687] **3429**

RENATO ROSALDO LECTURE SERIES MONOGRAPH (US/0883-3389) [12124168] **2272**

RENCANA KEGIATAN DAN RENCANA ANGGARAN PENDAPATAN DAN BELANJA (IO) [02239665] **125**

RENCONTRE - MOUVEMENT CHRETIEN DE PROFESSIONS SOCIALES (FR/0992-9215) [I09929215] **4992, 5304**

RENCONTRE (QUEBEC. EDITION ANGLAISE) (CN/0709-9495) [06213308] **4679**

RENCONTRE (QUEBEC. EDITION FRANCAISE) (CN/0709-9487) [06174003] **4679**

RENCONTRES GAIES (CN/0712-838X) [08861894] **2796**

RENCONTRES (IPN RWANDA) (RW) [07506597] **1777**

RENCONTRES PEDAGOGIQUES PARIS (FR/0762-3267) [I07623267] **1777**

RENDA E CIRCULACAO (BL) [09499775] **4744**

RENDAS ADUANEIRAS (BL) [02246892] **4744**

RENDEMENT. AMSTERDAM (NE/0926-3314) [I09263314] **884**

RENDER (US/0090-8932) [05122033] **2355**

RENDEZ-VOUS 76 MONTREAL (CN/0318-2843) [02441818] **4914**

RENDEZ-VOUS (QUEBEC) (CN/1184-6097) [23599113] **4149**

RENDEZVOUS & LONGRIFLES (CN/0828-4725) [11895276] **4914**

RENDEZVOUS (BRANTFORD) (CN/0712-7588) [08569853] **3174**

RENDEZVOUS (BUFFALO, N.Y.) (US/0484-3916) [03876764] **33**

RENDEZVOUS (FREDERICTON) (CN/0711-1177) [08651893] **3315**

RENDEZVOUS OF WESTERN ART (US/0095-702X) [01798482] **363**

RENDEZVOUS (POCATELLO, IDAHO) (US/0034-4400) [01853319] **3429**

RENDICONTI. A, SCIENZE MATEMATICHE E APPLICAZIONI / ISTITUTO LOMBARDO, ACCADEMIA DI SCIENZE E LETTERE (IT/0392-9523) [09467279] **3530**

RENDICONTI (ACCADEMIA NAZIONALE DEI LINCEI. CLASSE DI SCIENZE MORALI, STORICHE E FILOLOGICHE) (IT) [10150234] **3315, 2253**

RENDICONTI DEL CIRCOLO MATEMATICO DI PALERMO (IT/0009-725X) [01554745] **3531**

RENDICONTI DEL SEMINARIO DELLA FACOLTA DI SCIENZE DELL'UNIVERSITA DI CAGLIARI (IT/0370-727X) [03067656] **5145**

RENDICONTI DEL SEMINARIO MATEMATICO (IT) [05231117] **3531**

RENDICONTI DEL SEMINARIO MATEMATICO E FISICO DI MILANO (IT/0370-7377) [02448633] **3531**

RENDICONTI DELLA ACCADEMIA DI ARCHEOLOGIA LETTERE E BELLE ARTI NAPOLI (IT/0393-2931) [I03932931] 2853, **329**

RENDICONTI DELLA SOCIETA GEOLOGICA ITALIANA (IT/0392-3037) [05739747] **1394**

RENDICONTI DI MATEMATICA E DELLE SUE APPLICAZIONI (1981) (IT/1120-7183) [08099133] **3531**

RENDICONTI / INSTITUTO LOMBARDO ACCADEMIA DI SCIENZE E LETTERE, CLASSE DI LETTERE E SCIENZE MORALI E STORICHE (IT) [01798851] **2853**

RENDICONTI - ISTITUTO LOMBARDO, ACCADEMIA DI SCIENZE E LETTERE, B, SCIENZE CHEMICHE E FISICHE, GEOLOGICHE, BIOLOGICHE E MEDICHE (IT/0392-9531) [09568662] 471, **1394**

RENDICONTI - SEMINARIO MATEMATICO DELLA UNIVERSITA DI PADOVA (IT/0041-8994) [01761704] **3531**

RENDITIONS (HK/0377-3515) [01782164] **3429**

RENEGADE (BLOOMFIELD HILLS) (US) [05156587] 363, **3429**

RENEW AMERICA REPORT, THE (US/1050-4885) [19752702] **2241**

RENEWABLE ENERGY (UK/0960-1481) [23609608] **1954**

RENEWABLE ENERGY BULLETIN (UK/0306-364X) [01796124] **1954**

RENEWABLE ENERGY BULLETIN. A (UK) [07929582] **2128**

RENEWABLE ENERGY BULLETIN. B (UK) [07920763] **2128**

RENEWABLE ENERGY NEWS (CANADIAN ED.) (CN/0827-2093) [12064651] **1955**

RENEWABLE ENERGY NEWS NORTHEAST (US/0714-8615) [09373382] **1955**

RENEWABLE ENERGY RESOURCES INFORMATION CENTER See RERIC NEWS **1955**

RENEWABLE ENERGY RESOURCES INFORMATION CENTER (THAILAND) See RERIC HOLDINGS LIST : / AN OCCASIONAL PUBLICATION OF RERIC **1955**

RENEWABLE RESOURCES JOURNAL (US/0738-6532) [09500803] **2203**

RENEWABLE SOURCES OF ENERGY (IE/0790-0619) [11384353] **1955**

RENEWAL MAGAZINE (UK) **4992**

RENEWAL (WINCHESTER, VA.) (US/0279-0300) [07471861] **4493**

RENFRO VALLEY BUGLE (US/0034-4451) [03909885] **2544**

RENGONG JINGTI XUEBAO (CC/1000-985X) [I1000985X] **1033**

RENIN, ANGIOTENSIN & KININS (UK/0143-4284) [I01434284] **471**

RENKOU YANJIU (CC/1000-6087) [06077044] **4559**

RENKOU YU JINGJI (CC/1000-4149) [10669238] 1516, **4559**

RENLEIXUE XUEBAO (CC/1000-3193) [09362293] **244**

RENNINGER'S ANTIQUE GUIDE (US) [08971372] **252**

RENO (GW/0721-4588) [I07214588] **706**

RENO GAZETTE-JOURNAL (US/0745-1415) [08862461] **5708**

RENOVATEC BARCELONA (SP/0214-3127) [I02143127] **626**

RENOVATION BRICOLAGE (CN/0381-0992) [03230275] **626**

RENOVATOR, THE (CN/0836-5857) [17462530] **626**

RENOVER (OUTREMONT) **CEASED.** (CN/1187-0788) [25589834] **626**

RENSEIGNEMENTS AUX PARENTS / COMMISSION SCOLAIRE SAINT-EXUPERY (CN/0713-6994) [08936764] **1869**

RENSEIGNEMENTS SUR LES MEDICAMENTS (CN/1184-6968) [24986820] **4327**

RENSSELAER ENGINEER (US/0034-4508) [02266854] 5145, **1993**

RENT REVIEW & LEASE RENEWAL (UK/0263-7499) [I02637499] 2833, **4846**

RENT SUPPLEMENT HANDBOOK (US) [02924386] **2833**

RENTABILIDAD BRUTA DEL INVERSIONISTA EN BOLSA. BONOS DEL TESORO, OBLIGACIONES HIPOTECARIAS REAJUSTABLES, ACCIONES / BOLSA DE VALORES DE MONTEVIDEO (UY) [09699727] **912**

RENTABILITEIT EN FINANCIERING VAN DE BOOMKWEKERIJ IN NEDERLAND OVER (NE) [19049801] **2430**

RENTAL COMPILATION See RENTAL RATES COMPILATION **626**

RENTAL EQUIPMENT REGISTER (US/0034-4524) [05120777] **935**

RENTAL (FORT ATKINSON, WIS.) (US/0898-7106) [17886734] **707**

RENTAL MANAGEMENT (US/1042-9085) [19248168] **707**

●RENTAL PRODUCT NEWS (1992) (US/1067-0904) [27131415] **707**

RENTAL PRODUCT NEWS SHOWCASE (US) [07598091] **1624**

RENTAL RATE BLUE BOOK (US/0484-4041) [04485055] 626, 2030, **2128**

RENTAL RATE BLUE BOOK FOR OLDER EQUIPMENT (US/0277-2000) [07518965] **626**

RENTAL RATES COMPILATION (US/0164-0593) [04543644] **626**

RENTENVERSICHERUNG IM BEITRITTSGEBIET (GW) [24603189] **4679**

RENTGENOLOGIJA I RADIOLOGIJA (BU/0486-400X) [10595476] **3946**

RENVILLE COUNTY FARMER (US) [01763692] **5726**

RENVILLE COUNTY STAR FARMER NEWS (US) [20789332] **5698**

RENZU. / LENS (JA) [03285712] **4376**

REPAIR & REMODEL QUARTERLY (US) [20051279] **4846**

REPAIR CAR/NEW CAR DIRECTORY, THE (US/0885-1638) [07603804] **5424**

REPEAT (NE) 707, **1120**

REPERAGES NANTES. 1988 (FR/0989-1773) [I09891773] **3429**

●REPERE (MONTREAL. IMPRIME. 1994) (CN/1198-0281) [30633267] **423**

REPERES (FR) [10187464] **329**

REPERES, ESSAIS EN EDUCATION (CN/0821-1388) [10398352] **1778**

REPERES ET REFERENCES STATISTIQUES SUR LES ENSEIGNEMENTS ET LA FORMATION (FR/0761-3423) [12140763] 1778, **1796**

REPERES (MONTPELLIER) (FR/0395-9031) [06257814] 1516, **1538**

REPERTOIRE ALPHABETIQUE ET PHONETIQUE DES MARQUES INTERNATIONALES (BE) **3315**

REPERTOIRE ALPHAPHONETIQUE DES MARQUES FRANCAISES : RAMF (BE) **1308**

REPERTOIRE ANALYTIQUE DU BULLETIN JURIDIQUE / UCANSS, UNION DES CAISSES NATIONALES DE SECURITE SOCIALE (FR) [11087462] **5304**

REPERTOIRE ANNOTE DES PUBLICATIONS DES COMMISSIONS SCOLAIRES. NIVEAU SECONDAIRE (CN/0823-2776) [10057297] **1869**

REPERTOIRE ANNOTE DES PUBLICATIONS DES COMMISSIONS SCOLAIRES. NIVEAUX PRESCOLAIRE ET PRIMAIRE (CN/0823-2768) [10057304] **1869**

REPERTOIRE - ASSOCIATION CANADIENNE DE DEVELOPPEMENT INDUSTRIEL (1987) (CN/0842-1048) [19461825] **1624**

REPERTOIRE - ASSOCIATION DES INGENIEURS-CONSEILS DU QUEBEC (CN/0709-4787) [05767127] **1993**

REPERTOIRE BIBLIOGRAPHIQUE See ARGUS DU LIVRE DE COLLECTION **4823**

REPERTOIRE BIBLIOGRAPHIQUE DE LA PHILOSOPHIE (BE/0034-4567) [01713864] **4366**

REPERTOIRE BIBLIOGRAPHIQUE DES LIVRES IMPRIMES EN FRANCE AU SEIZIEME SIECLE (GW/0085-5499) [02251806] **423**

REPERTOIRE COMMERCIAL DE LA REGION DU SUD-EST (CN/0820-8522) [09551469] **849**

REPERTOIRE / COMMISSION ELECTROTECHNIQUE INTERNATIONALE (SZ) [10952724] **2079**

●REPERTOIRE / CORPORATION DES TRADUCTEURS, TRADUCTRICES, TERMINOLOGUES ET INTERPRETES DU NOUVEAU-BRUNSWICK (CN/1187-8711) [26497511] **3315**

REPERTOIRE D'ADRESSES - CONSEIL SUPERIEUR DU SPORT EN AFRIQUE (CM) [05863884] **4915**

REPERTOIRE DE DROIT COMMERCIAL (FR) [01781570] **3102**

REPERTOIRE DE LA LECTURE FRANCOPHONE, LE (CN/0823-969X) [11559814] **4819**

REPERTOIRE DE LA PRESSE SUISSE (SZ) [02441068] **2924**

REPERTOIRE DE LA VIE FRANCAISE EN AMERIQUE (CN/0708-1510) [05132946] **2544**

REPERTOIRE DE L'EDITION AU QUEBEC (CN/0315-5943) [02441571] **423**

REPERTOIRE DE L'ENSEIGNEMENT A DISTANCE EN FRANCAIS (CN/1183-1812) [25423725] **1844**

REPERTOIRE DE PROGRAMMES DE BOURSES INTERNATIONALES POUR LES CANADIENS ET LES RESSORTISSANTS ETRANGERS (CN/1183-1650) [24256728] **1844**

REPERTOIRE DE TARIFS D'AEROPORTS ET DE TARIFS D'INSTALLATIONS ET DE SERVICES DE NAVIGATION AERIENNE (CN) [06211829] **33**

REPERTOIRE DE VEDETTES-MATIERE (CN/0705-5455) [20779379] **1929**

REPERTOIRE DES ACTIVITES DE FORMATION ET D'INFORMATION (CN/0826-3116) [11085030] **2868**

REPERTOIRE DES ACTIVITES SCIENTIFIQUES DES MEMBRES / UNION INTERNATIONALE POUR L'ETUDE SCIENTIFIQUE DE LA POPULATION (BE) [05734730] **4559**

REPERTOIRE DES ARTISTES ET DES ARTISANS DE SAINT-EUSTACHE (CN/1186-1231) [24267114] **329**

REPERTOIRE — Alphabetical Title Index

REPERTOIRE DES ASSOCIATIONS (CN/0318-4595) [02248414] **707**

REPERTOIRE DES ASSOCIATIONS PATRONALES QUEBECOISES (CN/0714-8461) [09086770] **1706**

REPERTOIRE DES BANQUES DE DONNEES EN CONVERSATIONNEL (FR/0758-816X) [10873521] **3245**

REPERTOIRE DES BIBLIOTHEQUES UNIVERSITAIRES QUEBECOISES (CN/1187-0419) [24368377] 1844, **3245**

REPERTOIRE DES BIENS A STATUT PARTICULIER (CN/0834-9908) [11463202] 1778, **4846**

REPERTOIRE DES CENTRALES ELECTRIQUES (BE) [05320799] 2079, **2006**

REPERTOIRE DES CENTRES D'INFORMATION SUR L'ENERGIE DANS LE MONDE (FR) **1955**

REPERTOIRE DES CENTRES RESIDENTIELS COMMUNAUTAIRES AU CANADA (CN/0226-0492) [06213209] **5304**

REPERTOIRE DES ECOLES - CONSEIL SCOLAIRE DE L'ILE DE MONTREAL (CN/0824-0655) [11807700] **1778**

REPERTOIRE DES EDITEURS ET DE LEURS DISTRIBUTEURS (CN/0826-5631) [11847682] **4819**

REPERTOIRE DES ENSEIGNANTS ET CHERCHEURS DES INSTITUTIONS D'ENSEIGNEMENT SUPERIEUR MEMBRES DE L'AUPELF-UREF (AFRIQUE, CARAIBE, OCEAN INDIEN) (CN/1187-4112) [25423830] **1844**

REPERTOIRE DES ETABLISSEMENTS DE SANTE ET DE SERVICES SOCIAUX (CN/0318-6067) [02250058] **4798**

REPERTOIRE DES ETABLISSEMENTS D'ENSEIGNEMENT SUPERIEUR MEMBRES DE L'AUPELF-UREF (CN/1187-4090) [25423825] **1844**

REPERTOIRE DES ETABLISSEMENTS / SERVICE DES RECHERCHES ET DE LA STATISTIQUE, VILLE DE LAVAL (CN/0824-0507) [11575666] **707**

REPERTOIRE ... DES FICHIERS DES MINISTERES ET ORGANISMES DU GOUVERNEMENT DU QUEBEC (CN/0846-9709) [19052029] **4679**

REPERTOIRE DES GEOGRAPHES FRANCAIS PARIS (FR/1147-9558) [11479558] **2574**

REPERTOIRE DES INDUSTRIES MANUFACTURIERES DU NORD-OOUEST (CN/0849-0694) [22135700] **707**

REPERTOIRE DES INSTITUTIONS - ONTARIO. DIRECTION DE L'ACCES A L'INFORMATION ET DE LA PROTECTION DE LA VIE PRIVEE (CN/1183-5486) [25351964] **4679**

REPERTOIRE DES JOURNALISTES DU QUEBEC ET ANNUAIRE DES ENTREPRISES DE PRESSE (CN/1183-4978) [24368086] **2924**

REPERTOIRE DES LABORATOIRES D'ESSAIS ET D'ANALYSES DU QUEBEC ... (CN/0229-9534) [08875007] **1993**

REPERTOIRE DES MEMBRES - CORPORATION PROFESSIONNELLE DES DIETETISTES DU QUEBEC (CN/0226-2649) [06473944] **4198**

REPERTOIRE DES MEMBRES DE L'UNION DES ARTISTES (CN/0820-8425) [09547429] **388**

REPERTOIRE DES MEMBRES / ORDRE DES AGRONOMES DU QUEBEC (CN/0822-9430) [10926612] **125**

REPERTOIRE DES MEMBRES - ORDRE DES INGENIEURS FORESTIERS DU QUEBEC (CN/0836-5709) [17500070] **2392**

REPERTOIRE DES MUNICIPALITES DU QUEBEC (CN/0079-869X) [05842840] **4679**

REPERTOIRE DES MUNICIPALITES ET DES COMMISSIONS SCOLAIRES (CN) [01788460] **4679**

REPERTOIRE DES ORGANISATIONS INTERNATIONALES ET DE LEUR PERSONNEL PARTICIPANT AUX PROGRAMMES DE COOPERATION TECHNIQUE DES NATIONS-UNIES AU CAMEROUN / PROGRAMMES DES NATIONS UNIES POUR LE DEVELOPPEMENT, BUREAU DU REPRESENTANT RESIDENT, CAMEROUN (CM) [12152790] **4533**

REPERTOIRE DES ORGANISMES CULTURELS DE L'ABITIBI-TEMISCAMINGUE (CN/0831-9286) [15997582] **329**

REPERTOIRE DES ORGANISMES ET DES ECOLES / GOUVERNEMENT DU QUEBEC, MINISTERE DE L'EDUCATION, SERVICE DE L'INFORMATIQUE (CN) [08167880] **1778**

REPERTOIRE DES OUTILS DE REFERENCE (CN/0846-0698) [23658907] **423**

REPERTOIRE DES PRIX LITTERAIRES (CN/0715-1519) [09188476] **3429**

REPERTOIRE DES PRODUITS ET SERVICES HORTICOLES DE LAVAL (CN/0849-8334) [21530432] **2430**

REPERTOIRE DES PROJETS DE RECHERCHE DU PAREA (CN/1186-043X) [24280799] **1844**

REPERTOIRE DES PUBLICATIONS (CN) [01789891] **2203**

REPERTOIRE DES PUBLICATIONS OFFICIELLES, SERIES ET PERIODIQUES. ADMINISTRATIONS LOCALES DE L'ETAT / COMMISSION DE COORDINATION DE LA DOCUMENTATION ADMINISTRATIVE (FR) [07745987] **423**

REPERTOIRE DES RECHERCHES LATINO-AMERICANISTES EN FRANCE (FR) [06845586] **2705**

REPERTOIRE DES RESSOURCES CULTURELLES DES ILES-DE-LA-MADELEINE (CN/1183-6598) [24690503] **329**

REPERTOIRE DES RESSOURCES EN SEXUALITE, LE (CN/1184-020X) [23230629] 5304, **5188**

REPERTOIRE DES RESSOURCES FRANCO-ONTARIENNES (CN/0227-4442) [07805610] **2757**

REPERTOIRE DES SERVICES COMMUNAUTAIRES DE GRANBY ET DES ENVIRONS (CN/0315-8357) [02248228] **5304**

REPERTOIRE DES SERVICES COMMUNAUTAIRES DU GRAND MONTREAL. BIEN-ETRE. SANTE. LOISIRS (CN/0319-258X) [03199534] **5304**

REPERTOIRE DES SERVICES COMMUNAUTAIRES (SUDBURY) (CN/0823-891X) [11830192] **5305**

REPERTOIRE DES SERVICES MUNICIPAUX DE PREVENTION DES INCENDIES DU QUEBEC (CN) [05785852] **2292**

REPERTOIRE DES TAUX DE LOCATION (CN/0382-3547) [02729637] **2833**

REPERTOIRE DES THESES AFRICANISTES FRANCAISES / CENTRE D'ETUDES AFRICAINES - CARDAN, ECOLE DES HAUTES ETUDES EN SCIENCES SOCIALES (FR) [07295701] **5215**

REPERTOIRE DES USINES QUEBECOISES DE PLACAGES, DE CONTRE-PLAQUES ET DE PANNEAUX AGGLOMERES A BASE DE BOIS / MINISTERE DE L'ENERGIE ET DES RESSOURCES, DIRECTION DU DEVELOPPEMENT INDUSTRIEL (CN/1182-7556) [23264815] **4679**

REPERTOIRE DES VINS ET DES SPIRITUEUX, QUEBEC (CN/0715-6618) [09796188] **2370**

REPERTOIRE DESCRIPTIF. LE MONDE DE LA CULTURE AU QUEBEC *See* ART ET CULTURE AU QUEBEC **313**

REPERTOIRE DESCRIPTIF. LE MONDE DE LA SCIENCE ET DE LA TECHNOLOGIE AU QUEBEC *See* SCIENCE ET TECHNOLOGIE AU QUEBEC **5151**

REPERTOIRE DESCRIPTIF. LE MONDE DE L'ECONOMIE ET DES AFFAIRES AU QUEBEC *See* ECONOMIE ET AFFAIRES AU QUEBEC **671**

REPERTOIRE DESCRIPTIF. LE MONDE DE L'EDUCATION AU QUEBEC *See* EDUCATION ET FORMATION AU QUEBEC **1739**

REPERTOIRE DU NOTARIAT DEFRENOIS (FR) [04446972] **3037**

REPERTOIRE DU SERVICE DES DELEGUES COMMERCIAUX DU CANADA (CN/0845-1664) [I08451664] **850**

REPERTOIRE ET CARACTERISTIQUES DES PRINCIPAUX MATERIELS DE GENIE CIVIL (FR) [02686234] **626**

REPERTOIRE FISCAL *See* JOURNAL DE DROIT FISCAL **2986**

REPERTOIRE GENERAL DE LA PRODUCTION FRANCAISE, KOMPASS-FRANCE *See* KOMPASS-FRANCE **1571**

REPERTOIRE INTERNATIONAL DES DEPARTMENTS ET DES CENTRES DETUDES FRANCAISES (CN/1187-4104) [25423828] **3315**

REPERTOIRE INTERNATIONAL DES SOURCES MUSICALES. INTERNATIONALES QUELLENLEXICON DER MUSIK. SER. B: SERIE METHODIQUE (GW) [07064919] **4149**

REPERTOIRE INTERNATIONAL DES SOURCES MUSICALES. SERIES A. EINZELDRUCKE VOR 1800 (GW) [04573293] **4149**

REPERTOIRE / LA CHAMBRE DE COMMERCE DE LA PROVINCE DE QUEBEC (CN/0822-5389) [10105728] **821**

REPERTOIRE LEGISLATIF DE L'ASSEMBLEE DU QUEBEC (CN/0704-9730) [05873063] **3037**

REPERTOIRE MENSUEL DU MINISTERE DE L'INTERIEUR (FR/0240-4729) [07742837] **4680**

REPERTOIRE (MONTPELLIER, FRANCE) (FR/0987-6030) [17366983] 3429, **1929**

REPERTOIRE : MONTREAL METROPOLITAIN, CODE POSTAL (CN) [01794598] **1147**

REPERTOIRE OF THE PRACTICE OF THE SECURITY COUNCIL (US) [01644702] **3134**

REPERTOIRE PERMANENT DE L'ADMINISTRATION FRANCAISE (FR) [01866555] **4680**

●REPERTOIRE QUEBECOIS DES RECUPERATEURS ET DES RECYCLEURS, LE (CN/1193-2228) [26758336] **2241**

REPERTOIRE TELEPHONIQUE - QUEBEC (PROVINCE). MINISTERE DES AFFAIRES CULTURELLES (CN/1184-2326) [23455619] **4680**

REPERTOIRE THEMATIQUE DES DOCUMENTS STATISTIQUES DU SERVICE DE L'INFORMATIQUE DE GESTION ET DES STATISTIQUES, CENTRALISES PAR LE DEPARTEMENT DE LA DOCUMENTATION ET DE LA DIFFUSION DE L'INFORMATION STATISTIQUE / MINISTERE DE L'EDUCATION NATIONALE (FR) [10786155] 1778, **1796**

REPERTOIRE TLRC (CN/1186-8511) [24623677] **3245**

REPERTOIRE TOPONYMIQUE DU QUEBEC (1988) (CN/0848-2969) [20879805] **2574**

REPERTOIRE TOURISTIQUE (MONTREAL) (CN/1183-7489) [25423820] **5490**

REPERTOIRE / UNIVERSITE DE MONCTON (CN) [12409820] **1844**

REPERTOIRE (UNIVERSITE DU QUEBEC A MONTREAL) (CN/0715-8130) [10027671] **4832**

REPERTOIRE (UNIVERSITY OF CALGARY. FACULTY OF FINE ARTS) (CN/0712-6530) [09230787] **329**

REPERTOIRE VIDEO FEMMES (CN/0225-0632) [12064667] **423**

REPERTOIRES DES MEMBRES (CN/0822-9430) [11046467] **125**

REPERTORIEN ZUR DEUTSCHEN LITERATURGESCHICHTE (GW/0486-4166) [02844155] **3429**

REPERTORIO 4 CODICI TRIBUTARI (IT) **4744**

REPERTORIO AMERICANO (CR) [03111066] **3429**

REPERTORIO ASSOCIATE ANIMA (IT) [11952789] **1624**

REPERTORIO BOYACENSE (CK/0034-4605) [03500884] **2627**

REPERTORIO CHIMICO ITALIANO (IT) [07890240] **991**

REPERTORIO COMMERCIALE (IT) **707**

REPERTORIO DEL FILM INDUSTRIALE (IT) [01789186] **5145**

REPERTORIO DEL FORO ITALIANO; LEGISLAZIONE, BIBLIOGRAFIA, GIURISPRUDENZA (IT/0394-6347) [01775404] **3037**

REPERTORIO DELLA PRODUZIONE CHIMICA ITALIANA E DEL COMMERCIO CHIMICO *See* REPERTORIO CHIMICO ITALIANO **991**

REPERTORIO DELLE DECISIONI DELLA CORTE COSTITUZIONALE (IT) [13765171] **4680**

REPERTORIO DOGANALE CLASSIFICAZIONE MERCI (IT) **850**

REPERTORIO FARMACEUTICO ITALIANO : REFI *CEASED.* (IT) [20761116] **4327**

REPERTORIO GENERALE DELLA GIURISPRUDENZA ITALIANA (IT) [18305435] **3037**

REPERTORIO GIUSTIZIA CIVILE (IT) **3091**

REPERTORIO HISTORICO (CK) [02256839] **2757**

REPERTORIO LABORAL (ASUNCION, PARAGUAY) (PY) [08226397] **3153**

REPERTORIO LATINOAMERICANO (AG) [05120700] **3429**

REPERTORIO LE SOCIETA (IT) **935**

REPERTORIO LEGISLATIVO ACCION SOCIAL (SP) **5215**

REPERTORIO SIDERURGICO LATINOAMERICANO (CL) [04286993] 4017, **1624**

REPERTORIUM DER KIRCHENVISITATIONSKATEN (GW) **4992**

REPERTORIUM FONTIUM HISTORIAE MEDII AEVI (IT) [02266858] **2627**

REPERTORIUM PLANTARUM SUCCULENTARUM (NE/0486-4271) [02459631] **526**

REPERTORIUM (UTRECHT, NETHERLANDS) (NE) [16978280] **4327**

REPERTORIUM VAN BOEKEN EN TIJDSCHRIFTARTIKELEN BETREFFENDE DE GESCHIEDENIS VAN NEDERLAND (NE) [01763718] **2705**

Alphabetical Title Index — REPORT

REPINDEX : INDICE COMPUTARIZADO DE LA RED PANAMERICANA DE INFORMACION Y DOCUMENTACION EN INGENIERIA SANITARIA Y CIENCIAS DEL AMBIENTE (REPIDISCA) CEASED. (PE/0252-7987) [25007197] **2181**

REPLACEMENT ASSEMBLIES ESTIMATING GUIDE (US/1048-1036) [19674986] **5424**

REPLAY (US) [11502146] **4149**

REPLAY MAGAZINE See REPLAY **4149**

REPLICA (MIAMI, FLA. 1970) (US/0146-2008) [02884282] **2492**

REPLICA WRAP-UP, THE (US) [04377445] 4055, **375**

REPORT - ADMINISTRATIVE OFFICE OF PENNSYLVANIA COURTS (US/0148-9925) [03410216] **3142**

REPORT - ADVISORY COUNCIL ON HISTORIC PRESERVATION (US/0098-4035) [02241093] **2757**

REPORT - AGRICULTURAL ECONOMICS UNIT. UNIVERSITY OF EXETER (UK/0531-5344) [I05315344] **125**

REPORT / AGRICULTURAL RESEARCH COUNCIL, INSTITUTE OF ANIMAL PHYSIOLOGY (UK) [02243849] **5520**

REPORT - ALBERTA ENVIRONMENT. RESEARCH SECRETARIAT (CN/0707-9079) [04880338] **2181**

REPORT / ALBERTA LAW REFORM INSTITUTE (CN/0317-1604) [22963123] **3037**

REPORT - ALFRED P. SLOAN FOUNDATION (US/0065-6216) [01479090] **1516**

REPORT AM (NE) [11600700] **3531**

REPORT AND ACCOUNTS (UK) [01792666] **280**

REPORT AND ACCOUNTS - AIR TRAVEL RESERVE FUND AGENCY (UK) [04167490] 750, **33**

REPORT AND ACCOUNTS - ANDHRA PRADESH STATE FINANCIAL CORPORATION (II) [01790552] **807**

REPORT AND ACCOUNTS AT ... / INSURANCE CORPORATION OF BARBADOS (BB) [09921864] **2891**

REPORT AND ACCOUNTS - BANK OF ENGLAND (UK/0308-5279) [04282542] **807**

REPORT & ACCOUNTS / BARCLAYS BANK PLC (UK) [08678009] **807**

REPORT & ACCOUNTS - BERMUDA MONETARY AUTHORITY (BM) [06727504] **807**

REPORT & ACCOUNTS / BRITISH AGENCIES FOR ADOPTION AND FOSTERING (UK) [08334529] **5305**

REPORT AND ACCOUNTS - BRITISH TRANSPORT DOCKS BOARD (UK) [04815622] **5455**

REPORT AND ACCOUNTS - CALCUTTA ELECTRIC SUPPLY CORPORATION (II) [09601351] **1624**

REPORT & ACCOUNTS - CAPITAL DEVELOPMENT AUTHORITY (TZ) [02536890] **2833**

REPORT AND ACCOUNTS - CENTRAL ELECTRICITY GENERATING BOARD (LONDON) (UK/0528-4082) [02275292] 4762, **707**

REPORT AND ACCOUNTS - CREDITO ITALIANO (IT) [07365221] **807**

REPORT & ACCOUNTS FOR THE YEAR ENDED 30TH APRIL ... / THE MAURITIUS COMMERCIAL BANK LIMITED (MF) [10351625] **807**

REPORT AND ACCOUNTS FOR THE YEAR ENDED 30TH JUNE ... / AGRICULTURAL MARKETING AUTHORITY (RH) [07667041] **125**

REPORT AND ACCOUNTS FOR THE YEAR ENDED 30TH JUNE ... / PAKISTAN NATIONAL SHIPPING CORPORATION (PK) [11347392] **5455**

REPORT AND ACCOUNTS FOR THE YEAR ENDED 31ST DECEMBER ... / THE SECURITIES AND EXCHANGE COMMISSION (NIGERIA) (NR) [10855255] **912**

REPORT AND ACCOUNTS - GUYANA SUGAR CORPORATION (GY) [03693566] **2355**

REPORT AND ACCOUNTS ... : INCORPORATING THE REPORT AND ACCOUNTS OF DAIRY CREST LIMITED / MILK MARKETING BOARD (UK) [25635478] **198**

REPORT AND ACCOUNTS - ISTITUTO DI CREDITO PER LE IMPRESE DI PUBBLICA UTILITA (IT) [03599067] **807**

REPORT & ACCOUNTS / NATIONAL DEVELOPMENT BANK OF SRI LANKA (CE) [08721621] **807**

REPORT AND ACCOUNTS - NATIONAL DEVELOPMENT BANK, SIERRA LEONE (SL) [01784734] **807**

REPORT AND ACCOUNTS - SIERRA LEONE EXTERNAL COMMUNICATIONS LIMITED (SL) [03665409] **1162**

REPORT AND ACCOUNTS / SINGAPORE SHIPPING ASSOCIATION (SI) [11104001] **5455**

REPORT AND ACCOUNTS - SUTTON HOUSING TRUST (UK) [01795872] **4744**

REPORT & ACCOUNTS TO BE SUBMITTED AT THE ANNUAL GENERAL MEETING OF SHAREHOLDERS (FR) [02243224] **5455**

REPORT AND FINANCIAL STATEMENTS - RESERVE BANK OF AUSTRALIA (AT/0484-5412) [01853146] 807, **1516**

REPORT AND LIST OF SUBSCRIBER / LINCOLN RECORD SOCIETY See REPORT FOR THE YEAR ... / THE LINCOLN RECORD SOCIETY **2705**

REPORT AND MINUTES - ECONOMIC COMMISSION. INTERNATIONAL CIVIL AVIATION ORGANIZATION (CN/0828-2536) [11416135] **33**

REPORT AND RECOMMENDATIONS TO THE GOVERNOR AND THE GENERAL ASSEMBLY (US/0148-3633) [03302865] **3153**

REPORT AND RECOMMENDATIONS TO THE GOVERNOR AND THE GENERAL ASSEMBLY - ILLINOIS. COMMISSION ON THE STATUS OF WOMEN (US) [02661232] **5565**

REPORT AND RESOLUTIONS OF THE ... MEETING OF THE EXECUTIVE COMMITTEE (SZ) [08334239] **4992**

REPORT & REVIEW / WORLD FEDERATION OF ADVERTISERS, WFA (BE) [20380086] **765**

REPORT AND ROSTER : REGISTERED LAND SURVEYORS (US/0097-8817) [01798892] **2030**

REPORT AND STATEMENT OF ACCOUNT / THE MAURITIUS SUGAR SYNDICATE (MF) [10733603] **4680**

REPORT AND STATEMENT OF ACCOUNTS - BIRMINGHAM MUNICIPAL TRUSTEE SAVINGS BANK (UK) [03961191] **807**

REPORT AND STATEMENT OF ACCOUNTS - ENTERPRISE ULSTER (IE) [03890685] **1706**

REPORT AND STATEMENT OF ACCOUNTS FOR THE YEAR ENDED 30TH JUNE, ... / METROPOLITAN (PERTH) PASSENGER TRANSPORT TRUST (AT) [07320774] **5391**

REPORT AND STATEMENT OF ACCOUNTS - LIQUOR CONTROL COMMISSION (AT) [06933442] **3174**

REPORT AND STATEMENT OF THE PIPELINES AUTHORITY OF SOUTH AUSTRALIA (AT/0728-8093) [I07288093] **4276**

REPORT AND STATEMENTS OF ACCOUNTS OF THE ACCOUNTANT GENERAL FOR THE YEAR ENDED 31ST DECEMBER ... (AM) [10686370] **4744**

REPORT AND TRANSACTIONS - THE DEVONSHIRE ASSOCIATION FOR THE ADVANCEMENT OF SCIENCE, LITERATURE AND ART (UK/0309-7994) [01566555] 2853, **329**

REPORT - ANDHRA PRADESH (INDIA). LEGISLATURE. ESTIMATES COMMITTEE (II) [08246103] **4744**

REPORT : ANNUAL CONVENTION CEASED. (US) [05918116] **1869**

REPORT - ARTS COUNCIL OF GREAT BRITAIN (UK) [06409486] **329**

REPORT ASSESSING GLOBAL FOOD PRODUCTION AND NEEDS (US) [06162036] 1516, **125**

REPORT ASSISTANT MASTERS AND MISTRESSES ASSOCIATION (UK/0142-3134) [I01423134] **1778**

REPORT - ASSOCIATION FOR REPORT ON CONFEDERATION (CN/0708-9864) [05712118] **4680**

REPORT (ATOMIC ENERGY CONTROL BOARD) See RESEARCH REPORT / ATOMIC ENERGY CONTROL BOARD **1955**

REPORT - AUDUBON SOCIETY OF RHODE ISLAND (US/0274-502X) [06364545] 5620, **2203**

REPORT - AUSTRALIAN-AMERICAN EDUCATIONAL FOUNDATION (AT/1036-1499) [10361499] **1778**

REPORT, BASIC FACTS ABOUT MILITARY SERVICE (US) [02242515] **4055**

REPORT - BRITISH COLUMBIA. LEGISLATIVE ASSEMBLY. SELECT STANDING COMMITTEE ON FINANCE, CROWN CORPORATIONS AND GOVERNMENT SERVICES (CN/1186-0405) [24280781] 912, **807**

REPORT / BRITISH LIBRARY, RESEARCH AND DEVELOPMENT DEPARTMENT (UK) [24007021] **3245**

REPORT - BRITISH OVERSEAS TRADE BOARD (UK) [03338444] **850**

REPORT - BRITISH SCHOOLS EXPLORING SOCIETY (UK/0521-1573) [01795389] **5145**

REPORT - BROWN UNIVERSITY. DIVISION OF ENGINEERING (US/0736-6639) [09189255] **1993**

REPORT - BUCYRUS-ERIE COMPANY (US/0407-551X) [03038526] **707**

REPORT (BUSINESS INTELLIGENCE PROGRAM) (US) [18395561] **2181**

REPORT BY THE AUDITOR GENERAL FOR THE PERIOD ... / KINGDOM OF SWAZILAND (SQ) [27750150] **4744**

REPORT BY THE CHIEF INSPECTOR - GLASGOW. TRADING STANDARDS DEPARTMENT (UK) [05749205] **850**

REPORT BY THE INTERNATIONAL TELECOMMUNICATION UNION ON TELECOMMUNICATION AND THE PEACEFUL USES OF OUTER SPACE (SZ) [09587581] **1162**

REPORT BY THE SUB-COMMITTEE ON NUTRITIONAL SURVEILLANCE (LONDON) (UK/0301-4924) [07633394] **4198**

REPORT BY THE U. S. GENERAL ACCOUNTING OFFICE (US) [04819144] 4680, **750**

REPORT - CALIFORNIA WATER RESOURCES CENTER (US/0575-4968) [06066566] **5538**

REPORT - CANADA LAND INVENTORY (CN) [05722832] **4680**

●REPORT - CANADIAN RED CROSS SOCIETY. NEW BRUNSWICK DIVISION (CN/1188-2034) [26497581] **5305**

REPORT - CENTER FOR ENERGY STUDIES, KANSAS STATE UNIVERSITY (US/0145-0093) [02663240] **1994**

REPORT - CENTER FOR SOCIAL ORGANIZATION OF SCHOOLS, THE JOHNS HOPKINS UNIVERSITY (US/0160-1032) [05793433] **1778**

REPORT - CENTRAL SOYA, INC., FORT WAYNE IND (US/0411-4094) [03020855] **2627**

REPORT - CENTRE FOR OVERSEAS PEST RESEARCH (UK/0307-9082) [05640701] **4247**

REPORT / CHAMBER OF MINES, ZIMBABWE See ANNUAL REPORT / CHAMBRE DE MINES, ZIMBABWE **2133**

REPORT - CHEMICAL BANK NEW YORK TRUST COMPANY (US/0528-9300) [03132632] **807**

REPORT - CHUNG YANG YIN HANG (CH/0529-6676) [03145967] **807**

REPORT - CINCINNATI BAR ASSOCIATION (US/0732-0736) [08275718] **3037**

REPORT - CIRIA UNDERWATER ENGINEERING GROUP (UK/0305-4055) [05865385] **1994**

REPORT - COAL CORPORATION OF VICTORIA (AT/0816-9411) [I08169411] **2149**

REPORT / COLLEGE OF THE VIRGIN ISLANDS. AGRICULTURAL EXPERIMENT STATION (VI) [13506492] **125**

REPORT - COLUMBIA UNIVERSITY. CONSERVATION OF HUMAN RESOURCES PROJECT (US/0413-8465) [03232674] **1094**

REPORT - COMMISSION ON ACCREDITATION OF REHABILITATION FACILITIES (US/0045-7590) [03305422] **3792**

REPORT - COMMITTEE ON GOVERNMENT ASSURANCES (II) [03127577] 4680, **2892**

REPORT - COMMITTEE ON THE WELFARE OF SCHEDULED CASTES AND SCHEDULED TRIBES See REPORT - KARNATAKA LEGISLATURE, COMMITTEE ON THE WELFARE OF SCHEDULED CASTES & SCHEDULED TRIBES **5305**

REPORT / CONFERENCE OF AMERICAN STATES MEMBERS OF THE INTERNATIONAL LABOUR ORGANISATION (SZ) [07599474] **1706**

REPORT - CONFERENCE OF PRESIDENTS OF MAJOR AMERICAN JEWISH ORGANIZATIONS (US/0160-7057) [03731881] **5236**

REPORT / CONNECTICUT, JUDICIAL REVIEW COUNCIL (US) [08613504] **3142**

REPORT - COOPERATIVE ACCOUNTABILITY PROJECT (US/0360-4128) [02244509] **1869**

REPORT - COUNCIL FOR BRITISH ARCHAEOLOGY (UK/0589-9208) [03621337] **280**

REPORT (COUNCIL FOR MINERAL TECHNOLOGY (SOUTH AFRICA)) (SA/0254-1815) [09964971] 4017, **1444**

REPORT - COUNCIL ON LEGAL EDUCATION FOR PROFESSIONAL RESPONSIBILITY (US) [01565303] **3037**

REPORT - CSIRO CENTRE FOR IRRIGATION RESEARCH (AT) [18568576] **184**

REPORT / CSIRO, DIVISION OF ANIMAL HEALTH (AT/1031-1580) [18864832] **5520**

REPORT — Alphabetical Title Index

REPORT / CSIRO, DIVISION OF HUMAN NUTRITION (AT/0155-1507) [04544968] **4198**

REPORT / CSIRO DIVISION OF PLANT INDUSTRY (AT) [10497050] 125, **526**

REPORT - CSIRO MARINE LABORATORIES (AT/0725-4598) [08847833] 1455, **2311**

REPORT / CUCURBIT GENETICS COOPERATIVE (US/1064-5594) [10463197] **184**

REPORT / DALLAS HISTORICAL SOCIETY (US) [04921391] **2627**

REPORT - DELHI. PUBLIC LIBRARY (II/0418-5749) [01780848] **3245**

REPORT - DEPARTMENT OF ABORIGINAL AFFAIRS (AT) [02421004] **244**

REPORT / DEPARTMENT OF AGRICULTURAL ECONOMICS (US) [15371686] **125**

REPORT, DEPARTMENT OF DEFENSE CATALOGING AND STANDARDIZATION PROGRAMS *See* REPORT ON THE FEDERAL CATALOGING PROGRAM **4055**

REPORT - DEPARTMENT OF FOREIGN TRADE (II) [02178545] **850**

REPORT - DEPARTMENT OF PERSONNEL AND ADMINISTRATIVE REFORMS (ADMINISTRATIVE REFORMS) (MY) [02411133] **4680**

REPORT / DEPARTMENT OF RESOURCES AND ENERGY, BUREAU OF MINERAL RESOURCES, GEOLOGY AND GEOPHYSICS (AT/0084-7100) [06185101] 2149, **1394**

REPORT - DEPARTMENT OF SCIENCE, ANTARCTIC DIVISION (AT) [01795581] **5145**

REPORT - DEPARTMENT OF THE ENVIRONMENT AND CONSERVATION (AT) [02437428] 2203, **2181**

REPORT - DEPT. OF POSTS AND TELECOMMUNICATIONS (FJ) [01793710] **1147**

REPORT - DETROIT. METROPOLITAN AREA REGIONAL PLANNING COMMISSION (US) [04841010] **307**

REPORT - DEVELOPMENT STUDY UNIT, DEPARTMENT OF SOCIAL ANTHROPOLOGY, UNIVERSITY OF STOCKHOLM (SW/0284-9232) [02849232] **244**

REPORT - DIRECTOR OF MINES (HOBART) (AT/0155-1531) [07578241] **2149**

REPORT / DISTRICT OF COLUMBIA. PUBLIC DEFENDER SERVICE. BOARD OF TRUSTEES (US) [01566801] **3037**

REPORT - DIVISION OF ENVIRONMENTAL MECHANICS. CSIRO (CANBERRA) (AT/0312-567X) [02400914] **2181**

REPORT - DIVISION OF HEALTH SERVICES RESEARCH AND DEVELOPMENT, UNIVERSITY OF BRITISH COLUMBIA (CN/0225-901X) [06141484] **3917**

REPORT / DIVISION OF HORTICULTURAL RESEARCH (AT/0069-7435) [03190677] **2430**

REPORT / DIVISION OF MINERAL ENGINEERING (AT/0810-8862) [11033437] **2017**

REPORT : DRUG ABUSE PREVENTION PLAN (US) [04423897] **1348**

REPORT - DSIR CHEMISTRY (NZ/1170-9456) [I11709456] **991**

REPORT - DUBLIN. NATIONAL LIBRARY OF IRELAND. COUNCIL OF TRUSTEES (IE) [05351859] **3245**

REPORT - EARTHQUAKE ENGINEERING RESEARCH CENTER, COLLEGE OF ENGINEERING, UNIVERSITY OF CALIFORNIA, BERKELEY, CALIFORNIA (US/0271-0323) [04846178] **2030**

REPORT - EDUCATION COMMISSION OF THE STATES (US/0531-8335) [01780858] **1844**

REPORT - EDUCATION DEVELOPMENT CENTER (US/0899-0239) [14353880] **1778**

REPORT - EDUCATIONAL RECORDS BUREAU, NEW YORK. COMMITTEE ON SCHOOL AND COLLEGE RELATIONS (US) [05711873] **1844**

REPORT - EGYPT EXPLORATION SOCIETY (UK) [03903287] **2642**

REPORT : EXPENDITURE FROM THE CONSOLIDATED REVENUE FUND (AT) [02366155] **4744**

REPORT - FAMILY PLANNING ASSOCIATION OF INDIA (II) [01795888] **590**

REPORT - FEDERAL BAR ASSOCIATION. SECTION OF TAXATION (US/0742-5317) [10379090] 4744, **3037**

REPORT - FIJI NATIONAL TRAINING COUNCIL (FJ) [02659192] **1706**

REPORT - FLORIDA AGRICULTURAL AND MECHANICAL UNIVERSITY (US) [01325647] **1844**

REPORT - FLORIDA COUNCIL FOR THE BLIND (US) [01303869] **4393**

REPORT - FLORIDA. DEPARTMENT OF HEALTH AND REHABILITATIVE SERVICES. DIVISION OF MENTAL HEALTH (US) [01653093] **4798**

REPORT - FLORIDA. LEGISLATURE. JOINT INTERIM COMMITTEE ON MENTAL HEALTH (US/0428-6383) [01420930] 4798, **4680**

REPORT - FLORIDA. STATE BOARD OF BEAUTY CULTURE (US) [01330228] **405**

REPORT - FLORIDA. STATE DEPT. OF EDUCATION. PROFESSIONAL PRACTICES COUNCIL (US) [01319161] **1869**

REPORT - FLORIDA. STATE PERSONNEL BOARD (US) [01423674] **4705**

REPORT - FLORIDA. STATE UNIVERSITY, TALLAHASSEE. OCEANOGRAPHIC INSTITUTE (US) [01423808] **1456**

REPORT - FLORIDA. UNIVERSITY, GAINESVILLE. CANCER RESEARCH LABORATORY (US) [01330355] **3823**

REPORT FOR ... / C.A.B. INTERNATIONAL (UK) [19946554] **125**

REPORT FOR CALENDAR YEAR ... / CHIEF MINE INSPECTOR, DEPARTMENT OF MINES (US) [08296954] **2149**

REPORT FOR ... - INSTITUTE OF ARABLE CROPS RESEARCH (UK/0955-9051) [20689847] **184**

REPORT FOR THE DEPARTMENT OF SPORT AND RECREATION FOR THE YEAR ENDED *See* ANNUAL REPORT OF THE DEPARTMENT OF SPORT AND RECREATION FOR THE YEAR ENDED **4848**

REPORT FOR THE FINANCIAL YEAR ENDING 30 SEPTEMBER ... / WHEAT BOARD (SA) [07589570] 850, **4680**

● REPORT FOR THE FISCAL YEAR (UK) [30652853] **203**

REPORT FOR THE ... PERIOD OF THE AUSTRALIAN DRIED FRUITS CORPORATION FOR THE PERIOD ... (AT) [07902827] **126**

REPORT FOR THE PERIOD ... / REPUBLIC OF BOTSWANA, MINISTRY OF LOCAL GOVERNMENT AND LANDS, DEPARTMENT OF SURVEYS AND LANDS (BS) [19889076] **4680**

● REPORT FOR THE YEAR ... (AT) [27645542] **203**

REPORT FOR THE YEAR - BANGLADESH. UNIVERSITY GRANTS COMMISSION (II) [08366006] **1844**

REPORT FOR THE YEAR ... / BOARD OF FIRE COMMISSIONERS (FJ) [08545641] **2292**

REPORT FOR THE YEAR ... / DEPARTMENT OF TOURISM (AT) [08875116] **5490**

REPORT FOR THE YEAR ... / JANE AUSTEN SOCIETY (UK/0958-5443) [01921771] **3429**

REPORT FOR THE YEAR ... - MINERAL RESOURCES DEPARTMENT (FIJI) (FJ) [15491311] **1360**

REPORT FOR THE YEAR ... / THE LINCOLN RECORD SOCIETY (UK) [08460574] **2705**

REPORT FOR ... / UNITED STATES ATTORNEY, NORTHERN DISTRICT OF ILLINOIS (US/0731-1168) [06360651] **3038**

REPORT FOR YEAR ENDED 30TH JUNE ... / VICTORIAN DAIRY INDUSTRY AUTHORITY (AT/0157-5856) [10171676] **198**

REPORT / FOREIGN INVESTMENT REVIEW BOARD (AT/0155-0802) [07432375] **912**

REPORT - FOREST PEST MANAGEMENT INSTITUTE (CN/0704-772X) [04564189] 4248, **2392**

REPORT - FOREST SERVICE. SOUTHEASTERN AREA. DIVISION OF FOREST PEST MANAGEMENT (US) [01431136] **2392**

REPORT FROM ASPEN INSTITUTE BERLIN (US/0147-569X) [03198036] **2853**

REPORT FROM EUROPE (BE) [04075343] **1639**

REPORT FROM HEADQUARTERS (US/0162-0703) [04091639] **1706**

REPORT FROM STATE CIRCLE (US) **4680**

REPORT FROM THE CAPITAL (US/0364-6661) [01763721] **4992**

REPORT FROM THE COMMITTEE OF PUBLIC ACCOUNTS TOGETHER WITH THE PROCEEDINGS OF THE COMMITTEE AND THE MINUTES OF EVIDENCE TAKEN BY THE COMMITTEE OF PUBLIC ACCOUNTS ON (UK) [20151073] **4680**

REPORT FROM THE DEPARTMENT OF MATHEMATICS AND STATISTICS (CN/0824-4944) [11046435] **3531**

REPORT FROM THE DIRECTOR, NATIONAL INSTITUTE OF ALLERGY AND INFECTIOUS DISEASES (US/0161-3618) [03902284] 3676, **3715**

REPORT FROM THE INSTITUTE FOR PHILOSOPHY & PUBLIC POLICY (US/1051-6972) [21475926] **5215**

REPORT FROM THE LIBRARIES - NIGERIA. UNIVERSITY, NSUKKA (NR) [07036755] **3245**

REPORT FROM THE PUBLIC ACCOUNTS COMMITTEE UPON UNPAID ACCOUNTS (AT) [01795425] **4744**

REPORT FROM THE WHITE HOUSE CONFERENCE ON AGING (US/0278-517X) [07448625] **3754**

REPORT FROM WASHINGTON (ENGLEWOOD, COLO.) *See* COLORADO WHEAT GROWER **167**

REPORT - GEOLOGICAL SURVEY OF JAPAN (JA) [06201090] **1394**

REPORT / GEOLOGICAL SURVEY OF WESTERN AUSTRALIA (AT/0508-4741) [01774987] **1394**

REPORT - GOVERNMENT OF INDIA, DEPARTMENT OF POWER (II) [02357679] **2079**

REPORT - GOVERNMENT OF INDIA, MINISTRY OF INDUSTRY AND CIVIL SUPPLIES (II) [03287496] **4680**

REPORT, GOVERNMENT OF NAGALAND (II) [01784081] **4744**

REPORT, GOVERNMENT OF TAMIL NADU (II) [01784085] **4744**

REPORT, GOVERNMENT OF THE UNION TERRITORY OF GOA, DAMAN, AND DIU (II) [01784082] **4744**

REPORT, GOVERNMENT OF THE UNION TERRITORY OF PONDICHERRY (II) [05218509] **4744**

REPORT - GREAT BRITAIN. COMMITTEE ON SAFETY OF DRUGS (UK/0436-3779) [01470828] **4798**

REPORT (GREAT BRITAIN. ELECTRICAL EQUIPMENT CERTIFICATION MANAGEMENT BOARD) (UK) [10836933] **2079**

REPORT - GREAT BRITAIN. SCOTTISH DEVELOPMENT DEPT (UK) [06033650] **2833**

REPORT - GREAT LAKES INSTITUTE, UNIVERSITY OF TORONTO (CN/0082-5220) [01395740] **1417**

REPORT / GREAT LAKES SCIENCE ADVISORY BOARD (CN/0845-1214) [17970096] **5538**

REPORT - GREATER LONDON RECORD OFFICE AND LIBRARY (UK) [02243040] **2483**

REPORT - GROUP FOR THE ADVANCEMENT OF PSYCHIATRY (1984) (US/0888-3394) [11124689] **3935**

REPORT / HANNAH RESEARCH INSTITUTE (UK/0301-6315) [02658134] **198**

REPORT - HARVARD COLLEGE, CLASS OF 1959 (US/0438-6566) [02246379] **1844**

REPORT - HARVARD UNIVERSITY. CLASS OF 1936 (US) [05280214] **1844**

REPORT (HAWAII. LEGISLATURE. LEGISLATIVE REFERENCE BUREAU) (US) [02255715] **4680**

REPORT - HIGH SCHOOL NEWS SERVICE *See* REPORT, BASIC FACTS ABOUT MILITARY SERVICE **4055**

REPORT - HOSPITAL DESIGN AND EVALUATION UNIT, DEPARTMENT OF HEALTH (NZ/0110-6929) [04612425] **3792**

REPORT / HYDRAULICS RESEARCH STATION (UK/0958-1278) [10990248] **2095**

REPORT - IDAHO POTATO COMMISSION (US) [04223302] **184**

REPORT / IDAHO. PUBLIC UTILITIES COMMISSION (US) [01187129] **4680**

REPORT / IGER (UK/0961-6071) [24465497] 2220, 3696, **126**

REPORT - ILLINOIS NATURE PRESERVES COMMISSION (US) [05702236] **2203**

REPORT / INDIA. PLANNING COMMISSION (II) [08428358] **4680**

REPORT - INDIA (REPUBLIC) COFFEE BOARD (II/0445-5738) [03822064] **184**

REPORT / INSTITUTE FOR LAND AND WATER MANAGEMENT RESEARCH (ICW) (NE) [11084114] 2574, **5538**

REPORT - INSTITUTE FOR MANAGEMENT EDUCATION AND DEVELOPMENT (IO) [03725708] **884**

REPORT - INSTITUTE FOR THE FUTURE (US/0363-1109) [02410706] **5215**

REPORT (INSTITUTE OF GEOLOGICAL SCIENCES (GREAT BRITAIN). ENVIRONMENTAL PROTECTION UNIT) (UK) [07646752] 2181, **2241**

REPORT / INSTITUTE OF HYDROLOGY (UK/0264-8709) [09047561] **1417**

REPORT - INSTITUTE OF MINING RESEARCH, UNIVERSITY OF ZIMBABWE (RH) [08216113] **2149**

REPORT (INSTITUTE OF OCEANOGRAPHIC SCIENCES (GREAT BRITAIN)) (UK) [05206315] **1456**

REPORT

Alphabetical Title Index

REPORT - INSTITUTE OF SPACE AND ASTRONAUTICAL SCIENCE, TOKYO (JA/0285-6808) [08294633] **33**

REPORT - INSTITUTE OF THEORETICAL ASTROPHYSICS (NO/0078-6780) [01714907] **4419**

REPORT / INTELSAT (US) [12626907] **1162**

REPORT - INTERNATIONAL COMMISSION FOR THE CONSERVATION OF ATLANTIC TUNAS. ENGLISH VERSION (SP/0377-368X) [02441143] **2311**

REPORT - INTERNATIONAL CONGRESS ON PHYSICAL EDUCATION AND SPORTS FOR GIRLS AND WOMEN (ER) [02152855] **4915**

REPORT / INTERNATIONAL COUNCIL FOR RESEARCH IN AGROFORESTRY (KE) [11869240] **2392**

REPORT / INTERNATIONAL LABOUR CONFERENCE (SZ/0074-6681) [10410499] **1706**

REPORT - INTERNATIONAL LABOUR ORGANISATION, AFRICAN REGIONAL CONFERENCE (SZ/0255-349X) [I0255349X] **1706**

REPORT (INTERNATIONAL LABOUR ORGANISATION. ASIAN REGIONAL CONFERENCE) (US) [12112395] **1706**

REPORT IPD.TS - INDUSTRIAL PROCESSING DIVISION, DEPARTMENT OF SCIENTIFIC AND INDUSTRIAL RESEARCH (NZ/0110-9561) [09492041] **5145**

REPORT - IRELAND (EIRE). MERCHANDISE MARKS COMMISSICN (IE) [01787367] **850**

REPORT - ISRAEL ATOMIC ENERGY COMMISSION (IS/0367-6617) [I03676617] **4451**

REPORT - JAMMU AND KASHMIR. LEGISLATIVE ASSEMBLY. COMMITTEE ON PUBLIC UNDERTAKINGS (II) [01784206] **4680**

REPORT - JAMMU AND KASHMIR LEGISLATIVE COUNCIL, COMMITTEE ON PRIVILEGES (II/0448-2433) [01797756] **4680**

REPORT - JOINT COAL BOARD (AT/0312-6358) [02239103] **2149**

REPORT - JOINT COMMITTEE ON OFFICES OF PROFIT (II/0537-0280) [05543369] **4680**

REPORT / JOINT COMMITTEE ON THE SECONDARY LEGISLATION OF THE EUROPEAN COMMUNITIES (IE) [18762471] **2522**

REPORT (JOINT INSTITUTE FOR LABORATORY ASTROPHYSICS) (US/0732-7935) [08441131] **4419**

REPORT - KANSAS. STATE REGISTRATION AND EXAMINING BOARD FOR ARCHITECTS (US) [01782489] **307**

REPORT - KANSAS STATE UNIVERSITY. INSTITUTE FOR SYSTEMS DESIGN AND OPTIMIZATION (US/0453-249X) [01754988] **2017**

REPORT - KARNATAKA LEGISLATIVE ASSEMBLY, COMMITTEE OF PRIVILEGES (II) [02713927] **4680**

REPORT - KARNATAKA LEGISLATURE, COMMITTEE ON THE WELFARE OF SCHEDULED CASTES & SCHEDULED TRIBES (II) [02640920] **5305**

REPORT - KENTUCKY. DEPT. OF ECONOMIC SECURITY (US) [01782490] **5305**

REPORT - KENTUCKY. DEPT OF HEALTH (US) [01782520] **4798**

REPORT - KENTUCKY. DEPT. OF REVENUE (US) [01782266] **4745**

REPORT - KERALA, INDIA (STATE). LEGISLATIVE ASSEMBLY. BUSINESS ADVISORY COMMITTEE (II) [01784205] **3038**

REPORT - LOUISIANA DEPT. OF OCCUPATIONAL STANDARDS (US) [01783216] **1706**

REPORT - MAKERERE UNIVERSITY (UG) [02241878] **1844**

REPORT - MAKERERE UNIVERSITY COLLEGE See REPORT - MAKERERE UNIVERSITY **1844**

REPORT - MALAYA (FEDERATION) DEPT. OF SOCIAL WELFARE (MY) [04522581] **5305**

REPORT / MARKETING SCIENCE INSTITUTE (US/0733-5733) [05715224] **935**

REPORT - MARYLAND DIVISION OF CORRECTION (US/0362-9198) [02379998] **3174**

REPORT - MASSACHUSETTS. COMMISSIONER OF VETERANS' SERVICES (US) [06758439] **4055**

REPORT - MEDICAL RESEARCH COUNCIL (CN) [03520108] **3633**

REPORT - MEGHALAYA LEGISLATIVE ASSEMBLY, COMMITTEE ON PETITIONS (II) [01797745] **5305**

REPORT - MELBOURNE. UNIVERSITY. LIBRARY (AT) [06755992] **3245**

REPORT - MENNONITE CENTRAL COMMITTEE. PEACE SECTION TASK FORCE ON WOMEN IN CHURCH AND SOCIETY (US) [04039087] **4992**

REPORT - MICHIGAN STATE HOUSING DEVELOPMENT AUTHORITY (US) [01783860] **2833**

REPORT (MICHIGAN STATE UNIVERSITY. CENTER FOR RURAL MANPOWER & PUBLIC AFFAIRS) (US) [04977765] **126**, **1706**

REPORT - MISSISSIPPI. STATE VETERANS AFFAIRS BOARD (US) [06258384] **4055**

REPORT - MISSOURI. COMMISSION ON HUMAN RIGHTS (US) [06247090] **4512**

REPORT MITSG *CEASED.* (US) [01354745] **1456**

REPORT - MONTANA STATE BUREAU OF MINES AND GEOLOGY (US) [05984676] **1394**

REPORT - N.H. STATE PLANNING PROJECT (US/0090-4015) [01785043] **4854**

REPORT - NATIONAL ASSOCIATION OF MANUFACTURERS OF THE UNITED STATES OF AMERICA. POSTWAR COMMITTEE (US) [01644329] **3487**

REPORT - NATIONAL CENTER FOR STATE COURTS (US/0195-5241) [02045964] **3142**

REPORT / NATIONAL COUNCIL ON FAMILY RELATIONS (US/0278-6168) [09641069] **2285**

REPORT / NATIONAL COUNCIL ON HEALTH CARE TECHNOLOGY (US/0278-6354) [07844751] **3633**

REPORT - NATIONAL HEALTH COUNCIL (IE) [04209073] **4798**

REPORT - NATIONAL PARKS AUTHORITY OF W.A (AT) [04787320] **2203**

REPORT - NATIONAL RESEARCH COUNCIL OF CANADA (CN) [04262550] **5145**

REPORT - NATIONAL SOCIETY TO PREVENT BLINDNESS (US/0270-4234) [06201537] **3878**

REPORT / NEVADA BUREAU OF MINES AND GEOLOGY (US/0095-5264) [01796609] 2149, **1394**

REPORT - NEW ENGLAND INTERSTATE WATER POLLUTION CONTROL COMMISSION (US) [01759767] 5538, **2241**

REPORT - NEW HAMPSHIRE. BANK COMMISSIONER'S OFFICE (US) [04710364] **807**

REPORT - NEW ZEALAND. DEPT. OF HEALTH (NZ) [06342388] **4798**

REPORT OF THE DEPARTMENT OF LANDS AND SURVEY FOR THE YEAR ENDED ... (1958) See REPORT OF THE DEPARTMENT OF LANDS FOR THE YEAR ENDED ... **1580**

REPORT NO. TES (US/0093-8947) [01791455] 5391, **2241**

REPORT - NORTHEASTERN FOREST EXPERIMENT STATION (BROOMALL, PA.) (1977/78) (US/0731-8316) [05279216] **2392**

REPORT - NORTHERN TERRITORY GEOLOGICAL SURVEY, DEPARTMENT OF MINES AND ENERGY (AT/0814-7477) [I08147477] **1394**

REPORT OF A VANTAGE CONFERENCE (US/0748-0571) [10867307] **4533**

REPORT OF ACCOMPLISHMENTS, RHODE ISLAND (US/0147-3263) [03140014] 2203, **126**

REPORT OF ACHIEVEMENTS OF PROGRAMS FOR THE AGING (US/0090-2233) [01784805] **5305**

REPORT OF ACTIVITIES - CEDES (AG) [05996711] **5215**

REPORT OF ACTIVITIES / EUROPEAN UNIVERSITY INSTITUTE (LU) [11403853] **1844**

REPORT OF ACTIVITIES FOR THE STATE DEPARTMENT OF ART, HISTORICAL AND CULTURAL PRESERVATION (US/0095-2230) [01796346] **2853**

REPORT OF ACTIVITIES - MINERALS DIVISION (WINNIPEG) (CN/1184-8006) [23368488] 2149, **1394**

REPORT OF ACTIVITIES. MINNESOTA ENVIRONMENTAL QUALITY BOARD (US) [10157100] **2241**

REPORT OF ACTIVITIES - NEW MEXICO. DEPT. OF ALCOHOLIC BEVERAGE CONTROL (US) [01786599] **2370**

REPORT OF ACTIVITIES - NEW MEXICO FORESTRY DIVISION (US/0270-4080) [06379976] **2392**

REPORT OF ACTIVITIES (NOVA SCOTIA. MINES AND MINERALS BRANCH) (CN) [11407202] **1360**

● REPORT OF ACTIVITIES / WOMEN'S EDUCATIONAL EQUITY ACT PROGRAM (US) [27471737] 5565, **1778**

REPORT OF AIB CHAPTER PROGRAMS & ... ACTIVITIES (US/0735-7982) [08970473] **807**

REPORT OF AMERICAN BAR FOUNDATION, THE (US) [19656182] **3038**

REPORT OF ANNUAL SEMINAR ON ESTATE PLANNING (US/0145-5079) [02742914] **3119**

REPORT OF ANNUAL TRADES UNION CONGRESS (UK) [05279806] **1706**

REPORT OF ASSOCIATION FOR INVESTMENT MANAGEMENT AND RESEARCH CORPORATE INFORMATION COMMITTEE (US/1057-8927) [23999535] **912**

REPORT OF ATTORNEY GENERAL TO THE GOVERNOR AND THE LEGISLATURE (US) [04185612] **3142**

REPORT OF CASE DECISIONS (US/0147-3611) [05807345] **3153**

REPORT OF CASES DETERMINED IN THE SUPREME COURT AND COURT OF APPEALS OF THE STATE OF NEW MEXICO (US/0094-7148) [01794572] **3038**

REPORT OF COLORADO RIVER COMMISSION OF NEVADA See FINANCIAL REPORT - STATE OF NEVADA, DIVISION OF COLORADO RIVER RESOURCES **2089**

REPORT OF ... COMMISSIONER OF AGRICULTURE, FOOD AND RURAL RESOURCES TO THE ... REGULAR SESSION OF THE ... MAINE STATE LEGISLATURE (US/0738-8438) [09625080] **126**

REPORT OF CONSUMPTION AND ANALYSES SUMMARY OF COMMERCIAL FEED (US) [08581845] 850, **126**

REPORT OF COUNCIL (UK) [06418187] **3531**

REPORT OF COUNCIL, ACCOUNTS, AND MINUTES OF ANNUAL GENERAL MEETING (UK) [02242102] **2483**

REPORT OF CRIMINAL OFFENSES AND ARRESTS (US/1049-6785) [10970912] **3174**

REPORT OF DATA FROM FA-1 FORMS - NEW JERSEY. DIVISION OF TAXATION. LOCAL PROPERTY AND PUBLIC UTILITY BRANCH (US) [02245684] **4745**

REPORT OF DIRECTORS AND STATEMENT OF ACCOUNTS See INDO-BURMA PETROLEUM COMPANY LIMITED ANNUAL REPORT **4260**

REPORT OF E.D.P. BRANCH, MINISTRY OF FINANCE FOR THE YEAR ... (FJ) [08546086] **4745**

REPORT OF EDUCATION STATISTICS (US/0362-8787) [02378845] 1778, **1796**

REPORT OF EMPLOYMENT, VACANCIES, AND PAYROLL STATISTICS / COMPILED BY EMPLOYMENT AND EARNINGS STATISTICS SECTION, CENSUS AND STATISTICS DEPARTMENT, HONG KONG (HK) [17648150] **1706**

REPORT OF EVALUATION OF STUDENT FINANCIAL AID (HELENA) (US/0092-7910) [01789999] **1844**

REPORT OF EXAMINATION, PUBLIC EMPLOYEES' PENSION FUNDS (US) [08015665] **4680**

REPORT OF FINANCIAL CONDITION AND OPERATIONS OF THE COMMODITY CREDIT CORPORATION / UNITED STATES DEPARTMENT OF AGRICULTURE, COMMODITY CREDIT CORPORATION (US) [10356828] **807**

REPORT OF FINDINGS AND RECOMMENDATIONS / STATUTORY REVISION COMMITTEE (COLORADO) (US) [10481988] **3038**

REPORT OF FUNDS GRANTED TO DELAWARE DURING FISCAL YEAR ... BY STATE AGENCY AND BY FEDERAL PROGRAM (OMB NUMBER) (US) [09021855] **4745**

REPORT OF HEALTH, PHYSICAL EDUCATION, AND RECREATION RESEARCH PROJECTS COMPLETED OR IN PROGRESS IN THE STATE OF INDIANA, A (US/0275-7494) [07189181] **1857**

REPORT OF INVESTIGATION - FLORIDA GEOLOGICAL SURVEY (1987) (US/1053-0533) [20761168] **1394**

REPORT OF INVESTIGATION - GEOLOGICAL SURVEY (LANSING) (US/0543-8497) [01307323] **1394**

REPORT OF INVESTIGATION (ILLINOIS STATE WATER SURVEY) (US/0097-5672) [01590334] **5538**

REPORT OF INVESTIGATION - NORTH DAKOTA GEOLOGICAL SURVEY (US/0099-4227) [01269820] 2149, **1394**

REPORT OF INVESTIGATIONS - ALASKA. DIVISION OF GEOLOGICAL AND GEOPHYSICAL SURVEYS (US/0741-0832) [09599597] **1394**

REPORT OF INVESTIGATIONS - DELAWARE GEOLOGICAL SURVEY (US/0011-7749) [01345091] **1394**

REPORT — Alphabetical Title Index

REPORT OF INVESTIGATIONS - GEOLOGICAL SURVEY OF SOUTH AUSTRALIA (AT/0016-7681) [01347441] **1394**

REPORT OF INVESTIGATIONS / KENTUCKY GEOLOGICAL SURVEY (US/0075-5591) [01755097] **1394**

REPORT OF INVESTIGATIONS - MARYLAND GEOLOGICAL SURVEY (US/0076-4809) [01320776] **1394**

REPORT OF INVESTIGATIONS - MINNESOTA GEOLOGICAL SURVEY (US/0076-9177) [01306470] **1394**

REPORT OF INVESTIGATIONS - MISSISSIPPI MINERAL RESOURCES INSTITUTE (US/0732-8567) [08631161] **1444**

REPORT OF INVESTIGATIONS - MISSOURI DEPARTMENT OF NATURAL RESOURCES, DIVISION OF RESEARCH AND TECHNICAL INFORMATION, GEOLOGICAL SURVEY (US/0361-2554) [02359778] **1394**

REPORT OF INVESTIGATIONS / NEBRASKA GEOLOGICAL SURVEY (US/0548-0817) [04616437] **1394**

REPORT OF INVESTIGATIONS / NEW WORLD RESEARCH (US) [06534915] **280**

REPORT OF INVESTIGATIONS (OHIO. DIVISION OF GEOLOGICAL SURVEY) (US) [08322113] **1394**

REPORT OF INVESTIGATIONS - SOUTH DAKOTA GEOLOGICAL SURVEY (US) [01416789] **1394**

REPORT OF INVESTIGATIONS - STATE GEOLOGICAL AND NATURAL HISTORY SURVEY OF CONNECTICUT (US/0589-3739) [01564832] **1394**

REPORT OF INVESTIGATIONS - STATE OF OHIO, DEPARTMENT OF NATURAL RESOURCES, DIVISION OF GEOLOGICAL SURVEY (US/0097-5680) [01681512] **1394**

REPORT OF INVESTIGATIONS / STATE OF WEST VIRGINIA, GEOLOGICAL AND ECONOMIC SURVEY (US/0083-8543) [01309541] **1395**

REPORT OF INVESTIGATIONS - TENNESSEE DIVISION OF GEOLOGY (US/0497-2074) [01306631] **1395**

REPORT OF INVESTIGATIONS - UNITED STATES. BUREAU OF MINES (US/1066-5552) [27119144] **2149**

REPORT OF INVESTIGATIONS - UNITED STATES. BUREAU OF MINES (US/1066-5552) [01728640] 4017, **2149**

REPORT OF INVESTIGATIONS - UNIVERSITY OF TEXAS AT AUSTIN. BUREAU OF ECONOMIC GEOLOGY (US/0888-6725) [04471346] **1395**

REPORT OF INVESTIGATIONS (WASHINGTON STATE). DIVISION OF GEOLOGY AND EARTH RESOURCES (US) [07369243] 2203, **1395**

REPORT OF IPA GRANT ACTIVITY (US) [03458690] **4705**

REPORT OF MATERIALS SCIENCE AND TECHNOLOGY (JA /0916-6521) [21278723] **2108**

REPORT OF MEDICAL ASSISTANCE & COUNTY INDIGENT STATISTICS (US) [08329373] **4811**

REPORT OF NURSE POPULATION IN OKLAHOMA / OKLAHOMA BOARD OF NURSE REGISTRATION AND NURSING EDUCATION (US) [09635911] 3868, **1706**

REPORT OF OFFICERS TO THE ... REGULAR AND ... QUADRENNIAL CONVENTION (US) [25645275] **1706**

REPORT OF OPERATIONS : HIGHWAYS, BUSES, AERONAUTICS, RAILROADS (US) [01785215] **5391**

REPORT OF OUTSTANDING INDEBTEDNESS OF COUNTIES, CITIES, VILLAGES, TOWNSHIPS, SCHOOLS, SPECIAL DISTRICTS, AUTHORITIES, STATE BONDS (US/0147-975X) [03251782] **4745**

REPORT OF PENNSYLVANIA COUNCIL FOR SEXUAL MINORITIES (US) [04222907] **4559**

REPORT OF PERSONS DISCHARGED FROM PAROLE AND PERSONS VIOLATING PAROLE (US/0364-6580) [02667421] **3174**

REPORT OF PROBATION SUPERVISION WORKLOAD (US/0362-7489) [02315388] **3174**

● REPORT OF PROBATION SUPERVISION WORKLOAD (US/0362-7489) [06740129] **3174**

REPORT OF PROCEEDINGS. ANNUAL GENERAL MEETING - BRITISH COLUMBIA SCHOOL TRUSTEES ASSOCIATION (CN/0836-4486) [17236568] **1778**

REPORT OF PROCEEDINGS - COMMONWEALTH AGRICULTURAL BUREAUX REVIEW CONFERENCE (UK) [04093675] **126**

REPORT OF PROCEEDINGS / IISI ... ANNUAL MEETINGS AND CONFERENCE (BE) [18097504] **1624**

REPORT OF PROCEEDINGS / NEW IRELAND FORUM (IE) [10399405] **2705**

REPORT OF PROCEEDINGS OF THE CONGRESS OF THE UNIVERSITIES OF THE COMMONWEALTH (UK) [01564777] **1844**

REPORT OF PROCEEDINGS OF THE TAX CONFERENCE CONVENED BY THE CANADIAN TAX FOUNDATION (CN/0316-3571) [02442147] **4745**

REPORT OF PROCEEDINGS - TOWN AND COUNTRY PLANNING SUMMER SCHOOL (UK) [02144195] **2833**

REPORT OF PROGRESS BY THE ILLINOIS ENVIRONMENTAL PROTECTION AGENCY (US/0092-0770) [01786527] **2181**

REPORT OF PROGRESS - MERL (US/0193-3310) [04968956] **2241**

REPORT OF PROJECTS / LOUISIANA AGRICULTURAL EXPERIMENT STATION. DEPT. OF AGRONOMY (US/0456-5959) [05253572] **126**

REPORT OF PUBLICATION AND RESEARCH - GEORGIA STATE UNIVERSITY. COLLEGE OF BUSINESS ADMINISTRATION (US) [03804733] **707**

REPORT OF PUBLICATION BY THE FACULTY OF THE SCHOOL OF BUSINESS ADMINISTRATION, GEORGIA STATE UNIVERSITY **See** REPORT OF PUBLICATION AND RESEARCH - GEORGIA STATE UNIVERSITY. COLLEGE OF BUSINESS ADMINISTRATION **707**

REPORT OF RANDOM SAMPLE EGG PRODUCTION TESTS, UNITED STATES AND CANADA (US/0098-6836) [02240892] **126**

REPORT OF RECIDIVISTS COMMITTED TO THE VIRGINIA STATE PENAL SYSTEM (US/0363-0633) [02398966] **3174**

REPORT OF REGISTRATIONS (US) [11048383] **1955**

REPORT OF RESEARCH ACTIVITIES - DIVISION OF TECHNICAL SERVICES, QUEENSLAND DEPARTMENT OF FORESTRY (AT/0311-0893) [05060674] **2392**

REPORT OF RESEARCH CENTER OF ION BEAM TECHNOLOGY, HOSEI UNIVERSITY. SUPPLEMENT (JA) [09205482] **4419**

REPORT OF RESEARCH / COMMONWEALTH SCIENTIFIC AND INDUSTRIAL RESEARCH ORGANIZATION, AUSTRALIA, DIVISION OF FOOD RESEARCH (AT) [05155329] **2355**

REPORT OF RESEARCH - DIVISION OF FOOD RESEARCH (AT) [05668464] **2355**

REPORT OF SALARIES AND EMPLOYEE BENEFITS STATISTICS; MANAGERIAL AND PROFESSIONAL EMPLOYEES, EXCLUDING TOP MANAGEMENT (HK) [13557535] **1706**

REPORT OF SCIENTIFIC ACTIVITIES (PL) [01791433] **3633**

REPORT OF SOUTH DAKOTA'S PROFESSIONAL AND OCCUPATIONAL LICENSING BOARDS AND COMMISSIONS (US) [06745887] 4209, **4680**

REPORT OF ... SOYBEAN SEED RESEARCH CONFERENCE / ORGANIZED AND SPONSORED BY THE SOYBEAN SEED DIVISION OF THE AMERICAN SEED TRADE ASSOCIATION (US) [10462501] **184**

REPORT OF STUDENT PERFORMANCE (US) [05215320] **1778**

REPORT OF STUDY GROUP ON INTERNATIONAL ISSUES, FAPRC (JA/0915-5457) [l09155457] 2355, **126**

REPORT OF THE ADMINISTRATION OF COLOURED AFFAIRS FOR THE PERIOD ... (SA) [10279340] **2643**

REPORT OF THE ADMINISTRATOR / ALCOHOL, DRUG ABUSE, AND MENTAL HEALTH ADMINISTRATION (US/0193-0494) [05107791] 4798, **1348**

REPORT OF THE ADMINISTRATOR - UNITED STATES. HEALTH SERVICES ADMINISTRATION (US/0276-8321) [06884146] **4798**

REPORT OF THE ADVISORY PANEL ON ALZHEIMER'S DISEASE (US) [21237806] **3844**

REPORT OF THE AGRICULTURAL RESEARCH INSTITUTE OF ONTARIO (CN/0706-425X) [04526874] **126**

REPORT OF THE AGRICULTURE STUDY COMMITTEE OF SOUTH CAROLINA (US/0362-4226) [02338303] **126**

REPORT OF THE ... ANNUAL MEETING / FRANCISCAN EDUCATIONAL CONFERENCE (US) [01774934] **1778**

REPORT OF THE ATTORNEY GENERAL (US) [01757276] **3142**

REPORT OF THE ATTORNEY GENERAL OF NEW MEXICO **See** ANNUAL REPORT / OFFICE OF THE ATTORNEY GENERAL, DEPARTMENT OF JUSTICE, STATE OF NEW MEXICO **3139**

REPORT OF THE ATTORNEY GENERAL TO THE CONGRESS OF THE UNITED STATES ON THE ADMINISTRATION OF THE FOREIGN AGENTS REGISTRATION ACT, AS AMENDED, FOR THE CALENDAR YEAR ... (US) [02395037] **3142**

REPORT OF THE AUDITOR GENERAL (EDMONTON) (CN/0228-314X) [06861043] **4745**

REPORT OF THE AUDITOR-GENERAL FOR ... ON THE ACCOUNTS OF PARASTATAL BODIES (ZA) [08680798] 750, **4680**

REPORT OF THE AUDITOR GENERAL OF PRINCE EDWARD ISLAND TO THE LEGISLATIVE ASSEMBLY (CN/0318-8124) [11163518] **4745**

REPORT OF THE AUDITOR-GENERAL ON THE ACCOUNTS OF THE COTTON BOARD FOR THE FINANCIAL YEAR ... (SA) [15681777] **1580**

REPORT OF THE AUDITOR-GENERAL ON THE ACCOUNTS OF THE DAIRY BOARD FOR THE FINANCIAL YEAR ... (SA) [15901072] **198**

REPORT OF THE AUDITOR-GENERAL ON THE ACCOUNTS OF THE DECIDUOUS FRUIT BOARD AND THE SOUTH AFRICAN PLANT IMPROVEMENT ORGANISATION. VERSLAG VAN DIE OUDITEUR-GENERAAL VOR DIE REKENINGEN VAN DIE SAGTEVRUGTERAAD EN DIE SUID-AFRIKAANSE PLANT-VERBETERINGSORGANISASIE (SA) [03377289] 184, **4680**

REPORT OF THE AUDITOR-GENERAL ON THE ACCOUNTS OF THE DEPARTMENT OF POSTS AND TELECOMMUNICATIONS (SA) [06746751] **1162**

REPORT OF THE AUDITOR-GENERAL ON THE ACCOUNTS OF THE EGG BOARD FOR THE FINANCIAL YEAR ... / VERSLAG VAN DIE OUDITEUR-GENERAAL OOR DIE REKENINGS VAN DIE EIERRAAD VIR DIE BOEKJAAR ... (SA) [25912811] 750, **850**

REPORT OF THE AUDITOR-GENERAL ON THE ACCOUNTS OF THE LUCERNE SEED BOARD FOR THE FINANCIAL YEAR ... (SA) [22098509] **184**

REPORT OF THE AUDITOR-GENERAL ON THE ACCOUNTS OF THE MEAT BOARD FOR THE FINANCIAL YEAR ... (SA) [07251049] **2355**

REPORT OF THE AUDITOR-GENERAL ON THE ACCOUNTS OF THE OILSEEDS BOARD FOR THE FINANCIAL YEAR ... (SA) [15604617] **4680**

REPORT OF THE AUDITOR-GENERAL ON THE ACCOUNTS OF THE REPRESENTATIVE AUTHORITY OF THE OVAMBOS AND OF THE TRIBAL AUTHORITIES IN OVAMBO FOR THE FINANCIAL YEAR ... (SA) [15618743] **4745**

REPORT OF THE AUDITOR-GENERAL ON THE ACCOUNTS OF THE WHEAT BOARD FOR THE FINANCIAL YEAR ... (SA) [15701181] **1580**

REPORT OF THE AUDITOR GENERAL ON THE ACCOUNTS OF TRINIDAD AND TOBAGO (TR) [01787318] **4745**

REPORT OF THE AUDITOR GENERAL ON THE PUBLIC ACCOUNTS OF THE GOVERNMENT OF GUYANA FOR THE FINANCIAL YEAR ENDED 31ST DECEMBER ... / GUYANA (GL) [08616964] **4745**

REPORT OF THE AUDITOR GENERAL ON THE PUBLIC ACCOUNTS ... / PAPUA NEW GUINEA (PP) [09582283] **4745**

REPORT OF THE AUDITOR GENERAL ON THE ZANZIBAR SSTATE ENTERPRISES FOR THE PERIOD ENDED 31ST DECEMBER (ZA) [10062530] **4745**

REPORT OF THE AUDITOR GENERAL TO THE LEGISLATIVE ASSEMBLY (FREDERICTON) (CN/0382-1420) [01793340] **4745**

REPORT OF THE AUDITOR OF PUBLIC ACCOUNTS. AUDIT EXAMINATION OF THE GRAYSON COUNTY FISCAL COURT (US) [11486377] **4745**

REPORT OF THE AUDITOR OF PUBLIC ACCOUNTS. AUDIT EXAMINATIONS OF THE CUMBERLAND COUNTY FISCAL COURT, FISCAL YEAR ENDED JUNE 30 ... CUMBERLAND COUNTY CLERK, CALENDAR YEAR ... (US) [11486281] **4745**

REPORT OF THE AUSTRALIA AND NEW ZEALAND COMBINED DIALYSIS AND TRANSPLANT REGISTRY (AT/0727-3738) [l07273738] **3633**

REPORT OF THE BELFAST EDUCATION AND LIBRARY BOARD (IE) [03475538] **1903**

REPORT OF THE BENDEL STATE PUBLIC SERVICE COMMISSION (NR) [06380367] **4705**

REPORT OF THE BOARD OF DIRECTORS (TI) [11351863] **1516**

Alphabetical Title Index — REPORT

... REPORT OF THE BROADCASTING AUTHORITY ON THE PROGRESS OF TELEVISION BROADCASTING IN HONG KONG, THE (HK) [20708680] **1138**

REPORT OF THE BROADCASTING CORPORATION OF NEW ZEALAND (NZ) [06261885] **1138**

REPORT OF THE BROADCASTING TRIBUNAL FOR THE YEAR ENDED 31 MARCH ... (NZ) [10841442] **1138**

REPORT OF THE CANADIAN MULTICULTURALISM COUNCIL (CN/0846-9253) [22929901] **2757**

REPORT OF THE CARCINOGENESIS PROGRAM (US/0090-2403) [02638588] **3823**

REPORT OF THE CENTRAL COMMITTEE OF THE COMMUNIST PARTY OF UKRAINE TO THE CONGRESS OF THE COMMUNIST PARTY OF UKRAINE (UN) [03641663] **4546**

REPORT OF THE CHAIRMAN OF THE BOARD OF DIRECTORS - EMPORIKE TRAPEZA TES HELLADOS (GR) [01791497] **807**

REPORT OF THE CHAIRMAN - UNITED STATES. PRESIDENT'S CANCER PANEL (US/0739-9987) [09820159] **3823**

REPORT OF THE CHIEF ELECTORAL OFFICER OF CANADA (CN/0846-6351) [21095646] **4493**

REPORT OF THE CHIEF ELECTORAL OFFICER ON THE ... GENERAL ENUMERATION (CN/0708-3998) [05257913] **4680**

REPORT OF THE CHIEF INSPECTOR OF WEIGHTS & MEASURES, CITY OF BIRMINGHAM (UK) [02246963] **4032**

REPORT OF THE CHIEF OF THE SOIL CONSERVATION SERVICE (US) [01440366] **184**

REPORT OF THE CHIEF REGISTRAR / REGISTRY OF FRIENDLY SOCIETIES (UK) [07252588] **2892**

REPORT OF THE CO-ORDINATOR-GENERAL OF PUBLIC WORKS, QUEENSLAND (AT/0480-970X) [01190881] **4681**

REPORT OF THE CODEX COMMITTEE ON COCOA PRODUCTS AND CHOCOLATE (IT) [02554249] **2355**

REPORT OF THE COMMISSION ON HUMAN SETTLEMENTS (US) [06998541] **244**

REPORT OF THE COMMISSION ON TAXATION AND PRODUCTION OF IRON ORE AND OTHER MINERALS (US/0091-8229) [01787812] **4745**

REPORT OF THE COMMISSION TO STUDY THE ORGANIZATION OF PEACE (US) [01564388] **4533**

REPORT OF THE COMMISSIONER FOR RAILWAYS FOR THE YEAR ENDED 30TH JUNE . See ANNUAL REPORT FOR YEAR ENDED 30 JUNE ... / QUEENSLAND RAILWAYS **5429**

REPORT OF THE COMMISSIONER OF BANKS OF DEBT PRORATE COMPANIES LICENSED UNDER MINNESOTA STATUTES, CHAPTER 332 (US/0278-7571) [05038023] **807**

REPORT OF THE COMMISSIONER OF INSURANCE FOR THE YEAR ENDED ... / ZIMBABWE (RH) [27786457] **2892**

REPORT OF THE COMMISSIONER OF INSURANCE - KANSAS (US) [01782626] **2892**

REPORT OF THE COMMISSIONER OF POLICE OF THE METROPOLIS FOR THE YEAR (UK) [11313293] **3174**

REPORT OF THE COMMISSIONERS OF HIS MAJESTY'S INLAND REVENUE (UK) [01645882] **4745**

REPORT OF THE COMMISSIONERS OF THE STATE SINKING FUND TO THE GENERAL ASSEMBLY OF SOUTH CAROLINA See REPORT OF THE STATE BUDGET AND CONTROL BOARD, DIVISION OF SINKING FUNDS AND PROPERTY **4681**

REPORT OF THE COMMITTEE ON FOREIGN AFFAIRS FOR THE ... SESSION OF THE ... NATIONAL ASSEMBLY APPOINTED ON ... / REPUBLIC OF ZAMBIA (ZA) [08734158] **4533**

REPORT OF THE COMMITTEE ON GOVERNMENT ASSURANCES FOR THE ... SESSION OF THE ... NATIONAL ASSEMBLY, APPOINTED ON ... / REPUBLIC OF ZAMBIA (ZA) [08734697] **4681**

REPORT OF THE COMMITTEE ON INFECTIOUS DISEASES (US) [03679558] **3715**

REPORT OF THE COMMITTEE ON INFORMATION / UNITED NATIONS (US) [07122718] **4533**

REPORT OF THE COMMITTEE ON PUBLIC ACCOUNTS (II) [07445564] **4745**

REPORT OF THE COMMITTEE ON RULES (II) [02245604] **3038**

REPORT OF THE COMMONWEALTH MAGISTRATES' CONFERENCE (UK) [02240815] **3038**

REPORT OF THE COMPENSATION COMMISSIONER FOR OCCUPATIONAL DISEASES (SA/0377-970X) [02412123] **2868**

REPORT OF THE COMPTROLLER AND AUDITOR GENERAL OF INDIA FOR THE YEAR ... (COMMERCIAL), GOVERNMENT OF RAJASTHAN (II) [09396532] **4745**

REPORT OF THE COMPTROLLER AND AUDITOR GENERAL OF INDIA FOR THE YEAR ..., (REVENUE RECEIPTS) GOVERNMENT OF RAJASTHAN (II) [07141653] **4745**

REPORT OF THE COMPTROLLER AND AUDITOR-GENERAL OF INDIA. GOVERNMENT OF GUJARAT (II) [05506881] **4745**

REPORT OF THE COMPTROLLER AND AUDITOR GENERAL OF INDIA, GOVERNMENT OF KERALA, CIVIL (II) [03429025] **4745**

REPORT OF THE COMPTROLLER AND AUDITOR GENERAL OF INDIA GOVERNMENT OF TAMIL NADU : CIVIL (II) [02413975] **4745**

REPORT OF THE COMPTROLLER AND AUDITOR GENERAL OF INDIA, GOVERNMENT OF TAMIL NADU : REVENUE RECEIPTS (II) [02410598] **4745**

REPORT OF THE COMPTROLLER AND AUDITOR-GENERAL OF INDIA (REVENUE RECEIPTS) (II) [07042528] **4745**

REPORT OF THE COMPTROLLER AND AUDITOR GENERAL OF INDIA, UNION GOVERNMENT (RAILWAYS) (II) [05526525] **5436**

REPORT OF THE COMPTROLLER TO THE GOVERNOR OF VIRGINIA (US/0146-7387) [01241970] **4745**

REPORT OF THE COMPULSORY MOTOR VEHICLE INSURANCE SECTION AND OF THE MOTOR VEHICLE ASSURANCE FUND (SA) [02244919] **2892**

REPORT OF THE COMPUTER CENTRE, UNIVERSITY OF TOKYO (JA/0564-8742) [01963537] **1262**

REPORT OF THE CONFERENCE OF FAO (IT) [07706087] 126, **2355**

REPORT OF THE ... CONFERENCE / THE INTERNATIONAL LAW ASSOCIATION (UK/0074-6738) [01643078] **3134**

REPORT OF THE CONTROLLER AND AUDITOR-GENERAL ON THE ACCOUNTS OF THE ADMINISTRATION OF COLOURED AFFAIRS (SA) [01784914] **4745**

REPORT OF THE CONTROLLER AND AUDITOR-GENERAL ON THE ACCOUNTS OF THE LUCERNE SEED CONTROL BOARD (SA) [06985875] **1624**

REPORT OF THE CONTROLLER FOR THE PERIOD ENDED 30 JUNE / DEPARTMENT OF THE TREASURY, ROYAL AUSTRALIAN MINT (AT) [19831516] **4745**

REPORT OF THE CONTROLLER OF WORKS (RH) [01786500] **4681**

REPORT OF THE COUNCIL (AT) [02649184] **1844**

REPORT OF THE COUNCIL AND ABSTRACT OF THE ACCOUNTS / SELDEN SOCIETY (UK) [04551436] **3038**

REPORT OF THE COUNCIL FOR FRANCO-ONTARIAN EDUCATION (CN/0715-6510) [10167814] **1778**

REPORT OF THE COUNCIL FOR THE YEAR ... / SCIENCE AND ENGINEERING RESEARCH COUNCIL (UK/0261-7005) [08304224] **5145**

REPORT OF THE COUNCIL FOR TOBACCO RESEARCH--U.S.A., INC (US/0361-1612) [02239864] **5373**

REPORT OF THE COUNCIL / NATURAL ENVIRONMENT RESEARCH COUNCIL (UK/0072-7008) [01167737] **2181**

REPORT OF THE COUNCIL OF FAO (ENGLISH EDITION) (IT) [01473524] 2355, **126**

REPORT OF THE COUNCIL - ROYAL INSTITUTE OF CHEMISTRY, LONDON (UK/0557-4048) [01908254] **991**

REPORT OF THE CREDIT UNION SUPERVISOR (US) [09346144] **808**

REPORT OF THE DEPARTMENT OF CO-OPERATION AND DEVELOPMENT (SA) [06551788] **2643**

REPORT OF THE DEPARTMENT OF COMMUNITY SERVICES FOR THE YEAR ENDED 30 JUNE (AT) [15861868] **5305**

REPORT OF THE DEPARTMENT OF HEALTH PROFESSIONS, COMMONWEALTH OF VIRGINIA FOR THE ... BIENNIUM (US) [23810679] **4798**

REPORT OF THE DEPARTMENT OF LANDS AND SURVEY FOR THE YEAR ENDED . See REPORT OF THE DEPARTMENT OF SURVEY AND LAND INFORMATION FOR THE YEAR ENDED ... **2030**

REPORT OF THE DEPARTMENT OF LANDS FOR THE YEAR ENDED ... (NZ) [19650133] **1580**

REPORT OF THE DEPARTMENT OF PLURAL RELATIONS AND DEVELOPMENT (SA) [06832171] **4681**

REPORT OF THE DEPARTMENT OF SCIENTIFIC AND INDUSTRIAL RESEARCH (NZ) [05186284] **5145**

REPORT OF THE DEPARTMENT OF SURVEY AND LAND INFORMATION FOR THE YEAR ENDED ... (NZ) [20556160] **2030**

REPORT OF THE DEUTSCHE BUNDESBANK FOR THE YEAR (GW/0418-8306) [02538958] **808**

REPORT OF THE DIRECTOR (US) [13753993] **3245**

REPORT OF THE DIRECTOR - DEPARTMENT OF CHILDREN'S SERVICES (AT/0728-0645) [04074183] **5305**

REPORT OF THE DIRECTOR GENERAL OF HOUSING AND CONSTRUCTION FOR THE PERIOD FROM ... (AT) [20654395] **2833**

REPORT OF THE DIRECTOR GENERAL ON THE ACTIVITIES OF THE ORGANIZATION IN ... (FR) [02155400] **5236**

REPORT OF THE DIRECTOR, NATIONAL HEART, LUNG, AND BLOOD INSTITUTE (US/0193-7340) [03075833] 3710, **4798**

REPORT OF THE DIRECTOR OF AUDIT ON THE ACCOUNTS OF MAURITIUS FOR THE YEAR ENDED 30 JUNE ... (MF) [07511389] **4746**

REPORT OF THE DIRECTOR OF AUDIT ON THE RESULTS OF VALUE FOR MONEY AUDITS (HK) [20695762] **4681**

REPORT OF THE DIRECTOR OF ELECTIONS (JM) [19609457] **4493**

REPORT OF THE DIRECTOR OF FISHERY RESEARCH (UK) [01982653] **2311**

REPORT OF THE DIRECTOR OF MENTAL HEALTH SERVICES (AT) [05582464] **4798**

REPORT OF THE DIRECTOR OF MINES (HOBART. 1940) (AT) [02381373] **2150**

REPORT OF THE DIRECTOR OF NATIONAL ARCHIVES (RH) [02246091] **2483**

REPORT OF THE DIRECTOR OF UNIVERSITY LIBRARIES TO THE VICE PRESIDENT OF UNIVERSITY SERVICES (US/8756-2782) [11494701] **3245**

REPORT OF THE DIVISION OF CANCER TREATMENT, NCI See ANNUAL REPORT / NATIONAL CANCER INSTITUTE, DIVISION OF CANCER TREATMENT **3808**

REPORT OF THE DIVISION OF PUBLIC UTILITY CONTROL (CONNECTICUT) (US) [06402643] **4681**

REPORT OF THE ECONOMIC AND SOCIAL COUNCIL FOR THE YEAR ... UNITED NATIONS (US/0082-8203) [01589096] **5215**

REPORT OF THE ELECTION LAW ENFORCEMENT COMMISSION (US) [15192095] **4493**

REPORT OF THE FEDERAL HOME LOAN MORTGAGE CORPORATION (US/0094-7156) [01795164] **808**

REPORT OF THE FIREMASTER OF THE CITY OF GLASGOW (UK) [05519316] **2292**

REPORT OF THE FOREST SERVICE (WASHINGTON) (US/0272-1007) [04482233] **2392**

REPORT OF THE GAMING BOARD FOR GREAT BRITAIN (UK) [08864557] **4681**

REPORT OF THE GENERAL DIRECTOR - INTERAMERICAN CHILDREN'S INSTITUTE (UY) [01795706] **5305**

REPORT OF THE GEOMAGNETIC AND GEOELECTRIC OBSERVATIONS (JA) [08353066] **4445**

REPORT OF THE GOVERNMENT CHEMICAL LABORATORIES (AT/0511-7003) [01304707] **1018**

REPORT OF THE GOVERNMENT CHEMIST (UK) [02326344] **991**

REPORT OF THE GOVERNMENT COMPUTING SERVICE FOR THE YEAR ENDED 31 MARCH - NEW ZEALAND (NZ) [15155937] **4681**

REPORT OF THE GOVERNMENT OF THE UNITED STATES OF AMERICA TO THE FOOD AND AGRICULTURE ORGANIZATION OF THE UNITED NATIONS (US) [01475388] **126**

REPORT OF THE GOVERNOR'S EARTHQUAKE COUNCIL (US/0098-2717) [02240694] **5305**

REPORT OF THE GOVERNOR'S YOUTH COUNCIL (RICHMOND) (US/0094-4726) [05725308] **1068**

REPORT
Alphabetical Title Index

REPORT OF THE HOUGHTON POULTRY RESEARCH STATION (UK/0307-4927) [03633898] **220**

REPORT OF THE INSTITUTE OF INDUSTRIAL SCIENCE, UNIVERSITY OF TOKYO (JA/0040-9006) [02146989] **5146**

REPORT OF THE INSTITUTE OF OCEANOGRAPHIC SCIENCES DEACON LABORATORY FOR THE PERIOD 1ST APRIL ... TO 31ST MARCH ... (UK) [20573658] **1456**

REPORT OF THE INSURANCE DIVISION OF IOWA (US) [18892277] **2892**

REPORT OF THE INTERAGENCY TOXIC SUBSTANCES DATA COMMITTEE (US/0888-2681) [08547506] 4248, **3983**

REPORT OF THE INTERNATIONAL LABOUR ORGANIZATION TO THE UNITED NATIONS (SZ) [03025987] **1706**

REPORT OF THE INTERNATIONAL NARCOTICS CONTROL BOARD (US) [01182700] **1348**

REPORT OF THE INTERNATIONAL WHALING COMMISSION (UK/0143-8700) [06468892] **5596**

REPORT OF THE JOHNSONVILLE LICENSING TRUST FOR THE YEAR ENDED 31 MARCH ... (NZ) [10701285] **4681**

REPORT OF THE JOINT ENERGY COMMITTEE (US) [17286472] **1955**

REPORT OF THE JOINT LEGISLATIVE COMMITTEE ON MOTOR VEHICLES, HIGHWAY AND TRAFFIC SAFETY TO THE LEGISLATURE OF THE STATE OF NEW YORK (US/0731-6194) [05296373] 4798, **5391**

REPORT OF THE KOHALA TASK FORCE (US) [06720256] **1624**

REPORT OF THE LAW SOCIETY OF SCOTLAND ON THE LEGAL AID SCHEME (UK) [06030267] **3180**

REPORT OF THE LEGAL AID REVIEW COMMITTEE (AT) [02244012] **3180**

REPORT OF THE LEGISLATIVE INTERIM COMMITTEE ON EDUCATION (SALEM) (US/0093-1217) [01791369] **1778**

REPORT OF THE LIBRARIAN (US) [01782541] **3245**

REPORT OF THE LIBRARIAN TO THE PRESIDENT - ALLEGHENY COLLEGE, MEADVILLE, PA (US) [06240723] **3245**

REPORT OF THE LIBRARY COMMISSION OF MAINE (US) [07380622] **3245**

REPORT OF THE LIBRARY SCIENCE DEPARTMENT (PK) [02359797] **3245**

REPORT OF THE MANPOWER SURVEY (BM) [04937711] **1706**

REPORT OF THE MARINE POLLUTION LABORATORY (DK/0107-7430) [I01077430] 1456, 2241, **2220**

REPORT OF THE MARYLAND BOARD OF REVENUE ESTIMATES ON ESTIMATED MARYLAND REVENUES (US) [07890884] **4746**

REPORT OF THE MASSACHUSETTS COMMISSION ON INDIAN AFFAIRS (US) [03962225] 2272, **4681**

REPORT OF THE MEDICAL BUREAU FOR OCCUPATIONAL DISEASES (SA) [03503103] **2868**

REPORT OF THE MICHIGAN EDUCATIONAL ASSESSMENT PROGRAM (US/0090-2152) [01785744] **1870**

REPORT OF THE MIGRATORY BIRD CONSERVATION COMMISSION (US/0190-2245) [01047797] **5620**

REPORT OF THE MINISTRY OF AGRICULTURE AND FISHERIES (NZ) [02240761] 2311, **126**

REPORT OF THE MINISTRY OF CO-OPERATIVES AND CO-OPERATIVE DEVELOPMENT FOR PERIOD ... (MF) [07144024] **1543**

REPORT OF THE MINISTRY OF COLLEGES AND UNIVERSITIES (CN/0381-3878) [01786880] **1844**

REPORT OF THE MINISTRY OF EDUCATION, TE TAHUHU O TE MATAURANGA FOR THE 9 MONTHS FROM ... (NZ) [24604109] **1778**

REPORT OF THE MINISTRY OF RESEARCH, SCIENCE AND TECHNOLOGY FOR THE ... MONTHS ENDED 30 JUNE ... (NZ) [24160360] **471**

REPORT OF THE MINISTRY OF TRANSPORT (NZ) [01798869] **5391**

REPORT OF THE MISSISSIPPI RIVER PARKWAY COMMISSION OF MINNESOTA (US) [10297378] **4681**

REPORT OF THE MISSISSIPPI RIVER PARKWAY COMMISSION TO THE ... GENERAL ASSEMBLY OF ILLINOIS / MISSISSIPPI RIVER PARKWAY COMMISSION (US) [08100263] **5443**

REPORT OF THE MISSISSIPPI STATE HOSPITAL COMMISSION (US/0147-2607) [03134270] **3792**

REPORT OF THE MUNICIPAL COURT (SAN FRANCISCO) (US) [06956058] **3142**

REPORT OF THE NATIONAL CRITICAL TECHNOLOGIES PANEL (US) [23686795] **5146**

REPORT OF THE NATIONAL HEART, LUNG, AND BLOOD ADVISORY COUNCIL (US/0161-1917) [03603500] 3773, **3710**

REPORT OF THE NATIONAL HIKING WAY BOARD (SA) [05434120] **4878**

REPORT OF THE NATIONAL INSTITUTE OF GENETICS (JA/0077-4995) [01783000] **551**

REPORT OF THE NATIONAL MARINE FISHERIES SERVICE (US/0093-9412) [01791550] **2311**

REPORT OF THE NATIONAL MEETING OF THE CENTURY III LEADERS, THE (US/0192-608X) [05035370] **1870**

REPORT OF THE NATIONAL OBSERVATORY OF JAPAN (JA/0915-6321) **399**

REPORT OF THE NATIONAL POLICE COMMISSION (INDIA) (II) [07192080] **3174**

REPORT OF THE NATIONAL RESEARCH INSTITUTE FOR EARTH SCIENCE AND DISASTER PREVENTION (JA) 1073, **1410**

REPORT OF THE NATURE CONSERVATION COUNCIL FOR THE YEAR ENDED 31 MARCH ... (NZ) [08598211] **2203**

REPORT OF THE NATURE RESERVES COMMITTEE (UK) [02969183] **2203**

REPORT OF THE NEVADA INDIAN AFFAIRS COMMISSION (US/0548-3441) [01153976] **2272**

REPORT OF THE NEW MEXICO VETERANS' SERVICE COMMISSION (US/0094-7326) [01794531] 5215, 4055, **4681**

REPORT OF THE NEW SOUTH WALES STATE FISHERIES FOR THE YEAR ENDED ... (AT/0155-641X) [09332666] **2311**

REPORT OF THE NEW YORK CHAMBER OF COMMERCE AND INDUSTRY (US) [04506579] **821**

REPORT OF THE NEW ZEALAND FISHING INDUSTRY BOARD (NZ/0110-9618) [I01109618] **2311**

REPORT OF THE NODA INSTITUTE FOR SCIENTIFIC RESEARCH (JA/0078-0944) [01780288] 569, **493**

REPORT OF THE ... NORTH AMERICAN ALFALFA IMPROVEMENT CONFERENCE (US) [21130410] **184**

REPORT OF THE NUTRITION CENTER OF THE PHILIPPINES (PH) [02339008] **4198**

REPORT OF THE OAMARU LICENSING TRUST FOR THE YEAR ENDED (NZ) [15558923] **4681**

REPORT OF THE OFFICE OF THE PUBLIC COUNSEL, STATE OF MISSOURI (US) [04688374] **4681**

REPORT OF THE OFFICE OF THE PUBLIC DEFENDER FOR THE STATE OF MARYLAND (US/0093-2159) [01786336] **3108**

REPORT OF THE OHIO NURSING HOME COMMISSION TO THE GOVERNOR AND OHIO GENERAL ASSEMBLY (US) [05250476] **3792**

REPORT OF THE OMBUDSMAN (US/0073-1137) [01800016] **4681**

REPORT OF THE PATIENT REGISTRY (US/0197-7423) [05807504] **3801**

REPORT OF THE PERIOD ... / VERMONT BOARD OF REGISTRATION FOR LAND SURVEYORS (US) [11182488] **2030**

REPORT OF THE PFRA SHELTERBELT CENTRE / AGRICULTURE CANADA, PRAIRIE FARM REHABILITATION ADMINSTRATION (CN) [19233511] **2392**

REPORT OF THE PLANNING DIVISION, STATE DEPARTMENT OF FINANCE (US/0098-1338) [02240396] **4681**

REPORT OF THE POPULATION COMMISSION / ECONOMIC AND SOCIAL COUNCIL, UNITED NATIONS (US) [05289957] **4559**

REPORT OF THE PRESIDENT - MEDICAL RESEARCH COUNCIL OF CANADA (CN) [01597219] **3633**

REPORT OF THE PRESIDENT - MEDICAL RESEARCH COUNCIL (OTTAWA) (CN/0384-2029) [02442435] **3633**

REPORT OF THE PRESIDENT / NATURAL SCIENCES AND ENGINEERING RESEARCH COUNCIL CANADA (CN/0225-2376) [06082807] **4681**

REPORT OF THE PRESIDENT - UNIVERSITY OF MARYLAND (US/0147-3174) [03139918] **1844**

REPORT OF THE PRINCE EDWARD ISLAND HERITAGE FOUNDATION (CN) [03592910] **2757**

REPORT OF THE PROCEEDINGS : ANNUAL MEETING AND TECHNICAL FORUM (US/0428-5670) [01793580] **4569**

REPORT OF THE PROCEEDINGS - NATIONAL CENTER FOR A BARRIER FREE ENVIRONMENT, A (US/0270-9376) [06542662] **2181**

REPORT OF THE PROCEEDINGS OF THE ANNUAL MEETING OF THE ... MISSOURI BAR ASSOCIATION (US) [02360892] **3038**

REPORT OF THE PUBLIC ACCOUNTS COMMITTEE (ZA) [01796298] **4746**

REPORT OF THE PUBLIC AND POLICE SERVICE COMMISSIONS (MF) [28084625] **4681**

REPORT OF THE PUBLIC SERVICE COMMISSION (NR) [04941955] **4705**

REPORT OF THE PUBLIC SERVICE COMMISSION (MF) [03286016] **4681**

REPORT OF THE PUBLIC WORKS SUBCOMMITTEE OF FINANCE COMMITTEE APPOINTED TO REVIEW THE PUBLIC WORKS PROGRAMME (HK) [02313696] **4762**

REPORT OF THE ... RACING SEASON / MAINE STATE HARNESS RACING COMMISSION (US) [10214257] 2802, **4915**

REPORT OF THE REGISTRAR-GENERAL OF CEYLON ON VITAL STATISTICS FOR ... (CE/0254-0924) [07352970] **5337**

REPORT OF THE REGISTRAR OF BANKS AND FINANCIAL INSTITUTIONS (RH) [01785371] **808**

REPORT OF THE REGISTRAR OF BANKS AND FINANCIAL INSTITUTIONS AND REGISTRAR OF BUILDING SOCIETIES FOR THE YEAR ENDED DECEMBER 31 . *See* REPORT OF THE REGISTRAR OF BANKS AND FINANCIAL INSTITUTIONS AND REGISTRAR OF BUILDING SOCIETIES FOR THE YEAR ENDED DECEMBER 31 ... - (ZIMBABWE) **808**

REPORT OF THE REGISTRAR OF BANKS AND FINANCIAL INSTITUTIONS AND REGISTRAR OF BUILDING SOCIETIES FOR THE YEAR ENDED DECEMBER 31 ... - (ZIMBABWE) (RH) [07805765] **808**

REPORT OF THE REGISTRAR OF BUILDING SOCIETIES (IE) [05184877] **808**

REPORT OF THE REGISTRAR OF FRIENDLY SOCIETIES FOR THE YEAR ENDED 30 JUNE (AT) [20040749] **5236**

REPORT OF THE RESEARCH COMMITTEE (UK) [20861055] **1994**

REPORT OF THE RESEARCH LABORATORY OF ENGINEERING MATERIALS (TOKYO) (JA/0385-3799) [03356371] **2108**

REPORT OF THE ROAD TRANSPORT DEPARTMENT - SIERRA LEONE (SL) [06105172] **5391**

REPORT OF THE RURAL ASSISTANCE BOARD *SUSPENDED.* (AT) [02832676] **126**

REPORT OF THE SASKATCHEWAN SAFETY COUNCIL PUBLIC OPINION POLL, A (CN/0707-1973) [04875800] 5443, **4798**

REPORT OF THE SECRETARY FOR LANDS - RHODESIA, SOUTHERN (RH) [01785608] **2203**

REPORT OF THE SECRETARY FOR WATER DEVELOPMENT (RHODESIA) (RH) [05296815] 2095, **5538**

REPORT OF THE SECRETARY-GENERAL OF THE CARIBBEAN COMMUNITY (GY) [10443968] **1639**

REPORT OF THE SECRETARY OF AGRICULTURE (US/0082-9803) [01483840] **126**

REPORT OF THE SECRETARY OF DEFENSE TO THE PRESIDENT AND THE CONGRESS (US) [21061746] **4681**

REPORT OF THE SECRETARY OF THE COMMONWEALTH TO THE GOVERNOR AND GENERAL ASSEMBLY OF VIRGINIA (US/0145-1928) [01158566] **4681**

REPORT OF THE SECURITIES AND INVESTMENTS BOARD FOR ... (UK) [20770524] **912**

REPORT OF THE SECURITIES DIVISION (US) [01752609] **912**

REPORT OF THE SELECT COMMITTEE ON INSURANCE RATES, REGULATION AND RECODIFICATION OF THE INSURANCE LAW (US) [03283572] 2892, **3038**

REPORT OF THE SELECT COMMITTEE ON RAILWAY ACCOUNTS. VERSLAG VAN DIE GEKOSE KOMITEE OOR SPOORWEGREKENINGS (SA) [05902471] **5436**

REPORT OF THE SELECT STANDING COMMITTEE ON PUBLIC ACCOUNTS AND PRINTING, TOGETHER WITH MINUTES AND VERBATIM REPORT OF PROCEEDINGS (CN) [03300801] **4681**

Alphabetical Title Index — REPORT

REPORT OF THE SENATE DELEGATION ON THE MEETING-MEXICO-UNITED STATES INTERPARLIAMENTARY GROUP. DELEGATION FROM THE UNITED STATES (US/0539-6476) [01643582] **4533**

REPORT OF THE SESSION - ASIAN-AFRICAN LEGAL CONSULTATIVE COMMITTEE (II/0571-2726) [01748286] **3180**

REPORT OF THE ... SESSION / GENERAL FISHERIES COUNCIL FOR THE MEDITERRANEAN (IT/0072-0755) [05372505] **2311**

REPORT OF THE SESSION OF THE CODEX COMMITTEE ON FOODS FOR SPECIAL DIETARY USES (IT) [02555483] **2355**

REPORT OF THE ... SESSION OF THE COMMISSION FOR CONTROLLING THE DESERT LOCUST IN NORTHWEST AFRICA (IT) [04299122] **184**

REPORT OF THE ... SESSION OF THE CONSULTATIVE SUB-COMMITTEE ON THE ECONOMIC ASPECTS OF RICE TO THE COMMITTEE ON COMMODITY PROBLEMS (IT) [17312923] **1516**

REPORT OF THE SESSION OF THE JOINT ECE/CODEX ALIMENTARIUS GROUP OF EXPERTS ON STANDARDIZATION OF QUICK FROZEN FOODS (IT) [02658557] 2355, **3038**

REPORT OF THE SOIL CONSERVATION SERVICE OF NEW SOUTH WALES *See* ANNUAL REPORT / SOIL CONSERVATION SERVICE OF NSW **163**

REPORT OF THE SOUTH DAKOTA STATE PHARMACEUTICAL ASSOCIATION AND THE SOUTH DAKOTA BOARD OF PHARMACY (US/0095-3164) [01796349] **4327**

REPORT OF THE SOUTH PACIFIC CONFERENCE AND PROCEEDINGS OF THE SOUTH PACIFIC COMMISSION (NL) [01200163] **4681**

REPORT OF THE STANDING ADVISORY COMMISSION ON HUMAN RIGHTS (UK) [02715746] **4512**

REPORT OF THE STANDING COMMISSION ON REFORM OF THE ELECTORAL DISTRICTS (CN/0706-0890) [06270631] **4681**

REPORT OF THE STANDING JOINT COMMITTEE OF THE SENATE AND OF THE HOUSE OF COMMONS ON REGULATIONS AND OTHER STATUTORY INSTRUMENTS (CN) [03439850] **3038**

REPORT OF THE STATE AUDITOR OF MINNESOTA ON THE REVENUES, EXPENDITURES, AND DEBT OF THE CITIES AND VILLAGES IN MINNESOTA (US/0095-3199) [01796532] **4746**

REPORT OF THE STATE BANK COMMISSIONER AND SUPERVISOR OF HOMESTEAD AND BUILDING AND LOAN ASSOCIATIONS RELATIVE TO STATE BANKS, SAVINGS, BANKS AND TRUST COMPANIES, HOMESTEAD AND BUILDING AND LOAN ASSOCIATIONS, CREDIT UNIONS AND LICENSEES UNDER "LOUISIANA SMALL LOAN LAW" *See* BIENNIAL REPORT OF THE COMMISSIONER OF FINANCIAL INSTITUTIONS AND SUPERVISOR OF HOMESTEAD AND BUILDING AND LOAN ASSOCIATIONS **778**

REPORT OF THE STATE BOARD OF INDEPENDENT COLLEGES AND UNIVERSITIES (TALLAHASSEE) (US/0093-1071) [01792012] **1915**

REPORT OF THE STATE BUDGET AND CONTROL BOARD, DIVISION OF SINKING FUNDS AND PROPERTY (US) [12535432] **4681**

REPORT OF THE STATE CO-ORDINATION COUNCIL (AT) [08416528] **4681**

REPORT OF THE STATE COMMISSION ON EMINENT DOMAIN AND REAL PROPERTY TAX ASSESSMENT REVIEW (US) [03686481] 4746, **4846**

REPORT OF THE STATE EMPLOYEES RETIREMENT BENEFITS BOARD FOR THE YEAR ENDED 30 JUNE ... (AT) [10702138] **4681**

REPORT OF THE STATE FARMLAND EVALUATION ADVISORY COMMITTEE (US/0545-2376) [05395220] **126**

REPORT OF THE STATISTICAL COMMISSION. ECONOMIC AND SOCIAL COUNCIL, UNITED NATIONS (US) [05291159] **3082**

REPORT OF THE STEERING COMMITTEE TO THE STANDING COMMMITTEE ON PUBLIC ACCOUNTS (CN/0846-3336) [25067006] **4746**

REPORT OF THE ... STRATEGY FOR PEACE US FOREIGN POLICY CONFERENCE (US/0748-9641) [11039337] **4533**

REPORT OF THE ... SUMMER SESSION OF THE INTERNATIONAL OLYMPIC ACADEMY (GR/0538-8910) [02751603] 4915, **1857**

REPORT OF THE SUPERINTENDENT OF BANKS AND SMALL LOAN COMPANIES (US/0360-926X) [02245182] **808**

REPORT OF THE ... TAX CONFERENCE CONVENED BY THE CANADIAN TAX FOUNDATION *See* REPORT OF PROCEEDINGS OF THE TAX CONFERENCE CONVENED BY THE CANADIAN TAX FOUNDATION **4745**

REPORT OF THE TENNESSEE ALCOHOLIC BEVERAGE COMMISSION FOR THE YEAR JANUARY 1 ... DECEMBER 31 . *See* ANNUAL REPORT FOR THE YEAR JULY 1 ...-JUNE 30 ... / STATE OF TENNESSEE, ALCOHOLIC BEVERAGE COMMISSION **1340**

REPORT OF THE TOKYO UNIVERSITY OF FISHERIES (JA/0563-8372) [01790239] **2311**

REPORT OF THE TOMATO GENETICS COOPERATIVE (US/0495-8306) [01586446] **184**

REPORT OF THE TREASURER FOR THE FISCAL YEAR ENDED JUNE 30 ... / NATIONAL ACADEMY OF SCIENCES, INCLUDING NATIONAL ACADEMY OF ENGINEERING, NATIONAL RESEARCH COUNCIL AND INSTITUTE OF MEDICINE (US) [09448272] **5146**

REPORT OF THE TREASURER OF STATE - IOWA. DEPT. OF TREASURER OF STATE (US) [06132929] **4746**

REPORT OF THE TREASURER (ROCHESTER) (US/0483-2140) [01912381] **750**

REPORT OF THE TREE NUT AUTHORITY (CK) [03567808] **2430**

REPORT OF THE TROPICAL PRODUCTS INSTITUTE (UK/0458-2039) [02254599] **126**

REPORT OF THE TRUSTEES OF THE NATIONAL LIBRARY OF NEW ZEALAND AND OF THE NATIONAL LIBRARIAN (NZ) [06806390] **3245**

REPORT OF THE UNEMPLOYMENT INSURANCE FUND FOR THE YEAR ENDED ... / DEPARTMENT OF MANPOWER UTILISATION (SA) [06211999] 1707, **2892**

REPORT OF THE ... UNITED NATIONS ISSUES CONFERENCE (US/0743-9180) [10718415] **4533**

REPORT OF THE ... UNITED NATIONS OF THE NEXT DECADE CONFERENCE (US/0748-433X) [10945883] **4533**

REPORT OF THE UNITED NATIONS VISITING MISSION TO THE TRUST TERRITORY OF THE PACIFIC ISLANDS (XE) [01277005] **3134**

REPORT OF THE UNITED STATES ATTORNEY FOR THE DISTRICT OF CONNECTICUT FOR ... TO THE ATTORNEY GENERAL (US) [07092955] **3142**

REPORT OF THE UNIVERSITY GRANTS COMMITTEE (UG) [02246707] **1844**

REPORT OF THE UTAH CONSTITUTIONAL REVISION COMMISSION (US) [04050896] **4681**

REPORT OF THE VERMONT BICENTENNIAL COMMISSION (US) [04077781] **2757**

REPORT OF THE VIRGINIA ATHLETIC COMMISSION TO THE GOVERNOR OF VIRGINIA (US/0145-8191) [02793664] **4915**

REPORT OF THE VIRGINIA COUNCIL ON INDIANS TO THE GOVERNOR AND THE GENERAL ASSEMBLY (US) [21128618] **2757**

REPORT OF THE VIRGINIA HOUSING STUDY COMMISSION (US) [04025941] **2833**

REPORT OF THE VISA OFFICE (US/0566-0637) [01768687] **1921**

REPORT OF THE WEST VIRGINIA BOARD OF EXAMINERS FOR REGISTERED NURSES *See* REPORT OF THE WEST VIRGINIA BOARD OF EXAMINERS FOR REGISTERED PROFESSIONAL NURSES TO THE GOVERNOR ... FOR THE BIENNIUM PERIOD ENDING DECEMBER 31 ... **3868**

REPORT OF THE WEST VIRGINIA BOARD OF EXAMINERS FOR REGISTERED PROFESSIONAL NURSES TO THE GOVERNOR ... FOR THE BIENNIUM PERIOD ENDING DECEMBER 31 ... (US) [11512046] **3868**

REPORT OF THE WISCONSIN LEGISLATIVE COUNCIL *See* GENERAL REPORT OF THE LEGISLATIVE COUNCIL TO THE LEGISLATURE **4650**

REPORT OF THE WORKING PARTY ON PESTICIDE RESIDUES (UK) [10177817] **4248**

REPORT OF THE ... WORLD CONGRESS / INTERNATIONAL CONFEDERATION OF FREE TRADE UNIONS (BE) [09581457] 850, **4533**

REPORT OF VITAL STATISTICS FOR OHIO (US/0147-5614) [03197549] **4811**

REPORT OF WORK CARRIED OUT (UK/0573-0791) [01564454] **471**

REPORT - OFFICE OF ALCOHOLISM, DEPARTMENT OF HEALTH AND SOCIAL SERVICES, STATE OF ALASKA (US/0095-3318) [01796533] **1348**

REPORT - OFFICE OF ATHLETIC COMMISSIONER (LINCOLN) (US/0091-942X) [01788455] **4915**

REPORT - OFFICE OF STATE ARCHAEOLOGIST (US) [04986835] **280**

REPORT - OFFICE OF THE STATE CO-ORDINATOR OF INDIAN AFFAIRS (MONTANA) (US/0540-7109) [01758592] **2272**

REPORT / OHIO. STATE BOARD OF EDUCATION *See* SCHOOL SLATE **1871**

REPORT (OHIO STATE UNIVERSITY. BYRD POLAR RESEARCH CENTER) (US/0896-2472) [16970174] **5146**

REPORT ON ACTIVE AND PLANNED SPACECRAFT AND EXPERIMENTS (US) [08180882] 1929, **33**

REPORT ON ACTIVITIES / DEPARTMENT OF RESOURCES DEVELOPMENT, GOVERNMENT OF WESTERN AUSTRALIA (AT) [16558804] **2203**

REPORT ON ACTIVITIES / JOHN D. AND CATHERINE T. MACARTHUR FOUNDATION (US/0749-9701) [09228089] **4339**

REPORT ON ACTIVITIES OF THE AMERICAN CHAMBER OF COMMERCE FOR BRAZIL-SAO PAULO IN ... FOR PRESENTATION AT THE ... ANNUAL GENERAL MEETING (BL) [07953339] **821**

REPORT ON ACTIVITIES OF THE COUNTY GOVERNMENT DURING THE FISCAL YEAR, A (US) [03804864] **4681**

REPORT ON ACTIVITIES UNDER THE HIGHWAY SAFETY ACT OF 1966 AS AMENDED, A (US) [03330437] **5443**

REPORT ON ADMINISTRATIVE ADJUDICATION OF TRAFFIC INFRACTIONS (US/0363-0692) [02407038] **3038**

REPORT ON ADVERTISING REVENUES IN CANADA, A ***CEASED.*** (CN/0315-9779) [02247569] **765**

REPORT ON ALTERNATIVE RESIDENTIAL MODEL (ARM) RATES (US) [23473477] **4798**

REPORT ON ANDHRA PRADESH MINING CORPORATION (II) [02243618] 2150, **1624**

REPORT ON APPLICATIONS FOR ORDERS AUTHORIZING OR APPROVING THE INTERCEPTION OF WIRE, ORAL, OR ELECTRONIC COMMUNICATIONS (WIRETAP REPORT) FOR THE PERIOD ... (US) [20225421] **3038**

REPORT ON AT & T, THE (US/0741-8361) [10248788] **1162**

REPORT ON BUSINESS, CANADA COMPANY HANDBOOK (CN/0847-2831) [21201011] **707**

REPORT ON BUSINESS MAGAZINE (CN/0827-7680) [12043766] **707**

REPORT ON COMMUNITY DEVELOPMENT WEEK (II) [01732035] **5255**

REPORT ON COMPETITION POLICY (BE) [03886102] **3038**

REPORT ON CONFIDENTIAL ENQUIRIES INTO MATERNAL DEATHS IN ENGLAND AND WALES (UK/0072-6109) [00965756] **3633**

●REPORT ON CORPORATE EDUCATIONAL SUPPORT (US/1066-0151) [26829067] **1915**

REPORT ON COUNCIL ACTIVITY - CANADIAN ADVERTISING ADVISORY BOARD. ADVERTISING STANDARDS COUNCIL (CN/0227-6747) [08071283] **765**

REPORT ON CURRENCY AND FINANCE - RESERVE BANK OF INDIA (II) [01763784] **808**

REPORT ON DEFENSE PLANT WASTES (US/1043-268X) [19403255] 2242, **4055**

REPORT ON DEPARTMENT OF ECONOMIC DEVELOPMENT AND CONNECTICUT DEVELOPMENT AUTHORITY FOR FISCAL YEARS ENDED JUNE 30 ... (US) [07765577] **1581**

REPORT ON DEPARTMENT OF HEALTH, OFFICE OF MENTAL RETARDATION, NORTH CENTRAL REGIONAL CENTER (US/0362-8248) [02353776] **5305**

REPORT ON DEPARTMENT OF SOCIAL SERVICES (US) [04604186] **5305**

REPORT ON DEPARTMENT OF VETERANS' AFFAIRS FOR THE FISCAL YEARS ENDED JUNE 30 (US) [23915053] **4055**

REPORT ON DEVELOPMENT BANKING IN INDIA (II) [08832401] **808**

REPORT ON DIESEL AND GAS ENGINES POWER COSTS (US/0569-8243) [01360074] **2128**

REPORT ON DISABILITY PROGRAMS (US/1043-1209) [19036418] **4393**

REPORT
Alphabetical Title Index

REPORT ON DRIVING UNDER THE INFLUENCE OF ALCOHOL, OPERATING AFTER LICENSE SUSPENSION, AND HABITUAL OFFENDER REVOCATION VIOLATIONS (US) [16976450] 1348, **3174**

REPORT ON EASTERN EUROPE *See* RFE/RL RESEARCH REPORT **1138**

REPORT ON EDUCATION OF THE DISADVANTAGED (US/0034-4680) [01715182] **1884**

REPORT ON EDUCATION RESEARCH (US/0034-4699) [01026191] **1778**

REPORT ON EDUCATIONAL DEVELOPMENTS IN INDIA (II) [02418311] **1778**

REPORT ON ELECTRIC COMMERCE (US) 850, **1162**

REPORT ON ENVIRONMENTAL RADIATION SURVEILLANCE IN NORTH CAROLINA (US/0147-2887) [03139689] 4441, **2242**

REPORT ON ENVIRONMENTAL RESEARCH, TECHNOLOGY DEVELOPMENT AND AWARENESS ACTIVITIES (CN/1191-0305) [25652439] **2181**

REPORT ON EXECUTIVE PREREQUISITES (US/0195-9182) [05668272] 884, **1707**

REPORT ON EXECUTIVE REMUNERATION / WYATT DATA SERVICES, ECS (US) [24860166] **1707**

REPORT ON EXEMPT OVERTIME PLANS AND PRACTICES (US/1058-5109) [24206545] **1707**

REPORT ON FAMILY PLANNING SERVICES AND POPULATION RESEARCH, A (US/0275-2050) [07080553] 4559, **590**

REPORT ON FEDERAL FUNDS RECEIVED IN IOWA (US/0091-8695) [01788178] **4746**

REPORT ON FEDERAL GRANTS-IN-AID IN IOWA *See* REPORT ON FEDERAL FUNDS RECEIVED IN IOWA **4746**

REPORT ON FINANCE, COMMERCE, INDUSTRY - SOUTHEAST ASIA (MY) [04045174] **707**

REPORT ON FISHERIES IN NEW SOUTH WALES (1975/76) *See* REPORT OF THE NEW SOUTH WALES STATE FISHERIES FOR THE YEAR ENDED ... **2311**

REPORT ON FOREIGN CURRENCIES ACQUIRED BY THE UNITED STATES GOVERNMENT WITHOUT PAYMENT OF DOLLARS *See* REPORT ON FOREIGN CURRENCIES HELD BY THE U.S. GOVERNMENT **808**

REPORT ON FOREIGN CURRENCIES HELD BY THE U.S. GOVERNMENT (US/0098-3896) [02241090] **808**

REPORT ON FOREST RESEARCH (UK/0436-4120) [01431044] **2392**

REPORT ON FREEDOM (US) [06266106] **4493**

REPORT ON FRINGE BENEFITS AND RELATED PRACTICES AFFECTING GENERAL EMPLOYEES OF CITIES (US/0361-0314) [02244131] **4682**

REPORT ON FRINGE BENEFITS AND RELATED PRACTICES AFFECTING POLICEMEN (US/0147-5355) [03189747] **3174**

REPORT ON FUR FARMS *See* LIVESTOCK STATISTICS / STATISTICS CANADA, AGRICULTURE DIVISION, LIVESTOCK AND ANIMAL PRODUCTS SECTION **2247**

REPORT ON GREAT LAKES WATER QUALITY : REPORT TO THE INTERNATIONAL JOINT COMMISSION / GREAT LAKES WATER QUALITY BOARD (CN/0845-0919) [07296940] 4762, **5538**

REPORT ON GUATEMALA (US/1043-3856) [15566829] **5215**

REPORT ON HALF-YEARLY SURVEY OF WAGES, SALARIES, AND EMPLOYEE BENEFITS (HK) [24292969] **1707**

● REPORT ON HEALTHCARE INFORMATION MANAGEMNET (US/1071-006X) [28530168] **3792**

● REPORT ON HUMAN RESOURCES COMPENSATION (US/1063-1968) [25857010] **5305**

REPORT ON IBM, THE (US/0742-5341) [10361735] **1201**

REPORT ON INDUSTRIAL COMMUNICATIONS *See* AMR REPORT **860**

REPORT ON INDUSTRIAL COMMUNICATIONS, THE (US/0892-6158) [15248370] **884**

REPORT ON KANSAS LEGISLATIVE INTERIM STUDIES TO THE LEGISLATURE (US/0270-4331) [06380882] **3038**

REPORT ON KANSAS UNIFORM CONSUMER CREDIT CODE (US/0360-5663) [02242984] **808**

REPORT ON LEGISLATIVE ACTIVITIES OF THE COMMITTEE ON LABOR AND HUMAN RESOURCES, UNITED STATES SENATE DURING THE ... CONGRESS ... : PURSUANT TO SECTION 136 OF THE LEGISLATIVE REORGANIZATION ACT OF 1946, AS AMENDED BY THE LEGISLATIVE REORGANIZATION ACT OF 1970 (US) [24082791] 5305, 4682, **4798**

REPORT ON LITERACY PROGRAMS (US/1046-6150) [20017973] 1802, **5305**

REPORT ON LONDON G.C.E. EXAMINATION RESULTS (TR) [06435840] **1870**

REPORT ON LONG TERM CARE *CEASED.* (US) **3633**

REPORT ON MAIZE FOR THE FINANCIAL YEAR ... FOR SUBMISSION TO THE MINISTER OF AGRICULTURE / MAIZE BOARD (SA) [26102810] **126**

REPORT ON MANAGEMENT SUCCESSION (US/0486-4336) [01908045] **884**

REPORT ON MANDATES AND MEASURES AFFECTING LOCAL GOVERNMENT FISCAL CAPACITY / FLORIDA ADVISORY COUNCIL ON INTERGOVERNMENTAL RELATIONS (US) [09354608] **4682**

REPORT ON MEDICAL GUIDELINES & OUTCOMES RESEARCH. ANNOTATED DIRECTORY OF MEDICAL PRACTICE GUIDELINES (US/1064-4148) [24839309] **3633**

REPORT ON MEDICAL SCHOOL FACULTY SALARIES (US) [03806854] 3633, **1844**

REPORT ON MICROSOFT, THE (US/1072-9453) [29244692] **1201**

REPORT ON NEW ENROLMENTS IN WESTERN AUSTRALIAN TERTIARY EDUCATION INSTITUTIONS (AT) [02240412] **1844**

● REPORT ON OBJECT ANALYSIS AND DESIGN (US/1075-2528) [30067030] **1201**

REPORT ON OFFICE OF THE LIEUTENANT GOVERNOR - CONNECTICUT (US) [06688423] 750, **4682**

REPORT ON PARTICIPATION IN ASCS COUNTY PROGRAMS AND OPERATIONS BY RACIAL GROUPS (US/0361-2260) [02155419] **126**

REPORT ON PEDIATRIC INFECTIOUS DISEASES, THE (US/1050-964X) [21725412] 3911, **3715**

REPORT ON PRESCHOOL PROGRAMS : THE BIWEEKLY NEWSLETTER ON PROGRAMS FOR EARLY CHILDHOOD DEVELOPMENT (US) [10144601] **1805**

REPORT ON PRODUCTION AND EARNINGS OF RRS (US) **808**

REPORT ON PUBLIC EDUCATION IN VIRGINIA (US) [05071773] **1778**

REPORT ON PUBLICATIONS OF THE SCHOOL OF INTERNATIONAL AFFAIRS AND THE REGIONAL INSTITUTES (US/0084-8921) [01564256] **4533**

REPORT ON RADIOLOGICAL PROTECTION AND OCCUPATIONAL HEALTH FOR THE YEAR ... / UNITED KINGDOM ATOMIC ENERGY AUTHORITY (UK) [24280364] **4441**

REPORT ON REPORTS (US/0196-9382) [05917757] **935**

REPORT ON RESEARCH - PRAGUE. UNIVERSITA KARLOVA. USTAV GEOLOGICKYCH VED (XR) [05378018] **1360**

REPORT ON SALARIES (CN/0318-3734) [02441823] 1994, **1707**

REPORT ON SALARIES AND TOTAL PAY IN THE SMALLER MANUFACTURING COMPANY / ECS (US) [22357379] 1707, **3487**

REPORT ON SALARIES, FRINGE BENEFITS, AND RELATED PRACTICES AFFECTING CLASSIFIED SERVICE EMPLOYEES OF NEW YORK STATE (US/0095-7968) [03130680] **1707**

REPORT ON SALARIES IN OCCUPATIONS COMPARABLE TO STATE CIVIL SERVICE / PREPARED BY CALIFORNIA STATE PERSONNEL BOARD, PAY AND BENEFITS CENTER (US) [06218311] **1707**

REPORT ON SALARIES OF ADMINISTRATIVE FACULTY IN NURSING, EXCLUDING DEANS (US) [07960988] **3868**

REPORT ON SALARIES OF DEANS IN BACCALAUREATE AND GRADUATE PROGRAMS IN NURSING (US) [25065693] **1870**

REPORT ON SALARY SCHEDULES FOR FULL TIME NON-INSTRUCTIONAL EMPLOYEES OF SCHOOL DISTRICTS (US) [02882237] **1870**

REPORT ON SCHOOL AGE CHILD CARE *CEASED.* (US) **1805**

REPORT ON SCIENCE AND HUMAN RIGHTS (US/0895-5999) [16706971] **4512**

REPORT ON SHAREHOLDER PROPOSALS (US/0272-3948) [06782131] **1624**

REPORT ON SHORTAGE OCCUPATIONS (II) [01784277] **4209**

REPORT ON STATE COMPTROLLER - CONNECTICUT (US) [06415603] **4746**

REPORT ON STATE COMPTROLLER-RETIREMENT DIVISION. CONNECTICUT MUNICIPAL EMPLOYEES' RETIREMENT AND SOCIAL SECURITY SYSTEMS, FISCAL YEAR ENDED JUNE 30 ... (US) [09249981] **4682**

REPORT ON STATE COMPTROLLER. SPECIAL APPROPRIATIONS ADMINISTERED BY STATE COMPTROLLER, FISCAL YEAR ENDED JUNE 30 ... (US) [10315366] **4746**

REPORT ON STATE ELECTIONS COMMISSION - CONNECTICUT (US) [05215803] **4682**

REPORT ON SURVEY OF SHIPBUILDING AND REPAIR INDUSTRY *See* REPORT ON SURVEY OF U.S. SHIPBUILDING AND REPAIR FACILITIES **4182**

REPORT ON SURVEY OF U.S. SHIPBUILDING AND REPAIR FACILITIES (US/0193-3337) [04618057] **4182**

REPORT ON TELCO MARKETING, THE (US/8755-3511) [11183296] 935, **1163**

REPORT ON TELECOM ADVERTISING & PUBLISHING, TA (US/1071-4197) [28645983] **1120**

REPORT ON TELECOMMUNICATION AND THE PEACEFUL USES OF OUTER SPACE *See* REPORT BY THE INTERNATIONAL TELECOMMUNICATION UNION ON TELECOMMUNICATION AND THE PEACEFUL USES OF OUTER SPACE **1162**

REPORT ON TEXTILE PRODUCTION STATISTICS (HK) **5355**

REPORT ON THE ACTIVITIES OF COPPER PROMOTION CENTRES IN ... / CIPEC (FR) [09332628] **1624**

REPORT ON THE ACTIVITIES OF SPACE SCIENCE DEPARTMENT IN ... (FR) [09450104] **399**

REPORT ON THE ACTIVITIES OF THE IGU COMMISSION ON POPULATION GEOGRAPHY (FR) [02951873] **4559**

REPORT ON THE ACTIVITIES OF THE INTERNATIONAL TELECOMMUNICATION UNION (SZ) [02790320] **1163**

REPORT ON THE ADMINISTRATION OF THE EMERGENCY GOLD MINING ASSISTANCE ACT (CN) [01189701] **2150**

REPORT ON THE ADVISORY COMMITTEE TO THE PRIME MINISTER ON THE BUSINESS/GOVERNMENT EXECUTIVE EXCHANGE PROGRAM (CN/0842-6686) [19658872] **707**

REPORT ON THE AMERICAS (US/1058-5397) [23381668] **2757**

REPORT ON THE ... ANNUAL MEETING OF THE NIA GERIATRIC MEDICINE ACADEMIC AWARDEES (US) [07198078] **3754**

REPORT ON THE APPROPRIATION ACCOUNTS OF THE GOVERNMENT OF PUNJAB AND THE REPORTS OF THE COMPTROLLER AND AUDITOR GENERAL OF INDIA (II) [05095242] **4746**

REPORT ON THE BACKGROUND, CURRENT PROGRAMMES AND PLANNED DEVELOPMENT OF THE BANGLADESH INSTITUTE OF DEVELOPMENT STUDIES, A (BG) [02619423] **5215**

REPORT ON THE BIRDS OF THE DONCASTER DISTRICT (UK) [04386141] **5620**

REPORT ON THE BRITISH MUSEUM (NATURAL HISTORY) (UK/0524-6474) [02998773] 4095, **4171**

REPORT ON THE BUDGET FOR THE DEVELOPMENT USES OF UNEMPLOYMENT INSURANCE (CN/1191-3398) [25393211] 2892, **5305**

REPORT ON THE ... BUDGET FOR THE DEVELOPMENTAL USES OF UNEMPLOYMENT INSURANCE (CN/1191-3398) [26290422] **1707**

REPORT ON THE CANADIAN DRUG STORE MARKET, A (CN/0315-6311) [02247319] **4327**

REPORT ON THE CENSUS OF PRODUCTION. SUMMARY VOLUME (UK) [18239517] **1624**

REPORT ON THE CENTRE'S ACTIVITIES - PUSAT PENELITIAN ATMA JAYA (IO) [02741288] **1581**

REPORT ON THE CONDITION OF SAVINGS AND LOAN ASSOCIATIONS FOR THE YEAR ENDING ... (US) [05979537] **808**

REPORT ON THE DEMOGRAPHIC SITUATION IN CANADA (CN/0715-9293) [13031847] 4559, **4562**

REPORT ON THE DISEASE STATUS WORLDWIDE IN ... / OFFICE INTERNATIONAL DES EPIZOOTIES (FR) [20999710] 3716, **5520**

REPORT ON THE ECONOMY AND THE PROSPECTS (IE) [01795336] **1581**

REPORT ON THE ESTABLISHMENT AND WORK OF THE STATES POLICE FORCE (UK) [05378002] **3174**

Alphabetical Title Index — REPORT

REPORT ON THE FEDERAL CATALOGING PROGRAM (US) [08182513] **4055**

REPORT ON THE FINANCIAL YEAR - BERLINER HANDELS- UND FRANKFURTER BANK (GW) [07093553] **808**

REPORT ON THE FISCAL ... PAY INCREASE UNDER THE FEDERAL STATUTORY PAY SYSTEMS : ANNUAL REPORT OF THE ADVISORY COMMITTEE ON FEDERAL PAY (US) [09543927] **4682**

REPORT ON THE HEALTH, POPULATION AND NUTRITION ACTIVITIES OF THE AGENCY FOR INTERNATIONAL DEVELOPMENT, DEPARTMENT OF STATE (US/0503-485X) [02245676] **2911**

REPORT ON THE LABOUR FORCE SURVEY OF SINGAPORE (SI/0129-6965) [02310369] **1707**

REPORT ON THE MARKET MILK INDUSTRY IN WESTERN AUSTRALIA (AT) [05704591] 198, **1625**

REPORT ON THE NATIONAL LIBRARY SERVICE (BS) [02241958] **3245**

... REPORT ON THE PAY LEVEL SURVEY, THE (HK) [15532600] **4682**

REPORT ON THE ... PDCP SURVEY OF BUSINESS PERFORMANCE FOR MANILA, A (PH) [15567114] **707**

REPORT ON THE PROGRESS OF EDUCATION IN ORISSA *See* ANNUAL ADMINISTRATION REPORT ON THE PROGRESS OF EDUCATION IN ORISSA FOR THE YEAR ... **1724**

REPORT ON THE QUARTERLY INDEX OF INDUSTRIAL PRODUCTION (HK) [18810852] **1625**

REPORT ON THE ... SALARY BUDGET SURVEY (US/1041-6633) [17254090] **1707**

REPORT ON THE SCIENTIFIC SATELLITES OF THE EUROPEAN SPACE AGENCY *See* ACHIEVEMENTS OF ESA SCIENTIFIC SATELLITES, THE **3**

REPORT ON THE SITUATION OF THE COMMUNITY (US/0421-7381) [01627978] **1625**

REPORT ON THE STATE PROGRAM FOR THE UNEMPLOYED / [PREPARED BY OFFICE OF MANPOWER PLANNING] (US) [08978099] **1707**

REPORT ON THE SWAZILAND POPULATION CENSUS (SQ) [00132458] 4559, **4562**

REPORT ON THE ... SYRIA'S BUDGET (SY) [08685402] **4746**

REPORT ON THE TERMS OF CREDIT CARD PLANS (US) [21399409] **808**

REPORT ON THE USSR *See* RFE/RL RESEARCH REPORT **1138**

REPORT ON THE WORK OF ITS SESSIONS - UNITED NATIONS. COMMISSION ON INTERNATIONAL TRADE LAW (US) [01786113] 850, **3134**

REPORT ON THE WORK OF THE BUREAU SINCE THE PREVIOUS CONFERENCE (ML) [01782292] **4182**

REPORT ON THE WORK OF THE LIBRARY / UNIVERSITY COLLEGE OF SOUTH WALES AND MONMOUTHSHIRE (UK) [19098036] **3245**

REPORT ON THE WORKING OF THE PUBLIC SERVICE COMMISSION OF KENYA (KE) [03468005] **4682**

REPORT ON THE WORLD HEALTH SITUATION (SZ) [06956354] **4799**

REPORT ON THE WORLD SOCIAL SITUATION (US/0082-8068) [02246765] **5255**

REPORT ON TRAFFIC ACCIDENTS AND INJURIES (US/0735-8539) [07530933] **5443**

REPORT ON TRAVEL ON SASKATCHEWAN HIGHWAYS (CN/0701-6441) [03268108] **5443**

REPORT ON TREND AND PROGRESS OF BANKING IN INDIA (II) [06410086] **808**

REPORT ON UROLOGIC TECHNIQUES, THE *SUSPENDED.* (US/1052-3987) [22283740] **3993**

REPORT ON VARIABLE PAY PROGRAMS *See* SURVEY REPORT ON VARIABLE PAY PROGRAMS / WYATT DATA SERVICES, ECS **1713**

REPORT ON VISUAL IMPAIRMENT SERVICES TEAMS (US/0093-741X) [01798186] **4393**

REPORT ON VITAL STATISTICS & REGISTRATIONS (BB) [01786714] **5337**

REPORT ON WORLD AFFAIRS (UK/0034-4737) [03685986] **4533**

REPORT ORO (US/0272-4774) [05965246] 4276, **1955**

REPORT - PENNSYLVANIA CRIME COMMISSION (US/0091-4118) [01787071] **3174**

REPORT - PIPELINE AUTHORITY (AT) [02370050] **4682**

REPORT - PLANNING ADVISORY SERVICE (US/0160-8266) [04720796] **2833**

REPORT / POTATO MARKETING BOARD (UK/0309-2240) [09835019] **184**

REPORT PRESENTED TO THE HOUSE OF REPRESENTATIVES *See* REPORT OF THE OAMARU LICENSING TRUST FOR THE YEAR ENDED **4681**

REPORT - PROUDMAN OCEANOGRAPHIC LABORATORY (UK/0955-1603) [I09551603] **1456**

REPORT - PUBLIC ACCOUNTS COMMITTEE (II/0440-8411) [05199297] **4746**

REPORT : REVIEW BODY OF TOP SALARIES (UK) **1516**

REPORT - ROYAL COMMISSION ON ENERGY (OTTAWA) (CN/0527-8503) [01199997] **1955**

REPORT - ROYAL GREENWICH OBSERVATORY (UK/0308-3322) [02395107] **399**

REPORT / SARAWAK ELECTRICITY SUPPLY CORPORATION *See* ANNUAL REPORT **4759**

REPORT - SAVINGS BANKS GROUP OF THE EEC (BE) [02243183] **808**

REPORT - SCANDINAVIAN AIRLINES SYSTEM (SW) [06989259] **33**

REPORT SE (WORLD DATA CENTER A FOR SOLID EARTH GEOPHYSICS) (US/0271-4965) [03284011] **1410**

REPORT SERIES - AGRICULTURAL EXPERIMENT STATION, DIVISION OF AGRICULTURE, UNIVERSITY OF ARKANSAS (US/0097-5370) [01368259] **126**

REPORT SERIES (CANADA. INLAND WATERS DIRECTORATE) (CN/0318-5869) [01496486] **5538**

REPORT SERIES - UNIVERSITY OF ARKANSAS AGRICULTURAL EXPERIMENT STATION (US) [05163099] **126**

REPORT SERIES / UNIVERSITY OF OSLO, DEPARTMENT OF PHYSICS (NO/0332-5571) [11472756] **4419**

REPORT - SINGAPORE HINDUS RELIGIOUS AND CULTURAL SEMINAR (SI) [01783524] **5041**

REPORT - SOIL SURVEY OF GREAT BRITAIN *See* ANNUAL REPORT - SOIL SURVEY. ENGLAND AND WALES **163**

REPORT - SOUTH AFRICA. DRY BEAN BOARD (SA) [01784910] **4682**

REPORT / SPECIAL JOINT COMMITTEE OF THE GENERAL ASSEMBLY TO REVIEW RETIREMENT COST-OF-LIVING SUPPLEMENTS AND FUNDING SOURCES (US) [08859334] **4682**

REPORT - SPECIAL STUDIES SECTION, FIELD OPERATIONS DIVISION, TEXAS WATER QUALITY BOARD (US/0145-2215) [02711698] 5538, **4762**

REPORT - STAFF SELECTION COMMISSION (II) [07406045] **4705**

REPORT / STATE BANK OF NEW SOUTH WALES *CEASED.* (AT) [11742271] **808**

REPORT - STATE ENGINEER'S OFFICE, WYOMING WATER PLANNING PROGRAM (US/0160-8851) [03782935] **5538**

REPORT / STATE OF CALIFORNIA, MEDIATION/CONCILIATION SERVICE (US) [07522219] **1707**

REPORT / STATE OF NEBRASKA, INVESTMENT COUNCIL (US) [07664028] **4746**

REPORT, STATEMENTS, RETURNS, ETC., FOR THE YEAR ENDED 30TH JUNE ... / STATE BANK OF VICTORIA (AT) [11153009] **808**

REPORT - STATES OF MALAYA CHAMBER OF MINES. COUNCIL (MY) [01793282] **2150**

REPORT / SUPREME COURT, STATE OF ILLINOIS (US) [10172117] **3143**

REPORT, SURVEY OF METROPOLITAN JUVENILE COURTS / NATIONAL CENTER FOR STATE COURTS (US) [07260065] **3038**

REPORT - SWARTHMORE COLLEGE, SWARTHMORE, PENNSYLVANIA (US) [06241457] **3245**

REPORT - TAMIL NADU LEGISLATIVE ASSEMBLY COMMITTEE ON PUBLIC UNDERTAKINGS (II) [01797734] **4682**

REPORT - TASK FORCE HYDRO (CN) [03564203] **4682**

REPORT - TECHNICAL MEETING ON FISHERIES (PO) [02239433] **2311**

REPORT/TECHNICAL STUDY : REPORTED LOBBYING EXPENDITURES (US) [06896670] **4682**

REPORT - TENNESSEE HISTORICAL COMMISSION (US) [01793419] **2757**

REPORT - TEXAS MAPPING ADVISORY COMMITTEE (US/0095-3776) [01796390] **2583**

REPORT - TEXAS TECH UNIVERSITY, WATER RESOURCES CENTER (US/0163-1160) [04277994] **5538**

REPORT - THE COMMONWEALTH FOUNDATION (UK) [01793414] **1707**

REPORT / THE OHIO GENEALOGICAL SOCIETY (US) [14215830] **2470**

REPORT TO CONGRESS, ADMINISTRATION OF THE WILD FREE-ROAMING HORSE AND BURRO ACT (US/0739-3989) [08134916] **4682**

REPORT TO CONGRESS BY THE SECRETARY OF THE INTERIOR AND THE SECRETARY OF AGRICULTURE ON ADMINISTRATION OF THE WILD FREE-ROAMING HORSE AND BURRO ACT, PUBLIC LAW 92-195 *See* REPORT TO CONGRESS, ADMINISTRATION OF THE WILD FREE-ROAMING HORSE AND BURRO ACT **4682**

REPORT TO CONGRESS CONCERNING THE DEMONSTRATION OF FARE-FREE MASS TRANSPORTATION (US/0360-750X) [02244628] **5391**

REPORT TO CONGRESS ON ABNORMAL OCCURRENCES (US/0748-4151) [02263393] **2158**

REPORT TO CONGRESS ON ADMINISTRATION OF OCEAN DUMPING ACTIVITIES. PUBLIC LAW 92-532, MARINE PROTECTION, RESEARCH, AND SANCTUARIES ACT OF 1972 (US/0163-4755) [04290974] **2242**

REPORT TO CONGRESS ON THE ECONOMIC IMPACT OF ENERGY ACTIONS *CEASED.* (US/0361-6126) [04950417] 1516, **1955**

REPORT TO COUNCIL ON AGING (US/0277-660X) [07365330] **5305**

REPORT TO EXECUTIVES ON LARGE COMPANIES' BANKING PRACTICES (US/0883-4644) [12110493] **808**

REPORT TO EXECUTIVES ON MIDDLE MARKET FINANCIAL MANAGEMENT (US/0748-7541) [10978656] **808**

REPORT TO FARMERS ... ANNUAL SWINE FIELD DAY (US) [01391389] **5596**

REPORT TO MEMBERS (US) **707**

REPORT TO MEMBERS - MANITOBA TEACHERS' RETIREMENT ALLOWANCES FUND (CN/0228-3875) [09200943] **1870**

REPORT TO SENATE / UNIVERSITY OF MALAWI LIBRARIES (MW) [11274651] **3245**

REPORT TO STOCKHOLDERS (US) [04771335] **913**

REPORT TO THE ADMINISTRATOR ON THE SKYLAB PROGRAM (US/0090-5453) [01785176] **33**

REPORT TO THE ALASKA LEGISLATURE - DIVISION OF OCCUPATIONAL SAFETY AND HEALTH (US) [06990838] **2869**

REPORT TO THE BOARD OF GOVERNORS ON THE INSTITUTE'S WORK (NR) [06269410] **184**

REPORT TO THE BOARD OF HIGHER EDUCATION ON THE RESULTS OF THE NEW JERSEY COLLEGE BASIC SKILLS PLACEMENT TESTING AND RECOMMENDATIONS ON INSTRUCTION AND CURRICULUM DEVELOPMENT / NEW JERSEY BASIC SKILLS COUNCIL (US) [09787923] **1844**

REPORT TO THE COLORADO WATER QUALITY CONTROL COMMISSION (US/0733-3633) [08556366] 2242, **5538**

REPORT TO THE CONGRESS - LISTER HILL NATIONAL CENTER FOR BIOMEDICAL COMMUNICATIONS (US/0095-0831) [01795471] **3633**

REPORT TO THE CONGRESS OF THE UNITED STATES ON URBAN TRANSPORTATION POLICIES & ACTIVITIES (US/0098-0617) [02246592] **5391**

REPORT TO THE CONGRESS ON OCEAN POLLUTION AND OFFSHORE DEVELOPMENT (US/0277-2868) [06774228] 2181, 2242, **1456**

REPORT TO THE GOVERNOR (US) [19289665] **4682**

REPORT TO THE GOVERNOR AND THE LEGISLATURE - STATE OF CALIFORNIA, DEPARTMENT OF CONSUMER AFFAIRS (US/0360-8050) [02245008] **1299**

REPORT TO THE GOVERNOR - ARIZONA DEPARTMENT OF EDUCATION (US/0360-084X) [02240028] **1778**

REPORT TO THE GOVERNOR FROM THE MANPOWER SERVICES COUNCIL, THE (US) [02613830] **1707**

REPORT TO THE GOVERNOR - NEW YORK STATE FACILITIES DEVELOPMENT CORPORATION (US/0145-7306) [02920436] **4799**

REPORT TO THE GOVERNOR OF IDAHO AND THE LEGISLATURE FROM THE IDAHO POTATO COMMISSION (US/0097-8280) [01799433] **184**

REPORT

Alphabetical Title Index

REPORT TO THE GOVERNOR - WASHINGTON (STATE). STATE EMPLOYMENT DEVELOPMENT SERVICES COUNCIL (US) [02709104] **1707**

REPORT TO THE GOVERNORS (US/0882-679X) [11931044] **4682**

REPORT TO THE HEADS OF GOVERNMENT BY THE COMMONWEALTH SECRETARY-GENERAL (UK) [02239539] **4682**

REPORT TO THE HONORABLE ... GOVERNOR OF THE STATE OF ALABAMA AND MEMBERS OF THE ALABAMA LEGISLATURE, A (US) [07366458] **2242**

REPORT TO THE JOINT STANDING COMMITTEE ON PUBLIC UTILITIES, MAINE LEGISLATURE (US) [09579304] **4682**

REPORT TO THE LEGISLATIVE ASSEMBLY OF BRITISH COLUMBIA ON THE PUBLIC ACCOUNTS (CN/1193-2430) [26758338] **4746**

REPORT TO THE LEGISLATURE - MINNESOTA. DEPT. OF ECONOMIC SECURITY (US) [04663178] **1707**

REPORT TO THE NATION ON THE MANAGEMENT OF METRIC IMPLEMENTATION, A (US/0098-1443) [02240318] **4032**

REPORT TO THE PEOPLE (US) [05108230] 4799, **5443**

REPORT TO THE PEOPLE / YOUTH FOR CHRIST KINGSTON (CN/0829-3724) [15809360] **4992**

REPORT TO THE PEOPLE / YOUTH FOR CHRIST/VANCOUVER (CN/0228-8044) [08063779] **4992**

REPORT TO THE PRESIDENT AND CONGRESS / NATIONAL AGRICULTURAL RESEARCH AND EXTENSION USERS ADVISORY BOARD (US/1045-1579) [07537641] **126**

REPORT TO THE PRESIDENT AND TO THE COUNCIL ON ENVIRONMENTAL QUALITY (US/0148-0596) [01774176] **2181**

REPORT TO THE SECRETARY, DEPARTMENT OF HEALTH, EDUCATION, AND WELFARE (U.S. ARTHRITIS INTERAGENCY COORDINATING COMMITTEE) (US/0193-9998) [05250782] **3806**

REPORT TO THE SENATE AND HOUSE COMMITTEES ON THE BUDGET, A (US/0898-7491) [12980317] 4746, **1516**

REPORT TO THE SENATE ON THE JURISDICTION AND A SUMMARY OF ACTIVITIES OF THE COMMITTEE ON AGRICULTURE, NUTRITION, AND FORESTRY FOR THE ... CONGRESS (US) [19762356] 126, **4198**

REPORT TO THE SOUTH PACIFIC COMMISSION (NL) [01167142] **4682**

REPORT TO THE STATE BANKING BOARD, STATE CREDIT UNION BOARD, AND TO THE GOVERNOR (US) [08869033] **808**

REPORT TO THE STATE BOARD OF EQUALIZATION (US) [04724342] **4746**

REPORT TO THE STOCKHOLDERS (US) [09286976] **4746**

REPORT TO THE TRUSTEES, A (US) [03805265] **1844**

REPORT TO THE UNIVERSITY COURT (UK) [01788776] **1844**

REPORT TO THE VERMONT GENERAL ASSEMBLY (US/0362-7209) [02323752] **1844**

REPORT - TRINITY WESTERN UNIVERSITY (CN/0848-8533) [21353583] **1094**

REPORT : UNION GOVERNMENT (POSTS AND TELEGRAPHS) (II) [05218541] **1147**

REPORT - UNITED NATIONS' COUNCIL FOR NAMIBIA (US) [01788439] **3134**

REPORT - UNIVERSITY OF CONNECTICUT. INSTITUTE OF WATER RESOURCES (US/0069-9063) [01187438] **5538**

REPORT - UNIVERSITY OF NATAL, AGRICULTURAL CATCHMENTS RESEARCH UNIT (SA) [08122613] **1417**

REPORT (UNIVERSITY OF NEW SOUTH WALES. WATER RESEARCH LABORATORY) (AT/0548-6882) [01080071] 5538, **1417**

REPORT - UNIVERSITY OF NEWCASTLE UPON TYNE. DEPARTMENT OF AGRICULTURAL AND FOOD MARKETING *See* REPORT - UNIVERSITY OF NEWCASTLE UPON TYNE. DEPARTMENT OF AGRICULTURAL ECONOMICS AND FOOD MARKETING **126**

REPORT - UNIVERSITY OF NEWCASTLE UPON TYNE. DEPARTMENT OF AGRICULTURAL ECONOMICS AND FOOD MARKETING (UK/0963-6536) [I09636536] **126**

REPORT - UNIVERSITY OF TEXAS AT AUSTIN. ATMOSPHERIC SCIENCE GROUP (US/0738-5803) [09001876] **1434**

REPORT (UNIVERSITY OF TEXAS. ATMOSPHERIC SCIENCE GROUP) *See* REPORT - UNIVERSITY OF TEXAS AT AUSTIN. ATMOSPHERIC SCIENCE GROUP **1434**

REPORT / UNIVERSITY OF THE WITWATERSRAND, BUREAU FOR MINERALS STUDIES (SA) [07064526] **2150**

REPORT UPON THE OPERATIONS OF THE SUB-DEPARTMENTS OF NATIVE AFFAIRS, EVENTIDE (SANDGATE), EVENTIDE (CHARTERS TOWERS), EVENTIDE (ROCKHAMPTON), INSTITUTION FOR INEBRIATES (MARBURG), AND QUEENSLAND INDUSTRIAL INSTITUTION FOR THE BLIND (SOUTH BRISBANE) (AT) [21010266] 4682, **5305**

REPORT - URANIUM ADVISORY COUNCIL (AT/0158-5088) [I01585088] **4017**

REPORT - USDA FOREST SERVICE, NORTHERN REGION, STATE AND PRIVATE FORESTRY (US) [03743193] **2392**

REPORT - VICTORIA, AUSTRALIA. NATIONAL PARKS ADVISORY COMMITTEE (AT) [01791386] **2203**

REPORT - VIRGINIA. STATE BOARD OF NURSING (US/0749-3746) [09365871] **3868**

REPORT - VISUAL ARTS (EDMONTON) (CN/0226-1391) [06273637] **363**

REPORT (WASHINGTON (STATE). COUNCIL FOR POSTSECONDARY EDUCATION) (US) [04416010] **1845**

●REPORT, WASHINGTON STATE TRANSPORTATION PLAN UPDATE (US) [08838517] **5391**

REPORT - WASHINGTON UNIVERSITY (ST. LOUIS, MO.) (US) [06241440] **3245**

REPORT - WATER RESEARCH COMMISSION (SA) [02240461] **5538**

REPORT - WATER RESOURCES RESEARCH INSTITUTE, CLEMSON UNIVERSITY (US/0069-4657) [01145487] **5538**

REPORT / WATER RESOURCES RESEARCH INSTITUTE OF THE UNIVERSITY OF NORTH CAROLINA (US/0078-1525) [01185881] **5538**

REPORT - WATT COMMITTEE ON ENERGY (UK/0141-9676) [I01419676] **1955**

REPORT / WELLAND CANALS SOCIETY (CN/1181-7070) [24256724] **1625**

REPORT - WELSH SOILS DISCUSSION GROUP (UK/0083-7938) [02768190] **184**

REPORT / WESTERN PREMIERS' TASK FORCE ON CONSTITUTIONAL TRENDS (US) [07943213] **4682**

REPORT - WOOD UTILISATION RESEARCH CENTRE, DEPARTMENT OF CONSERVATION AND LAND MANAGEMENT (AT/1032-0407) [I10320407] 2203, **2404**

REPORT - WORKSHOP FOR CHILD CARE STAFF OF FLORIDA'S CHILD CARING FACILITIES (US/0091-8482) [01788023] **5305**

REPORT - WORLD BANK (US/0252-5097) [05719726] **808**

REPORT - WORLD METEOROLOGICAL ORGANIZATION (SZ/0084-1994) [01718948] **1434**

REPORT WRITING UPDATE *CEASED.* (US/0892-9378) [15296516] **3174**

REPORTABLE DISEASE BULLETIN / N. DAK. STATE DEPARTMENT OF HEALTH (US) [08818743] **3716**

REPORTAGE; THE INTERNATIONAL MAGAZINE OF PHOTOJOURNALISM (UK/1350-4010) 4376, **2924**

REPORTAJES; DOCUMENTOS PARA LA HISTORIA (BO) [01785654] **2757**

REPORTE ANUAL / SOUTHERN PERU COPPER CORPORATION, SUCURSAL DEL PERU (PE) [08773568] **4017**

REPORTE DE INVESTIGACION DEL INSTITUTO DE INVESTIGACIONES FUNDAMENTALES EN AGRICULTURA TROPICAL (CU) [09842636] **126**

REPORTE TEATRAL / COORDINACION GENERAL DE EXTENSION UNIVERSITARIA Y DIFUSION CULTURAL, EL (MX) [25495750] **5367**

REPORTED ARTHROPOD-BORNE ENCEPHALITIDES IN HORSES AND OTHER EQUIDAE (US) [02241069] **5520**

REPORTED DECISIONS OF THE SOCIAL SECURITY COMMISSIONER. SOCIAL SECURITY, CHILD BENEFIT, FAMILY INCOME SUPPLEMENTS, AND SUPPLEMENTARY BENEFIT ACTS / DEPARTMENT OF HEALTH AND SOCIAL SECURITY (UK) [10331416] **5305**

REPORTED MORBIDITY AND MORTALITY IN TEXAS, ANNUAL SUMMARY (US/0273-5202) [05665765] 3716, **4799**

REPORTED OCCUPATIONAL INJURIES AND ILLNESSES, SOUTH DAKOTA (US) [06675791] **2869**

REPORTER (US/1053-9972) [22718349] **5770**

REPORTER (US/0360-7119) [01895297] **946**

REPORTER (US) [21314763] **5698**

REPORTER (ALLISTON) (CN/0710-0949) [08124180] **5794**

REPORTER - AMERICAN PUBLIC WORKS ASSOCIATION (US/0092-4873) [01789483] **4682**

REPORTER AND FARMER AND THE WEBSTER JOURNAL (US) [13554646] **5744**

REPORTER ARGUS (US) [16810402] **5739**

REPORTER - BRITISH COLUMBIA LIBRARY ASSOCIATION (CN/1184-9703) [24690833] **3245**

REPORTER (CASEY, ILL.) (US/8750-2380) [11148110] **5661**

REPORTER - CHICAGO REGIONAL MARKETING AREA (US/0731-6097) [04386144] **935**

REPORTER DISPATCH, THE (US) [09579610] **5720**

REPORTER (EMMETSBURG, IOWA) (US/1042-1203) [16513692] **5672**

REPORTER (FOND DU LAC, WIS.), THE (US/0749-7172) [11167238] **5770**

REPORTER FOR CONSCIENCE' SAKE, THE (US/0034-4796) [02244974] **4055**

REPORTER (GRANADA HILLS), THE (US/0149-8754) [02588368] **5236**

REPORTER (LANSDALE, PA.), THE (US/0890-8443) [14553736] **5739**

REPORTER (LONDON) (CN/0828-6248) [12045312] **5794**

REPORTER (LONG BEACH, CALIF.) (US/0738-8527) [09626971] **1707**

REPORTER (LONG BEACH, CALIF.), THE (US/0746-5688) [10150278] **5639**

REPORTER (LOS ANGELES, CALIF.) (US/0739-3121) [09797241] **2924**

REPORTER (MARTINSVILLE, IND.) (US) [13503719] **5667**

REPORTER (NATIONAL CENTER FOR RESEARCH RESOURCES (U.S.)) *See* NCRR REPORTER / NATIONAL CENTER FOR RESEARCH RESOURCES **3619**

REPORTER - NATIONAL CENTER FOR RESEARCH RESOURCES (U.S.) (US/1057-9400) [23835252] **3634**

REPORTER - NEW JERSEY ASSOCIATION FOR HEALTH, PHYSICAL EDUCATION AND RECREATION, THE (US/0034-477X) [04130004] **4799**

REPORTER (O'FALLON, ILL.), THE (US/0889-5090) [13920061] **3038**

REPORTER ON HUMAN REPRODUCTION AND THE LAW (US/8756-2057) [05251544] 590, **3038**

REPORTER ON THE LEGAL PROFESSION (US/8755-7509) [05377199] **3038**

REPORTER - ONTARIO ENGLISH CATHOLIC TEACHERS' ASSOCIATION (CN/0384-5648) [03232972] **1903**

REPORTER (PATERSON), THE (US/0484-4610) [02241921] **3038**

REPORTER (PORT ELGIN) (CN/0380-8874) [02603870] **5794**

REPORTER. ROCKLEDGE EDITION, THE (US/0740-4166) [09974557] **5651**

REPORTER (SUPPLY AND SERVICES CANADA) (CN/0710-815X) [08271634] **4682**

REPORTER, THE (US) [17820187] **5753**

REPORTER TRES (BL) [05339493] **2552**

REPORTER (UTICA, N.Y.) (US/0277-6537) [04560186] **3245**

REPORTER (VACAVILLE, CALIF.) (US/0746-4193) [10029579] **5639**

REPORTER (WASHINGTON. 1977), THE (US/0193-8134) [04828331] **3183**

REPORTING CASH PAYMENTS OF OVER $10,000 (RECEIVED IN A TRADE OR BUSINESS) (US) [25483007] **707**

REPORTING CLASSROOM RESEARCH (CN/0315-369X) [02131709] **1778**

REPORTING FROM THE RUSSELL SAGE FOUNDATION (US/0736-217X) [09078559] **5236**

REPORTING ON READING (US/0196-0164) [04249781] **1778**

REPORTORIO GENERALE ANNUALE GIURISPRUDENZA ITALIANA (IT) **3038**

REPORTS (US) [06133441] **1845**

REPORTS. A - INTER-AFRICAN CONFERENCE. AGRICULTURE (UK/0414-0494) [01146024] **126**

REPORTS AND BALANCE SHEET PRESENTED TO THE SHAREHOLDERS AT THEIR GENERAL MEETING (BE) [01795962] **808**

REPORTS AND MEMOIRS (IT/0577-3199) [01553726] **280**

REPORTS AND PAPERS IN THE SOCIAL SCIENCES (US/0080-1348) [01614177] **5215**

Alphabetical Title Index — REPRODUCTIVE

REPORTS AND PAPERS ON MASS COMMUNICATION (FR/0080-1356) [01611405] **1120**

REPORTS AND PUBLICATIONS - PACIFIC FORESTRY CENTRE (CN/0846-6610) [22159259] **2392**

REPORTS AND RECOMMENDATIONS ... / KENTUCKY. STATE PARK COMMISSION (US) [06450833] **4708**

REPORTS AND SUMMARIES OF DISCUSSIONS / INTERNATIONAL SOCIAL SECURITY ASSOCIATION, COMMITTEE ON PROVIDENT FUNDS (II) [12176743] **4682, 2892**

REPORTS AND TESTIMONY / UNITED STATES GENERAL ACCOUNTING OFFICE, OFFICE OF PUBLIC AFFAIRS (US) [20707570] **4746**

REPORTS - BRITISH COLUMBIA ASSOCIATION OF HOSPITALS AND HEALTH ORGANIZATIONS (CN/0384-0883) [03235692] **3792**

REPORTS - CALIFORNIA COOPERATIVE OCEANIC FISHERIES INVESTIGATIONS (US/0575-3317) [01997942] **2311**

REPORTS DE L'ISE (BE) **1707**

... REPORTS / DEPARTMENT OF CORRECTIONS AND PAROLE BOARD, COMMONWEALTH OF VIRGINIA, THE (US) [08710612] **3175**

REPORTS : E (UK/0414-0508) [01146013] **1516**

REPORTS / EDUCATIONAL RESEARCH INSTITUTE OF BRITISH COLUMBIA (CN/0710-0809) [08936802] **1778**

REPORTS FROM GENERAL PRACTICE (UK/0557-3912) [09379736] **3739**

REPORTS FROM THE KEVO SUBARCTIC RESEARCH STATION (FI/0453-7831) [02572435] **4171**

REPORTS FROM THE PSYCHOLOGY DEPARTMENT, UNIVERSITY OF SOUTH AFRICA (SA) **4615**

REPORTS : IE (UK) [01145998] **1543**

REPORTS : L (UK/0414-0516) [01145984] **1707**

REPORTS LIST - EDUCATIONAL RESEARCH INSTITUTE OF BRITISH COLUMBIA (CN/0706-9944) [04590142] **1778**

REPORTS / MINORITY RIGHTS GROUP (UK/0305-6252) [02432544] 2272, **4512**

REPORTS - NATIONAL CENTER FOR SCIENCE EDUCATION (U.S.) (US/1064-2358) [20001950] 5146, **1778**

REPORTS / NEW YORK STATE, PUBLIC SERVICE COMMISSION (US) [05207830] **4682**

REPORTS OF CASES ARGUED AND DETERMINED IN THE COURTS OF APPEALS OF OHIO (US) [24785189] **3038**

REPORTS OF CASES ARGUED AND DETERMINED IN THE SUPERIOR COURT, APPELLATE DIVISION, CHANCERY DIVISION, LAW DIVISION, AND IN THE COUNTY COURTS OF THE STATE OF NEW JERSEY (US) [04863112] **3038**

REPORTS OF CASES ARGUED AND DETERMINED IN THE SUPREME COURT OF OHIO (US) [25178110] **3038**

REPORTS OF CASES ARGUED AND DETERMINED IN THE TAX COURT OF NEW JERSEY (US/0731-2954) [08138532] **3038**

REPORTS OF CASES BEFORE THE COURT OF JUSTICE AND THE COURT OF FIRST INSTANCE (LU/0378-7591) [24776691] **3038**

REPORTS OF CASES DECIDED IN THE APPELLATE DIVISION OF THE SUPREME COURT, STATE OF NEW YORK (US/0276-9581) [04644440] **3039**

REPORTS OF FAMILY LAW (CN/0317-4859) [01784937] **3122**

REPORTS OF H.M. INSPECTORS OF MINES AND QUARRIES UNDER THE MINES AND QUARRIES ACT 1954 : SOUTH WALES DISTRICT **CEASED.** (UK) [02246946] **2150**

REPORTS OF H. M. INSPECTORS OF MINES AND QUARRIES UNDER THE MINES AND QUARRIES ACT 1954 : THE NORTH OF ENGLAND DISTRICT (UK) [02611925] **2150**

REPORTS OF IMPORTANT DECISIONS BY THE EMPLOYMENT APPEALS TRIBUNAL UNDER THE UNFAIR DISMISSALS ACT, 1977 (IE) [11511965] **3153**

REPORTS OF INTERNATIONAL ARBITRAL AWARDS - UNITED NATIONS (US/0251-7833) [01751691] **3134**

REPORTS OF INVESTIGATIONS - INSTITUTE FOR THE STUDY OF EARTH AND MAN (US) [05024762] **4358**

REPORTS OF INVESTIGATIONS - SOUTHERN METHODIST UNIVERSITY. INSTITUTE FOR THE STUDY OF EARTH AND MAN (US/0885-8373) [02206851] **5146**

REPORTS OF MASSACHUSETTS APPELLATE DIVISION (MONTHLY) (US/0279-9413) [07368580] **3039**

REPORTS OF MEETINGS OF EXPERTS AND EQUIVALENT BODIES (FR/1014-9538) [I10149538] **1456**

● REPORTS OF MISCELLANEOUS CASES ARGUED AND DETERMINED IN THE COURTS OF OHIO: OTHER THAN THE SUPREME COURT AND THE COURTS OF APPEALS OF OHIO (US) [25778123] **3039**

REPORTS OF NATIONAL RESEARCH INSTITUTE OF POLICE SCIENCE (JA) **3175**

REPORTS OF OFFICERS AND PROCEEDINGS OF THE SUPREME LODGE OF THE ANCIENT ORDER OF UNITED WORKMEN (US/0090-8010) [01785605] **5236**

REPORTS OF PATENT, DESIGN AND TRADE MARK CASES (LONDON, ENGLAND : 1964) (UK) [01751438] **3039**

REPORTS OF PROCEEDINGS OF ANNUAL MEETING - WESTERN CANADIAN SOCIETY FOR HORTICULTURE (CN/0083-8810) [01713955] **2430**

REPORTS OF RESEARCH INSTITUTE FOR APPLIED MECHANICS, KYUSHU UNIVERSITY (JA/0023-6195) [01782738] **1994**

REPORTS OF TAX CASES (UK) [07446515] **4746**

REPORTS OF THE BOARD OF DIRECTORS AND STATUTORY AUDITORS TO SHAREHOLDERS **See** OPERATING YEAR ANNUAL REPORT **5422**

REPORTS OF THE BOARD OF DIRECTORS AND THE AUDITORS, STATEMENT OF CONDITION, PROFIT AND LOSS STATEMENT, RESOLUTIONS **See** REPORT OF THE BOARD OF DIRECTORS **1516**

REPORTS OF THE FACULTY OF SCIENCE AND ENGINEERING, SAGA UNIVERSITY MATHEMATICS (JA/0387-8538) [09859995] **3531**

REPORTS OF THE ODONATA SPECIALIST GROUP, SPECIES SURVIVAL COMMISSION, INTERNATIONAL UNION FOR THE CONSERVATION OF NATURE AND NATURAL RESOURCES (I.U.C.N.) (NE) [10217970] **5596**

REPORTS OF THE PRESIDENT AND THE TREASURER - JOHN SIMON GUGGENHEIM MEMORIAL FOUNDATION (US/0190-227X) [01123066] **5236**

REPORTS OF THE RESEARCH COMMITTEE OF THE SOCIETY OF ANTIQUARIES OF LONDON (UK) [01588329] **2705**

REPORTS OF THE RESEARCH INSTITUTE FOR STRENGTH AND FRACTURE OF MATERIALS, TOHOKU UNIVERSITY (JA/0563-6590) [02128467] **1994**

REPORTS OF THE STATE BIOLOGICAL SURVEY OF KANSAS (US/0885-8306) [06021666] **471**

REPORTS OF THE UNITED STATES TAX COURT (US/8755-6294) [07910015] 4746, **3039**

REPORTS OF THE UNIVERSITY GRANTS COMMITTEE AND UNIVERSITY INSTITUTIONS (NZ) [02246048] **1845**

REPORTS ON HEALTH AND SOCIAL SUBJECTS (UK/0300-8045) [01695539] **4799**

REPORTS ON INTERNATIONAL COMPENSATION : ARGENTINA (US/0095-4144) [01796761] **1707**

REPORTS ON INTERNATIONAL COMPENSATION : BRAZIL (US) [02506503] 884, **1707**

REPORTS ON MARINE SCIENCE AFFAIRS (SZ) [01789706] **1434**

REPORTS ON MATHEMATICAL LOGIC (PL/0137-2904) [01853538] **3531**

REPORTS ON MATHEMATICAL PHYSICS (PL/0034-4877) [02244613] 3531, **4419**

REPORTS ON NIUE AND THE TOKELAU ISLANDS (NZ) [02240023] **4682**

REPORTS ON PHILOSOPHY (PL/0324-8712) [03837977] **4358**

REPORTS ON PROGRESS IN PHYSICS (UK/0034-4885) [01607643] **4419**

REPORTS ON PROGRESS IN POLYMER PHYSICS IN JAPAN (JA/0486-4476) [01763731] **1057**

REPORTS ON PUBLIC BILLS (BOUND) (HOUSE AND SENATE) (US) [05795577] **3039**

REPORTS ON RESEARCH ASSISTED BY THE PETROLEUM RESEARCH FUND (US/0190-8715) [04012170] 4276, **1029**

REPORTS ON RESEARCH - WOODS HOLE OCEANOGRAPHIC INSTITUTION (US/1062-2160) [24241374] **1456**

REPORTS ON RHEUMATIC DISEASES (1985) (UK/0957-0381) [14912776] **3806**

REPORTS ON RHEUMATIC DISEASES (1985) (UK/0957-0381) [14912706] **3806**

REPORTS ON SCIENCE AND TECHNOLOGY / LINDE (GW) [30859430] **5146**

REPORTS ON SURGERY OF THE HAND (PL) [02208487] **3973**

REPORTS ON THE WORKING OF GOVERNMENT DEPARTMENTS FOR THE YEAR ... (MM) [09586476] **4682**

REPORTS SERVICE: NORTH AFRICA SERIES **See** NORTH AFRICA SERIES **2642**

REPORTS SERVICE: WEST AFRICA SERIES **See** WEST AFRICA SERIES **2644**

REPORTS : SS (UK/0414-0524) [01146031] **5215**

REPORTS : ST (UK/0414-0532) [01146064] **5337**

REPORTS : TO (UK) [01146053] **3175**

REPORTS TO THE GENERAL ASSEMBLY OF THE UNITED FREE CHURCH OF SCOTLAND (UK) [07035119] **4992**

REPORTS - UNITED STATES. TAX COURT (US/0040-0017) [07329854] 4746, **3039**

REPOSITORIO DE TRABALHOS DO L.N.I.V (PO/0870-1067) [03575900] **5520**

REPOSITORY (CANTON, OHIO), THE (US/0745-7545) [09424923] **5730**

REPPAL / CENTRE D'ETUDES PHENICIENNES-PUNIQUES ET DES ANTIQUITES LIBQUES (TI/0330-843X) [15188091] 363, 1079, **280**

REPRESENTABLE COMPENSATION PLAN - OREGON. EXECUTIVE DEPT. PERSONNEL DIVISION. OPERATIONS AND DEVELOPMENT UNIT (US) [06866097] **4683**

REPRESENTATIONS (BERKELEY, CALIF.) (US/0734-6018) [08781433] **2853**

REPRESENTATIVE AMERICAN SPEECHES (US/0197-6923) [01330654] **3429**

REPRESENTATIVE, FOX LAKE, WISCONSIN, THE (US/8755-4011) [11292013] **5770**

REPRESENTATIVE RESEARCH IN SOCIAL PSYCHOLOGY (US/0034-4907) [01763735] 5255, **4615**

REPRESENTING PROFESSIONAL ATHLETES AND TEAMS (US/0276-7627) [06594520] 4915, **3039**

REPRESENTING PUBLICLY TRADED CORPORATIONS (US/0276-6639) [04701481] **3102**

REPRESION (PE) [06007184] **4512**

REPRINT (US) [01549558] **5443**

REPRINT / KENTUCKY GEOLOGICAL SURVEY (US/0075-5605) [08502091] **1395**

REPRINT - RESOURCES FOR THE FUTURE (US/0486-5553) [01184540] **2203**

REPRINT SERIES - CANADIAN SOCIETY OF PETROLEUM GEOLOGISTS (CN/0704-7614) [04530837] **1395**

REPRINT SERIES - GEOLOGICAL SURVEY OF ALABAMA (US/0568-7896) [01478906] **1395**

REPRINT SERIES - INDUSTRIAL RELATIONS CENTRE. QUEEN'S UNIVERSITY (CN/0075-6156) [02248223] 1516, **1707**

REPRINT SERIES / SOCIETY FOR CENTRAL ASIAN STUDIES (UK) [15061282] **2663**

REPRINTED ACTS OF THE PARLIAMENT OF WESTERN AUSTRALIA (AT) [01640974] **3039**

REPRINTS FROM THE SOVIET PRESS **SUSPENDED.** (US/0034-4931) [01763736] 4493, **1516**

REPRODUCCION (MADRID) (SP/0303-5220) [00978810] **3767**

REPRODUCER, THE (US/0742-9088) [10470510] 1138, **2777**

REPRODUCTION (UK/0034-4958) [10119951] **4569**

REPRODUCTION BULLETIN (US/0736-1238) [07380611] **4238**

REPRODUCTION, FERTILITY, AND DEVELOPMENT (AT/1031-3613) [19505713] **586**

REPRODUCTION HUMAINE ET HORMONES (FR/0994-3919) [I09943919] **3733**

REPRODUCTION IN DOMESTIC ANIMALS 1990 (GW/0936-6768) [21265026] **5520**

REPRODUCTION, NUTRITION, DEVELOPMENT (FR) [20224294] 220, **4198**

REPRODUCTIVE MEDICINE (US/0732-1279) [08276411] **3767**

● REPRODUCTIVE MEDICINE REVIEW (UK/0962-2799) [26353176] **3767**

REPRODUCTIVE PHYSIOLOGY (US/0266-6499) [02572370] **586**

REPRODUCTIVE — Alphabetical Title Index

REPRODUCTIVE TOXICOLOGY (ELMSFORD, N.Y.) (US/0890-6238) [14286647] **3983**

REPRODUIRE (FR) **4376**

REPROGRAF, DER (GW) [01791714] **4376**

REPROGRAF UND LICHTPAUSER *See* REPROGRAF, DER **4376**

REPROGRAPHICS & DESIGN IMAGING *CEASED.* (US/1069-1510) [27403667] 626, 2030, **4569**

REPROGRAPHICS QUARTERLY (UK/0306-2880) [01794260] **4569**

REPS BODYBUILDING AUSTRALIA (AT/1033-5609) [I10335609] **2601**

REPSOL (FIRM) *See* ANNUAL REPORT - REPSOL (FIRM) **4250**

REPTILE & AMPHIBIAN MAGAZINE (US/1059-0668) [21252741] **5596**

●REPTILES (IRVINE, CALIF.) (US/1068-1965) [27466924] **4287**

REPUBBLICA (ROME, ITALY) (IT) [11003889] **5805**

REPUBLIC (COLUMBUS, IND.) (US) [12166653] **5667**

REPUBLIC (MEYERSDALE, PA.) (US) [14877435] **5739**

REPUBLIC OF CHINA YEARBOOK (CH/1013-0942) [20987680] **2663**

REPUBLIC OF TRINIDAD AND TOBAGO CONSOLIDATED INDEX OF PUBLIC ACTS & SUBSIDIARY LEGISLATION TO ... / COMPILED AT THE FACULTY OF LAW LIBRARY, UNIVERSITY OF THE WEST INDIES, BARBADOS (BB) [25416810] **3039**

REPUBLIC OF ZAMBIA, FINANCIAL REPORT / BANK OF ZAMBIA (ZA) [09934866] **808**

REPUBLICA DE LAS LETRAS : ORGANO DE LA ASOCIACION COLEGIAL DE ESCRITORES DE ESPANO (SP) [14874024] 1308, **3429**

REPUBLICA, LA (CK) [12608216] **5799**

REPUBLICAN ALMANAC (US/0363-9290) [02593987] **4493**

REPUBLICAN CHINA (US/0893-2344) [10690060] **2663**

REPUBLICAN (DANVILLE, IND.) (US) [11285350] **5667**

REPUBLICAN JOURNAL (BELFAST, ME.) (US/0034-5075) [02266886] **5685**

REPUBLICAN JOURNAL, BELMONT SUCCESS, THE OLD SETTLER, SCHULLSBURG PICK AND GAD (US) [13460076] **5770**

REPUBLICAN UPDATE (US/1056-9278) [23899502] **4493**

REPUBLICANS ABROAD (US/0738-193X) [09518710] **4683**

REPUBLICCKI ZAVOD ZA ZASTITU SPOMENIKA KULTURE *See* SAOPSTENJA - REPUBLICKI ZAVOD ZA ZASTITU SPOMENIKA KULTURE SR SRBIJE **308**

REPUBLICKI ZAVOD ZA STATISTIKU SR HRVATSKE *See* ZNANSTVENOISTRAZIVACKE I RAZVOJNE ORGANIZACIJE **5173**

REPUBLICKI ZAVOD ZA STATISTIKU SR SRBIJE *See* JAVNI VODOVOD I KANALIZACIJA U NASELJIMA SR SRBIJE **5535**

REPUBLICKI ZAVOD ZA STATISTIKU SR SRBIJE *See* OPSTINE U SR SRBIJI **5335**

REPUBLICKI ZAVOD ZA STATISTIKU SR SRBIJE. STATISTICKI POKAZATELJI O OPSTINAMA *See* OPSTINE U SR SRBIJI **5335**

REPUBLIK KOREA : ENERGIEWIRTSCHAFT (GW) [05235232] **1955**

REPUBLIK KOREA : WIRTSCHAFTLICHE ENTWICKLUNG (GW) [03463625] **1581**

REPUBLIK KOREA : WIRTSCHAFTSDATEN UND WIRTSCHAFTSDOKUMENTATION (GW) [06259659] **1581**

REPUBLIK SUDAFRIKA : ENERGIEWIRTSCHAFT (GW) [04338284] **1955**

REPULESI SZAKIRODALMI TAJEKOZTATO (HU/0231-3928) [I02313928] **33**

REQUEST (MINNEAPOLIS, MINN.) (US/1045-0084) [19987622] **4149**

REQUESTS FOR INTERPRETATIONS AND POLICY STATEMENTS (US/0148-5520) [03333604] **4705**

REQUIREMENTS FOR CERTIFICATION OF TEACHERS, COUNSELORS, LIBRARIANS, ADMINISTRATORS FOR ELEMENTARY AND SECONDARY SCHOOLS (US/1047-7071) [20002492] **1870**

REQUIREMENTS FOR TEACHING CERTIFICATES IN CANADA (CN/0080-1437) [09977370] **1778**

REREPORT, THE (UK/0143-9669) [06254023] **2892**

RERIC HOLDINGS LIST : / AN OCCASIONAL PUBLICATION OF RERIC (TH) [09474644] **1955**

RERIC INTERNATIONAL ENERGY JOURNAL (TH) [18806453] **1955**

RERIC NEWS (TH) [04757355] **1955**

RERUM ECCLESIASTICARUM DOCUMENTA. SERIES MAIOR: FONTES (IT/0484-4823) [05230255] **5035**

RERUNS *SUSPENDED.* (US/0278-6397) [07842826] **1138**

RES BUREAUX *See* RES BUREAUX BULLETIN **4358**

RES BUREAUX BULLETIN (CN/0383-6150) [03520257] **4358**

RES (CAMBRIDGE, MASS.) (US/0277-1322) [07569829] **244**

RES GESTA (AG) [04981347] **2757**

RES GESTAE (INDIANAPOLIS, IND.) (US/0557-9295) [01763748] **3039**

RES. PUB. (NATIONAL GEOGRAPHICAL SOCIETY OF INDIA) (II) [09311179] 4559, **2574**

RES PUBLICA (SA) [03170777] **3039**

RES PUBLICA (PL/0860-4592) [17347250] **2492**

RES PUBLICA (CLAREMONT) (US/0092-671X) [01791293] **4683**

RES PUBLICA LITTERARUM (IT/0275-4304) [04752662] **1079**

RESARUN (II) [07812630] **2663**

RESCENT *SUSPENDED.* (AT/0155-1078) [I01551078] **1845**

RESCUE-EMS MAGAZINE (US/1073-9998) [26030061] **4799**

RESCUE MAGAZINE (US/1041-0651) [18621066] **4799**

RESCUE NEWS *See* RESCUE-EMS MAGAZINE **4799**

RESCUE NEWS (UK/0950-5830) [I09505830] **280**

RESCUE (SOLANA BEACH, CALIF.) (US/1045-0246) [20344402] **3634**

RESEARCH (UK) [01791799] **1707**

RESEARCH ABSTRACTS (ANN ARBOR) (US/0362-7535) [02300970] **423**

RESEARCH ACCOMPLISHED (SOUTHERN FOREST EXPERIMENT STATION) *See* RECENT PUBLICATIONS (SOUTHERN FOREST EXPERIMENT STATION (NEW ORLEANS, LA.)) **2392**

RESEARCH ACCOMPLISHMENTS - WILDLIFE RESEARCH CENTER (DENVER) (US) [01541807] **2203**

RESEARCH ACCOMPLISHMENTS - WILDLIFE RESEARCH LABORATORY *See* RESEARCH ACCOMPLISHMENTS - WILDLIFE RESEARCH CENTER (DENVER) **2203**

RESEARCH ACTIVITIES IN ATMOSPHERIC AND OCEANIC MODELLING (SZ) [11646030] 1456, **1434**

RESEARCH ACTIVITIES OF THE INSTITUTE OF ATOMIC ENERGY, KYOTO UNIVERSITY (JA/0386-0752) [04645871] **1955**

RESEARCH ACTIVITIES / SWEDISH NATIONAL INDUSTRIAL BOARD (SW) [17987999] **4683**

RESEARCH ACTIVITY CATALOGUE (SW) [19215918] **2181**

RESEARCH ADVANCES IN ALCOHOL AND DRUG PROBLEMS (US/0093-9714) [02239425] **1348**

RESEARCH ALERT (US) [12412277] **1299**

RESEARCH ALERT (US) 3245, **3259**

RESEARCH AND ADVANCED STUDIES BULLETIN / UNIVERSITY OF STRATHCLYDE, DEPARTMENT OF ARCHITECTURE AND BUILDING SCIENCE (UK) [19841195] 307, **626**

RESEARCH AND APPLICATIONS IN MUSIC EDUCATION *CEASED.* (US/0883-9700) [12267492] **4149**

RESEARCH AND CLINICAL FORUMS (UK/0143-3083) [05104213] **3634**

RESEARCH & CREATIVE ACTIVITY (US/0731-4981) [06857269] 1845, **5146**

RESEARCH AND CURRENT ISSUES SERIES - INDUSTRIAL RELATIONS CENTRE. QUEEN'S UNIVERSITY (CN/0317-2546) [02248085] 1516, **1707**

RESEARCH AND DEVELOPMENT - AMERICAN GAS ASSOCIATION (US/0091-2786) [01786727] **4276**

RESEARCH AND DEVELOPMENT ASSOCIATES FOR MILITARY FOOD AND PACKAGING SYSTEMS *See* ACTIVITIES REPORT OF THE R & D ASSOCIATES **2326**

RESEARCH & DEVELOPMENT (BARRINGTON, ILL.) (US/0746-9179) [10366267] **5146**

RESEARCH AND DEVELOPMENT FOR THE ADVANCEMENT OF EDUCATION (US) [01785996] **1903**

RESEARCH AND DEVELOPMENT IN INDUSTRY (WASHINGTON, D.C. : 1966) (US) [01269747] **1625**

RESEARCH AND DEVELOPMENT MONOGRAPH - UNIVERSITY OF NEW SOUTH WALES, CENTRE FOR MEDICAL EDUCATION, RESEARCH AND DEVELOPMENT (AT/0157-745X) [09262815] **3634**

RESEARCH AND DEVELOPMENT NEWS (US/0486-476X) [01644850] **5538**

RESEARCH AND DEVELOPMENT PAPER - TERTIARY EDUCATION RESEARCH CENTRE. UNIVERSITY OF NEW SOUTH WALES (AT/0313-5543) [I03135543] **1845**

RESEARCH AND DEVELOPMENT PROGRAM FOR OUTER CONTINENTAL SHELF OIL AND GAS OPERATIONS, TECHNICAL REPORT (US) [06187570] **4276**

RESEARCH AND DEVELOPMENT PROGRAMS GUIDE *CEASED.* (US/0163-0202) [04264982] **4055**

RESEARCH AND DEVELOPMENT PROGRESS REPORT / OFFICE OF SALINE WATER (US/0500-2230) [01482668] **2203**

RESEARCH AND DEVELOPMENT PROJECTS IN AGING (US/0271-2784) [05047343] **5305**

RESEARCH AND DEVELOPMENT : R & D (JA/0373-8868) [10447217] **2108**

RESEARCH AND DEVELOPMENT REPORT - OFFICE OF COAL RESEARCH, DEPARTMENT OF THE INTERIOR (US/0083-260X) [01727788] **2150**

RESEARCH AND DEVELOPMENT REPORTER (II/0257-3245) [I02573245] **5146**

RESEARCH & DEVELOPMENT. TELEPHONE DIRECTORY (US) [10529806] 5146, **1929**

RESEARCH & EDUCATION NETWORKING (US/1051-4791) [21974448] 1244, 1276, **1221**

RESEARCH AND EVALUATION PLAN / NATIONAL INSTITUTE OF JUSTICE (US) [25897402] **3175**

RESEARCH & EXPLORATION (US/1056-800X) [23250636] **4171**

RESEARCH AND EXPOSITION IN MATHEMATICS (GW) [11843795] **3531**

RESEARCH AND INDUSTRY (II/0034-513X) [01696874] **5146**

RESEARCH AND INVENTION (US/0276-0401) [02266897] **5146**

RESEARCH AND PUBLICATIONS (KE) [05352137] 5215, **1516**

RESEARCH AND PUBLICATIONS (BIRMINGHAM, WEST MIDLANDS, ENGLAND) *See* RESEARCH & PUBLICATIONS REPORT (BIRMINGHAM, WEST MIDLANDS, ENGLAND) **1845**

RESEARCH & PUBLICATIONS REPORT (BIRMINGHAM, WEST MIDLANDS, ENGLAND) (UK) [10242116] **1845**

RESEARCH & SOCIETY (US/1052-3707) [20512568] **5215**

RESEARCH AND STUDIES - CARLETON UNIVERSITY (CN/0319-6143) [02627470] **1845**

RESEARCH & SURVEY IN NATURE CONSERVATION (UK/0952-4738) [I09524738] **2203**

RESEARCH & TEACHING IN DEVELOPMENTAL EDUCATION (US/1046-3364) [13405225] **1884**

RESEARCH AND TECHNOLOGY ANNUAL REPORT (US/0277-7290) [07606801] **5146**

RESEARCH AND TECHNOLOGY PROGRAM (US/0740-9443) [07342526] **2833**

RESEARCH & TECHNOLOGY TRANSPORTER / U.S. DEPARTMENT OF TRANSPORTATION, FEDERAL HIGHWAY ADMINISTRATION (US) [24048295] **5391**

RESEARCH ANIMALS IN CANADA (CN/0229-1223) [07849842] **226**

RESEARCH ASSOCIATION (ANTHROPOLOGY) *See* RESEARCH BULLETIN - RESEARCH ASSOCIATION (ANTHROPOLOGY) **244**

RESEARCH AT LOS BANOS (PH) [11264675] **127**

RESEARCH AT LSE (UK) [17419557] 4493, **1517**

RESEARCH BIWEEKLY (CN/1185-1902) [24257165] **1517**

RESEARCH (BLACKSBURG, VA.) (US/0731-9649) [08314454] **1845**

RESEARCH BRANCH REPORT (CANADA. AGRICULTURE CANADA. RESEARCH BRANCH) *See* DIRECTORY OF RESEARCH / RESEARCH BRANCH / ANNUAIRE DE LA RECHERCHE / DIRECTION GENERALE DE LA RECHERCHE **79**

RESEARCH BRANCH REPORT - RESEARCH STATION, SUMMERLAND, BRITISH COLUMBIA (CN/0845-9630) [11387164] **184**

RESEARCH

RESEARCH BULLETIN (II) [25679374] **127**

RESEARCH BULLETIN (US) [26236312] **127**

RESEARCH BULLETIN - ALABAMA AGRICULTURAL AND MECHANICAL UNIVERSITY, SCHOOL OF AGRICULTURE AND ENVIRONMENTAL SCIENCE (US) [03172225] **127**

RESEARCH BULLETIN / BRITISH LIBRARY RESEARCH AND DEVELOPMENT DEPARTMENT (UK/0952-2832) [17340722] **3245**

RESEARCH BULLETIN (CANADA PARKS) (CN) **2757**

RESEARCH BULLETIN (CENTRE OF ARABIC DOCUMENTATION) (NR/0536-2288) [02109463] **2770**

RESEARCH BULLETIN - CITY OF TORONTO PLANNING AND DEVELOPMENT. RESEARCH AND INFORMATION SECTION (CN/0828-4121) [11847745] **2833**

RESEARCH BULLETIN - COMMONWEALTH OF MASSACHUSETTS, DEPARTMENT OF EDUCATION, DIVISION OF RESEARCH AND STATISTICS (US/0465-1588) [02247009] 1778, **1796**

RESEARCH BULLETIN - DEPARTMENT OF AGRICULTURAL ECONOMICS AND FARM MANAGEMENT. FACULTY OF AGRICULTURE. UNIVERSITY OF MANITOBA (CN/0316-8816) [02247371] 1517, **127**

RESEARCH BULLETIN - DEPARTMENT OF CONSERVATION AND LAND MANAGEMENT WESTERN AUSTRALIA (AT/1032-8106) [21247334] **2203**

RESEARCH BULLETIN - DEPARTMENT OF TECHNICAL AND FURTHER EDUCATION SOUTH AUSTRALIA (AT/0815-7650) [I08157650] **1778**

RESEARCH BULLETIN - FLORIDA EDUCATIONAL RESEARCH AND DEVELOPMENT COUNCIL (US) [01326047] **1778**

RESEARCH BULLETIN (GREAT BRITAIN. HOME OFFICE. RESEARCH AND PLANNING UNIT) (UK/0305-9871) [09244038] **3175**

RESEARCH BULLETIN - INDIAN INSTITUTE OF TECHNOLOGY, BOMBAY (II) [03697536] **5146**

RESEARCH BULLETIN - INSTITUTE FOR THE STUDY OF WORSHIP AND RELIGIOUS ARCHITECTURE (UK/0305-2206) [06317347] **307**

RESEARCH BULLETIN - INTERNATIONAL CROPS RESEARCH INSTITUTE FOR THE SEMI-ARID TROPICS (II/0257-8441) [08272132] **184**

RESEARCH BULLETIN / MASSACHUSETTS AGRICULTURAL EXPERIMENT STATION (US/0271-7212) [05804084] **127**

RESEARCH BULLETIN - NATIONAL HORTICULTURAL RESEARCH INSTITUTE (NR/0795-414X) [I0795414X] **2430**

RESEARCH BULLETIN - NEW YORK (STATE). DEPT. OF COMMERCE (US/0077-9156) [06283903] **850**

RESEARCH BULLETIN OF THE FACULTY OF AGRICULTURE, GIFU UNIVERSITY (JA/0435-9844) [01458603] **127**

RESEARCH BULLETIN OF THE INSTITUTE OF COST AND WORKS ACCOUNTANTS OF INDIA (II) [09104939] **750**

RESEARCH BULLETIN OF THE NATIONAL INSTITUTE FOR EDUCATIONAL RESEARCH (JA/0085-378X) [01755221] **1779**

RESEARCH BULLETIN OF THE PANJAB UNIVERSITY. SCIENCE (II/0555-7631) [06035601] **5146**

RESEARCH BULLETIN / OHIO AGRICULTURAL RESEARCH AND DEVELOPMENT CENTER (US/0078-3951) [02229920] **127**

RESEARCH BULLETIN - OHIO EDUCATION ASSOCIATION (US/0092-458X) [01789672] **1779**

RESEARCH BULLETIN (OREGON STATE UNIVERSITY. FOREST RESEARCH LABORATORY) *See* RESEARCH CONTRIBUTION **2392**

RESEARCH BULLETIN / PAPUA NEW GUINEA DEPT. OF AGRICULTURE AND LIVESTOCK (PP) [21201039] **127**

RESEARCH BULLETIN (PEEL (ONT. : REGIONAL MUNICIPALITY). BOARD OF EDUCATION) (CN/0845-4485) [20125732] **1779**

RESEARCH BULLETIN - PENNSYLVANIA GAME COMMISSION (US) [01348070] **2203**

RESEARCH BULLETIN - RESEARCH ASSOCIATION (ANTHROPOLOGY) (II) [02311403] **244**

RESEARCH BULLETIN. SCIENCE SECTION (II) [01763173] **5146**

RESEARCH BULLETIN - ST. THOMAS PSYCHIATRIC HOSPITAL (CN/0711-6926) [10420570] **3935**

RESEARCH BULLETIN - STATE OF NEVADA, DEPARTMENT OF EDUCATION, OFFICE OF TECHNICAL ASSISTANCE (US) [02245064] **1870**

RESEARCH BULLETIN - UNIVERSITY OF MANITOBA (CN) **1845**

RESEARCH BULLETIN - UNIVERSITY OF MISSOURI-COLUMBIA. AGRICULTURAL EXPERIMENT STATION (US) [06987271] **127**

RESEARCH BULLETIN - WASHINGTON STATE UNIVERSITY. COLLEGE OF AGRICULTURE AND HOME ECONOMICS. RESEARCH CENTER (US/1059-8022) [20576064] **127**

RESEARCH CENTER FOR THE ARTS AND HUMANITIES REVIEW *SUSPENDED.* (US/8755-3864) [09091976] 2853, **329**

RESEARCH CENTERS DIRECTORY (US/0080-1518) [03765777] **3634**

RESEARCH CHRONICLE (UK) [07823904] **4149**

RESEARCH COMMUNICATIONS IN CHEMICAL PATHOLOGY & PHARMACOLOGY *See* RESEARCH COMMUNICATIONS IN MOLECULAR PATHOLOGY & PHARMACOLOGY **4327**

●RESEARCH COMMUNICATIONS IN ALCOHOL AND SUBSTANCES OF ABUSE (US) **1348**

RESEARCH COMMUNICATIONS IN CHEMICAL PATHOLOGY AND PHARMACOLOGY (US/0034-5164) [01763760] **4327**

●RESEARCH COMMUNICATIONS IN MOLECULAR PATHOLOGY & PHARMACOLOGY (US) **4327**

RESEARCH COMMUNICATIONS IN PSYCHOLOGY, PSYCHIATRY AND BEHAVIOR (US/0362-2428) [02185143] 3935, **4615**

RESEARCH COMMUNICATIONS IN SUBSTANCES OF ABUSE (US/0193-0818) [09106238] **1348**

●RESEARCH CONTRIBUTION (US) [28276410] **2392**

RESEARCH CONTRIBUTIONS OF THE AMERICAN BAR FOUNDATION (US) [01763761] **3039**

RESEARCH CORPORATION OF THE UNIVERSITY OF HAWAII *See* RESEARCH CORPORATION OF THE UNIVERSITY OF HAWAII ANNUAL REPORT, THE **5146**

RESEARCH CORPORATION OF THE UNIVERSITY OF HAWAII *See* RCUH ANNUAL REPORT **5145**

RESEARCH CORPORATION OF THE UNIVERSITY OF HAWAII ANNUAL REPORT, THE (US) [10918870] **5146**

RESEARCH COUNCIL OF ALBERTA *See* MINES AND MINERAL RESOURCES **1358**

RESEARCH, DEMONSTRATION AND EVALUATION STUDIES ON CHILD ABUSE AND NEGLECT (US/0362-8221) [02354327] **5305**

RESEARCH DIGEST - LATINO INSTITUTE (RESTON, VA.) (US/0276-0509) [07250928] **2757**

RESEARCH DIRECTORY - MEMORIAL UNIVERSITY OF NEWFOUNDLAND. OFFICE OF RESEARCH (CN/0704-7452) [03956434] **1845**

RESEARCH DIRECTORY OF THE REHABILITATION RESEARCH AND TRAINING CENTERS (US/0096-1531) [01234251] **4382**

RESEARCH DISCLOSURE (UK/0374-4353) [03782901] **5146**

RESEARCH DIVISION BULLETIN (VIRGINIA POLYTECHNIC INSTITUTE AND STATE UNIVERSITY. RESEARCH DIVISION) (US/0090-8134) [02718590] **1845**

RESEARCH EVALUATION (UK/0958-2029) [24868193] **5146**

RESEARCH, EVALUATION, AND DEMONSTRATION PROJECT (US) [17667324] **1707**

RESEARCH EXTENSION SERIES / HAWAII INSTITUTE OF TROPICAL AGRICULTURE AND HUMAN RESOURCES (US/0271-9916) [06740170] **127**

RESEARCH FIELDS IN PHYSICS AT UNITED KINGDOM UNIVERSITIES AND POLYTECHNICS (UK/0308-9290) [03089290] **4419**

RESEARCH FIELDS IN PHYSICS AT UNITED KINGDOM UNIVERSITIES AND POLYTECHNICS (UK) **4419**

RESEARCH FILE, THE (CN/1188-6641) [26497911] **2601**

RESEARCH FOR DEVELOPMENT : THE JOURNAL OF THE NIGERIAN INSTITUTE OF SOCIAL & ECONOMIC RESEARCH (NR/0189-0085) [08842615] **1517**

RESEARCH FROM WALL STREET *See* INFORMATION CATALOG, THE **682**

RESEARCH FRONTS IN ISI/BIOMED (US/0732-5606) [08407407] **5146**

RESEARCH FRONTS IN ISI. COMPUMATH (US/0735-794X) [08996281] 1201, **3531**

RESEARCH (GOTTINGEN, GERMANY) *CEASED.* (GW/0722-6349) [09193292] **244**

RESEARCH GRANTS, TRAINING AWARDS, SUMMARY TABLES (US/0277-3090) [07525725] **3844**

RESEARCH GRANTS / [PREPARED BY NATIONAL INSTITUTES OF HEALTH, DIVISION OF RESEARCH GRANTS, STATISTICS AND ANALYSIS BRANCH] (US) [04408614] 5305, **3634**

RESEARCH HIGHLIGHTS (CENTRAL POTATO RESEARCH INSTITUTE (INDIA)) (II) [11188980] **184**

RESEARCH HIGHLIGHTS (EDINBURGH) *See* RESEARCH HIGHLIGHTS IN SOCIAL WORK **5255**

RESEARCH HIGHLIGHTS IN AGING (US/0499-9797) [05014353] **3754**

RESEARCH HIGHLIGHTS IN SOCIAL WORK (UK/0955-7970) [I09557970] **5255**

RESEARCH IN ACCOUNTING REGULATION (US/1052-0457) [17786278] **750**

RESEARCH IN AFRICAN LITERATURES (US/0034-5210) [00834085] **3429**

RESEARCH IN ASIAN ECONOMIC STUDIES (US/1047-126X) [20510796] **1639**

RESEARCH IN BIOLOGICAL AND MEDICAL SCIENCES *See* ANNUAL PROGRESS REPORT / WALTER REED ARMY INSTITUTE OF RESEARCH **3550**

RESEARCH IN BIOPOLITICS (US) [25157560] **4493**

RESEARCH IN COMMUNITY AND MENTAL HEALTH (US/0192-0812) [04801197] **4615**

RESEARCH IN COMMUNITY SOCIOLOGY (US/1058-5028) [22216311] **5255**

RESEARCH IN CONSUMER BEHAVIOR (US/0885-2111) [12376636] **935**

RESEARCH IN CONTEMPORARY AND APPLIED GEOGRAPHY (US/1055-9914) [06952081] **2574**

RESEARCH IN CORPORATE SOCIAL PERFORMANCE AND POLICY (US/0191-1937) [04587718] 1625, **5255**

RESEARCH IN DEVELOPMENTAL DISABILITIES (US/0891-4222) [14765885] **4615**

RESEARCH IN DEVELOPMENTAL EDUCATION *See* REVIEW OF RESEARCH IN DEVELOPMENTAL EDUCATION **1780**

RESEARCH IN DOMESTIC AND INTERNATIONAL AGRIBUSINESS MANAGEMENT (US/0276-1653) [07189216] 127, **707**

RESEARCH IN ECONOMIC ANTHROPOLOGY (US/0190-1281) [04429847] **244**

RESEARCH IN ECONOMIC HISTORY (US/0363-3268) [02764097] **1581**

RESEARCH IN EDUCATION (MANCHESTER) (UK/0034-5237) [01115183] **1779**

RESEARCH IN EDUCATION SERIES (CN) [05821443] **1779**

RESEARCH IN ENGINEERING DESIGN (US/0934-9839) [20509228] **1994**

RESEARCH IN EXPERIMENTAL ECONOMICS (US/0193-2306) [05133224] **1517**

RESEARCH IN EXPERIMENTAL MEDICINE (GW/0300-9130) [01785668] **3634**

RESEARCH IN FINANCE (US/0196-3821) [05711941] **808**

RESEARCH IN FINANCE. SUPPLEMENT (US/0882-3138) [11115123] 1517, **808**

RESEARCH IN FINANCIAL SERVICES (US/1052-7788) [21286890] **808**

RESEARCH IN FISHERIES (US/0083-7555) [09251248] **2311**

RESEARCH IN GLOBAL STRATEGIC MANAGEMENT (US/1064-4857) [22213484] **884**

RESEARCH IN GOVERNMENTAL AND NONPROFIT ACCOUNTING (US/0884-0741) [11850438] **4746**

RESEARCH IN HIGHER EDUCATION (US/0361-0365) [01604288] **1845**

RESEARCH IN HUMAN CAPITAL AND DEVELOPMENT (US/0194-3960) [05340715] **1517**

RESEARCH IN HUMAN REPRODUCTION / WHO SPECIAL PROGRAMME OF RESEARCH, DEVELOPMENT, AND RESEARCH TRAINING IN HUMAN REPRODUCTION (SZ) [18440435] **591**

RESEARCH IN HUMANITIES COMPUTING : SELECTED PAPERS FROM THE AALC/ACH CONFERENCE (UK) [24868195] 1201, **2853**

RESEARCH IN IMMUNOLOGY (PARIS) (FR/0923-2494) [19340081] **3676**

RESEARCH

RESEARCH IN INEQUALITY AND SOCIAL CONFLICT (US/1048-1222) [20743498] **1581**

RESEARCH IN INORGANIC MATERIALS (CC) [09530204] 1037, **2593**

RESEARCH IN INTERNATIONAL BUSINESS AND FINANCE (US/0275-5319) [04660568] **1639**

RESEARCH IN INTERNATIONAL BUSINESS AND INTERNATIONAL RELATIONS (US/1053-1254) [13724865] 4533, **1639**

RESEARCH IN LABOR ECONOMICS (US/0147-9121) [03244461] **1707**

RESEARCH IN LABOR ECONOMICS. SUPPLEMENT (US/0194-3057) [05273826] **1707**

RESEARCH IN LAW AND ECONOMICS (US/0193-5895) [05036108] 1517, **3039**

RESEARCH IN LAW AND POLICY STUDIES (US/0898-0179) [15524836] **3039**

RESEARCH IN MARKETING (US/0191-3026) [04630931] **935**

RESEARCH IN MARKETING. SUPPLEMENT (US) [08941453] **935**

RESEARCH IN MEDICAL EDUCATION : PROCEEDINGS OF THE ... ANNUAL CONFERENCE (US) [19418275] 3634, **1845**

RESEARCH IN MELANESIA (PP/0254-0665) [02464815] **244**

RESEARCH IN MICROBIOLOGY (FR/0923-2508) [19340093] **569**

RESEARCH IN MICROPOLITICS (US/1041-5858) [14198626] **4493**

RESEARCH IN MINISTRY (US) [08676866] **4992**

RESEARCH IN MOLECULAR BIOLOGY (GW/0340-5400) [02111674] **471**

RESEARCH IN NONDESTRUCTIVE EVALUATION (US/0934-9847) [19559216] **1994**

RESEARCH IN NURSING & HEALTH (US/0160-6891) [03731905] **3868**

RESEARCH IN ORGANIZATIONAL BEHAVIOR (US/0191-3085) [04660463] **5255**

RESEARCH IN ORGANIZATIONAL CHANGE AND DEVELOPMENT (US/0897-3016) [16503730] **884**

RESEARCH IN PARAPSYCHOLOGY (US/0093-4798) [01787390] **4243**

RESEARCH IN PERSONNEL AND HUMAN RESOURCES MANAGEMENT (US/0742-7301) [10283374] **946**

RESEARCH IN PHENOMENOLOGY (US/0085-5553) [01763770] **4358**

RESEARCH IN PHILOSOPHY & TECHNOLOGY (US/0161-7249) [03949539] **5147**

RESEARCH IN PHILOSOPHY & TECHNOLOGY. SUPPLEMENT (US/8756-9299) [11412432] **5147**

RESEARCH IN POLITICAL ECONOMY (US/0161-7230) [03699481] **1581**

RESEARCH IN POLITICAL SOCIOLOGY (US/0895-9935) [12636986] 4493, **5255**

RESEARCH IN POLITICS AND SOCIETY (US/0885-212X) [12417217] **4493**

RESEARCH IN POPULATION ECONOMICS (US/0163-7878) [04380889] **4559**

●RESEARCH IN PROGRESS (US) [28139802] **5305**

RESEARCH IN PROGRESS. PHYSICS, CHEMISTRY, BIOLOGICAL SCIENCES, MATHEMATICS, ENGINEERING SCIENCES, METALLURGY AND MATERIALS SCIENCE, GEOSCIENCES, ELECTRONICS, EUROPEAN RESEARCH PROGRAM / U.S. ARMY RESEARCH OFFICE (US) [09089366] **5147**

RESEARCH-IN-PROGRESS (WASHINGTON, D.C. : 1983) *See* RESEARCH IN PROGRESS **5305**

RESEARCH IN PUBLIC ADMINISTRATION (US) [23468704] **4683**

RESEARCH IN PUBLIC POLICY ANALYSIS AND MANAGEMENT (US/0732-1317) [07650349] **5215**

RESEARCH IN RACE AND ETHNIC RELATIONS (US/0195-7449) [05366335] 5255, **2272**

RESEARCH IN READING AND THE LANGUAGE ARTS (US/0360-4063) [02244180] 1903, **3315**

RESEARCH IN REAL ESTATE : A RESEARCH ANNUAL (US/0731-7999) [08183533] **4846**

●RESEARCH IN RELIGION AND FAMILY--BLACK PERSPECTIVES (US/1055-1158) [23077466] 4992, **2272**

RESEARCH IN RURAL SOCIOLOGY AND DEVELOPMENT (US/1057-1922) [11821740] **5255**

RESEARCH IN SCIENCE & TECHNOLOGICAL EDUCATION (UK/0263-5143) [09614922] **5147**

RESEARCH IN SCIENCE EDUCATION (AT/0157-244X) [I0157244X] **1779**

RESEARCH IN SOCIAL MOVEMENTS, CONFLICTS AND CHANGE (US/0163-786X) [04325657] **5255**

RESEARCH IN SOCIAL POLICY (US/1048-1591) [17450775] **5255**

RESEARCH IN SOCIAL PROBLEMS AND PUBLIC POLICY (US/0196-1152) [05585436] **5255**

RESEARCH IN SOCIAL STRATIFICATION AND MOBILITY (US/0276-5624) [07237098] **5255**

RESEARCH IN SOCIOLOGY OF EDUCATION AND SOCIALIZATION (US/0197-5080) [06029944] 1903, **5255**

RESEARCH IN SURFACE FORCES / KONFERENTSIIA PO POVERKHNOSTYM SILAM (US) [01588876] **4419**

RESEARCH IN SURGERY (SP/0214-5987) [21375819] **3973**

RESEARCH IN SURGERY. SUPLEMENTO (SP/0214-5995) [21376465] **3973**

RESEARCH IN TEXT THEORY (GW/0179-4167) [04952625] **3315**

RESEARCH IN THE HISTORY OF ECONOMIC THOUGHT AND METHODOLOGY (US/0743-4154) [10513955] **1594**

RESEARCH IN THE INTERWEAVE OF SOCIAL ROLES *See* CURRENT RESEARCH ON OCCUPATIONS AND PROFESSIONS **4203**

RESEARCH IN THE SCHOOL OF BUSINESS (MADISON) (US/0094-5803) [02224289] **1517**

RESEARCH IN THE SOCIAL SCIENTIFIC STUDY OF RELIGION (US/1046-8064) [20407149] **4992**

RESEARCH IN THE SOCIOLOGY OF HEALTH CARE (US/0275-4959) [07107096] 3634, **5255**

RESEARCH IN THE SOCIOLOGY OF ORGANIZATIONS (US/0733-558X) [08605489] **5255**

RESEARCH IN THE SOCIOLOGY OF WORK (US/0277-2833) [07518509] **5255**

RESEARCH IN THE TEACHING OF ENGLISH (US/0034-527X) [01763773] 3315, **1903**

RESEARCH IN THIRD WORLD ACCOUNTING (US/1058-1995) [24104296] **750**

RESEARCH IN UNEMPLOYMENT INSURANCE. CHARACTERISTICS OF THE INSURED UNEMPLOYED (US) [07353267] **2892**, 1707

RESEARCH IN URBAN ECONOMICS (US/0277-0121) [07465125] **1517**

RESEARCH IN URBAN POLICY (US) [11845450] **2833**

RESEARCH IN URBAN SOCIOLOGY (US/1047-0042) [19818669] **5255**

RESEARCH IN VETERINARY SCIENCE (UK/0034-5288) [01644503] **5520**

RESEARCH IN VIROLOGY (PARIS) (FR/0923-2516) [19408546] **569**

RESEARCH INDEX (UK/0034-5296) [06681760] **707**

RESEARCH INDEX INDUSTRIES AMALGAMATION (UK) **1625**

RESEARCH INFORMATION NOTE - FORESTRY COMMISSION RESEARCH & DEVELOPMENT DIVISION (UK/0267-2375) [03640733] **2392**

RESEARCH INSTITUTE LAWYERS TAX ALERT, THE (US/0163-9994) [04553788] 4746, **3039**

RESEARCH INSTITUTE MASTER FEDERAL TAX MANUAL WITH FEDERAL TAX COORDINATOR 2D REFERENCES (US) [15673151] 4746, **3039**

RESEARCH INSTITUTE OF AMERICA, INC *See* EXECUTIVE WEALTH ADVISORY **674**

RESEARCH INSTITUTE OF AMERICA, INC *See* REGULATORY ALERT **3037**

RESEARCH INSTITUTE OF AMERICA, INC *See* TAX YEAR IN REVIEW, THE **752**

RESEARCH INSTITUTE OF AMERICA, INC *See* RESEARCH INSTITUTE LAWYERS TAX ALERT, THE **3039**

RESEARCH INSTITUTE OF AMERICA, INC *See* TAX ALERT FOR MANAGEMENT **4751**

RESEARCH INSTITUTE OF AMERICA, INC *See* TAX GUIDE. WEEKLY ALERT **4752**

RESEARCH INSTITUTE OF AMERICA, INC. RESEARCH INSTITUTE RECOMMENDATIONS *See* RESEARCH RECOMMENDATIONS **707**

RESEARCH INTO HIGHER EDUCATION ABSTRACTS (UK/0034-5326) [01587632] 1845, **1797**

RESEARCH INTO PRACTICE DIGEST, THE *CEASED.* (US/0885-2324) [12597978] **1904**

RESEARCH INVENTORY / MEMORIAL UNIVERSITY OF NEWFOUNDLAND, OFFICE OF RESEARCH (CN/0229-2599) [08010302] **1845**

RESEARCH ISSUES (US/0360-7631) [01924505] **1348**

RESEARCH ISSUES AND SUPPORTING RESEARCH OF THE NATIONAL PROGRAM ON CARBON DIOXIDE, ENVIRONMENT AND SOCIETY (US) [08561204] **2242**

RESEARCH JOURNAL : HUMANITIES & SOCIAL SCIENCE (II) [01642424] **2853**

RESEARCH JOURNAL OF PHILOSOPHY & SOCIAL SCIENCES (II/0048-7325) [01866363] **4358**

RESEARCH JOURNAL OF PLANT AND ENVIRONMENT (II/0970-3845) [26001914] **526**

RESEARCH JOURNAL OF SPORTS MEDICINE AND BIOMECHANICS (II) **3955**

RESEARCH JOURNAL OF THE WATER POLLUTION CONTROL FEDERATION *See* WATER ENVIRONMENT RESEARCH MICROFORM: A RESEARCH PUBLICATION OF THE WATER ENVIRONMENT FEDERATION **5542**

RESEARCH JOURNAL. SCIENCE / UNIVERSITY OF INDORE (II/0253-9306) [10407851] 1094, **5147**

RESEARCH LETTERS ON ATMOSPHERIC ELECTRICITY (JA/0286-6188) [08859368] **1434**

RESEARCH LIBRARIES GROUP *See* RESEARCH LIBRARIES GROUP NEWS, THE **3245**

RESEARCH LIBRARIES GROUP NEWS, THE (US/0196-173X) [05761609] **3245**

RESEARCH LIBRARY JOURNAL OF ABSTRACTS (AT) [03505878] **3767**

RESEARCH LIBRARY, RECENT ACQUISITIONS (US/0145-0301) [07125600] **3245**

RESEARCH MANAGEMENT REVIEW (US) **707**

RESEARCH MANUSCRIPT SERIES - INSTITUTE OF ARCHEOLOGY AND ANTHROPOLOGY, UNIVERSITY OF SOUTH CAROLINA (US) [05977014] 244, **280**

RESEARCH MEMORANDUM (UK) [19080431] **4683**

RESEARCH MEMORANDUM - MUNICIPAL RESEARCH AND SERVICES CENTER OF WASHINGTON (SEATTLE) (US/0092-5500) [01789880] **4683**

RESEARCH METHODS IN NEUROCHEMISTRY (US/0096-2902) [01589260] 586, **3844**

RESEARCH MONEY (CN/0833-1677) [17748677] **4339**

RESEARCH MONITOR (US) [04993182] **4683**

RESEARCH MONITOR; PROFILES (US) [04993313] **4683**

RESEARCH MONOGRAPH (TH) [16636836] **5147**

RESEARCH MONOGRAPH (US) [06680367] **707**

RESEARCH MONOGRAPH - CENTER FOR SOUTH AND SOUTHEAST ASIA STUDIES, UNIVERSITY OF CALIFORNIA (US) [04346771] **2663**

RESEARCH MONOGRAPH - CONNECTICUT OFFICE OF VETERANS AFFAIRS FOR EDUCATION (US) [04127690] **4055**

RESEARCH MONOGRAPH - NATIONAL INSTITUTE ON ALCOHOL ABUSE AND ALCOHOLISM (US/0270-7772) [06444696] **1348**

RESEARCH MONOGRAPH SERIES - NATIONAL INSTITUTE ON DRUG ABUSE (US/0361-8595) [02208524] **1348**

RESEARCH MONOGRAPH - UNIVERSITY OF TEXAS AT AUSTIN. BUREAU OF BUSINESS RESEARCH (US) [07013884] **707**

RESEARCH MONOGRAPHS IN BANKING AND FINANCE (UK/0950-849X) [I0950849X] **808**

RESEARCH MONOGRAPHS IN CELL AND TISSUE PHYSIOLOGY (NE/0378-6129) [03170308] **586**

RESEARCH MONOGRAPHS IN IMMUNOLOGY (NE/0167-6091) [06128819] **3676**

RESEARCH MONOGRAPHS IN PARALLEL AND DISTRIBUTED COMPUTING (UK/0953-7767) [I09537767] **1201**

RESEARCH NEWS - DIVISION OF RESEARCH DEVELOPMENT AND ADMINISTRATION (US/0093-7991) [02358400] **5147**

Alphabetical Title Index — **RESEARCH**

RESEARCH NEWS - FAMILY HISTORY WORLD *CEASED*. (US/0884-3716) [12541461] **2470**

RESEARCH NEWSLETTER - FACULTY OF HOME ECONOMICS, UNIVERSITY OF ALBERTA (CN/0709-9045) [06032898] **2792**

RESEARCH NOTE - BUREAU OF ECONOMIC GEOLOGY, UNIVERSITY OF TEXAS AT AUSTIN (US/0147-6823) [03217811] **1395**

RESEARCH NOTE FPL (US/0163-3643) [04347434] **2392**

RESEARCH NOTE INT (US/0099-3468) [08257538] **2392**

RESEARCH NOTE - MINERAL EXPLORATION RESEARCH INSTITUTE (1977) (CN/0714-4857) [09086733] **2150**

RESEARCH NOTE NC (US/0361-2449) [01489305] **2393**

RESEARCH NOTE PNW (US/0737-7150) [07115514] **2393**

RESEARCH NOTE (PROBLEM-DRINKER DRIVER PROJECT (NEW YORK)) *See* DRINKING, DRUGS & DRIVING **1343**

RESEARCH NOTE - PROVINCE OF BRITISH COLUMBIA, MINISTRY OF FORESTS (CN/0226-9368) [05790865] **2393**

RESEARCH NOTE PSW (US/0196-3376) [05782605] **2393**

RESEARCH NOTE RM (US/0277-5794) [04926155] **2393**

RESEARCH NOTE SE (US/0748-1217) [10891683] **2393**

RESEARCH NOTE SO (US/0197-8373) [03339458] **2393**

RESEARCH NOTE (UNIVERSITY OF CALIFORNIA, LOS ANGELES. CENTER FOR INTERNATIONAL AND STRATEGIC AFFAIRS) (US) [10806058] **4534**

●RESEARCH NOTES (US/1062-9300) [25812067] **4534**

RESEARCH NOTES AND MEMORANDA OF APPLIED GEOMETRY FOR PREVENIENT NATURAL PHILOSOPHY (JA) [17289555] 1994, **5147**

RESEARCH NOTES IN NEURAL COMPUTING (US/0939-4818) [20423404] **3845**

RESEARCH NOTES (LIVINGSTONE MUSEUM) (ZA) [11465240] 4171, **4095**

RESEARCH ON AGING (US/0164-0275) [04556801] **3754**

RESEARCH ON CHEMICAL INTERMEDIATES (NE/0922-6168) [19110149] **1057**

RESEARCH ON DEMOCRACY AND SOCIETY (US) [28654895] **5255**

RESEARCH ON ECONOMIC INEQUALITY (US/1049-2585) [20905248] **1517**

RESEARCH ON LANGUAGE AND SOCIAL INTERACTION (CN/0835-1813) [16013947] 1121, **3315**

RESEARCH ON LATIN AMERICA IN THE HUMANITIES AND SOCIAL SCIENCES IN THE UNIVERSITIES AND POLYTECHNICS OF THE UNITED KINGDOM (UK/0956-9014) [22162630] 5215, **2853**

RESEARCH ON NEGOTIATION IN ORGANIZATIONS (US/1040-9556) [15068846] 1581, **884**

RESEARCH ON READING IN SECONDARY SCHOOLS (US) [05702524] **1779**

RESEARCH ON SOCIAL WORK PRACTICE (US/1049-7315) [21286635] **5305**

RESEARCH ON TECHNOLOGICAL INNOVATION MANAGEMENT AND POLICY (US/0737-1071) [09286885] 5147, **884**

RESEARCH ON THE SOVIET UNION AND EASTERN EUROPE (US) [23881772] **5255**

RESEARCH OPPORTUNITIES IN RENAISSANCE DRAMA (US/0098-647X) [02241673] 5367, **3429**

RESEARCH OUTLOOK / UNITED STATES ENVIRONMENTAL PROTECTION AGENCY, RESEARCH AND DEVELOPMENT (US/0192-8376) [04683957] **2203**

RESEARCH PAMPHLET - FOREST RESEARCH INSTITUTE (MY) [05717721] **2393**

RESEARCH PAPER (JA) [22389709] **127**

RESEARCH PAPER (AT/1035-9796) [29435332] **2393**

RESEARCH PAPER - CENTRE FOR URBAN AND COMMUNITY STUDIES. UNIVERSITY OF TORONTO (CN/0316-0068) [02247328] **2833**

RESEARCH PAPER. FOREST SERIES (NR/0331-6793) [05463871] **2393**

RESEARCH PAPER FPL (US/0163-3376) [04332644] **2393**

RESEARCH PAPER (GREAT BRITAIN. HEALTH AND SAFETY EXECUTIVE) (UK/0265-9581) [08457821] **2869**

RESEARCH PAPER - HEBREW UNIVERSITY OF JERUSALEM, SOVIET AND EAST EUROPEAN RESEARCH CENTRE (IS) [04826248] **4534**

RESEARCH PAPER INT (US/0886-7380) [08167655] **2393**

RESEARCH PAPER NC (US/0888-9686) [08016582] **2393**

RESEARCH PAPER - NEVADA ARCHEOLOGICAL SURVEY (US/0270-5486) [02918189] **280**

RESEARCH PAPER PNW-RP / UNITED STATES, DEPARTMENT OF AGRICULTURE, FOREST SERVICE, PACIFIC NORTHWEST RESEARCH STATION (US) [24880367] **2393**

RESEARCH PAPER PSW (US/0196-1993) [05754854] **2393**

RESEARCH PAPER (QUEENSLAND. DEPT. OF FORESTRY) *See* RESEARCH PAPER **2393**

RESEARCH PAPER - RESEARCH GROUP ON LEISURE AND CULTURAL DEVELOPMENT, UNIVERSITY OF WATERLOO (CN/0821-1299) [09929516] **5269**

RESEARCH PAPER RM (US/0502-5001) [04926167] **2393**

RESEARCH PAPER SE (US/0888-9678) [09074010] **2393**

RESEARCH PAPER SO (US/0748-1225) [07208609] **2393**

RESEARCH PAPER - UNIVERSITY OF MELBOURNE, DEPARTMENT OF ECONOMICS (AT/0819-2642) [108192642] **1517**

RESEARCH PAPER (UNIVERSITY OF WISCONSIN--MADISON. TENURE CENTER) (US/0090-7170) [02253533] **1517**

RESEARCH PAPERS AND POLICY STUDIES / INSTITUTE OF EAST ASIAN STUDIES, UNIVERSITY OF CALIFORNIA, BERKELEY (US) [09812135] **2663**

RESEARCH PAPERS (CENTRE FOR THE STUDY OF ISLAM AND CHRISTIAN-MUSLIM RELATIONS (BIRMINGHAM, WEST MIDLANDS, ENGLAND)) *CEASED*. (UK/0260-3772) [08408051] **5044**

RESEARCH PAPERS - DEPARTMENT OF TAMIL, UNIVERSITY OF KERALA (II) [03251183] 3429, **3315**

RESEARCH PAPERS / HISTORY OF MEDICINE ASSOCIATES (US) [23465190] **3634**

RESEARCH PAPERS IN BANKING AND FINANCE (UK/0269-3933) [I02693933] **808**

RESEARCH PAPERS IN EDUCATION (UK/0267-1522) [13485318] **1779**

RESEARCH PAPERS : SERIES C - THE GENEALOGICAL DEPARTMENT OF THE CHURCH OF JESUS CHRIST OF LATTER-DAY SAINTS (US) [06826197] **2470**

RESEARCH PERSPECTIVES (RALEIGH, N.C.) (US/0732-4766) [07994748] **127**

RESEARCH POLICY (NE/0048-7333) [01039880] **5147**

RESEARCH, POLICY AND PLANNING : THE JOURNAL OF THE SOCIAL SERVICES RESEARCH GROUP (UK/0264-519X) [12259689] **5215**

RESEARCH, PROGRAM DEVELOPMENT, AND EVALUATION IN CALIFORNIA SPECIAL EDUCATION (US/0145-2169) [02711667] **1884**

RESEARCH PROGRAM PROSPECTUS / APPALACHIAN REGIONAL COMMISSION (US) [09036722] **4683**

RESEARCH PROGRAMS GUIDELINES (US) [04928097] 2853, **329**

RESEARCH PROGRAMS - NATIONAL ENDOWMENT FOR THE HUMANITIES (US/0147-0922) [03023041] 1845, **2853**

RESEARCH PROGRAMS / NATIONAL INSTITUTE OF ENVIRONMENTAL HEALTH SCIENCES (US/0148-5547) [03333425] **2242**

RESEARCH PROGRAMS OF THE NATIONAL INSTITUTE OF CHILD HEALTH AND HUMAN DEVELOPMENT. NUTRITION AND ENDOCRINOLOGY (US) [09538899] 3733, **4198**

RESEARCH PROGRESS REPORT - WESTERN SOCIETY OF WEED SCIENCE (US/0090-8142) [01769766] **185**

RESEARCH PROJECT (NZ/0069-3774) [03123003] 5256, **4615**

RESEARCH PROSPECTUS - GULF STATES MARINE FISHERIES COMMISSION (US/0434-9490) [01343783] **2311**

RESEARCH PUBLICATION (US/0079-063X) [01158930] **2203**

RESEARCH PUBLICATION (COLORADO. GENERAL ASSEMBLY. LEGISLATIVE COUNCIL) (US/0413-768X) [01564151] **3039**

RESEARCH PUBLICATIONS - ASSOCIATION FOR RESEARCH IN NERVOUS AND MENTAL DISEASE (US/0091-7443) [01777389] 3935, **3845**

RESEARCH PUBLICATIONS OF THE WELLCOME UNIT FOR THE HISTORY OF MEDICINE (UK/0143-7984) [08434093] **3634**

RESEARCH QUARTERLY FOR EXERCISE AND SPORT (US/0270-1367) [06247027] **1858**

RESEARCH RECOMMENDATIONS (US/0893-4347) [15523106] **707**

RESEARCH REGISTER LIST / THE SOCIETY OF ARCHITECTURAL HISTORIANS OF GREAT BRITAIN (UK) [04392699] **307**

RESEARCH REGISTER / UNIVERSITY OF STRATHCLYDE (UK) [16887891] **5147**

RESEARCH REPORT (US) [07013173] **185**

RESEARCH REPORT (NZ/0113-4485) [24634077] **127**

RESEARCH REPORT (SW/0080-6714) [01781912] **5215**

●RESEARCH REPORT (US) [26460073] **127**

RESEARCH REPORT AFDC (US/0091-5823) [01787649] **5306**

RESEARCH REPORT - AGRICULTURAL EXPERIMENT STATION (US/0548-5967) [01449070] **127**

RESEARCH REPORT - AGRICULTURAL EXPERIMENT STATION, UTAH STATE UNIVERSITY (US/0094-3878) [05691771] **127**

RESEARCH REPORT / ARCHITECTURAL AND ARCHAEOLOGICAL SOCIETY OF DURHAM AND NORTHUMBERLAND (UK) [19117900] 280, **307**

RESEARCH REPORT / ATOMIC ENERGY CONTROL BOARD (CN/0825-0162) [16916344] 4451, **1955**

RESEARCH REPORT - AUSTRALIAN ARMY PSYCHOLOGICAL RESEARCH UNIT (AT/0155-3453) [I01553453] **4615**

RESEARCH REPORT - AUSTRALIAN ROAD RESEARCH BOARD (AT) [06208102] **5443**

RESEARCH REPORT / CANADIAN ELECTRICAL ASSOCIATION (CN/0823-2660) [10446119] **2079**

RESEARCH REPORT / CANADIAN STUDIES COMMITTEE, FACULTY OF ARTS, FACULTY OF GRADUATE STUDIES AND RESEARCH, MCGILL UNIVERSITY (CN/0822-9546) [10680884] **423**

RESEARCH REPORT / COUNCIL FOR BRITISH ARCHAEOLOGY (UK/0589-9036) [08185916] **280**

RESEARCH REPORT - CSIRO DIVISION OF ANIMAL PRODUCTION (AT/0155-7742) [04841380] **220**

RESEARCH REPORT - CSIRO DIVISION OF MINERAL AND PROCESS ENGINEERING (AT/1033-3908) [I10333908] **2150**

RESEARCH REPORT / CSIRO DIVISION OF OCEANOGRAPHY (AT/1031-9964) [21253003] **1456**

RESEARCH REPORT / DEPARTMENT OF CIVIL ENGINEERING, UNIVERSITY OF QUEENSLAND (AT) [05843008] **2030**

RESEARCH REPORT - DEPARTMENT OF ELECTRICAL ENGINEERING. UNIVERSITY OF TORONTO (CN/0082-514X) [03245042] **2079**

RESEARCH REPORT - DEPARTMENT OF MOTOR VEHICLES. RESEARCH AND TECHNOLOGY DIVISION (OLYMPIA) (US/0092-3583) [01786974] **5424**

RESEARCH REPORT - DIVISION OF APPLIED ORGANIC CHEMISTRY (AT/0312-8466) [03145513] **1047**

RESEARCH REPORT ... / DIVISION OF MANUFACTURING TECHNOLOGY, COMMONWEALTH SCIENTIFIC AND INDUSTRIAL RESEARCH ORGANIZATION (AT/0812-2660) [13716469] **3487**

RESEARCH REPORT / DIVISION OF TECHNICAL SERVICES (RESEARCH AND UTILIZATION), QUEENSLAND DEPARTMENT OF FORESTRY (AT/0311-0893) [16641191] **2393**

RESEARCH REPORT - EXPERT COMMITTEE ON WEEDS. EASTERN CANADA SECTION (CN/0829-6200) [04564331] **127**

RESEARCH REPORT - EXPERT COMMITTEE ON WEEDS. WESTERN CANADA SECTION (CN/0829-7584) [04564330] **127**

RESEARCH REPORT - FEDERAL RESERVE BANK OF BOSTON (US/0430-1897) [01569013] **809**

RESEARCH REPORT - FEDERATION OF TAX ADMINISTRATORS (US) [01775563] **4746**

RESEARCH REPORT - FORESTRY COMMISSION OF N.S.W (AT) [04238602] **2393**

RESEARCH — Alphabetical Title Index

RESEARCH REPORT FROM THE MICHIGAN STATE UNIVERSITY AGRICULTURAL EXPERIMENT STATION, EAST LANSING (US/0543-8233) [03365839] **127**

RESEARCH REPORT - HEALTH EFFECTS INSTITUTE (US/1041-5505) [17543392] **2242**

RESEARCH REPORT - ILLINOIS COMMUNITY COLLEGE BOARD (US/0099-1341) [02240690] **1845**

RESEARCH REPORT - ILLINOIS STATE WATER SURVEY (US/1059-826X) [24685551] **5538**

RESEARCH REPORT - INSTITUTE FOR RESEARCH ON POVERTY (MADISON) (US/0092-847X) [05652366] **1581, 5215**

RESEARCH REPORT - INSTITUTE OF INTERNAL AUDITORS (US) [04197757] **750**

RESEARCH REPORT (INSTITUTE OF JEWISH AFFAIRS) (UK) [04394341] **4534, 5052**

RESEARCH REPORT (INSTYTUT IMMUNOLOGII I TERAPII DOSWIADCZALNEJ IM. LUDWIKA HIRSZFELDA) (PL) [20999650] **3676**

RESEARCH REPORT / INTERNATIONAL FOOD POLICY RESEARCH INSTITUTE (US/0886-7372) [06024207] **2355**

RESEARCH REPORT - LAPPEENRANTA UNIVERSITY OF TECHNOLOGY. DEPARTMENT OF INFORMATION TECHNOLOGY (FI/0783-8069) [I07838069] **5147**

RESEARCH REPORT - MISSISSIPPI AGRICULTURAL & FORESTRY EXPERIMENT STATION (US/0147-2186) [02352217] **2393, 128**

RESEARCH REPORT - MONASH UNIVERSITY (AT) [02376437] **1845**

RESEARCH REPORT / NATIONAL COUNCIL OF TEACHERS OF ENGLISH (US/0085-3739) [02848930] **3315**

RESEARCH REPORT / NEW HAMPSHIRE AGRICULTURAL EXPERIMENTAL STATION (US/0077-832X) [04876168] **128**

RESEARCH REPORT - NEW YORK CITY COMMISSION ON HUMAN RIGHTS (US/0545-4158) [03182640] **4512**

RESEARCH REPORT - NORTH CENTRAL WEED SCIENCE SOCIETY (U.S.) (US/1062-421X) [21458342] **128**

RESEARCH REPORT - OKLAHOMA MEDICAL RESEARCH FOUNDATION (US/0193-2209) [05083846] **3634**

RESEARCH REPORT OR OCCASIONAL PAPER / THE UNIVERSITY OF NEWCASTLE, DEPARTMENT OF ECONOMICS (AT/0812-1664) [05432590] **1517**

RESEARCH REPORT P (US/0361-5804) [02092756] **128**

RESEARCH REPORT (PHILIPPINE NORMAL COLLEGE. GRADUATE SCHOOL) (PH) [08312576] **1845**

RESEARCH REPORT - ROYAL PRINCE ALFRED HOSPITAL (AT/1031-4717) [16921138] **3634**

RESEARCH REPORT SERIES (US) [10045048] **128**

RESEARCH REPORT SERIES - BROCK GEOLOGICAL SCIENCES. STUDIES IN ENVIRONMENTAL EARTH SCIENCES (CN/0824-3220) [10339554] **1360**

RESEARCH REPORT SERIES - BROCK UNIVERSITY. DEPARTMENT OF GEOLOGICAL SCIENCES. STUDIES IN LANDSCAPE GEOCHEMISTRY (CN/0824-328X) [10339572] **1395**

RESEARCH REPORT SERIES - BROCK UNIVERSITY. DEPARTMENT OF GEOLOGICAL SCIENCES. STUDIES IN PALEOECOLOGY (CN/0824-3271) [10339548] **1395**

RESEARCH REPORT SERIES - BROCK UNIVERSITY. DEPARTMENT OF GEOLOGICAL SCIENCES. STUDIES IN PALEOZOIC STRATIGRAPHIC INVESTIGATIONS (CN/0824-3247) [10339561] **1395**

RESEARCH REPORT SERIES - BROCK UNIVERSITY. DEPARTMENT OF GEOLOGICAL SCIENCES. STUDIES IN SEDIMENTARY PROCESSES (CN/0824-3239) [10339565] **1459**

RESEARCH REPORT SERIES. GENERAL / BROCK UNIVERSITY, DEPARTMENT OF GEOLOGICAL SCIENCES (CN/0704-7592) [10179150] **1395**

RESEARCH REPORT (STEEL FOUNDERS' SOCIETY OF AMERICA) (US) [01794186] **4018**

RESEARCH REPORT - SUPERVISING SCIENTIST FOR THE ALLIGATOR RIVERS REGION (AT/0810-9966) [I08109966] **5147**

RESEARCH REPORT - TRANSPORT AND ROAD RESEARCH LABORATORY (UK/0266-5247) [I02665247] **5391**

RESEARCH REPORT (TROPICAL FRUIT RESEARCH STATION (N.S.W.)) (AT/0725-9492) [11377821] **185**

RESEARCH REPORT - U. S. LAND LOCOMOTION RESEARCH LABORATORY, CENTER LINE, MICHIGAN (US/0503-5562) [01542334] **5424, 1994**

RESEARCH REPORT - UNITED STATES DEPARTMENT OF THE INTERIOR, BUREAU OF RECLAMATION (US/0501-7467) [01541508] **2203**

RESEARCH REPORT (UNITED STATES. EQUAL EMPLOYMENT OPPORTUNITY COMMISSION) (US) [03371636] **1708**

RESEARCH REPORT (UNIVERSITY OF GEORGIA. COLLEGE OF AGRICULTURE. EXPERIMENT STATIONS) *See* RESEARCH REPORT **127**

RESEARCH REPORT / UNIVERSITY OF KENTUCKY, WATER RESOURCES INSTITUTE (US/0453-5669) [01247707] **5539**

RESEARCH REPORT - UNIVERSITY OF MANITOBA, CENTRE FOR TRANSPORTATION STUDIES (CN/0316-7984) [02248014] **5391**

RESEARCH REPORT - UNIVERSITY OF MICHIGAN. POPULATION STUDIES CENTER (US/0886-9014) [13043472] **4559**

RESEARCH REPORT (UNIVERSITY OF SYDNEY. DEPT. OF AGRICULTURAL ECONOMICS) (AT) [05002503] **128**

RESEARCH REPORT / UNIVERSITY OF TEXAS, MD ANDERSON CANCER CENTER (US) [20185136] **3823**

RESEARCH REPORT / UNIVERSITY OF WARWICK, DEPARTMENT OF COMPUTER SCIENCE (UK) [20002464] **1201**

RESEARCH REPORT - WATER RESOURCES RESEARCH CENTER (US) [01541687] **5539**

RESEARCH REPORT WI (US) [05629643] **5539**

RESEARCH REPORT - WISCONSIN. DEPT. OF NATURAL RESOURCES (US/0084-0556) [01342743] **2204**

RESEARCH REPORT - YORK UNIVERSITY. SOCIAL PSYCHOLOGY RESEARCH PROGRAMME. INSTITUTE FOR BEHAVIOURAL RESEARCH (CN/0316-070X) [02247658] **5256**

RESEARCH REPORTING SERIES. 9, MISCELLANEOUS REPORTS (US) [03455389] **2181**

RESEARCH REPORTS: AMERICAN INSTITUTE FOR ECONOMIC RESEARCH (US/0034-5407) [02085233] **707, 1517**

RESEARCH REPORTS AND TECHNICAL NOTES - BOSTON UNIVERSITY. HUMAN RELATIONS CENTER (US/0524-1286) [05201022] **1845**

RESEARCH REPORTS (COLORADO STATE UNIVERSITY. DEPT. OF ATMOSPHERIC SCIENCE) *See* ATMOSPHERIC SCIENCE PAPER **1420**

RESEARCH REPORTS / DEPARTMENT OF ANTHROPOLOGY, UNIVERSITY OF MASSACHUSETTS, AMHERST (US) [06880526] **244**

RESEARCH REPORTS DIGEST / NATURE CONSERVANCY COUNCIL (UK/0143-0386) [10462494] **2204**

RESEARCH REPORTS IN EDUCATION (II) [01790487] **1904**

RESEARCH REPORTS - INTERNATIONAL INSTITUTE FOR APPLIED SYSTEMS ANALYSIS (AU/0378-9004) [04915712] **5147**

RESEARCH REPORTS OF THE FACULTY OF ENGINEERING, MIE UNIVERSITY (JA) [14218639] **1994**

RESEARCH REPORTS / SMITHSONIAN INSTITUTION (US/0364-0175) [01421167] **5147**

RESEARCH RESOURCES INFORMATION CENTER *See* MINORITY BIOMEDICAL SUPPORT PROGRAM : A DIRECTORY OF THE RESEARCH PROJECTS **3617**

RESEARCH RESULTS DIGEST / NATIONAL COOPERATIVE HIGHWAY RESEARCH PROGRAM (US/0547-5554) [01695325] **5443**

RESEARCH REVIEW / ACIRL COAL RESEARCH (AT) [18400335] **2150**

RESEARCH REVIEW - COLORADO. DIVISION OF WILDLIFE (US/1055-4238) [23169508] **4878**

RESEARCH REVIEW / DIVISION OF CHEMICAL AND WOOD TECHNOLOGY (AT/0814-9992) [11692973] **2393, 991**

RESEARCH REVIEW - INSTITUTE OF AFRICAN STUDIES (GH/0020-2703) [04277170] **2643**

RESEARCH REVIEW - LITTLE BIG HORN ASSOCIATES (US/0195-8224) [03352555] **2757**

RESEARCH ROUNDUP (US/8755-2590) [11258156] **1870**

RESEARCH SAFETY MONOGRAPH SERIES (US/0894-0983) [10939292] **3823**

RESEARCH SERIES (US/0882-2042) [11788834] **244, 280**

RESEARCH SERIES (US/0577-7127) [03079077] **2663**

RESEARCH SERIES (CENTRE FOR ENVIRONMENTAL STUDIES (GREAT BRITAIN)) (UK) [05299080] **2181**

RESEARCH SERIES - INDUSTRIAL RELATIONS CENTRE. QUEEN'S UNIVERSITY (CN/0075-6164) [02248173] **1708**

RESEARCH SERIES - TENNESSEE RESEARCH COORDINATING UNIT FOR VOCATIONAL EDUCATION (US) [01794023] **1915**

RESEARCH SERIES / UNIVERSITY OF ARKANSAS, FAYETTVILLE. AGRICULTURAL EXPERIMENT STATION (US/1051-3140) [13227652] **128**

RESEARCH SERIES - UNIVERSITY OF CALIFORNIA, BERKELEY. INSTITUTE OF INTERNATIONAL STUDIES (US/0068-6093) [08097267] **4534**

RESEARCH SERIES (UNIVERSITY OF OKLAHOMA. ARCHAEOLOGICAL RESEARCH AND MANAGEMENT CENTER) (US/0160-3086) [03657021] **280**

RESEARCH SERVICE DIRECTORY *See* MRA BLUE BOOK, RESEARCH SERVICES DIRECTORY **933**

RESEARCH SERVICE DIRECTORY (NEW YORK, N.Y.) (US/0748-089X) [08310470] **935**

RESEARCH SERVICE - RESEARCH DEPARTMENT. BOARD OF EDUCATION FOR THE CITY OF TORONTO (CN/0316-8786) [02593320] **1779**

RESEARCH SERVICES DIRECTORY (US/0278-1743) [07729449] **5147**

RESEARCH SOCIETY OF PAKISTAN *See* JOURNAL OF THE RESEARCH SOCIETY OF PAKISTAN **5207**

RESEARCH STRATEGIES (US/0734-3310) [08724152] **3245**

RESEARCH STUDY / AGRARIAN RESEARCH AND TRAINING INSTITUTE (CE) [11679488] **128**

RESEARCH STUDY - DIVISION OF BUSINESS AND ECONOMIC RESEARCH, COLLEGE OF BUSINESS ADMINISTRATION, UNIVERSITY OF NEW ORLEANS (US/0362-7217) [02396557] **1581**

RESEARCH STUDY - EXECUTIVE SUPPORT SERVICE, EDUCATION DEPARTMENT OF TASMANIA (AT/0819-5404) [I08195404] **1845**

RESEARCH STUDY SERIES (AGRARIAN RESEARCH AND TRAINING INSTITUTE) *See* RESEARCH STUDY / AGRARIAN RESEARCH AND TRAINING INSTITUTE **128**

RESEARCH STUDY TD/RS (UK) [04782975] **2404**

RESEARCH SUMMARIES IN CANADIAN BUSINESS EDUCATION (CN/0709-2938) [08659471] **1779, 707**

RESEARCH SUMMARY / DIVISION OF BIOLOGICAL AND MEDICAL RESEARCH, ARGONNE NATIONAL LABORATORY (US) [12640980] **5147**

RESEARCH SUPPLEMENT / THE PHYSICAL EDUCATION ASSOCIATION OF GREAT BRITAIN AND NORTHERN IRELAND (UK) [18265724] **1858**

RESEARCH SUPPORTED BY THE ECONOMIC AND SOCIAL RESEARCH COUNCIL (UK/0266-2159) [11965252] **5215**

RESEARCH TECHNIQUES IN NONDESTRUCTIVE TESTING (US) [04790436] **1994**

RESEARCH TECHNOLOGY MANAGEMENT (US/0895-6308) [16714322] **5147**

RESEARCH (TORONTO BOARD OF EDUCATION. RESEARCH DEPT.) (CN/0712-1709) [08720466] **1779**

RESEARCH TRIANGLE INSTITUTE *See* HYPOTENUSE **3508**

RESEARCH UPDATE (US) [14263095] **3245**

RESEARCH VOLUME OF THE SURREY ARCHAEOLOGICAL SOCIETY (UK) [02002178] **280**

RESEARCHER (JACKSON, MISS.) (US/0271-5058) [06631407] **2627, 1845**

RESEARCHER (SUDBURY) *CEASED.* (CN/0225-3798) [06156826] **5019**

RESEARCHES ON POPULATION ECOLOGY (JA/0034-5466) [01763782] **2220**

RESEARCHIN' OUACHITA-CALHOUN COUNTIES, AR (US/8756-9817) [07725222] **2470**

RESEAU (CN/0700-6004) [02753597] **5147**

●RESEAU - ASSOCIATION DES ENSEIGNANTES ET DES ENSEIGNANTS FRANCO-ONTARIENS (CN/1192-2796) [27203212] **1779**

RESEAU D'ACTION ET D'INFORMATION POUR LES FEMMES *See* R A I F. RESEAU D'ACTION ET D'INFORMATION POUR LES FEMMES **5565**

Alphabetical Title Index

RESEAU D'INFORMATION COMPTABLE AGRICOLE. REGION BRETAGNE (FR) [11086317] **128**

RESEAU D'INFORMATION COMPTABLE AGRICOLE. REGION CENTRE (FR/0243-8941) [11770644] **128**

RESEAU (MONTREAL) (CN/0704-0539) [03956620] **4992**

RESEAU PLEIN-AIR (CN/0711-2572) [08422698] **4878**

RESEAU PRESSE (CN/1183-6415) [25313925] **1625**

RESEAU (TORONTO) (CN/0825-0332) [11283961] **2601**

RESEAUX (BE) [01877717] **4359**

RESEAUX DE CHALEUR FRANCAIS (FR) **1955**

RESEAUX ET CHALEUR (ORLEANS) *CEASED.* (FR/0993-3522) [21434101] **1955**

RESEAUX PARIS. 1989 *CEASED.* (FR/1142-2815) [11422815] **3245**

RESELLER MANAGEMENT (US/1042-7325) [19116809] **1239**

RESENA (AG) [01787322] **1779**

RESENA DE ACTIVIDADES - CENEP (AG) [05901616] **4559**

RESENA DE LA ACTIVIDAD DURANTE EL EJERCICIO (UY) [04095739] **1581**

RESENHA DE LIVROS PARA A INFANCIA E JUVENTUDE (BL) [18996343] 1068, **3429**

RESENHA ESTATISTICA DO RIO GRANDE DO SUL / SECRETARIA DE COORDENACAO E PLANEJAMENTO, FUNDACAO DE ECONOMIA E ESTATISTICA (BL/0102-0226) [05968838] 1581, **1538**

RESERVE BANK OF AUSTRALIA *See* REPORT AND FINANCIAL STATEMENTS - RESERVE BANK OF AUSTRALIA **1516**

RESERVE BANK OF AUSTRALIA *See* OCCASIONAL PAPER - RESERVE BANK OF AUSTRALIA **732**

RESERVE BANK OF AUSTRALIA. STATISTICAL BULLETIN - RESERVE BANK OF AUSTRALIA *See* BULLETIN / RESERVE BANK OF AUSTRALIA **781**

RESERVE BANK OF FIJI *See* ANNUAL REPORT / RESERVE BANK OF FIJI **772**

RESERVE BANK OF INDIA *See* STATISTICAL STATEMENTS RELATING TO THE COOPERATIVE MOVEMENT IN INDIA **156**

RESERVE BANK OF INDIA *See* REPORT ON CURRENCY AND FINANCE - RESERVE BANK OF INDIA **808**

RESERVE BANK OF INDIA. AGRICULTURAL CREDIT BOARD *See* PROCEEDINGS OF THE ... MEETING OF THE AGRICULTURAL CREDIT BOARD **804**

RESERVE BANK OF INDIA BULLETIN (II/0034-5512) [01763783] **809**

RESERVE BANK OF NEW ZEALAND *See* BULLETIN - RESERVE BANK OF NEW ZEALAND **781**

RESERVE FORCES ALMANAC (US/0363-860X) [03257623] **4055**

RESERVE FORCES MANPOWER CHARTS (US/0193-1008) [03172793] **4055**

RESERVE MARINE, THE (US/0034-5547) [01763785] **4055**

RESERVEOFFICEREN (DK) [02242022] **4055**

RESERVEOFFICERSFORENINGEN I DANMARK *See* RESERVEOFFICEREN **4055**

RESERVES OF COAL, PROVINCE OF ALBERTA (CN/0380-4275) [02443985] **1955**

RESERVOIR ANNUAL (1977) (CN/0707-2562) [04747336] **4276**

RESERVOIR ENGINEERING DIGEST. GAS FIELDS (CN) **4276**

RESERVOIR ENGINEERING DIGEST. OIL FIELDS (CN) **4276**

RESERVOIR PERFORMANCE CHARTS: GAS POOLS (CN) [02249310] **4276**

RESERVOIR PERFORMANCE CHARTS: OIL POOLS (CN) [02249311] **4276**

RESIDENCE & MIGRATION OF COLLEGE STUDENTS (US) [02485000] **1845**

RESIDENCY DIRECTORY (US) [08821231] **4327**

RESIDENT ABROAD (UK) **4559**

RESIDENT AND OFF-CAMPUS ENROLLMENT, VIRGINIA STATE-CONTROLLED INSTITUTIONS OF HIGHER EDUCATION (US/0091-6951) [01786260] **1845**

RESIDENT & RECORDED LIVE BIRTHS, INFANT DEATHS, AND DEATHS FOR ILLINOIS LARGER CITIES / ILLINOIS DEPARTMENT OF PUBLIC HEALTH (US) [08310981] **5337**

RESIDENT AND STAFF PHYSICIAN (US/0034-5555) [01763788] **3634**

RESIDENTIAL ACCOMMODATION FOR ELDERLY PEOPLE WITH PHYSICAL OR VISUAL DISABILITIES / WELSH OFFICE (UK/0958-9775) [28877554] **4393**

RESIDENTIAL ACCOMODATION FOR THE ELDERLY, BLIND, AND PHYSICALLY DISABLED *See* RESIDENTIAL ACCOMMODATION FOR ELDERLY PEOPLE WITH PHYSICAL OR VISUAL DISABILITIES / WELSH OFFICE **4393**

RESIDENTIAL BUILDERS COMPENSATION SURVEY (US/0735-5068) [08921096] 626, **1708**

RESIDENTIAL BUILDING COST GUIDE (MILWAUKEE, WIS. : 1986) (US/1053-2986) [13567436] **626**

RESIDENTIAL CARE FACILITIES, AGED / STATISTICS CANADA, CANADIAN CENTRE FOR HEALTH INFORMATION (CN/1195-4167) [29562928] **3754**

RESIDENTIAL CARE FACILITIES, MENTAL / STATISTICS CANADA, CANADIAN CENTRE FOR HEALTH INFORMATION (CN/1195-4175) [29562942] **5306**

RESIDENTIAL CONSTRUCTION IN SOUTHEAST MICHIGAN (US/0362-3424) [04215085] **626**

RESIDENTIAL CONSTRUCTION NEWS *See* DEVELOPERS AND BUILDERS NEWS **2821**

RESIDENTIAL ENERGY CONSUMPTION SURVEY. HOUSING CHARACTERISTICS (US/0741-725X) [09861462] **2834**

RESIDENTIAL ENERGY CONSUMPTION SURVEY [COMPUTER FILE] / ENERGY INFORMATION ADMINISTRATION, OFFICE OF ENERGY MARKETS AND END USE, ENERGY END USE DIVISION (US) [24681603] 2834, **1955**

RESIDENTIAL ENERGY CONSUMPTION SURVEY [COMPUTER FILE] / ENERGY INFORMATION ADMINISTRATION, OFFICE OF ENERGY MARKETS AND END USE, ENERGY END USE DIVISION (US) [24681951] **1955**

RESIDENTIAL FELLOWSHIPS FOR COLLEGE TEACHERS. SEMINAR DESCRIPTIONS (US) [06721999] **1845**

RESIDENTIAL FLORIDA REAL ESTATE (US/1042-0517) [18924636] **4846**

RESIDENTIAL GAS MARKET SURVEY (US) [23913738] **4277**

RESIDENTIAL GENERAL CONTRACTORS AND DEVELOPERS (CN/0835-1074) [15806991] 2834, **626**

RESIDENTIAL LAND AND HOUSING SURVEY / THE CITY OF CALGARY, PLANNING DEPARTMENT (CN/0712-6468) [09964620] **2834**

RESIDENTIAL TREATMENT FOR CHILDREN & YOUTH (US/0886-571X) [12930238] **5306**

RESIDENTS IN WISCONSIN ADULT CORRECTIONAL FACILITIES ON ... WITH FIVE-YEAR TRENDS FOR ... (US) [09341696] **3175**

RESIDENTS IN WISCONSIN ADULT CORRECTIONAL INSTITUTIONS (US) [05229944] **3175**

RESIDENTS IN WISCONSIN JUVENILE CORRECTIONAL INSTITUTIONS (1979) (US/0732-0787) [07430003] **3175**

●RESIDENTS' PRESCRIBING REFERENCE (US/1061-6632) [25391487] **3634**

RESIDUAL VALUE FORECASTS FOR DEC SYSTEMS AND PERIPHERALS (US) **1249**

RESIDUAL VALUE FORECASTS FOR IBM SYSTEMS AND PERIPHERALS (US) **1249**

RESILOG (CN/0225-5804) [06167348] **5306**

RESIST (SOMERVILLE, MASS.) (US/0897-2613) [12175902] **4493**

RESISTANCE NEWS / NATIONAL RESISTANCE COMMITTEE (US) [09841074] **4493**

RESISTANCE (VANCOUVER) (CN/0824-586X) [10805465] **4493**

RESISTENCIA (PO) [04694689] **2705**

RESMEDICA (US/0738-0496) [09513045] **3634**

RESOCONTI DELLE GIUNTE E DELLE COMMISSIONI. TIPO II (IT) **3039**

RESOCONTO SOMMARIO AULA E BOLLETTINO DELLE GIUNTE E COMMISSIONI PARLAMENTARI (IT) **4493**

RESOLUTION (US/1050-3978) [21474912] **1201**

RESOLUTION OF CORRECTIONAL PROBLEMS AND ISSUES (US/0095-3180) [01796581] **3175**

RESOLUTION - PARLIAMENTARY ASSEMBLY OF THE COUNCIL OF EUROPE (FR) [02243515] **4683**

RESOLUTION TRUST REPORTER (US/1045-0130) [19968724] **809**

RESOLUTIONS AND DECISIONS ADOPTED BY THE GENERAL ASSEMBLY DURING ITS ... SESSION - UNITED NATIONS (US/0252-7014) [03783691] **3134**

RESOLUTIONS AND DECISIONS, ANNEXES / WORLD HEALTH ORGANIZATION, EXECUTIVE BOARD (SZ) [12869891] **4799**

RESONNANCES (FR) [09764973] **3429**

RESORT & HOTEL MANAGEMENT *CEASED.* (US/0886-9863) [12995889] 2809, **884**

RESORT CONDOMINIUMS INTERNATIONAL. ANNUAL DIRECTORY EDITION *See* ENDLESS VACATION - RESORT CONDOMINIUMS INTERNATIONAL, THE **5469**

RESORT DEVELOPMENT & OPERATION (US/8750-1252) [22146029] **2809**

RESORTS & GREAT HOTELS (US/0897-5833) [17563898] **2809**

RESOUND (US/0749-2472) [10204552] 2272, **4149**

RESOURCE (CN/0832-9354) [16349305] **4992**

RESOURCE

●RESOURCE AND ENERGY ECONOMICS (NE/0928-7655) [28176146] **1955**

RESOURCE (ATLANTA, GA.) (US/0887-1752) [07440029] **2892**

RESOURCE ATLAS - UNIVERSITY OF NEBRASKA, CONSERVATION AND SURVEY DIVISION (US/0160-3094) [02251289] **2574**

●RESOURCE BOOK, REAL ESTATE. LOS ANGELES COUNTY (US/1059-3047) [24561492] **4846**

●RESOURCE BOOK, REAL ESTATE. ORANGE, RIVERSIDE & SAN BERNARDINO COUNTIES (US/1060-3948) [24959097] **4846**

RESOURCE BULLETIN INT (US/0748-1241) [08569238] **2393**

RESOURCE BULLETIN NC (US/0887-7130) [08278430] **2204**

RESOURCE BULLETIN NE (US/0748-1357) [08300014] **2393**

RESOURCE BULLETIN PNW (US/0748-1284) [06238241] **2393**

RESOURCE BULLETIN RM (US/0888-9708) [06635872] **2393**

RESOURCE BULLETIN SE (US/0885-8381) [10486683] **2393**

RESOURCE BULLETIN SO (US/0887-4832) [08904591] 2204, **2394**

RESOURCE CENTER BULLETIN (US) [20785157] **1779**

RESOURCE-DATA BOOK (US/0091-3758) [01785409] **5337**

RESOURCE DIRECTORY FOR THE APPLE COMPUTER, THE (US/0740-7866) [09988172] **1239**

RESOURCE DIRECTORY, HEALTH INFORMATION SHARING PROJECT (US/0190-3527) [04635658] **4799**

RESOURCE DIRECTORY OF DOE INFORMATION ORGANIZATIONS (US/0748-7231) [08704984] **1955**

RESOURCE DIRECTORY. PRESENTERS OF PERFORMING ARTS (US) [08354972] **388**

RESOURCE DIRECTORY (TORONTO) (CN/0822-2479) [10634819] **2903**

RESOURCE DIRECTORY. TOURING PERFORMING COMPANIES (US/0738-3681) [09563657] **388**

RESOURCE (DON MILLS, ONT.) (CN/0828-9522) [13529612] **4846**

RESOURCE GUIDE AND DIRECTORY - ALBERTA CHAMBER OF RESOURCES (CN/0849-2409) [23231499] **4277**

RESOURCE GUIDE TO READING & LANGUAGE ARTS PROGRAMS & MATERIALS (US/0092-4423) [01789809] **3336**

RESOURCE (KANSAS CITY, MO.) (US/0745-1164) [08828467] **5067**

RESOURCE-MAG *CEASED.* (CN/0712-7243) [08936689] 936, **2924**

RESOURCE MANAGEMENT (US/0893-1828) [15372966] **4055**

RESOURCE MANAGEMENT AND OPTIMIZATION (UK/0142-2391) [06389965] **2204**

RESOURCE MANAGEMENT REPORT (CN) [01790014] 2311, **2204**

RESOURCE MATERIAL SERIES (JA/0256-5471) [02562496] **3175**

RESOURCE MATERIALS : ESTATE PLANNING IN DEPTH (US/0272-264X) [06778255] **3119**

RESOURCE NOTES (US) **5539**

RESOURCE NOTES / UNIVERSITY OF NEBRASKA--LINCOLN, CONSERVATION AND SURVEY DIVISION (US/1049-524X) [13897659] **1395**

RESOURCE/ONE Alphabetical Title Index

RESOURCE/ONE ONDISC [COMPUTER FILE] (US) 2492, **2497**

RESOURCE (OTTAWA) (CN/0700-5237) [03300391] **227**

RESOURCE PUBLICATION - U.S. FISH AND WILDLIFE SERVICE (US/0163-4801) [03152558] **2204**

RESOURCE RECOVERY REPORT (US/0735-3081) [08910738] **2242**

RESOURCE RECYCLING / NORTH AMERICA'S RECYCLING JOURNAL (US/0744-4710) [08324305] **2242**

RESOURCE RECYCLING'S BOTTLE/CAN RECYCLING UPDATE (US/1052-4916) [22348589] **2242**

RESOURCE RECYCLING'S PLASTICS RECYCLING UPDATE (US/1052-4908) [22715090] 2242, **4460**

RESOURCE REPORT / DEPARTMENT OF RESOURCES AND ENERGY, BUREAU OF MINERAL RESOURCES, GEOLOGY & GEOPHYSICS (AT) [15638552] **1360**

RESOURCE REPORT / UNIVERSITY OF NEBRASKA CONSERVATION AND SURVEY DIVISION (US/0548-0825) [01759553] **2204**

RESOURCE REVIEW (US/0277-7819) [07632964] **5762**

RESOURCE REVIEW (ANCHORAGE, ALASKA) (US/8755-1918) [11264258] **2204**

RESOURCE RICHMOND (AT/1031-3796) [10313796] **5777**

●RESOURCE (SAINT JOSEPH, MICH.) (US/1076-3333) [30454689] **1994**

RESOURCE SERIES - COLORADO GEOLOGICAL SURVEY, DEPARTMENT OF NATURAL RESOURCES, STATE OF COLORADO (US/0197-7490) [03783665] **1395**

RESOURCE SHARING & INFORMATION NETWORKS (US/0737-7797) [09454342] **3245**

RESOURCE [SOUND RECORDING]: A MONTHLY AUDIO DIGEST OF CURRENT ISSUES IN HEALTH CARE RISK MANAGEMENT/ PRODUCED BY THE RISK MANAGEMENT FOUNDATION OF THE HARVARD MEDICAL INSTITUTIONS (US) [23063176] **4799**

RESOURCEBOOK (CN/0709-0439) [05258049] **1625**

RESOURCES (KE) [24959356] **2204**

RESOURCES 2000 *CEASED.* (CN/1188-2522) [25652253] **1121**

RESOURCES AND ENERGY (NE/0165-0572) [04864018] **1517**

RESOURCES AND ENERGY ECONOMICS (NE) **1517**

RESOURCES AND LIABILITIES OF ILLINOIS STATE BANKS AT THE CLOSE OF BUSINESS ON ... (US) [08731624] **809**

RESOURCES ASIA *See* ASIAN OIL & GAS **4251**

RESOURCES - CANADIAN INSTITUTE OF RESOURCES LAW (CN/0714-5918) [09313052] **3116**

RESOURCES, CONSERVATION AND RECYCLING (NE/0921-3449) [17900061] **2204**

RESOURCES FOR AMERICAN LITERARY STUDY (US/0048-7384) [01534143] **3351**

RESOURCES FOR CHILD CARE (US/1051-3469) [21936005] **2285**

RESOURCES FOR FEMINIST RESEARCH : RFR (CN/0707-8412) [05585549] **5565**

RESOURCES FOR HEALTH R & D REPORT (US/0360-7933) [02176600] **4799**

RESOURCES FOR THE FUTURE *See* ANNUAL REPORT - RESOURCES FOR THE FUTURE **2187**

RESOURCES FOR THE FUTURE, INC *See* REPRINT - RESOURCES FOR THE FUTURE **2203**

RESOURCES IN AGING (US/0892-0818) [15160127] **5306**

RESOURCES IN EDUCATION (US/0098-0897) [02241688] **1779**

RESOURCES IN EDUCATION. ANNUAL CUMULATION (US/0197-9973) [06876178] 1779, **1797**

RESOURCES IN HUMAN NURTURING MONOGRAPH (US/0198-9774) [06257557] **3767**

RESOURCES IN LIBRARY AND INFORMATION SCIENCE (US/0197-4742) [04481002] **3246**

RESOURCES PAPER - UNIVERSITY OF BRITISH COLUMBIA, DEPARTMENT OF ECONOMICS (CN/0381-0410) [03348927] **1517**

RESOURCES POLICY (UK/0301-4207) [01318559] **2204**

RESOURCES (WASHINGTON, D.C. 1959) (US/0048-7376) [01763792] **2204**

RESPA SPECIAL REPORT AND OPINION LETTERS (US) **809**

RESPIRATION (SZ/0025-7931) [01763797] **3951**

RESPIRATION PHYSIOLOGY (NE/0034-5687) [01763798] **586**

RESPIRATORY CARE (US/0020-1324) [01598077] **3951**

●RESPIRATORY CARE MANAGER (US/1076-6030) [27196076] **3951**

RESPIRATORY DISEASE IN PRACTICE (UK/0262-7043) [14380082] 3739, **3951**

RESPIRATORY DISEASES RESEARCH CENTER (KE) **3951**

RESPIRATORY MEDICINE (UK/0954-6111) [19320532] **3951**

RESPIRATORY PHYSIOLOGY (UK/0149-2950) [02572358] **3951**

RESPIRATORY PROTECTION NEWSLETTER *CEASED.* (US/0882-0953) [11777940] **2869**

RESPIRATORY SYSTEM (UK/0142-8780) [01428780] **3951**

RESPIRER (FR/0754-9245) [I07549245] **3951**

RESPIROLOGIE (POINTE-CLAIRE) *CEASED.* (CN/0848-7421) [23242770] **3951**

RESPITE CARE SERVICES FOR SENIORS IN METROPOLITAN TORONTO (CN/1186-2246) [24368331] **5181**

RESPONSA MERIDIANA (SA/0486-5588) [01606976] **3039**

RESPONSABILITA CIVILE E PREVIDENZA (IT) [01763799] 2892, **3039**

RESPONSE (CINCINNATI) (US/0034-5725) [01714948] **5067**

RESPONSE (LEBANON, PA.) (US/1040-3957) [18396210] **3634**

RESPONSE (LOS ANGELES, CALIF.) *CEASED.* (US/1055-3703) [23137286] **2272**

RESPONSE (NEW YORK. 1967) (US/0034-5709) [01303078] **5052**

RESPONSE! (ROCKVILLE, MD.) *CEASED.* (US/1056-2214) [23600115] **4339**

RESPONSE (SOLANA BEACH, CALIF.) (US/0732-2933) [08369303] **4799**

RESPONSE TO THE ... REPORT OF THE AUDITOR GENERAL - PROVINCE OF BRITISH COLUMBIA. FINANCE AND CORPORATE RELATIONS (CN/0835-7366) [18059961] **809**

RESPONSE TO THE VICTIMIZATION OF WOMEN AND CHILDREN (US/0894-7597) [11717158] 5565, **5306**

RESPONSE (WASHINGTON, D.C.) (US/0276-6043) [07386805] **4277**

RESPONSIVE COMMUNITY, THE (US/1053-0754) [22448114] **5256**

RESPONSIVE PHILANTHROPY (US/1065-0008) [14918859] **4339**

RESPUBLIKANS KA ONOMASTYCHNA (HIDRONIMICHNA) NARADA *See* MATERIALY - RESPUBLIKANSKA ONOMASTYCHNA (HIDRONIMICHNA) NARADA **4664**

RESPUESTA (US/0744-0251) [07123294] **4993**

RESSI REVIEW (US/0199-3534) [04247221] 913, **4846**

RESSOURCE (OTTAWA) (CN/0700-5245) [03399710] **227**

RESSOURCES CULTURELLES DES FRANCOPHONES HORS QUEBEC (CN/0710-1287) [08185753] **2757**

RESSOURCES EN EAU DE TUNISIE (TI/0330-0005) [01795767] **5539**

RESSOURCES ET VOUS (CN/0714-4288) [09046733] **3175**

RESSOURCES INFORMATIQUES (FR) **4209**

RESSOURCES (TORONTO) (CN/0227-6313) [07869919] **1625**

RESTANT (BE/0771-095X) [I0771095X] **3315**

RESTATEMENT OF THE LAW SECOND: TRUSTS / SUBMITTED TO THE MEMBERS BY THE COUNCIL (US) [08472924] **3039**

RESTATEMENT, THE (US/0484-5765) [02255139] **3039**

RESTAURANT AND FOOD BUSINESS PUBLICATIONS, NEWSLETTERS, ETC. - A REFERENCE (US) **5072**

RESTAURANT & FOODSERVICES ASSOCIATION OF BRITISH COLUMBIA *See* ROSTER / RESTAURANTS & FOODSERVICES ASSOCIATION OF BRITISH COLUMBIA **5073**

RESTAURANT- & HOTEL-MANAGEMENT (GW/0344-4422) [I03444422] 5072, **2809**

RESTAURANT ASSOCIATION OF MARYLAND *See* RAM UPDATE **5072**

RESTAURANT BUSINESS (US/0097-8043) [01793763] **5072**

RESTAURANT BUYERS GUIDE (US/0270-4161) [06416449] 5072, **951**

RESTAURANT, CATERER AND TAVERN STATISTICS (CN/0226-2320) [07761826] **5073**

RESTAURANT EXECUTIVE (US/0095-5159) [01793718] 884, **5072**

RESTAURANT HOSPITALITY (US/0147-9989) [01780348] **5072**

RESTAURANT/HOTEL DESIGN INTERNATIONAL (US/0898-9079) [17944086] **307**

RESTAURANT INDEX (US/1041-2840) [18708849] **5072**

RESTAURANT MANAGEMENT INSIDER (US/1052-4088) [22283663] **5072**

RESTAURANT MANAGEMENT TODAY *See* RESTAURANT MANAGEMENT INSIDER **5072**

●RESTAURANT MARKETING STRATEGIES (US/1063-942X) [25936015] 885, **5072**

●RESTAURANT SERVICE REPORT (US/1062-2322) [25540730] **5073**

RESTAURANT WINE (US/1040-7030) [18504970] **5073**

RESTAURANTS & INSTITUTIONS (CHICAGO, ILL.) (US/0273-5520) [07076392] **5073**

RESTAURANTS & INSTITUTIONS MARKETPLACE (US) **5073**

RESTAURANTS (QUEBEC) (CN/0849-0538) [22154448] **5073**

RESTAURANTS USA (US/0890-5584) [14090572] **5073**

RESTAURATOR (DK/0034-5806) [01696160] **2483**

RESTAURO (IT) [15066667] **307**

RESTAURO & CITTA *CEASED.* (IT) [13019569] **308**

RESTAURO MUNCHEN (GW/0933-4017) [I09334017] **363**

RESTAVRATSIIA, ISSLEDOVANIE I KHRANENIE MUZEINYKH KHUDOZHESTVENNYKH TSENNOSTEI (RU) [03045376] **363**

RESTO DEL CARLINO (IT) **5805**

RESTORATION (CN) [01608264] **5035**

RESTORATION AND 18TH CENTURY THEATRE RESEARCH (US/0034-5822) [04212379] **5368**

RESTORATION & MANAGEMENT NOTES (US/0733-0707) [07722299] **2204**

RESTORATION HERALD (US/0034-5830) [03910204] **4993**

RESTORATION (KNOXVILLE) (US/0162-9905) [04095276] 2705, **3429**

RESTORATION OF LOST OR OBLITERATED CORNERS AND SUBDIVISION OF SECTIONS (US) [01633110] **2574**

RESTORATION QUARTERLY (US/0486-5642) [01776685] **4993**

RESTORATION SERIALS INDEX (US/1070-8073) [17414422] **4993**

RESTORATION (TUCSON, ARIZ.) *SUSPENDED.* (US/0736-5934) [09170783] 5424, **252**

RESTORATION WITNESS (US/0191-0167) [04770222] **4993**

●RESTORATIVE ECOLOGY (US/1061-2971) [25233064] **2220**

RESTORATIVE NEUROLOGY (NE/0169-0833) [12495013] **3845**

RESTORATIVE NEUROLOGY AND NEUROSCIENCE (NE/0922-6028) [21370874] **3845**

RESTORER (ROWLETT, TEX.), THE (US/0279-8042) [07312131] **4993**

RESTORICA (SA) [05421902] **626**

RESULTATE DER MATHEMATIK (SZ/0378-6218) [04606790] **3531**

RESULTATER AF MANUELLE TRAFIKTLLINGER I ... I FASTE PUNKTER PA VEJNETTET / VEJDIREKTORATET, ARBEJDSGRUPPEN OM MANUELLE TRAFIKTLLINGER (DK) [11407306] **5443**

RESULTATERNE AF KONJUNKTURUNDERSGELSEN HOS VIRKSOMHEDSLEDERE I FLLESSKABET (LU/0378-4479) [04123276] **1581**

RESULTATS DE L'ENQUETE ANNUELLE SUR LA COOPERATION AGRICOLE (FR) [07040982] **128**

RESULTATS DEFINITIFS DE L'ENQUETE SUR LE CHEPTEL BOVIN (FR) [06998275] **220**

RESULTATS DES ETABLISSEMENTS DE CREDIT (FR) **809**

RESULTATS / ELECTRICITE DE FRANCE, DIRECTION REGIONALE POUR LES DEPARTEMENTS D'OUTRE-MER (FR) [09157688] **2079**

RESULTATS FINANCIERS (FR) [20026538] **1163**

RESULTATS : SOCIETES D'ETUDES ET DE CONSEILS, INGENIEURS-CONSEILS (FR) [03466197] **1994**

RESULTS AND PROBLEMS IN CELL DIFFERENTIATION (US/0080-1844) [01763805] **540**

RESULTS ... ANNUAL SURVEY OF CORPORATE RELOCATION POLICIES (US/1048-1311) [18659323] 5391, **707**

RESULTS (FORSKNINGSSTIFTELSEN SKOGSARBETEN) (SW/0280-1892) [08932791] **2394**

RESULTS FROM THE COOPERATIVE COORDINATED OAT BREEDING NURSERIES, AND THE UNIFORM WINTER-HARDINESS NURSERIES (US/0733-9283) [08649289] 2430, **1543**

RESULTS FROM THE WIND PROJECT PERFORMANCE REPORTING SYSTEM (US) [13222822] **1955**

RESULTS OF GEOMAGNETIC OBSERVATIONS, BELSK (PL) [04196218] **4445**

RESULTS OF RESEARCH RELATED TO STRATOSPHERIC OZONE PROTECTION / PREPARED FOR CONGRESS OF THE UNITED STATES ; PREPARED BY OFFICE OF RESEARCH AND DEVELOPMENT, U.S. ENVIRONMENTAL PROTECTION AGENCY (US) [08595874] **2242**

●RESUME D'ENQUETE (CN/1193-0667) [26290286] **4248**

RESUME (DENVER) (US/0270-7527) [06462059] **4277**

RESUME DES RECHERCHES - STATION DE RECHERCHES. SAINT-JEAN, QUEBEC (CN/0827-4339) [08086803] **128**

RESUME OF BUSINESS TRANSACTED DURING SESSION OF THE MEGHALAYA LEGISLATIVE ASSEMBLY, ASSEMBLED UNDER THE DEMOCRATIC CONSTITUTION OF INDIA (II) [01784265] **4494**

RESUME OF WORK FOR THE PERIOD ... / COMMONWEALTH OF AUSTRALIA, COMMONWEALTH SCIENTIFIC AND INDUSTRIAL RESEARCH ORGANIZATION, DIVISION OF FOREST PRODUCTS (AT) [16957157] **1625**

RESUMEN ECONOMICO FINANCIERO (VE) [03768025] **1581**

RESUMEN (MIAMI) (US/0034-5865) [02240986] **329**

RESUMENES ANALITICOS EDUCATIVOS / CENTRO BOLIVIANO DE INVESTIGACION Y ACCION EDUCATIVAS (BO) [12220008] **1779**

RESUMENES ANALITICOS EN EDUCACION (CL/0716-0151) [02922886] **1797**

RESUMENES ANALITICOS SOBRE PASTOS TROPICALES (CK/0120-2944) [09312805] **128**

RESUMENES SOBRE POBLACION DOMINICANA (DR) [12952999] **4559**

RESUMES DE JURISPRUDENCE PENALE DU QUEBEC (CN/0822-7616) [10681001] 3108, **3083**

RESUMES DES DECISIONS RECENTES RENDUES PAR LA COMMISSION D'APPEL DE L'IMMIGRATION (CN/0225-2651) [06461353] 3039, **1921**

RESUMOS - CONGRESSO BRASILEIRO DE PESQUISAS CAFEEIRAS (BL) [05589792] 2370, **185**

RESURGENCE (UK/0034-5970) [01763807] **4494**

RESURRECTION BULLETIN, THE (CN/0714-7686) [09543097] **4993**

RESURRECTION PARIS (FR/0484-5854) [04845854] **5035**

RESURSY BIOSFERY (RU) [02436556] **471**

RESUSCITATION (IE/0300-9572) [01778838] **3951**

RETAIL (UK) **956**

RETAIL AD WEEK (US/0735-7087) [08619693] **765**

RETAIL & BUSINESS REVIEW (US/0034-6004) [04426010] **956**

RETAIL ATTRACTION (UK) [17428910] **956**

RETAIL AUTOMATION (UK/0263-1377) [02631377] **707**

RETAIL BAKING TODAY (US/0146-2210) [02881658] **2356**

RETAIL BANK CREDIT REFERRAL DIRECTORY (US/0272-0000) [06659509] **809**

RETAIL BANKER INTERNATIONAL (LONDON EDITION) (UK/0261-1740) [07788314] **809**

RETAIL BANKING PRODUCTS SURVEY (AT) **809**

RETAIL BANKING PRODUCTS SURVEY. AT CALL DEPOSITS (AT/1032-870X) [I1032870X] **809**

RETAIL BANKING PRODUCTS SURVEY. CONTINUING CREDIT (AT/1032-8726) [I10328726] **809**

RETAIL BANKING PRODUCTS SURVEY. CREDIT CARDS (AT/1032-8742) [I10328742] **809**

RETAIL BANKING PRODUCTS SURVEY. TERM DEPOSITS (AT/1032-8718) [I10328718] **809**

RETAIL BANKING PRODUCTS SURVEY. TERM LOANS (AT/1032-8734) [I10328734] **809**

RETAIL BANKING REPORT (US/1058-885X) [24269704] **809**

RETAIL BANKING REVOLUTION : AN INTERNATIONAL PERSPECTIVE, THE (UK) [20525588] **809**

RETAIL BANKING SOURCEBOOK (US) **809**

RETAIL BREAKTHROUGHS INTERNATIONAL (UK) **956**

RETAIL BUSINESS. MARKET REPORTS See RETAIL BUSINESS. MARKET SURVEYS / ECONOMIST INTELLIGENCE UNIT **956**

RETAIL BUSINESS. MARKET REPORTS / ECONOMIST INTELLIGENCE UNIT (UK) [16685933] 936, **956**

●RETAIL BUSINESS. MARKET SURVEYS / ECONOMIST INTELLIGENCE UNIT (UK/0951-9734) [29886966] **956**

RETAIL BUSINESS. RETAIL TRADE REVIEWS / ECONOMIST INTELLIGENCE UNIT (UK) [16685912] 936, **956**

RETAIL CHAIN AND DEPARTMENT STORES (CN/0227-017X) [08290035] **956**

RETAIL CHALLENGE (US) **956**

RETAIL CONTROL (US/0034-6047) [01763809] **956**

RETAIL CREDIT SURVEY FOR SEVENTH FEDERAL RESERVE DISTRICT (US/0195-7414) [05578370] **809**

RETAIL DESIGN INTERNATIONAL **SUSPENDED.** (UK) **956**

RETAIL DIRECTORY (UK) [15511589] **956**

RETAIL ESTABLISHMENTS AND SELECTED SERVICE ESTABLISHMENTS, HOTELS AND ACCOMMODATION, TASMANIA / AUSTRALIAN BUREAU OF STATISTICS (AT/0725-9379) [08960068] **2809**

RETAIL FOOD PRICE INDEXES (CN) [01793929] 2356, **956**

RETAIL INFO SYSTEMS NEWS (US/1060-3808) [24947992] **956**

RETAIL INTELLIGENCE (UK) **957**

RETAIL JEWELLER (UK/0034-6063) **2915**

RETAIL LEASING REPORTER See DEALMAKERS (BELLE MEAD, N.J.), THE **4836**

RETAIL MARKET PRICES OF SOME FOOD ITEMS IN PLATEAU STATE, SELECTED FROM SOME LOCAL GOVERNMENT IN THE STATE (NR) [04939947] **2356**

RETAIL MARKETING & MANAGEMENT (UK) [18934551] **936**

RETAIL MONITOR See RETAIL MONITOR INTERNATIONAL **957**

RETAIL MONITOR INTERNATIONAL (UK/0968-8234) [I09688234] **957**

RETAIL NEWS LETTER ED. FRANCAISE (FR/1017-785X) [I1017785X] **957**

RETAIL NEWS WEST (US/8750-4286) [11388170] **957**

RETAIL OUTLETS FOR THE SALE OF DISTILLED SPIRITS (US/0416-0525) [02246501] 2370, **957**

RETAIL PRICES AND INDEXES OF FUELS AND UTILITIES (US/0160-9882) [02371429] **4683**

RETAIL PRICES IN THE EEC (UK) [02241302] **1625**

●RETAIL PROFIT FORUM (US/1057-7033) [24098411] **957**

RETAIL SALES AND MARKETING IDEA EXCHANGE (US) **936**

RETAIL SALES AND USE TAX See RETAIL SALES AND USE TAX REPORT **4746**

RETAIL SALES AND USE TAX REPORT (US) [05723738] **4746**

RETAIL SALES OUTLOOK (US) **957**

RETAIL SECURITY DIGEST (US/0735-8520) [08978358] 957, **3039**

RETAIL SECURITY MANAGEMENT LETTER (US/0883-2234) [12091124] 957, **3175**

RETAIL STORE IMAGE (US/1047-8841) [20805254] **2903**

RETAIL SYSTEMS ALERT (US/0898-8439) [17930682] **957**

RETAIL TECHNOLOGY (US/0731-1303) [08127873] **957**

RETAIL TENANT DIRECTORY (US/0887-0470) [10667427] 4846, **957**

RETAIL TRADE INTERNATIONAL (UK) [03615893] **957**

RETAIL TRADE (MONTHLY ED.) (CN/0380-6146) [03661707] **957**

RETAIL WEEK (UK) **957**

RETAIL WORLD (AT) [10126541] **957**

RETAILER AND MARKETING NEWS (US/0192-9151) [05137917] **936**

RETAILER NEWS (US/8750-4391) [11404078] **957**

RETAILER (RALEIGH), THE (US/0161-5688) [03977359] **957**

RETAILERS' MICROCOMPUTER MARKET PLACE **CEASED.** (US/0000-0833) [12404937] 1289, **1272**

RETAILING IN TENNESSEE (US/0361-0020) [02245121] **957**

RETAILING TODAY (US/0360-506X) [01922125] **957**

RETAINER See PHILADELPHIA BAR REPORTER **3029**

RETAINER, THE (US/0145-3491) [02698683] **3039**

RETENCION Y DESGRANAMIENTO : EDUCACION PRIMARIA, EDAD ESCOLAR (AG) [04327723] 1779, **1797**

RETFRD ARHUS (DK/0105-1121) [I01051121] **3039**

RETHINKING CORPORATE STRATEGY FOR AFRICA : OPPORTUNITIES AND RISKS IN A FAST-CHANGING ENVIRONMENT (UK) [22685523] **707**

RETHINKING MARXISM (US/0893-5696) [15581396] **1594**

RETHINKING SCHOOLS (US/0895-6855) [16400631] **1779**

RETI **CEASED.** (IT) [17534854] **5565**

RETINA (MX) [06179698] **3878**

RETINA (PHILADELPHIA, PA.) (US/0275-004X) [07066692] **3878**

RETIRED MILITARY ALMANAC (US/0149-7197) [03547298] **4055**

RETIRED OFFICER (ALEXANDRIA, VA.) See RETIRED OFFICER MAGAZINE (ALEXANDRIA, VA.), THE **4055**

RETIRED OFFICER (ALEXANDRIA, VA.), THE (US/0034-6160) [08401755] **4055**

RETIRED OFFICER MAGAZINE (ALEXANDRIA, VA.), THE (US/1061-3102) [25238526] **4055**

RETIREE NEWSLETTER (US) [08035939] **5181**

RETIREMENT GUIDE **CEASED.** (CN/1184-0765) [23302770] **5181**

RETIREMENT HOUSING BUSINESS REPORT (US/1062-7316) [25705535] **2834**

RETIREMENT HOUSING REPORT See RETIREMENT HOUSING BUSINESS REPORT **2834**

RETIREMENT INDUSTRY JOURNAL, THE (AT) 3792, **5181**

RETIREMENT LETTER (US/0093-5352) [01330131] **5181**

RETIREMENT LIFE (US/0034-6179) [03267351] **4683**

RETIREMENT LIFESTYLE (CN/0844-5982) [20254095] **5181**

RETIREMENT OPPORTUNITIES (US/1058-1359) [24225578] **885**

RETIREMENT PLANNING (UK) **4746**

RETIREMENT PLANS BULLETIN (US) **913**

RETIREMENT PLANS FOR THE SELF-EMPLOYED : FOR USE IN PREPARING ... RETURNS (US) [23289789] **1708**

RETIREMENT PROCEEDINGS (US/0278-3304) [04155498] **5181**

RETRAITE, LE (CN/0317-9222) [02442277] **3175**

RETREADER'S JOURNAL (US/0482-430X) [03910387] 5077, **707**

... RETREAT DIRECTORY, THE (US/0749-0593) [11051044] **4993**

RETRIBUCIONES, INDUSTRIA Y SERVICIOS VERDIENSTE, PRODUZIERENDES GEWERBE UND DIENSTLEISTUNGEN EARNINGS, INDUSTRY AND SERVICES / [EUROSTAT] (LU/0259-0492) [15178566] **1708**

RETRIEVAL CODE INDEX - DATA RESOURCES OF CANADA (CN/0823-9592) [11559749] **3246**

RETROFIT OF BUILDING ENERGY SYSTEMS AND PROCESSES (US/0742-731X) [10382272] **2608**

RETROSPECTIVE INDEX - WEST AFRICA RICE DEVELOPMENT ASSOCIATION (LB) [04648233] **128**

RETROSPECTIVE PERSPECTIVES (CN) [11108243] **750**

RETROSPEKTIVNAIA — Alphabetical Title Index

RETROSPEKTIVNAIA I SRAVNITELNAIA POLITOLOGIIA (RU) [25178737] **4494**

RETROVIRUS (FR) [20350930] **3676**

RETTENS GANG (NO) [01800002] **3039**

RETTUNGSDIENST (GW/0178-2525) [13340448] **3634**

RETURN OF OUTSTANDING DEBT (ENGLAND AND WALES) (UK) [02241329] **4746**

RETURN TO THE SOURCE (US/0743-1244) [10498471] 4359, **4993**

RETURN (WASHINGTON, D.C.), THE *SUSPENDED.* (US/1050-0022) [18631469] **2272**

REUMATISMO (IT/0048-7449) [I00487449] **3806**

REUMATIZAM (CI) [12032822] **3806**

REUMATOLOGIA (PL/0034-6233) [08397560] **3634**

REUMATOLOGO : PUBBLICA IL BOLLETTINO DELLA SOCIETA ITALIANA DI REUMATOLOGIA, IL (IT/0391-8963) [18526387] **3806**

REUNION (UY) [01792443] **2079**

REUNION; ANNUAIRE DEPARTEMENTAL PRIVE *See* ANNUAIRE DEPARTEMENTAL PRIVE : ILE DE LA REUNION **4626**

REUNION ANNUELLE DES SCIENCES DE LA TERRE. RESUMES DES COMMUNICATIONS (FR) [01798683] **1395**

REUNION ANUAL - AAEP (AG) [06849719] **1594**

REUNION - COMITE INTERNATIONAL DES POIDS ET MESURES, COMITE CONSULTATIF POUR LES ETALONS DE MESURE DES RAYONNEMENTS IONISANTS, SECTION II (FR/0379-5640) [01795731] **4451**

REUNION - COMITE INTERNATIONAL DES POIDS ET MESURES, COMITE CONSULTATIF POUR LES ETALONS DE MESURE DES RAYONNEMENTS IONISANTS, SECTION III (FR/0379-5659) [01795733] **4032**

REUNION DES SCIENCES DE LA TERRE (FR/0249-7557) [20572705] **1360**

REUNION. DIRECTION DEPARTEMENTALE DES AFFAIRES SANITAIRES ET SOCIALES *See* RAPPORT ANNUEL / DIRECTION DEPARTEMENTALE DES AFFAIRES SANITAIRES ET SOCIALES **4798**

REUNION LATINOAMERICANA DE PRODUCCION ANIMAL *See* MEMORIA - REUNION LATINOAMERICANA DE PRODUCCION ANIMAL **2746**

REUNION (REGION). PREFECTURE *See* RECUEIL DES ACTES ADMINISTRATIFS DE LA PREFECTURE DE LA REUNION **3093**

REUNION (REGION). PREFECTURE. RECUEIL DES ACTES ADMNISTRATIFS *See* RECUEIL DES ACTES ADMINISTRATIFS DE LA PREFECTURE DE LA REUNION **3093**

REUNIONES BIBLIOTECOLOGICAS (US/0078-639x) [04250557] **3246**

REUNIONES REGIONALES DE UROLOGIA (SP) **3993**

REUNIONS (MILWAUKEE, WIS.) (US/1046-5235) [20436740] **2470**

REUSE/RECYCLE (US/0048-7457) [01838474] **2242**

REUSSIR (FR) **5215**

REUSSIR- LAIT ELEVAGE (FR/0995-6492) [25361521] **198**

REVE JAARBOEK *CEASED.* (NE) [10940352] **3429**

REVEIL A CHICOUTIMI, LE (CN/0228-6653) [07802388] **5794**

REVEIL A JONQUIERE, LE (CN/0228-636X) [08071744] **5794**

REVEIL A LA BAIE, LE (CN/0228-6661) [07818055] **5794**

REVEIL ANARCHISTE, LE (FR) [11017241] **4546**

REVEIL DU PONTIAC, LE (CN/0229-0936) [08072114] **5794**

REVEIL MISSIONNAIRE (CN/0034-6284) [I00346284] **4993**

REVEILLE (AT) [07062386] **4055**

REVEILLE, THE (US) [06256202] **5684**

REVELSTOKE TIMES (CN) **5794**

REVENEWS (US/0160-0818) [02652219] **4746**

REVENGE (MONTREAL, QUEBEC) *See* CREATEURS QUEBECOIS **372**

REVENGE (MONTREAL, QUEBEC) *See* CREATEURS QUEBECOIS **372**

REVENU FRANCAIS (FR) **4746**

REVENUE (US) [08480934] **4746**

REVENUE COMPARISON WITH FY ... AND FY ... ESTIMATES (US) [08922153] **4746**

REVENUE ESTIMATE AND ECONOMIC OUTLOOK *See* OUTLOOK, THE REVENUE PICTURE FOR ... **1594**

REVENUE ESTIMATES - GREATER LONDON COUNCIL (UK) [03570486] **4746**

REVENUE LAW JOURNAL (AT/1034-7747) [23687335] **4746**

REVENUE LONDON (UK/0963-1046) [I09631046] **3039**

REVENUE MORTGAGE AND BOND PROJECTS UNDER THE INDUSTRIAL AND COMMERCIAL AUTHORITY LAW, SUMMARY OF LOANS ... / COMMONWEALTH OF PENNSYLVANIA, DEPARTMENT OF COMMERCE (US) [07666933] **913**

REVENUE NEWS (US/0147-3344) [03143321] **4747**

REVENUE REPORT - MAINE (US) [05094239] **4747**

REVIEW AND ANALYSIS OF ARCHEOLOGY PROGRAM (US/0565-8802) [01157732] **280**

REVIEW AND EVALUATION OF THE NUCLEAR REGULATORY COMMISSION SAFETY RESEARCH PROGRAM (US/0193-1970) [05132941] **2158**

REVIEW AND EXPOSITOR (BERNE) (US/0034-6373) [03876993] **5067**

REVIEW & PERSPECTIVE / COLLEGE OF BUSINESS AND ECONOMICS, UNIVERSITY OF KENTUCKY (US) [16860026] **1581**

REVIEW AND RECOMMENDATIONS ... OPERATING BUDGET REQUEST FOR WASHINGTON PUBLIC HIGHER EDUCATION (US) [10296395] **1845**

REVIEW - ANDHRA PRADESH, INDIA. LEGISLATURE. LEGISLATIVE COUNCIL (II) [01784190] **4683**

REVIEW BULLETIN (AT/0812-1567) [I08121567] **3246**

REVIEW / BURLINGTON CHAMBER OF COMMERCE (CN/0227-681X) [08078834] **850**

REVIEW / CHAMBER OF MINES OF SOUTH AFRICA (SA) [17629049] 2150, **1444**

REVIEW (CHARLOTTESVILLE) (US/0190-3233) [05197736] **3351**

REVIEW - COLE HARBOUR RURAL HERITAGE SOCIETY (CN/0821-7335) [09819101] **2757**

REVIEW / CUSTOMS AND EXCISE DEPARTMENT (HK) [12015394] **4747**

REVIEW / FEDERAL RESERVE BANK OF ST. LOUIS (US/0014-9187) [01569030] **809**

REVIEW - FERNAND BRAUDEL CENTER FOR THE STUDY OF ECONOMIES, HISTORICAL SYSTEMS, AND CIVILIZATIONS (US/0147-9032) [03245339] 2627, **1517**

REVIEW FOR ... / AGRICULTURAL RESEARCH INSTITUTE (CY/0070-2307) [25741249] **128**

REVIEW FOR ... / AGRICULTURAL RESEARCH INSTITUTE, REPUBLIC OF CYPRUS (CY) [25361775] **128**

REVIEW FOR RELIGIOUS (US/0034-639X) [01590021] **5035**

RE:VIEW - FRIENDS OF PHOTOGRAPHY (US/0891-5326) [14879921] **4376**

REVIEW-HERALD, THE (US/1052-5300) [22296608] **5639**

REVIEW IN ENGLISH LANGUAGE TEACHING (UK) **1779**

REVIEW ... INCLUDING ACCOUNTS FOR YEAR TO 31 DECEMBER ... / AN FORAS FORBARTHA (IE) [11070694] **1581**

REVIEW / INSTITUTE FOR THE HISTORY OF TECHNOLOGY & INDUSTRIAL ARCHAEOLOGY (US) [25754878] **2627**

● REVIEW - INSTITUTE OF NUCLEAR POWER OPERATIONS (U.S.) (US/1061-6411) [25384197] **4451**

REVIEW (INSTITUTE OF NUCLEAR POWER OPERATIONS (U.S.): 1981) *See* REVIEW - INSTITUTE OF NUCLEAR POWER OPERATIONS (U.S.) **4451**

REVIEW (INTERNATIONAL AIR TRANSPORT ASSOCIATION) (SZ) [13345839] **33**

REVIEW (INTERNATIONAL COMMISSION OF JURISTS (1952-)) (SZ/0020-6393) [01605495] **3134**

REVIEW JOURNAL OF PHILOSOPHY & SOCIAL SCIENCE (II/0258-1701) [04358708] 5216, **4359**

REVIEW : LATIN AMERICAN LITERATURE AND ARTS (US) [17010872] 3429, **329**

REVIEW - NAVAL RESEARCH LABORATORY (U.S.) (US/0736-4849) [09120136] **4182**

REVIEW (NEW ZEALAND MOUNTAIN LANDS INSTITUTE) (NZ/0114-7366) [21566670] **2204**

● REVIEW - NORTH-SOUTH INSTITUTE (OTTAWA) (CN/1188-4347) [26497771] **1625**

REVIEW / OAK RIDGE NATIONAL LABORATORY (US/0362-0751) [02432795] **4451**

● REVIEW OF ACCOUNTING STUDIES (NE/1380-6653) **751**

REVIEW OF AFRICAN POLITICAL ECONOMY (UK/0305-6244) [02243506] 4494, **1581**

REVIEW OF AGRICULTURAL ECONOMICS (US/1058-7195) [23748167] **128**

REVIEW OF AGRICULTURAL ECONOMICS MALAYSIA (MY/0034-6403) [02407196] 1517, **128**

REVIEW OF AGRICULTURAL ENTOMOLOGY (UK/0957-6762) [21107651] 5613, **5604**

REVIEW OF AGRICULTURAL PROGRAMMES AND ADVISORY ACTIVITIES / ROYAL TROPICAL INSTITUTE (NE) [11151057] **128**

REVIEW OF ANTI-SEMITISM IN CANADA, THE (CN) [12045276] **5216**

REVIEW OF ARCHAEOLOGY, THE (US/1050-4877) [21003857] **280**

REVIEW OF ARCHITECTURE AND LANDSCAPE ARCHITECTURE (CN/0705-1913) [04589984] **308**

● REVIEW OF AROMATIC AND MEDICINAL PLANTS (UK) **2430**

REVIEW OF AUSTRIAN ECONOMICS, THE (US/0889-3047) [13844230] **1517**

REVIEW OF BANKING & FINANCIAL SERVICES, THE (US/1051-1741) [20211631] 809, **3040**

REVIEW OF BIOLOGICAL RESEARCH IN AGING (US/0736-5055) [09181226] **3754**

REVIEW OF BLACK POLITICAL ECONOMY, THE (US/0034-6446) [01763818] 2272, **1517**

REVIEW OF BOOKS IN EDUCATION (US/1055-7784) [23298250] **1779**

REVIEW OF BOOKS ON THE BOOK OF MORMON (US/1050-7930) [21613842] **4993**

REVIEW OF ... / BRITISH RED CROSS (UK) [17376868] **5306**

REVIEW OF BUSINESS (US/0034-6454) [04533100] **708**

● REVIEW OF BUSINESS STUDIES, THE (US/1047-4595) [20697049] **708**

● REVIEW OF CENTRAL AND EAST EUROPEAN LAW (NE/0925-9880) [26238839] **3135**

REVIEW OF CLINICAL PHARMACOLOGY AND PHARMACOKINETICS (GR) **4327**

REVIEW OF COMPARATIVE LAW, THE (PL/0860-8156) [19735487] **3040**

REVIEW OF CONTEMPORARY FICTION (US/0276-0045) [07321196] **3351**

REVIEW OF CURRENT DHEW RESEARCH RELATED TO TOXICOLOGY *See* REVIEW OF CURRENT DHHS, DOE, AND EPA RESEARCH RELATED TO TOXICOLOGY **3983**

REVIEW OF CURRENT DHHS, DOE, AND EPA RESEARCH RELATED TO TOXICOLOGY (US/0737-0547) [08935145] **3983**

REVIEW OF CURRENT RESEARCH (US/0160-1091) [03610405] **3175**

REVIEW OF DERIVATIVES RESEARCH (NE/1380-6645) **991**

REVIEW OF ECONOMIC CONDITIONS (TU/0034-6500) [01642260] **1581**

REVIEW OF ECONOMIC INTEGRATION ACTIVITIES WITHIN THE EAST AFRICAN COMMUNITY (TZ) [03512043] **1581**

REVIEW OF ECONOMIC STUDIES, THE (UK/0034-6527) [01639811] **1517**

REVIEW OF ECONOMICS AND STATISTICS, THE (NE) [02360756] **1538**

REVIEW OF EDUCATION *See* REVIEW OF EDUCATION/PEDAGOGY/CULTURAL STUDIES, THE **1779**

● REVIEW OF EDUCATION/PEDAGOGY/CULTURAL STUDIES, THE (SZ/1071-4413) [28641886] **1779**

REVIEW OF EDUCATION, THE (US/0098-5597) [02239674] **1779**

REVIEW OF EDUCATIONAL PROVISION IN WALES / BY HM INSPECTORATE (WALES) (UK) [20115617] **1779**

REVIEW OF EDUCATIONAL RESEARCH (US/0034-6543) [01588319] **1779**

REVIEW OF EMPLOYMENT IN MADRAS STATE *See* REVIEW OF EMPLOYMENT IN TAMIL NADU **1708**

REVIEW OF EMPLOYMENT IN TAMIL NADU (II) [01784225] **1708**

Alphabetical Title Index — REVIEWS

REVIEW OF ENGLISH STUDIES (UK/0034-6551) [01589305] **3429**

● REVIEW OF EUROPEAN COMMUNITY AND INTERNATIONAL ENVIRONMENTAL LAW (UK/0962-8797) [25990329] **3116**

REVIEW OF EXISTENTIAL PSYCHOLOGY AND PSYCHIATRY (1972) (US/0361-1531) [01775405] **4615**

REVIEW OF FINANCIAL ECONOMICS (US/1058-3300) [24265098] **1518**

REVIEW OF FINANCIAL STUDIES, THE (US/0893-9454) [15703588] **809**

REVIEW OF FISHERIES IN OECD MEMBER COUNTRIES (FR/0078-6241) [01799915] **2311**

REVIEW OF FOREIGN TRADE (PK) [03238248] **850**

REVIEW OF GHANA LAW (GH/0034-6578) [01785313] **3040**

REVIEW OF HIGHER EDUCATION (US/0162-5748) [04179660] **1845**

REVIEW OF IBERIAN LATIN AMERICAN DERMATOLOGY **CEASED**. (BL/0101-9872) [15551817] **3722**

REVIEW OF INCOME AND WEALTH, THE (US/0034-6586) [01930976] **1518**

REVIEW OF INDONESIAN AND MALAYSIAN AFFAIRS (AT/0815-7251) [10954306] **4494**

REVIEW OF INDUSTRIAL ORGANIZATION (US/0889-938X) [11006084] **1625**

REVIEW OF INSTITUTIONAL THOUGHT, THE **CEASED**. (US/0735-8563) [08970234] **1594**

REVIEW OF INTERNATIONAL AFFAIRS (YU/0486-6096) [01605801] **4534**

REVIEW OF INTERNATIONAL BROADCASTING (US/0149-9971) [03600318] **1138**

REVIEW OF INTERNATIONAL COOPERATION (SZ) **1518**

REVIEW OF INTERNATIONAL ECONOMICS (UK/0965-7576) **1639**

REVIEW OF INTERNATIONAL POLITICAL ECONOMY (UK/0969-2290) **4534**

REVIEW OF INTERNATIONAL STUDIES (UK/0260-2105) [07310718] **4534**

REVIEW OF JAPANESE CULTURE AND SOCIETY (JA/0913-4700) [17312209] **2663**

REVIEW OF LATIN AMERICAN STUDIES **SUSPENDED**. (US) [19230297] **2757**

REVIEW OF LEGAL EDUCATION IN THE UNITED STATES, A (US/0163-8831) [04307086] 1846, **3040**

REVIEW OF LITIGATION, THE (US/0734-4015) [06317797] **3040**

REVIEW OF MAJOR INVESTMENT PROJECTS IN CANADA (CN/0824-362X) [10392609] **913**

REVIEW OF MARKETING AND AGRICULTURAL ECONOMICS (AT/0034-6616) [05379877] 1518, **128**

REVIEW OF MEDICAL AND VETERINARY ENTOMOLOGY (UK/0957-6770) [21218773] 5613, **5604**

REVIEW OF MEDICAL AND VETERINARY MYCOLOGY (UK/0034-6624) [07084319] 576, 5520, **5528**

REVIEW OF MEDICAL PHYSIOLOGY (US/0892-1253) [07588988] **586**

REVIEW OF METAPHYSICS, THE (US/0034-6632) [01763830] **4359**

REVIEW OF NATIONAL LITERATURES (US/0034-6640) [00827303] **3351**

REVIEW OF OPERATIONS - WESTERN AUSTRALIAN URBAN LANDS COUNCIL (AT) [06507254] **1518**

REVIEW OF PALAEOBOTANY AND PALYNOLOGY (NE/0034-6667) [01606995] **4230**

REVIEW OF PARLIAMENT AND PARLIAMENTARY DIGEST (UK) [01789934] **4683**

REVIEW OF PERSONALITY AND SOCIAL PSYCHOLOGY **CEASED**. (US/0270-1987) [06366592] 5256, **4615**

REVIEW OF PLANT PATHOLOGY (UK/0034-6438) [01796486] 526, **479**

REVIEW OF POLAROGRAPHY. PORAROGURAFII (JA/0034-6691) [09994585] **1018**

REVIEW OF POLITICAL ECONOMY (UK/0953-8259) [19769201] 1518, **4494**

REVIEW OF POLITICS, THE (US/0034-6705) [01607479] **4494**

REVIEW OF POPULATION REVIEWS (FR/0377-8967) [06773779] **4559**

REVIEW OF PROFESSIONAL EMPLOYMENT (CN/0840-7231) [21493441] **1708**

REVIEW OF PROFESSIONAL MANPOWER (CN/0229-0324) [07817398] **1708**

REVIEW OF PROGRESS IN COLORATION AND RELATED TOPICS (UK/0557-9325) [01606403] **1029**

REVIEW OF PROGRESS IN QUANTITATIVE NONDESTRUCTIVE EVALUATION (US/0743-0760) [09630386] **1994**

REVIEW OF PSYCHIATRY (US/1041-5882) [18023105] **3935**

REVIEW OF PUBLIC PERSONNEL ADMINISTRATION (US/0734-371X) [07330673] **4705**

REVIEW OF QUANTITATIVE FINANCE AND ACCOUNTING (US/0924-865X) [24469942] **751**

REVIEW OF RADICAL POLITICAL ECONOMICS, THE (US/0486-6134) [01590098] **1594**

REVIEW OF REGIONAL STUDIES, THE (US/0048-749X) [01697247] **2834**

REVIEW OF RELIGIOUS (PK/0034-6721) [01639594] **4993**

REVIEW OF RELIGIOUS RESEARCH (US/0034-673X) [01018815] **4993**

REVIEW OF RESEARCH IN DEVELOPMENTAL EDUCATION (US/0894-3907) **1780**

REVIEW OF RESEARCH IN EDUCATION (US/0091-732X) [01783674] **1904**

REVIEW OF RURAL AND URBAN PLANNING IN SOUTHERN AND EASTERN AFRICA : JOURNAL OF THE ASSOCIATION OF RURAL & URBAN PLANNERS IN SOUTHERN & EASTERN AFRICA (RH/1016-2240) [25071446] **2834**

REVIEW OF SCIENTIFIC INSTRUMENTS (US/0034-6748) [01763839] **5147**

REVIEW OF SCOTTISH CULTURE (UK/0267-6834) [11076460] 5269, **2705**

REVIEW OF SECURITIES & COMMODITIES REGULATION, THE (US/0884-2426) [11773427] 913, **3040**

REVIEW OF SECURITY AND THE STATE (UK/0143-0556) [04511586] **4683**

REVIEW OF SOCIAL ECONOMY (UK/0034-6764) [01763841] 1595, **1581**

REVIEW OF SOCIALIST LAW See REVIEW OF CENTRAL AND EAST EUROPEAN LAW **3135**

REVIEW OF SPECIAL EDUCATION CASES (US) [23735230] **1884**

REVIEW OF TAXATION OF INDIVIDUALS, THE **CEASED**. (US/0147-9229) [03076729] 4747, **3119**

REVIEW OF TEXAS BOOKS (US/0892-6212) [13692734] 3351, **4832**

REVIEW OF THE AUDIT OF THE NATIONAL CONSUMER COOPERATIVE BANK'S FINANCIAL STATEMENTS (US/0741-529X) [10150315] **809**

REVIEW OF THE COMMODITY CREDIT CORPORATION'S FINANCIAL STATEMENTS (US/8756-0763) [10192974] **809**

REVIEW OF THE ECONOMIC CONDITIONS IN ITALY (IT/0034-6799) [06392682] **1581**

REVIEW OF THE ECONOMIC SITUATION OF MEXICO (MX/0014-3960) [02323111] 1518, **1581**

REVIEW OF THE ECONOMY AND EMPLOYMENT (UK/0265-9387) [20978722] **1708**

REVIEW OF THE ELECTRICAL COMMUNICATION LAB (JA) **2079**

REVIEW OF THE FEDERAL CROP INSURANCE CORPORATION'S FINANCIAL STATEMENTS (US/0741-4676) [10144669] **809**

REVIEW OF THE GEOGRAPHICAL INSTITUTE OF THE UNIVERSITY OF ISTANBUL (TU/0535-8361) [06678248] **2574**

REVIEW OF THE INTERNATIONAL BOND MARKETS, A (UK) [16988574] **913**

REVIEW OF THE LITERATURE ON PULP AND PAPER EFFLUENT MANAGEMENT (US) [02438974] **4238**

REVIEW OF THE MAIZE POSITION (SA) [01787065] **128**

REVIEW OF THE MINERAL INDUSTRY IN TANZANIA (TZ) [01796692] **1444**

REVIEW OF THE NATIONAL RESEARCH COUNCIL (OTTAWA) (CN/0373-5303) [06860820] **573**

REVIEW OF THE NEW ZEALAND COUNCIL FOR RECREATION AND SPORT (NZ) [11070867] **4854**

REVIEW OF THE REGULAR PROGRAMME (IT) [06806400] **128**

REVIEW OF THE RIVER PLATE, THE (AG/0325-7487) [01681149] **1581**

REVIEW OF THE SOCIETY FOR THE HISTORY OF CZECHOSLOVAK JEWS (US) [17853339] **2627**

REVIEW OF THE U.S. ECONOMY (US/0743-7323) [10417159] **1518**

REVIEW OF THE UNITED STATES SYNTHETIC FUELS CORPORATIONS FINANCIAL STATEMENTS (US/0738-842X) [08897489] **4683**

REVIEW OF THE WORLD WHEAT SITUATION **CEASED**. (UK/0539-1318) [02785022] **203**

REVIEW OF THE YEAR - HAWAII COMMUNITY DEVELOPMENT AUTHORITY See ANNUAL REPORT **2814**

REVIEW OF TROPICAL PLANT PATHOLOGY (II) [11871893] **526**

REVIEW OF URBAN AND REGIONAL DEVELOPMENT STUDIES: RURDS (JA) [20864503] **2834**

REVIEW / OHIO COUNCIL FOR THE SOCIAL STUDIES, THE (US/1050-2130) [21431375] 5216, **4494**

REVIEW ... OUTLOOK ... See REVIEW - NORTH-SOUTH INSTITUTE (OTTAWA) **1625**

REVIEW PAPER - UNIVERSITY OF NEW SOUTH WALES, CENTRE FOR MEDICAL EDUCATION RESEARCH AND DEVELOPMENT (AT/0157-9347) [09262980] **3634**

● REVIEW - PATIENT FOCUSED CARE ASSOCIATION (US/1063-1356) [25897486] **5306**

REVIEW (PLYMOUTH, WIS.) (US) [13289743] **5770**

REVIEW / QUEENSLAND ENERGY ADVISORY COUNCIL (AU) [12641977] 4277, **1955**

REVIEW / REMUNERATION TRIBUNAL (AT) [07367688] **3040**

REVIEW REPORT - FORINTEK CANADA CORP., EASTERN LABORATORY (CN/0824-2135) [10092647] **2394**

REVIEW-REPUBLICAN, THE (US) [13199440] **5667**

REVIEW - SASKATCHEWAN ASSOCIATION ON HUMAN RIGHTS (CN/0713-0287) [08720658] **4512**

REVIEW (SHIDLER, OKLA.), THE (US/8750-8508) [11861211] **5732**

REVIEW / SOCIETY OF ARCHITECTURAL HISTORIANS, SOUTHERN CALIFORNIA CHAPTER (US/0734-3884) [08548183] **308**

REVIEW: STATE OF THE INDUSTRY See INDUSTRY REVIEW **5360**

REVIEW, THE (UK/0034-6349) [04268944] **2892**

REVIEW, THE (PH) [04336393] **1779**

REVIEW, THE (PH/0115-3870) [09306711] **2508**

REVIEW, THE (US/0891-8716) [12646729] **5647**

REVIEW, THE MAGAZINE FOR ALABAMIANS (US) [05792396] **2757**

REVIEW : THE QUARTERLY JOURNAL OF RENEWABLE ENERGY (UK) [18356067] 2204, **1956**

REVIEW / UKRAINIAN CANADIAN PROFESSIONAL AND BUSINESS FEDERATION (CN/0822-9740) [11046592] **708**

REVIEW - VETERINARY INSTITUTE FOR TROPICAL AND HIGH ALTITUDE RESEARCH, SAN MARCOS UNIVERSITY INVESTIGATION CENTRE (PE) [01242119] **5520**

RE:VIEW (WASHINGTON, D.C.) (US/0899-1510) [18008651] **4393**

REVIEW / WASHINGTON STATE REFORMATORY (US) [23361774] **3175**

REVIEW (WINSLOW, WASH.), THE (US/1053-2889) [22503145] **5762**

REVIEWERS' CONSENSUS (US/0164-341X) [04407922] **3351**

REVIEWING AND PROCESSING COMMUNITY DEVELOPMENT BLOCK GRANT ENTITLEMENT APPLICATIONS (US) [04988663] **2834**

REVIEWING SOCIOLOGY : A REVIEW JOURNAL FROM THE SCHOOL OF SOCIOLOGICAL STUDIES (UK/0261-0272) [11479414] **5256**

REVIEWPOINT **CEASED**. (AT) **3246**

REVIEWS IN AMERICAN HISTORY (US/0048-7511) [01783629] **2757**

REVIEWS IN AMERICAN STUDIES (II) [03564166] **2757**

REVIEWS IN ANALYTICAL CHEMISTRY (IS/0048-752X) [01790773] **1018**

REVIEWS IN ANTHROPOLOGY (US/0093-8157) [01784390] **244**

REVIEWS IN BIOCHEMICAL TOXICOLOGY (US/0163-7673) [04471386] **3983**

REVIEWS IN CANCER EPIDEMIOLOGY (US/0166-8544) [05782748] 3736, **3823**

REVIEWS IN CHEMICAL ENGINEERING (UK/0264-8431) [09572045] **2017**

REVIEWS IN CLINICAL GERONTOLOGY (UK/0959-2598) [24485866] **3754**

REVIEWS — Alphabetical Title Index

REVIEWS IN CONTEMPORARY PHARMACOTHERAPY (UK/0954-8602) [23110506] **4328**

REVIEWS IN ECONOMIC GEOLOGY (US/0741-0123) [10063506] **1395**

REVIEWS IN FISH BIOLOGY AND FISHERIES (UK/0960-3168) [25494913] **2311**

● REVIEWS IN FISHERIES SCIENCE (US/1064-1262) [26210450] **2312**

REVIEWS IN INORGANIC CHEMISTRY (LONDON, ENGLAND) (UK/0193-4929) [05206270] **1037**

REVIEWS IN LEUKAEMIA AND LYMPHOMA (NE/0377-7855) [01490103] **3823**

REVIEWS IN MATHEMATICAL PHYSICS (SI/0129-055X) [20915895] **3531, 4419**

REVIEWS IN MEDICAL MICROBIOLOGY : A JOURNAL OF THE PATHOLOGICAL SOCIETY OF GREAT BRITAIN AND IRELAND (UK/0954-139X) [21749775] **3634**

REVIEWS IN MEDICAL VIROLOGY (UK/1052-9276) [22415937] **569**

REVIEWS IN MINERALOGY (US/0275-0279) [07050441] **1444**

REVIEWS IN MODERN ASTRONOMY (GW) [19893151] **399**

REVIEWS IN PERINATAL MEDICINE (US/0362-5699) [02541887] **3767**

REVIEWS IN PESTICIDE TOXICOLOGY (US/1062-3965) [25615574] **4248**

REVIEWS IN RURAL SCIENCE (AT) [02253342] **5147**

REVIEWS IN THE NEUROSCIENCES (UK/0334-1763) [14986663] **3845**

REVIEWS - INSTITUTE OF OCCUPATIONAL HEALTH (FI/0357-5993) [09509006] **2869**

REVIEWS JOURNAL (AT/0157-3705) [07483158] **3351**

REVIEWS OF CLINICAL INFECTIOUS DISEASES (US/0731-9266) [08271903] **3716**

REVIEWS OF ENVIRONMENTAL CONTAMINATION AND TOXICOLOGY (US/0179-5953) [15106798] **2242**

REVIEWS OF GEOPHYSICS (1985) (US/8755-1209) [11240991] **1410**

REVIEWS OF HEMATOLOGY (US/0272-507X) [06860222] **3773**

REVIEWS OF INFECTIOUS DISEASES *See* CLINICAL INFECTIOUS DISEASES **3712**

REVIEWS OF INFRARED AND MILLIMETER WAVES (US/0743-0752) [09989359] **4441**

REVIEWS OF MAGNETIC RESONANCE IN MEDICINE (US/0883-8291) [12225696] **3849**

REVIEWS OF MODERN PHYSICS (US/0034-6861) [05975699] **4419**

REVIEWS OF NATIONAL POLICIES FOR EDUCATION (FR) [01761455] **1780**

REVIEWS OF OCULOMOTOR RESEARCH (NE/0168-8375) [12291470] **3879**

REVIEWS OF PHYSIOLOGY, BIOCHEMISTRY AND PHARMACOLOGY (GW/0303-4240) [01795836] **493, 4328, 586**

REVIEWS OF RENEWABLE ENERGY RESOURCES (US/8756-5501) [10994628] **1956**

REVIEWS OF RESEARCH AND PRACTICE OF THE INSTITUTE FOR RESEARCH INTO MENTAL AND MULTIPLE HANDICAP (UK/0307-238X) [02826100] **4393, 3935**

REVIEWS OF RESEARCH FOR PRACTITIONERS AND PARENTS (US) [05812280] **4615**

REVIEWS OF THE SOLID STATE SCIENCE *CEASED.* (SI/0218-1029) [17870842] **4419**

REVIEWS OF WEED SCIENCE (US/1042-4148) [12636269] **2430**

REVIEWS ON CANCER (NE/0304-419X) [04969902] **3823**

REVIEWS ON CARDS (US) **3246**

REVIEWS-ON-CARDS (US) [02253491] **3246**

REVIEWS ON ENVIRONMENTAL HEALTH (IS/0048-7554) [01790775] **2181**

REVIEWS ON HETEROATOM CHEMISTRY (JA) [19402153] **991, 1057**

REVIEWS ON IMMUNOASSAY TECHNOLOGY (UK/0952-7168) [19884740] **3676**

REVIEWS ON POWDER METALLURGY AND PHYSICAL CERAMICS *CEASED.* (UK/0379-0002) [07046808] **2593, 4018**

REVIJA (CI) [02246694] **2705**

REVIJA OBRAZOVANJA (YU) [06887737] **1780**

REVIJA RADA (YU/0350-4557) [03338277] **1708**

REVIJA ZA KRIMINALISTIKO IN KRIMINOLOGIJO (YU/0034-690X) [I0034690X] **3175**

REVIJA ZA NARODNOSTNA VPRASANJA (XV) [18540011] **2272**

REVIJA ZA PSIHOLOGIJU (CI/0352-1605) [04578860] **4615**

REVIJA ZA SOCIOLOGIJU (CI/0350-154X) [01142600] **5256**

REVISATA DE DERECHO PROCESAL (SP/0213-1137) [24366128] **3040**

REVISED CODE OF AMERICAN SAMOA. CUMULATIVE SUPPLEMENT (US) [01480699] **3040**

REVISED NATIONAL BUDGET / ROYAL NORWEGIAN MINISTRY OF FINANCE, THE (NO) [24682989] **4747**

REVISED PLAN FOR EQUALIZING EDUCATIONAL OPPORTUNITY IN PUBLIC HIGHER EDUCATION IN FLORIDA (US) [07472507] **1846**

REVISED STATUTES OF NEBRASKA, 1943 (US) [01759556] **3040**

REVISED STATUTES OF SASKATCHEWAN (CN) **4683**

REVISION (CAMBRIDGE, MASS.) (US/0275-6935) [04484113] **4243, 4359, 3429**

REVISION SERVICE FOR FEDERAL REGULATORY LIBRARY WITH I ADS. INSPECTIONS AIRWOTHINESS & DIRECTIVES (US) **33**

REVISIONES EN CANCER (SP) **3823**

REVISIONING PHILOSOPHY (US/0899-9937) [18285888] **4359**

REVISIONIST LETTERS (US/1045-5299) [20185517] **2627**

REVISIONS (UNIVERSITY OF NOTRE DAME PRESS) (US) [08093243] **4359**

REVISOR (AMSTERDAM) (GW/0302-8852) [01793404] **3429**

REVISTA A.I.T (SP/0378-3294) [I03783294] **5391**

REVISTA ABOP (BL) [03150554] **4747**

REVISTA ABP-APAL (BL/0102-7646) [I01027646] **3935**

REVISTA ADEMI (BL) [06495755] **626**

REVISTA ADM (MX/0001-0944) [11989667] **1334**

REVISTA AEREA (US/0279-4519) [07894851] **33**

REVISTA AEREA LATINOAMERICANA *See* REVISTA AEREA **33**

REVISTA AERONAUTICA (BO) [02243023] 33, **4055**

REVISTA AGUSTINIANA (SP) [11774558] **5035**

REVISTA AIBDA (CR/0250-3190) [06899586] **3246**

REVISTA AIT (SP) [04263315] **5436**

REVISTA ALICANTINA DE ESTUDIOS INGLESES (SP/0214-4808) [I02144808] **3429, 3315**

REVISTA AMAZONENSE DE DESENVOLVIMENTO (BL) [10041266] **1625**

REVISTA AMRIGS (BL/0102-2105) [05828990] **3634**

REVISTA ANDI (CK) [05184935] **1625**

REVISTA ANDINA (PE) [10142753] **5216**

REVISTA ANTIOGUENA DE ECONOMIA Y DESARROLLO (CK/0121-0017) [01210017] **1518**

REVISTA ARGENTINA DE CARDIOLOGIA (AG/0034-7000) [01778845] **3710**

REVISTA ARGENTINA DE CIRUGIA (AG) [06362996] **3973**

REVISTA ARGENTINA DE DERMATOLOGIA (AG/0325-2787) [I03252787] **3722**

REVISTA ARGENTINA DE ECONOMIA AGRARIA (AG) [17191652] **128**

REVISTA ARGENTINA DE ESTUDIOS ESTRATEGICOS : R.A.E.E *SUSPENDED.* (AG/0326-6427) [11779805] **4055**

REVISTA ARGENTINA DE LINGUISTICA (AG/0326-6400) [12957786] **3315**

REVISTA ARGENTINA DE MICOLOGIA : ORGANO DE DIFUSION DE LA SOCIEDAD ARGENTINA DE MICOLOGIA (AG/0325-4755) [27150835] **576**

REVISTA ARGENTINA DE MICROBIOLOGIA (AG/0325-7541) [06213126] **569**

REVISTA ARGENTINA DE POLITICA Y TEORIA (AG) [10343229] **4494**

REVISTA ARGENTINA DE PRODUCCION ANIMAL (AG/0326-0550) [I03260550] 2356, **5520**

REVISTA ARGENTINA NUCLEAR (AG/0326-7873) [15809069] **2158**

REVISTA ARHIVELOR (RM/0034-7043) [01869401] 2470, **2483**

REVISTA ARVORE (BL/0100-6762) [09519938] **2394**

REVISTA (ASSOCIACAO BRASILEIRA DAS INDUSTRIAS DA ALIMENTACAO. SETOR DE ALIMENTOS CALORICO-PROTEICOS) *See* ALIMENTACAO (SAO PAULO) **2326**

REVISTA ASTRONOMICA (AG/0374-4272) [05521432] **399**

REVISTA AVICULTURA (CU/0257-9162) [02569555] **220**

REVISTA BARACOA (CU) [27843501] **2394**

REVISTA BIBLICA (AG/0034-7078) [05427627] **5019**

REVISTA BIBLICA BRASILEIRA (BL) [29384187] **5035**

REVISTA BIMESTRAL - SERVICO DE ADMINISTRACAO MILITAR *See* REVISTA TRIMESTRAL - SERVICO DE ADMINISTRACAO MILITAR **4055**

REVISTA BIOLOGIA / UNIVERSIDAD DE LA HABANA (CU) [19415471] 586, **471**

REVISTA BOLIVIANA DE CIENCIAS PENALES / SOCIEDAD BOLIVIANA DE CIENCIAS PENALES (BO) [06473054] **3175**

REVISTA BOLIVIANA DE QUIMICA (BO/0250-5460) [08205462] **991**

REVISTA - BOLSA DE VALORES DE SAO PAULO (BL) [01789510] **913**

REVISTA BRASILEIRA DE ANESTESIOLOGIA (BL/0034-7094) [01778849] **3684**

REVISTA BRASILEIRA DE BIOLOGIA (BL/0034-7108) [01645004] **471**

REVISTA BRASILEIRA DE BOTANICA (BL/0100-8404) [04573686] **526**

REVISTA BRASILEIRA DE CIENCIA DO SOLO (BL/0100-0683) [03974080] **185**

REVISTA BRASILEIRA DE CIENCIAS DO ESPORTE (BL/0101-3289) [I01013289] **4915**

REVISTA BRASILEIRA DE CIRURGIA (BL/0034-7124) [01763855] **3973**

REVISTA BRASILEIRA DE CLINICA E TERAPEUTICA (BL/0100-3232) [14189562] **3634**

REVISTA BRASILEIRA DE CRESCIMENTO E DESENVOLVIMENTO HUMANO (BL) [25785051] **1805**

REVISTA BRASILEIRA DE DIREITO PROCESSUAL (BL) [02244125] **3040**

REVISTA BRASILEIRA DE ECONOMIA (BL/0034-7140) [00834113] **1518**

REVISTA BRASILEIRA DE ENGENHARIA. CADERNO DE ENGENHARIA QUIMICA / ASSOCIACAO BRASILEIRA DE ENGENHARIA QUIMICA (BL/0102-2687) [16694659] **2017**

REVISTA BRASILEIRA DE ENGENHARIA QUIMICA (BL/0102-9843) [14777802] **2017**

REVISTA BRASILEIRA DE ENTOMOLOGIA (BL/0085-5626) [01695292] **5613**

REVISTA BRASILEIRA DE ESTATISTICA (BL/0034-7175) [01763858] **5337**

REVISTA BRASILEIRA DE ESTUDOS DE POPULACAO (BL/0102-3098) [12497506] **4560**

REVISTA BRASILEIRA DE ESTUDOS PEDAGOGICOS (BL/0034-7183) [01881383] **1780**

REVISTA BRASILEIRA DE ESTUDOS POLITICOS (BL/0034-7191) [01763859] 3093, **4494**

REVISTA BRASILEIRA DE FARMACIA (BL/0370-372X) [09490065] **4328**

REVISTA BRASILEIRA DE FARMACOGNOSIA (BL/0102-695X) [I0102695X] **4328**

REVISTA BRASILEIRA DE FILOSOFIA (BL/0034-7205) [02266955] **4359**

REVISTA BRASILEIRA DE FISICA (BL/0374-4922) [01908610] **4420**

REVISTA BRASILEIRA DE FISIOLOGIA VEGETAL (BL/0103-3131) [24057671] **526**

REVISTA BRASILEIRA DE GENETICA (BL/0100-8455) [05059741] **551**

REVISTA BRASILEIRA DE GEOCIENCIAS (BL/0375-7536) [04556417] **1360**

REVISTA BRASILEIRA DE GEOGRAFIA (BL/0034-723X) [01763860] **2574**

REVISTA BRASILEIRA DE HISTORIA / ORGAO DA ASSOCIACAO NACIONAL DOS PROFESSORES UNIVERSITARIOS DE HISTORIA, ANPUH (BL) [09257060] **2627**

REVISTA BRASILEIRA DE LINGUA E LITERATURA (BL/0101-8248) [05304701] 3429, **3315**

REVISTA BRASILEIRA DE LITERATURA COMPARADA (BL/0103-6963) [24959960] **3429**

Alphabetical Title Index **REVISTA**

REVISTA BRASILEIRA DE MALARIOLOGIA E DOENCAS TROPICAIS *CEASED.* (BL/0034-7256) [01640510] **3634**

REVISTA BRASILEIRA DE MEDICINA (BL/0034-7264) [01763862] **3634**

REVISTA BRASILEIRA DE MEDICINA. PSIQUIATRIA (BL/0100-7343) [06836141] **3935**

REVISTA BRASILEIRA DE MERCADO DE CAPITAIS (BL/0102-9797) [02242351] **913**

REVISTA BRASILEIRA DE MUSICA (BL/0486-6398) [05200548] **4149**

REVISTA BRASILEIRA DE NEUROLOGIA : ORGAO OFICIAL DO INSTITUTO DE NEUROLOGIA DEOLINDO COUTO, UNIVERSIDADE FEDERAL DO RIO DE JANEIRO (BL/0101-8469) [23361701] **3845**

REVISTA BRASILEIRA DE OTO-RINO-LARINGOLOGIA (BL/0034-7299) [01778851] **3891**

REVISTA BRASILEIRA DE OTTALMOLOGIA (BL/0034-7280) [07544269] **3879**

REVISTA BRASILEIRA DE PATOLOGIA CLINICA (BL/0034-7302) [03566154] **3897**

REVISTA BRASILEIRA DE PLANEJAMENTO (BL) [03005701] **2834**

REVISTA BRASILEIRA DE POLITICA INTERNACIONAL (BL/0034-7329) [01868574] **4534**

REVISTA BRASILEIRA DE PSICANALISE (BL/0486-641X) [03545671] **4615**

REVISTA BRASILEIRA DE QUIMICA (BL/0370-3797) [06078453] **991**

REVISTA BRASILEIRA DE REPRODUCAO ANIMAL (BL/0102-0803) [24600702] **5520**

REVISTA BRASILEIRA DE SAUDE OCUPACIONAL (BL/0303-7657) [01135248] 3635, **2869**

REVISTA BRASILEIRA DE SOCIOLOGIA (BL/0103-2402) [I01032402] **5256**

REVISTA BRASILEIRA DE TECNOLOGIA (BL/0100-6711) [01590774] **5147**

REVISTA BRASILEIRA DE TELEDUCACAO (BL) [02241280] 1138, **1904**

REVISTA BRASILEIRA DE TRANSPORTES (BL) [01796732] **5391**

REVISTA BRASILEIRA DE ZOOLOGIA (BL/0101-8175) [10199649] **5596**

REVISTA CAFETALERA *See* CAFETAL: REVISTA BIMESTRAL DE ANACAFE **2365**

REVISTA CAFETERA DE COLOMBIA (CK) [02409140] **185**

REVISTA - CALI, COLOMBIA. UNIVERSIDAD DEL VALLE. DIVISION DE INGENIERIA (CK/0590-9120) [03077057] **1994**

REVISTA / CAMARA DE COMERCIO DE BOGOTA (CK/0120-4289) [02891275] **4683**

REVISTA - CAMERA DE COMERCIANTES EN ARTEFACTOS PARA EL HOGAR (AG) [01788543] **2907**

REVISTA CANADIENSE DE ESTUDIOS HISPANICOS (CN/0384-8167) [02774273] **3429**

REVISTA CANARIA DE ESTUDIOS INGLESES (SP/0211-5913) [12967920] 3430, **3315**

REVISTA CARTOGRAFICA (MX/0080-2085) [01763863] **2583**

REVISTA CASA DE LAS AMERICAS, LA (CU/0008-7157) [27230617] **3430**

REVISTA CATALANA DE GEOGRAFIA (SP) [07239070] **2705**

REVISTA CATALANA DE PSICOANALISI (SP/0212-9205) [I02129205] **4616**

REVISTA CATALANA DE TEOLOGIA (SP/0210-5551) [02957660] **4993**

REVISTA CENIC *SUSPENDED.* (CU/1015-8553) [19745149] **991**

REVISTA CENIC (CU/0253-5688) [18694665] **471**

REVISTA CENTROAMERICANA DE ADMINISTRACION PUBLICA (CR) [09151277] **4683**

REVISTA CENTROAMERICANA DE ECONOMIA (HO/0254-4210) [05962976] **1581**

REVISTA CENTROAMERICANA DE NUTRICION Y CIENCIAS DE ALIMENTOS (GT/0304-4033) [02407208] **4198**

REVISTA CERES (BL/0034-737X) [01770935] **128**

REVISTA CHAPINGO (MX/0186-3231) [09009966] **128**

REVISTA CHILENA DE DERECHO (CL) [04201572] **3040**

REVISTA CHILENA DE DERECHOS HUMANOS (CL) [13018325] **4512**

REVISTA CHILENA DE EDUCACION FISICA *See* EDUCACION FISICA, CHILE / UNIVERSIDAD DE CHILE, FACULTAD DE EDUCACION, DEPARTAMENTO DE EDUCACION FISCA, DEPORTES Y RECREATION **1855**

REVISTA CHILENA DE ENTOMOLOGIA (CL/0034-740X) [01695858] **5613**

REVISTA CHILENA DE HISTORIA DEL DERECHO (CL/0716-5447) [01587179] **3040**

REVISTA CHILENA DE HISTORIA NATURAL PURA Y APLICADA *See* REVISTA CHILENA DE HISTORIA NATURAL (VALPARAISO, CHILE : 1983) **4171**

REVISTA CHILENA DE HISTORIA NATURAL (VALPARAISO, CHILE : 1983) (CL/0716-078X) [01763865] **4171**

REVISTA CHILENA DE HISTORIA Y GEOGRAFIA (CL/0716-2812) [01763866] 2574, **2757**

REVISTA CHILENA DE LITERATURA (CL/0048-7651) [01763867] **3430**

REVISTA CHILENA DE NEURO-PSIQUIATRIA (CL/0034-7388) [06415368] 3845, **3935**

REVISTA CHILENA DE NUTRICION : ORGANO OFICIAL DE LA SOCIEDAD CHILENA DE NUTRICION, BROMATOLOGIA Y TOXICOLOGIA (CL/0716-1549) [27264142] **4198**

REVISTA CHILENA DE OBSTETRICIA Y GINECOLOGIA (CL/0048-766X) [09562197] **3767**

REVISTA CHILENA DE PEDIATRIA (CL/0370-4106) [01714488] **3911**

REVISTA CHILENA DE PSICOLOGIA (CL/0716-3630) [I07163630] **4616**

REVISTA CIAF (CK) [03566124] **1395**

REVISTA CIENCIAS TECNICAS AGROPECUARIAS (CU) [24765802] 1994, **129**

REVISTA CLINICA ESPANOLA. NUEVOS ARCHIVOS DE LA FACULTAD DE MEDICINA (SP) **3635**

REVISTA COAHUILENSE DE HISTORIA (MX) [04579084] **2757**

REVISTA COLOMBIANA DE ANTROPOLOGIA (CK/0486-6525) [01130757] **244**

REVISTA COLOMBIANA DE CIENCIAS QUIMICO-FARMACEUTICAS (CK/0034-7418) [05214800] **991**

REVISTA COLOMBIANA DE EDUCACION (BOGOTA, COLOMBIA : 1978) (CK) [04358732] **1780**

REVISTA COLOMBIANA DE ENTOMOLOGIA (CK) [04017566] **5613**

REVISTA COLOMBIANA DE ESTADISTICA (CK/0120-1751) [I01201751] **5337**

REVISTA COLOMBIANA DE MATEMATICAS (CK/0034-7426) [04670163] **3531**

REVISTA COLOMBIANA DE OBSTETRICIA Y GINECOLOGIA (CK/0034-7434) [06034303] **3768**

REVISTA COLOMBIANA DE PSIQUIATRIA (CK/0034-7450) [06020360] **3935**

REVISTA COLOMBIANA DE QUIMICA (CK/0120-2804) [05522470] **991**

REVISTA COLOMBIANA DE SOCIOLOGIA / DEPARTAMENTO DE SOCIOLOGIA, UNIVERSIDAD NACIONAL (CK/0120-159X) [08247491] **5256**

REVISTA COMERCIO *See* COMERCIO **828**

REVISTA COMPLUTENSE DE HISTORIA DE AMERICA (SP) [I11328312] **2757**

REVISTA COMPLUTENSE DE HISTORIA DE AMERICA / DEPARTAMENTO DE HISTORIA DE AMERICA I (SP/0211-6111) [28469355] **2757**

REVISTA COMUNICACOES E ARTES (BL/0102-0897) [09569179] 329, **1121**

REVISTA COOPERTIVA PUERTORRIQUENA (PR) [26268038] **1518**

REVISTA COSTARRICENSE DE CIENCIAS MEDICAS (CR/0253-2948) [09149045] **3635**

REVISTA CRITICA DE CIENCIAS SOCIAIS (PO) [06914122] **5216**

REVISTA CUBA ECONOMICA *SUSPENDED.* (CU) [25968378] **1518**

REVISTA. CUBAN GENEALOGICAL SOCIETY (US) **2470**

REVISTA CUBANA ALIMENTACION Y NUTRICION (CU/0864-2133) [23968257] **4198**

REVISTA CUBANA CARDIOLOGIA Y CIRURGIA CARDIOVASCULAR (CU) [19523188] **3710**

REVISTA CUBANA CIENCIAS DE LA INFORMACION (CU) **3246**

REVISTA CUBANA DE CIENCIA AVICOLA (CU/0303-5239) [00978828] **220**

REVISTA CUBANA DE CIENCIAS SOCIALES (CU/0138-6425) [10463651] **4546**

REVISTA CUBANA DE CIENCIAS VETERINARIAS *SUSPENDED.* (CU/0048-7678) [01763876] **5520**

REVISTA CUBANA DE CIRUGIA (CU/0034-7493) [01624135] **3973**

REVISTA CUBANA DE CONSTRUCCION NAVAL; REVISTA CIENTIFICO TECNICA *SUSPENDED.* (CU/0864-2621) 626, **5455**

REVISTA CUBANA DE DERECHO *CEASED.* (CU) [01791480] **3040**

REVISTA CUBANA DE EDUCACION SUPERIOR : RCES (CU/0257-4314) [07557875] **1846**

REVISTA CUBANA DE ENFERMERIA (CU) [24561443] **3868**

REVISTA CUBANA DE ESTOMATOLOGIA (CU/0034-7507) [02067562] **1334**

REVISTA CUBANA DE FISICA (CU/0253-9268) [08125427] **4420**

REVISTA CUBANA DE HEMATOLOGIA INMUNOLOGIA Y HEMOTERAPIA (CU/1012-3172) [20043572] **3635**

REVISTA CUBANA DE HIGIENE Y EPIDEMIOLOGIA (CU/0253-1151) [02082867] 4799, **3736**

REVISTA CUBANA DE INVESTIGACIONES BIOMEDICAS (CU/0864-0300) [17799891] **3635**

REVISTA CUBANA DE INVESTIGACIONES PESQUERAS / CENTRO DE INVESTIGACIONES PESQUERAS, MIRAMAR, LA HABANA, CUBA *CEASED.* (CU/0138-8452) [05347084] **2312**

REVISTA CUBANA DE MEDICINA *SUSPENDED.* (CU/0034-7523) [01778853] **3635**

REVISTA CUBANA DE MEDICINA GENERAL INTEGRAL (CU) [18656885] **3739**

REVISTA CUBANA DE MEDICINA TROPICAL (CU/0375-0760) [01778854] **3986**

REVISTA CUBANA DE OBSTETRICIA Y GINECOLOGIA (CU) [04558518] **3768**

REVISTA CUBANA DE OFTALMOLOGIA *CEASED.* (CU) [01763877] **3879**

REVISTA CUBANA DE ONCOLOGIA (CU) **3823**

REVISTA CUBANA DE PEDIATRIA (CU/0034-7531) [I00347531] **3911**

REVISTA CUBANA DE PSICOLOGIA / UNIVERSIDAD DE LA HABANA (CU/0257-4322) [18321016] **4616**

REVISTA CUBANA DE QUIMICA (CU/0258-5995) [14758046] **991**

REVISTA CUBANA DE REPRODUCCION ANIMAL *CEASED.* (CU/0258-6495) [10035899] **220**

REVISTA CUBANA DE SALUD PUBLICA (CU/0864-3466) [19277497] **4799**

REVISTA CULTURAL LOTERIA (PN) [23025839] **2757**

REVISTA DA ACADEMIA GOIANA DE LETRAS (BL) [02244255] **3430**

REVISTA DA ACADEMIA PAULISTA DE LETRAS (BL/0001-3846) [03262996] **2853**

REVISTA DA ACADEMIA PERNAMBUCANA DE LETRAS (BL) [02240957] **3430**

REVISTA DA ACADEMIA SOBRALENSE DE ESTUDOS E LETRAS (BL) [06996905] **2757**

REVISTA DA ADISMAR *CEASED.* (BL) [02241159] **4182**

REVISTA DA ASSOCIACAO DOS MAGISTRADOS, PARANA (BL) [03921919] **3040**

●REVISTA DA ASSOCIACAO MEDICA BRASILEIRA (BL) [28357928] **3635**

REVISTA DA BIBLIOTECA NACIONAL (LISBOA) (PO/0251-1711) [08272574] **3260**

REVISTA DA ESCOLA DE BIBLIOTECONOMIA DA UFMG (BL/0100-0829) [02387360] **3246**

REVISTA DA FACULDADE DE CIENCIAS (PO) [03178079] **5147**

REVISTA DA FACULDADE DE DIREITO DE PORTO ALEGRE (BL) [02414877] **3040**

REVISTA DA FACULDADE DE DIREITO DE SAO PAULO (BL) [07571232] **3040**

REVISTA DA FACULDADE SALESIANA (BL/0302-0959) [01792862] **2552**

REVISTA DA FUNDACAO JONES DOS SANTOS NEVES (BL) [05769513] **2834**

REVISTA DA FUNDACAO SESP (BL/0304-2138) [01216343] 3716, **4799**

REVISTA DA PROCURADORIA FISCAL (BL) [05322670] **4747**

REVISTA DA PROCURADORIA GERAL DO ESTADO (BL) [07142729] **3040**

REVISTA DA PROCURADORIA GERAL DO ESTADO DE SAO PAULO (BL) [01799610] **3040**

REVISTA DA PROCURADORIA GERAL DO ESTADO (MATO GROSSO DO SUL (BRAZIL). PROCURADORIA GERAL DO ESTADO) (BL) [07413673] **3040**

REVISTA DA PROCURADORIA-GERAL DO ESTADO (RIO GRANDE DO SUL (BRAZIL)) (BL) [07480925] **3143**

REVISTA DA SBPH / SOCIEDADE BRASILEIRA DE PESQUISA HISTORICA (BL) [12756039] **2627**

REVISTA DA SOCIEDADE BRASILEIRA DE CIRURGIA PLASTICA (BL) [19021905] **3973**

REVISTA DA SOCIEDADE BRASILEIRA DE MEDICINA TROPICAL (BL/0037-8682) [21075903] **3986**

REVISTA DA SOCIEDADE BRASILEIRA DE ZOOTECNIA (BL/0100-4859) [02379654] **5596**

REVISTA DA UNIVERSIDADE CATOLICA DE PETROPOLIS (BL) [03146555] **4616**

REVISTA DA UNIVERSIDADE SAO FRANCISCO (BL) [16265494] **1846**

REVISTA DE ACTUALIDAD ODONTOESTOMATOLOGICA ESPANOLA (SP) [21744410] **1334**

REVISTA DE ACUSTICA (SP) [06161703] **5318**

REVISTA DE ADMINISTRACAO DE EMPRESAS (BL/0034-7590) [01865030] **885**

REVISTA DE ADMINISTRACAO MUNICIPAL (BL) [03098262] **4683**

REVISTA DE ADMINISTRACAO PARA O DESENVOLVIMENTO (BL) [04726064] **4683**

REVISTA DE ADMINISTRACAO PUBLICA (RIO DE JANEIRO) (BL/0034-7612) [01172572] **4683**

REVISTA DE ADMINISTRACION GALEGA (SP) [19788873] **4683**

REVISTA DE ADMINISTRACION PUBLICA *CEASED*. (MX/0482-5209) **4683**

REVISTA DE ADMINISTRACION PUBLICA (MADRID, SPAIN) (SP/0034-7639) [01865245] **4683**

REVISTA DE ADMINISTRACION Y DESARROLLO *See* ADMINISTRACION Y DESARROLLO (1981) **4624**

REVISTA DE AERONAUTICA Y ASTRONAUTICA (SP) [06369151] **33**

REVISTA DE AFRICA Y MEDIO ORIENTE (CU/0864-4403) [18107480] **4494**

REVISTA DE AGRICULTURA (BL/0034-7655) [01607437] **129**

REVISTA DE AGROQUIMICA Y TECNOLOGIA DE ALIMENTOS *See* REVISTA ESPANOLA DE CIENCIA Y TECNOLOGIA DE ALIMENTOS / EDITADA POR EL CONSEJO SUPERIOR DE INVESTIGACIONES CIENTIFICAS **2356**

REVISTA DE ANALISIS ECONOMICO / PROGRAMA DE POSTGRADO EN ECONOMIA, ILADES / GEORGETOWN UNIVERSITY (CL/0716-5927) [20382444] 1846, **1595**

REVISTA DE ANTROPOLOGIA (EC) [04315226] **244**

REVISTA DE ANTROPOLOGIA (SAO PAULO) (BL/0034-7701) [01869324] **244**

REVISTA DE ANTROPOLOGIA SOCIAL / DEPARTAMENTO DE ANTROPOLOGIA SOCIAL, FACULTAD DE CIENCIAS POLITICAS Y SOCIOLOGIA, UNIVERSIDAD COMPLUTENSE DE MADRID (SP/1131-558X) [25757377] **244**

REVISTA DE ANTROPOLOGIA Y ARQUEOLOGIA (CK) [24582018] 280, **244**

REVISTA DE ARCHIVOS BIBLIOTECAS Y MUSEOS (MADRID, SPAIN : 1897) *SUSPENDED*. (SP/0034-771X) [06340930] 4095, **3246**

REVISTA DE ARQUEOLOGIA AMERICANA / INSTITUTO PANAMERICANO DE GEOGRAFIA E HISTORIA (MX/0188-3631) [22690608] **280**

REVISTA DE ARQUEOLOGIA (MADRID, SPAIN) (SP/0212-0062) [13844307] **280**

REVISTA DE ARQUEOLOGIA (RIO DE JANEIRO, BRAZIL) (BL) [11580690] **280**

REVISTA DE ASCOLBI / ASOCIATION COLOMBIANA DE BIBLIOTECOLOGOS Y DOCUMENTALISTAS, ASCOLBI (CK/0121-0203) [19015161] **3246**

REVISTA DE ATUALIDADE INDIGENA (BL) [03341104] **2757**

REVISTA DE BELLAS ARTES (MEXICO, D.F.) (MX/0185-3570) [02266971] 308, **363**

REVISTA DE BIBLIOTECONOMIA DE BRASILIA (BL/0100-7157) [01794712] **3246**

REVISTA DE BIOLOGIA DEL URUGUAY (UY/0304-971X) [04031518] **471**

REVISTA DE BIOLOGIA (LISBOA) (PO/0034-7736) [02396171] **471**

REVISTA DE BIOLOGIA MARINA (CL/0080-2115) [02549008] **557**

REVISTA DE BIOLOGIA TROPICAL (CR/0034-7744) [01763881] **3986**

REVISTA DE BIOLOGIA Y MEDICINA NUCLEAR (AG) [03043643] **3849**

REVISTA DE CERAMICA EN LA CONSTRUCCION (AG/0325-1594) [03251594] **626**

REVISTA DE CHIMIE (RM/0034-7752) [01908597] **991**

REVISTA DE CHIRURGIE ONCOLOGIE, RADIOLOGIE, O.R.L., OFTALMOLOGIE, STOMATOLOGIE. ONCOLOGIA (RM/0377-4724) [01535523] **3823**

REVISTA DE CHIRURGIE ONCOLOGIE, RADIOLOGIE, O.R.L., OFTALMOLOGIE, STOMATOLOGIE. OTO-RINO-LARINGOLOGIA (RM/0377-7863) [01373108] **3891**

REVISTA DE CHIRURGIE, ONCOLOGIE, RADIOLOGIE, O.R.L. OFTALMOLOGIE, STOMATOLOGIE. SERIA : STOMATOLOGIE (RM/0377-7871) [01214815] **3635**

REVISTA DE CIENCIA POLITICA (SANTIAGO) (CL/0716-1417) [06188521] **4494**

REVISTA DE CIENCIAS DE LA EDUCACION (SP) [01795418] **1780**

REVISTA DE CIENCIAS ECONOMICAS *See* CIENCIAS ECONOMICAS **1590**

REVISTA DE CIENCIAS FARMACEUTICAS (BL/0101-3793) [09359696] **4328**

REVISTA DE CIENCIAS HISTORICAS : [PUBLICACAO DO DEPARTAMENTO DE CIENCIAS HISTORICAS DA UNIVERSIDADE PORTUCALENSE] (PO/0871-2352) [18048237] **2705**

REVISTA DE CIENCIAS HUMANAS (BL) [09725560] **5216**

● REVISTA DE CIENCIAS HUMANAS : REVISTA DA UFPR (BL/0104-0111) [27823410] 329, **2853**

REVISTA DE CIENCIAS MATEMATICAS (MZ/1010-5980) [03887036] **3531**

REVISTA DE CIENCIAS PENALES (CL) [06367539] **3175**

REVISTA DE CIENCIAS SOCIAIS (BL/0303-9862) [02161411] **5216**

REVISTA DE CIENCIAS SOCIALES (UY) [17218002] **5216**

REVISTA DE CIENCIAS SOCIALES (RIO PIEDRAS, P.R.) (PR/0034-7817) [01763885] **5216**

REVISTA DE CIENCIAS SOCIALES (SAN JOSE) (CR/0482-5276) [01387827] **5216**

REVISTA DE CIENCIAS SOCIALES (UNIVERSIDAD DE VALPARAISO. FACULTAD DE CIENCIAS JURIDICAS, ECONOMICAS Y SOCIALES) (CL) [09301692] 5216, **3040**

REVISTA DE CONTROL FISCAL (VE) [02177497] **4747**

REVISTA DE COSTA RICA (CR) [02255884] **2757**

REVISTA DE CRITICA LITERARIA LATINOAMERICANA (PE/0252-8843) [02276527] **3351**

REVISTA DE CULTURA BRASILENA (SP/0034-785X) [01781382] **329**

REVISTA DE CULTURA VOZES *See* VOZES CULTURA **5225**

REVISTA DE DERECHO (EC) [02239794] **3040**

REVISTA DE DERECHO ADMINISTRATIVO (AG/0327-2265) [24149210] **3040**

REVISTA DE DERECHO AMBIENTAL (SP/0214-4042) [02144042] **3040**

REVISTA DE DERECHO COMERCIAL *See* REVISTA DE DERECHO COMERCIAL Y DE LA EMPRESA **3102**

REVISTA DE DERECHO COMERCIAL Y DE LA EMPRESA (UY) [04403065] **3102**

REVISTA DE DERECHO ECONOMICO (CL) [07129761] **1518**

REVISTA DE DERECHO FINANCIERO Y DE HACIENDA PUBLICA (SP) [06685066] 4747, **3040**

REVISTA DE DERECHO, JURISPRUDENCIA Y CIENCIAS SOCIALES Y GACETA DE LOS TRIBUNALES *See* REVISTA DE DERECHO Y JURISPRUDENCIA Y GACETA DE LOS TRIBUNALES. (1979) **3041**

REVISTA DE DERECHO MERCANTIL (SP) [01763892] **3102**

REVISTA DE DERECHO PENAL (FUNDACION DE CULTURA UNIVERSITARIA) (SP) [08224896] **3108**

REVISTA DE DERECHO POLITICO (SP/0210-7562) [09117583] **3094**

REVISTA DE DERECHO PRIVADO (CARACAS, VENEZUELA) (VE) [11451680] **3091**

REVISTA DE DERECHO PRIVADO; PUBLICACION MENSUAL PARA EL ESTUDIO DE LAS CUESTIONES PRACTICAS DEL DERECHO ESPANOL, CIVIL, MERCANTIL, ETC (SP) [01763893] **3040**

REVISTA DE DERECHO PROCESAL (CL) [02350333] **3040**

REVISTA DE DERECHO PROCESAL IBEROAMERICANA (SP) [01763894] **3040**

● REVISTA DE DERECHO PUBLICO (UY) [26487481] **3040**

REVISTA DE DERECHO PUBLICO (VE) [12573044] **3040**

REVISTA DE DERECHO PUERTORRIQUENO (PR/0034-7930) [01763895] **3040**

REVISTA DE DERECHO URBANISTICO (SP) **3041**

REVISTA DE DERECHO Y CIENCIAS POLITICAS (PE/0034-7949) [01326267] 4494, **3041**

REVISTA DE DERECHO Y JURISPRUDENCIA (PY) [06767883] **3041**

REVISTA DE DERECHO Y JURISPRUDENCIA Y GACETA DE LOS TRIBUNALES. (1979) (CL) [09843393] **3041**

REVISTA DE DERECHO Y JURISPRUDENCIA Y GACETA DE LOS TRIBUNALES (1981) (CL) **3041**

REVISTA DE DIAGNOSTICO BIOLOGICO (SP/0034-7973) [I00347973] **471**

REVISTA DE DIALECTOLOGIA Y TRADICIONES AND POULARES (SP/0034-7981) [01763898] **2324**

REVISTA DE DIALECTOLOGIA Y TRADICIONES POPULARES (SP/0034-7981) [09244636] 3315, **2324**

REVISTA DE DIREITO AGRARIO (BL) [01791672] 129, **3041**

REVISTA DE DIREITO CIVIL (BL) [04327617] **3091**

REVISTA DE DIREITO DA PROCURADORIA-GERAL DA JUSTICA DO ESTADO DO RIO DE JANEIRO (BL) [02687117] **3041**

REVISTA DE DIREITO DO COMERCIO DAS RELACOES INTERNACIONAIS (BL) [25266754] 850, **3135**

REVISTA DE DIREITO DO TRABALHO (SAO PAULO) (BL/0102-8774) [02744483] **3153**

REVISTA DE DIREITO MUNICIPAL (BL) [06780819] **3041**

REVISTA DE DIREITO PUBLICO (BL/0034-8015) [06272944] **3041**

REVISTA DE DIVULGACAO CULTURAL / FURB (BL) [10156808] **2757**

REVISTA DE DOCUMENTACAO DE ESTUDOS EM LINGUISTICA TEORICA E APLICADA (BL/0102-4450) [17554326] **3315**

REVISTA DE DOUTRINA E JURISPRUDENCIA / TRIBUNAL DE JUSTICA DO DISTRITO FEDERAL E DOS TERRITORIOS (BL/0101-8868) [10327614] **3041**

REVISTA DE ECONOMIA E FINANCAS (BL) [07110513] **4747**

REVISTA DE ECONOMIA E SOCIOLOGIA RURAL / SOCIEDADE BRASILEIRA DE ECONOMIA E SOCIOLOGIA RURAL (BL) [20396960] **129**

REVISTA DE ECONOMIA POLITICA (CENTRO DE ECONOMIA POLITICA (SAO PAULO, BRAZIL) (BL/0101-3157) [07727267] **1518**

REVISTA DE EDUCACION (CL) [02266994] **1780**

REVISTA DE EDUCACION (SPAIN. MINISTERIO DE EDUCACION NACIONAL) (SP/0034-8082) [02291860] **1780**

REVISTA DE ESPIRITUALIDAD (SP/0034-8147) [01639624] **5035**

REVISTA DE ESTETICA (AG) [12071113] **329**

REVISTA DE ESTUDIOS COLOMBIANOS Y LATINOAMERICANOS / ASOCIACION DE COLOMBIANISTAS NORTEAMERICANOS (US) [26023155] **3430**

REVISTA DE ESTUDIOS DE JUVENTUD (SP/0211-4364) [16397004] **1068**

REVISTA DE ESTUDIOS DEL PACIFICO (CL) [01785318] **1582**

REVISTA DE ESTUDIOS EXTREMENOS (SP/0210-2854) [02157699] **2705**

REVISTA DE ESTUDIOS FRANCISCANOS *See* ESTUDIOS FRANCISCANOS **5327**

REVISTA DE ESTUDIOS HISPANICOS (RIO PIEDRAS, P.R.) (PR/0378-7974) [00998931] 3430, **3315**

REVISTA DE ESTUDIOS HISPANICOS (UNIVERSITY, AL.) (US/0034-818X) [01586909] 3430, **3315**

REVISTA DE ESTUDIOS HISTORICO-JURIDICOS (CL/0716-5455) [02969768] 2627, **3041**

REVISTA DE ESTUDIOS HISTORICOS DE LA GUARDIA CIVIL (SP/0210-038X) [I0210038X] **2627**

REVISTA DE ESTUDIOS PENITENCIARIOS (1961) **CEASED.** (SP/0210-6035) [10521547] **3175**

REVISTA DE ESTUDIOS POLITICOS (SP/0048-7694) [01589742] **4494**

REVISTA DE ESTUDIOS REGIONALES (SP/0213-7585) [07627322] **5216**

REVISTA DE ESTUDIOS SINDICALES (SP) [02270865] **1708**

REVISTA DE ESTUDIOS SOCIALES (MADRID, SPAIN) (SP/0303-9889) [02267001] **5256**

REVISTA DE ESTUDOS DE ADMINISTRACAO (BL) [02649020] **885**

REVISTA DE ETNOGRAFIE SI FOLCLOR (RM/0034-8198) [04744077] 2324, **244**

REVISTA DE EXTENSION AGRARIA (SP/0210-1742) [13540080] **129**

REVISTA DE FARMACIA E BIOQUIMICA BELO HORIZONTE (BL/0301-7052) [I03017052] **4328**

REVISTA DE FARMACIA E BIOQUIMICA DA UNIVERSIDADE DE SAO PAULO (BL/0370-4726) [02709880] **4328**

REVISTA DE FARMACOLOGIA CLINICA Y EXPERIMENTAL **CEASED.** (SP) [13864068] **4328**

REVISTA DE FILOLOGIA DE LA UNIVERSIDAD DE LA LAGUNA (SP) [11409043] **3315**

REVISTA DE FILOLOGIA ESPANOLA (SP/0210-9174) [01200564] **3316**

REVISTA DE FILOLOGIA ROMANICA / SECCION DE FILOLOGIA ROMANICA (SP) [11297009] 3316, **1079**

REVISTA DE FILOLOGIA Y LINGUISTICA DE LA UNIVERSIDAD DE COSTA RICA (CR) [03579288] **3316**

REVISTA DE FILOSOFIA (VE) [05111088] **4359**

REVISTA DE FILOSOFIA (CL) [07157885] **4359**

REVISTA DE FILOSOFIA (MX/0185-3481) [01881281] **4359**

REVISTA DE FILOSOFIA DE LA UNIVERSIDAD DE COSTA RICA (CR/0034-8252) [01714432] **4359**

REVISTA DE FILOSOFIA MARACAIBO (VE/0798-1171) [I07981171] **4359**

REVISTA DE FIZICA SI CHIMIE (RM) [02243903] 991, **4420**

REVISTA DE FIZICA SI CHIMIE. SERIA A **See** REVISTA DE FIZICA SI CHIMIE **4420**

REVISTA DE FIZICA SI CHIMIE. SERIA B **See** REVISTA DE FIZICA SI CHIMIE **4420**

REVISTA DE FOMENTO SOCIAL (SP/0015-6043) [I00156043] **5216**

REVISTA DE GASTROENTEROLOGIA DE MEXICO (MX/0375-0906) [01778857] **3747**

REVISTA DE GEOFISICA (SP/0034-8279) [01884584] **1410**

REVISTA DE GEOGRAFIA (SP/0048-7708) **2574**

REVISTA DE GEOGRAFIA CANARIA (SP) [20061425] **2522**

REVISTA DE GIRONA (SP/0211-2663) [07494390] **2705**

REVISTA DE GUIMARAES (PO/0871-0759) [01880863] **2705**

REVISTA DE HACIENDA AUTONOMICA Y LOCAL **See** REVISTA DE HACIENDA LOCAL **809**

REVISTA DE HACIENDA LOCAL (SP) **809**

REVISTA DE HISTORIA (NQ) [23461478] **2757**

REVISTA DE HISTORIA AMERICANA Y ARGENTINA **CEASED.** (AG/0556-5960) [04734643] **2758**

REVISTA DE HISTORIA CANARIA (SP) [01644085] **2705**

REVISTA DE HISTORIA DE AMERICA (MX/0034-8325) [01763914] **2758**

REVISTA DE HISTORIA DE LA PSICOLOGIA (SP/0211-0040) [10378665] **4616**

REVISTA DE HISTORIA DE LAS IDEAS (EC/0556-5987) [02267011] **4359**

REVISTA DE HISTORIA DE ROSARIO (AG/0556-5995) [04595680] **2758**

REVISTA DE HISTORIA DEL DERECHO (AG) [02430491] **3041**

REVISTA DE HISTORIA ECONOMICA (SP/0212-6109) [10614873] **1582**

REVISTA DE HISTORIA ECONOMICA E SOCIAL (PO) [05152915] **1582**

REVISTA DE HISTORIA (HEREDIA) (CR/1012-9790) [02659621] **2758**

REVISTA DE HISTORIA JERONIMO ZURITA (SP) [19688843] **2705**

REVISTA DE HISTORIA MILITAR (SP/0482-5748) [05698980] **4055**

REVISTA DE HISTORIA MODERNA : ANALES DE LA UNIVERSIDAD DE ALICANTE (SP) [17642641] **2705**

REVISTA DE HISTORIA NAVAL (SP) [10366014] **4182**

REVISTA DE HISTORIA (SAO PAULO) (BL/0034-8309) [01164118] **2627**

REVISTA DE HISTORIA UNIVERSAL (AG) [20328141] **2627**

REVISTA DE IGIENA, BACTERIOLOGIE, VIRUSOLOGIE, PARAZITOLOGIE, EPIDEMIOLOGIE, PNEUMOFTIZIOLOGIE. SERIA : IGIENA (RM/0303-8440) [01204603] **4799**

REVISTA DE INDIAS (SP/0034-8341) [01639881] **2758**

REVISTA DE INFORMACAO LEGISLATIVA (BL/0034-835X) [01377317] **3041**

REVISTA DE INFORMACION CIENTIFICA Y TECNICA CUBANA (CU) [03084869] **5148**

REVISTA DE INSTITUCIONES EUROPEAS (SP/0210-0924) [01795416] **1582**

REVISTA DE INTERLINGUA (SZ) [08467067] **3316**

REVISTA DE INTERPRETACAO BIBLICA LATINO-AMERICANA : RIBLA (CR) [22690505] **5019**

REVISTA DE INTERPRETACION BIBLICA LATINOAMERICANA : RIBLA (CR/1018-5763) [19054396] **5019**

REVISTA DE INVESTIGACION (PE) [01786654] **5035**

REVISTA DE INVESTIGACION CLINICA (MX/0034-8376) [01763918] **3801**

REVISTA DE INVESTIGACION Y DESARROLLO PESQUERO (AG/0325-6375) [07251484] **2312**

REVISTA DE INVESTIGACIONES HISTORICAS / SEMINARIO DE HISTORIA (MX) [08567838] **2758**

REVISTA DE INVESTIGACIONES JURIDICAS (MX) [04956127] **3041**

REVISTA DE INVESTIGACIONES MARINAS (CU/0252-1962) [07557742] **557**

REVISTA DE ISTORIE SI TEORIE LITERARA (RM/0034-8392) [01884479] **3351**

REVISTA DE ISTORIE SI TEORIE LITERARA. SUPLIMENT (RM) [19419364] **3430**

REVISTA DE JURISPRUDENCIA DO TRIBUNAL DE JUSTICA DE MATO GROSSO DO SUL / RESPONSABILIDADE DE COMISSAO TECNICA PERMANENTE DE BIBLIOTECA E PUBLICACOES (BL) [07106104] **3041**

REVISTA DE JURISPRUDENCIA FISCAL (PE) [07600854] 4747, **3041**

REVISTA DE JURISPRUDENCIA Y DOCTRINA (UY) [10639760] **3041**

REVISTA DE LA ACADEMIA CANARIA DE CIENCIAS (SP/1130-4723) [11304723] **5148**

REVISTA DE LA ACADEMIA COLOMBIANA DE HISTORIA ECLESIASTICA (CK/0120-8268) [05178507] **2758**

REVISTA DE LA ACADEMIA DE CIENCIAS EXACTAS, FISICO-QUIMICAS Y NATURALES DE ZARAGOZA (SP/0370-3207) [03459967] **5148**

REVISTA DE LA ACADEMIA HONDURENA DE GEOGRAFIA E HISTORIA (HO/1013-2163) [03510456] **2483**

REVISTA DE LA ASOCIACION ARGENTINA DE MINERALOGIA, PETROLOGIA Y SEDIMENTOLOGIA (AG/0325-0253) [06513355] 1444, **1395**

REVISTA DE LA ASOCIACION BIOQUIMICA ARGENTINA (AG/0004-4768) [04879540] **493**

REVISTA DE LA ASOCIACION CASTELLANA DE APARATO DIGESTIVO (SP/0213-1463) [I02131463] **3801**

REVISTA DE LA ASOCIACION CASTELLANA DE APARATO DIGESTIVO (SP) **3635**

REVISTA DE LA ASOCIACION ESPANOLA DE A.T.S. EN UROLOGIA (SP) **3993**

REVISTA DE LA ASOCIACION ESPANOLA DE FARMACEUTICOS DE HOSPITALES (SP/0210-6329) [18307060] **4328**

REVISTA DE LA ASOCIACION ESPANOLA DE NEUROPSIQUIATRIA (SP/0211-5735) [26146657] **3935**

REVISTA DE LA ASOCIACION ODONTOLOGICA ARGENTINA (AG/0004-4881) [01514475] **1334**

REVISTA DE LA BIBLIOTECA, ARCHIVO Y MUSEO DEL AYUNTAMIENTO DE MADRID (SP) [05044330] 4095, **3246**

REVISTA DE LA BIBLIOTECA NACIONAL **See** DESLINDES : REVISTA DE LA BIBLIOTECA NACIONAL **3380**

REVISTA DE LA BIBLIOTECA NACIONAL JOSE MARTI (CU/0006-1727) [02454556] **423**

REVISTA DE LA BIBLIOTECA NACIONAL JOSE MARTI (CU) [01751866] 3430, **3246**

REVISTA DE LA CAMARA DE AGRICULTURA DE LA PRIMERA ZONA. ANO (EC) [01643945] **129**

REVISTA DE LA CEPAL (CL) [03113531] **1582**

REVISTA DE LA CORTE ESPANOLA DE ARBITRAJE (SP) [20288651] **3041**

● REVISTA DE LA DIRECCION DE EDUCACION (UY/0797-6275) [28307103] **1780**

REVISTA DE LA ECONOMIA SOCIAL Y DE LA EMPRESA (SP/1130-9121) [I11309121] **1518**

REVISTA DE LA EDUCACION SUPERIOR (MX) [02243059] **1846**

REVISTA DE LA ESCUELA DE DERECHO **See** REVISTA DE LA FACULTAD DE DERECHO **3041**

REVISTA DE LA ESCUELA DE DERECHO Y CIENCIAS SOCIALES (MX) [02394008] **3041**

REVISTA DE LA FACULTAD DE AGRONOMIA **SUSPENDED.** (VE/0041-8285) [01489269] **129**

REVISTA DE LA FACULTAD DE AGRONOMIA. ALCANCE **See** REVISTA DE LA FACULTAD DE AGRONOMIA DE LA UNIVERSIDAD CENTRAL DE VENEZUELA. ALCANCE **129**

REVISTA DE LA FACULTAD DE AGRONOMIA DE LA UNIVERSIDAD CENTRAL DE VENEZUELA. ALCANCE (VE/0376-0030) [14877585] **129**

REVISTA DE LA FACULTAD DE AGRONOMIA / FACULTAD DE AGRONOMIA, UNIVERSIDAD DE BUENOS AIRES (AG/0325-9250) [12685250] **129**

REVISTA DE LA FACULTAD DE CIENCIAS AGRARIAS, UNIVERSIDAD NACIONAL DE CUYO (AG/0370-4661) [I03704661] **129**

REVISTA DE LA FACULTAD DE CIENCIAS ECONOMICAS (AG) [02410209] **1595**

REVISTA DE LA FACULTAD DE CIENCIAS JURIDICAS Y POLITICAS (VE) [08001146] 4494, **3041**

REVISTA DE LA FACULTAD DE CIENCIAS MEDICAS DE CORDOBA (AG/0014-6722) [06241493] **3635**

REVISTA DE LA FACULTAD DE CIENCIAS VETERINARIAS : ORGANO DE LA FACULTAD DE CIENCIAS VETERINARIAS (VE) [08772021] **5520**

REVISTA DE LA FACULTAD DE DERECHO (VE) [03592658] **3041**

REVISTA DE LA FACULTAD DE DERECHO (MX) [16962283] **3041**

REVISTA DE LA FACULTAD DE DERECHO DE LA UNIVERSIDAD COMPLUTENSE (SP) [04874781] **3041**

REVISTA DE LA FACULTAD DE DERECHO DE MADRID **See** REVISTA DE LA FACULTAD DE DERECHO DE LA UNIVERSIDAD COMPLUTENSE **3041**

REVISTA DE LA FACULTAD DE DERECHO DE MEXICO (MX/0185-1810) [01590837] **3041**

REVISTA DE LA FACULTAD DE DERECHO : PUBLICACION DE LA FACULTAD DE DERECHO DE LA UNIVERSIDAD NACIONAL DE ROSARIO (AG/0325-9471) [09627040] **3041**

REVISTA DE LA FACULTAD DE DERECHO (ROSARIO, ARGENTINA) **See** REVISTA DE LA FACULTAD DE DERECHO : PUBLICACION DE LA FACULTAD DE DERECHO DE LA UNIVERSIDAD NACIONAL DE ROSARIO **3041**

REVISTA DE LA FACULTAD DE FARMACIA (VE/0041-8307) [03829183] **4328**

REVISTA DE LA FACULTAD NACIONAL DE SALUD PUBLICA (CK/0120-386X) [12644743] **4799**

REVISTA DE LA FEDERACION MEXICANA DE QUIMICOS Y TECNICOS DEL CUERO (MX) [08646924] **3185**

REVISTA DE LA IMAGEN Y EL SONIDO: EIKONOS (SP) [03462455] **4376**

REVISTA DE LA INTEGRACION Y EL DESARROLLO DE CENTROAMERICA (HO/0252-8762) [03686119] **1518**

REVISTA DE LA JUNTA DE ESTUDIOS HISTORICOS DE MENDOZA (AG/0076-6380) [01782315] **4171**

REVISTA DE LA MEDICINA TRADICIONAL CHINA (SP/1130-4405) [I11304405] **3635**

REVISTA DE LA REAL ACADEMIA DE CIENCIAS EXACTAS, FISICAS Y NATURALES DE MADRID (SP/0034-0596) [01460615] **5148**

REVISTA DE LA REAL ACADEMIA DE FARMACIA DE BARCELONA (SP/0375-9709) [I03759709] **4328**

REVISTA — Alphabetical Title Index

REVISTA DE LA REAL ACADEMIA DE MEDICINA DE BARCELONA (SP) **3635**

REVISTA DE LA SANIDAD DE LA POLICIA NACIONAL DEL PERU (PE/1018-6212) [I10186212] **4799**

REVISTA DE LA SANIDAD DE LAS FUERZAS POLICIALES (PE/0254-3435) [08502567] **3635**

REVISTA DE LA SOCIEDAD ANDALUZA DE PATOLOGIA DIGESTIVA (SP) **3897**

REVISTA DE LA SOCIEDAD ANDALUZA DE TRAUMATOLOGIA Y ORTOPEDIA (SP/0212-0771) [18307300] **3635**

REVISTA DE LA SOCIEDAD BOLIVARIANA (VE/0798-0019) [02992853] **2758**

REVISTA DE LA SOCIEDAD BOLIVIANA DE HISTORIA NATURAL (BO) [02241330] **4171**

REVISTA DE LA SOCIEDAD CIENTIFICA DEL PARAGUAY (PY/0379-9123) [02554619] **5148**

REVISTA DE LA SOCIEDAD COLOMBIANA DE ENDOCRINOLOGIA (CK/0120-1182) [07373124] **3733**

REVISTA DE LA SOCIEDAD CUBANA DE HISTORIA DE LA MEDICINA (CU/0037-847X) [07098738] **3635**

REVISTA DE LA SOCIEDAD DE OBSTETRICIA Y GINECOLOGIA DE BUENOS AIRES (AG/0037-8542) [I00378542] **3768**

REVISTA DE LA SOCIEDAD ENTOMOLOGICA ARGENTINA (AG/0373-5680) [01765729] **5596**

REVISTA DE LA SOCIEDAD ESPANOLA DE DIALISIS Y TRANSPLANTE *SUSPENDED*. (SP/0210-3451) [06128933] **3635**

REVISTA DE LA SOCIEDAD ESPANOLA DE NUTRICION PARENTERAL Y ENTERAL (SP) **4198**

REVISTA DE LA SOCIEDAD ESPANOLA DE QUIMICA CLINICA (SP/0213-8514) [20351017] **1018**

REVISTA DE LA SOCIEDAD MEDICO-QUIRURGICA DEL HOSPITAL DE EMERGENCIA "PEREZ DE LEON." (VE/0378-1852) [02125815] **3973**

REVISTA DE LA SOCIEDAD MEXICANA DE LEPIDOPTEROLOGIA (MX) [02477279] **5596**

REVISTA DE LA SOCIEDAD QUIMICA DE MEXICO (MX/0583-7693) [02753875] **991**

REVISTA DE LA UNACH / UNIVERSIDAD AUTONOMA DE CHIAPAS (MX) [16755776] **2272**

REVISTA DE LA UNION MATEMATICA ARGENTINA (1968) (AG/0041-6932) [01473532] **3531**

REVISTA DE LA UNIVERSIDAD AUTONOMA DE YUCATAN (MX) [12677795] **2853**

REVISTA DE LA UNIVERSIDAD CATOLICA DE LA PLATA (AG) [07816521] **1846**

REVISTA DE LA UNIVERSIDAD DE MEXICO (MX) [01715145] **1846**

REVISTA DE LA UNIVERSIDAD DE SAN CARLOS / USAC (GT) [16977927] **3430**

REVISTA DE LA UNIVERSIDAD NACIONAL DE RIO CUARTO (AG/0325-9587) [10208872] **5216**

REVISTA DE LA UNIVERSIDAD NACIONAL DEL CENTRO DE LA PROVINCIA DE BUENOS AIRES (AG) [03903729] **2552**

REVISTA DE LA UNIVERSIDAD POLITECNICA DE PUERTO RICO (PR) [24609097] **5148**

REVISTA DE LENGUA Y LITERATURA CATALANA, GALLEGA Y VASCA (SP/1130-8508) [111308508] **3316**

REVISTA DE LENGUAS EXTRANJERAS (AG) [05347309] **3316**

REVISTA DE LETRAS (FORTALEZA) (BL/0101-8051) [10630620] **3351**

REVISTA DE LETRAS (MARILIA) (BL/0101-3505) [01884268] **3316**

REVISTA DE LIBRERIA ANTIQUARIA (SP) [08256790] 4832, **3246**

REVISTA DE LITERATURA (SP/0034-849X) [01198143] 3430, **3459**

REVISTA DE LITERATURA CUBANA *SUSPENDED*. (CU) [09634896] **3351**

REVISTA DE LITERATURA HISPANOAMERICANA *SUSPENDED*. (VE) [01716222] **3430**

REVISTA DE LITERATURAS MODERNAS *SUSPENDED*. (AG/0556-6134) [01775058] **3430**

REVISTA DE LLENGUA I DRET (SP/0212-5056) [18095476] 3316, **1079**

REVISTA DE LOGOPEDIA, FONIATRIA Y AUDIOLOGIA / ASOCIACION ESPANOLA DE LOGOPEDIA, FONIATRIA Y AUDIOLOGIA (SP) [14508816] **3891**

REVISTA DE LOS CREA (AG/0325-9846) [03663507] **129**

REVISTA DE MARINA (CL/0034-8511) [07165899] **4055**

REVISTA DE MARINHA (PO) [06677968] **4182**

REVISTA DE MATEMATICA E ESTATISTICA / UNIVERSIDADE ESTADUAL PAULISTA (BL/0102-0811) [14346536] **3531**

REVISTA DE MATEMATICAS APLICADAS (CL/0716-5803) [I07165803] **3531**

REVISTA DE MEDICINA DE LA UNIVERSIDAD DE NAVARRA (SP/0556-6177) [01644425] **3973**

REVISTA DE MEDICINA GERIATRICA (SP) **3755**

REVISTA DE MEDICINA INTERNA, NEUROLOGIE, PSIHIATRIE, NEUROCHIRURGIE, DERMATO-VENEROLOGIE. DERMATO-VENEROLOGIE (RM/0377-4988) [01664157] **3635**

REVISTA DE MEDICINA-INTERNA, NEUROLOGIE, PSIHIATRIE, NEUROCHIRURGIE, DERMATO-VENEROLOGIE. NEUROLOGIE, PSIHIATRIE, NEUROCHIRURGIE (RM/0377-497X) [01284567] 3845, **3935**

REVISTA DE MEDICINA INTERNA, NEUROLOGIE, PSYHIATRIE, NEUROCHIRURGIE, DERMATO-VENERALOGIE. MEDICINA INTERNA *See* MEDICINA INTERNA (BUCHAREST, ROMANIA : 1991) **3799**

REVISTA DE MEDICINA VETERINARIA (AG/0325-6391) [01588492] **5520**

REVISTA DE METALURGIA (MADRID) (SP/0034-8570) [01799341] **4018**

REVISTA DE MICROBIOLOGIA (BL/0001-3714) [02409321] **569**

REVISTA DE MUSICA LATINOAMERICANA (US/0163-0350) [04287713] **4149**

REVISTA DE MUSICOLOGIA / SOCIEDAD ESPANOLA DE MUSICOLOGIA (SP) [07056859] **4150**

REVISTA DE NEFROLOGIA, DIALISIS Y TRANSPLANTE : PUBLICACION CONJUNTA DE LA ASOCIACION REGIONAL DE DIALISIS Y TRASPLANTES RENALES DE CAPITAL FEDERAL Y PROVINCIA DE BUENOS AIRES Y LA SOCIEDAD ARGENTINA DE NEFROLOGIA (AG/0326-3428) [24034643] 3973, **3635**

REVISTA DE NEURO-PSIQUIATRIA (PE/0034-8597) [01778860] 3936, **3845**

REVISTA DE NEUROLOGIA (SP/0210-0010) [03259542] **3845**

REVISTA DE OBRAS PUBLICAS (SP/0034-8619) [05373355] **2030**

REVISTA DE OCCIDENTE (SP/0034-8635) [06407611] **3351**

REVISTA DE ODONTOLOGIA DA UNESP (BL/0101-1774) [10037565] **1334**

REVISTA DE ODONTOLOGIA DA UNIVERSIDADE DE SAO PAULO (BL/0103-0663) [19021850] **1334**

REVISTA DE ORIENTE (PR) [04760782] **2508**

REVISTA DE ORTOPEDIA Y TRAUMATOLOGIA (SP/0482-5985) [01780349] **3884**

REVISTA DE PASTORAL JUVENIL (SP) **5035**

REVISTA DE PATOLOGIA TROPICAL (BL/0301-0406) [10283125] **3986**

REVISTA DE PEDAGOGIA (DR) [05805897] **1780**

REVISTA DE PEDAGOGIA (SANTO DOMINGO, DOMINICAN REPUBLIC) *See* REVISTA DE PEDAGOGIA **1780**

REVISTA DE PEDAGOGIE (RM) [02139616] **1780**

REVISTA DE PEDIATRIA PREVENTIVA E SOCIALE. NIPIOLOGIA (IT/0392-4416) [07798382] **3911**

REVISTA DE PEDIATRIE, OBSTETRICA SI GINECOLOGIE. OBSTETRICA SI GINECOLOGIE (RM/0377-4961) [01847383] **3768**

REVISTA DE PLANEACION Y DESARROLLO *See* PLANEACION & DESARROLLO **1578**

REVISTA DE PLASTICOS MODERNOS (SP/0034-8708) [02450169] **4460**

REVISTA DE POESIA E CRITICA (BL) [03529762] **3470**

REVISTA DE POLITICA COMPARADA (SP/0211-5581) [08482864] **4494**

REVISTA DE POLITICA INTERNACIONAL (SP/0034-8716) [01881179] **4494**

REVISTA DE POLITICA SOCIAL (SP/0034-8724) [01714642] **5216**

REVISTA DE PRE-HISTORIA (BL) [07290457] **2758**

REVISTA DE PREVENCION (SP/0034-8732) [10260000] **4799**

REVISTA DE PREVIDENCIA SOCIAL (BL) [07798881] **5306**

REVISTA DE PROCESSO (BL) [02744504] **3091**

REVISTA DE PROTECCION VEGETAL (CU/1010-2752) [I10102752] 2356, **185**

REVISTA DE PSICOANALYSIS (AG/0034-8740) [02567936] **4616**

REVISTA DE PSICOLOGIA (FORTALEZA, BRAZIL) (BL) [11395484] **4616**

REVISTA DE PSICOLOGIA GENERAL Y APLICADA (SP/0373-2002) [01874040] **4616**

REVISTA DE PSICOLOGIA SOCIAL (SP/0213-4748) [I02134748] **4616**

REVISTA DE PSICOLOGIA SOCIAL Y PERSONALIDAD (MX) [18352746] **4616**

REVISTA DE PSICOTERAPIA PSICOANALITICA (UY/0255-8327) [I02558327] **4616**

REVISTA DE PSIHOLOGIE (RM/0034-8759) [02924276] **4616**

REVISTA DE PSIQUIATRIA CLINICA DEL DEPARTAMENTO DE PSIQUIATRIA Y SALUD MENTAL, DIVISION DE CIENCIAS MEDICAS NORTE, FACULTAD DE MEDICINA, UNIVERSIDAD DE CHILE (CL/0716-1220) [24034594] **3936**

REVISTA DE PSIQUIATRIA DE LA FACULTAD DE MEDICINA DE BARCELONA (SP/0210-1793) [20051506] **3936**

REVISTA DE PSIQUIATRIA Y PSICOLOGIA MEDICA DE EUROPA Y AMERICA LATINAS *CEASED*. (SP) 4616, **3936**

REVISTA DE QUIMICA E FARMACIA RIO DE JANEIRO (BL/0370-6907) [I03706907] **4328**

REVISTA DE QUIMICA INDUSTRIAL (BL/0370-694X) [02450170] **1018**

REVISTA DE QUIMICA TEXTIL (SP/0300-3418) [01426396] **5355**

REVISTA DE REVISTAS; EL SEMANARIO NACIONAL (MX) [02682804] **2492**

REVISTA DE REVISTAS : SEMENARIO DE EXCELSIOR (MX) [04289310] **2544**

REVISTA DE ROBOTICA (SP/0212-3754) [I02123754] **2128**

REVISTA DE SALUD ANIMAL (CU/0253-570X) [07267384] **4799**

REVISTA DE SALUD PUBLICA DE CASTILLA Y LEON (SP) **4799**

REVISTA DE SANIDAD E HIGIENE PUBLICA (SP/0034-8899) [01607193] **4799**

REVISTA DE SANIDAD MILITAR (SP) [01794708] 4055, **3635**

REVISTA DE SAUDE PUBLICA (BL/0034-8910) [01586554] **4799**

REVISTA DE SEGURANCA & I.E. E PREVENCAO (BL) [02880629] **2869**

REVISTA DE SEGURIDAD SOCIAL (SP) [07040011] **5306**

REVISTA DE SENOLOGIA Y PATOLOGIA MAMARIA (SP) **3897**

REVISTA DE SERVICIOS SOCIALES Y POLITICA SOCIAL (SP) **5216**

REVISTA DE SOLDADURA (SP/0048-7759) [I00487759] **4027**

REVISTA DE TEATRO (BL/0034-8953) [05394952] **5368**

REVISTA DE TOXICOLOGIA (SP/0212-7113) [22887293] **3983**

REVISTA DE TRABAJO (MADRID) (SP/0034-897X) [05821302] **1708**

REVISTA DE TRABAJO Y SEGURIDAD SOCIAL (CK) [02245802] **1708**

REVISTA DEL ARCHIVO GENERAL DE LA NACION (LIMA) (PE/0259-2371) [01796583] **2483**

REVISTA DEL ARCHIVO HISTORICO DEL CUZCO (PE/0590-4609) [05461853] **2758**

REVISTA DEL ARCHIVO HISTORICO DEL GUAYAS (EC) [02242923] 2758, **2483**

REVISTA DEL ARCHIVO NACIONAL (CR/0034-9003) [03998357] 2758, **2483**

REVISTA DEL ARCHIVO NACIONAL (CK) [04367195] **2483**

REVISTA DEL ARCHIVO NACIONAL (SAN JOSE) (CR/0034-9003) [02255654] **2758**

REVISTA DEL BANCO DE LA REPUBLICA (CK/0005-4828) [02052647] **810**

REVISTA DEL CENTRO DE ESTUDIOS CONSTITUCIONALES (SP/0214-6185) [22966605] **3094**

REVISTA DEL CENTRO DE ESTUDIOS GENEALOGICOS DE BUENOS AIRES (AG) [05351475] **2470**

REVISTA DEL CENTRO NACIONAL DE INVESTIGACIONES GENEALOGICAS Y ANTROPOLOGICAS. SECCION GENEALOGIA (EC) [10615820] **2470**

REVISTA DEL DERECHO COMERCIAL Y DE LAS OBLIGACIONES (AG/0556-6428) [01763944] **3102**

REVISTA DEL DERECHO INDUSTRIAL (AG/0326-0763) [06461124] 1308, **3041**

Alphabetical Title Index

REVISTA

REVISTA DEL ESTUDIANTE UNIVERSITARIO LATINOAMERICANO (CL) [25117046] **1780**

REVISTA DEL FORO (PE) [01623576] **3041**

REVISTA DEL HOSPITAL DE NINOS (BUENOS AIRES) (AG/0521-517X) [06412843] **3911**

REVISTA DEL HOSPITAL PSIQUIATRICO DE LA HABANA (CU/0440-436X) [02628430] **3936**

REVISTA DEL IDIEM (CL/0034-9069) [I00349089] **1994**

REVISTA DEL INSTITUTO COLOMBIANO DE DERECHO PROCESAL (CK) [11838508] **3041**

REVISTA DEL INSTITUTO DE CULTURA PUERTORRIQUENA (PR/0020-3815) [01933454] **2758**

REVISTA DEL INSTITUTO DE ESTUDIOS ECONOMICOS (SP) [14983030] **1518**

REVISTA DEL INSTITUTO DE ESTUDIOS HISTORICO-MARITIMOS DEL PERU (PE) [05325002] **2758**

REVISTA DEL INSTITUTO DE ESTUDIOS ISLAMICOS (SP) **5044**

REVISTA DEL INSTITUTO DE HISTORIA DEL DERECHO RICARDO LEVENE (AG/0325-061X) [01537622] **3041**

REVISTA DEL INSTITUTO DE LA JUVENTUD (SP) [01796199] **1068**

REVISTA DEL INSTITUTO EGIPCIO DE ESTUDIOS ISLAMICOS EN MADRID (SP/0541-8585) [08619054] **2705**

REVISTA DEL INSTITUTO GENEALOGICO E HISTORICO LATINOAMERICANO (US/8755-3384) [11283984] **2470**

REVISTA DEL INSTITUTO JUAN CESAR GARCIA (EC) [25643191] **4800**

REVISTA DEL INSTITUTO MEXICANO DEL PETROLEO (MX/0538-1428) [01571069] **4277**

REVISTA DEL INSTITUTO NACIONAL DE CANCEROLOGIA (MX/0076-7131) [10262598] **3823**

REVISTA DEL INSTITUTO NACIONAL DE MEDICINA LEGAL DE COLOMBIA (CK/0120-0097) [03977601] **3742**

REVISTA DEL INSTITUTO URUGUAYO DE DERECHO PENAL (UY) [08256933] **3108**

REVISTA DEL JARDIN BOTANICO NACIONAL (CU/0253-5696) [0798093C] **526**

REVISTA DEL MEXICO AGRARIO (MX/0034-9097) [02267039] **129**

REVISTA DEL MINISTERIO DE JUSTICIA (VE/0506-5798) [03078732] **3041**

REVISTA DEL MINISTERIO PUBLICO : ORGANO DE DIVULGACION DEL MINISTERIO PUBLICO DE LA REPUBLICA DE VENEZUELA (VE) [09204556] **3042**

REVISTA DEL MUSEO ARGENTINO DE CIENCIAS NATURALES "BERNARDINO RIVADAVIA" E INSTITUTO NACIONAL DE INVESTIGACI,ON DE LAS CIENCIAS NATURALES. BOTANICA (AG/0376-2793) [03806781] **526**

REVISTA DEL MUSEO DE LA PLATA. SECCION ZOOLOGIA (AG/0372-4638) [06162070] 5596, **4095**

REVISTA DEL MUSEO HISTORICO REGIONAL (PE) [05283963] **4095**

REVISTA DEL MUSEO NACIONAL (LIMA) *SUSPENDED.* (PE/0304-2367) [01755923] 280, **244**

REVISTA DEL PENSAMIENTO CENTROAMERICANO (NQ/0378-3340) [01785539] **2512**

REVISTA DEL PODER JUDICIAL DEL ESTADO DE TLAXCALA (MX) [04781704] **3042**

REVISTA DEL SINASBI (VE) [05366880] **3246**

REVISTA DEL TRIBUNAL FISCAL DEL ESTADO DE MEXICO (MX) [07382090] **4747**

REVISTA DESARROLLO (SP) **5216**

REVISTA DI METEOROLOGIA AERONAUTICA (IT/0035-6328) [06363410] **1434**

REVISTA DIFUSION FISCAL (MX) [04083258] **4747**

REVISTA DIPLOMATICA E INTERNACIONAL (BO) [02240863] **3135**

REVISTA DO BRASIL (PO) [04575671] **2758**

REVISTA DO BRASIL (RIO DE JANEIRO, BRAZIL : 1984) (BL) [10892984] **2552**

REVISTA DO CENTRO DE ARTES E LETRAS / UNIVERSIDADE FEDERAL DE SANTA MARIA, CENTRO DE ARTES E LETRAS (BL) [09961996] **329**

REVISTA DO CENTRO DE CIENCIAS RURAIS (BL/0085-5901) [02477833] **129**

REVISTA DO CENTRO DE ESTUDOS DEMOGRAFICOS (PO/0079-4082) [06577203] **4560**

REVISTA DO COLEGIO BRASILEIRO DE CIRURGIOES (BL/0100-6991) [04677539] **3973**

REVISTA DO DER PERNAMBUCO (BL) [03276974] **5443**

REVISTA DO FRIO (BL) [01788512] **2608**

REVISTA DO GAS (BL) [01799197] **4277**

REVISTA DO HCPA & FACULDADE DE MEDICINA DA UNIVERSIDADE FEDERAL DO RIO GRANDE DO SUL (BL/0101-5575) [I01015575] **3635**

REVISTA DO HOSPITAL DAS CLINICAS (BL/0041-8781) [01763948] **3635**

REVISTA DO HOSPITAL DE EGAS MONIZ (PO) [19475509] **3635**

REVISTA DO INSTITUTO ADOLFO LUTZ (BL/0073-9855) [05159607] **4800**

REVISTA DO INSTITUTO DE ANTIBIOTICOS (BL) [06468965] **4328**

REVISTA DO INSTITUTO DE DIREITO DA ENERGIA (BL) [02410032] **3042**

REVISTA DO INSTITUTO DE ESTUDOS BRASILEIROS (BL/0020-3874) [01380556] **5216**

REVISTA DO INSTITUTO DE LATICINIOS CANDIDO TOSTES (BL/0100-3674) [08413534] **2356**

REVISTA DO INSTITUTO DE MEDICINA TROPICAL DE SAO PAULO (BL/0036-4665) [01765017] **3986**

REVISTA DO INSTITUTO DOS ADVOGADOS BRASILEIROS (BL/0100-1752) [01795239] **3042**

REVISTA DO INSTITUTO FLORESTAL (BL/0103-2674) [22897819] **2394**

REVISTA DO INSTITUTO GENEALOGICO BRASILEIRO (BL) [06843626] **2470**

REVISTA DO INSTITUTO HISTORICO DE OEIRAS (BL) [10641065] **2758**

REVISTA DO INSTITUTO HISTORICO E GEOGRAFICO BRASILEIRO (BL/0101-4366) [07253615] **2552**

REVISTA DO INSTITUTO HISTORICO E GEOGRAFICO DE SAO PAULO (BL) [02409403] 2574, **2758**

REVISTA DO IRB / INSTITUTO DE RESSEGUROS DO BRASIL (BL/0019-0446) [10357109] **2892**

● REVISTA DO MASP / MUSEU DE ARTE DE SAO PAULO (BL) [26383333] **363**

● REVISTA DO MERCOSUL (BL) [28056858] **4494**

REVISTA DO MINISTERIO PUBLICO DE PERNAMBUCO (BL) [02244054] **3042**

REVISTA DO MUSICO (BL) [02241621] **4150**

REVISTA DO PATRIMONIO HISTORICO E ARTISTICO NACIONAL (BL/0102-2571) [09096350] **308**

REVISTA DO SECTOR DE CIENCIAS AGRARIAS (BL/0100-607X) [08412386] **129**

REVISTA DO TRIBUNAL DE CONTAS DO DISTRITO FEDERAL (BL) [03143382] **4747**

REVISTA DO TRIBUNAL DE CONTAS DO ESTADO DA BAHIA (BL) [03697060] **751**

REVISTA DO TRIBUNAL DE CONTAS DO ESTADO DE SAO PAULO: JURISPRUDENCIA E INSTRUCOES (BL) [03530993] **4747**

REVISTA DO TRIBUNAL DE CONTAS DO MUNICIPIO DO RIO DE JANEIRO (AG) [10319643] 4747, **3042**

REVISTA DO TRIBUNAL DE JUSTICA (BL) [02773413] **3042**

REVISTA DOCPOP (BL/0101-7217) [11926506] **4560**

REVISTA DOMINICANA DE ANTROPOLOGIA E HISTORIA (DR) [08019001] **2758**

REVISTA ECONOMICA DO NORDESTE (BL/0100-4956) [02241866] **1582**

REVISTA ECUATORIANA DE HIGIENE Y MEDICINA TROPICAL (EC/0048-7775) [02398513] **3986**

REVISTA ECUATORIANA DE MEDICINA Y CIENCIAS BIOLOGICAS *SUSPENDED.* (EC/0034-9313) [04597110] **3635**

REVISTA ECUATORIANA DE NEUROLOGIA (EC/1019-8113) [I10198113] **3845**

REVISTA EL MONITOR DE LA FARMACIA (SP) **4328**

REVISTA ESCOLA DE MINAS : REM (BL) [10622496] **2150**

REVISTA ESPANOLA DE ALERGOLOGIA E INMUNOLOGIA CLINICA : ORGANO OFICIAL DE LA SOCIEDAD ESPANOLA DE ALERGOLOGIA E INMUNOLOGIA CLINICA (SP/0214-1477) [26319103] **3676**

REVISTA ESPANOLA DE ANESTESIOLOGIA Y REANIMACION (SP/0034-9356) [01778128] **3684**

REVISTA ESPANOLA DE ANTROPOLOGIA AMERICANA (SP/0556-6533) [01763949] **244**

REVISTA ESPANOLA DE CARDIOLOGIA (SP/0300-8932) [02267057] **3710**

● REVISTA ESPANOLA DE CIENCIA Y TECNOLOGIA DE ALIMENTOS / EDITADA POR EL CONSEJO SUPERIOR DE INVESTIGACIONES CIENTIFICAS (SP/1131-799X) [27132659] **2356**

REVISTA ESPANOLA DE CIRUGIA CARDIACA, TORACICA Y VASCULAR *CEASED.* (SP/0211-089X) [I0211089X] **3973**

REVISTA ESPANOLA DE CIRUGIA DE LA MANO (SP/0210-2323) [I02102323] **3973**

REVISTA ESPANOLA DE CIRUGIA ORAL Y MAXILOFACIAL (SP) [24034623] **3973**

REVISTA ESPANOLA DE DEFENSA (SP) [25703770] **4055**

REVISTA ESPANOLA DE DERECHO CANONICO (SP/0034-9372) [05787040] **4993**

REVISTA ESPANOLA DE DERECHO CONSTITUCIONAL (SP/0211-5743) [08612934] **3094**

REVISTA ESPANOLA DE DERECHO INTERNACIONAL (SP/0034-9380) [01763950] **3135**

REVISTA ESPANOLA DE DOCUMENTACION CIENTIFICA (SP/0210-0614) [07578980] **3246**

REVISTA ESPANOLA DE DROGODEPENDENCIAS (SP/0213-7615) [19022211] **1348**

REVISTA ESPANOLA DE ECONOMIA (SP) [01787549] **1595**

REVISTA ESPANOLA DE ELECTRONICA (SP/0482-6396) [06742143] **2079**

REVISTA ESPANOLA DE ENFERMEDADES DIGESTIVAS (SP/1130-0108) [22257976] **3747**

REVISTA ESPANOLA DE EPILEPSIA *CEASED.* (SP/0213-4241) [I02134241] **3845**

REVISTA ESPANOLA DE ESTOMATOLOGIA (SP) **3801**

REVISTA ESPANOLA DE FINANCIACION Y CONTABILIDAD (SP) **751**

REVISTA ESPANOLA DE FISIOLOGIA (SP/0034-9402) [01763951] **586**

REVISTA ESPANOLA DE FONIATRIA (SP) [19022236] **3845**

REVISTA ESPANOLA DE GERIATRIA Y GERONTOLOGIA (SP/0211-139X) [06869221] **3755**

REVISTA ESPANOLA DE INVESTIGACIONES SOCIOLOGICAS (SP/0210-5233) [07315209] **5256**

REVISTA ESPANOLA DE LECHERIA (SP/0300-5550) [06262210] **198**

REVISTA ESPANOLA DE LINGUISTICA (SP/0210-1874) [01775062] **3316**

REVISTA ESPANOLA DE MEDICINA LEGAL (SP/0377-4732) [01388192] **3742**

REVISTA ESPANOLA DE MEDICINA NUCLEAR (SP) [06146774] **3849**

REVISTA ESPANOLA DE MEDICINA NUCLEAR. SUPLEMENTO (SP/0213-814X) [I0213814X] **3849**

REVISTA ESPANOLA DE MICROBIOLOGIA CLINICA *CEASED.* (SP/0213-4829) [26050126] **569**

REVISTA ESPANOLA DE MICROPALEONTOLOGIA (SP/0556-655X) [01763952] **4230**

REVISTA ESPANOLA DE NEUROLOGIA (SP/0213-4233) [18306902] **3845**

REVISTA ESPANOLA DE OBSTETRICIA Y GINECOLOGIA (SP/0034-9445) [01645792] **3768**

REVISTA ESPANOLA DE ORTODONCIA (SP) **1334**

REVISTA ESPANOLA DE OTO-NEURO-OFTALMOLOGIA Y NEUROCIRUGIA *CEASED.* (SP/0034-9453) [01778133] **3845**

REVISTA ESPANOLA DE PALEONTOLOGIA (SP) [17666913] **4230**

REVISTA ESPANOLA DE PEDAGOGIA (SP/0034-9461) [04442349] **1780**

REVISTA ESPANOLA DE PEDIATRIA (SP/0034-947X) [01763953] **3911**

REVISTA ESPANOLA DE QUIMIOTERAPIA : PUBLICACION OFICIAL DE LA SOCIEDAD ESPANOLA DE QUIMIOTERAPIA (SP/0214-3429) [24034627] **3823**

REVISTA ESPANOLA DE REUMATISMO Y ENFERMEDADES OSTEOARTICULARES (SP/0048-7791) [10758645] **3635**

REVISTA — Alphabetical Title Index

REVISTA ESPANOLA DE REUMATOLOGIA : ORGANO OFICIAL DE LA SOCIEDAD ESPANOLA DE REUMATOLOGIA (SP/0304-4815) [26350008] **3806**

REVISTA ESPANOLA DE TEOLOGIA (SP/0210-7112) [01884217] **4993**

REVISTA ESPANOLA ONCOLOGIA (SP/0482-640X) [06687143] **3823**

REVISTA EUROPEA DE ESTUDIOS LATINOAMERICANOS Y DEL CARIBE. EUROPEAN REVIEW OF LATIN AMERICAN AND CARIBBEAN STUDIES (NE/0924-0608) [21104781] **5216**

REVISTA EUROPEA DE ODONTO-ESTOMATOLOGIA (SP) [19808371] **1334**

REVISTA FACULTAD DE ADMINISTRACION PUBLICA Y COMERCIO (PN) [02472844] **4683**

REVISTA FACULTAD NACIONAL DE AGRONOMIA, MEDELLIN (CK/0304-2847) [01564113] **129**

REVISTA FARABUNDO MARTI (CR) [08966561] **4494**

REVISTA FARMACEUTICA DE PUERTO RICO *See* REVISTA FARMACEUTICA (SAN JUAN, P.R.) **4328**

REVISTA FARMACEUTICA (SAN JUAN, P.R.) (PR/1070-5015) [28391613] **4328**

REVISTA - FEDERACION ARGENTINA DE COLEGIOS DE ABOGADOS (AG/0430-1420) [01445960] **3042**

REVISTA FORENSE (BL) [07718289] **3042**

REVISTA FORESTAL BARACOA (CU/0138-6441) [I01386441] **2394**

REVISTA FORESTAL DEL PERU (PE) [01585873] **2394**

REVISTA FORESTAL VENEZOLANA (VE/0556-6606) [02996931] **2394**

REVISTA FOTO SL (SP) **4376**

REVISTA FRUTICOLA (CL/0716-534X) [21345072] **129**

REVISTA GALEGA DE ESTUDIOS AGRARIOS (SP) [19988427] **129**

REVISTA GALLEGA DE PATOLOGIA DIGESTIVA (SP/1131-9178) [I11319178] **3897**

REVISTA GENERAL DE DERECHO (SP) [01763954] **3042**

REVISTA GENERAL DE LEGISLACION Y JURISPRUDENCIA (SP/0210-8518) [01763955] **3042**

REVISTA GENERAL DE MARINA (MX/0188-1477) [07210103] **4182**

REVISTA GEOFISICA (MX/0252-9769) [03595022] **1410**

REVISTA GEOGRAFICA DE AMERICA CENTRAL / ESCUELA DE GEOGRAFIA, FACULTAD DE CIENCIAS DE LA TIERRA Y EL MAR (CR) [06494375] **2574**

REVISTA GEOGRAFICA DE CHILE TERRA AUSTRALIS (CL/0378-8482) [01641350] **2574**

REVISTA GEOGRAFICA DEL INSTITUTO PANAMERICANO DE GEOGRAFIA E HISTORIA (MX/0031-0581) [06923519] **2575**

REVISTA GEOGRAFICA UNIVERSAL (AG) [02400855] **2575**

REVISTA GEOGRAFICA VENEZOLANA (VE/1012-1617) [13501309] **2575**

REVISTA GEOLOGICA DE CHILE (CL/0378-6617) [03575257] **1395**

REVISTA GOIANA DE MEDICINA (BL/0034-9585) [06526675] **3636**

REVISTA GUIA REX (BL) [02239813] **2552**

REVISTA GUIA REX (BL) [04731375] **2758**

REVISTA GUIA REX (EDICAO ESPECIAL). REVISTA GUIA REX *See* REVISTA GUIA REX **2758**

REVISTA HISPANICA MODERNA (US/0034-9593) [01605271] **3430**

REVISTA HISTORICA (UY/0252-8983) [06476735] **2758**

REVISTA HISTORICA (MONTEVIDEO) (UY/0252-8983) [09711771] **2758**

REVISTA IBERICA DE MICOLOGIA (SP) [12098752] **576**

REVISTA IBERO-AMERICANA DE ORTODONICA (SP/0212-193X) [11374286] **1334**

REVISTA IBEROAMERICANA (US/0034-9631) [01763960] **3430**

REVISTA IBEROAMERICANA DE CORROSION Y PROTECCION *CEASED*. (SP/0210-6604) [10560495] **2017**

REVISTA IBEROAMERICANA DE FERTILIDAD Y REPRODUCCION HUMANA (SP) **3636**

REVISTA IBEROAMERICANA DE FERTILIDAD Y REPRODUCCION HUMANA : OORH (SP) [23968379] **3768**

REVISTA IBEROAMERICANA DE MICOLOGIA (SP/1130-1406) [I11301406] **576**

REVISTA IBEROAMERICANA DE TROMBOSIS Y HEMOSTASIA (SP) **3636**

REVISTA ICA : PUBLICACION CIENTIFICA DEL INSTITUTO COLOMBIANO AGROPECUARIO (CK) [19548517] **129**

REVISTA IDEA / INSTITUTO PARA EL DESARROLLO DE EMPRESARIOS EN LA ARGENTINA (AG) [10033999] **1582**

REVISTA IIDH / INSTITUTO INTERAMERICANO DE DERECHOS HUMANOS (CR) [14160808] **4512**

REVISTA IMPOSTO FISCAL *See* IMPOSTO FISCAL **4731**

REVISTA INDUSTRIAL DE SERGIPE (BL) [01791684] **1582**

REVISTA INDUSTRIAL Y AGRICOLA DE TUCUMAN (AG/0370-5404) [01763962] **129**

REVISTA INIDEF (VE) [03696771] **2324, 4150**

REVISTA INOVACAO (PO/0871-2221) [23107043] **1780**

REVISTA (INSTITUTO GEOGRAFICO E CADASTRAL (PORTUGAL)) (PO/0870-9351) [08491367] **2583**

REVISTA - INSTITUTO NACIONAL DE PREVIDENCIA SOCIAL. PROCURADORIA-GERAL (BL) [01788605] **5306**

REVISTA INTERAMERICANA DE BIBLIOGRAFIA (1972) (US/0020-4994) [07483363] **423**

REVISTA INTERAMERICANA DE BIBLIOTECOLOGIA / UNIVERSIDAD DE ANTIOQUIA, ESCUELA INTERAMERICANA DE BIBLIOTECOLOGIA *CEASED*. (CK/0120-0976) [04310095] **3246**

REVISTA INTERAMERICANA DE DIREITO INTELECTUAL : RIDI (BL) [07089965] **1308**

REVISTA INTERAMERICANA DE DIREITO PROCESSUAL PENAL (BL) [06742301] **3108**

REVISTA INTERAMERICANA DE PLANIFICACION (US/0185-1861) [01785552] **2834**

REVISTA INTERAMERICANA DE PSICOLOGIA (US/0034-9690) [01763963] **4616**

REVISTA INTERAMERICANA DE SOCIOLOGIA (MX/0187-8468) [02267066] **5256**

REVISTA INTERCONTINENTAL DE PSICOLOGIA Y EDUCACION (MX/0187-7690) [I01877690] **4616**

REVISTA INTERNACIONAL DE CIENCIAS ADMINISTRATIVAS (BE) [07270673] **5216**

REVISTA INTERNACIONAL DE CIENCIAS SOCIALES (SP/0379-0762) [I03790762] **5216**

REVISTA INTERNACIONAL DE CONTAMINACION AMBIENTAL (MX/0188-4999) [I01884999] **2242**

REVISTA INTERNACIONAL DE ESTUDOS AFRICANOS (PO) [11665361] **5216**

REVISTA INTERNACIONAL DE METODOS NUMERICOS PARA CALCULO Y DISENO EN INGENIERIA (SP/0213-1315) [16783940] **2099**

REVISTA INTERNACIONAL DE METODOS NUMERICOS PARA CALCULO Y DISEƑNO EN INGENIERIA (SP/0213-1315) [I02131315] **1994**

REVISTA INTERNACIONAL DE SEGURIDAD SOCIAL (AG/0250-605X) [I0250605X] **1708**

REVISTA INTERNACIONAL DE SOCIOLOGIA (SP/0034-9712) [01590269] **5256, 5216**

REVISTA INTERNACIONAL DEL TRABAJO (SZ/0378-5548) [I03785548] **1708**

REVISTA INVESTIGACION OPERACIONAL (CU) [13163728] **3531, 2099**

REVISTA ISTORICA / ACADEMIA ROMANA, INSTITUTUL DE ISTORIE "N. IORGA." (RM) [23198336] **2627**

REVISTA JAVERIANA (BOGOTA) (CK/0120-3088) [05987710] **4494, 2552**

REVISTA - JUNTA DE ESTUDIOS HISTORICOS DE ENTRE RIOS (AG) [02998847] **2758**

REVISTA JURIDICA (CU) [07720339] **3042**

REVISTA JURIDICA ARGENTINA LA LEY (AG) [02703471] **3042**

REVISTA JURIDICA (CUBA. MINISTERIO DE JUSTICIA. DEPTO. DE DIVULGACION) (CU/0864-0831) [15342128] **3042**

REVISTA JURIDICA (CURITIBA, BRAZIL) (BL) [10240069] **3042**

REVISTA JURIDICA DE CATALUNYA (SP) **3042**

REVISTA JURIDICA DE LA UNIVERSIDAD DE PUERTO RICO (PR/0886-2516) [01763967] **3042**

REVISTA JURIDICA DE LA UNIVERSIDAD INTERAMERICANA DE PUERTO RICO (PR/0041-851X) [02254903] **3042**

REVISTA JURIDICA DEL PERU *CEASED*. (PE) [01713558] **3042**

REVISTA JURIDICA DO MINISTERIO PUBLICO CATARINENSE (BL) [10339557] **3042**

REVISTA JURIDICA ESPANOLA LA LEY (SP/0211-2744) [I02112744] **5810**

REVISTA JURIDICA LEMI. EDICAO MENSAL: SAO PAULO *See* REVISTA JURIDICA LEMI. EDICAO NACIONAL **3042**

REVISTA JURIDICA LEMI. EDICAO NACIONAL (BL) [01799138] **3042**

REVISTA JURIDICA LEMI. LEGISLACAO ESTADUAL. MINAS GERAIS (BL) [10381833] **3042**

REVISTA JURISDICCION CONTENCIOSA ADMINISTRATIVA (SP) **3042**

REVISTA LATINA DE CARDIOLOGIA EUROAMERICANA (SP/0210-8755) [11203582] **3710**

REVISTA LATINOAMERICANA DE ACUICULTURA (PE/0250-2135) [10498314] **2312**

REVISTA LATINOAMERICANA DE ADMINISTRACION PUBLICA (MX) [02479738] **4683**

REVISTA LATINOAMERICANA DE CIENCIAS AGRICOLAS (VE/0250-5479) [03800616] **129**

REVISTA LATINOAMERICANA DE DOCUMENTACION (BL/0101-3394) [09688902] **3246**

REVISTA LATINOAMERICANA DE ESTUDIOS EDUCATIVOS (MX/0185-1284) [04949106] **1780**

REVISTA LATINOAMERICANA DE ESTUDIOS ETNOLINGUISTICOS (PE) [08607984] **3316**

REVISTA LATINOAMERICANA DE FILOSOFIA (AG/0325-0725) [04312604] **4359**

REVISTA LATINOAMERICANA DE MICROBIOLOGIA (1970) (MX/0187-4640) [01763969] **569**

REVISTA LATINOAMERICANA DE PATOLOGIA (VE/0300-9068) [10214689] **3897**

REVISTA LATINOAMERICANA DE PSICOLOGIA (CK/0120-0534) [01763970] **4616**

REVISTA LATINOAMERICANA DE QUIMICA (MX/0370-5943) [01786826] **493, 1047**

REVISTA LATINOAMERICANA DE SALUD (MX) [11080751] **4800**

REVISTA LATINOAMERICANA DE SEXOLOGIA (CK/0120-7458) [I01207458] **4616**

REVISTA LATINOAMERICANA DE TEOLOGIA (ES) [12070733] **4993**

REVISTA LETRARO-ARTISTIKE (AA) [30829852] **2522**

REVISTA LETRAS (CURITIBA) (BL/0100-0888) [06441141] **3316**

REVISTA LTR (BL/0048-7813) [08518291] **3153**

REVISTA M (VE) [03216094] **2552**

REVISTA MANRESA (SP) **2522**

REVISTA MARITIMA BRASILEIRA (BL/0034-9860) [02862715] **4182**

REVISTA MATEMATICA DE LA UNIVERSIDAD COMPLUTENSE DE MADRID / FACULTAD DE CIENCIAS MATEMATICAS, UNIVERSIDAD COMPLUTENSE DE MADRID (SP/0214-3577) [21542350] **3531**

REVISTA MATEMATICA IBEROAMERICANA (SP/0213-2230) [12178861] **3531**

REVISTA MEDICA DA BAHIA (BL) [06538755] **3636**

REVISTA MEDICA DE CHILE (CL/0034-9887) [01640625] **3801**

REVISTA MEDICA DE COSTA RICA (CR/0034-9909) [07367178] **4800, 3636**

REVISTA MEDICA DE MOCAMBIQUE (MZ) [22457197] **4800, 3636**

REVISTA MEDICA DE PANAMA (PN/0379-1629) [03419164] **3636**

REVISTA MEDICA DE VALPARAISO (CL) [06526780] **3636**

REVISTA MEDICA DEL HOSPITAL COLONIA (MX/0018-5604) [05261918] **3636**

REVISTA MEDICA DO ESTADO DO RIO DE JANEIRO (BL/0100-0195) [05878669] **3636**

REVISTA MEDICA (LA PAZ) (BO/0482-6760) [04128482] **3636**

REVISTA MEDICA (MEXICO) (MX/0484-7849) [10512384] **3636**

REVISTA MEDICALA ROMANA (RM) [25837729] **3636**

REVISTA MEDICALA (TIRGU-MURES) (RM/0034-995X) [01607731] **4328**

REVISTA MEDICO-CHIRURGICALA (RM) [01778136] **3636**

REVISTA MEDICO-CHIRURGICALA A SOCIETATII DE MEDICI SI NATURALISTI DIN IASI (RM/0300-8738) [01357865] **3973**

REVISTA MENSAJE (CL) 5256, **4993**

REVISTA MEXICANA DE ANALISIS DE LA CONDUCTA (MX) [02879185] **4616**

REVISTA MEXICANA DE ANESTESIOLOGIA Y REANIMACION (MX/0185-1012) **3684**

REVISTA MEXICANA DE ASTRONOMIA Y ASTROFISICA (MX/0185-1101) [02250553] 4420, **399**

REVISTA MEXICANA DE CIENCIAS POLITICAS Y SOCIALES (MX/0185-1918) [02435215] **5216**

REVISTA MEXICANA DE CIRUGIA, GINECOLOGIA Y CANCER (MX/0034-9984) [01778137] 3823, **3768**

REVISTA MEXICANA DE COMUNICACION (MX/0187-8190) [22197707] **1121**

REVISTA MEXICANA DE DERECHO PENAL (MX/0034-9992) [02251816] **3108**

REVISTA MEXICANA DE FISICA (MX/0035-001X) [02450175] **4420**

REVISTA MEXICANA DE FITOPATOLOGIA (MX/0185-3309) [15500829] **526**

REVISTA MEXICANA DE INGENIERIA Y ARQUITECTURA : ORGANO DE LA ASSOCIACION DE INGENIEROS Y ARQUITECTOS DE MEXICO (MX/0035-0028) [05935815] 308, **1994**

REVISTA MEXICANA DE JUSTICIA (MX) [07970597] **3042**

REVISTA MEXICANA DE LA PROPIEDAD INDUSTRIAL Y ARTISTICA **CEASED.** (MX) [06429394] **1308**

REVISTA MEXICANA DE MICOLOGIA (MX/0187-3180) [13735025] **576**

REVISTA MEXICANA DE PEDIATRIA (MX/0035-0052) [01644151] **3911**

REVISTA MEXICANA DE POLITICA EXTERIOR (MX/0185-6022) [11940454] **2758**

REVISTA MEXICANA DE PSICOLOGIA (MX/0035-0079) [02872439] **4616**

REVISTA MEXICANA DE RADIOLOGIA (MX/0370-6486) [03706486] **3946**

REVISTA MEXICANA DE RELACIONES PUBLICAS (MX) [06441790] **765**

REVISTA MICROSOFT PARA PROGRAMADORES (SP/1130-622X) [l1130622X] **1239**

REVISTA MILITAR (PO) [06751596] **4055**

REVISTA MINELOR (RM) [25465831] 4277, **2150**

REVISTA MINERALOGICA ITALIANA (IT/0391-9641) [08205365] **1444**

REVISTA MONUMENTELOR ISTORICE / COMISIA NATIONALA A MONUMENTELOR, ASAMBLURILOR SI SITURILOR ISTORICE (RM) [26813729] 363, **2705**

REVISTA MUNDIAL (SZ) [01792545] **2758**

REVISTA MUSICAL CHILENA (CL/0716-2790) [01590560] **4150**

REVISTA MUSICAL DE VENEZUELA / INSTITUTO LATINOAMERICANO DE INVESTIGACIONES Y ESTUDIOS MUSICALES VICENTE EMILIO SOJO (VE) [08910641] **4150**

REVISTA MUZEELOR (RM) [22877667] **4095**

REVISTA NACIONAL DE AGRICULTURA (BOGOTA) (CK/0035-0222) [01763981] **129**

REVISTA NACIONAL DE CULTURA (PN) [04525571] **2758**

REVISTA NACIONAL DE CULTURA (CARACAS, VENEZUELA) (VE/0035-0230) [01639896] **5216**

REVISTA NACIONAL DE TELECOMUNICACOES (BRAZILIAN EDITION) See RNT **1163**

REVISTA NACIONAL DE TELECOMUNICACOES (INTERNATIONAL EDITION) (BL) [08072118] **1163**

REVISTA NEUROLOGICA ARGENTINA (AG/0325-0938) [01265990] **3845**

REVISTA NICARAGUENSE DE ENTOMOLOGIA (NQ/1021-0296) [I10210296] **5613**

REVISTA OBSTETRICIA Y GINECOLOGIA DE VENEZUELA (VE/0048-7732) [03996028] **3768**

REVISTA ODONTOLOGICA ECUATORIANA (EC/0484-8020) [11374032] **1334**

REVISTA OFICIAL DE LA ASOCIACION GENERAL DE AUTORES DEL URUGUAY (UY) [03029196] **3430**

REVISTA OLIMPICA (SZ/1018-1008) [I10181008] **4915**

REVISTA ORL (AG/0326-7067) [09601805] **3891**

REVISTA PADURILOR (BUCHAREST, ROMANIA : 1986) (RM) [14090467] **2394**

REVISTA PANAMENA DE ANTROPOLOGIA : PUBLICACION DE LA ASOCIACION PANAMENA DE ANTROPOLOGIA (PN) [07633456] **244**

REVISTA PARA NOVIAS (US) **2285**

REVISTA PARAENSE DE MEDICINA (BL/0101-5907) [08161721] **3636**

REVISTA PARAGUAYA DE SOCIOLOGIA (PY/0035-0354) [01763982] **5216**

REVISTA PAULISTA DE HOSPITAIS (BL/0048-7864) [01763983] **3636**

REVISTA PAULISTA DE MEDICINA (BL/0035-0362) [01763984] **3636**

REVISTA PEDAGOGJIKE (AA) [01786932] **1780**

REVISTA PERUANA DE CIENCIAS SOCIALES : RPCS (PE/1011-0410) [19095417] **5216**

REVISTA PERUANA DE DERECHO DE LA EMPRESA (PE) [11302684] **3042**

REVISTA PERUANA DE ENTOMOLOGIA (PE/0080-2425) [02405084] **5613**

●REVISTA PERUANA DE POBLACION (PE) [28491002] **4560**

REVISTA PESTALOZZI (BL) [08138653] **1884**

REVISTA POLICIA NACIONAL DE COLOMBIA (CK) [03341055] **3175**

REVISTA PORTUGUESA DE CARDIOLOGIA (PO/0870-2551) [16806739] **3710**

REVISTA PORTUGUESA DE CIENCIAS VETERINARIAS (PO/0035-0389) [06284461] **5520**

REVISTA PORTUGUESA DE ESTOMATOLOGIA E CIRURGIA MAXILO-FACIAL (PO/0035-0397) [07584456] **1334**

REVISTA PORTUGUESA DE FARMACIA (PO/0484-811X) [I0484811X] **4328**

REVISTA PORTUGUESA DE FILOLOGIA (PO/0870-4139) [01883842] **3316**

REVISTA PORTUGUESA DE FILOSOFIA (PO/0870-5283) [01881118] **4359**

REVISTA PORTUGUESA DE FILOSOFIA. SUPLEMENTO BIBLIOGRAFICO (PO/0556-6940) [01881051] **4359**

REVISTA PORTUGUESA DE HEMORREOLOGIA : ORGAO OFICIAL DA SOCIEDADE PORTUGUESA DE HEMORREOLOGIA / SOCIEDADE PORTUGUESA DE HEMORREOLOGIA (PO/0871-4649) [24908001] **3773**

REVISTA PORTUGUESA DE HISTORIA (PO/0253-1658) [01763987] **2706**

REVISTA PORTUGUESA DE QUIMICA (PO/0035-0419) [09542561] **991**

REVISTA PORTUGUESA DE SAUDE PUBLICA / ESCOLA NACIONAL DE SAUDE PUBLICA (PO/0870-9025) [27159295] **4800**

REVISTA - PROCURADORIA GERAL DO ESTADO (BL) [03237682] **3042**

REVISTA PROMOCAO SOCIAL SAO PAULO (BL) [02662025] **5306**

REVISTA PUERTORRIQUENA DE PSICOLOGIA (PR) [21125976] 3936, **4616**

REVISTA/REVIEW INTERAMERICANA (PR/0360-7917) [04161507] **5216**

REVISTA RODOVIARIA (BL) [01787228] **5443**

REVISTA ROL DE ENFERMERIA (SP/0210-5020) [10331573] **3868**

REVISTA ROMANA DE STATISTICA : ORGAN AL COMISIEI NATIONALE PENTRU STATISTICA (RM) [22723492] **5337**

REVISTA SEGURIDAD (SP/0378-9551) [I03789551] **1708**

REVISTA SIEMENS (PORTUGUESE EDITION) (GW/0937-9649) 1230, **2079**

REVISTA SIGNOS (CL/0035-0451) [02959106] 3430, **3316**

REVISTA SINDICAL (MX) [05814029] **4683**

REVISTA SINTAXIS (UY) [02436305] **3316**

REVISTA SOBRE RELACIONES INDUSTRIALES Y LABORALES / UNIVERSIDAD CATOLICA ANDRES BELLO (VE) [07878206] **1708**

REVISTA TAMAULIPAS (MX) [07371924] **2544**

REVISTA TECNICA DE LA FACULTAD DE INGENIERIA, UNIVERSIDAD DEL ZULIA (VE/0254-0770) [10032759] **1994**

REVISTA TECNICA DO TRABALHO (PO) [07678145] **3153**

REVISTA TECNICA INTEVEP (VE/0251-4478) [08563498] **4277**

REVISTA TECNOLOGICA (CU/0029-5736) [04011135] **5148**

REVISTA TELEBRAS (BL) [03632747] **1163**

REVISTA TELEGRAFICA ELECTRONICA (AG/0035-0516) [07389024] **2079**

REVISTA TEOLOGICA See REVISTA TEOLOGICA LIMENSE **5035**

REVISTA TEOLOGICA LIMENSE (PE) [05698875] **5035**

REVISTA TRANSPORTURILOR SI TELECOMUNICATIILOR (RM/0379-2390) [03048423] 1163, **5391**

REVISTA TRIBUTARIA (UY) [02821745] 4747, **3042**

REVISTA TRIMESTRAL / BANCO CENTRAL DE RESERVA DE EL SALVADOR (ES) [13740975] **810**

REVISTA TRIMESTRAL - SERVICO DE ADMINISTRACAO MILITAR (PO) [02240685] **4055**

REVISTA TROHPOS (MX) [10623423] **2544**

REVISTA TU (US) 405, **5565**

REVISTA UNIVERSIDAD DE ANTIOQUIA (CK/0120-2367) [14093368] **1094**

REVISTA UNIVERSIDAD DE LA HABANA (CU) **5217**

REVISTA / UNIVERSIDAD DE LA REPUBLICA, ESCUELA UNIVERSITARIA DE BIBLIOTECOLOGIA Y CIENCIAS AFINES "ING. FEDERICO E. CAPURRO," BIBLIOTECA (UY/0304-4343) [21022806] **3246**

REVISTA UNIVERSIDAD EAFIT (CK/0120-033X) [11416266] **4683**

REVISTA UNIVERSIDAD LA GRAN COLOMBIA (CK) [02246271] **1846**

REVISTA UNIVERSIDAD PONTIFICIA BOLIVARIANA (CK/0120-1115) [06036750] **2492**

REVISTA - UNIVERSIDADE DE UBERLANDIA FACULDADE DE DIREITO (BL) [01786383] **3042**

REVISTA UNIVERSITARIA (CL/0250-3670) [05285745] **1846**

REVISTA UPADI (MX) [03466164] **1994**

REVISTA URUGUAYA DE CIENCIAS SOCIALES (UY) [01784722] **5217**

REVISTA URUGUAYA DE DERECHO CONSTITUCIONAL Y POLITICO (UY/0256-0151) [11587405] **3094**

REVISTA URUGUAYA DE DERECHO PROCESAL (UY) [04376780] **3042**

REVISTA URUGUAYA DE ESTUDIOS ADMINISTRATIVOS (UY) [04237029] **3094**

REVISTA URUGUAYA DE ESTUDIOS INTERNACIONALES (UY) [09531431] **4534**

REVISTA URUGUAYA DE PSICOANALISIS (UY/0484-8268) [08758566] **4616**

REVISTA URUGUAYA DE PSICOLOGIA (UY) [06598310] **4616**

REVISTA USEM (MX) [04481797] **885**

REVISTA VALENCIANA DE FILOLOGIA (SP/0556-705X) [04601262] **3316**

REVISTA VENEZOLANA DE CIENCIA POLITICA (VE) [20241500] 2758, 4683, **4494**

REVISTA VENEZOLANA DE DESARROLLO ADMINISTRATIVO (VE) [10260432] **4683**

REVISTA VENEZOLANA DE FOLKLORE (VE/0035-0575) [04626332] **2324**

REVISTAS ESPANOLAS CON ISSN / INSTITUTO BIBLIOGRAFICO HISPANICO, CENTRO NACIONAL ESPANOL ISDS (SP) [07706528] 3246, **423**

REVISTERO. INTERNATIONAL PERIODICALS DIRECTORY (US/0085-5642) [01792122] **423**

REVISTI DI ARCHEOLOGIA CRISTIANA (VC/0035-6042) [01641389] **281**

REVITALIZED SIGNS (US) [18649878] **4616**

REVMATOLOGIJA (RU/0256-5528) [10332298] **3636**

REVMEDIA LONDON (UK/0955-8500) [I09558500] **1183**

REVOLTES (MONTREAL, QUEBEC) (CN/0834-0366) [15624764] **4494**

REVOLUCION Y CULTURA (HAVANA, CUBA : 1984) (CU) [12096488] **329**

REVOLUCIONES POR MINUTO : RPM (SP) **4150**

REVOLUTION (FR) [06836704] **2522**

REVOLUTION AFRICAINE
(AE/0035-0621) [02916999] **4494**

REVOLUTION (CHICAGO)
(US/0193-3612) [05215888] **4494**

REVOLUTION ET TRAVAIL
(AE/0484-8365) [05686045] **1708**

REVOLUTION PROLETARIENNE
(MONTREAL) (CN/0229-0693)
[08854772] **4546**

REVOLUTION (STATEN ISLAND, N.Y.)
(US/1059-0927) [24478003] **3868**

REVOLUTIONARY AGE (US/0556-7165)
[02381341] **4546**

REVOLUTIONARY RUSSIA
(UK/0954-6545) [19907619] **2706**

REVOLUTIONARY WAR MAGAZINE
CEASED. (US/0888-2258) [13503448]
2758

REVOLUTIONARY WORKER
(US/0193-3485) [05214537] **5661**

REVOLUTIONARY ZIMBABWE (UK)
[03217498] **4494**

REVS (AT) **4082**

REVTECH (US) **1202**

REVUE A. C. C. S (CN/0226-5931)
[06859268] 5035, **3792**

REVUE ACEDA (CN/0382-7976)
[16856771] 4393, **1884**

REVUE / ADMINISTRATION DE
L'ORGANISATION DES ETUDES (BE)
[24477246] **1780**

REVUE ADMINISTRATIVE, LA
(FR/0035-0672) [01908657] 3042, **4683**

REVUE AFRICAINE DE THEOLOGIE
(CG/1016-2461) [03463480] **4993**

REVUE AFRICAINE ET MALGACHE DE
PSYCHOLOGIE (SG) [01785825] **4616**

REVUE AGRICOLE ET SUCRIERE DE
L'ILE MAURICE (MF/0370-3576)
[04071453] **129**

REVUE ALERTE (CN/1191-9191)
[27725101] **4800**

REVUE ALGERIENNE DES SCIENCES
JURIDIQUES, ECONOMIQUES ET
POLITIQUES (AE/0035-0699)
[01588128] **3042**

REVUE ANDRE MALRAUX
SUSPENDED. (CN/0839-458X)
[17166009] **3351**

REVUE ANNUELLE - INDUSTRIE ET
COMMERCE (CN) [01795200] **850**

REVUE ANNUELLE - LOTO
ATLANTIQUE, CANADA
(CN/0848-6727) [23264604] **4683**

REVUE ARACHNOLOGIQUE
(FR/0398-4346) [05656053] **471**

REVUE ARBIDO (SZ/0258-0772)
[13980037] **3246**

REVUE ARCHEOLOGIQUE
(FR/0035-0737) [01639074] **281**

REVUE ARCHEOLOGIQUE DE
BORDEAUX (FR/1154-1342) [22574697]
281

REVUE ARCHEOLOGIQUE DE 'EST ET
DU CENTRE EST SUPPLEMENT
(FR/0220-7796) [I02207796] **281**

REVUE ARCHEOLOGIQUE DE L'EST
ET DU CENTRE-EST (FR/0035-0745)
[01713683] **281**

REVUE ARCHEOLOGIQUE DE
L'OUEST (FR/0767-709X) [13076124]
281

REVUE ARCHEOLOGIQUE DE
L'OUEST. SUPPLEMENT
(FR/1166-8261) [I11668261] **281**

REVUE ARCHEOLOGIQUE DE
NARBONNAISE (FR/0557-7705)
[01878228] **281**

REVUE ARCHEOLOGIQUE DE
NARBONNAISE. SUPPLEMENT (FR)
[02941523] **281**

REVUE ARCHEOLOGIQUE DE
PICARDIE (FR/0752-5656) [11002610]
281

REVUE ARCHEOLOGIQUE DU
CENTRE DE LA FRANCE
(FR/0220-6617) [07767190] **281**

REVUE AUTOCHTONE (CN/0226-7284)
[06511828] 2272, **3042**

REVUE BALTIQUE : THE JOURNAL OF
COOPERATION OF THE BALTIC
STATES (LI) [26799730] **2522**

REVUE BELGE D'ACUPUNCTURE
(BE/0250-488X) [05268094] **3636**

REVUE BELGE D'ARCHEOLOGIE ET
D'HISTOIRE DE L'ART (BE/0035-077X)
[01607886] **330**

REVUE BELGE DE DROIT
INTERNATIONAL (BE/0035-0788)
[01715592] **3135**

REVUE BELGE DE GEOGRAPHIE
(BE/0035-0796) [01764007] **2575**

REVUE BELGE DE LA COMPTABILITE
(BE) [06589867] **751**

REVUE BELGE DE MEDECINE
DENTAIRE 1984 (BE/0775-0293)
[I07750293] **1334**

REVUE BELGE DE MUSICOLOGIE
(BE/0771-6788) [01681218] **4150**

REVUE BELGE DE NUMISMATIQUE ET
DE SIGILLOGRAPHIE (BE/0774-5885)
[I07745885] **2783**

REVUE BELGE DE PHILOLOGIE ET
D'HISTOIRE (BE/0035-0818) [01641459]
3316

REVUE BELGE DE PSYCHANALYSE
(BE) [12775609] **4616**

REVUE BELGE DE SECURITE
SOCIALE (BE/0771-1530) [05703620]
2892, **5306**

REVUE BELGE D'HISTOIRE
CONTEMPORAINE (BE) [01880932]
2706

REVUE BELGE D'HISTOIRE MILITAIRE
(BE/0035-0877) [I00350877] **4056**

REVUE BELGE D'HOMOEOPATHIE
(BE/0035-0885) [02850573] **3775**

REVUE BELGE DU CINEMA
(BE/0774-0115) [20379503] **4077**

REVUE BELGE DU FEU (BE/0771-4033)
[I07714033] **2292**

REVUE BENEDICTINE (BE/0035-0893)
[05822236] **4993**

REVUE BENINOISE DE SCIENCES
JURIDIQUES ET ADMINISTRATIVES
(DM) [11252787] **3094**

REVUE BIBLIOGRAPHIQUE DE
SINOLOGIE (FR/0080-2484) [01764013]
2853, **2857**

REVUE BIBLIOGRAPHIQUE DU
MOYEN ORIENT *See* ...
BIBLIOGRAPHY OF THE MIDDLE EAST
: A COMPLETE AND CLASSIFIED LIST
OF ALL THE BOOKS PUBLISHED IN
ABOUT TEN MIDDLE EASTERN
COUNTRIES, THE **2634**

REVUE BIBLIOGRAPHIQUE -
TOXIBASE LYON (FR/0996-8393)
[I09968393] 1348, **1350**

REVUE BIBLIOGRAPHIQUE -
TOXIBASE (LYON) *See* REVUE
DOCUMENTAIRE - TOXIBASE LYON
3983

REVUE BIBLIQUE (FR/0035-0907)
[08461065] **5019**

REVUE BURKINABE DE DROIT
(UV/0773-8439) [15243234] **3042**

REVUE CAMEROUNAISE DE DROIT
(CM) [01791017] **3042**

REVUE CANADIENNE DE
LIPIDOLOGIE (CN/1185-720X)
[25313980] **3636**

REVUE CANADIENNE DE
PSYCHO-EDUCATION (CN/0080-2492)
[02971877] **1780**

REVUE CANADIENNE D'ETUDES
CINEMATOGRAPHIQUES
(CN/0847-5911) [22425888] **4077**

REVUE CANADIENNE D'ETUDES DU
DEVELOPPEMENT (CN/0225-5189)
[06860387] **1639**

REVUE CANADIENNE DU DROIT
D'AUTEUR (CN/0227-2180) [08436278]
1308

REVUE CELFAN (US/0890-6998)
[08331697] **3430**

REVUE CHIBRET D'OPHTALMOLOGIE
(FR/0338-9987) [06036083] **3879**

REVUE CHIEN 2000 (FR/0397-6866)
[I03976866] **4287**

REVUE COMMERCE 500 (CN) **850**

REVUE COMMERCE & INDUSTRIE
(CN/1184-6364) [24266604] 1625, **850**

REVUE COMMERCE (MONTREAL.
1975) (CN/0380-9811) [02775663] **850**

REVUE CREDIT (CN/0715-6669)
[09523785] **885**

REVUE CRITIQUE DE DROIT
INTERNATIONAL PRIVE
(FR/0035-0958) [01587183] **3135**

REVUE CRITIQUE DE
JURISPRUDENCE BELGE
(BE/0035-0966) [02715421] **3042**

REVUE CULINAIRE, LA (FR) **2792**

REVUE CURLING QUEBEC, LA
(CN/1187-4627) [25796388] **4915**

REVUE D'ACTION SOCIALE : AS (BE)
[07649256] **5306**

REVUE D'ALLEMAGNE (FR/0035-0974)
[01879980] **2706**

REVUE D'ALSACE (FR/0181-0448)
[06827362] 281, **2706**

REVUE D'ARCHEOLOGIE MODERNE
ET D'ARCHEOLOGIE GENERALE :
RAMAGE (FR/0294-0965) [16896449]
4993, **281**

REVUE D'ARCHEOMETRIE
(FR/0399-1237) [04752625] **281**

REVUE D'ASSYRIOLOGIE ET
D'ARCHEOLOGIE ORIENTALE
(FR/0373-6032) [01764026] **281**

REVUE D'ASSYRIOLOGIE ET
D'ARCHEOLOGIE ORIENTALE (LH)
[10135206] **3316**

REVUE D'AUVERGNE (FR/0035-1008)
[01880817] **2706**

REVUE DE BELLES-LETTRES
(SZ/0035-1016) [01883251] **3430**

REVUE DE BIBLIOLOGIE
(FR/0982-6548) [18366300] 3316, **3430**

REVUE DE BIOTHERAPIE
VETERINAIRE (FR/1151-3551)
[I11513551] **5520**

REVUE DE CARTO-QUEBEC
(CN/1184-1885) [23686571] **2583**

REVUE DE CHIRURGIE
ORTHOPEDIQUE ET REPARATRICE
DE L'APPAREIL MOTEUR
(FR/0035-1040) [01764032] **3973**

REVUE DE CHIRURGIE
ORTHOPEDIQUE ET
TRAUMATOLOGIQUE (FR) **3884**

REVUE DE COMMINGES
(FR/0035-1059) [02058893] 281, **2706**

REVUE DE CYTOLOGIE ET DE
BIOLOGIE VEGETALES - LE
BOTANISTE (FR/0181-7582) [04014742]
526

REVUE DE DROIT CANONIQUE
(FR/0556-7378) [01871222] **4993**

REVUE DE DROIT COMMERCIAL
BELGE (BE) [09375907] **3102**

REVUE DE DROIT DES AFFAIRES
INTERNATIONALES (FR/0295-5830)
[I02955830] **3102**

REVUE DE DROIT DES AFFAIRES
INTERNATIONALES. INTERNATIONAL
BUSINESS LAW JOURNAL (FR)
[12688443] 4747, **3135**

REVUE DE DROIT FRANCAIS
COMMERCIAL, MARITIME ET FISCAL
(FR) [02708973] **3182**

REVUE DE DROIT IMMOBILIER
(FR/0180-9869) **3042**

REVUE DE DROIT INTELLECTUAL
L'INGENIEUR-CONSEIL (BE)
[14627809] 3042, **1308**

REVUE DE DROIT INTERNATIONAL,
DE SCIENCES DIPLOMATIQUES ET
POLITIQUES (SZ/0035-1091)
[01764037] **3135**

REVUE DE DROIT INTERNATIONAL ET
DE DROIT COMPARE (BE/0775-4663)
[02267111] **3135**

REVUE DE DROIT JUDICIAIRE
(CN/0822-5117) [09812345] **3091**

REVUE DE DROIT MEDIA &
COMMUNICATIONS (CN/1180-4831)
[22961333] **1163**

REVUE DE DROIT MILITAIRE ET DE
DROIT DE LA GUERRE (BE/0556-7394)
[20876240] **3183**

REVUE DE DROIT PENAL ET DE
CRIMINOLOGIE (BE) [01764040] **3175**

REVUE DE DROIT PROSPECTIF *See*
REVUE DE LA RECHERCHE
JURIDIQUE, DROIT PROSPECTIF /
PUBLIEE PAR LA FACULTE DE DROIT
ET DE SCIENCE POLITIQUE
D'AIX-MARSEILLE **3043**

REVUE DE DROIT RURAL (FR) **3042**

REVUE DE DROIT SANITAIRE ET
SOCIAL (FR/0245-9469) [07266028]
4800

REVUE DE DROIT (SHERBROOKE)
(CN/0317-9656) [02442844] **3043**

REVUE DE DROIT SOCIAL (BE)
[05523799] **3043**

REVUE DE DROIT UNIFORME (IT)
[01795168] **3091**

REVUE DE DROIT [FRENCH EDITION]
(SHERBROOKE) (CN/0317-9656)
[01764035] **3043**

REVUE DE GEMMOLOGIE A.F.G
(FR/0398-9011) [03726447] **2915**

REVUE DE GEOGRAPHIE ALPINE
(FR/0035-1121) [08226396] **2575**

REVUE DE GEOGRAPHIE DE LYON
(FR/0035-113X) [01764045] **2575**

REVUE DE GEOGRAPHIE DU MAROC
(MR/0035-1156) [02267112] **2575**

REVUE DE GEOGRAPHIE.
MADAGASCAR (MG/0047-5416)
[01756394] **2575**

REVUE DE GEOMORPHOLOGIE
DYNAMIQUE (FR/0556-7432)
[01764047] **2575**

REVUE DE GERIATRIE, LA
(FR/0397-7927) [03179755] **3755**

REVUE DE JURISPRUDENCE
COMMERCIALE (FR/0048-7937)
[I00487937] **3043**

REVUE DE L ASSOCIATION
FRANCAISE DES AMIS DES CHEMINS
DE FER (FR/0760-548X) [I0760548X]
5436

REVUE DE LA BANQUE BANK EN
FINANCIENWEZEN REVUE AND
CAHIERS *See* BANK EN
FINANCIENWEZEN **774**

REVUE DE LA BANQUE, LA (BE)
[06751384] **810**

REVUE DE LA BIBLIOTHEQUE
NATIONALE *CEASED.* (FR/0249-7344)
[08257687] **3246**

REVUE DE LA CERAMIQUE ET DU
VERRE, LA (FR/0294-202X) [24072857]
281, **2593**

REVUE DE LA CERAMIQUE, LA (FR)
[08998012] 281, **2593**

Alphabetical Title Index — REVUE

REVUE DE LA CHAMBRE DE COMMERCE ET D'INDUSTRIE DE LA REUNION (1980) (FR) [07532310] **821**

REVUE DE LA CINEMATHEQUE, LA (CN/0843-6827) [20111004] **4077**

REVUE DE LA CONCURRENCE ET DE LA CONSOMMATION (FR/0220-9896) [18199092] **3103**

REVUE DE LA HAUTE-AUVERGNE (FR/1141-1325) [02879671] **2853**

REVUE DE LA MANCHE (FR/1161-7721) [24868199] **281**

REVUE DE LA NAVIGATION, PORTS & INDUSTRIES (FR/0767-094X) [14584235] **5455**

REVUE DE LA POLICE NATIONALE (FR/0035-1237) [10854680] **3175**

REVUE DE LA PROTECTION CIVILE, LA (CN/0837-5771) [18420529] **5256**

REVUE DE LA RECHERCHE JURIDIQUE, DROIT PROSPECTIF, PUBLIEE PAR LA FACULTE DE DROIT ET DE SCIENCE POLITIQUE D'AIX-MARSEILLE (FR) [09287267] **3043**

REVUE DE LA SAINTONGE ET DE L'AUNIS (FR/0399-0184) [I03990184] **363**

REVUE DE LA SOCIETE DES AMIS DU MUSEE DE L'ARMEE (FR/0758-881X) [0758881X] 4095, 2628, **4056**

REVUE DE LA SOCIETE D'HISTOIRE ET D'ART DE LA BRIE ET DU PAYS DE MEAUX (FR/0338-5256) [02628285] 363, **2706**

REVUE DE LA SOCIETE HISTORIQUE DU MADAWASKA (1982) (CN/0820-0793) [09379201] **2758**

REVUE DE LA SOUDURE (BRUXELLES) (BE/0035-127X) [06683284] **4027**

REVUE DE L'ACADEMIE DU CENTRE (FR/0243-8410) [I02438410] **2706**

REVUE DE L'ACLA (CN/1193-1493) [I11931493] **3316**

REVUE DE L'ACTIVITE DANS L'INDUSTRIE DE LA CONSTRUCTION / OFFICE DE LA CONSTRUCTION DU QUEBEC, SERVICE RECHERCHE ET DEVELOPPEMENT (CN/0714-4237) [12993671] **626**

REVUE DE L'AEFA (FR) **4915**

REVUE DE L'AGENAIS (FR) [02917818] **2706**

REVUE DE L'AGRICULTURE (BE/0035-1296) [01639722] **129**

REVUE DE L'AIDE-SOIGNANTE, AS *See* AIDE-SOIGNANTE, L' **3850**

REVUE DE L'ALCOOLISME, LA *CEASED.* (FR/0035-130X) [06415226] **1348**

REVUE DE L'ALIMENTATION ANIMALE (FR/0242-6595) [08380090] **220**

REVUE DE L'AMEUBLEMENT, LA (FR/0242-8903) [I02428903] **2907**

●REVUE DE L'AMIE (CN/1192-3636) [27391212] **5306**

REVUE DE L'ARBITRAGE (FR/0556-7440) [02969562] **3043**

REVUE DE L'ART (FR/0035-1326) [01645554] **363**

REVUE DE LARYNGOLOGIE, D'OTOLOGIE ET DE RHINOLOGIE (FR/0035-1334) [01589656] **3891**

REVUE DE L'ATEQ, LA (CN/0835-0868) [16687601] **1870**

REVUE DE L'AVRANCHIN ET DU PAYS DE GRANVILLE (FR/0035-1342) [I00351342] **330**

REVUE DE L'ECONOMIE MERIDIONALE : REM (FR) [17253278] **1518**

REVUE DE L'ECONOMIE SOCIALE, LA *CEASED.* (FR/0755-8902) [14955707] **1518**

REVUE DE L'EDUCATION PHYSIQUE (BE) [05856852] **1858**

REVUE DE L'ENERGIE (FR/0303-240X) [01798174] **1956**

REVUE DE L'HABITAT FRANCAIS (FR/0048-7953) [I00487953] **4846**

REVUE DE L'HISTOIRE DES RELIGIONS (FR/0035-1423) [01764060] **4993**

REVUE DE L'IMPERIALE (CN/0848-8835) [21515203] **4277**

REVUE DE L'INFIRMIERE ET DE L'ASSISTANTE SOCIALE (FR/0397-7900) [I03977900] **4393**

REVUE DE L'INFIRMIERE. INFORMATIONS (FR/0397-7897) [07544386] **3868**

REVUE DE LINGUISTIQUE ROMANE (FR/0035-1458) [01681180] **3316**

REVUE DE L'INSTITUT DE SOCIOLOGIE (BE/0771-6796) [01398157] **5217**

REVUE DE L'INSTITUT FRANCAIS DU PETROLE (FR/0020-2274) [01969459] **4277**

REVUE DE L'INSTITUT NAPOLEON (1954) (FR/0395-921X) [04821132] **2706**

REVUE DE L'IRES, LA (FR/1145-1378) [26123000] **1518**

REVUE DE LITTERATURE COMPAREE (FR/0035-1466) [01764063] **3430**

REVUE DE L'OCEAN INDIEN (MG) [10935166] **2628**

REVUE DE L'OCEAN INDIEN, ECONOMIE (MG) [10932051] **1518**

REVUE DE L'OPHTALMOLOGIE FRANCAISE & ANNUELLE (FR) **3879**

REVUE DE L'OTAN (BE/0251-3722) [I02513722] **4494**

REVUE DE L'UNIVERSITE DE BRUXELLES (BE/0378-4606) [01537523] **5148**

REVUE DE L'UNIVERSITE DE MONCTON (1976) (CN/0316-6368) [09698162] 2853, **1846**

REVUE DE L'UNIVERSITE NATIONALE DU ZAIRE, CAMPUS DE LUBUMBASHI. SERIE A : LETTRES (CG) [02239959] **1846**

REVUE DE L'UNIVERSITE NATIONALE DU ZAIRE, CAMPUS DE LUBUMBASHI. SERIE B : SCIENCES (CG) [01798450] **5148**

REVUE DE L'UNIVERSITE SAINTE-ANNE (CN/0706-8115) [04433073] **1846**

REVUE DE MATHEMATIQUES SPECIALES (FR/0035-1504) [01644920] **3531**

REVUE DE MEDECINE DE TOURS (FR/0557-7721) [09490030] **3636**

REVUE DE MEDECINE DU TRAVAIL (FR/0300-0559) [10138524] **3636**

REVUE DE MEDECINE INTERNE, LA (FR/0248-8663) [07373286] **3801**

REVUE DE MEDECINE PSYCHOSOMATIQUE (1985) (FR/0298-3850) [14282540] **4616**

REVUE DE MEDECINE VETERINAIRE (FR/0035-1555) [06274197] **5520**

REVUE DE METALLURGIE. CAHIERS & MEMOIRES (FR) **4018**

REVUE DE METALLURGIE (PARIS) (FR/0035-1563) [06344737] **4018**

REVUE DE METAPHYSIQUE ET DE MORALE (PARIS, FRANCE : 1945) (FR/0035-1571) [05748737] **4359**

REVUE DE MICROPALEONTOLOGIE (FR/0035-1598) [01764074] 1395, **4230**

REVUE DE MORET ET DE SA REGION, LA (FR/0557-773X) [I0557773X] **2706**

REVUE DE MUSICOLOGIE (FR/0035-1601) [10789222] **4150**

REVUE DE NEMATOLOGIE *See* FUNDAMENTAL AND APPLIED NEMATOLOGY **456**

REVUE DE NEUROPSYCHIATRIE DE L'OUEST (FR/0035-161X) [I0035161X] **3936**

REVUE DE NEUROPSYCHOLOGIE / SOCIETE DE NEUROPSYCHOLOGIE DE LANGUE FRANCAISE (FR/1155-4452) [25047218] 4616, **3845**

REVUE DE PALEOBIOLOGIE (SZ) [09071337] **4230**

REVUE DE PAPINEAU, LA (CN/0226-9945) [08078721] **5794**

REVUE DE PAU ET DU BEARN (FR/0241-7413) [06446086] 2628, **363**

REVUE DE PEDAGOGIE APPLIQUEE (CG) [01792470] **1780**

REVUE DE PHILOLOGIE, DE LITTERATURE ET D'HISTOIRE ANCIENNES (FR/0035-1652) [01764077] **3316**

REVUE DE PHONETIQUE APPLIQUEE (BE/0035-1660) [02916930] **3316**

REVUE DE PLANIFICATION FISCALE ET SUCCESSORALE (US/0708-5079) [05765446] **3119**

REVUE DE PNEUMOLOGIE CLINIQUE : LE POUMON ET LE COEUR (FR/0761-8417) [11000447] **3951**

REVUE DE PODOLOGIE (FR/0300-1296) [01498194] **3918**

REVUE DE POLITIQUE INTERNATIONALE. FRENCH EDITION, LA *SUSPENDED.* (YU) **4534**

REVUE DE PRATICIEN. MEDECINE GENERALE, LA (FR) [19273377] **3636**

REVUE DE PRESSE - CHAMBRE D'INDUSTRIES DE COTE D'IVOIRE. SERVICE DOCUMENTATION (IV) [05669478] **1582**

REVUE DE PRESSE CHAMPAGNE-ARDENNE ACTUALITES (FR/0980-2282) [I09802282] **708**

REVUE DE PRESSE DU ... FESTIVAL D'ETE DE QUEBEC, LA (CN/0822-8701) [10638747] **5269**

REVUE DE PRESSE / FEDERATION DES CAISSES POPULAIRES DESJARDINS DE MONTREAL ET DE L'OUEST-DU-QUEBEC (CN/0714-3559) [08985191] 1543, **810**

REVUE DE PSYCHOLOGIE (BUCHAREST, ROMANIA) *See* REVUE ROUMAINE DE PSYCHOLOGIE / ACADEMIE ROUMAINE **4617**

REVUE DE QUMRAN (FR/0035-1725) [01764081] **5052**

REVUE DE SCIENCE CRIMINELLE ET DE DROIT PENAL COMPARE (FR/0035-1733) [01764082] **3108**

REVUE DE STATISTIQUE APPLIQUEE (FR/0035-175X) [01886864] **5337**

REVUE DE STOMATOLOGIE ET DE CHIRURGIE MAXILLO-FACIALE (FR/0035-1768) [01764084] **3973**

REVUE DE SYNTHESE (FR/0035-1776) [01714801] **2628**

REVUE DE THEOLOGIE ET DE PHILOSOPHIE (SZ/0035-1784) [05922006] 4993, **4359**

REVUE DE TOURISME (SZ/0251-3102) [06782978] **5490**

REVUE D'ECOLOGIE (FR/0249-7395) [10047191] 2204, **2220**

REVUE D'ECOLOGIE ET DE BIOLOGIE DU SOL *See* EUROPEAN JOURNAL OF SOIL BIOLOGY **171**

REVUE D'ECONOMIE DU DEVELOPPEMENT (FR) **1518**

REVUE D'ECONOMIE DU DEVELOPPEMENT (FR) **1518**

REVUE D'ECONOMIE FINANCIERE (FR/0987-3368) [I09873368] **1518**

REVUE D'ECONOMIE INDUSTRIELLE (FR/0154-3229) [12855244] **1582**

REVUE D'ECONOMIE POLITIQUE (FR/0373-2630) [01715792] **1595**

REVUE D'ECONOMIE REGIONAL ET URBAINE (FR) [09430314] **2834**

REVUE D'EDUCATION MEDICALE (FR/0242-9454) [17355341] 1780, **3636**

REVUE D'EGYPTOLOGIE (FR/0035-1849) [01883330] **2628**

REVUE D'ELEVAGE ET DE MEDECINE VETERINAIRE DE NOUVELLE CALEDONIE (NL/0767-7189) [I07677189] **5520**

REVUE D'ELEVAGE ET DE MEDECINE VETERINAIRE DES PAYS TROPICAUX (FR/0035-1865) [01639737] **5521**

REVUE D'EPIDEMIOLOGIE ET DE SANTE PUBLIQUE (US/0398-7620) [02509902] 4800, **3736**

REVUE DES AFFAIRES EUROPEENNES (FR/1152-9172) [I11529172] **4534**

REVUE DES AGRICULTEURS DE FRANCE (FR) **129**

REVUE DES ARCHEOLOGUES ET HISTORIENS D'ART DE LOUVAIN (BE/0080-2530) [01893853] **281**

REVUE DES COMITES D'ENTREPRISE & EQUIVALENTS (FR) **5217**

REVUE DES DEUX MONDES (1982) (FR/0750-9278) [08797804] **3430**

REVUE DES ECHANGES DE L'ASSOCIATION FRANCOPHONE INTERNATIONALE DES DIRECTEURS D'ETABLISSEMENTS SCOLAIRES, LA (CN/0822-8329) [11085009] **1780**

REVUE DES ETUDES ANCIENNES (FR/0035-2004) [01196181] **1079**

REVUE DES ETUDES ARMENIENNES (PARIS) (FR/0080-2549) [01605433] **2663**

REVUE DES ETUDES AUGUSTINIENNES (FR/0035-2012) [01764098] 3430, **4993**

REVUE DES ETUDES BYZANTINES (FR/0373-5729) [01770939] **2706**

REVUE DES ETUDES COOPERATIVES MUTUALISTES ET ASSOCIATIVES (FR) [14988458] **1543**

REVUE DES ETUDES GEORGIENNES ET CAUCASIENNES (FR/0373-1537) [17212250] **3316**

REVUE DES ETUDES GRECQUES (FR/0035-2039) [01764100] **3316**

REVUE DES ETUDES ISLAMIQUES (FR/0336-156X) [01641951] **5044**

REVUE DES ETUDES ITALIENNES (FR/0035-2047) [01764102] **3430**

REVUE DES ETUDES JUIVES (FR/0484-8616) [06478285] **5052**

REVUE DES ETUDES LATINES (FR/0373-5737) [01152816] 3430, **3316**

REVUE DES ETUDES MAISTRIENNES (FR/0184-7015) [04268118] **3430**

REVUE DES ETUDES ROUMAINES (FR) [01764106] **2706**

REVUE DES ETUDES SLAVES (FR/0080-2557) [01764107] **2706**

REVUE DES ETUDES SUD-EST EUROPEENNES (RM/0035-2063) [01891785] **2706**

REVUE DES INDUSTRIES D'ART (FR/0295-5849) [I02955849] **363**

REVUE DES INGENIEURS (FR) **1360**

REVUE DES LABORATOIRES D'ESSAIS, LA (FR/0296-5321) [I02965321] **5148**

REVUE — Alphabetical Title Index

REVUE DES LANGUES ROMANES (FR/0223-3711) [01764110] **3316**

REVUE DES LETTRES MODERNES (FR/0035-2136) [01764111] **3430**

REVUE DES LETTRES MODERNES. JEAN GIONO, LA (FR/0180-9423) [01798337] **3430**

REVUE DES LIVRES POUR ENFANTS, LA (FR) [03995153] **3351**

REVUE DES LOYERS ET DES FERMAGES, DE LA PROPRIETE COMMERCIALE, DES FONDS DE COMMERCE, DE LA CONSTRUCTION ET DE LA COPROPRIETE IMMOBILIERES (FR/0242-5629) [02425629] 2834, **4846**

REVUE DES MALADIES RESPIRATOIRES (FR/0761-8425) [10804108] **3951**

REVUE DES MARCHES PUBLICS (FR) **936**

REVUE DES MST ET DU SIDA / REVUE INTERNE DE DERMATOLOGIE ET DU SIDA (FR) **3722**

REVUE DES OENOLOGUES ET DES TECHNIQUES VITIVINICOLES ET OENOLOGIQUES (FR/0760-9868) [07609868] **185**

REVUE DES PAYS DE L'EST (BE/0303-9617) [01886938] 1582, **4534**

REVUE DES QUESTIONS SCIENTIFIQUES (BE/0035-2160) [01607009] **5148**

REVUE DES REVUES, LA (FR/0980-2797) [20655145] **424**

REVUE DES ROULEMENTS, LA (SW) [02241394] **2128**

REVUE DES SCIENCES DE L'EAU (PARIS) (FR/0992-7158) [18764874] **5539**

REVUE DES SCIENCES DE L'EDUCATION (CN/0318-479X) [02442006] **1780**

REVUE DES SCIENCES HUMAINES (FR/0035-2195) [06165010] **4359**

REVUE DES SCIENCES MORALES & POLITIQUES (FR/0751-5804) [09310551] **4494**

REVUE DES SCIENCES PHILOSOPHIQUES ET THEOLOGIQUES (PARIS : 1947) (FR/0035-2209) [08226517] 4993, **4359**

REVUE DES SCIENCES RELIGIEUSES (FR/0035-2217) [01764116] **4993**

REVUE DES SCIENCES SOCIALES DE LA FRANCE DE L'EST (FR/0336-1578) [01998831] **5217**

REVUE DES SOCIETES. JOURNAL DES SOCIETES (FR) [02979756] **3043**

●REVUE DES TELECOMMUNICATIONS PARIS. 1992 (FR/1243-7492) [112437492] **1163**

REVUE DESJARDINS, LA **CEASED.** (CN/0035-2284) [02133235] **810**

REVUE D'ESTHETIQUE (FR) [02933706] **4359**

REVUE D'ETUDES (FR/0764-6232) [02881130] **1780**

REVUE D'ETUDES COMPARATIVES EST-OUEST (FR/0338-0599) [02355464] **4546**

REVUE D'ETUDES PALESTINIENNES (LE/0252-8290) [08686972] **4534**

REVUE D'HISTOIRE COMPAREE (FR) [05210747] **2976**

REVUE D'HISTOIRE DE BAYONNE, DU PAYS BASQUE ET DU BAS-ADOUR (FR/1240-2419) [112402419] **330**

REVUE D'HISTOIRE DE LA COTE-NORD (CN/0828-9468) [14879648] **2758**

REVUE D'HISTOIRE DE LA MEDECINE HEBRAIQUE (FR/0035-2330) [01884585] **3636**

REVUE D'HISTOIRE DE L'AMERIQUE FRANCAISE (CN/0035-2357) [01764125] **2758**

REVUE D'HISTOIRE DES FACULTES DE DROIT ET DE LA SCIENCE JURIDIQUE (FR) [16654090] **3043**

REVUE D'HISTOIRE DES FACULTES DE DROIT ET DE LA SCIENCE JURIDIQUE (FR/0989-7925) [09897925] **3043**

●REVUE D'HISTOIRE DES MATHEMATIQUES (FR) **3531**

REVUE D'HISTOIRE DES SCIENCES (FR/0151-4105) [01222770] **5148**

REVUE D'HISTOIRE DES TEXTES (FR/0373-6075) [01697089] 2483, **3316**

REVUE D'HISTOIRE DIPLOMATIQUE (FR/0035-2365) [01764127] **4534**

REVUE D'HISTOIRE DU BAS ST-LAURENT (CN/0381-8454) [06020396] **2758**

REVUE D'HISTOIRE DU THEATRE (FR/0035-2373) [01589751] **5368**

REVUE D'HISTOIRE ECCLESIASTIQUE (BE/0035-2381) [01644972] 4993, **5013**

REVUE D'HISTOIRE ET DE PHILOSOPHIE RELIGIEUSES (FR/0035-2403) [01764128] **4993**

REVUE D'HISTOIRE LITTERAIRE DE LA FRANCE (FR/0035-2411) [01238324] **3430**

REVUE D'HISTOIRE LITTERAIRE DU QUEBEC ET DU CANADA FRANCAIS **CEASED.** (CN/0713-7958) [09050353] 2759, **3430**

REVUE D'HISTOIRE MAGHREBINE (TI) [01880745] **2643**

REVUE D'HISTOIRE MODERNE ET CONTEMPORAINE (FR/0048-8003) [01604668] **2628**

REVUE D'HYDROBIOLOGIE TROPICALE (FR/0240-8783) [07831236] **471**

REVUE D'IMAGERIE MEDICALE (FR/0998-4321) [22154881] **3946**

REVUE D'INTEGRATION EUROPEENNE (CN/0703-6337) [04093765] 1518, **4494**

REVUE D'INTELLIGENCE ARTIFICIELLE ET SYSTEMS EXPERTS (FR) **1216**

REVUE DIPLOMATIQUE DE L'OCEAN INDIEN (MG) [10935345] **4534**

REVUE DOCUMENTAIRE - CENTRE TECHNIQUE DU BOIS ET DE L'AMEUBLEMENT (FR/0295-5717) [02955717] **5337**

●REVUE DOCUMENTAIRE - TOXIBASE LYON (FR/1240-2494) [112402494] **3983**

REVUE D'ODONTO-STOMATOLOGIE (FR/0300-9815) [01185118] **1334**

REVUE D'ODONTO-STOMATOLOGIE DU MIDI DE LA FRANCE (FR/0035-2470) [03996053] **1334**

REVUE D'ORTHOPEDIE DENTO-FACIALE (FR/0337-9736) [07074052] **1334**

REVUE DROMOISE (FR/0398-0022) [03142978] **281**

REVUE DU BARREAU (CN/0383-669X) [20838830] **3043**

REVUE DU BARREAU, LA (CN/0383-669X) [03222671] **3043**

REVUE DU BOIS ET DE SES APPLICATIONS (FR/0373-5133) [09558866] **2404**

REVUE DU BOIS STRASBOURG (FR/0984-2810) [09842810] **2404**

REVUE DU CARDIOLOGUE PRATICIEN, LA (FR) [26500326] **3710**

REVUE DU CHEVAL ARABE DU QUEBEC, LA (CN/1184-2059) [23294606] **2802**

REVUE DU CINEMA **See** MENSUEL DU CINEMA, LE **4074**

REVUE DU CINEMA (PARIS. 1969) (FR/0019-2635) [01877838] **4077**

REVUE DU CLERGE AFRICAIN (CG) [01795359] **4994**

REVUE DU DROIT DE LA PROPRIETE INTELLECTUELLE (FR) [24946505] **1308**

REVUE DU DROIT PUBLIC ET DE LA SCIENCE POLITIQUE EN FRANCE ET A L'ETRANGER (FR/0035-2578) [01764041] 4494, **3135**

REVUE DU FINANCIER, LA (FR) [10987177] **810**

REVUE DU GAZ DANS LA CONSTRUCTION (FR) [04459173] **2150**

REVUE DU GYNECOLOGUE OBSTETRICIEN (FR/1141-5886) [21455050] **3768**

REVUE DU JOUET, LA (FR/0035-2594) [00352594] 1068, **2585**

REVUE DU LITTORAL (FR/1152-8400) [27420902] **4616**

REVUE DU MARCHE ALIMENTAIRE (CN/0709-5856) [06082800] **129**

REVUE DU MARCHE COMMUN ET DE L'UNION EUROPEENNE (FR) [25646426] **1582**

REVUE DU MARCHE UNIQUE EUROPEEN (FR/1155-4274) [24488504] **1639**

REVUE DU MONDE MUSULMAN ET DE LA MEDITERRANEE (FR/0997-1327) [19690412] **5044**

REVUE DU MOYEN AGE LATIN (FR) [01607615] **3317**

REVUE DU NORD (FR/0035-2624) [01764146] **2706**

REVUE DU NOTARIAT, LA (CN/0035-2632) [10578797] **3043**

REVUE DU NOUVEL ONTARIO (CN/0708-1715) [05527560] **2759**

REVUE DU PALAIS DE LA DECOUVERTE (FR/0339-7521) [05351909] **5148**

REVUE DU PEDIATRE (FR) [20626800] **3911**

REVUE DU PRACTICIEN, LA (FR/0035-2640) [01764149] **3636**

REVUE DU RHUMATISME ET DES MALADIES OSTEO-ARTICULAIRES (FR/0035-2659) [01778153] **3806**

●REVUE DU RHUMATISME : MALADIES DES OS ET DES ARTICULATIONS (FR/0035-2659) [28711850] **3806**

REVUE DU ROSAIRE (FR) **5035**

REVUE DU ROUERGUE (FR/0035-2667) [05399255] **2706**

REVUE DU SCOM (FR/0181-0855) [05112210] **4683**

REVUE DU TARN (FR) [02921422] 2483, **2706**

REVUE DU TRAVAIL (BE) [02939034] **5217**

REVUE DU TRESOR, LA (FR/0035-2713) [18530191] 4747, **751**

REVUE DU VIN DE FRANCE (ENGLISH EDITION) (FR/0035-273X) [01764151] **2370**

REVUE DU VIVARAIS (FR/0035-2748) [00352748] 2853, **330**

REVUE E 1989 (BE/0777-2181) [07772181] **2079**

REVUE ECONOMIQUE (FR/0035-2764) [01681181] **1595**

REVUE ECONOMIQUE - CHAMBRE DE COMMERCE DE LAVAL (CN/0825-0707) [11193113] **1518**

REVUE ECONOMIQUE DE L'OCDE (PARIS) (FR/0255-0830) [02550830] **1956**

REVUE ECONOMIQUE DU SUD-OUEST **CEASED.** (FR/0395-9007) [04928301] **1582**

REVUE ECONOMIQUE ET SOCIALE (LAUSANNE) (SZ/0035-2772) [01880013] **1595**

REVUE ECONOMIQUE FRANCO-SUISSE (FR/0035-2799) [00352799] **821**

REVUE ECONOMIQUE TRIMESTRIELLE (OTTAWA) **CEASED.** (CN/0837-5836) [17662024] **1518**

REVUE EGYPTIENNE DE DROIT INTERNATIONAL (UA/0080-259X) [01285400] **3135**

●REVUE ELECTORALE, SYNTHESES ET DOCUMENTS, LA (CN/1188-6161) [26758256] **4495**

REVUE ENERGIE PRIMAIRE **CEASED.** (BE/0556-7734) [07411209] **1956**

REVUE ET BULLETIN DE L'ASSOCIATION CANADIENNE DES ENSEIGNANTS NOIRS (CN/0712-1350) [08790856] 2272, **1780**

REVUE EUROPEENNE DE DERMATOLOGIE ET DE MST (FR/1140-5325) [111405325] **3722**

REVUE EUROPEENNE DE DROIT DE LA CONSOMMATION (FR/0775-3209) [07753209] **3043**

REVUE EUROPEENNE DE DROIT PUBLIC (UK/1105-1590) [21172191] 4747, **3094**

REVUE EUROPEENNE DES MIGRATIONS INTERNATIONALES (FR/0765-0752) [14690071] **1921**

REVUE FIDUCIAIRE. FEUILLETS HEBDOMADAIRES D'INFORMATION **See** REVUE FIDUCIAIRE. INFORMATION HEBDOMADAIRES **3043**

REVUE FIDUCIAIRE. INFORMATION HEBDOMADAIRES (FR) [03564345] **3043**

REVUE FISCAL **See** JOURNAL DE DROIT FISCAL **2986**

REVUE FORESTIERE FRANCAISE (FR/0035-2829) [01764159] **2394**

REVUE FRANCAISE D'ADMINISTRATION PUBLIQUE (FR/0152-7401) [03442521] **4684**

REVUE FRANCAISE D'ALLERGOLOGIE ET D'IMMUNOLOGIE CLINIQUE (FR/0335-7457) [00977077] **3676**

REVUE FRANCAISE D'APICULTURE (FR/0035-2853) [01764160] **130**

REVUE FRANCAISE D'AQUARIOLOGIE, HERPETOLOGIE (FR/0399-1075) [07242465] **557**

REVUE FRANCAISE D'AUTOMATIQUE, INFORMATIQUE, RECHERCHE OPERATIONNELLE (FR) [01775409] **1202**

REVUE FRANCAISE DE COMPTABILITE (FR/0484-8764) [12763513] **751**

REVUE FRANCAISE DE COOPERATION ECONOMIQUE AVEC ISRAEL **See** SHEKEL / CHAMBRE DE COMMERCE FRANCE-ISRAEL **821**

REVUE FRANCAISE DE DIETETIQUE (FR) **4198**

REVUE FRANCAISE DE DROIT ADMINISTRATIF (FR/0763-1219) [12013278] **3094**

REVUE FRANCAISE DE DROIT AERIEN ET SPATIAL (FR) [20653234] **33**

REVUE FRANCAISE DE DROIT CONSTITUTIONNEL (FR) [22202667] **3094**

REVUE FRANCAISE DE FINANCES PUBLIQUES (FR/0294-0833) [10016083] **4747**

REVUE FRANCAISE DE GASTRO-ENTEROLOGIE (FR/0035-2888) [00352888] **3747**

REVUE FRANCAISE DE GEOTECHNIQUE (FR/0181-0529) [04242118] 2128, **1395**

REVUE FRANCAISE DE GESTION (FR/0338-4551) [02395927] **885**

REVUE FRANCAISE DE GESTION INDUSTRIELLE (FR/0242-9780) [25293713] **885**

REVUE FRANCAISE DE GYNECOLOGIE ET D'OBSTETRIQUE (FR/0035-290X) [01764161] **3768**

REVUE FRANCAISE DE L'AUDIT INTERNE (FR) **4747**

REVUE FRANCAISE DE LOGISTIQUE (FR/0297-4592) [I02974592] **5148**

REVUE FRANCAISE DE PEDAGOGIE (FR) [05856978] **1780**

REVUE FRANCAISE DE PSYCHANALYSE : ORGANE OFFICIEL DE LA SOCIETE PSYCHANALYTIQUE DE PARIS (FR/0035-2942) [08739201] **4616**

REVUE FRANCAISE DE PSYCHOSOMATIQUE (FR) [26671675] **4616**

REVUE FRANCAISE DE SCIENCE POLITIQUE (FR/0035-2950) [01764164] **4495**

REVUE FRANCAISE DE SERVICE SOCIAL, LA (FR) [09508869] **5306**

REVUE FRANCAISE DE SOCIOLOGIE (FR/0035-2969) [01639264] **5256**

REVUE FRANCAISE DE TRANSFUSION ET D'HEMOBIOLOGIE *See* TRANSFUSION CLINIQUE ET BIOLOGIQUE **3774**

REVUE FRANCAISE DE TRANSFUSION ET D'HEMOBIOLOGIE : BULLETIN DE LA SOCIETE NATIONALE DE TRANSFUSION SANGUINE (FR/1140-4639) [19743466] **3773**

REVUE FRANCAISE D'ENDOCRINOLOGIE CLINIQUE, NUTRITION ET METABOLISME (FR/0048-8062) [01778155] **3733**

REVUE FRANCAISE D'ENDODONTIE (FR/0294-1813) [11039325] **1334**

REVUE FRANCAISE DES AFFAIRES SOCIALES (FR/0035-2985) [05345206] **1708**, **5256**

REVUE FRANCAISE DES CORPS GRAS (FR/0035-3000) [01775175] **1047**

REVUE FRANCAISE D'ETUDES AMERICAINES (FR/0397-7870) [02657592] **2759**

REVUE FRANCAISE D'ETUDES POLITIQUES MEDITERRANEENNES (FR/0338-2060) [02241953] **2706**

REVUE FRANCAISE D'HISTOIRE D'OUTRE-MER (FR/0300-9513) [09407381] **2706**

REVUE FRANCAISE D'HISTOIRE DU LIVRE (FR/0037-9212) [01791119] **2706**, **3430**

REVUE FRANCAISE D'OENOLOGIE (FR/0395-899X) [I0395899X] **2370**

REVUE FRANCAISE DU DOMMAGE CORPOREL (FR/0337-730X) [16076499] **2601**, **2892**

REVUE FRANCAISE DU MARKETING (FR/0035-3051) [01877884] **936**

REVUE FRANCOPHONE DE LA DEFICIENCE INTELLECTUELLE (CN/0847-5733) [22632168] **3936**, **3845**

REVUE FRANCOPHONE DE LOUISIANE (US/0890-9555) [13416331] **3431**

REVUE FRONTENAC (CN/0715-9994) [10857633] **3431**

REVUE GABONAISE D'POLITIQUES, ECONOMIQUES, ET JURIDIQUES (GO/1016-2410) [08512016] **4684**

REVUE / GENDARMERIE NATIONALE, LA (FR) [19320216] **4056**

REVUE GENERAL DES ASSURANCES ET DE RESPONSABILITIES (BE) **2892**

REVUE GENERAL NUCLEAIRE (FR/0335-5004) [03287321] **2158**, **1956**

REVUE GENERALE (1985) (BE/0770-8602) [13378189] **2492**

REVUE GENERALE AFRICAINE DES TRAVAUX PUBLICS, DE L'INDUSTRIE ET DES MINES (TG) [02243361] **1582**

REVUE GENERALE DE DROIT (CN/0035-3086) [01764174] **3043**

REVUE GENERALE DE DROIT INTERNATIONAL PUBLIC (FR/0373-6156) [01764176] **3135**

REVUE GENERALE DE FISCALITE (BE) [09559778] **4747**, **3043**

REVUE GENERALE DE HOTELLERIE (FR) **5490**

REVUE GENERALE DE L'AIR ET DE L'ECSPACE (FR) [02240118] 33, **3043**

REVUE GENERALE DE L'ELECTRICITE (FR/0035-3116) [01642009] **2079**

REVUE GENERALE DE L'ETANCHEITE ET DE L'ISOLATION (FR/0035-3132) [I00353132] **2628**

REVUE GENERALE DE SECURITE (FR) **2869**

REVUE GENERALE DE THERMIQUE (FR/0035-3159) [02450216] **2128**

REVUE GENERALE DES CAOUTCHOUCS & PLASTIQUES (FR/0035-3175) [24098975] **5077**

REVUE GENERALE DES CHEMINS DE FER (1924) (FR/0035-3183) [02450217] **5436**

REVUE GENERALE DES ROUTES ET DES AERODROMES (FR/0035-3191) [06127188] 33

REVUE GENERALE DU FROID, LA (FR/0035-3205) [08484107] **2608**

REVUE GENERALE DU GAZ *CEASED.* (BE/0373-5001) [06751522] **4277**

REVUE GENERALE. PERSPECTIVES EUROPEENES DES SCIENCES HUMAINES (BE/0035-306X) [01764173] **5217**

REVUE GEOGRAPHIQUE DE L'EST (FR/0035-3213) [01764183] **2575**

REVUE GEOGRAPHIQUE DES PYRENEES ET DU SUD-OUEST (FR/0035-3221) [02267148] **2575**

●REVUE GERMANIQUE INTERNATIONALE (FR) **2706**

REVUE HEBDOMADAIRE DES INDUSTRIES CHIMIQUES (FR) **2017**

REVUE HELLENIQUE DE DROIT INTERNATIONAL (GR/0035-3256) [10594893] **3135**

REVUE HIPPIQUE, LA (CN/0380-2736) [02110116] **2802**

REVUE HISTORIQUE (FR/0035-3264) [01764185] **2628**

REVUE HISTORIQUE ARDENNAISE (FR/0035-3272) [01881436] 281, **2706**

REVUE HISTORIQUE DE BORDEAUX ET DU DEPARTEMENT DE LA GIRONDE (FR) [01764186] **2706**

REVUE HISTORIQUE DE DROIT FRANCAIS ET ETRANGER (FR/0035-3280) [05907525] **3043**

REVUE HISTORIQUE DES ARMEES (FR/0035-3299) [01794161] **4056**

REVUE HISTORIQUE ET ARCHEOLOGIQUE DU LIBOURNAIS ET DE LA VALLEE DE LA DORDOGNE (FR) [27910221] 281, **2706**

REVUE HISTORIQUE VAUDOISE (SZ/1013-6924) [01645559] 281, **2706**

REVUE HITTITE ET ASIANIQUE *SUSPENDED.* (FR/0080-2603) [01764190] **2663**

REVUE HOLSTEIN QUEBEC, LA (CN/0821-770X) [09863907] **198**

REVUE HORTICOLE SUISSE (SZ/0370-5323) [02431024] **2430**

REVUE HOSPITALIERE DE FRANCE (FR/0397-4626) [01764191] **3792**

REVUE IBEROAMERICANA DE CIRUGIA ORAL MAXILOFACIAL (SP) **3974**

REVUE INFORMATIQUE ET STATISTIQUE DANS LES SCIENCES HUMAINES (BE) [12105679] **3531**

REVUE INTERDISCIPLINAIRE D'ETUDES JURIDIQUES (BE) [10578897] **3043**

REVUE INTERNATIONALE D'ACTION COMMUNAUTAIRE (MONTREAL) (CN/0707-9699) [05720110] **2834**

REVUE INTERNATIONALE DE C.F.A.O. ET D'INFOGRAPHIE (FR/0298-0924) [I02980924] **1121**

REVUE INTERNATIONALE DE CRIMINOLOGIE ET DE POLICE TECHNIQUE (FR/0035-3329) [04999683] **3175**

REVUE INTERNATIONALE DE DROIT COMPARE (FR/0035-3337) [01764195] **3135**

REVUE INTERNATIONALE DE DROIT ECONOMIQUE (BE) [16641980] **2869**

REVUE INTERNATIONALE DE DROIT PENAL / DIRIGEE PAR J.A. ROUX, L. HUGUENEY, H. DONNEDIEU DE VABRES (FR/0223-5404) [01764196] **3109**

REVUE INTERNATIONALE DE LA CONCURRENCE (FR) [07318199] **3103**

REVUE INTERNATIONALE DE LA CROIX-ROUGE (SZ) [08044081] **2911**

REVUE INTERNATIONALE DE LA PROPRIETE INDUSTRIELLE *See* REVUE INTERNATIONALE DE LA PROPRIETE INDUSTRIELLE ET ARTISTIQUE : RIPIA **1308**

REVUE INTERNATIONALE DE LA PROPRIETE INDUSTRIELLE ET ARTISTIQUE : RIPIA (FR/0242-1623) [07333835] **1308**

REVUE INTERNATIONALE DE PARODONTIE & DENTISTERIE RESTAURATRICE (FR/0721-0078) [I07210078] **1335**

REVUE INTERNATIONALE DE PEDIATRIE (FR) **3911**

REVUE INTERNATIONALE DE PHILOSOPHIE (BE/0048-8143) [01462200] **4359**

REVUE INTERNATIONALE DE POLICE CRIMINELLE (FR/0035-3396) [I00353396] **3175**

REVUE INTERNATIONALE DE PROTECTION CIVILE (SZ) [19036951] **4800**

REVUE INTERNATIONALE DE PSYCHOLOGIE SOCIALE (FR/0992-986X) [26321842] **4617**

REVUE INTERNATIONALE DE PSYCHOPATHOLOGIE PARIS (FR/1150-6652) [I11506652] **3936**

REVUE INTERNATIONALE DE RHUMATOLOGIE *CEASED.* (FR/0294-474X) [11203917] **3807**

REVUE INTERNATIONALE DE SECURITE SOCIALE (SZ/0379-0312) [I03790312] **5306**

REVUE INTERNATIONALE DE SYSTEMIQUE (FR/0980-1472) [16893647] **1252**

REVUE INTERNATIONALE DES DROITS DE L'ANTIQUITE. 3E SERIE (BE) [01588100] **3043**

REVUE INTERNATIONALE DES HAUTES TEMPERATURES ET DES REFRACTAIRES (US/0035-3434) [02450226] **4432**, **1057**

REVUE INTERNATIONALE DES SCIENCES DE L'EAU (CN/0830-9590) [14954922] **1417**

REVUE INTERNATIONALE DES SCIENCES SOCIALES (FR/0304-3037) [I03043037] **5217**

REVUE INTERNATIONALE DES SERVICES DE SANTE DES FORCES ARMEES : ORGANE DU COMITE INTERNATIONAL DE MEDECINE ETUDE PHARMACIE MILITAIRES (BE/0259-8582) [16529776] **4056**, **3636**

REVUE INTERNATIONALE D'HISTOIRE PSYCHANALYSE *CEASED.* (FR) **4617**

REVUE INTERNATIONALE D'OCEANOGRAPHIE MEDICALE (FR/0035-3493) [01764207] **3636**

REVUE INTERNATIONALE D'ONOMASTIQUE *CEASED.* (FR) [01605655] **2470**

REVUE INTERNATIONALE DU DROIT D'AUTEUR (FR/0035-3515) [01764208] **1308**

REVUE INTERNATIONALE DU TRACHOME ET DE PATHOLOGIE OCULAIRE TROPICALE ET SUBTROPICALE ET DE SANTE PUBLIQUE (FR/0246-0831) [08631325] **3636**, **3879**

REVUE INTERNATIONALE DU TRAVAIL (SZ/0378-5599) [I03785599] **1708**

REVUE INTERNATIONALE P M E (BE) **708**

REVUE INTERNATIONALE POUR L'ENSEIGNEMENT COMMERCIAL. INTERNATIONAL REVIEW FOR BUSINESS EDUCATION. INTERNATIONAL ZEITSCHRIFT FUR KAUFMANNISCHES BILDUNGSWESEN. RIVISTA INTERNAZIONALE PER LA CULTURA COMMERCIALE. REVISTA INTERNACIONAL PARA LA ENSENANZA COMMERCIAL (SZ/0035-354X) [02255887] **1780**, **708**

REVUE IVOIRIENNE DE DROIT ECONOMIQUE ET COMPTABLE (IV) [27457009] **1518**

REVUE JEUNESSE (CN/0711-3455) [08649633] **4865**

REVUE JURIDIQUE DE L'ENVIRONNEMENT (FR) [06874320] **3116**

REVUE JURIDIQUE DES ETUDIANTS ET ETUDIANTES DE L'UNIVERSITE LAVAL, LA (CN/0845-9401) [20777943] **3043**

REVUE JURIDIQUE DU BURUNDI (BD) [08997587] **3043**

REVUE JURIDIQUE DU CENTRE QUEST (FR/0985-2549) [20288602] **3043**

REVUE JURIDIQUE DU CONGO *See* REVUE JURIDIQUE DU ZAIRE **3043**

REVUE JURIDIQUE DU RWANDA. IGAZETI ISOBANURA AMATEGEKO MU RWANDA (NR) [05250882] **3043**

REVUE JURIDIQUE DU ZAIRE (CG) [01785166] **3043**

REVUE JURIDIQUE DU ZAIRE; DROIT ECRIT ET DROIT COUTUMIER (CG) [01643106] **3043**

REVUE JURIDIQUE ET POLITIQUE, INDEPENDANCE ET COOPERATION (FR/0035-3574) [02977450] **3043**

REVUE JURIDIQUE, POLITIQUE, ET ECONOMIQUE DU MAROC (MR/0251-4761) [15097733] **3043**

REVUE JURIDIQUE THEMIS (1970) (CN/0556-7963) [01587856] **3044**

REVUE JURIDIQUE THEMIS (1970) (CN/0556-7963) [10256132] **3044**

REVUE - LA COMMISSION NATIONALE DE LA REPUBLIQUE SOCIALISTE DE ROUMANIE. JOURNAL - THE NATIONAL COMMISSION OF THE SOCIALIST REPUBLIC OF ROMANIA (RM) [04486208] **4684**

REVUE — Alphabetical Title Index

REVUE LAITIERE FRANCAISE (FR/0035-3590) [02955466] **220**

REVUE LE PAYSAN FRANCAIS (FR) [13882066] **130**

REVUE LITTERAIRE DU C.E.G.E.P. DE GRANBY (CN/0229-2297) [07888509] **3351**

REVUE MABILLON (FR/0035-3620) [01883449] 5035, **4994**

REVUE MABILLON: REVUE INTERNATIONAL D'HISTOIRE ET DE LITERATURE RELIGIEUSES (BE) 4994, **2706**

REVUE MARITIME 1990, LA (FR/1146-2132) [I11462132] **4182**

REVUE MARIVAUX (FR) [23275242] **3431**

REVUE MAROCAINE DE MEDECINE ET SANTE (MR/0251-0758) [06964544] **3636**

REVUE MEDICALE DE BRUXELLES (BE/0035-3639) [06292525] **3636**

REVUE MEDICALE DE LA SUISSE ROMANDE (SZ/0035-3655) [01764216] **3637**

REVUE MEDICALE DE L'ASSURANCE MALADIE (FR/0767-2004) [07672004] **3637**

REVUE MEDICALE DE LIEGE (BE/0370-629X) [04521524] **3637**

REVUE MENSUELLE DE FABRIMETAL MAGAZINE See FABRIMETAL **3478**

REVUE MILITAIRE SUISSE (SZ) [07367540] **4056**

REVUE MOTO TECHNIQUE BOULOGNE-SUR-SEINE (FR/0150-7214) [I01507214] 5424, **1625**

REVUE MUNICIPALE. ANNUAIRE (MONTREAL) (CN/0317-5510) [02248353] **4684**

REVUE MUNICIPALE (MONTREAL) (CN/0035-3728) [02110184] **4684**

REVUE MUSICALE DE SUISSE ROMANDE (SZ) [09077868] **4150**

REVUE NATIONALE DE LA CHASSE (FR) **4878**

REVUE NEUROLOGIQUE (FR/0035-3787) [01605920] **3845**

REVUE - NEW YORK UNIVERSITY. INSTITUTE OF FRENCH STUDIES (US/1058-1278) [24238749] **2706**

●REVUE NOIRE (FR/1157-4127) [24056710] **330**

REVUE NOUVELLE, LA (BE/0035-3809) [02593996] **2522**

REVUE NUMISMATIQUE (FR/0484-8942) [01607866] **2783**

REVUE OBHCODU, PRUMYSLU, HOSPODARSTVI (XR/0139-7036) [06158585] **1582**

REVUE - OFFICE INTERNATIONAL DES EPIZOOTIES (FR/0253-1933) [08941771] **5521**

REVUE OFFICIELLE DE LA SOCIETE FRANCAISE D'ORL ET DE PATHOLOGIE CERVICO-FACIALE (FR/1155-1087) **3891**

REVUE OLYMPIQUE (SZ/0251-3498) [I02513498] **4915**

REVUE... OPTIQUE... See REVUE : UN BULLETIN DE L'INSTITUT NORD-SUD **1625**

REVUE PARLEMENTAIRE CANADIENNE (CN/0229-2556) [07869871] **4684**

REVUE PENITENTIAIRE ET DE DROIT PENAL (1940) (FR) [07512479] **3175**

REVUE PHARMACOCINETIQUE (CN/0821-5987) [09774926] **4328**

REVUE PHILOSOPHIQUE (FR) **4359**

REVUE PHILOSOPHIQUE DE LA FRANCE ET DE L'ETRANGER (FR/0035-3833) [01764234] **4359**

REVUE PHILOSOPHIQUE DE LOUVAIN (BE/0035-3841) [04734362] **4360**

REVUE POLITIQUE ET PARLEMENTAIRE (FR/0035-385X) [01605422] **5217**

REVUE POLYTECHNIQUE (SZ/0374-4256) [I03744256] **5148**

REVUE PRACTIQUE DE DROIT SOCIAL (FR) [05804931] **3044**

REVUE PRATIQUE DE CONTROLE INDUSTRIEL 1984 (FR/0766-5210) [I07665210] **3487**

REVUE PRATIQUE DE PSYCHOLOGIE DE LA VIE SOCIALE ET DE L'HYGIENE MENTALE (FR) **4617**

REVUE PRATIQUE DES SOCIETES CIVILES & COMMERCIALES (BE) **3044**

REVUE PRATIQUE DU FROID ET DU CONDITIONNEMENT DE L'AIR (FR/0370-6699) [03056928] **2608**

REVUE PRESCRIRE, LA (FR/0247-7750) [I02477750] **3637**

REVUE QUART MONDE (FR) **4512**

REVUE QUEBECOISE DE BRIDGE, LA (CN/0828-5012) [12093237] **4865**

REVUE QUEBECOISE DE DROIT INTERNATIONAL (CN/0828-9999) [13541392] **3135**

REVUE QUEBECOISE DE LINGUISTIQUE THEORIQUE ET APPLIQUEE (CN/0835-3581) [15514507] **3317**

REVUE QUEBECOISE DE PSYCHOLOGIE (CN/0225-9885) [06563065] **4617**

REVUE QUEBECOISE DE SCIENCE POLITIQUE (CN/1189-9565) [30530892] **4495**

REVUE QUEBECOISE DE SEXOLOGIE **SUSPENDED.** (CN/0707-9516) [05761596] **5188**

REVUE QUEBECOISE D'ERGOTHERAPIE (CN/1192-0238) [11920238] **4382**

REVUE QUEBECOISE D URBANISME (CN/0842-957X) [19491117] **2834**

REVUE RECHERCHES (FR) **5148**

REVUE REFORMEE, LA (FR/0035-3884) [01774098] **5067**

REVUE RESSOURCES HUMAINES (FR) **947**

REVUE ROMANE (DK/0035-3906) [01695833] **3317**

REVUE ROUMAINE DE BIOCHIMIE (RM/0001-4214) [01608084] **493**

REVUE ROUMAINE DE BIOLOGIE. SERIE DE BIOLOGIE ANIMALE (RM/0377-8142) [02715717] **472**

REVUE ROUMAINE DE BIOLOGIE. SERIE DE BIOLOGIE VEGETALE (GW/0250-5517) [03231171] **526**

REVUE ROUMAINE DE CHIMIE (RM/0035-3930) [01590062] **991**

REVUE ROUMAINE DE GEOLOGIE / ACADEMIA ROMANA (RM) [25662371] **1395**

REVUE ROUMAINE DE GEOPHYSIQUE / ACADEMIE ROUMAINE (RM) [25662339] **1410**

REVUE ROUMAINE DE LINGUISTIQUE (RM/0035-3957) [03364106] **3317**

REVUE ROUMAINE DE MATHEMATIQUES PURES ET APPLIQUEES (RM/0035-3965) [06047747] **3531**

REVUE ROUMAINE DE MECANIQUE APPLIQUE (RM) **2128**

REVUE ROUMAINE DE MEDECINE INTERNE (1990) (RM/1220-4749) [27979017] **3801**

REVUE ROUMAINE DE NEUROLOGIE ET PSYCHIATRIE (1990) (RM/1017-5644) [22592732] 3936, **3845**

REVUE ROUMAINE DE PHILOSOPHIE / ACADEMIA ROMANA (RM) [25357299] **4360**

REVUE ROUMAINE DE PHYSIOLOGIE (BUCHAREST, ROMANIA : 1990) See ROMANIAN JOURNAL OF PHYSIOLOGY : PHYSIOLOGICAL SCIENCES / [ACADEMIA DE STIINTE MEDICALE] **586**

REVUE ROUMAINE DE PHYSIOLOGIE / ROMANIAN JOURNAL OF PHYSIOLOGY (RM) [22397776] **586**

REVUE ROUMAINE DE PHYSIQUE (RM/0035-4090) [01764242] **4420**

●REVUE ROUMAINE DE PSYCHOLOGIE / ACADEMIE ROUMAINE (RM/1220-5419) [27909195] **4617**

REVUE ROUMAINE DE VIROLOGIE (1990) (RM/1018-0532) [22807860] **569**

REVUE ROUMAINE D'EMBRYOLOGIE ET DE CYTOLOGIE. SERIE DE CYTOLOGIE (RM/0035-4007) [01774099] **540**

REVUE ROUMAINE DES SCIENCES SOCIALES. SERIE DE SCIENCES JURIDIQUES (RM/0035-4023) [01644989] **5217**

REVUE ROUMAINE DES SCIENCES TECHNIQUES SERIE DE MECANIQUE APPLIQUE See REVUE ROUMAINE DE MECANIQUE APPLIQUE **2128**

REVUE ROUMAINE DES SCIENCES TECHNIQUES. SERIE DE MECANIQUE APPLIQUEE (RM/0035-4074) [01586790] **2128**

REVUE ROUMAINE DES SCIENCES TECHNIQUES. SERIE ELECTROTECHNIQUE ET ENERGETIQUE (RM/0035-4066) [06130732] **4420**

REVUE ROUMAINE D'ETUDES INTERNATIONALES (RM/0048-8178) [02979721] **4534**

REVUE ROUMAINE D'HISTOIRE (RM/0556-8072) [01764247] **2706**

REVUE ROUMAINE D'HISTOIRE DE L'ART. SERIE BEAUX-ARTS (RM/0080-262X) [01881514] **330**

REVUE ROUMAINE D'HISTOIRE DE L'ART. SERIE THEATRE, MUSIQUE, CINEMA (RM) [01931226] **388**

REVUE ROUMAINE ELECTROTECHNIQUE ET ENERGETIQUE (RM) **4420**

REVUE S.A.M.U, LA (FR/0399-0265) [I03990265] **1068**

REVUE SAINTE ANNE, LA (CN/0831-0777) [13784779] **5035**

REVUE SAVOISIENNE (FR) [01764248] **2707**

REVUE SCHWEIZ (SZ) **708**

REVUE SCIENCE ET TECHNIQUE. SERIE SCIENCES AGRONOMIQUES ET ZOOTECHNIQUES (CM/0257-3385) [16162969] 5596, **185**

REVUE SCIENTIFIQUE ET TECHNIQUE DE LA DEFENSE (FR/0994-1541) [19084667] **4056**

REVUE SENEGALAISE DE DROIT (SG/0035-4112) [01764251] **3044**

REVUE SIEMENS (GW) [09092088] **2079**

REVUE STATISTIQUE DU CANADA. SUPPLEMENT (CN/0823-311X) [06149448] **5337**

REVUE STOMATO ODONTOLOGIQUE DU NORD DE LA FRANCE (FR/0035-4147) [I00354147] **1335**

REVUE SUISSE D'AGRICULTURE (SZ/0375-1325) [02409262] **130**

REVUE SUISSE DE NUMISMATIQUE (SZ) [01929354] **2783**

REVUE SUISSE DE VITICULTURE, ARBORICULTURE, HORTICULTURE (SZ/0375-1430) [02405133] **2430**

REVUE SUISSE DE ZOOLOGIE (SZ/0035-418X) [01587502] **5596**

REVUE SYNDICALE SUISSE (SZ/0035-421X) [05651968] **1708**

REVUE TECHNIQUE AUTOMOBILE (FR/0017-307X) [I0017307X] **5424**

REVUE TECHNIQUE CARROSSERIE (FR/0150-7206) [I01507206] **5424**

REVUE TECHNIQUE DE BATIMENT ET DES CONSTUCTIONS INDUSTRIELLES (FR/0397-9296) [I03979296] **2030**

REVUE TECHNIQUE DE LA VIANDE ET DES ABATTOIRS (FR) **220**

REVUE TECHNIQUE DIESEL (FR/0037-2579) [05261776] **5424**

REVUE TECHNIQUE EQUIP HOTEL (FR) **2809**

REVUE TECHNIQUE ET ECONOMIQUE DE L'INDUSTRIE ALIMENTAIRE See R.I.A. (PARIS, 1977) **2355**

REVUE TECHNIQUE - GEC ALSTHOM (FR/1148-2893) [I11482893] 5148, **2079**

REVUE TECHNIQUE LUXEMBOURGEOISE (LU/0035-4260) [02450231] **5148**

REVUE TECHNIQUE MACHINISME AGRICOLE (FR/0223-0135) [I02230135] 161, **5424**

REVUE TECHNIQUE THOMSON-CSF (FR/0035-4279) [01764253] **2079**

REVUE THEOLOGIQUE DE LOUVAIN (BE/0080-2654) [01776690] **4994**

REVUE THOMISTE (FR/0035-4295) [01764254] 4360, **4994**

REVUE TIRES A PART (CN/0843-5952) [24266599] **4617**

REVUE TRIMESTRIELLE DE DROIT CIVIL (PARIS, FRANCE : 1980) (FR/0397-9873) [07209609] **3091**

REVUE TRIMESTRIELLE DE DROIT COMMERCIAL ET DE DROIT ECONOMIQUE (FR/0244-9358) [06743630] **3103**

REVUE TRIMESTRIELLE DE DROIT EUROPEEN (COURT OF JUSTICE OF THE EUROPEAN COMMUNITIES) (FR/0035-4317) [08166379] **3044**

REVUE TRIMESTRIELLE DE DROIT FAMILIAL (BE) [05069987] **3122**

REVUE TRIMESTRIELLE DES DROITS DE L'HOMME (BE/0777-3579) [22795673] **4512**

REVUE TRIMESTRIELLE D'INFORMATION TECHNIQUE ET ECONOMIQUE (UV) [04984608] **220**

REVUE TUNISIENNE DE COMMUNICATION (TI/0330-8480) [11751514] **1121**

REVUE TUNISIENNE DE DROIT (TI) [01716631] **3044**

REVUE TUNISIENNE DE GEOGRAPHIE (TI) [05383618] **2575**

REVUE TUNISIENNE DE L'EQUIPEMENT (TI) [02241026] **2030**

REVUE TUNISIENNE DE SCIENCES SOCIALES (TI/0035-4333) [01770946] **5217**

●REVUE : UN BULLETIN DE L'INSTITUT NORD-SUD (CN/1188-4347) [26497773] **1625**

REVUE UNIVERSELLE DES DROITS DE L'HOMME (GW/0937-714X) [22929658] **4512**

REVUE UNIVERSITAIRE DE LIEGE (BE) [01640598] **1846**

REVUE VERVIETOISE D'HISTOIRE NATURELLE (BE/0375-1465) [09618745] **4171**

REVUE VINICOLE INTERNATIONALE. THE INTERNATIONAL WINE REVIEW (FR) [04077297] **2370**

REVUE VOILE QUEBEC, LA (CN/0820-4969) [16728223] **595**

REVUE VOYAGEUR, LA *CEASED.* (CN/0824-1309) [11825478] **5490**

REVUE ZAIROISE DE PSYCHOLOGIE ET DE PEDAGOGIE (CG) [01787867] **4617**

REVUE ZAIROISE DES SCIENCES NUCLEAIRES (CG/0252-1091) [10927415] **4451**

REVUSER (PHILADELPHIA, PA.) (US/1051-8118) [22133925] **1281, 1289**

REWIA ROZRYWKI (PL/0137-8295) [101378295] **4865**

REXBURG STANDARD/JOURNAL, THE (US) [11148048] **5657**

REXDALE TIMES REVIEW (CN/0316-5442) [02247479] **5794**

REYNOLDS COUNTY COURIER (ELLINGTON, MO.) (US) [19565393] **5704**

REYNOLDS RECORDS (US/1057-6010) [24056747] **2470**

REYNOLDSVILLE STAR, THE (US) [15681465] **5739**

REZA KAGAKU KENKYU (JA) [10387164] **4441**

REZA KENKYU (JA/0387-0200) [10463717] **4441**

REZO (CN/0711-1258) [08794451] **330**

REZULTATI SAMOPOPISIVANJA I POSTANSKIH METODA U BEOGRADU ... GODINE (YU) [08331094] **4560**

RFBH *See* BIJOUTIER : REVUE FRANCAISE DES BIJOUTIERS HORLOGERS, LE **2916**

RFD NEWS *See* NATIONAL RURAL LETTER CARRIER, THE **1146**

RFD (WOLF CREEK) (US/0149-709X) [03534835] **2796**

RFE. REVISTA FORESTAL ESPANOLA (SP/1130-958X) [I1130958X] 2220, **2394**

RFE/RL RESEARCH REPORT *CEASED.* (GW/0941-505X) [25118443] **1138**

RFL. RUNDSCHAU FUER FLEISCHUNTERSUCHUNG UND LEBENSMITTELUBERWACHUNG (GW/0178-2010) [01782010] **5521**

RFM REVUE FRANCAISE DES METALLURGISTES (FR/0988-629X) [I0988629X] **4018**

RG (CN/0831-375X) [15060075] **2796**

● RHEEDEA (CALICUT) (II/0971-2313) [25908359] **526**

RHEIN-MAINISCHE FORSCHUNGEN (GW/0080-2662) [02884316] **2575**

RHEINFELDER NEUJAHRSBLATTER (SZ) [06715658] **2707**

RHEINISCH-WESTFALISCHE AKADEMIE DER WISSENSCHAFTEN *See* VORTRAGE - RHEINISCH-WESTFALISCHE AKADEMIE DER WISSENSCHAFTEN, N, NATUR-, INGENIEUR- UND WIRTSCHAFTSWISSENSCHAFTEN **5169**

RHEINISCH-WESTFALISCHES INSTITUT FUR WIRTSCHAFTSFORSCHUNG ESSEN *See* KONJUNKTUR IM HANDWERK, DIE **1615**

RHEINISCHE AUSGRABUNGEN (GW) [06980742] **281**

RHEINISCHE LANDESMUSEUM BONN, DAS (GW/0524-0344) [I05240344] **4096**

RHEINISCHE LEBENSBILDER (GW/0080-2670) [06640731] **2628**

RHEINISCHE POST (GW) [12258850] **5802**

RHEINISCHE VIERTELJAHRSBLATTER (GW/0035-4473) [01641060] **2707**

RHEINISCHES JAHRBUCH FUER VOLKSKUNDE (GW/0080-2697) [04595767] **2324**

RHEINISCHES MUSEUM FUER PHILOLOGIE (GW/0035-449X) [06314167] **3317**

RHEINLAND-PALATINATE (GERMANY). LANDTAG *See* GLIEDERUNG DES LANDTAGS RHEINLAND-PFALZ ... WAHLPERIODE **4650**

RHEINSTAHL AKTIENGESELLSCHAFT *See* RHEINSTAHL TECHNIK **4018**

RHEINSTAHL TECHNIK (GW) [04250355] **4018**

RHENIUM (US) [03058486] 1444, **2150**

RHEOLOGICA ACTA (GW/0035-4511) [01764267] **4420**

RHEOLOGY (GW) **4429**

RHEOLOGY ABSTRACTS (UK/0035-452X) [01764268] **4429**

RHEOLOGY GERMANY (GW/0103-6440) [26760493] **1335**

RHEOLOGY SERIES (NE) [10836473] **4420**

RHETORIC REVIEW (US/0735-0198) [08832040] **3317**

RHETORIC SOCIETY QUARTERLY (US/0277-3945) [03350240] **3317**

RHETORICA (US/0734-8584) [08854766] **3317**

RHETORIK (GW/0720-5775) [07663756] **3317**

RHEUMA (MADRID) (SP/0211-7274) [I02117274] **3637**

RHEUMA, SCHMERZ & ENTZUNDUNG (GW/0721-8222) [09144917] **3637**

RHEUMATIC DISEASE CLINICS OF NORTH AMERICA (US/0889-857X) [14091867] **3807**

RHEUMATOLOGY (SZ/0080-2727) [01764270] **3807**

RHEUMATOLOGY FORUM (UK/0268-747X) [19349367] **3807**

RHEUMATOLOGY INTERNATIONAL (GW/0172-8172) [07936681] **3807**

RHEUMATOLOGY REVIEW (EDINBURGH) (UK/0958-2584) [I09582584] **3807**

RHINELAND-PALATINATE *See* STAATS-ZEITUNG; STAATSANZEIGER FUER RHEINLANDJ-PFALZ (MICROFICHE) **4687**

RHINELAND-PALATINATE. (GERMANY). MINISTERIUM FUR SOZIALES, GESUNDHEIT UND SPORT *See* LANDESJUGENDPLAN : DURCHFUHRUNGSPLAN **5294**

RHINELAND-PALATINATE. (GERMANY). MINISTERIUM FUR SOZIALES, GESUNDHEIT UND SPORT *See* JAHRESHERICHT - RHEINLAND PFALZ, MINISTERIUM FUER SOZIALES, GESUNDHEIT UND SPORT **5205**

RHINOLOGY (NE/0300-0729) [07633948] **3891**

RHINOLOGY. SUPPLEMENT (NE/1013-0047) [16814668] **3897**

RHODANIE (FR/0751-2325) [I07512325] **2628**

RHODE ISLAND *See* PUBLIC LAWS OF THE STATE OF RHODE ISLAND AND PROVIDENCE PLANTATIONS PASSED AT THE GENERAL ASSEMBLY **3033**

RHODE ISLAND *See* GENERAL LAWS OF RHODE ISLAND **2973**

RHODE ISLAND ANNUAL HIGHWAY SAFETY REPORT (US) [13318389] **4800**

RHODE ISLAND BAR JOURNAL (US/0556-8595) [01764296] **3044**

RHODE ISLAND BASIC ECONOMIC STATISTICS (US/0361-0632) [02784501] **1518**

RHODE ISLAND BUSINESS DIRECTORY (US/1048-7166) [21010830] **708**

RHODE ISLAND CASE NAMES CITATOR (US) **3044**

RHODE ISLAND DENTAL JOURNAL, THE (US/0091-8903) [04091899] **1335**

RHODE ISLAND. DEPARTMENT OF ECONOMIC DEVELOPMENT *See* RHODE ISLAND DEPARTMENT OF ECONOMIC DEVELOPMENT ANNUAL REPORT **1582**

RHODE ISLAND DEPARTMENT OF ECONOMIC DEVELOPMENT ANNUAL REPORT (US) [02468112] **1582**

RHODE ISLAND. DEPT. OF CORRECTIONS *See* CORRECTIONS, STATE OF RHODE ISLAND **3161**

RHODE ISLAND. DEPT. OF EMPLOYMENT SECURITY *See* STATISTICAL AND FISCAL DIGEST - RHODE ISLAND. DEPT. OF EMPLOYMENT SECURITY **1538**

RHODE ISLAND. DEPT. OF HEALTH *See* ANNUAL REPORT - RHODE ISLAND. DEPT. OF HEALTH (1979) **4766**

RHODE ISLAND. DEPT. OF MENTAL HEALTH, RETARDATION AND HOSPITALS *See* MENTAL HEALTH, RETARDATION AND HOSPITALS (CRANSTON) **3789**

RHODE ISLAND. DEPT. OF SOCIAL AND REHABILITATIVE SERVICES *See* SOCIAL AND REHABILITATIVE SERVICES (CRANSTON) **5308**

RHODE ISLAND. DEPT. OF STATE *See* MANUAL - THE STATE OF RHODE ISLAND AND PROVIDENCE PLANTATIONS **4664**

RHODE ISLAND. DEPT. OF TRANSPORTATION *See* DEPARTMENT OF TRANSPORTATION, STATE OF RHODE ISLAND **5381**

RHODE ISLAND. DEVELOPMENT COUNCIL. REPORT *See* RHODE ISLAND DEPARTMENT OF ECONOMIC DEVELOPMENT ANNUAL REPORT **1582**

RHODE ISLAND DIRECTORY OF MANUFACTURERS (US/0361-5103) [06608918] **3487**

RHODE ISLAND. DIVISION OF FISH AND GAME *See* DIVISION OF FISH AND GAME **2191**

RHODE ISLAND. ECONOMIC RESEARCH DIVISION *See* RHODE ISLAND BASIC ECONOMIC STATISTICS **1518**

RHODE ISLAND GENEALOGICAL REGISTER (US/0190-3055) [04660587] **2470**

RHODE ISLAND. GOVERNOR *See* STATE OF RHODE ISLAND AND PROVIDENCE PLANTATIONS, BUDGET IN BRIEF **4749**

RHODE ISLAND. GOVERNOR'S COUNCIL ON MENTAL HEALTH *See* ANNUAL REPORT - RHODE ISLAND GOVERNOR'S COUNCIL ON MENTAL HEALTH **4766**

● RHODE ISLAND HEALTH CARE IN PERSPECTIVE (US/1065-4402) [26606636] **4800**

RHODE ISLAND HISTORY (US/0035-4619) [01696593] **2759**

RHODE ISLAND IN PERSPECTIVE (US/1065-5670) [26662113] **5337**

RHODE ISLAND JEWISH HISTORICAL NOTES (US/0556-8609) [01764299] **2272**

RHODE ISLAND LAWYERS WEEKLY (US/0279-0882) [07518649] **3044**

RHODE ISLAND LIBRARY ASSOCIATION *See* RILA BULLETIN **3247**

RHODE ISLAND MAGAZINE *CEASED.* (US/0199-526X) [05965142] **2544**

RHODE ISLAND MEDICAL JOURNAL *See* RHODE ISLAND MEDICINE **3637**

● RHODE ISLAND MEDICINE (US/1061-222X) [25125272] **3637**

RHODE ISLAND MONTHLY (US/1041-1380) [18499849] **5490**

RHODE ISLAND QUERIES (US/0893-181X) [15372185] **2470**

RHODE ISLAND RESOURCES (US/0035-4635) [04574535] **130**

RHODE ISLAND ROOTS (US/0730-1235) [07936145] **2470**

RHODE ISLAND SCHOOL OF DESIGN. MUSEUM OF ART *See* MUSEUM NOTES (PROVIDENCE, R.I.) **359**

RHODES TODAY (US/0891-6446) [14939453] **1094**

RHODESIA. MINISTRY OF WATER DEVELOPMENT *See* REPORT OF THE SECRETARY FOR WATER DEVELOPMENT (RHODESIA) **5538**

RHODESIA RAILWAYS MAGAZINE *See* NATIONAL RAILWAYS OF ZIMBABWE **5433**

RHODESIA, SOUTHERN. AGRICULTURAL RESEARCH COUNCIL *See* TECHNICAL REPORT - AGRICULTURAL RESEARCH COUNCIL OF RHODESIA **140**

RHODESIA, SOUTHERN. DEPT. OF WORKS *See* REPORT OF THE CONTROLLER OF WORKS **4681**

RHODESIA, SOUTHERN. MINISTRY OF LANDS *See* REPORT OF THE SECRETARY FOR LANDS - RHODESIA, SOUTHERN **2203**

RHODESIAN RIDGEBACK QUARTERLY, THE (US/8750-3549) [11269381] **4287**

RHODESIANS WORLDWIDE (UK) [16883308] 2272, **2500**

RHODODENDRON, THE (AT/0485-0637) [02271462] **2430**

RHODODENDRON UND IMMERGRUNE LAUBGEHOLZE (GW/0482-9905) [12337545] **526**

RHODODENDRON UND IMMERGRUNE LAUBGEHOLZE JAHRBUCH (GW/0482-9905) [02522083] **2430**

RHODORA (US/0035-4902) [01764319] **526**

RHOMBUS (AT/0310-7205) [I03107205] **3532**

RHONDA WHITE-WARNER'S TIDBITS (US/1041-9799) [18894720] **2492**

RHUMATOLOGIE (AIX-LES-BAINS) (FR/0249-7581) [07635440] **3807**

RHYTHM (SASKATOON) (CN/0820-9626) [09631173] **4150**

RIA INTERNATIONAL, REVUE DES INDUSTRIES D'ART EXPORT (FR) [02173895] 850, **363**

RIA, LE TECHNICIEN DU LAIT (FR/0295-4303) [13320730] **198**

RIA, REVUE DES INDUSTRIES D'ART EXPORT *See* RIA INTERNATIONAL, REVUE DES INDUSTRIES D'ART EXPORT **363**

RIA ROBOTICS GLOSSARY (US/0741-9473) [10240903] **1216**

RIABILITAZIONE (IT/0557-9430) [I05579430] **4393**

RIABILITAZIONE E APPRENDIMENTO (IT/0393-7518) [I03937518] **4382**

RIABILITAZIONE, LA (IT) **3637**

RIABILITAZIONE OGGI (IT) **4382**

RIALTO, THE (UK/0268-5981) [12993011] **3470**

RIAS QUARTAL (GW) [07720607] **1138**

RIAZI (PK/0255-7568) [09998283] **3532**

● RIBA JOURNAL (UK) [28912371] **308**

RIBA MEMBERS (UK) [22844494] **308**

RIBC BISCUITERIE CHOCOLATERIE (FR) **2356**

RIBERUTERU (JA) [02779120] **4546**

RIBOSOMES & TRANSLATION (UK/0952-0414) [I09520414] **551**

RIC; REPERTOIRE BIBLIOGRAPHIQUE DES INSTITUTIONS CHRETIENNES (FR) [04828141] **4994**

RIC SUPPLEMENT (FR) [01589230] **4994**

RICARDA HUCH, STUDIEN ZU IHREM LEBEN UND WERK (GW) [19081011] **3431**

RICARDIAN (UK/0048-8267) [11995669] **5236**

RICE ABSTRACTS (UK/0141-0164) [04065534] 130, **1012**

RICE COUNTY HISTORIAN (US) **2470**

RICE CROP QUALITY (US/0193-1032) [05112050] **185**

RICE FARMING AND RICE INDUSTRY NEWS (US/0194-0929) [05321039] **185**

RICE JOURNAL (1938), THE (US/0035-4961) [05267092] **185**

RICE MARKET NEWS (US/0364-8087) [01607377] **130**

RICE MARKET REPORT (US/8750-460X) [11460616] **185**

RICE PLUS (US/0887-753X) [13377665] **1625**

RICE REVIEW / COMPILED BY RURAL ECONOMICS DIVISION, JCRR (CH) [01786628] **185**

RICE STOCKS (US/1057-7920) [02643480] **185**

RICE UNIVERSITY ALUMNI DIRECTORY (US) [05178295] **1102**

RICE WORLD (US) **185**

RICE WORLD & SOYBEAN NEWS *See* RICE WORLD **185**

RICE WORLD & SOYBEAN NEWS, THE (US/0738-5943) [09451675] **185**

RICERCA & PRATICA (IT/1120-379X) [I1120379X] **3637**

RICERCA E INNOVAZIONE (IT) **5148**

RICERCA EDUCATIVA (IT) **1780**

RICERCA FOLKLORICA, LA (IT/0391-9099) [07352741] **2324**

RICERCA; MATEMATICHE PURE ED APPLICATE (IT/0048-8283) [02604763] **3532**

RICERCA SOCIALE, LA (IT) [04479646] **5256**

RICERCHE DI BIOLOGIA DELLA SELVAGGINA (IT/0375-0736) [02002365] **5596**

RICERCHE DI MATEMATICA (IT/0035-5038) [01640734] **3532**

RICERCHE DI PSICOLOGIA (IT/0391-6081) [04896083] **4617**

RICERCHE DI STORIA DELL'ARTE (IT/0392-7202) [05070547] **363**

RICERCHE DI STORIA SOCIALE E RELIGIOSA (IT) [01786292] **4994**

RICERCHE DIDATTICHE (IT/0035-5046) [I00355046] **1781**

RICERCHE ECONOMICHE (IT/0035-5054) [13213808] **1518**

RICERCHE PEDAGOGICHE (IT) **1781**

RICERCHE SLAVISTICHE (IT/0391-4127) [01623993] **3317**

RICERCHE STORICHE (IT) [02245188] **2707**

RICERCHE STORICHE SALESIANA / A CURA DELL'ISTITUTO STORICO SALESIANO (IT) [10713108] **5035**

RICERCHE STORICO BIBLICHE : RSB (IT/0394-980X) [20974376] **5019**

RICERCHE SUL 600 NAPOLETANO (IT) **2628**

RICERCHE SUL SEI-SETTECENTO IN PUGLIA (IT) [08483534] **363**

RICERCHE SULLE DIMORE RURALI IN ITALIA (IT/0080-2964) [05701685] **308**

RICH MAC MAGAZINE (IT) **991**

RICH VIVONE'S INSIGHT INTO GOVERNMENT (CN/0849-567X) [21349168] **4684**

RICHARD C. YOUNG'S INTELLIGENCE REPORT (US/0884-3031) [12358031] **810**

RICHARD C YOUNG'S INTERNATIONAL GOLD REPORT (US/0895-1306) [16507826] **1518**

● RICHARD E PIGGLE. STUDI PSICOANALITICI DEL BAMBINO E DELL'ADOLESCENTE (IT) 1068, **4617**

RICHARD STRAUSS-BLATTER (AU) [03572957] **4150**

RICHARD STRAUSS JAHRBUCH (GW) [04534715] **2492**

RICHARDSON CONSTRUCTION COST TREND REPORTER, THE (US/0744-9240) [07297034] **626**

RICHARDSON ENGINEERING SERVICES *See* RICHARDSON CONSTRUCTION COST TREND REPORTER, THE **626**

RICHARDSON FAMILY RESEARCHER AND HISTORICAL NEWS (US/0147-2488) [03125966] **2470**

RICHARDSON NEWS (US/1045-4004) [20104812] **5754**

RICHFIELD REAPER, THE (US/0746-6730) [10214260] **5757**

● RICHLAND COUNTY NEWS-MONITOR (US/1061-1029) [25181444] **5726**

RICHLAND OBSERVER (RICHLAND CENTER, WIS.) (US) [13042773] **5770**

RICHLAND REVIEW (US) [16996285] **5762**

RICHLANDS NEWS PRESS (US) **5759**

RICHMOND AFRO-AMERICAN AND RICHMOND PLANET (RICHMOND, VA. : 1941) (US/0893-0805) [10702414] **5687**

RICHMOND BUSINESS JOURNAL, THE (US/0889-3357) [13848679] **708**

RICHMOND COUNTY HISTORY (US/0035-5119) [01887411] **2759**

RICHMOND HISTORIAN, THE (US/0360-1978) [02244213] **2759**

RICHMOND NEWS-LEADER, THE *CEASED.* (US) [09447277] **5759**

RICHMOND POLICE ACTIVITIES LEAGUE : REPORT TO THE LEGISLATURE / SUBMITTED BY DEPARTMENT OF THE YOUTH AUTHORITY, RESEARCH DIVISION *CEASED.* (US) [26320722] **3175**

RICHMOND POST (US) [10546247] **5639**

RICHMOND QUARTERLY, THE *SUSPENDED.* (US/0276-6515) [06911695] **3431**

RICHMOND REGISTER (RICHMOND, KY.) (US) [13674346] **5682**

RICHMOND SURROUNDINGS (US/1064-1785) [20116153] **4854**

RICHMOND TIMES-DISPATCH (US) [09493729] **5759**

RICHTON DISPATCH, THE (US) [16275770] **5701**

RICKEY ROOTS & REVELS (US/1058-0263) [22369063] **2470**

RICO LAW REPORTER (US/0889-0641) [12063742] **3103**

RICOCHET (NEW YORK, N.Y.) *SUSPENDED.* (US/0894-3737) [16067027] **330**

RID, RIVISTA ITALIANA DI DIALETTOLOGIA, SCUOLA, SOCIETA, TERRITORIO (IT) [05581004] **3317**

RID RIVISTA ITALIANA DIFESA (IT) **4056**

RIDDELL, RIDDLE, RUDDELL TRAIL, THE (US/0737-6758) [07406281] **2470**

RIDDICK-NORTON, GLENDA. GLENDA RIDDICK PRESENTS THE RESOURCE DIRECTORY FOR LOS ANGELES COUNTY *See* SOCIAL SERVICE RESOURCE DIRECTORY FOR LOS ANGELES COUNTY **5308**

RIDEAU (CN/0319-7131) [02443271] **388**

RIDEAU TRAIL NEWSLETTER, THE (CN/0709-7085) [05761624] **4878**

RIDEAU TRIAL ASSOCIATION *See* RIDEAU TRAIL NEWSLETTER, THE **4878**

RIDECAB, BOLETIN INFORMATIVO (PE) [08626189] **1781**

RIDER (US/0095-1625) [01794813] **4082**

RIDER COLLEGE (US/1060-4316) [24993202] **1102**

RIDERANNUAL (US/0278-596X) [07827119] **4082**

RIDERS CLUB TOKYO. 1978 (JA/0386-7137) [I03867137] **4854**

RIDGE RUNNERS, THE (US/0093-6987) [01792368] **2470**

RIDGEFIELD PRESS (US) [27538491] **5646**

RIDGWAY RECORD (US) [15349789] **5739**

RIDIM/RCMI NEWSLETTER (US/0360-8727) [02158955] 4150, **363**

RIDING (UK) **2802**

RIDING LINE (US/0556-9931) [02267208] **2628**

RIDNA SHKOLA (NEW YORK, N.Y.) (US/0278-7679) [07861947] **1781**

RIDOTTO (IT) [02267209] **5368**

RIEI INFORMATION LETTER (US) **626**

RIESEL RUSTLER, THE (US) [14687887] **5754**

RIETI (IT) [02240780] **2707**

RIFIUTI OGGI (IT) **2220**

RIFLE (US/0162-3583) [03911073] **4915**

● RIFLE & SHOTGUN ANNUAL (US/1059-5759) [24639044] 2777, **4915**

RIFLEMAN (UK) **4915**

RIFORMA MEDICA (IT/0035-5259) [01764336] **3637**

RIFORMA TRIBUTARIA : CASI E QUESTIONI (IT) **751**

RIFORMA UNIVERSITARIA (IT) [01785506] **1846**

RIG (SW/0035-5267) [01764338] **2707**

RIG LOCATOR (CN/0711-0901) [26714810] **4277**

RIG MARKET FORECAST (UK/0960-7315) [I09607315] **4277**

RIGA. POLITEHNISKAIS INSTITUTS. KAFEDRA PROMYSHLENNOI TEPLOENERGETIKI *See* TEPLOPROVODNOST' I DIFFUZIIA **4432**

RIGHT COLLEGE, THE (US/0899-1588) [16735608] **1846**

● RIGHT GUIDE (ANN ARBOR, MICH.), THE (US/1064-7414) [26391706] **4495**

RIGHT HERE (US/0895-3139) [16567833] **2492**

RIGHT OF AESTHETIC REALISM TO BE KNOWN, THE (US/0882-3731) [11833078] **4360**

RIGHT OF WAY (US/0035-5275) [01764345] **4846**

RIGHT ON (HOLLYWOOD, CALIF.) (US/0048-8305) [03453711] **1068**

RIGHT START (UK/0957-3704) [I09573704] **1068**

RIGHT STUFFED. CD-ROM, THE (US) **1289**

RIGHT TO KNOW & THE FREEDOM TO ACT *See* FBI NEWS **4508**

RIGHT TO KNOW & THE FREEDOM TO ACT : NCARL'S FIRST AMENDMENT MONITORING SERVICE, THE (US) [18375840] **4512**

RIGHT TO KNOW COMPLIANCE ADVISOR *CEASED.* (US/0888-8582) [13746108] **2869**

RIGHT-TO-KNOW PLANNING REPORT : CHEMICAL HAZARD COMMUNICATION AND EMERGENCY PLANNING (US) [17247612] 1073, **2869**

RIGHT TO WORK NATIONAL NEWSLETTER *See* NATIONAL RIGHT TO WORK NEWSLETTER **1692**

RIGHT TRACK (TORONTO) (CN/0824-4812) [10845142] **2802**

RIGHT WOMAN, THE (US/0162-9328) [04257668] **5565**

RIGHTING WORDS (US/0892-581X) [15232709] **2924**

RIGHTS AND HUMANITY (UK/0950-8465) [I09508465] **4512**

RIGHTS AND LIBERTIES (CN/1187-3272) [25589929] **4512**

RIGHTS (GENEVA, SWITZERLAND) *CEASED.* (SZ/1011-0240) [17396212] **1308**

RIGHTS (NEW YORK, N.Y. 1953) (US/0035-5283) [01764346] **4512**

RIGID DISK DRIVE MAGNETIC HEAD/MEDIA MARKET, AND TECHNOLOGY UPDATE (US) [18342924] **1202**

RIGID INSULATING BOARD, WOOD FIBRE AND MINERAL PRODUCTS (CN/0829-8653) [02443542] **2404**

RIISTA- JA KALATALOUDEN TUTKIMUSLAITOS. KALANTUKIMUSOSASTO *See* TIEDONANTOJA - RIISTA- JA KALATALOUDEN TUTKIMUSLAITOS KALANTUKIMUSOSASTO **2315**

RIJKSINSTITUUT VOOR NATUURBEHEER *See* JAARVERSLAG / RIJKSINSTITUUT VOOR NATUURBEHEER **4166**

RIJKSMUSEUM (NETHERLANDS) *See* BULLETIN VAN HET RYKSMUSEUM **4086**

RIJKSMUSEUM VAN NATUURLIJKE HISTORIE TE LEIDEN *See* ZOOLOGISCHE MEDEDELINGEN **5603**

RIJKSPOLITIE MAGAZINE (NE) **3175**

RIJKSPROEFSTATION VOOR ZAADONDERZOEK (NETHERLANDS) *See* JAARVERSLAG / RIJKSPROEFSTATION VOOR ZAADONDERZOEK **175**

RIJKSPROGRAMMA WELZIJN MINDERHEDEN / MINISTERIE VAN WELZIJN, VOLKSGEZONDHEID EN CULTUUR, HOOFDAFDELING WELZIJN MINDERHEDEN (NE) [19026968] **2707**

RIJKSUNIVERSITEIT TE GENT. FACULTEIT VAN DE LANDBOUWWETENSCHAPPEN *See* MEDEDELINGEN VAN DE FACULTEIT LANDBOUWWETENSCHAPPEN, RIJKSUNIVERSITEIT, GENT **3694**

RIJKSUNIVERSITEIT TE LEIDEN. AFRIKA-STUDIECENTRUM *See* DOCUMENTATIEBLAD **415**

RIKA GAKU KENKYUSHO HOKOKU *CEASED.* (JA/0020-3084) [07256595] 991, **4420**

RIKKA (CN) [05584146] **3352**

RIKKYO KEIZAIGAKU KENKYU (JA/0035-5356) [01906589] **1519**

RIKSREVISIONSVERKETS TAXERINGSSTATISTISKA UNDERSOKNING TAXERINGSARET ... (SW) [10336005] 4747, **4699**

RIKUSUIGAKU ZASSHI (JA/0021-5104) [01608284] **472**

RILA BULLETIN (US/0146-8685) [03049744] **3247**

RILCE : REVISTA DE FILOLOGIA HISPANICA (SP) [22418098] 3317, **3431**

RILEVAZIONE DEI PREZZI ALL INGROSSO : ASSOMET (IT) **4018**

RILISAR BULLETIN : QUARTERLY JOURNAL OF RANGANATHAN INSTITUTE OF LIBRARY AND INFORMATION SCIENCE FOR APPLIED RESEARCH (II) [14705966] **3247**

RILKE-GESELLSCHAFT *See* BLATTER DER RILKE-GESELLSCHAFT **3367**

RILM ABSTRACTS (US/0033-6955) [01853507] 4150, **4160**

RIM OF THE WORLD NEWS *See* CRESTLINE COURIER-NEWS **5634**

RIMBA INDONESIA (IO/0035-5372) [01905970] **2394**

RIMBAUD VIVANT (FR) [04676896] **3352**

RIMBEY RECORD (CN) **5794**

RINASCIMENTO (IT/0080-3073) [01764351] **2853**

RINBOKU IKUSHUJO KENKYU HOKOKU (JA/0287-5136) [13763626] **2394**

RINDERRASSENERHEBUNG (AU) [02805979] 220, **156**

RING-A-WORD PUZZLES (US/0194-3189) [05430255] **4865**

RING (NEW YORK), THE (US/0035-5410) [01764353] **4915**

RING OF FIRE *SUSPENDED.* (US/0892-6255) [15248625] 5256, **244**

RING. SERIES B, THE (PL) [06327800] **5620**

RING SYSTEMS HANDBOOK (US/0742-5996) [10386298] **1047**

RING SYSTEMS HANDBOOK. SUPPLEMENT (US/8756-565X) [11589280] **1047**

RING, THE (CN/0380-8149) [02583612] **1846**

RING (WASHINGTON), THE (US/0098-1788) [02241290] **4150**

RINGDOC (UK) [09446984] 4328, **4334**

RINGETTE CANADA *See* OFFICIAL RULES / RINGETTE CANADA **4910**

RINGETTE REVIEW (CN/0821-5782) [09658239] **4865**

RINGGOLD COUNTY GENEALOGICAL SOCIETY *See* RINGGOLD ROOTS **2470**

RINGGOLD ROOTS (US/8756-3819) [11508306] **2470**

RINGING & MIGRATION (UK/0307-8698) [02381523] **5620**

RINGING WORLD, THE (UK) [07083430] **4150**

RINGKAMPF (GW) **4915**

RINGMERKING AV FORSKJELLIGE FUGLEARTER (NO) [03390607] **5620**

RINGSTED DISPATCH (US) [16474513] **5672**

RINGYO KEIZAI (JA/0388-8614) [09543531] **2394**

RINGYO SEISAN TOKEI NEMPO (JA) [01797051] **2394**

RINGYO SHIKENJO JIHO (JA) [02255757] **2394**

RINGYO SHIKENJO KENKYU HOKOKU (JA/0082-4720) [08544150] **2394**

RINPAGAKU (JA/0910-4186) [28101475] **3676**

RINRIGAKU NEMPO (JA) [06872845] **2253**

RINSAN SHIKENJO KENKYU HOKOKU (JA) [10292703] **2394**

RINSAN SHIKENJOHO (JA/0913-140X) [18168553] **2394**

RINSHO BYORI (JA/0047-1860) [04161170] **3897**

RINSHO EIYO (JA/0485-1412) [10452382] **4198**

RINSHO FUJINKA SANKA (JA/0386-9865) [10387307] **3768**

RINSHO GANKA (JA/0370-5579) [07558251] **3879**

RINSHO HOSHASEN. JAPANESE JOURNAL OF CLINICAL RADIOLOGY (JA/0009-9252) [03828647] **3946**

RINSHO KAGAKU (JA/0370-5633) [02044788] **991**

RINSHO KENSA (JA/0485-1420) [10408221] **3637**

RINSHO KETSUEKI (JA/0485-1439) [08088970] **3774**

RINSHO SHIKA (JA/0035-5488) [01764357] **1335**

RINSHO SHINKEIGAKU (JA/0009-918X) [04301256] **3845**

RINSHO YAKURI (JA/0388-1601) [10452273] **4328**

RINSHO HINYUOKIKA (JA/0385-2393) [03852393] **3993**

RINTISAINS (MY) [01796547] **5148**

RIO DE JANEIRO. BIBLIOTECA NACIONAL *See* ANAIS DA BIBLIOTECA NACIONAL **3457**

RIO DE JANEIRO (BRASIL : STATE) *See* LEGISLACAO DO ESTADO DO RIO DE JANEIRO / SECRETARIA DE ESTADO DE JUSTICA, DIVISAO DE DIVULGACAO **3001**

RIO DE JANEIRO (BRAZIL : STATE) *See* D.O., DIARIO OFICIAL, ESTADO DO RIO DE JANEIRO. PARTE I **2958**

RIO DE JANEIRO (BRAZIL : STATE) *See* D.O., DIARIO OFICIAL, ESTADO DO RIO DE JANEIRO. PARTE II **4471**

RIO DE JANEIRO (BRAZIL : STATE) *See* D.O., DIARIO OFICIAL, ESTADO DO RIO DE JANEIRO. PARTE III **2958**

RIO DE JANEIRO (BRAZIL : STATE) *See* D.O., DIARIO OFICIAL, ESTADO DO RIO DE JANEIRO. PARTE IV **2958**

RIO DE JANEIRO (BRAZIL : STATE) *See* D.O., DIARIO OFICIAL, ESTADO DO RIO DE JANEIRO. PARTE V **2958**

RIO DE JANEIRO (BRAZIL : STATE) *See* QUADROS DE DETALHAMENTO DAS DESPESAS / GOVERNO DO ESTADO DO RIO DE JANEIRO **4743**

RIO DE JANEIRO (BRAZIL : STATE). D.O. DIARIO OFICIAL, ESTADO DO RIO DE JANEIRO. PARTES IV E V *See* D.O., DIARIO OFICIAL, ESTADO DO RIO DE JANEIRO. PARTE V **2958**

RIO DE JANEIRO (BRAZIL : STATE). D.O. DIARIO OFICIAL, ESTADO DO RIO DE JANEIRO. PARTES IV E V *See* D.O., DIARIO OFICIAL, ESTADO DO RIO DE JANEIRO. PARTE IV **2958**

RIO DE JANEIRO (BRAZIL : STATE). INSPETORIA GERAL DE FINANCAS *See* PRESTACAO DE CONTAS DA GESTACAO DO EXERCICIO DE ... **4741**

RIO DE JANEIRO (BRAZIL : STATE). TRIBUNAL DE JUSTICA *See* EMENTARIO DE JURISPRUDENCIA DO TRIBUNAL DE JUSTICA DO ESTADO DO RIO DE JANEIRO **2965**

RIO DE JANEIRO. MUSEU HISTORICO NACIONAL *See* ANAIS DO MUSEU HISTORICO NACIONAL **2720**

RIO DE JANEIRO (STATE) *See* LEGISLACAO DO ESTADO DO RIO DE JANEIRO **3001**

RIO DE JANEIRO (STATE). DEPARTAMENTO DE ESTRADAS DE RODAGEM. PROCURADORIA GERAL *See* BOLETIM DA PROCURADORIA GERAL **2942**

RIO DE JANEIRO (STATE). PROCURADORIA-GERAL DA JUSTICA *See* REVISTA DE DIREITO DA PROCURADORIA-GERAL DA JUSTICA DO ESTADO DO RIO DE JANEIRO **3041**

RIO DE JANEIRO (STATE). SECRETARIA DE EDUCACAO E CULTURA. INSTITUTO DE INFORMATICA *See* DADOS ESTATISTICOS - SECRETARIA DE EDUCACAO E CULTURA, INSTITUTO DE INFORMATICA **1794**

RIO DE JANEIRO (STATE). SUPERINTENDENCIA ESTUDUAL DE RIOS E LAGOAS *See* SINOPSE DE ATIVIDADES - SERLA **134**

RIO DE LA PLATA (FR/0982-0582) [15071472] **3431**

RIO GRANDE CHAPTER BULLETIN (US/0272-9644) [06977488] **3247**

RIO GRANDE DO NORTE, BRAZIL (STATE). COMISSAO ESTADUAL DE PLANEJAMENTO AGRICOLA *See* PLANO ESTADUAL PARA APLICACAO DE CREDITO RURAL NO RIO GRANDE DO NORTE **803**

RIO GRANDE DO SUL (BRAZIL) *See* DIARIO OFICIAL: INDUSTRIA & [I.E. E] COMERCIO **1555**

RIO GRANDE DO SUL, BRAZIL (STATE). DEPARTAMENTO AUTONOMO DE ESTRADAS DE RODAGEM *See* CONTAGENS DE TRAFEGO: TEMPORADA DE VERAO **5439**

RIO GRANDE DO SUL, BRAZIL (STATE). SECRETARIA DE COORDENACAO E PLANEJAMENTO. SUPERINTENDENCIA DE PLANEJAMENTO GLOBAL *See* MOVIMENTO SINDICAL **1691**

RIO GRANDE DO SUL, BRAZIL (STATE). UNIDADE DE ECONOMIA AGRICOLA *See* CONJUNTURA AGRICOLA **76**

RIO GRANDE DO SUL, BRAZIL (STATE). UNIVERSIDAD FEDERAL. INSTITUTO DE ESTUDOS E PESQUISAS ECONOMICAS *See* SONDAGEM CONJUNTURAL **1584**

RIO GRANDE DO SUL, BRAZIL (STATE). UNIVERSIDADE FEDERAL. FACULDADE DE DIREITO *See* REVISTA DA FACULDADE DE DIREITO DE PORTO ALEGRE **3040**

RIO GRANDE HISTORY *SUSPENDED.* (US/0146-1869) [02868949] **2759**

RIO GRANDE SUN (US) [10288712] **5713**

RIO GRANDE VALLEY HORTICULTURAL SOCIETY *See* JOURNAL OF THE RIO GRANDE VALLEY HORTICULTURAL SOCIETY **2421**

RIOTUR (BL) [02477763] **2759**

RIOTUR (FIRM) *See* RIOTUR **2759**

RIP (LOS ANGELES, CALIF.) (US/0889-5791) [13941892] **4150**

RIP OFF COMIX (US) [04146875] **4865**

RIPLEY BEE (RIPLEY, OHIO : 1887) (US) [09680138] **5730**

RIPLEY P. BULLEN MONOGRAPHS IN ANTHROPOLOGY AND HISTORY (US/0271-6925) [05654077] 2628, **245**

RIPON COLLEGE *See* RIPON COLLEGE MAGAZINE **1094**

RIPON COLLEGE MAGAZINE (US/0300-7928) [01327124] **1094**

RIPON COLLEGE UPDATE (US/0744-7450) [08525759] **1846**

RIPON COMMONWEALTH-PRESS, THE (US/0748-6863) [11002649] **5770**

RIPON FORUM (US/0035-5526) [04734472] **4495**

RIPOSTE (1980) (CN/0227-1184) [06563182] **1299**

RIPOTI YA UTEKELEZAJI WA MPANGO WA MAENDELEO / SERIKALI YA MAPINDUZI YA ZANZIBAR, WIZARA YA ELIMU (TZ) [10855913] **1781**

RIPOTI YA UTEKELEZAJI WA MPANGO WA MAENDELEO / SERIKALI YA MAPINDUZI YA ZANZIBAR, WIZARA YA HABARI, UTAMADUNI, NA MICHEZO (TZ) [10889160] **4684**

RIRON TO HOHO (JA/0913-1442) [I09131442] **5256**

RIS (BROOKSIDE, N.J.) *See* RETAIL INFO SYSTEMS NEWS **956**

RIS-R (DK/0106-2840) [12573206] **1956**

RIS : RIVISTA ITALIANA DE STOMATOLOGIA (IT) [15229862] **3898**

RISALAH (RABAT, MOROCCO) (MR) [11182931] **5044**

RISALAT AFRIQIYA (UA) [04222676] **2643**

RISALAT AL-AZHAR (UA) [08070389] **5044**

RISALAT AL-BATRUL AL-ARABI (LE) [03268308] **4277**

RISALAT AL-ISLAM (CAIRO, EGYPT : 1983) (UA) [11103933] **5044**

RISALAT AL-MAAHID AL-ILMIYAH / TASDURU AN MAHAD AL-RIYAD AL-ILMI (SU) [07801349] **5045**

RISALAT AL-MAKTABAH (JO) [03428966] **3247**

RISALAT AL-MUALLIM (SJ) [03494414] **1781**

RISALAT AL-MURABBI (TI) [07800782] **1781**

RISALAT AL-TARBIYAH (LY) [05854480] **1781**

RISALAT MAHAD AL-TURATH AL-ILMI AL-ARABI (SY) [04145879] **5148**

RISALAT SL-JIHAD (LY) [11077747] **5045**

RISC MANAGEMENT (US/1051-1393) [21879038] **1202**

RISC MANAGEMENT : ANALYSIS & COMMENT ON THE IMPACT OF RISC TECHNOLOGY *See* INSIDE THE NEW COMPUTER INDUSTRY **1189**

RISC USER (UK/0966-1913) [I09661913] **1202**

RISC WORLD (US/1059-9975) [24842203] **1265**

RISCONTRI (IT) [06645515] **2522**

RISCPT BULLETIN (FR/0250-4219) [I02504219] **2181**

RISING STAR (RISING STAR, TEX. : 1965) (US) [16953289] **5754**

RISING SUN RECORDER, THE (US) [11177229] **5667**

RISING SUN, THE (US) [01784107] **4495**

RISING TIDE, THE (US/0364-7668) [02653864] **4512**

RISK ABSTRACTS (CN/0824-3336) [10926533] 4800, **4811**

RISK — Alphabetical Title Index

RISK ANALYSIS (US/0272-4332) [06842248] 5148, **4800**

RISK & BENEFITS JOURNAL, THE (US/1053-556X) [22576471] 885, **2892**

RISK & BENEFITS MANAGEMENT **CEASED.** (US/0893-2654) [15482490] **2892**

RISK & INSURANCE (US/1050-9232) [21707909] **2892**

RISK BOOK SERIES (SZ) [05850972] **4994**

●RISK (CONCORD, N.H.) (US/1073-8673) [29540922] **5148**

RISK, ISSUES IN HEALTH & SAFETY (US/1047-0484) [20589168] **4800**

RISK LINE (US/0743-9458) [08527204] **2892**

RISK (LONDON. 1987) (UK/0952-8776) [18802972] **810**

RISK MANAGEMENT (US/0035-5593) [00818354] **2892**

RISK MANAGEMENT (NE) 885, **708**

RISK MANAGEMENT AND INSURANCE AUDIT TECHNIQUES (US) **2892**

●RISK MANAGEMENT FOR EXECUTIVE WOMEN (US/0732-2666) [08333572] 5565, **2892**

RISK MANAGEMENT LETTER, THE (US/1070-0102) [24294038] **2892**

RISK MANAGEMENT MANUAL (US) [03352493] **708**

RISK MANAGEMENT NEWSLETTER **CEASED.** (US/0740-1396) [09938835] **2892**

RISK MANAGEMENT REPORT, MEDICAL RECORDS, THE (US/0273-3617) [07048929] **3637**

RISK MANAGEMENT REPORTER FOR THE HEALTH CARE PROFESSIONAL, THE (US/0893-8245) [15649628] 3637, **3044**

RISK MANAGEMENT REPORTS (US/0199-6827) [03592818] **2892**

RISK MANAGER LAW BULLETIN (US) [25444762] **2892**

RISK MANAGER'S LAW ALERT **CEASED.** (US/1062-2624) [25561733] **3044**

RISK MEASUREMENT SERVICE (UK/0261-3344) [I02613344] 810, **1519**

RISK MEASUREMENT SERVICE KENSINGTON (AT/0812-8901) [I08128901] **885**

RISK REPORT, THE (US/0197-7539) [21769334] **2892**

RISK UPDATE (UK) **2893**

RISORGIMENTO (GROUPE EUROPEEN DE RECHERCHE ET D'INFORMATION SUR L'ITALIE CONTEMPORAINE) **SUSPENDED.** (BE) [08956538] **2707**

RISORGIMENTO, IL (IT/0035-5607) [02267224] **2707**

RISORSA UOMO (IT) **708**

RISPARMIO, IL (IT) [01881353] **810**

RISPOSTE (IT) **2492**

RISQUE PAYS (FR) **1639**

RISQUES DU METIER **See** PREVENIR LES RISQUES DU METIER **2868**

RISSHO DAIGAKU. JIMBUN KAGAKU KENKYUJO **See** RISSHO DAIGAKU JIMBUN KAGAKU KENKYUJO NEMPO. / ANNUAL REPORT OF THE INSTITUTE OF CULTURAL SCIENCES, RISSHO UNIVERSITY **5217**

RISSHO DAIGAKU JIMBUN KAGAKU KENKYUJO NEMPO. / ANNUAL REPORT OF THE INSTITUTE OF CULTURAL SCIENCES, RISSHO UNIVERSITY (JA) [05084655] **5217**

RISSHO DAIGAKU JINBUN KAGAKU KENKYUJO NENPO. BESSATSU (JA/0389-9535) [09106841] **2853**

RISSHO DAIGAKU KYOYOBU RONSHU. LOTUS (JA) [06076232] **5236**

RISSHO DAIGAKU, TOKYO. KYOYOBU **See** RISSHO DAIGAKU KYOYOBU RONSHU. LOTUS **5236**

RISSHO JOSHI DAIGAKU. TANKI DAIGAKUBU **See** KENKYU KIYO - RISSHO JOSHI DAIGAKU TANKI DAIGAKUBU **5232**

RISSHO KEIEI RONSHU (JA) [04735123] **1625**

RISSHO SHIGAKU (JA/0386-8966) [09543708] **2663**

RISTORAZIONE COLLETTIVA (IT/1120-6039) [I11206039] **2356**

RISVEGLIO MUSICALE : RM (IT) [09526526] **4150**

RIT FISKIDEILDAR (IC/0484-9019) [01982959] **2312**

RITCHIE GAZETTE AND THE CAIRO STANDARD (US) [13201534] **5765**

RITE IDEAS (US/8750-5703) [11544751] **4994**

RITM PERESTROIKI (RU) [18510716] 4684, **4495**

RITMO (SP) [09985581] **4150**

RITMO (MEXICO CITY, MEXICO) **CEASED.** (MX) [09212823] **4150**

RITSUMEIKAN KEIZAIGAKU (JA) [06714938] **1595**

RITTENHOUSE : JOURNAL OF THE AMERICAN SCIENTIFIC INSTRUMENT ENTERPRISE (US) [15011793] **2099**

RITZVILLE ADAMS COUNTY JOURNAL, THE (US) [17006052] **5762**

RIUNIONE ANNUALE - ATICELCA (IT) [07038999] **4238**

RIVE CULTURELLE **CEASED.** (CN/1186-8368) [24623509] **388**

RIVE DROITE **CEASED.** (MC) [23235983] **3431**

RIVER CIRCULAR, THE (US/0739-9790) [09833411] **2759**

RIVER CITIES **CEASED.** (US/0744-7418) [07994130] 708, **1299**

RIVER CITY LIBRARY TIMES (US/0270-9104) [05013969] **3247**

RIVER CITY (MEMPHIS, TENN.) (US/1048-129X) [20432242] **3431**

RIVER CITY REVIEW (LOUISVILLE, KY.) **CEASED.** (US/0734-497X) [08755577] **3431**

RIVER CITY (WICHITA, KAN.) (US/0360-4381) [02244670] **4150**

RIVER COUNTIES, THE **SUSPENDED.** (US/8756-0798) [05962585] **2470**

RIVER CURRENTS (ST. LOUIS, MO. : 1981) (US/0145-0689) [07866245] **4182**

RIVER FALLS JOURNAL (RIVER FALLS, WIS. : 1872) (US) [11795398] **5770**

RIVER FORECASTS PROVIDED BY THE NATIONAL WEATHER SERVICE (US/0093-7177) [01792239] **1417**

RIVER GROVE MESSENGER **CEASED.** (US/0744-5369) [08337858] **5662**

RIVER NEWS-HERALD **See** RIVER NEWS HERALD & ISLETON JOURNAL, THE **5639**

RIVER NEWS HERALD & ISLETON JOURNAL, THE (US) [28898973] **5639**

RIVER PARISHES GUIDE (US/0747-1955) [10632377] **5684**

RIVER PRESS, THE (US) [12280160] **5706**

RIVER QUALITY REPORT (US/0742-4426) [09049048] **2242**

RIVER REPORTER, THE (US) [15740951] **5720**

RIVER RUNNER MAGAZINE (US) [12331489] **595**

RIVER STYX (US/0149-8851) [03573826] 330, **3431**

RIVER SUMMARY AND FORECAST **See** WEEKLY RIVER SUMMARY AND FORECAST **1401**

RIVERDALE PRESS, THE (US) [09813447] **5720**

RIVERINA LIBRARY REVIEW (AT/0812-7352) [24572340] **3247**

RIVERINE GRAZIER, THE (AT) [11628165] **5777**

RIVERLANDER (AT) [02937524] **5539**

RIVERS (FORT COLLINS, COLO.) (US/0898-8048) [17913190] **5539**

RIVERS STATE TRADE DIRECTORY (NR) [02242076] **850**

RIVERSEDGE (US/0272-9598) [04447874] **3431**

RIVERSIDE COUNTY RECORD-NEWS (US/8750-7986) [11775079] **5639**

RIVERSIDE COUNTY STREET ATLAS AND DIRECTORY (US/0883-5225) [10904937] **2575**

RIVERSIDE QUARTERLY (US/0889-2326) [01764378] **3431**

●RIVERSIDE SOUTH FORUM (US) [26221973] **2834**

RIVERTON RANGER, THE (US) [22425674] **5772**

RIVERVIEW GAZETTE, THE (CN/0823-7573) [10398403] **5794**

RIVISTA ABRUZZESE (IT/0035-5739) [11057130] **2853**

RIVISTA AERONAUTICA (IT) [01680901] 4056, **33**

RIVISTA AMMINISTRATIVA DELLA REPUBBLICA ITALIANA (IT) [04925372] **4684**

RIVISTA ARCHEOLOGICA DELLA PROVINCIA E ANTICA DIOCESI DI COMO (IT/0080-3235) [I00803235] **281**

RIVISTA BANCARIA (IT) [01881263] **810**

RIVISTA BIBLICA (IT/0035-5798) [06009063] **5019**

RIVISTA CISTERCENSE (IT/0394-3275) [15619951] **5035**

RIVISTA CONSULTORIO FAMILIARE (IT) **3739**

RIVISTA CONSULTORIO FAMILIARE (IT) **2285**

RIVISTA CRITICA DEL DIRITTO PRIVATO (IT) [12212467] **3091**

RIVISTA DALMATICA, LA (IT/0393-4624) [I03934624] **2707**

RIVISTA D'ARTE (IT) [12193632] **363**

RIVISTA DEGLI INFORTUNI E DELLE MALATTIE PROFESSIONALI (IT/0035-5836) [09510782] **3637**

RIVISTA DEGLI STUDI ORIENTALI (IT/0392-4866) [01586706] **3317**

RIVISTA DEI COMBUSTIBILI (IT/0370-5463) [02450254] **4277**

RIVISTA DEI DOTTORI COMMERCIALISTI (IT) **3044**

RIVISTA DEI LIBRI, LA (IT) [25027819] **4832**

RIVISTA DEL CATASTO E DEI SERVIZI TECNICI ERARIALI **See** RIVISTA DEL DIPARTIMENTO DEL TERRITORIO **2583**

RIVISTA DEL CATASTO E DEI SERVIZI TECNICI ERARIALI (IT/0373-367X) [08338740] **2030**

RIVISTA DEL CINEMATOGRAFO (IT/0035-5879) [05981503] **4077**

RIVISTA DEL CLERO ITALIANO, LA (IT/0042-7586) [09227936] **4994**

RIVISTA DEL CLUB ALPINO ITALIANO (IT/0392-9221) [09551861] **4915**

RIVISTA DEL COLORE, VERNICIATURA INDUSTRIALE, LA (IT/0048-8348) [11520923] **4225**

RIVISTA DEL CONSIGLIO, LA (IT) **3044**

●RIVISTA DEL DIPARTIMENTO DEL TERRITORIO (IT) [29827618] **2583**

RIVISTA DEL DIRITTO COMMERCIALE E DEL DIRITTO GENERALE DELLE OBBLIGAZIONI (IT/0035-5887) [01764380] **3103**

RIVISTA DEL MEDICO PRATICO, LA (IT) **3637**

RIVISTA DEL NOTARIATO (IT) **3044**

RIVISTA DEL NUOVO CIMENTO (IT/0035-5917) [01764381] **4420**

RIVISTA DEL PERSONALE DELL'ENTE LOCALE (IT/0394-8439) [I03948439] **4684**

RIVISTA DEL PORTO DI NAPOLI, LA (IT/0035-5925) [I00355925] **850**

RIVISTA DEL VETRO (IT) **2593**

RIVISTA DELLA BORSA **SUSPENDED.** (IT/1120-5318) [I11205318] **821**

RIVISTA DELLA CORTE DEI CONTI (IT) **3044**

RIVISTA DELLA GUARDIA DI FINANZA (IT/0035-595X) [I0035595X] **4056**

RIVISTA DELLA SOCIETA ITALIANA DI SCIENZA DELL'ALIMENTAZIONE, LA (IT/0391-4887) [02473653] 4199, **2356**

RIVISTA DELLA STAZIONE SPERIMENTALE DEL VETRO (IT) [08998046] **5148**

RIVISTA DELLA STRADA **See** VIE E TRASPORTI **5399**

RIVISTA DELLA TUBERCOLOSI E DELLE MALATTIE DELL'APPARATO RESPIRATORIO (IT) **3952**

RIVISTA DELL'ARBITRATO / ASSOCIAZIONE ITALIANA PER L'ARBITRATO (IT) [26845164] **3044**

RIVISTA DELLE SOCIETA (IT/0035-6018) [01714760] **3103**

RIVISTA DELLE TECNOLOGIE TESSILI (IT/0394-5413) [I03945413] **5355**

RIVISTA DELL'INFERMIERE (IT) [11086314] 4800, **3792**

RIVISTA DELL'ISTITUTO NAZIONALE D'ARCHEOLOGIA E STORIA DELL'ARTE (IT) [09907537] **281**

RIVISTA DELL'ISTRUZIONE (IT) [17534941] **1781**

RIVISTA D'EUROPA (IT) [05300402] **2707**

RIVISTA DI AGRICOLTURA SUBTROPICALE E TROPICALE (IT/0035-6026) [04711562] **130**

RIVISTA DI AGRONOMIA (IT/0035-6034) [02404967] **130**

RIVISTA DI ANTROPOLOGIA (IT) [01585625] **245**

RIVISTA DI ARCHEOLOGIA (IT/0392-0895) [06177485] **281**

RIVISTA DI AVICOLTURA (IT) [04380836] **220**

RIVISTA DI BERGAMO (IT) **2492**

RIVISTA DI BIOLOGIA (IT/0035-6050) [02243195] **472**

RIVISTA DI BIOLOGIA NORMALE E PATOLOGICA (IT/0391-1551) [03881079] **472**

RIVISTA DI CARDIOLOGIA PREVENTIVA E RIABILITATIVA : ORGANO DELL'ASSOCIAZIONE NAZIONALE DEI CENTRI PER LE MALATTIE CARDIOVASCOLARI (IT/0393-2028) [20999813] **3710**

Alphabetical Title Index — RIVISTA

RIVISTA DI CHIMICA (IT) **992**

RIVISTA DI CHIRURGIA DELLA MANO (IT/0080-3243) [I00803243] **3974**

RIVISTA DI CONSULENZA AZIENDALE (IT) **885**

RIVISTA DI CULTURA CLASSICA E MEDIOEVALE (IT/0035-6085) [01881362] 3317, **3431**

RIVISTA DI DIRITTO AGRARIO MILANO (IT/0391-8696) [I03918696] **3044**

RIVISTA DI DIRITTO CIVILE (IT/0035-6093) [01681268] **3091**

RIVISTA DI DIRITTO ED ECONOMIA VALUTARIA (IT) [07912490] **3088**

RIVISTA DI DIRITTO EUROPEO (IT/0035-6123) [01764386] **3044**

RIVISTA DI DIRITTO INDUSTRIALE (IT/0035-614X) [01644110] **1308**

RIVISTA DI DIRITTO INTERNAZIONALE (IT/0035-6158) [01696695] **3135**

RIVISTA DI DIRITTO INTERNAZIONALE PRIVATO E PROCESSUALE (IT/0035-6174) [01764387] **3135**

RIVISTA DI DIRITTO PROCESSUALE (IT) [01606069] **3044**

RIVISTA DI DIRITTO SPORTIVO (IT) **3044**

RIVISTA DI DIRITTO TRIBUTARIO (IT/1121-4074) [I11214074] **3044**

RIVISTA DI DIRITTO VALUTARIO E DI ECONOMIA INTERNAZIONALE (IT) [09848995] **1639**

RIVISTA DI ECONOMIA AGRARIA (IT/0035-6190) [02431192] **130**

RIVISTA DI EMOTERAPIA ED IMMUNOEMATOLOGIA (IT/0035-6204) [I00356204] **3676**

RIVISTA DI ESTETICA (IT/0035-6212) [01894787] **4360**

RIVISTA DI FILOLOGIA E DI ISTRUZIONE CLASSICA (IT) [15038209] **3317**

RIVISTA DI FILOSOFIA (IT/0035-6239) [01643215] **4360**

RIVISTA DI FILOSOFIA NEO-SCOLASTICA (IT/0035-6247) [01780366] **4360**

RIVISTA DI FRUTTICOLTURA E D ORTOFLORICOLTURA (IT) [09786330] **2430**

RIVISTA DI GASTRO-ENTEROLOGIA (IT/0035-6255) [09554788] **3747**

RIVISTA DI GIURISPRUDENZA TRIBUTARIA (IT) **3044**

RIVISTA DI GIUSTIZIA AMMINISTRATIVA DELLA LOMBARDIA ***CEASED.*** (IT) **3044**

RIVISTA DI GRAMMATICA GENERATIVA (IT) [04820786] **3317**

RIVISTA DI IDROBIOLOGIA (IT/0048-8399) [02497392] **1417**

RIVISTA DI IMPIANTI INDUSTRIALI (IT) [01786746] **3487**

RIVISTA DI INFETTIVOLOGIA PEDIATRICA (IT) **3911**

RIVISTA DI INFORMATICA (IT/0390-668X) [I0390668X] **1202**

RIVISTA DI INFORMAZIONI MARITTIME (IT/0390-3842) [02438949] **3182**

RIVISTA DI INGEGNERIA AGRARIA (IT/0034-916X) [01184760] **1994**

RIVISTA DI INGEGNERIA AGRARIA (IT/0304-0593) [I03040593] **34**

RIVISTA DI LEGISLAZIONE FISCALE (IT) **3044**

RIVISTA DI LETTERATURA ITALIANA (IT) [10380666] **3431**

RIVISTA DI LETTERATURE MODERNE E COMPARATE (IT/0391-2108) [07387359] **3431**

RIVISTA DI LINGUISTICA (IT) [21180249] **3317**

RIVISTA DI MATEMATICA DELLA UNIVERSITA DI PARMA (IT/0035-6298) [01716082] **3532**

RIVISTA DI MATEMATICA PER LE SCIENZE ECONOMICHE E SOCIALI / ASSOCIAZIONE PER LA MATEMATICA APPLICATA ALLE SCIENZE ECONOMICHE E SOCIALI (IT) [05297908] **3532**

RIVISTA DI MATEMATICA PURA ED APPLICATA (IT) [17858553] **3532**

RIVISTA DI MATHEMATICA DELLA UNIVERSITA DI PARMA. SERIE 4 (IT) [10341588] **3532**

RIVISTA DI MECCANICA (IT/0035-6301) [11521064] **2128**

RIVISTA DI MEDICINA DEL LAVORO ED IGIENE INDUSTRIALE (IT/0391-2825) [09479512] 3637, **2869**

RIVISTA DI MERCEOLOGIA (IT/0392-064X) [11520554] **1625**

RIVISTA DI NEUROBIOLOGIA (IT/0035-6336) [01125279] **3845**

RIVISTA DI NEUROPSICHIATRIA E SCIENZE AFFINI (IT/0035-6352) [09510856] **3845**

RIVISTA DI NEURORADIOLOGIA (IT) [19961524] 3946, **3845**

RIVISTA DI OSTETRICIA GINECOLOGIA PRATICA E MEDICINA PERINATALE ***SUSPENDED.*** (IT/0391-0970) [04080129] **3768**

RIVISTA DI PARASSITOLOGIA (IT/0035-6387) [01787891] **569**

RIVISTA DI PASTORALE LITURGICA (IT/0035-6395) [I00356395] **4994**

RIVISTA DI PATOLOGIA E CLINICA (IT/0035-6417) [09554798] **3898**

RIVISTA DI PATOLOGIA E CLINICA DELLA TUBERCOLOSI E DI PNEUMOLOGIA ***SUSPENDED.*** (IT/0302-4717) [11318056] **3952**

RIVISTA DI PATOLOGIA NERVOSA E MENTALE ***SUSPENDED.*** (IT/0035-6433) [01764398] **3936**

RIVISTA DI PATOLOGIA VEGETALE (IT/0035-6441) [02396127] **526**

RIVISTA DI PEDAGOGIA E SCIENZE RELIGIOSE ***See*** RIVISTA DI SCIENZE DELL'EDUCAZIONE **1781**

RIVISTA DI POLITICA AGRARIA (IT/0035-645X) [02430204] **130**

RIVISTA DI POLITICA AGRARIA. RASSEGNA DELLA AGRICOLTURA ITALIANA (IT/0393-4810) [I03934810] **130**

RIVISTA DI POLITICA ECONOMICA (IT/0391-6170) [05267449] **1595**

RIVISTA DI POLIZIA (IT) **4056**

RIVISTA DI PSICHIATRIA (IT/0035-6484) [00972393] **3936**

RIVISTA DI PSICOANALISI (IT/0035-6492) [I00356492] **4617**

RIVISTA DI PSICOLOGIA ANALITICA (IT/0392-9787) [08228964] **4617**

RIVISTA DI PSICOLOGIA CLINICA (IT) [18453796] **4617**

RIVISTA DI PSICOLOGIA DELL'ARTE (IT) [07769833] 4617, **330**

RIVISTA DI RAGIONERIA E TECNICA COMMERCIALE (IT) **751**

RIVISTA DI SCIENZE DELL'EDUCAZIONE (IT) [01795805] **1781**

RIVISTA DI SCIENZE PREISTORICHE (IT/0035-6514) [01886664] **281**

RIVISTA DI SERVIZIO SOCIALE, LA (IT/0035-6522) [I00356522] **5306**

RIVISTA DI SESSUOLOGIA ROMA (IT/0392-1670) [I03921670] **5188**

RIVISTA DI STATISTICA APPLICATA (IT/0035-6549) [I00356549] **5337**

RIVISTA DI STORIA CONTEMPORANEA (IT/0391-4240) [01904749] **2522**

RIVISTA DI STORIA DEL DIRITTO ITALIANO (IT) [01764402] **3044**

RIVISTA DI STORIA DELLA CHIESA IN ITALIA (IT/0035-6557) [01589073] **4994**

RIVISTA DI STORIA DELLA FILOSOFIA (MILAN, ITALY : 1984) (IT) [10782838] **4360**

RIVISTA DI STORIA DELLA STORIOGRAFIA MODERNA (IT) [09470625] **2628**

RIVISTA DI STORIA DELL'AGRICOLTURA (IT/0557-1359) [02459181] **130**

RIVISTA DI STORIA E CRITICA DELLA FOTOGRAFIA (IT) [07543292] **4376**

RIVISTA DI STORIA E LETTERATURA RELIGIOSA (IT/0035-6573) [01589334] **4994**

RIVISTA DI STORIA ECONOMICA (IT/0393-3415) [01645190] 5217, **1582**

RIVISTA DI STORIA ECONOMICA. INTERNATIONAL ISSUE (IT) [12178787] **1519**

RIVISTA DI STUDI ANGLO-AMERICANI (IT) [08236332] **2759**

RIVISTA DI STUDI BIZANTINI E NEOELLENICI (IT/0557-1367) [10090579] **2628**

RIVISTA DI STUDI CANADESI (IT/1120-3420) [19496210] **3431**

RIVISTA DI STUDI FENICI (IT) [02438951] 2663, **281**

RIVISTA DI STUDI ITALIANI (CN/0821-3216) [10051568] 3317, **3431**

RIVISTA DI STUDI LIGURI (FR/0035-6603) [01910030] **281**

RIVISTA DI STUDI POLITICI INTERNAZIONALI (IT/0035-6611) [01764403] **4534**

RIVISTA DI SUINICOLTURA (IT) [06778824] **220**

RIVISTA DI TEOLOGIA MORALE (IT) [01798253] **4994**

RIVISTA DI TOSSICOLOGIA : SPERIMENTALE E CLINICA (IT/0390-6019) [02417212] **3983**

RIVISTA DI VITA SPIRITUALE (IT/0035-6638) [06036817] **4994**

RIVISTA DI ZOOTECNIA E VETERINARIA (IT/0304-0607) [01713673] **5521**

RIVISTA DIRITTO FINANZIARIO E SCIENZA DELLE FINANZE (IT) **3088**

RIVISTA ECONOMICA DEL MEZZOGIORNO : TRIMESTRALE DELLA SVIMEZ, ASSOCIAZIONE PER LO SVILUPPO DELL'I1NDUSTRIA NEL MEZZOGIORNO (IT) [21867282] **1582**

RIVISTA EUROPEA PER LE SCIENZE MEDICHE E FARMACOLOGICHE (IT/0392-291X) [07288973] **4328**

RIVISTA GENERALE ITALIANA DI CHIRURGIA (IT/0035-6689) [I00356689] **3974**

RIVISTA GEOGRAFICA ITALIANA (IT/0035-6697) [01397791] **2575**

RIVISTA GIURDICA DELL IMPRESA ***See*** QUADERNI GIURIDICI DELL IMPRESA **883**

RIVISTA GIURIDICA DEGLI UFFICI DI CONCILIAZIONE (IT) **3044**

RIVISTA GIURIDICA DEL LAVORO (IT/0392-7229) [01764406] 3153, **1708**

RIVISTA GIURIDICA DEL LAVORO E DELLA PREVIDENZA SOCIALE. DOTTRINA ***See*** RIVISTA GIURIDICA DEL LAVORO E DELLA PREVIDENZA SOCIALE. DOTTRINA, GIURISPRUDENZA **3154**

RIVISTA GIURIDICA DEL LAVORO E DELLA PREVIDENZA SOCIALE. DOTTRINA, GIURISPRUDENZA (IT) [07752739] **3154**

RIVISTA GIURIDICA DEL LAVORO E DELLA PREVIDENZA SOCIALE: GIURISPRUDENZA (IT) [03277040] **3154**

RIVISTA GIURIDICA DEL LAVORO E DELLA PREVIDENZA SOCIALE: PREVIDENZA (IT) [06032579] **3154**

RIVISTA GIURIDICA DEL MEZZOGIORNO : TRIMESTRALE DELLA SVIMEZ, ASSOCIAZIONE PER LO SVILUPPO DELL'INDUSTRIA NEL MEZZOGIORNO (IT) [21417433] **1519**

RIVISTA GIURIDICA DELLA CIRCOLAZIONE E DEI TRASPORTI : ORGANO DELLA COMMISSIONE GIURIDICA DELL'AUTOMOBILE CLUB D'ITALIA (IT) [12128604] **5424**

RIVISTA GIURIDICA DELL'AMBIENTE (IT) [17823913] **3116**

RIVISTA GIURIDICA DELL'EDILIZIA (IT) [18078387] 626, **3044**

RIVISTA GIURIDICA DI POLIZIA LOCALE (IT/0394-834X) [I0394834X] **3044**

RIVISTA GIURIDICA DI URBANISTICA (IT) [17807630] **3044**

RIVISTA GIURIDICA SARDA (IT/0394-0942) [I03940942] **3044**

RIVISTA GIURUDICA DELLA SCUOLA (IT/0391-1845) [I03911845] **1870**

RIVISTA ILLUSTRATA DEL MUSEO TEATRALE ALLA SCALA, LA (IT) [20967906] **5368**

RIVISTA INGAUNA E INTEMELIA (IT) [01910029] **281**

RIVISTA INTERNAZIONALE DEI DIRRITI DELL'UOMO (IT) **4512**

RIVISTA INTERNAZIONALE DI ECONOMIA DEI TRASPORTI (IT/0303-5247) [02239831] 5391, **1519**

RIVISTA INTERNAZIONALE DI FILOSOFIA DEL DIRITTO (IT/0035-6727) [01645979] 4360, **3044**

RIVISTA INTERNAZIONALE DI MUSICA SACRA (IT/0394-6282) [08224012] **4150**

RIVISTA INTERNAZIONALE DI PARODONTOLOGIA & ODONTOIATRIA RICOSTRUTTIVA (IT) **1335**

RIVISTA INTERNAZIONALE DI SCIENZE ECONOMICHE E COMMERCIALI (IT/0035-6751) [01912265] 708, **1519**

RIVISTA INTERNAZIONALE DI SCIENZE SOCIALI (IT/0035-676X) [06778413] **5217**

RIVISTA INTERNAZIONALE DIRITTO COMUNE (IT/1120-5695) **3045**

RIVISTA ITALIANA DEGLI ODONTOTECNICI (IT/0391-5611) [04571491] **1335**

RIVISTA ITALIANA DEL DISTURBO INTELLETTIVO : ORGANO UFFICIALE DEL GRUPPO ITALIANO PER LO STUDIO SCIENTIFICO E TERAPIA DELL'INSUFFICIENZA MENTALE, MONGOLISMO E AUTISMO INFANTILI (IT) [19485085] **3936**

RIVISTA ITALIANA DEL LEASING E DELL INTERMEDIAZIONE FINANZIARIA ***CEASED.*** (IT) [19739251] **708**

RIVISTA ITALIANA DELLA SALDATURA (IT/0035-6794) [06679926] **4027**

RIVISTA ITALIANA DELLE SOSTANZE GRASSE (IT/0035-6808) [01775180] **1029**

RIVISTA ITALIANA DI ACQUACOLTURA / ASSOCIAZIONE PISCICOLTORI ITALIANI (A.P.I.) (IT/1120-9151) [26093850] **557**

RIVISTA ITALIANA DI BIOLOGIA E MEDICINA (IT/0393-1137) [11118019] **472**

RIVISTA ITALIANA DI CHIRURGIA MAXILLO-FACCIALE (IT/1120-7558) [I11207558] **3974**

RIVISTA ITALIANA DI CHIRURGIA PLASTICA (IT/0391-2221) [03658532] **3974**

RIVISTA ITALIANA DI COLON-PROCTOLOGIA (IT) [13405496] **3974**

RIVISTA ITALIANA DI DIRITTO DEL LAVORO (IT/0393-2494) [08722252] **3154**

RIVISTA ITALIANA DI DIRITTO E PROCEDURA PENALE (IT) [01588198] **3109**

RIVISTA ITALIANA DI DIRITTO PUBBLICO COMUNITARIO (IT) [26288264] **3045**

RIVISTA ITALIANA DI ECONOMIA, DEMOGRAFIA E STATISTICA (IT/0035-6832) [08229661] **1519**

RIVISTA ITALIANA DI GEOTECNICA (IT/0557-1405) [06572363] **1395**

RIVISTA ITALIANA DI GRUPPOANALISI (IT) **4617**

RIVISTA ITALIANA DI MEDICINA LEGALE : DOTTRINA, CASISTICA, RICERCA SPERIMENTALE, GIURISPRUDENZE E LEGISLAZIONE (IT) [08939530] **3742**

RIVISTA ITALIANA DI MUSICOLOGIA (IT/0035-6867) [01764409] **4150**

RIVISTA ITALIANA DI NUMISMATICA E SCIENZE AFFINI (IT) [02898087] **2783**

RIVISTA ITALIANA DI NUTRIZIONE PARENTERALE ED ENTERALE : ORGANO UFFICIALE DELLA SOCIETA ITALIANA DI NUTRIZIONE PARENTERALE ED ENTERALE, SINPE - GASAPE (IT/0393-5582) [18466823] **4199**

RIVISTA ITALIANA DI ODONTOIATRIA INFANTILE : ORGANO UFFICIALE DELLA SOCIETA ITALIANA DI ODONTOIATRIA INFANTILE (IT) [24317899] **1335**

RIVISTA ITALIANA DI ORNITOLOGIA (IT/0035-6875) [01714546] **472**

RIVISTA ITALIANA DI ORTOPEDIA E TRAUMATOLOGIA (IT) **3884**

RIVISTA ITALIANA DI ORTOPEDIA E TRAUMATOLOGIA PEDIATRICA (IT) **3884**

RIVISTA ITALIANA DI OTORINOLARINGOLOGIA, AUDIOLOGIA E FONIATRIA (IT/0392-1360) [12608606] **3891**

RIVISTA ITALIANA DI PALEONTOLOGIA E STRATIGRAFIA (IT/0035-6883) [01910036] **4230**

RIVISTA ITALIANA DI PALEONTOLOGIA E STRATIGRAFIA. MEMORIA (IT/0375-9784) [05069404] **4230**

RIVISTA ITALIANA DI RAGIONERIA E DI ECONOMIA AZIENDALE (IT) **751**

RIVISTA ITALIANA DI SCIENZA POLITICA (IT/0048-8402) [02267241] **4495**

RIVISTA ITALIANA DI STUDI NAPOLENOICI (IT/0035-6913) [06748983] **2707**

RIVISTA ITALIANA D'IGIENE (IT/0035-6921) [06723214] **4800**

RIVISTA ITALIANA EPPOS (IT/0392-0445) [08298277] **405**

RIVISTA ITALIANA ESSENZE, PROFUMI, PIANTE OFFICINALI, AROMI, SAPONI, COSMETICI, AEROSOL (IT/0035-6948) [I00356948] **1029**

RIVISTA LITURGICA (IT/0035-6956) [01774101] **5035**

RIVISTA MARITTIMA (IT/0035-6964) [06723138] **4182**

RIVISTA MILITARE (IT/0035-6980) [02239101] **4056**

RIVISTA MUSICALE ITALIANA *See* NUOVA RIVISTA MUSICALE ITALIANA **4142**

RIVISTA PENALE (IT) **3045**

RIVISTA PENALE ECONOMIA (IT) **3045**

RIVISTA ROSMINIANA DI FILOSOFIA E DI CULTURA (IT/0035-7030) [01910037] **586**

RIVISTA SPERIMENTALE DI FRENIATRIA E MEDICINA LEGALE DELLE ALIENAZIONI MENTALI (IT/0370-7261) [01778171] **3936**

RIVISTA STORICA CALABRESE (IT/0393-022X) [17535012] **2707**

RIVISTA STORICA DELL'ANTICHITA (IT/0300-340X) [01445612] **2628**

RIVISTA STORICA ITALIANA (IT/0035-7073) [01695357] **2707**

RIVISTA SVIZZERA SICUREZZA LAVORO (SZ) **2869**

RIVISTA TRASPORTI (IT) **5391**

RIVISTA TRIMESTRALE DEGLI APPALTI (IT) **821**

RIVISTA TRIMESTRALE DI DIRITTO E PROCEDURA CIVILE (IT) [01715349] **3045**

RIVISTA TRIMESTRALE DI DIRITTO PENALE DELL'ECONOMIA (IT) [21500934] **3045**

RIVISTA TRIMESTRALE DI DIRITTO PUBBLICO (IT/0557-1464) [01608229] **3094**

RIVISTA TRIMESTRALE DI SCIENZA DELLA AMMINISTRAZIONE (IT/0391-190X) [01887425] **4684**

RIVISTERIA (IT/0393-5914) [12574701] **2492**

RIVOLI 15 (IT) **2492**

RIV'ON LE-MEHKAR HEVRATI (IS/0334-4762) [01904726] **5217**

RIVON LI-STATISTIKAH SHEL TAHBURAH (IS) [01798344] **5401**

RIYONG HUAXUE GONGYE (CC/1001-1803) [I10011803] **1029**

RIZA PSICOSOMATICA (IT/0394-9982) [I03949982] **3637**

RLA, REVISTA DE LINGUISTICA TEORICA Y APLICADA (CL/0033-698X) [01868170] **3317**

RLE CURRENTS (US/1040-2012) [18045848] **1216**

RLE PROGRESS REPORT (US/0163-9218) [03909536] **2079**

RLJ. ROSKILL'S LETTER FROM JAPAN (UK/0143-4861) [I01434861] **4018**

RM MARIANNHILL (CN/0712-1695) [08790866] **4994**

RM MENSARIO: RADIO MOCAMBIQUE (MZ) [02478017] **1138**

RM1 : RIVISTA DELLA MAGLIERIA (IT) **1087**

RMA ANNUAL STATEMENT STUDIES (US) [07376161] **708**

RMCLAS NEWSLETTER *See* RMCLAS REVIEW **2552**

RMCLAS REVIEW (US/0749-9728) [09230956] **2552**

●RMI ... REVIEW OF HIV & AIDS RESEARCH (US) [26038488] 3716, **3676**

RMS NEWS (CN/0824-5665) [11802877] **2272**

RN (US/0033-7021) [01695783] **3868**

RN-AIDSLINE *CEASED*. (US/1049-8966) [21344761] 3676, **3868**

RN & WPL ENCYCLOPEDIA / THE SALESMAN'S GUIDE, INC (US) [10881654] 1087, **5355**

RN-ECONOMICO (BL) [02172455] **1582**

RN IDAHO (US/0192-298X) [04949825] **3868**

RN MAGAZINE-NCLEX REVIEW (US) **3868**

RN NURSING OPPORTUNITIES : THE ... JOB MARKET (US) [24587129] **3868**

●RNA. THE OFFICIAL PUBLICATION OF THE RNA SOCIETY (US/1355-8382) **3637**

RNAM NEWSLETTER (TH/0252-3582) [I02523582] **161**

RNT (BL) [09965917] **1163**

ROAD ACCIDENTS GREAT BRITAIN (UK) [04123704] **5443**

ROAD ACCIDENTS, WALES (UK/0263-9653) [10204751] **5443**

ROAD & MOTOR SPORT (CN/0702-7885) [03409692] **4915**

ROAD & REC (US/1055-7725) [21729663] **5391**

ROAD AND TRACK (US/0035-7189) [01764416] **5424**

ROAD & TRACK ROAD ATLAS & TRAVEL GUIDE (US/0198-0386) [05188780] **5490**

●ROAD & TRANSPORT RESEARCH : [A JOURNAL OF AUSTRALIAN AND NEW ZEALAND RESEARCH AND PRACTICE] (AT/1037-5783) [26087078] **5443**

ROAD APPLE REVIEW (US/0035-7200) [00966970] **3352**

ROAD ATLAS : UNITED STATES, CANADA, AND MEXICO (US/0361-6509) [01697184] **1929**

ROAD HOME, THE (JA/0917-0863) [I09170863] **5443**

ROAD/HOUSE (US/0148-3730) [03295382] **3470**

ROAD LAW (UK) [19557347] **5443**

ROAD LAW AND ROAD LAW REPORTS (UK/1352-0717) **5443**

ROAD LENGTHS IN GREAT BRITAIN (UK) [20431968] **5443**

ROAD MOTOR VEHICLES. FUEL SALES (CN/0703-654X) [03520123] **5391**

ROAD MOTOR VEHICLES. REGISTRATIONS (CN/0706-067X) [04623740] **5443**

ROAD OF THE PARTY *CEASED*. (CN/0227-6089) [08036609] **4546**

ROAD RACE MANAGEMENT (US/0739-3784) [09722817] **4915**

ROAD RACE MANAGEMENT ... GUIDE TO ELITE ATHLETES AND PRIZE MONEY RACES (US) [17016189] **4915**

ROAD RESEARCH LABORATORY *See* WARTIME ROAD NOTE **5446**

ROAD RESEARCH LABORATORY *See* SUMMARIES OF LABORATORY NOTES **5445**

ROAD RIDER (US/0035-7243) [03916002] **4082**

ROAD RIDER'S MOTORCYCLE CONSUMER NEWS (US/1067-8697) [27365207] **5391**

ROAD ROUGHNESS PROFILES. MAIN ROADS / ADVANCE PLANNING SECTION, MAIN ROADS DEPARTMENT, WESTERN AUSTRALIA (AT) [16857935] **5443**

ROAD SAFETY AND THE ROAD USER BIENNIAL SYMPOSIUM PROCEEDINGS (UK) **5443**

ROAD SAFETY ANNUAL REPORT (CN/0317-8196) [01796705] 4800, **5443**

ROAD STATISTICS IN KARNATAKA STATE (II) [02246226] **5402**

ROAD TRAFFIC ACCIDENTS INVOLVING CASUALTIES (AT) [02241976] **5443**

ROAD TRAFFIC ACCIDENTS INVOLVING CASUALTIES, TASMANIA (AT) [06481723] **5443**

ROAD TRAFFIC ACCIDENTS (PRETORIA, SOUTH AFRICA) (SA) [01786691] **5443**

ROAD TRAFFIC INDICATOR (UK) **3045**

ROAD TRAFFIC LAW BULLETIN (UK/0265-7937) [18353605] **5443**

ROAD TRAFFIC REPORTS (UK/0306-5286) [02991248] **5444**

ROAD TRAFFIC SAFETY RESEARCH COUNCIL REPORT (NZ) [03212107] 4800, **5444**

ROAD TRANSPORT OPERATION; EMPLOYMENT LAW (UK) **5391**

ROAD WAY, THE (UK) [06712774] **5391**

ROADRUNNER REFUNDER *CEASED*. (US/0196-383X) [05815558] **1299**

ROADS (ALBANY, N.Y. : 1953) (US) [06288550] **5444**

ROADS & BRIDGES (DES PLAINS, ILL.) (US/8750-9229) [11660022] **2030**

ROADS AND TRANSPORTATION ASSOCIATION OF CANADA *See* ANNUAIRE - ASSOCIATION DES ROUTES ET TRANSPORTS DU CANADA **5376**

ROAMING ROOTS (CN/1180-5714) [23238170] **2470**

ROANE COUNTY REPORTER (US) [13201575] **5765**

ROANOKE BEACON, THE (US) [26101652] **5724**

ROANOKE REVIEW (US/0035-7367) [02896521] **3431**

ROANOKE TIMES & WORLD-NEWS (US) [09725349] **5759**

ROANOKER, THE (US/0274-9734) [05168127] **2544**

ROASTING PLANT (ZIMBABWE) *See* ANNUAL REPORT / THE ROASTING PLANT **3998**

ROB TUCKER'S MEMORY LANE (US/0274-7960) [06600877] **4077**

ROBB REPORT, THE (US/0279-1447) [07586419] **2492**

ROBERT CAMPBELL'S SOUP TO NUTS (CN/0227-5953) [07966552] **4865**

ROBERT FINIGAN'S PRIVATE GUIDE TO RESTAURANTS *SUSPENDED*. (US/0162-1319) [04103730] **5073**

ROBERT FROST REVIEW, THE (US/1062-6999) [25699763] **3431**

ROBERT FULLER REAL ESTATE REPORT (US) [13179420] **4846**

ROBERT G. ALLEN'S REAL ESTATE ADVISOR (US/8756-7784) [11653165] **4847**

ROBERT MORRIS ASSOCIATES *See* MEMBER ROSTER - ROBERT MORRIS ASSOCIATES **797**

ROBERT-SCHUMANN-GESELLSCHAFT *See* SAMMELBANDE DER ROBERT-SCHUMANN-GESELLSCHAFT **4151**

ROBERT-Z'BERG URBAN OPEN SPACE AND RECREATION PROGRAM ANNUAL REPORT (US) [11462068] **2834**

ROBERTS REGISTER (US/8756-7741) [11652939] **2470**

ROBERTSON REPORT (US/0898-5448) [13233293] **2470**

ROBERTSON'S CURRENT COMPETITION (US/1055-9450) [23373536] **2080**

ROBES COUTURE (SZ) **1087**

ROBES MANTEAUX (SZ) **1087**

ROBESON COUNTY REGISTER, THE (US/0888-3807) [13312304] **2470**

ROCKY

ROBESONIAN, THE (US) [10467669] **5724**

ROBINSON JEFFERS NEWSLETTER (US/0300-7936) [01342915] 3352, **434**

ROBINSON/ROBISON RESEARCHER, THE (US/8755-3589) [11268668] **2470**

ROBINSON'S FORTNIGHTLY (CN/0704-6472) [03979905] **2544**

ROBINSON'S HOWARD COUNTY, INDIANA RURAL DIRECTORY (US) [05507842] **2575**

●ROBINSONS REDBOOK. A NATIVE AMERICAN GUIDE TO WASHINGTON D.C (US) 2272, **4684**

ROBOT (SA) [04552557] 4800, **5444**

ROBOT EXPERIMENTER *CEASED*. (US/0884-1012) [12305777] **1216**

●ROBOT EXPLORER (US/1060-4375) [25028040] **1202**

ROBOT INSIDER *CEASED*. (US/0743-0701) [10560412] 1216, **1221**

ROBOT (TOKYO, 1971) (JA/0387-1940) [10713099] 1221, **1216**

ROBOTER (GW/0724-1712) [l07241712] 1221, **1216**

ROBOTERSYSTEME (GW/0178-0026) [16734507] 1221, **1216**

ROBOTICA (UK/0263-5747) [09734967] **1216**

ROBOTICS ABSTRACTS *CEASED*. (US/0000-1139) [18543950] 1216, **1209**

ROBOTICS AND AUTONOMOUS SYSTEMS (NE/0921-8890) [17828049] **1216**

ROBOTICS AND COMPUTER-INTEGRATED MANUFACTURING (US/0736-5845) [09171554] 3487, **1216**

ROBOTICS AND EXPERT SYSTEMS *SUSPENDED*. (US/0891-4621) [13027974] **1216**

ROBOTICS CAD/CAM MARKET PLACE *CEASED*. (US) [11674594] 1235, **1216**

ROBOTICS PRODUCT DATABASE *CEASED*. (US) [17747979] **1216**

ROBOTICS REPORT, THE (US/0889-5759) [08342310] **1216**

ROBOTICS TODAY (US) [19413505] 1221, **1216**

ROBOTICS TODAY (ANNUAL ED.) (US/0734-287X) [08701234] **1216**

ROBOTICS UPDATE (US/0737-5700) [09405074] **1216**

ROBOTICS WORLD (US/0737-7908) [09444716] **1216**

ROBOTICS WORLD DIRECTORY (US) [12437555] **1216**

ROBOTNIK ROLNY (PL) [04077566] **130**

ROBOTS (CERGY) *See* PRODUCTIQUE AFFAIRES PARIS **1216**

ROBOTS CERGY (FR/0752-4978) [l07524978] 1221, **1217**

ROBOTS EXPERT PARIS (FR/0989-7100) [l09897100] **1230**

ROCAS Y MINERALES (SP/0378-3316) [I03783316] **2150**

ROCCA (IT/0391-108X) [I0391108X] **4994**

ROCENKA KATEDER RUSISTIKY NA FILOZOFICKE A PEDAGOGICKE FAKULTE UNIVERZITY PALECKEHO (XR) [05580797] **3317**

ROCENKA - KRAJSKE KULTURNI STREDISKO V BRNE (XR) [02246960] **2707**

ROCENKA OBECNYCH DEJIN (XR/0862-9773) [24730255] **2628**

ROCENKA OKRESNIHO ARCHIVU V OPAVE (XR) [10713446] **2483**

ROCHAS DE QUALIDADE (BL) [03308821] **2150**

ROCHE HANDBOOK OF DIFFERENTIAL DIAGNOSIS (US) [05823879] **4328**

ROCHES CRISTALLINES. F42 (FR) **1033**

ROCHES SEDIMENTAIRES GEOLOGIE MARINE, F43 (FR) **1395**

ROCHESTER ACADEMY OF SCIENCE, ROCHESTER, N.Y *See* PROCEEDINGS OF THE ROCHESTER ACADEMY OF SCIENCE **5141**

ROCHESTER BUSINESS JOURNAL (ROCHESTER, N.Y. : 1987) (US/0896-3274) [15553720] **708**

ROCHESTER ECCENTRIC (US/0194-1917) [05342343] **5693**

ROCHESTER ENGINEER, THE (US/0035-7405) [05736520] **1994**

ROCHESTER GOLF WEEK & SPORTS LEDGER (US) **4915**

●ROCHESTER HISTORY (US/0035-7413) [01764433] **2759**

ROCHESTER LIVING (US) [10613797] **2544**

ROCHESTER SENTINEL (ROCHESTER, IND. : DAILY : 1961) (US) [15118201] **5667**

ROCHESTER TIMES, THE (US/0192-6535) [05071422] **5720**

ROCK & FOLK PARIS. 1966 (FR/0048-8445) [I00488445] **4150**

ROCK & GEM (US/0048-8453) [03876808] **1444**

ROCK & ICE (US/0885-5722) [12661931] **4878**

●ROCK & RAP CONFIDENTIAL (US/1068-7653) [26998298] **4150**

ROCK & ROLL CONFIDENTIAL (US/0891-9372) [11101276] **4150**

ROCK & ROLL INTERNATIONAL MAGAZINE (NE) [03496978] **4150**

ROCK & SOUL *CEASED*. (US/8756-3487) [11509588] **4150**

ROCK ART RESEARCH (AT/0813-0426) [17668761] **281**

ROCK CARLING FELLOWSHIP (UK) [05272339] **3637**

●ROCK CREEK CURRENT, THE (US/1062-2721) [25568033] **5647**

ROCK DE LUX (SP) **4150**

ROCK FLUFF (CN/0381-6613) [03079316] **5794**

●ROCK HEROES PRESENTS ... (US/1059-5279) [24617385] **4150**

ROCK MAGAZINE (BEVERLY HILLS, CALIF.) (US/0739-408X) [09719050] **4150**

ROCK MAGNETISM AND PALEOGEOPHYSICS (JA/0385-2520) [04206430] 1395, **1410**

ROCK MECHANICS AND ROCK ENGINEERING (AU/0723-2632) [09515010] 1459, **2150**

ROCK MECHANICS. SUPPLEMENT *CEASED*. (AU/0080-3375) [03866244] **1994**

ROCK (NEW YORK) (US/0092-0401) [01789177] **4150**

ROCK-OUT! (RIVER EDGE, N.J.) (US/1045-6376) [20178292] **4150**

ROCK POSTER MAGAZINE (US/8755-8661) [11423293] **4151**

ROCK SCENE *SUSPENDED*. (US/0090-3353) [01785131] **4151**

ROCK SPRINGS DAILY ROCKET-MINER (US/0893-3650) [15512358] **5772**

ROCK STAR BAZAAR (US/0735-8326) [08971524] **4151**

ROCKAMERICA GUIDE TO VIDEO/MUSIC, THE (US/0883-6469) [12175531] **4151**

ROCKBILL *CEASED*. (US/0890-460X) [14256661] **4151**

ROCKBOTTOM (US/0146-1419) [02858965] **3431**

●ROCKBRIDGE DAILY PRESS (US/1064-7740) [25924968] **5759**

ROCKBRIDGE HISTORICAL SOCIETY *See* PROCEEDINGS OF THE ROCKBRIDGE HISTORICAL SOCIETY **2755**

ROCKCASTLE REMINISCENCE (US) **2628**

ROCKDALE CITIZEN, THE (US/1050-1401) [19989792] **5654**

ROCKDALE NEIGHBOR, THE (US/0199-6282) [06065869] **5654**

ROCKDALE REPORTER AND MESSENGER, THE (US) [14227772] **5754**

ROCKEFELLER ARCHIVE CENTER NEWSLETTER (US/1041-6862) [12865793] **2483**

ROCKEFELLER INSTITUTE BULLETIN (US) [24997893] **4684**

ROCKERILLA (IT) **4151**

ROCKERS (KINGSTON, JAMAICA) (JM) [09150461] **4151**

ROCKET-COURIER (US) [13614438] **5739**

ROCKET-JET FLYING (US/0035-7499) [01764459] **34**

ROCKET (SEATTLE, WA) (US) **4151**

ROCKFORD LABOR NEWS (MICROFICHE) (US) [04127953] **1708**

ROCKFORD MAGAZINE (US/0899-9414) [15301048] **1299**

ROCKFORD MAP PUBLISHERS *See* TRIENNIAL ATLAS & PLAT BOOK, RICE COUNTY, MINNESOTA **2577**

ROCKFORD REGISTER STAR (US) [05004029] **5662**

ROCKFORD SQUIRE, THE (US/0747-1815) [10621238] **5693**

ROCKIN' 50'S (US/0738-7717) [15135753] **4151**

ROCKINGCHAIR (US/0146-1885) [02868658] **4151**

ROCKLAND COUNTY TIMES, THE (US) [09889767] **5720**

ROCKLAND JOURNAL-NEWS (US) [23137874] **5720**

ROCKPORT PILOT, THE (US) [14627400] **5754**

ROCKS AND MINERALS (US/0035-7529) [01764460] **1444**

ROCKS AND MINERALS IN CANADA (CN/0035-7537) [03439496] **1444**

ROCKSTAR (IT) **4151**

ROCKTON-ROSCOE HERALD (US/0894-7465) [16207721] **5662**

ROCKVILLE CENTRE'S LONG ISLAND NEWS AND THE OWL (US/1076-3740) [11425332] **5720**

ROCKVILLE INTERNATIONAL (NE) [01792556] **4151**

ROCKVILLE REMINDER *See* REMINDER **5646**

ROCKWALL COUNTY JOURNAL-SUCCESS (US) **5754**

ROCKWALL COUNTY JOURNAL-SUCCESS (US/1048-8227) [21051043] **5754**

ROCKWALL TEXAS SUCCESS *See* ROCKWALL COUNTY JOURNAL-SUCCESS **5754**

ROCKWALL TEXAS SUCCESS, THE (US/0882-4940) [11859576] **5754**

ROCKY FORD DAILY GAZETTE, THE (US) [21427046] **5644**

ROCKY HILL POST, THE (US) [27857076] **5646**

ROCKY MOUNTAIN AMERICAN BAPTIST (US/0745-3884) [01696530] **5067**

ROCKY MOUNTAIN BAPTIST (US/0485-294X) [01604597] **5067**

ROCKY MOUNTAIN CAVING (US/8756-033X) [10654292] **1410**

ROCKY MOUNTAIN ENERGY DIRECTORY (US/0730-0891) [07919564] 2128, **1956**

ROCKY MOUNTAIN FEED AND LIVESTOCK JOURNAL *See* ROCKY MOUNTAIN LIVESTOCK JOURNAL **220**

ROCKY MOUNTAIN FOOD DEALER BULLETIN : NEWSLETTER FOR MEMBERS OF THE ROCKY MOUNTAIN FOOD DEALERS ASSOCIATION, THE (US/1044-8330) [19944681] **2356**

ROCKY MOUNTAIN FOREST AND RANGE EXPERIMENT STATION (FORT COLLINS, COLO.) *See* RESOURCE BULLETIN RM **2393**

ROCKY MOUNTAIN GAME & FISH (US/1056-0114) [23446470] **4878**

ROCKY MOUNTAIN GARDENER (US/1054-9552) [23033964] **2430**

ROCKY MOUNTAIN HIGH TECHNOLOGY DIRECTORY (US/0883-8046) [12227572] **5148**

ROCKY MOUNTAIN HOUSE LIEU HISTORIQUE NATIONAL (CN/1187-3280) [25351900] **2759**

ROCKY MOUNTAIN HOUSE NATIONAL HISTORIC SITE (CN/1187-3299) [25351898] **2759**

ROCKY MOUNTAIN JEWISH HISTORICAL NOTES (US) [06966352] **5052**

ROCKY MOUNTAIN JOURNAL OF MATHEMATICS, THE (US/0035-7596) [01764461] **3532**

●ROCKY MOUNTAIN LIVESTOCK JOURNAL (US/1072-5636) [29014051] **220**

ROCKY MOUNTAIN MAGAZINE ... MEETING AND CONVENTION GUIDE TO THE ROCKY MOUNTAIN REGION (US/0731-1737) [08129969] **5490**

●ROCKY MOUNTAIN MAGAZINE (STAMFORD, CONN.) (US/1075-7856) [30150062] **2544**

ROCKY MOUNTAIN MAGAZINE ... WINTER GUIDE, THE (US/0278-0194) [07684741] **4878**

ROCKY MOUNTAIN MEDIEVAL AND RENAISSANCE ASSOCIATION *See* JOURNAL OF THE ROCKY MOUNTAIN MEDIEVAL AND RENAISSANCE ASSOCIATION **2621**

ROCKY MOUNTAIN MINERAL LAW FOUNDATION *See* AMERICAN LAW OF MINING **2932**

ROCKY MOUNTAIN MINERAL LAW FOUNDATION *See* GOWER FEDERAL SERVICE: MINING **2975**

ROCKY MOUNTAIN MINERAL LAW INSTITUTE *See* PROCEEDINGS OF THE ANNUAL INSTITUTE - ROCKY MOUNTAIN MINERAL LAW INSTITUTE **3115**

ROCKY MOUNTAIN MUSICAL EXPRESS (US/0148-7493) [03357607] **4151**

ROCKY MOUNTAIN NEWS (DENVER, COLO. : 1937) (US) [03946163] **5644**

ROCKY MOUNTAIN PAY DIRT (US/0886-0912) [12770772] **2150**

ROCKY MOUNTAIN PETROLEUM DIRECTORY (US/0278-9299) [05045386] **4277**

ROCKY MOUNTAIN QUARTER HORSE (US/0738-8381) [09694696] **2802**

ROCKY MOUNTAIN REVIEW OF LANGUAGE AND LITERATURE (US/0361-1299) [01910486] **3431**

ROCKY MOUNTAIN SPORTSMAN (COLORADO SPRINGS, COLO.) **CEASED.** (US/0893-746X) [15636287] **4878**

ROCKY MOUNTAIN UNION FARMER (US/0035-7650) [03916223] **130**

ROCKY VIEW FIVE VILLAGE WEEKLY (CN/0821-7262) [10415786] **5794**

ROCKY VIEW TIMES, THE (CN/0715-4992) [09538839] **5794**

ROCZNIK BIAOSTOCKI (PL/0080-3421) [02896641] **2707**

ROCZNIK DOLNOSLASKI (PL) [01787497] **1582**

ROCZNIK GDANSKI (PL/0080-3456) [02896788] **2707**

ROCZNIK HISTORII SZTUKI (PL/0080-3472) [01764466] **363**

ROCZNIK HYDROLOGICZNY WOD PODZIEMNYCH (PL) **1417**

ROCZNIK HYDROLOGICZNY WOD POWIERZCHNIOWYCH. DORECZE ORDY I RZEKI PRZYMORA MIEDZY ODRA I WISLA (PL) **1417**

ROCZNIK HYDROLOGICZNY WOD POWIERZCHNIOWYCH. DORZECZE WISLY I RZEKI PRZYMORZA NA WSCHOD OD WISLY (PL) **1417**

ROCZNIK INSTYTUTU RYNKU WEWNETRZNEGO I KONSUMPCJI (PL) [11881981] **957, 1519**

ROCZNIK KRAKOWSKI (PL/0080-3499) [02890539] **2707**

ROCZNIK METEOROLOGICZNY (PL) **1434**

ROCZNIK METEOROLOGICZNY STACJI ARCTOWSKIEGO (PL) **1434**

ROCZNIK METEOROLOGICZNY STACJI HORNSUNDU (PL) **1434**

ROCZNIK MUZEUM ETNOGRAFICZNEGO W KRAKOWIE (PL/0454-482X) [04079926] **245**

ROCZNIK MUZEUM GORNOSLASKIEGO W BYTOMIU. ENTOMOLOGIA (PL/0867-1966) [23227615] **5613**

ROCZNIK MUZEUM NARODOWEGO W KIELCACH (PL/0137-2866) [05885427] **4096**

ROCZNIK MUZEUM NARODOWEGO W WARSZAWIE (PL/0509-6936) [03192960] **4096**

ROCZNIK MUZEUM W TORUNIU (PL/0495-923X) [I0495923X] **4096**

ROCZNIK MUZEUM WSI LUBELSKIEJ / MUZEUM WSI LUBELSKIEJ (PL) [10128578] **2707**

ROCZNIK ORIENTALISTYCZNY (PL/0080-3545) [01764468] **2663**

ROCZNIK POLSKIEGO TOWARZYSTWA GEOLOGICZNEGO (PL/0079-3663) [01386781] **1395**

ROCZNIK SLAWISTYCZNY (PL/0080-3588) [01910013] **3317**

ROCZNIK STATYSTYCZNY (PL) [03504413] **5337**

ROCZNIK STATYSTYCZNY BUDOWNICTWA (PL) [05924969] **1582**

ROCZNIK STATYSTYCZNY FINANSOW (PL/0079-2640) [05821462] **4747**

ROCZNIK STATYSTYCZNY GOSPODARKI MORSKIEJ (PL/0079-2667) [05956159] **4182**

ROCZNIK STATYSTYCZNY / GOWNY URZAD STATYSTYCZNY (PL) [01223593] **5337**

ROCZNIK STATYSTYCZNY INWESTYCJI / GOWNY URZAD STATYSTYCZNY (PL) [17009281] **913**

ROCZNIK STATYSTYCZNY KULTURY (PL) [03986050] **5337**

ROCZNIK STATYSTYCZNY MIAST / GOWNY URZAD STATYSTYCZNY (PL/0208-838X) [08204978] **5337**

ROCZNIK STATYSTYCZNY MIASTA NYSY (PL) [01785004] **5337**

ROCZNIK STATYSTYCZNY MIASTA PIOTRKOWA TRYBUNALSKIEGO (PL) [01786238] **5337**

ROCZNIK STATYSTYCZNY MIASTA WROCAWIA See ROCZNIK STATYSTYCZNY WOJEWODZTWA WROCAWSKIEGO I MIASTA WROCAWIA / WOJEWODZKI URZAD STATYSTYCZNY WE WROCAWIU **5337**

ROCZNIK STATYSTYCZNY OCHRONY ZDROWIA (POLAND. GOWNY URZAD STATYSTYCZNY : 1974) (PL) [07567206] **4800**

ROCZNIK STATYSTYCZNY POWIATU KROSNO (PL) [01793532] **5337**

ROCZNIK STATYSTYCZNY PRACY (PL) [18196180] **5337**

ROCZNIK STATYSTYCZNY ROLNICTWA I GOSPODARKI ZYWNOSCIOWEJ (PL) [05955430] **130**

ROCZNIK STATYSTYCZNY SZKOLNICTWA (PL) [05821452] **1781**

ROCZNIK STATYSTYCZNY TRANSPORTU (PL) [02292262] **5392**

ROCZNIK STATYSTYCZNY WOJEWODZTW (PL/0208-9300) [04532711] **5337**

ROCZNIK STATYSTYCZNY WOJEWODZTWA WROCAWSKIEGO See ROCZNIK STATYSTYCZNY WOJEWODZTWA WROCAWSKIEGO I MIASTA WROCAWIA / WOJEWODZKI URZAD STATYSTYCZNY WE WROCAWIU **5337**

ROCZNIK STATYSTYCZNY WOJEWODZTWA WROCAWSKIEGO I MIASTA WROCAWIA / WOJEWODZKI URZAD STATYSTYCZNY WE WROCAWIU (PL) [09307839] **5337**

ROCZNIK STATYSTYKI MIEDZYNARODOWEJ (PL) [04619319] **5338**

ROCZNIK WARSZAWSKI (PL/0080-360X) [01642729] **2707**

ROCZNIKI AKADEMII MEDYCZNEJ W BIAYMSTOKU (PL/0067-6489) [24034936] **3637**

ROCZNIKI AKADEMII ROLNICZEJ W POZNANIU. OGRODNICTWO (PL/0137-1738) [I01371738] **130**

ROCZNIKI AKADEMII ROLNICZEJ W POZNANIU - WYDZIA ZOOTECHNICZNY (PL) [01795505] **220**

ROCZNIKI DZIEJOW SPOECZNYCH I GOSPODARCZYCH (PL/0080-3634) [01904732] **1582**

ROCZNIKI FILOSOFICZNE (PL/0035-7685) [01910012] **4360**

ROCZNIKI GLEBOZNAWCZE (PL/0080-3642) [02460608] **185**

ROCZNIKI HUMANISTYCZNE (PL/0035-7707) [01894692] **2853**

ROCZNIKI NAUK ROLNICZYCH. SERIA A. PRODUKCJA ROSLINNA (PL/0080-3650) [02472344] **130**

ROCZNIKI NAUK ROLNICZYCH. SERIA A, PRODUKCJA ROSLINNA / KOMITET UPRAWY I HODOWLI ROSLIN POLSKIEJ AKADEMII NAUK (PL/0080-3650) [20278796] **130**

ROCZNIKI NAUK ROLNICZYCH. SERIA B. ZOOTECHNICZNA (PL/0080-3669) [02482294] **130**

ROCZNIKI NAUK ROLNICZYCH. SERIA C. TECHNIKA ROLNICZA (PL/0080-3677) [04362036] **130**

ROCZNIKI NAUK ROLNICZYCH. SERIA E: OCHRONA ROSLIN (PL/0080-3693) [01788681] **527**

ROCZNIKI NAUK ROLNICZYCH. SERIA H. RYBACTWO (PL/0080-3723) [02515449] **2312**

ROCZNIKI NAUK SPOECZNYCH (PL) [02671811] **5217**

ROCZNIKI NAUKOWE (PL) [02242702] **2601**

ROCZNIKI NAUKOWE ZOOTECHNIKI (PL/0137-1657) [02707460] **5521**

ROCZNIKI NAUKOWE ZOOTECHNIKI. MONOGRAFIE I ROZPRAWY (PL/0137-1665) [03008630] **5521**

ROCZNIKI PANSTWOWEGO ZAKADU HIGIENY (PL/0035-7715) [10110246] **4800**

ROCZNIKI POLSKOGO TOWARZYSTWA MATEMATYCZNEGO, SERIA 2. WIADOMOSCI MATEMATYCZNE (PL/0373-8302) [06214994] **3532**

ROCZNIKI POLSKOGO TOWARZYSTWA MATEMATYCZNEGO, SERIA 3: MATEMATYKA STOSOWANA (PL/0137-2890) [01788300] **3532**

ROCZNIKI POMORSKIEJ AKADEMII MEDYCZNEJ IM. GEN. KAROLA SWIERCZEWSKIEGO W SZCZECINIE (PL/0066-1945) [02267267] **3987**

ROCZNIKI STATYSTYCZNE (PL/0867-082X) **5338**

ROCZNIKI STATYSTYCZNE. DEMOGRAFIA / GOWNY URZAD STATYSTYCZNY (PL) [23858112] **4560**

ROCZNIKI STATYSTYCZNE. DOCHOD NARODOWY / GOWNY URZAD STATYSTYCZNY (PL) [27139758] **1519**

ROCZNIKI STATYSTYCZNE. FINANSE / GOWNY URZAD STATYSTYCZNY (PL) [26849160] **810**

ROCZNIKI STATYSTYCZNE. PRZEMYS / GOWNY URZAD STATYSTYCZNY (PL) [25209512] **1582**

ROCZNIKI STATYSTYCZNE. SZKOLNICTWO / GOWNY URZAD STATYSTYCZNY (PL) [26176714] **1781**

ROCZNIKI SZTUKI SLASKIEJ (PL/0557-2231) [01910506] **363**

● ROCZNIKI TEOLOGICZNE (PO) [28094604] **4994**

ROCZNIKI TEOLOGICZNO-KANONICZNE See ROCZNIKI TEOLOGICZNE **4994**

ROD & CUSTOM (1990) (US/1053-2064) [22474893] **5424**

● ROD & CUSTOM ANNUAL (US/1060-6831) [25052338] **5424**

ROD SERLING'S THE TWILIGHT ZONE MAGAZINE **CEASED.** (US/0279-6090) [07120361] **3431**

RODALE'S AMERICAN WOODWORKER (US/1074-9152) [29876055] **635**

RODALE'S FOOD AND NUTRITION LETTER **CEASED.** (US/1051-6646) [22038543] **4199**

● RODALE'S SCUBA DIVING (US/1060-9563) [25124800] **4915**

RODALE'S STRAIGHT TALK (US/1057-9753) [24166059] **1068**

RODALE'S STRAIGHT TALK See STRAIGHT TALK (PLEASANTVILLE, N.Y.) **1069**

RODDY REPORT. BOULDER COUNTY (US) **4847**

RODDY REPORT. DALLAS COUNTY, THE (US/0889-1842) [09193124] **4847**

RODDY REPORT. TARRANT COUNTY, THE (US) [10142867] **4847**

RODEO NEWS (US/0149-6425) [02251830] **4915**

RODEO TIMES /NATIONAL HIGH SCHOOL RODEO ASSOCIATION (US) [08290991] **4915**

RODINA (RU/0235-7089) [19560543] **3352**

RODNA GRUDA See RODNA GRUDA SLOVENIJA **2272**

RODNA GRUDA SLOVENIJA (XV/0557-2282) [08091298] **5490, 2272**

RODNA RECH (BU) [04611032] **3317**

● RODNAE SLOVA (BW) [26758951] **3317**

RODO KAGAKU (JA/0035-7774) [02263083] **1708**

RODO KAGAKU KENKYUJO See NEMPO **1693**

RODO KANKEI BUNKEN SAKUIN (JA) [02541551] **3154**

RODO KEIZAI TOKEI NENPO (JA) [11935321] **1708**

RODO MONDAI KENKYU (JA) [02244253] **1708**

RODO NENKAN (JA) [11445430] **1708**

RODO SEISANSEI TOKEI CHOSA HOKOKU (JA) [01790114] **1582**

RODO SHIRYO JOHO (JA) [01796852] **1708**

RODO TOKEI NENPO (JA) [02239261] **1708**

RODO UNDO HAKUSHO (JA) [07115856] **1708**

RODOLIUBIE (BU/0324-1629) [09582450] **2707**

RODOPI PERSPECTIVES ON MODERN LITERATURE (NE/0923-0416) [I09230416] **3431**

RODORYOKU CHOSA NEMPO / HENSHU SORIFU TOKEIKYOKU (JA) [08054332] **1708**

RODOSHA BUNGAKU (JA) [07370463] **3431**

RODOSHA FUKUSHI SOGO CHOSA HOKOKU (JA) [02808990] **1708**

RODOSHO SANGYO IGAKU SOGO KENKYUJO See SANGYO IGAKU SOGO KENKYUJO NEMPO **2870**

RODRIGUES ALMANACH (MF) [09561528] **2643**

RODZINA (PL/0137-8287) [I01378287] **2285**

● RODZINY : THE JOURNAL OF THE POLISH GENEALOGICAL SOCIETY OF AMERICA (PL/0735-9349) [28531952] **2470**

ROELAND PARK SUN, THE (US) [11956493] **5678**

ROEMISCHE QUARTALSCHRIFT FUER CHRISTLICHE ALTERTUMSKUNDE UND KIRCHENGESCHICHTE (IT/0035-7812) [02450280] **4994**

ROENI U SR SRBIJI / SOCIJALISTICKA REPUBLIKA SRBIJA, REPUBLICKI ZAVOD ZA STATISTIKU (CI) [08296560] **5338**

ROEPER REVIEW (US/0278-3193) [05091964] **1885**

ROESSLERIA (BL/0101-7616) [03663898] **2220, 2204**

ROESTVAST STAAL (NE) **5148**

ROETZER HEIMATKUNDLICHE ARBEITEN (AU) [21016280] **2707**

ROFO. FORTSCHRITTE AUF DEM GEBIETE DER RONTGENSTRAHLEN UND DER NEUEN BILDGEBENDEN VERFAHREN (GW/0936-6652) [21064492] **3946**

ROGER EBERT'S MOVIE HOME COMPANION / BY ROGER EBERT (US) [14762276] **4376, 4077**

● ROGER EBERT'S VIDEO COMPANION (US/1072-561X) [29012835] **4077**

ROGER RABBIT (US/1050-2602) [21433039] **1068**

ROGER RABBIT'S TOONTOWN (US/1058-8248) [24395718] **4865**

ROGER! ROGER! (US/1055-1727) [23102336] **2544**

ROGER TORY PETERSON INSTITUTE'S BIRDS, BATS & BUTTERFLIES (US/1062-5232) [25651344] **5620**

ROGERIAN NURSING SCIENCE NEWS (US/1050-9089) [21456121] **3869**

ROGUE DIGGER (US/0048-8534) [07745404] **2470**

ROGUES 'N RASCALS (US/0094-0445) [05705220] **1846**

ROHMER REVIEW, THE (US/0145-5753) [02749477] **3431**

ROHRBLATT : MAGAZIN FUER OBOE, KLARINETTE, FAGOTT UND SAXOPHON (GW/0944-0291) [29163888] **4151**

ROHSSKA KONSTSLOJDMUSEETS ARSBOK (SW/0347-9374) [02045692] **375**

ROHSTOFFPREISINDEX (GW) **1519**

ROHWEDDER (US/0892-6956) [15246649] **3470**

ROJIN IRYO JIGYO NENPO (JA) [19299906] **5181**

ROJIN MONDAI KENKYU (JA/0286-8539) [11119230] **5181**

ROKYOIKU KAGAKU (JA) [06756082] **5306**

ROLAND OFFSET REVUE See M.A.N-ROLAND REVUE **4566**

ROLE OF BEHAVIORAL SCIENCE IN PHYSICAL SECURITY, THE (US/0271-3144) [05062868] **3175**

ROLE OF VIRUSES IN HUMAN CANCER, THE (US/0270-2118) [06381507] **3823**

ROLIG-PAPIR (DK/0106-0821) [08103098] **3317**

ROLL CALL (WASHINGTON, D.C.) (US/0035-788X) [02251832] **4495**

ROLL OF THE ORDER - THE PRIORY OF CANADA (CN/0315-9701) [07298831] **3175**

ROLLCALL (CN/0707-3542) [04784044] **3917**

ROLLER SKATING BUSINESS (US/0191-7617) [04913176] **4854**

ROLLERCOASTER! MAGAZINE (US/0896-7261) [17283449] **4865**

ROLLIN' HOMES (CN/0703-8674) [03960037] **5490**

ROLLING EAST (CN/0828-5993) [12093211] **4083**

ROLLING STONE (US/0035-791X) [01787396] **4151**

ROLLING STONE REVIEW, THE (US/8755-6324) [11362421] **4151**

●ROLLING VENTURES (US/1060-8893) [25100510] **708**

ROLLINS SANDSPUR (US/0035-7936) [03916295] **1094**

ROLLS-ROYCE OWNERS' CLUB See DIRECTORY AND REGISTER / ROLLS-ROYCE OWNERS' CLUB **5413**

ROLNICTWO / AKADEMIA ROLNICZA W SZCZECINIE (PL) [10969596] **130**

ROLNIK SPOLDZIELCA (PL) [04077592] **5306**

ROM NEWSLETTER; A NEWS REPORT ON COM APPLICATIONS FOR LIBRARIES (US) [05470173] **3247**

ROMA (II) [02240238] **2628**

ROMA COMUNE (IT/0391-8017) [I03918017] **2492**

ROMA NEL RINASCIMENTO : RR (IT) [13138421] **424**

ROMACAPITALE (IT) **2492**

ROMAGNA ARTE E STORIA (IT) [12184740] **363**

ROMAN CEASED. (FR) [09337110] **3431**

ROMAN 20-50 (FR/0295-5024) [21016294] **3431**

ROMAN-GAZETA (RU/0131-6044) [04612962] **3352**

ROMANA : BOLLETTINO DELLA PRELATURA DELLA SANTA CROCE E OPUS DEI (IT) **4994**

ROMANCE (CN/0228-0205) [06703430] **3431, 5074**

ROMANCE LINGUISTICS & LITERATURE REVIEW (US) [19074344] **3431, 3317**

ROMANCE MONOGRAPHS, INC. (SERIES) (US) [02901041] **3317, 3352**

ROMANCE NOTES (US/0035-7995) [01208053] **3318**

ROMANCE OF LIFE (US/1061-124X) [25184274] 3996, **5565**

ROMANCE PACKAGE / SPANISH LANGUAGE POPULAR FICTION (US) **3431, 5074**

ROMANCE PHILOLOGY (US/0035-8002) [01208043] **3318**

ROMANCE QUARTERLY (US/0883-1157) [12066070] 3431, **3318**

ROMANCE STUDIES : A JOURNAL OF THE UNIVERSITY OF WALES (UK/0263-9904) [09798987] **1846**

ROMANES LECTURES (UK) [01764485] **1846**

ROMANFUEHRER, DER (GW/0557-2614) [I05572614] **424**

ROMANIA See BULETINUL OFICIAL AL REPUBLICII SOCIALISTE ROMANIA. PARTEA A III-A. SUPLIMENT **2944**

ROMANIA See COLECTIA DE HOTARIRI ALE CONSILIULUI DE MINISTRI SI ALTE ACTE NORMATIVE **4639**

ROMANIA See MONITORUL OFICIAL AL ROMANIEI. PATRTEA 1. PUBLICATII SI ANUNTURI **4666**

ROMANIA (FR/0035-8029) [01606691] **3318**

ROMANIA (FR) **2853**

ROMANIA APICOLA (RM) [24914854] **130**

ROMANIA, DOCUMENTS, EVENTS / ROMANIAN NEWS AGENCY, AGERPRES (RM/0048-8658) [04340090] **2522**

ROMANIA. INSTITUTUL DE CERCETARI PENTRU PROTECTIA PLANTELOR See ANALELE - INSTITUTULUI DE CERCETARI PENTRU PROTECTIA PLANTELOR, ACADEMIA DE STIINTE AGRICOLE SI SILVICE **498**

ROMANIA LITERARA (RM/0048-8550) [02267274] 2853, **3431**

ROMANIA VIEWPOINTS (RM) [05041423] **4534**

●ROMANIAN ASTRONOMICAL JOURNAL (RM/1220-5168) [I12205168] **399**

ROMANIAN BOOKS IN FOREIGN LANGUAGES (RM) [01787463] **4822**

ROMANIAN BULLETIN (US/0035-8053) [02733243] **3318**

ROMANIAN ECONOMIC NEWS (RM) [02267278] **1582**

ROMANIAN ENGINEERING (RM) [07373370] **2128**

ROMANIAN FILM, THE (RM/0557-2630) [07213944] **4077**

ROMANIAN FOREIGN TRADE CEASED. (RM) [02267279] 708, **1519**

ROMANIAN JOURNAL OF CHEMISTRY (RM/0370-6273) [05418145] **992**

●ROMANIAN JOURNAL OF ENDOCRINOLOGY / SPONSORE [SIC] BY THE ACADEMY OF MEDICAL SCIENCES (RM) [28382737] **3733**

ROMANIAN JOURNAL OF GERONTOLOGY AND GERIATRICS (RM/0254-2307) [08071847] **3755**

●ROMANIAN JOURNAL OF MINERAL DEPOSITS (RM/1220-5648) [27911461] **1396**

ROMANIAN JOURNAL OF MORPHOLOGY AND EMBRYOLOGY (RM/1220-0522) [23814167] 541, **540**

●ROMANIAN JOURNAL OF PALEONTOLOGY (RM/1220-5656) [27919603] **4230**

ROMANIAN JOURNAL OF PHYSICS / ROMANIAN ACADEMY (RM) [28349152] **4420**

●ROMANIAN JOURNAL OF PHYSIOLOGY : PHYSIOLOGICAL SCIENCES / [ACADEMIA DE STIINTE MEDICALE] (RM) [31093279] **586**

ROMANIAN MEDICAL REVIEW (RM/0048-8585) [01764495] **3637**

ROMANIAN NEWS AND WORLD REPORT (US/0045-2351) [01640006] **2707**

ROMANIAN NEWS (BUCHAREST, ROMANIA) (RM) [04409508] **2522**

ROMANIAN PHILATELIC STUDIES (US/0748-2930) [10906060] **2787**

●ROMANIAN REPORTS IN PHYSICS (RM/1221-1451) [29553239] **4420**

ROMANIAN REVIEW OF MILITARY HISTORY (RM) [19068841] **4056**

ROMANIAN SOURCES (US/0098-6054) [01205122] **2707**

ROMANIC REVIEW (US/0035-8118) [01715699] 3318, **3431**

ROMANICA GANDENSIA (BE/0080-3855) [01590471] 3432, **3318**

ROMANICA GOTHOBURGENSIA (SW/0080-3863) [02888187] 3432, **3318**

ROMANICA HELVETICA (SZ/0080-3871) [01764496] **3318**

ROMANICA VULGARIA : QUADERNI (IT) [15916249] **2628**

ROMANISCHE BIBLIOGRAPHIE / BIBLIOGRAPHIE ROMANE / ROMANCE BIBLIOGRAPHY (GW) [02381586] **3336**

ROMANISCHE FORSCHUNGEN (GW/0035-8126) [01764498] 3432, **3318**

ROMANISTISCHE ARBEITSHEFTE (GW) [12405669] 3318, **3432**

ROMANISTISCHE ZEITSCHRIFT FUER LITERATURGESCHICHTE (GW/0343-379X) [04101230] 3432, **3318**

ROMANISTISCHES JAHRBUCH (GW/0080-3898) [01200525] **3318**

ROMANOBARBARICA (IT) [05690787] **1079**

ROMANOSLAVICA / ASOCIATIA SLAVISTILOR DIN REPUBLICA POPULARA ROMINA (RM/0557-272X) [04344255] **3318**

ROMANSKOE I GERMANSKOE IAZYKOZNANIE (BW/0134-9619) [01910020] **3318**

ROMANTIC MOVEMENT (US/0557-2738) [01910011] 3432, **3459**

ROMANTIC REASSESSMENT (AU/1019-1135) [16820910] **3432**

ROMANTIC SHELTERS (US) **2628**

ROMANTIC TIMES (US/0747-3370) [08985074] **5074**

ROMANTISME (FR/0048-8593) [00931119] 2628, **3432**

ROMANTIST, THE (US/0161-682X) [03987764] **3432**

ROMANTZO (GR) **5074**

ROMBO (IT) **5424**

ROME (FR) [05122502] **5490**

ROME (CITY). PONTIFICIA UNIVERSITA GREGORIANA. FACOLTA DI STORIA ECCLESIASTICA See MISCELLANEA HISTORIAE PONTIFICIAE **4977**

ROME (PARIS, FRANCE) (UK) [13723605] **5490**

ROMEO-WASHINGTON ADVISOR NEWSPAPER, THE (US/0192-8082) [05103731] **5693**

ROMISCHE HISTORISCHE MITTEILUNGEN (AU/0080-3790) [01908267] **2707**

ROMISCHES JAHRBUCH DER BIBLIOTHECA HERTZIANA (GW/0342-2046) [21208043] **363**

ROMISCHES OSTERREICH (AU/1012-5833) [03675637] 282, **2707**

ROMU KENKYU (JA) [05699309] **947**

RON JANOFF'S GUIDE TO COMMERCIAL REAL ESTATE (US/0194-3723) [05368511] **4847**

RON PAUL'S FUTURE FOOD TRENDS See AMERICA'S FUTURE FOOD TRENDS **2326**

RON SSHU - KOMAZAWA DAIGAKU GAIKOKUGOBU (JA) [04471902] **3318**

RONALD ANDERSON AND ASSOCIATES See RONALD ANDERSON'S PRIMARY INDUSTRY NEWSLETTER **130**

RONALD ANDERSON'S PRIMARY INDUSTRY NEWSLETTER (AT) [03962622] **130**

ROND DE TAFEL (NE/0035-8169) [08630302] **4994**

RONDA LITERARIA (AG) [05388860] **3352**

RONDEVLEI BIRD SANCTUARY See WARDEN'S ... ANNUAL REPORT ON THE RONDEVLEI BIRD SANCTUARY FOR THE YEAR ... / RONDEVLEI BIRD SANCTUARY, THE **2208**

RONDOM GEZIN (BE/0773-4239) [I07734239] **2285**

RONDOM HET WOORD (NE) [05154246] **5067**

RONMUNJIB - CUNNAM DAIHAGGYO GONNEB GYONYUG NYENGUSO (KO/0253-6315) [10560615] **5148**

RONSHU (JA) [02108149] **5269**

RONTGEN-BERICHTE (GW/0302-7813) [10110272] **3946**

RONTGENPRAXIS (STUTTGART) (GW/0035-7820) [01778176] **3946**

ROOF (UK) [06839982] **2834**

ROOF (US/0163-0687) [04271863] **3470**

ROOFER MAGAZINE, THE (US/0279-4616) [07893327] 626, **3487**

ROOFING, CLADDING & INSULATION (UK) **626**

ROOFING MATERIALS GUIDE (US/1061-8953) [15578617] **627**

ROOKIE AND RECORD BOOK See AMERICAN LEAGUE REDBOOK **4882**

ROOKS COUNTY RECORD (STOCKTON, KAN. : 1931) (US) [12487890] **5678**

ROOM OF ONE'S OWN (CN/0316-1609) [02248303] 5565, **3432**

ROOPA-LEKHA (II/0035-8215) [01697061] **363**

ROOSEVELT RECORD (US) [17311738] **5762**

ROOT AND BRANCH (UK/0306-9958) [I03069958] **2470**

ROOT CELLAR PRESERVES (US/0748-6251) [10969147] **2470**

ROOT CROPS DIGEST (PH/0116-4325) [14118304] **130**

ROOT'S AND BRANCHES (US) [13405229] **2470**

ROOTS & BRANCHES (US/0893-4150) [15537457] **2471**

ROOTS & BRANCHES (US/1057-2570) [23946627] **5338**

ROOTS AND LEAVES (US/0748-2485) [07400991] **2471**

ROOTS & SHOOTS QUARTERLY (US/0738-2391) [09539610] **2471**

ROOTS, BRANCHES AND TWIGS (ONTARIO GENEALOGICAL SOCIETY. KENT COUNTY BRANCH) (CN/0831-5930) [14473743] **2471**

ROOTS DIGEST (US/8755-8343) [11412592] **2471**

ROOTS (ST. PAUL, MINN.) *CEASED.* (US/0148-6659) [01775185] **2759**

ROOTS TRACER (US/0736-802X) [17203318] **2471**

ROPA A UHLIE (XO/0035-8231) [09696255] 1956, **4277**

ROPER REPORTS (US/0196-3589) [02241701] **5256**

ROPERS SPORTS NEWS (US/8750-3417) [11253518] **5639**

RORAIMA (US) [03216723] **4546**

ROSA CUBICA (SP) [19224476] **3470**

ROSE FAMILY BULLETIN (US/0748-7827) [05896614] **2471**

ROSEAU TIMES-REGION (US) [01695574] **5698**

ROSEBUD COUNTY PRESS (US/8750-2097) [11108194] **5706**

ROSEBUD NEWS, THE (US) [14703185] **5754**

ROSEMERE-NOUVELLES (CN/0712-2993) [08890869] **4684**

ROSEMONT EDITION OF THE TIMES (US/0895-0113) [16401547] **5662**

ROSEMONT PROGRESS *CEASED.* (US/0744-5407) [08337825] **5662**

ROSEVILLE PRESS-TRIBUNE (US) [27481186] **5639**

ROSICRUCIAN DIGEST (US/0035-8339) [02714902] **4243**

ROSKILDE UNIVERSITETSCENTER *See* BERETNING FOR ... / ROSKILDE UNIVERSITETSCENTER **1811**

ROSKILDE UNIVERSITETSCENTER. INSTITUT FOR GEOGRAFI, SAMFUNDSANALYSE OG DATALOGI *See* ARSBERETNING / ROSKILDE UNIVERSITETSCENTER, INSTITUT FOR GEOGRAFI, SAMFUNDSANALYSE OG DATALOGI **5191**

ROSKILDE UNIVERSITETSCENTER. INSTITUT FOR SAMFUNDSKONOMI OG PLANLGNING *See* ARSBERETNING **1546**

ROSPA BULLETIN (UK/0143-3377) [I01433377] **4800**

ROSS COUNTY GENEALOGICAL SOCIETY *See* NEWSLETTER / ROSS COUNTY GENEALOGICAL SOCIETY **2464**

ROSS COUNTY GENEALOGICAL SOCIETY. NEWSLETTER *See* RCGS NEWSLETTER **2469**

ROSS REPORTS TELEVISION (US/0035-8355) [05247997] **1138**

ROSSFORD RECORD JOURNAL (US) [10245164] **5730**

ROSSICA OLOMUCENSIA (XR) [04870601] 3352, **3318**

ROSSIIA MOLODAIA (RU/0234-1727) [22355223] **130**

ROSSIIANE (RU/0320-1031) [24362315] **3432**

●ROSSIISKAIA FEDERATSIIA (RU) [29572372] **4684**

●ROSSIISKAIA IUSTITSIIA (RU) [30571246] **3045**

ROSSIISKIE VESTI : EZHENEDELNAIA GAZETA PRAVITELSTVA ROSSIISKOI FEDERATSII (RU) [24323192] **5809**

●ROSSIISKII EKONOMICHESKII ZHURNAL / VYSSHII EKONOMICHESKII SOVET PRI PREZIDIUME VERKHOVNOGO SOVETA ROSSIISKOI FEDERATSII, MINISTERSTVO NAUKI, VYSSHEI SHKOLY I TEKHNICHESKOI POLITIKI ROSSIISKOI FEDERATSII [I] GOSUDARSTVENNAIA AKADEMIIA UPRAVLENIIA (RU) [26487343] **1519**

●ROSSIISKII VESTNIK PERINATOLOGII I PEDIATRII / MINISTERSTVO ZDRAVOOKHRANENIIA ROSSIISKOI FEDERATSII, MOSKOVSKII NII PEDIATRII I DETSKOI KHIRURGII, MOSKOVSKII OBLASTNOI NII AKUSHERSTVA I GINEKOLOGII (RU) [30684345] **3911**

●ROSSISKII MEDITSINSKII ZHURNAL : ORGAN MINISTERSTVA ZDRAVOOKHRANENIIA RSFSR (RU/0869-2106) [26104244] **3637**

ROSSLAND AND DISTRICT WEEKLY, THE (CN/0383-8153) [03232889] **5794**

ROSSOSCUOLA (IT) **1781**

ROST KRISTALLOV / AKADEMIIA NAUK SSSR, INSTITUT KRISTALLOGRAFII IM. A.V. SHUBNIKOVA (RU/0485-4802) [06610987] **1033**

ROSTER - AMERICAN INSTITUTE OF CERTIFIED PLANNERS (US/0271-0188) [06514480] **1582**

ROSTER AND LIST OF COMMITTEES OF THE GENERAL ASSEMBLY OF MARYLAND (US) [06191236] **4684**

ROSTER AND STATISTICS OF OKLAHOMA PUBLIC AND INSTITUTIONAL LIBRARIES (US) **3247**

ROSTER - ARIZONA STATE BOARD OF ACCOUNTANCY (US/0363-2954) [02437904] **751**

ROSTER - ASSOCIATED GENERAL CONTRACTORS OF AMERICA. CAROLINAS BRANCH (US/8756-3800) [11508946] **627**

ROSTER DE L'ACTL (CN/0823-4639) [10440754] **3637**

ROSTER - FLORIDA STATE BOARD OF ARCHITECTURE (US) [01304575] **308**

ROSTER/INDUSTRY DIRECTORY (US/0197-1565) [03982925] **2370**

ROSTER ISSUE OF THE NORTH CAROLINA MEDICAL JOURNAL (US) **3637**

ROSTER NO. ... OF LICENSED CONTRACTORS IN THE STATE OF ALABAMA / STATE LICENSING BOARD FOR GENERAL CONTRACTORS (US) [09559894] **2030**

ROSTER OF BLACK ELECTED OFFICIALS IN THE SOUTH (US/0093-9951) [01793610] 2272, **4684**

ROSTER OF CURRENT LICENSES - GEORGIA. STATE BOARD OF REGISTRATION FOR FORESTERS (US) [04794833] **2394**

ROSTER OF DENTISTS AND DENTAL HYGIENISTS REGISTERED IN THE STATE OF MINNESOTA (US/0360-5582) [02244102] **1335**

ROSTER OF DEPARTMENTS OF GEOGRAPHY, CANADIAN UNIVERSITIES AND COLLEGES (CN/0710-5754) [08716845] 1846, **2575**

ROSTER OF LICENSED CONTRACTORS IN THE STATE OF MISSISSIPPI (US) [20719881] **627**

ROSTER OF LICENSED CONTRACTORS IN THE STATE OF SOUTH CAROLINA (US/0561-0214) [06783008] **2030**

ROSTER OF LICENSED PROFESSIONAL ENGINEERS (US/0149-3035) [03454010] **1994**

ROSTER OF LICENSED REAL ESTATE BROKERS AND SALESMEN BY COMPANY (US/0098-0315) [01799053] **4847**

ROSTER OF LICENSED RESIDENTIAL HOME BUILDERS IN THE STATE OF SOUTH CAROLINA (US) [05933715] **627**

ROSTER OF MEMBERS (US) [02255224] 1202, **1209**

ROSTER OF MEMBERS - ASSOCIATION FOR HOSPITAL MEDICAL EDUCATION (US/0160-9440) [03764442] **3637**

ROSTER OF MEMBERSHIP AND RESOURCE GUIDE / EMPLOYEE RELOCATION COUNCIL (US/1053-2374) [22467591] **1929**

ROSTER OF PROFESSIONAL ENGINEERS AND LAND SURVEYORS (US) [09736269] **1994**

ROSTER OF QUALIFIED ENGINEERING AND LAND SURVEYING FIRMS / LOUISIANA STATE BOARD OF REGISTRATION FOR PROFESSIONAL ENGINEERS AND LAND SURVEYORS (US/8756-2251) [11482145] **2030**

ROSTER OF REAL ESTATE BROKERS AND SALESMEN *See* ROSTER OF LICENSED REAL ESTATE BROKERS AND SALESMEN BY COMPANY **4847**

ROSTER OF REAL ESTATE LICENSEES (IOWA) (US) [06567114] **4847**

ROSTER OF REGISTERED ARCHITECTS AND LANDSCAPE ARCHITECTS YEAR ENDING JUNE 30 ... / MAINE STATE BOARD FOR REGISTRATION OF ARCHITECTS AND LANDSCAPE ARCHITECTS (US) [07417563] **308**

ROSTER OF REGISTERED ARCHITECTS (AUSTIN) (US/0149-0486) [03417169] **308**

ROSTER OF REGISTERED ARCHITECTS / MISSISSIPPI STATE BOARD OF ARCHITECTURE (US) [09481063] **308**

ROSTER OF REGISTERED FORESTERS OF MISSISSIPPI (US/0196-7533) [05876044] **2394**

ROSTER OF REGISTERED FORESTERS : STATE OF ALABAMA (US) [05959756] **2394**

ROSTER OF REGISTERED LANDSCAPE ARCHITECTS, COMMONWEALTH OF KENTUCKY (US) [10088004] **2430**

ROSTER OF REGISTERED PRACTITIONERS OF THE HEALING ART, IN ACTIVE PRACTICE IN VIRGINIA *See* ROSTER OF REGISTERED PRACTITIONERS OF THE HEALING ARTS LICENSED AND REGISTERED IN THE STATE OF VIRGINIA **3917**

ROSTER OF REGISTERED PRACTITIONERS OF THE HEALING ARTS LICENSED AND REGISTERED IN THE STATE OF VIRGINIA (US/0097-9147) [02241205] **3917**

ROSTER OF REGISTERED PROFESSIONAL ENGINEERS AND LAND SURVEYORS (US) [04840739] **2030**

ROSTER OF REGISTERED PROFESSIONAL ENGINEERS AND LAND SURVEYORS : ANNUAL REPORT (US/0361-8161) [02247050] **2030**

ROSTER OF TEACHING PERSONNEL IN COLLEGES OF PHARMACY (US) [06643670] 1846, **4328**

ROSTER OF WOMEN AND MINORITY ENGINEERING AND TECHNOLOGY STUDENTS (US/0147-555X) [03197190] **1995**

ROSTER : REGISTERED ARCHITECTS, FIRMS, PROFESSIONAL CORPORATIONS, BUSINESS CORPORATIONS, AND PARTNERSHIPS (US) [25003433] **308**

ROSTER, REGISTERED ENGINEERS AND LAND SURVEYORS *See* BIENNIAL ROSTER OF REGISTERED PROFESSIONAL ENGINEERS AND LAND SURVEYORS AND ALABAMA LAW REGULATING PRACTICE OF ENGINEERING AND LAND SURVEYING **1966**

ROSTER / RESTAURANTS & FOODSERVICES ASSOCIATION OF BRITISH COLUMBIA (CN/0714-315X) [09156955] **5073**

ROSTER - STATE BOARD OF REGISTRATION OF PROFESSIONAL ENGINEERS, ARCHITECTS AND LAND SURVEYORS (US) [05793956] 308, **1995**

ROSTER - TENNESSEE STATE BOARD OF ARCHITECTURAL AND ENGINEERING EXAMINERS (US/0737-2329) [06253184] 1995, **308**

ROSTER / THE BIRMINGHAM GENEALOGICAL SOCIETY, INC (US/8756-4351) [05928354] **2471**

ROSTLINNA VYROBA (XR/0370-663X) [02403782] **130**

ROSTOCKER AGRARWISSENSCHAFTLICHE BEITRAEGE (GW/0138-3299) [10832060] **131**

ROSTOCKER MATHEMATISCHES KOLLOQUIUM (GW) [03568723] **3532**

ROSTOCKER PHYSIKALISCHE MANUSKRIPTE (GW/0138-3140) [09450645] **4420**

ROSTRUM (CAPE TOWN, SOUTH AFRICA) (SA) [11218590] **1781**

ROSTRUM, THE (US) [04521616] **1121**

ROSWELL DAILY RECORD, THE (US) [13454297] **5713**

ROSWELL MUSEUM AND ART CENTER *See* QUARTERLY BULLETIN / ROSWELL MUSEUM AND ART CENTER **4095**

ROSWELL NEIGHBOR, THE (US/0192-2637) [04978753] **5655**

ROTA-GENE (US/0730-5168) [07990684] **2471**

ROTACION (SP/0211-2892) [I02112892] **5455**

ROTAE ROMANAE DECISIONES SEU SENTENTIA SACRA ROMANA ROTA (IT) **4994**

ROTARIAN, THE (US/0035-838X) [01764547] **5236**

ROTARY CLUB OF ALBANY *See* CAPITAL COGS **5229**

ROTARY RIGS ACTUALLY MAKING HOLE IN THE US & CANADA (US) **2095**

ROTARY ROCKET (US/0194-6439) [04905023] **5424**

ROTE LISTE (GW) [01623766] **4328**

ROTEIRO DA CIDADE DE LOURENCO MARQUES (MZ) [02653802] **2643**

ROTHENBERG POLITICAL REPORT (US) **4495**

ROTHMANS FOOTBALL YEARBOOK (UK) [01786715] **4915**

ROTHNIUM MAGAZINE (CN/0702-7303) [03781548] **3432**

●ROTISSERIE LEAGUE FOOTBALL (US) [24133005] **4865**

ROTKIN REVIEW, THE *SUSPENDED.* (US/0883-735X) [12223384] 363, **4376**

ROTOR (ALEXANDRIA, VA.) (US/0897-831X) [17636743] **34**

ROTOR & WING (1992) (US/1066-8098) [27052632] **34**

Alphabetical Title Index — ROYAL

ROTOR & WING INTERNATIONAL (US/0191-6408) [04965712] **34**

ROTOR ROSTER (US) [18399727] **34**

ROTORCRAFT (CLINTON, LA.) (US/1041-2735) [18704813] **34**

ROTTERDAM. GEMEENTELIJK BUREAU VOOR ONDERZOEK EN STATISTIEK *See* DEMOGRAFISCHE GEGEVENS **5326**

ROTTERDAMS JAARBOEKJE (NE/0923-6287) [I09236287] **2707**

ROTUNDA (TORONTO) (CN/0035-8495) [01898685] **4096**

ROUFF & ROPER REGISTERED CONVEYANCING (UK) **3045**

ROUGE (UK/0958-188X) [23717866] **2796**

ROUGE (FR) **2853**

ROUGE & VERT (FR) [20655075] **4546**

ROUGE (BATON ROUGE, LA.) *CEASED.* (US/0896-0712) [16899161] **2492**

ROUGE VALLEY, PARK FORUM (CN/0846-3948) [25352143] **4708**

ROUGE VALLEY PARK PROJECT (ONT.) *See* ROUGE VALLEY, PARK FORUM **4708**

ROUGH NOTES CO *See* WHAT IT COSTS **2896**

ROUGH NOTES (INDIANAPOLIS) (US/0035-8525) [02253922] **2893**

ROUGHNECK, THE (CN/0048-864X) [02110447] **4277**

●ROULANT MA BOSSE, EN (CN/1188-9926) [26776214] **1519**

ROULEZ SANS VOUS FAIRE ROULER. GUIDE DES VOITURES D'OCCASION (CN/0820-0270) [09456902] **5424**

ROUMANIAN ARCHIVES OF MICROBIOLOGY AND IMMUNOLOGY (RM/1220-8485) [25545262] 570, **3676**

ROUND BOBBIN (US/1076-058X) [30379376] **5185**

ROUND QUARTER SERIES OF NEW POETS & ARTISTS (US/0483-4240) [08872045] **3470**

ROUND ROCK LEADER (US/0164-9124) [04233027] **5754**

ROUND TABLE (BARRIE) (CN/0384-0123) [03244972] **3247**

ROUND TABLE NEWS (CN/1186-0308) [24296309] 2181, **1519**

ROUND TABLE SERIES / ROYAL SOCIETY OF MEDICINE SERVICES (UK/0268-3091) [13659203] **3637**

ROUND TABLE, THE (UK/0035-8533) [01764559] **4534**

ROUND THE TABLE (US/0161-7125) [04010310] **2893**

ROUND UP (UNIVERSITY PARK, N.M.) (US/0744-5555) [06926596] **5713**

ROUNDEL (US/0889-3225) [13856048] **5424**

ROUNDTABLE (US) [08578284] **4994**

ROUNDTABLE (BOSTON, MASS.) *See* UNITED FLY TYERS' ROUNDTABLE **2315**

ROUNDTABLE REPORT *CEASED.* (US/0272-0515) [06744205] 5565, **4800**

ROUNDUP / LOW INCOME HOUSING INFORMATION SERVICE (US) [26046390] **2834**

●ROUNDUP MAGAZINE / WESTERN WRITERS OF AMERICA, THE (US) [28942729] **3432**

ROUNDUP (MINNEAPOLIS, MINN.), THE (US/0485-5140) [01791737] **1314**

ROUNDUP QUARTERLY *See* ROUNDUP MAGAZINE / WESTERN WRITERS OF AMERICA, THE **3432**

ROUNDUP QUARTERLY, THE (US/1041-5289) [18707949] **3432**

ROUNDUP RECORD-TRIBUNE & WINNETT TIMES (US/0890-9660) [13054725] **5706**

ROUNDUP (WASHINGTON, D.C.), THE (US/0738-8497) [07743066] **2759**

ROUSSILLON AGRICOLE (FR/0298-119X) [24905125] **131**

ROUSTABOUT, THE (US/0279-1943) [07624752] **1956**

ROUTES ET TRANSPORTS (CN/0319-3780) [02442873] **5392**

ROUTES PARIS. 1986 (FR/1011-1891) [I10111891] 5444, **1995**

ROUTES QUEBECOISES, LES (CN) [01789717] **5444**

ROUTIERS, LES (FR/0243-6795) [I02436795] **5444**

ROUTING (UK) **635**

ROUX'S ARCHIVES OF DEVELOPMENTAL BIOLOGY (GW/0930-035X) [13079525] **541**

ROUYN (QUEBEC) *See* TRAIT D'UNION (ROUYN) **4691**

ROV REVIEW (UK/0893-4665) [14170849] **2095**

ROVER REGISTER, THE (US/1060-5932) [25044238] **5392**

ROVESNIK (RU/0485-5167) [01906234] **1068**

ROW (PETALUMA, CALIF.) (US/1043-2345) [19356808] **4915**

ROWAN COUNTY REGISTER (US/0885-8454) [12763834] **2471**

ROWENA PRESS, THE (US) [17186835] **5754**

ROWETT RESEARCH INSTITUTE *See* ANNUAL REPORT / THE ROWETT RESEARCH INSTITUTE **5503**

ROWETT RESEARCH INSTITUTE, ABERDEEN, SCOTLAND *See* ANNUAL REPORT OF STUDIES IN ANIMAL NUTRITION AND ALLIED SCIENCES **206**

ROWING (UK) **595**

ROWLETT RECORD AMERICAN (US/0886-3733) [12873413] **5754**

ROY ANDERSON'S ROAD WORK SAFETY REPORT (US/1054-5050) [22902739] 2869, **5444**

ROYAL AERONAUTICAL SOCIETY. COUNCIL *See* ANNUAL REPORT OF THE COUNCIL **11**

ROYAL AERONAUTICAL SOCIETY. ENGINEERING SCIENCES DATA UNIT. INDEX *See* INDEX - ENGINEERING SCIENCES DATA UNIT **1977**

ROYAL AGRICULTURAL SOCIETY OF ENGLAND *See* JOURNAL OF THE ROYAL AGRICULTURAL SOCIETY OF ENGLAND **101**

ROYAL AIR FORCE COLLEGE JOURNAL, THE (UK/0035-8606) [12170237] **1094**

ROYAL AIR FORCE NEWS (UK) **4056**

ROYAL AIR FORCE RETIRED LIST, THE (UK) [01795440] **4056**

ROYAL AIR FORCE YEARBOOK (UK/0954-092X) **34**

ROYAL AMBASSADOR LEADERSHIP (US/0893-5246) [15562546] **4994**

ROYAL ASIATIC SOCIETY OF GREAT BRITAIN AND FINLAND. MALAYSIAN BRANCH *See* MONOGRAPHS - ROYAL ASIATIC SOCIETY OF GREAT BRITAIN AND FINLAND. MALAYSIAN BRANCH **2659**

ROYAL ASIATIC SOCIETY OF GREAT BRITAIN AND IRELAND *See* JOURNAL OF THE ROYAL ASIATIC SOCIETY OF GREAT BRITAIN & IRELAND **2769**

ROYAL ASIATIC SOCIETY OF GREAT BRITAIN AND IRELAND. SRI LANKA BRANCH *See* JOURNAL OF THE SRI LANKA BRANCH OF THE ROYAL ASIATIC SOCIETY **2656**

ROYAL ASTRONOMICAL SOCIETY *See* QUARTERLY JOURNAL OF THE ROYAL ASTRONOMICAL SOCIETY, THE **399**

ROYAL ASTRONOMICAL SOCIETY OF CANADA *See* JOURNAL OF THE ROYAL ASTRONOMICAL SOCIETY OF CANADA, THE **396**

ROYAL ASTRONOMICAL SOCIETY OF NEW ZEALAND VARIABLE STAR MONTHLY CIRCULARS M (NZ) **399**

ROYAL AUSTRALIAN CHEMICAL INSTITUTE *See* CHEMISTRY IN AUSTRALIA **970**

ROYAL AUSTRALIAN MINT *See* REPORT OF THE CONTROLLER FOR THE PERIOD ENDED 30 JUNE / DEPARTMENT OF THE TREASURY, ROYAL AUSTRALIAN MINT **4745**

ROYAL AUTOMOBILE CLUB OF QUEENSLAND *See* QUEENSLAND ACCOMMODATION AND CARAVANNING DIRECTORY **5489**

ROYAL BANK LETTER, THE (CN/0229-0243) [06741156] 810, **1582**

ROYAL BANK OF CANADA *See* INTERNATIONAL DIRECTORY - ROYAL BANK OF CANADA **792**

ROYAL BANK OF SCOTLAND REVIEW, THE *CEASED.* (UK) [12895603] 1519, **810**

ROYAL BANK TRENDICATOR REPORT (CN/0383-9834) [10259938] **1582**

ROYAL BOTANIC GARDENS (KEW, SURREY) *See* FLORA OF TROPICAL EAST AFRICA **511**

ROYAL BOTANICAL GARDENS (HAMILTON, ONT.) *See* ANNUAL REPORT - ROYAL BOTANICAL GARDENS **499**

ROYAL BRITISH LEGION *See* JOURNAL - ROYAL BRITISH LEGION **5232**

ROYAL CANADIAN ACADEMY OF ARTS *See* CATALOGUE OF THE EXHIBITION - ROYAL CANADIAN ACADEMY OF ARTS **347**

ROYAL CANADIAN COLLEGE OF ORGANISTS *See* YEARBOOK - ROYAL CANADIAN COLLEGE OF ORGANISTS (1978) **4159**

ROYAL CANADIAN MILITARY INSTITUTE *See* ROYAL CANADIAN MILITARY INSTITUTE YEARBOOK **4056**

ROYAL CANADIAN MILITARY INSTITUTE YEARBOOK (CN/0315-6451) [02624634] **4056**

ROYAL CANADIAN MOUNTED POLICE *See* QUARTERLY / ROYAL CANADIAN MOUNTED POLICE, THE **3174**

ROYAL CENTER RECORD (US) [15614886] **5667**

ROYAL COLLEGE OF GENERAL PRACTITIONERS *See* QUALITY IN PRACTICE : A BULLETIN FROM THE ROYAL COLLEGE OF GENERAL PRACTITIONERS **3739**

ROYAL COLLEGE OF MUSIC (GREAT BRITAIN) *See* ROYAL COLLEGE OF MUSIC MAGAZINE **4151**

ROYAL COLLEGE OF MUSIC MAGAZINE (UK) [05790761] **4151**

ROYAL COLLEGE OF PHYSICIANS OF LONDON *See* JOURNAL OF THE ROYAL COLLEGE OF PHYSICIANS OF LONDON **3599**

ROYAL COLLEGE OF PSYCHIATRISTS *See* MEMBERSHIP LIST - ROYAL COLLEGE OF PSYCHIATRISTS **3930**

ROYAL COLLEGE OF SURGEONS OF ENGLAND *See* ANNALS OF THE ROYAL COLLEGE OF SURGEONS OF ENGLAND **3959**

ROYAL COLLEGE OF SURGEONS OF ENGLAND. CALENDAR OF THE ROYAL COLLEGE OF SURGEONS OF ENGLAND *See* HANDBOOK LONDON. ROYAL COLLEGE OF SURGEONS OF ENGLAND **3965**

ROYAL COLLEGE OF VETERINARY SURGEONS *See* REGISTERS AND DIRECTORY - ROYAL COLLEGE OF VETERINARY SURGEONS **5520**

ROYAL COMMISSION ON HISTORICAL MONUMENTS (ENGLAND) *See* ANNUAL REPORT / ROYAL COMMISSION ON THE HISTORICAL MONUMENTS OF ENGLAND **2675**

ROYAL COMMISSION ON HISTORICAL MONUMENTS (ENGLAND). ANNUAL REVIEW *See* ANNUAL REPORT / ROYAL COMMISSION ON THE HISTORICAL MONUMENTS OF ENGLAND **2675**

ROYAL ENGINEERS JOURNAL, THE (UK/0035-8878) [05156485] 4056, **1995**

ROYAL ENTOMOLOGICAL SOCIETY SYMPOSIUM (UK) **5597**

ROYAL GAZETTE (CN) [02588367] 4684, **3045**

ROYAL GAZETTE. NEW BRUNSWICK (CN/0703-8623) [09523722] **4684**

ROYAL GAZETTE. PRINCE EDWARD ISLAND (CN/0035-8908) [02249494] **2544**

ROYAL GAZETTE, THE (BM) [09462864] **5778**

ROYAL GREENWICH OBSERVATORY *See* REPORT - ROYAL GREENWICH OBSERVATORY **399**

ROYAL HISTORICAL SOCIETY (GREAT BRITAIN) *See* TRANSACTIONS OF THE ROYAL HISTORICAL SOCIETY **2713**

ROYAL HISTORICAL SOCIETY (LONDON, ENGLAND) *See* GUIDES AND HANDBOOKS **2617**

ROYAL HISTORICAL SOCIETY STUDIES IN HISTORY (UK/0269-2244) [12763984] **2707**

ROYAL HORTICULTURAL SOCIETY (GREAT BRITAIN) *See* WISLEY HANDBOOK **2433**

ROYAL INSTITUTE OF BRITISH ARCHITECTS *See* RIBA MEMBERS **308**

ROYAL INSTITUTE OF CHEMISTRY, LONDON *See* REPORT OF THE COUNCIL - ROYAL INSTITUTE OF CHEMISTRY, LONDON **991**

ROYAL INSTITUTE OF CHEMISTRY. MONOGRAPHS FOR TEACHERS *See* MONOGRAPHS FOR TEACHERS **986**

ROYAL INSTITUTE OF PHILOSOPHY LECTURES *CEASED.* (UK/0080-4436) [01764595] **4360**

ROYAL INSTITUTE OF PUBLIC ADMINISTRATION. SOCIAL WORK EDUCATION COMMITTEE *See* SOCIAL WORK EDUCATION **5309**

ROYAL INSTITUTION OF CHARTERED SURVEYORS *See* YEAR BOOK - THE ROYAL INSTITUTION OF CHARTERED SURVEYORS **2579**

ROYAL INSTITUTION OF CORNWALL *See* JOURNAL OF THE ROYAL INSTITUTION OF CORNWALL **2695**

ROYAL INSTITUTION OF NAVAL ARCHITECTS *See* TRANSACTIONS OF THE ROYAL INSTITUTION OF NAVAL ARCHITECTS **310**

ROYAL INSTITUTION OF NAVAL ARCHITECTS *See* SUPPLEMENTARY PAPERS - ROYAL INSTITUTION OF NAVAL ARCHITECTS **4183**

ROYAL IRISH ACADEMY *See* PROCEEDINGS OF THE ROYAL IRISH ACADEMY. SECTION B. BIOLOGICAL, GEOLOGICAL AND CHEMICAL SCIENCE **470**

ROYAL — Alphabetical Title Index

ROYAL IRISH ACADEMY *See* PROCEEDINGS OF THE ROYAL IRISH ACADEMY. SECTION A. MATHEMATICAL AND PHYSICAL SCIENCES **3528**

ROYAL IRISH ACADEMY *See* PROCEEDINGS OF THE ROYAL IRISH ACADEMY. SECTION C. ARCHAEOLOGY, CELTIC STUDIES, HISTORY, LINGUISTICS AND LITERATURE **279**

ROYAL IRISH ACADEMY *See* PROCEEDINGS OF THE ROYAL IRISH ACADEMY **3425**

ROYAL IRISH ACADEMY. PROCEEDINGS OF THE ROYAL IRISH ACADEMY, SECTION B. BIOLOGICAL, GEOLOGICAL AND CHEMICAL SCIENCE *See* BIOLOGY AND ENVIRONMENT : PROCEEDINGS OF THE ROYAL IRISH ACADEMY **446**

ROYAL LEPAGE SURVEY OF CANADIAN HOUSE PRICES (CN/0831-148X) [14181531] **2834**

ROYAL LIFE SAVING SOCIETY CANADA. B.C. & YUKON BRANCH *See* WEST COAST LIFELINER **4807**

ROYAL LIFE SAVING SOCIETY CANADA. SASKATCHEWAN BRANCH *See* LIFELINES SASKATCHEWAN (1981) **4789**

ROYAL LIFE SAVING SOCIETY LIFESAVER UK, THE (UK) **4800**

ROYAL METEOROLOGICAL SOCIETY (GREAT BRITAIN) *See* QUARTERLY JOURNAL OF THE ROYAL METEOROLOGICAL SOCIETY **1434**

ROYAL MICROSCOPICAL SOCIETY, LONDON *See* PROCEEDINGS - ROYAL MICROSCOPICAL SOCIETY **573**

ROYAL MILITARY POLICE JOURNAL (UK) **3183**

ROYAL MUSICAL ASSOCIATION *See* ANNUAL REPORT AND ACCOUNTS FOR ... / ROYAL MUSICAL ASSOCIATION **4100**

ROYAL NEIGHBOR, THE (US/0035-905X) [01608090] **5236**

ROYAL NETHERLANDS TUBERCULOSIS ASSOCIATION *See* SELECTED PAPERS **3952**

ROYAL NUMISMATIC SOCIETY (GREAT BRITAIN) *See* COIN HOARDS **2780**

ROYAL ONTARIO MUSEUM *See* ATRIA **4084**

ROYAL ONTARIO MUSEUM *See* ANNUAL REPORT - ROYAL ONTARIO MUSEUM **4084**

ROYAL ONTARIO MUSEUM *See* ANNUAL REPORT / ROYAL ONTARIO MUSEUM **4084**

ROYAL OPERA HOUSE (LONDON, ENGLAND) *See* ROYAL OPERA HOUSE PRESENTS, THE **4151**

ROYAL OPERA HOUSE PRESENTS, THE (UK) [11539183] **4151**

ROYAL PHARMACEUTICAL SOCIETY OF GREAT BRITAIN *See* CALENDAR / ROYAL PHARMACEUTICAL SOCIETY OF GREAT BRITAIN **4295**

ROYAL POLICE FORCE OF ANTIGUA AND BARBUDA MAGAZINE ..., THE (AQ) [19371489] **3175**

ROYAL RED BALL OUTDOOR SPORTSMAN (US/0197-1883) [05966088] **4878**

ROYAL SCHOOL OF CHURCH MUSIC (WARREN, CONN.) *See* DIRECTORY OF MEMBERS AND FRIENDS / RSCM **4114**

ROYAL SERVICE (US/0035-9084) [06753248] **5067**

ROYAL SHAKESPEARE COMPANY *See* ROYAL SHAKESPEARE COMPANY ; A COMPLETE RECORD OF THE YEAR'S WORK **5368**

ROYAL SHAKESPEARE COMPANY ; A COMPLETE RECORD OF THE YEAR'S WORK (UK/0142-9434) [05967470] **5368**

ROYAL SOCIETY FOR THE PROTECTION OF BIRDS *See* RSPB BIRD LIFE **5620**

ROYAL SOCIETY (GREAT BRITAIN) *See* NOTES AND RECORDS OF THE ROYAL SOCIETY OF LONDON **5134**

ROYAL SOCIETY (GREAT BRITAIN) *See* PROCEEDINGS. MATHEMATICAL AND PHYSICAL SCIENCES / THE ROYAL SOCIETY **4417**

ROYAL SOCIETY (GREAT BRITAIN) *See* YEAR-BOOK OF THE ROYAL SOCIETY OF LONDON **5237**

ROYAL SOCIETY (GREAT BRITAIN) *See* PROCEEDINGS. BIOLOGICAL SCIENCES / THE ROYAL SOCIETY **469**

ROYAL SOCIETY (GREAT BRITAIN) *See* DECENNIAL INDEX ... : INDEX OF AUTHORS IN PROCEEDINGS, PHILOSOPHICAL TRANSACTIONS, AND BIOGRAPHICAL MEMOIRS **432**

ROYAL SOCIETY OF ANTIQUARIES OF IRELAND *See* JOURNAL OF THE ROYAL SOCIETY OF ANTIQUARIES OF IRELAND, THE **2695**

ROYAL SOCIETY OF ARTS (GREAT BRITAIN) *See* RSA JOURNAL **5149**

ROYAL SOCIETY OF CANADA *See* PRESENTATION - SOCIETE ROYALE DU CANADA **5235**

ROYAL SOCIETY OF CANADA *See* PROCEEDINGS OF THE ROYAL SOCIETY OF CANADA. DELIBERATIONS DE LA SOCIETE ROYALE DU CANADA **5235**

ROYAL SOCIETY OF CANADA *See* TRANSACTIONS OF THE ROYAL SOCIETY OF CANADA **2855**

ROYAL SOCIETY OF CANADA. ACADEMY OF SCIENCE *See* COMPTES RENDUS MATHEMATIQUES DE L'ACADEMIE DES SCIENCES **3501**

ROYAL SOCIETY OF EDINBURGH *See* YEAR BOOK OF THE ROYAL SOCIETY OF EDINBURGH **5237**

ROYAL SOCIETY OF LITERATURE OF THE UNITED KINGDOM, LONDON *See* ESSAYS BY DIVERS HANDS **3385**

ROYAL SOCIETY OF LONDON *See* SELECTED LECTURES OF THE ROYAL SOCIETY **570**

ROYAL SOCIETY OF LONDON *See* BIOGRAPHICAL MEMOIRS OF FELLOWS OF THE ROYAL SOCIETY **430**

ROYAL SOCIETY OF MEDICINE (GREAT BRITAIN) *See* JOURNAL OF THE ROYAL SOCIETY OF MEDICINE **3599**

ROYAL SOCIETY OF NEW SOUTH WALES, SYDNEY *See* JOURNAL AND PROCEEDINGS OF THE ROYAL SOCIETY OF NEW SOUTH WALES **5118**

ROYAL SOCIETY OF NEW ZEALAND *See* PROCEEDINGS OF THE ROYAL SOCIETY OF NEW ZEALAND **5141**

ROYAL SOCIETY OF NEW ZEALAND *See* BULLETIN - ROYAL SOCIETY OF NEW ZEALAND **5091**

ROYAL SOCIETY OF QUEENSLAND *See* PROCEEDINGS OF THE ROYAL SOCIETY OF QUEENSLAND **5141**

ROYAL SOCIETY OF SOUTH AFRICA *See* TRANSACTIONS OF THE ROYAL SOCIETY OF SOUTH AFRICA **5167**

ROYAL SOCIETY OF SOUTH AUSTRALIA *See* TRANSACTIONS OF THE ROYAL SOCIETY OF SOUTH AUSTRALIA **5167**

ROYAL SOCIETY OF TASMANIA *See* PAPERS AND PROCEEDINGS OF THE ROYAL SOCIETY OF TASMANIA **5137**

ROYAL SOCIETY OF TROPICAL MEDICINE AND HYGIENE *See* TRANSACTIONS OF THE ROYAL SOCIETY OF TROPICAL MEDICINE AND HYGIENE **3987**

ROYAL SOCIETY OF VICTORIA (MELBOURNE, VIC.) *See* PROCEEDINGS OF THE ROYAL SOCIETY OF VICTORIA **5141**

ROYAL STATISTICAL SOCIETY (GREAT BRITAIN) *See* JOURNAL OF THE ROYAL STATISTICAL SOCIETY. SERIES B (METHODOLOGICAL) **5330**

ROYAL STATISTICAL SOCIETY (GREAT BRITAIN) *See* JOURNAL OF THE ROYAL STATISTICAL SOCIETY. SERIES A (GENERAL) **5330**

ROYAL THAI GOVERNMENT GAZETTE (TH) [02101074] **4684**

ROYAL UNITED SERVICES INSTITUTE FOR DEFENCE STUDIES *See* R.U.S.I. AND BRASSEY'S DEFENCE YEARBOOK **4054**

ROYAL UNITED SERVICES INSTITUTE FOR DEFENCE STUDIES *See* R.U.S.I. AND BRASSEY'S DEFENCE YEARBOOK **4054**

ROYAL UNITED SERVICES INSTITUTE FOR DEFENCE STUDIES. R.U.S.I. AND BRASSEY'S DEFENCE YEARBOOK *See* BRASSEY'S DEFENCE YEARBOOK / EDITED BY THE CENTRE FOR DEFENCE STUDIES **4038**

ROYAL WESTERN AUSTRALIAN HISTORICAL SOCIETY *See* ROYAL WESTERN AUSTRALIAN HISTORICAL SOCIETY'S NEWSLETTER **2671**

ROYAL WESTERN AUSTRALIAN HISTORICAL SOCIETY'S NEWSLETTER (AT/0557-4242) [04010692] **2671**

ROYAL YACHTING ASSOCIATION (GREAT BRITAIN) *See* YEAR BOOK - ROYAL YACHTING ASSOCIATION **597**

ROYALTON REVIEW (US/0300-6093) [01327222] **1846**

●ROYALTY DIGEST (UK/0967-5744) [I09675744] **2522**

ROYALTY MANAGEMENT PROGRAM (U.S.) *See* MINERAL REVENUES : THE ... REPORT ON RECEIPTS FROM FEDERAL AND INDIAN LEASES **2198**

ROYALTY MONTHLY (UK/0950-3439) [I09503439] **2707**

ROYALTY, PEERAGE AND ARISTOCRACY OF THE WORLD *See* ROYALTY, PEERAGE AND NOBILITY OF THE WORLD, THE **2471**

ROYALTY, PEERAGE AND NOBILITY OF THE WORLD, THE (UK) [03528239] **2471**

ROYAUME (LIMOILOU, QUEBEC) (CN/0713-3413) [09145864] **4994**

ROYCE QUARTERLY, THE (US/0749-1867) [11069770] **2471**

ROYCROFT REVIEW, THE (US/1056-5841) [23742150] **3432**, **363**

ROZETA : KULTURNI ZAPISNIK RUZE (XR) [25419592] **3432**

ROZHLAD ; CASOPIS ZA SERBSKU KULTURU (SZ) [04684462] **2522**

ROZHLAS (XR) [01785476] **1138**

ROZHLEDY V CHIRURGII (XR/0035-9351) [01639078] **3974**

ROZPRAVY CESKOSLOVENSKE AKADEMIE VED. RADA MATEMATICKYCH A PRIRODNICH VED (XR) [12028926] **5149**, **3532**

ROZPRAVY CESKOSLOVENSKE AKADEMIE VED. RADA SPOLECENSKYCH VED (XR/0069-2298) [02255252] **5217**

ROZPRAVY. RADA MATEMATICKYCH A PRIRODNICH VED (XR/0069-228X) [03010529] **5149**

ROZPRAVY. RADA TECHNICKYCH VED (XR) [03014256] **5149**

ROZPRAWY - AKADEMIA ROLNICZA W SZCZECINIE (PL) [02228978] **2312**, **131**

ROZPRAWY INZYNIERSKIE *See* ENGINEERING TRANSACTIONS **1974**

ROZPRAWY KOMISJI HISTORII SZTUKI (PL/0084-2982) [I00842982] **2707**

ROZPRAWY KOMISJI JEZYKOWEJ. ODZKIE TOWARZYSTWO NAUKOWE (PL/0076-0390) [03136362] **3318**

ROZPRAWY MATEMATYCZNE (PL/0860-2581) [04748572] **3532**

ROZRYWKA (PL/0137-8252) [I01378252] **4865**

RPCV WRITERS & READERS (US/1062-4694) [25635613] **3432**

RPCVOICE (US/0892-1008) [15103916] **5256**

RPNABC PROFILE (CN/1187-0400) [25066272] **3936**, **3869**

RQ (US/0033-7072) [01852823] **3247**

RRC *See* IGCAR **2156**

RRM REPORT (CN/0847-1398) [20878836] **3792**

RR'S PHILIPPINE ALMANAC (PH) [23747479] **1929**

RRT (CN/0831-2478) [14955328] **3952**

RRUGA E PARTISE (AA) [03829021] **4546**

RS (CENTRO DE ARTE REINA SOFIA) (SP) [23026991] **4096**, **363**

RS. CUADERNOS DE REALIDADES SOCIALES (SP/0302-7724) [01792791] **5256**

●RS/MAGAZINE (BROOKLINE, MASS.) (US/1061-0030) [25153416] **1202**

R'S RELATIVES, THE (US/1058-6148) [24329524] **2471**

RS. RIFIUTI SOLIDI (IT/0394-5391) [I03945391] **2242**

RS-SERIES (US/0145-2320) [02711256] **1709**

RSA 2000 *See* AFRIKA 2001 **5081**

RSA CALLING (SA) [03012943] **2643**

RSA JOURNAL (IT) [24031643] **2759**

RSA JOURNAL (UK) [17404748] **5149**

RSA NEWSLETTER, THE (US/1046-6045) [20469192] **1121**

RSA WORLD (SA) [02637112] **4495**

RSAP NEWSLETTER (US/1057-8188) [24123192] **3247**, **3260**

RSCA (AG/0325-1179) [01792346] **308**

RSCJ: A JOURNAL OF REFLECTION (US/0272-0418) [06722894] **5035**

RSG. RICHTING SPORT-GERICHT (NE/0926-7638) [I09267638] **4915**, **1904**

RSGB AMATEUR RADIO CALL BOOK (UK) **1138**

RSI. ROOFING SIDING INSULATION (US/0033-7129) [04242246] **627**

RSI STUDENT NEWSLETTER (AT/0819-0283) [I08190283] **1709**

RSP-BULLETIN LELYSTAD (NE/0927-0655) [I09270655] **131**

RSPB BIRD LIFE (UK) [02675748] **2204**, **5620**

RSPB CONSERVATION REVIEW (UK) [19587453] **5620**, **2204**

RSRI ABSTRACTS (US) [03928135] **2834**

RSRI DISCUSSION PAPER SERIES (US/0485-8255) [03735194] **5149**

RSSI. RECHERCHES SEMIOTIQUES. SEMIOTIC INQUIRY (CN/0229-8651) [08956099] **3318**

RT IMAGE (US/1041-2182) [18679974] **3946**

RT (LOS ANGELES, CALIF.) (US/1040-6050) [18474188] **3952**

RT RECRUITER (US/1048-227X) [20871598] **3946**

RT&S, RAILWAY TRACK & STRUCTURES (US) [04677355] **5436**

RTC PROPERTY DISPOSITION REPORT (US/1049-7013) [21277873] **4847**

RTC REPORT (US) **4847**

RTFI INDEX, THE (US/0898-1515) [17728594] **810**

RTR. RAILWAY TECHNICAL REVIEW (GW/0079-9548) [I00799548] **5436**

RTTY JOURNAL (US/0033-7161) [13749431] **1163**

RTW REVIEW (US/0887-3003) [13171629] 957, **1087**

RUA, A (PO) [02459650] **2522**

RUACH SERIES (US) [03949041] **4994**

RUBBER AND PLASTIC PRODUCTS INDUSTRIES (CN/0835-0027) [17718281] 4460, **5077**

RUBBER & PLASTICS NEWS (US/0300-6123) [01332635] 4460, **5077**

RUBBER & PLASTICS NEWS II (US/0197-2219) [05634009] 4460, **5077**

RUBBER & PLASTICS WEEKLY *See* PLASTICS & RUBBER WEEKLY **4457**

RUBBER & RUBBER PRODUCTS (US) **5077**

RUBBER BOARD BULLETIN (II/0970-4124) [I09704124] **5077**

RUBBER BOARD BULLETIN (II/0537-0507) [01752813] **5077**

RUBBER CHEMISTRY AND TECHNOLOGY (US/0035-9475) [01764630] 992, **5077**

RUBBER DEVELOPMENTS (UK/0035-9483) [01905947] **5077**

RUBBER INDIA (II/0035-9491) [06674168] **5077**

RUBBER NEWS (II/0035-9513) [06456643] **5077**

RUBBER, PRODUCTION, SHIPMENTS, AND STOCKS (US/0738-033X) [08862076] 1625, **5078**

RUBBER PRODUCTS GUIDE (US) [05898392] **5078**

RUBBER RED BOOK (US/0361-0640) [01910016] **5078**

RUBBER RESEARCH INSTITUTE OF MALAYA *See* R.R.I.M. PLANTING MANUAL **184**

RUBBER RESEARCH INSTITUTE OF MALAYSIA *See* PLANTER'S BULLETIN (RUBBER RESEARCH INSTITUTE OF MALAYSIA) **5076**

RUBBER RESEARCH INSTITUTE OF SRI LANKA *See* JOURNAL - RUBBER RESEARCH INSTITUTE OF SRI LANKA **177**

RUBBER STATISTICAL BULLETIN (UK/0035-9548) [01898023] **5078**

RUBBER STATISTICAL NEWS SHEET *See* INTERNATIONAL RUBBER DIGEST **5076**

RUBBER TRENDS (UK/0035-9564) [06393082] **5078**

RUBBER WORLD (US/0035-9572) [01716692] 2017, **5078**

RUBBERSTAMPMADNESS (US/0746-7672) [10259548] **2777**

RUBBERVERWERKENDE INDUSTRIE / CENTRAAL BUREAU VOOR DE STATISTIEK, HOOFDAFDELING STATISTIEKEN VAN INDUSTRIE EN BOUWNIJVERHEID (NE/0168-4965) [11878923] 5078, **3487**

RUBBICANA (US) [03759244] **5078**

RUBBICANA. EUROPE (UK) [11353186] 4460, **5078**

RUBY'S PEARLS ELECMAG (US/1079-6673) **3432**

RUCH FILOSOFICKY (XR) [04681682] **4360**

RUCH MUZYCZNY (WARSAW, POLAND) (PL/0035-9610) [05183799] **4151**

RUCH PRAWNICZY, EKONOMICZNY I SOCJOLOGICZNY (PL/0035-9629) [02456808] **5217**

RUCH ZATRUDNIONYCH W GOSPODARCE USPOECZNIONEJ (PL) [02247006] **1709**

RUCKERT ZU EHREN : EINE SCHRIFTENREIHE DER RUCKERT-GESELLSCHAFT (GW/0933-9094) [18453735] **3470**

RUDARSKO-METALURSKI ZBORNIK (XV/0035-9645) [01588531] **4018**

RUDE (CN/0705-3444) [06703029] **2544**

RUDE PRAVO (XR) [02267332] **5799**

RUDERSPORT (GW/0342-8281) [I03428281] **595**

RUDOOBRAZOVATELNI PROCESI I MINERALNI NAHODISCA (BU/0204-5311) [02148794] **1444**

RUE DESCARTES (FR) [24843363] **4360**

RUE, LA (FR/0035-970X) [06655997] **3352**

RUEIL-MALMAISON, FRANCE. INSTITUT FRANCAIS DU PETROLE *See* REVUE DE L'INSTITUT FRANCAIS DU PETROLE **4277**

RUFANTHOLOGY (CN/0381-1158) [03222647] **3432**

RUFF TIMES (1986), THE (US/0891-5547) [14968760] **913**

RUFUS, THE (US/0147-1163) [03099136] **3470**

RUG HOOKER NEWS & VIEWS, THE *CEASED.* (US/0745-6905) [09395901] **5185**

RUG HOOKING (US/1045-4373) [20114477] **375**

RUG NEWS (US/0278-9795) [07938166] **5355**

RUGBEIAN (US) **2759**

RUGBY (FR) **4915**

RUGBY FOOTBALL LEAGUE OFFICIAL GUIDE (UK) **4915**

RUGBY FOOTBALL UNION *See* LAWS OF THE GAME OF RUGBY FOOTBALL WITH INSTRUCTIONS AND NOTES FOR GUIDANCE OF REFEREES **4903**

RUGBY FOOTBALL UNION *See* HANDBOOK - RUGBY FOOTBALL UNION **4898**

RUGBY LEAGUE WEEK (AT/0035-9742) [I00359742] **4915**

RUGBY (NEW YORK) (US/0162-1297) [04103824] **4915**

RUGBY WORLD (UK/0035-9777) [05296426] **4915**

RUGBY WORLD & POST (UK) [12841835] **4915**

RUHR-UNIVERSITAT BOCHUM *See* JAHRBUCH - RUHR-UNIVERSITAT BOCHUM **1831**

RUIDOSO NEWS (US/0745-5402) [09273506] **5713**

RUIMTE VOOR CULTUUR *CEASED.* (BE) **2853**

RUIMTELIJKE VERKENNINGEN (NE) [16768969] **2834**

RUIMTEVAART (NE) [01797976] **34**

RUIZIA (SP/0212-9108) [11858673] **527**

RUKOPISNAIA I PECHATNAIA KNIGA V FONDAKH (RU) [05637737] **424**

RULE BOOK / CANADIAN VOLLEYBALL ASSOCIATION (CN/0834-2946) [16349378] **4915**

RULE BOOK - MIDWEST 4 WHEEL DRIVE ASSOCIATION (US/0278-615X) [07841314] **4915**

RULES AND BY-LAWS / CANADIAN TRACK AND FIELD ASSOCIATION (CN/0710-4383) [08458450] **4915**

RULES AND DIRECTORY (US) [01782261] **4684**

RULES AND PROCEDURES FOR OPERATION OF TEACHERS' RETIREMENT SYSTEM OF OKLAHOMA (US/0094-4319) [01800263] 1870, **1709**

RULES AND REGULATIONS (US) [05337289] 1121, **3045**

RULES AND REGULATIONS ... AND STATEMENTS OF PROCEDURE / NATIONAL LABOR RELATIONS BOARD (US) [05666351] **3154**

RULES AND REGULATIONS - FEDERAL COMMUNICATIONS COMMISSION. VOLUME 1 (US) [02824597] **1121**

RULES AND REGULATIONS - FEDERAL COMMUNICATIONS COMMISSION. VOLUME 2 (US) [02824735] **1121**

RULES AND REGULATIONS - FEDERAL COMMUNICATIONS COMMISSION. VOLUME 3 (US) [02824786] **1121**

RULES AND REGULATIONS - FEDERAL COMMUNICATIONS COMMISSION. VOLUME 4 (US) [02824849] **1121**

RULES AND REGULATIONS - FEDERAL COMMUNICATIONS COMMISSION. VOLUME 5 (US) [02825006] **1121**

RULES AND REGULATIONS - FEDERAL COMMUNICATIONS COMMISSION. VOLUME 7 (US) [02825211] **1121**

RULES AND REGULATIONS - FEDERAL COMMUNICATIONS COMMISSION. VOLUME 8 (US) [02826349] **1121**

RULES AND REGULATIONS - FEDERAL COMMUNICATIONS COMMISSION. VOLUME 9 (US) [02826430] **1121**

RULES AND REGULATIONS - FEDERAL COMMUNICATIONS COMMISSION. VOLUME 10 (US) [02826616] **1121**

RULES AND REGULATIONS - FEDERAL COMMUNICATIONS COMMISSION. VOLUME 11 (US) [02826709] **1121**

RULES AND REGULATIONS FOR THE CLASSIFICATION OF SHIPS / LLOYD'S REGISTER OF SHIPPING (UK) [04477383] **5455**

RULES AND REGULATIONS - NATIONAL CREDIT UNION ADMINISTRATION (US) [03458837] **810**

RULES AND REGULATIONS OF THE NEW YORK STATE THRUWAY AUTHORITY (US/0362-1103) [02441131] **3045**

RULES AND REGULATIONS. PART 99, DISASTER COMMUNICATIONS SERVICE (US/0737-7649) [03139664] **1121**

RULES AND REGULATIONS - SOUTH CAROLINA. RESIDENTIAL HOME BUILDERS COMMISSION (US) [04316028] 627, **3045**

RULES AND REGULATIONS / UNITED STATES NUCLEAR REGULATORY COMMISSION (US) [02782157] **3045**

RULES AND STANDING ORDERS OF THE INTERNATIONAL TENNIS FEDERATION (UK) [07584828] **4915**

RULES BOOK OF THE FEDERATION OF CANADIAN ARCHERS (CN/0226-773X) [06515921] **4916**

RULES COMPENDIUM UNDER CENTRAL ACTS (II/0485-9383) [01763414] **3045**

RULES FOR CERTIFICATION OF CARGO CONTAINERS (US/0740-7297) [09978546] **4221**

RULES FOR INBOARD, INBOARD ENDURANCE, UNLIMITED RACING (US/0272-3468) [06781958] 4916, **595**

RULES FOR OUTBOARD PERFORMANCE, CRAFT AND DRAG RACING (US/0272-3514) [06793748] 4916, **595**

RULES FOR STOCK OUTBOARD, PRO OUTBOARD, MODIFIED OUTBOARD (US/0272-3476) [06793707] 4916, **595**

RULES GOVERNING THE COURTS OF THE STATE OF NEW JERSEY, 1969 REVISION, AS AMENDED (US/0193-967X) [05274085] **3143**

RULES OF CONDUCT. BYLAWS AND IMPLEMENTING RESOLUTIONS OF COUNCIL (US/0270-1510) [06333193] **751**

RULES OF COURT (US) **3045**

RULES OF GOLF AS APPROVED BY THE UNITED STATES GOLF ASSOCIATION AND THE ROYAL AND ANCIENT GOLF CLUB OF ST. ANDREWS, SCOTLAND, THE (US) [03498516] **4916**

●RULES OF GOLF FOR ... AND THE RULES FOR AMATEUR STATUS (US) [25909639] **4916**

RULES OF STANDARDBRED RACING (CN/0708-5125) [12198124] 4916, **2802**

RULES OF TENNIS (UK) [07578363] **4916**

RULES OF THE AIR; INTERNATIONAL STANDARDS. ANNEX 2 TO THE CONVENTION ON INTERNATIONAL CIVIL AVIATION (CN) [01716510] **34**

RULES OF THE SUPREME COURT OF LOUISIANA, ADOPTED AUGUST 31, 1973, EFFECTIVE JANUARY 1, 1974 AS AMENDED ... (US) [06661076] **3143**

RULES OF THOROUGHBRED RACING (CN/0707-8919) [05765955] 4916, **2802**

RULES, REGULATIONS AND LAW REGULATING BOXING AND WRESTLING MATCHES IN CALIFORNIA *See* STATE LAWS GOVERNING BOXING AND WRESTLING IN CALIFORNIA, WITH RULES AND REGULATIONS **3058**

RULES UPDATES (US) **3045**

RULINGS. CUMULATIVE EDITION : SOCIAL SECURITY RULINGS ON FEDERAL OLD-AGE, SURVIVORS, DISABILITY, SUPPLEMENTAL SECURITY INCOME, AND BLACK LUNG BENEFITS (US) [08540051] **5306**

RULINGS ENFORCEMENT ACTIONS, ADVISORY OPINIONS / STATE ETHICS COMMISSION (US) [18768309] **3045**

RUMAH TANGGA DAN KESEHATAN (IO/0485-6015) [01906521] **4800**

RUMANIAN REVIEW (RM/0035-8088) [05350807] **3352**

RUMANIEN: VOLKSWIRTSCHAFTSPLAN UND BUDGETDATEN (GW) [05277411] **1582**

RUMIPAMBA (EC) [11387901] **131**

RUMO PARANAENSE (BL) [02556796] **2759**

RUN *CEASED.* (US/0741-4285) [10151803] **1272**

RUNA — Alphabetical Title Index

RUNA (AG/0325-1217) [01910682] **245**

RUNDBRIEF (GW) [01784940] **2643**

RUNDFUNK UND FERNSEHEN (GW/0035-9874) [01696127] **1138**

RUNDFUNKTECHNISCHE MITTEILUNGEN (GW/0035-9890) [03711416] **1138**

RUNDOWN (US) **1138**

RUNDSCHAU FUER FLEISCHBESCHAUER, TRICHINENSCHAUER UND GEFLUGELFLEISCHKONTROLLEURE (GW/0340-1219) [01344112] **4800**

RUNDSCHAU FUER FLEISCHUNTERSUCHUNG UND LEBENSMITTELUBERWACHUNG (GW/0341-0668) [04746075] **2356**

RUNDSCHAU FUER INTERNATIONALE DAMENMODE MIT DOB- + HAKA-PRAXIS (GW/0722-2858) [I07222858] **1087**

RUNDSCHAU FUER INTERNATIONALE HERRENMODE MIT DOB- + HAKA-PRAXIS (GW/0722-2866) [I07222866] **1087**

RUNDSCHAU FUER UMSATZSTEUER (COLOGNE, GERMANY : 1983). RUNDSCHAU FUER UMSATZSTEUER See UMSATZSTEUER-RUNDSCHAU (COLOGNE, GERMANY : 1986) **3067**

RUNDT'S ASIAN INTELLIGENCE See ASIAN INTELLIGENCE **4464**

RUNDT'S WEEKLY INTELLIGENCE See RUNDT'S WORLD BUSINESS INTELLIGENCE **1519**

RUNDT'S WORLD BUSINESS INTELLIGENCE **1519**

●RUNGH (VANCOUVER) (CN/1188-9950) [28395936] **330**

RUNHUA YU MIFENG (CC/0254-0150) [09849250] **1995**

RUNNER (EDMONTON) (CN/0707-3186) [04755117] **1858**

RUNNER YEARBOOK, THE (US/0272-0353) [06720496] **4916**

RUNNERS (NE) **2777**

RUNNER'S GAZETTE (US/0199-6983) [06083043] **2601, 4916**

RUNNING (UK) **4916**

RUNNING & FITNEWS (US/0898-5162) [12273052] **4916, 2601**

RUNNING BOARD, THE (CN/0048-8771) [02110561] **252, 5424**

RUNNING JOURNAL (US/0892-5038) [15209634] **4916**

RUNNING RESEARCH NEWS (US/0887-7033) [13343142] **3974, 4916**

RUNNING TIMES (US/0147-2968) [03143282] **2601, 4916**

●RUNNING WILD (US/1067-5094) [27253063] **4916**

RUNZHEIMER GUIDE TO FLEET MANAGEMENT (US) **708, 5392**

RUNZHEIMER MEAL LODGING COST INDEX (US) **5490, 1299**

RUNZHEIMER ON CARS & LIVING COSTS (US/0730-8647) [08086123] **5424, 1299**

RUNZHEIMER REPORTS ON RELOCATION (US/0731-9150) [08269399] **708, 4847**

RUNZHEIMER REPORTS ON TRANSPORTATION (US/0730-8655) [08085899] **708, 5392**

RUNZHEIMER REPORTS ON TRAVEL MANAGEMENT (US/0730-8663) [08078899] **708, 5490**

RUPERTO CAROLA (GW/0035-998X) [01764643] **1846**

RUPERT'S LAND NEWS (CN/0228-8095) [08063663] **4994**

RUPPO SIDAE (KO) [11803095] **3432**

RUPTURE (TORONTO) (CN/0822-9600) [09865721] **3432**

RURAL ADVOCATE, THE (US) [23672039] **2834**

RURAL AFRICANA (US/0085-5839) [01764644] **1582**

RURAL AND SMALL LIBRARY SERVICES NEWSLETTER (US) [20863533] **3247**

RURAL ARKANSAS (US/0048-878X) [03916544] **2544**

RURAL BANK LIMITED See ANNUAL REPORT / RURAL BANK LIMITED **772**

RURAL BUILDER (US/0888-3025) [13544260] **627**

RURAL BUSINESS MAGAZINE (AT/1031-3079) [I10313079] **131**

RURAL CONDITIONS AND TRENDS (US/1063-5866) [22237857] **131**

RURAL COUNCILLOR, THE (CN/0036-0007) [02110780] **131**

RURAL DELIVERY (CN/0703-7724) [03439570] **2544**

RURAL DEMOGRAPHY (BG/1010-3783) [02438772] **4560**

RURAL DEVELOPMENT ABSTRACTS / [PREPARED BY THE COMMONWEALTH BUREAU OF AGRICULTURAL ECONOMICS] (UK/0140-4768) [04017470] **2834, 2840**

RURAL DEVELOPMENT AND CORPORATION OF ZAMBIA. ANNUAL REPORT See ANNUAL REPORT AND ACCOUNTS FOR THE YEAR ENDED 31ST MARCH ... - RURAL DEVELOPMENT CORPORATION OF ZAMBIA **60**

RURAL DEVELOPMENT CORPORATION OF ZAMBIA See ANNUAL REPORT AND ACCOUNTS FOR THE YEAR ENDED 31ST MARCH ... - RURAL DEVELOPMENT CORPORATION OF ZAMBIA **60**

RURAL DEVELOPMENT COUNCIL PUBLICATION (FAIRBANKS) (US/0197-4904) [03297116] **2834**

RURAL DEVELOPMENT NEWS (US/0886-8611) [07015810] **4847**

RURAL DEVELOPMENT PERSPECTIVES (US/0271-2172) [11564450] **131**

RURAL DEVELOPMENT PROGRESS (US/0161-7273) [03474615] **5256**

RURAL DEVELOPMENT RESEARCH REPORT (US/0886-7585) [04476214] **131**

RURAL DEVELOPMENT STUDIES (SW/0346-7287) [08122222] **2834**

RURAL DEVELOPMENT STUDIES (UNIVERSITY OF RAJSHAHI. DEPT. OF ECONOMICS) (BG) [05621660] **2834**

RURAL DEVELOPMENT WORKING PAPER / NATIONAL CENTRE FOR DEVELOPMENT STUDIES, THE AUSTRALIAN NATIONAL UNIVERSITY (AT/0816-5173) [14061412] **1582**

RURAL ECONOMY AND SOCIETY (CC/1002-8889) [27804003] **5256, 1519**

RURAL EDUCATION AND DEVELOPMENT ASSOCIATION See ALBERTA RURAL DEVELOPMENT STUDIES **57**

RURAL EDUCATION NEWS (RURAL EDUCATION ASSOCIATION : 1980) (US) [07830886] **1781**

RURAL EDUCATION REVIEW (AT/0811-1057) [I08111057] **1781**

RURAL EDUCATOR (FORT COLLINS), THE (US/0273-446X) [06455568] **1781**

RURAL ELECTRIC NEWS LETTER (US/0747-4784) [02251921] **1543, 4684**

RURAL ELECTRIFICATION MAGAZINE (1987) (US/1054-0474) [15585785] **1543**

RURAL ENTERPRISE (MENOMONEE FALLS, WIS.) SUSPENDED. (US/1057-1930) [15724525] **131**

RURAL ENVIRONMENTAL CONSERVATION PROGRAM See OHIO INSTRUCTIONAL GRANTS ANNUAL REPORT **1838**

RURAL GLEANINGS (CN/0700-3897) [03264621] **4994**

RURAL HEALTH NEWS (US) **4800**

RURAL HERITAGE (US/0889-2970) [13841581] **252**

RURAL HISTORY (UK/0956-7933) [21916010] **5256**

RURAL INDIA (II/0036-0058) [01644145] **5256**

RURAL INDUSTRIES (KONEDOBU, PAPUA NEW GUINEA) (PP) [01783584] **1625**

RURAL KENTUCKIAN See KENTUCKY LIVING **2536**

RURAL LIBRARIES (US/0276-2048) [06098371] **3247**

RURAL LIFE (UK/0036-0074) [02271320] **5256**

RURAL LIVING (A&N ELECTRIC COOPERATIVE ED.) (US/1054-4801) [05845162] **2544, 131**

●RURAL LIVING (LANSING, MICH.) (US/0743-9962) [26077841] **2544, 131**

RURAL LIVING (LANSING, MICH. : 1981) See RURAL LIVING (LANSING, MICH.) **131**

RURAL MISSOURI (US/0164-8578) [04309326] **2544**

RURAL MONTANA (US/0199-6401) [06071165] **131**

RURAL NEW ENGLAND MAGAZINE (US) **131**

RURAL PROGRESS (ET) [03910078] **2834**

RURAL REAL ESTATE MARKET IN NEW ZEALAND (WELLINGTON, N.Z. : 1981) (NZ/0549-0111) [09801370] **4847**

RURAL RECONSTRUCTION AUTHORITY OF WESTERN AUSTRALIA See ANNUAL REPORT - RURAL RECONSTRUCTION AUTHORITY OF WESTERN AUSTRALIA **4629**

RURAL RECONSTRUCTION BOARD See ANNUAL REPORT AND STATEMENT OF ACCOUNTS - RURAL RECONSTRUCTION BOARD (HOBART) **2814**

RURAL RECONSTRUCTION (NEW DELHI) (II/0557-6644) [02267337] **2835**

RURAL RESEARCH (AT/1034-6074) [00994400] **131**

RURAL ROUTE (WALLACEBURG, ONT.) (CN/0715-5271) [09538798] **5794**

RURAL SOCIETY (AT) **5257**

RURAL SOCIOLOGIST, THE (US/0279-5957) [07107956] **5257**

RURAL SOCIOLOGY (US/0036-0112) [01604686] **5257**

RURAL SOCIOLOGY RESEARCH REPORT (US) [22669053] **5257**

RURAL SPECIAL EDUCATION QUARTERLY (US/8756-8705) [11679951] **1885**

RURAL SYSTEMS (II) [12688149] **2835**

RURAL TELECOMMUNICATIONS (US/0744-2548) [08134713] **1163**

RURAL TELEPHONE BANK See ANNUAL REPORT OF THE BOARD OF DIRECTORS OF THE RURAL TELEPHONE BANK **1149**

RURAL UPDATE (AT/0818-1713) [I08181713] **131**

RURAL-URBAN RECORD (US/0192-9771) [05139285] **5730**

RURAL UTILITIES NEWSLETTER (CN/0226-658X) [06512713] **4684**

RURAL VOICE (BLYTH) (CN/0700-5385) [03291580] **131**

RURALITE (US) [08790803] **2080**

RURALTER : REVISTA DE DESARROLLO RURAL ALTERNATIVO / CENTRO INTERNACIONAL DE COOPERACION PARA EL DESARROLLO AGRICOLA, CICDA (PE) [15598055] **2835**

RURDS. REVIEW OF URBAN AND REGIONAL DEVELOPMENT STUDIES (JA/0917-0553) [I09170553] **2835**

RUSH COUNTY NEWS (LA CROSSE, KAN.) (US) [08808022] **5678**

RUSHLIGHT (VERNON), THE (US/0148-3501) [03295339] **2080**

RUSHMORE PRESS See PENNINGTON COUNTY NEWS **5744**

RUSHVILLE REPUBLICAN (RUSHVILLE, IND. : 1930 : DAILY) (US/8756-6443) [11308229] **5667**

RUSI JOURNAL / ROYAL UNITED SERVICES INSTITUTE FOR DEFENCE STUDIES, THE (UK) [17818978] **4056**

RUSISTIKA : THE RUSSIAN JOURNAL OF THE ASSOCIATION FOR LANGUAGE LEARNING (UK/0957-1760) [22774547] **3318**

RUSK CHEROKEEAN, THE (US) **5754**

RUSKIN NEWSLETTER, THE (UK/0953-1130) [05585521] **4096**

RUSLAND MONITOR (NE) [20865421] **5806**

RUSSELL (CN/0036-0163) [01764659] **4360**

RUSSELL COUNTY NEWS (JAMESTOWN, KY.), THE (US/8750-1651) [11058525] **5682**

RUSSELL DAILY NEWS (US) [08801282] **5678**

RUSSELL RECORD (RUSSELL, KAN. : 1905) (US) [12564752] **5678**

RUSSELL REGISTER, THE (US) [04249572] **2471**

RUSSELL'S OFFICIAL NATIONAL MOTOR COACH GUIDE (US/0036-0171) [01894673] **5392**

RUSSELL'S OFFICIAL NATIONAL MOTOR COACH GUIDE (US/0036-0171) [17458982] **5392**

RUSSIA (1923- U.S.S.R.). VERKHOVNYI SUD See BIULLETEN VERKHOVNOGO SUDA SSSR **2942**

RUSSIA & CIS TODAY See RUSSIA & CIS TODAY / COMPILED BY WHAT THE PAPERS SAY **2707**

●RUSSIA & CIS TODAY / COMPILED BY THE RFE/AL RESEARCH INSTITUTE MONITORING UNIT (GW) [25646910] **2707**

●RUSSIA & CIS TODAY / COMPILED BY WHAT THE PAPERS SAY (RU) [26118314] **2707**

RUSSIA AND COMMONWEALTH BUSINESS LAW REPORT (US/1064-637X) [25381246] **3103**

●RUSSIA & EURASIA DOCUMENTS ANNUAL (US) [30082913] **2508**

●RUSSIA AND HER NEIGHBORS (US/1066-0127) [26348684] **5217**

RUSSIA & REPUBLICS NUCLEAR INDUSTRY (UK) **708**

RUSSIA AND THE SUCCESSOR STATES BRIEFING SERVICE (UK/0967-2265) [28728133] **4495**

●RUSSIA, EURASIAN STATES, AND EASTERN EUROPE (US/1062-3574) [25596196] **2522, 2508**

RUSSIA EXPRESS (UK/0957-0853) [I09570853] **1625**

RUSSIA, SIBERIA, MONGOLIA, AND NORTH KOREA TRAVEL NEWS (AT/1321-2923) **5490**

●RUSSIA (SYRACUSE, N.Y.) (US/1060-8753) [25097929] **1595**

●RUSSIAN AERONAUTICS (US/1068-7998) [27389628] **34**

RUSSIAN AEROSPACE & TECHNOLOGY (US) [25761456] **34**

●RUSSIAN AGRICULTURAL SCIENCES (US/1068-3674) [27660643] **131**

●RUSSIAN & EAST EUROPEAN FINANCE AND TRADE (US/1061-2009) [25215976] 1639, **850**

RUSSIAN AND EAST EUROPEAN STUDIES (US) **4495**

●RUSSIAN AND EAST EUROPEAN STUDIES IN AESTHETICS AND THE PHILOSOPHY OF CULTURE (US/1065-9374) [26797491] 4360, **363**

RUSSIAN ARCHIVES OF INTERNAL MEDICINE *CEASED.* (RU) **3801**

●RUSSIAN BIOTECHNOLOGY (US/1068-3682) [27660810] **3696**

●RUSSIAN BUSINESS REPORTS (US/1060-569X) [25037734] **708**

●RUSSIAN CASTINGS TECHNOLOGY (US/1068-3690) [27660915] **4018**

●RUSSIAN CHEMICAL BULLETIN (US/1066-5285) [26982030] **992**

●RUSSIAN CHEMICAL INDUSTRY (US/1068-3704) [27660985] **1029**

RUSSIAN CHEMICAL REVIEWS (UK/0036-021X) [01764671] **992**

RUSSIAN COMMONWEALTH BUSINESS LAW REPORT (US/1065-2868) [25307230] **3103**

●RUSSIAN ECONOMIC TRENDS (UK/0967-0793) [I09670793] **1583**

●RUSSIAN ECONOMY AND BUSINESS DIGEST (US/1060-5894) [25039991] 708, **1519**

●RUSSIAN EDUCATION AND SOCIETY (US/1060-9393) [25118804] **1781**

●RUSSIAN ELECTRICAL ENGINEERING (US/1068-3712) [27661171] **2080**

RUSSIAN ELECTROCHEMISTRY (US/1070-3276) [28321132] **1035**

●RUSSIAN ENGINEERING RESEARCH (US/1068-798X) [27652372] **2128**

●RUSSIAN FAR EAST UPDATE (US/1061-5679) [25376247] **1519**

●RUSSIAN FIBER OPTICS AND TELECOMMUNICATIONS BUSINESS (US/1066-9612) [27097239] **1163**

●RUSSIAN FOREST SCIENCES (US/1068-669X) [26692504] **2394**

●RUSSIAN GEOLOGY AND GEOPHYSICS (US/1068-7971) [27637569] 1410, **1396**

●RUSSIAN GOVERNMENT TODAY (US/1069-1081) [27844206] **4684**

RUSSIAN HISTORY (PITTSBURGH) (US/0094-288X) [01680895] **2707**

●RUSSIAN JOURNAL OF APPLIED CHEMISTRY (US/1070-4272) [28365232] **992**

●RUSSIAN JOURNAL OF BIOORGANIC CHEMISTRY (US/1068-1620) [27457013] **493**

●RUSSIAN JOURNAL OF COMPUTATIONAL MECHANICS (RU/1061-7566) [25441595] 3532, **2128**

●RUSSIAN JOURNAL OF COORDINATION CHEMISTRY (US/1070-3284) [28318564] **992**

●RUSSIAN JOURNAL OF DEVELOPMENTAL BIOLOGY (US/1062-3604) [25596343] **472**

●RUSSIAN JOURNAL OF ECOLOGY (US/1067-4136) [27206248] **2220**

●RUSSIAN JOURNAL OF ELECTROCHEMISTRY (US) [28442034] **1035**

RUSSIAN JOURNAL OF ENGINEERING THERMOPHYSICS *CEASED.* (US/1051-8053) [22123505] 4420, **1995**

●RUSSIAN JOURNAL OF GENERAL CHEMISTRY (US/1070-3632) [28355338] **992**

RUSSIAN JOURNAL OF GENETICS (US) **551**

●RUSSIAN JOURNAL OF HEAVY MACHINERY (US/1068-3720) [27661240] **2128**

RUSSIAN JOURNAL OF INORGANIC CHEMISTRY (UK/0036-0236) [01764675] **1037**

●RUSSIAN JOURNAL OF MARINE BIOLOGY (US/1063-0740) [25850781] **557**

●RUSSIAN JOURNAL OF MATHEMATICAL PHYSICS (RU/1061-9208) [25491433] 3532, **4420**

●RUSSIAN JOURNAL OF NON-FERROUS METALS (US/1067-8212) [27361458] **4018**

●RUSSIAN JOURNAL OF NONDESTRUCTIVE TESTING (US/1061-8309) [25474132] **2128**

RUSSIAN JOURNAL OF NUMERICAL ANALYSIS AND MATHEMATICAL ANALYSIS (NE/0927-6467) [25660194] **3532**

RUSSIAN JOURNAL OF PHYSICAL CHEMISTRY (UK/0036-0244) [01606200] **1057**

RUSSIAN JOURNAL OF PLANT PHYSIOLOGY : A COMPREHENSIVE RUSSIAN JOURNAL ON MODERN PHYTOPHYSIOLOGY (US/1021-4437) [28686279] **527**

RUSSIAN LANGUAGE JOURNAL (US/0036-0252) [04288322] **3318**

●RUSSIAN LIFE (US/1066-999X) [28135590] **2522**

RUSSIAN LINGUISTICS (NE/0304-3487) [02241057] **3318**

RUSSIAN LITERATURE (NE/0304-3479) [01779371] **3432**

RUSSIAN MATHEMATICAL SURVEYS (UK/0036-0279) [01588215] **3532**

●RUSSIAN MATHEMATICS (US/1066-369X) [26866999] **3532**

RUSSIAN METALLURGY (UK/0036-0295) [01911260] **4018**

●RUSSIAN METEOROLOGY AND HYDROLOGY (US/1068-3739) [27661524] 1417, **1434**

●RUSSIAN MICROELECTRONICS (US/1063-7397) [26134131] **1202**

●RUSSIAN OIL & GAS GUIDE (US/1064-9697) [26478181] **4277**

RUSSIAN ORTHODOX JOURNAL, THE (US/0036-0317) [01715477] **5040**

RUSSIAN PETROLEUM INTELLIGENCE *See* RUSSIAN PETROLEUM INVESTOR **4277**

RUSSIAN PETROLEUM INVESTOR (US/1072-155X) [28876906] **4277**

RUSSIAN PHARMACOLOGY AND TOXICOLOGY (UK/0036-0325) [08163441] 3983, **4328**

●RUSSIAN PHYSICS JOURNAL (US/1064-8887) [26443086] **4420**

RUSSIAN PLANT PHYSIOLOGY (US/1070-3292) [28318519] 586, **527**

●RUSSIAN POLITICS AND LAW (US/1061-1940) [25215676] 4495, **3045**

●RUSSIAN PROGRESS IN VIROLOGY (US/1068-3747) [27661794] **570**

RUSSIAN REVIEW (STANFORD), THE (US/0036-0341) [01894664] **2708**

●RUSSIAN SOCIAL SCIENCE REVIEW (US/1061-1428) [25189454] **5217**

●RUSSIAN STUDIES IN HISTORY (US/1061-1983) [25215861] **2628**

●RUSSIAN STUDIES IN LITERATURE (US/1061-1975) [25215816] **3432**

●RUSSIAN STUDIES IN PHILOSOPHY (US/1061-1967) [25215755] **4360**

●RUSSIAN THEATRE ARCHIVE (US/1068-8161) [27821429] **5368**

RUSSIAN TRAVEL NEWS *See* RUSSIA, SIBERIA, MONGOLIA, AND NORTH KOREA TRAVEL NEWS **5490**

RUSSIAN ULTRASONICS (UK) [02450325] **4453**

RUSSISCHUNTERRICHT *See* FREMDSPRACHENUNTERRICHT **1879**

RUSSISTIK (GW/0935-8072) [20609519] **3318**

RUSSKAIA MYSL (FR) [01968946] **5801**

RUSSKAIA PRAVOSLAVNAIA TSERKOV. MOSKOVSKAIA PATRIARKHIIA *See* ZURNAL MOSKOVSKOJ PATRIARHII **5040**

RUSSKAIA PRAVOSLAVNAIA TSERKOV. MOSKOVSKAIA PATRIARKHIIA *See* JOURNAL OF THE MOSCOW PATRIARCHATE, THE **5039**

RUSSKAIA RECH (RU/0036-0368) [01696025] **3318**

●RUSSKAIA SLOVESNOST (RU) [28475290] **3318**

RUSSKAIA SOVETSKAIA LITERATURA (RU) [19822316] **3432**

RUSSKAIA ZHIZN (US) [27376932] **5639**

RUSSKAJA LITERATURA (LENINGRAD. 1958) (RU/0131-6095) [01590682] **3432**

RUSSKII GOLOS (NEW YORK, N.Y.) (US/0036-0406) [03917186] **2272**

RUSSKII GOROD (RU) [11963462] **2835**

RUSSKII IAZYK I LITERATURA V UZBEKSKOI SHKOLE (RU) [04360019] 3432, **3318**

RUSSKII IAZYK V ESTONSKOI SHKOLE (ER) [04266748] **3319**

RUSSKII IAZYK V MOLDAVSKOI SHKOLE : [UCHEBNO-METODICHESKII ZHURNAL MINISTERSTVA PROSVESHCHENIIA MOLDAVSKOI SSR] (MV/0202-5418) [07893708] **3319**

RUSSKII IAZYK V SNG (RU) [26152131] **3319**

RUSSKII IAZYK V SSSR *See* RUSSKII IAZYK V SNG **3319**

RUSSKII VODEVIL (RU) [03212998] **5368**

RUSSKIJ FOLKLOR (RU/0136-7447) [01478842] **2324**

RUSSKIJ JAZYK ZA RUBEZOM (RU/0036-0384) [01764688] **3319**

RUSSKOE PROSHLOE (RU/0869-1177) [25472597] **2708**

RUSSKOE VOZROZHDENIE (US/0222-1543) [04680360] 3432, **5040**

RUSTON DAILY LEADER, THE (US/0891-8708) [15047087] **5684**

RUSTUNGSBESCHRANKUNG UND SICHERHEIT (GW/0080-4800) [01607409] **4056**

RUSYCYSTYCZNE STUDIA LITERATUROZNAWCZE (PL) [04657300] **3432**

RUTAS GUIA TURISTICA DE BARCELONA (SP) [02239446] **5490**

RUTGERS ART REVIEW, THE (US/0194-049X) [05319937] **363**

RUTGERS COMPUTER & TECHNOLOGY LAW JOURNAL (US/0735-8938) [08496275] **1202**

RUTGERS LAW JOURNAL (US/0277-318X) [07383073] **3045**

RUTGERS LAW REVIEW (US/0036-0465) [00998909] **3045**

RUTGERS LAW SCHOOL (NEWARK, N.J.) *See* ALUMNAE/I DIRECTORY - RUTGERS LAW SCHOOL (NEWARK, N.J.) **1097**

RUTGERS PROFESSIONAL PSYCHOLOGY REVIEW (US/0277-4240) [07579983] **4617**

RUTGERS UNIVERSITY. BUREAU OF BIOLOGICAL RESEARCH *See* ANNUAL RESEARCH CONFERENCES OF THE BUREAU OF BIOLOGICAL RESEARCH, THE **442**

RUTGERS UNIVERSITY. INSTITUTE OF JAZZ STUDIES *See* IJS JAZZ REGISTER **4122**

RUTGERS UNIVERSITY, NEW BRUNSWICK, N.J. CENTER FOR COMPUTER AND INFORMATION SERVICES *See* CCIS NEWSLETTER **1173**

RUTGERS UNIVERSITY, NEW BRUNSWICK, N.J. CENTER OF ALCOHOL STUDIES. PUBLICATIONS DIVISION *See* DRINKERS, DRINKING AND ALCOHOL-RELATED MORTALITY AND HOSPITALIZATIONS **1343**

RUTGERS UNIVERSITY, NEW BRUNSWICK, NEW JERSEY *See* WILLIAM L. HUTCHESON MEMORIAL FOREST BULLETIN **2398**

RUTGERS UNIVERSITY STUDIES IN CLASSICAL HUMANITIES. HUMANITIES (US/0732-9814) [08496817] **1079**

RUTH L RATNY'S SCREEN *See* SCREEN (CHICAGO, ILL.) **4077**

RUTHERFORD APPLETON LABORATORY (UK/0263-8355) [I02638355] **5149**

RUTLAND DAILY HERALD (RUTLAND, VT. : 1885) (US) [11902841] **5757**

RUTLAND HISTORICAL SOCIETY QUARTERLY (US/0748-2493) [03497046] **2759**

RUTLAND RECORD (UK/0260-3322) [07698491] **2708**

RUXTON REPORT, THE (US/1040-2241) [18354279] **751**

RV BUYERS GUIDE (US/0742-6208) [10351957] **5392**

RV: THE FAMILY CAMPING VEHICLES YEAR END REPORT (US) **5490**

RV TRADE DIGEST (CHICAGO, ILL. 1981) (US/0745-0389) [08741842] **5392**

RV WEST MAGAZINE (US/1041-9772) [18894506] **4854**

RV WORLD (US) [01786475] 5392, **4854**

RVBUSINESS. ANNUAL DIRECTORY AND BUYER'S GUIDE (US) [09400909] **5424**

RVBUSINESS / FROM THE EDITORS OF TL ENTERPRISES (US/0744-9569) [08682942] **5392**

R:VIEW (TACOMA, WASH.) *CEASED.* (US/0897-1129) [17403269] **1202**

RWANDA. DIRECTION DE LA STATISTIQUE ET DE LA DOCUMENTATION *See* BULLETIN DE STATISTIQUE - DIRECTION DE LA STATISTIQUE ET DE LA DOCUMENTATION. SUPPLEMENT ANNUEL (RWANDA) **5324**

RWANDA. DIRECTION DE LA STATISTIQUE ET DE LA DOCUMENTATION *See* BULLETIN DE STATISTIQUE - DIRECTION DE LA STATISTIQUE ET DE LA DOCUMENTATION (RWANDA) **5324**

RWANDA. MINISTERE DE LA SANTE PUBLIQUE *See* RAPPORT ANNUEL - MINISTERE DE LA SANTE PUBLIQUE **4798**

RWANDA — Alphabetical Title Index

RWANDA. PRESIDENCE See DISCOURS ET ENTRETIENS - PRESIDENCE DE LA REPUBLIQUE **4644**

RWDSU RECORD (US/0033-7196) [02267363] 957, **1709**

RWI-KONJUNKTURBERICHTE (GW/0931-8801) [I09318801] **1625**

RWI-MITTEILUNGEN (GW/0933-0089) [I09330089] 992, **3637**

RX BEING WELL (US/0886-9766) [13084356] **4328**

RX CONSULTANT, THE (US/1066-7741) [27046123] **4328**

RX ET CETERA (US/0744-7736) [08549240] **4328**

RX REPORT (US/1056-4985) [23725735] **4329**

RYAN ADVISORY FOR HEALTH SERVICES GOVERNING BOARDS, THE (US/0161-7680) [03990767] **4800**

RYBOLOV (RU/0233-7754) [11940972] **2312**

RYDE RECORDER, THE (AT/0048-8879) [05573978] **2671**

RYE CHRONICLE, THE (US/0893-4401) [10085103] **5720**

RYERSON POLYTECHNICAL INSTITUTE See BRIEF TO THE ONTARIO COUNCIL ON UNIVERSITY AFFAIRS / RYERSON POLYTECHNICAL INSTITUTE **1812**

RYERSON REVIEW OF JOURNALISM (CN/0838-0651) [19462041] **2924**

RYNKI ZAGRANICZNE (PL/0036-052X) [I0036052X] **708**

RYTMY (PL) [01789174] **4151**

RYUKOKU KIYO (JA/0289-0917) [17632797] 5149, **2853**

RYUKOSHOKU. FASHION COLORS (JA) **1087**

RYUKYU DAIGAKU. HO-BUNGAKUBU See RYUKYU DAIGAKU KOKUBUNGAKU TETSUGAKU RON SHU **3352**

RYUKYU DAIGAKU. HO-BUNGAKUBU See RYUKYU DAIGAKU HO-BUNGAKUBU KIYO : KOKUBUNGAKU RONSHU **3432**

RYUKYU DAIGAKU HO-BUNGAKUBU KIYO : KOKUBUNGAKU RONSHU (JA) [06829832] **3432**

RYUKYU DAIGAKU IGAKKAI ZASSHI (JA/0289-1530) [I02891530] **3638**

RYUKYU DAIGAKU KOKUBUNGAKU TETSUGAKU RON SHU (JA) [01799689] **3352**

RYUKYU DAIGAKU. NOGAKUBU See RYUKYU DAIGAKU NOGAKUBU GAKUJUTSU HOKOKU **131**

RYUKYU DAIGAKU NOGAKUBU GAKUJUTSU HOKOKU (JA/0370-4246) [01790225] **131**

RYUKYU DAIGAKU RIGAKUBU KIYO (JA/0286-9640) [10052826] 472, **1456**

RYUMACHI (JA/0300-9157) [01351146] **3807**

RYUSAN TO KOGYO (JA/0370-8047) [09490209] **1029**

RYUTSU SHISUTEMU JOHO GAIDOBUKKU / RYUTSU SHISUTEMU KAIHATSU SENTA HEN (JA) [11734553] **732**

RZECZPOSPOLITA WARSZAWA (PL/0208-9130) [I02089130] **5808**

S.A.A.D. DIGEST (UK/0049-1160) [07595030] **1335**

S.A. ARGIEFBLAD (SA/1012-2796) [I10122796] **2483**

S.A.E. AUSTRALASIA (AT/0373-3173) [08620474] **5424**

S A F T T A NEWSLETTER (SA) 1138, **4077**

S.A. JOURNAL FOR RESEARCH IN SPORT PHYSICAL EDUCATION AND RECREATION (SA/0379-9069) [I03799069] **1858**

S. A. L. T. NEWSLETTER (CN/0702-7745) [03412166] **3247**

S.A. LAW LIBRARIANS BULLETIN (AT/0818-3236) [I08183236] 3045, **3247**

S.A.M. ADVANCED MANAGEMENT JOURNAL (1984) (US/0749-7075) [11220842] **885**

S.A.M.P.E. QUARTERLY (US/0036-0821) [01787138] **1995**

S.A.P.A. POULTRY BULLETIN, THE (SA/0257-201X) [I0257201X] **220**

S & B REPORT (US) **2903**

S & D : MAANDBLAD VAN DE WIARDI BECKMAN STICHTING (NE) [25952470] **4546**

S & L MUSEUM NEWSLETTER (CN/0715-5034) [09499086] 5436, **4096**

S & L- SAVINGS BANK FINANCIAL QUARTERLY (US/1051-9939) [16716750] **810**

S & P'S INSURER SOLVENCY REVIEW (LIFE-HEALTH ED.) (US/1059-0447) [23594203] **2893**

S & P'S INSURER SOLVENCY REVIEW (PROPERTY-CASUALTY ED.) (US/1059-0455) [23591127] **2893**

S.C.A.N. : SIMCOE COUNTY ANCESTORS' NEWS (CN/0823-9533) [11426748] **2471**

S D; SPACE DESIGN (JA/0563-0991) [04864450] 2903, **308**

S.E.M. NEWSLETTER (1981) (US/0739-9103) [08767081] 2272, **4151**

S + F (GW/0175-274X) [12617973] **4534**

●S.H.A.R.E. (TUKWILA, WASHINGTON) (US/1062-2640) [25562945] **5306**

S.I.T.R.A.M. RESULTATS GENERAUX, TRAFIC INTERIEUR ET INTERNATIONAL / MINISTERE DES TRANSPORTS, DEPARTEMENT DES STATISTIQUES DES TRANSPORTS (FR) [09787719] **5392**

S.I.T.R.A.M., TRAFIC INTERNATIONAL / MINISTERE DE L'EQUIPEMENT, DU LOGEMENT, DE L'AMENAGEMENT DU TERRITOIRE ET DES TRANSPORTS, DEPARTEMENT DES SYNTHESES STATISTIQUES ET ECONOMIQUES (FR/0762-0616) [19056147] **5392**

S. KLEIN DIRECTORY OF COMPUTER GRAPHICS SUPPLIERS, THE (US/0732-9199) [08402039] **1235**

S. KLEIN NEWSLETTER ON COMPUTER GRAPHICS, THE (US/0731-9207) [08264934] **1235**

S. L. A. N. T. : SAANEN, LAMANCHA, ALPINE, NUBIAN, TOGGENBURG (CN/0318-6806) [02442160] **221**

S. M. STUDY (CN/0318-3122) [02441767] **2108**

S/N. SPEECHWRITER'S NEWSLETTER (US/0272-8079) [06947986] 2924, **1121**

S. O. N. G. SHEET (CN/0225-4042) [06136410] **1709**

S.O.S (US/0891-866X) [15046998] **5306**

S O S GARDERIES (CN/0700-9666) [03406018] **1805**

S O S GARDERIES (ORGANISME) See S O S GARDERIES **1805**

S.P.A. JOURNAL (US/0036-181X) [03478544] **2787**

S.P.E.A. BULLETIN / THE SASK. PHYSICAL EDUCATION ASSOC (CN/0828-6132) [12069444] **1858**

S P E A Q JOURNAL (CN/0225-3550) [06034902] **3319**

S.P.E.L.D - INFORMATION (FR/0038-7282) [01604328] 1519, 5217, **3045**

S P E REPRINT SERIES (US) [01606784] **4277**

S P K W KANADZIE (CN/0381-5145) [02171651] **5236**

S R F B NEWSLETTER (CN/0382-1153) [02607481] **34**

S-R-S; SAFETY RESPONSIBILITY SUSPENSIONS (US) [25848321] **5424**

S.S.A. NEWSLETTER : A PUBLICATION OF THE SUDAN STUDIES ASSOCIATION (US/0899-3785) [13819261] **2500**

S S G M. SERVICE STATION & GARAGE MANAGEMENT (CN/0381-548X) [02604419] **5424**

S.S. HUEBNER FOUNDATION MONOGRAPH SERIES (US/0146-292X) [02900525] **2893**

S.T.A.L (FR/0339-722X) [04695073] **5521**

S.T.P. PHARMA PRATIQUES : TECHNIQUES REGLEMENTATIONS (FR/1157-1497) [23741218] **4329**

S.T.P. PHARMA SCIENCES (FR) [23741225] **4329**

S9 HOBBY RADIO (US/0193-7014) [05244910] 2777, **1138**

SA (US/0162-1270) [04104528] **2512**

SA BUILDER (SA) **627**

SA BUILDING WORKER (AT/0816-3103) [I08163103] **1709**

SA HIKER See HIKING AFRICA **4873**

SA JOURNAL OF FOOD SCIENCE AND NUTRITION, THE (SA/1013-3666) [I10133666] **4199**

SA JOURNAL OF LINGUISTICS (SA) [13714880] **3319**

SA MERCANTILE LAW JOURNAL / SA TYDSKRIF VIR HANDELSREG (SA/1015-0099) [20961487] **3045**

SA POLICE (AT) **3176**

SA PUBLIEKREG (SA/0258-6568) [16073334] **3045**

SA - VERBRUIKER, DIE (SA/0379-8992) [I03798992] **1299**

SA WATER BULLETIN (SA/0258-2244) [I02582244] **5539**

SAA AGE See STRATEGIC SYSTEMS **1249**

SAA NEWSLETTER (US/0091-5971) [02906584] **2483**

SAA PLACEMENT NEWSLETTER See SAA NEWSLETTER **2483**

SAAD (IS) [01784350] **5306**

SAAGVERKEN (SW) [01066842] **2404**

SAALBURG-JAHRBUCH (GW) [01917452] **282**

SAAMIS SEEKER (CN/0229-7205) [08486123] **2471**

SAARBRUCKEN. UNIVERSITAT DES SAARLANDES See VERBLEIB DER ABGEWIESENEN STUDIENBEWERBER **1853**

SAARBRUCKER BEITRAEGE ZUR ALTERTUMSKUNDE (GW/0080-5180) [02924819] **245**

SAARBRUCKER HEFTE (GW/0036-2115) [01917399] **2708**

SAARLAND (GERMANY). STATISTISCHES AMT See STATISTISCHE BERICHTE DES STATISTISCHEN AMTES DES SAARLANDES **5343**

SAARLAND HEUTE (GW) [04621488] **5338**

SAARLAND. STATISTISCHES AMT See SAARLANDISCHE KREBSDOKUMENTATION **3823**

SAARLANDISCHE ARBEITNEHMER See ARBEITNEHMER **1651**

SAARLANDISCHE KREBSDOKUMENTATION (GW) [02483246] **3823**

SAARLANDISCHE KREISZAHLEN (GW/0486-7890) [10616905] **5338**

SAARLANDISCHES ARZTEBLATT (GW/0340-644X) [04648581] **3638**

SAAS BULLETIN, BIOCHEMISTRY AND BIOTECHNOLOGY (US/1052-6781) [19500840] 131, **3696**

SABAH. DEPT. OF AGRICULTURE See TECHNICAL BULLETIN - DEPARTMENT OF AGRICULTURE, SABAH, MALAYSIA **139**

SABAH. DEPT. OF AGRICULTURE See AGRICULTURAL STATISTICS OF SABAH **150**

SABAH MUSEUM AND ARCHIVES JOURNAL (MY) [18819459] **4171**

SABAH (NICOSIA, CYPRUS) (CY) [11097889] **2663**

SABAH. PUBLIC SERVICE COMMISSION See LAPURAN TAHUNAN SURUHANJAYA PERKHIDMATAN AWAM NEGERI SABAH **4661**

SABAH SOCIETY See SABAH SOCIETY JOURNAL **2663**

SABAH SOCIETY JOURNAL (MY/0036-2131) [02017243] **2663**

SABAH. SURUHANJAYA PERKHIDMATAN AWAM NEGERI See LAPURAN TAHUNAN - SURUHANJAYA PERKHIDMATAN AWAM NEGERI SABAH **4704**

SABBATH RECORDER (NEW YORK, N.Y.) See SABBATH RECORDER, THE **5067**

SABBATH RECORDER, THE (US/0036-214X) [01775195] **5067**

SABBATH WATCHMAN, THE (US/0098-9517) [02242578] **5067**

SABENA REVUE (BE/0036-2158) [01775196] **34**

SABER LEER (SP/0213-6449) [15709110] **3352**

SABETHA HERALD (SABETHA, KAN. : 1905) (US) [11985915] **5678**

●SABIAN NEWS BEAT CATALOG (CN/1191-2642) [26497810] **4151**

SABINE INDEX (MANY, LA. : 1879) (US/0739-0017) [09701076] **5684**

SABINE/MAGAZINE (CN/0227-2261) [06635434] **3247**

SABISU SANGYO NENKAN / HENSHU, TSUSHO SANGYOSHO SANGYO SEISAKUKYOKU SHOMU SABISU SANGYOSHITSU (JA) [10221885] **1625**

SABO SAMYANG See SAMYANG SABO **1625**

SABO TONGBU (KO) [10088267] **1625**

SABORD, LE (CN/0822-2908) [10436282] **330**

SABRAO JOURNAL (CH/1010-3902) [05179155] **527**

SABRETACHE (AT/0486-8013) [02939111] **4056**

SAC ECONOMIC REPORT (UK/0953-4148) [I09534148] 1519, **131**

●SAC NEWS MONTHLY (US) 375, **5684**

SACCHARUM (PE/0379-5829) [03353305] **185**

SACCHARUM STAB (BL/0100-6223) [09051705] **992**

SACHGUETERERZEUGUNG SCHNELLBERICHT (AU) [04969836] **3487**

SACHSISCHE AKADEMIE DER WISSENSCHAFTEN, LEIPZIG. PHILOGOGISCHE-HISTORISCHE KLASSE See ABHANDLUNGEN DER SACHSISCHEN AKADEMIE DER WISSENSCHAFTEN ZU LEIPZIG, PHILOLOGISCH-HISTORISCHE KLASSE **2671**

SACHSISCHE AKADEMIE DER WISSENSCHAFTEN ZU LEIPZIG See JAHRBUCH - SACHSISCHE AKADEMIE DER WISSENSCHAFTEN ZU LEIPZIG **1831**

SACHSISCHE AKADEMIE DER WISSENSCHAFTEN ZU LEIPZIG See ABHANDLUNGEN DER SACHSISCHEN AKADEMIE DER WISSENSCHAFTEN ZU LEIPZIG. MATHEMATISCH-NATURWISSENSCHAFTLICHE KLASSE **5079**

SACHUNTERRICHT UND MATHEMATIK IN DER PRIMARSTUFE (GW/0170-0944) [I01700944] **3532**

SACOGE NEWS (US/8756-6907) [11605577] **2471**

SACRA DOCTRINA (IT/0036-2190) [06057637] **4995**

SACRAMENTAL LIFE (US/0899-2061) [17988385] **4995**

SACRAMENTO BANK FOR COOPERATIVES See REPORT TO STOCKHOLDERS **913**

SACRAMENTO BEE, THE (US/0890-5738) [08800746] **5639**

SACRAMENTO BUSINESS **CEASED.** (US/0036-2204) [03917366] **708**

SACRAMENTO (JONSSON COMMUNICATIONS CORPORATION) (US/0747-8712) [10806585] **2544**

SACRAMENTO MEDICINE (US/0886-2826) [12858960] **3638**

SACRAMENTO NEWS & REVIEW (US/1065-3287) [26583644] **2544**

SACRAMENTO NEWSLETTER, THE (US/0486-8161) [04079434] 4684, **3045**

SACRAMENTO OBSERVER, THE (US/0036-2212) [03917415] **5639**

SACRAMENTO PRESS-JOURNAL See DAILY RECORDER, THE **2958**

SACRAMENTO-SAN JOAQUIN DELTA WATER QUALITY SURVEILLANCE PROGRAM : MONITORING RESULTS PURSUANT TO CONDITIONS SET FORTH IN DELTA WATER RIGHTS DECISION ... / STATE OF CALIFORNIA, THE RESOURCES AGENCY, DEPARTMENT OF WATER RESOURCES (US) [07616135] **5539**

SACRAMENTO SPORTS (US/0746-1585) [09816794] **4916**

SACRAMENTO VALLEY UNION LABOR BULLETIN (US/0036-2247) [03917449] **1709**

SACRED ART JOURNAL (US/0741-9163) [08962851] 5040, **364**

SACRED BOOKS OF THE BUDDHISTS (UK) [04440345] **5022**

SACRED HEART UNIVERSITY REVIEW (US/0276-7643) [07364962] **1094**

SACRED MUSIC (US/0036-2255) [01764721] 4151, **5035**

SACRED ORGAN JOURNAL, THE (US/0036-2263) [08028619] **4151**

SACRED RIVER (US/1062-6298) [24131471] **5565**

SACRIS ERUDIRI (NE/0771-7776) [01773347] **4995**

SAD NOWOCZESNY (PL/0137-4788) [02059879] **185**

SADA AL-USBU (BA) [03301827] **2508**

SADA-YI BALTISTAN (PK) [01764723] **2663**

SADAN (KO) [10067026] **4376**

SADCC DIRECTORY AND TRADERS GUIDE (RH) **708**

SADDLE AND BRIDLE (US/0036-2271) [01764724] **2802**

SADDLE & STRIKER (1990) (CN/1184-1508) [23598663] **382**

SADDLE HORSE REPORT (US/0161-7842) [04025894] **2802**

SADEX (US/0276-1629) [06522531] **1583**

SADHANA (BANGALORE) (II/0256-2499) [11386328] **1995**

SADOVODSTVO (RU/0131-3568) [02853976] **2430**

SADOVODSTVO I VINOGRADARSTVO (RU/0235-2591) [18528809] **2430**

SADOVOE ZAVEDENIE SINOP See KATALOG SADOVOE ZAVEDENIE "SINOP" E I.V. VELIKAGO KNIAZIA ALEKSANDRA MIKHAILOVICHA **2422**

SADTLER RESEARCH LABORATORIES See SADTLER ULTRA VIOLET STANDARD SPECTRA **1019**

SADTLER RESEARCH LABORATORIES See STANDARD INFRARED PRISM SPECTRA **1019**

SADTLER RESEARCH LABORATORIES See SADTLER STANDARD CARBON-13 NMR SPECTRA **1019**

SADTLER RESEARCH LABORATORIES See STANDARD GRATING SPECTRA **1019**

SADTLER RESEARCH LABORATORIES See PROTON NMR COLLECTION. CUMULATIVE CHEMICAL CLASS INDEX **4450**

SADTLER STANDARD CARBON-13 NMR SPECTRA (US) [05348206] 1047, **1019**

SADTLER ULTRA VIOLET STANDARD SPECTRA (US) [01764729] 1047, **1019**

SAE GROUND VEHICLE STANDARDS INDEX (US/0891-995X) [15056875] **5424**

SAE HANDBOOK (US/0362-8205) [01764702] **5424**

SAE KAJONG (KO) [05189698] **2285**

SAE MAUL UNDONG YONGU (HANSA TAEHAK. SAE MAUL UNDONG YONGUSO) (KO) [10236488] **2835**

SAE MAUL YONGU (KO) [08365291] **131**

SAE MAUL YONGU (CHONNAM TAEHAKKYO. SAE MAUL YONGUSO) (KO) [08695567] **5257**

SAE MAUM NONMUNJIP (KO) [23029030] **2835**

SAE MULGYOL (KO) [05020007] **2526**

SAE MULLI (KO/0374-4914) [10153078] **4420**

SAE NONGSA (KO) [10261655] **2430**

SAE OMIN (KO) [07714673] **2312**

SAE, SAMMLUNG ARBEITSRECHTLICHER ENTSCHEIDUNGEN (GW) [06134159] **3154**

SAE TECHNICAL LITERATURE ABSTRACTS (US/0741-2029) [08559705] 5424, **1995**

SAE TECHNICAL PAPER SERIES (US/0148-7191) [08540031] **2128**

SAE TRANSACTIONS (US) [01765907] 1995, **5424**

SAE TRANSACTIONS (US/0096-736X) [05771020] **5425**

SAE TRANSACTIONS AND LITERATURE DEVELOPED DURING (US) [06901711] 1995, **5425**

SAEBYOK (CATHOLIC CHURCH. ARCHDIOCESE OF SEOUL (KOREA). HANGBOGUK) (KO) [09567417] **5036**

SAECHSISCHE AKADEMIE DER WISSENSCHAFTEN, LEIPZIG. PHILOLOGISCH-HISTORISCHE KLASSE See SITZUNGSBERICHTE DER SAECHSISCHE AKADEMIE DER WISSENSCHAFTEN, LEIPZIG, PHILOLOGISCH-HISTORISCHE KLASSE **3321**

SAECULUM (GW/0080-5319) [01764733] **2628**

SAEM I KIPPUN MUL (KO) [11525951] **2508**

SAEMTLICHE WERKE. ANTON BRUCKNER (GW) **4151**

SAEMTLICHE WERKE. ARNOLD SCHOENBERG (GW) **4151**

SAEMTLICHE WERKE. GUSTAV MAHLER (GW) **4151**

SAEMTLICHE WERKE. ORLANDO DE LASSUS (GW) **4151**

SAEMTLICHE WERKE. RICHARD WAGNER (GW) **4151**

SAEMTO (KO) [05134789] **2508**

SAENGHWAHAK NYUSU (KO/1016-0884) [I10160884] **3696**

SAENGHWAL CHIDO YONGU (KO) [08336746] **1870**

SAENGMYONG POHOM SEMU (KO) [11446845] **2893**

SAENGSAN KISUL YONGU (KO) [08365072] **5149**

SAEOPP JOURNAL (US/0730-7365) [08054110] **1870**

SAFARI (TUCSON, ARIZ.) (US/0199-5316) [05518865] 4878, **4916**

SAFE ASSOCIATION (U.S.). SYMPOSIUM See PROCEEDINGS OF THE ANNUAL SYMPOSIUM, SAFE ASSOCIATION **32**

SAFE BULLETIN : SCAM AND FRAUD EXCHANGE, THE (US/1059-6178) [24647703] **3176**

SAFE DRIVER (US/0898-8749) [09718006] 4800, **5425**

SAFE, EFFECTIVE AND THERAPEUTICALLY EQUIVALENT PRESCRIPTION DRUGS (US/0273-0820) [04636763] **4329**

SAFE ENERGY & ENVIRONMENT (II/0971-118X) [I0971118X] **1956**

SAFE FOREMAN (US) **2869**

SAFE JOURNAL (US/0191-6319) [04947749] **34**

SAFE MONEY REPORT (US/1068-4034) [27667271] **708**

SAFE WORKER (US/0896-9051) [02450337] **2869**

SAFETY ALERT (US/0748-1403) [08276970] **2869**

SAFETY AND EMC (UK) **2080**

SAFETY AND ENVIRONMENTAL PROTECTION DIVISION PROGRESS REPORT (US/0160-8290) [03765821] **2181**

SAFETY & HEALTH (US/0891-1797) [14641468] **2869**

SAFETY AND HEALTH AT WORK : ILO-CIS BULLETIN (SZ/1010-7053) [16865108] 2869, **2872**

SAFETY & HEALTH PRACTITIONER (UK/0958-479X) [I0958479X] **4800**

SAFETY AND SECURITY FOR SUPERVISORS (US/1040-4236) [12148376] **885**

SAFETY AND TRAINING NEWS (AT/1032-0024) [I10320024] **2869**

SAFETY AT SEA INTERNATIONAL (UK) [26866896] **5455**

SAFETY BRIEF (US/1041-9489) [18888263] **4801**

● SAFETY BRIEFS. WESTERN REGION (US/1062-5828) [25670364] **5257**

SAFETY EFFECTIVENESS EVALUATION : REPORT NO. NTSB-SEE (US) [04271250] **4801**

SAFETY, ENVIRONMENTAL PROTECTION, AND ANALYSIS (UK/0938-5215) **2181**

SAFETY IN THE CHEMICAL LABORATORY (US) **992**

SAFETY INFOGRAM (CN/0835-8184) [19317786] **2869**

SAFETY MANAGEMENT (SA/0377-8592) [03742079] **2869**

SAFETY MANAGEMENT LONDON (UK) [I09512624] **4801**

SAFETY MANAGEMENT NEWSLETTER (US/0740-1426) [09939001] **4801**

SAFETY MANAGEMENT PROGRAM (US) **885**

SAFETY MANAGEMENT (WATERFORD, CONN.) (US/1069-2118) [04105262] **2869**

SAFETY MANUAL / HELICOPTER ASSOCIATION INTERNATIONAL (US/0882-858X) [12004984] **34**

SAFETY NEWS (DENVER) (US/0270-4447) [06401757] **2869**

SAFETY PRACTITIONERS' YEAR BOOK, THE (UK) [14198350] **2869**

SAFETY PRODUCTION PLAN PROGRAM (US) **2869**

SAFETY RECOMMENDATIONS / NATIONAL TRANSPORTATION SAFETY BOARD (US) [06684840] **4801**

SAFETY RELATED RECALL CAMPAIGNS FOR MTOR VEHICLES AND MOTOR VEHICLE EQUIPMENT, INCLUDING TIRES: DETAILED REPORTS (US/0146-7026) [03012925] 4801, **5425**

SAFETY RESEARCH NEWS (FR/0765-913X) [I0765913X] **2869**

SAFETY SADISTICS **SUSPENDED.** (US/0147-3743) [03160044] 5444, **4801**

SAFETY SCIENCE (NE/0925-7535) [23966897] **2869**

SAFETY SMARTS (CN/0842-5477) [19770068] **2869**

SAFETY TALKS (CN) **2870**

SAFETY UPDATE (CN/0704-4739) [06132177] **4801**

SAFETY (WATERFORD, CONN.) (US/1069-2037) [14756070] **2870**

SAFETYLINE / NAVAL SAFETY CENTER (US/1073-9335) [24182777] **4182**

SAFEWORKER (US) **2870**

SAFRA (US/0733-9062) [07972450] **5052**

SAFRICAN NEWS (CN/0708-1960) [04955156] **4495**

SAFYBI (AG/0558-1265) [I05581265] **4329**

SAG HARBOR EXPRESS (US) [21488509] **5720**

SAGA (US) [06963231] **2492**

SAGA-BOOK (UK/0305-9219) [13077954] 3319, 2708, **3432**

SAGA DAIGAKU NOGAKUBU IHO (JA/0581-2801) [08559911] **131**

SAGA DAIGAKU. RIKOGAKUBU See SAGA DAIGAKU RIKOGAKUBU SHUHO **1995**

SAGA DAIGAKU RIKOGAKUBU SHUHO (JA/0385-6186) [03426700] 3532, **1995**

● SAGA DIRECTORY OF INTERNATIONAL AVIATION PRODUCTS AND SERVICES (US/1065-951X) [26815287] **34**

SAGA — Alphabetical Title Index

●SAGA INTERNATIONAL AVIATOR (US/1065-9501) [26815319] **34**

SAGA KENRITSU HAKUBUTSUKAN *See* SAGA KENRITSU HAKUBUTSUKAN NEMPO **4096**

SAGA KENRITSU HAKUBUTSUKAN NEMPO (JA) [01799691] **4096**

SAGA NATIONAL PRINT EXHIBITION (US/0163-4577) [04373170] **382**

SAGA OCH SED (SW/0586-5360) [01776038] **1094**

SAGA OF SOUTHERN ILLINOIS (US/0740-154X) [05867855] **2471**

SAGAMI JOSHI DAIGAKU KIYO (JA/0286-6250) [10439099] **1094**

SAGAMI JOSHI DAIGAKU KOKUBUN KENKYUKAI *See* SAGAMI KOKUBUN **3319**

SAGAMI KOKUBUN (JA) [01797266] **3319**

SAGAMIE (CN/0229-7698) [08143833] **4854**

SAGAMIEN (CN/0226-2169) [06859928] **2575**

SAGAMORE ARMY MATERIALS RESEARCH CONFERENCE PROCEEDINGS (US/0197-2790) [06005364] **4056**

●SAGAMORE PUBLISHING'S BOOK LOOK (US/1062-3418) [25590047] **3247**

SAGARA (NP) [08722125] **2663**

SAGARIN REVIEW, THE (US/1056-2591) [23603965] **2272**, **3432**

SAGA'S UFO REPORT *See* UFO REPORT (BROOKLYN) **38**

SAGE ANNUAL REVIEW OF SOCIAL AND EDUCATIONAL CHANGE *CEASED.* (UK/0140-2196) [03225029] **1781**

SAGE ANNUAL REVIEWS OF COMMUNICATIONS RESEARCH (US/0099-1414) [01674526] **1121**

SAGE ANNUAL REVIEWS OF COMMUNITY MENTAL HEALTH (US/0739-7283) [07383862] **4801**

SAGE (ATLANTA, GA.) *CEASED.* (US/0741-8639) [10219211] **2272**, **5565**

SAGE CRIMINAL JUSTICE SYSTEM ANNUALS (US) [04894608] **3176**

SAGE FAMILY STUDIES ABSTRACTS (US/0164-0283) [04556827] **2285**, **2287**

SAGE HUMAN SERVICES GUIDES (US) [06291749] **5306**

SAGE LIBRARY OF SOCIAL RESEARCH (US) [05859770] **5217**

SAGE PUBLIC ADMINISTRATION ABSTRACTS (US/0094-6958) [01794378] **4684**, **4699**

SAGE RACE RELATIONS ABSTRACTS (UK/0307-9201) [02163916] **5257**, **5266**

SAGE STUDIES IN 20TH CENTURY HISTORY *CEASED.* (UK) [02924771] **2628**

SAGE STUDIES IN INTERNATIONAL SOCIOLOGY (UK) [06031951] **5257**

SAGE URBAN STUDIES ABSTRACTS (US/0090-5747) [01785574] **2835**, **2840**

SAGE YEARBOOKS IN POLITICS AND PUBLIC POLICY (US/0275-5297) [05032109] **4684**, **4495**

SAGE YEARBOOKS IN WOMEN'S POLICY STUDIES (US/0275-5300) [03825395] **5565**

SAGES FEMMES *CEASED.* (FR/0180-0612) [04042890] **3768**

SAGETRIEB (US/0735-4665) [08598971] **3470**

SAGGI (IT) **3638**

SAGGI DI LETTERE ITALIANE (IT) **3432**

SAGGI E MEMORIE DI STORIA DELL'ARTE (IT/0392-713X) [01764742] **364**

SAGGI E RICERCHE DI LETTERATURA FRANCESE (IT/0581-2917) [01916507] **3432**

SAGGI NEUROPSICOLOGIA INFANTILE PSICOPEDAGOGIA RIABILITAZIONE (IT/0390-5179) [03905179] **4617**

SAGINAW, BAY CITY, MIDLAND LABOR MARKET REVIEW *See* SAGINAW-BAY-MIDLAND'S LABOR MARKET NEWS **1709**

●SAGINAW-BAY-MIDLAND'S LABOR MARKET NEWS (US) [25954788] **1709**

SAGINAW NEWS (1929) (US) [09872938] **5693**

SAGSET JOURNAL *See* SIMULATION/GAMES FOR LEARNING **1905**

SAGUARO (US/0885-5013) [11311933] **3432**

SAGUAROLAND BULLETIN (US/0275-6919) [02586116] **527**

SAGUENAYENSIA (CN/0581-295X) [01764743] **2759**

SAHARA (FR) [05526897] **4495**

SAHARA-INFO (FR) [07878017] **2643**

SAHARA INFO (FR/0150-262X) [l0150262X] **4495**

SAHARA (SEGRATE) (IT/1120-5679) [19791371] **2492**

SAHARIEN, LE (FR/0581-2976) [02939976] **2500**

SAHIFAT AL-MAKTABAH (UA) [03412066] **3247**

SAHITYA (II) [03443584] **3433**

SAHITYA AKADEMI *See* MONTHLY NEWS BULLETIN **3413**

SAHITYA SANKETA (II) [08383624] **3433**

SAHITYA-SAURABHA (II) [01784124] **3433**

SAHITYALOCANA (II) [02239575] **3433**

SAHITYATIRTHA (II) [09503956] **3433**

SAHKO TELE (FI/0036-2670) [23598546] **2080**

SAHOE KWAHAK NONCHONG (KO) [08731119] **5217**

SAHOE KWAHAK NONMUNJIP (MYONGJI TAEHAKKYO. SAHOE KWAHAK YONGUSO) (KO) [10672860] **5217**

SAHOE KWAHAK (YONGNAM TAEHAKKYO. SAHOE KWAHAK YONGUSO) (KO) [07756343] **5217**

SAHOE KWAHAK YONGU (YONGNAM TAEHAKKYO. SAHOE KWAHAK YONGUSO) (KO) [09068091] **5217**

SAHOE POKCHI (KO) [10620259] **5306**

SAHOVSKI GLASNIK (CI) [06411442] **4865**

SAHOVSKI INFORMATOR (CI/0351-1375) [03699388] **4865**

SAHPERD JOURNAL (US) **1858**

SAIASII TRIBUNA (KG) [25058810] **4546**

SAIBO (JA/0386-4766) [10438006] **472**

SAIBO KOGAKU (JA/0287-3796) [10392676] **472**

SAID MALTA COIN, BANKNOTE, AND MEDAL CATALOGUE (MM) [09581996] **2783**

SAIKIN NO ASUFARUTO JIJO (JA) [12033590] **1625**

SAIKO TO HOAN *CEASED.* (JA/0370-8217) [10463991] **2870**

SAIL (US/0036-2700) [01605174] **595**

SAIL BOARDER INTERNATIONAL *CEASED.* (US/0886-9626) [13083542] **4916**

SAIL INDEX (US/0733-0383) [08496880] **595**

SAILBOARD EXTRA (AT/0817-2773) [l08172773] **4916**

SAILBOARD RETAILER (US/1063-8180) [26142389] **4916**

SAILBOAT & EQUIPMENT DIRECTORY (US/0148-8732) [03400643] **596**

SAILBOAT & SAILING JOURNAL (US/0738-5242) [09599487] **596**

SAILBOAT TRADE-IN GUIDE, BLUE BOOK (US/0742-0447) [10232120] **596**

SAILING (US/0036-2719) [01642789] **596**

SAILING CANADA (CN/0709-4744) [05712364] **596**

SAILING DIRECTIONS (ENROUTE) FOR NEWFOUNDLAND, LABRADOR AND HUDSON BAY (US) [04344227] **5455**

SAILING DIRECTIONS (ENROUTE) FOR NOVA SCOTIA, AND THE ST. LAWRENCE (US) [04344209] **5392**

●SAILING DIRECTIONS. GENERAL INFORMATION. ATLANTIC COAST (CN) [25598736] **596**

SAILING DIRECTIONS. GULF AND RIVER OF ST. LAWRENCE *See* SAILING DIRECTIONS. GULF OF ST. LAWRENCE **4182**

●SAILING DIRECTIONS. GULF OF ST. LAWRENCE (CN) [26727308] **4182**

SAILING DIRECTIONS, LABRADOR AND HUDSON BAY (CN/0823-3799) [06887096] **596**

●SAILING DIRECTIONS. ST. LAWRENCE RIVER. CAP-ROUGE TO MONTREAL (CN) [25598605] **4182**

●SAILING DIRECTIONS. ST. LAWRENCE RIVER. ILE VERTE TO QUEBEC (CN) [25598722] **4183**

SAILING LIFE (CN/0821-4670) [09562891] **596**

SAILING QUARTERLY (US/1071-1392) [28399676] **596**

SAILING WORLD (US/0889-4094) [13895691] **596**

SAILOR (US) [21793000] **5698**

SAILPLANE & GLIDING (UK/0036-2735) [02267383] **34**

SAINIK SAMACHAR (II/0022-2743) [06681033] **4056**

SAINNYAG HAGHOI JI (SENUR) (KO/0253-3073) [08239952] **4329**

SAINS MALAYSIANA (MY/0126-6039) [01790699] **5149**

SAINT BARTHOLOMEW'S HOSPITAL JOURNAL (UK/0036-2778) [01681403] **3638**

SAINT CHRISTOPHER AND NEVIS CONSOLIDATED INDEX OF STATUTES AND SUBSIDIARY LEGISLATION TO ... (BB) [13919487] **3135**

SAINT CLAIR COUNTY (ILL.) *See* JOURNAL OF THE ST. CLAIR COUNTY HISTORICAL SOCIETY **2742**

SAINT-DENIS (REUNION) *See* ANNUAIRE MUNICIPAL DE SAINT DENIS **5023**

SAINT-ETIENNE-DE-BEAUMONT (QUEBEC) *See* CHESNAIE **4637**

SAINT-HUBERT D'ARDENNE (BE) [07117864] **2708**

SAINT-HUBERT, NOTRE VILLE (CN/0712-7308) [08584536] **4684**

SAINT-HUBERT (QUEBEC) *See* SAINT-HUBERT, NOTRE VILLE **4684**

SAINT JO TRIBUNE, THE (US) [14703124] **5754**

SAINT JOHN BUSINESS TODAY (CN) [20266823] **708**

●SAINT JOHN CITY DIRECTORY (1992) (CN/1191-940X) [27725196] **2575**

SAINT JOHN FOLK CLUB RAG, THE (CN/0715-4976) [09543089] **4151**

SAINT JOHN, NEW BRUNSWICK, CITY DIRECTORY *See* SAINT JOHN CITY DIRECTORY (1992) **2575**

SAINT KITTS-NEVIS-ANGUILLA *See* LAWS OF ST. CHRISTOPHER, NEVIS & ANGUILLA **2997**

SAINT-LAURENT (ILE-DE-MONTREAL, QUEBEC) *See* PROGRAMME DES ACTIVITES CULTURELLES ET SPORTIVES **4913**

SAINT-LAURENT JOURNAL (CN/0829-4941) [16656521] **4684**

SAINT LAWRENCE COUNTY HISTORICAL ASSOCIATION *See* QUARTERLY - ST. LAWRENCE COUNTY HISTORICAL ASSOCIATION, THE **2756**

SAINT LEO COLLEGE (ST. LEO, FLA.) *See* ALUMNI DIRECTORY / SAINT LEO COLLEGE **1099**

SAINT LEONARD (LE-DE-MONTREAL, QUEBEC) *See* FEUILLET D'INFORMATION DE LA VILLE DE SAINT-LEONARD, LE **4649**

SAINT LOUIS LUTHERAN (US) **5067**

SAINT LOUIS UNIVERSITY LAW JOURNAL (US/0036-3030) [01764812] **3045**

SAINT LOUIS UNIVERSITY PUBLIC LAW REVIEW (US/0898-8404) [14769913] **3045**

SAINT LUCIA CONSOLIDATED INDEX OF STATUTES AND SUBSIDIARY LEGISLATION TO ... (BB) [13309349] **3135**

SAINT MARGARET'S-MCTERNAN (SCHOOL) *See* ALUMNI DIRECTORY / SAINT MARGARET'S-MCTERNAN **1099**

SAINT PAUL LEGAL LEDGER (US) [01589554] **5698**

SAINT PAUL PIONEER PRESS (SAINT PAUL, MINN. : 1990 : A.M. ED.) (US/1050-0405) [21278702] **5698**

SAINT PETER HERALD (US) [01764928] **5698**

SAINT VINCENT AND THE GRENADINES *See* ACTS FOR THE YEAR ... / ST. VINCENT & THE GRENADINES **2927**

SAINT VINCENT AND THE GRENADINES CONSOLIDATED INDEX OF STATUTES AND SUBSIDIARY LEGISLATION TO ... (BB) [12608681] **3135**

SAINT VINCENT HOSPITAL (OTTAWA, ONT.). LIBRARY *See* LISTE DES NOUVELLES ACQUISITIONS - HOPITAL SAINT-VINCENT, OTTAWA, ONT. BIBLIOTHEQUE **3605**

SAINT VINCENT. LAWS, ETC. ACTS *See* ACTS FOR THE YEAR ... / ST. VINCENT & THE GRENADINES **2927**

SAINTPAULIA INTERNATIONAL NEWS (US) [20766660] **2430**

SAINTS HERALD (US/0036-3251) [12218970] **5067**

SAIOAK (SP) [03979376] **2708**

SAIONSU (KO) [10149514] **5149**

SAIPA (SA/0036-0767) [06138336] **4684**

SAIRAANHOITAJA / SUOMEN SAIRAANHOITAJALIITTO RY (FI/0785-7527) [24905462] **3869**

SAIRR ANNUAL REPORT (SA) **5257**

SAIS REVIEW (JOHNS HOPKINS UNIVERSITY. SCHOOL OF ADVANCED INTERNATIONAL STUDIES: 1981) (US/0036-0775) [07251414] **4534**

SAISEKI TOKEI NENPO / TSUSHO SANGYO DAIJIN KANBO CHOSA TOKEIBU HEN (JA) [09141715] **1625**

SAISENKAI SHIRYO (JA) [09930299] **2663**

SAISHIN CHUKAI SHOBO HOREI (JA) [03189688] **2292**

SAISHIN IGAKU (JA/0370-8241) [I03708241] **3638**

SAISHIN TOKI ROPPO / TODA SHUZO KANSHU (JA) [08880562] **3091**

SAISON EN EUROPE ET DANS LE MONDE FESTIVALS (FR) **5269**

●SAISONBEREINIGTE WIRTSCHAFTSZAHLEN / DEUTSCHE BUNDESBANK (GW/0943-8785) [28010664] 1519, **1538**

SAISONS D'ALSACE STRASBOURG (FR/0048-9018) [I00489018] **2522**

SAISONS DE LA DANSE, LES (FR) [24042707] **1314**

SAITABI (SP/0210-9980) [04254320] 364, **2708**

SAITAMA DAIGAKU KIYO. SOGO HEN (JA) [11109249] **5236**

SAITAMA IKA DAIGAKU ZASSHI (JA/0385-5074) [05621642] **3638**

SAITAMA-KEN EISEI KENKYUJO *See* SAITAMA-KEN EISEI KENKYUJO HO **4801**

SAITAMA-KEN EISEI KENKYUJO HO (JA) [05699629] **4801**

SAITAMA-KEN ENGEI SHIKENJO KENKYU HOKOKU (JA/0385-3675) [10288198] **2430**

SAITAMA-KEN (JAPAN). KANKYOBU. KANKYO KANRIKA *See* KANKYO HAKUSHO **2234**

SAITAMA KENRITSU MINZOKU BUNKA SENTA *See* SHOHO **2664**

SAITAMA MATHEMATICAL JOURNAL (JA/0289-0739) [10221196] **3532**

SAITEI CHINGIN KETTEI YORAN / RIDOSHO ROKIKYOKU CHINGIN FUKUSHIBU CHINGINKA HEN (JA) [11745118] **1709**

SAITENSPIEL (GW) [03261016] **4151**

SAITO MOKICHI TSUIBO KASHU (JA) [08160410] **3470**

SAJER (AT/0155-3259) [I01553259] **1781**

SAJIT (IT) [01797727] **2663**

SAJJANAGADA (II) [03762145] **4684**

SAKARTVELOS SSR MECNIEREBATA AKADEMIIS MACNE. BIOLOGIIS SERIA (GS/0321-1665) [01988215] **472**

SAKHARNAIA SVEKLA--PROIZVODSTVO I PERERABOTKA *CEASED.* (RU/0235-2583) [18202516] **2356**

SAKKA MAGAJIN (JA) **4916**

SAKKELET (HU/0237-2525) [I02372525] **4865**

SAKONNET TIMES (US) [24982081] **5741**

SAKSHARATA SANDESA (II) [10909756] **5257**

SAKTI VANI (II) [02240205] **2080**

SAKUMOTSU TOKEI / NORINSHO. NORIN KEIZAIKYOKU TOKEI CHOABU (JA) [02243083] **185**

SAKUN THAI (TH) [02012180] **2508**

●SAL-NEWS (ROCKVILLE, MD.) (US/1062-9130) [25806667] **1519**

SAL TERRAE (SP) [06029373] **4995**

SAL VUOSIKIRJA (FI) [09856374] **2924**

SALA PROVINCIA *See* ANALES - SALA PROVINCIA **336**

SALAC SIGNAL (AT/0812-7301) [I08127301] **3247**

SALALM NEWSLETTER (US/0098-6275) [01834040] **3247**

SALAM (MONTREAL) (CN/0710-023X) [08770506] **5036**

SALAMANCA PRESS (US/8755-9110) [11217777] **5720**

SALAMANDRA (FRANKFURT-AM-MAIN) (GW/0036-3375) [02293029] **5597**

SALAR (CN/0827-3472) [11856751] **2312**

SALARIES & BENEFITS IN BOAT MANUFACTURING (US/0147-2305) [03126238] 596, **1709**

SALARIES AND RELATED MATTERS IN THE SERVICE DEPARTMENT (US/0160-516X) [03686054] **1709**

SALARIES AND SALARY GUIDES FOR SUPPORTIVE SCHOOL PERSONNEL: CUSTODIAL, MAINTENANCE, TRANSPORTATION, AND CAFETERIA (US) [04381240] **1870**

SALARIES AND SALARY GUIDES FOR SUPPORTIVE SCHOOL PERSONNEL: SECRETARIAL AND CLERICAL (US) [04381299] **1870**

SALARIES AND SALARY SCALES OF FULL-TIME TEACHING STAFF AT CANADIAN UNIVERSITIES (SUPPLEMENT TO PRELIMINARY ED.) (CN/0225-3704) [07886055] **1846**

SALARIES & WAGES IN MAINE PUBLIC SCHOOLS (US) [04138322] **1870**

SALARIES & WAGES IN PENNSYLVANIA PUBLIC SCHOOLS : A COOPERATIVE STUDY OF THE PENNSYLVANIA SCHOOL BOARDS ASSOCIATION AND THE EDUCATIONAL RESEARCH SERVICE, WITH THE ENDORSEMENT OF THE PENNSYLVANIA ASSOCIATION OF SCHOOL ADMINISTRATORS, CONDUCTED AS A COMPONENT OF THE ERS NATIONAL SURVEY OF SALARIES AND WAGES IN PUBLIC SCHOOLS (US) [11724782] **1870**

SALARIES & WAGES IN WYOMING PUBLIC SCHOOLS (US) [03818884] 1870, **1709**

SALARIES (CAMBRIDGE, MASS.) (US/0732-099X) [08311963] **1709**

SALARIES OF CERTIFICATED EMPLOYEES IN CALIFORNIA PUBLIC SCHOOLS (US/0092-5357) [02243284] **1709**

SALARIES OF ENGINEERS IN EDUCATION (US/0742-6143) [08756513] **1995**

SALARIES OF SCIENTISTS, ENGINEERS AND TECHNICIANS (US/0146-5015) [02949698] **1709**

SALARIES PAID PRINCIPALS AND ASSISTANT PRINCIPALS (US) [17888832] **1870**

SALARIES SCHEDULED FOR ADMINISTRATIVE AND SUPERVISORY PERSONNEL IN PUBLIC SCHOOLS (US/0093-8742) [01792431] **1870**

SALARIES, WAGES AND FRINGE BENEFITS OF OKLAHOMA CITIES AND TOWNS (US/0147-7080) [03215639] 1709, **1538**

SALARY ADMINISTRATION POLICIES AND PRACTICES IN CANADA (CN/1184-0900) [23659061] **1709**

SALARY & BENEFITS SURVEY (US/0196-867X) [05904800] **1709**

SALARY INFORMATION FOR WORD PROCESSING PERSONNEL, UNITED STATES, CANADA (US) [04519116] 4209, **1292**

SALARY ORDINANCE OF THE COUNTY OF LOS ANGELES (US) [06845114] **4705**

SALARY PLAN, STATE OF NORTH CAROLINA (US/0099-0477) [02246608] **4684**

SALARY STRATIFICATION REPORT / UNIVERSITY OF WASHINGTON PAYROLL/PERSONNEL SYSTEM (US) [23278898] **1709**

SALARY STUDY (US) [25212596] 2853, **5306**

SALARY STUDY / DIVISION OF COMPUTER SERVICES AND STATISTICAL REPORTS (US) [07605430] **1870**

SALARY SURVEY. ADMINISTRATIVE, FINANCE, AND DATA PROCESSING REPORT (CN/0711-3196) [08469902] **1709**

SALARY SURVEY, CONNECTICUT PUBLIC LIBRARIES (US) [12095840] **3247**

SALARY SURVEY (LOS GATOS) (US/0149-4309) [03484321] **1709**

SALARY SURVEY (NEW YORK) (US/0145-3947) [02731351] **1709**

SALARY SURVEY OF MIDDLE MANAGEMENT AND SUPERVISORY PERSONNEL. SOUTHERN CALIFORNIA (US/0276-4822) [07352040] 947, **1709**

SALARY SURVEY OF STATE GOVERNMENT EMPLOYERS (PHOENIX) (US/0091-5599) [01786517] **1709**

SALARY SURVEY OF SUPERVISORY AND NON-SUPERVISORY PROFESSIONAL ENGINEERS (US/0190-5732) [04714729] **1709**

SALARY SURVEY (SOCIETY OF THE PLASTICS INDUSTRY OF CANADA) (CN/0229-4575) [08368432] 4460, **1709**

SALE & PEPE (IT) **5565**

SALE CATALOGUES OF LIBRARIES OF EMINENT PERSONS (UK) [02253244] **3247**

SALE - D & J RITCHIE (CN/0824-6823) [11108247] **364**

SALE - SOTHEBY, PARKE-BERNET, LOS ANGELES (US/0360-2303) [02244091] **364**

SALEM DEMOCRAT (SALEM, IND. : 1874) (US) [11190236] **5667**

SALEM LEADER (SALEM, INC. : 1959) (US) [12144680] **5667**

SALEM NEWS, THE (US) [09994387] **5730**

SALEM OBSERVER (US) [21554538] **5709**

SALEMBA (IO) [04427616] **1846**

SALES AIDS HOTLINE, THE (US/0743-1171) [10539509] **708**

SALES AND LEASING MONITOR (AT) **708**

SALES & MARKETING ANALYSIS (US/8755-5654) [08571843] **936**

SALES & MARKETING MANAGEMENT (US/0163-7517) [02246178] 885, **936**

SALES & MARKETING NOTES (US) **913**

●SALES & MARKETING ONE HUNDRED NEWSLETTER (US/1064-4466) [26287627] **936**

SALES & MARKETING SURVEY / SHESHUNOFF (US/1060-2860) [24864254] 765, **936**

SALES & USE TAX ALERT (US/1054-6812) [22937239] **4747**

SALES FORCE COMPENSATION *See* DARTNELL'S ... SALES FORCE COMPENSATION SURVEY **1662**

●SALES IMPROVEMENT FOR PROFESSIONALS (US/1063-1445) [25901774] **708**

SALES LEADS (RIVIERA BEACH, FLA.) (US/0889-4779) [14074225] **708**

SALES MANAGER'S BUDGET PLANNER *CEASED.* (US) [24079722] **936**

SALES MANAGER'S BULLETIN (US/0036-3421) [04038702] **885**

SALES MANAGER'S GUIDE TO THE U.S. SCHOOL MARKET *See* MARKET DATA RETRIEVAL'S SALES MANAGER'S GUIDE TO THE U.S. SCHOOL MARKET **1763**

SALES MANAGER'S HANDBOOK, THE *See* DARTNELL SALES MANAGER'S HANDBOOK, THE **664**

SALES MEMORY JOGGER (US) **708**

SALES MOTIVATION (SANTA MONICA, CALIF.) (US/0892-8193) [15605013] 947, **709**

SALES OF DISTILLED SPIRITS (US/0741-6288) [06528483] 957, **2370**

SALES PAY AND PRODUCTIVITY TRENDS (US) [15205267] **936**

SALES PRO (US) **2356**

●SALES PRODUCTIVITY REVIEW!, THE (US/1063-6587) [26103860] **885**

SALES PROFI (GW) **709**

SALES PROMOTION MONITOR (US/0891-1622) [14687541] **709**

SALES RATIO STUDY; RESIDENTIAL AND COMMERCIAL PROPERTIES (US/0095-1056) [01795406] **4747**

SALES REP'S ADVISOR, THE (US/0278-5048) [07828622] **885**

SALES SOFTWARE SUPPLIERS DIRECTORY / COMPILED BY THE SALES AUTOMATION ASSOCIATION (US) [25615986] **1202**

SALES TAX AFFAIRS (II) [02245607] **4747**

SALES TAX TOTALS BY KIND FOR ... / STATE OF FLORIDA, DEPARTMENT OF REVENUE (US) [01656050] **4747**

SALES TAXES (US) [03259130] **751**

SALES TRAINING & DEVELOPMENT (US/0095-3962) [01796646] **936**

SALES TRAINING AND DEVELOPMENT DIRECTORY (AT) **709**

SALES UPBEAT (US/0889-3209) [13854728] **709**

●SALESFYI (CHICAGO, ILL.) (US/1061-8465) [25480686] **885**

SALESIAN (US/0036-3480) [04039253] **4995**

SALESIANUM (IT/0036-3502) [01781185] **5036**

SALESMAN'S GUIDE NATIONWIDE DIRECTORY: MAJOR MASS MARKET MERCHANDISERS (EXCLUSIVE OF NEW YORK METROPOLITAN AREA), THE (US) [05579099] **709**

SALESMAN'S INSIDER (US/0738-6362) [09655122] 936, **709**

SALG NEWSLETTER (UK/0307-1456) [08424687] **3247**

SALINA JOURNAL, THE (US/0745-127X) [08801309] **5678**

SALINA SUN (SALINA, UTAH : 1918) (US) [12879162] **5757**

SALINE REPORTER (US) **5693**

SALINE, THE (US/0893-3057) [15513501] **2471**

SALING AKTIENFUHRER (GW) [04603699] **596**

SALISBURY POST, THE (US/0747-0738) [10534469] **5724**

SALISBURY PRESS-SPECTATOR (US) [13741123] **5704**

SALISBURY REVIEW, THE (UK/0265-4881) [10947279] **3352**

SALIX (GW/0178-7969) [21076901] **3638**

SALLIM (KO) [11312459] **2394**

SALLY ANN (CN/0838-7397) [18112290] **4995**

SALMAGUNDI
Alphabetical Title Index

SALMAGUNDI (SARATOGA SPRINGS) (US/0036-3529) [00859916] **2853**

SALMANTICENSIS (SP/0036-3537) [05931290] **5036**

SALMO SALAR (CN/0703-5810) [03951117] **2312**

SALMON AND TROUT MAGAZINE See YEARBOOK - SALMON AND TROUT ASSOCIATION **2316**

SALMON AND TROUT MAGAZINE, THE (UK/0036-3545) [01764944] **2312**

SALMON ARM AND DISTRICT CHAMBER OF COMMERCE BUSINESS DIRECTORY (CN/1185-3360) [24368259] **821**

SALMON FARMING (UK/0951-9882) [21266632] **2312**

●SALMON MAGAZINE (US/1063-9624) [26204812] **2312**

SALMON NET (UK/0962-6484) [l09626484] **2312**

SALMON RIVER NEWS (US/0193-0311) [05144709] **5720**

SALMON TROUT STEELHEADER (US/0029-3431) [03918913] 2312, **4854**

SALMONID (HARPERS FERRY, W.VA.) (US/1071-1635) [03190560] **2312**

SALOME (CHICAGO, ILL.) (US/0749-6435) [03438038] **1314**

SALON DE LA JEUNE SCULPTURE See SALON DE LA JEUNE SCULPTURE. CATALOGUE **364**

SALON DE LA JEUNE SCULPTURE. CATALOGUE (FR) [06681000] **364**

SALON DU LIVRE DE MONTREAL See SALON DU LIVRE DE MONTREAL **4832**

SALON DU LIVRE DE MONTREAL (CN/0822-5443) [10061759] **4832**

●SALON MAGAZINE (CN/1197-1495) [29396176] **405**

SALON NEWS MAGAZINE (US/1044-8616) [19930003] **405**

SALON TODAY (US/0743-6394) [10625627] **405**

SALONFOTO INDONESIA (IO) [02240286] **4376**

SALT (CHICAGO, ILL.) (US/0883-2587) [09150974] **4995**

SALT CITY SONG MINERS TRADITIONAL FOLK MUSIC CLUB OF CENTRAL NEW YORK See NEWSLETTER - SALT CITY SONG MINERS TRADITIONAL FOLK MUSIC CLUB OF CENTRAL NEW YORK **4141**

SALT (EDMONTON) (CN/0709-616X) [05696310] **4995**

SALT (KENNEBUNK) (US/0160-7537) [03741189] 5217, **1094**

SALT LAKE TRIBUNE (SALT LAKE CITY, UTAH : 1890) (US/0746-3502) [08086936] **5757**

SALT / THE SISTERS OF CHARITY (US) **4995**

SALT / U.S. DEPARTMENT OF THE INTERIOR, BUREAU OF MINES (US) [25793261] **1625**

SALT WATER SPORTSMAN (US/0036-3618) [03525186] **4916**

SALUBRITAS (ENGLISH EDITION) CEASED. (US/0191-5789) [04846881] **4801**

SALUD (SP) **2601**

SALUD BUCAL (AG/0325-0741) [11535242] **1335**

SALUD MENTAL (MEXICO) (MX/0185-3325) [11227829] **3936**

SALUD RURAL. T.S.R (SP) **3638**

SALUD Y TRABAJO (MADRID) (SP/0210-6612) [04896102] **2870**

SALUDOS HISPANOS (US/0898-4875) [17834835] **2492**

SALUT LES COPAINS (FR/0036-3650) [03377889] **4495**

SALUT MONTREAL! (ED. FRANCAISE) (CN/1180-3916) [23242604] **2759**

SALUT!... PARIS (FR/0397-7854) [l03977854] **1068**

SALUTE E TERRITORIO (IT/0392-4505) [19261996] **3638**

SALUTE UMANA, LA (IT/0391-223X) [03349876] **4801**

SALVADOR. CAMARA DE COMERCIO E INDUSTRIA, SAN SALVADOR See CARTA INFORMATIVA PARA LOS SOCIOS **818**

SALVADOR. DIRECCION GENERAL DE ESTADISTICA. BOLETIN ESTADISTICO See BOLETIN ESTADISTICO - DIRECCION GENERAL DE ESTADISTICA Y CENSOS **5323**

SALVADOR. DIRECCION GENERAL DE ESTADISTICA Y CENSOS, EL See BOLETIN ESTADISTICO - DIRECCION GENERAL DE ESTADISTICA Y CENSOS **5323**

SALVATION ARMY YOUTH (US/0744-5083) [08383224] **5306**

SALYERSVILLE INDEPENDENT (US) [13153890] **5682**

SALZBURG. HAUS DER NATUR See BERICHT AUS DEM HAUS DER NATUR IN SALZBURG **4162**

SALZBURG STUDIES IN ENGLISH LITERATURE (AU) [01779343] **3433**

SALZBURG STUDIES IN ENGLISH LITERATURE. POETIC DRAMA & POETIC THEORY (AU) [13153326] **3433**

SALZBURGER JAHRBUCH FUER PHILOSOPHIE (AU/0080-5696) [01917404] **4360**

SALZBURGER STUDIEN ZUR ANGLISTIK UND AMERIKANISTIK (AU/0080-5718) [04900124] **3319**

SAM ADVANCED MANAGEMENT JOURNAL (US) [02450357] **885**

SAM-CD : SCIENTIFIC AMERICAN MEDICINE ON CD-ROM (US) **3638**

SAM FOCUS ON MANAGEMENT (US) **885**

SAM HOUSTON STATE UNIVERSITY. CRIMINAL JUSTICE CENTER. INTERAGENCY WORKSHOP See PROCEEDINGS OF THE INTERAGENCY WORKSHOP **3173**

SAM HOUSTON STATE UNIVERSITY. CRIMINAL JUSTICE CENTER. SURVEY RESEARCH PROGRAM See TEXAS CRIME POLL **3177**

SAM HOUSTON STATE UNIVERSITY. NATIONAL EMPLOYMENT LISTING SERVICE FOR THE CRIMINAL JUSTICE SYSTEM See NATIONAL EMPLOYMENT LISTING SERVICE FOR THE CRIMINAL JUSTICE SYSTEM. SPECIAL EDITION: EDUCATIONAL OPPORTUNITIES **4206**

SAM KINCH'S TEXAS WEEKLY (US/0890-5924) [12761107] **5754**

SAM NA SAM (PL/0867-4310) [l08674310] **4865**

SAM NAGAGAMA'S ECONOMIC PERSPECTIVES (US/1071-0450) [28565214] **1519**

SAM. SUBSTANCE ABUSE MONTHLY (AT/0814-2025) [l08142025] **1348**

SAMAB SUSPENDED. (SA/0370-8314) [02243875] **4096**

SAMACARA (KE) [08487170] **2500**

SAMADARSI (II) [11349380] **3433**

SAMAKALINA BHARATIYA SAHITYA (II) [08619502] **3433**

SAMAKALINA TISARI DUNIYA (II) [08352693] **2628**

SAMARU: JOURNAL OF AGRICULTURE RESEARCH (NR/0331-7285) [09835017] **131**

SAMATALA (II) [10510621] **2663**

SAMAVETA SVARA (II) [01784166] **3433**

SAMBAHAYAN (PH) **2835**

SAMBIA : ENERGIEWIRTSCHAFT (GW) [05209208] **1625**

SAMBIA, WIRTSCHAFTSDATEN UND WIRTSCHAFTSDOKUMENTATION / BUNDESSTELLE FUER AUSSENHANDELSINFORMATION (GW) [11085692] **1583**

SAMBODA (NP) [25536919] **5022**

SAMBODHANA (II) [06467976] **3433**

SAMBODHI (II) [01790478] **4360**

SAME-DAY SURGERY (US/0190-5066) [04694012] **3974**

SAMFERDSEL (1979) (NO/0332-8988) [10682575] **5392**

SAMFERDSEL TRANSPORT (NO/0036-3774) [01914559] **5392**

SAMHALLSVETENSKAPLIGA STUDIER (SW) [01715218] **5217**

●SAMHSA NEWS / SUBSTANCE ABUSE AND MENTAL HEALTH SERVICES ADMINISTRATION (US) [27703026] **1349**

SAMID (LE) [05974738] **4534**

SAMIKSA (II/0304-5110) [02267432] **4617**

SAMIKSHA (II) [01774443] **3433**

SAMIR HUSNI'S GUIDE TO NEW MAGAZINES See SAMIR HUSNI'S GUIDE TO THE NEW CONSUMER MAGAZINES PUBLISHED IN ... **1299**

●SAMIR HUSNI'S GUIDE TO THE NEW CONSUMER MAGAZINES PUBLISHED IN ... (US) [27856378] **1299**

SAMISDAT (US/0226-840X) [06468498] **3352**

SAMJ. SOUTH AFRICAN MEDICAL JOURNAL (SA/0256-9574) [l02569574] **3638**

SAML: SOUTH-EAST ASIA MINING LETTER (UK) **2150**

SAMLAREN (UPPSALA) (SW/0348-6133) [01623854] **3433**

SAMLING AF ARSBERETNINGER FRA INSTITUTTERNE VED DEN POLYTEKNISKE LREANSTALT, DANMARKS TEKNISKE HJSKOLE I PERIODEN . See ARSBERETNINGER FRA AFDELINGER, INSTITUTTER OG LABORATORIER VED DEN POLYTEKNISKE LREANSTALT, DANMARKS TEKNISKE HJSKOLE GLDENDE FOR PERIODEN FRA ... / DEN POLYTEKNISKE LREANSTALT, DANMARKS TEKNISKE HJSKOLE **1875**

SAMMAMISH VALLEY NEWS (US) [13407871] **5762**

SAMMANFATTNING AV ARTIKLARNA (FI/0355-0656) [02395854] 4878, **4916**

SAMMELBANDE DER ROBERT-SCHUMANN-GESELLSCHAFT (GE/0557-1634) [01713714] 434, **4151**

SAMMELBANDE ZUR MUSIKGESCHICHTE DER DEUTSCHEN DEMOKRATISCHEN REPUBLIK (GE) [02067890] **4151**

SAMMLUNG DER EIDGENOSSISCHEN GESETZE (SZ) [01767022] **3045**

SAMMLUNG GELTENDER STAATSANGEHARIGKEITSGESETZE (GW/0080-5823) [01604933] **3045**

SAMMLUNG GEOGRAPHISCHER FUHRER (GW/0344-6565) [06873959] **2575**

SAMMLUNG GEOLOGISCHER FUHRER (GW/0343-737X) [06417942] **1396**

SAMMLUNG METZLER (GW/0558-3667) [06415799] **3433**

SAMMLUNG PROFILE (GW) [16132969] 3433, **434**

SAMNA WARQ (US/0891-9119) [15029265] **2643**

SAMOA NEWS (AS) [13415768] **5777**

SAMOSTIINA UKRAINA (US/0036-3847) [04702171] **2272**

SAMOUPRAVLJANJE (BELGRADE, SERBIA) (YU/0350-2546) [02017350] **885**

SAMOUPRAVLJANJE U BANKAMA I ZAJEDNICAMA OSIGURANJA (YU) [08237024] 810, **733**

SAMOUPRAVLJANJE U PRIVREDI (YU) [01789035] 1709, **1538**

SAMOUPRAVLJANJE U USTANOVAMA DRUSTVENIH SLUZBI (YU) [01795720] **5338**

SAMOUPRAVNE INTERESNE ZAJEDNICE (YU) [02241762] **5227**

SAMP CATALOG : SUPPLEMENT (US/0271-7603) [04324272] **3247**

SAMPAN (US/0738-4467) [09407395] **4684**

SAMPE JOURNAL (US/0091-1062) [01786354] **1995**

SAMPLE CASE, THE (US/0036-3898) [03918939] **709**

SAMPLE SURVEYS OF CURRENT INTEREST (US) [01607535] **5338**

SAMPLER & ANTIQUE NEEDLEWORK QUARTERLY CEASED. (US/1061-6756) [24159290] **375**

SAMPLINGS (CN/0711-1827) [08569893] **3433**

SAMPSON INDEPENDENT, THE (US) [13264721] **5724**

SAMRIG (ORGANIZATION : BRAZIL) See RELATORIO DA DIRETORIA / SAMRIG **1624**

SAMS AUTO RADIO SERVICE DATA (US/0163-3627) [04343577] **2080**

SAMS PHOTOFACT CB RADIO SERIES (US/0581-4693) [01586947] **1138**

SAMS PHOTOFACT TAPE RECORDER SERIES See SAMS TAPE RECORDER SERVICE DATA **5318**

SAMS TAPE RECORDER SERVICE DATA (US/0162-2447) [04106488] **5318**

SAMS TRANSISTOR RADIO (US) [01783659] **5149**

SAMS VIDEOCASSETTE RECORDER SERVICE DATA (US) [08721361] **5318**

SAMSAM (NE) [04323164] **2912**

SAMSKRTA-RATNAKARAH (II) [02240219] **2508**

SAMSKRTA SAHITYA PARISHAT (II) [01696345] **3319**

SAMSKRTAPRATIBHA (II/0558-3764) [01774445] 3433, **3319**

SAMSKRTASAKETAH (AT) [01784290] **2508**

SAMSKRTAVIMARSAH (II) [01797690] **3319**

SAMSON PERSONAL COMPUTER (BE) **1290**

SAMSUN SANAYI REHBERI (TU) [20677675] **709**

SAMTIDEN (NO/0036-3928) [01764959] **2522**

SAMUEL BUTLER NEWSLETTER, THE SUSPENDED. (US/0278-7350) [07870571] **3433**

SAMUEL FRENCH, INC See SAMUEL FRENCH'S BASIC CATALOGUE OF PLAYS **424**

SAMUEL FRENCH'S BASIC CATALOGUE OF PLAYS (US/0361-6495) [01971317] **424**

SAMUEL H. KRESS FOUNDATION *See* ANNUAL REPORT - SAMUEL H. KRESS FOUNDATION **5273**

SAMUEL SCHEIDT WERKE (GW) **4151**

SAMYA SHAKTI : A JOURNAL OF WOMEN'S STUDIES (II/0970-5880) [10176291] **5566**

SAMYANG SABO (KO) [10318650] **1625**

SAN (US/0049-1152) [01943814] **2783**

SAN ANGELO STANDARD-TIMES (US) [14363271] **5754**

SAN ANTONIO (US/0899-5826) [18098176] **2544**

SAN ANTONIO BUSINESS JOURNAL (US/0895-1551) [15172788] **709**

SAN ANTONIO EXECUTIVE (US) **709**

SAN ANTONIO EXPRESS-NEWS (US/1065-7908) [26736280] **5754**

SAN ANTONIO LIGHT (SAN ANTONIO, TEX.: 1911) *CEASED.* (US) [12225885] **5754**

SAN ANTONIO PERSPECTIVE (US/0895-6898) [16744735] **1519**

SAN AUGUSTINE TRIBUNE (US) [14758733] **5754**

SAN BERNARDINO COUNTY SUN, THE (US) [20396165] **5639**

SAN BERNARDINO, RIVERSIDE COUNTIES STREET ATLAS AND DIRECTORY (ZIP CODE ED.) (US/0883-0118) [11899341] **2575**

SAN BERNARDINO STREET ATLAS. ZIP CODE EDITION (US/0733-2297) [08545391] **1147**

SAN DIEGO BULLETIN *See* SAN DIEGO ECONOMIC BULLETIN **1519**

SAN DIEGO BUSINESS JOURNAL (US/8750-6890) [09871886] **709**

SAN DIEGO COMMERCE (US/1063-5513) [26059016] 4847, **850**

SAN DIEGO CONSUMER'S VOICE (US/0276-4601) [07363857] **1299**

SAN DIEGO COUNTY BUSINESS DIRECTORY (US/1047-9619) [20832027] **709**

SAN DIEGO COUNTY, CALIFORNIA. DEPARTMENT OF EDUCATION *See* EDUCATION SAN DIEGO COUNTY **1740**

SAN DIEGO COUNTY DIRECTORY OF MANUFACTURERS AND INDUSTRIAL DISTRIBUTORS (US/0273-3447) [07037873] 3487, **1625**

SAN DIEGO DAILY TRANSCRIPT (US) **5639**

SAN DIEGO DAILY TRANSCRIPT (US) **5639**

SAN DIEGO ECONOMIC BULLETIN (US/1068-7319) [12060974] **1519**

SAN DIEGO EXECUTIVE (US/1067-6384) [27316232] **709**

SAN DIEGO HOME / GARDEN (US) [06346713] 2430, **2792**

● SAN DIEGO HOME/GARDEN LIFESTYLES (US/1073-6891) [29513674] 2430, **2792**

● SAN DIEGO JUSTICE JOURNAL (US/1073-676X) [28172800] **3046**

SAN DIEGO LAW REVIEW, THE (US/0036-4037) [01716838] **3046**

SAN DIEGO LEAVES & SAPLINGS (US/0740-4417) [08905420] **2471**

SAN DIEGO LOG (US/0193-3183) [05173752] **2544**

SAN DIEGO MAGAZINE (1949) (US/0036-4045) [03249973] **2544**

SAN DIEGO MAGAZINE (1968) (US/0734-6727) [08683108] **2545**

SAN DIEGO MUSEUM PAPERS (US) [04634259] 282, **245**

SAN DIEGO PHYSICIAN (US) [07622568] **3638**

SAN DIEGO SOUND POST, THE (US/0036-407X) [04732449] **4151**

SAN DIEGO SOURCE BOOK (US/0196-8564) [05913878] **5236**

SAN DIEGO SPORTS DIGEST (US/0193-7332) [05241986] **4916**

SAN DIEGO TRIBUNE (US) [21351098] **5639**

SAN DIEGO UNION AND DAILY BEE *See* SAN DIEGO UNION (SAN DIEGO, CALIF. : 1930) **5639**

SAN DIEGO UNION (SAN DIEGO, CALIF.: 1930) *See* SAN DIEGO UNION-TRIBUNE (1992) **5639**

SAN DIEGO UNION (SAN DIEGO, CALIF. : 1930) (US) [13155544] **5639**

● SAN DIEGO UNION-TRIBUNE (1992) (US/1063-102X) [25257675] **5639**

SAN DIEGO WRITERS MONTHLY (US/1054-6774) [22937439] 3433, **2924**

SAN DIMAS PRESS, THE (US) [15624051] **5639**

SAN FERNANDO POETRY JOURNAL (US/0196-2884) [05789506] **3470**

SAN FERNANDO VALLEY APARTMENT OWNER BUILDER (US/0192-1738) [05120317] **2835**

SAN FERNANDO VALLEY SUN (US) **5639**

SAN FRANCISCO ATTORNEY, THE (US/0744-9348) [08440635] **3046**

SAN FRANCISCO BARRISTER (US/0744-3072) [08178031] **3046**

SAN FRANCISCO BAY ARCHITECTS' REVIEW *CEASED.* (US/0748-3899) [10062422] **308**

SAN FRANCISCO BAY AREA JOB BANK (US) [18978671] **4209**

SAN FRANCISCO/BAY AREA POWER BOOK, THE (US/1040-113X) [18328863] **2759**

SAN FRANCISCO BAY GUARDIAN, THE (US/0036-4096) [01775414] **2545**

SAN FRANCISCO BAY TIMES (US) **5639**

SAN FRANCISCO BUSINESS *CEASED.* (US/0036-410X) [03919073] **709**

SAN FRANCISCO BUSINESS TIMES (US/0890-0337) [14122657] **709**

SAN FRANCISCO CHRONICLE (US) [08812614] **5639**

SAN FRANCISCO CHRONICLE INDEX (US/0893-2425) [15502397] **5814**

SAN FRANCISCO DAILY JOURNAL (1990) (US/1059-2636) [22620370] **3046**

SAN FRANCISCO EXAMINER, THE (US) [01764973] **5639**

SAN FRANCISCO FOCUS (US/0274-5933) [06441561] **2545**

SAN FRANCISCO JOURNAL. CHINESE EDITION, THE *CEASED.* (US/0199-462X) [05910056] **5639**

SAN FRANCISCO JOURNAL, THE (US) [05073028] **5639**

SAN FRANCISCO JUNG INSTITUTE LIBRARY JOURNAL, THE (US/0270-6210) [06459370] **4617**

SAN FRANCISCO KEEPER'S VOICE, THE (US/0581-5029) [03441041] **2545**

SAN FRANCISCO MEDICINE (US/0361-705X) [02104951] **3638**

SAN FRANCISCO. MUNICIPAL COURT *See* REPORT OF THE MUNICIPAL COURT (SAN FRANCISCO) **3142**

SAN FRANCISCO OPERA (US/0892-7189) [15301396] **4151**

SAN FRANCISCO PERFORMING ARTS LIBRARY AND MUSEUM JOURNAL *See* SAN FRANCISCO PERFORMING ARTS LIBRARY AND MUSEUM SERIES **388**

● SAN FRANCISCO PERFORMING ARTS LIBRARY AND MUSEUM SERIES (US/1060-6858) [25052289] **388**

SAN FRANCISCO PLANNING AND URBAN RENEWAL ASSOCIATION *See* SPUR REPORT **2836**

SAN FRANCISCO POST (US) [10546260] **5639**

SAN FRANCISCO PROGRESS, THE *CEASED.* (US/0191-8192) [05265935] **5639**

SAN FRANCISCO REVIEW OF BOOKS (US/0194-0724) [04163281] **330**

SAN FRANCISCO SENTINEL (US) [26102329] 2796, **5639**

SAN FRANCISCO SYMPHONY MAGAZINE (US) [03758075] **4151**

SAN FRANCISCO THEATRE (US/0146-9576) [03535580] **5368**

SAN FRANCISCO WHOLESALE ORNAMENTAL CROPS REPORT (US/0273-6004) [07464916] **2430**

SAN GABRIEL VALLEY DAILY TRIBUNE (US/8755-9595) [09292694] **5639**

SAN JACINTO VALLEY REGISTER *CEASED.* (US) **5639**

SAN JOAQUIN AGRICULTURAL LAW REVIEW (US/1055-422X) [23169389] 131, **3046**

SAN JOAQUIN VALLEY POST-PROJECT ECONOMIC IMPACT / DEPARTMENT OF WATER RESOURCES, SAN JOAQUIN DISTRICT (US) [08379400] **2095**

SAN JOSE MERCURY NEWS (US/0747-2099) [10553708] **5639**

SAN JOSE POST-RECORD, THE (US/0036-4185) [03919141] **5640**

SAN JOSE STUDIES (US/0097-8051) [01799416] 330, **2854**

SAN JUAN RECORD (1953), THE (US/0894-3273) [13979339] **5757**

SAN JUAN STAR, THE (PR/8750-6122) [02267443] **5808**

SAN LUIS OBISPO COUNTY GENEALOGICAL SOCIETY, INC (US/1047-5893) [18516130] **2471**

SAN LUIS OBISPO COUNTY GENEALOGICAL SOCIETY, INC *See* BULLETIN (CALIFORNIA CENTRAL COAST GENEALOGICAL SOCIETY : 1993) **2440**

SAN LUIS OBISPO COUNTY TELEGRAM-TRIBUNE (US) **5640**

SAN MARCOS COURIER (US/0273-9259) [07039842] **5640**

SAN MARCOS NEWS (US/0746-8156) [10304620] **5754**

SAN MARCOS NEWS REPORTER (US) **5640**

SAN MARCOS OUTLOOK *See* SAN MARCOS NEWS REPORTER **5640**

SAN MARCOS RECORD, THE (US) [14396425] **5754**

SAN MATEO COUNTY COMMERCE & INDUSTRY DIRECTORY (US/1060-7951) [21814940] **1625**

SAN PATRICIO COUNTY NEWS (US) [14154752] **5754**

SAN SABA NEWS AND STAR, THE (US) [14874900] **5754**

SAN WEN (CC) [06807228] **3433**

SAN WEN HSUAN (CH) [10706238] **3433**

SANA UPDATE NEWSLETTER (AT/0811-2711) [I08112711] **4056**

SANANJALKA (FI/0558-4639) [01917496] **3319**

SANARE INFIRMOS (IT) **3638**

SANAVI TALIM (PK) [11645910] **1781**

SANAVIK COOPERATIVE *See* SANAVIK COOPERATIVE BAKER LAKE PRINTS **382**

SANAVIK COOPERATIVE BAKER LAKE PRINTS (CN/0319-5465) [02443106] **382**

SANBORN MANHATTAN LAND BOOK OF THE CITY OF NEW YORK (US/0362-3106) [02081683] **2575**

SANBORN PIONEER, THE (US) [16261875] **5672**

SANCARA MANTRALAYA KI ANUDANOM KI MANGEM (II) [01784101] **1121**

SANCTUAIRE DE NOTRE-DAME DE LOURDES, RIGAUD, QUEBEC *See* VOIX DU SANCTUAIRE **5008**

SANCTUARY ASIA (II) [08418374] 5597, **2204**

SANCTUARY (DENVER, COLO.) (US/1061-2165) [25217772] **5036**

SANCTUARY (LINCOLN, MASS.) (US/0272-8966) [06809373] 2204, **4171**

SAND CASTLES (US) [03441166] **3470**

SAND GEORGES 1804-1876 CORRESPONDANCE (FR) **3433**

SAND MOUNTAIN REPORTER (US/0890-1724) [13507950] **5628**

SAND PATTERNS (CN/0316-5167) [02247434] **3433**

SAND SPRINGS LEADER (US) [13663999] **5732**

SANDALION (IT) [05262412] **2628**

SANDARA (US/8750-2348) [09493846] **5662**

SANDARBHA (NP) [06693919] **2663**

SANDE MAINICHI (JA) [17597567] **131**

SANDERS COUNTY LEDGER (THOMPSON FALLS, MONT. : 1959) (US) [14056635] **5706**

SANDERSON TIMES (US) [08565067] **5754**

SANDERSVILLE PROGRESS, THE (US/0747-3710) [10788611] **5655**

SANDESH (WINNIPEG) (CN/0380-2949) [02940859] **2272**

SANDGROUSE (UK/0260-4736) [07500311] **5620**

SANDHILL CITIZEN AND NEWS OUTLOOK *See* CITIZEN NEWS-RECORD (COUNTY ED.), THE **5723**

● SANDHILLS REVIEW, THE (US/1061-3579) [25264237] **3433**

SANDHILLS/ST. ANDREWS REVIEW *See* SANDHILLS REVIEW, THE **3433**

SANDIA LABORATORIES *See* SANDIA TECHNOLOGY **5149**

SANDIA SCIENCE NEWS (US/0276-3672) [05044372] **5149**

SANDIA TECHNOLOGY (US/0734-5879) [05916847] **5149**

SANDLAPPER (1990) (US/1046-3267) [20379166] **2628**

SANDMAN, THE (US) [13784956] **4865**

SANDPOINT DAILY BEE (US) **5657**

S&P'S HIGH YIELD QUARTERLY (US/1049-3263) [20771283] **913**

SANDRA : TOLLE STRICKMODE (GW) 1087, **5185**

SANDS AND CORAL (PH) [02017222] **3433**

SANDUSKY REGISTER (SANDUSKY, OHIO : 1957) (US) [16632152] **5730**

SANDY PARKER REPORTS (US/1064-0029) [26187811] **3185**

SANDY — Alphabetical Title Index

SANDY PARKER'S FUR WORLD (US/0747-3753) [10787894] **3185**

SANDY SPRINGS NEIGHBOR, THE (US/0192-0715) [05010535] **5655**

SANEFREEZE NEWS / CAMPAIGN FOR GLOBAL SECURITY (US/0036-4304) [22758334] **4056**

SANFORD EVANS GOLD BOOK OF MOTORCYCLE DATA AND USED PRICES (CN/0705-1840) [03991821] **4083**

SANFORD EVANS GOLD BOOK OF OUTBOARD MOTOR DATA AND USED PRICES (CN/0705-2065) [03991823] **596**

SANFORD EVANS GOLD BOOK OF SNOWMOBILE DATA AND USED PRICES *See* SANFORD EVANS GOLD BOOK, OFFICIAL SNOWMOBILE DATA AND USED PRICES **5392**

SANFORD EVANS GOLD BOOK OF USED CAR PRICES (CN/0381-8179) [02154939] **5425**

●SANFORD EVANS GOLD BOOK, OFFICIAL SNOWMOBILE DATA AND USED PRICES (CN/1187-4562) [25796385] **4854, 5392**

SANFORD HERALD (SANFORD, FLA.) (US/0893-3642) [15512259] **5651**

SANFUJINKA CHIRYO (JA/0558-471X) [10412069] **3768**

SANFUJINKA NO SEKAI (JA/0386-9873) [10412100] **3768**

SANG-I MIL (PK) [02300028] **2324**

SANG-LIENS (CN/1184-0188) [23230616] **5306**

SANG, THROMBOSE, VAISSEAUX : STV (FR/0999-7385) [26585610] **3774, 3710**

SANGAKU SHASHIN NENKAN (JA) [01797269] **4376**

SANGAT (II) [02240271] **2508**

SANGAT (PK) [02239404] **4685**

SANGEET NATAK (II/0036-4339) [01605157] **4152**

SANGER HERALD (US) [27878817] **5640**

SANGIIN GIIN SENKYO NO KIROKU (JA) [05218505] **4685**

SANGKAKALA PERADILAN (IO) [01792956] **3046**

SANGO (BRONX) (US/0092-9719) [01791314] **2759**

SANGYO ANZEN KENKYUJO TOKUBETSU KENKYU HOKOKU (JA) [08349861] **2870**

SANGYO GIJUTSU SOGO KENKYUJO HOKOKU (JA/0914-854X) [19580397] **5149**

SANGYO IGAKU (JA/0047-1879) [07609479] **2870**

SANGYO IGAKU JANARU (JA/0388-337X) [10388603] **2870**

SANGYO IGAKU SOGO KENKYUJO NEMPO (JA) [04381146] **2870**

SANGYO KEIEI (JA) [06601947] **1626**

SANGYO KOGAI BOSHI NO GIJUTSU (JA) [02245335] **2242**

SANGYO KOZO NO CHOKI BIJON (JA) [02245423] **4685, 1626**

SANGYO KOZO SHINGIKAI (JAPAN) *See* SANGYO KOZO NO CHOKI BIJON **1626**

SANGYO SEMINA (JA) [07934644] **1583**

SANGYO SHARYO *CEASED.* (JA) [02247055] **5392**

SANGYO TO KANKYO (JN/0285-5380) [07310689] **2181, 2242**

SANGYO TO KYOIKU (JA) [06940184] **1781**

SANHAK HYOPTONG NONCHONG (KO) [08058315] **1904**

SAN'IN CHIIKI KENKYU (JA/0911-615X) [I0911615X] **2394**

SAN'IN CHIIKI KENKYU. SHIRO-HEN (JA/0911-6168) [I09116168] **2394**

SANITA PUBBLICA (IT/0393-4101) [16806678] **4685**

SANITA SCIENZA E STORIA *CEASED.* (IT) **5149**

SANITAR UND HEIZUNGSTECHNIK (GW/0036-4401) [07402924] **2608**

SANITARY ENGINEERING PAPERS (US/0069-6129) [01541524] **2242**

SANITARY LANDFILLS (US/0190-7670) [04705761] **2185**

SANITARY MAINTENANCE (US/0036-4436) [05069724] **2242**

SANJONG YON'GU (KO) [04277533] **1583**

SANKALANA (II) [11803063] **3433**

SANKAYA PATRIKA (II) [11195043] **4995**

SANKEN GIHO (JA/0285-9815) [27410992] **5149**

SANKHYA. SERIES A (II/0581-572X) [01606529] **5338**

SANKHYA. SERIES B (II/0581-5738) [01764992] **5338**

SANKHYIKIYA PUSTIKA (II) [05033802] **1519, 1538**

SANKOFA JOURNAL : THE AUTHENTIC VOICE OF THE TRADITIONAL HEALERS OF AFRICA (US/1060-5703) [25036526] **4329**

SANKT PETERBURGSKAIA PANORAMA (RU) [25492282] **627, 308**

SANKT-PETERBURGSKIE VEDOMOSTI (RU) [24980263] **5809**

SANKYO KENKYUJO NENPO (JA/0080-6064) [09769854] **5149**

SANNEB MISAINMURHAG HOIJI (KO/0257-2389) [08897511] **3638**

SANOP DIJAIN (KO) [10331088] **2099**

SANOP KISUL (KO) [04538624] **5149**

SANOP, KISUL TONGHYANG (KO) [11411814] **5149**

SANOP KISUL YON'GUSO NONMUNJIP (KO) [04691810] **1995**

SANOP KWAHAK KISUL YONGUSO NONMUNJIP (KO) [12960965] **5149**

SANOP KYONGJE YONGU (KO) [04360519] **1626**

SANOP MUNJE NONJIP (KO) [05927179] **885**

SANOP SAENGSAN YONBO *CEASED.* (KO) [04687662] **1626**

SANOP YONGU INDUSTRIAL STUDIES (KO) [12225319] **1626**

SANOP YONGWANPYO CHAKSONG POGO (KO) [10352890] **1583**

SANS FRONTIERES :LES FORCES PSYCHOLOGIQUES (CN) [16349391] **4617**

●SANSEVIERIA JOURNAL, THE (US/1062-8908) [25793733] **2430**

SANSHAIN KEIKAKU NYUSU (JA) [04601220] **2128**

SANSHI SHIKENJO NEMPO (JA) [02512531] **5597**

SANSON SHINKO KONSARUTANTO IKENSHO SORAN (JA) [01797103] **131**

SANT PAU (SP/0211-0873) [19169850] **3638**

SANTA BARBARA HISTORICAL SOCIETY *See* NOTICIAS - SANTA BARBARA HISTORICAL SOCIETY **2751**

SANTA BARBARA MAGAZINE (US/0744-5199) [07904406] **2545**

SANTA BARBARA MUSEUM OF ART *See* BIENNIAL REPORT / SANTA BARBARA MUSEUM OF ART **4084**

SANTA BARBARA MUSEUM OF ART NEWSLETTER (US) **4096**

SANTA BARBARA NEWS & REVIEW (MICROFICHE) (US/02935726) **5640**

SANTA BARBARA NEWS-PRESS (1932) (US) [08769683] **5640**

●SANTA BARBARA REVIEW (US/1068-8617) [27829521] **3433**

SANTA BARBARA SENIOR WORLD, THE (US/0276-0800) [07297265] **5181**

SANTA CATARINA, BRAZIL. MINISTERIO PUBLICO. ASSOCIACAO CATARINENSE DO MINISTERIO PUBLICO *See* INFORMATIVO - ASSOCIACAO CATARINENSE DO MINISTERIO PUBLICO **2982**

SANTA CATARINA, BRAZIL. SECRETARIA DA SAUDE *See* RECURSOS HUMANOS **3917**

SANTA CATARINA (BRAZIL : STATE). GOVERNOR *See* PRESTACAO DE CONTAS **4741**

SANTA CATARINA (BRAZIL : STATE). TRIBUNAL DE JUSTICA *See* JURISPRUDENCIA CATARINENSE **2991**

SANTA CLARA COMPUTER AND HIGH-TECHNOLOGY LAW JOURNAL (US/0882-3383) [11765510] **1202, 3046**

SANTA CLARA COUNTY CONNECTIONS (US/0895-6103) [16716875] **2471**

SANTA CLARA COUNTY POPULAR STREET ATLAS (ZIP CODE ED.) (US/0733-740X) [08652604] **2575**

SANTA CLARA LAW REVIEW (US/0146-0315) [02842601] **3046**

SANTA CLAUS (US) [24570772] **5185, 375**

SANTA CRUZ SENTINEL (SANTA CRUZ, CALIF. : DAILY) (US) [10317299] **5640**

SANTA FE INSTITUTE STUDIES IN THE SCIENCES OF COMPLEXITY. LECTURES (US) [20778878] **5149**

SANTA FE LITERARY REVIEW (US/1055-8446) [23359142] **3352**

SANTA FE NEW MEXICAN, THE (US) [26180871] **5713**

SANTA FE REPORTER, THE (US/0744-477X) [07618579] **5713**

SANTA FE ROUTE, THE (US/0738-9892) [09674265] **5436**

SANTA FEAN MAGAZINE (SANTA FE, N.M.) (US/1046-2708) [08176091] **2545**

SANTA GERTRUDIS ANNUAL *CEASED.* (AT) [03495006] **221**

SANTA GERTRUDIS JOURNAL, THE (US/0036-455X) [02420430] **221**

SANTA GERTRUDIS TRIBUNE (US/8750-3743) [11349408] **221**

SANTA MARIA, BRAZIL (RIO GRANDE DO SUL). UNIVERSIDADE FEDERAL. CENTRO DE CIENCIAS RURAIS *See* REVISTA DO CENTRO DE CIENCIAS RURAIS **129**

SANTA MARIA TIMES (US/0745-6166) [09399346] **5640**

SANTA MONICA REVIEW : SMR (US/0899-9848) [18282989] **3433**

SANTA PAULA CHRONICLE *CEASED.* (US) [13115456] **5640**

SANTA ROSA FREE PRESS (US/0273-5857) [07082433] **5651**

SANTA ROSA NEWS (1987) (US/0894-783X) [16238282] **5713**

SANTA ROSA REPUBLICAN (SANTA ROSA, CALIF. : DAILY) *See* PRESS DEMOCRAT (SANTA ROSA, CALIF.) **5638**

SANTA SANDESA (II) [02240237] **4995**

SANTAJIWA (MY/0586-9412) [02732733] **2508**

SANTE (CN/0832-6770) [20665768] **2601, 5566**

SANTE 2000 MEDECINE (FR/0293-5945) [09483581] **3638**

SANTE CULTURE (CN/0833-8590) [15241405] **245**

SANTE CULTURE (CN/0833-8590) [15264471] **3936**

SANTE DE L'ECOLIER (FR) **4801**

SANTE DE L'ECOLIER (FR) 3739, **4617**

SANTE DE L'HOMME, LA (FR) [08580435] **4801**

SANTE DU MONDE (SZ/0250-9326) [I02509326] **4801**

SANTE ET SPORTS (FR) **4916**

SANTE MAGAZINE (FR/0397-0329) [I03970329] **4801**

SANTE MENTALE AU CANADA (CN/0707-2910) [05072486] **4801**

SANTE MENTALE AU QUEBEC (CN/0383-6320) [03248244] **3936**

SANTE PUBLIQUE, LA (RM/0048-9107) [02457977] **4801**

SANTE QUEBEC : REVUE DE LA CORPORATION PROFESSIONNELLE DES INFIRMIERES ET INFIRMIERS AUXILIAIRES DU QUEBEC (CN/1180-3983) [23238095] **3869**

SANTE SOCIETE *CEASED.* (CN/0832-8048) [17863915] **5306**

SANTIAGO (CU/0048-9115) [02267452] **3433**

SANTIAGO DE CHILE. INSTITUTO FORESTAL *See* MANUAL - INSTITUTO FORESTAL, CHILE **2387**

SANTIAGO DEL ESTERO, ARGENTINE REPUBLIC (PROVINCE). DIRECCION GENERAL DE INVESTIGACIONES, ESTADISTICA Y CENSOS. DIVISION ECONOMICOS Y FINANCIEROS *See* FLUCTUACIONES MONETARIAS; METODO GENERAL DE ACTUALIZACION **1561**

SANTO DOMINGO NEWS (DR) [05097008] **5799**

SANTO, IL (IT/0391-7819) [01918915] **364, 4995**

SANTO TOMAS JOURNAL OF MEDICINE (PH/0371-3520) [01643353] **3638**

SANYO DENKI KABUSHIKI KAISHA *See* ANNUAL REPORT ... FOR THE YEAR ENDED NOVEMBER 30 ... / SANYO DENKI KABUSHIKI KAISHA **2035**

SAO PAULO, BRAZIL (CITY). INSTITUTO ADOLFO LUTZ *See* REVISTA DO INSTITUTO ADOLFO LUTZ **4800**

SAO PAULO, BRAZIL (CITY). UNIVERSIDADE. FACULDADE DE FARMACIA E BIOQUIMICA. REVISTA *See* REVISTA DE FARMACIA E BIOQUIMICA DA UNIVERSIDADE DE SAO PAULO **4328**

SAO PAULO, BRAZIL (CITY). UNIVERSIDADE. INSTITUTO DE GEOGRAFIA *See* CLIMATOLOGIA (SAO PAULO, BRAZIL) **1422**

SAO PAULO (BRAZIL). SECRETARIA DAS FINANCAS *See* FINANCAS PUBLICAS MUNICIPAIS **4724**

SAO PAULO (BRAZIL). SECRETARIA MUNICIPAL DA ADMINISTRACAO *See* BOLETIM INFORMATIVO **4633**

SAO PAULO, BRAZIL (STATE) *See* DIARIO OFICIAL, ESTADO DE SAO PAULO: DIARIO DA JUSTICA **2960**

SAO PAULO, BRAZIL (STATE) *See* DIARIO OFICIAL, ESTADO DE SAO PAULO : INEDITORIAIS **2960**

Alphabetical Title Index — SASKATCHEWAN

SAO PAULO (BRAZIL : STATE). FUNDACAO SISTEMA ESTADUAL DE ANALISE DE DADOS See PERFIL MUNICIPAL **5336**

SAO PAULO (BRAZIL : STATE). IMPRENSA OFICIAL DO ESTADO See DIARIO OFICIAL, ESTADO DE SAO PAULO. PODER JUDICIARIO **2960**

SAO PAULO (BRAZIL : STATE). PROCURADORIA DE ASSISTENCIA JURIDICA AOS MINICIPIOS MUNICIPIOS See MUNICIPIO PAULISTA : ASPECTOS JURIDICOS **3102**

SAO PAULO, BRAZIL (STATE). PROCURADORIA GERAL See REVISTA DA PROCURADORIA GERAL DO ESTADO DE SAO PAULO **3040**

SAO PAULO (BRAZIL : STATE). PROCURADORIA GERAL DO ESTADO. CENTRO DE ESTUDOS See BOLETIM - CENTRO DE ESTUDOS, PROCURADORIA GERAL DO ESTADO **2942**

SAO PAULO, BRAZIL (STATE). SECRETARIA DA AGRICULTURA. COORDENADORIA DE ASSISTENCIA TECNICA INTEGRAL See BOLETIM TECNICO - COORDENDORIA DE ASSISTENCIA TECNICA INTEGRAL **67**

SAO PAULO (BRAZIL : STATE). SECRETARIA DA PROMOCAO SOCIAL. SOCIAL See RELATORIO SETORIAL, GOVERNO DO ESTADO DE SAO PAULO **5304**

SAO PAULO (BRAZIL : STATE). SECRETARIA DE ECONOMIA E PLANEJAMENTO See ORCAMENTO PROGRAMA DE ... / GOVERNO DO ESTADO DE SAO PAULO, SECRETARIA DE ECONOMIA E PLANEJAMENTO **4739**

SAO PAULO, BRAZIL (STATE). TRIBUNAL DE CONTAS See REVISTA DO TRIBUNAL DE CONTAS DO ESTADO DE SAO PAULO: JURISPRUDENCIA E INSTRUCOES **4747**

SAO PAULO (BRAZIL : STATE). TRIBUNAL DE IMPOSTOS E TAXAS See EMENTARIO DO TIT **2965**

SAO PAULO YEAR BOOK (BL) [08375072] **850**

SAO TOME AND PRINCIPE See DIARIO DA REPUBLICA **2960**

SAO TOME E PRINCIPE. REPARTICAO PROVINCIAL DOS SERVICOS DE ESTATISTICA See BOLETIM TRIMESTRAL DE ESTATISTICA - INSTITUTO NACIONAL DE ESTATISTICA. DELEGACAO SE S. TOME E PRINCIPE **5323**

SAOBRACAJ I VEZE (YU) [01785881] **5338**

SAOBRACAJNE NEZGODE NA PUTEVIMA (YU) [06800552] **5402**

SAOPSTENJA - REPUBLICKI ZAVOD ZA ZASTITU SPOMENIKA KULTURE SR SRBIJE (YU/0409-008X) [03324455] **2708, 308**

SAOTHAR (IE/0332-1169) [06470111] **1709**

SAP, SPECTRA OF ANTHROPOLOGICAL PROGRESS (II) [06696872] **245**

SAPERE (IT/0036-4681) [I00364681] **5149**

SAPEUR-POMPIER, LE (FR/0036-469X) [I0036469X] **2292**

SAPIENTIA (AG/0036-4703) [01914988] **4360**

SAPIENZA (IT/0036-4711) [01779344] **4995, 4360**

SAPPORO IGAKU ZASSHI (JA/0036-472X) [06437404] **3638**

SAPPORO IKA DAIGAKU JINBUN SHIZEN KAGAKU KIYO (JA/0389-3944) [10327913] 1094, **3638**

SAPPORO, JAPAN. HOKKAIDO UNIVERSITY. FACULTY OF AGRICULTURE See JOURNAL OF THE FACULTY OF AGRICULTURE. HOKKAIDO UNIVERSITY **101**

SAPPORO KOKUZEIKYOKU TOKEISHO (JA) [02245280] **4747**

SAPPORO-SHI BUNKAZAI CHOSA HOKOKUSHO (JA) [11737449] **2508**

SAPTAHA (II) [03428987] **2508**

SAPTAHIKA HINDUSTANA **SUSPENDED.** (II/0581-734X) [01643098] **2508**

SAQ BULLETIN (SZ) [10837562] **885**

●SAR AND QSAR IN ENVIRONMENTAL RESEARCH (UK/1062-936X) [25812280] **992**

SAR MAGAZINE, THE (US/0161-0511) [03818950] **5236**

SAR STATISTICS (US/0163-2833) [04257851] **5392, 5402**

SARA INNUN ADONG MUNHAK (KO) [11175210] **3433**

SARAGOSSA. UNIVERSIDAD. DEPARTAMENTO DE HISTORIA MODERNA See ESTUDIOS - DEPARTAMENTO DE HISTORIA MODERNA, UNIVERSIDAD DE ZARAGOZA **2615**

SARAH STAMBLER'S MARKETING WITH TECHNOLOGY NEWS (US/1070-809X) [28473437] **936**

SARAJEVO. GAZI HUSREV-BEGOVA BIBLIOTEKA See ANALI GAZI HASREV-BEGOVE BIBLIOTEKE **2673**

SARAN (IO) [09186411] **2663**

SARANCE (EC) [03495292] **2759**

SARASANDHANA : JATIBHEDABIRO-DHISAMITIRAMUKHAPATRA (II) [10615603] **2663**

SARASOTA MAGAZINE (US/1048-2245) [20909844] **2545**

SARASVATI-SUSHAMA (II) [03224990] **3433**

SARATOGA NEWS (US/0745-6255) [09314253] **5640**

SARATOGA (RHINEBECK, N.Y.), THE (US/0740-9702) [10068178] **2471**

SARATOGA SUN (SARATOGA, WYO.), THE (US/0740-4948) [09965363] **5772**

SARATOGIAN (SARATOGA SPRINGS, N.Y., 1910), THE (US/1071-4448) [11062597] **5720**

SARATOVSKII SELSKOKHOZIAISTVENNYI INSTITUT See SARATOVSKII SELSKOKHOZIAISTVENNYI INSTITUT. TRUDY **131**

SARATOVSKII SELSKOKHOZIAISTVENNYI INSTITUT. TRUDY (RU) [04066696] **131**

SARAWAK See ANGGARAN HASIL DAN PERBELANJAAN BAGI TAHUN ... (MICROFORM) **4709**

SARAWAK ELECTRICITY SUPPLY CORPORATION See ANNUAL REPORT **4759**

SARAWAK MUSEUM JOURNAL, THE (MY/0581-7897) [02017321] **4096**

SARAWAK MUSEUM, KUCHING See SARAWAK MUSEUM JOURNAL, THE **4096**

SARCOIDOSIS (IT/0393-1447) [11762575] **3638**

SARCOPHAGUS (US/0271-2342) [06577453] **3470**

SARGETIA (RM/1013-4255) [I10134255] **4096**

SARHAD JOURNAL OF AGRICULTURE (PK/1010-6103) [14393251] **132**

SARI KARANGAN INDONESIA (IO/0216-4167) [10496307] **5149**

SARINAH (IO) [10774858] **2663**

SARJANA : JURNAL FAKULTI SASTERA DAN SAINS SOSIAL, UNIVERSITI MALAYA (MY) [09925206] **2663**

SARMATIAN REVIEW, THE (US/1059-5872) [19380654] **2708**

SARNIA PHARMACY BULLETIN (CN) **4329**

SARSIA (NO/0036-4827) [01590751] **557**

SARVEKSHANA (II) [04627468] **5338**

SARVODAYA (II/0036-4835) [10073789] **4832**

SAS BULLETIN (US/0899-8922) [18249578] **282**

SAS COMMUNICATIONS (US/0270-9422) [06542847] **1121**

SAS INSTITUTE See AUTHORLINE - SAS INSTITUTE **3365**

SAS INSTITUTE See SAS COMMUNICATIONS **1121**

SASBO NEWS (SA) [02244529] **810**

SASEBO KOGYO KOTO SENMON GAKKO KENKYU HOKOKU (JA/0386-4391) [10442827] 1094, **5149**

SASEBO SHIRITSU SOGO BYOIN IGAKU GYOSEKI SHU (JA) [05621731] **3638**

SASH (SA/0036-4843) [05686626] **4512**

SASK. REPORT (CN/0820-5043) [16688237] **2545**

●SASK RIGHTS (CN/1191-0933) [26290508] **4512**

SASK TEL. WELLNESS CONNECTION See HEALTHY INTERCHANGE **4782**

SASK-TRENDS MONITOR (CN/0830-0143) [16656336] **1519**

SASKATCHEWA. ANNUAL REPORT FOR THE DEPARTMENT OF HEALTH See ANNUAL REPORT FOR THE YEAR ENDING MARCH 31 ... / SASKATCHEWAN HEALTH **4765**

SASKATCHEWAN See SASKATCHEWAN GAZETTE **4685**

SASKATCHEWAN See STATUTES OF SASKATCHEWAN **3059**

SASKATCHEWAN See PUBLIC ACCOUNTS (REGINA) **4743**

SASKATCHEWAN See ANNUAL REPORT. JUDGES OF THE PROVINCIAL COURT SUPERANNUATION FUND **3139**

SASKATCHEWAN See SASKATCHEWAN GAZETTE, THE **4685**

SASKATCHEWAN See SUPPLEMENTARY INFORMATION ..., PAYMENTS TO INDIVIDUALS **813**

SASKATCHEWAN See ANNUAL REPORT ... SASKATCHEWAN AGRICULTURAL RETURNS STABILIZATION FUND **61**

SASKATCHEWAN. ADVISORY COUNCIL ON THE STATUS OF WOMEN See PUBLICATION - SASKATCHEWAN ADVISORY COUNCIL ON THE STATUS OF WOMEN **5565**

SASKATCHEWAN ANGLICAN (CN/0703-9433) [03960053] **4995**

SASKATCHEWAN ARCHAEOLOGICAL SOCIETY See NEWSLETTER - SASKATCHEWAN ARCHAEOLOGICAL SOCIETY **276**

SASKATCHEWAN ARCHAEOLOGY (CN/0227-5872) [07817294] **282**

SASKATCHEWAN ASSOCIATION OF LIBRARY TECHNICIANS See S. A. L. T. NEWSLETTER **3247**

SASKATCHEWAN ASSOCIATION OF SOCIAL WORKERS NEWSLETTER (CN) **5306**

SASKATCHEWAN BULLETIN, THE (CN/0036-4886) [02134881] **1781**

SASKATCHEWAN. BUREAU OF STATISTICS See MONTHLY STATISTICAL REVIEW - SASKATCHEWAN. BUREAU OF STATISTICS (1978) **5333**

SASKATCHEWAN BUSINESS (CN/0709-0854) [05362475] **709**

SASKATCHEWAN BUSINESS BULLETIN **CEASED.** (CN/0228-1953) [06859711] **709**

SASKATCHEWAN CENTRE OF THE ARTS See ANNUAL REPORT - SASKATCHEWAN CENTRE OF THE ARTS **313**

SASKATCHEWAN CHINESE TELEPHONE DIRECTORY **CEASED.** (CN/0849-0252) [22104245] **1163**

SASKATCHEWAN COMPUTER UTILITY CORPORATION See ANNUAL REPORT OF THE SASKATCHEWAN COMPUTER UTILITY CORPORATION OF THE PROVINCE OF SASKATCHEWAN **1235**

SASKATCHEWAN COUNCIL OF SOCIAL STUDIES TEACHER (CN/0711-3021) [08537542] 1904, **5217**

SASKATCHEWAN CRIMES COMPENSATION BOARD See SASKATCHEWAN CRIMES COMPENSATION BOARD ANNUAL REPORT **3176**

SASKATCHEWAN CRIMES COMPENSATION BOARD ANNUAL REPORT (CN/1185-9164) [25468257] **3176**

SASKATCHEWAN DECISIONS, CIVIL AND CRIMINAL CASES (CN/0319-7999) [02627314] **3046**

SASKATCHEWAN. DEPARTMENT OF NATURAL RESOURCES See ANNUAL REPORT OF THE DEPARTMENT OF NATURAL RESOURCES (REGINA) **2186**

SASKATCHEWAN. DEPT. OF SOCIAL SERVICES. PLANNING AND EVALUATION DIVISION See PROBATION & PAROLE STATISTICS (REGINA) **3082**

SASKATCHEWAN DEVELOPMENT FUND CORPORATION See ANNUAL REPORT OF THE SASKATCHEWAN DEVELOPMENT FUND CORPORATION OF THE PROVINCE OF SASKATCHEWAN **772**

SASKATCHEWAN ECONOMIC REVIEW (CN/0558-6976) [08598235] **1519**

SASKATCHEWAN EDUCATIONAL ADMINISTRATOR, THE (CN/0709-8146) [06166702] **1870**

SASKATCHEWAN FOOD PROCESSORS DIRECTORY (CN/0848-5313) [22716471] **2356**

SASKATCHEWAN GAME MANAGEMENT (CN/1185-4839) [13807338] 2204, **4878**

SASKATCHEWAN GAZETTE (CN/0036-4894) [09688401] **4685**

SASKATCHEWAN GAZETTE, THE (CN/0036-4894) [02249508] **4685**

SASKATCHEWAN GENEALOGICAL SOCIETY See BULLETIN - SASKATCHEWAN GENEALOGICAL SOCIETY **2441**

SASKATCHEWAN GENEALOGICAL SOCIETY See SURNAME EXCHANGE / SASKATCHEWAN GENEALOGICAL SOCIETY **2474**

SASKATCHEWAN GEOLOGICAL SOCIETY See SPECIAL PUBLICATION - SASKATCHEWAN GEOLOGICAL SOCIETY **1398**

SASKATCHEWAN GEOLOGICAL SURVEY See SUMMARY OF INVESTIGATIONS BY THE SASKATCHEWAN GEOLOGICAL SURVEY **1399**

SASKATCHEWAN — Alphabetical Title Index

SASKATCHEWAN HEALTH MANPOWER REPORT (CN/0824-8451) [06048122] **3917**

SASKATCHEWAN HEALTH RESEARCH BOARD *See* ANNUAL REPORT / SASKATCHEWAN HEALTH RESEARCH BOARD **4766**

SASKATCHEWAN. HEARING AID PLAN *See* ANNUAL REPORT - SASKATCHEWAN HEALTH, HEARING AID PLAN **4383**

SASKATCHEWAN HISTORY (CN/0036-4908) [02443952] **2759**

SASKATCHEWAN. HOG MARKETING COMMISSION *See* ANNUAL REPORT - SASKATCHEWAN HOG MARKETING COMMISSION **206**

SASKATCHEWAN HORIZONTAL WELL SUMMARY (CN/1182-9125) [23264898] **2150**

SASKATCHEWAN HUMAN RIGHTS COMMISSION *See* ANNUAL REPORT / SASKATCHEWAN HUMAN RIGHTS COMMISSION **4504**

SASKATCHEWAN HUMAN RIGHTS COMMISSION *See* SASK RIGHTS **4512**

SASKATCHEWAN INDIAN FEDERATED COLLEGE JOURNAL *SUSPENDED.* (CN/0828-3907) [14398452] **2759**

SASKATCHEWAN. LABOUR RELATIONS BOARD *See* ANNUAL REPORT - SASKATCHEWAN. LABOUR RELATIONS BOARD **1650**

SASKATCHEWAN LABOUR REPORT, THE (CN/0317-7335) [02443861] **1709**

SASKATCHEWAN LAW REVIEW (CN/0036-4916) [01765046] **3046**

SASKATCHEWAN. LEGISLATIVE ASSEMBLY. SELECT STANDING COMMITTEE ON PUBLIC ACCOUNTS AND PRINTING *See* REPORT OF THE SELECT STANDING COMMITTEE ON PUBLIC ACCOUNTS AND PRINTING, TOGETHER WITH MINUTES AND VERBATIM REPORT OF PROCEEDINGS **4681**

SASKATCHEWAN. LEGISLATIVE LIBRARY *See* ANNUAL REPORT / SASKATCHEWAN LEGISLATIVE LIBRARY **4629**

SASKATCHEWAN MEDICAL JOURNAL (CN/1182-0063) [22366806] **3638**

SASKATCHEWAN MULTICULTURAL MAGAZINE (CN/0714-9050) [09166835] 1781, **2272**

SASKATCHEWAN MUNICIPAL DIRECTORY (CN/0581-8435) [02441690] **4685**

SASKATCHEWAN NATURAL HISTORY SOCIETY *See* SPECIAL PUBLICATION - SASKATCHEWAN NATURAL HISTORY SOCIETY **4172**

SASKATCHEWAN POETRY BOOK (CN/0080-6560) [02441572] **3470**

SASKATCHEWAN PORK PRODUCERS MARKETING BOARD *See* ANNUAL REPORT OF THE SASKATCHEWAN PORK PRODUCERS MARKETING BOARD **2327**

SASKATCHEWAN PROVINCIAL HIGHWAYS ACCIDENT STATISTICS (CN/0318-2819) [06170176] **5402**

SASKATCHEWAN. PUBLIC AND PRIVATE RIGHTS BOARD *See* ANNUAL REPORT / PUBLIC AND PRIVATE RIGHTS BOARD **2935**

SASKATCHEWAN PUBLIC UTILITIES REVIEW COMMISSION *See* SASKATCHEWAN TELECOMMUNICATIONS / SASKATCHEWAN PUBLIC UTILITIES REVIEW COMMISSION **1163**

SASKATCHEWAN PULSE CROP DEVELOPMENT BOARD NEWSLETTER (CN) **132**

SASKATCHEWAN RAIL COMMITTEE *See* NEWS BULLETIN - SASKATCHEWAN RAIL COMMITTEE **5433**

SASKATCHEWAN REPORTS (CN/0713-7095) [06025305] **3046**

SASKATCHEWAN ROUGHRIDERS (FOOTBALL TEAM) *See* FACT BOOK - SASKATCHEWAN ROUGHRIDERS, FOOTBALL TEAM **4894**

SASKATCHEWAN ROUND TABLE ON ENVIRONMENT AND ECONOMY *See* UPDATE / SASKATCHEWAN ROUND TABLE ON ENVIRONMENT AND ECONOMY **2183**

SASKATCHEWAN SAFETY COUNCIL *See* REPORT OF THE SASKATCHEWAN SAFETY COUNCIL PUBLIC OPINION POLL, A **4798**

SASKATCHEWAN. SASKATCHEWAN COMMUNITY SERVICES *See* COMMUNITY SCENE **5280**

SASKATCHEWAN. SASKATCHEWAN ENVIRONMENT AND PUBLIC SAFETY *See* ANNUAL REPORT / SASKATCHEWAN ENVIRONMENT AND PUBLIC SAFETY **4766**

SASKATCHEWAN. SASKATCHEWAN HEALTH *See* ANNUAL REPORT FOR THE YEAR ENDING MARCH 31 ... / SASKATCHEWAN HEALTH **4765**

SASKATCHEWAN SCHEDULE OF WELLS (CN) 1995, **1396**

SASKATCHEWAN STATE OF THE ENVIRONMENT REPORT (CN/1186-8090) [24571305] **2204**

SASKATCHEWAN TELECOMMUNICATIONS / SASKATCHEWAN PUBLIC UTILITIES REVIEW COMMISSION (CN/0844-7020) [11967321] **1163**

SASKATCHEWAN TRADE DIRECTORY (1986) (CN/0831-9057) [15226825] **3487**

SASKATCHEWAN TRAFFIC ACCIDENT FACTS (CN/0711-9178) [07936418] **5444**

SASKATCHEWAN. TRIPARTITE BEEF ADMINISTRATION BOARD *See* ANNUAL REPORT - SASKATCHEWAN. TRIPARTITE BEEF ADMINISTRATION BOARD **206**

SASKATCHEWAN VETERINARY MEDICAL ASSOCIATION NEWSLETTER (CN/0711-2467) [08767094] **5521**

SASKATCHEWAN WATER NEWS (CN/0822-7551) [10392314] **5539**

SASKATCHEWAN WHEAT POOL *See* ANNUAL REPORT - SASKATCHEWAN WHEAT POOL **163**

SASKATOON BUSINESS DIRECTORY (CN/0714-8607) [09096522] **709**

SASKATOON HEALTH SERVICES AUTHORITY *See* ANNUAL REPORT / SASKATOON HEALTH SERVICES AUTHORITY **4766**

SASKATOON HISTORY REVIEW (CN/0843-6002) [19915004] **2759**

SASKATOON, SASKATCHEWAN, CITY DIRECTORY (CN/0228-9695) [07857818] **2575**

SASKATOON THE BEAUTIFUL (CN/0827-2956) [11816153] **5490**

SASP NEWSLETTER *See* CONTEMPORARY SSOCIAL PSYCHOLOGY **4582**

SASSY (NEW YORK, N.Y. 1988) (US/0899-9953) [18284013] **1068**

SAT AUDIO VIDEO (PL/1230-395X) [I1230395X] **5318**

SAT SANDESH (MONTREAL) (CN/0714-8003) [09084924] **4995**

SAT-VIEW *CEASED.* (US/1060-3581) [24946268] **34**

SATARANGI CAMALA (II) [10690733] **3319**

SATCOM QUARTERLY / JET PROPULSION LABORATORY (US) [24866217] **1163**

SATELLITE (IT) **1138**

SATELLITE BUSINESS NEWS (US/1043-0865) [19295191] **1121**

SATELLITE COMMUNICATIONS (US/0147-7439) [03880460] **1163**

SATELLITE DATA USERS BULLETIN (US) [06729076] **1434**

SATELLITE DIRECT (US/0892-3329) [15161170] **1626**

SATELLITE DIRECTORY AND BUYERS GUIDE (US/0742-7077) [10446724] **1163**

SATELLITE INDUSTRY UPDATE *See* DOWNLINK : SATELLITE & CABLE INDUSTRY NEWS **1153**

SATELLITE LEARNING (US/1054-9935) [23035233] **1846**

SATELLITE NEWS (US/0161-3448) [03905729] **1163**

SATELLITE NEWS (UK) [I03072932] **34**

SATELLITE ORBIT (US/0732-7668) [08423766] **1163**

SATELLITE RETAILER (US/0890-1252) [14179865] **957**

SATELLITE SERVICES SOURCEBOOK, THE (US/0737-9250) [08913535] **1163**

SATELLITE SITUATION REPORT (US) [02600845] **1163**

SATELLITE SYSTEMS HANDBOOK (US) **1163**

SATELLITE TECHNOLOGY (UK/0267-6389) [12357641] **34**

SATELLITE TIMES *CEASED.* (US/0890-1260) [14178880] **1626**

SATELLITE TIMES (UK) **1138**

SATELLITE TV EUROPE (UK/0268-8425) [I02688425] **1121**

SATELLITE TV FINANCE (UK) **1138**

SATELLITE TV PRE-VUE *CEASED.* (US/0896-3673) [17010501] **1138**

SATELLITE TV WEEK. NORTH AMERICAN EDITION (US/0744-7841) [08563844] **1163**

SATELLITE WEEK (US/0193-2861) [05150932] **1163**

SATERN (US/8756-1476) [11500815] **5307**

SATHER CLASSICAL LECTURES (US/0080-6684) [01605462] **1080**

● SATISFACTION (EVANS, GA.) (US/1063-9004) [26174547] 5307, **3792**

SATMER ED. FRANCAISE (FR/0294-1910) [I02941910] **1434**

SATORI *CEASED.* (US/0898-3011) [17781946] **2492**

SATTARA DASAKA (II) [02285177] **1335**

SATURDAY CENTRE *See* SCOPP : SATURDAY CENTRE OF PROSE & POETRY **3470**

SATURDAY EVENING POST (1839), THE (US/0048-9239) [02267483] **2492**

SATURDAY NIGHT (CN/0036-4975) [04448686] **2545**

SATYAKATHA (II/0581-8575) [06728501] **424**

● SAUDE E SOCIEDADE (BL/0104-1290) [I01041290] **4801**

SAUDI ARABIA MONITOR *See* BUSINESS MIDDLE EAST **650**

SAUDI ARABIA QUARTERLY (UK) 4495, **1583**

SAUDI ARABIA, RECORD OF ECONOMIC DEVELOPMENT (LE) [09460048] **1583**

SAUDI-ARABIEN: ENERGIEWIRTSCHAFT (GW) [05064300] **1956**

SAUDI-ARABIEN: WIRTSCHAFTLICHE ENTWICKLUNG (GW) [03231061] **1519**

SAUDI BULLETIN OF OPHTHALMOLOGY : OFFICIAL JOURNAL OF THE SAUDI OPHTHALMOLOGICAL SOCIETY (SU) [22380346] **3879**

SAUDI ECONOMIC SURVEY (SU) [06950313] **1583**

SAUDI GAZETTE (SU) **5810**

SAUDI MEDICAL JOURNAL (SU/0379-5284) [05237763] **3638**

SAUDI REPORT (US/0278-8772) [07885194] **2663**

SAUDI TRADE DIRECTORY FOR RIYADH (PK) [08001275] **850**

SAUF-CONDUIT (SZ) [19821754] **330**

SAUGETIERKUNDLICHE MITTEILUNGEN *SUSPENDED.* (GW/0036-2344) [01764736] 5597, **472**

SAUK-PRAIRIE STAR, THE (US) [11311066] **5770**

SAUL BELLOW JOURNAL (US/0735-1550) [08859104] 3352, **434**

SAUMONS (FR) [01796220] **2312**

SAUNDERS MONOGRAPHS IN CLINICAL ORTHOPAEDICS *CEASED.* (US/0195-9565) [05583245] **3884**

SAUNDERS MONOGRAPHS IN CLINICAL RADIOLOGY *CEASED.* (US/0277-853X) [03259618] **3946**

SAUSSUREA (SZ/0373-2525) [01788998] **527**

SAUTI YA KERICHO (KE) [10790139] **2643**

SAUVAGE, LE (FR) [01795686] **5257**

SAUVEGARDE DE L'ART FRANCAIS (ASSOCIATION) *See* CAHIER - LA SAUVRGARDE DE L'ART FRANCAIS **346**

SAUVEGARDE DE L'ENFANCE (FR/0036-5041) [06504739] **5307**

SAUVEGARDE DES CHANTIERS (FR/0036-505X) [I0036505X] **627**

SAUVETAGE : REVUE DE LA SOCIETE NATIONALE DE SAUVETAGE EN MER (FR) 4183, **4801**

SAVACOU (JM/0036-5068) [01765065] **364**

SAVAGE FAMILY DEPOSITORY NEWSLETTER (US/0739-6651) [09780540] **2471**

SAVANNA (NR/0331-0523) [01343161] 2835, **1519**

SAVANNA RESEARCH SERIES (CN/0079-7758) [02441852] **2575**

SAVANNAH COURIER (US) [19175383] **5746**

SAVANNAH EVENING PRESS (US/8750-4685) [08773622] **5655**

SAVANNAH MORNING NEWS, SAVANNAH EVENING PRESS (COASTAL EMPIRE ED.) (US/8750-8273) [11856954] **5655**

SAVANNAH RIVER LABORATORY *See* SAVANNAH RIVER LABORATORY QUARTERLY REPORT, WASTE MANAGEMENT **2242**

SAVANNAH RIVER LABORATORY QUARTERLY REPORT, WASTE MANAGEMENT (US) [06683282] **2242**

SAVANNAH VALLEY AUTHORITY (S.C.) *See* ANNUAL REPORT / SAVANNAH VALLEY AUTHORITY **5529**

SAVARIA (HU/0230-1954) [01795151] **2708**

SAVE ON SHOPPING DIRECTORY (US/0276-6701) [07233445] **957**

SAVE PROCEEDINGS (US/0163-6707) [04423378] **1626**

SAVE THE BULKLEY NEWSLETTER (CN/0713-5866) [08981143] **2204**

SAVE THE PLANET ... [COMPUTER FILE] (US) [25321249] **2181**

SAVE THE SCHOOLS (US/0277-7096) [07625318] **1781**

SAVENZI ZAVOD ZA STATISTIKU (YUGOSLAVIA) *See* KOMUNALNI FONDOVI U GRADSKIM NASELJIMA **4698**

SAVENZI ZAVOD ZA STATISTIKU (YUGOSLAVIA) *See* INDUSTRIJA **1611**

SAVENZI ZAVOD ZA STATISTIKU (YUGOSLAVIA) *See* STRUCNI ISPITI RADNIKA **1916**

SAVENZI ZAVOD ZA STATISTIKU (YUGOSLAVIA) *See* RATARSTVO, VOCARSTVO I VINOGRADARSTVO **125**

SAVENZI ZAVOD ZA STATISTIKU (YUGOSLAVIA) *See* INDUSTRIJSKE ORGANIZACIJE **1611**

SAVENZI ZAVOD ZA STATISTIKU (YUGOSLAVIA) *See* INDUSTRIJSKI PROIZVODI **730**

SAVEZNE OMLADINSKE RADNE AKCIJE U ... GODINI / SOCIJALISTICKA REPUBLIKA SRBIJA, REPUBLICKI ZAVOD ZA STATISTIKU (YU) [08342522] **1709**

SAVEZNI ZAVOD ZA STATISTIKU (YUGOSLAVIA) *See* DRUSTVENA POLJOPRIVREDNA GAZDINSTVA **80**

SAVEZNI ZAVOD ZA STATISTIKU (YUGOSLAVIA) *See* RADNE ORGANIZACIJE VANPRIVREDNIH DELATNOSTI **5337**

SAVEZNI ZAVOD ZA STATISTIKU (YUGOSLAVIA) *See* ZAPOSLENO OSOBLJE I NETO LICNI DOHOCI PO GRUPAMA DELATNOSTI **1720**

SAVEZNI ZAVOD ZA STATISTIKU (YUGOSLAVIA) *See* DELEGACIJE OSNOVNIH SAMOUPRAVNIH ORGANIZACIJA I ZAJEDNICA I SKUPSTINE DRUSTVENO-POLITICKIH ZAJEDNICA **4697**

SAVEZNI ZAVOD ZA STATISTIKU (YUGOSLAVIA) *See* INDUSTRIJSKA PREDUZECA **5328**

SAVEZNI ZAVOD ZA STATISTIKU (YUGOSLAVIA) *See* SAMOUPRAVLJANJE U USTANOVAMA DRUSTVENIH SLUZBI **5338**

SAVEZNI ZAVOD ZA STATISTIKU (YUGOSLAVIA) *See* ANKETA O PRIHODIMA, RASHEDIMA I POTRESNJI DOMACINSTAVA **1528**

SAVEZNI ZAVOD ZA STATISTIKU (YUGOSLAVIA) *See* STATISTICAL REPORT **733**

SAVEZNI ZAVOD ZA STATISTIKU (YUGOSLAVIA) *See* ANKETA O SEOSKIM DOMACINSTVIMA **5321**

SAVEZNI ZAVOD ZA STATISTIKU (YUGOSLAVIA) *See* TURIZAM **5498**

SAVEZNI ZAVOD ZA STATISTIKU (YUGOSLAVIA) *See* MESNE ZAJEDNICE **4664**

SAVEZNI ZAVOD ZA STATISTIKU (YUGOSLAVIA) *See* SAOBRACAJ I VEZE **5338**

SAVEZNI ZAVOD ZA STATISTIKU (YUGOSLAVIA) *See* DRUSTVENE ZANATSKE ORGANIZACIJE **728**

SAVEZNI ZAVOD ZA STATISTIKU (YUGOSLAVIA) *See* ANKETA O OSTVARIVANJU PRAVA RADNIKA IZ RADNOG ODNOSA **1528**

SAVEZNI ZAVOD ZA STATISTIKU (YUGOSLAVIA) *See* OSNOVNE I SREDNJE SKOLE **1796**

SAVEZNI ZAVOD ZA STATISTIKU (YUGOSLAVIA) *See* ANKETA O PORODICNIM BUDZETIMA RADNICKIH DOMACINSTAVA **5321**

SAVEZNI ZAVOD ZA STATISTIKU (YUGOSLAVIA) *See* DRUSTVENI PROIZVOD I NARODNI DOHODAK **1556**

SAVEZNI ZAVOD ZA STATISTIKU (YUGOSLAVIA) *See* IMENOVANJE DIREKTORA RADNIH ORGANIZACIJA **681**

SAVEZNI ZAVOD ZA STATISTIKU (YUGOSLAVIA) *See* OSTRUCAVANJE RADNIKA U RADNIM ORGANIZACIJAMA **1537**

SAVEZNI ZAVOD ZA STATISTIKU (YUGOSLAVIA) *See* ZAPOSLENO OSOBLJE **1720**

SAVEZNI ZAVOD ZA STATISTIKU (YUGOSLAVIA) *See* UCENICI U PRIVREDI **1798**

SAVEZNI ZAVOD ZA STATISTIKU (YUGOSLAVIA) *See* SAMOUPRAVLJANJE U PRIVREDI **1538**

SAVEZNI ZAVOD ZA STATISTIKU (YUGOSLAVIA) *See* TROMESECNI PREGLED MEUNARODNE STATISTIKE **5345**

SAVEZNI ZAVOD ZA STATISTIKU (YUGOSLAVIA) *See* LICNI DOHOCI **1535**

SAVEZNI ZAVOD ZA STATISTIKU (YUGOSLAVIA) *See* SAMOUPRAVNE INTERESNE ZAJEDNICE **5227**

SAVEZNI ZAVOD ZA STATISTIKU (YUGOSLAVIA) *See* AKTIVNOST MESNIH ZAJEDNICA **4696**

SAVEZNI ZAVOD ZA STATISTIKU (YUGOSLAVIA) *See* NEKI POKAZATELJI TEHNICKOG RAZVOJA PRIVREDE JUGOSLAVIJE **1536**

SAVING AND PRESERVING ARTS AND CULTURAL ENVIRONMENTS (US/0748-8378) [10684835] **330**

SAVING ENERGY (US/0279-2338) [07143959] **1956**

SAVING HEALTH (UK/0036-5106) [06361132] **4995**

●SAVINGS & COMMUNITY BANKER (US/1067-1757) [27000216] **810**

SAVINGS AND DEVELOPMENT (IT) [04753784] 913, **1519**

SAVINGS & HOME FINANCING SOURCE BOOK (US) [00997489] **810**

SAVINGS AND LOAN MARKET STUDY (US/0163-6782) [03883547] **810**

SAVINGS BANK AND SAVINGS AND LOAN ASSOCIATION SURVEY OF SALARIES AND PERSONNEL PRACTICES (US/0738-1123) [09500178] 810, **1709**

SAVINGS BANKS FOREIGN BUSINESS DIRECTORY (SZ) [20188962] **810**

SAVINGS BANKS INTERNATIONAL (SZ/1010-4038) [03178842] **810**

SAVINGS INSTITUTIONS (US/0746-1321) [09754856] **810**

SAVOIR MARIN, LE (FR/0182-4708) [I01824708] **4854**

SAVOIRS ET FORMATION (FR/0769-6094) [I07696094] **2792**

SAVOIRS LASALLE (FR/0997-5373) [I09975373] **245**

SAVON LUONTO (FI) [03131584] **4171**

SAVREMENA POLJOPRIVREDNA TEHNIKA (YU/0350-2953) [I03502953] 1995, **132**

SAVREMENIK (YU/0036-519X) [04770809] **3433**

SAVVY BUSINESS TRAVELER (US) 5490, **709**

SAVVY MANAGEMENT MONTHLY (US/0883-8720) [12255222] **885**

SAVVY SHOPPER, THE (US/1057-3275) [24018012] **5490**

SAWADDI (TH/0581-8893) [02024277] **2663**

SAWMILL HYDROSTATION REDEVELOPMENT ... ANNUAL REPORT (US) [07828111] **2095**

SAWMILL TECHNIQUES FOR SOUTHEAST ASIA (US/0190-7379) [04728523] **2404**

SAWT AL-ASIFAH (LE) [10940014] **2663**

SAWT AL-BILAD (CY) [11085608] **2663**

SAWT AL-FANNANIN (CY) [23209072] **4152**

SAWT AL-JABHAH : NASHRAT AL-JABHAH AL-WATANIYAH AL-QAWMIYAH AL-DIMUQRATIYAH FI AL-IRAQ, MAKTAB URUBBA AL-GHARBIYAH (LANDAN) (UK) [11248989] **2628**

SAWT AL-SHAB AL-LIBI (UA) [04126829] **2643**

SAWT AL-SHAHADAH (IR) [09850811] **2663**

SAWT AL-SIRYANI (IQ) [05900645] **2663**

SAWT AL-TAAWUN (CAIRO, EGYPT) (UA) [09547634] **1626**

SAWT AL-TALIAH (PARIS, FRANCE) (US) [11054287] **2643**

SAWT AL-URUBAH (TURANTU) (CN/0821-6428) [09770525] **5794**

SAWT FILASTIN (UA) [07417969] **2663**

SAWT KANADA (CN/1183-2274) [24571003] **2545**

SAWTRI SPECIAL PUBLICATION (SA/0258-4565) [10833902] **5355**

SAXOPHONE JOURNAL (US/0276-4768) [07198516] **4152**

SAXOPHONE SYMPOSIUM, THE (US/0271-3705) [05190155] **4152**

SAYAMA-SHI BUNKAZAI CHOSA HOKOKU (JA) [01799706] **2663**

SAYBROOK REVIEW *CEASED.* (US/0740-0853) [09809701] **4617**

SAYERS REVIEW, THE (US) [06994742] **3433**

SAYING IT BETTER (US/1070-7395) [28460466] **3319**

SAYYIDATI (UK/0265-5780) [09724939] 5566, **2601**

SAZZ (NEW YORK, N.Y.) (US/1046-5790) [20450885] 2272, **5566**

SB. SPORTSTATTENBAU UND BADERANLAGEN (GW/0036-102X) [I0036102X] 4854, **627**

SBA PUBLICATIONS. SBA 115A : FREE MANAGEMENT ASSISTANCE PUBLICATIONS (US) [06368867] **885**

SBANE ENTERPRISE (US/8750-3158) [11251793] **709**

SBC TODAY *See* BAPTISTS TODAY **4938**

SBIC DIGEST (US/0149-2500) [02758503] **913**

SBN UPDATE (US/1059-8413) [24781668] **1121**

SBORNIK AGRONOMICKA FAKULTA V CESKYCH BUDEJOVICICH FYTOTECHNICKA RADA (XR) [20576415] **185**

SBORNIK ANNOTACIJ NAUCNO-ISSLEDOVATELSKIH RABOT - TOMSKIJ POLITEHNICESKIJ INSTITUT IM. S.M. KIROVA (RU/0131-1638) [03009776] **5149**

SBORNIK ARCHIVNICH PRACI (XR/0036-5246) [01929362] 2708, **2483**

SBORNIK ASPIRANTSKIKH RABOT: TEORIIA PLASTIN I OBOLOCHEK (RU) [05885793] **1995**

SBORNIK CESKE GEOGRAFICKE SPOLECNOSTI (XR/1210-115X) [26671877] **2576**

SBORNIK. CHEMICKE INZENYRSTVI A AUTOMATIZACE (XR) [06653553] **2017**

SBORNIK FILOZOFICKEJ FAKULTY UNIVERZITY KOMENSKEHO. PSYCHOLOGICA (XO/0083-419X) [06678500] **4617**

SBORNIK GEOLOGICKYCH VED. ANTROPOZOIKUM (XR/0036-5270) [01924277] **1396**

SBORNIK GEOLOGICKYCH VED. HYDROGEOLOGIE INZENYRSKA GEOLOGIE (XR/0036-5289) [01159394] **1417**

SBORNIK GEOLOGICKYCH VED. LOZISKOVA GEOLOGIE, MINERALOGIE (XR/0581-9180) [03615563] **1444**

SBORNIK GEOLOGICKYCH VED. PALEONTOLOGIE (XR/0036-5297) [01924294] **4230**

SBORNIK GEOLOGICKYCH VED. TECHNOLOGIE, GEOCHEMIE (XR/0036-5300) [01931004] 992, **1444**

SBORNIK GPO (XR/0139-7834) [02683548] **1396**

SBORNIK HISTORICKY (XR/0577-3725) [01646030] **2628**

SBORNIK INFORMATSII O DEIATELNOSTI ORGANOV SEV (RU) [01794372] **1583**

SBORNIK JEDNOTY STARYCH CESKYCH RODU V PRAZE (XR) [18707511] **2471**

SBORNIK K DEJINAM 19. A 20. STOLETI (XR) [05968426] **2628**

SBORNIK LEKARSKY (XR/0036-5327) [07100965] **3638**

●SBORNIK. MATHEMATICS (US/1064-5616) [26329563] **3532**

SBORNIK MECHANIZACNI FAKULTY VYSOKE SKOLY ZEMEDELSKE V PRAZE (XR) [07242867] **132**

SBORNIK MUZEIA ANTROPOLOGII I ETNOGRAFII / AKADEMIIA NAUK SSSR, INSTITUT ETNOGRAFII IM. MIKLUKHO-MAKLAIA (RU) [00986013] **245**

SBORNIK NARODNIHO MUZEA V PRAZE. RADA A, HISTORIE (XR/0036-5335) [05002332] **2628**

SBORNIK NARODNIHO MUZEA V PRAZE. RADA B, PRIRODNI VEDY (XR) [15012965] **4171**

SBORNIK NARODNIHO MUZEA V PRAZE. RADA C, LITERARNI HISTORIE (XR/0036-5351) [05690901] **3433**

SBORNIK NAUCHNO-PRAKTICHESKIKH RABOT - MINISTERSTVO ZDRAVOOKHRANENIIA RSFSR, CHETVERTOE GLAVNOE UPRAVLENIE (RU) [07030116] **3638**

SBORNIK NAUCHNYKH RABOT SIBNIVI (RU) [02758126] **5521**

SBORNIK NAUCHNYKH TRUDOV / MINISTERVO RYBNOGO KHOZIAISTVA RSFSR, GOSUDARSTVENNYI NAUCHNO-ISSLEDOVATELSKII INSTITUT OZERNOGO I RECHNOGO RYBNOGO KHOZIAISTVA (RU/0367-7974) [09419417] **2312**

SBORNIK NAUCHNYKH TRUDOV MONIIAG (RU/0301-1909) [01428071] **5149**

SBORNIK NAUCHNYKH TRUDOV / VSESOIUZNAIA ORDENA LENINA I ORDENA TRUDOVOGO KRASNOGO ZNAMENI AKADEMIIA SELSKOKHOZIAISTVENNYKH NAUK IMENI V.I. LENINA, GOUDARSTVENNYI ORDENA TRUDOVOGO KRASNOGO ZNAMENI NIKITSKII BOTANICHESKII SAD (UN/0201-7997) [17347326] 2431, **527**

SBORNIK NAUCHNYKH TRUDOV (VSESOIUZNYI) (RU) [10674580] **551**

SBORNIK — Alphabetical Title Index

SBORNIK NAUCHNYKH TRUDOV (VSESOIUZNYI NAUCHNO-ISSLEDOVATELSKII INSTITUT FIZIOLOGII, BIOKHIMII I PITANIIA) (RU/0136-3751) [15056703] 5521, **221**

SBORNIK NAUCHNYKH TRUDOV / VSESOIUZNYI NAUCHNO-ISSLEDOVATELSKII INSTITUT LIUMINOFOROV I OSOBO CHISTYKH VESHCHESTV, VNIILIUMINOFOROV (RU/0371-1722) [11094704] **4441**

SBORNIK NAUCHNYKH TRUDOV / VSESOIUZNYI NAUCHNO-ISSLEDOVATELSKII INSTITUT MONOKRISTALLOV, STSINTILLIATSIONNYKH MATERIALOV I OSOBO CHISTYKH KHIMICHESKIKH VESHCHESTV (VNII MONOKRISTALLOV) (UN) [17255429] **992**

SBORNIK NAUCHNYKH TRUDOV (VSESOIUZNYI NAUCHNO-ISSLEDOVATELSKII INSTITUT SADOVODSTVA IM. I.V. MICHURINA) (RU/0375-2232) [11046892] **2431**

SBORNIK NAUCHNYKH (VETERINARNAIA AKADEMIIA) (RU/0130-8734) [09214833] **5521**

SBORNIK NAUCNYH TRUDOV - KLINIKA NERVNYH BOLEZNEJ IRKUTSKOGO MEDICINSKOGO INSTITUTA (RU/0300-0168) [01370107] **3638**

SBORNIK NAUCNYH TRUDOV - MAGNITOGORSKIJ GORNOMETALLURGICESKIJ INSTITUT IM. G. J. NOSOVA (RU/0320-0132) [03110892] **4018**

SBORNIK PEDAGOGICKE FAKULTY UNIVERSITY KARLOVY. HISTORIE (XR) [02468723] **2628**

SBORNIK PEDAGOGICKE FAKULTY UNIVERZITY KARLOVY. BIOLOGIE (XR/0231-7753) [07078267] **472**

SBORNIK PEDAGOGICKE FAKULTY V PLZNI. CIZI JAZYKY (XR) [08089612] **3319**

SBORNIK PEDAGOGICKE FAKULTY V PLZNI. ELEKTRONIKA (XR) [21006364] **2080**

SBORNIK PEDAGOGICKE FAKULTY V USTI NAD LABEM. RADA CIZICH JAZYKU (XR) [09247313] **3319**

SBORNIK PRACI (CS) [14375675] **2576**

SBORNIK PRACI FILOSOFICKE FACULTY BRNENSKE UNIVERSITY (XR/0068-2705) [02723893] **1904**

SBORNIK PRACI FILOSOFICKE FAKULTY BRNENSKE UNIVERSITY. A, RADY JAZYKOVEDNE (XR/0231-7567) [03037247] **3319**

SBORNIK PRACI FILOSOFICKE FAKULTY BRNENSKE UNIVERSITY. C, RADY HISTORICKA (XR/0231-7710) [03037224] **2629**

SBORNIK PRACI FILOZOFICKE FAKULTY BRNENSKE UNIVERZITY. RADA ARCHEOLOGICKO-KLASICKA (XR/0231-7915) [I02317915] **282**

SBORNIK PRACI FILOZOFICKE FAKULTY BRNENSKE UNIVERZITY. RADA UMENOVEDNA (XR/0231-5025) [I02315025] 2629, **364**

SBORNIK PRACI HISTORICKYCH (XR) [08694277] **2708**

SBORNIK PRACI. MARXISMUS-LENINISMUS (XR) [02663105] **4546**

SBORNIK PRACI TEORIE KULTURY (XR) [12444735] **5257**

SBORNIK PRACI UVP (XR) [24894126] **4277**

SBORNIK PRACI VYCHODOCESKYCH ARCHIVU (XR) [03055125] **2483**

SBORNIK RABOT / MINISTERSTVO SLSKOGO KHOZIAISTVA SSSR, LENINGRADSKII VETERINARNYI INSTITUT (RU/0371-0955) [10477895] **5521**

SBORNIK RABOT PO TEORII OPTIMALNYKH PROTSESSOV (RU) [02244376] **3532**

SBORNIK RABOT TOLJATTINSKOJ GIDROMETEOROLOGICESKOJ OBSERVATORII (RU/0303-5840) [01793642] **1417**

SBORNIK. RADA C: LITERARNI HISTORIE (XR) [06701145] **3433**

SBORNIK STATEI PO FRANTSUZSKOI LINGVISTIKE I METODIKE PREPODAVANIIA INOSTRANNOGO IAZYKA V VUZE (RU) [05881695] **3319**

SBORNIK TRUDOV - BELORUSSKII NAUCHNO-ISSLEDOVATEL'SKII INSTITUT ZHIVOTNOVODSTVA (BW) [03618315] **221**

SBORNIK TRUDOV CENTRALNOGO NAUCNO-ISSLEDOVATELSKOGO INSTITUTA BUMAGI (RU/0371-3733) [10158671] **4238**

SBORNIK TRUDOV CHELIABINSKOGO ELEKTROMETALLURICHESKOGO KOMBINATA (RU) [03715349] **4018**

SBORNIK TRUDOV - GOSUDARSTVENNYJ VSESOJUZNYJ NAUCNO--ISSLEDOVATELSKIJ INSTITUT STROITELNYH MATERIALOV I KONSTRUKCIJ IM. P.P. BUDNIKOVA (RU/0370-9906) [10859107] **627**

SBORNIK TRUDOV (VSESOIUZNYI NAUCHNO-ISSLEDOVATELSKII INSTITUT PRIKLADNYKH AVTOMATIZIROVANNYKH SISTEM (SOVIET UNION) (RU/0233-6944) [20344852] **1221**

SBORNIK TRUDOV ZOOLOGICHESKOGO MUZEIA (RU) [02807399] **5597**

SBORNIK. UMENI (XR) [06712826] **4152**

SBORNIK UVTI. ZAHRADNICTVI (XR/0231-567X) [05997111] **2431**

SBORNIK VEDECKYCH PRAC (XO/0452-6171) [05268475] **1995**

SBORNIK VEDECKYCH PRACI LEKARSKE FAKULTY KARLOVY UNIVERSITY V HRADCI KRALOVE (XR/0049-5514) [01778386] **3638**

SBORNIK VEDECKYCH PRACI. RADA HUTNICKA. DOKLADY. SERIIA METALLURGICHESKAIA. TRANSACTIONS. METALLURGICAL SERIES (XR/0474-8484) [02221655] **4018**

SBORNIK VEDECKYCH PRACI USTREDNIHO STATNIHO VETERINARNIHO USTAVU (XR/0139-5297) [I01395297] **5521**

SBORNIK VEDECKYCH PRACI. VYSOKA SKOLA BANSKA, OSTRAVA. RADA HORNICKO-GEOLOGICKA (XR/0474-8476) [06586331] 2150, **1396**

SBORNIK VEDECKYCH PRACI / VYSOKA SKOLA CHEMICKO-TECHNOLOGICKA PARDUBICE (XR/0553-2124) [11580199] **1029**

SBORNIK VEDECKYCH PRACI VYSOKE SKOLY BANSKE V OSTRAVE. RADA STROJNICKA (XR) [10846380] **2128**

SBORNIK VYSOKE SKOLY CHEMICKO-TECHNOLOGICKE V PRAZE. A (XR/0139-9683) [27163418] **992**

SBORNIK VYSOKE SKOLY CHEMICKO-TECHNOLOGICKE V PRAZE. AUTOMATIZOVANE SYSTEMY RIZENI A VYPOCETNI METODY. SBORNIK PRAZHSKOGO KHIMIKO-TEKHNOLOGICHESKOGO INSTITUTA. AVTOMATIZIROVANNYE SISTEMY UPRAVLENIIA I VYCHISLITELNYE METODY. SCIENTIFIC PAPERS OF THE PRAGUE INSTITUTE OF CHEMICAL TECHNOLOGY. AUTOMATIC CONTROL SYSTEMS AND COMPUTING METHODS (XR/0139-973X) [06272800] **2017**

SBORNIK VYSOKE SKOLY CHEMICKO-TECHNOLOGICKE V PRAZE. B, ANORGANICKA CHEMIE A TECHNOLOGIE (XR/0551-8393) [11577463] **1037**

SBORNIK VYSOKE SKOLY CHEMICKO-TECHNOLOGICKE V PRAZE. C, ORGANICKA CHEMIE A TECHNOLOGIE (XR/0554-9728) [11577295] **1047**

SBORNIK VYSOKE SKOLY CHEMICKO-TECHNOLOGICKE V PRAZE. D, TECHNOLOGIE PALIV (XR/0554-9736) [10406089] **4277**

SBORNIK VYSOKE SKOLY CHEMICKO-TECHNOLOGICKE V PRAZE. FIZIKA MATERIALU A MERICI TECHNIKA. SBORNIK PRAZHSKOGO KHIMIKO-TECHNOLOGICHESKOGO INSTITUTA. FIZIKA MATERIALOV I IZMERITELNAIA TEKHNIKA. SCIENTIFIC PAPERS OF THE PRAGUE INSTITUTE OF CHEMICAL TECHNOLOGY. MATERIAL SCIENCE AND MEASUREMENT TECHNIQUE (XR/0139-7575) [05589659] **2108**

SBORNIK VYSOKE SKOLY CHEMICKO-TECHNOLOGICKE V PRAZE. FIZIKALNI CHEMIE. SBORNIK PRAZHSKOGO KHIMIKO-TECHNOLOGICHESKOGO INSTITUTA. FIZICHESKAIA KHIMIIA. SCIENTIFIC PAPERS OF THE PRAGUE INSTITUTE OF CHEMICAL TECHNOLOGY. PHYSICAL CHEMISTRY (CZ/0139-682X) [05630916] **1057**

SBORNIK VYSOKE SKOLY CHEMICKO-TECHNOLOGICKE V PRAZE. G, MINERALOGIE (XR/0551-8407) [11580195] **1444**

SBORNIK VYSOKE SKOLY CHEMICKO-TECHNOLOGICKE V PRAZE. POLYMERY-CHEMIE, VLASTNOSTI A ZPRACOVANI (XR/0139-908X) [06360228] **1047**

SBORNIK VYSOKE SKOLY CHEMICKO-TECHNOLOGICKE V PRAZE ... POTRAVINY (XR/0554-9701) [07303686] **2356**

SBORNIK VYSOKE SKOLY ZEMEDELSKE V PRAZE, FAKULTA AGRONOMICKA. RADA A-C, ROSTLINNA VYROBA-ZEMEDELSKE MELIORACE A STAVBY (XR) [23978333] **132**

SBORNIK VYSOKE SKOLY ZEMEDELSKE V PRAZE, FAKULTA AGRONOMICKA. RADA B. ZIVOCISNA VYROBA (XR) [07591426] **221**

SBORNIK VYSOKE SKOLY ZEMEDELSKE V PRAZE, FAKULTA AGRONOMICKA. RADA C: ZEMEDELSKE MELIORACE, ZEMEDELSKE STAVBY (XR) [03008343] **132**

SBORNIK ZA NARODNI UMOTVORENIJA I NARODOPIS (BU/0205-2679) [02710688] 3433, **3319**

SCA, STATE & COUNTY ADMINISTRATOR (US/0363-9401) [02570943] **4685**

SCA TECHNICAL REPORT SERIES (AT) [11899875] **132**

SCABBARD AND BLADE See SCABBARD AND BLADE JOURNAL **4056**

SCABBARD AND BLADE JOURNAL (US/0036-5408) [03919502] **4056**

SCAD BULLETIN (BE) [14709130] **424**

SCAD+CD (NE) **424**

SCAG: A RECORD OF ACCOMPLISHMENT (US) [01786477] 2835, **4685**

SCAG TELECOMMUNITY *CEASED.* (US/0889-5856) [12044978] **1163**

SCALA (GW/0303-4232) [01793068] **2522**

SCALA DEUTSCHE AUSGABE (GW/0340-0441) [I03400441] **2522**

SCALA INTERNATIONAL (GW/0581-9385) [01765074] **2522**

SCALE AIRCRAFT MODELLING (UK) 34, **2777**

SCALE AUTO ENTHUSIAST (US) [05374458] **2777**

SCALE CABINETMAKER, THE (US/0145-8213) [02792355] **2777**

SCALE MODELER (US/0036-5424) [03919544] **34**

SCALE MODELS INTERNATIONAL (UK/0269-834X) [18181122] **2778**

SCALE R/C MODELER (US/0199-7327) [06109167] **2778**

SCALE RAILROADING, O *See* GAUGE RAIL-ROADING, O **2773**

SCALE SHIP MODELER (US/0194-780X) [05015459] **4183**

SCALE WOODCRAFT *CEASED.* (US/8750-4871) [11434433] **375**

SCALL NEWSLETTER / SOUTHERN CALIFORNIA ASSOCIATION OF LAW LIBRARIES (US) [09704294] 3046, **3247**

SCALPEL (BRONXVILLE, N.Y.) (US) [02267502] **3638**

SCAMBI COMMERCIALI CON L'ESTERO, GLI *CEASED.* (IT) [08996345] **850**

SCAMBI COMMERCIALI ITALIA-U.S.A (IT) [07898086] **850**

SCAN (US) **4847**

SCAN-ENERGY ENGLISH ED (DK/0905-5606) [I09055606] **1956**

SCAN MAGAZINE (US/0745-0923) [08808841] **1139**

SCAN NEWSLETTER (US/0273-3080) [07046880] **1221**

SCAN (NORTH SYDNEY) (AT/0726-4127) [I07264127] **1904**

SCAN : SUMMARISING CONTEXTS, ACTION AND NETWORKS (AT/0818-3317) [I08183317] **1710**

SCAN (WAGENINGEN) (NE/0925-1413) [23377900] 132, **2204**

SCANDAL SHEET (US/1054-7789) [22969857] **4865**

SCANDALE (MONTREAL) (CN/0712-6026) [09313066] **5188**

SCANDALOUS INTERNATIONAL NEWS (CN/0820-7887) [09981952] **4535**

SCANDIA JOURNAL (US) [12411785] **5678**

SCANDINAVIA ON $ ... A DAY: DENMARK, SWEDEN, FINLAND, NORWAY AND ICELAND (US) [05383350] **5490**

SCANDINAVIAN ACTUARIAL JOURNAL (SW/0346-1238) [01924284] **2893**

SCANDINAVIAN AIRLINES SYSTEM *See* REPORT - SCANDINAVIAN AIRLINES SYSTEM **33**

SCANDINAVIAN AND EUROPEAN SHIPPING REVIEW *See* INTERNATIONAL SHIPPING REVIEW **5450**

SCANDINAVIAN ATLAS OF HISTORIC TOWNS (DK/0108-7827) [08092944] **2708**

SCANDINAVIAN AUDIOLOGY (SW/0105-0397) [01798471] **3891**

Alphabetical Title Index — SCHEDULE

SCANDINAVIAN AUDIOLOGY. SUPPLEMENTUM (SW/0107-8593) [01607416] **3891**

SCANDINAVIAN CANADIAN BUSINESSMAN (CN/0048-928X) [02128148] **709**

SCANDINAVIAN-CANADIAN STUDIES (CN/0823-1796) [10789201] **2759**

SCANDINAVIAN COUNCIL FOR APPLIED RESEARCH *See* ARSBERATTELSE - NORDFORSK **5086**

SCANDINAVIAN DAIRY INFORMATION (SW/1101-2706) [24927395] **198**

SCANDINAVIAN DAIRY INFORMATION - SDI (SW/1101-2706) [15925822] **198**

SCANDINAVIAN ECONOMIC HISTORY REVIEW, THE (SW/0358-5522) [01765081] **1583**

SCANDINAVIAN FOREST ECONOMICS (FI/0355-032X) [05182741] 1520, **2394**

SCANDINAVIAN FORUM (CN/0836-2149) [16861037] **2272**

SCANDINAVIAN HOUSING AND PLANNING RESEARCH (SW/0281-5737) [10868744] **2835**

SCANDINAVIAN INDUSTRY REVUE : SIR *CEASED.* (NO) [08299833] **1626**

SCANDINAVIAN INSTITUTE OF ASIAN STUDIES *See* OCCASIONAL PAPERS / SCANDINAVIAN INSTITUTE OF ASIAN STUDIES **2661**

SCANDINAVIAN INTERNATIONAL BUSINESS REVIEW (UK/0962-9262) [I09629262] **709**

SCANDINAVIAN INTERNATIONAL BUSINESS REVIEW *See* INTERNATIONAL BUSINESS REVIEW **683**

SCANDINAVIAN JOURNAL OF BEHAVIOUR THERAPY (SW/0284-5717) [I02845717] **4617**

SCANDINAVIAN JOURNAL OF CARING SCIENCES (SW/0283-9318) [17726555] **3869**

SCANDINAVIAN JOURNAL OF CLINICAL & LABORATORY INVESTIGATION (UK/0036-5513) [01623860] **586**

SCANDINAVIAN JOURNAL OF DENTAL RESEARCH (DK/0029-845X) [01713707] **1335**

SCANDINAVIAN JOURNAL OF DEVELOPMENT ALTERNATIVES (SW/0280-2791) [09834662] **4535**

SCANDINAVIAN JOURNAL OF ECONOMICS, THE (UK/0347-0520) [02328521] **1520**

SCANDINAVIAN JOURNAL OF EDUCATIONAL RESEARCH (UK/0031-3831) [01765082] **1781**

SCANDINAVIAN JOURNAL OF FOREST RESEARCH (SW/0282-7581) [13163184] **2394**

SCANDINAVIAN JOURNAL OF GASTROENTEROLOGY (NO/0036-5521) [01765083] **3747**

SCANDINAVIAN JOURNAL OF GASTROENTEROLOGY (EDICION ESPANOLA) (SP) **3801**

SCANDINAVIAN JOURNAL OF GASTROENTEROLOGY. SUPPLEMENT (NO/0085-5928) [01112719] **3747**

SCANDINAVIAN JOURNAL OF HISTORY (SW/0346-8755) [02767018] **2708**

SCANDINAVIAN JOURNAL OF IMMUNOLOGY (UK/0300-9475) [01793076] **3676**

SCANDINAVIAN JOURNAL OF IMMUNOLOGY. SUPPLEMENT (NO/0301-6323) [01171063] **3676**

SCANDINAVIAN JOURNAL OF INFECTIOUS DISEASES (NO/0036-5548) [01765084] **3716**

SCANDINAVIAN JOURNAL OF INFECTIOUS DISEASES. SUPPLEMENTUM (SW/0300-8878) [03972313] **3716**

SCANDINAVIAN JOURNAL OF INFORMATION SYSTEMS (DK/0905-0167) [27835470] **1249**

SCANDINAVIAN JOURNAL OF LABORATORY ANIMAL SCIENCE (DK/0901-3393) [19264379] **5521**

SCANDINAVIAN JOURNAL OF MANAGEMENT (UK/0956-5221) [19121871] **885**

SCANDINAVIAN JOURNAL OF MATERIALS ADMINISTRATION (NO/0332-6039) [I03326039] **709**

SCANDINAVIAN JOURNAL OF METALLURGY (SW/0371-0459) [01765085] **4018**

●SCANDINAVIAN JOURNAL OF NUTRITION NARINGSFORSKNING (SW/1102-6480) [I11026480] **4199**

SCANDINAVIAN JOURNAL OF OCCUPATIONAL THERAPY (NO/1103-8128) **3639**

SCANDINAVIAN JOURNAL OF PLASTIC AND RECONSTRUCTIVE SURGERY AND HAND SURGERY (SW/0284-4311) [15688269] **3974**

SCANDINAVIAN JOURNAL OF PRIMARY HEALTH CARE (SW/0107-833X) [10680310] **3739**

SCANDINAVIAN JOURNAL OF PRIMARY HEALTH CARE. SUPPLEMENT (SW/0281-3432) [19475937] **3739**

SCANDINAVIAN JOURNAL OF PSYCHOLOGY (SW/0036-5564) [01645705] **4617**

SCANDINAVIAN JOURNAL OF REHABILITATION MEDICINE (SW/0036-5505) [01765087] **3639**

SCANDINAVIAN JOURNAL OF REHABILITATION MEDICINE. SUPPLEMENT (SW/0346-8720) [01778247] **3639**

SCANDINAVIAN JOURNAL OF RHEUMATOLOGY (SW/0300-9742) [01773365] **3807**

SCANDINAVIAN JOURNAL OF RHEUMATOLOGY. SUPPLEMENT (SW/0301-3847) [01588104] **3807**

SCANDINAVIAN JOURNAL OF SOCIAL MEDICINE (SW/0300-8037) [01443254] **3639**

SCANDINAVIAN JOURNAL OF SOCIAL MEDICINE. SUPPLEMENTUM (SW/0301-7311) [01777771] **3639**

●SCANDINAVIAN JOURNAL OF SOCIAL WELFARE (DK/0907-2055) [28610425] **5307**

SCANDINAVIAN JOURNAL OF STATISTICS (SW/0303-6898) [02243570] **5338**

SCANDINAVIAN JOURNAL OF THE OLD TESTAMENT : SJOT (DK/0901-8328) [16313081] **5019**

SCANDINAVIAN JOURNAL OF THORACIC AND CARDIOVASCULAR SURGERY (SW/0036-5580) [01588502] **3974**

SCANDINAVIAN JOURNAL OF THORACIC AND CARDIOVASCULAR SURGERY. SUPPLEMENTUM (SW/0586-9587) [01778249] **3710**

SCANDINAVIAN JOURNAL OF UROLOGY AND NEPHROLOGY (SW/0036-5599) [01641524] **3993**

SCANDINAVIAN JOURNAL OF UROLOGY AND NEPHROLOGY. SUPPLEMENT (SW/0300-8886) [01778250] **3993**

SCANDINAVIAN JOURNAL OF WORK, ENVIRONMENT & HEALTH (FI/0355-3140) [01683585] **2870**

SCANDINAVIAN OIL-GAS MAGAZINE (NO/0332-5334) [I03325334] **4277**

SCANDINAVIAN PERIODICALS INDEX IN ECONOMICS AND BUSINESS : SCANP (FI) [07859915] 1520, **1538**

SCANDINAVIAN POLITICAL STUDIES (NO/0080-6757) [01586864] **4495**

SCANDINAVIAN PSYCHOANALYTIC REVIEW, THE (NO/0106-2301) [04547219] **4617**

SCANDINAVIAN PUBLIC LIBRARY QUARTERLY (DK/0036-5602) [01713716] **3247**

SCANDINAVIAN PULP & PAPER MAGAZINE (SW/0284-6454) [18348110] **4239**

SCANDINAVIAN REVIEW (US/0098-857X) [02243489] **2272**

SCANDINAVIAN REVIEW [MICROFORM] (US) [06460539] **2272**

SCANDINAVIAN SHIPPING GAZETTE (DK) [06706393] **5455**

SCANDINAVIAN STUDIES IN CRIMINOLOGY (NO) [01765092] **3176**

SCANDINAVIAN STUDIES IN LAW (SW/0085-5944) [01606375] **3135**

SCANDINAVIAN STUDIES: PUBLICATION OF THE SOCIETY FOR THE ADVANCEMENT OF SCANDINAVIAN STUDY (US/0036-5637) [01765091] 5218, **3433**

SCANDINAVIAN TRADE CENTER FOR HOME FURNISHINGS *See* STC NEWS **2907**

SCANDINAVIAN WORKING PAPERS ON BILINGUALISM (SW/0280-7750) [13119422] **3319**

SCANDINAVICA (UK/0036-5653) [01338346] **3433**

SCANDO-SLAVICA (DK/0080-6765) [01765094] 3433, **3319**

SCANDO-SLAVICA. SUPPLEMENTUM (DK) [05995367] 3433, **3319**

SCANFAX (US/0018-9227) [04062694] **2080**

SCANNER AND KING COUNTY LABOR NEWS, THE (US/8750-1708) [11087308] **1710**

SCANNER (TORONTO) (CN/0318-014X) [02128164] **2759**

SCANNING (US/0161-0457) [03819106] **574**

SCANNING MICROSCOPY (US/0891-7035) [14972781] **574**

SCANNING SOURCEBOOK, THE (US) [20844379] **1202**

SCANORAMA (SW/0346-7775) [I03467775] **709**

SCAPE (LOS ANGELES, CALIF.) (US/1049-7455) [21310042] **2492**

SCARBORO CONSUMER (CN/0225-2074) [06156774] **5794**

SCARBORO MISSIONS (CN/0700-6802) [02803403] **4995**

SCARBOROUGH HISTORICAL NOTES & COMMENTS (CN/0712-4961) [09157005] **2759**

SCARBOROUGH NEWS (CN/0834-7131) [16386130] **5794**

SCARLET & GOLD (CN/0316-4209) [02441689] **3176**

SCARLET & GRAY ILLUSTRATED (US/0899-9066) [18261043] **4916**

SCARLET STREET (US/1058-8612) [24435311] **3433**

SCARLET WOMAN (AT/0313-4423) [04647078] **5566**

SCARSDALE INQUIRER, THE (US) [09932929] **5721**

SCAS & VSCAS COMPANIES' ACCOUNTS DISCLOSURE CHECKLIST (UK) **751**

SCAW NEWSLETTER (US/1052-7559) [20104149] 5521, **227**

SCBS BILKALENDER (SW) [10652899] **5402**

SCCUQ-INFO (CN/1184-9312) [24570990] **1710**

SCEA EMPHASIS *CEASED.* (US/0273-7906) [05321360] **1870**

SCENA (PL) [05341784] **5368**

SCENA ILLUSTRATA (IT/0036-5742) **2492**

SCENARIO : IL NURSING DELLA SOPRAVVIVENZA *CEASED.* (IT) **3869**

SCENE *See* TV 2 (SAINT PAUL, MINN.) **1141**

SCENE CHANGES (CN/0381-8098) [02168586] **5368**

SCENE ENTERTAINMENT WEEKLY (US/1064-6116) [25111701] 4152, **330**

SCENIC TRIPS TO THE GEOLOGIC PAST (US/0548-5983) [01673156] **1396**

SCENTERPIECE UPDATE (US) **375**

SCHAAK JAARBOEK (NE) [05873578] **4866**

SCHACH (GW/0048-9328) [I00489328] **4866**

SCHACH ECHO *See* SCHACH MAGAZIN 64 SCHACH ECHO **4916**

SCHACH GERMANY (GW) **4866**

SCHACH MAGAZIN 64 *See* SCHACH MAGAZIN 64 SCHACH ECHO **4916**

SCHACH MAGAZIN 64 SCHACH ECHO (GW) **4916**

SCHAFFHAUSER BEITRAGE ZUR GESCHICHTE (SZ/0259-3599) [01929460] **2708**

SCHALLPLATTEN ABC. SINGLE SCHALLPLATTEN, GESAMTVERZEICHNIS, DAS (GW) [10568821] **4152**

SCHALLPLATTEN ZUM AUSLEIHEN *See* CDS ZUM AUSLEIHEN **4160**

SCHALLPLATTEN ZUM AUSLEIHEN, NEUERWERBUNGEN / PHONOTHEK, BERLINER STADTBIBLIOTHEK (GW) [10340435] **4160**

SCHALLPLATTENRING ILLUSTRIERTE *See* MELODIE **4130**

SCHARTZER-SCHERTZER CONNECTION, THE (US/0882-5890) [11907333] **2471**

SCHATZKAMMER DER DEUTSCHEN SPRACHE, DICHTUNG UND GESCHICHTE (US/0740-1965) [09926503] 1904, **3433**

SCHAU-IN'S-LAND *See* ZEITSCHRIFT DES BREISGAU-GESCHICHTSVEREINS SCHAUINSLAND **2716**

SCHAU INS LAND. SOUND RECORDING (US/1041-2018) [15528112] **2522**

SCHAULADE, DIE (GW) [07045638] 2585, **2593**

SCHAUPLATZ KOLN (GW) [14929428] **2522**

SCHAUSPIELFUHRER, DER (GW) [02251664] **5372**

SCHEBEN NEWS (GW) **765**

SCHEDARIO (IT/0036-5955) [I00365955] **4819**

SCHEDARIO DELLA NORMATIVA CONSOB (IT) **810**

SCHEDE (IT) [03025981] **2030**

SCHEDE MEDIEVALI (IT/0392-5404) [09879133] **2708**

SCHEDULE & RULE BOOK - NATIONAL HOCKEY LEAGUE (CN/0842-0947) [19573574] **4916**

SCHEDULE — Alphabetical Title Index

SCHEDULE B, STATISTICAL CLASSIFICATION OF DOMESTIC AND FOREIGN COMMODITIES EXPORTED FROM THE UNITED STATES / U.S. DEPARTMENT OF COMMERCE, BUREAU OF THE CENSUS (US) [09876150] 850, **733**

SCHEDULE C-I, CLASSIFICATION OF COUNTRY AND TERRITORY DESIGNATIONS FOR U.S. IMPORT STATISTICS (US/0191-4057) [02558468] 850, **733**

SCHEDULE-INDUCED BEHAVIOR. RESEARCH & THEORY (CN/0704-500X) [03530648] **4617**

SCHEDULE OF NIH CONFERENCES (US/0733-4397) [08007929] **3639**

SCHEDULE OF WELLS *See* SASKATCHEWAN SCHEDULE OF WELLS **1396**

●SCHEDULED AND CHARTER FREIGHT TRAFFIC FORECAST (SZ) **34**

SCHEDULED AND CHARTER FREIGHT TRAFFIC FORECAST (SZ) [24878306] **34**

SCHEDULED CARGO TRAFFIC & REVENUE (US) [03457995] **34**

SCHEDULED PASSENGER TRAFFIC FORECAST (SZ) [17002568] **34**

SCHEDULED SALARIES FOR PROFESSIONAL PERSONNEL IN PUBLIC SCHOOLS (US/0742-0862) [04378293] 1870, **1710**

SCHEMI DI LAVORO (IT) **1710**

SCHERZO (US/1048-2180) [20869937] **4152**

SCHIESSPORTSCHULE DIALOGUES (US/0160-1253) [03617141] **4916**

SCHIFANOIA : NOTIZIE DELL'ISTITUTO DI STUDI RINASCIMENTALI DI FERRARA (IT) [16661078] **330**

SCHIFF & HAFEN/SEEWIRTSCHAFT (GW/0938-1643) [23997347] **5455**

SCHIFF REPORT, THE (US/1055-8969) [23366760] **4801**

SCHIFFBAUFORSCHUNG (GW/0036-6056) [07124635] **4183**

SCHIFFBAUTECHNISCHE GESELLSCHAFT *See* JAHRBUCH DER SCHIFFBAUTECHNISCHEN GESELLSCHAFT **4177**

SCHILLER PARK INDEPENDENT *CEASED.* (US/0744-5377) [08338895] **5662**

SCHILLERS WERKE (GW) **3470**

SCHIP EN WERF DE ZEE (NE/0926-4213) [25139628] **4183**

SCHIPHOLLAND (NE) **34**

SCHIST (WILLIMANTIC) (US/0092-9425) [01791362] **3470**

SCHISTO UPDATE (US/0197-7210) [06121165] 3639, **3661**

SCHIZOPHRENIA BULLETIN (US/0586-7614) [01345919] **3936**

SCHIZOPHRENIA RESEARCH (NE/0920-9964) [17726734] **3936**

SCHLERN, DER (IT/0036-6145) [05634548] **2708**

SCHLESIEN (GW/0036-6153) [01590215] **2708**

SCHLESWIG-HOLSTEIN (GW/0937-7247) [23753524] **2708**

SCHLESWIG LEADER, THE (US) [16687875] **5672**

SCHMAGG (CN/0706-8387) [08003108] **2545**

SCHMALENBACHS ZEITSCHRIFT FUER BETRIEBSWIRTSCHAFTLICHE FORSCHUNG (GW/0341-2687) [12125117] **850**

SCHMERZ, DER (GW/0932-433X) [19961434] **3639**

SCHMERZDIAGNOSTIK UND THERAPIE (GW/0178-692X) [13039143] **3639**

SCHMERZSTUDIEN (GW/0170-0596) [04855473] **3639**

SCHMITZ (R. M.) & COMPANY *See* REPORT ON MANAGEMENT SUCCESSION **884**

SCHNAUZER SHORTS (US/0276-1521) [07313739] **4288**

SCHNEIDER CONNECTIONS (US/0882-5904) [11907271] **2471**

SCHOCH LETTER, THE (US/0487-6520) [02904452] **3722**

SCHOENER WOHNEN (GW/0036-6277) [01765105] **2903**

SCHOENINDUSTRIE / CENTRAAL BUREAU VOOR DE STATISTIEK, HOOFDAFDELING STATISTIEKEN VAN INDUSTRIE EN BOUWNIJVERHEID (NE) [10608254] **1087**

SCHOFFE, DER (GW/0036-6250) [03032449] **3046**

SCHOHARIE COUNTY HISTORICAL REVIEW (US/0361-8528) [06514139] **2759**

SCHOLAR AND EDUCATOR (US/0149-3299) [03457665] **1781**

SCHOLAR CRITIC (II) [08279039] **3434**

SCHOLARLY BOOKS IN AUSTRALIA *CEASED.* (AT) [04274741] **4832**

SCHOLARLY INQUIRY FOR NURSING PRACTICE (US/0889-7182) [14039516] **3869**

SCHOLARLY PUBLISHING (CN/0036-634X) [01765109] **4819**

SCHOLARS' CHOICE (US/0558-8766) [01776698] 4995, **5013**

SCHOLARS' FACSIMILES AND REPRINTS (SERIES) (US/0161-7729) [04026772] 2854, 4360, **3319**

SCHOLARS OF EARLY MODERN STUDIES (US/1059-9185) [24808128] **2708**

SCHOLARSHIPS AND LOANS FOR NURSING EDUCATION (US/0891-7884) [11487879] 1846, **3869**

SCHOLARSHIPS, FELLOWSHIPS AND LOANS (US) **1846**

SCHOLARSHIPS GUIDE FOR COMMONWEALTH POSTGRADUATE STUDENTS *See* AWARDS FOR POSTGRADUATE STUDY AT COMMONWEALTH UNIVERSITIES **1811**

SCHOLARSHIPS, STUDENT AID & LOANS *See* GRANT$ FOR SCHOLARSHIPS, STUDENT AID & LOANS **4337**

SCHOLASTIC ACTION (US/0163-3570) [04398414] **1904**

●SCHOLASTIC ART (US/1060-832X) [25113273] **364**

SCHOLASTIC CHOICES (US/0883-475X) [12141402] **2792**

SCHOLASTIC COACH (US/0036-6382) [01765112] **4917**

●SCHOLASTIC COACH AND ATHLETIC DIRECTOR (US/1077-5625) [30834945] **4917**

SCHOLASTIC DYNAMATH (US/0732-7773) [08423656] 1904, **3532**

●SCHOLASTIC EARLY CHILDHOOD TODAY (US/1070-1214) [28280530] **1805**

SCHOLASTIC MATH MAGAZINE (US/0198-8379) [06232436] 1904, **3532**

SCHOLASTIC MATH POWER (US/1055-1212) [23086149] **3533**

SCHOLASTIC NEWS (CITIZEN ED.) (US/0736-0614) [09071437] **1781**

SCHOLASTIC NEWS (EXPLORER EDITION) (US/0736-0592) [09071854] **1781**

SCHOLASTIC NEWS (PILOT EDITION) (US/0736-0533) [08651817] **1094**

SCHOLASTIC NEWS (RANGER EDITION) (US/0736-055X) [09072502] **1781**

SCHOLASTIC NEWSTIME (1989) (US/1058-1537) [24228439] **1781**

SCHOLASTIC PRE-K TODAY (US/0888-3009) [13528433] **1781**

SCHOLASTIC SCOPE (US/0036-6412) [01765114] **1094**

SCHOLASTIC SEARCH *CEASED.* (US/0163-4798) [07707161] **1781**

SCHOLASTIC UPDATE (US/0745-7065) [09384159] 2760, **1782**

SCHOLASTIC UPDATE (TEACHERS' ED.) (US/0886-4551) [09416891] **2545**

SCHOLASTIC VOICE *CEASED.* (US/0032-6380) [02240075] **3319**

SCHOLASTIC WHEELS *See* NEW DRIVER (HIGHLAND PARK, ILL.) **5421**

SCHOLE : A JOURNAL OF LEISURE STUDIES AND RECREATION EDUCATION (US) [20843972] **4854**

SCHOLIASTIS (GR) **4819**

SCHOMBERG-NOBLETON NEWS (CN/0229-6071) [08036524] **5794**

SCHOMBURG CENTER FOR RESEARCH IN BLACK CULTURE *See* BIBLIOGRAPHIC GUIDE TO BLACK STUDIES **2276**

SCHOMBURG CENTER JOURNAL, THE (US/0883-3400) [10982996] **2272**

SCHONSTEN BUCHER OSTERREICHS, DIE (AU) [01071104] **4832**

SCHOOL (NE) [01794830] **1782**

SCHOOL ACHIEVEMENT IN EARLY CHILDHOOD EDUCATION (US/0145-2150) [02711678] **1805**

SCHOOL ADMINISTRATOR (WASHINGTON) (US/0036-6439) [01791849] **1870**

SCHOOL AGE NOTES (US/0278-3126) [07787987] **1782**

SCHOOL AND COLLEGE (CLEVELAND, OHIO) (US/1045-3970) [18007512] **1846**

SCHOOL AND COMMUNITY (COLUMBIA) (US/0036-6447) [06374265] **1782**

SCHOOL AND COMMUNITY NEWS CANBERRA (AT/0314-1543) [I03141543] 4685, **1782**

SCHOOL AND DISTRICT REPORTS. EXPLANATORY MATERIALS (US/0148-513X) [03317974] **1870**

SCHOOL & UNIVERSITY REVIEW (US) [04099515] **1846**

SCHOOL ARTS (US/0036-6463) [05457273] 1904, **364**

SCHOOL BELL (AT) **1871**

SCHOOL BOARD NEWS (ALEXANDRIA, VA.) (US/1045-8115) [11561660] **1871**

SCHOOL BOND GUIDE (US) [10250376] **1871**

SCHOOL BUILDING CONSTRUCTION NEEDS (US) [05058348] **1904**

SCHOOL BULLETIN, MINNEAPOLIS PUBLIC SCHOOLS (US) [01757565] **1782**

SCHOOL BUS FLEET (US/0036-6501) [05321218] **5392**

SCHOOL BUS FLEET FACT BOOK (US) **5392**

SCHOOL BUS PURCHASES (US) [01797990] 5392, **1871**

SCHOOL BUS TRANSPORTATION *See* SCHOOL BUS FLEET **5392**

SCHOOL BUSINESS ADMINISTRATION PUBLICATION (SACRAMENTO) (US/0487-6776) [01789791] **1871**

SCHOOL BUSINESS AFFAIRS (US/0036-651X) [01765121] **1871**

SCHOOL CALENDAR (TORONTO) (CN/0382-7879) [02813707] **1871**

SCHOOL CENSUS FOR THE STATE OF ARKANSAS (US/0571-0227) [03332025] **1871**

SCHOOL CHILD CARE REPORT *See* REPORT ON SCHOOL AGE CHILD CARE **1805**

SCHOOL COMMUNITY JOURNAL, THE (US/1059-308X) [24562552] **1782**

SCHOOL COUNSELOR, THE (US/0036-6536) [01639814] **1885**

SCHOOL CRIME IN CALIFORNIA FOR THE ... SCHOOL YEAR (US) [22749177] 1782, **3176**

SCHOOL DIRECTORY / MASSACHUSETTS DEPARTMENT OF EDUCATION (US) [22534188] **1782**

SCHOOL DIRECTORY (TRENTON, N.J.) (US) [12027325] **1782**

SCHOOL DISTRICT, COLLEGE AND INSTITUTE CONTINUING EDUCATION DATA (CN/0713-4010) [07964853] **1802**

SCHOOL DISTRICT PROFILES (US) [07769519] **1871**

SCHOOL DISTRICTS THAT WERE GRANTED WAIVERS OF ADMINISTRATOR-TEACHER RATIO LIMITS (US/0146-8766) [03058035] **1871**

SCHOOL DROPOUTS BY REASON (US) [07506859] **1782**

SCHOOL EDUCATION NEWS (AT/1036-5141) [I10365141] **1782**

SCHOOL EFFECTIVENESS AND SCHOOL IMPROVEMENT (NE/0924-3453) [21454519] **1871**

SCHOOL EMPLOYERS ASSOCIATION *See* SEA REPORTER **1872**

SCHOOL EN COMPUTER *CEASED.* (BE) **1224**

SCHOOL EN WET (NE) [07025098] **1782**

SCHOOL ENROLLMENT, SOCIAL AND ECONOMIC CHARACTERISTICS OF STUDENTS / BUREAU OF THE CENSUS, POPULATION DIVISION (US) [08620158] **1871**

SCHOOL EXECUTIVE (PHILADELPHIA, PA.) (US/1058-6431) [24345997] **1871**

SCHOOL FINANCE FACTS (US) [08359223] **1846**

SCHOOL FOOD SERVICE DIRECTOR (US/0741-4838) [10155592] 1871, **2356**

SCHOOL FOOD SERVICE JOURNAL (US/0160-6271) [03562551] **2356**

SCHOOL FOOD SERVICE : STATE PLAN FOR FISCAL YEAR ... (US) [04341899] **1782**

●SCHOOL FOODSERVICE & NUTRITION (US/1075-3885) [30045014] **2356**

SCHOOL FOODSERVICE RESEARCH REVIEW (US/0149-6808) [03520378] **2356**

SCHOOL GOVERNOR'S MANUAL (UK) **1871**

SCHOOL GUIDE (US) [03295387] **1846**

SCHOOL HEALTH ALERT (US/1048-3896) [15207786] 3869, **1782**

SCHOOL INTERVENTION REPORT (US/0894-5152) [16119088] **1782**

SCHOOL LAW BULLETIN (BOSTON, MASS.) (US/8755-8297) [05663683] **1871**

Alphabetical Title Index — SCHRIFTENREIHE

SCHOOL LAW BULLETIN (CHAPEL HILL, N.C.) (US/0886-2508) [03076780] **1871**

SCHOOL LAW COMMENTARY (CN/0833-0875) [16074614] **1782**, **3046**

SCHOOL LAW DIGEST See SCHOOL LAW / WASHINGTON STATE SCHOOL DIRECTORS' ASSOCIATION **3046**

SCHOOL LAW NEWS (US/0194-2271) [03744278] **1871**

SCHOOL LAW NEWSLETTER (VERNON, TEX.), THE (US/0891-5474) [04277683] **1782**, **3046**

SCHOOL LAW REPORTER (US/1059-4094) [16660907] **1782**, **3046**

●SCHOOL LAW / WASHINGTON STATE SCHOOL DIRECTORS' ASSOCIATION (US) [26715238] **1782**, **3046**

SCHOOL LAWS OF THE STATE OF WYOMING (US) [02480647] **1871**

SCHOOL LAWYER, THE (US/0197-3541) [06006436] **1871**

SCHOOL LEADER (US) [05217341] **1871**

SCHOOL LIBRARIAN, THE (UK/0036-6595) [02461665] **3247**

SCHOOL LIBRARIAN'S WORKSHOP, THE (US/0271-3667) [06629733] **3247**

SCHOOL LIBRARIES IN CANADA (CN/0227-3780) [07805889] **3248**

SCHOOL LIBRARY ADVOCATE (CN/1181-9979) [24265858] **3248**

SCHOOL LIBRARY ASSOCIATION See SCHOOL LIBRARY NEWSLETTER **3248**

SCHOOL LIBRARY FORUM (AT/0814-334X) [I0814334X] **1782**, **3248**

SCHOOL LIBRARY JOURNAL (NEW YORK, N.Y.) (US/0362-8930) [01798621] **3248**

SCHOOL LIBRARY MEDIA ACTIVITIES MONTHLY (US/0889-9371) [12257564] **3248**

SCHOOL LIBRARY MEDIA ANNUAL (US/0739-7712) [09809890] **3248**

SCHOOL LIBRARY MEDIA FOLDERS OF IDEAS FOR LIBRARY EXCELLENCE (US/1042-4245) [19039773] **3248**

SCHOOL LIBRARY MEDIA QUARTERLY (US/0278-4823) [07831305] **3248**

SCHOOL LIBRARY NEWS (AT/0814-8392) [I08148392] **1782**, **3248**

SCHOOL LIBRARY NEWSLETTER (CN/0706-2915) [05072594] **3248**

SCHOOL MAGAZINE (AT) [07723596] **1095**

SCHOOL MANAGEMENT SYSTEMS NEWSLETTER (AT/0814-5571) [I08145571] **1871**

SCHOOL MARKETING NEWSLETTER (US) **1782**, **936**

SCHOOL MATES (US/1040-7707) [18519075] 1068, **4866**

SCHOOL MUSIC NEWS, THE (US/0036-6668) [02450412] **4152**

SCHOOL OF COMPUTER SCIENCE. UNIVERSITY OF WINDSOR (CN/0316-8573) [02247241] **1202**

SCHOOL OF INDUSTRIAL RELATIONS RESEARCH ESSAY SERIES (CN) [15861372] **1626**

SCHOOL ORGANISATION (UK/0260-1362) [12515064] **1871**

SCHOOL ORGANISATION & MANAGEMENT ABSTRACTS (UK/0261-2755) [08906001] **1871**, **1797**

SCHOOL PRESS REVIEW See STUDENT PRESS REVIEW **2924**

SCHOOL PSYCHOLOGIST, THE (US/0160-5585) [03876627] **4618**

SCHOOL PSYCHOLOGY INTERNATIONAL (UK/0143-0343) [05924545] **4618**

SCHOOL PSYCHOLOGY QUARTERLY (US/1045-3830) [20083181] **1782**, **4618**

SCHOOL PSYCHOLOGY REVIEW (US/0279-6015) [06061214] 1904, **4618**

SCHOOL RACIAL-ETHNIC CENSUS (US/0145-8353) [02822603] 2272, **1782**

SCHOOL RETIREMENT SYSTEM OF THE STATE OF NEBRASKA See ACTUARIAL REPORT FOR STATE FISCAL YEAR ENDING ..., AND SYSTEM PLAN YEAR BEGINNING ... / SCHOOL RETIREMENT SYSTEM OF THE STATE OF NEBRASKA **1642**

SCHOOL RETIREMENT SYSTEM OF THE STATE OF NEBRASKA. SYSTEM ACTUARY'S REPORT, ACTUARIAL VALUATION See ACTUARIAL REPORT FOR STATE FISCAL YEAR ENDING ..., AND SYSTEM PLAN YEAR BEGINNING ... / SCHOOL RETIREMENT SYSTEM OF THE STATE OF NEBRASKA **1642**

SCHOOL SAFETY : NATIONAL SCHOOL SAFETY CENTER NEWSJOURNAL (US) [13182697] 4801, **1782**

SCHOOL SAFETY WORLD NEWSLETTER / SCHOOL AND COLLEGE DEPARTMENT, NATIONAL SAFETY COUNCIL (US) [07146554] **4801**

SCHOOL SCIENCE (II/0036-679X) [02455987] **5149**

SCHOOL SCIENCE AND MATHEMATICS (US/0036-6803) [04295250] 1904, **5149**

SCHOOL SCIENCE REVIEW (UK/0036-6811) [01640642] 1904, **5149**

SCHOOL SECURITY REPORT (US/1060-426X) [24989622] **1871**

SCHOOL SELECTION GUIDE See BAKER & TAYLOR'S SCHOOL SELECTION GUIDE **1727**

SCHOOL SHOP/TECH DIRECTIONS (US/1050-3749) [21471941] **1915**

SCHOOL SLATE (US/0890-8419) [04742219] **1871**

SCHOOL SOCIAL WORK JOURNAL (US/0161-5653) [02961486] **1871**

SCHOOL STAFFING RATIOS (US/0735-6625) [06002726] **1872**

SCHOOL TRANSPORTATION (US/0273-0936) [07004463] **5392**

SCHOOL TRANSPORTATION NEWS (US/1070-3586) [28347399] **5392**

SCHOOL TRANSPORTATION SUMMARY (US/0361-2287) [02246310] **1872**

SCHOOL TRUSTEE (REGINA) (CN/0036-6854) [02128849] **1872**

SCHOOL UNIVERSE DATA BOOK See CIC'S SCHOOL DIRECTORY. NORTH CAROLINA **1891**

SCHOOLMATCH [COMPUTER FILE] (US) [19946883] **1782**

SCHOOLS ABROAD OF INTEREST TO AMERICANS (US/0899-2002) [02950193] **1782**

SCHOOLS ADVOCATE, THE (US/0890-1236) [14179934] 1885, **3046**

SCHOOLS & STAFFING (AT) [01783728] **1782**

SCHOOLS AND THE COURTS, THE (US/0164-3851) [04697050] **1872**

SCHOOLS, AUSTRALIA (AT) [22341667] **1782**, **1797**

SCHOOLS, AUSTRALIA ... PRELIMINARY (AT/1034-5671) [I10345671] **1782**, **1797**

SCHOOLS IN THE MIDDLE (US/0276-4482) [07370677] **1872**

SCHOOLS OF ENGLAND, WALES, SCOTLAND AND IRELAND, THE (UK) [02946083] **1782**

SCHOOLS (OLYMPIA, WASH.) (US) [09450028] **1847**

SCHOOLTECHNEWS *CEASED.* (US/0740-185X) [09888918] **1782**

SCHOOLWORD See UNDERCURRENTS: MYSTIC MARINELIFE AQUARIUM QUARTERLY **5599**

SCHOTT-FORSCHUNGSBERICHTE (GW/0343-9356) [03439356] **1995**

SCHRIFTEN (GW) [01649132] **4495**

SCHRIFTEN (GW) [03279581] **2708**

SCHRIFTEN AUS DER FORSTLICHEN FAKULTAT DER UNIVERSITAT GOTTINGEN UND DER NIEDERSACHSISCHEN FORSTLICHEN VERSUCHSANSTALT (GW/0344-5666) [05913003] **2395**

SCHRIFTEN DER GOETHE-GESELLSCHAFT (GW) [01640168] 434, **3434**

SCHRIFTEN DER MAINZER PHILOSOPHISCHEN FAKULTATSGESELLSCHAFT E. V (GW/0170-3609) [01703609] **4360**

SCHRIFTEN DER MONUMENTA GERMANIAE HISTORICA (DEUTSCHES INSTITUT FUR ERFORSCHUNG DES MITTELALTERS) (GW/0080-6951) [04107974] **2708**

SCHRIFTEN DER SCHWEIZERISCHEN GESELLSCHAFT FUER VOLKSKUNDE (SZ/0080-732X) [03047140] 5269, **2324**

SCHRIFTEN DER THEODOR-STORM-GESELLSCHAFT (GW/0082-3880) [01258447] **3434**

SCHRIFTEN DES ARBEITSKREISES SELBSTANDIGER KULTUR-INSTITUTE (GW/0176-9472) [18230075] **2492**

SCHRIFTEN DES HISTORISCHEN MUSEUMS FRANKFURT AM MAIN (GW/0342-2038) [08909126] **364**

SCHRIFTEN DES INSTITUTES FUER OESTERREICHKUNDE (AU) [21244364] **2708**

SCHRIFTEN DES LIMESMUSEUMS AALEN (GW) [17006220] **4096**

SCHRIFTEN DES VEREINS FUER GESCHICHTE DES BODENSEES UND SEINER UMGEBUNG (GW) [02158016] **2708**

SCHRIFTEN DES ZENTRALINSTITUTS FUER WIRTSCHAFTWISSENSCHAFTEN BEI AKADEMIE DER WISSENSCHAFT (GW) **1520**

SCHRIFTEN - GESELLSCHAFT FUER SOZIALEN FORTSCHRITT (GW/0435-8287) [01454753] **5257**

SCHRIFTEN UND QUELLEN DER ALTEN WELT (GW/0080-696X) [01765146] 3319, **1080**

SCHRIFTEN ZU REGIONAL- UND VERKEHRSPROBLEMEN IN INDUSTRIE- UND ENTWICKLUNGSLANDERN (GW/0582-0170) [02936816] **1583**

SCHRIFTEN ZUM BURGERLICHEN RECHT (GW) [01765147] **3091**

SCHRIFTEN ZUM DEUTSCHEN UND EUROPAISCHEN ZIVIL, -HANDELS- UND PROZESSRECHT (GW) [01765148] **3046**

SCHRIFTEN ZUM OFFENTLICHEN RECHT (GW) [01765149] **3046**

SCHRIFTEN ZUM PROZESSRECHT (GW) [01765150] **3046**

SCHRIFTEN ZUM STRAFRECHT (GW) [01590653] **3109**

SCHRIFTEN ZUM VERGLEICH VON WIRTSCHAFTSORDNUNGEN (GW/0582-0243) [02936791] **1595**

SCHRIFTEN ZUM WIRTSCHAFTSRECHT (GW) [01765151] **1520**

SCHRIFTEN ZUR ANTIKEN MYTHOLOGIE (GW) [02936841] **2324**

SCHRIFTEN ZUR EUROPAISCHEN SOZIAL- UND VERFASSUNGSGESCHICHTE (GW/0723-4880) [14870297] **5218**

SCHRIFTEN ZUR KIRCHEN- UND RECHTGESCHICHTE (GW/0582-0367) [02946335] **2708**

SCHRIFTEN ZUR KULTURSOZIOLOGIE (GW) [18269320] **5257**

SCHRIFTEN ZUR LITERATUR- UND GEISTESGESCHICHTE (GW) [17391514] **2854**

SCHRIFTEN ZUR NATURWISSENSCHAFTS- UND TEHNIKGESCHICHTE (GW) [21006922] **5150**

SCHRIFTEN ZUR QUANTITATIVEN WIRTSCHAFTSFORSCHUNG (GW) [16161247] **1520**

SCHRIFTEN ZUR RECHTSGESCHICHTE (GW) [07029166] **3046**

SCHRIFTEN ZUR RECHTSTHEORIE (GW) [01589155] 2253, **3046**

SCHRIFTEN ZUR UR- UND FRUEHGESCHICHTE (GW) [01781359] **2629**

SCHRIFTEN ZUR VERFASSUNGSGESCHICHTE (GW/0582-0553) [01695371] **4495**

SCHRIFTEN ZUR VOLKSMUSIK (AU) [01589777] **4152**

SCHRIFTEN ZUR WIRTSCHAFTS- UND SOZIALGESCHICHTE (GW/0582-0588) [03053737] **5218**

SCHRIFTENREHE DES STADTARCHIVS ROSTOCK (GW) [20782432] **2708**

SCHRIFTENREICHE, N.F See SCHRIFTENREIHE DER HOCHSCHULE FUER POLITIK MUNCHEN **4495**

SCHRIFTENREIHE (GW) [01791614] **1029**

SCHRIFTENREIHE (GW/0417-1500) [04870128] **2835**

SCHRIFTENREIHE (GW/0522-9545) [02766974] **1847**

SCHRIFTENREIHE ANGEWANDTE VERSICHERUNGSMATHEMATIK (GW/0178-8116) [I01788116] **3533**

SCHRIFTENREIHE BEITRAGE ZUM SONDERSCHULWESEN UND ZUR REHABILITATIONSPADAGOGIK (GW/0138-1725) [04758643] **1885**

SCHRIFTENREIHE DER AGRARWISSENSCHAFTLICHEN FAKULTAT DER UNIVERSITAT KIEL (GW) [08760042] **132**

SCHRIFTENREIHE DER AKADEMIE FUR OEFFENTLICHES GESUNDHEITSWESEN IN DUSSELDORF (GW/0172-2131) [06796969] **4801**

SCHRIFTENREIHE DER BUNDESANSTALT FEUR ARBEITSSCHUTZ. REGELWERKE (GW/0932-478X) [I0932478X] **4801**

SCHRIFTENREIHE DER BUNDESANSTALT FEUR ARBEITSSCHUTZ. SONDERSCHRIFT (GW/0932-481X) [I0932481X] **4801**

SCHRIFTENREIHE DER BUNDESANSTALT FEUR AGRARWIRTSCHAFT (AU) [18925765] **132**

SCHRIFTENREIHE DER BUNDESANSTALT FEUR ARBEITSSCHUTZ. FORSCHUNG (GW/0932-3856) [I09323856] **4801**

SCHRIFTENREIHE — Alphabetical Title Index

SCHRIFTENREIHE DER BUNDESANSTALT FUER ARBEITSSCHUTZ. FORSCHUNGSANWENDUNG (GW/0932-4836) [27068343] **4801**

SCHRIFTENREIHE DER BUNDESANSTALT FUER ARBEITSSCHUTZ. GEFAHRLICHE ARBEITSSTOFFE (GW/0932-4712) [16167186] **2870**

SCHRIFTENREIHE DER BUNDESANSTALT F...UR ARBEITSSCHUTZ. TAGUNGSBERICHT (GW/0932-4828) [I09324828] **4801**

SCHRIFTENREIHE DER BUNDESAPOTHEKERKAMMER ZUR WISSENSCHAFTLICHEN FORTBILDUNG. GRUNE REIHE (GW/0721-1457) [09428875] **4329**

SCHRIFTENREIHE DER DEUTSCHEN GESELLSCHAFT FUER MEDIZINISCHE DOKUMENTATION, INFORMATIK UND STATISTIK E. V (GW/0174-4771) [06573710] **3639**

SCHRIFTENREIHE DER DEUTSCHEN GESELLSCHAFT FUER PHOTOGRAPHIE (GW) [17150020] **4376**

SCHRIFTENREIHE DER FORSCHUNGSGESELLSCHAFT FUER AGRARPOLITIK UND AGRARSOZIOLOGIE E.V. BONN (GW/0179-4485) [26046825] **5257**

SCHRIFTENREIHE DER GDMB GESELLSCHAFT DEUTSCHER METALLHUTTEN- UND BERGLEUTE (GW/0720-1877) [04739648] 2150, **4018**

SCHRIFTENREIHE DER HOCHSCHULE FUER POLITIK MUNCHEN (GW) [08332739] **4495**

SCHRIFTENREIHE DER LANDESANSTALT FUER IMMISSIONSSCHUTZ DES LANDES NORDRHEIN-WESTFALEN, ESSEN (GW/0342-9474) [03581688] **2242**

SCHRIFTENREIHE DER LANDSMANNSCHAFT DER BANATER SCHWABEN (GW) [23275337] **2272**

SCHRIFTENREIHE DES BAYERISCHEN LANDESAMTES FUER WASSERWIRTSCHAFT (GW/0172-665X) [02355920] 5539, **1417**

SCHRIFTENREIHE DES BUNDESMINISTERS FOR ERNAHRUNG, LANDWIRTSCHAFT UND FORSTEN. REIHE A, ANGEWANDTE WISSENSCHAFT (GW/0723-7847) [09855749] **132**

SCHRIFTENREIHE DES BUNDESMINISTERS FUER ERNAHRUNG, LANDWIRTSCHAFT UND FORSTEN. REIHE B, FLURBEREINIGUNG (GW/06995478] **132**

SCHRIFTENREIHE DES DEUTSCHEN KINDERHILFSWERKES E.V (GW/0933-3525) [16076418] **3911**

SCHRIFTENREIHE DES DEUTSCHEN STADTE- UND GEMEINDEBUNDES (GW) [04682451] **4685**

SCHRIFTENREIHE DES DEUTSCHEN VERBANDES FUER WASSERWIRTSCHAFT UND KULTURBAU (GW/0170-8147) [06909690] **5539**

SCHRIFTENREIHE DES DEUTSCHEN WOLLFORSCHUNGS INSTITUTES AN DER TECHNISCHEN HOCHSCHULE AACHEN (GW/0170-6322) [11286099] **5150**

SCHRIFTENREIHE DES FACHBEREICHS INTERNATIONALE AGRARENTWICKLUNG (GW/0177-6673) [25088034] **132**

SCHRIFTENREIHE DES IFO-INSTITUT FUER WIRTSCHAFTSFORSCHUNG (GW/0445-0736) [02100899] **1396**

SCHRIFTENREIHE DES INSTITUTS FUER DEUTSCHE GESCHICHTE, UNIVERSITAT TEL AVIV (GW) [04740471] **2708**

SCHRIFTENREIHE DES ISWW KARLSRUHE (GW) [26658936] 2242, **5539**

SCHRIFTENREIHE DES KULTURINSTITUTS DER DONAUSCHWABEN IN WIEN (GW) [21015095] **2272**

SCHRIFTENREIHE DES MATHEMATISCHEN INSTITUTS DER UNIVERSITAT MUNSTER (GW/0077-1961) [06417840] **3533**

SCHRIFTENREIHE DES STAATSARCHIVS DRESDEN (GW/0584-9993) [05849509] 2708, **2483**

SCHRIFTENREIHE DES VEREINS FUER RHEINISCHE KIRCHENGESCHICHTE (GW) [03188663] **4995**

SCHRIFTENREIHE DES VEREINS FUER WASSER-, BODEN- UND LUFTHYGIENE (GW/0300-8665) [01507925] **1360**

SCHRIFTENREIHE - DEUTSCHE GESELLSCHAFT FUR VOLKSKUNDE. KOMMISSION FUR OSTDEUTSCHE VOLKSKUNDE (GW/05202843] **2324**

SCHRIFTENREIHE FUER GEOLOGISCHE WISSENSCHAFTEN (GW/0323-8946) [05338087] **1396**

SCHRIFTENREIHE FUER GESCHICHTE DER NATURWISSENSCHAFTEN (GW) **5150**

SCHRIFTENREIHE FUER LANDSCHAFTSPFLEGE UND NATURSCHUTZ (GW/02391338] **2205**

SCHRIFTENREIHE FUER NATURSCHUTZ UND LANDSCHAFTSPFLEGE (GW) [04319400] **2242**

SCHRIFTENREIHE FUR SPORTWISSENSCHAFT UND SPORTPRAXIS See SPORTWISSENSCHAFT UND SPORTPRAXIS **4923**

SCHRIFTENREIHE INFANS CEREBROPATHICUS (AU/1012-912X) [11120086] **3936**

SCHRIFTENREIHE - INSTITUT FUER PHOTOGRAMMETRIE DER UNIVERSITAT STUTTGART (GW) [05904585] **4376**

SCHRIFTENREIHE INTENSIVMEDIZIN, NOTFALLMEDIZIN, ANASTHESIOLOGI (GW/0342-4448) [04240026] **3684**

SCHRIFTENREIHE KUNSTOFF -FORSCHUNG (GW/0174-4003) [08161708] **4460**

SCHRIFTENREIHE LEBENSMITTELCHEMIE, LEBENSMITTELQUALITAT (GW/0724-8784) [10437592] **2356**

SCHRIFTENREIHE LINGUISTIK (GW) [21015112] **3319**

SCHRIFTENREIHE NEUROLOGIE (GW/0080-715X) [01623628] **3845**

SCHRIFTENREIHE ZUR BAYERISCHEN LANDESGESCHICHTE (GW) [02958014] **2708**

SCHRIFTENREIHE ZUR GESCHICHTE UND POLITISCHEN BILDUNG (GW/0080-7168) [01765156] **4495**

SCHRIFTENREIHE ZUR MATHEMATIK CEASED. (GW) [05904631] **3533**

SCHRIFTTUM DER AGRARWIRTSCHAFT, DAS (AU/0036-6986) [02576501] **132**

SCHRIFTTUM UND PRAXIS (AU/0586-7703) [11602721] **3722**

SCHRIFTTUM ZUR DEUTSCHEN KUNST (GW/0080-7176) [01566490] 330, **334**

SCHRIFTTUMSUBERSICHT LARMMINDERUNG (GW/04451424] 2181, **2185**

SCHROEDER'S ANTIQUES PRICE GUIDE (US) [11342137] **252**

SCHS STUDIES (US) [07706497] **4801**

SCHUHTECHNIK 1987 (GW/0933-808X) [I0933808X] **1087**

SCHULBIBLIOTHEK AKTUELL (GW/0341-471X) [I0341471X] **3248**

SCHULDEN DES LANDES, DER GEMEINDEN, GEMEINDEVERBANDE UND ZWECKVERBANDE AM ..., DIE (GW) [11352137] 4747, **4699**

SCHULDEN DES LANDES, DER GEMEINDEN, SAMTGEMEINDEN UND LANDKREISE (GW) [02776376] **4747**

SCHULDEN DES LANDES, DER GEMEINDEN UND GEMEINDEVERBANDE See SCHULDEN DES LANDES, DER GEMEINDEN, GEMEINDEVERBANDE UND ZWECKVERBANDE AM ..., DIE **4699**

SCHULE UND MUSEUM (GW) [04904767] **4096**

SCHULE UND PSYCHOLOGIE See PSYCHOLOGIE IN ERZIEHUNG UND UNTERRICHT **1903**

SCHULEN & SPORTSTAETTEN (AU) **1782**

SCHULENBURG STICKER, THE (US/0895-4275) [14074451] **5754**

SCHULER- UND ABSOLVENTENPROGNOSE (GW) [17975078] **1782**

SCHULERFRONT (AU) [01799066] **1095**

SCHULVERZEICHNIS ... REALSCHULEN, ABENDREALSCHULEN, WIRTSCHAFTSSCHULEN, FACHOBERSCHULEN, GYMNASIEN, ABENDGYMNASIEN, GESAMTSCHULEN, KOLLEGS (GW) [10528603] **1782**

SCHUMPERT MEDICAL QUARTERLY CEASED. (US/0731-5406) [08212237] **3639**

SCHUSS (UK/0048-9492) [03920862] **1904**

SCHUSS UND WAFFE (SZ) [20256876] **2812**

SCHUTZ-JAHRBUCH (GW) [06609031] **4152**

SCHUTZ SOCIETY REPORTS : NEWSLETTER OF THE AMERICAN HEINRICH SCHUTZ SOCIETY (US) [20606901] **4152**

SCHUYLER SUN, THE (US) [10589506] **5707**

SCHWABISCHE CHRONIKEN DER STAUFERZEIT (GW) [16273509] **2708**

SCHWALBE (GW) **4917**

●SCHWANN OPUS (US/1066-2138) [26898861] **5318**

●SCHWANN SPECTRUM (US/1065-9161) [26790231] **5318**

SCHWARZWAELDER BOTE (GW) **5802**

SCHWEDEN FORST- UND HOLZWIRTSCHAFT / BUNDESSTELLE FUR AUSSENHANDELSINFORMATION (GW) [08917898] **2395**

SCHWEDEN : WIRTSCHAFT IN ZAHLEN UND WIRTSCHAFTSDOKUMENTATION (GW) [06267231] **1583**

SCHWEDEN : WIRTSCHAFTLICHE ENTWICKLUNG (GW) [05136271] **1583**

SCHWEINE-ZUCHT (GW) **132**

SCHWEINEZUCHT UND SCHWEINEMAST (GW/0036-7176) [I00367176] **132**

SCHWEISSEN UND SCHNEIDEN (GW/0036-7184) [02450417] **4027**

SCHWEISSTECHNIK (VIENNA) (AU/0253-5262) [09426619] **1995**

SCHWEIZ : ENERGIEWIRTSCHAFT (GW) [04221174] **1956**

SCHWEIZ IN KURVEN, DIE (SZ) [06504821] **5338**

SCHWEIZ; LA SUISSE; LA SVIZZERA; SWITZERLAND, DIE (SZ/0036-7230) [03213798] **5490**

SCHWEIZ, WIRTSCHAFT IN ZAHLEN UND WIRTSCHAFTSDOKUMENTATION / BUNDESSTELLE FUER AUSSENHANDELSINFORMATION (GW) [11364247] **1583**

SCHWEIZER ALUMINIUM RUNDSCHAU CEASED. (SZ/0036-7257) [08665141] **4018**

SCHWEIZER ANGLISTISCHE ARBEITEN (SZ/0080-7214) [02955714] **3434**

SCHWEIZER ARCHIV FUER TIERHEILKUNDE (SZ/0036-7281) [01765165] **5521**

SCHWEIZER ARCHIV FUR NEUROLOGIE UND PSYCHIATRIE (ZURICH, SWITZERLAND : 1985) (SZ) [12085146] 3936, **3845**

SCHWEIZER ASIATISCHE STUDIEN. STUDIENHEFTE (SZ) [14221289] **2663**

SCHWEIZER BAUMARKT (SZ/0255-688X) [17685929] **308**

SCHWEIZER BAUWIRTSCHAFT (SZ/0376-6853) [10935033] **627**

SCHWEIZER BRAUNVIEH (SZ) [12629286] **198**

SCHWEIZER BUCH (SZ/0036-732X) [04289116] **424**

SCHWEIZER ILLUSTRIERTE. SIE + I.E. UND ER (SZ) [05363785] **2522**

SCHWEIZER ILLUSTRIERTE ZEITUNG (SZ/0036-7362) [01765167] **2522**

SCHWEIZER INGENIEUR UND ARCHITEKT (SZ/0251-0960) [04863797] 308, **1995**

SCHWEIZER INGENIEUR UND ARCHITEKT (SZ/0251-0960) [06468243] 308, **2030**

SCHWEIZER JAHRBUCH DES OFFENTLICHEN LEBENS See PUBLICUS (BASEL, SWITZERLAND) **4677**

SCHWEIZER JAHRBUCH FEUR MUSIKWISSENSCHAFT (SZ) [08632137] **4152**

SCHWEIZER KUNST (SZ/1016-2879) [I10162879] **364**

SCHWEIZER LANDTECHNIK (SZ) [13764677] 1995, **132**

●SCHWEIZER LOGISTIK-KATALOG / SWISS LOGISITICS CATALOGUE (SZ) **1929**

SCHWEIZER MONATSHEFTE (SZ/0036-7400) [05383987] **2522**

SCHWEIZER MONATSSCHRIFT FUER ZAHNMEDIZIN (SZ/1011-4203) [16529581] **1335**

SCHWEIZER MUNZBLATTER (SZ/0487-8019) [01919645] **2783**

SCHWEIZER MUSIK AUF SCHALLPLATTEN. MUSIQUE SUISSE SUR DISQUES. SWISS MUSIC ON RECORDS (SZ) [05324023] **4152**

SCHWEIZER NATURSCHUTZ PROTECTION DE LA NATURE (SZ) [06785514] **2205**

SCHWEIZER OPTIKER. L'OPTICIEN SUISSE. L'OTTICO SVIZZERO, DER (SZ) [03615524] **4217**

SCHWEIZER SOLDAT See SCHWEIZER SOLDAT + MFD **4056**

SCHWEIZER SOLDAT + MFD (SZ) [17855586] **4056**

SCHWEIZER SPITAL (SZ/0304-4432) [09249062] **3792**

SCHWEIZER UHR See UHREN RUNDSCHAU. REVUE DE LA MONTRE **2916**

SCHWEIZER VERPACKUNGS- UND TRANSPORTKATALOG See SCHWEIZER VERPACKUNGSKATALOG **4222**

SCHWEIZER VERPACKUNGSKATALOG (SZ) [08912706] **4222**

SCHWEIZER VOLKSKUNDE (SZ/0048-9522) [01765168] 5269, **2324**

SCHWEIZER WAFFEN-MAGAZIN (SZ/0253-4878) [I02534878] 4917, **4056**

SCHWEIZERISCHE AKADEMIE DER NATURWISSENSCHAFTEN See JAHRBUCH **5117**

SCHWEIZERISCHE APOTHEKER-ZEITUNG. GIORNALE SVIZZERO DI FARMACIA (SZ/0036-7508) [01765170] **4329**

SCHWEIZERISCHE BEITRAGE ZUR ALTERTUMSWISSENSCHAFT (GW/0080-7273) [01604961] **2629**

SCHWEIZERISCHE BIBLIOTHEKEN (SZ) [06344216] 3248, **3260**

SCHWEIZERISCHE BIENEN-ZEITUNG (SZ/0036-7540) [01604830] **5597**

SCHWEIZERISCHE BLASMUSIKZEITUNG (SZ) [01589509] **4152**

SCHWEIZERISCHE EINKAUFSFUHRER, DER (SZ) [11274676] **850**

SCHWEIZERISCHE ENTOMOLOGISCHE GESELLSCHAFT See MITTEILUNGEN DER SCHWEIZERISCHEN ENTOMOLOGISCHEN GESELLSCHAFT **5612**

SCHWEIZERISCHE GEOTECHNISCHE KOMMISSION See BEITRAGE ZUR GEOLOGIE DER SCHWEIZ. GEOTECHNISCHE SERIE **1367**

SCHWEIZERISCHE GESELLSCHAFT FUER VOLKSKUNDE See SCHRIFTEN DER SCHWEIZERISCHEN GESELLSCHAFT FUER VOLKSKUNDE **2324**

SCHWEIZERISCHE GESELLSCHAFT FUR GESCHICHTE DER MEDIZIN UND DER NATURWISSENSCHAFTEN See VEROFFENTLICHUNGEN **3649**

SCHWEIZERISCHE GESELLSCHAFT FUR MARKETING See GESCHAFTSBERICHT UBER DIE TATIGKEIT DER GESELLSCHAFT **924**

SCHWEIZERISCHE GESELLSCHAFT FUR UR- UND FRUHGESCHICHTE See JAHRBUCH DER SCHWEIZERISCHEN GESELLSCHAFT FUER UR- UND FRUHGESCHICHTE **270**

SCHWEIZERISCHE GESELLSCHAFT FUR UR- UND FRUHGESCHICHTE See JAHRBUCH DER SCHWEIZERISCHEN GESELLSCHAFT FUER UR- UND FRUHGESCHICHTE **270**

SCHWEIZERISCHE HILFE FUR ENTWICKLUNGSLANDER / PUBLIE PAR SWISSAID (SZ) [03602096] **1583**

SCHWEIZERISCHE LANDWIRTSCHAFTLICHE FORSCHUNG (SZ/0036-763X) [02469733] **132**

● SCHWEIZERISCHE LEHRERINNEN- UND LEHRER-ZEITUNG: SLZ (SZ) [25879903] **1782**

SCHWEIZERISCHE LEHRERZEITUNG See SCHWEIZERISCHE LEHRERINNEN- UND LEHRER-ZEITUNG: SLZ **1782**

SCHWEIZERISCHE MEDIZINISCHE WOCHENSCHRIFT (SZ/0036-7672) [01765180] **3639**

SCHWEIZERISCHE MEDIZINISCHE WOCHENSCHRIFT. SUPPLEMENTUM (SZ/0250-5525) [03259710] **3639**

SCHWEIZERISCHE MILCHZEITUNG (SZ) [04081140] **198**

SCHWEIZERISCHE MINERALOGISCHE UND PETROGRAPHISCHE MITTEILUNGEN (SZ/0036-7699) [01640739] 1459, **1444**

SCHWEIZERISCHE NATURFORSCHENDE GESELLSCHAFT See DENKSCHRIFTEN DER SCHWEIZERISCHEN NATURFORSCHENDEN GESELLSCHAFT **5099**

SCHWEIZERISCHE PALAEONTOLOGISCHE ABHANDLUNGEN (SZ/0080-7389) [01929495] **4230**

SCHWEIZERISCHE POST, TELEFON UND TELEGRAFENBETRIEBE See RAPPORT DE GESTION ET COMPTE FINANCIER DES PTT / PTT **1147**

SCHWEIZERISCHE POST-, TELEFON- UND TELEGRAFENBETRIEBE See PTT-GESCHAFTSBERICHT UND FINANZRECHNUNG / PTT **1147**

SCHWEIZERISCHE POST-, TELEPHON- UND TELEGRAPHENBETRIEBE. GENERALDIREKTION See POST-, TELEFON- UND TELEGRAFEN-AMTSBLATT. FEUILLE OFFICIELLE DES POSTES, TELEPHONES ET TELEGRAPHES. FOGLIO UFFICIALE DELLE POSTE, DEI TELEFONI E DEI TELEGRAFI **1162**

SCHWEIZERISCHE REEDEREI UND NEPTUN AG See GESCHAFTSBERICHT (SCHWEIZERISCHE REEDEREI UND NEPTUN AG) **5449**

SCHWEIZERISCHE RUNDSCHAU FUER MEDIZIN PRAXIS (SZ/1013-2058) [02679732] **3801**

SCHWEIZERISCHE TECHNISCHE ZEITSCHRIFT (SZ/0040-151X) [07101887] **5150**

SCHWEIZERISCHE VERSICHERUNGS ZEITSCHRIFT. REVUE SUISSE D'ASSURANCES (SZ) [04772511] **2893**

SCHWEIZERISCHE VERSICHERUNGSZEITSCHRIFT. REVUE SUISSE D'ASSURANCES (SZ) [07050001] **2893**

SCHWEIZERISCHE ZEITSCHRIFT FUER GESCHICHTE (SZ/0036-7834) [01642701] **2708**

SCHWEIZERISCHE ZEITSCHRIFT FUER HYDROLOGIE (SZ/0036-7842) [01765186] **1417**

SCHWEIZERISCHE ZEITSCHRIFT FUER INTERNATIONALES UND EUROPAISCHES RECHT (SZ) [24664969] **3135**

● SCHWEIZERISCHE ZEITSCHRIFT FUER MEDIZIN UND TRAUMATOLOGIE (SZ/1022-6699) [30470405] **3955**

SCHWEIZERISCHE ZEITSCHRIFT FUER MILITAR- UND KATASTROPHENMEDIZIN (SZ/0377-8347) [02417277] **3725**

SCHWEIZERISCHE ZEITSCHRIFT FUER OBST- UND WEINBAU (SZ/0371-4942) [02520613] **2431**

SCHWEIZERISCHE ZEITSCHRIFT FUER PILZKUNDE (SZ/0373-2959) [02534714] **527**

SCHWEIZERISCHE ZEITSCHRIFT FUER PSYCHOLOGIE (SZ) [18249905] **4618**

SCHWEIZERISCHE ZEITSCHRIFT FUER PSYCHOLOGIE UND IHRE ANWENDUNGEN. BEIHEFT (SZ) [03049220] **4618**

SCHWEIZERISCHE ZEITSCHRIFT FUER SOZIALVERSICHERUNG UND BERUFLICHE VORSORGE (SZ/0255-9072) [09296351] 5307, **2893**

SCHWEIZERISCHE ZEITSCHRIFT FUER SOZIOLOGIE (SZ/0379-3664) [03289712] **5257**

SCHWEIZERISCHE ZEITSCHRIFT FUER SPORTMEDIZIN (SZ/0036-7885) [01643258] **3955**

SCHWEIZERISCHE ZEITSCHRIFT FUER SPORTMEDIZIN See SCHWEIZERISCHE ZEITSCHRIFT FUER MEDIZIN UND TRAUMATOLOGIE **3955**

SCHWEIZERISCHE ZEITSCHRIFT FUER STRAFRECHT (SZ/0036-7893) [01605626] **3176**

SCHWEIZERISCHE ZEITSCHRIFT FUER VOLKSWIRTSCHAFT UND STATISTIK (SZ/0303-9692) [09406862] 1520, **1538**

SCHWEIZERISCHER APOTHEKER-VEREIN. WISSENSCHAFTLICHE ZENTRALSTELLE See INDEX NOMINUM / ELBORE PAR LE CENTRE SCIENTIFIQUE DE LA SOCIETE SUISSE DE PHARMACIE **4307**

SCHWEIZERISCHER ELECTROTECHNISCHER VEREIN (SZ) **2080**

SCHWEIZERISCHER ELEKTROTECHNISCHER VEREIN See BULLETIN DES SCHWEIZERISCHEN ELEKTROTECHNISCHEN VEREINS (ZURICH) **2037**

SCHWEIZERISCHER GEWERKSCHAFTSBUND See RAPPORT D'ACTIVITE / UNION SYNDICALE SUISSE **1705**

SCHWEIZERISCHES ARCHIV FUER VOLKSKUNDE (SZ/0036-794X) [01715665] **2324**

SCHWEIZERISCHES GUTENBERGMUSEUM (SZ) [03127885] **709**

SCHWEIZERISCHES IDIOTIKON. WORTERBUCH DER SCHWEIZERDEUTSCHEN SPRACHE (SZ) [05910317] **3319**

SCHWEIZERISCHES PRIVATRECHT (SZ) **3046**

SCHWEIZERISCHES ROTES KREUZ See JAHRESBERICHT / SCHWEIZERISCHES ROTES KREUZ **5291**

SCHWEIZERISCHES ZENTRALBLATT FUR STAATS- UND GEMEINDEVERWALTUNG See SCHWEIZERISCHES ZENTRALBLATT FUER STAATS- UND VERWALTUNGSRECHT **3046**

SCHWEIZERISCHES ZENTRALBLATT FUER STAATS- UND VERWALTUNGSRECHT (SZ) [20591345] **3046**

SCHWENDEMAN'S DIRECTORY OF COLLEGE GEOGRAPHY OF THE UNITED STATES (US/0734-8185) [05089220] 1847, **2576**

SCHWENKFELDIAN, THE (US/0036-8032) [01776822] **5067**

SCHWERPUNKT MEDIZIN (GW/0722-3625) [09878506] **3639**

SCHWERPUNKTE DES KARTELLRECHTS (GW) [04206420] **3103**

SCHWESTER. DER PFLEGER, DIE (GW/0340-5303) [I03405303] **3639**

SCI JCR [MICROFORM] (US) [23953801] **5150**

SCI NEWS *CEASED.* (US) [04752505] **5150**

SCI NURSING (US/0888-8299) [12085705] **3869**

SCI RECORD BOOK OF TROPHY ANIMALS, THE (US/0195-7538) [05624476] 4917, **4878**

SCI-TECH NEWS (US/0036-8059) [06658893] **3248**

SCIARE (IT) **4917**

SCICAT SCIENCE REFERENCE AND INFORMATION SERVICE (UK/0966-114X) [I0966114X] **992**

SCIENCAJ KOMUNIKAJOJ - BUDAPESTA TERITORIA KOMITATO DE HUNGARA ESPERANTO-ASOCIO (HU/0133-1027) [I01331027] **5150**

SCIENCE ACTIVITIES (US/0036-8121) [01781192] 1904, **5150**

SCIENCE & BUSINESS (UK) [19052810] 709, **5150**

SCIENCE AND CHILDREN (US/0036-8148) [01607110] 5150, **1904**

SCIENCE & CHRISTIAN BELIEF (UK/0954-4194) [19839650] 5150, **4995**

SCIENCE AND CIVILISATION IN CHINA (UK) [20994534] **5150**

SCIENCE & CULTURE (II/0036-8156) [01765191] **5150**

SCIENCE & EDUCATION (NE/0926-7220) 4360, 3533, **1904**

SCIENCE AND ELECTRONICS See COMMUNICATIONS WORLD **1130**

SCIENCE & ENGINEERING (II/0036-8164) [02450432] 1995, **5150**

SCIENCE & ENGINEERING INDICATORS (US/1048-6313) [17847129] 5150, **1996**

SCIENCE AND ENGINEERING OF COMPOSITE MATERIALS (IS/0792-1233) [I07921233] **2108**

SCIENCE AND ENGINEERING PERSONNEL (US/0278-9620) [07908865] **5150**

SCIENCE AND ENGINEERING RESEARCH COUNCIL (GREAT BRITAIN) See REPORT OF THE COUNCIL FOR THE YEAR ... / SCIENCE AND ENGINEERING RESEARCH COUNCIL **5145**

SCIENCE AND ENVIRONMENT (II/0970-5139) [09108032] 2243, **5150**

SCIENCE & GLOBAL SECURITY (US/0892-9882) [15307789] 4056, **4535**

SCIENCE & GOVERNMENT REPORT (US/0048-9581) [02267544] **5150**

SCIENCE AND INDUSTRY (NE/0925-5842) [05326528] **5150**

SCIENCE & LIVING TOMORROW (US/0272-4510) [06793113] **5150**

SCIENCE AND PRACTICE OF AGROFORESTRY (KE) [16928426] 2395, **132**

SCIENCE AND PRACTICE OF SURGERY (US/0731-1680) [08124547] **3974**

SCIENCE AND PUBLIC AFFAIRS (LONDON, ENGLAND) (UK/0268-490X) [14578330] **5218**

SCIENCE & PUBLIC POLICY (UK/0302-3427) [01793567] 5150, **4685**

SCIENCE & RELIGION NEWS (US/1048-8642) [21063849] 5150, **4995**

SCIENCE AND SOCIETY (NEW YORK. 1936) (US/0036-8237) [01644619] **5218**

SCIENCE & SPORTS (FR/0765-1597) [16179395] **3956**

SCIENCE AND TECHNOLOGY : A REPORT TO THE CONGRESS (US) [27369390] **5150**

SCIENCE AND TECHNOLOGY DATA BOOK (US/0895-2000) [10511043] **5150**

SCIENCE AND TECHNOLOGY DATA BOOK See SCIENCE AND TECHNOLOGY POCKET DATA BOOK / DIVISION OF SCIENCE RESOURCES STUDIES, NATIONAL SCIENCE FOUNDATION **5150**

SCIENCE & TECHNOLOGY IN JAPAN (TOKYO. 1982) (JA/0286-0406) [08713147] **5150**

SCIENCE AND TECHNOLOGY INFORMATION BULLETIN. B10. FISH DISEASES (AT/0314-4984) [I03144984] **2312**

SCIENCE — Alphabetical Title Index

SCIENCE & TECHNOLOGY LIBRARIES (NEW YORK, N.Y.) (US/0194-262X) [05364880] 5150, **3248**

SCIENCE AND TECHNOLOGY MICROFORM / NEWSBANK, INC (US) [21191081] **5150**

● SCIENCE AND TECHNOLOGY OF BUILDING SEALS, SEALANTS, GLAZING AND WATERPROOFING (US/1062-967X) [25821811] **5150**

SCIENCE AND TECHNOLOGY PLAN (NZ) [11724905] **5150**

SCIENCE AND TECHNOLOGY POCKET DATA BOOK / DIVISION OF SCIENCE RESOURCES STUDIES, NATIONAL SCIENCE FOUNDATION (US) [27568593] **5150**

SCIENCE AND TECHNOLOGY POLICY (UK/0952-9616) [20382399] **5151**

SCIENCE AND TECHNOLOGY POLICY (FR) [25597052] **5151**

SCIENCE & TECHNOLOGY QUARTERLY *CEASED.* (SI) [08483008] **5151**

SCIENCE AND TECHNOLOGY REPORT AND OUTLOOK (US) [22981335] **5151**

SCIENCE AND TECHNOLOGY SERIES (US/0278-4017) [07800518] **34**

SCIENCE AND TECHNOLOGY YEARBOOK (BE/0377-7901) [01799480] **5151**

SCIENCE & VIE JUNIOR (FR/0992-5899) [I09925899] **5151**

SCIENCE & VIE. MICRO (FR/0760-6516) [I07606516] **5151**

SCIENCE AS CULTURE (UK/0950-5431) [17195407] **5151**

SCIENCE BOOKS & FILMS (US/0098-342X) [02246677] **5151**

SCIENCE BUDGET (IE/0332-1126) [07885953] **5151**

SCIENCE BULLETIN (OTTAWA) (CN/1184-227X) [25423651] **4495**

SCIENCE CITATION INDEX (COMPACT DISC ED.) (US/1044-6052) [20113418] 5151, **5176**

SCIENCE CITATION INDEX. GUIDE AND LISTS OF SOURCE PUBLICATIONS (US/0036-827X) [04216639] **5151**

SCIENCE CITATION INDEX (PRINT ED.) (US/0036-827X) [01604320] 5151, **5176**

● SCIENCE CITATION INDEX WITH ABSTRACTS (US/1061-1290) [25184798] 5151, **5176**

● SCIENCE COMMUNICATION (US/1075-5470) [30083948] **5151**

SCIENCE COUNCIL OF CANADA *See* IN TOUCH (OTTAWA) **5112**

SCIENCE COUNCIL OF CANADA *See* ANNUAL REVIEW - SCIENCE COUNCIL OF CANADA **5084**

SCIENCE COUNCIL OF CANADA *See* ANNUAL REPORT - SCIENCE COUNCIL OF CANADA **5084**

SCIENCE COUNCIL OF CANADA REPORT (1979) (CN/0820-9219) [09639242] **5151**

SCIENCE CURRICULUM IMPROVEMENT STUDY *See* SCIS NEWSLETTER **5156**

SCIENCE DILIMAN (PH/0115-7809) [11447060] **5151**

SCIENCE DU SOL (1984) (FR/0767-5319) [18648455] **185**

SCIENCE DU SOL (PLAISIR, FRANCE : 1984) *See* EUROPEAN JOURNAL OF SOIL SCIENCE **171**

SCIENCE DU SPORT (CN/0822-6792) [10356326] 3956, **1858**

SCIENCE EDUCATION IN THE REGION (UK) [01783758] 5151, **1847**

SCIENCE EDUCATION INTERNATIONAL (US/1022-6117) [23524837] 5151, **1782**

SCIENCE EDUCATION NEWS (AT) 1904, **5151**

SCIENCE EDUCATION (SALEM, MASS.) (US/0036-8326) [01697181] 1782, **5151**

SCIENCE ET COMPORTEMENT (CN/0841-7741) [19116261] **4618**

SCIENCE ET ESPRIT (CN/0316-5345) [08000724] 4995, **4360**

SCIENCE ET FRANCOPHONIE (CN/0825-9879) [12151235] **5151**

SCIENCE ET MOTRICITE : SM : REVUE SCIENTIFIQUE DE L'A.C.A.P.S., ASSOCIATION DES CHERCHEURS EN ACTIVITES PHYSIQUES ET SPORTIVES (FR) [18657008] **3956**

SCIENCE ET RECHERCHE (FR/0243-7694) [11189582] **5151**

SCIENCE ET TECHNIQUE DU FROID / REFRIGERATION SCIENCE AND TECHNOLOGY (FR/0151-1637) [04925914] **2608**

● SCIENCE ET TECHNOLOGIE AU QUEBEC (CN/1188-4290) [31000977] **5151**

SCIENCE ET TECHNOLOGIE DE LA CONSERVATION ET DE LA RESTAURATION DES OEUVRES D'ART ET DU PATRIMOINE (FR) [22465609] **4096**

SCIENCE ET VIE (FR/0036-8369) [08354153] **5151**

SCIENCE ET VIE. MICROFORM *CEASED.* (US/0036-8369) [14075748] **5151**

SCIENCE ET VIE. NUMERO HORS SERIE (FR/0151-0282) [I01510282] **5151**

SCIENCE FICTION (AT/0314-6677) [05620671] **3434**

● SCIENCE FICTION AGE (HERNDON, VA.) (US/1065-1829) [26520385] **3434**

SCIENCE FICTION & FANTASY BOOK REVIEW ANNUAL (US/1040-192X) [18340859] **3434**

SCIENCE FICTION AND FANTASY BOOK REVIEW INDEX (US/1046-1922) [12153161] 3434, **3459**

SCIENCE FICTION & FANTASY FORUM (US/0897-1072) [17401883] **3434**

SCIENCE FICTION AND FANTASY RESEARCH INDEX (PAPER ED.) (US) [10249579] **3434**

SCIENCE FICTION CHRONICLE (US/0195-5365) [05509898] 4819, **3434**

SCIENCE FICTION EYE (US/1071-3018) [22440318] **3434**

SCIENCE FICTION, FANTASY, & HORROR (US/0898-4077) [16845495] **3434**

SCIENCE FICTION REVIEW MONTHLY, THE (US/0361-7009) [02109172] **3434**

SCIENCE-FICTION STUDIES (CN/0091-7729) [01787622] **3434**

SCIENCE FILM (FR) [02246146] 4077, **5151**

SCIENCE FOR PEOPLE (LONDON) *SUSPENDED.* (UK/0144-8447) [11942371] **5151**

SCIENCE GLOBAL SECURITY MONOGRAPH SERIES (UK/1048-7042) [21016270] **5151**

SCIENCE/HEALTH ABSTRACTS (US/0890-7110) [14363807] **5152**

SCIENCE ILLUSTREE BAGNOLET (FR/0999-7342) [I09997342] **5152**

SCIENCE IN CHINA. SERIES A, MATHEMATICS, PHYSICS, ASTRONOMY & TECHNOLOGICAL SCIENCES (CC/1001-6511) [19752353] 3533, **5152**

SCIENCE IN CHINA. SERIES B, CHEMISTRY, LIFE SCIENCES & EARTH SCIENCES (CC/1001-652X) [19908874] 992, **5152**

SCIENCE IN CONTEXT (UK/0269-8897) [16060175] **5152**

SCIENCE IN NEW GUINEA (PP/0310-4303) [04081653] **5152**

SCIENCE IN PARLIAMENT (UK/0263-6271) [21943056] **5152**

● SCIENCE IN RUSSIA / RUSSIAN ACADEMY OF SCIENCES (RU) [28131825] **5152**

SCIENCE IN USSR (RU/0203-4638) [07936689] **5152**

SCIENCE INTERNATIONAL LAHORE (PK/1013-5316) [I10135316] **5152**

SCIENCE IS ELEMENTARY (US/1064-7015) [26459929] 1797, **5152**

SCIENCE LINK (CN/0821-7246) [09818992] **2924**

SCIENCE MONOGRAPH (US/0084-3156) [01736534] **132**

SCIENCE MUSEUM OF MINNESOTA *See* SCIENTIFIC PUBLICATIONS OF THE SCIENCE MUSEUM OF MINNESOTA **5155**

SCIENCE NEWS (WASHINGTON) (US/0036-8423) [02367617] **5152**

SCIENCE NOTES (US) [01606569] **5152**

SCIENCE OF BIOLOGY JOURNAL (US/0098-5600) [02241562] **472**

SCIENCE OF CERAMICS (NE/0080-7575) [01587143] **2594**

SCIENCE OF COMPUTER PROGRAMMING (NE/0167-6423) [08038828] **1281**

SCIENCE OF COOKERY. CHORI KAGAKU (JA) **2356**

SCIENCE OF FOOD AND AGRICULTURE (US/0738-9310) [18610691] 132, **2356**

SCIENCE OF MIND (US/0036-8458) [03920979] 4995, **4360**

SCIENCE OF SINTERING (YU/0350-820X) [01782172] **4018**

SCIENCE OF THE TOTAL ENVIRONMENT, THE (NE/0048-9697) [01642328] **2181**

SCIENCE OF TSUNAMI HAZARDS (US/8755-6839) [11097742] **1456**

SCIENCE POLICY DIGEST (SA) **5152**

SCIENCE POLICY IN THE NETHERLANDS (NE/0811-4536) [14336430] **5152**

SCIENCE POLICY STUDIES AND DOCUMENTS (FR) [01768103] **5152**

SCIENCE PROBE! *CEASED.* (US/1049-7730) [21308689] **5152**

SCIENCE PROGRESS (1916) (UK/0036-8504) [04295306] **5152**

SCIENCE QUEST (US/0090-9378) [01786011] **5153**

SCIENCE REPORT / HERMAN RESEARCH LABORATORY (AT) [08268734] **5153**

SCIENCE REPORT OF THE FACULTY OF EDUCATION, GIFU UNIVERSITY (NATURAL SCIENCE) (JA) [03489775] **5153**

SCIENCE REPORTER (II/0036-8512) [04782353] **5153**

SCIENCE REPORTS OF NIIGATA UNIVERSITY. SERIES D (BIOLOGY) (JA/0371-2672) [05793728] **472**

SCIENCE REPORTS OF THE HIROSAKI UNIVERSITY (JA/0367-6439) [04874908] **5153**

SCIENCE REPORTS OF THE INSTITUTE OF GEOSCIENCE, UNIVERSITY OF TSUKUBA. SECTION B, GEOLOGICAL SCIENCES (JA/0388-6182) [07303067] **1396**

SCIENCE REPORTS OF THE KANAZAWA UNIVERSITY, THE (JA/0022-8338) [02098504] **5153**

SCIENCE REPORTS OF THE RESEARCH INSTITUTES. SERIES A, PHYSICS, CHEMISTRY, AND METALLURGY (JA/0040-8808) [01695387] **5153**

SCIENCE REPORTS OF THE RESEARCH INSTITUTES. SERIES C, MEDICINE, THE (JA/0371-2761) [01608175] 3952, **3716**

SCIENCE REPORTS OF THE TOHOKU UNIVERSITY. EIGHTH SERIES. PHYSICS AND ASTRONOMY, THE (JA/0388-5607) [07502839] 399, **4420**

SCIENCE REPORTS OF THE TOHOKU UNIVERSITY. FIFTH SERIES, TOHOKU GEOPHYSICAL JOURNAL (JA) [07995556] **1410**

SCIENCE REPORTS OF THE TOHOKU UNIVERSITY. SERIES 7. GEOGRAPHY (JA/0375-7854) [01767550] **2576**

SCIENCE REPORTS OF THE YOKOHAMA NATIONAL UNIVERSITY. SECTION I : MATHEMATICS, PHYSICS, CHEMISTRY (JA) [02599943] **5153**

SCIENCE REPORTS OF THE YOKOHAMA NATIONAL UNIVERSITY. SECTION II: BIOLOGY AND GEOLOGY / FACULTY OF EDUCATION, YOKOHAMA NATIONAL UNIVERSITY (JA) [08479454] **472**

SCIENCE REPORTS OF TOKYO WOMAN'S CHRISTIAN COLLEGE *See* SCIENCE REPORTS OF TOKYO WOMAN'S CHRISTIAN UNIVERSITY **5153**

SCIENCE REPORTS OF TOKYO WOMAN'S CHRISTIAN UNIVERSITY (JA/0386-4006) [10461301] **5153**

SCIENCE REPORTS - OSAKA UNIVERSITY. COLLEGE OF GENERAL EDUCATION (JA/0474-781X) [01784645] 5153, **1858**

SCIENCE REPORTS, TOHOKU UNIVERSITY, SERIES 3, MINERALOGY, PETROLOGY, ECONOMIC GEOLOGY (JA/0371-3903) [06574197] **1360**

SCIENCE RESEARCH ANNUAL (US) [08177704] **5153**

SCIENCE RESOURCES STUDIES HIGHLIGHTS *CEASED.* (US/0566-9995) [03159753] **5153**

SCIENCE REVIEW (CALCUTTA) (II/0253-6684) [09179076] **5153**

SCIENCE REVIEW (DARTMOUTH) (CN/0846-9121) [21814754] **1456**

SCIENCE SCOPE (WASHINGTON, D.C.) (US/0887-2376) [10518686] 1904, **5153**

SCIENCE SERIES (LOS ANGELES) (US/0076-0943) [01730107] **4171**

SCIENCE STATISTICS (CN/0706-0793) [05843057] 5153, **5176**

SCIENCE TEACHER (WASHINGTON, D.C.), THE (US/0036-8555) [06445543] 1782, **5153**

SCIENCE, TECHNOLOGY & DEVELOPMENT (UK/0950-0707) [23069984] **5153**

SCIENCE, TECHNOLOGY & HUMAN VALUES (US/0162-2439) [04127609] **5153**

SCIENCE, TECHNOLOGY & SOCIETY (US/0275-8075) [07228298] 1904, **5153**

SCIENCE TODAY (UK) **5153**

SCIENCE TOOLS (SW/0036-8598) [01765211] **5153**

SCIENCE TRENDS (US/0043-0749) [01197317] **5153**

SCIENCE UPDATE (US/0163-4720) [04343381] **5154**

SCIENCE UPDATE (YELLOWKNIFE) (CN/0848-6832) [23242826] **5154**

SCIENCE (WASHINGTON, D.C.) (US/0036-8075) [01644869] **5154**

SCIENCE WATCH (US/1047-8043) [20443835] **5154**

SCIENCE WEEKLY. LEVEL A (US/0748-8904) [11025579] **1904**

SCIENCE WEEKLY. LEVEL B (US/8756-176X) [11479061] **1904**

SCIENCE WEEKLY. LEVEL C (US/8756-1778) [11479085] **1904**

SCIENCE WEEKLY. LEVEL D (US/8756-1786) [11479103] **1904**

SCIENCE WEEKLY. LEVEL E (US/8756-1794) [11479120] **1904**

SCIENCE WEEKLY. LEVEL F (US/1043-0997) [19298219] **1904**

SCIENCE WEEKLY. LEVEL PRE-A (US/0890-0388) [14122743] **1904**

SCIENCE WORLD (US/0036-8601) [01765212] **5154**

SCIENCE WORLD (US) [17516179] **5154**

SCIENCE WORLD (1987) (US/1041-1410) [17516197] **5154**

SCIENCE YEAR (US/0080-7621) [02251937] **5154**

SCIENCELAND (US/0147-3654) [03148602] 1068, **5154**

SCIENCES AGRONOMIQUES. PRODUCTIONS VEGETALES. T280 (FR) **185**

SCIENCES & AVENIR. HORS SERIE (FR/1142-4877) [I11424877] **5154**

SCIENCES & TECHNOLOGIES (FR) [18141829] **5154**

SCIENCES DE LA TERRE. INFORMATIQUE GEOLOGIQUE (FR/0335-9255) [02130428] **1396**

SCIENCES DE LA TERRE. MEMOIRES (FR/0582-2300) [03215044] **1396**

SCIENCES DE LA VIE. LEXIQUE (FR/0154-0319) [07087649] **5154**

SCIENCES DE L'ART (FR) [01697217] **364**

SCIENCES DE L'EDUCATION POUR L'ERE NOUVELLE, LES (FR/0755-9593) [I07559593] **1783**

SCIENCES DE L'INGENIEUR. LEXIQUE (FR/0154-0351) [07088173] **5154**

SCIENCES DES ALIMENTS (FR/0240-8813) [08120369] **2356**

SCIENCES ET AVENIR (FR/0036-8636) [03768333] **5154**

SCIENCES ET NATURE (FR/0987-0717) [I09870717] **5154**

SCIENCES ET TECHNIQUES DE L'EAU (CN) [10935318] **1418**

SCIENCES ET TECHNIQUES EN PERSPECTIVE (FR/0294-0264) [10540007] 3533, **5154**

SCIENCES GEOLOGIQUES (FR/0302-2684) [03235516] **1396**

SCIENCES GEOLOGIQUES. BULLETIN (FR/0302-2692) [01793250] **1396**

SCIENCES (NEW YORK), THE (US/0036-861X) [00856129] **5154**

SCIENCES SOCIALES ET SANTE (FR/0294-0337) [16529665] **4801**

SCIENCES SOCIALES PANORAMA : REVUE TRIMESTRIELLE EDITEE SOUS L'EGIDE DU MINISTERE DE L'ENSEIGNEMENT SUPERIEUR ET DE LA RECHERCHE SCIENTIFIQUE, O.N.R.S (AE) [10544832] **5218**

SCIENCES, TECHNIQUES, INFORMATIONS CRIAC (CG/0377-5135) [02161686] **5154**

SCIENCES VETERINAIRES, MEDECINE COMPAREE (FR/0750-7682) [09035070] **5521**

SCIENCETECH BULLETIN (II) [04912965] **5154**

●SCIENTIA AGRICOLA (BL/0103-9016) [27786385] **4171**

SCIENTIA AGRICULTURAE BOHEMOSLOVACA (XR/0582-2343) [01589936] **132**

SCIENTIA CANADENSIS (CN/0829-2507) [11305775] **5154**

SCIENTIA ELECTRICA *CEASED*. (US/0036-8695) [01919623] **2080**

SCIENTIA ET PRAXIS (PE/0559-1414) [02267556] **5218**

SCIENTIA HORTICULTURAE (NE/0304-4238) [02242207] **2431**

SCIENTIA IURIDICA (PO) [19099699] **3046**

SCIENTIA MARINA (SP/0214-8358) [20873235] **557**

SCIENTIA PAEDAGOGICA EXPERIMENTALIS (BE/0582-2351) [01605110] **1783**

SCIENTIA PHARMACEUTICA (AU/0036-8709) [01620123] **4329**

SCIENTIA. SERIES A. MATHEMATICAL SCIENCES (CL/0716-8446) [I07168446] **3533**

SCIENTIAE (IO) [05769605] **5154**

SCIENTIAE *CEASED*. (SA/0036-8717) [06992563] **1639**

SCIENTIFIC ACTIVITIES : FEDERAL GOVERNMENT COSTS AND EXPENDITURES (CN) [01789285] **5154**

SCIENTIFIC ACTIVITIES OF THE POLISH ACADEMY OF SCIENCES, INSTITUTE OF FUNDAMENTAL TECHNOLOGICAL RESEARCH (PL/0079-323X) [05152167] **5155**

SCIENTIFIC AMERICAN (US/0036-8733) [01775222] **5155**

●SCIENTIFIC AMERICAN FRONTIERS (MAGAZINE) (US/1068-6738) [27754320] **3639**

SCIENTIFIC AMERICAN LIBRARY SERIES (US/1040-3213) [16876289] **5155**

SCIENTIFIC AMERICAN MEDICINE (US/0194-9063) [05092670] **3639**

SCIENTIFIC AMERICAN RESOURCE LIBRARY (US) [01765225] **472**

SCIENTIFIC AMERICAN RESOURCE LIBRARY. READINGS IN PSYCHOLOGY (US/0586-5719) [02465251] **4618**

●SCIENTIFIC AMERICAN SCIENCE & MEDICINE (US/1068-6746) [27755260] **3639**

SCIENTIFIC AMERICAN. SPECIAL ISSUE (US/1048-0943) [20849843] **5155**

SCIENTIFIC AMERICAN SURGERY (US) **3974**

SCIENTIFIC & APPLIED PHOTOGRAPHY (US/1063-4088) [25999053] **4376**

SCIENTIFIC AND TECHNICAL AEROSPACE REPORTS (US/0036-8741) [01645472] **35**

SCIENTIFIC AND TECHNICAL BOOKS AND SERIALS IN PRINT (US/0000-054X) [03548752] **5176**

SCIENTIFIC AND TECHNICAL INFORMATION PROCESSING (US/0147-6882) [01591736] **3248**

SCIENTIFIC AND TECHNICAL ORGANIZATIONS AND AGENCIES DIRECTORY (US/0889-1729) [12747221] **5155**

SCIENTIFIC AND TECHNICAL PUBLICATIONS OF THE ENVIRONMENTAL RESEARCH LABORATORIES (US/0146-7956) [03048280] **2181**

SCIENTIFIC AND TECHNICAL SURVEYS - BRITISH FOOD MANUFACTURING INDUSTRIES RESEARCH ASSOCIATION (UK/0144-2074) [07801040] **2357**

SCIENTIFIC ANGLERS FLY FISHING HANDBOOK *CEASED*. (US/0271-5104) [06621328] **2312**

SCIENTIFIC AWAKENING IN THE RESTORATION (US/0882-2034) [11777913] **5155**

SCIENTIFIC BULLETIN OF THE ATOMIC ENERGY ORGANIZATION OF IRAN (IR) [19299463] 1956, **4420**

SCIENTIFIC COMPUTING & AUTOMATION (US/0891-9003) [12132234] 1245, **1221**

SCIENTIFIC COUNCIL REPORTS (CN/0250-6416) [08288854] **2312**

SCIENTIFIC COUNCIL STUDIES (CN/0250-6432) [08277599] **2312**

SCIENTIFIC DIRECTORY AND ANNUAL BIBLIOGRAPHY (US) [08066977] **5176**

SCIENTIFIC DRILLER, THE (US) [16766931] **1996**

SCIENTIFIC DRILLING (GW/0934-4365) [22349035] **1410**

SCIENTIFIC, ENGINEERING, AND MEDICAL SOCIETIES PUBLICATIONS IN PRINT *CEASED*. (US/0277-7355) [04128002] **5155**

SCIENTIFIC, ENGINEERING, TECHNICAL MANPOWER COMMENTS (US/0036-8768) [01642284] 1996, **5155**

SCIENTIFIC ET TECHNICAL RES (FR) **5155**

SCIENTIFIC HONEYWELLER (US/0196-8440) [05910661] **5155**

SCIENTIFIC INFORMATION BULLETIN *CEASED*. (US/1048-5678) [18061227] **5155**

SCIENTIFIC INTEGRITY *SUSPENDED*. (US) [14181471] 1904, **472**

SCIENTIFIC INVESTMENT (US/1067-6090) [27307184] **913**

SCIENTIFIC JOURNAL OF ORIENTEERING (SW/1012-0602) [I10120602] **4917**

SCIENTIFIC MANPOWER (US/0565-8306) [01253303] **5155**

SCIENTIFIC MANPOWER COMMISSION *See* SALARIES OF SCIENTISTS, ENGINEERS AND TECHNICIANS **1709**

SCIENTIFIC MANPOWER COMMISSION *See* DRAFT FACTS FOR GRADUATES AND GRADUATE STUDENTS **4043**

SCIENTIFIC MEETINGS (US/0487-8965) [03055496] **5155**

SCIENTIFIC PAPERS / ILLINOIS STATE MUSEUM (US/0445-3395) [01741077] **1360**

SCIENTIFIC PAPERS OF THE COLLEGE OF ARTS AND SCIENCES, THE UNIVERSITY OF TOKYO (JA/0289-7520) [09935039] **5155**

SCIENTIFIC PAPERS OF THE INSTITUTE OF ALGOLOGICAL RESEARCH, FACULTY OF SCIENCE, HOKKAIDO UNIVERSITY (JA/0385-6054) [01752186] **527**

SCIENTIFIC PRESENTATIONS OF THE ANNUAL MEETING - AMERICAN ANIMAL HOSPITAL ASSOCIATION (US/0164-1999) [01999159] **5521**

SCIENTIFIC PROCEEDINGS / AMERICAN COLLEGE OF VETERINARY INTERNAL MEDICINE (CN) [05737605] **5521**

●SCIENTIFIC PROGRAMMING (US/1058-9244) [24433883] **5155**

SCIENTIFIC PUBLICATION - FRESHWATER BIOLOGICAL ASSOCIATION (UK/0367-1887) [01570187] **472**

SCIENTIFIC PUBLICATIONS AND PRESENTATIONS RELATING TO PLANETARY QUARANTINE (US/0160-581X) [03696099] **41**

SCIENTIFIC PUBLICATIONS FROM EASTMAN KODAK LABORATORIES (US/0424-2017) [02468616] **4376**

SCIENTIFIC PUBLICATIONS OF THE SCIENCE MUSEUM OF MINNESOTA (US/0161-4452) [02637049] **5155**

SCIENTIFIC REPORT - FOX CHASE CANCER CENTER (US/1040-0303) [18310558] **3823**

SCIENTIFIC REPORT / INTERNATIONAL PACIFIC HALIBUT COMMISSION (US/0304-016X) [01714847] **2312**

SCIENTIFIC REPORT - MCGILL UNIVERSITY, STORMY WEATHER GROUP (CN/0076-180X) [02247773] **1434**

SCIENTIFIC REPORT / NUTRITION FOUNDATION OF INDIA (II) [23296482] **4199**

SCIENTIFIC REPORTS OF CETACEAN RESEARCH (JA/0917-0537) [23210021] 557, **5597**

SCIENTIFIC REPORTS OF THE HOKKAIDO SALMON HATCHERY (JA/0441-0769) [06009579] **2312**

SCIENTIFIC REVIEWS ON ARID ZONE RESEARCH (II/0254-0568) [10063474] 1360, **2220**

SCIENTIFIC SALARIES' SURVEY / PREPARED BY D. DIETRICH ASSOCIATES, INC (US) [22252356] **5155**

SCIENTIFIC SERIALS REVIEW. BIOMEDICINE *CEASED*. (UK/0884-8319) [12488739] 3639, **472**

SCIENTIFIC SERIES / ENVIRONMENT CANADA (CN) [27837778] **5155**

SCIENTIFIC SERIES (OTTAWA) (CN) [01497671] **1418**

SCIENTIFIC SLEUTHING REVIEW (US/1043-4224) [19484043] **5155**

SCIENTIFIC WORLD *CEASED*. (UK/0036-8857) [01918724] **5156**

SCIENTIFUR (DK/0105-2403) [04373466] **3186**

SCIENTIST OF PHYSICAL SCIENCES (II) [22443108] **5156**

SCIENTIST (PHILADELPHIA, PA.), THE (US/0890-3670) [14207826] **5156**

SCIENTOMETRICS (NE/0138-9130) [04846912] **5156**

SCIENZA & VITA NUOVA (IT/0393-7917) [I03937917] **4171**

SCIENZA E DIABETE (IT) **3733**

SCIENZA E TECNICA AGRARIA (IT) **132**

SCIENZA E TECNICA LATTIERO-CASEARIA (IT) [I03906361] **198**

SCIENZASOCIETA (IT/0392-7946) [15188388] **5156**

SCIENZE QUADERNI, LE (IT) **5156**

SCIFANT (US/0882-1348) [11768150] 3434, **5074**

SCIMA (II) [01784149] **1252**

SCIMITAR AND SONG ANTHOLOGY (US) [03683301] **4152**

SCIMP SELECTIVE CO-OPERATIVE INDEX OF MANAGEMENT PERIODICALS *CEASED*. (FI/0782-2979) [04904871] 885, **733**

SCINTEIA *CEASED*. (RM) [02267562] **5808**

SCINTILLA (TORONTO) (CN/0824-6009) [11564267] 2629, **3434**

SCIOS (AT/0157-6488) [01576488] 1904, **5156**

SCIPHERS
Alphabetical Title Index

SCIPHERS (COLLEGE STATION, TEX.) (US/1071-4103) [11435283] 5156, **2924**

SCIS NEWSLETTER (US/0036-8288) [01765240] **5156**

SCISEARCH [ONLINE DATABASE] (US) 5156, **5176**

SCITECH BOOK NEWS (US/0196-6006) [05855961] **5156**

SCITECH REFERENCE PLUS (US/1063-8717) [22477458] 5156, **5176**

SCITECH TECHNOLOGY DIRECTORY (AT/1030-4649) [I10304649] **5156**

SCLC (ATLANTA, GA.) (US/0735-7443) [08614912] **4995**

SCLEOA UPDATE (US/8750-3808) [11352169] **3176**

SCN NEWS / UNITED NATIONS, ADMINISTRATIVE COMMITTEE ON COORDINATION, SUBCOMMITTEE ON NUTRITION (US) [19120851] **4199**

SCN : THE SHOPPING CENTRE NEWSLETTER (CN/0843-1507) [19746803] **957**

SCO MAGAZINE *CEASED*. (US/1060-1074) [24880620] **1249**

SCODA NEWSLETTER : STANDING CONFERENCE ON DRUG ABUSE (UK) **1349**

SCOLAG : SCOTTISH LEGAL ACTION GROUP BULLETIN (UK/0264-8717) [21947708] **3046**

SCOLIES (FR) [01925854] **3352**

SCOOP (CN) **2835**

SCOPE *See* LOUPE (SANTA MONICA, CALIF.) **2915**

SCOPE/36 (US/0887-9338) [13471594] **1202**

SCOPE (CHICHESTER) (UK/0271-972X) [05261199] 5156, **2221**

SCOPE MISCELLANEOUS PUBLICATION (US/0275-7389) [05869830] **2181**

SCOPE NOTE / JOSEPH AND ROSE KENNEDY INSTITUTE OF ETHICS, GEORGETOWN UNIVERSITY (US) [18695203] 2253, **3639**

SCOPE NOTES (EDMONTON) (CN/0709-4027) [09586163] **2483**

SCOPP : SATURDAY CENTRE OF PROSE & POETRY (AT/0313-685x) [05201037] **3470**

SCOPUS (IS) [01604773] 2854, **1095**

SCORE (NE) **4866**

SCORE (NASHVILLE, TENN.) (US/1074-5769) [28825640] 4995, **4152**

SCORE (TORONTO) (CN/0711-3226) [08454709] **4917**

SCOREBOARD (OWINGS MILLS, MD. NORTHWEST ED.) (US/1055-8608) [23362084] **4917**

SCORP DIGEST (US) [07289729] **4878**

SCOT LIT (UK) [20666571] **3434**

SCOTIA (US/0273-0693) [04622028] **2709**

SCOTLAND. CROFTERS COMMISSION *See* APUA NEWSLETTER **62**

SCOTLAND, HOTELS & GUEST HOUSES (UK) [22523765] **2809**

SCOTLAND, WHERE TO STAY, HOTELS AND GUEST HOUSES (UK) [06125309] **2809**

SCOTLANDS (UK/1350-7508) **2854**

SCOTLANDS REGIONS (UK/0305-6562) [01826634] **4685**

SCOTLAND'S TOP 1000 COMPANIES (UK) [21200945] **709**

SCOTLIT ABERDEEN (UK/0957-5499) [I09575499] **3434**

SCOTS LAW TIMES; LYON COURT REPORTS, THE (UK/0036-908X) [03032462] **3046**

SCOTS LAW TIMES; NOTES OF RECENT DECISIONS, THE (UK/0036-908X) [03032468] **3046**

SCOTS LAW TIMES; REPORTS, THE (UK/0036-908X) [03032481] **3047**

SCOTS LAW TIMES; SCOTTISH LAND COURT REPORTS, THE (UK/0036-908X) [03032467] **3047**

SCOTS LAW TIMES; SHERIFF COURT REPORTS, THE (UK/0036-908X) [03032469] **3047**

SCOTS LAW TIMES, THE (UK/0036-908X) [01765265] **3046**

SCOTS LAW TIMES; THE LANDS TRIBUNAL FOR SCOTLAND REPORTS, THE (UK/0036-908X) [03032465] **3047**

SCOTS MAGAZINE, THE (UK) [01717026] **2522**

SCOTS MERCANTILE LAW STATUTES (UK/0308-1176) [01799994] **3103**

SCOTSMAN, THE (UK) [03856993] **5813**

SCOTT CATALOGUE SPECIALISE DES TIMBRES CANADIENS *See* UNITRADE CATALOGUE SPECIALISE DES TIMBRES CANADIENS **2788**

SCOTT COUNTY IOWAN (US/1046-1027) [08467720] **2760**

SCOTT COUNTY JOURNAL (SCOTTSBURG, IND.), THE (US/0740-4573) [09952883] **5667**

SCOTT COUNTY TIMES (FOREST, MISS.) (US) [15103981] **5701**

SCOTT COUNTY VIRGINIA STAR (US/8750-3832) [11408199] **5759**

SCOTT, JOE (JOSEPH III) JOE SCOTT'S THE POLITICAL ANIMAL *See* POLITICAL ANIMAL (1993), THE **4488**

SCOTT KING'S DIABETES INTERVIEW (US/1058-6598) [24383648] **3676**

SCOTT NEWSLETTER, THE (UK/0264-2522) [09456956] **3434**

SCOTT PUBLISHING CO *See* SCOTT STANDARD POSTAGE STAMP CATALOGUE **2787**

SCOTT PUBLISHING CO *See* STANDARD ... U.S. COIN CATALOGUE **2783**

SCOTT SPECIALIZED CATALOGUE OF CANADIAN STAMPS *See* UNITRADE SPECIALIZED CATALOGUE OF CANADIAN STAMPS **2788**

SCOTT SPECIALIZED CATALOGUE OF UNITED STATES STAMPS (US) [04866770] **2787**

SCOTT STAMP MONTHLY (US/0737-0741) [08932842] **2787**

SCOTT STANDARD POSTAGE STAMP CATALOGUE (US/0161-5084) [01775223] **2787**

SCOTTISH ABSTRACT OF STATISTICS (UK) [01942159] **5338**

SCOTTISH AGRICULTURAL DEVELOPMENT COUNCIL *See* ANNUAL REPORT - SCOTTISH AGRICULTURAL DEVELOPMENT COUNCIL **61**

SCOTTISH-AMERICAN GENEALOGIST (US/0271-5031) [06611014] **2471**

SCOTTISH ARCHAEOLOGICAL FORUM (UK) [01925910] **282**

SCOTTISH ARCHAEOLOGICAL NEWS (UK/0958-2002) [21360752] **282**

SCOTTISH ARCHAEOLOGICAL REVIEW : SAR (UK/0262-4389) [08967035] **282**

SCOTTISH ARCHITECTS DIRECTORY, THE (UK) [07112114] **308**

SCOTTISH ART REVIEW *SUSPENDED*. (UK/0036-911X) [01641720] **364**

SCOTTISH BANKER : MAGAZINE OF THE INSTITUTE OF BANKERS IN SCOTLAND, THE (UK) [17275229] **810**

SCOTTISH BANNER, THE (CN/0707-073X) [05018478] 2472, **2272**

SCOTTISH BAPTIST MAGAZINE (UK/0036-9136) [01776699] **5067**

SCOTTISH BEE JOURNAL (UK) **132**

SCOTTISH BEEKEEPER (UK/0370-8918) [02457943] **132**

SCOTTISH BIRDS (UK/0036-9144) [02500837] **5620**

SCOTTISH BOOK COLLECTOR (UK/0954-8769) [19348898] 3434, **4819**

SCOTTISH BUILDING AND CIVIL ENGINEERING YEAR BOOK (UK/0085-6002) [01793161] 2030, **627**

SCOTTISH BULLETIN OF EVANGELICAL THEOLOGY, THE (UK/0265-4539) [12603222] **4995**

SCOTTISH BUSINESS INSIDER (UK/0952-1488) [I09521488] **709**

SCOTTISH CIVIC TRUST *See* ANNUAL REPORT / THE SCOTTISH CIVIC TRUST **2815**

SCOTTISH CIVIL LAW REPORTS (UK/0951-0443) [16118205] **3091**

SCOTTISH CLANS & THEIR TARTANS, THE (UK) [05690452] **2472**

SCOTTISH CROP RESEARCH INSTITUTE *See* ANNUAL REPORT / SCOTTISH CROP RESEARCH INSTITUTE **163**

SCOTTISH CURRENT LAW YEAR BOOK (UK) [01765281] **3047**

SCOTTISH ECONOMIC & SOCIAL HISTORY (UK/0269-5030) [09296306] **5218**

SCOTTISH ECONOMIC BULLETIN (UK/0952-6498) [01941185] **1583**

SCOTTISH EDUCATIONAL REVIEW (UK/0141-9072) [04187845] **1783**

SCOTTISH FIELD (GLASGOW) (UK/0036-9209) [03884481] **2709**

SCOTTISH FISH FARMER (UK) **2312**

SCOTTISH FISHERIES INFORMATION PAMPHLET (UK/0309-9105) [05857243] **2312**

SCOTTISH FISHERIES RESEARCH REPORT (UK) [03201453] **2312**

SCOTTISH FOLK DIRECTORY (UK) [01788834] **4152**

SCOTTISH FORESTRY (UK/0036-9217) [01587336] **2395**

SCOTTISH GAELIC STUDIES (UK/0080-8024) [01765282] 3434, **3319**

SCOTTISH GENEALOGIST, THE (UK/0300-337X) [01453474] **2472**

SCOTTISH GEOGRAPHICAL MAGAZINE (UK/0036-9225) [01604208] **2576**

SCOTTISH GEORGIAN SOCIETY *See* BULLETIN OF THE SCOTTISH GEORGIAN SOCIETY **294**

SCOTTISH GOVERNMENT YEARBOOK, THE (UK) [03945806] **4495**

SCOTTISH HISTORICAL REVIEW, THE (UK/0036-9241) [01585736] **2709**

SCOTTISH HISTORY SOCIETY (SERIES) (UK) [07825578] **2709**

SCOTTISH HOME AND COUNTRY (UK) [04084297] **2903**

SCOTTISH HOUSING STATISTICS / SCOTTISH DEVELOPMENT DEPARTMENT (UK) [06052230] 2835, **2840**

SCOTTISH INDUSTRIAL HISTORY (UK/0266-7428) [I02667428] **1626**

SCOTTISH INSTITUTE OF MISSIONARY STUDIES *See* BULLETIN OF THE SCOTTISH INSTITUTE OF MISSIONARY STUDIES, THE **4941**

SCOTTISH JOURNAL OF GEOLOGY (UK/0036-9276) [01765283] **1396**

SCOTTISH JOURNAL OF PHYSICAL EDUCATION (UK/0140-2315) [I01402315] **1858**

SCOTTISH JOURNAL OF POLITICAL ECONOMY (UK/0036-9292) [01749755] **1595**

SCOTTISH JOURNAL OF RELIGIOUS STUDIES, THE (UK/0143-8301) [06681799] **4995**

SCOTTISH JOURNAL OF THEOLOGY (UK/0036-9306) [01765285] **4995**

SCOTTISH LANGUAGE (UK/0264-0198) [09392022] **3319**

SCOTTISH LAW COMMISSION *See* ANNUAL REPORT / SCOTTISH LAW COMMISSION **2935**

SCOTTISH LAW DIRECTORY FOR ..., THE (UK/0080-8083) [04084856] **3047**

SCOTTISH LAW GAZETTE, THE (UK/0036-9314) [21947430] **3047**

SCOTTISH LIBRARIES (1987) (UK/0950-0189) [15627052] **3248**

SCOTTISH LIBRARY AND INFORMATION RESOURCES (UK) [12250367] **3248**

SCOTTISH LIBRARY ASSOCIATION *See* PROCEEDINGS OF THE ANNUAL CONFERENCE **3242**

SCOTTISH LICENSED TRADE DIRECTORY *See* NATIONAL GUARDIAN DIRECTORY OF THE SCOTTISH LICENSED TRADE, THE **847**

SCOTTISH LICENSED TRADE NEWS (UK/0036-9322) [I00369322] **851**

SCOTTISH LITERARY JOURNAL (UK/0305-0785) [02243778] **3434**

SCOTTISH LITERARY JOURNAL. SUPPLEMENT (UK/0952-6439) [03405014] **3434**

SCOTTISH LITERARY JOURNAL. THE YEAR'S WORK IN SCOTTISH LITERARY AND LINGUISTIC STUDIES (UK) [18156529] **3319**

SCOTTISH MEDICAL JOURNAL (UK/0036-9330) [01765290] **3639**

SCOTTISH PETROLEUM ANNUAL (UK) [17561793] **4277**

SCOTTISH PHOTOGRAPHY BULLETIN (UK/0269-1787) [19781141] **4376**

●SCOTTISH PLANNING & ENVIRONMENTAL LAW (UK/0144-8196) [28581627] **2835**

SCOTTISH PLANNING LAW & PRACTICE (UK/0144-8196) [06937651] **3047**

SCOTTISH RECORD SOCIETY : PUBLICATIONS (UK) [02949792] **2472**

SCOTTISH RITE JOURNAL (US/0279-7011) [05665677] **5236**

SCOTTISH ROCK GARDEN CLUB *See* JOURNAL OF THE SCOTTISH ROCK GARDEN CLUB, THE **2422**

SCOTTISH SEA FISHERIES STATISTICAL TABLES (UK/0080-8202) [01765255] **2317**

SCOTTISH SHORT STORIES (UK) [02822009] **3434**

SCOTTISH SLAVONIC REVIEW (UK/0265-3273) [10153704] 2709, **3319**

SCOTTISH STAMP NEWS (EDINBURGH, SCOTLAND : 1987) (UK) [16170993] **2787**

SCOTTISH STUDIES (EDINBURGH) (UK/0036-9411) [01604178] **3434**

SCOTTISH TEACHERS' SALARIES MEMORANDUM (UK/0308-406X) [01799996] 1904, **1710**

SCOTTISH TERRIER QUARTERLY, THE (US/0747-3532) [10760813] **4288**

Alphabetical Title Index — SEA

SCOTTISH TRADITION (CN/0703-1580) [03363143] **2545**

SCOTTISH UNIVERSITIES COUNCIL ON ENTRANCE *See* COMPENDIUM OF INFORMATION - SCOTTISH UNIVERSITIES COUNCIL ON ENTRANCE **1818**

SCOTTISH UNIVERSITIES ENTRANCE GUIDE (UK) [08070053] **1847**

SCOTTISH WORLD (UK/0955-7024) [19692338] **5813**

SCOTT'S DIRECTORIES, ATLANTIC MANUFACTURERS (CN/0831-1854) [14398226] 1626, **3487**

SCOTT'S DIRECTORIES. ONTARIO MANUFACTURERS (CN/0830-9272) [11628675] 1626, **3487**

SCOTT'S DIRECTORIES, WESTERN MANUFACTURERS (CN/0829-2248) [11302089] **3487**

SCOTT'S REPERTOIRES, FABRICANTS DU QUEBEC (CN/0829-2221) [13207278] 1626, **3487**

SCOTTSBLUFF DAILY STAR-HERALD (US) [10575499] **5707**

SCOTTSDALE MAGAZINE (US) **2545**

SCOTTSDALE PROGRESS (US/0888-0271) [13451457] **5630**

SCOUT FOUR WHEEL DRIVE ANNUAL (US/0147-3506) [03144483] **5425**

SCOUT-JEUNESSE (CN/0383-0853) [02745927] **4878**

SCOUT MAGAZINE (AT) **4878**

SCOUT MID-RANGE SOFTWARE DIRECTORY (US/1047-1812) [20437750] **1202**

SCOUTING MAGAZINE (NE) 1068, **4878**

SCOUTING NEWS (CN/0318-3521) [02441705] **5236**

SCOUTING (NORTH BRUNSWICK) (UK/0036-9500) [01605593] **5236**

SCOUTING REPORT, THE (US/0743-1309) [09508462] **4917**

SCP JOURNAL (US/0883-1300) [05768591] **4995**

SCP NEWSLETTER (US/0883-1319) [12143835] **4996**

SCPF INFORMATION (SW/0283-0280) [28461800] **4239**

SCRANTON TIMES (SCRANTON, PA. : 1891 : DAILY) (US) [10432698] **5739**

SCRANTONIAN, THE (US) [15349864] **5739**

SCRAP PROCESSING AND RECYCLING (US/0898-0756) [17403817] **4018**

SCRAP TIRE NEWS (US) **2181**

SCRAP TIRE USERS DIRECTORY (US) **2181**

SCRAPBOOK PAGES (US/0890-8281) [14404278] **2760**

SCRAPE (PHOENIX, ARIZ.) (US/1058-0395) [24198951] **2545**

SCRATCHING RIVER POST, THE (CN/0707-2333) [04754940] **5794**

SCREAM (OTTAWA, ONT.) (CN/0828-6604) [12097952] **4535**

SCREAMING EAGLE, THE (US) [18472960] **4056**

SCREE (US/0360-2672) [01866095] **3352**

SCREEN (UK/0036-9543) [01765300] **4077**

SCREEN ACTOR (US/0036-956X) [02062664] **4077**

SCREEN ACTOR HOLLYWOOD (US/0890-5266) [14252551] 388, **4077**

SCREEN AND DISPLAY (UK) **1202**

●SCREEN (CHICAGO, ILL.) (US/1070-7573) [28471950] 1139, **4077**

SCREEN DIGEST (UK) [06097086] 4077, **1139**

SCREEN FINANCE (UK/0965-9587) [I09659587] **4077**

SCREEN IMAGING TECHNOLOGY FOR ELECTRONICS *CEASED.* (US/0885-5005) [12654614] **2080**

SCREEN INTERNATIONAL (UK/0307-4617) [02459245] 1139, **4077**

SCREEN INTERNATIONAL & CINEMA TV TODAY *See* SCREEN INTERNATIONAL **4077**

SCREEN INTERNATIONAL FILM AND TV YEAR BOOK (UK) [09704261] **4077**

●SCREEN INTERNATIONAL. THE INTERNATIONAL FILM & TELEVISION DIRECTORY (UK) [28552054] **4077**

SCREEN PLAY (DALLAS, TEX.) (US/1051-1032) [21834209] **388**

SCREEN PRINTER & T-SHIRT RETAILER MAGAZINE *See* IMPRINTING BUSINESS **1085**

SCREEN PRINTING (US) **4569**

SCREEN PRINTING TECHNIQUES (US/0362-160X) [02274165] **4569**

SCREEN PRINTING TECHNOLOGY AND MANAGEMENT *See* SCREEN PRINTING **4569**

SCREEN PRINTING TODAY *See* V.P.I.'S IMPRINTABLES TODAY **4570**

SCREEN PROCESS PRINTING (UK/0487-9775) [06184937] **4569**

SCREEN WORLD (II) [23313625] **4077**

SCREEN WORLD (US) [09152081] **4077**

●SCREENING: JOURNAL OF THE INTERNATIONAL SOCIETY OF NEONATAL SCREENING (NE/0925-6164) [25904632] 3911, **3768**

SCREENPRINT WEAR *See* PRINTWEAR & PROMOTION **4569**

SCREENPRINTING (UK) [17985022] **4569**

SCREW WEST (US/0199-042X) [05533235] **2492**

SCRIBE (US) [25603297] **3639**

SCRIBE (VAL-DAVID) (CN/0383-7262) [03278833] **4685**

SCRIBE (VANCOUVER) (CN/0824-6947) [12644000] **2760**

●SCRIBE (WASHINGTON, D.C.), THE (US/1060-5606) [25036090] **2273**

SCRIBES JOURNAL OF LEGAL WRITING, THE (US/1049-5177) [21245968] **3047**

SCRIBLERIAN AND THE KIT-CATS, THE (US/0190-731X) [02759643] **2854**

SCRIP MAGAZINE (UK) **4329**

SCRIP REPORT ON HYPERTENSION (UK) **3710**

SCRIP (RICHMOND) (UK/0143-7690) [06797243] **4329**

SCRIPPS CLINIC UPDATE (US) **3639**

SCRIPPS INSTITUTION OF OCEANOGRAPHY *See* ANNUAL REPORT - SCRIPPS INSTITUTION OF OCEANOGRAPHY (1984) **1446**

SCRIPPS INSTITUTION OF OCEANOGRAPHY. ANNUAL REPORT *See* EXPLORATIONS (LA JOLLA, CALIF.) **1449**

SCRIPSI (AT/0725-0096) [10387216] **3434**

SCRIPT (PARIS, 1988) (FR/0993-2097) [I09932097] **4077**

SCRIPT USER'S GUIDE (CN/0229-1231) [07822611] **1281**

SCRIPTA CLASSICA ISRAELICA (IS/0334-4509) [02243078] **3320**

SCRIPTA ETHNOLOGICA (AG) [01925800] **245**

SCRIPTA FACULTATIS SCIENTIARUM NATURALIUM UNIVERSITATIS PURKYNIANAE BRUNENSIS. BIOLOGIA (XR/0231-5777) [02707517] **472**

SCRIPTA FACULTATIS SCIENTIARUM NATURALIUM UNIVERSITATIS PURKYNIANAE BRUNENSIS. GEOGRAPHIA (XR/0324-6566) [02704401] **2576**

SCRIPTA GEOLOGICA (NE/0375-7587) [01918943] **1360**

SCRIPTA HIEROSOLYMITANA : PUBLICATIONS OF THE HEBREW UNIVERSITY, JERUSALEM (IS/0080-8369) [01681034] **1847**

SCRIPTA HISTORICA (FI/0358-710X) [08657060] **2629**

SCRIPTA HUMANISTICA (US) [15479342] 3320, **3434**

SCRIPTA ISLANDICA (SW/0582-3234) [01639075] **2709**

SCRIPTA LIMNOLOGICA UPSALIENSIA. COLLECTIO (SW/0586-4291) [01348059] **1418**

SCRIPTA MEDITERRANEA (CN/0226-8418) [07821345] **2854**

SCRIPTA MERCATURAE (GW/0036-973X) [01589367] **1583**

SCRIPTA METALLURGICA ET MATERIALIA (US/0956-716X) [21003869] **4018**

SCRIPTA SCIENTIFICA MEDICA (BU/0582-3250) [07722869] **3639**

SCRIPTA SERIES IN MATHEMATICS (US/0276-9670) [07468149] **3533**

SCRIPTA THEOLOGICA (SP/0036-9764) [02450471] **4996**

SCRIPTORES LATINI HIBERNIAE (IE/0332-4214) [I03324214] **3434**

SCRIPTORIUM (BE/0036-9772) [01714630] **3435**

SCRIPTORIUM (IT) **1080**

SCRIPTUM GERIATRICUM (GW/0172-1364) [04797227] **3755**

SCRIPTURA (SA/0254-1807) [08701896] **5019**

SCRIPTURE BULLETIN (UK/0036-9780) [01765310] **5019**

SCRIPTURE COMES ALIVE (US/0747-0207) [10470912] **5019**

SCRIPTURE IN CHURCH (IE/0332-1150) [01587123] **4996**

SCRIPTWRITERS MARKET (US/0748-6456) [09460558] 936, **4077**

SCRITTURA E CIVILTA (IT/0392-1697) [03977022] **3320**

SCRIVENER (CN/0227-5090) [07821182] **3435**

SCROGGINS NATIONAL LAW ENFORCEMENT DIRECTORY (US/0882-1909) [11674073] **3176**

SCROLL (MALVERNE, N.Y.) (US/0890-524X) [14256533] **1292**

SCRUTINY (SASKATOON, SASK.) (CN/0838-4525) [18810046] **1783**

SCS-TP (UNITED STATES. SOIL CONSERVATION SERVICE) (US/0270-9538) [02431063] **185**

SCTA HI LIGHTS (US) **5392**

SCUBA DIVER (AT/0729-5529) [I07295529] **4917**

SCUBA TIMES (US/0739-568X) [09455291] **4917**

SCUGOG CITIZEN [MICROFORM] (CN/1186-4907) [25796338] **5794**

SCULPTORS (US/0090-404X) [01785068] **2783**

●SCULPTURE MAQUETTE : A PUBLICATION OF THE INTERNATIONAL SCULPTURE CENTER (US) [25324401] **364**

SCULPTURE REVIEW (US/0747-5284) [09107554] **364**

SCULPTURE (WASHINGTON, D.C.) (US/0889-728X) [14039712] **364**

SCUOLA ARCHEOLOGICA ITALIANA DI ATENE *See* ANNUARIO DELLA SCUOLA ARCHEOLOGICA DI ATENE E DELLE MISSIONI ITALIANE IN ORIENTE **255**

SCUOLA CATTOLICA, LA (IT/0036-9810) [05933321] **5036**

SCUOLA DELLO SPORT : RIVISTA DI CULTURA SPORTIVA (IT) **4917**

SCUOLA DELLO SPORT RIVISTA DI CULTURA SPORTIVA (IT) **4917**

SCUOLA E CITTA (IT/0036-9853) [02293932] **1783**

SCUOLA E DIDATTICA (IT/0036-9861) [I00369861] **1872**

SCUOLA E L'UOMO (IT) **1872**

SCUOLA ITALIANA MODERNA (IT/0036-9888) [I00369888] **1904**

SCUOLA MATERNA (IT) **1068**

SCUOLA NORMALE SUPERIORE (ITALY). CLASSE DI SCIENZE *See* ANNALI DELLA SCUOLA NORMALE SUPERIORE DI PISA, CLASSE DI SCIENZE **3493**

SCUOLA SE (IT) **1872**

SCUOLA VIVA (IT) **1872**

SCUOLAOFFICINA (IT) [17419771] **5156**

SCUOLINFANZIA (IT) **1872**

SCWDC (US/0883-6817) [12200986] **4917**

SDA NEWS / SURFACE DESIGN ASSOCIATION (US) [28735464] **2778**

SDA WORKING PAPER SERIES (US/1014-739X) [20973444] **2912**

●SDB/PRIMES (US/1065-6286) [26659374] **709**

SDC INFORMATIONS (CN/0823-2040) [10517727] **1543**

SDI MONITOR (US/0886-7607) [12984477] **4056**

SDM FIELD GUIDE (US) **5177**

SDSVENSKA ORTNAMNSSALLSKAPET *See* ARSSKRIFT - SYDSVENSKA ORTNAMNSSALLSKAPETS **3267**

SE COMPRENDRE PARIS (FR/0245-7458) [I02457458] **4996**

SEA ABSTRACTS (PH) 5156, **5176**

SEA AND INLAND FISHERIES REPORT FOR ... / AN ROINN IASCAIGH AGUS FORAOISEACHTA (DEPT. OF FISHERIES AND FORESTRY) (IE) [07852479] **2313**

SEA-AR/BLM COOPERATIVE STUDIES. REYNOLDS CREEK WATERSHED INTERIM REPORT / NORTHWEST WATERSHED RESEARCH CENTER, WESTERN REGION, AGRICULTURAL RESEARCH, SCIENCE AND EDUCATION ADMINISTRATION, U.S. DEPARTMENT OF AGRICULTURE (US) [07832054] **132**

SEA BREEZE (BOSTON, MASS.) (US) [01590161] **5455**

SEA BREEZES (UK/0036-9977) [01765313] **5455**

SEA CHEST (BUXTON) (US/0364-9172) [02694028] **2760**

SEA CHEST, THE (US/0582-3471) [02955748] **2760**

SEA CLASSICS (US/0048-9867) [03922521] **4183**

SEA
Alphabetical Title Index

SEA COAST ECHO, THE (US) [14470132] **5701**

SEA COMBAT *See* SEA CLASSICS **4183**

SEA COMBINED WITH RUDDER (US) [04701326] **596**

SEA FRONTIERS (1988) (US/0897-2249) [17315312] **1456**

SEA GRANT BIENNIAL REPORT / U.S. DEPARTMENT OF COMMERCE, NATIONAL OCEANIC AND ATMOSPHERIC ADMINISTRATION, NATIONAL SEA GRANT COLLEGE PROGRAM (US/0277-5581) [07579861] **1456**

SEA GRANT PROGRAM REPORT (US) [18349420] 557, **1456**

SEA GRANT PUBLICATION (LA JOLLA) (US) [02801343] **1456**

SEA GRANT REPORT (COLLEGE) (US/0271-7069) [04092579] **2313**

SEA HERITAGE NEWS *SUSPENDED.* (US/0270-5524) [06457942] **2545**

SEA HISTORY (US/0146-9312) [03064427] **4183**

SEA HISTORY GAZETTE (US/0896-1646) [16941651] **5455**

SEA KAYAKER (US/0829-3279) [13529656] 4917, **596**

SEA (LOS ANGELES, CALIF.) (US/0746-8601) [10339454] 4917, **596**

SEA PEN (CN/0700-9275) [03399852] **557**

SEA POWER (1971) (US/0199-1337) [03324011] **4183**

SEA REPORTER (US/0193-1644) [05120806] **1872**

SEA SWALLOW, THE (UK) [05781696] **5620**

SEA TECHNOLOGY (US/0093-3651) [01788841] **1456**

SEA TECHNOLOGY. BUYERS GUIDE, DIRECTORY (US) [03510126] **1456**

SEA-TOWN CRIER (US) [25703746] **5307**

SEA WIND (CN/1011-1603) [17463626] **2205**

SEA WORLD (US/0162-8291) [04225396] **557**

SEABURY JOURNAL, THE *CEASED.* (US/0747-864X) [10143696] **4996**

SEABY COIN & MEDAL BULLETIN *See* CLASSICAL NUMISMATIC REVIEW **2780**

SEABY COINS SUBSCRIPTION (UK) **2783**

SEABY'S STANDARD CATALOGUE OF BRITISH COINS *See* STANDARD CATALOGUE OF BRITISH COINS **2783**

SEACOAST LIFE *CEASED.* (US/0885-6435) [12690494] **2545**

SEAFARER (HAWKESBURY, ONT.) (CN/0711-379X) [08681043] **596**

SEAFARER (LONDON) (UK/0037-007X) [06963204] 5455, **4183**

SEAFDEC NEWSLETTER / SOUTHEAST ASIAN FISHERIES DEVELOPMENT CENTER (TH) [05898822] **2313**

SEAFOOD AMERICA (US/0272-4294) [06849031] **2357**

SEAFOOD AUSTRALIA (AT/1320-9663) **2357**

SEAFOOD BUSINESS (CAMDEN, ME.) (US/0889-3217) [13767012] **2357**

SEAFOOD EXPORT JOURNAL (II/0037-010X) [05173568] **2313**

SEAFOOD INTERNATIONAL (UK/0268-1293) [13857978] **2313**

SEAFOOD LEADER (US/0744-4664) [08297292] **2313**

SEAFOOD NEWS FOR UK AND IRELAND (UK/0958-3246) [22723412] **2357**

SEAFOOD PRICE - CURRENT (US/0270-417X) [06416140] **2357**

SEAFOOD TREND NEWSLETTER (US/1057-2708) [23995934] **2357**

SEAFOOD YELLOW PAGES (US/1048-1303) [20859147] **2313**

SEAFORD HISTORICAL SOCIETY QUARTERLY *SUSPENDED.* (US/0737-9889) [09091706] **2760**

SEAHORSE / INTERNATIONAL YACHT RACING (UK) **596**

SEAISI DIRECTORY (MY) [10981682] **4019**

SEAISI QUARTERLY (SI/0129-5721) [01784308] **4019**

SEALING TECHNOLOGY (UK/1350-4789) **1029**

SEALS OF THE U.S. GOVERNMENT. CD-ROM (US) **382**

SEALY NEWS (SEALY, TEX. : 1915) (US) [14868555] **5754**

SEAMAN, THE *CEASED.* (UK/0037-0142) [05951192] **1710**

SEAMEO QUARTERLY / SOUTHEAST ASIAN MINISTERS OF EDUCATION ORGANIZATION (TH/0857-0361) [05081722] **1783**

SEAMIC HEALTH STATISTICS (JA) [06834718] 4811, **4562**

SEAMIC INFORMATION RETRIEVAL ON CURRENT LITERATURE. SERIES A: TYPHOID AND PARA-TYPHOID FEVERS, AND SALMONELLA FOOD POISONING (JA/1013-834X) [05767668] **4802**

SEAMIC INFORMATION RETRIEVAL ON CURRENT LITERATURE. SERIES F: HEALTH STATUS INDICATORS (JA/0254-2870) [06988471] **4802**

SEAMIC INFORMATION RETRIEVAL ON CURRENT LITERATURE. SERIES H, ENTEROTOXIGENIC COLI (JA) [07798533] **4802**

SEAMIC INFORMATION RETRIEVAL ON CURRENT LITERATURE. SERIES I, CAMPYLOBACTER (JA/1012-8638) [08090412] **4802**

SEAMIC INFORMATION RETRIEVAL ON CURRENT LITERATURE. SERIES J, VIRAL DIARRHEA (JA/1012-8646) [08985953] 3801, **4802**

SEAMIC INFORMATION RETRIEVAL ON CURRENT LITERATURE. SERIES K, DYSENTERY, BACILLARY (JA/1012-8654) [08987393] 3801, **4802**

SEAMIC INFORMATION RETRIEVAL ON CURRENT LITERATURE. SERIES L. VENEREAL DISEASE, GONORRHEA (JA/0254-8720) [09300176] 3716, **4802**

SEAMIC INFORMATION RETRIEVAL ON CURRENT LITERATURE. SERIES M, MALARIA (JA/1010-5441) [08987563] **4802**

SEAMIC NEWS LETTER.B (JA/0387-737X) [06644847] **3640**

SEAPORT (US/0743-6246) [04511066] **2760**

SEAPORTS AND THE SHIPPING WORLD (CN/0037-0150) [02509749] **5455**

SEAPORTS AND THE SHIPPING WORLD. SPRING ISSUE (CN) [02442906] **5455**

SEAPORTS OF THE WESTERN HEMISPHERE *CEASED.* (US/0899-1936) [13020202] **5455**

SEAPOSTER (US) [07425703] **2787**

SEARCH AND RESCUE; INTERNATIONAL STANDARDS AND RECOMMENDED PRACTICES. ANNEX 12 TO THE CONVENTION ON INTERNATIONAL CIVIL AVIATION (CN) [01753449] **35**

SEARCH AND RESCUE MAGAZINE (US/0092-5136) [01789747] **4802**

SEARCH AND SEIZURE BULLETIN (US/0037-0193) [03076806] **3176**

SEARCH AND SEIZURE LAW REPORT (US/0095-1005) [01794204] **3047**

●SEARCH AND SEIZURE LAW REPORTER, THE (CN/1188-6137) [26714899] **3047**

SEARCH AT THE STATE UNIVERSITY OF NEW YORK (US/0360-8476) [02359362] **5156**

SEARCH (DEVON, PA.) (US/1043-0946) [19277180] 308, **2903**

SEARCH (DUBLIN) (IE/0332-0618) [04106974] 1783, **4996**

SEARCH (FAIRFIELD, CONN.) (US/0739-0645) [09692671] **710**

SEARCH MAGAZINE (AMHERST) (US/0037-0290) [04167139] **35**

SEARCH (MIAMI), THE *CEASED.* (US/0272-5827) [06703295] **2664**

SEARCH (NASHVILLE) *CEASED.* (US/0048-9913) [02251943] **5067**

SEARCH (NEW YORK, N.Y. 1991) (US/1054-9358) [23024331] **3640**

SEARCH (NILES, ILL.) *CEASED.* (US/0277-5727) [07604326] **2472**

SEARCH (SANTA CLARA, CALIF.) (US/0886-1560) [12862401] **3248**

SEARCH (SYDNEY) (AT/0004-9549) [01765319] **5156**

SEARCH YORK (UK/0958-3467) [I09583467] **5307**

SEARCHER (UK) **2778**

●SEARCHER (MEDFORD, N.J.) (US/1070-4795) [28109010] **1202**

SEARCHER : OFFICIAL MONTHLY PERIODICAL OF THE SOUTHERN CALIFORNIA GENEALOGICAL SOCIETY, THE (US/01765321] **2472**

SEARCHERS & RESEARCHERS OF ELLIS COUNTY, TEXAS (US/0732-2879) [06680123] **2472**

SEARCHING TOGETHER (US/0739-2281) [09481068] **5067**

SEARCHLIGHT (US) [03188793] **3176**

SEARCHLIGHT (BLOOMFIELD, ONT.) (CN/0229-2637) [08605076] **2472**

SEARCHLIGHT (CULBERTSON, MONT.) (US) [11887583] **5706**

SEARCHLIGHT (LONDON) (UK/0262-4591) [I02624591] 4535, **5257**

SEARCHLIGHT SOUTH AFRICA *CEASED.* (UK/0954-3384) [20609533] **4546**

SEARL NATIONAL SPACE RESEARCH CONSORTIUM. UNITED KINGDOM DIVISION *See* NEWSLETTER - SEARL NATIONAL SPACE RESEARCH CONSORTIUM, UNITED KINGDOM DIVISION **30**

SEARMG NEWSLETTER (AT/0158-1953) [09080034] **2854**

SEARS (US/0193-4384) [01765324] **1299**

SEARS LIST OF SUBJECT HEADINGS (US) [07142014] **424**

SEARS, ROEBUCK AND COMPANY *See* SEARS **1299**

SEASON SUMMARY - OREGON BARTLETT PEAR COMMISSION (US/0091-567X) [01787537] 133, **2431**

SEASONAL FRUIT AND VEGETABLE REPORT (CN/0474-1560) [02240418] **133**

SEASONAL FRUIT & VEGETABLE REPORT (ANNUAL SUMMARY) (CN/0317-350X) [02955590] **2431**

SEASONALLY ADJUSTED TRAFFIC AND CAPACITY. MAJORS, SCHEDULED SERVICE, SYSTEM, DOMESTIC AND INTERNATIONAL OPERATIONS (US/0737-1969) [07332096] **5444**

SEASONS (CN/0227-793X) [06257356] **4171**

SEASONS IN ART (US/0272-0620) [06313770] **364**

SEASONS NORTH (CN/0225-6339) [06034744] **2760**

SEASONS (OAKLAND, CALIF.) (US/1047-4609) [20701178] 2273, **4802**

SEAT MARKET, THE (US/0743-7943) [10676930] **810**

SEATRAD BULLETIN (MY/0126-9860) [19366221] **2150**

SEATRAD CENTRE *See* ANNUAL REPORT / SEATRAD CENTRE **2134**

SEATRADE BUSINESS REVIEW *See* SEATRADE REVIEW **5455**

SEATRADE GERMAN SHIPPING REPORT *See* SEATRADE REVIEW **5455**

●SEATRADE REVIEW (UK/0964-8895) [25163203] 851, **5455**

SEATRADE WEEK (US/0891-2319) [13776058] **5455**

●SEATRADE WEEK NEWSFRONT (HK) [28159519] **5455**

●SEATTLE (US) [27899323] **2545**

SEATTLE & AREA AIRPORT BUSINESS DIRECTORY (CN/1183-0115) [23598358] **710**

SEATTLE ART MUSEUM *See* SEATTLE ART MUSEUM **4096**

SEATTLE ART MUSEUM *See* SEATTLE ART MUSEUM NEWSLETTER **4096**

SEATTLE ART MUSEUM (US) [06210065] 364, **4096**

SEATTLE ART MUSEUM NEWSLETTER (US/0197-5242) [04412621] **4096**

SEATTLE BRANCH BULLETIN *See* SEATTLE BRANCH NEWSLETTER / AMERICAN ASSOCIATION OF UNIVERSITY WOMEN **1847**

●SEATTLE BRANCH NEWSLETTER / AMERICAN ASSOCIATION OF UNIVERSITY WOMEN (US) [26409466] 5566, **1847**

SEATTLE DAILY JOURNAL OF COMMERCE (US) [19913186] **5762**

SEATTLE FOLKLORE SOCIETY *See* SFS FLYER **2324**

SEATTLE GENEALOGICAL SOCIETY *See* BULLETIN - SEATTLE GENEALOGICAL SOCIETY **2441**

SEATTLE HOME AND GARDEN (US) [20998799] **2431**

SEATTLE MARKETING DIRECTORY *See* SEATTLE METRO BUSINESS DIRECTORY **710**

SEATTLE MEDIUM, THE (US/0746-5394) [10124671] **5762**

●SEATTLE METRO BUSINESS DIRECTORY (US) [26458942] **710**

SEATTLE OPERA MAGAZINE (US) [18155751] **4152**

SEATTLE POST-INTELLIGENCER (1921) (US/0745-970X) [03734418] **5762**

SEATTLE REVIEW, THE (US/0147-6629) [03547595] **3435**

SEATTLE TIMES, THE (US/0745-9696) [09198928] **5762**

SEATTLE TRAFFIC ACCIDENT SUMMARY (US) [10320954] **5444**

●SEATTLE UNIVERSITY LAW REVIEW (US) **3047**

SEATTLE WEEKLY (US/0898-0845) [17527271] **5762**

Alphabetical Title Index — SECURITIES

SEATTLE'S CHILD (US/1064-4512) [22427235] **2286**

SEAWATCH *See* UNDERCURRENTS: MYSTIC MARINELIFE AQUARIUM QUARTERLY **5599**

SEAWATER AND DESALTING *CEASED*. (GW/0720-0773) [07866542] **2243**

SEAWAY MARITIME DIRECTORY (US/0582-3668) [05997019] **5456**

SEAWAY REVIEW (US/0037-0487) [01337219] **5456**

SEAWAYS (1980) (UK/0144-1019) [07003121] **4183**

SEAWAYS (SALT LAKE CITY, UTAH) *See* SEAWAYS' SHIPS IN SCALE **4183**

●SEAWAYS' SHIPS IN SCALE (US/1065-8904) [26732016] **4183**

SEAWORLD (MYSTIC) (US/0273-4168) [04811403] **1456**

SEBREE BANNER, THE (US) [14125089] **5682**

SEBRING NEWS *See* NEWS-SUN (SEBRING, FLA.), THE **5650**

SEBRING TIMES, THE (US) [11027893] **5730**

SEC ACCOUNTING & REPORTING UPDATE SERVICE (US/1045-1439) [20022688] **751**

SEC ACCOUNTING REPORT (US/0146-485X) [02952322] **751**

SEC CORPORATION INDEX (US/0193-0192) [04634351] **913**

SEC DOCKET (US/0091-4061) [08174967] **913**

SEC GUIDELINES, RULES, AND REGULATIONS (US) [12200737] **3088**

SEC NO-ACTION LETTERS INDEX AND SUMMARIES (US/0162-2838) [04146044] **4685**

SEC QUARTERLY BULLETIN, THE (PH) [05145007] **3047**

SEC REPORT (US/0885-9078) [12758470] **4917**

SEC SPEAKS IN ..., THE (US/0145-8744) [11285827] **3047**

SEC TODAY, THE (US/0745-2667) [09009233] **913**

SECHERESSE MONTROUGE (FR/1147-7806) [11477806] 2221, **1360**

SECHZIG - NA UND ? (GW) **5181**

SECIN ABSTRACTS / SPONSORED BY INTERNATIONAL DEVELOPMENT RESEARCH CENTRE (JM) [10569143] **1520**

SECOL REVIEW, THE (US/0730-6245) [08037568] **3320**

SECOLAS ANNALS (US/0081-2951) [07508671] **2760**

SECOLUL 20 (RM/0037-0517) [02272558] **3352**

SECOND BOAT, THE (US/0274-6441) [06492283] **2472**

SECOND CENTURY (ABILENE, TEX.) *See* JOURNAL OF EARLY CHRISTIAN STUDIES **4968**

SECOND CENTURY (ABILENE, TEX.), THE (US/0276-7899) [07421980] **4996**

SECOND CIRCUIT DIGEST (US/0746-5254) [06865503] **3047**

SECOND CIRCUIT REDBOOK (US/0146-163X) [02878995] **3143**

SECOND LANGUAGE INSTRUCTION/ACQUISITION ABSTRACTS (US/1055-4750) [23188519] **3320**

SECOND LANGUAGE RESEARCH (UK/0267-6583) [13540902] **3320**

SECOND LINE, THE (US/0037-0576) [05182807] **4152**

SECOND MESSENGER AND PHOSPHOPROTEINS (US/0895-7479) [16780926] 4329, **586**

SECOND OPINION (PARK RIDGE, ILL.) (US/0890-1570) [13672283] 2253, 4996, **3640**

SECOND OPINION (SAN FRANCISCO, CALIF.) (US/0748-9528) [11039823] 3716, **4802**

SECOND OPINIONS ON HEALTH CARE ISSUES *CEASED*. (US/0738-8802) [09673369] **3640**

SECOND ORDER (NR/0331-3379) [01923365] **4360**

SECOND SOURCE BIOMEDICAL (US/1053-6868) [22607492] **3696**

SECOND SOURCE IMAGING (US/1053-6876) [22607530] **3640**

SECOND STONE, THE (US/1047-3971) [20690040] **2796**

SECONDARY ALUMINIUM, EUROPE, JAPAN, USA (GW) [20008573] **4019**

SECONDARY EDUCATION TODAY (US/0160-6778) [02455957] **1783**

SECONDARY INDUSTRIES (PORT MORESBY, PAPUA NEW GUINEA) (PP) [13344043] **1626**

SECONDARY INDUSTRIES. PRELIMINARY STATEMENT (PP) [09821485] **1626**

●SECONDARY MARKET ANNUAL GUIDE, THE (US) **1299**

SECONDARY MARKET REPORTER *See* MORTGAGE MARKETPLACE, THE **800**

SECONDARY MARKETING EXECUTIVE (US/0891-2947) [14709371] **936**

SECONDARY MORTGAGE MARKETS (US/0740-4271) [09952788] 2835, **810**

SECONDARY RECOVERY AND PRESSURE MAINTENANCE OPERATIONS IN LOUISIANA (US) [06497893] **2150**

SECONDARY RECOVERY REPORT (US/0148-3285) [03297203] **2150**

SECONDARY SCHOOLS FOR INTERNATIONAL STUDENTS, U.S.A (US/0149-4538) [03484865] **1847**

SECONDARY TEACHER (AT/0155-588X) [0155588X] **1905**

●SECONDO RINASCIMENTO, IL (IT) [26102978] **2854**

SECONDS (NEW YORK, N.Y.) (US/1052-5025) [22408751] 330, **4152**

SECRECY & GOVERNMENT BULLETIN (US/1061-0340) [25161579] **4685**

●SECRET GUIDE TO MUSIC AND OTHER GREAT STUFF YOU'RE UNLIKELY TO FIND ANYWHERE ELSE, THE (US/1065-2981) [26569282] **4152**

●SECRET OF THE PROS, THE (US/1064-3257) [26346117] **2778**

SECRET PARIS (FR/1163-2747) [11632747] **710**

SECRETAIRE INFO (FR) **710**

SECRETAIRE MODERNE (1988) (CN/0842-1935) [19465214] **710**

SECRETARESSE MAGAZINE (NE) **4209**

SECRETARIA EJECUTIVA PERMANENTE DEL CONVENIO ANDRES BELLO *See* INFORME DE LABORES DE LA SECRETARIA EJECTIVA DEL CONVENIO ANDRES BELLO **5203**

SECRETARIAL ADMINISTRATION RELEASES *See* GORE-BROWNE ON COMPANIES **2975**

SECRETARIAL CONSULTANT, THE *CEASED*. (US/0892-6123) [15248300] **710**

SECRETARIAL SERVICES TODAY (US/8755-4038) [11291974] **4214**

SECRETARIAT PAPER - INTERNATIONAL WHEAT COUNCIL (UK) [01587623] 851, **203**

SECRETARY-GENERAL'S REPORT (MY) [04824425] **4685**

SECRETARY GENERAL'S REPORT FOR THE YEAR ... / INTERNATIONAL INSTITUTE OF HUMANITARIAN LAW, THE (IT) [20105613] **4512**

SECRETARY OF STATE'S BOOKSTORE CATALOG, THE (US) [10304820] **424**

SECRETARY, THE (US/0037-0622) [01765338] **4209**

SECRETARY, THE (US/0037-0622) [07072678] **710**

SECRETARY'S ALUMNAE PROGRAM (US) **4209**

SECRETARY'S IMPROVEMENT PROGRAM (US) [03467284] **710**

SECRETARY'S LETTER (ENGLEWOOD, N.J.) (US/1040-4708) [18425860] 710, **4209**

SECRETARY'S SEMIANNUAL REPORT TO THE CONGRESS, THE (US) [23231716] **5392**

SECRETARY'S UPDATE *See* ADMINISTRATIVE ASSISTANT'S UPDATE **859**

SECRETARY'S WORKSHOP (US) **4209**

SECRETARY'S WORLD *CEASED*. (NE) **4209**

SECRETORY PROCESS, THE (NE/0167-8523) [09635699] 3733, **3640**

SECRETS (NEW YORK, N.Y.) *CEASED*. (US/0037-0649) [03922781] **2545**

SECRETS OF WINNERS *SUSPENDED*. (US/0883-8941) [12245936] **4618**

SECTANTE (HO) [04388309] **2760**

SECTEURS D'EXPERIMENTATION DE BOBO-DIOULASSO ET DE OUAGADOUGOU : CAMPAGNE COTONNIERE (UV) [03411790] **185**

●SECTION 504 COMPLIANCE HANDBOOK. SUPPLEMENT (US/1068-6533) [27690808] **4393**

SECTION 802(C)(2) : INTEREST SUBSIDY GRANTS PROCESSING HANDBOOK (US) [03116588] **2835**

SECTION A - REVUE D'ARCHITECTURE (CN/0715-9781) [09809094] **308**

SECTION : CONSTRUCTION ELECTRIQUE (BE) [02475215] **2080**

SECTION OF ADMINISTRATIVE LAW DIRECTORY (US/0749-6613) [11085903] **3094**

SECTION OF TAXATION NEWSLETTER / ABA (US/0277-2361) [07967875] 4747, **3047**

SECTOR ELECTRICO (MX) [08046577] **4685**

SECTOR SOCIAL (MX) [23092178] **1710**

SECULAR DEMOCRACY (II/0582-3730) [01779927] **4685**

SECULAR ORGANIZATIONS FOR SOBRIETY *See* SOS INTERNATIONAL NEWSLETTER **1349**

SECULO ILUSTRADO, O (PO) [05880043] **2522**

●SECURE RETIREMENT (US/1069-6911) [27483685] **913**

SECURED CREDITORS AND LESSORS UNDER THE BANKRUPTCY REFORM ACT (US) [06856889] **3088**

SECURED LENDER, THE (US/0888-255X) [13212238] **811**

SECURED LENDING ALERT (US/0895-5492) [11913665] **811**

SECURING CALIFORNIA'S ENERGY FUTURE : ... BIENNIAL REPORT TO THE GOVERNOR AND THE LEGISLATURE / CALIFORNIA ENERGY COMMISSION (US) [10210196] **1956**

SECURITAIRE (CN/0822-7853) [11543818] **4917**

●SECURITE (FR) [28312095] **2870**

SECURITE & STRATEGIES, ASIE (CN/1183-2754) [25313919] **4535**

SECURITE CIVILE ET INDUSTRIELLE (FR/0222-559X) [0222559X] **1073**

SECURITE, ENVIRONEMENT (SZ/1015-6356) [20008291] **2870**

SECURITE ET CONTROLE DES EXPLOSIFS AU CANADA (CN/0848-5704) [22928203] **2150**

SECURITE ET MEDECINE DU TRAVAIL (FR/0755-2386) [07552386] **2870**

SECURITE SICHERHEIT SAFETY REPORT *CEASED*. (NE) **710**

SECURITECH (UK/0307-7780) [03077780] **2080**

SECURITIES AND CAPITAL MARKETS LAW REPORTS (UK) **3047**

SECURITIES AND EXCHANGE COMMISSION REPORT TO CONGRESS ON THE ACCOUNTING PROFESSION AND THE COMMISSION'S OVERSIGHT ROLE / PREPARED FOR THE SUBCOMMITTEE ON GOVERNMENTAL EFFICIENCY AND THE DISTRICT OF COLUMBIA OF THE COMMITTEE ON GOVERNMENTAL AFFAIRS, UNITED STATES SENATE, BY THE SECURITIES AND EXCHANGE COMMISSION (US) [05859561] **751**

SECURITIES AND FEDERAL CORPORATE LAW REPORT (US/0273-0685) [04650642] **3103**

SECURITIES & INSIDER TRADING LITIGATION REPORTER (US) [16069155] 913, **3047**

SECURITIES AND INVESTMENT BOARD (UK) **913**

SECURITIES AND INVESTMENTS BOARD (GREAT BRITAIN) *See* REPORT OF THE SECURITIES AND INVESTMENTS BOARD FOR ... **912**

SECURITIES ARBITRATION (US/1042-3184) [18055638] 913, **3047**

SECURITIES CREDIT TRANSACTIONS HANDBOOK. TRANSMITTAL / BOARD OF GOVERNORS OF THE FEDERAL RESERVE SYSTEM (US) [08775328] **811**

SECURITIES EXCHANGE OF THAILAND *See* HANDBOOK - SECURITIES EXCHANGE OF THAILAND **900**

SECURITIES INDUSTRY DATABANK (US) **913**

SECURITIES INDUSTRY REVIEW (SI) [02685691] **913**

SECURITIES INDUSTRY TRENDS (US/0276-2749) [04990389] **913**

SECURITIES INDUSTRY YEARBOOK (US/0730-5796) [06803229] **913**

SECURITIES INTERNATIONAL *CEASED*. (US/0894-2803) [15972553] **1520**

SECURITIES JOURNAL (HK) **811**

SECURITIES JOURNAL (HK) **913**

SECURITIES LAW HANDBOOK / BY HAROLD S. BLOOMENTHAL (US/0731-5805) [05375846] **3103**

SECURITIES LAW REVIEW (US/0080-8474) [01695631] **3103**

SECURITIES MARKET IN JAPAN (JA) [01787637] **913**

●SECURITIES MARKETING NEWS (US/1074-8385) [29859112] **811**

SECURITIES OPERATIONS MAGAZINE (US/1055-0720) [23068052] **913**

SECURITIES — Alphabetical Title Index

SECURITIES : PUBLIC AND PRIVATE OFFERINGS (US) [04252366] **710**

SECURITIES REGULATION (US) [01771114] **811**

SECURITIES REGULATION & LAW REPORT (US/0037-0665) [01795438] **913, 3088**

SECURITIES REGULATION LAW ALERT *CEASED.* (US/8756-209X) [10988102] **3047**

SECURITIES REGULATION LAW JOURNAL (US/0097-9554) [01799365] **3047**

SECURITIES REGULATION (NEW YORK, N.Y.) (US) [06561699] **3047**

SECURITIES WEEK (US/0149-3582) [03475680] **913**

● SECURITIZATION DIRECTORY & HANDBOOK (US/1062-5135) [25264451] **811**

SECURITIZATION HANDBOOK *See* SECURITIZATION DIRECTORY & HANDBOOK **811**

SECURITY AFFAIRS (US/0889-4876) [14083483] **4535**

SECURITY AND LAW ENFORCEMENT NEWS *See* SECURITY AUSTRALIA **5177**

SECURITY & PROTECTION (CN/0826-1083) [10845365] **5177**

SECURITY & PROTECTION EQUIPMENT (UK) **3176**

SECURITY AND SPECIAL POLICE LEGAL UPDATE (US/0741-482X) [10142784] **3176**

SECURITY, ANTI-TERRORISM AND LOSS PREVENTION EQUIPMENT AND DEVICES BUYERS GUIDE *CEASED.* (US/0747-6205) [10768240] **5177**

SECURITY AUSTRALIA (AT) **5177**

SECURITY AUSTRALIA DIRECTORY (AT) **5177**

SECURITY CLINIC (US/0746-2921) [09930319] **710**

SECURITY DEALER (US/0164-3320) [04619660] **5177**

● SECURITY DIALOGUE (UK/0967-0106) [26717433] **4495**

● SECURITY DIRECTOR'S DIGEST (US) **3176**

SECURITY DISTRIBUTING & MARKETING (US/0049-0016) [04650852] **5177**

SECURITY FACTS (US/0743-5207) [10634842] **885**

● SECURITY FOR BUYERS OF PRODUCTS, SYSTEMS AND SERVICES (US) [25517191] **5177**

SECURITY GAZETTE (UK/0049-0024) [I00490024] **5177**

SECURITY INDUSTRY BUYERS GUIDE (US) [17781411] **5177**

SECURITY INTELLIGENCE (US) [25833979] **4056**

SECURITY INTELLIGENCE REPORT *See* SECURITY INTELLIGENCE **4056**

SECURITY JOURNAL (US/0955-1662) [18647546] **3176**

SECURITY LAW NEWSLETTER (US/0889-0625) [11097936] **3176**

SECURITY LETTER (US/0363-4922) [02435463] **2893, 947**

SECURITY LETTER SOURCE BOOK (US/0736-0401) [09068932] **3176, 5177**

SECURITY MANAGEMENT (ARLINGTON, VA.) (US/0145-9406) [02807178] **885**

SECURITY MANAGEMENT BULLETIN (US/1062-1628) [25535106] **5177, 886**

SECURITY MANAGEMENT, PROTECTING PROPERTY, PEOPLE & ASSETS *See* SECURITY MANAGEMENT BULLETIN **886**

SECURITY MANAGEMENT, PROTECTING PROPERTY, PEOPLE ASSETS (US/0745-6093) [09359243] **710**

SECURITY (NEWTON, MASS.) (US/0890-8826) [14232908] **3176**

SECURITY (NEWTON, MASS.) *See* SECURITY FOR BUYERS OF PRODUCTS, SYSTEMS AND SERVICES **5177**

SECURITY REGISTER *SUSPENDED.* (US/0092-7740) [01791535] **5307**

SECURITY SALES (US/1045-831X) [20257391] **5177**

SECURITY SPECIFIER (UK) **5177**

SECURITY STUDIES (UK/0963-6412) [24993106] **4535**

SECURITY SYSTEMS ADMINISTRATION *CEASED.* (US/0745-6751) [08978398] **5177**

● SECURITY TECHNOLOGY NEWS (US/1068-8374) [27825445] **5177, 1227**

SECURITY TRADERS HANDBOOK (US/0885-2693) [12598353] **1520**

SECUTITIES TRADERS' MONTHLY *CEASED.* (US/0738-4351) [09600113] **913**

SEDAN TIMES-STAR, THE (US) [09899362] **5678**

SEDAROT STATISTIYOT (IS) [01792915] **133, 156**

SEDES SAPIENTIAE (FR/0751-6681) [I07516681] **5036**

SEDGEWICK PANTAGRAPH (SEDGEWICK, KAN. : 1947) *See* HARVEY COUNTY INDEPENDENT, THE **5676**

SEDIMENTA (US/0272-6084) [03987482] **557**

SEDIMENTARY GEOLOGY (NE/0037-0738) [01606241] **1396**

SEDIMENTOLOGICAL NEWSLETTER (AT/0725-7392) [06417018] **1396**

SEDIMENTOLOGY (UK/0037-0746) [01765340] **1410**

SEDIMENTOLOGY RESEARCH LABORATORY CONTRIBUTION (US/0275-4282) [04795148] **1396**

SEDME (II) [01799864] **886**

SEDOC NEWSLETTER (ET) [11526135] **5156**

SEDONA RED ROCK NEWS (US/1044-7555) [10705462] **5630**

SEDOS BULLETIN (IT) **4996**

SEDUTA INAUGURALE - SOCIETA NAZIONALE DI SCIENZE, LETTERE E ARTI IN NAPOLI (IT) [07335007] **330**

SEE (AT) **2511**

SEE THE MUSIC (CN/0826-5216) [11245814] **388, 4152**

SEE THE TREASURE COAST (US/0746-3944) [10013193] **5490**

SEE VERO BEACH, FT. PIERCE, STUART RESORT AREA *See* SEE THE TREASURE COAST **5490**

SEE WHAT'S HAPPENING *SUSPENDED.* (US) [10401572] **1068, 4393**

SEED ABSTRACTS (UK/0141-0180) [04530755] **185, 156**

SEED ANALYSIS REPORT (US/0149-1296) [03428863] **2431**

● SEED & CROPS INDUSTRY (US/1065-5980) [26647129] **186**

SEED CROPS. ANNUAL SUMMARY (US/0733-2726) [01643648] **186**

SEED CROPS. VEGETABLE SEED REPORT (US/0190-7948) [02715542] **186**

SEED INDUSTRY JOURNAL *See* SEED & CROPS INDUSTRY **186**

SEED PATHOLOGY AND MICROBIOLOGY (UK) [26181465] **133**

SEED REPORT (US/0740-2996) [09901885] **133**

SEED RESEARCH (II/0379-5594) [04103149] **186**

SEED SAVERS EXCHANGE (US) [06544768] **2431**

SEED SCIENCE AND TECHNOLOGY (NE/0251-0952) [01789062] **186**

SEED SCIENCE RESEARCH (UK/0960-2585) [25362907] **133**

SEED TRADE BUYERS' GUIDE (US/0080-8504) [01765343] **186**

SEED TRADE NEWS (US/0037-0789) [03922850] **133**

SEED WORLD (US/0037-0797) [01645357] **186**

SEEDBED (US/0363-5074) [02184666] **2273, 4996**

SEEDHEAD NEWS, THE (US) [10080763] **2431**

SEEDS (CN/0714-3338) [09021880] **1885**

SEEDS & FARMS *CEASED.* (II) [10676911] **133**

SEEDS & SOWERS (CN/0843-5197) [20601362] **4996, 1905**

SEEDS (DECATUR, GA.) (US/0194-4495) [04654450] **5307, 2912**

SEEDS OF PEACE (TH) [12728429] **4512**

SEEDSTOCK EDGE (US) **5521**

SEEGUTERUMSCHLAG IN SEEHAFEN DER BUNDESREPUBLIK DEUTSCHLAND IM JAHRE ..., DER (GW) [19001875] **851**

SEEING EYE GUIDE (US/0037-0819) [01765344] **4393**

SEEK-A-WORD (US/1059-8359) [24779565] **4866**

SEEKER (PITTSBURG), THE (US/0363-4590) [02476321] **2472**

SEEKER (SARNIA) (CN/0318-9279) [02441910] **4854**

SEEKING N SEARCHING ANCESTORS (US) **2472**

SEEMS (US/0095-1730) [01796283] **3470**

SEFARAD (SP/0037-0894) [01640500] **3320, 5052**

SEG ABSTRACTS (US/0737-0164) [09983013] **4420, 1396**

SEG REPORT *See* ISEGR REPORT **1568**

SEGAL, MURRAY D., 1949- ANNOTATED RULES OF CRIMINAL PRACTICE *See* ANNOTATED ONTARIO RULES OF CRIMINAL PRACTICE **3105**

SEGES (FRIBOURG) (SZ/0582-3951) [02974384] **3435, 3320**

SEGNI E COMPRENSIONE (IT) [18279895] **4360**

SEGNO PESCARA (IT/0391-3910) [I03913910] **330**

SEGNOCINEMA (IT/0393-3865) [09612583] **4077**

SEGRETISSIMO (IT) **3470**

SEGURIDAD SOCIAL (MX/0379-0304) [01534212] **2893, 1710**

SEGYE CHONOL (KO) [09054937] **1583**

SEGYE KYONGJE CHUBO (KO) [04854303] **710**

SEGYE (YONHAP TONGSIN (FIRM)) (KO) [07989316] **2492**

SEI MARIANNA IKA DAIGAKU ZASSHI (JA/0387-2289) [01397494] **3640**

SEI SUBSCRIBER PROGRAM (US) **5156**

SEIBUTSU BUTSURI (JA/0582-4052) [09787072] **472, 4420**

SEIBUTSU-BUTSURI-KAGAKU (JA/0031-9082) [04319770] **1057, 493**

SEIBUTSU KAGAKU / NIHON SEIBUTSU KAGAKUSHA KYOKAI HENSHU (JA/0045-2033) [09538482] **472**

SEIBUTSU KAGAKU SOGO KENKYU KIKO (JAPAN) *See* SEIBUTSU KAGAKU SOGO KENKYU KIKO YORAN **472**

SEIBUTSU KAGAKU SOGO KENKYU KIKO KISO SEIBUTSUGAKU KENKYUJO YORAN (JA) [04222179] **472**

SEIBUTSU KAGAKU SOGO KENKYU KIKO SEIRIGAKU KENKYUJO YORAN (JA) [04222354] **586**

SEIBUTSU KAGAKU SOGO KENKYU KIKO YORAN (JA) [04222117] **472**

SEIBUTSU KANKYO CHOSETSU (JA) [01200277] **472**

● SEIBUTSU KOGAKKAI SHI / SEIBUTSU-KOGAKU KAISHI (JA/0919-3758) [28655092] **3696**

SEIBUTSUGAKUSHI KENKYU JAPANESE JOURNAL OF THE HISTORY OF BIOLOGY / NIHON KAGAKUSHU GAKKAI SEIBUTSUGAKUSHI BUNKAKAI HENSHU (JA/0386-9539) [12061088] **473**

SEICHE, THE (US/8755-4682) [03259805] **2205**

SEIDENKI GAKKAI KOEN RONBUNSHU : SEIDENKI GAKKAI ZENKOKU TAIKAI (JA) [09861009] **4445**

SEIDENKI GAKKAI SHI (JA/0386-2550) [09517485] **4445**

SEIFU KANKOBUTSU SHIMBUN (JA) [04793522] **4699**

SEIFU KANKOBUTSU TO SOGO MOKUROKU (JA) [07722178] **4685**

SEIFU KOHO YOTEI JIKO (JA) [01799719] **4685**

SEIGNEURIE DE LAUZON (CN/0229-074X) [08003238] **2760**

SEIJI HANDOBUKKU (JA) [01797063] **4495**

SEIJI KEIZAI SORAN (JA) [10802354] **1639**

SEIJI KENKYU (JA) [05669582] **4495**

SEIJIGAKU RONSHU (JA) [03085218] **4495**

SEIJO BUNGEI (JA) [04430453] **330, 5236**

SEIJO DAIGAKU KEIZAI KENKYU (JA) [04217161] **1595**

SEIKABUTSU NISUGATA CHOSA KEKKA (JA) [01799718] **1626**

SEIKABUTSU SEISAN SHUKKA TOKEI (JA/0303-5859) [01797239] **1520**

SEIKAGAKU (JA/0037-1017) [07888711] **493**

SEIKAN YORAN (JA) [12166172] **4685**

SEIKATSU EISEI (JA/0582-4176) [10400620] **4802**

SEIKATSU-GAKU (JA) [03082148] **5257**

SEIKATSU KAGAKU KENKYUJO KENKYU HOKOKU (JA/0386-7536) [10461341] **5218, 5156**

SEIKATSU TO KANKYO (JA) [01263260] **2181**

SEIKEI BAIGAKU, TOKYO. KEIZAIGAKUBU *See* SEIKEI DAIGAKU KEIZAIGAKUBU RONSHU **1520**

Alphabetical Title Index — SELECTED

SEIKEI DAIGAKU IPPAN KENKYU HOKOKU (JA) [04755416] **1847**

SEIKEI DAIGAKU KEIZAIGAKUBU RONSHU (JA) [03534941] **1520**

SEIKEI DAIGAKU KOGAKUBU KOGAKU HOKOKU (JA/0582-4184) [10411074] **5156**

SEIKEI DAIGAKU, TOKYO See SEIKEI DAIGAKU IPPAN KENKYU HOKOKU **1847**

SEIKEI GEKA MOOK (JA) [04694708] **3884**

SEIKEI KENKYUJO See YAKUIN NO HOSHU SHOYO NENSHU **4759**

SEIKEI KENKYUJO See YADUIN NO HOSHU SHOYO CHOSA HOKOKUSHO **1720**

SEIKEI KENKYUJO See YAKUIN NO HOSHU SHOYO TO KIMEKATA **1589**

SEIKEI RONSO (JA) [22621532] **5218**

SEIKEN ZIHO (JA/0080-8539) [08740463] **473**

SEIKYO HODO SHASHINSHU (JA) [02244217] **5022**

SEIMEI HOKEN KEIEI (JA/0287-2641) [09276466] **2893**

SEIMITSU CHOSA HOKOKUSHO. HIDA CHIIKI (JA) [10410829] **2150**

SEIMITSU CHOSA HOKOKUSHO: JOZANKEI CHIIKI (JA) [02477836] **2151**

SEIMITSU CHOSA HOKOKUSHO. NISHIKIGAWA CHIIKI (JA) [10411352] **2151**

SEIMITSU KOGAKKAI SHI (JA/0912-0289) [16778353] **1996**

SEIN PARIS, LE (FR/1163-1961) [I11631961] **3640**

SEINAN DAIGAKU KEIZAIGAKU RON SHU (JA) [02243867] **1595**

SEINAN GAKUIN DAIGAKU BUNRI RON SHU (JA) [02243865] **5236**

SEINAN GAKUIN DAIGAKU EIGO EIBUNGAKU RON SHU (JA) [02246925] **3320**

SEINAN GAKUIN DAIGAKU. GAKUJUTSU KENKYUJO See SEINAN GAKUIN DAIGAKU SHOGAKU RON SHU **1626**

SEINAN GAKUIN DAIGAKU. GAKUJUTSU KENKYUJO See SEINAN GAKUIN DAIGAKU KEIZAIGAKU RON SHU **1595**

SEINAN GAKUIN DAIGAKU. GAKUJUTSU KENKYUJO See SEINAN GAKUIN DAIGAKU BUNRI RON SHU **5236**

SEINAN GAKUIN DAIGAKU. GAKUJUTSU KENKYUJO See SEINAN GAKUIN DAIGAKU EIGO EIBUNGAKU RON SHU **3320**

SEINAN GAKUIN DAIGAKU SHOGAKU RON SHU (JA) [02243866] **1626**

SEINEN SHINRI (JA) [03437145] **4618**

SEIRBHIS PHOIBLI : JOURNAL OF THE DEPARTMENT OF THE PUBLIC SERVICE (IE/0332-2688) [12209810] **4705**

SEIRI GIJUTSU ZENKOKU KAIGI GIJUROKU (JA) [01797058] **3248**

SEIRI SHINRIGAKU TO SEISHIN SEIRIGAKU (JA/0289-2405) [I02892405] **4618**

SEIRIGAKU GIJUTSU KENKYUKAI HOKOKU (JA/0285-3299) [27408953] **5156**

SEIRIGAKU KENKYUJO GIJUTSUKA HOKOKU (JA/0913-0322) [I09130322] **5156**

SEIRIGAKU KENKYUJO (JAPAN) See SEIBUTSU KAGAKU SOGO KENKYU KIKO SEIRIGAKU KENKYUJO YORAN **586**

SEIRIGAKU KENKYUJO NENPO (JA) [07628026] **587**

SEIRON (JA) [01797061] **4495**

SEISAKU SHIRYO (JA) [01797367] **4685**

SEISAN KENKYU (JA/0037-105X) [09769936] **5156**

SEISAN NOGYO SHOTOKU TOKEI (JA) [02247012] **133**

SEISHIN EISEI SHIRYO (JA/0454-2010) [03278049] **4802**

SEISHIN HOKEN KENKYU (JA) [23173932] **3936**

SEISHOGAKU RONSHU / NIHON SEISHOGAKU KENKYUJO HEN (JA) [09856102] **5019**

SEISHONEN MONDAI CHOSA NENPO (JA) [23117930] **1068**

SEISMIC ENGINEERING PROGRAM REPORT (US/0361-6614) [02617648] **1396**

SEISMIC INSTRUMENTS (US/0747-9239) [07225539] 1418, **1410**

SEISMOLOGIC SERIES (SA) [01953168] **1410**

SEISMOLOGICAL BULLETIN OF ABUYAMA SEISMOLOGICAL OBSERVATORY, KYOTO UNIVERSITY (JA) [02441464] **1410**

SEISMOLOGICAL RESEARCH LETTERS (US/0895-0695) [15287881] **1397**

SEISMOLOGICAL SOCIETY OF AMERICA See BULLETIN OF THE SEISMOLOGICAL SOCIETY OF AMERICA **1403**

SEISO GIHO (JA/0385-1907) [03304833] **2243**

SEITAI BOGYO (JA/0910-3627) [27475210] **473**

SEITAI JOHO KAGAKU KENKYU (JA) [03285892] **3640**

SEITAI KAGAKU (JA/0386-8141) [10448660] 992, **2221**

SEITAI NO KAGAKU (JA/0370-9531) [09733628] 5597, **473**

SEITAI ZAIRYO (JA) [19261440] **473**

SEITAIGAKU KENKYU (JA/0371-0548) [01567356] **527**

SEITO GIJUTSU KENKYUKAI See SEITO GIJUTSU KENKYUKAI SHI **133**

SEITO GIJUTSU KENKYUKAI SHI (JA/0370-9841) [09531386] **133**

SEITOKU EIYO TANKI DAIGAKU KIYO (JA/0286-6366) [10387844] 1095, **4199**

SEIVA **SUSPENDED.** (BL/0037-1122) [05166212] **133**

SEIYO SHIGAKU / NIHON SEIYOSHI GAKKAI (JA/0386-9253) [08831929] **2629**

●SEIZURE (LONDON, ENGLAND) (UK/1059-1311) [24484471] **3846**

SEJOURS A LA FERME (CN/0713-6048) [08878555] **1626**

SEKAI (JA/0582-4532) [01765350] **2629**

SEKAI CD-ROM SORAN / CD-ROM DIRECTORY OF THE WORLD (JA) [26147913] 1244, **1255**

SEKAI KARA (JA) [06076378] **2629**

SEKAI KIGYO YORAN (JA) [02240172] **811**

SEKAI KONPYUTA NENKAN (JA) [08875457] **1202**

SEKAI NI HIRAKU MADO (JA) [02998287] **2664**

SEKAI NO KIGYO NO KEIEI BUNSEKI: KOKUSAI KEIEI HIKAKU (JA) [01797172] **811**

SEKAI NO KUNI ICHIRANHYO (JA) [07341759] **2576**

SEKIGAISEN GIJUTSU (JA/0386-8044) [16781157] **4441**

SEKIRAH AL MEHKARIM BE-HINUKH SHE-NEERKHU BE-YISRAEL (IS) [03930135] **1905**

SEKIRAH AL PEULOT MISRAD HA-PITUAH VE-HEVROT HA-PITUAH (IS) [02239848] **1583**

SEKITAN KENKYU SHIRYO SOSHO (JA) [07777945] **2151**

SEKIYU GAKKAI SHI (JA/0582-4664) [10075296] **4278**

SEKIYU GIJUTSU KYOKAI See SEKIYU GIJUTSU KYOKAISHI **4278**

SEKIYU GIJUTSU KYOKAISHI (JA/0370-9868) [03527537] **4278**

SEKIYU KOGYO GIJUTSU KOZA See SEKIYU KOGYO GIJUTSU KOZA: KISOHEN **2151**

SEKIYU KOGYO GIJUTSU KOZA: KISOHEN (JA) [01797160] **2151**

SEKIYU KOGYO REMMEI. KIKAKU CHOSABU See WAGA KUNI SEKIYU KAIHATSU NO GENJO **4281**

SEKIYU NENKAN (JA) [07499309] **4278**

SEKIYU SHUNJU (JA) [10345129] **4278**

SEKIYU TO SHOHI DOTAI TOKEI GEPPO. SHO-KO-KOGYO / [HENSHU] TSUSHO SANGYO DAIJIN KANBO CHOSA TOKEIBU (JA/0285-4031) [11482686] **710**

SEKIYU TO SHOHI DOTAI TOKEI NENPO, SHO-KO-KOGYO / TSUSHO SANGYO DAIJIN KANBO CHOSA TOKEIBU HEN (JA) [12009047] **4278**

SEKKO TO SEKKAI (JA/0559-331X) [09558784] **1029**

SEKRETARIAT (GW/0171-4937) [I01714937] **710**

SEKRETY HISTORII (PL/0867-5864) [I08675864] **2629**

SEKSA KHMER (FR/0248-8515) [10451959] **2664**

SEL & POIVRE (CN/0714-6116) [09084883] **5073**

SELBYANA (US/0361-185X) [02245195] **527**

SELCUK UNIVERSITESI ILAHIYAT FAKULTESI DERGISI (TU) [20570476] **5045**

SELCUKLU ARASTRMALAR DERGISI (TU) [01787806] **2664**

SELDEN SOCIETY See PUBLICATIONS, LIST OF MEMBERS AND RULES / SELDEN SOCIETY **3033**

SELDEN SOCIETY See REPORT OF THE COUNCIL AND ABSTRACT OF THE ACCOUNTS / SELDEN SOCIETY **3038**

SELDEN SOCIETY, LONDON See PUBLICATIONS OF THE SELDEN SOCIETY, THE **3033**

SELECAO DE PARECERES E ESTUDOS DA COORDENACAO DE LEGISLACAO E NORMAS DE ENSINO (BL) [05259109] **3047**

SELECCIONES AVICOLAS (SP/0582-4818) [09723148] **221**

SELECCIONES DE AIR UNIVERSITY REVIEW (US/0362-8647) [02314756] **35**

SELECCIONES DE FRANCISCANISMO (SP) [12697902] **4996**

SELECCIONES DE TEOLOGIA (SP/0037-119X) [01696854] **4996**

SELECCIONES DEL READER'S DIGEST (UNITED STATES ED.) (US/0885-0496) [01765354] **2492**

SELECT HOMES See CANADIAN SELECT HOMES **2899**

SELECT HOMES & FOOD (CN/0848-8258) [21212499] 2903, **2792**

SELECT INFORMATION EXCHANGE See SIE GUIDE TO BUSINESS & INVESTMENT BOOKS **914**

SELECT : NATIONAL BIBLIOGRAPHIC SERVICE NEWSLETTER (UK/0960-1570) [22215180] **3248**

SELECT NOTES ON THE INTERNATIONAL SUNDAY SCHOOL LESSONS. IMPROVED UNIFORM SERIES See PELOUBET'S SELECT NOTES ON THE INTERNATIONAL BIBLE LESSONS FOR CHRISTIAN LIVING. UNIFORM SERIES **5018**

SELECT : THE PHOTOGRAPHIC SHOWCASE (GW) **4376**

SELECTA (IO) [06324603] **2508**

SELECTA (CORVALLIS, OR.) (US/0277-0598) [07473153] **3320**

SELECTA / DAS WOCHENMAGAZIN DES ARZTES (GW/0852-4877) **3640**

SELECTA MATHEMATICA (SZ) [28100347] **3533**

SELECTA MATHEMATICA. NEW SERIES (SZ) **3533**

SELECTA MATHEMATICA SOVIETICA (US/0272-9903) [06979605] **3533**

SELECTA MEDICA. GASTROENTEROLOGIA (IT) **3640**

SELECTA PLANEGG (GW/0582-4877) [I05824877] **3640**

SELECTA (PLANEGG, GERMANY) (GW/0721-8184) [11170949] **3640**

SELECTED ABSTRACTS OF COMPLETED RESEARCH STUDIES / U.S. SMALL BUSINESS ADMINISTRATION, ECONOMIC RESEARCH DIVISION, OFFICE OF ADVOCACY (US) [08349789] **710**

SELECTED ABSTRACTS ON OCCUPATIONAL DISEASES (UK/0262-9836) [I02629836] 2870, **2872**

SELECTED ACCESSIONS (GREAT BRITAIN. DIRECTORATE OF MILITARY SURVEY. MAP LIBRARY) See GREAT BRITAIN. DIRECTORATE OF MILITARY SURVEY. MAP LIBRARY. SELECTED ACCESSIONS **2565**

SELECTED ACQUISITIONS See SELECTED NEW ACQUISITIONS / CALIFORNIA ACADEMY OF SCIENCES, LIBRARY **3248**

SELECTED ACQUISITIONS BULLETIN - UNIVERSITY OF KENTUCKY. LIBRARIES. MAP DEPT (US/0749-3207) [10593562] **2576**

SELECTED ACQUISITIONS - ENGINEERING SOCIETIES LIBRARY. ACQUISITIONS DEPT **CEASED.** (US/0891-3218) [09013118] **1996**

SELECTED AND ANNOTATED BIBLIOGRAPHY OF REFERENCE MATERIAL IN CONSUMER FINANCE (US/0077-4014) [02195688] **811**

SELECTED ANNOTATED BIBLIOGRAPHY OF POPULATION STUDIES IN THE NETHERLANDS (NE/0167-4757) [03143244] **4562**

SELECTED ANNOTATED BIBLIOGRAPHY OF RECENT ... NATURAL HAZARDS PUBLICATIONS (US) [16843258] **1410**

SELECTED ANNOTATED BIBLIOGRAPHY ON THE ANALYSIS OF WATER RESOURCE SYSTEMS, A (US) [03786012] **5549**

SELECTED ANNUAL REVIEWS OF THE ANALYTICAL SCIENCES (UK/0300-9963) [01787437] **1019**

SELECTED ARTICLES FROM LANGUAGE LEARNING (US/0559-3468) [08854293] **3320**

SELECTED ATOMIC ENERGY PRODUCTS (US/0736-0657) [03059763] **1956**

SELECTED AUDIOVISUAL MATERIALS PRODUCED BY THE UNITED STATES GOVERNMENT (US/0748-4836) [10935309] **1139**

SELECTED BIBLIOGRAPHIES IN LANGUAGE AND LITERATURE **CEASED.** (US) [08248388] **3336**

SELECTED
Alphabetical Title Index

SELECTED BIBLIOGRAPHIES ON AGEING (UK/0267-0348) [15552641] 3755, **3661**

SELECTED BIBLIOGRAPHY OF ARAB EDUCATIONAL MATERIALS / COMPILED BY DOCUMENTATION CENTRE FOR EDUCATION (UA) [07910672] **1797**

SELECTED BIBLIOGRAPHY OF MATERIALS AND RESOURCES ON WOMEN, A (BB/1043-6359) [18492077] **5566**

SELECTED BIBLIOGRAPHY OF POLISH EDUCATIONAL MATERIALS (PL) [05874590] 1783, **1797**

SELECTED BIBLIOGRAPHY ON INCOME TAX ADMINISTRATION IN DEVELOPED AND DEVELOPING COUNTRIES (NE) [21215053] **4747**

SELECTED BIBLIOGRAPHY ON IRRIGATION MANAGEMENT, A (CE/1015-1680) [21432528] **186**

SELECTED BORROWINGS IN IMMEDIATELY AVAILABLE FUNDS OF LARGE MEMBER BANKS (US) [06190942] **811**

SELECTED CHARACTERISTICS OF PUBLIC ASSISTANCE RECIPIENTS IN NEW YORK CITY BY COMMUNITY DISTRICT (US) [07053252] **5307**

SELECTED COMPUTER ARTICLES / NATIONAL DEFENSE UNIVERSITY, DEPARTMENT OF DEFENSE COMPUTER INSTITUTE (US/0743-6599) [03489878] **1262**

SELECTED DATA ON FEDERAL R & D FUNDING BY BUDGET FUNCTION (US) [25043068] **4747**

SELECTED DATA ON MIXTURES. SER. A. THERMODYNAMIC PROPERTIES OF NON-REACTING BINARY SYSTEMS OF ORGANIC SUBSTANCES (US/0147-1503) [03114400] **1057**

SELECTED DECISIONS AND SELECTED DOCUMENTS OF THE INTERNATIONAL MONETARY FUND (US) [22945551] **811**

SELECTED DECISIONS OF THE INTERNATIONAL MONETARY FUND AND SELECTED DOCUMENTS (US/0094-1735) [01793843] **811**

SELECTED ECONOMIC DATA FOR DULUTH AND NORTHEASTERN MINNESOTA THROUGH ... (US) [09131226] **1583**

SELECTED EDUCATIONAL OPPORTUNITIES (US/0098-4256) [03179408] **1915**

SELECTED EDUCATIONAL STATISTICS (II) [27047461] **1783**

SELECTED EDUCATIONAL STATISTICS (II) [03882733] 1783, **1797**

SELECTED ELECTRONIC AND ASSOCIATED PRODUCTS, INCLUDING TELEPHONE AND TELEGRAPH APPARATUS (US/0276-5535) [03054257] **2080**

SELECTED ENERGY STATISTICS : SOUTH AFRICA (SA) 1956, **1963**

SELECTED FEDERAL AND STATE BOOK PROGRAM INFORMATION (US/0278-0518) [07681973] **3248**

SELECTED FINANCIAL AND ENROLLMENT DATA, MARYLAND COMMUNITY COLLEGES / MARYLAND STATE BOARD FOR COMMUNITY COLLEGES (US) [10115612] **1847**

SELECTED FORESTRY STATISTICS, CANADA (CN/0834-938X) [12936624] **2395**

SELECTED INDUSTRIAL AIR POLLUTION CONTROL EQUIPMENT (US/0195-7228) [03885426] **2243**

SELECTED INFORMATION ON SCHOOL EDUCATION IN INDIA (II) [02418915] **1783**

SELECTED INSTRUMENTS AND RELATED PRODUCTS (US/0744-2440) [03054635] **1626**

SELECTED INTEREST & EXCHANGE RATES (US/0364-8370) [02575437] **811**

SELECTED INTEREST RATES (MONTHLY) (US) [06164603] **811**

SELECTED INTEREST RATES (WEEKLY) (US) [05904589] **811**

SELECTED IRRIGATION RETURN FLOW QUALITY ABSTRACTS (US/0090-6808) [01784727] **2095**

SELECTED JAPANESE FEATURE FILMS (JA) [08436211] **4077**

SELECTED JUDGEMENTS OF THE HIGH COURT OF LAGOS STATE (NR) [12646866] **3047**

SELECTED JUDGEMENTS OF THE OGUN STATE HIGH COURT / OGUN STATE OF NIGERIA (NR) [07816622] **3047**

SELECTED LECTURES OF THE ROYAL SOCIETY (UK/0557-4129) [02251918] **570**

SELECTED LIBRARY ACQUISITIONS (US/0145-9309) [02782237] 5392, **3248**

SELECTED LIST OF ACQUISITIONS CATALOGED (US/0537-9342) [02242778] **3047**

SELECTED LIST OF FEDERAL LAWS AND TREATIES RELATING TO SPORT FISH AND WILDLIFE (US/0093-4631) [01791147] **3116**

SELECTED LIST OF NURSING BOOKS AND JOURNALS (US) [21051644] **3869**

SELECTED MANPOWER STATISTICS (US/0501-9427) [05161731] 1710, 4056, **4062**

SELECTED MEDICAL CARE STATISTICS (US/0884-1152) [09139259] 3661, **4062**

SELECTED MFRS. INDEX SURVEY (US/0740-5030) [07906516] **1710**

SELECTED MONOGRAPHS ON TAXATION (NE) [02383578] **4747**

●SELECTED NEW ACQUISITIONS / CALIFORNIA ACADEMY OF SCIENCES, LIBRARY (US/1065-7703) [26731912] **3248**

SELECTED NEW TITLES / LEGISLATIVE LIBRARY OF MANITOBA (CN/0711-8066) [08486076] **424**

SELECTED PAPERS (US/0069-3359) [03077163] **710**

SELECTED PAPERS (NE/0166-056X) [01644195] **3952**

SELECTED PAPERS (US/0069-3359) **2709**

SELECTED PAPERS FROM THE ENGLISH INSTITUTE (US/0423-183X) [03877011] **5218**

SELECTED PAPERS FROM THE TRANSPORTATION SEMINAR SERIES (CN/0229-8627) [08091269] **5392**

SELECTED PAPERS FROM THE WEST VIRGINIA SHAKESPEARE AND RENAISSANCE ASSOCIATION (US/0885-9574) [08620887] **3435**

SELECTED PAPERS IN SCHOOL FINANCE (US/0162-9697) [03012653] **1783**

SELECTED PAPERS PRESENTED AT THE ANNUAL MEETING - SOUTHERN REGIONAL SCIENCE ASSOCIATION (US) [04944999] **2835**

SELECTED PERINATAL STATISTICS (US) **5338**

SELECTED PUBLICATIONS - NATIONAL CLEARINGHOUSE FOR ALCOHOL INFORMATION (US) [02406738] **1349**

SELECTED RAND ABSTRACTS (US/0037-1343) [01588318] **424**

SELECTED READINGS IN GENERAL SURGERY (US) [01608036] **3974**

SELECTED READINGS IN ORAL AND MAXILLOFACIAL SURGERY (US/1044-7032) [19869466] **1335**

SELECTED READINGS IN PLASTIC SURGERY (US/0739-5523) [09780448] **3974**

SELECTED REFERENCE (US) **1626**

SELECTED REFERENCES - INDUSTRIAL RELATIONS SECTION, PRINCETON UNIVERSITY (US/0037-1351) [01644742] **1538**

●SELECTED REPORTABLE DISEASES BY HEALTH JURISDICTION (US) [25680356] 4802, **3716**

SELECTED REPORTS IN ETHNOMUSICOLOGY (US/0361-6622) [02387345] 2273, **4152**

SELECTED REVENUE DATA AND EQUALIZED MILLS FOR PENNSYLVANIA PUBLIC SCHOOLS (US) [11505245] **1872**

SELECTED SCHOOL CHARACTERISTICS. REPORT ON THE CITY-WIDE TESTING PROGRAM. REPORT ON PER PUPIL STAFFING COSTS : ELEMENTARY SCHOOLS (US/0098-9029) [03179980] **1783**

SELECTED SERIAL RESOURCES FOR QUEENSLAND PUBLIC LIBRARIES (AT) [04108704] **424**

SELECTED STATE DEPARTMENT PUBLICATIONS / UNITED STATES DEPARTMENT OF STATE, BUREAU OF PUBLIC AFFAIRS (US) [06591103] **4685**

SELECTED STATISTICAL DATA - MARYLAND STATE BOARD FOR COMMUNITY COLLEGES (US/0099-2089) [02239741] 1847, **1797**

SELECTED STATISTICS ON STUDENTS AND STAFF IN NEW YORK CITY SCHOOL DISTRICTS (US/0099-0485) [03180100] 1783, **1797**

SELECTED STATISTICS ON TECHNOLOGICAL INNOVATION IN INDUSTRY (CN/0318-7101) [02241025] 1626, **1538**

SELECTED STATISTICS ON THE OFFICE OF ATTORNEY GENERAL (US/0145-2436) [02716427] 3143, **3083**

SELECTED STUDIES IN MEDICAL CARE AND MEDICAL ECONOMICS (US/0361-3046) [02246075] **3640**

SELECTED TABLES IN MATHEMATICAL STATISTICS (US/0094-8837) [01790875] 3533, **3542**

SELECTED TOPICS IN GRAPH THEORY (UK) [10940035] **3533**

SELECTED TRADE AND ECONOMIC DATA OF THE CENTRALLY PLANNED ECONOMIES (US/0160-5968) [03130713] **851**

SELECTED TRANSLATIONS IN MATHEMATICAL STATISTICS AND PROBABILITY (US/0065-9274) [01765361] **3533**

SELECTED URBAN STORM WATER RUNOFF ABSTRACTS (US) [01800092] **5539**

SELECTED WATER-LEVEL RECORDS FOR OKLAHOMA / UNITED STATES DEPARTMENT OF THE INTERIOR, GEOLOGICAL SURVEY (US) [06319027] **1418**

SELECTIEF DEN HAAG. 1991 (NE/0926-4183) [I09264183] **5156**

SELECTION DE FILMS POUR LA JEUNESSE (FR) [11408764] **1069**

SELECTION DE PRESSE / CLUB MULTI-SPORTS INTERNATIONAL DE MONTREAL (CN/0226-8728) [07817343] **4917**

SELECTION DU READER'S DIGEST (EDITION CANADIENNE) (CN/0037-1378) [01642311] **2492**

SELECTION DU READER'S DIGEST PARIS (FR/0037-1386) [I00371386] **2522**

SELECTION OF INTERNATIONAL ROAD TRANSPORT DOCUMENTATION (SZ) **5444**

SELECTION OF RECENT ACQUISITIONS - CANADIAN IMPERIAL BANK OF COMMERCE, INFORMATION CENTRE, A (CN/0383-2392) [02879888] **1520**

SELECTIONS FROM THE ANNALES, ECONOMIES, SOCIETES, CIVILISATIONS (US) [02956686] 2629, **5218**

SELECTIONS (GRADUATE MANAGEMENT ADMISSION COUNCIL) (US/0882-0228) [11688662] **886**

SELECTIONS - MODERN LANGUAGES SERVICES BRANCH (RICHMOND) *CEASED.* (CN/0826-3310) [11221721] **3459**

SELECTIVE ACQUISITIONS (CN/0846-9415) [23247765] **3248**

SELECTIVE CANCER THERAPEUTICS *See* CANCER BIOTHERAPY **3810**

SELECTIVE DIGEST OF THE LAW OF INSURANCE AND RELATED TOPICS (US) [12336016] **2893**

SELECTIVE ELECTRODE REVIEWS *CEASED.* (US/0894-3923) [16068694] **1035**

SELECTIVE SERVICE NEWS (US/0361-2716) [01765365] **4056**

SELECTWARE SYSTEM. CD-ROM (US) 1290, **1239**

SELEKTSIIA I NASINNYTSTVO *See* SELEKTSIIA I SEMENOVODSTVO (KIEV) **186**

SELEKTSIIA I SEMENOVODSTVO (RU/0037-1459) [02252717] 551, **527**

SELEKTSIIA I SEMENOVODSTVO (KIEV) (UN/0582-5075) [09723799] **186**

SELENIUM AND TELLURIUM ABSTRACTS (US/0037-1467) [01791907] **1037**

SELEPLAST (IT) **4460**

SELESTAT, ALSACE. BIBLIOTHEQUE HUMANISTE. SOCIETE DES AMIS *See* ANNUAIRE - LES AMIS DE LA BIBLIOTHEQUE HUMANISTE DE SELESTAT **3190**

SELEZIONE DAL READER'S DIGEST (IT/0037-1483) [01765367] **2522**

SELEZIONE DI ELETTRONICA (IT) **2080**

SELEZIONE VETERINARIA (IT/0037-1521) [09723868] **5521**

SELF ADHESIVE MATERIALS & MARKETS BULLETIN (UK) 1029, **4222**

SELF DETERMINATION QUARTERLY JOURNAL, THE (US/0148-2653) [03279485] **4685**

SELF EMPLOYMENT UPDATE (US/0736-1912) [09091494] **710**

SELF-HELP GROUP DIRECTORY (US/0740-7548) [10009722] **5307**

SELF-HELP SOURCEBOOK, THE (US/8756-1425) [11482429] **4618**

SELF-IN-PROCESS SERIES (US/0160-4430) [03657725] **4618**

SELF (NEW YORK) (US/0149-0699) [04268816] 405, **5566**

SELF PUBLISHING UPDATE (US/0736-1882) [09091444] **710**

SELF-PUBLISHING WRITER, THE (US/0091-6226) [01786253] **4819**

SELF-REALIZATION (US/0037-1564) [04167134] **4360**

●SELF-STARTER (MARKHAM) (CN/1188-2980) [25883029] **765**

●SELF-STORAGE RENTAL GUIDE (SOUTHERN CALIFORNIA ED.) (US/1059-5384) [24622642] **1299**

SELINSGROVE TIMES-TRIBUNE, THE (US) [14391220] **5739**

SELLER/SERVICER UPDATE (US) **811**

SELLER'S GUIDE TO GOVERNMENT PURCHASING (US/1052-7443) [22366783] **4747**

SELLERS LETTERS (US/0740-2740) [09906223] **2472**

SELLING (US) **957**

SELLING ADVANTAGE, THE (US/1046-9036) [20555704] **886**

● SELLING EDGE, THE (US/1065-3066) [26570067] **710**

SELLING INSURANCE *See* LIFE INSURANCE SELLING **2887**

SELLING KNACKS (US) [14139914] **957**

SELLING MAGAZINE (US) **936**

SELLING TO THE OTHER EDUCATIONAL MARKETS (US/1054-4593) [22894012] **1783, 936**

SELLOWIA (BL/0375-1651) [07642662] **527**

SELL'S BRITISH EXPORTERS (1980) (UK/0140-5772) [06433480] **851**

● SELL'S BUILDING & CONSTRUCTION INDEX (UK/0966-0399) [26035965] **627**

SELL'S BUILDING INDEX *See* SELL'S BUILDING & CONSTRUCTION INDEX **627**

SELL'S PRODUCTS AND SERVICES DIRECTORY (UK) [20437647] **1626**

SELMA ENTERPRISE, THE (US) [27954166] **5640**

SELMA TIMES-JOURNAL, THE (US/1043-9129) [14480779] **5628**

SELON SA PAROLE (CN/0701-4260) [03564249] **4996**

SELSKAIA MOLODEZH (RU) [04084374] **1069**

SELSKAIA ZHIZN (RU) [04084479] **5809**

SELSKIE ZORI (RU/0131-6273) [09729283] **133**

SELSKII KALENDAR (RU) [09729338] **133**

SELSKOE KHOZIAISTVO UZBEKISTANA (UZ/0131-6370) [03093283] **133**

SELSKOE STROITELSTVO (RU/0201-4211) [04088032] **627**

SELSKOHOZJAJSTVENNAJA BIOLOGIJA *CEASED.* (RU/0131-6397) [01641384] **473**

SELSKOKHOZIAISTVENNAIA LITERATURA SSSR (RU/0037-1688) [02460430] **133**

SELSKOKHOZIAISTVENNOE PROIZVODSTVO SEVERNOGO KAVKAZA I TSCHO *See* SELSKIE ZORI **133**

SELSKOSTOPANSKA NAUKA : ORGAN NA PREZIDIUMA NA ASN (BU/0002-1636) [03816644] **133**

SELSKOSTOPANSKA TEKHNIKA (BU/0037-1718) [03816862] **161**

SEM DNEI (US) [10465404] **2492**

SEMA (TORONTO) (CN/1183-160X) [25796307] **5257**

SEMAINE AMEUBLEMENT INFORMATION, LA (FR/0990-6029) [I09906029] **2903**

SEMAINE DE L'EMIGRATION : ORGANE DE L'AMICALE DES ALGERIENS EN EUROPE, LA (FR) [09401514] **1921**

SEMAINE DES HOPITAUX (FR/0037-1777) [01765372] **3792**

SEMAINE DES HOPITAUX. THERAPEUTIQUE (FR/0302-9271) [06439156] **3792**

SEMAINE INTERNATIONALE, LA (CN/0711-0510) [08858475] **2629**

SEMAINE JUDICIAIRE, LA (SZ) [08154291] **3047**

SEMAINE JURIDIQUE, LA (FR) [01765373] **3047**

SEMAINE RELIGIEUSE D'ANGERS, LA (FR) **4996**

SEMAINE VETERINAIRE, LA (FR/0396-5015) [I03965015] **5521**

SEMANA (IS) [05780384] **2508**

SEMANA (BOGOTA, COLOMBIA : 1982) (CK) [09401505] **2552**

SEMANA ECONOMICA (PE) [09651333] **1520**

SEMANA ECONOMICA / APOYO (PE) [19901873] **1583**

SEMANA LATINOAMERICANA (AG) [05245037] **2512**

SEMANA LATINOAMERICANA. AGENCIA LATINOAMERICANA DE SERVICIOS (MX) [14962764] **2552**

SEMANA MEDICA (BUENOS AIRES, ARGENTINA : 1894) (AG) [07451079] **3640**

SEMANA MEDICA DE MEXICO (MX/0037-1823) [03547859] **3640**

SEMANA NACIONAL DE FILOSOFIA NO BRASIL: ANAIS (BL) [07107695] **4360**

SEMANA VITIVINICOLA, LE (SP/0037-184X) [14395316] **2370**

SEMANARIO (PO) **3996**

SEMANARIO ALTERNATIVA (CK) [03143422] **2552**

SEMANARIO DEPORTIVO LPV (CU) [02727359] **4917**

SEMANAS ESPANOLAS DE MISIONOLOGIA (SP) **4996**

SEMANTIKOS (FR/0395-3556) [06248513] **3320**

SEMBAI TOKEI NEMPO (JA) [02852027] **1626**

SEMC JOURNAL (US) [04414939] **4096**

SEMEIA (US/0095-571X) [01853840] **5019**

SEMENARSTVO ZAGREB (YU/0352-3047) [01353047] **133**

SEMENCE, LA (CN/0228-670X) [07802284] **5019**

SEMENCES ET PROGRES (FR/0395-8930) [I03958930] **5156**

SEMENTI ELETTE (IT/0037-1890) [02455386] **186**

SEMENTI SILE : CATALOGO (IT) [12057687] **2431**

SEMENTI SILE (FIRM) *See* SEMENTI SILE : CATALOGO **2431**

SEMENTO KONKURITO (JA/0371-0718) [09498426] **627**

SEMENTO KONKURITO RONBUNSHU (JA/0916-3182) [22753342] **627**

SEMER (SP) **3640**

SEMESTER REVIEW, THE (US/0009-871X) [02077072] **308, 1847**

SEMESTRE HISTORICO (VE) [02404465] **2760**

SEMI-ANNUAL BOOKLIST (US/0883-9565) [12171250] **3470**

SEMI-ANNUAL ELECTRIC POWER SURVEY *See* ELECTRIC POWER SURVEY (TOKYO, JAPAN) **2044**

SEMI-ANNUAL GEOGRAPHICAL INDEX OF SPECIALTY ADVERTISING DISTRIBUTORS (US/0360-1501) [02244089] **765**

SEMI-ANNUAL REPORT OF THE INSPECTOR GENERAL, U.S. SMALL BUSINESS ADMINISTRATION (US/0742-3802) [06849983] **3103**

SEMI DIRECTORY (US/0146-4264) [02957605] **2080**

SEMI MEMBERSHIP DIRECTORY (US) [09672209] **5156**

SEMI-MONTHLY MEANS OF SEA SURFACE TEMPERATURE, WEST COAST (US) [09821037] **2313**

SEMIANNUAL REPORT - DIVISION OF AIR POLLUTION CONTROL (US) [01794607] **2243**

SEMIANNUAL REPORT / NEW YORK STATE ENERGY RESEARCH AND DEVELOPMENT AUTHORITY (US) [23716025] **1956**

SEMIANNUAL REPORT TO CONGRESS ON THE EFFECTIVENESS OF THE CIVIL AVIATION SECURITY PROGRAM / U.S. DEPARTMENT OF TRANSPORTATION, FEDERAL AVIATION ADMINISTRATION (US) [09136527] **35**

SEMIANNUAL REPORT TO THE CONGRESS / OFFICE OF INSPECTOR GENERAL (US) [09796288] **4685**

SEMIANNUAL REPORT TO THE CONGRESS - UNITED STATES. DEPT. OF TRANSPORTATION. OFFICE OF INSPECTOR GENERAL (1981) (US/8755-4836) [10654707] **5392**

SEMIANNUAL REPORT - UNITED STATES. DEPT. OF AGRICULTURE. OFFICE OF THE INSPECTOR GENERAL (US/0740-168X) [09873465] **133**

SEMIANNUAL REPORT - UNITED STATES. DEPT. OF LABOR. OFFICE OF THE INSPECTOR GENERAL (US/0275-5076) [10307271] **1710**

SEMICONDUCTOR CURRENTS (US) **2080**

SEMICONDUCTOR DATA UPDATE *CEASED.* (US) **2080**

SEMICONDUCTOR EQUIPMENT AND MATERIALS INSTITUTE *See* SEMI DIRECTORY **2080**

SEMICONDUCTOR EQUIPMENT AND MATERIALS INSTITUTE *See* SEMI MEMBERSHIP DIRECTORY **5156**

SEMICONDUCTOR EQUIPMENT AND MATERIALS INSTITUTE *See* BOOK OF SEMI STANDARDS **2037**

SEMICONDUCTOR HEAT SINK, SOCKET & ASSOCIATED HARDWARE D.A.T.A. BOOK (US/0092-6302) [01789375] **2080**

SEMICONDUCTOR INDUSTRY AND BUSINESS SURVEY (US/0730-1014) [07941411] **2080**

SEMICONDUCTOR INDUSTRY ASSOCIATION *See* YEARBOOK AND DIRECTORY / SEMICONDUCTOR INDUSTRY ASSOCIATION **2086**

SEMICONDUCTOR INTERNATIONAL (US/0163-3767) [04359854] **2080**

SEMICONDUCTOR PACKAGING UPDATE (US/0889-9193) [14117055] **4222**

SEMICONDUCTOR SCIENCE AND TECHNOLOGY (UK/0268-1242) [13719465] **4420**

SEMICONDUCTOR SILICON (US/0091-391X) [01783373] **2080**

SEMICONDUCTOR TECHNIQUE (JA) **2080**

SEMICONDUCTOR WORLD (JA) [10509873] **2108**

SEMICONDUCTORS AND INSULATORS *See* ELECTRIC POWER *CEASED.* (US/0309-5991) [03007520] **4421**

SEMICONDUCTORS AND SEMIMETALS (US/0080-8784) [02252113] **2080**

● SEMICONDUCTORS (NEW YORK, N.Y.) (US/1063-7826) [26137247] **4421**

SEMIGROUP FORUM (US/0037-1912) [01697128] **3533**

SEMINA (FI/0049-0164) [I00490164] **4329**

SEMINA (LONDRINA) (BL/0101-3742) [06258016] **133**

SEMINAIRE CHOQUET. EXPOSES (FR) [02468065] **3533**

SEMINAIRE D'ANALYSE (CLERMONT-FERRAND, FRANCE) (FR/0985-0732) [19051540] **1847**

SEMINAIRE DE MATHEMATIQUE (FR/0772-2257) [09954060] **3533**

SEMINAIRE DE THEORIE DES NOMBRES / SEMINAIRE DELANGE-PISOT-POITOU (US/1046-5952) [08342824] **3533**

SEMINAIRE DE THEORIE DU POTENTIEL, PARIS : EXPOSES (GW) [03566816] **3533**

SEMINAIRE EQUATIONS AUX DERIVEES PARTIELLES / ECOLE POLYTECHNIQUE, CENTRE DE MATHEMATIQUES (FR) [18102969] **3533**

SEMINAIRE PAUL KREE *See* SEMINAIRE PAUL KREE. EXPOSES **3533**

SEMINAIRE PAUL KREE. EXPOSES (FR) [02441448] **3533**

SEMINAIRE SUR LES EQUATIONS AUX DERIVEES PARTIELLES (FR/0553-2264) [06047748] **3533**

SEMINAR (II/0037-1947) [01605255] **5156**

SEMINAR ANNUAL - ONTARIO GENEALOGICAL SOCIETY (CN/0824-7331) [11245830] **2472**

SEMINAR IMENI I. G. PETROVSKOGO *See* TRUDY SEMINARA IMENI I. G. PETROVSKOGO **3539**

SEMINAR LECTURE NOTES / SID, SOCIETY FOR INFORMATION DISPLAY (US/0887-915X) [13415080] **1202**

SEMINAR ON MATHEMATICAL SCIENCES (JA) [07819542] **3533**

SEMINAR ON THE ACQUISITION OF LATIN AMERICAN LIBRARY MATERIALS *See* SALALM NEWSLETTER **3247**

SEMINAR PAPERS - ASSOCIATION OF ONTARIO HOUSING AUTHORITIES (CN/0705-1506) [05761437] **2835**

SEMINAR PAPERS - DEPARTMENT OF GEOGRAPHY. UNIVERSITY OF NEWCASTLE UPON TYNE (UK/0307-3246) [I03073246] **2576**

SEMINAR PAPERS (LONDON, 1972-) (UK) [02026884] **710**

SEMINAR PROCEEDINGS FROM THE SCANDINAVIAN INSTITUTE OF AFRICAN STUDIES (SW/0281-0018) [12108716] **2500**

SEMINAR REPORTEUR (II) [11931205] **5157**

SEMINAR SERIES (SOCIETY FOR EXPERIMENTAL BIOLOGY (GREAT BRITAIN)) (UK/0309-6831) [02909139] **473**

SEMINAR SOPHUS LIE : DARMSTADT, ERLANGEN, GREIFSWALD, LEIPZIG (GW/0940-2268) [26136917] **3533**

SEMINAR (TORONTO) (CN/0037-1939) [01765379] **3320**

SEMINARIO DE ARTE ARAGONES (SP/0487-3491) [02952298] **364**

SEMINARIO MATEMATICO E FISICO DI MILANO *See* RENDICONTI DEL SEMINARIO MATEMATICO E FISICO DI MILANO **3531**

SEMINARIO SULLA EVOLUZIONE BIOLOGICA E I GRANDI PROBLEMI DELLA BIOLOGIA : ATTI (IT/0391-8041) [08300937] **551**

SEMINARIOS DE ROENTGENELOGIA (SP) **3640**

SEMINARIOS DO MUSEU DA CASA BRASILEIRA: BOLETIM (BL) [02999275] **4096**

SEMINARIUM (VC/0582-6314) [01773376] **5036**

SEMINARS — Alphabetical Title Index

SEMINARS DIRECTORY (US/1042-1866) [18671220] **710**

●SEMINARS FOR NURSE MANAGERS (US/1066-3851) [26937747] **3869**

SEMINARS IN ANESTHESIA (US/0277-0326) [07484013] **3684**

SEMINARS IN ARTHRITIS AND RHEUMATISM (US/0049-0172) [01714527] **3807**

SEMINARS IN ARTHROPLASTY (US/1045-4527) [20116321] **3974**

●SEMINARS IN AVIAN AND EXOTIC PET MEDICINE (US/1055-937X) [23369196] **5522**

SEMINARS IN CANCER BIOLOGY (US/1044-579X) [19834549] **3824**

SEMINARS IN CELL BIOLOGY (US/1043-4682) [19481113] **473**

SEMINARS IN CHIROPRACTIC *CEASED.* (US/1047-1227) [20609460] **3640**

SEMINARS IN COLON & RECTAL SURGERY (US/1043-1489) [19329190] **3974**

SEMINARS IN DENTAL HYGIENE (US/1042-718X) [19114816] **1335**

SEMINARS IN DERMATOLOGY (US/0278-145X) [07719685] **3722**

SEMINARS IN DERMATOLOGY ED. ITALIANA (IT/1121-1881) [I11211881] **3722**

SEMINARS IN DEVELOPMENTAL BIOLOGY (US/1044-5781) [19834499] **473**

SEMINARS IN DIAGNOSTIC PATHOLOGY (US/0740-2570) [09903028] **3898**

SEMINARS IN DIALYSIS (US/0894-0959) [15794263] **3640**

SEMINARS IN GASTROINTESTINAL DISEASE (US/1049-5118) [21245329] **3748**

●SEMINARS IN HEADACHE MANAGEMENT (CN/1198-7340) **3640**

SEMINARS IN HEARING (US/0734-0451) [08674511] **3891**

SEMINARS IN HEMATOLOGY (US/0037-1963) [01605802] **3774**

SEMINARS IN IMMUNOLOGY (UK/1044-5323) [19834417] **3676**

SEMINARS IN INTERVENTIONAL RADIOLOGY (US/0739-9529) [09839229] **3946**

●SEMINARS IN LAPAROSCOPIC UURGERY (US/1071-5517) [28678849] **3974**

SEMINARS IN LIVER DISEASE (US/0272-8087) [06939715] **3801**

SEMINARS IN NEPHROLOGY (US/0270-9295) [06520430] **3993**

SEMINARS IN NEUROLOGICAL SURGERY (US/0160-2489) [03646344] **3974**

SEMINARS IN NEUROLOGY (US/0271-8235) [06688999] **3846**

SEMINARS IN NEUROSCIENCES (US/1044-5765) [19834446] **3846**

SEMINARS IN NUCLEAR MEDICINE (US/0001-2998) [01765387] **3849**

SEMINARS IN NUTRITION (US/0898-5995) [13199115] **4199**

SEMINARS IN ONCOLOGY (US/0093-7754) [01793234] **3824**

SEMINARS IN ONCOLOGY NURSING (US/0749-2081) [11087679] **3824**, **3869**

SEMINARS IN OPHTHALMOLOGY (US/0882-0538) [11729970] **3879**

●SEMINARS IN ORTHODONTICS (US) [29559242] **3640**

SEMINARS IN ORTHOPAEDICS (US/0882-052X) [11729708] **3884**

SEMINARS IN OTOLARYNGIC ALLERGY (CN/1198-7421) **3891**, **3676**

SEMINARS IN PEDIATRIC GASTROENTEROLOGY AND NUTRITION (CN/1188-0244) [25652226] **3748**, **3911**

SEMINARS IN PEDIATRIC INFECTIOUS DISEASES (US/1045-1870) [20030821] **3911**, **3716**

●SEMINARS IN PEDIATRIC NEUROLOGY (US/1071-9091) [28762888] **3846**

●SEMINARS IN PEDIATRIC SURGERY (US/1055-8586) [23359248] **3911**, **3974**

SEMINARS IN PERINATOLOGY (US/0146-0005) [02824346] **3768**

●SEMINARS IN PERIOPERATIVE NURSING (US/1056-8670) [23887081] **3869**

SEMINARS IN RADIATION ONCOLOGY (US/1053-4296) [22529258] **3946**, **3824**

●SEMINARS IN RADIOLOGIC TECHNOLOGY (US/1070-535X) [28399564] **3946**

SEMINARS IN REPRODUCTIVE ENDOCRINOLOGY (US/0734-8630) [08815474] **3768**, **3733**

●SEMINARS IN RESPIRATORY AND CRITICAL CARE MEDICINE (US/1069-3424) [27994776] **3952**

SEMINARS IN RESPIRATORY INFECTIONS (US/0882-0546) [11729844] **3952**

SEMINARS IN RESPIRATORY MEDICINE (US/0192-9755) [05139998] **3952**

SEMINARS IN SPEECH AND LANGUAGE (US/0734-0478) [08674477] **3320**

SEMINARS IN SPINE SURGERY (US/1040-7383) [18507805] **3974**

SEMINARS IN SURGICAL ONCOLOGY (US/8756-0437) [11454466] **3974**, **3824**

SEMINARS IN THORACIC AND CARDIOVASCULAR SURGERY (US/1043-0679) [19290629] **3974**

SEMINARS IN THROMBOSIS AND HEMOSTASIS (US/0094-6176) [01015454] **3774**

SEMINARS IN ULTRASOUND, CT, AND MR (US/0887-2171) [10871915] **3946**

SEMINARS IN UROLOGY (US/0730-9147) [08094127] **3993**

SEMINARS IN VASCULAR SURGERY (US/0895-7967) [16798604] **3974**

SEMINARS IN VETERINARY MEDICINE AND SURGERY (SMALL ANIMALS) (US/0882-0511) [11730163] **5522**

SEMINARS IN VIROLOGY (US/1044-5773) [19834473] **570**

SEMINARUL DE OPERATORI LINIARI SI ANALIZA ARMONICA (RM) [09406830] **3533**

SEMINARUL DE TEORIA STRUCTURILOR / UNIVERSITATEA DIN TIMISOARA, FACULTATEA DE STIINTE ALE NATURII, SECTIA MATEMATICA (RM) [09406872] **3533**

SEMINARY NEWS (ENID, OKLA.) (US/0745-5518) [09285571] **4996**

SEMINARY TIMES, THE *CEASED.* (US/0899-6199) [18160698] **4996**

SEMINER (TU) [20222968] **5218**

SEMINOLE OUTLOOK (US/8750-2070) [11110585] **5651**

SEMINOLE TRIBUNE, THE (US/0891-8252) [15026238] **5651**

SEMIOSIS (MX) [05453520] **3320**

SEMIOSIS (GW/0170-219X) [05883051] **3435**, **3320**

SEMIOSIS (PARIS, FRANCE) (FR) [19085332] **3320**, **3435**

SEMIOTEXTE (NEW YORK) (US/0093-9579) [01793151] **5257**

SEMIOTIC CROSSROADS (NE/0922-5072) [20020983] **3320**

SEMIOTIC REVIEW OF BOOKS (CN/0847-1622) [22135108] **1121**

SEMIOTIC SOCIETY OF AMERICA. MEETING *See* SEMIOTICS **3320**

SEMIOTIC WEB, THE (GW) [17821098] **3320**

SEMIOTICA (NE/0037-1998) [01765390] **3320**

SEMIOTICS *CEASED.* (US/0742-7611) [10212912] **3320**

SEMIOTICS AND THE HUMAN SCIENCES (US/1054-8386) [22994208] **5218**

SEMIOTIKA I INFORMATIKA (RU) [02945386] **3533**

SEMIOTIQUE ET BIBLE (FR/0154-6902) [03944614] **4996**

SEMIOTIQUES / CENTRE NATIONAL DE LA RECHERCHE SCIENTIFIQUE, INSTITUT NATIONAL DE LA LANGUE FRANCAISE, URL7-ANALYSE DU DISCOURS (FR/1160-9907) [26910898] **3320**

SEMITIC STUDY SERIES (NE) [01765391] **5052**

SEMITICA (FR/0373-630X) [01605916] **5052**, **3320**

SEMITICA VIVA-SERIES DIDACTICA (GW/0935-7556) **3320**

SEMJA I SKOLA (RU/0131-7377) [02046120] **1783**

SEMMON TOSHOKAN (JA) [01797131] **3249**

SEMPAKU GIJUTSU KENKYUJO (JAPAN) *See* SENPAKU GIJUTSU KENKYUJO HOKOKU **4183**

SEMPAKU ROPPO (JA) [03528437] **3182**

SEMPAKU SETSUBI KANKEI HOREI (JA) [05277320] **5456**

●SEMPER REFORMANDA (US/1065-3783) [26602806] **4996**

SEMPEX (FR) **710**

SEMPRE (IT) **5307**

SEMSCOPE, THE (US/0361-1310) [01914533] **4685**

SEN TEX (US/1055-2820) [23138622] **5181**

SENALES (AG/0037-2099) [05698195] **424**

SENARA (SP/0211-464X) [I0211464X] **1080**, **3320**

SENARAI PERJAWATAN DI KEMENERIAN-KEMENTERIAN DAN JABATAN-JABATAN DALAM ANGGARAN PERBELANJAAN PERSEKUTUAN (MY) [23174543] **4685**

SENATE AND HOUSE JOURNALS OF THE ... LEGISLATURE OF THE STATE OF MONTANA COMMENCING IN SPECIAL SESSION ... AND ENDING ... (US) [08744637] **4495**

SENATE ELECTION LAW GUIDEBOOK (US/0740-9834) [06255037] **3047**

SENATE HISTORY / SENATE HISTORICAL OFFICE, OFFICE OF THE SECRETARY, UNITED STATES SENATE (US) [08486407] **2760**

SENATE ISSUES YEARBOOK (US/0271-4280) [06612829] **4685**

SENATE JOURNAL OF THE ... LEGISLATURE OF THE STATE OF MONTANA (US) [08227927] **4495**

SENCKENBERGIANA BIOLOGICA (GW/0037-2102) [01714447] **4172**

SENCKENBERGIANA LETHAEA (GW/0037-2110) [01383196] **4230**

SENCKENBERGIANA MARITIMA (GW/0080-889X) [02520714] **557**, **1456**

SENDEBAR : BOLETIN DE LA E.U.T.I. DE GRANADA (SP) [23599739] **3320**

SENDERO : ORGANO DE LA CONFERENCIA EPISCOPAL PARAGUAYA (PY) [09472767] **5036**

SENECA COUNTY FARM & HOME NEWS (US) [08465140] **133**

SENECA REVIEW, THE (US/0037-2145) [01717000] **3435**

SENECA SEARCHERS (US/1046-5545) [10551575] **2472**

SENEGAL *See* LISTE DU CORPS DIPLOMATIQUE - REPUBLIQUE DU SENEGAL **3132**

SENEGAL. DIRECTION DE L'INDUSTRIE *See* RAPPORT ANNUEL DE LA DIRECTION DE L'INDUSTRIE / REPUBLIQUE DU SENEGAL, MINISTERE DU DEVELOPPEMENT INDUSTRIEL ET L'ARTISANAT, DIRECTION DE L'INDUSTRIE **1623**

SENEGAL. DIRECTION GENERALE DE LA PRODUCTION AGRICOLE *See* RAPPORT SUR LA CULTURE DU RIZ PLUVIAL AU SENEGAL ORIENTAL **124**

SENEGAL EN CHIFFRE, LE (SG) [02728721] **1583**

SENEGAL : ENERGIEWIRTSCHAFT (GW) [05064238] **1956**

SENEGAL : WIRTSCHAFTLICHE ENTWICKLUNG (GW) [02356583] **1583**

SENEGAL. WIRTSCHAFTSDATEN UND WIRTSCHAFTSDOKUMENTATION / BUNDESSTELLE FUR AUSSENHANDELSINFORMATION (GW) [07677523] **1583**

SENEY NEWSLETTER (CN/0828-9980) [15059891] **2472**

SENGO RODO UNDOSHI KENKYU (JA) [11221930] **1710**

SENGONG KEJI TONGXUN (CC/0253-3669) [08107605] **2395**

SENI GAKKAI SHI (JA/0037-9875) [02450497] **5355**

SENI KAGAKU (JA/0286-987X) [10481047] **5355**

SENI KIKAI GAKKAI SHI (JA/0371-0580) [01790253] **5355**

SEN'I KOBUNSHI ZAIRYO KENKYUJO (JAPAN) *See* SEN'I KOBUNSHI ZAIRYO KENKYUJO NENPO **3487**

SEN'I KOBUNSHI ZAIRYO KENKYUJO NENPO (JA) [10643663] **3487**

SENI KOBUNSHI ZAIRYO KENKYUSHO KENKYU HOKOKU (JA/0371-0807) [10047396] 1996, **5355**

SEN'I KOGYO SHIKENJO NENPO *See* SEN'I KOBUNSHI ZAIRYO KENKYUJO NENPO **3487**

SENI SEIHIN SHOHI KAGAKU (JA/0037-2072) [10440749] **5355**

SENIN RODO TOKEI (JA) [01790275] **1710**

SENIN ROPPO (JA) [03518838] **4183**

SENIN TOKEI (JA) [01797228] **1710**

SENIOR ADULT STUDENT *See* SENIOR ADULT STUDENT GUIDE **4996**

●SENIOR ADULT STUDENT GUIDE (US/1059-3381) [24565214] **4996**

SENIOR ADVOCATE (SACRAMENTO, CALIF.), THE *CEASED.* (US/0740-7122) [08859988] **5181**

SENIOR CARE PROFESSIONAL (US/1051-6913) [22092401] **5181**

SENIOR CARE PROFESSIONAL *See* AGING NEWS ALERT : THE SENIOR SERVICES & FUNDING REPORT **5178**

SENIOR CITIZENS ADVOCATE AND ASPECTS OF AGING (US/0882-9403) [10937359] **5181**

SENIOR CITIZENS' CONSULTANTS OF ST. CATHARINES INC (CN/0714-5756) [09088987] **5181**

SENIOR CITIZENS NEWS (WASHINGTON, D.C.) (US/0559-4677) [02251947] **5181**

SENIOR CITIZENS TODAY (US/0049-0199) [04040171] **5181**

SENIOR CITIZENS WORLD (US/0883-1939) [12089326] **5181**

SENIOR DIGEST (US) **5181**

SENIOR ECONOMIST (US) **1520**

SENIOR HEALTH CARE *CEASED.* (US/1044-548X) [19829608] 5181, **4802**

SENIOR HEALTH DIGEST (US/1044-209X) [19730621] 5181, **4802**

SENIOR HIGH SCHOOL LIBRARY CATALOG (US) [01641840] **3249**

SENIOR HIGH TEACHER'S GUIDE (US/0162-9298) [04267903] **1905**

SENIOR LAW REPORT (US/1050-3250) [20139755] 5181, **3048**

SENIOR LIFE (US/0160-4783) [03688572] **5181**

SENIOR MEDIA GUIDE (US/1050-3803) [21472683] **936**

SENIOR MUSICIAN (US) 5067, **4152**

SENIOR NEWS (SA/0037-2234) [I00372234] 3755, **5181**

SENIOR NURSE (UK/0265-9999) [10934969] **3869**

SENIOR SCENE (CN/0714-5624) [09340505] **5182**

SENIOR SCENE (AT) **5182**

SENIOR SENTINEL (CN) **5182**

SENIOR SPECTRUM (US) 3755, **5182**

SENIOR TEXANS EMPLOYMENT PROGRAM *See* SENIOR TEXANS EMPLOYMENT PROGRAM ANNUAL REPORT TO GOVERNOR'S COMMITTEE ON AGING **1710**

SENIOR TEXANS EMPLOYMENT PROGRAM ANNUAL REPORT TO GOVERNOR'S COMMITTEE ON AGING (US/0149-161X) [03433734] **1710**

SENIOR TIMES (WELLESLEY, MASS.), THE (US/0890-4200) [14231428] **2545**

SENIOR TRIBUNE, THE (US/0149-7413) [03547179] **5182**

SENIOR VOICE (ANCHORAGE, ALASKA) (US/0741-2894) [10139859] **2545**

SENIOR WORLD (US/0146-2539) [02892692] **5182**

SENIOR WORLD NEWSMAGAZINE (US) **5182**

SENIOR WORLD QUARTERLY *SUSPENDED.* (CN/0714-8798) [09106578] **5182**

SENIOR YELLOW PAGES (US/1055-0933) [23072278] **424**

SENIORS TODAY (CN/0715-4046) [09157026] **5182**

SENIORVIEW (US) **5182**

SENKYO KAIUM NEMPO (JA) [01797315] **5456**

SENKYO NO AYUMI (JA) [08819419] **4685**

SENMON SHINBUN YORAN (JA) [10339693] **2924**

SENOLOGIA (FR/0395-0506) [05307883] **3824**

SENPAKU GIJUTSU KENKYUJO HOKOKU (JA/0495-775X) [09696352] **4183**

SENPAKU KAIYO KOGAKU GIJUTSU BUNKEN SOKUHO (JA/0385-1176) [09310478] **4185**

SENPAKU SEIBI KODAN GYOMU YORAN (JA) [08731163] **5456**

SENPAKU SEIBI KODAN (JAPAN) *See* SENPAKU SEIBI KODAN GYOMU YORAN **5456**

SENPE. REVISTA DE LA SOCIEDAD ESPANOLA DE NUTRICION PARENTERAL Y ENTERAL (SP/0212-4637) [I02124637] **4199**

SENRI ETHNOLOGICAL STUDIES (JA/0387-6004) [05246082] **245**

SENRYO TO YAKUHIN TOKYO. 1956 (JA/0370-9671) [I03709671] **1029**

SENRYU NENKAN (JA) [01797044] **3435**

SENS DES AFFAIRES (OTTAWA. PRINTEMPS 1990) (CN/1183-580X) [24256449] **3917**

SENS DU NON-SENS, LE *See* PARADOXIST MOVEMENT, THE **4354**

SENSHOKU KENKYU (JA/0389-6277) [10440804] **1029**

SENSHOKU KOGYO (JA/0370-9574) [10440892] **1029**

SENSHOKU-TAI (JA/0385-4655) [02251462] **551**

SENSIBLE SOUND, THE (US/0199-4654) [05901907] **5318**

SENSOR BUSINESS DIGEST (US/1060-1902) [24924621] 710, **3487**

SENSOR GIJUTSU: SENSOR TECHNOLOGY (JA) 1221, 4421, **1252**

SENSOR MAGAZINE (GW) **5157**

SENSOR REVIEW (UK/0260-2288) [07757536] **5157**

SENSOR TECHNOLOGY (US/8756-4017) [11569401] **2080**

SENSORS AND ACTUATORS. A, PHYSICAL (SZ/0924-4247) [21400903] **2080**

SENSORS AND ACTUATORS. B, CHEMICAL (SZ/0925-4005) [21252574] **2081**

SENSORS AND MATERIALS (JA/0914-4935) [I09144935] **1996**

SENSORS BUYER'S GUIDE (US/1042-2757) [18609737] 1996, **3488**

SENSORS (PETERSBOROUGH, N.H.) (US/0746-9462) [10406972] **1996**

SENSORY INTEGRATION SPECIAL INTEREST SECTION NEWSLETTER (US/0279-4128) [07841389] **1885**

SENSORY PERCEPTION AND INFORMATION PROCESSING (UK/0143-7526) [I01437526] **4618**

SENSORY SYSTEMS (US/0894-4520) [16101856] **587**

SENSUS VAN EKSEKUTEURSKAMERS EN TRUSTMAATSKAPPYE *See* CENSUS OF BOARDS OF EXECUTORS AND TRUST COMPANIES **782**

SENSUS VAN MYNWESE / REPUBLIEK VAN SUID-AFRIKA, DEPARTEMENT VAN STATISTIEK CENSUS OF MNING / REPUBLIC OF SOUTH AFRICA, DEPARTMENT OF STATISTICS (SA) [10742109] **1444**

SENTA REPOTO / BUNSHI KAGAKU KENKYUJO DENSHI KEISANKI SENTA (JA) [07628484] **1058**

SENTA TSUSHIN (JA) [08286329] **2664**

SENTAN GIJUTSU KAIHATSU SORAN (JA) [12189936] **5157**

SENTEI JIDO TOSHO MOKUROKU (JA) [06601874] **3435**

SENTEN IJO *See* CONGENITAL ANOMALIES **543**

SENTENCES (US/0732-8907) [08484221] **3176**

SENTENCES ARBITRALES DE LA FONCTION PUBLIQUE (CN/0823-3322) [10915385] **1710**

SENTENCIAS EN APELACION DE LAS AUDIENCIAS PROVINCIALES EN MATERIA CIVIL Y PENAL (SP) [02246340] **3048**

SENTENCING STATISTICS, HIGHER CRIMINAL COURTS, VICTORIA (AT/0725-654X) [09872475] 3176, **3083**

SENTENZE DELLA CORTE COSTITUZIONALE NEL ..., LE (IT) [09935423] **3048**

SENTIER CHASSE-PECHE (CN/0711-7957) [09067707] **4878**

SENTINEL (CARLISLE, PA.), THE (US/0887-0802) [13079923] **5739**

SENTINEL (CHICAGO, ILL.) (US/0037-2331) [03923054] **5662**

SENTINEL (EAST BRUNSWICK, N.J. : 1973) (US/0194-3537) [05422139] **5711**

SENTINEL-ECHO (LONDON, KY.), THE (US/0898-9311) [12401020] **5682**

SENTINEL LEADER, THE (US) [13723731] **5732**

SENTINEL (LEWISTOWN, PA.) (US) [13391942] **5739**

SENTINEL (MADISON, WIS.), THE (US) [08751374] **1885**

SENTINEL-NEWS, THE (US) [13323225] **5682**

SENTINEL OF THE BLESSED SACRAMENT *CEASED.* (US) [01607714] **4996**

SENTINEL (OTTAWA. 1973) *CEASED.* (CN/0037-2315) [02248975] **4056**

SENTINEL (POINTE CLAIRE) (CN/0037-2307) [02174057] 1783, **5067**

SENTINEL (RADCLIFF, KY.) (US) [13904975] **5682**

SENTINEL-RECORD, THE (US) [19988226] **5632**

SENTINEL (RIDGEWAY) (CN/0225-512X) [06141386] **4996**

SENTINEL (SHILLINGTON, PA.), THE (US/0747-1610) [10622787] **5739**

SENTINEL-STANDARD (US/0745-2128) [08917393] **5693**

SENTINEL, THE (US) [09106593] **2893**

SENTINEL (TORONTO. 1957) (CN/0049-0202) [02174718] **5067**

SENTINEL WELLINGTON. 1989 (NZ/0114-412X) [I0114412X] **133**

SENTINELLA DEL CANAVESE (IT) **2492**

SENUR DAIHAGGYO NYAGHAG KOMMUNJIB (KO/0250-3336) [04507397] **4329**

SENZA SORDINO (US) [04771507] **4152**

SEOUL JOURNAL OF ECONOMICS (KO) [20684216] **1520**

SEOUL JOURNAL OF MEDICINE, THE (KO) [18305317] **3640**

SEOUL NATIONAL UNIVERSITY FACULTY PAPERS : BIOLOGY AND AGRICULTURE SERIES (KO/0377-5232) [02246044] **473**

SEOUL NATIONAL UNIVERSITY FACULTY PAPERS : HUMANITIES AND SOCIAL SCIENCE SERIES, A & B (KO/0377-5240) [02241760] 2854, **1847**

SEPA (CL) [01787712] **2760**

SEPARATION *See* INTERNATIONAL LABMATE **1015**

SEPARATION AND PURIFICATION METHODS (SOFTCOVER ED.) (US/0360-2540) [01909666] **1029**

SEPARATION SCIENCE AND TECHNOLOGY (US/0149-6395) [03535090] **1029**

SEPARATIONS, STATE SERVICE (US) [04986735] **4705**

SEPARATIONS TECHNOLOGY (US/0956-9618) [23239860] **1996**

SEPHARDI WORLD (JERUSALEM) (US) [07525965] **2273**

SEPIA (FORT WORTH, TEX.) (US/0037-2374) [01765397] **2760**

SEPM FIELD TRIP GUIDEBOOK (US) [15122076] 1445, **1397**

SEPM JOURNAL (US) 1445, **4230**

SEPM REPRINT SERIES (US/0731-759X) [08251834] 1445, **4230**

SEPM SHORT COURSE NOTES (US/1050-9763) [08235661] 1445, **4230**

SEPTS (SAINT PAUL, MINN.), THE (US/1049-1783) [21076002] **2472**

SEPTUAGINTA : VETUS TESTAMENTUM GRACUM (GW) **4996**

SEPU (CC/1000-8713) [12783801] **1019**

SEQUELS (TORONTO) (CN/1181-9677) [24623637] **3435**

SEQUENCES (FR/0559-4871) [01927253] **3471**

SEQUENCES (MONTREAL) (CN/0037-2412) [04332993] **4077**

SEQUENTIAL ANALYSIS (US/0747-4946) [10728140] **3533**

SEQUOIA (SAN FRANCISCO) (US/0199-8153) [06183121] **4996**

SEQUOIA (STANFORD, CALIF.) (US/0037-2420) [02951847] 1095, **3435**

SER-BULLETIN (NE/0920-4849) [I09204849] **1710**

SER PADRES HOY (SP) **2286**

SERAMIKKUSU (JA/0009-031X) [11570349] **2594**

SERAMIKKUSU KENKYU SHISETSU NENPO / ANNUAL REPORT OF THE CERAMICS RESEARCH LABORATORY, NAGOYA INSTITUTE OF TECHNOLOGY (JA) [27063613] **2594**

SERAPIS (US/0586-7924) [03923432] **2643**

SERAPYUTIKKU RISACHI (JA/0289-8020) [12608784] **3640**

SERB WORLD U.S.A (US/8756-5579) [11563440] 2709, **2760**

SERBIAN STUDIES (US/0742-3330) [07936680] **2709**

SERDIKA (BU/0204-4110) [04360527] **3533**

SERDTSE ROSII (RU) [04919562] **3471**

SERENA, CHILE. MUSEO ARQUEOLOGICO *See* BOLETIN **262**

SERENDIPTY / NEWSLETTER FOR THE SOUTH DAKOTA STATE POETRY SOCIETY (US) [04292706] **3471**

SERENITY'S NEW LIFE (US) **4802**

SERGEANTS (US/0360-7364) [02244622] **4057**

SERGER UPDATE, THE (US/0899-8302) [18235650] **5185**

SERGIO ARAGONES GROO THE WANDERER (NEW YORK, N.Y.) (US/0887-5952) [12655341] **4866**

SERGIPE (BRAZIL). SECRETARIA DO PLANEJAMENTO *See* PLANO OPERATIVO ANUAL / GOVERNO DO ESTADO DE SERGIPE, SECRETARIA DO PLANEJAMENTO **4741**

SERGIPE, BRAZIL (STATE). TRIBUNAL DE JUSTICA *See* REVISTA DO TRIBUNAL DE JUSTICA **3042**

SERGIPE (BRAZIL). SUPERINTENDENCIA DA AGRICULTURA E PRODUCAO *See* PLANO ANUAL DE TRABALO - SUDAP **120**

SERI JOURNAL (US/0278-601X) [07727235] **1956**

SERI PMST (IO/0302-8879) [01790719] **4685**

SERI SCIENCE & TECHNOLOGY IN REVIEW *See* NREL SCIENCE & TECHNOLOGY IN REVIEW **1951**

SERI STATISTIK PENGANGKUTAN KERETA API. RAILWAYS STATISTICS (IO/0445-9474) [02813662] **5402**

SERIA ARCHEOLOGIA / UNIWERSYTET IM. ADAMA MICKIEWICZA W POZNANIU, WYDZIA FILOZOFICZNO-HISTORYCZNY (PL/0554-8195) [05653762] **282**

SERIA CHEMIA (PL) [03476709] **3534**

SERIA EKONOMIA (PL) [13024408] **1639**

SERIA FIZYKA / UNIWERSYTET IM. ADAMA MICKIEWICZA W POZNANIU, WYDZIA MATEMAYKI, FIZYKI, CHEMII (PL) [05293529] **4421**

SERIA HISTORYCZNA (PL) [01795588] **133**

SERIA KONFERENCJE (PL) [04550762] **308**

SERIA MATEMATYKA / UNIWERSYTET IM. ADAMA MICKIEWICZA W POZNANIU (PL) [27800588] **3534**

SERIA MONOGRAFIE - POLITECHNIKA WROCAWSKA, INSTYTUT CYBERNETYKI TECHNICZNEJ (PL) [03269573] **2128**

SERIA MONOGRAFIE - POLITECHNIKA WROCAWSKA, INSTYTUT MATEMATYKI (PL/0324-9603) [03262595] **3534**

SERIA STUDIA I MATERIAY - POLITECHNIKA WROCAWSKA, INSTYTUT MATEMATYKI (PL/0324-9611) [03265338] 2128, **3534**

SERIAL ARTICLES PUBLISHED IN NEWSPAPERS / STATE LIBRARY OF PENNSYLVANIA, LIBRARY SERVICES DIVISION, NEWSPAPER SECTION (US) [10964782] **5739**

SERIAL HOLDINGS (US) [04239966] **3249**

SERIAL HOLDINGS IN NEWFOUNDLAND LIBRARIES (CN/0709-0536) [05258038] **3249**

SERIAL NUMBER GUIDE (US/8756-2987) [10982669] **627**

SERIAL PUBLICATIONS CURRENTLY RECEIVED AND ON ORDER - EASTERN VIRGINIA MEDICAL SCHOOL, NORFOLK, VA. MOORMAN MEMORIAL LIBRARY (US) [05359300] 3640, **3249**

SERIAL PUBLICATIONS IN THE BRITISH MUSEUM, NATURAL HISTORY LIBRARY ON MICROFICHE (UK/0267-3347) [15695247] 3249, **4172**

SERIAL SOURCES OF THE BIOSIS PREVIEWS DATABASE (US/1044-4297) [19783880] **473**

SERIAL TITLES IN THE HUMANITIES AND SOCIAL SCIENCES (WINDSOR) (CN/0316-8379) [02624101] 5218, **2854**

SERIAL TITLES IN THE PURE AND APPLIED SCIENCES (WINDSOR) (CN/0316-8395) [02247201] **5157**

SERIALS & NEWSPAPERS IN MICROFORM (US/1063-0546) [25848988] **424**

SERIALS DIRECTORY (BIRMINGHAM, ALA. PRINT ED.), THE (US/0886-4179) [12884328] **3249**

SERIALS DIRECTORY / EBSCO CD-ROM, THE (US) **3249**

SERIALS HOLDINGS LIST (US) [04485421] **424**

SERIALS HOLDINGS MICROFORM / WILFRID LAURIER UNIVERSITY (CN/0823-5406) [10451497] **424**

SERIALS IN MICROFORM (US/0361-2740) [01935734] **424**

● SERIALS IN MICROFORM (ANN ARBOR, MICH. 1993) (US/1069-6164) [28122850] **3249**

SERIALS IN THE BRITISH LIBRARY (UK/0260-0005) [07979766] **424**

SERIALS LIBRARIAN, THE (US/0361-526X) [02705084] **3249**

SERIALS LIST / ERINDALE COLLEGE LIBRARY (CN/0229-1681) [08070619] **424**

SERIALS LIST MICROFORM / UNIVERSITY OF SASKATCHEWAN LIBRARY (CN/0227-6143) [07857974] **424**

SERIALS LIST - UNIVERSITY OF REGINA, LIBRARY (CN/0318-1529) [02441763] **424**

SERIALS M.I.T. LIBRARIES (US/0542-9560) [01796551] **3249**

SERIALS MASTER LIST (US) [03972598] **3249**

SERIALS (OXFORD, ENGLAND) (UK/0953-0460) [17801374] **3249**

SERIALS PERSPECTIVE (US/0747-5411) [10744896] **424**

SERIALS RECORD FILE / UNIVERSITY OF LETHBRIDGE LIBRARY (CN/0228-9156) [08071791] **424**

SERIALS REVIEW (US/0098-7913) [01562672] **3249**

SERICHAI (US/0888-238X) [13510631] **5640**

SERIDIM (IS) [09305877] **5052**

SERIE BIBLIOTECOLOGIA Y DOCUMENTACION (CR) [09456942] **133**

SERIE CIENCIAS ECONOMICAS Y EMPRESARIALES (SP) [04864601] **1520**

SERIE CIENTIFICA. INSTITUTO ANTARTICO CHILENO (CL/0073-9871) [04912781] **1360**

SERIE COSTA CENTRAL / TALLER DE ESTUDIOS ANDINOS (PE) [06562101] **5218**

SERIE DE CUENTOS PARA LA JUVENTUD (VE/0503-8308) [01487531] **1069**

SERIE DE DOCUMENTACION / CORPORACION NACIONAL DE INVESTIGACION Y FOMENTO FORESTAL (CK/0121-0254) [24905226] **2395**

SERIE DE FOLLETOS - FONDO MONETARIO INTERNACIONAL *CEASED.* (US/0252-2993) [07971493] **1520**

SERIE DE GEOFISICA (CU/0253-5718) [07556522] **1411**

SERIE DE INFORMES TECNICOS DE LA OMS (SZ) **2912**

SERIE DE INGENIERIA DE LA CALIDAD (SP) [01793300] **5355**

SERIE DE PLANEAMIENTO (CK/0588-3954) [03201913] **1583**

SERIE DESARROLLO RURAL. BOLETIN (CL) [06725154] **133**

SERIE DIDACTICA - FACULTAD DE AGRONOMIA Y ZOOTECNIA. UNIVERSIDAD NACIONAL TUCUMAN (AG/0325-2493) [09753133] **133**

SERIE ESTADISTICA (MENDOZA) (ARGENTINA : PROVINCE). (DIRECCION AGROPECUARIA) (AG) [10935255] 133, **156**

SERIE ESTUDOS PARA O PLANEAMENTO (BL) [02455691] **886**

SERIE ETUDES ET RECHERCHES / MINISTERE DE L'AGRICULTURE, INSTITUT NATIONAL DE LA RECHERCHE AGRONOMIQUE (FR) [05619501] **133**

SERIE : ETUDES SYNDICALES (FR/0577-1145) [03041700] **1710**

SERIE ICONOGRAPHIQUE (FR) **375**

SERIE INFORMACION ECONOMICA. PRECIOS *See* INDICES DE PRECIOS **1534**

SERIE INFORMACION ECONOMICA. SECTOR EXTERNO *See* INDICADORES DEL SECTOR EXTERNO **840**

SERIE "INFORMACION Y DOCUMENTACION" (CL) [04899061] **5157**

SERIE INSTRUMENTOS DE POLITICA AGRARIA (CK/0588-3970) [03201564] **133**

SERIE INTERNATIONALE D'ANALYSE NUMERIQUE (SZ/0373-3149) [02252933] **3534**

SERIE LINGUISTICA (BL/0102-6526) [02241766] **3320**

SERIE LINGUISTICA PERUANA (PE/0885-8691) [02955291] **3321**

SERIE MEMORIAS DE EVENTOS CIENTIFICOS COLOMBIANOS (CK/0120-5099) [20952360] 5157, **527**

SERIE NOTES ET DOCUMENTS / MINISTERE DE L'AGRICULTURE, INSTITUT NATIONAL DE LA RECHERCHE AGRONOMIQUE (FR) [05010999] **133**

SERIE ORIENTALE ROMA (IT/0582-7906) [01713993] **2664**

SERIE: PRODUCCION ANIMAL (SP) [02521860] **133**

SERIE : RECURSOS NATURALES (SP) [02242714] **133**

SERIE SEPARATAS / CENTRO DE ESTUDOS DE HISTORIA E CARTOGRAFIA ANTIGA (PO/0870-6735) [26134627] **2709**

SERIE U.R.S.S (FR) [02778927] **5218**

SERIES 2 : RESEARCH REPORTS - CENTER FOR SETTLEMENT STUDIES, UNIVERSITY OF MANITOBA (CN/0076-3934) [02247823] **5257**

SERIES A. MASTERWORKS OF YESTERDAY (US/0588-490X) [03257246] **4152**

SERIES ENTOMOLOGICA (NE/0924-4611) [05781852] **5613**

SERIES ESTADISTICAS DEL GRUPO ICO / INSTITUTO DE CREDITO OFICIAL (SP) [18664608] **811**

● SERIES IN CHICANA CRITICAL ISSUES (US/1065-688X) [26678127] **2760**

SERIES IN CLINICAL AND COMMUNITY PSYCHOLOGY, THE (US/0146-0846) [02851754] **4618**

SERIES IN FOOD MATERIAL SCIENCE (NE) [01933823] **1520**

SERIES IN GEOTECHNICAL ENGINEERING (US/0272-3980) [06833064] **1996**

SERIES IN HEALTH PSYCHOLOGY AND BEHAVIORAL MEDICINE, THE (US/8756-467X) [11566199] **4618**

SERIES IN MODERN APPLIED MATHEMATICS (SI/0217-8281) [10175554] **3534**

SERIES IN PSYCHOSOCIAL EPIDEMIOLOGY (US/1044-5633) [10408524] **3936**

SERIES IN PURE MATHEMATICS (SI) [12204382] **3534**

SERIES IN RADIOLOGY (NE/0167-465X) [05251222] **3947**

SERIES IN REAL ANALYSIS (SI) [19371495] **3534**

SERIES IN SOCIAL STUDIES : OCCASIONAL PAPER (RH) [04423732] **5218**

SERIES IN THEORETICAL AND APPLIED MECHANICS (SI) [15500278] **2128**

SERIES IN THERMAL AND TRANSPORT SCIENCES (US/0276-9662) [07468189] **5157**

SERIES OF MANUALS (HU) [20649945] 5539, **1418**

SERIES OF MONOGRAPHS ON SELECTED TOPICS IN SOLID STATE PHYSICS (NE) [01765400] **4421**

SERIES OF PROMINENT JUDGEMENTS OF THE SUPREME COURT UPON QUESTIONS OF CONSTITUTIONALITY (JA) [06885669] **3048**

SERIES OF SPECIAL REPORTS, A (US) [19246691] **1996**

SERIES ON EDUCATIONAL CHANGE (US) [01781332] **1783**

SERIES ON NURSING ADMINISTRATION (US/0895-4364) [16639198] **3869**

SERIES ON PROGRESS IN HIGH TEMPERATURE SUPERCONDUCTIVITY (SI) [19023531] **4421**

SERIES ON ROCK AND SOIL MECHANICS (US/0080-9004) [01773379] 2030, **1397**

SERIES ON THE DEVELOPMENT OF SOCIETIES (NE) [05256849] **5257**

SERIES - PACIFIC GROUP FOR POLICY ALTERNATIVES (CN/0824-135X) [11807715] **5307**

SERIES PAEDOPSYCHIATRICA (SZ/0080-9012) [01778260] **3936**

SERIES "REPORTS AND DOCUMENTS" / INTER-PARLIAMENTARY UNION (SZ) [08716502] **4685**

SERIES VI PAMPHLET. KENTUCKY GEOLOGICAL SURVEY (US) [06046357] **1397**

SERIF SERIES, THE *CEASED.* (US) [01604860] **3459**

SERIGRAFIA (MILANO, ITALY) (IT) [11367257] **4569**

● SERIIA 6, FILOSOFIIA, POLITOLOGIIA, SOTSIOLOGIIA, PSIKHOLOGIIA, PRAVO (RU) [25527106] 4495, **4360**

SERIIA 6, FILOSOFIIA, POLITOLOGIIA, TEORIIA I ISTORIIA SOTSIALIZMA, SOTSIOLOGIIA, PSIKHOLOGIIA, PRAVO *See* SERIIA 6, FILOSOFIIA, POLITOLOGIIA, SOTSIOLOGIIA, PSIKHOLOGIIA, PRAVO **4360**

SERIIA MATEMATICHESKIKH NAUK (RU) [05912487] **3534**

SERINFAR : A REGISTRAZIONE E PRODUZIONE SPECIALITA MEDICINALI (IT) **4329**

SERINFAR : B, PRESIDI MEDICO CHIRURGICI REGISTRAZIONE PRODUZIONE PUBBLICITA (IT) **4329**

SERINFAR DIETETICI : AUTORIZZAZIONE PRODUZIONE PUBBLICITA (IT) **4329**

SERINGUEIRA: RESUMOS INFORMATIVOS (BL) [06235703] **186**

SERLIN REPORT ON PARALLEL PROCESSING, THE (US/0894-2226) [15924385] **1202**

SERMENT DES HORACES : REVUE D'ART INTERNATIONALE, LE *SUSPENDED.* (FR) [20282837] **364**

SERMON BUILDER, THE (US) [06286177] **4996**

SERODIAGNOSIS AND IMMUNOTHERAPY IN INFECTIOUS DISEASE (UK/0888-0786) [13461226] 3716, **570**

SEROLOGICAL MUSEUM BULLETIN, THE *CEASED.* (US) [06152786] **4096**

SERON CHOSA NENKAN. ZENKOKU SERON CHOSA NO GENKYO (JA) [04008195] **5257**

SERPE (IT/0037-2498) [10409274] **3435**

Alphabetical Title Index — SESSIONAL

SERRA D'OR (SP/0037-2501) [04839802] **3352**

SERTEK (CN/0317-0322) [02441625] **3249**

SERTOMAN (US/0744-2807) [03462809] **5307**

SERVAMUS (SA) [06720450] **3176**

SERVANT, THE (CN/0705-6338) [04129863] **4996**

SERVANT (THREE HILLS) (CN/0848-1741) [21190700] **4996**

SERVANTESOVSKIE CHTENIIA (RU) [19504469] **3435**

SERVICE AND METHODS DEMONSTRATION PROGRAM ANNUAL REPORT. EXECUTIVE SUMMARY (US/0196-6405) [05452503] **5392**

●SERVICE & SUPPORT MANAGEMENT (US/1068-2902) [27566785] **710**

SERVICE BULLETIN (SAN JOSE, CALIF.) (US/0731-471X) [08158614] **5425**

SERVICE BUREAU NEWSLETTER (US/0892-5631) [15264878] **1626**

SERVICE BUSINESS (US/0736-5764) [09160264] 4209, **710**

SERVICE CANADIEN DES PARCS See NORTHERN YUKON NATIONAL PARK **4707**

SERVICE CIRCULAR - LEARN (CN/0821-221X) [09502190] **1783**

SERVICE CLUBS IN HAMILTON-WENTWORTH (CN/0712-7642) [08584661] **5307**

SERVICE COMMERCIAL DU CANADA A L'ETRANGER (CN/0822-1839) [10343961] **851**

SERVICE CORPORATION DIRECTORY (US/0272-3484) [06792996] 4847, **811**

SERVICE DE LA BIBLIOTHEQUE : SUPPLEMENT AU GUIDE DE L'USAGER (CN/0705-8322) [04653846] **3661**

SERVICE DEALER'S NEWSLETTER. SDN (US/0739-6236) [09772904] **5739**

SERVICE DELIVERY AREAS PROFILES (US) **1710**

SERVICE DES BIBLIOTHEQUES DE L'ONTARIO, NORD See BIBLIOTHEQUE POSTALE (1989) **3195**

SERVICE EDGE, THE (US/1053-1734) [18344761] **886**

SERVICE EMPLOYEES UNION (US/1062-4597) [17786893] **1710**

SERVICE GROUPE (FR) **886**

SERVICE INDUSTRIES JOURNAL, THE (UK/0264-2069) [11180504] **1626**

●SERVICE INDUSTRIES USA (US/1058-1626) [24233790] **1626**

SERVICE INDUSTRY NEWSLETTER (US/1048-3462) [20866400] **710**

SERVICE INSIDER (NORWALK, CONN.) (US/1047-7187) [20780139] **886**

SERVICE MANAGEMENT (UK/0953-9212) [I09539212] **5157**

SERVICE MANAGEMENT EUROPE (UK) **886**

SERVICE MANUAL (US) [23822598] **5425**

SERVICE MANUAL. CAMARO (US/1041-4282) [18686074] **5425**

SERVICE NEWS PARIS (FR/1144-2433) [11442433] **886**

SERVICE NEWS (YARMOUTH, ME.) (US/1046-1965) [19169704] **2081**

SERVICE PUBLIC D'EDUCATION ET D'INFORMATION JURIDIQUES DU NOUVEAU-BRUNSWICK See ACTIVITY REPORT - PUBLIC LEGAL EDUCATION AND INFORMATION SERVICE OF NEW BRUNSWICK **4624**

●SERVICE QUALITY B.C. UPDATE (CN/1193-2724) [26776096] **4685**

SERVICE REPORTER (US/0193-2128) [05166153] **2608**

SERVICE SAVVY (US/1049-5967) [21260798] **886**

SERVICE SAVVY See QUALITY SERVICE UPDATE **884**

SERVICE SHOP See PROFESSIONAL ELECTRONICS / THE OFFICIAL JOURNAL OF NESDA AND ISCET **2077**

SERVICE SOCIAL DANS LE MONDE (BE/0037-2641) [I00372641] **5307**

SERVICE SOCIALE (QUEBEC) (CN/0037-2633) [07508564] **5307**

SERVICE STATION (AT) 5425, **5392**

SERVICE STATION MANAGEMENT (US/0488-3896) [04879650] 4278, **5425**

SERVICE STATION SHOPPER SURVEY (UK) 936, **1299**

SERVICE TO REFUGEES See SERVICE TO REFUGEES : PROJECTS BOOK **4996**

SERVICE TO REFUGEES; PROGRESS REPORT (KE) [03257076] **4996**

SERVICE TO REFUGEES; PROJECT LIST (KE) [03249759] **4996**

SERVICE TO REFUGEES : PROJECTS BOOK (KE) [06242736] **4996**

SERVICE (TORONTO) (CN/0227-034X) [08701051] **5307**

SERVICEMEN'S AND VETERAN'S GROUP LIFE INSURANCE PROGRAMS, ANNUAL REPORT (US/0732-104X) [08139345] 2893, **4057**

SERVICES AUX MEMBRES - ASSOCIATION DE LA CONSTRUCTION DE MONTREAL ET DU QUEBEC (CN/0710-5630) [08713470] 627, **1710**

SERVICES FOR CHILDREN (UK) **5307**

SERVICES FOR SENIORS (CN/0820-8530) [09551464] **5307**

SERVICES FOR STUDENTS WITH DISABILITIES IN CALIFORNIA PUBLIC HIGHER EDUCATION (US) [22691672] 4393, **1847**

SERVICES FOR TEXAS CHILDREN / TEXAS DEPARTMENT OF COMMUNITY AFFAIRS, CHILDREN AND YOUTH SERVICES DIVISION (US) [06362640] **5307**

SERVICES HANDBOOK - ARIZONA DEPARTMENT OF EDUCATION (US/0149-6786) [03520415] **1783**

SERVICES LAW CASES (II/0304-100X) [01797743] **4705**

SERVICES LAW REPORTER (II) [01765407] **3048**

SERVICES MARKETING NEWSLETTER (US/0891-0952) [11361102] 936, **886**

SERVICES MARKETING TODAY (US) [24182323] **936**

SERVICES POSTE AERIENNE (FR) 1147, **2492**

SERVICES (VIENNA, VA.) (US/0279-0548) [07480166] **4214**

SERVICIO DE DOCUMENTACION SOCIAL (UY) [04459515] **5218**

SERVICIO DE INFORMACIONES RELIGIOSAS (SP/0326-6702) [I03266702] **4996**

SERVICIO EN LA INFORMACION / SERVICIO PAZ Y JUSTICIA EN AMERICA LATINA (AG) [15249661] **4513**

●SERVICIO INFORMATIVO / ALAI, AGENCIA LATINOAMERICANA DE INFORMACION (EC) [26229750] **1583**

SERVICIO MAREOGRAFICO NACIONAL (MEXICO) See TABLAS DE PREDICCION DE MAREAS : PUERTOS DEL OCEANO PACIFICO **4184**

SERVICIO MENSUAL DE INFORMACION Y DOCUMENTACION See SERVICIO INFORMATIVO / ALAI, AGENCIA LATINOAMERICANA DE INFORMACION **1583**

SERVICIO MENSUAL DE INFORMACION Y DOCUMENTACION - AGENCIA LATINOAMERICANA DE INFORMACION (CN/0827-5564) [12258582] **2760**

SERVICIO NACIONAL DE ADIESTRAMIENTO RAPIDO DE LA MANO DE OBRA EN LA INDUSTRIA. CENTRO DE INFORMACION Y DOCUMENTACION See INDICE BIBLIOGRAFICO - ARMO **417**

SERVICIOS PUBLICOS, DESARROLLO NACIONAL See DESARROLLO NACIONAL **5099**

SERVICIOS SOCIALES Y POLITICA SOCIAL (SP) **5307**

SERVICIOS Y ESTADOS FINANCIEROS (PN) [08557077] **811**

SERVICO DE DOCUMENTACAO (BL) [03020349] **5036**

SERVICO SOCIAL DA INDUSTRIA See RELATORIO ANUAL DE ATIVIDADES **5304**

SERVICO SOCIAL DA INDUSTRIA. DEPARTAMENTO REGIONAL DO ESTADO DO RIO DE JANEIRO See RELATORIO ANUAL DE ATIVIDADES REFERENTE AO EXERCICIO DE ... / SESI, DEPARTAMENTO REGIONAL DO ESTADO DO RIO DE JANEIRO **1706**

SERVICO SOCIAL DA INDUSTRIA. DEPARTAMENTO REGIONAL DO ESTADO DO RIO DE JANEIRO. RELATORIO DO EXECICIO See RELATORIO ANUAL DE ATIVIDADES REFERENTE AO EXERCICIO DE ... / SESI, DEPARTAMENTO REGIONAL DO ESTADO DO RIO DE JANEIRO **1706**

SERVICO SOCIAL DA INDUSTRIA. DEPARTAMENTO REGIONAL DO RIO GRANDE DO NORTE See RELATORIO ANUAL DE ATIVIDADES REFERENTE AO EXERCICIO DE ... / SERVICO SOCIAL DA INDUSTRIA, DEPARTAMENTO REGIONAL DO RIO GRANDE DO NORTE **1706**

SERVICO SOCIAL DA INDUSTRIA. DEPARTAMENTO REGIONAL DO RIO GRANDE DO NORTE See RELATORIO ANUAL DE ATIVIDADES **5304**

SERVICO SOCIAL DO COMERCIO See UNIDADES OPERACIONAIS: ENDERECOS **5313**

SERVICO SOCIAL DO COMERCIO See ANUARIO ESTATISTICO **5266**

SERVICO SOCIAL DO COMERCIO. ADMINISTRACAO NACIONAL See RELATORIO ANUAL / SERVICO SOCIAL DO COMERCIO, ADMINISTRACAO NACIONAL **5304**

SERVICO SOCIAL DO COMERCIO. ADMINISTRACAO REGIONAL DE MATO GROSSO See RELATORIO ANUAL / SERVICO SOCIAL DO COMERCIO, ADMINISTRACAO REGIONAL DE MATO GROSSO **1706**

SERVICO SOCIAL DO COMERCIO. ADMINISTRACAO REGIONAL EMMINAS GERAIS See ANUARIO ESTATISTICO - SERVICO SOCIAL DO COMERCIO, ADMINISTRACAO REGIONAL EM MINAS GERAIS **5266**

SERVICO SOCIAL DO COMERCIO. ADMINISTRACAO REGIONAL NO ESTADO DE GOIAS See RELATORIO DE ATIVIDADES - SERVICO SOCIAL DO COMERCIO, ADMINISTRACAO REGIONAL NO ESTADO DE GOIAS **5304**

SERVICO SOCIAL DO COMERCIO. ADMINISTRACAO REGIONAL NO ESTADO DE SAO PAULO See RELATORIO ANUAL **5304**

SERVICO SOCIAL DO COMERCIO. ADMINISTRACAO REGIONAL NO ESTADO DO PARA See RELATORIO ANNUAL - SERVICO SOCIAL DO COMERCIO, ADMINISTRACAO REGIONAL NO ESTADO DO PARA **5304**

SERVICO SOCIAL E SOCIEDADE (BL/0101-6628) [07365534] **5307**

SERVING YOU IN BOTH OFFICIAL LANGUAGES / TREASURY BOARD OF CANADA (CN) [10697885] **4685**

SERVIZI DEMOGRAFICI (IT) **4560**

SERVIZI SOCIALI (IT) **4685**

SERVIZIO DELLA PAROLA (IT/0037-2773) [I00372773] **4996**

SERVIZIO INFORMAZIONI AVIO (IT) **1872**

SERVO LOISIR (CN/0380-3082) [02442937] **4917**

SES CANADA FOCUS *CEASED*. (CN/1185-3425) [24368208] **2760**

SESAC, INC See RECORD-A-REF. SUPPLEMENT; COMMERCIAL RECORD REFERENCE **1928**

SESAME BULLETIN (UK/0950-2025) [15625810] **3321**

SESAME (MEDFORD, OR.) (US/0883-1467) [12158883] **4819**

SESAME STREET MAGAZINE (US/0049-0253) [01696325] **1069**

SESAME STREET PARENTS (US) **2286**

SESAME STREET PARENT'S GUIDE (US) **2286**

SESCHELLEN, WIRTSCHAFTLICHE ENTWICKLUNG / BUNDESSTELLE FUER AUSSENHANDELSINFORMATION (GW) [10931133] **1583**

SESIA (IT) **2492**

SESION INAUGURAL - REAL ACADEMIA DE FARMACIA DE BARCELONA (SP/0515-1147) [07418267] **4329**

SESITY / USTAV PRO FILOSOFII A SOCIOLOGII CSAV (XR) [20188832] 5257, **4361**

SESJA NAUKOWA (PL/0239-9342) [12638175] **134**

SESQUIANNUAL REPORT - FLORIDA COMMISSION ON HUMAN RELATIONS (US/0097-9244) [01798429] **4513**

SESSER-VALIER TIMES (US/1061-320X) [25251883] **5662**

SESSION BUDGETAIRE / GRAND CONSEIL DE L'AFRIQUE EQUATORIALE FRANCAISE (FR) [19111648] **4747**

SESSION / COMITE INTERNATIONAL DES POIDS ET MESURES, COMITE CONSULTATIF DE THERMOMETRIE (FR) [11320371] **4032**

SESSION D'ETUDES BIENNALE DE PHYSIQUE NUCLEAIRE (FR/1149-0276) [I11490276] **4451**

SESSION LAWS AND DIGEST (AS) [06254834] **3048**

SESSION LAWS OF THE STATE OF SOUTH DAKOTA (US) [09871393] **3048**

SESSION LAWS OF THE VIRGIN ISLANDS (US) [01713960] **3048**

SESSION REPORT / STATE PLANNING AND COMMUNITY AFFAIRS COMMITTEE (US) [12245724] **4685**

SESSION WEEKLY (US/1049-8176) [10580057] **4686**

SESSIONAL PAPER - SRI LANKA (CE) [05651867] **4686**

SESSIONAL — Alphabetical Title Index

SESSIONAL YEARBOOK ... AND DIRECTORY OF MEMBERS (UK/0073-9847) [13655272] **2030**

SESSIONS DE FORMATION... / COSE (CN/0712-7227) [08716910] **886**

SESTAVA ORGANOV SAMOUPRAVNIH INTERESNIH SKUPNOSTI / ZAVOD SR SLOVENIJE ZA STATISTIKO (XV) [12186730] **4686**

SET HAWTHORN **CEASED.** (AT/0725-4873) [I07254873] **1783**

SET: RESEARCH INFORMATION FOR TEACHERS (AT) **1905**

SET-VALUED ANALYSIS (NE/0927-6947) **3534**

SETCHAKU (JA/0037-0495) [10448002] **1030**

SETHALA : THE VOICE OF LESOTHO (LO) **2500**

SETO NAIKAI CHOSEKIHYO (JA) [01797152] **1456**

SETO NAIKAI REKISHI MINZOKU SHIRYOKAN NEMPO (JA) [08271841] **2664**

SETO NAIKAI RENGO KAIKU GYOGYO CHOSEI IINKAI GIJIROKU (JA) [03773250] **2313**

SETO NAIKAI SAIBAI GYOGYO HORYU GIJUTSU KAIHATSU CHOSA (JA) [05714915] **2313**

SETON HALL JOURNAL OF SPORT LAW (US/1059-4310) [23352654] 4917, **3048**

SETON HALL LAW REVIEW (US/0586-5964) [01765410] **3048**

SETON HALL LEGISLATIVE JOURNAL (US/0361-8951) [02397767] **3048**

SETTE E RELIGIONI (IT) **4996**

SETTER MAGAZINE, THE (US/0164-372X) [04636090] **4288**

SETTIMANA ENIGMISTICA (IT) **4854**

SETTIMANA GIURIDICA, LA (IT/0392-7253) [I03927253] **3048**

SETTIMANE DI STUDIO DEL CENTRO ITALIANO DI STUDI SULL'ALTO MEDIOEVO (IT/0528-5666) [01553722] **2709**

SETTING MUNICIPAL PRIORITIES (US/0272-8362) [06615286] **4747**

SETTLER (TOWANDA, PA. 1952), THE (US/0488-4965) [06684424] **2760**

SETTLERS OF NORTHEAST ALABAMA **See** NORTHEAST ALABAMA SETTLERS **2464**

SETUBAL ARQUEOLOGICA (PO) [04788721] **282**

SEURA 1979 (FI/0358-8017) [I03588017] **2522**

SEVARTHAM (II/0970-8324) [03779771] **4996**

SEVEC SUMMER INDIVIDUAL EXCHANGE PROGRAM, ... HANDBOOK **See** GENERAL INFORMATION AND GUIDELINES FOR THE SUMMER INDIVIDUAL EXCHANGE PROGRAM **1748**

SEVEN COUNTY FARM AND HOME NEWS (US/0192-4184) [05066404] **134**

SEVEN STARS (US/0146-695X) [03005013] **3471**

SEVENTEEN (US/0037-301X) [01643827] **1069**

SEVENTEENTH-CENTURY FRENCH STUDIES (UK/0265-1068) [10908934] 2709, **3435**

SEVENTEENTH CENTURY NEWS (US/0037-3028) [01765415] 2709, **3435**

SEVENTEENTH CENTURY, THE (UK/0268-117X) [13345307] 3435, **2709**

SEVENTH CIRCUIT DIGEST (US/0747-9387) [05951123] **3048**

SEVENTH-DAY ADVENTIST PERIODICAL INDEX (US/0270-3599) [05977061] 5067, **5013**

SEVENTH-DAY ADVENTISTS. ATLANTIC UNION CONFERENCE **See** ATLANTIC UNION GLEANER, THE **4936**

SEVENTIES, THE (US/0037-5969) [01100612] **3471**

SEVENTY SIX (US/0582-8872) [05107335] **4278**

SEVERN-WASHAGO MIRROR (CN/0704-0431) [03960158] **5794**

SEVERO-VOSTOCHNYI KOMPLEKSNYI NAUCHNO-ISSLEDOVATELSKII INSTITUT (AKADEMIIA NAUK SSSR) **See** TRUDY SEVERO-VOSTOCHNOGO KOMPLEKSNOGO NAUCHNO-ISSLEDOVATELSKOGO INSTITUTA **5167**

SEVERO-ZAPAD EVROPEISKOI CHASTI SSSR (RU/0582-8902) [04902302] **134**

SEVIER COUNTY HISTORICAL SOCIETY NEWSLETTER (US) **2472**

SEW (NE) [03890649] 1639, **3136**

SEW BEAUTIFUL (US/1063-9160) [17484158] **5185**

SEW BUSINESS (US/0029-4292) [04922114] **5186**

SEW BUSINESS MAGAZINE **See** CRAFTRENDS SEW BUSINESS **5183**

SEW IT BEGINS **CEASED.** (CN/0821-4247) [10224862] **5186**

SEW IT SEAMS (US/0888-577X) [13675284] **5186**

SEW NEWS (US/0273-8120) [06952826] **5186**

SEW TIJDSCHRIFT VOOR EUROPEES EN ECONOMISCH RECHT (NE) **3136**

SEWAGE TREATMENT CONSTRUCTION GRANTS MANUAL **CEASED.** (US/0149-5879) [03518695] **2243**

SEWANEE MEDIAEVAL STUDIES (US/0896-1638) [16935639] **2709**

SEWANEE NEWS, THE (US/0037-3044) [03923168] **1095**

SEWANEE REVIEW, THE (US/0037-3052) [01936968] **3352**

SEWANEE REVIEW [MICROFORM] (US) **3352**

SEWANEE THEOLOGICAL REVIEW (US/1059-9576) [24479030] **4996**

SEWARD PHOENIX LOG (US) **5629**

SEWICKLEY HERALD (1968), THE (US/1047-0697) [02267641] **5739**

SEWING DECOR (US) **5186**

SEWING UPDATE, THE (US/0899-8310) [18243438] **5186**

SEWTRADE C F I YEARBOOK AND DIRECTORY (AT/1035-1272) [I10351272] **1087**

SEX EDUCATION COALITION NEWS (US/0741-9686) [09812654] **1783**

SEX INFORMATION AND EDUCATION COUNCIL OF THE U.S **See** SIECUS REPORT **5188**

SEX NEWS (US) [01643729] **5188**

SEX OVER FORTY (US/0740-3593) [09954343] **5188**

SEX ROLES (US/0360-0025) [02243426] **5257**

SEXE PLUS (CN/0712-6034) [09313086] **5188**

SEXTANT (SEPT-ILES) (CN/0711-0774) [08981049] **5794**

SEXTANT (WASHINGTON, D.C.) **CEASED.** (US/0731-2180) [08139760] 1249, **1272**

SEXUAL ABUSE (US) 5218, **4802**

●SEXUAL ABUSE : A JOURNAL OF RESEARCH AND TREATMENT (US) 5188, **4618**

SEXUAL AND MARITAL THERAPY (UK/0267-4653) [13502187] 5188, **2286**

SEXUAL BEHAVIOR (NEW YORK, N.Y. : 1982) (US/0739-7321) [08898028] **5188**

SEXUAL COERCION & ASSAULT (US/0884-4372) [12412434] 5188, 5566, **5257**

SEXUAL FREEDOM (US) [02243641] **5188**

SEXUAL HEALTH AND RELATIONSHIPS (US/0148-7914) [03571072] **5188**

SEXUAL PLANT REPRODUCTION (GW/0934-0882) [18677388] **527**

SEXUAL POLITICS IN BRITAIN; A BIBLIOGRAPHICAL GUIDE WITH HISTORICAL NOTES (UK) [06301676] **4496**

SEXUAL SCIENCE (JA/0917-7507) [I09177507] **5188**

SEXUALITE NOUVELLE (CN/1191-1131) [25796556] **5188**

SEXUALITY AND DISABILITY (US/0146-1044) [03547569] 5188, **4393**

SEXUALITY AND LITERATURE (US/0893-6889) [15626407] **3435**

SEXUALITY (BOCA RATON) (US/0273-2564) [06941616] **5188**

SEXUALLY TRANSMITTED DISEASES (US/0148-5717) [03346945] 3716, **4802**

SEXUALLY TRANSMITTED DISEASES IN CANADA (CN/0711-8929) [08741196] 3716, 3736, **4802**

SEXUALMEDIZIN **CEASED.** (GW/0341-4884) [02208551] **3768**

SEXUOLOGIE (GW/0944-7105) 3640, **5188**

SEXY LAFFS (US/1059-3217) [24562848] **2545**

SEYBOLD DATA SHEETS **See** DURBIN DATA SHEETS **378**

SEYBOLD REPORT ON DESKTOP PUBLISHING, THE (US/0736-7260) [14109188] **1263**

SEYBOLD REPORT ON PUBLISHING SYSTEMS, THE (US/0889-9762) [08140742] **4819**

SEYCHELLES **See** TRADE REPORT - SEYCHELLES **854**

SEYCHELLES. ELECTRICITY DEPT. ANNUAL REPORT **See** ANNUAL REPORT OF THE ELECTRICITY DIVISION FOR THE YEAR ... (SEYCHELLES) **4628**

SEYCHELLES. ELECTRICITY DIVISION **See** ANNUAL REPORT OF THE ELECTRICITY DIVISION FOR THE YEAR ... (SEYCHELLES) **4628**

SEYCHELLES. LAWS, STATUTES, ETC **See** ORDINANCES **3023**

SEYMOUR BRITCHKY'S RESTAURANT LETTER **CEASED.** (US/0196-5220) [05835976] **5073**

SEYMOUR DAILY TRIBUNE (US) [12282697] **5667**

SEYMOUR HERALD, THE (US) [15325637] **5672**

SEZ (US/0190-3640) [04710326] **3435**

SEZAM (PL/0137-8694) [I01378694] **5566**

SEZD MONGOLSKOI NARODNO-REVOLIUTSIONNOI PARTII (RU) [06030528] **4546**

SEZNAM PLATNYCH CESKOSLOVENSKYCH STATNICH A OBOROVYCH NOREM (XR) [01789022] **5157**

SEZNAM PLATNYCH CESKOSLOVENSKYCH STATNICH NOREM **See** SEZNAM PLATNYCH CESKOSLOVENSKYCH STATNICH A OBOROVYCH NOREM **5157**

SEZNAM PREDNASEK LEKARSKE FAKULTY V HRADCI KRALOVE VE STUDIJNIM ROCE ... (XR) [24445843] **2522**

SEZNAM PREJETIH KNJIG, REVIJ IN STATISTICNIH PULIKACIJ V . **See** SEZNAM PREJETIH STATISTICNIH PUBLIKACIJ, KNJIG IN REVIJ V ... / ZAVOD SR SLOVENIJE ZA STATISTIKO **5338**

SEZNAM PREJETIH STATISTICNIH PUBLIKACIJ, KNJIG IN REVIJ V ... / ZAVOD SR SLOVENIJE ZA STATISTIKO (XV) [07934716] **5338**

SF CAMERAWORK QUARTERLY **See** CAMERAWORK **4368**

SF (LOS ANGELES, CALIF.) **See** SF UNIQUE VACATION SELECTIONS **5491**

SF NEWSLETTER (US) [03236407] **2404**

●SF UNIQUE VACATION SELECTIONS (US/1070-5856) [28402169] **5491**

SF WEEKLY (SAN FRANCISCO, CALIF.) (US/1060-2526) [22683610] **5640**

SFERA ROMA **CEASED.** (IT) [I11203145] **2854**

SFI BULLETIN (US/0085-6592) [01607740] **4917**

SFINX (DK/0105-7618) [I01057618] **2629**

SFOGLIALIBRO (IT/1120-253X) [I1120253X] **4819**

SFP (MONTREAL) (CN/1181-8522) [24368169] **4152**

SFPE HANDBOOK OF FIRE PROTECTION ENGINEERING (US) **2292**

SFRA NEWSLETTER **See** SFRA REVIEW **3435**

●SFRA REVIEW (US) [25620630] **3435**

SFS FLYER (US) [05979840] **2324**

SFS-LUETTELO (FI) [04316139] **2030**

SFT. SMARTER FINANCIAL TECHNOLOGIES ENGLISH ED (FR/0765-0418) [I07650418] **811**

SFWA BULLETIN **See** BULLETIN OF THE SCIENCE FICTION WRITERS OF AMERICA **3370**

SGA NEWSLETTER (US) [05284353] **2483**

SGM QUARTERLY (UK) [26883403] **570**

SGNA NEWS (US/1057-9095) [24152833] **3748**

SGPB ALERT (US/8755-7282) [11453271] **1520**

SHA **CEASED.** (JA) [02247139] **245**

SHAA (US/0743-4189) [03795384] 1885, **4393**

SHAANXI YIXUE ZAZHI (CC/1000-7377) [I10007377] **3640**

SHABAB AL-ARAB (LY) [11104343] **2664**

SHABAB WA-AL-RIYADAH (MAJLIS AL-ALA LIL-SHABAB WA-LA-RIYADAH (YEMEN). ALAQAT WA-AL-ILAM) (YE) [09788064] **4917**

SHABAB WA-AL-RIYADAH (TUNIS, TUNISIA) (TI) [11168011] **4917**

SHABAB WADI AL-DHAHAB (MR) [09986583] **4917**

SHABBAT SHALOM (US) [13452768] **5067**

SHADE TREE : MONTHLY BULLETIN OF THE NEW JERSEY FEDERATION OF SHADE TREE COMMISSIONS, THE (US) [09780270] **2431**

SHADES (CN/0228-3115) [06960303] **4152**

SHADES VALLEY SUN, THE *CEASED.* (US/0896-615X) [12046754] **5628**

SHADOW PLAY (US/1046-5243) [20436773] **3435**

SHADOW : THE NEWSLETTER OF THE TRADITIONAL COSMOLOGICAL SOCIETY (UK/0266-8599) [13844476] **399**

SHADOWS CHRIST CHURCH (NZ/1170-9758) [I11709758] **3947**

SHAHID (TEHRAN, IRAN : 1983) (IR) [19568494] **2493**

SHAHID (TRIPOLI, LIBYA) (LY) [10218016] **2643**

SHAIR INTERNATIONAL FORUM (CN/1185-3158) [24368138] **2545**

SHAKAI BUNKA KENKYU (JA) [02878463] **5218**

SHAKAI FUKUSHI NO DOKO (JA) [01797096] 2893, **5307**

SHAKAI FUKUSHI ROPPO / KOSEISHO SHAKAIKYOKU JIDO KATEIKYOKU ENGOKYOKU KANSHU (JA) [08884249] **5307**

SHAKAI FUKUSHI SHISETSU CHOSA KOKOKU (JA) [06469154] **5307**

SHAKAI HOKEN ROMU HANDOBUKKU (JA) [05916588] 1710, **5307**

SHAKAI HOKEN ROMU ROPPO (JA) [03528404] **3154**

SHAKAI HYORON (JA) [03249901] **1710**

SHAKAI JINRUIGAKU NENPO (JA) [02485916] **245**

SHAKAI KAGAKU KENKYU (TOKYO. 1948) (JA/0387-3307) [01765427] **5218**

SHAKAI KAGAKU RON SHU (JA) [01797414] **5218**

SHAKAI KAGAKU TOKYU (JA) [02243524] **5218**

SHAKAI KEIZAI SHIGAKU (JA/0038-0113) [01765428] **1583**

SHAKAI MONDAI KENKYU (JA) [03012682] **5307**

SHAKAI-RONENGAKU (JA) [02432700] **5182**

SHAKAI SEIKATSU TOKEI SHIHYO (JA) [10514589] **5257**

SHAKAI SHISO SHI KENKYU (JA) [04222251] **5218**

SHAKAI SHUGI KEIEI GAKKAI (JAPAN) *See* SHAKAI SHUGI KEIEI GAKKAI KENKYU NENPO **1626**

SHAKAI SHUGI KEIEI GAKKAI KENKYU NENPO (JA) [09456082] **1626**

SHAKAIGAKU HYORON (JA/0021-5414) [01765429] **5258**

SHAKAIGAKU KENKYUJO KIYO (JA/0285-4015) [08699258] **5218**

SHAKAIGAKU NENSHI (JA) [01790081] **5258**

SHAKAIKA KYOIKU KENKYU / NIHON SHAKAIKA KYOIKU GAKKAI HENSHU (JA) [09407886] **5218**

SHAKAIKA KYOIKU RONSO : NIHON SHAKAIKA KYOIKU KENKYUKAI NENPO (JA) [09030933] **5218**

SHAKAISHI KENKYU (JA) [09144111] **5258**

SHAKER MESSENGER, THE (US/0270-9368) [04368270] **2760**

SHAKER QUARTERLY, THE (US/0582-9348) [01681198] **4997**

SHAKESPEARE ASSOCIATION (GREAT BRITAIN) *See* SHAKESPEARE QUARTO FACSIMILES **5368**

SHAKESPEARE BULLETIN (US/0748-2558) [10918867] 388, **5368**

SHAKESPEARE IN SOUTHERN AFRICA : JOURNAL OF THE SHAKESPEARE SOCIETY OF SOUTHERN AFRICA (SA/1011-582X) [18672420] 3435, **5368**

SHAKESPEARE JAHRBUCH (GW/0080-9128) [01765433] **3435**

SHAKESPEARE NEWSLETTER, THE (US/0037-3214) [01765434] **3352**

SHAKESPEARE ON FILM NEWSLETTER (US/0739-6570) [03665688] **3435**

SHAKESPEARE QUARTERLY (US/0037-3222) [01644507] **3435**

SHAKESPEARE QUARTO FACSIMILES (UK) [01765431] 3435, **5368**

SHAKESPEARE STUDIES (JA/0582-9402) [01937004] **3435**

SHAKESPEARE SURVEY (CAMBRIDGE) (UK/0080-9152) [01765436] 3352, **434**

SHAKESPEARE YEARBOOK (US/1045-9456) [20292484] **3435**

SHAKESPEAREAN CRITICISM (DETROIT, MICH.) (US/0883-9123) [10658787] **3352**

SHAKHMATY V SSSR (RU/0132-0947) [06077742] **4866**

SHAKHTNYI I KARERNYI TRANSPORT (RU) [02716416] **2151**

SHAKOPEE VALLEY NEWS, THE (US) [01765441] **5698**

SHALE SHAKER (US/0037-3257) [02267649] 4278, **1397**

SHALOM (UK) [05713560] **5052**

SHAMA (TORONTO) (CN/0712-5704) [09336350] **2273**

SHAMAN'S DRUM (US/0887-8897) [13441208] **4997**

SHAMROCK TEXAN, THE (US) [13877376] **5754**

SHAN CHA (CC) [06875085] 2324, **3435**

SHAN HAI CHING (CC) [11394453] **2508**

SHAN-HSI CHIAO YU (CC) [10064255] **1783**

SHAN-HSI CHIAO YU (TAI-YUAN SHIH, CHINA) (CC) [10790953] **3249**

SHAN-HSI CHUNG I (CH) [08995986] **3640**

SHAN-HSI HSI CHU (CC) [09220599] **5368**

SHAN-HSI LIN YEH KO CHI (CC) [22355004] **2395**

SHAN-HSI SHIH TA HSUEH PAO. CHE HSUEH SHE HUI KO HSUEH PAN (CC) [09262513] **5218**

SHAN-HSI TA HSUEH HSUEH PAO. CHE HSUEH SHE HUI KO HSUEH PAN (CC) [09188517] **5218**

SHAN-HSI WEN HSUEH (CC) [08631202] **3435**

SHAN-TUNG HUA PAO (CC) [06664955] **2508**

SHAN-TUNG TA HSUEH HSUEH PAO. TZU JAN KO HSUEH PAN / ZIRAN KEXUE BAN. SHANDONG DAXUE XUEBAO (CC) [21707958] **5157**

SHAN-TUNG WEN HSUEH (CH) [09142134] **3436**

SHAN YEN WEN CHE *CEASED.* (US) [02245494] **2508**

SHANDONG HAIYANGXUE YUAN XUEBAO (CC/0253-3588) [08725053] **1457**

SHANDONG YIKE DAXUE XUEBAO (CC/1000-0496) [21632027] **3640**

SHANG-HAI CHEN CHIU TSA CHIH (CC) [09667900] **3640**

SHANG-HAI CHI YEH (CH) [11101108] **710**

SHANG-HAI CHIAO YU. KUNG NUNG CHIAO YU PAN (CC) [11656769] **1783**

SHANG-HAI HSI CHU (CC) [06683063] **5368**

SHANG-HAI HUA PAO (CC) [09005017] **2664**

SHANG-HAI I SHU CHIA (CC/0257-5639) [19804496] **364**

SHANG-HAI KUAI CHI (CC) [09493531] **751**

SHANG-HAI MEI SHU NIEN KAN / SHANG-HAI MEI SHU NIEN KAN PIEN CHI TSU PIEN (CC) [11093436] **364**

SHANG-HAI PO WU KUAN CHI KAN (CC) [11135413] **2664**

SHANG-HAI SHIH CHUNG HSIAO HSUEH CHIAO YU KUNG TSO CHING CHUNG HSIAO HSUEH CHIAO YU KUNG TSO CHING YEN HSUAN PIEN. HSIAO HSUEH FEN TSE / SHANG-HAI SHIH CHIAO YU CHU PIEN (CC) [11853120] **1783**

SHANG-HAI SHIH CHUNG HSIAO HSUEH CHIAO YU KUNG TSO CHING YEN HSUAN PIEN. CHUNG HSUEH LI KO FEN TSE / SHANG-HAI SHIH CHIAO YU HU PIEN (CC) [11848826] **5157**

SHANG-HAI SHIH CHUNG HSIAO HSUEH CHIAO YU KUNG TSO CHING YEN HSUAN PIEN. CHUNG HSUEH TSUNG HO FEN TSE / SHANG-HAI SHIH CHIAO YU CHU PIEN (CC) [11848712] **1783**

SHANG-HAI SHIH CHUNG HSIAO HSUEH CHIAO YU KUNG TSO CHING YEN HSUAN PIEN. CHUNG HSUEH WEN KO FEN TSE / SHANG-HAI SHIH CHIAO YU CHU PIEN (CC) [11848928] **1783**

SHANG-HAI SHIH HSIAO HSUEH CHIAO YU KUNG TSO CHING YEN HSUAN PIEN / SHANG-HAI SHIH CHIAO YU CHU PIEN (CC) [11848621] **1783**

SHANG-HAI TIEN WEN TAI NIEN KAN (CH) [08797845] **399**

SHANG-HAI WEN HSUEH (CC) [06955944] **3436**

SHANGHAI HUANJING KEXUE (CC/1000-3975) [I10003975] **2181**

SHANGHAI JIAOTONG DAXUE XUEBAO (CC/0253-9942) [06658674] 1095, **5157**

SHANGHAI KEJI DAXUE XUEBAO (CC/0258-7041) [11594959] **5157**

SHANGHAI MIANYIXUE ZAZHI (CC/1001-2478) [I10012478] **3676**

SHANGHAI NONGXUEYUAN XUEBAO (CC/1000-193X) [I1000193X] **134**

SHANGHAI NONYE XUEBAO (CC/1000-3924) [21587671] **134**

SHANGHAI PICTORIAL (CC) [10967962] **2508**

SHANGHAI YIKE DAXUE XUEBAO (CC/0257-8131) [17725035] **3640**

SHANGHAI YIXUE (CC/0253-9934) [04893619] **3640**

●SHANGRI-LA (WASHINGTON, D.C.) (US/1061-3919) [25285370] **3471**

SHANKAR'S CHILDREN'S ART NUMBER (II) [24395710] 1069, **330**

SHANNON COUNTY CURRENT WAVE (US) [22992158] **5704**

SHANTIH (US/0037-329X) [02878781] **3436**

SHANXI DAXUE XUEBAO. ZIRAN KEXUE BAN (CC/0253-2395) [08863269] **5157**

SHANXI XIN YIYAO (CH/0253-9853) [08933872] **3641**

SHAO NIEN KO CHI (CH) [04265133] **5157**

SHAO NIEN KO HSUEH (CC) [07986478] **5157**

SHAO NIEN TAN SO CHE / KUANG-TUNG SHENG KO PU CHUANG TSO HSIEH HUI (CH) [11006755] **5157**

SHAONIEN ZHONGGUO (SAN FRANCISCO, CALIF.) (US/0749-7679) [09861800] **5640**

SHAPE (SEATTLE, WASH.) (US/0890-3131) [14222777] **4802**

SHAPE (WOODLAND HILLS, CALIF.) (US/0744-5121) [08391872] 5566, **2601**

SHAPE WRITE UP *See* PERSONAL BEST **2600**

SHARDS NEWSLETTER, THE (US/0272-1910) [06444477] **2594**

SHARE (BERKELEY, CALIF.) (US/0273-2343) [07068989] **3249**

SHARE INTERNATIONAL (NE/0169-1341) [11177417] **4186**

SHARE THE WORD (US/0199-5049) [05951162] 5036, **5019**

SHARE (TORONTO) (CN/0709-4647) [05696329] **5794**

SHARED VOICES (CN/1193-8315) [27725103] **3471**

SHAREHOLDER REMEDIES IN CANADA (CN) **3103**

SHAREOWNERSHIP (US/0278-1514) [02975793] **913**

SHAREWARE GRAB-BAG [COMPUTER FILE] (US) [25777876] **1290**

SHAREWARE MAGAZINE *CEASED.* (US/1042-0681) [17444429] **1202**

SHARIKAH AL-TUNISIYAH LIL-BANK. CONSEIL D'ADMINISTRATION *See* REPORT OF THE BOARD OF DIRECTORS **1516**

SHARING IDEAS (US/0886-1501) [12866887] **2545**

SHARING OUR CARING *CEASED.* (US) **1885**

SHARING THE PRACTICE (US/0193-8274) [03695107] **4997**

SHARING THE VICTORY (US/0745-1245) [08853421] 4997, **4917**

SHARKARA : QUARTERLY BULLETIN OF THE NATIONAL SUGAR INSTITUTE, KANPUR (II) [09780353] **2357**

SHARON REPORTER, THE (US) [12294325] **5770**

SHARP GIHO (JA/0285-0362) [09579631] **5157**

SHARP NEWS (US) 4819, **4822**

SHARQ (CAIRO, EGYPT) (UA/0582-9615) [01931993] **2664**

SHARQ IULDUZI (UZ/0488-549X) [04796238] **3436**

SHASHIN KOGYO (JA/0371-0106) [I03710106] **4376**

SHASHKEVYCHIIANA (CN) [04964033] 3436, **3321**

SHAVER NEWS (CN/0037-3338) [02155336] **221**

SHAVIAN (LONDON) (UK/0037-3346) [01938305] **3436**

SHAVUA BA-KIBUTS HA-ARTSI *See* SHAVUA, HA- **4546**

SHAVUA, HA- (IS) [02245698] **4546**

SHAW (US/0741-5842) [07556559] **3352**

SHAW UNIVERSITY *See* ALUMNI DIRECTORY / SHAW UNIVERSITY **1099**

SHAWANO EVENING LEADER (US/0749-7148) [11167328] **5770**

SHAWNEE COUNTY HISTORICAL SOCIETY *See* BULLETIN - SHAWNEE COUNTY HISTORICAL SOCIETY **2725**

SHAWNEE-CRIDERSVILLE PRESS (US/0274-9408) [06727555] **5730**

SHAWNEE — Alphabetical Title Index

SHAWNEE NEWS-STAR (US) [12110604] **5732**

SHAWNEE SUN (SHAWNEE, OKLA.), THE (US/1056-7550) [23845643] **5732**

SHAW'S DIRECTORY OF COURTS IN ENGLAND AND WALES (UK/0307-3343) [02243179] **3048**

SHAW'S DIRECTORY OF COURTS IN THE UNITED KINGDOM (UK) [11225932] **3048**

SHD (UK) [06971616] 5157, **1202**

SHE (UK) [02996597] **5566**

SHE (AUSTRALIAN EDITION) (AT) **5566**

SHE HUI FU LI CHIH PIAO. SOCIAL WELFARE INDICATORS REPUBLIC OF CHINA (CH) [03212952] **5307**

SHE HUI HSUEH KAN (CH/0077-5851) [02014916] **5258**

SHE HUI KO HSUEH CHI KAN (LIAO-NING SHE HUI KO HSUEH YUAN) (CC) [07220402] **5218**

SHE HUI KO HSUEH HSUEH PAO / HSIANG-TAN TA HSUEH (CC) [11418997] **1847**

SHE HUI KO HSUEH / SHANG-HAI SHE HUI KO HSUEH YUAN, SHE HUI KO HSUEH PIEN WEI HUI (CC) [06656558] **5219**

SHE HUI KO HSUEH YEN CHIU (CHENG-TU, CHINA) (CC) [11265288] **5236**

SHE HUI PAO HSIEN NIEN KAN (CH) [04542221] **5307**

SHE HULK (US) **4866**

SHE YING CHIA TSO HSIN SHANG (HK) [04421141] **4376**

SHE YING SHIH CHIEH (HK) [01790381] **4376**

SHE YING TSUNG KAN (CC) [08630642] **4376**

SHEARS See BOXBOARD CONTAINERS **4218**

SHEBA (UK) [06851699] **2493**

SHEBOYGAN FALLS NEWS, THE (US/0897-4543) [13067451] **5770**

SHEBOYGAN PRESS (SHEBOYGAN, WIS. : 1924) (US/0749-7121) [11167357] **5770**

SHEEP AND GOAT, WOOL AND MOHAIR (US/0895-1500) [08617047] **221**

SHEEP AND GOATS (US/0094-3851) [02456023] **221**

SHEEP AND LAMBS ON FEED / IOWA CROP AND LIVESTOCK REPORTING SERVICE (US) [06230744] **221**

SHEEP AND WOOL / IOWA CROP AND LIVESTOCK REPORTING SERVICE (US) [06411528] **221**

SHEEP BREEDER AND SHEEPMAN MAGAZINE (US/0037-3400) [08311017] **221**

SHEEP CANADA MAGAZINE (CN/0702-8881) [03520236] **221**

SHEEP DAIRY NEWS (UK/0952-1380) [l09521380] 198, **221**

SHEEP FOCUS "N" FACTS (CN/0228-2933) [07314012] **221**

SHEEP INDUSTRY REVIEW VICTORIA (AT) [03759926] **221**

SHEEP MAGAZINE (US/0279-9200) [07244997] **221**

SHEEP RESEARCH JOURNAL (US/1057-1809) [21475788] **221**

SHEEP RETURNS (NZ) [02240644] **221**

SHEET - CSIRO, DIVISION OF BUILDING RESEARCH (AT/0314-5956) [05973771] **627**

SHEET METAL AUSTRALIA See METALWORKING AUSTRALIA **4011**

SHEET METAL INDUSTRIES (UK/0037-3435) [01915395] **4019**

SHEET METAL INDUSTRIES YEARBOOK (UK/0305-7798) [01798957] **4019**

SHEET METAL WORKERS JOURNAL (US/0037-3451) [03923231] **4019**

SHEET MUSIC EXCHANGE, THE (US/0741-7780) [10203485] **4152**

SHEET MUSIC MAGAZINE. EASY PLAY (US/1045-3911) [20086298] **4153**

SHEET MUSIC MAGAZINE. STANDARD PIANO See SHEET MUSIC MAGAZINE. STANDARD PIANO/GUITAR **4153**

SHEET MUSIC MAGAZINE. STANDARD PIANO/GUITAR (US/0273-6462) [06782319] **4153**

SHEETS, PILLOWCASES, AND TOWELS CEASED. (US/0145-496X) [02541411] **5355**

SHEFFIELD AND SOUTH YORKSHIRE CHAMBERS OF COMMERCE See SHEFFIELD AND SOUTH YORKSHIRE CHAMBERS OF COMMERCE DIRECTORY **851**

SHEFFIELD AND SOUTH YORKSHIRE CHAMBERS OF COMMERCE DIRECTORY (UK/0950-8945) [16878281] **851**

SHEHUI KEXUE LUNCONG (CH/0077-5835) [02021831] **5219**

SHEKEL / CHAMBRE DE COMMERCE FRANCE-ISRAEL (FR) [26122735] **821**

SHEKEL (PARIS, FRANCE) See MAISON FRANCE ISRAEL / CHAMBRE DE COMMERCE FRANCE-ISRAEL **844**

SHEKSPIROVSKIE CHTENIIA (RU) [07295378] **3436**

SHELBURNE COUNTY TELECASTER (CN/0319-5570) [02442273] **1139**

SHELBURNE HISTORICAL SOCIETY (NEWSLETTER) (CN/0822-4080) [09859827] **2760**

SHELBY COUNTY ANCESTORS (US/8756-131X) [11452323] **2472**

SHELBY COUNTY REPORTER (1955) (US/1063-9489) [11832262] **5628**

SHELBY EXCHANGE (US) **2472**

SHELBY PROMOTER, THE (US) [14146472] **5706**

SHELBY REPORT OF THE SOUTHEAST, THE (US/0194-1968) [05356127] **2357**

SHELBY REPORT OF THE SOUTHWEST (US/0192-916X) [05137919] **2357**

SHELBY STAR, THE (US/1043-1950) [13294279] **5724**

SHELBYVILLE TIMES-GAZETTE (US) [13518744] **5746**

SHELDON'S MAJOR STORES AND CHAINS (US) **957**

SHELDON'S RETAIL DIRECTORY OF THE UNITED STATES AND CANADA (US) [05088986] **1087**

SHELDON'S RETAIL DIRECTORY OF THE UNITED STATES AND CANADA AND PHELON'S RESIDENT BUYERS AND MERCHANDISE BROKERS (US/0094-0453) [01793585] **957**

SHELF LISTING - MIDWESTERN REGIONAL LIBRARY SYSTEM (CN/0710-6564) [08144131] **5794**

SHELL AGRICULTURE 1988 (UK/0953-9026) [l09539026] **134**

SHELL MANAGEMENT ANNUAL REPORT (US/0276-2137) [07310342] **2313**

SHELL NEWS (US/0275-3243) [05082408] **4278**

SHELL (WABAN) (US/0146-3985) [02934559] **3471**

SHELLFISH MARKET REVIEW (US/0191-2054) [04791489] **2313**

SHELLS AND SEA LIFE CEASED. (US/0747-6078) [10756383] **5597**

SHELTER (AT) [01791552] **2835**

SHELTER (GERMANTOWN) (US/0164-6559) [04420731] **627**

SHELTER ISLAND REPORTER (US/0746-066X) [09723302] **5721**

SHELTER SENSE (US/0734-3078) [05630107] 4288, **5307**

SHELTER TROPICS (NR) [03301021] **308**

SHELTERFORCE (US/0885-9612) [04416845] **2835**

SHELTIE INTERNATIONAL (US/0745-2012) [08913019] **4288**

SHELTIE PACESETTER (US/0744-6608) [08483092] **4288**

SHELTON-MASON COUNTY JOURNAL, THE (US) [17319687] **5762**

SHEM TOV (CN/0843-6924) [23598982] **2472**

SHEMAKHA, RUSSIA. ASTROFIZICHESKAIA OBSERVATORIIA See TSIRKULIAR-ASTROFIZICHESKAIA OBSERVATORIIA, SHEMAKHA, RUSSIA **401**

SHEN HUA / SHEN HUA (CC) [09257050] **3436**

SHEN PIEN TI KO HSUEH (CH) [08752288] **5157**

SHEN-YANG NUNG YEH TA HSUEH HSUEH PAO (CC) [17691231] **134**

SHEN-YANG SHIH FAN HSUEH YUAN HSUEH PAO. CHE HSUEH SHE HUI KO HSUEH PAN (CC) [10600847] **5236**

SHENANDOAH (US/0037-3583) [01765447] **3436**

SHENANDOAH HERALD See SHENANDOAH HERALD, SHENANDOAH VALLEY, THE **5759**

SHENANDOAH HERALD, SHENANDOAH VALLEY, THE (US/0746-6846) [10221055] **5759**

SHENATON LE-MIKRA ULE-HEKER HA-MIZRAH HA-KADUM (IS) [02310423] **5019**

SHENG HSUEH HSUEH PAO (CC/0371-0025) [08277194] **4453**

SHENG HUO YU CHIEN KANG (HK) [02917709] **4802**

SHENG LI CHIH KUANG (CH/0582-9860) [01765449] **2664**

SHENG LI HSUEH PAO (CC/0371-0874) [02245467] **587**

SHENG LI KO HSUEH CHIN CHAN (CC/0559-7765) [07506671] **587**

SHENG TAI HSUEH PAO (CC/1000-0933) [10575846] **2221**

SHENG TAI HSUEH TSA CHIH / CHUNG-KUO SHENG TAI HSUEH HUI CHU PAN (CC) [12969258] **2221**

SHENG WU FANG CHIH TUNG PAO (CC) **473**

SHENG WU HSUEH TUNG PAO (CC/0006-3193) [10476873] **473**

SHENGTAIXUE ZAZHI (CH/1000-4890) [l10004890] **2221**

SHENGWU FANGZHI TONGBAO (CH/1000-1034) [l10001034] **473**

SHENGWU GONGCHENG XUEBAO (CC/1000-3061) [21722531] **3696**

SHENGWU HUAXUE YU SHENGWU WULI JINZHAN (CH/0253-9918) [03622235] **473**

SHENGWU HUAXUE ZAZHI (CC/1000-8543) [14997587] **3696**

SHENGWU SHUXUE XUEBAO (CH/1001-9626) [l10019626] 473, 3641, **3534**

SHENGZHI YU BIYUN (CC/0253-357X) [08725157] 3768, **591**

SHENJING JINGSHEN JIBING ZAZHI (CC/1000-2464) [11171085] **3846**

SHENYANG YAOXUEYUAN XUEBAO (CC/1000-1727) [21663394] **4329**

SHEPARD'S ACTS AND CASES BY POPULAR NAMES, FEDERAL AND STATE (US/0080-9233) [01765454] **3048**

SHEPARD'S ALABAMA CASE NAMES CITATOR (US) [14442988] **3048**

SHEPARD'S ALABAMA CITATIONS (US/0730-3572) [05729958] **3048**

● SHEPARD'S ALABAMA CODE CITATIONS (US) [27064228] **3048**

SHEPARD'S ALABAMA EXPRESS CITATIONS CEASED. (US/1056-8980) [23890954] **3048**

SHEPARD'S ALASKA CASE NAMES CITATOR (US) [1052-5696) [22328505] **3048**

SHEPARD'S ALASKA CITATIONS (US/0488-6097) [20591246] **3048**

SHEPARD'S ARIZONA CASE NAMES CITATOR (US) [14482371] **3048**

SHEPARD'S ARIZONA CITATIONS (US/0730-3629) [10852159] **3048**

SHEPARD'S ARIZONA EXPRESS CITATIONS (US/1055-2510) [22959325] **3048**

SHEPARD'S ARKANSAS CASE NAMES CITATOR (US) [14443040] **3048**

SHEPARD'S ARKANSAS CITATIONS (US/0730-3637) [08044605] **3048**

SHEPARD'S ATLANTIC REPORTER CITATIONS (ADVANCE SHEET EDITION) (US) [02349575] **3048**

SHEPARD'S BANKING LAW CITATIONS CEASED. (US) [20579050] **3088**

SHEPARD'S BANKRUPTCY CASE NAMES CITATOR (US/1048-0587) [20844770] **3048**

SHEPARD'S BANKRUPTCY CITATIONS (US/0730-1936) [20654925] **3048**

SHEPARD'S CALIFORNIA CASE NAMES CITATOR (US/1048-0757) [12737361] **3049**

SHEPARD'S CALIFORNIA CITATIONS (1919) (US/0730-3661) [10868144] **3049**

SHEPARD'S CALIFORNIA CONSTRUCTION LAW REPORTER (US/1055-9469) [23377978] **3049**

SHEPARD'S CALIFORNIA ENVIRONMENTAL LAW & REGULATION REPORTER (US/1059-5414) [24453530] **3116**

SHEPARD'S CALIFORNIA EXPRESS CITATIONS CEASED. (US/1053-8283) [22650576] **3049**

SHEPARD'S CALIFORNIA REPORTER CITATIONS (US/0559-7781) [20378776] **3049**

SHEPARD'S CITATIONS FOR ANNOTATIONS (US/1047-9163) [20778867] **3049**

SHEPARD'S CITATIONS OF ALL CASES IN THE FEDERAL REPORTER WHICH HAVE HAD A SUBSEQUENT CITATION See SHEPARD'S FEDERAL CITATIONS **3050**

● SHEPARD'S CLEAN AIR ACT REPORTER (US/1068-235X) [27483627] **3116**

SHEPARD'S CODE OF FEDERAL REGULATIONS CITATIONS (US/0730-465X) [10070302] **3049**

SHEPARD'S COLORADO CASE NAMES CITATOR (US/1052-5653) [22328386] **3049**

Alphabetical Title Index — SHEPARD'S

SHEPARD'S COLORADO CITATIONS (US/0730-2096) [07964774] **3049**

SHEPARD'S COLORADO EXPRESS CITATIONS *CEASED.* (US/1056-4217) [23175853] **3049**

SHEPARD'S CONNECTICUT CASE NAMES CITATOR (US) [12593049] **3049**

SHEPARD'S CONNECTICUT CITATIONS (US/0730-3688) [05729929] **3049**

SHEPARD'S CONNECTICUT EXPRESS CITATIONS (US/1055-9507) [23373705] **3049**

SHEPARD'S CORPORATION LAW CITATIONS *CEASED.* (US/8750-1104) [11006967] **3103**

SHEPARD'S CORPORATION LAW CITATIONS : A COMPILATION OF CITATIONS TO DECISIONS OF THE UNITED STATES SUPREME COURT, LOWER FEDERAL COURTS, AND STATE COURTS IN CORPORATION CASES, TO CORPORATION PROVISIONS OF STATE CODES, AND TO THE MODEL BUSINESS CORPORATION ACT *CEASED.* (US) [13026349] **3103**

SHEPARD'S CRIMINAL JUSTICE CITATIONS (US/0363-0978) [01951002] **3109**

SHEPARD'S DAKOTA CITATIONS AND KEY NUMBER ANNOTATIONS *See* SHEPARD'S SOUTH DAKOTA CITATIONS **3054**

SHEPARD'S DELAWARE CITATIONS (US/0730-5869) [10852155] **3049**

SHEPARD'S DISTRICT OF COLUMBIA CITATIONS (US) [01765458] **3049**

SHEPARD'S ELDER CARE/LAW NEWSLETTER (US/1056-1218) [23721333] 5182, **3119**

SHEPARD'S ENVIRONMENTAL LIABILITY, ENFORCEMENT & PENALTIES REPORTER (US/1068-5804) [27707269] **3116**

SHEPARD'S ENVIRONMENTAL LIABILITY IN COMMERCIAL TRANSACTIONS REPORTER (US/1054-4771) [22901903] **3116**

●SHEPARD'S ENVIRONMENTAL REGULATION SUMMARIES (US/1070-213X) [28303421] **3116**

●SHEPARD'S EVIDENCE CITATIONS (US/1060-7625) [25058656] **3049**

SHEPARD'S FEDERAL CASE NAMES CITATOR, DISTRICT OF COLUMBIA CIRCUIT CASES (US/1048-0331) [20842107] **3049**

SHEPARD'S FEDERAL CASE NAMES CITATOR, EIGHTH CIRCUIT CASES (US/1048-0250) [20841568] **3049**

SHEPARD'S FEDERAL CASE NAMES CITATOR, ELEVENTH CIRCUIT CASES (US) [17355851] **3049**

SHEPARD'S FEDERAL CASE NAMES CITATOR, FIFTH CIRCUIT CASES (US/1048-0102) [20840126] **3049**

SHEPARD'S FEDERAL CASE NAMES CITATOR, FIRST CIRCUIT CASES (US) [16687571] **3049**

SHEPARD'S FEDERAL CASE NAMES CITATOR, FOURTH CIRCUIT CASES (US/1048-0099) [20840097] **3049**

SHEPARD'S FEDERAL CASE NAMES CITATOR : NINTH CIRCUIT CASES (US) [15610118] **3049**

SHEPARD'S FEDERAL CASE NAMES CITATOR, SECOND CIRCUIT CASES (US) [16262836] **3049**

SHEPARD'S FEDERAL CASE NAMES CITATOR, SEVENTH CIRCUIT CASES (US/1048-0242) [20841523] **3049**

SHEPARD'S FEDERAL CASE NAMES CITATOR, SIXTH CIRCUIT CASES (US/1048-0234) [20841481] **3049**

SHEPARD'S FEDERAL CASE NAMES CITATOR, TENTH CIRCUIT CASES (US) [16687341] **3049**

SHEPARD'S FEDERAL CASE NAMES CITATOR, THIRD CIRCUIT CASES (US/1048-0080) [20840066] **3050**

SHEPARD'S FEDERAL CIRCUIT CASE NAMES CITATOR (US/1048-034X) [20842081] **3050**

SHEPARD'S FEDERAL CIRCUIT TABLE (US/0730-7039) [22328582] **3050**

SHEPARD'S FEDERAL CITATIONS (US/0730-4633) [08202143] **3050**

SHEPARD'S FEDERAL ENERGY LAW CITATIONS (QUARTERLY) (US/0746-312X) [09931256] 1956, **3050**

SHEPARD'S FEDERAL LABOR LAW CASE NAMES CITATOR (US/1048-0579) [20844741] **3154**

SHEPARD'S FEDERAL LABOR LAW CITATIONS (US/0559-779X) [08039684] **3154**

SHEPARD'S FEDERAL LAW CITATIONS IN SELECTED LAW REVIEWS (US/0094-9531) [01795840] **3050**

SHEPARD'S FEDERAL MERIT SYSTEMS CITATIONS *CEASED.* (US/1053-5799) [22587932] **3050**

SHEPARD'S FEDERAL OCCUPATIONAL SAFETY AND HEALTH CITATIONS (US/0732-7722) [08092781] 2870, **3050**

SHEPARD'S FEDERAL RULES CITATIONS : A COMPILATION OF CITATIONS TO THE FEDERAL RULES OF CIVIL PROCEDURE . . (US) [17861438] **3143**

SHEPARD'S FEDERAL TAX CITATIONS (US/0732-7714) [18578575] 4747, **3050**

SHEPARD'S FEDERAL TAX LOCATOR *CEASED.* (US/0730-4714) [01604757] 4747, **3050**

SHEPARD'S FLORIDA CASE NAME CITATOR (US/1048-096X) [12174656] **3050**

SHEPARD'S FLORIDA CITATIONS (US/0730-3718) [03363189] **3050**

SHEPARD'S FLORIDA EXPRESS CITATIONS *CEASED.* (US/1050-9100) [21680597] **3050**

SHEPARD'S GEORGIA CASE NAME CITATOR (US/8750-1074) [10988514] **3050**

SHEPARD'S GEORGIA CITATIONS (US/0730-3742) [08041393] **3050**

SHEPARD'S GEORGIA CODE CITATIONS (US) [27064283] **3050**

SHEPARD'S GEORGIA EXPRESS CITATIONS *CEASED.* (US/1058-9732) [24448853] **3050**

SHEPARD'S HAWAII CASE NAMES CITATOR (US/1052-5920) [22332383] **3050**

SHEPARD'S HAWAII CITATIONS (US/0730-5885) [20586689] **3050**

SHEPARD'S IDAHO CITATIONS (US/0730-5893) [08036999] **3050**

SHEPARD'S ILLINOIS CASE NAMES CITATOR (US) [12780413] **3050**

SHEPARD'S ILLINOIS CITATIONS (US/0730-3904) [08077744] **3050**

SHEPARD'S ILLINOIS EXPRESS CITATIONS *CEASED.* (US/1057-3380) [23866566] **3050**

SHEPARD'S ILLINOIS TORT REPORTER (US/1053-1769) [22237124] **3050**

SHEPARD'S IMMIGRATION AND NATURALIZATION CITATIONS (US) [09164159] 1921, **3050**

SHEPARD'S INDIANA CASE NAMES CITATOR (US/1052-5939) [22332431] **3050**

SHEPARD'S INDIANA CITATIONS (US/0730-3831) [08044422] **3051**

●SHEPARD'S INDIANA EXPRESS CITATIONS (US/1071-961X) [28359928] **3051**

SHEPARD'S INSURANCE LAW CITATIONS *CEASED.* (US/1048-082X) [20850110] **3051**

SHEPARD'S IOWA CASE NAMES CITATOR (US) [12564321] **3051**

SHEPARD'S IOWA CITATIONS (US/0730-3866) [03921929] **3051**

SHEPARD'S KANSAS CASE NAMES CITATOR (US/1052-5955) [12498168] **3051**

SHEPARD'S KANSAS CITATIONS (US/0730-3947) [08019738] **3051**

●SHEPARD'S KANSAS EXPRESS CITATIONS (US/1069-0506) [27750680] **3051**

SHEPARD'S KENTUCKY CASE NAMES CITATOR (US) [14443120] **3051**

SHEPARD'S KENTUCKY CITATIONS (US/0730-3971) [08039106] **3051**

SHEPARD'S KENTUCKY EXPRESS CITATIONS *CEASED.* (US/1058-9600) [24356589] **3051**

SHEPARD'S LABOR ARBITRATION CITATIONS (US/1049-5096) [21207202] **3154**

SHEPARD'S LAW REVIEW CITATIONS (US/0582-9887) [20654236] **3051**

SHEPARD'S LOUISIANA CASE NAMES CITATOR (US/1048-0773) [20849086] **3051**

SHEPARD'S LOUISIANA CITATIONS (US/0730-4005) [08042113] **3051**

SHEPARD'S MAINE CASE NAMES CITATOR (US/1052-5971) [22332615] **3051**

SHEPARD'S MAINE CITATIONS (US/0730-5923) [01716794] **3051**

SHEPARD'S MANUAL OF FEDERAL PRACTICE / EDITORIAL STAFF, EDITOR IN CHIEF, RUDOLPH W. FISCHER ... [ET AL.] (US) [09483107] **3051**

SHEPARD'S MARYLAND CASE NAMES CITATOR (US) [13111885] **3051**

SHEPARD'S MARYLAND CITATIONS (US/0730-403X) [08024358] **3051**

●SHEPARD'S MARYLAND CODE CITATIONS (US) [27064099] **3051**

●SHEPARD'S MARYLAND EXPRESS CITATIONS (US/1072-1622) [28873767] **3051**

SHEPARD'S MASSACHUSETTS CASE NAMES CITATOR (US) [12593171] **3051**

SHEPARD'S MASSACHUSETTS CITATIONS (US/0730-4064) [08024911] **3051**

SHEPARD'S MASSACHUSETTS EXPRESS CITATIONS (US/1053-5780) [22298414] **3051**

SHEPARD'S MEDICAL MALPRACTICE CITATIONS (US/1048-0846) [20850143] 3641, **3051**

SHEPARD'S MICHIGAN CASE NAMES CITATOR (US/1048-0684) [12708144] **3051**

SHEPARD'S MICHIGAN CITATIONS (US/0730-4102) [08025590] **3051**

●SHEPARD'S MICHIGAN EXPRESS CITATIONS (US/1065-8815) [26785078] **3051**

SHEPARD'S MILITARY JUSTICE CITATIONS (US/0163-1101) [04086792] **3183**

SHEPARD'S MINNESOTA CASE NAMES CITATOR (US) [14443094] **3052**

SHEPARD'S MINNESOTA CITATIONS (US/0730-4145) [08025818] **3052**

●SHEPARD'S MINNESOTA EXPRESS CITATIONS (US/1068-4077) [27388345] **3052**

SHEPARD'S MISSISSIPPI CASE NAMES CITATOR (US) [14511311] **3052**

SHEPARD'S MISSISSIPPI CITATIONS (US/0488-6119) [08672622] **3052**

SHEPARD'S MISSOURI CASE NAMES CITATOR (US) [13771223] **3052**

SHEPARD'S MISSOURI CITATIONS (US/0730-417X) [08018860] **3052**

SHEPARD'S MISSOURI EXPRESS CITATIONS (US/1053-6892) [22328715] **3052**

SHEPARD'S MONTANA CITATIONS (US/0730-5931) [11182052] **3052**

SHEPARD'S NEBRASKA CASE NAMES CITATOR (US/1052-6315) [22337989] **3052**

SHEPARD'S NEBRASKA CITATIONS (US/0730-594X) [08038306] **3052**

SHEPARD'S NEVADA CASE NAMES CITATOR (US/1052-6307) [22338003] **3052**

SHEPARD'S NEVADA CITATIONS (US/0730-5974) [10104286] **3052**

SHEPARD'S NEW HAMPSHIRE CASE NAMES CITATOR (US) [14996181] **3052**

SHEPARD'S NEW HAMPSHIRE CITATIONS (US/0730-5982) [10102600] **3052**

SHEPARD'S NEW JERSEY CASE NAMES CITATOR (US) [15160753] **3052**

SHEPARD'S NEW JERSEY CITATIONS (US/0730-420X) [08043347] **3052**

SHEPARD'S NEW JERSEY EXPRESS CITATIONS (US/1060-3697) [24946813] **3052**

SHEPARD'S NEW JERSEY INSURANCE LAW & REGULATION REPORTER (US/1055-8667) [23362047] 2893, **3052**

SHEPARD'S NEW MEXICO CASE NAMES CITATOR (US) [14697243] **3052**

SHEPARD'S NEW MEXICO CITATIONS (US/0730-6008) [10065006] **3052**

SHEPARD'S NEW YORK COURT OF APPEALS CASE NAMES CITATOR (US) [14443196] **3052**

SHEPARD'S NEW YORK COURT OF APPEALS CITATIONS (US/0730-4277) [20607232] **3052**

SHEPARD'S NEW YORK MISCELLANEOUS CASE NAMES CITATOR (US/1046-7092) [20499069] **3052**

SHEPARD'S NEW YORK MISCELLANEOUS CITATIONS (US/0730-4269) [20940352] **3052**

SHEPARD'S NEW YORK STATUTE CITATIONS (US/0730-4242) [20381828] **3052**

●SHEPARD'S NEW YORK STATUTE EXPRESS CITATIONS (US/1061-7906) [25312751] **3053**

SHEPARD'S NEW YORK SUPPLEMENT CITATIONS (US/0730-4234) [20382063] **3053**

●SHEPARD'S NEW YORK SUPPLEMENT EXPRESS CITATIONS (US/1061-7914) [25361782] **3053**

SHEPARD'S NEW YORK SUPREME COURT APPELLATE DIVISION CASE NAMES CITATOR (US/1048-079X) [20849174] **3053**

SHEPARD'S NEW YORK SUPREME COURT CITATIONS (US) [01639006] **3053**

SHEPARD'S NORTH CAROLINA CASE NAMES CITATOR (US) [12593975] **3053**

SHEPARD'S NORTH CAROLINA CITATIONS (US/0730-2126) [07964606] **3053**

SHEPARD'S NORTH CAROLINA EXPRESS CITATIONS (US/1060-7633) [24989848] **3053**

SHEPARD'S Alphabetical Title Index

●SHEPARD'S NORTH CAROLINA STATUTES CITATIONS (US/1069-9511) [28202398] **3053**

SHEPARD'S NORTH DAKOTA CITATIONS (US/0730-6016) [01765476] **3053**

SHEPARD'S NORTHEASTERN REPORTER CITATIONS (US/0730-1979) [10104193] **3053**

SHEPARD'S NORTHWESTERN REPORTER CITATIONS (US/0730-4706) [10102756] **3053**

SHEPARD'S OHIO CASE NAMES CITATOR (US) [13112149] **3053**

SHEPARD'S OHIO CITATIONS (US/0730-4293) [08020373] **3053**

SHEPARD'S OHIO EXPRESS CITATIONS *CEASED*. (US/1050-9119) [21434889] **3053**

SHEPARD'S OKLAHOMA CASE NAMES CITATOR (US) [14479614] **3053**

SHEPARD'S OKLAHOMA CITATIONS (US/0730-4323) [08022148] **3053**

SHEPARD'S OKLAHOMA EXPRESS CITATIONS *CEASED*. (US/1054-903X) [22717161] **3053**

SHEPARD'S OREGON CASE NAMES CITATOR (US) [14481759] **3053**

SHEPARD'S OREGON CITATIONS (US/0730-4358) [03921897] **3053**

●SHEPARD'S OREGON EXPRESS CITATIONS (US/1069-7853) [28097172] **3053**

SHEPARD'S PACIFIC REPORTER CITATIONS; A COMPILATION OF CITATIONS TO ALL CASES REPORTED IN THE PACIFIC REPORTER. [COMPILED BY THE PUBLISHERS EDITORIAL STAFF] (US) [09474083] **3053**

SHEPARD'S PARTNERSHIP LAW CITATIONS *CEASED*. (US/8750-1112) [11006929] **3103**

SHEPARD'S PENNSYLVANIA CASE NAMES CITATOR (US) [13111989] **3053**

SHEPARD'S PENNSYLVANIA CITATIONS (US/0730-4382) [08022794] **3053**

SHEPARD'S PENNSYLVANIA EXPRESS CITATIONS *CEASED*. (US/1057-8161) [24122215] **3053**

SHEPARD'S PRODUCTS LIABILITY CITATIONS (US) [11006845] **3053**

SHEPARD'S PROFESSIONAL AND JUDICIAL CONDUCT CITATIONS (US/0730-6229) [07104931] **3143**

SHEPARD'S PUERTO RICO CASE NAMES CITATOR (US/1052-6641) [22342585] **3053**

SHEPARD'S PUERTO RICO CITATIONS (US/0730-6261) [10104224] **3054**

SHEPARD'S RESTATEMENT OF THE LAW CITATIONS (US/0730-4641) [20674319] **3054**

SHEPARD'S RHODE ISLAND CITATIONS (US/0730-6024) [10869860] **3054**

SHEPARD'S SOUTH CAROLINA CASE NAMES CITATOR (US) [14702472] **3054**

SHEPARD'S SOUTH CAROLINA CITATIONS (US/0730-6059) [08039322] **3054**

SHEPARD'S SOUTH DAKOTA CITATIONS (US/0730-6032) [10870093] **3054**

SHEPARD'S SOUTHEASTERN REPORTER CITATIONS (US/0730-4692) [10102955] **3054**

SHEPARD'S SOUTHERN REPORTER CITATIONS (US/0730-1944) [10044774] **3054**

SHEPARD'S SOUTHWESTERN REPORTER CITATIONS (US/0730-1952) [10065412] **3054**

SHEPARD'S ... TAX DICTIONARY (US) [23243235] **4747**

SHEPARD'S TENNESSEE CASE NAMES CITATOR (US/1052-6668) [22342654] **3054**

SHEPARD'S TENNESSEE CITATIONS (US/0730-4439) [08023070] **3054**

SHEPARD'S TENNESSEE CODE CITATIONS (US) [27064050] **3054**

●SHEPARD'S TENNESSEE EXPRESS CITATIONS *CEASED*. (US/1067-2591) [26998283] **3054**

SHEPARD'S TEXAS CASE NAMES CITATOR (US/8750-1120) [11006095] **3054**

SHEPARD'S TEXAS CITATIONS (US/0730-4463) [04960733] **3054**

SHEPARD'S TEXAS EXPRESS CITATIONS *CEASED*. (US/1056-8204) [23830680] **3054**

SHEPARD'S UNIFORM COMMERCIAL CODE CASE CITATIONS (US/1048-1273) [19249716] **3054**

SHEPARD'S UNIFORM COMMERCIAL CODE CITATIONS (US/0745-5925) [11967809] **3054**

SHEPARD'S UNITED STATES ADMINISTRATIVE CITATIONS (US/0582-9909) [10044812] **3054**

SHEPARD'S UNITED STATES CITATIONS (US) [09482996] **3054**

SHEPARD'S UNITED STATES CITATIONS. CASES (US/0730-2061) [22291349] **3054**

SHEPARD'S UNITED STATES CITATIONS: STATUTES (US) [01607359] **3054**

SHEPARD'S UNITED STATES PATENTS AND TRADEMARKS CITATIONS (US/0582-9917) [20382736] **3054**

SHEPARD'S UNITED STATES SUPREME COURT CASE NAMES CITATOR (US) [15134428] **3054**

SHEPARD'S VERMONT CITATIONS (US/0730-6091) [01640930] **3055**

SHEPARD'S VIRGINIA CASE NAMES CITATOR (US/1052-6676) [22342677] **3055**

SHEPARD'S VIRGINIA CITATIONS (US/0730-4498) [08024008] **3055**

●SHEPARD'S VIRGINIA CODE CITATIONS (US) [27064181] **3055**

SHEPARD'S VIRGINIA EXPRESS CITATIONS (US/1060-4774) [24497729] **3055**

SHEPARD'S WASHINGTON CASE NAMES CITATOR (US) [12593252] **3055**

SHEPARD'S WASHINGTON CITATIONS (US/0730-4528) [08042271] **3055**

●SHEPARD'S WASHINGTON EXPRESS CITATIONS (US/1066-1298) [10661298] **3055**

SHEPARD'S WEST VIRGINIA CASE NAMES CITATOR (US/1052-6684) [22342710] **3055**

SHEPARD'S WEST VIRGINIA CITATIONS (US/0730-4579) [08054335] **3055**

SHEPARD'S WISCONSIN CASE NAMES CITATOR (US/1052-5718) [11435148] **3055**

SHEPARD'S WISCONSIN CITATIONS (US) [01587159] **3055**

SHEPARD'S WISCONSIN EXPRESS CITATIONS *CEASED*. (US/1055-4629) [23185391] **3055**

SHEPARD'S WYOMING CITATIONS (US/0730-6105) [10852145] **3055**

SHEPHERD EXPRESS (US/1071-5185) [17851141] **5770**

SHEPHERD (NEW WASHINGTON, OHIO), THE (US/8750-7897) [11779312] **221**

SHEPHERD SYSTEM, THE (US) **3641**

SHEPHERD'S FRIEND : FOR THOSE WHO CARE FOR SHEEP, THE (US) [12316935] **221**

●SHEPPARD'S BOOK DEALERS IN EUROPE (UK/0963-0171) [24433759] **4819, 4832**

SHEPPARD'S BOOK DEALERS IN NORTH AMERICA (UK/0269-1469) [13854446] **4832**

SHEPPARD'S BOOK DEALERS IN THE BRITISH ISLES (UK/0950-0715) [15080008] **4832**

SHEPPARD'S EUROPEAN BOOK DEALERS *See* SHEPPARD'S BOOK DEALERS IN EUROPE **4832**

SHEPPARD'S INTERNATIONAL DIRECTORY OF PRINT AND MAP SELLERS (UK) [17390263] **2576**

SHERBURNE NEWS, THE (US) [09927494] **5721**

SHERIDAN HEADLIGHT, THE (US) [19816817] **5632**

SHERIDAN NEWS, THE (US/8750-0213) [10911446] **5667**

SHERIDAN PRESS (SHERIDAN, WYO.), THE (US/1074-682X) [22723737] **5772**

SHERIFF (ALEXANDRIA, VA.) (US/1070-8170) [23124286] **3176**

SHERIFF'S STAR (TALLAHASSEE, FLA.), THE (US/0488-6186) [06785342] **3176**

SHERLOCK HOLMES. CD-ROM (US) **3436**

SHERLOCK HOLMES JOURNAL, THE (UK/0037-3621) [01695466] **3436**

SHERLOCKIAN TIDBITS (US/1040-4937) [18432495] **3436**

SHERMAN COUNTY HERALD (US) [12621856] **5678**

SHERMAN DEMOCRAT (SHERMAN, TEX.) (US) [14918651] **5754**

SHERMAN SENTINEL, THE (US/1071-4480) [26892412] **2493**

●SHERMAN'S COMPLETE GUIDE TO BUSINESS LOAN SOURCES (US/1065-8467) [26778236] **811**

SHESHUNOFF BANKS OF CALIFORNIA (US) [12305404] **811**

SHEVET ROMANIA (IS) [05784435] **2709**

SHEVILEY HA-HINNUKH *SUSPENDED*. (US/0037-3656) [03923604] **5052**

SHEVILIN (IS) [05468018] **4997**

SHHH (US/0883-1688) [08385602] **4393**

SHHH NEWS (AT/1033-792X) **4393**

SHI CHI HANG KUNG (CH) [07025906] **35**

SHI - NIHON GANSEKI, KOBUTSU, KOSHOGAKKAI. JOURNAL OF THE JAPANESE ASSOCIATION OF MINERALOGISTS, PETROLOGISTS AND ECONOMIC GEOLOGISTS (JA/0021-4825) [04626393] **1360**

SHIAWASSEE COUNTY JOURNAL (US/0746-9055) [10384066] **5693**

SHIAWASSEE STEPPIN' STONES (US/0735-8016) [08060212] **2472**

SHIBAKUSA KENKYU (JA/0285-8800) [06190020] **134**

SHIBAO ZHOU KAN (MEIZHOU-BAN) (US/0883-6655) [12219676] **5721**

SHIBORUTO KENKYU : HOSEI DAIGAKU FON SHIBORUTO KENKYUKAI KAISHI (JA) [09901971] **2664**

SHICHO (JA) [06073130] **2629**

SHICHOSONBETSU KOCHI MENSEKI TOKEI (JA) [05204822] **1520**

SHIDO GIJUTSU KENKYUKAI (JAPAN) *See* SHINDO GIJUTSU KENKYUKAI-SHI **4019**

SHIELD FOR CIVIL SERVICE NEWS, THE *CEASED*. (US) [13878337] **5711**

SHIELD : THE INTERNATIONAL MAGAZINE OF THE BP GROUP *CEASED*. (US) [24349963] **4278**

SHIEN (TOKYO. 1928) (JA/0386-9318) [08921173] **2629**

SHIFT IN THE WIND : THE HUNGER PROJECT NEWSPAPER : A PROGRESS REPORT ON THE END OF HUNGER AND STARVATION, A (US) [05356309] **1639**

SHIFT (SAN FRANCISCO, CALIF.) *CEASED*. (US/0895-8351) [16820921] **330**

SHIFTWORK MANAGERS NEWSLETTER (US) **1710**

SHIFTWORK MANAGERS NEWSLETTER (US) **886**

SHIGA IKA DAIGAKU ZASSHI (JA/0912-3016) [09123016] **3641**

SHIGA, JAPAN. SEIKATSU KANKYOBU. KANKYO HOZENKA *See* KANKYO HAKUSHO **2235**

SHIGA KENRITSU EISEI KANKYO SENTA *See* SHIGA KENRITSU EISEI KANKYO SENTA SHOHO **4802**

SHIGA KENRITSU EISEI KANKYO SENTA SHOHO (JA) [07952536] **2243, 4802**

SHIGAKU (JA) [02243648] **2629**

SHIGAKU KENKYU (HIROSHIMA. 1929) (JA/0386-9342) [06077815] **2664**

SHIGAKU ZASSHI (JA/01715643] **2664**

SHIGEN CHOSAJO *See* KAGAKU GIJUTSUCHO SHIGEN CHOSAJO KIHO. / THE QUARTERLY REPORT OF [THE] NATIONAL INSTITUTE OF RESOURCES **2197**

SHIGEN JOHO (JA) [08858367] **1583**

SHIGEN TO SOZAI (JA/0916-1740) [22738027] **4019, 2151**

●SHIGEN TO TANKYO (JA/0916-9997) [29735597] **2205**

SHIGEN TOKEI GEPPO (JA) [02954464] **1626, 1445**

SHIGEN TOKEI NEMPO. YEARBOOK OF MINING, NON-FERROUS METALS, AND PRODUCTS STATISTICS (JA) [05224350] **1445, 4019, 4026**

SHIH CHI KAN KAO / KUO LI CHENG-KUNG TA HSUEH LI SHIH HSUEH HSI SHIH CHI YEN CHIU SHIH PIEN (CH) [09747500] **2664**

SHIH CHIEH CHIH SHIH / SHIJIE ZHISHI (CC) [01765505] **4535**

SHIH CHIEH CHING CHI (CHUNG-KUO SHIH CHIEH CHING CHI HSUEH HUI) (CC) [05140753] **1583**

SHIH CHIEH CHING KUNG (CH) [10665189] **1626**

SHIH CHIEH LI SHIH TSA CHIH (CC) [11976946] **2508**

SHIH CHIEH LIN YEH CHIU (CC) **2395**

SHIH CHIEH MEI SHU (CC) [06660428] **330**

SHIH CHIEH TSUNG CHIAO TZU LIAO (CC) [07254266] **4997**

SHIH CHIEH WEN HSUEH (CC) [07253541] **3436**

SHIH FANG YUEH KAN (CH) [11685230] **5022**

SHIH HSUAN (TAIPEI, TAIWAN) (CH) [11093519] **3471**

SHIH HSUEH (CH) [01797595] **2629**

SHIPS

SHIH HSUEH CHING PAO / CHUNG-KUO SHIH HSUEH HUI, CHUNG-KUO LI SHIH HSUEH NIEN CHIEN PIEN CHI PU PIEN (CC) [08868383] **2664**

SHIH HSUEH SHIH YEN CHIU (CC) [18170868] **2664**

SHIH KAN (CC/0583-0230) [05431306] **3471**

SHIH KUNG CHI SHU (CC) [10050003] **627**

SHIH PIN KO CHI (CH) [09220772] **2792**

SHIH TAI CHI YEH (CH) [01797512] **1626**

SHIH TAI PI PING (HK) [01604298] **2664**

SHIH TAI WEN CHAI (CH) [08148657] **2508**

SHIH TAXNG (US/0731-0897) [08119964] **3436**

SHIH TING CHIAO YU SHUANG YUEH KAN (CH) [03028287] **1905**

SHIH TZU REPORTER, THE (US/1040-5801) [18454655] **4288**

SHIH YEN SHENG WU HSUEH PAO (CC/0001-5334) [02450521] **473**

SHIH YU TI CHIU WU LI KAN TAN (CC) [07720410] 4278, **2151**

SHIH YUEH / SHIYUE (CC) [05436498] **3436**

SHIH YUNG CHIH SHIH (CH) [10862886] **1929**

SHIJIE LINYE YANJIU (CH/1001-4241) [I10014241] **2395**

SHIJIE LISHI (CC/1002-011X) [05348117] **2629**

SHIJIE RIBAO (HOUSTON, TEX.) (US/0887-5634) [13292339] **5754**

SHIJIE RIBAO (SAN FRANCISCO, CALIF.) (US/0747-5071) [09657772] **5640**

SHIKA GAKUHO (JA/0037-3710) [02267668] **1335**

SHIKA GIKO (JA/0389-1895) [10439146] **1335**

SHIKA IGAKU. DENTAL MEDICINE (JA) [07622228] **1335**

SHIKA JANARU (JA/0386-4715) [I03864715] **1335**

SHIKA KISO IGAKKAI ZASSHI (JA/0385-0137) [10453574] **1335**

SHIKA YAKUBUTSU RYOHO (JA/0288-1012) [I02881012] **4329**

SHIKA ZAIRYO, KIKAI (JA/0286-5858) [10388072] **1335**

SHIKAI (JA) [01799699] **3471**

SHIKAN (JA/0386-9350) [06073343] **2629**

SHIKEN HOKOKU (NIHON SENBAI KOSHA. HIRATSUKA SEIZO SHIKENJO) (JA/0389-2263) [10671380] **3488**

SHIKEN KENKYU NENPO : BYOGAI, CHUGAI HEN *CEASED*. (JA) [06653671] **186**

SHIKENJO NENPO (JA) [03718487] **2095**

SHIKI NO ATORIE (JA) [10662153] **2508**

SHIKIHAKU DAYORI (JA) [12003424] **4361**

SHIKIZAI KYOKAISHI (JA/0010-180X) [09959284] **1030**

SHIKOKU ACTA MEDICA (JA) [01765511] **3641**

SHIKOKU IGAKU ZASSHI (JA/0037-3699) [02267669] **3641**

SHIKOKU KOKENKAIHO (JA/0912-8859) [I09128859] **1996**

SHIKOKU NOGYO SHIKENJO *See* SHIKOKU NOGYO SHIKENJO HOKOKU **134**

SHIKOKU NOGYO SHIKENJO HOKOKU (JA/0037-3702) [02245252] **134**

SHIKOKU YUSEI TOKEI NEMPO (JA) [01797054] **1147**

SHIKYO KENKYU (JA/0911-1557) [03116481] **3436**

SHILAP. SOCIEDAD HISPANO-LUSO-AMERICANA DE LEPIDOPTEROLOGIA (SP/0300-5267) [I03005267] **5613**

SHILPAKALA (BG) [06613682] **330**

SHIMA MARINRANDO *See* SHIMA MARINRANDO KENKYU HOKOKU **5157**

SHIMA MARINRANDO KENKYU HOKOKU (JA/0385-1109) [04162718] **5157**

SHIMANE DAIGAKU CHISHITSUGAKU KENKYU HOKOKU (JA) [10485158] **1397**

SHIMANE DAIGAKU HOBUNGAKUBU KIYO. BUNGAKUKA HEN (JA) [07389305] **3436**

SHIMANE DAIGAKU, MATSUE, JAPAN. NOGAKUBU *See* SHIMANE DAIGAKU NOGAKUBU KENKYU HOKOKU **134**

SHIMANE DAIGAKU, MATSUE, JAPAN. NOGAKUBU *See* SHIMANE DAIGAKU NOGAKUBU ENSHURIN HOKOKU **2395**

SHIMANE DAIGAKU NOGAKUBU ENSHURIN HOKOKU (JA) [02244987] **2395**

SHIMANE DAIGAKU NOGAKUBU KENKYU HOKOKU (JA/0370-940X) [05471855] **134**

SHIMANE DAIGAKU RIGAKUBU KIYO (JA/0387-9925) [08672066] **5157**

SHIMANE-KEN NOGYO SHIKENJO KENKYU HOKOKU (JA/0388-905X) [10444339] **134**

SHIMANE NO KYOIKU (JA) [02245310] **1783**

SHIMAZAKI TOSON KENKYU (JA) [03865497] **3436**

SHIMAZU HYORON (JA/0371-005X) [10475823] **5157**

SHIMBUN GEPPO SHA *See* NEMPO - SHIMBUN GEPPO SHA **2660**

SHIMIZU TECHNICAL RESEARCH BULLETIN (JA) [10174736] **5157**

SHIMOTSUKE KOKOGAKU (JA) [08253684] **282**

SHIMPO (JA) [05952972] **5258**

SHIN BOEI RONSHU (JA) [01797285] **4057**

SHIN-ENERUGI SOGO KAIHATSU KIKO (JAPAN) *See* KENKYU SEIKA NENPO **2119**

SHIN KINZOKU KOGYO (JA/0583-0419) [10399392] **4019**

SHIN MITSUBISHI JUKOGYO KABUSHIKI KAISHA *See* TECHNICAL REVIEW - MITSUBISHI HEAVY INDUSTRIES **1629**

SHIN NIHON RETTO (JA) [01799698] **1626**

SHIN TOSHI (JA) [02541569] **2835**

SHINAGAWA GIHO (JA) [04203855] **1996**

SHINBUN NO KOTOBA JITEN / ASAHI SHINBUNSHA HEN (JA) [11886810] **1929**

SHINBUNGAKU HYORON (JA) [08787410] **3321**

SHINDAN TO CHIRYO (JA/0370-999X) [I0370999X] **3641**

SHINDIG IN THE BARN (US/0093-1950) [01791959] **4153**

SHINDO GIJUTSU KENKYUKAI-SHI (JA/0370-985X) [10454919] **4019**

SHINER GAZETTE (US) [14868691] **5754**

SHINGEKI *See* RE SUPEKKU **329**

SHINGLE, THE (US/0037-377X) [01590464] **3055**

SHINING LIGHT (US) **4997**

SHINING MOUNTAIN SENTINEL (US/0192-687X) [05053891] **2545**

SHINING STAR (CARTHAGE, ILL.) (US/0884-5514) [12389401] **1905**

SHINKEI GANKA (JA/0289-7024) [I02897024] **3879**

SHINKEI KENKYU NO SHIMPO (JA/0001-8724) [02255155] **3641**

SHINKEI NAIKA (JN/0386-9709) [01524393] **3846**

SHINKEI SEISHIN YAKURI (JA/0388-7588) [10399206] 4329, 4618, **3846**

SHINKEN KAWARABAN (SHUSATSUBAN) (JA) [11818307] **4686**

SHINKIN TO SHINKINSHO (JA/0583-0516) [10454792] **576**

SHINKU (JA/0559-8516) [10468028] **4429**

SHINKU TANKU NEMPO (JA) [08178129] **5157**

SHINON KEITOBETSU ZEN JOJO KAISHA SHURAN (JA) [08880092] **1626**

SHINRIGAKU (JA) [01799745] **4618**

SHINRIGAKU HYORON (JA/0386-1058) [01796992] **4618**

SHINRIGAKU KENKYU (JA/0021-5236) [02232640] **4618**

SHINRIN BOEKI (JA) [01797284] **2395**

SHINRIN REKURIESHON KENKYU (JA/0385-9088) [05671752] **2395**

SHINRIN SOGO KENKYUJO KENKYU HOKOKU (JA/0916-4405) [I09164405] **2395**

SHINSHIN IGAKU (JA/0385-0307) [02778186] 4618, **3641**

SHINSHU DAIGAKU (JAPAN). KEIZAIGAKUBU *See* SHINSHU DAIGAKU KEIZAIGAKUBU RONSHU **1595**

SHINSHU DAIGAKU KEIZAIGAKUBU RONSHU *See* SHINSHU DAIGAKU KEIZAIGAKUBU RONSHU **1595**

SHINSHU DAIGAKU KEIZAIGAKUBU RONSHU (JA) [06592071] **1595**

SHINSHU DAIGAKU. NOGAKUBU *See* SHINSHU DAIGAKU NOGAKUBU KIYO **134**

SHINSHU DAIGAKU NOGAKUBU KIYO (JA/0583-0621) [01773382] **134**

SHINSHU IGAKU ZASSHI (JA/0037-3826) [09498491] **3641**

SHINSHU MEDICAL JOURNAL (JA/0037-3826) [01778262] **3641**

SHINSHU MISO KENKYUJO KENKYU HOKOKU (JA) [10454734] **134**

SHINSHUGAKU (JA) [04764951] **5022**

SHINTAFFER NEWSLETTER, THE (US/0748-5166) [10944112] **2472**

SHINTO KOTEN KENKYU : KAIHO / SHINTO KOTEN KENKYUKAI (JA) [10167318] **4997**

SHINTO SHUKYO (JA) [02435375] **4997**

SHINYAKU TO RINSHO (JA/0559-8672) [10351123] **3641**

SHINZO PESHINGU (JA/0911-0836) [19078334] **3710**

SHIONOGI KENKYUSHO NENPO (JA/0559-8680) [I05598680] **5157**

SHIP & BOAT INTERNATIONAL (UK/0037-3834) [06002026] **5456**

SHIP & BOAT INTERNATIONAL. ANNUAL GUIDE (UK) [10193228] **4183**

SHIP-BY-TRUCK OFFICIAL ONTARIO DIRECTORY AND BUYER'S GUIDE (CN/0711-303X) [08458447] **5392**

SHIP TECHNOLOGY RESEARCH (GW) [23807413] **5456**

SHIPBROKER, THE *CEASED*. (UK/0142-6680) [06963254] **5456**

SHIPBUILDING & SHIPREPAIR (UK/0966-8330) [I09668330] **5456**

SHIPCARE & MARITIME MANAGEMENT (UK/0263-7944) [05690648] **5456**

SHIPIN YU FAXIAO GONGYE (CC/0253-990X) [10351605] **2357**

SHIPMATE (ANNAPOLIS, MD.) (US/0488-6720) [03489925] **4183**

SHIPMENTS OF PLASTIC FILM AND BAGS MANUFACTURED FROM RESIN (CN/0823-0900) [10827016] **4460**

SHIPMENTS OF SOLID FUEL BURNING HEATING PRODUCTS (CN/0713-6196) [09407493] **1956**

SHIPMENTS OF STEEL PRODUCTS: ALL GRADES INCLUDING CARBON, ALLOY AND STAINLESS (US) [03834788] **4019**

SHIPMENTS TO FEDERAL GOVERNMENT AGENCIES (US/0275-4533) [07117980] **3488**

SHIPPERS' TIMES (SI/0217-1139) [09490220] **5456**

SHIPPING (GR) [07654019] **5456**

SHIPPING AND AIR CARGO COMMODITY STATISTICS, AUSTRALIA *See* FOREIGN TRADE AUSTRALIA, INTERNATIONAL CARGO **5401**

SHIPPING AND CARGO MOVEMENTS (NZ/0110-5698) [08641710] **5456**

SHIPPING & MARINE INDUSTRIES JOURNAL (II/0970-0285) [02239578] **5456**

SHIPPING & TRADE NEWS (JA) 851, **5456**

SHIPPING BOURNEMOUTH (UK/0958-7683) [I09587683] **5456**

SHIPPING, COMMERCE AND INDUSTRY (AT) [01789129] 5456, **851**

SHIPPING DIGEST (US/0037-3893) [02460688] **5456**

SHIPPING IN CANADA (CN/0835-5533) [18490555] **5456**

SHIPPING MARKS ON TIMBER (UK/0080-9284) [I00809284] 4239, **5456**

SHIPPING STATISTICS (GW) [05937798] **5402**

SHIPPING STATISTICS AND ECONOMICS (UK/0306-1817) [07064233] **5402**

●SHIPPING STATISTICS AND MARKET REVIEW (GW) [30338140] **5456**

SHIPPING STATISTICS (BREMEN, GERMANY) *See* SHIPPING STATISTICS AND MARKET REVIEW **5456**

SHIPPING STATISTICS OF FIJI (FJ) [11829588] **5402**

SHIPPING STATISTICS (SUVA, FIJI) *See* SHIPPING STATISTICS OF FIJI **5402**

SHIPPING STATISTICS YEARBOOK (GW/0721-3220) [03563316] **5456**

SHIPPING STATISTICS (ZEITSCHRIFT) (GW/0721-3751) [08359868] **5456**

SHIPPING WORLD & SHIPBUILDER (UK/0037-3931) [06660842] **5456**

SHIPS AND AIRCRAFT OF THE UNITED STATES FLEET, THE (US/0080-9292) [05274395] 4183, **4057**

SHIPS — Alphabetical Title Index

SHIPS ATLAS, THE (UK) [16180895] **5456**

SHIP'S LOG (AMHERSTBURG) (CN/1183-5400) [24368655] **4183**

SHIPS MONTHLY (UK/0037-394X) [02960189] **4183**

SHIPS OF THE WORLD: SEKAI NO KANSEN (JA) **5456**

SHIPWRECKS & TREASURE MAGAZINE (US/0893-5777) [15585491] **5456**

●SHIPYARD CHRONICLE (US/1061-9224) [25188643] **4183**

SHIPYARD WEEKLY *See* SHIPYARD CHRONICLE **4183**

SHIRASAKI, ASAKICHI: ENSHU SOZOKUZEIHO *See* SOZOKUZEIHO ENSHU, RIRON TO KEISAN **3119**

SHIRE & MUNICIPAL RECORD, THE *CEASED.* (AT) [02957821] **4686**

SHIRE EGYPTOLOGY (UK) [19358039] **282**

SHIRIM (US/0894-606X) [09551461] **5052**, **3471**

SHIRIN (KYOTO. 1916) (JA/0386-9369) [01608044] **2664**

SHIRITSU TANKI DAIGAKU TOKYO NYUGAKU ANNAI (JA) [01797370] **1847**

SHIROARI (JA) [02245312] **4248**

SHIRON (TOKYO. 1953) (JA/0386-4022) [02245729] **2629**

SHIRYO HENSHUSHITSU KIYO (JA) [19597764] **2664**

SHIRYO KANKO ANNAI (JA) [02519587] **1584**

SHIRYO KENKYU HOKOKU (JA) [09364029] **203**

SHIRYO SHOHISHA GYOSEI (JA) [01796866] **1299**

SHISHA (JA) [05720009] **3436**

SHISHA CHIHOKYOKU TABAKO KOSAKU SHIKEH SEISEKI (JA) [02972625] **5373**

SHISO (TOKYO, JAPAN : 1921) (JA) [01715130] **4361**

SHISUTEMU, SEIGYO, JOHO (JA/0374-4507) [20988734] **886**

SHITENNOJI KOKUSAI BUKKYO DAIGAKU BUNGAKUBU KIYO (JA/0286-4185) [09128483] **5022**

SHITSUGI OTO (JA) [02245284] **3641**

SHITSURYO BUNSEKI (JA/0542-8645) [07396256] **1019**

SHIVA MATHEMATICS SERIES (UK) [16935172] **3534**

SHIYOU HUAGONG (CC/1000-8144) [15863402] **4278**

SHIYOU KANTAN KAIFA (CC/1000-0747) [07792001] **4278**

SHIYOU LIANZHI (CH/1001-4101) [10014101] **4278**

SHIYOU XUEBAO (CC/0253-2697) [07728755] **4278**

SHIYOU XUEBAO. SHIYOU JIAGONG (CC/1001-8719) [21741195] **4278**

SHIYOU YU TIANRANQI DIZHI (CC/0253-9985) [07720383] **4278**

SHIZEN HOGO KOZA *See* SHIZEN HOGO KOZA JISSHI HOKOKUSHO **2205**

SHIZEN HOGO KOZA JISSHI HOKOKUSHO (JA) [06569249] **2205**

SHIZEN KAGAKU RONSO (JA) [11819008] **5157**

SHIZENSHI KENKYU. / OCCASIONAL PAPERS FROM THE OSAKA MUSEUM OF NATURAL HISTORY (JA) [04180354] **4172**

SHIZUOKA DAIGAKU. DENSHI KOGAKU KENKYUJO *See* SHIZUOKA DAIGAKU DENSHI KOGAKU KENKYUJO KENKYU HOKOKU **2081**

SHIZUOKA DAIGAKU DENSHI KOGAKU KENKYUJO KENKYU HOKOKU (JA/0286-3383) [03500937] **2081**

SHIZUOKA DAIGAKU. HOKEI TANKI DAIGAKUBU *See* HOKEI RON SHU: KENKYU KIYO **2978**

SHIZUOKA DAIGAKU KOGAKUBU KENKYU HOHOKU (JA/0583-0915) [10437301] **1996**

SHIZUOKA DAIGAKU KYOYOBU KENKYU HOKOKU. JINBUN SHAKAI KAGAKU HEN (JA/0285-0427) [11340385] **2854**

SHIZUOKA DAIGAKU KYOYOBU KENKYU HOKOKU. SHIZEN KAGAKU HEN (JA) [08077155] **2854**

SHIZUOKA DAIGAKU NOGAKUBU KENKYU HOKOKU (JA/0559-8850) [09989216] **134**

SHIZUOKA JOSHI TANKI DAIGAKU, HAMAMATSU, JAPAN *See* KENKYU KIYO - SHIZUOKA JOSHI TANKI DAIGAKU **1833**

SHIZUOKA-KEN NOGYO SHIKENJO KENKYU HOKOKU (JA/0583-094X) [01423752] **134**

SHIZUOKA-KEN SHIZUOKA KOGYO GIJUTSU SENTA KENKYU HOKOKU (JA/0916-6572) [09166572] **5157**

SHKENCA DHE JETA (AA) [02554346] **5157**

SH'MA (PORT WASHINGTON, N.Y.) (US/0049-0385) [02450510] **4361**

SHMATE *CEASED.* (US/0885-8659) [08441686] **2629**

SHO-BAN NEWS, THE (US/0197-7954) [04574547] **5657**

SHO ENERUGI (JA/0387-1819) [08023860] **1956**

SHO-ENERUGI SORAN / SHIGEN ENERUGICHO SHO-ENERUGI TAISAKUKA KANSHU (JA) [09812914] **1956**

SHO-KEI RONSO (JA) [02243702] **1595**

SHO TO KIROKU NO JIMMEI JITEN (JA) [01790306] **5236**

SHOAL LAKE STAR (CN) **5794**

SHOALS NEWS, THE (US) [12212982] **5667**

SHOBO KENKYUJO HOKOKU (JA/0426-2700) [10481170] **2292**

SHOCK AND VIBRATION (US/1070-9622) [28522622] **1996**

SHOCK AND VIBRATION DIGEST, THE (US/0583-1024) [01928382] 2128, **2006**

SHOCK AND VIBRATION MONOGRAPH SERIES (US/0583-1032) [02879061] **2128**

SHOCK AND VIBRATION TECHNOLOGY REVIEW (US/1058-0670) [24154545] **1996**

SHOCK WAVES (GW/0938-1287) [24558784] 4453, **4429**

SHOCKS (US/0360-912X) [02244970] **3471**

SHOE FACTORY BUYERS' GUIDE (US) [08096543] **1087**

SHOES AND SLIPPERS, BY TYPE OF CONSTRUCTION AND PRICE LINE (US) [03053756] **1087**

SHOESTRING MARKETER, THE *CEASED.* (US/0882-3448) [11808066] **936**

SHOESTRING PRESS (CN/0383-8161) [03230480] **5794**

SHOFAR (MELVILLE, N.Y.) (US/0748-9706) [10502868] 5052, **1069**

SHOFAR (WASHINGTON, D.C.), THE (US/0745-9327) [09612556] **5052**

SHOFAR (WEST LAFAYETTE, IND.) (US/0882-8539) [10494580] **5052**

SHOHIN KENKYU (JA/0286-2212) [10409078] **851**

SHOHISHA SODAN JIREI SHU (JA) [06570811] **1299**

SHOHO (JA) [09122524] **2664**

SHOIN LITERARY REVIEW (JA/0288-6154) [02886154] **3352**

SHOJINKAI IGAKUSHI (JA/0388-9734) [03889734] **3641**

SHOKA TO KYUSHU (JA/0389-3626) [27465446] **3748**

SHOKAKI GEKA (JA/0387-2645) [19021792] **3748**

SHOKEN IHO (JA/0287-069X) [10190521] **3055**

SHOKEN KEIZAI JIHO (JA) [01790304] **913**

SHOKEN KEIZAIGAKKAI (JAPAN) *See* SHOKEN KEIZAIGAKKAI NEMPO **913**

SHOKEN KEIZAIGAKKAI NEMPO (JA/0388-1458) [08089734] **913**

SHOKIGYO NO KEIEI SHIHYO / KOKUMIN KINYU KOKO CHOSABU HEN (JA) [10356228] **851**

SHOKO NENKAN (PO) [05525851] **710**

SHOKU NO KAGAKU (JA/0287-1734) [10399018] **2357**

SHOKUBA NO ANZEN KANRI OYOBI EISEI KANRI NI KANSURU SOGO JITTAI CHOSA KEKKA HOKOKUSHO (JA) [01797213] **2870**

SHOKUBAI (JA/0559-8958) [I05598958] **1058**

SHOKUBUTSU BOEKI (JA/0037-4091) [09534007] **134**

SHOKUBUTSU BOEKIJO CHOSA KENKYU HOKOKU (JA/0387-0707) [05703407] **2431**

SHOKUBUTSU KENKYU ZASSHI (JA/0022-2062) [05158666] **527**

SHOKUBUTSU NO KAGAKU CHOSETSU (JA/0388-9130) [10398955] **527**

SHOKUBUTSUGAKU ZASSHI (JA/0006-808X) [01536894] **527**

SHOKUHIN EISEI KANKEI JIGYO HOKOKU (JA) [03502009] **4802**

SHOKUHIN EISEI KENKYU (JA/0559-8974) [04856482] 2357, **4802**

SHOKUHIN EISEIGAKU ZASSHI (JA/0015-6426) [08978734] **4803**

SHOKUHIN KAIHATSU (JA/0583-1121) [10398905] **2357**

SHOKUHIN KAIHATSU. UP-TO-DATE FOOD PROCESSING (JA) [03302597] **2357**

SHOKUHIN KIKAI SOCHI (JA) [10411271] **2357**

SHOKUHIN KOGYO. THE FOOD INDUSTRY (JA/0559-8990) [02096781] **2357**

SHOKUHIN SANGYO SENTA GIJUTSU KENKYU HOKOKU (JA/0388-3388) [10411339] **2357**

SHOKUHIN SHOSHA (JA/0387-1975) [03635203] **2357**

SHOKUHIN TO BISEIBUTSU (JA/0910-8637) [27457617] **2357**

SHOKUHIN TO KAGAKU (JA) [10451935] **2357**

SHOKUIN JIMU HANDOBUKKU (JA) [02245394] **4686**

SHOKUNIKU RYUTSU TOKEI GEPPO / HENSHU, NORIN SUISANSHO KEIZAIKYOKU TOKEI JOHOBU (JA) [08448161] **1626**

SHOKURYO KEIZAI HAKUSHO (JA) [02713213] **2357**

SHOKURYO KEIZAI NENKAN (JA) [01790287] **811**

SHOKURYO SEISAKU KENKYU (JA/0387-9836) [02706728] **2357**

SHONI GEKA (JA/0385-6313) [05083927] 3974, **3911**

SHONI NAIKA (JA/0385-6305) [04767273] **3911**

SHONIKA KIYO (JA/0003-4495) [01778263] **3911**

SHOOT (NEW YORK, N.Y.) (US/1074-5297) [29740221] 1139, **765**

SHOOTER'S BIBLE, THE (US/0080-9365) [04426243] **4917**

●SHOOTER'S GUIDE (CALIFORNIA ED.) (US/1053-0304) [22441428] **4878**

●SHOOTER'S RAG (US/1058-2789) [24252243] **4376**

SHOOTING & CONSERVATION (UK) [07956213] **2205**

SHOOTING INDUSTRY, THE (US/0037-4148) [05362640] **4917**

SHOOTING SPORTS RETAILER (US/0887-9397) [13416318] 4917, **957**

SHOOTING SPORTS USA (US/1069-6822) [22473793] 4878, **4917**

SHOOTING SPORTSMAN (WILLIAMSPORT, PA.) (US/1050-5717) [21540193] **4878**

SHOOTING STAR REVIEW (US/0892-1407) [15095791] **3436**

SHOOTING TIMES (US/0038-8084) [03259870] 4878, **4917**

SHOOTING TIMES HANDGUN QUARTERLY *See* HANDGUNNING **4898**

SHOP (DON MILLS) *CEASED.* (CN/0381-8667) [02172259] **2128**

SHOP EQUIPMENT & SHOPFITTING NEWS (UK) **308**

SHOP MANUAL. CAPRICE, MONTE CARLO, EL CAMINO (US) [13507606] **5425**

SHOP 'TIL YA DROP (US/1056-6473) [23753047] **1299**

●SHOPNOTES (DES MOINES, IOWA) (US/1062-9696) [25823325] **375**

SHOPPER & OBSERVER NEWS, THE (US) [08449152] **1299**

SHOPPER'S GUIDE (COLORADO SPRINGS, COLO.), THE (US/1055-2324) [23123650] **1299**

SHOPPERS' GUIDE TO CANADIAN LIFE INSURANCE PRICES (SUDBURY, ONT. : 1980) (CN/0705-1786) [09519524] **2893**

SHOPPING CENTER DIGEST (US/0885-209X) [09583615] **957**

●SHOPPING CENTER DIRECTORY (US/1066-9701) [26715676] **1299**

SHOPPING CENTER WORLD (US/0049-0393) [01765515] **4847**

SHOPPING CENTER WORLD PRODUCT AND SERVICE DIRECTORY (US/0049-0393=) **957**

SHOPPING CENTERS IN THE DETROIT REGION (US/0417-1225) [04841120] **2835**

SHOPPING CENTERS TODAY (US/0885-9841) [10203511] **957**

SHOPPING CENTRE CANADA (CN/0226-7551) [06512196] **958**

SHOPPING CENTRE NEWS (AT) **1299**

SHOPPING : OPCOES DE COMPRA PARA A GRANDE RIO (BL) [03147674] **710**

SHOPPING : OPCOES DE COMPRA PARA A GRANDE SAO PAULO (BL) [02711333] **710**

SHOPPING : OPCOES DE COMPRA PARA O INTERIOR DE SAO PAULO (BL) [02718962] **710**

SHOPTALK (US) [12617102] 2273, **405**

SHORASHIM (IS) [06575548] **2273**

SHORE AND BEACH (US/0037-4237) [01928404] **2205**

SHORE LINE, THE (CN/0380-8866) [02577932] **2783**

SHORE LINE TIMES (US/0887-7912) [07793338] **5646**

SHORE LINES (US/0745-4430) [09178749] **5019**

SHORELINE BUSINESS MONTHLY (US) **710**

SHORELINE LEADER, THE (US/0749-7156) [11167286] **5770**

SHORELINER (US/0162-0282) [04082856] **5436**

SHORELINER SUPPLEMENT (US/0162-0746) [04082629] **5436**

SHOREVIEW PRESS (US) **5698**

SHOROPPO (JA) [03530214] **3055**

SHORT BOOK REVIEWS / INTERNATIONAL STATISTICAL INSTITUTE (NE) [10091904] 4819, **4822**

SHORT COURSE IN AIRPORT MANAGEMENT (US/0402-1681) [03175982] **35**

SHORT FICTION BY WOMEN (US) [26471034] **3436**

SHORT LINE, THE (US/0199-4050) [05844626] **5436**

SHORT NOTES ON ALASKAN GEOLOGY (US/0162-5551) [04168393] **1397**

"SHORT PLAY" SERIES, THE (US/0083-9403) [02955664] **5368**

SHORT STORY (US) [01772434] **3436**

SHORT STORY (COLUMBIA, S.C.) (US/1052-648X) [22340948] **3436**

SHORT STORY CRITICISM (US/0895-9439) [16857629] **3436**

SHORT STORY INDEX (US/0360-9774) [02245062] **3459**

SHORT STORY INTERNATIONAL. SEEDLING SERIES (US/0732-5266) [08379653] **1069**

SHORT STORY INTERNATIONAL. STUDENT SERIES (US/0732-5274) [08377327] **1069**

SHORT STORY REVIEW, THE (US) [16324659] **3436**

SHORT-TERM ECONOMIC INDICATORS, CENTRAL AND EASTERN EUROPE *See* SHORT-TERM ECONOMIC INDICATORS, TRANSITION ECONOMIES / CENTRE FOR CO-OPERATION WITH THE ECONOMIES IN TRANSITION / INDICATEURS ECONOMIQUES A COURT TERME, ECONOMIES EN TRANSITION / CENTRE POUR LA COOPERATION AVEC LES ECONOMIES EN TRANSITION **1520**

●SHORT-TERM ECONOMIC INDICATORS, TRANSITION ECONOMIES / CENTRE FOR CO-OPERATION WITH THE ECONOMIES IN TRANSITION / INDICATEURS ECONOMIQUES A COURT TERME, ECONOMIES EN TRANSITION / CENTRE POUR LA COOPERATION AVEC LES ECONOMIES EN TRANSITION (FR/1019-9829) [29608141] **1520**

SHORT-TERM ENERGY OUTLOOK *See* SHORT-TERM ENERGY OUTLOOK. VOLUME II, METHODOLOGY **1956**

SHORT-TERM ENERGY OUTLOOK. QUARTERLY PROJECTIONS (US/0743-0604) [10488812] **1956**

SHORT-TERM ENERGY OUTLOOK. VOLUME II, METHODOLOGY (US/0743-0620) [10488896] **1956**

SHORT TITLE CATALOG OF BOOKS PRINTED IN ENGLAND, SCOTLAND, IRELAND, WALES, AND BRITISH AMERICA AND OF ENGLISH BOOKS PRINTED IN OTHER COUNTRIES (US) **3459**

SHORT WAVE MAGAZINE (UK/0037-4261) [06963301] **1139**

SHORTCUT2 (US) **2893**

SHORTHORN COUNTRY (US/0149-9319) [02455714] **221**

SHORTHORN NEWS (CN/0037-427X) [02172278] **221**

SHORTHORN, THE (US/0892-6603) [15264897] **1095**

SHOSETSU GENDAI (SA/0559-9202) [06073097] **5074**

SHOSETSU SHINCHO (JA) [02267672] **3436**

SHOSHI NENKAN (JA) [10713379] **424**

SHOSHI SAKUIN TEMBO (JA) [03618391] **3249**

SHOSHIGEN/SHOENERUGI GIJUTSU KOGAI BOSHI GIJUTSU RISUTO (JA) [07242611] 1956, **2205**

SHOSHONE NEWS-PRESS (US/1044-9353) [19117419] **5657**

SHOSOIN NEMPO (JA) [07342490] **364**

SHOTGUN NEWS (US/0049-0415) **4917**

SHOTGUN SPORTS (US/0744-3773) [08228447] **4917**

SHOTOKUZEI HOREI SHU (JA) [03573339] **4748**

SHOTOKUZEIHO SOCHIHO SANRIN SHOTOKU JOTO SHOTOKU KIHON TSUTATSU (JA) [03530595] **4686**

SHOTS (DANVILLE, KY.) (US/1048-793X) [17240714] **4376**

SHOU HUO (CC) [06955917] **3436**

SHOU I KO CHI TSA CHIH (CH/0254-0142) [08996008] **3641**

SHOU LEI HSUEH-PAO (CC) [08968228] **5597**

SHOUDU YIXUEYUAN XUEBAO (CC/1001-2389) [I10012389] **3641**

●SHOUT! (NEW YORK, N.Y.) (US/1059-4817) [24640047] **4153**

SHOW HORSE (BANGOR, ME.) (US/8755-3929) [11292147] **2802**

SHOW MAGAZINE (FR/0151-979X) **5368**

SHOW-ME LIBRARIES (US/0037-4326) [01641473] **3249**

SHOW-ME UNDERWRITER, THE (US/0883-6825) [12201511] **2893**

SHOW MUSIC (US/8755-9560) [11454970] 5368, **4153**

SHOW PRESS (SP) **4153**

SHOW RING (CN/0701-0001) [03279438] **4288**

SHOW STEER, THE (US/0195-2463) [05424466] **221**

SHOWA IGAKKAI *See* SHOWA IGAKKAI ZASSHI **3641**

SHOWA IGAKKAI ZASSHI (JA/0037-4342) [01779937] **3641**

SHOWA SHIGAKKAI ZASSHI (JA/0285-922X) [09531143] **1335**

SHOWA UNIVERSITY JOURNAL OF MEDICAL SCIENCES, THE (JA/0915-6380) [22178102] **3641**

SHOWBOATS INTERNATIONAL (US/0749-2952) [11107118] **596**

SHOWCASE (SI) [04403292] **851**

SHOWCASE (US/0743-7609) [08604147] **382**

SHOWCASE (MINNEAPOLIS) (US/0196-1586) [02255900] **4153**

SHOWCASE (NEW YORK) (US/0361-3232) [02376367] **3186**

SHOWCASE U.S.A (US/0164-3215) [04693230] **851**

SHOWCAST *CEASED.* (AT) [16238994] 5368, **388**

SHOWPAGE *CEASED.* (US/0893-5335) [15564448] **1202**

SHOWPLACE (GRAND RAPIDS, MICH.) (US/0897-8875) [17656136] **2545**

SHOWS & EXHIBITIONS (CN/0845-8448) [20444543] **766**

SHOYAKUGAKU ZASSHI (JA/0037-4377) [09770356] **4329**

SHOZO GIJUTSU JOHO SHIRYO ICHIRAN (JA) [06932150] **1457**

SHP NEWS (CC/0256-3118) [I02563118] **2095**

SHQIPTARJA E RE *CEASED.* (AA) **5566**

SHREE GURUDEV-VANI (II) [01790442] **4997**

SHREVEPORT JOURNAL (SHREVEPORT, LA. : 1895) (US) [15695258] **5684**

SHRIMP LANDINGS, ANNUAL SUMMARY (US/0559-9296) [04030067] **2313**

●SHRIMP NEWS INTERNATIONAL (US/1076-7568) [29905779] **2313**

SHROPSHIRE ARCHAEOLOGICAL AND HISTORICAL SOCIETY *See* TRANSACTIONS OF THE SHROPSHIRE ARCHAEOLOGICAL AND HISTORICAL SOCIETY **284**

SHROPSHIRE FAMILY HISTORY JOURNAL (UK/0261-135X) [I0261135X] **2472**

SHROUD SPECTRUM INTERNATIONAL (US/0738-6524) [08881303] **5157**

SHU FA (CC) [04320847] **382**

SHU FA TSUNG KAN / WEN WU PIEN CHI WEI YUAN HUI PIEN (CC) [08515266] **375**

SHU HSUEH HSUEH PAO (CC/0583-1431) [02011986] **3534**

SHU HSUEH WU LI HSUEH PAO (CC) [07934585] 3534, **4421**

SHU HSUEH YEN CHIU YU PING LUN (CC) [08779818] **3534**

SHU HUA CHIA (CH) [11178672] **382**

SHU PU *CEASED.* (HK) [01799810] **375**

SHU YU HUA (CC) [11477560] **382**

SHUCHO (JA) [01784060] **4686**

SHUFA (CC) **364**

SHUFAR : NASHRIYAH-I FIDIRASYUN-I YAHUDIYAN-I IRANI (US) [10259044] **2273**

SHUFU NO TOMO (JA) **5566**

SHUHO. BULLETIN OF THE HOKKAIDO PREFECTURAL AGRICULTURAL EXPERIMENT STATIONS (JA/0441-0807) [03337705] **134**

SHUI DONGLIXUE YANJIU YU JINZHAN (CC/1000-4874) [I10004874] **1418**

SHUI LI SHUI TIEN CHI SHU (CH) [08917475] **2095**

SHUI TU PAO CHIH TUNG PAO (CC) [11948300] **2095**

SHUI WU HSUN KAN (CH/0559-9407) [02017265] **4748**

SHUICHAN XUEBAO (CC/1000-0615) [09026347] **557**

SHUILI XUEBAO (CC/0559-9350) [10476869] **2095**

SHUKAN ASAHI (JA) [01765529] **2508**

SHUKAN BOEI TOKUSHIN (JA) [01790260] **4057**

SHUKAN SHAKAI HOSHO (JA) [04551925] **5307**

SHUKAN SHINCHO (JA/0488-7484) [06122354] **2508**

SHUKAN TOCHO (JA) [07411961] **5805**

SHUKAN TOYO KEIZAI (JA) [09497817] 1640, **1584**

SHUKAN TOYOGAKU (JA) [01765530] **2664**

SHUKAN YOMIURI (JA) [23125007] **134**

SHUNKI CHINAGE KANKEI SHUYO SANKO SHIRYO (JA) [05719365] **1710**

SHUNKI CHINGIN KOSHO SHIRYO (JA) [01799652] **1710**

SHUO FANG (CC) [07220564] **330**

SHUPIHUI (PE/0254-2021) [05366640] **2273**

SHURA (EDMONTON, ALTA.) (CN) [09159462] **2760**

SHUROT (IS) [02242663] **1710**

SHURTAH (SHURTAT JUMHURIYAT AL-SUDAN AL-DIMUQRATIYAH. QISM AL-ALAQAT AL-AMMAH) (SJ) [09247526] **3176**

SHUSHI RONBUN YOROKU / KOBE DAIGAKU DAIGAKUIN KYOIKUGAKU KENKYUKA (JA) [10873178] **1847**

SHUSHO NEMPO - HOMUSHO HOMU TOSHOKAN (JA) [03438064] **3055**

SHUTOKEN TOKEI YORAN (JA) [01799736] **5338**

SHUTTERBUG (US/0895-321X) [16570793] **4376**

SHUTTERBUG ADS PHOTOGRAPHIC NEWS *See* SHUTTERBUG **4376**

SHUTTLE (CN/0712-5801) [09250152] **4917**

SHUTTLE, SPINDLE & DYEPOT (US/0049-0423) [02244941] **375**

SHUUN AL-MARAH (WJ) [24853273] **5566**

SHUUN AL-SAAH (UK) [08392552] **2664**

SHUUN ARABIYAH (TI) [08159259] **2664**

SHUUN FILASTINIYAH (LE) [03338180] **2770**

SHUXUE WULI XUEBAO (CC/0252-9602) [I02529602] **3534**

SI BUSINESS (CN/0849-1801) [23237030] **1239**

SI..., ENTONCES... (SP/1130-149X) [I1130149X] **4618**

SI (MADRID, SPAIN) (SP) [16714316] **3471**

SI QUE *CEASED.* (CN/0229-5776) [08478785] **3436**

SI-RIVISTA STUDI SOCIALI DEL VENETO (IT) **5258**

SI YU YAN (CH/0258-8412) [01766391] 5219, **2854**

SIA FACT BOOK (US) **913**

SIA INTERNATIONAL CAPITAL MARKETS REVIEW *CEASED.* (US) **914**

SIA MUNICIPAL STATISTICAL BULLETIN *See* MUNICIPAL MARKET DEVELOPMENTS **908**

SIA ON THE HILL: A GRASSROOTS REPORT (US) 4653, **2975**

SIA POLICIES AND POSITIONS (US) **914**

SIA WASHINGTON REPORT (US) 4686, **3055**

SIAJ - JOURNAL OF THE SINGAPORE INSTITUTE OF ARCHITECTS (SI/0049-0520) [02038904] **308**

SIAL (IT) [02240881] **1445**

SIALIA (US/0890-7021) [12925441] **5597**

SIAM (IT) 811

SIAM-AMS PROCEEDINGS (US/0080-5084) [01480368] **3534**

SIAM DIRECTORY *CEASED.* (TH) [02026847] **2576**

SIAM JOURNAL ON APPLIED MATHEMATICS (US/0036-1399) [01765537] **3534**

SIAM JOURNAL ON COMPUTING (US/0097-5397) [01080306] **3534, 1262**

SIAM JOURNAL ON CONTROL AND OPTIMIZATION (US/0363-0129) [02014747] **3534**

SIAM JOURNAL ON DISCRETE MATHEMATICS (US/0895-4801) [16655673] **3534**

SIAM JOURNAL ON MATHEMATICAL ANALYSIS (US/0036-1410) [01765884] **3534**

SIAM JOURNAL ON MATRIX ANALYSIS AND APPLICATIONS (US/0895-4798) [16655630] **3534**

SIAM JOURNAL ON NUMERICAL ANALYSIS (US/0036-1429) [06035777] **3535**

SIAM JOURNAL ON OPTIMIZATION (US/1052-6234) [22338945] **3535**

SIAM JOURNAL ON SCIENTIFIC AND STATISTICAL COMPUTING (US/0196-5204) [05842767] **3535**

●SIAM JOURNAL ON SCIENTIFIC COMPUTING (US/1064-8275) [26409689] **3535**

SIAM NEWS : A PUBLICATION OF SOCIETY FOR INDUSTRIAL AND APPLIED MATHEMATICS (US) [04964580] **1202, 3535**

SIAM REVIEW (US/0036-1445) [01589229] **3535**

SIAM SOCIETY *See* JOURNAL OF THE SIAM SOCIETY, THE **2656**

SIAM SOCIETY *See* NATURAL HISTORY BULLETIN (BANGKOK) **4168**

SIARA (II) [02441077] **3436**

SIARAN PEKEBUN (MY) [06964688] **2431**

SIARAN PERANGKAAN TAHUNAN, SABAH. ANNUAL BULLETIN OF STATISTICS, SABAH (MY) [04565793] **5338**

SIARAN UMUM - DEPARTEMEN PENERANGAN R.I (IO) [04763057] **4686**

SIB PUBLISHING COMPANY *See* LEGAL ACTION IN NEW SOUTH WALES **2999**

SIBBALD GUIDE. PROFILES OF THE TOP COMPANIES & FINANCIAL INSTITUTIONS IN: OKLAHOMA, LOUISIANA, ARKANSAS, THE (US/0736-4172) [09122809] **811**

SIBBALD GUIDE, THE (US/0197-3029) [06081496] **811**

SIBBALD GUIDE TO THE TEXAS TOP TWO-FIFTY, THE (US/0278-3266) [07778105] **710**

SIBERIAN ADVANCES IN MATHEMATICS (US/1055-1344) [23092076] **3535**

●SIBERIAN BAM RAILWAY GUIDE : A HANDBOOK TO THE SECOND TRANS-SIBERIAN RAILWAY FOR RAIL ENTHUSIASTS AND TRAVELLERS, THE (AT) **5491**

SIBERIAN HUSKY CLUB OF AMERICA *See* NEWSLETTER - SIBERIAN HUSKY CLUB OF AMERICA **4287**

●SIBERIAN JOURNAL OF COMPUTER MATHEMATICS (US/1062-8053) [25744648] **1202, 3535**

SIBERIAN JOURNAL OF DIFFERENTIAL EQUATIONS (US) **3535**

SIBERIAN MATHEMATICAL JOURNAL (US/0037-4466) [01765539] **3535**

SIBERIAN QUARTERLY, THE (US/0274-7286) [06537436] **4288**

SIBERIANA / CENTRE REGIONAL DE PUBLICATION DE PARIE, CENTRE D' ETUDES ARCTIQUES (C.N.R.S.-E.H.E.S.S.) (FR) [10732523] **1360**

SIBERICA *See* SIBIRICA : THE JOURNAL OF SIBERIAN STUDIES **2664**

●SIBIRICA : THE JOURNAL OF SIBERIAN STUDIES (UK) [30537939] **2664**

SIBIRSKAIA GAZETA (RU) [17824684] **5809**

SIBIRSKIE OGNI (RU) [02045986] **2522**

SIBIRSKII NAUCHNO-ISSLEDOVATELSKII VETERINARNYI INSTITUT *See* SBORNIK NAUCHNYKH RABOT SIBNIVI **5521**

SIBIRSKII VESTNIK SELSKOKHOZIAISTVENNOI NAUKI (RU/0370-8799) [10124277] **134**

SIBIRSKIJ MATEMATICESKIH ZURNAL (RU/0037-4474) [01716701] **3535**

SIBLEY'S HARVARD GRADUATES (US) [06524674] **435**

SIBLING INFORMATION NETWORK NEWSLETTER (US) **2286**

SIBRIUM (IT/0559-9628) [I05599628] **282**

SIBSON & COMPANY *See* ANNUAL MANAGEMENT COMPENSATION STUDY **1645**

SIBYL-CHILD (US/0161-715X) [02568590] **330**

SIC (VE/0049-0431) [01928390] **1520, 4496**

SIC INFORMATIVO (BL) [01791015] **1584**

SICANGU SUN TIMES (US/1070-7786) [25598476] **2273**

SICGRAPH NEWSLETTER *CEASED.* (US) [04657736] **1235**

SICHER IST SICHER (GW/0037-4504) [I00374504] **2870**

SICHERE CHEMIEARBEIT (GW/0341-1990) [I03411990] **992**

SICHERHEIT IM BERGLAND (AU) [07102730] **4918, 4878**

SICHERHEIT IN CHEMIE UND UMWELT (GW/0720-1370) [08461252] **992**

SICHERHEITS-BERATER (GW/0344-8746) [I03448746] **947**

SICHERHEITSBEAUFTRAGTER (GW/0300-3337) [01426461] **3176**

SICHERHEITSINGENIEUR (GW/0300-3329) [01448650] **2870**

SICHERHEITSTECHNIK (GW) [05914167] **5177, 3176**

SICHUAN NONGYE DAXUE XUEBAO (CH/1000-2650) [I10002650] **134**

SICILIA (IT) [06059175] **5805**

SICILIA PARRA (US/8755-6987) [11456401] **2273**

SICK PAY BULLETIN (UK) [09064667] **1710**

SICKNESS & WELLNESS PUBLICATIONS (US/1041-2832) [18708816] **3641**

SICULORUM GYMNASIUM (IT/0037-458X) [01936976] **2854**

SICUREZZA E PREVENZIONE (IT) **1626**

SICUREZZA E PREVENZIONE: ANTICRIMINE, ANTINCENDIO, ANTINFORTUNISTICA (IT/0392-9000) [I03929000] **3176**

SICUREZZA NOTIZIE (IT) **4803**

SID CATO'S NEWSLETTER ON ANNUAL REPORTS (US) **914**

SID RESEARCH JOURNAL (US) [18109118] **221**

SIDA, BOTANICAL MISCELLANY (US/0883-1475) [12226138] **527**

SIDA, CONTRIBUTIONS TO BOTANY (US/0036-1488) [01765542] **527**

SIDA RAPPORT (SW/0282-6011) [15533179] **2912**

SIDAHORA :UN PROYECTO DEL DEPARTAMENTO DE PUBLICACIONES DEL PWA COALITION, NY (SP) [21516958] **3716, 3677**

SIDAMERICA (US) **3716, 3677**

SIDAPRESS (SP) **3641**

SIDDHA VANI (II) [01790530] **5041**

SIDE EFFECTS OF DRUGS ANNUAL (NE/0378-6080) [03182460] **4329**

SIDE-SADDLE NEWS (US/0744-3056) [08181893] **2802**

SIDE SHOW: AN ANNUAL OF CONTEMPORARY SHORT STORIES (US) [24893647] **3436**

SIDE STREETS OF THE WORLD *CEASED.* (US/0741-7624) [10237114] **5491**

SIDELINE VIEW (US) **4918**

SIDELINES *CEASED.* (US) **4918**

SIDERURGIA (BUENOS AIRES) (AG/0325-0520) [02245007] **4019**

SIDERURGIA LATINOAMERICANA (CL/0379-7759) [04375500] **4019**

SIDERURGIA LATINOAMERICANA EN ... Y SUS PERSPECTIVAS, LA (CL) [10616704] **1626, 4019**

SIDETREKKED (CN/0715-3007) [10436262] **3436**

SIDEWALKS (ANOKA, MINN.) (US/1059-2210) [24572183] **3436**

SIDEWINDER STUDIES IN HISTORY AND SOCIOLOGY (US) **5258, 2629**

SIDIC (ENGLISH ED.) (IT) [03793557] **4997**

SIDING & WINDOW CONTRACTOR (CN/0848-7677) [23238224] **627**

SIDNEY ARGUS-HERALD, THE (US) [15728734] **5672**

SIDNEY HERALD-LEADER (US) [17717958] **5706**

SIDNEY TELEGRAPH (SIDNEY, NEB. : 1951) (US) [13400546] **5707**

SIDWAYA (UV/1013-655X) [I1013655X] **5779**

SIE GUIDE TO BUSINESS & INVESTMENT BOOKS (US/0361-3917) [02169844] **914**

SIE UND ER *See* SCHWEIZER ILLUSTRIERTE. SIE + I.E. UND ER **2522**

SIEB + RAKEL *See* SIEBDRUCK, DER **4569**

SIEBDRUCK, DER (GW/0178-2835) [I01782835] **4569**

SIEBENBURGISCHES ARCHIV (GW/0583-1938) [02959139] **2709**

SIECCAN JOURNAL *See* CANADIAN JOURNAL OF HUMAN SEXUALITY, THE **5187**

SIECUS REPORT (US/0091-3995) [00906552] **5188**

SIEGENER PERIODICUM ZUR INTERNATIONALEN EMPIRISCHEN LITERATURWISSENSCHAFT (GW/0722-7833) [09385821] **3436**

SIEGRUNEN (US/0733-0367) [08505316] **2709**

SIEMENS AKTIENGESELLSCHAFT *See* ANNUAL REPORT - SIEMENS AKTIENGESELLSCHAFT **1598**

SIEMENS COMPONENTS. DEUTSCHE AUSGABE (GW/0173-1726) [I01731726] **2081**

SIEMENS COMPONENTS. ENGLISH AUSGABE (GW/0173-1734) [11240609] **2081**

SIEMENS REVIEW (GW/0302-2528) [01765545] **2081**

SIEMENS ZEITSCHRIFT (GW/0302-251X) [01589834] **2081**

SIEMPRE ADELANTE! (CK) [24013568] **1885**

SIENA. ACCADEMIA MUSICALE CHIGIANA *See* QUADERNI DELL'ACCADEMIA CHIGIANA **4148**

SIENA COLLEGE *See* ALUMNI DIRECTORY / SIENA COLLEGE **1099**

SIERRA (US/0161-7362) [03799993] **2205**

SIERRA CLUB YODELER (US/8750-5681) [11521263] **2205**

SIERRA COOPERATIVE PILOT PROJECT (U.S.) *See* STATUS REPORT - SIERRA COOPERATIVE PILOT PROJECT **1435**

SIERRA COUNTY SENTINEL (US) [27194670] **5713**

SIERRA HERITAGE (US/0886-6503) [12953591] **5491**

SIERRA LEONE EXTERNAL TELECOMMUNICATIONS LIMITED *See* REPORT AND ACCOUNTS - SIERRA LEONE EXTERNAL COMMUNICATIONS LIMITED **1162**

SIERRA LEONE LIBRARY JOURNAL, THE (SL/0377-5275) [01796638] **3249**

SIERRA LEONE NEWSLETTER (WASHINGTON, D.C.) *See* SIERRA LEONE REVIEW, THE **2643**

●SIERRA LEONE REVIEW, THE (US/1066-4947) [26963716] **2643**

●SIERRA LEONE REVIEW, THE (US/1062-0109) [25504107] **2643**

SIERRA LEONE. ROAD TRANSPORT DEPT *See* REPORT OF THE ROAD TRANSPORT DEPARTMENT - SIERRA LEONE **5391**

SIERRA LEONE, WIRTSCHAFTSDATEN UND WIRTSCHAFTSDOKUMENTATION BUNDESSTELLE FUER AUSSENHANDELSINFORMATION (GW) [12070478] **1584**

SIERRA NORTH STAR (US/0746-1682) [01590614] **2545**

SIERRA SOURCEBOOK : ELECTRONICS INDUSTRY MARKET DATA (US) [01789748] **2081**

SIERRA SUN (US) [14511009] **5640**

SIERRA VISTA HERALD (US/8750-3891) [11270339] **5630**

SIETE DIAS (BUENOS AIRES, ARGENTINA : 1979) (AG) [06362255] **2552**

SIETE DIAS ILUSTRADOS (AG) [07559269] **2552**

SIF TIDNINGEN (SW) [06368659] **1710**

SIFKU-INFORMATIONEN (GW/0170-8694) [07979052] **5307**

SIFRUT HA-TSIYONIT / ZIONIST LITERATURE, HA- (IS) [22973701] **4997**

SIFRUT YELADIM VA-NOAR (IS/0334-276X) [02243917] **1069**

SIG FORTH (US/1047-4544) [20412235] **1281**

SIG NEWSLETTER (US) [07451092] **3249**

SIG SECURITY, AUDIT & CONTROL REVIEW (US/0277-920X) [07661727] **1262**

SIGACT NEWS (US/0163-5700) [03824060] **1202**

Alphabetical Title Index — SILLON

SIGART BULLETIN (US/1053-4830) [22091943] **1217**

SIGBIO NEWSLETTER (US/0163-5697) [04411991] 3641, **1203**

SIGCAPH NEWSLETTER (US/0163-5727) [02054033] 4393, **1225**

SIGCHI BULLETIN (US/0736-6906) [08814572] 5219, **1249**

SIGCSE BULLETIN (US/0097-8418) [02286014] **1262**

SIGCUE OUTLOOK (US/0893-2999) [14047984] **1225**

SIGDA NEWSLETTER (US/0163-5743) [02989213] **1221**

SIGE ENERGIE BULLETIN (NE) **1956**

SIGERT'S FACHMAGAZIN FUER DIE UNTERHALTUNGS-GASTRONOMIE (GW) [15792340] **4153**

SIGERT'S FACHMAGAZIN FUR DIE UNTERHALTUNGS-GASTRONOMIE *See* DISCO-MAGAZIN **4115**

SIGHT AND SOUND (LONDON) (UK/0037-4806) [01645027] **4078**

SIGHT & SOUND MARKETING (US/0037-4814) [05190157] **936**

SIGHT & SOUND (MISSISSAUGA) (CN/0703-1408) [03782158] **4078**

SIGHTHOUND REVIEW (US/8750-1953) [11106471] **4288**

SIGHTLINE : JOURNAL OF THE ASSOCIATION OF BRITISH THEATRE TECHNICIANS **SUSPENDED.** (UK/0265-9808) [06354691] **388**

SIGHTLINES (NEW YORK, N.Y.) **CEASED.** (US/0037-4830) [01765552] **4078**

SIGICE BULLETIN (US) 1274, **1272**

SIGIR FORUM (US/0163-5840) [03824251] **1276**

●SIGLINK NEWSLETTER: QUARTERLY NEWSLETTER OF THE SPECIAL INTEREST GROUP ON HYPERTEXT, ASSOCIATION FOR COMPUTING MACHINERY (US) [25770340] **1249**

SIGLO XIX. CUADERNOS DE HISTORIA (MX) [25881040] **2629**

SIGLO XX (LINCOLN, NEB.) (US/0740-946X) [10060202] **3436**

SIGMA (AT/0314-7606) [03147606] **3535**

SIGMA (NE) **710**

SIGMA ALPHA IOTA : ZETA CHAPTER, INDIANAPOLIS ALUMNAE, PATRONESS CLUB (US) [09106918] **1847**

SIGMA ALPHA IOTA. ZETA CHAPTER (JORDAN COLLEGE OF FINE ARTS) *See* SIGMA ALPHA IOTA : ZETA CHAPTER, INDIANAPOLIS ALUMNAE, PATRONESS CLUB **1847**

SIGMA AUSTRALIA *See* CROSS SECTION **3502**

SIGMA PHI EPSILON *See* SIGMA PHI EPSILON JOURNAL **1872**

SIGMA PHI EPSILON JOURNAL (US/0097-6563) [01794447] **1872**

SIGMA SERIES IN APPLIED MATHEMATICS (GW) [15533015] **3535**

SIGMA SERIES IN PURE MATHEMATICS (GW) [10088315] **3535**

SIGMA SIGMA SIGMA *See* ALUMNAE DIRECTORY / SIGMA SIGMA SIGMA **1096**

SIGMA : THE BULLETIN OF EUROPEAN STATISTICS (LU/1018-5739) [24985966] **5338**

SIGMICRO CONFERENCE PROCEEDINGS (US) **1281**

SIGMICRO NEWSLETTER *See* SIGMICRO CONFERENCE PROCEEDINGS **1281**

SIGMICRO NEWSLETTER (1988) (US/1050-916X) [17990452] **1281**

SIGMOD RECORD (US/0163-5808) [03611577] **1255**

SIGMUND FREUD HOUSE BULLETIN (AU) [14908846] **4618**

SIGMUND FREUD SOCIETY *See* SIGMUND FREUD HOUSE BULLETIN **4618**

SIGN AND DISPLAY (JA) **766**

SIGN BUSINESS (US/0893-9888) [15721296] **710**

SIGN LANGUAGE STUDIES (US/0302-1475) [01779938] **3321**

SIGN WORLD (UK/0049-0466) **766**

SIGNA (US) [03292010] **2431**

SIGNAAL ABONNEMENT (NE) **1520**

SIGNAGE QUARTERLY (US/0196-5050) [05825996] **766**

SIGNAL (YU) [01791004] **3471**

SIGNAL (US) [04452461] **3436**

SIGNAL (1950) (US/0037-4938) [01353952] **1121**

SIGNAL (AMBERLEY) (UK/0037-4954) [01765555] **3437**

SIGNAL (EMMETT, IDAHO), THE **SUSPENDED.** (US/1040-4724) [18426008] **3437**

SIGNAL-ENTERPRISE, THE (US) [12760103] **5678**

SIGNAL HILL (CALIF.). REDEVELOPMENT AGENCY *See* TWO YEAR BUDGET / SIGNAL HILL REDEVELOPMENT AGENCY **2837**

SIGNAL (LISBON, OHIO) (US/0893-4592) [15547337] **5730**

SIGNAL (LONDON, ONT.) (CN/1185-1759) [24257181] **3249**

SIGNAL (MONONA, WIS.) (US/8750-2208) [11135270] **1783**

SIGNAL (MONTREAL) (CN/0037-4911) [02247534] **4803**

SIGNAL PROCESSING (NE/0165-1684) [04987231] **2081**

SIGNAL PROCESSING. IMAGE COMMUNICATION (NE/0923-5965) [20227008] **2081**

SIGNAL (QUEBEC) (CN/0316-361X) [02442239] **4997**

SIGNAL (RYCROFT) (CN/0712-1296) [08693681] **5794**

●SIGNAL TRANSDUCTION & CYCLIC NUCLEOTIDES (UK/0964-7589) [29706051] 540, 587, **493**

SIGNAL UND DRAHT (GW/0037-4997) [10563071] **5436**

SIGNAL (WINNIPEG) (CN/0228-3824) [08394503] **5393**

SIGNALEMENTEN (NE) **424**

SIGNALMAN'S JOURNAL, THE (US/0037-5020) [02450547] **5436**

SIGNALNAYA INFORMATSIYA KATALIZ I KATALIZATORY (RU/0234-9736) **1058**

SIGNALNAYA INFORMATSIYA KHIMIYA VYSOKIKH ENERGII (RU/0234-968X) **992**

SIGNALNAYA INFORMATSIYA NAPOLNENNYE I ARMIROVANNYE PLASTIKI (RU/0234-971X) **992**

SIGNALNAYA INFORMATSIYA NEIROPEPTIDY (RU/0234-9752) **587**

SIGNALNAYA INFORMATSIYA OCHISTKA I UTILIZATSIYA OTKHODOV KHIMICHESKIK PROIZVODSTV (RU/0234-9701) **992**

SIGNALNAYA INFORMATSIYA SORBENTY POVERKHNOSTNO-AKTIVNYE VESHCHESTVA (RU/0234-9698) **992**

SIGNALS (US) [21994349] 2924, **134**

SIGNATURE (US) [06010120] **3437**

SIGNATURE : A JOURNAL OF THEORY AND CANADIAN LITERATURE **CEASED.** (CN/0843-6290) [20606617] **3437**

SIGNATURE (PRAIRIE VILLAGE, KAN.) **CEASED.** (US/1068-1957) [27466208] **4569**

SIGNATURE (TORONTO) (CN/1183-5559) [24623407] **4819**

SIGNATURE (VANCOUVER) (CN/0708-515X) [05528115] **4819**

SIGNATURES (US) [16220898] **1095**

SIGNCRAFT (US/0270-4757) [06770111] **382**

SIGNE DE PISTE (CN/0820-0424) [09379170] **5236**

SIGNES D'AUJOURD'HUI PARIS (FR/0338-2052) [03382052] **5036**

SIGNES DU PRESENT **SUSPENDED.** (MR) [18370875] **5219**

SIGNIFICACAO (BL) [02243793] **3321**

SIGNIFICANT FEATURES OF FISCAL FEDERALISM (US/0146-9002) [03049237] **4748**

SIGNIFICANT ISSUES FACING DIRECTORS (US/0193-4201) [05215770] **886**

SIGNIFICANT ISSUES SERIES (US/0736-7163) [09206029] **4535**

SIGNIFICANT SEC FILINGS REPORTER (US/0199-6177) [06053218] 4496, **3055**

SIGNO (LA PAZ, BOLIVIA) (BO) [02267699] **2493**

SIGNOS (CL/0035-0451) [01773536] **330**

SIGNOS (PY) [04424899] **330**

SIGNOS UNIVERSITARIOS : REVISTA DE LA UNIVERSIDAD DEL SALVADOR (AG) [08079232] **1847**

SIGNPOST (UK) [01783238] **2809**

SIGNPOST FOR NORTHWEST TRAILS (1988) (US/1069-2177) [26835911] **4878**

SIGNPOSTS : A DIGEST OF RESEARCHED INFORMATION FOR CONCERNED CITIZENS (SA) [14589268] **4997**

SIGNS (CHICAGO, ILL.) (US/0097-9740) [01362618] **5566**

SIGNS OF THE TIMES (MOUNTAIN VIEW) (US/0037-5047) [01589555] **5067**

SIGNUM (FI/0355-0036) [12310203] **3249**

SIGNUM NEWSLETTER (US/0163-5778) [04387518] 3535, **1203**

SIGOIS BULLETIN (US/0894-0819) [14991329] **1249**

SIGOPS BULLETIN *See* OPERATING SYSTEMS REVIEW **1248**

SIGSAM BULLETIN (US/0163-5824) [03062933] 3535, **1203**

SIGSMALL/PC NOTES (US/0893-2875) [11658153] 1274, **1272**

SIGTC CONNECTIONS (US/1048-8340) [21052840] **1225**

SIGUCCS NEWSLETTER (US/0736-6892) [08266573] **1244**

SII VOUS INFORME (CN/0821-1442) [09770530] **4997**

SIIRTOLAISUUS / SIIRTOLAISUUSINSTITUUTTI (FI/0355-3779) [08608512] **1921**

SIJO MUNHAK (KO) [05277157] **3321**

SIK-RAPPORT (SW/0436-2071) [06797888] 2357, **4199**

SIK-SVENSKA LIVSMEDELSINSTITUTET *See* ARSBERATTELSE - SIK-SVENSKA LIVSMEDELSINSTITUTET **2327**

SIK-SVENSKA LIVSMEDELSINSTITUTET *See* SIK-RAPPORT **4199**

SIKH COURIER, THE (UK) [02246316] **4997**

SIKH DHARMA BROTHERHOOD (US/0364-8206) [02662617] **4997**

SIKH REVIEW, THE (II/0037-5128) [01534202] **4997**

SIKOKU KOGYO GIZYUTU SIKENSYO *See* TSUSHO SANGYOSHO KOGYO GIJUTSUIN SHIKOKU KOGYO GIJUTSU SHIKENJO YORAN **5167**

SIKPUM KONGOP (KO) [11054534] **2357**

SIKPUM KWAHAK (KO) [04856310] **2357**

SIKSI : THE NORDIC ART REVIEW (FI/0782-7423) [13620582] **330**

SIL - AAIB OCCASIONAL PAPERS (AT/1036-1243) [I10361243] **3321**

SILENCE -- ON TOURNE (MONTREAL) (CN/1188-0007) [25423683] **388**

SILENCIUM (GW) **2809**

SILENO (IT) [08609318] **3321**

SILENT ADVOCATE, THE (US/0037-5187) [03924660] **4393**

SILENT FLIGHT (UK) **2778**

SILENT NEWS (US/0049-0490) [04979221] **5721**

SILENT PARTNER, THE (US/0361-3291) [02039847] **4217**

SILENT PICTURE, THE (US/0037-5209) [01937000] **4078**

SILESIA ANTIQUA (PL/0080-9594) [01936955] 282, **2709**

SILHOUETTE DESIRE (US) **5075**

SILHOUETTE (IDAHO FALLS, IDAHO), THE (US/0744-866X) [08605558] **5657**

SILHOUETTE INTIMATE MOMENTS (US) **5075**

SILHOUETTE ROMANCE (US) **5075**

SILHOUETTE SPECIAL EDITIONS (US) **5075**

SILI ZHONGGUO YIYAO XUEYUAN YANJIU NIANBAO (CH/0254-0088) [06310113] 1847, **3641**

SILICATES INDUSTRIELS (BE/0037-5225) [02450551] **2594**

SILICATES INDUSTRIELS (FR) **2594**

SILICON CHIP (AT/1030-2662) [I10302662] **2081**

SILICON GRAPHICS WORLD (US/1057-7041) [24098453] **1235**

SILICON IN ... - U.S. DEPARTMENT OF THE INTERIOR, BUREAU OF MINES (US) [09936218] 4019, **4026**

SILICON MOUNTAIN REPORT **SUSPENDED.** (US/0748-6081) [10972481] **1626**

SILIKAT JOURNAL (GW) [04295946] **2594**

SILIKATTECHNIK **CEASED.** (GW/0037-5233) [06957890] **1030**

SILK EXPORT BULLETIN (II) [09210446] 5356, **851**

SILLAGES (FR) [01585739] **3437**

SILLERY VOUS INFORME (CN/0713-682X) [08980996] **4686**

SILLIMAN JOURNAL (PH/0037-5284) [01909529] **2854**

SILLON BELGE, LE (BE) **4496**

SILPAKALA : BAMLADESA SILPAKALA EKADEMIRA SHANMASIKA MUKHAPATRA (BG) [10168006] **330**

SILSBEE BEE, THE (US) [11615661] **5754**

SILSKI VISTI (UN) [04091124] **134**

SILSOE LINK (UK/0965-8106) [I09658106] **134**

SILVA BELGICA (BE) [19949477] **2395**

SILVA FENNICA (HELSINKI, FINLAND : 1926) (FI) [01643886] **2395**

SILVAE GENETICA (GW/0037-5349) [11054817] 2395, **528**

SILVER & GOLD REPORT (US/0195-8054) [05688387] 4019, **914**

SILVER AUCTION RECORDS (UK) [05186554] **375**

SILVER CITY DAILY PRESS (1963) (US/0891-7981) [10676257] **5713**

SILVER INSTITUTE *See* SILVER INSTITUTE LETTER **4019**

SILVER INSTITUTE LETTER (US/0730-8132) [01765562] **4019**

SILVER, KEMPE, BRUYN & FULGINITI'S HANDBOOK OF PEDIATRICS (US) [23763926] **3911**

SILVER MAGAZINE *See* SILVER (WHITTIER, CALIF.) **4019**

... SILVER SPRUCE YEARBOOK, THE (US) [10936234] **1847**

SILVER STATE POST, THE (US) [11514824] **5706**

SILVER SURFER (US/0897-9111) [17661540] **4866**

SILVER VAIN (US/0147-6122) [03199732] **3437**

SILVER (WHITTIER, CALIF.) (US/0899-6105) [13858326] **4019**

SILVERFISH REVIEW (US/0164-1085) [04579112] **3437**

SILVERPLATTER EXCHANGE, THE (US/0896-4068) [17064504] **1203**

SILVERTON STANDARD AND THE MINER, THE (US) [11285317] **5644**

SILVICULTURAL OPERATIONS NEWSLETTER (CN) **2395**

SILVOENERGIA (CR) [25088289] **134**

SIM INDUSTRIAL MICROBIOLOGY NEWS (US/1043-4976) [19479259] **2017**

SIM NOW (CN/0711-6683) [08142944] **4997**

SIMAN KERIAH (IS) [01784356] **3352**

SIMANTIKA (US/8755-7517) [11412941] **3437**

SIMBABWE, ENERGIEWIRTSCHAFT / BUNDESSTELLE FUER AUSSENHANDELSINFROMATION (GW) [10931212] **1957**

SIMBABWE, WIRTSCHAFTLICHE ENTWICKLUNG / BUNDESSTELLE FUER AUSSENHANDELSINFORMATION (GW) [10931369] **1584**

SIMBABWE, WIRTSCHAFTSDATEN UND WIRTSCHAFTSDOKUMENTATION / BUNDESSTELLE FUER AUSSENHANDELSINFORMATION (GW) [10931261] **1584**

SIMCOE MIRROR, THE (CN/0712-5569) [09159522] **5794**

SIMCOE REVIEW (CN/0226-3424) [07294904] **3352**

SIMENTU KAGONGOP (KO) [10125364] **5157**

SIMERA (QUEBEC) (CN/0707-1078) [05376711] **2545**

SIMERINI (CY) **5799**

SIMG : MEDICINA GENERALE (IT/1120-673X) **3641**

SIMIENTE (CL/0037-5403) [02805125] **134**

SIMIENTES (CU) [14116440] **1805**

SIMIOLUS (NE/0037-5411) [01928395] **364**

SIMMEL NEWSLETTER / [PRESENTED BY THE GEORG SIMMEL-GESELLSCHAFT E V., BIELEFELD] (GW/0939-2327) [24900328] **5258**

SIMMENTAL COUNTRY (CN/0225-7211) [05805542] **221**

SIMMENTAL JOURNAL (US) [01953315] **221**

SIMMENTAL SHIELD *CEASED.* (US/0192-3072) [04993402] **221**

SIMMONS-BOARDMAN MARINE DIRECTORY *See* MARINE DIRECTORY **5452**

SIMMONS KINFOLK (US/0146-9649) [03093384] **2472**

SIMMONS REVIEW, THE (US/0049-0512) [03924737] **1095**

SIMNENTAL SHIELD UPDATE (US) [04919953] **221**

SIMON AND SCHUSTER CROSSWORD PUZZLE BOOK (US/0196-7231) [05870103] **4866**

SIMON AND SCHUSTER, INC *See* SIMON AND SCHUSTER CROSSWORD PUZZLE BOOK **4866**

SIMON GREENLEAF LAW REVIEW : A PUBLICATION OF THE SIMON GREENLEAF SCHOOL OF LAW, THE (US/0882-181X) [09454479] **4513**

SIMON STEVIN (BE/0037-5454) [00829715] **3535**

SIMON WIESENTHAL CENTER ANNUAL *SUSPENDED.* (US/0741-8450) [10222225] **2709**

SIMON'S TAX CASES (UK) [03457757] **4748**

SIMON'S TAX INTELLIGENCE (UK) [02239960] **4748**

SIMON'S TAXES (UK) 4748, **3055**

SIMPLICIANA (SZ/0259-6415) [06219937] **3437**

SIMPLICITY FASHIONS (US/0091-1879) [01786735] **5186**

SIMPLICITY (NEW YORK, N.Y. : 1951) *See* SIMPLICITY FASHIONS **5186**

SIMPLICITY PATTERN CO *See* SIMPLICITY SCHOOL CATALOG **5186**

SIMPLICITY SCHOOL CATALOG (US/0488-8812) [02917768] **5186**

SIMPLIFIER, THE (US) **851**

●SIMPLY CROSS STITCH (US/1061-3234) [25258746] **5186**

SIMPLY LIVING (AT/0314-3155) [I03143155] **2182**

SIMPLY SEAFOOD (US/1056-8611) [23884619] **2357**

SIMPLY STATED *CEASED.* (US/0731-2016) [07291936] **3437**

SIMPOSIO (BL) [10927119] **4997**

●SIMPSON 7 : REVISTA DE LA SOCIEDAD DE ESCRITORES DE CHILE (CL) [25823733] **3437**

SIMPSON COUNTY NEWS (US) [15714639] **5701**

SIMPSONS ILLUSTRATED *CEASED.* (US/1054-8491) [22994123] **388**

SIMS SEEKER, THE (US/1045-9987) [20306111] **2472**

SIMSANG (KO) [01797430] **3471**

SIMSBURY NEWS, THE (US/0891-9542) [14633520] **5646**

SIMULATION & GAMING (US/1046-8781) [20550385] 5219, **1283**

SIMULATION DIGEST (US/1060-3689) [18902998] **1283**

SIMULATION/GAMES FOR LEARNING *CEASED.* (UK/0142-9361) [07917632] **1905**

SIMULATION PRACTICE AND THEORY (NE/0928-4869) **1244**

SIMULATION (SAN DIEGO, CALIF.) (US/0037-5497) [00992556] **1283**

SIMULATION SERIES (US/0735-9276) [08875970] **1283**

SIMULATIONS AND GAMING YEARBOOK (UK) **1783**

SIMUNHAK (KO) [04452690] **3437**

SIN CENSURA (BUENOS AIRES, ARGENTINA) (AG) [10109029] **2760**

SIN CENSURA (WASHINGTON, D.C.) (US/1060-5525) [06587769] **2760**

SIN CHEPUM, SIN KISUL (KO) [05136088] **5157**

SIN INGAN (KO) [08491108] **2854**

●SIN INTERNATIONAL (US/1070-2199) [28304099] **4153**

SIN KYOYUK YONGU (KO) [10175647] **1783**

SIN YOSONG (KO) [09231623] **2508**

SINAG-AGHAM (PH/0115-8864) [14348484] **5157**

SINAI (IS) [01765573] **5052**

SINAL, REGISTRO DE MARCAS E SIMBOLOS (BL) [02553751] **1308**

SINANG SEGYE (KO) [11332373] **4997**

SINAR DARUSSALAM (IO) [01795381] **5045**

SINAR ISLAM (IO) [05725323] **5045**

SINAR ZAMAN (MY) [02239417] **2664**

SINATRA INTERNATIONAL (AT/0810-5200) [I08105200] **435**

SIND JOURNAL OF POLITICAL SCIENCE & MODERN HISTORY / SPONSORED BY THE DEPARTMENTS OF POLITICAL SCIENCE AND MODERN HISTORY, UNIVERSITY OF SIND (PK) [05914110] **4496**

SIND (PAKISTAN). FINANCE DEPT *See* SUPPLEMENTARY STATEMENT OF EXPENDITURE **4751**

SIND, PAKISTAN. PROVINCIAL ASSEMBLY *See* DEBATES : OFFICIAL REPORT - PROVINCIAL ASSEMBLY OF SIND **4471**

SIND UNIVERSITY RESEARCH JOURNAL. SCIENCE SERIES (PK/0080-9624) [02256267] **5158**

SINDHOLOGICAL STUDIES (PK) [04851679] **2664**

SINDICALISMO EN ESPANA (SP) [02240827] **1710**

SINDICATO DOS BANCOS DO ESTADO DA GUANABARA *See* PANORAMA ESTATISTICO DO SETOR BANCARIO **732**

SINDICATO UNICO TRABAJADORES ESPECTACULO PUBLICO *See* MEMORIA Y BALANCE **1690**

SINE (HESPERIA, CALIF.) (US/1055-209X) [23121741] **2081**

SINERGIE (IT/0393-5108) [13540829] **886**

SINFONIAN (1980), THE (US/8750-5347) [08767026] 5236, **4153**

SING HEAVENLY MUSE! (US/0198-9855) [06265954] 5566, **3437**

SING OUT (US/0037-5624) [01695404] **4153**

SING OUT BULLETIN, THE (US/0737-1705) [08904742] **4153**

SING OUT EAST DONCASTER (AT/0818-0555) [I08180555] **4153**

SINGA (SI/0129-9387) [07802157] **5258**

SINGAPORE *See* BUDGET FOR THE FINANCIAL YEAR / REPUBLIC OF SINGAPORE, THE **780**

SINGAPORE ACCOUNTANT, THE (SI/0080-9640) [02038860] **751**

SINGAPORE AIRLINES *See* ANNUAL REPORT **11**

SINGAPORE BALANCE OF PAYMENTS (SI) [02683229] **811**

SINGAPORE BANKING AND FINANCE (SI) [04187728] **811**

SINGAPORE BOOK WORLD (SI/0080-9659) [02038692] **4832**

SINGAPORE BOOKS IN PRINT (SI/0129-4431) [05160058] **4832**

SINGAPORE BUILDER DIRECTORY *See* SINGAPORE BUILDERS DIRECTORY **627**

SINGAPORE BUILDERS DIRECTORY (SI) [11987095] **627**

SINGAPORE BULLETIN (SI) [01793568] **1584**

SINGAPORE BUSINESS (SI/0129-2951) [03066722] **851**

SINGAPORE CHINESE CHAMBER OF COMMERCE & INDUSTRY *See* HUI YUAN MING LU **820**

SINGAPORE (CITY) UNIVERSITY POLITICAL SCIENCE SOCIETY *See* JOURNAL OF THE POLITICAL SCIENCE SOCIETY **4479**

SINGAPORE COMMUNITY HEALTH BULLETIN, THE (SI/0129-7457) [05105316] **4803**

SINGAPORE COMPUTER SOCIETY *See* JOURNAL - SINGAPORE COMPUTER SOCIETY **1261**

SINGAPORE. DEPT. OF STATISTICS *See* MONTHLY DIGEST OF STATISTICS **5333**

SINGAPORE. DEPT. OF STATISTICS *See* SINGAPORE BALANCE OF PAYMENTS **811**

SINGAPORE DIRECTORY OF ADULT EDUCATION AGENCIES (SI) [03058706] **1802**

SINGAPORE. DIRECTORY OF ISTANA NEGARA, JUDICIAL, CABINET, LEGISLATIVE ASSEMBLY, PUBLIC SERVICE COMMISSION, AUDIT, MINISTERIES, INDUSTRIAL ARBITRATION COURT, STATUTORY BOARDS, ADVISORY COMMITTEES, UNIVERSITIES, POLYTECHNIC, COMMONWEALTH REPRESENTATIVES AND FOREIGN CONSULS *See* SINGAPORE GOVERNMENT DIRECTORY **4686**

SINGAPORE ECONOMIC REVIEW (SI/0217-5908) [10678845] **1584**

SINGAPORE FAMILY PHYSICIAN, THE (SI/0377-5305) [01673212] **3739**

SINGAPORE GOVERNMENT DIRECTORY (SI) [02285239] **4686**

SINGAPORE INDIAN CHAMBER OF COMMERCE *See* DIRECTORY - SINGAPORE INDIAN CHAMBER OF COMMERCE **819**

SINGAPORE INPUT-OUTPUT TABLES (SI/0217-6181) [10936320] **1584**

SINGAPORE INSTITUTE OF ARCHITECTS *See* SIAJ - JOURNAL OF THE SINGAPORE INSTITUTE OF ARCHITECTS **308**

SINGAPORE INSTITUTE OF PLANNERS *See* SIP JOURNAL **2835**

SINGAPORE. INTERNATIONAL CHAMBER OF COMMERCE *See* ECONOMIC BULLETIN - SINGAPORE INTERNATIONAL CHAMBER OF COMMERCE **819**

SINGAPORE INTERNATIONAL CHAMBER OF COMMERCE *See* INVESTOR'S GUIDE (SINGAPORE) **903**

Alphabetical Title Index

SINGAPORE INTERNATIONAL CHAMBER OF COMMERCE See ANNUAL REPORT / SINGAPORE INTERNATIONAL CHAMBER OF COMMERCE **818**

SINGAPORE INTERNATIONAL CHAMBER OF COMMERCE. INVESTOR'S GUIDE See INVESTOR'S GUIDE TO SINGAPORE, THE **903**

SINGAPORE JOURNAL OF EDUCATION *CEASED*. (SI/0129-4776) [05198442] **1784**

SINGAPORE JOURNAL OF LEGAL STUDIES (SI/0218-2173) [24914783] **3055**

SINGAPORE JOURNAL OF OBSTETRICS & GYNAECOLOGY (SI/0129-3273) [07064590] **3768**

SINGAPORE JOURNAL OF PHYSICS (SI/0217-4251) [16781207] **4421**

SINGAPORE JOURNAL OF PRIMARY INDUSTRIES (SI/0129-6485) [02239525] 2313, **134**

SINGAPORE JOURNAL OF TROPICAL GEOGRAPHY (SI/0129-7619) [06884190] **2576**

●SINGAPORE LAW REPORTS, THE (SI/0218-3161) [27749086] **3055**

SINGAPORE LAW REVIEW (SI/0080-9705) [01765576] **3055**

SINGAPORE LIBRARIES (SI/0085-6118) [02036083] **3249**

SINGAPORE MANAGEMENT REVIEW (SI) [05993361] **886**

SINGAPORE MANUFACTURERS AND PRODUCTS DIRECTORY (SI) [05242909] **3488**

SINGAPORE MEDICAL JOURNAL (SI/0037-5675) [01781205] **3641**

SINGAPORE. MINISTRY OF LABOUR See REPORT ON THE LABOUR FORCE SURVEY OF SINGAPORE **1707**

SINGAPORE. MINISTRY OF SCIENCE AND TECHNOLOGY See NATIONAL SURVEY OF SCIENTIFIC MANPOWER **1693**

SINGAPORE. MINISTRY OF SCIENCE AND TECHNOLOGY See NATIONAL SURVEY OF ENGINEERING MANPOWER **1693**

SINGAPORE NATIONAL ACADEMY OF SCIENCE See JOURNAL OF THE SINGAPORE NATIONAL ACADEMY OF SCIENCE **5121**

SINGAPORE NATIONAL BIBLIOGRAPHY (SI/0080-9713) [01643623] **424**

SINGAPORE NATIONAL INSTITUTE OF CHEMISTRY See BULLETIN **963**

SINGAPORE PERIODICALS INDEX (SI/0377-7928) [05705342] **1929**

SINGAPORE POLICE JOURNAL (SI) [01784317] **3176**

SINGAPORE PROFESSIONALS : JOURNAL OF THE SINGAPORE PROFESSIONAL CENTRE, THE (SI) [06928695] **1710**

SINGAPORE REPORT ON THE GROWTH TRIANGLE (US/1060-250X) [24924100] **851**

SINGAPORE SCIENTIST (SI/0217-1880) [02171880] **5158**

SINGAPORE SHIPPING & AIR TRANSPORTATION INDUSTRIES DIRECTORY (SI) [01797929] **5393**

SINGAPORE SHIPPING ASSOCIATION See REPORT AND ACCOUNTS / SINGAPORE SHIPPING ASSOCIATION **5455**

SINGAPORE SHIPPING 'N' SHIPBUILDER (SI) [01797873] **5457**

SINGAPORE (SINGAPORE) (SI) [03286392] **5491**

SINGAPORE STAMP CATALOGUE IN FULL COLOUR (MY/0127-1563) [09499354] **2787**

SINGAPORE STANDARDS YEARBOOK (SI/0129-6256) [11117044] **4032**

SINGAPORE STATISTICAL NEWS : SSN (SI/0217-4316) [10920308] **5338**

SINGAPORE TRADE STATISTICS. IMPORTS AND EXPORTS (SI) [21264201] **851**

SINGAPORE VETERINARY JOURNAL (SI/0129-3826) [06805387] **5522**

SINGAPORE'S JUDICIAL & LEGAL DIRECTORY (SI) [10294769] **3055**

SINGAPUR : ENERGIEWIRTSCHAFT (GW) [06597786] **1957**

SINGAPUR : WIRTSCHAFTLICHE ENTWICKLUNG (GW) [05217816] **1584**

SINGENDE KIRCHE (AU/0037-5721) [04977052] **4153**

SINGER REPORT ON MANAGED CARE SYSTEMS AND TECHNOLOGY, THE (US/1071-1910) [28566288] **5158**

SINGING NEWS MAGAZINE, THE (US/1060-3956) [11331629] **4153**

SINGLE (US/0091-8652) [01788094] **5258**

SINGLE ADULT MINISTRY INFORMATION See SINGLES & LEADERS NEWSLETTER **4997**

SINGLE ADULT MINISTRY INFORMATION (US/0887-1167) [13103216] **4997**

SINGLE AUDIT INFORMATION SERVICE (US/8756-3886) [I87563886] 751

SINGLE DAD'S LIFESTYLE (US/0739-8719) [06685987] **2286**

SINGLE DAD'S MAGAZINE (US/1040-6557) [18473916] **2286**

SINGLE FAMILY COINSURANCE PROGRAM (US) [02927565] **2893**

SINGLE FAMILY HOME PLANS (US) [19789422] **308**

SINGLE GENTLEMEN & WOMEN (US) 5566, **3996**

SINGLE HOUND (US/1044-8934) [19937491] **3471**

SINGLE LIVING MAGAZINE : AN IOWA PERSPECTIVE (US) **2493**

SINGLE MARKET COMMUNICATIONS LIMITED (UK) **1121**

SINGLE MARKET MONITOR (UK) **1627**

●SINGLE-PARENT FAMILY (US/1077-4092) [30803243] **2286**

SINGLE PARENT, THE (US/0037-5748) [08660434] **2286**

SINGLE STYLE FOR WRITERS DIALOGUE GROUP (US/1055-3401) [23157328] **3437**

SINGLE (TAMPA, FLA.) (US/0747-3184) [10739238] **5258**

SINGLE TODAY (LAPORTE, IND.) (US/1047-9066) [20809645] **2493**

SINGLELIFE (MILWAUKEE, WIS.) (US/8756-0380) [11464043] **2493**

SINGLES & LEADERS NEWSLETTER (US/1077-0887) [30696652] **4997**

SINGLES CHOICE (US/1058-0638) [24189068] 5566, **3996**

SINGLES SOLUTIONS (US/1057-2015) [23979300] 5566, **3996**

SINGMUL CHOJIK PAEYANG See SINGMUL CHOJIK PAEYANG HAKHOE CHI **528**

SINGMUL CHOJIK PAEYANG HAKHOE CHI (KO) [09316826] **528**

SINGMUL HAKHOE CHI (KO/0583-421X) [04677525] **528**

SINGMUL PULLYU HAKHOE CHI (KO) [07817397] **528**

SINGULARITE LYON (FR/1143-7723) [I11437723] **3535**

SINHAK CHONMANG (KO) [04427531] **5036**

SINHAK KWA SONKYO (KO) [04507390] **4997**

SINICA LEIDENSIA (NE/0169-9563) [01765578] **2664**

SINISTER WISDOM (US/0196-1853) [03451636] 3437, **2796**

SINK *CEASED*. (US/0891-298X) [14714811] **3437**

SINMIN (KO) [09606657] **2508**

SINMUN KWA PANGSONG (KO) [04403323] **3321**

SINN UND FORM (GW/0037-5756) [01604875] **2522**

SINO-AMERICAN RELATIONS (CH) [02243610] **4535**

SINO-JAPANESE STUDIES (US) [20977878] **2664**

SINO-PLATONIC PAPERS (US) [15688628] **3321**

●SINO-U.S. TRADING ALMANAC (US/1066-1816) [26885860] **851**

SINO-US TRADE STATISTICS (US/0196-4607) [05815334] 851, **733**

SINO-WESTERN CULTURAL RELATIONS JOURNAL (US/1041-875X) [18865015] **4535**

SINOPSE DE ATIVIDADES - SERLA (BL) [04146303] **134**

SINOPSE ESTATISTICA DA REGIAO NORTE / SECRETARIA DE PLANEJAMENTO DA PRESIDENCIA DA REPUBLICA, FUNDACAO INSTITUTO BRASILEIRO DE GEOGRAFIA E ESTATISTICA, IBGE (BL) [08916937] **5338**

SINOPSE ESTATISTICA DA REGIAO SUL / SECRETARIA DE PLANEJAMENTO DA PRESIDENCIA DA REPUBLICA, FUNDACAO INSTITUTO BRASILEIRO DE GEOGRAFIA E ESTATISTICA, IBGE (BL) [10024809] **5338**

SINSEAR (IE/0332-2653) [09726429] **2324**

SINTAK (KO) [04403366] **811**

SINTE GLESDA COLLEGE NEWS (US/8755-1322) [08641098] **1095**

SINTESE (BL/0103-4332) [02241876] **5219**

SINTESIS (MX) [05285182] **2552**

SINTESIS CULTURAL (ILCE (INSTITUTE)) (MX) [08945191] **2545**

SINTESIS ECONOMICA (BOGOTA, COLOMBIA) (CK) [04999083] **1584**

SINTESIS ESTADISTICA - MINISTERIO DI ECONOMIA, JUNTA NACIONAL DE CARNES DE LA REPUBLICA ARGENTINA (AG) [01744541] 222, **156**

SINTESIS GEOGRAFICA : REVISTA DE LA ESCUELA DE GEOGRAFIA, UNIVERSIDAD CENTRAL DE VENEZUELA (VE) [10755701] **2576**

SINTESIS INFORMATIVA (AG) [03399243] **1584**

SINTESIS INFORMATIVA IBEROAMERICANA (SP) [02245039] **2760**

SINTESIS (MADRID, SPAIN) (SP) [17202068] **1584**

SINTEZA (XV/0049-0601) [10864299] **364**

SINTOMAS EN LA CIENCIA, LA CULTURA, Y LA TECNICA (AG) [08771026] **5219**

SINTRIA / GABINETE DE ESTUDOS DE ARQUEOLOGIA, ARTE E ETNOGRAFIA, MUSEU REGIONAL DE SINTRA OE MUSEU ARQUEOLOGICO DE SAO MIGUEL DE ODRINHAS (PO/0871-8148) [21500263] **282**

SINYONG KYONGJE (KO) [10570447] **811**

SINYONG SAHOE (KO) [08832030] **1627**

SIOUX CENTER NEWS (US) [16165913] **5672**

SIOUX CITY JOURNAL (SIOUX CITY, IOWA : 1887) (US) [15319768] **5673**

SIOUX COUNTY CAPITAL-DEMOCRAT, THE (US) [16160185] **5673**

SIOUX COUNTY INDEX-REPORTER, THE (US) [16160309] **5673**

SIOUX FALLS COLLEGE, SIOUX FALLS, S.D See BULLETIN - SIOUX FALLS COLLEGE (SIOUX FALLS, S.D.) **1813**

SIOUX RAPIDS BULLETIN-PRESS (US) [16671083] **5673**

●SIOUXLAND EVENTS (US/1060-376X) [24947777] **4854**

SIP JOURNAL (SI) [02037294] **2835**

SIP NEWSLETTER FROM SWEDEN (ENGLISH EDITION) (SW/0282-941X) [07972491] **2522**

SIPAPU (US/0037-5837) [01283113] **3352**

SIPARIO (IT) [01765584] 4078, **5368**

SIPISCOPE (US/0737-0350) [05159374] **5158**

SIPRI YEARBOOK 1987 (UK/0953-0282) [I09530282] **4535**

SIPRI YEARBOOK : WORLD ARMAMENTS AND DISARMAMENT (SW/0347-2205) [02211125] **4057**

SIR PRESENTS 2 BY 2 (US/0731-986X) [08287454] **2493**

SIR ROBERT MADGWICK LECTURE (AT/0816-2735) [19046669] **1847**

SIRALU (II) [12074721] **3437**

SIRE BOOK See STALLION DIRECTORY **2802**

SIRENA : PROLETARSKII DVUKHNEDELNIK (RU) [26992023] **4686**

SIRIUS (LOS ANGELES, CALIF.) (US/0738-2820) [09552027] **2500**

SIRJANA (NP/0049-0628) [01640222] **1584**

SIRS GLOBAL PERSPECTIVES (US/1058-1731) [24232675] **4535**

SISA CHUNCHU (KO) [25793577] **2493**

SISA ILBONO YONGU (KO) [11363578] **3321**

SISA NEWS (US/0199-6193) [06103050] **2493**

SISAC NEWS (US/0885-3959) [12627315] **3249**

SISKIYOU COUNTY (CA) SERIES (US/1040-3620) [18241214] **2545**

SISKIYOU PIONEER IN FOLKLORE, FACT AND FICTION, THE (US/0196-0725) [05754395] **2324**

SISMODINAMICA (DURHAM, N.H.) (US/1051-6441) [22008231] 1411, **2031**

SISSETON AMBASSADOR See SISSETON COURIER, THE **5744**

SISSETON COURIER, THE (US) [13554564] **5744**

SISSETON JOURNAL-PRESS See SISSETON COURIER, THE **5744**

SISSETON WEEKLY STANDARD See SISSETON COURIER, THE **5744**

SISSIONS (J. N.) LIMITED See SISSONS STAMP AUCTION **2787**

SISSONS — Alphabetical Title Index

SISSONS STAMP AUCTION (CN/0583-4465) [02248052] **2787**

SISSTA SUGAR JOURNAL (II) [10178028] **186**

SISTEMA CASSE (IT) **811**

SISTEMA DE INFORMACAO ESTATISTICA PARA A INDUSTRIA NACIONAL DE CALCADOS (BL) [01799135] **1087**

SISTEMA DE INFORMACAO ESTATISTICA PARA A INDUSTRIA NACIONAL DE COUROS : BOLETIM DE INFORMACOES (BL) [02244404] **3186**

SISTEMA FERROVIARIO DO BRASIL / REDE FERROVIARIA FEDERAL, S.A., DIRECTORIA DE PLANEJAMENTO, DEPARTAMENTO GERAL DE ESTATISTICA (BL) [05818288] **5436**

SISTEMA ITALIA (IT) **2081**

SISTEMA (MADRID) (SP/0210-0223) [01786986] **5219**

SISTEMA NACIONAL DE INFORMACION See INFORMATIVO - SNI **5113**

SISTEMA RODOVIARIO DO ESTADO DO PARANA / ESTADO DO PARANA, SECRETARIA DE ESTADO DOS TRANSPORTES, DEPARTAMENTO DE ESTRADAS DE RODAGEM (BL) [11502729] **5444**

SISTEMARICERCA (IT/0393-9472) [15648920] **5158**

SISTEMAS (BL) [02720054] **1262**

SISTEMATICA *SUSPENDED.* (IT/0037-5888) [01928419] **4361**

SISTEMI & IMPRESA (IT/0394-929X) [0394929X] **1627**

SISTEMI DI TELECOMUNICAZIONI (IT) **1163**

SISTEMI E IMPRESA (IT) **886**

SISTEMI INTELLIGENTI (IT) [22365655] **1217**

SISTEMI URBANI (IT) [07341915] **2835**

SISTEMNOE MODELIROVANIE See TRUDY VYCHISLITELNOGO TSENTRA SO RAN. SERIIA SISTEMNOE MODELIROVANIE / ROSSIISKAIA AKADEMIIA NAUK, SIBIRSKOE OTDELENIE, VYCHISLITELNYI TSENTR **3540**

SISTEMNOE OPISANIE LEKSIKI GERMANSKIKH IAZYKOV (RU) [06886524] **3321**

SISTEMY AVTOMATICHESKOGO UPRAVLENIIA / INSTITUT PROBLEM UPRAVLENIIA, NAUCHNO-TEKHNICHESKAIA BIBLIOTEKA (RU) [08139487] **1221**

SISTEMY I SREDSTVA INFORMATIKI (RU) [21006606] **1203**

SISTERS IN STYLE (US) **1087**

SISTERS PICTORIAL (HK) **5566**

SISTERS TODAY (US/0037-590X) [01714387] **5036**

SISTREN (JM) [14815449] **5566**

SITE (CN/0826-5356) [11245758] **627**

SITE AUDITING (CN) **2243**

SITE REGISTER / TOXICS CLEANUP PROGRAM, WASHINGTON STATE DEPARTMENT OF ECOLOGY (US) [23232044] **2243**

SITE REPORT, THE *CEASED.* (US/0275-1488) [07087647] 627, **3488**

SITE SELECTION (US) **2835**

SITE SELECTION & INDUSTRIAL DEVELOPMENT (US/1041-3073) [18676146] 711, **4247**

SITE SELECTION EUROPE See SITE SELECTION **2835**

SITE WORLD (US/1055-3584) [23158330] **914**

SITES ET MONUMENTS (FR/0489-0280) [02578322] **2709**

SITES (NEW YORK, N.Y.) (US/0747-9409) [09271032] **330**

SITREP (CN/0316-5620) [02247545] **4057**

SITREP (AT) [03506387] **5307**

SITTINGS - EUROPEAN PARLIAMENT, THE (LU) [01432277] **4686**

SITUACION (BILBAO, SPAIN) (SP) [15534777] **1640**

SITUACION COYUNTURAL DEL SECTOR AGROPECUARIO (AG/0325-9161) [18057110] 1520, **135**

SITUATION *CEASED.* (DK) [01799308] **1520**

SITUATION (FR/0530-9190) [02961784] **3352**

SITUATION AND OOUTLOOK REPORT. AGRICULTURAL RESOURCES See SITUATION AND OUTLOOK SUMMARY. AGRICULTURAL RESOURCES, AGRICULTURAL LAND VALUES / UNITED STATES DEPARTMENT OF AGRICULTURE, ECONOMIC RESEARCH SERVICE **135**

SITUATION AND OUTLOOK REPORT. AGRICULTURAL INCOME AND FINANCE / UNITED STATES DEPARTMENT OF AGRICULTURE, ECONOMIC RESEARCH SERVICE (US) [18493842] **135**

SITUATION AND OUTLOOK REPORT. AGRICULTURAL RESOURCES (US/1057-8447) [15032581] **135**

SITUATION AND OUTLOOK REPORT. COTTON AND WOOL (US/1051-7928) [13920661] **5356**

SITUATION AND OUTLOOK REPORT. DAIRY (US/1050-9151) [14237318] **198**

SITUATION AND OUTLOOK REPORT. DAIRY See LIVESTOCK, DAIRY AND POULTRY SITUATION AND OUTLOOK **105**

SITUATION AND OUTLOOK REPORT. FEED (US/1050-9143) [14237720] **203**

SITUATION AND OUTLOOK REPORT. FRUIT AND TREE NUTS (US/1051-7901) [17793374] **135**

SITUATION AND OUTLOOK REPORT. LIVESTOCK AND POULTRY See LIVESTOCK, DAIRY AND POULTRY SITUATION AND OUTLOOK **105**

SITUATION AND OUTLOOK REPORT. LIVESTOCK AND POULTRY (US/1054-0849) [14076955] **222**

SITUATION AND OUTLOOK REPORT. OIL CROPS (US/1049-488X) [15046921] 186, **4278**

SITUATION AND OUTLOOK REPORT. RICE (US/1051-9149) [13994301] **135**

SITUATION AND OUTLOOK REPORT. SUGAR AND SWEETENER (US/0896-0240) [14395120] **135**

SITUATION AND OUTLOOK REPORT. TOBACCO (US/0893-8946) [14076280] **5373**

SITUATION AND OUTLOOK REPORT. VEGETABLES AND SPECIALTIES (US/1049-3352) [17735337] **2431**

SITUATION AND OUTLOOK REPORT. WHEAT (US/0895-1454) [13897055] **135**

SITUATION AND OUTLOOK SERIES. CHINA AGRICULTURE AND TRADE REPORT (US/1051-8703) [18669557] **135**

SITUATION AND OUTLOOK SERIES. DEVELOPING ECONOMIES AGRICULTURE AND TRADE REPORT / UNITED STATES DEPARTMENT OF AGRICULTURE, ECONOMIC RESEARCH SERVICE (US) [20521767] **135**

SITUATION AND OUTLOOK SERIES. PACIFIC RIM AGRICULTURE AND TRADE REPORT (US/1051-869X) [18669772] **135**

SITUATION AND OUTLOOK SERIES. WESTERN EUROPE AGRICULTURE AND TRADE REPORT (US/1051-791X) [18762707] **135**

SITUATION AND OUTLOOK SUMMARY. AGRICULTURAL RESOURCES, AGRICULTURAL LAND VALUES / UNITED STATES DEPARTMENT OF AGRICULTURE, ECONOMIC RESEARCH SERVICE *CEASED.* (UK) [24047681] **135**

SITUATION AND OUTLOOK. WOOL / BUREAU OF AGRICULTURAL ECONOMICS, CANBERRA (AT) [05089356] 1520, **135**

SITUATION ECONOMIQUE A L'ETRANGER ET LES STATISTIQUES MONETAIRES ET FINANCIERES TRIMESTRIELLES See BULLETIN DE LA BANQUE DE FRANCE **780**

SITUATION ECONOMIQUE AU DEBUT DE ... / REPUBLIQUE MALGACHE, SERVICE DE LA STATISTIQUE ET DES ETUDES SOCIO-ECONOMIQUES (MG) [19052081] **1520**

SITUATION ECONOMIQUE ET PERSPECTIVES D'AVENIR (FR) [04919055] 821, **1584**

SITUATION ECONOMIQUE, FINANCIERE ET SOCIALE DE LA REPUBLIQUE GABONAISE (GO) [02243117] **4748**

SITUATION ECONOMIQUE SUISSE ET LES PERSPECTIVES, LA (SZ) [06178393] **1584**

SITUATION (ENCINITAS, CALIF.), THE (US/1058-5044) [24316340] **811**

SITUATION ET PERSPECTIVES DANS LE COMMERCE D'APRES LES CHEFS D'ENTREPRISE (FR) [02766969] **1584**

SITUATION FINANCIERE DES REGIONS DE PROVINCE : OPERATIONS DES RESIDENTS (FR) [01793662] **811**

SITUATION MONDIALE DE L'ALIMENTATION ET DE L'AGRICULTURE, LA (IT/0251-1460) [I02511460] **135**

SITUATION REPORT - SECURITY AND INTELLIGENCE FOUNDATION (WASHINGTON, D.C.) (US/0892-5917) [15250388] **4686**

SITUATIONS (FR/0761-3857) [I07613857] **1710**

●SITUATIONS DIGEST (US/1059-1958) [24506926] **2545**

SITUATIONS WANTED; JOBS WANTED (US/0739-2222) [09700876] **4209**

SITUATSIIA (RU) [24299373] **5809**

SITUAZIONE ECONOMICA PROVINCIALE (IT) [02999594] **135**

SITULA (XV/0583-4554) [01941282] **2709**

SITZUNGBERICHTE (AU) [01478735] **5236**

SITZUNGS-BERICHTE DER GESELLSCHAFT NATURFORSCHENDER FREUNDE ZU BERLIN (GW/0433-8731) [01751186] **4172**

SITZUNGSBERICHTE. ABT. 1, BIOLOGISCHE WISSENSCHAFTEN UND ERDWISSENSCHAFTEN (AU/0723-791X) [09536203] **5158**

SITZUNGSBERICHTE DER BAYERISCHEN AKADEMIE DER WISSENSCHAFTEN. PHILOSOPHISCH-HISTORISCHE KLASSE (GW/0342-5991) [08465232] 2854, **1080**

SITZUNGSBERICHTE DER HEIDELBERGER AKADEMIE DER WISSENSCHAFTEN, MATHEMATISCH-NATURWISSENSCHAFTLICHE KLASSE (GW/0371-0165) [01751943] 3535, **5158**

SITZUNGSBERICHTE DER SACHSISCHEN AKADEMIE DER WISSENSCHAFTEN. MATHEMATISCH-NATURWISSENSCH AFTLICHE KLASSE (GW/0371-327X) [06240034] 5158, **3535**

SITZUNGSBERICHTE DER SACHSISCHEN AKADEMIE DER WISSENSCHAFTEN ZU LEIPZIG, PHILOLOGISCH-HISTORISCHE KLASSE (GW/0138-3957) [07771850] 2629, **4361**

SITZUNGSBERICHTE DER SAECHSISCHE AKADEMIE DER WISSENSCHAFTEN, LEIPZIG, PHILOLOGISCH-HISTORISCHE KLASSE (GW/0080-5300) [01715535] **3321**

SITZUNGSBERICHTE / KUNSTGESCHICHTLICHE GESELLSCHAFT ZU BERLIN (GW) [21399105] **364**

SITZUNGSBERICHTE / OSTERREICHISCHE AKADEMIE DER WISSENSCHAFTEN, PHILOSOPHISCH-HISTORISCHE KLASSE (AU/0029-8832) [08742492] 1080, **2629**

SIUSA NEWS (US) [13729465] **4513**

SIVAM (II) [11195297] **3437**

SIX, CINQ ET APRES : INNOVATIONS DANS L'ECONOMIE MUNICIPALE (CN/0822-9589) [10845315] **4748**

SIX, FIVE AND COUNTING : INNOVATIONS IN MUNICIPAL ECONOMY (CN/0822-9597) [10845309] **4748**

SIX-YEAR CAPITAL IMPROVEMENT PROGRAM See CAPITAL IMPROVEMENT PROGRAM **5379**

SIX-YEAR CAPITAL IMPROVEMENT PROGRAM, THE (US) [17009003] 4686, **5393**

SIXTEENTH CENTURY BIBLIOGRAPHY (US/0885-9302) [02255157] 2629, **2636**

SIXTEENTH CENTURY JOURNAL, THE (US/0361-0160) [01039942] **2629**

SIXTH CIRCUIT REVIEW (US/0889-356X) [04057792] **3055**

SIXTH GENERATION SYSTEMS (US) [22336734] **1203**

SIXTY CANADIAN MAGAZINES (CN/0318-3114) [02248390] **2546**

SIYASAL BILGILER FAKULTESI DERGISI (TU) [05291207] **4496**

SIYYON (IS/0044-4758) [01495197] **5052**

SIZZLE SHEET, THE (US/0738-6516) [08726909] 4214, **936**

SJFARTSHISTORISK ARBOK (NO) [05722874] **4183**

SKAD OSOBOWY W ROKU AKADEMICKIM ... / POLITECHNIKA ODZKA (PL) [10105693] **5158**

SKADNICA KSIEGARSKA, PANSTWOWE PRZEDSIEBIORSTWO, WARSAW See ALFABETYCZNY KATALOG SKADOWY **407**

SKADNICA KSIEGARSKA, PANSTWOWE PRZEDSIEBIORSTWO, WARSAW See PRZEDMIOTOWY KATALOG SKADOWY **422**

SKADNICA KSIEGARSKA, PANSTWOWE PRZEDSIEBIORSTWO, WARSAW See DZIAOWY KATALOG NOWOSCI **415**

SKAGEN FUGELSTATION (DK) [02618316] **5620**

SKAGIT ARGUS, THE (US) [17359408] **5721**

SKAGIT VALLEY HERALD (US/1071-197X) [17347816] **5762**

SKAGWAY NEWS, THE (US/0745-872X) [09526778] **5629**

SKALA (DK/0900-0518) [15563839] **309**

SKALDSKAPARMAL (IC) [23602426] **3437**

SKALK (DK/0560-1894) [06107433] **282**

SKANDINAVISKA ENSKILDA BANKEN *See* QUARTERLY REVIEW - SKANDINAVISKA ENSKILDA BANKEN **1580**

SKANDINAVISTIK (GW/0342-8427) [01641954] **3437**

SKANDINAVSKIJ SBORNIK (ER/0320-6432) [01765599] **3321**

SKANNER, THE (US) [12566075] **5734**

SKATING (US/0037-6132) [01587897] **4918**

SKATTER OG AFGIFTER (DK/0105-1164) [04352278] 4847, **4748**

SKATTERETT (NO/0333-2810) [11201821] **3055**

SKATTESTATISTIK (LU) [03438091] 4748, **4699**

SKATTESTATISTIKK: KOMMUNER OG HANDELSDISTRIKTER (NO) [01794519] **4748**

SKB TECHNICAL REPORT (SW/0284-3757) [16167033] **5158**

SKEET SHOOTING REVIEW (US/0037-6140) [03926287] **4918**

SKEETER, THE (US/0745-8517) [09512361] 4878, **4918**

SKELETAL RADIOLOGY (US/0364-2348) [02575772] 3807, **3947**

SKENECTADA (US/0270-2614) [06344580] **4172**

●SKEPTIC (ALTADENA, CALIF.) (US/1063-9330) [26183324] 4243, **5158**

SKEPTICAL INQUIRER, THE (US/0194-6730) [04081591] **4243**

SKEPTIKER (GW/0936-9244) [I09369244] **4243**

SKI AREA MANAGEMENT (US/0037-6175) [02450569] 886, **4918**

SKI BUSINESS (US/0037-6191) [05096296] **4918**

SKI CANADA (CN/0702-701X) [03409852] **4918**

SKI INDUSTRY BULLETIN (CN/0229-1940) [08071948] **4918**

SKI INDUSTRY LETTER, THE (US/0197-3479) [06002715] 711, **4918**

SKI NAUTIQUE NEWS (CN/0714-8267) [09106455] **4918**

SKI (NEW YORK, N.Y.) (US/0037-6159) [01765601] **4918**

SKI PATROL MAGAZINE (US/0890-6076) [14352768] 4918, **4803**

SKI QUEBEC (SAINT-LAURENT) (CN/0703-2056) [03827648] **4918**

SKI RACING (US/0037-6213) [03873841] **4918**

SKI RACING REDBOOK (US/0091-1461) [01786514] 4878, **4918**

SKI RUN (US/0195-5640) [05582743] **4918**

SKI TECH (US/1058-3246) [24266538] **4918**

SKI TRADE NEWS *See* STN (NEW YORK, N.Y.) **4924**

SKI TRAILS (VANCOUVER, B.C. : CA. 1978) (CN/0710-0523) [08315814] **4918**

SKI WELT *See* SPORT MAGAZIN **4920**

SKI X-C (US/0161-1054) [03831831] **4918**

SKIBSTILSYNETS MEDDELELSER / STATENS SKIBSTILSYN (DK) [09561732] **4183**

SKIERS ADVOCATE (US/0195-1300) [05299776] **4918**

SKIER'S HOLIDAY GUIDE (UK) [01799378] 4878, **4918**

●SKIING FOR WOMEN (US) [29259751] **4918**

SKIING (NEW YORK, N.Y.) (US/0037-6264) [02450570] **4918**

SKIING TRADE NEWS (US/0037-6299) [04146562] **4918**

SKILL (IT) **2493**

SKILL (DETROIT, MICH.) (US/0279-2028) [07624585] **1710**

SKILLED WORKER EMERITUS PROGRAM / NEW YORK STATE JOB TRAINING PARTNERSHIP COUNCIL (US) [23675194] **5307**

SKILLINGS' MINING REVIEW (US/0037-6329) [01765605] **2151**

SKILLS LETTER (CN/0835-2453) [17240533] **1710**

●SKILLSLINK LISTER NEWS (CN/1188-9705) [26498117] **1802**

SKIN & ALLERGY NEWS (US/0037-6337) [04276282] 3677, **3722**

SKIN CANCER LISBOA (PO/0871-2549) [I08712549] **3824**

SKIN DIVER (US/0037-6345) [01963767] **4918**

SKIN INC (US/0898-6525) [17882206] **3722**

SKIN PHARMACOLOGY (SZ/1011-0283) [18582120] **3723**

●SKIN RESEARCH AND TECHNOLOGY (DK) 1996, **473**

SKINNED KNUCKLES (US/0164-3509) [04629063] 2778, **5425**

SKINNER'S BRITISH TEXTILE REGISTER (UK) [01794093] **5356**

SKIP (NO/0300-3310) [01453459] **5457**

SKIPJACK SURVEY AND ASSESSMENT PROGRAMME *See* ANNUAL REPORT FOR THE YEAR ENDING ... / SKIPJACK SURVEY AND ASSESSMENT PROGRAMME **2294**

SKIPPER'S ALMANAC (SOUTHERN U.S. ED.) (US/1050-5199) [21510206] **4183**

SKIPPING STONES (US/0899-529X) [18124075] **1069**

SKLAR A KERAMIK *CEASED.* (XR/0037-637X) [08205256] **2594**

SKOG & FORSKNING (SW/1101-9506) [24289838] **2395**

SKOG INDUSTRI (NO/0800-8582) [12098099] **4239**

SKOGSINDUSTRIERNA (SW/1101-3354) [I11013354] **4239**

SKOL VREIZH (FR/0755-8848) [I07558848] **1784**

SKOLEBIBLIOTEKSARBOG (DK) [02959301] **3250**

SKOLER, ABBOTT, HAYES & PRESSER'S MASSACHUSETTS EMPLOYMENT LAW LETTER (US/1049-2062) [21174841] **3154**

SKOOP *CEASED.* (NE) [13712467] **4078**

SKOPJE, YUGOSLAVIA. ARHEOLOSKI MUZEJ *See* ZBORNIK - ARHEOLOSKI MUZEJ NA MAKEDONIJA. RECUEIL DES TRAVAUX **286**

SKRIEN (NE) [13441894] **4078**

SKRIF EN KERK (SA/0257-8891) [09237547] **4997**

SKRIFTER (NO/0458-7073) [02501014] **2709**

SKRIFTER (KONGELIGE NORSKE VIDENSKABERS SELSKAB) (NO/0368-6310) [09060299] **5158**

SKRIFTER - NORDISKA GENBANKEN (SW/1100-3456) [I11003456] **551**

SKRIFTER - NORSK POLARINSTITUTT (NO/0369-5417) [01653796] **5158**

SKRIFTER - NORSK SPRAKRAD (NO) [02858417] **3321**

SKRIFTER UTGIVNA AV INSTITUTIONEN FOR NORDISKA SPRAK VID UPPSALA UNIVERSITET (SW/0083-4661) [01605899] **3321**

SKRIFTER UTGIVNA AV LITTERATURVETENSKAPLIGA INSTITUTIONEN VID UPPSALA UNIVERSITET (SW/0346-7856) [08134132] 3321, **3437**

SKRIFTER UTGIVNA AV SVENSKA KYRKOHISTORISKA FOERENINGEN / PUBLICATIONS OF THE SWEDISH SOCIETY OF CHURCH HISTORY (SW) [07524609] **4997**

SKRIFTER UTGIVNA AV SVENSKA LITTERATURSALLSKAPET I FINLAND (FI/0039-6842) [01714428] **3437**

SKRIFTSERIE (NO) [02594479] **811**

SKULL BASE SURGERY (US/1052-1453) [22195072] **3974**

SKY AND TELESCOPE (US/0037-6604) [01765612] **399**

SKY CALENDAR (US/0733-6314) [08637780] **399**

SKY-HI NEWS (US) [23131352] **5644**

SKY INTERNATIONAL (UK/0955-6915) [I09556915] **2493**

SKY LETTERS (CN/0700-4834) [03956710] **3471**

SKY (NEW YORK, N.Y. : 1971) (US/0734-8967) [08658141] **35**

SKYBOX (CINCINNATI, OHIO) (US/1050-7078) [21577422] 711, **4918**

SKYDIVING (US/0192-7361) [05089179] **4918**

SKYLINE (HAMILTON) (CN/0227-6550) [08205804] **2760**

SKYLINE (PITTSBURGH, PA.) (US/0037-6639) [02254489] **35**

SKYLINES (WASHINGTON, D.C.) (US/0892-7847) [14585043] **4847**

SKYSAILOR (AT/0313-363X) [I0313363X] **4919**

SKYWATCHER'S ALMANAC (US/0889-9614) [14114302] **399**

SKYWAYS *SUSPENDED.* (II) [02619391] **35**

SKYWAYS (POUGHKEEPSIE, N.Y.) (US/1051-6956) [20462369] **35**

SKYWAYS: THE JOURNAL OF THE AIRPLANE 1920-1940 (US) **35**

SL RIVISTA DI ORGANIZZAZIONE (IT) **1520**

SLA BIENNIAL SALARY SURVEY / SPECIAL LIBRARIES ASSOCIATION (US) [23034244] **3250**

SLABOPROUDY OBZOR (XR/0037-668X) [11570991] **5158**

SLACAD NEWSLETTER (AT/0156-5281) [I01565281] **3250**

SLACHTOFFERS VAN MISDRIJVEN / CENTRAAL BUREAU VOOR DE STATISTIEK, HOOFDAFDELING STATISTIEKEN VAN CRIMINALITEIT EN RECHTSPELGING (NE) [11351633] **3176**

SLACKWATER REVIEW, THE (US/0160-7677) [03762937] **3437**

SLAGER (NE) **2357**

SLAKT OCH HAVD (SW/0489-1090) [06206803] **2472**

●SLAM (NEW YORK, N.Y.) (US/1072-625X) [29062984] **4919**

SLAM, TRADE YEAR BOOK OF AFRICA (SP) [04992815] **851**

SLAMMER (CN/0381-6699) [02802380] **3176**

SLANT *See* WOMAN'S TOUCH **5569**

SLAP (US/1076-9110) **4854**

SLASKI KWARTALNIK HISTORYCZNY SOBOTKA / WROCAWSKIE TOWARZYSTWO MIOSNIKOW HISTORII (PL/0037-7511) [12282575] **2629**

SLASKIE SPRAWOZDANIA ARCHEOLOGICZNE (PL/0520-9250) [02591918] **282**

SLATE NEWSLETTER *See* SUPPORT FOR THE LEARNING AND TEACHING OF ENGLISH **3327**

SLATE (TORONTO) (CN/0821-2287) [09502144] 364, **4096**

SLATON SLATONITE, THE (US) [14362835] **5754**

SLAVE RIVER JOURNAL (CN/0707-4964) [04754893] **5794**

SLAVERY & ABOLITION (UK/0144-039X) [07062044] **4513**

SLAVIA (XR/0037-6736) [01765618] **3321**

SLAVIA ANTIQUA (PL/0080-9993) [01775072] 2273, **282**

SLAVIA OCCIDENTALIS (PL/0081-0002) [01941278] **3321**

SLAVIA ORIENTALIS (PL/0037-6744) [05658416] **3321**

SLAVIANE (RU) [26365351] **5809**

●SLAVIANOVEDENIE (RU/0869-544X) [26273801] **2709**

●SLAVIANSKII MIR : VESTNIK PRAZDNIKA SLAVIANSKOI PISMENNOSTI I KULTURY I MEZHDUNARODNOGO KONGRESSA SLAVIANSKIKH KULTUR (RU) [26791709] **3321**

SLAVIC AND EAST EUROPEAN ARTS (US/0737-7002) [09253770] **330**

SLAVIC AND EAST EUROPEAN JOURNAL (US/0037-6752) [04530337] **3321**

●SLAVIC AND EAST EUROPEAN PERFORMANCE (US/1069-2800) [25978895] **5368**

SLAVIC AND SOVIET SERIES (IS) [02264438] **2709**

SLAVIC REVIEW (US/0037-6779) [05537901] **2854**

SLAVIC SYNTAX NEWSLETTER, THE (US/1070-5775) [26711072] **3321**

SLAVICA HELSINGIENSIA (FI/0780-3281) [14584415] **3321**

SLAVICA LUNDENSIA (SW) [02256596] **3321**

SLAVICA OTHINIENSIA (DK/0106-1313) [05810248] **3321**

SLAVICA PRAGENSIA (XR/0583-5380) [01935818] **3321**

SLAVICA SLOVACA (XO/0037-6787) [01928410] 3437, **3321**

●SLAVICA TAMPERENSIA (FI/0789-2764) [25810022] **3322**

SLAVISTICNA REVIJA (XV/0350-6894) [01929285] 3437, **3322**

SLAVISTISCHE FORSCHUNGEN (GW/0583-5437) [01765623] **2709**

SLAVNA NADEJE (CN/0700-5202) [27725192] **5067**

SLAVONIC AND EAST EUROPEAN REVIEW, THE (US/0037-6795) [06130663] **2629**

SLB BURIER : NACHRICHTEN AUS DER SACHSISCHEN LANDESBIBLIOTHEK DRESDEN (GW/0863-0682) [22038340] **3437**

SLEEP (NEW YORK, N.Y.) (US/0161-8105) [04024329] **3641**

SLEEP RESEARCH (US/0093-0407) [01437355] **4618**

SLEEP WATCHERS (US/0748-5352) [10963035] **3641**

SLEEPWALKER (NEW YORK, N.Y.) (US/1058-3475) [23706562] **4866**

SLEEPY EYE HERALD-DISPATCH (US) [01605090] **5698**

SLENDER SENSE (US/1056-7488) [24490729] **2601**

SLEVARENSTVI (XR/0037-6825) [09546467] **4019**

SLEZSKY SBORNIK (XR/0037-6833) [05578420] 2629, **5258**

●SLIDE ATLAS OF CURRENT CARDIOLOGY (UK/1064-5969) [26335313] **3710**

SLIDE ATLAS OF CURRENT OPHTHALMOLOGY (UK/1055-6575) [23251538] **3879**

SLIDE ATLAS OF CURRENT RADIOLOGY **CEASED.** (UK/1055-6567) [23251517] **3947**

●SLIDE ATLAS OF OPHTHALMIC LASER SURGERY (US/1064-5446) [26326351] 3975, **3879**

●SLIDE GUITARIST (US/1055-0135) [23055866] **4153**

SLIM FAST MAGAZINE **CEASED.** (US/1055-5552) [23235779] **2601**

SLIP OPINION / SUPREME COURT OF THE UNITED STATES (US) [05129852] **3055**

SLIPSTREAM (HAYWARDS HEATH, ENGLAND) See AIRCRAFT VALUE NEWSLETTER **9**

SLIPSTREAM (NIAGARA FALLS, N.Y.) (US/0749-0771) [08160209] **3471**

SLM ENGINEERING JOURNAL (SZ) **1996**

SLO PITCH (US/0149-3620) [03505741] **4919**

SLOAN MANAGEMENT REVIEW (US/0019-848X) [01765629] **886**

SLOANE REPORT, THE **CEASED.** (US/0882-5939) [11905940] 1300, **1203**

SLOAN'S GREEN GUIDE TO ANTIQUES DEALERS. NEW ENGLAND See SLOAN'S GREEN GUIDE TO ANTIQUING IN NEW ENGLAND **252**

●SLOAN'S GREEN GUIDE TO ANTIQUING IN NEW ENGLAND (US/1051-6719) [22044080] **252**

SLOBODA (CHICAGO, ILL.) (US/0037-6868) [03926459] **3353**

SLOBODNA DALMACIJA (CI/0350-4662) [I03504662] **5799**

SLOT MACHINE-JUKE BOX COLLECTOR (US/1058-8256) [24395730] **2778**

SLOVACI V ZAHRANICI : ZBORNIK USTAVU PRE ZAHRANICNYCH SLOVAKOV MS (XO) [04877224] **2709**

SLOVAK CATHOLIC FALCON (US/0897-8107) [17636428] **5036**

SLOVAK MUSIC (XO/0862-0407) [03143355] **4153**

●SLOVAK REVIEW (XO) [27899421] 1080, **3437**

SLOVAK SOCIALIST REPUBLIC (CZECHOSLOVAKIA) See USTREDNY VESTNIK SLOVENSKEJ SOCIALISTICKEJ REPUBLIKY **3070**

SLOVAK SOCIALIST REPUBLIC. MINISTERSTVO STAVEBNICTVA See SPRAVODAJCA MINISTERSTVA STAVEBNICTVA SLOVENSKEJ SOCIALISTICKEJ REPUBLIKY **628**

SLOVAK V AMERIKE (US/0199-6819) [02267741] **5739**

SLOVAKIA (WEST PATERSON, N.J.) (US/0583-5623) [01941355] **2709**

SLOVANSKE HISTORICKE STUDIE (XR/0081-007X) [01589665] **2709**

SLOVANSKE STUDIE (NE/0583-564X) [01932020] **2709**

SLOVANSKY PREHLED (XR/0037-6922) [01941337] **4496**

SLOVENE STUDIES (US/0193-1075) [05138033] 3322, **2710**

SLOVENI IN ITALIA (IT) [02592630] **2273**

SLOVENIA See URADNI LIST REPUBLIKE SLOVENIJE **3070**

SLOVENIJA (SLOVENSKA IZSELJENSKA MATICA) (XV) [18279807] **2273**

SLOVENSKA AKADEMIA VIED. GEOFYZIK ALNYUSTAV See CONTRIBUTIONS OF THE GEOPHYSICAL INSTITUTE OF THE SLOVAK AKADEMY OF SCIENCES. SERIES OF METEOROLOGY **1424**

SLOVENSKA AKADEMIA VIED. USTAV METEOROLOGIE A KLIMATOLOGIE See CONTRIBUTIONS OF THE INSTITUTE OF METEOROLOGY AND CLIMATOLOGY OF THE SLOVAK ACADEMY OF SCIENCES **1424**

SLOVENSKA ARCHEOLOGIA (XO/0037-6949) [01765634] **282**

SLOVENSKA ARCHIVISTIKA (XO/0583-6123) [01941325] **2483**

SLOVENSKA DRZAVA (CN/0037-6957) [06438655] **4496**

SLOVENSKA LITERATURA (XO/0037-6973) [01929277] **3437**

SLOVENSKA NARODNA BIBLIOGRAFIA. SERIA A : KNIHY (XO) [01789152] **424**

SLOVENSKA NARODNA BIBLIOGRAFIA. SERIA B-J, PERIODIKA, MAPY, DIZERTACNE PRACE, SPECIALNE TLACE, FIREMNA LITERATURA. GRAFIKA, HUDOBNINY, OFICIALNE DOKUMENTY, AUDIOVIZUALNE DOKUMENTY (XO/0231-973X) [I0231973X] **424**

SLOVENSKA NARODNA BIBLIOGRAFIA. SUPIS PERIODIK A ZBORNIKOV VYCHADZAJUCICH NA SLOVENSKU V ROKU (XO) [04394916] **424**

SLOVENSKA REC (XO/0037-6981) [01929294] **3322**

SLOVENSKE DIVADLO (XO/0037-699X) [05585200] **5368**

SLOVENSKE NARODNE MUZEUM See ZBORNIK SLOVENSKEHO NARODNEHO MUZEA. HISTORIA. ANNALES MUSEI NATIONALIS SLOVACI **2716**

SLOVENSKE NARODNE MUZEUM See ZBORNIK SLOVENSKEHO NARODNEHO MUZEA **4097**

SLOVENSKE NOVICE (XV/0354-1088) [I03541088] **5810**

SLOVENSKO ETNOLOSKO DRUSTVO See GLASNIK SLOVENSKEGA ETNOLOSKEGA DRUSTVA **237**

SLOVENSKO; KULTURNO-SPOLECENSK MESACNIK (XO) [06546121] **2710**

SLOVENSKY DENNIK (XO) [28185737] **5810**

SLOVENSKY NARODOPIS (XO/0037-7023) [01588888] **245**

SLOVNIK JAZYKA STAROSLOVENSK'EHO (XR) [05704346] 3437, **3322**

SLOVO (RU/0868-4855) [20614349] **3437**

SLOVO (RU/0235-4276) [22839147] **3437**

SLOVO A SLOVESNOST (GW/0037-7031) [01935810] **3322**

SLOVO KYRGYZSTANA : ORGAN TSENTRALNOGO KOMITETA KOMPARTII KYRGYZSTANA, VERKHOVNOGO SOVETA I KABINETA MINISTROV RESPUBLIKI KYRGYZSTAN (KG) [24137859] **5806**

SLOVO (LONDON, ENGLAND) (UK/0954-6839) [18390195] **4496**

SLOVO V SISTEMNYKH OTNOSHENIIAKH (RU) [02652240] **3322**

SLOVO (ZAGREB) (CI/0583-6255) [01765638] **3322**

SLOVOOBRAZOVANIE I EGO MESTO V KURSE OBUCHENIIA INOSTRANNOMU IAZYKU (RU) [23919039] **3322**

SLOW DANCER (UK/0143-1412) [08187411] **3471**

SLOWAKEI (MUNICH, GERMANY) See SLOVAK REVIEW **3437**

SLR CAMERA See POPULAR PHOTOGRAPHY'S SLR PHOTOGRAPHY **4375**

SLR PHOTOGRAPHY See PHOTO ANSWERS **4372**

●SLS REPORT, THE (US/1060-9458) [25119330] **3975**

SLUDGE (US/0148-4125) [03313537] **2243**

SLUDGE MANAGEMENT SERIES (US/0893-5793) [15869301] **2243**

SLUZBA ROLNA (PL/0137-4796) [02116440] **135**

●SLUZBENI LIST SAVEZNE REPUBLIKE JUGOSLAVIJE (YU) [26840905] **3055**

SLUZBENI LIST SOCIJALISTICKE FEDERATIVNE REPUBLIKE JUGOSLAVIJE See SLUZBENI LIST SAVEZNE REPUBLIKE JUGOSLAVIJE **3055**

SLVGS NEWS, THE (US/0890-1287) [13337430] **2472**

SLVGS QUERY QUARTERLY, THE (US/1051-9912) [13337444] **2472**

SM PAPER (CN/0317-7130) [02247935] **2129**

SM REPORT (BLUE SERIES) (CN/0317-7114) [02248029] **2129**

SMALL AIR COOLED ENGINES SERVICE MANUAL (US) [07560650] **2129**

SMALL ANIMAL ABSTRACTS BIBLIOGRAPHY (UK) 5522, **5528**

●SMALL ANIMAL MEDICINE (US) **5522**

SMALL ANIMAL PRACTICE **CEASED.** (US/0894-3710) [16060312] **5522**

SMALL ANIMALS (UK/0961-3501) [23945094] **5522**

SMALL ARMS IN PROFILE (GARDEN CITY, N.Y.) (US/0090-2276) [01784809] **4057**

●SMALL BLOCK CHEVY (US/1059-5724) [24638952] **5425**

SMALL BUSINESS, A CANADIAN VIEWPOINT (CN/0383-719X) [03248144] **711**

SMALL BUSINESS ADMINISTRATION AND INVESTMENT ACT WITH AMENDMENTS (US/0502-2150) [01189555] **711**

SMALL BUSINESS CHRONICLE (US) **711**

SMALL BUSINESS COMPUTER NEWS (US/0736-6957) [05011168] 711, 1274, **1272**

SMALL BUSINESS CONTROLLER, THE (US/1053-766X) [22637079] **711**

SMALL BUSINESS ECONOMICS (NE/0921-898X) [20141957] 711, **1520**

SMALL BUSINESS EMPLOYEE ASSISTANCE (US/1060-8184) [25073400] **711**

SMALL BUSINESS EXCHANGE (US/0892-5992) [15265492] **711**

SMALL BUSINESS FORUM (US/1053-4695) [21539121] **711**

●SMALL BUSINESS HEALTH REFORM WATCH (US/1076-4488) [30487172] 711, **4803**

SMALL BUSINESS IN WESTERN AUSTRALIA (AT/0817-5764) [I08175764] **711**

SMALL BUSINESS INVESTMENT COMPANY DIRECTORY AND HANDBOOK (US) **914**

SMALL BUSINESS JOURNAL (US) **711**

SMALL BUSINESS LETTER, THE (US/1059-6550) [24661672] **711**

SMALL BUSINESS PREFERENTIAL SUBCONTRACT OPPORTUNITIES MONTHLY (US/0887-4050) [13238173] **711**

SMALL BUSINESS REGISTER (US) [12634021] **711**

SMALL BUSINESS REPORT (MONTEREY, CALIF.) **CEASED.** (US/0164-5382) [04264164] **711**

SMALL BUSINESS REPORT (OTTAWA) (CN/0824-3719) [10392461] **711**

SMALL BUSINESS REVIEW (US) **711**

SMALL BUSINESS SOURCEBOOK (US/0883-3397) [09834543] **711**

●SMALL BUSINESS SPOTLIGHT NEWS (US/1063-0252) [25844444] **711**

SMALL BUSINESS START-UP INDEX **CEASED.** (US/1049-9636) [21359121] **711**

SMALL BUSINESS SUBCONTRACTING DIRECTORY (US/0741-4811) [10143103] **711**

SMALL BUSINESS TAX REVIEW, THE (US/0276-5322) [07268919] 711, **4748**

SMALL BUSINESS TAX SAVER (US/0732-5525) [08384521] **4748**

SMALL BUSINESS TODAY (US) **711**

SMALL BUSINESS WORLD MAGAZINE **SUSPENDED.** (CN/0835-4251) [17748666] **711**

SMALL BUSINESSMAN'S CLINIC (US/0094-2464) [03791962] **711**

SMALL CITY AND REGIONAL COMMUNITY, THE (US/0194-2735) [05113869] **2835**

SMALL CLAIMS COURT PRACTICE IN THE ONTARIO COURT (GENERAL DIVISION) See ONTARIO SMALL CLAIMS COURT PRACTICE **3023**

SMALL COMPANY INVESTOR (UK) **914**

SMALL COMPUTERS IN BIOMEDICAL RESEARCH (US/0743-8656) [10690037] 1272, **3696**

SMALL COMPUTERS IN THE ARTS NEWS (US/0748-2043) [10899835] 1203, **330**

SMALL CRAFT (UK/0306-0209) [11179393] **596**

SMALL ENTERPRISE DEVELOPMENT (UK/0957-1329) [24806928] 1627, **711**

SMALL ENTERPRISE IN THE ECONOMY (US/0362-417X) [02338251] 711, **1521**

SMALL FARM PROGRAMS AND ACTIVITIES, STATE REPORTS (US/0273-5237) [06777823] **135**

SMALL FARM, THE (US/0161-5270) [02973343] **3471**

SMALL FARMER See FORD FERGIE FARMER **88**

SMALL FARMER'S JOURNAL (US/0743-9989) [05083722] **135**

SMALL FLOWS (US) [19695109] **2243**

SMALL FRUIT CROPS, DISEASE IDENTIFICATION SHEET / CORNELL COOPERATION EXTENSION (US) [25511983] **135**

SMALL FRUIT INFORMATION LETTER (CN/0227-8863) [06965621] **135**

SMALL GRAINS (US/0270-0409) [06310999] **186**

SMALL GROUP RESEARCH (US/1046-4964) [20429782] **5258**

SMALL INDUSTRY BULLETIN FOR ASIA AND THE PACIFIC (US/0252-3426) [03667552] **711**

SMALL LAW OFFICE MANAGEMENT REPORT (US/0887-2481) [13152200] **3055**

SMALL MARKETERS AIDS (US/0081-0177) [02450581] **851**

SMALL MARKETERS AIDS (US/0081-0169) [02111344] **936**

SMALL POND *See* SMALL POND MAGAZINE OF LITERATURE, THE **3437**

SMALL POND MAGAZINE OF LITERATURE, THE (US/0737-1535) [06528202] **3437**

SMALL PRESS (US/0000-0485) [10026859] **4569**

SMALL PRESS BOOK REVIEW, THE *SUSPENDED.* (US/8756-7202) [11666313] **4832**

SMALL PRESS RECORD OF BOOKS IN PRINT (US/0148-9720) [03387232] **4832**

SMALL PRESS REVIEW (US/0037-7228) [01608098] **3353**

SMALL PRESS YEARBOOK (UK) [19240107] **4819**

SMALL RUMINANT RESEARCH (NE/0921-4488) [18081750] **5597**

SMALL SCALE FORESTRY (SW/0283-1007) [14990952] **2395**

SMALL SHIPS (UK/0262-480X) [18891029] **5457**

SMALL SIBLINGS (US/0897-7860) [15722034] **2472**

SMALL STREET JOURNAL (COLORADO SPRINGS, COLO.) *CEASED.* (US/0894-9239) [16314891] **2924**

SMALL TOWN (US/0196-1683) [02254050] **2835**

●SMALL TOWN OBSERVER, THE (US/1061-9933) [25513194] **2835**

SMALL WARS AND INSURGENCIES (UK/0959-2318) [21769758] **4057**

SMALL WORLD (GUILFORD) (US/0037-7260) [04947217] 2585, **2907**

SMALLER COMPANIES HANDBOOK (UK) **851**

SMALLER MANUFACTURER *See* DYNAMIC BUSINESS : A PUBLICATION OF THE SMALLER MANUFACTURER'S COUNCIL **670**

SMALLHOLDER, THE (CN/0383-6312) [03222629] **135**

SMALLMOUTH (EDGEFIELD, S.C.) (US/1042-8569) [19230921] **2313**

●SMALLTALK REPORT, THE (US/1056-7976) [23854476] **1281**

SMALTO (IT) [26507572] **4225**

SMALTO E SMALTATURA TECNOLOGIE E MERCATI (IT) **851**

SMARANDACHE FUNCTION JOURNAL (US/1053-4792) [22537752] **3536**

SMAR'S INDUSTRIAL DIRECTORY OF PAKISTAN (PK) [02246799] **1627**

SMAR'S INDUSTRIAL DIRECTORY OF WEST PAKISTAN *See* SMAR'S INDUSTRIAL DIRECTORY OF PAKISTAN **1627**

●SMART ACCESS (US/1066-7911) [27049384] **1255**

SMART BUYING (US) **951**

SMART CARD MONTHLY (US/0893-9462) [15703548] **1203**

SMART CARDS AND COMMENTS (US/0882-665X) [11910308] **1227**

●SMART DRUG NEWS (US/1060-8427) [25071625] **3641**

SMART LIVING (US/0884-4976) [12408322] **2546**

●SMART MATERIALS AND STRUCTURES (UK) [25792628] 2031, **2081**

SMART MONEY (US) **914**

SMART (NEW YORK, N.Y.) *SUSPENDED.* (US/0899-2347) [18040428] **2546**

SMART WOMAN & PORTFOLIO (AT) **5566**

SMARTMEDIA BUSINESS *CEASED.* (US) **1203**

●SMARTMONEY (NEW YORK, N.Y.) (US/1069-2851) [26559282] **712**

SMART'S INSURANCE BULLETIN (US/0736-8348) [09229806] **2893**

SMASH (US/0360-6074) [02241161] **3437**

SMASH HITS (UK/0260-3004) [I02603004] **1300**

SMATV NEWS (US/0734-5399) [08760846] **1139**

SMC NATIONAL REPORT (CN/0711-3102) [08486301] **2835**

SMDI INTERNATIONAL NEWSLETTER (CN/0840-8386) [19925331] 4393, **3807**

SME TECHNICAL DIGEST (US) [04935620] **1996**

SMENA (RU) [02054112] **2523**

SMFA ACTUALITES PARIS (FR/1156-2897) [I11562897] **627**

SMG MARKET LETTER (US) **3792**

SMITH ALUMNAE QUARTERLY (US) [06477002] **1103**

SMITH & HOGAN : CRIMINAL LAW - CASES AND MATERIALS (UK) **3109**

SMITH COLLEGE. SCHOOL FOR SOCIAL WORK *See* SMITH COLLEGE STUDIES IN SOCIAL WORK **5307**

SMITH COLLEGE STUDIES IN HISTORY (US/0897-6619) [01765644] **2629**

SMITH COLLEGE STUDIES IN SOCIAL WORK (US/0037-7317) [01765645] **5307**

SMITH COUNTY HISTORICAL & GENEALOGICAL SOCIETY (US) **2472**

SMITH COUNTY REFORMER, THE (US) [16275485] **5701**

SMITH FUNDING REPORT (US/0739-2184) [09700829] 4339, **1847**

SMITH PAPERS (US/0278-3134) [07256160] **2472**

SMITHS FALLS STAR (CN/0381-8365) [02588131] **5794**

SMITH'S TABLES (US/8756-3436) [11572201] **627**

SMITHSONIAN (US/0037-7333) [01359769] 5158, 5219, **4172**

SMITHSONIAN CONTRIBUTIONS TO ANTHROPOLOGY (US/0081-0223) [01167079] **245**

SMITHSONIAN CONTRIBUTIONS TO BOTANY (US/0081-024X) [01425854] **528**

SMITHSONIAN CONTRIBUTIONS TO PALEOBIOLOGY (US/0081-0266) [01382955] **4230**

SMITHSONIAN CONTRIBUTIONS TO THE EARTH SCIENCES (US/0081-0274) [01374743] **1360**

SMITHSONIAN CONTRIBUTIONS TO THE MARINE SCIENCES (US/0196-0768) [03477024] **1457**

SMITHSONIAN CONTRIBUTIONS TO ZOOLOGY (US/0081-0282) [01417272] **5597**

SMITHSONIAN FOLKLIFE STUDIES (US) [07938085] **5219**

SMITHSONIAN INSTITUTION *See* NATIONAL MUSEUM ACT; GUIDELINES FOR GRANT PROGRAMS **4093**

SMITHSONIAN INSTITUTION *See* SMITHSONIAN YEAR (1980) **5158**

SMITHSONIAN INSTITUTION *See* SMITHSONIAN STUDIES IN HISTORY AND TECHNOLOGY **2629**

SMITHSONIAN INSTITUTION LIBRARIES RESEARCH GUIDE (US/0732-7447) [08416061] **3250**

SMITHSONIAN INSTITUTION. TRAVELING EXHIBITION SERVICE *See* UPDATE (SMITHSONIAN INSTITUTION. TRAVELING EXHIBITION SERVICE) **4097**

SMITHSONIAN INSTITUTION. TRAVELING EXHIBITION SERVICE. CATALOGUE *See* UPDATE (SMITHSONIAN INSTITUTION. TRAVELING EXHIBITION SERVICE) **4097**

SMITHSONIAN OPPORTUNITIES FOR RESEARCH AND STUDY IN HISTORY, ART, SCIENCE (US/0093-8335) [01789143] **2854**

SMITHSONIAN RUNNER (US) **2273**

SMITHSONIAN STUDIES IN HISTORY AND TECHNOLOGY (US/0081-0258) [02879100] 5158, **2629**

SMITHSONIAN YEAR (1980) *CEASED.* (US/0273-4982) [06389115] **5158**

SMOKE SIGNAL *See* WYOMING ARCHAEOLOGIST, THE **285**

SMOKE SIGNAL (TUCSON), THE (US/0583-6573) [01932002] **2629**

SMOKE SIGNALS FROM THE ASSINIBOINE GENEALOGICAL SOCIETY (US/0748-5034) [10940848] **2472**

SMOKE SIGNALS (MARYVILLE, MO.) (US/8756-3517) [11502402] **2472**

SMOKESHOP (US/0146-9266) [03063086] 5373, **712**

SMOKEY'S TALE *See* TENNESSEE VOLUNTEERS MAGAZINE **1095**

SMOKIE REVIEW (US/0192-2742) [05422787] **5662**

SMOKING AND HEALTH BULLETIN (US/0081-0363) [01606820] 5373, **4803**

SMOKY LAKE SIGNAL (CN/0229-7949) [08292874] **5794**

SMOKY MOUNTAIN HISTORICAL SOCIETY NEWSLETTER (US/0884-6111) [09109478] 2473, **2760**

SMOKY RIVER NEWS, THE (CN/0227-9304) [09106557] **5794**

SMOLENSKII GOSUDARSTVENNYI MEDITSINSKII INSTITUT. NAUCHNOE STUDENCHESKOE OBSCHESTVO *See* MATERIALY NAUCNOJ STUDENCESKOJ KONFERENCII **5127**

SMOOTH MUSCLE (UK/0261-4928) [I02614928] 540, **3807**

SMPTE JOURNAL (1976) (US/0036-1682) [02093452] **4078**

SMRC-NEWSLETTER (US/0584-5025) [05025189] **2760**

SMRE DIGEST : ELECTRICAL HAZARDS (UK) [02302823] **2081**

SMT TRENDS (US/0890-7900) [14440741] 5158, **2081**

●SMU LAW REVIEW (US/1066-1271) [26738382] **3056**

SMU LAW SCHOOL STUDY, AN (US) [01561563] **3056**

SMYRNA NEIGHBOR, THE (US/0191-5487) [05010981] **5655**

SMYTH COUNTY NEWS (US/0744-0766) [08014619] **5759**

SN DISTRIBUTION STUDY OF GROCERY STORE SALES (US/0736-122X) [06257097] **2357**

SNA COMMUNICATIONS REPORTATIONS *See* MAINFRAME COMMUNICATIONS **1194**

SNA MONTHLY REVIEW (US/0893-0406) [15338395] **1203**

SNA PERSPECTIVE (US/0270-7284) [06492187] **1249**

SNA UPDATE (UK) **1281**

SNACK FOOD (US/0037-7406) [04241427] **2358**

SNACK FOOD BLUE BOOK *CEASED.* (US/0148-8872) [03391295] **2358**

SNACK FOOD INTERNATIONAL (UK/0957-4581) [25962341] **936**

SNACK FOOD MANUFACTURE AND MARKETING *See* SNACK FOOD INTERNATIONAL **936**

SNACK KOERIER (NE) **2358**

SNACK WORLD (US/0896-1670) [16938211] **2358**

SNACKS MAGAZINE, THE (UK) **2358**

SNAFU (LOW) (CN/0715-5522) [09340478] **4866**

SNAIL'S PACE REVIEW : A BIANNUAL LITTLE MAGAZINE OF CONTEMPRARY POETRY, THE (US/1054-1632) [22772583] **3471**

SNAKE (JA/0386-3425) [02531360] **5597**

SNAKE RIVER ECHOES (US/0882-374X) [06036627] **2760**

SNAKEROOTS (US) [03455560] **2761**

SNB QUARTALSHEFT (SZ) **2854**

SNE COMMUNICATOR *CEASED.* (US/0744-2343) [08125743] **4199**

SNEA IMPACT (US/0199-9044) [06276756] **1784**

SNIPPETS (US/0197-6818) [06076842] 1543, **936**

SNIPS (US/0037-7457) [02251952] **2608**

SNIPS (FREDERICTON, N.B.) (CN/0710-2216) [08340791] **5158**

SNOHOMISH COUNTY TRIBUNE (US) [17359892] **5762**

SNOP DEGLI AMBIENTI (IT) **2221**

SNOQUALMIE NORTH BEND VALLEY RECORD (US) [17242878] **5762**

SNOQUALMIE VALLEY REPORTER (US/1063-7567) [23117096] **5762**

SNOW BOARDER (US/1046-0403) [20313533] **4919**

SNOW COUNTRY (US/0896-758X) [17283087] **4919**

SNOW COUNTRY BUSINESS (US) 712, **4919**

SNOW COVER SURVEYS (US/0883-4482) [12075880] **1418**

SNOW-GOER (CN/0711-6454) [08489327] **4919**

SNOW GOER (US/0191-8095) [01695644] **4919**

SNOW GOER (WAYZATA, MINN.) (US/1056-4209) [23716100] **4919**

SNOW GOER'S WATER GOER (CN/0841-2014) [20008219] **596**

SNOW LAKE NEWS (CN/0826-2241) [10926447] **5794**

SNOW SURVEY BULLETIN (CN/0045-303X) [02934669] **5539**

SNOWMAN NEWS (CN/0833-2010) [15060023] 4854, **4919**

SNOWMOBILE & ATV SPORTS (US) [19766971] **4919**

SNOWMOBILE ANNUAL (CN/0700-3315) [03279256] **4919**

SNOWMOBILE (MILWAUKEE) (US/0274-8363) [06644858] **4919**

SNOWMOBILE TRADE-IN GUIDE BLUE BOOK (US) [10784260] **4854**

●SNOWWEST SNOWMOBILE WEST MAGAZINE (US) **4854**

SNOWY EGRET (US/0037-7473) [03455636] 4878, **4172**

SNYDER DAILY NEWS, THE (US) [14868536] **5754**

SNYDER MANAGEMENT ADVISORY (US) **886**

SO & SO (US/0272-6459) [06895669] 5368, **3471**

SOAP, COSMETICS, CHEMICAL SPECIALTIES (US/0091-1372) [06441847] **1030**

SOAP NEWSLETTER (US) 3768, **3641**

●SOAP OPERA BOOK, THE (US/1065-402X) [26607277] **2546**

SOAP OPERA DIGEST (US/0164-3584) [04630971] **2546**

●SOAP OPERA ILLUSTRATED (US/1063-9055) [26176287] **2546**

SOAP OPERA MAGAZINE (US/0274-7383) [06544149] **2546**

SOAP OPERA MAGAZINE (LANTANA, FLA.) (US/1057-9192) [24170281] **2546**

SOAP OPERA NOW (US/0883-6930) [12229216] **2546**

SOAP OPERA PANORAMA (US/1058-8647) [24412454] **2546**

SOAP OPERA PHOTOROMANCE (US/0889-6569) [13987376] **2546**

SOAP OPERA STARS (US/0199-3003) [05764091] **1139**

SOAP OPERA UPDATE (US/0898-1485) [17735668] **2546**

SOAP OPERA WEEKLY (US/1047-7128) [20771494] **2546**

SOAP OPERA WORD-FIND (US/1049-0159) [21108888] **4866**

SOAP OPERA WORD-FIND HIDDEN WORD PUZZLES (US/0194-3197) [05430270] **4866**

SOAP OPERA WORLD (US/0746-9381) [10392918] **2546**

SOAPS, DETERGENTS & TOILETRIES REVIEW (II/0379-5608) [11671517] **1030**

SOARING (US/0037-7503) [01765666] **35**

SOBANG ANJON FIRE SAFETY JOURNAL (KO) [10062836] **2292**

SOBER TIMES (US/1059-6259) [24649964] **1349**

SOBERING THOUGHTS (US/1071-4111) [25244472] **1349**

SOBESEDNIK (ANNUAL) (RU) [08161555] **3437**

SOBO (KO) [05045476] **4183**

SOBORNOST (UK/0144-8722) [05383853] **5040**

SOBRE LOS DERIVADOS DE LA CANA DE AZUCAR (CU/0049-0849) [02468042] 2358, **135**

SOBRE LOS DERIVADOS DE LA CANA DE AZUCAR (HAVANA, CUBA : 1983) (CU) [11303990] **2358**

SOBRETODO (UY) [27102386] **2552**

SOBREVIVENCIA (BL) [02439019] **2205**

SOCCER AMERICA (US/0163-4070) [03552631] **4919**

SOCCER CANADA (CN/0227-1834) [06562613] **4919**

SOCCER DIGEST (EVANSTON) (US/0149-2365) [03505755] **4919**

SOCCER ILLUSTRATED (TORONTO) (CN/0710-2577) [08340655] **4919**

SOCCER INTERNATIONAL (US/1053-4199) [22538661] **4919**

SOCCER JOURNAL (US/0560-3617) [05730634] **4919**

●SOCCER JR (US/1060-9911) [25148104] 4919, **1069**

●SOCCER MAGAZINE (TITUSVILLE, FLA.) (US/1070-9754) [28523786] **4919**

SOCCER MATCH (US/0744-964X) [08682482] **4919**

SOCCER RULE BOOK (US/0731-9541) [06109945] **4919**

●SOCCER RULES (US/1072-0170) [28825701] **4919**

SOCCER TEXAS (US/0882-9632) [12046508] **4919**

SOCCER WORLD (US/0098-8707) [01599837] **4919**

SOCEIDAD DE FOMENTO FABRIL (CHILE) *See* MEMORIA ANUAL - SOCIEDAD DE FOMENTO FABRIL **1914**

SOCHI SHIKENJO KENKYU HOKOKU (JA/0385-0196) [02472176] **136**

SOCHI SHIKENJO, TOCHIGI, JAPAN *See* SOCHI SHIKENJO KENKYU HOKOKU **136**

SOCIAAL (BE) **5219**

SOCIAAL BESTEK (NE) [05630878] **5258**

SOCIAAL-CULTUREEL KWARTAALBERICHT (NE) [07417889] **5258**

SOCIAAL-ECONOMISCHE WETGEVING. EUROPA/BENELUX/NEDERLAND *See* SEW **3136**

SOCIAAL EN CULTUREEL RAPPORT (NE) [02243965] **5258**

SOCIAAL MAANDBLAD-ARBEID (NE) [05686167] **1710**

SOCIAAL RECHT (NE/0920-2870) [I09202870] **5308**

SOCIAL ACCOUNTING FOR OREGON : SOCIO-ECONOMIC INDICATORS (US) [04625952] **1584**

SOCIAL ACTION & THE LAW *CEASED.* (US/0272-765X) [06949398] 5219, **3056**

SOCIAL ACTION (NEW DELHI) (II/0037-7627) [01644495] **5258**

SOCIAL ACTIVITIES FOR ADULTS (CN/0712-3205) [08898808] **4854**

SOCIAL ALTERNATIVES (AT/0155-0306) [05291478] 4496, **5258**

SOCIAL ANALYSIS (ADELAIDE, S. AUST.) (AT/0155-977X) [06807167] 245, **5219**

SOCIAL ANARCHISM (US/0196-4801) [05824297] **4546**

SOCIAL AND BEHAVIORAL SCIENCES JOURNAL (US) [27005014] **5219**

SOCIAL AND CULTURAL REPORT (NE) [03819888] **5258**

SOCIAL AND ECONOMIC STUDIES (JM/0037-7651) [01644922] **5219**

SOCIAL AND LABOUR BULLETIN *CEASED.* (US/0377-5380) [02240359] **1710**

●SOCIAL & LEGAL STUDIES (UK/0964-6639) [25566142] **3056**

SOCIAL AND POLICY ISSUES IN EDUCATION (US) **1784**

SOCIAL AND REHABILITATIVE SERVICES (CRANSTON) (US/0092-5128) [01789715] **5308**

●SOCIAL ANTHROPOLOGY : THE JOURNAL OF THE EUROPEAN ASSOCIATION OF SOCIAL ANTHROPOLOGISTS (UK/0964-0282) [27344144] **245**

SOCIAL ATTITUDES IN NORTHERN IRELAND (IE) [24692202] 4618, **5258**

SOCIAL AUDIT (UK) [01791972] **4686**

SOCIAL BEHAVIOR AND PERSONALITY (NZ/0301-2212) [01788339] 4618, **5258**

SOCIAL BIOLOGY (US/0037-766X) [01796753] **551**

SOCIAL BIOLOGY AND HUMAN AFFAIRS (UK/0143-5051) [07267313] **5258**

SOCIAL CHANGE (II/0049-0857) [01608049] **5308**

SOCIAL CHANGE AND DEVELOPMENT (RH) [09965287] **4546**

SOCIAL CHOICE AND WELFARE (GW/0176-1714) [10835904] **5308**

SOCIAL COGNITION (US/0278-016X) [07684865] **5258**

SOCIAL COMPASS (UK/0037-7686) [01765673] 4997, **5219**

SOCIAL CONCEPT *CEASED.* (US/0737-7762) [09454383] 1521, **5219**

SOCIAL DEFENCE (II/0037-7716) [03201609] **3177**

●SOCIAL DEVELOPMENT (UK/0961-205X) [25699606] **1805**

SOCIAL DEVELOPMENT ACTIVITIES IN LATIN AMERICA PROMOTED BY THE INTER-AMERICAN FOUNDATION (US/0091-6234) [01787758] **1584**

SOCIAL DEVELOPMENT ISSUES (US/0147-1473) [03502489] **5308**

SOCIAL DEVELOPMENT NEWSLETTER (BANGKOK (THAILAND)) (TH) [02267763] **5308**

SOCIAL DEVELOPMENT OVERVIEW *CEASED.* (CN/0822-711X) [10451185] **5308**

SOCIAL DIRECTORY OF HOUSTON (US/0489-2593) [07298060] 2473, **2546**

SOCIAL DYNAMICS (SA/0253-3952) [02592702] **5258**

SOCIAL, ECONOMIC AND POLITICAL STUDIES OF THE MIDDLE EAST (NE) [01644767] 1521, 4496, **2770**

SOCIAL EDUCATION (US/0037-7724) [01682295] 1905, **5219**

SOCIAL EPISTEMOLOGY (UK/0269-1728) [14374770] 5258, **4361**

SOCIAL EUROPE (LU/0255-0776) [10916137] **1711**

SOCIAL EUROPE. SUPPLEMENT / COMMISSION OF THE EUROPEAN COMMUNITIES, DIRECTORATE-GENERAL FOR EMPLOYMENT, SOCIAL AFFAIRS AND EDUCATION (LU) [15527642] **1711**

SOCIAL FORCES (US/0037-7732) [04670293] **5258**

SOCIAL FORECASTING: DOCUMENTATION (IT) [01796632] **5219**

SOCIAL HISTORY (LONDON) (UK/0307-1022) [03066708] **2630**

SOCIAL HISTORY OF ALCOHOL REVIEW, THE (US/0887-2783) [13199817] **1349**

SOCIAL HISTORY OF MEDICINE : THE JOURNAL OF THE SOCIETY FOR THE SOCIAL HISTORY OF MEDICINE (UK/0951-631X) [18236809] **3641**

SOCIAL HISTORY OF MODERN ART, A (US) [16902619] **364**

SOCIAL HOUSING (UK/1351-4288) **5308**

●SOCIAL IDENTITIES (UK/1350-4630) **5259**

SOCIAL IMPACT ASSESSMENT (US/0741-5761) [05256738] 2182, **5259**

SOCIAL INDICATORS (AT) [03398045] **5308**

SOCIAL INDICATORS FOR FIJI (FJ) [03960741] **5259**

SOCIAL INDICATORS NETWORK NEWS (US/0885-6729) [11646224] **5219**

SOCIAL INDICATORS OF DEVELOPMENT (US/1012-8026) [17941932] **1521**

SOCIAL INDICATORS OF PAKISTAN (PK) [14245688] **5259**

SOCIAL INDICATORS RESEARCH (NE/0303-8300) [01794824] 2854, **5219**

SOCIAL INFOPAC (TORONTO) (CN/0712-6867) [09379158] **2761**

SOCIAL INTELLIGENCE *See* JOURNAL OF ECONOMIC AND SOCIAL INTELLIGENCE **5206**

SOCIAL INVENTIONS (UK/0954-206X) [I0954206X] **5259**

SOCIAL ISSUES NEWS (CN/1183-4986) [24368150] **4997**

SOCIAL ISSUES RESOURCES SERIES (US/0740-3127) [03640616] **5308**

SOCIAL JUSTICE RESEARCH (NEW YORK, N.Y.) (US/0885-7466) [12712767] **5219**

SOCIAL JUSTICE REVIEW (US/0037-7767) [01765681] **5036**

SOCIAL JUSTICE (SAN FRANCISCO, CALIF.) (US/1043-1578) [18176236] **3177**

SOCIAL KRITIK (DK/0904-3535) [20655163] **5259**

SOCIAL LIST OF WASHINGTON AND SOCIAL PRECEDENCE IN WASHINGTON *See* SOCIAL LIST OF WASHINGTON, D.C. AND SOCIAL PRECEDENCE IN WASHINGTON, THE **4686**

SOCIAL LIST OF WASHINGTON, D.C. AND SOCIAL PRECEDENCE IN WASHINGTON, THE (US/1063-7516) [14288747] **4686**

SOCIAL MARKETING FORUM *CEASED.* (US) [13832427] **591**

SOCIAL MARKETING UPDATE (US/0882-3529) [11809178] **5219**

SOCIAL MARKETING UPDATE (US/0882-3510) [11827685] **936**

SOCIAL MARKETING UPDATE (US/0882-2255) [11789372] **936**

SOCIAL MIRROR, THE (BG) [04199662] **5259**

SOCIAL NETWORKS (SZ/0378-8733) [04262583] **5259**

SOCIAL ONCOLOGY NETWORK ... NEWSLETTER (US/0882-4398) [11854952] 3824, **5259**

SOCIAL PERSPECTIVES ON EMOTION (US) **5259**

SOCIAL PHARMACOLOGY (US/0891-5180) [14874832] **4329**

SOCIAL PHILOSOPHY & POLICY (UK/0265-0525) [10500490] **5219**

SOCIAL PLANNING, POLICY & DEVELOPMENT ABSTRACTS (US/1042-8380) [11252412] 5308, **5266**

SOCIAL POLICY (US/0037-7783) [01765683] **5259**

SOCIAL POLICY & ADMINISTRATION (UK/0144-5596) [05294514] 5308, **4686**

Alphabetical Title Index — SOCIALISM

SOCIAL POLICY RESEARCH MONOGRAPHS SERIES (UK/0276-9654) [07506828] **5219**

SOCIAL POLICY REVIEW (UK) [20085521] **5308**

●SOCIAL POLITICS (US/1072-4745) [28959388] 4496, **5259**

SOCIAL PRACTICE (US/0192-8686) [05077266] **5220**

SOCIAL PRATIQUE (FR) **5259**

SOCIAL PROBLEMS (US/0037-7791) [01667861] **5220**

SOCIAL PROBLEMS (GUILFORD) (US/0272-4464) [06808821] **5259**

SOCIAL PROCESS IN HAWAII (1979) (US/0737-6871) [09047228] **5220**

SOCIAL PSYCHIATRY AND PSYCHIATRIC EPIDEMIOLOGY (GW/0933-7954) [17661557] 3736, **3936**

SOCIAL PSYCHOLOGY (GUILFORD, CONN.) (US/0730-6962) [08039334] **4618**

SOCIAL PSYCHOLOGY QUARTERLY (US/0190-2725) [04692447] 4618, **5259**

SOCIAL QUESTIONS BULLETIN (1981) (US/0731-0234) [08097967] **4997**

SOCIAL REGISTER (US/1071-3905) [03545748] **425**

SOCIAL REGISTER NEW ORLEANS (US/0360-831X) [02245020] **2473**

SOCIAL RESEARCH (US/0037-783X) [01664336] **5220**

SOCIAL RESEARCH METHODOLOGY ABSTRACTS (NE/0167-8477) [07681316] 5220, **5227**

SOCIAL RESOURCES INVENTORY. CALGARY REGION (CN/0835-9296) [17682202] **5308**

SOCIAL RESOURCES INVENTORY. EDMONTON REGION (CN/0228-1333) [10871659] **5308**

SOCIAL RESOURCES INVENTORY. NORTHEASTERN REGION (CN/0228-1325) [09873559] **5308**

SOCIAL RESPONSIBILITY, BUSINESS, JOURNALISM, LAW, MEDICINE (US/0883-9395) [11779989] **3103**

SOCIAL SCIENCE & MEDICINE (1982) (US/0277-9536) [07667666] 3642, **5220**

SOCIAL SCIENCE COMPUTER REVIEW (US/0894-4393) [16077884] 5220, **1272**

SOCIAL SCIENCE HISTORY (US/0145-5532) [02761258] **5220**

SOCIAL SCIENCE INFORMATION (UK/0539-0184) [02450595] **5220**

SOCIAL SCIENCE INTERNATIONAL (II/0970-1087) [20397872] **5220**

SOCIAL SCIENCE JOURNAL (FORT COLLINS), THE (US/0362-3319) [01949554] **5220**

SOCIAL SCIENCE MONITOR (US/0195-7791) [05669906] 766, **5220**

SOCIAL SCIENCE PROBINGS (II) [11086423] **5220**

SOCIAL SCIENCE QUARTERLY (US/0038-4941) [04708543] **5220**

SOCIAL SCIENCE RECORD (US/0037-7872) [01149651] **5221**

SOCIAL SCIENCE RESEARCH (US/0049-089X) [01765694] **5221**

SOCIAL SCIENCE RESEARCH COUNCIL (GREAT BRITAIN). POSTGRADUATE TRAINING DIVISION *See* SSRC STUDENTSHIP HANDBOOK. POSTGRADUATE STUDENTSHIPS IN THE SOCIAL SCIENCES **5223**

SOCIAL SCIENCE RESEARCH COUNCIL (U.S.) *See* ANNUAL REPORT - SOCIAL SCIENCE RESEARCH COUNCIL (NEW YORK) **5191**

SOCIAL SCIENCE RESEARCH COUNCIL (U.S.) *See* ITEMS - SOCIAL SCIENCE RESEARCH COUNCIL (U.S.) **5205**

SOCIAL SCIENCE REVIEW (TH) [02805839] **5221**

SOCIAL SCIENCE REVIEW (SOCIAL SCIENTISTS ASSOCIATION OF SRI LANKA) (CE) [07578130] **5221**

●SOCIAL SCIENCE SOURCE (US/1063-9802) [26185110] 5221, **5227**

SOCIAL SCIENCE STUDIES (US) [03081450] **5221**

SOCIAL SCIENCE TEACHER (UK/0309-7544) [I03097544] 5221, **1905**

SOCIAL SCIENCE TEACHER SYDNEY (AT/0312-1844) [I03121844] 1905, **5221**

SOCIAL SCIENCES (RU/0134-5486) [01937044] **5221**

SOCIAL SCIENCES AND HUMANITIES IN RUSSIA / RUSSIAN ACADEMY OF SCIENCES, INSTITUTE OF SCIENTIFIC INFORMATION ON SOCIAL SCIENCES (RU) [29503657] **5221**

SOCIAL SCIENCES AND HUMANITIES RESEARCH COUNCIL OF CANADA *See* SSHRC NEWS **5223**

SOCIAL SCIENCES CITATION INDEX (COMPACT DISC ED.) (US/1044-6044) [19840922] **5221**

SOCIAL SCIENCES CITATION INDEX (PRINT ED.) (US/0091-3707) [01784460] 5221, **5228**

●SOCIAL SCIENCES CITATION INDEX WITH ABSTRACTS (US/1061-1282) [25184737] **5221**

SOCIAL SCIENCES IN CHINA (CC/0252-9203) [06481371] **5221**

●SOCIAL SCIENCES IN HEALTH (UK/1352-4127) **5221**

SOCIAL SCIENCES INDEX (US/0094-4920) [02244928] 5221, **5228**

SOCIAL SCIENCES INDEX (CD-ROM ED.) (US/1063-3308) [22294451] **5228**

SOCIAL SCIENCES INDEX / FULLTEXT (US) 5221, **5228**

SOCIAL SCIENCES RESEARCH JOURNAL (II) [05088936] **5221**

SOCIAL SCIENCES (SWINDON, WILTSHIRE, ENGLAND) (UK) [20675276] **5221**

SOCIAL SCIENTIST (NEW DELHI) (II/0970-0293) [01784228] **5221**

SOCIAL SCISEARCH (US) **5221**

SOCIAL SECURITY ALERT (1985) (US/0882-6234) [12118366] **2893**

SOCIAL SECURITY AND MEDICARE EXPLAINED *See* SOCIAL SECURITY EXPLAINED **5308**

SOCIAL SECURITY BULLETIN. ANNUAL STATISTICAL SUPPLEMENT *See* ANNUAL STATISTICAL SUPPLEMENT, ... TO THE SOCIAL SECURITY BULLETIN **5273**

SOCIAL SECURITY BULLETIN (WASHINGTON, D.C. : 1938) (US/0037-7910) [01640226] **5308**

SOCIAL SECURITY DOCUMENTATION. AFRICAN SERIES (SZ/0379-704X) [07685106] **5308**

SOCIAL SECURITY DOCUMENTATION : ASIAN SERIES (II) [08857445] **5308**

SOCIAL SECURITY DOCUMENTATION. ASIAN SERIES (II/0250-4057) [21501228] **2893**

SOCIAL SECURITY DOCUMENTATION. EUROPEAN SERIES (SZ) **2893**

SOCIAL SECURITY DOCUMENTATION. PACIFIC SERIES (II/1013-4492) [I10134492] **1711**

SOCIAL SECURITY EXPLAINED (US/0277-0539) [05713006] **5308**

SOCIAL SECURITY FORUM (US/0735-3812) [08608453] **5308**

SOCIAL SECURITY JOURNAL (AT/0726-1195) [09654358] 2893, **5308**

SOCIAL SECURITY MANUAL (US/0148-1967) [03278622] **5308**

SOCIAL SECURITY REPORTER (AT) [09177222] **5308**

SOCIAL SECURITY RESEARCH REPORTS (CN) [04589367] **1711**

SOCIAL SECURITY STATISTICS (UK/0950-7515) [01791562] 5308, **5267**

SOCIAL SERVICE ABSTRACTS (LONDON) (UK/0309-4693) [08359957] **5267**

SOCIAL SERVICE DELIVERY SYSTEMS *CEASED*. (US/0271-4086) [03599905] **5221**

SOCIAL SERVICE JOBS (US) [05639288] **5308**

●SOCIAL SERVICE RESOURCE DIRECTORY FOR LOS ANGELES COUNTY (US) [23134219] **5308**

SOCIAL SERVICE REVIEW (CHICAGO), THE (US/0037-7961) [01765700] **5309**

SOCIAL SERVICES BLOCK GRANT APPLICATION, WASHINGTON STATE (US) [11203428] **5309**

SOCIAL SERVICES EMPLOYMENT BULLETIN (US/1054-3384) [22850037] 4209, **5309**

SOCIAL SERVICES, INCOME SECURITY PROGRAMS *See* INCOME SECURITY PROGRAMS **5289**

SOCIAL SERVICES PERSONNEL IN NORTH CAROLINA COUNTIES (US/0099-2070) [02243253] **5309**

SOCIAL SERVICES RESEARCH (UK) [12989806] **5221**

SOCIAL SERVICES RESEARCH JOURNAL (UK/0265-6957) **5309**

SOCIAL SERVICES STATISTICS *See* ASSISTANCE PAYMENTS STATISTICS **5266**

SOCIAL STUDIES 30 BULLETIN (CN/0848-7537) [23263612] **5221**

SOCIAL STUDIES AND THE YOUNG LEARNER (US/1056-0300) [18519446] 1905, **5221**

SOCIAL STUDIES JOURNAL (PENNSYLVANIA COUNCIL FOR THE SOCIAL STUDIES) (US/0886-9286) [13045768] **5221**

SOCIAL STUDIES OF SCIENCE (UK/0306-3127) [02242476] **5221**

SOCIAL STUDIES (PHILADELPHIA, PA. : 1953) (US/0037-7996) [08622753] **5222**

SOCIAL STUDIES PROFESSIONAL, THE (US/0586-6235) [02593514] 1905, **5222**

SOCIAL STUDIES REVIEW *CEASED*. (UK/0267-0712) [13548925] **5259**

SOCIAL STUDIES REVIEW (MILLBRAE, CALIF.) (US/1056-6325) [03494042] **5222**

SOCIAL STUDIES REVIEW (NEW YORK, N.Y.) (US/1047-7217) [20764664] **5222**

SOCIAL STUDIES TEXAN, THE (US/1056-4675) [20803206] **5222**

SOCIAL SURVEY (AT/0037-8011) [07393312] **5259**

SOCIAL TEXT (US/0164-2472) [04617572] **5259**

SOCIAL THEORY (US/0887-3577) [13195794] **5228**

SOCIAL THEORY AND PRACTICE (US/0037-802X) [00830969] **5222**

●SOCIAL THOUGHT: JOURNAL OF RELIGION IN THE SOCIAL SERVICES (US) 5309, **4997**

SOCIAL THOUGHT (WASHINGTON, D.C.) *SUSPENDED*. (US/0099-183X) [02243359] **4997**

SOCIAL TRENDS (IT) **5222**

SOCIAL TRENDS (UK/0306-7742) [01946609] **5267**

SOCIAL WELFARE (II/0037-8038) [01765702] **5309**

SOCIAL WELFARE HISTORY GROUP *See* NEWSLETTER-SOCIAL WELFARE HISTORY GROUP **5299**

SOCIAL WORK (SI) [01784305] **5309**

●SOCIAL WORK ABSTRACTS (US/1070-5317) [28398789] 5309, **5267**

SOCIAL WORK AND CHRISTIANITY (US/0737-5778) [06012277] 4998, **5309**

SOCIAL WORK AND SOCIAL SCIENCES REVIEW (UK/0953-5225) [20456474] **5309**

SOCIAL WORK EDUCATION (UK/0261-5479) [I02615479] **5309**

SOCIAL WORK EDUCATION REPORTER (US/0037-8062) [00871444] **5309**

SOCIAL WORK IN HEALTH CARE (US/0098-1389) [02246514] 3936, **5309**

SOCIAL WORK INFORMATION BULLETIN *CEASED*. (UK/0144-0969) [I01440969] **5309**

SOCIAL WORK (MANILA) *SUSPENDED*. (PH/0583-7057) [02033168] **5309**

SOCIAL WORK (NEW YORK) (US/0037-8046) [01605893] **5309**

SOCIAL WORK PAPERS OF THE SCHOOL OF SOCIAL WORK, UNIVERSITY OF SOUTHERN CALIFORNIA *CEASED*. (US/0272-9016) [06949782] **5309**

SOCIAL WORK PERSPECTIVES (CN) **5259**

●SOCIAL WORK RESEARCH (US/1070-5309) [28398727] **5309**

SOCIAL WORK RESEARCH & ABSTRACTS (US/0148-0847) [03264044] 5310, **5267**

SOCIAL WORK RESEARCH AND ABSTRACTS *See* SOCIAL WORK RESEARCH **5309**

SOCIAL WORK RESEARCH AND ABSTRACTS *See* SOCIAL WORK ABSTRACTS **5267**

SOCIAL WORK REVIEW (NEWTON, AUCKLAND, N.Z.) (NZ/0111-7351) [19101083] **5310**

SOCIAL WORK STELLENBOSCH (SA/0037-8054) [I00378054] **5310**

SOCIAL WORK TODAY (UK/0037-8070) [02253712] **5310**

SOCIAL WORK TODAY *See* COMMUNITY CARE **5279**

SOCIAL WORK WITH GROUPS (NEW YORK. 1978) (US/0160-9513) [03788764] **5310**

SOCIAL WORKER. TRAVAILLEUR SOCIAL (CN/0037-8089) [02888936] **5310**

SOCIALE VERSEKERING, PENSIOENVERSEKERING, LEVENSVERZEKERING / CENTRAAL BUREAU VOOR DE STATISTIEK (NE) [07890508] 2893, **5310**

SOCIALFORSAKRING / RIKSFORSAKRINGSVERKET (SW) [29738145] **5310**

SOCIALISM AND DEMOCRACY *CEASED*. (US/0885-4300) [12646102] **4546**

●SOCIALISM OF THE FUTURE (UK) **4546**

SOCIALISM, THEORY AND PRACTICE *CEASED*. (RU/0583-7138) [02241665] **4546**

SOCIALISME (BRUXELLES) (BE/0037-8127) [05918437] **4546**

SOCIALISME EN DEMOCRATIE (NE) [01936015] **4546**

SOCIALISME MONDIAL (CN/0318-1685) [02441770] **4546**

SOCIALISMO OGGI (IT) [11576490] **4535**

SOCIALISMO Y PARTICIPACION (PE) [04526590] **4546**

SOCIALIST ACTION (UK) [10797906] **4547**

SOCIALIST ACTION (SAN FRANCISCO, CALIF.) (US/0747-4237) [10842708] **4496**

SOCIALIST AFFAIRS AND WOMEN & POLITICS (UK) [23446011] **4547**

SOCIALIST CHALLENGE (UK) [05920226] **4547**

SOCIALIST CHALLENGE (MONTREAL) (CN/0821-4980) [10634706] **4547**

SOCIALIST FULCRUM (CN/0707-5472) [04653834] **4547**

SOCIALIST LAWYER (UK/0954-3635) [I09543635] **3056**, **4547**

SOCIALIST (LOS ANGELES, CALIF.) (US/0884-6154) [12403398] **4547**

SOCIALIST PERSPECTIVE (II) [01797721] **4547**

SOCIALIST POLITICS **SUSPENDED.** (NZ) [05933561] **4547**

SOCIALIST REGISTER (UK/0081-0606) [01643733] **4547**

SOCIALIST REPUBLIC See PEOPLE FOR A NEW SYSTEM **4544**

SOCIALIST REVIEW (UK) [24476058] **4547**

SOCIALIST REVIEW (SAN FRANCISCO) (US/0161-1801) [03504884] **4547**

SOCIALIST STANDARD (UK/0037-8259) [01765716] **4547**

SOCIALIST STUDIES/ETUDES SOCIALIST: A CANADIAN ANNUAL (CN) 2854, **5222**

SOCIALIST WORKER (UK) **1711**

SOCIALIST WORKER (CHICAGO, ILL.), THE (US/0885-1468) [06777117] **4547**

SOCIALIST WORKER (TORONTO) (CN/0836-7094) [17759100] **4547**

SOCIALIST WORLD PERSPECTIVES (II) [04584746] **4547**

SOCIALISTA (P.S.O.E. (POLITICAL PARTY) : WEEKLY) (SP) [08376757] **4547**

SOCIALISTICKA EKONOMICKA INTEGRACE (XR) [10199274] **1584**

SOCIALISTISCHE STANDPUNTEN (BE) [05821267] **4547**

SOCIALISTISCHE WELZIJNSWERK (BE) **5310**

SOCIALNI POLITIKA (XO) [05381727] **5259**

SOCIALNYTT (SW/0037-7619) [03755850] **4803**

SOCIEDAD AMERICANA DE OFTALMOLOGIA Y OPTOMETRIA See ARCHIVOS - SOCIEDAD AMERICANA DE OFTALMOLOGIA Y OPTOMETRIA **3872**

SOCIEDAD ARGENTINA DE ANTROPOLOGIA, BUENOS AIRES See RELACIONES DE LA SOCIEDAD ARGENTINA DE ANTROPOLOGIA **244**

SOCIEDAD ARGENTINA DE BOTANICA See BOLETIN DE LA SOCIEDAD ARGENTINA DE BOTANICA **502**

SOCIEDAD BOLIVARIANA DE VENEZUELA See REVISTA DE LA SOCIEDAD BOLIVARIANA **2758**

SOCIEDAD BOLIVARIANA DEL PARAGUAY See BOLETIN DE LA SOCIEDAD BOLIVARIANA DEL PARAGUAY **2724**

SOCIEDAD BOLIVIANA DE HISTORIA NATURAL See REVISTA DE LA SOCIEDAD BOLIVIANA DE HISTORIA NATURAL **4171**

SOCIEDAD BOTANICA DE MEXICO See BOLETIN DE LA SOCIEDAD BOTANICA DE MEXICO **503**

SOCIEDAD CASTELLONENSE DE CULTURA See BOLETIN DE LA SOCIEDAD CASTELLONENSE DE CULTURA **2843**

SOCIEDAD CENTRAL DE ARQUITECTOS, BUENOS AIRES See RSCA **308**

SOCIEDAD CIENTIFICA ARGENTINA See ANALES DE LA SOCIEDAD CIENTIFICA ARGENTINA **5082**

SOCIEDAD CIENTIFICA ARGENTINA See CICLO DE CONFERENCIAS **5094**

SOCIEDAD CIENTIFICA DEL PARAGUAY See REVISTA DE LA SOCIEDAD CIENTIFICA DEL PARAGUAY **5148**

SOCIEDAD COLOMBIANA DE PLANIFICACION See CUADERNOS **1478**

SOCIEDAD CUBANA DE HISTORIA DE LA MEDICINA See REVISTA DE LA SOCIEDAD CUBANA DE HISTORIA DE LA MEDICINA **3635**

SOCIEDAD DE CIENCIAS NATURALES LA SALLE, CARACAS See MEMORIA - SOCIEDAD DE CIENCIAS NATURALES LA SALLE **5128**

SOCIEDAD DE INGENIEROS, LIMA See INFORMACIONES Y MEMORIAS DE LA SOCIEDAD DE INGENIEROS DEL PERU **1978**

SOCIEDAD ENTOMOLOGICA ARGENTINA See REVISTA DE LA SOCIEDAD ENTOMOLOGICA ARGENTINA **5596**

SOCIEDAD ESPANOLA DE HISTORIA DE LA FARMACIA See BOLETIN DE LA SOCIEDAD ESPANOLA DE HISTORIA DE LA FARMACIA **4294**

SOCIEDAD GEOGRAFICA DE COLOMBIA See BOLETIN DE LA SOCIEDAD GEOGRAFICA DE COLOMBIA **2556**

SOCIEDAD GEOGRAFICA DE LIMA See BOLETIN DE LA SOCIEDAD GEOGRAFICA DE LIMA **2556**

SOCIEDAD GEOGRAFICA, MADRID See BOLETIN DE LA REAL SOCIEDAD GEOGRAFICA **2556**

SOCIEDAD GEOLOGICA DEL PERU See BOLETIN DE LA SOCIEDAD GEOLOGICA DEL PERU **1367**

SOCIEDAD MATEMATICA MEXICANA See BOLETIN DE LA SOCIEDAD MATEMATICA MEXICANA **3497**

SOCIEDAD MEXICANA DE LEPIDOPTEROLOGIA See REVISTA DE LA SOCIEDAD MEXICANA DE LEPIDOPTEROLOGIA **5596**

SOCIEDAD PRIVADA MUNICIPAL TRANSPORTES DE BARCELONA See DATOS - SOCIEDAD PRIVADA MUNICIPAL TRANSPORTES DE BARCELONA **5380**

SOCIEDAD PRIVADA MUNICIPAL TRANSPORTES DE BARCELONA See BALANCE PREVENTIVO - SOCIEDAD PRIVADA MUNICIPAL TRANSPORTES DE BARCELONA **5377**

SOCIEDAD QUIMICA DE MEXICO See REVISTA DE LA SOCIEDAD QUIMICA DE MEXICO **991**

SOCIEDAD Y POLITICA (PE) [01786166] **4496**

SOCIEDADE BRASILEIRA (BL) [01792268] **2761**

SOCIEDADE BRASILEIRA DE CULTURA JAPONESA See RELATORIO ANUAL - SOCIEDADE BRASILEIRA DE CULTURA JAPONESA **2756**

SOCIEDADE BRASILEIRA DE GEOLOGIA. NUCLEO DO NORDESTE See BOLETIM DO NUCLEO DO NORDESTE DA SOCIEDADE BRASILEIRA DE GEOLOGIA **1367**

SOCIEDADE BRASILEIRA DE MATEMATICA See BOLETIM DA SOCIEDADE BRASILEIRA DE MATEMATICA **3497**

SOCIEDADE BRASILEIRA DE PESQUISA HISTORICA. REUNIAO See ANAIS DA ... REUNIAO / SOCIEDADE BRASILEIRA DE PESQUISA HISTORICA, SBPH **2720**

SOCIEDADE BROTERIANA See MEMORIAS DA SOCIEDADE BROTERIANA **518**

SOCIEDADE BROTERIANA See BOLETIM DA SOCIEDADE BROTERIANA **502**

SOCIEDADE E ESTADO : REVISTA SEMESTRAL DO DEPARTAMENTO DE SOCIOLOGIA DA UNB (BL/0102-6992) [16104371] **5259**

SOCIEDADE E TERRITORIO (PO) [20081422] **2835**

SOCIEDADE ENTOMOLOGICA DO BRASIL See ANAIS DA SOCIEDADE ENTOMOLOGICA DO BRASIL **5605**

SOCIEDADE GEOLOGICA DE PORTUGAL See BOLETIM DA SOCIEDADE GEOLOGICA DE PORTUGAL **1367**

SOCIEDADE PORTUGUESA DE ANTROPOLOGIA E ETNOLOGIA See TRABALHOS DE ANTROPOLOGIA E ETNOLOGIA **246**

SOCIEDADES POR ACOES (BL) [04080286] **3103**

SOCIETA ASTRONOMICA ITALIANA See MEMORIE DELLA SOCIETA ASTRONOMICA ITALIANA **397**

SOCIETA BILANCIO E CONTABILITA (IT/0394-3631) [I03943631] **751**

SOCIETA DEI NATURALISTI E MATEMATICI DI MODENA See ATTI DELLA SOCIETA DEI NATURALISTI E MATEMATICI DI MODENA **5086**

SOCIETA DI STUDI VALDESI See BOLLETTINO DELLA SOCIETA DI STUDI VALDESI **4939**

SOCIETA E SALUTE **SUSPENDED.** (IT/0391-5913) [04851547] **4803**

SOCIETA E STORIA (IT) [05343571] **2630**

SOCIETA ENTOMOLOGICA ITALIANA See BOLLETTINO DELLA SOCIETA ENTOMOLOGICA ITALIANA **5606**

SOCIETA ENTOMOLOGICA ITALIANA See MEMORIE DELLA SOCIETA ENTOMOLOGICA ITALIANA **5612**

SOCIETA GEOGRAFICA ITALIANA See MEMORIE DELLA SOCIETA GEOGRAFICA ITALIANA **2569**

SOCIETA GEOLOGICA ITALIANA See RENDICONTI DELLA SOCIETA GEOLOGICA ITALIANA **1394**

SOCIETA GEOLOGICA ITALIANA See BOLLETTINO DELLA SOCIETA GEOLOGICA ITALIANA **1368**

SOCIETA ISTRIANA DI ARCHEOLOGIA E STORIA PATRIA See ATTI E MEMORIE DELLA SOCIETA ISTRIANA DI ARCHEOLOGIA E STORIA PATRIA **260**

SOCIETA ITALIANA DE SCIENZA DELL'ALIMENTAZIONE See RIVISTA DELLA SOCIETA ITALIANA DI SCIENZA DELL'ALIMENTAZIONE, LA **2356**

SOCIETA ITALIANA DI BIOLOGIA SPERIMENTALE See BOLLETTINO DELLA SOCIETA ITALIANA DI BIOLOGIA SPERIMENTALE **449**

SOCIETA ITALIANA PER L'ORGANIZZAZIONE INTERNAZIONALE. CONSIGLIO DIRETTIVO See RELAZIONE PROVVISORIA DEL CONSIGLIO DIRETTIVO PER L'ANNO **3134**

SOCIETA / ITALY, LE (IT) **3056**

SOCIETA, LE (IT) [10523099] **3103**

SOCIETA LIGURE DI STORIA PATRIA See ATTI DELLA SOCIETA LIGURE DI STORIA PATRIA **2677**

SOCIETA MAGNA GRECIA, ROME See ATTI E MEMORIE DELLA SOCIETA MAGNA GRECIA **2611**

SOCIETA NAZIONALE DI SCIENZE, LETTERE E ARTI IN NAPOLI See SEDUTA INAUGURALE - SOCIETA NAZIONALE DI SCIENZE, LETTERE E ARTI IN NAPOLI **330**

SOCIETA PALEONTOLOGICA ITALIANA See BOLLETTINO DELLA SOCIETA PALEONTOLOGICA ITALIANA **4226**

SOCIETA PAVESE DI STORIA PATRIA See BOLLETTINO DELLA SOCIETA PAVESE DI STORIA PATRIA **2679**

SOCIETA PELORITANA DI SCIENZE See ATTI DELLA SOCIETA PELORITANA DI SCIENZE **5086**

SOCIETA RETO-ROMANTSCHA See ANNALAS DALA SOCIETAD RHAETO-ROMANSCHA. NSS **2674**

SOCIETA STORICA MAREMMANA See BOLLETTINO DELLA SOCIETA STORICA MAREMMANA **2679**

SOCIETA TIBURTINA DI STORIA E D'ARTE See ATTI E MEMORIE DELLA SOCIETA TIBURTINA DI STORIA E D'ARTE **2611**

SOCIETAIRE (MONTREAL) (CN/0846-1961) [24368717] **2893**

SOCIETAS PRO FAUNA ET FLORA FENNICA See MEMORANDA SOCIETATIS PRO FAUNA ET FLORA FENNICA **518**

SOCIETATEA DE MEDICI SI NATURALISTI DIN IASI See REVISTA MEDICO-CHIRURGICALA A SOCIETATII DE MEDICI SI NATURALISTI DIN IASI **3973**

SOCIETATEA DE STIINTE FILOLOGICE DIN REPUBLICA SOCIALISTA ROMANIA See LIMBA SI LITERATURA ROMANA / SOCIETATEA DE STIINTE FILOLOGICE **3298**

SOCIETATEA DE STIINTE FILOLOGICE DIN REPUBLICA SOCIALISTA ROMANIA See LIMBA SI LITERATURA / SOCIETATEA DE STIINTE ISTORICE SI FILOLOGICE **3298**

SOCIETATEA DE STIINTE ISTORICE DIN REPUBLICA SOCIALISTA ROMANIA See STUDII SI ARTICOLE DE ISTORIE **2711**

SOCIETE ARCHEOLOGIQUE DE NAMUR See ANNALES DE LA SOCIETE ARCHEOLOGIQUE DE NAMUR **2674**

SOCIETE ARCHEOLOGIQUE DU FINISTERE See BULLETIN DE LA SOCIETE ARCHEOLOGIQUE DU FINISTERE **263**

SOCIETE ARCHEOLOGIQUE DU MIDI DE LA FRANCE See MEMOIRES DE LA SOCIETE ARCHEOLOGIQUE DU MIDI DE LA FRANCE **274**

SOCIETE ARCHEOLOGIQUE ET HISTORIQUE DU LIMOUSIN, LIMOGES See BULLETIN DE LA SOCIETE ARCHEOLOGIQUE ET HISTORIQUE DU LIMOUSIN **263**

SOCIETE ARCHEOLOGIQUE, HISTORIQUE, LITTERAIRE ET SCIENTIFIQUE DU GERS See BULLETIN DE LA SOCIETE ARCHEOLOGIQUE, HISTORIQUE, LITTERAIRE & SCIENTIFIQUE DU GERS **5193**

SOCIETE BELGE DE GEOLOGIE See BULLETIN DE LA SOCIETE BELGE DE GEOLOGIE **1368**

SOCIETE

SOCIETE BELGE D'ETUDES GEOGRAPHIQUES *See* BULLETIN DE LA SOCIETE BELGE D'ETUDES GEOGRAPHIQUES **2556**

SOCIETE BELGE D'HISTOIRE DES HOPITAUX *See* ANNALES DE LA SOCIETE BELGE D'HISTOIRE DES HOPITAUX **3776**

SOCIETE BELGE D'OPHTALMOLCGIE *See* BULLETIN DE LA SOCIETE BELGE D'OPHTALMOLOGIE **3873**

SOCIETE BELGE D'UROLOGIE *See* ACTA UROLOGICA BELGICA **3987**

SOCIETE BOTANIQUE DE FRANCE *See* LETTRES BOTANIQUES (PARIS) **517**

SOCIETE BOTANIQUE DE FRANCE. BULLETIN DE LA SOCIETE BOTANIQUE DE FRANCE. LETTRES BOTANIQUES *See* ACTA BOTANICA GALLICA : BULLETIN DE LA SOCIETE BOTANIQUE DE FRANCE **496**

SOCIETE CANADIENNE DE LA CROIX-ROUGE *See* RAPPORT SUR LES PROJETS / LA SOCIETE CANADIENNE DE LA CROIX-ROUGE **5304**

SOCIETE CANADIENNE DE LA SURETE INDUSTRIELLE *See* MEMBERSHIP DIRECTORY / CANADIAN SOCIETY FOR INDUSTRIAL SECURITY **2865**

SOCIETE CANADIENNE D'HYPOTHEQUES ET DE LOGEMENT *See* STRATEGIC PLAN - CANADA MORTGAGE AND HOUSING CORPORATION **4689**

SOCIETE CHATEAUBRIAND, CHATENAY-MALABRY, FRANCE *See* BULLETIN - SOCIETE CHATEAUBRIAND **3370**

SOCIETE D'AGRICULTURE, COMMERCE, SCIENCES ET ARTS DU DEPARTEMENT DE LA MARNE, CHALONS-SUR-MARNE *See* MEMOIRES DE LA SOCIETE D'AGRICULTURE, COMMERCE, SCIENCES ET ARTS DU DEPARTEMENT DE LA MARNE **107**

SOCIETE D'AGRICULTURE, SCIENCES ET ARTS DE LA SARTHE *See* BULLETIN DE LA SOCIETE D'AGRICULTURE, SCIENCES ET ARTS DE LA SARTHE **316**

SOCIETE D'AMENAGEMENT ET D'EXPLOITATION DES TERRES DU DELTA *See* RAPPORT D'ACTIVITES - SOCIETE D'AMENAGEMENT ET D'EXPLOITATION DES TERRES DU DELTA **124**

SOCIETE D'ARCHEOLOGIE D'HISTOIRE ET DE FOLKLORE DE NIVELLES ET DU BRABANT WALLON *See* ANNALES - SOCIETE D'ARCHEOLOGIE D'HISTOIRE ET DE FOLKLORE DE NIVELLES ET DU BRABANT WALLON **2674**

SOCIETE D'ARCHITECTURE DE MONTREAL *See* COMMUNIQUE - SOCIETE D'ARCHITECTURE DE MONTREAL **295**

SOCIETE D'ART ET D'HISTOIRE DU DIOCESE DE LIEGE *See* BULLETIN DE LA SOCIETE D'ART ET D'HISTOIRE DU DIOCESE DE LIEGE **2843**

SOCIETE DE BIOGEOGRAPHIE *See* COMPTE RENDU DES SEANCES DE LA SOCIETE DE BIOGEOGRAPHIE **2558**

SOCIETE DE BIOGEOGRAPHIE. COMPTE RENDU DES SEANCES DE LA SOCIETE DE BIOGEOGRAPHIE *See* BIOGEOGRAPHICA : COMPTE-RENDU DES SEANCES DE LA SOCIETE DE BIOGEOGRAPHIE **444**

SOCIETE DE BIOLOGIE, (PARIS, FRANCE) *See* COMPTES RENDUS DES SEANCES DE LA SOCIETE DE BIOLOGIE ET DE SES FILIALES **452**

SOCIETE DE CHIMIE ORGANIQUE ET BIOLOGIQUE. DEPARTEMENT ALIMENTATION ANIMALE *See* INFORMATIONS - AEC, DEPARTEMENT ALIMENTATION ANIMALE **5512**

SOCIETE DE DEVELOPPEMENT CULTUREL DE SAINT-EUSTACHE *See* REPERTOIRE DES ARTISTES ET DES ARTISANS DE SAINT-EUSTACHE **329**

SOCIETE DE DEVELOPPEMENT DU NKAM *See* COMPTES DE RESULTATS D'EXECUTION DU BUDGET / MINISTERE DE L'ECONOMIE ET DU PLAN, SOCIETE DE DEVELOPPEMENT DU NKAM **784**

SOCIETE DE DEVELOPPEMENT DU NKAM *See* BUDGET / MINISTERE DE L'ECONOMIE ET DU PLAN, SOCIETE DE DEVELOPPEMENT DU NKAM **780**

SOCIETE DE DEVELOPPEMENT DU NKAM *See* PROGRAMME D'ACTIVITES SODENKAM **804**

SOCIETE DE DEVELOPPEMENT INDUSTRIEL DU QUEBEC *See* RAPPORT ANNUEL - SOCIETE DE DEVELOPPEMENT INDUSTRIEL DU QUEBEC **806**

SOCIETE DE GEOGRAPHIE DE MARSEILLE *See* BULLETIN DE LA SOCIETE DE GEOGRAPHIE DE MARSEILLE **2556**

SOCIETE DE L'AIDE A L'ENFANCE D'OTTAWA *See* COMMUNIQUE - CHILDREN'S AID SOCIETY OF OTTAWA **5279**

SOCIETE DE L'HISTOIRE DE L'ART FRANCAIS (PARIS, FRANCE) *See* BULLETIN DE LA SOCIETE DE L'HISTOIRE DE L'ART FRANCAIS **345**

SOCIETE DE L'HISTOIRE DE PARIS ET DE L'ILE-DE-FRANCE, PARIS *See* BULLETIN DE LA SOCIETE DE L'HISTOIRE DE PARIS ET DE L'ILE-DE-FRANCE **2680**

SOCIETE DE LINGUISTIQUE DE PARIS *See* BULLETIN DE LA SOCIETE DE LINGUISTIQUE DE PARIS **3270**

SOCIETE DE MUSIQUE D'AUTREFOIS *See* ANNALES MUSICOLOGIQUES, MOYEN-AGE ET RENAISSANCE **4100**

SOCIETE DE PHILOSOPHIE DU QUEBEC *See* BULLETIN DE LA SOCIETE DE PHILOSOPHIE DU QUEBEC **4343**

SOCIETE DE STATISTIQUE DE PARIS *See* JOURNAL DE LA SOCIETE DE STATISTIQUE DE PARIS **5329**

SOCIETE D'EMULATION DE LA VENDEE 1971 (FR/0767-9203) [I07679203] **364**

SOCIETE D'EMULATION DES COTES-D'AMOUR (FR/1251-9103) [I12519103] **2630**

SOCIETE D'EMULATION DES COTES DU NORD *See* SOCIETE D'EMULATION DES COTES-D'AMOUR **2630**

SOCIETE D'ENERGIE DE LA BAIE JAMES *See* PROGRESS REPORT - SOCIETE D'ENERGIE DE LA BAIE JAMES **705**

SOCIETE DES ACIENCES, DES ARTS ET DES LETTRES DU HAINAUT *See* MEMOIRES ET PUBLICATIONS DE LA SOCIETE DES SCIENCES, DES ARTS ET DES LETTRES DU HAINAUT **325**

SOCIETE DES ALCOOLS DU QUEBEC *See* RAPPORT ANNUEL - SOCIETE DES ALCOOLS DU QUEBEC (1986?) **4678**

SOCIETE DES AMERICANISTES DE PARIS *See* JOURNAL DE LA SOCIETE DES AMERICANISTES **271**

SOCIETE DES AMIS DES ARTS ET SCIENCES DE TOURNUS (FR/0153-9353) [I01539353] **2854**

SOCIETE DES ANCIENS TEXTES FRANCAIS PUBLICATIONS (FR) **3322**

SOCIETE DES JEUX DU QUEBEC *See* BULLETIN - SOCIETE DES JEUX DU QUEBEC **4858**

SOCIETE DES LETTRES, SCIENCES ET ARTS DE LA CORREZE *See* BULLETIN DE LA SOCIETE DES LETTRES, SCIENCES ET ARTS DE LA CORREZE **2843**

SOCIETE DES OCEANISTES *See* JOURNAL DE LA SOCIETE DES OCEANISTES **238**

SOCIETE DES TEXTES FRANCAIS MODERNES (PARIS, FRANCE) *See* PUBLICATIONS - SOCIETE DES TEXTES FRANCAIS MODERNES **3313**

SOCIETE DES TRADUCTEURS DU QUEBEC *See* GUIDE DES MEMBRES DE LA STQ (FRENCH EDITION) **3284**

SOCIETE D'ETUDE D'HISTOIRE ECONOMIQUE ET SOCIALE DE LA FRANCE *See* BULLETIN BIBLIOGRAPHIQUE **411**

SOCIETE D'ETUDES DES HAUTES-ALPES *See* BULLETIN DE LA SOCIETE D'ETUDES DES HAUTES-ALPES **2680**

SOCIETE D'ETUDES ET DE DOCUMENTATION ECONOMIQUES, INDUSTRIELLES ET SOCIALES *See* ANALYSES DE LA S.E.D.E.I.S **1461**

SOCIETE D'ETUDES POUR LA CONNAISSANCE D'EDOUARD MANET *See* BULLETIN DE LA SOCIETE D'ETUDES POUR LA CONNAISSANCE D'EDOUARD MANET **1729**

SOCIETE DEVELOPPEMENT DU CACAO *See* RAPPORT D'ACTIVITES - SOCIETE DEVELOPPEMENT DU CACAO **1623**

SOCIETE D'EXPANSION TECHNIQUE ET ECONOMIQUE (FRANCE) *See* INFORMATIONS CHIMIE (EDITION FRANCAISE) **978**

SOCIETE D'HISTOIRE DE L'EGLISE D'ALSACE *See* ARCHIVES DE L'EGLISE D'ALSACE **5023**

SOCIETE D'HISTOIRE DU PROTESTANTISME BELGE *See* BULLETIN - SOCIETE D'HISTOIRE DU PROTESTANTISME BELGE **5057**

SOCIETE D'HISTOIRE DU VAL DE LIEPVRE (FR/0299-8556) [I02998556] **2710**

SOCIETE D'HISTOIRE DU VAL ET DE LA VILLE DE MUNSTER *See* ANNUAIRE DE LA SOCIETE D'HISTOIRE DU VAL ET DE LA VILLE DE MUNSTER **2674**

SOCIETE D'HISTOIRE ET D'ARCHEOLOGIE DE BRETAGNE *See* MEMOIRES DE LA SOCIETE D'HISTOIRE ET D'ARCHEOLOGIE DE BRETAGNE **274**

SOCIETE D'HISTOIRE ET D'ARCHEOLOGIE DE CHALON-SUR-SAONE *See* MEMOIRES DE LA SOCIETE D'HISTOIRE ET D'ARCHEOLOGIE DE CHALON-SUR-SAONE **274**

SOCIETE D'HISTOIRE ET D'ARCHEOLOGIE DE COLMAR *See* ANNUAIRE - SOCIETE D'HISTOIRE ET D'ARCHEOLOGIE DE COLMAR **2675**

SOCIETE D'HISTOIRE ET D'ARCHEOLOGIE DE DAMBACH-LA-VILLE, BARR, OBERNAI *See* ANNUAIRE DE LA SOCIETE D'HISTOIRE ET D'ARCHEOLOGIE DE DAMBACH-LA-VILLE, BARR, OBERNAI **2674**

SOCIETE D'HISTOIRE ET D'ARCHEOLOGIE DE GAND *See* HANDELINGEN DER MAATSCHAPPIJ VOOR GESCHIEDENIS EN OUDHEIDKUNDE TE GENT **2617**

SOCIETE D'HISTOIRE ET D'ARCHEOLOGIE DE GENEVE *See* MEMOIRES ET DOCUMENTS PUBLIES PAR LA SOCIETE D'HISTOIRE ET D'ARCHEOLOGIE DE GENEVE **2482**

SOCIETE D'HISTOIRE ET D'ART DE LA BRIE ET DU PAYS DE MEAUX *See* REVUE DE LA SOCIETE D'HISTOIRE ET D'ART DE LA BRIE ET DU PAYS DE MEAUX **2706**

SOCIETE D'HISTOIRE MODERNE (PARIS, FRANCE) *See* BULLETIN DE LA SOCIETE D'HISTOIRE MODERNE **2612**

SOCIETE D'HISTOIRE NATURELLE DE L'AFRIQUE DU NORD, ALGIERS *See* BULLETIN DE LA SOCIETE D'HISTOIRE NATURELLE DE L'AFRIQUE DU NORD **4163**

SOCIETE D'HISTOIRE NATURELLE DE TOULOUSE *See* BULLETIN DE LA SOCIETE D'HISTOIRE NATURELLE DE TOULOUSE **4163**

SOCIETE D'HORTICULTURE ET D'HISTOIRE NATURELLE DE L'HERAULT *See* ANNALES DE LA SOCIETE D'HORTICULTURE ET D'HISTOIRE NATURELLE DE L'HERAULT **2408**

SOCIETE DU QUEBECOISE D'INITIATIVES AGRO-ALIMENTAIRES *See* RAPPORT ANNUEL - SOCIETE QUEBECOISE D'INITIATIVES AGRO-ALIMENTAIRES **124**

SOCIETE ENTOMOLOGIQUE DE FRANCE *See* ANNALES DE LA SOCIETE ENTOMOLOGIQUE DE FRANCE **5575**

SOCIETE ENTOMOLOGIQUE DE FRANCE *See* BULLETIN DE LA SOCIETE ENTOMOLOGIQUE DE FRANCE **5606**

SOCIETE ENTOMOLOGIQUE DU QUEBEC *See* MEMOIRES DE LA SOCIETE ENTOMOLOGIQUE DU QUEBEC **5591**

SOCIETE FINANCIERE EUROPEENNE *See* WORLD MONEY OUTLOOK **817**

SOCIETE FRANCAISE (FR) **5222**

SOCIETE FRANCAISE DE BIOMETRIE *See* BIOMETRIE ET ECOLOGIE **2212**

SOCIETE FRANCAISE DE NUMISMATIQUE *See* BULLETIN DE LA SOCIETE FRANCAISE DE NUMISMATIQUE **2780**

SOCIETE FRANCAISE DE PHILOSOPHIE *See* BULLETIN DE LA SOCIETE FRANCAISE DE PHILOSOPHIE **4343**

SOCIETE FRANCAISE DE PHOTOGRAMMETRIE ET DE TELEDETECTION *See* BULLETIN - SOCIETE FRANCAISE DE PHOTOGRAMMETRIE ET DE TELEDETECTION **4367**

SOCIETE FRANCAISE D'ETUDE DU XVIIIE SIECLE *See* BULLETIN DE LA SOCIETE FRANCAISE D'ETUDE DU DIX-HUITIEME SIECLE **2680**

SOCIETE FRANCAISE D'HISTOIRE DES HOPITAUX *See* BULLETIN **3777**

SOCIETE FRANCAISE D'OPHTALMOLOGIE *See* BULLETINS ET MEMOIRES **3873**

SOCIETE GENEALOGIQUE CANADIENNE-FRANCAISE *See* MEMOIRES DE LA SOCIETE GENEALOGIQUE CANADIENNE-FRANCAISE **2460**

SOCIETE GENERALE DE BANQUES EN COTE D'IVOIRE *See* ECONOMIE IVOIRIENNE, L' **1558**

SOCIETE GEOLOGIQUE DE BELGIQUE *See* ANNALES DE LA SOCIETE GEOLOGIQUE DE BELGIQUE **1365**

SOCIETE GEOLOGIQUE DE FRANCE *See* LISTE DES MEMBRES DE LA SOCIETE GEOLOGIQUE DE FRANCE AU **1386**

SOCIETE GEOLOGIQUE DE FRANCE *See* LISTE DES MEMBRES DE LA SOCIETE GEOLOGIQUE DE FRANCE **1386**

SOCIETE GEOLOGIQUE DU NORD *See* MEMOIRES DE LA SOCIETE GEOLOGIQUE DU NORD **1358**

SOCIETE — Alphabetical Title Index

SOCIETE GEOLOGIQUE DU NORD (LILLE, FRANCE) *See* ANNALES DE LA SOCIETE GEOLOGIQUE DU NORD **1365**

SOCIETE GEOLOGIQUE ET MINERALOGIQUE DE BRETAGNE *See* MEMOIRES DE LA SOCIETE GEOLOGIQUE ET MINERALOGIQUE DE BRETAGNE **1358**

SOCIETE GEOLOGIQUE ET MINERALOGIQUE DE BRETAGNE *See* BULLETIN **1352**

SOCIETE HISTORIQUE ACADIENNE *See* CAHIERS--SOCIETE HISTORIQUE ACADIENNE, LES **2725**

SOCIETE HISTORIQUE DE QUEBEC *See* TEXTES - SOCIETE HISTORIQUE DE QUEBEC **2763**

SOCIETE HISTORIQUE DE SAINT-BONIFACE *See* BULLETIN DE LA SOCIETE HISTORIQUE DE SAINT-BONIFACE **2681**

SOCIETE HISTORIQUE DU CANADA *See* DIRECTORY OF MEMBERS / THE CANADIAN HISTORICAL ASSOCIATION **2731**

SOCIETE HISTORIQUE ET ARCHEOLOGIQUE DE LANGRES *See* BULLETIN DE LA SOCIETE HISTORIQUE ET ARCHEOLOGIQUE DE LANGRES **2681**

SOCIETE HISTORIQUE ET ARCHEOLOGIQUE DE L'ORNE (FR/0154-0505) [I01540505] **282, 2710**

SOCIETE HISTORIQUE ET ARCHEOLOGIQUE DE PONTOISE, DU VAL-D'OISE ET DU VEXIN *See* MEMOIRES DE LA SOCIETE HISTORIQUE ET ARCHEOLOGIQUE DE PONTOISE, DU VAL-D'OISE ET DU VEXIN **2698**

SOCIETE HISTORIQUE ET SCIENTIFIQUE DES DEUX-SEVRES, NIORT *See* BULLETIN DE LA SOCIETE HISTORIQUE ET SCIENTIFIQUE DES DEUX-SEVRES **2681**

SOCIETE J.-K. HUYSMANS *See* BULLETIN **5229**

SOCIETE JEAN BODIN POUR L'HISTOIRE COMPARATIVE DES INSTITUTIONS *See* RECUEILS DE LA SOCIETE JEAN BODIN POUR L'HISTOIRE COMPARATIVE DES INSTITUTIONS **5215**

SOCIETE LAMY *See* LAMY FISCAL **2993**

SOCIETE LINNEENNE DE LYON *See* BULLETIN MENSUEL DE LA SOCIETE LINNEENNE DE LYON **4164**

SOCIETE LINNEENNE DE NORMANDIE, CAEN *See* MEMOIRES DE LA SOCIETE LINNEENNE DE NORMANDIE. SECTION BOTANIQUE **517**

SOCIETE NATIONALE DE COMMERCE ET DE PRODUCTION (NIGER) *See* BILAN AU 30 SEPTEMBRE ... / SOCIETE NATIONALE DE COMMERCE ET DE PRODUCTION **824**

SOCIETE NATIONALE DES CHEMINS DE FER BELGES. DIRECTION DU PERSONNEL ET DES SERVICES SOCIAUX *See* DOCUMENTATION - SNCB, DIRECTION DU PERSONNEL ET DES SERVICES SOCIAUX **5431**

SOCIETE NATIONALE D'ETUDES ET DE PROMOTION INDUSTRIELLE *See* GUIDE DE L'INVESTISSEUR INDUSTRIEL AU SENEGAL **1565**

SOCIETE NATIONALE DU LOGEMENT *See* VERSLAG VAN DE RAAD VAN BEHEER OVER DE VERRICHTINGEN **2838**

SOCIETE NATIONALE DU LOGEMENT (BELGIUM) *See* RAPPORT DU CONSEIL D'ADMINISTRATION SUR LES OPERATIONS DE L'EXERCICE ... / SOCIETE NATIONALE DU LOGEMENT **1705**

SOCIETE NATIONALE INDUSTRIELLE AEROSPATIALE *See* COMPTES DE L'EXERCICE / SOCIETE NATIONALE INDUSTRIELLE AEROSPATIALE **17**

SOCIETE NEUCHATELOISE DE GEOGRAPHIE *See* BULLETIN DE LA SOCIETE NEUCHATELOISE DE GEOGRAPHIE **2556**

SOCIETE PAUL CLAUDEL (FRANCE) *See* BULLETIN DE LA SOCIETE PAUL CLAUDEL **3369**

SOCIETE POUR LA PROMOTION DE L'ENSEIGNEMENT DE L'ANGLAIS (LANGUE SECONDE) AU QUEBEC *See* S P E A Q JOURNAL **3319**

SOCIETE POUR L'HISTOIRE DU DROIT ET DES INSTITUTIONS DES ANCIENS PAYS BOURGUIGNONS, COMTOIS ET ROMANDS, DIJON *See* MEMOIRES DE LA SOCIETE POUR L'HISTOIRE DES ANCIENS PAYS BOURGUIGNONS, COMTOIS ET ROMANDS **3009**

SOCIETE PREHISTORIQUE FRANCAISE *See* BULLETIN DE LA SOCIETE PREHISTORIQUE FRANCAISE **263**

SOCIETE QUEBECOISE DE SPELEOLOGIE *See* PROGRAMMES - SOCIETE QUEBECOISE DE SPELEOLOGIE **1409**

SOCIETE QUEBECOISE D'INFORMATION JURIDIQUE *See* DECISIONS DISCIPLINAIRES CONCERNANT LES CORPORATIONS PROFESSIONNELLES **665**

SOCIETE QUEBECOISE D'INFORMATION JURIDIQUE *See* RAPPORT ANNUEL / SOCIETE QUEBECOISE D'INFORMATION JURIDIQUE **3243**

SOCIETE RENCESVALS *See* BULLETIN BIBLIOGRAPHIQUE DE LA SOCIETE RENCESVALS **3369**

SOCIETE ROUMAINE DE LINGUISTIQUE ROMANE *See* BULLETIN **3270**

SOCIETE ROYALE BELGE D'ENTOMOLOGIE *See* BULLETIN & I.E. ET ANNALES DE LA SOCIETE ROYALE BELGE D'ENTOMOLOGIE **5579**

SOCIETE ROYALE BELGE DES ELECTRICIENS *See* BULLETIN **2037**

SOCIETE ROYALE D'ARCHEOLOGIE DE BRUXELLES *See* ANNALES DE LA SOCIETE ROYALE D'ARCHEOLOGIE DE BRUXELLES **255**

SOCIETE ROYALE D'ASTRONOMIE DU CANADA. CENTRE DE QUEBEC *See* ALMANACH-GRAPHIQUE - CENTRE DE QUEBEC, SOCIETE ROYALE D'ASTRONOMIE DU CANADA **391**

SOCIETE ROYALE D'ASTRONOMIE DU CANADA. CENTRE DE QUEBEC *See* BULLETIN DU CENTRE DE QUEBEC DE LA S R A C **394**

SOCIETE ROYALE D'ECONOMIE POLITIQUE DE BELGIQUE (SERIES) (BE/0303-9609) [18530038] **1521**

SOCIETE ROYALE DES SCIENCES DE LIEGE *See* BULLETIN DE LA SOCIETE ROYALE DES SCIENCES DE LIEGE **5090**

SOCIETE SAINT-JEAN-BAPTISTE DE QUEBEC *See* PROCES-VERBAL DU CONGRES GENERAL ANNUEL - SOCIETE SAINT-JEAN-BAPTISTE DE QUEBEC **5235**

SOCIETE SCIENTIFIQUE DE BRETAGNE *See* BULLETIN DE LA SOCIETE SCIENTIFIQUE DE BRETAGNE **5090**

SOCIETE SCIENTIFIQUE, HISTORIQUE ET ARCHEOLOGIQUE DE LA CORREZE *See* BULLETIN DE LA SOCIETE SCIENTIFIQUE HISTORIQUE ET ARCHEOLOGIQUE DE LA CORREZE **263**

SOCIETE VAUDOISE DES SCIENCES NATURELLES, LAUSANNE *See* MEMOIRES DE LA SOCIETE VAUDOISE DES SCIENCES NATURELLES **5128**

SOCIETE VAUDOISE DES SCIENCES NATURELLES, LAUSANNE *See* BULLETIN DE LA SOCIETE VAUDOISE DES SCIENCES NATURELLES **4163**

SOCIETE VETERINAIRE PRATIQUE DE FRANCE *See* BULLETIN MENSUEL DE LA SOCIETE VETERINAIRE PRATIQUE DE FRANCE **5506**

SOCIETE ZOOLOGIQUE DE FRANCE *See* BULLETIN DE LA SOCIETE ZOOLOGIQUE DE FRANCE **5579**

SOCIETES CONTEMPORAINES (FR) [24031649] **5259**

SOCIETES DE SERVICE ET CONSEIL EN INFORMATIQUE, LES (FR) [02239881] **712**

SOCIETIES (PARIS, FRANCE) (FR/0765-3697) [13119183] **5259**

● SOCIETY & ANIMALS (UK/1063-1119) [25866594] **5222**

SOCIETY & COMMERCE (II) [01784114] **851**

SOCIETY AND CULTURE (II/0037-9662) [01765874] **5259**

SOCIETY & NATURAL RESOURCES (US/0894-1920) [15863293] **2205**

● SOCIETY AND NATURE (US/1062-9599) [25815341] **2182**

SOCIETY AND WELFARE (IS) [07633906] **5222**

SOCIETY FOR AFRICAN CHURCH HISTORY *See* BULLETIN OF THE SOCIETY FOR AFRICAN CHURCH HISTORY, THE **4941**

SOCIETY FOR ANCIENT NUMISMATICS *See* SAN **2783**

SOCIETY FOR ARMY HISTORICAL RESEARCH (LONDON, ENGLAND) *See* JOURNAL OF THE SOCIETY FOR ARMY HISTORICAL RESEARCH **4048**

SOCIETY FOR ASIAN AND COMPARATIVE PHILOSOPHY *See* MONOGRAPH ... OF THE SOCIETY FOR ASIAN AND COMPARATIVE PHILOSOPHY **4353**

SOCIETY FOR CALIFORNIA ARCHAEOLOGY. MEETING *See* PROCEEDINGS OF THE SOCIETY FOR CALIFORNIA ARCHAEOLOGY **279**

SOCIETY FOR DEVELOPMENTAL BIOLOGY. SYMPOSIUM *See* ... SYMPOSIUM OF THE SOCIETY FOR DEVELOPMENTAL BIOLOGY, THE **474**

SOCIETY FOR EARLY HISTORIC ARCHAEOLOGY *See* NEWSLETTER AND PROCEEDINGS OF THE S.E.H.A **276**

SOCIETY FOR ECONOMIC BOTANY NEWSLETTER *See* PLANTS & PEOPLE : SOCIETY FOR ECONOMIC BOTANY NEWSLETTER **525**

SOCIETY FOR EDUCATIONAL VISITS AND EXCHANGES IN CANADA *See* GENERAL INFORMATION AND GUIDELINES FOR THE SUMMER INDIVIDUAL EXCHANGE PROGRAM **1748**

SOCIETY FOR EDUCATIONAL VISITS AND EXCHANGES IN CANADA *See* GENERAL INFORMATION AND GUIDELINES FOR THE SUMMER INDIVIDUAL EXCHANGE PROGRAM **1748**

SOCIETY FOR ENDOCRINOLOGY *See* MEMOIRS OF THE SOCIETY FOR ENDOCRINOLOGY **3731**

SOCIETY FOR ETHNOMUSICOLOGY *See* SPECIAL SERIES / SOCIETY FOR ETHNOMUSICOLOGY **4154**

SOCIETY FOR EXPERIMENTAL BIOLOGY AND MEDICINE (NEW YORK, N.Y.) *See* PROCEEDINGS OF THE SOCIETY FOR EXPERIMENTAL BIOLOGY AND MEDICINE **3630**

SOCIETY FOR EXPERIMENTAL BIOLOGY (GREAT BRITAIN) *See* SYMPOSIA OF THE SOCIETY FOR EXPERIMENTAL BIOLOGY **474**

SOCIETY FOR EXPERIMENTAL MECHANICS (U.S.) *See* PROCEEDINGS OF THE SOCIETY FOR EXPERIMENTAL MECHANICS **4429**

SOCIETY FOR FORENSIC HAEMOGENETICS. CONGRESS *See* ADVANCES IN FORENSIC HAEMOGENETICS **3770**

SOCIETY FOR GENERAL MICROBIOLOGY *See* SOCIETY FOR GENERAL MICROBIOLOGY QUARTERLY, THE **570**

SOCIETY FOR GENERAL MICROBIOLOGY QUARTERLY *See* SGM QUARTERLY **570**

SOCIETY FOR GENERAL MICROBIOLOGY QUARTERLY, THE (UK/0142-7547) [04628174] **570**

SOCIETY FOR GERMAN-AMERICAN STUDIES NEWSLETTER (US/0741-5753) [10030054] **2273**

SOCIETY FOR HISTORIANS OF AMERICAN FOREIGN RELATIONS *See* NEWSLETTER - SOCIETY FOR HISTORIANS OF AMERICAN FOREIGN RELATIONS **4530**

SOCIETY FOR HISTORICAL ARCHAEOLOGY CONFERENCE UNDERWATER PROCEEDINGS (US) **282**

SOCIETY FOR INDUSTRIAL AND APPLIED MATHEMATICS *See* SIAM REVIEW **3535**

SOCIETY FOR INDUSTRIAL AND APPLIED MATHEMATICS *See* SIAM JOURNAL ON COMPUTING **1262**

SOCIETY FOR INDUSTRIAL AND APPLIED MATHEMATICS *See* SIAM JOURNAL ON APPLIED MATHEMATICS **3534**

SOCIETY FOR INDUSTRIAL AND APPLIED MATHEMATICS *See* SIAM JOURNAL ON NUMERICAL ANALYSIS **3535**

SOCIETY FOR INDUSTRIAL AND APPLIED MATHEMATICS *See* SIAM JOURNAL ON SCIENTIFIC AND STATISTICAL COMPUTING **3535**

SOCIETY FOR INDUSTRIAL AND APPLIED MATHEMATICS *See* SIAM JOURNAL ON CONTROL AND OPTIMIZATION **3534**

SOCIETY FOR INDUSTRIAL AND APPLIED MATHEMATICS *See* SIAM JOURNAL ON MATHEMATICAL ANALYSIS **3534**

SOCIETY FOR INDUSTRIAL ARCHAEOLOGY *See* NEWSLETTER - SOCIETY FOR INDUSTRIAL ARCHAEOLOGY **276**

SOCIETY FOR INDUSTRIAL ARCHAEOLOGY NEWSLETTER (US/0160-1067) [03617218] **309, 282**

SOCIETY FOR ITALIAN HISTORICAL STUDIES (U.S.) *See* MEMBERS IN GOOD STANDING AS OF ... / SOCIETY FOR ITALIAN HISTORICAL STUDIES **2698**

SOCIETY FOR ITALIC HANDWRITING *See* JOURNAL OF THE SOCIETY FOR ITALIC HANDWRITING, THE **380**

SOCIETY FOR NEUROSCIENCE *See* ABSTRACTS - SOCIETY FOR NEUROSCIENCE **3825**

SOCIETY FOR NURSING HISTORY GAZETTE, THE (US/0886-9278) [12243428] **3869**

SOCIETY FOR OLD TESTAMENT STUDY *See* BOOK LIST / SOCIETY FOR OLD TESTAMENT STUDY **5012**

SOCIETY FOR OLD TESTAMENT STUDY *See* MONOGRAPH SERIES **5018**

Alphabetical Title Index — SOCIETY

SOCIETY FOR ORGANIC PETROLOGY. MEETING See ANNUAL MEETING OF THE SOCIETY FOR ORGANIC PETROLOGY. ABSTRACTS AND PROGRAM **1458**

SOCIETY FOR ORGANIC PETROLOGY NEWSLETTER, THE (US/0743-3816) [10565252] **1459**

SOCIETY FOR PSYCHICAL RESEARCH (LONDON, ENGLAND) See PROCEEDINGS OF THE SOCIETY FOR PSYCHICAL RESEARCH **4609**

SOCIETY FOR PSYCHICAL RESEARCH (LONDON, ENGLAND) See JOURNAL OF THE SOCIETY FOR PSYCHICAL RESEARCH **4242**

SOCIETY FOR PSYCHOANALYTIC PSYCHOTHERAPY BULLETIN See INTERNATIONAL JOURNAL OF COMMUNICATIVE PSYCHOANALYSIS AND PSYCHOTHERAPY, THE **3927**

SOCIETY FOR SOCIAL RESPONSIBILITY IN SCIENCE See SSRS NEWSLETTER **5160**

SOCIETY FOR SOUTH INDIA STUDIES See NEWSLETTER OF THE SSIS **2660**

SOCIETY FOR SPANISH AND PORTUGUESE HISTORICAL STUDIES See BULLETIN - SOCIETY FOR SPANISH AND PORTUGUESE HISTORICAL STUDIES (U.S.) **2681**

SOCIETY FOR STUDY OF STATE GOVERNMENTS See JOURNAL OF THE SOCIETY FOR STUDY OF STATE GOVERNMENTS **4659**

SOCIETY FOR TECHNICAL COMMUNICATION. CONFERENCE See PROCEEDINGS / STC, SOCIETY FOR TECHNICAL COMMUNICATION ANNUAL CONFERENCE **5142**

SOCIETY FOR THE ADVANCEMENT OF FOOD SERVICE RESEARCH See PROCEEDINGS OF THE CONFERENCE - SOCIETY FOR THE ADVANCEMENT OF FOOD SERVICE RESEARCH **2354**

SOCIETY FOR THE ADVANCEMENT OF GIFTED EDUCATION. CONFERENCE See CONFERENCE PROCEEDINGS - SOCIETY FOR THE ADVANCEMENT OF GIFTED EDUCATION. CONFERENCE **1877**

SOCIETY FOR THE ADVANCEMENT OF MATERIAL AND PROCESS ENGINEERING See S.A.M.P.E. QUARTERLY **1995**

SOCIETY FOR THE ADVANCEMENT OF MATERIAL AND PROCESS ENGINEERING See SAMPE JOURNAL **1995**

SOCIETY FOR THE PRESERVATION OF LONG ISLAND ANTIQUITIES See NEWSLETTER - SOCIETY FOR THE PRESERVATION OF LONG ISLAND ANTIQUITIES **251**

SOCIETY FOR THE SCIENTIFIC STUDY OF RELIGION See MONOGRAPH SERIES / SOCIETY FOR THE SCIENTIFIC STUDY OF RELIGION **4979**

SOCIETY FOR THE STUDY OF HUMAN BIOLOGY SYMPOSIUM SERIES (UK/0954-7800) [13039141] **473**

SOCIETY FOR THE STUDY OF INBORN ERRORS OF METABOLISM See SYMPOSIA OF THE SOCIETY FOR THE STUDY OF INBORN ERRORS OF METABOLISM **3644**

SOCIETY FOR THE STUDY OF MIDWESTERN LITERATURE (U.S.) See NEWSLETTER - SOCIETY FOR THE STUDY OF MIDWESTERN LITERATURE (U.S.) **3417**

SOCIETY FOR THE STUDY OF SOUTHERN LITERATURE See NEWS-LETTER OF THE SOCIETY FOR THE STUDY OF SOUTHERN LITERATURE, THE **3416**

SOCIETY (MONTREAL) (CN/0381-1794) [04129343] **5260**

SOCIETY (NEW BRUNSWICK) (US/0147-2011) [02162353] **5222**

SOCIETY NEWS (BROOMALL, PA.) (US/8756-8861) [11608084] 388, **4153**

SOCIETY NEWS - SOCIETY OF ONTARIO HYDRO MANAGEMENT AND PROFESSIONAL STAFF (CN/0715-5212) [09502238] **1627**

SOCIETY OF ACTUARIES See TRANSACTIONS - SOCIETY OF ACTUARIES **2895**

SOCIETY OF ACTUARIES See YEAR BOOK / SOCIETY OF ACTUARIES **2896**

SOCIETY OF ACTUARIES. MEETING See RECORD - SOCIETY OF ACTUARIES. MEETING **2891**

SOCIETY OF AIRWAY PIONEERS See YEAR BOOK & DIRECTORY - SOCIETY OF AIRWAY PIONEERS **40**

SOCIETY OF AMERICAN ARCHIVISTS See MEMBERSHIP DIRECTORY - SOCIETY OF AMERICAN ARCHIVISTS **2482**

SOCIETY OF AMERICAN FORESTERS. NORTHERN CALIFORNIA SECTION See PROCEEDINGS ANNUAL MEETING / SOCIETY OF AMERICAN FORESTERS, NORTHERN CALIFORNIA SECTION **2391**

SOCIETY OF AMERICAN GRAPHIC ARTISTS See SAGA NATIONAL PRINT EXHIBITION **382**

SOCIETY OF AMERICAN TRAVEL WRITERS See DIRECTORY OF MEMBERS / SOCIETY OF AMERICAN TRAVEL WRITERS **5468**

SOCIETY OF AMERICAN TRAVEL WRITERS. ROSTER OF MEMBERS See DIRECTORY OF MEMBERS / SOCIETY OF AMERICAN TRAVEL WRITERS **5468**

SOCIETY OF AMERICAN VALUE ENGINEERS See SAVE PROCEEDINGS **1626**

SOCIETY OF ANTIQUARIES OF LONDON. RESEARCH COMMITTEE See REPORTS OF THE RESEARCH COMMITTEE OF THE SOCIETY OF ANTIQUARIES OF LONDON **2705**

SOCIETY OF ARCHER-ANTIQUARIES See JOURNAL OF THE SOCIETY OF ARCHER-ANTIQUARIES **4902**

SOCIETY OF ARCHITECTURAL HISTORIANS See JOURNAL OF THE SOCIETY OF ARCHITECTURAL HISTORIANS **302**

SOCIETY OF ARCHITECTURAL HISTORIANS See MEMBERSHIP DIRECTORY / SOCIETY OF ARCHITECTURAL HISTORIANS **303**

SOCIETY OF ARCHITECTURAL HISTORIANS See NEWSLETTER - THE SOCIETY OF ARCHITECTURAL HISTORIANS **304**

SOCIETY OF ARCHIVISTS (GREAT BRITAIN) See JOURNAL OF THE SOCIETY OF ARCHIVISTS **2482**

SOCIETY OF AUTOMOTIVE ENGINEERS See PROGRESS IN TECHNOLOGY **5142**

SOCIETY OF AUTOMOTIVE ENGINEERS See SAE TRANSACTIONS **5424**

SOCIETY OF AUTOMOTIVE ENGINEERS See SAE TRANSACTIONS **5425**

SOCIETY OF AUTOMOTIVE ENGINEERS See PREPRINTS OF PAPERS OF THE SAE TRANSACTIONS **1991**

SOCIETY OF AUTOMOTIVE ENGINEERS See SOCIETY OF AUTOMOTIVE ENGINEERS **1996**

SOCIETY OF AUTOMOTIVE ENGINEERS See AEROSPACE MATERIAL SPECIFICATIONS **5**

SOCIETY OF AUTOMOTIVE ENGINEERS (US/0099-5908) [07964893] 5425, **1996**

SOCIETY OF BIBLICAL LITERATURE See SOCIETY OF BIBLICAL LITERATURE SEMINAR PAPERS **5019**

SOCIETY OF BIBLICAL LITERATURE See MEMBER'S HANDBOOK / SOCIETY OF BIBLICAL LITERATURE **5018**

SOCIETY OF BIBLICAL LITERATURE. ABSTRACTS See ABSTRACTS / AMERICAN ACADEMY OF RELIGION **4931**

SOCIETY OF BIBLICAL LITERATURE DISSERTATION SERIES (US/0145-2770) [02997976] **5019**

SOCIETY OF BIBLICAL LITERATURE MONOGRAPH SERIES (US/0145-269X) [01587005] **5019**

SOCIETY OF BIBLICAL LITERATURE SEMINAR PAPERS (US/0145-2711) [03247598] **5019**

SOCIETY OF BOOKBINDERS AND BOOK RESTORERS See BOOKBINDER : JOURNAL OF THE SOCIETY OF BOOKBINDERS AND BOOK RESTORERS **4825**

SOCIETY OF CHARTERED PROPERTY AND CASUALTY UNDERWRITERS See CPCU NEWS **2878**

SOCIETY OF CHARTERED PROPERTY AND CASUALTY UNDERWRITERS See CPCU JOURNAL **2878**

SOCIETY OF CHEMICAL INDUSTRY (GREAT BRITAIN) See BULLETIN **963**

SOCIETY OF CHRISTIAN ETHICS (U.S.) See ANNUAL OF THE SOCIETY OF CHRISTIAN ETHICS, THE **4935**

SOCIETY OF CHRISTIAN POETS DIRECTORY (US) [11286717] **3471**

SOCIETY OF CLERKS-AT-THE-TABLE IN COMMONWEALTH PARLIAMENTS See TABLE (LONDON. 1953) **4689**

SOCIETY OF COMPETITIVE INTELLIGENCE PROFESSIONALS See COMPETITIVE INTELLIGENCE REVIEW **659**

SOCIETY OF COSMETIC CHEMISTS (U.S.) See MEMBERSHIP DIRECTORY / SOCIETY OF COSMETIC CHEMISTS **1027**

SOCIETY OF COUNTY TREASURERS See WASTE DISPOSAL STATISTICS BASED ON ESTIMATES **2185**

SOCIETY OF CRITICAL CARE MEDICINE See CRITICAL CARE **3569**

SOCIETY OF DAIRY TECHNOLOGY See JOURNAL OF THE SOCIETY OF DAIRY TECHNOLOGY **196**

SOCIETY OF DYERS AND COLOURISTS See JOURNAL OF THE SOCIETY OF DYERS AND COLOURISTS **1026**

SOCIETY OF ECONOMIC PALEONTOLOGISTS AND MINERALOGISTS. SEPM SHORT COURSE See SEPM SHORT COURSE NOTES **4230**

SOCIETY OF EXPERIMENTAL TEST PILOTS See COCKPIT (LANCASTER, CALIF.) **16**

SOCIETY OF EXPERIMENTAL TEST PILOTS. SYMPOSIUM See SYMPOSIUM PROCEEDINGS - SOCIETY OF EXPERIMENTAL TEST PILOTS. SYMPOSIUM **37**

SOCIETY OF EXPLORATION GEOPHYSICISTS See INDEX OF WELLS SHOT FOR VELOCITY **4260**

SOCIETY OF FLIGHT TEST ENGINEERS. NATIONAL SYMPOSIUM See ANNUAL SYMPOSIUM PROCEEDINGS / SOCIETY OF FLIGHT TEST ENGINEERS **12**

SOCIETY OF FRIENDS. NEW YORK YEARLY MEETING See YEARBOOK - NEW YORK YEARLY MEETING, RELIGIOUS SOCIETY OF FRIENDS **5069**

SOCIETY OF FRIENDS. PHILADELPHIA YEARLY MEETING See PYM NEWS: A PUBLICATION OF THE RELIGIOUS SOCIETY OF FRIENDS **4988**

SOCIETY OF ILLUSTRATORS (US) **375**

SOCIETY OF INDUSTRIAL ACCOUNTANTS OF CANADA See SPECIAL STUDY - SOCIETY OF INDUSTRIAL ACCOUNTANTS OF CANADA **751**

SOCIETY OF INDUSTRIAL AND COST ACCOUNTANTS OF CANADA. SPECIAL STUDY See SPECIAL STUDY - SOCIETY OF INDUSTRIAL ACCOUNTANTS OF CANADA **751**

SOCIETY OF INDUSTRIAL REALTORS See PHOTO ROSTER **4842**

SOCIETY OF MAGNETIC RESONANCE IN MEDICINE (U.S.). MEETING BOOK OF ABSTRACTS See PROCEEDINGS OF THE SOCIETY OF MAGNETIC RESONANCE IN MEDICINE **4445**

SOCIETY OF MALAWI JOURNAL, THE (MW/0037-993X) [05703599] **2643**

SOCIETY OF MANUFACTURING ENGINEERS See TECHNICAL PAPER - SOCIETY OF MANUFACTURING ENGINEERS (MF) **3488**

SOCIETY OF MANUFACTURING ENGINEERS See TECHNICAL DIGEST **2099**

SOCIETY OF MANUFACTURING ENGINEERS See TECHNICAL PAPER - SOCIETY OF MANUFACTURING ENGINEERS. TE **1998**

SOCIETY OF MANUFACTURING ENGINEERS See TECHNICAL PAPER - SOCIETY OF MANUFACTURING ENGINEERS. EM **1998**

SOCIETY OF MANUFACTURING ENGINEERS See SME TECHNICAL DIGEST **1996**

SOCIETY OF MANUFACTURING ENGINEERS See TECHNICAL PAPER - SOCIETY OF MANUFACTURING ENGINEERS. EE **2130**

SOCIETY OF MOTION PICTURE AND TELEVISION ENGINEERS See DIRECTORY FOR MEMBERS - SOCIETY OF MOTION PICTURE AND TELEVISION ENGINEERS, INC **4067**

SOCIETY OF NAVAL ARCHITECTS AND MARINE ENGINEERS (U.S.) See TRANSACTIONS - THE SOCIETY OF NAVAL ARCHITECTS AND MARINE ENGINEERS **4184**

SOCIETY OF NUCLEAR MEDICINE (1953-). MEDICAL INTERNAL RADIATION DOSE COMMITTEE See MIRD PAMPHLETS **3944**

SOCIETY OF NUCLEAR MEDICINE (1963-) See MITGLIEDERVERZEICHNIS - GESELLSCHAFT FUR NUCLEARMEDIZIN **3944**

SOCIETY OF NUCLEAR MEDICINE. SOUTHEASTERN CHAPTER See CONTINUING EDUCATION LECTURES **3568**

SOCIETY OF ONTARIO HYDRO MANAGEMENT AND PROFESSIONAL STAFF See SOCIETY NEWS - SOCIETY OF ONTARIO HYDRO MANAGEMENT AND PROFESSIONAL STAFF **1627**

SOCIETY OF ONTARIO NUT GROWERS See SONG NEWS **187**

SOCIETY OF PETROLEUM ENGINEERS OF AIME See S P E REPRINT SERIES **4277**

SOCIETY OF PETROLEUM ENGINEERS (U.S.) See SPE MEMBERSHIP DIRECTORY **4279**

SOCIETY OF PHILATELIC AMERICANS See S.P.A. JOURNAL **2787**

SOCIETY OF PHYSICS STUDENTS See SPS CHAPTER LIST **4422**

SOCIETY OF PLASTICS ENGINEERS. TECHNICAL CONFERENCE *See* CONFERENCE PROCEEDINGS / ANTEC **4454**

SOCIETY OF PROFESSIONAL WELL LOG ANALYSTS *See* TRANSACTIONS OF THE SPWLA ANNUAL LOGGING SYMPOSIUM **4280**

SOCIETY OF PROSPECTIVE MEDICINE. MEETING *See* PROCEEDINGS OF THE ... ANNUAL MEETING OF THE SOCIETY OF PROSPECTIVE MEDICINE **3630**

SOCIETY OF THE PLASTICS INDUSTRY OF CANADA *See* SPI CANADA ... PROGRAM, ... ACCOMPLISHMENTS **4460**

SOCIETY OF TRIBOLOGISTS AND LUBRICATION ENGINEERS SPECIAL PUBLICATIONS (US) **1996**

SOCIETY OF VACUUM COATERS *See* PROCEEDINGS OF THE ANNUAL TECHNICAL CONFERENCE **3486**

SOCIETY OF VERTEBRATE PALEONTOLOGY *See* ADDRESS DIRECTORY / SOCIETY OF VERTEBRATE PALEONTOLOGY **4226**

SOCIETY OF VERTEBRATE PALEONTOLOGY MEMOIR (US/1062-161X) [24171875] **4231**

SOCIETY OF WIRELESS PIONEERS *See* YEARBOOK - SOCIETY OF WIRELESS PIONEERS **2087**

SOCIETY OF WIRELESS PIONEERS *See* WIRELESS REGISTER. WORLD WIDE EDITION, THE **1143**

SOCIETY OF WIRELESS PIONEERS *See* AMATEUR CALL BOOK, THE **1148**

SOCIETY PAGE (US/0038-0075) [03926649] **2893**

SOCIJALIZAM (CI/0560-6675) [01534319] **4547**

SOCIJALNA PSIHIJATRIJA (CI/0303-7908) [01112665] **3937**

SOCIO-ECONOMIC FACTBOOK FOR SURGERY (US/0193-3302) [05049313] 1521, **3975**

SOCIO-ECONOMIC PLANNING SCIENCES (US/0038-0121) [01765941] 5260, **1521**

SOCIO-ECONOMIC REVIEW: GUJARAT STATE (II/0533-5884) [01586435] **1584**

SOCIO-ECONOMIC STUDIES (FR) [07426797] 5260, **1521**

SOCIO-ECONOMICS DEPARTMENT RESEARCH PROGRAMME (ET) [07724165] **136**

SOCIOBIOLOGY (US/0361-6525) [02247124] **5597**

SOCIOCRITICISM (US/1041-9861) [13001594] 245, **5260**

SOCIOCRITICISM MONTPELLIER (FR/0985-5939) [I09855939] **3437**

SOCIOCRITICISM (NEW YORK, N.Y.) (US/1043-5727) [19488961] **5260**

SOCIOECONOMIC CHARACTERISTICS OF MEDICAL PRACTICE (US/0742-2709) [10269501] **3917**

SOCIOECONOMIC ISSUES OF HEALTH (US/0198-7399) [05917991] 5260, **4803**

SOCIOECONOMIC REPORT (US/0575-5964) [04363077] **3642**

SOCIOFILE DATABASE [COMPUTER FILE], THE (US) [20839793] **5260**

SOCIOLINGUISTICA (GW/0933-1883) [17864624] 5260, **3322**

SOCIOLINGUISTICS (CN/0257-7135) [I02577135] **3322**

SOCIOLOGIA (XO/0049-1225) [06246425] **5260**

SOCIOLOGIA (IT/0038-0156) [04345239] **5260**

SOCIOLOGIA (BL) [04941611] **5260**

SOCIOLOGIA DEL DIRITTO (IT/0390-0851) [02242692] **3056**

SOCIOLOGIA DEL LAVORO (IT/0392-5048) [08341318] 1711, **5260**

SOCIOLOGIA DEL TRABAJO (MADRID, SPAIN) (SP) [11911202] **5260**

SOCIOLOGIA DELLA COMUNICAZIONE (IT) [09847848] **1121**

SOCIOLOGIA DELLA LETTERATURA (IT) [05256935] **3437**

SOCIOLOGIA E RICERCA SOCIALE (IT) [09398049] **5260**

SOCIOLOGIA INDICA (II) [04766918] **5260**

SOCIOLOGIA INTERNATIONALIS (GW/0038-0164) [01765942] **5260**

SOCIOLOGIA RURALIS (NE/0038-0199) [01641341] **5260**

SOCIOLOGICA (MX/0187-0173) [19866665] **5260**

SOCIOLOGICAL ABSTRACTS (US/0038-0202) [01624065] 5260, **5267**

SOCIOLOGICAL ANALYSIS (US/0038-0210) [02608224] **4998**

SOCIOLOGICAL BULLETIN (II/0038-0229) [01774470] **5260**

SOCIOLOGICAL CONTRIBUTIONS FROM FLANDERS (BE) [03469623] **5260**

SOCIOLOGICAL FOCUS (KENT, OHIO) (US/0038-0237) [01034960] **5260**

SOCIOLOGICAL FORUM (RANDOLPH, N.J.) (US/0884-8971) [12534133] **5260**

●SOCIOLOGICAL IMAGINATION (US/1077-5048) [30338387] **5260**

SOCIOLOGICAL INQUIRY (US/0038-0245) [00830574] **5260**

SOCIOLOGICAL METHODOLOGY (US/0081-1750) [01765945] **5260**

SOCIOLOGICAL METHODS & RESEARCH (US/0049-1241) [01765946] **5261**

SOCIOLOGICAL OBSERVATIONS (US/0149-4872) [03535604] **5261**

SOCIOLOGICAL PERSPECTIVES (US/0731-1214) [08123782] **5261**

SOCIOLOGICAL PRACTICE *CEASED*. (US/0163-8505) [04517465] **5261**

SOCIOLOGICAL PRACTICE REVIEW *CEASED*. (US/1050-6306) [21567436] **5261**

SOCIOLOGICAL QUARTERLY (US/0038-0253) [01644316] **5261**

●SOCIOLOGICAL RESEARCH (US/1061-0154) [25153252] **5261**

SOCIOLOGICAL REVIEW MONOGRAPH, THE (UK/0081-1769) [03115287] **5261**

SOCIOLOGICAL REVIEW, THE (UK/0038-0261) [01654047] **5261**

SOCIOLOGICAL SPECTRUM (US/0273-2173) [07023725] **5261**

SOCIOLOGICAL STUDIES (US) [03459042] **5261**

SOCIOLOGICAL STUDIES OF CHILD DEVELOPMENT (US/1058-8930) [14561161] **5261**

SOCIOLOGICAL STUDIES OF CHILDREN (US) **5261**

SOCIOLOGICAL THEORY (UK/0735-2751) [08900405] **5261**

●SOCIOLOGICAL THEORY ABSTRACTS (US/1070-1192) [28286908] 5267, **5261**

SOCIOLOGICAL VIEWPOINTS (US/1060-0876) [20558053] **5261**

SOCIOLOGICKY CASOPIS (XR/0038-0288) [01943837] **5261**

SOCIOLOGIE DU TRAVAIL (PARIS) (FR/0038-0296) [01961168] **1711**

SOCIOLOGIE ET SOCIETES (CN/0038-030X) [06365938] **5262**

SOCIOLOGIE ROMANEASCA (RM) [02267857] **5262**

SOCIOLOGIE SANTE (FR/0998-0113) [24189682] **4803**

SOCIOLOGIJA (YU/0038-0318) [01955791] **5262**

SOCIOLOGIJA SELA (CI/0038-0326) [04942180] **5262**

SOCIOLOGISCHE GIDS (BE/0038-0334) [01946447] **5262**

SOCIOLOGISK FORSKNING (SW/0038-0342) [05821064] **5262**

SOCIOLOGISKE MEDDELELSER (DK/0038-0350) [01587376] **5262**

SOCIOLOGUS; ZEITSCHRIFT FUER EMPIRISCHE ETHNOSOZIOLOGIE UND ETHNOPSYCHOLOGIE. JOURNAL FOR EMPIRICAL ETHNO-SOCIOLOGY AND ETHNO-PSYCHOLOGY (GW/0038-0377) [02056407] **5262**

SOCIOLOGY AND RELATED DISCIPLINES / INTERNATIONAL CURRENT AWARENESS SERVICES *CEASED*. (UK/0960-1546) [23888210] **5262**

SOCIOLOGY AND SOCIAL RESEARCH *CEASED*. (US/0038-0393) [05088377] **5262**

SOCIOLOGY ETHNOLOGY BULLETIN (ET) [25760565] 5262, **245**

SOCIOLOGY (GUILFORD, CONN.) (US/0277-9315) [06523081] **5262**

SOCIOLOGY OF EDUCATION (US/0038-0407) [01765952] 5262, **1784**

SOCIOLOGY OF EDUCATION ABSTRACTS (UK/0038-0415) [01644626] 1784, **1797**

SOCIOLOGY OF HEALTH & ILLNESS (UK/0141-9889) [05308133] 4803, **5262**

●SOCIOLOGY OF RELIGION (US/1069-4404) [27909994] 5262, **4998**

SOCIOLOGY OF SPORT JOURNAL (US/0741-1235) [10094521] **4919**

SOCIOLOGY OF THE SCIENCES (NE/0167-2320) [04014321] **5158**

SOCIOLOGY (OXFORD) (UK/0038-0385) [01765950] **5262**

SOCIOLOGY REVIEW (UK/0959-8499) [I09598499] **5262**

SOCIOLOSKI PREGLED (YU/0085-6320) [01955420] **5262**

SOCIOMETRY MONOGRAPHS (US) [01680851] **5262**

SOCIONOMEN 1987 (SW/0283-1929) [I02831929] **5310**

SOCM SENTINEL, THE (US/0889-2415) [13825259] **2205**

SODA TO ENSO (JA/0371-3768) [10411942] **2371**

SODAN (JA) [09491695] **425**

SODOBNOST (XV/0038-0482) [05898319] **2523**

SOEDRA SKOG (SW) **2395**

SOETMUL (KO) [08364493] **4019**

SOFIA NEWS *SUSPENDED*. (BU) [02475919] **4496**

SOFT & MICRO (FR/0755-3579) [I07553579] 1290, **1272**

SOFT DRINKS MANAGEMENT INTERNATIONAL (UK/0953-4776) [17748545] **2371**

SOFT-LETTER (US/0882-3499) [11809137] **1290**

SOFT TECHNOLOGY (AT/0810-1434) [I08101434] 2205, **1957**

●SOFT WATCH (US/1064-8860) [26450381] 1290, **1209**

SOFTART PRESS (SZ/0255-9773) [I02559773] **364**

●SOFTAWARENESS (AUSTIN, TEX.) (US/1065-7290) [26708901] **1290**

SOFTDISK (US/0886-4152) [16006209] **1203**

SOFTSEL RESELLER (UK) **1203**

SOFTWARE ABC (GW) **1290**

SOFTWARE ABSTRACTS FOR ENGINEERS : SAFE (IE/0790-150X) [10976577] 1230, 1290, **1210**

SOFTWARE - CONCEPTS AND TOOLS (GW) **1290**

●SOFTWARE CONNECTION, DOS (US/1065-0776) [26515587] **1290**

SOFTWARE DEVELOPER'S MONTHLY (US) [12004097] **1290**

●SOFTWARE DEVELOPMENT (US/1070-8588) [28480726] **1290**

SOFTWARE DEVELOPMENT AND COMPUTER SERVICE INDUSTRY / STATISTICS CANADA, SERVICES, SCIENCE AND TECHNOLOGY DIVISION (CN/1181-9847) [29384148] **1203**

SOFTWARE DEVELOPMENT MONITOR (UK/0964-6841) **1290**

SOFTWARE DIGEST (US) **1290**

SOFTWARE DIGEST RATINGS REPORT (US/0893-6455) [15125611] **1290**

SOFTWARE DIRECTORY. DATACENTER MANAGER *See* SOFTWARE DIRECTORY. SYSTEMS & UTILITIES **1290**

SOFTWARE DIRECTORY FOR THE OFFSHORE INDUSTRY (UK) 4278, **1290**

SOFTWARE DIRECTORY. MASTER INDEX *CEASED*. (US/1057-798X) [24118099] **1290**

SOFTWARE DIRECTORY. SYSTEM BUILDER *See* SOFTWARE DIRECTORY. SYSTEMS & UTILITIES **1290**

●SOFTWARE DIRECTORY. SYSTEMS & UTILITIES (US/1071-3441) [27262729] **1290**

●SOFTWARE ECONOMICS LETTER (US/1065-6146) [26648835] **1290**

SOFTWARE. EDUCATION ADMINISTRATION *CEASED*. (US/0882-7702) [11989467] 1872, **1290**

SOFTWARE ENCYCLOPEDIA, THE (US/0000-006X) [12402610] **1210**

SOFTWARE ENGINEERING *CEASED*. (US/1053-6760) [22137113] 1203, **1996**

SOFTWARE ENGINEERING JOURNAL (UK/0268-6961) [13295958] 1290, **1996**

SOFTWARE ENGINEERING NOTES (US/0163-5948) [02989202] 1290, **1230**

SOFTWARE ENGINEERING STRATEGIES *CEASED*. (US/1067-1293) [27141485] **1290**

SOFTWARE EXPRESS (US/0742-5058) [10344696] 1290, **1272**

SOFTWARE FOR ENGINEERING AND WORKSTATIONS (UK/0952-8768) [18352849] 1996, **1203**

SOFTWARE FOR ENGINEERING WORKSTATIONS *See* ADVANCES IN ENGINEERING SOFTWARE & WORKSTATIONS **1284**

SOFTWARE FUTURES (UK/0965-6545) [I09656545] **1290**

●SOFTWARE HANDBOOK (PLYMOUTH MEETING, PA.) (US/1063-147X) [25105297] **1290**

SOFTWARE INDUSTRY BULLETIN (US/0883-5772) [12210999] **1290**

Alphabetical Title Index — SOLAR

SOFTWARE INDUSTRY FACTBOOK (US) [22719556] **1290**

SOFTWARE INDUSTRY REPORT (US/1042-7252) [19117402] 1217, 1239, **1290**

SOFTWARE INVENTORY CATALOG (US) [05035032] **1203**

SOFTWARE JOURNAL, THE (US/0747-6027) [10762265] **1290**

SOFTWARE-KURIER FUER MEDIZINER UND PSYCHOLOGEN **CEASED.** (GW/0934-5841) [I09345841] **1203**

SOFTWARE LAW BULLETIN, THE (US/0897-2680) [17454638] 1290, **3056**

SOFTWARE LAW JOURNAL (US/0886-3628) [12873561] 1203, **3056**

SOFTWARE MAGAZINE (WESTBOROUGH, MASS.) (US/0897-8085) [17364022] **1290**

SOFTWARE MAINTENANCE NEWS (US/0741-4501) [10199668] **1291**

SOFTWARE MANAGEMENT (UK/0960-0906) [I09600906] **1291**

●SOFTWARE MANUFACTURING NEWS (US/1064-878X) [26447196] 1291, **1203**

●SOFTWARE MARKETING JOURNAL (US/1060-3964) [24990747] 936, **1291**

SOFTWARE : PRACTICE & EXPERIENCE (UK/0038-0644) [01639246] 1281, **1291**

SOFTWARE PROCESS IMPROVEMENT AND PRACTICE (UK) [30820251] **1203**

●SOFTWARE PROCESS, QUALITY & ISO 9000 (US/1070-5457) [28406657] **1291**

SOFTWARE PRODUCTIVITY REVIEW (AT/1032-1071) [I10321071] **1291**

SOFTWARE PROTECTION (US/0733-1274) [08534987] 1291, **1227**

SOFTWARE QUALITY & ISO 9000 **See** SOFTWARE PROCESS, QUALITY & ISO 9000 **1291**

●SOFTWARE QUALITY JOURNAL (UK/0963-9314) [26235616] **1203**

SOFTWARE QUALITY WORLD (US/1042-9255) [19252585] **1291**

SOFTWARE REFERENCE GUIDE (US) [16383597] **1291**

SOFTWARE RETAILING (US/0736-5675) [09139700] 1291, **1245**

SOFTWARE REVIEWS ON FILE (US/8755-7169) [11390111] 1281, **1291**

SOFTWARE SERIES - NEW YORK STATE GEOLOGICAL SURVEY (US/0891-6357) [14938300] **1397**

SOFTWARE STRATEGY SERVICE (US) **1291**

SOFTWARE SYSTEMS AND TECHNIQUES ABSTRACTS (UK/0958-465X) **1291**

SOFTWARE TAXATION LETTER (US/1048-521X) [20966930] **3056**

●SOFTWARE TESTING, VERIFICATION & RELIABILITY (UK/0960-0833) [27326681] **1291**

SOFTWARE USERS YEAR BOOK CD-ROM (UK) **1291**

SOFTWARE USER'S YEAR BOOK, THE (UK/0268-6708) [13488187] **1203**

SOFTWARE WORLD (UK/0038-0652) [04718377] 1281, **1291**

SOFTWARE WRITERS MARKET (POMONA, N.Y.) (US/8756-9833) [11522582] 1281, **1291**

SOFTWHERE. AGRI-BUSINESS (US/8756-1050) [11478464] 136, **1291**

SOFTWHERE. BANKING/FINANCE (US/8756-1069) [11161578] **812**

SOFTWHERE. EDUCATION COURSEWARE **CEASED.** (US/0882-7699) [11986940] 1784, **1291**

SOFTWHERE. ENGINEERING (US/8756-1085) [11161722] 1230, **1291**

SOFTWHERE. HEALTH CARE (US/8756-1077) [10844271] 1281, **1291**

SOFTWHERE. INSURANCE (US/8756-1093) [11478174] 2893, **1291**

SOFTWHERE. LEGAL (US/8756-1107) [11439585] 3056, **1291**

SOFTWHERE. MANUFACTURING (US/0882-7443) [11966111] 3488, **1291**

SOFTWHERE. REAL ESTATE (US/8755-6065) [11337903] **4847**

SOFW **See** SOFW JOURNAL **1030**

●SOFW JOURNAL (GW) [26340751] **1030**

●SOFWIN REPORTS (US/1070-101X) [28278221] **1203**

SOGANG OMUN (KO) [09522822] **3322**

SOGLASIE (RU/0868-8710) [24019630] **3437**

SOGO KENKYU KAIHATSU KIKO **See** NIRA SOGO KINKYU KAIHATSU KIKO ... NENJI HOKOKUSHO **5211**

SOGO KENKYU KAIHATSU KIKO (JAPAN) **See** NIRA REPORT **1576**

SOGO KENKYUJO HO (JA) [02435137] **2508**

SOGO-SHOSHA, JAPANESE GENERAL TRADING COMPANIES YEAR BOOK (JA) [02577478] **1627**

SOGO TOSHI KENKYU (JA) [05055989] **2835**

SOGO TOSHO MOKUROKU (JA) [02480513] **1538**

SOGYU (KO) [08880100] **4278**

SOGYU YONBO (KO) [09047724] **4278**

SOHIO NEWS (US/0273-1843) [05686178] **4278**

SOIL AND CROP SCIENCE SOCIETY OF FLORIDA. MEETING **See** PROCEEDINGS / THE SOIL AND CROP SCIENCE SOCIETY OF FLORIDA **183**

SOIL AND HEALTH (NZ/0038-0687) [19551138] **186**

SOIL & TILLAGE RESEARCH (NE/0167-1987) [07190117] **186**

SOIL & WATER CONSERVATION NEWS **CEASED.** (US/0199-9060) [06162905] **186**

SOIL BIOLOGY & BIOCHEMISTRY (UK/0038-0717) [01716162] **186**

SOIL DYNAMICS AND EARTHQUAKE ENGINEERING (1984) (UK/0267-7261) [11276156] **1996**

SOIL MECHANICS AND FOUNDATION ENGINEERING (US/0038-0741) [02184483] 2031, **2129**

SOIL MECHANICS & FOUNDATION ENGINEERING. JAPAN TSUCHI TO KISO (JA) **186**

SOIL MECHANICS SERIES (MONTREAL, QUEBEC) (CN/0541-6329) [02247267] **2031**

SOIL NOTE (AT/0811-2622) [19487005] **187**

SOIL RESEARCH REPORT (CC/0254-5616) [09480088] **187**

SOIL SCIENCE (US/0038-075X) [01765965] **187**

SOIL SCIENCE AND PLANT NUTRITION (TOKYO) (JA/0038-0768) [05146955] **187**

SOIL SCIENCE BULLETIN / INSTITUTE OF AGRICULTURAL RESEARCH (ET) [11793208] **187**

SOIL SCIENCE SOCIETY OF AMERICA **See** SOIL SCIENCE SOCIETY OF AMERICA JOURNAL **187**

SOIL SCIENCE SOCIETY OF AMERICA JOURNAL (US/0361-5995) [02093507] **187**

SOIL SURVEY BULLETIN (NEW SOUTH WALES) (AT/0727-9078) [11008690] **187**

SOIL SURVEY HORIZONS (US/0584-0554) [04163150] **187**

SOIL SURVEY INVESTIGATIONS REPORT (US/0083-3320) [01780629] **187**

SOIL SURVEY OF ENGLAND AND WALES **See** TECHNICAL MONOGRAPH - GREAT BRITAIN. SOIL SURVEY **189**

SOIL SURVEY OF ENGLAND AND WALES **See** ANNUAL REPORT - SOIL SURVEY. ENGLAND AND WALES **163**

SOIL TECHNOLOGY (GW/0933-3630) [18422718] **187**

SOIL USE AND MANAGEMENT (UK/0266-0032) [12054519] **187**

SOILLESS CULTURE **CEASED.** (NE/0256-9701) [13279037] **187**

SOILS AND FERTILIZERS (UK/0038-0792) [01765967] 187, **156**

SOILS AND FERTILIZERS IN TAIWAN (CH/0370-9779) [01765968] **187**

SOILS AND FOUNDATIONS (SA/0038-0806) [04991477] **2031**

SOILS AND FOUNDATIONS (JA/0385-1621) [11902012] **1996**

SOILS AND LAND USE SERIES (AT/0375-5754) [03642135] **187**

SOILS (INDEPENDENCE, MO.) (US/1056-0157) [23467895] **187**

SOILS NEWS (AT) [11123989] **187**

SOILUTIONS (EDMONTON) (CN/1182-7858) [23264543] **187**

SOINS (SZ) **2912**

SOINS. CARDIOLOGIE (FR/0755-1916) [11171277] **3710**

●SOINS. FORMATION, PEDAGOGIE, ENCADREMENT : AVEC LA PARTICIPATION DU CEEIEC (FR/1163-4723) [29522356] **3869**

SOINS. GYNECOLOGIE PUERICULTRICE (FR) **3768**

SOINS PARIS (FR/0038-0814) [I00380814] **3869**

SOINS. PSYCHIATRIE (FR/0241-6972) [08411693] **3937**

SOIS PRET (CN/0383-8587) [03406098] **5236**

SOJA : A NEWS BULLETIN OF THE NIGERIAN ARMY (NR) [11605789] **4057**

SOJOURN (SINGAPORE, SINGAPORE) (SI/0217-9520) [15188350] **5222**

SOJOURNER (CAMBRIDGE) (US/0191-8699) [04656277] **5566**

SOJOURNERS (US/0364-2097) [01995372] **4998**

SOKA GAKKAI **See** SOKA GAKKAI NEWS, THE **5022**

SOKA GAKKAI NEWS, THE (JA/0385-6321) [01946615] **5022**

SOKA GAKKAI NYUSU THE SOKAGAKKAI NEWS (JA) [08712167] **5022**

SOKA-SHI SHI KENKYU (JA) [08480204] **2664**

SOKEIZAI (JA) [11604963] **1521**

SOKUCHI GAKKAISHI (JA/0038-0830) [06119685] **2576**

SOKUGYO NORYOKU KAIHATSU JANARU / RODOSHO SHOKUGYO NORYOKU KAIHATSUKYOKU HEN (JA) [11994775] **1915**

SOL DE TEXAS, EL (US) [05285396] **5754**

SOL (HOUSTON, TEX.), EL (US/0891-818X) [05112974] **5754**

SOL MAYOR : REVISTA DE MUSICA (PE) [08601605] **4153**

SOL (NEW YORK), EL (UK/0038-0849) [04074371] **3322**

SOL (PHOENIX, ARIZ. : 1939) (US) [05086957] **5630**

SOL (WINNIPEG) (CN/0709-504X) [08770568] 2205, **1957**

SOL (ZAGREB) (CI/0352-8715) [22341014] **3322**

SOLANUS (UK/0038-0903) [01765971] 2710, **3250**

SOLAR BULLETIN (RAMSEY) (US/0271-8480) [04902175] **400**

SOLAR CELLS **See** SOLAR ENERGY MATERIALS AND SOLAR CELLS : AN INTERNATIONAL JOURNAL DEVOTED TO PHOTOVOLTAIC, PHOTOTHERMAL, AND PHOTOCHEMICAL SOLAR ENERGY CONVERSION **1957**

SOLAR CENSUS (US/0272-9776) [06887474] 309, 627, **1957**

SOLAR COLLECTOR MANUFACTURING ACTIVITY (US/0197-2022) [05904339] 1957, **1963**

SOLAR EARTHBUILDER INTERNATIONAL'S EARTH & SUN (US/0898-5065) [17403286] **627**

SOLAR ENERGY AND NONFOSSIL FUEL RESEARCH (US/0741-5419) [05835555] 1957, **136**

SOLAR ENERGY & RESEARCH DIRECTORY (US/0148-0871) [03262001] **1957**

SOLAR ENERGY HANDBOOK (US/0149-9238) [03556112] **1957**

SOLAR ENERGY MATERIALS **See** SOLAR ENERGY MATERIALS AND SOLAR CELLS : AN INTERNATIONAL JOURNAL DEVOTED TO PHOTOVOLTAIC, PHOTOTHERMAL, AND PHOTOCHEMICAL SOLAR ENERGY CONVERSION **1957**

●SOLAR ENERGY MATERIALS AND SOLAR CELLS : AN INTERNATIONAL JOURNAL DEVOTED TO PHOTOVOLTAIC, PHOTOTHERMAL, AND PHOTOCHEMICAL SOLAR ENERGY CONVERSION (NE/0927-0248) [25469470] **1957**

SOLAR ENERGY (PHOENIX, ARIZ.) (US/0038-092X) [04796733] **1957**

SOLAR ENERGY PROGRESS IN AUSTRALIA AND NEW ZEALAND (AT) [07547663] **1957**

SOLAR-GEOPHYSICAL DATA (US/0038-0911) [04692787] **1411**

SOLAR, GEOTHERMAL, ELECTRIC AND STORAGE SYSTEMS PROGRAM, SUMMARY DOCUMENT (US/0194-1046) [04607413] **1957**

SOLAR INDEX (US/0735-6862) [08560432] **1957**

SOLAR INDICES BULLETIN (US/1046-1914) [15235208] **1411**

SOLAR INDUSTRY JOURNAL (US/1050-5660) [21314081] **1957**

SOLAR LAW : CUMULATIVE SUPPLEMENT / PRESENT AND FUTURE : WITH PROPOSED FORMS. SANDY F. KRAEMER (US) [09269540] 1957, **3056**

SOLAR, MAN OF THE ATOM (US/1056-3938) [23703567] **4866**

SOLAR PHYSICS (NE/0038-0938) [01644783] 4421, **400**

SOLAR PROBE NEWSLETTER (US) [23882965] **1957**

SOLAR PROGRESS (AT/0729-6436) [I07296436] **1957**

SOLAR RADIATION AND RADIATION BALANCE DATA, THE WORLD NETWORK / USSR STATE COMMITTEE FOR HYDROMETEOROLOGY AND CONTROL OF NATURAL ENVIRONMENT, I. VOEIKOV MAIN GEOPHYSICAL OBSERVATORY (RU) [10179394] **1434**

SOLAR SYSTEM RESEARCH (US/0038-0946) [01765972] **400**

SOLAR TECHNICAL SERIES (OTTAWA) (CN/0709-4043) [05589732] **1957**

SOLAR TERRESTRIAL ENVIRONMENTAL RESEARCH IN JAPAN (JA/0386-5444) [04274833] **400**

SOLAR THERMAL ENERGY TECHNOLOGY (US/0741-5249) [10168016] **1957**

SOLAR THERMAL ENERGY UTILIZATION. CUMULATIVE VOLUME (US/0146-6909) [03006401] **1957**

SOLAR THERMAL POWER SYSTEMS. PROGRAM SUMMARY (US) [09151687] **1957**

SOLAR TIMES (MADISON, CONN.) (US/0888-4048) [05981243] **1957**

SOLAR TODAY (US/1042-0630) [15737630] **1957**

SOLAR WASHINGTON (US/0734-3949) [08480309] **1957**

SOLARIS (CN/0709-8863) [05842223] **3437**

SOLATHIA (IT) [14209614] **4832**

SOLDADURA Y TECNOLOGIAS DE UNION (SP/1130-0280) [I11300280] **4019**

SOLDAT UND TECHNIK (GW/0038-0989) [05740653] **4057**

SOLDATSKAIA SLAVA (RU) [05098196] **4057**

SOLDERING & SURFACE MOUNT TECHNOLOGY : JOURNAL OF THE SMART (SURFACE MOUNT & RELATED TECHNOLOGIES) GROUP (UK/0954-0911) [20425957] **4019**

SOLDIER (UK) [07359435] **4057**

SOLDIER OF FORTUNE (US/0145-6784) [02778757] **4057**

SOLDIER OF FORTUNE PRESENTS FIGHTING FIREARMS (US) [25567052] **4057**

●SOLDIERS TODAY (US/1059-194X) [24506932] **4057**

SOLDIERS (WASHINGTON) (US/0093-8440) [01644395] **4057**

SOLE 24 ORE (IT/0391-786X) [I0391786X] **5805**

SOLE PROPRIETOR, THE (US) [03455794] **712**

SOLEIL DE COLOMBIE, LE *See* SOLEIL DE COLOMBIE-BRITANNIQUE **5794**

●SOLEIL DE COLOMBIE-BRITANNIQUE (CN/1194-7098) [28824267] **5794**

SOLEIL DE HAUTE-VOLTA, LE (UV) [01788614] **2643**

SOLEIL DE TRIEST (CN/0229-3889) [08078710] **5310**

SOLETTER (US/0747-623X) [07492424] **1997**

SOLIA (US/0038-1039) [02180224] **4998**

SOLICITORS' AND BARRISTERS' DIRECTORY AND DIARY, THE (UK) [11908576] **3056**

SOLICITORS' JOURNAL (LONDON, ENGLAND : 1928) (UK/0038-1047) [11653888] **3056**

SOLICITORS' LIABILITY INDEX (CN/0821-5383) [11360446] **3056**

SOLID FUEL (UK) [07354470] **1030**

SOLID FUEL CHEMISTRY (US/0361-5219) [01947444] **1957**, **1030**

SOLID MECHANICS AND ITS APPLICATIONS (NE/0925-0042) [I09250042] **2129**

SOLID STATE AND SUPERCONDUCTIVITY ABSTRACTS (US/0896-5900) [17204816] **4429**, **4427**

SOLID STATE COMMUNICATIONS (US/0038-1098) [01717054] **4421**

SOLID-STATE ELECTRONICS (UK/0038-1101) [01765978] **2081**

SOLID STATE IONICS (NE/0167-2738) [06693627] **992**, **4421**

●SOLID STATE NUCLEAR MAGNETIC RESONANCE (NE/0926-2040) [26287056] **4421**

SOLID STATE PHYSICS : ADVANCES IN RESEARCH AND APPLICATIONS. SUPPLEMENT (US/0081-1955) [02337308] **4421**

SOLID STATE PHYSICS (NEW YORK. 1955) (US/0081-1947) [01623882] **4421**

SOLID STATE TECHNOLOGY (US/0038-111X) [01715701] **2081**

●SOLID STATE TECHNOLOGY ... BUYING GUIDE (US) [25937210] **2082**

SOLID STATE TECHNOLOGY ... PROCESSING & PRODUCTION BUYERS GUIDE *See* SOLID STATE TECHNOLOGY ... BUYING GUIDE **2082**

SOLID WASTE & POWER (US/1058-9074) [17896771] **2243**

SOLID WASTE MANAGEMENT ECONOMICS REPORT : SWMER (US/1055-1298) [23086888] **2243**

SOLID WASTE MANAGEMENT NEWSLETTER *CEASED.* (US) [03787780] **2243**

SOLID WASTE REPORT (US/0038-1128) [01765981] **2243**

SOLIDARIDAD (CL) [05248679] **5262**, **4513**, **4998**

SOLIDARIDAD (PH) [25357303] **4496**

SOLIDARIDAD SAN JUAN, METRO MANILA (PH/0117-3138) [I01173138] **4496**

SOLIDARIETA LOMBARDIA (IT) **2835**

SOLIDARITAT (GW) [04995805] **1584**

SOLIDARITE, SANTE. ETUDES STATISTIQUES / MINISTERE DES AFFAIRES SOCIALES ET DE LA SOLIDARITE NATIONALE (FR) [11987561] **2897**, **4811**

SOLIDARITES (CN/0383-6711) [03402850] **4998**

SOLIDARITY (DETROIT, MICH.) (US/0164-856X) [04309031] **1711**

SOLIDARITY (MANILA) (PH/0038-1160) [01775087] **4513**

SOLINEWS (US/0193-273X) [04115497] **3250**

SOLNECHNYE DANNYE (RU/0552-5829) [05186903] **400**

SOLNOTE (CN/0709-5031) [08063775] **2608**

SOLOINTIMO SOLOMARE (IT) **1087**

SOLOMON INTERNATIONAL TELEVISION NEWSLETTER, THE (US) **1139**

SOLOMON ISLANDS LAW REPORTS, THE (BP) [10470800] **3056**

SOLOMON ISLANDS. MINISTRY OF FINANCE *See* SOLOMON ISLANDS ... RECURRENT ESTIMATE **4748**

SOLOMON ISLANDS ... RECURRENT ESTIMATE (BP) [19212221] **4748**

SOLOMON VALLEY POST (US) [12101636] **5678**

SOLON ECONOMIST (SOLON, IOWA : 1981) (US) [11986927] **5673**

SOLON TIMES, THE (US/0194-3677) [05469223] **5730**

SOLOTEXTOS : REVISTA CULTURAL DEL DEPARTAMENTO DE LITERATURA DE LA CASA DE LA CULTURA ECUATORIANA, NUCLEO DEL AZUAY (EC) [26369841] **3438**

SOLPLAN REVIEW (CN/0828-6574) [15515279] **382**, **2835**

SOLS (FR/0038-1217) [01948013] **2031**

SOLSTICE (ANN ARBOR, MICH.) (US/1059-5325) [23375258] **3536**, **2576**

SOLSTICE NEWS (CN/0821-4743) [09692415] **4153**

SOLUBILITY DATA SERIES (UK/0191-5622) [04967896] **992**

SOLUTIONS (1980) (US/0199-9869) [05957710] **136**

SOLUTIONS (BOCA RATON, FLA.) *CEASED.* (US/0892-7413) [15347143] **886**

SOLUTIONS FOR BETTER HEALTH *SUSPENDED.* (US/1050-0219) [21378583] **4803**, **5222**

SOLUTIONS FOR LONG-TERM CARE ADMINISTRATION (US/1059-5023) [24608690] **3792**

SOLUTIONS (FREDERICTON) (CN/0710-779X) [08737571] **5158**

SOLUTIONS TELEMATIQUES PARIS (FR/1167-2501) [I11672501] **1121**

SOLVENT EXTRACTION AND ION EXCHANGE (US/0736-6299) [09189188] **1019**

SOLWEST (CN/0229-1959) [08010272] **1957**

SOLZHENITSYN STUDIES *SUSPENDED.* (US/0731-2261) [07821250] **156**

SOMA (SAN FRANCISCO, CALIF.) (US/0896-5005) [17193152] **2546**

SOMALI JOURNAL OF RANGE SCIENCE : PUBLICATION OF THE DEPARTMENT OF BOTANY AND RANGE SCIENCE, FACULTY OF AGRICULTURE, SOMALI NATIONAL UNIVERSITY (SO) [18726154] **4686**, **222**

SOMALIA : WIRTSCHAFTLICHE ENTWICKLUNG (GW) [03415499] **1521**

SOMALIA, WIRTSCHAFTSDATEN UND WIRTSCHAFTSDOKUMENTATION / BUNDESSTELLE FUER AUSSENHANDELSINFORMATION (GW) [10931577] **1584**

SOMATIC CELL AND MOLECULAR GENETICS (US/0740-7750) [10009256] **551**

SOMATICS (US/0147-5231) [03179870] **3937**, **4361**

SOMATOSENSORY & MOTOR RESEARCH (US/0899-0220) [17973711] **5597**

SOMATOTHERAPIES ET SOMATOLOGIE (FR) **3642**

SOMBRAS DEL PASADO (US/0272-8249) [06930141] **2761**

SOME DATA ABOUT SWEDEN (SW) [01783354] **2523**

SOME SOCIO-ECONOMIC TRENDS (PK) [01761729] **1584**

SOMENI (TZ) [07011745] **3250**

SOMERSET ARCHAEOLOGY AND NATURAL HISTORY (UK/0081-2056) [09242639] **282**

SOMERSET HERALD (PRINCESS ANNE, MD. : 1985) (US/8756-6397) [11627428] **5687**

SOMERSET INDUSTRIAL ARCHAEOLOGY SOCIETY *See* JOURNAL OF THE SOMERSET INDUSTRIAL ARCHAEOLOGICAL SOCIETY **272**

SOMERSET LEGAL JOURNAL (US) [03248775] **3056**

SOMERSET LEVELS PAPERS (UK) [02568311] **282**

SOMERSET MESSENGER GAZETTE (US) [11116539] **5711**

SOMERSET RECORD SOCIETY : [PUBLICATION] (UK) [03013459] **2630**

SOMETHING ABOUT THE AUTHOR (US/0276-816X) [01765991] **435**

SOMETHING ABOUT THE AUTHOR. AUTOBIOGRAPHY SERIES (US/0885-6842) [12708474] **3438**

SOMETHING ELSE YEARBOOK (US/0093-0776) [01783678] **331**

SOMETHING SPECIAL PATTERN CLUB (US/0883-3710) [12125174] **5186**

●SOMMAIRE - SYNDICAT DE L'ASSOCIATION DES JURISTES DE L'ETAT (CN/1193-414X) [27193650] **3056**

SOMMAIRE (SYNDICAT DES AVOCATS ET NOTAIRES DE LA FONCTION PUBLIQUE) *See* SOMMAIRE - SYNDICAT DE L'ASSOCIATION DES JURISTES DE L'ETAT **3056**

SOMMAIRES DE DROIT DU TRAVAIL (FR/0223-7164) [09718630] **3154**

SOMMAIRES DE SECURITE SOCIALE (FR/0755-7000) [I07557000] **5310**

SOMMERFELTIA (NO/0800-6865) [15106296] **528**

SOMOGYI MUZEUMOK KOZLEMENYEI (HU/0139-4983) [02242413] **2710**

●SOMOS (CU) [26790742] **1069**

SOMOS (BUENOS AIRES, ARGENTINA) *CEASED.* (AG) [03093612] **2552**

SOMOS JOVENES (CU/0864-0564) [13791076] **1069**

SOMYU YONGAM (KO) [07452021] **5356**

SON HI-FI VIDEO (CN/0831-0785) [13784493] **5319**

SON MAGAZINE *See* SON, VIDEO MAGAZINE **5319**

SON MISUL (KO) [05304419] **364**

SON, MUSIQUE, VIDEO MAG (FR/1148-4322) [25844978] **5319**, **4377**

SON OF THE STARS (US) [06989370] **5236**

SON, VIDEO MAGAZINE (FR/0765-3530) [11505925] **5319**

SONANCES *CEASED.* (CN/0712-2438) [08734097] **4153**

SONCINO HEBREW ENGLISH TALMUD (UK) **5053**

SONDAGEM CONJUNTURAL (BL) [03218007] **1584**

SONDAGEM CONJUNTURAL, INDUSTRIA DE TRANSFORMACAO / FUNDACAO INSTITUTO TECNICO DE ECONOMIA E PLANEJAMENTO (BL/0101-3351) [08336291] **1627**

SONDEI SOUL (KO) [07959932] **2508**

SONDERBAENDE ZUR STRAHLENTHERAPIE UND ONKOLOGIE (GW/0931-2447) [15285785] **3642**

SONDERHEFT (GW) [04096796] **4803**

SONDERHEFT - DEUTSCHE KERAMISCHE GESELLSCHAFT (GW/0417-2256) [05202693] **2594**

SONDERHEFTE ZUM ALLGEMEINEN STATISTISCHEN ARCHIV (GW) [05363206] **5338**

SONDERPADAGOGIK (GW) [01785645] **4393**, **1885**

SONDERREIHE, OFFENTLICHE VORTRAGE / UNIVERSITAT DES SAARLANDES (GW) [20441061] **5158**

SONDERSCHRIFT DES IFO-INSTITUTS FUR WIRTSCHAFTSFORSCHUNG (GW/0536-1613) [02130477] **1521**

SONDERVEROFFENTLICHUNG (BUNDESSTELLE FUR AUSSENHANDELSINFORMATION (GERMANY). LEGISLATIVER DIENST) See AUSLANDISCHES WIRTSCHAFTS- UND STEUERRECHT **2938**

SONECRAN (CN/0706-7410) [05018164] **331**

SONFLOWERS DISCIPLESHIP JOURNAL (US/0194-9179) [05109959] **4998**

●SONG HITS' HEARTBREAKERS (US/1053-7791) [22638150] **4153**

SONG NEWS (CN/0704-5859) [03887211] **187**

SONG (TORONTO) (CN/0822-4226) [09816289] **3471**

SONGAI HOKEN KENKYU (JA) [05593527] **2893**

SONGSIM CHUNGANG YUJI CHAEDAN YONBO (KO) [10197504] **4803**

SONGSO YONGU (KO) [10527446] **4998**

SONGWRITER (HOLLYWOOD) (US/0274-5917) [05960375] **4153**

SONGWRITER'S MARKET (US/0161-5971) [03979280] **4153**

SONGWRITER'S REVIEW *SUSPENDED.* (US/0038-1373) [01765994] **4153**

SONIDO (NEW YORK, N.Y.) (US/0734-2896) [08700925] **4153**

SONIX (US/0097-6008) [02241532] **3801**

SONNECK SOCIETY BULLETIN, THE (US) [15562358] **4153**

SONNENENERGIE & WARMEPUMPE (GW/0172-5912) [10450960] **1957**

SONO PARIS (FR/0243-4938) [I02434938] **4453**

SONOMA BUSINESS (US/0191-6327) [04947678] **712**

SONOMA INDEX-TRIBUNE, THE (US/8755-9498) [11429595] **5640**

SONOMA SEARCHER, THE (US/1065-1217) [11299185] **2473**

SONORA REVIEW (US/0275-5203) [07118676] **3353**

SONORAN QUARTERLY, THE (US) [23452826] **2431**

SONORENSE, EL (MX) [05651145] **2546**

SONORENSIS (US/0277-4887) [04347308] **4096**

SONOVISION PARIS (FR/0768-956X) [I0768956X] **1121**

SONS, CHIRURGIE (PARIS, FRANCE : 1982) (FR/0249-6429) [11171507] **3975**

SONS OF NORWAY VIKING, THE (US/0038-1462) [03926883] 2324, 2710, **2273**

SONS OF THE AMERICAN REVOLUTION See SAR MAGAZINE, THE **5236**

SONUS (US/0739-229X) [08289018] **4153**

SOO, THE (US/0733-5296) [08594939] **5436**

SOOBSCENIJA BJURAKANSKOJ OBSERVATORII (AI/0370-8691) [02723568] **400**

SOOBSHCHENIIA (RU) [02771790] **364**

SOOBSHCHENIIA (RU) [01755762] **1121**

SOOBSHCHENIIA AKADEMII NAUK GRUZII (GS) [27674274] **5158**

SOOCHOW JOURNAL OF MATHEMATICS (CH/0250-3255) [05622964] **3536**

SOOKE STANDARD, THE (CN/1182-9966) [23598193] **5794**

SOONER JAYCEE (US/0279-2451) [09242290] **5236**

SOONER POSTMASTER (US/0744-5644) [08353579] **1147**

SOONER, THE (US/0038-1497) [03789945] **1095**

SOP (MX) [02161751] **1627**

SOPERTON NEWS, THE (US) [08796129] **5655**

SOPHIA (AT/0038-1527) [02577658] 4361, **4998**

SOPHIA (JA) [12698051] **1080**

SOPHIA (GW/0584-1259) [05238519] **5040**

SOPHIA LINGUISTICA (JA/0287-5357) [03265731] **3322**

SOPHISTICATE'S BLACK HAIR STYLES AND CARE GUIDE (US/1042-5276) [19076658] **405**

SOPHISTICATE'S HAIRSTYLE GUIDE / 1,001 IDEAS (US) [09888600] **405**

SOPRODEN (SP/0213-831X) [22378835] **1584**

SOPRONI SZEMLE (HU/0133-0748) [I01330748] **2630**

SOPYONG MUNHWA (KO) [25496669] **4832**

SOREN TOO BOEKI CHOSA GEPPO (JA) [10861275] **851**

SOREN TOO / SOREN TOO KENKYUKAI HENCHO (JA) [09494567] **2710**

S'ORGANISER (CN/0714-3303) [08996000] **5794**

SORGHUM AND MILLETS ABSTRACTS *CEASED.* (UK/03082970) [02956988] 136, **156**

SORGHUM NEWSLETTER (US/0584-1321) [02516385] **136**

SORGO, UMA ALTERNATIVA ECONOMICA (BL) [02649539] **187**

SORIPAR (HU/0560-8538) [02352356] **2371**

SORKIN'S DIRECTORY OF BUSINESS & GOVERNMENT (KANSAS CITY ED.) (US/0894-1033) [15796733] 1627, **712**

SORKINS' DIRECTORY OF BUSINESS & GOVERNMENT (ST. LOUIS ED.) (US/0748-0458) [10869690] **712**

SORKINS' MAGAZINE (US/1057-9346) [24221395] **712**

SORONDA (PG) [17490720] **2643**

SOROPTIMIST OF THE AMERICAS, THE (US/0097-9562) [01799258] **5566**

SOROUSH / SURUSH (IR) [11189467] **2508**

SORRISI E CANZONI TV (IT/0038-156X) [I0038156X] **2493**

SORT IT OUT (CN/0229-6640) [08023769] **4153**

SORTIE (MONTREAL) (CN/0714-7376) [09543149] **2796**

SORTING CODE NUMBERS (UK) **812**

SORUI (JA/0038-1578) [02520764] **528**

SOS INTERNATIONAL NEWSLETTER (US/1071-1422) [28556976] **1349**

SOSALISTA PANORAMA (II) [02239365] **4547**

SOSEI TO KAKO : NIHON SOSEI KAKO GAKKAI SHI (JA/0038-1586) [10118790] **4460**

SOSHIKI KAGAKU / ORGANIZATION SCIENCE / HENSHU, SOSHIKI GAKKAI (JA/0286-9713) [11016975] **5158**

SOSHIOROJI (JA/0584-1380) [I05841380] **5262**

SOSHIRAN ENGLISH ED (JA/0910-5042) [I09105042] **3677**

SOSIAL TRYGD (NO) [07207964] 2893, **5310**

SOSIALKONOMEN (NO) [07207184] **1595**

SOSIALT FORUM/SOSIALT ARBEID (NO) [05843721] **4547**

SOSIALT UTSYN / SOCIAL SURVEY (NO) [04403773] **5222**

SOSIOLOGI I DAG (NO/0332-6330) [12499171] **5262**

SOSIOLOGIA (FI/0038-1640) [07200168] **5262**

SOSIOLOGISK TIDSSKRIFT (NO) **5222**

SOSOL MUNHAK (KO) [07386951] 3438, **3322**

SOT LA NAPE (IT) [17257962] 1080, **3322**

SOTAHISTORIALLINEN AIKAKAUSKIRJA (FI/0357-816X) [I0357816X] 2710, **4057**

SOTHEBY, PARKE-BERNET, LOS ANGELES See SALE - SOTHEBY, PARKE-BERNET, LOS ANGELES **364**

SOTHEBY'S ART AT AUCTION (UK) [17429721] **365**

SOTHEBY'S (FIRM) See SOTHERBY'S PREVIEW **365**

SOTHEBY'S (FIRM) See SOTHEBY'S ART AT AUCTION **365**

SOTHEBY'S IN IRELAND See CATALOG OF ... - SOTHEBY'S IN IRELAND **347**

SOTHERBY'S PREVIEW (UK) [20910416] **365**

SOTILASAVUSTUS (FI) [19244361] 4393, **4057**

SOTO STATES ANTHROPOLOGIST, THE (US/1056-5299) [22342967] **245**

SOTSIALISTICHESKAIA ZAKONNOST See ZAKONNOST **3179**

SOTSIALISTICHESKII OBRAZ ZHIZNI I IDEOLOGICHESKAIA BORBA / AKADEMIIA NAUK SSSR, INSTITUT NAUCHNOI INFORMATSII PO OBSHCHESTVENNYM NAUKAM (RU) [07634861] **1584**

SOTSIALISTICHESKII TRUD See CHELOVEK I TRUD **1659**

SOTSIALNO-EKONOMICHESKIE PROBLEMY NAUCHNO-TEKHNICHESKOGO PROGRESSA (RU) [02241931] **1627**

SOTSIALNO-EKONOMICHESKOE RAZVITIE MOSKVY I KRUPNEISHIKH GORODOV SSSR (RU) [20864064] **2835**

SOTSIALNO-POLITICHESKIE NAUKI (RU/0868-5797) [22190296] **4547**

●SOTSIALNO-POLITICHESKII ZHURNAL (RU) [27019348] **4547**

SOTSIALNOE OBESPECHENIE (RU) [02043546] **2894**

●SOTSIALNYE I GUMANITARNYE NAUKI. SERIIA 2, EKONOMIKA : OTECHESTVENNAIA I ZARUBEZHNAIA LITERATURA / ROSSIISKAIA AKADEMIIA NAUK, INSTITUT NAUCHNOI INFORMATSII PO OBSHCHESTVENNYM NAUKAM (RU) [29889183] **1521**

SOTSIALNYE I GUMANITARNYE NAUKI. SERIIA 3, FILOSOFSKIE NAUKI : OTECHENNAIA I ZARUBEZHNAIA LITERATURA / ROSSIISKAIA AKADEMIIA NAUK, INSTITUT NAUCHNOI INFORMATSII PO OBSHCHESTVENNYM NAUKAM (RU) [29893046] **4361**

●SOTSIALNYE I GUMANITARNYE NAUKI. SERIIA 4, GOSUDARSTVO I PRAVO. OTECHESTVENNAIA LITERATURA / ROSSIISKAIA AKADEMIIA NAUK, INSTITUT NAUCHNOI INFORMATSII PO OBSHCHESTVENNYM NAUKAM (RU) [29837663] 4496, **3056**

●SOTSIALNYE I GUMANITARNYE NAUKI. SERIIA 4, GOSUDARSTVO I PRAVO. ZARUBEZHNAIA LITERATURA / ROSSIISKAIA AKADEMIIA NAUK, INSTITUT NAUCHNOI INFORMATSII PO OBSHCHESTVENNYM NAUKAM (RU) 4496, **3056**

●SOTSIALNYE I GUMANITARNYE NAUKI. SERIIA 5, ISTORIIA. OTECHESTVENNAIA LITERATURA / ROSSIISKAIA AKADEMIIA NAUK, INSTITUT NAUCHNOI INFORMATSII PO OBSHCHESTVENNYM NAUKAM (RU) [29892935] **2630**

SOTSIALNYE I GUMANITARNYE NAUKI. SERIIA 6, I AZYKOZNANIE. OTECHESTVENNAIA LITERATURA / ROSSIISKAIA AKADEMIIA NAUK, INSTITUT NAUCHNOI INFORMATSII PO OBSHCHESTVENNYM NAUKAM (RU) [29904835] **3322**

SOTSIALNYE I GUMANITARNYE NAUKI. SERIIA 7, LITERATUROVEDENIE. ZARUBEZHNAIA LITERATURA (RU) [29990530] **3438**

●SOTSIALNYE I GUMANITARNYE NAUKI. SERIIA 8, NAUKOVEDENIE : OTECHESTVENNAIA I ZARUBEZHNAIA LITERATURA / ROSSIISKAIA AKADEMIIA NAUK, INSTITUT NAUCHNOI INFORMATSII PO OBSHCHESTVENNYM NAUKAM (RU/0202-2141) [29995818] **5158**

●SOTSIALNYE I GUMANITARNYE NAUKI. SERIIA 9, VOSTOKOVEDENIE I AFRIKANISTIKA. ZARUBEZHNAIA LITERATURA / ROSSIISKAIA AKADEMIIA NAUK, INSTITUT NAUCHNOI INFORMATSII PO OBSHCHESTVENNYM NAUKAM (RU) [29992488] 2643, **2664**

SOTSIOLOGICHESKI PROBLEMI (BU/0038-1683) [02049529] **5263**

SOTSIOLOGICHESKIE ISSLEDOVANIIA (RU/0132-1625) [01799314] **5263**

SOUDAGE ET TECHNIQUES CONNEXES (FR/0038-173X) [06006666] **4027**

SOUDER (FR/0246-1900) [10681243] **4027**

SOUDERTON INDEPENDENT (US) [13724602] **5739**

SOUDNI LEKARSTVI CESKOSLOVENSKA PATOLOGIE (XR) **3898**

SOUL & JAZZ RECORD, THE (US/0361-2619) [02246328] **4153**

SOUL CHOKSIPCHA PYONGWON See CHOKSIPCHA PYONGWON CHI **3563**

SOUL CHOKSIPCHA PYONGWON See YONBO **3794**

SOUL IN REVIEW (US/0098-0730) [01799458] **4153**

SOUL JOURNEY (US/0091-6323) [01787789] **5491**

SOUL SEARCHER (US/0275-6501) [04521935] **4243**

SOUL TAEHAKKYO See SEOUL NATIONAL UNIVERSITY FACULTY PAPERS : BIOLOGY AND AGRICULTURE SERIES **473**

SOUL TAEHAKKYO See SEOUL NATIONAL UNIVERSITY FACULTY PAPERS : HUMANITIES AND SOCIAL SCIENCE SERIES, A & B **1847**

SOUL TAEHAKKYO KONGDAE SOSIK (KO) [04863782] 1847, **1997**

SOUL TAEHAKKYO. KONGKWA TAEHAK See SOUL TAEHAKKYO KONGDAE SOSIK **1997**

SOUL TAEHAKKYO. KONGKWA TAEHAK See YONBO **5172**

SOUL TAEHAKKYO. KONGKWA TAEHAK See KONGHAK YON'GU POGO **1985**

SOUL Alphabetical Title Index

SOUL TAEHAKKYO. KONGKWA TAEHAK. KONGDAE YONGU POGO See KONGHAK YON'GU POGO **1985**

SOUL TAEHAKKYO NONGKWA TAEHAK YONSUMNIM YONGU POGO (KO) [10297193] **2395**

SOUL TAEHAKKYO. YAKHAK TAEHAK See SENUR DAIHAGGYO NYAGHAG KOMMUNJIB **4329**

SOUL UYY (KO) [07979971] **198**

SOUL YAKSAHOE CHI / JOURNAL OF THE SEOUL PHARMACEUTICAL ASSOCIATION (KO) [10225583] **4329**

SOULE NEWSLETTER (US/0584-164X) [03898202] **2473**

SOUND ADVICE (US/0733-4605) [08609791] 914, **4847**

SOUND & COMMUNICATIONS (US/0038-1845) [02461347] **1122**

SOUND & IMAGE (US/1050-2777) [21434038] 4078, **4154**

SOUND AND IMAGE. DEE WHY (AT/1032-3899) [I10323899] **1139**

SOUND & PICTURE TAPE RECORDING MAGAZINE See TAPE **5319**

SOUND & VIDEO CONTRACTOR (US/0741-1715) [10091293] **5319**

SOUND & VISION (TORONTO) (CN/0829-3678) [12565519] **1627**

SOUND CHECK CEASED. (NE) **4154**

SOUND CREATIVE. CD ROM (FR) **5319**

SOUND HERITAGE SERIES (CN/0228-7781) [07136846] **1997**

SOUND IMAGE (US/0362-3955) [02299610] **331**

SOUND INTERNATIONAL (UK/0144-6037) [07021497] **5319**

SOUND OF VIENNA, THE (US/0192-5180) [05053431] **2546**

SOUND POST (GRANITE FALLS, MINN.) (US/0749-0755) [11093479] **4154**

SOUND RECORDING (CN/0847-1223) [21577432] **5319**

●SOUND SAFETY (US/1062-581X) [25670390] **136**

SOUND TIMES (US/1059-0897) [24493587] **5319**

SOUND TRAX (US/0163-4607) [04420174] 5319, **4154**

SOUND WAVES : MONTHLY NEWSLETTER (US) **252**

SOUND WORDS (MIFFLINBURG, PA.) (US/8756-8756) [11673075] **4998**

SOUNDBOARD (US/0145-6237) [02763923] **4154**

SOUNDER NEWSLETTER (SNOQUALMIE, WASH. : 1980) (US) [08325576] **2761**

SOUNDER (RANDOM LAKE, WIS.) (US/8755-3686) [11283946] **5770**

SOUNDINGS EAST (US) [06395940] **3438**

SOUNDINGS (ESSEX, CONN.) (US) [08963517] **596**

SOUNDINGS FROM AROUND THE WORLD (US) **2836**

SOUNDINGS (KNOXVILLE, TENN.) (US/0038-1861) [02441097] 1784, **4998**

SOUNDINGS (MILWAUKEE, WIS.) (US/0888-4072) [11048469] 2761, **5457**

SOUNDINGS (NOTRE DAME) (US) [19060083] 2253, **712**

SOUNDINGS (SANTA BARBARA) (US/0038-1853) [01372274] **3250**

SOUNDINGS. TRADE ONLY (US/0194-8369) [05048524] **596**

●SOUNDNOTES (TORONTO) (CN/1183-7659) [25423680] **4154**

SOUNDS CEASED. (UK/0144-5774) [I01445774] **4154**

SOUNDS ABOUT SUNDAY (1981) CEASED. (CN/0712-5836) [09336352] **3056**

SOUNDS AUSTRALIAN : AUSTRALIAN MUSIC CENTRE JOURNAL (AT/0811-3149) [19096485] **4154**

SOUNDS OF GOSPEL RECORDINGS (US) **4998**

SOUNDS OF TRUTH AND TRADITION (US/0038-187X) [02338345] **5036**

SOUNDTRACK (BE/0771-6303) [I07716303] **5319**

SOUNDTRACK! (BE) [08698978] **4078**

SOUNDTRACK (RINGWOOD, N.J.) (US/1042-0649) [18929049] 4154, **5319**

SOUNDVIEW EXECUTIVE BOOK SUMMARIES (US/0747-2196) [10635421] **712**

SOUPISY RUKOPISNYCH FONDU (XR/0524-7349) [03029683] **425**

SOURCE BOOK MAGAZINE (US/1047-3890) [20707499] **886**

SOURCE BOOK (NEW YORK, N.Y. 1983), THE (US/0740-4549) [09961000] **5310**

SOURCE BOOK OF AMERICAN STATE LEGISLATION, THE (US/0730-1154) [06181988] **3056**

SOURCE BOOK OF HEALTH INSURANCE DATA (US/0073-148X) [01766014] **2894**

SOURCE BOOK OF MINICOMPUTERS (US/0194-018X) [05289508] **1274**

SOURCE BOOK OF PROJECTS, SCIENCE EDUCATION DEVELOPMENT AND RESEARCH (US/0273-3714) [07037691] **1872**

SOURCE BOOK PROFILES See FOUNDATION 1000, THE **4336**

SOURCE DATA : THE DATAPOINT CUSTOMER MAGAZINE CEASED. (US) [09956252] **1203**

SOURCE DIRECTORY : NATIVE AMERICAN OWNED AND OPERATED ARTS AND CRAFTS BUSINESSES / UNITED STATES DEPARTMENT OF THE INTERIOR, INDIAN ARTS AND CRAFTS BOARD (US) [05957271] **375**

SOURCE DIRECTORY OF PREDICASTS, INC, THE CEASED. (US/0092-7767) [01789377] **425**

SOURCE (EDMONTON) (CN/1186-723X) [24402157] **4686**

SOURCE FILE SUSPENDED. (US/0897-4128) [17497509] **1203**

SOURCE II, THE (US/0278-4386) [07806893] **5491**

SOURCE JOURNALS IN METALS & MATERIALS (UK/0968-1043) [I09681043] **4019**

SOURCE JOURNALS IN METALS & MATERIALS (US/1068-9397) [13872789] **4019**

SOURCE MATERIALS AND STUDIES IN ETHNOMUSICOLOGY (NE) **4154**

●SOURCE (MONTREAL. 1992) (CN/1188-4428) [26497521] **5310**

SOURCE (MONTREAL, QUEBEC) (CN/0704-6324) [08811611] **4998**

SOURCE (NEW YORK, N.Y.) (US) [07885191] **365**

SOURCE REFERENCES FOR FACTS AND FIGURES ON GOVERNMENT FINANCE (US/0494-8203) [02144430] **4748**

SOURCE (RIMOUSKI, QUEBEC) (CN/0712-3361) [08890915] **2221**

SOURCE SAMPLING NEWS CEASED. (US/0892-8436) [15268085] **2243**

SOURCE (SHAWNEE MISSION, KAN.) (US) [12071212] **2358**

SOURCE (TALLAHASSEE, FLA.) See ASSOCIATION SOURCE **640**

SOURCE, THE (CN) [03043808] **5794**

SOURCE (UNITED NATIONS DEVELOPMENT PROGRAMME) CEASED. (US) [20185005] **2243**

SOURCE (WINTER PARK, FLA.) (US/0898-8811) [17940838] **712**

SOURCEBOOK FOR SCIENCE, MATHEMATICS, AND TECHNOLOGY EDUCATION (US/1060-0973) [22548935] 3536, **5158**

SOURCEBOOK OF COUNTY DEMOGRAPHICS, THE (US) [21533711] **733**

SOURCEBOOK OF CRIMINAL JUSTICE STATISTICS (US/0360-3431) [02441090] 3177, **3083**

SOURCEBOOK OF LIBRARY TECHNOLOGY, THE (US/0275-6811) [03754804] **3250**

SOURCEBOOK OF ZIP CODE DEMOGRAPHICS, THE (US) [21427162] **733**

SOURCEBOOK ON FOOD AND NUTRITION CEASED. (US) [04259179] 2358, **4199**

SOURCEBOOK (WASHINGTON, D.C.), THE (US/0730-6164) [08037493] **309**

SOURCEMEX (ALBUQUERQUE, N.M.) (US/1054-8890) [23010578] **1521**

SOURCEMEX [COMPUTER FILE] (US/1054-8890) [23184079] **1521**

SOURCES (ALBUQUERQUE) (US/0094-9981) [02545905] **3250**

SOURCES & RESOURCES (BRITISH COLUMBIA SCHOOL LIBRARIANS' ASSOCIATION) (CN/0229-4605) [08036548] **3250**

SOURCES (B. ZWICKER : PUBLISHER) See DIRECTORY OF SOURCES FOR EDITORS, REPORTERS & RESEARCHERS, THE **2919**

SOURCES CANADA See MEN'S WEAR OF CANADA **1086**

SOURCES CHRETIENNES (FR/0750-1978) [03050258] **5040**

SOURCES D'HISTOIRE MEDIEVALE (FR/0398-3811) [01781364] **2710**

SOURCES-ENAP (CN/0841-2227) [20444418] **4686**

SOURCES ET SUPPLEMENT VIE DOMINICAINE (SZ) **4998**

SOURCES FOR SUCCESSFUL SMALL BUSINESS FINANCING IN CANADA (CN/1184-602X) [24265465] **712**

SOURCES FOR THE STUDY OF RELIGION IN MALAWI (MW) [05243147] **4998**

SOURCES FROM THE ANCIENT NEAR EAST (US/0732-6424) [03009923] **2664**

SOURCES IN THE HISTORY OF MATHEMATICS AND PHYSICAL SCIENCES (GW/0172-6315) [08459809] 5158, **3536**

SOURCES OF COMPILED LEGISLATIVE HISTORIES (US/0275-5157) [05795302] **3083**

SOURCES OF ORIENTAL LANGUAGES AND LITERATURES / DOGU DILLERI VE EDEBIYATLARNN KAYNAKLAR (US) [03010994] 3322, **2664**

SOURCES OF SUPPLY : BUYERS GUIDE (US/0190-8200) [03961686] **4239**

SOURCES OF VOLUNTARY AGENCY INCOME / SUSAN HADDOW, MARY ANN JONES CEASED. (US) [07760195] **5310**

SOURCES (PARIS) (FR/0765-0124) [12643288] **2630**

SOURCES: THE SECURITIES EXECUTIVE'S GUIDE TO PRODUCTS AND SERVICES (US) **766**

SOURCES (TORONTO) (CN/0700-480X) [09000488] **2924**

SOURCEWORLD (US/0270-496X) [06252881] **1276**

SOURCING DIRECTORY / AAMA (US) [18189499] **1087**

SOURD QUEBECOIS, LE (CN/0384-8779) [03258732] **5310**

●SOURDS DU CANADA (CN/1195-3349) [29736133] **4393**

SOUREMENNAIA VOSTOCHNAIA NOVELLA; SBORNIK PEREVODOV (RU) [02852934] **3438**

SOUROZH (UK/0950-2742) [10571481] **4998**

SOUS-TERRE (CN/0827-9772) [12782117] 4854, **1411**

SOUTH AFRICA See SUPPLEMENTARY ESTIMATE OF THE EXPENDITURE TO BE DEFRAYED FROM REVENUE, LOAN AND SOUTH-WEST AFRICA ACCOUNTS **4751**

SOUTH AFRICA See STAATSKOERANT. GOVERNMENT GAZETTE **4687**

SOUTH AFRICA (SA/0302-0681) [02280825] **2643**

SOUTH AFRICA See TREATY SERIES **3137**

SOUTH AFRICA See ESTIMATE OF THE ADDITIONAL EXPENDITURE TO BE DEFRAYED FROM STATE REVENUE ACCOUNT. BEGROTING VAN DIE ADDISIONALE UITGAWES WAT UIT STAATSINKOMSTEREKENING **4721**

SOUTH AFRICA See BEGROTING VAN INKOMSTE **4713**

SOUTH AFRICA See SUIDWES-AFRIKA REKENING : BEGROTING VAN INKOMSTE EN UITGAWES **4751**

SOUTH AFRICA See BUDGET : STATISTICAL SURVEY **4696**

SOUTH AFRICA. ADMINISTRATION OF COLOURED AFFAIRS See REPORT OF THE ADMINISTRATION OF COLOURED AFFAIRS FOR THE PERIOD ... **2643**

SOUTH AFRICA ALERT See BUSINESS AFRICA / ECONOMIST INTELLIGENCE UNIT **645**

SOUTH AFRICA. BLACK RESETTLEMENT BOARD See ANNUAL REPORT - BLACK RESETTLEMENT BOARD **4627**

SOUTH AFRICA. COMMITTEE OF HEADS OF EDUCATION See ANNUAL REPORT - COMMITTEE OF HEADS OF EDUCATION **1860**

SOUTH AFRICA. COMPENSATION COMMISSIONER FOR OCCUPATIONAL DISEASES See REPORT OF THE COMPENSATION COMMISSIONER FOR OCCUPATIONAL DISEASES **2868**

SOUTH AFRICA. CONTROLLER AND AUDITOR-GENERAL See VERSLAG VAN DIE OUDITEUR-GENERAAL OOR DIE REKENINGS VAN DIE SYBOKHAARRAAD. REPORT OF THE AUDITOR-GENERAL ON THE ACCOUNTS OF THE MOHAIR BOARD **4693**

SOUTH AFRICA. CONTROLLER AND AUDITOR-GENERAL See REPORT OF THE CONTROLLER AND AUDITOR-GENERAL ON THE ACCOUNTS OF THE LUCERNE SEED CONTROL BOARD **1624**

SOUTH AFRICA. CONTROLLER AND AUDITOR-GENERAL See REPORT OF THE AUDITOR-GENERAL ON THE ACCOUNTS OF THE DEPARTMENT OF POSTS AND TELECOMMUNICATIONS **1162**

Alphabetical Title Index — SOUTH

SOUTH AFRICA. CONTROLLER AND AUDITOR-GENERAL *See* MUVHIGO WA MULAULI NA MUTOLAMUVHALELANO MUHULU NGA HA MBALELANO DZA MUVHJSO WA VENDA NA WA MBALELANO DZA MIVHUSO MITUKU VHUPONI HAWO DZA NWAHA **4738**

SOUTH AFRICA. CONTROLLER AND AUDITOR-GENERAL *See* PEGO YA MOHLAKISI-MOGOLO KA DITSHUPAMOLATO TSA MMUSO WA LEBOWA LE YA DITSHUPAMOLATO TSA DIPUSWANA TIKOLOGONG MO NGWAGATSHELETENG **4740**

SOUTH AFRICA. DAIRY BOARD. ANNUAL REPORT - DAIRY BOARD *See* ANNUAL REPORT FOR THE YEAR ENDED ... / DAIRY CONTROL BOARD (SOUTH AFRICA) **191**

SOUTH AFRICA. DAIRY CONTROL BOARD *See* ANNUAL REPORT FOR THE YEAR ENDED ... / DAIRY CONTROL BOARD (SOUTH AFRICA) **191**

SOUTH AFRICA. DECENTRALISATION BOARD *See* DECENTRALISATION BOARD ANNUAL REPORT **2639**

SOUTH AFRICA. DECIDUOUS FRUIT BOARD *See* REPORT OF THE AUDITOR-GENERAL ON THE ACCOUNTS OF THE DECIDUOUS FRUIT BOARD AND THE SOUTH AFRICAN PLANT IMPROVEMENT ORGANISATION. VERSLAG VAN DIE OUDITEUR-GENERAAL VOR DIE REKENINGE VAN DIE SAGTEVRUGTERAAD EN DIE SUID-AFRIKAANSE PLANT-VERBETERINGSORGANISASIE **4680**

SOUTH AFRICA. DEPARTMENT OF POSTS AND TELECOMMUNICATIONS *See* ESTIMATES OF REVENUE AND EXPENDITURE - DEPARTMENT OF POSTS AND TELECOMMUNICATIONS **1145**

SOUTH AFRICA. DEPT. OF AGRICULTURE *See* ANNUAL REPORT OF THE DIRECTOR GENERAL, AGRICULTURE FOR THE PERIOD ... / REPUBLIC OF SOUTH AFRICA, DEPARTMENT OF AGRICULTURE **61**

SOUTH AFRICA. DEPT. OF AGRICULTURE AND FISHERIES *See* ANNUAL REPORT OF THE DIRECTOR GENERAL, AGRICULTURE AND FISHERIES FOR THE PERIOD 1 APRIL ... TO 31 MARCH / REPUBLIC OF SOUTH AFRICA **61**

SOUTH AFRICA. DEPT. OF BANTU EDUCATION *See* LIST OF SCHOOLS, ADDRESSES AND STATISTICS **1761**

SOUTH AFRICA. DEPT. OF BANTU EDUCATION *See* ANNUAL REPORT - DEPARTMENT OF BANTU EDUCATION **1725**

SOUTH AFRICA. DEPT. OF CO-OPERATION AND DEVELOPMENT *See* REPORT OF THE DEPARTMENT OF CO-OPERATION AND DEVELOPMENT **2643**

SOUTH AFRICA. DEPT. OF COLOURED RELATIONS AND REHOBOTH AFFAIRS *See* JAARVERSLAG - DEPARTEMENT VAN KLEURLING-, REHOBOTH - EN NAMABETREKKINGE **2640**

SOUTH AFRICA. DEPT. OF COMMUNITY DEVELOPMENT *See* VERSLAG VAN DIE DIREKTEUR-GENERAAL, GEMEENSKAPSONTWIKKELING VIR DIE TYDPERK ... **2839**

SOUTH AFRICA. DEPT. OF INFORMATION *See* PROGRESS IN INTER-GROUP AND RACE RELATIONS **5254**

SOUTH AFRICA. DEPT. OF JUSTICE *See* VERSLAG VIR DIE TYDPERK. DEPARTEMENT VAN JUSTISIE VAN DIE REPUBLIEK VAN SUID-AFRIKA **4693**

SOUTH AFRICA. DEPT. OF MANPOWER *See* JAARVERSLAG / DEPARTEMENT VAN MANNEKRAG / ANNUAL REPORT / DEPARTMENT OF MANPOWER **4658**

SOUTH AFRICA. DEPT. OF PLURAL RELATIONS AND DEVELOPMENT *See* REPORT OF THE DEPARTMENT OF PLURAL RELATIONS AND DEVELOPMENT **4681**

SOUTH AFRICA. DEPT. OF POSTS AND TELECOMMUNICATIONS *See* ESTIMATES OF ADDITIONAL EXPENDITURE - DEPARTMENT OF POSTS AND TELECOMMUNICATIONS **1154**

SOUTH AFRICA. DEPT. OF STATISTICS *See* 'N OORSIG VAN DIE REKENINGS VAN MYNMAATSKAPPYE **1443**

SOUTH AFRICA. DEPT. OF STATISTICS *See* LABOUR STATISTICS : WAGE RATES, EARNINGS AND AVERAGE HOURS WORKED IN THE PRINTING AND NEWSPAPER INDUSTRY, ENGINEERING INDUSTRY, BUILDING INDUSTRY AND COMMERCE **1535**

SOUTH AFRICA. DEPT. OF STATISTICS *See* STATISTIEKE VAN PLAASLIKE OWERHEDE, ORANJE-VRYSTAAT, TRANSVAAL **5342**

SOUTH AFRICA. DEPT. OF STATISTICS *See* TOERISME EN MIGRASIE **5492**

SOUTH AFRICA. DEPT. OF STATISTICS *See* STATISTIEKE VAN MOTORVOERTUIE : NUWE VOERTUIE GELISENSIEER **5426**

SOUTH AFRICA. DEPT. OF STATISTICS *See* STATISTIEKE VAN NUWE VOERTUIE GELISENSIEER **5402**

SOUTH AFRICA. DEPT. OF STATISTICS *See* ROAD TRAFFIC ACCIDENTS (PRETORIA, SOUTH AFRICA) **5443**

SOUTH AFRICA. DEPT. OF STATISTICS *See* KORTTERMYN EKONOMIESE AANWYSERS / REPUBLIEK VAN SUID-AFRIKA, BURO VIR STATISTIEK **1571**

SOUTH AFRICA. DEPT. OF STATISTICS *See* CENSUS OF BOARDS OF EXECUTORS AND TRUST COMPANIES **782**

SOUTH AFRICA. DEPT. OF THE AUDITOR-GENERAL *See* VERSLAG VAN DIE OUDITEUR-GENERAAL VOOR DIE REKENINGS VAN DIE SIGOREIRRAAD **753**

SOUTH AFRICA. DEPT. OF THE AUDITOR-GENERAL *See* VERSLAG VAN DIE OUDITEUR- GENERAAL VOOR DIE SUIDWES-AFRIKAREKENING WAT DEEL UITMAAK VAN DIE STAATSINKOMSTEFONDS VAN DIE REPUBLIEK VAN SUID-AFRIKA **4758**

SOUTH AFRICA. DEPT. OF THE AUDITOR-GENERAL *See* EHOKOLOLONINGOMWA LYOMTYEKINDJAYI LYOOLEKENENGA EPANGELO LYOWAMBO NODHOMALELO GIILONGO MOWAMBO MOLWEENDO LWOMUMVO GWEMBO ... **4721**

SOUTH AFRICA. DEPT. OF THE AUDITOR-GENERAL. EHOKOLOLONINGOMWA LYOMTYEKINDJAYI LYOOLEKENENGA EPANGELO LYOWAMBO NODHOMALELO GIILONGO MOWAMBO MOLWEENDO LWOMUMVO GWEMBO . *See* REPORT OF THE AUDITOR-GENERAL ON THE ACCOUNTS OF THE REPRESENTATIVE AUTHORITY OF THE OVAMBOS AND OF THE TRIBAL AUTHORITIES IN OVAMBO FOR THE FINANCIAL YEAR ... **4745**

SOUTH AFRICA. DEPT. OF THE CONTROLLER AND AUDITOR-GENERAL *See* INGXELO YOMLAWULI NOMPHICOTHI-ZINCWADI JIKELELE KWIIAKHAWUNTI ZORHULUMENTE WASECISKEI KUNYE NOOGUNYAZIWE ABANGEZANTSI KULOO MMANDLA **4732**

SOUTH AFRICA. DEPT. OF THE CONTROLLER AND AUDITOR-GENERAL *See* RAPORTA ZOMUKONAKONI NOMUTARELI-NTONI KOMBINGA ZOYIVARO YEPANGERO LYAKAVANGO KUMWE NEZI ZOMAPANGERO GORUDI MOSIRONGO ZOMUMVHO **4743**

SOUTH AFRICA. DEPT. OF THE CONTROLLER AND AUDTOR-GENERAL *See* REPORT OF THE CONTROLLER AND AUDITOR-GENERAL ON THE ACCOUNTS OF THE ADMINISTRATION OF COLOURED AFFAIRS **4745**

SOUTH AFRICA. DEPT. OF THE INTERIOR *See* ANNUAL REPORT - DEPARTMENT OF THE INTERIOR **4627**

SOUTH AFRICA. DEPT. OF TRANSPORT *See* REPORT OF THE COMPULSORY MOTOR VEHICLE INSURANCE SECTION AND OF THE MOTOR VEHICLE ASSURANCE FUND **2892**

SOUTH AFRICA. DRY BEAN BOARD *See* REPORT - SOUTH AFRICA. DRY BEAN BOARD **4682**

SOUTH AFRICA. EGG BOARD *See* REPORT OF THE AUDITOR-GENERAL ON THE ACCOUNTS OF THE EGG BOARD FOR THE FINANCIAL YEAR ... / VERSLAG VAN DIE OUDITEUR-GENERAAL OOR DIE REKENINGS VAN DIE EIERRAAD VIR DIE BOEKJAAR ... **850**

SOUTH AFRICA. FINANCIAL INSTITUTIONS OFFICE *See* ANNUAL REPORT OF THE REGISTRAR OF BANKS (SOUTH AFRICA) **772**

SOUTH AFRICA. FORESTRY COUNCIL *See* VERSLAG - BOSBOURAAD **2398**

SOUTH AFRICA INTERNATIONAL *CEASED.* (SA/0015-5055) [01766041] **2500**

SOUTH AFRICA JOURNAL OF PLANT AND SOIL (SA/0257-1862) [11230084] **187**

SOUTH AFRICA. LAW COMMISSION *See* JAARVERSLAG VAN DIE SUID-AFRIKAANSE REGSKOMMISSIE **2986**

SOUTH AFRICA. LAWS, STATUTES, ETC *See* INDUSTRIAL LAWS OF SOUTH AFRICA **3149**

SOUTH AFRICA. MAIZE BOARD *See* REVIEW OF THE MAIZE POSITION **128**

SOUTH AFRICA. MAIZE BOARD *See* REPORT ON MAIZE FOR THE FINANCIAL YEAR ... FOR SUBMISSION TO THE MINISTER OF AGRICULTURE / MAIZE BOARD **126**

SOUTH AFRICA. MEDICAL BUREAU FOR OCCUPATIONAL DISEASES *See* REPORT OF THE MEDICAL BUREAU FOR OCCUPATIONAL DISEASES **2868**

SOUTH AFRICA. NATIONAL MANPOWER COMMISSION *See* ANNUAL REPORT / NATIONAL MANPOWER COMMISSION **1649**

SOUTH AFRICA. NATIONAL MANPOWER COMMISSION. JAARVERSLAG *See* ANNUAL REPORT / NATIONAL MANPOWER COMMISSION **1649**

SOUTH AFRICA. NATIONAL TRAINING BOARD *See* JAARVERSLAG **1681**

SOUTH AFRICA. NATIVE AFFAIRS DEPT. REPORT *See* ANNUAL REPORT - DEPARTMENT OF BANTU EDUCATION **1725**

SOUTH AFRICA. OFFICE OF THE AUDITOR-GENERAL *See* REPORT OF THE AUDITOR-GENERAL ON THE ACCOUNTS OF THE REPRESENTATIVE AUTHORITY OF THE OVAMBOS AND OF THE TRIBAL AUTHORITIES IN OVAMBO FOR THE FINANCIAL YEAR ... **4745**

SOUTH AFRICA. OILSEEDS BOARD *See* FINANSIELE STATE VAN DIE OLIESADERAAD VIR DIE BOEKJAAR ... **1607**

SOUTH AFRICA. OILSEEDS BOARD *See* JAARVERSLAG VAN DIE OLIESADERAAD VIR DIE JAAR ... **175**

SOUTH AFRICA OILSEEDS CONTROL BOARD *See* ANNUAL REPORT OF THE OILSEED CONTROL BOARD FOR THE PERIOD ... / OILSEED CONTROL BOARD **4628**

SOUTH AFRICA. PARLIAMENT *See* DEBATES OF PARLIAMENT / REPUBLIC OF SOUTH AFRICA **4641**

SOUTH AFRICA. PARLIAMENT. HOUSE OF ASSEMBLY *See* DEBATTE VAN STAANDE KOMITEES / REPUBLIEK VAN SUID-AFRIKA, VOLKSRAAD **4471**

SOUTH AFRICA. PARLIAMENT. HOUSE OF ASSEMBLY. SELECT COMMITTEE ON PENSIONS *See* VERSLAE VAN DIE GEKOSE KOMITEE VOOR PENSIOENE **1716**

SOUTH AFRICA. PARLIAMENT. HOUSE OF ASSEMBLY. SELECT COMMITTEE ON POSTS AND TELECOMMUNICATIONS *See* VERSLAG VAN DIE GEKOSE KOMITEE OOR POS- EN TELEKOMMUNIKASIEWESE. REPORT OF THE SELECT COMMITTEE ON POSTS AND TELECOMMUNICATIONS **1147**

SOUTH AFRICA. PARLIAMENT. HOUSE OF ASSEMBLY. SELECT COMMITTEE ON RAILWAY ACCOUNTS *See* REPORT OF THE SELECT COMMITTEE ON RAILWAY ACCOUNTS. VERSLAG VAN DIE GEKOSE KOMITEE OOR SPOORWEGREKENINGS **5436**

SOUTH AFRICA. PARLIAMENT. HOUSE OF ASSEMBLY. SELECT COMMITTEE ON STATE-OWNED LAND *See* VERSLAE VAN DIE GEKOSE KOMITEE VOOR STAATSGROND **4693**

SOUTH AFRICA. PARLIAMENT. HOUSE OF ASSEMBLY. SELECT COMMITTEE ON THE COPYRIGHT BILL *See* VERSLAE VAN DIE GEKOSE KOMITEE OOR DIE WETSONTWERP OP OUTEURSREG. REPORTS OF THE SELECT COMMITTEE ON THE COPYRIGHT BILL **1309**

SOUTH AFRICA. PARLIAMENT. HOUSE OF ASSEMBLY. SELECT COMMITTEE ON THE FOREST BILL *See* VERSLAE VAN DIE GEKOSE KOMITEE VOOR DIE BOSWETSONTWERP **3071**

SOUTH AFRICA. PARLIAMENT. HOUSE OF ASSEMBLY. SELECT COMMITTEE ON THE MORATORIUM AMENDMENT BILL *See* VERSLAE VAN DIE GEKOSE KOMITEE OOR DIE MORATORIUMWYSIGINGSWETSONTWERP. REPORTS OF THE SELECT COMMITTEE ON THE MORATORIUM AMENDMENT BILL **3071**

SOUTH AFRICA. PARLIAMENT. HOUSE OF ASSEMBLY. STANDING COMMITTEE ON APPROPRIATION BILL *See* DEBATTE VAN DIE STAANDE KOMITEE VOOR BEGROTINGSWETSONTWERP **4642**

SOUTH AFRICA. POLICE. SAP *See* SERVAMUS **3176**

SOUTH AFRICA. PRESIDENT'S COUNCIL *See* DEBATTE VAN DIE PRESIDENTSRAAD **4642**

SOUTH AFRICA REPORTER (US/1053-5497) [14077755] 914, 1640, **851**

● SOUTH AFRICA / SOUTH AFRICA FOUNDATION (SA) [26781234] **2643**

SOUTH

Alphabetical Title Index

SOUTH AFRICA. STATE LIBRARY *See* CONTRIBUTIONS TO LIBRARY SCIENCE. BIBLIOTEEKKUNDIGE HYDRAES **3204**

SOUTH AFRICA. SUPREME COURT *See* SOUTH AFRICAN TAX CASES, INCLUDING DECISIONS OF THE SUPREME COURT OF SOUTH AFRICA, THE HIGH COURT OF ZIMBABWE AND THE SPECIAL COURTS FOR HEARING INCOME TAX APPEALS **3056**

SOUTH AFRICA. TREASURY *See* ESTIMATE OF THE ADDITIONAL EXPENDITURE TO BE DEFRAYED FROM REVENUE AND LOAN ACCOUNTS **4721**

SOUTH AFRICA. UNIVERSITY *See* PUBLICATIONS OF THE UNIVERSITY OF SOUTH AFRICA **423**

SOUTH AFRICA. WEATHER BUREAU *See* JAARLIKSE STRALINGSVERSLAG **4435**

SOUTH AFRICA. WHEAT BOARD *See* JAARVERSLAG - KORINGRAAD **1568**

SOUTH AFRICA. WHEAT BOARD *See* REPORT FOR THE FINANCIAL YEAR ENDING 30 SEPTEMBER ... / WHEAT BOARD **4680**

SOUTH AFRICA. WHEAT BOARD. ANNUAL REPORT *See* REPORT FOR THE FINANCIAL YEAR ENDING 30 SEPTEMBER ... / WHEAT BOARD **4680**

SOUTH AFRICA. WHEAT INDUSTRY CONTROL BOARD. JAARVERSLAG *See* JAARVERSLAG - KORINGRAAD **1568**

SOUTH AFRICAN ANIMAL LIFE (SW) [01321378] **5597**

SOUTH AFRICAN ARCHAEOLOGICAL BULLETIN, THE (SA/0038-1969) [02241322] **282**

SOUTH AFRICAN ARCHIVES OF OPHTHALMOLOGY (SA/0301-2131) [06478815] **3879**

SOUTH AFRICAN ASSOCIATION OF CONSULTING ENGINEERS *See* DIRECTORY OF MEMBERS' FIRMS - SOUTH AFRICAN ASSOCIATION OF CONSULTING ENGINEERS **1971**

SOUTH AFRICAN ASTRONOMICAL OBSERVATORY *See* CIRCULARS - SOUTH AFRICAN ASTRONOMICAL OBSERVATORY **394**

SOUTH AFRICAN BANKING MAGAZINE *See* SASBO NEWS **810**

SOUTH AFRICAN BEE JOURNAL (SA/0038-2019) [02481933] **5597**

SOUTH AFRICAN BUILDER, THE (SA) [05702502] **627**

SOUTH AFRICAN CLEANING REVIEW (SA) **1711**

SOUTH AFRICAN COMPUTER JOURNAL SUID-AFRIKAANSE REKENAARTYDSKRIF (SA/1015-7999) [25568934] **1203**

SOUTH AFRICAN COUNCIL FOR SCIENTIFIC AND INDUSTRIAL RESEARCH *See* CSIR RESEARCH REPORT **611**

SOUTH AFRICAN COUNCIL FOR SCIENTIFIC AND INDUSTRIAL RESEARCH *See* TI, TECHNICAL INFORMATION FOR INDUSTRY **5165**

SOUTH AFRICAN COUNCIL FOR SCIENTIFIC AND INDUSTRIAL RESEARCH *See* CSIR ANNUAL REPORT **5097**

SOUTH AFRICAN CULTURAL HISTORY MUSEUM ANNALS (SA) **2643**

SOUTH AFRICAN DEVELOPMENT TRUST CORPORATION *See* JAARVERSLAG / SUID-AFRIKAANSE ONTWIKKELINGSTRUSTKORPORASIE BEPERK (STK) **1568**

SOUTH AFRICAN EXPORTERS (SA) [04991306] **851**

SOUTH AFRICAN FISHING INDUSTRY HANDBOOK AND BUYER'S GUIDE, THE (SA/0080-5076) [02021316] **2313**

SOUTH AFRICAN FOOD REVIEW *See* FOOD REVIEW **2339**

SOUTH AFRICAN FORESTRY JOURNAL (SA/0038-2167) [01766049] **2395**

SOUTH AFRICAN GEOGRAPHICAL JOURNAL (SA/0373-6245) [01766050] **2576**

SOUTH AFRICAN HAIRDRESSING AND BEAUTY CULTURE (SA/0036-0759) [I00360759] **405**

SOUTH AFRICAN HISTORICAL JOURNAL (SA) [01952703] **2643**

SOUTH AFRICAN INSTITUTE OF ELECTRICAL ENGINEERS *See* TRANSACTIONS - THE SOUTH AFRICAN INSTITUTE OF ELECTRICAL ENGINEERS **2084**

SOUTH AFRICAN INSTITUTE OF INTERNATIONAL AFFAIRS *See* BIBLIOGRAPHICAL SERIES / SOUTH AFRICAN INSTITUTE OF INTERNATIONAL AFFAIRS / BIBLIOGRAFIESE REEKS / SUID-AFRIKAANSE INSTITUUT VAN INTERNASIONALE AANGELEENTHEDE **4501**

SOUTH AFRICAN INSTITUTE OF MINING AND METALLURGY *See* JOURNAL OF THE SOUTH AFRICAN INSTITUTE OF MINING & METALLURGY **2142**

SOUTH AFRICAN INSTITUTE OF RACE RELATIONS *See* SAIRR ANNUAL REPORT **5257**

SOUTH AFRICAN JOURNAL FOR ENOLOGY AND VITICULTURE (SA/0253-939X) [11294302] **2371**

SOUTH AFRICAN JOURNAL OF ANIMAL SCIENCE (SA/0375-1589) [02529228] **222**

SOUTH AFRICAN JOURNAL OF ANTARCTIC RESEARCH (SA/0081-2455) [01784901] **2576**

SOUTH AFRICAN JOURNAL OF ART AND ARCHITECTURAL HISTORY (SA/1018-0753) [22886787] **365**

SOUTH AFRICAN JOURNAL OF BOTANY (SA/0254-6299) [08631618] **528**

SOUTH AFRICAN JOURNAL OF BUSINESS MANAGEMENT (SA) [06211986] **886**

SOUTH AFRICAN JOURNAL OF CHEMICAL ENGINEERING (SA) [21491337] **2017**

SOUTH AFRICAN JOURNAL OF CHEMISTRY (SA/0379-4350) [03263150] **992**

SOUTH AFRICAN JOURNAL OF COMMUNICATION DISORDERS (SA/0379-8046) [04420584] **4394**, **3846**

SOUTH AFRICAN JOURNAL OF CRIMINAL JUSTICE (SA/1011-8527) [18145206] **3109**

SOUTH AFRICAN JOURNAL OF CULTURAL HISTORY (SA) [22634307] **2630**

SOUTH AFRICAN JOURNAL OF DAIRY SCIENCE *CEASED.* (SA/0258-3321) [14231008] **198**

SOUTH AFRICAN JOURNAL OF ECONOMIC HISTORY : [JOURNAL OF THE ECONOMIC HISTORY SOCIETY OF SOUTHERN AFRICA], THE (SA/1011-3436) [16310283] **1584**

SOUTH AFRICAN JOURNAL OF ECONOMICS, THE (SA/0038-2280) [01766055] **1521**

SOUTH AFRICAN JOURNAL OF EDUCATION (SA/0256-0100) [12800350] **1784**

SOUTH AFRICAN JOURNAL OF GEO INFORMATION (SA) **2583**

SOUTH AFRICAN JOURNAL OF GEOLOGY (SA/1012-0750) [16416271] **1397**

SOUTH AFRICAN JOURNAL OF HIGHER EDUCATION (SA/1011-3487) [I10113487] **1847**

SOUTH AFRICAN JOURNAL OF INTERNATIONAL AFFAIRS, THE (SA/1022-0461) [29983345] **4535**

SOUTH AFRICAN JOURNAL OF LIBRARY AND INFORMATION SCIENCE (SA/0256-8861) [11080287] **3250**

SOUTH AFRICAN JOURNAL OF MARINE SCIENCE / REPUBLIC OF SOUTH AFRICA, DEPARTMENT OF ENVIRONMENT AFFAIRS, SEA FISHERIES RESEARCH INSTITUTE (SA) [10576790] **557**

SOUTH AFRICAN JOURNAL OF MUSICOLOGY (SA/0258-509X) [09288323] **4154**

SOUTH AFRICAN JOURNAL OF PHILOSOPHY (SA/0258-0136) [11526275] **4361**

SOUTH AFRICAN JOURNAL OF PHOTOGRAMMETRY, REMOTE SENSING, AND CARTOGRAHPY *See* SOUTH AFRICAN JOURNAL OF GEO INFORMATION **2583**

SOUTH AFRICAN JOURNAL OF PHOTOGRAMMETRY, REMOTE SENSING, AND CARTOGRAPHY (SA) [08732086] **2583**

SOUTH AFRICAN JOURNAL OF PHOTOGRAMMETRY, THE (SA/0085-6398) [07426136] **2576**

SOUTH AFRICAN JOURNAL OF PHYSICS *CEASED.* (SA/0379-4377) [06409229] **4421**

SOUTH AFRICAN JOURNAL OF PHYSIOTHERAPY (SA/0379-6175) [I03796175] **587**, **3642**

SOUTH AFRICAN JOURNAL OF PSYCHOLOGY (SA/0081-2463) [01950667] **4619**

SOUTH AFRICAN JOURNAL OF SCIENCE (SA/0038-2353) [07471431] **5158**

SOUTH AFRICAN JOURNAL OF SURGERY (SA/0038-2361) [01766056] **3975**

SOUTH AFRICAN JOURNAL OF WILDLIFE RESEARCH (SA/0379-4369) [02534844] **2205**

SOUTH AFRICAN JOURNAL OF ZOOLOGY (SA/0254-1858) [05113936] **5597**

SOUTH AFRICAN JOURNAL ON HUMAN RIGHTS (SA/0258-7203) [12575425] **4513**

SOUTH AFRICAN LABOUR BULLETIN (SA/0377-5429) [01766475] **1711**

SOUTH AFRICAN LAUNDRY & CLEANING REVIEW *See* SOUTH AFRICAN CLEANING REVIEW **1711**

SOUTH AFRICAN LAW JOURNAL (SA/0038-2388) [01766057] **3056**

SOUTH AFRICAN LAW REPORTS; TRANSLATION OF AFRIKAANS PASSAGES IN REPORTED CASES, THE (SA) [03226739] **3056**

SOUTH AFRICAN LIBRARY *See* QUARTERLY BULLETIN OF THE SOUTH AFRICAN LIBRARY **3243**

SOUTH AFRICAN MACHINE TOOL REVIEW (SA/0036-0848) [I00360848] **2129**

SOUTH AFRICAN MECHANICAL ENGINEER, THE (SA/0038-2442) [02450700] **2129**

SOUTH AFRICAN MEDICAL JOURNAL (SA/0038-2469) [03582234] **3642**

SOUTH AFRICAN MINING WORLD (SA) **2151**

SOUTH AFRICAN MONITOR, THE (SA) [12116756] **2500**

SOUTH AFRICAN MUSEUM *See* ANNALS OF THE SOUTH AFRICAN MUSEUM **4083**

SOUTH AFRICAN MUSIC TEACHER (SA/0038-2493) [07215509] **4154**

SOUTH AFRICAN NATIONAL BIBLIOGRAPHY (SA/0036-0864) [01715459] **425**

SOUTH AFRICAN NATIONAL MUSEUM OF MILITARY HISTORY *See* ANNUAL REPORT - SOUTH AFRICAN NATIONAL MUSEUM OF MILITARY HISTORY **4084**

SOUTH AFRICAN NURSERYMAN : THE OFFICIAL JOURNAL OF SANA / DIE SUID-AFRIKAANSE KWEKER : DIE AMPTELIKE TYDSKRIF VAN DIE SAKU, THE (SA) [12223649] **2431**

SOUTH AFRICAN OBSERVER, THE (SA) [04337556] **2500**

SOUTH AFRICAN OPTOMETRIST, SUID-AFRIKAANSE OOGKUNDIGE, THE (SA/0378-9411) [05462749] **4217**

SOUTH AFRICAN ORCHID JOURNAL. SUID-AFRIKAANSE ORGIDEEJOERNAAL (SA) [06190628] **528**, **2431**

SOUTH AFRICAN OUTLOOK (SA/0038-2523) [01776708] **4998**

SOUTH AFRICAN PANORAMA (SA/0038-254X) [01766066] **4686**

SOUTH AFRICAN. PARLIAMENT. HOUSE OF ASSEMBLY. DEBATES *See* DEBATTE VAN STAANDE KOMITEES / REPUBLIEK VAN SUID-AFRIKA, VOLKSRAAD **4471**

SOUTH AFRICAN PHARMACEUTICAL & COSMETIC REVIEW *See* PHARMACEUTICAL & COSMETIC REVIEW **4320**

SOUTH AFRICAN PROGRESS (SA) [02393911] **1584**

SOUTH AFRICAN RAILWAYS AND HARBOURS *See* BEGROTING VAN DIE ADDISIONELE BEDRYFSUITGAWE. ESTIMATES OF THE ADDITIONAL WORKING EXPENDITURE **5429**

SOUTH AFRICAN RAILWAYS AND HARBOURS *See* THIS IS SAR & H : HARBOURS & PIPELINES HANDBOOK **5457**

SOUTH AFRICAN RAILWAYS AND HARBOURS *See* THIS IS SAR & H : ROAD TRANSPORT HANDBOOK **5394**

SOUTH AFRICAN RAILWAYS AND HARBOURS *See* THIS IS SAR & H : RAILWAYS HANDBOOK **5437**

SOUTH AFRICAN RESERVE BANK *See* QUARTERLY BULLETIN - SOUTH AFRICAN RESERVE BANK **805**

SOUTH AFRICAN REVIEW (JOHANNESBURG, SOUTH AFRICA: 1983) (SA) [10857702] **2643**

SOUTH AFRICAN SHIPPING NEWS AND FISHING INDUSTRY REVIEW, THE (SA/0038-2671) [07394454] **2313**, **5457**

SOUTH AFRICAN SOCIETY OF BANK OFFICIALS *See* SASBO NEWS **810**

SOUTH AFRICAN STATISTICAL JOURNAL (SA/0038-271X) [01766068] **3536**, **3542**

SOUTH AFRICAN SUGAR JOURNAL, THE (SA/0038-2728) [02457981] **187**

SOUTH AFRICAN SUGAR TECHNOLOGISTS' ASSOCIATION. CONGRESS *See* PROCEEDINGS OF THE ANNUAL CONGRESS OF THE SOUTH AFRICAN SUGAR TECHNOLOGISTS' ASSOCIATION **2353**

SOUTH AFRICAN SUGAR YEAR BOOK, THE (SA) [02554231] **2358**, **136**

SOUTH AFRICAN TAX CASES, INCLUDING DECISIONS OF THE SUPREME COURT OF SOUTH AFRICA, THE HIGH COURT OF ZIMBABWE AND THE SPECIAL COURTS FOR HEARING INCOME TAX APPEALS (SA/0038-2752) [01640152] **4748**, **3056**

SOUTH AFRICAN THEATRE JOURNAL : SATJ (SA) [19999467] **388**, **5368**

SOUTH

SOUTH AFRICAN TIDE TABLES (SA) [01788488] **4183**

SOUTH AFRICAN TRANSPORT SERVICES *See* BEDRYFSBEGROTINGS VIR DIE BOEKJARE WAT EINDIG OP ... **4632**

SOUTH AFRICAN TRANSPORT SERVICES *See* ANNUAL REPORT / THE SOUTH AFRICAN TRANSPORT SERVICES **5376**

SOUTH AFRICAN TRANSPORT SERVICES BOARD *See* VERSLAG VAN DIE RAAD VAN SUID-AFRIKAANSE VERVOERDIENSTE VIR DIE JAAR GEEINDIG ... **5399**

SOUTH AFRICAN TREASURER, THE (SA/0038-2779) [01640894] **4748**

SOUTH AFRICAN TUNNELLING (SA/0255-058X) [03118142] **2031**

SOUTH AFRICAN YEARBOOK OF INTERNATIONAL LAW (SA/0379-8895) [02979731] **3136**

SOUTH ALABAMIAN (JACKSON, ALA.), THE (US/0890-8168) [12494262] **5628**

SOUTH AMBOY CITIZEN (SOUTH AMBOY, N.J. 1884), THE (US/1041-2514) [12221786] **5711**

SOUTH AMERICA, CENTRAL AMERICA, AND THE CARIBBEAN (UK/0268-0661) [12956657] 1521, **2761**

SOUTH AMERICA TRAVEL DIGEST (US/0584-3103) [05153671] **5491**

SOUTH AMERICAN EXPLORER (US/0889-7891) [06116536] **4878**

SOUTH AMERICAN HANDBOOK (UK/0309-4529) [01766070] **5491**

SOUTH ASIA (AT/0085-6401) [01643654] **2664**

SOUTH ASIA BULLETIN (US/0732-3867) [07669783] **2665**

SOUTH ASIA CURRENTS [COMPUTER FILE] (US/1059-4981) [24606898] **2665**

SOUTH ASIA IN REVIEW *CEASED.* (US/0889-8650) [04087247] **2665**

SOUTH ASIA JOURNAL : QUARTERLY JOURNAL OF INDIAN COUNCIL FOR SOUTH ASIAN COOPERATION *CEASED.* (II) [18634114] **5222**

SOUTH ASIA LIBRARY NOTES & QUERIES (US/0197-5366) [05248576] **3250**

SOUTH ASIA NEWSLETTER (NE) **2273**

SOUTH ASIA RESEARCH (UK/0262-7280) [07950094] 5222, **2854**

SOUTH ASIAN ANTHROPOLOGIST (II/0257-7348) [07994287] **245**

SOUTH ASIAN HANDBOOK (NEW YORK, N.Y.) (US/1061-9836) [25499319] **5491**

SOUTH ASIAN LANGUAGE REVIEW (II) [24100079] **3322**

SOUTH ASIAN REVIEW (UK/0038-2841) [01798160] **2665**

SOUTH ASIAN REVIEW - SOUTH ASIAN LITERARY ASSOCIATION (US/0275-9527) [07251753] **3353**

SOUTH ASIAN STUDIES (JAIPUR) (II/0038-285X) [01605763] **2665**

SOUTH ASIAN STUDIES (SOCIETY FOR SOUTH ASIAN STUDIES) (UK/0266-6030) [13103013] **2665**

SOUTH ASIAN SURVEY (II) [02715655] **2665**

SOUTH ATLANTIC QUARTERLY, THE (US/0038-2876) [01642494] 3353, **2854**

SOUTH ATLANTIC REVIEW (US/0277-335X) [07142213] 3438, **3322**

SOUTH ATLANTIC URBAN STUDIES *CEASED.* (US/0147-8559) [03244610] **2836**

SOUTH AUSTRALIA *See* SOUTH AUSTRALIAN INDUSTRIAL GAZETTE **1711**

SOUTH AUSTRALIA *See* SOUTH AUSTRALIAN GOVERNMENT GAZETTE, THE **4496**

SOUTH AUSTRALIA. DEPT. OF FISHERIES *See* ANNUAL REPORT / DEPARTMENT OF FISHERIES **2294**

SOUTH AUSTRALIA. DEPT. OF TECHNICAL AND FURTHER EDUCATION *See* HANDBOOK / THE DEPARTMENT OF TECHNICAL AND FURTHER EDUCATION OF SOUTH AUSTRALIA **1749**

SOUTH AUSTRALIA. INDUSTRIAL COURT *See* SOUTH AUSTRALIAN INDUSTRIAL REPORTS **1711**

SOUTH AUSTRALIA. PARLIAMENT *See* OFFICIAL REPORTS OF THE PARLIAMENTARY DEBATES (HANSARD) **4671**

SOUTH AUSTRALIA. STATE LIBRARY. REFERENCE SERVICES BRANCH *See* REFERENCE SERVICES BIBLIOGRAPHIES **3259**

SOUTH AUSTRALIA. SUPREME COURT *See* SOUTH AUSTRALIAN STATE REPORTS, THE **3056**

SOUTH AUSTRALIAN ANGLER (AT) **4919**

SOUTH AUSTRALIAN DAIRY FARMER'S JOURNAL, THE (AT/0049-1446) [13529016] **199**

SOUTH AUSTRALIAN GENEALOGIST (AT/0311-2756) [I03112756] **2473**

SOUTH AUSTRALIAN GEOGRAPHER (AT) **2576**

SOUTH AUSTRALIAN GEOGRAPHICAL JOURNAL (AT/1030-0481) [18546220] 2671, **2576**

SOUTH AUSTRALIAN GOVERNMENT GAZETTE, THE (SA) [07498260] **4496**

SOUTH AUSTRALIAN HERPETOLOGIST *See* HERPETOFAUNA **5585**

SOUTH AUSTRALIAN INDUSTRIAL GAZETTE *CEASED.* (AT) [05026863] **1711**

SOUTH AUSTRALIAN INDUSTRIAL REPORTS (AT) [01766077] **1711**

SOUTH AUSTRALIAN MAJOR MANUFACTURING, MINING AND DEVELOPMENT PROJECTS (AT) [03257039] 2151, **3488**

SOUTH AUSTRALIAN MASTER BUILDER (AT) [07360128] **1627**

SOUTH AUSTRALIAN MUSEUM, ADELAIDE *See* RECORDS OF THE SOUTH AUSTRALIAN MUSEUM **4095**

SOUTH AUSTRALIAN NATURALIST; THE JOURNAL OF THE FIELD NATURALISTS' SECTION OF THE ROYAL SOCIETY OF SOUTH AUSTRALIA (AT/0038-2965) [01590217] **4172**

SOUTH AUSTRALIAN NEWSLETTER (AT/1036-918X) [I1036918X] **4496**

SOUTH AUSTRALIAN NUMISMATIC JOURNAL *See* AUSTRALIAN NUMISMATIC JOURNAL **2780**

SOUTH AUSTRALIAN ORNITHOLOGIST (AT/0038-2973) [02578732] **5620**

SOUTH AUSTRALIAN SCHOOL POST (AT) **1784**

SOUTH AUSTRALIAN SCIENCE TEACHERS JOURNAL (AT) **1905**

SOUTH AUSTRALIAN STATE REPORTS, THE (AT/0049-1470) [03229806] **3056**

SOUTH AUSTRALIAN YEAR BOOK (AT/0085-6428) [01949781] **1929**

SOUTH BEND AREA GENEALOGICAL SOCIETY (US/0737-2973) [09318418] **2473**

SOUTH BEND AREA GENEALOGICAL SOCIETY : [NEWSLETTER] *See* NEWSLETTER - SOUTH BEND AREA GENEALOGICAL SOCIETY **4555**

SOUTH BEND CIVIC PLANNING ASSOCIATION *See* CIVIC CINEMA **4638**

SOUTH BEND (ST. JOSEPH COUNTY, IND.) CITY DIRECTORY (US) [06372005] **2576**

SOUTH BEND TRIBUNE IRISH SPORTS REPORTS (US) **5667**

SOUTH BEND TRIBUNE, THE (US) [08793233] **5667**

SOUTH BUSINESS (US/0277-5344) [07143695] **712**

SOUTH CAROLINA *See* ACTS AND JOINT RESOLUTIONS OF THE GENERAL ASSEMBLY OF THE STATE OF SOUTH CAROLINA **4624**

SOUTH CAROLINA *See* CODE OF LAWS OF SOUTH CAROLINA; ANNOTATED **2952**

SOUTH CAROLINA ANNUAL STATE PLAN FOR VOCATIONAL-TECHNICAL EDUCATION (US/0272-1058) [06742225] **1915**

SOUTH CAROLINA APPELLATE DIGEST, THE (US/0743-2453) [10538448] **3057**

SOUTH CAROLINA BAPTIST HISTORICAL SOCIETY *See* JOURNAL OF THE SOUTH CAROLINA BAPTIST HISTORICAL SOCIETY **5062**

SOUTH CAROLINA. BOARD OF FINANCIAL INSTITUTIONS *See* ANNUAL REPORT OF THE STATE BOARD OF FINANCIAL INSTITUTIONS OF THE STATE OF SOUTH CAROLINA **772**

SOUTH CAROLINA. BUDGET COMMISSION *See* SOUTH CAROLINA STATE BUDGET FOR THE FISCAL YEAR ENDING ... **4748**

SOUTH CAROLINA BUSINESS (US/1050-7698) [07389778] **712**

SOUTH CAROLINA BUSINESS DIRECTORY (US/1046-0934) [18894598] **712**

SOUTH CAROLINA BUSINESS JOURNAL (US/0745-4473) [09181931] **712**

SOUTH CAROLINA. DEPT. OF ARCHIVES AND HISTORY *See* SOUTH CAROLINA HISTORIC PRESERVATION PLAN : ANNUAL PRESERVATION PROGRAM **2761**

SOUTH CAROLINA. DEPT. OF CONSUMER AFFAIRS *See* ANNUAL REPORT OF THE DEPARTMENT OF CONSUMER AFFAIRS OF THE STATE OF SOUTH CAROLINA **1293**

SOUTH CAROLINA. DEPT. OF EDUCATION *See* DATA REPORT ON PROGRAMS FOR THE HANDICAPPED **1877**

SOUTH CAROLINA. DEPT. OF EDUCATION. DIVISION OF ADMINISTRATION AND PLANNING *See* INDICATORS OF EDUCATIONAL QUALITY, SUMMARY **1752**

SOUTH CAROLINA. DEPT. OF EDUCATION. DIVISION OF ADMINISTRATION AND PLANNING *See* RANKINGS OF THE COUNTIES AND SCHOOL DISTRICTS OF SOUTH CAROLINA **1776**

SOUTH CAROLINA. DEPT. OF EDUCATION. OFFICE OF RESEARCH *See* SOUTH CAROLINA STATEWIDE TESTING PROGRAM, SUMMARY REPORT **1872**

SOUTH CAROLINA. DEPT. OF HEALTH AND ENVIRONMENTAL CONTROL. BUREAU OF LABORATORIES *See* NEWSLETTER - BUREAU OF LABORATORIES **2237**

SOUTH CAROLINA. DEPT. OF HIGHWAYS AND PUBLIC TRANSPORTATION *See* ANNUAL REPORT OF THE SOUTH CAROLINA DEPARTMENT OF HIGHWAYS AND PUBLIC TRANSPORTATION TO THE GENERAL ASSEMBLY **5438**

SOUTH CAROLINA. DEPT. OF VETERANS AFFAIRS *See* ANNUAL REPORT OF SOUTH CAROLINA DEPARTMENT OF VETERANS AFFAIRS **4035**

SOUTH CAROLINA. DEPT. OF YOUTH SERVICES *See* ANNUAL REPORT OF THE STATE DEPARTMENT OF YOUTH SERVICES FOR THE PERIOD BEGINNING JULY 1 ... AND ENDING JUNE 30 ... (SOUTH CAROLINA) **3157**

SOUTH CAROLINA. DIVISION OF BIOSTATISTICS *See* SOUTH CAROLINA VITAL AND MORBIDITY STATISTICS **5338**

SOUTH CAROLINA. DIVISION OF GAME AND FRESHWATER FISHERIES *See* ANNUAL PROGRESS REPORT - DIVISION OF GAME AND FRESHWATER FISHERIES **2294**

SOUTH CAROLINA DRIVER'S HANDBOOK (US) [04315955] **5425**

SOUTH CAROLINA ECONOMIC INDICATORS (US/0038-304X) [04044175] **1584**

SOUTH CAROLINA EDUCATION ASSOCIATION *See* SCEA EMPHASIS **1870**

SOUTH CAROLINA. EDUCATIONAL TELEVISION COMMISSION *See* ANNUAL REPORT OF THE SOUTH CAROLINA EDUCATIONAL TELEVISION COMMISSION **1725**

SOUTH CAROLINA EGGSAMINER (US) [04417439] **222**

● SOUTH CAROLINA EMPLOYMENT LAW LETTER (US/1064-461X) [26288854] **3154**

● SOUTH CAROLINA ENVIRONMENTAL COMPLIANCE UPDATE (US/1065-7975) [26739023] **2243**

SOUTH CAROLINA FACTS (US/1056-960X) [23903966] **2761**

SOUTH CAROLINA FARMER : THE SOUTH CAROLINA FARM BUREAU FEDERATION NEWS (US/0889-1834) [08859392] **136**

SOUTH CAROLINA FIREMAN MAGAZINE, THE (US/0744-3730) [08223416] **2292**

SOUTH CAROLINA FOOD AND AGRICULTURAL PRODUCTS : EXPORT DIRECTORY (US/0145-5796) [02773102] **2358**

SOUTH CAROLINA FORUM *See* SOUTH CAROLINA POLICY FORUM : A REVIEW OF PUBLIC AFFAIRS IN SOUTH CAROLINA, THE **4686**

SOUTH CAROLINA GAME & FISH (US/0897-9154) [17664786] **4878**

SOUTH CAROLINA. GENERAL ASSEMBLY *See* SOUTH CAROLINA LEGISLATIVE MANUAL / GENERAL ASSEMBLY OF SOUTH CAROLINA **4686**

SOUTH CAROLINA. GENERAL ASSEMBLY *See* LEGISLATIVE MANUAL - GENERAL ASSEMBLY OF SOUTH CAROLINA **4661**

SOUTH CAROLINA. GENERAL ASSEMBLY *See* DIGEST, HOUSE AND SENATE BILLS AND RESOLUTIONS (SOUTH CAROLINA) **2960**

SOUTH CAROLINA. GENERAL ASSEMBLY. AGRICULTURE STUDY COMMITTEE *See* REPORT OF THE AGRICULTURE STUDY COMMITTEE OF SOUTH CAROLINA **126**

SOUTH CAROLINA. GENERAL ASSEMBLY. DIGEST OF ACTION ON BILLS AND RESOLUTIONS *See* DIGEST, HOUSE AND SENATE BILLS AND RESOLUTIONS (SOUTH CAROLINA) **2960**

SOUTH
Alphabetical Title Index

SOUTH CAROLINA. GENERAL ASSEMBLY. HOUSE OF REPRESENTATIVES *See* JOURNAL OF THE HOUSE OF REPRESENTATIVES OF THE ... SESSION OF THE ... GENERAL ASSEMBLY OF THE STATE OF SOUTH CAROLINA **4659**

SOUTH CAROLINA. GENERAL ASSEMBLY. SENATE *See* JOURNAL OF THE SENATE OF THE GENERAL ASSEMBLY OF THE STATE OF SOUTH CAROLINA **4659**

SOUTH CAROLINA. GENERAL ASSEMBLY. STUDY COMMITTEE ON AGING *See* ANNUAL REPORT / SOUTH CAROLINA GENERAL ASSEMBLY. STUDY COMMITTEE ON AGING **3749**

SOUTH CAROLINA. GEOLOGICAL SURVEY *See* FIELD TRIP GUIDEBOOK (COLUMBIA) **1375**

SOUTH CAROLINA GEOLOGY SUSPENDED. (US/0272-9873) [06368845] **1397**

● SOUTH CAROLINA HEALTH CARE IN PERSPECTIVE (US/1065-4410) [26606675] **4803**

SOUTH CAROLINA HIGHWAY SAFETY PLAN (US) [05205791] **5444**

SOUTH CAROLINA HISTORIC PRESERVATION PLAN : ANNUAL PRESERVATION PROGRAM (US/0361-1639) [02246118] **2761**

SOUTH CAROLINA HISTORICAL ASSOCIATION *See* PROCEEDINGS OF THE SOUTH CAROLINA HISTORICAL ASSOCIATION, THE **2755**

SOUTH CAROLINA HISTORICAL MAGAZINE (US/0038-3082) [05622612] **2761**

SOUTH CAROLINA. HUMAN SERVICES COORDINATING COUNCIL *See* ANNUAL REPORT / SOUTH CAROLINA, HUMAN SERVICES COORDINATING COUNCIL **938**

SOUTH CAROLINA IN PERSPECTIVE (US/1065-5689) [26662177] **5338**

● SOUTH CAROLINA INDUSTRIAL DIRECTORY (US) [25193637] **1627**

SOUTH CAROLINA JOURNAL OF HEALTH, PHYSICAL EDUCATION, RECREATION AND DANCE (US/0740-8331) [08753971] **1784**

SOUTH CAROLINA LABOR MARKET REVIEW / SOUTH CAROLINA EMPLOYMENT SECURITY COMMISSION (US) [11034050] 1711, **1521**

SOUTH CAROLINA. LAND RESOURCES CONSERVATION COMMISSION *See* ANNUAL REPORT - SOUTH CAROLINA LAND RESOURCES CONSERVATION COMMISSION **2187**

SOUTH CAROLINA LANDINGS, ANNUAL SUMMARY (US/0148-5326) [03260002] **1457**

SOUTH CAROLINA LAW REVIEW (US/0038-3104) [01585980] **3057**

SOUTH CAROLINA LAWYER (US/1044-4238) [19782950] **3057**

SOUTH CAROLINA. LEGISLATIVE AUDIT COUNCIL *See* FISCAL ACCOUNTABILITY ACT; SUMMARY REPORT TO THE GENERAL ASSEMBLY **4726**

SOUTH CAROLINA LEGISLATIVE MANUAL / GENERAL ASSEMBLY OF SOUTH CAROLINA (US) [22966120] **4686**

SOUTH CAROLINA LIBRARY ASSOCIATION *See* NEWS & VIEWS OF THE SOUTH CAROLINA LIBRARY ASSOCIATION **3234**

SOUTH CAROLINA. LICENSING BOARD FOR CONTRACTORS *See* ROSTER OF LICENSED CONTRACTORS IN THE STATE OF SOUTH CAROLINA **2030**

SOUTH CAROLINA MAGAZINE OF ANCESTRAL RESEARCH, THE (US/0190-826X) [04748841] **2473**

SOUTH CAROLINA METALWORKING DIRECTORY (US/0363-5090) [02471886] **4019**

SOUTH CAROLINA MONTHLY LOCAL CLIMATOLOGICAL DATA. MICROFORM (US) [10859025] **1434**

SOUTH CAROLINA NEWS (CLEVELAND, TENN.) (US/0747-1130) [03778373] **4998**

SOUTH CAROLINA NEWS MEDIA DIRECTORY (US) **1122**

SOUTH CAROLINA NURSE, THE (US/1046-7394) [14523043] **3869**

SOUTH CAROLINA OCCUPATIONAL INJURIES AND ILLNESSES SURVEY (US) [09796599] **2870**

SOUTH CAROLINA. OFFICE OF VOCATIONAL EDUCATION *See* SOUTH CAROLINA ANNUAL STATE PLAN FOR VOCATIONAL-TECHNICAL EDUCATION **1915**

SOUTH CAROLINA OUT-OF-DOORS (US/0887-9249) [04545919] **2205**

● SOUTH CAROLINA POLICY FORUM : A REVIEW OF PUBLIC AFFAIRS IN SOUTH CAROLINA, THE (US) [25504960] **4686**

SOUTH CAROLINA PROGRAM FOR LIBRARY DEVELOPMENT, THE (US/1046-5553) [17513349] **3250**

SOUTH CAROLINA PUBLIC LIBRARY ANNUAL STATISTICAL SUMMARY (US) [07243545] 3250, **3260**

SOUTH CAROLINA. RESIDENTIAL HOME BUILDERS COMMISSION *See* RULES AND REGULATIONS - SOUTH CAROLINA. RESIDENTIAL HOME BUILDERS COMMISSION **3045**

SOUTH CAROLINA REVIEW, THE (US/0038-3163) [01786834] **3353**

SOUTH CAROLINA SCENE: ETV/RADIO GUIDE (US) [04417924] **1139**

SOUTH CAROLINA SCENE: ITV STAFF DEVELOPMENT SCHEDULE (US) [04231399] **1784**

SOUTH CAROLINA. STATE AUDITOR *See* SOUTH CAROLINA STATE PORTS AUTHORITY, CHARLESTON, SOUTH CAROLINA. REPORT OF STATE AUDITOR AND FINANCIAL STATEMENTS **5457**

SOUTH CAROLINA. STATE BOARD OF COSMETIC ART EXAMINERS *See* ANNUAL REPORT FOR THE YEAR ENDING JUNE 30 ... / SOUTH CAROLINA, STATE BOARD OF COSMETIC ART EXAMINERS **402**

SOUTH CAROLINA STATE BOARD OF EXAMINERS FOR NURSING HOME ADMINISTRATORS *See* ANNUAL REPORT FOR THE FISCAL YEAR ... / SOUTH CAROLINA STATE BOARD OF EXAMINERS FOR NURSING HOME ADMINISTRATORS **3776**

SOUTH CAROLINA STATE BOARD OF HEALTH *See* STATE PLAN FOR CONSTRUCTION AND MODERNIZATION OF HOSPITAL AND MEDICAL FACILITIES (COLUMBIA) **3792**

SOUTH CAROLINA. STATE BOARD OF MEDICAL EXAMINERS *See* DIRECTORY - STATE BOARD OF MEDICAL EXAMINERS OF SOUTH CAROLINA **3914**

SOUTH CAROLINA. STATE BUDGET AND CONTROL BOARD. DIVISION OF RESEARCH AND STATISTICAL SERVICES *See* QUARTERLY ECONOMIC REPORT **4743**

SOUTH CAROLINA. STATE BUDGET AND CONTROL BOARD. DIVISION OF RESEARCH AND STATISTICAL SERVICES *See* ECONOMIC REPORT, THE STATE OF SOUTH CAROLINA **1558**

SOUTH CAROLINA. STATE BUDGET AND CONTROL BOARD. DIVISION OF SINKING FUNDS AND PROPERTY *See* REPORT OF THE STATE BUDGET AND CONTROL BOARD, DIVISION OF SINKING FUNDS AND PROPERTY **4681**

SOUTH CAROLINA STATE BUDGET FOR THE FISCAL YEAR ENDING ... (US) [17726229] **4748**

SOUTH CAROLINA. STATE DEPT. OF EDUCATION *See* ANNUAL PROGRAM PLAN AMENDMENT FOR PART B (P.L. 94-142) **1725**

SOUTH CAROLINA. STATE DEPT. OF EDUCATION. OFFICE OF FEDERAL PROGRAMS *See* ECIA CHARTER 2, ANNUAL EVALUATION REPORT **1737**

SOUTH CAROLINA. STATE DEPT. OF EDUCATION. OFFICE OF RESEARCH *See* SUPPLEMENTAL SALARY STUDY, SELECTED SCHOOL, DISTRICT, AND COUNTY PERSONNEL **1873**

SOUTH CAROLINA. STATE DEPT. OF MENTAL HEALTH *See* STATE PLAN PROGRESS REPORT FOR FISCAL YEAR ... / SOUTH CAROLINA STATE DEPARTMENT OF MENTAL HEALTH **4804**

SOUTH CAROLINA. STATE DEPT. OF MENTAL HEALTH *See* STATE PLAN / SOUTH CAROLINA STATE DEPT OF MENTAL HEALTH **4804**

SOUTH CAROLINA STATE DEVELOPMENT BOARD NEWS (US) [05209988] **4686**

SOUTH CAROLINA STATE LIBRARY *See* CHECKLIST OF SOUTH CAROLINA STATE PUBLICATIONS **413**

SOUTH CAROLINA. STATE LIBRARY, COLUMBIA *See* ANNUAL PROGRAM; LIBRARY SERVICES AND CONSTRUCTION ACT - SOUTH CAROLINA. STATE LIBRARY, COLUMBIA **3190**

SOUTH CAROLINA. STATE LIBRARY, COLUMBIA *See* NEWS FOR SOUTH CAROLINA LIBRARIES **3234**

SOUTH CAROLINA STATE PLAN VOCATIONAL-EDUCATION PROGRAMS *See* SOUTH CAROLINA ANNUAL STATE PLAN FOR VOCATIONAL-TECHNICAL EDUCATION **1915**

SOUTH CAROLINA STATE PORTS AUTHORITY, CHARLESTON, SOUTH CAROLINA. REPORT OF STATE AUDITOR AND FINANCIAL STATEMENTS (US) [04792059] **5457**

SOUTH CAROLINA STATE REGISTER (US) [04044264] **3057**

SOUTH CAROLINA STATEWIDE TESTING PROGRAM, SUMMARY REPORT (US/0149-1865) [03435762] **1872**

SOUTH CAROLINA STATISTICAL ABSTRACT (US/0739-9308) [01783864] **5338**

SOUTH CAROLINA TAX COMMISSION. RESEARCH SECTION *See* BASIS AND RATES OF TAXES FOR FISCAL YEAR ... **4713**

SOUTH CAROLINA. UNIVERSITY. LIBRARY *See* SERIAL HOLDINGS **3249**

SOUTH CAROLINA VITAL AND MORBIDITY STATISTICS (US/0094-6338) [04030167] **5338**

SOUTH CAROLINA VOTER (US) **2493**

SOUTH CAROLINA WILDLIFE (US/0038-3198) [01643509] **2205**

SOUTH CAROLINA YOUNG FARMER AND FUTURE FARMER MAGAZINE (US/0038-3201) [03927978] **136**

SOUTH CAROLINA ZIP+4 STATE DIRECTORY (US) [11527167] **1147**

SOUTH CENTRAL BANNER (CN/0707-2295) [04754942] **5795**

SOUTH CENTRAL REVIEW (US/0743-6831) [10639393] **3322**

SOUTH CENTRAL SALES GUIDE TO HIGH-TECH COMPANIES (US/1040-0532) [18304488] **5159**

SOUTH CHINA MORNING POST (HK) [05340667] **5802**

SOUTH COAST POETRY JOURNAL (US/0887-2074) [13138275] **3471**

SOUTH COAST SPORTFISHING (US/0279-2249) [07646461] 4878, **4854**

SOUTH COAST WEEK (US/0744-785X) [08563903] **5734**

SOUTH CROW RIVER NEWS (US) [22333604] **5698**

SOUTH DADE NEWS LEADER (US/1048-5406) [10000063] **5651**

SOUTH DAKOTA (US/0038-3236) [03154864] **1521**

SOUTH DAKOTA *See* SESSION LAWS OF THE STATE OF SOUTH DAKOTA **3048**

SOUTH DAKOTA ACADEMY OF SCIENCE *See* PROCEEDINGS OF THE SOUTH DAKOTA ACADEMY OF SCIENCE **5142**

SOUTH DAKOTA ARCHAEOLOGY (US/0276-5543) [06539569] **282**

SOUTH DAKOTA AUTHORS' CATALOG (US/0742-8936) [08824902] **4832**

SOUTH DAKOTA BIRD NOTES (US/0038-3252) [01623603] **5620**

SOUTH DAKOTA BUSINESS REVIEW (US/0038-3260) [01766145] **4748**

SOUTH DAKOTA CASE NAMES CITATOR (US) **3057**

SOUTH DAKOTA CHURCHMAN (US) [04160547] **4998**

SOUTH DAKOTA. COMMISSION ON THE STATUS OF WOMEN *See* ANNUAL REPORT - COMMISSION ON THE STATUS OF WOMEN OF SOUTH DAKOTA **5550**

SOUTH DAKOTA CONSERVATION DIGEST (US/0038-3279) [01766146] **2205**

SOUTH DAKOTA COUNTY POOR RELIEF (US/0360-9022) [02244920] **5310**

SOUTH DAKOTA COURTS : THE STATE OF THE JUDICIARY AND ... ANNUAL REPORT OF THE SOUTH DAKOTA UNIFIED JUDICIAL SYSTEM (US) [24056758] **3057**

SOUTH DAKOTA. CRIMINAL JUSTICE COMMISSION *See* SUMMARY OF THE SOUTH DAKOTA CRIMINAL JUSTICE PLAN FOR ACTION, A **3177**

SOUTH DAKOTA CROP & LIVESTOCK REPORTER (US/1045-8999) [04277522] **136**

SOUTH DAKOTA DEPARTMENT OF SOCIAL SERVICES - PRE-EXPENDITURE REPORT FOR TITLE XX SOCIAL SERVICES BLOCK GRANT (US) **4748**

SOUTH DAKOTA. DEPT. OF COMMERCE AND CONSUMER AFFAIRS *See* REPORT OF SOUTH DAKOTA'S PROFESSIONAL AND OCCUPATIONAL LICENSING BOARDS AND COMMISSIONS **4680**

SOUTH DAKOTA. DEPT. OF EDUCATION AND CULTURAL AFFAIRS *See* FACILITIES INVENTORY & UTILIZATION STUDY **1746**

SOUTH DAKOTA. DEPT. OF GAME, FISH, AND PARKS *See* TECHNICAL BULLETIN - SOUTH DAKOTA DEPARTMENT OF GAME, FISH AND PARKS **2206**

SOUTH DAKOTA. DEPT. OF LABOR *See* CETA PRIME SPONSOR AGREEMENT AND TITLE I ANNUAL PLAN (SOUTH DAKOTA) **1658**

SOUTH DAKOTA. DEPT. OF LABOR *See* COMPREHENSIVE MANPOWER PLAN AND GRANT APPLICATION **1660**

SOUTH DAKOTA. DEPT. OF NATURAL RESOURCE DEVELOPMENT. ANNUAL REPORT OF THE DEPARTMENT OF NATURAL RESOURCE DEVELOPMENT ON THE WATER RESOURCES MANAGEMENT SYSTEM *See* ANNUAL REPORT OF THE DEPARTMENT OF WATER AND NATURAL RESOURCES ON THE WATER RESOURCES MANAGEMENT SYSTEM (SOUTH DAKOTA) **5529**

SOUTH DAKOTA. DEPT. OF SOCIAL SERVICES *See* SOUTH DAKOTA INDIAN RECIPIENTS OF SOCIAL WELFARE **5310**

SOUTH DAKOTA. DEPT. OF SOCIAL SERVICES *See* TITLE XX FINAL COMPREHENSIVE I.E. COMPREHENSIVE ANNUAL SERVICES PLAN **5312**

SOUTH DAKOTA. DEPT. OF SOCIAL SERVICES *See* MENTAL HEALTH STATE PLAN **5296**

SOUTH DAKOTA. DEPT. OF SOCIAL SERVICES *See* ANNUAL SERVICES PLAN - DEPARTMENT OF SOCIAL SERVICES **5273**

SOUTH DAKOTA. DEPT. OF SOCIAL SERVICES *See* SOUTH DAKOTA COUNTY POOR RELIEF **5310**

SOUTH DAKOTA. DEPT. OF SOCIAL SERVICES *See* ANNUAL STATISTICAL REPORT - SOUTH DAKOTA DEPARTMENT OF SOCIAL SERVICES **5266**

SOUTH DAKOTA. DEPT. OF SOCIAL SERVICES *See* STATE PLAN FOR CHILD WELFARE SERVICES **5311**

SOUTH DAKOTA. DEPT. OF WATER AND NATURAL RESOURCES *See* ANNUAL REPORT OF THE DEPARTMENT OF WATER AND NATURAL RESOURCES ON THE WATER RESOURCES MANAGEMENT SYSTEM (SOUTH DAKOTA) **5529**

SOUTH DAKOTA. DEPT. OF WILDLIFE, PARKS AND FORESTRY *See* ANNUAL FINANCIAL REPORT - SOUTH DAKOTA DEPARTMENT OF WILDLIFE, PARKS AND FORESTRY **4869**

SOUTH DAKOTA. DIVISION OF ELEMENTARY AND SECONDARY EDUCATION *See* EVALUATION : TITLE I **1746**

SOUTH DAKOTA. DIVISION OF ELEMENTARY AND SECONDARY EDUCATION *See* SOUTH DAKOTA EDUCATIONAL STATISTICS DIGEST **1797**

SOUTH DAKOTA. DIVISION OF ELEMENTARY AND SECONDARY EDUCATION. OFFICE OF AUXILIARY SERVICES *See* SOUTH DAKOTA ELEMENTARY AND SECONDARY EDUCATIONAL COMPARISONS **1784**

SOUTH DAKOTA. DIVISION OF HIGHWAY SAFETY *See* SOUTH DAKOTA HIGHWAY SAFETY WORK PROGRAM **5444**

SOUTH DAKOTA. DIVISION OF HIGHWAY SAFETY *See* SOUTH DAKOTA HIGHWAY SAFETY MANAGEMENT SYSTEM PLAN **5444**

SOUTH DAKOTA. DIVISION OF HIGHWAY SAFETY. STATE & COMMUNITY PROGRAMS *See* ANNUAL REPORT, SOUTH DAKOTA GOVERNOR'S TRAFFIC SAFETY PROGRAM **5438**

SOUTH DAKOTA. DIVISION OF LAW ENFORCEMENT ASSISTANCE *See* CRIMINAL JUSTICE IN SOUTH DAKOTA **3162**

SOUTH DAKOTA EDUCATIONAL DIRECTORY (US/0363-0137) [01781210] **1784**

SOUTH DAKOTA EDUCATIONAL STATISTICS DIGEST (US/0360-4772) [02243039] **1784**, **1797**

SOUTH DAKOTA ELEMENTARY AND SECONDARY EDUCATIONAL COMPARISONS (US) [06704724] **1784**

SOUTH DAKOTA EPISCOPAL CHURCH NEWS (US/0746-9276) [10395646] **4998**

SOUTH DAKOTA FARM & HOME RESEARCH (US/0038-3295) [01605145] **136**

SOUTH DAKOTA GENEALOGICAL SOCIETY (US) [13771321] **2473**

SOUTH DAKOTA GEOLOGICAL SURVEY *See* SPECIAL REPORT - SOUTH DAKOTA STATE GEOLOGICAL SURVEY **1398**

SOUTH DAKOTA GEOLOGICAL SURVEY *See* BIENNIAL REPORT OF THE STATE GEOLOGIST (VERMILLION), THE **1367**

SOUTH DAKOTA GEOLOGICAL SURVEY *See* REPORT OF INVESTIGATIONS - SOUTH DAKOTA GEOLOGICAL SURVEY **1394**

SOUTH DAKOTA. GOVERNOR *See* GOVERNOR'S BUDGET REPORT - SOUTH DAKOTA **4729**

SOUTH DAKOTA. GOVERNOR *See* STATE OF SOUTH DAKOTA GOVERNOR'S BUDGET **4749**

SOUTH DAKOTA. GOVERNOR'S ADVISORY COMMITTEE ON EMPLOYMENT OF THE HANDICAPPED *See* SOUTH DAKOTA GOVERNOR'S ADVISORY COMMITTEE ON EMPLOYMENT OF THE HANDICAPPED **4394**

SOUTH DAKOTA GOVERNOR'S ADVISORY COMMITTEE ON EMPLOYMENT OF THE HANDICAPPED (US/0147-474X) [03172417] **4394**

SOUTH DAKOTA. GOVERNOR'S BUDGET REPORT *See* STATE OF SOUTH DAKOTA GOVERNOR'S BUDGET **4749**

● SOUTH DAKOTA HALL OF FAME (US/1061-4427) [25308764] **2546**

● SOUTH DAKOTA HEALTH CARE IN PERSPECTIVE (US/1065-4429) [26606716] **4803**

SOUTH DAKOTA HERITAGE *See* SOUTH DAKOTA HALL OF FAME **2546**

SOUTH DAKOTA HIGH LINER (US/0038-3309) [03928018] **2082**

SOUTH DAKOTA HIGH LINER MAGAZINE (US/1067-4977) [27251086] **2493**

SOUTH DAKOTA HIGHWAY SAFETY MANAGEMENT SYSTEM PLAN (US) [02768598] **5444**

SOUTH DAKOTA HIGHWAY SAFETY WORK PROGRAM (US/0361-3461) [02246323] **5444**

SOUTH DAKOTA HISTORY (US/0361-8676) [01639290] **2761**

SOUTH DAKOTA HOUSING DEVELOPMENT AUTHORITY *See* ANNUAL REPORT - SOUTH DAKOTA HOUSING DEVELOPMENT AUTHORITY **2815**

SOUTH DAKOTA IN PERSPECTIVE (US/1065-5697) [26662275] **5338**

SOUTH DAKOTA INDIAN RECIPIENTS OF SOCIAL WELFARE (US/0094-372X) [01794234] **2273**, **5310**

SOUTH DAKOTA JOURNAL OF MEDICINE (US/0038-3317) [01766148] **3642**

SOUTH DAKOTA LAW REVIEW (US/0038-3325) [01642397] **3057**

SOUTH DAKOTA LEGISLATIVE MANUAL (US/0362-2738) [01588991] **3057**

SOUTH DAKOTA. LEGISLATURE *See* SOUTH DAKOTA LEGISLATIVE MANUAL **3057**

SOUTH DAKOTA. LEGISLATURE. STATE LEGISLATIVE RESEARCH COUNCIL *See* INTERIM REPORT TO THE ... LEGISLATURE **2983**

SOUTH DAKOTA LIBRARY DIRECTORY (US) [10812066] **3250**

SOUTH DAKOTA MAGAZINE (YANKTON, S.D.) (US/0886-2680) [12319446] **2546**

SOUTH DAKOTA MOTOR VEHICLE TRAFFIC ACCIDENT SUMMARY (US) [11313416] **5444**

SOUTH DAKOTA MUNICIPAL LEAGUE *See* LEGISLATION AFFECTING SOUTH DAKOTA MUNICIPALITIES **4661**

SOUTH DAKOTA MUNICIPALITIES (US/0300-6182) [01775089] **4686**

SOUTH DAKOTA MUSEUM, THE (US/0885-9140) [04421535] **4096**

SOUTH DAKOTA MUSICIAN (US/0038-3341) [04179372] **4154**

SOUTH DAKOTA NURSE, THE (US/0038-335X) [04165472] **3869**

SOUTH DAKOTA. OFFICE OF ADULT SERVICES AND AGING *See* STATE PLAN ON AGING UNDER TITLE III OF THE OLDER AMERICANS ACT FOR STATE OF SOUTH DAKOTA / DEPARTMENT OF SOCIAL SERVICES, OFFICE OF ADULT SERVICES & AGING **5311**

SOUTH DAKOTA. OFFICE OF ADULT SERVICES AND AGING. STATE PLAN ON AGING *See* STATE PLAN ON AGING UNDER TITLE III OF THE OLDER AMERICANS ACT FOR STATE OF SOUTH DAKOTA / DEPARTMENT OF SOCIAL SERVICES, OFFICE OF ADULT SERVICES & AGING **5311**

SOUTH DAKOTA PHARMACEUTICAL ASSOCIATION *See* REPORT OF THE SOUTH DAKOTA STATE PHARMACEUTICAL ASSOCIATION AND THE SOUTH DAKOTA BOARD OF PHARMACY **4327**

SOUTH DAKOTA PUBLIC TELEVISION *See* PROGRAM GUIDE - SOUTH DAKOTA PUBLIC TELEVISION **1136**

SOUTH DAKOTA REGISTER (US/0191-1104) [02711621] **3057**

SOUTH DAKOTA REVIEW (US/0038-3368) [01714208] **3438**

SOUTH DAKOTA STATE CEMENT PLANT RETIREMENT FUND ANNUAL FINANCIAL REPORT FOR THE PERIOD JANUARY 1, THROUGH DECEMBER 31 / BY THE STATE OF SOUTH DAKOTA, DEPARTMENT OF LEGISLATIVE AUDIT (US) [08556580] **1711**

SOUTH DAKOTA. STATE CENTER FOR HEALTH STATISTICS *See* REPORTED OCCUPATIONAL INJURIES AND ILLNESSES, SOUTH DAKOTA **2869**

SOUTH DAKOTA. STATE DIVISION OF VOCATIONAL EDUCATION *See* SOUTH DAKOTA STATE PLAN FOR VOCATIONAL-TECHNICAL EDUCATION **1915**

SOUTH DAKOTA. STATE ECONOMIC OPPORTUNITY OFFICE *See* ANNUAL CAUSES & CONDITIONS OF POVERTY IN SOUTH DAKOTA **5272**

SOUTH DAKOTA. STATE GEOLOGIST *See* INFORMATION PAMPHLET - SOUTH DAKOTA GEOLOGICAL SURVEY **1383**

SOUTH DAKOTA STATE GOVERNMENT PUBLICATIONS (US) [08139275] **425**

SOUTH DAKOTA STATE LIBRARY *See* STATISTICS OF SOUTH DAKOTA LIBRARIES **3260**

SOUTH DAKOTA STATE LIBRARY *See* SOUTH DAKOTA STATE GOVERNMENT PUBLICATIONS **425**

SOUTH DAKOTA STATE LIBRARY COMMISSION *See* STATISTICS OF SOUTH DAKOTA PUBLIC LIBRARIES **3260**

SOUTH DAKOTA STATE PLAN FOR VOCATIONAL-TECHNICAL EDUCATION (US/0363-7670) [02534827] **1915**

SOUTH DAKOTA STATE POETRY SOCIETY *See* SERENDIPTY / NEWSLETTER FOR THE SOUTH DAKOTA STATE POETRY SOCIETY **3471**

SOUTH DAKOTA. SUPREME COURT. OFFICE OF THE COURT ADMINISTRATOR *See* BENCHMARK **3139**

SOUTH DAKOTA. SUPREME COURT. OFFICE OF THE COURT ADMINISTRATOR *See* SOUTH DAKOTA COURTS : THE STATE OF THE JUDICIARY AND ... ANNUAL REPORT OF THE SOUTH DAKOTA UNIFIED JUDICIAL SYSTEM **3057**

SOUTH DAKOTA UNIFIED COURTS (US/0146-3241) [02925728] **3143**

SOUTH DAKOTA UNIFIED JUDICIAL SYSTEM (US) [04810942] **3143**

● SOUTH DAKOTA WRITERS (US/1062-063X) [25517172] **3438**

SOUTH DEKALB NEIGHBOR, THE (US/0199-6029) [06034450] **5655**

SOUTH DISTRICT JOURNAL (SEATTLE, WASH. : 1930) (US) [17292015] **5762**

SOUTH EAST ARTS REVIEW (UK) [06691559] **3438**

SOUTH EAST ASIA ACTIVITY REPORT (SI) **4278**

SOUTH EAST ASIA IRON AND STEEL INSTITUTE *See* SEAISI QUARTERLY **4019**

SOUTH EAST ASIA IRON AND STEEL INSTITUTE *See* SEAISI DIRECTORY **4019**

SOUTH-EAST ASIA LIBRARY GROUP *See* NEWSLETTER - SOUTH-EAST ASIA LIBRARY GROUP **3236**

SOUTH EAST ASIA MONITOR (UK/0959-2601) [22366612] **1584**

SOUTH EAST ASIA OIL SERVICE (UK) **4278**

SOUTH EAST ASIA RESEARCH (UK/0967-828X) [I0967828X] **2508**

SOUTH EAST ASIAN BUSINESS (SI) [03500853] **712**

SOUTH EAST ASIAN PRINTER MAGAZINE (SI/0129-1262) [I01291262] **4569**

SOUTH EAST ASIAN REVIEW, THE (II) [03391847] **2665**

SOUTH EAST ECONOMIC COMMISSION (N.B.) *See* REPERTOIRE COMMERCIAL DE LA REGION DU SUD-EST **849**

SOUTH EAST LANCE (CN/0384-7934) [03261396] **5795**

SOUTH EASTERN LATIN AMERICANIST (US/0049-1527) [03802207] **2761**

SOUTH-EASTERN STATE, NIGERIA *See* STAFF LIST - SOUTH-EASTERN STATE OF NIGERIA **4687**

SOUTH END NEWS (BOSTON, MASS.) (US/0738-9108) [09668887] **5690**

SOUTH FLORIDA (US/0895-5352) [16655691] **2546**

SOUTH FLORIDA BUSINESS JOURNAL (US/0746-2271) [09869577] **712**

● SOUTH FLORIDA CONTINUING EDUCATION NEWS (US/1064-5152) [26320604] **1802**

SOUTH FLORIDA ENVIRONMENTAL READER (ELECTRONIC ED.) (US/1044-3479) [19819642] **2243**

SOUTH FLORIDA ENVIRONMENTAL READER (PRINT ED.) (US/1044-3479) [19819510] **2243**

SOUTH FLORIDA HISTORY MAGAZINE : QUARTERLY OF THE HISTORICAL MUSEUM OF SOUTHERN FLORIDA *CEASED*. (US) [19380276] **2761**

SOUTH — Alphabetical Title Index

SOUTH FLORIDA MEDICAL REVIEW *CEASED.* (US/0886-2079) [12889973] **3642**

SOUTH FLORIDA PIONEERS (US/8756-2766) [04198445] **2473**

SOUTH FLORIDA POETRY REVIEW *SUSPENDED.* (US/0885-0720) [12561131] **3471**

SOUTH FLORIDA SHIPPER *See* FLORIDA SHIPPER, THE **5449**

SOUTH FLORIDA SPORTSCENE MAGAZINE (US/0194-8911) [05082610] **4919**

SOUTH FULTON NEIGHBOR, THE (US/0192-0693) [04995941] **5655**

SOUTH GEORGIA BUSINESS JOURNAL (US) **712**

SOUTH GIBSON STAR-TIMES (US) [29428481] **5667**

SOUTH HAMILTON RECORD/NEWS (JEWELL, IOWA : 1978) (US) [12610166] **5673**

SOUTH HAVEN DAILY TRIBUNE (US) [09344136] **5694**

SOUTH HAVEN NEW ERA (SOUTH HAVEN, KAN. : 1941) (US) [12686101] **5678**

SOUTH HILL ENTERPRISE, THE (US/0746-6676) [10214959] **5759**

SOUTH HILLS RECORD (US) [02267923] **5739**

SOUTH HOLLAND (NETHERLANDS) *See* BELEIDSNOTA VAN GEDEPUTEERDE STATEN **4713**

SOUTH IDAHO PRESS (US) [12292672] **5657**

SOUTH INDIA CHURCHMAN, THE (II) [06785010] **4998**

SOUTH INDIAN HORTICULTURE (II/0038-3473) [01772924] **2431**

SOUTH JERSEY MAGAZINE (US/0275-4423) [04782876] **2761**

SOUTH MILWAUKEE VOICE GRAPHIC (US) [16753747] **5770**

SOUTH-NORTH DIALOGUE IN KOREA (KO) [01789777] **4496**

SOUTH OF THE MOUNTAINS (US/0489-9563) [02566792] **2761**

SOUTH PACIFIC BIBLIOGRAPHY (FJ) [09921005] **425**

SOUTH PACIFIC COMMISSION *See* TECHNICAL PAPER - SOUTH PACIFIC COMMISSION **2671**

SOUTH PACIFIC COMMISSION *See* SOUTH PACIFIC COMMISSION FISHERIES NEWSLETTER, THE **2313**

SOUTH PACIFIC COMMISSION *See* REPORT TO THE SOUTH PACIFIC COMMISSION **4682**

SOUTH PACIFIC COMMISSION *See* INFORMATION CIRCULAR / SOUTH PACIFIC COMMISSION **96**

SOUTH PACIFIC COMMISSION FISHERIES NEWSLETTER, THE (NL) [03764435] **2313**

SOUTH PACIFIC CONFERENCE *See* REPORT OF THE SOUTH PACIFIC CONFERENCE AND PROCEEDINGS OF THE SOUTH PACIFIC COMMISSION **4681**

SOUTH PACIFIC JOURNAL OF NATURAL SCIENCE, THE (FJ/1013-9877) [08801553] **4172**

SOUTH PACIFIC JOURNAL OF TEACHER EDUCATION (UK/0311-2136) [03112136] **1847**

SOUTH PACIFIC LAW REPORTS (UK/0967-4136) [09674136] **3057**

SOUTH PACIFIC MAIL, THE (CL) [02267930] **5798**

SOUTH PACIFIC PERIODICALS INDEX (FJ/1011-5110) [11434038] **425**

SOUTH PACIFIC RESEARCH REGISTER (FJ/1011-5145) [10041123] **5159**

SOUTH PIERCE COUNTY DISPATCH, THE (US) [17331486] **5762**

SOUTH PITTSBURG HUSTLER (US) [19176322] **5746**

SOUTH PITTSBURGH REPORTER (US) [12178289] **5739**

SOUTH PLAINS ASSOCIATION OF GOVERNMENTS *See* PERSPECTIVE (LUBBOCK) **2830**

SOUTH-REPORTER (US) [15277687] **5701**

SOUTH SEA DIGEST, THE (AT) [07709134] **2511**

SOUTH SHORE (US/0149-6824) [03520690] **331**

SOUTH SHORE NEWS (CN/0710-0213) [08091316] **5795**

SOUTH SHORE NEWS (WEST HANOVER, MASS.) (US/0192-4869) [05081297] **5690**

SOUTH SHORE RECORD (US/0038-352X) [03928111] **2546**

SOUTH SHORE SCENE (US) [24314702] **5662**

SOUTH SIDE NEWS *See* ONONDAGA VALLEY NEWS **5719**

SOUTH SLAV JOURNAL, THE (UK) [06687185] **2710**

SOUTH STAFFORDSHIRE ARCHAEOLOGICAL AND HISTORICAL SOCIETY *See* TRANSACTIONS - SOUTH STAFFORDSHIRE ARCHAEOLOGICAL AND HISTORICAL SOCIETY **284**

SOUTH TEXAS AGRINEWS (US/0279-2486) [07678734] **136**

SOUTH TEXAS LAW REVIEW (US/1052-343X) [12795278] **3057**

SOUTH VANCOUVER REVUE (CN/0821-0187) [09666965] **5795**

SOUTH VOICE, THE (CN/0824-6726) [11096337] **5795**

SOUTH WEST AFRICA SERIES (SA/0377-7944) [05796129] **1397**

SOUTH WEST NOVA (CN/0708-9821) [05257093] **5491**

SOUTH WESTERN CATHOLIC HISTORY (UK/0269-8390) [18786573] **5036**

SOUTH WESTERN REGIONAL LIBRARY SYSTEM (ENGLAND) *See* ANNUAL REPORT - SOUTH WESTERN REGIONAL LIBRARY SYSTEM (ENGLAND) **3191**

SOUTH WHIDBEY RECORD (US/1064-0622) [17196117] **5762**

SOUTH YORKSHIRE (UK) [05754072] **4096**

SOUTHAMPTON MEDICAL JOURNAL (UK/0266-0342) [12005745] **3642**

SOUTHAMPTON PRESS, THE (US/0745-6484) [09320230] **5721**

SOUTHAMPTON RECORDS SERIES (UK/0584-4029) [01766164] **5236**

SOUTHEAST ALABAMA GENEALOGICAL SOCIETY QUARTERLY (US) **2473**

SOUTHEAST ASIA BUILDING *CEASED.* (SI/0129-6175) [18304351] **627**

SOUTHEAST ASIA DEVELOPMENT ADVISORY GROUP *See* CHAIRMAN'S REPORT - THE ASIA SOCIETY--SEADAG **1601**

SOUTHEAST ASIA HIGH TECH REVIEW (US/0892-1938) [15104827] **1627**

SOUTHEAST ASIA JOURNAL (PH/0038-3600) [02045971] **2508**

SOUTHEAST ASIA MICROFILMS NEWSLETTER (MY) [02036065] **2483**

SOUTHEAST ASIA PAPER (US) [06033037] **2665**

SOUTHEAST ASIA PETROLEUM EXPLORATION SOCIETY *See* PROCEEDINGS OF THE SOUTHEAST ASIA PETROLEUM EXPLORATION SOCIETY **4275**

SOUTHEAST ASIA PROGRAM SERIES (US) **2665**

SOUTHEAST ASIA SAWMILL SEMINAR *See* SAWMILL TECHNIQUES FOR SOUTHEAST ASIA **2404**

SOUTHEAST ASIAN AFFAIRS (SI/0377-5437) [01797870] **4496**

SOUTHEAST ASIAN ARCHIVES (MY/0085-6509) [02036042] **2484**

SOUTHEAST ASIAN BULLETIN OF MATHEMATICS (HK/0129-2021) [03578941] **3536**

SOUTHEAST ASIAN FISHERIES DEVELOPMENT CENTER. MARINE FISHERIES RESEARCH DEPT *See* MARINE FISHERIES RESEARCH DEPARTMENT ANNUAL REPORT **2308**

SOUTHEAST ASIAN JOURNAL OF EDUCATIONAL STUDIES (SI) [07142757] **1784**

SOUTHEAST ASIAN JOURNAL OF SOCIAL SCIENCE (SI) [01790717] **5222**

SOUTHEAST ASIAN JOURNAL OF SURGERY *See* ASIAN JOURNAL OF SURGERY **3960**

SOUTHEAST ASIAN JOURNAL OF TROPICAL MEDICINE AND PUBLIC HEALTH, THE (TH/0038-3619) [01766165] 3642, **4803**

SOUTHEAST ASIAN MINISTERS OF EDUCATION ORGANIZATION. SEAMEO DIGEST *See* SEAMEO QUARTERLY / SOUTHEAST ASIAN MINISTERS OF EDUCATION ORGANIZATION **1783**

SOUTHEAST ASIAN REVIEW OF ENGLISH (MY/0127-046X) [08138897] 3438, **3322**

SOUTHEAST CREATIVE DIRECTORY, THE (US/8756-5544) [11572670] **331**

SOUTHEAST DRAGSTER : AN NHRA PUBLICATION (US) [22692153] **4919**

SOUTHEAST FARM PRESS (US/0194-0937) [02082289] **136**

SOUTHEAST FOOD SERVICE NEWS (US/0199-2805) [05746676] **2358**

SOUTHEAST LOUISIANA DAIRY AND PASTURE EXPERIMENT STATION *See* ANNUAL PROGRESS REPORT - SOUTHEAST LOUISIANA DAIRY AND PASTURE EXPERIMENT STATION **191**

SOUTHEAST LOUISIANA HISTORICAL PAPERS (US/0897-3695) [16126296] **2761**

SOUTHEAST MESSENGER (US/0891-2289) [14703729] **5730**

SOUTHEAST MICHIGAN COUNCIL OF GOVERNMENTS *See* RESIDENTIAL CONSTRUCTION IN SOUTHEAST MICHIGAN **626**

SOUTHEAST MISSOURIAN (US/0746-4452) [10049209] **5704**

SOUTHEAST POWER REPORT (US/1062-5798) [25670384] **2082**

SOUTHEAST REAL ESTATE NEWS (US/0192-1630) [05120084] **4847**

SOUTHEAST SALES GUIDE TO HIGH-TECH COMPANIES (US/1040-0567) [18304546] **5159**

● ... SOUTHEAST SOURCEBOOK, THE (US/1057-6185) [24082750] **766**

SOUTHEAST SOUTH DAKOTA EXPERIMENT FARM *See* PROGRESS REPORT - SOUTHEAST SOUTH DAKOTA EXPERIMENT FARM **123**

SOUTHEAST WAVE STAR (US) [10535172] **5640**

SOUTHEAST ARCHAEOLOGY (US/0734-578X) [08771365] **282**

SOUTHEASTERN AREA SOUTHERN PINE BEETLE OUTBREAK STATUS (US) [01241945] **5613**

SOUTHEASTERN ASSOCIATION OF FISH AND WILDLIFE AGENCIES *See* PROCEEDINGS OF THE ... ANNUAL CONFERENCE SOUTHEASTERN ASSOCIATION OF FISH AND WILDLIFE AGENCIES **4913**

SOUTHEASTERN ASSOCIATION OF STATE HIGHWAY AND TRANSPORTATION OFFICIALS (U.S.). MEETING *See* PROCEEDINGS - SOUTHEASTERN ASSOCIATION OF STATE HIGHWAY AND TRANSPORTATION OFFICIALS (U.S.). MEETING **5390**

SOUTHEASTERN COLLEGE ART CONFERENCE REVIEW (US/1043-5158) [02081082] **331**

SOUTHEASTERN EUROPE (PITTSBURGH) (US/0094-4467) [01779959] **2523**

SOUTHEASTERN FOREST EXPERIMENT STATION (ASHEVILLE, N.C.) *See* FOREST RESEARCH IN THE SOUTHEAST **2381**

SOUTHEASTERN FRONT (US) [12871830] 365, **3438**

SOUTHEASTERN GEOGRAPHER (US/0038-366X) [01792028] **2576**

SOUTHEASTERN GEOLOGY (US/0038-3678) [01606985] **1397**

SOUTHEASTERN INSTITUTE OF MEDIEVAL AND RENAISSANCE STUDIES *See* MEDIEVAL AND RENAISSANCE STUDIES (DURHAM) **2698**

SOUTHEASTERN JOURNAL OF MUSIC EDUCATION (US/1047-9635) [20832121] **4154**

SOUTHEASTERN LAW LIBRARIAN (US/0272-7560) [03469161] **3250**

SOUTHEASTERN LIBRARIAN, THE (US/0038-3686) [01766169] **3250**

SOUTHEASTERN LIBRARY NETWORK *See* ANNUAL REPORT - SOUTHEASTERN LIBRARY NETWORK **3191**

SOUTHEASTERN MASSACHUSETTS BUSINESS DIGEST (US/1040-5380) [18435149] **712**

SOUTHEASTERN MUSEUMS CONFERENCE *See* INSIDE SEMC **4089**

SOUTHEASTERN MUSEUMS CONFERENCE, INC *See* SEMC JOURNAL **4096**

SOUTHEASTERN OUTLOOK (US/0887-0934) [13137403] 1103, **4998**

SOUTHEASTERN PEANUT FARMER (US/0038-3694) [01847351] **188**

SOUTHEASTERN POLITICAL REVIEW (US/0730-2177) [07579745] **4496**

SOUTHEASTERN REGULATORY ALERT *CEASED.* (US/1045-0459) [19985664] **3057**

SOUTHEASTERN REPORTER CASE NAMES CITATOR (US) **3057**

SOUTHEASTERN STATES MINING DIRECTORY (US/1060-8044) [25067358] **2151**

● SOUTHEASTERN STATES MINING DIRECTORY (US/1056-8638) [23881322] **2151**

SOUTHEASTERN VISUAL RESOURCES NEWSLETTER *CEASED.* (US/0889-0544) [13818598] **331**

SOUTHEASTERN WISCONSIN REGIONAL PLANNING COMMISSION *See* NEWSLETTER - SOUTHEASTERN WISCONSIN REGIONAL PLANNING COMMISSION **2829**

SOUTHEASTERN WISCONSIN REGIONAL PLANNING COMMISSION *See* TECHNICAL REPORT - SOUTHEASTERN WISCONSIN REGIONAL PLANNING COMMISSION **2836**

Alphabetical Title Index

SOUTHERN

SOUTHERLY (AT/0038-3732) [01766172] 3471, **3438**

SOUTHERN A.R.C (US/0197-5307) [06035236] **2761**

SOUTHERN ACCENTS (US/0149-516X) [03496530] 2431, **2903**

SOUTHERN AFRICA (DENVER, COLO.) (US/1061-723X) [25176082] **2643**

SOUTHERN AFRICA POLITICAL & ECONOMIC MONTHLY (RH) [20456790] **1521**

SOUTHERN AFRICA PROJECT ANNUAL REPORT *CEASED*. (US/0887-8706) [09365127] **4496**

SOUTHERN AFRICA RECORD (SA) [02243949] **4535**

SOUTHERN AFRICA REPORT (SA) [11305725] **2500**

SOUTHERN AFRICA REPORT (TORONTO) (CN/0820-5582)[14120311] **2643**

SOUTHERN AFRICA TEXTILES (SA) [07411167] **5356**

SOUTHERN AFRICAN AND INDIAN OCEAN ISLANDS TRAVEL INDUSTRY'S YEARBOOK, DIRECTORY AND WHO'S WHO, THE (SA) [04552763] **5491**

SOUTHERN AFRICAN ECONOMIST (RH) [18179370] **1521**

SOUTHERN AFRICAN JOURNAL OF AQUATIC SCIENCES (SA/1018-9688) [21741982] **2313**

SOUTHERN AFRICAN JOURNAL OF DEMOGRAPHY (SA) [20082376] **591**

SOUTHERN AFRICAN JOURNAL OF EPIDEMIOLOGY & INFECTION : OFFICIAL JOURNAL OF THE SEXUALLY TRANSMITTED DISEASES, INFECTIOUS DISEASES, AND EPIDEMIOLOGICAL SOCIETIES OF SOUTHERN AFRICA, THE (SA) [20101007] 3736, **3716**

SOUTHERN AFRICAN REVIEW OF BOOKS (SA/0952-8040) [17490746] **3438**

SOUTHERN AFRICAN STUDIES (SA) [15925894] **2643**

SOUTHERN AFRICAN UPDATE (SA/0258-9168) [15641047] **2500**

SOUTHERN ALBERTA ART GALLERY *See* GALLERY (LETHBRIDGE) **351**

SOUTHERN AND SOUTHWESTERN RAILWAY ASSOCIATION *See* PROCEEDINGS / SOUTHERN AND SOUTHWESTERN RAILWAY ASSOCIATION **5434**

SOUTHERN ANTHROPOLOGICAL SOCIETY PROCEEDINGS (US/0081-2994) [01766174] **245**

SOUTHERN ASSOCIATION OF AFRICANISTS (U.S.) *See* BULLETIN OF THE SOUTHERN ASSOCIATION OF AFRICANISTS, THE **2638**

SOUTHERN ASSOCIATION OF COLLEGES AND SCHOOLS *See* PROCEEDINGS - SOUTHERN ASSOCIATION OF COLLEGES AND SCHOOLS; THE SOUTHERN ASSOCIATION NEWSLETTER **1842**

SOUTHERN BANKER, THE *CEASED*. (US/0038-383X) [03484970] **812**

SOUTHERN BANKERS DIRECTORY (US/0734-7812) [03421478] **812**

SOUTHERN BAPTIST EDUCATOR, THE (US/0038-3848) [01715114] 1784, **5067**

SOUTHERN BAPTIST HANDBOOK (1991) (US/1058-319X) [24242214] **4998**

SOUTHERN BAPTIST JOURNAL (US/0199-8269) [01781213] **5067**

SOUTHERN BAPTIST PERIODICAL INDEX (US/0081-3028) [01696794] 4998, **5013**

SOUTHERN BEVERAGE JOURNAL (US/0193-0613) [05142680] **2371**

SOUTHERN BIRDS (SA) [02500850] **5620**

SOUTHERN BOATING (US/0192-3579) [05055193] **596**

SOUTHERN BODYBUILDER (US/0736-6280) [09170631] **2601**

SOUTHERN BRIDE *See* ELEGANT BRIDE **2278**

SOUTHERN BUILDING (US/0038-3864) [06105360] **628**

SOUTHERN BUILDING CODE CONGRESS INTERNATIONAL COMPLIANCE REPORT (US) **628**

SOUTHERN BUSINESS & ECONOMIC JOURNAL, THE (US/0743-779X) [15691661] 1521, **712**

SOUTHERN BUSINESS REVIEW (US/0884-1373) [08155647] **886**

●SOUTHERN BUSINESS REVIEW & FORECAST (US/1066-3754) [26926394] **712**

SOUTHERN CALIFORNIA ACADEMY OF SCIENCES, LOS ANGELES *See* MEMOIRS OF THE SOUTHERN CALIFORNIA ACADEMY OF SCIENCES **5128**

SOUTHERN CALIFORNIA ANTHOLOGY, THE (US/0743-1406) [10354791] **3438**

SOUTHERN CALIFORNIA ASSOCIATION OF GOVERNMENTS *See* SCAG: A RECORD OF ACCOMPLISHMENT **4685**

SOUTHERN CALIFORNIA ASSOCIATION OF LAW LIBRARIES *See* SCALL NEWSLETTER / SOUTHERN CALIFORNIA ASSOCIATION OF LAW LIBRARIES **3247**

SOUTHERN CALIFORNIA ASSOCIATION OF LAW LIBRARIES. NEWSLETTER *See* SCALL NEWSLETTER / SOUTHERN CALIFORNIA ASSOCIATION OF LAW LIBRARIES **3247**

SOUTHERN CALIFORNIA BEVERAGE BULLETIN (US/0192-1835) [05132592] **2371**

SOUTHERN CALIFORNIA BUSINESS (US/0038-3880) [04038257] **821**

●SOUTHERN CALIFORNIA BUSINESS DIRECTORY (US/1061-2181) [25999483] **712**

SOUTHERN CALIFORNIA BUSINESS DIRECTORY AND BUYERS GUIDE (US/0093-3090) [01792211] **712**

SOUTHERN CALIFORNIA DENTAL HYGIENISTS' ASSOCIATION JOURNAL *See* CALIFORNIA DENTAL HYGIENISTS' ASSOCIATION JOURNAL **1318**

SOUTHERN CALIFORNIA DENTAL LABORATORY ASSOCIATION *See* BULLETIN - SOUTHERN CALIFORNIA DENTAL LABORATORY ASSOCIATION **1318**

SOUTHERN CALIFORNIA EARLY MUSIC SOCIETY NEWSLETTER (US/0749-4106) [10481792] **4154**

SOUTHERN CALIFORNIA HOME & GARDEN (US/0199-896X) [06275992] 2903, **309**

SOUTHERN CALIFORNIA LAW REVIEW (US/0038-3910) [01766179] **3057**

●SOUTHERN CALIFORNIA LEGAL RESOURCE MANUAL (US/1056-2494) [23600139] **3057**

SOUTHERN CALIFORNIA MEDIA DIRECTORY (US) **1122**

●SOUTHERN CALIFORNIA MEDIA SOURCEBOOK (US/1071-4685) [28159290] **766**

SOUTHERN CALIFORNIA OCCASIONAL PAPERS IN LINGUISTICS (US) [03973743] **3322**

SOUTHERN CALIFORNIA PALEONTOLOGICAL SOCIETY *See* BULLETIN OF THE SOUTHERN CALIFORNIA PALEONTOLOGICAL SOCIETY **4226**

SOUTHERN CALIFORNIA QUARTERLY (US/0038-3929) [01695696] **2761**

SOUTHERN CALIFORNIA SENIOR LIFE (US) **5182**

SOUTHERN CALIFORNIA TDD COMMUNITY DIRECTORY (US/1044-6168) [19843014] **5310**

SOUTHERN CALIFORNIA TEAMSTER (US/0038-3953) [03928204] **1711**

SOUTHERN CALIFORNIA WOMEN'S CAUCUS FOR ART (US/0749-5528) [10068775] 5566, **365**

SOUTHERN CALIFORNIA WOODWORKER, THE (US/0898-3550) [17792851] 375, **635**

SOUTHERN CALIFORNIAN, THE (US) [19656814] **2761**

SOUTHERN CHANGES (US/0193-2446) [04810899] **4513**

SOUTHERN CITY (US/0361-7130) [01955685] **4686**

SOUTHERN COALITION REPORT ON JAILS AND PRISONS (US) [06799272] **3177**

SOUTHERN COLLEGIATE ACCOUNTANT, THE (US/1050-4524) [21121426] **751**

SOUTHERN COMMUNICATION JOURNAL, THE (US/1041-794X) [18653584] **1122**

SOUTHERN COMMUNITIES (US) 4513, **2836**

SOUTHERN COOPERATIVE SERIES BULLETIN (US/0096-8498) [01766183] **136**

SOUTHERN COUNTY NEWS, THE (US) [16842037] **5673**

SOUTHERN CREATIVITY ANNUAL (US/0095-4926) [01784453] **766**

SOUTHERN CROSS (SAN DIEGO, CALIF.) (US/0745-0257) [08730938] **5036**

SOUTHERN CROSS SYDNEY. 1961 (AT/0313-5861) [I03135861] **4998**

●SOUTHERN CULTURES (US/1068-8218) [27820539] **5263**

SOUTHERN DOG LOVERS DIGEST (US/0561-1245) [01795155] **4288**

SOUTHERN DUTCHESS NEWS (US/0192-9631) [05095560] **5721**

SOUTHERN ECHOES (US/0735-6870) [08793173] **2473**

SOUTHERN ECONOMIC JOURNAL (US/0038-4038) [01766186] **1521**

SOUTHERN ECONOMIC REVIEW (II) [01642141] **1521**

SOUTHERN ECONOMIST (II/0038-4046) [01644785] **1521**

SOUTHERN ELECTRICAL BUYERS' GUIDE (US/0145-8426) [02789750] **2082**

SOUTHERN EXPORTER, THE (US/0273-4303) [07054928] **851**

SOUTHERN EXPOSURE (DURHAM, N.C.) (US/0146-809X) [01798545] **2761**

SOUTHERN FOLKLORE (US/0899-594X) [18176287] 5269, **2324**

SOUTHERN FOLKLORE REPORTS (US) [05543197] **2324**

SOUTHERN FRIEND, THE (US/0743-7439) [07968538] **5067**

SOUTHERN FUNERAL DIRECTOR (US/0038-4135) [01643906] **2407**

SOUTHERN GAZETTE (CN/0319-6224) [02442834] **5795**

SOUTHERN GENEALOGICAL INDEX (US/8755-1748) [10918428] **2473**

SOUTHERN GENEALOGIST'S EXCHANGE QUARTERLY, THE (US/0584-4487) [05107619] **2473**

SOUTHERN GLENN GLEANINGS NEWSLETTER (US/1056-0874) [23461258] **2473**

SOUTHERN GOLF (US/0146-8251) [03036545] **4919**

SOUTHERN GOVERNORS' ASSOCIATION (U.S.). MEETING *See* SUMMARY OF PROCEEDINGS : ANNUAL MEETING OF THE SOUTHERN GOVERNORS' ASSOCIATION **4689**

SOUTHERN GOVERNORS' CONFERENCE. MEETING. SUMMARY OF PROCEEDINGS *See* SUMMARY OF PROCEEDINGS : ANNUAL MEETING OF THE SOUTHERN GOVERNORS' ASSOCIATION **4689**

SOUTHERN GRAPHICS (US/0274-774X) [06582613] **382**

SOUTHERN GROWTH ALERT (US) [25418783] **1522**

SOUTHERN HERALD (LIBERTY, MISS.), THE (US/0893-3790) [15500745] **5701**

SOUTHERN HISTORIAN, THE (US/0738-5102) [09612447] 1095, **2761**

SOUTHERN HISTORY (UK/0142-4688) [06001787] **2710**

SOUTHERN HOG PRODUCER *See* PREMIER HOG PRODUCER **219**

SOUTHERN HORSEMAN (US/0093-3929) [02253929] **2802**

SOUTHERN HOSPITALS *CEASED*. (US/0038-4178) [08246293] **3792**

SOUTHERN HUMANITIES REVIEW (US/0038-4186) [01643471] **2854**

SOUTHERN ILLINOIS UNIVERSITY AT CARBONDALE. SCHOOL OF LAW *See* SOUTHERN ILLINOIS UNIVERSITY LAW JOURNAL **3057**

SOUTHERN ILLINOIS UNIVERSITY LAW JOURNAL (US/0145-3432) [02569791] **3057**

SOUTHERN INDIAN STUDIES (US/0085-6525) [01766191] 2273, **2761**

SOUTHERN INDIANA GENEALOGICAL SOCIETY QUARTERLY (US/0747-8453) [06680289] **2473**

SOUTHERN INSURANCE (US/0038-4216) [03485573] **2894**

SOUTHERN JOURNAL OF AGRICULTURAL ECONOMICS (US/0081-3052) [01786622] 1522, **136**

SOUTHERN JOURNAL OF APPLIED FORESTRY (US/0148-4419) [03338121] **2395**

SOUTHERN JOURNAL OF OPTOMETRY (ATLANTA, GA. : 1983) (US) [12409465] **4217**

SOUTHERN JOURNAL OF PHILOSOPHY, THE (US/0038-4283) [01766192] **4361**

SOUTHERN LAW JOURNAL (ABILENE, TEX.) (US/1056-2184) [23598096] **3057**

SOUTHERN LAWNMOWERS DEALERS NEWSLETTER (US) **2431**

SOUTHERN LIBERTARIAN MESSENGER, THE (US) [13686085] 4496, **4686**

SOUTHERN LINKS (HILTON HEAD ISLAND, S.C.) (US/1043-6375) [19502164] 5491, **4919**

SOUTHERN LITERARY JOURNAL, THE (US/0038-4291) [01641372] **3438**

SOUTHERN LIVING (US/0038-4305) [02457928] **2546**

SOUTHERN LIVING ... ANNUAL RECIPES (US/0272-2003) [06545840] **2792**

SOUTHERN — Alphabetical Title Index

SOUTHERN LIVING ... GARDEN ANNUAL (US/1048-2318) [20874909] **2431**

SOUTHERN LOGGIN' TIMES (US/0744-2106) [08116867] **2404**

SOUTHERN LUMBERMAN (US/0038-4313) [01645923] **2404**

SOUTHERN MARKETING ASSOCIATION *See* PROCEEDINGS - SOUTHERN MARKETING ASSOCIATION **935**

SOUTHERN MEDIATOR (US) [12832408] **2273**

SOUTHERN MEDICAL JOURNAL (BIRMINGHAM) (US/0038-4348) [01766196] **3975**

SOUTHERN MEDICINE (US/0097-5419) [01378518] **3642**

SOUTHERN METHODIST UNIVERSITY *See* ALUMNI DIRECTORY / SOUTHERN METHODIST UNIVERSITY **1099**

SOUTHERN METHODIST UNIVERSITY *See* SOUTHERN METHODIST UNIVERSITY CONTRIBUTIONS IN ANTHROPOLOGY **245**

SOUTHERN METHODIST UNIVERSITY CONTRIBUTIONS IN ANTHROPOLOGY (US/0069-9632) [01561569] **245**

SOUTHERN METHODIST UNIVERSITY, DALLAS, TEXAS. INSTITUTE FOR THE STUDY OF EARTH AND MAN *See* REPORTS OF INVESTIGATIONS - INSTITUTE FOR THE STUDY OF EARTH AND MAN **4358**

SOUTHERN METHODIST UNIVERSITY. INSTITUTE FOR THE STUDY OF EARTH AND MAN. N *See* REPORTS OF INVESTIGATIONS - SOUTHERN METHODIST UNIVERSITY. INSTITUTE FOR THE STUDY OF EARTH AND MAN **5146**

SOUTHERN MICHIGAN REGIONAL INDUSTRIAL PURCHASING GUIDE (US/0737-0970) [08909080] **951**

SOUTHERN MOTOR CARGO (US/0038-4372) [05320989] **5425**

SOUTHERN MOTORACING (US/0049-1616) [03929841] **4919, 5425**

SOUTHERN NEIGHBORHOODS *See* SOUTHERN COMMUNITIES **2836**

SOUTHERN NEW JERSEY BUSINESS DIGEST (US/0892-8835) [15278381] **712**

SOUTHERN NURSERY DIGEST (US) [25485121] **2431**

SOUTHERN NURSERYMEN'S ASSOCIATION *See* SOUTHERN NURSERYMEN'S ASSOCIATION RESEARCH CONFERENCE, ANNUAL REPORT **2431**

SOUTHERN NURSERYMEN'S ASSOCIATION RESEARCH CONFERENCE, ANNUAL REPORT (US) [01691013] **2431**

SOUTHERN NURSEY DIGEST *See* LANDSCAPE & NURSERY DIGEST **2422**

SOUTHERN ONTARIO NEWSPAPER GUILD *See* S. O. N. G. SHEET **1709**

SOUTHERN OUTDOORS (MONTGOMERY) (US/0199-3372) [05796951] **4920, 4878**

SOUTHERN PACIFIC LOCOMOTIVE DIRECTORY (US/8756-8853) [11603820] **5436**

SOUTHERN PACIFIC MOTIVE POWER ANNUAL (US/0584-4568) [07355786] **5437**

SOUTHERN PARTISAN, THE (US/0739-1714) [06401604] **2761, 4496**

SOUTHERN PERU COPPER CORPORATION. SUCURSAL DEL PERU *See* REPORTE ANUAL / SOUTHERN PERU COPPER CORPORATION, SUCURSAL DEL PERU **4017**

SOUTHERN PHARMACY JOURNAL (US/0192-5792) [04636549] **4329**

SOUTHERN PLUMBING, HEATING, COOLING (US/0038-4461) [05430859] **2608**

SOUTHERN POETRY REVIEW (US/0038-447X) [01036277] **3471**

SOUTHERN POLITICAL REPORT (US/0739-3938) [08633023] **4496**

SOUTHERN POST, THE (US/0744-1118) [08035780] **5724**

SOUTHERN PURCHASOR (US/0049-1624) [05094106] **951**

SOUTHERN QUARTERLY, THE (US/0038-4496) [01644229] **331**

SOUTHERN QUERIES : THE CONTACT MAGAZINE FOR PEOPLE SEARCHING FOR THEIR SOUTHERN ANCESTORS (US/1048-8057) [21064213] **2473**

SOUTHERN RE-ENACTING VETERAN, THE (US/1063-9640) [26181729] **2761, 4854**

SOUTHERN READER (US/1042-6604) [19100987] **3438**

SOUTHERN REGIONAL COUNCIL *See* ANNUAL REPORT - THE SOUTHERN REGIONAL COUNCIL **2721**

SOUTHERN REGIONAL EDUCATION BOARD *See* SREB ANNUAL REPORT **1784**

SOUTHERN REGIONAL SCIENCE ASSOCIATION *See* SELECTED PAPERS PRESENTED AT THE ANNUAL MEETING - SOUTHERN REGIONAL SCIENCE ASSOCIATION **2835**

SOUTHERN REGISTER : THE NEWSLETTER OF THE CENTER FOR THE STUDY OF SOUTHERN CULTURE, THE UNIVERSITY OF MISSISSIPPI, THE (US/0895-5573) [09216674] **2761**

SOUTHERN REPORTER (SARDIS, MISS.) (US) [16308735] **5701**

SOUTHERN RESEARCH INSTITUTE (BIRMINGHAM, ALA.) *See* ANNUAL REPORT - SOUTHERN RESEARCH INSTITUTE **5084**

SOUTHERN REVIEW (ADELAIDE) (AT/0038-4526) [01766212] **3353**

SOUTHERN REVIEW (BATON ROUGE), THE (US/0038-4534) [01766210] **3438**

SOUTHERN RHODESIA. AGRICULTURAL MARKETING AUTHORITY *See* REPORT AND ACCOUNTS FOR THE YEAR ENDED 30TH JUNE ... / AGRICULTURAL MARKETING AUTHORITY **125**

SOUTHERN RHODESIA. CENTRAL STATISTICAL OFFICE *See* CENSUS OF LIVESTOCK IN EUROPEAN AREAS **209**

SOUTHERN RHODESIA. MINISTRY OF FINANCE *See* REPORT OF THE REGISTRAR OF BANKS AND FINANCIAL INSTITUTIONS **808**

SOUTHERN ROOTS AND SHOOTS (US/0895-2876) [13766455] **2473**

SOUTHERN RURAL SOCIOLOGY (US/0885-3436) [10736291] **5263**

SOUTHERN SCHOOL LAW DIGEST (US/0361-0861) [02244874] **1784, 3057**

SOUTHERN SEMINARY (US/1078-2613) [31034728] **4998**

SOUTHERN SENTINEL (RIPLEY, MISS.) (US) [16292022] **5702**

SOUTHERN SHIPPER (US/1054-7150) [22928442] **5457**

SOUTHERN SOCIAL STUDIES JOURNAL (US/1047-7942) [20788986] **5222**

SOUTHERN SOCIOLOGIST / THE SOUTHERN SOCIOLOGICAL SOCIETY, THE (US/0038-4577) [04045639] **5263**

SOUTHERN STANDARD (MCMINNVILLE, TENN.) (US) [14961576] **5746**

SOUTHERN STAR (US) [10944856] **5628**

SOUTHERN STARS (NZ/0049-1640) [06108757] **400**

SOUTHERN STRUGGLE (US/0199-8668) [03110992] **5263**

SOUTHERN STUDIES (US/0735-8342) [03262379] **2761**

SOUTHERN SUDAN (SJ) [08905654] **2508**

SOUTHERN TEXTILE NEWS (US/0038-4607) [03929924] **5356**

SOUTHERN THEATRE (US/0584-4738) [03959342] **5368**

SOUTHERN TIDINGS (US/0885-2421) [12049294] **4998**

SOUTHERN TOBACCO JOURNAL (US/0300-6239) [01332517] **5373**

SOUTHERN TRAVEL *See* TRAVEL SOUTH (1989) **2548**

SOUTHERN UNION WORKER *See* SOUTHERN TIDINGS **4998**

SOUTHERN UNIVERSITY AND A & M COLLEGE. SCHOOL OF LAW *See* SOUTHERN UNIVERSITY LAW REVIEW **3057**

SOUTHERN UNIVERSITY AT NEW ORLEANS *See* ALUMNI DIRECTORY / SOUTHERN UNIVERSITY AT NEW ORLEANS **1099**

SOUTHERN UNIVERSITY LAW REVIEW (US/0099-1465) [01466563] **3057**

SOUTHERN UTAH NEWS (US/0049-1659) [03929958] **5757**

SOUTHERN UTE DRUM, THE (US/0587-0674) [01773546] **2273**

SOUTHERN VERMONT *CEASED.* (US/0892-8789) [15278095] **2546**

SOUTHERN VINDICATOR *See* HAMMOND VINDICATOR, THE **5684**

SOUTHERN WASTE INFORMATION EXCHANGE CATALOG, THE (US/0892-5739) [15234227] **2243**

SOUTHERN WEED SCIENCE SOCIETY (U.S.) *See* PROCEEDINGS, SOUTHERN WEED SCIENCE SOCIETY **2429**

SOUTHFIELD ECCENTRIC (US) **5694**

SOUTHLAND TIMES (NZ/0112-9910) [I01129910] **5807**

SOUTHSCAN (UK/0952-7524) [17269680] **4496**

SOUTHSIDE AND FAYETTE SUN (US/0192-0774) [05010530] **5655**

SOUTHSIDE CHALLENGER, THE (US) [11541810] **5667**

SOUTHSIDE MIRROR, THE (CN/0701-1423) [03406550] **2546**

SOUTHSIDE VIRGINIAN, THE (US/0736-5683) [09139072] **2473**

SOUTHWEST & TEXAS WATER WORKS JOURNAL *CEASED.* (US/0196-0717) [05760951] **5539**

SOUTHWEST ART (US/0192-4214) [05143351] **365**

SOUTHWEST BUSINESS REVIEW (SAN MARCOS, TEX.) (US/1055-0119) [23055800] **713**

SOUTHWEST CONTRACTOR (PHOENIX, ARIZ.) (US/1064-6914) [10995097] **2031, 628**

SOUTHWEST DAILY TIMES, THE (US/0745-8916) [09316974] **5678**

SOUTHWEST DIGEST (US) [14399287] **5754**

SOUTHWEST DIRECTORY OF ADVERTISING AND PUBLIC RELATIONS AGENCIES (US/0361-3593) [02246266] **766**

SOUTHWEST ECONOMY & SOCIETY NEWSLETTER (US) [04564535] **1522**

SOUTHWEST FARM PRESS (US/0194-0945) [05320962] **136**

●SOUTHWEST (FLAGSTAFF, AZ.) (US/1065-0156) [26493964] **3438**

SOUTHWEST FLORIDA WATER MANAGEMENT DISTRICT *See* ANNUAL REPORT/SOUTHWEST FLORIDA WATER MANAGEMENT DISTRICT **5529**

SOUTHWEST GLOBE-TIMES (US) [12715088] **5739**

SOUTHWEST HARBOR NEWS (US) [24607978] **5393**

SOUTHWEST INTERNATIONAL WINE & FOOD REVIEW (US) [19716172] **2358**

SOUTHWEST JOURNAL OF BUSINESS AND ECONOMICS *CEASED.* (US/8750-4294) [10470150] **1522, 713**

SOUTHWEST JOURNAL OF LINGUISTICS (US/0737-4143) [09368210] **3322**

SOUTHWEST JOURNAL ON AGING, THE (US) [29451544] **3755**

SOUTHWEST MISSOURIAN *See* BRANSON TRI-LAKES DAILY NEWS **5702**

SOUTHWEST MUSEUM PAPERS (US/0076-0994) [01756162] **245, 282, 4096**

SOUTHWEST NEW MEXICO COUNCIL OF GOVERNMENTS *See* ANNUAL WORK PROGRAM - SOUTHWEST NEW MEXICO COUNCIL OF GOVERNMENTS **2815**

SOUTHWEST NEWS-HERALD (US/0038-4704) [03930056] **5662**

SOUTHWEST NEWS WAVE (US) [10535049] **5640**

SOUTHWEST NEWSWEEK, THE (US) [26791626] **2546**

●SOUTHWEST NEWSWEEK, THE (US/1064-1645) [26220513] **5682**

SOUTHWEST OIL AND GAS WORLD (US/1071-4804) [28354577] **4278**

SOUTHWEST OIL WORLD (US/0884-6219) [12403694] **4278**

SOUTHWEST PHILA. GLOBE TIMES *See* SOUTHWEST GLOBE-TIMES **5739**

SOUTHWEST PHILOSOPHICAL STUDIES (US/0885-9310) [03797676] **4361**

SOUTHWEST PHILOSOPHY REVIEW (US/0897-2346) [17435910] **4361**

SOUTHWEST PROFILE *SUSPENDED.* (US/0895-6049) [16223168] **2546**

SOUTHWEST PUBLISHING MARKET PLACE : A COMPREHENSIVE DIRECTORY OF MARKETS, RESOURCES, AND OPPORTUNITIES FOR WRITERS (US/1059-5341) [20289735] **4819**

SOUTHWEST PURCHASING (US/0274-8800) [06641177] **951**

SOUTHWEST REAL ESTATE NEWS (US/0192-9194) [04744770] **4847**

SOUTHWEST REFERENCE ... (US) [07841965] **188, 222**

SOUTHWEST REVIEW (US/0038-4712) [04670628] **3353**

SOUTHWEST SALES GUIDE TO HIGH-TECH COMPANIES (US/1040-0524) [18304466] **5159**

SOUTHWEST SAMPLER (US/1047-4242) [20689889] **2903**

SOUTHWEST STOCKMAN (US/1050-9526) [21720257] **222**

SOUTHWEST STORYTELLER'S GAZETTE (US/0891-8619) [15028111] **3438**

SOUTHWEST TECHNOLOGY REPORT (US/1041-2379) [13924011] **2082**

SOUTHWEST TIMES RECORD (US) [15172460] **5632**

SOUTHWEST TOPICS WAVE (US) [10535110] **5640**

SOUTHWEST VIRGINIA ENTERPRISE (US) **5759**

SOUTHWEST VIRGINIAN, THE (US/0740-7335) [07524720] **2473**

SOUTHWEST WAVE (US) [10535081] **5640**

SOUTHWEST WOMAN (US/0744-5938) [08420589] **5566**

SOUTHWESTERN (US/0038-4852) [04040385] **1095**

SOUTHWESTERN AMERICAN LITERATURE (US/0049-1675) [02180010] **3438**

SOUTHWESTERN ARCHIVIST (US/1056-1021) [23466655] **2484**, **3250**

SOUTHWESTERN ART (US/0038-4739) [02069888] **365**

SOUTHWESTERN ASSOCIATION OF LAW LIBRARIES *See* SWALL BULLETIN **3252**

SOUTHWESTERN BAPTIST THEOLOGICAL SEMINARY, FORT WORTH *See* SOUTHWESTERN NEWS **4998**

SOUTHWESTERN CAMPING & TRAILERING (US/0093-1977) [01791806] **4878**

SOUTHWESTERN (DENTON, TEX.), THE (US/1053-4911) [18287023] **5182**

SOUTHWESTERN ENTOMOLOGIST. SUPPLEMENT (WESLACO, TEX.) (US/1055-8799) [23273384] **5613**

SOUTHWESTERN ENTOMOLOGIST, THE (US/0147-1724) [02558451] **5613**

SOUTHWESTERN HISTORICAL QUARTERLY (US/0038-478X) [04707909] **2761**

SOUTHWESTERN JOURNAL OF ECONOMIC ABSTRACTS (US/8756-2278) [07119730] **1522**

SOUTHWESTERN JOURNAL OF SOCIAL EDUCATION *CEASED.* (US/0049-1683) [02584806] **5222**

SOUTHWESTERN JOURNAL OF THEOLOGY (US/0038-4828) [01776710] **5067**

SOUTHWESTERN LAW JOURNAL (US/0038-4836) [06026094] **3057**

SOUTHWESTERN LEGAL FOUNDATION *See* ANNUAL REPORT - THE SOUTHWESTERN LEGAL FOUNDATION **2935**

SOUTHWESTERN LORE (US/0038-4844) [01766228] **282**

SOUTHWESTERN MASS COMMUNICATION JOURNAL (US/0891-9186) [12675133] **1122**

SOUTHWESTERN MUSICIAN COMBINED WITH THE TEXAS MUSIC EDUCATOR, THE (US) [05214989] 1905, **4154**

SOUTHWESTERN NATURALIST, THE (US/0038-4909) [01606304] **4172**

SOUTHWESTERN NEWS (US/0038-4917) [01641579] **4998**

SOUTHWESTERN PAY DIRT (US/0886-0920) [12733904] **2151**

SOUTHWESTERN PEANUT GROWERS NEWS (US) [09106910] **188**

SOUTHWESTERN PHILOSOPHY OF EDUCATION SOCIETY *See* PROCEEDINGS OF THE ANNUAL MEETING - SOUTHWESTERN PHILOSOPHY OF EDUCATION SOCIETY **1774**

SOUTHWESTERN PHILOSOPHY OF EDUCATION SOCIETY. PROCEEDINGS OF THE ANNUAL MEETING *See* JOURNAL OF EDUCATIONAL PHILOSOPHY AND HISTORY : AN ANNUAL PUBLICATION OF THE SOUTHWESTERN PHILOSOPHY OF EDUCATION SOCIETY **1757**

SOUTHWESTERN REVIEW (LAFAYETTE, LA.), THE (US/0276-7155) [05064056] **3353**

SOUTHWESTERN STUDIES (US/0081-315X) [01766229] **2762**

SOUTHWESTERN SUN WAVE (US) [10535202] **2273**, **5640**

SOUTHWESTERN UNIVERSITY LAW REVIEW (US/0886-3296) [01766230] **3057**

SOUTHWINDS (CN/0712-9750) [09021900] **1784**

SOUVENANCE ANABAPTISTE (FR/0769-1734) [I07691734] **4999**

SOUVENIR BOOK (ROYAL BALLET) *See* YEARBOOK (ROYAL BALLET) **1314**

SOUVENIR NAPOLEONIEN, LE (FR/0246-1919) [01966610] **2630**

SOUVENIRS & NOVELTIES (US/0038-4968) [04352238] **2585**

SOU'WESTER (EDWARDSVILLE), THE (US/0038-4976) [02240372] **3438**

SOU'WESTER LITERARY QUARTERLY *See* SOU'WESTER (EDWARDSVILLE), THE **3438**

SOU'WESTER (RAYMOND, WASH.), THE (US/0038-4984) [05082814] **2546**

SOVERSHENSTVOVANIE PSIKHOLOGO-PEDAGOGICHESKOI PODGOTOVKI UCHITELIA (RU) [02390686] **1905**

SOVET EKONOMICHESKOI VZAIMOPOMOSHCHI *See* STATISTICAL YEARBOOK OF MEMBER STATES OF THE COUNCIL FOR MUTUAL ECONOMIC ASSISTANCE **5341**

SOVET EKONOMICHESKOI VZAIMOPOMOSHCHI. SEKRETARIAT *See* SURVEY OF CMEA ACTIVITIES **1523**

SOVET EKONOMICHESKOI VZAIMOPOMOSHCHI. SEKRETARIAT *See* SBORNIK INFORMATSII O DEIATELNOSTI ORGANOV SEV **1583**

SOVETIS HEYMLAND (RU/0134-4315) [04197319] **365**, **3438**

SOVETISH HEIMLAND *See* IDISHE GAS, DI **3395**

SOVETSKAA GRAFIKA (RU/0256-260X) [I0256260X] **365**

SOVETSKAA TURKOLOGIA (AJ/0131-677X) [02050407] **3322**

SOVETSKAIA ARKHEOLOGIIA (RU/0038-5034) [01586019] **283**

SOVETSKAIA BIBLIOGRAFIA (MOSKVA, R.S.F.S.R. : 1946) (RU/0301-0252) [01367461] **425**

SOVETSKAIA ESTRADA I TSIRK (RU/0584-522X) [02049590] **388**

SOVETSKAIA ISTORICHESKAIA ENTSIKLOPEDIIA (RU) [06296600] **1929**

SOVETSKAIA IUSTITSIIA (MOSCOW, R.S.F.S.R. : 1957) *See* ROSSIISKAIA IUSTITSIIA **3045**

SOVETSKAIA JENSCINA (RU) **5566**

SOVETSKAIA LITERATURA PO OBSHCHIM PROBLEMAM KULTURNO-PROSVETITELNOI RABOTY I KLUBOVEDENIIU (RU) [03195758] **5222**

SOVETSKAIA LITVA (LI) [04909282] **3438**

SOVETSKAIA MEDITSINA *See* ROSSIISKII MEDITSINSKII ZHURNAL : ORGAN MINISTERSTVA ZDRAVOOKHRANENIIA RSFSR **3637**

SOVETSKAIA MUZYKA *See* MUSIKALNAIA AKADEMIIA **4138**

SOVETSKAIA PEDAGOGIKA *See* PEDAGOGIKA **1772**

SOVETSKAIA SKULPTURA (RU) [03815542] **365**

SOVETSKAIA TORGOVLIA (RU/0371-1927) [02049378] **1522**, **851**

SOVETSKAIA ZHENSHCHINA *CEASED.* (RU/0201-6982) [01606325] **5566**

SOVETSKAIA ZHENSHCHINA *See* MIR ZHENSHCHINY **5561**

SOVETSKAJA GEOLOGIJA (RU/0038-5069) [08053904] **1397**

SOVETSKAJA JUSTICIJA (RU/0131-6761) [01642667] **3057**

SOVETSKIE KHUDOZHNIKI TEATRA I KINO (RU) [03815295] **4078**, **5368**

SOVETSKIE PROFSOIUZY (RU/0038-5174) [02267974] **1711**

SOVETSKII DAGESTAN *See* NASH DAGESTAN **2699**

SOVETSKII EKSPORT (RU) [02243516] **851**

SOVETSKII EZHEGODNIK MEZHDUNARODNOGO PRAVA / SOVETSKAIA ASSOTSIATSIIA MEZHDUNARODNOGO PRAVA *CEASED.* (RU/0584-5335) [01766242] **3136**

SOVETSKII MUZEI (1984) (RU/0208-2403) [10691648] **4096**

SOVETSKII MUZEI (1984) *See* MIR MUZEIA **4091**

SOVETSKII TEATR *CEASED.* (RU) [10651863] **5368**

SOVETSKII VOIN *CEASED.* (RU/0134-8140) [20177833] **4057**

SOVETSKOE BIBLIOTEKOVEDENIE *See* BIBLIOTEKOVEDENIE **3194**

SOVETSKOE BIBLIOTEKOVEDENIE (RU/0134-6695) [03284255] **3250**

SOVETSKOE DEKORATIVNOE ISKUSSTVO (RU/0256-2596) [04596392] **365**

SOVETSKOE GOSUDARSTVO I PRAVO (RU/0038-5204) [07606045] **3057**

SOVETSKOE ISKUSSTVOZNANIE (RU) [02240857] **365**

SOVETSKOE SLAVIANOVEDENIE (RU/0132-1366) [01766244] **2710**

SOVETSKOE SLAVIANOVEDENIE (MOSCOW, R.S.F.S.R. : 1965) *See* SLAVIANOVEDENIE **2709**

SOVETSKOE ZDRAVOOKHRANENIE (RU/0038-5239) [01766246] **4803**

SOVETSKOE ZDRAVOOKHRANENIE *See* PROBLEMY SOTSIALNOI GIGIENY I ISTORIIA MEDITSINY / NII SOTSIALNOI GIGIENY, EKONOMIKI I UPRAVLENIIA ZDRAVOOKHRANENIEM IM N.A. SEMASHKO RAMN, AO ASSOTSIATSIIA 'MEDITSINSKAIA LITERATURA.' **4796**

SOVIET AERONAUTICS *See* RUSSIAN AERONAUTICS **34**

SOVIET AEROSPACE & TECHNOLOGY (US/1049-5940) [21259669] **5159**

SOVIET AGRICULTURAL BIOLOGY. PART 1, PLANT BIOLOGY *CEASED.* (US/0892-6999) [15239111] **136**

SOVIET AGRICULTURAL SCIENCES (US/1055-0607) [07509867] **136**

SOVIET AGRICULTURAL SCIENCES (US/0735-2700) [05962132] **136**

SOVIET ANALYST (UK/0049-1713) [01715780] **4496**

SOVIET AND EAST EUROPEAN ACCOUNTING BULLETIN : QUARTERLY BULLETIN (UK) [08447011] **751**

SOVIET AND EAST EUROPEAN PERFORMANCE *See* SLAVIC AND EAST EUROPEAN PERFORMANCE **5368**

SOVIET AND EASTERN EUROPEAN FOREIGN TRADE (US/0038-5263) [04903178] **1640**

SOVIET & EASTERN EUROPEAN REPORT (UK/0963-7036) [I09637036] **1640**, **3136**

● SOVIET AND POST-SOVIET REVIEW, THE (US/1075-1262) [28282499] **4496**

SOVIET ANTHROPOLOGY AND ARCHAEOLOGY (US/0038-528X) [01639463] **283**, **245**

SOVIET ANTHROPOLOGY AND ARCHEOLOGY *See* ANTHROPOLOGY & ARCHEOLOGY OF EURASIA **229**

SOVIET APPLIED MECHANICS (US/0038-5298) [01792522] **2129**

SOVIET ARCHIVES OF INTERNAL MEDICINE (US/1054-6596) [22937559] **3801**

SOVIET ARMED FORCES REVIEW ANNUAL (US/0148-0928) [03260865] **4057**

SOVIET ARMY : A DIGEST FROM THE SOVIET PRESS, THE (IS/0334-5734) [12774036] **4057**

SOVIET ASTRONOMY (US/0038-5301) [01766248] **400**

SOVIET ASTRONOMY LETTERS (US/0360-0327) [02245131] **400**

SOVIET ATOMIC ENERGY (US/0038-531X) [01642867] **2158**

SOVIET BIOGRAPHICAL SERVICE (US) [12258522] **435**

SOVIET BIOLOGICAL RESEARCH ABSTRACTS (SZ/0885-5951) [12675465] **473**

SOVIET BUSINESS & TRADE (1982) *See* EAST/WEST BUSINESS & TRADE **832**

SOVIET BUSINESS & TRADE (1982) (US/0731-7727) [08248784] **851**

SOVIET BUSINESS LAW REPORT *See* RUSSIAN COMMONWEALTH BUSINESS LAW REPORT **3103**

SOVIET BUSINESS REPORT, THE (US/1057-7467) [24111728] **713**

SOVIET CASTINGS TECHNOLOGY (US/0891-0316) [14547233] **4019**

SOVIET CHEMICAL INDUSTRY *See* RUSSIAN CHEMICAL INDUSTRY **1029**

SOVIET CHEMICAL INDUSTRY, THE (US/0038-5344) [01623972] **1047**, **1038**

SOVIET CHRISTIAN PRISONER LIST (US/0278-1018) [07695728] **4999**

SOVIET ECONOMIC PERFORMANCE IN ... / NATO ECONOMIC COMMITTEE (BE) [26486139] **1584**

SOVIET ECONOMY (SILVER SPRING, MD.) *See* POST-SOVIET AFFAIRS **1513**

SOVIET ECONOMY (SILVER SPRING, MD.) (US/0882-6994) [11925361] **1640**

SOVIET EDUCATION *See* RUSSIAN EDUCATION AND SOCIETY **1781**

SOVIET ELECTRICAL ENGINEERING (US/0038-5379) [02450733] **2082**

SOVIET ELECTROCHEMISTRY (US/0038-5387) [01697209] **1035**

SOVIET ENGINEERING RESEARCH *See* RUSSIAN ENGINEERING RESEARCH **2128**

SOVIET FAR EAST UPDATE *See* RUSSIAN FAR EAST UPDATE **1519**

SOVIET — Alphabetical Title Index

SOVIET FILM *CEASED.*
(RU/0201-8373) [01774122] **4078**

SOVIET FOREIGN POLICY TODAY : REPORTS AND COMMENTARIES FROM THE SOVIET PRESS (US) [20276683] **4535**

SOVIET GENETICS (US/0038-5409) [01587761] **551**

SOVIET GEOGRAPHY *See* POST-SOVIET GEOGRAPHY **2573**

SOVIET GEOLOGY AND GEOPHYSICS (US/0361-7149) [01983332] 1411, **1397**

SOVIET HYDROLOGY *CEASED.* (US/0038-5425) [01766252] **1418**

SOVIET INDEPENDENT BUSINESS DIRECTORY : SIBD (US/1052-8156) [22393016] **713**

SOVIET INTELLIGENCE & ACTIVE MEASURES (US/1050-2866) [21438862] **4535**

SOVIET INVENTIONS ILLUSTRATED : PARTS I-III COMPLETE (UK) [02474062] **1308**

SOVIET INVENTIONS ILLUSTRATED. SECTIONS P, Q: GENERAL/MECHANICAL (UK) [06713311] **2129**

SOVIET JEWISH AFFAIRS *See* EAST EUROPEAN JEWISH AFFAIRS **5047**

SOVIET JOURNAL GLASS, PHYSICS AND CHEMISTRY *See* GLASS, PHYSICS & CHEMISTRY **4404**

SOVIET JOURNAL OF APPLIED PHYSICS *See* JOURNAL OF ENERGETICS AND FLUIDS ENGINEERING **2091**

SOVIET JOURNAL OF AUTOMATION AND INFORMATION SCIENCES *See* JOURNAL OF AUTOMATION AND INFORMATION SCIENCES **1220**

SOVIET JOURNAL OF BIOORGANIC CHEMISTRY (US/0360-4497) [02477462] **1047**

SOVIET JOURNAL OF COMMUNICATIONS TECHNOLOGY & ELECTRONICS (US/8756-6648) [12274591] **2082**

SOVIET JOURNAL OF COMPUTER AND SYSTEMS SCIENCES (US/0882-4002) [11825947] 1249, **1221**

SOVIET JOURNAL OF CONTEMPORARY PHYSICS (US/8755-4585) [11347236] **4421**

SOVIET JOURNAL OF COORDINATION CHEMISTRY (US/0364-4626) [02474541] **1058**

SOVIET JOURNAL OF DEVELOPMENTAL BIOLOGY *See* RUSSIAN JOURNAL OF DEVELOPMENTAL BIOLOGY **472**

SOVIET JOURNAL OF ECOLOGY *See* RUSSIAN JOURNAL OF ECOLOGY **2220**

SOVIET JOURNAL OF ECOLOGY, THE (US/0096-7807) [00983152] **2221**

SOVIET JOURNAL OF GLASS PHYSICS AND CHEMISTRY, THE (US/0360-5043) [03188356] **1030**

SOVIET JOURNAL OF HEAVY MACHINERY (US/1052-6196) [22337892] **2129**

SOVIET JOURNAL OF LOW TEMPERATURE PHYSICS (US/0360-0335) [02246326] **4432**

SOVIET JOURNAL OF MARINE BIOLOGY *See* RUSSIAN JOURNAL OF MARINE BIOLOGY **557**

SOVIET JOURNAL OF MARINE BIOLOGY, THE (US/0145-1456) [02245169] **557**

SOVIET JOURNAL OF NMERICAL ANALYSIS AND MATHEMATICAL MODELLING *See* RUSSIAN JOURNAL OF NUMERICAL ANALYSIS AND MATHEMATICAL ANALYSIS **3532**

SOVIET JOURNAL OF NONDESTRUCTIVE TESTING *See* RUSSIAN JOURNAL OF NONDESTRUCTIVE TESTING **2128**

SOVIET JOURNAL OF NONDESTRUCTIVE TESTING, THE (US/0038-5492) [01766253] **2031**

SOVIET JOURNAL OF NUCLEAR PHYSICS (US/0038-5506) [01766254] **4451**

SOVIET JOURNAL OF OPTICAL TECHNOLOGY (US) [27827913] **4441**

SOVIET JOURNAL OF PARTICLES AND NUCLEI (US/0090-4759) [01785102] **4451**

SOVIET JOURNAL OF PLASMA PHYSICS (US/0360-0343) [02246325] **4421**

SOVIET JOURNAL OF PSYCHOLOGY (US/0891-2726) [14689060] **4619**

SOVIET JOURNAL OF QUANTUM ELECTRONICS (US/0049-1748) [00850979] **2082**

SOVIET JOURNAL OF SUPERHARD METALS *See* JOURNAL OF SUPERHARD MATERIALS **4006**

SOVIET JOURNAL ON CONCRETE AND REINFORCED CONCRETE (NE) **2031**

SOVIET JOURNAL ON STRUCTURAL MECHANICS AND DESIGN OF STRUCTURES (NE) [24904714] 2129, **2031**

SOVIET LAW & BUSINESS NEWS (US/1055-4580) [23185549] **3103**

SOVIET LAW AND GOVERNMENT (US/0038-5530) [01607989] **3057**

SOVIET LIFE *See* RUSSIAN LIFE **2522**

SOVIET LIGHTWAVE COMMUNICATIONS *CEASED.* (UK/0960-0884) [25182538] **4441**

SOVIET LITERATURE (RU) [05879455] **3353**

SOVIET MATERIALS SCIENCE (US/0038-5565) [01766257] **2108**

SOVIET MATERIALS SCIENCE REVIEWS *CEASED.* (US/0888-689X) [13690136] 4019, **2129**

SOVIET MATHEMATICS - DOKLADY (US/0197-6788) [05417745] **3536**

SOVIET MEDICAL REVIEWS. SECTION A, CARDIOLOGY REVIEWS *CEASED.* (SZ/0888-0697) [13460881] **3710**

SOVIET MEDICAL REVIEWS. SECTION B, PHYSICOCHEMICAL ASPECTS OF MEDICINE REVIEWS *CEASED.* (SZ/0887-2392) [13153052] **3898**

SOVIET MEDICAL REVIEWS. SECTION C, HEMATOLOGY REVIEWS *CEASED.* (SZ/0888-3920) [13562230] **3774**

SOVIET MEDICAL REVIEWS. SECTION D, IMMUNOLOGY REVIEWS *CEASED.* (SZ/0887-3488) [13189698] **3677**

SOVIET MEDICAL REVIEWS. SECTION E, VIROLOGY REVIEWS *CEASED.* (SZ/0887-3496) [13189674] **570**

SOVIET MEDICAL REVIEWS. SECTION F, ONCOLOGY REVIEWS *CEASED.* (SZ/0888-0700) [13460896] **3824**

SOVIET MEDICAL REVIEWS. SECTION G, NEUROPHARMACOLOGY REVIEWS *CEASED.* (SZ/0896-8306) [17303036] 3846, **4330**

SOVIET MEDICAL REVIEWS SUPPLEMENT SERIES. SECTION D, IMMUNOLOGY (SZ/0896-601X) [17211255] **3677**

SOVIET METEOROLOGY AND HYDROLOGY (US/0146-4108) [02624387] 1418, **1434**

SOVIET MICROELECTRONICS (US/0363-8529) [02551381] **2082**

SOVIET MINING SCIENCE (US/0038-5581) [01766259] **2151**

SOVIET MUSLIMS BRIEF *See* CENTRAL ASIA BRIEF **5042**

SOVIET NEUROLOGY & PSYCHIATRY (US/0038-559X) [01766260] 3937, **3846**

SOVIET OBSERVER (NEW YORK, N.Y.) *CEASED.* (US/1060-9474) [22299799] **2710**

SOVIET PANORAMA (CN/0380-0660) [02625037] **2710**

SOVIET PERSPECTIVES *CEASED.* (US/1055-1042) [23072632] **2710**

SOVIET PHYSICS-ACOUSTICS (US/0038-562X) [01766261] **4453**

SOVIET PHYSICS-CRYSTALLOGRAPHY (US/0038-5638) [01766262] **1033**

SOVIET PHYSICS-DOKLADY (US/0038-5689) [01909463] **4421**

SOVIET PHYSICS-JETP (US/0038-5646) [01766264] **4421**

SOVIET PHYSICS JOURNAL (US/0038-5697) [01766266] **4421**

SOVIET PHYSICS-LEBEDEV INSTITUTE REPORTS (US/0364-2321) [02619065] **4422**

SOVIET PHYSICS-SEMICONDUCTORS (US/0038-5700) [01766265] **4422**

SOVIET PHYSICS-SOLID STATE (US/0038-5654) [01642598] **4422**

SOVIET PHYSICS-TECHNICAL PHYSICS (US/0038-5662) [01911544] **4422**

SOVIET PHYSICS-USPEKHI (US/0038-5670) [01642564] **4422**

SOVIET PLANT PHYSIOLOGY (US/0038-5719) [06012510] **528**

SOVIET POWDER METALLURGY AND METAL CERAMICS (US/0038-5735) [07884223] **4019**

SOVIET PROGRESS IN CHEMISTRY *See* UKRAINIAN CHEMISTRY JOURNAL **994**

SOVIET PSYCHOLOGY *See* JOURNAL OF RUSSIAN AND EAST EUROPEAN PSYCHOLOGY **4601**

SOVIET RADIOCHEMISTRY (US/0038-576X) [01766271] **992**

SOVIET REVIEW (AT/1033-6257) 4496, **1522**

SOVIET REVIEW INDIA (II/0038-5786) [07468187] **2710**

SOVIET REVIEW (WHITE PLAINS), THE (US/0038-5794) [01766272] **2523**

SOVIET SCIENTIFIC REVIEWS. SECTION A, PHYSICS REVIEWS (SZ/0143-0394) [05460967] **4422**

SOVIET SCIENTIFIC REVIEWS. SECTION B, CHEMISTRY REVIEWS *See* CHEMISTRY REVIEWS **971**

SOVIET SCIENTIFIC REVIEWS. SECTION C, MATHEMATICAL PHYSICS REVIEWS (SZ/0143-0416) [06998984] **4422**

SOVIET SCIENTIFIC REVIEWS. SECTION D, PHYSICOCHEMICAL BIOLOGY REVIEWS *CEASED.* (SZ/0734-9351) [08828488] 473, **5159**

SOVIET SCIENTIFIC REVIEWS. SECTION E, ASTROPHYSICS AND SPACE PHYSICS REVIEWS (SZ/0143-0432) [06998794] **400**

SOVIET SCIENTIFIC REVIEWS. SECTION F, PHYSIOLOGY AND GENERAL BIOLOGY REVIEWS (SZ/0888-4803) [13613986] **473**

SOVIET SCIENTIFIC REVIEWS. SECTION G, GEOLOGY REVIEWS (SZ/0896-7571) [17283050] **1397**

SOVIET SCIENTIFIC REVIEWS SUPPLEMENT SERIES. ASTROPHYSICS AND SPACE PHYSICS REVIEWS (US/0275-7281) [07227748] **35**

SOVIET SCIENTIFIC REVIEWS SUPPLEMENT SERIES. PHYSICOCHEMICAL BIOLOGY (SZ/0742-4256) [10354697] **496**

SOVIET SCIENTIFIC REVIEWS SUPPLEMENT SERIES. PHYSIOLOGY AND GENERAL BIOLOGY (UK/1040-3361) [18384548] 473, **587**

SOVIET SHIPBUILDING (US/0094-9892) [01794394] **4183**

SOVIET SOCIOLOGY *See* SOCIOLOGICAL RESEARCH **5261**

SOVIET SOIL SCIENCE (US/0038-5832) [01587583] **188**

SOVIET SPORTS REVIEW *See* FITNESS AND SPORTS REVIEW INTERNATIONAL **1855**

SOVIET STATUTES & DECISIONS *See* STATUTES & DECISIONS **3059**

SOVIET STUDIES (UK/0038-5859) [01606740] **4547**

SOVIET STUDIES IN HISTORY (US/0038-5867) [01766275] **2710**

SOVIET STUDIES IN LITERATURE *See* RUSSIAN STUDIES IN LITERATURE **3432**

SOVIET STUDIES IN PHILOSOPHY (US/0038-5883) [01496316] **4361**

SOVIET SURFACE ENGINEERING AND APPLIED ELECTROCHEMISTRY *See* SURFACE ENGINEERING AND APPLIED ELECTROCHEMISTRY **1997**

SOVIET SURFACE ENGINEERING & APPLIED ELECTROCHEMISTRY (US/8756-7008) [12190451] 1997, **1035**

SOVIET TECHNICAL PHYSICS LETTERS (US/0360-120X) [02247060] **4422**

SOVIET TECHNOLOGY ALERT (UK/0953-4016) [I09534016] **5159**

SOVIET TECHNOLOGY ALERT *See* ADVANCED RUSSIAN TECHNOLOGIES **5081**

SOVIET TECHNOLOGY DIGEST (UK) [20316158] **5159**

SOVIET TECHNOLOGY REVIEWS. SECTION A, ENERGY REVIEWS *CEASED.* (SZ/0275-7893) [07219597] 2129, **1957**

SOVIET TECHNOLOGY REVIEWS. SECTION B, THERMAL PHYSICS REVIEWS *CEASED.* (UK/0892-6808) [15234523] **4432**

SOVIET TECHNOLOGY REVIEWS. SECTION C, WELDING AND SURFACING REVIEWS (SZ/1040-7073) [18515759] **4027**

SOVIET UNION *See* SOVIET AND POST-SOVIET REVIEW, THE **4496**

SOVIET UNION AND EASTERN EUROPE *See* RUSSIA, EURASIAN STATES, AND EASTERN EUROPE **2508**

SOVIET UNION AND THE MIDDLE EAST *See* COMMONWEALTH OF INDEPENDENT STATES AND THE MIDDLE EAST **4518**

SOVIET UNION. GLAVNOE UPRAVLENIE GEODEZII I KARTOGRAFII *See* ZHELEZNYE DOROGI SSSR **5438**

SOVIET UNION. MINISTERSTVO FINANSOV. BIUDZHETNOE UPRAVLENIE *See* GOSUDARSTVENNYI BIUDZHET SSSR / MINISTERSTVO FINANSOV SSSR, BIUDZHETNOE UPRAVLENIE **1493**

SOVIET UNION. MINISTERSTVO VYSSHEGO I SPEDNEGO SPETSIALNOGO OBRAZOVANIIA. OBRAZOVANIIA *See* RADIOFIZIKA AND QUANTUM ELECTRONICS **4441**

SOVIET UNION. MINISTERSTVO VYSSHEGO I SREDNEGO SPETSIALNOGO OBRAZOVANIIA. IZVESTIIA VYSSHIKH UCHEBNYKH ZAVEDENII. MATEMATIKA. ENGLISH. SOVIET MATHEMATICS See RUSSIAN MATHEMATICS **3532**

SOVIET UNION. MINISTERSTVO VYSSHEGO OBRAZOVANI I A See NAUCHNYE DOKLADY VYSSHEI SHKOLY. BIOLOGICHESKIE NAUKI **466**

SOVIET UNION. POSOLSTVO (ITALY). UFFICIO STAMPA See URSS OGGI **2632**

SOVIET UNION. VERKHOVNYI SOVET See MATERIALY ... VERKHOVNOGO SOVETA SSSR **4481**

SOVIET UPDATE (US/1057-1531) [23958848] **2710**

SOVIET WEEKLY CEASED. (UK) [02267988] **2523**

SOVREMENNAIA KHUDOZHESTVENNAIA LITERATURA ZA RUBEZHOM (RU) [02081072] **1069**

SOVREMENNAIA LITERATURA ZA RUBEZHOM (RU/0584-5750) [04902764] **3438**

SOVREMENNAIA VYSSHAIA SHKOLA CEASED. (CU) [03522948] **1847**

SOVREMENNAIA VYSSHAIA SHKOLA (PL) [02246274] **1847**

SOVREMENNAIA ZARUBEZHNAIA FILOSOFIIA I SOTSIOLOGIIA (RU) [03458632] **4361**

SOVREMENNYE PROBLEMY ORGANICESKOJ HIMII (RU/0371-2192) [10866887] **1047**

SOWER, THE (UK/0049-1772) [01645566] **4999**

SOWJETSTUDIEN (GW/0038-5999) [04909009] **2710**

SOWJETUNION (MUNCHEN) (GW/0724-5823) [03127867] **2710**

SOWO LUDU (PL/0137-9275) [l01379275] **5808**

SOWO PODLASIA (PL/0208-4163) [l02084163] **2523**

SOWO POLSKIE (PL/0137-9291) [l01379291] **5808**

SOYA BLUEBOOK (US/0275-4509) [06591987] **188**

●SOYA WORLD (US/1041-0120) [18609891] **136**

SOYABEAN ABSTRACTS (UK/0141-0172) [03998835] **136, 156**

SOYBEAN DIGEST (US/0038-6014) [01604181] **188**

SOYBEAN GENETICS NEWSLETTER (US/1054-2116) [01600741] **188**

SOYBEAN RUST NEWSLETTER (CH/0258-3097) [11093547] 2358, **528**

SOYE (KO) [05432211] **382**

SOYFOODS (US/8755-9188) [07016493] **4199**

SOYFOODS INDUSTRY AND MARKET, DIRECTORY AND DATABOOK, THE (US/8755-1683) [10271969] **2358**

SOZEI TO ZAISEI NO ARAMASHI (JA) [02244602] **4748**

SOZEIHO KENKYU (JA) [02245348] **4748**

SOZIAL- UND PRAEVENTIVMEDIZIN (SZ/0303-8408) [01224881] **4803**

SOZIALANTHROPOLOGISCHE ARBEITSPAPIERE / FU BERLIN, INSTITUT FUER ETHNOLOGIE, SCHWERPUNKT SOZIALANTHROPOLOGIE (GW/0932-5476) [19006309] **245**

SOZIALDEMOKRATISCHE PARTEI DEUTSCHLANDS See JAHRBUCH DER SOZIALDEMOKRATISCHEN PARTEI DEUTSCHLANDS **4658**

SOZIALE ARBEIT (GW/0490-1606) [02179500] **5310**

SOZIALE BEWEGUNGEN : ANALYSE UND DOKUMENTATION DES IMSF (GW) [10357020] 5223, **1711**

SOZIALE SICHERHEIT (KOLN) (GW/0490-1630) [05742049] **5310**

SOZIALE SICHERHEIT (WIEN) (AU/0038-6065) [06364849] **5310**

SOZIALE WELT (GW/0038-6073) [01766284] **5223**

SOZIALER FORTSCHRITT (BERLIN) (GW/0038-609X) [01966595] **5223**

SOZIALISTISCHES MUSIKSCHAFFEN DER DEUTSCHEN DEMOKRATISCHEN REPUBLIK (GW) [08374857] **4154**

SOZIALLEISTUNGEN. REIHE 1: VERSICHERTE IN DER KRANKEN- UND RENTENVERSICHERUNG (GW/0173-394X) [04612667] 2894, **5310**

SOZIALLEISTUNGEN. REIHE 5.1, SCHWERBEHINDERTE / HERAUSGEBER, STATISTISCHES BUNDESAMT WIESBADEN (GW) [17240267] **4394**

SOZIALPADAGOGIK (GW) [07268122] **5263**

SOZIALPADAGOGISCHE BLATTER (GW) [05587807] **1784**

SOZIALPAEDIATRIE IN PRAXIS UND KLINIK (GW/0171-9327) [06322821] **3911**

SOZIALPAEDIATRIE UND KINDERAERZTLICHE PRAXIS (GW) **3911**

SOZIALPAEDIATRIES IN PRAXIS UND KLINIK See SOZIALPAEDIATRIE UND KINDERAERZTLICHE PRAXIS **3911**

SOZIALPOLITIK UND ARBEITSRECHT (AU) [06335180] **3154**

SOZIALPOLITISCHE SCHRIFTEN (GW/0584-5998) [03024603] **5223**

SOZIALVERSICHERUNGS-BERATER (GW/0936-9198) [l09369198] **5310**

SOZIALWISSENSCHAFTLICHE ABHANDLUNGEN DER GORRES-GESELLSCHAFT (GW) [17961163] **5223**

SOZIALWISSENSCHAFTLICHE ARBEITSMARKTFORSCHUNG (GW) [17570642] **1711**

SOZIALWISSENSCHAFTLICHE INFORMATIONEN (GW) [16840839] **5263**

SOZIALWISSENSCHAFTLICHER FACHINFORMATIONSDIENST. MIGRATION UND ETHNISCHE MINDERHEITEN : SOFID / INFORMATIONSZENTRUM SOZIALWISSENSCHAFTEN (GW/0938-6033) [23130229] **1921**

SOZIALWISSENSCHAFTLICHER FACHINFORMATIONSDIENST. SOZIALPOLITIK / INFORMATIONSZENTRUM SOZIALWISSENSCHAFTEN (GW/0938-6076) [23099170] **5263**

SOZIOLOGENKORRESPONDENZ (GW/0172-4797) [01724797] **5263**

SOZIOLOGIE CEASED. (GW/0340-918X) [06767006] **5263**

SOZIOLOGISCHE ABHANDLUNGEN (GW/0584-6048) [02758071] **5263**

SOZIOLOGISCHE REVUE (GW/0343-4109) [05000812] **5263**

SOZOKUZEIHO ENSHU, RIRON TO KEISAN (JA) [03610230] **3119**

SOZVEZDIE (RU) [01799388] **3438**

SP QUEBEC (CN/0822-5702) [10220868] **3846**

SPA AND SAUNA TRADE JOURNAL. BUYERS GUIDE (US) [08748658] **713**

SPAA PROVINCIAL NEWSLETTER (CN/1180-1913) [24368307] **1885**

SPAB NEWSLETTER / SOCIETY OF PSYCHOLOGISTS IN ADDICTIVE BEHAVIORS (US) [23274440] **4619**

SPACE (UK) [04850819] **3438**

SPACE 90 (US) **35**

●SPACE 2000 (US/1064-2064) [26230672] **1291**

SPACE ABSTRACTS ON DISKETTE (US) 35, **41**

SPACE ABSTRACTS ON MICROFICHE (US) 35, **41**

SPACE AGE NEWS (US/0091-0554) [01786355] **35**

SPACE AGE TIMES (US/0738-0968) [09519881] **35**

SPACE AND SECURITY NEWS (US/1071-2569) [28599313] **35**

●SPACE AVAILABLE (US/1068-0233) [27403654] **35**

SPACE (BEACONSFIELD) (UK/0267-954X) [12303505] **35**

SPACE BUSINESS NEWS (US/0738-9884) [09674313] **35**

SPACE CALENDAR (US/0741-1731) [09208762] **35**

SPACE COMMERCE (SZ/1043-934X) [19609582] **35**

SPACE COMMERCE BULLETIN See SPACE COMMERCE WEEK **35**

SPACE COMMERCE WEEK (US) **35**

SPACE COMMUNICATIONS (NE/0924-8625) [21022805] **1164**

SPACE ENTERPRISE TODAY (US/0743-3069) [10584044] **35**

SPACE ENTREPRENEURS DIRECTORY (US/0884-2337) [12359339] **1627**

SPACE EXPLORATION TECHNOLOGY (US/1052-3383) [22252884] **35**

SPACE FAX DAILY (US/1048-2652) [20881140] **36**

●SPACE FAX DAILY (GLOBAL ED.) (US/1074-8881) [29870897] **36**

SPACE IN JAPAN (JA) [01783734] **36**

SPACE INFORMATION REVIEW See SPACE ABSTRACTS ON MICROFICHE **41**

SPACE INSURANCE REPORT (UK/0957-0063) [l09570063] **2894**

SPACE : JOURNAL OF SCHOOL OF PLANNING AND ARCHITECTURE, NEW DELHI (II/0970-0501) [21509344] **309**

SPACE LETTER (US) **36**

SPACE NEWS (SPRINGFIELD, VA.) (US/1046-6940) [20496753] **36**

SPACE NUCLEAR POWER SYSTEMS (US/1041-2824) [17389524] **36**

SPACE POLICY (UK/0265-9646) [11742201] **36**

SPACE POWER (US/0883-6272) [12183760] **1958**

SPACE PRESS (US/0733-8678) [08672862] **36**

SPACE R & D ALERT (US/0743-8982) [10701966] **36**

SPACE RESEARCH IN BULGARIA (BU/0204-9104) [06103959] **400**

SPACE REVIEW (UK) **36**

SPACE SATELLITE HANDBOOK (US) [13749397] 1122, **36**

SPACE SCIENCE REVIEWS (NE/0038-6308) [01607933] **400**

SPACE SCIENCE TEXT SERIES (US/0195-4253) [05432701] **400**

●SPACE SHUTTLE DATABASE REPORT (US/1061-8686) [25484869] **36**

●SPACE STATION FREEDOM NEWS (US/1061-5350) [25344956] 5159, **36**

SPACE STATION NEWS (US/0895-8947) [16851116] **36**

SPACE STATISTICS REVIEW (UK) **36**

SPACE SYSTEMS FORECAST (US) **4057**

SPACE TECHNOLOGY (OXFORD) (UK/0892-9270) [15294716] **36**

SPACE TELESCOPE SCIENCE INSTITUTE SYMPOSIUM SERIES (UK) [18568344] **400**

SPACE TIMES (US) [15495928] **36**

SPACE TIMES (SEATTLE, WASH.) (US/1062-8762) [25776196] **36**

SPACE TODAY SUSPENDED. (US/0889-6054) [13990152] 5159, **400**

SPACE TRANSPORTATION SYSTEM USER HANDBOOK (US) [03454560] **36**

SPACE TRAVEL MAGAZINE (CN/0709-7999) [06082727] **36**

SPACE VOLUME (US/0561-3078) [06525035] **36**

SPACE YEAR (US/1058-2576) [22979546] **36**

SPACEBUSINESS CONFERENCE DIGEST, THE (US/8756-517X) [11589594] **1627**

SPAFOTO (SP) [01792788] **4377**

SPAIN See BOLETIN OFICIAL DEL ESTADO : GACETA DE MADRID **2942**

SPAIN See REGLAMENTACION DEL SECTOR LABORAL **3153**

SPAIN (UK) [02555546] **5491**

SPAIN AND MOROCCO ON $10 AND $15 A DAY (US) [03816517] **5491**

SPAIN. CENTRO DE ESTUDIOS HIDROGRAFICOS See PUBLICACIONES **1417**

SPAIN. CONSEJO SUPERIOR DE DEPORTES See BOLETIN DEL CONSEJO SUPERIOR DE DEPORTES **1855**

SPAIN. CORTES GENERALES See BOLETIN DE LEGISLACION DE LAS COMUNIDADES AUTONOMAS : BCA **4633**

SPAIN. DIRECCION GENERAL DE AGRICULTURA, SECCION 7A See CENSO DE MAQUINARIA AGRICOLA **158**

SPAIN. DIRECCION GENERAL DE EMPRESAS Y ACTIVIDADES TURISTICAS See VACACIONES EN CASAS DE LABRANZAS **2809**

SPAIN. DIRECCION GENERAL DEL TURISMO. HOTELES DE ESPANA See GUIA DE HOTELES : ESPANA **2806**

SPAIN. INSPECCION GENERAL DE MUSEOS ARQUELOGICOS See MEMORIAS DE LOS MUSEOS ARQUEOLOGICOS PROVINCIALES. (EXTRACTOS) **4091**

SPAIN. INSTITUTO NACIONAL DE ESTADISTICA See ESTADISTICA DEL SUICIDIO EN ESPANA **5327**

SPAIN. INSTITUTO NACIONAL DE ESTADISTICA See ESPANA, PANORAMICA SOCIAL **5244**

SPAIN. INSTITUTO NACIONAL DE ESTADISTICA See ESTADISTICAS JUDICIALES DE ESPANA **3080**

SPAIN. MINISTERIO DE ASUNTOS EXTERIORES See LISTA DEL CUERPO DIPLOMATICO **3132**

SPAIN. MINISTERIO DE DEFENSA See BOLETIN OFICIAL DEL MINISTERIO DE DEFENSA **4038**

SPAIN. MINISTERIO DE ECONOMIA Y HACIENDA See BOLETIN OFICIAL DEL MINISTERIO DE ECONOMIA Y HACIENDA **4633**

SPAIN — Alphabetical Title Index

SPAIN. MINISTERIO DE EDUCACION. BOLETIN OFICIAL, MINISTERIO DE EDUCACION. ACTOS ADMINISTRATIVOS See BOLETIN OFICIAL, MINISTERIO DE EDUCACION Y CIENCIA. ACTOS ADMINISTRATIVOS **2942**

SPAIN. MINISTERIO DE EDUCACION Y CIENCIA See BOLETIN OFICIAL, MINISTERIO DE EDUCACION Y CIENCIA. ACTOS ADMINISTRATIVOS **2942**

SPAIN. MINISTERIO DE EDUCACION Y CIENCIA. SECRETARIA GENERAL TECNICA See COURSES FOR FOREIGNERS IN SPAIN **3275**

SPAIN. MINISTERIO DE HACIENDA. SECRETARIA GENERAL TECNICA See PRESUPUESTO Y LA ECONOMIA ESPANOLA, EL **1579**

SPAIN. MINISTERIO DE INDUSTRIA. SECRETARIA GENERAL TECNICA See COYUNTURA INDUSTRIAL REGIONAL (SPAIN) **1603**

SPAIN. MINISTERIO DE LA VIVIENDA See BOLETIN DE JURISPRUDENCIA Y RESOLUCIONES ADMINISTRATIVAS SOBRE URBANISMO Y VIVIENDA **2942**

SPAIN. MINISTERIO DE SANIDAD Y CONSUMO See BOLETIN OFICIAL DEL MINISTERIO DE SANIDAD Y CONSUMO **1293**

SPAIN. MINISTERIO DE TRABAJO See ORDENANZAS LABORALES PARA LA INDUSTRIA Y COMERCIO : SEGURIDAD E HIGIENE EN EL TRABAJO, PLAN NACIONAL Y ORDENANZA GENERAL **2867**

SPAIN. MINISTERIO DE TRABAJO Y SEGURIDAD SOCIAL See BOLETIN DEL MINISTERIO DE TRABAJO Y SEGURIDAD SOCIAL **3144**

SPAIN. TRIBUNAL SUPREMO. SECRETARIA TECNICA See SENTENCIAS EN APELACION DE LAS AUDIENCIAS PROVINCIALES EN MATERIA CIVIL Y PENAL **3048**

●SPALDING BOOK OF RULES AND ... SPORTS ALMANAC (US/1065-4763) [26612494] **4920**

SPAN (NZ/0313-1459) [05298819] 3322, **3439**

SPAN (CHICAGO, ILL.) (US/0584-8016) [05095135] 4278, **914**

SPANG ROBINSON REPORT ON HIGH PERFORMANCE COMPUTING *CEASED.* (US/1053-1661) [22502096] **1203**

SPANG ROBINSON REPORT ON INTELLIGENT SYSTEMS, THE *CEASED.* (US/1060-0388) [24705832] **1217**

SPANIEN, EINFUERRGLOBALKONTINGENTE / BUNDESSTELLE FUER AUSSENHANDELSINFORMATION (GW) [10931403] **851**

SPANIEN, ENERGIEWIRTSCHAFT / BUNDESSTELLE FUER AUSSENHANDELSINFORMATION (GW) [10931173] **1958**

SPANIEN, FORSCHUNGSPOLITIK UND FORSCHUNGSPRAXIS / BUNDESSTELLE FUER AUSSENHANDELSINFORMATION (GW) [11454185] **1584**

SPANIEN, LAND- UND FORSTWIRTSCHAFT, FISCHEREI / BUNDESSTELLE FUER AUSSENHANDELSINFORMATION (GW) [11406672] 2313, 2395, **136**

SPANIEN, LANDWIRTSCHAFT / BUNDESSTELLE FUR AUSSENHANDELSINFORMATION (GW) [10931034] **136**

SPANIEN UND KANARISCHE INSELN, WIRTSCHAFT IN ZAHLEN UND WIRTSCHAFTSDOKUMENTATION / BUNDESSTELLE FUER AUSSENHANDELSINFORMATION (GW) [07787885] **1585**

SPANISCHE FORSCHUNGEN DER GORRES-GESELLSCHAFT. REIHE 2 (GW) [06936145] **2710**

SPANISH ECONOMIC NEWS SERVICE (SP) [02450758] **1522**

SPANISH FORK PRESS, THE (US/0892-435X) [12653543] **5757**

SPANISH-LANGUAGE PSYCHOLOGY (NE/0167-5311) [07495410] **4619**

SPANISH REAL ESTATE MAGAZINE (SP) **4847**

SPANISH STUDIES (UK) [07541597] 2854, **2710**

SPANISH TODAY *SUSPENDED.* (US/0049-1802) [02251976] **3439**

SPANNER (UK) [02239990] 3471, **365**

SPANZINE (VANCOUVER) (CN/1185-8834) [25423257] **4569**

SPARE RIB *CEASED.* (UK/0306-7971) [05237209] **5566**

SPARK (II) [07705525] **3471**

SPARK (CINCINNATI, OHIO) *CEASED.* (US/1057-5227) [24047770] **1069**

SPARK (NEW YORK. 1971) (US/0361-7866) [01966641] **1997**

SPARKASSE (GW/0038-6561) [07299117] **812**

SPARKS QUARTERLY, THE (US/0561-5445) [01604114] **2473**

SPARROW (US/1062-0478) [24336916] **3471**

SPARTA HERALD (SPARTA, WIS. : 1869) (US) [11800370] **5770**

SPARTACIST (US/0038-6596) [05425293] **4547**

SPARTACIST CANADA (CN/0229-5415) [08078650] **4547**

SPARTAN, THE (US/0147-3441) [03145504] 4057, **4866**

SPARTANBURG HERALD-JOURNAL (US/0740-4743) [09951368] **5743**

SPASTICS NEWS See DISABILITY NOW **4387**

SPATIAL VISION (NE/0169-1015) [13187095] **3536**

SPATZENPOST (AU) **1069**

SPAULDING & SLYE REPORT. GREATER BOSTON MARKET (BOSTON, MASS. : 1992) See SPAULDING & SLYE REPORT. GREATER BOSTON, THE **4847**

●SPAULDING & SLYE REPORT. GREATER BOSTON, THE (US/1063-9098) [26180855] **4847**

SPAULDING & SLYE REPORT. WASHINGTON, D.C. MARKET See SPAULDING & SLYE REPORT. WASHINGTON, D.C, THE **4847**

●SPAULDING & SLYE REPORT. WASHINGTON, D.C, THE (US/1063-9101) [26180902] **4847**

SPAZIO CASA (IT) **2907**

SPAZIO E SOCIETA (IT/0392-4947) [03928249] **309**

SPAZIO IMPRESA *CEASED.* (IT/0394-3127) [24692210] **1711**

SPAZIO SPORT (IT) **4920**

SPAZIO UMANO, LO (IT/0394-4816) [03944816] **331**

SPBR REVIEW (US) [06306414] **4705**

SPC. SOAP, PERFUMERY, AND COSMETICS (UK/0037-749X) [02430733] **405**

SPE COMPUTER APPLICATIONS (US/1064-9778) [19938279] **4278**

●SPE DRILLING AND COMPLETIONS (US/1064-6671) [26368701] **4278**

SPE DRILLING ENGINEERING (US/0885-9744) [12788115] **4278**

SPE FORMATION EVALUATION (US/0885-923X) [12788207] **4279**

SPE MEMBERSHIP DIRECTORY (US/1059-4507) [24595411] **4279**

SPE MONOGRAPH SERIES (US/0882-1100) [11965675] **1847**

●SPE PRODUCTION AND FACILITIES (US/1064-668X) [26368945] **4279**

SPE PRODUCTION ENGINEERING (US/0885-9221) [12764954] **4279**

SPE PRODUCTION ENGINEERING See SPE PRODUCTION AND FACILITIES **4279**

SPE RESERVOIR ENGINEERING (US/0885-9248) [12788379] **4279**

SPE : SOCIETY OF PETROLEUM ENGINEERS OF AIME (US/0560-642X) [07300710] **4279**

SPEAK OUT (RH) **5566**

SPEAK OUT FOR CHILDREN (US/1042-3559) [19032501] **2286**

SPEAK UP *CEASED.* (CN/0383-9370) [03222657] **2762**

SPEAK UP MILANO (IT/1120-4583) [I11204583] **3322**

SPEAK UP PARIS (FR/0982-3425) [I09823425] **3322**

SPEAKEASY (FR/0221-833X) [I0221833X] **3353**

SPEAKER AND GAVEL (US/0584-8164) [01766315] **3322**

SPEAKER BUILDER (US/0199-7920) [06159497] **5319**

SPEAKER REPORT, THE (US/0897-4349) [17527624] **3439**

SPEAKERS (US/0278-1387) [07708614] **5319**

SPEAKER'S DIGEST *CEASED.* (US/0883-8607) [12259681] **1122**

SPEAKER'S IDEA FILE (US) **1122**

SPEAKERS' OUTLINES, FEDERAL PRACTICE AND PROCEDURE (US) [08000257] **3091**

SPEAKIN' OUT NEWS (US) [21026715] **2273**

SPEAQ-OUT (CN/0229-6535) [08078556] **3323**

SPEAR (TORONTO) (CN/0315-0208) [02702254] **2273**

SPEARHEAD (UK) [05425302] **4535**

SPEARMAN REPORTER, THE (US) [14266213] **5754**

SPEARS AND ASSOCIATES See SPEARS REPORT, PRODUCTION **4279**

SPEARS AND ASSOCIATES See SPEARS REPORT, DRILLING **4279**

SPEARS REPORT, DRILLING (US/0163-1969) [04303889] **4279**

SPEARS REPORT, PRODUCTION (US/0193-2438) [05138981] **4279**

SPEARVILLE NEWS (SPEARVILLE, KAN. : 1899) (US) [11239451] **5678**

SPEC CHECK. BRITISH COLUMBIA & YUKON REPORT (CN/1184-2113) [23686636] **628**

SPEC CHECK. ONTARIO REPORT (CN/1184-2091) [23686638] **628**

SPEC CHECK. PRAIRIE & TERRITORIES REPORT (CN/1184-2105) [23686637] **628**

SPEC CHECK. QUEBEC & ATLANTIC REPORT (CN/1184-2083) [23686639] **628**

SPEC-COM (US/0883-2560) [12113815] **1139**

SPEC (NEW CARLISLE) (CN/0226-9120) [08071452] **5795**

SPEC NEWSLETTER (US/1068-557X) [26662905] **2082**

SPECCHECK (SAN JOSE, CALIF.) *CEASED.* (US) [12928679] **4214**

SPECCHIO ECONOMICO (IT) **1522**

SPECIAL, DOS See DOS-WIN SPECIAL **1183**

SPECIAL ASPECTS OF EDUCATION (US/0731-8413) [08261071] **1885**

SPECIAL BIBLIOGRAPHIES (ROCKVILLE) (US/0095-0572) [01108185] **1350**

SPECIAL BIBLIOGRAPHY (CN) [11652335] **156**

SPECIAL BIBLIOGRAPHY. PLASMA PHYSICS *CEASED.* (GW) [11092954] **4422**

SPECIAL BROADCASTING SERVICE (AUSTRALIA) See ETHNIC BROADCASTING IN AUSTRALIA **1132**

SPECIAL BULLETIN / MISSISSIPPI AGRICULTURAL AND FORESTRY EXPERIMENT STATION (US/1057-1663) [14283453] **136**

SPECIAL BULLETIN - MUNICIPAL FINANCE OFFICERS ASSOCIATION OF THE UNITED STATES AND CANADA (US/0196-9161) [04289587] **4748**

SPECIAL BULLETIN OF THE COLLEGE OF AGRICULTURE, UTSUNOMIYA UNIVERSITY (JA/0566-4683) [01768919] **136**

SPECIAL BULLETIN - PENNSYLVANIA. BUREAU OF TOPOGRAPHIC AND GEOLOGIC SURVEY (US/0734-6247) [01636466] **1397**

SPECIAL BULLETIN - THEATRE CANADA (CN/0703-5640) [04079812] **5368**

SPECIAL BULLETIN - VERMONT GEOLOGICAL SURVEY (US/0506-7553) [05105637] **1397**

SPECIAL CARE IN DENTISTRY (US/0275-1879) [07098243] **1335**

SPECIAL CHILDREN (BIRMINGHAM) (UK/0951-6875) [I09516875] **1885**

SPECIAL CIRCULAR - OHIO AGRICULTURAL EXPERIMENT STATION See SPECIAL CIRCULAR - OHIO AGRICULTURAL RESEARCH AND DEVELOPMENT CENTER **136**

SPECIAL CIRCULAR - OHIO AGRICULTURAL RESEARCH AND DEVELOPMENT CENTER (US/0736-8003) [05373918] **136**

SPECIAL CONNECTIONS NEWSLETTER (CN) **1847**

SPECIAL COURT NEWS (US/0275-2913) [06680005] **3143**

SPECIAL DATA ISSUE / ICMA (US) [15681827] **4686**

SPECIAL DELIVERY (WINNIPEG) (CN/0831-1994) [16207467] **3250**

SPECIAL EDITION (US) **1885**

SPECIAL EDUCATION AND THE HANDICAPPED (US/8756-3746) [12353530] 1885, **3057**

SPECIAL EDUCATION ASSOCIATION (B.C.) See NEWSLETTER - SPECIAL EDUCATION ASSOCIATION **1882**

SPECIAL EDUCATION BULLETIN BRISBANE (AT/0313-6728) [I03136728] **1885**

SPECIAL EDUCATION LAW UPDATE (US) 1885, **3057**

SPECIAL EDUCATION LEADERSHIP *CEASED.* (US/0896-7784) [17287180] **1885**

SPECIAL EDUCATION PROGRAMS/SERVICES (US/0099-0302) [02243240] **1885**

●SPECIAL EDUCATION REPORT: THE INDEPENDENT BI-WEEKLY NEWS SERVICE ON LEGISLATION, REGULATION AND FUNDING OF PROGRAMS FOR CHILDREN AND YOUTHS WITH DISABILITIES (US) [26058006] **4394**

SPECIAL EDUCATION, TEACHER (US/1049-2828) [21191989] **1885**

SPECIAL EDUCATIONAL NEEDS ABSTRACTS (UK/0954-0822) [20423360] **1885**, **1797**

SPECIAL EDUCATOR ... DESK BOOK, THE (US) [26297983] **1885**, **3057**

SPECIAL EDUCATOR, THE (US/1047-1618) [12719167] **1885**

SPECIAL EFFECTS *SUSPENDED.* (US/1045-8751) [20277135] **4078**

SPECIAL EFFECTS & STUNTS GUIDE (US/1045-0750) [20010950] **4078**

SPECIAL ENROLLMENT EXAMINATION. QUESTIONS AND ANSWERS (US) [08543470] **4748**

SPECIAL ENVIRONMENTAL REPORT - WORLD METEOROLOGICAL ORGANIZATION (SZ/0302-9328) [01792841] **1434**

SPECIAL EVENTS (US/0890-281X) [14192983] **2809**

●SPECIAL EVENTS NEWS (US/1066-1417) [26864466] 958, **2358**

SPECIAL FISHERIES REPORT - STATE OF ILLINOIS (US/0445-3042) [01331498] **2313**

SPECIAL GROUND-WATER REPORT (LITTLE ROCK) (US/0571-026X) [01146636] **5539**

SPECIAL-INTEREST AUTOS (US/0049-1845) [03266853] 2778, **5425**

SPECIAL INTEREST REPORT / THE AMERICAN COUNCIL FOR JUDAISM (US/0740-8528) [01479717] **5053**

SPECIAL ISSUES (CN/0843-7289) [21485647] **3250**

SPECIAL ISSUES (US/1043-6863) [19462097] **425**

●SPECIAL ISSUES IN GEOSCIENCE (US/1062-1407) [25532430] **1360**

SPECIAL LABOUR FORCE *See* SPECIAL LABOUR FORCE REPORT / REPUBLIC OF TRINIDAD & TOBAGO, CENTRAL STATISTICAL OFFICE **1711**

SPECIAL LABOUR FORCE REPORT / REPUBLIC OF TRINIDAD & TOBAGO, CENTRAL STATISTICAL OFFICE (TR) [20075231] **1711**

SPECIAL LAWS ENACTED BY THE REGULAR SESSION OF THE LEGISLATIVE ASSEMBLY, THE (US) [06068923] **3058**

SPECIAL LECTURES OF THE LAW SOCIETY OF UPPER CANADA (CN/0316-5310) [01755620] **3058**

SPECIAL LIBRARIES ASSOCIATION. BOSTON CHAPTER *See* NEWS BULLETIN - SPECIAL LIBRARIES ASSOCIATION, BOSTON CHAPTER **3234**

SPECIAL LIBRARIES ASSOCIATION. EASTERN CANADA CHAPTER *See* BULLETIN - SPECIAL LIBRARIES ASSOCIATION, EASTERN CANADA CHAPTER **3198**

SPECIAL LIBRARIES ASSOCIATION. EDUCATION DIVISION *See* BULLETIN - SPECIAL LIBRARIES ASSOCIATION. EDUCATION DIVISION **3198**

SPECIAL LIBRARIES ASSOCIATION. GEOGRAPHY AND MAP DIVISION *See* BULLETIN - SPECIAL LIBRARIES ASSOCIATION. GEOGRAPHY AND MAP DIVISION **2557**

SPECIAL LIBRARIES ASSOCIATION. NORTH CAROLINA CHAPTER *See* BULLETIN - SPECIAL LIBRARIES ASSOCIATION, NORTH CAROLINA CHAPTER **3198**

SPECIAL LIBRARIES ASSOCIATION. RIO GRANDE CHAPTER *See* RIO GRANDE CHAPTER BULLETIN **3247**

SPECIAL LIBRARIES ASSOCIATION. SAN FRANCISCO BAY REGION CHAPTER *See* BULLETIN - SPECIAL LIBRARIES ASSOCIATION. SAN FRANCISCO BAY REGION CHAPTER **3199**

SPECIAL LIBRARIES ASSOCIATION. VIRGINIA CHAPTER *See* VASLA **3255**

SPECIAL LIBRARIES IN QUEENSLAND (AT) [19532135] **3250**

SPECIAL LIBRARIES IN THE EDMONTON AREA (1981) (CN/0711-1770) [11278752] **3250**

SPECIAL MANAGEMENT BULLETIN (US/0094-7180) [01795089] **812**

SPECIAL MANPOWER RESEARCH REPORT (US) [04943002] **1711**

SPECIAL MAP / GEOLOGICAL SURVEY OF ALABAMA, ENERGY RESOURCES DIVISION (US/1058-2215) [22915916] **1397**

SPECIAL NEGO (CN/0714-7430) [09448560] **1711**

SPECIAL NOTICE - ONTARIO MUNICIPAL EMPLOYEES RETIREMENT BOARD (CN/1187-7316) [25608109] **4705**

SPECIAL PAPER - GEOLOGICAL SOCIETY OF AMERICA (US/0072-1077) [01570696] **1397**

SPECIAL PAPER - JOINT FAO/WHO/OAU REGIONAL FOOD AND NUTRITION COMMISSION FOR AFRICA (GH/0378-2239) [02490506] 4199, **2358**

SPECIAL PAPER (NIHON GINKO. CHOSA TOKEIKYOKU) (JA) [10271572] **1522**

SPECIAL PAPER (NIHON GINKO. CHOSA TOKEIKYOKU) *See* BANK OF JAPAN QUARTERLY BULLETIN **775**

SPECIAL PAPERS IN INTERNATIONAL ECONOMICS (US/0081-3559) [01762865] **1640**

SPECIAL PAPERS IN PALEONTOLOGY (UK/0038-6804) [02450768] **4231**

SPECIAL PROGRAMME OF RESEARCH, DEVELOPMENT, AND RESEARCH TRAINING IN HUMAN REPRODUCTION (WORLD HEALTH ORGANIZATION) *See* RESEARCH IN HUMAN REPRODUCTION / WHO SPECIAL PROGRAMME OF RESEARCH, DEVELOPMENT, AND RESEARCH TRAINING IN HUMAN REPRODUCTION **591**

SPECIAL PROGRAMME OF RESEARCH, DEVELOPMENT, AND RESEARCH TRAINING IN HUMAN REPRODUCTION (WORLD HEALTH ORGANIZATION) *See* BIENNIAL REPORT / SPECIAL PROGRAMME OF RESEARCH, DEVELOPMENT AND RESEARCH TRAINING IN HUMAN REPRODUCTION **588**

SPECIAL PUBLICATION - ACADEMY OF NATURAL SCIENCES OF PHILADELPHIA (US/0097-3254) [01460717] **1360**

SPECIAL PUBLICATION - AGRICULTURAL RESEARCH ORGANIZATION (IS/0334-2484) [11960047] **137**

SPECIAL PUBLICATION - AGRICULTURAL RESEARCH ORGANIZATION, THE VOLCANI CENTER (IS/0334-2484) [02649310] **137**

SPECIAL PUBLICATION / AGRONOMY SOCIETY OF NEW ZEALAND (NZ/0111-9184) [09997855] **137**

SPECIAL PUBLICATION - AMERICAN FISHERIES SOCIETY (US/0097-0638) [01437750] **2313**

SPECIAL PUBLICATION (AMERICAN SOCIETY OF ICHTHYOLOGISTS AND HERPETOLOGISTS) (US/0748-0539) [10870341] **5597**

SPECIAL PUBLICATION / AMERICAN SOCIETY OF MAMMALOGISTS (JS/0569-8219) [02229911] **5597**

SPECIAL PUBLICATION / AUSTRALIAN NATIONAL PARKS AND WILDLIFE SERVICE (AT) [08636486] **2205**

SPECIAL PUBLICATION - BERMUDA BIOLOGICAL STATION FOR RESEARCH, INC (BM/1012-0335) [02386386] **2221**

SPECIAL PUBLICATION - BRITISH CARBONIZATION RESEARCH ASSOCIATION (UK/0306-4352) [10972077] **992**

SPECIAL PUBLICATION - BRITISH CERAMIC RESEARCH ASSOCIATION (UK/0144-2147) [07791227] **2594**

SPECIAL PUBLICATION (BRITISH COKE RESEARCH ASSOCIATION) *See* SPECIAL PUBLICATION - BRITISH CARBONIZATION RESEARCH ASSOCIATION **992**

SPECIAL PUBLICATION - CALIFORNIA DIVISION OF MINES AND GEOLOGY (US/0147-6211) [02828679] **1397**

SPECIAL PUBLICATION - CALIFORNIA NATIVE PLANT SOCIETY (US/0190-8723) [04027150] **2431**

SPECIAL PUBLICATION - CARNEGIE MUSEUM OF NATURAL HISTORY (US/0145-9031) [02805072] 283, **4172**

SPECIAL PUBLICATION - COLORADO GEOLOGICAL SURVEY (US/0099-6459) [02534071] **1397**

SPECIAL PUBLICATION - COUNCIL FOR AGRICULTURAL SCIENCE AND TECHNOLOGY (US/0194-407X) [02915101] **137**

SPECIAL PUBLICATION - CUSHMAN FOUNDATION FOR FORAMINIFERAL RESEARCH (US/0070-2242) [01565719] **5597**

SPECIAL PUBLICATION / DEPARTMENT OF MINES AND ENERGY (AT/0726-1527) [09573457] **2151**

SPECIAL PUBLICATION - DIVISION OF FISH AND WILDLIFE, SECTION OF FISHERIES (US/0193-1245) [05116736] **2313**

SPECIAL PUBLICATION / EUROPEAN AQUACULTURE SOCIETY (BE/0774-0689) [15201996] **2313**

SPECIAL PUBLICATION - FLORIDA. BUREAU OF GEOLOGY (US/0085-0640) [02021410] 2205, **1397**

SPECIAL PUBLICATION / FOREST RESEARCH LAB, SCHOOL OF FORESTRY, OREGON STATE UNIVERSITY (US/1059-2512) [08445795] **2395**

SPECIAL PUBLICATION - FORINTEK CANADA CORP. EASTERN LABORATORY (CN/0824-2119) [10092645] **2404**

SPECIAL PUBLICATION (GASKELL (PUBLISHER)) (UK) [09727968] **3937**

SPECIAL PUBLICATION - GEOLOGICAL SOCIETY OF AUSTRALIA *CEASED.* (AT/0072-1085) [06184915] **1397**

SPECIAL PUBLICATION - GEOLOGICAL SOCIETY OF SOUTH AFRICA *CEASED.* (SA/0367-5335) [01695388] **1398**

SPECIAL PUBLICATION IFDC (US/0277-4305) [07568224] **188**

SPECIAL PUBLICATION--INSTITUTE OF BRITISH GEOGRAPHIES (UK/0073-9006) [02252783] **2576**

SPECIAL PUBLICATION - INSTITUTE OF OCEANOGRAPHIC AND FISHERIES RESEARCH (GR) [08599327] 2313, **1457**

SPECIAL PUBLICATION / INTERNATIONAL CENTRE FOR DIARRHOEAL DISEASE RESEARCH, BANGLADESH (BG/0255-7126) [09728085] **3801**

SPECIAL PUBLICATION / J. L. B. SMITH INSTITUTE OF ICHTHYOLOGY (SA/0075-2088) [05861933] **5598**

SPECIAL PUBLICATION. KENTUCKY GEOLOGICAL SURVEY (US/0075-5613) [05201702] **1398**

SPECIAL PUBLICATION - MINES & GEOLOGY DIVISION (JM) [03812621] **2151**

SPECIAL PUBLICATION - NEW MEXICO GEOLOGICAL SOCIETY (US/0548-6327) [02834526] **1398**

SPECIAL PUBLICATION OF THE AMERICAN ANTHROPOLOGICAL ASSOCIATION, A (US/0065-6941) [06681178] **245**

SPECIAL PUBLICATION ... OF THE BRITISH ECOLOGICAL SOCIETY, (UK/0262-7027) [09117794] **2221**

SPECIAL PUBLICATION ... OF THE INTERNATIONAL ASSOCIATION OF SEDIMENTOLOGISTS (UK/0141-3600) [02993725] **1398**

SPECIAL PUBLICATION OF THE PALAEONTOLOGICAL SOCIETY OF INDIA (II) [09424776] **4231**

SPECIAL PUBLICATION ... OF THE SOCIETY FOR GEOLOGY APPLIED TO MINERAL DEPOSITS (GW/0723-8835) [08362698] **1398**

SPECIAL PUBLICATION / OKLAHOMA GEOLOGICAL SURVEY (US/0275-0929) [07076910] **1398**

SPECIAL PUBLICATION (OREGON STATE UNIVERSITY. FOREST RESEARCH LABORATORY) *See* RESEARCH CONTRIBUTION **2392**

SPECIAL PUBLICATION. PALEONTOLOGICAL SOCIETY (US) [14372535] **4231**

SPECIAL PUBLICATION / ROYAL SOCIETY OF CHEMISTRY (UK/0260-6291) [07767597] **993**

SPECIAL PUBLICATION - SASKATCHEWAN GEOLOGICAL SOCIETY (CN/0704-7622) [01716168] **1398**

SPECIAL PUBLICATION - SASKATCHEWAN NATURAL HISTORY SOCIETY (CN/0080-6552) [01285497] **4172**

SPECIAL PUBLICATION / SEPM (SOCIETY FOR SEDIMENTARY GEOLOGY) (US) [24594702] **1360**

SPECIAL PUBLICATION SERIES (ATLANTIC SALMON FEDERATION) (US) [11336754] **2313**

SPECIAL PUBLICATION SERIES / GEOLOGICAL SURVEY OF INDIA (II/0254-0436) [08359497] **1398**

SPECIAL PUBLICATION SERIES - PYMATUNING LABORATORY OF ECOLOGY, UNIVERSITY OF PITTSBURGH (US/0192-5563) [04952987] **2221**

SPECIAL PUBLICATION / SOCIETY FOR SEDIMENTARY GEOLOGY (US/1060-071X) [24242821] 1445, **4231**

SPECIAL PUBLICATION - STATE OF MONTANA, BUREAU OF MINES AND GEOLOGY (US/0077-1139) [01758595] **1398**

SPECIAL PUBLICATION / THE GEOCHEMICAL SOCIETY (US) [18798756] **1360**

SPECIAL PUBLICATION / THE UNIVERSITY OF GEORGIA, COLLEGE OF AGRICULTURE, EXPERIMENT STATION (US/0748-0032) [04952679] **137**

SPECIAL PUBLICATION - U.N.M. INSTITUTE OF METEORITICS (US/0097-3866) [01640674] **1434**

SPECIAL PUBLICATION - UNITED STATES. BUREAU OF MINES (US/0731-762X) [08249849] 1445, **2151**

SPECIAL PUBLICATION - UNIVERSITY OF COLORADO, BOULDER. NATURAL HAZARDS RESEARCH AND APPLICATIONS INFORMATION CENTER (US/0749-9442) [09631588] **5310**

SPECIAL — Alphabetical Title Index

SPECIAL PUBLICATION - VERMONT GEOLOGICAL SURVEY (US/0083-5765) [02253656] **1398**

SPECIAL PUBLICATIONS (US/0067-6179) [01519634] **4096**

SPECIAL PUBLICATIONS / AMERICAN PHILOLOGICAL ASSOCIATION (US/0065-9703) [07767077] **3323**

SPECIAL PUBLICATIONS : GULF COAST ASSOCIATION OF GEOLOGICAL SOCIETIES (US/0733-8856) [04245896] **1398**

SPECIAL PUBLICATIONS IN ANTHROPOLOGY AND HISTORY *CEASED.* (US) [03365855] **245**

SPECIAL PUBLICATIONS - KROEBER ANTHROPOLOGICAL SOCIETY (US/0454-5419) [01784555] **246**

SPECIAL PUBLICATIONS - MISSOURI ARCHAEOLOGICAL SOCIETY (US/0735-5467) [09034600] **283**

SPECIAL PUBLICATIONS OF THE SOCIETY FOR GENERAL MICROBIOLOGY (UK/0197-1751) [05200572] **570**

SPECIAL PUBLICATIONS - THE MUSEUM, TEXAS TECH UNIVERSITY (US/0149-1768) [01521585] **4096**

SPECIAL PUBLICATIONS - TOKAI REGIONAL FISHERIES RESEARCH LABORATORY (JA/0493-4008) [02001579] **2313**

SPECIAL RECREATION DIGEST *SUSPENDED.* (US/0747-0185) [10471707] **4394, 4854**

SPECIAL REFERENCE BRIEFS (US/1052-536X) [11739950] **137**

SPECIAL REPORT (CH/0258-2708) [15059105] **137**

SPECIAL REPORT - AGRICULTURAL EXPERIMENT STATION, DIVISION OF AGRICULTURE, UNIVERSITY OF ARKANSAS, FAYETTEVILLE (US/0571-0189) [02496386] **137**

SPECIAL REPORT - ALASKA. DIVISION OF GEOLOGICAL AND GEOPHYSICAL SURVEYS (US/0360-3881) [06132462] **1398**

SPECIAL REPORT - AMERICAN PUBLIC WORKS ASSOCIATION (US/0065-9932) [03794780] **4686**

SPECIAL REPORT - AUSTRALIAN ROAD RESEARCH BOARD (AT/0572-144X) [I0572144X] **5444**

SPECIAL REPORT - CALIFORNIA DIVISION OF MINES AND GEOLOGY (US/0527-0014) [01552404] **1398**

SPECIAL REPORT / CENTER FOR GREAT LAKES STUDIES, UNIVERSITY OF WISCONSIN-MILWAUKEE (US/0512-5421) [01801538] **1847**

SPECIAL REPORT / COLORADO DIVISION OF WILDLIFE (US/0084-8875) [01377401] **2205**

SPECIAL REPORT - DEPARTMENT OF STATE, BUREAU OF PUBLIC AFFAIRS, OFFICE OF PUBLIC COMMUNICATION *See* SPECIAL REPORT - UNITED STATES DEPARTMENT OF STATE, BUREAU OF PUBLIC AFFAIRS **4535**

SPECIAL REPORT - DIVISION OF CORRECTION, A (US/0098-3845) [02241254] **3177**

SPECIAL REPORT ECOLOGY *See* ECOLOGY (HOUSTON) **2214**

SPECIAL REPORT, FICTION (US/1047-2886) [20654131] **3439**

SPECIAL REPORT (FOREST ENGINEERING RESEARCH INSTITUTE OF CANADA) (CN/0381-7733) [04207486] **2395**

SPECIAL REPORT IN APPLIED MARINE SCIENCE AND OCEAN ENGINEERING (US/0882-7427) [05687128] **1457, 2095**

SPECIAL REPORT - MARINE LABORATORY (GALVESTON) (US) [01138426] **1457**

SPECIAL REPORT - MONTANA FISH AND GAME DEPARTMENT (US/0099-5541) [01521725] **2313**

SPECIAL REPORT - NEW YORK STATE AGRICULTURAL EXPERIMENT STATION (US/0886-7623) [02858305] **137**

SPECIAL REPORT (NORTHERN ILLINOIS UNIVERSITY. CENTER FOR SOUTHEAST ASIAN STUDIES) (US/0073-4934) [02111921] **2665**

SPECIAL REPORT OF THE DIRECTOR-GENERAL ON THE APPLICATION OF THE DECLARATION CONCERNING ACTION AGAINST APARTHEID IN SOUTH AFRICA / INTERNATIONAL LABOUR OFFICE (SZ/0074-6681) [24220445] **2643**

SPECIAL REPORT ON FAMILY (US/1047-2878) [20654101] **2286**

SPECIAL REPORT ON HEALTH (US/1047-272X) [20600683] **4803**

SPECIAL REPORT ON LIVING (US/1047-0123) [20465932] **5263**

SPECIAL REPORT ON MUNICIPAL AFFAIRS FOR LOCAL FISCAL YEARS ENDED IN ... (US) [09172081] **4748**

SPECIAL REPORT ON PERSONALITIES (US/1047-286X) [20640977] **4619**

SPECIAL REPORT ON PUERTO RICO HIGHWAY AUTHORITY, A (PR) [01439672] **5444**

SPECIAL REPORT ON PUERTO RICO INDUSTRIAL DEVELOPMENT COMPANY (PRIDCO), A (PR) [01439653] **1585**

SPECIAL REPORT ON SAN JUAN, CAPITAL OF PUERTO RICO (PR) [01439747] **1585**

SPECIAL REPORT ON SPORTS *See* SPECIAL REPORT - WHITTLE COMMUNICATIONS **2546**

SPECIAL REPORT ON VETERANS (US) [06252902] **4057**

SPECIAL REPORT - OTTENBY BIRD OBSERVATORY (SW) **5598**

SPECIAL REPORT - REPUBLIC OF SOUTH AFRICA, DEPARTMENT OF ENVIRONMENT AFFAIRS, SEA FISHERIES RESEARCH INSTITUTE (SA) [12985650] **2313**

SPECIAL REPORT - SOUTH DAKOTA STATE GEOLOGICAL SURVEY (US/0561-0559) [01715063] **1398**

SPECIAL REPORT (STATE UNIVERSITY OF NEW YORK AT STONY BROOK. MARINE SCIENCES RESEARCH CENTER) (US/0196-2361) [03992894] **473**

SPECIAL REPORT - TRANSPORTATION RESEARCH BOARD, NATIONAL RESEARCH COUNCIL (US/0360-859X) [01696347] **5393**

SPECIAL REPORT - UNITED STATES DEPARTMENT OF STATE, BUREAU OF PUBLIC AFFAIRS (US/0271-1486) [06546228] **1640, 4535**

SPECIAL REPORT / UNIVERSITY OF MISSOURI--COLUMBIA, AGRICULTURAL EXPERIMENT STATION (US) [11634995] **137**

SPECIAL REPORT - UNIVERSITY OF WASHINGTON, DEPARTMENT OF OCEANOGRAPHY (US/0083-7547) [01166273] **1457**

SPECIAL REPORT - WATER RESOURCES AUTHORITY, A (PR) [02246603] **5539**

● SPECIAL REPORT - WHITTLE COMMUNICATIONS (US/1059-5201) [24614420] **2546**

SPECIAL REVIEW OF THE DEPARTMENT OF HEALTH AND SOCIAL SERVICES, DIVISION OF PUBLIC ASSISTANCE, MEDICAL ASSISTANCE PAYMENTS FOR ABORTIONS, A (US) [07363296] **2894, 5310**

SPECIAL SCIENTIFIC REPORT - NORTH CAROLINA. DIVISION OF MARINE FISHERIES (US/0734-3914) [07854352] **2313**

SPECIAL SERIES / SOCIETY FOR ETHNOMUSICOLOGY (US/0270-1766) [06351636] **2273, 4154**

SPECIAL STUDIES IN AGRICULTURAL ECONOMICS - UNIVERSITY OF READING, DEPARTMENT OF AGRICULTURAL ECONOMICS & MANAGEMENT (UK/0958-9732) [22695131] **137**

SPECIAL STUDIES - UTAH GEOLOGICAL AND MINERAL SURVEY (US/0098-115X) [02243995] **1445, 1398**

SPECIAL STUDY - SOCIETY OF INDUSTRIAL ACCOUNTANTS OF CANADA (CN) [02594620] **751**

SPECIAL STUDY - TEXAS DEPARTMENT OF CORRECTIONS, RESEARCH, PLANNING, AND DEVELOPMENT DIVISION (US) [06244120] **3177**

SPECIAL STUDY / UTAH GEOLOGICAL SURVEY (US) [25525172] **2151, 1398**

SPECIAL TECHNOLOGIES (US/1071-6092) [28694496] **5159**

SPECIAL TOPICS IN SUPERCOMPUTING (NE) [17302936] **1204**

SPECIAL TRADE CONTRACTORS (CN/0835-1090) [15871357] **628**

SPECIAL VEHICLE ENGINEER (UK/0957-7580) [I09577580] **1997**

SPECIAL VOLUME (CANADIAN INSTITUTE OF MINING AND METALLURGY : 1982) (CN/0826-6166) [11607599] **2151**

SPECIAL WARFARE : THE PROFESSIONAL BULLETIN OF THE JOHN F. KENNEDY SPECIAL WARFARE CENTER AND SCHOOL (US/1058-0123) [19478662] **4057**

SPECIALISED NATIONAL COUNCILS' MAGAZINE, THE (UA/1012-0319) [04583195] **5223**

SPECIALIST KARACHI (PK/1017-4699) [I10174699] **3642**

SPECIALIST (NEW YORK, N.Y.) (US/0273-9399) [06802958] **3251**

SPECIALIST PERIODICAL REPORTS (UK) **993**

SPECIALISTA (IT) **2129**

SPECIALISTE (GATINEAU, QUEBEC) (CN/0712-5151) [09223126] **5319**

SPECIALITY PAPER & BOARD MATERIALS & MARKETS BULLETIN (UK) **4222**

SPECIALIZZATA (IT) **628**

SPECIALMEDDELANDE / SVERIGES LANTBRUKSUNIVERSITET, INSTITUTIONEN FOR LANTBRUKETS BYGGNADSTEKNIK (SW/0348-0593) [06454585] **628**

SPECIALTY ADVERTISING BUSINESS (US/0195-0495) [05235685] **766**

SPECIALTY & CUSTOM DEALER (US/0193-7278) [05250351] **713, 5425**

● SPECIALTY AUTO MARKETPLACE (US/1063-0716) [25855161] **5425**

SPECIALTY AUTOMOTIVE PARTS AND ACCESSORIES (US/0894-7414) [16200412] **5425**

SPECIALTY BOOKSELLERS DIRECTORY (US/0895-254X) [16567320] **4832, 4820**

SPECIALTY CAR (US/1068-2627) [27520930] **5425**

SPECIALTY CHEMICALS (REDHILL) (UK/0262-2262) [11233072] **993**

SPECIALTY COOKING (US/1048-8413) [21052166] **2792, 4199**

SPECIALTY COVERAGE MARKET REPORTS : SCMR (US) [21369288] **2894**

SPECIALTY FOOD MERCHANDISING (US/0194-1429) [05267121] **2358**

SPECIALTY LAB UPDATE (US) **4377**

SPECIALTY LAW DIGEST. HEALTH CARE (ANNUAL) *CEASED.* (US/0276-3079) [07110782] **3742**

SPECIALTY LAW DIGEST. HEALTH CARE LAW (US) [30113217] **3742**

SPECIALTY NEWS (US/0886-2052) [12890077] **851**

SPECIALTY REFERENCES. APPLICATION NOTES (US/1059-3772) [21707896] **2082**

SPECIALTY STORE SERVICE BULLETIN *CEASED.* (US/1052-5564) [22301564] **1087, 958**

SPECIALTY TOOLS & FASTENERS DISTRIBUTORS ASSOCIATION *See* STAFDA ... DIRECTORY **1627**

SPECIALTY TRAVEL INDEX: THE DIRECTORY TO SPECIAL INTEREST TRAVEL (US/0889-7085) [09528403] **5491**

SPECIES (BROOKFIELD) (US/1016-927X) [13573321] **2205**

SPECIFICATION (UK) [04484406] **628**

SPECIFIED DOMESTIC ELECTRICAL APPLIANCES (UK/0410-5907) [02585592] **2812**

SPECIFIER'S GUIDE TO CONTRACT FLOOR COVERING (US) **628**

● SPECIFIER'S GUIDE TO HEATING, VENTILATING, AIR CONDITIONING AND REFRIGERATION (UK) [25332077] **2608**

SPECTACLE DU MONDE, LE (FR/0038-6944) [06353364] **3353**

SPECTACLE DU MONDE / PERSPECTIVES / REALITIES, LE (FR) [12769705] **3353**

SPECTACLE DU MONDE / REALITIES, LE *See* SPECTACLE DU MONDE / PERSPECTIVES / REALITIES, LE **3353**

SPECTACULAR SPIDER-MAN (US/0898-1833) [17742409] **4866**

SPECTATOR (BE) [01789675] **2523**

SPECTATOR (LONDON. 1828) (UK/0038-6952) [01766325] **2523**

SPECTATOR (LOS ANGELES, CALIF.) (US/1051-0230) [19842339] **1139, 4078**

SPECTATOR (SEATTLE), THE (US/0037-0479) [03922653] **1095**

SPECTATOR, THE (US) [18927531] **3177**

SPECTOR REPORT ALUMINUM INDUSTRY SERVICE (US) **4019**

SPECTRA BIOLOGIE (FR/0295-1967) [19078390] **3696**

SPECTRA (STONY BROOK, N.Y.) (US/0747-7775) [05626195] **331**

SPECTRA (SYRACUSE, N.Y.) (US/1042-3729) [15530872] **4096**

SPECTROCHIMICA ACTA. PART A : MOLECULAR SPECTROSCOPY (UK/0584-8539) [01766328] **4441**

SPECTROCHIMICA ACTA. PART B : ATOMIC SPECTROSCOPY (UK/0584-8547) [01766329] **1019, 4422**

SPECTROCHIMICA ACTA REVIEWS *CEASED.* (UK/0958-319X) [22102331] **4441**

SPECTROCHIMICA ACTA REVIEWS [MICROFORM] (US/0958-319X) [23200393] **4441**

SPECTROSCOPIA MOLECULAR (US/0038-6995) [02310122] **4441**

SPECTROSCOPIC PROPERTIES OF INORGANIC AND ORGANOMETALLIC COMPOUNDS (UK/0584-8555) [01586020] **1019**

Alphabetical Title Index SPINE

SPECTROSCOPY (US/0887-6703) [13258350] **4453**

●SPECTROSCOPY EUROPE (GW/0966-0941) [26040433] **4442**

SPECTROSCOPY INTERNATIONAL (US/1040-7669) [18519461] **993**

SPECTROSCOPY LETTERS (US/0038-7010) [01642104] **4442**

SPECTROSCOPY (OTTAWA, ONT.) (CN/0712-4813) [09635007] 473, **993**

SPECTROSCOPY SOCIETY OF CANADA *See* DIRECTORY / SPECTROSCOPY SOCIETY OF CANADA **4401**

SPECTROSCOPY WORLD *See* SPECTROSCOPY EUROPE **4442**

SPECTRUM (US/0892-9459) [15347151] **1122**

SPECTRUM (US) [06798579] **4096**

SPECTRUM 1: STOCK HOLDINGS SURVEY (US/0091-6854) [01787830] **914**

SPECTRUM 2: INVESTMENT COMPANY PORTFOLIOS (US/0091-6862) [01787835] **914**

SPECTRUM 3: 13 (F) INSTITUTIONAL STOCK HOLDINGS SURVEY (US) [13732388] 812, **914**

SPECTRUM 3 : 13(F) INSTITUTIONAL STOCK HOLDINGS SURVEY (US) [05518613] 812, **914**

SPECTRUM 3: BANK STOCK HOLDINGS SURVEY *See* SPECTRUM 3: 13 (F) INSTITUTIONAL STOCK HOLDINGS SURVEY **914**

SPECTRUM 3: BANK STOCK HOLDINGS SURVEY *See* SPECTRUM 3 : 13(F) INSTITUTIONAL STOCK HOLDINGS SURVEY **914**

SPECTRUM 4: 13(F) INSTITUTIONAL PORTFOLIOS (US) [13732402] **914**

SPECTRUM 5 (US) [10298711] **914**

SPECTRUM 6 (US) [10298729] **914**

SPECTRUM (ALBERTA SCHOOL TRUSTEES ASSOCIATION) (CN/0838-7605) [18371830] **1872**

SPECTRUM (CHATSWORTH, CALIF.) (US/1047-2371) [20643809] **4154**

SPECTRUM (CHATSWORTH, CALIF.) *See* SCHWANN SPECTRUM **5318**

SPECTRUM CONVERTIBLES -- 13 (F) INSTITUTIONAL HOLDINGS SURVEY OF CONVERTIBLE BONDS AND CONVERTIBLE PREFERRED STOCK (US) **914**

SPECTRUM (EXETER, DEVON) (US) [13716441] 1784, **4999**

●SPECTRUM (LEXINGTON, KY.) (US/1067-8530) [26815112] **4686**

SPECTRUM (MONTREAL. 1981) (CN/0228-8982) [08770492] **5223**

●SPECTRUM (NEW YORK, N.Y. : 1992) (US/1062-0958) [25523692] **2500**

SPECTRUM NEWSLETTER (US/0738-9051) [09674718] **1122**

●SPECTRUM : NEWSLETTER OF THE ROYAL OBSERVATORIES (UK/1353-7784) [30099712] **390**

SPECTRUM REPORT, THE *See* WASHINGTON TELECOM NEWS **1168**

SPECTRUM REPORT : NEWS AND ANALYSIS ON THE GLOBAL FREQUENCY ALLOCATION BATTLE, THE (US/1053-993X) [22715163] **1122**

SPECTRUM (ROCKVILLE, MD.) *CEASED.* (US/0738-470X) [09472813] **3642**

SPECTRUM (SANTA BARBARA, CALIF.) (US/0038-7061) [01983423] **1095**

SPECTRUM (ST. PAUL, MINN.) (US/0739-2559) [01613865] **1921**

SPECTRUM (TAKOMA PARK, MD.) (US/0890-0264) [03837502] **4999**

SPECTRUM (TEL AVIV, ISRAEL) (IS/0334-1046) [10903547] **1711**

SPECTRUM : THE QUARTERLY MAGAZINE OF THE INDEPENDENT TELEVISION COMMISSION (UK/0962-1830) [23674712] **1139**

SPECTRUM (TORONTO. 1979) (CN/0710-2224) [08562688] **812**

SPECTRUM (TORONTO. 1981) (CN/0226-9228) [08862005] 4394, **5311**

●SPECTRUM (WHEATON, ILL.) (US/1061-6160) [25380451] **4999**

SPECTRUM (WINTER HAVEN, FLA.) (US/0883-282X) [12041360] **4503**

SPECULATIONS IN SCIENCE AND TECHNOLOGY (UK/0155-7785) [04482694] **5159**

SPECULATOR (BUTTE, MONT.), THE (US/0882-3464) [11828638] **2762**

SPECULATORS MAGAZINE *CEASED.* (US/0894-8216) [16262351] **914**

SPECULUM (US/0038-7134) [01605897] 3353, **2710**

SPECULUM ANNIVERSARY MONOGRAPHS (US) [06082290] **2630**

SPECULUM (COLUMBUS, OHIO), THE (US/0739-3806) [01772943] **5522**

SPECULUM ORBIS (GW/0178-9902) [13453348] **2583**

SPEECH AND DRAMA (UK/0038-7142) [02239767] 1784, **5368**

SPEECH COMMUNICATION (NE/0167-6393) [08843982] **1122**

SPEECH COMMUNICATION ASSOCIATION *See* SPEECH COMMUNICATION DIRECTORY **1122**

SPEECH COMMUNICATION DIRECTORY (US/0190-2075) [00988638] **1122**

SPEECH, HEARING AND LANGUAGE (UK/0265-6191) [22530413] **3323**

SPEECH INDEX (US) [02253026] 3323, **3336**

SPEECH MAKERS NEWSLETTER (US/1060-9601) [25125508] **1122**

SPEECH TECHNOLOGY *CEASED.* (US/0744-1355) [08041398] **1122**

SPEED & CUSTOM DEALER *See* SPECIALTY & CUSTOM DEALER **5425**

SPEED (BELOIT) (US/0092-4229) [01789729] **1349**

SPEED MONITORING REPORT / PREPARED BY THE DEPARTMENT OF TRANSPORTATION, DIVISION OF DATA BASE GENERATION, BUREAU OF DATA RESOURCES (US) [09231181] **5444**

SPEEDHORSE (MONTHLY), THE (US/0364-9237) [02693854] **2802**

SPEEDNEWS (US/0271-2598) [06741671] **36**

SPEEDNEWS DEFENSE BIWEEKLY (US/1060-1368) [24880566] 4057, **36**

SPEEDWAY SCENE (US/0747-5403) [10768261] **4920**

SPEEDX (US/0882-8091) [11992179] **1122**

SPEEDXGRAM (US/0882-8199) [11991946] **1122**

SPEEDY BEE (US/0190-6798) [02253930] **5598**

SPEEGLE FAMILY QUARTERLY (US) [22255832] **2473**

SPEER'S DIGEST OF TOXIC SUBSTANCES STATE LAW (US/8756-7059) [10588657] 2243, **3116**

SPEKTATOR (NE/0165-084X) [01979036] 3323, **3439**

SPEKTROSKOPIJA GAZORAZRJADNOJ PLAZMY (RU/0134-9007) [04314586] **4445**

SPEKTRUM *CEASED.* (SZ/0038-7274) [05958874] 382, **3471**

SPEKTRUM DER AUGENHEILKUNDE : ZEITSCHRIFT DER OSTERREICHISCHEN OPHTHALMOLOGISCHEN GESELLSCHAFT, OOG (AU/0930-4282) [22893131] **3879**

SPEKTRUM DER WISSENSCHAFT (GW/0170-2971) [01702971] **5159**

SPELD (AT) **1885**

SPELEMANNSBLADET (NO/0333-0370) [08240195] **4154**

SPELEO DIGEST (US/0584-8717) [03313053] **1411**

SPELEO-QUEBEC (CN/0317-6215) [02248389] **1411**

SPELEOLOGIE - PREHISTOIRE, DIFFUSION SCIENTIFIQUE / SOCIETE ROYALE BELGE D'ETUDES GEOLOGIQUES ET ARCHEOLOGIQUES, ET- LES CHERCHEURS DE LA WALLONIE (BE) [17438760] **1411**

SPELEONEWS (US/0734-5895) [08781389] **4878**

SPELUNCA (FR/0376-2203) [02830973] **1411**

SPENCER COUNTY JOURNAL-DEMOCRAT, THE (US) [15345490] **5667**

SPENCER'S RESEARCH REPORTS ON EMPLOYEE BENEFITS (US) [14410342] **914**

SPENCER'S RETIREMENT PLAN SERVICE (US/0740-1329) [09940286] 914, **2894**

SPENSER NEWSLETTER (US/0038-7347) [01981052] **3471**

SPENSER STUDIES (US/0195-9468) [05736497] **3471**

SPENT FUEL AND RADIOACTIVE WASTE INVENTORIES, PROJECTIONS, AND CHARACTERISTICS (US) [10250601] **2243**

SPERRY LAWYER, THE (US/0148-0901) [03260978] **3103**

SPERRY NEW HOLLAND *See* SPERRY NEW HOLLAND NEWS **137**

SPERRY NEW HOLLAND NEWS (US) [04242766] **137**

●SPETSIALIST (RU) [25790814] **1915**

SPETTACOLO, LO (IT/0038-738X) [02268034] **331**

SPEUR- EN ONTWIKKELINGSWERK IN NEDERLAND / CENTRAAL BUREAU VOOR DE STATISTIEK, HOOFDAFDELING STATISTIEKEN VAN ONDERWIJS EN WETENSCHAPPEN (NE/0168-468X) [06401415] **5159**

SPEZIALINFORMATION DETERGENTIEN (GW) **993**

SPEZIALKATALOG UBER DIE BRIEFMARKEN DER SCHWEIZ UND VON LIECHTENSTEIN (SZ) [10611213] **2787**

SPEZIELLE PATHOLOGISCHE ANATOMIE (GW/0081-3699) [01590364] **3898**

SPGQ EN NEGOTIATION (CN/0714-7570) [09519510] **1711**

SPHAN PRO-MEMORIA / FUNDACAO NACIONAL PRO-MEMORIA, SECRETARIA DO PATRIMONIO HISTORICO E ARTISTICO NACIONAL, MINISTERIO DA EDUCACAO E CULTURA (BL) [10811066] **2630**

SPHENISCID PENGUIN NEWSLETTER : SPN (US/1045-0076) [19987025] **5598**

SPHINX (HELSINKI, FINLAND) (FI/0783-5892) [15025267] **5159**

SPHQ NOUVELLES (CN/0229-7655) [08099496] **2762**

SPI CANADA ... PROGRAM, ... ACCOMPLISHMENTS (CN/0714-346X) [08981072] **4460**

SPI STATISTICAL REPORT ON THERMOPLASTIC AND THERMOSETTING RESINS (US) **4460**

SPICE (US/0894-6183) [15240377] **4999**

SPICE (US) 2273, **1069**

SPICE NEWSLETTER (II) [01797733] **2358**

SPICILEGIO MODERNO (IT/0391-4216) [01983621] **3439**

SPICILEGIUM FRIBURGENSE (SZ/0561-6158) [05238566] **4999**

SPIDELL PUBLISHING INC *See* SPIDELL'S CALIFORNIA TAXLETTER **3058**

SPIDELL'S CALIFORNIA TAXLETTER (US/0194-8237) [05038476] 4748, **3058**

●SPIDER (PERU, ILL.) (US/1070-2911) [28312995] **1069**

SPIDR NEWS (US/0888-9325) [13756626] **1711**

●SPIE HOLOGRAPHICS INTERNATIONAL DIRECTORY & RESOURCE GUIDE (US/1058-045X) [24185661] **4442**

SPIEGEL DER LETTEREN (BE/0038-7479) [07198971] **3439**

SPIEGEL (HAMBURG), DER (GW/0038-7452) [04927901] **2523**

SPIEGEL HISTORIAEL (NE/0038-7487) [07199028] 283, **2630**

SPIEL SPORT FREIZEIT MODE (AU) **4854**

SPIELEN UND LERNEN (GW/0344-8754) [I03448754] **1784**

SPIELRAUM (GW/0934-4853) [I09344853] **2601**

SPIELZEUG, DAS (GW/0038-7525) [I00387525] **2585**

SPIL, STELLENBOSCH PAPERS IN LINGUISTICS (SA) [07118688] **3323**

SPILL SCIENCE AND TECHNOLOGY BULLETIN (UK/1353-2561) **2243**

SPILLWAY *See* PANAMA CANAL SPILLWAY, THE **5454**

SPIN (US) 4422, **4427**

SPIN (UK/0038-7533) [01717041] **2324**

SPIN (NEW YORK, N.Y.) (US/0886-3032) [12872607] **4154**

SPIN-OFF (LOVELAND, COLO.) (US/0198-8239) [03900873] 5186, **5356**

SPINA BIFIDA THERAPY (US/0160-9475) [03791784] **3807**

SPINAL COLUMNS (CN/1195-5767) **4394**

SPINAL CORD SOCIETY *See* NEWSLETTER (SPINAL CORD SOCIETY (U.S.)) **3843**

SPINAL CORD SOCIETY CANADA (CN/1184-8472) [24265963] **3642**

SPINAL CORD SOCIETY CANADA (BULLETIN) *See* CSRO. CANADIAN SPINAL RESEARCH ORGANIZATION **3569**

SPINAL MANIPULATION (US) [14879846] **3807**

SPINAL NETWORK EXTRA *See* SPINAL NETWORK'S NEW MOBILITY **3975**

SPINAL NETWORK'S NEW MOBILITY (US/1065-2124) [26529841] **3975**

SPINDRIFTER, THE (CN/0711-4826) [08651964] **3439**

●SPINE LETTER (US/1072-3730) [29485266] **3885**

Alphabetical Title Index

SPINE (PHILADELPHIA, PA. 1976) (US/0362-2436) [02589719] **3642**

SPINE (PHILADELPHIA, PA. 1986) (US/0887-9869) [13505881] **3975**

SPINE REHABILITATION *CEASED.* (US/1058-1421) [24233651] **3642**

SPINK & SON, LTD., LONDON *See* NUMISMATIC CIRCULAR, THE **2782**

SPINK NUMISMATIC CIRCULAR (UK/0263-7677) [09320197] **2783**

SPINNER (NEW BEDFORD, MASS.) (US/0730-2657) [07966715] **2762**

SPINOFF (US/0148-2203) [05183743] **5159**

SPIRALE (MONTREAL) (CN/0225-9044) [18346197] **4832, 365**

SPIRALE (MONTREAL) (CN/0225-9044) [06141466] **331**

SPIRALE (SHERBROOKE) (CN/0822-9252) [10669019] **4619**

SPIRALES (MILAN, ITALY) *See* SECONDO RINASCIMENTO, IL **2854**

SPIRALI DEL SECONDO RINASCIMENTO *See* SECONDO RINASCIMENTO, IL **2854**

SPIRE (US) 5067, **1103**

SPIRIT & LIFE (CLYDE, MO.) (US/0038-7592) [01589942] **4999**

SPIRIT CANADA (CN/0229-7930) [08124134] **4154**

SPIRIT OF CHRISTMAS (US) [11476171] **5269**

SPIRIT OF DEMOCRACY (WOODSFIELD, OHIO : 1844) (US) [11751867] **5730**

SPIRIT OF JEFFERSON FARMERS ADVOCATE (US) [12889829] **5765**

SPIRIT (PUNXSUTAWNEY, PA.) (US) [15088867] **5739**

SPIRIT (SISTERS, OR.) (US/0885-0291) [12542311] **4999**

SPIRIT (SOUTH ORANGE) (US/0038-7584) [01766343] **3471**

SPIRIT THAT MOVES US, THE (US/0364-4014) [04351246] **3439**

SPIRIT (WASHINGTON) (US/0160-7367) [03738309] **4999**

SPIRITS, WINE & BEER MARKETING IN MINNESOTA, NORTH AND SOUTH DAKOTA (US/0747-3206) [10740185] **2371**

SPIRITS, WINE & BEVERAGE MARKETING IN IOWA (US/0747-3214) [10740262] **2371**

SPIRITUAL FRONTIERS (US/0038-7614) [01590003] **4999**

SPIRITUAL INDIA (II) [01799483] **4999**

SPIRITUAL LIFE (WASHINGTON) (US/0038-7630) [01641952] **5036**

SPIRITUALITY TODAY *CEASED.* (US/0162-6760) [03922304] **5036**

SPIRITUS (FR/0038-7665) [02450783] **5036**

SPIROU (BE/0771-8071) [07718071] **5075**

SPISANIE NA BALGARSKOTO GEOLOGICESKO DRUZESTVO (BU/0007-3938) [02250678] **1398**

SPISANIE NA BULGARSKATA AKADEMIIA NA NAUKITE (BU/0007-3989) [03020575] **5159**

SPISOK NEOPUBLIKOVANNYKH BIBLIOGRAFICHESKIKH RABOT V BIBLIOTEKAKH I INFOMATSIONNYKH TSENTRAKH SSSR ZA ... GOD / AKADEMIIA NAUK SSSR, INSTITUT NAUCHNOI INFORMATSII PO OBSHCHESTVENNYM NAUKAM (RU) [07592429] **425**

SPISY UNIVERZITY J.E. PURKYNE V BRNE, FILOZOFICKA FAKULTA (XR) [03029651] **4361**

SPISY UNIVERZITY J. E. PURKYNE V BRNE, FILOZOFICKA FAKULTA. ETUDES ROMANES DE BRNO (XR/0531-1985) [02495387] **3323**

SPIT IN THE OCEAN (US/0095-0459) [01795113] **3439**

SPITBALL (US/8755-741X) [11247625] **4920, 3439**

SPIXIANA (GW/0341-8391) [04445276] **5598**

SPIXIANA. SUPPLEMENT (GW/0177-7424) [04445353] **5598**

SPLASH (ANAHEIM, CALIF.) (US/0898-8951) [17946917] **4920**

SPLASH / WORLD WATERPARK ASSOCIATION (US) [17899445] **4920**

SPLICE (NEW YORK, N.Y.) *CEASED.* (US/0892-5089) [15217224] **331**

SPLIT LEVEL (CN/0317-0039) [02624611] **3439**

SPLITTING HEIRS (CN) **2473**

SPM. SALUD PUBLICA DE MEXICO (MX/0185-2264) [03641376] **4803**

SPOKANE CHRONICLE (US) [17365219] **5762**

SPOKEN ENGLISH (UK/0038-772X) [07415347] 1784, **3323**

SPOKESMAN (EDMONTON) *SUSPENDED.* (CN/0700-5229) [03403022] 5182, **4394**

SPOKESMAN-REVIEW (1894), THE (US/1064-7317) [11102610] **5762**

SPOKESWOMAN FOR ABORTION LAW REPEAL (CN/0700-8279) [03423253] 3768, **3058**

SPOLETIUM (IT/0490-4788) [I04904788] **2710**

SPOLETO FESTIVAL U.S.A *See* OFFICIAL SOUVENIR PROGRAM OF SPOLETO FESTIVAL U.S.A, THE **386**

SPON'S ARCHITECT'S AND BUILDER'S PRICE BOOK (UK) [17691732] 309, **628**

SPON'S CIVIL ENGINEERING PRICE BOOK (UK) [19619359] **2031**

SPON'S INTERNATIONAL CONSTRUCTION COSTS HANDBOOK (UK) [19607400] **628**

SPON'S LANDSCAPE AND EXTERNAL WORKS PRICE BOOK (UK) [19248487] **2431**

SPON'S MECHANICAL ELECTRICAL SERVICES PRICE BOOK (UK) [17844264] 2082, **4429**

SPONSA REGIS *See* SISTERS TODAY **5036**

SPONSERING (NE) **766**

SPONSORED RESEARCH IN THE HISTORY OF ART (US/0742-0242) [09447156] **365**

SPONSORSHIP REPORT (CN) **936**

SPOON RIVER POETRY REVIEW (US) **3471**

SPOON RIVER QUARTERLY *See* SPOON RIVER POETRY REVIEW **3471**

SPOON RIVER QUARTERLY, THE (US/0738-8993) [03827225] **3353**

SPOONER ADVOCATE, THE (US/8755-6995) [11383969] **5770**

SPOR FAALIYETLERI VE TESISLERI (TU) [17653143] **4920**

SPOR KULUPLERI (TU) [17890725] 4920, **5236**

SPORE (ENGLISH ED.) (NE/1011-0054) [13841664] **137**

SPORE RESEARCH (UK/0306-2074) [01784398] **570**

SPORT (AU) [06005212] **4920**

SPORT (BE) **4920**

SPORT (UK) **4920**

SPORT A L'UNIVERSITE (FR) **4920**

SPORT ADMINISTRATOR, THE (CN/0824-7900) [12782113] **4920**

SPORT AEROBATICS (US/0161-5351) [03952088] 36, **4920**

SPORT ALBERTA NEWS (CN/0700-9046) [03279391] **4920**

SPORT AMERICANA BASEBALL CARD PRICE GUIDE, THE (US/0190-1389) [04643108] 4920, **2778**

SPORT AMERICANA BASEBALL MEMORABILIA AND AUTOGRAPH PRICE GUIDE, THE (US/0738-1212) [08887290] **4920**

SPORT AMERICANA BASKETBALL CARD PRICE GUIDE AND ALPHABETICAL CHECKLIST, THE (US) [25235455] **4854**

SPORT AMERICANA HOCKEY CARD PRICE GUIDE, THE (US) [24601016] 4920, **2778**

SPORT & LEISURE *CEASED.* (CN/0838-4061) [19642350] **4854**

SPORT AND LEISURE (UK) [06662442] 4854, **4920**

SPORT & MEDICINA (IT/0392-9647) [I03929647] **3956**

● SPORT AND SPORT 2 (UK) **4920**

SPORT AUTO (GW) [09176883] 5425, **4920**

SPORT AUTO, VIRAGE AUTO, CHAMPION (FR/0151-6353) [I01516353] 4920, **5425**

SPORT AVIATION (US/0038-7835) [06569714] 36, **4920**

SPORT B.C. GENERAL MEETING *See* PROCEEDINGS - SPORT B. C., ANNUAL GENERAL MEETING **4913**

SPORT-, BADER-, FREIZEIT-BAUTEN (GW/0344-6492) [I03446492] 4920, **628**

SPORT BOWLING (FR/0398-8341) [I03988341] **4920**

SPORT : COMMUNAUTE FRANCAISE DE BELGIQUE (BE) **4920**

SPORT COMPACT CAR (US/1062-9629) [25820927] **5425**

SPORT CONSTRUCTION BUYERS GUIDE (US) **2031**

SPORT DISCUS [COMPUTER FILE] (US) [22213809] 1858, **1797**

SPORT ET VIE DIJON (FR/1152-9563) [I11529563] 2601, **4920**

SPORT FLYER (US/8750-8117) [11799302] 36, **4920**

SPORT FLYING *See* AIR PROGRESS **8**

SPORT GERICHT (NE) **4920**

SPORT HEALTH (AT/0812-8308) [10661963] **3956**

SPORT / HERAUSGEGEBEN VOM SCHWEIZERISCHEN LANDESVERBAND FUER SPORT (SZ) [27893462] **4920**

SPORT INTERN (GW) **4920**

SPORT INTERNATIONAL (BE) **4920**

SPORT ITALIA (IT) **4920**

SPORT KARATE MAGAZINE *See* BOICE LYDELL'S SPORT KARATE INTERNATIONAL **4887**

SPORT KATOWICE (PL/0137-9305) [I01379305] **4920**

SPORT MAGAZIN (AU) **4920**

SPORT MAGAZINE (CN/1195-7956) **4920**

● SPORT MARKETING QUARTERLY (US/1061-6934) [25406101] 937, **4920**

SPORT MEDIA BUYERS GUIDE (US) **4920**

SPORT MEDICINE DIRECTORY (CN/0229-1541) [07857955] **3956**

SPORT (NEW YORK) (US/0038-7797) [03796670] **4920**

SPORT ONTARIO *See* SPORT ONTARIO NEWS **4921**

SPORT ONTARIO DIRECTORY OF SPORTS, RECREATION AND PHYSICAL EDUCATION (CN/0708-6113) [05071944] 1858, **4920**

SPORT ONTARIO NEWS (CN/0707-1906) [04754968] **4921**

SPORT PARACHUTIST (UK) [07436215] **4921**

SPORT PARACHUTIST'S SAFETY JOURNAL (US/0898-4301) [17810519] **4854**

SPORT PARTNER (NE) **4921**

SPORT PILOT HOT KITS & HOMEBUILTS (US/1040-5798) [18454632] **36**

SPORT PLACE INTERNATIONAL : AN INTERNATIONAL MAGAZINE OF SPORTS GEOGRAPHY (US) [19909122] **4921**

SPORT PRESTIGE (CN/0227-7417) [08649560] **4921**

SPORT PSYCHOLOGIST, THE (US/0888-4781) [13609726] 4921, **4619**

SPORT PSYCHOLOGY TRAINING BULLETIN (US/1044-3118) [19746075] 4619, **4921**

SPORT QUEBEC (CN/0700-8791) [03406479] **4921**

SPORT REPORT (AT) **4921**

● SPORT RIDER (US/1065-7649) [26725835] **4921**

SPORT ROCKETRY (US/1076-2701) [30444195] 36, **2778**

SPORT SCENE (US/0270-1812) [06353273] 1784, **4921**

● SPORT SCIENCE REVIEW (CHAMPAIGN, ILL.) (US/1056-6724) [23819653] 5159, **4921**

SPORT STYLE (US/0162-2242) [04124256] 4921, **1087**

SPORT TRUCK (US/1044-7903) [19901355] **5425**

SPORT WYCZYNOWY (PL/0239-4405) [I02394405] **4921**

SPORT ZA RUBEZHOM *CEASED.* (RU/0234-8004) **4921**

SPORTBIKE (NEW YORK, N.Y.) (US/1060-8419) [24405289] **4921**

SPORTBOSTON (PHILADELPHIA, PA.) (US/1047-210X) [20641787] **4921**

SPORTCARE & FITNESS *CEASED.* (US/0899-3815) [18091205] 2601, **4921**

SPORTDOKUMENTATION : LITERATUR DER SPORTWISSENSCHAFT *CEASED.* (GW/0170-2890) [06118720] 1858, **4921**

SPORTERZIEHUNG IN DER SCHULE (SZ) [04527757] **1858**

SPORTING CLASSICS (US) [07568005] **4921**

SPORTING CLASSICS (OTTAWA) *CEASED.* (CN/0846-1333) [25796310] 252, **5425**

SPORTING CLAYS (US/1061-2424) [25123371] **4879**

SPORTING GOODS BUSINESS (US/0146-0889) [02850764] 4921, **713**

SPORTING GOODS BUYERS. NATIONAL DIRECTORY (US) [27015756] **951**

SPORTING GOODS DEALER, THE (US/0038-8017) [01715986] **4921**

SPORTING GOODS INTELLIGENCE (US/1060-2550) [24923825] 4921, **937**

SPORTING GOODS INTELLIGENCE (BRY-SUR-MARNE) (FR/1143-2462) [I11432462] **4921**

Alphabetical Title Index — SPOTLIGHT

SPORTING GOODS MARKET IN ..., THE (US/0193-8401) [03903134] 4921, **4879**

SPORTING GOODS REGISTER, THE (US/0363-1478) [02434721] **4921**

SPORTING GOODS REVIEW (CN/0827-5726) [13511776] 1627, **4921**

SPORTING LIFE (WESTMOUNT, QUEBEC) (CN/0826-5992) [11355437] **4921**

SPORTING NEWS BASEBALL GUIDE AND REGISTER. CD-ROM (US) **4921**

SPORTING NEWS ... BASEBALL YEARBOOK, THE (US/0275-0732) [07075462] **4921**

SPORTING NEWS COLLEGE BASKETBALL, THE (US/0895-0598) [16415959] **4921**

SPORTING NEWS ... COLLEGE FOOTBALL YEARBOOK, THE (US/0733-2823) [08560656] **4921**

SPORTING NEWS ... FANTASY BASEBALL OWNER'S MANUAL, THE (US/1052-7591) [22369482] **4922**

SPORTING NEWS HOCKEY, THE (US/1051-6018) [21994438] **4922**

SPORTING NEWS INSIDER REPORT, THE *CEASED.* (US/1062-2071) [25538449] **4922**

●SPORTING NEWS NBA GUIDE, THE (US) [26863941] **4922**

●SPORTING NEWS OFFICIAL BASEBALL REGISTER, THE (US) [25798333] 4922, **4856**

SPORTING NEWS ... PRO BASKETBALL YEARBOOK, THE (US/0895-0601) [16415942] **4922**

SPORTING NEWS PRO FOOTBALL REGISTER, THE (US) [24558764] **4922**

SPORTING NEWS ... PRO FOOTBALL YEARBOOK, THE (US/0276-2307) [07378912] **4922**

SPORTING NEWS ROTISSERIE & FANTASY BASEBALL LEAGUE GUIDE, THE *CEASED.* (US/1046-7017) [20496296] **4922**

SPORTING NEWS SUPER BOWL BOOK, THE (US/0275-4487) [07138835] **4922**

SPORTING NEWS, THE (US/0038-805X) [01642745] **4921**

SPORTING SCENE (SCARBOROUGH, ONT.) (CN/0824-9849) [10624722] **4922**

SPORTING TIMES (VERNON) (CN/1180-5080) [23598413] **4922**

SPORTING TRADITIONS (AT/0813-2577) [I08132577] **4922**

SPORTMASSAGE (NE) **4922**

SPORTMEDINFO FROM THE SPORT MEDICINE COUNCIL OF CANADA (CN/0824-4219) [19597943] **3956**

SPORTORVOSI SZEMLE (HU/0209-682X) [07030947] **3956**

SPORTS (SI) [06843852] **4922**

SPORTS ADDRESS BIBLE (US) **4922**

SPORTS ADVANTAGE *CEASED.* (US/1064-573X) [24147653] 766, **4922**

SPORTS AFIELD (1940) (US/0038-8149) [02379636] **4922**

SPORTS AFIELD ALMANAC *See* SPORTS AFIELD OUTDOOR ALMANAC, THE **4879**

SPORTS AFIELD DEER (US/0160-1830) [03638560] 4922, **4879**

SPORTS AFIELD HUNTING ANNUAL *See* HUNTING (NEW YORK, N.Y.) **4899**

SPORTS AFIELD OUTDOOR ALMANAC, THE (US/0190-1249) [04619584] **4879**

SPORTS & LEISURE RETAILER (AT/1035-915X) [I1035915X] **958**

SPORTS AND THE COURTS (US/0733-0669) [06501658] 4922, **3058**

SPORTS (BOCA RATON) (US/0273-2572) [05164090] **4922**

SPORTS BUSINESS (CN/0830-1921) [14956118] **958**

SPORTS CAR (US/0300-6387) [01346934] **5425**

SPORTS CAR CLUB OF AMERICA *See* GENERAL COMPETITION RULES (DENVER) **5415**

SPORTS CAR INTERNATIONAL (US/1042-9662) [19260380] 4922, **5425**

●SPORTS CARD PRICE GUIDE MONTHLY (US/1061-5512) [25353778] 4854, **4922**

SPORTS CARD TRADER (US/1050-365X) [21469543] **2778**

SPORTS CARDS (US/1069-2282) [27781813] **2778**

SPORTS CARS IN REVIEW (US/0096-3313) [01798523] **5425**

SPORTS CLUB MAGAZINE (CN/0225-1876) [06020912] **4922**

SPORTS COACH (AT) [14755937] **4922**

SPORTS (COACHING ASSOCIATION OF CANADA : 1980) (CN/0820-6457) [09506647] 3956, 4922, **1858**

SPORTS COLLECTORS DIGEST (US/0278-2693) [07760556] **4922**

SPORTS COLLECTORS DIGEST FOOTBALL, BASKETBALL & HOCKEY PRICE GUIDE / BY THE STAFF OF SPORTS COLLECTORS DIGEST (US) [25080096] 4922, **2778**

SPORTS COUNCIL STUDY (UK) [17165294] 4854, **4922**

SPORTS DIRECTORY (CN/0380-5751) [02578706] **4922**

SPORTS DOCUMENTATION MONTHLY BULLETIN (UK) [08127368] **4922**

●SPORTS, EXERCISE AND INJURY (UK/1351-0029) 4922, **3058**

●SPORTS FAN'S CONNECTION (US/1059-0862) [24478649] **4922**

SPORTS FEDERATION OF CANADA *See* DIRECTORY - SPORTS FEDERATION OF CANADA **4893**

SPORTS HERITAGE (US/0895-0350) [16089278] **4922**

SPORTS HIGH (US/0733-8740) [08649298] **4922**

SPORTS ILLUSTRATED (US/0038-822X) [01766364] **4922**

SPORTS ILLUSTRATED FOR KIDS (US/1042-394X) [19017159] 4923, **1069**

●SPORTS ILLUSTRATED ... SPORTS ALMANAC, THE (US/1056-7887) [23853505] **4923**

SPORTS IN ROMANIA : MAGAZINE OF THE ROMANIAN OLYMPIC COMMITTEE (RM) [10603118] **4923**

SPORTS IN THE GDR *CEASED.* (GW/0584-9209) [05773937] **4923**

SPORTS INDUSTRY NEWS (US/0742-2024) [10304646] **4923**

SPORTS INSTRUCTION SERIES (NZ) [25858099] 1858, **4923**

SPORTS LAW AND FINANCE (UK) [I09686037] **4923**

SPORTS LAW REPORTER (US/0195-8623) [04394924] 4923, **3058**

SPORTS LITERATURE INDEX (US/0195-8100) [05664132] **4923**

SPORTS-LOISIRS (MONTREAL) (CN/0826-5305) [11895274] **4923**

SPORTS MARKET PLACE (US/1055-8020) [10549975] **4923**

SPORTS MARKETING NEWS *CEASED.* (US/0898-6541) [14699729] **4923**

●SPORTS MEDICINE AND ARTHROSCOPY REVIEW (US/1062-8592) [25771795] **3956**

SPORTS MEDICINE (AUCKLAND) (NZ/0112-1642) [10493825] **3956**

SPORTS MEDICINE BULLETIN (LONDON, ENGLAND) (UK/0952-4630) [18489097] **3956**

SPORTS MEDICINE DIGEST (US/0731-9770) [15811304] **3956**

SPORTS MEDICINE (MOUNT KISCO) (US/0271-2857) [05591748] **3956**

SPORTS MEDICINE NEWS (US) **3956**

SPORTS MEDICINE STANDARDS AND MALPRACTICE REPORTER, THE (US/1041-696X) [18826291] **3956**

SPORTS MEDICINE, TRAINING, AND REHABILITATION (SZ/1057-8315) [24124745] **3956**

SPORTS MEDICINE UPDATE (US) [21211957] **3956**

SPORTS. MIT SPORT ILLUSTRIERTE (GW) **4923**

●SPORTS-N-REVIEW (US/1062-8215) [25760544] **4923**

SPORTS 'N SPOKES (US/0161-6706) [03984111] 4394, **4923**

SPORTS NUTRITION (UK) 4923, **4199**

SPORTS, PARKS & RECREATION LAW REPORTER, THE (US/0893-8210) [15649531] 4708, **3058**

SPORTS PERIODICALS INDEX, THE *CEASED.* (US/0883-1580) [12074596] **4923**

SPORTS PHYSIOLOGY & MEDICINE (UK/0967-7755) **3956**

SPORTS PROFILES (US) **4923**

SPORTS QUARTERLY PRESENTS INSIDE HOCKEY (US/0732-0043) [08291829] **4923**

SPORTS REVIEW WRESTLING (AMBLER, PA.) (US/1073-1326) [29338635] **4923**

SPORTS : SCIENCE PERIODICAL ON RESEARCH AND TECHNOLOGY IN SPORT / COACHING ASSOCIATION OF CANADA *See* COACHES REPORT **1855**

SPORTS TRAINERS DIGEST : A CONTINUING EDUCATION SERVICE OF THE AUSTRALIAN SPORTS MEDICINE FEDERATION / NATIONAL SPORTS TRAINERS SCHEME (AT/1032-5506) [29705945] **3956**

SPORTS TRAINING, MEDICINE AND REHABILITATION *See* SPORTS MEDICINE, TRAINING, AND REHABILITATION **3956**

SPORTS TREND (US/0890-8745) [14442141] **958**

SPORTS TURF BULLETIN (UK/0490-5474) [I04905474] **4923**

SPORTS TURF RESEARCH INSTITUTE, BINGLEY, YORKSHIRE, THE *See* JOURNAL OF THE SPORTS TURF RESEARCH INSTITUTE, THE **4902**

SPORTS WEEKLY NEWSLETTER/BASKETBALL (US) **4923**

SPORTS WEEKLY NEWSLETTER/ FOOTBALL/ THE LITTLE GREEN SHEET (US) **4923**

SPORTSCAPE (US/0272-7579) [06912542] **4923**

SPORTSEARCH (US/0882-553X) [11881394] 1858, 4923, **4856**

SPORTSMAN PILOT (HALES CORNERS, WIS.) (US/0279-1749) [07602111] **36**

SPORTSMEDICINE DIGEST (US/0731-9770) [06767529] **3956**

SPORTSNETWORK (AT/1033-8977) [I10338977] **4923**

SPORTSTATTEN IN NORDRHEIN-WESTFALEN / HERAUSGEBER LANDESAMT FUR DATENVERARBEITUNG UND STATISTIK NORDRHEIN-WESTFALEN (GW) [08948643] **4923**

●SPORTSTURF (1992) (US/1061-687X) [25405114] **2431**

SPORTSTYLE (CONSUMER EDITION) (US/0733-8708) [08691602] **4923**

SPORTSWEAR INTERNATIONAL (U.S.A. ED.) (US/0743-1155) [10554400] **1087**

SPORTSWEAR INTERNATIONAL'S KIDS (US) 1069, **1087**

SPORTSWOMAN, THE (US/0099-0388) [02243208] 5566, **4923**

SPORTUNTERRICHT (GW/0342-2402) [01785956] 4923, **1858**

SPORTVERLETZUNG, SPORTSCHADEN (GW/0932-0555) [19345945] **3956**

SPORTVEZETO (HU) [04327451] **4923**

SPORTWISSENSCHAFT (GW) [01786141] **4923**

SPORTWISSENSCHAFT UND SPORTPRAXIS (GW) [06241192] **4923**

SPOSA (IT) **5566**

SPOSABELLA (IT/0394-3682) [I03943682] **1087**

SPOT (CI) [01785623] **4377**

SPOT (HOUSTON, TEX.) (US/1049-0450) [11646270] **4377**

SPOT RADIO (US/1066-2030) [26888671] **1139**

SPOT RADIO RATES AND DATA (US/0038-9560) [06225735] **766**

SPOT TELEVISION RATES AND DATA (US/0038-9552) [06273389] 1139, **766**

SPOT TV & CABLE SOURCE (US/1071-4596) [28934983] 766, **1139**

SPOTKANIA Z ZABYTKAMI (PL/0137-222X) [I0137222X] **283**

SPOTLIGHT (US) **2836**

SPOTLIGHT (DK) [01791985] 1139, **4078**

SPOTLIGHT. ACTORS (UK/0309-0183) [I03090183] **388**

SPOTLIGHT. ACTRESSES (UK/0308-9827) [I03089827] **388**

SPOTLIGHT (BROOKLYN, N.Y.) (US/1044-1247) [19688855] **2512**

"SPOTLIGHT" CASTING DIRECTORY, THE (UK) [06064019] **4078**

SPOTLIGHT CASTING MAGAZINE (US/1057-8234) [24123630] **4078**

SPOTLIGHT CONTACTS (UK/0010-7344) [06056635] **388**

SPOTLIGHT (INDIANAPOLIS, IND.) (US) [16403579] **5667**

SPOTLIGHT (NEW YORK) (US/0161-004X) [03804924] **2762**

SPOTLIGHT ON AFRICA (US/0584-9365) [04904157] **4496**

SPOTLIGHT ON AIDS (US/0895-755X) [16784764] 4803, **3677**

SPOTLIGHT ON CAREER PLANNING, PLACEMENT AND RECRUITMENT (US/0162-1068) [04100455] **4209**

SPOTLIGHT ON YOUTH SPORTS (US/0740-0802) [08216941] **4923**

SPOTLIGHT / SOUTH AFRICAN INSTITUTE OF RACE RELATIONS (SA) [24382096] 2273, **5263**

SPOTLIGHT (VANCOUVER) (CN/0821-4778) [09590440] **388**

SPOTLIGHT (WASHINGTON), THE (US/0191-6270) [02481738] **5648**

SPOTLIGHT — Alphabetical Title Index

SPOTLIGHT (WAYNE, N.J.) (US/0890-4170) [14231329] **1103**

SPOTLIGHTING PLAYS ON ALCOHOL AND OTHER DRUGS (CN/1189-3397) [25796788] 1349, **5368**

SPOTS (US/0095-7461) [01798310] **388**

SPOTTED NEWS (US/0038-8432) [01645796] **222**

SPR STUDENT PRESS REVIEW (US) **2924**

SPRACHDIENST, DER (GW/0038-8459) [05234423] **3323**

SPRACHE (AU/0376-401X) [01716759] **3323**

SPRACHE & KOGNITION (SZ/0253-4533) [09651478] 4619, **3323**

SPRACHE DER GEGENWART (GW) [03441320] **3323**

SPRACHE IM TECHNISCHEN ZEITALTER (GW/0038-8475) [01641356] 3439, **3353**

SPRACHE-STIMME-GEHOR (GW/0342-0477) [03793871] **4394**

SPRACHE UND DATENVERARBEITUNG (GW/0343-5202) [03714976] 1122, **3323**

SPRACHE UND DICHTUNG (SZ/0081-3826) [01587471] **3439**

SPRACHE UND INFORMATION (GW) [11929853] **3323**

SPRACHE UND LITERATUR IN WISSENSCHAFT UND UNTERRICHT (GW/0724-9713) [10157898] 3439, **3323**

SPRACHHEILPADAGOGE, DER (AU/0586-660X) [04116440] 1885, **4394**

SPRACHKUNST (AU/0038-8483) [01766370] 3439, **3323**

SPRACHMITTLER, DER (GW/0038-8505) [07513883] 3439, **3323**

SPRACHREPORT / INSTITUT FUER DEUTSCHE SPRACHE (GW) [16949224] **3323**

SPRACHSPIEGEL (SZ/0038-8513) [01977923] **3323**

SPRACHSTRUKTUREN. REIHE A: HISTORISCHE SPRACHSTRUKTUREN (GW) [03036326] 3323, **2630**

●SPRACHTYPOLOGIE UND UNIVERSALIENFORSCHUNG (GW/0942-2919) [28164484] **3323**

SPRACHWISSENSCHAFT (GW/0344-8169) [03921587] **3323**

SPRAK NYTT (NO) [04525976] **3323**

●SPRAK OCH STIL (SW/1101-1165) [27123923] **3323**

SPRAKVARD (SW/0038-8440) [07269256] **3323**

SPRAVNI PRAVO (XR/0139-6005) [10167506] **3094**

SPRAVODAJCA MINISTERSTVA STAVEBNICTVA SLOVENSKEJ SOCIALISTICKEJ REPUBLIKY (XO) [03635247] **628**

SPRAWOZDANIA ARCHEOLOGICZNE (PL/0081-3834) [01978166] **283**

SPRAWOZDANIA - POZNANSKIE TOWARZYSTWO PRZYJACIO NAUK. WYDZIA HISTORII I NAUK SPOECZNYCH (PL/0137-5857) [01375857] **2630**

SPRAWY I LUDZIE (PL) [09275050] **2523**

SPRAWY MIEDZYNARODOWE (PL/0038-853X) [01983309] **4535**

SPRAY TECHNOLOGY & MARKETING (US/1055-2340) [23123720] **4222**

SPREADING THE FAME OF CHRIST (US/0744-6780) [08489426] **4999**

SPRECHSAAL (GW/0341-0439) [04205498] **2594**

SPRECHSAAL 1976 (GW/0341-0676) [I03410676] 375, **2594**

SPRING (US/0362-0522) [01817223] **4619**

SPRING-AUTUMN PAPERS (US/0273-4532) [06997328] **2665**

SPRING CATALOGUE / BERKSHIRE GARDEN SUPPLY (US) [12006306] **2432**

SPRING FEVER (US/1055-4874) [23190811] **4866**

SPRING GROVE HERALD (US) [01766374] **5698**

SPRING (NEW YORK, N.Y. : 1982) (US/0735-6889) [08963944] **3472**

SPRING ... PRICE LIST - ECCLES NURSERIES (US) [12219728] **2432**

SPRING TESTING PROGRAM IN INDEPENDENT SCHOOLS AND SUPPLEMENTARY STUDIES (US/0093-6219) [01789725] **1784**

SPRING VALLEY SUN (SPRING VALLEY, WIS. : 1952) (US) [13049471] **5771**

SPRING VEGETABLES, SPRING MELONS See ACREAGE MARKETING GUIDES. SPRING VEGETABLES AND MELONS **2407**

SPRINGER PROCEEDINGS IN PHYSICS (GW/0930-8989) [11758206] **4422**

SPRINGER SEMINARS IN IMMUNOPATHOLOGY (US/0344-4325) [04212631] 3898, **3677**

SPRINGER SERIES, FOCUS ON WOMEN (US/0272-202X) [06617233] **5566**

SPRINGER SERIES IN BIOPHYSICS (GW/0932-2353) [15470847] **496**

SPRINGER SERIES IN BRAIN DYNAMICS (GW) [18466984] **3642**

SPRINGER SERIES IN CHEMICAL PHYSICS (GW/0172-6218) [04880076] **4442**

SPRINGER SERIES IN COMPUTATIONAL MATHEMATICS (GW/0179-3632) [10586583] **1262**

SPRINGER SERIES IN COMPUTATIONAL PHYSICS (GW/0172-5726) [08459956] **4422**

SPRINGER SERIES IN ELECTRONICS AND PHOTONICS (GW/0931-7260) [15469658] **2082**

SPRINGER SERIES IN EXPERIMENTAL ENTOMOLOGY (US/0172-6188) [06434514] **5613**

SPRINGER SERIES IN INFORMATION SCIENCES (GW/0720-678X) [07342909] **4619**

SPRINGER SERIES IN LANGUAGE AND COMMUNICATION (GW/0172-620X) [05655991] **3323**

SPRINGER SERIES IN MATERIALS SCIENCE (GW) [17021227] **2108**

SPRINGER SERIES IN MICROBIOLOGY (US/0172-6331) [07355452] **570**

SPRINGER SERIES IN OPTICAL SCIENCES (US/0342-4111) [03282621] **4442**

SPRINGER SERIES IN SOLID-STATE SCIENCES (GW/0171-1873) [06493285] 4422, **993**

SPRINGER SERIES IN SURFACE SCIENCES (GW/0931-5195) [13486681] **4422**

SPRINGER SERIES IN SYNERGETICS (GW/0172-7389) [06389779] **5159**

SPRINGER SERIES ON ADULTHOOD AND AGING CEASED. (US/0272-5835) [05154100] **3755**

SPRINGER SERIES ON ATOMS + PLASMAS (GW/0177-6495) [12232178] **4422**

SPRINGER SERIES ON BEHAVIOR THERAPY AND BEHAVIORAL MEDICINE (US/0278-6729) [07016988] **4619**

SPRINGER SERIES ON DEATH AND SUICIDE, THE (US/0271-1192) [05762983] 5263, **4361**

SPRINGER SERIES ON ENVIRONMENTAL MANAGEMENT (US/0172-6161) [07355469] 2314, **2206**

SPRINGER SERIES ON PSYCHIATRY (US/0740-4212) [08592191] **3937**

SPRINGER SERIES ON SOCIAL WORK (US/0891-9720) [11946165] **5311**

SPRINGER TRACTS IN MODERN PHYSICS (GW/0081-3869) [01766379] **4422**

SPRINGER TRACTS IN NATURAL PHILOSOPHY (GW/0081-3877) [02253591] **4361**

SPRINGER'S HANDBOOK OF NORTH AMERICAN CINDERELLA STAMPS, INCLUDING TAXPAID REVENUES (US/0738-2529) [09536828] **1147**

SPRINGFIELD ADVANCE-PRESS (US) [01588118] **5698**

SPRINGFIELD COLLEGE See ALUMNI DIRECTORY - SPRINGFIELD COLLEGE **1099**

SPRINGFIELD MAGAZINE (US/0164-6745) [04430317] **2546**

SPRINGFIELD MAGAZINE (SPRINGFIELD, MO.) (US/0195-0894) [05274029] **2546**

SPRINGFIELD NEWS-SUN (US/0744-6101) [08440215] **5730**

SPRINGFIELD SUN, THE (US) [13868417] **5682**

SPRINGHOUSE, THE (US/0888-3319) [11481647] **2324**

SPRINGS MAGAZINE (COLORADO SPRINGS, COLO.) (US/0748-6405) [10979189] **2546**

SPRINGS VALLEY HERALD (US) [12180220] **5667**

SPRINGVILLE HERALD (SPRINGVILLE, UTAH) (US) [13000326] **5757**

SPRINGWELLS UPDATE (US/1058-1820) [24236968] **1784**

SPRINKLER AGE (US/0896-2685) [09045823] **2292**

SPROG OG KULTUR CEASED. (DK/0038-8645) [01766382] **3323**

SPROUSE'S INCOME TAX HANDBOOK See MONEY INCOME TAX HANDBOOK, THE **4737**

SPS CHAPTER LIST (US/0197-6761) [06076561] **4422**

SPS NEWSREPORT CEASED. (US/0274-9777) [06826646] **2924**

SPSC LETTER (US/0891-608X) [10730564] **4496**

SPSM&H (US/0891-2378) [14689328] **3439**

SPUDMAN (US/0038-8661) [01766384] **137**

SPUMS JOURNAL (AT/0813-1988) [16986801] **3642**

SPUN YARN PRODUCTION (US/0277-0733) [03060422] 5356, **3488**

SPUNTI E RICERCHE (AT/0816-5432) [15334896] 3323, **3439**

SPUR AND PHOENIX, THE (US/0275-4525) [07117837] **2473**

SPUR (DELAPLANE) (US/0098-5422) [02240399] **2802**

SPUR OF VIRGINIA See SPUR (DELAPLANE) **2802**

SPUR REPORT (US/0361-6444) [01968998] **2836**

SPURS & FEATHERS (US/0745-4368) [09159805] **4923**

SPUTNIK (ANGL. JAZ.) (RU/0131-8721) [01680817] **2523**

SPUTNIK MOLODOGO RABOCHEGO (RU) [02242129] **5159**

SPUTNIK SELSKOI MOLODEZHI (RU) [02242130] **137**

SPW (GW/0170-4613) [08735143] **4547**

SPY (NEW YORK, N.Y.) (US/0890-1759) [14162898] **2546**

SPYGLASS (US/0272-619X) [06868717] **596**

SQL FORUM (US/1068-0950) [26707864] **1204**

SQUARE ONE SYDNEY (AT/0725-1092) [I07251092] **3536**

SQUASH LIFE (CN/0821-025X) [09658270] **4923**

SQUASH NEWS (HOPE VALLEY, R.I.) (US/0164-7148) [04415350] **4924**

SQUASH PLAYER INTERNATIONAL (UK) **4924**

SQUASH REVIEW (CN/0229-2351) [08072153] **4924**

SQUATCHBERRY JOURNAL, THE (CN/0383-283X) [03235575] **3439**

SR SUPPLEMENTS (CN) [05356320] **4999**

SR. TEXAS (US) **5182**

SRA JOURNAL (US/1062-8142) [24484610] **5159**

SRA "OUTFIT" NEWSLETTER (US/0149-1458) [03427447] **36**

SRASHTA (II) [08426626] **3439**

SRAVNITELNO LITERATUROZNANIE / [BULGARSKA AKADEMIIA NA NAUKITE, INSTITUT ZA LITERATURA] (BU/0205-0390) [09961494] **3439**

SRBIJA (WINONA) (CN/0715-5921) [10082503] **5795**

SRC BLUE BOOK OF 5-TREND CYCLI-GRAPHS, THE (US/8750-2356) [10992534] **914**

SRC GREEN BOOK OF 5-TREND 35-YEAR CHARTS, THE (US/0884-8475) [10907788] **914**

●SRC ORANGE BOOK OF 5-TREND LONG-TERM O-T-C CHARTS, THE (US/1063-5173) [26049468] **812**

SRC RED BOOK OF 5-TREND SECURITY CHARTS, THE (US/8750-2461) [10992597] **914**

SRC UNITED STATES FACULTY SOURCEBOOK, THE (US) [23238067] **1847**

SRD REPORT. UNITED KINGDOM ATOMIC ENERGY AUTHORITY, SAFETY AND RELIABILITY DIRECTORATE (UK/0372-4255) [I03724255] 1958, **4422**

●SRDS MEDIA & MARKET PLANNER. ARCHITECTURAL & CONSTRUCTION MARKETS (US/1064-5500) [26328858] 309, **628**

SRDS MEDIA & MARKET PLANNER. HEALTHCARE MARKETS (US/1064-4636) [26178313] 3792, **766**

SRDS REPORT, THE CEASED. (US/1047-0433) [19330609] **766**

SRDS SPOT RADIO SMALL MARKETS EDITION (US) [02980483] **766**

SRDS ... TRADESHOW CATALOG, THE CEASED. (US/1064-5748) [25994121] **766**

SREB ANNUAL REPORT (US) [06510437] **1784**

SREDNEE SPETSIALNOE OBRAZOVANIE See SPETSIALIST **1915**

SREDNEVEKOVYI GOROD (RU) [02239288] **2836**

Alphabetical Title Index — ST

●SREDNIE SPETSIALNYE UCHEBNYE ZAVEDENIIA PETERBURGA I OBLASTI (RU) [26738746] **1916**

SREDNIE VEKA (RU) [01840890] **2630**

SREDNIE VEKA (RU/0131-8780) [01793227] **2710**

SREDNIOWIECZE (PL/0079-3183) [I00793183] 1080, **2710**

SREDNJE USMERENO OBRAZOVANJE (PO REGIONIMA I OPSTINAMA) / SOCIJALISTICKA REPUBLIKA SRBIJA, REPUBLICKI ZAVOD ZA STATISTIKU (CI) [08287315] **5338**

SRI AUROBINDO CENTENARY ANNUAL (CE) [01788084] **4999**

SRI AUROBINDO INTERNATIONAL CENTRE OF EDUCATION, PONDICHERRY, INDIA See BULLETIN **4343**

SRI LANKA See SESSIONAL PAPER - SRI LANKA **4686**

SRI LANKA See STATE ACCOUNTS OF THE REPUBLIC OF SRI LANKA FOR THE YEAR ... **4748**

SRI LANKA ATTORNEY-AT-LAW, THE (CE) [02245580] **3058**

SRI LANKA (CEYLON) : WIRTSCHAFTLICHE ENTWICKLUNG (GW) [01798322] **1585**

SRI LANKA : ENERGIEWIRTSCHAFT (GW) [05691255] **1958**

SRI LANKA FORESTER, THE (CE/0258-624X) [02253139] **2396**

SRI LANKA HUMAN RIGHTS BULLETIN (AT/0816-7095) [I08167095] **4513**

SRI LANKA (ISBN) PUBLISHERS DIRECTORY (CE) [18993684] **3251**

SRI LANKA JATIKA GRANTHA NAMAVALIYA (CE/0253-8229) [03582032] **425**

SRI LANKA JOURNAL OF SOCIAL SCIENCES (CE/0258-9710) [06704315] **5223**

SRI LANKA JOURNAL OF TEA SCIENCE (CE/1010-4208) [14339711] **2371**

SRI LANKA JOURNAL OF THE HUMANITIES, THE (CE/0378-486X) [03058595] **2854**

SRI LANKA LABOUR GAZETTE (CE/0379-3737) [01790441] **1711**

SRI LANKA LIBRARY REVIEW (CE) [02550957] **3251**

SRI LANKA. NITI KOMISAN DEPARTAMENTUVA See ANNUAL REPORT / THE LAW COMMISSION, SRI LANKA **2935**

SRI LANKA POLICE JOURNAL (CE) [02245579] **3177**

SRI LANKA. RAJYA ARAKSAKE HA VIDESA KATAYUTU AMATYAMSAYA See DIPLOMATIC, CONSULAR AND OTHER REPRESENTATION IN THE DEMOCRATIC SOCIALIST REPUBLIC OF SRI LANKA **3127**

SRI LANKA. RAJYA PARIPALANA HA SVADESA KATAYUTU AMATYAMSAYA See PERFORMANCE REPORT - MINISTRY OF PUBLIC ADMINISTRATION AND HOME AFFAIRS **4673**

SRI LANKA. SRESTHADHIKARANAYA See MODERN LAW REPORTS, EMBODYING CASES DECIDED BY THE SUPREME COURT OF THE REPUBLIC OF SRI LANKA **3011**

SRI LANKA SURVEYOR : JOURNAL OF THE SURVEYORS' INSTITUTE OF SRI LANKA (CE) [18039858] **2031**

SRI LANKA. TAPAL HA VIDULI SANDESA AMATYAMSAYA See PERFORMANCE REPORT - MINISTRY OF POSTS & TELECOMMUNICATIONS **1161**

SRI LANKA VETERINARY JOURNAL : THE OFFICIAL JOURNAL OF THE SRI LANKA VETERINARY ASSOCIATION, THE (CE) [10691263] **5522**

SRI LANKA, WIRTSCHAFTSDATEN / BUNDESSTELLE FUER AUSSENHANDELSINFORMATION (GW) [11394358] **1585**

SRI LANKA, WIRTSCHAFTSDATEN UND WIRTSCHAFTSDOKUMENTATION / BUNDESSTELLE FUR AUSSENHANDELSINFORMATION (GW) [09047299] **1585**

SRI LANKA YEAR BOOK (CE/0256-808X) [04803845] **2526**

SRI LANKAN FAMILY PHYSICIAN (CE/0254-8623) [09149059] **3739**

SRI LANKAN JOURNAL OF AGRICULTURAL SCIENCES (CE) [10894076] **137**

SRI VARSHA SAPTAHIKA (II) [08353850] **2508**

SRINAGAR LAW JOURNAL (II) [07097080] **3058**

SRIRANGA (II) [02240253] **2665**

SRIS MICROFICHE CATALOGUE See SCICAT SCIENCE REFERENCE AND INFORMATION SERVICE **992**

SRM BIBLIOGRAPHY (NE) [05854276] **5263**

SRPSKA AKADEMIJA NAUKA I UMETNOSTI See BULLETIN - ACADEMIE SERBE DES SCIENCES ET DES ARTS. CLASSE DES SCIENCES SOCIALES **5193**

SRPSKA AKADEMIJA NAUKA I UMETNOSTI. GLAS. ODELJENJE TEHNICKIH NAUKA (YU/0374-0803) [01794027] 1997, **5159**

SRPSKA AKADEMIJA NAUKA I UMETNOSTI. ODELJENJE PRIRODNO-MATEMATICKIH NAUKA See BULLETIN - ACADEMIE SERBE DES SCIENCES ET DES ARTS, CLASSE DES SCIENCES NATURELLES ET MATHEMATIQUES. SCIENCES NATURELLES **5090**

SRPSKA AKADEMIJA NAUKA I UMETNOSTI. ODELJENJE PRIRODNO-MATEMATICKIKH NAUKA See GLAS - SRPSKA AKADEMIJA NAUKA I UMETNOSTI, ODELJENJE PRIRODNO-MATEMATICKIKH NAUKA **2589**

SRPSKA BORBA (US/0279-1293) [07590068] 5263, **2273**

SRPSKI ARHIV ZA CELOKUPNO LEKARSTVO. / ARCHIVES SERBES DE MEDECINE GENERAL / SERBIAN ARCHIVES OF GENERAL MEDICINE (YU/0049-0210) [01778400] **3642**

SRRT NEWSLETTER (CHICAGO, ILL.) (US/0749-1670) [11087358] **3251**

SSCI JCR [MICROFORM] / ISI (US) [23915248] **5223**

SSCR JOURNAL (UK/0959-2369) [I09592369] **283**

SSELECT (US/0895-7746) [16811539] **1204**

SSHA (RU/0321-2068) [02046098] **1595**

SSHOP NEWSLETTER (UK) [11603873] **4377**

SSHRC NEWS (CN/0839-4377) [18528428] 2855, **5223**

SSI (US/0160-0400) [03590415] **1272**

SSI RECIPIENTS BY STATE AND COUNTY (US) [25904700] **5311**

SSI, SHORT STORY INTERNATIONAL (US/0147-7706) [03224761] **3439**

SSI UPDATE (US/0898-8242) [17926403] 41, **36**

SSIAL UI SORI (KO) [05204497] **4361**

SSRC STUDENTSHIP HANDBOOK. POSTGRADUATE STUDENTSHIPS IN THE SOCIAL SCIENCES (UK) [07033157] **5223**

SSRS NEWSLETTER CEASED. (US/0036-1917) [01639939] **5160**

SSSA SPECIAL PUBLICATION (US/1063-2565) [25739543] **188**

SSSR, ADMINISTRATIVNO-TERRITORIALNO E DELENIE SOIUZNYKH RESPUBLIK (RU) [09546421] **4687**

SSSR I ZARUBEZHNYE STRANY (RU) [19504495] **1585**

SSSR KHALQ DEPUTATLARI SEZDI VA SSSR OLII SOVETINING AKHBOROTNOMASI (UZ/0207-7280) [23242613] **4497**

SSU-CHUAN CHIAO YU SICHUAN JIAOYU (CC) [08962535] **1784**

SSU-CHUAN HUA PAO (CC) [11654458] **2665**

SSU-CHUAN SHIH YUAN HSUEH PAO. SHE HUI KO HSUEH PAN / SICHUANSHI YUANXUEBAO (CC) [09232260] **2665**

SSU-CHUAN TA HSUEH HSUEH PAO. TZU JAN KO HSUEH PAN (CC/0490-6756) [09224395] 5160, **4172**

SSU-CHUAN TU SHU KUAN HSUEH PAO (CC) [08442524] **3251**

SSU-CHUAN WEN HSUEH (CC) [25315349] **3439**

ST. ALBANS DAILY MESSENGER See ST. ALBANS MESSENGER **5757**

ST. ALBANS MESSENGER (US) [11932116] **5757**

ST. ANDREW'S SOCIETY OF TORONTO See NEWS LETTER OF THE ST. ANDREW'S SOCIETY OF TORONTO **5234**

ST. ANTHONY MESSENGER (US/0036-276X) [01589392] **5036**

ST. ANTHONY'S ICD-9-CM CODING FOR PHYSICIAN REIMBURSEMENT (US) [20372189] **2894**

ST. BONIFACE GENERAL HOSPITAL See PERSPECTIVES - ST. BONIFACE GENERAL HOSPITAL **3791**

ST. CATHARINES (CN/0824-6572) [10926546] **5491**

ST. CHARLES JOURNAL (US) [20213561] **5704**

ST. CHARLES PRESS (US) [01716125] **5698**

ST. CLAIR COUNTY GENEALOGICAL SOCIETY QUARTERLY (US/0882-6528) [09113171] **2473**

ST. CLAIR NEWS-AEGIS (US/1044-1964) [12038473] **5628**

ST. CLAIR SERIES IN MANAGEMENT AND ORGANIZATIONAL BEHAVIOR, THE (US/0277-0458) [07487113] **886**

ST. CLOUD SMSA ANNUAL PLANNING INFORMATION REPORT See ST. CLOUD SMSA LABOR MARKET INFORMATION SUMMARY FOR ... **1711**

ST. CLOUD SMSA LABOR MARKET INFORMATION SUMMARY FOR ... (US) [09889481] **1711**

ST. CLOUD STATE UNIVERSITY CHRONICLE (US/0747-1025) [07881238] **1095**

ST. CLOUD TIMES (US/0899-5028) [18126925] **5698**

ST COMPUTER (GW) **1204**

ST. CROIX AVIS (VI) [10476288] **5813**

ST. CROIX COUNTY STAR (US/1053-539X) [22376539] **5771**

ST. CROIX REVIEW, THE (US/0093-2582) [01792218] **5223**

ST. CROIX VALLEY PRESS (US/0892-1784) [15144327] **5698**

ST. FRANCIS YACHT CLUB (SAN FRANCISCO, CALIF.) See MAINSHEET (SAN FRANCISCO, CALIF.) **594**

ST. GAME (US/0882-6862) [11806651] 1272, **1230**

ST. GEORGE MAGAZINE (US/0882-8741) [12001499] **5491**

ST. IGNACE NEWS (US) **5694**

ST. JAMES GUIDE TO BIOGRAPHY (US) 435, **439**

ST. JAMES MUTUAL FUND DIRECTORY / INVESTMENT COMPANY INSTITUTE (US) [23244011] **914**

●ST. JAMES WORLD FUTURES AND OPTIONS DIRECTORY (US) [23461409] **914**

ST. JOHN AMBULANCE. ONTARIO COUNCIL See ONTARIO COUNCIL BULLETIN **4671**

ST. JOHN NEWS (CN/0380-8181) [02111709] **5311**

ST. JOHN'S JOURNAL OF LEGAL COMMENTARY (US/1049-0299) [13432620] **3058**

ST. JOHN'S LAW REVIEW (US/0036-2905) [01764779] **3058**

ST. JOHN'S OBELISK, THE (US/1060-829X) [25069555] **1095**

ST. JOHNS REVIEW (1981), THE (US/0277-4720) [07481416] 2855, **1847**

ST. JOSEPH JOURNAL OF LIVESTOCK AND AGRICULTURE CEASED. (US/0162-5225) [01782095] **222**

●ST. JOSEPH NEWS-PRESS (1992) (US/1063-4312) [26027494] **5704**

ST. JOSEPH NEWS-PRESS/GAZETTE (US/0899-711X) [21981673] **5704**

ST. LAMBERT JOURNAL (CN/0826-4295) [11108253] **5795**

ST-LAURENT (CN/0228-7846) [08003195] **375**

●ST. LAWRENCE ISLANDS NATIONAL PARK, MANAGEMENT PLAN REVIEW (CN/1191-4718) [26758059] **4708**

ST. LAWRENCE SEAWAY DEVELOPMENT CORPORATION See ANNUAL REPORT / SAINT LAWRENCE SEAWAY DEVELOPMENT CORPORATION **5447**

ST. LAWRENCE UNIVERSITY, CANTON, N.Y. DEPT. OF GEOLOGY AND GEOGRAPHY See MONOGRAPH OF THE DEPARTMENT OF GEOLOGY AND GEOGRAPHY, ST. LAWRENCE UNIVERSITY **1388**

ST. LAWRENCE UPDATE (CN/1180-1220) [23243167] **5393**

ST. LOUIS CEASED. (US/0272-1279) [05297869] **2546**

ST. LOUIS ARGUS (US) [02934741] **5704**

ST. LOUIS ART MUSEUM See ST. LOUIS ART MUSEUM ANNUAL REPORT, THE **365**

ST. LOUIS ART MUSEUM ANNUAL REPORT, THE (US/0899-4730) [07032339] 4096, **365**

ST. LOUIS BAR JOURNAL (US/0581-3344) [03023880] **3058**

ST. LOUIS BUSINESS JOURNAL (US/0271-6453) [06674071] **713**

ST. LOUIS COMMERCE (US/0036-293X) [21301249] **851**

ST. LOUIS COUNTIAN, THE (US/0036-2948) [03918772] **5704**

ST. LOUIS DAILY RECORD (US) [04508937] **3058**

ST. LOUIS HOME/GARDEN (US/0190-4205) [04705431] 2432, **2903**

ST. LOUIS JOURNALISM REVIEW, THE (US/0036-2972) [01784457] **2924**

ST. LOUIS MANAGER *CEASED.* (US/0746-8903) [10377622] **886**

ST. LOUIS METRO MEDIA GUIDE (US/0276-1726) [07208984] **1122**

ST. LOUIS METROPOLITAN MEDICINE (US/0892-1334) [05174013] **3642**

ST. LOUIS. MISSOURI BOTANICAL GARDEN *See* MISSOURI BOTANICAL GARDEN BULLETIN **518**

ST. LOUIS POST-DISPATCH (US) [01764810] **5704**

ST. LOUIS REVIEW (US/0036-3022) [02267401] **5036**

ST. LOUIS SENTINEL (US) [02935779] **5704**

ST. LOUIS/SOUTHERN ILLINOIS LABOR TRIBUNE (US/0885-6869) [12709875] **1711**

ST. LOUIS SYMPHONY ORCHESTRA *See* [PROGRAMS] / ST. LOUIS SYMPHONY ORCHESTRA **4160**

ST. LOUIS UNIVERSITY (PHILIPPINES). GRADUATE SCHOOL OF ARTS AND SCIENCES *See* ST. LOUIS UNIVERSITY RESEARCH JOURNAL **2855**

ST. LOUIS UNIVERSITY RESEARCH JOURNAL (PH/0036-3014) [02024537] **2855**

ST. LOUIS UNIVERSITY. SCHOOL OF LAW *See* SAINT LOUIS UNIVERSITY LAW JOURNAL **3045**

ST-MAGAZIN 68000ER (GW/0934-3237) [I09343237] **1230**

ST MAGAZINE (FR/0980-5338) [I09805338] **4866**

ST. MARIES GAZETTE-RECORD (US) [13142084] **5657**

ST. MARK'S REVIEW (AT/0036-3103) [06285458] **4999**

ST. MARY'S LAW JOURNAL (US/0581-3441) [02643086] **3058**

ST. MARYS STAR (ST. MARYS, KAN. : 1978) (US) [12347845] **5678**

ST. MARY'S UNIVERSITY (SAN ANTONIO, TEX.). SCHOOL OF LAW *See* LAW ALUMNI DIRECTORY, ST. MARY'S UNIVERSITY SCHOOL OF LAW **2993**

ST NEWS (NE) **1204**

ST. PAUL RECORDER (US) [01715473] **5698**

ST. PAUL'S FAMILY MAGAZINE (US/0896-8276) [17302812] **3439**, **365**

ST. PETERSBURG BUSINESS GUIDE (UK) **713**

●ST. PETERSBURG MATHEMATICAL JOURNAL (US/1061-0022) [25170372] **3536**

ST. PETERSBURG TIMES (US) [05920090] **5651**

●ST. PETERSBURG UNIVERSITY MECHANICS BULLETIN (US/1068-8005) [27347042] **2129**

ST. RAPHAEL'S BETTER HEALTH (US) **4803**

ST. TAMMANY FARMER (US) [08807168] **5684**

ST. TAMMANY NEWS-BANNER, THE (US/0745-5526) [09286481] **5684**

ST. THOMAS COURIER (CN/1194-076X) [27203022] **5795**

ST. THOMAS LAW FORUM *See* ST. THOMAS LAW REVIEW **3058**

●ST. THOMAS LAW REVIEW (US/1065-318X) [26064140] **3058**

ST. THOMAS'S HOSPITAL GAZETTE (1981) (UK/0263-3507) [07891810] **3792**

ST. VINCENT UND DIE GRENADINEN, WIRTSCHAFTSDATEN / BUNDESSTELLE FUER AUSSENHANDELINFORMATION (GW) [11788252] **1585**

ST. VITAL LEADER (CN/0700-9518) [03279436] **5795**

ST. VLADIMIR'S THEOLOGICAL QUARTERLY (US/0036-3227) [01795586] **5040**

ST. WILLIBRORD STUDIES IN PHILOSOPHY AND RELIGION (US/1059-8375) [24779733] 4361, **4999**

ST WORLD (US/0888-1057) [13492544] **1265**

STA PHANTOM, THE (US/0890-3603) [14229502] **1627**

STA TODAY / SCIENCE AND TECHNOLOGY AGENCY, JAPAN (JA) [22226930] **5160**

STAAT, DER (GW/0038-884X) [03247406] **3094**

STAAT UND KIRCHE IM 19 UND 20 JAHRHUNDERT (GW) **2630**

STAATLICHE KUNSTSAMMLUNG IN BADEN-WURTTEMBERG *See* JAHRBUCH DER STAATLICHEN KUNSTSAMMLUNGEN IN BADEN-WURTTEMBERG **354**

STAATLICHE KUNSTSAMMLUNGEN DRESDEN *See* JAHRBUCH DER STAATLICHEN KUNSTSAMMLUNGEN DRESDEN **353**

STAATLICHE MUSEEN ZU BERLIN (GERMANY : EAST) *See* FORSCHUNGEN UND BERICHTE - STAATLICHE MUSEEN BERLIN **4088**

STAATLICHES INSTITUT FEUR MUSIKFORSCHUNG *See* JAHRBUCH DES STAATLICHEN INSTITUTS FUER MUSIKFORSCHUNG PREUSSISCHER KULTURBESITZ **4124**

STAATS- UND GEMEINDEFINANZEN IM RECHNUNGSJAHR, DIE (GW) [11669191] **4748**

STAATS- UND KOMMUNALVERWALTUNG *See* VERWALTUNGSRUNDSCHAU **889**

STAATS-ZEITUNG; STAATSANZEIGER FUER RHEINLANDJ-PFALZ (MICROFICHE) (GW) [04444315] **4687**

STAATSARCHIV DRESDEN *See* SCHRIFTENREIHE DES STAATSARCHIVS DRESDEN **2483**

STAATSBIBLIOTHEK PREUSSISCHER KULTURBESITZ. MITTEILUNGEN - STAATSBIBLIOTHEK PREUSSISCHER KULTURBESITZ *See* MITTEILUNGEN **3231**

STAATSBIBLIOTHEK ZU BERLIN--PREUSSISCHER KULTURBESITZ *See* MITTEILUNGEN **3231**

STAATSBURGERKUNDLICHE ARBEITSMAPPE (GW) **5539**

STAATSBURGERLICHE INFORMATION *See* INFORMATIONEN ZUR POLITISCHEN BILDUNG **4477**

STAATSCOURANT (NE/0169-5037) [I01695037] **4687**

STAATSKOERANT. GOVERNMENT GAZETTE (SA) [05351746] **4687**

STABILITY & APPLIED ANALYSIS OF CONTINUOUS MEDIA (IT/1120-4222) [I11204222] 4422, **3536**

●STABILIZATION AND SOLIDIFICATION OF HAZARDOUS, RADIOACTIVE, AND MIXED WASTES (US/1059-423X) [24585728] **2243**

STABLE & KENNEL NEWS OF THE SOUTH (US/0163-7649) [04470067] 4288, **2802**

STACCATO (TERRE HAUTE, IND.) (US/0889-3276) [13866113] **4154**

●STACKS (SAN FRANCISCO, CALIF.) (US/1070-8596) [28246889] **1244**

STACKS: THE NETWORK JOURNAL (US) **1204**

STAD OCH LAND (SW/0280-4549) [21075949] 2836, **2432**

STADEN-JAHRBUCH (BL/0582-1150) [01681141] **2762**

STADER JAHRBUCH (GW) [03041187] **2710**

STADION (COLOGNE, GERMANY) (GW/0172-4029) [03571864] 1858, **4924**

STADLER GENETICS SYMPOSIA (US/0081-4148) [01772954] **551**

STADS- OG HAVNEINGENIREN (DK) [07397633] **2243**

●STADSWERK (NE/0927-7641) [27038679] **2031**

STADT, REGION, LAND (GW) [06840509] **2836**

STADTBAUWELT (GW/0585-0096) [03113384] **2836**

STADTBIBLIOTHEK WINTERTHUR *See* AFRICANA-SAMMLUNG UND AFRICANA-KATALOG IN DER STADTBIBLIOTHEK WINTERTHUR **3262**

STADTEBAUBERICHT (GW) [02417007] **2836**

STADTGRUPPEN- UND MITGLIEDERVERZEICHNIS / DEUTSCHE GESELLSCHAFT FUER HERPETOLOGIE UND TERRARIENKUNDE E.V., DGHT (GW) [19483425] **2523**

STADTVERKEHR, DER (GW) [07406775] **5393**

STAEDEL-JAHRBUCH (GW/0585-0118) [02268074] **365**

STAEDTETAG (1948), DER (GW/0038-9048) [05697491] **4687**

STAFDA ... DIRECTORY (US/1051-2136) [21893640] 2129, **1627**

STAFF AND CLASS DATA FOR COLLEGES AND INSTITUTES (CN/0715-1942) [06902198] **1848**

STAFF BIOGRAPHIES, HONG KONG GOVERNMENT / COMPILED IN THE GOVERNMENT SECRETARIAT / HSIANG-KANG CHENG FU KUNG WU YUAN CHIEN CHIEH / PU CHENG SSU SHU PIEN (HK) [19100798] **4687**

STAFF COMMODITY WORKING PAPER - WORLD BANK (US/0253-3537) [08571310] **812**

STAFF DEVELOPMENT CALENDAR - ALBERTA. ALBERTA FAMILY AND SOCIAL SERVICES. STAFF DEVELOPMENT (CN/0848-7340) [23659128] **5311**

STAFF DEVELOPMENT IN AUSTRALIAN LIBRARIES *CEASED.* (AT/0817-5810) [I08175810] **3251**

STAFF LEADER (US/0897-8484) [17640581] **887**

STAFF LIST, HONG KONG GOVERNMENT (HK) [03219036] **4687**

STAFF LIST - MID-WESTERN STATE, NIGERIA. MINISTRY OF ESTABLISHMENTS (NR) [01785028] **4687**

STAFF LIST - SOUTH-EASTERN STATE OF NIGERIA (NR) [02308428] **4687**

STAFF NOTES (US/0146-5791) [02970379] **4154**

STAFF NOTES (US) **1434**

STAFF NOTES - WISCONSIN BOARD OF VOCATIONAL, TECHNICAL AND ADULT EDUCATION (US) [04302589] **1916**

STAFF OF SCOTTISH SOCIAL WORK DEPARTMENTS (UK/0144-5081) [07377534] **5311**

STAFF OF SOCIAL SERVICES DEPARTMENTS ... / WELSH OFFICE (UK) [07668245] **5311**

STAFF PAPER P (US/0090-1334) [03793724] **137**

STAFF PAPER SERIES / DEPARTMENT OF FOREST RESOURCES (US) [08632160] **2396**

STAFF PAPERS - INTERNATIONAL MONETARY FUND (US/0020-8027) [01753643] **812**

STAFF PAPERS SERIES / MISSISSIPPI AGRICULTURAL AND FORESTRY EXPERIMENT STATION. DEPT. OF AGRICULTURAL ECONOMICS (US) [08247482] **137**

STAFF PAPERS : UNIVERSITY OF ALBERTA. DEPARTMENT OF RURAL ECONOMY (CN) **137**

STAFF REPORTER (US/0013-8495) [06674322] **3251**

STAFF STUDIES FOR THE WORLD ECONOMIC OUTLOOK / BY THE RESEARCH DEPARTMENT OF THE INTERNATIONAL MONETARY FUND (US) [14956614] **1640**

STAFFETTA QUOTIDIANA PETROLIFERA (IT) [16726616] **4279**

STAFFORD COURIER (US) [12649692] **5678**

STAFFORDSHIRE ARCHAEOLOGICAL STUDIES (UK/0266-4992) [12934883] **283**

STAFFORDSHIRE RECORD SOCIETY *See* COLLECTIONS FOR A HISTORY OF STAFFORDSHIRE **2684**

STAFFORDSHIRE STUDIES (UK/0950-1630) [19677204] **2710**

STAFFRIDER SERIES (SA) [08054012] **3439**

STAGE AND TELEVISION TODAY, THE (UK/0038-9099) [05589877] **5368**

STAGE DIRECTIONS (WEST SACRAMENTO, CALIF.) (US/1047-1901) [20639756] **5368**

STAGE FIVE ADOLESCENCE (US/1057-2473) [21423046] **1069**

STAGES MELBOURNE (AT/1033-3975) [I10333975] **388**

STAGES (NORWOOD, N.J.) (US/1041-6048) [11275342] **5369**

STAHL MARKT (GW/0343-3862) [12759030] **1627**

STAHL UND EISEN (GW/0340-4803) [01766403] **4020**

STAHLBAU, DER (GW/0038-9145) [01766404] **628**

STAHLBAU RUNDSCHAU (AU/0561-7855) [07406680] **2031**

STAHLBERATUNG (GW/0138-1679) [06429920] **4020**

STAINED GLASS (US/0038-9161) [01766406] **2594**

STAINED GLASS (LEE'S SUMMIT, MO.) (US/1067-8867) [23962584] **2594**

STAINLESS (JA) **4020**

STAINLESS STEEL AND ALLOY TOOL STEEL: U.S. IMPORTERS' PRICES, UNSHIPPED ORDERS, AND INVENTORIES, ANNUAL SURVEY (US/0195-8747) [04584036] **4020**

STAINLESS STEEL DATABOOK (UK) [19597242] **4020**

STAINLESS STEEL EUROPE (NE) **1030**

STAINLESS STEEL INDUSTRY (UK/0306-2988) [06463203] 4020, **1627**

STAINLESS STEELS DIGEST (US/0730-8140) [08081603] **4020**

STAINLESS STEELS MONTHLY (UK/1355-5634) [I13555634] **4020**

STAKE (SAN FRANCISCO, CALIF.), THE (US/1060-4235) [24991312] **3439**

STAL (RU/0038-920X) [02122961] **4020**

STALETA PRAHA (XR/0231-6056) [06637631] **309**

STALKER (US/0882-7311) [11383307] **2473**

STALLION DIRECTORY (US/1055-2979) [18794151] **2802**

STALLION REGISTER FOR ... (US) [06253052] **2802**

STALSBY/WILSON'S PETROLEUM SUPPLY AMERICAS (US/1043-0369) [19284940] **4279**

STALSBY/WILSON'S PETROLEUM SUPPLY EUROPE (US/1043-0377) [19285030] **4279**

STALSBY WILSON'S WHO'S WHO IN FERTILIZER AND AG CHEMCIAL SUPPLY (US) **435**

STALSBY WILSON'S WHO'S WHO IN FERTILIZER AND AG-CHEMICAL SUPPLY (US) 137, **435**

STALSBY WILSON'S WHO'S WHO IN FERTILIZER SUPPLY See STALSBY WILSON'S WHO'S WHO IN FERTILIZER AND AG CHEMCIAL SUPPLY **435**

STALSBY/ WILSON'S WHO'S WHO IN NATURAL GAS SUPPLY (US/0897-2028) [17430977] **4279**

STAMFORD AMERICAN (STAMFORD, TEX. : 1965) (US) [17159672] **5754**

STAMFORD ANNUAL PLANNING INFORMATION See ANNUAL PLANNING INFORMATION FOR STAMFORD LABOR MARKET AREA **1646**

STAMM LEITFADEN DURCH PRESSE UND WERBUNG (GW/0341-7093) [04338718] 766, 5814, **5802**

STAMP AUCTION NEWS (US/0273-7078) [06852774] **2787**

STAMP BULLETIN (SOUTH MELBOURNE, VIC.) (AT) [17555711] **2787**

STAMP COLLECTOR (US/0277-3899) [06965286] **2787**

STAMP DEALER FORUM (US/8755-3139) [11269749] **2787**

STAMP LOVER, THE (UK/0038-9277) [10472328] **2787**

STAMP MAGAZINE (UK/0307-6679) [08875512] **2787**

STAMP WHOLESALER, THE (US/0038-9315) [03930838] **2787**

STAMPA, LA (IT) **5805**

STAMPA MEDICA (IT/0038-9323) [I00389323] **3642**

STAMPING QUARTERLY (US/1043-5093) [19481129] **4020**

STAMPS (NEW YORK, N.Y. 1932) (US/0038-9358) [02450813] **2787**

STAMPS (PETERBOROUGH, CAMBRIDGESHIRE) (UK) [15793650] **1147**

STAN HODOWLI I WYNIKI OCENY SWIN W ROKU (PL/0239-5096) [15095625] **5522**

STAND MAGAZINE (UK/0952-648X) [10317444] **3439**

STAND VAN ZAKEN See INZET AMSTERDAM **2910**

STAND ZIEKENGELDVERZEKERING VERSLAG OVER ... / SOCIALE VERZEKERINGSRAAD (NE) [08578925] **2894**

STANDARD AND OPTIONAL FORMS FACSIMILE HANDBOOK (US) [04016471] **4687**

STANDARD & POOR'S ... ANNUAL DIVIDEND RECORD See STANDARD & POOR'S QUARTERLY DIVIDEND RECORD **915**

STANDARD & POOR'S COMMERCIAL PAPER GUIDE (US/1057-3305) [24018756] **812**

STANDARD AND POOR'S CORPORATION See STOCKS IN THE STANDARD & POOR'S 500 **916**

STANDARD AND POOR'S CORPORATION See STANDARD & POOR'S STATISTICAL SERVICE: SECURITY PRICE INDEX RECORD **915**

STANDARD AND POOR'S CORPORATION See STANDARD & POOR'S DIVIDEND RECORD **915**

STANDARD AND POOR'S CORPORATION See STANDARD & POOR'S STOCK REPORTS: NEW YORK STOCK EXCHANGE **915**

STANDARD AND POOR'S CORPORATION See STANDARD & POOR'S WEEKLY DIVIDEND RECORD **915**

STANDARD AND POOR'S CORPORATION See STOCK GUIDE **916**

STANDARD AND POOR'S CORPORATION See STANDARD & POOR'S INTERNATIONAL STOCK REPORT **915**

STANDARD AND POOR'S CORPORATION See STANDARD & POOR'S STOCK REPORTS: OVER THE COUNTER **915**

STANDARD AND POOR'S CORPORATION See STANDARD AND POOR'S REGISTERED BOND INTEREST RECORD **915**

STANDARD AND POOR'S CORPORATION See STANDARD CORPORATION DESCRIPTIONS **916**

STANDARD AND POOR'S CORPORATION See DAILY STOCK PRICE RECORD. OVER-THE-COUNTER **896**

STANDARD AND POOR'S CORPORATION See STANDARD & POOR'S INDUSTRY SURVEYS **1522**

STANDARD AND POOR'S CORPORATION See STANDARD AND POOR'S DIRECTORY OF BOND AGENTS **915**

STANDARD AND POOR'S CORPORATION See STANDARD & POOR'S SEMI-WEEKLY CALLED BOND RECORD **915**

STANDARD AND POOR'S CORPORATION See STANDARD & POOR'S STATISTICAL SERVICE **1538**

STANDARD AND POOR'S CORPORATION See STANDARD & POOR'S STOCK REPORTS. AMERICAN STOCK EXCHANGE **915**

STANDARD AND POOR'S CORPORATION See TRENDS & PROJECTIONS **918**

STANDARD AND POOR'S CORPORATION See STANDARD & POOR'S STATISTICAL SERVICE CURRENT STATISTICS **733**

STANDARD AND POOR'S CORPORATION See OVER-THE-COUNTER AND REGIONAL EXCHANGE STOCK REPORTS **910**

STANDARD AND POOR'S CORPORATION See DAILY STOCK PRICE RECORD. AMERICAN STOCK EXCHANGE **896**

STANDARD AND POOR'S CORPORATION See BOND GUIDE **892**

STANDARD AND POOR'S CORPORATION See STANDARD & POOR'S REGISTER OF CORPORATIONS, DIRECTORS AND EXECUTIVES **713**

STANDARD AND POOR'S CORPORATION See DAILY STOCK PRICE RECORD. NEW YORK STOCK EXCHANGE **896**

STANDARD AND POOR'S CORPORATION. DAILY STOCK PRICE RECORD. OVER-THE-COUNTER See DAILY STOCK PRICE RECORD. NASDAQ **896**

STANDARD & POOR'S CORPORATION RECORDS. CURRENT NEWS EDITION (US/0196-4674) [04176525] **915**

STANDARD & POOR'S CREDITSTATS (US/1047-9341) [20793573] **812**

STANDARD & POOR'S CREDITWEEK (US/0731-1974) [07910037] **915**

STANDARD & POOR'S CREDITWEEK INTERNATIONAL (US) [23174279] **915**

STANDARD & POOR'S CREDITWEEK. MUNICIPAL (US/1058-6679) [24351747] **915**

STANDARD AND POOR'S DIRECTORY OF BOND AGENTS (US) [01794579] **915**

STANDARD & POOR'S DIRECTORY OF DIVIDEND REINVESTMENT PLANS (US/1062-5607) [25171472] **915**

STANDARD & POOR'S DIVIDEND RECORD (US/0196-4658) [03661098] **915**

STANDARD & POOR'S EMERGING & SPECIAL SITUATIONS (US/0882-5440) [11217594] **915**

●STANDARD & POOR'S GLOBAL SECTOR REVIEW (US/1076-0423) [30374595] **812**

●STANDARD AND POOR'S HIGH YIELD DIRECTIONS (US/1072-1290) [28867373] **1522**

STANDARD AND POOR'S HIGH YIELD QUARTERLY See STANDARD AND POOR'S HIGH YIELD DIRECTIONS **1522**

STANDARD & POOR'S INDUSTRY SURVEYS (US/0196-4666) [01766414] 812, **1522**

STANDARD & POOR'S INTERNATIONAL STOCK REPORT (US/0364-5711) [02665547] **915**

STANDARD & POOR'S/ LIPPER MUTUAL FUND PROFILES (US/0897-5108) [17371314] **915**

●STANDARD & POOR'S NASDAQ AND REGIONAL EXCHANGE PROFILES (US/1078-0262) [30925806] **915**

STANDARD & POOR'S OTC PROFILES (US/0733-205X) [07869406] **915**

●STANDARD & POOR'S QIB (US/1061-7043) [25422356] **915**

STANDARD & POOR'S QUARTERLY DIVIDEND RECORD (US) [05984998] **915**

●STANDARD & POOR'S RATINGS HANDBOOK (US/1061-0855) [25178288] **915**

STANDARD & POOR'S REGISTER OF CORPORATIONS, DIRECTORS AND EXECUTIVES (US/0361-3623) [01981061] **713**

STANDARD AND POOR'S REGISTERED BOND INTEREST RECORD (US/0162-6531) [04185673] **915**

STANDARD & POOR'S SECURITY DEALERS OF NORTH AMERICA (US) [03981508] **915**

STANDARD & POOR'S SEMI-WEEKLY CALLED BOND RECORD (US/0737-299X) [05110816] **915**

STANDARD & POOR'S STATISTICAL SERVICE (US) [05764537] **1538**

STANDARD & POOR'S STATISTICAL SERVICE CURRENT STATISTICS (US/0147-636X) [03211391] **733**

STANDARD & POOR'S STATISTICAL SERVICE: SECURITY PRICE INDEX RECORD (US/0272-0914) [05138502] **915**

STANDARD & POOR'S STOCK REPORTS. AMERICAN STOCK EXCHANGE (US/0191-1112) [02692476] **915**

STANDARD & POOR'S STOCK REPORTS: NEW YORK STOCK EXCHANGE (US/0160-4899) [02692502] **915**

STANDARD & POOR'S STOCK REPORTS: OVER THE COUNTER (US/0163-1993) [00928174] **915**

STANDARD & POOR'S STRUCTURED FINANCE (US/1056-9162) [23880145] **915**

STANDARD & POOR'S WEEKLY DIVIDEND RECORD (US) [03926655] **915**

STANDARD & TIMES See STANDARD AND TIMES LAUDERDALE COUNTY NEWS, THE **5628**

STANDARD AND TIMES LAUDERDALE COUNTY NEWS, THE (US) [21063999] **5628**

STANDARD BANK INTERNATIONAL BUSINESS REPORT See INTERNATIONAL BUSINESS REPORT **792**

STANDARD BEARER (GRAND RAPIDS), THE (US/0362-4692) [01586891] **4999**

STANDARD BEARER (SACRAMENTO), THE (US/0038-9447) [02863967] **4394**

STANDARD-BEARER, THE (US/0049-206X) [04425832] **4687**

STANDARD (BOSTON), THE (US/0038-9390) [03937994] **2894**

STANDARD CANADIAN PLATE BLOCK CATALOGUE, THE (CN/0700-5555) [03409837] **2787**

STANDARD CARRIER ALPHA CODE SCAS See DIRECTORY OF STANDARD MULTI-MODAL CARRIER AND TARIFF AGENT'S CODES. SCAC AND STAC **5381**

STANDARD CATALOG OF WORLD GOLD COINS / BY CHESTER L. KRAUSE AND CLIFFORD MISHLER (US) [12935228] **2783**

STANDARD CATALOGUE OF BRITISH COINS (UK) [04558828] **2783**

STANDARD CATALOGUE OF MALAYSIA-SINGAPORE-BRUNEI COINS AND PAPER MONEY (MY/0126-9682) [07429421] **2783**

STANDARD COMMERCIAL DIRECTORY (US/0147-8486) [03243351] **851**

STANDARD CORPORATION DESCRIPTIONS (US/0277-500X) [03827092] **916**

STANDARD DIRECTORY OF ADVERTISERS (BUSINESS CLASSIFICATIONS ED.) (US) [02111878] **766**

STANDARD DIRECTORY OF ADVERTISERS (CLASSIFIED ED.) See STANDARD DIRECTORY OF ADVERTISERS. TRADENAME INDEX **733**

STANDARD DIRECTORY OF ADVERTISERS (GEOGRAPHICAL ED.) See STANDARD DIRECTORY OF ADVERTISERS. TRADENAME INDEX **733**

STANDARD DIRECTORY OF ADVERTISERS (GEOGRAPHICAL ED.) (US/0081-4229) [05192359] **766**

●STANDARD DIRECTORY OF ADVERTISERS. TRADENAME INDEX (US) [25902166] 766, **733**

STANDARD DIRECTORY OF ADVERTISING AGENCIES (US/0085-6614) [05656494] **766**

●STANDARD DIRECTORY OF INTERNATIONAL ADVERTISERS & AGENCIES (US) [25107800] **766**

STANDARD (ELLIOT LAKE) (CN/0827-6609) [20660585] **5795**

STANDARD (EVANSTON, ILL.), THE (US/0038-9382) [01519163] **5068**

STANDARD-EXAMINER, THE (US) [12983206] **5757**

STANDARD FEDERAL TAX REPORTER (US) [04770057] **4748**

STANDARD

STANDARD FOR AUDITING COMPUTER APPLICATIONS, A (US/0741-336X) [10131426] 751, 1204, **812**

STANDARD FOR PORTABLE FIRE EXTINGUISHERS (US) **2292**

STANDARD FOR THE STORAGE AND HANDLING OF LIQUEFIED PETROLEUM GASES (US) 2292, **4279**

STANDARD FOR THE UNIFORM SCHEDULING OF DRUGS AND POISONS (AT/1032-6898) [I10326898] **4330**

STANDARD GAS CODE AMENDMENTS (US) **4279**

STANDARD GRATING SPECTRA (US) [03695856] 1047, **1019**

STANDARD GUIDEBOOK TO THE ISLES OF SCILLY, THE (UK) [02246623] **5491**

STANDARD HANDBOOK FOR ELECTRICAL ENGINEERS (US) [01772956] **2082**

STANDARD HIGHWAY MILEAGE GUIDE (US) [05760009] 5491, **1929**

STANDARD HIGHWAY SIGNS / AS SPECIFIED IN THE MANUAL ON UNIFORM TRAFFIC CONTROL DEVICES (US) [05880231] **5444**

STANDARD INDUSTRIAL CLASSIFICATION MANUAL / EXECUTIVE OFFICE OF THE PRESIDENT, OFFICE OF MANAGEMENT AND BUDGET (US) [05657351] **1627**

STANDARD INFRARED PRISM SPECTRA (US) [04064739] **1019**

STANDARD INSTRUMENT APPROACH PROCEDURES, TAKEOFF MINIMUMS/DEPARTURES, AND FIX ACTIONS / U.S. DEPARTMENT OF TRANSPORTATION, FEDERAL AVIATION ADMINISTRATION (US) [09834067] **37**

STANDARD MAGAZINE (US/0097-725X) [01799209] **2547**

STANDARD MECHANICAL CODE AMENDMENTS (US) **2608**

STANDARD METHODS FOR ANALYSIS AND TESTING OF PETROLEUM AND RELATED PRODUCTS (UK) [15681734] **4279**

STANDARD METHODS FOR THE EXAMINATION OF DAIRY PRODUCTS (1967) (US/8755-3554) [04696748] 199, **4803**

STANDARD METHODS FOR THE EXAMINATION OF WATER AND WASTEWATER (US/8755-3546) [03426044] **2243**

STANDARD METROPOLITAN STATISTICAL AREAS (US/0362-5397) [02298216] **5339**

STANDARD (NAIROBI, KENYA) (KE) [08103436] **5805**

STANDARD OBSERVER (IRWIN, PA. : 1979) (US) [14258491] **5739**

STANDARD OTC STOCK REPORTS (US) [04578675] **916**

STANDARD PERIODICAL DIRECTORY, THE (US/0085-6630) [01766421] **3251**

STANDARD PLUMBING CODE AMENDMENTS (US) **2608**

STANDARD RATE & DATA SERVICE See SRDS SPOT RADIO SMALL MARKETS EDITION **766**

STANDARD RATE & DATA SERVICE See CONSUMER MAGAZINE AND FARM PUBLICATION RATES AND DATA **758**

STANDARD RATE & DATA SERVICE SRDS SPOT RADIO SMALL MARKETS EDITION See SPOT RADIO **1139**

STANDARD-SPEAKER (US) [14767894] **5739**

STANDARD SPECIFICATIONS FOR HIGHWAY BRIDGES (US) [05326866] **2031**

STANDARD SPECIFICATIONS FOR HIGHWAY CONSTRUCTION (US) [03585901] 628, **5444**

STANDARD SPECIFICATIONS FOR TRANSPORTATION MATERIALS AND METHODS OF SAMPLING AND TESTING (US/0360-6902) [01196169] **2031**

STANDARD (SWAN RIVER) (CN/0702-7893) [03409704] **5795**

STANDARD TESTING METHODS (CN) **4239**

STANDARD-TIMES (NEW BEDFORD, MASS.), THE (US/0745-3574) [09087296] **5690**

STANDARD-TIMES (WAKEFIELD, R.I), THE (US/1040-3337) [18382790] **5741**

STANDARD TRADE & INDUSTRY DIRECTORY OF INDONESIA (IO) [08209903] **852**

STANDARD TRADE DIRECTORY OF INDONESIA (IO) [04934879] **852**

STANDARD TRADE INDEX OF JAPAN (JA/0585-0444) [01775099] **1595**

STANDARD TRANSPORTATION COMMODITY CODE (US/0160-6875) [03721840] **5437**

STANDARD TRANSPORTATION COMMODITY CODE. HAZARDOUS MATERIALS OR SUBSTANCES OR HAZARDOUS WASTES (US) [25523427] 5393, **2243**

STANDARD ... U.S. COIN CATALOGUE (US/0741-9236) [10112807] **2783**

STANDARD VIEW / STANVIEW (US) **1204**

STANDARDBRED SIRES AND DAMS (US/0083-3495) [04724274] **2802**

STANDARDBRED, THE (CN/0705-2553) [11856761] **2802**

STANDARDISIERUNG See STANDARDISIERUNG UND QUALITAT **4032**

STANDARDISIERUNG UND QUALITAT (GW) [01792962] **4032**

STANDARDIZAREA See STANDARDIZAREA ROMANA **4032**

STANDARDIZAREA ROMANA (RM) [04064941] **4032**

STANDARDIZATION NEWS : SN (US/0090-1210) [11951092] **4032**

STANDARDIZED REGULATIONS (US/1057-9990) [02268085] **4687**

STANDARDS ACTION (US/0038-9633) [02938364] **4032**

STANDARDS AND LABELING POLICY BOOK / UNITED STATES DEPARTMENT OF AGRICULTURE, FOOD SAFETY AND INSPECTION SERVICE, REGULATORY PROGRAMS, STANDARDS AND LABELING DIVISION (US) [26624913] **2358**

STANDARDS AND RECOMMENDED PRACTICES FOR INSTRUMENTATION AND CONTROL (US/1042-6019) [19090333] **1997**

STANDARDS ASSOCIATION OF AUSTRALIA See ANNUAL REPORT **1965**

STANDARDS ENGINEERING (US/0038-9668) [04040480] **4032**

STANDARDS ENGINEERING SOCIETY CONFERENCE See ANNUAL CONFERENCE PROCEEDINGS - STANDARDS ENGINEERING SOCIETY. CONFERENCE **1965**

STANDARDS FOR A BLOOD TRANSFUSION SERVICE See STANDARDS FOR BLOOD BANKS AND TRANSFUSION SERVICES **3774**

STANDARDS FOR BLOOD BANKS AND TRANSFUSION SERVICES (US/0730-6865) [06416305] **3774**

STANDARDS FOR OBSTETRIC, GYNECOLOGIC, AND NEONATAL NURSING (US/0276-6787) [07399180] 3869, **3768**

STANDARDS INDIA (II/0970-2628) [18308030] **4032**

STANDARDS INFOBRIEFS (US/0740-2961) [08458504] **2108**

STANDARDS MANUAL : EUROPEAN TYRE AND RIM TECHNICAL ORGANIZATION (BE) **4032**

STANDARDS MONITOR (US/0739-0564) [09701142] **3642**

● STANDARDS OF MEDICAL CARE (US/1062-7162) [25704747] **3642**

STANDARDTERM (AU/0258-837X) [19132793] **3323**

STANDARTY SEV I REKOMENDATSII SEV PO STANDARTIZATSII: UKAZATEL (RU) [03644635] **4032**

STANDBY (NE) **5160**

STANDING CONFERENCE OF LOCAL AND REGIONAL AUTHORITIES OF EUROPE See OFFICIAL REPORT OF DEBATES / COUNCIL OF EUROPE, STANDING CONFERENCE OF LOCAL AND REGIONAL AUTHORITIES OF EUROPE **4671**

STANDING CONFERENCE OF LOCAL AND REGIONAL AUTHORITIES OF EUROPE See ADOPTED TEXTS / STANDING CONFERENCE OF LOCAL AND REGIONAL AUTHORITIES OF EUROPE / TEXTES ADOPTES / CONFERENCE PERMANENTE DES POUVOIRS LOCAUX ET REGIONAUX DE L'EUROPE **4624**

STANDING ORDERS OF THE HOUSE OF COMMONS (UK) [02586081] **3136**

STANDORT CHEMIE (GW/0945-2737) **993**

STANDORT - ZEITSCHRIFT FUER ANGEWANDTE GEOGRAPHIE (GW) **2576**

STANDORTWAHL DER BETRIEBE IN DER BUNDESREPUBLIK DEUTSCHLAND UND BERLIN (WEST) / BUNDESMINISTER FUR ARBEIT UND SOZIALORDNUNG, DIE (GW) [09962327] **1585**

STANDOUT MAGAZINE (CN/0708-109X) [05072058] **2796**

STANDPUNTE (SA/0038-9730) [01983344] **3439**

STANFORD BUSINESS SCHOOL ALUMNI ASSOCIATION See STANFORD BUSINESS SCHOOL MAGAZINE **713**

STANFORD BUSINESS SCHOOL MAGAZINE (US/0883-265X) [12045802] **713**

STANFORD CHAPARRAL, THE (US) [07403411] **1095**

STANFORD ENVIRONMENTAL LAW JOURNAL (US/0892-7138) [15244703] **3116**

STANFORD FRENCH AND ITALIAN STUDIES (US/0886-0750) [07264182] **3439**

STANFORD FRENCH REVIEW CEASED. (US/0163-657X) [03248695] **3353**

STANFORD GERMAN STUDIES (SZ/0171-7219) [03042241] **3323**

STANFORD HUMANITIES REVIEW (US/1048-3721) [20548808] **2855**

STANFORD ITALIAN REVIEW CEASED. (US/0730-6857) [06245450] **3353**

STANFORD JOURNAL OF INTERNATIONAL LAW (US/0731-5082) [06715123] **3136**

● STANFORD LAW ALUM (US/1061-3447) [25257988] 1848, **3058**

STANFORD LAW & POLICY REVIEW (US/1044-4386) [19787565] **3058**

STANFORD LAW REVIEW (US/0038-9765) [01779979] **3058**

STANFORD LAWYER (US/0585-0576) [02255169] **3058**

STANFORD LITERATURE REVIEW CEASED. (US/0886-666X) [10926562] **3353**

STANFORD MAGAZINE, THE (US/0745-3981) [06318314] **1095**

STANFORD OBSERVER, THE (US/0038-979X) [03931606] **1095**

STANFORD REVIEW (US/0092-0258) [01788191] **1848**

STANFORD SLAVIC STUDIES (US/1048-4833) [16860856] **3324**

STANFORD UNIVERSITY. DEPT. OF CIVIL ENGINEERING See TECHNICAL REPORT (STANFORD UNIVERSITY. DEPT. OF CIVIL ENGINEERING) **2032**

STANFORD UNIVERSITY. LIBRARIES See SURVEY OF LIBRARY MATERIAL EXPENDITURES AT STANFORD UNIVERSITY LIBRARIES **3252**

STANFORD UNIVERSITY. LIBRARIES See ANNUAL REPORT / STANFORD UNIVERSITY LIBRARIES **3191**

STANFORD UNIVERSITY. NATURAL HISTORY MUSEUM See TECHNICAL REPORT - STANFORD UNIVERSITY, NATURAL HISTORY MUSEUM **4173**

STANFORD UNIVERSITY. OFFICE OF PUBLIC AFFAIRS See CAMPUS REPORT (STANFORD) **1090**

STANFORD UNIVERSITY PUBLICATIONS. GEOLOGICAL SCIENCES (US) [06588488] **1398**

STANGER REPORT, THE (US/0195-6620) [05528489] **916**

STANGER'S DRILLING FUND YEARBOOK (US/0739-5205) [09740666] **4279**

STANGER'S INVESTMENT ADVISOR (US/1052-5912) [21965917] **916**

STANGER'S PARTNERSHIP SPONSOR DIRECTORY DIRECTORIES BUSINESS (US/0884-1586) [11615698] **916**

STANGER'S SELLING MUTUAL FUNDS (US) [23831575] **916**

STANISLAUS FARM NEWS (US/8750-4960) [08397812] **137**

● STANISLAUS RESEARCHER / GENEALOGICAL SOCIETY OF STANISLAUS COUNTY, CA, INC (US) [27230517] **2473**

STANLEY & KILCULLEN'S FEDERAL INCOME TAX LAW (US/1066-1972) [09982395] 4748, **3058**

STANLEY GIBBONS, INC See PRICED CATALOGUE OF STAMPS OF FOREIGN COUNTRIES **2786**

STANLEY GIBBONS POSTCARD CATALOGUE (UK/0144-249X) [10294973] **2778**

STANLEY GIBBONS PUBLICATIONS LTD See STANLEY GIBBONS STAMP CATALOGUE. PART 1: BRITISH COMMONWEALTH **2787**

STANLEY GIBBONS SIMPLIFIED CATALOGUE STAMPS OF THE WORLD / STANLEY GIBBONS PUBLICATIONS (UK) [10010045] **2787**

STANLEY GIBBONS STAMP CATALOGUE. PART 1: BRITISH COMMONWEALTH (UK/0142-9752) [05539580] **2787**

STANLEY GIBBONS STAMP CATALOGUE. PART 16, CENTRAL ASIA (UK) [07918974] **2787**

STANLY COUNTY GENEALOGICAL SOCIETY JOURNAL, THE (US/0893-3359) [13770837] **2473**

STANOVNISTVO (YU/0038-982X) [05017512] **4560**

Alphabetical Title Index — STATE

STANOVNISTVO I DOMACINSTVA SR SRBIJE PREMA POPISU ... / REPUBLICKI ZAVOD ZA STATISTIKU SR SRBIJE I CENTAR ZA DEMOGRAFSKA ISTRAZIVANJA IDN (CI) [11453287] **1585**

STANSTEAD HISTORICAL SOCIETY *See* JOURNAL - STANSTEAD COUNTY HISTORICAL SOCIETY **2743**

STANYAN NEWS (US/0092-0398) [01788882] **4154**

STANZA (MEDFORD, N.J.) (US/1063-8377) [26152920] **3472**

STAPLES WORLD (US) [01766441] **5698**

STAPLREVIEW (US/0279-3148) [03149427] **188**

STAPP CAR CRASH AND FIELD DEMONSTRATION CONFERENCE (US) [02987403] **5425**

STAR (MW) [02857525] **2500**

STAR ALMANAC FOR LAND SURVEYORS / PREPARED BY H. M. NAUTICAL ALMANAC OFFICE, THE (UK) [04659935] **400**

STAR AND LAMP OF PI KAPPA PHI, THE (US/0038-9854) [07426561] 5236, **1095**

STAR & SKY (US/0164-5994) [04527763] **37**

STAR AUSTRALIS (AT/1033-8160) [I10338160] **1360**

STAR (CARVILLE), THE (US/0049-2116) [03743938] **3716**

STAR (CHICAGO HEIGHTS AREA ED.]), THE (US/0746-5181) [10134169] **5662**

STAR (CHICAGO HEIGHTS, ILL.), THE (US/8750-5932) [11586883] **5662**

STAR COUNTRYMAN (US) [11855864] **5771**

STAR-COURIER, THE (US) [27314941] **5662**

STAR-COURIER, THE (US) **5754**

STAR DATE : THE ASTRONOMY NEWS REPORT / THE UNIVERSITY OF TEXAS AT AUSTIN MCDONALD OBSERVATORY (US/0889-3098) [13562748] **400**

STAR-DEMOCRAT (EASTON, MD.), THE (US/1065-2345) [20400341] **5687**

STAR-ECHO, THE (US) [14525088] **5667**

STAR FILE ANNUAL (UK) [06570427] **4154**

STAR (FRANKFORT, ILL.), THE (US/0746-5742) [10149832] **5662**

STAR-GAZETTE (ELMIRA, N.Y.) (US) [11991828] **5721**

STAR-GAZETTE (HACKETTSTOWN, N.J.) (US) [12087128] **5711**

STAR GUIDE (US/1060-9997) [17016314] **2493**

STAR (HARVEY-MARKHAM AREA ED.), THE (US/0746-5173) [10129939] **5662**

STAR HERALD *See* STAR (TINLEY PARK ED.), THE **5662**

STAR-HERALD (KOSCIUSKO, MISS.), THE (US/1048-4116) [15584108] **5702**

STAR (JOHANNESBURG, SOUTH AFRICA) (SA) [08083390] **5810**

STAR JOURNAL (GULFPORT, MISS.) (US) [15273124] **5702**

STAR-JOURNAL (HOPE, IND.) (US) [12158666] **5667**

STAR (LAKEWOOD, COLO.), THE (US/0744-155X) [08073030] **5425**

STAR-LEDGER (NEWARK, N.J. : 1964) (US) [10944976] **5711**

STAR (LOS ANGELES, CALIF.) (US) [10990552] **2547**

STAR (NEW YORK, N.Y.), THE (US/0745-8509) [09500748] **2273**

STAR NEWS (MEDFORD, WIS.) (US) [14918007] **5771**

STAR NEWSLETTER / S.T.A.R. OF GUATEMALA, SOUTH TEXAS AID TO REFUGEES (US) [12207258] **4497**

STAR-PHOENIX (SASKATOON, SASK.) (CN/0832-4174) [16851731] **5795**

STAR PROGRESS, THE (US) [19366528] **5632**

STAR, THE (SA) [12279454] **5810**

STAR, THE (US/0049-2116) [04674100] **4803**

STAR (TINLEY PARK ED.), THE (US/0746-5157) [10149742] **5662**

●STAR TREK FEDERATION SCIENCE (EXHIBIT GUIDE) (US/1065-6928) [26678299] **5160**

●STAR TREK FEDERATION SCIENCE (TEACHER'S GUIDE) (US/1065-691X) [26678263] 1905, **5160**

STAR TREK III (US/0883-3125) [12115065] **4078**

STAR TREK : THE NEW VOYAGES (US) [05873676] **5075**

STAR TRIBUNE (ATTICA, IND.) (US/8750-6548) [11619848] **5667**

STAR TRIBUNE (ATTICA, IND.) *See* FOUNTAIN COUNTY NEIGHBOR **5664**

STAR TRIBUNE (MINNEAPOLIS, MINN.) (US/0895-2825) [16532336] **5699**

STAR VALLEY INDEPENDENT (US) [13322011] **5773**

STAR (VICTORIA) (CN/0824-7501) [11278700] **5795**

STAR-WEB PAPER (US/0146-2105) [02934215] **3439**

STARA PAZOVA, SERBIA (DISTRICT). NARODNI ODBOR *See* STATISTICKI GODISNJAK **5341**

STARBENE MILANO (IT/1120-527X) [I1120527X] **3642**

STARBUCK STAR, THE (US) [17023469] **5762**

STARCH TESTED COPY (US/1055-1026) [17456966] **766**

STARDOCK (OTTAWA) (CN/0228-9326) [08071766] **3439**

STARINAR (YU) [01586392] **283**

STARINE (CI/0351-272X) [01983554] **283**

STARINE CRNE GORE (YU/0585-0886) [05046424] 309, **2710**

STARKE, DIE (GW/0038-9056) [01587848] **993**

STARKE, DIE (GW/0038-9056) [06480942] **137**

STARKS OFF HIGHWAY LEDGER (US) **5393**

STARKVILLE DAILY NEWS (US/1044-3657) [16400779] **5702**

STARLIGHT (WILSON, N.C.) (US/0896-6095) [17235618] **4999**

STARMONT FACSIMILE FICTION (US/0893-5211) [15560109] **3439**

STARMONT HARDCOVER COLLECTION (US/0893-5203) [15560072] **3439**

STARMONT POPULAR CULTURE STUDIES (US/0890-6270) [14285091] **5223**

STARMONT POPULAR FICTION (US/0895-9323) [16855535] **3439**

STARMONT PULP AND DIME NOVEL STUDIES (US/0885-0658) [12566120] **3439**

STARMONT READER'S GUIDES *CEASED.* (US/0272-7730) [06929162] **3353**

STARMONT REFERENCE GUIDE (US/0738-0127) [09492754] **3439**

STARMONT STUDIES IN LITERARY CRITICISM (MERCER ISLAND, WASH.) (US/0737-1306) [09311803] **3353**

STAROHRVATSKA PROSVJETA (YU/0351-4536) [I03514536] **2710**

STARS AND STRIPES, THE NATIONAL TRIBUNE, THE (US/0894-8542) [08777119] **4057**

●STARS FOR STUDENTS, CLASS ACTS (US/1059-3519) [24578431] **1784**

STARS MARIEMBOURG (BE/0776-0698) [I07760698] **425**

STARS (SEATTLE, WASH.) (US/0740-0500) [09857289] 1069, **1905**

START BERLIN, DDR. 1986 (GW/0233-2736) [I02332736] **4924**

START (BIRMINGHAM, ALA.) (US/0162-6841) [04206393] **4999**

START OF MESSAGE (US/0361-0241) [01984865] **3251**

START (SAN FRANCISCO, CALIF.) *CEASED.* (US/0889-6216) [14047163] **1204**

START (ZAGREB, CROATIA) (CI) [10501893] **3353**

STARTER COLLECTION FOR JUNIOR HIGH SCHOOLS, A (CN/0823-7646) [10420495] **3251**

STARTEXT INK (US/0890-6688) [14340200] 1204, **1122**

STARTLING DETECTIVE (US/0038-996X) [07898315] **5075**

STASINOS, DELTION TOU SYNDESMOU HELLENON PHILOLOGON KYPROU (CY) [09650043] **1080**

STAT (US/0038-9986) [01280305] **3869**

STAT & STYRING (NO/0803-0103) [I08030103] **4687**

STAT BANK [COMPUTER FILE] (US) [24352223] **5339**

STAT NEWS (US/1064-0851) [26231116] **5373**

STAT (SANTA MONICA) (US/0272-555X) [05289664] **3725**

STAT (VANCOUVER) (CN/0844-3955) [19751331] **852**

STATE (CE) [02246797] **4548**

STATE 50 REPORT (US) **812**

STATE ACCOUNTS OF THE REPUBLIC OF SRI LANKA FOR THE YEAR ... (CE) [07017420] **4748**

STATE ACTION REPORTER, NATURAL GAS AND ELECTRIC POWER. ABSTRACTS/INDEX (US/0749-8527) [11353553] **4279**

STATE ADM REPORTS : ALCOHOLISM, DRUG ABUSE & MENTAL HEALTH / INTERGOVERNMENTAL HEALTH POLICY PROJECT (US) [23100373] 4804, **1349**

STATE ADMINISTRATIVE EXPENSE PLAN FOR FISCAL YEAR (US) **2358**

STATE ADMINISTRATIVE OFFICIALS CLASSIFIED BY FUNCTIONS (US/0191-9423) [03473338] **4687**

STATE ADVISORY COMMITTEE HANDBOOK / UNITED STATES COMMISSION ON CIVIL RIGHTS (US/0741-224X) [10094168] **4513**

STATE AGENCY EXPENDITURES BY COUNTY (US/0363-3381) [03184733] **4748**

STATE AID TO LOCAL GOVERNMENT (US) [01760123] **4748**

STATE AID TO MUNICIPALITIES FOR HIGHWAYS AND STREETS (BOSTON) (US/0091-6064) [01787025] **5444**

STATE AIR POLLUTION IMPLEMENTATION PLAN PROGRESS REPORT (US/0094-2871) [01793792] **2182**

STATE & AREA FORECASTING SERVICE (US/0147-6734) [03213482] **1522**

STATE & DISTRICT REPORT OF RESULTS *See* STATE, DISTRICT, AND REGIONAL REPORT OF STATEWIDE ASSESSMENT RESULTS **3536**

STATE AND LOCAL DOCUMENTS INDEX [MICROFORM] / BOSTON PUBLIC LIBRARY (US) [23158657] **4687**

STATE & LOCAL GOVERNMENT REVIEW (US/0160-323X) [02256696] **4687**

STATE AND LOCAL GRANT AWARDS (US/0195-7392) [04828920] **4749**

●STATE & LOCAL LAW NEWS (US) [29698661] **4687**

STATE AND LOCAL STATISTICS SOURCES *CEASED.* (US/1047-3394) [20668504] **4563**

STATE AND LOCAL TAX PERFORMANCE (US) [06524394] **4749**

STATE AND LOCAL TAXES; REPORT BULLETIN (US) [02268105] **4749**

STATE AND METROPOLITAN AREA DATA BOOK (US/0276-6566) [07113217] **5339**

STATE AND MUNICIPAL SALES AND USE TAX COLLECTION REPORTS (US) [03879128] **4749**

STATE AND REGIONAL ASSOCIATIONS OF THE UNITED STATES (US/1044-324X) [19254856] **713**

STATE AND REGIONAL DATA, FEDERALLY FUNDED COMMUNITY MENTAL HEALTH CENTERS (US/0095-3660) [03184749] **5311**

STATE AND REGIONAL ECONOMIC ILLINOIS DATA BOOK (US/0737-1543) [04007199] 1522, **1538**

●STATE AND REGIONAL PROGRAM/ NATIONAL ENDOWMENT FOR THE ARTS, OFFICE FOR PUBLIC PARTNERSHIP (US) [25362723] **331**

STATE AND REGIONAL PROJECTIONS. BULLETIN (AT/1032-8793) [I10328793] **4563**

STATE AND SOCIETY : QUARTERLY JOURNAL OF THE INDIAN INSTITUTE FOR REGIONAL DEVELOPMENT STUDIES (II) [09103814] **1585**

STATE-APPROVED SCHOOLS OF NURSING, L.P.N./L.V.N (US/0081-4423) [01212001] 1848, **3869**

STATE-APPROVED SCHOOLS OF NURSING-R.N (US/0081-4431) [03887145] 1848, **3869**

STATE ARCHIVES OF ASSYRIA (US) [18787901] **2484**

STATE AUDITOR'S OFFICE ANNUAL REPORT, FISCAL YEAR ENDED JUNE 30 ... (MASSACHUSETTS), THE (US) [10216730] **4749**

STATE AWARD SUMMARY, FISCAL YEAR / NATIONAL SCIENCE FOUNDATION (US) [25360401] **5160**

STATE BANK OF INDIA. ECONOMIC AND STATISTICAL RESEARCH DEPT *See* STATE BANK OF INDIA MONTHLY REVIEW **812**

STATE BANK OF INDIA MONTHLY REVIEW (II) [01640194] **812**

STATE BANK OF NEW SOUTH WALES *See* REPORT / STATE BANK OF NEW SOUTH WALES **808**

STATE BANK OF PAKISTAN *See* BULLETIN - STATE BANK OF PAKISTAN **781**

STATE BANK OF PAKISTAN BULLETIN - STATE BANK OF PAKISTAN *See* STATISTICAL BULLETIN / STATE BANK OF PAKISTAN **812**

STATE Alphabetical Title Index

STATE BANK OF PAKISTAN. DEPT. OF STATISTICS *See* BANKING STATISTICS OF PAKISTAN **726**

STATE BANK OF PAKISTAN. DEPT. OF STATISTICS *See* PAKISTAN'S BALANCE OF PAYMENTS **802**

STATE BANK OF PAKISTAN. DEPT. OF STATISTICS *See* STATISTICS ON SCHEDULED BANKS IN PAKISTAN **733**

STATE BANK OF PAKISTAN. DEPT. OF STATISTICS *See* EXPORT RECEIPTS **834**

STATE BANK OF PAKISTAN. DEPT. OF STATISTICS *See* INDEX NUMBERS OF STOCK EXCHANGE SECURITIES **901**

STATE BANK OF VICTORIA *See* REPORT, STATEMENTS, RETURNS, ETC., FOR THE YEAR ENDED 30TH JUNE ... / STATE BANK OF VICTORIA **808**

STATE BANKING, CREDIT UNION, AND SAVINGS, AND LOAN ASSOCIATION LEGISLATION (US/0884-8629) [06567511] **3088**

STATE BAR OF ARIZONA *See* DIRECTORY OF MEMBERS - STATE BAR OF ARIZONA **2962**

STATE BAR OF CALIFORNIA. PUBLIC LAW SECTION *See* PROCEEDINGS - PUBLIC LAW SECTION OF THE STATE BAR OF CALIFORNIA **3031**

STATE BAR OF GEORGIA *See* DIRECTORY - STATE BAR OF GEORGIA **2962**

STATE BAR OF GEORGIA *See* GEORGIA STATE BAR NEWS **2974**

STATE BAR OF GEORGIA *See* DIRECTORY & HANDBOOK / STATE BAR OF GEORGIA **2961**

STATE BAR OF GEORGIA. DIRECTORY - STATE BAR OF GEORGIA *See* DIRECTORY & HANDBOOK / STATE BAR OF GEORGIA **2961**

STATE BAR OF GEORGIA. HANDBOOK - STATE BAR OF GEORGIA *See* DIRECTORY & HANDBOOK / STATE BAR OF GEORGIA **2961**

STATE BAR OF NEW MEXICO. ATTORNEY DIRECTORY *See* DIRECTORY OF THE NEW MEXICO BENCH AND BAR **2962**

STATE BAR OF TEXAS *See* STATE BAR SECTION REPORT. NATURAL RESOURCES **2206**

STATE BAR OF TEXAS *See* STATE BAR SECTION REPORT. GENERAL PRACTICE **3058**

STATE BAR OF TEXAS. ANTITRUST AND TRADE REGULATION SECTION *See* TEXAS ANTITRUST BULLETIN **3104**

STATE BAR OF TEXAS. CORPORATE COUNSEL SECTION *See* CORPORATE COUNSEL : STATE BAR SECTION REPORT **3098**

STATE BAR OF TEXAS. PROFESSIONAL DEVELOPMENT PROGRAM *See* ANNUAL ADVANCED FAMILY LAW COURSE **3119**

STATE BAR SECTION REPORT. GENERAL PRACTICE (US) [06491254] **3058**

STATE BAR SECTION REPORT. NATURAL RESOURCES (US) [04571027] **2206**

STATE BIOLOGICAL SURVEY OF KANSAS *See* REPORTS OF THE STATE BIOLOGICAL SURVEY OF KANSAS **2**

STATE BUDGET - OFFICE OF FISCAL ANALYSIS (HARTFORD) (US/0093-5247) [01784617] **4749**

STATE BUDGET TRENDS (US/0272-7862) [04104097] **4749**

STATE BUILDING AUTHORITY, MICHIGAN (US) [11665081] **628**

STATE-BY-STATE SCHOOL GUIDE. ILLINOIS / QED (US) [22856009] **1784**

STATE-BY-STATE SCHOOL GUIDE. INDIANA / QED (US) [22857129] **1784**

STATE-BY-STATE SCHOOL GUIDE. IOWA / QED (US) [22856510] **1784**

STATE-BY-STATE SCHOOL GUIDE. KANSAS / QED (US) [22857175] **1784**

STATE-BY-STATE SCHOOL GUIDE. MICHIGAN / QED (US) [22856838] **1784**

STATE-BY-STATE SCHOOL GUIDE. MINNESOTA / QED (US) [22857054] **1784**

STATE-BY-STATE SCHOOL GUIDE. MISSOURI / QED (US) [22856638] **1784**

STATE-BY-STATE SCHOOL GUIDE. NEBRASKA / QED (US) [22856734] **1784**

STATE-BY-STATE SCHOOL GUIDE. OHIO / QED (US) [22856154] **1785**

STATE-BY-STATE SCHOOL GUIDE. WISCONSIN / QED (US) [22856074] **1785**

●STATE-BY-STATE SUMMARY OF SOFTWARE SALES & USE TAX (US/1063-2522) [25896812] **1204**

STATE (CHARLOTTE, N.C.), THE (US/0038-9994) [06986185] **2762**

STATE CHILD WELFARE SERVICES PLAN, STATE OF TENNESSEE (US) [06833372] **5311**

STATE/CITY LIST OF LENDERS (US/0193-8673) [04822956] **1848**

STATE CLIMATOLOGIST, THE (US/0883-9581) [09741273] **1434**

STATE CO-ORDINATION COUNCIL (VICTORIA) *See* REPORT OF THE STATE CO-ORDINATION COUNCIL **4681**

STATE COASTAL ZONE MANAGEMENT ACTIVITIES (US/0147-0566) [03085357] 852, **4687**

STATE (COLUMBIA, S.C. : 1891 : DAILY) (US) [05208681] **5743**

STATE CONSTITUTIONAL COMMENTARIES AND NOTES (US/1065-6839) [20816479] **3058**

STATE CONSTITUTIONAL CONVENTION STUDIES (US/0081-4474) [01759303] **4687**

STATE CONSTITUTIONAL LAW - CASES AND MATERIALS (US) **3094**

STATE CONSUMER ACTION (US/0190-2210) [01018391] **1300**

STATE COUNCIL OF HIGHER EDUCATION FOR VIRGINIA *See* RESIDENT AND OFF-CAMPUS ENROLLMENT, VIRGINIA STATE-CONTROLLED INSTITUTIONS OF HIGHER EDUCATION **1845**

STATE COUNCIL OF HIGHER EDUCATION FOR VIRGINIA *See* STUDENT ENROLLMENT **1848**

STATE COUNCIL OF HIGHER EDUCATION FOR VIRGINIA *See* VIRGINIA'S APPROPRIATIONS FOR HIGHER EDUCATION **1853**

STATE, COUNTY, AND MUNICIPAL COLLECTIVE BARGAINING AGREEMENTS ON FILE WITH THE BUREAU OF LABOR STATISTICS *See* BLS FILE OF STATE, COUNTY, AND MUNICIPAL COLLECTIVE BARGAINING AGREEMENTS **1655**

STATE COURT CASELOAD STATISTICS, ADVANCE REPORT (US) [06314789] 3058, **3083**

STATE COURT JOURNAL (US/0145-3076) [02712757] **3058**

STATE DATA AND DATABASE FINDER (US/1050-2378) [20521047] **1204**

STATE DATA CENTER DATA DEVELOPMENTS BULLETIN / STATE OF NEW YORK, DEPARTMENT OF COMMERCE (US) [11198583] **5339**

STATE DATA ON OCCUPATIONAL INJURIES AND ILLNESSES (US/0270-5273) [05920369] **2870**

STATE DATA PROFILES *See* STATE DATA PROFILES, CALENDAR YEAR **137**

STATE DATA PROFILES, CALENDAR YEAR (US/0277-9307) [07649313] **137**

STATE DIRECTORY OF HIGHER EDUCATION INSTITUTIONS AND AGENCIES IN MARYLAND (US/0098-4132) [02241350] **1848**

STATE DIRECTORY OF KENTUCKY (US/0585-1173) [01713915] **4687**

STATE DIRECTORY OF NEW ELECTRIC POWER PLANTS (US/1073-6646) [23812657] **4762**

STATE DIRECTORY OF O.G.S. INTEGRATED TELECOMMUNICATIONS SYSTEMS (US) [20348327] **1164**

STATE DIRECTORY OF PUBLIC OFFICIALS IN GEORGIA, THE (US/0099-0175) [02242950] **4687**

STATE, DISTRICT, AND REGIONAL REPORT OF STATEWIDE ASSESSMENT RESULTS (US) [11337672] 1905, **3536**

STATE EDUCATION JOURNAL INDEX AND EDUCATOR'S GUIDE TO PERIODICAL RESEARCH STRATEGIES (US) [13987869] **1785**

STATE EDUCATION LEADER (US/0736-7511) [08594394] **1785**

STATE EDUCATION REVIEW (US) [09623833] **1785**

STATE ELECTIVE OFFICIALS AND THE LEGISLATURES (1977) (US/0191-9466) [03336178] **4687**

STATE ELECTRICITY COMMISSION OF QUEENSLAND *See* ELECTRICITY SUPPLY INDUSTRY IN QUEENSLAND, FINANCIAL REPORT, THE **2046**

STATE ENERGY DATA REPORT / PREPARED BY STATISTICS BRANCH (US) [06366728] **1958**

STATE ENERGY PRICE AND EXPENDITURE REPORT (US) [11490280] **1958**

STATE ENVIRONMENT REPORT (US/1054-2604) [22590027] **3116**

STATE ENVIRONMENTAL IMPROVEMENT AUTHORITY *See* ANNUAL REPORT - STATE ENVIRONMENTAL IMPROVEMENT AUTHORITY **2224**

STATE EXECUTIVE DIRECTORY (US/0276-7163) [06582376] **4687**

●STATE EXECUTIVE DIRECTORY ANNUAL (US/1056-7011) [23820019] **4687**

STATE FACILITIES PLAN (OLYMPIA) (US/0092-5543) [01790969] **5311**

STATE FISHERIES DEVELOPMENT CORPORATION (CALCUTTA, INDIA) *See* ANNUAL REPORT / STATE FISHERIES DEVELOPMENT CORPORATION LIMITED (CALCUTTA, INDIA) **2295**

STATE FORMULA AIDS AND ENTITLEMENTS FOR ELEMENTARY AND SECONDARY EDUCATION IN NEW YORK STATE ... (US) [24351459] 4749, **1785**

STATE FUNDING CLAIMS PROCESSED AND PAID BY THE ILLINOIS COMMUNITY COLLEGE BOARD (US) [05624324] **1848**

STATE GEOLOGICAL AND NATURAL HISTORY SURVEY OF CONNECTICUT *See* BULLETIN - STATE GEOLOGICAL AND NATURAL HISTORY SURVEY OF CONNECTICUT **4164**

STATE GEOLOGICAL AND NATURAL HISTORY SURVEY OF CONNECTICUT *See* REPORT OF INVESTIGATIONS - STATE GEOLOGICAL AND NATURAL HISTORY SURVEY OF CONNECTICUT **1394**

STATE GEOLOGIST'S JOURNAL, THE (US/0039-0089) [01766458] **1398**

STATE GOVERNMENT FINANCES (US/0090-5895) [01785504] **4749**

STATE GOVERNMENT NEWS (US/0039-0119) [01716058] **4687**

STATE GOVERNMENT TAX COLLECTIONS IN ... (US/0270-0808) [04016982] **4749**

STATE GUIDE FOR RV MANUFACTURERS (US) [09903840] 5393, **3488**

STATE HEALTH NOTES (US) [08498359] **4804**

STATE HEALTH PLAN (LITTLE ROCK, ARK.) (US/0735-0880) [07818518] **4804**

STATE HIGHWAY IMPROVEMENT PROGRAM: PRIMARY SYSTEM (US/0146-0633) [02878533] **2031**

STATE HISTORICAL SOCIETY OF NORTH DAKOTA *See* INDEX TO THE JOURNALS OF THE NORTH DAKOTA HISTORICAL SOCIETY **2738**

STATE HOUSE WATCH (US/1070-7719) [09947526] 5311, **4687**

STATE INDUSTRIAL AND INVESTMENT CORPORATION OF MAHARASHTRA *See* ANNUAL REPORT **891**

STATE INFORMATION RESOURCE MANAGEMENT, STRUCTURE, AND ACTIVITIES *See* STATE IRM ORGANIZATIONAL STRUCTURES **4688**

STATE INHERITANCE TAXES (US) **4749**

STATE INVESTMENT PLAN (US/0196-1098) [05753958] **2836**

●STATE IRM ORGANIZATIONAL STRUCTURES (US/1066-842X) [26281987] **4688**

STATE JOURNAL-REGISTER, THE (US) [08821066] **5662**

STATE JOURNAL, THE (US) [12926204] **713**

STATE JOURNAL, THE (US) [08804393] **5682**

STATE JUDICIARY NEWS (US/0363-1362) [02255279] **3058**

STATE KOHALA TASK FORCE *See* REPORT OF THE KOHALA TASK FORCE **1624**

STATE LAWS AND PUBLISHED ORDINANCES, FIREARMS (US/0276-7651) [07301672] **3058**

STATE LAWS GOVERNING BOXING AND WRESTLING IN CALIFORNIA, WITH RULES AND REGULATIONS (US/0362-4579) [02285915] 4924, **3058**

STATE LEGAL ISSUES QUARTERLY (US) **3058**

STATE LEGISLATION ON SMOKING AND HEALTH (US/0146-017X) [02830145] **4804**

STATE LEGISLATIVE LEADERSHIP, COMMITTEES, AND STAFF (US/0195-6639) [05123302] **4688**

STATE LEGISLATIVE REPORT (US/0735-8733) [04751320] 3059, **4688**

STATE LEGISLATIVE SOURCEBOOK (US/0898-7297) [13051608] **4688**

STATE LEGISLATURES (US/0147-6041) [03208281] **4688**

STATE LIBRARIAN (UK/0305-9189) [08398467] **3251**

STATE LIBRARY AGENCIES, A SURVEY PROJECT REPORT, THE (US) [05308344] **3251**

STATE LIBRARY OF MASSACHUSETTS *See* MASSACHUSETTS STATE PUBLICATIONS, CHECKLIST **3230**

Alphabetical Title Index — STATE

STATE LIBRARY OF MASSACHUSETTS *See* MASSACHUSETTS STATE PUBLICATIONS **419**

STATE LIBRARY OF OHIO *See* OPERATING PLAN - STATE LIBRARY OF OHIO **3239**

STATE LIBRARY OF SOUTH AUSTRALIA. RESEARCH SERVICES BRANCH. RESEARCH SERVICE BIBLIOGRAPHIE *See* REFERENCE SERVICES BIBLIOGRAPHIES **3259**

STATE LIBRARY (SOUTH AFRICA) *See* INFORMAT **3215**

STATE LINE OBSERVER (US) [12264075] **5694**

STATE LINE TRIBUNE, THE (US) [14201455] **5754**

STATE LOCAL GOVERNMENT FUND, AMOUNTS DISTRIBUTED DIRECTLY TO MUNICIPALITIES LEVYING INCOME TAXES AND BASIS FOR DISTRIBUTION, BY MUNICIPALITY (US) [04397216] **4749**

STATE LOCAL GOVERNMENT FUND, AMOUNTS DISTRIBUTED TO COUNTIES AND BASIS FOR DISTRIBUTION, BY COUNTY (US) [04397241] **4749**

STATE MANPOWER REPORT TO THE GOVERNOR - IOWA (US) [06495695] **1711**

STATE MANPOWER REVIEW (US/0148-4567) [03295238] **1712**

STATE MEDICAL FACILITIES PLAN (RALEIGH, N.C.) (US/0741-0573) [10052724] **4804**

STATE MEMBER BANKS OF THE FEDERAL RESERVE SYSTEM AND NONMEMBER BANKS THAT MAINTAIN CLEARING ACCOUNTS WITH FEDERAL RESERVE BANKS AND CORPORATIONS DOING FOREIGN BANKING OR FINANCING THAT MAINTAIN RESERVE ACCOUNTS WITH FEDERAL RESERVE BANKS (US/0364-9601) [02710564] **812**

STATE MENTAL HOSPITALS (US/0162-2374) [04102603] 3937, **3792**

STATE MENTAL RETARDATION FACILITY DATA (US/0743-7676) [09023755] **5311**

STATE MUNICIPAL LEAGUE DIRECTORY (US/0898-8374) [04428745] **4688**

STATE NEWS (US) **5694**

STATE NURSING LEGISLATION QUARTERLY *CEASED*. (US/0891-8341) [13089061] 3870, **3059**

STATE OF ALASKA ALCOHOLISM AND DRUG ABUSE PLAN (US) [27871401] **1349**

STATE OF AMERICA'S CHILDREN (US/1055-9213) [23435393] **5311**

● STATE OF AMERICA'S CHILDREN YEARBOOK, THE (US) [30134774] **5311**

STATE OF ARKANSAS ... BIENNIAL BUDGET (US) [10601061] **4749**

STATE OF ART (IT) **331**

STATE OF BLACK AMERICA, THE (US/0148-6985) [03354443] **2273**

STATE OF CALIFORNIA TELEPHONE DIRECTORY (US) [04768765] **1164**

STATE OF CIVIL RIGHTS, THE (US/0161-9233) [03790722] **4513**

STATE OF COLORADO ANNUAL HIGHWAY SAFETY WORK PROGRAM (US/0097-000X) [03114334] 4804, **5444**

STATE OF COLORADO TELEPHONE DIRECTORY (US/1052-5114) [09245422] 1164, **766**

STATE OF CORRECTIONS, PROCEEDINGS, ACA ANNUAL CONFERENCES (US) [20397118] **3177**

STATE OF DELAWARE DEFERRED COMPENSATION COUNCIL'S ANNUAL REPORT FOR THE FISCAL YEAR ENDED JUNE 30 ... (US) [09015074] **4688**

STATE OF FLORIDA BUDGET RECOMMENDATIONS (US) [19638032] **4688**

STATE OF FLORIDA COMPREHENSIVE MANPOWER PLAN (US/0095-6430) [01795225] **1712**

STATE OF FLORIDA: LOCAL GOVERNMENT FINANCIAL REPORT (US/0146-7409) [03026830] **4749**

STATE OF FLORIDA PROPROSED COMPREHENSIVE ANNUAL SERVICES PROGRAM PLAN FOR SOCIAL SECURITY ACT TITLE XX (US) [04525420] **5311**

STATE OF FLORIDA TELEPHONE DIRECTORY (US) **1929**

STATE OF FOOD AND AGRICULTURE (KO) [10544873] 2358, **137**

STATE OF FOOD AND AGRICULTURE, THE (IT/0081-4539) [03909425] **137**

STATE OF GEORGIA ... OFFICIAL DIRECTORY OF UNITED STATES CONGRESSMEN, STATE AND COUNTY OFFICERS / OFFICE OF SECRETARY OF STATE (US) [25306405] **4688**

STATE OF HAWAII ANNUAL ACCOUNTABILITY REPORT FOR VOCATIONAL EDUCATION FOR THE ACADEMIC YEAR ... (US) [07797128] **1916**

STATE OF HAWAII DATA BOOK (US/0073-1080) [01783344] **5339**

STATE OF IDAHO ANNUAL WORK PROGRAM (US/0094-5706) [01793848] **5444**

STATE OF ILLINOIS PLAN FOR THE TREATMENT AND PREVENTION OF ALCOHOL ABUSE AND ALCOHOLISM (US/0736-766X) [07383425] **1349**

STATE OF ILLINOIS REPORT ON TITLE I, PUBLIC LAW 89-313 (US/0098-7468) [02241668] 4394, **1885**

STATE OF ILLINOIS STATISTICAL REPORT (US/0090-3787) [01784973] **5339**

STATE OF INDIANA FINAL COMPREHENSIVE ANNUAL SERVICES PLAN (US) [05422569] **5311**

STATE OF INDIA'S ENVIRONMENT : A CITIZEN'S REPORT, THE (II) [09201764] **2244**

STATE OF IOWA CLASSIFIED SERVICE PAY PLAN (US/0146-C65X) [02872129] **1712**

STATE OF IOWA SCHOLARSHIPS, TUITION GRANTS : ANNUAL REPORT (US) **1848**

STATE OF IOWA SCHOLARSHIPS, TUITION GRANTS, MEDICAL TUITION LOANS : BIENNIUM REPORT (US/0091-3588) [01766801] 4749, **1785**

STATE OF KANSAS BUDGET *See* GOVERNOR'S BUDGET REPORT PREPARED BY THE DIVISION OF THE BUDGET, THE **4729**

STATE OF LOUISIANA, ACTS OF THE LEGISLATURE (US) [05853960] **3059**

STATE OF MINNESOTA FINANCES (US) [17974439] **4749**

STATE OF MONTANA, BOARD OF EXAMINERS, REPORT ON EXAMINATION OF FINANCIAL STATEMENTS (US/0148-6306) [03341258] **4749**

STATE OF MONTANA, DEPARTMENT OF LABOR AND INDUSTRY, WORKMEN'S COMPENSATION DIVISION, REPORT ON REVIEW OF CERTAIN INSURANCE AND DISABILITY COMPENSATION OPERATIONS (US/0149-7617) [01799221] 2894, **1712**

STATE OF MONTANA DEPARTMENT OF NATURAL RESOURCES AND CONSERVATION : REPORT ON EXAMINATION OF FINANCIAL STATEMENT (US/0147-7617) [03231088] **2206**

STATE OF MONTANA OFFICE OF THE SUPERINTENDENT OF PUBLIC INSTRUCTION AND BOARD OF PUBLIC EDUCATION : REPORT ON AUDIT (US/0146-4914) [02952413] **4688**

STATE OF MUNICIPAL SERVICES, THE (US/0743-7447) [09889445] **4688**

STATE OF NEVADA BOND TRUST FUND AUDITOR REPORT (US/0097-8825) [01799251] **2894**

STATE OF NEVADA COMPREHENSIVE CRIMINAL JUSTICE PLAN *See* NEVADA COMPREHENSIVE CRIMINAL JUSTICE PLAN **3170**

STATE OF NEVADA COMPREHENSIVE CRIMINAL JUSTICE PROGRESS REPORT (US) [05186242] **3177**

STATE OF NEVADA, COMPUTER ACQUISITION SINKING FUND, AUDIT REPORT (US/0149-2179) [03440760] **4749**

STATE OF NEVADA, CONSOLIDATED BOND AND INTEREST REDEMPTION FUND, AUDIT REPORT (US/0149-2160) [03440732] **4749**

STATE OF NEVADA, DEPARTMENT OF CONSERVATION AND NATURAL RESOURCES, DIVISION OF STATE PARKS AUDIT REPORT (US) [04423251] **2206**

STATE OF NEVADA, DEPARTMENT OF PAROLE AND PROBATION, AUDIT REPORT (US/0149-2012) [03437462] **3177**

STATE OF NEVADA, DEPARTMENT OF PAROLE AND PROBATION, RESTITUTION TRUST FUND, AUDIT REPORT (US/0149-2144) [03440701] **3177**

STATE OF NEVADA, DEPARTMENT OF THE MILITARY, AUDIT REPORT (US) [06711673] **4057**

STATE OF NEVADA REVENUE SHARING TRUST FUND AUDIT REPORT (US/0094-517X) [01794616] **4749**

STATE OF NEVADA UNIFORM CRIME REPORTS ... ANNUAL REPORT (US) [07155706] **3177**

STATE OF NEW JERSEY COMPENSATION PLAN : HIGHER EDUCATION AND THE STATE COLLEGES; AN ALPHABETICAL LISTING OF CLASS TITLES AND RANGES, STANDARD WORK HOURS BY CLASS (US) [05119914] **1848**

STATE OF NEW MEXICO OFFICIAL RETURNS ... GENERAL AND PRIMARY RETURNS (US) [04914795] **4688**

STATE OF NEW MEXICO STATE INVESTMENT COUNCIL *See* FINANCIAL REPORT - STATE INVESTMENT COUNCIL **4725**

STATE OF NEW MEXICO STATE INVESTMENT COUNCIL *See* ANNUAL REPORT OF THE NEW MEXICO STATE PERMANENT FUND AND SEVERENCE TAX PERMANENT FUND **891**

STATE OF NEW YORK ANNUAL BUDGET MESSAGE *See* STATE OF NEW YORK EXECUTIVE BUDGET ... ANNUAL MESSAGE **4749**

STATE OF NEW YORK COMPREHENSIVE CRIME CONTROL PLAN (US/0360-0629) [02368493] **3177**

STATE OF NEW YORK EXECUTIVE BUDGET *See* STATE OF NEW YORK EXECUTIVE BUDGET, AGENCY PRESENTATIONS **4749**

● STATE OF NEW YORK EXECUTIVE BUDGET, AGENCY PRESENTATIONS (US) [23284418] **4749**

● STATE OF NEW YORK EXECUTIVE BUDGET ... ANNUAL MESSAGE (US) [23190018] **4749**

STATE OF NEW YORK EXECUTIVE BUDGET BRIEFING BOOK (US) [23284601] **4749**

STATE OF NORTH CAROLINA UNIFORM CRIME REPORT (US/0096-3208) [01798750] 3177, **3083**

STATE OF OKLAHOMA EXECUTIVE BUDGET (US) [07428206] **4749**

STATE OF OREGON COMPREHENSIVE DEVELOPMENTAL DISABILITIES PLAN (US/0149-9505) [03576810] **4394**

STATE OF RHODE ISLAND AND PROVIDENCE PLANTATIONS, BUDGET IN BRIEF (US) [06284580] **4749**

STATE OF SMALL BUSINESS, THE (US/0735-1437) [08277547] **713**

STATE OF SOUTH CAROLINA ROSTER OF REGISTERED ARCHITECTS, FIRMS, CORPORATIONS, AND PARTNERSHIPS *See* ROSTER : REGISTERED ARCHITECTS, FIRMS, PROFESSIONAL CORPORATIONS, BUSINESS CORPORATIONS, AND PARTNERSHIPS **308**

STATE OF SOUTH CAROLINA STATE ETHICS COMMISSION *See* NEWSLETTER - SOUTH CAROLINA STATE ETHICS COMMISSION **2252**

STATE OF SOUTH CAROLINA STATE ETHICS COMMISSION *See* ADVISORY OPINIONS OF THE STATE OF SOUTH CAROLINA STATE ETHICS COMMISSION **2248**

STATE OF SOUTH DAKOTA GOVERNOR'S BUDGET (US) [07542853] **4749**

STATE OF TEXAS/ENVIRONMENTAL PROTECTION AGENCY AGREEMENT FOR FISCAL YEAR ..., THE (US) [07999686] **2206**

STATE OF TEXAS PLAN FOR ENERGY CRISIS ASSISTANCE PROGRAM (ECAP) (US) [05918138] **1958**

STATE OF TEXAS WATER QUALITY MANAGEMENT, ANNUAL WORK PROGRAM, THE (US/0741-3386) [10125572] **5539**

STATE OF TEXAS WATER QUALITY MANAGEMENT PROGRAM (US/0160-6905) [04719128] **5539**

STATE OF THE ART REPORT *CEASED*. (UK/0276-8267) [07445304] **5160**

● STATE-OF-THE-ART RESEARCH SUMMARIES (US/1071-0000) [28528729] **3755**

● STATE OF THE ARTS : A PUBLICATION OF THE CALIFORNIA ARTS COUNCIL (US) [26670870] **365**

STATE OF THE COLORADO JUDICIARY, THE (US/0193-7081) [02948456] **3143**

STATE OF THE ENVIRONMENT, REPORT FOR MANITOBA (CN/1185-5762) [24986903] **2221**

STATE OF THE JUDICIARY REPORT (US) [11479665] **3143**

STATE OF THE STATES ON CRIME AND JUSTICE (US/0147-0434) [03081434] **3177**

STATE OF THE UNION ADDRESS (US) [06080809] **4688**

STATE OF THE UNION REPORT (US) [06860520] **2762**

STATE OF THE WORLD (US/0887-364X) [10478419] **1585**

STATE OF THE WORLD'S CHILDREN (OXFORD) (US/0265-718X) [09856203] **5311**

STATE OF UTAH BIENNIAL CAPITAL BUDGET ... (US) [11258546] **4749**

STATE OF WASHINGTON ECONOMIC AND REVENUE FORECAST / PREPARED BY OFFICE OF THE FORECAST COUNCIL (US) [18928952] **1522**

STATE — Alphabetical Title Index

STATE OF WASHINGTON ENVIRONMENTAL RADIATION PROGRAM ... ANNUAL REPORT (US) [17591276] **2244**

STATE OF WASHINGTON WATER RESEARCH CENTER *See* WASHINGTON STATE'S WATER **5541**

STATE OF WISCONSIN STATE SUMMARY. TYPE AND AMOUNT OF AIDS PAID TO ALL GOVERNMENTAL UNITS AND COUNTIES (US/0090-1067) [01784650] **5444**

STATE OF WORLD POPULATION / RAFAEL M. SALAS, EXECUTIVE DIRECTOR OF THE UNITED NATIONS FUND FOR POPULATION ACTIVITIES, THE (US) [14980317] 2576, **4560**

STATE OF WYOMING CHARACTERISTICS OF RECORDABLE OCCUPATIONAL INJURIES AND ILLNESSES (US) [17719759] 2870, **2872**

STATE-OWNED ENERGY ENTERPRISES (US/0742-8235) [10467966] **1958**

●STATE PARK AND RECREATION UPDATE (US/1056-8514) [23880481] **4708**

STATE PAYMENTS TO LOCAL GOVERNMENT (US/0360-2311) [02244097] **4749**

STATE PLAN ANNUAL REVISION, DEVELOPMENTAL DISABILITIES SERVICES AND FACILITIES CONSTRUCTION ACT OF 1970 (US) [02882540] **5311**

STATE PLAN FOR ALCOHOL PROBLEMS (US) [07368834] **1349**

STATE PLAN FOR CHILD WELFARE SERVICES (US/0146-5740) [02979982] **5311**

STATE PLAN FOR COMMUNITY COLLEGES IN MARYLAND (US) [05243881] **1848**

STATE PLAN FOR COMPREHENSIVE MENTAL HEALTH SERVICES : ANNUAL REVIEW AND PROGRESS REPORTS FOR THE STATE OF OKLAHOMA (US/0193-4260) [05178865] **4804**

STATE PLAN FOR CONSTRUCTION AND MODERNIZATION OF HOSPITAL AND MEDICAL FACILITIES (COLUMBIA) (US/0081-2692) [01789658] **3792**

STATE PLAN FOR DEVELOPMENTAL DISABILITIES (HARRISBURG, PA.) (US/0743-5916) [10607219] **4688**

STATE PLAN FOR HOSPITAL AND MEDICAL FACILITIES CONSTRUCTION (US/0091-1585) [01785431] **3792**

STATE PLAN FOR PROGRAMS ON AGING UNDER TITLE III AND TITLE VII OF THE OLDER AMERICANS ACT OF 1965 AS AMENDED FOR THE STATE OF NEW HAMPSHIRE (US/0148-9240) [03390654] **5311**

STATE PLAN FOR THE ADMINISTRATION OF VOCATIONAL EDUCATION UNDER THE VOCATIONAL EDUCATION AMENDMENTS OF 1968, AND PART F OF THE HIGHER EDUCATION ACT OF 1965 (SALEM) (US/0147-0000) [03076026] **1916**

STATE PLAN FOR THE ADMINISTRATION OF VOCATIONAL EDUCATION UNDER THE VOCATIONAL EDUCATION AMENDMENTS OF 1976. PUBLIC LAW 94-482, MISSISSIPPI : ANNUAL PLAN FOR FISCAL YEAR ... (US) [05159851] **1916**

STATE PLAN FOR THE IMPLEMENTATION OF THE COMPREHENSIVE ALCOHOL ABUSE AND ALCOHOLISM PREVENTION, TREATMENT AND REHABILITATION ACT OF 1970 *See* MISSOURI STATE PLAN FOR THE IMPLEMENTATION OF THE COMPREHENSIVE ALCOHOL ABUSE AND ALCOHOLISM PREVENTION, TREATMENT AND REHABILITATION ACT OF 1970 **1346**

STATE PLAN FOR TITLE IV OF THE ELEMENTARY AND SECONDARY EDUCATION ACT AS AMENDED, EDUCATIONAL IMPROVEMENT, RESOURCES, AND SUPPORT (US) [07263856] **1872**

STATE PLAN FOR VOCATIONAL EDUCATION (US) [13415383] **1916**

STATE PLAN FOR VOCATIONAL EDUCATION IN NORTH DAKOTA / STATE BOARD FOR VOCATIONAL EDUCATION (US/0743-653X) [10615987] **1916**

STATE PLAN OF SCHOOL NUTRITION PROGRAMS / BUREAU OF FOOD AND NUTRITION SERVICES (US) [07781895] 4199, **1872**

STATE PLAN ON AGING FOR THE STATE OF NEBRASKA (US) [05816993] **5311**

STATE PLAN ON AGING UNDER TITLE III OF THE OLDER AMERICANS ACT FOR SOUTH CAROLINA (US) [08198940] **5311**

STATE PLAN ON AGING UNDER TITLE III OF THE OLDER AMERICANS ACT FOR STATE OF SOUTH DAKOTA / DEPARTMENT OF SOCIAL SERVICES, OFFICE OF ADULT SERVICES & AGING (US) [08164684] **5311**

STATE PLAN PROGRESS REPORT FOR FISCAL YEAR ... / SOUTH CAROLINA STATE DEPARTMENT OF MENTAL HEALTH (US) [07525159] **4804**

STATE PLAN / SOUTH CAROLINA STATE DEPT OF MENTAL HEALTH (US) [08308640] **4804**

STATE POLICY REPORTS (US/8750-6637) [09408692] **4688**

STATE PORT PILOT, THE (US) [13277473] **5724**

STATE PROFILE (WASHINGTON, D.C. 1984) (US/1044-4947) [19817505] **1522**

STATE PROGRAM OVERVIEWS / U.S. DEPARTMENT OF THE INTERIOR, NATIONAL PARK SERVICE, DIVISION OF STATE PLANS AND GRANTS (US) [09400299] **2206**

STATE PUBLICATIONS DIRECTORY (US) [19017331] **425**

STATE PUBLICATIONS INDEX CEASED. (US/0197-5668) [06064446] **4497**

STATE RAIL PLAN, ANNUAL UPDATE (US) [05574859] **5437**

STATE RANKINGS (LAWRENCE, KAN.) (US/1057-3623) [21567547] **5339**

●STATE RECYCLING LAWS UPDATE (QUARTERLY ED.) (US/1070-3217) [28317558] **2244**

●STATE REFERENCE PUBLICATIONS (US/1057-0586) [23926319] **4688**

STATE, REGIONAL, AND NATIONAL MONTHLY AND ANNUAL TEMPERATURES WEIGHTED BY AREA (US) [05140145] **1434**

STATE REGISTER AND THE LEADER (US) [16073182] **5687**

STATE REGULATORY PERMITS INVENTORY / THE GOVERNOR'S DEVELOPMENT OFFICE (US) [06341910] **4688**

STATE REPORTER (US) **3059**

STATE REPORTER OF EDUCATION LAW (US) 3059, **1785**

STATE REPORTS, WESTERN AUSTRALIA (AT/0158-1996) [I01581996] **4688**

STATE REPRODUCTIVE HEALTH MONITOR (US/1046-6703) [20484871] **591**

STATE REVENUE NEWSLETTER, THE (US/0883-6760) [10989585] **2787**

STATE ROAD ANNUAL REPORT (US/0146-8359) [03037988] **5444**

●STATE RULES AND SCORECARDS FOR CALIFORNIA FAIRS (US) [26515850] 767, **137**

STATE SALARY SURVEY (US) [06510497] **1712**

STATE SALES TAX COLLECTIONS REPORT (US/0362-1367) [02396575] **4749**

STATE SERIES (US/0506-7588) [01510513] **4688**

STATE SERVICE (UK) [06506309] **4688**

STATE SERVICES FOR THE VISUALLY HANDICAPPED: RECOMMENDATIONS (US) [05363786] **4394**

STATE SUPERINTENDENT'S NEWSLETTER *See* SUPERINTENDENT'S NEWSLETTER **1873**

STATE SUPPORTED MINIMUM PROGRAM FOR UTAH PUBLIC SCHOOLS (US) [22426585] **1785**

STATE TAX NEWS (US) [03993166] **4749**

●STATE TAX NOTES (MICROFICHE) (US/1060-491X) [25011385] **4749**

STATE TAX NOTES (PRINT) (US/1057-8404) [24124673] **4750**

STATE TELEPHONE REGULATION REPORT (US/0741-8388) [10227176] **1164**

STATE TREASURER'S ANNUAL REPORT (US) [12390280] **4688**

STATE TREASURER'S ANNUAL REPORT (COLORADO) (US) [06211947] **4750**

●STATE TRENDS FORECASTS (US/1075-5209) [28628672] **4688**

STATE UNIVERSITY OF NEW YORK AT ALBANY *See* ALUMNI DIRECTORY / STATE UNIVERSITY OF NEW YORK AT ALBANY **1099**

STATE UNIVERSITY OF NEW YORK AT BUFFALO. UNIVERSITY LIBRARIES *See* REPORT OF THE DIRECTOR OF UNIVERSITY LIBRARIES TO THE VICE PRESIDENT OF UNIVERSITY SERVICES **3245**

STATE UNIVERSITY OF NEW YORK AT STONY BROOK. CENTER FOR CONTEMPORARY ARTS AND LETTERS *See* SPECTRA (STONY BROOK, N.Y.) **331**

STATE UNIVERSITY OF NEW YORK AT STONY BROOK. MARINE SCIENCES RESEARCH CENTER *See* TECHNICAL REPORT - MARINE SCIENCES RESEARCH CENTER, STATE UNIVERSITY OF NEW YORK **5162**

STATE UNIVERSITY OF NEW YORK AT STONY BROOK. MARINE SCIENCES RESEARCH CENTER *See* SPECIAL REPORT (STATE UNIVERSITY OF NEW YORK AT STONY BROOK. MARINE SCIENCES RESEARCH CENTER) **473**

STATE UNIVERSITY OF NEW YORK. ATMOSPHERIC SCIENCES RESEARCH CENTER *See* ASRC REPORT **1420**

STATE UNIVERSITY OF NEW YORK. ATMOSPHERIC SCIENCES RESEARCH CENTER. ANNUAL REPORT *See* ASRC REPORT **1420**

STATE UNIVERSITY OF NEW YORK COLLEGE AT BROCKPORT *See* ALUMNI DIRECTORY / THE STATE UNIVERSITY OF NEW YORK COLLEGE AT BROCKPORT **1099**

STATE UNIVERSITY OF NEW YORK. OFFICE OF INSTITUTIONAL RESEARCH *See* APPLICATION AND ENROLLMENT PATTERNS OF TRANSFER STUDENTS (ALBANY) **1810**

STATE UNIVERSITY OF NEW YORK RESEARCH (US/1041-9764) [18896572] **1848**

STATE VOCATIONAL REHABILITATION AGENCY PROGRAM DATA (US/0147-0914) [03063700] **5311**

STATE (WASHINGTON, D.C.) (US/0278-1859) [07189412] **4688**

STATE WATER PLAN PUBLICATION (LINCOLN) (US/0092-6442) [01788031] **5539**

STATE WATER PROGRAM; BIENNIAL REPORT (WASHINGTON (STATE)) (US) [01785516] **5539**

STATE WATER PROJECT ANNUAL REPORT OF OPERATIONS (US/0730-9864) [06804467] **5539**

STATE WORKERS' COMPENSATION LAWS / U.S. DEPARTMENT OF LABOR, EMPLOYMENT STANDARDS ADMINISTRATION, OFFICE OF STATE LIAISON AND LEGISLATIVE ANALYSIS, DIVISION OF STATE WORKERS' COMPENSATION PROGRAMS (US) [10305575] **3154**

STATE WORKMEN'S COMPENSATION LAWS *See* STATE WORKERS' COMPENSATION LAWS / U.S. DEPARTMENT OF LABOR, EMPLOYMENT STANDARDS ADMINISTRATION, OFFICE OF STATE LIAISON AND LEGISLATIVE ANALYSIS, DIVISION OF STATE WORKERS' COMPENSATION PROGRAMS **3154**

STATE YELLOW BOOK (US/0899-2207) [18035201] 4688, **1929**

STATEHOUSE OBSERVER, THE (US/0091-1402) [01785520] **4688**

STATEMENT (US) [24570378] **4750**

STATEMENT (FORT COLLINS, CO.) (US) [07481397] 1785, **3324**

STATEMENT OF FINANCIAL ACCOUNTING STANDARDS (US/0746-7486) [01781699] **751**

STATEMENT OF FINANCIAL OPERATIONS (CN/0228-7633) [02248464] **812**

STATEMENT OF FOREIGN CURRENCIES PURCHASED WITH DOLLARS (US/0275-9373) [06630729] **4750**

STATEMENT OF PUBLIC ACCOUNTS PREPARED BY THE TREASURER (AT) [07427148] **4750**

STATEMENT OF SUMS REQUIRED ON ACCOUNT (IE) [03050452] **4750**

STATEMENT OF TAX POLICY (US/0146-9797) [03063312] **4750**

STATEMENT OF THE LAWS OF ARGENTINA IN MATTERS AFFECTING BUSINESS (US) 713, **3059**

STATEMENT OF THE LAWS OF MEXICO IN MATTERS AFFECTING BUSINESS (US) 713, **3059**

●STATEMENT ON NATIONAL SECURITY / BY THE SOLICITOR GENERAL OF CANADA (CN/1191-4653) [26758036] **4058**

STATEMENT ON THE ... SUPPLEMENTARY ESTIMATES / BY THE MINISTER OF FINANCE (WS) [18672531] **4750**

STATEMENT SHOWING FINANCIAL RESULTS OF IMPORTANT SCHEMES OF GOVERNMENT INVOLVING TRANSACTIONS OF A COMMERCIAL OR SEMI-COMMERCIAL NATURE (II/0511-5299) [05156612] **713**

STATEMENT SHOWING THE SUPPLEMENTARY GRANTS (II) [01784169] **4750**

STATEMENTS AND RESOLUTIONS - INTERNATIONAL CHAMBER OF COMMERCE. CONGRESS (FR) [01753432] **821**

STATEMENTS AND SPEECHES / EXTERNAL AFFAIRS, CANADA (CN/0712-0761) [07037641] **4535**

STATEMENTS (CHICAGO, ILL. 1985) (US/1054-7746) [22970628] **309**

Alphabetical Title Index — STATISTICAL

STATEMENTS (CHICAGO, ILL. : 1985) *See* DESIGN STATEMENTS / AMERICAN CENTER FOR DESIGN **1233**

STATEMENTS OF POSITION OF THE ACCOUNTING STANDARDS DIVISION AS OF JANUARY 1 ... (US) [04148954] **751**

STATEMENTS SHOWING PROGRESS OF THE CO-OPERATIVE MOVEMENT IN INDIA *See* STATISTICAL STATEMENTS RELATING TO THE CO-OPERATIVE MOVEMENT IN INDIA, FOR THE YEAR ... **1539**

STATEN ISLAND ADVANCE (US) [11485841] **5721**

STATEN ISLAND HISTORIAN, THE (US/0039-0232) [01645365] **2762**

STATEN ISLAND INSTITUTE OF ARTS AND SCIENCES *See* PROCEEDINGS - STATEN ISLAND INSTITUTE OF ARTS AND SCIENCES **328**

STATEN ISLAND MAGAZINE (US/0279-9766) [07401758] **2547**

STATEN ISLAND REGISTER (US/0890-9881) [14575929] **5721**

STATENS INKOMSTER OCH UTGIFTER LANSVIS (FI) [10270067] **4750**

STATENS JARNVAGAR (SWEDEN) *See* ARSREDOVISNING / SJ **5429**

STATENS KONTROL MED DLE METALLER (DENMARK) *See* BERETNING OM VIRKSOMHEDEN I ... **3998**

STATENS PLANTEAVLSUDVALG BERETNING / UDARBEJDET AF INFORMATIONSTJENESTEN (DK/0106-2581) [12257089] **188**

STATENS PSYKOLOGISK-PEDAGOGISKA BIBLIOTEK *See* EDUCATIONAL RESEARCH IN SWEDEN **1742**

STATENS PSYKOLOGISK-PEDAGOGISKA BIBLIOTEK *See* SWEDISH BEHAVIORAL SCIENCE RESEARCH REPORTS **5224**

STATENS UDDANNELSESSTTTE (DENMARK) *See* REGELSAMLING FOR STTEARET ... **1903**

STATENS UDDANNELSESSTTTE (DENMARK). REGELSAMLING FOR UDDELINGSARET *See* REGELSAMLING FOR STTEARET ... **1903**

STATENS VILTUNDERSKELSER (NORWAY) *See* RINGMERKING AV FORSKJELLIGE FUGLEARTER **5620**

STATES AND SMALL BUSINESS, THE (US/0742-843X) [10165466] **713**

STATES-GRAPHIC *See* BROWNSVILLE STATES-GRAPHIC **5744**

STATES IN PROFILE (US/1053-7740) [22107788] **5339**

STATES OF MALAYA CHAMBER OF MINES. COUNCIL *See* REPORT - STATES OF MALAYA CHAMBER OF MINES. COUNCIL **2150**

STATESBORO HERALD (US/0746-4665) [10052780] **5655**

STATESMAN (II) [01604538] **5803**

STATESMAN-EXAMINER (COLVILLE, WASH.) (US) [17365635] **5762**

STATESMAN JOURNAL (US/0739-5507) [09769018] **5734**

STATESMAN (STONY BROOK, N.Y.) (US) [09096347] **1848**

STATESMAN, THE (PK/0039-0313) [01640497] **3353**

STATESMAN, THE (NR) [01785599] **4497**

STATESMAN'S YEAR BOOK OF NEW SOUTH WALES, AUSTRALIA *See* POCKET YEAR BOOK OF NEW SOUTH WALES, AUSTRALIA, THE **1928**

STATESMAN'S YEAR-BOOK, THE (US/0081-4601) [01238236] **4497**

STATESVILLE RECORD & LANDMARK (US/0745-7804) [09448940] **5724**

STATEVIEW (US) 4688, **3059**

STATEWAYS (US/0279-2133) [04124625] **852**

STATEWIDE AVERAGE CLIMATIC HISTORY. COLORADO (US) [10917036] **1435**

STATEWIDE AVERAGE CLIMATIC HISTORY. NORTH DAKOTA (US) [10872145] **1435**

STATEWIDE AVERAGE CLIMATIC HISTORY. WASHINGTON (US) [10879900] **1435**

STATEWIDE COMPREHENSIVE PLAN FOR FISH AND WILDLIFE ON THE NATIONAL FORESTS IN THE STATE OF OREGON, A (US) [05033297] **2206**

STATEWIDE SPACE SURVEY (US/0362-5524) [02343178] **1848**

STATEWIDE SUMMARY OF FIRE PROTECTION DISTRICT FINANCE IN ILLINOIS (US/0362-6008) [02307516] **2292**

STATEWIDE SYSTEM OF IN-SERVICE TRAINING : ANNUAL REPORT, A (US) [25622706] **3177**

STATION & STORE PRODUCTS *CEASED.* (US/1071-8419) [28738777] **4279**

STATION BIOLOGIQUE DU ST-LAURENT *See* CONTRIBUTIONS DE LA STATION BIOLOGIQUE DU ST-LAURENT A TROIS-PISTOLES, P. Q., CANADA **452**

STATION BULLETIN - AGRICULTURAL EXPERIMENT STATION (US/0362-8167) [02308802] **137**

STATION BULLETIN - NEW HAMPSHIRE AGRICULTURAL EXPERIMENT STATION (US/0077-8338) [09190545] **137**

STATION BULLETIN - OREGON STATE UNIVERSITY, AGRICULTURAL EXPERIMENT STATION (US/0096-1078) [01431305] **137**

STATION DE PHYTOPHARMACIE DE LETAT. NOTE TECHNIQUE *See* NOTE TECHNIQUE DU CENTRE DE RECHERCHES AGRONOMIQUE DE LETAT **115**

STATION MARINE DE VILLEFRANCHE-SUR-MER *See* TRAVAUX DE LA STATION MARINE DE VILLEFRANCHE-SUR-MER **5599**

STATION NOTE - UNIVERSITY OF IDAHO FOREST, WILDLIFE AND RANGE EXPERIMENT STATION (US/0073-4594) [02477125] **2206**

STATION PAPER - U. S. FOREST SERVICE. LAKE STATES FOREST EXPERIMENT STATION, ST. PAUL (US) [01540277] **2396**

STATION RELAY *See* RUSSIA AND HER NEIGHBORS **5217**

STATION RELAY, THE (US) [13440811] 246, **5223**

STATIONERY NEWS (AT/1033-758X) [I1033758X] **713**

STATIONERY TRADE NEWS (UK/0951-7820) [I09517820] 958, **713**

STATIONS (US/0090-4171) [01785157] **3472**

STATISTICA (IT/0390-590X) [01587415] **5339**

STATISTICA ANNUALE DEL COMMERCIO CON L'ESTERO (IT/0075-1871) [05203246] 852, **733**

STATISTICA ANNUALE DEL COMMERCIO CON L'ESTERO. TOMO 2. MERCI PER PAESI (IT/0390-6566) [03906566] **5339**

STATISTICA DEGLI INCIDENTI STRADALI (IT/0075-188X) [I0075188X] **5339**

STATISTICA DEL COMMERCIO CON L'ESTERO (ROME, ITALY : 1986) (IT) [16396975] **852**

STATISTICA NEERLANDICA (NE/0039-0402) [08096233] **5339**

STATISTICA SINICA (CN/1017-0405) [23609575] 3543, **3536**

STATISTICAL ABSTRACT - CENTRAL STATISTICAL OFFICE (KU) [01607406] **5339**

STATISTICAL ABSTRACT (DAR ES SALAAM, TANZANIA) (TZ) [01208130] **5339**

STATISTICAL ABSTRACT DUBLIN. 1986 (IE/0790-8970) [07908970] **5339**

STATISTICAL ABSTRACT - ETHIOPIA. CENTRAL STATISTICAL OFFICE (ET) [01077894] **5339**

STATISTICAL ABSTRACT, INDIA (II) [01590010] **5339**

STATISTICAL ABSTRACT - NEW YORK STATE DEPARTMENT OF STATE (US/0361-7475) [02246766] 4688, **4699**

STATISTICAL ABSTRACT OF COLORADO (US/0364-9202) [03268770] **5339**

STATISTICAL ABSTRACT OF ISRAEL (IS/0081-4679) [01640554] **5339**

STATISTICAL ABSTRACT OF LATIN AMERICA (US/0081-4687) [01695117] **5339**

STATISTICAL ABSTRACT OF LOUISIANA / COMPILED UNDER THE DIRECTION OF JAMES R. BOBO (US/0081-4695) [02661516] **5339**

STATISTICAL ABSTRACT OF MAHARASHTRA STATE (II) [01715711] **5339**

STATISTICAL ABSTRACT OF OHIO (US) [02421033] **5339**

STATISTICAL ABSTRACT OF OKLAHOMA (1972) (US/0191-0310) [03436814] **5339**

STATISTICAL ABSTRACT OF PUBLIC FINANCE OF HARYANA STATE (II) [01644130] **4699**

STATISTICAL ABSTRACT OF THE UNITED STATES (US/0081-4741) [01193890] **5339**

● STATISTICAL ABSTRACT OF THE UNITED STATES (ENLARGED PRINT ED.) (US/1063-1690) [25908131] **5340**

STATISTICAL ABSTRACT OF UTAH (SALT LAKE CITY, UTAH. 1987) (US/0898-3879) [16380003] 713, **733**

STATISTICAL ABSTRACT - STATISTICS AND RESEARCH DEPARTMENT (NICOSIA) (CY/0590-4862) [01154473] **5340**

STATISTICAL ANALYSIS OF ... DAIRY PROCESSOR DIRECTORY (US) [18269501] **199**

STATISTICAL ANALYSIS OF DAIRY PROCESSOR MARKET GUIDE *See* STATISTICAL ANALYSIS OF ... DAIRY PROCESSOR DIRECTORY **199**

STATISTICAL AND ACCOUNTING REPORT (US/0147-6807) [03213992] **4811**

STATISTICAL AND COST SUPPLEMENT TO A REPORT ON SCHOOL BUILDINGS IN UTAH. SEPTEMBER, 1975 (US) [06461053] 1785, **1797**

STATISTICAL AND FISCAL DIGEST - RHODE ISLAND. DEPT. OF EMPLOYMENT SECURITY (US) [06588011] 1712, **1538**

STATISTICAL ANNUAL / COFFEE, SUGAR & COCOA EXCHANGE INC (US/0731-9576) [08261630] 852, **733**

STATISTICAL ANNUAL - MINNEAPOLIS GRAIN EXCHANGE (US/0736-1092) [08331181] 203, **156**

STATISTICAL ANNUAL / THE WINNIPEG COMMODITY EXCHANGE (CN) [05087078] 852, **733**

STATISTICAL BASEBOOK SERIES - ECONOMICS SERVICE, DEPARTMENT OF FISHERIES OF CANADA (CN/0527-6942) [01201676] 2314, **2317**

STATISTICAL BULLETIN (IE/0790-8334) [17615971] **5340**

STATISTICAL BULLETIN (US) [16992466] **4279**

STATISTICAL BULLETIN - CANADIAN PULP AND PAPER ASSOCIATION (CN/0709-2253) [05765817] **4239**

STATISTICAL BULLETIN / CENTRAL BANK OF THE PHILIPPINES (PH) [03581840] 1522, **1538**

STATISTICAL BULLETIN - CIPEC DOCUMENTATION CENTRE (FR/0254-2552) [03500778] 4020, **1627**

STATISTICAL BULLETIN FOR PUBLIC LIBRARIES IN WESTERN AUSTRALIA (AT/0729-199X) [09256583] 3251, **3260**

STATISTICAL BULLETIN - METROPOLITAN LIFE INSURANCE COMPANY (1984) (US/0741-9767) [10269119] **2897**

STATISTICAL BULLETIN / NORTHWEST ATLANTIC FISHERIES ORGANIZATION (CN/0250-6394) [08429448] 2314, **2317**

STATISTICAL BULLETIN OF THE INTERNATIONAL SUGAR ORGANIZATION (UK) **1522**

STATISTICAL BULLETIN: PRODUCTION STATISTICS (JM) [03798703] **1538**

STATISTICAL BULLETIN / REPUBLIC OF BOTSWANA (BS) [07409965] **5340**

● STATISTICAL BULLETIN / STATE BANK OF PAKISTAN (PK) [29614922] **812**

STATISTICAL BULLETIN / UNITED STATES DEPARTMENT OF AGRICULTURE (US) [01188307] **156**

STATISTICAL CHANGES IN 1992 / CENTRAL STATISTICAL OFFICE (UK) [22839847] **5340**

STATISTICAL COMPILATION - ADMINISTRATIVE OFFICE OF THE COURTS (ANNAPOLIS) (US/0093-4186) [01792004] **3083**

STATISTICAL DATA (US/0145-8531) [02791037] 1349, **1350**

STATISTICAL DATA ON PERSONS RELEASED FROM PAROLE BY DISCHARGE AND VIOLATION (US/0097-7667) [02241409] 3177, **3083**

STATISTICAL DIGEST (BANK OF JAMAICA. RESEARCH AND DEVELOPMENT DIVISION) (JM) [15274594] 812, **733**

STATISTICAL DIGEST - LEGISLATIVE BUDGET AND FINANCE COMMITTEE (US) [04411140] 4750, **4699**

STATISTICAL ECOLOGY SERIES (US/0886-070X) [07128627] **2221**

STATISTICAL, ECONOMIC, AND SOCIAL RESEARCH AND TRAINING CENTRE FOR ISLAMIC COUNTRIES *See* ANNUAL ECONOMIC REPORT / STATISTICAL, ECONOMIC AND SOCIAL RESEARCH AND TRAINING CENTRE FOR ISLAMIC COUNTRIES, ORGANIZATION OF THE ISLAMIC CONFERENCE **1545**

STATISTICAL FACT BOOK - DIRECT MARKETING ASSOCIATION (U.S.) (US/1049-6092) [19259870] 937, **1300**

STATISTICAL HANDBOOK / NEW ZEALAND WOOD BOARD (NZ/0110-1242) [04981896] **5360**

STATISTICAL HANDBOOK - WEST BENGAL. BUREAU OF APPLIED ECONOMICS AND STATISTICS (II) [01784103] **5340**

STATISTICAL — Alphabetical Title Index

STATISTICAL INDICATORS FOR ASIA AND THE PACIFIC (TH) [04852898] 1585, **1538**

STATISTICAL INDICATORS OF SHORT TERM ECONOMIC CHANGES IN ECE COUNTRIES *CEASED.* (SZ) [01607939] **1538**

STATISTICAL INFORMATION ON THE FINANCIAL SERVICES INDUSTRY (US) [10766738] 812, **733**

STATISTICAL INFORMATION RELEVANT TO THE HEALTH SERVICES (IE) [03547395] 3642, **3661**

STATISTICAL INFORMATION SERVICE: PERSONAL SOCIAL SERVICES STATISTICS ACTUALS (UK) [03560413] 5311, **5267**

STATISTICAL INFORMATION SERVICE: POLICE FORCE AND REGIONAL CRIME SQUAD STATISTICS, ACTUALS (UK) [03426237] **3083**

STATISTICAL JOURNAL OF THE UNITED NATIONS ECONOMIC COMMISSION FOR EUROPE (NE/0167-8000) [09766942] **5340**

STATISTICAL MASTERFILE [COMPUTER FILE] (US) [24641318] **5340**

●STATISTICAL METHODS IN MEDICAL RESEARCH (UK/0962-2802) [26266301] **3642**

STATISTICAL NEWS (BB) [15498059] **5491**

●STATISTICAL NEWS (US) [29498755] **4811**

STATISTICAL NEWS FROM THE HEALTH DATA CENTER *See* STATISTICAL NEWS **4811**

STATISTICAL NEWS (GREAT BRITAIN. CENTRAL STATISTICAL OFFICE) (UK/0017-3630) [02268126] **5340**

STATISTICAL OFFICE OF THE EUROPEAN COMMUNITIES *See* FOREIGN TRADE OF THE PEOPLE'S REPUBLIC OF CHINA. LE COMMERCE EXTERIEUR DE LA REPUBLIQUE POPULAIRE DE CHINE **836**

STATISTICAL OFFICE OF THE EUROPEAN COMMUNITIES *See* EG-INDIZES DER EINKAUFSPREISE LANDWIRTSCHAFTLICHER BETRIEBSMITTEL **81**

STATISTICAL OFFICE OF THE EUROPEAN COMMUNITIES *See* EUROSTAT CATALOGUE : PUBLICATIONS AND ELECTRONIC SERVICES **5327**

STATISTICAL OFFICE OF THE EUROPEAN COMMUNITIES *See* FORSYNINGSBALANCER **1607**

STATISTICAL OFFICE OF THE EUROPEAN COMMUNITIES *See* FODERBALANCER : RESSOURCER **201**

STATISTICAL OFFICE OF THE EUROPEAN COMMUNITIES *See* KUL : MANEDSBULLETIN **1615**

STATISTICAL OFFICE OF THE EUROPEAN COMMUNITIES *See* KULBRINTER **4262**

STATISTICAL OFFICE OF THE EUROPEAN COMMUNITIES *See* NATIONAL ACCOUNTS ESA, AGGREGATES **4738**

STATISTICAL OUTLINE OF INDIA (II/0496-9464) [01607000] **1538**

STATISTICAL PAPERS (BERLIN, GERMANY) (GW/0932-5026) [19619791] **5340**

STATISTICAL PAPERS - UNITED NATIONS. SERIES D. COMMODITY TRADE STATISTICS (US/0010-3233) [03216741] 852, **733**

STATISTICAL PAPERS - UNITED NATIONS. STATISTICAL OFFICE (US) [01490247] **3083**

STATISTICAL POCKET BOOK, NEPAL (NP) [01797716] **5340**

STATISTICAL POCKET-BOOK OF AFGHANISTAN (AF) [01792425] **5340**

STATISTICAL POCKET BOOK OF BANGLADESH (BG) [06508001] **5340**

STATISTICAL POCKET BOOK OF THE DEMOCRATIC SOCIALIST REPUBLIC OF SRI LANKA (CE/0585-1777) [04417662] **5340**

STATISTICAL POCKET-BOOK OF YUGOSLAVIA (YU/0585-1815) [01215902] **5340**

STATISTICAL PROFILE - IOWA DEPARTMENT OF TRANSPORTATION (US/0160-1970) [03620206] **5402**

STATISTICAL PROFILE, NORTH CAROLINA PUBLIC SCHOOLS (US/0148-2742) [03286259] 1785, **1797**

STATISTICAL PROFILE OF ILLINOIS SCHOOL ADMINISTRATORS / ILLINOIS STATE BOARD OF EDUCATION (US) [07700848] 1872, **1797**

STATISTICAL PROFILE OF IOWA (US) [02245162] **1538**

STATISTICAL PROFILE OF ZAMBIAN EDUCATION (ZA) [04697956] 1785, **1797**

STATISTICAL RECORD, THE (UK) [03292136] 2802, **2803**

STATISTICAL REFERENCE BOOK OF INTERNATIONAL ACTIVITIES (US/0361-0764) [01950807] 1929, **1930**

STATISTICAL REFERENCE INDEX (US/0885-6834) [05951104] **5340**

STATISTICAL REFERENCE INDEX ... ANNUAL (US/0278-694X) [07568304] **5340**

STATISTICAL RELEASE / FEDERAL FINANCIAL INSTITUTIONS EXAMINATIONS COUNCIL (US) [08921855] **812**

STATISTICAL REPORT (US) [11530377] 4279, **4284**

STATISTICAL REPORT (PK) [01790651] 821, **733**

STATISTICAL REPORT (YU) [01789038] 916, 5340, **733**

STATISTICAL REPORT - ALBERTA ADVANCED EDUCATION AND MANPOWER (CN/0826-2004) [11135028] 1848, **1797**

STATISTICAL REPORT - AUSTRALIA. ARMY OFFICE. 1 PSYCHOLOGICAL RESEARCH UNIT (AT/1035-7602) [I10357602] **4619**

●STATISTICAL REPORT - CANADIAN ASSOCIATION FOR GRADUATE STUDIES (CN/1194-689X) [28745254] **1848**

STATISTICAL REPORT - CITY OF LOS ANGELES. SOCIAL SERVICE DEPARTMENT (US/0090-6565) [01785330] 5311, **5267**

STATISTICAL REPORT - EXECUTIVE OFFICE FOR U.S. ATTORNEYS (US/0740-8277) [06246026] 3059, **3083**

STATISTICAL REPORT, FISCAL YEAR ... : A REPORT ON THE YEAR OF TITLE I ELEMENTARY AND SECONDARY EDUCATION ACT OF 1965 (US) [05935805] **1785**

STATISTICAL REPORT - LOUISIANA, HEALTH AND SOCIAL AND REHABILITATION SERVICES ADMINISTRATION (ANNUAL) (US/0098-8057) [02239819] 3792, **3661**

STATISTICAL REPORT (MICHIGAN. LEGISLATURE. SENATE. FISCAL AGENCY) (US) [08022407] 4750, **4700**

STATISTICAL REPORT OF ACCIDENTS (CHARLESTON) (US/0093-2418) [01791742] **5402**

STATISTICAL REPORT OF GENERAL PROPERTY ASSESSMENT AND TAXATION *See* STATISTICAL REPORT OF PROPERTY ASSESSMENT AND TAXATION **4848**

STATISTICAL REPORT OF PROPERTY ASSESSMENT AND TAXATION (US/0098-0056) [01799152] **4848**

STATISTICAL REPORT ON MERGERS AND ACQUISITIONS (US/0731-0692) [04055476] 1627, **1539**

STATISTICAL REPORT ON THE NATIONAL AGRICULTURAL EXHIBITION / REPUBLIC OF TRINIDAD & TOBAGO, CENTRAL STATISTICAL OFFICE (SP) [08201493] 138, **156**

STATISTICAL REPORT. RURAL ELECTRIC BORROWERS / UNITED STATES DEPARTMENT OF AGRICULTURE, RURAL ELECTRIFICATION ADMINISTRATION (US) [08225439] 1627, **1539**

STATISTICAL REPORT. RURAL TELEPHONE BORROWERS (US/0731-8251) [08225079] 1164, **1125**

STATISTICAL REPORT SERIES - DIVISION OF EDUCATIONAL STATISTICS (US) [02242577] 1785, **1797**

STATISTICAL REPORT SERIES (WYOMING. STATE DEPT. OF EDUCATION. PLANNING & VOCATIONAL SERVICES DIVISION) (US) [11920440] 1872, **1797**

STATISTICAL REPORT - SOUTH CAROLINA DEPARTMENT OF SOCIAL SERVICES (US/0163-6898) [04419043] 5311, **5267**

STATISTICAL REPORT - STATE OF ALASKA, ALASKA OIL AND GAS CONSERVATION COMMISSION (US/0273-1916) [05654161] 1958, **2206**

STATISTICAL REPORT - STATE OF NEW YORK OFFICE OF COURT ADMINISTRATION (US/0098-2016) [02240447] **3083**

STATISTICAL REPORT (VIRGINIA. DEPT. OF SOCIAL SERVICES. BUREAU OF RESEARCH AND REPORTING) (US) [09590488] 5311, **5267**

STATISTICAL RESEARCH MONOGRAPHS (US/0081-5020) [01766472] **5340**

STATISTICAL REVIEW (AT) [27247779] **222**

STATISTICAL REVIEW - AUSTRALIAN TOURIST COMMISSION (AT) [03081991] **5491**

STATISTICAL REVIEW - EXPORT DEVELOPMENT CORPORATION (CN/0823-3454) [10343876] **852**

STATISTICAL REVIEW (JAMAICA. DEPT. OF STATISTICS) (JM) [08483235] **5340**

STATISTICAL REVIEW (NEW YORK) (US/0162-8097) [01510997] **4222**

STATISTICAL REVIEW OF COAL IN CANADA (CN/0707-2767) [04653994] 2151, **2006**

STATISTICAL REVIEW OF CRIME (AT) [02244995] 3177, **3083**

STATISTICAL REVIEW OF NORTHERN IRELAND AGRICULTURE / DEPARTMENT OF AGRICULTURE FOR NORTHERN IRELAND (IE) [06267175] 138, **156**

STATISTICAL REVIEW OF TOURISM, HONG KONG, A (HK) [14117548] **5500**

STATISTICAL ROUNDUP (US) [18501566] 2396, **2399**

STATISTICAL SCIENCE (US/0883-4237) [12143452] **5340**

STATISTICAL SERVICES DIRECTORY *CEASED.* (US/0732-6971) [08412651] **5340**

STATISTICAL SERVICES OF THE UNITED STATES GOVERNMENT (US/0362-4315) [03220181] **4700**

STATISTICAL SOFTWARE NEWSLETTER (GW/0173-5896) [10748537] 5340, **3536**

STATISTICAL SOURCE DIRECTORY FOR NEW JERSEY STATE GOVERNMENT (US/0147-5525) [03193773] **5340**

STATISTICAL STANDARDS AND STUDIES (US/0069-8458) [01564693] **2244**

STATISTICAL STATEMENTS RELATING TO THE CO-OPERATIVE MOVEMENT IN INDIA, FOR THE YEAR ... (II) [10755518] 1543, **1539**

STATISTICAL STATEMENTS RELATING TO THE COOPERATIVE MOVEMENT IN INDIA (II) [01585685] **156**

STATISTICAL SUMMARY : AIR CARRIER ENFORCEMENT CASES (US) [01784888] **41**

STATISTICAL SUMMARY - COMMONWEALTH OF VIRGINIA, STATE MILK COMMISSION (US/0363-0072) [02404664] 2371, **2362**

STATISTICAL SUMMARY / DEPARTMENT OF MINES, WESTERN AUSTRALIA (AT) [17987184] **2151**

STATISTICAL SUMMARY, FEDERAL MEAT AND POULTRY INSPECTION FOR FISCAL YEAR (US/0277-3724) [02290740] 2358, **2362**

STATISTICAL SUMMARY - FLORIDA CANNERS ASSOCIATION *CEASED.* (US/0430-7585) [02246900] 2358, **2362**

STATISTICAL SUMMARY - FLORIDA CITRUS PROCESSORS ASSOCIATION (US/0270-7691) [06469127] **2358**

STATISTICAL SUMMARY FOR THE PUBLIC SCHOOLS OF ARKANSAS (US) [01514111] 1785, **1797**

STATISTICAL SUMMARY OF DEPARTMENTAL ACTIONS (US) [05795120] 2836, **2840**

STATISTICAL SUMMARY OF PROGRAMS / NEW YORK STATE DIVISION OF HOUSING AND COMMUNITY RENEWAL (US) [11943220] 2836, **2841**

STATISTICAL SUMMARY OF THE COLORADO JUDICIARY (US/0731-6992) [06621263] 3059, **3083**

STATISTICAL SUMMARY OF THE OFFICE OF REGISTRATION AND RECORDS (US/0096-1264) [03201435] 1872, **1798**

STATISTICAL SURVEY OF CZECHOSLOVAKIA (XR) [01798393] **5340**

STATISTICAL TABLES (UK/0076-0234) [01782828] **5457**

STATISTICAL TABLES - DEPARTMENT OF EMPLOYMENT SECURITY (US/0095-1382) [01796157] 2894, **2898**

STATISTICAL TABLES FROM ANNUAL STATEMENTS (US) [04022000] 2894, **2898**

STATISTICAL THEORY AND METHOD ABSTRACTS (UK/0039-0518) [04323547] **5340**

STATISTICAL UPDATE (CN/1189-038X) [25352022] **5341**

STATISTICAL YEAR BOOK OF THE ELECTRIC UTILITY INDUSTRY (US/0361-3607) [01981103] 4762, **4700**

STATISTICAL YEAR BOOK, THAILAND (TH) [03128014] **5341**

STATISTICAL YEAR BOOK - THE AUSTRALIAN GAS INDUSTRY (AT/0466-2865) [01155109] **4284**

STATISTICAL YEARBOOK (UK) [22505010] **5341**

STATISTICAL YEARBOOK / ANNUAIRE STATISTIQUE / DEPARTMENT OF ECONOMIC AND SOCIAL INFORMATION AND POLICY ANALYSIS, STATISTICAL DIVISION (US/0082-8459) [30065137] **5341**

STATISTICAL YEARBOOK / CHICAGO MERCANTILE EXCHANGE (US/1046-820X) [13694199] **5356**

Alphabetical Title Index — STATISTICS

STATISTICAL YEARBOOK FOR ASIA AND THE PACIFIC (TH) [02247083] **5341**

STATISTICAL YEARBOOK / INTERNATIONAL NORTH PACIFIC FISHERIES COMMISSION (CN/0535-1588) [08960098] 2314, **2317**

STATISTICAL YEARBOOK - NEW YORK MERCANTILE EXCHANGE (US/0090-8991) [04240102] 916, **733**

STATISTICAL YEARBOOK OF BANGLADESH (BG) [04524797] **5341**

STATISTICAL YEARBOOK OF JAMAICA (JM) [01795189] **5341**

STATISTICAL YEARBOOK OF MEMBER STATES OF THE COUNCIL FOR MUTUAL ECONOMIC ASSISTANCE (UK) [03368954] **5341**

STATISTICAL YEARBOOK OF MUNICIPAL FINANCE *SUSPENDED*. (US/0740-5790) [08513912] 4750, **4700**

STATISTICAL YEARBOOK OF THE NETHERLANDS (NE/0303-6448) [01798543] **5341**

STATISTICAL YEARBOOK OF THE REPUBLIC OF CHINA (CH) [02591212] **5341**

STATISTICAL YEARBOOK OF THE SOCIALIST FEDERAL REPUBLIC OF YUGOSLAVIA / SOCIALIST FEDERAL REPUBLIC OF YUGOSLAVIA, FEDERAL STATISTICAL OFFICE (YU/0585-1858) [01180284] **5341**

STATISTICAL YEARBOOK OF THE SOCIALIST REPUBLIC OF ROMANIA (RM/0377-5739) [01223836] **5341**

STATISTICAL YEARBOOK OF THE WESTERN LUMBER INDUSTRY (US/0195-931X) [05740161] 2404, **2399**

STATISTICAL YEARBOOK OF ZIMBABWE (RH) [15079882] **5341**

STATISTICAL YEARBOOK (UNESCO) (FR/0082-7541) [01607331] **5341**

STATISTICALLY AUTHENTICATED USED BOAT PRICE GUIDE *See* BUC USED BOAT PRICE GUIDE **592**

STATISTICHE AMBIENTALI (IT) [12542281] **2182**

STATISTICHE CULTURALI (IT) [17212263] **5341**

STATISTICHE DALLA SANITA (IT/1121-1008) [23001954] **4804**

STATISTICHE DEI BILANCI DELLE AMMINISTRAZIONI REGIONALI, PROVINCIALI E COMUNALI (IT/0075-1820) [05235737] **4750**

STATISTICHE DEL COMMERCIO INTERNO (IT/0075-1782) [16795897] **5500**

STATISTICHE DEL MOVIMENTO PORTUALE DI LIVORNO (IT) [19254214] **5457**

STATISTICHE DEL TURISMO (IT) [20803427] **5491**

STATISTICHE DELLA CACCIA, PESCA E COOPERAZIONE (IT/0390-6426) [18525079] **138**

STATISTICHE DELLA NAVIGAZIONE MARITTIMA (IT) [19830242] **4183**

STATISTICHE DELLA PREVIDENZA, DELLA SANITA E DELL'ASSISTENZA SOCIALE (IT) [17303504] 5311, **5267**

STATISTICHE DELLA ZOOTECNICA, PESCA E CACCIA (IT) [20034627] **222**

STATISTICHE DELL'AGRICOLTURA, ZOOTECNIA E MEZZI DI PRODUZIONE *CEASED*. (IT/1120-8945) [20616011] **222**

STATISTICHE DELLE OPERE PUBBLICHE (IT) [20377669] **628**

STATISTICHE DEMOGRAFICHE (IT) [17571699] 4560, **4563**

STATISTICHE FORESTALI (IT) [18237485] **2396**

STATISTICHE GIUDIZIARIE (IT) [18484980] **5341**

STATISTICHE INDUSTRIALI *CEASED*. (IT) [18045869] **1585**

STATISTICHE METEOROLOGICHE (IT) [18365510] **1435**

STATISTICHE PER LA PREVENZIONE (IT) [04568488] **2870**

STATISTICHE UUBERSICHTEN : BESTAND UND BEDARF AN CHEMIKERN IN DER CHEMISCHEN INDUSTRIE DER BUNDESREPUBLIK DEUTSCHLAND (GW) [04286350] 1030, **1012**

STATISTICHESKI GODISHNIK NA REPUBLIKA BULGARIIA / TSENTRALNO STATISTICHESKO UPRAVLENIE (BU) [24041424] **5341**

STATISTICHESKI IZVESTIIA (BU) [06317710] **5341**

STATISTICHESKII BIULLETEN / VSEUKRAINSKII SOVET PROFESSIONALNHYKH SOIUZOV, NARODNYI KOMISSARIAT TRUDA UKRAINY (UN) [23987796] **5341**

STATISTICHESKII EZHEGODNIK (RU) [19691628] **5341**

STATISTICHESKOE UPRAVLENIE GORODA MOSKVY *See* MOSKVA V CIFRAH **5333**

STATISTICIAN, THE (UK/0039-0526) [03562541] **5341**

STATISTICKA REVIJA (YU/0039-0534) [01983440] **5341**

STATISTICKI GODISNJAK (YU) [02239160] **5341**

STATISTICKI GODISNJAK JUGOSLAVIJE (CI/0585-1920) [01214221] **5341**

STATISTICNI LETOPIS REPUBLIKE SLOVENIJE / REPUBLIKA SLOVENIJA, ZAVOD REPUBLIKE SLOVENIJE ZA STATISTIKO (XV) [23711880] **5341**

STATISTICS AND COMPUTING (UK/0960-3174) [25290806] **1210**

STATISTICS & DECISIONS (GW/0721-2631) [09172040] **5342**

STATISTICS & DECISIONS. SUPPLEMENT ISSUE (GW) [11950672] **5342**

STATISTICS & PROBABILITY LETTERS (NE/0167-7152) [08940061] **3536**

STATISTICS AT A GLANCE / REPUBLIC OF TRINIDAD AND TOBAGO, CENTRAL STATISTICAL OFFICE (TR) [16936526] **5342**

STATISTICS (BERLIN, DDR) (GW/0233-1888) [04029789] **3543**

STATISTICS : CALENDAR YEAR REVIEW (US/0362-0360) [02441486] 5311, **5267**

STATISTICS CANADA *See* INVESTISSEMENTS PRIVES ET PUBLICS AU CANADA : PERSPECTIVES **902**

STATISTICS CANADA. AGRICULTURE DIVISION. CROPS SECTION *See* FRUIT AND VEGETABLE PRODUCTION **172**

STATISTICS CANADA. AGRICULTURE DIVISION. CROPS SECTION *See* FIELD CROP REPORTING SERIES **171**

STATISTICS CANADA. BALANCE OF PAYMENTS DIVISION *See* CANADIAN BALANCE OF INTERNATIONAL PAYMENTS, THE **4716**

STATISTICS CANADA CATALOGUE (1988) (CN/0838-4223) [18201992] **4700**

STATISTICS CANADA. COMMUNICATIONS DIVISION *See* ANNUAL REPORT - STATISTICS CANADA **5321**

STATISTICS CANADA. COMMUNICATIONS SECTION *See* TELECOMMUNICATIONS STATISTICS **1125**

STATISTICS CANADA. COMMUNICATIONS SECTION *See* CABLE TELEVISION **1129**

STATISTICS CANADA. CONSUMER INCOME AND EXPENDITURE DIVISION *See* INCOME DISTRIBUTIONS BY SIZE IN CANADA **1533**

STATISTICS CANADA. CONSUMER INCOME AND EXPENDITURE DIVISION *See* FAMILY INCOMES. CENSUS FAMILIES **2287**

STATISTICS CANADA. CROPS SECTION. CROPS SECTION *See* GRAIN TRADE OF CANADA **202**

STATISTICS CANADA. ELEMENTARY-SECONDARY EDUCATION SECTION *See* ELEMENTARY-SECONDARY SCHOOL ENROLMENT **1794**

STATISTICS CANADA. GROSS NATIONAL PRODUCT DIVISION *See* NATIONAL INCOME AND EXPENDITURE ACCOUNTS **1575**

STATISTICS CANADA. LABOR INCOME SECTION *See* ESTIMATES OF LABOUR INCOME (OTTAWA) **1532**

STATISTICS CANADA. LIBRARY *See* LISTING OF SUPPLEMENTARY DOCUMENTS, SUPPLEMENT / STATISTICS CANADA, LIBRARY **3259**

STATISTICS CANADA. LIBRARY *See* LISTING OF SUPPLEMENTARY DOCUMENTS / STATISTICS CANADA, LIBRARY **3259**

STATISTICS CANADA. LIBRARY SERVICES DIVISION *See* STATISTICS CANADA CATALOGUE (1988) **4700**

STATISTICS CANADA. LIVESTOCK AND ANIMAL PRODUCTS SECTION *See* PRODUCTION AND STOCKS OF EGGS AND POULTRY **219**

STATISTICS CANADA. MANUFACTURING AND PRIMARY INDUSTRIES DIVISION *See* PRODUCTION, SHIPMENTS, AND STOCKS ON HAND OF SAWMILLS EAST OF THE ROCKIES **2404**

STATISTICS CANADA. MANUFACTURING AND PRIMARY INDUSTRIES DIVISION *See* HARDWARE, TOOL AND CUTLERY MANUFACTURERS (PRELIMINARY ED.) **2811**

STATISTICS CANADA. MANUFACTURING AND PRIMARY INDUSTRIES DIVISION *See* MANUFACTURERS OF SMALL ELECTRIC APPLIANCES **3483**

STATISTICS CANADA. MANUFACTURING AND PRIMARY INDUSTRIES DIVISION *See* PRODUCTION, SHIPMENTS AND STOCKS ON HAND OF SAWMILLS IN BRITISH COLUMBIA **1622**

STATISTICS CANADA. MANUFACTURING AND PRIMARY INDUSTRIES DIVISION *See* MINES DE CHARBON **2006**

STATISTICS CANADA. MANUFACTURING AND PRIMARY INDUSTRIES DIVISION *See* CANADA'S MINERAL PRODUCTION, PRELIMINARY ESTIMATES **2136**

STATISTICS CANADA. MANUFACTURING AND PRIMARY INDUSTRIES DIVISION *See* MANUFACTURERS OF ELECTRIC WIRE AND CABLE (PRELIMINARY ED.) **3483**

STATISTICS CANADA. MANUFACTURING AND PRIMARY INDUSTRIES DIVISION *See* GENERAL REVIEW OF THE MINERAL INDUSTRIES. MINES, QUARRIES AND OIL WELLS **1362**

STATISTICS CANADA. MANUFACTURING AND PRIMARY INDUSTRIES DIVISION *See* PULPWOOD AND WOOD RESIDUE STATISTICS **2404**

STATISTICS CANADA. MANUFACTURING AND PRIMARY INDUSTRIES DIVISION *See* WIRE AND WIRE PRODUCTS MANUFACTURERS (PRELIMINARY ED.) **4023**

STATISTICS CANADA. MANUFACTURING AND PRIMARY INDUSTRIES DIVISION *See* REFINED PETROLEUM PRODUCTS (MONTHLY ED.) **4276**

STATISTICS CANADA. MANUFACTURING AND PRIMARY INDUSTRIES DIVISION *See* MONTHLY REVIEW OF CANADIAN FISHERIES STATISTICS **2317**

STATISTICS CANADA. MANUFACTURING AND PRIMARY INDUSTRIES DIVISION *See* OTHER MISCELLANEOUS MANUFACTURING INDUSTRIES **3490**

STATISTICS CANADA. MANUFACTURING AND PRIMARY INDUSTRIES DIVISION *See* OIL PIPE LINE TRANSPORT (ANNUAL ED.) **4270**

STATISTICS CANADA. MANUFACTURING AND PRIMARY INDUSTRIES DIVISION *See* REFINED PETROLEUM PRODUCTS. VOLUME 2. CONSUMPTION OF PETROLEUM PRODUCTS **4276**

STATISTICS CANADA. MANUFACTURING AND PRIMARY INDUSTRIES DIVISION *See* CONCRETE PRODUCTS MANUFACTURERS (PRELIMINARY ED.) **3477**

STATISTICS CANADA MERCHANDISING AND SERVICES DIVISION *See* DIRECT SELLING IN CANADA **923**

STATISTICS CANADA. MERCHANDISING AND SERVICES DIVISION *See* TRAVELLER ACCOMMODATION STATISTICS **5501**

STATISTICS CANADA. MERCHANDISING AND SERVICES DIVISION. RESTAURANT STATISTICS *See* RESTAURANT, CATERER AND TAVERN STATISTICS **5073**

STATISTICS CANADA. PRICES DIVISION *See* CONSUMER PRICE INDEX (OTTAWA) **1471**

STATISTICS CANADA. PROVINCIAL GOVERNMENT SECTION *See* CONTROL AND SALE OF ALCOHOLIC BEVERAGES IN CANADA, THE **2366**

STATISTICS CANADA PUBLICATIONS LIST (CN/1180-548X) [23249080] **4822**

STATISTICS CANADA. STUDENT INFORMATION SECTION *See* TRAINING IN INDUSTRY **1715**

STATISTICS CANADA. SURFACE TRANSPORT SECTION *See* RAILWAY FREIGHT TRAFFIC (OTTAWA. QUARTERLY EDITION) **5435**

STATISTICS CANADA. SURFACE TRANSPORT SECTION *See* PUBLIC WAREHOUSING **705**

STATISTICS CANADA. TRANSPORTATION AND COMMUNICATIONS DIVISION *See* AIR CARRIER TRAFFIC AT CANADIAN AIRPORTS (QUARTERLY EDITION) **7**

STATISTICS CANADA. TRANSPORTATION AND COMMUNICATIONS DIVISION *See* COMMUNICATIONS (OTTAWA) **1152**

STATISTICS CANADA. TRANSPORTATION SECTION *See* MOTOR VEHICLE TRAFFIC ACCIDENTS **5442**

STATISTICS FOR MUNICIPAL AUTHORITIES IN PENNSYLVANIA (US/0147-4626) [03173537] 4750, **4700**

STATISTICS FROM RELIGIOUS ORGANIZATIONS (PP) [01791171] **5013**

STATISTICS IN MEDICINE (UK/0277-6715) [07625714] 3643, **3661**

STATISTICS INFOGRAM (CN/1181-781X) [23247982] **2870**

STATISTICS Alphabetical Title Index

STATISTICS / NEW MEXICO STATE DEPARTMENT OF EDUCATION, SCHOOL MANAGEMENT DIVISION, SCHOOL BUDGET PLANNING UNIT (US) [23473161] **1785**

STATISTICS OF CIVIL COURTS IN THE STATE OF TAMIL NADU FOR THE YEAR ... (II) [06719559] 3059, **3083**

STATISTICS OF COMMUNICATIONS COMMON CARRIERS (US/0161-5173) [03124984] **1164**

●STATISTICS OF EDUCATION AND TRAINING IN WALES. SCHOOLS / WELSH OFFICE / YSTADEGAU ADDYSG A HYFFORDDIANT YNG NGHYMRU. YSGOLION / Y SWYDDFA GYMREIG (UK/0968-5588) [29733222] **1785**

STATISTICS OF EDUCATION IN LAGOS STATE (NR/0331-0477) [02241654] 1785, **1798**

STATISTICS OF EDUCATION IN WALES. SCHOOLS See STATISTICS OF EDUCATION AND TRAINING IN WALES. SCHOOLS / WELSH OFFICE / YSTADEGAU ADDYSG A HYFFORDDIANT YNG NGHYMRU. YSGOLION / Y SWYDDFA GYMREIG **1785**

STATISTICS OF EDUCATION; SPECIAL SERIES - GREAT BRITAIN (UK) [05650910] 1785, **1798**

STATISTICS OF EMPLOYMENT IN LOCAL BODIES IN WEST BENGAL (II/0511-5507) [05161214] 1712, **1539**

STATISTICS OF EMPLOYMENT UNDER THE PUBLIC SERVICE ACT (AT) [01784701] **1539**

STATISTICS OF FOREIGN TRADE. STATISTIQUES DU COMMERCE EXTERIER. SERIES B. TRADE BY COMMODITIES: COUNTRY SUMMARIES. ECHANGES PAR PRODUITS: RESUME PAR PAYS (FR) [05228850] **733**

STATISTICS OF FRATERNAL BENEFIT SOCIETIES (US/0532-6109) [01766476] **2898**

STATISTICS OF HOSPITAL CASES DISCHARGED. BRITISH COLUMBIA (CN/0524-5354) [03436606] 3793, **3662**

STATISTICS OF HOSPITALIZED ACCIDENTS : BRITISH COLUMBIA (CN/0524-5451) [02250077] 3793, **3662**

STATISTICS OF IMPORTS AND EXPORTS See IMPORTS AND EXPORTS STATISTICS **5328**

STATISTICS OF INCOME. CORPORATION INCOME TAX RETURNS (US/0160-9920) [02687847] 4750, **4700**

STATISTICS OF INCOME : INCOME TAX RETURNS (US) [05020892] 4750, **4700**

STATISTICS OF INCOME. INDIVIDUAL INCOME TAX RETURNS (US) [02688571] 4750, **4700**

STATISTICS OF INCOME. PARTNERSHIP RETURNS (1977) (US/0734-1709) [07629528] 4750, **4700**

STATISTICS OF INCOME. SOI BULLETIN (US/0730-0743) [07904895] 4750, **4700**

STATISTICS OF INCOME. SOLE PROPRIETORSHIP RETURNS (US/0744-0030) [07538626] 4750, **4700**

STATISTICS OF INCOME. SUPPLEMENTAL REPORT. INTERNATIONAL INCOME AND TAXES. DOMESTIC INTERNATIONAL SALES CORPORATION RETURNS (US) [06634116] 4750, **4700**

STATISTICS OF MARINE PRODUCTS EXPORTS (II) [03520655] **2314**

STATISTICS OF MINES IN INDIA: COAL (II) [05507277] **2151**

STATISTICS OF MINES IN INDIA: NON-COAL (II) [05507287] **2151**

STATISTICS OF MISSOURI NONPUBLIC ELEMENTARY AND SECONDARY SCHOOLS (US/0090-7154) [01785245] 1785, **1798**

STATISTICS OF MONTANA PUBLIC LIBRARIES See MONTANA LIBRARY DIRECTORY, WITH STATISTICS OF MONTANA PUBLIC LIBRARIES **3259**

STATISTICS OF PAPER, PAPERBOARD AND WOOD PULP (US/0731-8863) [08018696] 4239, **4240**

STATISTICS OF PROMOTIONS AND APPEALS (AT) [01784702] **1539**

STATISTICS OF PUBLIC SCHOOL LIBRARIES / MEDIA CENTERS (US/0733-2041) [08515869] 3251, **3260**

STATISTICS OF PUBLIC SCHOOL SYSTEMS IN THE TWENTY LARGEST U.S. CITIES (US/0742-3888) [09773962] 1785, **1798**

STATISTICS OF SOUTH DAKOTA LIBRARIES (US) [03857442] 3251, **3260**

STATISTICS OF SOUTH DAKOTA PUBLIC LIBRARIES (US/0099-0655) [02242760] 3251, **3260**

STATISTICS OF SOUTH DAKOTA SCHOOL LIBRARIES (US) **3251**

STATISTICS OF THE AIR BORNE FOREIGN TRADE OF INDIA (II) [07053310] **41**

STATISTICS OF THE MISUSE OF DRUGS UNITED KINGDOM, SUPPLEMENTARY TABLES / HOME OFFICE (UK/0143-1463) [07394544] 1349, **1350**

STATISTICS OF TIMBER EXPORTS FROM SINGAPORE IN ... (SI) [08120240] **2404**

STATISTICS OF VIRGINIA PUBLIC LIBRARIES AND INSTITUTIONAL LIBRARIES (US/0731-8464) [08146368] 3251, **3260**

STATISTICS OF WESTERN AUSTRALIA. MINING See MINING, WESTERN AUSTRALIA / AUSTRALIAN BUREAU OF STATISTICS, WESTERN AUSTRALIAN OFFICE **2006**

STATISTICS OF WESTERN AUSTRALIA: RURAL INDUSTRIES (AT) [02829845] 138, **156**

STATISTICS OF WORLD TRADE IN STEEL (NEW YORK N.Y. : 1976) (US) [05328104] 4020, **1627**

STATISTICS ON ALCOHOL AND DRUG USE IN CANADA AND OTHER COUNTRIES (CN/0715-7657) [09986590] 1349, **1350**

STATISTICS ON EXTERNAL INDEBTEDNESS (PARIS, FRANCE : 1985) (FR) [17417207] **4750**

STATISTICS ON FUEL USED TO GENERATE ELECTRICITY BY THE ELECTRIC UTILITY INDUSTRY (US/1055-9698) [11856250] **1958**

STATISTICS ON OCCUPATIONAL WAGES AND HOURS OF WORK AND ON FOOD PRICES : OCTOBER INQUIRY RESULTS / INTERNATIONAL LABOUR OFFICE, GENEVA (SZ) [27209264] **1712**

STATISTICS ON OPERATIONS (US) [01787647] 1712, **1539**

STATISTICS ON SCHEDULED BANKS IN PAKISTAN (PK/0039-0577) [01774141] **733**

STATISTICS ON SOCIAL WORK EDUCATION IN THE UNITED STATES (US/0163-1403) [02255497] 5311, **5267**

STATISTICS ON THE OPERATION OF THE PREVENTION OF TERRORISM LEGISLATION (UK) 4535, **3059**

STATISTICS - ONTARIO MINISTRY OF NATURAL RESOURCES (CN/0383-5898) [02239756] 2206, **2185**

STATISTICS PUBLICATIONS CATALOGUE (NZ/0113-1133) [15527555] **5342**

STATISTICS QUARTERLY - BUREAU OF STATISTICS (YELLOWKNIFE) (CN/0225-9907) [06758359] **5342**

STATISTICS RELATING TO DGTD UNITS (II) [06634126] 1585, **1539**

STATISTICS RELATING TO REGIONAL AND MUNICIPAL GOVERNMENTS IN BRITISH COLUMBIA (CN/0702-0988) [01791352] 4750, **4700**

STATISTICS SOURCES (US/0585-198X) [01487829] **5342**

STATISTICS - STATE OF TENNESSEE, DEPARTMENT OF HUMAN SERVICES (US/0361-896X) [02441373] 5311, **5267**

STATISTICS, TEXTBOOKS AND MONOGRAPHS (US/1040-0672) [10560163] **5342**

●STATISTICS USERS NETWORK (US/1062-3507) [25590340] **5342**

STATISTICS WEEKLY (AT/1033-8640) [I10338640] **5342**

STATISTICS WITH DIRECTORY OF NEVADA LIBRARIES AND LIBRARY PERSONNEL See NEVADA LIBRARY DIRECTORY AND STATISTICS **3259**

STATISTIEK DER BRANDEN / CENTRAAL BUREAU VOOR DE STATISTIEK, HOOFDAFDELING STATISTIEKEN VAN RECHTSBESCHERMING EN VEILIGHEID (NE/0168-4639) [02500849] **2293**

STATISTIEK DER GEMEENTEBEGROTINGEN / CENTRAAL BUREAU VOOR DE STATISTIEK, HOOFDAFDELING FINANCIELE STATISTIEKEN (NE) [09983370] 4750, **4700**

STATISTIEK DER PROVINCIALE FINANCIEN / CENTRAAL BUREAU VOOR DE STATISTIEK (NE/0168-3837) [11737353] 4750, **4700**

STATISTIEK FINANCIEN VAN ONDERNEMINGEN, HANDEL / CENTRAAL BUREAU VOOR DE STATISTIEK, HOOFDAFDELING STATISTIEKEN VAN KAPITAALGOEDERENVOORRAAD EN BALANSEN (NE/0168-8405) [12269193] 852, **733**

STATISTIEK VAN DE BINNENVLOOT (NE) [06480217] **5457**

STATISTIEK VAN DE ELEKTRICITEITS--VOORZIENING IN NEDERLAND / CENTRAAL BUREAU VOOR DE STATISTIEK, HOOFDAFDELING STATISTIEKEN VAN INDUSTRIE EN BOUWNIJVERHEID (NE/0168-5163) [06402078] 4762, **4700**

STATISTIEK VAN DE LAND- EN TUINBOUW / CENTRAAL BUREAU VOOR DE STATISTIEK, HOOFDAFDELING LANDBOUWSTATISTIEKEN (NE) [05152074] 138, **156**

STATISTIEK VAN DE OPENBARE BIBLIOTHEKEN / CENTRAAL BUREAU VOOR DE STATISTIEK, HOOFDAFDELING SOCIAAL-CULTURELE STATISTIEKEN (NE/0168-3462) [02500888] 3251, **3260**

STATISTIEK VAN DE SCHEEPVAARTBEWEGING / CENTRAAL BUREAU VOOR DE STATISTIEK, HOOFDAFDELING STATISTIEKEN VAN VERKEER EN VERVOER (NE) [09954243] 5457, **5402**

STATISTIEK VAN DE SCHEEPVAARTBEWEGING IN NEDERLAND See STATISTIEK VAN DE SCHEEPVAARTBEWEGING / CENTRAAL BUREAU VOOR DE STATISTIEK, HOOFDAFDELING STATISTIEKEN VAN VERKEER EN VERVOER **5402**

STATISTIEK VAN DE VAN GEMEENTEWAGE PER LEERLING BESCHIKBAAR GESTELDE BEDRAGEN TER BESTRIJDING VAN DE MATERIELE EXPLOITATIEKOSTEN DER LAGERE SCHOLEN See PER LEERLING BESCHIKBAAR GESTELDE BEDRAGEN VOOR HET LAGER ONDERWIJS **1772**

STATISTIEK VAN HET AUTOPARK (NE) [02621488] **5402**

STATISTIEK VAN HET BASISONDERWIJS, HET SPECIAAL ONDERWIJS EN HET VOORTGEZET SPECIAAL ONDERWIJS. PERSONEEL (NE/0921-4828) [21682262] 1905, **1805**

STATISTIEK VAN HET BASISONDERWIJS, HET SPECIAAL ONDERWIJS EN HET VOORTGEZET SPECIAAL ONDERWIJS. SCHOLEN EN LEERLINGEN (NE/0921-0350) [19317329] **1785**

STATISTIEK VAN HET BEROEPSONDERWIJS. BEROEPSBEGELEIDEND ONDERWIJS EN VORMINGSEREK, CURSORISCH ONDERNEMERSONDERWIJS / CBS, CENTRAAL BUREAU VOOR DE STATISTIEK, HOOFDAFDELING STATISTIEKEN VAN ONDERWIJS EN WETENSCHAPPEN (NE/0921-0083) [19030924] **5342**

STATISTIEK VAN HET BEROEPSONDERWIJS. HUISHOUD- EN NIJVERHEIDSONDERWIJS / CENTRAAL BUREAU VOOR DE STATISTIEK, HOOFDAFDELING STATISTIEKEN VAN ONDERWIJS EN WETENSCHAPPEN (NE) [04486230] **1916**

STATISTIEK VAN HET CONSUMPTIEF KREDIET / CENTRAAL BUREAU VOOR DE STATISTIEK (NE) [11063093] 812, **733**

STATISTIEK VAN HET ERKENDE SCHRIFTELIJK ONDERWIJS / CENTRAAL BUREAU VOOR DE STATISTIEK, HOOFDAFDELING STATISTIEKEN VAN ONDERWIJS EN WETENSCHAPPEN (NE) [03602168] **1785**

STATISTIEK VAN HET HOGER BEROEPSONDERWIJS. INSTELLINGEN EN STUDENTEN / CBS, CENTRAAL BUREAU VOOR DE STATISTIEK, HOOFDAFDELING STATISTIEKEN VAN ONDERWIJS EN WETENSCHAPPEN (NE/0921-0091) [19273827] **1916**

STATISTIEK VAN HET LAGER BEROEPSONDERWIJS. PERSONEEL / CBS, CENTRAAL BUREAU VOOR DE STATISTIEK, HOOFDAFDELING STATISTIEKEN VAN ONDERWIJS EN WETENSCHAPPEN (NE/0924-0837) [21793417] **1785**

STATISTIEK VAN HET VREEMDELINGENVERKEER See STATISTIEK VREEMDELINGENVERKEER / CENTRAAL BUREAU VOOR DE STATISTIEK, HOOFDAFDELING SOCIAAL-CULTURELE STATISTIEKEN **5500**

STATISTIEK VAN HET VWO, HAVO EN MAVO : IN-, DOOR- EN UITSTROOM VAN DE LEERLINGEN (NE) [06538138] **1785**

STATISTIEK VAN HET WETENSCHAPPELIJK ONDERWIJS / CENTRAAL BUREAU VOOR DE STATISTIEK, HOOFDAFDELING STATISTIEKEN VAN ONDERWIJS EN WETENSCHAPPEN (NE/0168-5058) [01788865] 1848, **1798**

STATISTIEK VREEMDELINGENVERKEER / CENTRAAL BUREAU VOOR DE STATISTIEK, HOOFDAFDELING SOCIAAL-CULTURELE STATISTIEKEN (NE/0168-5538) [05795994] **5500**

STATISTIEKE VAN MOTOR- EN ANDER VOERTUIE SOOS OP ... / REPUBLIEK VAN SUID-AFRIKA, SENTRALE STATISTIEKDIENS (SA) [09508481] **5402**

Alphabetical Title Index — STATISTIQUES

STATISTIEKE VAN MOTORVOERTUIE : NUWE VOERTUIE GELISENSIEER (SA) [01786687] **5426**

STATISTIEKE VAN NUWE VOERTUIE GELISENSIEER (SA) [03214955] **5402**

STATISTIEKE VAN PLAASLIKE OWERHEDE, ORANJE-VRYSTAAT, TRANSVAAL (SA) [02242148] **5342**

STATISTIK BIOSKOP & REKREASI (IO) [08913391] **5342**

STATISTIK BONGKAR MUAT BARANG DI PELABUHAN INDONESIA (IO) [02439012] **5457**

STATISTIK COKLAT (IO) [02582204] 1627, **1539**

STATISTIK DER ALLGEMEINBILDENDEN SCHULEN IN NIEDERSACHSEN (GW) [04787967] 1785, **1798**

STATISTIK DER KOHLENWIRTSCHAFT See ZAHLEN ZUR KOHLENWIRTSCHAFT **1632**

STATISTIK DER KOMMUNALEN OFFENTLICHEN BIBLIOTHEKEN DER BUNDESREPUBLIK, REGIONALSTATISTIK (GW) [02243573] 3251, **3260**

STATISTIK DER ORTSKRANKENKASSEN IN DER BUNDESREPUBLIK DEUTSCHLAND : ALTERSGLIEDERUNG DER MITGLIEDER (GW) [01794492] 2894, **2898**

STATISTIK DES AUSLANDES. LANDERBERICHT. EG-STAATEN / HERAUSGEBER STATISTISCHES BUNDESAMT (GW) [11835445] **5342**

STATISTIK DES AUSLANDES. LANDERBERICHT. FINLAND (GW) [14576414] **2523**

STATISTIK DES AUSLANDES. LANDERBERICHT. HONDURAS (GW) [19948731] **2512**

STATISTIK DES AUSLANDES. LANDERBERICHT. IRAN See LANDERBERICHT. IRAN / STATISTISCHES BUNDESAMT **5331**

STATISTIK DES AUSLANDES. LANDERBERICHT. KATAR / HERAUSGEBER STATISTISCHES BUNDESAMT (GW) [11835789] 1585, **1539**

STATISTIK DES AUSLANDES. LANDERBERICHT. KOLOMBIEN / HERAUSGEBER STATISTISCHES BUNDESAMT (GW) [12225454] **5342**

STATISTIK DES AUSLANDES. LANDERBERICHT. OMAN / HERAUSGEBER STATISTISCHES BUNDESAMT (GW) [11780417] **5342**

STATISTIK DES AUSLANDES. LANDERBERICHT. SAMBIA / HERAUSGEBER STATISTISCHES BUNDESAMT (GW) [10648867] **5342**

STATISTIK DES AUSLANDES. LANDERBERICHT. SCHWEDEN (GW) [16401890] **2523**

STATISTIK DES AUSLANDES. LANDERBERICHT. ZYPERN / HERAUSGEBER STATISTISCHES BUNDESAMT (GW) [11780528] **5342**

STATISTIK DES AUSLANDES. LANDERKURZBERICHT. KARIBISCHE STAATEN / HERAUSGEBER STATISTISCHES BUNDESAMT (GW) [09983026] **5342**

STATISTIK DES AUSLANDES. LANDERKURZBERICHT. PAZIFISCHE STAATEN / HERAUSGEBER STATISTISCHES BUNDESAMT (GW) [09982421] **5342**

STATISTIK DES AUSLANDS. LANDERBERICHT (GW) [18012677] **1640**

STATISTIK DES HOCHSCHULWESENS IN DER SCHWEIZ (SZ) [03285580] **1848**

STATISTIK EKONOMI DAN KEUANGAN INDONESIA (IO) [16655078] **1585**

STATISTIK EKSPOR HASIL HUTAN BUKAN KAYU (IO) [02989502] 2396, **2399**

STATISTIK EKSPOR HASIL HUTAN NON KAYU See STATISTIK EKSPOR HASIL HUTAN BUKAN KAYU **2399**

STATISTIK ENERGI (IO) [09492137] 1958, **1963**

STATISTIK HARGA HARGA PROPINSI KALIMANTAN TIMUR (IO) [07510318] 1595, **1539**

STATISTIK HARGA ... SULAWESI SELATAN (IO) [11009756] 1522, **1539**

STATISTIK IN DER RENTENVERSICHERUNG (GW) [04851733] **5311**

STATISTIK INDONESIA See BUKU SAKU STATISTIK INDONESIA **5324**

STATISTIK INDONESIA. STATISTICAL YEARBOOK OF INDONESIA (IO/0126-2912) [03634681] **5342**

STATISTIK INDUSTRI BALI (IO) [09186074] 1585, **1539**

STATISTIK INDUSTRI KARET REMAH (CRUMB RUBBER) ... INDONESIA (IO) [11585880] **5078**

STATISTIK INDUSTRI KECIL (IO) [10252714] 1627, **1539**

STATISTIK - KAMMER DE GEWERBLICHEN WIRTSCHAFT FUR WIEN (AU) [03307296] **5342**

STATISTIK KENDARAAN BERMOTOR DAN PANJANG JALAN (IO) [02240296] **5402**

STATISTIK KEUANGAN DESA JAWA DAN MADURA (IO/0126-4397) [08258317] 4750, **4700**

STATISTIK KEUANGAN DESA. SULAWESI-MALUKU-BALI-NUSATENGGARA (IO) [09561341] 4750, **4700**

STATISTIK KEUANGAN PEMERINTAHAN DESA See STATISTIK KEUANGAN DESA. SULAWESI-MALUKU-BALI-NUSATENGGARA **4700**

STATISTIK KOTAMADYA PASURUAN (IO) [08489808] **5342**

STATISTIK KRIMINALITAS DKI JAKARTA (IO) [10238418] **5311**

STATISTIK LINGKUNGAN HIDUP INDONESIA (IO) [10252796] 1522, **1539**

STATISTIK OVER LUFTFARTSAKTIVITETER / LUFTFARTSDIREKTORATET (DK) [10319095] **5342**

STATISTIK OVER PENSIONSTAGARNA I FINLAND (FI/0780-7554) [11613556] 5312, **5267**

STATISTIK PENDIDIKAN DILUAR LINGKUNGAN DEPARTEMEN P & K (IO) [06602049] 1785, **1798**

STATISTIK PENDIDIKAN DILUAR LINGKUNGAN DEPARTEMEN P & K DI-SUMATERA UTARA (IO) [04589796] 1805, **1798**

STATISTIK PENDIDIKAN NON FORMIL, KURSUS-KURSUS DI DKI JAKARTA See PENDIDIKAN NON FORMIL DKI JAKARTA **1772**

STATISTIK PENDIDIKAN SMA SELURUH INDONESIA (IO) [02175003] 1785, **1798**

STATISTIK PENDIDIKAN ST SELURUH INDONESIA (IO) [02177111] **1916**

STATISTIK PENGADILAN NEGERI PROPINSI IRIAN JAYA MICROFORM (II) [18953090] **3177**

STATISTIK PERHUBUNGAN - BIRO PUSAT STATISTIK (LALU LINTAS ANGKUTAN BARANG ANTAR PULAU MENURUT JENIS PELAYARAN) (IO/0216-6909) [07242827] **5457**

STATISTIK PERJALANAN WISATAWAN DOMESTIK JAWA TENGAH (IO) [10252815] **5500**

STATISTIK PERKEBUNAN BESAR (IO) [11150760] **138**

STATISTIK PERUMAHAN DAN LINGKUNGANNYA (IO) [11598082] 2836, **2841**

STATISTIK RESTORAN : HASIL PELAKSANAAN SURVEI KHUSUS RESTORAN DI 12 PROPINSI (IO) [10946659] **5073**

STATISTIK (SWEDEN. STATISTISKA CENTRALBYRAN) (SW) [09665974] **5342**

STATISTIK TANAMAN BAHAN MAKANAN (IO) [09186120] 188, **156**

STATISTIK UBER DIE MONATSBEZUEGE DER ANGESTELLTEN See MONATSBEZUEGE DER ANGESTELLTEN IN DER INDUSTRIE OSTERREICHS **1691**

STATISTIK UBER NS-PROZESSE (GW) [04287832] 3059, **3083**

STATISTIK UNIVERSITAS SRIWIJAYA (IO) [03982393] **1848**

STATISTIK WILAYAH DKI JAKARTA (IO) [01795515] **5342**

STATISTIK--WIRTSCHAFTSKAMMER WIEN (AU) **5342**

STATISTIKA (XR/0585-2013) [01981211] **5342**

STATISTIKA (BU) [02690686] **5342**

STATISTIKA NOVE TEHNIKI See NEKI POKAZATELJI TEHNICKOG RAZVOJA PRIVREDE JUGOSLAVIJE **1536**

STATISTIKA RECHI I AVTOMATICHESKII ANALIZ TEKSTA (RU) [02936392] 3536, **3324**

STATISTIKAH SHEL SEHAR HUTS (IS) [03134720] **852**

STATISTIKE DEMOSION OIKONOMIKON (GR) [02244866] **4750**

STATISTIKE EPETERIS DEMOSION OIKONOMIKON (GR) [01791991] 4750, **4700**

STATISTIKE EPETERIS TES HELLADOS (GR/0072-7431) [01146775] **5342**

STATISTIKE TOU DELOTHENTOS EISODEMATOS PHYSIKON PROSOPON KAI TES PHOROLOGIAS AUTOU (GR) [01792743] 1585, **1539**

STATISTIKEN UBER DEN AUSSENHANDEL. ANALYTISCHE UBERSICHTEN: AUSFUHR (LU/0585-1661) [01249871] **852**

STATISTIKKEN. ARBEJDERLN (DK/0107-0851) [20077352] **5343**

STATISTIQUE AGRICOLE: CAHIERS See CAHIERS DE STATISTIQUES AGRICOLES **71**

STATISTIQUE AGRICOLE. PRINCIPAUX RENSEIGNEMENTS, REGIONS NORD-PAS DE CALAIS ET PICARDIE / MINISTERE DE L'AGRICULTURE, SERVICE REGIONAL DE STATISTIQUE AGRICOLE (FR/0243-7155) [09887799] **156**

STATISTIQUE AGRICOLE : REGION PARISIENNE (FR) [02243012] 5343, **157**

STATISTIQUE AGRICOLE. REGIONS NORD-PICARDIE See STATISTIQUE AGRICOLE. PRINCIPAUX RENSEIGNEMENTS, REGIONS NORD-PAS DE CALAIS ET PICARDIE / MINISTERE DE L'AGRICULTURE, SERVICE REGIONAL DE STATISTIQUE AGRICOLE **156**

STATISTIQUE ANNUELLE / CHARBONNAGES DE FRANCE, PLAN ETUDES INVESTISSEMENTS (FR) [28032760] **1445**

STATISTIQUE ANNUELLE DES VEHICULES NEUFS IMMATRICULES EN BELGIQUE. JAARLIJKSE STATISTIEK DER NIEUWE VOERTUIGEN IN BELGIE INGESCHREVEN (BE) [04564829] **5402**

STATISTIQUE - BUREAU DE LA STATISTIQUE DU QUEBEC (1981) (CN/0227-0668) [07964021] **5343**

STATISTIQUE CRIMINELLE DE LA BELGIQUE (BE) [01519449] **3083**

STATISTIQUE DE LA NAVIGATION MARITIME (BE) [06721614] **5457**

STATISTIQUE DU TRAFIC INTERNATIONAL DES PORTS (BE) [03298303] **5457**

STATISTIQUE DU TRAFIC INTERNATIONAL DES PORTS, U.E.B.L. / ROYAUME DE BELGIQUE, MINISTERE DES AFFAIRES ECONOMIQUES, INSTITUT NATIONAL DE BELGIQUE (BE) [04285828] **5402**

STATISTIQUE ET ANALYSE DES DONNEES (FR/0750-7364) [I07507364] **5343**

STATISTIQUE MEDICALE DANS LES ARMEES (FR/0291-851X) [11722274] 4058, **4062**

STATISTIQUE MENSUELLE DE L'ENERGIE / MINISTERE DU DEVELOPPEMENT INDUSTRIEL ET SCIENTIFIQUE, SECRETARIAT GENERAL DE L'ENERGIE ET SERVICE CENTRAL DE LA STATISTIQUE ET DES INFORMATIONS INDUSTRIELLES (FR) [01796683] 1958, **1963**

STATISTIQUE MENSUELLES DE LA DISTRIBUTION DES FUEL-OILS See STATISTIQUES F. O. A. : DISTRIBUTION DES FUELS-OILS **4284**

STATISTIQUES & ETUDES : MIDI-PYRENEES (FR/0396-0099) [06257549] **5343**

STATISTIQUES CORRECTIONNELLES QUEBECOISES (CN/0714-4555) [12676849] **3177**

STATISTIQUES CRIMINELLES INTERNATIONALES (FR) [01791611] 3177, **3083**

STATISTIQUES DE COMMERCE. EXTERIEUR DE LA FRANCE (FR) **852**

STATISTIQUES DE LA CONSTRUCTION (FR) [07031703] 628, **633**

STATISTIQUES DE LA CONSTRUCTION ET DU LOGEMENT (BE/0772-7712) [03424352] 628, **633**

STATISTIQUES DE LA JUSTICE : CONTINENT ET ILES ADJACENTES (PO/0253-0600) [03835732] 3059, **3083**

STATISTIQUES DE LA POPULATION ACTIVE (FR) **1712**

STATISTIQUES DE LA PRODUCTION MINERALE (CN) [03424967] 1627, **1398**

STATISTIQUES DE L'ADMISSION - UNIVERSITE DE MONTREAL. BUREAU DES ADMISSIONS (CN/1184-2970) [24265516] **1848**

STATISTIQUES DE L'AGRICULTURE, DES PECHES ET DE L'ALIMENTATION (CN/0828-2501) [11720589] 138, **157**

STATISTIQUES DE L'ENSEIGNEMENT (RW) [06987875] 1785, **1798**

STATISTIQUES DE L'ENSEIGNEMENT AU GABON (GO) [02246661] 1785, **1798**

STATISTIQUES DE L'ENSEIGNEMENT PRIMAIRE ET SECONDAIRE (CG) [01798285] **5036**

STATISTIQUES DE L'ENSEIGNEMENT SECONDAIRE (LU) [02240956] 1785, **1798**

STATISTIQUES DE L'INDUSTRIE GAZIERE EN FRANCE (FR) [02245962] 4279, **4284**

STATISTIQUES DE L'INSCRIPTION - UNIVERSITE DE MONTREAL, BUREAU DU REGISTRAIRE (CN/0225-9648) [06265016] **1848**

STATISTIQUES DE PERSONNEL / MINISTERE DES PTT, DIRECTION DU PERSONNEL ET DES AFFAIRES SOCIALES (FR) [09789472] 1147, **1125**

STATISTIQUES   Alphabetical Title Index

STATISTIQUES DE RECETTES PUBLIQUES DES PAYS MEMBRES DE L'OCDE: UNE CLASSIFICATION NORMALISEE (FR) [02471673] **4700**

STATISTIQUES DE TRAFIC (FR) [02441285] **41**

STATISTIQUES DE TRAFIC : GRANDS AEROPORTS DE L'OUEST DE L'EUROPE (FR/0078-947X) [03530041] **42**

STATISTIQUES DEMOGRAPHIQUES (BE/0067-5490) [02435958] 4560, **4563**

STATISTIQUES DES BENEFICIAIRES DE PRESTATIONS DE RETRAITE ET DE SURVIE (BE) [01787617] 1712, **1539**

STATISTIQUES DES COMPTES DES COMMUNES, DES DEPARTEMENTS ET DE LEURS ETABLISSEMENTS PUBLICS *See* STATISTIQUES DES COMPTES POUR L'EXERCICE ... DES COMMUNES, DES DEPARTEMENTS, DES REGIONS ET DES ETABLISSEMENTS PUBLICS LOCAUX **4700**

STATISTIQUES DES COMPTES POUR L'EXERCICE ... DES COMMUNES, DES DEPARTEMENTS, DES REGIONS ET DES ETABLISSEMENTS PUBLICS LOCAUX (FR) [10782466] 4750, **4700**

STATISTIQUES DES PERSONNES ASSUJETTIES AU STATUT SOCIAL DES TRAVAILLEURS INDEPENDANTS (NE) [01787675] 1712, **1539**

STATISTIQUES DES SOCIETES (PO) [26896081] 5343, **713**

STATISTIQUES DES SOCIETES. ESTATISTICAS DAS SOCIEDADES (PO/0870-3205) [03726819] **5343**

STATISTIQUES DES TRANSPORTS ET COMMUNICATIONS : CONTINENT, AZORES ET MADERE (PO/0377-2292) [04182322] **5402**

STATISTIQUES DIVERSES (FR) [09535441] 3059, **3083**

STATISTIQUES DU BATIMENT ET DE L'HABITATION : CONTINENT, AZORES ET MADERE (PO) [03950060] 1712, **1539**

STATISTIQUES DU COMMERCE EXTERIEUR DE LA FRANCE. IMPORTATIONS, EXPORTATIONS EN N.C.C.D (FR) [20311363] **852**

STATISTIQUES DU COMMERCE EXTERIEUR DE L'UNION ECONOMIQUE BELGO-LUXEMBOURGEOISE. ETATS DEVELOPPES / ROYAUME DE BELGIQUE, MINISTERE DES AFFAIRES ECONOMIQUES, INSTITUT NATIONAL DE STATISTIQUE *SUSPENDED.* (BE/0773-6215) [13072590] 852, **734**

STATISTIQUES DU COMMERCE EXTERIEUR DE L'UNION ECONOMIQUE BELGO-LUXEMBURGEOISE *SUSPENDED.* (BE/0772-6694) [12278335] 852, **734**

STATISTIQUES DU COMMERCE INTERIEUR ET DES TRANSPORTS / ROYAUME DE BELGIQUE, MINISTERE DES AFFAIRES ECONOMIQUES, INSTITUT NATIONAL DE STATISTIQUE (BE) [12210502] 852, **734**

STATISTIQUES DU TOURISME (FR) [05080259] **5501**

STATISTIQUES ELECTRICITE (FR) [01795830] **2082**

STATISTIQUES ENERGETIQUES PARIS (FR/0984-5259) [I09845259] **1963**

STATISTIQUES ET INDICATEURS DES REGIONS FRANCAISES (FR) [02357137] 1585, **1539**

STATISTIQUES ET RESULTATS COMPLEMENTAIRES (FR) [01799153] 2286, **2287**

STATISTIQUES F. O. A. : DISTRIBUTION DES FUELS-OILS (FR) [03347781] 4279, **4284**

STATISTIQUES FINANCIERES (BE) [02378027] 812, **734**

STATISTIQUES FINANCIERES (TI) [02242057] 812, **734**

STATISTIQUES FINANCIERES DU GOUVERNEMENT DU QUEBEC (CN/0705-579X) [11501642] 4750, **4700**

STATISTIQUES FINANCIERES EN ..., LES (CN/0846-8001) [09910165] 1712, 2894, **1539**

STATISTIQUES FINANCIERES INTERNATIONALES ANNUAIRE - FONDS MONETAIRE INTERNATIONAL *CEASED.* (US/0252-029X) [07960695] **812**

STATISTIQUES FINANCIERES INTERNATIONALES / FONDS MONETAIRE INTERNATIONAL (US/0252-2977) [08139835] 812, **734**

STATISTIQUES FORESTIERES EN ... / REPUBLIQUE FRANCAISE, MINISTERE DE L'AGRICULTURE, SERVICE CENTRAL DES ENQUETES ET ETUDES STATISTIQUES (FR) [20909659] **2396**

STATISTIQUES: HOUILLE, COKES, AGGLOMERES, METALLURGIE, CARRIERES. STATISTIEKEN: STEENKOLEN, COKES, AGGLOMERATEN, METAALNIJVERHEID, GROVEN (BE) [03266386] 2151, **2006**

STATISTIQUES INDUSTRIELLES (BE/0772-7704) [02258247] 1627, **1539**

STATISTIQUES JEUNESSE, SPORTS ET LOISIRS *See* ANNUAIRE (FRANCE. MINISTERE DE LA JEUNESSE, DES SPORTS ET DES LOISIRS. DIVISION DES ETUDES ET DE LA STATISTIQUE) **4883**

STATISTIQUES JUDICIAIRES (BE/0775-311X) [03424379] 3059, **3083**

STATISTIQUES MONETAIRES ET FINANCIERES *See* STATISTIQUES MONETAIRES ET FINANCIERES : CONTINENT ET REGIONS AUTONOMES DES AZORES ET MADERE **812**

STATISTIQUES MONETAIRES ET FINANCIERES : CONTINENT ET REGIONS AUTONOMES DES AZORES ET MADERE (PO) [06611354] **812**

STATISTIQUES POUR L'ECONOMIE NORMANDE (FR/0395-8973) [06260766] 1522, **1539**

STATISTIQUES PRINCIPALES, LEDUCATION A LELEMENTAIRE ET AU SECONDAIRE EN ONTARIO (CN/1180-5730) [24280794] **1805**

STATISTIQUES SCOLAIRES (FR) [01792793] 1785, **1798**

STATISTIQUES SOCIALES (BE/0067-5563) [02625453] 1712, **1539**

STATISTIQUES SUR LA RECHERCHE ET LE DEVELOPPEMENT INDUSTRIELS AU QUEBEC (CN/0715-7908) [09475909] **5160**

STATISTIQUES SUR L'INDUSTRIE DU MEUBLE (CN/1181-9464) [23599098] 2907, **635**

STATISTIQUES TEMPS LIBRE, JEUNESSE ET SPORTS (FR) [25059794] **4924**

STATISTIQUES - UNIVERSITE LAVAL (CN/0708-1545) [04879575] 1848, **1798**

STATISTISCH BULLETIN - CENTRAAL BUREAU VOOR DE STATISTIEK (NE) [06382773] **5343**

STATISTISCH TYDSCHRIFT (BE) **5343**

STATISTISCHE BEIHEFTE ZU DEN MONATSBERICHTEN DER DEUTSCHEN BUNDESBANK. REIHE 1 : BANKENSTATISTIK NACH BANKENGRUPPEN (GW/0419-9014) [01724217] 813, **734**

STATISTISCHE BEIHEFTE ZU DEN MONATSBERICHTEN DER DEUTSCHEN BUNDESBANK. REIHE 2 : WERTPAPIERSTATISTIK (GW/0418-8314) [01724238] **1539**

STATISTISCHE BEIHEFTE ZU DEN MONATSBERICHTEN DER DEUTSCHEN BUNDESBANK. REIHE 3 : ZAHLUNGSBILANZSTATISTIK (GW/0418-8322) [01724267] **5343**

STATISTISCHE BEIHEFTE ZU DEN MONATSBERICHTEN DER DEUTSCHEN BUNDESBANK. REIHE 4 : SAISONBEREINIGTE WIRTSCHAFTSZAHLEN (GW/0418-8330) [01724308] 1522, **1539**

STATISTISCHE BEIHEFTE ZU DEN MONATSBERICHTEN DER DEUTSCHEN BUNDESBANK. REIHE 5, DIE WAHRUNGEN DER WELT (GW) [01799057] **813**

STATISTISCHE BERICHTE DES STATISTISCHEN AMTES DES SAARLANDES (GW) [01793820] **5343**

STATISTISCHE DELL'ATTIVITA EDILIZIA (IT) [20501204] **628**

STATISTISCHE GEGEVENS BETREFFENDE HET GENEESHERENKORPS (BE) [05714084] **3917**

STATISTISCHE MITTEILUNGEN (GW/0175-7350) [11874940] **5343**

STATISTISCHE MITTEILUNGEN FREIER HANSESTADT BREMEN *See* STATISTISCHE MITTEILUNGEN **5343**

STATISTISCHE NACHRICHTEN - OSTERREICHISCHES STATISTISCHES ZENTRALAMT (AU/0029-9960) [01812571] **5343**

STATISTISCHE NACHRICHTEN (SAARLAND, GERMANY) (GW) [11284314] **5343**

STATISTISCHE RUNDSCHAU FUR DAS LAND NORDRHEIN-WESTFALEN *See* STATISTISCHE RUNDSCHAU NORDRHEIN-WESTFALEN **1522**

STATISTISCHE RUNDSCHAU NORDRHEIN-WESTFALEN (GW/0934-6767) [22165332] **1522**

STATISTISCHE UBERSICHTEN : CHEMIE AN DER HOCHSCHULEN DER BUNDESREPUBLIK DEUTSCHLAND (GW) [04187348] 993, **1012**

STATISTISCHE UBERSICHTEN FUR DAS JAHR (UNIVERSITAT KIEL. INSTITUTS FUR WELTWIRTSCHAFT. BIBLIOTHEK) (GW) [08520557] 3251, **3260**

STATISTISCHER WOCHENDIENST (GW/0431-6983) [01766479] **5343**

STATISTISCHES HANDBUCH FUER DIE REPUBLIK OESTERREICH (AU) [01518885] **5343**

STATISTISCHES HANDBUCH FUER DIE REPUBLIK OESTERREICH (1950) *See* STATISTISCHES JAHRBUCH FUER DIE REPUBLIK OESTERREICH / HERAUS-GEGELEN VON OESTERREICHISCHEN STATISTISCHEN ZENTRALANT **5343**

STATISTISCHES JAHRBUCH BERLIN (GW) [02244148] **5343**

STATISTISCHES JAHRBUCH DER NORDRHEIN-WESTFALISCHEN INDUSTRIE- UND HANDELSKAMMERN / HERAUSGEGEBEN UND BEARBEITET VON DER GEMEINSAMEN STATISTISCHEN STELLE DER NORDRHEIN-WESTFALISCHEN INDUSTRIE- UND HANDELSKAMMERN IN DORTMUND (GW) [10223833] 1522, **1539**

STATISTISCHES JAHRBUCH DER SCHWEIZ (SZ/0081-5330) [09279291] **5343**

STATISTISCHES JAHRBUCH DER STADT BERLIN *See* STATISTISCHES JAHRBUCH BERLIN **5343**

STATISTISCHES JAHRBUCH DEUTSCHER GEMEINDEN (GW/0081-5349) [01766481] **5343**

●STATISTISCHES JAHRBUCH FUER DIE REPUBLIK OESTERREICH / HERAUS-GEGELEN VON OESTERREICHISCHEN STATISTISCHEN ZENTRALANT (AU) [28310222] **5343**

STATISTISCHES JAHRBUCH NORDRHEIN-WESTFALEN (GW/0468-656X) [05912776] **5343**

STATISTISCHES LANDESAMT BADEN-WUERTTEMBERG *See* BAUWIRTSCHAFT, DIE **600**

STATISTISCHES LANDESAMT BADEN-WUERTTEMBERG *See* VEROEFFENTLICHUNGEN DES STATISTISCHEN LANDESAMTES BADEN-WUERTTEMBERG **5345**

STATISTISCHES LANDESAMT BADEN-WUERTTEMBERG. PREISE UND LOEHNE *See* PREISE, LOEHNE, WIRTSCHAFTSRECHNUNGEN **1537**

STATISTISCHES LANDESAMT BADEN-WUERTTEMBERG. VEROEFFENTLICHUNGSVERZEICHNIS *See* VEROEFFENTLICHUNGEN DES STATISTISCHEN LANDESAMTES BADEN-WUERTTEMBERG **5345**

STATISTISCHES LANDESAMT BADEN-WURTTEMBERG *See* DATEN ZUR SOZIALSTRUKTUR: DIE MATERIELLE LEBENSSICHERUNG **1479**

STATISTISCHES LANDESAMT BADEN-WURTTEMBERG *See* JAHRBUCHER FUR STATISTIK UND LANDESKUNDE VON BADEN-WURTTEMBERG **5329**

STATISTISCHES LANDESAMT BADEN-WURTTEMBERG *See* LAND- UND FORSTWIRTSCHAFT, DIE **154**

STATISTISCHES LANDESAMT BADEN-WURTTEMBERG *See* DATEN ZUR UMWELT **2227**

STATISTISCHES LANDESAMT BADEN-WURTTEMBERG *See* VERKEHRSWIRTSCHAFT, DIE **5402**

STATISTISCHES LANDESAMT BADEN-WURTTEMBERG *See* AUSSENHANDEL, DER **726**

STATISTISCHES LANDESAMT BEDEN-WURTTEMBERG *See* REGIONALSTRUKTUR BADEN-WURTTEMBERG: GEMEINDEN **5337**

STATISTISCHES LANDESAMT BREMEN *See* BEVOLKERUNGSSTAND UND BEVOLKERUNGSBEWEGUNG **1918**

STATISTISCHES LANDESAMT NORDRHEIN-WESTFALEN. KREISSTANDARDZAHLEN DES LANDES NORDRHEIN-WESTFALEN *See* KREISSTANDARDZAHLEN **5330**

STATISTISCHES MONATSHEFT / OESTERREICHISCHE NATIONALBANK (AU) [22503671] **5343**

STATISTISCHES TASCHENBUCH (GW) [06589844] **5343**

STATISTISK ARBOG (DK) [01642398] **5343**

STATISTISK ARBOG FOR NORGE (MICROFICHE) (NO) [04161149] **5343**

STATISTISK ARBOK (NO/0078-1932) [02417423] **5343**

STATISTISK ARSBOK FOER SVERIGE (SW/0081-5381) [01696681] **5343**

STATISTISK ARSBOK FOR FINLAND *See* SUOMEN TILASTOLLINEN VUOSIKIRJA **5344**

STATISTISK MANEDSHEFTE (NO/0029-3636) [01718595] **5344**

STATISTISK MANEDSOVERSIGT (DK/0108-5603) [10144910] 1522, **1539**

STATISTIK TIDSKRIFT (SW/0039-7261) [04060887] **5344**

STATISTISK VAREFORTEGNELSE FOR UTENRIKSHANDELEN (NO) [05981649] 852, **734**

Alphabetical Title Index — STEEL

STATISTISKA MEDDELANDEN (SW) [02239817] 5344

STATISTISKA MEDDELANDEN. P (SW) [09961218] 1595, **1540**

STATISTISKA MEDDELANDEN. SERIE BO (SW/0085-6991) [10270221] **628**

STATISTISKA MEDDELANDEN. T (SW/0082-0334) [10292894] 5402

STATISTISKE EFTERRETNINGER See STATISTISKE EFTERRETNINGER. SAMFRDSEL OG TURISME 5393

STATISTISKE EFTERRETNINGER. ARBEJDSMARKED (DK/0108-5514) [10816613] 1712, **1540**

STATISTISKE EFTERRETNINGER. BEFOLKNING OG VALG (DK/0108-5530) [10816659] 5344

STATISTISKE EFTERRETNINGER. BYGGE- OG ANLGSVIRKSOMHED (DK/0108-5549) [10816717] 5344

STATISTISKE EFTERRETNINGER. FRERNE OG GRNLAND (DK/0108-5557) [10816774] 5344

STATISTISKE EFTERRETNINGER. GENEREL ERHVERVSSTATISTIK OG HANDEL (DK/0108-5573) [10816826] 5344

STATISTISKE EFTERRETNINGER. INDKOMST, FORBRUG OG PRISER (DK/0108-5565) [10785727] 1522, **1540**

STATISTISKE EFTERRETNINGER. INDUSTRI OG ENERGI / DANMARKS STATISTIK (DK/0108-5468) [10812434] 1522, **1540**

STATISTISKE EFTERRETNINGER. LANDBRUG (DK/0108-5522) [10816869] **157**

STATISTISKE EFTERRETNINGER. NATIONALREGNSKAB, OFFENTLIGE FINANSER, BETALINGSBALANCE (DK/0108-545X) [10817214] 4750, **4700**

STATISTISKE EFTERRETNINGER. PENGE- OG KAPITALMARKED (DK/0108-5476) [10817251] 813, **734**

STATISTISKE EFTERRETNINGER. SAMFRDSEL OG TURISME (DK/0108-5484) [10744375] 5393

STATISTISKE EFTERRETNINGER. UDDANNELSE OG KULTUR (DK/0108-5492) [10817318] 1785, **1798**

STATISTISKE EFTERRETNINGER. UDENRIGSHANDEL / DANMARKS STATISTIK (DK/0108-5506) [10817353] 5344

STATISZTIKAI HAVI KOZLEMENYEK (HU/0018-781X) [01224960] 5344

STATISZTIKAI SZEMLE (HU/0039-0690) [08923000] 1522, **1540**

STATO CIVILE ITALIANO (IT) **4688**

STATO E MERCATO (IT/0392-9701) [08903673] 852, **1522**

STATO E PROSPETTIVE DELLA FORMAZIONE PROFESSIONALE IN ITALIA : RELAZIONE ANNUALE PRESENTATA DALL'ISFOL AL MINISTERO DEL LAVORO E DELLA PREVIDENZA SOCIALE IN ATTUAZIONE DELL'ART. 20 DELLA LEGGE-QUADRO SULLA FORMAZIONE PROFESSIONALE (IT/0390-3532) [07528958] **1712**

STATO OGGI (IT) **4688**

STATOIL MAGAZINE (NO) [24423656] 2082

STATS (SA) [03084212] 1522, **5344**

STATS (ALEXANDRIA, VA.) (US/1053-8607) [22215969] 5344

STATSFORETAG AB See PRODUKTPROGRAM, STATSFORETAGSGRUPPEN **1622**

STATSGARANTIANSTALTEN (FI) [02937876] **813**

STATSTILSKUD TIL PRODUKTUDVIKLING (DK) [06558273] **1627**

STATSVETENSKAPLIG TIDSKRIFT (SW/0039-0747) [01766484] **4497**

STATUS NEWS (US/0739-9146) [04065120] 5566, **2924**

STATUS OF ACTIVE FOREIGN CREDITS OF THE U.S. GOVT.: FOREIGN CREDITS BY U.S. GOVT. AGENCIES (US/0198-6716) [06184773] 4750

STATUS OF BILLS REPORT CEASED. (CN/0704-609X) [05787690] 3059

STATUS OF ELECTRIC POWER IN THE MISSOURI RIVER BASIN (US/0162-2927) [03625808] **2082**

STATUS OF EQUAL EMPLOYMENT OPPORTUNITY PROGRAM (WASHINGTON, D.C. : 1970) (US/0733-480X) [04864329] **4705**

STATUS OF MAJOR ACQUISITIONS AS OF ... (US) [09305631] 4688, **952**

STATUS OF NATIONAL DIRECT STUDENT LOAN DEFAULTS (US/0741-4528) [10131401] **1848**

STATUS OF OHIO'S CAPITAL AND OPERATING NEEDS FOR PUBLIC TRANSPORTATION, THE (US) [04841778] 5393

STATUS OF SCIENCE REVIEWS (US/0737-013X) [05932218] 5160

STATUS OF THE CONSUMER PRICE EQUALIZATION FUND ... / MINISTRY OF ENERGY (PH) [08077711] **4279**

STATUS OF THE FAMILY FARM, ANNUAL REPORT TO THE CONGRESS (US/0270-1154) [05919143] **138**

STATUS OF WATERFOWL AND FALL FLIGHT FORECASTS / C.U.S. FISH AND WILDLIFE SERVICE AND CANADIAN WILDLIFE SERVICE (US) [19751451] **5620**

STATUS, PROGRESS, AND PROBLEMS IN FEDERAL AGENCY ACCOUNTING (US/0730-3440) [07967194] 4750, **4701**

STATUS REPORT: CAPITAL IMPROVEMENT PROGRAM, BOND FUND SUMMARY (US/0364-8281) [02662561] **4750**

STATUS REPORT : CAPITAL IMPROVEMENTS PROGRAM, CONSTRUCTION SUMMARY (US/0095-8263) [01798236] **1627**

STATUS REPORT - COUNTY RESTRUCTURING STUDIES PROGRAM (CN/0382-1293) [02590085] **4688**

STATUS REPORT - FINANCIAL ACCOUNTING STANDARDS BOARD (US/0149-8452) [01370503] **751**

STATUS REPORT - INSURANCE INSTITUTE FOR HIGHWAY SAFETY (US/0018-988X) [01788367] **5444**

STATUS REPORT OF PUBLIC BROADCASTING (US) [04265581] **1139**

STATUS REPORT ON EDUCATION IN PENNSYLVANIA (US) [12659081] **1785**

STATUS REPORT ON SPEECH RESEARCH (US/0888-3971) [02275104] **3324**

STATUS REPORT ON THE ENERGY-RELATED INVENTIONS PROGRAM (US/0884-1810) [12205314] **1958**

STATUS REPORT - PENNSYLVANIA TRANSPORTATION INSTITUTE (US/0360-1188) [02242419] **5444**

STATUS REPORT - SIERRA COOPERATIVE PILOT PROJECT (US) [07338317] **1435**

STATUS REPORT / THE PREMIER'S COUNCIL ON THE STATUS OF PERSONS WITH DISABILITIES, ALBERTA, THE (CN/0844-8671) [20386571] **4394**

STATUS REPORT - UNITED STATES. HEALTH CARE FINANCING ADMINISTRATION. OFFICE OF RESEARCH AND DEMONSTRATIONS (US/0742-8871) [10452482] **3643**

STATUS (SCOTTSDALE) (US/0195-9190) [05668519] **2082**

STATUS (WASHINGTON) (US/0147-0477) [02548403] 1522, **1540**

STATUTE LAW OF TASMANIA, THE (AT) [09024589] **3059**

STATUTE LAW REVIEW (UK/0144-3593) [06780833] **3059**

● STATUTES & DECISIONS (US/1061-0014) [25157886] **3059**

STATUTES GOVERNING MUNICIPAL PLANNING AND ZONING (US) [03967887] **3059**

STATUTES OF ALBERTA (CN/0823-3489) [10398491] **3059**

STATUTES OF NEW BRUNSWICK (CN/0226-1219) [08877460] **3059**

STATUTES OF NEW ZEALAND (1947), THE (NZ) [06142193] **3059**

STATUTES OF SASKATCHEWAN (CN/0840-2043) [12003534] **3059**

STATUTES OF THE PROVINCE OF MANITOBA (CN) [01585878] **3059**

STATUTES OF THE PROVINCE OF NEWFOUNDLAND (CN) [04526924] **3059**

STATUTES OF THE YUKON TERRITORY (CN/0823-4949) [11134789] **3059**

STATUTORY INSTRUMENTS (UK) [01751483] **4689**

STATUTORY PUBLICATIONS, PRICE LIST - MANITOBA. OFFICE OF THE QUEEN'S PRINTER (ENGLISH EDITION) (CN/1185-9652) [25468444] **3059**

STATUTORY PUBLICATIONS, PRICE LIST - MANITOBA. OFFICE OF THE QUEEN'S PRINTER (FRENCH EDITION) (CN/1185-9652) [25468449] **3059**

STATUTORY REGULATIONS (NZ) [01760253] **3059**

STATUTORY RULES See STATUTORY RULES MADE DURING THE YEAR / OFFICE OF THE PARLIAMENTARY COUNSEL **4689**

STATUTORY RULES MADE DURING THE YEAR / OFFICE OF THE PARLIAMENTARY COUNSEL (AT) [19745033] **4689**

STATUTORY SALARIES, MISSOURI STATE OFFICIALS (US/0092-4687) [01788391] **4689**

STATUTS, LISTE DES MEMBRES - INSTITUT BELGE DU PETROLE (BE) [02240589] **4279**

STAUB, REINHALTUNG DER LUFT (GW/0039-0771) [02240395] **2244**

STAVEBNICKA ROCENKA (XO) [07234910] **628**

STAVEBNICKY CASOPIS (XO/0039-078X) [07113656] **628**

STAVIVO CEASED. (XR/0039-0801) [06428574] **628**

STAYING WELL SCHOOL NEWS CEASED. (US/0895-9579) [16865809] 4804, **1785**

STAYNER SUN (CN) **5795**

STAYNER SUN [MICROFORM], THE (CN/0834-7425) [16390984] **5795**

STC NEWS (DK) [01792797] **2907**

STEAM & FUEL USERS' JOURNAL See ENERGY & FUEL USERS' JOURNAL **1939**

STEAM CLASSIC (UK/0958-7373) [l09587373] **5437**

STEAM COAL (UK/0951-578X) [18615065] **852**

STEAM COAL WATCH (US/0735-8253) [09013391] **2151**

STEAM ELECTRIC MARKET ANALYSIS (US/1045-3148) [04479413] **1958**

STEAM-ELECTRIC PLANT FACTORS (US/0090-3884) [01785045] **1958**

STEAM PASSENGER SERVICE DIRECTORY (US/0081-542X) [02246874] 4096, **5437**

STEAMBOAT BILL (1958) (US/0039-0844) [04477747] 5393, **2762**

STEAMBOAT PILOT, THE (US) [21057056] **5644**

STEAMBOAT SPRINGS MAGAZINE (US/0743-2267) [10535892] **2493**

STEARMAN RESTORERS ASSOCIATION See SRA "OUTFIT" NEWSLETTER **36**

STEARNS-MORRISON ENTERPRISE (US) [02253820] **5699**

STEAUA (RM) [05001837] 365, **3353**

STEDMAN'S MEDICAL DICTIONARY (US) [04757691] **3643**

STEEL & MATERIALS TECHNOLOGY (GW/0941-388X) [I0941388X] 2108, **4020**

STEEL ARBITRATION DIGEST (US) [05656646] 1627, **1712**

STEEL COMPANY OF CANADA See STELCO TENDANCES **629**

STEEL CONSTRUCTION : JOURNAL OF THE AUSTRALIAN INSTITUTE OF STEEL CONSTRUCTION (AT/0049-2205) [11927088] **628**

STEEL CONSTRUCTION TODAY (UK) [17647499] **628**

STEEL DESIGN (CN/0712-9092) [08737639] **2031**

STEEL EMPLOYMENT NEWS (US/0892-1652) [15145544] **1712**

STEEL FOUNDERS' SOCIETY OF AMERICA See DISTRIBUTION OF STEEL CASTINGS SALES BY END USE OF PRODUCT **923**

STEEL GUITAR INTERNATIONAL NEWSLETTER (US) **4154**

STEEL HORIZONS (US/0039-0925) [01607975] **4020**

STEEL IN THE USSR See STEEL IN TRANSLATION **4020**

● STEEL IN TRANSLATION (US/0967-0912) [27394875] **4020**

STEEL INDIA (II/0970-1311) [14180093] **4020**

STEEL INDUSTRY MONITOR (US) [08314694] **1997**

STEEL INDUSTRY OF JAPAN, THE (JA) [06674171] 4020, **1627**

STEEL INDUSTRY REVIEW (US/0163-206X) [04307489] 4020, **1628**

STEEL INDUSTRY UPDATE (US/1063-4339) [26032535] **4020**

STEEL MARKET IN ... AND THE OUTLOOK FOR ... , THE (FR) [07383789] **4020**

STEEL MARKET IN ..., THE (US/0497-9478) [01785626] **1640**

STEEL MARKET PRICE DATA ON TELEFAX (UK) **4020**

STEEL MARKETS MONTHLY (UK/0964-7694) [I09647694] **4020**

STEEL METALS MONITOR (SA) **4020**

STEEL MILL PRODUCTS (LEXINGTON) (US/0148-2807) [03280111] 4020, **1628**

STEEL MILL PRODUCTS (WASHINGTON, D.C.) CEASED. (US/0275-6862) [03048771] **4020**

STEEL OUTLOOK (UK) **4020**

STEEL — Alphabetical Title Index

STEEL PRODUCTS MANUAL (US/0275-2239) [07095687] **4020**

STEEL PROFILE (AT/0726-0865) [I07260865] **4020**

STEEL RESEARCH (GW/0177-4832) [11859579] **4020**

STEEL RESEARCH FOR CONSTRUCTION; BULLETIN (US/0585-2382) [00991548] **628**

STEEL SHIPPING DRUMS AND PAILS (US) [02564084] 1628, **3488**

STEEL STATISTICAL YEARBOOK / INTERNATIONAL IRON AND STEEL INSTITUTE, COMMITTEE ON STATISTICS (BE/0771-2871) [12144060] **1628**

STEEL TECHNOLOGY INTERNATIONAL (UK/0953-2412) [21214794] 1628, **4020**

STEEL TIMES (UK/0039-095X) [05275010] **4020**

STEEL TIMES INTERNATIONAL (UK/0143-7798) [08819821] **4021**

STEEL TODAY & TOMORROW (SEMIANNUAL EDITION) (JA/0388-0923) [07938940] **4021**

STEEL (WASHINGTON, D.C. : 1976) (US/0730-8388) [02397689] **4021**

STEEL WIRE AND SPECIFIED WIRE PRODUCTS (CN/0380-0822) [02443639] **3488**

STEEL YACHT, THE (US/0744-8066) [08566627] **596**

STEELABOR (US/0883-3141) [06683590] 4021, **1712**

STEELHEAD HARVEST ANALYSIS (CN/0319-9436) [06557970] **2314**

STEELS ALERT (US/1048-0307) [11683714] **4021**

STEELS & MATERIAL TECHNOLOGY NOW RECYCLING PRAXIS (GW) **4021**

STEELVILLE STAR-CRAWFORD MIRROR (US) [21580185] **5704**

STEENSTRUPIA (DK/0375-2909) [01772965] **5598**

STEERING WHEEL (AUSTIN) *CEASED.* (US/0039-1298) [03931897] **5393**

STEFAN BANACH INTERNATIONAL MATHEMATICAL CENTER See BANACH CENTER PUBLICATIONS **3496**

STEIERMARKISCHE GEBIETSKRANKENKASSE FUR ARBEITER UND ANGESTELLTE See JAHRBUCH - STEIERMARKISCHE GEBIETSKRANKENKASSE FUR ARBEITER UND ANGESTELLTE **3591**

STEIERMARKISCHE GEBIETSKRANKENKASSE FUR ARBEITER UND ANGESTELLTE See JAHRESBERICHT - STEIERMARKISCHE GEBIETSKRANKENKASSE FUER ARBEITER UND ANGESTELLTE **1681**

STEIERMARKISCHE LANDESBAHNEN See GESCHAFTSBERICHT UND RECHNUNGSABSCHLUSS - STEIERMARKISCHE LANDESBAHNEN **5431**

STEINBECK QUARTERLY *CEASED.* (US/0039-100X) [01795730] 3353, **435**

STEINBRUCH UND SANDGRUBE (1952) (GW/0039-1018) [07406506] **2151**

STEINE SPRECHEN (AU) [05958971] **2836**

STEINWAY NEWS (US) [05182940] **4154**

STEIRERBLATT, DAS (AU) [20074585] **5778**

STEIRISCHE BEITRAEGE ZUR HYDROGEOLOGIE (AU/0376-4826) [01981963] **1418**

STEIRISCHE BEITRAGE ZUR ROHSTOFF- UND ENERGIEFORSCHUNG (AU) [10810976] 2206, **2151**

●STEIRISCHE BILDUNGSSTATISTIK (AU) [29514142] 1785, **1798**

STEIRISCHE SCHULSTATISTIK See STEIRISCHE BILDUNGSSTATISTIK **1798**

STEIRISCHE STATISTIKEN / AMT DER STEIERMAERKISCHEN LANDESREGIERUNG, PRAESIDIALABTEILUNG, REFERAT STATISTIK (AU/0039-1093) [02244429] **5344**

STEIRISCHES ARZTEJOURNAL : MITTEILUNGEN DER ARZTEKAMMER FUER STEIERMARK (AU) [27143434] **3643**

STEKLO I KERAMIKA (RU/0131-9582) [I01319582] **2594**

STEKLO, SITALLY I SILIKATY / MINISTERSTVO VYSSHEGO I SREDNOGO SPETSIALNOGO OBRAZOVANIIA BSSR, BELORUSSKII TEKHOLOGICHESKII INSTITUT IM. S.M. KIROVA (RU) [11248323] **5160**

STELCO INC (CN/1186-8619) [24571254] **4750**

STELCO TENDANCES (CN/0701-0176) [03406093] **629**

●STEM CELLS (DAYTON, OHIO) (US/1066-5099) [26971021] **540**

STEM-, SPRAAK- EN TAALPATHOLOGIE (NE/0924-7025) **4619**

STEM TO STERN (CLAYTON, CALIF.) *CEASED.* (US/1065-349X) [26577948] **4183**

STENDEK; SERVICIO INFORMATIVO (SP) [01787931] **37**

STENDHAL CLUB (GRENOBLE) (FR/0039-1158) [01987323] **3440**

STEP-BY-STEP ELECTRONIC DESIGN (US/1055-2774) [23131087] **1235**

STEP-BY-STEP GRAPHICS (US/0886-7682) [12747820] **382**

STEP-BY-STEP GUIDE TO LOWERING YOUR INCOME TAX 50-90%, THE (US/1055-3622) [23159931] **4750**

STEP GBRSC NEWS (JA) [25516015] **1411**

STEP UP YOUR AWARENESS (US/0145-4684) [02734352] **3251**

STEPFAMILIES (US/0195-5969) [20343171] **2286**

STEPFAMILIES & BEYOND (US) **2286**

STEPHEN BIRNBAUM TRAVEL GUIDE, A (US/0749-2561) [11105635] **5491**

●STEPHEN CRANE STUDIES (US/1061-6136) [25380597] **3440**

STEPHENS COLLEGE See ALUMNAE DIRECTORY / STEPHENS COLLEGE **1096**

●STEPHENS' OHIO PLASTICS DIRECTORY (US/1065-7142) [26684663] **4460**

STEPNYE PROSTORY (RU/0131-9140) [12069910] **138**

STEPPARENT NEWS See STEPFAMILIES & BEYOND **2286**

STEPPENWOLF (US/0081-5462) [01986487] **3472**

STEPPIN' OUT (SUDBURY) (CN/1181-6805) [23598867] **4154**

STEPPING BACK IN TIME (US/0894-8313) [16275281] **2473**

STEPPING OUT ARTS MAGAZINE (US) [18963642] **331**

STEPPING STONES (WARREN, PA.) (US) [02268143] **2762**

STEPPKE (GW/0938-0914) [I09380914] **1069**

STEPTEXT (TORONTO) (CN/1183-966X) [25423207] **5369**

STEREO (US) [02467873] **5319**

STEREO (GW/0340-0778) [01798324] 4154, **5319**

STEREO-ATLAS OF OSTRACOD SHELLS; EDITED BY P.C. SYLVESTER-BRADLEY AND DAVID J. SIVETER (UK) [02252009] **557**

STEREO DIRECTORY & BUYING GUIDE (US/0090-6786) [01785569] **5319**

STEREO FM RADIO (AT/0313-0797) [I03130797] **1139**

STEREO/HI-FI DIRECTORY See STEREO DIRECTORY & BUYING GUIDE **5319**

STEREO REVIEW (US/0039-1220) [01766502] **5319**

STEREO REVIEW'S STEREO ... BUYERS GUIDE (US/0736-6515) [08912357] **5319**

STEREO REVIEWS TAPE RECORDING BUYERS' GUIDE (US) [12538417] 2082, **5319**

STEREO TEST REPORTS (US/0194-1844) [05324573] **5319**

STEREO WORLD (US/0191-4030) [04863930] **4377**

STEREOCHEMISTRY, FUNDAMENTALS AND METHODS (GW) [04183298] **993**

STEREOCHEMISTRY OF ORGANOMETALLIC AND INORGANIC COMPOUNDS (NE/0924-3984) [14689273] **993**

STEREOFONIA (SP/0211-7045) [I02117045] **5319**

STEREOPHILE (US/0585-2544) [02255911] **5319**

STEREOPLAY (GW) [11328432] **5319**

STEREOTACTIC AND FUNCTIONAL NEUROSURGERY (SZ/1011-6125) [18665402] 3846, **3975**

STERFTETAFELS VOOR NEDERLAND AFGELEID UIT WAARNEMINGEN OVER DE PERIODE ... / CENTRAAL BUREAU VOOR DE STATISTIEK, HOOFDAFDELING BEVOLKINGSSTATISTIEKEN (NE) [10529516] **1595**

STERLING CITY NEWS-RECORD (US) [14236602] **5754**

STERN See STERN MAGAZIN **2523**

STERN MAGAZIN (GW) [06456854] **2523**

STERNE, DIE (GW/0039-1255) [05315237] **400**

STERNE UND WELTRAUM (GW/0039-1263) [01643045] **400**

STERN'S PERFORMING ARTS DIRECTORY (US) [18615924] 388, **1314**

STERN'S SOURCEFINDER (US/1052-4819) [22294377] **947**

STERNWARTE SONNEBERG See VEROFFENTLICHUNGEN DER STERNWARTE IN SONNEBERG **401**

STEROID RECEPTORS (UK/0142-8330) [I01428330] 3733, **540**

STEROIDS (US/0039-128X) [01766506] 993, **473**

STERRENGIDS (NE) [07363723] **400**

STET. TRICKS OF THE TRADE FOR WRITERS AND EDITORS (US) **4820**

STETSON LAW REVIEW (US/0739-9731) [04654025] **3059**

STEUBEN COURIER-ADVOCATE, THE (US) [10710331] **5721**

STEUBEN NEWS (US) [06437280] **4513**

STEUBENVILLE REGISTER, THE (US/0744-771X) [02268149] **5730**

STEUER UND WIRTSCHAFT (GW) [07444690] **4750**

STEUERAUFKOMMEN DER GEMEINDEN See STEUERAUFKOMMEN DER GEMEINDEN NIEDEROSTERREICHS, DAS **4750**

STEUERAUFKOMMEN DER GEMEINDEN NIEDEROSTERREICHS, DAS (AU) [02240898] **4750**

STEUERBELASTUNG IN DER SCHWEIZ (SZ) [19018907] **4751**

STEUERBERATER RECHTSHANDBUCH / DEUTSCHER STEUERBERATERVERBAND E.V (GW) [20979785] 3059, **4751**

STEUEREINNAHMEN DER GEMEINDEN IM JAHR ... / HERAUSGEBER, VERBINDUNGSSTELLE DER BUNDESLANDER BEIM AMT DER NIEDEROSTERREICHISCHEN LANDESREGIERUNG (AU) [19473775] **4751**

STEUERENTSCHEID : STE / HERAUSGEBER, PRAXIS IN DER WISSENSCHAFT, DER (SZ/0254-8992) [19103529] **1522**

STEVE FORRESTER'S NORTHWEST LETTER FROM WASHINGTON, D.C (US/0890-9776) [08675915] **4497**

STEVE WILSON REPORT, THE (US/1065-0865) [26497953] **3353**

STEVEN DWORMAN'S INFORMERCIAL MARKETING REPORT (US/1058-0344) [24202822] **937**

STEVEN SPIELBERG FILM SOCIETY NEWSLETTER, THE (US/0883-6094) [12173937] **4078**

STEVENS POINT JOURNAL (STEVENS POINT, WIS. : 1981 : DAILY) (US/0748-6332) [10979697] **5771**

STEVENSON CLASSICAL COMPACT DISC GUIDE (US/1048-7468) [20892931] **4154**

STEWARD ANTHROPOLOGICAL SOCIETY See JOURNAL OF THE STEWARD ANTHROPOLOGICAL SOCIETY **239**

STEWARDS' LEGISLATIVE HANDBOOK (CN/0380-8300) [02586363] **3154**

STEWARDSHIP REPORT, A (US/0362-6563) [02309435] **4708**

STEWARDSON CLIPPER See BEECHER CITY JOURNAL **5658**

STEWART ALSOP'S P.C. LETTER (US/8756-7822) [11653927] **1239**

STEWART'S GUIDE TO ANTIQUE & COLLECTIBLE SHOPS COVERING LOS ANGELES COUNTY (US/1047-885X) [20805350] **252**

STEWART'S GUIDE TO ANTIQUE & COLLECTIBLES SHOPS (US/1053-5918) [22583032] **252**

STEWARTVILLE STAR (US) [01639358] **5699**

STFI-MEDDELANDE. SERIE A *CEASED.* (SW/0348-2650) [09069564] **2404**

STI BULLETIN / NATIONAL AERONAUTICS AND SPACE ADMINISTRATION, SCIENTIFIC AND TECHNICAL INFORMATION BRANCH (US) [15723796] **37**

STI-RECON BULLETIN & TECHNICAL INFORMATION NEWS See STI BULLETIN / NATIONAL AERONAUTICS AND SPACE ADMINISTRATION, SCIENTIFIC AND TECHNICAL INFORMATION BRANCH **37**

STI REVIEW (FR) [15297148] 1712, **1628**

STI REVUE (INT/1010-5239) [I10105239] **5160**

STICHTING & VERENIGING (NE/0920-7783) [I09207783] **405**

Alphabetical Title Index
STOP

STICHTING FONDS VOOR DE LETTEREN (NETHERLANDS) See VERSLAG OVER HET JAAR ... / STICHTING FONDS VOOR DE LETTEREN **3450**

STICHTUNG GUA See GUA PAPERS OF GEOLOGY. SERIES 1 **1381**

STICHWORT OESTERREICH (AU) [05810101] **2710**

STICHWORT- UND TITEL-REGISTER (GW) [18724374] **4832**

STICKNEY ARGUS, THE (US) [13554588] **5744**

STICUSA JOURNAAL See JOURNAAL / UITGAVE STICHTING VOOR CULTURELE SAMENWERKING (STICUSA) **2694**

STIFTERVERBAND FUR DIE DEUTSCHE WISSENSCHAFT See BERICHT / STIFTERVERBAND FUR DIE DEUTSCHE WISSENSCHAFT **5087**

STIKHI, STIKHI (RU) [02245884] **3472**

STILL (US) [04403615] **4377**

STILL HERE : JOB/SCHOLARSHIP REFERRAL NEWSLETTER / SCHOOL OF COMMUNICATIONS, HOWARD UNIVERSITY *SUSPENDED.* (US) [08374507] **1122**

STILLWATER EVENING GAZETTE (US) [22533671] **5699**

STIMME DER ORTHODOXIE (GW/0562-0694) [01793471] **5040**

STIMME (VIENNA, AUSTRIA) (AU) [20360763] **5778**

STIMMEN DER ZEIT (FREIBURG) (GW/0039-1492) [01766529] **4999**

STIMULATION (BE) **4394**

STIMULATOR See SOSIALKONOMEN **1595**

STIMULOGRAPHY (FR/0989-2192) [20350918] **3710**

STING (CENTER SQUARE, PA.) *CEASED.* (US/8750-8974) [11890735] **3440**

STIR (II) [02441059] **4497**

STIRLING NEWS-ARGUS (CN) **5795**

STIRPES (US/0039-1522) [01589595] 2762, **2473**

STITCH 'N SEW QUILTS (US/0744-1649) [08077510] **5186**

STITCHES MAGAZINE (US/0899-5893) [18145987] **5356**

●STITCHES : THE JOURNAL OF MEDICAL HUMOUR (CN) [30471291] **3643**

STM INFORMATION BOOKLET (NE) [15024741] **4820**

STM NEWSLETTER 76 (NE) **887**

STN (NEW YORK, N.Y.) (US/1061-4524) [25321600] **4924**

●STN'S JOURNAL OF TRAUMA NURSING (US/1076-4747) [30492238] **3870**

STOCARSTVO (CI) [03826106] **138**

STOCHASTIC ANALYSIS AND APPLICATIONS (US/0736-2994) [09104615] 2031, **3536**

STOCHASTIC HYDROLOGY AND HYDRAULICS (GW/0931-1955) [15116316] **1418**

STOCHASTIC PROCESSES AND THEIR APPLICATIONS (NE/0304-4149) [01789401] **3536**

STOCHASTICA *CEASED.* (SP/0210-7821) [03054057] **3536**

STOCHASTICS AND STOCHASTICS REPORT (US/1045-1129) [19359428] 1204, **3536**

STOCK & LAND (AT/0039-1565) **138**

STOCK & WATSON INDICATOR REPORTS (US) **1585**

STOCK CAR CLASSIFICATION GUIDE (US/0731-2008) [08125386] 4924, **5426**

STOCK CAR RACING (US/0734-7340) [04350002] **4924**

STOCK EXCHANGE INVESTMENT LIST (UK) **916**

STOCK EXCHANGE (LONDON, ENGLAND) See MEMBERS AND FIRMS / THE STOCK EXCHANGE **906**

●STOCK EXCHANGE OFFICIAL YEARBOOK (UK) [25403590] **916**

STOCK EXCHANGE WEEKLY OFFICIAL INTELLIGENCE See WEEKLY OFFICIAL INTELLIGENCE **919**

STOCK EXCHANGE WEEKLY OFFICIAL INTELLIGENCE, THE (UK) [07476026] **916**

STOCK-FINDER, THE (US) [10165817] **5522**

STOCK GUIDE (US/0737-4135) [03633965] **916**

STOCK GUIDE (WILLIAMSTOWN) (CN/0844-9082) [20373067] **813**

STOCK JOURNAL (ADELAIDE, S. AUST.) (AT) [13853941] **222**

STOCK MARKET ENCYCLOPEDIA (1985) (US/0882-5467) [11884490] **916**

STOCK MARKET MAGAZINE, THE *SUSPENDED.* (US/0039-1638) [02251990] **916**

STOCK PHOTO DESKBOOK, THE (US/0897-6287) [17574858] **4377**

STOCK PICTURE, THE (US/0196-1705) [02003417] **916**

STOCK QUOTATIONS ON THE NEW YORK STOCK EXCHANGE (US/0562-083X) [08099393] **916**

STOCK SHOW, THE (US/0273-5776) [07082826] **222**

STOCK SURVEY See MOODY'S STOCK SURVEY **908**

STOCK-TAKING ON THE EUROPEAN CONVENTION ON HUMAN RIGHTS (FR/0252-0613) [16835280] **4513**

STOCK TRADER'S ALMANAC, THE (US) [03404291] **916**

STOCK VALUES AND DIVIDENDS FOR TAX PURPOSES (US/0081-5624) [01786072] **916**

STOCK WORKBOOK (US) **713**

STOCKGROWER DIGEST, THE (CN/0820-4683) [16667941] **222**

STOCKHOLDERS & CREDITORS NEWS SERVICE CONCERNING ASBESTOS BANKRUPTCIES (US/1078-313X) [29294969] **3103**

STOCKHOLDERS & CREDITORS NEWS SERVICE CONCERNING EASTERN AIRLINES, INC. / CONTINENTAL AIRLINES, INC *CEASED.* (US/1056-4292) [23738121] **37**

STOCKHOLDERS & CREDITORS NEWS SERVICE CONCERNING HILLSBOROUGH HOLDINGS CORPORATION See STOCKHOLDERS & CREDITORS NEWS SERVICE CONCERNING ASBESTOS BANKRUPTCIES **3103**

STOCKHOLDERS & CREDITORS NEWS SERVICE CONCERNING JOHNS-MANVILLE CORPORATION, ET AL See STOCKHOLDERS & CREDITORS NEWS SERVICE CONCERNING ASBESTOS BANKRUPTCIES **3103**

STOCKHOLDERS & CREDITORS NEWS SERVICE CONCERNING LTV CORPORATION, ET AL (US/1042-5772) [15799427] **3103**

STOCKHOLM CONTRIBUTIONS IN GEOLOGY (SW/0585-3532) [01643250] **1398**

STOCKHOLM ECONOMIC STUDIES (SW) [06109594] **1522**

STOCKHOLM FASTIGHETS KALENDER (SW) [05167365] **4847**

STOCKHOLM. STATENS INSTITUT FOR BYGGNADSFORSKNING See LITTERATUR/PUBLICATIONS **633**

STOCKHOLM. STATENS INSTITUT FOR BYGGNADSFORSKNING (SWEDEN) See VERKSAMHETEN **631**

STOCKHOLM STUDIES IN BALTIC LANGUAGES (SW/0281-5478) [I02815478] **3324**

STOCKHOLM STUDIES IN ENGLISH (SW/0346-6272) [01639479] **3324**

STOCKHOLM STUDIES IN HISTORY OF ART (SW/0491-0850) [01766567] **365**

STOCKHOLM STUDIES IN HISTORY OF LITERATURE (SW/0491-0869) [01766568] **3440**

STOCKHOLM STUDIES IN RUSSIAN LITERATURE (SW/0346-8496) [03058276] **3440**

STOCKHOLMER GERMANISTISCHE FORSCHUNGEN (SW/0491-0893) [01766571] **2710**

STOCKHOLMS HANDELSKAMMARE See MATRIKEL / STOCKHOLMS HANDELSKAMMARE **845**

STOCKHOLMS STADSBIBLIOTEK See WORK OF THE STOCKHOLM PUBLIC LIBRARY IN ..., THE **3256**

STOCKLISTS AND NEWS SERVICE FOR CARPET AND FLOORCOVERING BUYERS, THE (CN/1180-3908) [23598282] **5356**

STOCKMAN GRASS FARMER, THE (US/0899-1057) [15532653] **222**

STOCKS & BONDS (US) [04675106] **916**

STOCKS & BONDS ON THE NEW YORK STOCK EXCHANGE (US/0276-7740) [05715606] **916**

STOCKS, BONDS, BILLS, AND INFLATION YEARBOOK (US/1047-2436) [10609093] **916**

STOCKS IN THE STANDARD & POOR'S 500 (US/0163-6235) [04399557] **916**

STOCKS OF DAIRY AND FROZEN POULTRY PRODUCTS (CN) [02442606] 199, **222**

STOCKS OF FOOD COMMODITIES IN COLD STORAGE AND OTHER WAREHOUSES (CN/0527-6268) [02442609] 222, **199**

STOCKS OF FROZEN MEAT PRODUCTS *CEASED.* (CN/0703-7333) [02940614] **2358**

STOCKS OF FRUIT AND VEGETABLES *CEASED.* (CN/0705-4289) [02255617] **2358**

STOCKS OF GRAIN AT SELECTED TERMINAL & ELEVATOR SITES. WEEKLY ED (US/0889-0471) [08875409] **203**

STOCKS OF GRAINS, OILSEEDS, AND HAY, FINAL ESTIMATES BY STATES / UNITED STATES DEPARTMENT OF AGRICULTURE, STATISTICAL REPORTING SERVICE, CROP REPORTING BOARD (US) [11820660] **138**

STOCKS OF WOOL AND RELATED FIBERS (US/0149-0583) [03049677] **5356**

STOCKTON AREA LABOR MARKET BULLETIN (US) [18113240] **1712**

STOCKTON DAILY EVENING RECORD (US) [08786607] **5640**

STOCKTON RECORD (STOCKTON, CALIF.) (US) [15874901] **5640**

STOCKTON STATE COLLEGE See ALUMNI DIRECTORY / STOCKTON STATE COLLEGE **1099**

STOF & SAKS (DK) [05591978] **5186**

STOFF MISBRUK : INFORMASJON FRA SENTRALRADET FOR NARKOTIKAPROBLEMER (NO) [08240678] **1349**

STOFFWECHSELKRANKHEITEN (GW/0931-8283) [14521130] **3733**

STOKVIS STUDIES IN HISTORICAL CHRONOLOGY & THOUGHT (US/0270-5338) [06454598] **2630**

STOLICA (PL) [05022937] **2710**

STOMA (PO/0870-4287) [19584912] **1336**

STOMATOLOGIA MEDITERRANEA : SM (IT) [12608703] **1336**

STOMATOLOGIE (AU/0946-3151) **1336**

STOMATOLOGIJA (RU/0039-1735) [01639158] **1336**

STOMATOLOGIJA (SOFIJA) (BU/0491-0982) [07611568] **1336**

STOMATOLOSKI GLASNIK SRBIJE (YU/0039-1743) [10983619] **1336**

STONE AGE (US/0163-5891) [04444579] **713**

STONE COUNTRY *CEASED.* (US/0146-1397) [02859027] **3472**

STONE COUNTY CITIZEN (US) [24904493] **5632**

STONE COUNTY ENTERPRISE (US) [16577516] **5702**

STONE COUNTY LEADER (1956) (US/1066-3983) [19101101] **5632**

STONE IN AMERICA (US/0160-7243) [03735817] **365**

STONE INDUSTRIES (UK/0039-1778) [08177293] 629, **1445**

STONE JUSTICE MANUAL; BEING THE YEARLY JUSTICES' PRACTICE FOR 18 See STONE'S JUSTICES' MANUAL **3059**

STONE LION REVIEW (US/0747-6744) [04543904] **3440**

STONE MOUNTAIN DEKALB NEIGHBOR (US) [23849972] **5655**

STONE MOUNTAIN NEIGHBOR See STONE MOUNTAIN DEKALB NEIGHBOR **5655**

STONE REVIEW (US/8750-9210) [11936094] **2151**

STONE SOUP (SANTA CRUZ, CALIF.) (US/0094-579X) [01794077] **1069**

STONE, THE (US) [03464458] **3472**

STONE WORLD (US/1052-6994) [19058030] **2151**

STONEHAM CATALOGUE OF BRITISH STAMPS, THE (UK/0142-615X) [10944254] **2787**

STONEHAM INDEPENDENT, THE (US) [23075225] **5690**

STONEHENGE VIEWPOINT (US/0140-654X) [09035515] 400, 1398, **283**

STONES & BONES NEWSLETTER (US/0585-3699) [02003428] 283, **246**

STONE'S JUSTICES' MANUAL (UK) [02845363] **3059**

STONEY MONDAY (CN/0706-9006) [04518993] **3440**

STONY HILLS *SUSPENDED.* (US/0146-2067) [03715022] **3354**

STOOMKETEK- EN KRACHTWERKTUIGENINDUSTRIE / CENTRAAL BUREAU VOOR DE STATISTITEK, HOOFDAFDELING STATISTIEKEN VAN INDUSTRIE EN BOUWNIFVERHEID (NE/0168-3578) [10291335] **2129**

STOP (BRATISLAVA) (XO/0139-6501) [02243401] **5426**

STOP MILANO (IT/1121-1288) [11211288] **2523**

STOP — Alphabetical Title Index

STOP (MONTREAL) (CN/0831-0319) [14956195] **3440**

STOPPING AND RANGES OF IONS IN MATTER, THE (US/0891-5490) [03988152] **4422**

STOPWATCH (CN/0821-2503) [09654175] **1858**

STORAGE, HANDLING, DISTRIBUTION (UK) [02450859] **713**

STORAGE IN RESERVOIRS, DAILY DISCHARGE RECORDS OF MISCELLANEOUS STREAMS AND CANAL DIVERSIONS / STATE OF NEBRASKA, DEPARTMENT OF WATER RESOURCES (US) [06049817] **5539**

STORE CHECK REPORT (US) 958, **1291**

STORES (US/0039-1867) [01714651] **958**

STORES OF THE YEAR (US/0192-8732) [05089124] **2903**

STORIA ARCHITETTURA (IT/0390-4253) [04625675] **309**

STORIA CONTEMPORANEA (IT/0039-1875) [01984383] **2630**

STORIA CONTEMPORANEA IN FRIULI / ISTITUTO FRIULANO PER LA STORIA DEL MOVIMENTO DI LIBERAZIONE (IT) [03050353] **2630**

STORIA DEL PENSIERO ECONOMICO. BOLLETTINO DI INFORMAZIONE (IT) **1585**

STORIA DELLA CITTA *CEASED.* (IT/0391-3929) [03701592] **2836**

STORIA DELLA STORIOGRAFIA (IT) [09541298] **2630**

STORIA DELLARTE (IT/0392-4513) [01185167] **365**

STORIA DELLE RELAZIONI INTERNATIONALI (IT/1120-0677) [13297636] **4535**

STORIA E DOSSIER (IT/0394-0209) [16800148] **2630**

STORIA E MEDICINA POPOLARE (IT/0393-4292) [13130644] **3643**

STORIA E POLITICA (IT/0039-1905) [01996459] **2630**

STORIA IN LOMBARDIA (IT) [17558426] **2710**

STORIA (LONDON, ENGLAND) (UK) [19836847] **3440**

STORIA URBANA (IT) [04716674] **2836**

STORIES (BOSTON, MASS.) (US/0742-2113) [09841587] **3440**

STORIES (LOS ANGELES, CALIF.) (US/0895-7592) [16786898] **3440**

STORIES OF RESOURCE-FULL KANSAS (US/0562-1372) [02251454] **1398**

● STORIES THAT RHYME EVERY TIME KIDS PAGES (US/1063-1380) [25898605] 3440, **1069**

STORM DATA (US/0039-1972) [02468803] **1435**

STORM DATA FOR THE UNITED STATES (US/0748-268X) [10678061] **1435**

STORRS LECTURES ON JURISPRUDENCE (US) [01639079] **3059**

STORTINGET I NAVN OG TALL (NO) [15514175] **4689**

STORY ART; A MAGAZINE FOR STORYTELLERS (US/0039-1999) [06601037] **3440**

STORY CITY HERALD (STORY CITY, IOWA : 1892) (US) [11794673] **5673**

STORY PAPERS COLLECTORS DIGEST (UK) **2778**

STORY (SAINT PAUL, MINN.) (US/0883-7678) [11773276] **4999**

STORY SO FAR, THE (CN/0316-0645) [02246588] **3440**

STORY TIME STORIES THAT RHYME NEWSLETTER (US/1045-5515) [22457049] **1069**

STORY (VIENNA, AUSTRIA) (US/1045-0831) [01766582] **3440**

STORYBOARD (ANAHEIM HILLS, CALIF.) (US/1040-3167) [18374669] **388**

STORYBOARD (MANGILAO, GUAM) (GU/1059-7492) [24727081] **3440**

STORYQUARTERLY (NORTHBROOK, ILL.) (US/1041-0708) [02381158] **3440**

STORYTELLERS OF SAN DIEGO NEWSLETTER (US/0889-8812) [14137517] **3440**

STORYTELLING MAGAZINE (US/1048-1354) [20655043] **2324**

STORYVILLE (CHIGWELL) (UK/0039-2030) [03335747] **4154**

● STORYWORKS (NEW YORK, N.Y.) (US/1068-0292) [27407565] **1805**

STOUFFVILLE SUN (CN/0821-0225) [09929493] **5795**

STOUGHTON COURIER HUB (STOUGHTON, WIS. : 1981) (US/1049-0655) [11868122] **5771**

STOUT CENTRE REVIEW : JOURNAL OF THE STOUT RESEARCH CENTRE FOR THE STUDY OF NEW ZEALAND HISTORY AND CULTURE (NZ/1170-4616) [24637097] **2671**

STOUTONIA, THE (US) [04955223] **1095**

STOVE, FURNACE & ALLIED APPLIANCE WORKERS' JOURNAL (US) [05866892] **2812**

STOW SENTRY (US/0192-9410) [05134030] **5730**

STP NEWSLETTER / INTERNATIONAL COUNCIL OF SCIENTIFIC UNIONS, SCIENTIFIC COMMITTEE ON SOLAR-TERRESTRIAL PHYSICS (FR) [08362452] **4422**

STRAD, THE (UK/0039-2049) [01766587] **4154**

STRAFFORD FESTIVAL (CN/0085-6770) [02442907] **388**

STRAFRECHTLICHE ABHANDLUNGEN, NEUE FOLGE (GW) [01766589] **3060**

STRAFVERTEIDIGER (GW/0720-1605) [08863167] **3109**

STRAHLENSCHUTZ IN FORSCHUNG UND PRAXIS (GW/0081-5888) [06479006] **3947**

STRAHLENTHERAPIE UND ONKOLOGIE (GW/0179-7158) [13320934] **3824**

STRAHOVSKA KNIHOVNA (XR/0081-5896) [01605077] **3251**

STRAIGHT FACTS ON PHARMACEUTICAL PRICES, MANUFACTURING AND RESEARCH, THE (UK/1187-3787) [25314168] **4330**

STRAIGHT LINES (UK) [05920601] **3440**

● STRAIGHT TALK (PLEASANTVILLE, N.Y.) (US/1062-0095) [25503582] **1069**

STRAIGHTTALK -- FROM THE DESK OF THE CHIEF ECONOMIST .... (US/1051-9521) [22165143] **1522**

STRAIN (UK/0039-2103) [03793423] **2129**

STRAITS TIMES, THE (SI) [08572659] **5810**

STRANA I MIR *CEASED.* (GW) [11092622] **2523**

STRAND (CN/0710-4537) [08781414] **5795**

STRANGE MAGAZINE (US/0894-8968) [16307624] **2493**

STRANI JEZICI (CI/0351-0840) [01786665] **3440**

STRANI PRAVNI ZIVOT / INSTITUT ZA UPOREDNO PRAVO (YU/0039-2138) [10241042] **3060**

STRANY CHLENY SODRUZHESTVA NEZAVISIMYHK GOSUDARSTV (RU) **1540**

STRASSE UND AUTOBAHN (GW/0039-2162) [07286414] **2031**

STRASSE UND VERKEHR (SZ) [07267812] **5444**

STRASSEN, BRUCKEN UND PARKEINRICHTUNGEN (GW) [03675025] **4689**

STRASSEN- UND TIEFBAU (GW/0039-2197) [04270078] **2031**

STRASSEN- VERKEHRSTECHNIK (GW/0039-2219) [06525734] **5444**

STRASSENGUTERVERKEHR, DER (AU) [08161345] **5426**

STRASSENVERKEHRSSICHERHEIT IM JAHRE ... / HERAUSGEGEBEN VOM OSTERREICHISCHEN STATISTISCHEN ZENTRALAMT (AU) [07765500] **5444**

STRASSENVERKEHRSUNFAELLE (GW) [02776327] **5445**

STRASSENVERKEHRSUNFALLE IN DER SCHWEIZ (SZ) [10478386] **5445**

STRASSENVERKEHRSZAHLUNGEN (GW/0173-2501) [02642584] **5426**

STRAT FAN (US/1061-1037) [25180962] **4866**

STRATEGIA (IT) **767**

STRATEGIC ANALYSIS (II/0970-0161) [03714185] **4058**

● STRATEGIC APPROACHES OF THE NATIONAL ARCHIVES OF CANADA (CN/0844-7594) [20019473] **2484**

STRATEGIC APPROACHES OF THE PUBLIC ARCHIVES OF CANADA *See* STRATEGIC APPROACHES OF THE NATIONAL ARCHIVES OF CANADA **2484**

STRATEGIC DEFENSE *CEASED.* (US/0890-7331) [14369079] **4058**

STRATEGIC DEVELOPMENTS IN BIOTECHNOLOGY / NORTH CAROLINA BIOTECHNOLOGY CENTER (US/1055-7318) [23284257] **3696**

STRATEGIC DIGEST (II/0970-017X) [01784187] **4058**

● STRATEGIC DIRECTION (UK/0258-0543) [28712575] **713**

STRATEGIC HEALTH CARE MARKETING (US/0749-5153) [11136162] 937, **3793**

STRATEGIC INFORMATION ON US AIR TRAVEL (US) **5491**

STRATEGIC INSIGHTS INTO QUALITY (UK/0968-0829) **713**

STRATEGIC ISSUES FORUM REPORT (AT) **1585**

STRATEGIC MANAGEMENT JOURNAL (UK/0143-2095) [05468579] **887**

STRATEGIC MANAGEMENT, POLICY AND PLANNING (US) **887**

STRATEGIC PERSPECTIVES (PK) [25109850] **4058**

● STRATEGIC PLAN - CANADA MORTGAGE AND HOUSING CORPORATION (CN/1184-616X) [24280164] **4689**

STRATEGIC PLANNING AND ENERGY MANAGEMENT (US/8750-3204) [11251972] **1958**

STRATEGIC PLANNING FOR ENERGY AND THE ENVIRONMENT (US/1048-5236) [20967531] **1958**

STRATEGIC PLANNING MANAGEMENT (US/0748-4895) [10130293] **887**

STRATEGIC REVIEW (US/0091-6846) [01787813] **4058**

STRATEGIC REVIEW FOR SOUTHERN AFRICA (SA) [19036350] **5223**

STRATEGIC SURVEY (UK/0459-7230) [02003616] 4535, **4058**

● STRATEGIC SYSTEMS (US/1060-3751) [24947728] **1249**

STRATEGIC VAS - VANS REPORT *See* TELECOMMUNICATIONS STRATEGIES REPORT **1166**

STRATEGIE + (CN/0712-9130) [09414354] **713**

STRATEGIE ET DEFENSE (FR) [05454087] **4058**

STRATEGIE (TORONTO) (CN/0822-9694) [11147668] **916**

STRATEGIES (FR) **887**

STRATEGIES ALIMENTAIRES (FR) **138**

● STRATEGIES & SOLUTIONS (US/1067-9537) [27424470] 4619, **4804**

STRATEGIES (BIRMINGHAM) (UK/0959-8936) [I09598936] **1905**

STRATEGIES DU MANAGEMENT PARIS (FR/1148-750X) [I1148750X] **887**

STRATEGIES FOR HEALTHCARE EXCELLENCE (US/1058-7829) [24386676] **3793**

STRATEGIES FOR INSURANCE COVERAGES (US) **713**

STRATEGIES GOURMANDE *See* FILIERE GOURMANDE **2335**

STRATEGIES GOURMANDES PARIS (FR/0987-7541) [I09877541] **2358**

STRATEGIES (LOS ANGELES, CALIF.) *SUSPENDED.* (US/1040-2136) [18353123] **4497**

STRATEGIES PARIS (FR/0180-6424) [I01806424] **767**

STRATEGIES (RESTON, VA.) (US/0892-4562) [15194576] **1858**

STRATEGIQUE *CEASED.* (FR/0224-0424) [06004798] **4058**

STRATEGY & DEFENCE (IE/0307-4420) [11308804] **4058**

STRATEGY & TACTICS (CAMBRIA, CALIF.) (US/1040-886X) [18569083] **4058**

STRATEGY & TACTICS MAGAZINE (SPECIAL ED.) (US/0736-654X) [09181919] **4058**

STRATEGY (LIBRARIES & LEARNING, INC.) (CN/0227-4760) [10195125] **3251**

STRATEGY PAPERS (NATIONAL STRATEGY INFORMATION CENTER) (US/0580-4105) [01766606] **4535**

STRATEGY REPORT - MANITOBA. WASTE REDUCTION AND PREVENTION BRANCH (CN/1186-8392) [24571446] **2244**

STRATEGY (TORONTO) (CN/0229-0510) [08770534] **916**

STRATEGY (TORONTO. 1991) (CN/1187-4309) [25652220] **937**

STRATFORD BARD, THE (US) [26890069] **5646**

STRATFORD FESTIVAL (ONT.) *See* STRATFORD FESTIVAL STORY, THE **5369**

STRATFORD FESTIVAL (ONT.) *See* STRAFFORD FESTIVAL **388**

STRATFORD FESTIVAL STORY, THE (CN/0085-6789) [02441925] **5369**

STRATFORD FOR STUDENTS (CN/0822-9066) [10935295] **5369**

STRATFORD JOURNAL (STRATFORD, WIS.) (US) [15494184] **5771**

STRATFORD STAR, THE (US) [14642327] **5754**

STRATHCLAIR & DISTRICT REVIEW (CN/0229-6519) [08027993] **5795**

Alphabetical Title Index **STUDENT**

STRATIGRAPHIE GEOLOGIE REGIONALE GEOLOGIE GENERALE. F44 (FR) **2576**

●STRATIGRAPHY AND GEOLOGICAL CORRELATION (RU) [29573835] **1398**

STRATIGRAPHY AND PALEONTOLOGY OF CHINA / SPONSORED BY COMMISSION ON STRATIGRAPHY AND PALEONTOLOGY, GEOLOGICAL SOCIETY OF CHINA (CC) [26022506] **1398**

STRATTON MAGAZINE (US/1064-1629) [07299132] **4924**

STRAWBERRY POINT PRESS-JOURNAL (US) [15431560] **5673**

STREAM OF HISTORY, THE (US/0562-1690) [02766226] **2762**

STREAMLAND (NZ/0111-977X) [09265890] 5540, **188**

STREAMLINE UPDATE / DEPARTMENT OF RESOURCES AND ENERGY (AT/0812-7735) [11083580] **5540**

STREAMLINED SEMINAR (US/0735-0023) [08842978] **1872**

●STREET ADDRESS DIRECTORY, OTTAWA-HULL (ENGLISH EDITION 1992) (CN/1188-2794) [26497907] **425**

●STREET ADDRESS DIRECTORY, OTTAWA-HULL (FRENCH EDITION 1992) (CN/1188-2794) [26497908] **425**

STREET & DIRT (CN/0820-7224) [09635038] **4083**

STREET & SMITH'S PRO BASKETBALL (US) [18842760] **4924**

STREET BEAT (PITTSBURGH, PA.) (US/1069-5478) [27665176] 5312, **3440**

STREET FINANCE REPORT FOR IOWA CITIES (US) [06136017] **5445**

STREET MACHINE (CANOGA PARK, LOS ANGELES, CALIF.) (US/0164-3975) [18666398] **4866**

STREET MACHINE (LONDON, ENGLAND) (UK/0143-5949) [16016664] **5426**

STREET MACHINE SYDNEY (AT/0810-0187) [I08100187] **5393**

STREET MACHINES & BRACKET RACING (US/0192-1967) [04960010] 4924, **5426**

STREET MAGAZINE **CEASED.** (US/0190-1737) [03466591] **2547**

STREET NEWS (US) **2547**

STREET PHARMACOLOGIST NEWSLETTER (US) [17946765] **4330**

STREET ROD ACTION (US/1046-5367) [20324561] **5426**

●STREET ROD PICKUPS (US/1067-5256) [27298699] **5426**

STREET RODDER (US/0277-5735) [07605479] **4924**

STREET RODDING ILLUSTRATED **CEASED.** (US/8750-3298) [11256916] 2778, **5426**

STREET SONGS (US/1055-5854) [22037577] **3440**

STREET TALK (US) [05393919] **2836**

STREETBIKE (AT/1034-9294) [I10349294] **4083**

STREETSOUND (TORONTO) (CN/0841-2650) [20372111] **4155**

STREETWISE : THE MAGAZINE OF URBAN STUDIES (UK/0957-6517) [25226791] **2836**

STREIT (GW/0175-4467) [I01754467] **3060**

STREITBARBER MATERIALISMUS (GW) [18822262] **4497**

STREITKRAFTEVERGLEICH NATO-WARSCHAUER PAKT (GW) [12075695] **4535**

STRELEC (JERSEY CITY, N.J.) (US/0747-7287) [10810241] **3440**

STREM CHEMIKER, THE (US/0160-8614) [03795629] **993**

STRENGTH (CN/0383-6940) [03258553] **5566**

●STRENGTH AND CONDITIONING (US/1073-6840) [29509002] **1858**

STRENGTH AND HEALTH **CEASED.** (US/0039-2308) [02251991] 4199, **2601**

STRENGTH OF MATERIALS (US/0039-2316) [01766613] **2129**

STRESS AND COPING (US/0883-0908) [12055480] **4619**

STRESS AND EMOTION (US/1053-2161) [22481265] **4619**

STRESS IN MODERN SOCIETY (US/0884-870X) [12487069] **4619**

STRESS IN THE AMERICAN WORKPLACE (US) **947**

STRESS MANAGEMENT ADVISOR **CEASED.** (US/1056-5868) [23742930] **4619**

STRESS MEDICINE (UK/0748-8386) [11013263] **3643**

STREUDATEN DER SCHWEIZER PRESSE : ZEITUNGEN, ANZEIGER UND AMTSBLATTER (SZ) [03295763] **2924**

STRIAE (SW/0345-0074) [04030990] **1399**

STRICKLAND SCENE (US/0733-8392) [08131759] **2474**

STRICTLY U.S (US/0095-5418) [01445569] **2787**

STRIKEFORCE MORITURI **CEASED.** (US/0897-5760) [14641826] **4866**

STRIKES, STOPPAGES, AND BOYCOTTS (US/0272-6548) [03998257] **3154**

STRINDBERGIANA (SW/0282-8006) [13771678] **3440**

STRINGS (SAN ANSELMO, CALIF.) (US/0888-3106) [13532959] **4155**

STRINGYBARK & GREENHIDE (AT/0157-7832) [10113367] **4155**

STRIPED BASS MAGAZINE (US/0279-0610) [07491490] **2314**

STRIPER (US/0199-5634) [05987322] **2314**

STRIVE (OTTAWA) (CN/1185-3077) [24368134] **813**

STROEZ I FUNKCII NA MOZKA (BU/0204-4560) [10278244] **3846**

STROITEL (RU/0039-2375) [02049546] **629**

STROITELI MATERIALI I SILIKATNA PROMISLENOST (BU/0562-1836) [09997667] **629**

STROITELNYE MATERIALY (RU/0585-430X) [10215979] **629**

STROITELNYE MATERIALY I KONSTRUKTSII (RU/0136-7773) [03575123] **629**

STROITELSTVO (BU/0562-1852) [105621852] **629**

STROITELSTVO GELMINTOLOGICHESKOI NAUKI I PRAKTIKI V SSSR (RU) [05284057] **5598**

STROITELSTVO I ARKHITEKTURA LENINGRADA (RU/0039-2413) [02049409] **309**

STROITELSTVO I ARKHITEKTURA MOSKVY (RU/0039-2421) [01766615] **629**

STROITELSTVO TRUBOPROVODOV (RU/0039-2448) [05292297] **4279**

STROJARSTVO (CI/0562-1887) [10984017] **2244**

STROJIMPORT (XR) [13980132] 3186, **5356**

STROJIRENSKA VYROBA (XR) **2129**

STROJIRENSTVI (XR/0039-2464) [09490010] **2129**

STROJNICKY CASOPIS (XO/0039-2472) **1997**

STROJNISKI VESTNIK (XV/0039-2480) [10269822] **5160**

STROKE (1970) (US/0039-2499) [01714534] 3846, **3710**

●STROKE & DAGGER (US/1065-397X) [26602715] **388**

STROKE. CLINICAL UPDATES (US/1049-7463) [21288762] **3643**

STROKE CONNECTION (US/1047-014X) [20581150] **5312**

STROKING TIMES, THE (US/8756-0364) [11454720] **4382**

STROLLING ASTRONOMER, THE (US/0039-2502) [01766616] **400**

STROM + SEE (SZ/0039-2510) **5393**

STROMATA (AG/0049-2353) [04530692] **4999**

STROMUNGSMECHANIK UND STROMUNGSMASCHINEN (GW/0585-427X) [11095017] **2108**

STRONG-MOTION ACCELERATION RECORDS FROM PUBLIC WORKS IN JAPAN (JA) **1411**

STRONG-MOTION EARTHQUAKE RECORDS IN JAPAN (JA) **1411**

STRONGEST FUNDS, THE **See** MUTUAL FUND TRENDS **909**

STROPHES / NATIONAL FEDERATION OF STATE POETRY SOCIETIES, INC (US) [10118487] **3440**

STROUD'S JUDICIAL DICTIONARY OF WORDS & PHRASES (UK) **3060**

STRUCNI ISPITI RADNIKA (YU) [01789037] **1916**

STRUCTURAL CHANGE AND ECONOMIC DYNAMICS (UK/0954-349X) [23674765] **1522**

STRUCTURAL CHEMISTRY (US/1040-0400) [18299153] **993**

STRUCTURAL ENGINEER (LONDON, ENGLAND : 1988) (UK) [17408109] **2031**

STRUCTURAL ENGINEERING AND MECHANICS (KO/1225-4568) **1997**

STRUCTURAL ENGINEERING/EARTHQUAKE ENGINEERING (JA/0289-8063) [12729413] **2031**

STRUCTURAL ENGINEERING INTERNATIONAL : JOURNAL OF THE INTERNATIONAL ASSOCIATION FOR BRIDGE AND STRUCTURAL ENGINEERING (IABSE) (SZ/1016-8664) [23381143] 2031, **5393**

STRUCTURAL ENGINEERING REPORT (CN/0319-0110) [02442149] **2031**

STRUCTURAL ENGINEERING REVIEW (UK/0952-5807) [18680558] **2031**

●STRUCTURAL EQUATION MODELING (US/1070-5511) [28407358] **3536**

STRUCTURAL FOAM PLASTICS (US/8755-7371) [10434328] **4460**

STRUCTURAL OPTIMIZATION (GW/0934-4373) [21148715] **2129**

STRUCTURAL RESEARCH SERIES; REPORT (CN/0318-3378) [02441757] **2032**

STRUCTURAL SAFETY (NE/0167-4730) [09026645] 2032, **629**

STRUCTURAL SURVEY (US) [18923061] **629**

●STRUCTURE (UK/0969-2126) [28867361] **540**

STRUCTURE AND ACTIVITY OF INDUSTRY. DATA BY REGIONS (LU) [19959531] **1628**

STRUCTURE AND BONDING (BERLIN) (GW/0081-5993) [01766618] **1038**

STRUCTURE DES EXPLOITATIONS AGRICOLES TRADITIONNELLES DE LA REPUBLIQUE POPULAIRE DU BENIN (DM) [05055832] **138**

STRUCTURE DES LIQUIDES ET DES SOLIDES CRISTALLOGRAPHIE, E13 (FR) **1033**

STRUCTURE REPORTS (NE) [01766619] **1033**

STRUCTURED PROGRAMMING (US/0935-1183) [19453350] **1204**

STRUCTURES AND ENVIRONMENT HANDBOOK (US/0149-1245) [02256556] 138, **629**

STRUCTURES & TENDANCES DE LA DISTRIBUTION FRANCAISE, TABLEAU DE BORD / MINISTERE DU COMMERCE ET DE L'ARTISANAT, DIRECTION DU COMMERCE INTERIEUR, UNIVERSITE PARIS 9 DAUPHINE, UNITE D'ENSEIGNEMENT ET DE RECHERCHE SCIENCES DES ORGANISATIONS (FR) [09930370] **852**

STRUCTURES COST MANUAL; SQUARE FOOT COSTS FOR RESIDENTIAL, COMMERCIAL, INDUSTRIAL, AGRICULTURAL AND MILITARY BUILDINGS (US/0162-3508) [03860724] **629**

STRUCTURING COMMERCIAL REAL ESTATE WORKOUTS : ALTERNATIVES TO FORECLOSURE (US) **4847**

STRUCTURIST (CN/0081-6027) [02247321] **365**

STRUGGLE : MATHEMATICS FOR LOW ATTAINERS (UK) 3536, **1885**

STRUKTUR BIAYA BUS DAN TRUK UMUM (IO/0126-494X) [10945508] **5426**

STRUKTURNAIA I PRIKLADNAIA LINGVISTIKA (RU) [06344788] **3324**

STRUKTURTALL FOR KOMMUNENES KONOMI (NO) [03228220] 4751, **4701**

STRUMENTI CRITICI (IT/0039-2618) [01766622] **3440**

STRUMENTI DI CONTROLLO DIREZIONALE (IT) **887**

STRUMENTI MUSICALI (IT/0392-890X) [I0392890X] **4155**

STRUTTURE AMBIENTALI (IT) [01987354] **309**

●STS MISSION PROFILES : COMPLETE SPACE SHUTTLE MISSION COVERAGE **SUSPENDED.** (US/1066-1263) [26891525] **37**

STSENICHESKAIA TEKHNIKA I TEKHNOLOGIIA (RU) [05302083] **388**

STUART HERALD, THE (US) [16838700] **5673**

STUART NEWS, THE (US) [13020754] **5651**

STUBS (US/0081-6051) [01987383] **5369**

●STUCK, PUTZ, TROCKENBAU (GW/0941-7583) [I09417583] **3488**

STUDEBAKER FAMILY, THE (US) [01766625] **2474**

STUDENT ADVOCATE (OTTAWA) (CN/0703-2072) [03681034] **1848**

●STUDENT ADVOCATE (OTTAWA. 1992) (CN/1188-3960) [25882957] **1848**

●STUDENT ADVOCATE (OTTAWA. 1992) (CN/1188-3960) [25882958] **1848**

STUDENT AID NEWS (US/0194-2212) [05014059] **1785**

STUDENT ASSISTANCE JOURNAL (US/1042-6388) [19097417] 1786, **1349**

STUDENT CONTRIBUTION SERIES (US) [06246908] **3251**

STUDENT
Alphabetical Title Index

STUDENT COURSE EVALUATIONS, CORE CLERKSHIPS / HARVARD MEDICAL SCHOOL, COMMITTEE ON EDUCATIONAL EVALUATION (US) [23906027] **3643**

STUDENT DISCUSSION PAPER (CN/0383-9990) [03400138] **2221**

STUDENT DOCTOR (US/0274-6018) [06433774] **3643**

STUDENT DRUG USE IN AMERICA (US) [09036209] **1349**

STUDENT ENROLLMENT (US) [01785393] **1848**

STUDENT ENROLLMENT IN THE PUBLIC COMMUNITY COLLEGES OF ILLINOIS (US) [02240691] **1848**

STUDENT FINANCIAL AID ACTIVITY REPORT (US/0097-918X) [01799324] **1848**

STUDENT FINANCIAL AID BULLETIN (ATHENS, GA.) (US/0735-5963) [08622323] **1872**

STUDENT FINANCIAL AID BY SOURCE, TYPE, SECTOR AND LEVEL DURING FISCAL YEAR (US) [16949595] **1872**

STUDENT FINANCIAL AID PROGRAMS, ANNUAL REPORT (US) [12305724] **1848**

STUDENT GUIDE (NEW YORK, N.Y.), THE (US/0740-5413) [09960788] **1848**

STUDENT GUIDE TO: GRADUATE LAW STUDY PROGRAMS (US/0196-9773) [05930869] **3060**

STUDENT GUIDE TO MASS MEDIA INTERNSHIPS, THE (US/0730-5117) [03722874] **1122**

STUDENT GUIDE TO: SUMMER LAW STUDY PROGRAMS (US/0197-6656) [06074067] **1848, 3060**

STUDENT GUIDE TO THE SAT *CEASED.* (US/1043-8378) [19576230] **1848**

STUDENT HANDBOOK OF INFORMATION ON UNIVERSITY POLICIES AND PRACTICES (NR) [02382979] **1848**

STUDENT HANDBOOK - PRINCE GEORGE'S COMMUNITY COLLEGE (US/0148-8813) [03386847] **1849**

STUDENT LAWYER (CHICAGO. 1972) (US/0039-274X) [01773422] **3060**

STUDENT LEADER (MADISON, WIS.) (US/1057-8722) [24134326] **1786**

STUDENT LEADER NEWS SERVICE (US/1060-0353) [24862260] **1849**

STUDENT LEADERSHIP MAGAZINE (US) **1849**

STUDENT LIBRARY HANDBOOK (CN/1194-3963) [I11943963] **3251**

STUDENT LOAN PROGRAM, ANNUAL REPORT *See* STUDENT FINANCIAL AID PROGRAMS, ANNUAL REPORT **1848**

STUDENT (NASHVILLE), THE (US/0039-2685) [02924403] 1849, **5068**

STUDENT PERSONNEL ASSOCIATION FOR TEACHER EDUCATION *See* MONOGRAPH - STUDENT PERSONNEL ASSOCIATION FOR TEACHER EDUCATION **1836**

STUDENT PRESS BULLETIN, THE *CEASED.* (US/0274-8401) [06658694] **1095**

STUDENT PRESS LAW CENTER *See* STUDENT PRESS LAW CENTER REPORT **3060**

STUDENT PRESS LAW CENTER REPORT (US/0160-3825) [03658508] 2924, **3060**

STUDENT PRESS REVIEW (US) **2924**

STUDENT PRESS SERVICE *See* SPS NEWSREPORT **2924**

STUDENT PRESS, THE (US) [06172200] **2924**

STUDENT PUBLICATION OF THE SCHOOL OF DESIGN (US/0078-1444) [04417343] **309**

STUDENT SPORTS (CAL-HI SPORTS ED.) (US/1059-793X) [24767703] **4924**

STUDENT SUCCESS TUTOR DIRECTORY. SARASOTA COUNTY (US/0899-2355) [18041173] **1786**

STUDENT TIMES (MONTREAL) (CN/0712-7944) [08828223] **5795**

STUDENT TRAVELER (KNOXVILLE, TENN.) (US/1051-3868) [21946679] **5491**

STUDENT TRAVELS MAGAZINE (US) **5491**

STUDENT UND PRAKTIKANT (GW/0721-8672) [l07218672] 1905, **4330**

STUDENT VENTURE CAPITAL PROGRAM (CN/1184-0870) [23659372] **1522**

STUDENT VOICE (US/0039-2804) [03936762] **1095**

STUDENTS AID NEWSLETTER (US/1060-2275) [22696738] **1849**

STUDENTS' GUIDE TO GRADUATE STUDIES IN THE UK, THE (UK) [11567707] **1849**

STUDENTS LAW JOURNAL (MW) [08243582] **3060**

STUDENT'S QUARTERLY JOURNAL (UK) [20150740] **2082**

STUDI ALIMENTARI CU APA (RM/0521-3479) [03111623] **5540**

STUDI & NOTIZIE (IT) [06682134] **5160**

STUDI BITONTINI (IT/0392-1727) [18179558] **365**

STUDI CATTOLICI (IT/0039-2901) [01986582] **5036**

STUDI CLASSICI E ORIENTALI (IT/0081-6124) [01986519] 2665, **1080**

STUDI DANTESCHI (IT/0391-7835) [01200207] **1080**

STUDI DELL'ISTITUTO LINGUISTICO (IT) [07762752] **3324**

STUDI DI ANTICHITA CRISTIANA (IT) [05236095] **283**

STUDI DI ARCHITETTURA ANTICA (IT/0081-6140) [03067206] **283**

STUDI DI EGITTOLOGIA E DI ANTICHITA PUNICHE (IT) [19585606] **283**

STUDI DI ESTETICA : BOLLETTINO SEMESTRALE DELLA SEZIONE DI ESTETICA DEL DIPARTIMENTO DI FILOSOFIA DELL'UNIVERSITA DI BOLOGNA (IT/0585-4733) [04278112] **331**

STUDI DI FILOLOGIA ITALIANA (IT/0392-5110) [01200246] **3324**

STUDI DI FILOLOGIA TEDESCA (IT) [01606345] **3324**

STUDI DI GRAMMATICA ITALIANA (IT) [02015812] **3324**

STUDI DI LESSICOGRAFIA ITALIANA / A CURA DELL'ACCADEMIA DELLA CRUSCA (IT) [06695914] **3324**

STUDI DI LETTERATURA FRANCESE (IT/0585-4768) [03067007] **3440**

STUDI DI LETTERATURA ISPANO-AMERICANA (IT/0585-4776) [01766650] **3440**

STUDI DI PSICOLOGIA DELL EDUCAZIONE (IT/0393-6457) **4619**

STUDI DI PSICOLOGIA DELL'EDUCAZIONE (IT/0393-6163) [l03936163] **4619**

STUDI DI SCIENZE RELIGIOSE (IT) [28032058] 4361, **4999**

STUDI DI SOCIOLOGIA (IT/0039-291X) [01986575] **5263**

STUDI DI STORIA DELL'ARTE (IT) [25836326] **365**

STUDI DI STORIA DELLE ARTI / UNIVERSITA DI GENOVA, ISTITUTO DI STORIA DELL'ARTE (IT) [09916391] **365**

STUDI DI STORIA DELL'EDUCAZIONE (IT/0392-1948) [10860541] **1786**

STUDI DI STORIA MEDIOEVALE E DI DIPLOMATICA (IT) [04918965] **2630**

STUDI DI TEOLOGIA (IT) [26283262] **4999**

STUDI DI TEOLOGIA DOGMATICA (IT) [13409889] **4999**

STUDI D'ITALIANISTICA NELL'AFRICA AUSTRALE (SA/1012-2338) [20142654] **2273**

STUDI DONIZETTIANI (IT) [07957102] **4155**

STUDI E DOCUMENTI DEGLI ANNALI DELLA PUBBLICA ISTRUZIONE (IT) [18546091] **1786**

STUDI E DOCUMENTI DI ARCHITETTURA (IT/0301-6455) [02077083] **309**

STUDI E FONTI DI STORIA LOMBARDA : QUADERNI MILANESI (IT) **2630**

STUDI E MATERIALI DI STORIA DELLE RELIGIONI (L'AQUILA, ITALY : 1983) (IT) [12360111] **4999**

STUDI E PROBLEMI DI CRITICA TESTUALE (IT/0049-2361) [02000256] **3324**

STUDI E RICERCHE DELLA FACOLTA DI ECONOMIA E COMMERCIO (IT) [06617465] **1585**

STUDI E RICERCHE FRANCESCANE (IT) [05713835] **5036**

STUDI E RICERCHE / POLITECNICO DI MILANO, SCUOLA DI SPECIALIZZAZIONE IN COSTRUZIONI IN CEMENTO ARMATO (IT) [27423396] **629**

STUDI E RICERCHE SULL'ORIENTE CRISTIANO (IT) [06249259] **5040**

STUDI E SAGGI LINGUISTICI (IT/0085-6827) [01986540] **3324**

STUDI E TESTI (BARI, ITALY) (IT) [20081389] **3354**

STUDI EBLAITI / MISSIONE ARCHEOLOGICA ITALIANA IN SIRIA (IT) [07064147] 2665, **283**

STUDI ECONOMICI (IT/0029-2928) [10757675] **1522**

STUDI ECONOMICI E SOCIALI (IT/0391-8750) [l03918750] **1628**

STUDI ECUMENICI (IT/0393-3687) [11073370] **4999**

STUDI EMIGRAZIONE (IT/0039-2936) [01680971] **1921**

STUDI ETNO-ANTROPOLOGICI E SOCIOLOGICI / PUBBLICATA SOTTO GLI AUSPICI DEL CONSIGLIO NAZIONALE DELLE RICHERCHE (IT) [15686541] **246**

STUDI ETRUSCHI (IT/0391-7762) [01766651] **2711**

STUDI. FATTI. RICERCHE (IT/0393-3695) [l03933695] **2493**

STUDI FILOSOFICI (IT) [06779202] **4361**

STUDI FRANCESCANI (IT) [02006868] **4999**

STUDI FRANCESI (IT/0039-2944) [01766652] **3440**

STUDI GERMANICI (IT/0039-2952) [01766653] 3324, **3440**

STUDI GOLDONIANI (IT) [01800170] **3440**

STUDI GORIZIANI (IT) [01987327] **2855**

STUDI INTERDISCIPLINARI SULLA FAMIGLIA (IT) **2286**

STUDI ISPANICI (IT) [04676910] **3440**

STUDI ITALIANI DI FILOLOGIA CLASSICA (IT/0039-2987) [01588733] 3324, **1080**

STUDI LATINI E ITALIANI / UNIVERSITA DEGLI STUDI "LA SAPIENZA," DIPARTIMENTO DI LINGUE E CULTURE D'ITALIA DALLA LATINITA ALL'ETA CONTEMPORANEA (IT) [18230991] **3440**

STUDI LINGUISTICI ITALIANI (IT/0394-3569) [11215596] **3324**

STUDI LINGUISTICI SALENTINI (IT) [01786241] **3324**

STUDI LIVORNESI *See* NUOVI STUDI LIVORNESI / ASSOCIAZIONE DI STORIA, LETTERE E ARTI LIVORNESI **2851**

STUDI LIVORNESI / ASSOCIAZIONE DI STORIA, LETTERE E ARTI LIVORNESI (IT) [20716750] **2855**

STUDI LUNIGIANESI (IT) [19907584] **3354**

STUDI MAGREBINI (IT/0585-4954) [01996423] **2643**

STUDI MEDIOLATINI E VOLGARI (IT/0585-4962) [01604500] 5075, **3441**

STUDI MICENEI ED EGEO-ANATOLICI (IT) [02251993] **1080**

STUDI MONTEFELTRANI (IT/0394-5499) [l03945499] **2711**

STUDI MUSICALI (IT/0391-7789) [01824569] **4155**

STUDI NOVECENTESCHI (IT/0303-4615) [01005525] **5223**

STUDI ORGANIZZATIVI (IT) **887**

STUDI ORIENTALI E LINGUISTICI / ISTITUTO DI GLOTTOLOGIA, UNIVERSITA DEGLI STUDI DI BOLOGNA (IT) [13139013] **3324**

STUDI PARLAMENTARI E DI POLITICA COSTITUZIONALE (IT) **4497**

STUDI PER L'ECOLOGIA DEL QUATERNARIO : PERIODICO DEL CENTRO STUDI PER L'ECOLOGIA QUATERNARIO (IT) [10003508] **2221**

STUDI PETRARCHESCHI / ACCADEMIA PETRARCA DI LETTERE, ARTI E SCIENZE DI AREZZO (IT) [03212395] **3441**

STUDI PIEMONTESI (IT) [02002632] **2711**

STUDI ROMAGNOLI (IT/0081-6205) [02002169] **2711**

STUDI ROMANI (IT/0039-2995) [01984347] **2630**

STUDI SALENTINI (IT/0039-3002) [02002145] **2711**

STUDI SARDI (IT) [02673398] **2711**

STUDI SCIACCHIANI (IT) [15188614] **2855**

STUDI SECENTESCHI (IT/0081-6248) [02002158] **2711**

STUDI SENESI NEL CIRCOLO GIURIDICO DELLA R. UNIVERSITA (IT/0039-3010) [01643870] **3060**

STUDI SETTECENTESCHI (IT) [08105705] **2630**

STUDI STORICI (IT/0039-3037) [01586874] **2711**

STUDI STORICI DELL'ORDINE DEI SERVI DI MARIA (IT/0039-3045) [09564639] **5036**

STUDI STORICI LUIGI SIMEONI (IT) [09223473] **2630**

STUDI STORICI MERIDIONALI (IT) [08821717] **2630**

STUDI STORICI SULL'ORDINE DEI SERVI DI MARIA *See* STUDI STORICI DELL'ORDINE DEI SERVI DI MARIA **5036**

STUDI SUL BOCCACCIO (IT/0585-4997) [01987254] 3354, **435**

STUDIA

STUDI SULLA TOSCANA MEDICEA (IT) [06392626] **3643**

STUDI TASSIANI (IT/0081-6256) [02014629] **3441**

STUDI TRENTINI DI SCIENZE NATURALI. ACTA BIOLOGICA (IT/0392-0542) [04622517] **474**

STUDI TRENTINI DI SCIENZE NATURALI. ACTA GEOLOGICA (IT/0392-0534) [04622549] **1399**

STUDI TRENTINI DI SCIENZE NATURALI. SEZIONE B. BIOLOGICA (IT/0585-5616) [02822527] **5160**

STUDI TRENTINI DI SCIENZE STORICHE (IT/0392-0690) [01766659] **2855**

STUDI URBINATI. B, SCIENZE UMANE E SOCIALI (IT) [23072118] **2855**

STUDI VERDIANI (IT) [09678596] **4155**

STUDIA (PO/0870-0028) **2630**

STUDIA AFRICANA (US/0163-2965) [04099275] **2643**

STUDIA ALBANICA (AA/0585-5047) [01996482] **2711**

STUDIA ANGLICA POSNANIENSIA (PL/0081-6272) [01766662] **3324**

STUDIA ANGLISTICA UPSALIENSIA (SW/0562-2719) [01604290] **3441, 3324**

STUDIA ANSELMIANA; PHILOSOPHICA, THEOLOGICA (IT) [01772976] 5000, **4361**

STUDIA ANTHROPONYMICA SCANDINAVICA (SW/0280-8633) [11387708] **2474**

STUDIA BIBLIOLOGICA (CN/0229-6330) [09026032] **425**

STUDIA BIOPHYSICA **SUSPENDED.** (SZ/0081-6337) [03425207] **496**

STUDIA BOTANICA (SP/0211-9714) [09178804] **528**

STUDIA BOTANICA HUNGARICA (HU/0301-7001) [02500884] **528**

STUDIA CANONICA (CN/0039-310X) [01788951] **5036**

STUDIA CAUCASICA (BE/0081-6345) [02391141] **2711**

STUDIA CELTICA (UK/0081-6353) [02000313] 3441, **3324**

STUDIA CHEMICA (SP) [01607522] **993**

STUDIA CLASSICA (US/0899-9929) [18284080] **1080**

STUDIA COMENIANA ET HISTORICA (PN/0323-2220) [05907272] 4361, **1786**

STUDIA COMITATENSIA BUDAPEST (HU/0133-3046) [02243786] **4096**

STUDIA DEMOGRAFICZNE (PL/0039-3134) [01987292] **4560**

STUDIA DIPLOMATICA (BE/0770-2965) [01205196] **4497**

STUDIA DO DZIEJOW DAWNEGO UZBROJENIA I UNIFORMU WOJSKOWEGO (PL/0239-832X) [I0239832X] 4058, **2630**

STUDIA EKUMENICZNE (PL) [09823007] **5000**

STUDIA ESTETYCZNE (PL/0081-637X) [01987269] **2855**

STUDIA ET DOCUMENTA AD IURA ORIENTIS ANTIQUI PERTINENTIA (NE) [01766664] **3060**

STUDIA ET DOCUMENTA IURIS CANONICI (IT) [08574369] **5037**

STUDIA ETHNOGRAPHICA FRIBURGENSIA (SZ) [03113163] **246**

STUDIA FENNICA See STUDIA FENNICA. FOLKLORISTICA **2324**

STUDIA FENNICA See STUDIA FENNICA. ETHNOLOGICA **246**

●STUDIA FENNICA. ETHNOLOGICA (FI) [27749967] **246**

●STUDIA FENNICA. FOLKLORISTICA (FI/1235-1946) [28407377] **2324**

STUDIA FENNICA. LINGUISTICA (FI/1235-1938) [27750010] **3324**

STUDIA FILOZOFICZNE **CEASED.** (PL/0039-3142) [01996378] **4361**

STUDIA FORESTALIA SUECICA (SW/0039-3150) [01506775] **2396**

STUDIA GALLO-POLONICA (PL/0083-4351) [19027181] **2711**

STUDIA GEOBOTANICA (IT) [08362107] **528**

STUDIA GEOGRAPHICA (GE) [05236039] **2577**

STUDIA GEOGRAPHICA DEBRECEN (HU/0209-4835) [I02094835] **2577**

STUDIA GEOLOGICA See STUDIA GEOLOGICA SALMANTICENSIA **1399**

STUDIA GEOLOGICA POLONICA (PL/0081-6426) [01911467] **1399**

STUDIA GEOLOGICA SALMANTICENSIA (SP/0370-9957) [09752880] **1399**

STUDIA GEOMORPHOLOGICA CARPATHO-BALCANICA (PL/0081-6434) [06569344] **2577**

STUDIA GEOPHYSICA ET GEODAETICA (XR/0039-3169) [01624336] **1411**

STUDIA GEOTECHNICA ET MECHANICA (PL/0137-6365) [05584590] **1997**

STUDIA GERMANICA GANDENSIA (BE/0081-6442) [01996397] 3324, **3441**

STUDIA GERMANICA POSNANIENSIA (PL/0137-2467) [01988435] **3324**

STUDIA GERMANISTICA UPSALIENSIA (SW/0585-5160) [01714704] **3324**

STUDIA GRAMATYCZNE / POLSKA AKADEMIA NAUK, INSTYTUT JEZYKA POLSKIEGO (PL/0208-4074) [08964253] **3324**

STUDIA GRAMMATICA (GW/0081-6469) [01766669] **3324**

STUDIA GRATIANA (IT) [02268195] **3354**

STUDIA HIBERNICA (IE/0081-6477) [02242098] 3441, **3324**

STUDIA HISTORIAE OECONOMICAE (PL/0081-6485) [01645756] **1585**

STUDIA HISTORICA. HA. ANTIQUA (SP/0213-2052) [12643245] **2630**

STUDIA HISTORICA. HA. CONTEMPORANEA (SP/0213-2087) [23196542] **2631**

STUDIA HISTORYCZNE (PL/0025-1429) [02000435] **2631**

STUDIA I MATERIAY LUBELSKIE / MUZEUM OKREGOWE W LUBLINIE (PL/0585-5276) [12706043] **4096**

STUDIA I MATERIAY OCEANOLOGICZNE (PL/0208-421X) [11465394] **5160**

STUDIA I MATERIAY Z DZIEJOW NAUKI POLSKIEJ. SERIA C : HISTORIA NAUK MATEMATYCZNYCH, FIZYKO-CHEMICZNYCH I GEOLOGICZNO-GEOGRAFICZNYCH (PL/0081-6590) [02007334] **5160**

STUDIA I MATERIAY Z DZIEJOW NAUKI POLSKIEJ. SERIA II, HISTORIA NAUK SCISYCH, PRZYRODNICZYCH I TECHNICZNYCH (PL/0860-102X) [19666715] **5223**

STUDIA I MATERIAY Z DZIEJOW POLSKI LUDOWEJ (PL) [04919347] **2711**

STUDIA IN VETERIS TESTAMENTI PSEUDEPIGRAPHA (NE) [02013253] **5019**

STUDIA IRANICA (FR/0221-5004) [01787164] **2665**

STUDIA IRANICA (NE/0772-7852) **2665**

STUDIA ISLAMICA (FR/0585-5292) [01766673] **5045**

STUDIA ISLAMIKA (IO/0125-0492) [04699274] **5045**

STUDIA ISLANDICA (IC/0258-3828) [01766674] **3441**

STUDIA ITALO-POLONICA (PL) [10061763] **2711**

STUDIA IURIDICA SILESIANA / UNIWERSYTET SLASKI (PL) [07384303] **3060**

STUDIA JUDAICA; FORSCHUNGEN ZUR WISSENSCHAFT DES JUDENTUMS (GW/0585-5306) [03088017] **5053**

STUDIA LEIBNITIANA (GW/0039-3185) [01766677] **4361**

STUDIA LEIBNITIANA. SONDERHEFT (GW) [16901985] **4362**

STUDIA LEIBNITIANA. SUPPLEMENTA (GW/0303-5980) [01986284] **4362**

STUDIA LINGUISTICA (SW/0039-3193) [01717038] **3324**

STUDIA LINGUISTICA ET PHILOLOGICA (US/0886-0432) [05627218] **3324**

STUDIA LITTERARIA (HU/0562-2867) [01999496] **3441**

STUDIA LITURGICA (NE/0039-3207) [01766679] **5000**

STUDIA LITURGICZNE (PL) [20695084] **3441**

STUDIA LOGICA (PL/0039-3215) [01624491] **4362**

STUDIA MARINA (YU/0585-5349) [I05855349] **1457**

STUDIA MATHEMATICA (PL/0039-3223) [01588428] **3536**

STUDIA MEDIEWISTYCZNE (PL/0039-3231) [02000306] **5263**

STUDIA MISSIONALIA (IT/0080-3987) [01999451] **5000**

STUDIA MISSIONALIA UPSALIENSIA (SW/0585-5373) [03067065] **5000**

STUDIA MORALIA (IT/0081-6736) [04669141] **5000**

STUDIA MUSICOLOGICA. ACADEMIAE SCIENTIARUM HUNGARICA (HU/0039-3266) [01589216] **4155**

STUDIA MUSICOLOGICA NORVEGICA (NO/0332-5024) [01586982] **4155**

STUDIA MUZEALNE (PL/0137-5318) [I01375318] **4097**

STUDIA MYSTICA (US/0161-7222) [03786460] 5000, **3441**

STUDIA NAUK POLITYCZNYCH (PL/0511-1765) [04216057] **4497**

STUDIA NEOPHILOLOGICA (SW/0039-3274) [01766680] 3354, **3325**

STUDIA NORVEGICA See STUDIA NORVEGICA ETHNOLOGICA ET FOLKLORISTICA **2324**

STUDIA NORVEGICA ETHNOLOGICA ET FOLKLORISTICA **CEASED.** (NO) [02241037] **2324**

STUDIA OECOLOGICA (SP/0211-4623) [17991674] **2221**

STUDIA OLIVERIANA (IT) [09753799] **1080**

STUDIA ORIENTALIA (FI/0039-3282) [01639720] **3325**

STUDIA PALMYRENSKIE. ETUDES PALMYRENIENNES (PL/0081-6787) [04977835] **283**

STUDIA PATAVINA (IT/0039-3304) [01999239] 4362, **5000**

STUDIA PATRISTICA : PAPERS PRESENTED TO THE ... INTERNATIONAL CONFERENCE ON PATRISTIC STUDIES HELD (GW) [06005593] **5000**

STUDIA PHILOLOGIAE SCANDINAVICAE UPSALIENSIS (SW/0081-6809) [01766681] **3325**

STUDIA PHILONICA ANNUAL, THE (US/1052-4533) [20985182] **4362**

STUDIA PHILOSOPHIAE CHRISTIANAE (PL/0585-5470) [05251287] **4362**

STUDIA PHILOSOPHICA (SZ) [04423032] **4362**

STUDIA PHONETICA (CN/0829-2167) [03057455] **3325**

STUDIA PHONETICA POSNANIENSIA (PL/0861-2085) **3325**

STUDIA PHONOLOGICA (JA/0300-1067) [01796826] **3325**

STUDIA PICENA (IT) [02000396] **2711**

STUDIA PNEUMOLOGICA ET PHTISEOLOGICA CECHOSLOVACA (XO/0371-2222) [09531070] **3643**

STUDIA POHL; SERIES MAIOR (IT) [03055342] **5019**

STUDIA POST-BIBLICA (NE/0585-5500) [02010794] **5000**

STUDIA PRAEHISTORICA (BU) [05003783] **283**

STUDIA PRAWNICZE (PL/0039-3312) [04217794] **3060**

STUDIA PSYCHOLOGICA (XO) [07406005] **4619**

STUDIA PSYCHOLOGICA (CZ/0039-3320) [02450878] **4619**

STUDIA PSYCHOLOGICZNE (PL/0081-685X) [02006884] **4619**

STUDIA ROMANICA ET ANGLICA ZAGRABIENSIA (CI/0039-3339) [02014654] **3325**

STUDIA ROMANICA POSNANIENSIA (PL/0137-2475) [03058921] 3325, **5075**

STUDIA ROMANICA. SERIES LINGUISTICA (HU/0418-4564) [04852262] **3325**

STUDIA ROMANICA. SERIES LITTERARIA (HU/0418-4572) [04852307] **3441**

STUDIA ROMANICA UPSALIENSIA (SW/0562-3022) [01766682] **3441**

STUDIA ROSENTHALIANA (NE/0039-3347) [02002960] **2273**

STUDIA ROSSICA POSNANIENSIA (PL/0081-6884) [03057413] **3325**

STUDIA SCIENTIARUM MATHEMATICARUM HUNGARICA (HU/0081-6906) [02056432] **3537**

STUDIA SEMINARII LATINI UPSALIENSIS (SW/1100-8091) [22222527] 1080, **3325**

STUDIA SLAVICA ACADEMIAE SCIENTIARUM HUNGARICAE (HU/0039-3363) [01766683] **3325**

STUDIA SLAVICA FINLANDENSIA (FI/0781-3333) [14643439] 3441, **3325**

STUDIA SOCIETATIS SCIENTIARUM TORUNENSIS. SECTIO C. GEOGRAPHIA ET GEOLOGIA (PL/0082-5549) [03143417] 1399, **2577**

STUDIA SOCIETATIS SCIENTIARUM TORUNENSIS. SECTIO H, MEDICINA (PL/0860-9594) [I08609594] **3643**

STUDIA SOCJOLOGICZNE (PL/0039-3371) [01986570] **5223**

STUDIA SPINOZANA (GW) [13392459] **4362**

STUDIA STAROPOLSKIE (PL/0081-6949) [03075415] **3441**

STUDIA SWEDENBORGIANA (US/0361-6045) [01779271] **4362**

STUDIA THEOLOGICA (NO/0039-338X) [02247109] **5000**

STUDIA THEOLOGICA LUNDENSIA; UTG. AV TEOLOGISKA FAKULTETEN I LUND (SW) [01715390] **5000**

STUDIA — Alphabetical Title Index

STUDIA THEOLOGICA VARSAVIENSIA (PL/0585-5594) [07016321] **5000**

STUDIA UNIVERSITATIS BABES-BOLYAI. BIOLOGIA (RM/0039-3398) [05388813] **474**

STUDIA UNIVERSITATIS BABES-BOLYAI. CHEMIA (RM/0039-3401) [05526375] **993**

STUDIA UNIVERSITATIS BABES-BOLYAI. GEOGRAPHIA (RM) [26468253] **2577**

STUDIA UNIVERSITATIS BABES-BOLYAI. GEOLOGIA (RM) [25959742] **1399**

STUDIA UNIVERSITATIS BABES-BOLYAI. HISTORIA (RM) [05691112] **2711**

STUDIA UNIVERSITATIS BABES-BOLYAI : MATHEMATICA (RM/0373-1227) [02853160] **3537**

STUDIA UNIVERSITATIS BABES-BOLYAI. PHILOLOGIA (RM) [05924669] **3325**

STUDIA UNIVERSITATIS BABES-BOLYAI. PHYSICA (RM/0258-8730) [06140443] **4423**

STUDIA UNIVERSITATIS BABES-BOLYAI. SERIES PHILOLOGIA *See* STUDIA UNIVERSITATIS BABES-BOLYAI. PHILOLOGIA **3325**

STUDIA URBANIANA (IT) [16987781] **2631**

STUDIA Z DZIEJOW ROSJI I EUROPY SRODKOWO-WSCHODNIEJ / POLSKA AKADEMIA NAUK, INSTYTUT HISTORII, ZAKAD DZIEJOW EUROPY XIX I XX WIEKU (PL) [28490892] **2711**

STUDIA Z DZIEJOW ZSRR I EUROPY SRODKOWEJ *See* STUDIA Z DZIEJOW ROSJI I EUROPY SRODKOWO-WSCHODNIEJ / POLSKA AKADEMIA NAUK, INSTYTUT HISTORII, ZAKAD DZIEJOW EUROPY XIX I XX WIEKU **2711**

STUDIA Z HISTORII KAZNODZIEJSTWA I HOMILETYKI (PL) [02400098] **5000**

STUDIA Z HISTORII SZTUKI (PL/0081-7104) [03055472] **2631**

STUDIA ZAMORENSIA (SP/0214-736X) [10861584] **3325**

STUDIA ZRODOZNAWCZE. COMMENTATIONES (PL/0081-7147) [03085001] 1849, **2631**

STUDIE (IT/0450-9250) [01783564] **5000**

STUDIE A PRACE LINGUISTICKE (XR/0585-5675) [01645814] **3325**

STUDIE ET DOCUMENTA HISTORIAE ET IURIS (IT) [01987300] **3060**

STUDIEHANDBOK (SW) [02952018] **5160**

STUDIEINFORMATION (DK) [02244551] 1786, **309**

STUDIEKAMRATEN (SW/0039-3452) [01766687] **365**

STUDIEN UBER ASIEN, AFRIKA UND LATEINAMERIKA (GW) [03085062] **2631**

STUDIEN UBER WIRTSCHAFTS- UND SYSTEMVERGLEICHE (AU/0344-824X) [01607200] **1595**

STUDIEN UND ARBEITEN DER THEOLOGISCHEN FAKULTAT (AU/0579-7780) [02711352] **5000**

STUDIEN UND BERICHTE - MAX-PLANCK-INSTITUT FUR BILDUNGSFORSCHUNG (GW) [05088327] **1905**

STUDIEN UND MITTEILUNGEN ZUR GESCHICHTE DES BENEDIKTINER-ORDENS UND SEINER ZWEIGE (GW) [02050419] **5037**

STUDIEN UND QUELLEN (SZ) [03303043] **2711**

STUDIEN UND QUELLEN ZUR VERSGESCHICHTE (GW/0585-5810) [03058830] **3354**

STUDIEN UND TEXTE ZUR GEISTESGESCHICHTE DES MITTELALTERS (NE/0585-5837) [03058878] **2711**

STUDIEN UND TEXTE ZUR SOZIALGESCHICHTE DER LITERATUR (GW/0174-4410) [11625142] **3441**

STUDIEN ZU DEN BOGAZKOY-TEXTEN (GW/0585-5853) [03075531] **3325**

STUDIEN ZUM FRUHNEUHOCHDEUTSCHEN (GW) [05035605] 5019, **3325**

STUDIEN ZUM INTERNATIONALEN ROHSTOFFRECHT (GW) [19087139] 2206, **3060**

STUDIEN ZUM KLEINEN DEUTSCHEN SPRACHATLAS (GW) [10988018] **3325**

STUDIEN ZUM NEUEN TESTAMENT (GW) [02013292] **5019**

STUDIEN ZUM WANDEL VON GESELLSCHAFT UND BILDUNG IM NEUNZEHNTEN JAHRHUNDERT (GW) [03077825] **2631**

STUDIEN ZUR ALTAGYPTISCHEN KULTUR (GW/0340-2215) [03062685] **283**

STUDIEN ZUR BAYERISCHEN VERFASSUNGS- UND SOZIALGESCHICHTE (GW/0562-3251) [03064067] **2711**

STUDIEN ZUR DEUTSCHEN LITERATUR (GW/0081-7236) [01606092] **3441**

STUDIEN ZUR ENGLISCHEN PHILOLOGIE (GW/0081-7244) [01681269] **3325**

STUDIEN ZUR EUROPAISCHEN GESCHICHTE (GW) [03058898] **2711**

STUDIEN ZUR GERMANISTIK, ANGLISTIK UND KOMPARATISTIK (GW/0340-594X) [02013266] **3325**

STUDIEN ZUR GESCHICHTE DER AKADEMIE DER WISSENSCHAFTEN DER DDR (GW) [03084880] **5160**

STUDIEN ZUR GESCHICHTE DER KATH. MORALTHEOLOGIE (GW/0081-7295) [03086331] **5000**

STUDIEN ZUR HEIMATGESCHICHTE DER STADT BAD HONNEF AM RHEIN (GW) [21016008] **2711**

STUDIEN ZUR INDOLOGIE UND IRANISTIK (GW/0341-4191) [02247001] **2665**

STUDIEN ZUR INTEGRIERTEN LANDLICHEN ENTWICKLUNG (GW/0177-2503) [12753672] **138**

STUDIEN ZUR KRITISCHEN PSYCHOLOGIE (GW/0721-4502) [07365921] **4619**

STUDIEN ZUR KULTURKUNDE (GW) [03079326] **2273**

STUDIEN ZUR KUNSTGESCHICHTE (GE) [20921101] **365**

STUDIEN ZUR LITERATUR DER MODERNE (GW/0340-9023) [07644341] **3441**

STUDIEN ZUR MEDIZINGESCHICHTE DES NEUNZEHNTEN JAHRHUNDERTS (GW/0081-7333) [06409269] **3643**

STUDIEN ZUR MUSIKGESCHICHTE DES 19. JAHRHUNDERTS (GW/0081-7341) [02008257] **4155**

STUDIEN ZUR MUSIKWISSENSCHAFT (GW/0081-3222) [01766697] **4155**

STUDIEN ZUR OSTERREICHISCHEN PHILOSOPHIE (NE) [10801534] **4362**

STUDIEN ZUR PALAEGRAPHIE UND PAPYRUSKUNDE (SP) **3325**

STUDIEN ZUR PALEOGRAPHIE UND PAPYRUSKUNDE (GW) [01772977] **1080**

STUDIEN ZUR PHILOSOPHIE UND LITERATUR DES NEUNZEHNTEN JAHRHUNDERTS (GW/0081-735X) [01585762] **4362**

STUDIEN ZUR PROBLEMGESCHICHTE DER ANTIKEN UND MITTELALTERLICHEN PHILOSOPHIE (NE) [01586128] **4362**

STUDIEN ZUR REGIERUNGSLEHRE UND INTERNATIONALEN POLITIK (NE) [01766701] **4535**

STUDIEN ZUR THEORETISCHEN LINGUISTIK (GW/0178-126X) [17309479] **3325**

STUDIEN ZUR TRADITIONELLEN MUSIK JAPANS (GW) [04296362] **4155**

STUDIEN ZUR UMWELT DES NEUEN TESTAMENTS (GW/0585-6272) [02008271] **5000**

STUDIEN ZUR WERTUNGSFORSCHUNG (GW) [05072502] **4155**

STUDIEN ZUR WISSENSCHAFTS-, SOZIAL- UND BILDUNGSGESCHICHTE DER MATHEMATIK (GW) [18036824] **3537**

STUDIENFUHRER (GW) [05705248] **1849**

STUDIENMATERIAL - INSTITUT FUER MILITAERISCHE GRUNDLAGENFORSCHUNG (AU) [02660622] **4058**

STUDIENMATERIAL ZUR WEITERBILDUNG MEDIZINISCH-TECHNISCHER LABORASSISTENTEN (GW/0323-4126) [01064902] **3643**

STUDIENREIHE ROMANIA (GW) [06038072] **1080**

STUDIENSTIFTUNG *See* JAHRESBERICHT - STUDIENSTIFTUNG **1831**

STUDIER FRA SPROG- OG OLDTIDSFORSKNING (DK/0107-9212) [01766704] 2631, **3325**

STUDIER I ARBETARRORELSENS HISTORIA (SW/02547423) **1712**

STUDIER I MODERN SPRAKVETENSKAP (SW/0585-3583) [03100504] **3325**

STUDIER I NORDISK FILOLOGI (FI/0356-0376) [02017404] **3325**

STUDIEREN IM RUHRGEBIET / HERAUSGEBER, KOMMUNALVERBAND RUHRGEBIET (GW) [10446163] **1849**

STUDIEREN IN KOLN (GW) [24333407] **1095**

STUDIES (IE/0039-3495) [01586420] **2523**

STUDIES AND DOCUMENTS (US) [01997394] **2631**

STUDIES AND DOCUMENTS (US) [01913418] **4155**

STUDIES AND DOCUMENTS ON CULTURAL POLICIES (US/0251-575X) [04014770] **1885**

STUDIES AND REPORTS IN HYDROLOGY (FR/0081-7449) [01162482] **5540**

STUDIES AND RESEARCH - INTERNATIONAL SOCIAL SECURITY ASSOCIATION (SW/0254-3931) [l02543931] **1712**

STUDIES AND REVIEWS - GENERAL FISHERIES COUNCIL FOR THE MEDITERRANEAN (IT/0433-3519) [01435431] **2314**

STUDIES FOR TRADE UNIONISTS *CEASED.* (UK) [03896128] **1712**

STUDIES IN 20TH CENTURY LITERATURE (US/0145-7888) [02777062] **3354**

STUDIES IN ADULT EDUCATION (TZ) [05399526] **1802**

STUDIES IN AFRICAN AND AFRO-AMERICAN CULTURE (US/0890-4847) [14236632] **2643**

STUDIES IN AFRICAN LINGUISTICS (US/0039-3533) [01779272] **3325**

STUDIES IN AMERICAN DRAMA, 1945-PRESENT *SUSPENDED.* (US/0886-7097) [12964544] 3441, **5369**

STUDIES IN AMERICAN FICTION (US/0091-8083) [01787903] **3354**

STUDIES IN AMERICAN HUMOR (US/0095-280X) [01796470] **3441**

STUDIES IN AMERICAN INDIAN LITERATURE *See* DISPATCH - COLUMBIA UNIVERSITY. CENTER FOR AMERICAN CULTURE STUDIES, THE **2731**

STUDIES IN AMERICAN INDIAN LITERATURE (US) [07400425] **3441**

STUDIES IN AMERICAN JEWISH LITERATURE (ALBANY, N.Y.) (US/0271-9274) [06753496] **3441**

STUDIES IN AMERICAN LITERATURE (NIHON AMERIKA BUNGAKKAI) (JA/0385-6100) [08398253] **3441**

STUDIES IN AMERICAN POLITICAL DEVELOPMENT (US/0898-588X) [15122845] **4497**

STUDIES IN ANCIENT CHRONOLOGY (UK/0952-4975) [19006295] **2631**

STUDIES IN ANCIENT MEDICINE (NE/0925-1421) [24540694] **3643**

STUDIES IN ANCIENT ORIENTAL CIVILIZATION (US/0081-7554) [01554131] 2665, **283**

STUDIES IN ANTHROPOLOGY AND HISTORY (SW/1055-2464) [23124658] 2631, **246**

STUDIES IN APPLIED MATHEMATICS (CAMBRIDGE) (US/0022-2526) [02246121] **3537**

STUDIES IN APPLIED MECHANICS (US) [08427010] **2129**

STUDIES IN APPLIED PHILOSOPHY (UK) [15001107] **4362**

STUDIES IN ARABIC LITERATURE (NE) [27717139] **3441**

STUDIES IN ARGUMENTATION IN PRAGMATICS AND DISCOURSE ANALYSIS (NE) [12227394] **1122**

STUDIES IN ART EDUCATION (US/0039-3541) [01766713] 1786, **365**

STUDIES IN ART HISTORY PRESENTED AT THE MIDDLE ATLANTIC SYMPOSIUM IN THE HISTORY OF ART (US/0146-5244) [02974469] **366**

STUDIES IN ASIAN ART AND ARCHAEOLOGY (NE) 283, **366**

STUDIES IN AUSTRALIAN BIBLIOGRAPHY (AT/0562-3618) [03059844] **425**

STUDIES IN AUTOMATION AND CONTROL (NE) [17388091] **1221**

STUDIES IN AVIAN BIOLOGY (US/0197-9922) [04837306] **474**

STUDIES IN BIBLIOGRAPHY AND BOOKLORE (US/0039-3568) [01766714] **5013**

STUDIES IN BIBLIOGRAPHY (CHARLOTTESVILLE, VA.) (US/0081-7600) [06540977] **425**

STUDIES IN BRITISH ART (US) [03080754] **366**

STUDIES IN BROWNING AND HIS CIRCLE (US/0095-4489) [02239808] 3472, **435**

STUDIES IN BUSINESS EXPECTATIONS AND PLANNING (US) [01604796] **714**

STUDIES IN CANADIAN LITERATURE (FREDERICTON, N.B.) (CN/0380-6995) [02443352] **3441**

STUDIES IN CELTIC HISTORY (UK) [08841926] **2711**

STUDIES IN CENTRAL AND EAST ASIAN RELIGIONS : JOURNAL OF THE SEMINAR FOR BUDDHIST STUDIES, COPENHAGEN & AARHUS (DK/0904-2431) [22212184] 5000, **5022**

STUDIES IN CENTRAL AND EASTERN EUROPEAN MUSIC (HU) [15741290] **4155**

STUDIES IN CHRISTIAN ETHICS (UK) [20134784] **5000**

STUDIES IN CHRISTIAN MISSION (NE/0924-9389) [I09249389] **5000**

STUDIES IN CHRISTIANITY AND JUDAISM (CN/0711-5903) [10985711] **5000**

STUDIES IN CHURCH HISTORY (LONDON, ENGLAND) (UK/0424-2084) [01425545] **5000**

STUDIES IN CHURCH HISTORY: SUBSIDIA (UK) [05427442] **5000**

STUDIES IN CLASSICAL GREEK (US/0897-7828) [17624516] **1080**

STUDIES IN COMMUNICATION (NORWOOD, N.J.) (US) [12098060] **1122**

STUDIES IN COMMUNICATIONS (US/0275-7982) [07207450] **1122**

STUDIES IN COMPARATIVE COMMUNISM (UK/0039-3592) [01645170] **4548**

STUDIES IN COMPARATIVE INTERNATIONAL DEVELOPMENT (US/0039-3606) [01606394] **5223**

STUDIES IN COMPARATIVE LITERATURE (US/0077-9504) [02549500] **3441**

STUDIES IN COMPARATIVE LITERATURE (LUBBOCK, TEX.) (US/0899-2193) [18037027] **3441**

STUDIES IN COMPARATIVE RELIGION *CEASED.* (UK/0039-3622) [01695943] **5000**

STUDIES IN COMPUTATIONAL MATHEMATICS (NE) [15607005] **3537**

STUDIES IN COMPUTER SCIENCE AND ARTIFICIAL INTELLIGENCE (NE/0924-3542) [17402351] **1217**

●STUDIES IN CONFLICT AND TERRORISM (US/1057-610X) [24081047] **5263**

STUDIES IN CONSERVATION (UK/0039-3630) [01184472] 283, **366**

STUDIES IN CONTEMPORARY HISTORY (US) [07719730] **2631**

STUDIES IN CONTEMPORARY JEWRY (US/0740-8625) [10024129] 2273, **5053**

STUDIES IN CONTEMPORARY SATIRE (US/0163-4143) [03940724] **3441**

STUDIES IN CONTINUING EDUCATION (AT/0158-037X) [I0158037X] **1802**

STUDIES IN CULTURAL RESOURCE MANAGEMENT (US/0272-3298) [05857941] **2396**

STUDIES IN CURRICULUM DEVELOPMENT (TZ) [02721068] **1905**

STUDIES IN CURRICULUM HISTORY (UK) [15011367] **1905**

STUDIES IN CYBERNETICS (US/0275-5807) [07189237] **1252**

STUDIES IN DANCE HISTORY (US/1043-7592) [19549613] **1314**

●STUDIES IN DEFENCE ECONOMICS (US/1062-046X) [25510852] **1523**

STUDIES IN DEMOGRAPHY AT THE AUSTRALIAN NATIONAL UNIVERSITY (AT) [20287532] **4560**

STUDIES IN DESCRIPTIVE LINGUISTICS (GW) [11614749] **3325**

STUDIES IN DESIGN EDUCATION CRAFT & TECHNOLOGY *See* DESIGN TECHNOLOGY TEACHING **372**

STUDIES IN DEVELOPMENT AND PLANNING (ROTTERDAM) (NE) [03061154] **2912**

STUDIES IN EAST ASIAN BUDDHISM / KURODA INSTITUTE (US) [11042096] **5022**

STUDIES IN EAST EUROPEAN THOUGHT (NE/0925-9392) **4362**

STUDIES IN ECONOMIC ANALYSIS (US/0198-8263) [04475145] 1640, **1595**

STUDIES IN ECONOMICS (MENLO PARK) (US/0148-6535) [03350848] **1523**

STUDIES IN EDUCATION NUMBER *See* EMPORIA STATE RESEARCH STUDIES, THE **1744**

STUDIES IN EDUCATION (WICHITA) (US/0148-5458) [03336051] **1786**

STUDIES IN EDUCATIONAL ADMINISTRATION (AT) [21137564] **1872**

STUDIES IN EIGHTEENTH-CENTURY CULTURE (US/0360-2370) [02244225] **2631**

STUDIES IN ENGLISH AND AMERICAN (HU/0134-1790) [03817545] **3325**

STUDIES IN ENGLISH AND AMERICAN LITERATURE, LINGUISTICS, AND CULTURE (US) [11760876] 2855, 3325, **3442**

STUDIES IN ENGLISH LITERATURE, 1500-1900 (US/0039-3657) [01766723] **3442**

STUDIES IN ENGLISH LITERATURE & LINGUISTICS (CH) [07033215] **3325**

STUDIES IN ENGLISH LITERATURE (TOKYO. 1960) (JA/0387-3439) [01766722] **3442**

STUDIES IN ENVIRONMENTAL SCIENCE (AMSTERDAM) (NE/0166-1116) [04309186] **2221**

STUDIES IN EUROPEAN SOCIETY (NE) [03622673] **2711**

STUDIES IN EUROPEAN THOUGHT (US/1043-5786) [19490909] **5223**

STUDIES IN FAMILY PLANNING (US/0039-3665) [01651215] 4560, **591**

STUDIES IN FORMATIVE SPIRITUALITY (US/0193-2748) [05156328] **5037**

●STUDIES IN FRENCH THEATRE (US/1062-0591) [25517005] **5369**

STUDIES IN GERARD MANLEY HOPKINS (US/1043-5751) [19489065] **3472**

STUDIES IN GERMAN LITERATURE, LINGUISTICS AND CULTURE (US) [09915777] **3442**

STUDIES IN GREEK AND ROMAN RELIGION (NE) [07954105] 5000, **1080**

STUDIES IN HAMITO-SEMITIC (PL) [03054054] 3442, **3326**

STUDIES IN HEALTH AND HUMAN SERVICES (US/0891-849X) [11634823] 5312, **4804**

STUDIES IN HIGH ENERGY PHYSICS (SZ/0270-4730) [06462203] **4423**

STUDIES IN HISTORY AND PHILOSOPHY OF SCIENCE (UK/0039-3681) [01343146] **5160**

STUDIES IN HISTORY AND PHILOSOPHY OF SCIENCE. PART B : MODERN PHYSICS (UK/1355-2198) **4423**

STUDIES IN HISTORY AND SOCIAL SCIENCES (DK/0078-3307) [02740828] 5223, **2631**

STUDIES IN HISTORY NEW DELHI (II/0257-6430) [I02576430] **2665**

STUDIES IN HISTORY OF MEDICINE AND SCIENCE (II) [17947817] 5160, **3643**

STUDIES IN HISTORY (SAHIBABAD) (US/0258-1698) [06382566] **2665**

STUDIES IN HUMAN ECOLOGY (PL/0324-8666) [01798254] **246**

STUDIES IN HUMAN RIGHTS (US/0146-3586) [02918903] **4513**

STUDIES IN HUMAN SOCIETY (NE/0920-6221) [18276409] **5263**

STUDIES IN HUME AND SCOTTISH PHILOSOPHY (US) [06987136] **4362**

STUDIES IN ICONOGRAPHY (US/0148-1029) [02924022] **5000**

STUDIES IN INCOME AND WEALTH (US/0069-8652) [01564735] **1523**

STUDIES IN INDIAN PLACE NAMES (II) [14275974] **2577**

STUDIES IN INDUSTRIAL ORGANIZATION (US/0924-4646) [08462242] **887**

STUDIES IN INORGANIC CHEMISTRY (NE/0169-3158) [06978445] **1038**

STUDIES IN INTERACTIONAL SOCIOLINGUISTICS (UK) [09321503] **3326**

STUDIES IN INTERNATIONAL AFFAIRS *CEASED.* (US/0081-802X) [01657319] **4536**

STUDIES IN INTERNATIONAL AND COMPARATIVE POLITICS (US) [05364817] **4497**

STUDIES IN INTERNATIONAL ECONOMICS & GEOGRAPHY (SW/1100-1283) [I11001283] 2577, **1640**

STUDIES IN INTERRELIGIOUS DIALOGUE (NE/0926-2326) [I09262326] **5000**

STUDIES IN IRISH HISTORY *CEASED.* (UK/0081-8100) [03076238] **2711**

STUDIES IN ITALIAN CULTURE. LITERATURE IN HISTORY (US/1043-5794) [19490977] 3442, **246**

STUDIES IN JEWISH/CHRISTIAN RELATIONS (UK) [17606315] **5000**

STUDIES IN JEWISH EDUCATION / THE HEBREW UNIVERSITY OF JERUSALEM, THE MELTON CENTRE FOR JEWISH EDUCATION IN THE DIASPORA (IS/0333-9661) [09809048] 5053, **1786**

STUDIES IN JUDAICA AND THE HOLOCAUST (US/0884-6952) [12412036] **5053**

STUDIES IN LANGUAGE (NE/0378-4177) [03404175] **3326**

STUDIES IN LANGUAGE AND LINGUISTICS *CEASED.* (US/0586-6928) [01766731] **3326**

STUDIES IN LANGUAGE AND LITERATURE (CH) [14913750] **3326**

STUDIES IN LANGUAGE COMPANION SERIES : SLCS (NE/0165-7763) [10339553] **3326**

STUDIES IN LANGUAGE LEARNING (US/0736-9867) [05853194] **3326**

STUDIES IN LANGUAGE ORIGINS (NE/0378-4177) [21354614] **3326**

STUDIES IN LATIN AMERICAN POPULAR CULTURE (US/0730-9139) [08094310] 5223, **331**

STUDIES IN LAW AND PRACTICE FOR HEALTH SERVICE MANAGEMENT (UK/0263-8630) [06968459] 4804, **3060**

STUDIES IN LAW, POLITICS AND SOCIETY (US/1059-4337) [22500877] **5263**

STUDIES IN LIBRARIANSHIP (US) [04677798] **3251**

STUDIES IN LINGUISTICS (DK/0078-3315) [01681359] **3326**

STUDIES IN LINGUISTICS AND PHILOSOPHY (NE/0924-4662) [I09244662] 4362, **3326**

STUDIES IN LITERATURE (ODENSE) (DK/0078-3323) [02683051] **3442**

STUDIES IN LOGIC AND THE FOUNDATIONS OF MATHEMATICS (NE/0049-237X) [02908760] **3537**

STUDIES IN MANAGEMENT SCIENCE AND SYSTEMS (NE/0921-3163) [06179014] **887**

STUDIES IN MANAGERIAL AND FINANCIAL ACCOUNTING (US) **751**

STUDIES IN MARXISM (MINNEAPOLIS, MINN.) (US) [05039137] 4497, **5223**

STUDIES IN MATHEMATICAL AND MANAGERIAL ECONOMICS (NE/0081-8194) [03877811] 3537, **1523**

STUDIES IN MATHEMATICS (NEW HAVEN) (US/0585-6892) [00936268] **3537**

STUDIES IN MEDICAL GEOGRAPHY (US/0585-6906) [02211632] **3643**

STUDIES IN MEDIEVAL AND REFORMATION THOUGHT (NE/0585-6914) [01766733] **5000**

STUDIES IN MEDIEVAL AND RENAISSANCE HISTORY (US/0081-8224) [01766734] **2711**

STUDIES IN MEDIEVAL AND RENAISSANCE TEACHING (US/1050-9739) [08691683] **2711**

STUDIES IN MEDIEVAL CULTURE (US/0085-6878) [02007708] **2711**

STUDIES IN MEDIEVAL ENGLISH LANGUAGE AND LITERATURE (JA/0913-1507) [I09131507] 3442, **3326**

STUDIES IN MEDIEVALISM (UK/0738-7164) [06010661] 3442, **2711**

STUDIES IN MEDITERRANEAN ARCHAEOLOGY (SW/0081-8232) [01696636] **283**

STUDIES IN MEDITERRANEAN ARCHAEOLOGY AND LITERATURE. POCKET-BOOK (SW/0283-8494) [16473859] 3442, **283**

STUDIES IN MICROBIOLOGY (BERKELEY, CALIF.) (US/0273-3536) [06455016] **570**

STUDIES IN MIDDLE EASTERN LITERATURES (US) [03061834] **3442**

STUDIES IN MODERN ART (US/1058-997X) [24456502] 309, 4377, **331**

STUDIES IN MODERN EUROPEAN HISTORY AND CULTURE (US/0098-275X) [02241105] **2711**

STUDIES IN MODERN GERMAN LITERATURE (US/0888-3904) [13561993] **3442**

STUDIES IN MODERN INDIAN HISTORY (II) [01790523] **2665**

STUDIES IN MODERN THERMODYNAMICS (NE/0166-6061) [05922059] 4423, **1058**

STUDIES IN MUSEOLOGY (II/0081-8259) [01774481] **4097**

STUDIES IN MUSIC *CEASED.* (AT/0081-8267) [01792275] **4155**

STUDIES IN MUSIC FROM THE UNIVERSITY OF WESTERN ONTARIO (CN/0703-3052) [02878265] **4155**

●STUDIES IN MUSLIM-JEWISH RELATIONS (US/1061-9380) [25489421] **5000**

STUDIES IN MYCOLOGY (NE/0166-0616) [02604492] **576**

STUDIES IN NATURAL SCIENCES (US/0097-4412) [01434578] **4172**

STUDIES IN NEAR EASTERN CIVILIZATION (US/0081-8291) [02549421] **2665**

STUDIES IN OLD GERMANIC LANGUAGES AND LITERATURES (US/0899-9872) [18283234] **3442**

STUDIES IN OPERATIONS RESEARCH (UK/0141-1004) [03802616] **1204**

STUDIES — Alphabetical Title Index

STUDIES IN ORGANIC CHEMISTRY (AMSTERDAM) (NE/0165-3253) [05670547] **1047**

STUDIES IN ORIENTAL CULTURE (US/0081-8321) [01715593] **2665**

● STUDIES IN PHENOMENOLOGICAL THEOLOGY (US/1056-4969) [23725572] **5001**

STUDIES IN PHILANTHROPY (WASHINGTON, D.C.) (US/0882-5750) [11880423] **4339**

STUDIES IN PHILIPPINE LINGUISTICS (PH/0116-0516) [03738561] **3326**

STUDIES IN PHILOLOGY (US/0039-3738) [01766738] **3442, 3326**

STUDIES IN PHILOSOPHY (UK/0081-8399) [03066177] **4362**

STUDIES IN PHILOSOPHY AND EDUCATION (US/0039-3746) [01604448] 1786, **4362**

STUDIES IN PHILOSOPHY AND THE HISTORY OF PHILOSOPHY (US/0585-6965) [01766739] **4362**

STUDIES IN PHYSICAL AND THEORETICAL CHEMISTRY (NE/0167-6881) [06435241] **1058**

STUDIES IN PHYSICAL ANTHROPOLOGY (PL/0324-8291) [02243695] **246**

STUDIES IN PLANT ECOLOGY (SW/0282-8677) [14636014] **528**

STUDIES IN PLANT SCIENCE (NE) [25577777] **528**

STUDIES IN POLITICAL ECONOMY (CN/0707-8552) [05360662] 1523, **4497**

STUDIES IN POLYMER SCIENCE (NE/0922-5579) [21326397] **993**

STUDIES IN POPULAR CULTURE (US/0888-5753) [04948624] **2855**

STUDIES IN PRE-COLUMBIAN ART AND ARCHAEOLOGY (US/0585-7023) [01126794] **283**

STUDIES IN PRODUCTION AND ENGINEERING ECONOMICS (NE) [10469817] **1628**

STUDIES IN PROOF THEORY (IT) [12826411] **3537**

STUDIES IN QUALITATIVE METHODOLOGY (US/1042-3192) [18492029] **5223**

STUDIES IN RADIATION EFFECTS : SERIES A, PHYSICAL AND CHEMICAL (US) [01377680] **4442**

STUDIES IN RELIGION (CN/0008-4298) [01773426] **5001**

STUDIES IN RELIGION AND SOCIETY SERIES (US) [01624348] **5001**

STUDIES IN RENAISSANCE ART HISTORY (US) [10945122] **366**

STUDIES IN RESOURCE MANAGEMENT (NZ/0113-0994) [I01130994] **2206**

STUDIES IN ROMANCE LANGUAGES (LEXINGTON, KY.) (US/0085-6894) [02850547] **3442**

STUDIES IN ROMANTIC AND MODERN LITERATURE (US/0743-7889) [10686492] **3442**

STUDIES IN ROMANTICISM (US/0039-3762) [01766743] **3442**

STUDIES IN SCIENCE EDUCATION (UK/0305-7267) [02256286] **5160**

STUDIES IN SCOTTISH LITERATURE (US/0039-3770) [01766744] **3354**

STUDIES IN SECOND LANGUAGE ACQUISITION (US/0272-2631) [04536243] **3326**

STUDIES IN SHORT FICTION (US/0039-3789) [01605955] **3354**

STUDIES IN SIKHISM AND COMPARATIVE RELIGION (II) [09438808] **5001**

STUDIES IN SLAVIC AND GENERAL LINGUISTICS (NE/0169-0124) [07432249] **3326**

STUDIES IN SLAVIC LITERATURE AND POETICS (NE/0169-0175) [11703397] **3442**

STUDIES IN SOCIAL LIFE (NE/0081-8518) [03077545] **5223**

STUDIES IN SOCIAL POLICY AND WELFARE (UK) [11077576] **5312**

STUDIES IN SOCIAL WELFARE POLICIES AND PROGRAMS (US/8755-5360) [11336840] **5312**

STUDIES IN SOCIETY (US) [05747425] **5223**

STUDIES IN SOCIOLOGY (GEORGE ALLEN & UNWIN) (UK) [12563210] **5263**

STUDIES IN SOUTH ASIAN CULTURE (NE/0169-9865) [01608156] **2665**

STUDIES IN SOUTH INDIAN COINS (II) [23954938] **2783**

● STUDIES IN SOUTHERN ITALIAN AND ITALIAN AMERICAN CULTURE (US/1058-5621) [24329627] 5263, **2273**

STUDIES IN SOVIET THOUGHT (NE/0039-3797) [01716356] **4362**

STUDIES IN SPECULATIVE FICTION (US/1040-5119) [12239338] **3442**

STUDIES IN SPELEOLOGY (UK/0585-718X) [01996300] **1399**

STUDIES IN SPIRITUALITY (NE) **5001**

STUDIES IN STATISTICAL MECHANICS (NE/0081-8542) [06746747] **4429**

STUDIES IN SURFACE SCIENCE AND CATALYSIS (NE/0167-2991) [07144419] **1058**

STUDIES IN SYMBOLIC INTERACTION (US/0163-2396) [04292849] **5263**

STUDIES IN TECHNOLOGY AND SOCIAL CHANGE SERIES (US/0896-1905) [16946199] **5160**

● STUDIES IN TEXTILE AND COSTUME HISTORY (NE/0924-7696) [I09247696] **5356**

STUDIES IN THE AGE OF CHAUCER (US/0190-2407) [04676149] 3354, **435**

STUDIES IN THE AMERICAN RENAISSANCE (US/0149-015X) [03547435] **3354**

STUDIES IN THE BIBLE AND EARLY CHRISTIANITY (US/0894-6361) [09006870] **5019**

● STUDIES IN THE DECORATIVE ARTS (US/1069-8825) [28177905] **375**

STUDIES IN THE DEVELOPMENT OF MODERN MATHEMATICS (US/1040-6441) [18481084] **3537**

STUDIES IN THE EDUCATION OF ADULTS (UK/0266-0830) [11557715] **1802**

STUDIES IN THE HISTORY AND ARCHAEOLOGY OF JORDAN (JO) [10205021] **283**

STUDIES IN THE HISTORY OF AMERICAN EDUCATION (US/0195-430X) [06741742] **1786**

STUDIES IN THE HISTORY OF ART (US/0091-7338) [02061037] **366**

STUDIES IN THE HISTORY OF ART (WILLIAMSTOWN, MASS.) (US/0886-0424) [05327212] **366**

STUDIES IN THE HISTORY OF CHRISTIAN THOUGHT (NE/0081-8607) [02008182] **5001**

STUDIES IN THE HISTORY OF DISCOVERIES (US) [01644272] **2631**

STUDIES IN THE HISTORY OF MATHEMATICS AND PHYSICAL SCIENCES (US/0172-570X) [05217531] **3537**

STUDIES IN THE HISTORY OF MODERN SCIENCE *CEASED.* (NE/0169-5533) [04469863] **5160**

STUDIES IN THE HISTORY OF MUSIC (US/0743-9822) [10647746] **4155**

STUDIES IN THE HISTORY OF RELIGIONS (NE/0169-8834) [01608272] **5001**

STUDIES IN THE HISTORY OF THE ANCIENT NEAR EAST (NE) [09994867] **2770**

STUDIES IN THE HUMANITIES (US) [05719820] **2855**

STUDIES IN THE LINGUISTIC SCIENCES (US/0049-2388) [03118402] **3326**

STUDIES IN THE LITERARY IMAGINATION (US/0039-3819) [01605898] **3442**

STUDIES IN THE MANAGEMENT SCIENCES (NE/0378-3766) [05671670] 887, **5160**

STUDIES IN THE NOVEL (US/0039-3827) [01766749] **3354**

STUDIES IN THE REFORMATION (US) [03942530] **5001**

STUDIES IN THE ROMANTIC AGE (US/0897-9243) [17665023] **3442**

STUDIES IN THE SCIENCES OF LANGUAGE SERIES (NE) [12526475] **3326**

STUDIES IN THE SOCIAL SCIENCES (CARROLLTON, GA.) (US/0081-8682) [01448729] **5223**

STUDIES IN THE SPIRITUALITY OF JESUITS (US) [01779274] **5037**

STUDIES IN THIRD WORLD SOCIETIES (US/1056-9189) [02690895] **5223**

STUDIES IN TRANSNATIONAL LEGAL POLICY (US/1057-0551) [02385524] **3136**

STUDIES IN TROPICAL OCEANOGRAPHY (US/0081-8720) [01391276] **1457**

STUDIES IN VERMONT GEOLOGY (US/0081-8747) [01696549] **1399**

STUDIES IN WEIRD FICTION (US/1050-1045) [14903686] **3442**

STUDIES IN WELFARE POLICY (US/0149-2586) [03391454] **5312**

STUDIES IN WEST PATRICIA ARCHAEOLOGY (CN/0706-1226) [07635140] **283**

STUDIES IN WESTERN AUSTRALIAN HISTORY (AT) [05290386] **2671**

STUDIES IN WOMEN AND RELIGION (US) [05957506] 5001, **5566**

STUDIES IN ZIONISM (IS/0334-1771) [07937788] **5053**

STUDIES OF BRAIN FUNCTION (GW/0172-5742) [03814051] **3846**

STUDIES OF BROADCASTING (JA) [01791128] **1139**

● STUDIES OF ECONOMIES IN TRANSFORMATION (US/1014-997X) [26489169] **1523**

STUDIES OF HIGH TEMPERATURE SUPERCONDUCTORS (US/1050-3943) [20071857] 4432, **2082**

STUDIES OF HIGHER EDUCATION AND RESEARCH (SW/0283-7692) [I02837692] **1849**

STUDIES OF ISRAELI SOCIETY (US/0734-4937) [08760662] **5263**

STUDIES OF LAW IN SOCIAL CHANGE AND DEVELOPMENT (SW/0348-1964) [03811586] **3060**

STUDIES OF THE LABOR MARKET. REPORT (US) [03081533] **1712**

STUDIES OF THE SOCIAL SECURITY SYSTEM (UK) [13275248] **5263**

STUDIES OF THE WARBURG INSTITUTE (UK/0083-7199) [01715617] **2855**

● STUDIES OF VACUUM ULTRAVIOLET AND X-RAY PROCESSES (US/1065-7665) [26725676] **4442**

● STUDIES OF WORLD LITERATURE IN ENGLISH (US/1043-8580) [19582959] **3442**

STUDIES ON ASIAN TOPICS (UK/0142-6028) [09246096] **2508**

STUDIES ON CERVANTES AND HIS TIMES (US/1054-1403) [22761995] **3442**

STUDIES ON CRIME AND CRIME PREVENTION (SW/1102-3937) **3177**

STUDIES ON DEFENCE ECONOMICS (US/1062-8916) [25793828] 4058, **1523**

STUDIES ON DEVELOPMENT PROBLEMS IN COUNTRIES OF WESTERN ASIA *CEASED.* (US) [02766261] 1585, **4689**

STUDIES ON EAST ASIA (US) [07120742] **2665**

STUDIES ON LUCETTE DESVIGNES AND THE TWENTIETH CENTURY (US) [25559391] **3442**

● STUDIES ON MANUFACTURING ENGINEERING AND PRODUCTION MANAGEMENT (UK/1062-3949) [25610609] **1997**

STUDIES ON NEOTROPICAL FAUNA AND ENVIRONMENT (NE/0165-0521) [02455995] **5598**

● STUDIES ON RUSSIAN ECONOMIC DEVELOPMENT (RU) [27658002] **1585**

STUDIES ON SOUTHEAST ASIA (US) **2665**

STUDIES ON SOVIET ECONOMIC DEVELOPMENT (US/1054-6588) [22937587] **1640**

STUDIES ON TEACHING AND RESEARCH IN PHILOSOPHY THROUGHOUT THE WORLD (FR) [14039240] **4362**

STUDIES ON THE DEVELOPING COUNTRIES (PL/0137-9860) [01785885] **1628**

STUDIES ON THE FAUNA OF CURACAO AND OTHER ISLANDS (NE/0166-5189) [01385671] **5598**

STUDIES ON THE MORPHOLOGY AND SYSTEMATICS OF SCALE INSECTS (US/0271-6348) [05908233] **5613**

STUDIES ON THE SHOAH (US/1054-3120) [22841361] **2711**

STUDIES ON THE TEXTS OF THE DESERT OF JUDAH (US/0585-7457) [01606439] **5053**

STUDIES ON THEMES AND MOTIFS IN LITERATURE (US/1056-3970) [23703735] **3442**

STUDIES ON TROPICAL ANDEAN ECOSYSTEMS (LH) [11364385] **2221**

STUDIES ON VOLTAIRE AND THE EIGHTEENTH CENTURY (UK/0435-2866) [01766759] 2631, **3442**

STUDIES ON WOMEN ABSTRACTS (UK/0262-5644) [09447685] 5566, **5572**

STUDIES OVER DE SOCIAAL-ECONOMISCHE GESCHIEDENIS VAN LIMBURG (NE/0562-4231) [03116235] **1585**

STUDIES VAN HET CENTRUM VOOR LOGICA, WETENSCHAPSFILOSOFIE EN FILOSOFIE VAN DE TAAL, HOGER INSTITUUT VOOR WIJSBEGEERTE, K.U. LEUVEN (BE) [14076386] **4362**

STUDII DE DREPT ROMANESC / ACADEMIA ROMANA, INSTITUTUL DE CERCETARI JURIDICE (RM/0039-4041) [23369220] **3060**

STUDII DE ECONOMIA APELOR (RM) [01787873] **5540**

STUDII DE GRAMATICA (RM/0515-1694) [05624934] **3326**

STUDII DE ISTORIE A FILOZOFIEI UNIVERSALE (BUCHAREST, ROMANIA : 1974) (RM) [10111048] **4362**

Alphabetical Title Index — SUBMISSION

STUDII DE LITERATURA ROMANA SI COMPARATA / UNIVERSITATEA DIN TIMISOARA, FACULTATEA DE FILOLOGIE-ISTORIE (RM) [08710468] **3442**

STUDII DE LITERATURA UNIVERSALA (RM) [05032648] **3442**

STUDII - INSTITUTUL DE CERCETARI SI PROIECTARI PENTRU GOSPODARIREA APELOR. EPURAREA APELOR (RM/1011-9485) [02244151] **2244**

STUDII SI ARTICOLE DE ISTORIE (RM/0585-749X) [02441247] **2711**

STUDII SI CERCETARI DE ANTROPOLOGIE (RM) [01792891] **246**

STUDII SI CERCETARI DE BIOCHIMIE (RM) [04091212] **493**

STUDII SI CERCETARI DE BIOLOGIE. SERIA BIOLOGIE ANIMALA (RM/0377-8150) [02714950] **474**

STUDII SI CERCETARI DE BIOLOGIE. SERIA BIOLOGIE VEGETALA (RM/0377-8169) [02714884] **474**

STUDII SI CERCETARI DE FIZICA (RM/0039-3940) [01799109] **4423**

STUDII SI CERCETARI DE GEOFIZICA / ACADEMIA ROMANA (RM/1220-5265) [27178799] **1411**

STUDII SI CERCETARI DE GEOLOGIE, GEOFIZICA, GEOGRAFIE. SERIA GEOLOGIE (RM/0567-638X) [01787570] **1399**

STUDII SI CERCETARI DE ISTORIA ARTEI. SERIA ARTA PLASTICA (RM/0039-3983) [08243277] **366**

STUDII SI CERCETARI DE ISTORIA ARTEI. SERIA TEATRU, MUZICA, CINEMATOGRAFIE (RM/0039-3991) [05719772] **388**

STUDII SI CERCETARI DE ISTORIE VECHE SI ARHEOLOGIE (RM) [01794659] **283**

STUDII SI CERCETARI DE MECANICA APLICATA (RM/0039-4017) [02240635] **4429**

STUDII SI CERCETARI DE NUMISMATICA (RM) [02242230] **2783**

STUDII SI CERCETARI LINGVISTICE (RM/0039-405X) [01995191] **3326**

STUDII SI CERCETARI MATEMATICE (RM/0039-4068) [02450889] **3537**

STUDII SI MATERIALE DE ISTORIE CONTEMPORANA (RM) [04940136] **2711**

STUDII SI MATERIALE DE ISTORIE MEDIE (RM/0567-6312) [01787573] **2712**

STUDII SI MATERIALE DE ISTORIE MODERNA (RM/0567-6320) [02240420] **2712**

STUDII TEOLOGICE (RM/1011-8845) [07023513] **5040**

STUDIJNE ZVESTI ARCHEOLOGICKEHO USTAVU SLOVENSKEJ AKADEMIE VIED (XO) [09450196] **283**

STUDIME FILOLOGJIKE (AA/0563-5780) [02268583] **3326**

STUDIME HISTORIKE (AA/0563-5799) [03648264] **2712**

●STUDIO (CN) [31235273] **382**

STUDIO CENTRO *See* CATALOGO STUDIO CENTRO **347**

STUDIO FILE (CN/1185-3476) [24690883] **366**

STUDIO MAGAZINE (FR/0982-8354) **2903**

STUDIO MAGAZINE, THE (CN/0715-6626) [09658151] **382**

STUDIO NORTH (CN/1183-8965) [25590007] **574**

STUDIO ONE (US/0364-457X) [02638475] **331**

STUDIO PHOTOGRAPHY (US/0746-0996) [07439104] **4377**

STUDIO POTTER (US/0091-6641) [01788043] **2594**

STUDIO SOUND (SHAWNEE MISSION, KAN.) (US/1041-7699) [18843349] **5319**

STUDIUM (IT) [01785296] **3354**

STUDIUM BIBLICUM FRANCISCANUM *See* LIBER ANNUUS - STUDIUM BIBLICUM FRANCISCANUM **5017**

STUDIUM (MADRID) (SP/0585-766X) [02007673] **3443**

STUDIUM OPTHALMOLOGICUM (SP) **3879**

STUDSVIK ENERGITEKNIK AB *See* ANNUAL REPORT - STUDSVIK ENERGITEKNIK AB **4446**

STUDSVIK ENERGITEKNIK AB. STUDSVIK ENERGITEKNIK AB *See* ANNUAL REPORT - STUDSVIK ENERGITEKNIK AB **4446**

STUDY ABROAD (FR/0081-895X) [02014766] **1849**

STUDY BINDER - CHARTERED ACCOUNTANTS STUDENTS' ASSOCIATION OF ONTARIO (CN/0707-7653) [04747083] **751**

STUDY - CITIZENS' RESEARCH FOUNDATION (US/0578-3461) [01554775] **5160**

STUDY GROUP ON EIGHTEENTH-CENTURY RUSSIA *See* NEWSLETTER - STUDY GROUP ON EIGHTEENTH-CENTURY RUSSIA **2700**

●STUDY IN FINLAND: ENGLISH LANGUAGE PROGRAMMES AND STUDIES IN FINNISH UNIVERSITIES / MINISTRY OF EDUCATION (FI/0788-5695) [24635040] **3326**

STUDY OF FEDERAL TAX LAW. CASES AND MATERIALS. TAXATION OF BUSINESS ENTERPRISES, THE (US) [27966958] **3103**

STUDY OF FEDERAL TAX LAW. TAXATION OF BUSINESS ENTERPRISES *See* STUDY OF FEDERAL TAX LAW. CASES AND MATERIALS. TAXATION OF BUSINESS ENTERPRISES, THE **3103**

STUDY OF FEDERAL TAX LAW. TAXATION OF BUSINESS ENTERPRISES, THE (US) [17418484] **3103**

STUDY OF FEDERAL TAX LAW. TAXATION OF ESTATES, GIFTS, AND TRUSTS *See* TAXATION OF ESTATES, GIFTS, AND TRUSTS : CASES AND MATERIALS **4755**

STUDY OF PROPERTY VALUATIONS FOR THE TAX YEAR ... (US) [23955121] **4751**

STUDY OF THE ST. LAWRENCE RIVER; REPORT FOR THE FISCAL YEAR (CN) [02240137] **1418**

STUDY PAPER - CGIAR (US/0257-3148) [12303528] **138**

STUDY PAPER SERIES / CANADIAN CERTIFIED GENERAL ACCOUNTANTS' RESEARCH FOUNDATION (CN/0826-2926) [11050383] **752**

STUDY REPORT / INTERNATIONAL COUNCIL FOR BIRD PRESERVATION (UK) [16222087] 2206, **5620**

STUDY - ROYAL COMMISSION ON MATTERS OF HEALTH AND SAFETY ARISING FROM THE USE OF ASBESTOS IN ONTARIO (CN/0714-0169) [09399176] **4804**

STUDY SERIES (VICTORIA UNIVERSITY OF WELLINGTON. INSTITUTE OF CRIMINOLOGY) (NZ) [20404260] **3177**

STUDY TIME : A QUARTERLY LETTER OF NEWS AND COMMENT FOR THE AAA LABOR ARBITRATOR (US) [10010126] **3154**

STUDY/ UNIVERSITY OF READING, DEPARTMENT OF AGRICULTURAL ECONOMICS & MANAGEMEMT (UK) [21485978] 1523, **138**

STUDYING ADULT LIFE AND WORK LESSONS (US/0191-4219) [04893328] **2286**

STUFFED (US/0890-4782) [14256560] 2585, **1069**

STUK-A (FI/0781-1705) [I07811705] **3643**

STUKKATEUR (GEISLINGEN), DER *See* STUCK, PUTZ, TROCKENBAU **3488**

STUMPAGE PRICE REPORT (EUGENE, OR.) (US/0889-339X) [12297255] **2404**

STUNDE (VIENNA, AUSTRIA) (AU) [20360822] **5778**

STUPA (DK) [06608997] **5022**

STUPENI (RU/0869-0022) [23825722] **1069**

STURGIS DAILY JOURNAL (MICHIGAN EDITION) *See* STURGIS JOURNAL (MICHIGAN EDITION) **5694**

STURGIS JOURNAL (MICHIGAN EDITION) (US/0747-3230) [10742147] **5694**

STURGIS NEWS, THE (US) [12352775] **5682**

STURM DIETER'S RESTAURANT GUIDE, OKLAHOMA CITY (US/1053-0185) [22435161] **5073**

STURZA'S MEDICAL INVESTMENT LETTER (US/1060-4251) [24992955] **916**

STUTTGART. ARCHIV DER STADT STUTTGART *See* VEROFFENTLICHUNGEN DES ARCHIVES DER STADT STUTTGART **2714**

STUTTGART DAILY LEADER, THE (US) [21982065] **5632**

STUTTGART. UNIVERSITAT. INSTITUT FUR PHOTOGRAMMETRIE *See* SCHRIFTENREIHE - INSTITUT FUER PHOTOGRAMMETRIE DER UNIVERSITAT STUTTGART **4376**

STUTTGARTER ARBEITEN ZUR GERMANISTIK (GW/0179-2482) [03098331] 3326, **3443**

STUTTGARTER BEITRAEGE ZUR NATURKUNDE. SERIE A, BIOLOGIE (GW/0341-0145) [02461291] **474**

STUTTGARTER BEITRAEGE ZUR NATURKUNDE. SERIE B. GEOLOGIE UND PALAONTOLOGIE (GW/0341-0153) [02604395] **1399**

STUTTGARTER BEITRAEGE ZUR NATURKUNDE. SERIES C. ALLGEMEINVERSTAENDLICHE AUFSAETZE (GW/0341-0161) [02578961] **4172**

STUTTGARTER BEITRAGE ZUR GESCHICHTE UND POLITIK (GW/0585-7945) [03111054] **4497**

STUTTGARTER BERICHTE ZUR SIEDLUNGSWASSERWIRTSCHAFT (GW/0585-7953) [11348124] **5540**

STUTTGARTER BIBELSTUDIEN (GW/0585-7961) [02008196] **5020**

STUTTGARTER TEXBEITRAGE (GW) [19096330] **3443**

STUTTHOF / MUZEUM STUTTHOF W SZTUTOWIE (PL) [07260128] **4097**

STVDIA ET ACTA ORIENTALIA (RM/0585-511X) [04995907] **2665**

STYGOLOGIA *CEASED.* (NE/0169-3662) [12336323] **1418**

STYLE AUTO (IT/0039-4254) [I00394254] **5426**

STYLE (FAYETTEVILLE) (US/0039-4238) [01154245] 3326, **3443**

STYLE (MINNEAPOLIS, MINN.) (US) [11264189] **2924**

STYLE (TORONTO) (CN/0039-4246) [02160214] **1087**

STYLES MAGAZINE (US/1044-8608) [19930040] **405**

STYLISTE, LE (GW) **405**

SU MIAO (CC) [09372660] **382**

SU URUNLERI ISTATISTIKLERI (TU) [20182240] **2318**

SUARA (MY) [01800042] **5001**

SUARA AISYIYAH (MY) [02241932] **5566**

SUB-CELLULAR BIOCHEMISTRY (UK/0306-0225) [01786669] **540**

SUB-COMMITTEE OF THE STANDING COMMITTEE ON EXTERNAL AFFAIRS AND NATIONAL DEFENCE ON ARMED FORCES RESERVES (CN/0713-7508) [08977661] **4058**

SUB-SAHARAN MONITOR (US/1018-1520) [23915653] **1523**

SUB-STANCE (US/0049-2426) [01005599] **3443**

SUBAQUA MARSEILLE (FR/0990-0845) [I09900845] 4879, **4924**

SUBCHAPTER S ELECTION FOR "SMALL BUSINESS CORPORATIONS.", THE (US) [04389714] **714**

SUBCONTRACTING (US/0192-673X) [05043134] **3060**

SUBCONTRACTOR, THE (US/0195-1459) [05306762] **629**

SUBH-I ADAB (II) [02245590] **3443**

SUBJECT CATALOG OF THE LIBRARY. SUPPLEMENT (US/0099-0922) [02243170] **3251**

SUBJECT COLLECTIONS (US/0000-0140) [01514402] **3260**

SUBJECT DIRECTORY OF SPECIAL LIBRARIES AND INFORMATION CENTERS (US/0732-927X) [03816794] **3251**

SUBJECT GUIDE TO AUSTRALIAN BOOKS IN PRINT (AT) [22197191] **425**

●SUBJECT GUIDE TO AUSTRALIAN CHILDREN'S BOOKS IN PRINT (AT) **425**

SUBJECT GUIDE TO BOOK REVIEWS (US/8756-002X) [11466129] **3251**

SUBJECT GUIDE TO BOOKS IN PRINT (US/0000-0159) [01641085] 4832, **3459**

SUBJECT GUIDE TO IAC DATABASES (US) [09078489] **1204**

SUBJECT GUIDE TO MICROFORMS IN PRINT (UK) [02852398] **425**

SUBJECT HEADINGS IN MICROFORM (US/0361-5243) [03454199] **3251**

SUBJECT INDEX OF EXTRAMURAL RESEARCH ADMINISTERED BY THE NATIONAL CANCER INSTITUTE (US/0278-2529) [05375602] **3824**

SUBJECT INDEX TO THE ILLINOIS REGISTER, WITH TABLES (US/0273-3692) [05470357] **3083**

SUBJECT MATTER INDEX TO PUBLIC AND PRIVATE STATUTES OF NEW BRUNSWICK (CN/0713-8954) [07127660] **3060**

SUBJECT TO CHANGE (CN/0706-7992) [05071907] **3937**

SUBJECTS FROM DECISIONS OF DEPARTMENTAL APPEALS BOARD / U.S. DEPARTMENT OF HEALTH AND HUMAN SERVICES *CEASED.* (US) [19797121] **5312**

●SUBMARINE FIBER OPTIC COMMUNICATIONS SYSTEMS (US/1070-096X) [28277454] **1164**

SUBMISSION SOURCEBOOK FOR CREATIVE CLASSROOM PUBLISHING, THE (US/1045-2273) [20043446] 4820, **1786**

SUBMISSION
Alphabetical Title Index

SUBMISSION TO THE . *See* ABARE RESEARCH REPORT **42**

SUBMISSION TO THE GOVERNMENT OF NEW BRUNSWICK / NATIONAL FARMERS UNION, REGION 1 (CN/0714-4644) [09050426] **138**

SUBMISSION TO THE ONTARIO COUNCIL ON UNIVERSITY AFFAIRS (CARLETON UNIVERSITY) (CN/0225-9850) [06166656] **1849**

SUBNUCLEAR SERIES, THE (US/8756-4475) [09993448] **4451**

SUBSCRIBER AND PRIMARY AUDIENCE STUDY DIGEST, THE (US/0197-9892) [06148674] **2924**

SUBSCRIBER NEWS : PRACTICAL INFORMATION FOR USERS OF FATE, FET, FIT, AND FGT (US/1054-5417) [22916181] **1204**

SUBSCRIBERS DIRECTORY - TELEFLORA CANADA (CN/0824-0442) [11777590] **2436**

SUBSCRIBERS' INTEREST LIST ... / ULSTER GENEALOGICAL & HISTORICAL GUILD (UK) [11526229] **2474**

SUBSEA-DATA-BASE (HOUSTON, TEX.) (US/1055-1123) [23089109] **1523**

SUBSEA ENGINEERING NEWS (UK/0266-2205) [I02662205] **2095**

SUBSIDIA AL CORPUS PHILOSOPHORUM MEDII AEVI (IT/0394-4360) [08680960] **4362**

SUBSIDIA HAGIOGRAPHICA (BE) [03099408] 2631, **5037**

SUBSIDIA MEDIAEVALIA (CN) [03110179] **1080**

SUBSIDIOS PARA A FIXACAO DOS PRECOS MINIMOS / MINISTERIO DA AGRICULTURA, COMISSAO DE FINANCIAMENTO DA PRODUCAO (BL) [05721054] **138**

SUBSTANCE (US) **2855**

SUBSTANCE ABUSE (US/0889-7077) [14095074] **1349**

SUBSTANCE ABUSE FUNDING NEWS (US/1067-0165) [27120443] **1349**

SUBSTANCE ABUSE IN SCHOOLS (US/0895-8874) [16851247] 1786, **1349**

SUBSTANCE ABUSE LETTER (US/1076-979X) **1349**

SUBSTANCE ABUSE REPORT (NEW YORK, N.Y.) (US/1040-4163) [11178571] **1349**

SUBSTANCES ET SPECIALITES PHARMACEUTIQUES CLASSEES COMME STUPEFIANTS EN VENTE DANS 16 PAYS EUROPEENS (FR/0256-4378) [05465101] **4330**

SUBSURFACE GEOLOGY SERIES (US/0731-311X) [04406926] **1399**

SUBTERRANEAN SOCIOLOGY NEWSLETTER / SUBTERRANEAN SOCIOLOGICAL ASSOCIATION, THE (US/0039-4394) [03471301] **5263**

SUBTROPICHESKIE KULTURY (RU/0207-9224) [02457815] **188**

SUBURBAN. COTE DES NEIGES EDITION (CN/0229-2998) [08655583] **5795**

SUBURBAN (COTE-SAINT-LUC ED.) (CN/0226-9686) [08663159] **5795**

SUBURBAN. DOLLARD DES ORMEAUX EDITION (CN/0229-298X) [08777546] **5795**

SUBURBAN GAZETTE (US) [12093825] **5739**

SUBURBAN (LAVAL EDITION) (CN/0229-3048) [08693581] **2547**

SUBURBAN METRO TORONTO CRISS-CROSS DIRECTORY *See* SUBURBAN TORONTO CRISS-CROSS DIRECTORY **5491**

SUBURBAN MIRROR, THE (CN/0704-7363) [03890000] **5795**

SUBURBAN. NEW BORDEAUX, CARTIERVILLE EDITION (CN/0229-3013) [08584558] **5795**

SUBURBAN NEWS (US/0193-6492) [05231768] **5711**

SUBURBAN NEWS (FLINT), THE (US/0194-2751) [05359302] **5694**

SUBURBAN NEWS (FRANKLIN LAKES, N.J. : 1981) (US/0746-052X) [09701117] **5711**

SUBURBAN NEWS (READING), THE (US/0194-276X) [05359298] **5690**

SUBURBAN NEWSPAPERS OF AMERICA, CHICAGO, ILL *See* MEMBERSHIP DIRECTORY - SUBURBAN NEWSPAPERS OF AMERICA **5661**

SUBURBAN. NOTRE DAME DE GRACE EDITION (CN/0229-2971) [08693614] **5795**

SUBURBAN. ST. LAURENT EDITION (CN/0229-303X) [08663166] **5795**

●SUBURBAN TORONTO CRISS-CROSS DIRECTORY (CN/1193-1175) [26714675] **5491**

SUBURBAN. TOWN OF MOUNT ROYAL EDITION (CN/0229-3021) [08693574] **5795**

SUBURBAN TRIBUNE, THE (US/1063-0392) [16816023] **5755**

SUBURBAN (WESTMOUNT EDITION) (CN/0229-3005) [08693577] **5795**

SUBVENTIONS (CN/0822-5044) [11193215] **2836**

SUBVENTIONS A LA RECHERCHE, BOURSES D'EXCELLENCE ET SUBVENTIONS POUR ETUDESET ANALYSES (CN/0837-9971) [18334958] **5223**

SUBVENTIONS A LA RECHERCHE ET BOURSES / GOUVERNEMENT DU QUEBEC, CONSEIL QUEBECOIS DE LA RECHERCHE SOCIALE (CN) [11897201] **916**

SUCCES (LAVAL) (CN/1181-8514) [23236403] **331**

SUCCESS (CHICAGO, ILL.) (US/0745-2489) [08597853] **714**

SUCCESS GUIDE : THE GUIDE TO BLACK RESOURCES : CINCINNATI/DAYTON (US) [24729602] **2273**

SUCCESS, PROMOTION & PROFITS (CN/0830-8802) [15997117] **937**

SUCCESSFUL ADVERTISING STRATEGIES (US/0882-3502) [11809094] **767**

SUCCESSFUL AND UNSUCCESSFUL JOB SEARCH EXPERIENCE, AUSTRALIA (AT) [16935849] 1712, **1540**

SUCCESSFUL BUSINESS (US/0161-2042) [03862548] **714**

SUCCESSFUL CALIFORNIA ACCOUNTANT, THE (US) **752**

SUCCESSFUL CASH FLOW STRATEGIES (US/0736-5926) [09168324] 1523, **813**

SUCCESSFUL DEALER, THE (US/0161-6080) [03979377] **5393**

SUCCESSFUL FARMING (US/0039-4432) [01639325] **138**

●SUCCESSFUL FUND RAISING (US/1070-9061) [28060501] **4339**

SUCCESSFUL HORTICULTURE (AT) **2432**

SUCCESSFUL HOTEL MARKETER *See* TOTAL QUALITY IN HOSPITALITY **2809**

SUCCESSFUL HOTEL MARKETER, THE (US/1040-600X) [18474628] **2809**

SUCCESSFUL MAGAZINE PUBLISHING (US/0892-6581) [15265351] **4820**

SUCCESSFUL MARKETING TO SENIOR CITIZENS *CEASED.* (US/8755-321X) [11270014] 5182, **937**

SUCCESSFUL MEETINGS : SM (US/0148-4052) [01796640] **714**

SUCCESSFUL RESTRUCTURINGS (US/1071-7625) [28725266] **3091**

●SUCCESSFUL RETIREMENT (US/1063-5742) [26068095] **5182**

SUCCESSFUL SALESWOMAN (US/0886-1498) [12867585] 5567, **714**

SUCCESSFUL SELLING & MANAGING (AT/1036-1693) [I10361693] **937**

SUCCESSGUIDE: THE GUIDE TO BLACK RESOURCES (US) [24901716] **714**

SUCCESSO (IT) [02450899] **813**

SUCCULENTA (NE/0039-4467) [02591785] **528**

SUCCULENTARUM BIBLIOGRAPHIA (US) [02450900] **425**

SUCEAVA (RM/1016-460X) [I1016460X] **2712**

SUCHASNIST (US/0585-8364) [01380623] **3443**

SUCHT (GW/0939-5911) [I09395911] **3643**

SUCOLIAN (STONY BROOK, N.Y.) *See* STATESMAN (STONY BROOK, N.Y.) **1848**

SUCRERIE FRANCAISE (FR/0371-4020) [04109469] **993**

SUCRERIE MAGHREBINE (MR/0851-2582) [I08512582] **188**

SUD; INFORMATION ECONOMIQUE : PROVENCE ALPES COTE D'AZUR (FR) [05182953] **1585**

SUD (MARSEILLE) (FR/0049-2450) [03426251] **3443**

SUD-QUEST (FR) [20447477] **5801**

SUDAN JOURNAL OF ANIMAL PRODUCTION, THE (SJ/1016-5711) [I10165711] 2358, **5522**

SUDAN JOURNAL OF DEVELOPMENT RESEARCH (SJ) [04479394] **1585**

SUDAN JOURNAL OF FOOD SCIENCE AND TECHNOLOGY (SJ/0254-0789) [01791430] **2358**

SUDAN JOURNAL OF VETERINARY SCIENCE AND ANIMAL HUSBANDRY, THE (SJ/0562-5084) [01766772] **5522**

SUDAN NOTES AND RECORDS (SJ/0375-2984) [01730412] 1360, **2855**

SUDAN SILVA (SJ/0562-5122) [03246077] **2396**

SUDAN UPDATE (UK) **2493**

SUDAN, WIRTSCHAFTSDATEN UND WIRTSCHAFTSDOKUMENTATION / BUNDESSTELLE FUR AUSSENHANDELSINFORMATION (GW) [09147339] **1585**

SUDAN. WIZARAT AL-MALIYAG WA-AL-IQTISAD *See* CENTRAL BUDGET PROPOSALS - DEMOCRATIC REPUBLIC OF SUDAN, MINISTRY OF FINANCE & NATIONAL ECONOMY **4717**

SUDAN. WIZARAT AL-MALIYAH WA-AL-IQTISAD *See* MASHRU AL-MIZANIYAH AL-AMMAH WA-MIZANIYAT AL-TANMIYAH LIL-AM AL-MALI ... **4736**

SUDANIC AFRICA (US/0803-0685) [23201252] **2643**

SUDASIATISCHE SPRACHWISSENSCHAFTLICHE STUDIEN / AKADEMIE DER WISSENSCHAFTEN DER DDR, ZENTRALINSTITUT FUR SPRACHWISSENSCHAFT (GW/0138-4694) [09268270] **3326**

SUDBURY (ONT. : REGIONAL MUNICIPALITY). CLERK'S DEPT *See* INFORMATION LISTING / REGIONAL CLERK'S DEPT **4656**

SUDBURY PUBLIC LIBRARY *See* DIRECTORY OF COMMUNITY SERVICES (SUDBURY) **5282**

SUDEBNO-MEDICINSKAJA EKSPERTIZA (RU/0039-4521) [07101259] **3742**

SUDENE INFORMA (BL) [02168715] **1585**

SUDESTASIE MAGAZINE *SUSPENDED.* (FR) [12645948] **2665**

SUDETENDEUTSCHES ARCHIV *See* MITTEILUNGEN DES SUDETENDEUTSCHEN ARCHIVS **2699**

SUDETENLAND (GW/0585-8682) [01696131] **2712**

SUDHANIDHI (II) [02441079] **3643**

SUDHOFFS ARCHIV (GW/0039-4564) [08492419] **3643**

SUDKURIER (GW) [12102018] **5802**

SUDO KYOYUK (KO) [07989714] **1786**

SUDOST EUROPA : [MONATSSCHRIFT DER ABTEILUNG GEGENWARTSFORSCHUNG DES SUDOST-INSTITUTS] (GW/0722-480X) [08529924] 4497, **5224**

SUDOST-FORSCHUNGEN (GW/0081-9077) [02268237] **2712**

SUDOSTASIEN AKTUELL (GW/0722-8821) [12259585] **2665**

SUDOSTDEUTSCHE HISTORISCHE KOMMISSION *See* BUCHREIHE DER SUDOSTDEUTSCHEN HISTORISCHEN KOMMISSION **2680**

SUDOSTDEUTSCHE VIERTELJAHRESBLATTER (GW/0562-5297) [02002156] **2273**

SUDOSTDEUTSCHES ARCHIV (GW/0081-9085) [01995231] **2712**

SUDOSTEUROPA (GW) [06483363] 1523, **4497**

SUDOSTEUROPA-BIBLIOGRAPHIE. ERGANZUNGSBAND / HERAUSGEGEBEN VOM SUDOST-INSTITUT, MUNCHEN (GW) [23263968] **425**

SUDOSTEUROPA-GESELLSCHAFT (GERMANY) *See* TATIGKEITSBERICHT **715**

SUDOSTEUROPA-MITTEILUNGEN (GW/0340-174X) [03100353] **2712**

SUDOSTEUROPA-STUDIEN (GW) [03125325] **2712**

SUDOSTEUROPE-BIBLIOGRAPHIE (GW/0081-9131) [01604490] **425**

SUDOSTROENIE (UN) [02322951] **5457**

SUEDDEUTSCHE ZEITUNG (GW/0174-4917) [01586812] **5802**

SUELO Y PLANTA *CEASED.* (SP/1130-796X) [24103758] **188**

SUELOS (AG) [01794905] **188**

SUFFOLK BANNER *See* BANNER (CUBA, ILL.), THE **207**

SUFFOLK BANNER, THE (US/0194-7230) [04978971] **222**

SUFFOLK COUNTY AGRICULTURAL NEWS (US/0039-467X) [02591775] **138**

SUFFOLK COUNTY AGRICULTURAL NEWS (US) [07234270] **138**

SUFFOLK COUNTY ARCHAEOLOGICAL ASSOCIATION *See* NEWSLETTER / SUFFOLK COUNTY ARCHAEOLOGICAL ASSOCIATION **276**

SUFFOLK COUNTY LIFE (US/8750-7307) [11698195] 2547, **5721**

SUFFOLK COUNTY NEWS, THE (US/1065-1470) [10968247] **5721**

Alphabetical Title Index

SUFFOLK INSTITUTE OF ARCHAEOLOGY AND HISTORY *See* PROCEEDINGS OF THE SUFFOLK INSTITUTE OF ARCHAEOLOGY AND HISTORY **279**

SUFFOLK NEWS-HERALD (US/8750-9598) [11964820] **5759**

SUFFOLK RECORDS SOCIETY (SERIES) (UK/0585-878X) [01766781] **2712**

SUFFOLK REVIEW (1983) (UK) [11103463] **2523**

SUFFOLK SOURCE, THE (US/8750-0922) [10969409] **5721**

SUFFOLK TIMES, THE (US) [19319771] **5721**

SUFFOLK TRANSNATIONAL LAW JOURNAL (US/0886-2648) [03582953] **3136**

●SUFFOLK TRANSNATIONAL LAW REVIEW (US/0886-2648) [27857679] **3136**

SUFFOLK UNIVERSITY, BOSTON. LAW SCHOOL. SUFFOLK LAW ALUMNI ASSOCIATION *See* SUFFOLK UNIVERSITY LAW SCHOOL ALUMNI DIRECTORY **1103**

SUFFOLK UNIVERSITY LAW REVIEW (US/0039-4696) [01766782] **3060**

SUFFOLK UNIVERSITY. LAW SCHOOL *See* SUFFOLK UNIVERSITY LAW REVIEW **3060**

SUFFOLK UNIVERSITY LAW SCHOOL ALUMNI DIRECTORY (US/0196-318X) [05780031] 3060, **1103**

SUFFRAGES (FR/0751-5774) [l07515774] **405**

SUFI (UK) [21543336] **5045**

SUFISM (SAN RAFAEL, CALIF.) (US/0898-3380) [17787204] **5001**

SUGADAIRA KOGEN JIKKEN SENTA KENKYU HOKOKU (JA/0913-6800) [18240761] **4172**

SUGAKU EXPOSITIONS (US/0898-9583) [17959438] **3537**

SUGAKU (TOKYO. 1947) (JA/0039-470X) [07675560] **3537**

SUGAKUSHI KENKYU (JA/0386-9555) [10832028] **3537**

SUGANDHA (II) [07935519] **3443**

SUGAR BEET JOURNAL (US) [05213368] **188**

SUGAR BULLETIN, THE (US/0039-4726) [01789292] **2358**

SUGAR CANE (1983) (UK/0265-7406) [10239946] 4248, **188**

SUGAR CLUB *See* SUGAR CLUB ANNUAL, THE **2358**

SUGAR CLUB ANNUAL, THE (US/0585-881X) [01605039] **2358**

SUGAR INDUSTRY ABSTRACTS / [CAB INTERNATIONAL, BUREAU OF HORTICULTURE AND PLANTATION CROPS IN ASSOCIATION WITH TATE & LYLE PLC] (UK/0957-5022) [21396128] 188, **157**

SUGAR INDUSTRY BUYERS GUIDE (UK) [10953198] **1628**

SUGAR INDUSTRY TECHNOLOGISTS, INC *See* PUBLICATION OF TECHNICAL PAPERS AND PROCEEDINGS OF THE ANNUAL MEETING OF SUGAR INDUSTRY TECHNOLOGISTS, INC **2354**

SUGAR JOURNAL (US/0039-4734) [02211683] **188**

SUGAR NEWS *SUSPENDED.* (PH/0049-2477) [02038667] **188**

SUGAR PRODUCER, THE (US/0199-8498) [06212614] **2359**

SUGAR SERIES (NE) [09547402] **2359**

SUGAR SITUATION, THE (CN/0380-8378) [02586032] **2359**

SUGAR TECHNOLOGISTS' ASSOCIATION OF INDIA *See* PROCEEDINGS OF THE ANNUAL CONVENTION OF THE SUGAR TECHNOLOGISTS' ASSOCIATION OF INDIA **121**

SUGAR WORLD (CN/0229-737X) [08292886] 1712, **2359**

SUGAR Y AZUCAR (US/0039-4742) [01996568] 2359, **138**

SUGAR Y AZUCAR. YEARBOOK (US/0081-9212) [02601709] **2359**

SUGARBEET GROWER, THE (US/0039-4750) [01766784] **188**

SUGARLAND *CEASED.* (PH/0039-4777) [05884231] **188**

SUGGESTED LIST OF MEDICAL BOOKS & JOURNALS (CN/0821-1582) [09774750] **3662**

SUGGESTED RULES FOR CARE OF POWER BOILERS *See* RECOMMENDED RULES FOR CARE OF POWER BOILERS **2127**

SUGGESTED STATE LEGISLATION (1965) (US/0070-1157) [04796764] 4689, **3060**

SUGIA, SPRACHE UND GESCHICHTE IN AFRIKA (GW/0170-5946) [06097326] 2644, **3326**

SUHDANNE (FI/0303-8130) [01794893] **1586**

SUHYOP TONGGYE WOLBO (KO) [11092618] **2314**

SUICIDE & LIFE-THREATENING BEHAVIOR (US/0363-0234) [02705480] **4619**

SUID-AFRIKAAN, DIE (SA/1011-7547) [21057848] 4497, **1523**

SUID-AFRIKAANSE AKADEMIE VIR WETENSKAP EN KUNS *See* NUUSBRIEF **5234**

SUID-AFRIKAANSE BOSBOUTYDSKRIF (SA/0038-2167) [05666564] **2396**

SUID-AFRIKAANSE GEOGRAAF *CEASED.* (SA) [01785652] **2577**

SUID-AFRIKAANSE TEATERSUSTER (US) **3870**

SUID-AFRIKAANSE TYDSKRIF VIR AFRIKATALE (SA) [08683835] 3443, **3326**

SUID-AFRIKAANSE TYDSKRIF VIR AFRIKATALE. BYBLAD (SA) [08887253] 3327, **3443**

SUID-AFRIKAANSE TYDSKRIF VIR APTEEKWESE (SA/0038-2558) [05458111] **4330**

SUID-AFRIKAANSE TYDSKRIF VIR ETNOLOGIE (SA/0379-8860) [10521290] **246**

SUID.-AFRIKAANSE TYDSKRIF VIR LANDBOUVOORLIGTING (SA/0301-603X) [I0301603X] **138**

SUID-AFRIKAANSE TYDSKRIF VIR LANDBOUWETENSKAP *See* AGROPLANTAE **56**

SUID-AFRIKAANSE TYDSKRIF VIR NATUURWETENSKAP EN TEGNOLOGIE (SA/0254-3486) [09824372] **5160**

SUID-AFRIKAANSE TYDSKRIF VIR SOSIOLOGIE, DIE (SA/0258-0144) [04278989] **5263**

SUIDO JITSUMU ROPPO / KOSEISHO KANKYO EISEIKYOKU SUIDO KANKYOBU SUIDO SEIBIKA HENSHU (JA) [10105913] **5540**

SUIDWES-AFRIKA REKENING : BEGROTING VAN INKOMSTE EN UITGAWES (SA) [06832596] **4751**

SUIKERINDUSTRIE, ZETMEEL- EN ZETMEELDERIVATENINDUSTRIE (NE/0920-7554) [15734470] **1628**

S JIKO (JA) [08478975] **4183**

SUIRI KAGAKU. WATER SCIENCE (JA/0039-4858) [02573216] 1418, **5540**

SUIRI KOENKAI KOENSHU (JA) [02242956] **2095**

SUIRO (NIHON SUIRO KYOKAI) (JA) [08794666] **1457**

SUIROBU GIHO (JA) [10643564] **4183**

SUISAN DAIGAKKO KENKYU HOKOKU (JA/0370-9361) [07722770] **2314**

SUISAN FUKAJO KENKYU HOKOKU (JA/0286-6536) [10288038] **2314**

SUISAN KAIYO KENKYU (JA/0916-1562) [22737525] **2314**

SUISAN KOGAKU KENKYUJO HOKOKU (JA/0388-9718) [08286352] **2314**

SUISAN ZOSHOKU (JA) [04745675] **474**

SUISHITSU ODAKU KENKYU (TOKYO. 1978) (JA/0387-2025) [10153334] **2244**

SUIVRE, A (FR/0180-3840) [I01803840] **3354**

SUIYOKAI SHI (JA/0371-408X) [09726094] 4021, **2151**

SUIZO (JA/0913-0071) [I09130071] **3801**

SUJI DE MIRU JIDOSHA (JA) [02547176] **5445**

SUJI DE MIRU KOGAI (JA) [02561668] **2244**

SUJI DE MIRU MINTETSU (JA) [02639159] **5437**

SUJUN (KHARTOUM, SUDAN) (SJ) [08400989] **2500**

●SUKCES W AMERYCE (CN/1192-523X) [27898405] **4924**

SUKOVS-NUUS (SA) [01788329] **388**

SUKURIN (SEOUL, KOREA : 1984) (KO) [10727655] **4078**

SULFUR LETTERS (UK/0278-6117) [07856812] **1038**

SULFUR (PASADENA, CALIF.) (US/0730-305X) [07587450] **3443**

SULFUR REPORTS (SZ/0196-1772) [05761730] **1038**

SULFUR (UNITED STATES. BUREAU OF MINES) (US/0191-4383) [03321974] **1445**

SULIAO (BEIJING) (CC/1001-9456) [13521137] **4460**

SULLIVAN COUNTY DEMOCRAT (US) [18932481] **4497**

SULLIVAN DAILY TIMES, THE (US) [14814225] **5667**

SULLIVAN REVIEW (DUSHORE, PA. : 1958) (US) [14762058] **5739**

SULLIVAN'S LAW DIRECTORY FOR THE STATE OF ILLINOIS (US) [04578903] **3060**

SULLIVAN'S RETAIL PERFORMANCE MONITOR (US/1050-1789) [21423447] **958**

SULPHUR (UK/0039-4890) [09498394] **1030**

SULPHUR IN AGRICULTURE (US/0160-0680) [03458928] **188**

SULPHUR SPRINGS NEWS-TELEGRAM (US/0745-6425) [09319601] **5755**

SULUH HUKUM YUSTITIA (IO) [03882964] **3060**

SULUH PEPABRI (IO) [07684712] **2508**

SULZER TECHNICAL REVIEW (1985) (SZ) [13443014] **2129**

SUMARSKI LIST (CI/0373-1332) [03827034] **138**

SUMATERA UTARA, INDONESIA. DINAS KEHUTANAN *See* LAPORAN TAHUNAN - DINAS KEHUTANAN PROPINSI SUMATERA UTARA **2386**

SUMMARIES

SUMATERA UTARA (INDONESIA). DINAS SOSIAL *See* LAPORAN TAHUNAN / DINAS SOSIAL DAERAH TINGKAT I SUMATERA UTARA **5294**

SUMATERA UTARA, INDONESIA. KANTOR SENSUS DAN STATISTIK *See* STATISTIK PENDIDIKAN DILUAR LINGKUNGAN DEPARTEMEN P & K DI-SUMATERA UTARA **1798**

SUMATRA PLANTERS ASSOCIATION. RESEARCH INSTITUTE *See* DAFTAR PERBANDINGAN KONTROLE PENGOLAHAN KELAPA SAWIT **4254**

SUMATRA PLANTERS ASSOCIATION. RESEARCH INSTITUTE *See* RENCANA KEGIATAN DAN RENCANA ANGGARAN PENDAPATAN DAN BELANJA **125**

SUMER (BAGHDAD) (IQ/0081-9271) [01203076] **283**

SUMITOMO BANK ECONOMIC SURVEY (JA/0287-7406) [09144353] **1586**

SUMITOMO BYOIN IGAKU ZASSHI (JA/0285-8177) [10396558] **3643**

SUMITOMO ELECTRIC TECHNICAL REVIEW (JA) [12068002] **2082**

SUMITOMO JUKIKAI GIHO (JA/0387-1304) [10411426] **5160**

SUMITOMO KEIKINZOKU GIHO (JA/0039-4963) [10411502] **4021**

SUMITOMO KINZOKU (JA/0371-411X) [10412162] **4021**

SUMITOMO QUARTERLY (JA) [07450999] **1586**

SUMITOMO SANGYO EISEI (JA/0081-928X) [10411865] **2870**

SUMITOMO SEARCH, THE (JA/0585-9131) [02239521] **4021**

SUMITOMO TOKUSHU KINZOKU GIHO (JA) [10412204] **4021**

SUMLEN (SW/0346-8119) [05744782] **4155**

SUMMA (AG/0325-4615) [06574083] **309**

●SUMMA+ (AG/0327-9022) [30136167] **309**

SUMMA ARTIS, HISTORIA GENERAL DEL ARTE (SP) [04338924] **366**

SUMMA (BUENOS AIRES, ARGENTINA) *See* SUMMA+ **309**

SUMMA MUSICAE MEDII AEVI (GW/0585-9158) [01766792] **4155**

SUMMA PHYTOPATHOLOGICA (BL/0100-5405) [02309323] **2432**

SUMMARIES OF CONCLUSIONS AND RECOMMENDATIONS ON DEPARTMENT OF DEFENSE OPERATIONS : REPORT TO THE HOUSE AND SENATE COMMITTEES ON APPROPRIATIONS BY THE COMPTROLLER GENERAL OF THE UNITED STATES (US) [05143021] **4058**

SUMMARIES OF CONCLUSIONS AND RECOMMENDATIONS ON THE OPERATIONS OF CIVIL DEPARTMENTS AND AGENCIES (US/0193-2926) [05143070] **4689**

SUMMARIES OF DECISIONS / SOCIAL ASSISTANCE REVIEW BOARD (CN/1185-877X) [25352045] **5312**

SUMMARIES OF FOREIGN GOVERNMENT ENVIRONMENTAL REPORTS (US/0094-3142) [01794117] **2182**

SUMMARIES OF FY ... RESEARCH IN THE CHEMICAL SCIENCES (US/0195-7341) [05578342] **993**

SUMMARIES OF IMPORTANT LABOUR JUDGEMENTS (II) [02607701] **3154**

SUMMARIES OF LABORATORY NOTES (UK) [20316142] **5445**

SUMMARIES OF PHYSICAL RESEARCH IN THE GEOSCIENCES (US) [06777965] **1399**

SUMMARIES — Alphabetical Title Index

SUMMARIES OF PROJECTS COMPLETED (US/0161-4169) [03734795] **5160**

SUMMARIES OF PUBLICATIONS / DIPARTIMENTO DI INGEGNERIA STRUTTURALE, POLITECNICO DI MILANO (IT) [08136611] **2032**

SUMMARIES OF REPORTS OF THE ELECTROTECHNICAL LABORATORY (JA) [02623100] **2082**

SUMMARIES OF RESEARCH IN NUCLEAR PHYSICS (US) [04629583] **4451**

SUMMARIOS *CEASED.* (AG/0325-6448) [04765104] **309**

SUMMARY - ALBERTA SECURITIES COMMISSION (CN/0319-3667) [02244965] 916, **3060**

SUMMARY & ANALYSIS : CALIFORNIA FIRE INCIDENT REPORTING SYSTEM (US) [07036645] **2293**

SUMMARY AND ANALYSIS OF INTERNATIONAL TRAVEL TO THE U.S (US/0095-3482) [06325816] **5491**

SUMMARY AND OBJECTIVES (IS) [11412535] **5457**

SUMMARY - ANNUAL MEETING - NATIONAL ASSOCIATION OF STATE PURCHASING OFFICIALS (US) [04552952] **952**

SUMMARY DATA FROM THE CONSUMER PRICE INDEX NEWS RELEASE (US) [23232737] **1523**

SUMMARY INFORMATION ON MASTER OF SOCIAL WORK PROGRAMS (US/0145-7314) [02783273] **5312**

SUMMARY INSPECTION REPORT OF OFFICIAL SAMPLES ON SEED, FEED, FERTILIZER & AG-LIME (US/0193-8592) [05250753] **203**

SUMMARY JUDGEMENT (US/0738-1972) [09305814] **3060**

SUMMARY OF ACCIDENT DATA (RICHMOND) *CEASED.* (US/0146-7468) [03018798] **5445**

SUMMARY OF ACCIDENTS/INCIDENTS REPORTED BY ALL LINE-HAUL AND SWITCHING AND TERMINAL RAILROAD COMPANIES / DEPARTMENT OF TRANSPORTATION, FEDERAL RAILROAD ADMINISTRATION (US) [03457178] **5437**

SUMMARY OF ACCIDENTS INVESTIGATED BY THE FEDERAL RAILROAD ADMINISTRATION (US/0092-2781) [05314050] **5437**

SUMMARY OF ACCIDENTS INVOLVING THE DRINKING DRIVER (US/0146-1192) [02872081] **5445**

SUMMARY OF ACCOUNTS AND DEPOSITS IN ALL MUTUAL SAVINGS BANKS (US/0149-8282) [03131552] **813**

SUMMARY OF ACTION (US) [06782140] **3060**

SUMMARY OF ACTION TAKEN BY THE HOUSE OF DELEGATES OF THE AMERICAN BAR ASSOCIATION (US) [04060748] **3060**

SUMMARY OF ACTIVITIES - COMMITTEE ON ARMED SERVICES, UNITED STATES SENATE (US/0148-0693) [03122714] **3183**

SUMMARY OF ACTIVITIES / COMMONWEALTH OF AUSTRALIA, DEPARTMENT OF NATIONAL DEVELOPMENT (AT) [16939786] **4689**

SUMMARY OF ACTIVITIES - MENTAL HEALTH LAW PROJECT (US/0363-2687) [02255795] **3060**

SUMMARY OF ACTIVITIES OF THE WESTERN AUSTRALIAN MEAT INDUSTRY AUTHORITY FOR THE YEAR ENDED ... (AT) [09256547] **222**

SUMMARY OF ACTIVITIES, OFFICE OF RESEARCH (US) [05054632] **5393**

SUMMARY OF ACTUAL RECEIPTS AND EXPENDITURES FOR ... AND ANNUAL SCHOOL BUDGET FOR ... / JEFFERSON COUNTY BOARD OF EDUCATION (US) [10662509] **1872**

SUMMARY OF AIR QUALITY IN CALIFORNIA'S SOUTH COAST AIR BASIN (US) [11838626] **2244**

SUMMARY OF ALL REPORTED MOTOR VEHICLE TRAFFIC ACCIDENTS AND ACTIVITIES OF ALL FIELD PERSONNEL AND DRIVER SERVICES DIVISION IN THE STATE OF MISSISSIPPI (US) [04839793] **5445**

SUMMARY OF AWARDS, ... PROGRAM OF UNIVERSITY RESEARCH (US) [04024774] **5393**

SUMMARY OF BROADCASTS. PART 2, EASTERN EUROPE (UK) [06128295] **1139**

SUMMARY OF BUDGET REQUESTS - STATE BOARD OF REGENTS (US/0361-5014) [02246994] **1872**

SUMMARY OF CALIFORNIA LAW (US) [11612571] **3061**

SUMMARY OF CANADIAN TRANSIT STATISTICS (CN) [29894552] **5393**

SUMMARY OF CORRECTIONS : CHARTS (US) [09100181] **2577**

SUMMARY OF COTTON FIBER AND PROCESSING TEST RESULTS *CEASED.* (US/0565-2030) [02242069] **5356**

SUMMARY OF CRIMINAL COURT PROCEEDINGS, WESTERN AUSTRALIA (AT/1037-9177) **3109**

SUMMARY OF CROPS AUSTRALIA (AT/1033-8772) [20798416] 138, **157**

SUMMARY OF CROPS, WESTERN AUSTRALIA (AT/1037-5678) [10375678] 188, **157**

SUMMARY OF CURRENT INCOME TAX STATISTICS (NR/0331-0434) [01798225] 4751, **4701**

SUMMARY OF DECISIONS / WASHINGTON STATE PERSONNEL APPEALS BOARD (US) [10292399] **4705**

● SUMMARY OF ECONOMIC AND LOAD FORECASTS (CN/0825-6667) [13470478] **4762**

SUMMARY OF EDUCATION AND LIBRARY BOARDS' ACCOUNTS TOGETHER WITH THE REPORT OF THE COMPTROLLER AND AUDITOR GENERAL (IE) [03547465] **1872**

SUMMARY OF ELECTION LAWS ENACTED BY THE LEGISLATIVE ASSEMBLY - OREGON (US/0095-2796) [01783173] **3061**

SUMMARY OF ENACTMENTS (US/0098-759X) [02246628] **3061**

SUMMARY OF ENACTMENTS - TEXAS. LEGISLATURE. LEGISLATIVE COUNCIL (US) [06246073] **3061**

SUMMARY OF FEDERAL HUNTING REGULATIONS, ATLANTIC FLYWAY (US) [03114315] **4879**

SUMMARY OF FEDERAL HUNTING REGULATIONS, CENTRAL FLYWAY (US) [03114683] **4879**

SUMMARY OF FEDERAL HUNTING REGULATIONS, MISSISSIPPI FLYWAY (US) [03114770] **4879**

SUMMARY OF FEDERAL HUNTING REGULATIONS, PACIFIC FLYWAY (US) [03114734] **4879**

SUMMARY OF FINANCIAL OPERATIONS OF LICENSEES FOR THE YEAR ENDED ... (US) [09515874] **199**

SUMMARY OF FISCAL YEAR ... APPROPRIATIONS (US) [06372527] **4751**

SUMMARY OF GENERAL LEGISLATION (TALLAHASSEE) (US/0090-1520) [01784751] **4689**

SUMMARY OF GENERAL STATISTICS (US/0098-2725) [02240524] **4811**

SUMMARY OF GRANTS AND CONTRACTS ACTIVE ON ... (US/0094-7741) [03755459] **4804**

SUMMARY OF GROUND WATER DATA FOR TENNESSEE (US/0093-0539) [01791344] **5540**

SUMMARY OF HEALTH AND PERSONAL SOCIAL SERVICES ACCOUNTS (UK) [02775997] 5312, **4804**

SUMMARY OF HIV/AIDS LAWS FROM THE ... STATE LEGISLATIVE SESSIONS, A (US) [23808024] **3061**

SUMMARY OF HYDROLOGIC DATA COLLECTED IN DADE COUNTY, FLORIDA (US/0363-1958) [02460441] **1418**

SUMMARY OF INFORMATION RELATING TO THE SUBMISSION TO THE COMPETENT AUTHORITIES OF CONVENTIONS AND RECOMMENDATIONS ADOPTED BY THE INTERNATIONAL LABOR CONFERENCE (ARTICLE 19 OF THE CONSTITUTION) (US/0538-8341) [02211959] **1712**

SUMMARY OF INSIDER TRANSACTIONS (US) [10119246] **813**

SUMMARY OF INSTITUTIONAL REQUESTS FOR OPERATING FUNDS (US/0363-6682) [02556568] **1849**

SUMMARY OF INVESTIGATIONS BY THE SASKATCHEWAN GEOLOGICAL SURVEY (CN/0228-5657) [03021234] **1399**

SUMMARY OF INVESTIGATIONS RELATING TO READING (US/0197-5129) [06058201] 1905, **3327**

SUMMARY OF IOWA COUNTY ENGINEERS ANNUAL HIGHWAY REPORTS (US) [06664473] **5445**

SUMMARY OF KENTUCKY EDUCATION (US/0362-6679) [02338732] 1786, **1798**

SUMMARY OF LABOR ARBITRATION AWARDS (US/0039-5005) [01479309] **1712**

SUMMARY OF LEGISLATION (US) [06239442] **3061**

SUMMARY OF LEGISLATION APPROVED BY THE ... SESSION OF THE ... IOWA GENERAL ASSEMBLY MEETING IN THE YEAR ... (US) [04818293] **4689**

SUMMARY OF LEGISLATIVE ACTIVITIES - UNITED STATES. CONGRESS. HOUSE. COMMITTEE ON PUBLIC WORKS AND TRANSPORTATION (US/0740-9427) [09736483] 5393, **3061**

SUMMARY OF MEDICAL PROGRAMS (US) [07472005] **3643**

SUMMARY OF ... MOTOR VEHICLE LICENSE ISSUE AS COMPARED TO ... / COMMONWEALTH OF VIRGINIA, DIVISION OF MOTOR VEHICLES (US) [06260651] **5426**

SUMMARY OF MOTOR VEHICLE TRAFFIC ACCIDENTS. ALEXANDRIA (US/0741-448X) [10153564] **5445**

SUMMARY OF MOTOR VEHICLE TRAFFIC ACCIDENTS. BATON ROUGE (US/0741-4471) [10153513] **5445**

SUMMARY OF MOTOR VEHICLE TRAFFIC ACCIDENTS. GRETNA (US/0741-4455) [10153396] **5445**

SUMMARY OF MOTOR VEHICLE TRAFFIC ACCIDENTS INVESTIGATED / REPORTED BY STATE POLICE (US/0741-4366) [10152574] **5445**

SUMMARY OF MOTOR VEHICLE TRAFFIC ACCIDENTS. KENNER (US/0741-4439) [10153225] **5445**

SUMMARY OF MOTOR VEHICLE TRAFFIC ACCIDENTS. MONROE (US/0741-4404) [10153000] **5445**

SUMMARY OF MOTOR VEHICLE TRAFFIC ACCIDENTS. NEW IBERIA (US/0741-4390) [10152942] **5445**

SUMMARY OF MOTOR VEHICLE TRAFFIC ACCIDENTS. NEW ORLEANS (US/0741-4374) [10152774] **5445**

SUMMARY OF MOTOR VEHICLE TRAFFIC ACCIDENTS. STATEWIDE (US/0741-4358) [10152749] **5445**

SUMMARY OF MOTOR VEHICLE TRAFFIC ACCIDENTS. URBAN (US/0741-4331) [10152667] **5445**

SUMMARY OF NATURAL GAS STATISTICS / OHIO DEPARTMENT OF ENERGY (US) [08361000] 4280, **4284**

SUMMARY OF NEW MOTOR VEHICLES REGISTERED (PP) [01795752] **5426**

SUMMARY OF O-D TRIPS (ALL TRAINS) (US) [04144663] **5437**

SUMMARY OF OCCUPATIONAL INJURIES AND ILLNESSES (US) [22339418] **2870**

SUMMARY OF OIL FIELDS WELL CHANGES (US/0276-8453) [07432260] **4280**

SUMMARY OF ONGOING RESEARCH AND TECHNICAL ASSISTANCE PROJECTS IN AGRICULTURE (US) [02684617] **2912**

SUMMARY OF OPEN GAO RECOMMENDATIONS FOR LEGISLATIVE ACTION (US/0148-2599) [02869211] **752**

SUMMARY OF OPERATIONS / MINERAL RESOURCES DIVISION (CN/0825-6896) [13054479] **2151**

SUMMARY OF ORDERS AND APPROVALS - ENERGY RESOURCES CONSERVATION BOARD (CN/0709-3713) [05532432] **1958**

SUMMARY OF PRESCRIBED UNIT COST AND HOURLY RATE FOR RETURN ON INVESTMENT AND TAX ALLOWANCE (US) [04527048] **916**

SUMMARY OF PROCEEDINGS / AMERICAN NURSES' ASSOCIATION ... CONVENTION (US/0744-2580) [07917347] **3870**

SUMMARY OF PROCEEDINGS. ANNUAL CONFERENCE / AMERICAN THEOLOGICAL LIBRARY ASSOCIATION (US/0066-0868) [01480910] **3251**

SUMMARY OF PROCEEDINGS. ANNUAL CONVENTION - B.C. FEDERATION OF LABOUR (CLC) (CN/0229-365X) [07966416] **1712**

SUMMARY OF PROCEEDINGS : ANNUAL MEETING OF THE SOUTHERN GOVERNORS' ASSOCIATION (US/0278-4815) [07429985] **4689**

SUMMARY OF PROCEEDINGS. MANAGEMENT INSTITUTE (US/0276-5616) [06050505] **3143**

SUMMARY OF PROCEEDINGS OF THE ... ASSEMBLY / INTERNATIONAL RUBBER STUDY GROUP (UK) [08965658] **5078**

SUMMARY OF PROGRESS - NATIONAL COOPERATIVE HIGHWAY RESEARCH PROGRAM (US/0547-5562) [02246599] **5445**

SUMMARY OF PROJECTIONS OF ELECTRIC AND GAS GROSS LOAD REQUIREMENTS *See* SUMMARY OF ECONOMIC AND LOAD FORECASTS **4762**

SUMMARY OF PUBLIC ACTS (HARTFORD) (US/0093-9226) [01784607] **3061**

SUMMARY OF ... PUBLIC ACTS OF INTEREST TO TENNESSEE OFFICIALS *See* TENNESSEE PUBLIC ACTS : SUMMARIES OF INTEREST TO MUNICIPAL OFFICIALS **3063**

SUMMARY OF PUBLIC SECTOR LABOR RELATIONS POLICIES (US/0163-139X) [03689318] **3154**

SUMMARY OF RATE SCHEDULES OF NATURAL GAS PIPELINE COMPANIES AS FILED WITH FEDERAL POWER COMMISSION *See* SUMMARY OF RATE SCHEDULES OF NATURAL GAS PIPELINE COMPANIES AS FILED WITH THE FEDERAL ENERGY REGULATORY COMMISSION AND THE NATIONAL ENERGY BOARD OF CANADA **4284**

SUMMARY OF RATE SCHEDULES OF NATURAL GAS PIPELINE COMPANIES AS FILED WITH THE FEDERAL ENERGY REGULATORY COMMISSION AND THE NATIONAL ENERGY BOARD OF CANADA (US/0190-2997) [04633489] **4284**

SUMMARY OF REAL ESTATE ASSESSMENT/SALES RATIO STUDY / COMPILED BY STATE OF IOWA, DEPARTMENT OF REVENUE (US) [06412111] **4847**

SUMMARY OF RECEIPTS, DISBURSEMENTS, AND BALANCES (US) [01329362] **4804**

SUMMARY OF ... REDUCTIONS IN LOCAL GOVERNMENT FISCAL ASSISTANCE (US) [11779385] **4689**

SUMMARY OF REFERENCE DATA ON SCHOOL ADMINISTRATIVE UNITS / NEW HAMPSHIRE STATE DEPARTMENT OF EDUCATION, DIVISION OF ADMINISTRATION (US) [08855270] **1872**

SUMMARY OF REPORTS (ARTICLES 19, 22 AND 35 OF THE CONSTITUTION) (SZ/0074-6681) [08648416] **1712**

SUMMARY OF RESEARCH AWARDS (US/0743-6998) [10633941] **714**

SUMMARY OF RESEARCH WITHIN THE UNIT AND OF RESEARCH SUPPORTED BY GRANT (UK) [03159820] **3177**

●SUMMARY OF REVENUE PROPOSALS IN THE PRESIDENT'S ... BUDGET / PREPARED BY THE STAFF OF THE JOINT COMMITTEE ON TAXATION (US) [25619112] **4751**

SUMMARY OF REVENUE PROVISIONS IN THE PRESIDENT'S FISCAL YEAR ... BUDGET PROPOSAL *See* SUMMARY OF REVENUE PROPOSALS IN THE PRESIDENT'S ... BUDGET / PREPARED BY THE STAFF OF THE JOINT COMMITTEE ON TAXATION **4751**

SUMMARY OF SAFETY MANAGEMENT AUDITS (US/0748-2949) [10908150] **4804**

SUMMARY OF SCHOOL REFERENDA IN DELAWARE (US/0361-4549) [02246466] **1873**

SUMMARY OF SELECTED LEGISLATION RELATED TO THE HANDICAPPED, A (US/0148-625X) [03346244] **3061**

SUMMARY OF STATE LAWS AND REGULATIONS RELATING TO DISTILLED SPIRITS (US/0081-931X) [01003182] 2371, **3061**

SUMMARY OF STATE LIQUOR CONTROL LAWS AND REGULATIONS RELATING TO DISTILLED SPIRITS AS OF . *See* SUMMARY OF STATE LAWS AND REGULATIONS RELATING TO DISTILLED SPIRITS **3061**

SUMMARY OF STATE REGULATIONS AND LAWS AFFECTING GENERAL CONTRACTORS (US) [27837549] 629, **4751**

SUMMARY OF STATE REGULATIONS AND TAXES AFFECTING GENERAL CONTRACTORS *See* SUMMARY OF STATE REGULATIONS AND LAWS AFFECTING GENERAL CONTRACTORS **4751**

SUMMARY OF STATISTICS - AUSTRALIAN BUREAU OF STATISTICS. VICTORIAN OFFICE (AT/1033-3665) [I10333665] 4689, **4701**

SUMMARY OF STATISTICS. BUREAU OF STATISTICS, KONEDOBU (PP/0377-5844) [01791072] **5344**

SUMMARY OF SUPPLEMENTAL TYPE CERTIFICATES (US/0364-6416) [02576201] **37**

SUMMARY OF TAX EXEMPTION DEVICES / DIVISION OF RESEARCH AND ANALYSIS, DEPARTMENT OF REVENUE (US) [07095662] **4751**

SUMMARY OF TAXES IN ARKANSAS, A (US/0272-9318) [02144108] **4751**

SUMMARY OF TECHNICAL REPORT - FOREST ENGINEERING RESEARCH INSTITUTE OF CANADA (CN/0701-8347) [10840889] **2396**

SUMMARY OF THE ACTIVITY REPORT - CENTRE DE RECHERCHES MINERALES SAINTE-FOY (CN/0848-5771) [I08485771] **4394**

SUMMARY OF THE ANNUAL FINANCIAL REPORT, STATE OF TEXAS (US) [04674392] **4751**

SUMMARY OF THE DECISIONS TAKEN AT THE MEETINGS AND TEXTS OF THE RESOLUTIONS APPROVED (US/0250-6319) [05879585] **3136**

SUMMARY OF THE HUNTING REGULATIONS (TORONTO) (CN/0226-482X) [06965702] **4879**

SUMMARY OF THE SOUTH DAKOTA CRIMINAL JUSTICE PLAN FOR ACTION, A (US/0148-4273) [03301636] **3177**

SUMMARY OF TOTAL REVENUES COLLECTED BY THE SALES AND USE TAX SECTION FOR THE MONTH OF FISCAL YEAR ... / ARIZONA DEPARTMENT OF REVENUE (US) [11286876] **4751**

SUMMARY OF TRAFFIC ACCIDENTS INVOLVING TEEN-AGE DRIVERS *See* TEEN-AGE DRIVERS (OLYMPIA) **5445**

SUMMARY OF U.S. EXPORT CONTROL REGULATIONS, A (US) [08321674] **852**

SUMMARY OF UMTA'S TRANSIT ASSISTANCE PROGRAM (US/0277-5859) [07582973] **5393**

SUMMARY OF WATER QUALITY (US) [06805331] **5540**

SUMMARY OF WEATHER MODIFICATION ACTIVITIES REPORTED IN ... (US/0275-6137) [07121031] **1435**

SUMMARY OF WORLD BROADCASTS (UK) [10807079] **1139**

SUMMARY OF WORLD BROADCASTS. PART 1, THE USSR (UK) [02258594] **1139**

●SUMMARY OF WORLD BROADCASTS. PART 2, CENTRAL EUROPE, THE BALKANS. WEEKLY ECONOMIC REPORT : SWB (UK) [29541778] 1523, **1139**

SUMMARY OF WORLD BROADCASTS, PART 2, EASTERN EUROPE. WEEKLY ECONOMIC REPORT (UK) [17653909] 1523, **1139**

●SUMMARY OF WORLD BROADCASTS. PART 3, ASIA, PACIFIC / BBC MONITORING (UK) [28685680] **1139**

SUMMARY OF WORLD BROADCASTS. PART 4, MIDDLE EAST, AFRICA, AND LATIN AMERICA *See* SUMMARY OF WORLD BROADCASTS. PART 5, AFRICA, LATIN AMERICA AND THE CARIBBEAN : SWB **1140**

SUMMARY OF WORLD BROADCASTS. PART 4, MIDDLE EAST, AFRICA, AND LATIN AMERICA *See* SUMMARY OF WORLD BROADCASTS. PART 4, MIDDLE EAST : SWB **1140**

SUMMARY OF WORLD BROADCASTS. PART 4, MIDDLE EAST, AFRICA AND LATIN AMERICA. WEEKLY ECONOMIC REPORT *See* SUMMARY OF WORLD BROADCASTS. PART 4, THE MIDDLE EAST. WEEKLY ECONOMIC REPORT : SWB **1140**

SUMMARY OF WORLD BROADCASTS. PART 4, MIDDLE EAST, AFRICA AND LATIN AMERICA. WEEKLY ECONOMIC REPORT *See* SUMMARY OF WORLD BROADCASTS. PART 5, AFRICA, LATIN AMERICA AND THE CARIBBEAN. WEEKLY ECONOMIC REPORT : SWB **1140**

SUMMARY OF WORLD BROADCASTS. PART 4, THE MIDDLE EAST, AFRICA, AND LATIN AMERICA (UK) [11368732] **1139**

SUMMARY OF WORLD BROADCASTS. PART 4, THE MIDDLE EAST, AFRICA, AND LATIN AMERICA. WEEKLY ECONOMIC REPORT (UK) [11368765] **1140**

●SUMMARY OF WORLD BROADCASTS. PART 4, THE MIDDLE EAST : SWB (UK) [29235904] **1140**

SUMMARY OF WORLD BROADCASTS. PART 4, THE MIDDLE EAST. WEEKLY ECONOMIC REPORT : SWB (UK) [29529012] **1140**

●SUMMARY OF WORLD BROADCASTS. PART 5, AFRICA, LATIN AMERICA AND THE CARIBBEAN : SWB (UK) [29235884] **1140**

●SUMMARY OF WORLD BROADCASTS. PART 5, AFRICA, LATIN AMERICA AND THE CARIBBEAN. WEEKLY ECONOMIC REPORT : SWB (UK) [29528907] **1140**

SUMMARY OF WORLD BROADCASTS. PART 5, THE FAR EAST *See* SUMMARY OF WORLD BROADCASTS **1139**

SUMMARY OF WORLD BROADCASTS. PART III, FAR EAST *See* SUMMARY OF WORLD BROADCASTS. PART 3, ASIA, PACIFIC / BBC MONITORING **1139**

SUMMARY PROCEEDINGS OF THE ANNUAL CONFERENCE - FEDERATION OF CANADIAN MUNICIPALITIES (CN/0710-5134) [08559405] **4689**

SUMMARY PROCEEDINGS OF THE ANNUAL MEETING OF THE BOARD OF GOVERNORS. INTERNATIONAL MONETARY FUND (US/0074-7025) [04397587] **1523**

SUMMARY PROGRESS REPORT / U.S. GRAIN MARKETING RESEARCH LABORATORY (US/0277-2191) [07267670] **188**

SUMMARY REPORT, ASSETS AND LIABILITIES OF MEMBER BANKS (US) [03320295] **813**

SUMMARY REPORT ... CANADIAN REGIONAL CONFERENCE. COMMONWEALTH PARLIAMENTARY ASSOCIATION (CN/0830-9825) [13541647] **4497**

SUMMARY REPORT, DATA FORM THE NATIONAL DRUG ABUSE TREATMENT UTILIZATION SURVEY (NDATUS) (US/0161-5041) [03906428] **1349**

SUMMARY REPORT - FEDERAL WIND ENERGY PROGRAM (US) [03289359] **1958**

SUMMARY REPORT FOR THE PROFESSIONAL DEVELOPMENT AND PROGRAM IMPROVEMENT CENTERS PROGRAM (US/0277-0148) [07465279] **1873**

SUMMARY REPORT, INDIVIDUAL INCOME TAX RETURNS FILED (US) [05250416] **4751**

SUMMARY REPORT OF CAMPAIGN CONTRIBUTIONS AND EXPENDITURES, PRIMARY ELECTION (US/0148-9399) [03398682] **4497**

SUMMARY REPORT OF FOREIGN TRADE STATISTICS / COMMONWEALTH OF THE BAHAMAS (BF) [27332499] **852**

SUMMARY REPORT ON REAL PROPERTY OWNED BY THE UNITED STATES THROUGHOUT THE WORLD AS OF ... (US/0145-4595) [02739273] **4847**

SUMMARY REPORT - SOLAR THERMAL ENERGY CONVERSION PROGRAM (US) [03133032] **1958**

SUMMARY REPORTER (US/1061-0146) [24707091] **3061**

SUMMARY STATEMENTS OF NIEHS-SUPPORTED RESEARCH PROJECTS (US) [04761720] **4804**

SUMMER EMPLOYMENT DIRECTORY OF THE UNITED STATES (US) [01639797] **1712**

SUMMER IN CANADA (CN/0319-5082) [02443135] 4855, **1712**

SUMMER INSTITUTE OF LINGUISTICS *See* WORKPAPERS OF THE SUMMER INSTITUTE OF LINGUISTICS, UNIVERSITY OF NORTH DAKOTA **3333**

SUMMER INSTITUTE OF LINGUISTICS AND THE UNIVERSITY OF TEXAS AT ARLINGTON PUBLICATIONS IN LINGUISTICS (US/1040-0850) [20350407] **3327**

SUMMER JOBS, BRITAIN (UK/0143-3490) [11774362] **4209**

●SUMMER JOBS (PRINCETON, N.J.) (US/1064-6701) [26368207] **4209**

SUMMER LEGAL EMPLOYMENT GUIDE (US/0738-1921) [09120409] **3061**

SUMMER MINING INDUSTRY SURVEY (US/0731-3497) [08147021] **2152**

SUMMER NEWS SERVICE - CANADIAN UNIVERSITY PRESS (CN/0381-8411) [02606756] **1849**

SUMMER REVIEW SERVICE - CANADIAN UNIVERSITY PRESS (CN/0381-8403) [02606767] **1849**

SUMMER SEMINARS FOR COLLEGE TEACHERS. GUIDELINES AND APPLICATION FORM FOR DIRECTORS / NATIONAL ENDOWMENT FOR THE HUMANITIES, DIVISION OF FELLOWSHIPS AND SEMINARS (US) [09259385] **1905**

SUMMER SEMINARS FOR COLLEGE TEACHERS / NATIONAL ENDOWMENT FOR THE HUMANITIES (US) [09257880] **1905**

SUMMER SEMINARS FOR SCHOOL TEACHERS. GUIDELINES AND APPLICATION FORM FOR DIRECTORS (US) [17538242] **1786**

SUMMER STIPENDS. GUIDELINES & APPLICATION FORM (US) [10201721] **1905**

SUMMER THEATRE DIRECTORY (DORSET, VT.) (US/0884-5840) [10845354] **5369**

SUMMER THEATRES (US) [02470432] **5369**

SUMMER VISITATION AND OUTDOOR RECREATION STATISTICAL REPORT (CN/0846-7145) [21417343] **4879**

SUMMERFOLK MUSIC & CRAFTS FESTIVAL (CN/1182-6630) [23231266] 375, **4155**

SUMMERVILLE NEWS, THE (US) [20970318] **5655**

SUMMIT (BIG BEAR LAKE) (US/0039-5056) [03377954] **4879**

SUMMIT COUNTY BEE (COALVILLE, UTAH : 1964) (US) [12429116] **5757**

SUMMIT OXFORD *CEASED.* (UK/0958-6709) [I09586709] **3537**

SUMNER GAZETTE (SUMNER, IOWA) (US) [16067076] **5673**

SUMPTION TAXATION CAPITAL GAINS (UK) **813**

SUMTER COUNTY JOURNAL (US) [19260189] **5628**

SUMTER DAILY ITEM *See* ITEM, THE **5742**

SUMTER JOURNAL, THE (US/0747-0304) [10498003] **5651**

SUMULA TRIBUTARIA TRABALHISTA (SEMIMONTHLY) (BL) [08419197] 4751, **3154**

SUN (1993) (US/1072-8619) [28059845] **5721**

SUN-ADVOCATE, THE (US) [13039549] **5757**

SUN AT WORK IN EUROPE (UK/0269-1159) [17422430] **1958**

SUN (BALTIMORE, MD. : 1837) (US) [07909813] **5687**

SUN BELT BUILDINGS JOURNAL (US/0745-354X) [09086144] **4847**

SUN BELT FLOOR COVERING (US/0895-934X) [16859035] **2907**

SUN (BOLINBROOK EDITION) (US/0885-6389) [12680590] **5662**

SUN (BREMERTON, WASH.), THE (US/1050-3692) [17294017] **5762**

SUN (CHAPEL HILL, N.C.) (US/0744-9666) [06844086] **3443**

SUN CHRONICLE (ATTLEBORO, MASS.) (US/1053-7805) [16645175] **5690**

SUN CITIES GENEALOGIST, THE (US) [24674734] **2474**

SUN/COAST ARCHITECT/BUILDER (US/0744-8872) [08634864] 309, **629**

● SUN DANCER REVIEW (US/1062-6387) [25688711] 3354, **3443**

SUN-DIAMOND GROWER (US/0899-8809) [07695536] **2432**

SUN DOG (US/0735-7133) [08692007] **3443**

SUN-FLYER (US) [11628606] **5656**

SUN (FREDERICTON) (CN/0705-4033) [03960184] **5795**

SUN (GRAND CENTRE) (CN/0710-0019) [08192576] **5795**

SUN HERALD (BILOXI, MISS.) (US) [12788034] **5702**

SUN HERALD (CHARLOTTE ED.) (US/1055-7806) [23302696] **5651**

● SUN HERALD (ENGLEWOOD ED.) (US/1068-7939) [27804448] **5651**

SUN (HUMMELSTOWN, PA.) (US) [13030221] **5739**

SUN (LAGRANGE, ILL.), THE (US/8750-2003) [11110899] **5662**

SUN (LEAMINGTON) (CN/0380-8912) [02603975] **5795**

SUN (LONDON, ENGLAND) (UK) [16310628] **5813**

SUN (LOWELL, MASS. : 1946) (US) [13848471] **5690**

SUN MAGAZINE (US/0889-3497) [05282275] **4280**

SUN (MOUNT VERNON, IOWA : 1979) (US) [12364906] **5673**

SUN-NEWS (LOWDEN, IOWA) (US) [12206163] **5673**

SUN OBSERVER (U.S. ED.), THE (US/1058-5400) [20649973] **1204**

SUN-REPORTER, THE (US/0890-0930) [02268253] **5687**

SUN-SENTINEL (FORT LAUDERDALE, FLA.) (US/0744-8139) [08582345] **5651**

SUN, THE (YU) [25556878] **5567**

SUN-TIMES (HEBER SPRINGS, ARK.) (US/1050-5105) [21504909] **5632**

SUN TRACKS (US/0300-788X) [01335401] **3443**

SUN TRIBUNE (US) **5734**

SUNA (SJ) [02176756] **2644**

SUNAGAWA SHIRITSU BYOIN IGAKU ZASSHI (JA/0289-5102) [I02895102] **3643**

SUNATUINNARNIK QAUJISAQTULIRINIRMUT TUSAGAKSAIT (CN/0848-6840) [23242820] **5161**

SUNBELT FOODSERVICE (US/1069-3475) [25500963] **2359**

SUNBONNET CRAFTS **CEASED.** (US/1070-0560) [28221105] **5186**

SUNBOUND (US) [04122837] **5491**

SUNBURST (ROSEVILLE) (US/0274-9181) [06716170] **5224**

SUNBURY NEWS, THE (US) [18143465] **5730**

SUNCEN HYAN DAIHAG NONMUNJIB (KO/0253-3111) [08819500] **1095**

SUNCOAST THEATRE GRAPEVINE, THE (US/0887-3119) [13207429] **5369**

SUNDANCE (US/0049-2507) [01784781] **2547**

SUNDAY (ATLANTA, GA.) (US/0039-5161) [01607283] **5001**

SUNDAY BUSINESS POST, THE (IE/0791-2617) [I07912617] **5803**

SUNDAY BY SUNDAY (US/1057-3259) [24017628] **5001**

SUNDAY DISPATCH (PITTSON, PA.) (US) [15648046] **5740**

SUNDAY EXPONENT-TELEGRAM (CLARKSBURG, W.VA.) (US) [12877132] **5765**

SUNDAY EXPRESS (LONDON, ENGLAND) (UK) [18361126] **5813**

SUNDAY GAZETTE (CN/0711-2149) [08649576] **5795**

SUNDAY GAZETTE-MAIL (US) [09589515] **5765**

SUNDAY HOMILY HELPS (US) **5037**

SUNDAY INDEPENDENT (IE/0039-5218) **5803**

SUNDAY INDEPENDENT, THE (US/0744-883X) [08623167] **5682**

SUNDAY INDEPENDENT (WILKES-BARRE, PA.) (US) [15713964] **5740**

SUNDAY JOURNAL AND STAR (US) [10519294] **5707**

SUNDAY NEWS (LANCASTER, PA.) (US) [11379967] **5740**

SUNDAY NEWS SUN (US/0746-2182) [09864577] **5651**

SUNDAY REPUBLICAN (SPRINGFIELD, MASS.) (US/0191-281X) [04828215] **5690**

SUNDAY SCHOOL COUNSELOR (US/0039-5285) [03798860] **5068**

SUNDAY SCHOOL LEADER (LARGER CHURCH ED.), THE (US/1056-201X) [23541311] **5068**

SUNDAY SCHOOL LEADER. SMALLER CHURCH ED, THE (US/1056-2001) [23540788] **5068**

SUNDAY SCHOOL YOUTH TEACHER (US/0736-9174) [09264232] **5001**

SUNDAY SERMONS (US/0745-3558) [09086873] **5001**

SUNDAY STAR-NEWS, THE (US/0163-4038) [04376847] **5724**

SUNDAY SUN-JOURNAL (US/0747-1432) [10577235] **5685**

SUNDAY TELEGRAM, THE (US) [13173970] **5685**

SUNDAY TELEGRAPH (LONDON, ENGLAND) (UK) [12283056] **5813**

SUNDAY TIMES (SI) **5810**

SUNDAY TIMES (LONDON, ENGLAND : 1931) (UK) [16310772] **5813**

SUNDAY TIMES MAGAZINE, LONDON (UK) [05918601] **2523**

SUNDAY TIMES, MALAYSIA **See** NEW SUNDAY TIMES, MALAYSIA **5806**

SUNDAY TIMES (MICROFICHE) (SA) [03987602] **5810**

SUNDAY TIMES (SCRANTON, PA. : 1966) (US) [14562850] **5740**

SUNDAY TIMES, THE (UK) [06120768] **5813**

SUNDAY TRIBUNE (NR/0331-2569) [I03312569] **5807**

SUNDAY WORLD-HERALD (OMAHA, NEB. : 1937) (US) [09642169] **5707**

SUNDAY WYOMING TRIBUNE-EAGLE (US/8750-0809) [10745618] **5773**

SUNDEW GARDENS REPORTS **CEASED.** (US/1052-2247) [22218340] **2432**

SUNDHEDSTILSTANDEN I KBENHAVN ; STADSLGENS ARSBERETNING (DK) [05376304] **4804**

SUNDIAL (US) [23928354] **1997**

SUNDIAL (TORONTO) (CN/0827-312X) [11825455] **5001**

SUNEXPERT (BROOKLINE, MASS.) (US/1053-9239) [20842313] **1204**

SUNFLOWER COUNTY NEWS (US) [15079157] **5702**

SUNFLOWER (FARGO), THE (US/0192-8988) [04121293] **188**

SUNFLOWER NEWSLETTER, THE **CEASED.** (NE) [06319041] **2432**

SUNFLOWER WORLD (US/0273-7671) [06907666] **2432**

SUNG LIAO CHIN YUAN **See** JOURNAL OF SUNG-YUAN STUDIES **2505**

SUNGGONG NONMUNJIP (KO) [10741993] **4548**

SUNHWANGI (KO) [07762236] **3710**

SUNKIST GROWERS, INC. INFORMATION SYSTEMS DEPT **See** CITRUS FRUIT INDUSTRY STATISTICAL BULLETIN **2362**

SUNNYVALE VALLEY JOURNAL (US/0192-0278) [05094158] **5640**

SUNRISE (ALTADENA, CALIF.) (US/0562-6048) [03117123] 5001, **4362**

SUNRISE EXPRESS (CN/0821-3615) [09864041] **1070**

SUNSET (MENLO PARK, CALIF.) (US/0039-5404) [01766806] **2547**

SUNSHINE ARTISTS, U.S.A (US/0199-9370) [04895497] **375**

SUNSHINE CIRCLE TOUR MAGAZINE : SUNSHINE COAST AND VANCOUVER ISLAND, THE (CN/1186-7914) [24623442] **5491**

SUNSTONE (US/0363-1370) [02401028] **5001**

SUNSTONE REVIEW (SALT LAKE CITY, UTAH) (US/0731-6518) [08176109] **5068**

SUNTESTER BULLETIN **CEASED.** (US) [06562261] **2082**

SUNWORLD (AT/0149-1938) [02550065] **1958**

SUNWORLD. (PETERBOROUGH, N.H.) (US/1054-5980) [22922146] **1272**

SUNY GENESCO COMPASS (US/0745-4147) [09139613] 1849, **1095**

SUNYATA (VICTORIA) (CN/0384-8248) [03300897] **3443**

SUO (FI/0039-5471) [07211623] 2396, **138**

SUOMALAINEN TIEDEAKATEMIA **See** ANNALES ACADEMIAE SCIENTIARUM FENNICAE. SERIES A. VI: PHYSICA **4396**

SUOMALAINEN TIEDEAKATEMIA **See** ANNALES ACADEMIAE SCIENTIARUM FENNICAE. SERIES A. III : GEOLOGICA-GEOGRAPHICA **5083**

SUOMALAINEN TIEDEAKATEMIA **See** ANNALES ACADEMIAE SCIENTIARUM FENNICAE. SERIES B **254**

SUOMALAIS-UGRILAINEN SEURA **See** SUOMALAIS-UGRILAISEN SEURAN AIKAKAUSKIRJA **3443**

SUOMALAIS-UGRILAISEN SEURAN AIKAKAUSKIRJA (FI) [01641118] **3443**

SUOMALAIS-UGRILAISEN SEURAN TOIMITUKSIA / MEMOIRES DE LA SOCIETE FINNO-OUGRIENNE (FI) [01588779] **3327**

SUOMALAISEN KASVATUSALAN KIRJALLISUUDEN LUETTELO VUODELTA ... AIKAKAUSLEHTIARTIKKELIT (FI) [19176391] **425**

SUOMALAISEN KIRJALLISUUDEN SEURAN TOIMITUKSIA (FI) [03094531] **3443**

SUOMALAISTA TYOTERVEYS- JA TYOTURVALLISUUSALAN KIRJALLISUUTTA (FI) [19010443] **2871**

SUOMALAISTEN ANITTEIDEN LUETTELO. CATALOGUE OF FINNISH RECORDINGS (FI/0782-1875) [18764210] **4155**

SUOMEN 1500 I.E. VIISITOISTASATAA SUURINTA YRITYSTA (FI) [05280045] **714**

SUOMEN 2000 I.E. KAKSITUHATTA SUURINTA YRITYSTA (FI) [05667411] **1628**

SUOMEN AIKAKAUSLEHDENTOIMITTAJAIN LIITOO **See** SAL VUOSIKIRJA **2924**

SUOMEN AKATEMIAN JULKAISUJA (FI/0358-9153) [I03589153] **138**

SUOMEN ANTROPOLOGI : SUOMEN ANTROPOLOGISEN SEURAN JULKAISU (FI) [13051297] **246**

SUOMEN APTEEKKARILEHTI (FI/0355-533X) [I0355533X] **4330**

SUOMEN ELAINLAAKARILEHTI (FI/0039-5501) [01716646] **5522**

SUOMEN GEODEETTISEN LAITOKSEN TIEDONANTOJA (FI/0355-1962) [06201519] 3537, **1360**

SUOMEN GEOLOGINEN SEURA **See** BULLETIN OF THE GEOLOGICAL SOCIETY OF FINLAND **1370**

SUOMEN HAMMASLAAKARISEURAN TOIMITUKSIA **CEASED.** (FI/0039-551X) [03031294] **1336**

SUOMEN HISTORIALLINEN SEURA **See** HISTORIALLINEN ARKISTO **2691**

SUOMEN KALASTUSLEHTI (FI) [07368919] **2314**

SUOMEN KALATALOUS (FI/0085-6940) [02289508] **2314**

SUOMEN KAUPPALAIVASTO. FINLANDS HANDELSFLOTTA. THE FINNISH MERCHANT MARINE (FI) [07365039] **5457**

SUOMEN KAUPUNKILIITTO **See** TIETOJA KAUPUNGEISTA, KAUPPALOISTA JA KAUPUNKILIITOSTA **5264**

SUOMEN KIRJALLISUUS (FI/0355-001X) [01606212] **3459**

SUOMEN KIRJALLISUUS; VUOSILUETTELO (FI) [01794592] **425**

SUOMEN KULTTUURIRAHASTO **See** SUOMEN KULTTUURIRAHASTON VUOSIKATSAUS **2712**

SUOMEN KULTTUURIRAHASTON TOIMINTAKERTOMUS **See** SUOMEN KULTTUURIRAHASTON VUOSIKATSAUS **2712**

SUOMEN KULTTUURIRAHASTON VUOSIKATSAUS (FI) [09678774] **2712**

SUOMEN KUVALEHTI (FI/0039-5552) [01766827] **2523**

SUOMEN LAAKARILEHTI. FINLANDS LAKARTIDNING (FI/0039-5560) [06481449] **3643**

Alphabetical Title Index — SUPPLEMENT

SUOMEN LAAKETILASTO / LAAKEINFORMAATION JA -TILASTOINNIN YHTEISTYOTOIMIKUNTA (FI/0786-2180) [20387126] 3643, **3662**

SUOMEN MAKSUTASE (FI) [02241268] **813**

SUOMEN MATKAILU (FI/0359-0607) [09688884] 5491, **2523**

SUOMEN MUINAISMUISTOYHDISTYKSEN AIKAKAUSKIRJA (FI/0355-1822) [01716124] **283**

SUOMEN MUINAISMUISTOYHDISTYS See AIKAKAUSKIRJA **253**

SUOMEN MUINAISMUISTOYHDISTYS See KANSATIETEELLINEN ARKISTO ... **240**

SUOMEN MUSEO (FI/0355-1806) [03091905] **283**

SUOMEN OSUUSMEIJERIEN LIIKETILASTO / TOIMITTANUT VOINVIENTI -OSUUSLIIKE VALIO, R.L (FI) [19551281] **199**

SUOMEN RANNIKON LOISTOT (FI) [04560240] **4183**

SUOMEN SHAKKI (FI) [04044721] **4924**

SUOMEN STANDARDISOIMISLIITTO See SFS-LUETTELO **2030**

SUOMEN TEOLLISUUSLIITTO See JASENLUETTELO - SUOMEN TEOLLISUUSLIITTO **1569**

SUOMEN TIEDESEURA See COMMENTATIONES HUMANARUM LITTERARUM **3274**

SUOMEN TIEDESEURA. PARASITOLOGIAN LAITOS See CONTRIBUTION - SUOMEN TIEDESEURA. PARASITOLOGIAN LAITOS **452**

SUOMEN TILASTOLLINEN VUOSIKIRJA (FI) [04904475] **5344**

SUOMEN TUULIATLAS (FI) [24060917] **1435**

SUOMEN TYSUOJELUKIRJALLISUUS (FI) [20793599] **2871**

SUOMEN VIRALLINEN TILASTO. XXI B, SOSIAALIHUOLTO (FI) [08407001] 5312, **5267**

SUOMENKIELISIA KIRJOJA (CN/0710-5215) [09448371] **4832**

SUPER AUTOMOTIVE SERVICE CEASED. (US/0896-0437) [16888377] **5426**

SUPER BENEFITS (NZ) **1712**

SUPER BMX & FREESTYLE CEASED. (US/1040-8290) [12177417] **429**

SUPER BOWL FACT BOOK (US/0733-1630) [08516081] **4924**

SUPER CHEVY (US/0146-2628) [02902650] **5426**

SUPER EXPRESS (PL/0867-8723) [I08678723] **5808**

SUPER FORD (US/1054-318X) [21110620] **5426**

SUPER FORD MAGAZINE (US/0279-2184) [07642835] **5426**

SUPER GAMING (US/1060-4685) [24999201] **4866**

SUPER GROUP MAGAZINE (US/1043-2418) [19359546] **1204**

SUPER MAGAZINE (CN/0708-1561) [04879629] **2547**

SUPER MARKET INSTITUTE See ANNUAL FINANCIAL REVIEW - SUPER MARKET INSTITUTE **2327**

SUPER MAZE CRAZE PUZZLE PICTURES (US/0732-5657) [08413593] **4866**

●SUPER PROJECTS (US/1062-8398) [25763351] **1628**

SUPER SCIENCE (BLUE ED.) (US/1040-144X) [18334874] **4866**

SUPER SCIENCE (RED ED.) (US/1040-1431) [18334867] **4866**

SUPER SEXE (CN/0712-5984) [09313061] **5188**

SUPER SNACK NEWS (US/1066-2898) [25649214] 2792, **1070**

SUPER STOCK & DRAG ILLUSTRATED (US/0039-5692) [03937084] 5426, **4924**

SUPER STREET TRUCK CEASED. (US) [23281041] **5426**

SUPER TEEN (US/8750-1767) [11081735] **1070**

SUPERANNUATION FUND INVESTMENT TRUST (AUSTRALIA) See ANNUAL REPORT **891**

SUPERB CROSSWORDS (US/0894-6469) [16151089] **4866**

SUPERB FILL-IT-INS (US/0194-3227) [05430434] **4866**

SUPERB WORD-FIND PUZZLES (US/0194-3235) [05430573] **4866**

SUPERB WORD-TWISTS (US/0199-218X) [05718129] **4866**

SUPERBASE (UK) [18796301] **4058**

SUPERBRANDS (US) [22462491] **767**

SUPERCOMPUTER (NE/0168-7875) [15533021] **1204**

SUPERCOMPUTING PROCEEDINGS (US) **1204**

SUPERCOMPUTING REVIEW (US/1048-6836) [19229720] **1204**

SUPERCONDUCTIVE TECHNOLOGY IN REVIEW SUSPENDED. (US/0739-3350) [08711735] **5161**

SUPERCONDUCTIVITY ABSTRACTS SUSPENDED. (UK) **2082**

SUPERCONDUCTIVITY BULLETIN (US/1062-1776) [25536321] **1958**

SUPERCONDUCTIVITY FLASH REPORT (US/0896-3401) [17005410] **2082**

SUPERCONDUCTIVITY: PHYSICS, CHEMISTRY, TECHNIQUE (US/0235-8964) [22465522] **4423**

●SUPERCONDUCTIVITY REVIEW (US/1054-2698) [22806927] **2082**

SUPERCONDUCTOR INDUSTRY (US/1042-4105) [18679857] **5161**

SUPERCONDUCTOR PATENT PROFILE (UK) **4423**

SUPERCONDUCTOR SCIENCE & TECHNOLOGY (UK/0953-2048) [18126477] 4432, **4445**

SUPERCONDUCTOR WEEK (US/0894-7635) [16219723] **1997**

SUPERCONDUCTORS UPDATE CEASED. (US/0893-5297) [15559589] 2108, **2082**

●SUPERCROSS (US/1065-9234) [26793676] **4083**

SUPERCURRENTS CEASED. (US) [17999199] **2083**

SUPERCYCLE (HUNTINGTON BEACH) (US/0162-3923) [04162625] **4083**

SUPERFICIE DES PRINCIPALES GRANDES CULTURES (CN/0381-078X) [02240433] **189**

SUPERFICIE FORESTALE NELLE COMUNITA MONTANE AL 31 DICEMBRE, LA (IT) [20438781] **2396**

SUPERFUND (US/0892-2985) [15148153] **2244**

SUPERFUND WEEK (US) **2244**

SUPERFUNDS (AT/0729-3828) [I07293828] **4751**

SUPERGROWTH (US) **2894**

SUPERINTENDENCIA DOS SERVICOS DE ESTATISTICA. SERVICOS DE ESTATISTICA See PRODUCAO AGRICOLA **122**

SUPERINTENDENT'S DIGEST (US/0735-0082) [05534470] **1873**

SUPERINTENDENT'S NEWSLETTER (US/0149-2322) [03443308] **1873**

SUPERINTENDENTS ONLY (US) **1905**

SUPERLATTICES AND MICROSTRUCTURES (UK/0749-6036) [11171257] **5161**

SUPERMAGAZINE D'ARTISANAT LES MOUSTARTS (CN/0824-6254) [10852310] **376**

SUPERMARKET (SW/0039-5781) [I00395781] 952, **937**

SUPERMARKET ADVERTISING NEWSLETTER (US/0899-1898) [18028103] **767**

SUPERMARKET BUSINESS (US/0196-5700) [05737626] **2359**

SUPERMARKET FLORAL (US/1058-4803) [24307805] **2432**

SUPERMARKET HQ QUARTERLY CEASED. (US) [23673162] **714**

SUPERMARKET MANAGEMENT (US/0149-8894) [03567964] **887**

SUPERMARKET NEWS (US/0039-5803) [01781222] **2359**

SUPERMARKET NEWS (AT) **2359**

SUPERMARKET NEWS (US/0039-5803) [15980461] **2359**

SUPERMARKET SCOOP (US/1065-3260) [26596995] **2359**

SUPERMARKET SHOPPER (US/0163-9528) [04540860] **2359**

SUPERMARKET STRATEGIC ALERT (US/1053-3648) [22518554] **2359**

SUPERMARKETING AUCKLAND (NZ/0112-949X) [I0112949X] **2359**

SUPERMICRO See BUS DATABASE **1172**

SUPERPREP. AMERICA'S RECRUITING MAGAZINE (US) **4924**

SUPERSTAR WRESTLER (US/0887-1035) [13089802] **4866**

SUPERSTORE MANAGEMENT See SUPERSTORE MANAGEMENT INTERNATIONAL **958**

SUPERSTORE MANAGEMENT INTERNATIONAL (UK/0962-2225) [I0962 2225] **958**

SUPERTRAX (CN) **4855**

SUPERVAREJO (BL) [01787884] **2359**

SUPERVISION (BURLINGTON) (US/0039-5854) [01909510] **947**

SUPERVISOR (ENGLEWOOD, N.J.), EL (US/1043-2191) [04443574] **2871**

SUPERVISOR'S BULLETIN (US/0039-5889) [03937168] **947**

SUPERVISOR'S BULLETIN FOR ADMINISTRATION AND OFFICE SUPPORT GROUPS (US/0744-3625) [08217031] **887**

SUPERVISOR'S DEVELOPMENT PROGRAM (US) **887**

SUPERVISOR'S EEO REVIEW, THE (US/0362-5826) [02278760] 947, **1713**

SUPERVISOR'S ENVIRONMENTAL ALERT See ENVIRONMENTAL SAFETY ALERT **2229**

SUPERVISOR'S MEMORY JOGGER (US) **887**

SUPERVISOR'S MOTIVATION SERIES (US) **887**

SUPERVISOR'S NEWSLETTER, THE CEASED. (US/0740-0411) [09873741] **947**

SUPERVISOR'S QUALITY CLINIC (US/1054-3511) [22856891] **714**

SUPERVISORS REPORT (US/1061-7736) [25456038] **2871**

SUPERVISOR'S SAFETY CLINIC (US/0194-8717) [05066091] **4804**

SUPERVISORY AND MIDDLE MANAGEMENT SALARY SURVEY (LOS ANGELES) (US/0092-5802) [01799975] 887, **1713**

SUPERVISORY MANAGEMENT (1989) (US/1045-263X) [18946821] **947**

SUPERVISORY SENSE CEASED. (US/0274-645X) [06483443] **947**

SUPLEMENTO ANTROPOLOGICO - UNIVERSIDAD CATOLICA (PY/0378-9896) [01794765] **246**

SUPLEMENTO DE ATUALIZACAO : LIVLEX TRABALHISTA (BL) [03012784] **3154**

SUPLEMENTO TRABALHISTA LTR (BL) [10534187] **3154**

SUPLEMENTOS SOBRE EL SISTEMA FINANCIERO (SP/0212-5994) [17976579] **1586**

SUPOCHU REJO (KO) [10845267] **4924**

SUPOCHU SAJIN YONGAM (KO) [10265533] **4924**

SUPOSTAVITELNO EZIKOZNANIE (BU/0204-8701) [06067723] **3327**

SUPPLEMENT AU BULLETIN ANALYTIQUE PETROLIER (FR/0249-0420) [02490420] **4280**

SUPPLEMENT AUX ANNALES DU SERVICE DES ANTIQUTES DE L'EQYPTE (UA) [06879010] **283**

SUPPLEMENT BIJ DE SOCIAAL-ECONOMISCHE MAANDSTATISTIEK / CENTRAL BUREAU VOOR DE STATISTIEK (NE/0168-8456) [11660885] **5228**

SUPPLEMENT (DARMSTADT) CEASED. (GW/0930-4061) [16185678] **3643**

SUPPLEMENT ... DE LA NOMENCLATURE DES STATIONS DE RADIOREPERAGE ET DES STATIONS EFFECTUANT DES SERVICES SPECIAUX. ADDITIONS / UNION INTERNATIONALE DES TELECOMMUNICATIONS (SZ) [11451543] **1140**

SUPPLEMENT / DIOCESE DE SAINTE-ANNE-DE-LA-POCATIERE (CN/0820-9669) [09635043] **5037**

SUPPLEMENT, LE (FR/0750-1455) [05933439] **2253**

SUPPLEMENT (MONTREAL) (CN/0382-490X) [03029025] **1885**

SUPPLEMENT ONE, HEALTH SCIENCES BOOKS & JOURNALS (CN/0821-1590) [09774737] 3643, **4832**

SUPPLEMENT TO ATTORNEY'S GUIDE TO TRADE SECRETS (US) [07036835] **3061**

SUPPLEMENT TO BIBLIOGRAPHY ON LOGISTICS AND PHYSICAL DISTRIBUTION MANAGEMENT / BY BERNARD J. LALONDE (US) [13676272] **887**

SUPPLEMENT TO BIBLIOGRAPHY ON PHYSICAL DISTRIBUTION MANAGEMENT (US) [04822807] **734**

SUPPLEMENT TO BOOKS ON DEMAND (US/0734-8657) [08815344] **426**

SUPPLEMENT TO CAMPAIGN FINANCE LAW (US) [04889587] **3061**

SUPPLEMENT TO EMPLOYMENT AND EARNINGS, REVISED ESTABLISHMENT DATA See EMPLOYMENT AND EARNINGS / U.S. DEPARTMENT OF LABOR, BUREAU OF LABOR STATISTICS **1666**

SUPPLEMENT

Alphabetical Title Index

SUPPLEMENT TO EMPLOYMENT AND UNEMPLOYMENT IN STATES AND LOCAL AREAS (SUPPL. TO THE MONTHLY) (US) [11065328] **1713**

SUPPLEMENT TO EMPLOYMENT, HOURS, AND EARNINGS, STATES AND AREAS (US/8755-4712) [11249049] **1713**

SUPPLEMENT TO INTERNATIONAL JOURNAL OF GYNECOLOGY AND OBSTETRICS (IE/0924-8447) [20761200] **3768**

SUPPLEMENT TO ... JOURNAL OF NEMATOLOGY (US) [27015613] **5598**

SUPPLEMENT TO ORGANIZATION OF FEDERAL EXECUTIVE DEPARTMENTS AND AGENCIES (US/0730-983X) [04164566] **4689**

SUPPLEMENT TO THE ANNUAL ENERGY OUTLOOK (US/0742-7328) [09868493] **1958**

SUPPLEMENT TO THE BEAT INFLATION STRATEGY (US) [02771593] **916**

SUPPLEMENT TO THE DIRECTORY OF THE AMERICAN RIGHT (US/0164-2510) [04617526] **4497**

SUPPLEMENT TO THE INDEX OF FLUTE MUSIC (US) [03719973] **4155**

SUPPLEMENT ... TO THE JOURNAL MEDICAL ONCOLOGY AND TUMOR PHARMACOTHERAPY (UK) [19218522] **3824**

SUPPLEMENT ... TO THE JUSTICE OF THE PEACE AND LOCAL GOVERNMENT REVIEW *See* J.P. WEEKLY LAW DIGEST, THE **2986**

SUPPLEMENT TO THE NATIONAL BUILDING CODE OF CANADA, THE (CN/0826-6131) [11575683] **629**

SUPPLEMENT TO THE STATISTICAL YEARBOOK AND THE MONTHLY BULLETIN OF STATISTICS *CEASED.* (US/0503-4019) [01768087] **5344**

SUPPLEMENT ... TO WOMEN OF EUROPE (BE) [07684371] **5567**

SUPPLEMENTA ITALICA / UNIONE ACCADEMICA NAZIONALE (IT) [08340959] **2712**

SUPPLEMENTAL ANNUITY COLLECTIVE TRUST OF NEW JERSEY *See* ANNUAL REPORT / SUPPLEMENTAL ANNUITY COLLECTIVE TRUST FUND OF NEW JERSEY **4629**

SUPPLEMENTAL CLIMATOLOGICAL DATA, LATE REPORTS AND CORRECTIONS. ALASKA (US) [07765952] **1435**

SUPPLEMENTAL CLIMATOLOGICAL DATA, LATE REPORTS AND CORRECTIONS. CALIFORNIA (US/0730-2746) [07762165] **1435**

SUPPLEMENTAL CLIMATOLOGICAL DATA, LATE REPORTS AND CORRECTIONS. COLORADO (US/0730-661X) [07940760] **1435**

SUPPLEMENTAL CLIMATOLOGICAL DATA, LATE REPORTS AND CORRECTIONS. FLORIDA (US/0730-6601) [07762132] **1435**

SUPPLEMENTAL CLIMATOLOGICAL DATA, LATE REPORTS AND CORRECTIONS. KANSAS (US/0730-2843) [07786553] **1435**

SUPPLEMENTAL CLIMATOLOGICAL DATA, LATE REPORTS AND CORRECTIONS. KENTUCKY (US/0730-2851) [07786567] **1435**

SUPPLEMENTAL CLIMATOLOGICAL DATA, LATE REPORTS AND CORRECTIONS. LOUISIANA (US/0730-286X) [07786591] **1435**

SUPPLEMENTAL CLIMATOLOGICAL DATA, LATE REPORTS AND CORRECTIONS. MARYLAND & DELAWARE (US/0730-2878) [07786607] **1435**

SUPPLEMENTAL CLIMATOLOGICAL DATA, LATE REPORTS AND CORRECTIONS. NEBRASKA (US/0730-2835) [07777429] **1435**

SUPPLEMENTAL CLIMATOLOGICAL DATA, LATE REPORTS AND CORRECTIONS. NEW ENGLAND (US/0730-2797) [07777394] **1435**

SUPPLEMENTAL CLIMATOLOGICAL DATA, LATE REPORTS AND CORRECTIONS. NEW JERSEY (US/0730-2762) [07760509] **1435**

SUPPLEMENTAL CLIMATOLOGICAL DATA, LATE REPORTS AND CORRECTIONS. NEW MEXICO (US/0730-4927) [07940782] **1435**

SUPPLEMENTAL DIRECTORY OF CERTIFIED APPLIANCES AND ACCESSORIES / AMERICAN GAS ASSOCIATION LABORATORIES (US) [07163828] **2812**

SUPPLEMENTAL FINANCIAL DATA FOR THE FISCAL YEAR ENDED JUNE 30 ... / STATE OF MARYLAND (US) [08203207] **4751**

SUPPLEMENTAL GENERAL APPROPRIATIONS AND LEGISLATIVE INTENT FOR THE ... BIENNIUM (US) [08673109] **4751**

SUPPLEMENTAL MANAGEMENT FUND FOR SUBSIDIZED MULTIFAMILY PROJECTS (US) [03117957] **2836**

SUPPLEMENTAL SALARY STUDY, SELECTED SCHOOL, DISTRICT, AND COUNTY PERSONNEL (US/0148-3234) [03289565] **1873**

SUPPLEMENTAL SECURITY INCOME, STATE AND COUNTY DATA *See* SSI RECIPIENTS BY STATE AND COUNTY **5311**

SUPPLEMENTAL TIDAL PREDICTIONS, ANCHORAGE, NIKISHKA, SELDOVIA, AND VALDEZ, ALASKA (US/0270-8876) [06497549] **4183**

SUPPLEMENTAL YEAR BOOK - STATE BOARD OF PROFESSIONAL ENGINEERS AND LAND SURVEYORS (US/0095-0416) [01795305] **1997**

SUPPLEMENTARY BUDGET INFORMATION / WESTERN AUSTRALIA (AT) [19598138] **4751**

SUPPLEMENTARY BUDGET STATEMENT OF PAKISTAN RAILWAYS (PK) [03256552] 4751, **5437**

SUPPLEMENTARY CANADA PENSION PLAN CONTRIBUTION AND UNEMPLOYMENT INSURANCE PREMIUM TABLES (CN/0713-1763) [08828294] 2894, **1713**

SUPPLEMENTARY DIRECTORY OF THE AMERICAN BAPTIST CHURCHES IN THE U.S.A (US/0090-9459) [01785606] **5068**

SUPPLEMENTARY ESTIMATE OF THE EXPENDITURE TO BE DEFRAYED FROM REVENUE, LOAN AND SOUTH-WEST AFRICA ACCOUNTS (SA) [01788311] **4751**

●SUPPLEMENTARY INFORMATION FOR LEGISLATIVE REVIEW, EXPENDITURE ESTIMATES - MANITOBA., CIVIL SERVICE COMMISSION. EMPLOYEE BENEFITS AND OTHER PAYMENTS (CN/1189-0770) [25352186] **4689**

●SUPPLEMENTARY INFORMATION FOR LEGISLATIVE REVIEW, REVENUE ESTIMATES (CN/1187-5917) [25468471] **813**

SUPPLEMENTARY INFORMATION ..., PAYMENTS TO INDIVIDUALS (CN/1187-8266) [25796815] **813**

SUPPLEMENTARY PAPER - COMMITTEE FOR ECONOMIC DEVELOPMENT OF AUSTRALIA (AT/0591-0137) [03563748] **1523**

SUPPLEMENTARY PAPERS - ROYAL INSTITUTION OF NAVAL ARCHITECTS (UK/0373-529X) [02468613] **4183**

SUPPLEMENTARY SHEEP BRANDS AND MARKS DIRECTORY OF NEW SOUTH WALES (AT) [20177517] **222**

SUPPLEMENTARY STATEMENT OF EXPENDITURE (PK) [02245126] **4751**

SUPPLEMENTARY UNEMPLOYMENT INSURANCE PREMIUM TABLES ... PROVINCE OF QUEBEC (CN/0713-178X) [08741225] **2894**

SUPPLEMENTARY VOLUME - ARISTOTELIAN SOCIETY (UK/0309-7013) [03078135] **4363**

SUPPLEMENTARY VOLUME (CAMBRIDGE PHILOLOGICAL SOCIETY) (UK) [07723247] **3327**

SUPPLEMENTO ALLE RICERCHE DI BIOLOGIA DELLA SELVAGGINA / LABORATORIO DI ZOOLOGIA APPLICATA ALLA CACCIA (IT) [05359751] **5598**

SUPPLEMENTS TO NOVUM TESTAMENTUM (NE/0167-9732) [02621917] **5001**

SUPPLEMENTS TO VETUS TESTAMENTUM (NE/0083-5889) [03164594] **5001**

SUPPLEMENTS TO VIGILIAE CHRISTIANAE (NE/0920-623X) [16162642] **5001**

SUPPLEMENTUM EPIGRAPHICUM GRAECUM (NE/0920-8399) [01607583] 3327, **1080**

SUPPLEMENTUM SBORNIKU VEDECKYCH PRACI LEKARSKE FAKULTY UNIVERZITY KARLOVY V HRADCI KRALOVE (XR/0049-5522) [01778387] **3644**

SUPPLIER SELECTION & MANAGEMENT REPORT (US/1046-3771) [20398754] **887**

SUPPLIERS DIRECTORY (COLORADO SPRINGS, COLO.) (US/0739-2419) [07338027] 3443, **5001**

SUPPLY, DEMAND AND SALARIES; NEW GRADUATES OF UNIVERSITIES AND COMMUNITY COLLEGES (CN/0317-4697) [01795860] **1713**

SUPPLY HOUSE TIMES (US/0039-5935) [05150436] **2608**

SUPPLY LINE (US/8750-0124) [10917359] 5393, **4058**

SUPPORT FOR LEARNING (UK/0268-2141) [13406533] **1786**

SUPPORT FOR PROFESSIONAL ARTISTS (CN/1187-063X) [25079389] **331**

SUPPORT FOR THE LEARNING AND TEACHING OF ENGLISH (US/0738-1417) [09530677] 1905, **3327**

●SUPPORT LINE (CHICAGO, ILL.) (US/1067-3768) [26674007] **4199**

SUPPORT SERVICES SALARIES SURVEY (US/0730-6849) [07354352] **1713**

●SUPPORT@FTP.COM (WAKEFIELD, MASS.) (US/1064-1750) [26297869] **1204**

●SUPPORTIVE CARE IN CANCER : OFFICIAL JOURNAL OF THE MULTINATIONAL ASSOCIATION OF SUPPORTIVE CARE IN CANCER (GW/0941-4355) [27806812] **3824**

SUPPRESSED! (PLYMOUTH, MICH.) (US/1055-4831) [23189845] **2762**

●SUPRAMOLECULAR CHEMISTRY (SW/1061-0278) [25161155] **993**

SUPRAPHON *See* NUMERICAL LISTING OF SUPRAPHON LP RECORDS / SUPRAPHON **4142**

SUPREME COUNCIL FOR SPORT IN AFRICA *See* REPERTOIRE D'ADRESSES - CONSEIL SUPERIEUR DU SPORT EN AFRIQUE **4915**

SUPREME COURT BULLETIN (MANCHESTER, N.H.) (US/0199-5030) [05951094] **3061**

SUPREME COURT CASES, THE (II) [01607799] **3061**

SUPREME COURT DECISIONS : SUBJECT INDEX AND DIGESTS (PH) [06245620] **3061**

SUPREME COURT DOCTRINES (PH) [03225676] **3061**

SUPREME COURT ECONOMIC REVIEW (US/0736-9921) [09278961] 3061, **1523**

SUPREME COURT JOURNAL, THE (II) [01766855] **3061**

SUPREME COURT LAW JOURNAL (US/0893-9640) [15715692] **3061**

SUPREME COURT LAW REVIEW, THE (CN/0228-0108) [06472512] **3061**

SUPREME COURT MONTHLY REVIEW, THE (PK) [01766856] **3061**

SUPREME COURT OF CANADA DECISIONS. CIVIL AND CRIMINAL CASES (CN/0709-5600) [05528911] **3061**

SUPREME COURT PRACTICE, THE (UK/0039-5978) [02254079] **3143**

SUPREME COURT RECORD (US/0892-810X) [15262372] **3061**

SUPREME COURT REPORTS (II) [01752816] **3061**

SUPREME COURT REVIEW, THE (US/0081-9557) [01643150] **3061**

SUPREME COURT YEARBOOK, THE (US/1054-2701) [22806965] **3061**

SUR (BUENOS AIRES, ARGENTINA) *CEASED.* (AG/0035-0478) [01766859] **2552**

SUR L'EMPREMIER (CN/0228-9016) [07865701] **2762**

SUR MESURE (CN/0822-5257) [10763887] **1802**

SURA SAURABHA (II) [08620646] **3443**

SURABU KENKYU (JA/0562-6579) [06696149] **2712**

SURAJ (1984) (US/8750-6599) [11618925] **2273**

SURE : TOP LEVEL ENGLISH (IT) **3327**

SUREPAY UPDATE (US/0195-5225) [05590172] **813**

SURETE (CN/0820-6643) [09407581] **5312**

SURETE DU QUEBEC *See* RAPPORT D'ACTIVITE - SURETE DU QUEBEC **3174**

SURF (GW/0342-7560) [I03427560] **4879**

SURF REPORT, THE (US/0270-2630) [06374551] **4924**

SURF SKI QUARTERLY (AT) **4924**

SURFACE & COATINGS TECHNOLOGY (SZ/0257-8972) [13170399] **2108**

SURFACE AND COLLOID SCIENCE (US/0081-9573) [01604974] **1058**

SURFACE AND INTERFACE ANALYSIS : SIA (UK/0142-2421) [04995160] 1058, **1019**

SURFACE AND MARINE TRANSPORT (CN/0828-2897) [12490418] **5393**

SURFACE COATING & RAW MATERIAL DIRECTORY (UK/0268-9766) [02689766] **4225**

SURFACE COATINGS AUSTRALIA (AT/0815-709X) [11541591] **1030**

SURFACE COATINGS INTERNATIONAL : JOCCA, JOURNAL OF THE OIL AND COLOUR CHEMISTS' ASSOCIATION (UK/0964-928X) [23675823] **4225**

SURFACE DESIGN ASSOCIATION (U.S.) *See* SDA NEWS / SURFACE DESIGN ASSOCIATION **2778**

SURVEY

SURFACE DESIGN ASSOCIATION (U.S.) NEWSLETTER See SDA NEWS / SURFACE DESIGN ASSOCIATION **2778**

SURFACE DESIGN JOURNAL (US/0197-4483) [06035770] **5356**

SURFACE ENGINEERING (UK/0267-0844) [12223229] **1997**

●SURFACE ENGINEERING AND APPLIED ELECTROCHEMISTRY (US/1068-3755) [27661866] 1035, **1997**

SURFACE MODIFICATION TECHNOLOGY NEWS (US/1058-093X) [24207439] **1030**

SURFACE MOUNT TECHNOLOGY (US/0893-3588) [15495634] **2083**

SURFACE MOUNT TECHNOLOGY (UK) **2083**

SURFACE MOUNT TECHNOLOGY TODAY (US/0886-618X) [12955132] **4423**

SURFACE OBSERVATIONS IN HONG KONG / ROYAL OBSERVATORY, HONG KONG (HK) [19537907] **1435**

SURFACE SCIENCE (NE/0039-6028) [01766860] **1058**

SURFACE SCIENCE LETTERS (NE/0167-2584) [06620484] **5161**

SURFACE SCIENCE REPORTS (NE/0167-5729) [07969615] 4423, **2083**

●SURFACE SCIENCE SPECTRA (US/1055-5269) [23199889] **4442**

SURFACE TREATMENT TECHNOLOGY ABSTRACTS (UK) [14156834] 4021, **4026**

SURFACE WARFARE (US/0145-1073) [02663436] **4183**

SURFACE WATER DATA. BRITISH COLUMBIA (CN/0576-2367) [03233200] **5540**

SURFACE WATER DATA. ONTARIO (CN/0576-2383) [02246249] **1418**

SURFACE WATER DATA : SASKATCHEWAN (CN/0576-2405) [01552927] **1418**

SURFACE WAVE ABSTRACTS (UK/0049-2639) [04960128] **4453**

SURFACES (FR/0585-9840) [07027520] 4225, **4021**

SURFACES (MONTREAL) (CN/1188-2492) [25652130] **331**

SURFACES (MONTREAL) (CN/1188-2492) [25652132] **331**

SURFACING JOURNAL INTERNATIONAL (UK/0269-2848) [13897154] **993**

SURFACING (TORONTO) (CN/0847-0553) [20985291] **5356**

SURFACTANT SCIENCE SERIES (US/0081-9603) [01696169] 1058, **993**

SURFBOARD (US/0276-6582) [07368790] **4924**

SURFER (US/0039-6036) [03904860] **4924**

●SURFER'S JOURNAL, THE (US/1062-3892) [25603461] **4924**

SURFING (SAN CLEMENTE, CALIF.) (US/0194-9314) [05121960] **4924**

SURGELATION, LA (FR/0049-2647) [l00492647] **1628**

SURGERY (US/0039-6060) [01645314] **3975**

SURGERY ALERT **CEASED.** (US/0748-1942) [10897517] **3975**

SURGERY AND IMMUNITY (IT) [18838339] **3975**

SURGERY ANNUAL (US/0081-9638) [01605834] **3975**

SURGERY COMBINED (NO) **3975**

SURGERY, GYNECOLOGY & OBSTETRICS (US/0039-6087) [01766861] 3768, **3975**

SURGERY (OXFORD) (UK/0263-9319) [10642447] **3975**

SURGERY (SOUTHERN AFRICAN ED.) (SA/0254-6361) [l02546361] **3975**

SURGERY TODAY (GW/0941-1291) **3975**

SURGICAL AND RADIOLOGIC ANATOMY (ENGLISH ED.) (GW/0930-1038) [14037082] 3947, 3975, **3680**

SURGICAL CLINICS OF NORTH AMERICA, THE (US/0039-6109) [01714309] 3793, **3975**

SURGICAL ENDOSCOPY (GW/0930-2794) [18306633] **3976**

SURGICAL FORUM (US/0071-8041) [01479684] **3976**

SURGICAL FORUM (BIRMINGHAM) (US/0147-4154) [03155496] **3976**

SURGICAL GASTROENTEROLOGY (US/0730-2681) [07983420] **3748**

SURGICAL LAPAROSCOPY AND ENDOSCOPY (US/1051-7200) [22096181] **3976**

SURGICAL NEUROLOGY (US/0090-3019) [01784905] **3976**

SURGICAL NURSE (UK/0954-8947) [22238785] **3870**

●SURGICAL ONCOLOGY (UK/0960-7404) [25622778] 3976, **3824**

●SURGICAL ONCOLOGY CLINICS OF NORTH AMERICA (US/1055-3207) [23138755] **3824**

SURGICAL PATHOLOGY (US/0899-8175) [17804251] 3976, **3898**

SURGICAL PRODUCT NEWS (US/0279-4829) [07909289] **3684**

SURGICAL PRODUCTS (US/1062-4732) [25635696] **3976**

SURGICAL RESEARCH COMMUNICATIONS (SZ/0882-9233) [12009084] **3976**

SURGICAL RESIDENT, THE **CEASED.** (US/1063-8547) [26150055] **3976**

SURGICAL ROUNDS (US/0161-1372) [03676919] **3976**

SURGICAL ROUNDS FOR ORTHOPAEDICS **CEASED.** (US/0891-1800) [14639936] **3885**

SURGICAL STERILIZATION SURVEILLANCE. TUBAL STERILIZATION AND HYSTERECTOMY IN WOMEN AGED 15-44 (US/0743-6173) [10381099] **3768**

SURGICAL TECHNOLOGIST, THE (US/0164-4238) [04699434] 3976, **3644**

SURI KAGAKU (JA/0386-2240) [06923553] 1997, **3537**

SURINAM See ADVERTENTIEBLAD VAN DE REPUBLIEK SURINAME **4461**

SURINAM. GEOLOGISCHE MIJNBOUWKUNDIGE DIENST See MEDEDELING **1387**

SURINAM, WIRTSCHAFTSDATEN / BUNDESSTELLE FUER AUSSENHANDELSINFORMATION (GW) [09189678] **1586**

SURNAME AND PUBLICATION INDEX (US/0270-9856) [06514372] **2474**

SURNAME EXCHANGE / SASKATCHEWAN GENEALOGICAL SOCIETY (CN/0713-780X) [09071335] **2474**

SURNAME INDEX (WICHITA) (US/0091-6439) [01787473] **2474**

SURNAME RESEARCH DIRECTORY (US/0277-366X) [07541022] **2474**

SURNAMES (US) [16821995] **2474**

SURPLUS ET PENURIES DE MAIN-D OEUVRE PREVUS AU QUEBEC ET DANS SES REGIONS POUR ... **CEASED.** (CN) [15075367] **1713**

SURPLUS RECORD AND INDEX See SURPLUS RECORD, THE **2129**

SURPLUS RECORD, THE (US/0039-615X) [05510967] **2129**

SURPRISES (US/0890-3573) [14223811] **1070**

SURREALIST TRANSFORMA(C)TION (UK/0039-6168) [03470607] **366**

SURREY ARCHAEOLOGICAL COLLECTIONS (UK) [01641502] **283**

SURREY ARCHAEOLOGICAL SOCIETY See RESEARCH VOLUME OF THE SURREY ARCHAEOLOGICAL SOCIETY **280**

SURREY ARCHAEOLOGICAL SOCIETY, GUILFORD See SURREY ARCHAEOLOGICAL COLLECTIONS **283**

SURREY-DELTA MAGAZINE (JUNE 1990) (CN/1184-0269) [23302819] **2547**

SURREY/NORTH DELTA TODAY (CN/0712-1113) [08651992] **5795**

SURREY TIMES (CN/0229-6861) [08071007] **5795**

SURVEI PENDIDIKAN DKI JAKARTA. WILAYAH JAKARTA SELATAN (IO) [11494666] **1805**

SURVEI PERIKANAN LAUT (IO) [10283354] **2314**

SURVEILLANCE (CN/0833-7926) [16948221] **3644**

SURVEILLANCE REPORT (CN/0707-9796) [l07079796] **2182**

SURVEILLANCE (WELLINGTON) (NZ/0112-4927) [07106418] **5522**

SURVEILLANT (WASHINGTON, D.C.) (US/1051-0923) [21820898] **4058**

SURVEY AGRO EKONOMI INDONESIA See LAPORAN - SURVEY AGRO EKONOMI INDONESIA **104**

SURVEY AND ANALYSIS OF BUSINESS CAR POLICIES & COSTS (US/0278-422X) [06372083] 5426, **714**

SURVEY AND ANALYSIS OF BUSINESS TRAVEL POLICIES & COSTS (US/0735-0376) [08833272] 714, **5491**

SURVEY AND ANALYSIS OF EMPLOYEE RELOCATION POLICIES & COST (US) **714**

SURVEY ANGKUTAN UDARA (IO) [11374743] **37**

SURVEY ANNOUNCEMENT - KENTUCKY CROP & LIVESTOCK REPORTING SERVICE (US/0274-5410) [06387106] **222**

SURVEY METHODOLOGY (CN/0714-0045) [07123757] **5224**

SURVEY NOTES - UTAH GEOLOGICAL AND MINERAL SURVEY (US) [02286120] **1399**

SURVEY NOTES / UTAH GEOLOGICAL SURVEY (US/1061-7930) [25465406] 1418, **1399**

SURVEY OF ACCOUNTING AND REPORTING PRACTICES OF REAL ESTATE DEVELOPERS, A (US) [05539202] 752, **4847**

SURVEY OF AGRICULTURAL LOST TIME INJURIES (CN/0228-2305) [06966028] **138**

SURVEY OF ANESTHESIOLOGY (US/0039-6206) [01766867] **3684**

SURVEY OF ARAB AFFAIRS (IS) [12438382] 4536, **5053**

SURVEY OF ARCHITECTURAL DRAFTING & DESIGNERS' SALARIES (US/0275-9691) [07250434] **309**

SURVEY OF ARCHITECTURAL SALARIES (US/0739-9944) [05108074] **309**

SURVEY OF ARTS ADMINISTRATION TRAINING See GUIDE TO ARTS ADMINISTRATION TRAINING. / CENTER FOR ARTS ADMINISTRATION, GRADUATE SCHOOL OF BUSINESS, UNIVERSITY OF WISCONSIN - MADISON, AND ASSOCIATION OF ARTS ADMINISTRATION EDUCATORS **321**

SURVEY OF ARTS ADMINISTRATION TRAINING / CENTER FOR ARTS ADMINISTRATION, GRADUATE SCHOOL OF BUSINESS, UNIVERSITY OF WISCONSIN-MADISON, AND ASSOCIATION OF ARTS ADMINISTRATION EDUCATORS (US) [16162711] **331**

SURVEY OF BLACK BASS TOURNAMENT FISHING IN TEXAS, A (US) [06865828] **2314**

SURVEY OF BUILDING, CONSTRUCTION, AND REAL ESTATE SECTORS (HK) [11801918] 4847, **629**

SURVEY OF BUSINESS (US/0099-0973) [02080171] **1586**

SURVEY OF BUYING POWER (US/0361-1329) [01914575] **714**

SURVEY OF BUYING POWER DEMOGRAPHICS USA, THE (US) [24436583] **952**

SURVEY OF BUYING POWER FORECASTER'S HANDBOOK See ... SURVEY OF BUYING POWER FORECASTING SERVICE, THE **1523**

... SURVEY OF BUYING POWER FORECASTING SERVICE, THE (US/0735-9942) [08080428] 952, **1523**

SURVEY OF CANADIAN NURSERY TRADES INDUSTRY (CN/0318-5184) [02240588] **2432**

SURVEY OF CHAINS AND GROUPS (CN) [02604087] **2359**

SURVEY OF CMEA ACTIVITIES (RU) [01783816] **1523**

SURVEY OF CONTRACTING STATISTICS (US/0193-9327) [05260065] 4058, **4062**

SURVEY OF CURRENT AFFAIRS (UK/0039-6214) [01996367] **4497**

SURVEY OF CURRENT BUSINESS (US) [11034500] **714**

SURVEY OF CURRENT BUSINESS (US/0039-6222) [01697070] **714**

SURVEY OF CURRENT LITERATURE ON THE CHRISTIAN MISSION AND CHRISTIANITY IN THE NON-WESTERN WORLD (MICROFORM) (UK) [09748519] **5001**

SURVEY OF DATA PROCESSING SALARIES (US/0737-4887) [09363658] **1713**

SURVEY OF DENTAL PRACTICE (US/0517-1032) [03236419] **1336**

SURVEY OF DISTRIBUTIVE TRADE (FJ) [11620556] **958**

SURVEY OF DOMESTIC SPORT MARKET PRICES (US) **937**

SURVEY OF DRUG STORE TRENDS See ANNUAL SURVEY OF PRESCRIPTION AND OVER-THE-COUNTER DRUGS **4291**

SURVEY OF DRUG STORE TRENDS, A (CN/0832-8692) [16220374] **4330**

SURVEY OF EMPLOYMENT, EARNINGS AND HOURS OF WORK (GM) [19638528] **1713**

SURVEY OF ENGINEERING SALARIES See ENGINEERING SALARIES SURVEY / PREPARED BY D. DIETRICH ASSOCIATES, INC **1974**

SURVEY OF EXECUTIVE ENGINEERING COMPENSATION (US/1051-4716) [21959258] **1997**

SURVEY Alphabetical Title Index

SURVEY OF FINANCIAL REPORTING AND ACCOUNTING DEVELOPMENTS IN THE ENTERTAINMENT INDUSTRY, A (US) [04522091] 389, **752**

SURVEY OF FINANCIAL REPORTING AND ACCOUNTING DEVELOPMENTS IN THE PETROLEUM INDUSTRY, A (US) [04525096] **4280**

SURVEY OF FINANCIAL REPORTING AND ACCOUNTING DEVELOPMENTS IN THE PUBLIC UTILITY INDUSTRY, A (US) [04522110] 4689, **752**

SURVEY OF FINANCIAL REPORTING AND ACCOUNTING DEVELOPMENTS IN THE STEEL INDUSTRY OF AMERICA, A (US) [04525094] 1628, **752**

SURVEY OF FLORIDA'S LOCAL RETIREMENT SYSTEMS : REPORT TO THE FLORIDA LEGISLATURE, THE (US) [19701473] **4689**

SURVEY OF FUNDS (TORONTO. 1985) (CN/0834-0420) [13664105] **916**

SURVEY OF GENERATION AND TRANSMISSION COOPERATIVES (US/0197-6877) [06068672] **1543**

SURVEY OF GRANT-MAKING FOUNDATIONS WITH ASSETS OF OVER $1,000,000 OR GRANTS OF OVER $200,000 (US/0190-5163) [01187783] **4689**

SURVEY OF INCOME OF CIVIL SERVICE ANNUITANTS (WASHINGTON) (US/0093-7150) [01791040] **4689**

SURVEY OF INDIA'S IMPORTS (II) [01790449] **852**

SURVEY OF INDUSTRIAL PRODUCTION / CENSUS AND STATISTICS DEPARTMENT, HONG KONG (HK) [10635115] **1628**

SURVEY OF INDUSTRIALS (TORONTO. 1985) (CN/0833-9597) [12596441] **734**

SURVEY OF JAPANESE FINANCE AND INDUSTRY (JA/0039-6249) [02015727] **813**

SURVEY OF JEWISH AFFAIRS **CEASED.** (US/0741-6571) [10199866] **2274**

SURVEY OF JUDICIAL SALARIES (US/0276-2463) [04234903] **3143**

SURVEY OF LABORATORY TECHNICIAN SALARIES (US/0738-1832) [09520442] **1713**

SURVEY OF LAW (US/0271-2792) [05722830] **3061**

SURVEY OF LAW REVIEWS (US/0360-7372) [02244764] **3061**

SURVEY OF LIBRARY MATERIAL EXPENDITURES AT STANFORD UNIVERSITY LIBRARIES (US/0360-2435) [02441107] **3252**

SURVEY OF LIVING COSTS IN MAJOR CITIES WORLDWIDE (SZ) [02369745] **1713**

SURVEY OF MALAYSIAN LAW (MY/0217-3239) [08462211] **3061**

SURVEY OF MANUFACTURING CONDITIONS AND FUTURE PROSPECTS IN N.S.W (AT/0816-9128) [I08169128] **3488**

SURVEY OF MINES AND ENERGY RESOURCES (CN/0833-9600) [12650255] 1959, **2152**

SURVEY OF MOTOR VEHICLE USE (AT) [20270462] 5426, **5402**

SURVEY OF MUNICIPAL PLANNING AND REGULATORY ACTIVITY, A (US/0363-7514) [02533902] **2836**

SURVEY OF NON-US STOCK MARKET SUITABILITY (US) [23591605] **916**

SURVEY OF OFFICE SALARIES, PERSONNEL PRACTICES, AND BENEFITS (US/0737-4860) [06505574] **1713**

SURVEY OF OPERATING PERFORMANCE FOR MUSIC DEALERS (US) [18661477] **4155**

SURVEY OF OPHTHALMOLOGY (US/0039-6257) [01766871] **3879**

SURVEY OF OUT-OF-STATE PASSENGER CARS AND OUT-OF-STATE CAMPER VEHICLES ON INTERSTATE, ARTERIAL AND PRIMARY HIGHWAYS IN VIRGINIA, A (US/0363-4027) [02439071] **5445**

SURVEY OF PENSION PLANS IN CANADA (CN/0843-3097) [20273420] **1713**

SURVEY OF PHARMACY LAW (US/0098-714X) [01524284] 4330, **3061**

SURVEY OF PREDECESSOR AND DEFUNCT COMPANIES (1985) (CN/0832-0772) [13348678] **734**

SURVEY OF PRESS FREEDOM IN LATIN AMERICA, A (US/0743-4324) [10569274] **4497**

SURVEY OF PRODUCTION (CN/0068-7227) [02443643] **1628**

SURVEY OF REGIONAL LITERATURE, THE (US) [17564769] **2836**

SURVEY OF RETAIL SALES AND SELECTED SERVICES (PP) [02240877] **958**

SURVEY OF SECONDARY AND ENHANCED RECOVERY OPERATIONS IN TEXAS, A (US/0161-5920) [03674324] **4280**

SURVEY OF STATE INVOLVEMENT IN PUBLIC TRANSPORTATION (US/0743-4499) [09755469] **5393**

SURVEY OF STATE TRAVEL OFFICES (US/0361-8307) [02987988] **5491**

SURVEY OF STORAGE, COMMUNICATIONS, FINANCING, INSURANCE, AND BUSINESS SERVICES (HK) [14874268] **714**

SURVEY OF SUPERVISORY PERSONNEL SALARIES (US/0737-4879) [09363608] **1713**

SURVEY OF TEMPORARY AND EXEMPT EMPLOYMENT (AT) [01784700] **1713**

SURVEY OF TERMS OF BANK LENDING MADE DURING ... (US) [06308625] **813**

SURVEY OF THE AUSTRIAN ECONOMY (AU) [10991055] **1586**

SURVEY OF THE MINI/MICROCOMPUTER MARKET (US/0192-9690) [05090931] 1272, **1274**

SURVEY OF TOWN MILK PRODUCERS' INCOMES (NZ) [15372826] **1713**

SURVEY OF TRANSPORT & RELATED SERVICES / TRANSPORT AND SERVICES STATISTICS SECTION, CENSUS AND STATISTICS DEPARTMENT, HONG KONG (HK) [17538716] **5393**

SURVEY OF TRAVEL IN KENTUCKY (US/0146-4698) [02955299] **5492**

SURVEY OF WHOLESALE & RETAIL TRADE & RESTAURANTS (PK) [10351762] 5073, **958**

SURVEY OF WHOLESALE, RETAIL, AND IMPORT/EXPORT TRADES, RESTAURANTS AND HOTELS (HK) [08243630] **714**

SURVEY OF WORLD ADVERTISING EXPENDITURES **SUSPENDED.** (US/0894-5004) [09831567] **767**

SURVEY PERTANIAN (IO) [02441082] **138**

●SURVEY REPORT ON VARIABLE PAY PROGRAMS / WYATT DATA SERVICES, ECS (US) [25680798] 947, **1713**

SURVEY REVIEW - DIRECTORATE OF OVERSEAS SURVEYS (UK/0039-6265) [01607157] **2032**

SURVEY STATISTICIAN (FR) [05887351] **5344**

SURVEYING AND LAND INFORMATION SYSTEMS (US/1052-2905) [21396434] **2583**

SURVEYING AUSTRALIA (AT/0157-1672) [I01571672] **2032**

SURVEYING TECHNICIAN **CEASED.** (UK/0952-5793) [I09525793] **2032**

SURVEYOR (WALLINGTON, ENGLAND) (UK) [15789013] **1997**

SURVEYOR (WALLINGTON, ENGLAND : 1987) (UK) [19568901] **2032**

SURVEYS AND REFERENCE WORKS IN MATHEMATICS (US/0743-0345) [04815231] **3537**

SURVEYS IN DIFFERENTIAL GEOMETRY (US/1052-9233) [22416740] **3537**

SURVEYS IN GEOPHYSICS (NE/0169-3298) [13622401] **1411**

SURVEYS IN HIGH ENERGY PHYSICS (SZ/0142-2413) [05757563] **4451**

SURVEYS ON MATHEMATICS FOR INDUSTRY (AU/0938-1953) [26780638] 3537, **1997**

SURVEYS, POLLS, CENSUSES, AND FORECASTS DIRECTORY **CEASED.** (US/0737-545X) [09401878] **5344**

SURVIVAL IN THE 21ST CENTURY (JA) [13390569] **4513**

SURVIVAL INTERNATIONAL ANNUAL REVIEW (UK) [24877353] 246, **4513**

SURVIVAL (LONDON) (UK/0039-6338) [05010177] **4058**

SURVIVAL (NORTH AMERICAN EDITION) (CN/0300-7944) [02247705] **4497**

SURVIVAL : THE INTERNATIONAL NEWSLETTER OF SURVIVAL INTERNATIONAL (UK) [24535572] 246, **4513**

SURVIVAL TOMORROW (US/0273-2017) [07023846] **5264**

SURVIVE (VANCOUVER, B.C.) (CN/0229-1975) [08854770] **5001**

SURVIVING TOGETHER (US/0895-6286) [11981869] **4536**

●SURVOL CHAUDIERE-APPALACHES (CN/1183-627X) [24623513] **1628**

SURYA INDIA (II) [03473018] **2508**

SUSA (II) [03217060] **3443**

SUSANMUL KYETONG PANMAEGO TONGGYE YONBO (KO) [09075644] 2314, **2318**

SUSPECT CHEMICALS SOURCEBOOK. UPDATE SERVICE (US/0893-7044) [15636369] **1030**

SUSPOP NEWS (CN/1194-6164) [28474097] **4560**

SUSQUEHANNA COUNTY INDEPENDENT, THE (US) [15355945] **5740**

SUSSEX ARCHAEOLOGICAL COLLECTIONS (UK/0143-8204) [01608099] **284**

SUSSEX FAMILY HISTORIAN (UK) [03114152] **2474**

SUSSEX FOLK DIARY (UK) [01788972] **4155**

SUSSEX GENEALOGIST AND LOCAL HISTORIAN, THE (UK) [07808429] **2474**

SUSSEX RECORD SOCIETY **See** [PUBLICATIONS] / SUSSEX RECORD SOCIETY **2634**

SUSSEX-SURRY DISPATCH (US/0745-9467) [09613967] **5759**

SUSSIDI PATRISTICI (IT) [13570962] **3354**

SUSSWAREN (GW/0039-4653) [I00394653] **2359**

SUSSWAREN-ZEITUNG **See** FOOD + I.E. UND NONFOOD **2337**

SUSTAINABLE DEVELOPMENT **CEASED.** (CN/0840-4666) [19049225] **2206**

SUSTAINABLE DEVELOPMENT : QUARTERLY FORUM OF GLOBAL ENVIRONMENTAL CONSERVATION AND DEVELOPMENT (II) [28231262] **1628**

SUSTAINABLE FARMING (CN/1180-1506) [26066434] **138**

SUT JOURNAL OF MATHEMATICS (JA/0496-6597) [21615847] **3537**

SUTTON HOUSING TRUST **See** REPORT AND ACCOUNTS - SUTTON HOUSING TRUST **4744**

SUTTON SEARCHERS (US/1061-9992) [25471638] **2474**

SUUN CHOSA WOLBO (KO) [11201413] **1586**

SUVANNABHUMI (US) [21238300] **2665**

SUVREMENA METODIKA NASTAVE HRVATSKOGA JEZIKA (CI/0350-221X) [25669271] 3443, **3327**

SUVREMENNA MEDICINA (BU/0562-7192) [07633844] **3644**

SUVREMENNA ZHURNALISTIKA / [SBZH, NAUCHNO-INFORMATSIONEN TSENTUR] (BU/0205-1656) [09242349] **2924**

SUVREMENNI PROBLEMI NA NEVROMORFOLOGIIATA (BU/0324-0258) [01794478] 587, **3846**

SUZBA ZDROWIA (PL/0137-8686) [I01378686] **4804**

SV. SOUND AND VIBRATION (US/0038-1810) [01786054] 2182, **4453**

SVA BULLETIN : OFFIZIELLES ORGAN DER SVA UND DESOAF (SZ/0036-777X) [07889382] **4451**

SVAKALA (II) [10612607] **3443**

SVANTEVIT (DK/0106-5378) [07334401] 3443, **3327**

S'VARA (NEW YORK, N.Y.) **SUSPENDED.** (US/1044-0011) [19643453] 3061, 5053, **4363**

SVAROCNOE PROIZVODSTVO (RU/0491-6441) [10113991] **4028**

SVENSK BERGS- & BRUKSTIDNING (SW) [07290642] **2152**

SVENSK BOK-KATALOG (SW) [02023108] **426**

SVENSK BOKFORTECKNING (SW/0039-6443) [01642087] 3443, **3459**

SVENSK BOKHANDEL (SW/0039-6451) [01643023] **4832**

SVENSK BOTANISK TIDSKRIFT (SW/0039-646X) [01607330] **528**

SVENSK EXEGETISK ARSBOK (SW/1100-2298) [02246404] **5020**

SVENSK FARMACEUTIK TIDSKRIFT (SW/0039-6524) [01766883] **4330**

SVENSK FORSAKRINGS-ARSBOK. THE SWEDISH INSURANCE YEAR-BOOK (SW) [04316839] **2894**

SVENSK GEOGRAFISK ARSBOK (SW/0081-9808) [01607051] **2577**

SVENSK HUSDJURSKOTSEL **See** EFFEKTIVITETSKONTROL I MJOLKPRODUKTIONEN, RESULTAT OCH ANALYS **194**

SVENSK INDUSTRIKALENDER (SW) [01792728] **1628**

SVENSK JAKT (SW/0039-6583) [02578984] **4879**

SVENSK JAKTKALENDER (SW) [02242957] **4924**

SVENSK JURISTTIDNING (SW/0039-6591) [01587755] **3061**

SVENSK KYRKOMUSIK UPPL. A/B **See** KYRKOMUSIKERNAS TIDNING **4128**

Alphabetical Title Index — SWEDEN

SVENSK KYRKOMUSIK UPPL. B See KYRKOMUSIKERNAS TIDNING **4128**

SVENSK LANTMATERITIDSKRIFT (SW) [07438310] **2032**

SVENSK LITTERATURTIDSKRIFT (SW/0039-663X) [01606719] **3443**

SVENSK MISSIONSTIDSKRIFT (SW/0346-217X) [01776714] **5001**

SVENSK-OESTERBOTTINISKA SAMFUNDETS ASBOK (FI) [29855790] **2712**

SVENSK PAPPERSTIDNING (SW/0039-6680) [06399227] **4239**

SVENSK PAPPERSTIDNING. NORDISK CELLULOSA (SW/1101-766X) [25717185] **4239**

SVENSK SJOFARTSTIDNING (SW/0039-6702) [07419526] 852, **4184**

SVENSK TEOLOGISK KVARTALSKRIFT (SW/0039-6761) [01779285] **5001**

SVENSK TIDSKRIFT (SW/0039-677X) [01586291] **3354**

SVENSK TIDSKRIFT FOR MUSIKFORSKNING (SW/0081-9816) [01777574] **4155**

SVENSK TRAVARU- OCH PAPPERSMASSETIDNING (SW/0039-6796) [01766892] **2405**

SVENSK VETERINARTIDNING (SW/0346-2250) [01773001] **5522**

SVENSKA See SIF TIDNINGEN **1710**

SVENSKA DAGBLADET (SW) [12578509] **5811**

SVENSKA FORSKINGSINSTITUTET FOR CEMENT OCH BETONG See CBI RAPPORTER **2020**

SVENSKA KRAFTVERKSFORENINGEN See KRAFTARET : SVENSKA KRAFTVERKSFORENINGENS VERKSAMHETSBERATTELSE **2070**

SVENSKA LANDSMAL OCH SVENSKT FOLKLIV (SW/0347-1837) [10259133] 2324, **3327**

SVENSKA LANDSTINGSFORBUNDET See LANDSTINGENS PLANER **5294**

SVENSKA LANDSTINGSFORBUNDET See PERSONALSITUATIONEN **3626**

SVENSKA MARKNADEN, KNOW HOW, DEN (SW) [29780696] **767**

SVENSKA NATIONALKOMMITTEN FOR MEKANIK. SEKTIONEN FOR DETONIK OCH FORBRANNING See FOREDRAG VID PYROTEKNIKDAGEN **975**

SVENSKA PC-WORLD (SW/0281-9015) [I02819015] **1204**

SVENSKA TIDNINGSARTIKLAR (SW/0039-6907) [01641062] **426**

SVENSKA TIDSKRIFTSARTIKLAR (SW) [07302054] **426**

SVENSKA VAZTGEOGRAFISKA SALLSKAPET See ACTA PHYTOGEOGRAPHICA SUECICA **497**

SVENSKLARARFORENINGENS ARSSKRIFT (SW) [13650988] **1080**

SVENSKT MUSIKHISTORISKT ARKIV See BULLETIN - SVENSKT MUSIKHISTORISKT ARKIV **4106**

SVERDLOVSK, RUSSIA URALSKII GOSUDARSTVENNYI UNIVERSITET See LENINSKAIA TEORIIA OTRAZHENIIA I PROBLEMY PSIKHOLOGII **583**

SVERH-TVERDYE MATERIALY (UN/0203-3119) [06751839] **1997**

SVERIGE-NYTT (SW) [07414793] **426**

SVERIGEKONTAKT (SW) [01775111] **2523**

SVERIGES 1000 I.E. TUSEN STORSTA FORETAG (SW) [02415437] **1628**

SVERIGES FORFATTARFORBUND See MEDLEMSFORTECKNING **3410**

SVERIGES FRIMARKEN OCH HELSAKER / SVERIGES FILATELIST-FORBUND (SW/0347-1152) [10269056] **2787**

SVERIGES HANDELSKALENDER (SW) [01792711] **852**

SVERIGES LANTBRUKSUNIVERSITET. INSTITUTIONEN FOR EKONOMI OCH STATISTIK See RAPPORT - SVERIGES LANTBRUKSUNIVERSITET, INSTITUTIONEN FOR EKONOMI OCH STATISTIK. REPORT - DEPARTMENT OF ECONOMICS AND STATISTICS **1537**

SVERIGES LANTBRUKSUNIVERSITET. INSTITUTIONEN FOR MARKVETENSKAP See RAPPORTER FRAN JORDEBEARBETNINGSAVDELNINGEN, SVERIGES LANTBRUKSUNIVERSITET **184**

SVERIGES LANTBRUKSUNIVERSITET. INSTITUTIONEN FOR SKOGLIG GENETIK OCH VAXTFYSIOLOGI See RAPPORT - SVERIGES LANTBRUKSUNIVERSITET. INSTITUTIONEN FOR SKOGLIG GENETIK OCH VAXTFYSIOLOGI. REPORT - SWEDISH UNIVERSITY OF AGRICULTURAL SCIENCES, DEPARTMENT OF FOREST GENETICS AND PLANT PHYSIOLOGY **2392**

SVERIGES LANTBRUKSUNIVERSITET. INSTITUTIONEN FOR VAXT- OCH SKOGSSKYDD. KONSULENTAVDELNINGEN/VAXTSKYDD See VAXTSKYDDSRAPPORTER. JORDBRUK **529**

SVERIGES LANTBRUKSUNIVERSITET. INSTITUTIONEN FOR VIRKESLARA See RAPPORT - SVERIGES LANTBRUKSUNIVERSITET, INSTITUTION FOR VIRKESLARA **2391**

SVERIGES NATUR (SW/0039-6974) [01794821] **2206**

SVERIGES SKOGSVARDSFORBUND See SKOG & FORSKNING **2395**

SVERIGES UTSADESFORENING See SVERIGES UTSADESFORENINGS TIDSKRIFT **189**

SVERIGES UTSADESFORENINGS TIDSKRIFT (SW/0039-6990) [01773002] 528, **189**

SVERSTNIKI (RU) [06201817] **3443**

SVESKE ZADUZBINE IVE ANDRICA (YU) [10582463] **3327**

SVET (RU) [24536322] **2221**

SVET (BROOKLYN, NEW YORK, N.Y.) (RU/0731-3993) [08173952] **5053**

SVET LITERATURY (XR/0862-8440) **3443**

SVETOVA LITERATURA (XR/0039-7075) [I00397075] **3443**

SVETSAREN (SW/0346-8577) [02470460] **4028**

SVETSEN (SW/0039-7091) [09542292] **4028**

SVILUPPO E ORGANIZZAZIONE (IT/0391-7045) [I03917045] **887**

SVINOVODSTVO (MOSKVA) (RU/0039-713X) [10017335] **222**

SVJAZANNAJA VODA V DISPERSNYH SISTEMAH (RU/0371-4268) [10863553] **5540**

SVM MAC PARIS (FR/1166-4770) [I11664770] **1204**

SVOBODA (JERSEY CITY) (US/0274-6964) [01766932] **5711**

SVOBODNAIA GRUZIIA : ORGAN VERKHOVNOGO SOVETA RESPUBLIKI GRUZIIA (GS) [24167481] **5801**

SVOBODNAIA MYSL (RU) [24940226] **4497**

SVOBODNOE VREMIA I ORGANIZATSIIA DOSUGA V SOTSIALISTICHESKOM OBSHCHESTVE NA SOVREMENNOM ETAPE (RU) [20445868] **4855**

SVOBODNYJ MIR (US/0892-6379) [12994749] **426**

SVODNYI BIULLETEN NOVYKH INOSTRANNYKH KNIG, POSTUPIVSHIKH V BIBLIOTEKI SSSR: OBSHCHESTVENNYE NAUKI (RU) [04205328] **5224**

SVODNYI KATALOG BIBLIOGRAFICHESKIKH RABOT, VYPOLNENNYKH V SOVETSKOM SOIUZE: ESTESTVENNYE I FIZIKO-MATEMATICHESKIE NAUKI (RU) [02441227] 5161, **5176**

SVODNYI KATALOG INOSTRANNYH KART I ATLASOV, POLUCHENNYKH BIBLIOTEKAMI AKADEMII NAUK SSSR I BIBLIOTEKAMI AKADEMII NAUK SOIUZNYKH RESPUBLIK (RU) [02436987] **2577**

SVOISTVA POCHV I IKH PLODORODIE See POCHVOVEDENIE I AAGROKHIMIIA / BELORUSSKII NAUCHNO-ISSLEDOVATELSKII INSTITUT POCHVOVEDENIIA I AGROKHIMII **182**

SVOLTA DEL SIDACATO, LA SUSPENDED. (IT) **1713**

SVPW-JAHRBUCH ANNUAIRE ASSP (SZ) [19230577] **4497**

SVT. JULKINEN TALOUS (FI/0784-8323) [20142474] **5344**

SVT. KOULUTUS JA TUTKIMUS See KOULUTUS **1760**

SWAIA UPDATE (US/0892-6417) [09626031] **2274**

SWALL BULLETIN (US) [03478548] 3062, **3252**

SWAMP GAS JOURNAL, THE (CN/0707-7106) [04879600] **37**

SWAMP ROOT (US/1045-7682) [19486743] **3443**

SWAMP THING (US) [14641719] **4866**

SWAMPFOX (US/8756-0143) [11426792] **2762**

SWANN GALLERIES, INC See SWANN GALLERIES, INC **4832**

SWANN GALLERIES, INC (US/0193-5526) [02009467] **4832**

SWANSEA GEOGRAPHER (UK/0081-9980) [08641829] **2577**

SWARA / EAST AFRICAN WILD LIFE SOCIETY (KE) [05022641] **5598**

SWARAJYA (II) [03999897] **2665**

SWARTHMORE COLLEGE, SWARTHMORE, PENNSYLVANIA LIBRARY See REPORT - SWARTHMORE COLLEGE, SWARTHMORE, PENNSYLVANIA **3245**

●SWARTZLANDER DESCENDANTS, THE (US/1062-3930) [25610480] **2474**

SWASILAND : WIRTSCHAFTLICHE ENTWICKLUNG (GW) [05113825] **1586**

SWAZILAND REPORT BY THE AUDITOR GENERAL FOR THE PERIOD ... / KINGDOM OF SWAZILAND **4744**

SWAZILAND. CENTRAL STATISTICAL OFFICE See EMPLOYMENT AND WAGES **1666**

SWAZILAND. CENTRAL STATISTICAL OFFICE See EDUCATION STATISTICS - (SWAZILAND) **1794**

SWAZILAND. CENTRAL STATISTICAL OFFICE See BALANCE OF PAYMENTS **773**

SWAZILAND. CENTRAL STATISTICAL OFFICE See ANNUAL STATISTICAL BULLETIN - SWAZILAND. CENTRAL STATISTICAL OFFICE **5321**

SWAZILAND. DEPT. OF ESTABLISHMENT & TRAINING See OFFICE DIRECTORY - DEPT. OF ESTABLISHMENT & TRAINING **4670**

SWAZILAND. DEPT. OF POSTS AND TELECOMMUNICATIONS See POST OFFICE GUIDE **1146**

SWAZILAND. DEPT. OF STATISTICS. ANNUAL STATISTICAL BULLETIN - SWAZILAND See ANNUAL STATISTICAL BULLETIN - SWAZILAND. CENTRAL STATISTICAL OFFICE **5321**

SWAZILAND. GEOLOGICAL SURVEY AND MINES DEPT See ANNUAL REPORT OF THE GEOLOGICAL SURVEY AND MINES DEPARTMENT, SWAZILAND **1365**

SWAZILAND. GEOLOGICAL SURVEY AND MINES DEPT See BULLETIN - SWAZILAND, GEOLOGICAL SURVEY AND MINES DEPARTMENT **1370**

SWAZILAND GOVERNMENT GAZETTE (SQ) **5811**

SWAZILAND POPULATION CENSUS See REPORT ON THE SWAZILAND POPULATION CENSUS **4562**

●SWE (NEW YORK, N.Y.) (US/1070-6232) [28441347] **1997**

SWEA CITY HERALD-PRESS, THE (US) [16316672] **5673**

SWEATERS AND AFGHANS CEASED. (US/0278-7466) [07118337] **5186**

SWEDEN See LAGEN OM ALLMAN FORSAKRING OCH ANDRA FORFATTNINGAR OM SOCIALFORSAKRING M.M **5294**

SWEDEN See KONSUMENTVERKETS FOERFATTNINGSSAMLING **2993**

SWEDEN See FORFATTNINGAR OM UPPBORD M.M **4727**

SWEDEN. DELEGATIONEN FOR ENERGIFORSKNING See FORSKNING, UTVECKLING OCH DEMONSTRATION INOM ENERGIOMRADET--EN GLOBAL OVERSIKT **1944**

SWEDEN. DOMANVERKET See DOMANKONCERNEN **2378**

SWEDEN. EKONOMIDEPARTEMENTET See SWEDISH BUDGET, THE **4751**

SWEDEN. FINANSDEPARTEMENTET See DEPARTEMENTSNYTT **1591**

SWEDEN. GENERALTULLSTYRELSEN See GTM, GENERALTULLSTYRELSENS MEDDELANDEN **4729**

SWEDEN. GEOLOGISKA UNDERSOKNING See RAPPORTER OCH MEDDELANDEN - SVERIGES GEOLOGISKA UNDERSOKNING **1393**

SWEDEN INTERNATIONAL (SW/1101-4989) [I11014989] **714**

SWEDEN. KONSUMENTOMBUDSMANNEN See KO, KONSUMENTOMBUDSMANNEN. TIDSKRIFTEN **1571**

SWEDEN. KONSUMENTVERKET See VAD VI GOR **1300**

SWEDEN. KUNGL. PATENT- OCH REGISTRERINGSVERKET See PATENT **1307**

SWEDEN. LUFTFARTSVERKET See LUFTFARTSVERKET **28**

SWEDEN. RIKSARKIVET See MEDDELANDEN FRAN SVENSKA RIKSARKIVET **2482**

SWEDEN. RIKSDAGEN See FRAN RIKSDAG & I.E. OCH DEPARTEMENT **4727**

SWEDEN. RIKSREVISIONSVERKET See EA, BESTAMMELSER OM REDOVISNING, BOKFORING, REVISION, UPPHANDLING, ARKIVVARD M.M **743**

SWEDEN. RIKSSKATTEVERKET See ARSBOK - RIKSSKATTEVERKET **4711**

SWEDEN — Alphabetical Title Index

SWEDEN. SOCIALSTYRELSEN *See* ALKOHOLSTATISTIK **1350**

SWEDEN. SOCIALSTYRELSEN. NAMNDEN FOR HALSOUPPLYSNING *See* HALSOUPPLYSNING **4777**

SWEDEN. STATENS INDUSTRIVERK *See* RESEARCH ACTIVITIES / SWEDISH NATIONAL INDUSTRIAL BOARD **4683**

SWEDEN. STATENS KARNKRAFTINSPEKTION *See* ANSLAGSFRAMSTALLNING FOR BUDGETARET **2154**

SWEDEN. STATENS NATURVARDSVERK *See* RESEARCH ACTIVITY CATALOGUE **2181**

SWEDEN. STATENS RAD FOR BYGGNADSFORSKNING *See* CURRENT PROJECTS - SWEDISH COUNCIL FOR BUILDING RESEARCH **612**

SWEDEN. STATENS RAD FOR BYGGNADSFORSKNING *See* VERKSAMHETSPLAN - STATENS RAD FOR BYGGNADSFORSKNING **631**

SWEDEN. STATISTISKA CENTRALBYRAN *See* HAELSA OCH SJUKVAARDSKONSUMTION **4777**

SWEDEN. STATISTISKA CENTRALBYRAN *See* SYSSELSATTNING OCH ARBETSTIDER **1713**

SWEDEN. STATISTISKA CENTRALBYRAN *See* INVANDRARNAS LEVNADSFORHALLANDEN **1680**

SWEDEN. STATISTISKA CENTRALBYRAN *See* UTBILDNINGSSTATISTIK **1789**

SWEDEN. STATISTISKA CENTRALBYRAN *See* ALLMAN MANADSSTATISTIK **5320**

SWEDEN. STATISTISKA CENTRALBYRAN *See* KOMMUNERNAS FINANSER **4735**

SWEDEN. STATISTISKA CENTRALBYRAN *See* ARETS TRYCK **5322**

SWEDEN. STATISTISKA CENTRALBYRAN *See* FARSKA FAKTA OCH SORTERADE SIFFRUR **5327**

SWEDEN. STATISTISKA CENTRALBYRAN *See* FOLKMANGD **4562**

SWEDEN. STATISTISKA CENTRALBYRIAN *See* STATISTISK TIDSKRIFT **5344**

SWEDEN. TELEVERKET *See* ARSREDOVISNING - TELEVERKET **1149**

SWEDEN. TELEVERKET *See* ANNUAL REPORT - TELEVERKET **1149**

SWEDENBORG MOVEMENT NEWSLETTER *See* OUTLOOK NEW CHURCH. GENERAL CONFERENCE **4984**

SWEDISH AMERICAN GENEALOGIST (US/0275-9314) [07250412] **2474**

SWEDISH-AMERICAN HISTORICAL QUARTERLY (US/0730-028X) [07941673] **2762**

SWEDISH ARCHAEOLOGY *See* CURRENT SWEDISH ARCHAEOLOGY **266**

SWEDISH BEHAVIORAL SCIENCE RESEARCH REPORTS (SW) [02243271] **5224**

SWEDISH BOOK REVIEW (UK/0265-8119) [10318667] **3354**

SWEDISH BOOK REVIEW. SUPPLEMENT (UK/0265-8119) [11838017] **4832**

SWEDISH BUDGET, THE (SW) [04016439] **4751**

SWEDISH CONCRETE ASSOCIATION *See* BETONG **601**

SWEDISH DEFENCE MATERIEL ADMINISTRATION QUALIFIED PRODUCT LIST OF ELECTRONIC COMPONENTS : SE-MIL-QPL (SW/0283-8060) **2083**

SWEDISH DENTAL JOURNAL (SW/0347-9994) [03459473] **1336**

SWEDISH DENTAL JOURNAL. SUPPLEMENT (SW/0348-6672) [03956546] **1336**

SWEDISH ECONOMY (STOCKHOLM. 1961), THE (SW/0039-7296) [01587357] **1523**

SWEDISH EXPORT DIRECTORY (SW/0280-4344) [02009389] **852**

SWEDISH FILMS. FILMS SUEDOIS (SW) [06218328] **4078**

SWEDISH FOUNDATION (SW) [19880717] **189**

SWEDISH IMPRINTS : A RETROSPECTIVE NATIONAL BIBLIOGRAPHY (SW) **426**

SWEDISH JOURNAL OF AGRICULTURAL RESEARCH (SW/0049-2701) [01773003] **139**

SWEDISH JOURNAL OF ECONOMICS, THE (SW/0039-7318) [01641438] **1523**

SWEDISH SOCIETY FOR THE CONSERVATION OF NATURE *See* ACID RAIN **2185**

SWEDISH TOWN AND COUNTRY PLANNING REVIEW, THE (SW/0032-0560) [05331704] **2836**

SWEET BRIAR COLLEGE *See* ALUMNAE DIRECTORY OF SWEET BRIAR COLLEGE **1096**

SWEET BRIAR COLLEGE *See* ALUMNAE MAGAZINE - SWEET BRIAR COLLEGE **1808**

● SWEET B'S PAD (US/1064-5977) [26335347] 2274, **1070**

SWEET POTATO (US/0147-5282) [03190635] **4155**

● SWEETENER MARKET DATA / UNITED STATES DEPARTMENT OF AGRICULTURE, AGRICULTURAL STABILIZATION AND CONSERVATION SERVICE (US) [26190871] **2359**

SWEETGRASS (CN/0825-1886) [12991740] **2274**

SWEET'S CATALOG FILE. CONTRACT INTERIORS (US) [22994725] **629**

SWEET'S CATALOG FILE. GENERAL BUILDING & RENOVATION (US) [23458903] **629**

SWEET'S CATALOG FILE. HOMEBUILDING & REMODELING (US/1070-8324) [23166071] **629**

SWEET'S CATALOG FILE. PRODUCTS FOR ENGINEERING AND RETROFIT, ELECTRICAL AND RELATED PRODUCTS (US/1056-5647) [10701481] **2083**

SWEET'S CATALOG FILE. PRODUCTS FOR HOME BUILDING AND REMODELING (US/0743-5789) [10246317] **629**

SWEET'S CATALOG FILE : PRODUCTS FOR INDUSTRIAL CONSTRUCTION AND RENOVATION (US/0145-4870) [02744370] **629**

SWEET'S CATALOG FILE : PRODUCTS FOR INDUSTRIAL CONSTRUCTION AND RENOVATION, RENOVATION EXTENSION (US/0145-4889) [02743736] **629**

SWEET'S ELECTRICAL ENGINEERING & REPORT CATALOG FILE (US/1056-5426) [23723069] **2083**

SWEET'S ENGINEERING CATALOG FILE (US) [02245760] **629**

SWEET'S ENGINEERING MARKET (US/0146-8316) [03038262] **2032**

SWEET'S GENERAL BUILDING MARKET (US/0146-8456) [03036952] **630**

SWEET'S INDUSTRIAL CONSTRUCTION & RENOVATION CATALOG FILE (US/1056-5272) [22882461] 1628, **1997**

SWEET'S INDUSTRIAL CONSTRUCTION AND RENOVATION FILE *See* SWEET'S CATALOG FILE : PRODUCTS FOR INDUSTRIAL CONSTRUCTION AND RENOVATION **629**

SWEET'S INDUSTRIAL CONSTRUCTION & RENOVATION FILE WITH PLANT ENGINEERING EXTENSION MARKET LIST (US/0094-825X) [01794561] 2099, **630**

SWEET'S INDUSTRIAL CONSTRUCTION AND RENOVATION MARKET/RENOVATION EXTENSION (US/0146-8324) [03038313] **630**

SWEET'S INTERIORS MARKET (US/0146-8243) [03036917] **2903**

SWEET'S LIGHT RESIDENTIAL CONSTRUCTION MARKET (US/0146-8308) [03038091] **630**

SWEET'S PLANT ENGINEERING EXTENSION INDUSTRIAL CONSTRUCTION AND RENOVATION FILE (US/0092-8763) [01791657] **2099**

SWEET'S SHOWROOM (US/0364-7021) [02667527] **3488**

SWEET'S SHOWROOM MARKET LIST (US/0364-3654) [02636576] **630**

SWEETWATER REPORTER (SWEETWATER, TEX.: 1911) (US) [14396347] **5755**

SWENSON CENTER NEWS (US/0895-7126) [15146665] **2474**

SWFL BUSINESS VIEWS (US) **714**

SWIAT CISZY (PL/0238-9746) [I02389746] **4394**

● SWIAT KARATE (PL/0867-6410) [I08676410] **4924**

SWIAT MODYCH WARSZAWA. 1949 (PL/0137-9321) [I01379321] **1070**

SWIATOWIT (PL) [02011093] 4231, **284**

SWIERSZCZYK (PL/0491-8193) [I04918193] **3443**

SWIFT COUNTY MONITOR-NEWS (US/0747-1653) [10621845] **5699**

SWIFT STUDIES : THE ANNUAL OF THE EHRENPREIS CENTER (GW) [15737599] **3443**

SWIM (CN/0319-0560) [02442091] **4924**

SWIM (ARLINGTON, VA.) (US/8755-2027) [11275170] **4924**

SWIM FASHION QUARTERLY (US) **1087**

SWIMMING AND DIVING RULES (US/0163-2884) [04335705] **4925**

SWIMMING POOL AGE & SPA MERCHANDISER, DATA & REFERENCE ANNUAL (US) [08568002] **4855**

SWIMMING POOL & SPA INDUSTRY MARKET REPORT (US/1042-7074) [19092123] **1628**

SWIMMING POOL NEWS (UK) **4925**

SWIMMING POOL/SPA AGE (US/0899-1022) [17992066] **4855**

SWIMMING POOL WEEKLY AND SWIMMING POOL AGE REPLACEMENT PARTS GUIDE (US/0197-7997) [06112763] **630**

SWIMMING TEACHER (UK/0306-0403) [I03060403] **4925**

SWIMMING TECHNIQUE (US/0039-7415) [01696565] **4925**

SWIMMING TIMES (UK) [01773434] **4925**

SWIMMING WORLD (US) [01695073] **4925**

SWIMMING WORLD AND JUNIOR SWIMMER (1965) (US/0039-7431) [03794698] **4925**

● SWINE HEALTH AND PRODUCTION (US/1066-4963) [26966585] **222**

SWINGTIME NEWS (CN/0227-6836) [08072116] **5188**

SWISS AMERICAN HISTORICAL SOCIETY REVIEW (US) **2762**

SWISS AMERICAN HISTORICAL SOCIETY REVIEW (US) **2474**

SWISS AMERICAN REVIEW (US) [14081222] **5721**

SWISS ART GUIDE (SZ) [08376541] **366**

SWISS BANK CORPORATION *See* RAPPORT DU CONSEIL D'ADMINISTRATION A L'ASSEMBLEE GENERALE ORDINAIRE DES ACTIONNAIRES **806**

SWISS BIOTECH (SZ/0253-9675) [21969309] **3696**

SWISS BUSINESS (SZ) [16700118] 917, **714**

SWISS CHEM (SZ/0251-1703) [09028261] **993**

SWISS CONTAMINATION CONTROL (SZ/1011-6710) [I10116710] **2244**

SWISS DENT (SZ/0251-1657) [13909718] **1336**

SWISS ECONOMIC NEWS (SW/1019-1127) [08262611] **1523**

SWISS FINANCIAL YEAR BOOK. SCHWEIZERISCHES FINANZ-JAHRBUCH. ANNUAIRE FINANCIER SUISSE. ANNUARIO FINANZIARIO SVIZZERO (SZ) [05159572] **813**

SWISS FOOD (SZ/0251-1681) [09027873] **2359**

SWISS MATERIALS (SZ/1013-4476) [21980533] **1997**

SWISS MED (SZ/0251-1665) [08415202] **3644**

SWISS NEWS (BE/0770-996X) [I0770996X] **852**

SWISS PACKAGING CATALOGUE (SZ) **4222**

SWISS PHARMA (SZ/0251-1673) [08415241] **4330**

SWISS PLASTICS (SZ/0251-169X) [I0251169X] **2108**

SWISS PRESS REVIEW AND NEWS REPORT (SZ) **2712**

SWISS REVIEW OF WORLD AFFAIRS (SZ/0039-7490) [01604364] **4536**

SWISS VET (SZ/0254-6337) [I02546337] **5522**

SWISS WATCH *See* UHREN RUNDSCHAU. REVUE DE LA MONTRE **2916**

SWISS WATCH AND JEWELRY JOURNAL (SZ/0039-7520) [13100745] **2916**

SWITCHGEAR, SWITCHBOARD APPARATUS, RELAYS, AND INDUSTRIAL CONTROLS (US/0275-4932) [03061042] **2083**

SWITZERLAND *See* SAMMLUNG DER EIDGENÖSSISCHEN GESETZE **3045**

SWITZERLAND *See* RECUEIL OFFICIEL DES LOIS FEDERALES **3037**

SWITZERLAND *See* AMTLICHE SAMMLUNG DES BUNDESRECHTS **2933**

SWITZERLAND *See* FODOR'S SWITZERLAND **5473**

Alphabetical Title Index — SYNCHRO

SWITZERLAND. BUNDESAMT FUR SOZIALVERSICHERUNG *See* RAPPORT ANNUEL SUR L'ASSURANCE-VIEILLESSE, SURVIVANTS ET INVALIDITE FEDERALE ET SUR LE REGIME DES ALLOCATIONS EN FAVEUR DES MILITAIRES ET DES PERSONNES ASTREINTES A SERVIR DANS L'ORGANISATION DE LA PROTECTION CIVILE **5303**

SWITZERLAND. BUNDESAMT FUR STATISTIK *See* SCHWEIZERISCHE BIBLIOTHEKEN **3260**

SWITZERLAND. BUNDESGERICHT *See* ARRETS DU TRIBUNAL FEDERAL SUISSE. RECUEIL OFFICIEL **2937**

SWITZERLAND. BUNDESVERSAMMLUNG. NATIONALRAT *See* AMTLICHES BULLETIN DER BUNDESVERSAMMLUNG **4463**

SWITZERLAND DEMOCRAT (US) [11829574] **5667**

SWITZERLAND. DEPARTEMENT DES AUSWARTIGEN *See* LISTE DES MEMBRES DU CORPS CONSULAIRE **4662**

SWITZERLAND EDIGENOSSISCHE OBERZOLLDIREKTION *See* JAHRESSTATISTIK DES AUSSENHANDELS DER SCHWEIZ. STATISTIQUE ANNUELLE DU COMMERCE EXTERIEUR DE LA SUISSE **730**

SWITZERLAND. EIDGENOSSISCHE OBERZOLLDIREKTION *See* MONATSSTATISTIK DES AUSSENHANDELS DER SCHWEIZ. STATISTIQUE MENSUELLE DU COMMERCE EXTERIEUR DE LA SUISSE **846**

SWITZERLAND. EIDGENOSSISCHES STATISTISCHES AMT *See* STATISTIK DES HOCHSCHULWESENS IN DER SCHWEIZ **1848**

SWITZERLAND. EIDGENOSSISCHES STATISTISCHES AMT *See* EINGEFUHRTE MOTORFAHRZEUGE **5414**

SWITZERLAND. EIDGENOSSISCHES STATISTISCHES AMT *See* TOURISMUS IM KANTON GRAUBUNDEN **5494**

SWITZERLAND. EIDGENOSSISCHES STATISTISCHES AMT *See* TOURISMUS IN FREMDENORTEN UND STADTEN. TOURISME DANS QUELQUES CENTRES TOURISTIQUES ET VILLES **5494**

SWITZERLAND. GENERALDIREKTION DER POST-, TELEGRAPHEN UND TELEPHON-VERWALTUNG *See* TECHNISCHE MITTEILUNGEN DER SCHWEIZERISCHEN TELEGRAPHEN- UND TELEPHON-VERWALTUNG **5162**

SWITZERLAND. GENERALDIREKTION DER POST-, TELEGRAPHEN- UND TELEPHONVERWALTUNG. POST-, TELEGRAPHEN- UND TELEPHON-AMTSBLATT *See* POST-, TELEFON- UND TELEGRAFEN-AMTSBLATT. FEUILLE OFFICIELLE DES POSTES, TELEPHONES ET TELEGRAPHES. FOGLIO UFFICIALE DELLE POSTE, DEI TELEFONI E DEI TELEGRAFI **1162**

SWITZERLAND, JEWEL OF EUROPE (US/1057-0896) [23936408] **2712**

SWITZERLAND. KOMMISSION FUR KONJUNKTURFRAGEN *See* SITUATION ECONOMIQUE SUISSE ET LES PERSPECTIVES, LA **1584**

SWITZERLAND, LAWS, STATUTES, ETC *See* KOMMENTAR ZUM SCHWEIZERISCHEN ZIVILGESETZBUCH **2992**

SWITZERLAND. SCHWEIZERISCHE KARTELLKOMMISSION *See* VEROFFENTLICHUNGEN DER SCHWEIZERISCHEN KARTELLKOMMISSION **3071**

SWITZERLAND. STATISTISCHES AMT *See* TOURISME DANS LE CANTON DU VALAIS. TOURISMUS IM KANTON WALLIS **5493**

SWITZERLAND. STATISTISCHES AMT *See* MOTORFAHRZEUGBESTAND IN DER SCHWEIZ NACH KANTONEN UND ORTSCHAFTEN **5420**

SWITZERLAND. STATISTISCHES AMT *See* REISEVERKEHR DER SCHWEIZER IM AUSLAND **2574**

SWIZZLE STICK (US/0090-9009) [01786131] **852**

SWOP HI LO INK REFERENCE (US) **4569**

SWORD AND THE TROWEL, THE (UK) [06948418] **5001**

SWORD OF THE LORD, THE (US/0039-7547) [01776715] **5001**

SWORD. SIKH WORLD ORGANIZATION'S REVIEW AND DIGEST (CN/0828-9131) [12873938] **5001**

SWORDS & PLOUGHSHARES (US/1063-133X) [25897395] **4536**

SWS CONTRACT REPORT (US/0733-3927) [07995933] **1418**

SWS RUNDSCHAU (AU) [17543384] **5224**

SYARIKAT PERMODALAN KEMAJUAN PERUSAHAAN MALAYSIA BERHAD *See* MIDF MELAPURKAN **798**

SYBIRACY WARSZAWA (PL/0867-2814) [I08672814] **2274**

SYCAMORE REVIEW (US/1043-1497) [19329223] **3443**

SYD MATTHEWS & PARTNERS LIMITED *See* MATTHEWS' LIST **1116**

SYDNEY & LOUISBURG RAILWAY HISTORICAL SOCIETY *See* S & L MUSEUM NEWSLETTER **4096**

SYDNEY LAW REVIEW, THE (AT/0082-0512) [01767029] **3062**

SYDNEY MORNING HERALD, THE (AT) [01767031] **5777**

SYDNEY OBSERVATORY *See* SYDNEY OBSERVATORY PAPERS **401**

SYDNEY OBSERVATORY PAPERS (AT) [06103769] **401**

SYDNEY PAPERS, THE (AT/1035-7068) [25267606] **1640**

SYDNEY REVIEW 1988 (AT/1032-2892) [10322892] 2511, **331**

SYDNEY STUDIES IN ENGLISH (AT/0156-5419) [03304693] **3443**

SYDNEY STUDIES IN SOCIETY AND CULTURE (AT) [15325222] **5264**

SYDNEY. UNIVERSITY. AUSTRALIAN LANGUAGE RESEARCH CENTRE *See* OCCASIONAL PAPER - UNIVERSITY OF SYDNEY, AUSTRALIAN LANGUAGE RESEARCH CENTRE **3307**

SYDNEY. UNIVERSITY. SYDNEY UNIVERSITY UNION *See* UNION RECORDER, THE **1096**

SYDNEY'S CHILD (AT/1034-6384) [I10346384] **2286**

SYDOWIA (AU/0082-0598) [01767032] **528**

SYGEPLEJERSKEN (DK/0106-8350) [00931841] **3870**

SYLLABUS (US) 1905, **1225**

SYLLABUS (US) [07967958] **3062**

SYLLABUS / UNIVERSITY OF HEALING (US/0733-0375) [08519923] **1849**

SYLLECTA CLASSICA (US/1040-3612) [18390584] **1080**

SYLLOGE EXCERPTORUM E DISSERTATIONIBUS AD GRADUM DOCTORIS IN SACRA THEOLOGIA VEL IN IURE CANONICO CONSEQUENDUM CONSCRIPTIS (BE) [01604848] **5037**

SYLLOGE NUMMORUM GRAECORUM (NEW YORK) (US/0271-3993) [06636459] **2783**

SYLLOGEUS - NATIONAL MUSEUM OF NATURAL SCIENCES (CN/0704-576X) [02248669] 5161, **4097**

SYLVATROP (PH/0115-0022) [02805379] **2396**

SYLVESTER LOCAL NEWS, THE (US/8750-5312) [11477593] **5655**

SYLVIA PORTER'S PERSONAL FINANCE (US/0896-4106) [17064907] **917**

SYLWAN : CZASOPISMO MIESIECZNE DLA LESNIKOW I WASCICIELI ZIEMSKICH / ORGAN GALIC. TOWARZYSTWA LESNEGO (PL/0039-7660) [01607487] **2396**

SYMBIOSIS (PHILADELPHIA, PA.) (US/0334-5114) [12781550] **474**

SYMBOLA ET EMBLEMATA (NE/0923-9073) [I09239073] **2712**

SYMBOLAE BOTANICAE UPSALIENSIS (SW/0082-0644) [01589996] **528**

SYMBOLAE OSLOENSES (NO/0039-7679) [09089497] **3327**

SYMBOLIC INTERACTION (US/0195-6086) [05025923] **5264**

SYMBOLON *CEASED*. (GW/0082-0660) [01696943] 2855, 4363, **5001**

SYMBOLS (US/0889-7425) [06153607] 4097, **246**

SYMBOLS OF AMERICAN LIBRARIES (US/0095-0874) [03423023] **3252**

SYMMEIKTA / VASILIKON HIDRYMA EREUNON, KENTRON VYZANTINÂON EREUNON (GR) [06158118] **2712**

SYMPHONIUM (PITTSBURGH, PA.) (US/1052-7648) [22366551] **4155**

SYMPHONY OF VOICES : AN ASIAN AMERICAN WOMEN'S JOURNAL, A (US) [25514908] 2274, **5567**

SYMPHONY USER'S JOURNAL, THE *CEASED*. (US/8750-9415) [11950115] **1291**

SYMPHONY (WASHINGTON, D.C.) (US/1046-3232) [20183269] 389, **4155**

SYMPOSIA BIOLOGICA HUNGARICA *CEASED*. (HU/0082-0695) [01767039] **474**

SYMPOSIA IN NEUROSCIENCE (IT) [14986811] **3846**

SYMPOSIA MATHEMATICA (UK/0082-0725) [02253604] **3537**

SYMPOSIA MEDICA HOECHST (GW/0341-6321) [02530327] **3644**

SYMPOSIA OF THE GIOVANNI LORENZINI FOUNDATION (NE/0166-1167) [04012084] 493, **3644**

SYMPOSIA OF THE INSTITUTE OF BIOLOGY (UK/0537-9032) [07466967] **474**

SYMPOSIA OF THE JOURNAL OF APPLIED POLYMER SCIENCE (US) **994**

SYMPOSIA OF THE ROYAL ENTOMOLOGICAL SOCIETY OF LONDON (UK/0080-4363) [02450296] **5613**

SYMPOSIA OF THE SOCIETY FOR EXPERIMENTAL BIOLOGY (UK/0081-1386) [01697185] **474**

SYMPOSIA OF THE SOCIETY FOR GENERAL MICROBIOLOGY (UK) [08920293] **570**

SYMPOSIA OF THE SOCIETY FOR THE STUDY OF INBORN ERRORS OF METABOLISM (US/0081-1548) [04015558] **3644**

SYMPOSIA OF THE SWEDISH NUTRITION FOUNDATION (SW/0082-0415) [03754124] **4199**

SYMPOSIA OF THE ZOOLOGICAL SOCIETY OF LONDON (UK/0084-5612) [01417377] **5598**

SYMPOSIA ON FRONTIERS OF PHARMACOLOGY (US/0733-9321) [08693737] **4330**

SYMPOSION; PHILOSOPHISCHE SCHRIFTENREIHE (GW) [01767043] **4363**

SYMPOSIUM AT GUERNEVILLE *See* NEWSLETTER : CONCERT RECORDINGS **4141**

SYMPOSIUM / DEUTSCHKANADISCHE STUDIEN (CN/0823-2458) [10052309] 2631, **3443**

SYMPOSIUM - INTERNATIONAL ASTRONOMICAL UNION (NE/0074-1809) [01641452] **401**

SYMPOSIUM (INTERNATIONAL) ON COMBUSTION. PAPERS (US/0082-0784) [02052729] 994, **1997**

... SYMPOSIUM OF THE SOCIETY FOR DEVELOPMENTAL BIOLOGY, THE (US/0583-9009) [08851748] **474**

SYMPOSIUM ON CHEMICAL PROBLEMS CONNECTED WITH THE STABILITY OF EXPLOSIVES (SW/0348-7180) [I03487180] **994**

SYMPOSIUM ON FUSION ENGINEERING. PROCEEDINGS *See* IEEE/NPSS SYMPOSIUM FUSION ENGINEERING : PROCEEDINGS **1977**

SYMPOSIUM ON OCULAR THERAPY (US/0082-0873) [01589327] **3879**

SYMPOSIUM ON PETROLEUM ECONOMICS AND EVALUATION *See* SYMPOSIUM ON PETROLEUM ECONOMICS AND EVALUATION **4280**

SYMPOSIUM ON PETROLEUM ECONOMICS AND EVALUATION (US) [01644634] **4280**

SYMPOSIUM ON PRIVATE INVESTMENTS ABROAD. PRIVATE INVESTORS ABROAD *See* PRIVATE INVESTMENTS ABROAD. PROBLEMS AND SOLUTIONS IN INTERNATIONAL BUSINESS **1639**

SYMPOSIUM ON SALT (US/0277-4267) [01767051] **1399**

SYMPOSIUM PAPERS / INSTITUTION OF CHEMICAL ENGINEERS, NORTH WESTERN BRANCH (UK/0142-5811) [10970608] **2017**

SYMPOSIUM PROCEEDINGS - SOCIETY OF EXPERIMENTAL TEST PILOTS. SYMPOSIUM (US/0742-3705) [09212920] **37**

SYMPOSIUM RECORD / IEEE ... INTERNATIONAL SYMPOSIUM ON ELECTROMAGNETIC COMPATIBILITY (US) [12728643] 4445, **2083**

SYMPOSIUM SERIES (CN) [05931583] **1786**

SYMPOSIUM (SYRACUSE) (US/0039-7709) [02009385] 3354, **3327**

SYMPTOME (GW/0930-3472) [18058479] **4363**

SYN OG SEGN (NO/0039-7717) [01767053] **2523**

SYNAPSE (FR/0762-7475) [I07627475] **3846**

SYNAPSE CONNECTION *See* NEURAL TECHNOLOGY UPDATE **1243**

SYNAPSE (NEW YORK, N.Y.) (US/0887-4476) [13234053] **3801**

SYNAPSE (REGINA) (CN/0823-1435) [10195227] **4363**

SYNAPSE (SAN FERNANDO) (US/0145-5435) [02750689] **4156**

SYNAXIS (CN/0710-1627) [08415809] **5002**

SYNC (US/0279-5701) [07102506] **1272**

SYNCHRO (US/0746-5726) [06153921] **4925**

SYNCHROTRON   Alphabetical Title Index

SYNCHROTRON RADIATION NEWS (US/0894-0886) [15789018] **4442**

SYNDICAT DES FONCTIONNAIRES PROVINCIAUX DU QUEBEC *See* BULLETIN DES MEMBRES - SYNDICAT DES FONCTIONNAIRES PROVINCIAUX DU QUEBEC **1656**

SYNDICAT DES FONCTIONNAIRES PROVINCIAUX DU QUEBEC. CONGRES *See* RAPPORT DU PRESIDENT GENERAL - SYNDICAT DES FONCTIONNAIRES PROVINCIAUX DU QUEBEC **1705**

SYNDICATE NEWS (US) **752**

SYNDICATED COLUMNIST CONTACTS (US/1055-2723) [21469872] **2924**

SYNDICATION NEWS (US/1052-4290) [22291697] **1140**

SYNERGY (DALLAS) (US/0164-8993) [04297596] **3252**

SYNERJY (US/0163-2183) [02948005] **1959**

SYNESIS *CEASED.* (IT) 2631, **3444**

SYNFORM *CEASED.* (GW/0723-3655) [10698738] **1048**

SYNFUELS HANDBOOK (US/0732-1120) [08301670] **4280**

SYNLETT (GW/0936-5214) [20447347] **1048**

SYNOPSES FROM THE SWEDISH BUILDING RESEARCH (SW) [04068126] **630**

SYNOPSES OF THE BRITISH FAUNA (UK/0082-1101) [03290683] **5598**

SYNOPSIS OF BOILER AND PRESSURE VESSEL LAW RULES AND REGULATIONS (US) **3103**

SYNOPSIS OF FAMILY THERAPY PRACTICE (US/0162-7171) [04219052] 2286, **3937**

SYNOPSIS OF LAWS ENACTED BY THE STATE OF MARYLAND (US/0093-0520) [01789933] **3062**

SYNOPSIS OF THE HERPETOFAUNA OF MEXICO (US) [01714666] **5598**

SYNOPTIC *CEASED.* (CN/0049-2760) [02305997] **1786**

SYNOPTIC AND UPPER AIR OBSERVATIONS IN THE NETHERLANDS (NE/0470-7427) [02527188] **1435**

SYNTAGMA, TO (GR) [11383650] **3094**

SYNTAX AND SEMANTICS (US/0092-4563) [01783623] **3327**

SYNTAX QUARTERLY (US/0734-0133) [08672623] **1204**

SYNTEESI JYVASKYLA (FI/0359-5242) [03595242] **3444**

SYNTHESE (DORDRECHT) (NE/0039-7857) [02009440] **4363**

SYNTHESE (EDITIONS RECHERCHE SUR LES CIVILISATIONS) (FR/0291-1655) [13615113] **2712**

SYNTHESE FINANCIERE, LA (FR/0985-2174) [09852174] **813**

SYNTHESE HISTORICAL LIBRARY (NE/0082-111X) [11127906] **3252**

SYNTHESE LANGUAGE LIBRARY (NE) [12173372] **3252**

SYNTHESE LIBRARY (NE/0166-6991) [02591121] 5224, **4363**

SYNTHESIS AND REACTIVITY IN INORGANIC AND METAL-ORGANIC CHEMISTRY (US/0094-5714) [01792284] **994**

SYNTHESIS (ASHEVILLE, N.C.) (US/1042-0169) [18904443] 1849, **3062**

SYNTHESIS (BUCURESTI) (RM/0256-7245) [03011872] **3444**

SYNTHESIS (MINNEAPOLIS, MINN.) (US/0890-9687) [01586410] **4156**

SYNTHESIS OF HIGHWAY PRACTICE (US/0547-5570) [01605570] **5393**

SYNTHESIS (OTTAWA) (CN/1180-4734) [22630908] **1786**

SYNTHESIS (REDWOOD CITY) (US/0098-8634) [01574073] **4619**

SYNTHESIS (STUTTGART) (GW/0039-7881) [01430237] **1048**

SYNTHETIC COMMUNICATIONS (US/0039-7911) [01590411] **1048**

SYNTHETIC CRYSTALS NEWSLETTER (UK/0309-8133) [03098133] **1033**

SYNTHETIC FIBRES / ASSOCIATION OF SYNTHETIC FIBRE INDUSTRY (II) [09122786] **5356**

SYNTHETIC FUELS UPDATE (US/0273-2971) [07037268] **4280**

SYNTHETIC LUBRICATION (UK) **1030**

SYNTHETIC METALS (SZ/0379-6779) [05540596] **4021**

SYNTHETIC ORGANIC CHEMICALS. UNITED STATES PRODUCTION AND SALES (US/0082-1144) [02242455] **1628**

SYNTHETIC ORGANIC CHEMICALS. UNITED STATES PRODUCTION AND SALES OF PLASTICIZERS (US) [02344458] 1048, **4460**

SYOPA (FI/0356-3081) [05046075] **3824**

SYRACUSE BUSINESS (US) **714**

SYRACUSE CHEMIST, THE (US/0039-792X) [03246736] **994**

SYRACUSE HERALD-JOURNAL (US) [11178284] **5721**

SYRACUSE JOURNAL OF INTERNATIONAL LAW AND COMMERCE (US/0093-0709) [01787641] **3136**

SYRACUSE LAW REVIEW (US/0039-7938) [01767066] **3062**

SYRACUSE (N.Y.). DEPT. OF AVIATION *See* ANNUAL REPORT / SYRACUSE (N.Y.) DEPT. OF AVIATION **11**

SYRACUSE NEW TIMES (US/0893-844X) [15669760] **2493**

SYRACUSE NEWS (US/0272-2917) [05881812] **2083**

SYRACUSE UNIVERSITY ALUMNI NEWS (US) [03250432] **1103**

SYRACUSE UNIVERSITY. DEPT. OF GEOGRAPHY *See* DISCUSSION PAPER SERIES - DEPARTMENT OF GEOGRAPHY, SYRACUSE UNIVERSITY **2559**

SYRIA (FR/0039-7946) [00998956] 284, **2577**

SYRIA *See* SYRIA'S BUDGET **4751**

SYRIA *See* REPORT ON THE ... SYRIA'S BUDGET **4746**

SYRIA. KAMMER DER GEWERBLICHEN WIRTSCHAFT *See* LEHRLINGSSTATISTIK / KAMMER DER GEWERBLICHEN WIRTSCHAFT FUER STEIERMARK **1687**

SYRIA'S BUDGET (SY) [08683111] **4751**

SYRIE & MONDE ARABE (SY/0039-7962) [02268337] **1523**

SYRIEN : WIRTSCHAFTLICHE ENTWICKLUNG (GW) [03123121] **1586**

SYRO-MESOPOTAMIAN STUDIES (US/0732-6483) [04101377] **2665**

●SYS ADMIN (LAWRENCE, KAN.) (US/1061-2688) [25224543] **1249**

SYSDATA (SZ) 1249, **1262**

SYSSELSATTNING OCH ARBETSTIDER (SW) [04274606] **1713**

SYSTEEMTEORETISCH BULLETIN - INTERAKTIE AKADEMIE (BE/0775-5694) [07755694] **1886**

SYSTEM (ATLANTA, GA.) (US) [17730859] **1849**

SYSTEM DEVELOPMENT (US/0275-6617) [07193130] **1262**

SYSTEM DYNAMICS NEWSLETTER (US) [05157898] **5161**

SYSTEM DYNAMICS REVIEW (US/0883-7066) [12227562] 1283, **3537**

SYSTEM FAMILIE (GW/0933-3053) [18838350] **2286**

SYSTEM (LINKOPING) (UK/0346-251X) [03448460] **3327**

SYSTEM TREND SERVICE (US) [08934347] **1204**

SYSTEMA ASCOMYCETUM (UK/0280-8331) [09922180] **528**

SYSTEMA HELMINTHUM (US) [01456230] **5598**

SYSTEMATIC AND APPLIED MICROBIOLOGY (GW/0723-2020) [09416926] **570**

SYSTEMATIC AND ECOGEOGRAPHIC STUDIES ON CROP GENEPOOLS / INTERNATIONAL BOARD FOR PLANT GENETIC RESOURCES (IT/1017-5598) [14121118] **528**

●SYSTEMATIC BIOLOGY (US/1063-5157) [26048753] **474**

SYSTEMATIC BOTANY (US/0363-6445) [02531771] **528**

SYSTEMATIC BOTANY MONOGRAPHS (US/0737-8211) [09461671] **529**

SYSTEMATIC ENTOMOLOGY (UK/0307-6970) [02356912] **5613**

SYSTEMATIC PARASITOLOGY (NE/0165-5752) [05868970] **5598**

SYSTEMATIC ZOOLOGY *See* SYSTEMATIC BIOLOGY **474**

SYSTEMATISCHE VERZEICHNISSE. ALPHABETISCHES WARENVERZEICHNIS FUER DIE BINNENHANDELSSTATISTIK / HERAUSGEBER STATISTISCHES BUNDESAMT (GW) [11979980] 852, **734**

SYSTEME D PRATIQUE PARIS (FR/1154-2829) [11542829] **1886**

SYSTEMES DE PENSEE EN AFRIQUE NOIRE (FR/0294-7080) [09059869] **5002**

SYSTEMES EXPERTS PARIS (FR/0988-5730) [09885730] **5161**

SYSTEMES SOLAIRES (FR/0295-5873) [02955873] 2182, **1959**

SYSTEMLETTER (CN/0714-7864) [09499041] **1262**

SYSTEMS 3X/400 (US/1055-7768) [23298024] **1204**

SYSTEMS ANALYSIS, MODELLING, SIMULATION (GW/0232-9298) [11887695] 1283, **3537**

SYSTEMS AND COMPUTERS IN JAPAN (US/0882-1666) [11767891] **1249**

SYSTEMS & CONTROL LETTERS (NE/0167-6911) [07764076] **1998**

SYSTEMS & NETWORK INTEGRATION (US/1060-1384) [24880746] **1291**

SYSTEMS & SOFTWARE *CEASED.* (US/0745-0850) [08809644] 1273, 1291, **1249**

SYSTEMS ENGINEERING FOR POWER (US/0147-6068) [02961755] **2083**

SYSTEMS EXPERTS : APPLICATIONS TECHNOLOGIES ACTEURS (FR) **5161**

SYSTEMS INTEGRATION (US/1044-4262) [19540595] 1273, **1274**

SYSTEMS INTEGRATION BUSINESS *CEASED.* (US/1063-407X) [25920351] 1273, **1274**

SYSTEMS, MAN, AND CYBERNETICS REVIEW (US/0160-6409) [04024624] **1252**

SYSTEMS PRACTICE (US/0894-9859) [16389024] 2130, **1249**

SYSTEMS RESEARCH AND INFORMATION SCIENCE (US/0882-3014) [11804163] **3252**

SYSTEMS SCIENCE (PL/0137-1223) [02580682] 1998, 3538, **1249**

SYSTEMS SCIENCE AND MATHEMATICAL SCIENCES / EDITED BY INSTITUTE OF SYSTEMS SCIENCE, CHINESE ACADEMY OF SCIENCES (CC/1000-9590) [22783993] **3538**

SYSTEMS TECHNOLOGY *CEASED.* (UK/0039-8047) [02450959] **2158**

SYSTEMS THINKER, THE (US/1050-2726) [21433741] **887**

SYSTEMS USER *CEASED.* (US/0199-8951) [06275944] **1262**

SYSTEMTALK (US/0893-9586) [15716215] **1204**

SYYSRIISTATIEDUSTELU (FI) [19233609] **4925**

●SYZYGY (STANFORD, CALIF.) (US/1059-6860) [24679754] **5002**

SZABOLCS-SZATMAR MEGYEI KONYVTARI HIRADO (HU/0139-3499) [01393499] **3252**

SZABVANY ES VILAG (HU/0237-5265) [20557541] **4032**

●SZACHISTA WARSZAWA (PL/1230-2309) [I12302309] **4866**

SZACHY (PL) [04051459] 4925, **4866**

SZAKSZERVEZETI SZEMLE (HU) [01789595] **4548**

SZAMADAS (CN/0700-5199) [03399698] **2762**

SZAZADOK (HU/0039-8098) [02007784] **2631**

SZCZECIN (POLAND : VOIVODESHIP) *See* DZIENNIK URZEDOWY WOJEWODZTWA SZCZECINSKIEGO **5807**

SZCZECINSKIE ROCZNIKI NAUKOWE. NAUKI SPOECZNE (PL/0860-2212) [21074984] **5224**

SZEGED (HUNGARY). EGYETEM *See* ACTA MINERALOGICA-PETROGRAPHICA (SZEGED) **1437**

SZEGED, HUNGARY. TUDOMANYEGYETEM (FOUNDED 1940) *See* ACTA SCIENTIARUM MATHEMATICARUM **3490**

SZEGED, HUNGARY. TUDOMANYEGYETEM (FOUNDED 1940) *See* ACTA UNIVERSITATIS SZEGEDIENSIS. ACTA MINERALOGICA-PETROGRAPHICA **1437**

SZENE (SZ) [07308124] **3444**

SZEPMUVESZETI MUSEUM (HUNGARY) *See* BULLETIN DU MUSEE HONGROIS DES BEAUX-ARTS **4085**

SZESZIPAR (HU/0563-0746) [03602033] **1628**

SZILIKATIPARI ES SZILIKATTUDOMANYI KONFERENCIA (HU/0237-2169) [02372169] **2594**

SZILIKATTECHNIKA (HU/0586-3791) [08240301] **1030**

SZINHAZ (HU/0039-8136) [02007779] **5369**

SZIVARVANY (US/0270-5508) [06459281] **3444**

SZKIEKO I OKO (PL/0239-6653) [I02396653] **1070**

SZKO I CERAMIKA (PL/0039-8144) [05246235] **2594**

SZKOA GOWNA PLANOWANIA I STATYSTYKI (WARSAW, POLAND). INSTYTUT GOSPODARKI KRAJOW ROZWIJAJACYCH SIE *See* ECONOMIC PAPERS **1484**

SZKOA GOWNA PLANOWANIA STATYSTYKI (WARSAW, POLAND). INSTYTUT GOSPODARSTWA SPOECZNEGO. BIULETYN See BIULETYN IGS / SZKOA GOWNA HANDLOWA, INSTYTUT GOSPODARSTWA SPOECZNEGO **5193**

SZKOLA ZAWODOWA (PL/0137-8171) [I01378171] **4209**

SZOCIOLOGIA (BUDAPEST. 1972) (HU/0133-3461) [01681586] **5264**

SZOLNOK MEGYEI MUZEUMI EVKONYV (HU/0138-9947) [03428892] **4097**

SZOLOTERMEZTESES BORASZAT (UN/0230-2241) [03399817] 2432, **2371**

SZOVETKEZETEK ORSZAGOS SZOVETSEGE (HUNGARY) See SZOVOSZ TAJEKOZTATO KERESKEDELMI MELLEKLETE, A **852**

SZOVETKEZETI IPAR (HU) [01791009] **5356**

SZOVOSZ TAJEKOZTATO KERESKEDELMI MELLEKLETE, A (HU) [01784764] **852**

SZPILKI (PL/0039-8152) [05043719] **3354**

SZTANDAR MODYCH (PL/0557-9783) [I05579783] **1070**

SZTUKA (PL/0324-8232) [01796488] **366**

SZTUKA DLA DZIECKA (PL/0860-3464) [I08603464] **366**

SZW NIEUWS (NE) **4689**

T.A.C. NEWS (CN/1183-5532) [22737380] **5393**

T.A. INFORMATIONS See TRAITEMENT AUTOMATIQUE DES LANGUES : T.A.L **3327**

T A Q JOURNAL, A (CN/0706-9987) [04589531] **3327**

T A S A, TEACHING ATYPICAL STUDENTS IN ALBERTA (CN/0315-1808) [03079394] **1886**

T.& A.M. REPORT (US/0073-5264) [01378130] **2130**

● T & D (AT/1037-9687) [I10379687] **887**

T & G RECORD (UK) [10399565] **1713**

T & T. TRASPORTI E TRAZIONE (IT/1120-8732) [I11208732] **5393**

T.E.A.M (US) [06639457] **5312**

T.E.C. (PARIS) (FR/0397-6513) [07061181] **2244**

T.E.L. THE ELECTRIC LETTER CEASED. (US/0093-5379) [01425367] **2083**

T.E.M. TEXTE EN MAIN (FR/0761-8239) [13301351] **3444**

T.E. NOTES (US/1054-514X) [22904355] 435, **3354**

T. E. S. L. TALK (CN/0700-1584) [03282347] **1786**

T-GUIDE (UK) **852**

T.H.E. JOURNAL. SOURCE GUIDE OF HIGH-TECHNOLOGY PRODUCTS FOR EDUCATION (US/0898-3348) [14181798] 1905, **1225**

T H E S A NEWSLETTER (CN/0702-7133) [03412082] **2792**

T.I.E. NEWS (US/1048-8359) [21052785] 1786, **1164**

T-L NETWORK CEASED. (CN/0836-155X) [18241948] **3252**

T 'N T, TRUCK 'N TRAILER (CN/0703-6906) [03439343] **5394**

T-SHIRT TIMES, THE (US/0194-2794) [05357210] **1087**

T-SPORT (IT) 4855, **309**

T-SPORT (IT) **4925**

T-SPORT : INSERTI TECNICI CALCIO (IT) **4925**

T-SPORT : INSERTI TECNICI GESTIONE E MANUTENZIONE (IT) **4925**

T-SPORT : INSERTI TECNICI GLI SPORT TENNIS ATLETICA GOLF (IT) **4925**

T-SPORT : INSERTI TECNICI PALAZZETTI PALESTRE SALE SPORTIVE (IT) **4925**

T-SPORT : RACCOLTA SCHEDE TECNICHE (IT) **4925**

T.U.B.A. JOURNAL (US/0363-4787) [02831512] **4156**

T.U.B.A. MEMBERSHIP ROSTER (US/0163-5360) [04097233] **4156**

T V B (CN/0703-8178) [04098101] **4866**

T V HEBDO (MONTREAL) (CN/0039-8551) [02583545] **1140**

T V THIS WEEK (CN/0319-342X) [02442883] **1140**

T.V. VIDEO JAQUETTES (FR/0752-4757) [I07524757] **1122**

TA HISTORIKA (GR) [13453284] **2712**

TA JEN (CH) [02419913] **887**

TA-KUNG-PAO (HK/0039-8675) [01589481] **5802**

TA-LIEN KUNG HSUEH YUAN HSUEH PAO (CC/0253-0031) [09290164] **5111**

TA LU TSA CHIH (CH) [01607944] 284, **2666**

TA MA KO YU CHIH SHENG (MY) [01790394] **4156**

TA NEA (GR) [08935803] **5802**

TA TI SHENG HUO (CH) [09263015] **2509**

TA TOU KO HSUEH (CC) [13102402] **189**

TA TZU JAN (CC/0255-7800) [10648700] **4172**

TA TZU JAN (TAIPEI, TAIWAN) (CH) [11249063] **2206**

TA TZU JAN TAN SO (CH) [11093193] **5161**

TAA REPORT (US/1041-1453) [18658910] **4832**

TAAL EN TONGVAL (BE/0039-8691) [02056499] **3327**

TAAL EN TONGVAL. THEMANUMMER (BE) [20337237] **3327**

TAAMULI (TZ) [26785997] **4497**

TAARIFA YA TAKWIMU ROBO MWAKA (TZ) [17254375] **5344**

TAARIFA YA TARAKIMU (TZ) [01791537] **5344**

TAARS NEWS & NOTES (US/0740-0241) [07346202] **284**

TAATIGKEITSBERICHT DER OESTERREICHISCHEN AKADEMIE DER WISSENSCHAFTEN (AU/1017-1592) [07079016] **5161**

TAAWUM MIN AJLI AL-TANMIYAH (SJ) [11760287] **1523**

TAAWUN (KUWAIT, KUWAIT) (KU) [11251550] **5264**

TAAWUN (SANA, YEMEN) (YE) [09547454] **2666**

TABAC AU CANADA (CN/0713-5467) [09046601] **5373**

TABAK-JOURNAL INTERNATIONAL See TJI : TOBACCO JOURNAL INTERNATIONAL **5373**

TABEL AKHIR STATISTIK PENDIDIKAN SLTP/SLTA SMP SELURUH INDONESIA (IO) [02335369] 1786, **1798**

TABELLA REVISIONE PREZZI (IT) **852**

TABERNACLE AND PURGATORY See SPIRIT & LIFE (CLYDE, MO.) **4999**

TABER'S CYCLOPEDIC MEDICAL DICTIONARY (US/1065-1357) [02470615] **3644**

TABI (JA) [09251592] **5492**

TABLAS (CU) [09515534] **5369**

TABLAS DE PREDICCION DE MAREAS : PUERTOS DEL OCEANO PACIFICO (MX) [07039162] **4184**

TABLE DES DEBATS DU SENAT. TABLE DES MATIERES / ETABLIE PAR LE SERVICE DES ARCHIVES DU SENAT (FR) [07961332] **4689**

TABLE DES DEBATS DU SENAT. TABLE NOMINATIVE / ETABLIE PAR LE SERVICE DES ARCHIVES DU SENAT (FR) [07960962] **4689**

TABLE ET CADEAU, L'OBJET POUR LA MAISON (FR/0039-8780) [11476272] 2594, **2907**

TABLE (LONDON. 1953) (UK/0264-7133) [06540995] **4689**

TABLE OF GOVERNMENT ORDERS (UK) [03215787] **4689**

TABLE PAR DENOMINATIONS DE MARQUES DE FABRIQUE, DE COMMERCE OU DE SERVICE (FR) [11017624] **5161**

TABLE RONDE. CAHIERS, LA (FR) [01786040] **3444**

TABLE RONDE NATIONALE SUR L'ENVIRONNEMENT ET L'ECONOMIE (CANADA) See NATIONAL ROUND TABLE REVIEW **2178**

TABLE TENNIS TECHNICAL (CN/0828-4539) [11847735] **4925**

TABLEAU DE BORD CONJONCTUREL DU LOGEMENT (FR) [04459166] **2836**

TABLEAU DE BORD DE L'ECONOMIE / REPUBLIQUE GABONAISE, MINISTERE DE L'ECONOMIE ET DES FINANCES, DIRECTION GENERALE DE L'ECONOMIE (GB) [10337074] **1586**

TABLEAU DE BORD DE L'ENERGIE (FR) **1959**

TABLEAU DE BORD DU TRANSPORT AERIEN DANS LE MONDE / WORLD AIR TRANSPORT DATA GUIDE (FR) [20865424] **37**

TABLEAU DES MEMBRES - ORDRE DES ARCHITECTES DU QUEBEC (CN/0317-8854) [02624645] **309**

TABLEAU (UTRECHT) (NE/0166-4492) [08541868] **366**

TABLEAU (WINNIPEG, MAN.) (CN/0841-8012) [19038102] **366**

TABLEAUX DE L'ECONOMIE BRETONNE (FR/0395-871X) [18668949] **1586**

TABLEAUX DE L'ECONOMIE CALEDONIENNE (NL) [13604921] **5344**

TABLEAUX DE L'ECONOMIE CHAMPENOISE / INSEE, OBSERVATOIRE ECONOMIQUE DE CHAMPAGNE-ARDENNE (FR) [09754118] **5344**

TABLEAUX DE L'ECONOMIE DU POITOU-CHARENTES (FR) **1523**

TABLEAUX ECONOMIQUES DE MIDI-PYRENEES (FR) [09751830] 1523, **1540**

TABLES CHAMPETRES ET PROMENADES A LA FERME AU QUEBEC (CN/1187-2691) [25423631] **5073**

TABLES CHAMPETRES ET PROMENADES A LA FERME AU QUEBEC (CN/1187-2691) [25423627] **5073**

TABLES DES QUESTIONS ET DES REPONSES DES MINISTRES PUBLIEES DU ... / ETABLIES PAR LE SERVICE DES IMPRESSIONS, DE LA DOCUMENTATION PARLEMENTAIRE ET DE L'INFORMATIQUE (FR) [08937684] **4690**

TABLES DU JOURNAL LE TEMPS (FR) [07196061] **2493**

TABLES OF REDEMPTION VALUES FOR UNITED STATES SAVINGS BONDS FOR ALL MONTHS FROM ... SERIES EE (US) [06416203] **917**

TABLET (LONDON), THE (UK/0039-8837) [01767092] **5002**

TABLET, THE (US/0039-8845) [03938476] **5037**

TABLETALK (LAKE MARY, FLA.) (US/1064-881X) [09505762] **5002**

TABLEWARE INTERNATIONAL (UK/0143-7755) [04375547] **2594**

TABLOID (FAIRFAX, VA.), THE (US/0279-053X) [07483183] **4569**

TABULATION SHOWING ANNUAL AVERAGE DAILY TRAFFIC VOLUME AT RECORDER LOCATIONS AND PERCENT OF CHANGE IN VOLUME OVER PREVIOUS YEARS (US) [01328625] **5445**

TAC ATTACK (US/0494-3880) [05052890] **4058**

TAC PHAM MI (VM) [02106052] **3444**

● TAC TECHNICAL BULLETIN (CN/1188-8709) [26714915] **5394**

TAC/USA OFFICIAL RULES FOR ATHLETICS (US) [08001091] **4925**

TACD JOURNAL (US/1046-171X) [11160800] **4620**

TACHIKAWA TANDAI KIYO (JA/0286-7117) [10396345] **5161**

TACHYDROMOS (GR/0039-8888) [02268353] **2493**

TACK 'N TOGS MERCHANDISING (US/0149-3442) [01773179] **2802**

TACKLE TEST (US/1048-9215) [21075597] **2314**

● TACKLE TESTER (US/1068-5812) [27712273] 4879, **2778**

TACO TIMES (US/0747-2358) [10649452] **5651**

TACT : THE AIR CARGO TARIFF (NE) 37, **5394**

TACTICAL NOTEBOOK (US) **4058**

TACTICAL TECHNOLOGY (US/1059-0552) [24467094] **5161**

TACTICS (US) **3793**

TADRIS AL-ULUM WA-AL-RIYADIYAT (UA) [04161261] **5161**

TAE KWON DO TIMES (US/0741-028X) [10089520] 331, **4925**

TAE NYUYOK CHIGU HANILLOK (US) [08059527] **2547**

TAEGWANG CHONJA (KO) [10410745] **1586**

TAEHAK ANNAE CHARYO (KO) [10036722] **1849**

TAEHAN CHIKWA UISA HYOPHOE CHI (KO/0376-4672) [02040020] **1336**

TAEHAN CHONGHYONG OEKWA HAKHOE CHI (KO) [12071661] **3885**

TAEHAN CHON'GI HAKHOE See JOURNAL OF THE KOREAN INSTITUTE OF ELECTRICAL ENGINEERS **2070**

TAEHAN CHONGI HYOPHOE CHI (KO) [07820212] **2083**

TAEHAN HANGGONG HYOPHOE HOEBO (KO) [09383322] **37**

TAEHAN HANUI HAKHOE CHI (KO/1010-0695) [10631499] **3644**

TAEHAN Alphabetical Title Index

TAEHAN HWANGYONG KONGHAKHOE CHI (KO) [08240001] **2244**

TAEHAN HYORAEK HAKHOE CHI (KO) [16906652] **3774**

TAEHAN KAJONG HAHOE CHI (KO) [04841714] **2792**

TAEHAN KAJONG HAKHOE *See* TAEHAN KAJONG HAHOE CHI **2792**

TAEHAN KANHO (KO) [04474863] **3870**

TAEHAN KUMSOK HAKHOE *See* DAIHAN GUMSOG HAGHOI JI **4000**

TAEHAN KWANGSAN HAKHOE *See* DAIHAN GWANSANHAG HOI JI **2138**

TAEHAN MINGUK HAKSURWON *See* PROCEEDINGS, THE ... INTERNATIONAL SYMPOSIA **5142**

TAEHAN OEKWA HAKHOE *See* OEKWA HAKHOE CHI **3971**

TAEHAN PANGSASON HAKHOE CHI (KO/0301-2867) [01432411] **3947**

TAEHAN PANSSASFON HAKHOE *See* TAEHAN PANGSASON HAKHOE CHI **3947**

TAEHAN PIBU KWAHAKHOE CHI (KO/0494-4739) [I04944739] **3723**

TAEHAN PINYOGIKWA HAKHOE CHI (KO) [09602843] **3993**

TAEHAN SAENGHWAHAKHOE CHAPCHI *See* KOREAN JOURNAL OF BIOCHEMISTRY **490**

TAEHAN SAENGNI HAKHOE *See* TAEHAN SAENGNI HAKHOE CHI **587**

TAEHAN SAENGNI HAKHOE CHI (KO/0372-1582) [04856508] **587**

TAEHAN SANOP KONGHAKHOE *See* TAEHAN SANOP KONGHAKHOE CHI **2099**

TAEHAN SANOP KONGHAKHOE CHI (KO) [04887646] **2099**

TAEHAN SONHAE POHOM HYOPHOE *See* KOREA NON-LIFE INSURANCE INDUSTRY **1**

TAEHAN SUUI HAKHOE *See* TAEHAN SUUI HAKHOE CHI **5522**

TAEHAN SUUI HAKHOE CHI (KO) [04910846] **5522**

TAEHAN TOMOK HAKHOE *See* TAEHAN TOMOK HAKHOE CHI. JOURNAL OF THE KOREAN SOCIETY OF CIVIL ENGINEERS **2032**

TAEHAN TOMOK HAKHOE CHI. JOURNAL OF THE KOREAN SOCIETY OF CIVIL ENGINEERS (KO) [06566589] **2032**

TAEHAN UIHAK HYOPHOE *See* TAEHAN UIHAK HYOPHOE CHI **3644**

TAEHAN UIHAK HYOPHOE CHAPCHI (KO/0023-4028) [01778410] **3644**

TAEHAN UIHAK HYOPHOE CHI (KO) [04991237] **3644**

TAEHAN UIHAK HYOPHOE, SEOUL, KOREA *See* TAEHAN UIHAK HYOPHOE CHAPCHI **3644**

TAEHAN YAKHAKHOE *See* YAGHAG-HOI-JI **4333**

TAEHAN YEBANK UIHAKHOE *See* NYEIBAN NUIHAG HOI JI **3623**

TAEHWA (KO) [04856468] **2509**

TAEKWONDO WORLD (US/1043-1047) [19300019] **2601**

TAEPYONGYANG CHANGHAK MUNHWA CHAEDAN *See* YON'GU NONMUNJIP - TAEPYONGYANG CHANGHAK MUNHWA CHAEDAN **5237**

TAFE HANDBOOK - NSW DEPARTMENT OF TECHNICAL AND FURTHER EDUCATION *See* TAFE NSW HANDBOOK **1916**

TAFE HANDBOOKS (AT) **1916**

TAFE MAGAZINE (AT/0810-8749) [I08108749] **1916**

TAFE NSW HANDBOOK (AT/1037-9606) [I10379606] **1916**

TAFE STUDENT HANDBOOK (AT) **1786**

TAFE VIEW (AT/0157-4388) [I01574388] **1786**

TAFRIJA (TUCKER, GA.) (US/1070-7522) [26848095] **389**

●TAFT AND UNIVERSITY OF CINCINNATI SERIES IN LATIN AMERICAN AND HISPANIC AMERICAN THEATRE (US/1062-5453) [25660877] **5369**

TAFT DAILY MIDWAY DRILLER *See* DAILY MIDWAY DRILLER **5634**

TAFT FOUNDATION REPORTER *See* FOUNDATION REPORTER (1990) **4727**

TAFT GUIDE TO CORPORATE GIVING CONTACTS (US/1048-0374) [20001381] **5312**

TAFT NONPROFIT EXECUTIVE *See* NONPROFIT MANAGEMENT STRATEGIES **5299**

TAFT NONPROFIT EXECUTIVE, THE (US/0882-5521) [11881332] **887**

TAFT'S WEALTHWATCHER (US/1056-2206) [23600033] **714**

TAG DES HERRN (GW/0492-1283) [05243341] **5037**

TAG (STERLING, VA.) (US/1067-9197) [17152736] **1281**

TAG (VIENNA, AUSTRIA) *See* WIENER TAG, DER **5778**

TAGES ANZEIGER (SZ) **5811**

TAGESSPIEGEL, DER (GW) [12594004] **5802**

TAGLICHE HOHENKARTEN DER 30-MB-FLACHE SOWIE MONATLICHE MITTELKARTEN (GW) [06842829] **1435**

TAGLICHE HOHENKARTEN DER 50-MB-FLACHE SOWIE MONATLICHE MITTELKARTEN (GW) [04159218] **1435**

TAGLICHE PRAXIS (GW/0494-464X) [06565352] **3644**

TAGLINE (OLNEY) (UK/0968-0349) [I09680349] **1291**, **4820**

TAGS (US) [24704245] **1786**

TAG'S CHANNEL COMPASS (US/1073-6662) [29503792] **937**

TAGUNGSBAND - KAMMER DER TECHNIK SUHL (GW/0232-5683) [08324450] **5161**

TAHATA KAKAKU OYOBI KOSAKURYO SHIRABE (JA) [06500087] **139**

TAHAWWULAT (LE) [10424482] **3472**

TAHITI SUN PRESS (FP) [07894962] **5801**

TAHOE DAILY TRIBUNE AND THE LAKE TAHOE NEWS (US/8750-3948) [11407443] **5640**

TAHOE WORLD (US) [14510658] **5640**

TAHQIQAT-I ISLAMI (II) [11464675] **5045**

TAHSIS INLET OUTLET, THE (CN/0383-7343) [03248105] **5795**

TAHZIB AL-AKHLAQ (II) [11809251] **5045**

T'AI CHI (US/0730-1049) [07941596] **2601**

TAI CHUAN CHI KAN *See* CHUNG CHUAN CHI KAN **4175**

TAI-DIAN HENENG YUEKAN (CH/1017-0529) [09332741] **2159**

TAI I SHIH PARLIAMENTARIAN MAGAZINE (CC) [09689001] **2666**

TAI-NAN SHIH CAN HUEH YEN CHIU HUI CHI KAN (CH) [11901625] **1849**

TAI-PEI SHIH JEN SHOU PAO HSIEN SHANG YEH TUNG YEH KUNG HUI *See* JEN SHOU PAO HSIEN YEH WU TUNG CHI NIEN PAO **2885**

TAI-PEI TZU LAI SHUI CHANG. CHU CHI SHIH *See* TUNG CHI NIEN PAO - TAI-PEI TZU LAI SHUI CHANG CHU CHI SHIH **5541**

TAI-PEI TZU LAI SHUI CHANG. CHU CHI SHIH. TUNG CHI NIEN PAO *See* TAI-PEI TZU LAI SHUI SHIH YEH TUNG CHI NIEN PAO **5540**

TAI-PEI TZU LAI SHUI SHIH YEH TUNG CHI NIEN PAO (CH) [27084409] **5540**

TAI SHENG (CC) [11455249] **2666**

TAI-WAN CHING CHI YEN CHIU YUEH KAN (CH) [06652222] **1586**

TAI-WAN HSIAO SHUO HSUAN / YEH SHIH-TAO CHU PIEN (CH) [10979237] **3444**

T'AI-WAN HSU MU SHOU I HSUEH HUI *See* TAIWAN HSU MU SHOU I HSUEH HUI HUI PAO **5522**

TAI-WAN KO HSUEH (CH/0371-845X) [06767290] **5161**

TAI-WAN MAO I YAO LAN (CH) [01797497] **852**

TAI-WAN NUNG YEH (NAN-TOU HSIEN, TAIWAN : 1979) (CH/0253-276X) [08472426] **139**

TAI-WAN NUNG YEH NIEN PAO (CH/0429-1255) [01767105] **139**

●TAI-WAN PAO CHUANG CHI HSIEH PIEN LAN (CH) [26576114] 2130, **4222**

TAI-WAN SAN WEN HSUAN / CHI CHI CHU PIEN (CH) [11012509] **3444**

TAI-WAN SHENG HSU MU SHOU I HSUEH HUI *See* HUIBAO - TAIWAN UMU SHOUYI XUEHUI **5511**

TAI-WAN SHENG TAI-NAN CHU NUNG YEH KAI LIANG CHANG YEN CHIU HUI PAO (CH) [08093719] **139**

TAI-WAN SHENG YEN CHIU KUNG MAI CHU. YEN YEH SHIH YEN SO *See* TAIWAN SHENGYANJIU GONGMAIJU YONGYE SHIYAN-SUO YANJIU HUIBAO **5373**

TAI-WAN SHIH HSUAN / WU SHENG CHU PIEN (CH) [11522638] **3444**

TAI-WAN SHUI LI (CH) [10126380] **2244**

TAI-WAN SSU CHAO (US) [09107262] **2509**

TAI-WAN TA HSUEEH, TAI-PEI. COLLEGE OF MEDICINE *See* MEMOIRS OF THE COLLEGE OF MEDICINE OF THE NATIONAL TAIWAN UNIVERSITY **3616**

TAI-WAN TA HSUEH, TAI-PEI. KUNG HSUEH YUAN *See* KUO LI TAI-WAN TA HSUEH KUNG CHENG HSUEH KAN **1985**

TAI-WAN TANG YEH KU FEN YU HSIEN KUNG SSU. HSU CHAN YEN CHIU SO *See* YEN CHIU SHIH YEN PAO KAO - TAI-WAN TANG YEH KU FEN YU HSIEN KUNG SSU HSU CHAN YEN CHIU SO **224**

TAI-YUAN KUNG HSUEH YUAN HSUEH PAO *See* TAIYUAN GONGYE DAXUE XUEBAO **5161**

TAIDE (FI/0039-8977) [05131090] **366**

TAIDEHISTORIALLISIA TUTKIMUKSIA (FI/0355-1938) [05167597] **366**

TAIIKU KENKYUJO KIYO (JA/0286-6951) [11279465] 4925, **1858**

TAIIKUGAKU KENKYU. JAPANESE JOURNAL OF PHYSICAL EDUCATION (JA) [06907246] **1858**

TAIKABUTSU (JA/0039-8993) [06442367] **4021**

TAIKABUTSU GIJUTSU KYOKAI (JAPAN) *See* TAIKABUTSU **4021**

TAIKABUTSU OVERSEAS (JA/0285-0028) [09096234] **5161**

TAIKI OSEN GAKKAI SHI (JA/0386-7064) [10475337] **2244**

TAIKI OSEN JOJI SOKUTEIKYOKU SOKUTEI KEKKA HOKOKU. KEINENPO (JA) [10964472] **2244**

TAIKI OSEN JOJI SOKUTEIKYOKU SOKUTEI KEKKA HOKOKU. NENPO (JA) [10957346] **2244**

TAIKI OSEN NYUSU (JA) [02244740] **2244**

TAILING DISPOSAL TODAY (US/0270-9554) [06012872] **4021**

TAILS (PADUCAH, KY.) (US/1053-5578) [22576514] **1087**

TAINYAN NEINJI (KO/0253-3103) [06719168] **1959**

TAIPAN (US) **917**

TAIRYOKU KENKYU (JA/0389-9071) [10393837] **3644**

TAISEI KENSETSU GIJUTSU KENKYUJOHO (JA/0387-2254) [10468081] **5161**

TAISEI TECHNICAL RESEARCH REPORT (JA) **5161**

TAISHA (JA/0372-1566) [10475961] **3644**

TAISHO DAIGAKU KENKYU KIYO (JA) [08426969] **5022**

TAISHO DAIGAKU SOGO BUKKYO KENKYUJO NENPO (JA) [08416245] **5022**

TAISHO OYOBI TAISHOJIN (JA) [03954362] **2666**

TAISHOKUKIN TEINENSEI OYOBI NENKIN JIJO CHOSA (JA) [03407566] **5312**

TAITEEN KESKUSTOIMIKUNNAN KASIKIRJOJA (FI) [I07881429] **331**

TAITEEN KESKUSTOIMIKUNNAN TIEDOTUSLEHTI (FI) [02242304] **331**

TAITO (FI/0355-7421) [23737836] **376**

TAIWAN *See* BALANCE OF PAYMENTS / TAIWAN DISTRICT, THE REPUBLIC OF CHINA **773**

TAIWAN BUSINESS DIRECTORY (CH) [07259327] **714**

TAIWAN BUYERS' GUIDE (US/0082-1470) [02066409] 852, **3488**

TAIWAN CHURCH GROWTH BULLETIN (CC) [09586078] **5002**

TAIWAN COMMUNIQUE (US) [20999829] **4513**

TAIWAN COMMUNIQUE (NORTH AMERICAN EDITION) (NE) [12073943] **4513**

TAIWAN COMMUNIQUE (SEATTLE, WASH.) *See* TAIWAN COMMUNIQUE (NORTH AMERICAN EDITION) **4513**

TAIWAN ELECTRONICS INDUSTRY (CH/0257-8166) [I02578166] **2083**

TAIWAN ENTERPRISE (CH) [02246499] **1628**

TAIWAN EXPORTERS GUIDE (CH) [05023034] **853**

TAIWAN EXPORTS (CH) [01800273] **853**

TAIWAN FINANCIAL STATISTICS MONTHLY (CH/0496-7046) [01554328] **1540**

TAIWAN GIFTS BUYER'S GUIDE (CH) **2585**

TAIWAN GONGLUNBAO (US/0743-5355) [08048825] **5640**

TAIWAN HAIXIA (CC/1000-8160) [I10008160] **1457**

TAIWAN HSU MU SHOU I HSUEH HUI HUI PAO (CH/0258-526X) [02319417] **5522**

TAIWAN INDUSTRIAL PANORAMA (CH) [02247032] **917**

TAIWAN NONGYE (CH/0255-6103) [I02556103] **139**

Alphabetical Title Index — TAMPA

TAIWAN REGISTER (US/1044-470X) [19796222] 917, **4847**

TAIWAN REVIEW (US/8756-212X) [11509848] **3644**

TAIWAN SHENG CIA TING CI HA YEN CHIU SO *See* ANNUAL REPORT - TAIWAN PROVINCIAL INSTITUTE OF FAMILY PLANNING **588**

TAIWAN-SHENG TAIZHONG-QU NONGYE GAILIANG CHANG TEKAN ... HAO (CH/0258-2708) [18096572] **139**

TAIWAN SHENGYANJIU GONGMAIJU YONGYE SHIYAN-SUO YANJIU HUIBAO (CH/0379-4199) [03917197] **5373**

TAIWAN SHENXUE LUNKAN (CH/0251-4788) [07772232] **5002**

TAIWAN SHUICHANXUE HUI KAN (CH/0379-4180) [08286356] **558**

TAIWAN STATISTICAL DATA BOOK (CH) [01791857] **5344**

●TAIWAN STUDIES (US/1074-5599) [29744227] **2509**

TAIWAN STUDIES NEWSLETTER (US/1048-2342) [14083106] **2666**

TAIWAN SUGAR (CH/0492-1712) [01791619] **189**

TAIWAN TA HSUEH, TAI-PEI. NUNG HSUEH YUAN *See* YEN CHIU PAO KAO **148**

TAIWAN TRADE DIRECTORY (CH) [01797498] **853**

TAIWAN, WIRTSCHAFTSDATEN UND WIRTSCHAFTSDOKUMENTATION / BUNDESSTELLE FUER AUSSENHANDELSINFORMATION (GW) [11299158] **1586**

TAIWAN YELLOW PAGES *CEASED.* (CH) [04474192] 853, **2577**

TAIWAN YU SHIJIE (US/0737-6197) [09425575] **2666**

TAIWANIA (CH/0372-333X) [02450965] **529**

TAIYANG NENG XUEBAO (CC/0254-0096) [09233101] **1959**

TAIYO CHIKYU KEIHO EISEI CHOSA HOKOKU (JA) [09359473] **37**

TAIYO ENERUGI (TOKYO. 1975) (JA/0388-9564) [28108876] **1959**

TAIYO (HEIBONSHA) (JA) [05392696] **2509**

TAIYUAN GONGYE DAXUE XUEBAO (CC/1000-1611) [21743787] 1998, **5161**

TAKAHE CHRISTCHURCH (NZ/0114-4138) [I01144138] **3444**

TAKAMATSU KOGYO KOTO SEMMON GAKKO *See* TAKAMATSU KOGYO KOTO SENMON GAKKO KENKYU KIYO **5237**

TAKAMATSU KOGYO KOTO SENMON GAKKO KENKYU KIYO (JA/0389-9268) [01790113] **5237**

TAKAMATSU KOKUZEIKYOKU TOKEISHO (JA) [02245279] **4751**

TAKE FIVE (SASKATOON, SASK.) *CEASED.* (CN/0821-0160) [09692611] **2547**

TAKE OFF MAGAZINE (US) **37**

TAKE PRIDE IN AMERICA *See* AMERICAN SPIRIT / TAKE PRIDE IN AMERICA **2186**

TAKE PRIDE IN AMERICA *See* AMERICAN SPIRIT / TAKE PRIDE IN AMERICA **2186**

TAKEDA KENKYUJO HO (JA/0371-5167) [10467962] **5161**

TAKENAKA GIJUTSU KENKYU HOKOKU (JA/0374-4663) [09926471] **2032**

TAKENAKA TECHNICAL RESEARCH REPORT (JA) **5161**

TAKING CARE (US) [06151849] **4804**

●TAKING STOCK LONDON. 1992 (UK/0966-6745) [I09666745] **3252**

TAKTSIV LEUMI (IS) [01794152] **1586**

TALAI AL-FATIH (LY) [06109667] **2644**

TALANTA (OXFORD) (UK/0039-9140) [01767116] **1019**

TALBOT RESEARCH ORGANISATION *See* TALBOTANIA; THE BULLETIN OF THE TALBOT RESEARCH ORGANISATION **2474**

TALBOT TIMES (CN/0827-2816) [11739663] **2474**

TALBOTANIA; THE BULLETIN OF THE TALBOT RESEARCH ORGANISATION (UK) [07041870] **2474**

TALBOTTON NEW ERA (US/0885-6567) [12683669] **5655**

TALEN GRONINGEN (NE/0922-1166) [I09221166] **3327**

TALENT & BOOKING'S DISCO (US/0194-1771) [05344137] 1314, **4156**

TALENT CATALOGUE / ACTRA ATLANTIC CANADA (CN/1181-6090) [22934862] **389**

TALENT EDUCATION JOURNAL *CEASED.* (US/0889-4175) [13943598] 1786, **4156**

TALENTED (AT/0815-8150) [I08158150] **1849**

TALES OF PARADISE RIDGE (US/0496-7607) [02052111] **2631**

TALES OF THE NINJA WARRIORS (US/1043-4739) [18133666] **1070**

TALES OF THE TEEN TITANS *CEASED.* (US/0887-7114) [10915784] **4866**

TALES OF THE TWELVE (CN/0713-3901) [09086731] **4097**

TALIAH (PARIS, FRANCE) (FR) [11153822] **2666**

TALIB (MUTAMAR AL-AMM LI-TALABAT AL-JAMAHIRIYAH) (LY) [10940427] **2500**

TALIM AL-JAMAHIR (UA) [04450189] **1802**

TALISMAN (COLUMBUS, OHIO) (US/0749-5994) [11148948] **3472**

TALISMAN (HOBOKEN, N.J.) (US/0898-8684) [17938198] **3472**

TALK B.A.C (CN/1183-8728) [25313922] **331**

TALK (LONDON, ENGLAND) (UK) [10338220] **1122**

TALK (NEW YORK) (US/0164-8535) [04305125] **5264**

TALK OF THE MONTH (US/0743-1384) [10548841] 4243, **3444**

TALK OF THE THAMES (CN/0822-8043) [10517595] **5540**

TALK SHOW DIRECTORY (US/0731-9134) [07855160] **1140**

TALK SHOW "SELECTS" (US/1045-9553) [20293088] **1140**

TALKIN' TWINS BASEBALL (US/0899-6849) [18183073] **4925**

TALKIN' UNION (TAKOMA PARK MD.) *CEASED.* (US/0738-7911) [09425779] 4156, 2324, **1713**

TALKING BETTAS (US/1062-6425) [25690333] **4288**

TALKING BOOK TOPICS (US/0039-9183) [01644858] 4832, **4394**

TALKING BOOKS (CN/0225-5723) [07313540] **4832**

TALKING BOOKS AVAILABLE IN THE PUBLIC LIBRARIES OF METROPOLITAN TORONTO (CN/0700-3277) [03279185] **4832**

TALKING BOOKS CATALOGUE / LAKE ONTARIO REGIONAL LIBRARY SYSTEM (CN/0229-4915) [08028189] **426**

TALKING BOOKS CATALOGUE SUPPLEMENT (CN/0229-4028) [08192517] 4394, **4832**

TALKING BOOKS (THUNDER BAY) (CN/0842-5116) [19898475] **4833**

TALKING DRUMS (CN/0383-9192) [02918364] **2274**

TALKING DRUMS (LONDON, ENGLAND) (UK) [11319926] **2644**

TALKING LEAF (LOS ANGELES, CALIF. : 1972) (US/0300-6247) [01342763] **2274**

TALKING LEAVES (WARRENVILLE, ILL.) (US/0894-833X) [16275250] **2206**

TALKING POLITICS (UK/0955-8780) [18864420] **4497**

TALKING POLITICS (UK) [16441822] **4498**

TALKS OF POPE JOHN PAUL II (US) [04993826] **5037**

TALL NEWSLETTER (1984) (CN/0841-8195) [18903581] 3062, **3252**

TALL TIMBER FIRE ECOLOGY. CONFERENCE *See* PROCEEDINGS OF THE ANNUAL TALL TIMBER FIRE ECOLOGY CONFERENCE **2391**

TALLAHASSEE ADVERTISER, THE (US/0744-4400) [08265675] **5651**

TALLAHASSEE DEMOCRAT (US/0738-5153) [08253038] **5651**

TALLAHASSEE. TALL TIMBERS RESEARCH STATION *See* MISCELLANEOUS PUBLICATION - TALL TIMBERS RESEARCH STATION **465**

TALLASSEE TRIBUNE, THE (US) [12038421] **5628**

TALLASU HANIN CHUSO MIT OPSOROK (US/0742-7352) [10406508] **714**

TALLIN (ER) [06154058] **3444**

TALLINNA POLUTEHNILINE INSTITUUT. POLIITILISE OKONOOMIA KATEEDER *See* UURIMUSI **1596**

TALLINSKIE TETRADI (ER) [04897449] **3444**

TALLMADGE EXPRESS (US) [23455871] **5730**

TALLYBOARD (CN/0712-3094) [08981115] 4804, **2396**

TALMON STUDIES IN BIBLICAL LITERATURE (NE) 5002, **3444**

TALOHA (MG) [07520614] **2855**

TALON ANNUAL REPORT. SOUTH CENTRAL REGIONAL MEDICAL LIBRARY PROGRAM (US/0190-7565) [04701334] **3252**

TALON (AURORA, COLO.) (US/0892-6476) [15220309] 4172, 2221, **5598**

TALON (MILWAUKEE, WIS.), THE (US/0887-6339) [13322706] **4498**

TALON REGIONAL MEDICAL LIBRARY PROGRAM *See* TALON ANNUAL REPORT. SOUTH CENTRAL REGIONAL MEDICAL LIBRARY PROGRAM **3252**

TALON (WASHINGTON, D.C.) (US) [09508396] **1849**

TALONRAKENNUSYRITYSTEN TILINPAATOSTILASTO (FI/0784-9044) [19791158] **3488**

TAM-TAM *See* MESSAGE **1764**

TAM TAY (US/0191-0256) [04770806] **2509**

TAMA NEWS-HERALD, THE (US) [15923995] **5673**

TAMAGAWA DAIGAKU NOGAKUBU KENKYU HOKOKU (JA/0082-156X) [01767123] **139**

TAMAGAWA DAIGAKU, TOKYO. NOGAKUBU *See* TAMAGAWA DAIGAKU NOGAKUBU KENKYU HOKOKU **139**

TAMARACK (AUSTERLITZ, N.Y.) *SUSPENDED.* (US) [11861771] **3472**

TAMARAW TIMES (CN/0710-1112) [08185743] **5795**

TAMARIND PAPERS, THE (US/0276-3397) [04546587] **382**

TAMBAE (HANGUK YONCHO HAKHOE) (KO) [08539994] **5373**

TAMBAE YONGU NONMUNJIP (KO) [09074957] **5373**

TAMBARA (PH) [11938086] **5002**

TAMIL EELAM DOCUMENTATION BULLETIN (CN/0822-2762) [11278699] 4498, **4513**

TAMIL INFORMATION (II) [14924424] **2274**

TAMIL NADU (INDIA) *See* DETAILS OF WORKS FOR DEMANDS 39, ROADS AND BRIDGES AND 52, CAPITAL OUTLAY ON ROADS AND BRIDGES FOR THE YEAR ... **5440**

TAMIL NADU (INDIA) *See* DETAILED AGRICULTURE BUDGET **78**

TAMIL NADU (INDIA) *See* CATALOGUE OF GOVERNMENT PUBLICATIONS. GOVERNMENT OF TAMIL NADU **412**

TAMIL NADU (INDIA) *See* DETAILED IRRIGATION BUDGET FOR THE YEAR ... - TAMIL NADU (INDIA) **2088**

TAMIL NADU (INDIA). AGRICULTURE DEPT *See* ANNUAL ADMINISTRATION REPORT FOR THE YEAR ... / GOVERNMENT OF TAMIL NADU, AGRICULTURE DEPARTMENT **60**

TAMIL NADU (INDIA). CO-OPERATION DEPT *See* ADMINISTRATION REPORTS ON THE WORKING OF CO-OPERATIVE SOCIETIES IN TAMIL NADU / CO-OPERATION DEPARTMENT **1541**

TAMIL NADU. (INDIA). DIRECTOR OF EMPLOYMENT AND TRAINING *See* REVIEW OF EMPLOYMENT IN TAMIL NADU **1708**

TAMIL NADU (INDIA). LEGISLATURE. LEGISLATIVE COUNCIL *See* WHO IS WHO **435**

TAMIL NADU JOURNAL OF CO-OPERATION, THE (II/0377-8002) [01790459] **1543**

TAMIL NADU LABOUR JOURNAL (II) [05639115] **1713**

TAMIL NADU. LEGISLATURE. LEGISLATIVE ASSEMBLY. COMMITTEE ON PUBLIC UNDERTAKINGS *See* REPORT - TAMIL NADU LEGISLATIVE ASSEMBLY COMMITTEE ON PUBLIC UNDERTAKINGS **4682**

TAMIL NADU. LEGISLATURE. LEGISLATIVE COUNCIL. COMMITTEE ON GOVERNMENT ASSURANCES *See* REPORT - COMMITTEE ON GOVERNMENT ASSURANCES **2892**

TAMIL STUDIES (MADIRAI, INDIA) (II) [09915115] **2666**

TAMIL TIMES (UK/0266-4488) [13999855] **2666**

TAMIYA MODEL MAGAZINE INTERNATIONAL (JA/0912-9715) [I09129715] **2778**

TAMIYA MODEL MAGAZINE INTERNATIONAL FALQUEMONT (UK/1161-8566) [I11618566] **2778**

TAMKANG JOURNAL OF MATHEMATICS (CH/0376-4079) [04026879] **3538**

TAMKANG REVIEW (CH/0049-2949) [01642234] **3354**

TAMPA BAY BUSINESS JOURNAL (US/0896-467X) [17156648] **714**

TAMPA — Alphabetical Title Index

TAMPA BAY (CLEARWATER, FLA.) (US/0894-105X) [15806599] **2762**

TAMPA BAY HISTORY (US/0272-1406) [05879958] **2762**

TAMPA BAY LIFE (TAMPA, FLA.) *CEASED.* (US/1048-0056) [18775908] **2547**

TAMPA BAY REVIEW CHAPBOOK SERIES (US/1059-3527) [24578568] **3444**

TAMPA BAY SUNCOAST BUSINESS DIRECTORY, THE (US/0736-4652) [09134799] **715**

TAMPA DAILY TIMES, THE (US) [08790237] **5651**

TAMPA REVIEW (US/0896-064X) [16898687] **2547**

TAMPA TRIBUNE, THE (US/1042-3761) [08253122] **5651**

TAMRC INTERNATIONAL MARKET RESEARCH REPORT (US) [25360701] **853**

TAMS JOURNAL (US/0039-8233) [03938157] **2783**

TAMSIL (PK) [02239642] **2509**

TAMU (NP) [09094421] **2666**

TAN-CHIANG WEN LI HSUEH YUAN CHUNG WAI CHI KAN PAO CHIH MU LU. TAMKANG LIST OF SERIALS (CH) [07076622] **2924**

TAN MAGAZINE (US/1042-3036) [19003222] **4804, 405**

TANASENA (NP) [08151122] **3444**

TANDLAKARTIDNINGEN (SW/0039-6982) [01026811] **1336**

TANDLGERNES NYE TIDSSKRIFT (DK/0901-9898) [21455613] **1336**

TANE (NZ/0496-8026) [02244371] **474, 4172**

TANEY COUNTY REPUBLICAN *See* BRANSON TRI-LAKES DAILY NEWS **5702**

TANG SHIH TZU LIAO TSUNG KAN (CC) [10947034] **4690**

TANG SHIH YEN CHIU TZU LIAO / CHUNG-KUO KO MING PO WU KUAN TANG SHIH YEN CHIU SHIH PIEN (CH) [08809277] **4690**

TANG STUDIES (US/0737-5034) [09151673] **334**

TANG TAI (PEKING, CHINA) (CC) [05657357] **3444**

TANG TAI SHIH TZU (CC) [08818713] **3472**

TANG TAI WEN HSEUH (SIAN, CHINA) *See* TANG TAI WEN HSUEH LUN TSUNG / HSI PEI TA HSUEH CHUNG WEN HSI TANG TAI WEN HSUEH YEN CHIU SHIH, HSI PEI TA HSUEH HSUEH PAO PIEN CHI PU PIEN **3444**

TANG TAI WEN HSUEH (CC) [08483258] **3444**

TANG TAI WEN HSUEH LUN TSUNG / HSI PEI TA HSUEH CHUNG WEN HSI TANG TAI WEN HSUEH YEN CHIU SHIH, HSI PEI TA HSUEH HSUEH PAO PIEN CHI PU PIEN (CC) [10818939] **3444**

TANG TI CHIEN SHE DANGDE JIANSHE / CHUNG-KUO KUNG CHAN TANG KAN-SU SHENG WEI YUAN HUI CHU PAN (CC) [11618770] **4498**

TANGANYIKA. AIR SURVEY DIVISION *See* ANNUAL REPORT OF THE AIR SURVEY DIVISION **2554**

TANGANYIKA. LAND DIVISION *See* ANNUAL REPORT OF THE LAND DIVISION **2554**

TANGANYIKA. WATER DEVELOPMENT AND IRRIGATION DIVISION *See* ANNUAL REPORT OF THE WATER DEVELOPMENT AND IRRIGATION DIVISION (DAR ES SALAAM) **2087**

●TANGENCE (CN/1189-4563) [26715178] **3444**

TANGI TALK (US) [17426804] **5684**

TANGIBLE PERSONAL PROPERTY TAXES. TAXES LEVIED BY TYPE OF GOVERNMENTAL UNIT AND VALUE OF PROPERTY, BY COUNTY, CALENDAR YEAR ... OHIO DEPARTMENT OF TAXATION (US) [12166253] **4751**

TANGUK MUNHAK (KO) [08630606] **3444**

TANIGUCHI SYMPOSIA ON BRAIN SCIENCES *CEASED.* (JA) [16152470] **3846**

TANK (UK/0039-9418) **4058**

TANK CONTAINER WORLD (UK/0959-6089) [22049049] **5457**

TANK-, RESERVOIR- EN PIJPLEIDINGBOUW / CENTRAAL BUREAU VOOR DE STATISTIEK, HOOFDAFDELING STATISTIEKEN VAN INDUSTRIE EN BOUWNIJVERHEID (NE/0168-3179) [10340870] **1628**

TANK WORLD (UK) **5457**

TANKA GENDAI (JA) [03698842] **3472**

TANKER CHARTER RECORD (UK/0958-8787) [I09588787] **5457**

TANKER MARKET QUARTERLY REPORT (UK) **5457**

TANKER MARKET REPORT (UK) **5457**

TANKER REGISTER (UK/0305-179X) [06586626] **5457**

TANMIYAT AL-MUJTAMA (UA) [11306658] **2836**

TANNER LECTURES ON HUMAN VALUES, THE (US/0275-7656) [06940395] **2253**

TANNING TRENDS (US/0885-1522) [12568798] **1628**

TANPAKUSHITSU KAKUSAN KOSO (JA/0039-9450) [06539906] **474**

TANPAKUSHITSU KOGAKU KISO KENKYU SENTA DAYORI (JA/0916-1554) [24228004] **1048**

TANSANIA, ENERGIEWIRTSCHAFT / BUNDESSTELLE FUER AUSSENHANDELSINFORMATION (GW) [11175677] **1959**

TANSANIA: WIRTSCHAFTLICHE ENTWICKLUNG (GW) [01795575] **1586**

TANSANIA WIRTSCHAFTSDATEN UND WIRTSCHAFTSDOKUMENTATION / BUNDESSTELLE FUR AUSSENHANDELSINFORMATION (GW) [07369998] **1586**

TANSHOKUBAN NITTEN SHOSHU (JA) [10664989] **382**

TANSO (JA/0371-5345) [103715345] **994**

TANSY (LAWRENCE, KAN. : 1976) (US) [04161012] **3472**

TANTARA (MG) [03422259] **2671**

TANTRA (TORREON, N.M.) (US/1064-0584) [26208783] **4363**

TANTUR NEWSLETTER (IS) [03288916] **5002**

TANZ AKTUELL *See* BALLETT INTERNATIONAL, TANZ AKTUELL **1311**

TANZANIA *See* APPROPRIATION ACCOUNTS, REVENUE STATEMENTS, ACCOUNTS OF THE FUNDS AND OTHER PUBLIC ACCOUNTS OF TANZANIA, THE **4711**

TANZANIA *See* BACKGROUND TO THE BUDGET; AN ECONOMIC SURVEY **4712**

TANZANIA. ANNUAL PLAN *See* ANNUAL DEVELOPMENT PLAN FOR ... / PRODUCED BY THE MINISTRY OF FINANCE, ECONOMIC AFFAIRS AND PLANNING **1545**

TANZANIA BUREAU OF STANDARDS *See* ANNUAL REPORT / TANZANIA BUREAU OF STANDARDS **4029**

TANZANIA. BUREAU OF STATISTICS *See* TAARIFA YA TARAKIMU **5344**

TANZANIA. CAPITAL DEVELOPMENT AUTHORITY *See* REPORT & ACCOUNTS - CAPITAL DEVELOPMENT AUTHORITY **2833**

TANZANIA. CROP DEVELOPMENT DIVISION *See* NATIONAL AGRICULTURAL RESEARCH PROGRAMME **110**

TANZANIA. GEOLOGY AND MINES DIVISION *See* REVIEW OF THE MINERAL INDUSTRY IN TANZANIA **1444**

TANZANIA IMPORT, EXPORT DIRECTORY (TZ) [02245170] **853**

TANZANIA INDUSTRIAL STUDIES AND CONSULTING ORGANISATION *See* ANNUAL REPORT AND ACCOUNTS / TISCO **1597**

TANZANIA INDUSTRIAL STUDIES AND CONSULTING ORGANISATION. ANNUAL REPORT & ACCOUNTS *See* ANNUAL REPORT AND ACCOUNTS / TISCO **1597**

TANZANIA LIBRARY ASSOCIATION *See* FINANCIAL STATEMENT FOR THE PERIOD COVERING FROM 1ST JANUARY TO 31ST DECEMBER ... / TANZANIA LIBRARY ASSOCIATION **3210**

TANZANIA NATIONAL BIBLIOGRAPHY (ANNUAL) (TZ) [04331972] **426**

TANZANIA NATIONAL BIBLIOGRAPHY (MONTHLY) (TZ/0856-003X) [14169810] **426**

TANZANIA. PROTOCOL DIVISION. DIPLOMATIC MISSIONS, CONSULAR MISSIONS, TRADE AND INTERNATIONAL ORGANIZATIONS *See* LIST OF DIPLOMATIC AND CONSULAR MISSIONS, TRADE AND INTERNATIONAL ORGANIZATIONS / [ISSUED BY PROTOCOL DIVISION, MINISTRY OF FOREIGN AFFAIRS] **3132**

TANZANIA. SURVEY DIVISION *See* ANNUAL REPORT OF THE SURVEY DIVISION (TANZANIA) **2554**

TANZANIA TRADE CURRENTS : A JOURNAL OF THE BOARD OF EXTERNAL TRADE (TZ/0856-2105) [20024699] **853**

TANZANIA. WIZARA YA FEDHA, UCHUMI, NA MIPANGO *See* ANNUAL DEVELOPMENT PLAN FOR ... / PRODUCED BY THE MINISTRY OF FINANCE, ECONOMIC AFFAIRS AND PLANNING **1545**

TANZANIA. WIZARA YA MAMBO YA NJE *See* HOTUBA YA WAZIRI WA MAMBO YA NJE **3129**

TANZANIAN MATHEMATICAL BULLETIN / THE MATHEMATICAL ASSOCIATION OF TANZANIA, THE (TZ) [06025449] **3538**

TANZANIAN VETERINARY BULLETIN : THE TROPICAL VETERINARIAN / TANZANIA VETERINARY ASSOCIATION (TZ) [07558143] **5522**

TAO HUA YUAN (CC) [11265110] **3327**

TAOS MAGAZINE (US/0895-6065) [16699676] **2547**

TAOS NEWS (US) [11280710] **5713**

TAP CHI KHOA HOC KY THUAT (VM/0255-2876) [04922288] **5161**

TAP CHI NGI DAN (US/1065-6871) [26679570] **2666**

TAP CHI SINH HOC (VM/1019-1224) [I10191224] **474**

TAP CHI TOAN HOC (VM) [05001838] **3538**

TAP CHI VAN HOC (VM/0404-6928) [02100911] **3444**

TAP HOP (US) **2666**

TAP ROOTS (SHREVEPORT) (US/0147-6432) [03212327] **2474**

TAP ROOTS (TUSKEGEE) (US/0494-6944) [01789291] **2474**

TAPE (UK) [01791447] **5319**

TAPE BUSINESS *See* TAPE/DISC BUSINESS **1140**

TAPE DECK (US/0164-4602) [04743553] **5319**

TAPE/DISC BUSINESS (US) **1140**

TAPE/DISC DIRECTORY / BILLBOARD (US) [24021655] **4377, 5319**

TAPE RECORDER (NOVA SCOTIA TEACHERS UNION. TEACHERS ASSOCIATION FOR PHYSICAL EDUCATION) (CN/0823-8839) [11629662] **1858**

TAPE RECORDING & BUYING GUIDE *SUSPENDED.* (US/0093-996X) [01793417] **5319**

TAPER & SHAVE (US/1059-6364) [24652347] **4925**

TAPES BY MAIL CATALOGUE (CN/0822-9783) [10764065] **4160**

TAPIJT- EN VLOERMATTENINDUSTRIE / CENTRAAL BUREAU VOOR DE STATISTIEK, HOOFDAFDELING STATISTIEKEN VAN INDUSTRIE EN BOUWNIJVERHEID (NE) [10529320] **1586**

TAPJOE (US) **3472**

TAPORI (US/0882-5424) [11891222] **1070**

TAPPI JOURNAL (US/0734-1415) [08693713] **4239**

TAPPI MONOGRAPH SERIES (US/0097-2169) [01767210] **4239**

TAPPI : [PROCEEDINGS] (US) [22460224] **4239**

TAPPING THE NETWORK JOURNAL (US/1048-5198) [20962234] **887**

TAPROOT (US/0887-9257) [07943944] **3444**

TAPTOE (NE) **1070**

TAQRIR AN AL-TANMIYAH FI AL-ALAM (US/0271-1834) [05159889] **1586**

TAR HEEL JUNIOR HISTORIAN (US/0496-8913) [06740319] **2762**

TAR HEEL NURSE (US/0039-9620) [04769461] **3870**

TAR PAPER (EDMONTON) (CN/0704-9811) [04253030] **4280**

TAR RIVER POETRY (US/0740-9141) [05388650] **3472**

TAR, TENNESSEE ADMINISTRATIVE REGISTER. NOTICE SECTION (US/0149-9718) [03584470] **3062**

TARA (SZ) **4222**

TARAKAI (CE) [09104925] **331**

TARAKAN MUSIC LETTER, THE (US/0272-9520) [06984930] **4156**

TARAKHARA : BHO. JI. SAM. SA. ANERASVAVIYU KO MUKHAPATRA (NP) [08722079] **3444**

TARBIYAH (SANA, YEMEN) (YE) [07931708] **1786**

TARBIYAH (UNITED ARAB EMIRATES. QISM AL-ILAM AL-TARBAWI) (IS) [07800687] **1786**

TARBIZ; RIVON LE-MADE HA-YAHADUT (IS) [05470899] **3327, 5053**

TARBIZS (IS/0334-3650) [02056470] **5053**

TARBUT (NEW YORK, N.Y. : 1989) (US/0792-5891) [22144419] **331**

TAREAS (PN/0494-7061) [02240614] **5224**

Alphabetical Title Index — TAX

TARGET (NE/0924-1884) [20768955] **3327**

TARGET 92 See FRONTIER-FREE EUROPE / COMMISSION OF THE EUROPEAN COMMUNITIES, DIRECTORATE-GENERAL FOR AUDIOVISUAL MEDIA, INFORMATION, COMMUNICATION AND CULTURE **1562**

TARGET 92 / COMMISSION OF THE EUROPEAN COMMUNITIES, DIRECTORATE-GENERAL INFORMATION, COMMUNICATIONS, CULTURE (LU/0776-8508) [18717687] 3136, **1586**

TARGET ARSON / UPDATE (US) **3177**

TARGET GUN (UK/0143-8751) [I01438751] **4925**

TARGET MANAGEMENT DEVELOPMENT REVIEW (UK/0962-2519) [24270770] **887**

TARGET MARKETING (US/0889-5333) [13925680] **937**

TARGET (TORONTO) (CN/0712-2942) [08811537] **5002**

TARGET (WHEELING, ILL.) (US/1051-1636) [14954440] **4222**

TARGETED DIAGNOSIS AND THERAPY (US/1046-1906) [19906397] **3644**

TARHEEL BANKER, THE *CEASED.* (US/0039-9663) [03939705] **813**

TARHEEL HISTORIAN See TAR HEEL JUNIOR HISTORIAN **2762**

TARHEEL WHEELS (US/0039-968X) [03939741] **5394**

TARIF DES COLIS POSTAUX (FR) **1523**

TARIF DES DOUANES (FR) [03689263] **853**

TARIF DES SPECIALITES PHARMACEUTIQUES (BE/0770-1772) [05426575] **4330**

TARIF DOUANIER ALGERIEN (FR) **853**

TARIF EXPORT 25 (FR) **853**

TARIF MEDIA (FR/0038-9579) [I00389579] **767**

TARIF MEDIA MEDICAL (FR) **767**

TARIFAS HOTELERAS (CK) [02459410] **2809**

TARIFAS Y DATOS: MEDIOS IMPRESOS (MX) [06245259] **767**

TARIFF AMENDMENT See MODIFICATION AU TARIF **846**

TARIFF NEWS (US/1064-4199) [26282396] **5394**

TARIFFA DAZI DOGANALI (IT) **1640**

TARIFFA DOGANALE D'USO INTEGRATA (IT) **853**

TARIFFARIO DOGANALE TARIC (IT) **1523**

TARIH ENSTITUSU DERGISI (TU/1015-180X) [04384587] **2631**

TARIH INCELEMELERI DERGISI (TU) [17561896] **2712**

TARIH VE TOPLUM : AYLK ANSIKLOPEDIK DERGI (TU/1019-4681) [15377329] **2712**

TARIK (CHICAGO, ILL.) (US/1050-5369) [21533252] **1523**

TARIKH AL-ARAB WA-AL-ALAM (LE) [05671380] **2666**

TARIKHUNA (LE) [10079823] **2666**

TARIQ AL-SALAMAH / AL-JAMIYAH AL-URDUNIYAH LIL-WIQAYAH MIN HAWADITH AL-TURUQ (JO) [11861922] 4804, **5394**

TARIQ AL-THAWRAH (IR) [09201152] **2666**

TARKIO AVALANCHE, THE (US) [13663575] **5704**

TARLTON LAW LIBRARY See TARLTON LAW LIBRARY LEGAL BIBLIOGRAPHY SERIES **3083**

TARLTON LAW LIBRARY LEGAL BIBLIOGRAPHY SERIES (US/0085-7092) [02361542] **3083**

TARM, ORMAN, VE KOYISLERI BAKANLG DERGISI (TU) [19054285] 2396, **139**

TARM VE KOYISLERI BAKANLG DERGISI (TU) [25180536] 2396, **139**

TARSADALMI SZEMLE (HU/0039-971X) [02268387] **4548**

TARSADALOMKUTATAS (HU/0231-2522) [13297595] 3062, **5224**

TARSADALOMTUDOMANYI KOZLEMENYEK (HU) [04456467] **5224**

TARTAN, THE (US/0890-3107) [14223265] **1095**

$TARTING $MART (US/1042-9557) [19258796] **715**

TARTU. ASTRONOOMIA OBSERVATOORIUM. TARTU TAHETORNI KALENDER See TARTU TAHETORNI KALENDER **401**

TARTU TAHETORNI KALENDER (ER) [04840150] **401**

TARYBU LIETUVOS VISUOMENES MOKSLAI. MENOTYRA / LIETUVOS TSR MOKSLU AKADEMIJA, FILOSOFIJOS, SOCIOLOGIJOS IR TEISES INSTITUTAS, VISUOMENES MOKSLU INFORMACIJOS SEKTORIUS (LI) [19891106] **331**

TAS TOTS (AT) **1070**

TASB NEWS (US) [04269228] **1873**

TASCABILE TV (IT) **2493**

TASCHENBUCH FUER DAS GAS-UND WASSERFACH (GW) [20866192] 4280, **5540**

TASCHENBUCH INFORMATION & DOKUMENTATION (GW/0723-4074) [10661399] **3252**

TASCHENBUCH-KATALOG (GW) [11360610] **4833**

TASFORESTS (AT/1033-8306) [I10338306] **2396**

TASK FORCE REPORT (US/1048-4159) [02268391] **3937**

TASK FORCE REPORT / COUNCIL FOR AGRICULTURAL SCIENCE AND TECHNOLOGY (US/1057-7017) [20273029] **139**

TASKS FOR VEGETATION SCIENCE (US/0167-9406) [08964241] **5161**

TASMANIA See STATUTE LAW OF TASMANIA, THE **3059**

TASMANIA. CONSUMER AFFAIRS COUNCIL See ANNUAL REPORT OF THE CONSUMER AFFAIRS COUNCIL UPON THE ACTIVITIES OF THE COUNCIL **1293**

TASMANIA. CORPORATE AFFAIRS OFFICE See ANNUAL REPORT FOR THE YEAR ... / COMMISSIONER FOR CORPORATE AFFAIRS **3095**

TASMANIA. DEPT. OF MINES See REPORT OF THE DIRECTOR OF MINES (HOBART. 1940) **2150**

TASMANIA. DEPT. OF MINES See REPORT - DIRECTOR OF MINES (HOBART) **2149**

TASMANIA. DEPT. OF MINES. REPORT OF THE DIRECTOR OF MINES See REPORT - DIRECTOR OF MINES (HOBART) **2149**

TASMANIA. DEPT. OF THE TREASURY See STATEMENT OF PUBLIC ACCOUNTS PREPARED BY THE TREASURER **4750**

TASMANIA. DEPT. OF THE TREASURY See CONSOLIDATED REVENUE FUND : SUMMARY OF ESTIMATED EXPENDITURE (INCLUDING EXPENDITURE RESERVED BY LAW) AND ESTIMATED REVENUE **4718**

TASMANIA. DEPT. OF TOURISM See REPORT FOR THE YEAR ... / DEPARTMENT OF TOURISM **5490**

TASMANIA. FISHERIES DEVELOPMENT AUTHORITY See ANNUAL REPORT OF THE FISHERIES DEVELOPMENT AUTHORITY FOR THE YEAR ENDING 30 JUNE ... (TASMANIA) **2295**

TASMANIA. FORESTRY COMMISSION See ANNUAL REPORT / FORESTRY COMMISSION OF TASMANIA **2375**

TASMANIA. GEOLOGICAL SURVEY See GEOLOGICAL SURVEY BULLETIN (HOBART) **1378**

TASMANIA. OFFICE OF THE PARLIAMENTARY COUNSEL See STATUTORY RULES MADE DURING THE YEAR / OFFICE OF THE PARLIAMENTARY COUNSEL **4689**

TASMANIA. STATE LIBRARY SERVICE See ANNUAL REPORT FOR THE YEAR ENDED 30 JUNE ... **3190**

TASMANIA. TOURISM DEVELOPMENT AUTHORITY. REPORT FOR YEAR. See REPORT FOR THE YEAR ... / DEPARTMENT OF TOURISM **5490**

TASMANIAN ANCESTRY (AT/0159-0677) [I01590677] **2474**

TASMANIAN BUILDING JOURNAL (AT) **630**

TASMANIAN COUNTRY (AT) [I1320002X] **2511**

TASMANIAN FISHERIES RESEARCH (AT) [07424295] **2314**

TASMANIAN HISTORICAL RESEARCH ASSOCIATION See PAPERS AND PROCEEDINGS - TASMANIAN HISTORICAL RESEARCH ASSOCIATION **2670**

TASMANIAN POCKET YEAR BOOK (AT/1031-9573) [19117710] **1929**

TASMANIAN REPORTS, THE (AT/0085-7106) [10269353] **3062**

TASMANIAN STATE REPORTS, THE (AT) [01643603] **3062**

TASMANIAN YEAR BOOK (AT/0082-2116) [01639981] **2509**

TASPO MAGAZIN (GW/0177-5014) [02890655] **2432**

TASTE (US/0364-3824) [02627937] **2792**

TASTE FULL (US) 5492, **2359**

●TASTE OF HOME (US/1071-5878) [27481413] **2547**

TATAM (II) [08839377] **139**

TATARSKAIA ASSR (RU) [16640628] 2509, **376**

TATE (UK/1351-3737) **366**

TATE COUNTY DEMOCRAT, THE (US) [16396353] **5702**

TATE TRAILS (US/0893-309X) [09963401] **2474**

TATE'S DOCUMENTATION See TATE'S EXPORT **853**

TATE'S EXPORT (UK) **853**

TATIGKEITSBERICHT (GW) [19174424] **715**

TATIGKEITSBERICHT - BAYERISCHES STAATSINSTITUT FUR HOCHSCHULFORSCHUNG UND HOCHSCHULPLANUNG (GW) [02580161] **1849**

TATIGKEITSBERICHT - BUNDESANSTALT FUER GEOWISSENSCHAFTEN UND ROHSTOFFE (GW/0343-8147) [02767029] **1399**

TATIGKEITSBERICHT DER FORSCHUNGSGESELLSCHAFT FUR DAS STRASSENWESEN See FORSCHUNGSGESELLSCHAFT FUR STRASSEN- UND VERKEHRSWESEN (GERMANY) **5440**

TATIGKEITSBERICHT DER LANDARBEITERKAMMER FUR TIROL (GW) [03381982] **139**

TATIGKEITSBERICHT DES BUNDESVERSICHERUNGSAMTES (GW) [05815967] **1713**

TATIGKEITSBERICHT DES ILS (GW) [02341087] **2836**

TATIGKEITSBERICHT - GEOLOGISCHES LANDESAMT NORDRHEIN-WESTFALIA (GW/0939-4893) [03111166] **1399**

TATIGKEITSBERICHT / HAUPTVERBAND DER OSTERREICHISCHEN SPARKASSEN See JAHRESBERICHT - HAUPTVERBAND DER OSTERREICHISCHEN SPARKASSEN **793**

TATIGKEITSBERICHT - INSTITUT FUR REAKTORSICHERHEIT DER TECHNISCHEN UBERWACHUNGS-VEREINE (GW) [02246017] **2159**

TATIGKEITSBERICHT / KAMMER FUER ARBEITER UND ANGESTELLTE FUER VORARLBERG (AU) [12710800] **1713**

TATIGKEITSBERICHT / STIFTENVERBAND FUR DIE DEUTSCHE WISSENSCHAFT See BERICHT / STIFTERVERBAND FUR DIE DEUTSCHE WISSENSCHAFT **5087**

TATISTICS CANADA. MONTHLY EMPLOYMENT, PAYROLLS AND LABOUR INCOME SECTION See ESTIMATES OF EMPLOYEES BY PROVINCE AND INDUSTRY (CUMULATED EDITION) **1532**

TATLER & BYSTANDER See TATLER, THE **2523**

TATLER, THE (UK) [05822412] **2523**

TATSINANANA (MG) [01794466] **2644**

TATTI STUDIES, I (IT/0393-5949) [13745700] **2712**

TATTOO ADVOCATE (US/0896-8063) [17291265] **5269**

TATTOO (AGOURA HILLS, CALIF.) (US/1041-3146) [18762049] **2493**

TATTVALOKAH / TATTVALOKA (II) [08775117] **5041**

TAUBMAN CENTER ANNUAL REPORT, THE (US) [23829208] **4690**

TAUCHEN (GW) [04322329] **4925**

TAUCHER See TAUCHEN **4925**

TAUNTON DAILY GAZETTE (US) [09545291] **5690**

●TAUNTON'S FINE COOKING (US/1072-5121) [28989163] 2778, **2359**

TAVAN ATAL (RU/0206-4251) [19869407] **3444**

TAVERN SPORTS INTERNATIONAL (US) **4866**

TAVERNA DE AUERBACH, LA (IT/0394-3518) [20081305] **3472**

TAVISTOCK INSTITUTE OF HUMAN RELATIONS, LONDON See ANNUAL REVIEW - TAVISTOCK INSTITUTE OF HUMAN RELATIONS, LONDON **5191**

TAVLATOK (AU/1215-282X) [24470996] **5037**

TAVOLA, A (IT/0394-7181) [I03947181] **2359**

TAWHID (TEHRAN, IRAN) (IR) [10747295] **5045**

TAX ADMINISTRATORS NEWS (US/0039-9949) [01767153] **4751**

TAX ADVISER, THE (US/0039-9957) [01385149] **4751**

TAX AFFAIRS (II/0039-9965) [01767154] 4751, **3062**

TAX ALERT FOR MANAGEMENT (US/0196-8882) [05909785] **4751**

TAX — Alphabetical Title Index

TAX ANALYSTS' DAILY TAX HIGHLIGHTS & DOCUMENTS (US/0889-3055) [17687371] **4751**

TAX AND ACCOUNTING ASPECTS OF CORPORATE REORGANIZATIONS *See* TAX, SEC, AND ACCOUNTING ASPECTS OF CORPORATE ACQUISITIONS **3104**

TAX & INVESTMENT PROFILE. GERMANY (US) [09769392] 917, **4751**

TAX & TARIFF BULLETIN (CN/0820-0653) [09456920] **4752**

TAX ANGLES (US/0193-5771) [05231886] **4752**

TAX ASPECTS OF INTERNATIONAL TREASURY PLANNING (UK) **4752**

TAX AVOIDANCE DIGEST (US/0733-2254) [08535868] **4752**

TAX/BENEFIT POSITION OF PRODUCTION WORKERS, THE (FR) [11709034] **4752**

TAX BREAKS (CN/0846-1112) [24266783] **4752**

TAX BRIEFINGS LOOSELEAF (UK) **752**

TAX BRIEFS *CEASED.* (US) **752**

TAX BULLETIN (US) **4752**

TAX BURDEN ON TOBACCO, THE (US/0563-6191) [02993632] **5373**

TAX CLAIMS AND ELECTIONS (UK) **752**

TAX COLLECTORS MANUAL (US) [05986361] **4752**

TAX COMPANION, THE (US/0270-0077) [03336984] **4752**

TAX CONSULTANT (II) [01767155] **4752**

TAX COURT (US) **4752**

TAX COURT PETITIONS (US/1060-4944) [25011418] **4762**

TAX DIGEST (CORAL GABLES, FLA.) (US) [09039937] 4752, **3062**

TAX DIGEST (LONDON, ENGLAND) (UK) [08371814] 4752, **3062**

●TAX DIGEST (SANTA BARBARA, CALIF.) (US/1062-7308) [25717811] **3062**

TAX DIRECTORY, THE (US/0888-1243) [12905733] **4752**

TAX EXECUTIVE, THE (US/0040-0025) [01713725] **4752**

TAX EXEMPT FINANCING (US/1043-0873) [18530575] 4752, **3062**

TAX EXEMPT NEWS (US/0194-228X) [05373665] **4752**

TAX EXEMPTIONS (OLYMPIA, WASH.) (US) [09535634] 4752, **3062**

TAX EXPENDITURE BUDGET FOR THE STATE OF MINNESOTA, FISCAL YEARS (US) [16522025] **4752**

TAX FACT BOOK (UK) **4752**

TAX FACTS AND FIGURES (MONTREAL) (CN/0821-0780) [09678221] **4752**

●TAX FACTS. INSURANCE AND EMPLOYEE BENEFITS ED (US/1061-401X) [25302391] **2894**

●TAX FACTS. INVESTMENTS ED (US/1061-4028) [25302414] **917**

TAX FACTS ON INVESTMENTS (US/0739-6619) [09779635] 4752, **917**

TAX FACTS ON LIFE INSURANCE (US/0496-9685) [01608198] **2894**

TAX FEATURES (US/1069-711X) [28087007] **4752**

TAX FILE (UK) **4752**

TAX, FINANCIAL AND ESTATE PLANNING FOR THE OWNER OF A CLOSELY-HELD CORPORATION *CEASED.* (US/0194-8822) [05069499] **3119**

TAX FOUNDATION *See* TAX FOUNDATION'S LIBRARY BULLETIN **3252**

TAX FOUNDATION *See* SOURCE REFERENCES FOR FACTS AND FIGURES ON GOVERNMENT FINANCE **4748**

TAX FOUNDATION *See* FEDERAL BUDGET; FOCUS AND PERSPECTIVES, THE **4723**

TAX FOUNDATION'S LIBRARY BULLETIN (US/0736-6469) [09159548] 4752, **3252**

TAX FOUNDATION'S TAX FEATURES (US/0883-1335) [12170275] **4752**

TAX FREE INCOME BULLETIN (US) [16412665] **4752**

TAX GUIDE FOR COLLEGE TEACHERS AND OTHER COLLEGE PERSONNEL (US/0190-7522) [02878347] 1849, **4752**

TAX GUIDE FOR ENGINEERS (US/0146-8235) [02905306] 1998, **4752**

TAX GUIDE FOR INDIVIDUALS WITH INCOME FROM U.S. POSSESSIONS : FOR USE IN PREPARING ... RETURNS (US) [23277105] **4752**

TAX GUIDE FOR SMALL BUSINESS / DEPARTMENT OF THE TREASURY, INTERNAL REVENUE SERVICE (US/0083-1484) [01768450] **4752**

TAX GUIDE FOR U.S. CITIZENS ABROAD / DEPARTMENT OF THE TREASURY, INTERNAL REVENUE SERVICE (US) [01768451] **4752**

TAX GUIDE (NEW YORK, N.Y.) (US/1045-8484) [07880269] **4752**

TAX GUIDE. WEEKLY ALERT (US/0195-6531) [04813520] **4752**

TAX HAVEN & SHELTER REPORT. NORTH AMERICAN EDITION (US/0143-9677) [06258460] **4752**

TAX HAVEN ENCYCLOPEDIA (UK) **4753**

TAX HOTLINE (US/0279-4446) [07879487] **4753**

TAX IDEAS (US/0279-2109) [01716013] **4753**

TAX INFORMATION BULLETIN (CN/0713-7192) [08964026] **4753**

TAX INFORMATION FOR PERSONS WITH HANDICAPS OR DISABILITIES *See* INFORMATION FOR PERSONS WITH HANDICAPS OR DISABILITIES : FOR USE IN PREPARING ... RETURNS **4389**

TAX INSTITUTE, UNIVERSITY OF SOUTHERN CALIFORNIA *See* MAJOR TAX PLANNING **4736**

TAX JOURNAL, THE (UK/0954-7274) [22875958] **4753**

TAX LAW ANTHOLOGY *CEASED.* (US/0892-4430) [15192821] 4753, **3062**

TAX LAW REVIEW (US/0040-0041) [01767167] 4753, **3062**

TAX LAWS OF THE WORLD. CLASS B (US) 3136, **4753**

TAX LAWYER : BULLETIN OF THE SECTION OF TAXATION, AMERICAN BAR ASSOCIATION, THE (US/0040-005X) [01767168] 4753, **3062**

TAX LEVY AUTHORIZATIONS AND LIMITATIONS (US) [05386105] **4753**

TAX LITERATURE REPORT *CEASED.* (US/8755-0369) [10469860] 4753, **3062**

TAX MAGAZINE (US) **4753**

TAX MANAGEMENT COMPENSATION PLANNING JOURNAL (US/0747-8607) [10790924] **917**

TAX MANAGEMENT ESTATES, GIFTS, AND TRUSTS JOURNAL (US/0886-3547) [11351392] **3119**

TAX MANAGEMENT FINANCIAL PLANNING JOURNAL (US/8756-1360) [11481889] **4753**

TAX MANAGEMENT FOREIGN INCOME PORTFOLIOS (US) **4753**

TAX MANAGEMENT INTERNATIONAL FORUM, THE (UK/0143-7941) [06575860] **4753**

TAX MANAGEMENT INTERNATIONAL JOURNAL (US/0090-4600) [01785084] 4753, **887**

TAX MANAGEMENT INTERNATIONAL PORTFOLIOS (UK) **4753**

TAX MANAGEMENT INTERNATIONAL PROGRAM (UK) **4753**

TAX MANAGEMENT IRS FORMS (US) **4753**

TAX MANAGEMENT MEMORANDUM (US/0148-8295) [03387803] **4753**

TAX MANAGEMENT, PRIMARY SOURCES (US/0738-5285) [01795097] **4753**

TAX MANAGEMENT REAL ESTATE JOURNAL (US/8755-0628) [11247136] 4848, **3062**

TAX MANAGEMENT U.S. INCOME (US) **4753**

TAX MANAGEMENT WASHINGTON TAX REVIEW (US/0887-2562) [11510393] **4753**

TAX MANAGEMENT WEEKLY REPORT (US/0884-6057) [12401843] **4753**

TAX MEMO (PRICE WATERHOUSE (FIRM)) (CN/0712-6921) [09515287] **4753**

TAX MONTHLY FOR ASSOCIATIONS (US/0196-1950) [05780629] **4753**

TAX MONTHLY, THE (CE/0377-600X) [02245581] **4753**

TAX NEWS (US) [12576194] **4753**

TAX NEWS SERVICE (NE/0040-0076) [06697297] 4753, **3062**

TAX NOTES (US) [05851167] **4753**

TAX NOTES (ARLINGTON) (US/0270-5494) [01736719] **4753**

TAX NOTES (EDMONTON) (CN/0715-8556) [09594506] **4753**

TAX NOTES INTERNATIONAL (US/1048-3306) [19991830] **4753**

TAX NOTES INTERNATIONAL WEEKLY NEWS (US/1058-3971) [24292602] **3062**

TAX ON PROPERTY (UK) 4753, **4848**

TAX PENALTIES : THE COMPLETE GUIDE TO PENALTIES UNDER THE INTERNAL REVENUE SERVICE (US/1055-2456) [23124603] **4753**

TAX PLANNING CHECKLIST (CN/0821-0764) [09678197] 4753, **3062**

TAX PLANNING FOR THE TROUBLED BUSINESS (US/8756-5137) [10366088] 752, **715**

TAX PLANNING GUIDE (CN/0841-6621) [19032999] **4754**

TAX PLANNING IDEAS (US/0040-0092) [02668803] **4754**

TAX PLANNING INTERNATIONAL (UK) [03420986] **4754**

TAX PLANNING INTERNATIONAL REVIEW (UK/0309-7900) [08063073] **4754**

TAX POLICY AND THE ECONOMY (US/0892-8649) [15274143] **1595**

●TAX PRACTICE & CONTROVERSIES (US/1074-5858) [29627457] **752**

TAX PRACTICE AND PROCEDURE (US/0091-1178) [01786589] **4754**

TAX PRACTITIONER'S DIARY (UK/0269-3720) [l02693720] **4754**

TAX PREPARERS LIABILITY SERVICE (US/0279-7046) [07222580] 4754, **3062**

TAX PRINCIPLES TO REMEMBER (CN/0227-1265) [06562674] **4754**

TAX PROFILE (DON MILLS, ONT.) (CN/0827-3677) [11895310] **4754**

TAX RATES IN VIRGINIA TOWNS (US) [05112354] **4754**

TAX RATES IN VIRGINIA'S CITIES, COUNTIES, AND SELECTED TOWNS (US) [09179377] **4754**

TAX REFORM AND RETIREMENT SAVINGS (TORONTO) (CN/1186-1487) [24368026] **917**

TAX-RELATED ADMINISTRATIVE DOCUMENTS *See* TAX-RELATED DOCUMENTS **4754**

TAX-RELATED DOCUMENTS (US/1062-9106) [25770270] **4754**

TAX REPORTS, NEW ZEALAND (NZ/0110-0246) [02255920] 4754, **3062**

TAX RETURN PREPARER'S GUIDE (US/1059-0390) [24400692] **4754**

TAX RETURN PREPARER'S LETTER (US/1059-6356) [20276737] **4754**

TAX, SEC, AND ACCOUNTING ASPECTS OF CORPORATE ACQUISITIONS (US/8756-5412) [10784393] **3104**

TAX SERVICE FOR "C" CORPORATIONS (US) [25116508] **4754**

TAX SHELTER ANALYST (US/0742-888X) [10470467] 4754, **3062**

TAX SHELTER INSIDER *See* TAX FREE INCOME BULLETIN **4752**

TAX SHOP 1040 (US/0895-7266) [16755837] **4754**

TAX TIPS - DOANE, RAYMOND, PANNELL (CN/1187-4589) [25796387] **4754**

TAX TREATMENT OF CROSS-BORDER DONATIONS: INCLUDING THE TAX STATUS OF CHARITIES AND FOUNDATIONS, THE (NE) **4754**

TAX TREATMENT OF TRANSFER PRICING, THE (NE) [17289227] **4754**

TAX TREATY NETWORKS (SZ/0898-5081) [17833714] **3136**

TAX UPDATE FOR BUSINESS OWNERS (US/0746-0384) [09697098] **4754**

TAX YEAR IN REVIEW, THE (US/0163-9978) [03764426] 4754, **752**

TAXABLE AND NONTAXABLE INCOME : FOR USE IN PREPARING ... RETURNS (US) [23277175] **4754**

TAXABLE SALES IN CALIFORNIA. SALES AND USE TAX (ANNUAL) (US/0095-2753) [01796473] **4754**

TAXABLE SALES IN VIRGINIA COUNTIES & CITIES BASED ON RETAIL SALES TAX REVENUES (US/0095-7798) [01798796] **4754**

TAXATION (UK/0040-0149) [01767175] **4754**

TAXATION AND INVESTMENT IN CANADA (NE) [21632427] 917, **4754**

TAXATION AND INVESTMENT IN CENTRAL AND EAST EUROPEAN COUNTRIES (NE) 752, **4754**

TAXATION & INVESTMENT IN MEXICO (NE) 917, **4754**

TAXATION AND INVESTMENT IN SOUTH AFRICA (NE) 917, **4754**

TAXATION AND INVESTMENT IN THE CARIBBEAN (NE) **4754**

TAXATION AND MERGERS & ACQUISITIONS *CEASED.* (US/1049-9830) [21360061] **4755**

TAXATION (DON MILLS) (CN/0384-9201) [03797286] 3119, **4755**

TAXATION FOR ACCOUNTANTS (US/0040-0165) [01767177] 4755, **752**

TAXATION FOR LAWYERS (US/0161-178X) [01784881] 4755, **3062**

TAXATION IN AUSTRALIA (US) [10209291] **4755**

Alphabetical Title Index — TEACHERS'

TAXATION IN LATIN AMERICA (NE) [17008242] **4755**

TAXATION IN LATIN AMERICA. SUPPLEMENT (NE) [17498763] **4755**

TAXATION INTERNATIONAL (UK/0954-7053) [20439473] **4755**

TAXATION, KEY TO INCOME TAX AND SURTAX *See* KEY TO INCOME TAX **4735**

TAXATION LAW REPORTS, THE (II) [01773441] **3063**

TAXATION MANUAL (UK) **4755**

TAXATION OF COMPANIES IN EUROPE (NE) [20578141] **4755**

TAXATION OF CORPORATE LIQUIDATIONS (US) [16637759] **3104**

TAXATION OF ESTATES, GIFTS, AND TRUSTS : CASES AND MATERIALS (US) [28314768] 3119, **4755**

TAXATION OF INDIVIDUALS IN EUROPE (NE) **4755**

TAXATION OF MINING OPERATIONS (US) [09509365] 2152, **4755**

TAXATION OF PATENT ROYALTIES, DIVIDENDS, INTEREST IN EUROPE (NE) [01753425] **4755**

●TAXATION OF PERMANENT ESTABLISHMENTS, THE (NE) **4755**

TAXATION OF PRIVATE INVESTMENT INCOME (NE) [01752255] **4755**

TAXATION REVENUE, AUSTRALIA (AT) [07662005] 4755, **4701**

TAXATION STATISTICS (OTTAWA) (CN/0700-1665) [01552861] **4701**

TAXATION STATISTICS (PORT MORESBY, PAPUA NEW GUINEA) (PP) [02573646] 4755, **4701**

TAXATION TODAY (WINNIPEG) (CN/0840-5735) [19461996] **4755**

TAXES AND INVESTMENT IN ASIA AND THE PACIFIC (NE) **4755**

TAXES AND INVESTMENT IN THE MIDDLE EAST (NE) [04056961] **4755**

TAXES AND INVESTMENT IN THE MIDDLE EAST. SUPPLEMENT (NE) [14575409] 4755, **3104**

TAXES AND PLANNING (II/0304-1964) [01790559] **4755**

TAXES (CHICAGO, ILL.) (US/0040-0181) [06565278] **4755**

TAXES FEDERALES ET PROVINCIALES SUR LES PRODUITS PETROLIERS (CN/1182-5847) [23248037] **4280**

TAXES INTERPRETED (US/0040-0203) [04045742] **3063**

TAXES (MADISON, WIS.) (US) [10718953] **4755**

TAXI (MILAN, ITALY) *CEASED.* (IT) [14267929] **1087**

TAXIDERMY REVIEW (US/0199-2988) [05764027] **2778**

TAXIDERMY TODAY (US/0279-9731) [07405984] **2778**

TAXIDIA STEN EUROPE (GR) [01793390] **5426**

TAXIDIA STEN HELLADA KAI TEN KYPRO (GR) [01793526] **5426**

TAXLETTER (CN/0821-3704) [09929489] **917**

TAXLINE (UK) **752**

TAXLINE (CINCINNATI, OHIO) (US/1048-2121) [19772090] 3119, **4755**

TAXON (GW/0040-0262) [01767185] **529**

TAXPAYER (AT) [02438791] **4755**

TAXPAYER: ANNUAL TAXATION SUMMARY (AT) [05017208] 3063, **4755**

TAXPAYER, THE (CN) **4755**

TAXPAYERS BULLETIN *See* TAXPAYER **4755**

TAXWISE GIVING (US/0734-2349) [05523062] **4755**

TAY (II) [08839361] **3444**

TAYA YEI YA SA SAUNG (BR) [02652370] **3063**

TAYDENNYSKOULUTUS VUONNA ... (FI) [19860753] **3177**

TAYLOR QUARTERLY, THE (US/0735-9144) [09022515] **2474**

TAYLOR'S ENCYCLOPEDIA OF GOVERNMENT OFFICIALS, FEDERAL AND STATE (US/0082-2183) [01783247] **4498**

TAYLOR'S ENCYCLOPEDIA OF GOVERNMENT OFFICIALS, FEDERAL AND STATE. SUPPLEMENT (US/0733-0294) [05454330] **4498**

TAYLOR'S INDUSTRY DIGEST (CN/0700-3099) [03303900] 5394, **1628**

TAYLORSVILLE POST, THE (US) [16505268] **5702**

TAZEWELL GENEALOGICAL MONTHLY (1985) (US/1071-054X) [12001887] **2474**

TB (SOUTH DAKOTA AGRICULTURAL EXPERIMENT STATION) (US/0191-1716) [04814411] **139**

●TB WEEKLY (US/1065-982X) [26821018] 3952, **3716**

TBC NEWS (US/1046-8927) [20437631] **4394**

TBI'S WORLD GUIDE (US/1052-7192) [22258038] **1140**

TC MEMORANDUM DECISIONS : CONTAINING THE FULL TEXT OF ALL MEMORANDUM DECISIONS OF THE TAX COURT OF THE UNITED STATES RENDERED DURING ... (US) [06958102] **4756**

TC REPORTED DECISIONS; CONTAINING THE FULL TEXT OF ALL REPORTED DECISIONS OF THE TAX COURT OF THE UNITED STATES (US) [01489742] **4756**

TC. TWIN CITIES (US/0274-5151) [06370167] **2547**

●TCA JOURNAL (US) [26906768] 1886, **5312**

TCA REPORT (US/0163-772X) [04471457] **570**

TCF INDUSTRY ADVISOR (AT/1034-4837) [I10344837] **1087**

TCG THEATRE DIRECTORY (US) [08412071] **5369**

●TCI (NEW YORK, N.Y.) (US/1063-9497) [26180112] **5369**

TCM GROWER, THE (US/0747-0746) [10534420] **139**

TCNN RESEARCH BULLETIN (NR/0794-7046) [07361769] **5002**

TCS&D BUYERS' GUIDE (UK/0265-9441) [I02659441] **2359**

TD&T (NEW YORK, N.Y.) (US/1052-6765) [16582078] **5369**

TDR (1988) (US/1054-2043) [17893778] **5369**

TDR NEWS (SZ) [22097778] **3987**

TE & MS TELECOM ASIA (HK) **1164**

TE AO HOU; THE MAORI MAGAZINE (NZ/0570-4499) [01720883] **2671**

TE AVEIA (FP/0293-2547) [07729961] **1586**

TE PUNA MATAURANGA: THE NATIONAL LIBRARY OF NEW ZEALAND NEWSLETTER *CEASED.* (NZ/0114-1090) **3252**

TE REO (NZ/0494-8440) [01865511] **3327**

TEA (KE) [08472202] **189**

TEA & COFFEE TRADE JOURNAL, THE (US/0040-0343) [04922303] **2371**

TEA BOARD OF KENYA *See* ANNUAL REPORT & ACCOUNTS / THE TEA BOARD OF KENYA **60**

TEA BULLETIN (CE/1012-3962) [I10123962] **2371**

TEA DIRECTORY (II) [01800419] **2371**

TEA NEWS (NASHVILLE, TENN.) (US/0039-8292) [03938229] **1873**

TEA NEWS SYDNEY (AT/1033-0801) [I10330801] **3327**

TEA NEWSLETTER (US/0891-9674) [05899294] **1786**

TEA RESEARCH FOUNDATION OF CENTRAL AFRICA *See* QUARTERLY NEWSLETTER - TEA RESEARCH FOUNDATION OF CENTRAL AFRICA **183**

TEA RESEARCH FOUNDATION OF KENYA *See* ANNUAL REPORT FOR THE YEAR ... / TEA RESEARCH FOUNDATION OF KENYA **163**

TEA STATISTICS (CALCUTTA, INDIA : 1982) (II) [10900934] 2371, **2362**

TEACH (FORT WORTH, TEX.) (US/8755-8769) [11427555] 1786, **5002**

TEACHABLE MOMENTS *SUSPENDED.* (US) [20910322] **1786**

TEACHER CERTIFICATION REQUIREMENTS IN ALL FIFTY STATES (US/1063-7508) [21285988] **1905**

TEACHER EDUCATION (II/0312-4886) [02240732] **1905**

TEACHER EDUCATION & PRACTICE (US/0890-6459) [11324823] **1905**

TEACHER EDUCATION AND SPECIAL EDUCATION (US/0888-4064) [04625324] **1886**

TEACHER EDUCATION AT MAKERERE (UG/0377-6026) [02240862] **1905**

TEACHER EDUCATION CENTERS IN WEST VIRGINIA (US/0160-189X) [03620387] **1906**

TEACHER EDUCATION QUARTERLY (CLAREMONT, CALIF.) (US/0737-5328) [09404543] **1906**

TEACHER EDUCATION REPORTS (US) [06073629] **1906**

TEACHER EDUCATION RESEARCH SERIES (PENNSYLVANIA STATE UNIVERSITY. DEPT. OF AGRICULTURAL AND EXTENSION EDUCATION) (US) [09170498] 139, **1906**

TEACHER EDUCATOR, THE (US/0887-8730) [05786657] **1906**

TEACHER FEEDBACK (AT/0311-2772) [I03112772] **1906**

TEACHER (HALIFAX) (CN/0382-408X) [02300078] **1906**

TEACHER HOBART (AT/0813-6580) [I08136580] 1906, **1786**

TEACHER-LIBRARIAN, THE (AT) [11385447] 1786, **3252**

TEACHER MAGAZINE (US/1046-6193) [20311330] **1906**

TEACHER SALARY SCHEDULES, NEW HAMPSHIRE SCHOOL DISTRICTS / NEW HAMPSHIRE STATE DEPARTMENT OF EDUCATION, DIVISION OF ADMINISTRATION (US) [04180152] 1786, **1713**

TEACHER SALARY STUDY (US) [06524615] **1873**

TEACHER SUPPLY AND DEMAND IN FLORIDA ... ANNUAL REPORT (US) [10794660] **1873**

TEACHER SUPPLY AND DEMAND IN UNIVERSITIES, COLLEGES, AND JUNIOR COLLEGES (US) [02229875] **1849**

TEACHER TRAINER (UK/0951-7626) [I09517626] **1906**

TEACHER UNIONIST (AT/1030-7907) [I10307907] 1713, **1786**

TEACHER UPDATE *CEASED.* (US/0194-2859) [05370743] **1786**

TEACHER (VANCOUVER) (CN/0841-9574) [19277811] 1906, **1787**

TEACHER WRITER (US/0162-0002) [04365703] **2924**

TEACHERAID (US/0745-1059) [08820719] **1873**

TEACHERS & WRITERS (US/0739-0084) [06988737] 1906, **3444**

TEACHER'S ARTS AND CRAFTS WORKSHOP (US/0496-9944) [02450982] **376**

TEACHERS' ASSOCIATIONS. ASSOCIATIONS D'ENSEIGNANTS. ASOCIACIONES DE PERSONAL DOCENTE (FR/0082-2213) [01767196] **1906**

TEACHERS COLLEGE RECORD (1970) (US/0161-4681) [01590002] **1849**

TEACHERS COLLEGE SERIES IN SPECIAL EDUCATION (US) [01716056] **1886**

TEACHER'S GUIDE TO CLASSROOM MANAGEMENT *CEASED.* (US/1052-410X) [22284202] **1906**

TEACHERS' GUIDE TO TEACHING POSITIONS IN FOREIGN COUNTRIES (US) [05934771] **1906**

TEACHERS GUIDES TO TELEVISION *CEASED.* (US/0496-9960) [01411358] 1140, **1906**

TEACHER'S HELPER MAGAZINE : GRADE 1 EDITION (US) **1906**

TEACHER'S HELPER MAGAZINE : GRADES 2-3 EDITION (US) **1906**

TEACHER'S HELPER MAGAZINE : GRADES 4-5 EDITION (US) **1906**

TEACHER'S HELPER MAGAZINE : KINDERGARTEN EDITION (US) **1906**

●TEACHERS IN FOCUS (US/1065-5182) [26622610] 5002, **1787**

TEACHERS IN UNIVERSITIES (OTTAWA. 1976) (CN/0707-9737) [05257795] **1849**

TEACHERS INTERACTION (US/0894-7821) [16238689] **5002**

TEACHERS' JOURNAL (SQ) [03122481] **1906**

TEACHER'S LEGAL GUIDE (UK) 3063, **1906**

TEACHERS' MONEY MATTERS *SUSPENDED.* (CN/0829-917X) [13770189] **1713**

TEACHERS' NETWORK NEWSLETTER (US) [25538670] **1906**

TEACHERS OF ENGLISH TO SPEAKERS OF OTHER LANGUAGES *See* TESOL MEMBERSHIP DIRECTORY **3328**

TEACHERS OF HISTORY IN THE UNIVERSITIES AND POLYTECHNICS OF THE UNITED KINGDOM (UK/0085-7114) [13566697] 2631, **1849**

TEACHERS OF HOME ECONOMICS SPECIALISTS ASSOCIATION *See* T H E S A NEWSLETTER **2792**

TEACHERS OF RELIGION AND CHRISTIAN ETHICS IN SASKATCHEWAN *See* TRACES. TEACHERS OF RELIGION AND CHRISTIAN ETHICS IN SASKATCHEWAN **5005**

TEACHERS OF THE WORLD (GW/0492-4134) [02268406] **1906**

TEACHERS' RETIREMENT SYSTEM OF OKLAHOMA (US) [11330818] **1713**

TEACHERS' — Alphabetical Title Index

TEACHERS' RETIREMENT SYSTEM OF OKLAHOMA See RULES AND PROCEDURES FOR OPERATION OF TEACHERS' RETIREMENT SYSTEM OF OKLAHOMA **1709**

TEACHERS' RETIREMENT SYSTEM OF THE STATE OF ILLINOIS See COMPREHENSIVE ANNUAL FINANCIAL REPORT FOR THE YEAR ENDED JUNE 30 ... / STATE OF ILLINOIS. TEACHERS' RETIREMENT SYSTEM **1891**

●TEACHING AND CHANGE (US/1068-378X) [27667201] **1906**

TEACHING & LEARNING BULLETIN (UK/0968-2414) [I09682414] **1906**

TEACHING AND LEARNING IN MEDICINE (US/1040-1334) [18330866] **3644**

●TEACHING AND LEARNING LITERATURE WITH CHILDREN AND YOUNG ADULTS (US/1063-5092) [26048422] 3444, **1906**

TEACHING & LEARNING : THE JOURNAL OF NATURAL INQUIRY (US/0887-9486) [13438988] **1906**

TEACHING AND TEACHER EDUCATION (UK/0742-051X) [10259540] **1906**

TEACHING AND TRAINING IN GERIATRIC MEDICINE (SZ/1011-3738) [19668049] **3755**

TEACHING CASES & PREHOSPITAL CARE (US) **3644**

●TEACHING CHILDREN MATHEMATICS (US/1073-5836) [29484227] 1906, **3538**

TEACHING, COACHING, SUPERVISING NEWSLETTER SUSPENDED. (US/0896-3940) [17150667] **1906**

TEACHING EARTH SCIENCES (UK/0957-8005) [20062859] 1906, **1360**

TEACHING EDUCATION (COLUMBIA, S.C.) (US/1047-6210) [16014679] **1906**

TEACHING ELEMENTARY PHYSICAL EDUCATION (US/1045-4853) [20121171] 1907, **1805**

TEACHING ENGLISH IN THE TWO-YEAR COLLEGE (US/0098-6291) [02240087] 3327, **1850**

TEACHING ENGLISH TO DEAF AND SECOND-LANGUAGE STUDENTS CEASED. (US) [08891997] **1886**

TEACHING EXCEPTIONAL CHILDREN (US/0040-0599) [01680991] **1886**

TEACHING FOR EXCELLENCE (US/8755-3155) [11269532] **1907**

TEACHING FOR SUCCESS (US) **1850**

TEACHING FORUM (CN/0380-3589) [02443084] **1850**

TEACHING GEOGRAPHY (UK) [02779230] 2577, **1907**

●TEACHING HIGH SCHOOL PHYSICAL EDUCATION (US) **1858**

TEACHING HISTORY (EMPORIA, KAN.) (US/0730-1383) [02752174] 1907, **2631**

TEACHING HISTORY (LONDON) (UK/0040-0610) [01606761] 2631, **1907**

TEACHING HISTORY SYDNEY (AT/0040-0602) [I00400602] 2631, **1907**

TEACHING HOME, THE (US) [14409058] **1787**

TEACHING, LEARNING, COMPUTING : TLC (US/0742-4930) [10358590] 1907, **1225**

●TEACHING LEARNING PROCESS, THE (US/1059-6151) [24647344] **1907**

●TEACHING LIBRARIAN (CN/1188-679X) [26715050] 1787, **3252**

TEACHING MATHEMATICS (AT/0313-7767) [I03137767] 1907, **3538**

TEACHING MATHEMATICS AND ITS APPLICATIONS (UK/0268-3679) [09658755] 1907, **3538**

●TEACHING MIDDLE SCHOOL PHYSICAL EDUCATION (US) **1858**

●TEACHING MUSIC (US/1069-7446) [28167585] 1787, **4156**

TEACHING NOTES ON POPULATION (US/0363-3144) [02101110] **4560**

TEACHING OF ENGLISH (US) [01395718] 1907, **3327**

TEACHING OF ENGLISH (AT) **1907**

TEACHING OF PSYCHOLOGY (US/0098-6283) [01834160] 1907, **4620**

TEACHING OPPORTUNITIES (NORTH BRUNSWICK, N.J.) (US/1060-8958) [25103825] **1907**

TEACHING PHILOSOPHY (US/0145-5788) [02773264] 1907, **4363**

TEACHING PICTURES FOR BIBLE SEARCHERS (US/0040-0645) [04045830] 1907, **5020**

TEACHING POLITICS (II) [07217041] 1907, **4498**

TEACHING PRE-K-8 (US/0891-4508) [14778929] **1805**

TEACHING PROFESSOR, THE (US/0892-2209) [15124094] **1850**

TEACHING PUBLIC ADMINISTRATION : TPA (UK/0144-7394) [10354756] **4690**

TEACHING SCIENCE (UK/0028-0763) [09835394] 1907, **5161**

TEACHING SOCIOLOGY (US/0092-055X) [01789172] 1907, **5264**

TEACHING STATISTICS (UK/0141-982X) [07294450] 1907, **1798**

TEACHING THINKING & PROBLEM SOLVING (US/0887-0217) [12242989] **4620**

TEACHING TODAY (EDMONTON) (CN/0827-3049) [11847667] **1907**

●TEACHING TOLERANCE (US/1066-2847) [26707781] **5264**

TEAM (US) **3328**

TEAM AND TRAIL (US) **4925**

TEAM LEADER'S BRIEFING (UK) **947**

TEAM LICENSING BUSINESS (US/1065-738X) [26709269] **1628**

TEAM LICENSING BUSINESS MAGAZINE See TEAM LICENSING BUSINESS **1628**

TEAM MARKETING REPORT (US) [21028551] **4925**

●TEAM PERFORMANCE MANAGEMENT: AN INTERNATIONAL JOURNAL (UK/1352-7592) **947**

TEAM TORIZONS (US/0163-3422) [04336397] **5002**

TEAMREHAB REPORT (US/1053-5926) [22583697] **4382**

TEAMWORK IN INDUSTRY (CN) [01787662] **1713**

TEANGA - IRISH ASSOCIATION FOR APPLIED LINGUISTICS (IE/0332-205X) [I0332205X] **3328**

TEATAR (YU) [22905837] **5369**

TEATER-ET (DK/0905-3026) [22966185] **389**

TEATERRAADETS INDSTILLINGER, FORSLAG OG KONKLUSIONER (DK/0902-8234) [21370599] **5369**

TEATERTIDNINGEN (SW) [23917545] **5369**

TEATR (RU) [06307156] **5369**

TEATR LUDOWY See SCENA **5368**

TEATRALNO-KONTSERTNAIA MOSKVA (RU) [02314044] **389**

TEATRALNYI LENINGRAD (LENINGRAD, R.S.F.S.R. : 1956) (RU) [19804234] **5369**

TEATRO DEL SIGLO DE ORO (GW) [12711794] **5369**

TEATRO DEL SIGLO DE ORO. EDICIONES CRITICAS (GW) [12716634] **3354**

TEATRO DEL SIGLO DE ORO. ESTUDIOS DE LITERATURA (GW) [13173456] **3444**

TEATRO E STORIA (IT) [17212099] **5369**

TEATRO IN EUROPA : TE SUSPENDED. (IT) [18128064] **5369**

TEATRO IN ITALIA (IT) [21284664] **5369**

TEATRO, STUDI E TESTI (IT) [16397539] **5369**

TEATRUL AZI (RM) [22294478] **5369**

TEBANEWS (TU) **1714**

TEBIWA (US/0040-0823) [03300196] **4172**

●TECH DIRECTIONS (US/1062-9351) [25812296] **1916**

TECH-EUROPE (BE) [13442822] 1164, **3252**

TECH MARKET SOUTH (US/1056-2699) [23614010] **853**

TECH. MEMO. - UNIVERSITY OF GUELPH. DEPARTMENT OF LAND RESOURCE SCIENCE (CN/0710-9466) [08205651] **189**

TECH STREET JOURNAL CEASED. (US/0889-6461) [10480252] **5162**

TECH TALK (CAMBRIDGE, MASS.) (US) [08438395] **5162**

TECH TEACHER (AT/0812-6119) [I08126119] **1907**

TECH, THE (US/0148-9607) [03406944] **5690**

TECH TIPS (PH) **5162**

TECH WRITING TIPS SUSPENDED. (US/0887-5324) [13291891] **3328**

TECHJOURNAL (SANTA CLARA, CALIF.) CEASED. (US/1065-2590) [26539034] **2493**

TECHLETTER (US/0883-8828) [12246040] **4248**

TECHN. BIOL. - 1985 (FR/0766-5725) [15085380] **3644**

TECHNI-PORC (FR/0181-6764) [07481858] **222**

TECHNICA (BASEL) (BE/0040-0866) [07468028] **2915**

TECHNICAL ABSTRACT REPORT - DEPT. OF TRANSPORTATION. CLIMATIC IMPACT ASSESSMENT PROGRAM (US/0091-8644) [01786651] **1435**

TECHNICAL ABSTRACTS - U. S. GODDARD SPACE FLIGHT CENTER (US/0565-6141) [01541313] **37**

TECHNICAL AID TO THE DISABLED JOURNAL (AT/0725-2919) [I07252919] **4394**

TECHNICAL ANALYSIS OF STOCKS AND COMMODITIES (JOURNAL) (US/0738-3355) [09583112] **917**

TECHNICAL AND FURTHER EDUCATION. APPLIED SCIENCES : TAFE (AT) [12427186] **5162**

TECHNICAL AND FURTHER EDUCATION. ARCHITECTURAL AND BUILDING STUDIES (AT) [12801853] 1787, **309**

TECHNICAL AND FURTHER EDUCATION. ART, DESIGN AND FASHION (AT) [12801842] 1787, **366**

TECHNICAL AND FURTHER EDUCATION. DETAILS OF SUBJECTS (AT) [18656712] **1916**

TECHNICAL AND FURTHER EDUCATION. ENGINEERING (AT) [12801856] 1787, **1998**

TECHNICAL AND FURTHER EDUCATION. GENERAL STUDIES (AT) [12801859] **1787**

TECHNICAL AND FURTHER EDUCATION. HEALTH AND COMMUNITY CARE (AT) [12801863] 1787, **4804**

TECHNICAL AND FURTHER EDUCATION. HOSPITALITY AND TOURISM (AT) [12801873] 1787, **5492**

TECHNICAL AND FURTHER EDUCATION. MANAGEMENT, BUSINESS AND COMMERCIAL STUDIES (AT) [12801881] 1787, **715**

TECHNICAL & SKILLS TRAINING (US/1047-8388) [20792331] **4209**

TECHNICAL AND VOCATIONAL EDUCATION (FR) [09099095] **1916**

TECHNICAL ASSISTANCE BULLETIN (ANN ARBOR) (US/0190-2792) [02232928] **4879**

TECHNICAL ASSISTANCE INFORMATION CLEARING HOUSE See DEVELOPMENT ASSISTANCE PROGRAMS OF U. S. NON-PROFIT ORGANIZATIONS IN EL SALVADOR **2908**

TECHNICAL ASSISTANCE NOTIFICATIONS See NOTIFICATIONS / HCRS INFORMATION EXCHANGE **2201**

TECHNICAL ASSOCIATION OF THE GRAPHIC ARTS See PROCEEDINGS - TAGA **381**

TECHNICAL ASSOCIATION OF THE PULP AND PAPER INDUSTRY See ALKALINE PULPING CONFERENCE **4232**

TECHNICAL ASSOCIATION OF THE PULP AND PAPER INDUSTRY See TAPPI MONOGRAPH SERIES **4239**

TECHNICAL ASSOCIATION OF THE PULP AND PAPER INDUSTRY. MEETING See TAPPI : [PROCEEDINGS] **4239**

TECHNICAL BOOKS & MONOGRAPHS (US) [04296813] **5162**

TECHNICAL BRIEF (YALE SCHOOL OF DRAMA. DEPT. OF TECHNICAL DESIGN AND PRODUCTION) (US/1053-8860) [10661841] 5369, **389**

TECHNICAL BULLETIN (PK) [12682996] **139**

TECHNICAL BULLETIN (US) [23865417] **3252**

TECHNICAL BULLETIN (MF) [17986217] **139**

TECHNICAL BULLETIN (AT) [27995483] **139**

TECHNICAL BULLETIN (CN) [04627528] **2244**

TECHNICAL BULLETIN / AGRICULTURE CANADA (CN) [26265350] **139**

TECHNICAL BULLETIN - AGRICULTURE CANADA. RESEARCH BRANCH (CN/0825-2084) [I08252084] **139**

TECHNICAL BULLETIN / AIB RESEARCH DEPARTMENT (US) [08459040] **2359**

TECHNICAL BULLETIN - ASPAC, FOOD & FERTILIZER TECHNOLOGY CENTER (CH/0379-7627) [01606590] 139, **2359**

TECHNICAL BULLETIN - BRITISH GEOMORPHOLOGICAL RESEARCH GROUP (UK/0306-3380) [02505508] **1361**

TECHNICAL BULLETIN - CANADIAN CONSERVATION INSTITUTE (CN/0706-4152) [03254637] **2206**

TECHNICAL BULLETIN - CYPRUS AGRICULTURAL RESEARCH INSTITUTE (CY/0070-2315) [03431635] **139**

TECHNICAL BULLETIN - DEPARTMENT OF AGRICULTURE, SABAH, MALAYSIA (MY) [02352867] **139**

TECHNICAL

TECHNICAL BULLETIN (EGGS AUTHORITY) (UK/0263-5178) [10176214] **5162**

TECHNICAL BULLETIN - IFI RESEARCH CENTER (US/0095-666X) [01798405] **5356**

TECHNICAL BULLETIN - INSTITUTE FOR LAND AND WATER MANAGEMENT RESEARCH (NE/0074-042X) [01634281] 5540, **189**

TECHNICAL BULLETIN - INSTITUTE OF MUNICIPAL ASSESSORS OF ONTARIO (CN/0020-2991) [02443194] **4690**

TECHNICAL BULLETIN - MAINE AGRICULTURAL EXPERIMENT STATION (US/0734-9556) [08838989] **139**

TECHNICAL BULLETIN - MINISTRY OF AGRICULTURE, FISHERIES AND FOOD (UK/0072-6729) [01751492] 2314, **139**

TECHNICAL BULLETIN - MISSISSIPPI AGRICULTURAL AND FORESTRY EXPERIMENT STATION (US/0277-5506) [04830105] 2396, **139**

TECHNICAL BULLETIN - NATIONAL COUNCIL OF THE PAPER INDUSTRY FOR AIR AND STREAM IMPROVEMENT (U.S.) (1981) (US/0886-0882) [09899562] 2206, **4239**

TECHNICAL BULLETIN - NATIONAL HORTICULTURAL RESEARCH INSTITUTE (NR/0795-4131) [07954131] **2432**

TECHNICAL BULLETIN (NEW SOUTH WALES. DEPT. OF AGRICULTURE) (AT/0311-8576) [02566235] **139**

TECHNICAL BULLETIN (NORTHERN TERRITORY. ANIMAL INDUSTRY AND AGRICULTURE BRANCH) *See* TECHNICAL BULLETIN / NORTHERN TERRITORY, DEPARTMENT OF PRIMARY PRODUCTION **140**

TECHNICAL BULLETIN / NORTHERN TERRITORY, DEPARTMENT OF PRIMARY PRODUCTION (AT/0158-2763) [11584266] **140**

TECHNICAL BULLETIN / OKLAHOMA AGRICULTURAL AND MECHANICAL COLLEGE, AGRICULTURAL EXPERIMENT STATION (US/0362-8159) [02308738] **140**

TECHNICAL BULLETIN (SOUTH DAKOTA AGRICULTURAL EXPERIMENT STATION) *See* TB (SOUTH DAKOTA AGRICULTURAL EXPERIMENT STATION) **139**

TECHNICAL BULLETIN - SOUTH DAKOTA DEPARTMENT OF GAME, FISH AND PARKS (US) [01999404] **2206**

TECHNICAL BULLETIN / SOUTH PACIFIC APPLIED GEOSCIENCE COMMISSION (SOPAC) (FJ) [25418292] **1361**

TECHNICAL BULLETIN / UNITED STATES DEPARTMENT OF AGRICULTURE (US/0082-9811) [01681299] **140**

TECHNICAL BULLETIN - URBAN LAND INSTITUTE (US/0083-4718) [01494852] **2836**

TECHNICAL BULLETIN / WESTERN AUSTRALIAN DEPARTMENT OF AGRICULTURE (AT/0083-8675) [02768178] **140**

TECHNICAL BULLETIN - WISCONSIN DEPARTMENT OF NATURAL RESOURCES (US/0084-0564) [01590415] **2206**

TECHNICAL BULLETINS / ASSOCIATION OF OPERATIVE MILLERS (US) [07434219] **937**

TECHNICAL BULLETINS (INSTITUUT VOOR CULTUURTECHNIEK EN WATERHUISHOUDING : 1981) (NE) [09163537] **5540**

TECHNICAL BULLETINS / WORLD FERTILITY SURVEY (NE/1012-8727) [05192394] **4560**

TECHNICAL CERAMICS INTERNATIONAL (UK/0960-6661) [09606661] **2594**

TECHNICAL CIRCULAR - NEW HAMPSHIRE FISH AND GAME DEPARTMENT (US/0077-8389) [01510505] **4879**

●TECHNICAL COMMUNICATION QUARTERLY (US/1057-2252) [23980286] **1122**

TECHNICAL COMMUNICATION (SOUTH AFRICA. DEPT. OF AGRICULTURE AND WATER SUPPLY) (SA/1012-7100) [18314286] **140**

TECHNICAL COMMUNICATION (WASHINGTON) (US/0049-3155) [03316919] **5162**

TECHNICAL COMMUNIQUE - CANADIAN CABLE TELEVISION ASSOCIATION (CN/0710-2267) [08858360] **1122**

TECHNICAL COMPUTING (US/0891-303X) [14709443] **1204**

TECHNICAL COMPUTING (ALEXANDRIA) (AT/1038-5231) [10385231] **1204**

TECHNICAL CONFERENCE PROCEEDINGS / IRRIGATION ASSOCIATION (US/0160-7499) [03104936] **2095**

TECHNICAL DIAGNOSTICS AND NONDESTRUCTIVE TESTING (UK/0955-3835) **1998**

TECHNICAL DIGEST (US) [10731467] **2099**

TECHNICAL DIGEST - I.E.E.E. VEHICULAR TECHNOLOGY ANNUAL CONFERENCE (US/0092-3680) [01790880] 2083, **5426**

TECHNICAL DIGEST / INTERNATIONAL ELECTRON DEVICES MEETING (US/0163-1918) [03799851] **2083**

TECHNICAL DIGEST / NAVAL SURFACE WARFARE CENTER (US) [25680715] **4184**

TECHNICAL DOCUMENT / FAO REGIONAL OFFICE FOR ASIA AND THE PACIFIC. ASIA AND PACIFIC PLANT PROTECTION COMMISSION (TH/1014-3351) [12320787] **140**

TECHNICAL DOCUMENT - UNITED STATES. NAVAL OCEAN SYSTEMS CENTER (US/0277-8246) [07637857] **1457**

TECHNICAL EDUCATION ABSTRACTS (UK/0040-0920) [07444125] 1916, **1798**

TECHNICAL EDUCATION & TRAINING ABSTRACTS (UK) [27862509] 1916, **1798**

TECHNICAL EDUCATION NEWS *CEASED.* (US/0146-0137) [01767214] **1916**

TECHNICAL EDUCATION, VICTORIA (AT/0158-5428) [11562545] **1916**

TECHNICAL EMPLOYMENT NEWS (US) **947**

TECHNICAL FISHERY REPORT (US) [17929397] **2314**

TECHNICAL GUIDE - INTERNATIONAL LABOUR OFFICE (SZ) [05766271] **1714**

TECHNICAL GUIDE (QUATERNARY RESEARCH ASSOCIATION (GREAT BRITAIN)) (UK/0264-9241) [12005113] **1399**

TECHNICAL HANDBOOKS FOR MUSEUMS AND MONUMENTS (FR) [07089972] **4097**

TECHNICAL HIGHLIGHTS - NATIONAL MEASUREMENT LABORATORY (US/0271-969X) [06477483] **4032**

TECHNICAL INFORMATION BULLETIN - PARENTERAL DRUG ASSOCIATION (US/0736-0681) [09069056] **4330**

TECHNICAL INFORMATION SERVICE - CHARTERED INSTITUTE BUILDING (UK/0262-6632) [02626632] **630**

TECHNICAL INFORMATION SERVICE / ROYAL AUSTRALIAN HISTORICAL SOCIETY *CEASED.* (AT) [24452952] **2671**

TECHNICAL INSIGHTS ANNUAL REPORT ON GENETIC TECHNOLOGY (US/0741-3661) [10134316] 551, **3696**

TECHNICAL INSIGHTS ANNUAL REPORT ON INDUSTRIAL ROBOTS (US/0741-367X) [10134380] 1628, **1217**

TECHNICAL LEAFLET / AMERICAN ASSOCIATION FOR STATE AND LOCAL HISTORY (US/0516-9216) [01479343] **2631**

TECHNICAL LITERATURE ABSTRACTS (WARRENDALE, PA. : 1987) (US/0741-2029) [17801977] 5426, **1998**

TECHNICAL MANUAL (SY) [24386127] 189, **140**

TECHNICAL MANUAL ATM (AT/0313-895X) [I0313895X] **5445**

TECHNICAL MANUAL - CANADIAN SOCCER ASSOCIATION (CN/0705-7504) [04233429] **4925**

TECHNICAL MARKET SOCIETY OF AMERICA *See* TMSA AEROSPACE MARKET OUTLOOK **37**

TECHNICAL MEMORANDUM (AT) [21139476] 5540, **140**

TECHNICAL MEMORANDUM (UK) [21129255] **2359**

TECHNICAL MEMORANDUM - ASSOCIATE COMMITTEE ON GEOTECHNICAL RESEARCH (OTTAWA) (CN/0077-5428) [01586687] **2032**

TECHNICAL MEMORANDUM - SUPERVISING SCIENTIST FOR THE ALLIGATOR RIVERS REGION (AT/0810-9532) [08109532] **5162**

TECHNICAL METHODS BULLETIN - PARENTERAL DRUG ASSOCIATION (US/0271-325X) [06599999] **4330**

TECHNICAL MONOGRAPH - GREAT BRITAIN. SOIL SURVEY (UK/0072-7210) [03136578] **189**

TECHNICAL MONOGRAPH - PARENTERAL DRUG ASSOCIATION, INC (US/0196-3619) [05795045] **4330**

TECHNICAL NEWS - PERKIN-ELMER CORPORATION (US/0736-6965) [08996499] **5162**

TECHNICAL NOTE BRITISH CERAMIC RESEARCH ASSOCIATION (UK/0144-3631) [01443631] **2594**

TECHNICAL NOTE - FOREST ENGINEERING RESEARCH INSTITUTE OF CANADA (CN/0381-7741) [03520232] **2405**

TECHNICAL NOTE - FOREST ENGINEERING RESEARCH INSTITUTE OF CANADA (CN/0381-7741) [03418077] **2396**

TECHNICAL NOTE - GEOPHYSICS DIVISION (NZ/0110-7089) [02130724] **1411**

TECHNICAL NOTE - SCOTTISH AGRICULTURAL COLLEGES (UK/0142-7695) [01427695] **140**

TECHNICAL NOTE (UNITED STATES). BUREAU OF LAND MANAGEMENT) (US/0098-6860) [02242139] **5598**

TECHNICAL NOTE - WORLD METEOROLOGICAL ORGANIZATION (SZ/0084-201X) [01654259] **1435**

TECHNICAL NOTES : MEDLARS INDEXING INSTRUCTIONS : SUPPLEMENT (US) [05531595] **3644**

TECHNICAL NOTES - OCCUPATIONAL SAFETY AND HEALTH ADMINISTRATION (US/0145-0263) [02606267] **2871**

TECHNICAL NOTES - RCA (US/0483-7495) [03967698] **1140**

TECHNICAL NOTES - UNITED STATES. DEPT. OF HEALTH AND HUMAN SERVICES. DIVISION OF CHILDREN, YOUTH, AND FAMILY POLICY (US/0735-7966) [08268660] **5312**

TECHNICAL OFFICE, THE (US/8755-4526) [08172686] **1239**

TECHNICAL PAPER (AUSTRALIAN BUREAU OF AGRICULTURE AND RESOURCE ECONOMICS) *See* ABARE RESEARCH REPORT **42**

TECHNICAL PAPER - CENTRE FOR RESOURCE STUDIES, QUEEN'S UNIVERSITY (CN/0821-0675) [09929511] **1445**

TECHNICAL PAPER (COLORADO STATE UNIVERSITY. DEPT. OF ATMOSPHERIC SCIENCE) *See* ATMOSPHERIC SCIENCE PAPER **1420**

TECHNICAL PAPER / FLORIDA SEA GRANT COLLEGE (US) [13188652] **1457**

TECHNICAL PAPER - FORESTRY COMMISSION OF NEW SOUTH WALES (AT/0548-6807) [01759968] **2396**

TECHNICAL PAPER / NATIONAL HYDRAULIC RESEARCH CENTER (PH) [08247296] **2095**

TECHNICAL PAPER P - BUILDING RESEARCH ASSOCIATION OF NEW ZEALAND (NZ/0110-4403) [10660500] **630**

TECHNICAL PAPER SERIES - INSTITUTE FOR THE QUANTITATIVE ANALYSIS OF SOCIAL AND ECONOMIC POLICY, UNIVERSITY OF TORONTO (CN/0318-918X) [02442173] **1523**

TECHNICAL PAPER - SOCIETY OF MANUFACTURING ENGINEERS. EE (US/0191-0841) [04787402] **2130**

TECHNICAL PAPER - SOCIETY OF MANUFACTURING ENGINEERS. EM (US/0161-1852) [03857119] **1998**

TECHNICAL PAPER - SOCIETY OF MANUFACTURING ENGINEERS (MF) (US/0191-085X) [04787220] **3488**

TECHNICAL PAPER - SOCIETY OF MANUFACTURING ENGINEERS. TE (US/0161-1887) [03857377] **1998**

TECHNICAL PAPER - SOUTH PACIFIC COMMISSION (NL/0081-2862) [01123074] **2671**

TECHNICAL PAPER - U.S. ARMY, CORPS OF ENGINEERS, COASTAL ENGINEERING RESEARCH CENTER (US/0271-499X) [02902744] **1998**

TECHNICAL PAPER - U.S. DEPARTMENT OF COMMERCE, SOCIAL AND ECONOMICS STATISTICS ADMINISTRATION, BUREAU OF THE CENSUS (US/0082-9544) [02667066] **5344**

TECHNICAL PAPER (UNIVERSITY OF DAR ES SALAAM. DEPT. OF RURAL ECONOMY) (TZ) [11668720] **140**

TECHNICAL PAPERS (US) [23025846] **2583**

TECHNICAL PAPERS (US/0083-8837) [01924783] **2083**

TECHNICAL PAPERS / ASPRS-ACSM ANNUAL CONVENTION (US) [13416273] **2583**

TECHNICAL PAPERS IN HYDROLOGY (FR/0082-2310) [02441154] **1418**

TECHNICAL PAPERS - INTERNATIONAL FINANCE CORPORATION (US/1018-5097) [24336158] **813**

TECHNICAL PAPERS PRESENTED AT GENERAL SESSIONS AND COMMITTEE WORKSHOPS. ANNUAL MEETING (US/0730-935X) [08059382] **5437**

TECHNICAL PAPERS, REGIONAL TECHNICAL CONFERENCE (US/0099-3492) [02909292] **4460**

TECHNICAL Alphabetical Title Index

TECHNICAL PAPERS - SOCIETY OF EXPLORATION GEOPHYSICISTS. INTERNATIONAL MEETING AND EXPOSITION (US/0733-6063) [08191205] **1411**

● TECHNICAL PHYSICS (US/1063-7842) [26136881] **4423**

● TECHNICAL PHYSICS LETTERS (US/1063-7850) [26136316] **4423**

TECHNICAL PROCEEDINGS / ANNUAL CONFERENCE AND INTERNATIONAL TRADE FAIR OF THE NATIONAL WATER SUPPLY IMPROVEMENT ASSOCIATION (US/0278-6206) [07845793] **5540**

TECHNICAL PUBLICATION (AT) [01791793] **2396**

TECHNICAL PUBLICATION - COMMITTEE FOR COORDINATION OF JOINT PROSPECTING FOR MINERAL RESOURCES IN ASIAN OFFSHORE AREAS (CCOP) (TH) [06753607] **1445**

TECHNICAL PUBLICATION R8-TP / UNITED STATES DEPARTMENT OF AGRICULTURE, FOREST SERVICE, SOUTHERN REGION (US/0749-5536) [10062040] **2396**

TECHNICAL PUBLICATION SERIES - DEPARTMENT OF MECHANICAL ENGINEERING, UNIVERSITY OF TORONTO (CN/0082-5182) [02442263] **2130**

TECHNICAL PUBLICATION (UTAH. DEPT. OF NATURAL RESOURCES) (US/0096-5197) [01405520] **2206**

TECHNICAL PUBLICATIONS OF THE STATE BIOLOGICAL SURVEY OF KANSAS (US/0277-6553) [04582477] **474**

TECHNICAL RECORD (NATIONAL BUILDING TECHNOLOGY CENTRE (AUSTRALIA)) (AT) [13807982] **630**

TECHNICAL RELEASE (UK) **752**

TECHNICAL RELEASE - NATIONAL PEST CONTROL ASSOCIATION (US) [01759325] **4248**

TECHNICAL REPORT AFML-TR (US/0099-8508) [02592538] **4058**

TECHNICAL REPORT - AGRICULTURAL RESEARCH COUNCIL OF RHODESIA (RH) [05725321] **140**

TECHNICAL REPORT / AGRICULTURAL RESEARCH COUNCIL OF ZIMBABWE RHODESIA (RH) [07779111] **140**

TECHNICAL REPORT - BUREAU OF GOVERNMENTAL RESEARCH, UNIVERSITY OF NEVADA (US/0548-3646) [01238326] **4690**

TECHNICAL REPORT - CEMENT AND CONCRETE ASSOCIATION (UK/0528-3701) [03942442] **2594**

TECHNICAL REPORT CERC (US/0749-9477) [11143428] **1998**

TECHNICAL REPORT - CIVIL ENGINEERING LABORATORY, NAVAL CONSTRUCTION BATTALION CENTER, PORT HUENEME, CALIFORNIA (US/0502-3262) [06782641] 4184, **2032**

TECHNICAL REPORT - COASTAL ENGINEERING RESEARCH CENTER (U.S.) (US/0271-4981) [06668759] **1998**

TECHNICAL REPORT - COASTAL STUDIES INSTITUTE, CENTER FOR WETLAND RESOURCES, LOUISIANA STATE UNIVERSITY (US) [04829310] **2206**

TECHNICAL REPORT - COLLEGE OF MARINE STUDIES, UNIVERSITY OF DELAWARE (US/0149-3078) [03463437] **1457**

TECHNICAL REPORT (CONSERVATION COMMISSION OF THE NORTHERN TERRITORY) (AT/0729-9990) [18775708] **2206**

TECHNICAL REPORT (COOPERATIVE NATIONAL PARK RESOURCES STUDIES UNIT (DAVIS, CALIF.)) (US) [08077142] **2206**

TECHNICAL REPORT (COOPERATIVE NATIONAL PARK RESOURCES STUDIES UNIT (TUCSON, ARIZ.)) (US) [05231072] **2206**

TECHNICAL REPORT - COOPERATIVE NATIONAL PARK RESOURCES STUDIES UNIT, UNIVERSITY OF HAWAII AT MANOA (US) [04633595] **2206**

TECHNICAL REPORT - CORNELL UNIVERSITY WATER RESOURCES AND MARINE SCIENCES CENTER (US/0197-0526) [01209304] **5540**

TECHNICAL REPORT / DEPARTMENT OF AGRICULTURE, SOUTH AUSTRALIA (AT/0727-601X) [19931051] **140**

TECHNICAL REPORT - DEPARTMENT OF OCEANOGRAPHY (US/0407-4432) [01150836] **1457**

TECHNICAL REPORT - DEPARTMENT OF OCEANOGRAPHY. SCHOOL OF SCIENCE. OREGON STATE UNIVERSITY (US/0473-2170) [01141702] **1457**

TECHNICAL REPORT (FOREST ENGINEERING RESEARCH INSTITUTE OF CANADA) (CN/0318-7063) [02624833] **2396**

TECHNICAL REPORT - FORINTEK CANADA CORP., EASTERN LABORATORY (CN/0709-4523) [10220675] **2396**

TECHNICAL REPORT - INSTITUTE OF WATER RESEARCH (EAST LANSING) (US/0580-9746) [01090698] **5540**

TECHNICAL REPORT - INTERNATIONAL PACIFIC HALIBUT COMMISSION (US/0579-3920) [01771051] **2314**

TECHNICAL REPORT - LAMAR-MERIFIELD (US/0271-0358) [05299653] **1399**

TECHNICAL REPORT - LAMONT-DOHERTY GEOLOGICAL OBSERVATORY (US/0572-8258) [04317107] **1399**

TECHNICAL REPORT - LONG ASHTON RESEARCH STATION, WEED RESEARCH DEPARTMENT (UK/0959-2164) [24888884] **2432**

TECHNICAL REPORT - LOUISIANA WATER RESOURCES RESEARCH INSTITUTE (US/0459-8768) [01134138] 1418, **5540**

TECHNICAL REPORT - MARINE SCIENCES RESEARCH CENTER, STATE UNIVERSITY OF NEW YORK (US/0362-2886) [02215848] **5162**

TECHNICAL REPORT (NEW MEXICO. STATE ENGINEER OFFICE) (US/0545-3038) [02251306] **2095**

TECHNICAL REPORT - PARENTERAL DRUG ASSOCIATION (US/0277-3406) [07583200] **4330**

TECHNICAL REPORT / PLANT PHYSIOLOGY DIVISION (NZ/0110-0610) [10012405] **529**

TECHNICAL REPORT - PURDUE UNIVERSITY, WATER RESOURCES RESEARCH CENTER (US/0555-8026) [01185725] 570, 2095, **5540**

TECHNICAL REPORT : REPORT OF THE MICHIGAN EDUCATIONAL ASSESSMENT PROGRAM (US) [03851378] **1850**

TECHNICAL REPORT SAM-TR (US) [07070086] **3644**

TECHNICAL REPORT (SASKATCHEWAN. SASKATCHEWAN HIGHWAYS AND TRANSPORTATION) (CN/0709-9916) [02250191] **2032**

TECHNICAL REPORT - SCHOOL OF FOREST RESOURCES. NORTH CAROLINA STATE UNIVERSITY (US/0090-0664) [05540436] **2396**

TECHNICAL REPORT - SCHOOL OF FORESTRY, NORTH CAROLINA STATE UNIVERSITY *See* TECHNICAL REPORT - SCHOOL OF FOREST RESOURCES. NORTH CAROLINA STATE UNIVERSITY **2396**

TECHNICAL REPORT SERIES / ARTHUR RYLAH INSTITUTE FOR ENVIRONMENTAL RESEARCH (AT/0810-5774) [20084190] **2206**

TECHNICAL REPORT SERIES - FISHERIES LABORATORY (UK/0308-5589) [04403869] **2314**

TECHNICAL REPORT SERIES OF THE LABORATORY FOR RESEARCH IN STATISTICS AND PROBABILITY (CN/0823-1664) [11382038] **3538**

TECHNICAL REPORT SERIES P. PHYSICAL SCIENCES PUBLICATION (US/0077-796X) [01362475] **5162**

TECHNICAL REPORT SERIES (VICTORIA. DEPT. OF AGRICULTURE AND RURAL AFFAIRS) (AT/0815-2357) [16575635] **140**

TECHNICAL REPORT / SOUTH CAROLINA MARINE RESOURCES CENTER (US) [02534857] **2207**

TECHNICAL REPORT - SOUTHEASTERN WISCONSIN REGIONAL PLANNING COMMISSION (US/0584-4290) [02063782] **2836**

TECHNICAL REPORT SOUTHERN SOUTH ISLAND REGION, AGRICULTURAL RESEARCH DIVISION, MINISTRY OF AGRICULTURE & FISHERIES (NZ/0111-932X) [I0111932X] 2314, **140**

TECHNICAL REPORT (STANFORD UNIVERSITY. DEPT. OF CIVIL ENGINEERING) (US/0585-0738) [01534777] **2032**

TECHNICAL REPORT - STANFORD UNIVERSITY, NATURAL HISTORY MUSEUM (US) [01167917] **4173**

TECHNICAL REPORT - STATE RESOURCES PLANNING PROGRAM (US/0543-8330) [01171007] **1586**

TECHNICAL REPORT - TEXAS. UNIVERSITY AT AUSTIN. LABORATORIES FOR ELECTRONICS AND RELATED SCIENCE RESEARCH (US) [06317411] **2083**

TECHNICAL REPORT - TEXAS WATER RESOURCES INSTITUTE (US/0275-5483) [01785400] **5540**

TECHNICAL REPORT - U. S. ARMY RESEARCH INSTITUTE FOR THE BEHAVIORAL AND SOCIAL SCIENCES (US/0886-9324) [13046146] **4059**

TECHNICAL REPORT - U. S. WATERWAYS EXPERIMENT STATION, VICKSBURG, MISS (US/0500-473X) [01490127] **2095**

TECHNICAL REPORT - UNIVERSITY OF GUELPH, SCHOOL OF ENGINEERING (CN/0715-8629) [05533576] 140, **1998**

TECHNICAL REPORT (UNIVERSITY OF NEW BRUNSWICK. DEPT. OF SURVEYING ENGINEERING) (CN/0709-1222) [05376795] **2032**

TECHNICAL REPORT / UNIVERSITY OF TEXAS AT AUSTIN. ELECTRONICS RESEARCH CENTER *See* TECHNICAL REPORT - TEXAS. UNIVERSITY AT AUSTIN. LABORATORIES FOR ELECTRONICS AND RELATED SCIENCE RESEARCH **2083**

TECHNICAL REPORT (UNIVERSITY OF TORONTO. DEPT. OF COMPUTER SCIENCE) (CN/0042-0204) [02247284] **1262**

TECHNICAL REPORT - UNIVERSITY OF WATERLOO. DEPARTMENT OF ELECTRICAL ENGINEERING (CN/0711-4613) [08499660] **2083**

TECHNICAL REPORT - WASHINGTON DEPARTMENT OF FISHERIES (US/0083-7474) [01511614] **2314**

TECHNICAL REPORT - WATER AND ENERGY RESEARCH INSTITUTE, UNIVERSITY OF GUAM (GU/0272-9555) [04811896] **5540**

TECHNICAL REPORT - WATER RESOURCES RESEARCH CENTER, UNIVERSITY OF HAWAII (US/0272-8729) [06934948] **5540**

TECHNICAL REPORT (WESTERN AUSTRALIA. DEPT. OF CONSERVATION AND LAND MANAGEMENT) (AT/0816-6757) [15586349] **2207**

TECHNICAL REPORT / WOODS HOLE OCEANOGRAPHIC INSTITUTION (US/0730-9694) [08115923] **1457**

TECHNICAL REPORTS (BE) [06795681] **2017**

TECHNICAL REPORTS OF THE NATIONAL HIGHWAY TRAFFIC SAFETY ADMINISTRATION (US) [04455838] **5445**

TECHNICAL REPORTS SERIES / INTERNATIONAL ATOMIC ENERGY AGENCY (AU/0074-1914) [01642481] **1959**

TECHNICAL REPORTS (UNIVERSITY OF MICHIGAN. MUSEUM OF ANTHROPOLOGY) (US/0196-8297) [01781908] 246, **4097**

TECHNICAL RESEARCH REPORT OF HAZAMA-GUMI (JA) **5162**

TECHNICAL REVIEW & REGISTER (US/0065-7069) [01479344] **5356**

TECHNICAL REVIEW / GEC ALSTHOM (FR/0994-7590) [21897721] 5162, **2083**

TECHNICAL REVIEW - IETE (II/0255-9609) [11294462] **2083**

TECHNICAL REVIEW MIDDLE EAST (UK/0267-5307) [I02675307] 715, **5162**

TECHNICAL REVIEW - MITSUBISHI HEAVY INDUSTRIES (JA/0026-6817) [01758421] **1629**

TECHNICAL SECTION PROCEEDINGS (MONTREAL) (CN/0068-9521) [02441243] **4239**

TECHNICAL SERIES - FISHERIES SECTION (DES MOINES) (US) [01449024] **2314**

TECHNICAL SERIES / INTERGOVERNMENTAL OCEANOGRAPHIC COMMISSION (US/0074-1175) [08681769] **1457**

TECHNICAL SERIES (SOCIETY FOR APPLIED BACTERIOLOGY) (UK) [01643202] **570**

TECHNICAL SERVICES LAW LIBRARIAN (US/0195-4857) [05584876] 3063, **3252**

TECHNICAL SERVICES QUARTERLY (US/0731-7131) [08234865] **3252**

TECHNICAL SOARING (US/0744-8996) [08324471] **37**

TECHNICAL SUMMARY - GULF STATES MARINE FISHERIES COMMISSION (US/0434-9504) [01343774] **2314**

TECHNICAL SUPPORT (US/1052-2581) [15619940] **1249**

TECHNICAL TEXTILES (UK) [21967821] **5356**

● TECHNICAL TEXTILES INTERNATIONAL (UK/0964-5993) [I09645993] **5356**

TECHNICAL, TRADE, & BUSINESS SCHOOL DATA HANDBOOK. MIDWEST/WEST REGIONS (US/1044-9221) [18358270] **1916**

TECHNICAL, TRADE, & BUSINESS SCHOOL DATA HANDBOOK. NORTHEAST/SOUTHEAST REGIONS (US/1045-6171) [18364843] **1916**

TECHNICAL TRANSLATION BULLETIN *CEASED.* (UK/0497-0489) [06759278] **5162**

TECHNICAL TRENDS (US/0889-9525) [14108199] **917**

TECHNOLOGY

TECHNICAL WORKING PAPERS / NATIONAL BUREAU OF ECONOMIC RESEARCH (US) [07708999] **1524**

TECHNICAL WRITING TEACHER *See* TECHNICAL COMMUNICATION QUARTERLY **1122**

TECHNICALITIES (US/0272-0884) [06753722] **3252**

TECHNICIAN AND SKILLED TRADES PERSONNEL REPORT / EXECUTIVE COMPENSATION SERVICE, INC (US) [15669692] **1629, 1714**

TECHNICIAN ASSOCIATION NEWS (US) **2083**

TECHNICIANS TODAY (US) [20620014] **994**

TECHNICIEN D'AGRICULTURE TROPICALE, LE (FR) [14439415] **140**

TECHNICIEN DU FILM ET DE LA VIDEO, LA TECHNIQUE, L'EXPLOITATION CINEMAGRAPHIQUE, LE (FR) [08698884] **4078**

TECHNICKE PRIUCKY (STATNI VYZKUMNY USTAV PRO STAVBU STROJU) (XR/0231-5297) [10041784] **2130**

TECHNICKE ZPRAVY (CKD PRAHA (FIRM) : 1978) (XR/0322-8533) [10487140] **5162**

TECHNICKY SBORNIK - VYZKUMNY USTAV CKD (XR) [02243579] **2130**

TECHNICKY TYDENIK [MICROFORM] (US) [15268434] **1629**

TECHNICS AND LEISURES (IT) **4855**

TECHNICUIR (FR) [04092111] **3186**

TECHNIEK IN DE GGEZONDHEIDSZORG : BEHEER EN TOEPASSING (NE/0169-622X) [I0169622X] **5162**

TECHNIK, DIE (GW/0040-1099) [02058956] **5162**

TECHNIK REPORT (AU) [01798417] **5162**

TECHNIK UND GESELLSCHAFT (FRANKFURT AM MAIN, GERMANY) (GW/0723-0664) [10406735] **5162**

TECHNIKA (HU) [06024158] **5162**

TECHNIKA CHRONIKA EPISTEMONIKE EKDOSE. T.E.E. EPISTEMONIKE PERIOCHE A (GR/0250-9954) [13449020] **2032**

TECHNIKA CHRONIKA EPISTEMONIKE EKDOSE T.E.E. EPISTEMONIKE PERIOCHE B (GR/0251-0316) [13449038] **2130**

TECHNIKA CHRONIKA EPISTEMONIKE EKDOSE T.E.E. EPISTEMONIKE PERIOCHE C (GR/0251-0324) [13449066] **2017**

TECHNIKA LOTNICZA I ASTRONAUTYCZNA (PL/0040-1145) [11465752] **37**

TECHNIKAS APSKATS - LATVIESU INZENIERU APVIENIBA (CN/0381-5366) [02830738] **1998**

TECHNIKGESCHICHTE (GW/0040-117X) [07471031] **5162**

TECHNION (IS/0040-1188) [03466530] **5162**

TECHNIQUE AGRICOLE (SZ) **140**

TECHNIQUE CHAUSSURE (FR) **4879**

TECHNIQUE CHAUSSURE MAROQUINERIE MODE (FR/0985-5556) [I09855556] **3186**

TECHNIQUE DE L'EAU ET DE L'ASSAINISSEMENT, LA (BE/0040-120X) [02063128] **5540**

TECHNIQUE ET MANAGEMENT (BE) **887**

TECHNIQUE ET SCIENCE INFORMATIQUES : TSI (FR/0752-4072) [08892233] **1262**

●TECHNIQUE (HYATTSVILLE, MD.) (US/1076-0326) [30418496] **1122**

TECHNIQUE (INDIANAPOLIS, IND.) (US/0748-5999) [10975455] **4925**

TECHNIQUE LAITIERE (FR/0040-1242) [09574316] **199**

TECHNIQUE LAITIERE & MARKETING *See* PROCESS MAGAZINE : LE MENSUEL DES TECHNIQUES LAITIERES ET ALIMENTAIRES **2354**

TECHNIQUE MODERNE, LA (FR/0040-1250) [01767221] **5162**

TECHNIQUES AND APPLICATIONS IN ORGANIC SYNTHESIS SERIES (US) **1048**

TECHNIQUES AND COMMENTS (US/0730-6504) [07407096] **630**

TECHNIQUES & CULTURE (FR/0248-6016) [10782555] **5162**

TECHNIQUES & EQUIPEMENTS DE PRODUCTION PARIS (FR/0998-4909) [I09984909] **1629**

TECHNIQUES AND INSTRUMENTATION IN ANALYTICAL CHEMISTRY (NE/0167-9244) [05307386] **1019**

TECHNIQUES DE L'INGENIEUR / ANALYSE CHIMIQUE & CARACTERISATION PA (FR) **2017**

TECHNIQUES DE L'INGENIEUR / CONSTRUCTION CA (FR) **2032**

TECHNIQUES DE L'INGENIEUR. ELECTROTECHNIQUE (FR/0399-4112) [09050717] **2083**

TECHNIQUES DE L'INGENIEUR / GENERALITES GENIE INDUSTRIEL (FR) **1998**

TECHNIQUES DE L'INGENIEUR / GENIE ENERGETIQUE AND GENIE MECANIQUE (FR) **1998**

TECHNIQUES DE L'INGENIEUR / INFORMATIQUE HA (FR) **2083**

TECHNIQUES DE L'INGENIEUR. MESURES ET CONTROLE (FR/0399-4147) [09050645] **1998**

TECHNIQUES DE L'INGENIEUR. METALLURGIE (FR/0399-4139) [09519987] **4021**

TECHNIQUES DE L'INGENIEUR / METAUX & ALLIAGES MAB (FR) **4021**

TECHNIQUES DE L'INGENIEUR. PLASTIQUES (FR/0245-9574) [I02459574] **4460**

TECHNIQUES DE PECHE (CN/0225-199X) [06021144] **2314**

TECHNIQUES ET ARCHITECTURE (FR/0373-0719) [01589987] **309**

TECHNIQUES ET MANAGEMENT DES PROJETS INFORMATIQUES (FR) **5162**

TECHNIQUES FOR SUCCESS IN FUND-RAISING, MARKETING, AND PUBLIC RELATIONS FOR NONPROFIT ORGANIZATIONS (US/0738-9612) [09697511] **767**

TECHNIQUES FOR THE BENEFITS COMMUNICATOR (US) **1123**

TECHNIQUES IN DIAGNOSTIC PATHOLOGY (BALTIMORE, MD.) (US/1056-7208) [23460888] **3898**

TECHNIQUES IN NEUROSURGERY (US) **3846**

TECHNIQUES IN ORTHOPAEDICS (ROCKVILLE, MD.) (US/0885-9698) [12795612] **3885**

TECHNIQUES IN THE BEHAVIORAL AND NEURAL SCIENCES (NE/0921-0709) [18455050] **3846, 4620**

TECHNIQUES IN THE LIFE SCIENCES. BIOCHEMISTRY *CEASED.* (NE/0165-1064) [05369192] **493**

TECHNIQUES IN THE LIFE SCIENCES. CELL BIOLOGY *CEASED.* (IE/0165-1064) [12940543] **540**

TECHNIQUES IN THE LIFE SCIENCES. PHYSIOLOGY *CEASED.* (NE/0165-1064) [08418174] **587**

TECHNIQUES IN UROLOGY (US) **3993**

TECHNIQUES INDUSTRIELLES (FR) [05770727] **3488**

TECHNIQUES NOUVELLES (BE/0040-1382) [02813546] **2762**

TECHNIQUES NOUVELLES EN SCIENCES DE L'HOMME (FR) [13412432] **2855**

TECHNIQUES OF BIOCHEMICAL AND BIOPHYSICAL MORPHOLOGY (US/0082-2523) [01021945] **474**

TECHNIQUES OF CHEMISTRY (US/0082-2531) [02251912] **994**

TECHNIQUES OF METALS RESEARCH (US/0082-2558) [01459488] **4021**

TECHNIQUES OF PHYSICS (UK/0308-5392) [02294680] **4423**

TECHNIQUES OF WATER-RESOURCES INVESTIGATIONS OF THE UNITED STATES GEOLOGICAL SURVEY (US/0565-596X) [01727864] **5540**

TECHNIQUES, SCIENCES, METHODES : TSM (FR/0299-7258) [13743804] **2244**

TECHNIQUES TRESOR (FR/0223-5587) [I02235587] **887**

TECHNISCH-OEKONOMISCHE INFORMATION DER ZIVILEN LUFTFAHRT (GW) [06804862] **37**

TECHNISCH-PHYSISCHE DIENST TNO-TH *See* ANNUAL REPORT - TECHNISCH-PHYSISCHE DIENST TNO-TH **4397**

TECHNISCH-WISSENSFHAFTLICHE ABHANDLUNGEN DER OSRAM-GESELLSCHAFT (GW/0371-5264) [08536097] **5162**

TECHNISCHE BERICHTE - THYSSEN *CEASED.* (GW/0340-5060) [02242258] **2152, 4021**

TECHNISCHE DOCUMENTATIE- EN INFORMATIECENTRUM VOOR DE KRIJGSMACHT. LUCHTVAARTTECHNIEK *See* LUCHT- EN RUIMTEVAART TECHNIEK LITERATUUROVERZICHT / WETENSCHAPPELIJK EN TECHNIEK DOCUMENTATIE- EN INFORMATIECENTRUM VOOR DE KRIJGSMACHT **28**

TECHNISCHE GEMEINSCHAFT (GW) [08182969] **5162**

TECHNISCHE HOCHSCHULE DARMSTADT. LEHRSTUHL UND INSTITUT FUER MASSIVBAU *See* MITTEILUNGEN **621**

TECHNISCHE HOGESCHOOL DELFT. CENTRE FOR INTERNATIONAL CO-OPERATION AND APPROPRIATE TECHNOLOGY *See* ANNUAL REPORT - TECHNISCHE HOGESCHOOL DELFT **5084**

TECHNISCHE MITTEILUNGEN (SZ) [13830732] **4021**

TECHNISCHE MITTEILUNGEN DER SCHWEIZERISCHEN TELEGRAPHEN- UND TELEPHON-VERWALTUNG (SZ/0040-1471) [07529467] **5162**

TECHNISCHE MITTEILUNGEN FUER SAPPEURE, PONTONIERE, UND MINEURE (SZ) [07480107] **4059, 2032**

TECHNISCHE MITTEILUNGEN KRUPP (DEUTSCH AUSG.) (GW/0930-9276) [15552769] **1629**

TECHNISCHE MITTEILUNGEN KRUPP (ENGLISH ED.) (GW/0930-9284) [17899788] **4021**

TECHNISCHE PHYSIK IN EINZELDARSTELLUNGEN (GW/0082-2590) [08500606] **4423**

TECHNISCHE RUNDSCHAU (SZ/0040-148X) [10647100] **5163**

TECHNISCHE RUNDSCHAU (BERN, SWITZERLAND) *See* TR TRANSFER : TECHNISCHE RUNDSCHAU TRANSFER **5166**

TECHNISCHE UNIVERSITAT BERLIN. INSTITUT FUR SOZIALOKONOMIE DER AGRARENTWICKLUNG *See* ANNUAL REPORT (ABBREVIATED). TECHNISCHE UNIVERSITAT BERLIN. INSTITUT FUR SOZIALOKONOMIE DER AGRARENTWICKLUNG.-- **1809**

TECHNISCHE UNIVERSITAT CAROLO-WILHELMINA. LEICHTWEISS-INSTITUT FUR WASSERBAU *See* MITTEILUNGEN - LEICHTWEISS-INSTITUT FUER WASSERBAU DER TECHNISCHEN UNIVERSITAT BRAUNSCHWEIG **2093**

TECHNISCHE UNIVERSITAT DRESDEN *See* WISSENSCHAFTLICHE ZEITSCHRIFT DER TECHNISCHEN UNIVERSITAT DRESDEN **5170**

TECHNISCHE UNIVERSITAT WIEN. UNIVERSITATSBIBLIOTHEK *See* AUSWAHLLISTE DER NEUERWERBUNGEN **408**

TECHNISCHE VEREINIGUNG DER GROSSKRAFTWERKSBETREIBER E.V *See* VGB-KRAFTWERKSTECHNIK **2000**

TECHNISCHEN UNIVERSITAT HANNOVER SONDERFORSCHUNGSBEREICHS 79 *See* MITTEILUNGEN DES SONDERFORSCHUNGSBEREICHS 79 FUER WASSERFORSCHUNG IM KUSTENBEREICH DER TECHNISCHEN UNIVERSITAT HANNOVER **1452**

TECHNISCHES MESSE : TM (GW/0171-8096) [04781237] **4033**

TECHNO JAPAN (JA/0911-5544) [12935839] **5163**

TECHNOAMBIENTE (IT) **5163**

TECHNOCRACY DIGEST (CN/0040-1587) [01716498] **5224**

TECHNOLOGIA ALIMENTORUM (PL/0324-9212) [14200288] **2359**

TECHNOLOGIA DREWNA (PL) [01789194] **2405**

TECHNOLOGICAL FORECASTING AND SOCIAL CHANGE (US/0040-1625) [02397718] **5163**

TECHNOLOGICAL REPORT - COTTON TECHNOLOGICAL RESEARCH LABORATORY (II) [04538571] **189**

TECHNOLOGIE & MANAGEMENT (GW/0932-2558) [I09322558] **887**

TECHNOLOGIE ET THERAPIE DU COMPORTEMENT (CN/0831-6570) [14955458] **3937**

TECHNOLOGIE SCIENCES & TECHNIQUES INDUSTRIELLES (FR) **5163**

TECHNOLOGIES & FORMATIONS (FR) [13732929] **1787**

TECHNOLOGIES BANCAIRES (FR/0765-3069) [I07653069] **813**

TECHNOLOGIES DE L'INFORMATION ET SOCIETE (CN/0840-4836) [19793617] **5163**

TECHNOLOGIES MECANIQUES SENLIS (FR/0997-9565) [I09979565] **2130**

TECHNOLOGIES PARIS. 1988 (FR/0992-1788) [I09921788] **5163**

TECHNOLOGUE (CN/0825-5172) [12035521] **5163**

TECHNOLOGY ACCESS REPORT (US/1050-043X) [20665585] **5163**

TECHNOLOGY ALERT (PLANTATION, FLA.) (US/1054-4267) [22913296] **5163**

TECHNOLOGY ANALYSIS & STRATEGIC MANAGEMENT (UK/0953-7325) [20071548] **5163**

TECHNOLOGY & CONSERVATION (US/0146-1214) [02670402] **366**

TECHNOLOGY — Alphabetical Title Index

TECHNOLOGY AND CULTURE (US/0040-165X) [01640126] **5163**

TECHNOLOGY AND DISABILITY (US/1055-4181) [23169064] **4394**

TECHNOLOGY AND HEALTH CARE : OFFICIAL JOURNAL OF THE EUROPEAN SOCIETY FOR ENGINEERING AND MEDICINE (NE/0928-7329) [29259415] **3644**

TECHNOLOGY & LEARNING (US/1053-6728) [22361990] 1907, **1225**

TECHNOLOGY AND LEARNING *CEASED.* (US/0890-7889) [14440877] **5163**

TECHNOLOGY ASSESSMENT & FORECAST (US/0364-9105) [02712701] **5163**

TECHNOLOGY ASSESSMENT AND RESEARCH PROGRAM FOR OFFSHORE MINERALS OPERATIONS (US/0882-4584) [11805860] 4804, **2244**

TECHNOLOGY ASSESSMENT (COMPUTER/ELECTRONICS ED.) (US/0882-8660) [12020115] **5163**

TECHNOLOGY ASSESSMENT (NEW YORK, N.Y.) (US/0092-2234) [01788814] **5163**

TECHNOLOGY (BOCA RATON) (US/0273-2580) [06941588] **5163**

TECHNOLOGY BOOK GUIDE (US/0091-7885) [02244990] **5163**

TECHNOLOGY BUSINESS (US/0895-903X) [16852022] **5163**

TECHNOLOGY COMMERCIALISATION (EUROPE ED.) (UK/0965-0326) [24703602] **5163**

●TECHNOLOGY CONNECTION (US/1074-4851) [29735566] **1205**

●TECHNOLOGY DIRECTORY / ASSOCIATION FOR TECHNOLOGY IN MUSIC INSTRUCTION (US) [21931124] **4156**

TECHNOLOGY EXCHANGE BULLETIN (US/0163-2698) [04336750] **5163**

TECHNOLOGY FOR ANESTHESIA (US/8756-8578) [11693199] **3684**

TECHNOLOGY FOR CARDIOLOGY (US/8756-8586) [11693344] **3710**

TECHNOLOGY FOR CRITICAL CARE NURSES *CEASED.* (US/1055-9620) [23375499] **3870**

TECHNOLOGY FOR EMERGENCY CARE NURSES *CEASED.* (US/1059-454X) [24595590] **3870**

●TECHNOLOGY FOR HOME CARE (US/1051-5682) [21990645] **3644**

TECHNOLOGY FOR IMAGING AND RADIOLOGY *CEASED.* (US/0892-7340) [15248630] **3947**

TECHNOLOGY FOR LABORATORY MEDICINE *CEASED.* (US/0892-7332) [15248610] **3644**

TECHNOLOGY FOR MATERIALS MANAGEMENT *CEASED.* (US/8756-8608) [11693814] **3644**

TECHNOLOGY FOR NURSING *CEASED.* (US/0890-9059) [14448561] **3870**

TECHNOLOGY FOR RESPIRATORY THERAPY (US/8756-8616) [11693903] **3952**

TECHNOLOGY FOR SURGERY *CEASED.* (US/8756-8624) [11693668] **3976**

TECHNOLOGY FORECASTS AND TECHNOLOGY SURVEYS (US/0886-0890) [02395757] **5163**

TECHNOLOGY FUTURES NEWSLETTER (US/0896-744X) [17287955] **5163**

TECHNOLOGY IN SOCIETY (US/0160-791X) [04415904] **5164**

TECHNOLOGY IRELAND (IE/0040-1676) [07162865] 5176, **5164**

TECHNOLOGY MANAGEMENT ACTION (US/0886-103X) [12205485] **5164**

●TECHNOLOGY MANAGEMENT (NEW YORK, N.Y.) (US/1073-4457) [29407864] **888**

TECHNOLOGY NEWS - UNITED STATES. BUREAU OF MINES (US/0196-0792) [03457103] **2152**

TECHNOLOGY NOTEBOOK (TECHNICAL UNIVERSITY OF NOVA SCOTIA) *CEASED.* (CN/0824-0353) [11564263] **5164**

TECHNOLOGY NY REPORT (US/1058-2282) [18056013] **5164**

TECHNOLOGY REPORTS OF KANSAI UNIVERSITY (JA/0453-2198) [01783358] **1998**

TECHNOLOGY REPORTS OF THE OSAKA UNIVERSITY (JA/0030-6177) [02265558] 5164, **1998**

TECHNOLOGY REPORTS OF THE TOHOKU UNIVERSITY. LIST OF OTHER PUBLICATIONS, THE (JA) [08926221] **5164**

TECHNOLOGY REPORTS OF THE YAMAGUCHI UNIVERSITY (JA/0386-3433) [02320477] **5164**

TECHNOLOGY RESOURCE GUIDES (US) **5164**

TECHNOLOGY REVIEW (US/0040-1692) [01767230] **5164**

TECHNOLOGY SOURCES (GW) **5164**

TECHNOLOGY SPECIAL INTEREST SECTION NEWSLETTER (US/1059-0609) [24466975] 1886, **5164**

TECHNOLOGY STOCK MONITOR (US/0749-999X) [11241391] **917**

TECHNOLOGY STRATEGIES (UK/0258-0551) [I02580551] **5164**

TECHNOLOGY STUDIES (GW/0940-9467) **5164**

TECHNOLOGY TEACHER, THE (US/0746-3537) [09958429] **5164**

TECHNOLOGY TODAY (US) [05209114] **5164**

TECHNOLOGY TODAY (US/0148-3595) [02758966] **1916**

TECHNOLOGY TODAY (MISSISSAUGA) (CN/0712-9467) [08751932] **5164**

TECHNOLOGY TRACKING (US) **5164**

TECHNOLOGY TRANSFER ABSTRACTS (US/0889-0250) [13775169] **5164**

TECHNOLOGY TRANSFER INTERNATIONAL (UK) 1524, **715**

●TECHNOLOGY TRANSFER WEEK (US) [29701597] 5164, **4059**

TECHNOLOGY TUTORIALS ENTERPRISE NETWORKING (US/1058-6733) [24356919] **1244**

TECHNOLOGY UPDATE *CEASED.* (US/0732-5533) [08384432] **5164**

TECHNOLOGY UPDATE (PALO ALTO, CALIF.) (US/0896-8586) [12394539] 5312, **4394**

TECHNOLOGY WATCH FOR THE GRAPHIC ARTS AND INFORMATION INDUSTRIES (CN/0738-9507) [09708080] **382**

TECHNOLOGY WATCH (WILLOWDALE) (CN/1180-3703) [23598125] 1164, **1205**

TECHNOMETRICS (US/0040-1706) [01767231] **5176**

●TECHNOS (BLOOMINGTON, IND.) (US/1060-5649) [25036970] **1787**

TECHNOSTYLE (CN/0712-4627) [09046634] **3444**

TECHNOTE DARWIN (AT/0158-2755) [I01582755] **5164**

TECHNOTES DBASE IV *CEASED.* (US/1047-1367) [19036322] **1273**

TECHNOTES. REPORTS (FR) **5164**

TECHNOTRENDS NEWSLETTER (US) **5165**

TECHNOVA (HK) **1998**

TECHNOVATION (NE/0166-4972) [07471314] **1629**

TECHPAK (US/0892-7146) [15244367] **4222**

TECHQUA IKACHI (US) [05543502] **2274**

TECHSCAN (NEW YORK, N.Y.) (US/1054-979X) [23041578] **5165**

TECHTRADE (FR) **1205**

TECHTRANSFER NEWS (US/1049-4324) [21218009] **3644**

TECHTRENDS (US/8756-3894) [11557330] 1907, **1225**

TECHTRENDS (FR) **5165**

TECHTRENDS INTERNATIONAL (US/0891-267X) [14695390] **5165**

TECNEWS *CEASED.* (IT) **5165**

TECNICA AGRICOLA / EDITA A CURA DELL'ASSOCIAZIONE DEI DOTTORI IN SCIENZE AGRARIE DELLA PROVINCIA DI CATANIA (IT) [09542396] **140**

TECNICA CERAMICA (SP) [08165158] **2594**

TECNICA DEL CALZADO (SP) **1087**

TECNICA DEL NUOTO, LA (IT) **4925**

TECNICA DEL PUNTO (SP) **5165**

TECNICA DELLA CONFEZIONE E DELLA MAGLIERIA (IT/0392-8136) [I03928136] **5356**

TECNICA DELLA SCUOLA, LA (IT) **1873**

TECNICA E INDUSTRIA (AG) [07296679] **3488**

TECNICA E METODOLOGIA ECONOMALE (IT/0494-9501) [I04949501] **1629**

TECNICA INDUSTRIAL (MADRID) (SP/0040-1838) [02241125] **3488**

TECNICA ITALIANA (IT/0040-1846) [07469990] **2032**

TECNICA LISBOA (PO/0040-1714) [I00401714] **1998**

TECNICA METALURGICA (BARCELONA) (SP/0371-9537) [07507073] **4021**

TECNICA MOLITORIA (IT/0040-1862) [01644022] **204**

TECNICA OSPEDALIERA MILANO (IT/0392-4831) [I03924831] **3793**

TECNICA PECUARIA EN MEXICO (MX/0040-1889) [01696490] **222**

TECNICA PESQUERA *CEASED.* (MX) [07304691] **2314**

TECNICA POPULAR (CU/0138-8800) [19109627] **5165**

TECNICA SANITARIA E MEDICINA DI COMUNITA : ORGANO UFFICIALE DELL'ASSOCIAZIONE NAZIONALE UFFICIALI SANITARI, MEDICI IGIENISTI (IT/0392-8144) [18713562] **4804**

TECNICA TEXTIL INTERNACIONAL (SP/0040-1900) [I00401900] **5356**

TECNICA TOPOGRAFICA : REVISTA DEL COLEGIO OFICIAL DE INGENIEROS TECNICOS EN TOPOGRAFIA (SP) [11296874] **2577**

TECNICAS DE LABORATORIO (SP) **3644**

TECNICHE DELL AUTOMAZIONE & ROBOTICA (IT/0040-1927) 1217, **1221**

TECNICHE DELL IMBALLAGGIO (IT) **4222**

TECNICHE : DI PSICOTERAPIA (IT) **3937**

TECNICHE ED ECONOMIE (IT) **1629**

TECNICO COMERCIAL (AG) [02241336] **4280**

TECNOLOGIA (CK/0367-8210) [02432761] 994, **5165**

TECNOLOGIA (MX) [01642349] **246**

TECNOLOGIA & DEFESA (BL) [10328277] **4059**

TECNOLOGIA DEL AGUA (SP/0211-8173) [23031769] 1418, **5541**

TECNOLOGIA DELLA DEFORMAZIONE (IT) **5165**

TECNOLOGIA EDUCACIONAL (BL) [08097673] **1907**

TECNOLOGIA ELETTRICHE. INDUSTRIA ITALIANA ELETTROTECNICA ED ELETTRONICA (IT/0390-6698) [I03906698] **2083**

TECNOLOGIA MILITAR (GW/0722-2904) [09914164] **4059**

TECNOLOGIA Y ARQUITECTURA (SP/0214-4662) **5165**

TECNOLOGIA Y GESTION (AG) [07028796] **5165**

TECNOLOGIE BIOMEDICHE (IT) 3696, **3793**

TECNOLOGIE CHIMICHE (IT/0392-3452) [09051118] **994**

TECNOLOGIE DEI SERVIZI PUBBLICI (IT) 4804, **4690**

TECNOLOGIE MECCANICHE (IT/0391-1683) [I03911683] **2130**

TECNOLOGIE PER LA SANITA (IT) **5165**

TECOLOTE, EL (US/0741-0034) [05591052] **2493**

TECTONICS (WASHINGTON, D.C.) (US/0278-7407) [07871316] **1411**

TECTONIQUE, GEOPHYSIQUE INTERNE F45 (FR) **1205**

TECTONOPHYSICS (NE/0040-1951) [01767232] **1411**

TECUMSEH HERALD (TECUMSEH, MICH. : 1850) (US) [12277329] **5694**

●TED : THE ELECTRICAL DISTRIBUTORS MAGAZINE (US/1067-3806) [27128891] **2084**

TEDDY BEAR AND FRIENDS, THE (US/0745-7189) [09401541] **2778**

TEDDY BEAR REVIEW (US/0890-4162) [14222242] **376**

TEDENEN EN SCHILDEREN (NE) **382**

TEE SHORTS (US/1061-2254) [25266334] **3444**

TEELINE : THE SHORTHAND AND BUSINESS STUDIES MAGAZINE *CEASED.* (UK) **1850**

TEEN (IT) **1787**

'TEEN (US/0040-2001) [01641635] **1070**

TEEN-AGE DRIVERS (OLYMPIA) (US/0093-917X) [01792450] **5445**

TEEN ARTS CONNECTION/TORONTO (CN/1186-611X) [24368268] 1070, **366**

TEEN BAG (US/0731-9991) [08287184] **1070**

TEEN BEAT (US/1056-0513) [07869686] **1070**

TEEN BEAT ALL STARS (US/1056-0505) 4156, **1070**

TEEN GENERATION (CN/0843-4557) [04039718] **1070**

TEEN LEADER SYNDICATED STUDY (US/0741-7047) [10195450] **1300**

TEEN LIFE (SPRINGFIELD, MO.) (US/1076-9897) [30674073] **5002**

TEEN MACHINE *CEASED.* (US/0747-4695) [10894592] **1070**

Alphabetical Title Index — TELECOMMUNICATIONS

TEEN SET CEASED. (US/1058-9856) [24291826] **1070**

TEEN STUDENT See TEEN STUDENT GUIDE (SPRINGFIELD, MO.) **1070**

●TEEN STUDENT GUIDE (SPRINGFIELD, MO.) (US/1059-3349) [24568148] 5002, **1070**

TEEN TEACHER See TEEN TEACHER GUIDE (SPRINGFIELD, MO.) **5002**

●TEEN TEACHER GUIDE (SPRINGFIELD, MO.) (US/1059-3330) [24568122] 1787, **5002**

TEEN TEACHER'S MANUAL (US/0746-3057) [09926635] **1907**

TEEN TIMES (WASHINGTON, D.C.) (US/0735-6986) [01767238] 1070, **2792**

TEEN VOICES See TEEN VOICES MAGAZINE **1070**

TEEN VOICES MAGAZINE (US) [26441986] 5567, **1070**

TEEN WORLD, THE MAGAZINE FOR TOMORROW'S LEADERS CEASED. (US/1063-2492) **1070**

TEENAGE CHRISTIAN (US) 5002, **1070**

TEENAGE MUTANT NINJA TURTLES MAGAZINE CEASED. (US/1049-0183) [21109471] **4866**

TEENQUEST (US/0890-4006) [14222589] 5068, **1070**

●TEENSCOPE MAGAZINE (US/1059-3764) [24578531] **1070**

TEGLAND'S LITIGATION TODAY (US) [18448174] **3091**

TEHACHAPI NEWS, THE (US) [28310709] **5640**

TEHERAN. UNIVERSITY. VETERINARY FACULTY See NAMAH-I DANISHKADAH-I DAMPIZISHKI **5516**

TEHNICESKAJA ELEKTRODINAMIKA (UN/0204-3599) [06973083] **2084**

TEHNICESKAJA ESTETIKA (MOSKVA) (RU/0040-2230) [06463370] **1998**

TEHNIKA (BEOGRAD) (YU/0040-2176) [10618848] **5165**

TEHNOLOGIJA MESA (YU/0494-9846) [08614889] 2359, **3488**

TEHO / TYOTEHOSEURA (FI/0355-0567) [13529414] 2793, **140**

TEHRAN TIMES TEHRAN (IR/1017-9410) [I10179410] **1123**

TEHY (FI/0358-4038) [09942278] **3870**

TEIKOKU GINKO KAISHA NENKAN. HIGASHI NIHON (JA) [10660225] **1629**

TEIKOKU GINKO KAISHA NENKAN. NISHI NIHON (JA) [10662312] **1629**

TEIKOKU GINKO KAISHA YOROKU See TEIKOKU GINKO KAISHA NENKAN. HIGASHI NIHON **1629**

TEIKYO IGAKU ZASSHI (JA/0387-5547) [10394190] **3645**

TEIKYO WESTMAR UNIVERSITY See ALUMNI DIRECTORY / TEIKYO WESTMAR UNIVERSITY **1099**

TEILHARD REVIEW, THE CEASED. (UK/0040-2184) [20782475] 4363, **246**

TEILHARD STUDIES (US/0739-2303) [05577945] **4363**

TEILTON : SCHRIFTENREIHE DER HEINRICH-STROBEL-STIFTUNG (GW) [05897692] **4156**

TEINTURE ET APPRETS (FR/0040-2206) [11313999] **5356**

TEJAS See TEJAS JOURNAL OF AUDIOLOGY AND SPEECH PATHOLOGY **3891**

TEJAS JOURNAL OF AUDIOLOGY AND SPEECH PATHOLOGY (US/0738-8837) [09699345] **3891**

TEJIPAR (HU/0494-9900) [I04949900] **199**

TEKA (PL/0082-5514) [02146565] **2631**

TEKA KOMISJI URBANISTYKI I ARCHITEKTURY (PL/0079-3450) [I00793450] **309**

TEKAWENNAKE (CN/0300-3159) [01445615] **2547**

TEKHNICHESKIE KULTURY (RU/0235-2559) [19560279] **189**

TEKHNICHESKIE USLOVIIA NA METODY OPREDELENIIA VREDNYKH VESHCHESTV V VOZDUKHE (RU) [05967892] **2244**

TEKHNIKA I VOORUZHENIE : ORGAN NACHALNIKA VOORUZHENII RKKA CEASED. (RU/0201-7490) [10651920] **4059**

TEKHNIKA V SELSKOM KHOZIAISTE (RU/0040-2265) [01605430] **161**

TEKHNOLOGIA I OBORUDOVANIE DEREVOOBRABATYVAIUSHCHIKH PROIZVODSTV (RU/0321-382X) [03334034] **635**

TEKHNOLOGIIA TORFIANOGO PROIZVODSTVA I TORFIANYE MASHINY See MASINY I TEHNOLOGIJA TORFJANOGO PROIZVODSTVA **2143**

TEKI HISTORYCZNE / POLSKIE TOWARZYSTWO HISTORYCZNE W WIELKIEJ BRYTANII (UK/0085-4956) [05022898] **2631**

TEKNICHESKIE SREDSTVA OBUCHENIIA (LV) [02466121] **1907**

TEKNIIKAN SANASTOJA (FI) [19117652] **426**

TEKNIIKKA (FI/0040-2303) [07433609] **5165**

TEKNIK BULTEN (TU) [01784706] **2095**

TEKNIK FOR LANTBRUKET (SW/0282-6674) [I02826674] **140**

TEKNIK I TRANSPORT (SW/1100-4231) [I11004231] **5394**

TEKNISK TIDSKRIFT-NY TEKNIK (SW) [06206866] **5165**

TEKNISK TRAFIKRAPPORT (DK/0902-1116) [19453532] **5445**

TEKNISK UKEBLAD (NO/0800-532X) [12429819] **5165**

TEKNOLOGI (MY) [04842234] 1998, **5165**

TEKNOLOGI KOKO-KELAPA (MY/0127-7979) [25756867] **140**

TEKNOS (IT) **5165**

TEKSTIILI- JA VAATETUSTEOLLISUUS (FI/0785-0549) [19489037] **5356**

TEKSTIILILEHTI (FI) [07433659] **5356**

TEKSTIILITEOLLISUUDEN KONEKANTA. TEXTILINDUSTRINS MASKINER (FI) [02413095] **5356**

TEKSTIILITEOLLISUUDEN VUOSIKIRJA. TEXTILINDUSTRINS ARSBOK. THE TEXTILE INDUSTRY YEARBOOK (FI) [02415415] **5356**

TEKSTIL (CI/0492-5882) [I04925882] **5356**

TEKSTIL & TEKNIK (TU) **5165**

TEKSTILNAJA PROMYSLENNOST (RU/0040-2397) [04109787] **5357**

TEKSTY DRUGIE (PL/0867-0633) [22431786] **3444**

TEL AVIV (1974) (IS/0334-4355) [02050024] **284**

TEL AVIV REVIEW (TEL AVIV, ISRAEL : 1988) SUSPENDED. (IS) [18704438] 3444, **5053**

TEL AVIV UNIVERSITY STUDIES IN LAW (IS) [02256293] **3063**

TEL AVIVER JAHRBUCH FUR DEUTSCHE GESCHICHTE / HERAUSGEGEBEN VOM INSTITUT FUR DEUTSCHE GESCHICHTE (IS/0932-8408) [17303966] **5053**

TEL QUE NOUS LE PENSONS ET AVONS ENVIE DE LE DIRE (CN/0317-5243) [02248124] **5369**

TELCO COMPETITION REPORT (US) **1164**

TELCOM DATA REPORT (US) **1164**

TELCOM HIGHLIGHTS (US/0890-1198) [14181560] **1164**

TELCOM REPORT DEUTSCHE AUSGABE (GW/0344-4724) [I03444724] **1164**

TELCOM REPORT (ENGLISH EDITION) (GW/0344-4880) [04326720] **1164**

TELE (SZ/0040-2427) [07269950] **1164**

TELE 7 JOURS (FR/0153-0747) [I01530747] **1164**

TELE 7 VIDEO (PARIS) See TELE K7, TELE 7 VIDEO **1140**

TELE-AFRICA REVUE (GW) [05579359] **2644**

TELE-C.L.E.F (CN/0822-451X) [10420458] **3063**

TELE CONFERENCE (US/0739-7208) [09813619] **715**

TELE DES ENFANTS, LA (CN/0820-3334) [16582784] 1070, **1140**

TELE ENGLISH EDITION (SW/0495-0127) [I04950127] **1164**

TELE K7 (FR/0757-0112) [I07570112] **1140**

TELE K7 See TELE K7, TELE 7 VIDEO **1140**

●TELE K7, TELE 7 VIDEO (FR/1248-9948) [I12489948] **1140**

TELE SATELLIT (GW) **37**

TELE-TIPS LONG DISTANCE RATE COMPARISON CHART (US) **1164**

TELEBRAS See REVISTA TELEBRAS **1163**

TELEBRAS See RELATORIO DA ADMINISTRACAO - TELEBRAS **1162**

TELECAST AND BROADCAST (SP) **1140**

TELECOM (FR) **1164**

TELECOM ADVISOR, THE (CN/1195-5759) **1164**

TELECOM/EYE BEE EM (US/0888-7292) [13726496] **1164**

TELECOM INFO (FR/0339-9486) [I03399486] **1164**

TELECOM INSIDER (US/0742-6445) [09116474] **1164**

TELECOM MARKET LETTER See NORTHERN BUSINESS INFORMATION'S TELECOM PERSPECTIVES **1161**

TELECOM MARKET LETTER, THE (US/0712-3663) [09029866] **1164**

TELECOM OUTLOOK : THE TELECOMMUNICATIONS & DATA COMMUNICATIONS NEWSLETTER (US/1045-6562) [20185624] **1164**

TELECOM REPORTS WIRELESS NEWS (US) **1164**

TELECOM (SAINTE-FOY) (CN/0820-8018) [10314550] **1165**

●TELECOM STANDARDS NEWSLETTER (US/1064-1076) [26207325] **1165**

TELECOM STRATEGY LETTER See NORTHERN BUSINESS INFORMATION'S TELECOM PERSPECTIVES **1161**

TELECOM TEN YEAR CALENDAR (US/1057-6002) [24074220] **1165**

TELECOM TRIBUNE (JA) **1165**

TELECOM WORLD (UK/0963-0597) [24489689] **1165**

TELECOMBRIEF (NE) **1165**

TELECOMEUROPA'S COMMUNICATIONS NEWSLETTER (UK) **1123**

TELECOMEUROPA'S EASTERN EUROPE NEWSLETTER (UK/0962-3825) [I09623825] **1165**

TELECOMEUROPA'S ISDN NEWSLETTER (UK/0958-8515) [I09588515] **1165**

TELECOMEUROPA'S PERSONAL COMMUNICATIONS NEWSLETTER (UK/0958-8523) **1165**

TELECOMMAGAZINE (NE) **1165**

TELECOMMS ABSTRACTS (UK/0957-4611) [I09574611] **1165**

TELECOMMS REGULATION REVIEW (UK/0951-4686) [I09514686] **1165**

TELECOMMUNICATION JOURNAL (ENGLISH EDITION) (SZ/0497-137X) [01779312] **1165**

TELECOMMUNICATION JOURNAL OF AUSTRALIA, THE (AT/0040-2486) [07045759] **1165**

TELECOMMUNICATION SYSTEMS (NE/1018-4864) [I10184864] **1165**

TELECOMMUNICATIONS ALERT (US/0742-5384) [10370926] **1165**

TELECOMMUNICATIONS AND RADIO ENGINEERING (US/0040-2508) [01585957] **1165**

TELECOMMUNICATIONS CALENDAR (US) **1165**

TELECOMMUNICATIONS COST AND CALL MANAGEMENT CEASED. (US) [18104726] **1165**

TELECOMMUNICATIONS COUNSELOR (US/0735-388X) [08941811] **1165**

TELECOMMUNICATIONS DEVELOPMENT REPORT (US/0889-907X) [14109391] **1165**

●TELECOMMUNICATIONS DIRECTORY (DETROIT, MICH.) (US/1055-8454) [23359114] **1165**

TELECOMMUNICATIONS (EURO-GLOBAL ED.) (US/0192-6209) [05056192] **1165**

TELECOMMUNICATIONS - EXPORT LICENSING CONTROLS (US) 1165, **853**

TELECOMMUNICATIONS (GLOBAL ED.) CEASED. (US/0278-484X) [07832126] **1165**

TELECOMMUNICATIONS (INTERNATIONAL ED.) (US/0040-2494) [02195038] **1165**

TELECOMMUNICATIONS MANAGEMENT AND MARKETING NEWSLETTER (AT/1034-7496) [I10347496] 888, 937, **1165**

TELECOMMUNICATIONS NEWS (UK/0264-4568) [I02644568] **1165**

TELECOMMUNICATIONS (NORTH AMERICAN EDITION) (US/0278-4831) [07832220] **1166**

TELECOMMUNICATIONS POLICY (UK/0308-5961) [03116425] **1166**

TELECOMMUNICATIONS PRODUCT REVIEW (US/0736-4156) [09121279] **1166**

TELECOMMUNICATIONS REGULATORY MONITOR See WASHINGTON TELECOM NEWS **1168**

TELECOMMUNICATIONS REPORTS (US/0163-9854) [02404942] **1166**

TELECOMMUNICATIONS REPORTS INTERNATIONAL (US/1054-1942) [21990514] **1166**

TELECOMMUNICATIONS RETAILER : TCR (US) [09993517] **1166**

TELECOMMUNICATIONS SOURCEBOOK (US/0730-9872) [08072930] **1166**

TELECOMMUNICATIONS   Alphabetical Title Index

TELECOMMUNICATIONS STATISTICS **CEASED.** (CN/0703-7252) [01789703] 1166, **1125**

TELECOMMUNICATIONS STRATEGIES REPORT (AT/1322-3518) **1166**

TELECOMMUNICATIONS SYSTEMS AND SERVICES DIRECTORY **See** TELECOMMUNICATIONS DIRECTORY (DETROIT, MICH.) **1165**

TELECOMMUNICATIONS SYSTEMS GUIDE **CEASED.** (US) [18103945] **1166**

TELECOMMUNICATIONS WEEK (NEW YORK, N.Y.) (US/1040-418X) [10024019] **1166**

TELECOMMUNICATORS DISPATCH **See** DISPATCH CENTER MANAGEMENT **1153**

TELECOMMUNICATORS DISPATCH, THE (US/0887-1647) [13136939] **1166**

TELECOMMUTING REVIEW (US/8756-7431) [11770665] **1166**

TELECOMS MAGAZINE (FR) [22789035] **1166**

TELECOMS MAGAZINE / ENTREPRISE COMMUNICATION RESEAUX (FR) **1166**

TELECOMS RESEAUX INTERNATIONAL (FR/1163-9180) [11639180] **1166**

TELECOMUNICAZIONI (IT/0495-0186) [02715628] **1166**

TELECONFERENCING DIRECTORY (US/0889-5147) [10956626] **1166**

TELECONFERENCING NEWS (US/1065-3007) [26566369] **1166**

TELECONNECT (US/0740-9354) [09793356] **1166**

TELECONS (US) **1166**

TELEFACTS (UK) **1166**

TELEFAX INTERNATIONAL (GW) [13967233] **1166**

TELEFILM CANADA **See** ANNUAL REPORT / TELEFILM CANADA **4063**

TELEFLORA CANADA **See** SUBSCRIBERS DIRECTORY - TELEFLORA CANADA **2436**

TELEFOCUS (US/0743-541X) [10598866] **1166**

TELEFONNYI SPRAVOCHNIK : POLITICHESKIE PARTII I ORGANIZATSII (RU) [25330981] **4498**

TELEGRAFSKA AGENCIJA NOVA JUGOSLAVIJA **See** POSLOVNI DNEVNIK - TANJUG **1579**

TELEGRAM (UK) **1166**

TELEGRAM & GAZETTE (US/1050-4184) [20398430] **5690**

TELEGRAM (MECHANICSBURG, OHIO) (US) [17246670] **5730**

TELEGRAMADRESSEBOK FOR NORGE (NO) [02239793] **1166**

TELEGRAPH AFFARI ESTEUROPA (IT) **1123**

TELEGRAPH (ALTON, ILL.), THE (US/0897-456X) [17501868] **5662**

TELEGRAPH (BROWNSVILLE, PA.) (US) [15578732] **5740**

TELEGRAPH HERALD (1935) (US/1041-293X) [08814165] **5673**

TELEGRAPH (NORTH PLATTE, NEB.) (US/0747-4008) [10785399] **5707**

TELEKEHITYSKESKUS (FINLAND) **See** TOIMINTAKERTOMUS / TELEKEHITYSKESKUS **1168**

TELEKOM PRAXIS /HERAUSGEGEBEN IM BENEHMEN MIT DER FERNMELDETECHNISCHEN ZENTRALAMT (GW/0015-0118) [24516902] **1166**

TELEKOMUNIKACE (XR) [17701621] **1166**

TELEKTRONIKK (NO/0085-7130) [07504879] **2084**

TELEM (IS) [06566669] **5053**

TELEMA (KINSHASA) (CG/1013-7769) [07349228] **5002**

TELEMANAGEMENT (PICKERING) (CN/0840-5476) [19962524] **1167**

TELEMARKETER **See** 800 900 REVIEW **1148**

TELEMARKETING (US/0730-6156) [08036171] 937, **1167**

TELEMARKETING UPDATE (US/0736-167X) [09091801] 937, **767**

TELEMATICS AND INFORMATICS (US/0736-5853) [09171333] **1167**

TELEMATICS COMMUNICATIONS QUARTERLY (US) **1123**

TELEMATICS INDIA (II/0970-3934) [18452069] **1167**

TELEMATIQUE MAGAZINE **See** NOUVEL OBSERVATEUR ENTERPRISES ET TELECOMMUNICATIONS **1161**

● TELEMEDIA NEWS AND VIEWS (US/1071-135X) [28555790] **1167**

TELEMEDICINE (US) **3645**

TELEMETRY JOURNAL (US/0040-2621) [01785059] **2084**

TELENATION (CN/0315-8985) [02184258] **1140**

TELEPHONE AND SERVICE DIRECTORY / NATIONAL INSTITUTES OF HEALTH (US) [07809968] **4804**

TELEPHONE ANGLES (US/0270-4269) [06416484] **1167**

TELEPHONE BYPASS NEWS (US/0886-537X) [10266349] **1167**

TELEPHONE CONTACTS FOR DATA USERS / BUREAU OF THE CENSUS (US) [09927468] **1167**

TELEPHONE DIRECTORY (US) [06550017] **5312**

TELEPHONE DIRECTORY, CENTRAL OFFICE AND NATIONAL CAPITAL REGION (US) [06368293] **4690**

TELEPHONE DIRECTORY CENTRAL OFFICE AND REGION 3 (US) [02532698] **4690**

TELEPHONE DIRECTORY - DEPARTMENT OF DEFENSE (US/0363-6844) [02437003] **4059**

TELEPHONE DIRECTORY. GOVERNMENT OF ALBERTA AND THE LEGISLATIVE ASSEMBLY OF ALBERTA (CN/0701-7510) [07822815] **4690**

TELEPHONE DIRECTORY (GREATER VANCOUVER AND AREA EDITION) (CN/0710-8265) [08834591] **4690**

TELEPHONE DIRECTORY. MANITOBA GOVERNMENT (CN/0318-0255) [02441813] **4690**

● TELEPHONE DIRECTORY, OTTAWA-HULL (CN/1196-054X) [28036697] **4690**

TELEPHONE DIRECTORY / THE WORLD BANK (US) [04730077] **813**

TELEPHONE DIRECTORY - U.S. ENVIRONMENTAL PROTECTION AGENCY (US) [13909876] **2245**

TELEPHONE DIRECTORY / U.S. POSTAL SERVICE (US) [12088938] **1147**

TELEPHONE DIRECTORY / UNITED STATES DEPARTMENT OF THE INTERIOR, GEOLOGICAL SURVEY, CENTRAL REGION (US) [09832459] **1399**

TELEPHONE ENGINEER & MANAGEMENT (US/0040-263X) [06536000] 2084, **1167**

TELEPHONE ENGINEER & MANAGEMENT (US/0040-263X) [02451041] 1167, **2084**

TELEPHONE ENGINEER & MANAGEMENT DIRECTORY (US) [04153853] **1167**

● ... TELEPHONE INDUSTRY DIRECTORY / PHILLIPS BUSINESS INFORMATION, INC, THE (US) [27420299] **1167**

TELEPHONE MANAGEMENT STRATEGIST **CEASED.** (US/0886-9839) [13073814] **1167**

TELEPHONE MARKETING COUNCIL NEWSLETTER (US/0888-353X) [13562943] 1167, **937**

TELEPHONE NEWS (US/0271-5430) [06664359] **1167**

TELEPHONE SELLING REPORT (US/0882-1461) [11788956] 1167, **937**

TELEPHONE STATISTICS (CN/0380-7843) [02442613] 1167, **1125**

TELEPHONE STATISTICS (MONTHLY ED.) (CN/0707-9753) [05021397] 1167, **1125**

TELEPHONE STATISTICS : SELECTED FINANCIAL DATA FOR WISCONSIN TELEPHONE COMPANIES (US/0097-9198) [05082655] 1167, **1125**

● TELEPHONE WEEK (US/1062-4724) [25521838] **1167**

TELEPHONE WORKER **See** CWA NEWS **1662**

TELEPHONY (US/0040-2656) [01639138] **1167**

TELEPHONY'S BUYERS' INFORMATION **See** TELEPHONY'S PUBLIC NETWORK TECHNOLOGY SOURCE **1167**

TELEPHONY'S PUBLIC NETWORK TECHNOLOGY SOURCE **CEASED.** (US) [26679305] **1167**

TELEPIU MILANO (IT/1121-1814) [11211814] **2493**

TELEPROFESSIONAL (US/0886-9642) [13047403] 1167, **937**

TELEPUBLISHING REPORT **SUSPENDED.** (US/0894-9581) [16359851] **4820**

TELEPULESFEJLESZTES (HU/0230-4805) [16514463] **2836**

TELERAMA ED. PARISIENNE (FR/0040-2699) [I00402699] **1123**

TELERATE BANK REGISTER (UK) [18123945] **813**

TELESCOPE (JA) [18073348] **309**

TELESCOPE (DETROIT) (US/0040-2702) [02396149] **4184**

TELESCOPES, INSTRUMENTS, RESEARCH, AND SERVICES (UK) [15131641] **401**

TELESEMAINE (CN/0380-6073) [02578530] **1140**

TELESIS (CN/0040-2710) [03586736] **1167**

TELESNA VZGOJA, SPORT IN SPORTNA REKREACIJA (XV) [06523844] 4925, **1859**

TELESPAN (US/0743-2283) [10536014] **1167**

TELESPECTATEUR, LE **SUSPENDED.** (CN/0712-6891) [09590525] **1140**

TELETEKNIK (ENGLISH EDITION) (DK/0492-6110) [06878561] **2084**

TELEVIDENIE, RADIOVESHCHANIE (RU/0131-694X) [05067988] **1123**

TELEVISION AND CABLE ACTION UPDATE (US) [26969372] **1140**

TELEVISION & CABLE FACTBOOK (US/0732-8648) [08456263] **1140**

TELEVISION & CABLE UPDATE (US/1061-5741) [25279732] **1140**

TELEVISION ANNUAL (US) [23719541] **1140**

TELEVISION BROADCAST (US/0898-767X) [13141802] **1140**

TELEVISION BUSINESS INTERNATIONAL : TBI (UK/0953-6841) [19791303] 715, **1140**

TELEVISION BUYER (US) **1123**

TELEVISION CONTACTS **CEASED.** (US/0147-3352) [03144223] **1140**

TELEVISION DATATRAK (US/1056-0963) [23443724] **1140**

TELEVISION DIGEST WITH CONSUMER ELECTRONICS (1984) (US/0497-1515) [11585012] 2084, **1140**

TELEVISION DIRECTORS GUIDE (US/1055-0828) [23076404] **1140**

TELEVISION EQUIPMENT SPECIFICATION SERVICE (US/0735-567X) [08447297] **2084**

TELEVISION INDEX: NETWORK FUTURES, PROGRAM DEBUTS, RETURNS, SPECIALS AND CHANGES (US/0149-7375) [03526206] **1141**

TELEVISION LISTING CO (US/1058-1030) [24238534] **1141**

TELEVISION (LONDON) (UK/0308-454X) [02386325] **1141**

TELEVISION LONDON. 1970 (UK/0032-647X) [I0032647X] **1141**

TELEVISION MARKET INSIGHT (US/0894-5225) [16122491] **1167**

TELEVISION NETWORK MOVIES **CEASED.** (US/0149-7359) [03526404] **4078**

TELEVISION NEWS INDEX AND ABSTRACTS (US/0085-7157) [01795244] **1167**

TELEVISION NEWS INDEX AND ABSTRACTS : ANNUAL INDEX (US/0085-7157) [05225473] **1141**

TELEVISION QUARTERLY (BEVERLY HILL) (US/0040-2796) [01696403] **1141**

TELEVISION/RADIO AGE COMMUNICATIONS COURSEBOOK (US/0271-4809) [04693373] **1141**

TELEVISION; SERVICING, CONSTRUCTION, COLOUR, DEVELOPMENTS (UK) [17267570] 2812, **2084**

TELEVISION TRENDS (US/0887-1000) [13089939] **1141**

TELEVISION VIEWING (CN/1181-6643) [25066247] **4560**

TELEVISION WRITERS GUIDE (US/0894-8658) [16270187] **1141**

TELEVISUAL (UK) [17851616] 4377, **1141**

TELEVIZIIA, RADIO (BU) [05319514] **1141**

TELEX AFRICA (BE) [02481043] **4536**

TELEX COOPERAZIONE (IT) **4536**

TELEX DEVELOPMENT (BE) **4536**

TELEX DIRECTORY (US/0091-3170) [01786084] **1168**

TELEX MEDITERRANNEE (BE) **4536**

TELEXPORT : LES EXPORTATEURS ET IMPORTATEURS FRANCAIS (FR) [24314535] **853**

TELFAIR TIMES, THE (US) [22037710] **5655**

● TELINDE'S OPERATIVE GYNECOLOGY UPDATES (US/1060-5681) [25058644] **3769**

TELINDUS NEWS (NE) **1244**

TELL (AT/1030-8768) **5002**

● TELL (CINCINNATI, OHIO) (US/1063-9438) [26180243] **5002**

TELLER SENSE (US) **813**

Alphabetical Title Index — TENNESSEE

TELLER, THE (US) [02253143] **5726**

TELLER VISION (US/0895-1039) [16466804] **813**

TELLING AND DUXBURY : PLANNING LAW AND PROCEDURE (UK) 2836, **3063**

TELLTALES (STERLING, VA.) (US/1058-7136) [24362182] **1070**

TELLURIDE TIMES-JOURNAL, THE (US) [20272326] **5644**

TELLUS. SERIES A, DYNAMIC METEOROLOGY AND OCEANOGRAPHY (SW/0280-6495) [09220257] 1457, **1436**

TELLUS. SERIES B, CHEMICAL AND PHYSICAL METEOROLOGY (SW/0280-6509) [09311197] **1436**

TELMA (GW/0340-4927) [01906556] **189**

TELOCATOR See PCIA JOURNAL **1161**

TELOCATOR (US/0193-1458) [05138000] **1168**

TELOPEA (AT/0312-9764) [02620568] **2432**

TELOS (ST. LOUIS) (US/0090-6514) [01785433] **5224**

TELVA (SP) **1787**

TEMA CELESTE (IT) [18912515] **366**

TEMA / ITALY (IT) **309**

TEMA (RIO DE JANEIRO, BRAZIL) (BL) [12300868] **2762**

TEMA (SASKATOON) (CN/0381-9582) [02219075] **1787**

TEMAS ACTUALES DE MEDICINA GENERAL (SP) **3645**

TEMAS DE ANTROPOLOGIA ARAGONESA (SP) **246**

TEMAS DE CIENCIAS HUMANAS (BL) [03529740] **2552**

●TEMAS DE COMUNICACION (UY/0797-6488) [28174769] **1123**

●TEMAS DE COMUNICACION (VE) [29290569] **1123**

TEMAS DE DERECHO PENAL / LUIS A. BRAMONT ARIAS (PE) [09227353] **3109**

TEMAS DE GINECOLOGIA DE NORTEAMERICA (SP) **3769**

TEMAS DE LA LITERATURA INFANTIL (SP) **3444**

TEMAS DE PSICOLOGIA Y PSIQUIATRIA DE LA NINEZ Y ADOLESCENCIA (AG/0325-4437) [03659157] 4620, **3937**

TEMAS DE TRABAJO SOCIAL (CU/0256-2863) [07061396] **5312**

TEMAS EM FOCO (BL) [01788411] **5237**

TEMAS (NEW YORK, N.Y.) (US/0040-2869) [02395992] **2493**

TEMAT (PL) [06290289] **5165**

TEMATICA ECONOMICA POLITICA Y SOCIAL (MX) [02300533] **1524**

TEMENOS (FI/0497-1817) [01767248] **5002**

TEMENOS CEASED. (UK/0262-4524) [08180630] **332**

TEMES DE DISSENY (SP) [17394827] **366**

TEMI DI VITA ITALIANA (IT) **3354**

TEMI ROMANA (IT) **3063**

TEMI. TARNOWSKI MAGAZYN INFORMACYJNY (PL/0208-7006) [02087006] **2523**

TEMISCAMIEN (1976) (CN/0382-0653) [10314449] **5796**

TEMISCOUATA, LE (CN/0706-1757) [06515000] **2762**

TEMOIGNAGE MESSIANIQUE AU PEUPLE D'ISRAEL (FR) **5002**

TEMOIGNAGES ET DOSSIER (FR) **3063**

TEMPDIGEST (HOUSTON, TEX.) (US/0897-5574) [17556520] **4209**

TEMPE DAILY NEWS (US) [02914427] **5630**

TEMPERATURE CONTROLLED STORAGE AND DISTRIBUTION (UK/0143-750X) [I0143750X] **2359**

TEMPERATURE CONTROLLED STORAGE AND DISTRIBUTION (UK/0143-750X) **1629**

TEMPERATURE DEVELOPMENTS (US) [08314701] **4432**

TEMPI MODERNI (IT) [01792459] **1586**

TEMPI MODERNI DELL'ECONOMIA, DELLA POLITICA E DELLA CULTURA See TEMPI MODERNI **1586**

TEMPLE CITY TIMES (US/0191-7145) [04949185] **5640**

TEMPLE DAILY TELEGRAM (US) [14077736] **5755**

TEMPLE ENVIRONMENTAL LAW & TECHNOLOGY JOURNAL (US/0885-2987) [11393907] **3116**

TEMPLE INTERNATIONAL AND COMPARATIVE LAW JOURNAL (US/0889-1915) [13286647] **3136**

TEMPLE LAW REVIEW (US/0899-8086) [17759458] **3063**

●TEMPLE POLITICAL & CIVIL RIGHTS LAW REVIEW (US/1062-5887) [25677715] 3091, **4513**

TEMPO (PO) [03041181] **5808**

TEMPO (US/0896-386X) [04045893] **752**

TEMPO (MZ) [04283050] **2500**

TEMPO (IO) [03528922] **2509**

TEMPO (IT) **5805**

TEMPO (PK) [02240268] **4498**

TEMPO E O MODO, O (PO/0492-6749) [03217229] **1586**

TEMPO E PRESENCA (BL) [08308415] 4363, **4498**

TEMPO ECONOMICO (IT) **1524**

TEMPO KRAKOW (PL/0137-933X) [I0137933X] **4925**

TEMPO (LONDON) (UK/0040-2982) [01767255] **4156**

TEMPO MEDICAL INTERNATIONAL (FR/0378-8407) [I03788407] **3645**

TEMPO MEDICO (IT) **3645**

TEMPO PRESENTE (IT) **4498**

TEMPO (ROCKAWAY, N.J.) (US/0040-3016) [06767309] **4156**

TEMPO SOCIAL : REVISTA DE SOCIOLOGIA DA USP / UNIVERSIDADE DE SAO PAULO, FACULDADE DE FILOSOFIA, LETRAS E CIENCIAS HUMANAS, DEPARTAMENTO DE SOCIOLOGIA (BL/0103-2070) [21286459] **5264**

TEMPORALE (SZ/1016-0809) [13297352] **332**

TEMPORARY CULTURE (US/1055-7644) [23296231] **3444**

TEMPORARY MILITARY LODGING AROUND THE WORLD (US) **4059**

TEMPS DE L'UNION NATIONALE, LE (CN/0703-5578) [03951149] **4498**

TEMPS DE VIVRE (MONTREAL) (CN/0708-7632) [05694838] **5182**

TEMPS FORT (CN/0229-4052) [08308000] **4855**

TEMPS FOU, LE (CN/0705-694X) [04098000] **2547**

TEMPS LIBRE (LAUZON) (CN/0228-6629) [08469732] **4925**

TEMPS LIBRE (MONTREAL) (CN/0823-5708) [10634791] **5492**

TEMPS MELES, DOCUMENTS QUENEAU (FR) [07637975] **3444**

TEMPS MODERNES (FR/0040-3075) [01767256] **3354**

TEMPS STRATEGIQUE, LA (SZ) [10077062] **2493**

TEMPTATION OF SAINT ANTHONY, THE (US/1062-3981) [25611575] **4620**

TEN DIRECTIONS, THE (US) **5022**

TEN.8 (UK/0142-9663) [12002234] **4377**

TENAGAWAN (MY) [05760068] **1629**

TENANT (US/0040-3083) [03940220] **2836**

TENANTS BULLETIN (CN/1195-423X) **2836**

TENDANCES CHEZ LES OISEAUX (CN/1185-5959) [25351932] **5620**

TENDANCES DE LA CONJONCTURE. CAHIER 1, GRAPHIQUES SUR 10 ANS (FR/0754-1627) [11299552] **5344**

TENDANCES DE LA CONJONCTURE. CAHIER 2, GRAPHIQUES SUR 20 ANS (FR/0754-1619) [11299688] **5345**

TENDANCES DES MARCHES : BULLETIN DE L'INSTITUT TECHNIQUE DE L'AVICOLE, TDM (FR) **140**

TENDANCES DES MARCHES DES CAPITAUX (FR) [17278068] **813**

TENDANCES (MONTREAL. 1991) (CN/1188-0589) [25796545] **888**

TENDANCES SOCIALES CANADIENNES (CN/0831-5701) [16728275] **5264**

TENDENCIA (BL) [01792112] **1586**

TENDENCIAS PARA EL INVERSIONISTA (MX) [24223865] **917**

TENDENTSII MIROVOGO EKONOMICHESKOGO RAZVITIIA / AKADEMIIA NAUK SSSR, INSTITUT MIROVOI EKONOMIKI I MEZHDUNARODNYKH OTNOSHENII (RU) [25822646] **1586**

TENDER LOVING CARE PRACTICE PROMOTIONS (US/0898-0268) [17692022] **5522**

TENDERS AUSTRALIA (AT) **715**

TENDRIL CEASED. (US/0197-890X) [04443799] **3444**

TENGGARA (MY/0126-6373) [02129539] **3444**

TENINGUR (IC) [18054625] 366, **3445**

TENINO INDEPENDENT (TENINO, WASH. : 1968) (US) [17377149] **5762**

TENIS STOOWY (PL/0867-1486) [I08671486] **4925**

TENKAI (JA) [04355620] **401**

TENKAN KENKYU / NIHON TENKAN GAKKAI (JA) [11605171] **3846**

TENKANKI NI ARU SHUPPANGYOKAI (JA) [01799744] **4820**

TENKI (JA/0546-0921) [10464040] 1457, **1436**

TENNEN KINENBUTSU NARA NO SHIKA CHOSA HOKOKU (JA) [04206654] **5598**

TENNES-SIERRAN, THE (US/0274-6697) [06477593] **5237**

TENNESSEAN (1972), THE (US/1053-6590) [06431386] **5746**

TENNESSEE See PRIVATE ACTS OF THE STATE OF TENNESSEE PASSED BY THE GENERAL ASSEMBLY **4674**

TENNESSEE ACADEMY OF SCIENCE See JOURNAL OF THE TENNESSEE ACADEMY OF SCIENCE **5121**

TENNESSEE AGRICULTURAL STATISTICS (US/0497-2317) [02620553] 140, **157**

TENNESSEE. ALCOHOLIC BEVERAGE COMMISSION See ANNUAL REPORT FOR THE YEAR JULY 1 ...-JUNE 30 ... / STATE OF TENNESSEE, ALCOHOLIC BEVERAGE COMMISSION **1340**

TENNESSEE ANCESTORS (US/0882-0635) [11736928] **2474**

●TENNESSEE & KENTUCKY QUERIES (US/1068-0063) [27416492] **2474**

TENNESSEE ANTHROPOLOGICAL ASSOCIATION See NEWSLETTER - TENNESSEE ANTHROPOLOGICAL ASSOCIATION **242**

TENNESSEE ANTHROPOLOGIST (US/0892-7979) [02364872] **246**

TENNESSEE ARCHAEOLOGIST (US/0040-3180) [02050509] **284**

TENNESSEE ARCHIVISTS (US) [08335667] **5002**

TENNESSEE ARTS COMMISSION See ANNUAL REPORT - TENNESSEE ARTS COMMISSION **313**

TENNESSEE ATTORNEYS DIRECTORY (US/0742-4329) [08226138] **3063**

TENNESSEE ATTORNEYS MEMO (US/0194-1259) [I01941259] **3063**

TENNESSEE BANKER, THE (US/0040-3199) [03940278] **813**

TENNESSEE BAR ASSOCIATION See TENNESSEE BAR JOURNAL **3063**

TENNESSEE BAR JOURNAL (US/0497-2325) [01716386] **3063**

TENNESSEE BLUE BOOK (US/0364-5746) [02114654] **4690**

TENNESSEE. BUREAU OF MASS TRANSIT. ANNUAL REPORT OF THE BUREAU OF AREA MASS TRANSIT OF THE TENNESSEE DEPARTMENT OF TRANSPORTATION See ANNUAL REPORT OF THE COMMISSIONER OF TRANSPORTATION TO THE GOVERNOR **5376**

TENNESSEE BUSINESS AND INDUSTRIAL REVIEW (US) [06173416] **1629**

TENNESSEE BUSINESS (NASHVILLE, TENN.) (US/0745-1474) [08868245] **715**

TENNESSEE CODE ANNOTATED ADVANCE ANNOTATION SERVICE (US/0747-7074) [08073584] **3063**

TENNESSEE COMMUNICABLE DISEASE BULLETIN (US/0898-6967) [17884232] **4804**

TENNESSEE CONSERVATIONIST, THE (US/0040-3202) [02398884] **2207**

TENNESSEE COUNTY HISTORY SERIES CEASED. (US) [06820526] **2762**

TENNESSEE DAIRY STATISTICS (US/0748-4119) [06833404] 199, **157**

TENNESSEE. DEPARTMENT OF EDUCATION See DIRECTORY OF PUBLIC SCHOOLS **1736**

TENNESSEE. DEPT. OF COMMERCE AND INSURANCE See ANNUAL REPORT OF THE DEPARTMENT OF COMMERCE AND INSURANCE **823**

TENNESSEE. DEPT. OF EMPLOYMENT SECURITY See BIENNIAL REPORT / TENNESSEE DEPARTMENT OF EMPLOYMENT SECURITY **1655**

TENNESSEE. DEPT. OF FINANCIAL INSTITUTIONS See ANNUAL REPORT / STATE OF TENNESSEE, DEPARTMENT OF FINANCIAL INSTITUTIONS **772**

TENNESSEE. DEPT. OF HUMAN SERVICES See STATISTICS - STATE OF TENNESSEE, DEPARTMENT OF HUMAN SERVICES **5267**

TENNESSEE. DEPT. OF HUMAN SERVICES See RECORD - TENNESSEE DEPARTMENT OF HUMAN SERVICES, THE **5304**

TENNESSEE — Alphabetical Title Index

TENNESSEE. DEPT. OF PUBLIC WELFARE. TENNESSEE PUBLIC WELFARE RECORD See RECORD - TENNESSEE DEPARTMENT OF HUMAN SERVICES, THE **5304**

TENNESSEE. DEPT. OF REVENUE See BIENNIAL REPORT - TENNESSEE DEPARTMENT OF REVENUE **4713**

TENNESSEE. DEPT. OF REVENUE. BIENNIAL REPORT FOR THE FISCAL YEARS . See BIENNIAL REPORT - TENNESSEE DEPARTMENT OF REVENUE **4713**

TENNESSEE. DEPT. OF SAFETY See ANNUAL REPORT - DEPARTMENT OF SAFETY **5438**

TENNESSEE. DEPT. OF SAFETY. PLANNING AND RESEARCH SECTION See TENNESSEE MOTOR VEHICLE TRAFFIC ACCIDENT FACTS **5445**

TENNESSEE. DEPT. OF TRANSPORTATION See ANNUAL REPORT OF THE COMMISSIONER OF TRANSPORTATION TO THE GOVERNOR **5376**

TENNESSEE. DEPT. OF TRANSPORTATION. BUREAU OF PLANNING AND PROGRAMMING See TRUCK WEIGHT SURVEY **5398**

TENNESSEE. DIVISION OF GEOLOGY See BULLETIN - DIVISION OF GEOLOGY **1369**

TENNESSEE. DIVISION OF GEOLOGY See INFORMATION CIRCULAR - STATE OF TENNESSEE, DEPARTMENT OF CONSERVATION, DIVISION OF GEOLOGY **1383**

TENNESSEE. DIVISION OF GEOLOGY See LIST OF PUBLICATIONS / TENNESSEE DIVISION OF GEOLOGY **1386**

TENNESSEE. DIVISION OF PROPERTY ASSESSMENT See REPORT TO THE STATE BOARD OF EQUALIZATION **4746**

TENNESSEE. DIVISION OF STATE AUDIT See AUDIT REPORT, DEPARTMENT OF GENERAL SERVICES, MOTOR VEHICLE MANAGEMENT DIVISION **4631**

TENNESSEE. DIVISION OF STATE AUDIT See AUDIT REPORT. BOARD OF PSYCHOLOGY **4575**

TENNESSEE. DIVISION OF STATE AUDIT See AUDIT REPORT, DEPARTMENT OF EDUCATION, TENNESSEE SCHOOL FOR THE DEAF **1726**

TENNESSEE. DIVISION OF STATE AUDIT See AUDIT REPORT, COMMISSION TO CONTROL THE SUPREME COURT BUILDING AT NASHVILLE **4631**

TENNESSEE. DIVISION OF STATE AUDIT See AUDIT REPORT, COMMISSION ON AGING **5178**

TENNESSEE. DIVISION OF STATE AUDIT See AUDIT REPORT, DEPARTMENT OF EDUCATION, TENNESSEE ASSOCIATION OF THE FUTURE FARMERS OF AMERICA **63**

TENNESSEE. DIVISION OF STATE AUDIT See AUDIT REPORT, DEPARTMENT OF JUDICIAL, STATE PROSECUTIONS **3158**

TENNESSEE. DIVISION OF STATE AUDIT See AUDIT REPORT, DEPARTMENT OF INSURANCE, TENNESSEE BOARD OF BARBER EXAMINERS **4712**

TENNESSEE. DIVISION OF STATE AUDIT See AUDIT REPORT, DEPARTMENT OF INSURANCE, TENNESSEE REAL ESTATE COMMISSION **4834**

TENNESSEE. DIVISION OF STATE AUDIT See AUDIT REPORT, DEPARTMENT OF MILITARY - TENNESSEE DIVISION OF STATE AUDIT **4037**

TENNESSEE. DIVISION OF STATE AUDIT See AUDIT REPORT, BOARD OF PODIATRY **3554**

TENNESSEE. DIVISION OF STATE AUDIT See AUDIT REPORT, DEPARTMENT OF INSURANCE, STATE BOARD OF ACCOUNTANCY **739**

TENNESSEE. DIVISION OF STATE AUDIT See AUDIT REPORT, DEPARTMENT OF EDUCATION, ALVIN C. YORK AGRICULTURAL INSTITUTE **63**

TENNESSEE. DIVISION OF STATE AUDIT See AUDIT REPORT, DIVISION OF PRINTING **4631**

TENNESSEE. DIVISION OF STATE AUDIT See AUDIT REPORT, DEPARTMENT OF EDUCATION CENTRAL OFFICE **1726**

TENNESSEE. DIVISION OF STATE AUDIT See AUDIT REPORT. BOARD OF MEDICAL EXAMINERS **3554**

TENNESSEE. DIVISION OF THE STATE AUDIT See AUDIT REPORT, CLEVELAND STATE COMMUNITY COLLEGE (TENNESSEE) **1810**

TENNESSEE. DIVISION OF THE STATE AUDIT See AUDIT REPORT, DEPARTMENT OF EDUCATION, TENNESSEE SCHOOL FOR THE BLIND **1726**

TENNESSEE. DIVISION OF THE STATE AUDIT See AUDIT REPORT, DEPARTMENT OF EDUCATION, DIVISION OF VOCATIONAL TECHNICAL EDUCATION **1910**

TENNESSEE. DIVISION OF WATER RESOURCES See SUMMARY OF GROUND WATER DATA FOR TENNESSEE **5540**

TENNESSEE EDUCATION (US/0739-0408) [04266041] **1787**

TENNESSEE EMPLOYMENT LAW UPDATE, THE (US/0886-8557) [13017362] **3154**

TENNESSEE ENVIRONMENTAL LAW LETTER (US/1042-3168) [19008852] 2182, **3063**

TENNESSEE ENVIRONMENTAL REPORT (US/0892-5925) [15220427] **2182**

TENNESSEE ENVIRONMENTAL REPORT See PROTECT **2180**

TENNESSEE EXPORT / IMPORT TRADE DIRECTORY / EXPORT TRADE PROMOTION OFFICE, DEPARTMENT OF ECONOMIC AND COMMUNITY DEVELOPMENT, STATE OF TENNESSEE (US) [07594654] **853**

TENNESSEE FAMILY LAW LETTER (US/0890-5355) [14263990] **3122**

TENNESSEE FARM AND HOME SCIENCE (US/0040-3229) [01767279] **140**

TENNESSEE FARM FACTS (US/0744-7388) [08523195] **140**

TENNESSEE FARMER (NASHVILLE, TENN.) (US/0040-3245) [03940333] **140**

TENNESSEE. FILM, TAPE, AND MUSIC COMMISSION See ANNUAL REPORT / TENNESSEE FILM, TAPE, AND MUSIC COMMISSION **4063**

TENNESSEE FOLKLORE SOCIETY BULLETIN (US/0040-3253) [08948316] **2324**

TENNESSEE GOVERNMENT OFFICIALS DIRECOTRY UPDATE SERVICE (US) **4690**

TENNESSEE GROWER **SUSPENDED.** (US/0893-2891) [15496010] **189**

● TENNESSEE HEALTH CARE IN PERSPECTIVE (US/1065-4437) [26606752] **4804**

TENNESSEE. HIGHER EDUCATION COMMISSION See SUMMARY OF INSTITUTIONAL REQUESTS FOR OPERATING FUNDS **1849**

TENNESSEE HISTORICAL QUARTERLY (US/0040-3261) [01534246] **2762**

TENNESSEE ILLUSTRATED **CEASED.** (US/1047-2843) [18403433] **2493**

TENNESSEE IN PERSPECTIVE (US/1065-5700) [26662853] **5345**

TENNESSEE INDUSTRIES GUIDE, THE (US/0146-5325) [02970415] **1629**

TENNESSEE JOURNAL OF HEALTH, PHYSICAL EDUCATION, RECREATION, AND DANCE / TENNESSEE ASSOCIATION OF HEALTH, PHYSICAL EDUCATION, RECREATION, AND DANCE (US/0890-1597) [09867321] 1314, **1859**

TENNESSEE JOURNAL, THE (US/0194-1240) [05320141] 715, **4498**

TENNESSEE JUDICIAL NEWSLETTER (US) [11224974] **3063**

TENNESSEE LABOR MARKET INFORMATION DIRECTORY (US/0749-9930) [03804095] **1714**

TENNESSEE LAW ENFORCEMENT BULLETIN (US/1059-5082) [24613496] 3063, **3177**

TENNESSEE LAW ENFORCEMENT JOURNAL (US/0040-327X) [03940348] **3177**

TENNESSEE LAW REVIEW (US/0040-3288) [01606020] **3063**

TENNESSEE LEGISLATIVE RECORD (US) [04810467] **3063**

TENNESSEE LEGISLATIVE RESEARCHER (US/0164-4130) [04716772] **3063**

TENNESSEE LIBRARIAN (US/0162-1564) [01642282] **3252**

TENNESSEE LINGUISTICS (US/0740-8021) [09889973] **3328**

TENNESSEE MAGAZINE (US/0492-746X) [03940443] **2547**

TENNESSEE MANAGED CARE (US/1048-3926) [20939694] **3645**

TENNESSEE. MILITARY DEPT See AUDIT REPORT MILITARY DEPARTMENT OF TENNESSEE NASHVILLE TENNESSEE FOR THE YEAR ENDED JUNE 30 **4037**

TENNESSEE MOTOR VEHICLE TRAFFIC ACCIDENT FACTS (US/0360-5396) [02244575] **5445**

TENNESSEE MUSICIAN (US/0040-3334) [06811602] **4156**

TENNESSEE NEWS MEDIA DIRECTORY (US) **1123**

TENNESSEE NURSE (US/1055-3134) [23076168] **3870**

TENNESSEE NURSERY DIGEST (US/0731-6240) [07297992] **140**

TENNESSEE OUT OF DOORS (US/0190-2377) [04676211] **2207**

TENNESSEE PHARMACIST (US/1047-0166) [04124124] **4330**

TENNESSEE PHILOLOGICAL BULLETIN (US/0735-0783) [04110771] **3328**

TENNESSEE PROFESSIONAL ENGINEER, THE (US/0744-4044) [08247181] **1998**

● TENNESSEE PUBLIC ACTS : SUMMARIES OF INTEREST TO MUNICIPAL OFFICIALS (US) [27209701] **3063**

TENNESSEE PUBLIC WORKS (US/0892-5380) [14926397] **4690**

TENNESSEE QUERIES (US/0898-5472) [17846420] **2474**

TENNESSEE REAL ESTATE LAW LETTER (US/1059-5090) [10106075] 4848, **3063**

TENNESSEE REGISTER, THE (US/1041-1569) [18327378] 5037, **5746**

TENNESSEE REPUBLICAN (US) [11961057] **5746**

TENNESSEE RESEARCH COORDINATING UNIT FOR VOCATIONAL EDUCATION See RESEARCH SERIES - TENNESSEE RESEARCH COORDINATING UNIT FOR VOCATIONAL EDUCATION **1915**

TENNESSEE RESEARCHER (CHARLOTTESVILLE), THE (US/0163-2604) [04330283] **3063**

TENNESSEE RESTAURANTEUR (US) **5073**

TENNESSEE. SALES AND USE TAX DIVISION See RETAILING IN TENNESSEE **957**

TENNESSEE SCHOOL BOARDS JOURNAL (US/0747-6159) [10309006] **1873**

TENNESSEE SPORTSMAN (US/0161-3871) [06826439] **4879**

TENNESSEE. STATE BOARD FOR VOCATIONAL EDUCATION See INFORMATION SERIES - TENNESSEE STATE BOARD OF VOCATIONAL EDUCATION **1913**

TENNESSEE. STATE BOARD FOR VOCATIONAL EDUCATION See TENNESSEE STATE PLAN FOR THE ADMINISTRATION OF VOCATIONAL EDUCATION **1916**

TENNESSEE STATE BOARD OF ARCHITECTURAL AND ENGINEERING EXAMINERS See ROSTER - TENNESSEE STATE BOARD OF ARCHITECTURAL AND ENGINEERING EXAMINERS **308**

TENNESSEE. STATE DEPARTMENT See OFFICIAL COMPILATION RULES AND REGULATIONS OF THE STATE OF TENNESSEE; CONTAINING ALL OF THE RULES APPROVED FOR PRINTING BY THE SECRETARY OF STATE, DULY COMPILED, ARRANGED AND NUMBERED AS REQUIRED BY LAW **4670**

TENNESSEE. STATE DEPT. ADMINISTRATIVE PROCEDURE DIVISION See TAR, TENNESSEE ADMINISTRATIVE REGISTER. NOTICE SECTION **3062**

TENNESSEE. STATE HISTORICAL COMMISSION See REPORT - TENNESSEE HISTORICAL COMMISSION **2757**

TENNESSEE STATE PLAN FOR THE ADMINISTRATION OF VOCATIONAL EDUCATION (US) [01789850] **1916**

TENNESSEE STATE PLANNING OFFICE See ACTIVITIES - THE TENNESSEE STATE PLANNING OFFICE **2813**

TENNESSEE. STATE PLANNING OFFICE. MIDDLE TENNESSEE SECTION See PUBLICATION - MIDDLE TENNESSEE SECTION, TENNESSEE STATE PLANNING OFFICE **2832**

TENNESSEE STATISTICAL ABSTRACT (US/0082-2760) [02144377] **5345**

TENNESSEE STUDIES IN LITERATURE (US/0497-2384) [01605314] **3445**

TENNESSEE TAX GUIDE (US/0742-0757) [10131664] **4756**

TENNESSEE TEACHER (US/0040-3407) [02451055] **1907**

TENNESSEE TOWN & CITY (US/0040-3415) [01767285] **4690**

TENNESSEE TRUCKER, THE (US/0887-3526) [13228235] **5394**

TENNESSEE. UNIVERSITY. LIBRARIES See OCCASIONAL PUBLICATION **3238**

TENNESSEE VALLEY AUTHORITY See FACTS ABOUT TVA OPERATIONS **5245**

TENNESSEE VALLEY AUTHORITY See PRESS HANDBOOK **121**

TENNESSEE VALLEY AUTHORITY. DIVISION OF FORESTRY DEVELOPMENT. ANNUAL REPORT See ANNUAL REPORT - DIVISION OF FORESTRY, FISHERIES, AND WILDLIFE DEVELOPMENT, TENNESSEE VALLEY AUTHORITY **2374**

TENNESSEE VALLEY AUTHORITY. DIVISION OF FORESTRY, FISHERIES, AND WILDLIFE DEVELOPMENT See ANNUAL REPORT - DIVISION OF FORESTRY, FISHERIES, AND WILDLIFE DEVELOPMENT, TENNESSEE VALLEY AUTHORITY **2374**

TENNESSEE VALLEY AUTHORITY PRESS HANDBOOK See PRESS HANDBOOK **121**

TENNESSEE VALLEY ENGINEER (US) [06560505] **2032**

TENNESSEE VALLEY HISTORICAL REVIEW (US/0097-9708) [01799019] **2762**

TENNESSEE VOLUNTEERS MAGAZINE (US) **1095**

TENNESSEE WARBLER : NEWSLETTER OF THE TENNESSEE ORNITHOLOGICAL SOCIETY, THE (US) [09321423] **5620**

TENNESSEE WILDLIFE (NASHVILLE, TENN. 1977) (US/0886-1269) [04245320] **2207**

TENNESSEE'S BUSINESS (MURFREESBORO, TENN.) (US/0735-1135) [08851106] **715**

TENNIS (AT) **4925**

TENNIS BUYER'S GUIDE (NORWALK, CONN.) (US/0749-6478) [11152964] **4925**

TENNIS DE FRANCE (FR) **4925**

TENNIS ILLUSTRATED SUSPENDED. (US/1057-6851) [24096217] **4925**

TENNIS INDUSTRY (US/0191-5851) [05010582] **4925**

TENNIS ITALIANO, IL (IT/0393-0890) [03930890] **4925**

TENNIS LIFE (US/0279-9979) [07419978] **4925**

TENNIS LONDON. 1981 CEASED. (UK/0262-9224) [02629224] **4925**

TENNIS MAGAZINE (FR) **4926**

TENNIS MAGAZINE. AUSTRALIA (AT) **4926**

TENNIS (NORWALK, CONN.) (US/0040-3423) [03830751] **4926**

TENNIS TALK & SPORTS REVIEW (US/0745-1547) [08868624] **4926**

TENNIS WEEK (US/0194-9098) [05103788] **4926**

TENNIS WORLD (UK/0040-3474) [01607613] **4926**

TENNISPRO (US) **4926**

TENNOSEI KENKYU (JA) [06930987] **4690**

TENNYSON RESEARCH BULLETIN (UK/0082-2841) [02050498] **1850**

TENNYSON SOCIETY MONOGRAPHS (UK) [02050629] 3472, **3445**

TENOLAI (II) [03452475] **5176**

TENOR (II) [05997541] **3445**

TENRI JOURNAL OF RELIGION (JA/0495-1492) [02233361] **5002**

TENRIKYO (JA/0040-3482) [03295016] **5002**

TENRIKYO TOKEI NENKAN (JA) [01796920] **5002**

TENSIDE, SURFACTANTS, DETERGENTS (GW) [14231621] **1058**

TENSIOLOGIE SUSPENDED. (FR/0989-2672) [20856435] **3710**

TENSION ARTERIELLE QUEBEC See MULTI-FACT **3708**

TENSION CONTROL (US/0272-5398) [06839781] **4620**

TENSO (US/0890-3352) [14229620] **3445**

TENSOR (JA/0040-3504) [01767294] **3538**

TENTATIVE ... OIL AND GAS UNIT OF PRODUCTION VALUES (US/0883-7449) [12175435] **4280**

TENTATIVE RECOMMENDED PRACTICE (INSTRUMENT SOCIETY OF AMERICA) (US/0443-5443) [06694172] **3488**

TENTH DECADE (UK) [22613682] **3472**

TENTH MUSE, THE (US/0094-162X) [01793988] **3472**

TEOCOMUNICACAO (BL) [05774753] **5037**

TEOLLISUUSSANOMAT (FI/0300-3124) [01422910] **3488**

TEOLLISUUSYRITYSTEN TILINPAEAETOESTILASTO / BOKSLUTSSTATISTIK OEVER INDUSTRIFOERETAG / FINANCIAL STATEMENTS STATISTICS OF INDUSTRIAL ENTERPRISES (FI/0784-9079) [19819647] 1629, **1540**

TEOLOGIA (BRESCIA, ITALY) (IT) [05764468] **5037**

TEOLOGIA ESPIRITUAL (SP/0495-1549) [06129958] **5002**

TEOLOGIA Y VIDA (CL/0049-3449) [01715270] **5002**

TEOLOGINEN AIKAKAUSKIRJA. TEOLOGISK TIDSKRIFT (FI/0040-3555) [01713503] **5002**

TEOLOGISK FORUM (NO) [I08021457] **5002**

TEOREMA SUSPENDED. (SP/0210-1602) [01686288] **4363**

TEORETICESKAJA I EKSPERIMENTALNAJA HIMIJA (UN/0497-2627) [02128456] **994**

TEORETICESKAJA I MATEMATICESKAJA FIZIKA (RU/0564-6162) [02113576] **4423**

TEORETICESKAJA I PRIKLADNAJA MEHANIKA (MINSK) (BW/0137-0235) [06928243] **2130**

TEORETICESKIE OSNOVY HIMICESKOJ TEHNOLOGII (RU/0040-3571) [02113540] **994**

TEORETICHESKIE VOPROSY AVTOMATIZIROVANNYKH SISTEM UPRAVLENIIA (LV) [05738341] **1205**

TEORETICHNA I PRILOZHNA MEKHANIKA / BULGARSKA AKADEMIIA NA NAUKITE, NATSIONALEN KOMITET PO TEORETICHNA I PRILOZHNA MEKHANIKA (BU) [19704794] **4429**

TEORIA (IT) [27394590] **4363**

TEORIA E PRATICA DEGLI SCAMBI INTERNAZIONALI (IT) **853**

TEORIA E PRATICA DEGLI SCAMBI INTERNAZIONALI (IT) **1640**

TEORIA LITERARIA, TEXTO Y TEORIA (NE/0921-2523) [20311655] **3445**

TEORIA POLITICA (IT/0394-1248) [15188154] **4498**

TEORIA SOCIOLOGICA (IT) [29527861] **5264**

TEORIA Y PRACTICA (SP) [03624840] **5312**

TEORIE A PRAXE TELESNE VYCHOVY CEASED. (CS/0040-358X) [I0040358X] **2601**

TEORIE SOCIALISMU / USTAV MARKXISMU-LENINISMU UV KSC A USTAV MARXIZMU-LENINIZMU UV KSS (XR) [17701681] **4548**

TEORIE VEDY (XR) [24043093] **5165**

TEORIIA FUNKTSII KOMPLEKSNOGO PEREMENNOGO I KRAEVYE ZADACHI (RU) [01799387] **3538**

TEORIIA I PRAKTIKA NA PROPAGANDATA I AGITASIIA (BU) [02972944] **4548**

TEORIIA MASHIN METALLURGICHESKOGO I GORNOGO OBORUDOVANIIA (RU) [06401925] **2130**

TEORIIA OPERATOROV I TEORIIA FUNKTSII (RU/0207-9941) [10803401] **3538**

TEORIIA VEROIATNOSTEI I EE PRIMENENIIA (RU/0040-361X) [01589738] **3538**

TEORIJA FUNKCIJ, FUNKCIONALNYJ ANALIZ I IH PRILOZENIJA (HARKOV) (UN/0321-4427) [09205924] **3538**

TEORIJA I PRAKTIKA FIZICESKOJ KULTURY (RU/0040-3601) [06463422] **1859**

TEORIJA SLUCAINYH PROCESSOV (UN/0321-3900) [01788503] **3538**

TEORIJSKA I PRIMENJENA MEHANIKA (YU/0353-8249) [103538249] **4429**

TEOROS (CN/0712-8657) [08902999] **5492**

TEPLOENERGETIKA (MOSKVA, 1954) (RU/0040-3636) [01767295] **2130**

TEPLOFIZIKA VYSOKIKH TEMPERATUR (RU/0040-3644) [02113568] **4423**

TEPLOPROVODNOST' I DIFFUZIIA (LV) [05439185] **4432**

TEPSA JOURNAL (US/0300-6433) [01425325] **1873**

TEQUESTA (US/0363-3705) [02096319] **2762**

TER HERKENNING (NE) [04048024] **5002**

TERA ANALYSIS (US/0884-1780) [08180581] **1959**

TERAPEVTICESKIJ ARHIV (RU/0040-3660) [01586644] 4330, **3645**

TERAPEVTICHESKAIA STOMATOLOGIIA (UN/0303-8866) [01003212] **1336**

TERAPIA FAMILIARE : RIVISTA INTERDISCIPLINARE DI RICERCA ED INTERVENTO RELAZIONALES (IT/0391-2868) [27868483] **4620**

TERAPIA MODERNA (IT) [02831519] **3645**

TERATOGENESIS, CARCINOGENESIS, AND MUTAGENESIS (US/0270-3211) [06389392] **3824**

TERATOLOGY (PHILADELPHIA) (US/0040-3709) [01767298] **474**

TEREBIJON GAKKAISHI (JA/0386-6831) [16783909] 1141, **1998**

TERESIANUM (IT) [09564678] **5003**

TERM FREQUENCY LIST (US/1060-5304) [25036151] **4280**

TERMESZET VILAGA (HU/0040-3717) [04940595] **5165**

TERMINAL / INFORMATIQUE CULTURE SOCIETE (FR) **1205**

TERMINALS MAGAZINE (US) **4280**

TERMINATION OF EMPLOYMENT (US/0749-8233) [11194117] **3154**

TERMINOGRAMME (CN/0225-3194) [08079180] **3328**

TERMINOLOGIE (CN/0225-1981) [06141377] **3328**

TERMINOLOGIE COMPTABLE (CN/0705-3673) [03963616] **752**

TERMINOLOGIE ET TRADUCTION / COMMISSION DES COMMUNAUTES EUROPEENES, DIRECTION TRADUCTION, SERVICE TERMINOLOGIE ET APPLICATIONS INFORMATIQUES (LU/0256-7873) [12351895] **3328**

TERMINOLOGY (NE/0929-9971) **1123**

TERMINOLOGY BULLETIN (FOOD AND AGRICULTURE ORGANIZATION OF THE UNITED NATIONS. TERMINOLOGY AND REFERENCE SECTION) (IT) [03874245] **141**

TERMINUS BUSINESS DIRECTORY (US/0362-1995) [02304438] **715**

TERMINUS (MONTREAL) (CN/0822-3394) [11559795] **3445**

TERMNET NEWS : JOURNAL OF THE INTERNATIONAL NETWORK FOR TERMINOLOGY (TERMNET) (AU/0251-5253) [08690295] 3252, **3328**

TERMODINAMIKA ORGANICHESKIKH SOEDINENII (RU) [04283430] **1058**

TERMOTECNICA (IT/0040-3725) [07380467] **1998**

TERRA (FI/0040-3741) [08118795] **2577**

TERRA (IT) **2221**

TERRA AMERIGA SUSPENDED. (IT/0040-375X) [02068629] **2763**

TERRA E SOLE (IT/0040-3768) [I00403768] **161**

TERRA E VITA (IT/0040-3776) [13529439] **141**

TERRA ET AQUA (NE/0376-6411) [05389337] 2032, **2096**

TERRA GRISCHUNA (SZ) [10616389] **2712**

TERRA INDIGENA : BOLETIM MENSAL DO G.E.I. KURUMIM (BL) [13042040] **2274**

TERRA (LOS ANGELES, CALIF.) CEASED. (US/0040-3733) [05658917] **4173**

TERRA NOVA (UK/0954-4879) [19834283] **1411**

TERRA NOVA (WASHINGTON, D.C.) CEASED. (US/1056-8018) [23858374] **4536**

TERRAE INCOGNITAE (US/0082-2884) [00968369] 2763, **2577**

TERRAIN (PARIS, 1983) (FR/0760-5668) [10204938] **246**

TERRAVUE (CN/0714-4091) [10061800] **2032**

TERRAZZO (IT) [18850333] **309**

TERRE DE CHEZ NOUS. DOSSIER D'INFORMATION TECHNIQUE ET PROFESSIONNELLE, LA (CN/0823-2784) [10032138] 2396, **141**

TERRE DE CHEZ NOUS (MONTREAL) (CN/0040-3830) [02183774] **141**

TERRE D'IMAGES See ARTS ET TECHNIQUES GRAPHIQUES **376**

TERRE ET LA VIE, LA (FR/0040-3865) [01767300] **2221**

TERRE HAUTE GAZETTE (TERRE HAUTE, IND. : WEEKLY) (US/8755-934X) [11450258] **5667**

TERRE INFORMATION (FR/0758-4083) [I07584083] **2577**

TERRE SAUVAGE (FR) [06302298] **4173**

TERREBONNE LIFE LINES (US/0735-2794) [08882560] **2474**

TERRELL DAILY TRIBUNE See TERRELL TRIBUNE, THE **5755**

TERRELL STATE HOSPITAL See ANNUAL REPORT / TERRELL STATE HOSPITAL **3776**

TERRELL TRAILS (US/0884-2108) [12319125] **2474**

TERRELL Alphabetical Title Index

TERRELL TRIBUNE, THE (US) [14874943] **5755**

TERRESTRIAL ECOSYSTEMS NEWSLETTERS (SA/0250-0787) [18457885] **474**

TERRITOIRES (FR) **4498**

TERRITOIRES PARIS. 1988 (FR/0991-2428) [I09912428] **4690**

TERRITORIAL SEA JOUNRAL See OCEAN AND COASTAL LAW JOURNAL **3182**

TERRITORIAL SEA JOURNAL (US/1046-9680) [20576435] **3182**

TERRITORIAL, THE (US/0890-4235) [14231862] **2547**

TERRITORIO E AMBIENTE (IT) **2221**

TERRITORIO PARA LA PRODUCCION Y CRITICA EN GEOGRAFIA Y CIENCIAS SOCIALES (AG/0327-3210) [I03273210] 5224, **2577**

TERRITORY DIGEST CEASED. (AT) [07763089] **2671**

TERRITORY OF NORFOLK ISLAND; REPORT (AT) [01788594] **4690**

TERRITORY OF PAPUA GOVERNMENT GAZETTE See GOVERNMENT GAZETTE **4475**

TERROR AUSTRALIS: THE AUSTRALIAN HORROR & FANTASY MAGAZINE (AT/1031-3001) [I10313001] **3445**

TERROR FANTASTIC (SP) [01792186] **4078**

●TERROR, INC (US/1065-1764) [26519887] **4866**

TERRORICIEL (FR) **2523**

TERRORISM, AN INTERNATIONAL RESOURCE FILE. INDEX (US/1048-3276) [18281199] 4498, **4536**

TERRORISM AND POLITICAL VIOLENCE (UK/0954-6553) [20185510] **4536**

TERRORISM (MINNEAPOLIS, MINN.) (US/0278-663X) [13740413] **3177**

●TERRORISM, SECOND SERIES (US/1064-9352) [26464454] **4059**

TERRORIST GROUP PROFILES (US) **4536**

TERRRE, LA (FR) [03997491] **1361**

TERRY HEADLIGHT, THE (US) [16396120] **5702**

●TERRY SHANNON ON DEC (US/1068-8412) [26835474] **1205**

TERSKEL / MUSEET FOR SAMTIDSKUNST (NO/0802-7323) [22337351] **366**

TERTIARY AND RESIDENTIAL COLLEGE FEES CEASED. (AT) [02246857] **1850**

TERTIARY EDUCATION, TASMANIA / AUSTRALIAN BUREAU OF STATISTICS (AT/0705-5765) [07982228] **1850**

TERTIARY RESEARCH (NE/0308-9649) [03235641] **1399**

TERTIARY RESEARCH SPECIAL PAPER SUSPENDED. (UK/0308-7506) [03337732] **1399**

TERUEL (SP/0210-3524) [06546293] **2712**

TERVEYDENHUOLLON LAITOKSET JA VIRANOMAISET (FI) [09849748] **4804**

TERVEYDENHUOLLON ORGANISAATIO See TERVEYDENHUOLLON LAITOKSET JA VIRANOMAISET **4804**

TERVEYDENHUOLTO (FI/0303-2442) [05141026] **4804**

TERVUREN, BELGIUM. MUSEE ROYAL DE L'AFRIQUE CENTRALE. DEPARTEMENT DE GEOLOGIE ET DE MINERALOGIE See RAPPORT ANNUEL DU DEPARTEMENT DE GEOLOGIE ET DE MINERALOGIE DU MUSEE ROYAL DE L'AFRIQUE CENTRALE **1393**

TERZAFASE CEASED. (IT) **4498**

TERZAKE (NE) **752**

TERZIARIA (IT) **1524**

TERZO MONDO (IT/0040-392X) [02070059] 246, 4498, **5264**

TERZO MONDO INFORMAZIONI SUSPENDED. (IT) **2493**

TERZOOCCHIO (IT) [02243022] **366**

TESIS DOCTORALES (SP) [02243327] **1798**

TESL CANADA JOURNAL (CN/0826-435X) [11108232] **3328**

TESL MANITOBA (CN/1187-497X) [25652329] **1907**

TESL REPORTER (US/0886-0661) [05909606] **1787**

TESOL JOURNAL (US/1056-7941) [23853840] **1907**

TESOL MATTERS (US/1051-8886) [22143872] 3328, **1907**

TESOL MEMBERSHIP DIRECTORY (US/0730-9325) [03547819] **3328**

TESOL NEWS (AT/0810-6649) [I08106649] 3328, **1907**

TESOL QUARTERLY (US/0039-8322) [01767202] **3328**

TESSERA (BURNABY) (CN/0840-4631) [20493998] **3445**

TESSERACT. EARLY SCIENTIFIC INSTRUMENTS (US) **5165**

TEST (SZ) **1300**

TEST ACHATS MAGAZINE (BE/0772-9405) [I07729405] **1300**

TEST & MEASUREMENT WORLD (US/0744-1657) [08077236] **2084**

TEST : AUTONOMIE (IT) **4690**

TEST BERLIN, WEST. ZEITSCHRIFT (GW/0040-3946) [I00403946] **1300**

TEST CADMAT : INTERFACING DESIGN AND TEST (UK) **1205**

TEST CRITIQUES (US) [11945540] **4620**

TEST INDUSTRY REPORTER, THE (US/1053-9328) [22694647] **2130**

●TEST (MADRID) (SP/1133-0686) [I11330686] **5345**

TEST (OAKHURST, N.J.) (US/0193-4120) [05205505] **2130**

TEST SERVICES FOR SCHOOLS OF NURSING (US) [07288129] 1850, **3870**

TEST : TERZIARIO SERVIZI E TURISMO CEASED. (IT) **5492**

TESTAMENT (US/0743-572X) [10640274] **5003**

TESTI E COMMENTI (IT) [06767876] **3445**

TESTI E DOCUMENTI DE LETTERATURA E DI LINGUA (IT) [17827929] 3328, **3445**

TESTI E STUDI UMANISTICI (IT) [19965993] **3445**

TESTIMONIANZE (IT/0040-3989) [09004774] **5003**

TESTIMONIANZE SULL'EBRAISMO (IT) [19965933] **5053**

TESTIMONIO / COMISION POR LA DEFENSA DE LOS DERECHOS HUMANOS (EC) [19683801] **4513**

TESTIMONIO LATINOAMERICANO (SP) [08335872] **2763**

TESTIMONY OF TRUTH, THE (US/1045-3989) [18785663] **5003**

TESTMEVELES- ES SPORTEGESZSEGUGYI SZMELE (HU/0563-2013) [01345632] **3956**

TESTO A FRONTE : RIVISTA SEMESTRALE DI TEORIA E PRATICA DELLA TRADUZIONE LETTERARIA (IT) [21960016] **3445**

TESTO UNICO CODICE PENALE DELL IMPRESA (IT) **3063**

TESTO UNICO IMPOSTE DIRETTE (IT) 4756, **3063**

TESTO UNICO IVA (IT) **1524**

TESTO UNICO LEGISLAZIONE PENALE TRIBUTARIA (IT) **3063**

TESTS IN MICROFICHE (US/01612573) [04344835] 4620, **1886**

TESTS IN MICROFICHE : ANNOTATED INDEX (US/0161-2573) [02694430] **1873**

TESTS OF AGROCHEMICALS AND CULTIVARS (UK/0951-4309) [06457607] **4248**

TET : THE EAST TRADE (SP) 5357, **2903**

TETE-A-TETE (OTTAWA. 1991) (CN/1187-4848) [25314277] 1168, **1141**

TETE-A-TETE (OTTAWA. 1991) (CN/1187-4848) [25314280] **1141**

TETE, EN (CN/0822-8531) [10935324] **1850**

TETON SUSPENDED. (US/0049-3481) [02945901] **4879**

TETON VALLEY NEWS (US/0889-9851) [13107316] **5657**

TETRAHEDRON (UK/0040-4020) [01606999] **1048**

TETRAHEDRON, ASYMMETRY (UK/0957-4166) [20943807] **994**

TETRAHEDRON LETTERS (UK/0040-4039) [01714161] **1048**

TETRAHEDRON LETTERS (UK/0040-4039) [07522874] 493, **1048**

TETRAHEDRON. SUPPLEMENT (UK/0563-2072) [02134227] **994**

TETSU TO HAGANE (JA/0021-1575) [09698705] **4021**

TETSUDO GIJUTSU KENKYUJO, TOKYO See QUARTERLY REPORTS - RAILWAY TECHNICAL RESEARCH INSTITUTE **5434**

TETSUGAKU RONSO (JA) [05952233] **4363**

TETSUGAKU SHISO RONSHU (JA) [09890138] **4363**

TETTO, IL (IT) [07448992] **5037**

TEUBNER-TEXTE ZUR MATHEMATIK (GW) [09396097] **3538**

TEUTONIC UNITY (GW) [14064803] **4548**

TEVYNE (US/0040-4071) [03941231] **2274**

●TEX AND TUG NEWS (US/1065-240X) [26535895] **1205**

TEX HOME (IT) **5357**

TEX-RAYS : OFFICIAL JOURNAL TEXAS SOCIETY OF RADIOLOGIC TECHNOLOGISTS, INC (US) [07970878] **3947**

TEX TEXTILIS See CON TEXT MAGAZINE **1083**

TEX - TEXTILIS, DE (BE) [01112062] **5357**

TEXANA (US/0040-411X) [02058940] **2763**

TEXARKANA GAZETTE (US) [14908961] **5632**

TEXARKANA USA GENEALOGIST'S QUARTERLY, THE (US/0741-6105) [10135813] **2474**

TEXARKANA USA QUARTERLY (1987) (US/1067-1412) [24244500] **2474**

TEXAS See TEXAS SCHOOL LAW BULLETIN **3064**

TEXAS See TEXAS ELECTION LAW, INCLUDING POLITICAL CALENDER, CONSTITUTIONAL PROVISIONS, ELECTION CODE, AND STATUTES **3094**

TEXAS See TEXAS BUSINESS STATUTES AND SECURITIES RULES **3104**

TEXAS See PARKER'S BUSINESS STATUTES AND SECURITIES RULES OF TEXAS **3102**

TEXAS See GENERAL AND SPECIAL LAWS OF THE STATE OF TEXAS **2973**

TEXAS A & I UNIVERSITY See ALUMNI DIRECTORY / TEXAS A & I UNIVERSITY **1099**

TEXAS A & M BUSINESS FORUM CEASED. (US/0882-8849) [11982445] **715**

TEXAS. ADJUTANT-GENERAL'S DEPT See FINANCIAL REPORT / ADJUTANT-GENERAL'S DEPARTMENT (TEXAS) **4044**

TEXAS AGRICULTURAL AND MECHANICAL UNIVERSITY. MARINE LABORATORY See SPECIAL REPORT - MARINE LABORATORY (GALVESTON) **1457**

TEXAS AGRICULTURAL EXPERIMENT STATION See MISCELLANEOUS PUBLICATION - TEXAS AGRICULTURAL EXPERIMENT STATION **109**

TEXAS. AGRICULTURAL EXPERIMENT STATION See BEEF CATTLE RESEARCH IN TEXAS **207**

TEXAS. AGRICULTURAL EXPERIMENT STATION, COLLEGE STATION See BULLETIN - TEXAS AGRICULTURAL EXPERIMENT STATION **70**

TEXAS AGRICULTURAL EXPERIMENT STATION LEAFLET (US/0099-7730) [I00997730] **141**

TEXAS AGRICULTURAL EXPORT DIRECTORY (US/0735-1542) [07047007] 853, **141**

TEXAS AGRICULTURAL FACTS (US) [05131687] 141, **157**

TEXAS AGRICULTURE (NORTH TEXAS EDITION : 1987) (US) [15627146] **141**

TEXAS. AIR CONTROL BOARD See CONNIE DATA SUMMARIES **2226**

TEXAS AIRPORT DIRECTORY (US) [04085107] **37**

●TEXAS ALCALDE (US/1061-561X) [25361657] **1103**

TEXAS ALMANAC AND STATE INDUSTRIAL GUIDE (1967) (US/0363-4248) [02418737] **2547**

TEXAS ANIMAL HEALTH COMMISSION See FOURTH QUARTER AND ANNUAL REPORT ON THE TEXAS BOVINE BRUCELLOSIS PROGRAM / TEXAS ANIMAL HEALTH COMMISSION, AUSTIN TEXAS **211**

TEXAS ANIMAL HEALTH COMMISSION See ANNUAL FINANCIAL REPORT / TEXAS ANIMAL HEALTH COMMISSION **4709**

TEXAS ANNUAL PROGRAM PLAN FOR VOCATIONAL EDUCATION (US) [04904893] **1916**

TEXAS ANTITRUST BULLETIN (US/0271-1923) [03942901] **3104**

TEXAS APARTMENT ASSOCIATION See REDBOOK / TAA, TEXAS APARTMENT ASSOCIATION **2832**

TEXAS ARCHEOLOGICAL SOCIETY See BULLETIN OF THE TEXAS ARCHEOLOGICAL SOCIETY **264**

TEXAS ARCHEOLOGY (US/0082-2949) [02947123] **284**

Alphabetical Title Index

TEXAS

TEXAS ARCHITECT (US/0040-4179) [02144339] **310**

TEXAS ASSESSMENT OF BASIC SKILLS : TABS (US) [08312041] **1787**

TEXAS. ATTORNEY-GENERAL'S OFFICE *See* ANNUAL FINANCIAL REPORT FOR YEAR ENDING AUG. 31 ... - TEXAS. ATTORNEY-GENERAL'S OFFICE **4709**

TEXAS BANKING (US/0885-6907) [12699574] **813**

TEXAS BANKING REDBOOK (US) **813**

TEXAS BANKRUPTCY COURT REPORTER, THE (US/0895-2736) [15051269] **3088**

TEXAS BAPTIST HISTORY (US/0732-4324) [08324118] **5068**

TEXAS BAR JOURNAL (US/0040-4187) [01587278] **3063**

TEXAS BASKETBALL MAGAZINE (US) 1787, **4926**

TEXAS BICYCLIST (US) **429**

TEXAS BLUE BOOK OF LIFE INSURANCE STATISTICS (1982), THE (US/0739-4691) [09739143] **2898**

TEXAS BLUEGRASS ASSOCIATION *See* NEWSLETTER **4140**

TEXAS BOARD OF CHIROPRACTIC EXAMINERS *See* AUDIT REPORT, TEXAS BOARD OF CHIROPRACTIC EXAMINERS **4379**

TEXAS BOARD OF LICENSURE FOR NURSING HOME ADMINISTRATORS *See* ANNUAL REPORT / TEXAS BOARD OF LICENSURE FOR NURSING HOME ADMINISTRATORS **3776**

TEXAS BOARD OF LICENSURE FOR NURSING HOME ADMINISTRATORS *See* AUDIT REPORT. TEXAS BOARD OF LICENSURE FOR NURSING HOME ADMINISTRATORS **3777**

TEXAS BOND REPORTER (US) [09389967] **917**

TEXAS BOOKS IN REVIEW (US/0739-3202) [03654173] **4833**

TEXAS BRIEFCASE SHEPARD'S (US/0270-529X) [05457223] **3063**

TEXAS BUILDERS AND CONTRACTORS DIRECTORY (US/0731-4035) [08120068] **630**

TEXAS. BUREAU OF STATE HEALTH PLANNING & RESOURCE DEVELOPMENT *See* TEXAS COMPENDIUM OF HEALTH RELATED DATA **4804**

●TEXAS BUSINESS DIRECTORY (US/1053-6698) [22604991] **715**

TEXAS BUSINESS EDUCATION ASSOCIATION *See* TEXAS BUSINESS EDUCATION ASSOCIATION YEARBOOK **715**

TEXAS BUSINESS EDUCATION ASSOCIATION YEARBOOK (US/0196-3198) [05781229] **715**

TEXAS BUSINESS REVIEW (US/0040-4209) [01767348] 715, **1586**

TEXAS BUSINESS STATUTES AND SECURITIES RULES (US/1069-8434) [25978805] **3104**

TEXAS CANCER MORTALITY STATISTICS / TEXAS DEPARTMENT OF HEALTH, BUREAU OF DISEASE CONTROL AND EPIDEMIOLOGY, CANCER REGISTRY DIVISION (US) [17483353] **3824**

TEXAS CAVER, THE (US/0040-4233) [08252541] **1411**

TEXAS CERTIFIED SEED DIRECTORY (US/0095-1927) [01792421] **2432**

TEXAS CHILD CARE (US/1049-9466) [17949976] **1070**

TEXAS CHRISTIAN UNIVERSITY *See* ALUMNI DIRECTORY - TEXAS CHRISTIAN UNIVERSITY, THE **1099**

TEXAS CHURCH WOMAN (US/0746-9756) [10427417] **5003**

TEXAS CITRUS TREE INVENTORY SURVEY (US/0748-7746) [03617970] **189**

TEXAS CITY SUN (US) [15613603] **5755**

TEXAS COACH (US/0040-4241) [03941338] **4926**

TEXAS COASTAL AND MARINE COUNCIL *See* ANNUAL REPORT / TEXAS COASTAL AND MARINE COUNCIL **2815**

TEXAS. COASTAL FISHERIES BRANCH *See* SHELL MANAGEMENT ANNUAL REPORT **2313**

TEXAS COLLEGE ENGLISH (US/0889-6011) [14102885] **1850**

TEXAS COLLEGIATE EDUCATION DIRECTORY (US/0145-4242) [02735454] **1850**

TEXAS COMMERCIAL HARVEST STATISTICS (US/0734-7278) [08747448] 2314, **2318**

TEXAS. COMMISSION ON ALCOHOLISM *See* TEXAS STATE PLAN FOR THE PREVENTION, TREATMENT, AND CONTROL OF ALCOHOL ABUSE AND ALCOHOLISM **1349**

TEXAS COMMISSION ON ALCOHOLISM *See* AUDIT REPORT. TEXAS COMMISSION ON ALCOHOLISM **1341**

TEXAS COMMISSION ON JAIL STANDARDS *See* ANNUAL REPORT **3157**

TEXAS COMPENDIUM OF HEALTH RELATED DATA (US) [04993285] **4804**

TEXAS COMPREHENSIVE ANNUAL FINANCIAL REPORT / COMPTROLLER OF PUBLIC ACCOUNTS (US) [23292870] **813**

TEXAS. COMPTROLLER'S OFFICE *See* ANNUAL CASH REPORT / TEXAS COMPTROLLER OF PUBLIC ACCOUNTS **4709**

TEXAS. COMPTROLLER'S OFFICE *See* AUDIT REPORT, STATE COMPTROLLER OF PUBLIC ACCOUNTS, AUSTIN, TEXAS, YEAR ENDED AUGUST 31 ... **4712**

TEXAS. COMPTROLLER'S OFFICE *See* ANALYSIS - TEXAS. COMPTROLLER'S OFFICE **4709**

TEXAS. COMPTROLLER'S OFFICE *See* TEXAS COMPREHENSIVE ANNUAL FINANCIAL REPORT / COMPTROLLER OF PUBLIC ACCOUNTS **813**

TEXAS. COMPTROLLER'S OFFICE *See* ENERGY REPORT - TEXAS. COMPTROLLER'S OFFICE **1941**

TEXAS CONNECTION (US) **4339**

TEXAS CONSUMER LAW REPORTER (US) **1300**

TEXAS CONTRACTOR (US/0192-9216) [05137928] **630**

TEXAS COSMETOLOGY COMMISSION *See* GOVERNOR'S REPORT FOR THE PERIOD ... / TEXAS COSMETOLOGY COMMISSION **404**

TEXAS COUNTRY WESTERN MAGAZINE (US) [02421135] **4156**

TEXAS CRIME POLL (US) [05163860] **3177**

TEXAS CRIMINAL LAW AND MOTOR VEHICLE HANDBOOK (US/1055-1913) [23076839] **3109**

TEXAS CROP AND LIVESTOCK REPORTING SERVICE *See* TEXAS LIVESTOCK STATISTICS **157**

TEXAS CROP AND LIVESTOCK REPORTING SERVICE *See* TEXAS AGRICULTURAL FACTS **157**

TEXAS CROP AND LIVESTOCK REPORTING SERVICE *See* TEXAS FRUIT AND PECAN STATISTICS **2362**

TEXAS CRUISING GUIDE (US/0197-4114) [06010113] **4184**

TEXAS DENTAL ASSISTANTS ASSOCIATION BULLETIN (US/0049-3503) [01438886] **1336**

TEXAS DENTAL JOURNAL (US/0040-4284) [01643893] **1336**

TEXAS. DEPARTMENT OF AGRICULTURE *See* TEXAS LIVESTOCK MARKET NEWS **222**

TEXAS. DEPT. OF AGRICULTURE *See* TEXAS FAMILY LAND HERITAGE REGISTRY **141**

TEXAS. DEPT. OF AGRICULTURE *See* ANNUAL FINANCIAL REPORT **60**

TEXAS. DEPT. OF CORRECTIONS. RESEARCH, PLANNING, AND DEVELOPMENT DIVISION *See* SPECIAL STUDY - TEXAS DEPARTMENT OF CORRECTIONS, RESEARCH, PLANNING, AND DEVELOPMENT DIVISION **3177**

TEXAS. DEPT. OF HEALTH *See* BIENNIAL REPORT - TEXAS DEPARTMENT OF HEALTH **4768**

TEXAS. DEPT. OF HEALTH *See* ANNUAL FINANCIAL REPORT / TEXAS DEPARTMENT OF HEALTH **4765**

TEXAS. DEPT. OF HEALTH. AUDIT REPORT *See* ANNUAL FINANCIAL REPORT / TEXAS DEPARTMENT OF HEALTH **4765**

TEXAS. DEPT. OF HUMAN RESOURCES *See* TITLE XX, SOCIAL SERVICES **5312**

TEXAS. DEPT. OF LABOR AND STANDARDS *See* ANNUAL REPORT OF THE TEXAS DEPARTMENT OF LABOR AND STANDARDS **1649**

TEXAS. DEPT. OF MENTAL HEALTH AND MENTAL RETARDATION *See* TEXAS STATE PLAN FOR CONSTRUCTION OF COMMUNITY MENTAL HEALTH CENTERS **4805**

TEXAS. DEPT. OF MENTAL HEALTH AND MENTAL RETARDATION. CENTRAL OFFICE *See* ANNUAL REPORT FOR THE YEAR ENDED AUGUST 31 ... / CENTRAL OFFICE **5272**

TEXAS. DEPT. OF PUBLIC SAFETY *See* CRIME IN TEXAS **3080**

TEXAS. DEPT. OF PUBLIC SAFETY *See* S-R-S; SAFETY RESPONSIBILITY SUSPENSIONS **5424**

TEXAS. DEPT. OF PUBLIC SAFETY. DIVISION OF DISASTER EMERGENCY SERVICES *See* DIGEST - TEXAS. DEPT. OF PUBLIC SAFETY. DIVISION OF DISASTER EMERGENCY SERVICES, THE **4773**

TEXAS. DEPT. OF PUBLIC SAFETY. S-R SUSPENSIONS BY COUNTY *See* S-R-S; SAFETY RESPONSIBILITY SUSPENSIONS **5424**

TEXAS. DEPT. OF WATER RESOURCES *See* STATE OF TEXAS WATER QUALITY MANAGEMENT PROGRAM **5539**

TEXAS. DEPT. OF WATER RESOURCES *See* STATE OF TEXAS WATER QUALITY MANAGEMENT, ANNUAL WORK PROGRAM, THE **5539**

TEXAS. DEPT. OF WATER RESOURCES *See* LIBRARY BULLETIN - TEXAS DEPARTMENT OF WATER RESOURCES **5536**

TEXAS DO (US/0275-1453) [06904036] **3645**

TEXAS ECONOMIC FORECAST (US/0748-0008) [10867256] **1524**

TEXAS ECONOMIC INDICATORS (AUSTIN, TEX.: 1987) *CEASED.* (US/0896-0453) [16888785] **1586**

TEXAS. ECONOMIC OPPORTUNITY DIVISION *See* TEXAS FRONT IN THE NATION'S STRUGGLE AGAINST POVERTY : ANNUAL REPORT OF THE TEXAS DEPARTMENT OF COMMUNITY AFFAIRS' ECONOMIC OPPORTUNITY DIVISION, THE **5312**

TEXAS ECONOMIC QUARTERLY / COMPTROLLER OF PUBLIC ACCOUNTS (US) [23897471] **1524**

TEXAS EDUCATION AGENCY *See* ANNUAL PROGRAM PLAN FOR VOCATIONAL EDUCATION FOR FISCAL YEAR ... AND ACCOUNTABILITY REPORT FOR FISCAL YEAR ... (TEXAS) **1910**

TEXAS. EDUCATION AGENCY *See* RECOMMENDATIONS FOR LEGISLATIVE CONSIDERATION ON PUBLIC EDUCATION IN TEXAS **3036**

TEXAS EDUCATION AGENCY *See* TEXAS ANNUAL PROGRAM PLAN FOR VOCATIONAL EDUCATION **1916**

TEXAS EDUCATION AGENCY. DIVISION OF PROGRAM EVALUATION *See* ANNUAL RPEORT OF THE TEXAS MIGRANT PROGRAM, ESEA, TITLE I **1725**

TEXAS EDUCATION NEWS (US/8755-3147) [11269643] **1787**

TEXAS ELECTION LAW, INCLUDING POLITICAL CALENDER, CONSTITUTIONAL PROVISIONS, ELECTION CODE, AND STATUTES (US) [06407067] **3094**

TEXAS. EMPLOYMENT COMMISSION *See* ANNUAL PLANNING INFORMATION REPORT : BEAUMONT-PORT ARTHUR-ORANGE SMSA **1529**

TEXAS EMPLOYMENT COMMISSION *See* ANNUAL PLANNING INFORMATION REPORT: WACO SMSA **1647**

TEXAS. EMPLOYMENT COMMISSION *See* ANNUAL PLANNING INFORMATION REPORT: DALLAS-FORT WORTH SMSA **1529**

TEXAS EMPLOYMENT COMMISSION *See* AUDIT REPORT, TEXAS EMPLOYMENT COMMISSION **1654**

TEXAS EMPLOYMENT LAW LETTER (US/1046-9214) [20584366] **3154**

●TEXAS EMS MAGAZINE (US/1063-8202) [25761679] **4805**

TEXAS EMS MESSENGER (US/1048-8235) [20751677] **4805**

TEXAS ENERGY (1989) (US/1050-7116) [21309036] **1959**

TEXAS ENERGY ISSUES (US/0273-396X) [07038894] **1959**

TEXAS ENERGY REPORTER *CEASED.* (US/0739-8050) [09806736] **1959**

TEXAS ENVIRONMENT *SUSPENDED.* (US/1050-6403) [21569195] **2182**

●TEXAS ENVIRONMENTAL COMPLIANCE UPDATE (US/1075-2595) [29986567] **3116**

TEXAS. EQUAL EMPLOYMENT OPPORTUNITY OFFICE *See* AFFIRMATIVE ACTION REPORT - TEXAS. EQUAL EMPLOYMENT OPPORTUNITY OFFICE **4701**

TEXAS ETHICS COMMISSION *See* INDEX TO ... ETHICS ADVISORY OPINIONS **2251**

TEXAS EVIDENCE REPORTER (US/0266-0814) [10864076] **3063**

TEXAS. EXECUTIVE DEPT *See* ANNUAL FINANCIAL REPORT / EXECUTIVE DEPARTMENT **4626**

TEXAS FACT BOOK *CEASED.* (US/0163-4666) [04295721] **1586**

TEXAS FAMILY JOURNAL (US/0277-4100) [07546703] **2286**

TEXAS FAMILY LAND HERITAGE REGISTRY (US/0272-8400) [06930280] **141**

TEXAS
Alphabetical Title Index

TEXAS FAMILY LAW REPORTER (US/0743-9342) [09958525] **3122**

TEXAS FAMILY PHYSICIAN (US/0098-1052) [01372426] **3739**

TEXAS FARMER (US/8750-9873) [12005454] **141**

TEXAS FARMER STOCKMAN (US/0279-165X) [02807119] **141**

TEXAS FFA MAGAZINE (US/0893-8997) [15692501] **141**

TEXAS FIDDLER, THE (US/0148-270X) [03279498] **4156**

TEXAS FIREMEN (US/0278-9930) [07955786] **2293**

TEXAS FISH & GAME (US/0887-4174) [12659953] **4879**

TEXAS FISHERMAN (US/8750-7951) [11775509] **2314**

TEXAS FOOD MERCHANT (US/0040-4322) [03941472] **2359**

TEXAS FORESTRY (LUFKIN, TEX.) (US/0739-1463) [03949635] **2396**

TEXAS FRONT IN THE NATION'S STRUGGLE AGAINST POVERTY: ANNUAL REPORT OF TEXAS DEPARTMENT OF COMMUNITY AFFAIRS' TEXAS OFFICE OF ECONOMIC OPPORTUNITY See TEXAS FRONT IN THE NATION'S STRUGGLE AGAINST POVERTY : ANNUAL REPORT OF THE TEXAS DEPARTMENT OF COMMUNITY AFFAIRS' ECONOMIC OPPORTUNITY DIVISION, THE **5312**

TEXAS FRONT IN THE NATION'S STRUGGLE AGAINST POVERTY : ANNUAL REPORT OF THE TEXAS DEPARTMENT OF COMMUNITY AFFAIRS' ECONOMIC OPPORTUNITY DIVISION, THE (US) [03652466] **5312**

TEXAS FRUIT AND PECAN STATISTICS (US/0092-2005) [02239531] **2359, 2362**

TEXAS FUNERAL SERVICES DIRECTORY (US/1062-5909) [25625501] **2407**

TEXAS GARDENER (WACO, TX.) (US/0744-0987) [08028688] **2432**

TEXAS. GENERAL LAND OFFICE See ANNUAL REPORT ON THE GEOTHERMAL RESOURCES ACT OF 1975 (TEXAS) **2554**

TEXAS GOLF (US/0199-3062) [05768440] **4926**

TEXAS GOVERNMENT NEWSLETTER (US/0164-9221) [03959513] **4498**

TEXAS. GOVERNOR'S BUDGET OFFICE See STATE AGENCY EXPENDITURES BY COUNTY **4748**

TEXAS. GOVERNOR'S COORDINATING OFFICE FOR THE VISUALLY HANDICAPPED See STATE SERVICES FOR THE VISUALLY HANDICAPPED: RECOMMENDATIONS **4394**

TEXAS GULF HISTORICAL AND BIOGRAPHICAL RECORD, THE (US) [03641258] **2763**

● TEXAS HEALTH CARE IN PERSPECTIVE (US/1065-4445) [26606781] **4805**

TEXAS HEALTH FACILITIES COMMISSION See ANNUAL FINANCIAL REPORT - TEXAS HEALTH FACILITIES COMMISSION **3776**

TEXAS HEALTH LAW REPORTER CEASED. (US/0266-0806) [10811002] **4805, 3063**

TEXAS HEART INSTITUTE JOURNAL (US/0730-2347) [07979978] **3710**

TEXAS HEREFORD (US/0744-4761) [03959457] **222**

TEXAS HERITAGE (FORT WORTH) (US/0148-1983) [03276490] **2475**

TEXAS HIGH TECHNOLOGY DIRECTORY (US/0896-9779) [17350706] **5165**

TEXAS HIGHER EDUCATION COORDINATING BOARD See CB REPORT **1814**

TEXAS HIGHWAYS (AUSTIN, TEX.) (US/0040-4349) [01644197] **5492**

TEXAS HISTORIAN, THE (US/0022-6602) [02574475] **2763**

TEXAS HISTORICAL COMMISSION See AUDIT REPORT, TEXAS HISTORICAL COMMISSION **2722**

TEXAS. HISTORICAL COMMISSION See BIENNIAL REPORT - TEXAS HISTORICAL COMMISSION **2723**

TEXAS HORSE-TRADER, THE (US/0149-9920) [03638603] **2802**

TEXAS HORTICULTURIST, THE (US) [23031792] **2432**

TEXAS HOTEL REVIEW (SAN ANTONIO, TEX. : 1988) CEASED. (US) [17501183] **2809**

TEXAS HUNTER'S DIRECTORY (US/0748-9854) [10249363] **4879**

TEXAS IN PERSPECTIVE (US/1065-5719) [25319929] **5345**

TEXAS INDEPENDENT PRODUCERS AND ROYALTY OWNERS ASSOCIATION See TIPRO REPORTER **4280**

TEXAS INDEX (US/1045-764X) [18346346] **2763**

TEXAS INDUSTRIAL COMMISSION See TEXAS INDUSTRIAL COMMISSION ANNUAL REPORT **1629**

TEXAS INDUSTRIAL COMMISSION ANNUAL REPORT (US/0361-2597) [02246317] **1629**

TEXAS INDUSTRIAL EXPANSION (US/0040-4365) [02268493] **1629**

TEXAS INDUSTRY ENVIRONMENTAL ALERT (US/1055-2561) [23129248] **3116**

TEXAS INSTRUMENTS TECHNICAL JOURNAL (US/0893-7877) [14101014] **1230**

TEXAS INSURANCE FACT BOOK (US/0093-3368) [04168375] **2894**

TEXAS INSURANCE LAW REPORTER (US/0264-6307) [09942329] **2894, 3064**

TEXAS INTERNATIONAL LAW JOURNAL (US/0163-7479) [01767354] **3136**

TEXAS JEWISH POST, THE (US/0040-439X) [03941582] **5755**

TEXAS JOB FINDER CEASED. (US/1064-3850) [26251985] **1916, 4209**

TEXAS JOURNAL OF AGRICULTURE AND NATURAL RESOURCES (US/0891-5466) [14907343] **141**

TEXAS JOURNAL OF IDEAS, HISTORY, AND CULTURE (US/0894-3354) [13089582] **2855**

TEXAS JOURNAL OF POLITICAL STUDIES (US/0191-0930) [04560637] **4498**

TEXAS JOURNAL OF SCIENCE, THE (US/0040-4403) [01695517] **5165**

● TEXAS JOURNAL OF WOMEN AND THE LAW (US/1058-5427) [24329603] **3064, 5567**

TEXAS JUDICIAL COUNCIL See TEXAS JUDICIAL SYSTEM ANNUAL REPORT FISCAL YEAR **3083**

TEXAS JUDICIAL SYSTEM ANNUAL REPORT FISCAL YEAR (US) [23373644] **3064, 3083**

TEXAS JUVENILE PROBATION STATISTICAL REPORT : STATISTICAL AND OTHER DATA ON THE JUVENILE JUSTICE SYSTEM IN TEXAS FOR CALENDAR YEARS ... ABBREVIATED (US) [08986573] **3177, 3083**

TEXAS KIN SUSPENDED. (US/0748-2590) [05863038] **2475**

TEXAS LABOR MARKET REVIEW / TEXAS EMPLOYMENT COMMISSION (US) [05010162] **937**

TEXAS LAW REVIEW (US/0040-4411) [01767356] **3064**

TEXAS LAWMAN, THE (US/0040-442X) [03941629] **3178**

TEXAS LAWYER, THE (US/0267-8306) [11911875] **3064**

TEXAS LAWYER'S CIVIL DIGEST (US/0731-9088) [08108138] **3064**

TEXAS LEAGUE SAVINGS ACCOUNT (US/0882-0384) [11763898] **813**

TEXAS LEGAL DIRECTORY (US) [05584936] **3064**

TEXAS. LEGISLATIVE BUDGET BOARD See LEGISLATIVE BUDGET ESTIMATES **4736**

TEXAS. LEGISLATIVE BUDGET BOARD See PERFORMANCE REPORT TO THE LEGISLATURE- LEGISLATIVE BUDGET BOARD **4673**

TEXAS LEGISLATIVE HANDBOOK (US/0193-2322) [04721222] **4498**

TEXAS LEGISLATIVE SERVICE See FINAL REPORT - TEXAS LEGISLATIVE SERVICE **2970**

TEXAS. LEGISLATURE. LEGISLATIVE COUNCIL See EMPLOYMENT IN STATE GOVERNMENT; A STATISTICAL SURVEY BY ETHNIC ORIGIN AND SEX **1666**

TEXAS. LEGISLATURE. LEGISLATIVE COUNCIL See SUMMARY OF ENACTMENTS - TEXAS. LEGISLATURE. LEGISLATIVE COUNCIL **3061**

TEXAS. LIBRARY AND HISTORICAL COMMISSION See BIENNIAL REPORT OF THE TEXAS LIBRARY AND HISTORICAL COMMISSION **3195**

TEXAS LIBRARY ASSOCIATION See DIRECTORY / TEXAS LIBRARY ASSOCIATION **3208**

TEXAS LIBRARY JOURNAL (US/0040-4446) [01767360] **3253**

TEXAS LINGUISTIC FORUM (US/0741-2576) [05169377] **3328**

TEXAS LIST, THE CEASED. (US/0363-2474) [04605181] **1714**

TEXAS LIVESTOCK MARKET NEWS (US/0199-7041) [05131657] **222**

TEXAS LIVESTOCK STATISTICS (US/0091-1550) [01786577] **222, 157**

TEXAS LONE STAR (US/0749-9310) [09456906] **1873**

TEXAS LONGHORN JOURNAL (US/0747-1556) [10596056] **222**

TEXAS MANUFACTURERS REGISTER (US/0743-1163) [10528005] **3488**

TEXAS MAPPING ADVISORY COMMITTEE See REPORT - TEXAS MAPPING ADVISORY COMMITTEE **2583**

TEXAS MATHEMATICS TEACHER (US/0277-030X) [06076252] **1907, 3538**

TEXAS MEDIA GUIDE, THE (US/0749-9949) [08304060] **1123**

TEXAS MEDICAL ASSOCIATION See TMA ACTION **3646**

TEXAS MEDICINE (US/0040-4470) [01644122] **3645**

TEXAS MOHAIR WEEKLY (ROCKSPRINGS, TEX.) (US) [14472265] **5755**

TEXAS MONTHLY (AUSTIN) (US/0148-7736) [02592251] **2547**

TEXAS MONTHLY LOCAL CLIMATOLOGICAL DATA. MICROFORM (US) [10863287] **1436**

TEXAS MUNICIPAL LEAGUE See TML LEGISLATIVE REPORT **3065**

TEXAS MUNICIPAL RETIREMENT SYSTEM See COMPREHENSIVE ANNUAL, FINANCIAL REPORT **4639**

● TEXAS MUSIC INDUSTRY DIRECTORY, THE (US/1062-6646) [24393866] **4156**

TEXAS NATURAL HISTORY (US/0882-5335) [11884916] **4173**

TEXAS NATURAL RESOURCES REPORTER (US/0197-2340) [05307263] **4280**

TEXAS NEIGHBORS (US) [12718690] **141**

TEXAS NOTES ON PRECOLUMBIAN ART, WRITING, AND CULTURE (US) [28884857] **2763**

TEXAS NURSING (US/0095-036X) [01090189] **3870**

TEXAS OBSERVER, THE (US) [07101312] **5755**

TEXAS. OFFICE OF CONSUMER CREDIT COMMISSIONER See ANALYSIS OF ANNUAL REPORTS OF LICENSEES **770**

TEXAS. OFFICE OF ECONOMIC OPPORTUNITY See POVERTY IN TEXAS **5254**

TEXAS. OFFICE OF STATE-FEDERAL RELATIONS See GUIDE TO SERVICES **4653**

TEXAS. OFFICE OF THE STATE ARCHEOLOGIST See OFFICE OF THE STATE ARCHEOLOGIST REPORTS **277**

TEXAS. OFFICE OF THE STATE AUDITOR. SYSTEM/ADMINISTRATIVE SERVICES DIVISION See SOFTWARE INVENTORY CATALOG **1203**

TEXAS OFFICIAL FEES (US) [06611085] **3064**

TEXAS OIL REGISTER (US/0272-8915) [06962126] **853, 4280**

TEXAS OLD TIME FIDDLERS ASSOCIATION See TEXAS FIDDLER, THE **4156**

TEXAS OPTOMETRY (US/0738-7644) [05820029] **4217**

TEXAS ORNITHOLOGICAL SOCIETY See BULLETIN OF THE TEXAS ORNITHOLOGICAL SOCIETY **5616**

TEXAS OSTEOPATHIC MEDICAL ASSOCIATION See DIRECTORY - TEXAS OSTEOPATHIC MEDICAL ASSOCIATION **3572**

TEXAS OUTLOOK, THE (US/0040-4551) [01767362] **1787**

TEXAS PAN AMERICAN SERIES (US) **2763**

TEXAS PARKS & WILDLIFE (US/0040-4586) [01714625] **4708**

TEXAS. PARKS AND WILDLIFE DEPT See ANNUAL FINANCIAL REPORT OF THE TEXAS PARKS & WILDLIFE DEPARTMENT **2186**

TEXAS PERSONAL INJURY LAW REPORTER (US/0264-4770) [09765841] **3064**

TEXAS PHARMACY (US/0362-7926) [02306153] **4330**

TEXAS PLANNING COUNCIL FOR DEVELOPMENTAL DISABILITIES See ANNUAL REPORT TO THE GOVERNOR / TEXAS PLANNING COUNCIL FOR DEVELOPMENTAL DISABILITIES **5273**

TEXAS PLANNING INFORMATION (US) [17615952] **1714**

TEXAS POLICE JOURNAL (US/0040-4594) [03941700] **3178**

TEXAS PRESS ASSOCIATION See TPA MESSENGER **4820**

TEXAS PREVENTABLE DISEASE NEWS (US/8750-9474) [08692653] **4805**

TEXAS PRINTER (US/1043-2302) [19356928] **4570**

Alphabetical Title Index — TEXTES

TEXAS PROFESSIONAL ENGINEER (1981) (US/0747-1262) [08126741] **1998**

TEXAS PROFESSIONAL PHOTOGRAPHER (US) **4377**

TEXAS. PROSECUTOR COUNCIL *See* ANNUAL REPORT OF THE PROSECUTOR COUNCIL (TEXAS) **3105**

TEXAS PSYCHOLOGIST (US/0749-3185) [10614963] **4620**

TEXAS PUBLIC EMPLOYEE (US/0040-4640) [03943483] **1714**

TEXAS PUBLIC LIBRARY STATISTICS (US/0082-3120) [10330300] 3253, **3260**

TEXAS. PUBLIC UTILITY COMMISSION *See* AUDITED ANNUAL FINANCIAL REPORT / PUBLIC UTILITY COMMISSION OF TEXAS **4760**

TEXAS. PUBLIC UTILITY COMMISSION *See* PUC BULLETIN **4762**

TEXAS PUBLIC UTILITY NEWS (US/0744-7981) [08560342] **4762**

TEXAS. RAILROAD COMMISSION. LIQUEFIED PETROLEUM GAS DIVISION *See* ANNUAL REPORT - LIQUEFIED PETROLEUM GAS DIVISION OF THE RAILROAD COMMISSION OF TEXAS **4250**

TEXAS. RAILROAD COMMISSION. OIL AND GAS DIVISION *See* ANNUAL REPORT OF THE OIL AND GAS DIVISION (AUSTIN) **4250**

TEXAS. RAILROAD COMMISSION. OIL AND GAS DIVISION *See* INACTIVE OIL AND GAS FIELDS **4260**

TEXAS REAL ESTATE LAW REPORTER (US/0267-8896) [12638493] 4848, **3064**

TEXAS REGISTER (US/0362-4781) [02309724] **4690**

TEXAS. REHABILITATION COMMISSION *See* PROGRAM & FINANCIAL PLAN - TEXAS. REHABILITATION COMMISSION **1704**

TEXAS RESEARCH LEAGUE *See* TRL ANALYZES DEVELOPMENTS IN TEXAS STATE AND LOCAL GOVERNMENT **4691**

TEXAS RESEARCH LEAGUE *See* BENCH MARKS FOR SCHOOL DISTRICT BUDGETS IN TEXAS; A REPORT **1860**

TEXAS RETAIL GROCERS ASSOCIATION *See* ANNUAL DIRECTORY / TEXAS RETAIL GROCERS ASSOCIATION **2327**

TEXAS REVIEW (HUNTSVILLE, TEX.), THE (US/0885-2685) [06247600] **3354**

TEXAS RIVERS AND RAPIDS (US/0163-4771) [04180485] **4879**

TEXAS SAVINGS & LOAN DIRECTORY (US) [10361646] **813**

TEXAS SCHOOL ADMINISTRATOR'S LEGAL DIGEST (US/0882-021X) [11789236] 1873, **3064**

TEXAS SCHOOL BUSINESS (US/0563-2978) [04268972] **1787**

TEXAS SCHOOL DIRECTORY (US/0363-4566) [02474654] **1787**

TEXAS SCHOOL LAW BULLETIN (US/0362-6334) [04053675] 1787, **3064**

TEXAS SCHOOL LAW NEWS (AUSTIN, TEX. : 1980) (US/0275-4444) [10523063] 1787, **3064**

TEXAS. SECRETARY OF STATE *See* TEXAS REGISTER **4690**

TEXAS. SECRETARY OF STATE *See* ANNUAL REPORT - OFFICE OF THE SECRETARY OF STATE **4629**

TEXAS SHORES (US/0747-0959) [10545596] **1457**

TEXAS SOCIETY FOR ELECTRON MICROSCOPY *See* JOURNAL - TEXAS SOCIETY FOR ELECTRON MICROSCOPY **572**

TEXAS SPEECH COMMUNICATION JOURNAL (US/0363-8782) [02546388] **1123**

TEXAS SPORTSMAN (US/0279-8875) [07331514] **4879**

TEXAS SPORTSMAN MAGAZINE *See* TEXAS SPORTSMAN **4879**

TEXAS. STATE BOARD OF LANDSCAPE ARCHITECTS *See* ANNUAL ROSTER - TEXAS STATE BOARD OF LANDSCAPE ARCHITECTS **2409**

TEXAS STATE BOARD OF PUBLIC ACCOUNTANCY *See* DIRECTORY OF LICENSEES / TEXAS STATE BOARD OF PUBLIC ACCOUNTANCY **743**

TEXAS STATE BOARD OF PUBLIC ACCOUNTANCY. PERMIT HOLDERS *See* DIRECTORY OF LICENSEES / TEXAS STATE BOARD OF PUBLIC ACCOUNTANCY **743**

TEXAS. STATE DEPT. OF HIGHWAYS AND PUBLIC TRANSPORTATION *See* ANNUAL FINANCIAL REPORT FOR THE FISCAL YEAR ENDING AUGUST 31 ... - TEXAS. STATE DEPT. OF HIGHWAYS AND PUBLIC TRANSPORTATION **5376**

TEXAS. STATE DEPT. OF HIGHWAYS AND PUBLIC TRANSPORTATION. FINANCE DIVISION *See* BIENNIAL REPORT - STATE DEPARTMENT OF HIGHWAYS AND PUBLIC TRANSPORTATION **5377**

TEXAS STATE DIRECTORY (US/0363-7530) [02111112] **4690**

TEXAS STATE LIBRARY AND ARCHIVES COMMISSION *See* BIENNIAL REPORT OF THE TEXAS STATE LIBRARY AND ARCHIVES COMMISSION **3195**

TEXAS. STATE PENSION REVIEW BOARD *See* BIENNIAL REPORT **1655**

TEXAS STATE PLAN FOR CONSTRUCTION OF COMMUNITY MENTAL HEALTH CENTERS (US/0364-4642) [02634679] **4805**

TEXAS STATE PLAN FOR THE PREVENTION, TREATMENT, AND CONTROL OF ALCOHOL ABUSE AND ALCOHOLISM (US/0364-8850) [02665297] **1349**

TEXAS STATE PLAN FOR VOCATIONAL EDUCATION *See* TEXAS ANNUAL PROGRAM PLAN FOR VOCATIONAL EDUCATION **1916**

●TEXAS STATE PUBLICATIONS (US) [29349377] **4690**

TEXAS STATE PUBLICATIONS (US) [19769005] **4690**

TEXAS STATE PUBLICATIONS CLEARINGHOUSE *See* TEXAS STATE PUBLICATIONS **4690**

TEXAS STATE PUBLICATIONS CLEARINGHOUSE. TEXAS STATE PUBLICATIONS *See* TEXAS STATE PUBLICATIONS **4690**

TEXAS. STATE PURCHASING AND GENERAL SERVICES COMMISSION *See* OPERATING BUDGET - TEXAS. STATE PURCHASING AND GENERAL SERVICES COMMISSION **4671**

TEXAS STATE REPORTER *See* CAPITOL REPORTER **782**

TEXAS STATE TEACHERS ASSOCIATION BULLETIN *See* TEXAS OUTLOOK, THE **1787**

TEXAS STUDIES IN LITERATURE AND LANGUAGE (US/0040-4691) [01767367] 3328, **3445**

TEXAS STUDY OF SECONDARY EDUCATION (US) **1787**

TEXAS STUDY OF SECONDARY EDUCATION RESEARCH JOURNAL (US/0040-4705) [02396081] **1787**

TEXAS. SUPREME COURT *See* TEXAS SUPREME COURT JOURNAL, THE **3064**

TEXAS SUPREME COURT JOURNAL, THE (US/0492-973X) [06608937] **3064**

TEXAS TAX GUIDE UPDATES (US) **4756**

TEXAS TECH LAW REVIEW (US/0564-6197) [01767368] **3064**

TEXAS TECH UNIVERSITY. MUSEUM *See* SPECIAL PUBLICATIONS - THE MUSEUM, TEXAS TECH UNIVERSITY **4096**

TEXAS TECH UNIVERSITY. WATER RESOURCES CENTER *See* REPORT - TEXAS TECH UNIVERSITY, WATER RESOURCES CENTER **5538**

TEXAS TEEN! (US/1049-474X) [21233722] **1070**

TEXAS TELLER QUARTERLY NEWSLETTER (US/0892-5186) [15217136] **3445**

TEXAS THOROUGHBRED (WICHITA FALLS, KAN.) (US/0164-6168) [04481843] **2802**

TEXAS TRADE AND PROFESSIONAL ASSOCIATIONS AND OTHER SELECTED ORGANIZATIONS (US/0362-7519) [02144415] **715**

TEXAS TRAFFIC SAFETY REPORT (US) [03959549] **5445**

TEXAS TREES (US/1047-7667) [20793077] **2396**

TEXAS UNITED COMMUNITY SERVICES, INC *See* NEWSLETTER - TEXAS UNITED COMMUNITY SERVICES **5299**

TEXAS. UNIVERSITY AT AUSTIN. CENTER FOR RESEARCH IN WATER RESOURCES *See* ANNUAL REPORT - CENTER FOR RESEARCH IN WATER RESOURCES, THE UNIVERSITY OF TEXAS AT AUSTIN **5529**

TEXAS. UNIVERSITY AT AUSTIN. ELECTRONICS RESEARCH CENTER *See* ANNUAL REPORT ON ELECTRONICS RESEARCH AT THE UNIVERSITY OF TEXAS AT AUSTIN **2035**

TEXAS. UNIVERSITY AT AUSTIN. LABORATORIES FOR ELECTRONICS AND RELATED SCIENCE RESEARCH *See* TECHNICAL REPORT - TEXAS. UNIVERSITY AT AUSTIN. LABORATORIES FOR ELECTRONICS AND RELATED SCIENCE RESEARCH **2083**

●TEXAS VETERINARIAN (US/1071-0566) [28153317] **5522**

TEXAS VETERINARY BULLETIN *See* TEXAS VETERINARY MEDICAL JOURNAL **5522**

TEXAS VETERINARY MEDICAL JOURNAL (US/0040-4756) [03726750] **5522**

TEXAS WATER DEVELOPMENT BOARD *See* TEXAS WATER DEVELOPMENT BOARD PUBLICATIONS CATALOG **5541**

TEXAS WATER DEVELOPMENT BOARD PUBLICATIONS CATALOG (US/0564-7495) [02086961] **5541**

TEXAS. WATER QUALITY BOARD. FIELD OPERATIONS DIVISION. SPECIAL STUDIES SECTION *See* REPORT - SPECIAL STUDIES SECTION, FIELD OPERATIONS DIVISION, TEXAS WATER QUALITY BOARD **4762**

TEXAS WATER REPORT (US/0492-9829) [05202275] **5541**

TEXAS WATER RESOURCES (US/0744-1320) [02336522] **5541**

TEXAS. WILDLIFE DIVISION *See* ANNUAL REPORT OF THE WILDLIFE DIVISION, PARKS AND WILDLIFE DEPARTMENT **2186**

TEXAS WOMAN (FORT WORTH, TEX.) (US/0279-2443) [07663840] **5567**

TEXAS WORKERS COMPENSATION & SAFETY REPORTER (US) 4805, **1714**

TEXAS WRITER'S NEWSLETTER (US) [05012686] **3445**

TEXINCON (II) [23086747] **5357**

TEXINCON AHMEDABAD (II/0970-5686) [09705686] **5357**

TEXPRESS (NE) 715, **5357**

TEXREPORT (SA) **5357**

TEXT (SW) [01799164] **426**

TEXT & IMAGE NEWS (UK) 1263, 1292, **1277**

TEXT & KONTEXT (DK/0105-7014) [03081241] 3445, **3328**

TEXT AND PERFORMANCE QUARTERLY (US/1046-2937) [19298194] **389**

TEXT AND PRESENTATION (US/1054-724X) [22966665] **5369**

TEXT + KRITIK (GW/0040-5329) [01767372] **3445**

TEXT (NEW YORK, N.Y. : 1985) (US/0736-3974) [13587443] **3354**

TEXT OF "A" PAPERS FROM THE WINTER MEETING - IEEE POWER ENGINEERING SOCIETY (US/0195-6825) [03906266] **2084**

TEXT ON MICROFORM (US/0883-4261) [12298149] **3253**

TEXT TECHNOLOGY (US/1053-900X) [22687017] **1205**

TEXT (THE HAGUE) (NE/0165-4888) [07365246] **3328**

TEXTBOOK LETTER, THE (US) [23228649] **1787**

TEXTBOOK NEWS *CEASED.* (US/0733-8228) [08645985] 4833, **1787**

TEXTBOOK SERIES / AMERICAN PHILOLOGICAL ASSOCIATION (US/0278-6400) [07856397] **3328**

TEXTBOOKS SUITABLE FOR USE IN KANSAS SCHOOLS (US/0451-3665) [01782913] **1787**

TEXTCONTEXT (GW/0179-6844) [18409740] **3328**

TEXTE DER HETHITER (GW/0173-4865) [06046019] **1080**

TEXTE DES SPATEN MITTELALTERS UND DER FRUHEN NEUZEIT (GW/0563-3079) [01605165] **3445**

TEXTE (TORONTO) (CN/0715-8920) [09938312] **3354**

TEXTE UND KOMMENTARE; EINE ALTERTUMSWISSENSCHAFTLICHE REIHE (GW/0563-3087) [01695956] **284**

TEXTE UND UNTERSUCHUNGEN ZUR GESCHICHTE DER ALTCHRISTLICHEN LITERATUR (GW/0082-3589) [01695649] **3445**

TEXTE ZUR FORSCHUNG (GW/0174-0474) [01740474] 1850, **3445**

TEXTE ZUR GESCHICHTE DER PRAVENTIVMEDIZIN : TGP / HERAUSGEGEBEN VON ERWIN BRAUN GESELLSCHAFT FUR PRAVENTIVMEDIZIN (SZ/1013-2007) [11181569] **3645**

TEXTEN + SCHREIBEN (GW/0172-8288) [01728288] **1205**

TEXTES ARABES ET ETUDES ISLAMIQUES (UA) [07311246] **284**

TEXTES D'INTERET GENERAL (FR) [03884742] **3064**

TEXTES DU CINEMA FRANCAIS (FR) [09554447] **4078**

TEXTES ET DOCUMENTS - MINISTERE DES AFFAIRES ETRANGERES, DU COMMERCE EXTERIEUR ET DE LA COOPERATION AU DEVELOPPEMENT (BE) [03739255] **4536**

TEXTES ET DOCUMENTS POUR LA CLASSE (FR/0395-6601) [02396206] **2523**

TEXTES — Alphabetical Title Index

TEXTES ET LANGAGES (FR/0248-4579) [08539417] 3328, **3445**

TEXTES LITTERAIRES FRANCAIS (SZ/0257-4063) [10559877] **3445**

TEXTES PUBLIES PAR L'INSTITUT D'ETUDES SLAVES (FR/0079-001X) [06549924] 3445, **3328**

TEXTES REGLEMENTAIRES DU CINEMA FRANCAIS *See* TEXTES DU CINEMA FRANCAIS **4078**

TEXTES - SOCIETE HISTORIQUE DE QUEBEC (CN/0081-1130) [03290819] **2763**

TEXTIEL BEHEER (NE) [23193855] **5357**

TEXTIL (XR/0040-4829) [09555109] **5357**

TEXTIL- ES TEXTILRUHAZATI IPARI SZAKIRODALMI TAJEKOZTATO (HU/0209-9578) [I02099578] **5357**

TEXTIL MITTEILUNGEN : TM (GW) **5357**

TEXTIL PRAXIS INTERNATIONAL *CEASED.* (GW/0040-4853) [01791617] **5357**

TEXTIL-WIRTSCHAFT (FRANKFURT) (GW/0040-487X) [04114965] **5357**

TEXTILE ANALYSIS BULLETIN SERVICE (US/0894-8267) [09026204] **5357**

TEXTILE & APPAREL MANUFACTURER (AT/0810-574X) [09098866] **1087**

TEXTILE & TEXT *CEASED.* (US/1051-4090) [20468845] 376, **5357**

TEXTILE ASIA (HK/0049-3554) [04292727] 1088, **5357**

TEXTILE ASIA INDEX (HK) **5357**

TEXTILE ASSOCIATION (INDIA) *See* JOURNAL OF THE TEXTILE ASSOCIATION **5353**

TEXTILE BUSINESS OUTLOOK (US/0739-0491) [09691124] **5357**

TEXTILE CHALLENGER (US/0270-0786) [05180509] 5357, **1714**

TEXTILE CHEMIST AND COLORIST (US/0040-490X) [01767375] 994, **5357**

TEXTILE CLEANING TECHNOLOGY (US/0094-5781) [01793735] **5357**

TEXTILE DYER & PRINTER (II/0040-4926) [08536469] **5357**

TEXTILE DYER & PRINTER : ANNUAL NUMBER (II) [01790406] 1030, **5357**

TEXTILE EXPORTS OF JAPAN : COUNTRY BY COMMODITY (JA) [06325039] **5357**

TEXTILE FINANCIAL OUTLOOK. ENGINEERING (US/1054-982X) [23041660] **5357**

TEXTILE FLAMMABILITY DIGEST *CEASED.* (US/0738-9620) [04024274] 2293, **5357**

TEXTILE HISTORY (UK/0040-4969) [01767378] **5358**

●TEXTILE HORIZONS (UK/1351-0266) [30096906] **5358**

TEXTILE HORIZONS INTERNATIONAL (UK/1351-0266) [25562800] **5358**

TEXTILE INDUSTRIES DYEGEST OF SOUTHERN AFRICA (SA/0254-0533) [09477080] **5358**

TEXTILE INDUSTRY & TRADE JOURNAL (II/0040-4993) [02246734] **5358**

TEXTILE INSTITUTE (MANCHESTER, ENGLAND) *See* ANNUAL REPORT / THE TEXTILE INDUSTRY **5347**

TEXTILE INSTITUTE (MANCHESTER, ENGLAND) *See* ACCOUNTS **5347**

TEXTILE INSTITUTE (MANCHESTER, ENGLAND). CONFERENCE *See* PAPERS OF THE ... ANNUAL CONFERENCE OF THE TEXTILE INSTITUTE **5355**

TEXTILE INSTITUTE (MANCHESTER, GREATER MANCHESTER) *See* JOURNAL OF THE TEXTILE INSTITUTE **5353**

TEXTILE LEADER (SZ) [22366667] **5358**

TEXTILE MAGAZINE, THE (II/0040-5078) [09669381] **5358**

TEXTILE MANUAL (CN/0381-551X) [01787546] **5358**

TEXTILE MANUFACTURER & KNITTING WORLD (UK) [02244959] **5358**

TEXTILE MANUFATURING (US/1065-1713) [26567655] **5358**

TEXTILE MONTH (UK/0040-5116) [01604840] **5358**

TEXTILE MUSEUM JOURNAL (US/0083-7407) [01769413] 5358, **4097**

TEXTILE MUSEUM (WASHINGTON, D.C.) *See* TEXTILE MUSEUM JOURNAL **4097**

TEXTILE OUTLOOK INTERNATIONAL (UK/0268-4764) [15295869] **5358**

TEXTILE PRICING OUTLOOK (US/0739-4144) [09737187] **5358**

TEXTILE PRODUCTION *See* WORLD FIBRE NEWS **5360**

TEXTILE PRODUCTS INDUSTRIES (CN/0319-891X) [11454084] **5358**

TEXTILE PROGRESS (UK/0040-5167) [01767383] **5358**

TEXTILE RECORDER BOOK OF THE YEAR, THE (UK) [06631434] **5358**

TEXTILE RENTAL SERVICES ASSOCIATION OF AMERICA *See* TRSA ORGANIZATION **5359**

TEXTILE RESEARCH JOURNAL (US/0040-5175) [06456954] **5358**

TEXTILE TECHNOLOGY DIGEST (US/0040-5191) [01772712] 5358, **5360**

TEXTILE TECHNOLOGY INTERNATIONAL (UK/0953-2404) [I09532404] **5358**

TEXTILE TRENDS (II/0040-5205) [02624953] **5358**

TEXTILE VIEW MAGAZINE (NE) **5358**

TEXTILE WEEK (US/0161-9713) [04071584] **5358**

TEXTILE WORLD (US/0040-5213) [01605639] **5358**

TEXTILES (UK/0306-0748) [01772713] **5359**

TEXTILES AND APPAREL. APPAREL (US) **5359**

TEXTILES AND APPAREL. TEXTILES (US) **5359**

TEXTILES NEWS / INTERNATIONAL PRESS CUTTING SERVICE (II/0047-1119) [12727542] **5359**

TEXTILES PANAMERICANOS (US/0049-3570) [04725162] **5359**

TEXTILES PARA EL HOGAR (SP) **5359**

TEXTILES SUISSES (SZ/0040-5248) [01767386] **5359**

TEXTILFORUM (GW) [25521197] 376, **5359**

TEXTILIPARI KUTATO INTEZET KOZLEMENYEI (HU/0133-2082) [09519554] **5359**

TEXTILIPARI TERVGAZDAG (HU) **5359**

TEXTILVEREDLUNG (SZ/0040-5310) [02624977] **5359**

TEXTO CRITICO / CENTRO DE INVESTIGACIONES LINGUISTICO-LITERARIAS (MX/0185-0830) [02428035] **3445**

TEXTOS DE METODOS MATEMATICOS (BL/0103-491X) [I0103491X] **3538**

TEXTRACTS *CEASED.* (US/0495-3789) [02592444] **5359**

TEXTS ADOPTED BY THE ASSEMBLY - COUNCIL OF EUROPE. PARLIAMENTARY ASSEMBLY (FR/0377-6093) [02242267] **4690**

TEXTS AND DISSERTATIONS (UK/0957-0322) [05228019] **2855**

TEXTS AND MONOGRAPHS IN COMPUTER SCIENCE (US/0172-603X) [08498409] **1205**

TEXTS AND MONOGRAPHS IN PHYSICS (US/0172-5998) [08500537] **4423**

TEXTS AND STUDIES IN THE HISTORY OF MEDIAEVAL EDUCATION (US/0082-3732) [03125264] **1787**

TEXTS AND TRANSLATIONS (US/0145-3203) [02719339] **1080**

TEXTS FROM CUNEIFORM SOURCES (US/0082-3759) [01767388] **2631**

TEXTS FROM EXCAVATIONS (UK/0307-5125) [05632988] **284**

TEXTS IN APPLIED MATHEMATICS (US/0939-2475) [19936963] **4429**

TEXTUAL (PE) [01791419] **2552**

TEXTUAL PRACTICE (UK) [16744351] **3445**

TEXTUAL STUDIES IN CANADA (CN) [I1183854X] **3355**

●TEXTURE MINIATURE (US/1061-9887) [25512002] **3472**

TEXTURE (NORMAN, OKLA.) (US/1061-6365) [25387944] **3445**

TEXTURED YARN PRODUCTION *CEASED.* (US/0272-7439) [03060512] 5359, **3488**

TEXTURES AND MICROSTRUCTURES (US/0730-3300) [07988926] **1033**

TEXTUS (IS/0082-3767) [01767389] **5020**

TEXTUS PATRISTICI ET LITURGICI (GW/0082-3775) [05243622] **5003**

TEZUKAYAMA DAIGAKU *See* TEZUKAYAMA DAIGAKU RONSHU **2855**

TEZUKAYAMA DAIGAKU RONSHU (JA) [06853551] **2855**

TFP INFORME *CEASED.* (CN/0229-964X) [08295267] **5003**

TFP NEWSLETTER *CEASED.* (CN/0229-9631) [08295152] **5003**

TG. TAPICERIAS GANCEDO (SP/0210-3761) [I02103761] **376**

TGA-PC (ARLINGTON, VA.) (US/1047-045X) [20589332] **1850**

TGC TYPEFACE DIRECTORY (US) [05527195] **4570**

TGO. TIJDSCHRIFT VOOR THERAPIE, GENEESMIDDEL EN ONDERZOEK (NE/0921-562X) [15815424] **4330**

THACKERAY NEWSLETTER, THE (US/1064-2463) [09766536] **3445**

THAI ABSTRACTS. SERIES A: SCIENCE AND TECHNOLOGY (TH) [02243620] **5165**

THAI-AMERICAN BUSINESS (TH/0002-7855) [02113512] **853**

THAI BUILDER DIRECTORY (TH) [02515714] **630**

THAI CHAMBER OF COMMERCE. DIRECTORY *See* BUSINESS DIRECTORY **647**

THAI DEVELOPMENT NEWSLETTER (TH) [12126214] **5312**

THAI ECONOMY, THE (TH) [07808992] **1587**

THAI INDUSTRIAL DIRECTORY (TH) [03125930] **1629**

THAI INFORMATION BULLETIN (FR) [03632937] **4498**

THAI INFORMATION CENTER *See* TIC NEWS **2509**

THAI JOURNAL OF AGRICULTURAL SCIENCE (TH/0049-3589) [02233468] **141**

THAI JOURNAL OF SURGERY (TH/0125-6068) [08537122] **3976**

THAI LIFE (TH/0125-6637) [10845940] **2770**

THAI PHILATELY (US/0198-7992) [04362538] **2787**

THAILAND *See* ROYAL THAI GOVERNMENT GAZETTE **4684**

THAILAND BIBLE LITERATURE (US/0744-7248) [08514998] **5020**

THAILAND BUSINESS (TH) [04347747] **715**

THAILAND EXECUTIVES (TH) [09932217] **715**

THAILAND FOREIGN AFFAIRS NEWSLETTER / INFORMATION DEPARTMENT, MINISTRY OF FOREIGN AFFAIRS (TH/0125-6459) [10384991] **4498**

THAILAND GUIDEBOOK, THE (US/1055-8861) [23363694] **5492**

●THAILAND, INDOCHINA & BURMA HANDBOOK (US/1061-9844) [25499358] **5492**

THAILAND INVESTMENT (TH) [19380714] **917**

THAILAND INVESTMENT HANDBOOK AND DIRECTORY OF PROMOTED COMPANIES *See* THAILAND INVESTMENT **917**

THAILAND. KANFAIFA SUAN PHUMIPHAK *See* ANNUAL REPORT / PROVINCIAL ELECTRICITY AUTHORITY **4629**

THAILAND MANUFACTURERS AND PRODUCTS DIRECTORY (TH) [05004508] **3488**

THAILAND. NATIONAL STATISTICAL OFFICE *See* STATISTICAL YEAR BOOK, THAILAND **5341**

THAILAND PROFILES (CH) [11595035] **1629**

THAILAND TRAVEL TRADE YEARBOOK (TH) [06977910] **5492**

THAILAND : WIRTSCHAFTLICHE ENTWICKLUNG (GW) [03463898] **1587**

THAILAND, WIRTSCHAFTSDATEN UND WIRTSCHAFTSDOKUMENTATION / BUNDESSTELLE FUER AUSSENHANDELSINFORMATION (GW) [11296660] **1587**

THAILAND'S COMMODITY EXPORTS DIRECTORY (TH) [09705095] **853**

THAILAND'S EXPORTERS (TH) [02515728] **853**

THALASSAS : REVISTA DE CIENCIAS DEL MAR (SP) [13377311] **558**

THALASSIA JUGOSLAVICA (CI/0495-4025) [02625149] **5598**

THALASSOGRAFIKA (GR/0250-3298) [03466099] **2314**

THALIA (OTTAWA) (CN/0706-5604) [04589604] **3445**

THAMES POETRY *SUSPENDED.* (UK/0307-9562) [03801073] **3472**

THAMES RIVER REVIEW (CN/0823-9843) [11575670] **2207**

THAMES VALLEY TIMES (CN/0229-6594) [08099277] **5796**

THAMES WATER AUTHORITY. PLANNING DIRECTORATE. CENTRAL INFORMATION UNIT *See* THAMES WATER STATISTICS **5549**

THAMES WATER STATISTICS (UK) [03703561] **5549**

THAMESFORD TOWN CRIER (CN/0707-4794) [04754911] **5796**

THANATOLOGIE (PARIS) (FR/1157-0466) [I11570466] **4363**

THANATOLOGY ABSTRACTS (US/0196-0121) [16864414] 2855, **4620**

THANATOS (US/0160-8681) [03773273] **4363**

THANG-TIEN (US) [04248208] **4059**

THAQAFAH (TI) [01798392] **2644**

THAT WAS THE WEEK THAT WAS (CN/0820-8026) [10334913] **917**

THAT'S YUGOSLAVIA (GW/0179-3063) [I01793063] **2524**

THAWRAH (ROME, ITALY) (IT) [19926189] **2644**

THE B.C. HOME BUSINESS REPORT *See* BRITISH COLUMBIA & ALBERTA HOME BUSINESS REPORT **644**

●(THE) BRAVE NEW TICK (US/1070-0161) [28232350] **2796**

THE JOURNAL (US/0192-592X) [02252014] 1907, **1225**

THE POINT (HANCOCK, MICH.), TO (US/1058-5303) [24323186] **366**

THE POINT (VICTORIA), TO (CN/1186-0103) [24280754] **1787**

THE UNCANNY X-MEN (US/0274-5372) [06388417] **4867**

THEATER (GW) [06201089] **5369**

THEATER DER ZEIT (GW/0040-5418) [01713663] **5370**

THEATER FINANCIAL RECORD, THE (US) [17614432] **4078**

THEATER HEUTE (GW/0040-5507) [01773450] **5370**

THEATER IN OSTERREICH / WIENER GESELLSCHAFT FUER THEATERFORSCHUNG, INSTITUT FUER THEATERWISSENSCHAFT AN DER UNIVERSITAT WIEN (AU) [10534447] **5370**

THEATER (NEW HAVEN, CONN.) (US/0161-0775) [03563829] **5370**

THEATER RUNDSCHAU (GW) **5370**

THEATER THREE *CEASED.* (US/1052-0511) [14977767] **5370**

THEATER WEEK (US/0896-1956) [16987637] **5370**

THEATERWORK MAGAZINE (US/0735-1895) [08882897] **5370**

THEATERZEITSCHRIFT (GW/0723-1172) [10446930] 5370, **389**

THEATRE (UK) [04643037] **5370**

THEATRE & THERAPY *CEASED.* (UK) **5370**

THEATRE ANNUAL, THE (US/0082-3821) [01767400] **5370**

THEATRE CANADA *See* SPECIAL BULLETIN - THEATRE CANADA **5368**

THEATRE CLASSICS : THE LEAGUE OF HISTORIC AMERICAN THEATRES ANNUAL PUBLICATION (US) [20620897] **5370**

THEATRE CRAFTS (US/0040-5469) [01767402] **5370**

THEATRE CRAFTS DIRECTORY (US) [05003156] **5370**

THEATRE CRAFTS INTERNATIONAL (US/1060-3042) [24691354] **5370**

THEATRE, CZECH & SLOVAK (XR) [25504383] **5370**

THEATRE, DANSE, MUSIQUE, ARTS MULTIDISCIPLINAIRES ET MULTIMEDIAS (CN/1182-4948) [22769004] **332**

THEATRE DIRECTORY OF THE SAN FRANCISCO BAY AREA (US/0737-0172) [09286045] 389, **5370**

THEATRE/DRAMA ABSTRACTS (US) [03175337] **5370**

THEATRE EN POLOGNE, LE (PL/0040-5493) [02268525] **5370**

THEATRE HISTORY IN CANADA (CN/0226-5761) [07015618] **5370**

THEATRE HISTORY STUDIES (US/0733-2033) [07863668] **5370**

THEATRE INFORMATION BULLETIN (US/0040-5515) [01773451] **5370**

THEATRE INSIGHT (US) [19819526] **5370**

THEATRE IRELAND *CEASED.* (IE/0263-6344) [09222917] **5370**

THEATRE JOBLIST (US/0892-0796) [15186270] 1314, 4156, **389**

THEATRE JOURNAL (WASHINGTON, D.C.) (US/0192-2882) [04799124] **5371**

THEATRE, LE (FR/0563-3966) [05135540] **5370**

THEATRE NOTEBOOK (UK/0040-5523) [01767405] **5371**

THEATRE ORGAN (1970) (US/0040-5531) [04046918] 5371, **4156**

THEATRE PROFILES (US/0361-7947) [02247018] **5371**

THEATRE/PUBLIC (FR/0335-2927) [08586808] **5371**

THEATRE QUEBEC (CN/0825-4494) [10926552] **5371**

THEATRE (QUEBEC) (CN/0705-0453) [04875308] **5371**

THEATRE RECORD (UK/0962-1792) [23266174] **5371**

●THEATRE RESEARCH IN CANADA (CN/1196-1198) [28190633] **5371**

THEATRE RESEARCH INTERNATIONAL (UK/0307-8833) [02152713] **5371**

THEATRE REVIEW (UK) [01792959] **5371**

THEATRE SOUTHWEST (US/0743-5452) [04327105] **5371**

THEATRE STUDIES (US/0362-0964) [00943231] **5371**

THEATRE SURVEY (US/0040-5574) [01767408] **5371**

●THEATRE SYMPOSIUM (US/1065-4917) [26613915] **5371**

THEATRE TIMES *SUSPENDED.* (US/0732-300X) [08343331] **5371**

THEATRE TOPICS (US/1054-8378) [22994185] **5371**

THEATRE (WASHINGTON, D.C.) (US/8756-4335) [11382436] **5371**

THEATRE WORLD (NEW YORK, N.Y. : 1981) *CEASED.* (US) [10416424] **5371**

●THEATREFORUM (LA JOLLA, CALIF.) (US/1060-5320) [25036007] **5371**

THEATREPHILE (UK/0265-2609) [10747880] **5371**

THEATRICAL INDEX (US/1046-9869) [06835088] **5371**

THEATRIKA (GR) [01799302] **5371**

THEATRUM (TORONTO) (CN/0838-5696) [19603940] **5371**

THEILHEIMER'S SYNTHETIC METHODS OF ORGANIC CHEMISTRY (SZ/0253-200X) [08614846] **1048**

THEIR WORLD (US) [10669565] **1886**

THEM DAYS (CN/0381-6109) [02802258] 2324, **2763**

THEMA (METAIRIE, LA.) (US/1041-4851) [18859652] **3446**

THEMA UMWELT (OSNABRUCK) (GW/0939-8767) [I09398767] **426**

THEMATA CHOROU + TECHNON (GR/0074-1191) [05663412] 366, **310**

THEMATIC MAPPING BULLETIN (AT/0314-657X) [04554284] **2583**

THEMELIOS (UK/0307-8388) [01776720] **5003**

THEMEN DER PRAKTISCHEN THEOLOGIE, THEOLOGIA PRACTICA (GW/0720-9525) [09810059] **5003**

THEMES IN DRAMA *CEASED.* (UK/0263-676X) [05157358] 1080, **389**

THEODOR-STORM-GESELLSCHAFT *See* SCHRIFTEN DER THEODOR-STORM-GESELLSCHAFT **3434**

THEODORE ROOSEVELT ASSOCIATION *See* THEODORE ROOSEVELT ASSOCIATION JOURNAL **435**

THEODORE ROOSEVELT ASSOCIATION JOURNAL (US/0161-8423) [04029289] **435**

THEOLOGIA 21 (US/0362-0085) [02167325] **5003**

THEOLOGIA ATHENAI (GR/1105-154X) [I1105154X] **5003**

THEOLOGIA EVANGELICA (SA) [02686122] **5003**

THEOLOGIA REFORMATA (NE/0040-5612) [07035248] **5003**

THEOLOGIA VIATORUM (PIETERSBURG, SOUTH AFRICA) (SA) [05870047] **5003**

THEOLOGIAI SZEMLE (HU/0133-7599) [07471961] **5003**

THEOLOGICA XAVERIANA (CK) [03312565] **5037**

THEOLOGICAL BOOK REVIEW (UK/0954-2191) [I09542191] **5003**

THEOLOGICAL DIGEST & OUTLOOK (CN/1184-8901) [24368407] **5003**

THEOLOGICAL EDUCATION (US/0040-5620) [01773454] **5003**

THEOLOGICAL EDUCATOR, THE (US/0198-6856) [06217080] **5003**

THEOLOGICAL NEWS (UK) [03598499] **5003**

THEOLOGICAL REVIEW (BEIRUT, LEBANON) (LE/0379-9557) [04276887] **5003**

THEOLOGICAL STUDIES (BALTIMORE) (US/0040-5639) [01767417] **5003**

THEOLOGIE DER GEGENWART (GW) [07413985] **5003**

THEOLOGIE FUER DIE PARXIS (GW/0939-5121) [I09395121] **5003**

THEOLOGIE HISTORIQUE (FR/0563-4253) [03126416] **5003**

THEOLOGIE UND GLAUBE (GW/0049-366X) [01587738] **5003**

THEOLOGIE UND PHILOSOPHIE (GW/0040-5655) [03251843] 4363, **5003**

THEOLOGISCH-PRAKTISCHE QUARTALSCHRIFT (AU/0040-5663) [01773456] **5037**

THEOLOGISCHE BEITRAEGE (GW/0342-2372) [01782191] **5003**

THEOLOGISCHE BUCHEREI (GW/0563-430X) [05243754] **5004**

THEOLOGISCHE LITERATURZEITUNG (GW/0040-5671) [01767418] **5004**

THEOLOGISCHE QUARTALSCHRIFT (MUNCHEN) (GW/0342-1430) [01773457] **5004**

THEOLOGISCHE REALENZYKLOPADIE (GW) **1929**

THEOLOGISCHE REVUE (GW/0040-568X) [01696877] **5004**

THEOLOGISCHE RUNDSCHAU (GW/0040-5698) [01773458] **5004**

THEOLOGISCHE STUDIEN (SZ) [02068681] **5004**

THEOLOGISCHE ZEITSCHRIFT (SZ/0040-5701) [01773460] **5004**

THEOLOGISCHER HANDKOMMENTAR ZUM NEUEN TESTAMENT (GW) **5004**

THEOLOGISCHES WORTERBUCH ZUM ALTEN TESTAMENT (GW) **5004**

THEOLOGOS, HO (IT) [12617910] **5004**

THEOLOGY & LIFE (HONG KONG) (HK/0253-3812) [09199209] **5004**

THEOLOGY AND LIFE SERIES (US) [10808437] **5004**

THEOLOGY & PUBLIC POLICY (US/1052-9314) [20460775] 2253, **5004**

THEOLOGY AND SCIENCE AT THE FRONTIERS OF KNOWLEDGE (UK) [13896890] **5004**

THEOLOGY ANNUAL (HK) [09222283] **5037**

THEOLOGY DIGEST (US/0040-5728) [01642682] **5004**

THEOLOGY IN CONTEXT (GW/0176-1439) [11539169] **5004**

THEOLOGY (LONDON) (UK/0040-571X) [01767420] **5004**

THEOLOGY NEWS & NOTES (US) [04619469] **5004**

THEOLOGY TODAY (EPHRATA, PA.) (US/0040-5736) [01587753] **5004**

THEOLOGY TODAY. [MICROFILM] (US) [04063723] **5004**

THEORETIC PAPERS / INSTITUTE OF MATHEMATICS, UNIVERSITY OF OSLO (NO/0801-3128) [11163379] **3538**

THEORETICA CHIMICA ACTA (GW/0040-5744) [01585892] **1058**

THEORETICAL AND APPLIED CLIMATOLOGY (AU/0177-798X) [15035261] **1436**

THEORETICAL AND APPLIED FRACTURE MECHANICS (NE/0167-8442) [10758739] **4430**

THEORETICAL AND APPLIED GENETICS (GW/0040-5752) [04624238] **551**

THEORETICAL AND APPLIED MECHANICS (YU/0350-2708) [07562538] **4430**

THEORETICAL AND APPLIED MECHANICS (JA) [04281266] **2130**

THEORETICAL AND COMPUTATIONAL FLUID DYNAMICS (US/0935-4964) [19964607] **4423**

THEORETICAL AND EXPERIMENTAL CHEMISTRY (US/0040-5760) [01767423] **1058**

THEORETICAL AND MATHEMATICAL PHYSICS (US/0040-5779) [01767424] 3538, **4423**

THEORETICAL CHEMICAL ENGINEERING (UK/0960-5053) [I09605053] 1012, 2017, **2007**

THEORETICAL COMPUTER SCIENCE (NE/0304-3975) [02243959] **1205**

THEORETICAL FOUNDATIONS OF CHEMICAL ENGINEERING (US/0040-5795) [01767426] **2017**

THEORETICAL LINGUISTICS (GW/0301-4428) [02079248] **3328**

THEORETICAL MEDICINE (NE/0167-9902) [09352504] 4363, **3645**

THEORETICAL PARAPSYCHOLOGY *CEASED.* (US/0894-2528) [15909382] **4243**

THEORETICAL — Alphabetical Title Index

THEORETICAL POPULATION BIOLOGY (US/0040-5809) [00932477] 552, **4560**

THEORETICAL STUDIES IN SECOND LANGUAGE ACQUISITION (US/1051-6670) [22043857] **3328**

THEORETICAL SURGERY *CEASED*. (GW/0179-8669) [14521126] 3684, **3976**

THEORETISCHE GESCHIEDENIS (GW/0167-8310) [25357310] **2631**

THEORIA (SP/0495-4548) [12714148] 5165, **4363**

THEORIA (SW/0040-5825) [01435624] **4363**

THEORIA (DENTON, TEX.) (US) [12979399] **4156**

THEORIA (PIETERMARITZBURG) (SA/0040-5817) [01767428] 332, **2855**

THEORIA/PRAXIS: A GRADUATE JOURNAL OF THEORY AND CRITICISM (CN) 4363, **5224**

THEORIE UND PRAXIS DER SOZIALPADAGOGIK (GW/0342-7145) [I03427145] 1070, **5004**

THEORIES IN MARKETING SERIES (US/0272-4014) [06833300] **937**

THEORIES OF CONTEMPORARY CULTURE (US) [08072862] **5264**

THEORY AND DECISION (NE/0040-5833) [01604091] 5224, **4363**

THEORY AND DECISION LIBRARY (NE/0921-3376) [09986168] **3253**

THEORY AND PRACTICE : JOURNAL OF THE MUSIC THEORY SOCIETY OF NEW YORK STATE (US/0741-6156) [06704032] **4156**

● THEORY AND PRACTICE OF OBJECT SYSTEMS (US/1074-3227) [29681363] **1249**

THEORY & PSYCHOLOGY (UK/0959-3543) [23361233] **4620**

THEORY AND RESEARCH IN BEHAVIORAL PEDIATRICS (US/0735-6897) [08654620] **3912**

THEORY AND RESEARCH IN SOCIAL EDUCATION (US/0093-3104) [01792096] 1907, **5224**

THEORY AND SOCIETY (NE/0304-2421) [02252022] 4363, **5264**

THEORY, CULTURE & SOCIETY (UK/0263-2764) [09512993] **5224**

THEORY INTO PRACTICE (US/0040-5841) [01604387] **1907**

THEORY OF PROBABILITY AND ITS APPLICATIONS (UK/0040-585X) [01767431] **3538**

THEORY OF PROBABILITY AND MATHEMATICAL STATISTICS (US/0094-9000) [01795521] **3538**

THEORY OF STOCHASTIC PROCESSES (US/0095-7380) [01790826] **3538**

THEOSOPHICAL HISTORY (US/0951-497X) [22902594] **5004**

THEOSOPHICAL MOVEMENT, THE (II/0040-5884) [01681222] **5045**

THEOSOPHIST, THE (II/0040-5892) [01713828] **5004**

THEOSOPHY (US/0040-5906) [02078413] **4363**

THERAPEUTIC ABORTIONS - CANADIAN CENTRE FOR HEALTH INFORMATION (CN/1195-4078) [29562887] **3769**

● THERAPEUTIC CARE AND EDUCATION : THE JOURNAL OF THE ASSOCIATION OF WORKERS FOR CHILDREN WITH EMOTIONAL AND BEHAVIOURAL DIFFICULTIES (UK) [26878881] 3937, **4620**

THERAPEUTIC COMMUNITIES (UK/0964-1866) [I09641866] **3645**

THERAPEUTIC DRUG MONITORING (US/0163-4356) [04393066] 3645, **4330**

● THERAPEUTIC IMMUNOLOGY (UK/0967-0149) [30000188] **3677**

THERAPEUTIC RECREATION JOURNAL (US/0040-5914) [01775922] 4855, **4394**

● THERAPEUTIC WORK WITH CHILDREN (UK/1353-3347) **1886**

THERAPEUTIQUE (FR/0040-5922) [01778411] **3801**

THERAPEUTIQUE ACTUELLE : TA *SUSPENDED*. (FR/0989-6171) [20818189] **3645**

THERAPEUTISCHE KONZEPTE DER ANALYTISCHEN PSYCHOLOGIE C.G. JUNG (GW/0344-8967) [10007099] **4620**

THERAPEUTISCHE UMSCHAU (SZ/0040-5930) [01640440] **3976**

THERAPIA HUNGARICA (ENGLISH EDITION) (HU/0133-3909) [04173339] **3645**

THERAPIE (FR/0040-5957) [01645296] **4330**

THERAPIE COMPORTEMENT (FR) **4620**

THERAPIE DER GEGENWART *CEASED*. (GW/0040-5965) [01639172] **3645**

THERAPIE ET REEDUCATION PSYCHOMOTRICE (FR/0154-473X) [04371452] **3846**

THERAPIE FAMILIALE (SZ/0250-4952) [07254580] 2286, **4620**

THERAPIEWOCHE (GW/0040-5973) [01695148] **3645**

THERAPIEWOCHE OSTERREICH (AU/0258-848X) [I0258848X] **3645**

THERAPIEWOCHE SCHWEIZ (SZ/0256-6869) [I02566869] **3645**

● THERAPISTS AND ALLIED HEALTH PROFESSIONALS CAREER DIRECTORY (US/1070-7263) [28513877] **3917**

THERAPY OF INFECTIOUS DISEASES (IT/0394-025X) [I0394025X] **4805**

THERE IS (CN/0823-3276) [10638817] **3472**

THERIAULT'S BOOK OF DOLLS (US/0737-8904) [09461733] **376**

THERIAULT'S THE DOLLMASTERS *See* THERIAULT'S BOOK OF DOLLS **376**

THERIOGENOLOGY (US/0093-691X) [02504829] **5522**

THERIOS : REVISTA DE MEDICINA VETERINARIA Y PRODUCCION ANIMAL (AG) [10113857] **5523**

THERMAL ANALYSIS APPLICATION STUDY (US/0163-9595) [04544038] **1019**

THERMAL BELT NEWS JOURNAL (US/0746-2654) [09898481] **5724**

THERMAL CONDUCTIVITY (1975) (US/0163-9005) [03815736] **4432**

THERMAL ENGINEERING (UK/0040-6015) [01767435] **1998**

THERMOCHIMICA ACTA (NE/0040-6031) [00825205] **1058**

THERMOLOGY (US/0882-3758) [11821605] **3645**

THERMOPOLIS INDEPENDENT RECORD (US) [26817091] **5773**

THERMOTROL TECHNICIAN, THE (US/0161-5459) [03952345] **1336**

THESAURISMATA TOU HELLENIKOU INSTITOUTOU VYZANTINON KAI METAVYZANTINON SPOUDON (IT) [10766872] **2712**

THESAURUS (UK) [23709521] 4423, **2084**

THESAURUS - AMERICAN PETROLEUM INSTITUTE (US/0193-5151) [01793118] **3253**

THESAURUS DE DESCRIPTEURS SUR L'EDUCATION. LISTE ROTATIVE ET ADDITIONS ET CORRECTIONS (CN/0383-2910) [03233236] **1929**

THESAURUS - INSTITUTO CARO Y CUERVO (CK/0040-604X) [05542799] **3328**

THESAURUS LINGUAE GRAECAE; NEWSLETTER (US/0361-8641) [02054817] **1080**

THESAURUS LINGUAE LATINAE (GW) [02251881] **1929**

THESAURUS, MANUFACTURING ENGINEERING TERMS (US/0739-8778) [09326601] 3488, **3253**

THESAURUS OF ENGINEERED MATERIALS / MATERIALS INFORMATION (US) [20685551] **1999**

THESAURUS OF ERIC DESCRIPTORS (US/1051-2993) [04032031] 1787, **1798**

THESAURUS OF ERIC DESCRIPTORS. SUPPLEMENT (US) [09605504] 1787, **1929**

THESAURUS OF METALLURGICAL TERMS (US/1052-7877) [20685489] **4021**

THESAURUS OF PSYCHOLOGICAL INDEX TERMS (US) [05471840] **4620**

● THESE CELESTIAL TIMES (US/1062-4643) [25636098] **4243**

THESE TIMES (US/0040-6058) [02268533] **5004**

THESES AND DISSERTATIONS PRESENTED AND CURRENTLY BEING UNDERTAKEN IN GEOGRAPHY (AT) [03265405] **2577**

THESES IN LATIN AMERICAN STUDIES AT BRITISH UNIVERSITIES IN PROGRESS AND RECENTLY COMPLETED (UK) [08156745] **426**

THESES PUBLICATION SERIES (II/0533-652X) [01454832] **1850**

THESES ZOOLOGICAE (GW) [11431519] **5598**

THESINDEX MEDICAL (FR/0399-0648) [04798206] **3645**

THESIS (US/0892-2330) [15166679] **1850**

THESIS ABSTRACTS (INDIAN AGRICULTURAL UNIVERSITIES ASSOCIATION) (II) [09228129] **222**

THESIS ELEVEN (US/0725-5136) [09911231] 4548, **5264**

THESIS SERIES - KENTUCKY GEOLOGICAL SURVEY (US/0075-5621) [01715527] **1399**

THESOTHEQUE, LA (FR) [09249919] **3446**

THESSALIKE HESTIA (GR) [01798871] **2712**

THETA (DURHAM) *CEASED*. (US/0040-6066) [01767440] **4243**

THEY MULTIPLIED (US/0147-7048) [03215654] **2475**

THIEF RIVER FALLS TIMES (US/8750-3883) [01767443] **5699**

THIN SOLID FILMS (SZ/0040-6090) [01605925] **2084**

THIN-WALLED STRUCTURES (UK/0263-8231) [09638435] **2032**

THINK & GROW RICH NEWSLETTER (US/1053-718X) [22615466] **888**

THINK INDIA (II) [22505062] **2666**

THINK (SAN ANTONIO, TEX.) (US/1055-9272) [23368973] 1886, **1805**

● THINK TANK DIRECTORY (US/1063-3340) [25982856] **4690**

THINKING (US/0190-3330) [04692647] 4363, **1907**

THINKING FAMILIES *SUSPENDED*. (US/1046-0845) [19646592] **1787**

THIRD BRANCH, THE (US/0040-6120) [01767445] **3143**

THIRD COAST *CEASED*. (US/0744-9372) [07969831] **2547**

THIRD DECADE, THE (US/0888-5230) [11427923] **2763**

THIRD DEGREE (US) [05626677] **3446**

THIRD EYE (US/0198-800X) [04352355] **3472**

THIRD EYE (TORONTO) (CN/0229-0715) [08028075] **4394**

● THIRD FORCE (1993) (US/1067-3237) [27190971] **4513**

THIRD GRADE READING ACHIEVEMENT TEST RESULT REPORT *See* READING ACHIEVEMENT TEST REPORT **1903**

THIRD OPINION (AT/1030-5467) [10305467] **2511**

THIRD PRESS REVIEW OF THIRD WORLD DIPLOMACY (US) [08189398] **4536**

THIRD RAIL (LOS ANGELES, CALIF.) (US/0741-5958) [03474069] 332, **3446**

THIRD TEXT (UK/0952-8822) [19988920] **366**

● ... THIRD WAVE DEVELOPMENT AWARDS, THE (US) [26018664] **1524**

THIRD WAY (UK/0309-3492) [04283424] **5004**

THIRD WORLD (BOCA RATON) (US/0273-2599) [06941611] **2912**

THIRD WORLD ECONOMIC HANDBOOK (UK) 937, **715**

THIRD WORLD ECONOMICS (MY/0128-4134) [26242702] **1524**

THIRD WORLD FORUM (CN/0317-0659) [02247679] **4498**

THIRD WORLD GUIDE (UY) [14951673] **4536**

THIRD WORLD IN PERSPECTIVE (US/0885-2200) [12598424] **5224**

THIRD WORLD LEGAL STUDIES (US/0895-5018) [09404219] **3136**

THIRD WORLD LIBRARIES (US/1052-3049) [22248373] **3253**

THIRD WORLD PLANNING REVIEW (UK/0142-7849) [05733646] **2836**

THIRD WORLD QUARTERLY (UK/0143-6597) [05255600] 4498, **1587**

THIRD WORLD REPORTS (UK) [09455226] **2912**

THIRD WORLD REPORTS (UK/0049-3740) [05508450] 1640, **4498**

THIRD WORLD RESOURCES (US/8755-8831) [11427269] **2912**

THIRD WORLD RESURGENCE (MY/0128-357X) [25613020] **2855**

THIRD WORLD REVIEW, THE (PK) [02240265] **1587**

THIRD WORLD SCIENCE & ENVIRONMENT PERSPECTIVES (II/0970-860X) [21144684] 2182, **5165**

THIRD WORLD UNITY (II) [04469262] **4536**

THIRD WORLD WEEK *CEASED*. (US/0894-1319) [15806860] **2912**

THIRDWORLD (PK) [19470744] **2912**

THIRTEEN (PORTLANDVILLE, N.Y.) (US/0747-9727) [10870394] **3446**

THIRTEEN TOWNS, THE (US) [01605594] **5699**

THIS AUSTRALIA *CEASED*. (AT/0725-4946) [12297172] **2511**

THIS BUSINESS OF TRUCKING (CN/0229-0065) [08063959] **5394**

Alphabetical Title Index

THIS ENGLAND (UK/0040-6171) [01607845] **2524**

THIS IS ALASKA (US/8756-4920) [11562233] **5492**

THIS IS LAGUNA (US/1058-3378) [24269575] **5492**

THIS IS SAR & H : HARBOURS & PIPELINES HANDBOOK (SA) [06220017] **5457**

THIS IS SAR & H : RAILWAYS HANDBOOK (SA) [06220614] **5437**

THIS IS SAR & H : ROAD TRANSPORT HANDBOOK (SA) [06187150] **5394**

THIS IS THE VOICE OF CASA (CN/0703-9360) [03960085] **767**

THIS IS WEST TEXAS *CEASED.* (US/0040-6201) [03898977] **2547**

THIS MAGAZINE (CN/0381-3746) [01775434] **2493**

THIS MONTH ON LONG ISLAND (US/0896-4599) [17164995] **5492**

●THIS OLD TRUCK (US/1068-1744) [27458101] **5426**

THIS PEOPLE (US/0273-6527) [06798701] **5004**

THIS ROCK (US/1049-4561) [21256233] **5004**

THIS WEEK AT CARLETON (1987) (CN/0836-4400) [17241986] **1850**

THIS WEEK (HARROW) (CN/0821-2333) [09502161] **5796**

THIS WEEK IN CENTRAL AMERICA (GT) [21224797] **2512**

THIS WEEK IN FARM BUREAU (GLENMONT, N.Y.) *See* FARM BUREAU PERSPECTIVE **84**

THIS WEEK IN MIAMI BEACH *See* KEY. THIS WEEK IN MIAMI BEACH **5482**

THIS WEEK IN PEACHTREE CITY (US/1050-6012) [21547903] **5655**

THIS WEEK IN THE VALLEY OF THE SUN. KEY (US/0193-7510) [05247506] **2547**

THIS WEEK MAGAZINE (PORTLAND, ORE.) (US/0746-1100) [09764385] **5734**

THISTLE, THE (CN) [11209313] **2493**

THOI TAP (US) [02242039] **2509**

THOI-TIET DAI-LUOC NGUYET-SAN *See* THOI TIET NGUYET SAN **1436**

THOI TIET NGUYET SAN (VM) [02240759] **1436**

THOMAS BROS. MAPS *See* PIERCE COUNTY POPULAR STREET ATLAS (CENSUS TRACT ED.) **2572**

THOMAS BROS. MAPS *See* LOS ANGELES COUNTY POPULAR STREET ATLAS (CENSUS TRACT ED.) **2568**

THOMAS BROS. MAPS *See* CALIFORNIA ROAD ATLAS AND TRAVEL GUIDE. ZIP CODE EDITION **2557**

THOMAS BUFFINGTON & ASSOCIATES *See* CAREER EDUCATION (WASHINGTON) **1911**

THOMAS BURKE MEMORIAL WASHINGTON STATE MUSEUM *See* BIENNIAL REPORT **4084**

THOMAS COLLEGE (WATERVILLE, MAINE) *See* ALUMNI DIRECTORY / THOMAS COLLEGE, WATERVILLE, MAINE **1099**

THOMAS COOK BUSINESS TRAVELER (US/0731-728X) [08239673] **715, 5492**

THOMAS COOK EUROPEAN TIMETABLE (UK/0952-620X) [17394405] **5437**

THOMAS COOK OVERSEAS TIMETABLE (UK/0144-7475) [07370492] **5437, 5492**

THOMAS COOK RAILPASS GUIDE *CEASED.* (UK) [19642329] **5492**

THOMAS FOOD INDUSTRY REGISTER (US/1061-284X) [21665317] **2359**

THOMAS GROCERY REGISTER. FOOD MARKETERS' HANDBOOK (US/0894-184X) [15297028] **2360**

THOMAS HARDY ANNUAL (LONDON, ENGLAND) (UK/0264-9454) [09847112] **3446**

THOMAS HARDY JOURNAL, THE (UK/0268-5419) [13112901] **3446**

THOMAS HARDY YEAR BOOK (UK/0082-416X) [01767452] **3446**

THOMAS JEFFERSON UNIVERSITY *See* AFFIRMATIVE ACTION PLAN - THOMAS JEFFERSON UNIVERSITY **4503**

THOMAS M. COOLEY LAW REVIEW (US) [24272323] **3064**

THOMAS MANN-GESELLSCHAFT *See* BLATTER DER THOMAS MANN-GESELLSCHAFT **3367**

THOMAS MANN JAHRBUCH (GW) [19117812] **3446**

THOMAS MANN STUDIEN (SZ/0563-4822) [03127359] **3446**

THOMAS-MANN-STUDIEN (GW) [01587541] **3446**

THOMAS REGISTER OF AMERICAN MANUFACTURERS AND THOMAS REGISTER CATALOG FILE (US/0362-7721) [01767453] **3489**

THOMAS REGISTER'S INBOUND LOGISTICS (US/0888-8493) [12438777] **853**

THOMAS REGISTER'S MID-YEAR GUIDE TO FACTORY AUTOMATION PRODUCTS, SYSTEMS, SERVICES *CEASED.* (US/0894-4288) [12867890] **3489, 1235**

THOMAS WOLFE REVIEW, THE (US/0276-5683) [07329827] **3446**

THOMASTON TIMES AND THE FREE PRESS, THE (US) [19334376] **5655**

THOMASVILLE TIMES-ENTERPRISE (US/0746-4894) [10074865] **5655**

THOMASVILLE TIMES (THOMASVILLE, ALA.) (US) [12574361] **5628**

THOMIST, THE (US/0040-6325) [01645845] **5005, 4363**

THOMPSON COURIER (THOMPSON, IOWA : 1926) (US) [16830114] **5673**

THOMPSON-OKANAGAN DEVELOPMENT REGION MANUFACTURERS DIRECTORY (CN/1183-1448) [24571474] **3489**

THOMSON BANK DIRECTORY (US/1057-8986) [23882349] **814**

THOMSON CREDIT UNION DIRECTORY (US/1061-1681) [22913918] **814**

THOMSON-CSF *See* REVUE TECHNIQUE THOMSON-CSF **2079**

THOMSON DESKTOP FINANCIAL DIRECTORY : ROUTING NUMBER INDEX (US/1062-0729) [25101856] **814**

THOMSON SAVINGS DIRECTORY (US/1062-1717) [24019929] **814**

THOMSON'S CONSTRUCTION AUSTRALIA (AT/1030-7036) [I10307036] **630**

THOMSON'S INTERNATIONAL BANKING REGULATOR (UK/0958-353X) [21962459] **814**

THOMSON'S LIQUOR GUIDE (AT/0313-0568) [I03130568] **2371**

THORACIC AND CARDIOVASCULAR SURGEON, THE (GW/0171-6425) [04817311] **3976**

THORAX (UK/0040-6376) [01590818] **3952**

THOREAU RESEARCH NEWSLETTER (US/1055-7326) [23284750] **4363**

THOREAU SOCIETY *See* THOREAU SOCIETY BULLETIN, THE **3446**

THOREAU SOCIETY *See* THOREAU SOCIETY BOOKLET **3446**

THOREAU SOCIETY BOOKLET (US/0362-2835) [01767454] **3446**

THOREAU SOCIETY BULLETIN, THE (US/0040-6406) [01767455] **435, 3446**

THORESBY SOCIETY *See* PUBLICATIONS OF THE THORESBY SOCIETY **5235**

THORIKOS (BE) [02096602] **284**

THORNDIKE ENCYCLOPEDIA OF BANKING AND FINANCIAL TABLES, THE (US) [04712627] **814**

THORNDIKE ENCYCLOPEDIA OF BANKING AND FINANCIAL TABLES. YEARBOOK (US/0196-7762) [02216105] **814**

THORNDYKE FILE, THE (US/0145-5575) [02749398] **3446**

THORNHILL MONTH (CN/0229-7248) [08292868] **2547**

THORNY TRAIL, THE (US/0094-0844) [01793569] **2475**

THOROTON SOCIETY, NOTTINGHAM, ENG *See* TRANSACTIONS OF THE THOROTON SOCIETY OF NOTTINGHAMSHIRE **2713**

THOROUGH (CN/0707-3968) [06131755] **1999**

THOROUGHBRED & CLASSIC CARS (UK) [02694286] **5426**

THOROUGHBRED BUSINESS (US/0883-8038) [12228080] **2803**

THOROUGHBRED OF CALIFORNIA, THE (US/0049-3821) [03943697] **2803**

THOROUGHBRED RECORD (1967) (US/0162-3117) [04142630] **2803**

THOROUGHBRED RECORD. FOREIGN STATISTICAL REVIEW, THE (US) [11826383] **2803**

THOROUGHBRED STALLION RECORDS OF ... (US/0739-5809) [09591266] **2803**

THOROUGHBRED TIMES (US/0887-2244) [12704359] **2803**

THOROUGHBREDS (US/0160-418X) [03678958] **2803**

THORP COURIER, THE (US/0885-2375) [12603425] **5771**

THORPE ROM (US) **3253**

THOSE ANNOYING POST BROS *CEASED.* (CN/0827-4703) [11979847] **4867**

THOUGHT & ACTION (WASHINGTON, D.C.) (US/0748-8475) [11018391] **1850**

THOUGHT (NEW YORK) *CEASED.* (US/0040-6457) [01767458] **5005**

THOUGHTS FOR ALL SEASONS (US/0886-6481) [10367167] **3446**

THOUGHTS ON ECONOMICS (BG) [07664269] **5045, 1587**

THOUGHTS ON INTERNATIONAL DEVELOPMENT (CN/0707-7815) [02443520] **1640**

THOUSAND ISLANDS SUN AND ON THE ST. LAWRENCE (US) [25104593] **5721**

THRACO-DACIA (RM/0259-1081) [09491975] **2712**

THRASHER (SAN FRANCISCO, CALIF.) (US/0889-0692) [13789617] **4926**

THREADS LONDON (UK/0954-7096) [I09547096] **1205**

THREADS MAGAZINE (US/0882-7370) [11951760] **5359**

THREADS OF LIFE (US/0895-8416) [10865051] **2475**

THREE FORKS HERALD AND MANHATTAN INTERMOUNTAIN PRESS (US) [12965129] **5706**

THREE RIVERS HEALTH SYSTEMS AGENCY, INC *See* DRAFT, FULL DESIGNATION RENEWAL APPLICATION **3573**

THREE RIVERS POETRY JOURNAL *CEASED.* (US/0362-4846) [02079993] **3472**

THREE R'S FOR TEACHERS. RESEARCH, REPORTS, AND REVIEWS (US) **1907**

THREE SISTERS (US) [03130150] **2547**

THREE VILLAGE HERALD (US/1053-2684) [11062930] **5721**

THREE WIRE WINTER (US) [03772908] **2763**

THREE-YEAR REPORT / FUND FOR THE CITY OF NEW YORK (US/0741-8213) [09010428] **5312**

THREEPENNY REVIEW, THE (US/0275-1410) [07065494] **332, 3446**

THRESHOLD *CEASED.* (UK/0040-6562) [01767460] **3446**

THRESHOLD (CHICAGO, ILL.) *CEASED.* (US/0736-1149) [08852109] **310**

THRESHOLD LIMIT VALUES AND BIOLOGICAL EXPOSURE INDICES FOR ... (US) [20816059] **3983, 2871**

THRESHOLD OF FANTASY (US/0277-7800) [07643083] **3446**

THRESHOLDS IN EDUCATION (US/0196-9641) [04472889] **1787**

THRIFT REGULATOR (US) **814**

●THRIFT SHOPPING IN YOUR NEIGHBORHOOD (US/1060-961X) [25276209] **1300**

THRIFTY NICKEL WEEKLY NEWSPAPER. BIRMINGHAM (US) **5628**

THROCKMORTON TRIBUNE (US) [16686455] **5755**

THROMBOSIS AND HAEMOSTASIS (GW/0340-6245) [02208259] **3801**

THROMBOSIS RESEARCH (US/0049-3848) [00985997] **3710**

THROMBOSIS RESEARCH. SUPPLEMENT (US/0896-0569) [04140897] **3774**

THROMBOTIC AND HAEMORRHAGIC DISORDERS *CEASED.* (AU/0934-9669) [22449934] **3774**

THROMBOTIC AND HEMORRHAGIC DISORDERS (AU/0934-9669) **3645**

THROUGH THE LOUPE *See* LOUPE (SANTA MONICA, CALIF.) **2915**

THROUGH THE YEARS (CN/0826-4775) [11245844] **2763**

THRUPUT (US/0147-0698) [03079501] **814**

THRUST *CEASED.* (US/0190-3381) [04698325] **1714**

●THRUST (AUSTIN, TEX.) (US/1064-0126) [26190884] **3446**

THRUST FOR EDUCATIONAL LEADERSHIP (US/1055-2243) [22761173] **1873**

THS HEALTH SUMMARY (UK/0266-9056) [I02669056] **4805**

THUERINGER ZAHNAERZTEBLATT (GW/0939-5687) [I09395687] **1336**

THUMPER (ST. ALBERT, ALTA.) (CN/0821-7114) [10450911] **4926**

THUNDER BAY CAMPING GUIDE (CN/0380-6197) [02578680] **4879**

THUNDER BAY HISTORICAL MUSEUM SOCIETY *See* PAPERS AND RECORDS - THUNDER BAY HISTORICAL MUSEUM SOCIETY **4095**

THUNDER Alphabetical Title Index

THUNDER BAY MAGAZINE (CN/0823-6542) [09929599] **2547**

THUNDER BAY METRO TRADE INDEX (CN/1187-0796) [25066840] **853**

THUNDER BAY MUSEUM NEWSLETTER (CN/1184-6216) [24266547] **4097**

THUNDER COUNTRY OUTDOORS (CN/0318-8477) [02443167] **4879**

THUNDERBIRD ILLUSTRATED (US/0145-4110) [02732690] **5426**

THUNDERBIRD INTERNATIONAL, THE (US/0160-9823) [03795560] **888**

THUNDERBIRD (PULLMAN, WASH.), THE (US/0737-5557) [09248175] **284**

THUNDERCATS MAGAZINE *CEASED.* (US/0890-0256) [14122846] **1070**

THUNDERMUG REPORT (US/1055-0232) [23059609] **3446**

THURGOOD MARSHALL LAW REVIEW (US/0749-1646) [08824103] **3064**

THURIES MAGAZINE (FR/0989-6333) [I09896333] **2793**

THURN UND TAXIS-STUDIEN (GW/0563-4970) [02096590] **2631**

THURSDAY REPORT, THE (CN/0704-5506) [03797329] **1850**

THY KINGDOM COME (BURNABY, B.C.) (CN/0840-5778) [19962545] **5005**

THYME (CN/0705-9027) [04098096] **2763**

THYMUS (NE/0165-6090) [05871435] **3677**

THYMUS UPDATE (SZ/0896-341X) [17004985] **3645**

THYRISTOR DISCONTINUED DEVICES D.A.T.A BOOK *CEASED.* (US/0730-4838) [07319651] **2084**

THYRISTORS, RECTIFIERS, AND DIACS (US/0092-7228) [01791160] **2084**

THYROID HORMONES (UK/0142-8349) [I01428349] **3645**

THYROID (NEW YORK, N.Y.) (US/1050-7256) [21579335] **3733**

THYROID TODAY (US/0190-0625) [04127166] **3733**

THYSSEN EDELSTAHL TECHNISCHE BERICHTE (GW/0724-7265) [06597274] **4021**

TI CHEN (CH) [08752003] **1399**

TI CHEN KUNG CHENG YU KUNG CHENG CHEN TUNG (CC) [10476903] **1999**

TI CHEN YEN CHIU (CC) [10052702] **1411**

TI CHI TSE LIANG (CH) [10818360] **1999**

TI CHIU KO HSUEH : WU-HAN TI CHIH HSUEH YUAN HSUEH PAO (CC/1000-2383) [08595463] **1361**

TI. GESCHAFTSREISE (GW/0723-6875) [I07236875] **5492**

TI LI CHI KAN (SI) [02113410] **2577**

TI NEWS / THE TEXTILE INSTITUTE (UK) [17417993] **5359**

TI, TECHNICAL INFORMATION FOR INDUSTRY (SA) [02069884] **5165**

TI TSAO (CC) [11630396] **4926**

TI TZU KUAN TSE PAO KAO (CC) [08964285] **4445**

TI TZU KUAN TSE PAO KAO (KUANG-CHOU TI TZU TAI) (CH) [09040383] **4445**

TI YU KO HSUEH (CC) [11630313] 1859, **4926**

TIAC NEWSLETTER (CN/0701-1741) [11422266] **5492**

TIANJIN DAXUE XUEBAO (CC/0493-2137) [09027949] **5165**

TIANJIN YIYAO (CC/0253-9896) [01797481] 4330, **3645**

TIANTI WULI XUEBAO (CC/0253-2379) [08617689] 401, **4423**

TIAOWEI FUSHIPIN KEJI (CC/0253-6080) [08512413] **4199**

TIAZHELOE MASHINOSTROENIE (MOSCOW, R.S.F.S.R. : 1990) (RU) [22363697] **2130**

TIAZHELOE MASHINOSTROENIE (MOSCOW, RUSSIA : 1990). ENGLISH. SOVIET JOURNAL OF HEAVY MACHINERY *See* RUSSIAN JOURNAL OF HEAVY MACHINERY **2128**

TIBET JOURNAL, THE (II) [02641780] **2666**

TIBET PRESS WATCH (US/1049-2666) [21177493] **2666**

TIBETAN BULLETIN (II/0254-9808) [I02549808] 4363, **5005**

TIBETAN BULLETIN (DHARMSALA, INDIA : 1981) (II) [12735223] **2666**

TIBETAN MEDICINE (II/0970-1257) [08161953] **3645**

TIBETAN REVIEW (II/0040-6708) [01695364] 2509, **2577**

TIBIA (GW) [04351600] **4156**

TIC NEWS (US) [03860513] **2509**

TICKER TAPE PARADE (US/0883-5322) [12210439] **814**

TICKER TAPE (TORONTO) (CN/0710-5061) [08555926] **5005**

TICKETING HANDBOOK (CN/0256-4459) [07267355] **37**

TICKLEACE (CN/0823-6399) [09951436] **3472**

TICO TIMES, THE (CR) [05069394] **5799**

TIDAL CURRENT TABLES. ATLANTIC COAST OF NORTH AMERICA (US/0501-8234) [02458466] **4184**

TIDAL CURRENT TABLES. PACIFIC COAST OF NORTH AMERICA AND ASIA FOR THE YEAR ... (US) [02458480] **4184**

TIDAL GRAVITY CORRECTIONS FOR ... (NE) [02757358] **1411**

TIDAL PREDICTIONS AUSTRALIA, NORTH-WEST COAST FOR THE YEAR ... PUBLIC WORKS DEPARTMENT, WESTERN AUSTRALIA, HARBORS AND RIVERS BRANCH (AT) [21010290] **1457**

TIDE, DISTANCE AND SPEED TABLES (UK) [07184654] **4184**

TIDE (LEWISPORTE) (CN/0713-0562) [08584519] **5796**

TIDE TABLES, HIGH AND LOW WATER PREDICTIONS, EAST COAST OF NORTH AND SOUTH AMERICA, INCLUDING GREENLAND (US/0098-6488) [02242236] **1457**

TIDE TABLES ... HIGH AND LOW WATER PREDICTIONS, WEST COAST OF NORTH AND SOUTH AMERICA, INCLUDING THE HAWAIIAN ISLANDS (US) [02458490] **4184**

TIDE : TERI INFORMATION DIGEST ON ENERGY (II/0971-085X) [26906886] **1959**

TIDEPOOL (HAMILTON) (CN/0824-7579) [11431422] **3446**

TIDES OF CHANGE (CN/0841-7563) [18958369] **2207**

TIDEVANDSTABELLER. DANMARK (DK) [28768896] **4184**

TIDEWATER ADVANTAGE. NEWPORT NEWS EDITION, THE (US/0744-7116) [08508124] **5759**

●TIDEWATER VIRGINIA FAMILIES (US/1061-8678) [25484851] **2475**

TIDINGS INTERNATIONAL BUSINESS DIRECTORY (II) [09626770] **1587**

TIDINGS (LOS ANGELES) (US/0040-6791) [03943842] **5037**

TIDINGS, WEST LINN (US/0194-9640) [05159263] **5734**

TIDINGS (WESTERLY, R.I.) (US/0897-0335) [17404441] **2763**

TIDNINGEN BYGGINDUSTRIN (SW/0349-3733) [09539948] **630**

TIDSKRIFT FOR ARKITEKTURFORSKNING *See* NORDISK ARKITEKTURFORSKNING **305**

TIDSKRIFT FOR DOKUMENTATION (SW/0040-6872) [08592614] **3253**

TIDSKRIFT FOR LITTERATURVETENSKAP (SW/0282-7913) [01767474] **3446**

TIDSKRIFT FOR MEDICINSK OCH TEKNISK FOTOGRAFI (SW/1100-6323) [I11006323] 3645, **4377**

TIDSKRIFT FOR POSTVASENDET *See* NORDISK POSTTIDSKRIFT **1146**

TIDSKRIFT FOR RATTSSOCIOLOGI (SW) [10960177] **3064**

TIDSKRIFT I FORTIFIKATION (SW/0040-6937) [07498101] **4059**

TIDSKRIFT (SUOMEN LAINOPILLINEN YHDISTYS) (FI/0040-6953) [01605004] **3064**

TIDSSKRIFT FOR DANSK FAAREAVL (DK/0906-1746) [I09061746] **223**

TIDSSKRIFT FOR DANSKE SYGEHUSE (DK/0040-702X) [12291654] **3793**

TIDSSKRIFT FOR DEN NORSKE LAEGEFORENING; TIDSSKRIFT FOR PRAKTISK MEDISIN. THE JOURNAL OF THE NORWEGIAN MEDICAL ASSOCIATION (NO/0029-2281) [01639226] **3645**

TIDSSKRIFT FOR JORDEMODRE (DK) **141**

TIDSSKRIFT FOR NORSK PSYKOLOGFORENING (NO/0332-6470) [I03326470] **4620**

TIDSSKRIFT FOR PLANTEAVL (DK/0040-7135) [04689653] **189**

TIDSSKRIFT FOR RETTSVIDENSKAP (NO/0040-7143) [01767482] **3064**

TIDSSKRIFT FOR SAMFUNNSFORSKNING (NO/0040-716X) [01767483] **5224**

TIDSSKRIFT FOR SVSEN (DK/0040-7186) [07490438] **4184**

TIDSSKRIFT FOR TANDLGER (COPENHAGEN, DENMARK : 1981) (DK/0108-1284) [11529008] **1336**

TIDSSKRIFT FOR TEOLOGI OG KIRKE (NO/0040-7194) [01680955] **5005**

TIDSSKRIFTIE ANTROPOLOGI (DK) [24121286] **246**

TIE *See* SOUTHERN SEMINARY **4998**

TIE JA LIIKENNE (FI) [01795186] **2032**

TIE-LINES (US) **4805**

TIE (LOUISVILLE), THE (US/0040-7232) [01776727] **5005**

TIE REPORT (NE/0196-254X) [05786289] 1524, **1714**

TIEDONANTOJA - MAATALOUDEN TALOUDELLINEN TUTKIMUSLAITOS (FI/0788-5199) [I07885199] 1524, **141**

TIEDONANTOJA - RIISTA- JA KALATALOUDEN TUTKIMUSLAITOS KALANTUKIMUSOSASTO (FI/0355-0648) [02755324] **2315**

TIEDONANTOJA / VALTION MAITOTALOUDEN TUTKIMUSLAITOS (FI/0358-0202) [09091391] **199**

TIEDONANTOJA (VALTION MAITOTALOUSKOELAITOS (FINLAND)) *See* TIEDONANTOJA / VALTION MAITOTALOUDEN TUTKIMUSLAITOS **199**

TIEFBAU, INGENIEURBAU, STRASSENBAU (GW/0340-5079) [02886958] **2032**

TIEH TAO HSUEH PAO (CC) [20041095] **5437**

TIELIIKENNEONNETTOMUUDET (FI) [06876125] **5445**

TIEMPO ACTUAL / JUNTA DE PENSIONES Y JUBILACIONES DEL MAGISTERIO NACIONAL (CR) [07341191] **2524**

TIEMPO, EL (SP) **5810**

TIEMPO, EL (CK) [04650471] **5799**

TIEMPO LIBRE / PUBLICACION SEMANAL DE UNO MAS UNO (MX) [09746257] **4855**

TIEMPOS MEDICOS DE ESPANA (SP/0210-9999) [I02109999] **1788**

TIEN-CHIN CHIAO YU (CH) [09289335] **1788**

TIEN-CHIN WEN SHIH TZU LIAO HSUAN CHI (CC) [07480105] **2666**

TIEN CHING (CC) [11685336] **4926**

TIEN HSIA TSA CHIH (CH) [09702824] **715**

TIEN HSIN CHI SHU (JEN MIN YU TIEN CHU PAN SHE) (CH) [09456222] **2084**

TIEN HSIN CHI SHU TELECOMS TECHNICAL QUARTERLY (CH) [08706211] **5165**

TIEN PHONG (US/0191-2097) [04781014] **2509**

TIEN SHENG CHIEH (HK) [03325016] **2084**

TIEN WEN HSUEH PAO (CC/0001-5245) [02093782] **401**

T'IEN WEN T'UNG HSUN (CC) [05188988] **401**

TIEN YING TSO PIN (CH) [08966293] **4078**

TIERARZTLICHE PRAXIS (GW/0303-6286) [01150159] **5523**

TIERARZTLICHE PRAXIS. SUPPLEMENT (GW/0930-6447) [15689330] **5523**

TIERARZTLICHE UMSCHAU (GW/0049-3864) [01641014] **5523**

TIERERNAHRUNG UND FUTTERUNG (GW/0138-4309) [04677671] **204**

TIERFREUND NURNBERG (GW/0342-3018) [I03423018] 474, 5598, **1070**

TIERHALTUNG (SZ) [03693088] **223**

TIERLABORATORIUM / HERAUSGEGEBEN VON DEN ZENTRALEN TIERLABORATORIEN UND DEM INSTITUT FUER VERSUCHSTIERKUNDE DER FREIEN UNIVERSITAT BERLIN (GW) [06794654] 3646, **5523**

TIERRA AMIGA (UY) [27787445] **2182**

TIERRA NUEVA (CL) [01792131] 5264, **5005**

TIERRA (SOUTHERN TEXAS ARCHAEOLOGICAL ASSOCIATION), LA (US/0163-0695) [04283371] **284**

TIERRA Y LIBERTAD (US) [06987392] **4513**

TIERRAS DE LEON (SP/0495-5773) [07486535] **2712**

TIERS MONDE INGENIERIE : TMI (FR) **1999**

TIERS MONDE (PARIS) (FR/0040-7356) [04605769] **1640**

TIERZUCHT (GW/0373-1677) [02618534] **223**

TIERZUCHTER, DER (GW/0040-7364) [02618492] **223**

TIES (PHILADELPHIA, PA.) (US/1041-6587) [18821597] **5165**

Alphabetical Title Index — TIMBERLINE

TIETOJA KAUPUNGEISTA, KAUPPALOISTA JA KAUPUNKILIITOSTA (FI) [02242718] **5264**

TIETOPALVELU (FI/0782-825X) [I0782825X] **3253**

TIFA SASTRA (IO) [03147096] **3446**

TIFTON GAZETTE (DAILY), THE (US/1065-2884) [19227197] **5655**

TIG BRIEF : THE INSPECTOR GENERAL (US/8750-376X) [09449760] **4059**

TIGARD TIMES (US/8750-0841) [10961165] **5734**

TIGER BEAT (US/0040-7380) [02250584] 4156, **1070**

TIGER-CAT FACT BOOK / TIGER-CATS FOOTBALL (CN/0710-1643) [08205643] **4926**

TIGER RAG (US/0744-7604) [04919464] **4926**

●TIGER TRIBE (US/1065-6650) [26668233] **5523**

TIGERPAPER (TH) [04599926] **2207**

TIGHTWAD GAZETTE (US/1065-366X) [24182829] 2221, **2793**

TIGHTWIRE (CN/0702-9004) [18110446] **3178**

TIJARAT AL-ARAB (UA) [05268948] **853**

TIJARAT AL-JUMLAH FI AL-QUITA AL-KHASS ADA SHARIKAT AL-MUSAHAMAH WA-DHAT AL-MASULIYAH AL-MAHDUDAH WA-AL-TAWSIYAH BI-AL-ASHUM WA-FURU AL-SHARIKAT AL-AJNABIYAH / AL-JIHAZ AL-MARKAZI LIL-TABIAH AL-AMMAH WA-AL-IHSA (UA) [08815825] **715**

TIJARAT AL-TAJZIAH FI AL-QUITA AL-KHASS, KHAMSAT MUSHTAGHILIN FA-AKTHAR, ADA AL-SHARIKAT AL-MUSAHIMAH WA-DHAT AL-MASULIYAH AL-MAHDUDAH WA-AL-TAWSIYAH BI-AL-ASHUM WA-FURU AL-SHARIKAT AL-AJNABIYAH / AL-JIHAZ AL-MARKAZI LIL-TABIAH AL-AMMAH (UA) [09352064] **958**

TIJDSCHRIFT FINANCIEEL MANAGEMENT (NE/0167-0581) [I01670581] **814**

TIJDSCHRIFT HOGER ONDERWIJS (NE) **1850**

TIJDSCHRIFT INKOOP EN LOGISTIEK (NE) **952**

TIJDSCHRIFT KANKER (NE/0166-3925) [04701250] **3824**

TIJDSCHRIFT RECHTSDOCUMENTATIE (BE/0771-0704) [08735285] **3064**

TIJDSCHRIFT VAN DE NATIONALE BANK VAN BELGIE (BE/0772-2621) [I07722621] **814**

TIJDSCHRIFT VAN DE NEDERLANDSE VERENIGING VOOR KLINISCHE CHEMIE (NE/0168-8472) [14943305] **994**

TIJDSCHRIFT VAN DE VERENIGING VOOR NEDERLANDSE MUZIEKGESCHIEDENIS (NE/0042-3874) [09199441] **4156**

TIJDSCHRIFT VOOR ADMINISTRATEURS EN CONTROLLERS (NE) **752**

TIJDSCHRIFT VOOR AGOLOGIE (NE/0168-8626) [21546253] **5224**

TIJDSCHRIFT VOOR ALCOHOL, DRUGS EN ANDERE PSYCHOTROPE STOFFEN (NE/0378-2778) [02909432] **1349**

TIJDSCHRIFT VOOR ANTILLIAANS RECHT, JUSTICIA / UITGEVER STICHTING TIJDSCHRIFT VOOR ANTILLIAANS RECHT, JUSTICIA (NA) [14977858] **3064**

TIJDSCHRIFT VOOR ARBEIDSVRAAGSTUKKEN (NE/0169-2216) [I01692216] **947**

TIJDSCHRIFT VOOR ARBITRAGE (NE/0167-1359) [I01671359] **3064**

TIJDSCHRIFT VOOR BELGISCH BURGERLIJK RECHT : TBBR (BE/0775-2814) [17685676] **3091**

TIJDSCHRIFT VOOR BESTUURSWETENCHAPPEN EN PUBLEKRECHT (BE/0040-7437) [I00407437] **3064**

TIJDSCHRIFT VOOR BESTUURSWETENSCHAPPEN See TIJDSCHRIFT VOOR BESTUURSWETENCHAPPEN EN PUBLEKRECHT **3064**

TIJDSCHRIFT VOOR BESTUURSWETENSCHAPPEN EN PUBLEKRECHT (BE) **4690**

TIJDSCHRIFT VOOR CONSUMENTENRECHT (NE/0169-1570) [19089018] **1300**

TIJDSCHRIFT VOOR CRIMINOLOGIE (NE/0165-182X) [03603181] **3178**

TIJDSCHRIFT VOOR DE GESCHIEDENIS DER GENEESKUNDE, NATUURWETENSCHAPPEN, WISKUNDE EN TECHNIEK See GEWINA **5108**

TIJDSCHRIFT VOOR DE STUDIE VAN DE VERLICHTING See TIJDSCHRIFT VOOR DE STUDIE VAN DE VERLICHTING EN HET VRIJE DENKEN **3446**

TIJDSCHRIFT VOOR DE STUDIE VAN DE VERLICHTING EN HET VRIJE DENKEN (BE) [07965469] **3446**

TIJDSCHRIFT VOOR DIERGENEESKUNDE (NE/0040-7453) [01767489] **5523**

TIJDSCHRIFT VOOR ECONOMIE EN MANAGEMENT (BE/0772-7674) [02243213] **1524**

TIJDSCHRIFT VOOR ECONOMISCHE EN SOCIALE GEOGRAFIE : TESG (NE/0040-747X) [07668711] 2837, 2577, **1524**

TIJDSCHRIFT VOOR ENTOMOLOGIE (NE/0040-7496) [01588093] **5614**

TIJDSCHRIFT VOOR ERGONOMIE (NE/0921-4348) [I09214348] **2130**

TIJDSCHRIFT VOOR FAMILIE- EN JEUGDRECHT (NE) [07288756] **3122**

TIJDSCHRIFT VOOR FILOSOFIE (BE/0040-750X) [02079217] **4364**

TIJDSCHRIFT VOOR GENEESKUNDE (BE/0371-683X) [01778416] **3802**

TIJDSCHRIFT VOOR GENEESKUNDE & ETHIEK (NE/0925-2819) [I09252819] **3646**

TIJDSCHRIFT VOOR GERONTOLOGIE EN GERIATRIE (NE/0167-9228) [08625701] **3755**

TIJDSCHRIFT VOOR GESCHIEDENIS (1920) (NE/0040-7518) [07508094] **2631**

●TIJDSCHRIFT VOOR HYGIENE EN INFEKTIEPREVENTIE (NE/0928-2998) [I09282998] **3793**

TIJDSCHRIFT VOOR KINDERGENEESKUNDE (NE/0376-7442) [02680500] **3912**

TIJDSCHRIFT VOOR KREATIEVE THERAPIE (NE) **5188**

TIJDSCHRIFT VOOR MARKETING (NE) **937**

TIJDSCHRIFT VOOR MILIEU EN RECHT (NE/0165-1137) [02658575] **3116**

TIJDSCHRIFT VOOR NEDERLANDSE TAAL-EN LETTERKUNDE (NE/0040-7550) [08964106] **3328**

TIJDSCHRIFT VOOR ONDERWIJSRESEARCH (NE/0166-591X) [07048087] **5165**

TIJDSCHRIFT VOOR OPENBAAR BESTUUR See OPENBAAR BESTUUR **4671**

TIJDSCHRIFT VOOR OUDE MUZIEK (NE/0920-0649) [I09200649] **4156**

TIJDSCHRIFT VOOR PARAPSYCHOLOGIE (NE) [03138342] **4243**

TIJDSCHRIFT VOOR PHILOSOPHIE (BE) [10152740] **4364**

TIJDSCHRIFT VOOR PRIVAATRECHT (BE) [01794685] **3091**

TIJDSCHRIFT VOOR PSYCHIATRIE (NE/0303-7339) [00947250] **3937**

TIJDSCHRIFT VOOR PSYCHOTHERAPIE (NE/0165-1188) [I01651188] **4620**

TIJDSCHRIFT VOOR PSYCHOTHERAPIE (NE) **3937**

TIJDSCHRIFT VOOR RECHTSGESCHIEDENIS (NE/0040-7585) [01585956] **3064**

TIJDSCHRIFT VOOR SEKSUOLOGIE (NE/0167-5915) **5188**

TIJDSCHRIFT VOOR SKANDINAVISTIEK (NE/0168-2148) [10932205] 3446, **3328**

TIJDSCHRIFT VOOR SOCIAAL WETENSCHAPPELIJK ONDERZOEK VAN DE LANDBOUW (NE/0921-481X) [I0921481X] 1524, **141**

TIJDSCHRIFT VOOR SOCIALE GESCHIEDENIS (NE/0303-9935) [02242869] **4548**

TIJDSCHRIFT VOOR SOCIALE GEZONDHEIDSZORG : TSG : 14-DAAGS BLAD VAN DE ALGEMENE NEDERLANDSE VERENIGING VOOR SOCIALE GEZONDHEIDSZORG (NE/0920-0517) [19743605] **4805**

TIJDSCHRIFT VOOR SOCIALE WETENSCHAPPEN (BE/0040-7615) [02079897] **5224**

TIJDSCHRIFT VOOR SOCIOLOGIE (BE) [09698667] **5264**

TIJDSCHRIFT VOOR THEOLOGIE (NE/0168-9959) [01774143] **5005**

TIJDSCHRIFT VOOR VERVOERSWETENSCHAP (NE/0040-7623) [07498126] **5394**

TIJDSCHRIFT VOOR VERZORGENDEN (NE/0921-5832) [18418513] **4805**

TIJDSCHRIFT VOOR VROUWENSTUDIES (NE) [07989954] **5567**

TIJDSCHRIFT VOOR WELZIJNSWERK (BE) **5312**

TIJDSCHRIFTERN VOOR OPPERVLAKTETECHNIEKEN EN CORROSIEBERSTRIJDING (NE) **4022**

TIJUANA MAGAZINE (US/0274-6859) [06504453] **2547**

TIKALIA (GT) [10585116] **141**

TIKHOOKEANSKAIA GEOLOGIA (RU/0207-4028) [08490626] **1399**

TIKHOOKEANSKAIA GEOLOGIIA. ENGLISH (SZ/8755-755X) [11412708] **1399**

TIKKER (NE/0165-0890) 1070, **3446**

TIKKUN (US/0887-9982) [13451367] **2274**

TILASTOKATSAUKSIA (FI/0015-2390) [04552653] **5345**

TILASTOKIRJASTO (FINLAND) See ULKOMAISET TILASTOKAUSIJULKAISUT **5345**

TILASTOTIEDOTUS. KT (FI/0355-2276) [06157201] **1587**

TILASTOTIEDOTUS. VL (FI/0358-6243) [19481202] **5345**

TILASTOTIEDOTUS. YR See TUKKUKAUPAN TILINPAATOSTILASTO **855**

●TILBURG FOREIGN LAW REVIEW (NE/0926-874X) [25895676] 3136, **3064**

TILBURY TIMES (CN) **5796**

TILBURY TIMES (CN/0834-7344) [16396183] **5796**

TILE & BRICK INTERNATIONAL (GW/0938-9806) [I09389806] **630**

TILE & DECORATIVE SURFACES (US/0192-9550) [05095483] **2907**

●TILE DESIGN & INSTALLATION (US/1077-6974) [30859401] **2594**

TILE ITALIA (IT/1120-7884) [11207884] **2594**

TILE WORLD See TILE DESIGN & INSTALLATION **2594**

TILIFIZYUN AL-KHALIJ (SU) [11154777] **1141**

TILK : NELJANNESVUOSIKATSAUS (FI) [06501559] **5345**

TILLER (ALEXANDRIA, VA.), THE (US/1068-896X) [15183567] **4184**

TILLER AND TOILER (1986), THE (US/0888-1189) [13521179] **5678**

TILR. TRANSNATIONAL IMMIGRATION LAW REPORTER (US/0271-2202) [05121266] **1921**

TIM : TRAVEL INFORMATION MANUAL (NE) [09537780] **5492**

TIMARIT MALS OG MENNINGAR (IC) [09505571] **3355**

TIMBER BULLETIN (SZ/0255-4356) [12129772] **2405**

TIMBER DEVELOPMENT ASSOCIATION OF INDIA See JOURNAL - TIMBER DEVELOPMENT ASSOCIATION OF INDIA **2402**

TIMBER ECONOMY (UK) [20299016] **2405**

TIMBER FOR ARCHITECTS (UK) 310, **2405**

TIMBER FRAME HOMES (US/1054-1136) [22752900] **630**

TIMBER GROWER (UK/0040-7763) [02256605] **2396**

TIMBER HARVESTING (US/0160-6433) [03536224] 4239, **2405**

TIMBER MART-SOUTH (US/0194-5955) [04844296] **2405**

TIMBER MART-SOUTH ... YEARBOOK (US/0882-732X) [11102252] **2405**

TIMBER NOTE (AT) [09525821] **2397**

TIMBER PROCESSING (US/0885-906X) [12758347] **2405**

TIMBER PRODUCER, THE (US/0886-1242) [11438496] **2405**

TIMBER RESEARCH AND DEVELOPMENT ASSOCIATION See TRADA : REPORT OF THE DIRECTOR OF THE TIMBER RESEARCH AND DEVELOPMENT ASSOCIATION **2405**

TIMBER RESEARCH AND DEVELOPMENT ASSOCIATION See RESEARCH STUDY TD/RS **2404**

TIMBER REVIEW (US/0748-9129) [11005787] **2405**

●TIMBER TIMES (US/1065-7010) [26684392] **2405**

TIMBER TRADE REVIEW (MY) [01784321] 2405, **1629**

TIMBER TRADES JOURNAL & WOOD PROCESSING (UK) [07163869] **2405**

TIMBER TRAILS (US/0735-018X) [07193983] **2475**

TIMBER UPDATE, TIMBER MARKETS THROUGH 1990 (US/0740-9877) [10041977] **2405**

TIMBER/WEST (US/0192-0642) [05065344] **2405**

TIMBERLINE (PEMBROKE) (CN/1183-9686) [25652181] **2475**

TIMBERLINES — Alphabetical Title Index

TIMBERLINES (CN/0833-0689) [15063183] **2397**

TIMBERTALK (US/0744-8511) [08598353] **2405**

TIMBERTOWN LOG (US/0740-5367) [04955512] **2475**

TIMBERTRADER NEWS (1990) (AT/1035-4298) [I10354298] **2405**

TIMBRE (WOODINVILLE, WASH.) (US/8750-782X) [11759737] **4156**

TIMBUKTU *CEASED.* (US/0896-3878) [17061982] **3446**

● TIME & SOCIETY (UK/0961-463X) [25927736] **4364**

TIME & TIDE (II/0040-7836) [01797739] 1141, **4078**

TIME ANNUAL : THE YEAR IN REVIEW / BY THE EDITORS OF TIME (US) [05280441] **2631**

TIME AUSTRALIA (AT/0818-0628) [I08180628] **2511**

TIME BARRIER EXPRESS (US/0099-0396) [02242511] **4156**

TIME (CHICAGO, ILL.) (US/0040-781X) [01767509] **2493**

TIME FINANCE ADJUSTERS (FIRM) *See* OFFICIAL GUIDE - TIME FINANCE ADJUSTERS (FIRM) **802**

TIME-LIFE ACCESS. APPLE *CEASED.* (US/0743-5878) [10613856] **1273**

TIME-LIFE ACCESS. IBM (US/0743-5886) [10613846] **1273**

TIME-LIFE FILMS *See* TLF QUARTERLY **4079**

TIME MANAGEMENT LETTER (AT) **888**

TIME MANAGEMENT REPORT (CN/0228-4189) [07822633] **888**

TIME OUT (UK/0049-3910) [13914830] **2524**

TIME OUT (KANNAPOLIS, N.C.) (US/8756-8497) [11695411] **4926**

TIME-SENSITIVE DELIVERY GUIDE *CEASED.* (US/0731-0722) [07921094] **5394**

TIME SERIES OF OCEAN MEASUREMENTS (FR) [10809280] **1457**

● TIME TABLE OF HISTORY. BUSINESS, POLITICS, AND MEDIA (US/1054-5042) [22904579] **2631**

TIME TABLE OF HISTORY. SCIENCE AND INNOVATION (US/1041-2891) [18721984] **715**

TIMEKEEPER'S HANDBOOK (US) [04051929] **2837**

TIMELINE (US/0748-9579) [11039559] **2763**

● TIMELINE (PALO ALTO, CALIF.) (US/1061-2734) [25226179] **4498**

● TIMELINES (EUGENE, OR) (US/1074-1593) [29610894] **2253**

TIMEPIECE (UK) [08138728] **2916**

TIMEPIECE (NAPLES, FLA.) (US/0748-8637) [08558408] **2763**

TIMER DIGEST (US) **917**

TIMES 500 *See* TIMES 1000, THE **715**

TIMES 1000, THE (UK) [04923752] **715**

TIMES AND DEMOCRAT, THE (US) [13640331] **5743**

TIMES ARGUS (BARRE, VT.) (US) [13687824] **5757**

TIMES-ARGUS (CENTRAL CITY, KY) (US) [08807549] **5682**

TIMES-BULLETIN, THE (US/8750-1503) [11058353] **5730**

TIMES BUSINESS DIRECTORY OF SINGAPORE (SI) [10524794] **715**

TIMES (CANAL WINCHESTER, OHIO) (US/0884-4135) [12560151] **5730**

TIMES-CHRONICLE (US/0746-4606) [10053098] **5740**

TIMES CLARION (HARLOWTON, MONT.), THE (US/0889-5627) [13776802] **5706**

TIMES COLONIST (VICTORIA) (CN/0839-427X) [18604674] **5796**

TIMES-COURIER (US) [20982178] **5662**

TIMES DIGEST, THE (CE) [01797710] **2666**

TIMES DISPATCH, THE (US) [08776992] **5632**

TIMES EDUCATIONAL SUPPLEMENT, THE (UK/0040-7887) [02239057] **1788**

TIMES FEMNIST (CN/1184-0455) [23598138] 4513, **5567**

TIMES (FRANKFORT, IND.) (US) [15244665] **5667**

TIMES-GAZETTE (US) [25264483] **5741**

TIMES-GEORGIAN (CARROLLTON, GA.) (US/1049-9458) [19493296] **5655**

TIMES HERALD (CARROLL, IOWA) (US) [16830253] **5673**

TIMES-HERALD (FORREST CITY, ARK.) (US) [22949416] **5632**

TIMES HERALD (NORRISTOWN, PA.) (US) [15475975] **5740**

TIMES HERALD (OLEAN, N.Y.) (US) [11103257] **5721**

TIMES HERALD RECORD, THE (US) [22233819] **5721**

TIMES HIGHER EDUCATION SUPPLEMENT *See* HIGHER [MICROFORM], THE **1828**

TIMES INDEX, THE (UK/0260-0668) [02897414] **5813**

TIMES INTERNATIONAL (LAGOS, NIGERIA : 1979) (NR) [12048199] **2644**

TIMES-JOURNAL (US) [17512177] **5721**

TIMES-JOURNAL (FORT PAYNE, ALA.) (US) [13364148] **5628**

TIMES JOURNAL (RUSSELL SPRINGS, KY.) (US) [14208294] **5682**

TIMES JOURNAL SPOTLIGHT (US) [19647011] **5655**

TIMES (KATY, TEX.) (US) [17392178] **5755**

TIMES LAW REPORTS (UK/0958-0441) [21503990] **3065**

TIMES-LEADER (MARTINS FERRY, OHIO) (US) [17235009] **5730**

TIMES-LEADER, THE (US) [08814951] **5662**

● TIMES-LEADER, THE (US) [26792059] **5682**

TIMES LEADER (WILKES-BARRE, PA.) (US/0896-4084) [12378393] **5740**

TIMES (LONDON, ENGLAND: 1788) (UK/0140-0460) [06967919] **5813**

TIMES (LONDON, ENGLAND), THE (UK) **5813**

TIMES MAGAZINE (WASHINGTON), THE (US/0097-8833) [03187985] **2547**

TIMES-MAIL, THE (US) [13449666] **5667**

TIMES (MOORESVILLE, IND.) (US) [11351666] **5667**

TIMES-NEWS (US) [13917626] **5682**

TIMES-NEWS (HENDERSONVILLE, N.C.) (US/1042-2323) [13285937] **5724**

TIMES-NEWS (LEHIGHTON, PA.) (US) [15101379] **5740**

TIMES-NEWS (TWIN FALLS, IDAHO) (US) [12292697] **5657**

TIMES OF BUCHAREST (RM) **5809**

TIMES OF DOWNTOWN LONDON, THE (CN/0715-450X) [09166960] **2547**

TIMES OF FOUNTAIN HILLS, THE (US) **5630**

TIMES OF INDIA (II) [18036893] **5803**

TIMES OF NORTH AND WEST VANCOUVER, THE (CN/0380-4569) [02443255] **5678**

TIMES OF NORTHEAST BENTON COUNTY, THE (US/8750-3921) [11407203] **5632**

TIMES OF OMAN (MK) **5807**

TIMES OF SRI LANKA, THE (CN/1185-1880) [24257156] **5796**

TIMES OF THE AMERICAS, THE *CEASED.* (US/0040-7917) [01767518] **2552**

TIMES OF TI (US/0746-0392) [09697060] **5721**

TIMES OF ZAMBIA, THE (ZA) [03145688] **5813**

TIMES (PAWTUCKET, R.I.), THE (US/1060-2747) [24900988] **5741**

TIMES-PICAYUNE (NEW ORLEANS, LA. 1986), THE (US/1055-3053) [15937704] **5684**

TIMES-PICAYUNE, THE (US) [22423974] **5632**

TIMES-PLAIN DEALER, THE (US) [15528574] **5673**

TIMES-POST (US/0746-3901) [10014121] **5672**

TIMES PRESS HARTFORD PUBLICATIONS (US) **5771**

TIMES PRESS (SEYMOUR, WIS. : 1978) (US) [12291459] **5771**

TIMES-PRESS (STREATOR, ILL.) (US/0745-5542) [09286311] **5662**

TIMES RECORD (BRUNSWICK, ME), THE (US/0747-1300) [10561177] **5685**

TIMES RECORD NEWS (US/0895-6138) [16700583] **5755**

TIMES-RECORD (SPENCER, W.VA.) (US) [13201617] **5765**

TIMES-RECORD, THE (US) [08821392] **5662**

TIMES-RECORD, THE (US) [12046616] **5628**

TIMES RECORDER (ZANESVILLE, OHIO : 1965) (US) [17358777] **5730**

TIMES-REGISTER, THE (US) [12948683] **5760**

TIMES-REPUBLICAN (CORYDON, IOWA : 1973) (US) [15307723] **5673**

TIMES-REPUBLICAN (MARSHALLTOWN, IOWA : 1974) (US) [11826853] **5673**

TIMES (SHREVEPORT, LA.) (US) [09866167] **5684**

TIMES (SMITHFIELD, VA) (US) **5760**

TIMES STANDARD, THE (US) [27389437] **5640**

TIMES-SUN, THE (US) [14288474] **5740**

TIMES, THE (US) [22518339] **5699**

TIMES, THE (US) [19960343] **5655**

TIMES (TRENTON, N.J. PRINCETON METRO ED.), THE (US/8750-9083) [11947025] **5711**

TIMES TRIBUNE (CORBIN, KY.) (US) [14252720] **5682**

TIMES-UNION (ALBANY, N.Y.) (US) [06228404] **5721**

TIMES-UNION (ROCHESTER, N.Y.) (US/0744-1851) [06028045] **5721**

TIMES-UNION (WARSAW, IND.) (US) [15467243] **5667**

TIMES (WAITSBURG, WASH.) (US) [17390356] **5762**

TIMES (WALWORTH, WIS.) (US) [13459583] **5771**

TIMES (WEBSTER, MASS.), THE (US/0747-2900) [10698320] **5690**

TIMES-WEST VIRGINIAN (FAIRMONT, W.VA. : DAILY) (US) [13032698] **5765**

TIMES (WINNIPEG) (CN/0821-2473) [09428067] **5796**

TIMESDAILY (REGIONAL ED.) (US/0743-152X) [10536023] **5628**

TIMESDAILY (SHOALS EDITION) (US/0743-1511) [09867255] **5628**

TIMESHARING LAW REPORTER (WASHINGTON, D.C. : 1987) (US) [16530080] 4848, **3065**

TIMINN REYKJAVIK (IC/1021-8459) [I10218459] **5802**

TIMIX BUYERS' GUIDE (US) **1245**

TIMMINS PORCUPINE NEWS (CN/0316-6872) [02247748] **5796**

TIMMINS TIMES, THE (CN/1191-0771) [25652386] **5796**

TIMS (HK) **3646**

TIMS/ORSA BULLETIN (US/0161-0295) [02471224] **1629**

TIMTARIKITA (II) [08714559] **2509**

TIN AND ITS USES (UK/0040-7941) [01589312] **4022**

TIN INTERNATIONAL (UK/0040-795X) [01096935] **2152**

TIN NEWS *CEASED.* (US/0040-7968) [01772724] **4022**

TIN STATISTICS (UK) [02217194] 4022, **4026**

TIN TYPE (US) [05862851] **4022**

TIN TYPE : AMHERSTBURG HISTORIC SITES ASSOCIATION NEWSLETTER (CN/1188-0376) [25314056] **2763**

TIN (UNITED STATES. BUREAU OF MINES) (US/0364-7935) [02256331] **4022**

TIN (WASHINGTON, D.C. ANNUAL) (US/0886-1331) [09915272] **2152**

TINBERGEN INSTITUTE RESEARCH BULLETIN (NE) [20640456] 715, **1524**

TINCTORIA (IT/0040-7984) [09542765] **5359**

TINDERBOX (US) [06401659] **3472**

TINGKAT PENGHUNIAN KAMAR HOTEL (IO) [07514380] **2809**

TINIG (CN/0229-7795) [05470084] **2509**

TINJAUAN EKONOMI (IO/0216-7050) [I02167050] **814**

TINKLE (II) **1070**

TINS PRODUCT DIRECTORY (UK) [17690213] **3846**

TINTA (SANTA BARBARA, CALIF.) (US/0739-7003) [09809917] 3329, **3446**

TINY TOON ADVENTURES MAGAZINE *CEASED.* (US/1050-7760) [21588578] **4867**

TINY WAILS (CN/1191-0909) [25882954] **366**

TIP (NE) **2360**

TIP APPLICATIONS (UK) 1205, **3253**

TIP DUNYASI (TU) [07105677] **3646**

TIPOLOGIIA I VZAIMOSVIAZI V RUSSKOI I ZARUBEZHNOI LITERATURE (RU) [04723067] **3446**

TIPPERARY HISTORICAL JOURNAL (IE) [27332506] **2712**

TIPPS (CN/0714-3788) [09457073] **2778**

TIPPS DIRECTORY OF TALENT, INFORMATION, PROPS, PLACES, SERVICES FOR ADVERTISING, FILM AND THEATRE (US) [14095227] **389**

TIPRO REPORTER (US/0039-8403) [03938261] **4280**

TIPS & TOPICS (CN/0381-9345) [02228762] **5394**

TIPS & TOPICS (LUBBOCK, TEX.) *CEASED.* (US) [08564744] **2793**

TIPS FOR PRINCIPALS FROM NASSP (US) [09134441] **1873**

TIPTON CONSERVATIVE AND ADVERTISER, THE (US) [12006491] **5673**

TIPTON COUNTY TRIBUNE (US/0746-0619) [09714649] **5667**

TIRADE (NE/0165-5094) [02079881] **5237**

TIRATURE (IT) [27420911] **3446**

TIRDO (ORGANIZATION) *See* ANNUAL REPORT AND ACCOUNTS / TANZANIA INDUSTRIAL RESEARCH AND DEVELOPMENT ORGANIZATION **5083**

TIRDO (ORGANIZATION). ANNUAL REPORT AND ACCOUNTS FOR THE PERIOD . *See* ANNUAL REPORT AND ACCOUNTS / TANZANIA INDUSTRIAL RESEARCH AND DEVELOPMENT ORGANIZATION **5083**

TIRE A PART - ECOLE DE RELATIONS INDUSTRIELLES, UNIVERSITE DE MONTREAL (CN/0319-3845) [02442965] **947**

TIRE BUSINESS (US) [25225039] **715, 5078**

TIRE RETREADING/REPAIR JOURNAL, THE (US/1046-7157) [20500529] **5078**

TIRE REVIEW (1966) (US/0040-8085) [05294276] **5078**

TIRE SCIENCE & TECHNOLOGY (US/0090-8657) [01785640] **5426**

●TIRE TALK (CN/1187-967X) [26290469] **5312**

TIRES (US/0095-2001) [01796231] **5426, 4805**

TIROLER GEBIETSKRANKENKASSE *See* JAHRESBERICHT DER TIROLER GEBIETSKRANKENKASSE **2885**

TIROLER GEBIETSKRANKENKASSE FUR ARBIETER UND ANGESTELLTE. JAHRESBERICHT *See* JAHRESBERICHT DER TIROLER GEBIETSKRANKENKASSE **2885**

TIROLER HEIMAT (AU/1013-8919) [I10138919] 2324, **2712**

TIROLER VERKEHRSWIRTSCHAFTLICHE ZAHLEN (AU) [01784873] **5492**

●TIRRA LIRRA (AT/1038-8400) **3446**

TIRUNILAKANTAN (II) [11266340] **2666**

TISCHTENNIS (GW/0138-1547) **4926**

TISGLOW NEW DELHI (II/0970-9703) [I09709703] **2182**

TISHOMINGO COUNTY NEWS. THE VIDETTE AND BELMONT NEWS (US) [15300474] **5702**

TISSUE & CELL (UK/0040-8166) [01681062] **540**

TISSUE ANTIGENS (DK/0001-2815) [01767531] **3802**

TISSUE CULTURE ASSOCIATION *See* TCA REPORT **570**

TISSUE CULTURE SHEFFIELD (UK/0142-8810) [I01428810] **540**

●TISSUE ENGINEERING (US/1076-3279) [30453761] **3646**

TISTA-SUNAKOSA (II) [08354083] **3446**

TITLE 38, UNITED STATES CODE, VETERANS' BENEFITS (US) [03181727] **4059**

TITLE I IN ACTION (US/0146-6984) [03013637] **1788**

TITLE I, PART A, HIGHER EDUCATION ACT OF 1965 ANNUAL PROGRAM PLAN AMENDMENT TO WASHINGTON STATE PLAN FOR COMMUNITY SERVICE, CONTINUING EDUCATION AND PLANNING FOR RESOURCE MATERIALS SHARING PROGRAMS (US) [04911069] **1850**

TITLE III ESEA MINI-GRANT PROJECT ABSTRACTS (US/0097-7497) [01798330] **1788**

TITLE INDEX OF CURRENT REVIEWS (US/0739-4616) [08726915] **426**

TITLE LIST OF DOCUMENTS MADE PUBLICLY AVAILABLE (US/1054-2914) [05182879] **4691**

TITLE LISTING - MIDWESTERN REGIONAL LIBRARY SYSTEM (CN/0710-6572) [08144110] **426**

TITLE MASTER (US/0747-6418) [10765065] **426**

TITLE NEWS (US/0040-8190) [01767533] **2894**

TITLE VARIES (US/0092-6108) [01779330] **3253**

TITLE VI-B, EDUCATION OF THE HANDICAPPED ACT : ANNUAL PROGRAM PLAN (US) [04552432] **1886**

TITLE XX COMPREHENSIVE ANNUAL SERVICES PROGRAM PLAN (US) [09824060] **5312**

TITLE XX FINAL COMPREHENSIVE I.E. COMPREHENSIVE ANNUAL SERVICES PLAN (US) [03773400] **5312**

TITLE XX NEEDS ASSESSMENT, FISCAL YEAR ... - BUREAU OF PLANNING ANALYSIS, DIVISION OF PLANNING SERVICES, IOWA DEPARTMENT OF SOCIAL SERVICES (US) [07208544] **5312**

TITLE XX, SOCIAL SERVICES (US) [04252076] **5312**

TITLE XX SOCIAL SERVICES BLOCK GRANT REPORT (US) [09672381] **5312**

TITLES IN SERIES / A HANDBOOK FOR LIBRARIANS AND STUDENTS (US/0082-4526) [01039577] **3253**

TITLES MAGAZINE *SUSPENDED.* (US/1049-2704) [21190996] **2925**

TITOLO (IT) **4833**

TITOLO : RIVISTA SCIENTIFICO-CULTURALE D'ARTE CONTEMPORANEA (IT/1120-5539) [26335973] **366**

TITONKA TOPIC (US/0745-7405) [09420521] **5673**

TITRA *CEASED.* (FR) [28951745] **3446**

TITUS TRAIL, THE (US/0271-2830) [06583355] **2475**

TITUSVILLE HERALD, THE (US) [12396338] **5740**

TIURKOLOGIIA (AJ) [27588891] **3329**

TIZ (GW/0722-9488) [07535016] **2152**

TIZ INTERNATIONAL POWDER & BULK MAGAZINE (GW) **2152**

TIZ PULVER + SCHUETTGUT MAGAZIN (GW/0942-8194) **2152**

TJENESTEYTING, FORRETNINGSMESSIG TJENESTEYTING, UTLEIE AV MASKINER OG UTSTYR, RENOVASJON OG REINGJRING, VASKERI- OG RENSERIVIRKSOMHET (NO) [09395704] **5360**

TJFR BUSINESS NEWS REPORTER (US) **2925**

TJFR HEALTH NEWS REPORTER (US) 1123, **3646**

TJI : TOBACCO JOURNAL INTERNATIONAL (GW/0721-5185) [10896493] **5373**

TJS SPEC. PUBL (US/0145-0123) [02664331] **5166**

TJURUNGA; AN AUSTRALASIAN BENEDICTINE REVIEW (AT) [04387182] **5037**

TJUSTBYGDEN (SW) [06396239] **2712**

TK REPORT (GW/0723-5054) [18533522] **2360**

TKG : FACHZEITSCHRIFT FUR DIE TECHNIK IN DER KERAMIK, GLAS UND EMAIL INDUSTRIE (LH) [06563053] 3489, **2594**

TLA NEWSLETTER (1983) (TZ/0378-3375) [11750129] **3253**

TLALOCAN *SUSPENDED.* (MX/0185-0989) [01767534] **246**

TLC -- FOR PLANTS (CN/0835-3271) [18595946] **2432**

TLC MONTHLY (US) **2494**

TLF QUARTERLY (US/0092-9263) [01788509] 1141, **4079**

TLRC DIRECTORY (CN/1186-8503) [24623680] **2585**

TLS, THE TIMES LITERARY SUPPLEMENT INDEX (UK) [06720096] **3446**

TLS. TIMES LITERARY SUPPLEMENT (UK/0307-661X) [02241740] 3447, **4820**

TLS, TIMES LITERARY SUPPLEMENT MICROFORM (UK) [09444486] **4833**

TLTA NEWS (US) [19365440] **2894**

TM. TEKNIIKAN MAAILMA (FI/0355-4287) [I03554287] **5166**

TM, TRADEMARK DIRECTORY (US/0148-3498) [01640274] **1308**

TM. TROPICAL AGRONOMY TECHNICAL MEMORANDUM (AT/0157-9711) [10064038] **529**

TMA ACTION (US) [05119135] **3646**

TMA JOURNAL (US) **888**

TMB (AGENCY : BARCELONA, SPAIN) *See* PLAN DE EMPRESA **5389**

TMJ UPDATE (US/0885-9191) [12770818] **1336**

TML LEGISLATIVE REPORT (US) [05304822] **3065**

TML TEXAS TOWN & CITY (US/1040-6565) [12138967] **4691**

TMO UPDATE (US/0270-0123) [06327374] **4033**

TMR, TRAVEL MARKETING REPORT (US/0197-6753) [06077385] **1999**

TMS-LETTER, THE *SUSPENDED.* (US/0893-1259) [15364302] **937**

TMS PAPER SELECTION (US/0197-1689) [05970712] **4022**

TMSA AEROSPACE MARKET OUTLOOK *CEASED.* (US/0271-7417) [06686801] 937, **37**

TNC'S BULLETIN (XR) [19001091] **1714**

TO CHO, I (JA/0536-2180) [05579067] **3748**

TO DENTRO (GR) [21744618] **332**

TO KALAMI (GR) [20571847] **2712**

TO QUOC (VM) [01796000] **2509**

TO SHIN, HAI (JA/0440-0852) [I04400852] 3711, **3646**

TO TETARTO (GR) [13998726] **5372**

TO (TORONTO, ONT.) *CEASED.* (CN/0823-9452) [12846783] **2547**

TO VIMA (GR) **5802**

TO YOUR GOOD HEALTH (US/0882-522X) [11892073] **4805**

TO YOUR HEALTH (US/0891-1304) [14638089] **4805**

TO YUN (CC) [08752391] **366**

TOA (JA) [07023750] **1999**

TOASTMASTER, THE (US/0040-8263) [02252026] **1123**

TOBA SHOSEN KOTO SEMMON GAKKO *See* KIYO - TOBA SHOSEN KOTO SEMMON GAKKO **1833**

TOBACCO (UK/0040-8271) [06216041] **5373**

TOBACCO ABSTRACTS (US/0040-8298) [01589110] **5373**

TOBACCO ALLOTTED, BY COUNTIES AND KINDS (US) [03803169] **5373**

●TOBACCO & HEALTH (US/1064-8577) [26434659] 4805, **5373**

TOBACCO AND YOUTH REPORTER *See* TOBACCO-FREE YOUTHREPORTER **5373**

●TOBACCO CONTROL (UK/0964-4563) [26106320] **4805**

TOBACCO FARMER / GEORGIA AGRICULTURAL COMMODITY COMMISSION FOR TOBACCO. --, THE (US) [09242162] **5373**

●TOBACCO-FREE YOUTHREPORTER (US/1064-2072) [26230885] **5373**

TOBACCO GROWER, THE (US/8756-4750) [11566104] **5374**

TOBACCO IN CANADA (CN/0713-5459) [09046596] **5374**

TOBACCO INDUSTRY LITIGATION REPORTER (US/0887-7831) [12958122] 5374, **3065**

TOBACCO INTERNATIONAL (US/0049-3945) [03247550] **5374**

TOBACCO MARKET REVIEW. BURLEY (US/0742-1869) [10234661] **5374**

TOBACCO MARKET REVIEW. FIRE-CURED AND DARK AIR-CURED (US/0272-2771) [04166118] **5374**

TOBACCO MARKET REVIEW. FLUE-CURED (US/0193-6514) [03076318] **5374**

TOBACCO MARKET REVIEW. SOUTHERN MARYLAND (US/0364-7420) [02671878] **5374**

●TOBACCO NEWS (RH) [26496443] **5374**

TOBACCO NEWS / TOBACCO BOARD INDIA (II) [11861393] **5374**

TOBACCO QUARTERLY *CEASED.* (UK/0142-1913) [07479012] **5374**

TOBACCO REPORTER (US/0040-8328) [02247090] **5374**

TOBACCO REPRINT SERIES *CEASED.* (US/0743-4707) [06697169] **5374**

TOBACCO RESEARCH (II/0379-055X) [02200777] **5374**

TOBACCO ROOT GEOLOGICAL SOCIETY. CONFERENCE *See* ABSTRACTS OF PAPERS PRESENTED AT THE ... TOBACCO ROOT GEOLOGICAL SOCIETY CONFERENCE **1364**

TOBACCO STOCKS (US) [02255937] 5374, **917**

TOBACCO TRADE DIRECTORY AND DIARY *See* TOBACCO TRADE MARKETING DIRECTORY **5374**

TOBACCO TRADE MARKETING DIRECTORY (UK/0954-9773) **5374**

TOBACCO VALLEY NEWS (US/8750-2925) [11249654] **5706**

●TOBACCO, WORLD MARKETS & TRADE / UNITED STATES DEPARTMENT OF AGRICULTURE, FOREIGN AGRICULTURAL SERVICE (US) [30521977] **5374**

TOBAGI (KO) [11382696] **2666**

TOBIQUER (CN/0709-0846) [05527720] **2763**

TOBOGGAN TOULOUSE (FR/0248-2339) [I02482339] **4926**

TOCCOA Alphabetical Title Index

TOCCOA RECORD, THE (US) [22045276] **5655**

TOCCUPATIONAL COMPENSATION SURVEY--PAY AND BENEFITS. AUSTIN, TX See OCCUPATIONAL COMPENSATION SURVEY--PAY ONLY. AUSTIN, TX / U.S. DEPARTMENT OF LABOR, BUREAU OF LABOR STATISTICS **1697**

TOCHER; TALES, SONGS, TRADITION (UK/0049-397X) [05243554] **4156**

TOCHI HAKUSHO / KOKUDOCHO HEN (JA) [23073369] **4848**

TOCHI SHISHU (JA) [01790274] **3472**

TOCHI ZOSEI KOGAKU KENKYU SHISETSU HOKOKU (JA/0288-6502) [10399172] **1999**

TOCHIGI, JAPAN (PREFECTURE) EISEI KANKYOBU See KANKYO HAKUSHO **2234**

TOCHKA OPORY (RU) [18606290] **3447**

TOCQUEVILLE REVIEW, THE (US/0730-479X) [06336786] **5224**

TOCQUEVILLE SOCIETY See TOCQUEVILLE REVIEW, THE **5224**

TODA SHISHI KENKYU (JA) [03714159] **2666**

TODAY (UK) **5068**

TODAY (FR) **2494**

TODAY CEDAR HILL (US/1065-2876) [26566247] **5755**

TODAY IN HEALTH PLANNING (US/0164-498X) [04765407] **4805**

TODAY IN MEDICINE. CARDIOVASCULAR DISEASE (US/1042-2455) [18978941] **3711**

TODAY IN MEDICINE DIABETOLOGY AND ENDOCRINOLOGY (US/1042-2838) [18997016] **3733**

TODAY IN MEDICINE. FAMILY PRACTICE (US/1054-8521) [22994594] **3739**

TODAY IN MEDICINE. OPHTHALMOLOGY (US) [18999603] **3879**

TODAY IN MEDICINE. RESPIRATORY DISEASE (US/1042-2846) [18997098] **3952**

TODAY IN MISSISSIPPI (US/1052-2433) [22222163] **2084**

TODAY ITALIA (IT) **2494**

● TODAY LANCASTER (US/1065-0644) [26496965] **5755**

TODAY MONA VALE CEASED. (AT/1034-5337) [10345337] **2182**

TODAY NEWS (US/0899-6687) [18181174] **5630**

TODAY ON THE COLORADO RIVER See TODAY NEWS **5630**

TODAY'S AQUARIST (DEVON, CONN.) (US/1040-2098) [18352730] **4879**

TODAY'S ASTROLOGER (US/1067-1439) [25472768] **390**

● TODAY'S BEAUTY TRENDS (US/1062-2748) [25568189] **405**

TODAY'S BEST NONFICTION (US/0893-9373) [15699502] **3447**

TODAY'S BRIDE (DON MILLS) (CN/0226-1758) [06468246] **2286**

TODAY'S CATHOLIC (SAN ANTONIO, TEX.) (US/0745-3612) [09094200] **5037**

TODAY'S CATHOLIC TEACHER (US/0040-8441) [01588037] **1873**

TODAY'S CHEMIST See TODAY'S CHEMIST AT WORK **994**

● TODAY'S CHEMIST AT WORK (US/1062-094X) [25523449] **994**

TODAY'S CHICAGO WOMAN (US/1071-3786) [09636949] **5567**

TODAY'S CHIROPRACTIC (US/0091-2360) [02766507] **3646**

TODAY'S CHRISTIAN WOMAN (US/0163-1799) [04324198] 5567, **5005**

TODAY'S CLINICIAN (US/0147-4782) [03383503] **3646**

TODAY'S COLLECTOR CEASED. (US/1060-4502) [24995677] **752**

● TODAY'S COLLECTOR (IOLA, WIS.) (US/1066-7423) [27038317] **2778**

TODAY'S CPA (US/0889-4337) [13895868] **752**

TODAY'S DAILY NEWS. (LAKE HAVASU CITY) (US/1068-1876) [27463963] **5630**

TODAY'S DELINQUENT SUSPENDED. (US/0733-6551) [08632340] **3178**

TODAY'S DISTRIBUTOR (US/0898-5561) [17850471] **1629**

TODAY'S ECONOMY (DENVER, COLO.) (US/1043-2671) [19379117] **1524**

TODAY'S EDUCATION. SOCIAL STUDIES EDITION CEASED. (US/0272-3581) [06849249] **1907**

● TODAY'S EGG PRODUCER (CN/1195-1877) [29205945] **223**

TODAY'S EXECUTIVE (US/0887-5200) [06391839] **888**

TODAY'S FACILITY MANAGER (US/1059-0307) [24461480] **2903**

TODAY'S FAMILY HOME PLANS (US/1059-5252) [14248101] **310**

TODAY'S FAMILY (ST. PAUL, MINN.) (US/1055-3169) [23138681] **2286**

TODAY'S FARMER (US/0739-0092) [09710388] **141**

TODAY'S FDA (US/1048-5317) [20968047] **1336**

TODAY'S FEED LOTTING (AT/1034-6147) [I10346147] **223**

TODAY'S FILM MAKER (US/0193-6085) [02253252] **4079**

TODAY'S HEALTH REPORT CEASED. (CN) **3646**

TODAY'S HEALTH (TORONTO) (CN/0821-6819) [09774752] **4805**

TODAY'S HEALTHCARE MANAGER (US/1054-5204) [22913835] **3793**

TODAY'S HERBS (US) 2432, **3775**

TODAY'S IMAGE (US/0898-1434) [17724320] 937, **715**

TODAY'S INVESTOR (US/1042-8127) [19218776] **917**

● TODAY'S JEWISH FAMILY (US/1056-8492) [23880557] **5053**

TODAY'S LIFE SCIENCE (AT/1033-6893) [22926381] **5166**

● TODAY'S MANAGER (US/1055-0844) [23070508] **888**

TODAY'S MINISTRY (NEWTON CENTRE, MASS. : 1983) (US/0563-637X) [09410069] **5005**

TODAY'S MISSAL (US/0199-8803) [06242064] **5037**

TODAY'S MOTOR (AT/1033-1069) [I10331069] **2130**

TODAY'S OR NURSE (US/0194-5181) [04786409] 3976, **3870**

TODAY'S PARENT (CN/0823-9258) [13843559] **2286**

TODAY'S PARISH (US/0040-8549) [01640538] **5005**

TODAY'S PARTS MANAGER (US/1060-2534) [24923386] **1999**

TODAY'S PROFESSIONALS (US/0163-299X) [04432878] **4209**

TODAY'S REFINERY (US/1048-0935) [20858424] 2033, **4280**

TODAY'S RUNNER (UK/0268-4977) [I02684977] **4926**

● TODAY'S SCIENCE ON FILE (US/1059-9274) [24811706] **5166**

TODAY'S SENIORS (CN/0827-6854) [14153820] **5182**

TODAY'S SENIORS HOUSING CHOICES GUIDE (CN/1187-5887) [25423596] 5182, **2837**

TODAY'S SINGLE (US/0748-7355) [10993058] 3996, **5567**

TODAYS SKATER (CN/1181-6341) [22569792] **4926**

TODAY'S SPIRIT (US/8755-9315) [11450700] **5467**

TODAY'S SUNBEAM (US/0890-9830) [14513784] **5711**

TODAY'S SUPERVISOR (US/0734-3302) [08724128] **2871**

TODAY'S TEAM (US/1059-0242) [24462489] **3646**

TODAY'S THERAPEUTIC TRENDS (US/0741-2320) [10010328] **3646**

● TODAY'S TIMES (CN/1193-171X) [I1193171X] **5182**

TODAY'S TRANSPORT INTERNATIONAL CEASED. (US/0040-859X) [01795296] **853**

TODAY'S TRIVIA (US/0748-2256) [10908094] **2494**

TODAY'S TRUCKING (CN/0837-1512) [17883872] **5394**

TODAY'S WOMAN (US/1054-9587) [23032487] **5567**

TODAY'S WOODWORKER (US/1041-8113) [18851831] **635**

TODD COUNTY STANDARD, THE (US) [14037791] **5683**

TODD COUNTY TRIBUNE (US) [01643883] **5744**

TODO (BL) [02651976] **853**

TODO ES HISTORIA CEASED. (AG/0040-8611) [03139396] **2763**

TODO HOSPITAL (SP) [12186710] **3793**

TODO NATURAL DE NUEVA YORK (US/8755-1063) [11270750] **4330**

TODO, O MERCADO DO BRASIL PARA O INTERIOR DO ESTADO DO RIO E ESPIRITO SANTO (BL) [03603231] **1587**

TODOS AMIGOS (IT) **1788**

TOEGEPASTE WETENSCHAP (NE) [12015684] **3646**

TOERISME EN MIGRASIE (SA) [03641291] **5492**

TOERTENELMI SZEMLE (HU/0040-9634) [02078399] **2631**

TOGA, LA (PR) [02441293] **3065**

TOGA VERDE : DIRITTO E AMBIENTE (IT) **3065**

TOGETHER (UK) [05671388] **5068**

TOGETHER (INFORMATION CENTER FOR INDIVIDUALS WITH DISABILITIES (BOSTON, MASS.)) See DISABILITY ISSUES **4387**

TOGETHER (MONROVIA, CALIF.) (US/0742-1524) [10304014] **2912**

TOGETHER (OTTAWA) (CN/1180-0852) [23247916] **5264**

TOGIL MUNHAK (KO) [07681765] 3447, **3329**

TOGO. DIRECTION DE LA STATISTIQUE See INDICATEURS DE L'ECONOMIE TOGOLAISE **1567**

TOGO. DIRECTION DE LA STATISTIQUE See PRIX, INDICES DES PRIX ET COUT DE LA VIE A LOME **1513**

TOGO : ENERGIEWIRTSCHAFT (GW) [05691289] **1959**

TOGO. MINISTERE DE L'EDUCATION NATIONALE. DIRECTION DE LA PLANIFICATION, DES STATISTIQUES ET DE LA CONJONCTURE See STATISTIQUES SCOLAIRES **1798**

TOGO. MINISTERE DU PLAN, DU DEVELOPPEMENT INDUSTRIEL ET DE LA REFORME ADMINISTRATIVE See BUDGET D'INVESTISSEMENT ET D'EQUIPEMENT **4714**

TOGO : WIRTSCHAFTLICHE ENTWICKLUNG (GW) [06246874] **1587**

TOGO : WIRTSCHAFTSDATEN UND WIRTSCHAFTSDOKUMENTATION (GW) [06229668] **1587**

TOHO GAKUEN DAIGAKU See TOHO GAKUEN DAIGAKU KENKYU KIYO **2509**

TOHO GAKUEN DAIGAKU KENKYU KIYO (JA) [02943243] **2509**

TOHO IGAKKAI See TOHO IGAKKAI ZASSHI **3646**

TOHO IGAKKAI ZASSHI (JA/0040-8670) [01778417] **3646**

TOHO SHUKYO (JA) [03045564] **5005**

TOHOGAKU (JA/0495-7199) [01714204] **2666**

TOHOKAI (JA) [01797095] **5022**

TOHOKU CHIHO KOGYO KAIHATSU YORAN (JA) [02245774] **1629**

TOHOKU DAIGAKU See SCIENCE REPORTS OF THE RESEARCH INSTITUTES. SERIES C, MEDICINE, THE **3716**

TOHOKU DAIGAKU See SCIENCE REPORTS OF THE TOHOKU UNIVERSITY. SERIES 7. GEOGRAPHY **2576**

TOHOKU DAIGAKU RIGAKUBU CHISHITSUGAKU KOSEIBUTSUGAKU KYOSHITSU KENKYU HOBUN HOKOKU (JA/0082-4658) [01711132] 4231, **1399**

TOHOKU DAIGAKU, SENDAI, JAPAN. GENSHIKAKU RIGAKU KENKYU SHISETSU See KAKURIKEN KEDKYU HOKOKU **4448**

TOHOKU DAIGAKU, SENDAI, JAPAN. KOGAKUBU. ZAIRYO KYODO KENKYU SHISETSU See REPORTS OF THE RESEARCH INSTITUTE FOR STRENGTH AND FRACTURE OF MATERIALS, TOHOKU UNIVERSITY **1994**

TOHOKU DAIGAKU, SENDAI, JAPAN. RIGAKUBU. CHISHITSUGAKU KOSEIBUTSUGAKU KYOSHITSU See TOHOKU DAIGAKU RIGAKUBU CHISHITSUGAKU KOSEIBUTSUGAKU KYOSHITSU KENKYU HOBUN HOKOKU **1399**

TOHOKU GAKUIN DAIGAKU RONSHU. EIGO, EIBUNGAKU (JA/0385-406X) [I0385406X] 3329, **3447**

TOHOKU JOURNAL OF AGRICULTURAL RESEARCH (JA/0040-8719) [01767555] **141**

TOHOKU JOURNAL OF EXPERIMENTAL MEDICINE, THE (JA/0040-8727) [01767556] **3646**

TOHOKU KOGYO DAIGAKU KIYO. 2, JIMBUN SHAKAI KAGUKU HEN (JA) [07999933] **1850**

TOHOKU KOGYO DAIGAKU KIYO. SERIES 1. RIKOGAKUEN (JA/0285-3817) [08000587] **2033**

TOHOKU KOGYO GIJUTSU SHIKENJO See YORAN- [TOHOKU KOGYO GIJUTSU SHIKENJO] **5172**

TOHOKU KOGYO GIJUTSU SHIKENJO See TOHOKU KOGYO GIJUTSU SHIKENJO HOKOKU **5166**

TOHOKU KOGYO GIJUTSU SHIKENJO HOKOKU (JA) [02244307] **5166**

TOHOKU MATHEMATICAL JOURNAL (JA/0040-8735) [01642556] **3538**

TOHOKU NOGYO SHIKENJO See MISCELLANEOUS PUBLICATION OF THE TOHOKU NATIONAL AGRICULTURAL EXPERIMENT STATION **109**

TOHOKU NOGYO SHIKENJO, MORIOKA, JAPAN See KENKYU HOKOKU TOHOKU NOGYO SHIKENJO **102**

TOHOKU PSYCHOLOGICA FOLIA (JA/0040-8743) [01040785] **4620**

TOILETRY AND BEAUTY AIDS MARKET (US/0273-4540) [07043842] **405**

TOIMIALALUOKITUS (TOL) (FI) [20977594] 1629, **1540**

TOIMINTAKERTOMUS (FI) [19090943] **814**

TOIMINTAKERTOMUS / KORKEIN HALLINTO-OIKEUS (FI/0357-9190) [10225972] **3143**

TOIMINTAKERTOMUS / MERENTUTKIMUSLAITOS (FI) [19855769] **1457**

TOIMINTAKERTOMUS / TELEKEHITYSKESKUS (FI) [24236514] **1168**

TOIMIPISTEET HELSINGISSA (FI) [19901424] **1714**

TOK BLONG PASIFIK (CN) **2671**

TOK BLONG SPPF See TOK BLONG PASIFIK **2671**

TOKAI DAIGAKU KIYO. GAIKOKUGO KYOIKU SENTA (JA/0389-3081) [08208534] **3329**

TOKAI DAIGAKU KIYO : KAIYOGAKUBU (JA/0375-3271) [09050690] **474**

TOKAI DAIGAKU KIYO : KOGAKUBU (JA) [03910349] **5166**

TOKAI DAIGAKU KIYO : KYOYO GAKUBU (JA) [03759491] **2509**

TOKAI DAIGAKU KIYO. RIGAKUBU. PROCEEDINGS OF THE FACULTY OF SCIENCE OF TOKAI UNIVERSITY See PROCEEDINGS OF THE SCHOOL OF SCIENCE OF TOKAI UNIVERSITY **5142**

TOKAI DAIGAKU KIYO: TAIIKUGAKUBU (JA) [03452026] **1859**

TOKAI DAIGAKU. KOGAKUBU See PROCEEDINGS OF THE FACULTY OF ENGINEERING OF TOKAI UNIVERSITY **1991**

TOKAI DAIGAKU. KYOYO GAKUBU See TOKAI DAIGAKU KIYO : KYOYO GAKUBU **2509**

TOKAI DAIGAKU. RIGAKUBU See HAKUJU GAKUI ROMBUN NO GAIYO OYOBI SHINSA NO YOSHI **5109**

TOKAI DAIGAKU. RIGAKUBU See PROCEEDINGS OF THE FACULTY OF SCIENCE OF TOKAI UNIVERSITY **5140**

TOKAI DAIGAKU. TAIIKUGAKUBU See TOKAI DAIGAKU KIYO: TAIIKUGAKUBU **1859**

TOKAI HOKURIKU TSUSAN TOKEI NEMPO (JA) [02245322] **1587**

TOKAI JOURNAL OF EXPERIMENTAL AND CLINICAL MEDICINE (JA/0385-0005) [03155885] **3646**

TOKAI-KU SUISAN KENKYUJO See TOKAI-KU SUISAN KENKYUJO GYOSEKISHU **2315**

TOKAI-KU SUISAN KENKYUJO See SPECIAL PUBLICATIONS - TOKAI REGIONAL FISHERIES RESEARCH LABORATORY **2313**

TOKAI-KU SUISAN KENKYUJO GYOSEKI MOKUROKU (JA) [01797139] **2315**

TOKAI-KU SUISAN KENKYUJO GYOSEKISHU (JA/0495-7490) [02011364] **2315**

TOKAI-KU SUISAN KENKYUJO, TOKYO See TOKAI-KU SUISAN KENKYUJO GYOSEKI MOKUROKU **2315**

TOKAI NORIN SUISAN TOKEI (JA) [02243339] **141**

TOKAI SHIGAKU (JA) [03111614] **2631**

TOKEI CHOSA SORAN (JA) [02302271] **5345**

TOKEI SURI (JA/0912-6112) [16851629] **3538**

TOKEI SURI KENKYUJO NENPO (JA) [01797355] **3538**

TOKEI SURI KENKYUJO, TOKYO See TOKEI SURI KENKYUJO NENPO **3538**

TOKEI SURI KENKYUJO (TOKYO, JAPAN) See ANNALS OF THE INSTITUTE OF STATISTICAL MATHEMATICS **3542**

●TOKELAU NATIONAL BIBLIOGRAPHY / FAKAMAUMAUGA O NA TUHITUHIGA O TOKELAU (NZ) [26738203] **426**

TOKEN AND MEDAL SOCIETY See TAMS JOURNAL **2783**

TOKEN PERSPECTIVES NEWSLETTER (US/0886-2362) [12894136] **1205**

TOKISHIKOROJI FORAMU (JA/0287-8712) [10394442] **3983**

TOKO-GINECOLOGIA PRACTICA (SP) **3646**

TOKO-GINECOLOGIA PRACTICA (SP/0040-8867) [I00408867] **3769**

TOKOH P2 S POLITIK MALAYSIA (MY) [08138382] **2666**

TOKTOKKIE AFRIKAANSE ED (SA/0256-6095) [I02566095] 1070, **2207**

TOKUBETSUKU KUSEI GAIYO (JA) [05795885] **1587**

TOKUSHIMA DAIGAKU See JOURNAL OF MATHEMATICS, TOKUSHIMA UNIVERSITY **3514**

TOKUSHIMA DAIGAKU KYOYOBU KIYO. SHIZEN KAGAKU (JA/0563-6981) [10480591] **5166**

TOKUSHIMA JOURNAL OF EXPERIMENTAL MEDICINE, THE (JA/0040-8875) [01767565] **3646**

TOKUSHU KYOIKU KANKEI KIKAN DANTAI NI YORU SHUPPANBUTSU ZASSHI TO MOKUROKU (JA) [02246497] 4394, **1886**

TOKUSHU KYOIKU KENKYU SHISETSU MOKUROKU (JA/0386-3271) [05845415] **1886**

TOKUSHU KYOKUGAKU KENKYU (JA/0387-3374) [05043710] 4394, **1886**

TOKUSHUKO (JA/0495-7644) [10465757] **4022**

TOKUTEI SABISUGYO JITTAI TOKEI CHOSA HOKOKUSHO (JA) [02245356] **1629**

TOKUTEI SANGYO SHOKIBO KIGYO RODO JOKEN JITTAI CHOSA HOKOKU (JA) [07498897] 1629, **1714**

TOKYO BUSINESS TODAY (JA/0911-7008) [13317809] **715**

TOKYO CHIKU KOKURITSU DAIGAKU TOSHOKAN NETTOWAKU KENKYUKAI KENKYU HOKOKU (JA) [09495653] **3253**

TOKYO CHUO YUBINKYOKU See GYOMU GAIYO **1145**

TOKYO DAIGAKU. AMERIKA KENKYU SHIRYO SENTA See TOKYO DAIGAKU AMERIKA KENKYU SHIRYO SENTA NEMPO **2763**

TOKYO DAIGAKU AMERIKA KENKYU SHIRYO SENTA NEMPO (JA) [06714049] **2763**

TOKYO DAIGAKU. BUSSEI KENKYUJO See BUSSEIKEN DAYORI (TOKYO) **4427**

TOKYO DAIGAKU. CHOKOATSU DENSHI KEMBIKYOSHITSU See TOKYO DAIGAKU CHOKOATSU DENSHI KEMBIKYOSHITSU NEMPO **574**

TOKYO DAIGAKU CHOKOATSU DENSHI KEMBIKYOSHITSU NEMPO (JA) [05593159] **574**

TOKYO DAIGAKU. GENSHIKAKU KENKYUJO See ANNUAL REPORT - INSTITUTE FOR NUCLEAR STUDY, UNIVERSITY OF TOKYO **4445**

TOKYO DAIGAKU. GENSHIKAKU KENKYUJO. KAIROSHITSU See KAIROSHITSU GIHO - TOKYO DAIGAKU GENSHIKAKU KENKYUJO KAIROSHITSU **2156**

TOKYO DAIGAKU. HYAKUNENSHI HENSHUSHITSU See TOKYO DAIGAKU SHI KIYO **1850**

TOKYO DAIGAKU. KAIYO KENKYUJO See BULLETIN OF THE OCEAN RESEARCH INSTITUTE, UNIVERSITY OF TOKYO **1447**

TOKYO DAIGAKU. KOGAKUBU See JOURNAL OF THE FACULTY OF ENGINEERING, UNIVERSITY OF TOKYO. SERIES A, ANNUAL REPORT **1983**

TOKYO DAIGAKU. KOGAKUBU See JOURNAL OF THE FACULTY OF ENGINEERING, UNIVERSITY OF TOKYO. SERIES B **1983**

TOKYO DAIGAKU. KYOYO GAKUBU. SHINRIGAKU KENKYUSHITSU See SHINRIGAKU **4618**

TOKYO DAIGAKU NOGAKUBU ENSHURIN HOKOKU (JA/0371-6007) [I03716007] **2397**

TOKYO DAIGAKU. NOGAKUBU. EXPERIMENTAL FOREST See BULLETIN OF THE TOKYO UNIVERSITY FORESTS **2377**

TOKYO DAIGAKU. NOGAKUBU. EXPERIMENTAL FOREST See MISCELLANEOUS INFORMATION, THE TOKYO UNIVERSITY FORESTS **2388**

TOKYO DAIGAKU. OGATA KEISANKI SENTA See NEMPO - TOKYO DAIGAKU OGATA KEISANKI SENTA **1261**

TOKYO DAIGAKU. RIGAKUBU See JOURNAL OF THE FACULTY OF SCIENCE, UNIVERSITY OF TOKYO. SECTION III : BOTANY **5120**

TOKYO DAIGAKU. RIGAKUBU. CHIRIGAKU KYOSHITSU See BULLETIN OF THE DEPARTMENT OF GEOGRAPHY, UNIVERSITY OF TOKYO **2557**

TOKYO DAIGAKU SHI KIYO (JA) [05190031] **1850**

TOKYO DAIGAKU. SOGO KENKYU SHIRYOKAN See TOKYO DAIGAKU SOGO KENKYU SHIRYOKAN YORAN **4097**

TOKYO DAIGAKU. SOGO KENKYU SHIRYOKAN See UNIVERSITY MUSEUM, THE UNIVERSITY OF TOKYO, THE **4097**

TOKYO DAIGAKU SOGO KENKYU SHIRYOKAN YORAN (JA) [01799731] **4097**

TOKYO DAIGAKU. UCHU KOKU KENKYUJO See TOKYO DAIGAKU UCHU KOKU KENKYUJO TEIKI HOKOKU **37**

TOKYO DAIGAKU UCHU KOKU KENKYUJO TEIKI HOKOKU (JA) [03075037] **37**

TOKYO DENKI DAIGAKU KOGAKUBU KENKYU HOKOKU (JA/0389-617X) [10388288] **1999**

TOKYO EISEI SHIKENJO. EISEI SHIKENJO IHO See EISEI SHIKENJO HOKOKU **4774**

TOKYO. EISEIKYOKU. KANKYO EISEIBU See SHOKUHIN EISEI KANKEI JIGYO HOKOKU **4802**

TOKYO FINANCIAL REVIEW (JA/0387-6896) [04254175] **814**

TOKYO GAIKOKUGO DAIGAKU See RONSHU **5269**

TOKYO IKA DAIGAKU See TOKYO IKA DAIGAKU ZASSHI **3646**

TOKYO IKA DAIGAKU ZASSHI (JA/0040-8905) [06403937] **3646**

TOKYO IKA SHIKA DAIGAKU See BULLETIN OF TOKYO MEDICAL AND DENTAL UNIVERSITY, THE **3561**

TOKYO (JAPAN) See TOSEI **4691**

TOKYO, JAPAN. SENKYO KANRI IINKAI See SANGIIN GIIN SENKYO NO KIROKU **4685**

TOKYO (JAPAN). SHOBOCHO See TOKYO SHOBOCHO JIMU NENKAN **630**

TOKYO JIKEIKAI IKA DAIGAKU ZASSHI (JA/0375-9172) [09733756] **3646**

TOKYO JOSHI IKA DAIGAKU ZASSHI (JA/0040-9022) [09534004] **3646**

TOKYO JOURNAL OF MATHEMATICS (JA/0387-3870) [04602814] **3538**

TOKYO KASEI DAIGAKU See TOKYO KASEI DAIGAKU KENKYU KIYO **2793**

TOKYO KASEI DAIGAKU KENKYU KIYO (JA/0371-831X) [02245319] **2793**

TOKYO. KENSETSUKYOKU. KASENBU. BOSAIKA See TOKYO-TO SUIBO KEIKAKU **2096**

TOKYO KODAI KURONIKURU GAKUJUTSU SOKUHO (JA) [01790098] **5166**

TOKYO. KOGAIKYOKU. SOMUBU. SODANKA See KOGAI NO ARAMASHI **2235**

TOKYO KOGYO DAIGAKU See BULLETIN OF THE TOKYO INSTITUTE OF TECHNOLOGY **5091**

TOKYO KOGYO DAIGAKU See TOKYO KOGYO DAIGAKU JIMBUN RONSO **2509**

TOKYO KOGYO DAIGAKU See TOKYO KODAI KURONIKURU GAKUJUTSU SOKUHO **5166**

TOKYO KOGYO DAIGAKU JIMBUN RONSO (JA) [02958989] **2509**

TOKYO KOKURITSU BUNKAZAI KENKYUJO See TOKYO KOKURITSU BUNKAZAI KENKYUJO YORAN **310**

TOKYO KOKURITSU BUNKAZAI KENKYUJO YORAN (JA) [01797215] **310**

TOKYO KOYO DAIGAKU. KOGYO ZAIRYO KENKYUJO See REPORT OF THE RESEARCH LABORATORY OF ENGINEERING MATERIALS (TOKYO) **2108**

TOKYO. MAISON FRANCO-JAPONAISE See BULLETIN DE LA MAISON FRANCO-JAPONAISE **2843**

TOKYO METROPOLITAN NEWS : A QUARTERLY JOURNAL OF THE TOKYO METROPOLITAN GOVERNMENT (JA/0040-893X) [24153899] **4691**

TOKYO. MINSEIKYOKU See MINSEI IIN JIDO IIN NO TEBIKI **5296**

TOKYO. MINSEIKYOKU. SOMUBU. KIKAKUKA See SHAKAI FUKUSHI SHISETSU CHOSA KOKOKU **5307**

TOKYO NO HIKO SHONEN (JA) [01797062] **3178**

TOKYO NO IKEBANA (JA) [02579969] **2432**

TOKYO NOGYO DAIGAKU See MEMOIRS OF THE TOKYO UNIVERSITY OF AGRICULTURE **108**

TOKYO NOGYO DAIGAKU NOGAKU SHUHO (JA/0375-9202) [I03759202] **141**

TOKYO NOGYO DAIGAKU NOGAKU SHUHO (JA/0447-8959) [01624247] **141**

TOKYO NOKO DAIGAKU HOKEN TAIIKUGAKU RON SHU (JA) [01790298] **1859**

TOKYO
Alphabetical Title Index

TOKYO NOKO DAIGAKU. IPPAN KYOIKUBU. HOKEN TAIIKUGAKU KYOSHITSU See TOKYO NOKO DAIGAKU HOKEN TAIIKUGAKU RON SHU **1859**

TOKYO NORIN SUISAN TOKEI NEMPO (JA) [01790329] **141**

TOKYO. SEISOKYOKU See PUBLIC CLEANSING SERVICE IN TOKYO **4676**

TOKYO. SEISOKYOKU See SEISO GIHO **2243**

TOKYO. SENKYO KANRI IINKAI See TOKYO TOGIKAI GIIN SENKYO NO KIROKU **4691**

TOKYO SHIKA DAIGAKU See BULLETIN OF TOKYO DENTAL COLLEGE, THE **1318**

TOKYO SHOBOCHO JIMU NENKAN (JA) [05199881] **630**

TOKYO SHOKEN TORIHIKIJO See FACT BOOK - TOKYO SHOKEN TORIHIKIJO **728**

TOKYO SHOKO RISACHI See TOSHO SHINYOROKU. KANTO-BAN **814**

TOKYO. SOMUKYOKU. TOKEIBU See TOKYO-TO TOKEI CHOSA ICHIRAN **5345**

TOKYO SUISAN DAIGAKU See REPORT OF THE TOKYO UNIVERSITY OF FISHERIES **2311**

TOKYO SUISAN DAIGAKU See JOURNAL OF THE TOKYO UNIVERSITY OF FISHERIES **2307**

TOKYO-TO CHUO OROSHIURI SHIJO See TOKYO-TO CHUO OROSHIURI SHIJO GAIYO **715**

TOKYO-TO CHUO OROSHIURI SHIJO GAIYO (JA) [01797351] **715**

TOKYO-TO GAKKO MEIBO (JA) [02959278] **1788**

TOKYO-TO HAIKU REMMEI See TOKYO-TO HAIKU REMMEI TAIKAI KUSHU **3447**

TOKYO-TO HAIKU REMMEI TAIKAI KUSHU (JA) [05951725] **3447**

TOKYO-TO KOBUNSHOKAN See TOKYO-TO KOBUNSHOKAN NENPO **4691**

TOKYO-TO KOBUNSHOKAN NENPO (JA) [10670121] **4691**

TOKYO-TO KOGAI KENKYUJO See ANNUAL REPORT - TOKYO-TO KOGAI KENKYUJO **2224**

TOKYO-TO KOGAT KENKYUJO See KOGAI KENKYU NEMPO **2235**

TOKYO-TO ROJIN SOGO KENKYUJO See TOKYO-TO ROJIN SOGO KENKYUJO NEMPO **3755**

TOKYO-TO ROJIN SOGO KENKYUJO NEMPO (JA) [03800774] **3755**

TOKYO-TO SHIKEN KENKYU KIKAN NO KENKYU KEIKAKU (JA) [06569318] **5166**

TOKYO-TO SHINKEI KAGAKU SOGO KENKYUJO See TOKYO-TO SHINKEI KAGAKU SOGO KENKYUJO NEMPO **3846**

TOKYO-TO SHINKEI KAGAKU SOGO KENKYUJO NEMPO (JA/0301-5041) [01790268] **3937**, **3846**

TOKYO-TO SHINSHIN SHOGAISHA FUKUSHI SENTA See KENKYU HOKOKU SHU - TOKYO-TO SHINSHIN SHOGAISHA FUKUSHI SENTA **5294**

TOKYO-TO SHOHISHA SENTA See SHOHISHA SODAN JIREI SHU **1299**

TOKYO-TO SUIBO KEIKAKU (JA) [06706132] **2096**

TOKYO-TO TOKEI CHOSA ICHIRAN (JA) [05634092] **5345**

TOKYO TOGIKAI GIIN SENKYO NO KIROKU (JA) [01800118] **4691**

TOKYO TORITSU DAIGAKU. KOGAKUBU See MEMOIRS OF FACULTY OF TECHNOLOGY, TOKYO METROPOLITAN UNIVERSITY **1987**

TOKYO TORITSU EISEI KENKYUJO KENKYU NEMPO (JA/0082-4771) [09959495] **4805**

TOKYO TORITSU KOGYO GIJUTSU SENTA KENKYU HOKOKU (JA) [08105775] **5166**

TOKYO YESTERDAY, TODAY AND TOMORROW (JA) [20559188] **2666**

TOKYO YUSEIKYOKU TOKEI NEMPO (JA) [01797121] **1147**

TOLDETATEN (DK) [10386217] **853**

TOLDOT HA-DOAR SHEL ERETS YISRAEL (IS) [06634672] **1147**, **2787**

TOLDVAESENET (DK) [01787992] **4756**

TOLE WORLD (US/0199-4514) [05884606] **332**

TOLEDO AREA ABORIGINAL RESEARCH BULLETIN *CEASED*. (US/0145-5443) [02750672] **2763**

TOLEDO BUSINESS JOURNAL (US) **715**

TOLEDO-LUCAS COUNTY PUBLIC LIBRARY See COUNTY LINE, THE **3204**

TOLEDO SPORTSMAN, THE (US/8750-6726) [11682012] **4926**

TOLEDO TECHNICAL TOPICS (US/0745-9297) [08217010] **5166**

TOLEDO UNION JOURNAL (US/0745-1989) [06483970] **5731**

TOLEDOT (US/0146-9568) [03129026] **2475**

TOLERIE PONTAULT-COMBAULT (FR/0985-5637) [I09855637] **4022**

TOLETUM (SP/0210-6310) [I02106310] **2855**

TOLIATTINSKAIA GIDROMETEOROLOGICHESKAIA OBSERVATORIIA See SBORNIK RABOT TOLJATTINSKOJ GIDROMETEOROLOGICESKOJ OBSERVATORII **1417**

TOLILALAR PATAI (CE) [09600269] **141**, **1714**

TOLL FREE BUSINESS (US/0146-6801) [03443441] **1168**

TOLL FREE DIGEST *SUSPENDED*. (US/0363-2962) [02451796] **1168**

TOLL-FREE TRAVEL/VACATION PHONE DIRECTORY (US/0739-1420) [08526777] **5492**

TOLLEY PUBLISHING COMPANY See TOLLEY'S CORPORATION TAX **4756**

TOLLEY'S CAPITAL ALLOWANCES (UK) **3065**

TOLLEY'S CAPITAL GAINS TAX / DAVID G. YOUNG, DAVID R. HARRIS (UK) [08601701] **4756**, **3065**

TOLLEY'S CAPITAL TRANSFER TAX (UK) [08248984] **3065**

● TOLLEY'S COMPUTER LAW AND PRACTICE (UK/0266-4801) [25714146] **1239**, **1227**

TOLLEY'S CORPORATION TAX (UK) [07722031] **4756**

TOLLEY'S EMPLOYMENT HANDBOOK (UK) **1714**

● TOLLEY'S IMMIGRATION AND NATIONALITY LAW AND PRACTICE (UK/0269-5774) [25865541] **1921**

TOLLEY'S INCOME TAX (UK/0305-893X) [01798640] **3065**, **4756**

TOLLEY'S INHERITANCE TAX (UK) **4756**

TOLLEY'S JOURNAL OF MEDIA LAW AND PRACTICE (UK) [25161986] **3065**

TOLLEY'S LAW DATA (UK) **3065**

TOLLEY'S NATIONAL INSURANCE CONTRIBUTIONS (UK) **2894**

TOLLEY'S OFFICIAL TAX STATEMENTS (UK) [19746654] **4756**

TOLLEY'S PRACTICAL TAX (UK) **4756**

TOLLEY'S PRACTICAL VAT (UK) **3065**

TOLLEY'S PROFESSIONAL NEGLIGENCE (UK) [25720179] **3065**

TOLLEY'S PROPERTY TAXES (UK) **4756**

TOLLEY'S SOCIAL SECURITY AND STATE BENEFITS (UK) **2894**

TOLLEY'S STAMP DUTIES & STAMP DUTY RESERVE TAX (UK) **4756**

TOLLEY'S TAX CASES (UK) [07212494] **4756**, **3065**

TOLLEY'S TAX COMPUTATIONS (UK) **4756**

TOLLEY'S TAX DATA (UK) [09227430] **4756**

TOLLEY'S TAX PLANNING (UK) **4756**

TOLLEY'S TAX TABLES (UK) [01793918] **4756**

TOLLEY'S TAXATION IN THE CHANNEL ISLANDS AND ISLE OF MAN (UK) [06245721] **4756**

TOLLEY'S TAXATION IN THE REPUBLIC OF IRELAND / BY NIGEL A.D. LAMBERT LLM, BARRISTER & ERIC L. HARVEY, FCA AITI (UK) [08268477] **4756**, **3065**

TOLLEY'S TRADING IN EUROPE (UK) **4756**, **853**

TOLLEY'S TRUST LAW INTERNATIONAL (UK) [29778598] **917**

TOLLEY'S VALUE ADDED TAX (UK) **4756**

TOLLEY'S VAT CASES (UK) **4756**

TOLNA MEGYEI KONYVTAROS (HU/0133-8358) [I01338358] **3253**

TOLSTOY STUDIES JOURNAL (US/1044-1573) [19694467] **3447**

TOLUENE XYLENES ANNUAL (US/0271-2660) [06566224] **1030**

TOLUENE-XYLENES ANNUAL WORLD SURVEY See TOLUENE XYLENES ANNUAL **1030**

TOM GENERAL INDEX (US) **2494**, **2497**

TOM PETERS ON ACHIEVING EXCELLENCE (US/0887-5332) [13291952] **888**

TOM TAC, LE REGIONAL (CN/1187-0672) [24570874] **5796**

TOMAHAWK (ELLWOOD CITY, PA.), THE (US/0741-5435) [10157257] **1850**

TOMAHAWK OF ALPHA SIGMA PHI See TOMAHAWK (ELLWOOD CITY, PA.), THE **1850**

TOMART'S ACTION FIGURE DIGEST (US/1056-8697) [23886979] **2778**

TOMATO GENETICS COOPERATIVE See REPORT OF THE TOMATO GENETICS COOPERATIVE **184**

TOMBALL SUN, THE (US/8750-619X) [11595460] **5755**

TOMBE D'ETA SAITICA A SAQQARA (IT) [10544623] **284**

TOMBSTONE, THE *SUSPENDED*. (US/0893-7664) [10035058] **2475**

TOMBSTONE TRAILS (US/0738-1808) [09518805] **2475**

TOMIN FUJIN NO GONJO (JA) [05780676] **5567**

TOMIN FUJIN NO ISHIKI TO JITTAI CHOSA HOKOKUSHO (JA) [02474633] **5567**

TOMLINSON'S LONE STAR BOOK OF TEXAS RECORDS (US/0271-0218) [06520803] **2763**

TOMMASO NATALE, IL (IT) [05722851] **3109**

TOMORROW : THE GLOBAL ENVIRONMENT MAGAZINE (SW) [24616749] **2182**

TOMORROW'S JOBS, TOMORROW'S WORKERS. CAPITAL REGION (US) [24839734] **1595**

TOMORROW'S JOBS, TOMORROW'S WORKERS. CENTRAL NEW YORK REGION / NEW YORK STATE DEPARTMENT OF LABOR, DIVISION OF RESEARCH AND STATISTICS (US) [24692712] **1714**

TOMORROW'S JOBS, TOMORROW'S WORKERS. FINGER LAKES REGION (US) [25014564] **1714**

TOMORROW'S JOBS, TOMORROW'S WORKERS. HUDSON VALLEY REGION / NEW YORK STATE DEPARTMENT OF LABOR, DIVISION OF RESEARCH AND STATISTICS (US) [24839838] **1714**

TOMORROW'S JOBS, TOMORROW'S WORKERS. LONG ISLAND REGION / NEW YORK STATE DEPARTMENT OF LABOR, DIVISION OF RESEARCH AND STATISTICS (US) [24852820] **1714**

TOMORROW'S JOBS, TOMORROW'S WORKERS. MOHAWK VALLEY REGION / NEW YORK STATE DEPARTMENT OF LABOR, DIVISION OF RESEARCH AND STATISTICS (US) [24692828] **1714**

TOMORROW'S JOBS, TOMORROW'S WORKERS. NEW YORK CITY / NEW YORK STATE DEPARTMENT OF LABOR, DIVISION OF RESEARCH AND STATISTICS (US) [24585657] **1714**

TOMORROW'S JOBS, TOMORROW'S WORKERS. NORTH COUNTRY REGION (US) [24692903] **1714**

TOMORROW'S JOBS, TOMORROW'S WORKERS. SOUTHERN TIER REGION / NEW YORK STATE DEPARTMENT OF LABOR, DIVISION OF RESEARCH AND STATISTICS (US) [24565013] **1714**

TOMORROW'S JOBS, TOMORROW'S WORKERS. WESTERN NEW YORK REGION / NEW YORK STATE DEPARTMENT OF LABOR, DIVISION OF RESEARCH AND STATISTICS (US) [24604288] **1714**

TOMORROW'S NATION *CEASED*. (US/1068-1817) [27464168] **5699**

TOMORROW'S OFFICE (CN/0821-4905) [09590456] **888**

TOMPKINS COUNTY HOME & GARDEN (US) [09521230] **2432**, **2793**

TOMPKINSVILLE NEWS, THE (US) [14184639] **5683**

TOMSKII POLITEKHNICHESKII INSTITUT IM. S.M. KIROVA See SBORNIK ANNOTACIJ NAUCNO-ISSLEDOVATELSKIH RABOT - TOMSKIJ POLITEHNICESKIJ INSTITUT IM. S.M. KIROVA **5149**

TON AMI (CN/0824-1422) [12266713] **5005**

TON REPORT (GW) [05896228] **5319**

TONAM HAKPO (KO) [05861012] **3329**

TONAWANDA NEWS (US) [17869395] **5721**

TONEEL TEATRAAL (NE/0040-9170) [03643656] **389**

TONER TECHNOLOGY MONTHLY (US/1066-0011) [26822552] **4214**

TONGA KURUP (KO) [07983155] **1629**

TONGA PAEKHWAJOM SABO (KO) [10257709] **716**

TONGA YONGU (KO) [09530320] **2666**

TONGBANG HAKCHI (KO) [08479788] **2666**

TONGBANG PYONGNON : THE ORIENTAL REVIEW (KO) [10153783] **2509**

TONGGANG SI / TONGGANG SI TONGINHOE (KO) [10596292] **3472**

Alphabetical Title Index   TORGOVLIA

TONGGWANG (KO) [05059851] **2509**

TONGHAK SASANG NONCHONG (KO) [10469665] **5005**

TONGIL MUNJE YONGU (CHOSON TAEHAKKYO. TONGIL MUNJE YONGUSO) (KO) [08365168] **2666**

TONGIL MUNYE (CN) [07659123] **3447**

TONGIL SEGYE (KO) [11378034] **5068**

TONGIL (SEOUL, KOREA) (KO) [08239586] **2666**

TONGNYOK CHAWON (KO) [13324262] 2152, **1959**

TONGNYOK CHAWON YONGU (KO) [08293605] **2084**

TONGUN. TONGA (KO) [04283678] **1629**

TONIC (ROBERT SIMPSON SOCIETY) (UK/0260-7425) [09492310] **4156**

TONINDUSTRIE ZEITUNG FACHBERICHTE (GW) [04977358] **2594**

TONKAWA NEWS, THE (US) [13621324] **5732**

TONNAGE OF FERTILIZER SOLD IN MISSISSIPPI (US) [03773205] **141**

TONNAGE OF FERTILIZER SOLD IN MISSISSIPPI BY GRADES (US) [04576678] **141**

TONOPAH TIMES-BONANZA AND GOLDFIELD NEWS (US) [13622476] **5708**

TONUS DENTAIRE (FR) **1336**

TONUS MEDICAL (FR) **3646**

TONUS PHARMACIE PRATIQUE (FR) **4330**

TONYOBYO (JA/0021-437X) [10465490] **3733**

TOOELE TRANSCRIPT-BULLETIN (US) [13018879] **5757**

TOOL & ALLOY STEELS (II/0377-9408) [02747483] **2130**

● TOOL WATCH (US/1063-2662) [25958428] **1205**

TOOLING & PRODUCTION (US/0040-9243) [05095461] **2130**

TOOLS & TILLAGE (DK/0563-8887) [00975392] **141**

TOOLS & TRADES (UK/0266-1756) [16850854] **635**

TOOSHI KENKYU (JA/0386-6904) [05591950] **2712**

TOP 10'S AND TRIVIA OF ROCK & ROLL AND RHYTHM & BLUES *CEASED.* (US) [09578808] **4156**

TOP 100 BUSINESS LIBRARIES (UK/0967-6368) 716, **3253**

TOP 100 COOPERATIVES FINANCIAL PROFILE / UNITED STATES DEPARTMENT OF AGRICULTURE, AGRICULTURAL COOPERATIVE SERVICE (US) [09232801] **1543**

TOP 3,000 DIRECTORIES & ANNUALS : A GUIDE TO THE MAJOR TITLES USED IN BRITISH LIBRARIES, THE (UK) [12964796] **1929**

TOP AGRAR : DAS MAGAZIN FUR MODERNE LANDWIRTSCHAFT (GW) [08139008] **141**

TOP BID (US) **5166**

TOP BULLETIN : A JOINT ACTIVITY OF THE U.S. DEPARTMENT OF COMMERCE AND THE U.S. FOREIGN SERVICE--U.S. DEPARTMENT OF STATE (US) [04506981] **853**

TOP-BUSINESS (GW) [25897880] 888, **1629**

TOP ... CREDIT UNION INVESTORS IN BANKS AND S&L'S (US) [18145438] **814**

TOP CULTURES (FRANCE) (FR/1156-1602) [23922614] **141**

TOP EXECUTIVE COMPENSATION (US) [02246598] **716**

TOP FIVE CONTRACTORS RECEIVING THE LARGEST DOLLAR VOLUME OF PRIME CONTRACT AWARDS IN EACH STATE (US/0743-5010) [10362904] **1629**

TOP GENERATION NEWSLETTER (CN/0229-2602) [08028036] **5182**

TOP HAIR (GW/0178-9805) [01789805] **405**

TOP LINE (US/0738-6699) [09627117] **888**

TOP MANAGEMENT DIGEST *See* EXECUTIVE DEVELOPMENT **867**

TOP MUSIQUE (FR) [02242699] **4157**

TOP PAY UNIT REVIEW : MONTHLY REVIEW OF SALARIES AND BENEFITS *See* MANAGEMENT PAY REVIEW **1689**

TOP SECURITY (UK) [04028169] **3178**

TOP SHELF *CEASED.* (US/1040-0885) [18315422] **5073**

TOP STORIES *SUSPENDED.* (US) [10178036] **3472**

TOP VENTES BOULOGNE-BILLANCOURT (FR/0996-8067) [I09968067] **716**

TOP VIDEO (IT) **4079**

TOPEKA BUSINESS REPORT, THE (US/0889-6992) [12994822] **716**

TOPEKA CAPITAL-JOURNAL (TOPEKA, KAN. : MORNING ED.) (US/1067-1994) [08787195] **5678**

TOPEKA GENEALOGICAL SOCIETY QUARTERLY, THE (US/0734-8495) [08315996] **2475**

TOPEKA MAGAZINE (US/0192-3080) [04993528] **2548**

TOPIC (VANCOUVER) (CN/0710-2135) [08418977] **5068**

TOPIC (WASHINGTON) *SUSPENDED.* (US/0049-4127) [01586535] **2855**

TOPIC WINDSOR (UK/0953-895X) [I0953895X] **1788**

TOPICAL BRIEFS, FISH AND WILDLIFE RESOURCES AND ELECTRIC POWER GENERATION / BIOLOGICAL SERVICES PROGRAM (US) [07626323] **2207**

TOPICAL HANDBOOK *See* ATA HANDBOOK **2784**

TOPICAL INDEX FOR THE ANNUAL EDITIONS BASIC REFERENCE LIBRARY (US) [05237502] **3253**

TOPICAL ISSUES IN PROCUREMENT SERIES (US) 1073, 3065, **952**

TOPICAL LAW *CEASED.* (UK/0265-9735) [11330100] **3065**

TOPICAL LAW REPORTS (CN) [21149714] **853**

TOPICAL NEW ISSUES (US/0090-7286) [01783743] **2788**

TOPICAL REVIEWS IN VASCULAR SURGERY (UK/0264-3014) [09452583] **3976**

TOPICAL STUDIES (US) [07002582] **2763**

TOPICAL TIME (US/0040-9332) [02252027] **2788**

TOPICATOR (US/0040-9340) [01781584] 1123, **1125**

TOPICS (UK) **4209**

TOPICS AND TEXTS IN MATHEMATICS (UK) [12707421] **3539**

TOFICS CATALOG (US/1050-1398) [21417752] **1141**

TOPICS IN ACUTE CARE AND TRAUMA REHABILITATION *CEASED.* (US/0885-971X) [12794205] **3646**

TOPICS IN ANTIBIOTIC CHEMISTRY *CEASED.* (UK/0140-0843) [03597604] **4331**

TOPICS IN APPLIED PHYSICS (GW/0303-4216) [00944392] **4423**

TOPICS IN BIOELECTROCHEMISTRY AND BIOENERGETICS (UK/0160-3183) [03451033] 1035, **493**

TOPICS IN CARBON-13 NMR SPECTROSCOPY (US/0093-2221) [01984471] **1019**

TOPICS IN CATALYSIS (NE) **994**

TOPICS IN CHEMICAL ENGINEERING (US/0277-5883) [07610882] **2017**

● TOPICS IN CLINICAL CHIROPRACTIC (US/1073-2837) [29382113] **3807**

TOPICS IN CLINICAL NUTRITION (US/0883-5691) [12173391] **4199**

TOPICS IN CURRENT CHEMISTRY (GW/0340-1022) [01793926] **994**

TOPICS IN CURRENT PHYSICS (GW/0342-6793) [03219145] **4423**

TOPICS IN EARLY CHILDHOOD SPECIAL EDUCATION (US/0271-1214) [06550492] 1805, **1886**

TOPICS IN EMERGENCY MEDICINE (US/0164-2340) [04617701] **3725**

TOPICS IN ENGINEERING (UK/0952-5300) [20738535] **1999**

TOPICS IN ENVIRONMENTAL HEALTH (NE/0166-2082) [04924992] 2182, **4805**

TOPICS IN ENVIRONMENTAL PHYSIOLOGY AND MEDICINE (US/0172-6048) [08498770] **2182**

TOPICS IN ENZYME AND FERMENTATION BIOTECHNOLOGY *CEASED.* (UK/0140-0835) [03152954] **3696**

TOPICS IN FAMILY PSYCHOLOGY AND COUNSELING *CEASED.* (US/1058-9864) [24451486] **4620**

TOPICS IN GASTROENTEROLOGY (UK/0307-6598) [01650312] **3748**

TOPICS IN GEOBIOLOGY (US/0275-0120) [07062829] **475**

TOPICS IN GERIATRIC REHABILITATION (US/0882-7524) [11961054] **3755**

TOPICS IN HEALTH CARE FINANCING (US/0095-3814) [01535495] 3793, **814**

TOPICS IN HEALTH INFORMATION MANAGEMENT (US/0270-5230) [06454717] **3793**

● TOPICS IN HEALTH INFORMATION MANAGEMENT (US/1065-0989) [26450644] **4805**

TOPICS IN HEALTH RECORD MANAGEMENT *See* TOPICS IN HEALTH INFORMATION MANAGEMENT **4805**

TOPICS IN HORMONE CHEMISTRY (UK/0271-9282) [04174146] **587**

TOPICS IN HOSPITAL PHARMACY MANAGEMENT (US/0271-1206) [06550764] 888, **4331**

TOPICS IN INORGANIC AND GENERAL CHEMISTRY (NE/0082-495X) [02993105] **1038**

TOPICS IN LANGUAGE DISORDERS (US/0271-8294) [06690806] 4394, **3329**

TOPICS IN LIPID CHEMISTRY *CEASED.* (US) [06027130] **1048**

TOPICS IN MAGNETIC RESONANCE IMAGING (US/0899-3459) [18068151] **3947**

TOPICS IN MOLECULAR AND STRUCTURAL BIOLOGY (UK/0265-4377) [12428973] **475**

TOPICS IN MOLECULAR PHARMACOLOGY (NE/0167-7101) [08411746] **4331**

TOPICS IN MYCOBIOLOGY (CN) [04573293] **576**

TOPICS IN NEUROCHEMISTRY AND NEUROPHARMACOLOGY *CEASED.* (UK/0952-2638) [19485337] **3846**

TOPICS IN PAIN MANAGEMENT (US/0882-5645) [11880370] **3646**

TOPICS IN PEDIATRICS. / MINNEAPOLIS CHILDREN'S HEALTH CENTER (US/0892-0435) [11181757] **3912**

TOPICS IN PHOTOSYNTHESIS (NE/0378-6099) [03410454] **529**

TOPICS IN PHYSICAL ORGANOMETALLIC CHEMISTRY (UK) [14947831] **994**

TOPICS IN SOCIOLINGUISTICS (NE) [18377948] **3329**

TOPICS IN STEREOCHEMISTRY (US/0082-500X) [01767613] **1058**

● TOPICS IN STROKE REHABILITATION (US/1074-9357) [29887968] **4382**

TOPICS IN THE NEUROSCIENCES (US/0897-3946) [14990765] **3846**

TOPICS IN TOTAL COMPENSATION *CEASED.* (US/0888-6032) [13661031] **888**

TOPICS IN VETERINARY MEDICINE (US/1064-5101) [22504252] **5523**

TOPICS ON THE CULTURE OF THE AMERICAN SOUTH (US/1051-371X) [21940049] **2548**

TOPIQUE (FR/0040-9375) [02080118] **4620**

TOPLUM VE BILIM (TU) [05223673] **5224**

TOPOI (NE/0167-7411) [09508371] **4364**

● TOPOLOGICAL METHODS IN NONLINEAR ANALYSIS (PO/1230-3429) [30406136] **3539**

TOPOLOGIE STRUCTURALE STRUCTURAL TOPOLOGY (CN/0226-9171) [05586203] 2033, **3539**

TOPOLOGY AND ITS APPLICATIONS (NE/0166-8641) [05843055] **3539**

TOPOLOGY (BERLIN, WEST) (GW/0720-2571) [09319669] **3539**

TOPOLOGY (OXFORD) (UK/0040-9383) [01714618] **3539**

TOPOLOGY PROCEEDINGS (US/0146-4124) [03645676] **3539**

TOPONYME, LE (CN/0822-7373) [10915401] **2577**

TOPPS MAGAZINE *CEASED.* (US/1047-1871) [20619575] **4926**

TOPS IDEAS (US/0748-0245) [10873122] **2601**

TOPURON SOSIK (KO) [10149582] 1123, **716**

TOR (SW/0495-8772) [01767615] **2712**

TORAH EDUCATION (US) [07026899] **5053**

TORAH U-MADDA JOURNAL, THE (US/1050-4745) [21491917] 5053, **5005**

TORAIBOROJISUTO (JA/0915-1168) [22412094] **2130**

TORCH (INDIANAPOLIS, IND.) (US/8755-3600) [11269666] **5237**

TORCH (WASHINGTON, D.C. : 1980), THE (US/0730-2231) [07228799] **2548**

TOREX *See* COLLECTABLES AUCTION **2772**

TOREX *See* PHILATELIC AUCTION - TOREX **2786**

TOREX *See* MILITARIA AUCTION - TOREX **2781**

TOREX *See* JEWELLERY AUCTION - TOREX **2914**

TORGOVAIA GAZETA (RU) [25544648] **5809**

● TORGOVLIA (RU) [26275485] **853**

TORINO — Alphabetical Title Index

TORINO MOTORI See MOTORI **5420**

TORO KYOTONG (KO) [09224651] **4805**, **5445**

TORONTO & AREA AIRPORT BUSINESS DIRECTORY (CN/0822-7748) [10768413] **37**

TORONTO ARGONAUT FOOTBALL CLUB See TORONTO ARGONAUTS FACT BOOK **4926**

TORONTO ARGONAUTS FACT BOOK (CN/0227-6526) [08302644] **4926**

TORONTO BIOSCAN (CN) **3697**

TORONTO BOARD OF EDUCATION. RESEARCH DEPT See RESEARCH SERVICE - RESEARCH DEPARTMENT. BOARD OF EDUCATION FOR THE CITY OF TORONTO **1779**

TORONTO CHILDREN'S CHORUS See TORONTO CHILDREN'S CHORUS **4157**

TORONTO CHILDREN'S CHORUS (CN/0844-5818) [19995619] 1070, **4157**

TORONTO CHRONICLE, THE (CN/0821-6312) [09796028] **2548**

TORONTO CLARION (CN/0229-3196) [08072184] **5796**

TORONTO CONSTRUCTION NEWS (CN/0712-5895) [09375344] **630**

TORONTO CONSTRUCTION TRENDS (CN/0827-407X) [12168387] **630**

TORONTO FILMMAKERS' CO-OPERATIVE See TORONTO FILMMAKERS' CO-OP **4079**

TORONTO FILMMAKERS' CO-OP (CN/0704-5816) [03790874] **4079**

TORONTO FINANCIAL INSTITUTIONS TELEPHONE DIRECTORY, METRO TORONTO AND VICINITY (CN/0843-221X) [20121209] **814**

TORONTO HERALD, THE (US/0899-9635) [13554609] **5744**

TORONTO IRISH NEWS (CN/0821-2740) [09448454] **2763**

TORONTO JOURNAL OF THEOLOGY (CN/0826-9831) [12735972] **5005**

TORONTO LEGAL DIRECTORY (CN/0317-588X) [02248356] **3065**

TORONTO LIFE (CN/0049-4194) [02545264] **2548**

TORONTO LIFE FASHION (CN/0821-7955) [09938493] **406**

TORONTO MEDIEVAL BIBLIOGRAPHIES (CN/0082-5042) [01781585] **426**

TORONTO MEDIEVAL LATIN TEXTS (CN) [03136319] 2712, **3447**

TORONTO MUSIC GUIDE (CN/0049-4208) [02624928] **4157**

●TORONTO REGION TOP EMPLOYERS GUIDE (CN/1199-6579) [31095556] **1629**

●TORONTO REVIEW OF CONTEMPORARY WRITING ABROAD, THE (CN) [29698699] **3447**

TORONTO ROYALIST (CN) **2494**

TORONTO SOUTH ASIAN REVIEW See TORONTO REVIEW OF CONTEMPORARY WRITING ABROAD, THE **3447**

TORONTO SOUTH ASIAN REVIEW, THE (CN/0714-3508) [09075022] **3447**

TORONTO STAR (CN/0319-0781) [01767637] **5796**

TORONTO STOCK EXCHANGE See TORONTO STOCK EXCHANGE '300' STOCK PRICE INDEX SYSTEM, THE **917**

TORONTO STOCK EXCHANGE See TORONTO STOCK EXCHANGE REVIEW, THE **917**

TORONTO STOCK EXCHANGE '300' STOCK PRICE INDEX SYSTEM, THE (CN/0703-7716) [03645252] **917**

TORONTO STOCK EXCHANGE REVIEW, THE (CN/0049-4216) [02079838] **917**

TORONTO STUDIES IN RELIGION (US/8756-7385) [11637842] **5005**

TORONTO STUDIES IN THEOLOGY. BONHOEFFER SERIES (US) [10114586] **5005**

TORONTO SUN. MICROFORM, THE (CN/0837-3175) [18110480] **5796**

TORONTO THEATRE REVIEW (CN/0225-638X) [06156783] **5372**

TORONTO TONIGHT CEASED. (CN/0827-4207) [12199556] **4855**

TORONTO TREE (CN/0381-9167) [02199642] **2475**

TORONTO. UNIVERSITY. ALEXANDER FOUNDATION See ALEXANDER LECTURES, THE **3359**

TORONTO'S WEDDING BELLS (CN/0831-2184) [15046050] 5269, **2286**

TORRE DE PAPEL (IOWA CITY, IOWA) (US/1056-8336) [23872071] **3447**

TORRE (RIO PIEDRAS (SAN JUAN), P.R.), LA (PR/0040-9588) [01767638] 3329, **3447**

TORRENS (SP) [11334252] 284, **2713**

TORREY BOTANICAL CLUB See BULLETIN OF THE TORREY BOTANICAL CLUB, THE **505**

TORREY BOTANICAL CLUB See MEMOIRS OF THE TORREY BOTANICAL CLUB **518**

TORRINGTON TELEGRAM (US) [25575099] **5773**

TORRINGTON VOICE, THE (US) [30323217] **2548**

TORT & INSURANCE LAW JOURNAL (US/0885-856X) [12763429] **3065**

TORT LAW LETTER, THE (US/0094-7849) [01795051] **3065**

TORTS (US/0098-7611) [02239700] **3065**

TORYO WA TOJANG (KO) [10053987] **4225**

TOSCANA QUI (IT) **332**

TOSCANAVERDE See VERDEDOMANI **2222**

TOSEI (JA) [05780800] **4691**

TOSHI JUTAKU CEASED. (JA) [10582939] **310**

TOSHI KENKYU HOKOKU (JA) [02473346] **2837**

TOSHIBA'S SELECTED PAPERS ON SCIENCE & TECHNOLOGY (JA/0916-1465) [I09161465] **5166**

TOSHIBA'S SELECTED PAPERS ON SCIENCE & TECHNOLOGY / TOSHIBA (JA) [20438296] **2084**

TOSHIBETSU KEIZAI SHIHYO (JA) [01797069] **853**

TOSHIKA NO TAME NO GYOKAI BUNSEKI (JA) [12089551] 1629, **716**

TOSHO (JA) [01589505] 3253, **4833**

TOSHO MOKUROKU - KOKU IGAKU JIKKENTAI (JA) [02244380] **3662**

TOSHO SHINYOROKU. KANTO-BAN (JA) [02174176] **814**

TOSHOKAN JANARU (JA) [02245331] **3253**

TOSHOKAN JOHO DAIGAKU KENKYU HOKOKU (JA/0287-0010) [10946703] **3253**

TOSHOKAN KYORYOKU TSUSHIN (JA/0913-8005) **3253**

TOSHOKAN NENKAN / HENSHU, NIHON TOSHOKAN KYOKAI TOSHOKAN NENKAN HENSHU IINKAI (JA) [08994959] **3253**

TOSHOKAN ZASSHI (JA/0385-4000) [01476453] **3253**

TOSHOKANGAKU NEMPO / DOSHISHA DAIGAKU (JA) [07480939] **3253**

TOSHOKANHO (JA) [03973224] **3253**

TOSHOKANKAI (JA/0040-9669) [10713331] **3253**

TOSOGWAN (KO) [04115200] **3253**

TOSOGWAN HWICHONG (KO) [11014359] **3253**

TOSOGWAN MUNHWA (KO) [22159677] **3253**

TOT (IT) **1788**

TOT TALK (CN/0824-507X) [10638782] **4805**

TOTAH TRACINGS (US) **2475**

TOTAL AIDS CASES, UTAH AND UNITED STATES (US) [21359022] 3677, 3716, **4805**

TOTAL COMPAGNIE FRANCAISE DES PETROLES See TOTAL COMPAGNIE FRANCAISE DES PETROLIS IN ... **4280**

TOTAL COMPAGNIE FRANCAISE DES PETROLIS IN ... (FR) [14396020] **4280**

TOTAL COMPLIANCE (US) **4805**

TOTAL EMPLOYEE INVOLVEMENT (US/0896-7776) [17287221] 1714, **888**

TOTAL FOOD SERVICE : TFS (US/1060-8966) [25101733] **2360**

TOTAL HEALTH (US/0274-6743) [06478806] **4805**

TOTAL INFORMATION (FR/0152-6189) [12952195] **4280**

TOTAL PRODUCTIVE MAINTENANCE : TPM (US/1054-1233) [22754551] 3489, **888**

TOTAL QUALITY & SITE-BASED MANAGEMENT JOURNAL (US) **888**

TOTAL QUALITY ENVIRONMENTAL MANAGEMENT (US/1055-7571) [23302474] **2182**

●TOTAL QUALITY IN HOSPITALITY (US/1069-5591) [28102744] **2809**

TOTAL QUALITY MANAGEMENT (UK/0954-4127) [22150210] **888**

TOTAL QUALITY NEWSLETTER (US/1053-1718) [22196780] **888**

TOTAL QUALITY REVIEW, THE (US/1075-2056) [29959823] **888**

●TOTAL TRIATHLON ALMANAC, THE (US/1065-1977) [26522714] **4926**

TOTEM (OLYMPIA) (US/0040-9723) [01713574] **2207**

TOTH-MAATIAN REVIEW, THE (US/0740-7564) [09390129] **2494**

TOTLINE (US/0734-4473) [08470174] **1908**

TOTTORI DAIGAKU KYOIKUGAKUBU KENKYU HOKOKU. SHINZEN KAGAKU (JA/0371-5965) [09845776] **1850**

TOTTORI DAIGAKU. NOGAKU-BU See TOTTORI DAIGAKU NOGAKUBU KENKYU HOKOKU **142**

TOTTORI DAIGAKU. NOGAKUBU See JOURNAL OF THE FACULTY OF AGRICULTURE, TOTTORI UNIVERSITY **101**

TOTTORI DAIGAKU NOGAKUBU KENKYU HOKOKU (JA/0372-0349) [I03720349] **142**

TOTTORI DAIGAKU NOGAKUBU KENKYU HOKOKU (JA) [04100986] **142**

TOTTORI DAIGAKU. TOSHOKAN See TOSHOKANHO **3253**

TOTTORI-KEN KOGYO SHIKENJO KENKYU HOKOKU (JA) [07387757] **5166**

TOTTORI-KEN YASAI SHIKENJO KENKYU HOKOKU (JA/0387-6993) [10387936] **189**

TOTUS HOMO (IT/0390-6604) [02082127] **4620**

TOUCHDOWN (PHOENIX, ARIZ.) (US/0090-4228) [01785085] **4926**

TOUCHING (US/0738-6311) [09659826] **2912**

TOUCHSTONE (US) **5005**

TOUCHSTONE (CHICAGO, ILL. 1986) (US/0897-327X) [17460057] **5005**

TOUCHSTONE (MARSHALL, TEX.) (US/0740-8986) [09743908] **2763**

TOUCHSTONE / UNIVERSITY OF WISCONSIN-MADISON, UNIVERSITY-INDUSTRY RESEARCH PROGRAM (US) [09401855] **5166**

TOUCHSTONE (WINNIPEG) (CN/0827-3200) [11732902] **5005**

TOUGH PUZZLES (UK) **4867**

TOULADI (CN/0712-3299) [08898734] **5796**

TOUNG PAO (NE/0082-5433) [01767648] **2666**

TOUR & TRAVEL NEWS (US/0889-3349) [13848895] **5492**

TOUR BOOK : ALABAMA, LOUISIANA, MISSISSIPPI (US/0361-4948) [02246516] **5492**

TOUR BOOK : ARIZONA, NEW MEXICO (US/0362-3599) [02326485] **5492**

TOUR BOOK : ARKANSAS, KANSAS, MISSOURI, OKLAHOMA (US/0363-1486) [02414046] **5492**

TOUR BOOK : ATLANTIC PROVINCES AND QUEBEC (US/0363-1788) [02420565] **5492**

TOUR BOOK: CONNECTICUT, MASSACHUSETTS, RHODE ISLAND (US/0363-1494) [02414050] **5492**

TOUR BOOK : GEORGIA, NORTH CAROLINA, SOUTH CAROLINA (US/0361-4956) [02246961] **5492**

TOUR BOOK : HAWAII (US/0160-6921) [03711487] **5492**

TOUR BOOK : IDAHO, MONTANA, WYOMING (US/0363-2695) [02457388] **5492**

TOUR BOOK : ILLINOIS, INDIANA, OHIO (US/0363-1508) [02414088] **5492**

TOUR BOOK: KENTUCKY-TENNESSEE (US/0361-4964) [02246517] **5492**

TOUR BOOK: MAINE, NEW HAMPSHIRE, VERMONT (US/0363-1516) [02434680] **5492**

TOUR BOOK: MICHIGAN, WISCONSIN (US/0363-1524) [02414096] **5493**

TOUR BOOK: NEW JERSEY, PENNSYLVANIA (US/0363-1532) [02414091] **5493**

TOUR BOOK: NEW YORK (US/0363-1540) [02414100] **5493**

TOUR BOOK: OREGON, WASHINGTON (US/0363-1567) [02414084] **5493**

TOUR BOOK : TEXAS (US/0363-1575) [02414106] **5493**

TOUR BOOK, THE (US/0146-1796) [02879730] **4926**

TOUR BOOK : WESTERN CANADA AND ALASKA (US/0362-3602) [02326444] **5493**

TOUR BRITISH COLUMBIA (CN/0226-3513) [06514477] **5493**

TOUR DE SUTTON, LE (CN/0826-5224) [11245772] **4855**

TOUR DES PONTS, LE (CN/1183-1936) [24256533] **5796**

TOURBILLON DE LA SQTRP, LE (CN/0836-7655) [17835588] **3646**

TOURBOOK: COLORADO, UTAH (US/0362-9821) [03188027] **5493**

TOURBOOK: MID-ATLANTIC (US/0364-0086) [02586647] **5493**

Alphabetical Title Index — TOXICOLOGY

TOURBOOK. NORTH CENTRAL (US/0733-8368) [04763799] **5493**

TOURING (FR) [03402181] **5493**

TOURING AMERICA (US/1055-6850) [23269557] **5493**

TOURISM & HOTEL SECURITY WORLDWIDE MAGAZINE (SZ) [22779741] **2809**

TOURISM AND HOTEL SERVICES STATISTICS QUARTERLY (IS) [07116201] 2809, 5493, **5501**

TOURISM AND TRAVEL DUBLIN (IE/0791-3443) [I07913443] **5493**

TOURISM ASIA (SI) **5493**

●TOURISM ECONOMICS (UK/1354-8166) 5493, **1524**

TOURISM IN CANADA (CN/0838-3863) [19962998] **5493**

TOURISM IN ENGLISH (UK) [03054165] **5493**

TOURISM IN JAPAN (JA) [11346724] **5493**

TOURISM INTELLIGENCE QUARTERLY (UK/0309-8958) [04646688] **5493**

TOURISM MANAGEMENT (1982) (UK/0261-5177) [08435547] 5493, **888**

TOURISM MARKET TRENDS (SP) **5493**

TOURISM MARKETPLACE *CEASED.* (UK) **5493**

TOURISM POLICY AND INTERNATIONAL TOURISM IN OECD MEMBER COUNTRIES (FR) [01796328] **5493**

TOURISM RECREATION RESEARCH (II) [05957959] **5493**

TOURISM TO THE YEAR 2000 AND BEYOND; QUALITATIVE ASPECTS (SP) **5493**

TOURISM TO THE YEAR 2000 AND BEYOND; REGIONAL FORECAST STUDIES (SP) **5493**

TOURISM TODAY OTTAWA (CN/1191-789X) [I1191789X] **5493**

TOURISME (FR) **5493**

TOURISME DANS LE CANTON DU VALAIS. TOURISMUS IM KANTON WALLIS (SZ) [05071635] **5493**

TOURISME EN BELGIQUE, LE (BE) [11017791] **5493**

TOURISME EN FRANCE, LE (FR) [10048740] **5493**

TOURISME+, LE JOURNAL DES VOYAGES (CN/0836-205X) [16856724] **5493**

TOURISME OUTAOUAIS BONJOUR (CN/0848-9815) [21924465] **5493**

TOURISM'S TOP TWENTY (US/1050-6152) [11511745] **5494**

TOURISMUS IM KANTON GRAUBUNDEN (SZ) [02241196] **5494**

TOURISMUS IN DER SCHWEIZ IN DER HOTELLERIE UND DEN UBRIGEN BEHERBERGUNGSFORMEN (SZ) [03536690] 5494, **2809**

TOURISMUS IN FREMDENORTEN UND STADTEN. TOURISME DANS QUELQUES CENTRES TOURISTIQUES ET VILLES (SZ) [03278131] **5494**

TOURISMUS IN FREMDENVERKEHRSORTEN UND STADTEN (SZ) [26902052] 853, **5494**

TOURIST & HOTEL GUIDE FOR LEBANON (LE) [01792320] 2809, **5494**

TOURIST ATTRACTIONS & PARKS (US/0194-4894) [04765438] 5494, **4855**

TOURIST BULGARIA (BU) [08487139] **5494**

TOURIST COUNCIL NEWS (CN/0824-6114) [10832007] **5494**

TOURIST GUIDE BOOK (UA) [01786404] **5494**

TOURIST GUIDE BOOK OF ONTARIO (CN/0319-0439) [02442042] **5494**

TOURIST GUIDE, GREATER QUEBEC AREA (CN/1180-0186) [22632253] **5494**

TOURIST GUIDE, LANAUDIERE (CN/1180-0313) [23242618] 2548, **5494**

TOURIST RECEPTION CENTRE SURVEY (CN/0846-9717) [11680480] **5494**

TOURIST REPORT - MALAWI. NATIONAL STATISTICAL OFFICE (MW) [01784634] **5494**

TOURIST TRADE OF INDIA (II) [01784113] **5494**

TOURISTIC ANALYSIS REVIEW *CEASED.* (FR) [07102147] **5494**

TOURISTICS (AT/0815-1318) [15680242] **5494**

TOURISTISCHE NACHFRAGE DER BUNDESDEUTSCHEN IN DER SCHWEIZ, DIE (SZ) [11901727] **5494**

TOURNAMENT CHESS (UK/0276-7090) [07414608] **4867**

TOURNAMENTS ILLUMINATED (US/0732-6645) [08398140] **2713**

TOURO JOURNAL OF TRANSNATIONAL LAW (US/1046-3445) [19738745] **3136**

TOURO LAW REVIEW (US/8756-7326) [11638260] **3065**

TOUROPINDEX *See* AGENT'S HOTEL GAZETTEER : TOURIST CITIES OF EUROPE, THE **2803**

TOURPLUS (CN) **389**

TOURS & RESORTS (US/0890-2852) [14103671] **5494**

TOURS AND VISITS DIRECTORY (US/0278-467X) [07827788] **5494**

TOURS ON MOTORCOACH (CN/0847-9348) [20781854] **5494**

TOUS LES FILMS (FR) [06829412] **4079**

TOUT A LOISIR (CN/0822-5524) [10105659] **4855**

TOUT EN CARTES (FR/0988-8233) [I09888233] **1524**

TOUT PREVOIR (FR) **3646**

TOUTE JUSTICE (OTTAWA, ONT.), EN (CN/0824-2801) [10156754] 4394, **3065**

TOUTE LA BRODERIE (FR) **5186**

TOUTE LA BRODERIE LE JOURNAL DES BRODEUSES (FR) **2793**

TOUTES LES NOUVELLES DE L'HOTELLERIE ET DU TOURISME (FR/0150-7540) [I01507540] 5494, 5073, **2809**

●TOWARD AN ELECTRONIC PATIENT RECORD (US/1063-973X) [26183426] 1210, **1205**

TOWARD CLOSER TIES (US/0882-9012) [11076636] **1850**

TOWARD FREEDOM (US/0040-9898) [01767652] **4536**

TOWARD FREEDOM (1990) (US/1063-4134) [24507237] **4536**

TOWARD FREEDOM EUROFILE (US) [22151703] **4536**

TOWARD INTERAGENCY COORDINATION: FEDERAL RESEARCH AND DEVELOPMENT ON ADOLESCENCE (US/0193-1385) [04727738] **2286**

TOWARD INTERAGENCY COORDINATION: FEDERAL RESEARCH AND DEVELOPMENT ON EARLY CHILDHOOD (US/0275-133X) [04727752] **1788**

TOWARDS WHOLENESS (UK) [04522406] **5005**

TOWARZYSTWO D/S UCHOCZCOW W NANAIMO (CN/0824-5177) [10857677] **5312**

TOWARZYSTWO NAUKOWE W TORUNIU *See* STUDIA SOCIETATIS SCIENTIARUM TORUNENSIS. SECTIO C. GEOGRAPHIA ET GEOLOGIA **2577**

TOWARZYSTWO NAUKOWE W TORUNIU. KOMISJA HISTORII SZTUKI *See* TEKA **2631**

TOWARZYSTWO NAUKOWE W TORUNIU. WYDZIA NAUK HISTORYCZNYCH *See* ZAPISKI HISTORYCZNE **2716**

TOWER (HAMILTON) (CN/0495-9701) [02731787] **3472**

TOWERS CLUB USA *See* TOWERS CLUB USA NEWSLETTER **2925**

TOWERS CLUB USA NEWSLETTER (US/0193-4953) [06058093] 937, **2925**

TOWN & COUNTRY BED & BREAKFAST IN B.C., CANADA *CEASED.* (CN/0823-8502) [11629641] **5494**

TOWN AND COUNTRY FARMER (AT/0814-4540) [I08144540] **142**

TOWN AND COUNTRY (LANSDALE, PA.) (US/0888-9996) [13781301] **5740**

●TOWN AND COUNTRY MAGAZINE PERSONAL NAME INDEX (US/1064-9654) [26478002] **426**

TOWN & COUNTRY NEEDLECRAFT (AT) **5186**

TOWN & COUNTRY (NEW YORK, N.Y.) (US/0040-9952) [05878257] **2548**

TOWN & COUNTRY PLANNING (UK/0040-9960) [01714593] **4691**

TOWN AND COUNTRY PLANNING ASSOCIATION *See* PLANNING BULLETIN **2831**

TOWN AND COUNTRY PLANNING ASSOCIATION (GREAT BRITAIN) *See* ANNUAL REPORT - TOWN AND COUNTRY PLANNING ASSOCIATION **2815**

TOWN AND COUNTRY PLANNING SUMMER SCHOOL *See* REPORT OF PROCEEDINGS - TOWN AND COUNTRY PLANNING SUMMER SCHOOL **2833**

TOWN & VILLAGE (US/0040-9979) [03950210] **5721**

TOWN COUNCILS ESTIMATES OF EXPENDITURE AND INCOME, RECURRENT BUDGET AND CAPITAL BUDGETS *See* TOWN COUNCILS ESTIMATES OF REVENUE AND EXPENDITURE, RECURRENT BUDGET **4756**

TOWN COUNCILS ESTIMATES OF REVENUE AND EXPENDITURE, RECURRENT BUDGET *CEASED.* (BS) [01795531] **4756**

TOWN CRIER (COCHRANE) (CN/0710-541X) [08700999] **5796**

TOWN HALL JOURNAL (US/0732-4049) [08064286] **4691**

TOWN HISTORY SERIES (UK) [12223891] **2631**

TOWN MEETING (US) **5694**

TOWN OF MOUNT ROYAL WEEKLY POST (CN/0834-700X) [22478676] **5796**

TOWN OF VAUGHAN VANGUARD, THE (CN/0701-0869) [03406341] **2548**

TOWN OF VAUGHAN WEEKLY, THE (CN/0380-3694) [02443366] **5796**

TOWN-PLANNING AND LOCAL GOVERNMENT GUIDE, THE (AT/0040-9995) [02079855] 3065, **2837**

TOWN PLANNING MANUAL (NR/0331-0485) [01786573] **2837**

TOWN PLANNING REVIEW (UK/0041-0020) [01641371] **2837**

TOWN SQUIRE (US) **2494**

TOWN TOPICS (US) [23720743] **4691**

TOWN TOPICS (PRINCETON, N.J.) (US/0191-7056) [04926661] **5711**

TOWN, VILLAGE AND CITY TAXES (US) [04510022] **4756**

TOWNE COURIER (US/1062-4279) [10243885] **5694**

TOWNER COUNTY RECORD HERALD (US) [01767657] **5726**

TOWNSEND STAR (US) [14077917] **5706**

TOWNSFOLK (US/0892-0443) [15103867] **2494**

TOWNSHIPS CROSSROADS (CN/0228-6858) [09318285] **5224**

TOWNSHIPS SUN, THE (CN/0316-022X) [02247308] **5796**

TOWNSMAN (BRIDGEWATER, MASS.) *See* BRIDGEWATER TOWNSMAN, THE **5688**

TOWPATHS (US/0890-7129) [05858773] **5394**

TOWSON STATE JOURNAL OF INTERNATIONAL AFFAIRS (US/0041-0063) [02246816] **4536**

TOWSON STATE UNIVERSITY JOURNAL OF PSYCHOLOGY (US/0161-7648) [04026807] **4620**

TOXIC AND HAZARDOUS INDUSTRIAL CHEMICALS SAFETY MANUAL (JA) **2871**

TOXIC AND HAZARDOUS WASTE DISPOSAL (US/0271-9371) [04660694] **2245**

TOXIC CHEMICALS LITIGATION REPORTER (US/0737-8513) [09462769] **3116**

TOXIC CONTROL (US/0276-2242) [07265249] 2245, **3983**

●TOXIC CRUSADERS (US/1064-4261) [26281415] **4867**

TOXIC MATERIALS NEWS (US/0093-5891) [03320970] **2245**

TOXIC MATERIALS TRANSPORT (US/0275-3766) [06895575] 2245, **5394**

TOXIC REAL ESTATE MANUAL (CN) **2182**

●TOXIC SUBSTANCE MECHANISMS (UK/1076-9188) [30636522] **3983**

TOXIC SUBSTANCES BULLETIN (UK/0953-7414) [I09537414] **3983**

TOXIC SUBSTANCES CONTROL ACT (US/0883-0576) [10872766] **3116**

TOXIC SUBSTANCES JOURNAL (US/0199-3178) [05461500] **2871**

TOXIC TIMES (US) [21067185] **2245**

TOXICOLOGIC PATHOLOGY (US/0192-6233) [05035503] 3984, **3898**

TOXICOLOGICAL AND ENVIRONMENTAL CHEMISTRY (UK/0277-2248) [07442593] **3984**

TOXICOLOGICAL EUROPEAN RESEARCH (FR/0249-6402) [04644299] **3984**

TOXICOLOGICAL EVALUATIONS (US) **3984**

TOXICOLOGIST, THE (US/0731-9193) [08268758] **3984**

TOXICOLOGY ABSTRACTS (US/0140-5365) [04219757] 3984, **3662**

TOXICOLOGY (AMSTERDAM) (IE/0300-483X) [01792578] **3984**

TOXICOLOGY AND APPLIED PHARMACOLOGY (US/0041-008X) [01695655] 4331, **3984**

●TOXICOLOGY AND ECOTOXICOLOGY NEWS (UK/1350-4592) **3984**

TOXICOLOGY AND INDUSTRIAL HEALTH (US/0748-2337) [10906396] 2871, **3984**

TOXICOLOGY — Alphabetical Title Index

TOXICOLOGY IN VITRO (UK/0887-2333) [13144158] **3984**

TOXICOLOGY LETTERS (NE/0378-4274) [03180425] **3984**

TOXICOLOGY METHODS (US/1051-7235) [22096208] **3984**

TOXICON (OXFORD) (UK/0041-0101) [01767658] **3984, 4331**

TOXICON. SUPPLEMENT (OXFORD) (UK/0190-5368) [04658496] **4331**

TOXICS LAW REPORTER (US/0887-7394) [13348208] **3116**

TOXICS NEWS See ENVIRONMENTAL ISSUES REPORT **2168**

TOXICS PROGRAM COMMENTARY. FLORIDA (US) **2182**

TOXICS PROGRAM COMMENTARY. ILLINOIS (CN) **2182**

TOXICS PROGRAM COMMENTARY. MASSACHUSETTS (CN) **2182**

TOXICS PROGRAM COMMENTARY. NEW JERSEY (CN) **2182**

TOXICS PROGRAM COMMENTARY. NEW YORK (CN) **2182**

TOXICS PROGRAM COMMENTARY. OHIO (CN) **2182**

TOXICS PROGRAM COMMENTARY. PENNSYLVANIA (CN) **2182**

TOXICS PROGRAM COMMENTARY. TEXAS (CN) **2182**

TOXICS PROGRAM MATRIX (CN) **2182**

TOXICS PROGRAM MATRIX. MASSACHUSETTS (CN) **2182**

TOXICS PROGRAM MATRIX. NEW YORK (CN) **2182**

TOXICS PROGRAM MATRIX. TEXAS (US) **2182**

TOY & HOBBY RETAILER (AT/1035-9176) [10359176] **2778, 2585**

●TOY & HOBBY WORLD (1993) (US/1073-8932) [29545554] **2778, 2585**

TOY & HOBBY WORLD INTERNATIONAL (US/1069-3254) [27991359] **2778, 2585**

TOY & HOBBY WORLD. WEEKLY MARKET REPORT CEASED. (US) [29546375] **2778, 2585, 958**

TOY BOOK, THE (US/0885-3991) [12630224] **2585**

●TOY COLLECTOR (US) [25664125] **2585**

●TOY COLLECTOR & PRICE GUIDE (US/1069-1685) [27954267] **2585**

TOY COLLECTOR MAGAZINE See TOY COLLECTOR **2585**

TOY COLLECTORS DIRECTORY (US) [14408489] **2778**

TOY FARMER, THE (US/0894-5055) [16117697] **2778**

TOY REPORT (US) **2585**

TOY REPORT (CN/0229-8422) [08079011] **2585**

TOY SHOP (US/0898-5650) [17850372] **2585**

TOY TRADER (UK) **2585**

TOY TRADER YEAR BOOK (UK) [02239884] **2585**

TOY TRAIN OPERATING SOCIETY See DIRECTORY / TOY TRAIN OPERATING SOCIETY **2584**

TOY TRUCKER & CONTRACTOR (US/1051-2187) [21893172] **2778**

TOYAMA DAIGAKU JINBUN GAKUBU KIYO (JA/0386-5975) [08660147] **2855**

TOYAMA DAIGAKU KYOIKU GAKUBU KIYO. A, BUNKAKEI (JA) [09047511] **1788**

TOYAMA DAIGAKU KYOIKU GAKUBU KIYO. B, RIKAKEI (JA/0285-9610) [09047436] **5166**

TOYAMA DAIGAKU. NIHONKAI KEIZAI KENKYUJO See KENKYU NEMPO - TOYAMA DAIGAKU NIHONKAI KEIZAI KENKYUJO **1570**

TOYAMA DAIGAKU TORICHIUMU KAGAKU SENTA KENKYU HOKOKO (JA/0287-1408) [09293066] **1038**

TOYAMA DAIGAKU. WAKAN-YAKU KENKYUJO See WAKAN-YAKU KENKYUJO NEMPO **4332**

TOYAMA KENRITSU GIJUTSU TANKI DAIGAKU KENKYU HOKOKU (JA/0389-9330) [10400788] **5166**

TOYAMA SHOSEN KOTO SEMMON GAKKO See TOYAMA SHOSEN KOTO SEMMON GAKKO KENKYU SHUROKU **4184**

TOYAMA SHOSEN KOTO SEMMON GAKKO KENKYU SHUROKU (JA) [01790118] **4184**

TOYO BUNKA (JA/0564-0202) [01714722] **2666**

TOYO BUNKA KENKYUJO KIYO (JA/0563-8089) [02111131] **2666**

TOYO BUNKA KENKYUJO SHOHO (JA) [09328717] **2666**

TOYO DAIGAKU, TOKYO. AJIA-AFURIKA BUNKA KENKYUJO See AJIA-AFURIKA BUNKA KENKYUJO KENKYU NEMPO **2645**

TOYO IGAKU (JA) **3646**

TOYO IGAKU (JA/0385-4469) [03854469] **3646**

TOYO KYOIKUSHI KENKYU (JA) [09544116] **2666**

TOYO ONGAKU KENKYU (JA/0039-3851) [01695347] **4157**

TOYO SODA KENKYU HOKOKU (JA/0041-0144) [09277544] **3489**

TOYOGAKU BUNKEN RUIMOKU (JA) [05121740] **2666**

TOYOTA KOGYO KOTO SEMMON GAKKO See KENKY KIYO - TOYOTA KOGYO KOTO SEMMON GAKKO **1833**

TOYS & GAMES (CN/0381-9930) [02211165] **4867, 2585**

TOYS AND PLAYTHINGS (UK/0041-0187) [00410187] **4867**

TOYS & PRICES See TOY COLLECTOR & PRICE GUIDE **2585**

TOYS COLLECTOR MAGAZINE See TOY COLLECTOR & PRICE GUIDE **2585**

TOYS INTERNATIONAL & TOY BUYER See TOY TRADER **2585**

TP. IL GIORNALE DELLA TRASMISSIONE DI POTENZA CEASED. (IT/0394-512X) [0394512X] **1999**

TP, TECHNIQUES PETROMONDE (FR) [03927334] **4280**

TP. TELEPROGRAMA (SP/0040-2672) [00402672] **1141**

TP; TREFPUNT VAN CULTUUR, RECREATIE EN MAATSCHAPPELIJK WERK See TREFPUNT **2713**

TPA MESSENGER (US/0194-9802) [05174379] **4820**

TPH. THERAPEUTIQUE ET PRATIQUE HOSPITALIERES PARIS (FR/1142-2866) [11422866] **3646**

TPS ET LES TAXES A LA CONSOMMATION, LA (CN/1183-0042) [24266624] **4756**

TPUG MAGAZINE (CN/0825-0367) [11147561] **1205**

●TQM IN HIGHER EDUCATION (US/1065-6774) [26677202] **1850**

TQM MAGAZINE See TOTAL QUALITY REVIEW, THE **888**

TQM MAGAZINE (INTERNATIONAL ED.) (UK/0954-478X) [22272165] **888**

TQS NEWS (US/1045-8875) [20150467] **2274**

TQS : TOTAL QUALITY SALES CEASED. (US) **767**

TR NEWS (US/0738-6826) [09316459] **5394**

TR. TELEVIZIIA, RADIO See TELEVIZIIA, RADIO **1141**

●TR TRANSFER : TECHNISCHE RUNDSCHAU TRANSFER (SZ) [29833869] **5166**

TRA DIGEST (US/0360-7534) [02157806] **5494**

TRA FOODSERVICE DIGEST (US/0890-5134) [07413148] **2360**

TRABAJADORES (CU) [05980988] **5799**

TRABAJO (HO) [05045465] **1714**

TRABAJO SOCIAL Y SALUD (SP/1130-2976) [11302976] **5312**

TRABAJOS & NEGOCIOS (CL) [22919621] **1714**

TRABAJOS DE ARQUEOLOGIA NAVARRA (SP) [08657808] **284**

TRABAJOS DE ESTADISTICA (MADRID. 1986) See TEST (MADRID) **5345**

TRABAJOS DE INVESTIGACION OPERATIVA (SP/0213-8204) [16406276] **3539**

TRABAJOS DE PREHISTORIA (SP/0082-5638) [03449477] **284**

TRABAJOS DEL INSTITUTO CAJAL SUSPENDED. (SP/0211-8343) [12745447] **3847, 540**

TRABAJOS DEL SANATORIO NACIONAL DE FONTILLES See FONTILLES **3720**

TRABAJOS Y COMUNICACIONES / FACULTAD DE HUMANIDADES Y CIENCIAS DE EDUCACION, INSTITUTO DE INVESTIGACIONES HISTORICAS (AG) [01154267] **2631**

TRABALHOS DE ANTROPOLOGIA E ETNOLOGIA (PO) [05738952] **246**

TRABALHOS EM LINGUISTICA APLICADA (BL/0103-1813) [01031813] **3329**

TRABALHOS TECNICOS - FUNDACAO INSTITUTO BRASILEIRO DE GEOGRAFIA E ESTATISTICA, SUPERINTENDENCIA DE CARTOGRAFIA (BL) [02989625] **2577**

TRAC, TRENDS IN ANALYTICAL CHEMISTRY (NE/0167-2940) [09521237] **1019**

TRAC, TRENDS IN ANALYTICAL CHEMISTRY (PERSONAL EDITION) (NE/0165-9936) [08086251] **1019**

TRACCE (IT) [09836503] **4498**

TRACE ELEMENTS IN ELECTROLYTES (GW) **3647**

TRACE ELEMENTS IN MEDICINE (GW/0174-7371) [10781336] **3647**

TRACE (MEXICO CITY, MEXICO) (MX/0185-6286) [15063228] **5224**

TRACE MINERALS, FOOD AND HEALTH (CN/0843-6584) [20135494] **4199**

TRACE NEWSLETTER - TORONTO REGION AGGREGATION OF COMPUTER ENTHUSIASTS (CN/0827-2131) [11564272] **1205**

TRACE SUBSTANCES IN ENVIRONMENTAL HEALTH (UK) **2221**

TRACE SUBSTANCES IN ENVIRONMENTAL HEALTH (UK/0361-5162) [01564743] **2221**

TRACER - OHIO GENEALOGICAL SOCIETY. HAMILTON COUNTY CHAPTER, THE (US/8756-8462) [08469158] **2475**

TRACES (FR/0248-496X) [09204838] **3447**

TRACES; LINGUISTIQUE SEMIOTIQUE (MR) [07019855] **3329**

TRACES (MONTREAL) (CN/0841-6397) [19027096] **2631, 1908**

TRACES OF INDIANA AND MIDWESTERN HISTORY (US/1040-788X) [18532930] **2763**

TRACES OF SOUTH CENTRAL KENTUCKY (US/0882-2158) [08377388] **2475**

TRACES. TEACHERS OF RELIGION AND CHRISTIAN ETHICS IN SASKATCHEWAN (CN/0704-6421) [03790843] **1788, 5005**

TRACINGS CEASED. (US/0738-4130) [06495550] **3253**

TRACK (KE) [01792179] **4926**

TRACK AND FIELD AND CROSS COUNTRY RULE BOOK (US/1042-878X) [17409284] **4926**

TRACK & FIELD NEWS (US/0041-0284) [01767664] **4926**

TRACK & FIELD QUARTERLY REVIEW (US/0041-0292) [01775440] **4926**

TRACK NEWSLETTER (US/0041-0306) [01767665] **4927**

TRACK TECHNIQUE (US/0742-3918) [01337298] **4927**

TRACKER, THE (US/0041-0330) [01767666] **4157**

TRACKING EASTERN EUROPE (US/1051-7197) [22096148] **917**

TRACKING THE UPCOMING BESTSELLERS CEASED. (US/1044-7644) [19889560] **4833**

TRACKKER (FORT WORTH, TEX.) (US/1056-9782) [23915837] **752**

TRACKS (AT) **4927**

TRACKS AND TRACES (US) [11297349] **2475**

TRACKS (LANSING, MICH.) (US/0738-8810) [09673276] **2207**

TRACS JOURNAL SUSPENDED. (US/0885-7393) [12709460] **1886**

TRACT (CHICOUTIMI) (CN/0713-5726) [08967835] **5796**

TRACTEURS & MACHINES AGRICOLES PARIS (FR/0754-121X) [0754121X] **161**

TRACTION (BE) **4536**

TRACTION YEARBOOK (US/0730-5400) [07894986] **5394**

TRACTOR AND FARM IMPLEMENT LUBRICATION GUIDE (US/0162-3427) [04153121] **161**

TRACTOR DIGEST (US/0731-4698) [08197997] **161**

TRACTOR MAGAZINE, THE (US/1057-0306) [23914077] **161**

TRACTOROEXPORT (RU) [04275158] **161**

TRACTORS, EXCEPT GARDEN TRACTORS (US/0145-5249) [02545236] **1629**

TRACTRIX (NE/0924-0829) [21989474] **5166**

TRACY HEADLIGHT-HERALD (US) [01695405] **5699**

TRADA : REPORT OF THE DIRECTOR OF THE TIMBER RESEARCH AND DEVELOPMENT ASSOCIATION (UK) [04223967] **2405**

TRADE (US/1054-7452) [22964278] **2548**

TRADE AND COMMERCE (WINNIPEG) (CN/0049-4321) [02131149] **853**

Alphabetical Title Index — TRAFFIC

TRADE AND DEVELOPMENT REPORT : REPORT BY THE SECRETARIAT OF THE UNITED NATIONS CONFERENCE ON TRADE AND DEVELOPMENT (US) [07973397] 1524, **853**

TRADE AND EMPLOYMENT (US/1057-9702) [12031776] **853**

TRADE AND INDUSTRIAL DIRECTORY OF NEPAL (NP) [02630667] **854**

TRADE & INDUSTRY ASAP [ONLINE DATABASE] (US) 854, 1630, **734**

TRADE & INDUSTRY IN UGANDA (UG) [03197147] **854**

TRADE & INDUSTRY INDEX [ONLINE DATABASE] (US) 1630, **854**

TRADE AND PROFESSIONAL ASSOCIATIONS IN CALIFORNIA : A DIRECTORY (US) [05004034] **1300**

TRADE AND SHIPPING STATISTICS (IE) [01228082] **5402**

TRADE ASIAN DIRECTORY OF EXPORTERS, IMPORTERS & MANUFACTURERS *See* TRADO, ASIAN AFRICAN DIRECTORY OF EXPORTERS-IMPORTERS & MANUFACTURERS **854**

TRADE ASSOCIATIONS AND PROFESSIONAL BODIES OF THE UNITED KINGDOM (UK) [06998059] **716**

TRADE CASES *CEASED.* (US/1045-5191) [01564341] **3104**

TRADE CONNECTIONS (CN/0713-634X) [08936731] **854**

TRADE CONTACTS IN WEST AFRICAN COUNTRIES (UK) [05279781] **854**

TRADE DEVELOPMENT AUTHORITY *See* ANNUAL REPORT - TRADE DEVELOPMENT AUTHORITY (NEW DELHI) **823**

TRADE DIRECTORIES OF THE WORLD (US/0564-0482) [02254671] **854**

TRADE DIRECTORY (MM) [05984168] **854**

TRADE DIRECTORY - COMMERCIAL BANK OF ETHIOPIA S. C (ET) [01799326] **854**

TRADE DIRECTORY, MEMBERSHIP LIST - ELECTRONIC INDUSTRIES ASSOCIATION (US/0091-9519) [01786173] **2084**

TRADE FINANCE (UK) [22773736] 814, **854**

TRADE FINANCE REVIEW (UK) **4756**

TRADE FLASH BRUXELLES (BE/0775-2911) [07752911] **888**

TRADE INDICES *See* INDICES OF EXTERNAL TRADE **840**

TRADE INTELLIGENCE BULLETIN (II) **854**

TRADE LEADS *CEASED.* (US) [22842922] **142**

TRADE-MARK REPORTER, THE (US/0041-056X) [01716530] **1308**

TRADE MARKETING (IT) **937**

TRADE MARKS JOURNAL (OTTAWA) (CN/0041-0438) [03963661] **1309**

TRADE MARKS JOURNAL, THE (UK) [02447283] **1309**

● TRADE NEWS / OAS (US) [29592133] **854**

TRADE NEWS SERVICE, THE (US/1071-0604) [12187714] **1630**

TRADE POLICY AGENDA AND ... ANNUAL REPORT OF THE PRESIDENT OF THE UNITED STATES ON THE TRADE AGREEMENTS PROGRAM (US) [12331859] **4691**

TRADE POLICY REVIEW. CHILE (SZ) [25107012] **854**

TRADE POLICY REVIEW. HUNGARY (SZ) [24421872] **854**

TRADE POLICY REVIEW. INDONESIA (SZ) [24600640] **854**

TRADE POLICY REVIEW. NIGERIA (SZ) [25302795] **1640**

TRADE POLICY REVIEW. NORWAY (SZ) [25305338] **854**

TRADE POLICY REVIEW. SWITZERLAND (SZ) [25303180] **854**

TRADE POLICY REVIEW. THAILAND (SZ) [25303050] **854**

TRADE POLICY REVIEW. THE EUROPEAN COMMUNITIES (SZ) [24397042] **854**

TRADE POLICY REVIEW. THE EUROPEAN COMMUNITIES (SZ/1014-7411) [25058793] **854**

TRADE PRACTICES COMMISSION BULLETIN (AT/0818-044X) [0818044X] 3104, **3065**

TRADE REPORT FOR THE BRITISH VIRGIN ISLANDS (VB) [01798536] **854**

TRADE REPORT SERVICE: WEEKLY TRADE REPORT (US) [13519015] **142**

TRADE REPORT - SEYCHELLES (SE) [03603286] **854**

TRADE REVIEW (SP) [06463135] **854**

TRADE SECRET LAW REPORTER (US/8756-1492) [11482379] **3065**

TRADE SECRETS (US) [01757472] **3104**

TRADE SHOW & CONVENTION GUIDE (US/0743-9709) [09789730] **767**

TRADE SHOWS WORLDWIDE (US/1046-4395) [20424996] **767**

TRADE STATISTICS OF IRELAND (IE/0790-5122) [11303962] 854, **734**

TRADE + TECHNICAL REVIEW *See* GDR MARKET **1492**

TRADE TIMES (JA) [07449461] **854**

TRADE UNION INFORMATION (IE) [06201585] **1714**

TRADE UNION INFORMATION BULLETIN (BE) [19547972] **1714**

TRADE UNION RECORD (II) [03142321] **1714**

TRADE UNION STATISTICS: AUSTRALIA (AT) [01796339] 1715, **1540**

TRADE UNIONS & EMPLOYERS ORGANIZATIONS (UK) **1715**

TRADE UNIONS INTERNATIONAL OF WORKERS IN COMMERCE *See* NOUVELLES - UNION INTERNATIONALE DES LSYNDICATS DES TRAVAILLEURS DU COMMERCE **1695**

TRADE WINDS INDUSTRY WEEKLY (CH) 1640, **854**

TRADE WINDS MONTHLY (CH/0259-9880) [I02599880] 1640, **854**

TRADE WINDS WEEKLY *See* TRADE WINDS INDUSTRY WEEKLY **854**

TRADE WINNERS COMPUTERS (CH) **1205**

TRADE WINNERS CONSUMERS ELECTRONICS (CH) **2084**

TRADE WITH GREECE (GR/0041-0543) [05038150] **854**

TRADEASIA MAGAZINE *CEASED.* (CN/0829-8157) [13490325] **854**

TRADEMARK INFORMATION FOR TRAVELERS / U.S. CUSTOMS SERVICE (US) [10451287] **5494**

TRADEMARK LAW HANDBOOK (US/0731-5813) [07209557] **1309**

TRADEMARK MANUAL OF EXAMINING PROCEDURE (TMEP) (US) [04506599] **1309**

TRADEMARK REGISTER OF THE UNITED STATES, THE (US/0082-5786) [01772735] **1309**

TRADEMARK RULES OF PRACTICE OF THE PATENT AND TRADEMARK OFFICE WITH FORMS AND STATUTES (US/0149-6387) [03457889] **1309**

TRADEMARK TRENDS (US/1062-7766) [08326608] **1309**

TRADEMARK WORLD (UK/0950-2564) [18448666] **1309**

TRADEMARKS, COPYRIGHTS, AND UNFAIR COMPETITION : ALI-ABA COURSE OF STUDY MATERIALS (US) [21082660] **1309**

TRADER *See* CROSS SECTION **830**

TRADERS DIRECTORY, THE (UK) [16965675] **1640**

● TRADES (NEW ORLEANS, LA.) (US/1060-8249) [25065421] **854**

TRADES UNION CONGRESS *See* REPORT OF ANNUAL TRADES UNION CONGRESS **1706**

TRADESHOW & EXHIBIT MANAGER (US/0893-2662) [15482453] **767**

TRADESHOW (LOS ANGELES, CALIF.) (US/0145-5559) [02763492] **767**

TRADESHOW WEEK (US/0733-0170) [08508297] **767**

TRADESHOW WEEK DATA BOOK, THE (US/0000-1023) [12158504] **734**

TRADESHOW WEEK'S MAJOR EXHIBIT HALL DIRECTORY (US) [10244694] **767**

TRADESHOW WEEK'S ... TRADESHOW SERVICES DIRECTORY (US) [17636829] **767**

... TRADESHOWS & EXHIBITS SCHEDULE, THE (US) [17498474] **767**

TRADESWOMEN (US/0739-344X) [09726358] **5567**

TRADEWEEK (CH) [08482942] **854**

TRADEWEEK (LOS ANGELES, CALIF.) (US/1056-8301) [23861366] **854**

TRADEWINDS (SAINT JOHN, V.I.) (VI/0895-0970) [10488783] **5813**

TRADICION POPULAR, LA (GT) [02434746] **2324**

TRADICIONES DE GUATEMALA (GT/0564-0571) [04348412] **2325**

TRADING CARDS (US/1060-9970) [24160283] **2778**

TRADING CYCLES *CEASED.* (US/0892-3280) [15175974] **917**

TRADING LAW (UK/0262-9240) [08425545] **3136**

● TRADING LAW AND TRADING LAW REPORTS (UK/1352-061X) [30592844] **3104**

TRADING LAW REPORTS (UK) [10656656] **3104**

TRADING POST (COLUMBIA, MD.) (US/1043-7665) [07160518] **4059**

TRADING STANDARDS REVIEW: THE MONTHLY JOURNAL OF THE INSTITUTE OF TRADING STANDARDS ADMINISTRATION, THE (UK) [18057847] **4033**

TRADING SYSTEMS TECHNOLOGY (US/0892-5542) [15214409] **1249**

TRADING TRENDS (CN/0846-0469) [23598405] **917**

TRADISJON (NO/0332-5997) [02094342] **2325**

TRADITIO (US/0362-1529) [01767676] **2713**

TRADITION D'AVENIR (CN/1183-2215) [24690495] **1095**

TRADITION MAGAZINE (FR/0980-8493) [I0980849318493] **4157**

TRADITION (NEW YORK) (US/0041-0608) [01776823] **5053**

TRADITION (WALNUT, IOWA) (US/1071-1864) [28564598] **4157**

TRADITIONAL ARCHERY (US/0888-5443) [13663468] **4927**

TRADITIONAL BOWHUNTER (US) **4927**

TRADITIONAL CHINESE MEDICINE DIGEST *CEASED.* (CC/0258-8803) [14219084] **3647**

TRADITIONAL DWELLINGS AND SETTLEMENTS REVIEW (US/1050-2092) [21021078] **5225**

TRADITIONAL HOME (US/0883-4660) [12120606] **2903**

TRADITIONAL HOMES (UK/0950-2181) [19931185] **2903**

TRADITIONAL INTERIOR DECORATION (UK/0950-219X) [I0950219X] **2903**

TRADITIONAL KENT BUILDINGS (UK/0260-4116) [I02604116] **310**

TRADITIONAL MEDICAL SYSTEMS (II/0025-7109) [06832319] **3647**

TRADITIONAL MUSIC (UK/0306-7440) [10892012] **4157**

TRADITIONAL MUSICLINE, THE (US/1059-5953) [24536284] **4157**

TRADITIONAL QUILTWORKS (US/1050-4435) [21491411] **5186**

TRADITIONAL TAEKWON-DO *CEASED.* (US/0745-2365) [08968798] 2601, **4927**

TRADITIONES (XV) [01785957] **2713**

TRADO, ASIAN AFRICAN DIRECTORY OF EXPORTERS-IMPORTERS & MANUFACTURERS (II) [09551198] **854**

TRADUCTIONS (FR) **2096**

TRADUIRE / SOCIETE FRANCAISE DES TRADUCTEURS (FR/0395-773X) [10600840] **3329**

TRAER STAR-CLIPPER, THE (US) [15924055] **5673**

TRAFFIC ACCIDENT FACTS (US) [10297426] **5445**

TRAFFIC ACCIDENT FACTS (DOVER, DEL.) (US/0738-3657) [09564806] **5446**

TRAFFIC AND OPERATING DATA OF AEA AIRLINES (BE) [04689108] **37**

TRAFFIC BULLETIN - WILDLIFE TRADE MONITORING UNIT (UK/0267-4297) [I02674297] **2207**

TRAFFIC BY FLIGHT STAGE / TRAFFIC PAR ETAPES (CN) [04771169] **37**

TRAFFIC CRASH DATA / FLORIDA DEPARTMENT OF HIGHWAY SAFETY AND MOTOR VEHICLES (US) [27800007] **5446**

TRAFFIC CRASH FACTS (US) [31318645] **5446**

TRAFFIC DATA FROM AUTOMATIC TRAFFIC RECORDER STATIONS (US) [01786962] **5446**

TRAFFIC ENGINEERING & CONTROL (UK/0041-0683) [01645844] **5394**

TRAFFIC FLOW (CN) [02503209] **37**

TRAFFIC LAW REPORTS (US/0893-3030) [15513593] 5446, **3065**

TRAFFIC MANAGEMENT (US/0041-0691) [01767683] **5394**

TRAFFIC SAFETY (CHICAGO, ILL.) (US/0041-0721) [06553278] 4805, **5446**

TRAFFIC SAFETY SERIES (US) **5446**

TRAFFIC TOPICS *CEASED.* (US/0735-7613) [08156620] **5394**

TRAFFIC VOLUMES AND SUPPLEMENTARY DATA, CENTRAL MOUNTAINS DIVISION AND COLO-GOSFORD SHIRES *See* TRAFFIC VOLUMES AND SUPPLEMENTARY DATA, CENTRAL MOUNTAINS DIVISION, CITY OF GOSFORD AND SHIRE OF COLO / DMR **5446**

TRAFFIC

Alphabetical Title Index

TRAFFIC VOLUMES AND SUPPLEMENTARY DATA, CENTRAL MOUNTAINS DIVISION AND SHIRE OF HAWKESBURY (AT) [16726593] **5446**

TRAFFIC VOLUMES AND SUPPLEMENTARY DATA, CENTRAL MOUNTAINS DIVISION, CITY OF GOSFORD AND SHIRE OF COLO / DMR (AT) [08755716] **5446**

TRAFFIC VOLUMES ON THE CALIFORNIA STATE HIGHWAY SYSTEM (US/0145-9813) [02830978] **5446**

TRAFFIC WORLD, THE (US/0041-073X) [04563352] **5394**

TRAFIC (FR) [02802797] **5457**

TRAFIC INTERNATIONAL DU FRET (FR) [04198784] **38**

TRAFIC ROUTIER (MONTREAL. 1981) (CN/0229-6497) [08072048] **5394**

TRAFICS (CN/0712-7391) [08996020] **332**

TRAFIK-SKADOR (SW/0347-6359) [15613797] **5446**

TRAFODION ANRHYDEDDUS GYMDEITHAS Y CYMMRODORION (UK/0959-3632) [01565736] **3447**

TRAGICORUM GRAECORUM FRAGMENTA (GW) **1080**

TRAI TIM DU'C ME (US/0744-6128) [08440149] **5005**

TRAIL & LANDSCAPE (CN/0041-0748) [02192306] **4173**

TRAIL AND TIMBERLINE (US/0041-0756) [01607304] **4879**

TRAIL BLAZER (PASO ROBLES) (US/0274-8274) [06644807] **4927**, **2803**

TRAIL BREAKERS (US/0362-0344) [02441280] **2475**

TRAIL CAMPING (US/0090-2241) [01784810] **4879**

TRAIL DAILY TIMES (CN) **5796**

TRAIL RIDER MAGAZINE (US/0892-3922) [15207838] **4855**

TRAIL SEEKERS (US/0739-6643) [08252460] **2475**

TRAIL TALES (US) **2475**

TRAIL WALKER (US/0749-1352) [11105229] **2548**

TRAILER BOATS (US/0300-6557) [01422924] **596**

TRAILER/BODY BUILD (US/0041-0772) [02451217] 3489, **5394**

TRAILER BOOK, THE *See* COMMERCIAL TRAILER BLUE BOOK **949**

TRAILER LIFE (US/0041-0780) [03950471] **4855**

TRAILER LIFE'S RV CAMPGROUND & SERVICES DIRECTORY (US/0099-0191) [02240779] **4879**

TRAILHEAD (US) **2397**

TRAILL COUNTY TRIBUNE (US) [01767685] **5726**

TRAILS-A-WAY. OHIO EDITION (US/0194-5394) [04802336] **4879**

TRAILS AND TALES (US/0091-6455) [01787539] **2475**

TRAILS (WINDSOR) (CN/1195-4906) [18881815] **2475**

TRAIN COLLECTORS QUARTERLY, THE (US/0041-0829) [02252031] 2585, **2778**

TRAIN DISPATCHER (BERWYN), THE (US/0041-0837) [03950878] **1715**

TRAINDUSTRIN (STOCKHOLM) (SW/0346-2846) [03462846] **635**

TRAINEES AND FELLOWS SUPPORTED BY THE NATIONAL INSTITUTE OF DENTAL RESEARCH AND TRAINED DURING FISCAL YEAR ... (US/0145-9724) [02791423] **1336**

TRAINER'S WORKSHOP **CEASED.** (US/0888-5893) [13521675] **947**

TRAINING AIDS DIGEST *See* CJ MANAGEMENT & TRAINING DIGEST **3160**

TRAINING & CONDITIONING (US/1058-3548) [24278150] **2601**

TRAINING AND DEVELOPMENT ALERT (US/0192-0596) [04975964] **947**

TRAINING & DEVELOPMENT (ALEXANDRIA, VA.) (US/1055-9760) [23436259] **947**

TRAINING AND DEVELOPMENT IN AUSTRALIA (AT/0310-4664) [l03104664] **716**

TRAINING AND DEVELOPMENT LITERATURE INDEX **CEASED.** (US/0895-1748) [16507663] **947**

TRAINING AND DEVELOPMENT ORGANIZATIONS DIRECTORY (US/0278-5749) [07435404] **888**

TRAINING AND DEVELOPMENT YEARBOOK (US/1049-3875) [21214150] 947, **734**

TRAINING AND EMPLOYMENT REPORT OF THE SECRETARY OF LABOR **CEASED.** (US) [17722624] **1715**

TRAINING & MANAGEMENT DEVELOPMENT METHODS (UK) **888**

TRAINING AND MANPOWER DEVELOPMENT ACTIVITIES (US/0161-8288) [04023153] 5182, **5312**

TRAINING & METHODS SERIES (US/0084-0823) [01780642] **1524**

TRAINING AWARDS, FELLOWSHIP AWARDS ... DATA BOOK / NATIONAL INSTITUTE OF NEUROLOGICAL AND COMMUNICATIVE DISORDERS AND STROKE (US) [04694194] **3847**

TRAINING DIGEST (UK/0141-7134) [I01417134] **947**

TRAINING DIGEST EUROPE (UK) 1587, **716**

TRAINING DIRECTORS' FORUM NEWSLETTER (US/1050-6160) [12185883] **947**

TRAINING DIRECTORY FOR BUSINESS AND INDUSTRY (US/1044-1840) [19643356] 1630, **716**

TRAINING DIRECTORY, THE (UK) [20212580] 948, **4209**

TRAINING FOR AGRICULTURE AND RURAL DEVELOPMENT (IT/0251-1495) [02441278] **142**

TRAINING FOR QUALITY (UK/0968-4875) [l09684875] **948**

TRAINING FOR SOCIAL WELFARE (US) [07033821] **5313**

TRAINING IDEAS **CEASED.** (CN/0828-1742) [13297693] **1916**

TRAINING IN INDUSTRY (CN/0318-7225) [01786277] **1715**

TRAINING KEY (US/0564-0881) [03298985] **3178**

TRAINING MATTERS (UK/0967-3962) [l09673962] **332**

●TRAINING MEDIA REVIEW (US/1072-3188) [28911486] **1123**

TRAINING (MINNEAPOLIS) (US/0095-5892) [01795129] **948**

TRAINING NETWORK (UK) **948**

TRAINING OFFICER, THE (UK/0041-090X) [10756102] **948**

TRAINING SOLUTIONS / DIGITAL CONTROLS (US/0887-1450) [13136632] **1205**

TRAINING TECHNOLOGY (UK) **1205**

TRAINING TOMORROW (UK/0957-0004) [27870102] **4691**

TRAINING WORLD (US/0193-2136) [05165993] **1123**

TRAINS (US/0041-0934) [06163876] **5437**

TRAIT D'UNION - FEDERATION DES CAISSES POPULAIRES ACADIENNES (CN/0822-3521) [11245949] **1543**

TRAIT D'UNION JEUNESSE, LE **CEASED.** (CN/0225-7416) [06299428] **5005**

TRAIT D'UNION (MASCOUCHE) (CN/0227-5562) [08078848] **5796**

TRAIT D'UNION (OTTAWA) (CN/0225-2627) [06167106] **4691**

TRAIT D'UNION (QUEBEC) (CN/0707-8633) [06960200] **1850**

TRAIT D'UNION (ROUYN) (CN/0820-7720) [09467643] **4691**

TRAITE D'ANATOMIE HUMAINE (FR) **3647**

TRAITE DE LA SECURITE SOCIALE (FR/0767-1822) [I07671822] **5313**

TRAITE DE ZOOLOGIE (FR) [04182121] **5598**

●TRAITEMENT AUTOMATIQUE DES LANGUES : T.A.L (FR) [29514389] **3327**

TRAITEMENT DE TEXTE (FR) **1205**

TRAITEMENT DU SIGNAL (FR/0765-0019) [12675508] **2159**

TRAITEMENT THERMIQUE (FR/0041-0950) [07483227] **4022**

TRAITEMENTS, SOLDES ET INDEMNITES DES FONCTIONNAIRES A COMPTER DU ... / JOURNAL OFFICIEL DE LA REPUBLIQUE FRANCAISE (FR) [07318096] **3065**

TRAITS : BULLETIN LITTERAIRE DE LA LIBRAIRIE LIBRIS (BE) [08256907] **3447**

●TRAJECTA (BE/0778-8304) [26741203] **5037**

TRAJECTOIRES (CN) [05258040] **332**

TRAJEKT (GW) [01786057] **3447**

TRAKCJA I WAGONY (PL) [06410746] **5437**

TRAKTANDUM MAGAZIN (SZ) [27332175] **4691**

TRAKTANDUM PERSONLICH (SZ) [27331667] **4691**

TRAKTORY I SELSKOKHOZIAISTVENNYE MASHINY (RU/0235-8573) [26163995] **161**

TRAM- EN AUTOBUSBEDRIJVEN / CENTRAAL BUREAU VOOR DE STATISTIEK, HOOFDAFDELING STATISTIEKEN VAN VERKEER EN VERVOER (NE/0168-5775) [05964974] **5394**

TRAM : HENA OCHEMA (GR) [10750843] **3447**

TRAMES (MONTREAL) (CN/0847-9119) [20676786] **2837**

TRAMOYA (MX) [03678365] **5372**

TRANCIATURA STAMPAGGIO (IT/0041-1027) [07448966] **4022**

TRANEL (SZ) [13419728] **3329**

TRANET (US/0739-0971) [09309349] 1959, **2207**

TRANS ACTION / CALIFORNIA DEPARTMENT OF TRANSPORTATION, DISTRICT 7 (US) [13085432] **5394**

TRANS F M (CN/0704-478X) [06511493] **1141**

TRANS RURAL EXPRESS (FR/0766-8007) [l07668007] **5395**

TRANS TASMAN (NZ/1171-2961) [I11712961] **854**

TRANSACTION (CN/0714-8100) [09106405] 5395, **5068**

TRANSACTIONAL ANALYSIS JOURNAL (US/0362-1537) [01774150] **4620**

TRANSACTIONS (UK) [02429948] **2713**

TRANSACTIONS - AMERICAN BRONCHO-ESOPHAGOLOGICAL ASSOCIATION. MEETING (US/0891-8295) [09611717] **3952**

TRANSACTIONS - AMERICAN CRYSTALLOGRAPHIC ASSOCIATION (US/0065-8006) [03598414] **1033**

TRANSACTIONS - AMERICAN GEOPHYSICAL UNION *See* PROCEEDINGS OF THE WESTERN SNOW CONFERENCE **1359**

TRANSACTIONS AND DIRECTORY (US) [01929336] **1850**

TRANSACTIONS AND INTENTIONS REPORT (US) **917**

TRANSACTIONS AND PROCEEDINGS OF THE PALAEONTOLOGICAL SOCIETY OF JAPAN (JA/0031-0204) [02449413] **4231**

TRANSACTIONS & STUDIES OF THE COLLEGE OF PHYSICIANS OF PHILADELPHIA (US/0010-1087) [01604550] **3647**

TRANSACTIONS - ANGLESEY ANTIQUARIAN SOCIETY AND FIELD CLUB (UK/0306-5790) [01796373] **2713**

TRANSACTIONS - ASSOCIATION FOR STUDIES IN THE CONSERVATION OF HISTORIC BUILDINGS (UK/0142-5803) [07863820] **310**

TRANSACTIONS - BIRMINGHAM AND WARWICKSHIRE ARCHAEOLOGICAL SOCIETY (UK) [02551539] **284**

TRANSACTIONS - BRISTOL AND GLOUCESTERSHIRE ARCHAEOLOGICAL SOCIETY (UK/0068-1032) [01537100] 2713, **284**

TRANSACTIONS BULLETIN - INDUSTRIAL HYGIENE FOUNDATION OF AMERICA (US) [01197503] **2871**

TRANSACTIONS - CAERNARVONSHIRE HISTORICAL SOCIETY (UK/0144-0098) [I01440098] **2713**

TRANSACTIONS - CANADIAN INSTITUTE OF MINING AND METALLURGY (CN) [04179722] **2152**

TRANSACTIONS - CONGRESS ON IRRIGATION AND DRAINAGE (II/0589-3127) [01564778] **2096**

TRANSACTIONS - DESERT BIGHORN COUNCIL (US/0418-7598) [02013961] 5598, **2207**

TRANSACTIONS (DOKLADY) OF THE USSR ACADEMY OF SCIENCES. EARTH SCIENCE SECTIONS (US/0891-5571) [14962377] **1361**

TRANSACTIONS - ENGINEERING AND OPERATING DIVISION. CANADIAN ELECTRICAL ASSOCIATION (CN/0576-5161) [04518900] **2084**

TRANSACTIONS - ENGLISH CERAMIC CIRCLE (UK) [08351144] **2594**

TRANSACTIONS - GEOTHERMAL RESOURCES COUNCIL (US/0193-5933) [03719487] **1959**

TRANSACTIONS - GULF COAST ASSOCIATION OF GEOLOGICAL SOCIETIES (US/0533-6562) [07887134] **1400**

TRANSACTIONS - INSTITUTE OF BRITISH GEOGRAPHERS (1965) (UK/0020-2754) [02167081] **2577**

TRANSACTIONS / INSTITUTE OF MARINE ENGINEERS (UK) [20027192] 5457, **1999**

TRANSACTIONS / INSTITUTION OF ENGINEERS AND SHIPBUILDERS IN SCOTLAND (UK) [07113860] 5457, **1999**

Alphabetical Title Index — TRANSACTIONS

TRANSACTIONS - INSTITUTION OF ENGINEERS OF IRELAND (IE) [05109921] **1999**

TRANSACTIONS - LEICESTERSHIRE ARCHAEOLOGICAL AND HISTORICAL SOCIETY (UK/0140-3990) [I01403990] 2713, **284**

TRANSACTIONS - NEWCOMEN SOCIETY FOR THE STUDY OF THE HISTORY OF ENGINEERING AND TECHNOLOGY (UK/0372-0187) [01760302] **5166**

TRANSACTIONS - NORTH CAROLINA MEDICAL SOCIETY (US/0361-5537) [02246835] **3647**

TRANSACTIONS - NORTH EAST COAST INSTITUTION OF ENGINEERS AND SHIPBUILDERS *CEASED.* (UK/0029-280X) [02449169] **1999**

TRANSACTIONS - NORTHEAST FISH & WILDLIFE CONFERENCE [06694149] **2315**

TRANSACTIONS OF DIESEL ENGINEERS & USERS ASSOCIATION (UK/0261-0345) [I02610345] **2100**

TRANSACTIONS OF INDIAN SOCIETY OF DESERT TECHNOLOGY (II/0970-3918) [21066909] **142**

TRANSACTIONS OF JWRI (JA/0387-4508) [02176492] **4022**

TRANSACTIONS OF POWDER METALLURGY ASSOCIATION OF INDIA (II/0377-9416) [02747542] **4022**

TRANSACTIONS OF SHASE JAPAN (JA/0081-1610) [01784597] **2608**

TRANSACTIONS OF SOCIETY FOR MINING, METALLURGY, AND EXPLORATION, INC (US) [23460424] **2152**

● TRANSACTIONS OF THE ACADEMY OF INSURANCE MEDICINE: 1992, VOLUME LXXVI (US/1064-4709) [26293875] 3647, **2894**

TRANSACTIONS OF THE AMERICAN ASSOCIATION OF COST ENGINEERS (US) [22338183] **2100**

TRANSACTIONS OF THE AMERICAN CLINICAL AND CLIMATOLOGICAL ASSOCIATION (US/0065-7778) [01479671] **3647**

TRANSACTIONS OF THE AMERICAN CRYSTALLOGRAPHIC ASSOCIATION (US/0065-8006) [01479745] **1033**

TRANSACTIONS OF THE AMERICAN ENTOMOLOGICAL SOCIETY (1890) (US/0002-8320) [06273198] **5614**

TRANSACTIONS OF THE AMERICAN FISHERIES SOCIETY (1900) (US/0002-8487) [06445080] **2315**

TRANSACTIONS OF THE AMERICAN FOUNDRYMEN'S SOCIETY (ANNUAL) (US/0065-8375) [07367031] **4022**

TRANSACTIONS OF THE AMERICAN GYNECOLOGICAL AND OBSTETRICAL SOCIETY (US/0892-1962) [10555974] **3769**

TRANSACTIONS OF THE AMERICAN INSTITUTE OF MINING, METALLURGICAL AND PETROLEUM ENGINEERS (US) [01480064] **1999**

TRANSACTIONS OF THE AMERICAN MATHEMATICAL SOCIETY (US/0002-9947) [01480369] **3539**

TRANSACTIONS OF THE AMERICAN MICROSCOPICAL SOCIETY *See* INVERTEBRATE BIOLOGY **459**

TRANSACTIONS OF THE AMERICAN NUCLEAR SOCIETY (US/0003-018X) [01252341] **2159**

TRANSACTIONS OF THE AMERICAN OPHTHALMOLOGICAL SOCIETY ANNUAL MEETING (US/0065-9533) [01480500] **3879**

TRANSACTIONS OF THE AMERICAN OTOLOGICAL SOCIETY (US/0096-6851) [01480516] **3891**

TRANSACTIONS OF THE AMERICAN PHILOLOGICAL ASSOCIATION (1974) (US/0360-5949) [03131421] **3329**

TRANSACTIONS OF THE AMERICAN PHILOSOPHICAL SOCIETY (US/0065-9746) [02382293] **4364**

TRANSACTIONS OF THE AMERICAN SOCIETY FOR NEUROCHEMISTRY (US/0066-0132) [02781989] 1012, **3847**

TRANSACTIONS OF THE AMERICAN SOCIETY OF CIVIL ENGINEERS (US/0066-0604) [01480786] 2033, **2007**

TRANSACTIONS OF THE AMERICAN SOCIETY OF MECHANICAL ENGINEERS (US/0097-6822) [01480830] **2130**

TRANSACTIONS OF THE ANCIENT MONUMENTS SOCIETY (UK/0951-001X) [02219745] **366**

TRANSACTIONS OF THE ... ANNUAL MEETING OF THE BIOELECTRICAL REPAIR AND GROWTH SOCIETY (US/0892-2020) [12651317] **475**

TRANSACTIONS OF THE ANNUAL MEETING OF THE ORTHOPAEDIC RESEARCH SOCIETY (US/0149-6433) [03519893] **3885**

TRANSACTIONS OF THE ... ANNUAL SCIENTIFIC PROGRAM OF THE AMERICAN COLLEGE OF VETERINARY OPHTHALMOLOGISTS (US) [18798560] **5523**

TRANSACTIONS OF THE ARCHITECTURAL AND ARCHAEOLOGICAL SOCIETY OF DURHAM AND NORTHUMBERLAND (UK/0066-6203) [01715508] **284**

TRANSACTIONS OF THE ASAE (US/0001-2351) [01772174] 142, **1999**

TRANSACTIONS OF THE ASIATIC SOCIETY OF JAPAN (JA) [01514456] **2509**

TRANSACTIONS OF THE ASSOCIATION OF AMERICAN PHYSICIANS (US/0066-9458) [01514571] **3647**

TRANSACTIONS OF THE ASSOCIATION OF LIFE INSURANCE MEDICAL DIRECTORS OF AMERICA, ANNUAL MEETING (US/0066-9598) [05841953] 3647, **2894**

TRANSACTIONS OF THE BOSE RESEARCH INSTITUTE, CALCUTTA (II/0006-7903) [01536836] **475**

TRANSACTIONS OF THE CAMBRIDGE BIBLIOGRAPHICAL SOCIETY (UK/0068-6611) [01552627] **426**

TRANSACTIONS OF THE CANADIAN SOCIETY FOR MECHANICAL ENGINEERING (CN/0315-8977) [01978304] **2130**

TRANSACTIONS OF THE CHARLES S. PIERCE SOCIETY (US/0009-1774) [01553904] **4364**

TRANSACTIONS OF THE CITRUS ENGINEERING CONFERENCE (US/0412-6300) [03227694] **189**

TRANSACTIONS OF THE CUMBERLAND & WESTMORLAND ANTIQUARIAN & ARCHAEOLOGICAL SOCIETY (UK/0309-7986) [I03097986] 284, **2713**

TRANSACTIONS OF THE DELAWARE ACADEMY OF SCIENCE (US/0093-6456) [01784458] **5166**

TRANSACTIONS OF THE FACULTY OF ACTUARIES (UK/0071-3686) [03786019] **2894**

TRANSACTIONS OF THE GAELIC SOCIETY OF INVERNESS (UK/0958-5451) [01643898] 3447, **3329**

TRANSACTIONS OF THE HISTORIC SOCIETY OF LANCASHIRE AND CHESHIRE FOR THE YEAR (UK/0140-332X) [04962016] **2713**

TRANSACTIONS OF THE HISTORICAL SOCIETY OF GHANA (GH/0073-2648) [00978171] **2667**

TRANSACTIONS OF THE HUGUENOT SOCIETY OF SOUTH CAROLINA (US/0363-3152) [01641684] **5237**

TRANSACTIONS OF THE ILLINOIS STATE ACADEMY OF SCIENCE (US/0019-2252) [01588890] **5166**

TRANSACTIONS OF THE ILLINOIS STATE HORTICULTURAL SOCIETY FOR THE YEAR (US) [28863795] **2432**

TRANSACTIONS OF THE INDIAN CERAMIC SOCIETY (II/0371-750X) [02447549] **2594**

TRANSACTIONS OF THE INDIAN INSTITUTE OF METALS (II/0019-493X) [01605477] **4022**

TRANSACTIONS OF THE INSTITUTE OF INDIAN GEOGRAPHERS (II) [08151597] **2577**

TRANSACTIONS OF THE INSTITUTE OF MEASUREMENT AND CONTROL (UK/0142-3312) [04950987] **2131**

TRANSACTIONS OF THE INSTITUTE OF METAL FINISHING (UK/0020-2967) [07730294] **4022**

TRANSACTIONS OF THE INSTITUTION OF ENGINEERS, AUSTRALIA. CIVIL ENGINEERING (AT/0159-2068) [06175149] **2033**

TRANSACTIONS OF THE INSTITUTION OF ENGINEERS, AUSTRALIA. MECHANICAL ENGINEERING (AT/0727-7369) [06599384] **2131**

TRANSACTIONS OF THE INSTITUTION OF ENGINEERS, AUSTRALIA. MULTI-DISCIPLINARY ENGINEERING (AT/0812-3314) [10546732] **1999**

TRANSACTIONS OF THE INSTITUTION OF ENGINEERS IN SCOTLAND, WITH WHICH IS INCORPORATED THE SCOTTISH SHIPBUILDERS' ASSOCIATION *See* TRANSACTIONS / INSTITUTION OF ENGINEERS AND SHIPBUILDERS IN SCOTLAND **1999**

TRANSACTIONS OF THE INSTITUTION OF PROFESSIONAL ENGINEERS NEW ZEALAND, CIVIL ENGINEERING SECTION (NZ/0111-9508) [09542850] **2033**

TRANSACTIONS OF THE INSTITUTION OF PROFESSIONAL ENGINEERS NEW ZEALAND, ELECTRICAL/MECHANICAL/CHEMICAL ENGINEERING SECTION (NZ/0111-946X) [09291366] **1999**

TRANSACTIONS OF THE INSTITUTION OF PROFESSIONAL ENGINEERS NEW ZEALAND. GENERAL SECTION (NZ/0114-1562) [I01141562] **2182**

TRANSACTIONS OF THE INTERNATIONAL ASTRONOMICAL UNION (UK/0251-107X) [02720263] **401**

TRANSACTIONS OF THE INTERNATIONAL CONFERENCE OF ORIENTALISTS IN JAPAN (JA/0538-6012) [02697720] **3329**

TRANSACTIONS OF THE INTERNATIONAL CONFERENCE ON ENDODONTICS (US/0074-3054) [03384105] **1337**

TRANSACTIONS OF THE IRON AND STEEL INSTITUTE OF JAPAN (JA/0021-1583) [01760381] **4022**

TRANSACTIONS OF THE IRON & STEEL SOCIETY (US/1051-0508) [19450584] **4022**

TRANSACTIONS OF THE JAPAN CONCRETE INSTITUTE (JA) [10474059] 310, **2033**

TRANSACTIONS OF THE JAPAN FOUNDRYMEN'S SOCIETY (JA/0287-041X) [12096335] **4022**

TRANSACTIONS OF THE JAPAN SOCIETY FOR AERONAUTICAL AND SPACE SCIENCES (JA/0549-3811) [03282709] **38**

TRANSACTIONS OF THE JAPAN WELDING SOCIETY (JA/0385-9282) [08205408] **4028**

TRANSACTIONS OF THE KANSAS ACADEMY OF SCIENCE (1903) (US/0022-8443) [01280185] **5166**

TRANSACTIONS OF THE KENTUCKY ACADEMY OF SCIENCE (US/0023-0081) [01782274] **5166**

TRANSACTIONS OF THE LANCASHIRE AND CHESHIRE ANTIQUARIAN SOCIETY (UK/0950-4699) [01755501] **2713**

TRANSACTIONS OF THE LINNAEAN SOCIETY OF NEW YORK (US/0075-9708) [01586414] **529**

TRANSACTIONS OF THE LONDON & MIDDLESEX ARCHAEOLOGICAL SOCIETY (UK/0076-0501) [01756125] **284**

TRANSACTIONS OF THE MARTIN CENTRE FOR ARCHITECTURAL & URBAN STUDIES (UK) [04282364] 2837, **310**

TRANSACTIONS OF THE MEDICAL SOCIETY (UK/0076-6011) [01757021] **3647**

TRANSACTIONS OF THE MEDICAL SOCIETY OF THE STATE OF NORTH CAROLINA *See* TRANSACTIONS - NORTH CAROLINA MEDICAL SOCIETY **3647**

TRANSACTIONS OF THE MEETING OF THE AMERICAN SURGICAL ASSOCIATION (US/0066-0833) [01480882] **3976**

TRANSACTIONS OF THE MISSOURI ACADEMY OF SCIENCE (US/0544-540X) [02281457] **5166**

TRANSACTIONS OF THE MONUMENTAL BRASS SOCIETY (UK/0143-1250) [07366387] **284**

TRANSACTIONS OF THE MORAVIAN HISTORICAL SOCIETY (US/0886-1730) [01681332] **5068**

TRANSACTIONS OF THE MOSCOW MATHEMATICAL SOCIETY (US/0077-1554) [01696584] **3539**

TRANSACTIONS OF THE NATIONAL ACADEMY OF SCIENCE AND TECHNOLOGY (PH/0115-8848) [09818217] **5166**

TRANSACTIONS OF THE NATURAL HISTORY SOCIETY OF NORTHUMBRIA (UK/0144-221X) [02666234] **4173**

TRANSACTIONS OF THE NEBRASKA ACADEMY OF SCIENCES AND AFFILIATED SOCIETIES (US/0163-9013) [04525861] **5167**

TRANSACTIONS OF THE NEW ORLEANS ACADEMY OF OPHTHALMOLOGY (US/0077-8605) [02306067] **3879**

TRANSACTIONS OF THE ... NORTH AMERICAN WILDLIFE AND NATURAL RESOURCES CONFERENCE (US/0078-1355) [01606992] **2207**

TRANSACTIONS OF THE NORTHEAST SECTION OF THE WILDLIFE SOCIETY *See* NORTHEAST WILDLIFE **2201**

TRANSACTIONS OF THE ORIENTAL CERAMIC SOCIETY (UK/0306-0926) [01589063] **2595**

TRANSACTIONS OF THE PACIFIC COAST OBSTETRICAL AND GYNECOLOGICAL SOCIETY (US/0078-7442) [01761667] **3769**

TRANSACTIONS OF THE PHILOLOGICAL SOCIETY (UK/0079-1636) [01762269] **3329**

TRANSACTIONS OF THE ... PRAGUE CONFERENCE ON INFORMATION THEORY, STATISTICAL DECISION FUNCTIONS, RANDOM PROCESSES (XR/0231-9969) [02071058] **3539**

TRANSACTIONS OF THE RADNORSHIRE SOCIETY, THE (UK/0306-848X) [17732832] **2713**

TRANSACTIONS OF THE ROYAL ASIATIC SOCIETY, KOREA BRANCH (KO) [08377416] **2509**

TRANSACTIONS — Alphabetical Title Index

TRANSACTIONS OF THE ROYAL HISTORICAL SOCIETY (UK/0080-4401) [01715427] **2713**

TRANSACTIONS OF THE ROYAL INSTITUTION OF NAVAL ARCHITECTS (UK/0035-8967) [06288314] **310**

TRANSACTIONS OF THE ROYAL SOCIETY OF CANADA (CN/0035-9122) [02441526] **2855**

TRANSACTIONS OF THE ROYAL SOCIETY OF EDINBURGH. EARTH SCIENCES (UK/0263-5933) [06471346] **1361**

TRANSACTIONS OF THE ROYAL SOCIETY OF SOUTH AFRICA (SA/0035-919X) [01604900] 4173, **5167**

TRANSACTIONS OF THE ROYAL SOCIETY OF SOUTH AUSTRALIA (AT/0372-1426) [06271809] **5167**

TRANSACTIONS OF THE ROYAL SOCIETY OF TROPICAL MEDICINE AND HYGIENE (UK/0035-9203) [01640202] **3987**

TRANSACTIONS OF THE SAEST (II/0036-0678) [10762784] **1035**

TRANSACTIONS OF THE SHIKOKU ENTOMOLOGICAL SOCIETY (JA/0037-3680) [01765512] **5598**

TRANSACTIONS OF THE SHROPSHIRE ARCHAEOLOGICAL AND HISTORICAL SOCIETY (UK/0143-5175) [21401707] 4173, **284**

TRANSACTIONS OF THE SOCIETY FOR COMPUTER SIMULATION (US/0740-6797) [09991936] **1283**

TRANSACTIONS OF THE SOCIETY OF ACTUARIES COMMITTEE REPORTS (US) **2895**

TRANSACTIONS OF THE SOCIETY OF PETROLEUM ENGINEERS (US/8756-8152) [10932119] **4280**

TRANSACTIONS OF THE SPWLA ANNUAL LOGGING SYMPOSIUM (US/0081-1718) [03794769] **4280**

TRANSACTIONS OF THE THOROTON SOCIETY OF NOTTINGHAMSHIRE (UK/0309-9210) [01772717] **2713**

TRANSACTIONS OF THE UNITARIAN HISTORICAL SOCIETY (UK/0082-7800) [02526807] **5068**

TRANSACTIONS OF THE WESTERMARCK SOCIETY (FI/0357-1823) [01772756] 246, **5264**

TRANSACTIONS OF THE WESTERN SECTION OF THE WILDLIFE SOCIETY (US/0893-214X) [15472310] **2207**

TRANSACTIONS OF THE WISCONSIN ACADEMY OF SCIENCES, ARTS, AND LETTERS (US/0084-0505) [01589638] **5167**

TRANSACTIONS OF THE WORCESTERSHIRE ARCHAEOLOGICAL SOCIETY (UK/0143-2389) [l01432389] **284**

TRANSACTIONS OF THE YORKSHIRE DIALECT SOCIETY (UK/0954-6316) [01773083] **3329**

TRANSACTIONS OF THE ZIMBABWE SCIENTIFIC ASSOCIATION (RH/0254-2765) [07252407] **5167**

●TRANSACTIONS ON COMPONENTS, PACKAGING & MANUFACTURING TECHNOLOGY PART B : TRANSACTIONS ON COMPONENTS, PACKAGING & ADVANCED PACKAGING (US/1070-9894) [28525078] **4222**

●TRANSACTIONS ON COMPUTER-HUMAN INTERACTION (US/1073-0516) [29297317] **1221**

TRANSACTIONS - PIONEER AMERICA SOCIETY (US/0884-3309) [03987720] **2763**

TRANSACTIONS. SECTION A, MINING INDUSTRY / INSTITUTION OF MINING & METALLURGY (UK/0371-7844) [02401163] **2152**

TRANSACTIONS - SOCIETY OF ACTUARIES (US/0037-9794) [01765899] **2895**

TRANSACTIONS - SOUTH STAFFORDSHIRE ARCHAEOLOGICAL AND HISTORICAL SOCIETY (UK/0457-7817) [01786327] 2713, **284**

TRANSACTIONS - THE ISRAEL NUCLEAR SOCIETY, THE ISRAEL HEALTH PHYSICS SOCIETY, RADIATION RESEARCH SOCIETY OF ISRAEL, THE ISRAEL SOCIETY OF MEDICAL PHYSICS, THE ISRAEL SOCIETY OF NUCLEAR MEDICINE (IS) [05186134] 3849, **4451**

TRANSACTIONS - THE SOCIETY OF NAVAL ARCHITECTS AND MARINE ENGINEERS (US/0081-1661) [01765929] **4184**

TRANSACTIONS - THE SOUTH AFRICAN INSTITUTE OF ELECTRICAL ENGINEERS (SA/0038-2221) [02933788] **2084**

TRANSACTIONS. TRAFODION (UK) [03289669] **2484**

TRANSACTOR, THE (CN/0827-2530) [11607550] **1273**

TRANSAFETY REPORTER (US/0884-612X) [10939033] 5446, **4805**

TRANSAFRICA FORUM (US/0730-8876) [08077914] **4536**

TRANSAFRICAN JOURNAL OF HISTORY (KE/0251-0391) [01767693] **2644**

TRANSAKTIE : PUBLIKATIE VAN HET POLEMOLOGISCH INSTITUUT VAN DE RIJKSUNIVERSITEIT GRONINGEN (NE/0165-2230) [17423834] **4536**

TRANSATLANTIC PERSPECTIVES (US/0192-477X) [05042829] 4536, **4339**

TRANSCEND (US) **1070**

●TRANSCENDING LIMITS (US/1061-6683) [25394844] **4243**

TRANSCRIBINGS, ANNUAL CONFERENCE - AMERICAN SOCIETY OF PENSION ACTUARIES (US/0094-422X) [01784533] 2895, **1715**

TRANSCRIPT (US) [22536703] **5690**

TRANSCRIPT (US/1040-4848) [18427389] **1123**

TRANSCRIPT (US/0577-7135) [03079106] **2667**

●TRANSCRIPT OF SELECT COMMITTEE ON THE CONSTITUTION (FRENCH EDITION) (CN/1191-4254) [26621249] **4691**

●TRANSCRIPT OF STANDING COMMITTEE ON PUBLIC ACCOUNTS (CN/1189-4210) [26290753] **4756**

TRANSCRIPT, THE **SUSPENDED.** (US) [06648123] 1788, **1123**

TRANSCRIPTASE : REVUE CRITIQUE DE L'ACTUALIT,E SCIENTIFIQUE INTERNATIONALE SUR LE SIDA (FR/1166-5300) [26850577] **3677**

TRANSCULTURAL PSYCHIATRIC RESEARCH REVIEW (CN/0041-1108) [00987512] **3937**

TRANSDEX (US) [04482583] **426**

TRANSDEX INDEX (US/1041-6714) [11028910] **426**

TRANSDUCER TECHNOLOGY (UK/0143-7275) [11084500] **5167**

TRANSESCENCE (US) [01721502] **1788**

TRANSEUPHRATENE PARIS (FR/0996-5904) [l09965904] **2632**

TRANSEUROPEENNES (SZ) **2713**

TRANSFER (SANTA BARBARA, CALIF.) (US/0898-2333) [17748273] 1244, **1205**

TRANSFER STUDENTS DEGREE DIRECTORY (US) **1850**

TRANSFER STUDENTS DIRECTORY (US) **1788**

TRANSFERENCIA (MX) [22416817] **1630**

TRANSFERT (CN/0713-4355) [08902956] **1886**

TRANSFERT (MONTREAL. 1979) **See** REVUE QUEBECOISE D'ERGOTHERAPIE **4382**

TRANSFIL EUROPE PARIS (FR/1143-3760) [l11433760] 4442, **1168**

TRANSFORMACAO (BL/0101-3173) [02385331] **4364**

TRANSFORMACION (MX/0041-1124) [04559818] **1630**

TRANSFORMATION (EXETER) (UK/0265-3788) [11004341] **5005**

TRANSFORMATION OF THE CLASSICAL HERITAGE, THE (US) [07935486] **1080**

TRANSFORMATIONS (PARIS) (FR/1148-7194) [21324808] **310**

TRANSFORMATIONS (WAYNE, N.J.) (US/1052-5017) [22296121] **5225**

TRANSFORMERS (US/0744-0650) [07257373] **2085**

TRANSFORMING ANTHROPOLOGY : A PUBLICATION OF THE ASSOCIATION OF BLACK ANTHROPOLOGISTS (US/1051-0559) [21864128] **246**

●TRANSFUSION CLINIQUE ET BIOLOGIQUE (FR) [30108497] **3774**

TRANSFUSION MEDICINE (UK/0958-7578) [26133630] **3802**

TRANSFUSION MEDICINE REVIEWS (US/0887-7963) [13351558] **3647**

TRANSFUSION MEDICINE. SUPPLEMENT (UK/0960-5592) [l09605592] 3802, **3774**

TRANSFUSION (PHILADELPHIA) (US/0041-1132) [01604474] **3774**

TRANSFUSION SCIENCE (UK/0955-3886) [20059785] **3647**

TRANSGENIC RESEARCH (UK/0962-8819) [25352579] **552**

●TRANSGENICA (LEVITTOWN, PA) (US/1051-9688) [22159991] **3697**

TRANSILVANIA (RM) [02272679] **2713**

TRANSISTOR D.A.T.A. BOOK (US) [01711453] **2085**

TRANSISTOR DISCONTINUED DEVICES D.A.T.A. BOOK **CEASED.** (US/0730-4846) [06812879] **2085**

TRANSISTOR SUBSTITUTION HANDBOOK (US) [04722639] **2085**

TRANSIT (GW) [20031623] **2524**

TRANSIT AUSTRALIA (AT/0818-5204) [l08185204] **5395**

TRANSIT CONNECTIONS (US) **5437**

TRANSIT FACT BOOK (WASHINGTON, D.C.) (US/0149-3132) [01443256] **5395**

TRANSIT LAW REVIEW (US/0149-0656) [03422042] **5395**

TRANSIT NEWS CANADA **CEASED.** (CN/0712-8355) [08040472] **5395**

TRANSIT OPERATING REPORT (US/0361-6371) [02247022] **5395**

TRANSIT POSTMARK COLLECTOR (US/0041-1175) [05854702] **1147**

TRANSIT PULSE (US/0748-7347) [10993102] **5395**

●TRANSIT RESEARCH ABSTRACTS (1992) (US/1062-9483) [25816715] **5395**

TRANSITION (GY/1012-8263) [04728328] **5225**

TRANSITION (AT/0157-7344) [09301388] **310**

TRANSITION (US) [24483612] **4498**

TRANSITION (LONDON, ENGLAND) **CEASED.** (UK/0267-8950) [13443299] **1917**

TRANSITION METAL CHEMISTRY (US/0082-5921) [01330684] **1038**

TRANSITION METAL CHEMISTRY (UK/0340-4285) [02885834] **4022**

TRANSITION NEWS (AT/0811-0336) [l08110336] **1908**

TRANSITION (OTTAWA) (CN/0049-4429) [02227569] **2286**

TRANSITION : REVUE INTERNATIONALE D'ASEPSI DU CHANGEMENT PSYCHIATRIQUE ET SOCIAL (FR) **3937**

TRANSITION : THE NEWSLETTER ABOUT REFORMING ECONOMIES / TRANSITION AND MACRO-ADJUSTMENT, COUNTRY ECONOMICS DEPARTMENT, WORLD BANK (US) [23172930] **1640**

TRANSITION (WASHINGTON) (US/0049-4437) [01798046] **1524**

●TRANSITIONS (BE) [28032201] 1587, 5225, **4536**

TRANSITIONS ABROAD (US/1061-2343) [12378882] 5494, **1788**

TRANSITIONS (CINCINNATI, OHIO) (US/0278-2804) [07718349] 4691, **5395**

TRANSITIONS IN MENTAL RETARDATION (US/0749-3924) [11120822] **4620**

TRANSIZIONE (IT) [17257966] **5225**

TRANSKEI. NATIONAL ASSEMBLY **See** DEBATES OF THE NATIONAL ASSEMBLY **4471**

TRANSLATING AND THE COMPUTER : PROCEEDINGS OF A CONFERENCE JOINTLY SPONSORED BY ASLIB, THE ASSOCIATION FOR INFORMATION MANAGEMENT; THE ASLIB TECHNICAL TRANSLATION GROUP; THE TRANSLATORS' GUILD (UK) [17900883] **1205**

●TRANSLATION AND LITERATURE (UK/0968-1361) [26025417] **3447**

TRANSLATION - BUREAU OF RECLAMATION (US) [01542218] **4691**

TRANSLATION - NAVAL OCEANOGRAPHIC OFFICE (US) [01167204] **1457**

TRANSLATION (NEW YORK) (US/0093-9307) [01793246] **3447**

TRANSLATION PERSPECTIVES (US/0890-4758) [14337251] **3329**

TRANSLATION REVIEW (US/0737-4836) [04282678] 3447, **3329**

TRANSLATION SERVICES DIRECTORY (US/0738-4750) [09604040] **3329**

TRANSLATION - UNITED KINGDOM ATOMIC ENERGY AUTHORITY, RESEARCH GROUP, CULHAM LABORATORY (UK/0372-3666) [l03723666] 1959, **4423**

TRANSLATIONS - AMERICAN MATHEMATICAL SOCIETY (US/0065-9290) [01480371] **3539**

TRANSLATIONS INDEX (AMERICAN SOCIETY FOR METALS) **CEASED.** (US/0278-4238) [07490675] **4022**

TRANSLATIONS OF MATHEMATICAL MONOGRAPHS (US/0065-9282) [01767701] **3539**

TRANSLATIONS ON JAPAN (US) [02370919] **4536**

TRANSLATIONS ON NARCOTICS AND DANGEROUS DRUGS (US) [02370800] **1350**

TRANSLATIONS ON NORTH KOREA (US/0196-8386) [01944273] **2667**

TRANSLATIONS ON USSR AGRICULTURE (US) [02370673] **142**

TRANSLATIONS ON USSR ECONOMIC AFFAIRS (US) [02370978] **1524**

TRANSLATOR REFERRAL, TRANSLATION SERVICES DIRECTORY (US/0730-3327) [07986856] **3329**

TRANSLATORS' SOCIETY OF QUEBEC *See* GUIDE DES MEMBRES DE LA STQ **3284**

TRANSLINK'S 1992 M & A MONTHLY *CEASED.* (UK) [21668109] 917, **716**

TRANSLOG (WASHINGTON, D.C.) (US/0041-1639) [15666584] **4059**

TRANSMARGE (CN/0823-9274) [11873820] **5264**

TRANSMISSION & DISTRIBUTION (US/0041-1280) [04964736] **2085**

TRANSMISSION & DISTRIBUTION INTERNATIONAL (US/1050-8686) [21664152] **2085**

TRANSMISSION DIGEST (US/0277-8300) [07643183] **5426**

TRANSMISSION/DISTRIBUTION HEALTH & SAFETY REPORT (US/0737-5743) [09395412] 4805, **2085**

TRANSMISSION (MONTREAL) (CN/0824-510X) [10620208] **3329**

TRANSMISSION SERVICE & REPAIR IMPORTED CARS & TRUCKS *See* IMPORTED CARS & TRUCKS, TRANSMISSION SERVICE & REPAIR **5416**

TRANSMITTERS RECEPTORS & SYNAPSES (UK/0143-4241) [I01434241] **4331**

TRANSNATIONAL ASSOCIATIONS (BE/0020-6059) [14578454] **4691**

●TRANSNATIONAL CORPORATIONS (US/1014-9562) [25854186] **716**

TRANSNATIONAL DATA AND COMMUNICATIONS REPORT (US/0892-399X) [13296400] 1239, **1168**

TRANSNATIONAL LAW & CONTEMPORARY PROBLEMS : A JOURNAL OF THE UNIVERSITY OF IOWA COLLEGE OF LAW (US/1058-1006) [23887639] **3136**

TRANSNATIONAL LAWYER, THE (US/1045-8905) [16752042] 3104, **3136**

TRANSNATIONAL PERSPECTIVES *CEASED.* (SZ/0376-6403) [02240634] **3136**

TRANSPAC ACTUALITES (FR/0764-809X) [I0764809X] **5395**

TRANSPACIFIC (VENICE, CALIF.) (US/1047-7977) [20478242] **2274**

TRANSPATENT (GW) **1309**

●TRANSPLANT IMMUNOLOGY (US/0966-3274) [28552018] **3677**

TRANSPLANT INTERNATIONAL (GW/0934-0874) [19743737] **3976**

TRANSPLANTATION (US/0041-1337) [01767703] **3647**

TRANSPLANTATION AND IMMUNOLOGY LETTER (US/0748-1861) [10896896] 3677, **3976**

TRANSPLANTATION, IMPLANTATION TODAY *CEASED.* (CN/0849-1070) [23302578] 3977, **540**

TRANSPLANTATION PROCEEDINGS (US/0041-1345) [01767705] **3977**

TRANSPLANTATION REVIEWS (ORLANDO, FLA.) (US/0955-470X) [17000036] **3977**

TRANSPLANTATION SOCIETY *See* TRANSPLANTATION TODAY **3977**

TRANSPLANTATION TODAY *CEASED.* (US/0091-2719) [02743920] **3977**

TRANSPO *SUSPENDED.* (CN/0706-3954) [04441648] **5395**

TRANSPORT-ACTION (CN/0227-3020) [08124207] **5395**

TRANSPORT AND COMMUNICATIONS INDICATORS (AT/1033-9752) [I10339752] 1123, **5395**

TRANSPORT & TOURISM JOURNAL (II) [01797812] 5494, **5395**

TRANSPORT CANADA CORPORATE PRIORITIES (CN/0842-6546) [19824768] **854**

TRANSPORT CANADIEN (1963) *CEASED.* (CN/0381-5404) [02177136] **5437**

TRANSPORT (DE)REGULATION REPORT (US/0733-0197) [08509028] **5395**

TRANSPORT-DIENST *See* TRANSPORT-DIENST + WIRTSCHAFTS-CORRESPONDENT **5395**

TRANSPORT-DIENST + WIRTSCHAFTS-CORRESPONDENT *CEASED.* (GW) [08211816] **5395**

TRANSPORT ECHO ED. BILINGUE (BE/0009-6083) [I00096083] **5395**

TRANSPORT ECONOMICS (US/0041-1434) [01542281] **5395**

TRANSPORT EN OPSLAG (NE) 5395, **716**

TRANSPORT ENGINEER, THE (UK/0020-3122) [06359636] 5395, **1999**

TRANSPORT ENGINEER'S HANDBOOK, THE (UK) [11563122] **1999**

TRANSPORT ET TOURISME (BE/0041-1442) [I00411442] **5494**

TRANSPORT HISTORY (UK/0041-1469) [01605940] **5395**

●TRANSPORT HISTORY MONOGRAPH (US/1049-1422) [21141493] **5437**

TRANSPORT IN POROUS MEDIA (NE/0169-3913) [13826607] **994**

TRANSPORT IN THE LIFE SCIENCES (US/0271-6208) [06682121] **540**

TRANSPORT LOGISTICS (NE/0929-9645) **5395**

TRANSPORT (LONDON. 1980) (UK/0144-3453) [06538506] 888, **5395**

TRANSPORT MAGAZINE PARIS (FR/1162-387X) [I1162387X] 1524, **5395**

TRANSPORT MANAGEMENT; THE BRITISH JOURNAL OF TRADE AND TRANSPORT (UK/0041-1515) [01767706] 854, **5395**

TRANSPORT MANAGER'S HANDBOOK, THE (UK) [01786357] **5395**

TRANSPORT MIEJSKI (PL/0209-0333) [24521290] **5395**

TRANSPORT OF DANGEROUS GOODS (US) [01476708] **5395**

TRANSPORT OF THUNDER BAY (CN/0822-580X) [10235741] **5395**

●TRANSPORT POLICY (UK/0967-070X) [29485010] **5395**

TRANSPORT POLICY AND DECISION MAKING (NE/0166-1957) [06631556] **5395**

TRANSPORT PUBLIC (FR/0249-5643) [I02495643] **5395**

TRANSPORT RESEARCH & CONSULTANCY BRIEFING (UK/0265-9301) [I02659301] **5396**

TRANSPORT REVIEW (UK) [02480199] **5396**

TRANSPORT REVIEWS (UK/0144-1647) [07802200] **5396**

TRANSPORT ROUTIER DU QUEBEC *CEASED.* (CN/0049-447X) [02304542] **5396**

TRANSPORT STATISTICS (BS) [06952258] **5402**

TRANSPORT STATISTICS IN THE UNITED STATES (US) [03187705] **5402**

TRANSPORT THEORY AND STATISTICAL PHYSICS (US/0041-1450) [01695230] 3539, **4430**

TRANSPORT TOPICS (US/0041-1558) [02705369] **5396**

TRANSPORT USERS CONSULTATIVE COMMITTEE FOR WALES *See* ANNUAL REPORT - TRANSPORT USERS CONSULTATIVE COMMITTEE FOR WALES **5429**

TRANSPORT WORKERS UNION OF AMERICA *See* TWU EXPRESS **1715**

TRANSPORTATION & DISTRIBUTION (US/0895-8548) [16787126] **5457**

TRANSPORTATION AND STORAGE (US) [03930901] 1959, 4280, **1963**

TRANSPORTATION AND TRAVEL : OFFICIAL TABLE OF DISTANCES, FOREIGN TRAVEL (US/0197-3320) [05986305] 5396, **5494**

TRANSPORTATION (BOCA RATON) (US/0273-2602) [04454464] **5396**

TRANSPORTATION BUILDER (US/1043-4054) [19451392] **5396**

TRANSPORTATION (CLEVELAND, OHIO) (US/1041-9136) [12429049] **5396**

TRANSPORTATION COMMISSION UPDATE (US) **5396**

TRANSPORTATION COMMUNICATIONS INTERNATIONAL UNION *See* REPORT OF OFFICERS TO THE ... REGULAR AND ... QUADRENNIAL CONVENTION **1706**

TRANSPORTATION; CURRENT LITERATURE (US/0091-1410) [01785536] **5396**

TRANSPORTATION (DORDRECHT) (NE/0049-4488) [01624097] **5396**

TRANSPORTATION ENERGY RESEARCH (US/0885-8330) [12745360] 1959, **5396**

TRANSPORTATION EQUIPMENT INDUSTRIES (1986) (CN/0835-0140) [16955520] **5396**

TRANSPORTATION FOCUS (US/0098-0129) [01794916] **5396**

TRANSPORTATION IN AMERICA (US/0889-0889) [09605139] 5396, **5402**

TRANSPORTATION JOURNAL (US/0041-1612) [01588960] **5396**

TRANSPORTATION LAW JOURNAL, THE (US/0049-450X) [01767710] 5396, **3065**

TRANSPORTATION LINES OF THE UNITED STATES (US) [12645227] 5457, **5396**

TRANSPORTATION LINES ON THE ATLANTIC, GULF, AND PACIFIC COASTS (US/0361-9125) [02441467] **5457**

TRANSPORTATION LINES ON THE GREAT LAKES SYSTEM (US/0361-8978) [02247135] **5457**

TRANSPORTATION LINES ON THE MISSISSIPPI RIVER SYSTEM AND THE GULF INTRACOASTAL WATERWAY (US/0361-8986) [02441468] **5457**

TRANSPORTATION MONITORING REPORT (US/0162-699X) [04196828] **5396**

TRANSPORTATION NEWS DIGEST, THE (US/1047-062X) [20590829] **5396**

TRANSPORTATION NOTICE OF HEARING *CEASED.* (US) **4280**

TRANSPORTATION / NTIS *See* NTIS ALERT. TRANSPORTATION **5388**

TRANSPORTATION OF DANGEROUS GOODS REGULATIONS (CN/1193-8250) [27649213] **2245**

TRANSPORTATION PLANNING AND TECHNOLOGY (US/0308-1060) [01767712] **5396**

TRANSPORTATION PLANNING SYSTEMS (UK/0962-7146) [I09627146] **5396**

TRANSPORTATION PRACTITIONERS JOURNAL (US/8756-9302) [11465395] **5396**

TRANSPORTATION QUARTERLY (US/0278-9434) [07938948] **5397**

TRANSPORTATION REPORT FOR UNIFIED SCHOOL DISTRICTS (US) [04281399] **1908**

TRANSPORTATION RESEARCH IN CANADA (CN/0381-8284) [02604160] **5446**

TRANSPORTATION RESEARCH. PART A: GENERAL *See* TRANSPORTATION RESEARCH. PART A, POLICY AND PRACTICE **5397**

●TRANSPORTATION RESEARCH. PART A, POLICY AND PRACTICE (US/0965-8564) [25574875] **5397**

TRANSPORTATION RESEARCH. PART B : METHODOLOGICAL (UK/0191-2615) [04827986] **5397**

●TRANSPORTATION RESEARCH. PART C, EMERGING TECHNOLOGIES (US/0968-090X) [27960434] **5397**

TRANSPORTATION RESEARCH RECORD (US/0361-1981) [01259379] **5397**

TRANSPORTATION REVIEW (US/0197-419X) [06011253] **5397**

TRANSPORTATION SCIENCE (US/0041-1655) [01767714] **5397**

... TRANSPORTATION SYSTEM MANAGEMENT REPORT FOR NORTHEASTERN ILLINOIS, THE (US/0741-2266) [09405405] **5397**

TRANSPORTATION TELEPHONE TICKLER (US) [01211312] **5397**

TRANSPORTATION WORLDWIDE (US/8750-8397) [11848195] **854**

TRANSPORTE MODERNO *See* MOTRIX **5421**

TRANSPORTE Y VIAS DE COMUNICACION (CU) [08885130] **5397**

TRANSPORTES, EL TURISMO Y LAS COMUNICACIONES EN ... Y PRIMER SEMESTRE DE, LOS (SP) [13036243] **5397**

TRANSPORTES Y LAS COMUNICACIONES / [MOPT, MINISTERIO DE OBRAS PUBLICAS Y TRANSPORTES], LOS (SP) [28323026] 1123, **5446**

TRANSPORTEUR, LE (CN/0229-4362) [08028140] **5005**

●TRANSPORTING HAZARDOUS MATERIALS (US/1061-3595) [25265715] **2245**

TRANSPORTING PERSONAL FIREARMS (US/0883-0932) [11880491] **5397**

TRANSPORTRECHT (GW/0174-559X) [10055819] 5397, **3066**

TRANSPORTS (FR/0564-1373) [07487147] **5397**

TRANSPORTS ACTUALITES (FR) **5397**

TRANSPORTS EN EUROPE; BIBLIOGRAPHIE, LES (FR/0525-9363) [03991531] **5402**

TRANSPORTS ROUTIERS DE MARCHANDISES (FR) [03439373] **5397**

TRANSPORTS SCOLAIRES / MINISTERE DES TRANSPORTS, DEPARTEMENT DES STATISTIQUES DES TRANSPORTS, LES (FR) [07719859] **1873**

TRANSPUTER AND OCCAM ENGINEERING SERIES (NE/0925-4986) [I09254986] **1249**

●TRANSPUTER COMMUNICATIONS (UK/1070-454X) [28369576] **1205**

TRANSURANIUM PROCESSING PLANT SEMIANNUAL REPORT OF PRODUCTION, STATUS, AND PLANS (US) [05906345] **1959**

TRANSWORLD — Alphabetical Title Index

TRANSWORLD IDENTITY SERIES (US/0890-1562) [14173300] **246**

TRANSWORLD SKATEBOARDING (US/0748-7401) [10993467] **4927**

TRANSWORLD SNOWBOARDING (US/1046-4611) [20411289] **4927**

TRANSYLVANIA TIMES, THE (US) [13285957] **5724**

TRAP & FIELD (US/0041-1760) [03950950] **4927**

TRAPPER AND PREDATOR CALLER, THE (US/8750-233X) [11140981] **3186**

TRAPPER (NORTH BATTLEFORD. 1990) (CN/1184-7417) [24266837] **4879**

TRAPPEUR QUEBECOIS, LE *CEASED.* (CN/0836-7248) [17631633] **4879**

TRAPPING SEASONS AND REGULATIONS / STATE OF WASHINGTON, DEPARTMENT OF GAME (US) [11580713] **4879**

TRASFUSIONE DEL SANGUE (IT/0041-1787) [11520558] **3802**

TRASGRESSIONI (IT) [17367068] **4498**

TRASMISSIONI DATI E TELECOMUNICAZIONI (IT) **1168**

TRASPLANTE OF ORGANS AND TISSUES (SP/0214-820X) [I0214820X] **3977**

TRASPORTI INDUSTRIALI (IT/0041-1809) [I00411809] **5397**

TRASPORTI MARE TERRITORIO (IT) **5458**

TRASPORTI NEWS (IT) **5397**

TRATTAMENTI E FINITURA (IT/0041-1833) [I00411833] **4022**

TRATTATO ENCICLOPEDICO DI ANESTESIA RIANIMAZIONE E TERAPIA INTENSIVA (IT) **3647**

TRAUMA (NEW YORK, N.Y.) (US/0564-1470) [01767722] **3742**

TRAUMA (PRINCETON, N.J.) (US/0883-0304) [12046878] **3977**

TRAUMA QUARTERLY *CEASED.* (US/0743-6637) [10634793] **3977**

TRAUVUX SCIENTIFIQUES DU PARC NATIONAL DE LA VANOISE (FR/0180-961X) [01795585] **4173**

TRAVAIL & SECURITE (FR/0373-1944) [01796024] **2871**

TRAVAIL DANS LE MONDE, LE (INT/0255-5506) [I02555506] **5494**

TRAVAIL ET EMPLOI (FR/0224-4365) [11096436] **3154**

TRAVAIL ET MAITRISE (FR/0750-8964) [06694586] 1524, **948**

TRAVAIL ET METHODES (FR/0041-185X) [01586271] **888**

TRAVAIL ET SANTE (CN/0829-0369) [14556404] **2871**

TRAVAIL ET SOCIETE *CEASED.* (SZ/0378-5424) [I03785424] 5225, **1715**

TRAVAIL HUMAIN, LE (FR/0041-1868) [01767724] **4620**

TRAVAIL (PARIS, FRANCE) (FR/0757-3065) [20795744] **1715**

TRAVAIL PROTEGE NIORT (FR/0397-0264) [I03970264] **4209**

TRAVAIL SOCIAL 1981 (SZ/0255-9641) [I02559641] **5313**

TRAVAIL SOCIAL ACTUALITES PARIS (FR/0753-9711) [I07539711] **5313**

TRAVAILLEUR (QUEBEC) (CN/0707-7017) [04755042] **1715**

TRAVAUX (FR) **5225**

TRAVAUX (FR/0041-1906) [01767725] **1999**

TRAVAUX (FR/0079-0028) [01589609] **2713**

TRAVAUX DE DIDACTIQUE DU FRANCAIS LANGUE ETRANGERE (FR/0765-1635) [I07651635] **3329**

TRAVAUX DE DROIT, D'ECONOMIE, DE SOCIOLOGIE ET DE SCIENCES POLITIQUES (SZ) [07429894] 5264, **1524**

TRAVAUX DE JURIDICTION INTERNATIONALE (SZ/0082-6030) [01767726] **3137**

TRAVAUX DE LA STATION MARINE DE VILLEFRANCHE-SUR-MER (FR) [04542509] 2221, **5599**

TRAVAUX DE L'ASSOCIATION HENRI CAPITANT DES AMIS DE LA CULTURE JURIDIQUE FRANCAISE (FR) [13646268] **3066**

TRAVAUX DE L'ASSOCIATION HENRI CAPITANT POUR LA CULTURE JURIDIQUE FRANCAISE (FR/0399-1466) [06481814] 1524, **1300**

TRAVAUX DE L'ATELIER PROUDHON / ECOLE DES HAUTES ETUDES EN SCIENCES SOCIALES, LES (FR) [17343093] **4548**

TRAVAUX DE LINGUISTIQUE (BE) [05064779] **3329**

TRAVAUX DE LINGUISTIQUE ET DE PHILOLOGIE (FR) [20436965] **3447**

TRAVAUX DE LINGUISTIQUE QUANTITATIVE (FR) [13097546] **3329**

TRAVAUX DE LINGUISTIQUE QUEBECOISE (CN/0710-2534) [06005558] **3329**

TRAVAUX DE L'INSTITUT D'ART PREHISTORIQUE (FR) [05522965] **246**

TRAVAUX DE L'INSTITUT D'ART PREHISTORIQUE *SUSPENDED.* (FR) [02602728] **367**

TRAVAUX DE L'INSTITUT DE GEOGRAPHIE DE REIMS (FR/0048-7163) [I00487163] **2577**

TRAVAUX DE L'INSTITUT DE PHONETIQUE D'AIX (FR/0750-6112) [02710114] **3329**

TRAVAUX DE L'INSTITUT DE PHONETIQUE DE STRASBOURG REVUE (FR/0039-2235) [I00392235] **3329**

TRAVAUX DE L'INSTITUT DE SPEOLOGIE EMILE RACOVITZA (RM/0301-9187) [01792865] **4173**

TRAVAUX DE L'INSTITUT D'HISTOIRE DE L'ART DE LYON (FR/0181-4400) [06651948] **367**

TRAVAUX DE LITTERATURE : T.L (FR/0995-6794) [20938824] **3447**

TRAVAUX DE RECHERCHE - BANQUE DU CANADA (CN/0228-3573) [06965406] **814**

TRAVAUX DES CAMPEUSES D'ETE AU CAMP ROLLAND-GERMAIN (1976) (CN/0704-1993) [03890144] **4173**

TRAVAUX D'HISTOIRE ETHICO-POLITIQUE (SZ/0082-6073) [03142787] **2632**

TRAVAUX D'HUMANISME ET RENAISSANCE (SZ/0082-6081) [01590480] **2713**

TRAVAUX DU CENTRE DE DOCUMENTATION ET DE BIBLIOGRAPHIE PHILOSOPHIQUES DE BESANCON (FR) [05802192] **3253**

TRAVAUX DU CENTRE DE RECHERCHES ET D'ETUDES OCEANOGRAPHIQUES (FR/0008-9680) [01161446] **1457**

TRAVAUX DU COMITE FRANCAIS DE DROIT INTERNATIONAL PRIVE (FR) [01564288] **3137**

TRAVAUX DU LABORATOIRE D'ANTHROPOLOGIE, DE PREHISTOIRE ET D'ETHNOLOGIE DES PAYS DE LA MEDITERRANEE OCCIDENTALE *See* PREHISTOIRE ANTHROPOLOGIE MEDITERRANEENNES **243**

TRAVAUX DU LABORATOIRE D'ANTHROPOLOGIE ET DE PREHISTOIRE DES PAYS DE LA MEDITERRANEE OCCIDENTALE (FR/1148-2141) [I11482141] **246**

TRAVAUX EN COURS (FR/0766-9968) [18583796] **3539**

TRAVAUX ET ACQUISITIONS DU MUSEUM NATIONAL D'HISTOIRE NATURELLE (FR) [04815694] **4173**

TRAVAUX ET DOCUMENTS (FR/0298-8879) [14102677] **4536**

TRAVAUX ET DOCUMENTS (CN/0079-8339) [02794786] **2763**

TRAVAUX ET DOCUMENTS / INSTITUT NATIONAL D'ETUDES DEMOGRAPHIQUES (FR/0071-8823) [01570032] **4560**

TRAVAUX ET MEMOIRES (FR) [06528153] **1850**

TRAVAUX ET MEMOIRES (CENTRE DE RECHERCHE D'HISTOIRE ET CIVILISATION DE BYZANCE (PARIS, FRANCE)) (FR) [06063895] **2713**

TRAVAUX ET MEMOIRES DE L'INSTITUT D'ETHNOLOGIE (FR) [01761900] 247, **5225**

TRAVAUX ET RECHERCHES - CENTRE DE RECHERCHES RELATIONS INTERNATIONALES DE L'UNIVERSITE DE METZ (FR) [05756544] **4536**

TRAVAUX ET RECHERCHES GRIC / GROUPE DE RECHERCHE EN INFORMATION ET COMMUNICATION (CN/0703-1297) [10763934] **3253**

TRAVAUX / UNIVERSITE JEAN MONNET-SAINT-ETIENNE, CENTRE INTERDISCIPLINAIRE D'ETUDE ET DE RECHERCHE SUR L'EXPRESSION CONTEMPORAINE (FR) [26776265] 3447, **3329**

TRAVEL 50 & BEYOND (US/1049-6211) [21265717] **5494**

TRAVEL 800 (US/0192-155X) [03472768] **5494**

TRAVEL A LA CARTE (CN/0836-7353) [17759139] **5494**

TRAVEL AGENCY (UK/0041-1981) [I00411981] **5494**

TRAVEL AGENT (US/1053-9360) [22693677] **5494**

TRAVEL AGENT INTERNACIONAL, EL (US/0194-620X) [04889254] **5495**

TRAVEL AGENT. PERSONNEL DIRECTORY *See* TRAVEL INDUSTRY PERSONNEL DIRECTORY **5496**

TRAVEL AGENTS' ANNUAL PRODUCTION, UNITED STATES ONLY (US/8755-7738) [11382822] **5495**

TRAVEL ALERT BULLETIN (US/1068-7416) [27786098] **5495**

TRAVEL AND DESCRIPTION SERIES (US) [01760809] **2763**

TRAVEL AND ENTERTAINMENT, BUSINESS OR PLEASURE? (US/0733-0030) [08487966] **4756**

TRAVEL & HOSPITALITY CAREER DIRECTORY (US/1048-1079) [20614704] **4209**

TRAVEL & LEARNING ABROAD (US/0748-7398) [10993428] **5495**

TRAVEL & LEISURE (US/0041-2007) [01588756] **5495**

TRAVEL & LEISURE'S WORLD TRAVEL OVERVIEW *CEASED.* (US/0895-2698) [15747067] **5495**

TRAVEL & TOURISM ANALYST (UK/0269-3755) [15606526] **5495**

TRAVEL AND TOURISM BAROMETER : TTB (SP/1014-7306) [24237837] **5495**

TRAVEL & TOURISM EXECUTIVE REPORT (US/1070-8855) [15273289] **5495**

TRAVEL AND TOURISM INDEX, THE *SUSPENDED.* (US/1040-8142) [12439159] **5495**

TRAVEL & TOURISM LAW BIBLIOGRAPHY (US/0897-389X) [17486207] 5501, **3083**

TRAVEL AND TOURISM RESEARCH ASSOCIATION (U.S.) *See* ANNUAL CONFERENCE / TRAVEL AND TOURISM RESEARCH ASSOCIATION **5461**

TRAVEL AUSTRALIA SYDNEY (AT/0817-2935) [I08172935] **5495**

TRAVEL BOOKS WORLDWIDE (US/1058-7098) [24361981] **5495**

TRAVEL BUSINESS ANALYST ASIA ED (HK/1011-7768) [I10117768] 716, **5495**

TRAVEL BUSINESS ANALYST EUROPE ED (HK/0256-419X) [I0256419X] 716, **5495**

TRAVEL BUSINESS MANAGER, THE (US/0886-6147) [12953185] 716, **5495**

TRAVEL BUSINESS REPORT *CEASED.* (US/0884-0687) [12298789] 716, **5495**

TRAVEL CHINA NEWSLETTER (CN/0834-258X) [16309481] **5495**

TRAVEL CLUB (UK) **5495**

TRAVEL COLLECTOR *CEASED.* (US/1040-0001) [18286686] 5495, **2778**

... TRAVEL CONSULTANTS DIRECTORY, THE (US/1053-721X) [22616695] **5495**

TRAVEL COURIER (TORONTO) (CN/1182-9699) [21053807] **5495**

TRAVEL EXPENSE MANAGEMENT (US/0272-569X) [06876972] **5495**

TRAVEL GUIDE FLORISSON (US/0277-4097) [07546462] **5495**

TRAVEL GUIDE, MEXICO (US/0732-2313) [08298613] **5495**

TRAVEL GUIDE, MEXICO AND CENTRAL AMERICA (US/0732-0434) [04791898] **5495**

TRAVEL GUIDE TO MEXICO, CENTRAL AMERICA AND SOUTH AMERICA, A (CN/0711-4710) [08499927] **5495**

TRAVEL HANDBOOK (US) [04169625] **5495**

TRAVEL HOLIDAY (US/0199-025X) [05519926] **5495**

TRAVEL IDEAS (US/0085-7351) [01785332] **5495**

TRAVEL IN VIRGINIA (US) [11790022] **5495**

TRAVEL INDUSTRY ASSOCIATION OF CANADA *See* TIAC NEWSLETTER **5492**

TRAVEL INDUSTRY INDICATORS (US/8756-8799) [11689886] **5495**

TRAVEL INDUSTRY MONITOR (UK/0959-6186) [22589657] **5496**

TRAVEL INDUSTRY PERSONNEL DIRECTORY (US/0082-6146) [06444702] **5496**

TRAVEL INDUSTRY WORLD YEARBOOK (US/0738-9515) [09579105] **5496**

TRAVEL ITEMS AND COURIER WEEKLY *See* TRAVEL WEEKLY **5497**

TRAVEL JOURNAL (JA) **5496**

TRAVEL JOURNAL INTERNATIONAL: TJI (JA) **5496**

TRAVEL JOURNALIST, THE (BE/0772-0033) [I07720033] **5496**

TRAVEL LEISURE & ENTERTAINMENT NEWS MEDIA (US/1041-5203) [18767022] 4855, **5496**

TRAVEL-LOG (CN/0713-2840) [15509008] **5496**

TRAVEL MANAGEMENT DAILY (US) **5496**

TRAVEL MANAGEMENT NEWSLETTER (US) **5496**

TRAVEL MARKET REPORT : NATIONAL TRAVEL SURVEY TABULATIONS AND ANALYSIS (US/0737-2620) [22424796] **5496**

TRAVEL MARKETING AND AGENCY MANAGEMENT GUIDELINES (US/0275-3545) [07118862] 937, **5496**

TRAVEL MASTER (US/0145-7810) [02781636] 5496, **2809**

TRAVEL MEDICINE ADVISOR (US) **3647**

TRAVEL MEDICINE INTERNATIONAL (UK/0267-3606) [11255264] 5496, **3647**

● TRAVEL MEXICO EVENTS (US/1048-5139) [20961546] **5496**

● TRAVEL MEXICO MAGAZINE (US/1048-5163) [20961664] **5496**

● TRAVEL MEXICO UPDATE (US/1048-5155) [20961625] **5496**

● TRAVEL NEWS AMERICAS (US/1069-286X) [27970515] **5496**

TRAVEL NEWS ASIA (HK) **5496**

TRAVEL NORTH AMERICA (US/0147-1422) [03114552] **5496**

TRAVEL PREVIEW (US/0898-0055) [17691313] **5496**

TRAVEL PRINTOUT (US/0744-6233) [03616462] **5496**

TRAVEL PUBLISHING NEWS *CEASED*. (US/1043-6138) [19497762] **5496**

TRAVEL RESEARCH ASSOCIATES *See* TRA DIGEST **5494**

TRAVEL REVIEW, THE *CEASED*. (US/1053-1998) [22473658] **5496**

TRAVEL SCOOP (CN/0822-9228) [10680921] **5496**

TRAVEL SMART (US/0741-5826) [04616809] **5496**

TRAVEL SMART FOR BUSINESS (US/0741-5818) [10204477] 716, **5496**

TRAVEL SMARTER (US/1055-0488) [23065219] **5496**

TRAVEL SOUTH (1989) (US/1041-3642) [18733132] **2548**

TRAVEL STATISTICS (JO) [02240489] **5501**

TRAVEL STATISTICS, JAMAICA (JM) [07800485] **5501**

TRAVEL TIDINGS (US/0895-4135) [16644779] **5496**

TRAVEL TO THE USSR (RU/0320-0167) [01792178] **5496**

TRAVEL TRADE DIRECTORY (UK) [08525812] **5497**

● TRAVEL TRADE GAZETTE DIRECTORY (UK) [26280936] **5497**

TRAVEL TRADE (NEW YORK, N.Y.) (US/0041-2066) [03384361] **5497**

TRAVEL TRAILERS, 5TH WHEEL TRAILERS, CAMPING TRAILERS RV GUIDE, NEW & USED VALUES (US/0145-3785) [02729049] **5397**

TRAVEL TRENDS IN THE UNITED STATES AND CANADA (US) [04058484] **5497**

TRAVEL WEEKLY (US/0041-2082) [03951062] **5497**

TRAVEL WEEKLY'S WORLD TRAVEL DIRECTORY *CEASED*. (US/0739-5698) [04155799] **5497**

TRAVELAGE EAST (US/0041-2104) [03387160] **5497**

TRAVELAGE MIDAMERICA (US/0744-1606) [08073104] **5497**

TRAVELAGE WEST (US/0041-1973) [04935230] **5497**

● TRAVELAMERICA (EVANSTON, ILL.) (US/1068-2554) [27505529] **5497**

TRAVELCADE MAGAZINE (US/0363-1796) [02431221] **5497**

TRAVELER'S ALMANAC (US/0161-8075) [04019345] **5497**

● TRAVELER'S GUIDE TO ART MUSEUM EXHIBITIONS (US) [25535853] **367**

TRAVELER'S GUIDE TO MUSEUM EXHIBITIONS *See* TRAVELER'S GUIDE TO ART MUSEUM EXHIBITIONS **367**

TRAVELER'S GUIDE TO WORLD RADIO (US/1062-9181) [22998866] **1141**

TRAVELER'S INFORMATION EXCHANGE *See* FOREIGN LODGING LIST **2805**

TRAVELER'S TOLL-FREE TELEPHONE DIRECTORY (US/0146-5988) [02990668] **5497**

TRAVELIFE (CN/0228-5916) [08332575] **5497**

TRAVELIN' (EUGENE, OR.) (US/1051-9335) [22151663] **5497**

TRAVELIN TALK NEWSLETTER, THE (US/1052-1615) [22200226] 4394, **5497**

TRAVELING HEALTHY NEWSLETTER (US/0899-2169) [18035360] **5497**

TRAVELLER ACCOMMODATION STATISTICS (CN/0380-5956) [02443717] **5501**

TRAVELLER MAGAZINE (US) **5497**

TRAVELLERS AGENDA (US/1045-5841) [20173484] **5497**

TRAVELLER'S GUIDE TO THE MIDDLE EAST (UK) [06234598] **5497**

TRAVELNEWS ASIA (HK/0252-9629) [I02529629] **5497**

TRAVELOGUE MAGAZINE (US) **5497**

TRAVELORE REPORT, THE (US/0270-2398) [06389440] **5497**

TRAVELTRADE (AT) **5497**

TRAVELVISION *See* EXXON TRAVEL CLUB MEXICO VACATION TRAVEL GUIDE **2805**

TRAVELWARE (US/0747-475X) [10891570] 3186, **1630**

TRAVELWEEK BULLETIN (CN/0225-6207) [07293923] **5497**

TRAVELWRITER MARKETLETTER (US/0738-9094) [09668929] **2925**

TRAVERS LES VIGNES, A (CN/0824-1465) [11825449] **2371**

TRAVERSE, THE MAGAZINE *See* TRAVERSE (TRAVERSE CITY, MICH.) **2494**

TRAVERSE (TRAVERSE CITY, MICH.) (US/1071-3719) [28626122] **2494**

TRAVERSES *CEASED*. (FR/0336-9730) [05095082] **367**

TRAVERSIERS, PONTS ET CROISIERES (CN/0708-3319) [08271687] **855**

TRAVERSO (CLAVERACK, N.Y.) (US/1041-7494) [18839327] **4157**

TRAVESSIA (BL/0101-9570) [09725537] **3447**

TRAVIS COUNTY BUSINESS GUIDE (US/0749-5498) [10135317] **716**

TRAVLTIPS (US/0162-9816) [03951095] **5497**

TRAWICK'S FLORIDA PRACTICE AND PROCEDURE (US/0191-7684) [04913052] **3066**

TRC SPECTRAL DATA--INFRARED (US) [12374979] **1019**

TRC SPECTRAL DATA--ULTRAVIOLET (US) [13085550] **1020**

TRC THERMODYNAMIC TABLES NON-HYDROCARBONS (US) **4432**

TRC THERMODYNAMIC TABLES - HYDROCARBONS (US) **4432**

TREASURE (US/0049-4593) [03951146] **2779**

TREASURE CHEST (NEW YORK, N.Y.) (US/0897-814X) [17631445] **252**

TREASURE CHEST NEWS (US/0882-1178) [11744935] **2475**

TREASURE FACTS (US/1054-8246) [22979044] **4855**

TREASURE HUNTING (UK/0140-4539) [I01404539] **2779**

TREASURE STATE LINES (US) [04579771] **2475**

● TREASURE TRAILS (CN/1188-9918) [26776213] **5497**

TREASURER (UK/0264-0937) [I02640937] **1524**

TREASURES IN NEEDLEWORK *CEASED*. (US/1059-2466) [24521504] **376**

TREASURY AND CIVIL SERVICE COMMITTEE (UK) **4691**

TREASURY AND RISK MANAGEMENT (US/1067-0432) [27131223] **1524**

TREASURY BULLETIN *CEASED*. (UK/0960-8532) [22159422] **4757**

TREASURY BULLETIN (US/0041-2155) [02451358] **814**

TREASURY DEPARTMENT TELEPHONE DIRECTORY (US) [03458507] **4691**

● TREASURY MANAGEMENT INTERNATIONAL (UK/0967-523X) [29155314] **814**

TREASURY MANAGER (UK) **814**

TREASURY MANAGER, THE (US/0896-2987) [16994841] **888**

● TREASURY MANAGER'S REPORT (US/1071-8532) [28740759] **814**

TREASURY TODAY (UK/0961-5261) [I09615261] **752**

TREASURY TODAY (UK) **752**

TREATIES AND OTHER INTERNATIONAL ACTS SERIES (US/0083-0186) [01774183] **4537**

TREATIES IN FORCE. COPY A (US) [01768353] **4537**

TREATING ABUSE TODAY (US/1052-3995) [22283793] **5313**

TREATISE OF PETROLEUM GEOLOGY REPRINT SERIES (US/1046-0144) [17409457] **4280**

TREATISE ON ADHESION AND ADHESIVES (US/0082-6235) [01783203] **1058**

TREATISE ON ENVIRONMENTAL LAW (US) [04553490] **3116**

TREATMENT : HANDBOOK OF DRUG THERAPY (UK) **4331**

TREATMENT IN GENERAL PRACTICE (US) [05038736] **3802**

TREATMENT ISSUES (US/1050-625X) [19715391] 3716, **3677**

TREATY SERIES (SA) [03013972] **3137**

TREATY SERIES - UNITED NATIONS (US/0379-8267) [01768015] **3137**

TREBEDE : REVISTA DE POESIA (SP) **3472**

TREBLE POETS (UK) [03789290] **3472**

TREE (US/0041-2171) [03490879] **3447**

TREE CLIMBER (SALINA, KAN.) (US/0737-9226) [08863830] **2475**

TREE NUT AUTHORITY *See* REPORT OF THE TREE NUT AUTHORITY **2430**

TREE PHYSIOLOGY (CN/0829-318X) [13989514] 529, **2397**

TREE PLANTER, THE (US/0732-0329) [08290172] **2397**

TREE PLANTERS' NOTES (US/0096-8714) [01767732] **2397**

TREE PLANTING IN THE UNITED STATES / UNITED STATES DEPARTMENT OF AGRICULTURE, FOREST SERVICE, STATE AND PRIVATE FORESTRY, COOPERATIVE FORESTRY (US) [23997715] **2397**

TREE-RING BULLETIN (US/0041-2198) [01767733] **2397**

TREE SHAKER / EASTERN KENTUCKY GENEALOGICAL SOCIETY (US/0893-2069) [10296417] **2475**

TREE TALK (JACKSONVILLE, TEX.) (US/0736-7678) [09198319] **2475**

TREE TIPS (1982) *See* NORTHBOUND (EAGLE RIVER, WIS.) **2201**

TREE TRACER (CN/0841-2642) [20372089] **2475**

TREE TRACERS, THE (US/0162-1440) [04099212] **2475**

TREE TRIMMER, THE *CEASED*. (US/0892-774X) [15347279] **3647**

TREELINE (CN/0710-4375) [08811683] **3447**

TREES AND NATURAL RESOURCES (AT/0814-4680) [12276556] **2207**

TREES (BERLIN, WEST) (GW/0931-1890) [16576511] **2397**

TREES FROM THE GROVE (US/1046-6339) [20443127] **2476**

TREES IN SOUTH AFRICA (SA/0041-2236) [07165068] **2397**

TREESEARCHER, THE (US) [07578226] **2476**

TREESPEAK ADELAIDE (AT/1032-6111) [I10326111] **2207**

TREFF AND WUNDERWELT *See* TREFF WUNDERWELT **1524**

TREFF WUNDERWELT (AU) **1524**

TREFILE, LE (GW/0374-2261) [03694900] **4022**

TREFPUNT (NE) [01793336] **2713**

TREGANZA ANTHROPOLOGY MUSEUM *See* TREGANZA ANTHROPOLOGY MUSEUM PAPERS **247**

TREGANZA ANTHROPOLOGY MUSEUM PAPERS (US) [03148107] **247**

TREK, LIFE-CENTERED BIBLE STUDY FOR JUNIOR HIGHS. STUDENTS LEAFLETS (US/1056-2311) [23592023] 1070, **5020**

TREK, LIFE-CENTERED BIBLE STUDY FOR JUNIOR HIGHS. TEACHER IDEA BOOK (US/1056-232X) [23592107] **5005**

TREK, LIFE-CENTERED BIBLE STUDY FOR SENIOR HIGHS. STUDENTS LEAFLETS (US/1056-229X) [23591950] **5020**

TREK, LIFE-CENTERED BIBLE STUDY FOR SENIOR HIGHS. TEACHER IDEA BOOK (US/1056-2303) [23591991] **5020**

TREKWEST (SACRAMENTO, CALIF.) (US/1056-8298) [23859481] **5497**

TRELLIS (CN/0380-1470) [02443331] **2432**

TRELLIS (SAN MARINO) *See* EDITOR'S DIGEST **4814**

TREMBLAIE (CN/0713-4282) [08902930] **2476**

TREMPLIN AVERBODE (BE/0041-2279) [I00412279] **1070**

● TRENCHLESS TECHNOLOGY (US/1064-4156) [26280441] **5167**

TREND (AU) [07558807] **1587**

TREND (XR) [02497076] **5167**

TREND (II) [01790417] **2667**

TREND IN ENGINEERING AT THE UNIVERSITY OF WASHINGTON, THE (US/0362-0018) [02162933] **2000**

TREND — Alphabetical Title Index

TREND OF EMPLOYMENT AND UNEMPLOYMENT, THE (IE) [06140867] **1715**

TREND (POINTE-CLAIRE) (CN/0041-2295) [01606940] **4239**

TRENDEX NEWSLETTER (AT) **716**

TRENDLETTER (GW/0935-5596) **716**

TRENDLETTER MEGATRENDS AKTUELL (GW) 716, **1524**

TRENDLINE CORPORATION *See* TRENDLINE'S CURRENT MARKET PERSPECTIVES **918**

TRENDLINE DAILY ACTION STOCK CHARTS (US/0277-4968) [06366835] **917**

TRENDLINE'S CURRENT MARKET PERSPECTIVES (US/0041-2333) [04741345] **918**

TRENDS :AMERICAN SOCIETY OF ALLIED HEALTH PROFESSIONS (US) [13098367] **3647**

TRENDS AND ALTERNATIVES IN TESTING (CN/1191-1700) [25883028] **2253**

TRENDS AND APPLICATIONS (US) [04145651] **1205**

TRENDS AND ISSUES IN CRIME AND CRIMINAL JUSTICE (AT/0817-8542) [I08178542] **3178**

TRENDS AND PERSPECTIVES IN PARASITOLOGY (UK/0260-6763) [07654173] **475**

TRENDS AND POLICIES IN PRIVATISATION / CENTRE FOR CO-OPERATION WITH EUROPEAN ECONOMIES IN TRANSITION / TENDANCES ET POLITIQUES DES PRIVATISATIONS / CENTRE POUR LA COOPERATION AVEC LES ECONOMIES EUROPEENNES EN TRANSITION (FR/1021-3287) [28627151] **1524**

TRENDS & PROJECTIONS (US) [03776034] **918**

TRENDS & TECHNIQUES IN THE CONTEMPORARY DENTAL LABORATORY (US/0746-8962) [10378256] **1337**

TRENDS & WORDS (IT) 1524, **937**

TRENDS, BIOTECHNOLOGY : INFORMATION AND ISSUES FOR PHARMACISTS (US/1061-6314) [25381622] 3697, **4331**

TRENDS--CONSUMER ATTITUDES AND THE SUPERMARKET ... UPDATE (US/0278-6346) [07819893] **2360**

TRENDS DATA (US/0740-1027) [09859825] **4059**

TRENDS IN BHPR PROGRAM STATISTICS. GRANTS, AWARDS, LOANS (US) [07526047] 3647, **3662**

TRENDS IN BIOCHEMICAL SCIENCES (AMSTERDAM. REFERENCE EDITION) (NE/0376-5067) [02452307] **493**

TRENDS IN BIOCHEMICAL SCIENCES (AMSTERDAM. REGULAR ED.) (UK/0167-7640) [02131214] **493**

TRENDS IN BIOTECHNOLOGY (PERSONAL EDITION) (NE/0167-7799) [09897803] **3697**

TRENDS IN BIOTECHNOLOGY (REFERENCE ED.) (NE/0167-9430) [10619726] **3697**

TRENDS IN CARDIOVASCULAR MEDICINE (US/1050-1738) [21431144] **3711**

TRENDS IN CELL BIOLOGY (UK) [24312489] **540**

TRENDS IN COLLEGE MEDIA (US/1046-2163) [20365403] 1851, **2925**

TRENDS IN COMMUNIST MEDIA (US) [03458681] **2925**

TRENDS IN CONSUMPTION OF LEAD AND ZINC (UK) **1630**

TRENDS IN ECOLOGY & EVOLUTION (AMSTERDAM) (UK/0169-5347) [14100627] **2221**

TRENDS IN EMPLOYMENT & WAGES COVERED BY UNEMPLOYMENT INSURANCE (US) [21346847] **2895**

TRENDS IN END-USE MARKETS FOR PLASTICS (US/0013-7154) [02484630] **4460**

TRENDS IN ENDOCRINOLOGY AND METABOLISM (US/1043-2760) [19370142] **3733**

TRENDS IN FOOD SCIENCE & TECHNOLOGY (UK/0924-2244) [22444833] **2360**

TRENDS IN GENETICS (LIBRARY ED.) (NE/0168-9479) [13784832] **552**

TRENDS IN GOVERNMENT *See* NATIONAL VOTER, THE **4483**

TRENDS IN HAMILTON-WENTWORTH (CN/1187-0877) [25066831] **5264**

●TRENDS IN HEALTH CARE, LAW & ETHICS (US/1062-5364) [25651315] 3066, **2253**

TRENDS IN HIGH SCHOOL MEDIA (US/1046-2155) [20365337] **2925**

TRENDS IN HOUSING (US/0300-6026) [01101428] **2837**

TRENDS IN INTERNATIONAL BANKING AND CAPITAL MARKETS (UK/0309-8001) [04824255] **814**

TRENDS IN LAW LIBRARY MANAGEMENT AND TECHNOLOGY (US/0893-6773) [15633326] 3066, **3254**

TRENDS IN LEGAL SERVICES (US/0098-8995) [02240486] **3066**

TRENDS IN LIFE SCIENCES (II/0970-2504) [15923484] **493**

TRENDS IN LINGUISTICS. STATE-OF-THE-ART REPORT (NE) [06739064] **3330**

TRENDS IN LINGUISTICS. STUDIES AND MONOGRAPHS (NE) [04949797] **3330**

TRENDS IN LINGUISTICS. DOCUMENTATION (GW) [14100654] **3330**

●TRENDS IN MICROBIOLOGY (REGULAR ED.) (UK/0966-842X) [28154412] **570**

TRENDS IN NEUROSCIENCES (REFERENCE ED.) (UK/0378-5912) [04582412] **3847**

TRENDS IN NEUROSCIENCES (REGULAR ED.) (NE/0166-2236) [04124768] **3847**

TRENDS IN PHARMACOLOGICAL SCIENCES (REFERENCE ED.) (UK/0167-7691) [07024534] **4331**

TRENDS IN PHARMACOLOGICAL SCIENCES (REGULAR ED.) (UK/0165-6147) [05224752] **4331**

TRENDS IN POLYMER SCIENCE REGULAR ED (UK/0966-4793) [I09664793] **994**

TRENDS IN PRIVATE INVESTMENT IN DEVELOPING COUNTRIES (US/1018-208X) [23961987] 814, **918**

TRENDS IN PRODUCTION OF LEAD AND ZINC (UK) 1445, **2152**

TRENDS IN ROMANCE LINGUISTICS AND PHILOLOGY (US) [08336727] **3330**

●TRENDS IN SOCIAL SECURITY (SZ/1019-4126) [26676632] 2895, **1715**

TRENDS IN TECHNOLOGY (PH) [01786252] **5167**

TRENDS IN TELECOMMUNICATIONS (NE/0920-2706) [16778568] **1168**

●TRENDS IN THE CANADIAN PC MARKET (CN/1193-1477) [26714959] **1273**

TRENDS IN THE HOTEL INDUSTRY. INTERNATIONAL EDITION *See* INTERNATIONAL HOTEL TRENDS **2807**

TRENDS IN THE HOTEL INDUSTRY. INTERNATIONAL EDITION (US/0278-3983) [07231811] **2809**

TRENDS IN THE HOTEL INDUSTRY. USA EDITION (US/0276-5357) [07049408] **2809**

●TRENDS IN U.S. R & D FUNDING FOR ... (US) [30387631] **5167**

●TRENDS JOURNAL (RHINEBECK, N.Y.), THE (US/1065-2094) [26529577] **1524**

TRENDS MAGAZINE (US/1062-8266) [21389250] **5523**

TRENDS (NORTH CAROLINA. LABOR MARKET INFORMATION DIVISION) (US) [08122170] **1715**

TRENDS (PARK PRACTICE PROGRAM (U.S.)) (US) [07343465] **4708**

TRENDS (SCARBOROUGH) (CN/1183-1855) [24267085] **716**

TRENDS (SCOTTSDALE, ARIZ.) (US/0742-034X) [10265863] **332**

TRENDS-TENDANCES (BRUXELLES) (BE/0776-3395) [06080439] **1587**

TRENDS THROUGH ... (US/0893-1976) [15434334] **1587**

TRENDS UPDATE (NEW YORK, N.Y.) (US/0731-5589) [08215000] **4833**

TRENER (XO) **4855**

TRENIE I IZNOS (US/0733-1924) [07810251] **2108**

TRENIE I IZNOS (BW) [06896899] **2033**

TRENO, IL (IT) [06410740] **5437**

●TRENT-SEVERN WATERWAY, MANAGEMENT PLANNING (CN/1191-4750) [26758071] **4691**

TRENT UNIVERSITY. AUDIO LIBRARY PROGRAMME *See* MASTER TAPE LIST OF EDUCATIONAL TEXTS FOR THE VISUALLY AND PHYSICALLY HANDICAPPED ... **1882**

TRENTON (US/0041-2449) [01789576] **855**

TRENTONIAN (TRENTON, N.J.), THE (US/1064-3567) [15342162] **5711**

TREOIR (IE/0790-004X) [01788835] **4157**

TRESORERIE PARIS (FR/0996-8407) [I09968407] **4691**

TRESORS MONETAIRES (FR/0223-4300) [06830175] **2783**

TREUBIA : RECUEIL DE TRAVAUX ZOOLOGIQUES, HYDROBIOLOGIQUES ET OCEANOGRAPHIQUES (IO/0082-6340) [01716369] **475**

TREYNOR RECORD, THE (US) [16838587] **5673**

●TRI-CITY COMPUTING MAGAZINE (US) **1205**

TRI-CITY GENEALOGICAL SOCIETY *See* TRI-CITY GENEALOGICAL SOCIETY BULLETIN, THE **2476**

TRI-CITY GENEALOGICAL SOCIETY BULLETIN, THE (US/0496-1803) [07578237] **2476**

TRI-CITY LEDGER (FLOMATON), THE (US/0889-0676) [13593092] **5628**

TRI-CITY NEWS, THE (US) [14994871] **5683**

TRI-CITY REPORTER, THE (US) [19259040] **5746**

TRI-CITY TRIBUNE (US) [24773072] **5632**

TRI-COUNTY BANNER (US) [13750427] **5667**

TRI-COUNTY FREE-PRESS, THE (US/0192-8600) [05081878] **2494**

TRI-COUNTY GENEALOGY (US/0896-419X) [17155267] **2476**

TRI-COUNTY JOURNAL (US/0746-1712) [09819367] **5704**

TRI-COUNTY NEWS (FENTON) (US/0194-892X) [05083362] **5694**

TRI-COUNTY NEWS (OSSEO, WIS.), THE (US/0749-7040) [08786679] **5771**

TRI-COUNTY NEWS (SOUTH BEND, IND.) (US) [15567338] **5667**

TRI-COUNTY NEWS (WASHINGTON, IND.) (US) [14283701] **5667**

TRI-COUNTY NEWS (ZEARING, IOWA. 1986), THE (US/0890-4626) [11986651] **5673**

TRI-COUNTY PRESS (US) [12830047] **5771**

TRI-COUNTY RECORD (US) [01767741] **5699**

TRI-COUNTY RESEARCHER (US) **2476**

TRI-COUNTY SEARCHER, THE (US/0742-5015) [09482185] **2476**

TRI-COUNTY SUN (FORDVILLE, N.D.) (US) [01589052] **5726**

TRI-COUNTY TIMES, THE (US) [11770685] **5673**

TRI-LAKE RECORDER, THE (CN/0710-0221) [08294941] **5796**

TRI NEWS AND RESEARCH BRIEFS (US) [09073659] **5359**

TRI-OLOGY TECHNICAL REPORT (US/0041-2481) [02468216] **142**

TRI-S SPOT-LIGHT (US) [16567976] **1123**

TRI-STATE FOOD NEWS (US/0041-249X) [05250709] **2360**

TRI-STATE GAZETTE, THE (US) [15740955] **5721**

TRI-STATE HORSEMEN'S ASSOCIATION *See* NEWSLETTER / TRI-STATE HORSEMEN'S ASSOCIATION **2801**

TRI STATE LIVESTOCK NEWS (US) **223**

TRI-STATE PACKET OF THE TRI-STATE GENEALOGICAL SOCIETY, THE (US/0740-896X) [06746434] **2476**

TRI-STATE REAL ESTATE JOURNAL (CHERRY HILL, N.J.) (US/8750-5088) [11464156] **4848**

TRI-STATE TRADER ANTIQUE GUIDE TO OVER 3,000 LISTINGS OF ANTIQUE SHOPS *See* ANTIQUE SHOP GUIDE **249**

TRI-STATE UNIVERSITY (U.S.) *See* ALUMNI DIRECTORY / TRI-STATE UNIVERSITY **1099**

TRI-TOWN NEWS, THE (US) [11425222] **5721**

TRI-VALLEY HERALD (1990) (US/1051-5739) [21994149] **5641**

TRIAD BUSINESS (US/0897-0408) [17373652] **716**

TRIAD (FARMINGTON, MICH.) (US/1046-4948) [20427584] **3647**

TRIAD (OHIO MUSIC EDUCATION ASSOCIATION) (US/0041-2511) [02594274] 1788, **4157**

TRIAKEL GRONINGEN (NE/0922-1611) [I09221611] **3870**

TRIAL (US/0041-2538) [01767746] **3066**

TRIAL ADVOCATE QUARTERLY (US/0743-412X) [08145172] **3066**

TRIAL AND TORT TRENDS (US/0564-2108) [01767748] **3066**

TRIAL BAR NEWS (SAN DIEGO, CALIF.) (US/0732-5959) [08371928] **3066**

TRIAL COURT REPORTER / OFFICE OF THE CHIEF ADMINISTRATIVE JUSTICE, THE TRIAL COURT, THE (US) [07155126] **3066**

TRIAL DIPLOMACY JOURNAL (US/0160-7308) [03745259] **3066**

TRIAL JUDGES NEWS / NATIONAL CONFERENCE OF STATE TRIAL JUDGES (US) [07957033] **3143**

TRIAL LAWYER'S GUIDE, THE (US/0041-2546) [01767750] **3066**

TRIAL LAWYERS QUARTERLY (US/0041-2554) [01767752] **3066**

TRIAL LAWYERS SECTION DIGEST (US) [16466834] **3066**

TRIAL LAWYERS SECTION NEWSLETTER *See* TRIAL LAWYERS SECTION DIGEST **3066**

TRIAL OF ACCIDENT CASES (US) [01765160] **3066**

TRIAL TACTICS AND TECHNIQUES *CEASED.* (US/0887-4212) [13221970] **3066**

TRIAL TALK (US/0747-1378) [08723431] **3066**

TRIALOG (GW/0724-6234) [14269359] **630**

TRIALOGUE (US/0275-5351) [03792901] 4498, **1640**

TRIANGLE BUSINESS (US/0891-0022) [14516543] **5724**

TRIANGLE D'OR, LE (CN/0701-1512) [03406533] **1524**

TRIANGLE (ENGLISH EDITION) (SZ/0041-2597) [01767754] **3647**

TRIANGLE NEWS (CORONACH) (CN/0823-6925) [10032107] **5796**

TRIANGLE OF MU PHI EPSILON, THE (US/0041-2600) [01775930] **4157**

TRIATHLETE (ALLENTOWN, PA.) (US/0898-3410) [14347887] **4927**

TRIATHLON SPORTS (AT) **4927**

TRIATHLON UND SPORTWISSENSCHAFT (GW/0931-3850) [19477078] **4927**

TRIBAL AND BUREAU LAW ENFORCEMENT SERVICES AUTOMATED DATA REPORT: BILLINGS AREA (US) [06308605] **3178**

TRIBAL AND BUREAU LAW ENFORCEMENT SERVICES AUTOMATED DATA REPORT: NAVAJO AREA (US/0198-8891) [06238849] 2274, **3178**

TRIBAL AND BUREAU LAW ENFORCEMENT SERVICES AUTOMATED DATA REPORT: TOTAL ALL AREAS (US/0198-8905) [06238851] 2274, **3178**

TRIBAL ARTS SALES CATALOGUE (FR) **367**

TRIBAL COLLEGE (US/1052-5505) [22301094] **1851**

TRIBAL DIRECTORY (US) [01128422] **2274**

TRIBAL RESEARCH AND DEVELOPMENT INSTITUTE *See* BULLETIN OF THE TRIBAL RESEARCH AND DEVELOPMENT INSTITUTE BHOPAL **1549**

TRIBAL TRIBUNE (US) [06168837] **5733**

TRIBE (BALTIMORE, MD.) (US/1046-9613) [20574425] **2796**

TRIBOLIUM INFORMATION BULLETIN (US/0082-6391) [01715688] **5604**

TRIBOLOGIA (FI/0780-2285) [I07802285] **2000**

TRIBOLOGIE UND SCHMIERUNGSTECHNIK (GW/0724-3472) [10236022] **1048**

TRIBOLOGY AND CORROSION ABSTRACTS *CEASED.* (UK/0962-7189) [24188115] **2017**

TRIBOLOGY INTERNATIONAL (UK/0301-679X) [01390164] **2108**

TRIBOLOGY TRANSACTIONS (US/1040-2004) [17407825] **2000**

TRIBOMATERIALS NEWS (US/1063-9195) [26183115] **4424**

TRIBORO BANNER (US/1055-9590) [15214806] **5740**

TRIBOROUGH BRIDGE AND TUNNEL AUTHORITY *See* EXECUTIVE BUDGET AND FINANCIAL PLAN / TRIBOROUGH BRIDGE AND TUNNEL AUTHORITY **4722**

TRIBOROUGH BRIDGE AND TUNNEL AUTHORITY *See* FINANCIAL PLAN AND ... EXECUTIVE BUDGET / TRIBOROUGH BRIDGE AND TUNNEL AUTHORITY **4725**

TRIBOROUGH BRIDGE AND TUNNEL AUTHORITY. BUDGET AND ... FINANCIAL PLAN *See* FINANCIAL PLAN AND ... EXECUTIVE BUDGET / TRIBOROUGH BRIDGE AND TUNNEL AUTHORITY **4725**

TRIBOROUGH BRIDGE AND TUNNEL AUTHORITY. FINANCIAL PLAN AND ...EXECUTIVE BUDGET *See* EXECUTIVE BUDGET AND FINANCIAL PLAN / TRIBOROUGH BRIDGE AND TUNNEL AUTHORITY **4722**

TRIBUN (IO) [01790741] **2509**

TRIBUNA COSTENA (SP) [02505504] **2713**

TRIBUNA DA JUSTICA (BL) [09499696] **3143**

TRIBUNA DA JUSTICA. SUPLEMENTO DE JURISPRUDENCIA (BL) [09499653] **3066**

TRIBUNA D'ARQUEOLOGIA / DIRECCIO GENERAL DEL PATRIMONI ARTISTIC, SERVEI D'ARQUEOLOGIA (SP) [13347960] **284**

TRIBUNA DE NEW YORK & NEW JERSEY, LA (US) [18515819] **5712**

TRIBUNA DI TREVISO, LA (IT) **5805**

TRIBUNA DO ADVOGADO (BL) [04844695] **3066**

TRIBUNA ECONOMICA : PUBLICATIE A ECONOMISTILOR DIN ROMANIA (RM) [21492443] **1587**

TRIBUNA FARMACEUTICA (BL/0371-6619) [06262023] **4331**

TRIBUNA INFORMATICA (SP) **716**

TRIBUNA ITALIANA, LA (CN/0049-464X) [02233452] **2524**

TRIBUNA LITERARIA (AG) [04187824] **3447**

TRIBUNA POSTALE E DELLE TELECOMUNICAZIONI (IT/0390-5187) [I03905187] 1168, **1147**

TRIBUNA STAMPA (IT/0391-2159) [I03912159] **4570**

TRIBUNAL CANADIEN DU COMMERCE EXTERIEUR *See* DECISION - TRIBUNAL CANADIEN DU COMMERCE EXTERIEUR **2959**

TRIBUNALI AMMINISTRATIVI REGIONALI, I (IT) [03577545] **3094**

TRIBUNAUX CORRECTIONNELS, COURS D'APPEL, CONSEILS DE GUERRE ET COUR MILITAIRE (BE) [09534812] 3066, **3083**

TRIBUNE (UK/0041-2821) [05685666] 1715, **5813**

TRIBUNE (GW/0041-2716) [02083976] **2632**

TRIBUNE AFRICAINE (FR) [09708994] **2644**

TRIBUNE BUSINESS WEEKLY (US/1051-7367) [22098820] **716**

TRIBUNE (COSHOCTON, OHIO) (US) [17415337] **5731**

TRIBUNE-COURIER (1989) (US/1046-302X) [19943648] **5683**

TRIBUNE D'ALLEMAGNE, LA *CEASED.* (GW/0344-9041) [I03449041] **2524**

TRIBUNE DE L'EAU / MINISTERE DE LA REGION WALLONNE, UNION WALLONNE DES ENTREPRISES, [ET] CEBEDEAU (BE) [18660242] 5541, **2245**

TRIBUNE DE L'EXPANSION, LA (FR/0989-1323) [I09891323] **855**

TRIBUNE DE L'ORGUE, LA (SZ/1013-6835) [03048858] **4157**

TRIBUNE-DEMOCRAT (JOHNSTOWN, PA.) (US) [02262950] **5740**

TRIBUNE DES INDUSTRIES DE LA LANGUE, LA (FR/1148-7666) [27495878] **3330**

TRIBUNE DES MEMOIRES ET THESES (FR) **426**

TRIBUNE (GRAVELBOURG) (CN/0829-6650) [19099291] **5796**

TRIBUNE - INTERNATIONAL WOMEN'S TRIBUNE CENTRE (FEB. FRANCAISE), LA (US/0748-4593) [10953239] **5567**

TRIBUNE - INTERNATIONAL WOMEN'S TRIBUNE CENTRE, THE (US/0738-9779) [08339405] **5567**

TRIBUNE INTERNATIONALE LA VERITE (FR) **2494**

TRIBUNE (NEW ALBANY, IND.) (US) [11810337] **5667**

TRIBUNE-NEWS (SOUTH WHITLEY, IND.) (US) [15159389] **5667**

TRIBUNE NEWS WAVE (US) [10536932] **5641**

TRIBUNE PARIS. 1992, LA (FR/1168-6944) [I11686944] **855**

TRIBUNE-PHONOGRAPH (US) [11339697] **5771**

TRIBUNE PRESS REPORTER (US) [11251759] **5771**

TRIBUNE RECORD-GLEANER, THE (US) [15275668] **5771**

TRIBUNE-REVIEW (GREENSBURG, PA.) (US) [17240557] **5740**

TRIBUNE-REVIEW (GREENSBURG, PA. : ALLEGHENY EAST ED.) (US) [17240577] **5740**

TRIBUNE-REVIEW (GREENSBURG, PA. : FAY-WEST ED.) (US) [17240572] **5740**

TRIBUNE-REVIEW (GREENSBURG, PA. : WESTERN ED.) (US) [17240568] **5740**

TRIBUNE (SCRANTON, PA.) (US) [15061214] **5662**

TRIBUNE (SCRANTON, PA. 1990), THE (US/1062-5844) [21587797] **5740**

TRIBUNE (SHERBROOKE QUEBEC), LA (CN) **5796**

TRIBUNE SOCIALISTE (FR) [04108999] **4548**

TRIBUNE-STAR, THE (US/0745-9599) [09616458] **5667**

TRIBUNE SYOSSET, JERICHO (US/1052-374X) [22267004] **5721**

TRIBUNE (TABOR CITY), THE (US/1063-7702) [26136062] **5724**

TRIBUNE, THE (US) [23096510] **5644**

● TRIBUNE, THE *SUSPENDED.* (CN) [26050154] **5796**

TRIBUNE-TIMES (US/0747-1165) [10554051] **5743**

TRIBUS (GW/0082-6413) [03146144] **247**

TRIBUTACION (DR) [05985412] 4757, **3066**

TRIBUTE GOES TO THE MOVIES (CN/0826-1210) [10832021] **4079**

TRIBUTE MAGAZINE (CN/0823-678X) [10057324] **4079**

TRIBUTE TO BAHRAIN (BA) [07181224] **2667**

TRIBUTI (IT) **752**

TRICHINOSIS SURVEILLANCE, ANNUAL SUMMARY (US) [01770695] **4805**

TRICOLORUL (CN/0228-250X) [07821082] **2713**

TRICONTINENTAL BIBLIOGRAPHICAL REVIEW *See* NORTH / SOUTH ISSUES : BIBLIOGRAPHY OF THEORETICAL AND CURRENT EVENT ANALYSIS **421**

TRICOT- EN KOUSENINDUSTRIE / CENTRAAL BUREAU VOOR DE STATISTIEK, HOOFDAFDELING STATISTIEDEN VAN INDUSTRIE EN BOUWNIJVERHEID (NE/0168-4469) [10291225] **1088**

TRICOT SELECTION (FR) **1088**

TRICYCLE (NEW YORK, N.Y.) (US/1055-484X) [23189884] **5022**

TRIDENT (HALIFAX) (CN/0025-3413) [03438171] **4059**

TRIDENT (WASHINGTON, D.C.) (US/0882-1674) [11770014] 2783, **2788**

TRIENNIAL ASSESSMENT OF THE TENNESSEE VALLEY AUTHORITY (US/0272-2623) [06773292] **4691**

TRIENNIAL ATLAS & PLAT BOOK, RICE COUNTY, MINNESOTA (US) [08562195] **2577**

TRIENNIAL REPORT : A SURVEY OF PUBLIC EDUCATION IN THE NATION'S URBAN SCHOOL DISTRICTS, THE (US/0272-8656) [06945331] **1788**

TRIENNIAL REPORT - BOTANY DIVISION (NZ/0548-9547) [01791320] **529**

TRIENNIAL REPORT / INDIANA CIVIL RIGHTS COMMISSION (US) [07560634] **4513**

TRIENNIAL REPORT ON WATER RESOURCES DEVELOPMENT (US/0091-1593) [01785801] **5541**

TRIENNIAL REPORT - TRANSPORT WORKERS UNION (IO) [03731924] **1715**

TRIERER STUDIEN ZUR LITERATUR (GW/0721-4294) [06882040] **3447**

TRIERER THEOLOGISCHE STUDIEN (GW) [06440076] **5005**

TRIERER THEOLOGISCHE ZEITSCHRIFT (GW/0041-2945) [01643159] **5006**

TRIERER ZEITSCHRIFT FUER GESCHICHTE UND KUNST DES TRIERER LANDES UND SEINER NACHBARGEBIETE (GW/0041-2953) [02092948] 284, **2713**

TRIESTE ECONOMICA (IT) **1524**

TRIFLUVIEN (TROIS-RIVIERES. 1990) (CN/0849-1127) [23302604] **4691**

TRIINU (CN/0702-8679) [03439492] **2763**

TRILOGY (US/1046-5693) [20450656] **5648**

TRILOGY (LEXINGTON, KY.) *SUSPENDED.* (US/1050-8031) [21615386] **5313**

TRIMENIAIO PERIODIKO TES CHRISTIANIKES EPISTEMES. BIBLIKA MATHEMATA (US/0145-9503) [02813754] **5006**

TRIMESTRE DELL IVA (IT) **752**

TRIMESTRE DELLE IMPOSTE INDIRETTE (IT) **752**

TRIMESTRE ECONOMICO, EL (MX/0041-3011) [01767764] **1640**

TRIMESTRE GEOGRAFICO (CK/0120-8098) [I01208098] **2578**

TRIMESTRE POLITICO (MX/0185-1039) [02093494] **4498**

TRINIDAD AND TOBAGO *See* ESTIMATES OF EXPENDITURE (TRINIDAD AND TOBAGO) **4722**

TRINIDAD — Alphabetical Title Index

TRINIDAD AND TOBAGO. AUDITOR GENERAL'S DEPT See REPORT OF THE AUDITOR GENERAL ON THE ACCOUNTS OF TRINIDAD AND TOBAGO **4745**

TRINIDAD AND TOBAGO BUSINESS DIRECTORY AND GUIDE TO THE LOME CONVENTION (TR) [07369583] **716**

TRINIDAD AND TOBAGO. CENTRAL STATISTICAL OFFICE See REPORT ON LONDON G.C.E. EXAMINATION RESULTS **1870**

TRINIDAD AND TOBAGO. CENTRAL STATISTICAL OFFICE See LABOUR FORCE BY SEX **1535**

TRINIDAD AND TOBAGO. CENTRAL STATISTICAL OFFICE See MANPOWER INCOME REPORT **1689**

TRINIDAD AND TOBAGO. CENTRAL STATISTICAL OFFICE See FINANCIAL STATISTICS **729**

TRINIDAD AND TOBAGO. CENTRAL STATISTICAL OFFICE See ESTIMATED INTERNAL MIGRATION BULLETIN (PORT OF SPAIN) **4552**

TRINIDAD AND TOBAGO. CENTRAL STATISTICAL OFFICE See QUARTERLY ECONOMIC REPORT **1514**

TRINIDAD AND TOBAGO NATIONAL BIBLIOGRAPHY (TR) [02791259] **426**

TRINIDAD & TOBAGO QUARTERLY ECONOMIC REPORT (SP) **1524**

TRINIDAD & TOBAGO REVIEW (TR) [04880960] **2763**

TRINIDAD GUARDIAN (TR) [12086429] **5811**

TRINIDAD NATURALIST MAGAZINE See NATURALIST (TRINIDAD AND TOBAGO) **4168**

TRINIDAD UND TOBAGO : ENERGIEWIRTSCHAFT (GW) [06597707] **1959**

TRINIDAD UND TOBAGO : WIRTSCHAFTLICHE ENTWICKLUNG (GW) [04508292] **1525**

TRINIDAD UND TOBAGO, WIRTSCHAFTSDATEN / BUNDESSTELLE FUER AUSSENHANDELSINFORMATION (GW) [11297013] **1587**

TRINITE, LIBERTE (CN/0318-0573) [02441641] **5006**

TRINITY (US/0564-2744) [02096308] **2632**

TRINITY COLLEGE (HARTFORD, CONN.) See ALUMNI DIRECTORY - TRINITY COLLEGE (HARTFORD, CONN.) **1099**

TRINITY COLLEGE OF QUEZON CITY See JOURNAL - TRINITY COLLEGE OF QUEZON CITY **1833**

TRINITY COLLEGE RECORD (US/0041-3054) [03491123] **1851**

TRINITY DIGEST (US) **2925**

●TRINITY FORUM READING, THE (US/1062-2527) [25559425] **3447**

TRINITY JOURNAL (US/0360-3032) [02243858] 5006, **2925**

TRINITY PAPERS, THE (US/0736-2439) [08501770] **1095**

TRINITY THEOLOGICAL COLLEGE See TRINITY THEOLOGICAL COLLEGE ANNUAL **5006**

TRINITY THEOLOGICAL COLLEGE ANNUAL (SI) [06960868] **5006**

TRINITY WEEKLY JOURNAL (US) [08786458] **5641**

TRINITY WORLD FORUM (US) [09879256] **5068**

TRINITY'S WELLSPRING (US) **5006**

TRIO. TRAFFIC RULINGS, INTERPRETATIONS, OPINIONS (US) [04924749] **5446**

TRIOLO (FR) **4855**

TRIP (MONTREAL) (CN/0380-0954) [02443302] **2548**

TRIPLE A (AT/0816-9837) [16994860] **815**

TRIPLE I (SI) **716**

TRIPOD (HK) **5006**

TRIPOD. CHRISTIANITY AND CONTEMPORARY CHINA (HK) **5006**

TRIPURA DARPANA (II) [10612554] **3447**

TRIQUARTERLY / NORTHWESTERN UNIVERSITY (US/0041-3097) [05937719] **3447**

TRIQUARTERLY SERIES ON CRITICISM AND CULTURE (US) [12811691] **5269**

TRISAKTI (IO) [03460315] **3066**

TRISTANIA (US/0360-3385) [02441372] **3448**

TRITON See DIVER **4893**

TRIUMPH (LOS ANGELES, CALIF.) (US/8750-2542) [11189392] **5641**

TRIVENETO (IT) [02802873] **1715**

TRIVENI (GUNTUR) (II/0041-3135) [01779339] 2713, **367**

TRIVIA (US/0736-928X) [09247235] 5567, **3355**

TRIVIUM (CARDIFF, WALES) (UK/0082-660X) [02096204] **5225**

TRL ANALYZES DEVELOPMENTS IN TEXAS STATE AND LOCAL GOVERNMENT (US) [05505167] **4691**

TRO OCH LIV (SW/0346-2803) [07561836] **5006**

TROBE UNIVERSITY. SCHOOL OF ECONOMICS, LA See DISCUSSION PAPER **1480**

TROIS (CN/0829-4275) [14708952] **3448**

TROIS MOIS DE NOUVEAUTES (FR/0294-0035) [10768703] **4833**

TROLLEY COACH NEWS (US/0890-5029) [11184037] **5397**

TROLLEY TALK (US/0148-8406) [03380939] **5437**

TROLLOPIANA (UK) [24278563] **3448**

TROMESECNI PREGLED MEUNARODNE STATISTIKE (YU) [01795637] **5345**

TROMS MUSEUM See ARSBERETNING / TROMS MUSEUM **4084**

TROMURA. KULTURHISTOIRE : TROMS MUSEUMS RAPPORTSERIE (NO/0333-2802) [12281862] **2713**

TROMURA. NATURVITENSKAP (NO/0332-6195) [08092790] **4097**

TRONDHEIM. NORGES TEKNISKE HGSKOLE. DET FYSISKE SEMINAR See ARKIV FOR DET FYSISKE SEMINAR I TRONDHEIM **4398**

TROPAG & RURAL [COMPUTER FILE] (US) [25512421] **142**

TROPENBOS SCIENTIFIC SERIES (NE) [18182424] **2222**

TROPENLANDWIRT, DER (GW/0041-3186) [14444262] **142**

TROPHY BIG GAME INVESTIGATIONS AND HUNTING SEASON RECOMMENDATIONS / STATE OF NEVADA, DEPARTMENT OF WILDLIFE, DIVISION OF GAME (US/0883-2951) [12013795] **4927**

TROPIC ISLE PUBLISHERS See YACHTSMAN'S GUIDE TO THE GREATER ANTILLES **5500**

TROPICAL AGRICULTURE (UK/0041-3216) [01767777] **142**

TROPICAL AGRICULTURE RESEARCH SERIES (JA/0388-9386) [07138312] **142**

TROPICAL AGRICULTURIST (CE/0041-3224) [01695244] **142**

TROPICAL AND GEOGRAPHICAL MEDICINE (NE/0041-3232) [01767778] **3987**

TROPICAL AND SUBTROPICAL FISHERIES TECHNOLOGICAL SOCIETY OF THE AMERICAS. CONFERENCE See PROCEEDINGS ... ANNUAL CONFERENCE OF THE TROPICAL AND SUBTROPICAL FISHERIES TECHNOLOGICAL SOCIETY OF THE AMERICAS **2310**

TROPICAL ANIMAL HEALTH AND PRODUCTION (UK/0049-4747) [01767779] **5523**

●TROPICAL BIODIVERSITY (US/0854-1566) [28861120] **2207**

TROPICAL BIOMEDICINE (MY/0127-5720) [12391449] **3987**

TROPICAL BRYOLOGY (GW/0935-5626) [21204529] **529**

TROPICAL DEVELOPMENT AND RESEARCH INSTITUTE (GREAT BRITAIN) LIBRARY See ACCESSIONS BULLETIN / TROPICAL DEVELOPMENT AND RESEARCH INSTITUTE, LIBRARY **3186**

TROPICAL DEVELOPMENT AND RESEARCH INSTITUTE (SERIES G) CEASED. (UK/0264-763X) [10040528] **142**

TROPICAL DISEASES BULLETIN (UK/0041-3240) [01643371] 3987, **3662**

TROPICAL DOCTOR (UK/0049-4755) [02268729] **3987**

TROPICAL ECOLOGY (II/0564-3295) [07821257] **2222**

TROPICAL FISH HOBBYIST (US/0041-3259) [01767781] **2315**

TROPICAL FORESTRY PAPERS (UK/0141-9668) [02637062] **2397**

TROPICAL FORESTRY REPORTS (FI/0786-8170) [07868170] **2397**

TROPICAL FRESHWATER BIOLOGY (NR/0795-0101) [19299341] **475**

TROPICAL GASTROENTEROLOGY (II/0250-636X) [07891871] **3987**

TROPICAL GRASSLANDS (AT/0049-4763) [01767784] **189**

TROPICAL LEPIDOPTERA (US/1048-8138) [21067139] **5614**

TROPICAL MEDICINE AND HYGIENE NEWS (US/0041-3275) [01716994] **3987**

TROPICAL MEDICINE AND PARASITOLOGY (GW/0177-2392) [11990104] **3987**

TROPICAL PEST MANAGEMENT (UK/0143-6147) [06349167] **4248**

TROPICAL PRODUCTS INSTITUTE (GREAT BRITAIN) See REPORT OF THE TROPICAL PRODUCTS INSTITUTE **126**

TROPICAL PRODUCTS INSTITUTE LIBRARY See ACCESSIONS BULLETIN - TROPICAL PRODUCTS INSTITUTE, LIBRARY **42**

●TROPICAL PRODUCTS, WORLD MARKETS AND TRADE / UNITED STATES DEPARTMENT OF AGRICULTURE, FOREIGN AGRICULTURAL SERVICE (US) [30338199] **189**

TROPICAL RESOURCE MANAGEMENT PAPERS (NE/0926-9495) [09269495] **142**

TROPICAL SCIENCE (UK/0041-3291) [01767785] **142**

TROPICAL TIMBERS (UK/0269-980X) [0269980X] 937, **2399**

TROPICAL VETERINARIAN (NR/0253-4851) [10002026] **3987**

TROPICAL VETERINARIAN IBADAN CEASED. (NR/0794-4845) [I07944845] **3987**

TROPICAL ZOOLOGY (IT/0394-6975) [18888732] **5599**

TROPICO SEMI-ARIDO : RESUMOS INFORMATIVOS (BL) [06621717] **142**

TROPICULTURA (BE/0771-3312) [21282952] **142**

TROPICUS (US) [18487950] **2207**

TROPISMES / CENTRE DE RECHERCHES ANGLO-AMERICAINES (FR/0761-2591) [18796126] **3448**

TROPMED NEWSLETTER (TH/0858-0375) [26101154] **3987**

TROPOS (EAST LANSING, MICH.) (US/1044-8209) [07754300] **3330**

TROPSOILS TECHNICAL REPORT (US) [16150153] **189**

TROT (CN/0704-0733) [03979996] **2803**

TROTSKYIST INTERNATIONAL (UK/0953-7554) [I09537554] **4548**

TROTTEUR DE FRANCE (FR) **142**

TROTTEUR DU MAQUIGNON (CN/0383-1086) [03196194] **2548**

TROUBADOUR : BULLETIN BIMESTRIEL (CN/0826-2918) [11081741] **332**

TROUBADOUR (FREDERICTON) (CN/0713-8113) [08996243] **4157**

TROUBLE AND STRIFE (UK) [16406843] **5567**

●TROUBLED COMPANY PROSPECTOR, THE (US/1062-2330) [25540693] **716**

TROUBLESOME CREEK TIMES (US) [14509947] **5683**

TROUT AND SALMON (UK/0041-3372) [04125121] **2315**

TROUT FISHERMAN (UK) 2315, **4879**

TROUT NEWS (UK/0954-7037) [I09547037] **2315**

TROUVAILLES PARIS. 1976 (FR/0396-6356) [I03966356] **367**

TROUW. DAGBLAD (NE) **5807**

TROY DAILY NEWS (US) [17420181] **5731**

TROY GAZETTE-REGISTER (US) [14409038] **5740**

TRSA ORGANIZATION (US/0748-7142) [10994304] **5359**

TRUBUS (IO/0126-0057) [01795603] **142**

TRUCK (UK) [02951315] **5426**

TRUCK & BUS BUILDER (UK/0263-6263) [I02636263] 5426, **3489**

TRUCK & TRAILER BUYER'S GUIDE SUSPENDED. (US/8756-5129) [11552554] **5397**

TRUCK & TRANSPORT (NE) **5397**

TRUCK AUSTRALIA (AT) **5397**

TRUCK BLUE BOOK (US/0273-9402) [04093453] **5426**

TRUCK BLUE BOOK LEASE GUIDE, RESIDUAL PROJECTIONS, THE (US/8756-4041) [11556836] **5397**

TRUCK BROKER DIRECTORY (US/0362-5737) [02304223] **5398**

TRUCK CAMPER TRADE-IN GUIDE CEASED. (US/0749-4548) [10897266] **5398**

TRUCK CANADA (CN/0315-5501) [02196622] **5398**

TRUCK DATA BOOK (CN/0564-3392) [02441629] **5426**

TRUCK EN TRANSPORT MANAGEMENT (NE) **5398**

TRUCK ENGINEERING (US/1048-9584) [20860947] **5426**

TRUCK IDENTIFICATION BOOK (US/0889-3888) [13900795] **5427**

TRUCK LUBRICATION GUIDE (US/0162-3435) [04153198] **5398**

TRUCK NEWS (TORONTO) (CN/0712-2683) [08781341] **5398**

TRUCK OPERATING COSTS (NZ) [07039933] **5398**

TRUCK SAFETY NEWS (US/1047-7535) [20770605] **5398**

TRUCK SALES & LEASING (US/1053-5942) [22587368] **5398**

TRUCK TAXES BY STATES (US/0517-5666) [02636523] **5398**

TRUCK TRAILERS (US/0145-5001) [07182412] **5398**, **3489**

●TRUCK, VAN AND 4X4 BOOK (US/1062-2578) [29875188] **5427**

TRUCK, VAN, AND 4X4 BOOK (NEW YORK : 1994) *See* TRUCK, VAN AND 4X4 BOOK **5427**

TRUCK, VAN, AND 4X4 BOOK, THE (US/1050-9259) [21708065] **5427**

TRUCK WEIGHT STUDY (JACKSON) (US/0364-703X) [02667495] **5398**

TRUCK WEIGHT SURVEY (US/0360-7399) [02244635] **5398**

TRUCKER'S ALMANAC (US/0743-5525) [10597430] **5398**

TRUCKERS/USA (TUSCALOOSA, ALA.) (US/0897-9219) [17664374] **5398**

TRUCKIN (US/0277-5743) [07605554] **5398**

TRUCKIN' LIFE (AT/0155-9648) [01559648] **5398**

TRUCKING IN CANADA (CN/0829-8947) [14096372] **5398**

TRUCKS *CEASED*. (US/0884-8947) [12533915] **5398**

TRUCKS 26,000 PLUS (US/0146-9622) [03093445] **5398**

TRUCKSTOP WORLD (US/0894-962X) [16366051] **5073**, **5398**

TRUD (RU) [02268732] **5809**

●TRUDEL, NADEAU INFO (CN/1188-7702) [26715166] **3066**

TRUDOVE NA NAUCHEN TSENTUR ZA PLANIRANE (RU) [05305913] **1587**

TRUDY - AKADEMIA NAUK SSSR, INSTITUT BIOLOGII VNUTRENNIH VOD (RU/0568-5656) [01396032] **475**

TRUDY ARKHIVA (RU) [01478814] **2484**

TRUDY ASTROFIZICESKOGO INSTITUTA (RU/0131-3940) [10863339] **4424**, **38**

TRUDY ASTRONOMICHESKOI OBSERVATORII (LENINGRAD, R.S.F.S.R.) (RU/0201-6745) [06108760] **401**

TRUDY - AZOVO-CHERNOMORSKI I NAUCHNO-ISSLEDOVATEL-SKI I INSTITUT MORSKOGO RYBNOGO KHOZIAISTVA I OKEANOGRAFII (RU) [01395384] **558**

TRUDY - BAKINSKII NAUCHNO-ISSLEDOVATEL'SKII INSTITUT TRAVMATOLOGII I ORTOPEDII (AJ) [06011634] **3885**

TRUDY (CHUVASHSKAIA A.S.S.R. (R.S.F.S.R.)) (RU) [04372896] **2713**

TRUDY EREVANSKOGO ZOOVETERINARNOGO INSTITUTA (AI/0371-6562) [11063113] **5599**

TRUDY FIZICHESKOGO INSTITUTA / AKADEMIIA NAUK SSSR, FIZICHESKII INSTITUT IM. P.N. LEBEDEVA (RU/0132-0114) [06071743] **4424**

TRUDY GELMINTOLOGICHESKOI LABORATORII (RU/0568-5524) [01478826] **5599**

TRUDY GEOMETRICHESKOGO SEMINARA (RU/0256-341X) [04919118] **3539**

TRUDY GOSUDARSTVENNOGO OKEANOGRAFICESKOGO INSTITUTA (RU/0371-7119) [09358804] **1457**

TRUDY - GOSUDARSTVENNYJ NAUCNO-ISSLEDOVATELSKIJ I PROEKTNYJ INSTITUT NEFTJANOJ PROMYSLENNOSTI (RU/0131-1689) [03026743] **4280**

TRUDY INSTITUTA (AVTOMATIKA GITAHETAZOTAKAN INSTITUT. OTDEL NAUCHNO-TEKHNICHESKOI INFORMATSII) (RU) [09189030] **1030**

TRUDY INSTITUTA GEOLOGII (RU/0568-6156) [01835346] **1400**

TRUDY INSTITUTA GEOLOGII I GEOFIZIKI (NOVOSIBIRSK) (RU/0568-658X) [03778312] **1411**, **1400**

TRUDY INSTITUTA IMENI PASTERA (RU/0202-1447) [03917292] **570**, **3736**

TRUDY INSTITUTA - NAUCNO-ISSLEDOVATELSKIJ INSTITUT KLINICESKOJ I EKSPERIMENTALNOJ HIRURGII M.Z. S.S.S.R (RU/0302-8402) [00933319] **3977**

TRUDY INSTITUTA - NAUCNO-ISSLEDOVATELSKIJ INSTITUT PROMYSLENNOGO STROITELSTVA (RU/0206-1074) [02962343] **630**

TRUDY INSTITUTA OKEANOLOGII IM. P.P. SHIRSHOVA (RU/0375-8419) [01241846] **1458**

TRUDY INSTITUTA POCHVOVEDENIIA I AGROKHIMII / MINISTERSTVO SEL'SKOGO KHOZIAISTVA ARM SSR; NAUCHNO-ISSLEDOVATEL'SKII INSTITUT POCHVOVEDENIIA I AGROKHIMIA [AND] ARMIANSKII FILIAL VSESOIUZNOGO OBSHCHESTVA POCHVOVEDOV (AI) [10976426] **189**

TRUDY INSTITUTOV INZHENEROV ZHELEZNODOROZHNOGO TRANSPORTA (RU) [05773546] **5437**

TRUDY (INSTITUTUL AGRIKOL M.V. FRUNZE) (MV/0371-8794) [07059763] **142**

TRUDY KLINICHESKOGO OTDELA INSTITUTA (AI) [05967985] **2871**

TRUDY KOMI NAUCHNOGO TSENTRA URO AN SSSR / AKADEMIIA NAUK SSSR, URALSKOE OTDELENIE, KOMI NAUCHNYI TSENTR (RU/0135-5813) [18472248] **5599**

TRUDY LENINGRADSKOGO NAUCHNO-ISSLEDOVATELSKOGO PSIKHONEVROLOGICHESKOGO INSTITUTA IM. V. M. BEKHTEREVA (RU/0455-6550) [06080900] **3937**, **3847**

TRUDY LESOSTEPNOI NAUCHNO-ISSLEDOVATELSKOI STANTSII LENINGRADSKOGO UNIVERSITETA "LES NA VORSKLE." (RU) [03049310] **2397**

TRUDY LSKHA (LV) [21021553] **142**

TRUDY MAGADANSKOGO ZONALNOGO NAUCHNO-ISSLEDOVATELSKOGO INSTITUTA SELSKOGO KHOZIAISTVA SEVERO-VOSTOKA (RU) [08138914] **143**

TRUDY. MEMOIRS (UN) [04848325] **1400**

TRUDY ORDENA LENINA GIDROMETEOROLOGICESKOGO NAUCNO-ISSLEDOVATELSKOGO CENTRA SSSR (RU/0371-7089) [09067715] **1436**

TRUDY ORDENA LENINA MATEMATICESKOGO INSTITUTA IM. V.A. STEKLOVA (RU/0371-9685) [C1830887] **4424**, **3539**

TRUDY ORDENA LENINA MATEMATICESKOGO INSTITUTA IMENI V. A. STEKLOVA (US/0081-5438) [0¯404256] **3539**

TRUDY OTDELA DREVNERUSSKOJ LITERATURY. AKADEMIIA NAUK SSSR; INSTITUT RUSSKOJ LITERATURY. PUSKINSKIJ DOM (RU/0253-259X) [01478843] **3448**

TRUDY PALEONTOLOGICHESKOGO INSTITUTA (RU/0376-1444) [01399274] **4231**

TRUDY PO PRIKLADNOJ BOTANIKE. GENETIKE I SELEKCII (RU/0372-0586) [15470271] **529**

TRUDY SAMARKANDSKOGO GOSUDARSTVENNOGO UNIVERSITETA. IM. ALISERA NAVOI. ISSLEDOVANIA PO RUSSKOMU I SLAVANSKOMU AZYKOZNANIIU (RU/0320-0892) [I03200892] **3330**

TRUDY SEKTSII ARKHEOLOGII (RU) [16584060] **285**

TRUDY SEMINARA IMENI I. G. PETROVSKOGO (RU/0321-2971) [04318457] **3539**

TRUDY SEMINARA PO KRAEVYM ZADACHAM / KAZANSKII ORDENA TRUDOVOGO KRASNOGO ZNAMENI GOSUDARSTVENNYI UNIVERSITET IM. V.I. ULIANOVA-LENINA (RU) [05037075] **1908**, **3539**

TRUDY SEMINARA PO VEKTORNOMU I TENZORNOMU ANALIZU (RU/0373-4870) [06343321] **3540**

TRUDY ... SESSII VSESOIUZNOGO PALEONTOLOGICHESKOGO OBSHCHESTVA (RU/0506-2160) [06764462] **4231**

TRUDY SEVERO-VOSTOCHNOGO KOMPLEKSNOGO NAUCHNO-ISSLEDOVATELSKOGO INSTITUTA (RU) [02240969] **5167**

TRUDY SEZDA MIKROBIOLOGOV UKRAINY (UN) [03735065] **570**

TRUDY SOVETSKOI ANTARKTICHESKOI EKSPEDITSII / ARKTICHESKII I ANTARKTICHESKII NAUCHNO-ISSLEDOVATELSKII INSTITUT (RU) [21024348] **2578**

TRUDY TSNIITMASH (RU) [02163168] **2131**

TRUDY VIEV (RU/0203-6703) [10784700] **5523**

TRUDY VSESOIUZNOGO ENTOMOLOGICHESKOGO OBSHCHESTVA (RU/0373-1278) [06369356] **5599**

TRUDY - VSESOIUZNYI NAUCHNO-ISSLEDOVATELSKII INSTITUT PO PERERABOTKE NEFTI (RU) [03728590] **4280**

TRUDY VSESOJUZNOGO NAUCNO-ISSLEDOVATELSKOGO INSTITUTA GIDROMETEOROLOGICESKOJ INFORMACII-MIROVOGO CENTRA DANNYH (RU/0201-9957) [10796748] **1436**

TRUDY VSESOJUZNOGO NAUCNO-ISSLEDOVATELSKOGO INSTITUTA ZELEZNODOROZNOGO TRANSPORTA (RU/0372-3305) [10981403] **5437**

TRUDY - VSESOJUZNYJ NAUCNO-ISSLEDOVATELSKIJ INSTITUT GIDROGEOLOGIII INZENERNOJ GEOLOGII (RU/0541-1025) [11081644] **1400**

TRUDY - VSESOJUZNYJ NAUCNO-ISSLEDOVATELSKIJ INSTITUT MORSKOGO RYBNOGO HOZJAISTVA I OKEANOGRAFII (RU/0372-2864) [02086556] **2315**

TRUDY VSESOUZNOGO NAUCNO-ISSLEDOVATELSKOGO INSTITUTA ZERNOVOGO HOZAJSTVA (RU/0372-3283) [01791333] **143**

TRUDY VSESOYUZNOGO INSTITUTA GELMINTOLOGII IM K. I. SKRYABINA (RU/0372-2996) [I03722996] **1445**

TRUDY VYCHISLITELNOGO TSENTRA / AKADEMIIA NAUK AZERBAIDZHANSKOI SSR (AJ) [16798751] **1281**, **1205**

●TRUDY VYCHISLITELNOGO TSENTRA SO RAN. SERIIA SISTEMNOE MODELIROVANIE / ROSSIISKAIA AKADEMIIA NAUK, SIBIRSKOE OTDELENIE, VYCHISLITELNYI TSENTR (RU) [31093125] **3540**

TRUDY ZOOLOGICHESKOGO INSTITUTA (RU/0206-0477) [01405158] **5599**

TRUDY'S TIME-PERIODS (US/1061-3587) [25265173] **3448**

TRUE & FAIR (UK) [05299315] **752**

TRUE CITIZEN, THE (US) [19530958] **5655**

TRUE CONFESSIONS (NEW YORK) (US/0041-3488) [03951319] **2494**

TRUE DETECTIVE (US/0041-350X) [03951344] **5075**

TRUE EXPERIENCE (NEW YORK) (US/0199-0012) [05506891] **2494**

TRUE LOVE (NEW YORK) (US/0199-0004) [05506910] **5075**

TRUE NEWS (NEW YORK, N.Y.) *CEASED*. (US/1064-8232) [26409592] **2548**

TRUE NORTH (CN/0319-7956) [02442957] **5796**

TRUE NORTH / DOWN UNDER (CN/0823-1508) [10057190] **3448**

TRUE ROMANCE (NEW YORK) (US/0199-0020) [05506922] **5075**

TRUE ROMANCES (UK/0262-415X) [I0262415X] **5075**

TRUE STORY LONDON (UK/0262-4125) [I02624125] **5567**, **2494**

TRUE STORY (NEW YORK) (US/0195-3117) [05510186] **5075**

TRUE VINE (US/1043-7878) [19563293] **5040**

TRUE WEST (US/0041-3615) [01585787] **2764**

TRUITE OMBRE SAUMON (FR/0396-518X) [I0396518X] **2315**

TRULY PORTABLE (US/0749-5897) [11172181] **1273**

TRUMANN DEMOCRAT, THE (US) [21064045] **5632**

TRUMANSBURG FREE PRESS (US) [21127194] **5721**

TRUMBULL TIMES, THE (US) [27909069] **5646**

TRUMPETER (LONDON) (CN/0148-673X) [03355143] **2788**

TRUMPETER (VICTORIA) (CN/0832-6193) [15644792] **2222**

TRUNKLINE CARRIER DOMESTIC PASSENGER ENPLANEMENTS (US/0148-9356) [03198046] **38**

TRUPPENPRAXIS (GW) [07506486] **4059**

TRURO AND DISTRICT, NOVA SCOTIA, CITY DIRECTORY (CN/0227-8464) [06858488] **2578**

TRUSST TIMES (US/0888-2266) [13505343] **5398**

TRUST : A QUARTERLY FROM THE NATIONAL TRUST OF AUSTRALIA (VICTORIA) (AT) [13026393] **2671**

TRUST ADMINISTRATION AND TAXATION (US) [01715205] **4757**

TRUST FUNDS (US/0149-6468) [03520355] **5068**

TRUST INDENTURE ACT OF 1939 RELEASE (US) [04245645] **3066**

TRUST LAW INTERNATIONAL *See* TOLLEY'S TRUST LAW INTERNATIONAL **917**

TRUST LAW INTERNATIONAL : PENSION FUNDS, COMMERCIAL TRUSTS, AND CHARITIES (UK/0962-2624) [25443301] **918**

TRUST MONITOR & GRANT NEWS (UK/0968-8137) [I09688137] **815**

TRUST NEWS (AT) [06263358] **2207**

TRUST TERRITORY BUDGET PLAN (FM) [02241078] **4757**

TRUSTED PENSION FUNDS FINANCIAL STATISTICS (CN/0835-4634) [17313425] **918**

TRUSTEE (US/0041-3674) [01681272] **3793**

TRUSTEE (EDMONTON, ALTA.) *CEASED.* (CN/0229-4141) [08469736] **1873**

TRUSTEE NEWS / SASKATCHEWAN SCHOOL TRUSTEES ASSOCIATION (CN/0228-8826) [07888593] **1873**

TRUSTEE'S LETTER, THE (US/1044-6370) [19855845] **1788**

●TRUSTEESHIP (WASHINGTON, D.C.) (US/1068-1027) [27425469] **1851**

TRUSTS (US) [02239696] **3066**

TRUSTS & ESTATES (US/0041-3682) [05508974] **3119**

TRUTH AT LAST, THE (US) [19251233] **4498**

TRUTH (PHILADELPHIA), THE (US/0041-3690) [03952308] **2274**

TRUTH SEEKER (SAN DIEGO, CALIF.), THE (US/0041-3712) [03952366] **5006**

TRUXBOOK (CN/0820-5655) [16849648] 5398, **855**

●TRW REDI REALTY REPORT (US/1075-3664) [28741065] 630, **4848**

TRW SOFTWARE SERIES : INDEX TO PUBLICATIONS IN PRINT (US/0095-4179) [03183707] 1292, **1210**

TRY US (US/0191-6106) [03737746] 716, **2274**

TRYBUNA (PL) [21204293] **5808**

TRYBUNA SAMORZADU ROBOTNICZEGO (PL) [01787092] **1715**

TRYBUNA SLASKA 1990 (PL/0867-4507) [I08674507] **5808**

TRYBUNA WABRZYSKA (PL/0208-6956) [I02086956] **2524**

TRYON DAILY BULLETIN, THE (US) [11921827] **5724**

TRYON TIMES, THE (US/0899-7462) [18203714] **2476**

TRZODA CHLEWNA (PL) [16311763] **223**

TS, TRIBUNE SOCIALISTE *See* TRIBUNE SOCIALISTE **4548**

TSA' ASZI' *CEASED.* (US) [04588873] **2274**

TSA LA GI (US/0148-2769) [03279726] **1851**

TSAI CHENG (CC) [02268745] **4757**

TSAI CHENG NIEN CHIEN (US) [04831570] **4757**

TSAI CHENG YEN CHIU (CC) [11228577] **4757**

TSAI CHING KO HSUEH (CC/1000-8306) [21436987] 815, **1525**

TSAI CHING YEN CHIU (CC) [02268748] 815, **1525**

TSAI HSING SHIH CHIEH (CC) [02245453] **1587**

TSAI MAO CHING CHI (CC) [10854630] **4757**

TSAI WU YU KUAI CHI / CAIWU YUKUAIJI (CN) [11976640] **815**

TSAO KEN JEN (CH) [11680817] **4855**

TSCA CHEMICALS IN PROGRESS BULLETIN (US) [07420075] **994**

TSCHECHOSLOWAKISCHE WIRTSCHAFTSRUNDSCHAU (XR) [01788783] **1587**

TSE HUI HSUEH PAO (CC) [01797447] **2583**

TSE LIANG CHI SHU TUNG PAO (CH) [01797666] **2033**

TSE LIANG CHIH TU HSUEH PAO *See* TSE HUI HSUEH PAO **2583**

●TSELLIULOZA, BUMAGA, KARTON (RU) [27255590] **4239**

TSEMENT (RU/0041-4867) [05244746] **630**

TSENTRALNYI NAUCHNO-ISSLEDOVATELSKII INSTITUT TEKHNOLOGII I MASHINOSTROENIIA *See* TRUDY TSNIITMASH **2131**

TSENTRALNYI NAUCHNO-ISSLEDOVATELSKII INSTITUT TEKHNOLOGII I MASHINOSTROENIIA. (SOVIET UNION) [TRUDY] *See* TRUDY TSNIITMASH **2131**

TSERKOVNYI VESTNIK : CERKIEWNY WIESTNIK (PL) [11708425] **5040**

TSERKOVNYI VESTNIK (PRAVOSLAVNAIA TSERKV V POLSHE) *See* TSERKOVNYI VESTNIK : CERKIEWNY WIESTNIK **5040**

TSERKOVNYI VISNYK / UKRAINSKA KATOLYTSKA PARAFIIA SVIATYKH VOLODYMYRA I OLHY V CHIKAGO (US) [08941719] **5037**

TSETSE AND TRYPANOSOMIASIS INFORMATION QUARTERLY (UK/0142-193X) [06032415] 5523, **5599**

TSI JOURNAL OF PARTICLE INSTRUMENTATION (US) [15378655] **994**

TSIG NEWSLETTER (CN/1181-9839) [24256702] **3254**

TSIKLON (IS) [03237544] **2632**

TSIRKULIAR-ASTROFIZICHESKAIA OBSERVATORIIA, SHEMAKHA, RUSSIA (AJ/0135-0420) [06099712] **401**

TSITOLOGIIA (RU/0041-3771) [02255514] **540**

TSIYUR U-FISUL (IS) [01784357] **367**

TSK. KPSS. VYSSHAIA PARTIINAIA SHKOLA *See* UCHENYE ZAPISKI / ORDENA LENINA VYSSHAIA PARTIINAIA SHKOLA PRI TSK KPSS **4548**

TSO WU HSUEH PAO (CC/0496-3490) [10386670] **189**

TSO WU PIN CHUNG TZU YUAN (CC/1000-6435) [23181449] **189**

TSOFAR (IS) [06381627] **5053**

TSR HOTLINE (US/8755-4380) [11308224] **888**

TSU CHIU SHIH CHIEH / CHUNG-KUO TSU CHIU HSIEH HUI CHU PAN (CC) [09650381] **4927**

TSUCHI TO BISEIBUTSU (JA/0912-2184) [I09122184] **190**

TSUDA-JUKU DAIGAKU *See* TSUDA-JUKU DAIGAKU KIYO **2855**

TSUDA-JUKU DAIGAKU KIYO (JA/0287-7805) [02243652] **2855**

TSUKO SEMPAKU JITTAI CHOSA HOKOKUSHO (JA) [02245303] **5458**

TSUKUBA CHUGOKU BUNKA RONSO / TSUKUBA DAIGAKU CHUGOKU BUNKA KENKYU PUROJEKUTO (JA/0286-9675) [10523320] **3448**

TSUKUBA DAIGAKU. GAKKO KYOIKUBU *See* TSUKUBA DAIGAKU GAKKO KYOIKUBU KIYO **1788**

TSUKUBA DAIGAKU GAKKO KYOIKUBU KIYO (JA) [06653185] **1788**

TSUKUBA DAIGAKU. TAIIKU KAGAKUKEI *See* TSUKUBA DAIGAKU TAIIKU KAGAKUKEI KIYO **1859**

TSUKUBA DAIGAKU TAIIKU KAGAKUKEI KIYO (JA/0386-7129) [05041204] **1859**

TSUKUBA FORAMU. TSUKUBA FORUM (JA) [07187227] **1851**

TSUKUBA JIKKEN SHOKUBUTSUEN KENKYU HOKOKU (JA/0289-3568) [10903593] **2432**

TSUKUBA JOURNAL OF MATHEMATICS (JA/0387-4982) [04098420] **3540**

TSUNAMI NEWSLETTER (US/0259-3637) [09120554] **1412**

TSUNG CHIAO SHIH CHIEH (CH) [06520122] **5006**

TSUNG HENG YUEH KAN (HK) [02683615] **2509**

TSURUMI DAIGAKU KIYO. DAI 1-BU, KOKUGO KOKUBUNGAKU HEN (JA/0389-8008) [10232146] **3330**

TSURUMI DAIGAKU KIYO. DAI 2-BU, GAIKOKUGO GAIKOKU BUNGAKU HEN (JA/0389-8016) [10577993] **3330**

TSURUMI DAIGAKU KIYO. DAI 3-BU, HOIKU HOKEN SHIKA HEN (JA) [10231911] **1851**

TSURUMI DAIGAKU KIYO. DAI 4-BU, JINBUN SHAKAI HEN (JA/0389-8032) [10231931] **2855**

TSUSAN HANDOBUKKU (JA) [03215504] **855**

TSUSAN TOKEI. INDUSTRIAL STATISTICS MONTHLY (JA/04207771] **1540**

TSUSANSHO KOHO (JA) [03265153] **1587**

TSUSHIN SOGO KENKYUJO KIHO (JA/0914-9279) [19525090] **1123**

TSUSHO NEMPO (JA) [01797289] **855**

TSUSHO SANGYOSHO KOGYO GIJUTSUIN SHIKOKU KOGYO GIJUTSU SHIKENJO YORAN *CEASED.* (JA) [02247106] **5167**

TSUSHO SANGYOSHO TOSHOKAN TOSHO MOKUROKU (JA) [02952308] **1596**

TSVETNYE METALLY (ENGLISH TRANSLATION ED.) (US/0038-5484) [01715651] **4023**

TT REVUE / HERAUSGEBER, VERBAND OFFENTLICHER VERKEHR VOV ... ET AL (SZ) [18592326] **5398**

TTC : REVISTA DEL MINISTERIO DE TRANSPORTES, TURISMO Y COMUNICACIONES (SP) [16882157] **5497**

TTG ITALIA : TRAVEL TRADE GAZETTE (IT) **5497**

TTG. TRAVEL TRADE GAZETTE. EUROPA (UK/0262-5709) [I02625709] **5497**

TTG. TRAVEL TRADE GAZETTE. U.K. AND IRELAND (UK/0262-4397) [I02624397] **5498**

●TTJ (UK) [26409555] **2405**

TTJ TELEPHONE ADDRESS BOOK (UK/0141-5735) [26689473] **2405**

TTR : TRADUCTION, TERMINOLOGIE, REDACTION (CN/0835-8443) [19751437] **3330**

TTS BLUE BOOK OF TRUCKING COMPANIES (US/1056-0440) [23435784] **5398**

TTS NATIONAL MOTOR CARRIER DIRECTORY (US/1061-477X) [25321296] **5398**

TTT, INTERDISCIPLINAIR TIJDSCHRIFT VOOR TAAL- & TEKSTWETENSCHAP (NE/0167-4773) [10544963] **3330**

TTUV NEWS (AT/0728-487X) [I0728487X] **1908**

TU (GW/0376-1185) [09578330] **5523**

TU CHE WEN CHAI (HK/0041-3836) [04258507] **2509**

TU DO / TRIBUNE DES VIETNAMIENS LIBRE (BE) **4498**

TU JANG (CC/0253-9829) [04873878] **190**

TU JANG TUNG PAO (CC/0564-3945) [19545510] **190**

TU MU SHUI LI (CH/0253-3804) [09220183] 2096, **2033**

TU PO (GW) [01797594] **2509**

TU SHU KUAN HSUEH YU TZU HSUN KO HSUEH (CH/0363-3640) [02123285] **3254**

TU SHU KUAN TSA CHIH (CC/1000-4254) [08964823] **3254**

TU TANGATA (NZ/0111-5871) [08548683] **2671**

TUAN PIEN HSIAO SHUO HSUAN (PEKING, CHINA) (CC) [08146719] **3448**

TUAN PIEN HSIAO SHUO NIEN PIEN (CC) [09552822] **3448**

TUATARA *CEASED.* (NZ/0041-3860) [01767810] **475**

TUBE & PIPE QUARTERLY, THE (US/1051-4120) [21956697] **4023**

TUBE & PIPE TECHNOLOGY (UK/0953-2366) [I09532366] **4023**

TUBE INTERNATIONAL (UK/0263-6794) [08973143] 3489, **4023**

TUBE SUBSTITUTION HANDBOOK (US) [04871886] **2085**

TUBERCLE *See* TUBERCLE AND LUNG DISEASE : THE OFFICIAL JOURNAL OF THE INTERNATIONAL UNION AGAINST TUBERCULOSIS AND LUNG DISEASE **3952**

●TUBERCLE AND LUNG DISEASE : THE OFFICIAL JOURNAL OF THE INTERNATIONAL UNION AGAINST TUBERCULOSIS AND LUNG DISEASE (UK/0962-8479) [25531569] **3952**

TUBERCULOSE. TUBERCULOSIS (FR) [06868221] **3952**

TUBERCULOSIS BEDS IN HOSPITALS (US/0095-1129) [01795898] 3793, **3952**

TUBERCULOSIS BEDS IN HOSPITALS AND SANATORIA *See* TUBERCULOSIS BEDS IN HOSPITALS **3952**

TUBERCULOSIS IN INDIANA (US/0092-959X) [01789584] **3952**

TUBERCULOSIS PROGRAMS (US/0090-9351) [01785544] **3952**

TUBERCULOSIS STATISTICS / STATISTICS CANADA, CANADIAN CENTRE FOR HEALTH INFORMATION (CN/1195-4086) [29880386] **3662**

TUBINGEN. UNIVERSITAT. BOTANISCHER GARTEN. SEMENVERZEICHNIS *See* HORTUS TUBIGENSIS INDEX SEMINUM **2420**

TUBINGER BEITRAGE ZUR LINGUISTIK (GW/0564-7959) [03157476] **3330**

TUBINGER GEOGRAPHISCHE STUDIEN (GW/0564-4232) [01642375] **2578**

TUBINGER RECHTSWISSENSCHAFTLICHE ABHANDLUNGEN (GW/0082-6731) [01767821] **3066**

TUBINGER STUDIEN ZUR DEUTSCHEN LITERATUR (GW/0171-7235) [15271210] **3448**

TUBINGER WIRTSCHAFTSWISSENSCHAFTLICHE ABHANDLUNGEN (GW/0564-4291) [03154382] **1525**

TUBISTS UNIVERSAL BROTHERHOOD ASSOCIATION *See* T.U.B.A. MEMBERSHIP ROSTER **4156**

TUBISTS UNIVERSAL BROTHERHOOD ASSOCIATION *See* T.U.B.A. JOURNAL **4156**

TUBULAR STRUCTURES (UK/0041-3909) [02828568] **630**

Alphabetical Title Index — TURISMO

TUCH LITERACKI (KRAKOW, POLAND) (PL/0035-9602) [01764633] **3448**

TUCKERTON BEACON (TUCKERTON, N.J. : 1985) (US/0882-9616) [12046339] **5712**

TUCSON CITIZEN (1977) (US/0888-5478) [08879411] **5630**

TUCSON EDUCATION ASSOCIATION *See* TEA NEWSLETTER **1786**

TUCSON GUIDE *See* TUCSON GUIDE QUARTERLY **2548**

TUCSON GUIDE QUARTERLY (US) [21541680] **2548**

TUCSON METROPOLITAN CHAMBER OF COMMERCE *See* MEMBERSHIP DIRECTORY & BUYERS GUIDE **820**

TUCSON'S MOUNTAIN NEWSREAL *See* NEWSREAL **4817**

TUCUMCARI LITERARY REVIEW (US) [19227115] **3448**

TUDO E HISTORIA; CADERNOS DE PESQUISA (BL) [04980968] **2764**

TUDOMANYOS ES MUSZAKI TAJEKOZTATAS (HU/0041-3917) [02638239] **3254**

TUDOMANYOS KOZLEMENYEK (HU) [05346570] 4927, **1859**

TUEBOR TERRA *CEASED.* (US/1058-7381) [21985376] **2207**

TUESDAY BULLETIN (US) **1095**

TUESDAY LETTER (US/0047-8733) [05786136] **2207**

TUEXEMIA (GW/0772-494X) **2222**

TUFF STUFF (US/1041-4258) [18764752] 4927, **2779**

TUFTS KINSMEN (US/0149-2438) [03467441] **2476**

TUFTS UNIVERSITY DIET & NUTRITION LETTER (US/0747-4105) [10401443] **4199**

TUG & SALVAGE WORLD (UK) **5458**

TUG LINES *CEASED.* (US/0892-4961) [11137921] 1273, **1281**

TUGBOAT (PROVIDENCE, R.I.) (US/0896-3207) [07705797] **1249**

TUGON (PH/0116-4260) [15988737] **5006**

TUIJIN JISHU (CC/1001-4055) [I10014055] **2000**

TUIN EN LANDSCHAP (NE) [10842172] **2432**

TUINBOUW VISIE (BE/0776-4472) [I07764472] **2432**

TUINBOUWCIJFERS (NE/0440-0771) [02616903] 2432, **2434**

TUINBOUWMAGAZINE (BE) **2432**

TUITION AND LIVING ACCOMMODATION COSTS AT CANADIAN UNIVERSITIES *CEASED.* (CN/0318-2991) [01795227] **1851**

TUITION AND REQUIRED FEES AND ROOM AND BOARD CHARGES AT INSTITUTIONS OF HIGHER EDUCATION IN PENNSYLVANIA (US/0275-9543) [07238910] **1851**

TUITIONS AND SALARIES (US) [26435205] **1873**

TUJA SINTAK / INVESTMENT TRUST (KO) [10057271] **918**

TUKHOCHONG YONBO (KO) [08835486] **1309**

TUKKUKAUPAN TILINPAATOSTILASTO (FI/0784-9095) [19926967] **855**

TUKOR *See* UJ TUKOR **2524**

TUKSU KYOYUK HAKHOE CHI (KO) [08998278] **1886**

TULANE CIVIL LAW FORUM (US/1045-8891) [01644396] **3091**

TULANE ENVIRONMENTAL LAW JOURNAL (US/1047-6857) [18410317] **3117**

TULANE EUROPEAN AND CIVIL LAW FORUM (US) [29569025] **3091**

TULANE LAW REVIEW (US/0041-3992) [01644207] **3066**

TULANE LAW REVIEW. TEN YEAR INDEX VOLUMES 46-55 (US) [09520895] **3066**

TULANE LAWYER (US) [05703884] **3066**

TULANE MARITIME LAW JOURNAL (US/1048-3748) [18148927] **3182**

TULANE STUDIES IN GEOLOGY AND PALEONTOLOGY (US/0041-4018) [01786412] 4231, **1400**

TULANE STUDIES IN POLITICAL SCIENCE (US/0082-6744) [01767832] **4498**

TULANE STUDIES IN ROMANCE LANGUAGES AND LITERATURE (US/0564-4380) [01639409] **3448**

TULANE STUDIES IN ZOOLOGY AND BOTANY (US/0082-6782) [01422955] 529, 2222, **5599**

TULANIAN, THE (US/0041-4026) [03952454] **1095**

TULARE COUNTY FARM BUREAU NEWS (US/0744-7086) [08508442] **143**

TULASI PRAJNA (II) [04261466] **5006**

TULIA HERALD, THE (US) [14266363] **5755**

TULIAO GONGYE (CH/0253-4312) [09028058] **4225**

TULIMULD (SW/0041-4034) [05066428] 367, **3448**

TULIP TIDINGS (US/0163-0059) [02629770] **2433**

TULL TRACING (US/0161-2719) [03877038] **2476**

TULSA ANNALS (US/0564-4437) [07092839] **2476**

TULSA BUSINESS CHRONICLE *CEASED.* (US/0745-5747) [08782811] **5733**

TULSA ECONOMIC OUTLOOK (US) [06843085] **1587**

TULSA KIDS (US/1043-5999) [19531412] **1071**

TULSA LAW JOURNAL (US/0041-4050) [01767838] **3067**

TULSA STUDIES IN WOMEN'S LITERATURE (US/0732-7730) [08426594] 5567, **3448**

TULSA SUNDAY WORLD *See* COUNTRY WORLD **2486**

TULSA TRIBUNE, THE *CEASED.* (US) [09259084] **5733**

TULSA WORLD (TULSA, OKLA.) (JS/8750-5959) [11587000] **5733**

TULSALETTER (1976) (US/0193-9467) [C5275166] **4281**

TUMBLEWEED (CN/0380-1667) [02443363] **5237**

TUMBUH (MY) [02438907] **143**

TUMOR BIOLOGY (SZ/1010-4283) [I10104283] **3824**

TUMOR RESEARCH (JA/0041-4093) [05229340] **3824**

● TUMOR TARGETING (UK/1351-8488) **3647**

TUMORDIAGNOSTIK & THERAPIE (GW/0722-219X) [10815600] **3824**

TUMORI (IT/0300-8916) [01767840] **3824**

TUMOUR BIOLOGY (SZ/0289-5447) [11080830] **475**

TUMOUR MARKER UPDATE (UK/0955-5102) [24378673] **3825**

TUN-HUANG YEN CHIU / TUN-HUANG WEN WU YEN CHIU SO PIEN (CC/1000-4106) [09301047] **2667**

TUNA CATCH AND EFFORT, AND SIZE DATA FOR ... LONGLINE FISHERY, COLLECTED AT TRANSSHIPMENT PORTS IN THE ATLANTIC (SP) [07321077] **2315**

TUNDRA DRUMS, THE (US) [12812838] **5629**

TUNDRA TIMES (US/0049-4801) [02712152] **5629**

TUNE UP (US/0161-3081) [03888077] **4157**

TUNG CHI NIEN PAO - TAI-PEI TZU LAI SHUI CHANG CHU CHI SHIH (CH) [02246566] **5541**

TUNG FANG (HANG-CHOU SHIH, CHINA) (CH) [09458542] **3448**

TUNG HAI / CHE-CHIANG SHENG WEN HSUEH I SHU CHIEH LIEN HO HUI CHU PAN (CC) [11459688] **3330**

TUNG HAI HSU MU (CH) [06909187] **223**

TUNG HAI SHE HUI KO HSUEH HSUEH PAO (CH) [11228776] **5225**

TUNG HSUEH PAO, TA (CH/0379-7309) [03043731] **5237**

TUNG HUA (CH) [09300933] **3448**

TUNG-PEI KAO KU YU LI SHIH (CC) [11870725] **285**

TUNG-PEI LIN YEH TA HSUEH PAO (CC/1000-5382) [14714442] **2397**

TUNG-PEI SHIH TA HSUEH PAO. CHE HSUEH SHE HUI KO HSUEH PAN (CC) [10304296] 5225, **4364**

● TUNG-PEI TA HSUEH HSUEH PAO. TZU JAN KO HSUEH PAN (CC/1005-3026) [30490484] **5167**

● TUNG WU CHE HSUEH CHUAN HSI LU / TUNG WU TA HSUEH (CH/1010-0725) [26175263] **4364**

● TUNG WU CHENG CHIH HSUEH PAO (CH) [26440787] **4498**

TUNG WU CHENG CHIH SHE HUI HSUEH PAO (CH) [05359454] 5264, **4498**

TUNG WU CHI KUAN (CH) [07027020] **889**

TUNG WU FA LU HSUEH PAO (CH) [03762645] **3067**

TUNG WU HSUEH PAO (CC/0001-7302) [02100915] **5599**

● TUNG WU SHE HUI HSUEH PAO (CH/1019-0449) [26440779] **5264**

TUNGSTEN NEWS (US/0049-481X) [01767846] **4023**

TUNICA TIMES-DEMOCRAT, THE (US) [16505345] **5702**

TUNING BOARD, THE (US/0362-6091) [02308145] **4157**

TUNIS. AL-JAMIAH AL-TUNISIYAH *See* HAWLIYAT AL-JAMIAH AL-TUNISIYAH **2652**

TUNIS AL-KHADRA (TI) [04392018] **143**

TUNISIA. SERVICE DES STATISTIQUES. BULLETIN MENSUEL DE STATISTIQUE *See* BULLETIN MENSUEL DE STATISTIQUE - INSTITUT NATIONAL DE LA STATISTIQUE (AL-MAHAD) **5324**

TUNISIAN HIGHLIGHTS (TI) [05507972] **2644**

TUNISIE MEDICALE, LA (TI/0041-4131) [02268769] **3647**

TUNNEL (GW) 2000, **630**

TUNNELING TECHNOLOGY NEWSLETTER *CEASED.* (US/0095-2664) [01795667] **2033**

TUNNELLING (UK/0143-3911) [07903344] **2152**

TUNNELLING AND UNDERGROUND SPACE TECHNOLOGY (UK/0886-7798) [12986247] **2033**

TUNNELS & TUNNELLING (UK/0041-414X) [01716744] **2033**

TUNNELS & TUNNELLING. WORLD PROFILE OF CONTRACTORS (UK) [08433919] **2033**

TUNNELS. ET OUVRAGES SOUTERRAINS (FR) [I03390834] **2033**

TUNNELS ET OUVRAGES SOUTERRAINS VILLEURBANNE (FR/0399-0834) [I03990834] **2033**

TUNUM : TUNABYGDENS FORNMINNES- OCH HEMBYGDSFORENINGS ARSSKRIFT (SW) [07805196] **2713**

TUOMIOISTUIMISSA KASITELLYT RIKOS-, SIVIILI- JA HALLINTOOIKEUDELLISET ASIAT (FI/0355-2187) [08180065] 3067, **3084**

TUOMIOISTUINTEN TUTKIMAT RIKOKSET (FI) [03936716] 3067, **3084**

TUPAKKATILASTO (FI/0784-8412) [19484228] **5374**

TUPAKKATUOTTEIDEN KULUTUS (FI) [10574394] **5374**

TUPPER LAKE FREE PRESS AND TUPPER LAKE HERALD (US) [10886322] **5721**

TURANG XUEBAO (CC/0564-3929) [04341147] **190**

TURATHUNA (IR) [12795247] **5045**

● TURBOFORCE (LOMBARD, ILL.) (US/1063-8334) [26174189] **4867**

TURBOJET/TURBOFAN AIRCRAFT OPERATING COST AND PERFORMANCE TRENDS. DOMESTIC OPERATIONS OF TRUNK AND LOCAL SERVICE CARRIERS (US) [05435823] **38**

TURBOMACHINERY DESIGN DIGEST *See* TURBOMACHINERY DIGEST **2131**

TURBOMACHINERY DIGEST (US) [15172210] **2131**

TURBOMACHINERY INTERNATIONAL (US/0149-4147) [03472381] **2131**

TURBOMACHINERY INTERNATIONAL HANDBOOK (US/0748-0903) [07485994] **2131**

TURBULENCE / [INITIATED BY THERMAL MACHINERY INSTITUTE, TECHNICAL UNIVERSITY OF CZESTOCHOWA, POLAND] (PL/0860-7222) [24538554] **2856**

TURCICA (PARIS) (BE/0082-6847) [02057385] **3330**

TURF *See* TURF WEST **2433**

TURF *See* TURF NORTH **2433**

● TURF & ORNAMENTAL CHEMICALS REFERENCE: T&OCR (US/1056-2648) [23612180] **143**

TURF & RECREATION (CN/1186-0170) [24266666] **2433**

TURF AND SPORT DIGEST (US/0041-4158) [01681305] **4927**

TURF CENTRAL (US/1059-6348) [24652062] **2433**

TURF CRAFT AUST (AT/0819-8632) [I08198632] **4927**

TURF MANAGEMENT (UK/0262-0669) [I02620669] **2433**

TURF NEWS (US/0899-417X) [05909026] **2433**

TURF NORTH (US) **2433**

TURF WEST (US/1071-4995) [28464005] **2433**

TURIA (SP/0213-4373) [15232753] **3448**

TURISMO D'ITALIA (IT) 5073, **2809**

TURISMO DOMANI (IT) **5498**

TURISMO ED AMBIENTE (IT) **5498**

TURISMO

TURISMO, ENCUESTA (NQ) [03006580] **5498**

TURISMO NEL CANTONE TICINO, IL (SZ) [03289760] **5498**

TURIZAM (YU) [01787785] **5498**

TURK ANESTEZIYOLOJI VE REANIMASYON CEMIYETI MECMUASI (TU/1016-5150) [I10165150] **3684**

TURK DILI VE EDEBIYAT DERGISI (TU) [02093394] **3330**

TURK EDEBIYATI DERGISI (TU) **3330**

TURK HIJIYEN VE DENEYSEL BIYOLOJI DERGISI (TU) [10017327] **4805**, **3648**

TURK KARDIYOLOJI DERNEGI ARSIVI (TU/1016-5169) [I10165169] **3711**

TURK KOYUNDE MODERNLESME EGILIMLERI ARASTRMAS (TU) [01786712] **1587**

TURK KUTUPHANECILIGI (TU) [20725907] **3254**

TURK TARIH KURUMU See BELLETEN **2611**

TURKEI, EINFUHRREGELUNG / BUNDESSTELLE FUER AUSSENHANDELSINFORMATION (GW) [11296969] **855**

TURKEI, ENERGIEWIRTSCHAFT / BUNDESSTELLE FUER AUSSENHANDELSINFORMATION (GW) [11175752] **1959**

TURKEI, WIRTSCHAFT IN ZAHLEN UND WIRTSCHAFTSDOKUMENTATION / BUNDESSTELLE FUER AUSSENHANDELSINFORMATION (GW) [11778338] **1587**

TURKEY & TURKEY HUNTING (US/1067-4942) [24336003] **4879**

TURKEY (ANKARA, TURKEY) (TU) [20907520] **2524**

TURKEY CALL (US/1064-6094) [10139766] **4879**

TURKEY. GELIRLER UMUM MUDURLUGU See BUTCE GELIRLERI YLLG **4716**

TURKEY HATCHERY (WASHINGTON, D.C.) (US) [12252355] **223**

TURKEY HUNTER, THE (US/0896-1786) [16942668] **4880**

TURKEY MONITOR (UK/0950-3234) [I09503234] **1525**, **4757**

TURKEY MONITOR See BUSINESS MIDDLE EAST **650**

TURKEY NEWSLETTER : MONTHLY PUBLICATION OF THE COMMITTEE FOR DEFENCE OF DEMOCRATIC RIGHTS IN TURKEY (UK) [22391210] **4548**

TURKEY. TOPRAKSU GENEL MUDURLUGU See GENEL YAYIN - TURKEY. TOPRASKU GENEL MUDURLUGU **172**

TURKEY WORLD (1968) (US/0041-4271) [05002848] **223**

TURKEY YEAR BOOK (US/0161-8903) [04029328] **2713**

TURKEYS (UK/0041-428X) [02638632] **223**

TURKEYS (1985) (US/1057-7858) [13200690] **223**

TURKEYS, FINAL ESTIMATES FOR ... (US) [08384153] **223**

TURKISH DEFENCE & AEROSPACE UPDATE (TU) 38, **4059**

TURKISH EXPORT NEWS (TU) **855**

TURKISH JOURNAL OF NUCLEAR SCIENCES (TU/0254-5446) [09776229] **4451**

TURKISH JOURNAL OF PEDIATRICS, THE (TU/0041-4301) [01715230] **3912**

TURKISH JOURNAL OF SPORTS MEDICINE (TU) **3956**

TURKISH NEUROSURGERY (TU/1019-5149) [I10195149] **3847**

TURKISH PUBLIC ADMINISTRATION ANNUAL (TU/0251-2955) [02083822] **4691**

TURKISH REVIEW QUARTERLY DIGEST (TU) [13151568] **2667**

TURKISH SHIPPING (UK/0266-7193) [11357598] **5458**

TURKISH STUDIES ASSOCIATION See TURKISH STUDIES ASSOCIATION BULLETIN **3355**

TURKISH STUDIES ASSOCIATION BULLETIN (US/0275-6048) [05207280] **3355**

TURKIYE BITKI KORUMA DERGISI (TU/0254-5454) [07938117] **143**

TURKIYE ENTOMOLOJI DERGISI (TU/1010-6960) [I10106960] **5614**

TURKIYE IS BANKAS See ECONOMIC REPORT - TURKIYE IS BANKAS A.S **1558**

TURKIYE IS BANKASI See REVIEW OF ECONOMIC CONDITIONS **1581**

TURKIYE ISTATISTIK YLL. STATISTICAL YEARBOOK OF TURKEY (TU) [04265945] **5345**

TURKIYE OZETLI NUFUS BIBLIOGRAFYAS (TU) [01783782] **4563**

TURKIYE TICARET ODALAR, SANAYI ODALAR VE TICARET BORSALAR BIRLIGI See ARAP ULKELERI EKONOMIK RAPORU **1546**

TURKIYE'YE AMERIKAN IKTISAD YARDMLAR (TU) [20539957] **2912**

TURKMENISTAN SSR YLYMLAR AKADEMIIASY See IZVESTIIA AKADEMII NAUK TURKMENSKOI SSR. SERIIA BIOLOGICHESKIKH NAUK **459**

TURKMENISTAN YLYMLAR AKADEMIIASYNYNG KHABARLARY. BIOLOGIK YLYMLARYNG SERIIASY (TK) [26714341] **143**, **475**

TURKMENISTAN YLYMLAR AKADEMIIASYNYNG KHABARLARY. GUMANITAR YLYMLARY (TK) [26265502] **2856**, **5225**

TURKMENSKAIA ISKRA : ORGAN TSENTALNOGO KOMITETA KOMMUNISTICHESKOI PARTII TURKMENISTANA (TK) [14122992] **5811**

TURKS AND CAICOS ISLANDS See NATIONAL DEVELOPMENT PROGRAMME / GOVERNMENT OF THE TURKS AND CAICOS ISLANDS, BRITISH WEST INDIES **2911**

TURKS AND CAICOS ISLANDS CONSOLIDATED INDEX OF STATUTES AND SUBSIDIARY LEGISLATION TO ... / COMPILED AT THE FACULTY OF LAW LIBRARY, UNIVERSITY OF THE WEST INDIES, BARBADOS (BB) [11845858] **3137**

TURLOCK JOURNAL (US) [20380657] **5641**

TURNABOUT (US/0148-7388) [03356755] **5188**

TURNAROUND LETTER, THE (US/1056-0173) [23456367] **918**

TURNAROUNDS & WORKOUTS (US/0889-1699) [13801118] **815**

TURNAROUNDS & WORKOUTS. EUROPE (US/1061-4176) [25305180] **815**

TURNAROUNDS & WORKOUTS. SURVEY (US/1061-4184) [25305235] **4848**

TURNBULL LIBRARY RECORD, THE (NZ/0110-1625) [02093774] **3254**

TURNER STUDIES CEASED. (UK/0260-597X) [07605713] **367**

TURNING POINTS (CHESHIRE) (US/0274-8894) [06679254] **716**

TURNOUT, THE (CN/0227-244X) [07313475] **5437**

TURNSTILE (NEW YORK, N.Y.) (US/0896-5951) [17211563] **3448**

TUROK'S CHOICE (US/1052-3170) [22257738] **4157**

TUROV ON OPTIONS AND HEDGING (US/0148-5911) [03456730] **918**

TURQUOISE (TU) [20579971] **2667**

TURRIALBA : REVISTA INTERAMERICANO DE CIENCIAS AGRICOLAS (CR/0041-4360) [01695176] **143**

TURTLE MAGAZINE FOR PRESCHOOL KIDS (US/0191-3654) [04852794] **1071**

TURTLE MOUNTAIN STAR (US) [01767865] **5726**

TURTLE NEWS (US/8755-8645) [11456039] **1851**

TURTLE QUARTERLY (US/0896-2022) [15074805] 332, **2274**

TURTOX NEWS (US/0096-3895) [01767866] **475**

TURUN HISTORIALLINEN ARKISTO (FI/0085-7440) [100857440] **2713**

TURUN YLIOPISTO See TURUN YLIOPISTON JULKAISUJA SARJA B: HUMANIORA **2856**

TURUN YLIOPISTO. HISTORIAN LAITOS. YLEINEN HISTORIA See PUBLICATIONS OF THE INSTITUTE OF HISTORY, GENERAL HISTORY, UNIVERSITY OF TURKU, FINLAND **2626**

TURUN YLIOPISTON JULKAISUJA. SARJA A 2, BIOLOGICA. GEOGRAPHICA. GEOLOGICA (FI/0082-6979) [22660349] 2578, **475**

TURUN YLIOPISTON JULKAISUJA SARJA B: HUMANIORA (FI/0082-6987) [01767862] **2856**

TUSAGATSAIT (YELLOWKNIFE) (CN/1185-6084) [25066919] **3330**

TUSAN (KO) [10090240] **1300**

TUSCALOOSA NEWS, THE (US) [18329797] **5628**

TUSCIA (IT) [04171592] **2713**

TUSKEGEE INSTITUTE. HUMAN RESOURCES DEVELOPMENT CENTER See ANNUAL REPORT - TUSKEGEE INSTITUTE. HUMAN RESOURCES DEVELOPMENT CENTER **5239**

TUSTIN NEWS, THE (US/0892-6441) [15307712] **5641**

TUT. TEXTILES A USAGES TECHNIQUES (FR/1161-9317) [11161317] **5359**

TUTELA (IT/0393-7798) [I03937798] **5313**

TUTKIMAS JA TEKNIIKKA (FI/0784-1469) [07841469] 5167, **5176**

TUTKIMUKSIA (VALTION TEKNILLINEN TUTKIMUSKESKUS) (FI/0358-5077) [08874218] **5167**

TUTORIAL ESSAYS IN PSYCHOLOGY (US/0277-2639) [03974557] **4621**

TUTORIAL MONOGRAPHS IN COGNITIVE SCIENCE (US) **4621**

TUTORIAL (UNIVERSITY OF ALBERTA. COMPUTING SERVICES) (CN/0821-1043) [09743054] **1262**

TUTTI FOTOGRAFI (IT/0041-4395) [I00414395] **4377**

TUTTI GLI ATTI PARLAMENTARI (IT) **3067**

TUTTI INSIEME PARIS (FR/0984-1466) [I09841466] **2494**

TUTTITALIA (UK) [I09571752] **3330**

TUTTO DIABETE (IT) **3802**

TUTTO SCUOLA (IT) **1788**

TUTTO TRASPORTI PASSEGGERI (IT/1121-5593) [I11215593] **5398**

TUTTOLAZIO (IT) **2494**

TUTTOLIBRI (IT) [02511620] **4820**

TUTTONORMEL (IT) **3489**

TUTTOPARLAMENTO (IT) **4691**

TUTTOTRASPORTI ROZZANO (IT/1121-5585) [I11215585] **5427**

TUTTOTURISMO (IT/0392-8020) [I03928020] **5498**

TUUMBA (US/0146-2083) [02881575] **3448**

TUV AUTO-REPORT (GW) [02459358] **5427**

TV 2 (SAINT PAUL, MINN.) (US/1059-9657) [24821618] **1141**

● TV BLUEPRINT (US/1064-9433) [26470558] **1141**

TV BROADCAST FINANCIAL DATA (US) [03163803] **1141**

TV CROSSWORDS (US/0734-5585) [08767965] **4867**

TV ENTERTAINMENT (US/1049-1163) [21137568] **1141**

TV ETC (US/1054-2329) [22253953] **1141**

TV EXECUTIVE, THE (US/0736-2986) [09104165] **1141**

TV EXPRESS (BE) **1141**

TV FACTS, FIGURES & FILM CEASED. (US) [15479552] **1141**

TV GAME SHOW MAGAZINE CEASED. (US/0884-4992) [12384905] **4867**

TV GUIDE (US/0039-8543) [01585969] **1141**

TV GUIDE MONTHLY (UK) **2494**

TV HOREN UND SEHEN (GW) [04686999] **1141**

TV LINK (US/0744-5504) [08349396] **1141**

TV NEWS CONTACTS CEASED. (US/1051-3590) [13239179] **1141**

TV PICTURE LIFE, METAL EDGE See METAL EDGE **4131**

TV PRO-LOG (US) [07934991] **1141**

TV PROGRAM INVESTOR (US/0885-2340) [12603628] **1141**

TV PROGRAM STATS (US/1040-6123) [18460607] **1141**

TV STAR PARADE (US/0041-4530) [03938423] **1142**

● TV STATION LOG (US/1061-8317) [25473937] **1142**

TV TECHNOLOGY (US/0887-1701) [13136451] **1168**

TV. THE TELEVISION ANNUAL (US) [06268763] **1142**

TV TIMES (UK/0039-8624) **1142**

TV TNT (US) [08872423] **1142**

● TV VIDEO (US/1064-2676) [26239690] **1142**

TV WEEK MELBOURNE (AT/0810-249X) [I0810249X] **1142**

TV WORLD (UK/0142-7466) [06497377] **1142**

TV WORLD (US/0199-4484) [03956783] **1142**

TV Y NOVELAS (MX/0188-0683) [I01880683] **2494**

TV ZONE (UK/0957-3844) [I09573844] **1142**

TVARSNITT (SW/0348-7997) [10737408] **2856**

TVERDYI ZNAK (RU) [25351768] **3448**

Alphabetical Title Index — U

TVI REPORT (US/1041-8474) [13212553] **4537**

TVIS NEWS / THE TROPICAL VEGETABLE INFORMATION SERVICE (CH) [12338850] **190**

TVMS TIGER BEAT (US) **1071**

TVORCHESTVO (RU/0041-4565) [04099208] **332**

TVORCHESTVO A. P. CHEKHOVA (RU) [04268788] **3448**, **3330**

TVZ : VAKBLAD VOOR DE VERPLEGKUNDIGEN (NE/0303-6456) [20423259] **3870**

TW DERMATOLOGIE : ARZTLICHE KOSMETOLOGIE (GW/0939-0448) [27143460] **406**

TW NEUROLOGIE, PSYCHIATRIE (GW/0935-3224) [24625843] **3937**, **3847**

TW-PADIATRIE (GW/0935-3216) [I09353216] **3648**

TW. TAGUNGS-WIRTSCHAFT TW, TAG.-WIRTSCH (GW/0342-7951) [I03427951] **1525**

TW (TORONTO, ONT.) (CN/0711-7426) [08559373] **5567**

TW-UROLOGIE, NEPHROLOGIE (GW/0936-2002) [I09362002] **3993**

TWAYNE'S ENGLISH AUTHOR SERIES (US/0564-559X) [01767869] **3355**, **435**

TWAYNE'S MASTERWORK STUDIES (US) [14866230] **3448**

TWAYNE'S UNITED STATES AUTHORS SERIES (US/0496-6015) [01605729] **3448**

TWAYNE'S WORLD AUTHORS SERIES (US/0564-5603) [02046937] **3448**

TWENTIETH CENTURY AMERICAN JEWISH WRITERS (US/0897-7844) [17624785] **3448**

TWENTIETH-CENTURY CHILDREN'S WRITERS (US) **3448**

TWENTIETH-CENTURY CRIME AND MYSTERY WRITERS (US) **3448**

TWENTIETH CENTURY FUND *See* ANNUAL REPORT - TWENTIETH CENTURY FUND **5228**

TWENTIETH-CENTURY LITERARY CRITICISM (US/0276-8178) [04254388] **3355**

TWENTIETH CENTURY LITERATURE (US/0041-462X) [01713698] **3355**

TWENTIETH CENTURY PETROLEUM STATISTICS (US/1048-4825) [07404652] **4281**, **4285**

TWENTIETH-CENTURY ROMANCE & HISTORICAL WRITERS (US) **3448**

TWENTIETH-CENTURY SCIENCE-FICTION WRITERS (US) **3448**

TWENTIETH CENTURY VIEWS (US/0496-6058) [03472850] **3448**

TWENTIETH CENTURY WATCH (US/0276-6604) [07368754] **5068**

TWENTIETH-CENTURY WESTERN WRITERS (US) **3448**

TWENTY YEAR HIGHWAY NEEDS STUDY (US/0090-5879) [01784604] **5446**

● TWI JOURNAL (UK/0963-6927) [I09636927] **4028**

TWICE (US/0892-7278) [15247994] **2085**

TWICE WEEKLY INDEPENDENT *See* COLUMBIA COUNTY INDEPENDENT, THE **5715**

TWIGS MAGAZINE *CEASED.* (US/0891-3706) [14387746] **2476**

TWILIGHT WORLD (NE) **3448**

TWILIGHT ZONE *See* TWILIGHT WORLD **3448**

TWIN CIRCLE *See* CATHOLIC TWIN CIRCLE **5026**

TWIN CITIES CHRISTIAN, THE (US/0745-8606) [04445412] **5006**

TWIN CITIES EPICURE (US/0198-7895) [04456879] **2548**

TWIN CITIES READER (US/0193-2802) [05165132] **2548**

TWIN CITY NEWS (CHATTAHOOCHEE, FLA.) (US/0889-2245) [13819745] **5651**

TWIN FALLS TIMES-NEWS (US) [22066173] **5657**

TWIN FIDDLE TREASURY, THE (US/0731-7469) [05176495] **4157**

TWIN PLANT NEWS (US/1046-9427) [17347728] **855**

TWIN TERRITORIES (MUSKOGEE, OKLA. 1990) (US/1071-2895) [23030277] **2494**

TWIN VALLEY TIMES AND GARY GRAPHIC, THE (US) [21209650] **5699**

TWINE LINE : OHIO SEA GRANT PROGRAM NEWSLETTER (US/1064-6418) [17754129] **5549**, **2315**

TWINS (US/0890-3077) [13241073] **2286**

TWINS LETTER, THE (US/0743-748X) [10661800] **4621**

TWIST & SHOUT (CN/0710-3476) [08319687] **4157**

TWO AND A BUD (II/0496-6201) [01772745] **143**

TWO MOUNTAINS JOURNAL (CN/0229-7957) [08099487] **5796**

TWO THIRDS (CN/0705-3452) [04098105] **2912**

TWO THOUSAND TWENTY-NINE : 2029 (GW) **367**

TWO-WAY RADIO DEALER *CEASED.* (US/0191-5436) [04350066] **1142**

TWO WHEELS (AT/0041-4700) [I00414700] **4083**

● TWO YEAR BUDGET/ CITY OF PALO ALTO (US) [22856728] **4757**

TWO YEAR BUDGET / SIGNAL HILL REDEVELOPMENT AGENCY (US) [22939651] **2837**

TWORCZOSC (PL/0041-4727) [01767892] **3448**

TWOS AND THREES TEACHER (US/0744-7620) [08530836] **1908**

TWR'S INSIDER REPORT (US) **716**, **5567**

TWU EXPRESS (US/0039-8659) [02451258] **1715**

TYDENIK OBCHODU A PODNIKANI (XR) [22917904] **5799**

TYDSKRIF VAN DIE TANDHEELKUNDIGE VERENIGING VAN SUID AFRIKA (SA/0011-8516) [01029329] **1337**

TYDSKRIF VIR CHRISTELIKE WETENSKAP (SA/1013-1116) [I10131116] **5006**

TYDSKRIF VIR DIE SUID-AFRIKAANSE REG (SA) [04412595] **3067**

TYDSKRIF VIR GEESTESWETENSKAPPE (SA/0041-4751) [05162103] **2856**

TYDSKRIF VIR LETTERKUNDE (SA/0041-476X) [03173189] **2315**

TYDSKRIF VIR REGSWETENSKAP (SA/0258-252X) [04286817] **3067**

TYDSKRIF VIR STUDIES IN EKONOMIE EN EKONOMETRIE (SA/0379-6205) [09364443] **1525**

TYDSKRIF VIR VOLKSKUNDE EN VOLKSTAAL (SA/0049-4933) [03304678] **2325**

TYGODNIK CIECHANOWSKI (PL/0239-6807) [I02396807] **2524**

TYGODNIK LUDOWY (PL/0209-2166) [I02092166] **2524**

TYGODNIK NADWISLANSKI (PL/0208-8622) [I02088622] **2524**

TYGODNIK PILSKI (PL/0138-0710) [I01380710] **2524**

TYGODNIK PIOTRKOWSKI (PL/0208-6980) [I02086980] **2524**

TYGODNIK POCKI (PL/0208-6972) [I02086972] **2524**

TYGODNIK POPULARNY ZWIAZKOWIEC (PL/0867-5961) [I08675961] **1715**

TYGODNIK POWSZECHNY (PL) [12072556] **5808**

TYGODNIK SIEDLECKI (PL/0239-684X) [I0239684X] **2524**

TYGODNIK SOLIDARNOSC (PL/0208-8045) [07993192] **5808**

TYLER COURIER-TIMES-TELEGRAPH (US) [13594544] **5755**

TYLER COURIER-TIMES, THE (US) [18506489] **5755**

TYLER MORNING TELEGRAPH (US) [14248248] **5755**

TYLER TODAY (US) **2548**

TYLER WEEKLY COURIER-TIMES (US) [13695346] **5755**

TYLERTOWN TIMES, THE (US/0738-9930) [09674391] **5702**

TYMBAL / AUCHENORRHYNCHA NEWSLETTER (UK) **5614**

TYNDALE BULLETIN (1966) (UK/0082-7118) [03147286] **5006**

TYO TERVEYS TURVALLISUUS (FI/0041-4816) [01204480] **2871**

TYOKANSAN KALENTERI (CN) [08562323] **1929**

TYOLLISYYSKURSSIN SUORITTANEET (FI) [05508061] **1715**

TYOMARKKINATIETOJA (FI) [03061265] **5345**

TYOPAPEREITA - TAITEEN KESKUSTOIMIKUNTA (FI/0788-5318) [I07885318] **332**

TYOTEHOSEURAN JULKAISUJA (FI/0355-0710) [09843595] **2397**, **143**

TYOTERVEISET (FI/0359-1255) [I03591255] **2871**

TYOTERVEYSLAITOS *See* ANNUAL REPORT / INSTITUTE OF OCCUPATIONAL HEALTH **2859**

TYOTERVEYSPAIVAT (FI/0780-5292) [10578186] **1587**

TYOTERVEYSSAATIO *See* OCCUPATIONAL HEALTH FOUNDATION, INSTITUTE OF OCCUPATIONAL HEALTH **2866**

TYOVOIMA-ARVIO (FI) [02243047] **1715**

TYPE CERTIFICATE DATA SHEETS AND SPECIFICATIONS. VOLUME 1, SINGLE-ENGINE AIRPLANES *See* AIRCRAFT TYPE CERTIFICATE DATA SHEETS AND SPECIFICATION. VOLUME I, SINGLE-ENGINE AIRPLANES **9**

TYPE CERTIFICATE DATA SHEETS AND SPECIFICATIONS. VOLUME VI, AIRCRAFT LISTING & AIRCRAFT ENGINE & PROPELLER LISTING (US/0278-3037) [03014436] **38**

TYPE REPORTER, THE (US/8756-4963) [12354170] **4621**

TYPE WORLD (US/0194-4851) [03688234] **1263**, **4570**

TYPEX (FR) **1123**

TYPOGRAF-TIDENDE *See* DANSK GRAFIA **4564**

TYPOGRAFISCHE MONATSBLATTER (SZ) [06078011] **382**, **4570**

TYPOGRAPHIC SOCIETY OF TYPOGRAPHIC DESIGNERS (UK/0143-7623) [I01437623] **4570**

TYPOGRAPHIC : THE JOURNAL OF THE SOCIETY OF TYPOGRAPHIC DESIGNERS (UK) **4570**

TYPOGRAPHICS COMMUNICATIONS, INC *See* TGC TYPEFACE DIRECTORY **4570**

TYPOGRAPHISCHE MONATSBLATTER *See* TYPOGRAFISCHE MONATSBLATTER **4570**

TYPOGRAPHY (NEW YORK, N.Y.) (US/0275-6870) [07071162] **4570**

TYPOLOGICAL STUDIES IN LANGUAGE (NE/0167-7373) [10388792] **3330**

TYPOLOGIE DES SOURCES DU MOYEN AGE OCCIDENTAL (BE/0775-3381) [I07753381] **2713**

TYRES AND ACCESSORIES (UK/0041-4859) [I00414859] **5078**

TYRES, BATTERIES, AND EXHAUSTS (UK) **5427**

TYRONE DAILY HERALD (US) [12684400] **5740**

TZ FUER METALLBEARBEITUNG *CEASED.* (GW/0170-9577) [05319023] **3489**, **4023**

TZ. TYGODNIK ZAMOJSKI (PL/0138-0729) [I01380729] **2524**

TZU-CHIN SHAN T'IEN WEN T'AI, NANKING *See* T'IEN WEN T'UNG HSUN **401**

TZU HSUEH (CC) [09147885] **3448**

TZU HSUEH (PEKING, CHINA) (CC) [11459774] **3540**

TZU JAN KO HSUEH NIEN CHIEN (CH) [09833646] **5167**

TZU JAN TZU YUAN HSUEH PAO / CHUNG-KUO TZU JAN TZU YUAN YEN CHIU HUI PIEN CHI (CC) [17815621] **2207**

TZU LIAO HUI PIEN (CH) [09552762] **3330**

TZU LIU (CC) [11535578] **3449**

TZU SHU YEN CHIU (CC) [06212525] **3330**

TZU TIEN YEN CHIU TSUNG KAN (CH) [08739733] **3330**

TZU TUNG HUA HSUEH PAO (CC/0254-4156) [09477676] **1221**

TZU YU JEN (US) [02114928] **2274**

U.A.R. TOURISM IN THE FOREIGN PRESS (UA) [05173814] **5498**

U AND I CULTIVATOR, THE (US) [07510422] **190**

U & LC (US/0362-6245) [02328696] **4570**

U.B.C. PLANNING PAPERS. CANADIAN PLANNING ISSUES (CN/0828-2390) [14960832] **2837**

U.B.C. PLANNING PAPERS. COMPARATIVE URBAN & REGIONAL STUDIES (CN/0828-2404) [15128002] **1587**

U.B.C. PLANNING PAPERS. DISCUSSION PAPERS (CN/0828-2412) [16458771] **1587**

U. B. C. REPORTS (CN/0497-2929) [02225698] **1851**

U B LIBRARIES FACULTY NEWSLETTER, I (US) **3254**

U.C. DAVIS LAW REVIEW (US/0197-4564) [06033027] **3067**

U C L A GENERAL CATALOG (US) [06168446] **1851**

U C P A JOURNAL (CN/0709-2490) [06017240] **1851**

U. C. REVIEW (CN/0226-3440) [06511728] **3449**

Alphabetical Title Index

U-CHOOSE (CN/0706-4713) [07972990] **1095**

U F O UPDATE (CN/0227-1559) [06635132] **38**

U.G.T. : BOLETIN DE LA UNION GENERAL DE TRABAJADORES DE ESPANA (FR) [02636535] **1715**

U.I.T. JOURNAL (GW) [08163475] **4927**

U.K. MAGAZINE (US/8750-1082) [10988555] **2524**

U.K. PETROLEUM INDUSTRY STATISTICS. CONSUMPTION AND REFINERY PRODUCTION (UK/0141-4305) [08458470] 4281, **4285**

U K UPSTREAM PETROLEUM DATABASE (UK) **4281**

U L C NEWS (EDITION FRANCAISE) (CN/0700-9623) [03412063] **4033**

U. L. SCIENCE MAGAZINE (LB) [05351848] **5167**

U-M COMPUTING NEWS See INFORMATION TECHNOLOGY DIGEST/ INFORMATION TECHNOLOGY DIVISION, UNIVERSITY OF MICHIGAN **1268**

U MUT MAYA : AN UNOFFICIAL COLLECTION OF PAPERS, REPORTS, AND READINGS BY ATTENDANTS OF THE ... ADVANCED SEMINAR ON MAYA HIEROGLYPHIC WRITING HELD AT THE UNIVERSITY OF TEXAS AT AUSTIN ... (US) [23057815] 285, **2764**

U N B ENGINEERING NEWSLETTER (CN/0708-1995) [05257997] **2000**

U.N.B. TEMPERANCE UNION See NEWSLETTER / U.N.B. TEMPERANCE UNION **5299**

U.N. OBSERVER & INTERNATIONAL REPORT (US/1014-6539) [05536266] **3137**

U OF T WOMAN'S NEWSMAGAZINE (CN/0228-9024) [07817152] **5567**

U.S.A./AUSTRALIA TRADE DIRECTORY / AMCHAM (AT) [25650669] 855, **435**

●U.S.A. GULF COAST OIL & GAS INDUSTRY DIRECTORY (US/1056-795X) [23853882] **4281**

U.S.A.N. AND THE U.S.P. DICTIONARY OF DRUG NAMES (US/0090-6816) [01783667] **4331**

U.S.A. OIL INDUSTRY DIRECTORY (US/0082-8599) [02050691] **4281**

●U.S.A. OIL INDUSTRY'S ENVIRONMENTAL DIRECTORY (US/1062-0605) [25517229] **4281**

U.S.A. OILFIELD SERVICE, SUPPLY, AND MANUFACTURERS DIRECTORY (US) [12004834] **4281**

U.S. AGRICULTURAL POLICY GUIDE (US/0895-545X) [16665669] 143, **4691**

U S AIRBOAT (US) **596**

U.S. ALPHABETICAL PHYSICIAN REFERENCE LISTING (US/0098-8413) [02242710] **3917**

U.S. & FOREIGN DIPLOMATIC CONTACTS (US/1052-5238) [22294963] **4691**

U.S. AND INTERNATIONAL BOND MARKETS (US) [19330781] **815**

U.S. & WORLD FERTILIZER SERVICE SHORT-TERM FORECAST AND ANALYSIS (US) [16171101] **1525**

U.S. AND WORLD STEEL EXECUTIVE REPORT (US) [24836680] **4023**

U.S. AND WORLD WIDE TRAVEL ACCOMMODATIONS GUIDE (US/0898-4247) [10015995] **5498**

U.S.-ARAB CHAMBERS OF COMMERCE TRADE DIRECTORY (US) [15065045] **855**

U.S.-ARAB COMMERCE (US/0886-3717) [08535839] **855**

U.S. ARMS CONTROL AND DISARMAMENT AGENCY ANNUAL REPORT (US) [03079003] **4059**

U.S. ARMY COLD REGIONS RESEARCH AND ENGINEERING LABORATORY See CRREL REPORT **5097**

U.S. ARMY COMMUNICATIONS-ELECTRONICS ENGINEERING INSTALLATION AGENCY See AIR/GROUND SKY-WAVE PROPAGATION CHARTS FOR SELECTED WORLD WIDE STATIONS **7**

U.S. ARMY RESEARCH INSTITUTE FOR THE BEHAVIORAL AND SOCIAL SCIENCES See ABSTRACTS OF ARI RESEARCH PUBLICATIONS **5189**

U.S. ART (US/0899-1782) [18025453] **367**

U.S. AUTOMOBILE INDUSTRY, THE (US) [08102381] **5427**

U.S. AUTOMOTIVE SERVICES BULLETIN (US/0734-6573) [08770517] **5427**

U.S. BEER MARKET (US/1059-6887) [23904183] **2371**

U. S. BLACK BUSINESS (US/0091-4622) [01787168] **716**

U.S. BOAT & SHIP MODELER (US/0899-496X) [18111901] **2779**

U.S. BUDGET RECOMMENDATIONS (US/0095-8069) [01798654] **4757**

U.S. BUSINESS OUTLOOK, LONG-TERM See U.S. LONG-TERM REVIEW **1540**

U.S. CAMERA (US) [01695152] **4377**

U.S./CANADA PROFILES (US/1058-4722) [24300362] **5498**

U.S. CATHOLIC (US/0041-7548) [01795167] **5037**

U.S. CATHOLIC HISTORIAN (US/0735-8318) [07526668] **5037**

U.S. CENTRAL STATION NUCLEAR ELECTRIC GENERATING UNITS, SIGNIFICANT MILESTONES (US/0193-8657) [05899725] **2159**

U.S. CHEMICAL INDUSTRY STATISTICAL HANDBOOK (US/1061-9143) [22980986] **1030**

U.S. CHEMICAL PATENT INDEX (US/0362-4358) [02359702] **1309**

U.S.-CHINA ECONOMIC JOURNAL (US/0888-0476) [13451844] **1525**

U.S. CHINA RELATIONS. NOTES FROM THE NATIONAL COMMITTEE (US) [03813159] **4537**

U.S. CIVIL AIRMEN STATISTICS (US/0364-927X) [02693825] **42**

U.S. CLEAN COAL TECHNOLOGY DEMONSTRATION PROGRAM See PROGRAM UPDATE ... AS OF DECEMBER 31 ... / CLEAN COAL TECHNOLOGY DEMONSTRATION PROGRAM **1444**

U. S. COAL MINE PRODUCTION BY SEAM (US) [04741636] **2152**

U. S. COAL PRODUCTION BY COMPANY : BITUMINOUS, ANTHRACITE, LIGNITE (US/0097-8477) [01800141] **1630**

U.S. COINS, CURRENCY & STAMPS CEASED. (US/0743-9350) [10699271] 2788, **2783**

U.S. COINS OF VALUE (US/0271-3969) [05215611] **2783**

●U.S. COLLEGE HOCKEY MAGAZINE (US/1076-0008) [30351979] **4927**

U.S. CONGRESS HANDBOOK, THE (US/0196-7614) [04296035] **4691**

U.S. CONGRESSMAN JACK BRINKLEY REPORTS FROM WASHINGTON (US/0735-6021) [08681416] **4691**

U.S. CONSTITUTION REVIEW, THE (US/1055-0801) [23070244] **3067**

U.S. CONSUMER PRODUCT SAFETY COMMISSION See ANNUAL REPORT TO CONGRESS / UNITED STATES CONSUMER PRODUCT SAFETY COMMISSION **1293**

U.S. CONSUMER PRODUCT SAFETY COMMISSION. ANNUAL REPORT See ANNUAL REPORT TO CONGRESS / UNITED STATES CONSUMER PRODUCT SAFETY COMMISSION **1293**

U.S. CORPORATIONS DOING BUSINESS ABROAD (US/1066-1778) [07650561] **716**

U.S. CRUDE OIL DISTILLATION REFINING CAPACITY SURVEY FOR ... CEASED. (US/0740-9966) [06698190] **4281**

U.S. CRUDE OIL, NATURAL GAS, AND NATURAL GAS LIQUIDS RESERVES, ANNUAL REPORT (US/0731-924X) [08172489] **4281**

U.S. CRUDE OIL, NATURAL GAS, AND NATURAL GAS LIQUIDS RESERVES [COMPUTER FILE] / U.S. DEPARTMENT OF ENERGY (US) [25361431] **4281**

U.S. CUSTOM HOUSE GUIDE (US) [17432316] 855, **4757**

U.S. CUSTOMS DIRECTORY (US) [05896103] **4692**

U.S.D.A. FOREST SERVICE RESEARCH NOTE FPL See RESEARCH NOTE FPL **2392**

U.S.D. REPORT ON ENROLLMENTS AND GENERAL FUND BUDGET PER PUPIL (US) [07591716] 4692, **1788**

U.S. DAIRY, LIVESTOCK, AND POULTRY TRADE See DAIRY, LIVESTOCK AND POULTRY, U.S. TRADE AND PROSPECTS / UNITED STATES DEPARTMENT OF AGRICULTURE, FOREIGN AGRICULTURAL SERVICE **193**

U.S. DAIRY, LIVESTOCK, AND POULTRY TRADE / UNITED STATES DEPARTMENT OF AGRICULTURE, FOREIGN AGRICULTURAL SERVICE (US) [28358055] **143**

U.S. DECENNIAL LIFE TABLES. ACTUARIAL TABLES BASED ON UNITED STATES LIFE TABLES (US) [03067940] 2895, **2898**

U.S. DECENNIAL LIFE TABLES. METHODOLOGY OF THE NATIONAL AND STATE LIFE TABLES FOR THE UNITED STATES (US) [03319728] 2895, **2898**

U.S. DEFENSE BUDGET FORECAST (US) **4059**

U.S. DEPARTMENT OF ENERGY BUDGET TO CONGRESS : BUDGET HIGHLIGHTS (US/0193-1040) [04648062] 1959, **4692**

U.S. DEPARTMENT OF LABOR PROGRAM HIGHLIGHTS (US) [03457269] **1715**

U.S. DEPARTMENT OF STATE INDEXES OF LIVING COSTS ABROAD, QUARTERS ALLOWANCES, AND HARDSHIP DIFFERENTIALS (US/1058-0018) [09358077] 4692, **4560**

U.S. DEPARTMENT OF THE INTERIOR NATIONAL PARK SERVICE TRANSACTIONS AND PROCEEDINGS SERIES (US/0270-8655) [05384320] **2207**

U.S. DIRECT INVESTMENT ABROAD (US/0730-9848) [07832049] **918**

U.S. DIRECTORY OF POULTRY & EGG PROCESSING PLANTS (US) [02209313] **223**

U.S. DIRECTORY OF VENDORS See CAD/CAM, CAE, SURVEY, REVIEW, AND BUYERS' GUIDE **1173**

U.S. DISTILLED SPIRITS MARKET (US) [20512976] **2371**

U.S. DISTRICT COURT FEDERAL FILINGS ALERT CEASED. (US/0742-1087) [05874442] **3067**

U.S. ELECTRONICS INDUSTRY DIRECTORY See ELECTRONICS MANUFACTURERS DIRECTORY **3478**

U.S. EMPLOYMENT OPPORTUNITIES (US/0890-5959) [13342222] 1715, **4209**

U.S. ENERGY INDUSTRY FINANCIAL DEVELOPMENTS (US) [24046815] **1959**

U.S. ENVIRONMENTAL PROTECTION AGENCY LIBRARY SYSTEM BOOK CATALOG (US/0161-5645) [03012961] 2182, **3214**

U.S. EXPORT AND IMPORT PRICE INDEXES (US) [05186965] **5345**

U.S. EXPORT SALES (US/0145-0352) [02582283] **855**

U.S. EXPORTS AND IMPORTS OF GOLD (US/0098-7751) [02166563] **855**

U.S. EXPORTS. DOMESTIC MERCHANDISE, SIC-BASED PRODUCTS BY WORLD AREA (US/0098-5325) [03148347] **855**

U.S. EXPORTS. HARMONIED SCHEDULE B COMMODITY BY COUNTRY (US) [22723161] **855**

U.S. EXPORTS OF MERCHANDISE (US/1057-8773) [23886398] **855**

U.S. EXPORTS. SCHEDULE E COMMODITY BY COUNTRY (US) [09473778] **855**

U.S. FACILITIES AND PROGRAMS FOR CHILDREN WITH SEVERE MENTAL ILLNESSES : DIRECTORY (US/0160-676X) [03718110] 4805, **3912**

U.S. FARM NEWS (US/0041-7637) [03952779] **143**

U.S. FATS AND OILS STATISTICS (US/0146-8782) [03057218] 143, **157**

U.S. FINANCIAL DATA (US) [05962005] **1525**

U.S. FIRMS IN TAIWAN : DIRECTORY (CH) [07413690] **716**

U.S. FISH AND WILDLIFE SERVICE See CATALOG OF TRAINING / FISH AND WILDLIFE SERVICE, U.S. DEPARTMENT OF THE INTERIOR **2212**

U.S. FOAMED PLASTICS MARKETS & DIRECTORY (US/0083-0968) [02243447] **4460**

U. S. FOOD PRODUCTS DIRECTORY, THE BLUE BOOK OF FOOD PACKERS AND DISTRIBUTORS (US) [01496685] **2360**

U.S. FOREIGN TRADE: CONCORDANCE OF STATISTICAL CLASSIFICATIONS OF DOMESTIC AND FOREIGN COMMODITIES EXPORTED FROM THE UNITED STATES (US/0193-1687) [04796117] 855, **734**

U. S. FOREST SERVICE RESEARCH NOTE NOR (US/0502-3548) [01747473] **2397**

U.S.G. NEWSLETTER (CN/0229-5334) [06676167] **2578**

U.S. GELATIN-GLUE-BONES. IMPORTS (US/0747-6264) [10766612] **855**

U.S. GENERAL IMPORTS. SCHEDULE A, COMMODITY GROUPINGS BY WORLD AREA AND COUNTRY (US/0899-515X) [12208222] **855**

U.S. GEODYNAMICS COMMITTEE See GEODYNAMICS PROJECT : U.S. PROGRESS REPORT **1376**

U.S. GEOLOGICAL SURVEY BULLETIN (US/8755-531X) [10956746] **1400**

U.S. GEOLOGICAL SURVEY CIRCULAR (US/1067-084X) [10956655] **1400**

U.S. GEOLOGICAL SURVEY IN ALASKA ...., PROGRAMS, THE (US/0278-0747) [06660878] **1400**

U.S. GEOLOGICAL SURVEY PROFESSIONAL PAPER (US/1044-9612) [10957100] **1400**

Alphabetical Title Index U

U.S. GEOLOGICAL SURVEY WATER-SUPPLY PAPER (US/0886-9308) [13028128] **1400**

U.S. GLASS, METAL & GLAZING (US/0041-7661) [02451361] **2595**

U.S. GOVERNMENT AGENCY SECURITY MARKET REPORT : FORECASTS AND ANALYSES, THE (US/0272-8427) [06930026] **815**

U. S. GOVERNMENT RESEARCH AND DEVELOPMENT REPORTS. GOVERNMENT-WIDE INDEX TO FEDERAL RESEARCH AND DEVELOPMENT REPORTS (US) [01541368] **4692**

U.S. GRAIN MARKETING RESEARCH LABORATORY *See* SUMMARY PROGRESS REPORT / U.S. GRAIN MARKETING RESEARCH LABORATORY **188**

U.S. GREAT LAKES PORTS (US/0145-1308) [02672574] **5398**

U.S.H.L. YEARBOOK (US/0363-7050) [02534458] **4927**

U. S. HEALTH CARE FINANCING ADMINISTRATION. OFFICE OF SPECIAL PROGRAMS *See* END-STAGE RENAL DISEASE ANNUAL REPORT TO CONGRESS **3989**

U.S. HOUSING MARKETS (US/0502-9716) [04293261] **2837**

U.S. IDENTIFICATION MANUAL (US/0732-6688) [08428629] **3178**

●U.S. IMMIGRATION (US/1055-8276) [23352222] **1921**

U.S. IMPORT AND EXPORT PRICE INDEXES (US) [05528603] **855**

U.S. IMPORTS. CONSUMPTION AND GENERAL SIC-BASED PRODUCTS BY WORLD AREAS (US/0095-5485) [01037363] **855**

U.S. IMPORTS OF MERCHANDISE (US/1057-8765) [23886474] **855**

U.S. INDIAN POLICE TRAINING CENTER *See* TRIBAL AND BUREAU LAW ENFORCEMENT SERVICES AUTOMATED DATA REPORT: BILLINGS AREA **3178**

U.S. INDIAN POLICE TRAINING CENTER *See* TRIBAL AND BUREAU LAW ENFORCEMENT SERVICES AUTOMATED DATA REPORT: NAVAJO AREA **3178**

U.S. INDIAN POLICE TRAINING CENTER *See* TRIBAL AND BUREAU LAW ENFORCEMENT SERVICES AUTOMATED DATA REPORT: TOTAL ALL AREAS **3178**

U.S. INDUSTRIAL DIRECTORY (US/0095-7046) [03061101] **1630**

U.S. INDUSTRIAL OUTLOOK (1984) (US/0748-2671) [10482680] **1630**

U.S. INTERNATIONAL AIR TRAVEL STATISTICS (CALENDAR YEAR) (US) [08274678] **42**

... U.S. INVESTMENT TAX CREDIT INDEX, THE (US/0275-1755) [07093916] **918**

U.S.-JAPAN COOPERATIVE CANCER RESEARCH PROGRAM *See* PROGRESS REPORT / THE UNITED STATES-JAPAN COOPERATIVE CANCER RESEARCH PROGRAM **3822**

U.S./JAPAN OUTLOOK (US/0091-407X) [01786975] 1640, **855**

U.S.-JAPAN WOMEN'S JOURNAL. ENGLISH SUPPLEMENT (US/1059-9770) [24838451] **5567**

U.S. JOINT PUBLICATIONS RESEARCH SERVICE *See* TRANSLATIONS ON NARCOTICS AND DANGEROUS DRUGS **1350**

U.S. JOURNAL OF DRUG AND ALCOHOL DEPENDENCE, THE (US/0148-8619) [03115443] **1350**

U.S. KIDS (US/0895-9471) [16858972] **1071**

... U.S.-KUWAITI TRADE DIRECTORY, THE (US) [24608105] **855**

U S L HISTORY SERIES, THE (US) [01780997] **2764**

U.S. LICENSING INDUSTRY BUYERS GUIDE *See* NORTH AMERICAN LICENSING INDUSTRY BUYERS GUIDE **934**

U.S. LONG-TERM REVIEW (US/0734-4449) [08735951] 1525, **1540**

U.S. MANUFACTURERS DIRECTORY *See* AMERICAN MANUFACTURERS DIRECTORY **3475**

U.S. MARITIME MONTHLY (US/0744-8651) [08605331] **4184**

U.S. MAYOR (US/1049-2119) [20848636] **4692**

U.S. MEDICAL DIRECTORY (US/0091-8393) [01799972] **3793**

U.S. MEDICAL LICENSURE STATISTICS ... AND LICENSURE REQUIREMENTS ... (US/0741-6326) [09263123] 3917, **3662**

U.S. MEDICINE (US/0191-6246) [01767913] **3917**

U.S. MERCHANDISE TRADE (US/1057-9680) [21282434] **1630**

U.S. MERCHANDISE TRADE, SELECTED HIGHLIGHTS (US) [24165617] **856**

U.S. METRIC BOARD ANNUAL REPORT (US/0270-4838) [06118668] **4033**

U.S.-MEXICO FREE TRADE REPORTER (US/1064-802X) [24594933] **856**

U.S. MILITARY AIRCRAFT DATA BOOK (US/1064-1459) [02737842] **38**

U.S. MISSILE DATA BOOK (US/0360-7801) [02158145] **4059**

U.S. MOPED, 3 & 4 WHEELER, MOTOR SCOOTERS, ETC. IMPORTS (US/0742-4523) [10357399] 821, **5375**

U.S. NEWS & WORLD REPORT (US/0041-5537) [07786209] **2494**

U.S. NUCLEAR REGULATORY COMMISSION *See* NRC TELEPHONE DIRECTORY **4670**

U.S. NUCLEAR REGULATORY COMMISSION *See* BUDGET ESTIMATES - U.S. NUCLEAR REGULATORY COMMISSION **4634**

U.S. NUCLEAR REGULATORY COMMISSION *See* ANNUAL REPORT / U.S. NUCLEAR REGULATORY COMMISSION **2154**

U.S. NUCLEAR REGULATORY COMMISSION *See* NUCLEAR REGULATORY COMMISSION ISSUANCES **1952**

U.S. NUCLEAR REGULATORY COMMISSION *See* NUREG/CR (UNITED STATES. NUCLEAR REGULATORY COMMISSION) **2158**

U.S. NUCLEAR REGULATORY COMMISSION *See* AGENDA OF REGULATIONS **2153**

U.S. NUCLEAR REGULATORY COMMISSION. ADVISORY COMMITTEE ON REACTOR SAFEGUARDS *See* REVIEW AND EVALUATION OF THE NUCLEAR REGULATORY COMMISSION SAFETY RESEARCH PROGRAM **2158**

U.S. NUCLEAR REGULATORY COMMISSION. DIVISION OF TECHNICAL INFORMATION AND DOCUMENT CONTROL *See* NUCLEAR REGULATORY COMMISSION ISSUANCES : OPINIONS AND DECISIONS OF THE NUCLEAR REGULATORY COMMISSION WITH SELECTED ORDERS **4670**

U.S. NUCLEAR REGULATORY COMMISSION. OFFICE OF ENFORCEMENT *See* ENFORCEMENT ACTIONS **2155**

U.S. NUCLEAR REGULATORY COMMISSION. OFFICE OF NUCLEAR REGULATORY RESEARCH *See* LONG-RANGE RESEARCH PLAN **2156**

U.S. NUCLEAR REGULATORY COMMISSION. OFFICE OF STANDARDS DEVELOPMENT *See* REGULATORY GUIDE / U.S. NUCLEAR REGULATORY COMMISSION, OFFICE OF STANDARDS DEVELOPMENT **2868**

U.S. NUCLEAR REGULATORY COMMISSION. OFFICE OF THE EXECUTIVE LEGAL DIRECTOR *See* UNITED STATES NUCLEAR REGULATORY COMMISSION STAFF PRACTICE AND PROCEDURE DIGEST **4692**

U.S. NUCLEAR REGULATORY COMMISSION. REGULATORY PUBLICATIONS BRANCH *See* REGULATORY AND TECHNICAL REPORTS (ABSTRACT INDEX JOURNAL) **2158**

U.S. OIL WEEK (US/0502-9767) [04071378] **4281**

U.S. PARTICIPATION IN THE UN (US/0083-0208) [02939249] **4537**

U.S. PATENT CLASSIFICATION - NUMERIC LISTING (US) [05995538] **1309**

U.S. PHARMACEUTICAL MARKET. DRUG STORES (US/0275-5181) [07123866] 937, **4331**

U.S. PHARMACIST (US/0148-4818) [03295771] **4331**

U.S. PHYSICIAN REFERENCE LISTING (US/0098-986X) [02242711] **3917**

U.S. PRESS (US/8755-2663) [11258468] **5687**

U.S. PRODUCTION OF FISH FILLETS AND STEAKS, ANNUAL SUMMARY (US/0148-5318) [03298052] **2315**

U.S. PUBLICITY DIRECTORY. BUSINESS & FINANCE *CEASED*. (US/0196-5093) [05848200] **2925**

U.S. PUBLICITY DIRECTORY. COMMUNICATION SERVICES (US/0196-5107) [05848270] **2925**

U.S. PUBLICITY DIRECTORY. MAGAZINES (US/0196-5085) [05848225] **2925**

U.S. PUBLICITY DIRECTORY. NEWSPAPERS (US/0196-5077) [05848297] **2925**

U.S. PUBLICITY DIRECTORY. RADIO & TV *CEASED*. (US/0196-5069) [05848188] **1142**

U.S. RAG *CEASED*. (US/0892-6530) [15236161] **3449**

U.S. RAIL NEWS *CEASED*. (US/0743-7994) [09912381] **5437**

U.S. RAIL NEWS (US/0275-3758) [06270959] **5437**

U.S. / R&D (US) [02147820] **5167**

U.S. REAL ESTATE REGISTER (US/8755-1608) [10985244] **4848**

U.S. REGIONAL (US/8755-7398) [11308328] **5345**

U.S. REGULATORY REPORTER (US/0749-5005) [11136422] 4331, 2360, **5313**

U.S. ROLLER SKATING (US/1044-0801) [19681558] **4927**

U.S.S.R. COMPUTATIONAL MATHEMATICS AND MATHEMATICAL PHYSICS *See* COMPUTATIONAL MATHEMATICS AND MATHEMATICAL PHYSICS **3501**

U.S.S.R. MONITOR *See* FORMER U.S.S.R. MONITOR **2688**

U S S R REPORT: MATERIALS SCIENCE (US) **5167**

U.S. SCIENTISTS AND ENGINEERS (US/0163-2302) [02812399] **5167**

U.S. SECONDARY FIBRE STUDY (US/0741-823X) [10187027] **4239**

U.S. SEED EXPORTS (US) [16641032] 143, **856**

U.S. STATISTICS (US/0888-7926) [13718312] **5345**

U.S. STEP NEWSLETTER (US) [23840945] **1959**

U.S. TAPE IMPORTS (MANIFEST EDITION) (US/8756-8055) [11666474] **856**

U.S. TAPE IMPORTS (STATISTICAL ED.) (US/8756-8063) [11666556] **856**

U.S. TAX CASES (US/0277-402X) [03157871] **4757**

U.S. TELECOMMUNICATIONS (US) **1168**

U.S. TERMINAL PROCEDURES. ALASKA (US) [23937667] **38**

U.S. TERMINAL PROCEDURES. CHANGE NOTICE (CN) (US) [23937687] **38**

U.S. TERMINAL PROCEDURES. EAST CENTRAL (EC) (US) [23936551] **38**

U.S. TERMINAL PROCEDURES. NORTH CENTRAL (NC) (US) [23936398] **38**

U.S. TERMINAL PROCEDURES. NORTHEAST (NE) (US) [23936605] **38**

U.S. TERMINAL PROCEDURES. SOUTH CENTRAL (SC) (US) [23935366] **38**

U.S. TERMINAL PROCEDURES. SOUTHWEST (SW) (US) [23935098] **38**

U.S.-THIRD WORLD POLICY PERSPECTIVES (US) [11870719] **4537**

U.S. TOY COLLECTOR MAGAZINE (US/1044-1344) [19692053] 2779, **2585**

U.S. TRADE AND PROSPECTS, DAIRY, LIVESTOCK, AND POULTRY PRODUCTS *See* U.S. DAIRY, LIVESTOCK, AND POULTRY TRADE / UNITED STATES DEPARTMENT OF AGRICULTURE, FOREIGN AGRICULTURAL SERVICE **143**

U.S. TRADE AND PROSPECTS, DAIRY, LIVESTOCK, AND POULTRY PRODUCTS / UNITED STATES DEPARTMENT OF AGRICULTURE, FOREIGN AGRICULTURAL SERVICE (US) [24493823] 223, **199**

U.S. TRADE SHIFTS IN SELECTED COMMODITY AREAS (US/0736-3397) [07871964] 856, **1525**

U.S. TRADE STATUS WITH SOCIALIST COUNTRIES (US) [02458431] 1640, **856**

U.S. TRADE WITH PUERTO RICO AND U.S. POSSESSIONS *CEASED*. (US/0565-1204) [01294492] **856**

U.S. TRADE WITH THE COMMUNIST COUNTRIES BY SEVEN DIGIT COMMODITY CODE FOR ... (US/0196-3953) [05794358] **856**

U.S. UNION SOURCEBOOK (US/0897-1439) [12640277] **1715**

U.S. WATER NEWS (US/0749-1980) [11087857] **5541**

U.S. WATERBORNE EXPORTS AND GENERAL IMPORTS (US) [01796564] **856**

U.S. WEAPON SYSTEMS COSTS (US/1064-1467) [12736262] **4059**

U.S. WINE MARKET (US/0163-9544) [21346958] **2371**

U.S. WOMAN ENGINEER (US/0272-7838) [06380740] **2000**

U-T LAWYER, THE (US/0041-560X) [01495294] **3067**

U : THE NATIONAL COLLEGE NEWSPAPER (US) **5641**

U TURN *CEASED*. (US/0734-8401) [08811755] **367**

U W GUIDELINES (CN/0700-3692) [03279319] **1851**

UA JOURNAL (US/0095-7763) [01796419] **1715**

U&C UNIFICAZIONE & CERTIFICAZIONE (IT/0394-9605) **630**

UANG & EFEK (PERSERIKATAN PERDAGANGAN UANG DAN EFEK-EFEK (INDONESIA) : 1982) (IO) [09185268] **918**

UAW FACTS (US/0890-040X) [14126634] 5427, **1715**

UB NEWS (CN/0229-6756) [08072022] **223**

UBC DATA LIBRARY CATALOGUE. MICROFORM (CN/0713-8172) [09086740] **3254**

UBC LIBRARY BULLETIN (CN/0229-5954) [08375633] **3254**

UBD AUSTRALIA WIDE BUSINESS AND STREET DIRECTORY: BUNDABERG (AT) [05145328] **716**

UBD AUSTRALIA WIDE BUSINESS AND STREET DIRECTORY: GLADSTONE (AT) [05145475] **716**

UBD AUSTRALIA WIDE BUSINESS AND STREET DIRECTORY : GOLD COAST (AT) [05145363] 1929, **716**

UBD AUSTRALIA-WIDE BUSINESS AND STREET DIRECTORY. SOUTH AUSTRALIA, SOUTH AND EAST See UBD BUSINESS TO BUSINESS. SOUTH AUSTRALIA COUNTRY BUSINESS & STREET DIRECTORY **717**

UBD AUSTRALIA WIDE BUSINESS AND STREET DIRECTORY: TOOWOOMBA DISTRICT (AT) [05145419] **717**

UBD AUSTRALIA WIDE BUSINESS AND STREET DIRECTORY: WARWICK, STANTHORPE, GOONDIWINDI, ST. GEORGE (AT) [05145572] **717**

UBD BUSINESS & STREET DIRECTORY: BRISBANE, CITY & SUBURBAN (AT) [07352761] **717**

UBD BUSINESS & STREET DIRECTORY, WESTERN AUSTRALIAN COUNTRY TOWNS (AT) [03721586] **717**

UBD BUSINESS TO BUSINESS DIRECTORY (AT) **717**

UBD BUSINESS TO BUSINESS. SOUTH AUSTRALIA COUNTRY BUSINESS & STREET DIRECTORY (AT) [15481363] 2578, **717**

UBD CONFERENCE DIRECTORY (AT) **717**

UBERSEE RUNDSCHAU (GW/0041-5707) [02125885] 1640, **856**

UBERSETZUNGEN, KERNTECHNISCHE REGELN (GW) [03305183] **2159**

UBERSICHT UBER DIE BISHERIGEN ARBEITEN (GW) [01789409] **1788**

UBEZPIECZENIA MAJATKOWE I OSOBOWE (PL) [01799134] **2895**

UBS INTERNATIONAL FINANCE (SZ) [20794195] **1640**

UBU REPERTORY THEATER PUBLICATIONS (US/0738-4009) [09584315] 3449, **5372**

UBUMWE (BD) [01788441] **5779**

UC CLIP SHEET *SUSPENDED.* (US/0745-3213) [09067923] **1851**

UCAP WEEKLY BULLETIN (PH) **190**

UCC BULLETIN (US/1062-7693) [23752291] 815, **3067**

UCC INTERCHANGE (US/1059-4558) [24600022] **889**

UCEBNI POMUCKY : UP (XR) [11243265] **1886**

UCEBNI POMUCKY VE SKOLE A V OSVETE See UCEBNI POMUCKY : UP **1886**

UCENICI U PRIVREDI (YU) [01785884] 1788, **1798**

UCENYE ZAPISKIE CAGI (RU/0321-3439) [02555400] **38**

● UCGM (NORTH CHARLESTON, S.C.) (US/1059-7182) [24642084] **4157**

UCHENYE ZAPISKI KAFEDR MARKSISTSKO-LENINSKOI FILOSOFII VYSSHEI PARTIINOI SHKOLY PRI TSK KPSS I MESTNYKH VYSSHIKH PARTIINYKH SHKOL (RU/0502-9988) [02172342] 4548, **4364**

UCHENYE ZAPISKI LENINGRADSKOGO ORDENA LENINA GOSUDARSTVENNOGO UNIVERSITETA IMENI A.A. ZHDANOVA. SERIIA MATEMATICHESKIKH NAUK (RU/0136-8109) [10427657] **5167**

UCHENYE ZAPISKI / ORDENA LENINA VYSSHAIA PARTIINAIA SHKOLA PRI TSK KPSS (RU) [02244991] **4548**

UCHENYE ZAPISKI PO NOVOI I NOVEISHEI ISTORII (RU) [05194803] **2632**

UCHENYE ZAPISKI PO STATISTIKE (RU/0503-0021) [01607670] **5345**

UCHENYE ZAPISKI TARTUSKOGO GOSUDARSTVENNOGO UNIVERSITETA. TRUDY PO TSITOLOGII I GENETIKE TARTU RIIKLIKU ULIKOOLI TOIMETISED. TSUTOLOOGIA- JA GENEETIKA-ALASED TOOD (ER) [03429112] **541**

UCHITELSKAIA GAZETA (RU) [04740889] **5809**

UCHU KAGAKU KENKYUJO HOKOKU. TOKUSHU (JA/0285-2853) [08574879] **401**

UCHU KAGAKU KENKYUJO (JAPAN) See UCHU KAGAKU KENKYUJO NENJI YORAN **401**

UCHU KAGAKU KENKYUJO NENJI YORAN (JA) [12166299] **401**

UCHU KAIHATSU HANDOBUKKU (JA) [01800025] **38**

UCHU KAIHATSU JIGYODAN GIJUTSU HOKOKU (JA) [10437102] **38**

UCHU KAIHATSU SUISHIN KAIGI See UCHU KAIHATSU HANDOBUKKU **38**

UCHU KOKU KANKYO IGAKU (JA/0387-0723) [10475509] **3648**

UCI JOURNAL (US/0896-9299) [17336113] **1095**

UCL NEWSLETTER (TH) [15249412] **4513**

UCLA BUSINESS FORECAST FOR CALIFORNIA, THE (US/0740-851X) [09773556] 717, **1525**

UCLA BUSINESS FORECAST FOR THE NATION AND CALIFORNIA / UCLA BUSINESS FORECASTING PROJECT, THE (US) [26086179] 717, **1525**

UCLA CAMPUS PROFILE (US) [24160720] **1851**

UCLA FAMILY MEDICINE NEWS (US) [21476098] **3739**

UCLA HISTORICAL JOURNAL (US/0276-864X) [07071835] **2632**

UCLA JOURNAL OF DANCE ETHNOLOGY (US/0884-3198) [11639436] **1314**

UCLA JOURNAL OF ENVIRONMENTAL LAW & POLICY (US/0733-401X) [07066735] **3117**

UCLA LATIN AMERICAN STUDIES (US/1046-9176) [01755561] **2764**

UCLA LAW REVIEW (US/0041-5650) [00820597] **3067**

UCLA LIBRARIAN (US) [02268801] **3254**

UCLA MAGAZINE (1989) (US/1075-2749) [19572789] **1103**

UCLA MINORITY AND WOMEN-OWNED SMALL BUSINESS DIRECTORY See BUSINESS AFFIRMATIVE ACTION DIRECTORY **1600**

UCLA OCCASIONAL PAPERS IN LINGUISTICS (US) [26748452] **3330**

UCLA PACIFIC BASIN LAW JOURNAL (US/0884-0768) [08405602] **3067**

UCLA UAF BIBLIOGRAPHY IN MENTAL RETARDATION (US) [05218361] **3662**

UCLA WOMEN'S LAW JOURNAL (US) [24105198] 5567, **3067**

UCLA WORKING PAPERS IN PHONETICS (US/1067-9030) [16275199] **3330**

UCMP QUARTERLY (US/0276-7570) [05038545] **3254**

UDDANNELSESINSTITUTIONER OVER GRUNDSKOLENIVEAU (DK) [09968052] **1788**

UDENRIGS (DK/0903-7845) [19239775] **4498**

UDENRIGSMINISTERIETS TIDSSKRIFT: NYT FRA EKSPORTMARKEDERNE (DK) [06546483] **856**

UDGIFTSANALYSER (DK/0905-7544) [25067904] **4757**

UDI WHO'S WHO IN COGENERATION & INDEPENDENT POWER (US) [25252624] **4762**

UDS AIR QUALITY CONTROL DIGEST *CEASED.* (US) [04880430] **2245**

UDT NEWSLETTER (CN/1010-9501) [16886075] **3254**

UDVALGSLISTE OVER ORKESTERMATERIALE (DK) [05665725] **4157**

UDVIKLING (DK) [01799300] **1587**

UDYANIKA / RAJASTHAN HORTICULTURAL SOCIETY (II) [09586149] **2433**

UDYOGA VYAPARA SAMIKSHA (NP) [11984563] **856**

UE NEWS (U.S. EDITION) (US/0041-5065) [01493026] **1715**

UEA ACTION (US/0042-1413) [03952659] **1788**

UEA PAPERS IN LINGUISTICS (UK/0951-2292) [02754198] **3330**

UFAHAMU (US/0041-5715) [01126753] **2500**

UFANISI (KE) [01796591] **856**

UFCW ACTION (US/0195-0363) [05226648] 717, **1715**

UFCW LEADERSHIP UPDATE (US/8750-328X) [11256975] **1715**

UFCW LOCAL 1428 MESSENGER (US/1060-3840) [24955241] **1715**

UFF REACH (US/8755-1845) [08029906] **1715**

UFFICIO MODERNO, L' See UOMO MANAGER **3996**

UFFICIO TECNICO, L' (IT/0394-8293) [03948293] **5167**

UFFICIOSTILE (IT) **310**

UFFICIOSTILE (IT/0503-0455) [I05030455] **2903**

UFO ANNUAL (BROOKLYN) (US/0162-8046) [04212573] **38**

UFO BIAYSTOK (PL/0867-2490) [I08672490] **4186**

UFO CONTACT (DK) [01788792] **38**

UFO REPORT (BROOKLYN) (US/0148-6438) [03340683] **38**

UFO TIMES (UK/0958-4846) [I09584846] **38**

UFONTAS, AS (BL) [05721078] **38**

UFPA DIGEST See DIGEST **4067**

UFPSS FRIENDSHIP (US/1055-5293) [23199971] **3449**

UGANDA ECONOMIC JOURNAL, THE (UG) [01786219] **1525**

UGANDA : ENERGIEWIRTSCHAFT (GW) [05064252] **1959**

UGANDA FRESHWATER FISHERIES RESEARCH ORGANIZATION See ANNUAL REPORT / UGANDA FRESHWATER FISHERIES RESEARCH ORGANIZATION **2295**

UGANDA JOURNAL *SUSPENDED.* (UG/0041-574X) [01644239] **2644**

UGANDA LAW FOCUS, THE (UG) [01791651] **3067**

UGANDA LIBRARIES See JOURNAL OF UGANDAN LIBRARIES **3221**

UGANDA. MINISTRY OF FINANCE, PLANNING AND ECONOMIC DEVELOPMENT. STATISTICS DIVISION See MONTHLY TRADE BULLETIN - MINISTRY OF FINANCE, PLANNING AND ECONOMIC DEVELOPMENT, STATISTICS DIVISION **731**

UGANDA. OFFICE OF THE PRESIDENT. STATISTICS DIVISION See MONTHLY/QUARTERLY TRADE BULLETIN **846**

UGANDA. PUBLIC LIBRARIES. BOARD See PROCEEDINGS OF THE PUBLIC LIBRARIES BOARD STAFF CONFERENCE AND SEMINAR **3242**

UGARIT-FORSCHUNGEN (GW/0342-2356) [01468917] **3330**

UGAZINE (US/0733-9712) [08131731] **1095**

UGESKRIFT FOR JORDBRUG See JORD OG VIDEN **98**

UGESKRIFT FOR LAGER (DK/0041-5782) [01767927] **3648**

UGESKRIFT FOR RETSVAESEN (DK) [01639080] **3067**

UGOL (RU/0041-5790) [02451264] **2152**

UGRA MITTEILUNGEN (SZ/1019-4754) [I10194754] **4570**

UGYVITEL ES INFORMACIO AZ ALLAMIGAZGATASBAN (HU/0302-9778) [01793947] **4692**

UHANDISI (TZ) [02951523] **2000**

UHF. ULTRA HIGH FIDELITY (CN/0847-1851) [20873492] **5319**

UHLI (PRAGUE, CZECHOSLOVAKIA : 1959) See UHLI, RUDY **2152**

UHLI, RUDY (XR/0041-5812) [25840027] 1400, **2152**

● UHLI- RUDY- GEOLOGICKY PRUZKUM (XR/1210-7697) [I12107697] **1400**

UHREN 1992 (GW/0942-2366) [I09422366] **367**

UHREN, JUWELEN, SCHMUCK (GW) [01785277] **2916**

UHREN RUNDSCHAU. REVUE DE LA MONTRE (SZ) [01785876] **2916**

UHREN UND SCHMUCK (SZ) [07536618] **4023**

UHS BULLETIN See HIAS BULLETIN **1919**

UHUD (II) [02240195] **5045**

UHURU (DAR ES SALAAM, TANZANIA) (TZ) [02268813] **5811**

UIA INFORMATION (FR) [02610657] **310**

UICC MONOGRAPH SERIES (GW/0074-9214) [01753747] **3825**

UICC NEWS : INTERNATIONAL UNION AGAINST CANCER NEWSLETTER (SZ) [26028783] **3825**

UIJONG (KO) [04507340] **2667**

UINTA COUNTY HERALD (US) [12306077] **5773**

UINTAH BASIN STANDARD, THE (US) [12358626] **5757**

UIRUSU (JA/0042-6857) [01593783] **3648**

UIRYO POHOM TONGGYE YONBO (KO) [14994932] **2895**

UIRYO POHOM YONBO (KO) [08858393] 3648, **2895**

UIRYU KISUL (KO) [10125795] **1088**

UIS BULLETIN (AU/0254-9824) [02549824] **1400**

UIS NEWSLETTER *See* INFORMATION TECHNOLOGY DIGEST/ INFORMATION TECHNOLOGY DIVISION, UNIVERSITY OF MICHIGAN **1268**

UIT EUROPOORTKRINGEN (NE) 717, **5458**

UIT HET NIEUWS GLICHT : KNIPSELKRANT (NE) **3716**

UITGAVE VAN DE VERENIGING REMBRANDT / VERENIGING REMBRANDT, NATIONAAL FONDS KUNSTBEHOUD (NE) [27047193] **367**

UITGAVEN VAN DE NATUURWETENSCHAPPELIJKE STUDIEKRING VOOR SURINAME EN DE NEDERLANDSE ANTILLEN. NATUURHISTORISCHE REEKS (NE) [06441706] **4173**

UITGAVEN VAN DE NATUURWETENSCHAPPELIJKE WERKGROEP NEDERLANDSE ANTILLEN (NE/0470-3995) [01685694] **4173**

UITP BIBLIO-INDEX. TRANSPORT-VERKEHR (BE/0041-5146) [10073814] **5398**

UITVOERINGSORGANEN BUURT- EN KLUBHUISWERK (NE) [04259421] **4855**

UITVOERINGSPROGRAMMA BELEIDSPLAN MILIEUHYGIENE (NE) [18726522] **2182**

UIW NEWSLETTER (US/0745-0052) [08717960] **1715**

UIYAK CHONGBO (KO) [11379705] **4331**

UJ ELET (CN) [02254682] **332**

UJ ERDEKES UJSAG (HU/0865-9435) [108659435] **4855**

UJ FORRAS (HU/0133-5332) [18946207] **3449**

UJ MAGYAR HIREK *CEASED.* (HU/0866-4749) [24234671] **2524**

UJ TUKOR *CEASED.* (HU) [04733408] **2524**

UJAMAA (FR) **2500**

UK BUSINESS FINANCE DIRECTORY (UK) [22165255] **815**

UK CHRISTIAN HANDBOOK (UK) [14641757] **5068**

UK ELECTRICITY / ELECTRICITY ASSOCIATION (UK) [25334221] 2085, **4762**

UK FILM INITIATIVES (UK) **4079**

UK INTERNATIONAL TRAVEL MONITOR (UK) **5498**

UK OFFSHORE LEGISLATION GUIDE (UK) **4692**

UK OFFSHORE LEGISLATION UPDATES (UK) **4281**

UK OFFSHORE OIL & GAS DIRECTORY (UK) [09046997] **4281**

UK OIL & GAS LAW (UK) 4281, **3067**

UK PESTICIDE GUIDE, THE (UK/0952-7788) [23474395] **4248**

UK PRESS GAZETTE (UK) [I00415170] **2926**

UK PUBLISHERS DIRECTORY (US) **4820**

UK TELECOMMUNICATIONS POLICY REVIEW (UK) [24993896] **1168**

UK TRADE BULLETIN IMPORTS & EXPORTS OF FISH & FISH PRODUCTS (UK/0963-9446) [I09639446] **2315**

UK VENTURE CAPITAL JOURNAL (UK/0265-8364) [12710890] **815**

UKAEA UNDERLYING RESEARCH PROGRAMME, ANNUAL REPORT (UK) [20148609] **1959**

UKIAH DAILY JOURNAL (US) [28464153] **5641**

UKIC GRAPEVINE (UK/0957-0578) [I09570578] **4097**

UKIRT NEWSLETTER (1993) *See* SPECTRUM : NEWSLETTER OF THE ROYAL OBSERVATORIES **390**

UKIYOE GEIJUTSU (JA) [04348941] **367**

UKOLN. OFFICE FOR LIBRARY AND INFORMATION NETWORKING (UK) **3254**

●UKRAINE BUSINESS REVIEW (UK/0969-3483) [I09693483] **717**

UKRAINE. KABINET MINISTRIV *See* ZIBRANNIA POSTANOV URIADU UKRAINY **3078**

UKRAINE (KIEV, UKRAINE) (UN) [02268816] **2524**

●UKRAINE (SYRACUSE, N.Y.) (US/1061-1304) [25185030] 4498, **1587**

UKRAINIAN ACADEMY OF ARTS AND SCIENCES IN THE UNITED STATES *See* ANNALS OF THE UKRAINIAN ACADEMY OF ARTS AND SCIENCES IN THE UNITED STATES **2842**

UKRAINIAN BIOCHEMISTRY *CEASED.* (US/1055-7954) [20999919] **494**

UKRAINIAN BUSINESS DIGEST (US/1053-4237) [22529113] **717**

UKRAINIAN CANADIAN COMMITTEE *See* BJULETEN' - KOMITETU UKRAJINCIV KANADY **2723**

UKRAINIAN CANADIAN CONGRESS *See* KONGRES UKRAJINCIV KANADY **2743**

●UKRAINIAN CANADIAN HERALD (CN/1193-2813) [26715046] **5796**

●UKRAINIAN CHEMISTRY JOURNAL (US/1063-4568) [26040169] **994**

UKRAINIAN CLASSICS IN TRANSLATION (US) [03178819] **1080**

UKRAINIAN MATHEMATICAL JOURNAL (US/0041-5995) [01496592] **3540**

●UKRAINIAN MATHEMATICS JOURNAL (US/1069-5346) [28093980] **3540**

UKRAINIAN ORTHODOX WORD *SUSPENDED.* (US/0147-1015) [03098875] **5040**

UKRAINIAN QUARTERLY, THE (US/0041-6010) [01767936] **4498**

UKRAINIAN REPORTER (UN/0964-4326) [25067905] **4537**

UKRAINIAN REVIEW (LONDON, ENGLAND) (UK/0041-6029) [01779352] **4499**

UKRAINIAN WEEKLY, THE (US/0273-9348) [07042061] **2274**

UKRAINSKA BIBLIOTEKA IMENY S. PETLIURY V PARYZHI *See* INFORMATSIINYI BIULETEN - UKRAINSKA BIBLIOTEKA IMENY S. PETLIURY V PARYZHI **3217**

UKRAINSKA KNYHA (US/0190-7115) [03735350] **426**

UKRAINSKA KULTURA (UN/0868-9644) [24040944] **2524**

UKRAINSKA MOVA I LITERATURA V SHKOLI (UN/0130-5263) [02178353] 3330, **3449**

UKRAINSKA RSR (UN) [05217058] **5398**

UKRAINSKE LITERATUROZNAVSTVO (UN) [01643417] **3449**

UKRAINSKE MIKROBIOLOHICHNE TOVARYSTVO *See* TRUDY SEZDA MIKROBIOLOGOV UKRAINY **570**

UKRAINS'KE MOVOZNAVSTVO (UN/0320-3077) [02407002] **3330**

UKRAINSKE MUZYKOZNAVSTVO (UN/0566-6155) [02218431] **4157**

UKRAINSKE VIDRODZHENNJA (CN/0824-6238) [10852431] **2714**

UKRAINSKI VISTI (EDMONTON) (CN/0041-6002) [22569391] **5796**

UKRAINSKII BIOKHIMICHESKII ZHURNAL (UN/0201-8470) [04383010] **494**

UKRAINSKII BOTANICHNII ZHURNAL (UN/0372-4123) [07342915] **529**

UKRAINSKII MATEMATICHESKII ZHURNAL *See* UKRAINSKYI MATEMATYCHNYI ZHURNAL **3540**

UKRAINSKIJ FIZICESKIJ ZURNAL (KIEV, 1967) (UN/0503-1265) [02163454] **4424**

UKRAINSKIJ HIMICESKIJ ZURNAL (UN/0041-6045) [18210374] **995**

UKRAINSKIJ ISTORICNIJ ZURNAL (UN/0130-5247) [01767930] **2632**

UKRAINSKYI BOTANICHNYI ZHURNAL (UN/0041-6118) [01767938] **529**

UKRAINSKYI BOTANICHNYI ZHURNAL / AKADEMIIA NAUK UKRAINSKOI RSR, INSTYTUT BOTANIKY (UN/0372-4123) [17636449] **529**

UKRAINSKYI FILATELIST / SOIUZ UKRAINSKYKH FILATELISTIV I NUMIZMATYKIV (US/0198-6252) [09012804] 2783, **2788**

UKRAINSKYI INSTYTUT SV. VOLODYMYRA *See* VISTI - INSTYTUTU SV. VOLODYMYRA **2275**

UKRAINSKYI ISTORYK (US/0041-6061) [02256614] **2714**

●UKRAINSKYI MATEMATYCHNYI ZHURNAL (UN) [27335196] **3540**

UKRAINSKYI SAMOSTIINYK. UKRAINSKYJ SAMOSTIJNYK (GW) [05160917] **2714**

UKRAINSKYI TEATR (UN) [05170078] **5372**

UKRAINSKYI VISNYK (FR) [05197606] **3449**

UKRAJINSKYJ ZURNALIST (CN/0380-1403) [02578514] **2925**

UK'S ... LARGEST COMPANIES (UK) [13769234] **717**

UKTUBIR (UA) [03393257] **2644**

UKULIMA WA KISASA (TZ/0856-0838) [20064936] **143**

UKW-BERICHTE (GW/0177-7513) [I01777513] **4442**

UKY BU (UNIVERSITY OF KENTUCKY) (US/0270-6504) [06573232] **2000**

UL TRENDS (US) [09016157] **2895**

ULAGASHEVSKIE CHTENIIA / GORNO-ALTAISKII NAUCHNO-ISSLEDOVATELSKII INSTITUT ISTORII, IAZYKA I LITERATURY (RU) [06515609] **3449**

ULAKA ITAYA OLI (II) (02441078] **2509**

ULASAN GETAH MALAYSIA (MY/0126-9089) [03249210] **5078**

ULCN. UNION LIST OF CANADIAN NEWSPAPERS (CN/0840-5832) [19317856] **3254**

ULEN UNION, THE (US) [01714882] **5699**

ULI MARKET PROFILES (US/0894-6108) [14054076] **4848**

ULKOMAANKAUPPA (FI/0355-0249) [03523009] **856**

ULKOMAANKAUPPA; KUUKAUSIJULKAISU. UTRIKESHANDEL MANADSPUBLIKATION (FI) [02704385] **856**

ULKOMAISET TILASTOKAUSIJULKAISUT (FI) [19417728] **5345**

ULLMANN'S ENCYCLOPEDIA OF INDUSTRIAL CHEMISTRY (GW) **1030**

ULM. UNIVERSITAT *See* FORSCHUNGSBERICHT - UNIVERSITAT ULM **5105**

ULRF REPORTS (US/0364-443X) [02220993] **2837**

ULRICH'S INTERNATIONAL PERIODICALS DIRECTORY (US/0000-0175) [02521849] **3254**

ULRICH'S NEWS *CEASED.* (US/0000-1163) [17602057] **3254**

ULRICH'S ON MICROFICHE (US/0000-0981) [15534616] **3254**

ULRICH'S PLUS (US/1068-0500) [18363931] **3254**

ULRICH'S UPDATE (US/0000-1074) [17683073] **3254**

ULSTER-AMERICAN NEWSLETTER (US/0733-8686) [08672960] **2764**

ULSTER COUNTY GENIE (US) **2476**

ULSTER FOLK AND TRANSPORT MUSEUM *See* YEAR BOOK - ULSTER FOLK AND TRANSPORT MUSEUM **4097**

ULSTER FOLKLIFE (NL/0082-7347) [01497279] **2325**

ULSTER GENEALOGICAL & HISTORICAL GUILD *See* SUBSCRIBERS' INTEREST LIST ... / ULSTER GENEALOGICAL & HISTORICAL GUILD **2474**

ULSTER JOURNAL OF ARCHAEOLOGY (UK/0082-7355) [01562885] **285**

ULSTER MEDICAL JOURNAL (UK/0041-6193) [01778194] **3648**

●ULTIMATE FANTASY FOOTBALL LEAGUE ... GUIDE AND HANDBOOK, THE (US) [26698567] **4927**

ULTIMATE FITNESS FOR A LIFETIME (US/1056-4780) [23722982] **2601**

●ULTIMATE GUIDE TO BUYING WINE / THE WINE SPECTATOR (US) [27464308] **2371**

ULTIMATE ISSUES (US/0888-3440) [11990860] **5053**

ULTIMATE NETWORKING DIRECTORY, THE (US/1044-3312) [19756197] **1205**

ULTIMATE REALITY AND MEANING (CN/0709-549X) [04942980] **4364**

ULTIMISSIME PELLICCERIA (IT) 1088, **3186**

●ULTRA CYCLING (US/1063-9349) [26183242] **4927**

ULTRA FIT *See* ULTRAFIT AUSTRALIA **2601**

●ULTRA HAWK (US/1062-9122) [25806686] **382**

ULTRA (HOUSTON, TEX.) *SUSPENDED.* (US/0279-4322) [07868708] **2548**

ULTRACENTRIFUGE APPLICATIONS; A CONTINUING BIBLIOGRAPHY (US) [02253351] **426**

ULTRAFIT AUSTRALIA (AT) **2601**

ULTRAHIGH- AND HIGH-SPEED PHOTOGRAPHY, VIDEOGRAPHY, AND PHOTONICS (US/1018-7928) [24728114] **4377**

ULTRALIGHT PILOT (US/0736-2447) [09078445] **38**

ULTRAMICROSCOPY — Alphabetical Title Index

ULTRAMICROSCOPY (NE/0304-3991) [02246092] **574**

ULTRANUTRITION DIGEST (US/0270-7918) [06498595] **4199**

ULTRAPURE WATER (US/0747-8291) [10808727] **5541**

ULTRARUNNING (US/0744-3609) [08217166] **4927**

ULTRASCHALL IN DER MEDIZIN (GW/0172-4614) [09718856] **3648**

ULTRASCHALL IN KLINIK UND PRAXIS (GW/0930-8040) [18306750] **3648**

ULTRASONIC IMAGING (US/0161-7346) [04015539] **3802**

ULTRASONICA (IT/0393-7801) [18418660] **3769**

ULTRASONICS (UK/0041-624X) [01607881] **4424**

●ULTRASONICS SONOCHEMISTRY (UK/1350-4177) [30502153] **4424**

ULTRASONIDOS *CEASED.* (SP/0211-9099) [17726459] **2000**

ULTRASOUND IN MEDICINE (US/0098-0382) [02239681] **3648**

ULTRASOUND IN MEDICINE & BIOLOGY (US/0301-5629) [01789455] 475, **3648**

ULTRASOUND IN OBSTETRICS AND GYNAECOLOGY (UK/0960-7692) [23968529] **3769**

ULTRASOUND QUARTERLY (US/0894-8771) [16274495] **3648**

ULTRASOUND SOURCEBOOK & REFERENCE GUIDE (US/1055-7997) [23265611] **3648**

ULTRASTRUCTURAL PATHOLOGY (US/0191-3123) [04848588] **3898**

ULTRASTRUCTURAL PATHOLOGY PUBLICATION SERIES, AN *CEASED.* (US/0730-6482) [08030687] **3898**

ULULA (US/0747-8011) [10807375] **3449**

ULYSSES NEWS, THE (US) [08821148] **5678**

UMAK NONDAN. JOURNAL OF THE SCIENCE AND PRACTICE OF MUSIC (KO) [12324608] **4157**

UMAK SEGYE (KO) [11304848] **4157**

UMAK TONGA (KO) [10842869] **4157**

UMAK YONGU (KO) [08724008] **4157**

UMANA AVVENTURA, L' (IT) [16799798] **367**

UMAP JOURNAL, THE (US/0197-3622) [06008117] 1788, **3540**

UMAP MODULES (US) [08600023] 3540, **3543**

UMBEN (PP) 1525, **5264**

UMBRA (US/0016-6618) [03494085] **5237**

UMBRAE CODICUM OCCIDENTALIUM (NE/0503-1486) [01779354] **2632**

UMBRAL 2000 I.E. DOS MIL (AG) [01789957] **3254**

UMBRELLA (BELLEVILLE) (CN/1183-1839) [24266017] **332**

UMBRELLA (GLENDALE) (US/0160-0699) [03611863] **367**

UMD STATESMAN (US) [01758010] **5699**

UME TRENDS (US) **3540**

UMEA PSYCHOLOGICAL REPORTS (SW/0375-4561) [01767944] **4621**

UMEA STUDIES IN SOCIOLOGY / UNIVERSITY OF UMEA (SW) [19964697] **5264**

UMENI (XR/0049-5123) [02123295] **367**

UMENI A REMESLA (XR/0139-5815) [08998157] **376**

UMFORMTECHNIK (GW/0300-3167) [01449794] **2131**

UMI ABI/INFORM--BUSINESS PERIODICALS ONDISC (US/1064-5381) [26326812] 717, **734**

UMI TO SORA (JA) [01498066] **1361**

UMI'S SOUTHEASTERN BASKETBALL HANDBOOK (US) [17973536] **4927**

UMKC LAW REVIEW (US/0047-7575) [02059813] **3067**

UMMAH (DAWHAH, QATAR) (QA) [07849099] **5045**

UMODZI (MW) [11247018] **1851**

UMPQUA FREE PRESS (US/0745-7588) [09428544] **5734**

UMPQUA TRAPPER, THE (US/0041-6339) [03157975] **2764**

UMSATZSTEUER-RUNDSCHAU (COLOGNE, GERMANY : 1986) (GW/0341-8669) [14139265] **3067**

UMTA UNIVERSITY RESEARCH AND TRAINING PROGRAM : ABSTRACTS FOR UNIVERSITY RESEARCH PROJECTS / DEPARTMENT OF TRANSPORTATION, URBAN MASS TRANSPORTATION ADMINISTRATION, OFFICE OF POLICY AND PROGRAM DEVELOPMENT, UNIVERSITY RESEARCH AND TRAINING DIVISION (US) [05788811] **1851**

UMTRI RESEARCH REVIEW, THE (US/0739-7100) [09187496] **5398**

UMUM NEWSLETTER / BLACK HISTORY MUSEUM (US) [03674556] **5264**

UMUNYAMUYANGO (RW) [05204381] 1543, **143**

UMWELT (DUSSELDORF) (GW/0041-6355) [04088503] **2245**

UMWELT UND ENERGIE (GW/0173-8720) [01738720] **1959**

UMWELTDATEN (AU) [05715156] **2245**

UMWELTFORSCHUNGSKATALOG (GW) [02939444] **2245**

UMWELTHYGIENE (ESSEN) (GW/0174-3244) [09383546] **2245**

UMWELTMAGAZIN WURZBURG (GW/0173-363X) [0173363X] **2182**

UMWELTWISSENSCHAFTEN UND SCHADSTOFF-FORSCHUNG : ORGAN DER ARBEITSGEMEINSCHAFT UMWELTCHEMIE UND OKOTOXIKOLOGIE DER GESELLSCHAFT DEUTSCHER CHEMIKER (GW/0934-3504) [24914356] **2245**

UN AN DE NOUVEAUTES (FR/0294-1090) [08241549] **4833**

UN CHRONICLE (US/0251-7329) [04268996] **4537**

●UN-COMMON SENSE (LONG BEACH, CALIF.) (US/1062-080X) [25521139] **3648**

UNA SANCTA (METTINGEN) (GW/0342-1465) [01777332] **5006**

UNABASHED LIBRARIAN, THE (US/0049-514X) [01645097] **3254**

UNAK (TORONTO) (CN/0044-1384) [03113924] **1071**

UNARVU (MADRAS, INDIA) (II) [08714552] **2667**

UNASYLVA (IT/0041-6436) [01589480] **2397**

UNB FORESTRY FOCUS (CN/0707-1957) [09511207] **2397**

UNB LAW JOURNAL (CN/0836-6632) [17636313] **3067**

UNB PERSPECTIVES (CN/0229-4680) [08028209] **1851**

UNC NOTIZIE (IT) **1300**

UNCAPTIVE MINDS (US/0897-9669) [17679781] **2714**

UNCENSORED POLAND NEWS BULLETIN / INFORMATION CENTRE FOR POLISH AFFAIRS (U.K.), STUDIUM SPRAW POLSKICH (WLK. BRYTANIA) (UK/0264-6501) [09749793] **2714**

UNCLASSIFIED ACCESSION LIST (US/0094-8292) [08235757] **426**

UNCLASSIFIED (WASHINGTON, D.C.) (US/1062-3450) [21209865] **5177**

UNCOVER D.C (US/0361-5731) [02166596] **2548**

UNCOVERINGS (US/0277-0628) [07495216] **5186**

UNCRD WORKING PAPERS (JA) [12415131] **2837**

UNCTAD BULLETIN (SZ) [09864497] **1640**

UNCTAD COMMODITY YEARBOOK / UNITED NATIONS CONFERENCE ON TRADE AND DEVELOPMENT (US) [15687375] **856**

UNCTAD REVIEW (SZ/1014-370X) [20456690] **1640**

UNDER AFRIKAS SOL (DK) [01782527] **5006**

UNDER CONSTRUCTION (US/0740-4409) [09934116] **2476**

UNDER WESTERN SKIES (US/0279-6244) [07120292] **4079**

UNDERCAR DIGEST (US/0893-6943) [15626862] **5427**

UNDERCURRENT (NEW YORK) (US/0192-0871) [06741821] **4927**

UNDERCURRENTS (UK) [01785579] **5167**

●UNDERCURRENTS: MYSTIC MARINELIFE AQUARIUM QUARTERLY (US/1061-5776) [25363355] **5599**

UNDERGLAZE DECORATION (US/0009-0328) **2595**

UNDERGRADUATE CHEMISTRY (US/1040-3396) [14136031] **995**

UNDERGRADUATE RESEARCH PARTICIPATION. GUIDE FOR PREPARATION OF PROPOSALS AND PROJECT OPERATION (US) [06586655] **1851**

UNDERGRADUATE TEXTS IN MATHEMATICS (US/0172-6056) [08498500] **3540**

UNDERGROUND AND ALTERNATIVE PRESS IN BRITAIN, THE (UK) [04402008] **2925**

UNDERGROUND EVANGELISM MAGAZINE (US/0097-6784) [01799143] **5006**

UNDERGROUND GRAMMARIAN, THE *SUSPENDED.* (US) [05852525] **1788**

UNDERGROUND SHOPPER. NEW YORK CITY, THE (US/0191-3549) [04853302] **2793**

UNDERGROUND STORAGE OF NATURAL GAS BY INTERSTATE PIPELINE COMPANIES (US/0193-5658) [03170276] **4281**

UNDERGROUND STORAGE TANK GUIDE (US/1055-4246) [21457458] **1929**

UNDERGROUND TANK TECHNOLOGY UPDATE (US) **2000**

UNDERGROUND WINE JOURNAL, THE (US/1047-6865) [19675782] **2371**

UNDERHILL SOCIETY OF AMERICA *See* BULLETIN - UNDERHILL SOCIETY OF AMERICA **2725**

UNDERLINE (US/0276-0398) [07302511] **310**

●UNDERSEA & HYPERBARIC MEDICINE (US/1066-2936) [26915585] **3697**

UNDERSEA BIOMEDICAL RESEARCH (US/0093-5387) [02068005] **3697**

UNDERSEA JOURNAL, THE (US/0740-1930) [05967265] 4927, **4855**

UNDERSTANDING FINANCIAL STATEMENTS (US/0147-4774) [03172182] **752**

UNDERSTANDING FINANCIAL SUPPORT OF PUBLIC SCHOOLS (US/0362-3610) [02367249] **1873**

UNDERSTANDING HEALTH (US/0278-6435) [07853515] **4805**

UNDERSTANDING JAPAN (JA/0041-6576) [02129506] **2509**

●UNDERSTANDING JAPAN (DENVER, COLO.) (US/1070-5198) [26328718] **2667**

UNDERSTANDING OUR GIFTED (US/1040-1350) [18333074] **1886**

UNDERSTANDING PEOPLE (US) **4621**

UNDERSTANDING TAXES. FARM SUPPLEMENT ... EDITION (US) [02629742] **4757**

UNDERVISNINGSSTATISTIKK : AVSLUTTET UTDANNING (NO) [01786999] 1788, **1798**

UNDERWATER AND HYPERBARIC MEDICINE (US) [17192810] **3648**

UNDERWATER DEFENSE LETTER *See* UNDERWATER LETTER, THE **1458**

UNDERWATER LETTER, THE (US/0041-6592) [13872797] 5541, **1458**

UNDERWATER MEDICINE AND RELATED SCIENCES (US/0191-2534) [04797921] **3648**

●UNDERWATER NEWS & TECHNOLOGY (US/1069-6547) [28130426] **1458**

UNDERWATER USA (US/0749-1794) [11104151] **4927**

UNDERWATER WORLD (MARCH 1982) *See* DIVER **4893**

UNDERWOOD ANNALS (US/0099-1473) [02242083] **2476**

UNDERWOOD NEWS, THE (US/8750-7285) [11698447] **5726**

UNDERWRITER ALERT (US/1062-6441) [25690729] **2895**

UNDERWRITERS' HANDBOOK (US) **2895**

UNDERWRITERS' LABORATORIES OF CANADA *See* LIST OF EQUIPMENT AND MATERIALS **619**

UNDERWRITERS' LABORATORIES OF CANADA *See* U L C NEWS (EDITION FRANCAISE) **4033**

UNDERWRITERS' LABORATORIES OF CANADA *See* GUIDES OF UNDERWRITERS' LABORATORIES OF CANADA **2881**

UNDERWRITERS' REPORT (US/0041-6622) [05092656] **2895**

UNDERWRITING : TECHNICAL DIRECTION FOR PROJECT MORTGAGE INSURANCE (US) [03116443] **2895**

●UNDISCOVERED COUNTRIES JOURNAL (US/1068-3267) [27648263] **3449**

UNDOC: CURRENT INDEX. UNITED NATIONS DOCUMENTS INDEX (US/0250-5584) [05587478] **4503**

UNDP BUSINESS BULLETIN (US/0379-1645) [01874019] **1525**

UNDRO NEWS (SZ/0250-9377) [06498708] **2912**

UNDRO NEWS *See* DHA UNDRO NEWS / UNITED NATIONS, DEPT. OF HUMANITARIAN AFFAIRS **4519**

UNDZER SHTIME (IS) [08518282] **4692**

UNDZER VEG (TORONTO) *CEASED.* (CN/0382-0610) [01796795] **2274**

UNE (SP) [07980911] **4033**

UNEMPLOYMENT INSURANCE PREMIUM TABLES ... PROVINCE OF QUEBEC (CN/0713-1771) [08741215] **2895**

Alphabetical Title Index — UNION

UNEMPLOYMENT INSURANCE QUALITY APPRAISAL RESULTS (US/8756-9892) [10494019] **2895**

UNEMPLOYMENT INSURANCE STATISTICS. ANNUAL SUPPLEMENT (OTTAWA) (CN/0828-3176) [134€1272] **2895**

UNEMPLOYMENT INSURANCE STATISTICS (OTTAWA) (CN/0829-1098) [13460937] 1715, **2895**

UNEP, ASIA-PACIFIC REPORT (TH) [17590698] **2182**

UNEP-ASIA REPORT (TH) [07192032] **2245**

UNEP ENVIRONMENTAL MANAGEMENT GUIDELINES (KE/1014-949X) [17168688] **2208**

UNEP REGIONAL SEAS REPORTS AND STUDIES (SZ/1014-8647) [I10148647] **1458**

UNESCO *See* UNESCO TECHNICAL PAPERS IN MARINE SCIENCE **1458**

UNESCO *See* COPYRIGHT LAWS AND TREATIES OF THE WORLD **1303**

UNESCO *See* CATALOGUE OF UNESCO PUBLICATIONS **413**

UNESCO *See* CATALOGUE DES PUBLICATIONS UNESCO **412**

UNESCO *See* REPORT OF THE DIRECTOR GENERAL ON THE ACTIVITIES OF THE ORGANIZATION IN ... **5236**

UNESCO *See* UNESCO LIST OF DOCUMENTS AND PUBLICATIONS **426**

UNESCO *See* MONOGRAPHS ON EDUCATION **1765**

UNESCO *See* CORREO, EL **2845**

UNESCO *See* LITERACY **1881**

UNESCO ADULT EDUCATION INFORMATION NOTES (FR/0376-4907) [03067987] **1802**

UNESCO AUSTRALIA / AUSTRALIAN NATIONAL COMMISSION FOR UNESCO (AT/1033-1891) [20785141] 2671, **3137**

UNESCO BULLETIN (NP) [05218398] **3137**

UNESCO COURIER, THE (FR/0041-5278) [19993541] **2856**

UNESCO. EDUCATION SECTOR. DOCUMENTATION AND COMPUTER-ASSISTED MANAGEMENT SERVICE *See* CATALOGUE OF DOCUMENTS AND PUBLICATIONS / EDUCATION SECTOR, DOCUMENTATION AND COMPUTER-ASSISTED MANAGEMENT SERVICE **1173**

UNESCO FEATURES (FR) [01470255] **5237**

UNESCO. GENERAL CONFERENCE *See* RECORDS OF THE GENERAL CONFERENCE OF THE UNITED NATIONS EDUCATIONAL, SCIENTIFIC AND CULTURAL ORGANIZATION **5235**

UNESCO. GENERAL INFORMATION PROGRAMME *See* GENERAL INFORMATION PROGRAMME. UNISIST NEWSLETTER **5107**

UNESCO KOERIER (BE/0304-3169) [I03043169] 2632, **332**

UNESCO LIST OF DOCUMENTS AND PUBLICATIONS (FR/0377-631X) [02147771] **426**

UNESCO. PRINCIPAL REGIONAL OFFICE FOR ASIA AND THE PACIFIC. LIBRARY *See* LIBRARY ACCESSIONS LIST / UNESCO PRINCIPAL REGIONAL OFFICE FOR ASIA AND THE PACIFIC **3223**

UNESCO PRIZE FOR PEACE EDUCATION (FR) [08864800] **4537**

UNESCO. REGIONAL OFFICE OF SCIENCE AND TECHNOLOGY FOR AFRICA. OFFICE OF SCIENCE AND TECHNOLOGY FOR AFRICA *See* BULLETIN OF THE UNESCO REGIONAL OFFICE OF SCIENCE AND TECHNOLOGY FOR AFRICA **5091**

UNESCO REPORTS IN MARINE SCIENCE (FR) [05272685] 558, **1458**

UNESCO SOURCES (FR) [19968245] **1929**

UNESCO TECHNICAL PAPERS IN MARINE SCIENCE (FR/0503-4299) [01779110] **1458**

UNESCO WORLD REVIEW (FR) [01470319] **2632**

UNFAIR DISMISSAL (UK) [19538353] **1715**

UNFALLCHIRURG, DER (GW/0177-5537) [11776707] **3725**

UNFALLCHIRURGIE (GW/0340-2649) [05730429] **3977**

UNFALLVERHUTUNGSBERICHT STRASSENVERKEHR : BERICHT DES BUNDESMINISTERS FUER VERKEHR UBER MASSNAHMEN AUF DEM GEBIET DER UNFALLVERHUTUNG IM STRASSENVERKEHR (GW/0722-8333) [11080623] **5398**

UNFILLED JOB OPENINGS (US) [03801368] **1715**

UNGARISCHE WIRTSCHAFTSHEFTE (HU/0237-1545) [I02371545] **937**

UNGDOMSSKOLEN (DENMARK. UNDERVISNINGSMINISTERIET. KONOMISK--STATISTISK KONTOR) (DK/0903-6296) [19482294] **1788**

UNGI RAPPORT (SW) [05279580] **2578**

UNGYONG MULLI (KO/1013-7009) [I10137009] **4424**

UNHAENGGYE (KO) [05156460] **815**

UNHCR INFORMATION (SZ/0251-6497) [I02516497] **1921**

UNI HANNOVER (GW/0171-2268) [07053446] **1851**

UNIBODY & CHASSIS, DIMENSION & SPECIFICATION CHARTS. DOMESTIC CARS & TRUCKS (US) [20161719] **5427**

UNIBODY & CHASSIS, DIMENSION & SPECIFICATION CHARTS. IMPORT CARS & TRUCKS (US) [19341026] **5427**

UNICAMERAL UPDATE (US/1063-0813) [05299979] **4692**

UNICE *See* UNICE INFORMATION **1715**

● UNICE INFORMATION (BE) [26676567] **1715**

UNICEF *See* ANNUAL REPORT / UNICEF **3123**

UNICEF HISTORY SERIES (SZ) [15323712] **5313**

UN'CIV REPORT (AT) [20316301] **2033**

UNICO (BL) [01798091] **717**

UNICORN (CARLTON, TAS.) (AT/0311-4775) [17503173] **1788**

UNICORN TIMES (US/0192-0375) [05002250] **2548**

UNIDAD DE PROMOCION VOLUNTARIA DEL IMSS : REVISTA (MX) [06064551] 4805, **5313**

UNIDAD INDIGENA (CK/0121-2354) [I01212354] **247**

UNIDADES OPERACIONAIS: ENDERECOS (BL) [01790909] **5313**

UNIDEX QUARTERLY (US) **815**

UNIDEX REPORTS (US) **815**

UNIDIR NEWSLETTER / UNITED NATIONS INSTITUTE FOR DISARMAMENT RESEARCH (SZ/1012-4934) [18485497] 4537, **4059**

UNIDO MONOGRAPHS ON INDUSTRIAL DEVELOPMENT (US/0082-8262) [01591830] **1641**

UNIDO NEWSLETTER (AU/0049-5387) [02325575] **1630**

● UNIDOS : JOURNAL OF OPPORTUNITY (US) 5567, **717**

UNIE GOODWOOD, DIE (SA/0259-5591) [I02595591] **1908**

UNIFICATION NEWS (US/1061-0871) [09046492] **5006**

UNIFIED ISSUANCES SYSTEM (US) [02932889] **2837**

UNIFIED SCHOOL DISTRICT WEALTH (US) [04391475] **1873**

UNIFIED WORK PROGRAM (US/0361-9079) [02441357] **5398**

UNIFORM BUILDING CODE (US) [02723175] **630**

UNIFORM BUILDING CODE STANDARDS (US/0896-9663) [07295934] **630**

UNIFORM COMMERCIAL CODE LAW JOURNAL (US/0041-672X) [01608148] **3104**

UNIFORM COMMERCIAL CODE LAW LETTER, THE (US/0503-1966) [03469049] **3067**

UNIFORM COMMERCIAL CODE REPORTING SERVICE (US/0501-1183) [06868490] **3067**

UNIFORM CPA EXAMINATION. QUESTIONS AND UNOFFICIAL ANSWERS (US/0742-6216) [01480030] **752**

UNIFORM CRIME REPORT ARREST INFORMATION RELATING TO SUBSTANCE ABUSE IN SOUTH CAROLINA (US) [11429272] **3178**

UNIFORM CRIME REPORT FOR THE STATE OF MICHIGAN (US/0360-9146) [02244582] 3178, **3084**

UNIFORM CRIME REPORTING (US) [05658956] **3178**

UNIFORM CRIME REPORTS (US) [03457182] **3178**

UNIFORM CRIME REPORTS, COMMONWEALTH OF PENNSYLVANIA (US/0095-5752) [01798191] 3178, **3084**

UNIFORM CRIME REPORTS FOR THE UNITED STATES (US/0082-7592) [02165904] **3084**

UNIFORM CRIME REPORTS, STATE OF FLORIDA. LAW ENFORCEMENET OFFICERS KILLED AND ASSAULTED, ANNUAL REPORT (US) [19789835] **3178**

UNIFORM CRIME REPORTS, STATE OF FLORIDA. LAW ENFORCEMENT EMPLOYEE DATA ANNUAL REPORT / COMPILED BY THE FLORIDA DEPARTMENT OF LAW ENFORCEMENT (US) [19794597] **3178**

UNIFORM CRIME REPORTS, STATE OF NEW JERSEY (US/0548-5851) [01641471] 3178, **3084**

UNIFORM FINAL EXAMINATION REPORT / THE INSTITUTES OF CHARTERED ACCOUNTANTS IN CANADA AND BERMUDA (CN/0713-357X) [08723570] **752**

UNIFORM FIRE CODE (US/0896-9736) [04680423] **2293**

UNIFORM FIRE CODE STANDARDS (US/0896-9744) [05810379] **2293**

UNIFORM HOUSING CODE (US/0501-1213) [05701007] 2837, **631**

UNIFORM LAW CONFERENCE OF CANADA. MEETING *See* PROCEEDINGS OF THE ... ANNUAL MEETING / UNIFORM LAW CONFERENCE OF CANADA **3031**

UNIFORM MECHANICAL CODE (US/0896-9671) [04680501] **631**

UNIFORM PLUMBING CODE (US/0733-2335) [04128086] **2608**

UNIFORM PRACTICES FOR THE CLEARANCE AND SETTLEMENT OF MORTGAGE-BACKED SECURITIES (US) **815**

UNIFORM SIGN CODE (US/0896-9701) [07296105] **631**

UNIFORM SYSTEM OF ACCOUNTS PRESCRIBED FOR NATURAL GAS COMPANIES (US) [01243288] **4281**

UNIFORM ZONING CODE (US/1060-4014) [24987200] **631**

UNIFORMED SERVICES ALMANAC (US/0503-1982) [02535681] **4059**

UNIFORMED SERVICES MEDICAL/DENTAL FACILITIES IN THE U.S.A (US) [08014008] **3648**

UNIFORMED SERVICES UNIVERSITY OF THE HEALTH SCIENCES *See* GRADUATE EDUCATION BULLETIN **3579**

UNIFORMES (FR) **2632**

UNIFORMES MILITARES ESPANOLES (SP) **4059**

UNIFORUM PRODUCTS DIRECTORY *See* OPEN SYSTEMS PRODUCTS DIRECTORY **1198**

UNIFUHRER / ALLGEMEINER STUDENTENAUSSCHUSS DER UNIVERSITAT KOLN (GW) [10407282] **1851**

UNIGEO - SBORNIK PRACI (XR) **5167**

UNIGRAM. X (UK/0952-3359) [I09523359] **1249**

UNILET INFORMATIONS / UNION NATIONALE INTERPROFESSIONNELLE DES LEGUMES TRANFORMES (FR) [23105096] 2360, **143**

UNILETRAS (BL/0101-8698) [I01018698] **3449**

UNILETRAS : REVISTA DO DEPARTAMENTO DE LETRAS DA UEPG (BL) [10270837] 3330, **3449**

UNILIT (SECUNDERABAD) (II/0041-6762) [01696179] **3449**

UNIMA CANADA *See* UNIMA CANADA **389**

UNIMA CANADA *See* UNIMA CANADA NOUVELLES **389**

UNIMA CANADA *CEASED*. (CN/0708-5745) [05584995] **389**

UNIMA CANADA NOUVELLES (CN/0380-3252) [02443181] **389**

UNIMA INFORMATIONS (FR) [09703566] **389**

UNIMETRO : ORGANO DE INFORMACION E INVESTIGACION (CK/0120-7504) [23968234] **3648**

UNION (1987), THE (US/1050-7906) [21613794] **5641**

UNION ADVOCATE (US/8750-1562) [01767972] **5699**

UNION BANNER (US) [25278798] **5662**

UNION CANADIENNE DES RELIGIEUSES CONTEMPLATIVES *See* BOTTIN / UNION CANADIENNE DES RELIGIEUSES CONTEMPLATIVES **4940**

UNION CATALOG OF MAPS (BERKELEY) (US/0094-4033) [01794313] **2578**

UNION CITY DAILY MESSENGER *See* DAILY MESSENGER (UNION CITY, TENN.) **5745**

UNION CONTRACT EXPIRATIONS IN THE NORTH CENTRAL REGION 5 (US/0362-4188) [02359700] **1716**

UNION COUNTY ADVOCATE (MORGANFIELD, KY.) (US) [14106494] **5683**

UNION COUNTY LEADER, THE (US) [15270622] **5713**

UNION Alphabetical Title Index

UNION (CRANFORD) (US/0098-9525) [02242836] **2548**

UNION DAILY TIMES, THE (US) [13088988] **5743**

UNION DE PRODUCTEURS AGRICOLES *See* ORIENTATIONS ET POLITIQUES DE L'U P A **117**

UNION DEMOCRACY REVIEW (US) [01645880] **1716**

UNION DEMOCRAT, THE (US) [28541808] **5641**

UNION DES ARTISTES *See* BULLETIN DE L'UNION DES ARTISTES, LE **1656**

UNION DES ARTISTES *See* REPERTOIRE DES MEMBRES DE L'UNION DES ARTISTES **388**

UNION DES ARTISTES *See* UNION EXPRESS, L' **1716**

UNION DES CAISSES CENTRALES DE LA MUTUALITE AGRICOLE *See* MUTUALITE SOCIALE AGRICOLE, STATISTIQUES, LA **5297**

UNION DES ECRIVAINES ET ECRIVAINS QUEBECOIS *See* ANNUAIRE - UNION DES ECRIVAINES ET ECRIVAINS QUEBECOIS **2917**

UNION DES ECRIVAINS QUEBECOIS (CN/0709-9118) [08036643] **1716**

UNION DES MUNICIPALITES DE LA PROVINCE DE QUEBEC *See* BULLETIN D'INFORMATION - UNION DES MUNICIPALITES DE LA PROVINCE DE QUEBEC **4634**

UNION DES MUNICIPALITES REGIONALES DE COMTE ET DES MUNICIPALITES LOCALES DU QUEBEC *See* INFORMATION U.M.R.C **4656**

UNION DES PRODUCTEURS AGRICOLES *See* UNION DES PRODUCTEURS AGRICOLES **1716**

UNION DES PRODUCTEURS AGRICOLES (CN/0317-2279) [02248024] 143, **1716**

UNION ECONOMIQUE, L' (MG) [01786403] **1587**

UNION EXPRESS, L' (CN/0715-6359) [09590484] **1716**

UNION FOR THE COORDINATION OF THE PRODUCTION AND TRANSPORT OF ELECTRIC POWER *See* RAPPORT ANNUEL - UNION POUR LA COORDINATION DE LA PRODUCTION ET DU TRANSPORT DE L'ELECTRICITE **2078**

UNION GENERAL DE TRABAJADORES DE ESPANA *See* U.G.T. : BOLETIN DE LA UNION GENERAL DE TRABAJADORES DE ESPANA **1715**

UNION (GRASS VALLEY-NEVADA CITY, CALIF.) (US) [15340619] **5641**

UNION INTERNATIONALE DES MARIONETTES *See* UNIMA INFORMATIONS **389**

UNION ISSUES (AT/1033-2391) [I10332391] **1716**

UNION, L' (HT) [28397061] **5802**

UNION, L' (GO) [03759576] **5801**

UNION LABOR ADVOCATE. DEVOTED TO THE INTEREST OF ALL UNION LABOR AND LABELS (US) [01473365] **1716**

UNION LABOR JOURNAL (US/0894-7775) [11216116] **1716**

UNION LABOR NEWS (MADISON, WIS.) (US/0041-6924) [01513121] **1716**

UNION LABOR REPORT (US/0091-5459) [01786751] **3155**

UNION LABOR REPORT WEEKLY NEWSLETTER (US/0190-5260) [04725498] **3155**

UNION LEADER (US/0161-9292) [04067339] **2548**

UNION LEADER (MANCHESTER, N.H. : STATE EDITION), THE (US) [08597404] **5709**

UNION LIST OF LEGAL PERIODICALS, DISTRICT OF COLUMBIA AREA (US) [01643052] **3067**

UNION LIST OF LEGISLATIVE HISTORIES (US) [01645861] **3084**

UNION LIST OF PERIODICALS / CASLIS, CALGARY CHAPTER (CN/0822-1685) [10935376] **3254**

UNION LIST OF PERIODICALS IN EUROPEAN BUSINESS SCHOOLS (UK) [04851617] **426**

UNION LIST OF PERIODICALS - TORONTO HEALTH LIBRARIES ASSOCIATION (CN/1187-7723) [25796392] **426**

UNION LIST OF SCIENTIFIC SERIALS IN CANADIAN LIBRARIES (CN/0082-7657) [03473030] **5176**

UNION LIST OF SERIALS IN MONTREAL HOSPITAL LIBRARIES (CN/0316-5043) [02247198] **426**

UNION LIST OF SERIALS IN THE SOCIAL SCIENCES AND HUMANITIES HELD BY CANADIAN LIBRARIES (CN/0227-3187) [08871399] **5228**

UNION MATEMATICA ARGENTINA *See* REVISTA DE LA UNION MATEMATICA ARGENTINA (1968) **3531**

UNION MEDICALE BALKANIQUE *See* ARCHIVES **3552**

UNION MEDICALE DU CANADA (CN/0041-6959) [01767980] **3648**

UNION NATIONALE DES ASSOCIATIONS DE PARENTS D'ENFANTS INADAPTES *See* CAHIERS DE L'EUROPE PARIS **5276**

UNION NATIONALE (PARTI POLITIQUE) *See* TEMPS DE L'UNION NATIONALE, LE **4498**

UNION-NEWS (US) [23434909] **5690**

UNION OF SOCIALIST GEOGRAPHERS *See* U.S.G. NEWSLETTER **2578**

UNION OF THE CAPITALS OF THE EUROPEAN COMMUNITY *See* EUROPA DES CAPITALES **2822**

UNION PARIS. 1972 (FR/0750-3555) [I07503555] **717**

UNION POSTALE (SZ) [03157938] **1147**

UNION PRESS-COURIER (US) [15133261] **5740**

UNION RECORDER (US) [20300854] **5655**

UNION RECORDER (AT/0041-7017) [04175586] **1096**

UNION RECORDER, THE (AT) [06473711] **1096**

UNION REGISTER, THE (US/0274-970X) [06517460] **2405**

UNION REPORTER (DIAMOND BAR, CALIF.) (US/0744-9658) [05467987] **1716**

UNION ROUTIERE DE FRANCE *See* CIRCULATION ROUTIERE: FAITS ET CHIFFRES, LA **5439**

UNION SENEGALAISE DE BANQUE POUR LE COMMERCE ET L'INDUSTRIE *See* RAPPORT DU CONSEIL D'ADMINISTRATION, BILAN, RESOLUTIONS DE L'ASSEMBLEE GENERALE ORDINAIRE / UNION SENEGALAISE DE BANQUE POUR LE COMMERCE ET L'INDUSTRIE **1515**

UNION SPRINGS HERALD (US) [10993099] **5628**

UNION-SUN AND JOURNAL (US/0747-3788) [10790598] **5721**

UNION TEILT MIT (SZ) [08179086] **2524**

UNION, THE (US) [27732634] **5641**

UNION-TRIBUNE'S REVIEW OF SAN DIEGO BUSINESS, THE (US) [10962663] **717**

UNION WAGES AND HOURS : GROCERY STORES (US/0093-0784) [01786603] **1716**

UNION WOMAN *SUSPENDED.* (CN/0707-0063) [04590159] 5567, **1716**

UNION WRITES NEWSLETTER (US/0748-6839) [11001814] **1716**

UNIONE DEGLI INDUSTRIALI DELLA PROVINCIA DI TORINO *See* NOTIZIARIO GIURIDICO REGIONALE **3019**

UNIONE SARDA, L' (IT) **5805**

UNIONIST, THE (BB) [05395638] **1716**

UNIPUB *See* UNIPUB BULLETIN **2494**

UNIPUB BULLETIN (US) [06358725] **2494**

UNIQUE 3-IN-1 RESEARCH & DEVELOPMENT DIRECTORY (US/0080-1461) [01868656] **5167**

UNIQUE (EAST HANOVER, N.J.) *CEASED.* (US/0736-4083) [09121159] 1273, **1244**

UNIQUE HOMES (US/0747-7465) [08780691] **310**

UNIQUE OPPORTUNITIES (US/1059-6100) [24647512] **3793**

UNIREA. ALMANAC. CALENDARUL. UNIREA (US) [05533772] **5037**

UNISA ENGLISH STUDIES (SA/0041-5359) [02452184] **3449**

UNISA PSYCHOLOGIA (SA) [05854323] **4621**

UNISCOPE (HULL) (CN/0847-4109) [22378739] **1851**

UNISPHERE (US/0279-1579) [07598014] 1262, **1249**

UNISSON (CN/0229-4397) [08360291] **1873**

UNISURV REPORT S (AT) [05123104] 2000, **1361**

UNISYS WORLD (US/0892-2845) [15145738] **1206**

UNISYS WORLD. EUROPE *CEASED.* (US/0895-0334) [16414166] **1239**

UNISYS WORLD OPEN SYSTEMS NEWS (US/1059-9967) [24841890] **1206**

UNIT COST ANALYSIS IN THE PUBLIC COMMUNITY COLLEGES OF ILLINOIS *See* FY ... UNIT COST REPORT FOR THE PUBLIC COMMUNITY COLLEGES OF ILLINOIS **1825**

UNIT INVESTMENT TRUSTS DISTRIBUTIONS (US/0747-5713) [10742606] **918**

UNIT PICTURE COLLECTIONS AND ART PRINTS (US) [01328414] **367**

UNITA (MICROFICHE), L' (IT) [04287657] **5805**

UNITARIAN HISTORICAL SOCIETY, LONDON *See* TRANSACTIONS OF THE UNITARIAN HISTORICAL SOCIETY **5068**

UNITARIAN QUEST (AT) [02514708] **1071**

UNITARIAN SERVICE COMMITTEE OF CANADA *See* USC COUNTRY PROFILE. SWAZILAND **2912**

UNITARIAN SERVICE COMMITTEE OF CANADA *See* USC COUNTRY PROFILE. NEPAL **2912**

UNITARIAN SERVICE COMMITTEE OF CANADA *See* USC COUNTRY PROFILE. MALI **2912**

UNITARIAN SERVICE COMMITTEE OF CANADA *See* USC COUNTRY PROFILE. INDONESIA **2912**

UNITARIAN SERVICE COMMITTEE OF CANADA *See* USC COUNTRY PROFILE. LESOTHO **2912**

UNITARIAN UNIVERSALISM (US/0882-4029) [11826567] **5068**

UNITARIAN UNIVERSALIST ASSOCIATION *See* DIRECTORY (UNITARIAN UNIVERSALIST ASSOCIATION : 1965) **5059**

UNITARIAN UNIVERSALIST ASSOCIATION. MASSACHUSETTS BAY DISTRICT *See* NEWSLETTER - MASSACHUSETTS BAY DISTRICT, UNITARIAN UNIVERSALIST CHURCHES **4981**

UNITARIAN UNIVERSALIST CHRISTIAN, THE (US/0362-0492) [01953024] **5068**

UNITARIAN UNIVERSALIST PSI SYMPOSIUM : NEWSLETTER (US) [09841933] **4243**

UNITAS FRATRUM (GW/0344-9254) [04582800] **5068**

UNITAS (MANILA) (PH/0041-7149) [01774163] **1096**

UNITE CHRETIENNE (FR) [03831111] **5006**

UNITE DES CHRETIENS (FR) **5006**

UNITE PROLETARIENNE (CN/0707-7696) [05018401] **4548**

UNITED & BABSON INVESTMENT REPORT (US/0895-5689) [15050025] **918**

UNITED ARAB EMIRATES. MAJLIS AL-NAQD *See* BULLETIN - UNITED ARAB EMIRATES CURRENCY BOARD **1549**

UNITED ARAB EMIRATES. MAJLIS AL-NAQD *See* AL-TAQRIR AL-SANAWI - MAJLIS AL-NAQD **769**

UNITED ARAB REPUBLIC JOURNAL OF PHYSICS *See* EGYPTIAN JOURNAL OF PHYSICS **4402**

UNITED ASIA (BOMBAY) (II/0041-7173) [01774164] **2667**

UNITED ASSOCIATION OF JOURNEYMEN AND APPRENTICES OF THE PLUMBING AND PIPE FITTING INDUSTRY *See* JOURNAL - UNITED ASSOCIATION OF JOURNEYMEN AND APPRENTICES OF THE PLUMBING AND PIPE FITTING INDUSTRY **1682**

UNITED BAPTIST CONVENTION OF THE ATLANTIC PROVINCES *See* YEAR BOOK OF THE UNITED BAPTIST CONVENTION OF THE ATLANTIC PROVINCES **5069**

UNITED BIBLE SOCIETIES *See* BULLETIN - UNITED BIBLE SOCIETIES **5015**

UNITED CAPRINE NEWS (US/0164-9353) [04116692] **223**

UNITED CHURCH BOARD FOR WORLD MINISTRIES *See* ANNUAL REPORT - UNITED CHURCH BOARD FOR WORLD MINISTRIES **4935**

UNITED CHURCH BOARD FOR WORLD MINISTRIES *See* FINANCIAL STATEMENTS AND SCHEDULES : (WITH ACCOUNTANTS' REPORT THEREON) / UNITED CHURCH BOARD FOR WORLD MINISTRIES **4959**

UNITED CHURCH NEWS (NATIONAL EDITION) (US/0882-7214) [11986005] 5068, **5731**

UNITED CHURCH OBSERVER, THE (CN/0041-7238) [01776736] **5006**

UNITED CHURCH OF CANADA *See* YEAR BOOK AND DIRECTORY - UNITED CHURCH OF CANADA **5010**

UNITED CHURCH OF CANADA. GENERAL COUNCIL *See* RECORD OF PROCEEDINGS - GENERAL COUNCIL. UNITED CHURCH OF CANADA **5066**

UNITED CHURCH OF CHRIST *See* PENSION BOARDS **5065**

UNITED CHURCH OF CHRIST. GENERAL SYNOD *See* MINUTES / THE ... GENERAL SYNOD OF THE UNITED CHURCH OF CHRIST **5064**

UNITED DAILY NEWS (CH) [01768005] **5799**

Alphabetical Title Index — UNITED

UNITED DAUGHTERS OF THE CONFEDERACY MAGAZINE (US) [01768006] **2764**

UNITED EVANGELICAL (US/0041-7262) [03953362] **5040**

UNITED EVANGELICAL ACTION *CEASED.* (US/0041-7270) [01768007] **5006**

UNITED FLY TYERS' ROUNDTABLE (US/0747-9832) [10813926] **2315**

UNITED FOOD AND COMMERCIAL WORKERS UNION. LOCAL 1428 *See* UFCW LOCAL 1428 MESSENGER **1715**

UNITED FREE CHURCH OF SCOTLAND *See* HANDBOOK OF THE UNITED FREE CHURCH OF SCOTLAND, THE **5061**

UNITED FREE CHURCH OF SCOTLAND *See* REPORTS TO THE GENERAL ASSEMBLY OF THE UNITED FREE CHURCH OF SCOTLAND **4992**

UNITED HIAS SERVICE *See* HIAS BULLETIN **1919**

UNITED ISRAEL APPEAL *See* ANNUAL REPORT / UIA, UNITED ISRAEL APPEAL, INC **5273**

UNITED KINGDOM AIRPORTS - ACCOUNTS AND STATISTICS (UK/0260-9967) [22369964] **42**

UNITED KINGDOM ANTARCTIC RESEARCH REPORT (UK/0308-1192) [01786512] **1361**

UNITED KINGDOM ATOMIC ENERGY AUTHORITY NORTHERN DIVISION REPORT (UK/0142-288X) [I0142288X] **1959**

UNITED KINGDOM ATOMIC ENERGY AUTHORITY. PROGRAMME PLANNING GROUP *See* UKAEA UNDERLYING RESEARCH PROGRAMME, ANNUAL REPORT **1959**

UNITED KINGDOM BALANCE OF PAYMENTS (UK) [02052925] **5345**

UNITED KINGDOM GEODESY REPORT (UK) [01787435] **2578**

UNITED KINGDOM INSTITUTE FOR CONSERVATION OF HISTORIC AND ARTISTIC WORKS *See* CONSERVATION NEWS (LONDON) **4087**

UNITED KINGDOM MEAT MARKET REVIEW (UK/0954-5875) [I0954587S] **2360**, **223**

UNITED KINGDOM NATIONAL ACCOUNTS (UK/0267-8691) [11426993] **1525**

UNITED KINGDOM OIL AND GAS (UK/0963-8156) [I09638156] **4757**, **4281**

UNITED KINGDOM REPORT ON ANTARCTIC RESEARCH *See* UNITED KINGDOM ANTARCTIC RESEARCH REPORT **1361**

UNITED KINGDOM, THE COMMONWEALTH OF NATIONS, A DIRECTORY OF GOVERNMENTS, THE (US/0193-4783) [05206383] **4499**

UNITED METHODIST BOARD OF HIGHER EDUCATION AND MINISTRY (U.S.) *See* OCCASIONAL PAPERS - UNITED METHODIST BOARD OF HIGHER EDUCATION AND MINISTRY **1838**

UNITED METHODIST CHRISTIAN ADVOCATE, THE (US/8750-7668) [11271540] **5068**

UNITED METHODIST CHURCH (U.S.). NORTH MISSISSIPPI CONFERENCE *See* JOURNAL OF THE NORTH MISSISSIPPI CONFERENCE OF THE UNITED METHODIST CHURCH ... : SESSION SINCE MERGER OF THE UPPER MISSISSIPPI CONFERENCE (ORGANIZED IN 1891) AND THE NORTH MISSISSIPPI CONFERENCE (ORGANIZED IN 1870) **5062**

UNITED METHODIST CHURCH (UNITED STATES). PROGRAM-CURRICULUM COMMITTEE *See* PROGRAM-CURRICULUM PLANS **5066**

UNITED METHODIST NEWSCOPE, THE (US) [02777452] **5068**

UNITED METHODIST REPORTER (DALLAS, TEX.), THE (US/0737-5581) [08881339] **5068**

UNITED METHODIST RURAL FELLOWSHIP *See* UNITED METHODIST RURAL FELLOWSHIP BULLETIN **5068**

UNITED METHODIST RURAL FELLOWSHIP BULLETIN (US) [06595416] **5068**

UNITED MINE WORKERS JOURNAL (US/0041-7327) [01644288] **1716**

UNITED MINE WORKERS OF AMERICA *See* UNITED MINE WORKERS JOURNAL **1716**

UNITED MINE WORKERS OF AMERICA HEALTH AND RETIREMENT FUNDS *See* BASIC DRUG LIST **4293**

UNITED MUTUAL FUND SELECTOR *CEASED.* (US/0740-557X) [06714256] **918**

UNITED NATIONS *See* YEARBOOK OF THE UNITED NATIONS **3138**

UNITED NATIONS *See* TREATY SERIES - UNITED NATIONS **3137**

UNITED NATIONS *See* UNITED NATIONS JURIDICAL YEARBOOK **3137**

UNITED NATIONS. ADMINISTRATIVE TRIBUNAL *See* JUDGEMENTS OF THE UNITED NATIONS ADMINISTRATIVE TRIBUNAL **3131**

UNITED NATIONS AND SPECIALISED AGENCIES HANDBOOK *See* UNITED NATIONS HANDBOOK **4537**

UNITED NATIONS ASSOCIATION IN CANADA *See* BULLETIN - UNITED NATIONS ASSOCIATION IN CANADA **3125**

UNITED NATIONS CENTRE FOR HUMAN SETTLEMENTS *See* PROJECT INFORMATION REPORT **2832**

UNITED NATIONS CENTRE FOR REGIONAL DEVELOPMENT *See* BULLETIN / UNITED NATIONS CENTRE FOR REGIONAL DEVELOPMENT **2816**

UNITED NATIONS. COMMISSION ON HUMAN SETTLEMENTS *See* REPORT OF THE COMMISSION ON HUMAN SETTLEMENTS **244**

UNITED NATIONS COMMISSION ON INTERNATIONAL TRADE LAW *See* YEARBOOK / UNITED NATIONS COMMISSION ON INTERNATIONAL TRADE LAW **3138**

UNITED NATIONS. COMMISSION ON INTERNATIONAL TRADE LAW *See* REPORT ON THE WORK OF ITS SESSIONS - UNITED NATIONS. COMMISSION ON INTERNATIONAL TRADE LAW **3134**

UNITED NATIONS. COMMISSION ON NARCOTIC DRUGS *See* ANNUAL SUMMARY OF LAWS AND REGULATIONS RELATING TO THE CONTROL OF NARCOTIC DRUGS **3123**

UNITED NATIONS. COMMITTEE OF EXPERTS ON THE TRANSPORT OF DANGEROUS GOODS. (1953-1956) *See* TRANSPORT OF DANGEROUS GOODS **5395**

UNITED NATIONS CONFERENCE ON TRADE AND DEVELOPMENT *See* OPERATION AND EFFECTS OF THE GENERALIZED SYSTEM OF PREFERENCES **848**

UNITED NATIONS CONFERENCE ON TRADE AND DEVELOPMENT *See* HANDBOOK OF INTERNATIONAL TRADE AND DEVELOPMENT STATISTICS **1533**

UNITED NATIONS CONFERENCE ON TRADE AND DEVELOPMENT. TRADE AND DEVELOPMENT BOARD *See* REPORT **850**

UNITED NATIONS. COUNCIL FOR NAMIBIA *See* REPORT - UNITED NATIONS' COUNCIL FOR NAMIBIA **3134**

UNITED NATIONS. DEPARTMENT OF ECONOMIC AND SOCIAL AFFAIRS *See* CASE STUDIES OF ARRANGEMENTS FOR EVALUATION AND UTILIZATION OF POPULATION CENSUS RESULTS; REPORT **4550**

UNITED NATIONS. DEPARTMENT OF ECONOMIC AND SOCIAL AFFAIRS *See* INTERNATIONAL FLOW OF PRIVATE CAPITAL, THE **901**

UNITED NATIONS. DEPARTMENT OF PUBLIC INFORMATION *See* UNITED NATIONS PUBLICATIONS **4692**

UNITED NATIONS. DEPT. OF ECONOMIC AND SOCIAL AFFAIRS *See* TRIENNIAL REPORT ON WATER RESOURCES DEVELOPMENT **5541**

UNITED NATIONS. DEPT. OF ECONOMIC AND SOCIAL AFFAIRS *See* TRAINING FOR SOCIAL WELFARE **5313**

UNITED NATIONS. DEPT. OF ECONOMIC AND SOCIAL AFFAIRS *See* POPULATION STUDIES - UNITED NATIONS **4558**

UNITED NATIONS. DEPT OF POLITICAL AND SECURITY COUNCIL AFFAIRS *See* REPERTOIRE OF THE PRACTICE OF THE SECURITY COUNCIL **3134**

UNITED NATIONS. DEPT. OF PUBLIC INFORMATION *See* BASIC FACTS ABOUT THE UNITED NATIONS **3124**

UNITED NATIONS DEVELOPMENT PROGRAMME *See* COMPENDIUM OF PROJECTS AS OF 31 DECEMBER ... **1633**

UNITED NATIONS DEVELOPMENT PROGRAMME *See* FINANCIAL REPORT AND AUDITED FINANCIAL STATEMENTS FOR THE YEAR ENDED 31 DECEMBER ... AND REPORT OF THE BOARD OF AUDITORS / UNITED NATIONS DEVELOPMENT PROGRAMME **1635**

UNITED NATIONS DEVELOPMENT PROGRAMME *See* UNDP BUSINESS BULLETIN **1525**

UNITED NATIONS DEVELOPMENT PROGRAMME *See* UNITED NATIONS TELEPHONE DIRECTORY. FIJI, FEDERATED STATES OF MICRONESIA, KIRIBATI, MARSHALL ISLANDS, NAURU, SOLOMON ISLANDS, TONGA, TUVALU, VANUATU AND PACIFIC REGIONAL PROGRAMMES **1168**

UNITED NATIONS DISARMAMENT YEARBOOK, THE (US) [03557808] **4537**

UNITED NATIONS. ECONOMIC AND SOCIAL COMMISSION FOR ASIA AND THE PACIFIC *See* ECONOMIC AND SOCIAL SURVEY OF ASIA AND THE PACIFIC **5199**

UNITED NATIONS. ECONOMIC AND SOCIAL COMMISSION FOR ASIA AND THE PACIFIC *See* SMALL INDUSTRY BULLETIN FOR ASIA AND THE PACIFIC **711**

UNITED NATIONS. ECONOMIC AND SOCIAL COMMISSION FOR ASIA AND THE PACIFIC *See* ELECTRIC POWER IN ASIA AND THE PACIFIC **2043**

UNITED NATIONS. ECONOMIC AND SOCIAL COMMISSION FOR ASIA AND THE PACIFIC *See* ANNUAL REPORT - ECONOMIC AND SOCIAL COMMISSION FOR ASIA AND THE PACIFIC **5191**

UNITED NATIONS. ECONOMIC AND SOCIAL COUNCIL *See* OFFICIAL RECORDS - ECONOMIC AND SOCIAL COUNCIL **4530**

UNITED NATIONS. ECONOMIC AND SOCIAL COUNCIL *See* REPORT OF THE ECONOMIC AND SOCIAL COUNCIL FOR THE YEAR ... UNITED NATIONS **5215**

UNITED NATIONS. ECONOMIC AND SOCIAL COUNCIL. POPULATION COMMISSION *See* REPORT OF THE POPULATION COMMISSION / ECONOMIC AND SOCIAL COUNCIL, UNITED NATIONS **4559**

UNITED NATIONS. ECONOMIC AND SOCIAL COUNCIL. STATISTICAL COMMISSION *See* REPORT OF THE STATISTICAL COMMISSION. ECONOMIC AND SOCIAL COUNCIL, UNITED NATIONS **3082**

UNITED NATIONS. ECONOMIC COMMISSION FOR AFRICA *See* ANNUAL REPORT - UNITED NATIONS, ECONOMIC COMMISSION FOR AFRICA **1462**

UNITED NATIONS. ECONOMIC COMMISSION FOR AFRICA *See* BIENNIAL REPORT OF THE EXECUTIVE SECRETARY **1548**

UNITED NATIONS. ECONOMIC COMMISSION FOR AFRICA *See* FOREIGN TRADE STATISTICS FOR AFRICA. SERIES A: DIRECTION OF TRADE. STATISTIQUES AFRICAINES DU COMMERCE EXTERIEUR. SERIE. ECHANGES PAR PAYS **729**

UNITED NATIONS. ECONOMIC COMMISSION FOR AFRICA *See* DEVINDEX AFRICA / UNITED NATIONS, ECONOMIC COMMISSION FOR AFRICA **1479**

UNITED NATIONS. ECONOMIC COMMISSION FOR AFRICA. LIBRARY *See* PERIODICALS RECEIVED IN THE UNECA LIBRARY **422**

UNITED NATIONS. ECONOMIC COMMISSION FOR AFRICA. SOCIAL DEVELOPMENT SECTION *See* DIRECTORY OF REGIONAL SOCIAL WELFARE ACTIVITIES **5283**

UNITED NATIONS. ECONOMIC COMMISSION FOR ASIA AND THE FAR EAST *See* CASE HISTORIES OF OIL AND GAS FIELDS IN ASIA AND THE FAR EAST **4253**

UNITED NATIONS. ECONOMIC COMMISSION FOR ASIA AND THE FAR EAST *See* REGIONAL ECONOMIC CO-OPERATION SERIES **1516**

UNITED NATIONS. ECONOMIC COMMISSION FOR ASIA AND THE FAR EAST *See* MINERAL RESOURCES DEVELOPMENT SERIES **2198**

UNITED NATIONS. ECONOMIC COMMISSION FOR ASIA AND THE FAR EAST. REPORT *See* ANNUAL REPORT - ECONOMIC AND SOCIAL COMMISSION FOR ASIA AND THE PACIFIC **5191**

UNITED NATIONS. ECONOMIC COMMISSION FOR EUROPE *See* ANNUAL BULLETIN OF HOUSING AND BUILDING STATISTICS FOR EUROPE **2839**

UNITED NATIONS. ECONOMIC COMMISSION FOR EUROPE *See* STEEL MARKET IN ..., THE **1640**

UNITED NATIONS. ECONOMIC COMMISSION FOR EUROPE *See* ANNUAL BULLETIN OF ELECTRIC ENERGY STATISTICS FOR EUROPE **2035**

UNITED NATIONS. ECONOMIC COMMISSION FOR EUROPE *See* ANNUAL BULLETIN OF GENERAL ENERGY STATISTICS FOR EUROPE / ECONOMIC COMMISSION FOR EUROPE **1961**

UNITED NATIONS. ECONOMIC COMMISSION FOR EUROPE *See* ANNUAL REVIEW OF THE CHEMICAL INDUSTRY **1598**

UNITED — Alphabetical Title Index

UNITED NATIONS. ECONOMIC COMMISSION FOR EUROPE See ANNUAL BULLETIN OF TRADE IN CHEMICAL PRODUCTS. BULLETIN ANNUEL DU COMMERCE DES PRODUITS CHIMIQUES. EZHEGODNYI BIULLETEN EVROPEISKOI TORGOVLI KHIMICHESKMI PRODUKTAMI **1597**

UNITED NATIONS. ECONOMIC COMMISSION FOR EUROPE See PRICES OF AGRICULTURAL PRODUCTS AND SELECTED INPUTS IN EUROPE AND NORTH AMERICA **121**

UNITED NATIONS. ECONOMIC COMMISSION FOR EUROPE See BULLETIN OF STATISTICS ON WORLD TRADE IN ENGINEERING PRODUCTS **2002**

UNITED NATIONS. ECONOMIC COMMISSION FOR EUROPE See ANNUAL BULLETIN OF STEEL STATISTICS FOR EUROPE **4025**

UNITED NATIONS. ECONOMIC COMMISSION FOR EUROPE See ECONOMIC SURVEY OF EUROPE **1485**

UNITED NATIONS. ECONOMIC COMMISSION FOR EUROPE See ANNUAL BULLETIN OF COAL STATISTICS FOR EUROPE **1961**

UNITED NATIONS. ECONOMIC COMMISSION FOR EUROPE See ANNUAL BULLETIN OF TRANSPORT STATISTICS FOR EUROPE. BULLETIN ANNUEL DE STATISTIQUES DE TRANSPORTS POUR L'EUROPE. EZHEGODNYI BIULLETEN' EVROPEISKOI STATISTIKI TRANSPORTA **5376**

UNITED NATIONS. ECONOMIC COMMISSION FOR EUROPE See HALF-YEARLY BULLETIN OF ELECTRIC ENERGY STATISTICS FOR EUROPE. BULLETIN SEMESTRIEL DE STATISTIQUES DE L'ENERGIE ELECTRIQUE POUR L'EUROPE. POLUGODOVOI BIULLETEN EVROPEISKOI STATISTIKI ELECTROENERGII **1962**

UNITED NATIONS. ECONOMIC COMMISSION FOR EUROPE. ANNUAL BULLETIN OF ELECTRIC ENERGY STATISTICS FOR EUROPE See ANNUAL BULLETIN OF ELECTRIC ENERGY STATISTICS FOR EUROPE AND NORTH AMERICA / BULLETIN ANNUEL DE STATISTIQUES DE L'ENERGIE ELECTRIQUE POUR L'EUROPE ET L'AMERIQUE DU NORD / EZHEGODNYI BIULLETEN' STATISTIKI ELEKTROENERGII DLIA EVROPY I SEVERNOI AMERIKI **2035**

UNITED NATIONS. ECONOMIC COMMISSION FOR LATIN AMERICA See CEPAL REVIEW **1551**

UNITED NATIONS. ECONOMIC COMMISSION FOR LATIN AMERICA See REVISTA DE LA CEPAL **1582**

UNITED NATIONS. ECONOMIC COMMISSION FOR WESTERN ASIA See STUDIES ON DEVELOPMENT PROBLEMS IN COUNTRIES OF WESTERN ASIA **4689**

UNITED NATIONS EDUCATIONAL, SCIENTIFIC AND CULTURAL ORGANIZATION See LIST OF DOCUMENTS AND PUBLICATIONS IN THE FIELD OF MASS COMMUNICATION **1115**

UNITED NATIONS EDUCATIONAL, SCIENTIFIC AND CULTURAL ORGANIZATION. DEPT. OF MASS COMMUNICATIONS See REPORTS AND PAPERS ON MASS COMMUNICATION **1120**

UNITED NATIONS EDUCATIONAL, SCIENTIFIC AND CULTURAL ORGANIZATION. GENERAL CONFERENCE See MANUAL - UNITED NATIONS EDUCATIONAL, SCIENTIFIC AND CULTURAL ORGANIZATION. GENERAL CONFERENCE **5233**

UNITED NATIONS EDUCATIONAL, SCIENTIFIC AND CULTURAL ORGANIZATION. GENERAL CONFERENCE See PROVISIONAL VERBATIM RECORD, PLENARY MEETING **5142**

UNITED NATIONS EDUCATIONAL, SCIENTIFIC AND CULTURAL ORGANIZATION. SOCIAL SCIENCE CLEARING HOUSE See REPORTS AND PAPERS IN THE SOCIAL SCIENCES **5215**

UNITED NATIONS ENVIRONMENT PROGRAMME See EVALUATION REPORT : REPORT OF THE EXECUTIVE DIRECTOR **2193**

UNITED NATIONS. ESTUDIO ECONOMICO DE AMERICA LATINA See ESTUDIO ECONOMICO DE AMERICA LATINA Y EL CARIBE / COMISION ECONOMICA PARA AMERICA LATINA Y EL CARIBE **1489**

UNITED NATIONS. GENERAL ASSEMBLY See RESOLUTIONS AND DECISIONS ADOPTED BY THE GENERAL ASSEMBLY DURING ITS ... SESSION - UNITED NATIONS **3134**

UNITED NATIONS. GENERAL ASSEMBLY. COMMITTEE ON INFORMATION See REPORT OF THE COMMITTEE ON INFORMATION / UNITED NATIONS **4533**

UNITED NATIONS HANDBOOK (NZ/0110-1951) [01799412] **4537**

UNITED NATIONS. INDUSTRIAL DEVELOPMENT ORGANIZATION See UNIDO MONOGRAPHS ON INDUSTRIAL DEVELOPMENT **1641**

UNITED NATIONS INDUSTRIAL DEVELOPMENT ORGANIZATION See DOCUMENTS LIST **4502**

UNITED NATIONS. INTERNATIONAL LAW COMMISSION See YEARBOOK OF THE INTERNATIONAL LAW COMMISSION **3138**

UNITED NATIONS JURIDICAL YEARBOOK (US/0082-8297) [01768110] **3137**

UNITED NATIONS LAW REPORTS (US) [01642111] **3137**

UNITED NATIONS LEGISLATIVE SERIES (US/0082-8300) [01606729] **3137**

UNITED NATIONS LIBRARY (GENEVA, SWITZERLAND) See MONTHLY BIBLIOGRAPHY. PT 1 : BOOKS, OFFICIAL DOCUMENTS, SERIALS **420**

UNITED NATIONS LIBRARY (GENEVA, SWITZERLAND) See LIBRARY NEWS **3226**

UNITED NATIONS LIBRARY (GENEVA, SWITZERLAND) See MONTHLY BIBLIOGRAPHY. PART II, SELECTED ARTICLES / UNITED NATIONS, LIBRARY **4529**

UNITED NATIONS LIST OF NATIONAL PARKS AND PROTECTED AREAS (SZ) [10169676] **2208**

UNITED NATIONS NEWS DIGEST (US) [11872506] **4537**

UNITED NATIONS. OFFICE OF LEGAL AFFAIRS See REPORTS OF INTERNATIONAL ARBITRAL AWARDS - UNITED NATIONS **3134**

UNITED NATIONS. OFFICE OF PUBLIC INFORMATION See INTERNATIONAL COURT OF JUSTICE **3130**

UNITED NATIONS. OFFICE OF THE UNITED NATIONS HIGH COMMISSIONER FOR REFUGEES See VOLUNTARY FUNDS ADMINISTERED BY THE UNITED NATIONS HIGH COMMISSIONER FOR REFUGEES ACCOUNTS, AND REPORT OF THE BOARD OF AUDITORS **3137**

UNITED NATIONS POPULATION FUND (UNFPA) See POPULI / UNITED NATIONS POPULATION FUND **4559**

UNITED NATIONS PUBLICATIONS (US) [01695100] **4692**

UNITED NATIONS RELIEF AND WORKS AGENCY FOR PALESTINE REFUGEES IN THE NEAR EAST See UNRWA : RESUME DU RAPPORT **5313**

UNITED NATIONS RESOLUTIONS ON PALESTINE AND ARAB-ISRAELI CONFLICT (LE) [04163764] **3137**

UNITED NATIONS RESOLUTIONS ON PALESTINE AND THE ARAB-ISRAELI CONFLICT (LE) [07965725] **3137**

UNITED NATIONS RESOLUTIONS. SERIES 2, RESOLUTIONS AND DECISIONS OF THE SECURITY COUNCIL (US/0898-2929) [17780463] **3137**

●UNITED NATIONS RESOLUTIONS.SERIES 3, RESOLUTIONS AND DECISIONS OF THE ECONOMIC AND SOCIAL COUNCIL (US/1051-399X) [21952689] **4537**

UNITED NATIONS REVIEW (AT/0817-9751) [18969540] **4537**

UNITED NATIONS. SECURITY COUNCIL See UNITED NATIONS RESOLUTIONS. SERIES 2, RESOLUTIONS AND DECISIONS OF THE SECURITY COUNCIL **3137**

UNITED NATIONS. SECURITY COUNCIL See OFFICIAL RECORDS. SUPPLEMENT FOR ... / UNITED NATIONS, SECURITY COUNCIL **4530**

UNITED NATIONS SPECIAL FUND See UNITED NATIONS SPECIAL FUND, THE **1587**

UNITED NATIONS SPECIAL FUND, THE (US/0498-0085) [01490081] **1587**

UNITED NATIONS. STATISTICAL OFFICE See POPULATION AND VITAL STATISTICS REPORT (NEW YORK, N.Y.) **4562**

UNITED NATIONS. STATISTICAL OFFICE See STATISTICAL PAPERS - UNITED NATIONS. STATISTICAL OFFICE **3083**

UNITED NATIONS. STATISTICAL OFFICE See SUPPLEMENT TO THE STATISTICAL YEARBOOK AND THE MONTHLY BULLETIN OF STATISTICS **5344**

UNITED NATIONS. STATISTICAL OFFICE See STATISTICAL YEARBOOK / ANNUAIRE STATISTIQUE / DEPARTMENT OF ECONOMIC AND SOCIAL INFORMATION AND POLICY ANALYSIS, STATISTICAL DIVISION **5341**

UNITED NATIONS SYSTEM OF ORGANIZATIONS ... AND DIRECTORY OF SENIOR OFFICIALS (US/1015-2199) [03834738] **3137**

UNITED NATIONS TELEPHONE DIRECTORY. FIJI, FEDERATED STATES OF MICRONESIA, KIRIBATI, MARSHALL ISLANDS, NAURU, SOLOMON ISLANDS, TONGA, TUVALU, VANUATU AND PACIFIC REGIONAL PROGRAMMES (FI) [23156603] **1168**

UNITED NATIONS. TRUSTEESHIP COUNCIL See REPORT OF THE UNITED NATIONS VISITING MISSION TO THE TRUST TERRITORY OF THE PACIFIC ISLANDS **3134**

UNITED NATIONS VOLUNTEERS See UNVNEWS / THE UNITED NATIONS VOLUNTEERS PROGRAMME **2912**

UNITED PLANNING ORGANIZATION See COMMUNITY UPO **2818**

UNITED PLANTERS' ASSOCIATION OF SOUTHERN INDIA. SCIENTIFIC DEPT See BULLETIN - UNITED PLANTERS' ASSOCIATION OF SOUTHERN INDIA, SCIENTIFIC DEPARTMENT **165**

UNITED PLANTING ASSOCIATION OF MALAYSIA See ANNUAL REPORT - UNITED PLANTING ASSOCIATION OF MALAYSIA **61**

UNITED PRESBYTERIAN CHURCH IN THE U.S.A. GENERAL ASSEMBLY See MINUTES - UNITED PRESBYTERIAN CHURCH IN THE U.S.A **5064**

UNITED REFORMED CHURCH See YEAR BOOK - UNITED REFORMED CHURCH **5069**

UNITED REFORMED CHURCH HISTORY SOCIETY See JOURNAL - UNITED REFORMED CHURCH HISTORY SOCIETY **5062**

UNITED RETIREMENT BULLETIN CEASED. (US) [04568019] **5182**

UNITED RUBBER, CORK, LINOLEUM AND PLASTIC WORKERS OF AMERICA See UNITED RUBBER WORKER: URW, THE **5078**

UNITED RUBBER WORKER See UNITED RUBBER WORKER: URW, THE **5078**

UNITED RUBBER WORKER: URW, THE (US/0162-3869) [04160644] **1630**, **5078**

UNITED SENIOR CITIZENS OF ONTARIO See VOICE OF UNITED SENIOR CITIENS OF ONTARIO, INC **5182**

UNITED SENIORS HEALTH REPORT (US/1043-9250) [19604237] **4806**, **5182**

UNITED SOCIETY FOR THE PROPAGATION OF THE GOSPEL ISSUES (UK/0958-2789) **5006**

UNITED SPANISH WAR VETERANS. DEPT. OF MICHIGAN See ANNUAL REPORT AND PROCEEDINGS OF THE ANNUAL ENCAMPMENT (LANSING) **4034**

UNITED SPANISH WAR VETERANS. DEPT. OF MICHIGAN. PROCEEDINGS ... ANNUAL ENCAMPMENT See ANNUAL REPORT AND PROCEEDINGS OF THE ANNUAL ENCAMPMENT (LANSING) **4034**

UNITED STATES See HARMONIZED TARIFF SCHEDULE OF THE UNITED STATES **4730**

UNITED STATES See SMALL BUSINESS ADMINISTRATION AND INVESTMENT ACT WITH AMENDMENTS **711**

UNITED STATES See TREATIES AND OTHER INTERNATIONAL ACTS SERIES **4537**

UNITED STATES See MUTUAL SECURITY PROGRAM FOR FISCAL YEAR 1952-, THE **4052**

UNITED STATES See ENVIRONMENTAL STATUTES **3112**

UNITED STATES See UNITED STATES TREATIES AND OTHER INTERNATIONAL AGREEMENTS **3137**

UNITED STATES See UNITED STATES CODE CONGRESSIONAL AND ADMINISTRATIVE NEWS **4692**

UNITED STATES See LEGISLATIVE STATUS REPORT - UNITED STATES. VETERANS ADMINISTRATION **3002**

UNITED STATES See TITLE 38, UNITED STATES CODE, VETERANS' BENEFITS **4059**

UNITED STATES See PUBLIC LAWS **3033**

UNITED STATES See INTERNAL REVENUE CODE **4732**

UNITED STATES See FEDERAL LABOR LAWS **3148**

UNITED STATES See FEDERAL RESERVE ACT OF 1913, WITH AMENDMENTS AND LAWS RELATING TO BANKING, THE **3086**

UNITED STATES ACHIEVEMENT ACADEMY NATIONAL AWARDS (US/0738-176X) [09471751] **435**

UNITED STATES. ACTION See ACTION NEWS DIGEST **1460**

UNITED STATES. ADJUTANT-GENERAL'S OFFICE. CLUB AND COMMUNITY ACTIVITIES MANAGEMENT DIRECTORATE See ARMY CLUB SYSTEM ANNUAL REPORT, FISCAL YEAR ... **4036**

Alphabetical Title Index

UNITED

UNITED STATES. ADJUTANT-GENERAL'S OFFICE. NONAPPROPRIATED FUND FINANCIAL MANAGEMENT DIRECTORATE See ARMY MORALE, WELFARE, AND RECREATION 4036

UNITED STATES. ADMINISTRATION FOR CHILDREN, YOUTH, AND FAMILIES See CHILD ABUSE AND NEGLECT GRANTS PROGRAM 5277

UNITED STATES. ADMINISTRATION ON AGING See RESEARCH AND DEVELOPMENT PROJECTS IN AGING 5305

UNITED STATES. ADMINISTRATION ON AGING See GUIDELINES FOR PREPARATION OF GRANT APPLICATIONS. RESEARCH AND DEVELOPMENT PROJECTS IN AGING, TITLE IV-B OF THE OLDER AMERICANS ACT 3752

UNITED STATES. ADMINISTRATION ON AGING See INFORMATION STATEMENT FOR APPLICANTS AND GRANTEES MODEL PROJECTS ON AGING 5179

UNITED STATES. ADMINISTRATION ON AGING. DIVISION OF MANPOWER RESOURCES See TRAINING AND MANPOWER DEVELOPMENT ACTIVITIES 5312

UNITED STATES. ADMINISTRATIVE CONFERENCE See NEWS - ADMINISTRATIVE CONFERENCE OF THE UNITED STATES 4669

UNITED STATES. ADVISORY COMMISSION ON INTERGOVERNMENTAL RELATIONS See ANNUAL REPORT - ADVISORY COMMISSION ON INTERGOVERNMENTAL RELATIONS 4626

UNITED STATES ADVISORY COMMITTEE ON FEDERAL PAY See REPORT ON THE FISCAL ... PAY INCREASE UNDER THE FEDERAL STATUTORY PAY SYSTEMS : ANNUAL REPORT OF THE ADVISORY COMMITTEE ON FEDERAL PAY 4682

UNITED STATES. ADVISORY COMMITTEE ON THE LAW OF THE SEA See ANNUAL REPORT - ADVISORY COMMITTEE ON THE LAW OF THE SEA 3180

UNITED STATES. ADVISORY COUNCIL ON HISTORIC PRESERVATION See REPORT - ADVISORY COUNCIL ON HISTORIC PRESERVATION 2757

UNITED STATES. AGENCY FOR INTERNATIONAL DEVELOPMENT See REPORT ON THE HEALTH, POPULATION AND NUTRITION ACTIVITIES OF THE AGENCY FOR INTERNATIONAL DEVELOPMENT, DEPARTMENT OF STATE 2911

UNITED STATES. AGENCY FOR INTERNATIONAL DEVELOPMENT See FOREIGN ASSISTANCE PROGRAM 2909

UNITED STATES. AGENCY FOR INTERNATIONAL DEVELOPMENT See A.I.D. BIBLIOGRAPHY SERIES : DEVELOPMENT ADMINISTRATION 1528

UNITED STATES. AGENCY FOR INTERNATIONAL DEVELOPMENT See SUMMARY OF ONGOING RESEARCH AND TECHNICAL ASSISTANCE PROJECTS IN AGRICULTURE 2912

UNITED STATES. AGENCY FOR INTERNATIONAL DEVELOPMENT. OFFICE OF U.S. FOREIGN DISASTER ASSISTANCE See OFDA ANNUAL REPORT / OFFICE OF U.S. FOREIGN DISASTER ASSISTANCE, AGENCY FOR INTERNATIONAL DEVELOPMENT 2911

UNITED STATES. AGENCY FOR INTERNATIONAL DEVELOPMENT. STATISTICS AND REPORTS DIVISION See GROSS NATIONAL PRODUCT GROWTH RATES AND TREND DATA BY REGION AND COUNTRY 1564

UNITED STATES. AGENCY FOR INTERNATIONAL DEVELOPMENT. STATISTICS AND REPORTS DIVISION See A.I.D. ECONOMIC DATA BOOK, LATIN AMERICA 1459

UNITED STATES. AGENCY FOR INTERNATIONAL DEVELOPMENT. STATISTICS AND REPORTS DIVISION See A.I.D. ECONOMIC DATA BOOK. AFRICA 1459

UNITED STATES. AGENCY FOR INTERNATIONAL DEVELOPMENT. STATISTICS AND REPORTS DIVISION See A.I.D. ECONOMIC DATA BOOK, EAST ASIA 1459

UNITED STATES. AGENCY FOR INTERNATIONAL DEVELOPMENT. STATISTICS AND REPORTS DIVISION See A.I.D. ECONOMIC DATA BOOK, NEAR EAST AND SOUTH ASIA 2913

UNITED STATES. AGRICULTURAL MARKETING SERVICE See POULTRY MARKET STATISTICS 156

UNITED STATES. AGRICULTURAL MARKETING SERVICE See BROILER MARKETING FACTS 922

UNITED STATES. AGRICULTURAL MARKETING SERVICE. COTTON DIVISION. MARKET NEWS SECTION See ESTIMATED GRADE AND STAPLE OF UPLAND COTTON GINNED IN THE UNITED STATES 171

UNITED STATES. AGRICULTURAL MARKETING SERVICE. FRUIT AND VEGETABLE DIVISION See FVUS 89

UNITED STATES. AGRICULTURAL MARKETING SERVICE. LIVESTOCK DIVISION See INSTITUTIONAL MEAT PURCHASE SPECIFICATIONS 213

UNITED STATES. AGRICULTURAL MARKETING SERVICE. TOBACCO DIVISION. TOBACCO STOCKS See TOBACCO STOCKS 917

UNITED STATES. AGRICULTURAL RESEARCH SERVICE See ARS 43 / AGRICULTURAL RESEARCH SERVICE, UNITED STATES DEPARTMENT OF AGRICULTURE 63

UNITED STATES. AGRICULTURAL RESEARCH SERVICE See ARS 41 63

UNITED STATES. AGRICULTURAL RESEARCH SERVICE See ARS-H 63

UNITED STATES. AGRICULTURAL RESEARCH SERVICE See DIRECTORY OF THE AGRICULTURAL RESEARCH SERVICE 79

UNITED STATES. AGRICULTURAL RESEARCH SERVICE See VEGETABLES FOR THE HOT, HUMID TROPICS 144

UNITED STATES. AGRICULTURAL RESEARCH SERVICE See A.R.S. S. AGRICULTURAL RESEARCH SERVICE. SOUTHERN REGION 42

UNITED STATES. AGRICULTURAL RESEARCH SERVICE See ARS DIRECTORY / UNITED STATES DEPARTMENT OF AGRICULTURE, AGRICULTURAL RESEARCH SERVICE 63

UNITED STATES. AGRICULTURAL RESEARCH SERVICE DIRECTORY OF THE AGRICULTURAL RESEARCH SERVICE See ARS DIRECTORY / UNITED STATES DEPARTMENT OF AGRICULTURE, AGRICULTURAL RESEARCH SERVICE 63

UNITED STATES. AGRICULTURAL RESEARCH SERVICE. EASTERN MARKETING AND NUTRITION RESEARCH DIVISION. EMN PUBLICATION See ERRL PUBLICATION 82

UNITED STATES. AGRICULTURAL RESEARCH SERVICE. EASTERN REGIONAL RESEARCH CENTER See PUBLICATIONS AND PATENTS - UNITED STATES. AGRICULTURAL RESEARCH SERVICE. EASTERN REGIONAL RESEARCH CENTER (1981) 1308

UNITED STATES. AGRICULTURAL RESEARCH SERVICE. EASTERN REGIONAL RESEARCH LABORATORY See ERRL PUBLICATION 82

UNITED STATES. AGRICULTURAL RESEARCH SERVICE. EASTERN UTILIZATION RESEARCH AND DEVELOPMENT DIVISION See PUBLICATIONS AND PATENTS OF THE EASTERN UTILIZATION RESEARCH AND DEVELOPMENT DIVISION 123

UNITED STATES. AGRICULTURAL STABILIZATION AND CONSERVATION SERVICE See NEW YORK ANNUAL PROGRAM SUMMARY 112

UNITED STATES. AGRICULTURAL STABILIZATION AND CONSERVATION SERVICE See REPORT OF ACCOMPLISHMENTS, RHODE ISLAND 126

UNITED STATES. AGRICULTURAL STABILIZATION AND CONSERVATION SERVICE. AERIAL PHOTOGRAPHY FIELD OFFICE See COMPREHENSIVE LISTING OF AERIAL PHOTOGRAPHY 2558

UNITED STATES. AID MISSION TO TURKEY. ECONOMIC ANALYSIS STAFF See ECONOMIC AND SOCIAL INDICATORS-TURKEY 1556

UNITED STATES AIR FORCE ACADEMY See ANNUAL BULLETIN - UNITED STATES AIR FORCE ACADEMY 4034

UNITED STATES AIR FORCE ACADEMY JOURNAL OF PROFESSIONAL MILITARY ETHICS (US/0731-2865) [08138741] 2253, 4059

UNITED STATES. AIR FORCE. JUDGE ADVOCATE GENERAL See CIVIL LAW OPINIONS OF THE JUDGE ADVOCATE GENERAL, UNITED STATES AIR FORCE 3089

UNITED STATES. AIR FORCE MATERIALS LABORATORY, DAYTON, OHIO See TECHNICAL REPORT AFML-TR 4058

UNITED STATES. AIR FORCE. OFFICE OF THE DEPUTY FOR COST AND ECONOMICS See UNITED STATES AIR FORCE STATISTICAL DIGEST (ABRIDGED) FISCAL YEAR ... ESTIMATE / PREPARED BY DEPUTY ASSISTANT SECRETARY (COST AND ECONOMICS), ASSISTANT SECRETARY OF THE AIR FORCE (FINANCIAL MANAGEMENT AND COMPTROLLER OF THE AIR FORCE) 4059

UNITED STATES AIR FORCE STATISTICAL DIGEST (ABRIDGED) FISCAL YEAR ... ESTIMATE / PREPARED BY DEPUTY ASSISTANT SECRETARY (COST AND ECONOMICS), ASSISTANT SECRETARY OF THE AIR FORCE (FINANCIAL MANAGEMENT AND COMPTROLLER OF THE AIR FORCE) (US) [22901463] 4757, 4059

UNITED STATES. AIR FORCE. SYSTEMS COMMAND See YEAR IN REVIEW / AIR FORCE SYSTEMS COMMAND, THE 4061

UNITED STATES. AIR FORCE. SYSTEMS COMMAND. COMPTROLLER See ACQUISITION FINANCIAL STATUS / AFSC COMPTROLLER 3

UNITED STATES AIR FORCE YEARBOOK (UK/0956-2828) 4059

UNITED STATES. ALCOHOL, DRUG ABUSE, AND MENTAL HEALTH ADMINISTRATION See REPORT OF THE ADMINISTRATOR / ALCOHOL, DRUG ABUSE, AND MENTAL HEALTH ADMINISTRATION 1348

UNITED STATES. ALCOHOL, DRUG ABUSE, AND MENTAL HEALTH ADMINISTRATION See ADAMHA DATA BOOK 1338

UNITED STATES. ANIMAL AND PLANT HEALTH INSPECTION SERVICE See REPORTED ARTHROPOD-BORNE ENCEPHALITIDES IN HORSES AND OTHER EQUIDAE 5520

UNITED STATES. ANIMAL AND PLANT HEALTH INSPECTION SERVICE See APHIS 91 62

UNITED STATES. ANIMAL AND PLANT HEALTH INSPECTION SERVICE See DEVELOPMENTAL STUDIES AND LABORATORY INVESTIGATIONS CONDUCTED BY VETERINARY SERVICES DIAGNOSTIC LABORATORIES 5508

UNITED STATES. ANIMAL AND PLANT HEALTH INSPECTION SERVICE See APHIS 82 5504

UNITED STATES. ANIMAL AND PLANT HEALTH INSPECTION SERVICE. VETERINARY SERVICES See GUIDE FOR ACCREDITED VETERINARIANS, A 5510

UNITED STATES. ANIMAL AND PLANT HEALTH SERVICE. A GUIDE FOR ACCREDITED VETERINARIANS See GUIDE FOR ACCREDITED VETERINARIANS, A 5510

UNITED STATES ANIMAL HEALTH ASSOCIATION See PROCEEDINGS, ANNUAL MEETING OF THE UNITED STATES ANIMAL HEALTH ASSOCIATION 5519

UNITED STATES. ARCHITECT OF THE CAPITOL See ANNUAL REPORT OF THE ARCHITECT OF THE CAPITOL FOR THE PERIOD ... 287

UNITED STATES. ARMED SERVICES BOARD OF CONTRACT APPEALS See BOARD OF CONTRACT APPEALS DECISIONS 3182

UNITED STATES. ARMS CONTROL AND DISARMAMENT AGENCY See U.S. ARMS CONTROL AND DISARMAMENT AGENCY ANNUAL REPORT 4059

UNITED STATES ARMY AVIATION DIGEST (US) [01606792] 4059, 38

UNITED STATES. ARMY. CORPS OF ENGINEERS See OFFICER AND WARRANT OFFICER DIRECTORY 4053

UNITED STATES. ARMY. CORPS OF ENGINEERS See TRANSPORTATION LINES ON THE MISSISSIPPI RIVER SYSTEM AND THE GULF INTRACOASTAL WATERWAY 5457

UNITED STATES. ARMY. CORPS OF ENGINEERS See REPORT TO CONGRESS ON ADMINISTRATION OF OCEAN DUMPING ACTIVITIES. PUBLIC LAW 92-532, MARINE PROTECTION, RESEARCH, AND SANCTUARIES ACT OF 1972 2242

UNITED STATES. ARMY. CORPS OF ENGINEERS See OFFICIAL DIRECTORY / U.S. ARMY CORPS OF ENGINEERS 4053

UNITED STATES. ARMY. CORPS OF ENGINEERS See TRANSPORTATION LINES ON THE ATLANTIC, GULF, AND PACIFIC COASTS 5457

UNITED STATES. ARMY. CORPS OF ENGINEERS. DETROIT DISTRICT See NAVIGATION SEASON EXTENSION DEMONSTRATION PROGRAM. DRAFT ENVIRONMENTAL STATEMENT 4180

UNITED STATES ARMY INFANTRY CENTER See HISTORY; ANNUAL SUPPLEMENT 4045

UNITED STATES. ARTHRITIS INTERAGENCY COORDINATING COMMITTEE See REPORT TO THE SECRETARY, DEPARTMENT OF HEALTH, EDUCATION, AND WELFARE (U.S. ARTHRITIS INTERAGENCY COORDINATING COMMITTEE) 3806

UNITED STATES. ARTHRITIS INTERAGENCY COORDINATING COMMITTEE See ARTHRITIS INTERAGENCY COORDINATING COMMITTEE ANNUAL REPORT TO THE SECRETARY, U.S. DEPARTMENT OF HEALTH, EDUCATION, AND WELFARE 3803

UNITED STATES. ATMOSPHERIC WATER RESOURCES PROGRAM See PROJECT SKYWATER; BIENNIAL REPORT 1433

UNITED
Alphabetical Title Index

UNITED STATES. ATTORNEY (CONNECTICUT) *See* REPORT OF THE UNITED STATES ATTORNEY FOR THE DISTRICT OF CONNECTICUT BY ... TO THE ATTORNEY GENERAL 3142

UNITED STATES. ATTORNEY (ILLINOIS : NORTHERN DISTRICT) *See* REPORT FOR ... / UNITED STATES ATTORNEY, NORTHERN DISTRICT OF ILLINOIS 3038

UNITED STATES ATTORNEYS BULLETIN (US/0566-0785) [03350999] 3067

UNITED STATES ATTORNEYS' MANUAL (US) [06057034] 3067

UNITED STATES. AVIATION FORECAST BRANCH *See* IFR AIRCRAFT HANDLED 23

UNITED STATES. AVIATION FORECAST BRANCH *See* PROFILES OF SCHEDULED AIR CARRIER PASSENGER TRAFFIC, TOP 100 U.S. AIRPORTS 32

UNITED STATES. AVIATION FORECAST BRANCH *See* PROFILES OF SCHEDULED AIR CARRIER OPERATIONS BY STAGE LENGTH 32

UNITED STATES BANKER (COS COB) (US/0148-8848) [03386992] 815

UNITED STATES. BEACH EROSION BOARD. TECHNICAL REPORT - BEACH EROSION BOARD *See* TECHNICAL REPORT - COASTAL ENGINEERING RESEARCH CENTER (U.S.) 1998

UNITED STATES BIOCHEMICAL CORPORATION *See* ENZYMES & REAGENTS FOR MOLECULAR BIOLOGY 454

UNITED STATES BIOCHEMICAL CORPORATION *See* USB MOLECULAR BIOLOGY REAGENTS/PROTOCOLS 475

UNITED STATES BIOCHEMICAL CORPORATION. ENZYMES & REAGENTS FOR MOLECULAR BIOLOGY *See* USB MOLECULAR BIOLOGY REAGENTS/PROTOCOLS 475

UNITED STATES. BOARD FOR INTERNATIONAL BROADCASTING *See* BUDGET - BOARD FOR INTERNATIONAL BROADCASTING 1128

UNITED STATES. BOARD FOR INTERNATIONAL BROADCASTING *See* ANNUAL REPORT ON RADIO FREE EUROPE/RADIO LIBERTY 1126

UNITED STATES. BOARD OF ENGINEERS FOR RIVERS AND HARBORS. TRANSPORTATION LINES ON THE ATLANTIC, GULF, AND PACIFIC COASTS *See* TRANSPORTATION LINES ON THE ATLANTIC, GULF, AND PACIFIC COASTS 5457

UNITED STATES. BOARD OF GOVERNORS OF THE FEDERAL RESERVE SYSTEM *See* OFFICIAL HOLIDAYS TO BE OBSERVED BY FEDERAL RESERVE OFFICES DURING THE YEAR ... 802

UNITED STATES BOARD ON GEOGRAPHIC NAMES *See* DECISIONS ON GEOGRAPHIC NAMES IN THE UNITED STATES 2559

UNITED STATES. BOARD ON GEOGRAPHIC NAMES *See* OFFICIAL STANDARD NAMES GAZETTEER 2571

UNITED STATES. BOARD ON GEOGRAPHIC NAMES *See* GAZETTEER - UNITED STATES BOARD ON GEOGRAPHIC NAMES 2561

UNITED STATES. BONNEVILLE POWER ADMINISTRATION *See* ANNUAL REPORT / BONNEVILLE POWER ADMINISTRATION 2035

UNITED STATES. BONNEVILLE POWER ADMINISTRATION *See* PROPOSED FISCAL YEAR ... PROGRAM. FINAL ENVIRONMENTAL IMPACT STATEMENT / BONNEVILLE POWER ADMINISTRATION 2240

UNITED STATES. BONNEVILLE POWER ADMINISTRATION *See* ISSUE UPDATE / BONNEVILLE POWER ADMINISTRATION 2067

UNITED STATES. BROOKHAVEN NATIONAL LABORATORY, UPTON, N.Y. SAFETY AND ENVIRONMENTAL PROTECTION DIVISION *See* SAFETY AND ENVIRONMENTAL PROTECTION DIVISION PROGRESS REPORT 2181

UNITED STATES. BUREAU OF ALCOHOL, TOBACCO, AND FIREARMS *See* QUARTERLY BULLETIN - UNITED STATES. BUREAU OF ALCOHOL, TOBACCO AND FIREARMS 4677

UNITED STATES. BUREAU OF EXECUTIVE PERSONNEL *See* EXECUTIVE PERSONNEL IN THE FEDERAL SERVICE 4647

UNITED STATES. BUREAU OF EXPORT ADMINISTRATION *See* EXPORT ADMINISTRATION REGULATIONS 2968

UNITED STATES. BUREAU OF HEALTH RESOURCES DEVELOPMENT. DIVISION OF NURSING *See* NURSE TRAINING 3863

UNITED STATES. BUREAU OF HIGHER AND CONTINUING EDUCATION *See* FACTBOOK - BUREAU OF HIGHER AND CONTINUING EDUCATION 1823

UNITED STATES. BUREAU OF HIGHER AND CONTINUING EDUCATION. DIVISION OF STUDENT SERVICES AND VETERANS PROGRAMS *See* DIRECTORY OF FUNDED PROJECTS 1821

UNITED STATES. BUREAU OF INDIAN AFFAIRS. OFFICE OF TRUST RESPONSIBILITIES. BRANCH OF INVESTMENTS *See* INDIAN TRUST FUNDS INVESTMENT OPERATIONS 901

UNITED STATES. BUREAU OF JUSTICE STATISTICS *See* BUREAU OF JUSTICE STATISTICS ANNUAL REPORT / U.S. DEPARTMENT OF JUSTICE, BUREAU OF JUSTICE STATISTICS 3079

UNITED STATES. BUREAU OF LABOR STATISTICS *See* STATE DATA ON OCCUPATIONAL INJURIES AND ILLNESSES 2870

UNITED STATES. BUREAU OF LABOR STATISTICS *See* PROFESSIONAL, ADMINISTRATIVE, TECHNICAL AND CLERICAL PAY IN NEW YORK 1703

UNITED STATES. BUREAU OF LABOR STATISTICS *See* EMPLOYEE COMPENSATION IN THE PRIVATE NONFARM ECONOMY 1665

UNITED STATES. BUREAU OF LABOR STATISTICS *See* AREA WAGE SURVEY : BIRMINGHAM, ALABAMA, METROPOLITAN AREA 1652

UNITED STATES. BUREAU OF LABOR STATISTICS *See* INDUSTRY WAGE SURVEY : NONFERROUS FOUNDRIES 1679

UNITED STATES. BUREAU OF LABOR STATISTICS *See* OCCUPATIONAL INJURIES AND ILLNESSES. SUMMARY (WASHINGTON) 2867

UNITED STATES. BUREAU OF LABOR STATISTICS *See* CURRENT WAGE DEVELOPMENTS 1662

UNITED STATES. BUREAU OF LABOR STATISTICS *See* LOCKHEED AIRCRAFT CORPORATION 1536

UNITED STATES. BUREAU OF LABOR STATISTICS *See* AREA WAGE SURVEY : WESTCHESTER COUNTY, NEW YORK 1653

UNITED STATES. BUREAU OF LABOR STATISTICS *See* AREA WAGE SURVEY : FORT LAUDERDALE-HOLLYWOOD AND WEST PALM BEACH, FLORIDA, METROPOLITAN AREAS 1652

UNITED STATES. BUREAU OF LABOR STATISTICS *See* AVERAGE ANNUAL WAGES (ANNUAL PAYROLL DIVIDED BY EMPLOYMENT) AND WAGE ADJUSTMENT INDEX FOR CETA PRIME SPONSORS 1654

UNITED STATES. BUREAU OF LABOR STATISTICS *See* INDUSTRY WAGE SURVEY : METAL MINING 1679

UNITED STATES. BUREAU OF LABOR STATISTICS *See* AVERAGE RETAIL PRICES OF SELECTED COMMODITIES AND SERVICES 1590

UNITED STATES. BUREAU OF LABOR STATISTICS *See* AREA WAGE SURVEY : STAMFORD, CONNECTICUT, METROPOLITAN AREA 1653

UNITED STATES. BUREAU OF LABOR STATISTICS *See* DISTRIBUTION OF OCCUPATIONAL EMPLOYMENT IN STATES AND AREAS BY RACE AND SEX 1663

UNITED STATES. BUREAU OF LABOR STATISTICS *See* DEPARTMENT STORE INVENTORY PRICE INDEXES / U.S. DEPARTMENT OF LABOR, BUREAU OF LABOR STATISTICS 953

UNITED STATES. BUREAU OF LABOR STATISTICS *See* NEWS - BUREAU OF LABOR STATISTICS 1537

UNITED STATES. BUREAU OF LABOR STATISTICS *See* CHARTBOOK ON PRICES, WAGES, AND PRODUCTIVITY 1590

UNITED STATES. BUREAU OF LABOR STATISTICS *See* WAGE DIFFERENCES AMONG METROPOLITAN AREAS : SUMMARY 1717

UNITED STATES. BUREAU OF LABOR STATISTICS *See* UNION WAGES AND HOURS : GROCERY STORES 1716

UNITED STATES. BUREAU OF LABOR STATISTICS *See* AREA WAGE SURVEY : AUSTIN, TEXAS, METROPOLITAN AREA 1652

UNITED STATES. BUREAU OF LABOR STATISTICS *See* HOURLY EARNINGS INDEX, THE 1677

UNITED STATES. BUREAU OF LABOR STATISTICS *See* WAGE CHRONOLOGY SERIES. SER 4, THE 1717

UNITED STATES. BUREAU OF LABOR STATISTICS *See* U.S. EXPORT AND IMPORT PRICE INDEXES 5345

UNITED STATES. BUREAU OF LABOR STATISTICS *See* MAJOR PROGRAMS, BUREAU OF LABOR STATISTICS 1536

UNITED STATES. BUREAU OF LABOR STATISTICS *See* CETA AREA EMPLOYMENT AND UNEMPLOYMENT 1658

UNITED STATES. BUREAU OF LABOR STATISTICS *See* CHARTBOOK ON OCCUPATIONAL INJURIES AND ILLNESSES 2860

UNITED STATES. BUREAU OF LABOR STATISTICS *See* AREA WAGE SURVEY: THE RALEIGH-DURHAM, NORTH CAROLINA, METROPOLITAN AREA 1653

UNITED STATES. BUREAU OF LABOR STATISTICS *See* BLS FILE OF STATE, COUNTY, AND MUNICIPAL COLLECTIVE BARGAINING AGREEMENTS 1655

UNITED STATES. BUREAU OF LABOR STATISTICS *See* WAGE CHRONOLOGY : BERKSHIRE HATHAWAY AND THE CLOTHING AND TEXTILE WORKERS 1717

UNITED STATES. BUREAU OF LABOR STATISTICS *See* WAGE CHRONOLOGY : THE BOEING CO., WASHINGTON PLANTS, AND INTERNATIONAL ASSOCIATION OF MACHINISTS 1717

UNITED STATES. BUREAU OF LABOR STATISTICS. AREA WAGE SURVEY: THE DURHAM, NORTH CAROLINA, METROPOLITAN AREA *See* AREA WAGE SURVEY: THE RALEIGH-DURHAM, NORTH CAROLINA, METROPOLITAN AREA 1653

UNITED STATES. BUREAU OF LABOR STATISTICS. AREA WAGE SURVEY: THE RALEIGH, NORTH CAROLINA, METROPOLITAN AREA *See* AREA WAGE SURVEY: THE RALEIGH-DURHAM, NORTH CAROLINA, METROPOLITAN AREA 1653

UNITED STATES. BUREAU OF LABOR STATISTICS. BUSINESS RESEARCH ADVISORY COUNCIL *See* DIRECTORY OF THE BUSINESS RESEARCH ADVISORY COUNCIL TO THE BUREAU OF LABOR STATISTICS 1531

UNITED STATES. BUREAU OF LABOR STATISTICS. EMPLOYMENT AND UNEMPLOYMENT *See* EMPLOYMENT AND UNEMPLOYMENT TRENDS 1666

UNITED STATES. BUREAU OF LAND MANAGEMENT *See* ANNUAL FIRE REPORT (WASHINGTON) 2288

UNITED STATES. BUREAU OF LAND MANAGEMENT *See* MANAGING THE NATION'S PUBLIC LANDS : A PROGRAM REPORT PREPARED PURSUANT TO REQUIREMENTS OF THE FEDERAL LAND POLICY AND MANAGEMENT ACT OF 1976 878

UNITED STATES. BUREAU OF LAND MANAGEMENT *See* RESTORATION OF LOST OR OBLITERATED CORNERS AND SUBDIVISION OF SECTIONS 2574

UNITED STATES. BUREAU OF LAND MANAGEMENT. UTAH STATE OFFICE *See* BLM FACTS & FIGURES FOR UTAH 4633

UNITED STATES. BUREAU OF MEDICINE AND SURGERY *See* HANDBOOK OF THE HOSPITAL CORPS, UNITED STATES NAVY 4177

UNITED STATES. BUREAU OF MINES *See* NEW PUBLICATIONS OF THE BUREAU OF MINES 2147

UNITED STATES. BUREAU OF MINES *See* BITUMINOUS COAL AND LIGNITE DISTRIBUTION 1599

UNITED STATES. BUREAU OF MINES *See* PREPRINT FROM THE BUREAU OF MINES MINERALS YEARBOOK 2148

UNITED STATES. BUREAU OF MINES *See* OPEN-FILE REPORT - BUREAU OF MINES 2147

UNITED STATES. BUREAU OF MINES *See* MINING RESEARCH REVIEW 2146

UNITED STATES. BUREAU OF MINES *See* MINERAL PERSPECTIVES 1441

UNITED STATES. BUREAU OF MOTOR CARRIER SAFETY *See* PHYSICAL CONDITION REPORT OF COMMERCIAL DRIVERS INVOLVED IN ACCIDENTS 5389

UNITED STATES. BUREAU OF NAVAL PERSONNEL *See* REGISTER OF COMMISSIONED AND WARRANT OFFICERS OF THE UNITED STATES NAVY AND MARINE CORPS 4182

UNITED STATES. BUREAU OF NAVAL PERSONNEL *See* BUREAU OF NAVAL PERSONNEL MANUAL 939

UNITED STATES. BUREAU OF POSTSECONDARY EDUCATION *See* BASIC EDUCATIONAL OPPORTUNITY GRANT PROGRAM HANDBOOK 1727

UNITED STATES. BUREAU OF RADIOLOGICAL HEALTH. OFFICE OF MANAGEMENT AND SYSTEMS. TECHNICAL INFORMATION STAFF *See* BUREAU OF RADIOLOGICAL HEALTH PUBLICATIONS SUBJECT INDEX 3939

UNITED STATES. BUREAU OF RECLAMATION *See* TRANSLATION - BUREAU OF RECLAMATION 4691

Alphabetical Title Index

UNITED

UNITED STATES. BUREAU OF RECLAMATION *See* ANNUAL PROJECT HISTORY : MANN CREEK PROJECT **2087**

UNITED STATES. BUREAU OF RECLAMATION *See* BUREAU OF RECLAMATION PROGRESS **70**

UNITED STATES. BUREAU OF RECLAMATION *See* ANNUAL PROJECT HISTORY : PACIFIC NORTHWEST-PACIFIC SOUTHWEST INTERTIE, ARIZONA, CALIFORNIA, NEVADA **2035**

UNITED STATES. BUREAU OF RECLAMATION *See* RESEARCH REPORT - UNITED STATES DEPARTMENT OF THE INTERIOR, BUREAU OF RECLAMATION **2203**

UNITED STATES. BUREAU OF RECLAMATION *See* ANNUAL OPERATING PLAN, WESTERN DIVISION, MISSOURI RIVER BASIN **2087**

UNITED STATES. BUREAU OF RECLAMATION *See* MID-PACIFIC REGION REPORT **2093**

UNITED STATES. BUREAU OF RECLAMATION *See* ANNUAL REPORT. OPERATION OF THE COLORADO RIVER BASIN. PROJECTED OPERATIONS **2087**

UNITED STATES. BUREAU OF RECLAMATION *See* PLS LISTING. POWER FACILITIES OPERATED BY THE BUREAU OF RECLAMATION **2075**

UNITED STATES. BUREAU OF SPORT FISHERIES AND WILDLIFE *See* NATIONAL WILDLIFE REFUGES **2199**

UNITED STATES. BUREAU OF SPORT FISHERIES AND WILDLIFE *See* SELECTED LIST OF FEDERAL LAWS AND TREATIES RELATING TO SPORT FISH AND WILDLIFE **3116**

UNITED STATES. BUREAU OF THE CENSUS *See* U.S. EXPORTS AND IMPORTS OF GOLD **855**

UNITED STATES. BUREAU OF THE CENSUS *See* CURRENT POPULATION REPORTS : FARM POPULATION. SERIES P-27 **4551**

UNITED STATES. BUREAU OF THE CENSUS *See* FACTFINDER FOR THE NATION **4553**

UNITED STATES. BUREAU OF THE CENSUS *See* CURRENT BUSINESS REPORTS: MONTHLY WHOLESALE TRADE, SALES AND INVENTORIES **663**

UNITED STATES. BUREAU OF THE CENSUS *See* CENSUS OF TRANSPORTATION **5379**

UNITED STATES. BUREAU OF THE CENSUS *See* RECENT SOCIAL AND ECONOMIC TRENDS **1515**

UNITED STATES. BUREAU OF THE CENSUS *See* UNITED STATES FOREIGN TRADE : BUNKER OIL AND COAL LADEN IN THE UNITED STATES ON VESSELS ENGAGED IN FOREIGN TRADE **856**

UNITED STATES. BUREAU OF THE CENSUS *See* CENSUS OF SELECTED SERVICE INDUSTRIES **4637**

UNITED STATES. BUREAU OF THE CENSUS *See* CENSUS OF MINERAL INDUSTRIES **1438**

UNITED STATES. BUREAU OF THE CENSUS *See* ELECTRIC LAMPS (ANNUAL) **2043**

UNITED STATES. BUREAU OF THE CENSUS *See* GOVERNMENTAL FINANCE **4728**

UNITED STATES. BUREAU OF THE CENSUS *See* CONGRESSIONAL DISTRICT ATLAS **2559**

UNITED STATES. BUREAU OF THE CENSUS *See* FLOUR MILLING PRODUCTS **201**

UNITED STATES. BUREAU OF THE CENSUS *See* STEEL SHIPPING DRUMS AND PAILS **3488**

UNITED STATES. BUREAU OF THE CENSUS *See* SCHEDULE B, STATISTICAL CLASSIFICATION OF DOMESTIC AND FOREIGN COMMODITIES EXPORTED FROM THE UNITED STATES / U.S. DEPARTMENT OF COMMERCE, BUREAU OF THE CENSUS **733**

UNITED STATES. BUREAU OF THE CENSUS *See* CONSTRUCTION REPORTS: VALUE OF NEW CONSTRUCTION PUT IN PLACE **610**

UNITED STATES. BUREAU OF THE CENSUS *See* TELEPHONE CONTACTS FOR DATA USERS / BUREAU OF THE CENSUS **1167**

UNITED STATES. BUREAU OF THE CENSUS *See* U.S. FOREIGN TRADE: CONCORDANCE OF STATISTICAL CLASSIFICATIONS OF DOMESTIC AND FOREIGN COMMODITIES EXPORTED FROM THE UNITED STATES **734**

UNITED STATES. BUREAU OF THE CENSUS *See* FATS AND OILS. PRODUCTION, CONSUMPTION, AND FACTORY AND WAREHOUSE STOCKS (ANNUAL) **1606**

UNITED STATES. BUREAU OF THE CENSUS *See* COUNTY BUSINESS PATTERNS **662**

UNITED STATES. BUREAU OF THE CENSUS *See* CENSUS BUREAU METHODOLOGICAL RESEARCH **4550**

UNITED STATES. BUREAU OF THE CENSUS *See* DIRECTORY OF DATA FILES **4643**

UNITED STATES. BUREAU OF THE CENSUS *See* GOVERNMENTAL FINANCES AND EMPLOYMENT AT A GLANCE **4728**

UNITED STATES. BUREAU OF THE CENSUS *See* CONSTRUCTION REPORTS: NEW ONE-FAMILY HOMES SOLD AND FOR SALE **2819**

UNITED STATES. BUREAU OF THE CENSUS *See* FLUORESCENT LAMP BALLASTS **1607**

UNITED STATES. BUREAU OF THE CENSUS *See* CENSUS OF RETAIL TRADE **952**

UNITED STATES. BUREAU OF THE CENSUS *See* CENSUS OF WHOLESALE TRADE **826**

UNITED STATES. BUREAU OF THE CENSUS *See* CHART BOOK OF GOVERNMENTAL DATA: ORGANIZATION, FINANCES AND EMPLOYMENT **4717**

UNITED STATES. BUREAU OF THE CENSUS *See* U.S. WATERBORNE EXPORTS AND GENERAL IMPORTS **856**

UNITED STATES. BUREAU OF THE CENSUS. CHART BOOK ON GOVERNMENTAL FINANCES AND EMPLOYMENT *See* CHART BOOK OF GOVERNMENTAL DATA: ORGANIZATION, FINANCES AND EMPLOYMENT **4717**

UNITED STATES. BUREAU OF THE CENSUS. DATA USER SERVICES DIVISION *See* CATALOG OF TRAINING ACTIVITIES / U.S. DEPARTMENT OF COMMERCE, BUREAU OF THE CENSUS **5194**

UNITED STATES. BUREAU OF THE CENSUS. DATA USER SERVICES DIVISION *See* DATA USER EDUCATION & TRAINING ACTIVITIES **5326**

UNITED STATES CATHOLIC CONFERENCE *See* PUBLICATIONS IN PRINT (WASHINGTON, D.C.) **5035**

UNITED STATES CATHOLIC HISTORICAL SOCIETY *See* MONOGRAPH SERIES - UNITED STATES HISTORICAL SOCIETY **2747**

UNITED STATES CATHOLIC MISSION COUNCIL *See* MISSION HAND BOOK **4978**

UNITED STATES. CENTRAL INTELLIGENCE AGENCY *See* REFERENCE AID, CHIEFS OF STATE, AND CABINET MEMBERS OF FOREIGN GOVERNMENTS **4493**

UNITED STATES. CENTRAL INTELLIGENCE AGENCY *See* USSR : HARD CURRENCY TRADE AND PAYMENTS **856**

UNITED STATES. CENTRAL INTELLIGENCE AGENCY. DIRECTORATE OF INTELLIGENCE *See* CIA PUBLICATIONS RELEASED TO THE PUBLIC THROUGH LIBRARY OF CONGRESS DOCEX **4638**

UNITED STATES. CITIZENS' ADVISORY COMMITTEE ON ENVIRONMENTAL QUALITY *See* REPORT TO THE PRESIDENT AND TO THE COUNCIL ON ENVIRONMENTAL QUALITY **2181**

UNITED STATES. CITIZENS' ADVISORY COUNCIL ON THE STATUS OF WOMEN *See* WOMEN (WASHINGTON) **5570**

UNITED STATES. CIVIL AERONAUTICS BOARD *See* ECONOMIC REGULATIONS. PT. 214. TERMS, CHARTERS, AND LIMITATIONS OF FOREIGN AIR CARRIER PERMITS AUTHORIZING CHARTER TRANSPORTATION ONLY **18**

UNITED STATES. CIVIL AERONAUTICS BOARD *See* PRODUCTIVITY AND COST OF EMPLOYMENT. LOCAL SERVICE CARRIERS **1703**

UNITED STATES. CIVIL AERONAUTICS BOARD *See* REGULATIONS OF THE CIVIL AERONAUTICS BOARD **33**

UNITED STATES. CIVIL AERONAUTICS BOARD *See* LEGISLATIVE HISTORY OF CAB REGULATIONS **3002**

UNITED STATES. CIVIL AERONAUTICS BOARD *See* ORIGIN-DESTINATION SURVEY OF AIRLINE PASSENGER TRAFFIC - DOMESTIC **31**

UNITED STATES. CIVIL AERONAUTICS BOARD. BUREAU OF OPERATING RIGHTS *See* LOCAL SERVICE CARRIERS PASSENGER ENPLANEMENTS **27**

UNITED STATES. CIVIL AERONAUTICS BOARD. BUREAU OF OPERATING RIGHTS. STANDARDS DIVISION *See* TRUNKLINE CARRIER DOMESTIC PASSENGER ENPLANEMENTS **38**

UNITED STATES. CIVIL SERVICE COMMISSION *See* EMPLOYMENT OF DISABLED AND VIETNAM ERA VETERANS IN THE FEDERAL GOVERNMENT **4702**

UNITED STATES. CIVIL SERVICE COMMISSION *See* SURVEY OF INCOME OF CIVIL SERVICE ANNUITANTS (WASHINGTON) **4689**

UNITED STATES. CIVIL SERVICE COMMISSION. BUREAU OF INTERGOVERNMENTAL PERSONNEL PROGRAMS *See* GRANT AWARDS - UNITED STATES CIVIL SERVICE COMMISSION, BUREAU OF INTERGOVERNMENTAL PERSONNEL PROGRAMS **4704**

UNITED STATES. CIVIL SERVICE COMMISSION. BUREAU OF INTERGOVERNMENTAL PERSONNEL PROGRAMS *See* REPORT OF IPA GRANT ACTIVITY **4705**

UNITED STATES. CIVIL SERVICE COMMISSION. BUREAU OF INTERGOVERNMENTAL PERSONNEL PROGRAMS *See* IPA INTERGOVERNMENTAL ASSIGNMENT PROGRAM : REPORT, THE **4658**

UNITED STATES CIVIL SERVICE COMMISSION. BUREAU OF TRAINING *See* INTERAGENCY TRAINING PROGRAMS CATALOG **4704**

UNITED STATES. CIVIL SERVICE COMMISSION. BUREAU OF TRAINING *See* INTERGOVERNMENTAL AFFAIRS FELLOWSHIP PROGRAM **4657**

UNITED STATES. CIVIL SERVICE COMMISSION. GENERAL MANAGEMENT TRAINING CENTER *See* GMT CALENDAR OF COURSES **1676**

UNITED STATES CIVIL SERVICE COMMISSION. LIBRARY *See* MANPOWER PLANNING AND UTILIZATION **1689**

UNITED STATES. CIVIL SERVICE COMMISSION. LIBRARY *See* POSITION CLASSIFICATION, PAY, AND EMPLOYEE BENEFITS **1702**

UNITED STATES. CIVIL SERVICE COMMISSION. PERSONNEL MANAGEMENT TRAINING CENTER *See* PERSONNEL MANAGEMENT TRAINING CENTER COURSE CATALOGUE **4704**

UNITED STATES. CIVIL SERVICE COMMISSION. PERSONNEL RESEARCH AND DEVELOPMENT CENTER *See* PERSONNEL RESEARCH AND DEVELOPMENT CENTER OF THE U. S. CIVIL SERVICE COMMISSION, THE **4704**

UNITED STATES CLAIMS COURT DIGEST (US/8755-5980) [09869804] **3067**

UNITED STATES CLAIMS COURT REPORTER (US) [10684454] **3067**

UNITED STATES CLAIMS COURT REPORTER (ANNUAL) *See* FEDERAL CLAIMS REPORTER **2969**

UNITED STATES COAL PRODUCTION BY COMPANY (US) [01768739] **2152**

UNITED STATES. COAST GUARD *See* REGISTER OF OFFICERS - COAST GUARD **4182**

UNITED STATES. COAST GUARD *See* MARINE SAFETY MANUAL **4179**

UNITED STATES. COAST GUARD *See* LIST OF INSPECTED TANK BARGES & TANKSHIPS **5451**

UNITED STATES. COAST GUARD *See* REGISTER OF RESERVE OFFICERS **4182**

UNITED STATES. COAST GUARD, ACADEMY, NEW LONDON, CONN. ALUMNI ASSOCIATION *See* DIRECTORY - U. S. COAST GUARD ACADEMY ALUMNI ASSOCIATION **1101**

UNITED STATES. COAST GUARD ACADEMY, NEW LONDON, CONN. ALUMNI ASSOCIATION *See* BULLETIN - U.S. COAST GUARD ACADEMY ALUMNI ASSOCIATION **1101**

UNITED STATES. COAST GUARD AUXILIARY *See* AUXILIARY, BIBLIOGRAPHY OF PUBLICATIONS **408**

UNITED STATES COAST PILOT. 1, ATLANTIC COAST. EASTPORT TO CAPE COD (US/0363-3209) [02406679] **4059, 4184**

UNITED STATES COAST PILOT. 2, ATLANTIC COAST. CAPE COD TO SANDY HOOK (US/0363-695X) [02458451] **4184**

UNITED STATES COAST PILOT. 3, ATLANTIC COAST. SANDY HOOK TO CAPE HENRY (US/0363-3217) [02406894] **4184**

UNITED STATES COAST PILOT. 4, ATLANTIC COAST. CAPE HENRY TO KEY WEST (US/0362-7713) [07293708] **4184**

UNITED STATES COAST PILOT. 5, ATLANTIC COAST. GULF OF MEXICO, PUERTO RICO, AND VIRGIN ISLANDS (US/0360-0149) [02243296] **4184**

UNITED STATES COAST PILOT. 6, GREAT LAKES, LAKES ONTARIO, ERIE, HURON, MICHIGAN, AND SUPERIOR AND ST. LAWRENCE RIVER (US/0161-4444) [03922256] **4184**

UNITED — Alphabetical Title Index

UNITED STATES COAST PILOT. 8, PACIFIC COAST. ALASKA, DIXON ENTRANCE TO CAPE SPENCER (US/0163-9471) [04534194] **4184**

UNITED STATES COAST PILOT. 9, PACIFIC AND ARCTIC COASTS. ALASKA, CAPE SPENCER TO BEAUFORT SEA (US/0278-0089) [01188015] **4184**

UNITED STATES CODE ANNOTATED (US) [01642535] **3067**

UNITED STATES CODE CONGRESSIONAL AND ADMINISTRATIVE NEWS (US) [01768740] **4692**

UNITED STATES. COMMISSION ON CIVIL RIGHTS *See* STATE OF CIVIL RIGHTS, THE **4513**

UNITED STATES COMMISSION ON CIVIL RIGHTS *See* STATE ADVISORY COMMITTEE HANDBOOK / UNITED STATES COMMISSION ON CIVIL RIGHTS **4513**

UNITED STATES. COMMODITY FUTURES TRADING COMMISSION *See* ANNUAL REPORT / COMMODITY FUTURES TRADING COMMISSION **891**

UNITED STATES. COMMODITY FUTURES TRADING COMMISSION *See* CFTC DATABOOK **894**

UNITED STATES. COMMUNITY RELATIONS SERVICE *See* ANNUAL REPORT OF THE COMMUNITY RELATIONS SERVICE **4628**

UNITED STATES. COMMUNITY SERVICES ADMINISTRATION *See* FEDERAL OUTLAYS IN TERRITORIES AND OTHER AREAS ADMINISTERED BY THE U.S **1490**

UNITED STATES CONFERENCE OF MAYORS *See* OFFICIAL POLICY RESOLUTIONS ADOPTED AT THE ANNUAL CONFERENCE OF MAYORS **4671**

UNITED STATES CONFERENCE OF MAYORS *See* FEDERAL BUDGET AND THE CITIES - UNITED STATES CONFERENCE OF MAYORS, THE **4647**

UNITED STATES. CONGRESS *See* CONGRESSIONAL RECORD (PERMANENT ED.) **2955**

UNITED STATES. CONGRESS *See* HOUSE AND SENATE REPORTS ON PUBLIC BILLS (NUMBERED, UNBOUND) **2979**

UNITED STATES. CONGRESS *See* REPORTS ON PUBLIC BILLS (BOUND) (HOUSE AND SENATE) **3039**

UNITED STATES. CONGRESS *See* OFFICIAL CONGRESSIONAL DIRECTORY **4670**

UNITED STATES. CONGRESS *See* CONGRESSIONAL RECORD (DAILY ED.) **2955**

UNITED STATES. CONGRESS *See* CONGRESSIONAL RECORD [COMPUTER FILE] : PROCEEDINGS AND DEBATES OF THE ... CONGRESS **2955**

UNITED STATES. CONGRESS. HOUSE *See* CALENDARS OF THE UNITED STATES HOUSE OF REPRESENTATIVES AND HISTORY OF LEGISLATION **4635**

UNITED STATES. CONGRESS. HOUSE *See* CONSTITUTION, JEFFERSON'S MANUAL, AND RULES OF THE HOUSE OF REPRESENTATIVES OF THE UNITED STATES **4640**

UNITED STATES. CONGRESS. HOUSE. COMMITTEE ON BANKING, FINANCE, AND URBAN AFFAIRS *See* LEGISLATIVE CALENDAR / UNITED STATES HOUSE OF REPRESENTATIVES, COMMITTEE ON BANKING, FINANCE, AND URBAN AFFAIRS **4661**

UNITED STATES. CONGRESS. HOUSE. COMMITTEE ON ENERGY AND COMMERCE *See* LEGISLATIVE CALENDAR / COMMITTEE ON ENERGY AND COMMERCE **4661**

UNITED STATES. CONGRESS. HOUSE. COMMITTEE ON FOREIGN AFFAIRS *See* VIEWS AND ESTIMATES OF THE COMMITTEE ON FOREIGN AFFAIRS ON THE BUDGET **3137**

UNITED STATES. CONGRESS. HOUSE. COMMITTEE ON GOVERNMENT OPERATION *See* FEDERAL REAL AND PERSONAL PROPERTY INVENTORY REPORT (CIVILIAN AND MILITARY) OF THE UNITED STATES GOVERNMENT COVERING ITS PROPERTIES LOCATED IN THE UNITED STATES, IN THE TERRITORIES, AND OVERSEAS **4648**

UNITED STATES. CONGRESS. HOUSE. COMMITTEE ON GOVERNMENT OPERATIONS *See* ACTIVITIES OF THE HOUSE COMMITTEE ON GOVERNMENT OPERATIONS **4623**

UNITED STATES. CONGRESS. HOUSE. COMMITTEE ON GOVERNMENT OPERATIONS. ACTIVITIES REPORT *See* ACTIVITIES OF THE HOUSE COMMITTEE ON GOVERNMENT OPERATIONS **4623**

UNITED STATES. CONGRESS. HOUSE. COMMITTEE ON INTERIOR AND INSULAR AFFAIRS *See* ACCOMPLISHMENTS OF THE COMMITTEE ON INTERIOR AND INSULAR AFFAIRS OF THE HOUSE OF REPRESENTATIVES DURING THE ... CONGRESS **4461**

UNITED STATES. CONGRESS. HOUSE. COMMITTEE ON PUBLIC WORKS AND TRANSPORTATION *See* SUMMARY OF LEGISLATIVE ACTIVITIES - UNITED STATES. CONGRESS. HOUSE. COMMITTEE ON PUBLIC WORKS AND TRANSPORTATION **3061**

UNITED STATES. CONGRESS. HOUSE. COMMITTEE ON RULES *See* LEGISLATIVE CALENDAR / UNITED STATES HOUSE OF REPRESENTATIVES, COMMITTEE ON RULES **4661**

UNITED STATES. CONGRESS. HOUSE. COMMITTEE ON THE BUDGET *See* LEGISLATIVE CALENDAR / UNITED STATES HOUSE OF REPRESENTATIVES, COMMITTEE ON THE BUDGET **4736**

UNITED STATES. CONGRESS. HOUSE. COMMITTEE ON THE DISTRICT OF COLUMBIA *See* ACTIVITIES AND SUMMARY REPORT OF THE COMMITTEE ON THE DISTRICT OF COLUMBIA, HOUSE OF REPRESENTATIVES **4623**

UNITED STATES. CONGRESS. HOUSE. COMMITTEE ON THE DISTRICT OF COLUMBIA *See* ACTIVITIES OF THE COMMITTEE ON THE DISTRICT OF COLUMBIA, HOUSE OF REPRESENTATIVES **4623**

UNITED STATES. CONGRESS. HOUSE. COMMITTEE ON THE DISTRICT OF COLUMBIA. ACTIVITIES AND SUMMARY REPORT OF THE COMMITTEE ON THE DISTRICT OF COLUMBIA, HOUSE OF REPRESENTATIVES *See* ACTIVITIES OF THE COMMITTEE ON THE DISTRICT OF COLUMBIA, HOUSE OF REPRESENTATIVES **4623**

UNITED STATES. CONGRESS. HOUSE. COMMITTEE ON VETERANS' AFFAIRS *See* LEGISLATIVE CALENDAR / UNITED STATES HOUSE OF REPRESENTATIVES, COMMITTEE ON VETERAN AFFAIRS **4661**

UNITED STATES. CONGRESS. JOINT COMMITTEE ON PRINTING *See* GOVERNMENT PRINTING & BINDING REGULATIONS **4565**

UNITED STATES. CONGRESS. JOINT COMMITTEE ON PRINTING *See* GOVERNMENT PAPER SPECIFICATION STANDARDS **4651**

UNITED STATES. CONGRESS. JOINT ECONOMIC COMMITTEE *See* ECONOMIC REPORT OF THE PRESIDENT; HEARINGS BEFORE THE JOINT ECONOMIC COMMITTEE, CONGRESS OF THE UNITED STATES **1557**

UNITED STATES. CONGRESS. JOINT ECONOMIC COMMITTEE *See* JOINT ECONOMIC REPORT, THE **1498**

UNITED STATES. CONGRESS. OFFICE OF TECHNOLOGY ASSESSMENT *See* ANNUAL REPORT TO THE CONGRESS BY THE OFFICE OF TECHNOLOGY ASSESSMENT **5084**

UNITED STATES. CONGRESS. OFFICE OF TECHNOLOGY ASSESSMENT *See* ASSESSMENT ACTIVITIES **5086**

UNITED STATES. CONGRESS. OFFICE OF TECHNOLOGY ASSESSMENT *See* CATALOGUE OF OTA PUBLICATIONS **5174**

UNITED STATES. CONGRESS. OFFICE OF TECHNOLOGY ASSESSMENT. CATALOG OF PUBLICATIONS *See* CATALOGUE OF OTA PUBLICATIONS **5174**

UNITED STATES. CONGRESS. SENATE *See* JOURNAL OF THE SENATE OF THE UNITED STATES OF AMERICA **4479**

UNITED STATES. CONGRESS. SENATE *See* UNITED STATES SENATE TELEPHONE DIRECTORY **4692**

UNITED STATES. CONGRESS. SENATE. COMMITTEE ON AGRICULTURE, NUTRITION, AND FORESTRY *See* LEGISLATIVE CALENDAR - UNITED STATES SENATE. COMMITTEE ON AGRICULTURE, NUTRITION, AND FORESTRY **4661**

UNITED STATES. CONGRESS. SENATE. COMMITTEE ON AGRICULTURE, NUTRITION, AND FORESTRY *See* REPORT TO THE SENATE ON THE JURISDICTION AND A SUMMARY OF ACTIVITIES OF THE COMMITTEE ON AGRICULTURE, NUTRITION, AND FORESTRY FOR THE ... CONGRESS **4198**

UNITED STATES. CONGRESS. SENATE. COMMITTEE ON ARMED SERVICES *See* SUMMARY OF ACTIVITIES - COMMITTEE ON ARMED SERVICES, UNITED STATES SENATE **3183**

UNITED STATES. CONGRESS. SENATE. COMMITTEE ON BANKING, HOUSING, AND URBAN AFFAIRS *See* MONETARY POLICY REPORT FROM THE COMMITTEE ON BANKING, HOUSING, AND URBAN AFFAIRS, UNITED STATES SENATE **799**

UNITED STATES. CONGRESS. SENATE. COMMITTEE ON GOVERNMENTAL AFFAIRS *See* LEGISLATIVE CALENDAR - UNITED STATES SENATE. COMMITTEE ON GOVERNMENTAL AFFAIRS **4661**

UNITED STATES. CONGRESS. SENATE. COMMITTEE ON INTERIOR AND INSULAR AFFAIRS *See* CONFERENCE WITH THE DIRECTORS OF THE NATIONAL RECLAMATION ASSOCIATION **2088**

UNITED STATES. CONGRESS. SENATE. COMMITTEE ON LABOR AND HUMAN RESOURCES *See* REPORT ON LEGISLATIVE ACTIVITIES OF THE COMMITTEE ON LABOR AND HUMAN RESOURCES, UNITED STATES SENATE DURING THE ... CONGRESS ... : PURSUANT TO SECTION 136 OF THE LEGISLATIVE REORGANIZATION ACT OF 1946, AS AMENDED BY THE LEGISLATIVE REORGANIZATION ACT OF 1970 **4798**

UNITED STATES. CONGRESS. SENATE. COMMITTEE ON LABOR AND HUMAN RESOURCES *See* LEGISLATIVE REVIEW ACTIVITY - UNITED STATES. CONGRESS. SENATE. COMMITTEE ON LABOR AND HUMAN RESOURCES **3002**

UNITED STATES. CONGRESS. SENATE. HISTORICAL OFFICE *See* SENATE HISTORY / SENATE HISTORICAL OFFICE, OFFICE OF THE SECRETARY, UNITED STATES SENATE **2760**

UNITED STATES. CONGRESS. SENATE. SELECT COMMITTEE ON INTELLIGENCE *See* LEGISLATIVE CALENDAR / SELECT COMMITTEE ON INTELLIGENCE, UNITED STATES SENATE **4661**

UNITED STATES. CONGRESS. SENATE. SPECIAL COMMITTEE ON AGING *See* DEVELOPMENT IN AGING **5178**

UNITED STATES. CONGRESSIONAL BUDGET OFFICE *See* ADVANCE BUDGETING. A REPORT TO THE CONGRESS **4624**

UNITED STATES. CONGRESSIONAL BUDGET OFFICE *See* ANALYSIS OF THE PRESIDENT'S BUDGETARY PROPOSALS, AN **4709**

UNITED STATES. CONGRESSIONAL BUDGET OFFICE *See* LIST OF PUBLICATIONS - UNITED STATES. CONGRESSIONAL BUDGET OFFICE **4736**

UNITED STATES. CONSUMER AND MARKETING SERVICE *See* EGG MARKETING GUIDE **2334**

UNITED STATES. CONSUMER AND MARKETING SERVICE *See* ACREAGE-MARKETING GUIDES, WINTER VEGETABLES AND POTATOES **2325**

UNITED STATES. CONSUMER PRODUCT SAFETY COMMISSION *See* CONSUMER PRODUCT HAZARD INDEX **4772**

UNITED STATES. CONSUMER PRODUCT SAFETY COMMISSION *See* BUDGET REQUEST - U.S. CONSUMER PRODUCT SAFETY COMMISSION **4634**

UNITED STATES CONTRIBUTIONS TO INTERNATIONAL ORGANIZATIONS (US/0499-1583) [03257295] **1641**

UNITED STATES CONVENTIONS AND TRADE SHOWS (US) [01783852] **5167**

UNITED STATES. COST OF LIVING COUNCIL *See* ECONOMIC STABILIZATION PROGRAM **1485**

UNITED STATES COTTON QUALITY REPORT FOR GINNINGS (US/0093-4429) [02585867] **5359**, **190**

UNITED STATES COURT DIRECTORY (UNITED STATES. ADMINISTRATIVE OFFICE OF THE UNITED STATES COURTS) (US/0162-8674) [04010539] **3143**

UNITED STATES. COURT OF INTERNATIONAL TRADE *See* UNITED STATES COURT OF INTERNATIONAL TRADE REPORTS **3137**

UNITED STATES COURT OF INTERNATIONAL TRADE REPORTS (US/0740-9540) [09359546] **856**, **3137**

UNITED STATES. COURTS *See* BENDER'S FEDERAL PRACTICE MANUAL **3139**

UNITED STATES COURTS (PICTORIAL SUMMARY), THE (US/0732-7900) [08407333] **3143**

UNITED STATES. CROP REPORTING BOARD *See* CROP PRODUCTION (WASHINGTON, D.C.) **169**

UNITED STATES. CROP REPORTING BOARD *See* WINTER WHEAT AND RYE SEEDINGS **191**

UNITED STATES. CROP REPORTING BOARD *See* EGG PRODUCTS **210**

UNITED STATES. CROP REPORTING BOARD *See* DIGEST FOR REPORTERS **170**

UNITED STATES. CUSTOMS SERVICE *See* CUSTOMS REGULATIONS OF THE UNITED STATES **2958**

Alphabetical Title Index — UNITED

UNITED STATES. CUSTOMS SERVICE *See* U.S. CUSTOMS DIRECTORY **4692**

UNITED STATES. DEFENSE CONTRACT ADMINISTRATION SERVICES *See* DCAS MANUFACTURING COST CONTROL DIGEST **3477**

UNITED STATES. DEFENSE CONTRACT AUDIT AGENCY *See* DCAA CONTRACT AUDIT MANUAL **4040**

UNITED STATES. DEFENSE CONTRACT AUDIT AGENCY *See* INDEX OF DCAA NUMBERED PUBLICATIONS AND MEMORANDUMS **745**

UNITED STATES. DEFENSE CONTRACT AUDIT AGENCY *See* CONTRACT AUDIT MANUAL **4040**

UNITED STATES. DEFENSE CONTRACT AUDIT AGENCY *See* INDEX OF DCAA MEMORANDUMS FOR REGIONAL DIRECTORS (MRDS) **4045**

UNITED STATES. DEFENSE CONTRACT AUDIT AGENCY *See* DIRECTORY OF DCAA OFFICES **4643**

UNITED STATES. DEFENSE CONTRACT AUDIT AGENCY *See* INDEX OF DCAA MEMORANDUMS FOR REGIONAL DIRECTORS (MRDS) **4045**

UNITED STATES. DEFENSE LOGISTICS STUDIES INFORMATION EXCHANGE *See* QUARTERLY SUPPLEMENT TO THE ... ANNUAL DEPARTMENT OF DEFENSE BIBLIOGRAPHY OF LOGISTICS STUDIES AND RELATED DOCUMENTS / DEFENSE LOGISTICS STUDIES INFORMATION EXCHANGE **4054**

UNITED STATES. DEFENSE MAPPING AGENCY. HYDROGRAPHIC CENTER *See* RADIO NAVIGATIONAL AIDS : ATLANTIC AND MEDITERRANEAN AREA **4182**

UNITED STATES. DEFENSE MAPPING AGENCY HYDROGRAPHIC/TOPOGRAPHIC CENTER *See* LIST OF LIGHTS AND FOG SIGNALS **4178**

UNITED STATES. DEFENSE MAPPING AGENCY. HYDROGRAPHIC/TOPOGRAPHIC CENTER *See* UNCLASSIFIED ACCESSION LIST **426**

UNITED STATES. DEFENSE MAPPING AGENCY. TOPOGRAPHIC CENTER. UNCLASSIFIED ACCESSION LIST *See* UNCLASSIFIED ACCESSION LIST **426**

UNITED STATES. DEFENSE SUPPLY AGENCY *See* DCAS MANAGEMENT SYNOPSIS EXECUTIVE SUMMARY **4040**

UNITED STATES. DEPARTMENT OF DEFENSE *See* TELEPHONE DIRECTORY - DEPARTMENT OF DEFENSE **4059**

UNITED STATES DEPARTMENT OF HOUSING AND URBAN DEVELOPMENT ANNUAL REPORT / U.S. DEPARTMENT OF HOUSING AND URBAN DEVELOPMENT, THE (US) [16948382] **4692**

UNITED STATES. DEPARTMENT OF HOUSING AND URBAN DEVELOPMENT. FINANCIAL MANAGEMENT BRANCH *See* ALL LOW-RENT PUBLIC HOUSING PROGRAMS, REGION 2: NEW YORK **2813**

UNITED STATES. DEPARTMENT OF HOUSING AND URBAN DEVELOPMENT. FINANCIAL MANAGEMENT BRANCH *See* ALL LOW-RENT PUBLIC HOUSING PROGRAMS, REGION 1: BOSTON **2813**

UNITED STATES. DEPARTMENT OF HOUSING AND URBAN DEVELOPMENT. FINANCIAL MANAGEMENT BRANCH *See* ALL LOW-RENT PUBLIC HOUSING PROGRAMS, REGION 6: FORT WORTH **2813**

UNITED STATES. DEPARTMENT OF HOUSING AND URBAN DEVELOPMENT. FINANCIAL MANAGEMENT BRANCH *See* ALL LOW-RENT PUBLIC HOUSING PROGRAMS, REGION 5: CHICAGO **2813**

UNITED STATES. DEPARTMENT OF HOUSING AND URBAN DEVELOPMENT. FINANCIAL MANAGEMENT BRANCH *See* ALL LOW-RENT PUBLIC HOUSING PROGRAMS, REGION 9: SAN FRANCISCO **2813**

UNITED STATES. DEPARTMENT OF HOUSING AND URBAN DEVELOPMENT. FINANCIAL MANAGEMENT BRANCH *See* ALL LOW-RENT PUBLIC HOUSING PROGRAMS, REGION 3: PHILADELPHIA **2813**

UNITED STATES. DEPARTMENT OF HOUSING AND URBAN DEVELOPMENT. FINANCIAL MANAGEMENT BRANCH *See* ALL LOW-RENT PUBLIC HOUSING PROGRAMS, REGION 4: ATLANTA **2813**

UNITED STATES. DEPARTMENT OF STATE. OFFICE OF THE LEGAL ADVISER *See* TREATIES IN FORCE. COPY A **4537**

UNITED STATES. DEPARTMENT OF THE INTERIOR *See* PROPOSED LEGISLATIVE PROGRAM - DEPARTMENT OF THE INTERIOR **3032**

UNITED STATES. DEPT. FOR ENERGY. OFFICE OF THE ASSISTANT SECRETARY FOR MANAGEMENT AND ADMINISTRATION *See* NATIONAL TELEPHONE DIRECTORY / DEPARTMENT OF ENERGY **4668**

UNITED STATES. DEPT. OF AGRICULTURE *See* ISSUE BRIEFING PAPER / UNITED STATES DEPARTMENT OF AGRICULTURE **98**

UNITED STATES. DEPT. OF AGRICULTURE *See* CODE OF FEDERAL REGULATIONS. 7, AGRICULTURE **2951**

UNITED STATES. DEPT. OF AGRICULTURE *See* ANNUAL REPORT - UNITED STATES. DEPT. OF AGRICULTURE **61**

UNITED STATES. DEPT. OF AGRICULTURE *See* PROGRESS REPORT ON PESTICIDES AND RELATED ACTIVITIES **4247**

UNITED STATES. DEPT. OF AGRICULTURE *See* PRODUCTION RESEARCH REPORT - UNITED STATES DEPARTMENT OF AGRICULTURE **122**

UNITED STATES. DEPT. OF AGRICULTURE *See* AGRICULTURE DECISIONS **53**

UNITED STATES. DEPT. OF AGRICULTURE *See* REPORT OF THE SECRETARY OF AGRICULTURE **126**

UNITED STATES. DEPT. OF AGRICULTURE. ECONOMIC RESEARCH SERVICE *See* AGRICULTURAL FINANCE STATISTICS **726**

UNITED STATES. DEPT. OF AGRICULTURE. ECONOMIC RESEARCH SERVICE *See* COSTS OF FOODS PURCHASED BY USDA AND LOCAL SCHOOL SYSTEMS **1862**

UNITED STATES. DEPT. OF AGRICULTURE. ECONOMIC RESEARCH SERVICE *See* AGRICULTURAL SITUATION IN THE SOVIET UNION, THE **52**

UNITED STATES. DEPT. OF AGRICULTURE. ECONOMIC RESEARCH SERVICE *See* U.S. FATS AND OILS STATISTICS **157**

UNITED STATES. DEPT. OF AGRICULTURE. ECONOMIC RESEARCH SERVICE *See* COST OF STORING AND HANDLING COTTON AT PUBLIC STORAGE FACILITIES **77**

UNITED STATES. DEPT. OF AGRICULTURE. ECONOMIC RESEARCH SERVICE *See* AGRICULTURAL SITUATION IN THE PEOPLE'S REPUBLIC OF CHINA AND OTHER COMMUNIST ASIAN COUNTRIES, THE **52**

UNITED STATES. DEPT. OF AGRICULTURE. ECONOMIC, STATISTICS, AND COOPERATIVES SERVICE *See* REPORT ASSESSING GLOBAL FOOD PRODUCTION AND NEEDS **125**

UNITED STATES. DEPT. OF AGRICULTURE. ECONOMICS, STATISTICS, AND COOPERATIVES SERVICE *See* ERS **82**

UNITED STATES. DEPT. OF AGRICULTURE. ECONOMICS, STATISTICS, AND COOPERATIVES SERVICE *See* WORLD ECONOMIC CONDITIONS IN RELATION TO AGRICULTURAL TRADE **1641**

UNITED STATES. DEPT. OF AGRICULTURE. ECONOMICS, STATISTICS, AND COOPERATIVES SERVICE *See* FOREIGN AGRICULTURAL ECONOMIC REPORT **88**

UNITED STATES. DEPT. OF AGRICULTURE. ECONOMICS, STATISTICS, AND COOPERATIVES SERVICE *See* ECONOMICS, STATISTICS, COOPERATIVES; PROGRAM RESULTS AND PLANS **1532**

UNITED STATES. DEPT. OF AGRICULTURE. ECONOMICS, STATISTICS, AND COOPERATIVES SERVICE. NATIONAL ECONOMICS DIVISION *See* STATUS OF THE FAMILY FARM, ANNUAL REPORT TO THE CONGRESS **138**

UNITED STATES. DEPT. OF AGRICULTURE. ECONOMICS, STATISTICS AND COOPERATIVES SERVICE. NATURAL RESOURCE ECONOMICS DIVISION *See* AGESCS **45**

UNITED STATES. DEPT. OF AGRICULTURE. OFFICE OF EQUAL OPPORTUNITY *See* EQUAL OPPORTUNITY REPORT USDA PROGRAMS **1667**

UNITED STATES. DEPT. OF AGRICULTURE. OFFICE OF THE INSPECTOR GENERAL *See* OFFICE OF INSPECTOR GENERAL SEMIANNUAL REPORT TO CONGRESS / UNITED STATES DEPARTMENT OF AGRICULTURE, OFFICE OF INSPECTOR GENERAL **116**

UNITED STATES. DEPT. OF AGRICULTURE. OFFICE OF THE INSPECTOR GENERAL *See* SEMIANNUAL REPORT - UNITED STATES. DEPT. OF AGRICULTURE. OFFICE OF THE INSPECTOR GENERAL **133**

UNITED STATES. DEPT. OF AGRICULTURE. OFFICE OF THE SECRETARY *See* FOREIGN MEAT INSPECTION **211**

UNITED STATES. DEPT. OF AGRICULTURE. OFFICE OF THE SECRETARY *See* RURAL DEVELOPMENT PROGRESS **5256**

UNITED STATES. DEPT. OF AGRICULTURE. RESEARCH AND EDUCATION COMMITTEE *See* ANNUAL REPORT ON THE FOOD AND AGRICULTURAL SCIENCES, FROM THE SECRETARY OF AGRICULTURE TO THE PRESIDENT AND THE CONGRESS OF THE UNITED STATES **61**

UNITED STATES. DEPT. OF AGRICULTURE. SCIENCE AND EDUCATION ADMINISTRATION. FEDERAL RESEARCH *See* MANAGEMENT REVIEW **878**

UNITED STATES. DEPT. OF DEFENSE *See* QUADRENNIAL REVIEW OF MILITARY COMPENSATION **4054**

UNITED STATES. DEPT. OF DEFENSE *See* JOINT TRAVEL REGULATIONS. VOLUME 2, DEPARTMENT OF DEFENSE CIVILIAN PERSONNEL **943**

UNITED STATES. DEPT. OF DEFENSE *See* PRIME CONTRACT AWARDS IN LABOR SURPLUS AREAS **4054**

UNITED STATES. DEPT. OF DEFENSE *See* DEFENSE ACQUISITION CIRCULAR **4040**

UNITED STATES. DEPT. OF DEFENSE *See* DEFENSE CONTRACT AUDIT MANUAL **4041**

UNITED STATES. DEPT. OF DEFENSE *See* REPORT OF THE SECRETARY OF DEFENSE TO THE PRESIDENT AND THE CONGRESS **4681**

UNITED STATES. DEPT. OF DEFENSE *See* PRIME CONTRACT AWARDS BY SERVICE CATEGORY AND FEDERAL SUPPLY CLASSIFICATION **4054**

UNITED STATES. DEPT. OF DEFENSE *See* COMMERCIAL ACTIVITIES INVENTORY REPORT AND FIVE-YEAR REVIEW SCHEDULE / DEPARTMENT OF DEFENSE **4039**

UNITED STATES. DEPT. OF DEFENSE *See* INDEX OF SPECIFICATIONS AND STANDARDS **4045**

UNITED STATES. DEPT. OF DEFENSE *See* JOINT TRAVEL REGULATIONS. VOLUME 1. MEMBERS OF UNIFORMED SERVICES: ARMY, NAVY, MARINE CORPS, AIR FORCE, COAST GUARD, NATIONAL OCEANIC AND ATMOSPHERIC ADMINISTRATION CORPS, PUBLIC HEALTH SERVICE **4048**

UNITED STATES. DEPT OF DEFENSE *See* PRIME CONTRACT AWARDS BY STATE **4674**

UNITED STATES. DEPT. OF DEFENSE *See* REPORT ON THE FEDERAL CATALOGING PROGRAM **4055**

UNITED STATES. DEPT. OF DEFENSE. HIGH SCHOOL NEWS SERVICE *See* REPORT, BASIC FACTS ABOUT MILITARY SERVICE **4055**

UNITED STATES. DEPT. OF DEFENSE. WASHINGTON HEADQUARTERS SERVICES. DIRECTORATE FOR INFORMATION OPERATIONS AND REPORTS *See* PRIME CONTRACT AWARDS BY REGION AND STATE **4054**

UNITED STATES. DEPT. OF DEFENSE. WASHINGTON HEADQUARTERS SERVICES. DIRECTORATE FOR INFORMATION OPERATIONS AND REPORTS *See* NATO MUTUAL SUPPORT ACT, AS AMENDED (ACQUISITION AND CROSS SERVICING AGREEMENTS WITH NATO ALLIES AND OTHER COUNTRIES); REPORT OF AGREEMENTS AND TRANSACTIONS / DEPARTMENT OF DEFENSE **4052**

UNITED STATES. DEPT. OF EDUCATION *See* ANNUAL REPORT / U.S. DEPARTMENT OF EDUCATION **1725**

UNITED STATES. DEPT. OF EDUCATION *See* JUSTIFICATIONS OF APPROPRIATION ESTIMATES FOR COMMITTEES ON APPROPRIATIONS - UNITED STATES DEPT. OF EDUCATION **1865**

UNITED STATES. DEPT. OF EDUCATION *See* ADMINISTRATION OF PUBLIC LAWS 81-874 & 81-815 **1859**

UNITED STATES. DEPT. OF EDUCATION. OFFICE OF INTERNATIONAL EDUCATION *See* OPPORTUNITIES ABROAD FOR TEACHERS **1902**

UNITED STATES. DEPT. OF ENERGY *See* ANNUAL PROCUREMENT AND FEDERAL ASSISTANCE REPORT **4626**

UNITED STATES. DEPT. OF ENERGY *See* DOE TELEPHONE DIRECTORY **4645**

UNITED STATES. DEPT. OF ENERGY See DEPARTMENT OF ENERGY SOLAR ENERGY OBJECTIVES 1936

UNITED STATES. DEPT. OF ENERGY See DOE NEWS / U.S. DEPARTMENT OF ENERGY 1936

UNITED STATES. DEPT. OF ENERGY See U.S. DEPARTMENT OF ENERGY BUDGET TO CONGRESS : BUDGET HIGHLIGHTS 4692

UNITED STATES. DEPT. OF ENERGY See TECHNICAL BOOKS & MONOGRAPHS 5162

UNITED STATES. DEPT. OF ENERGY See CONGRESSIONAL BUDGET REQUEST 1936

UNITED STATES. DEPT. OF ENERGY See DOE NEW TECHNOLOGY 1936

UNITED STATES. DEPT. OF ENERGY. ASSISTANT SECRETARY FOR CONSERVATION AND SOLAR ENERGY See SOLAR THERMAL POWER SYSTEMS. PROGRAM SUMMARY 1957

UNITED STATES. DEPT. OF ENERGY. ASSISTANT SECRETARY FOR ENVIRONMENT. OFFICE OF PROGRAM COORDINATION See COMPREHENSIVE ENVIRONMENT, HEALTH, AND SAFETY PROGRAM REPORT 4772

UNITED STATES. DEPT. OF ENERGY. ASSISTANT SECRETARY FOR ENVIRONMENTAL PROTECTION SAFETY, AND EMERGENCY PREPAREDNESS See ENVIRONMENT, SAFETY, HEALTH AT DOE FACILITIES 2861

UNITED STATES. DEPT. OF ENERGY. BOARD OF CONTRACT APPEALS See GUIDE TO PRACTICE AND PROCEDURE, U.S. DEPARTMENT OF ENERGY, BOARD OF CONTRACT APPEALS, CONTRACT ADJUSTMENT BOARD, FINANCIAL ASSISTANCE APPEALS BOARD, INVENTION LICENSING APPEALS BOARD 1945

UNITED STATES. DEPT. OF ENERGY. DEPUTY ASSISTANT SECRETARY FOR NUCLEAR REACTOR PROGRAMS See FISSION ENERGY PROGRAM OF THE U.S. DEPARTMENT OF ENERGY 1944

UNITED STATES. DEPT. OF ENERGY. DIVISION OF ENVIRONMENTAL CONTROL TECHNOLOGY See ANNUAL STATUS REPORT ON THE INACTIVE URANIUM MILL TAILINGS SITES REMEDIAL ACTION PROGRAM 2224

UNITED STATES. DEPT. OF ENERGY. DIVISION OF NUCLEAR PHYSICS See SUMMARIES OF RESEARCH IN NUCLEAR PHYSICS 4451

UNITED STATES. DEPT. OF ENERGY. DIVISION OF SOLAR ENERGY See ENVIRONMENTAL AND RESOURCE ASSESSMENT PROGRAM; PROGRAM SUMMARY 2192

UNITED STATES. DEPT. OF ENERGY. DIVISION OF SOLAR ENERGY See ANNUAL COLLECTION AND STORAGE OF SOLAR ENERGY FOR THE HEATING OF BUILDINGS 1931

UNITED STATES. DEPT. OF ENERGY. EDUCATION PROGRAMS DIVISION See GUIDE FOR THE PREPARATION OF PROPOSALS FOR FACULTY DEVELOPMENT PROJECTS IN ENERGY EDUCATION 1945

UNITED STATES. DEPT. OF ENERGY. OFFICE OF ANALYTICAL SERVICES See REPORT TO CONGRESS ON THE ECONOMIC IMPACT OF ENERGY ACTIONS 1955

UNITED STATES. DEPT. OF ENERGY. OFFICE OF CONSERVATION AND SOLAR APPLICATIONS See ENVIRONMENTAL ASSESSMENT. ELECTRIC HYBRID VEHICLE RESEARCH, DEVELOPMENT AND DEMONSTRATION PROGRAM 2228

UNITED STATES. DEPT. OF ENERGY. OFFICE OF CONSERVATION AND SOLAR APPLICATIONS. OFFICE OF BUSINESS ASSISTANCE PROGRAMS See VOLUNTARY INDUSTRIAL ENERGY CONSERVATION 1960

UNITED STATES. DEPT. OF ENERGY. OFFICE OF CONSERVATION AND SOLAR APPLICATIONS. OFFICE OF STATE AND LOCAL PROGRAMS See ANNUAL REPORT TO THE PRESIDENT AND THE CONGRESS ON THE WEATHERIZATION ASSISTANCE PROGRAM 1932

UNITED STATES. DEPT. OF ENERGY. OFFICE OF CONSERVATION AND SOLAR ENERGY. OFFICE OF STATE AND LOCAL ASSISTANCE PROGRAMS See DOE STATE & LOCAL ASSISTANCE PROGRAMS 1936

UNITED STATES. DEPT. OF ENERGY. OFFICE OF ENERGY RESEARCH See DOE/ER (UNITED STATES. DEPT. OF ENERGY. OFFICE OF ENERGY RESEARCH) 1936

UNITED STATES. DEPT. OF ENERGY. OFFICE OF ENERGY TECHNOLOGY See ENVIRONMENTAL DEVELOPMENT PLAN (EDP). INDUSTRIAL ENERGY CONSERVATION 1943

UNITED STATES. DEPT. OF ENERGY. OFFICE OF ENERGY TECHNOLOGY See SOLAR, GEOTHERMAL, ELECTRIC AND STORAGE SYSTEMS PROGRAM, SUMMARY DOCUMENT 1957

UNITED STATES. DEPT. OF ENERGY. OFFICE OF ENERGY TECHNOLOGY See ENVIRONMENTAL DEVELOPMENT PLAN. WIND ENERGY CONVERSION 1943

UNITED STATES. DEPT. OF ENERGY. OFFICE OF ENERGY TECHNOLOGY See ENVIRONMENTAL DEVELOPMENT PLAN (EDP). ELECTRIC ENERGY SYSTEMS 2053

UNITED STATES. DEPT. OF ENERGY. OFFICE OF ENERGY TECHNOLOGY See ENVIRONMENTAL DEVELOPMENT PLAN. BIOMASS ENERGY SYSTEMS 2167

UNITED STATES. DEPT. OF ENERGY. OFFICE OF ENERGY TECHNOLOGY See ENVIRONMENTAL DEVELOPMENT PLAN (EDP). WIND ENERGY CONVERSION 1943

UNITED STATES. DEPT. OF ENERGY. OFFICE OF ENERGY TECHNOLOGY See ENVIRONMENTAL DEVELOPMENT PLAN (EDP). ENHANCED GAS RECOVERY 4255

UNITED STATES. DEPT. OF ENERGY. OFFICE OF ENERGY TECHNOLOGY See ENVIRONMENTAL DEVELOPMENT PLAN (EDP). DIRECT COMBUSTION PROGRAM 1943

UNITED STATES. DEPT. OF ENERGY. OFFICE OF ENERGY TECHNOLOGY See ENVIRONMENTAL DEVELOPMENT PLAN (EDP). ENERGY STORAGE SYSTEMS 1943

UNITED STATES. DEPT. OF ENERGY. OFFICE OF ENERGY TECHNOLOGY See ENVIRONMENTAL DEVELOPMENT PLAN. OCEAN THERMAL ENERGY CONVERSION 1943

UNITED STATES. DEPT. OF ENERGY. OFFICE OF ENERGY TECHNOLOGY See ENVIRONMENTAL DEVELOPMENT PLAN. SOLAR HEATING AND COOLING OF BUILDINGS 1943

UNITED STATES. DEPT. OF ENERGY. OFFICE OF ENERGY TECHNOLOGY See FOSSIL ENERGY RESEARCH AND DEVELOPMENT PROGRAM OF THE U.S. DEPARTMENT OF ENERGY 1944

UNITED STATES. DEPT. OF ENERGY. OFFICE OF ENERGY TECHNOLOGY See DOE/ET 5101

UNITED STATES. DEPT. OF ENERGY. OFFICE OF FACILITY PLANNING AND SUPPORT See FY ANNUAL REPORT ON IN-HOUSE ENERGY MANAGEMENT 1945

UNITED STATES. DEPT. OF ENERGY. OFFICE OF FUSION ENERGY See MAGNETIC FUSION ENERGY; PROGRAM SUMMARY DOCUMENT 1950

UNITED STATES. DEPT. OF ENERGY. OFFICE OF FUSION ENERGY See MAGNETIC FUSION PROGRAM SUMMARY DOCUMENT 4444

UNITED STATES. DEPT. OF ENERGY. OFFICE OF HEALTH AND ENVIRONMENTAL RESEARCH See CARBON DIOXIDE EFFECTS RESEARCH AND ASSESSMENT PROGRAM. CARBON DIOXIDE RESEARCH PROGRESS REPORT 2226

UNITED STATES. DEPT. OF ENERGY. OFFICE OF NUCLEAR WASTE MANAGEMENT See NUCLEAR WASTE MANAGEMENT PROGRAM SUMMARY DOCUMENT 2237

UNITED STATES. DEPT. OF ENERGY. OFFICE OF SOLAR APPLICATIONS See ENVIRONMENTAL DEVELOPMENT PLAN. INDUSTRIAL PROGRAMS 1943

UNITED STATES. DEPT. OF ENERGY. OFFICE OF THE ASSISTANT SECRETARY FOR ENVIRONMENT See ENVIRONMENTAL DEVELOPMENT PLAN. URANIUM MINING, MILLING, AND CONVERSION 2167

UNITED STATES. DEPT. OF ENERGY. OFFICE OF THE ASSISTANT SECRETARY FOR ENVIRONMENT See OFFICE OF ENVIRONMENT STATEMENT OF PROGRAMS 2179

UNITED STATES. DEPT. OF ENERGY. OFFICE OF THE ASSISTANT SECRETARY FOR ENVIRONMENT See ENVIRONMENTAL DEVELOPMENT PLAN. DECONTAMINATION AND DECOMMISSIONING 2228

UNITED STATES. DEPT. OF ENERGY. OFFICE OF THE CONTROLLER See BUDGET IN BRIEF / U.S. DEPARTMENT OF ENERGY 4714

UNITED STATES. DEPT. OF ENERGY. OFFICE OF THE CONTROLLER See DEPARTMENT OF ENERGY FY ... OBLIGATIONS AND COSTS BY STATE 1936

UNITED STATES. DEPT. OF ENERGY. OFFICE OF THE CONTROLLER See BUDGET HIGHLIGHTS - UNITED STATES. DEPT. OF ENERGY. OFFICE OF THE CONTROLLER 4634

UNITED STATES. DEPT. OF ENERGY. PROCUREMENT MANAGEMENT SYSTEMS AND ANALYSIS DIVISION See COMPENDIUM OF PUBLICLY AVAILABLE REPORTS ON PROCUREMENT AND FINANCIAL ASSISTANCE AWARDS - (DEPT OF ENERGY) 1935

UNITED STATES. DEPT. OF ENERGY. TECHNICAL INFORMATION CENTER See RESOURCE DIRECTORY OF DOE INFORMATION ORGANIZATIONS 1955

UNITED STATES. DEPT. OF HEALTH AND HUMAN SERVICES See HHS FELLOWS PROGRAM, THE 5287

UNITED STATES. DEPT. OF HEALTH AND HUMAN SERVICES See CODE OF FEDERAL REGULATIONS. 42, PUBLIC HEALTH 2952

UNITED STATES. DEPT. OF HEALTH AND HUMAN SERVICES See ANNUAL REPORT FROM THE SECRETARY OF THE DEPARTMENT OF HEALTH AND HUMAN SERVICES TO THE PRESIDENT AND CONGRESS OF THE UNITED STATES : DRUG ABUSE PREVENTION, TREATMENT, AND REHABILITATION 1341

UNITED STATES. DEPT. OF HEALTH AND HUMAN SERVICES See PUBLICATION CATALOG OF THE U.S. DEPARTMENT OF HEALTH AND HUMAN SERVICES 5303

UNITED STATES. DEPT. OF HEALTH AND HUMAN SERVICES See TELEPHONE DIRECTORY 5312

UNITED STATES. DEPT. OF HEALTH AND HUMAN SERVICES. OFFICE OF INSPECTOR GENERAL See ABBREVIATED ANNUAL REPORT / U.S. DEPARTMENT OF HEALTH AND HUMAN SERVICES, OFFICE OF INSPECTOR GENERAL 4623

UNITED STATES. DEPT. OF HEALTH, EDUCATION, AND WELFARE See HEALTH STATISTICS PLAN 4810

UNITED STATES. DEPT. OF HEALTH, EDUCATION AND WELFARE See SUMMARY OF SELECTED LEGISLATION RELATED TO THE HANDICAPPED, A 3061

UNITED STATES. DEPT. OF HEALTH, EDUCATION, AND WELFARE. INTRADEPARTMENTAL COMMITTEE ON CHILD ABUSE AND NEGLECT See RESEARCH, DEMONSTRATION AND EVALUATION STUDIES ON CHILD ABUSE AND NEGLECT 5305

UNITED STATES. DEPT. OF HEALTH, EDUCATION, AND WELFARE. REGION III See DEMOGRAPHIC REPORT, HEW 4552

UNITED STATES. DEPT. OF HEALTH, EDUCATION, AND WELFARE. VOCATIONAL REHABILITATION ADMINISTRATION See VRA BULLETIN BOARD 4694

UNITED STATES. DEPT. OF HOUSING AND URBAN DEVELOPMENT See INTERMEDIATE MINIMUM PROPERTY STANDARDS FOR SOLAR HEATING AND DOMESTIC HOT WATER SYSTEMS 2606

UNITED STATES. DEPT. OF HOUSING AND URBAN DEVELOPMENT See MANUAL OF ACCEPTABLE PRACTICES 2827

UNITED STATES. DEPT. OF HOUSING AND URBAN DEVELOPMENT See UNITED STATES DEPARTMENT OF HOUSING AND URBAN DEVELOPMENT ANNUAL REPORT / U.S. DEPARTMENT OF HOUSING AND URBAN DEVELOPMENT, THE 4692

UNITED STATES. DEPT. OF HOUSING AND URBAN DEVELOPMENT See ANNUAL AWARDS CEREMONY / U.S. DEPARTMENT OF HOUSING AND URBAN DEVELOPMENT 2814

UNITED STATES. DEPT. OF HOUSING AND URBAN DEVELOPMENT See MINIMUM PROPERTY STANDARDS FOR ONE-AND TWO-FAMILY DWELLINGS 2828

UNITED STATES. DEPT. OF HOUSING AND URBAN DEVELOPMENT See MINIMUM PROPERTY STANDARDS FOR CARE-TYPE HOUSING 2828

UNITED STATES. DEPT. OF HOUSING AND URBAN DEVELOPMENT See PRESIDENT'S NATIONAL URBAN POLICY REPORT, THE 2831

UNITED STATES. DEPT. OF HOUSING AND URBAN DEVELOPMENT See MINIMUM PROPERTY STANDARDS FOR MULTIFAMILY HOUSING 2828

UNITED STATES. DEPT. OF HOUSING AND URBAN DEVELOPMENT. ASSISTED HOUSING BRANCH See LOCAL AUTHORITIES PARTICIPATING IN LOW-RENT HOUSING PROGRAMS 2827

UNITED STATES. DEPT. OF HOUSING AND URBAN DEVELOPMENT. FINANCIAL MANAGEMENT BRANCH See ALL LOW-RENT PUBLIC HOUSING PROGRAMS, REGION 7: KANSAS CITY 2813

UNITED STATES. DEPT. OF HOUSING AND URBAN DEVELOPMENT. FINANCIAL MANAGEMENT BRANCH See ALL LOW-RENT PUBLIC HOUSING PROGRAMS, REGION 10: SEATTLE **2813**

UNITED STATES. DEPT. OF HOUSING AND URBAN DEVELOPMENT. FINANCIAL MANAGEMENT BRANCH See ALL LOW-RENT PUBLIC HOUSING PROGRAMS, REGION 8: DENVER **2813**

UNITED STATES. DEPT. OF HOUSING AND URBAN DEVELOPMENT. OFFICE OF ADMINISTRATION See PROCUREMENT POLICIES AND PROCEDURES **2832**

UNITED STATES. DEPT. OF HOUSING AND URBAN DEVELOPMENT. OFFICE OF ADMINISTRATION See CLAIMS COLLECTION HANDBOOK **2818**

UNITED STATES. DEPT. OF HOUSING AND URBAN DEVELOPMENT. OFFICE OF FINANCE AND ACCOUNTING See FINANCIAL STATEMENTS - DEPARTMENT OF HOUSING AND URBAN DEVELOPMENT, OFFICE OF FINANCE AND ACCOUNTING **2822**

UNITED STATES. DEPT. OF HOUSING AND URBAN DEVELOPMENT. OFFICE OF GENERAL COUNSEL See LEGAL OPINIONS OF THE OFFICE OF GENERAL COUNSEL - UNITED STATES. DEPT. OF HOUSING AND URBAN DEVELOPMENT **3000**

UNITED STATES. DEPT. OF HOUSING AND URBAN DEVELOPMENT. OFFICE OF HOUSING See ADVANCES FOR PUBLIC WORKS PLANNING PROGRAM **2813**

UNITED STATES. DEPT. OF HOUSING AND URBAN DEVELOPMENT. OFFICE OF HOUSING See APPLICATION THROUGH INSURANCE, SINGLE FAMILY, SECTION 203(N) **2815**

UNITED STATES. DEPT. OF HOUSING AND URBAN DEVELOPMENT. OFFICE OF INSPECTOR GENERAL See AUDIT GUIDE FOR AUDITS OF HUD APPROVED NONSUPERVISED MORTGAGES FOR USE BY INDEPENDENT PUBLIC ACCOUNTANTS **739**

UNITED STATES. DEPT. OF HOUSING AND URBAN DEVELOPMENT. OFFICE OF INSPECTOR GENERAL See ANNUAL AUDIT PLAN **2814**

UNITED STATES. DEPT. OF HOUSING AND URBAN DEVELOPMENT. OFFICE OF INTERNATIONAL AFFAIRS See HUD INTERNATIONAL INFORMATION SERIES **2825**

UNITED STATES. DEPT. OF HOUSING AND URBAN DEVELOPMENT. OFFICE OF POLICY DEVELOPMENT AND RESEARCH See COMPENDIUM OF RESEARCH CONTRACTS AND REPORTS - (DEPT. OF HOUSING AND URBAN DEVELOPMENT) **2819**

UNITED STATES. DEPT. OF HOUSING AND URBAN DEVELOPMENT. OFFICE OF POLICY DEVELOPMENT AND RESEARCH See EVALUATION OF THE URBAN HOMESTEADING DEMONSTRATION PROGRAM, ANNUAL REPORT **2822**

UNITED STATES. DEPT. OF HOUSING AND URBAN DEVELOPMENT. OFFICE OF POLICY DEVELOPMENT AND RESEARCH See PDR, RESEARCH AND TECHNOLOGY PROGRAM **2830**

UNITED STATES. DEPT. OF HOUSING AND URBAN DEVELOPMENT. OFFICE OF THE SPECIAL ASSISTANT TO THE SECRETARY FOR INDIAN AND ALASKA NATIVE PROGRAMS See DEPARTMENT OF HOUSING AND URBAN DEVELOPMENT ANNUAL REPORT TO CONGRESS ON INDIAN AND ALASKA NATIVE HOUSING AND COMMUNITY DEVELOPMENT PROGRAMS **2820**

UNITED STATES. DEPT. OF JUSTICE See JUSTICE (WASHINGTON, D.C.) **2992**

UNITED STATES. DEPT. OF JUSTICE See PROGRAM AND RESOURCE DIGEST, THE **4675**

UNITED STATES. DEPT. OF JUSTICE See JURIS NEWSLETTER **2990**

UNITED STATES. DEPT. OF JUSTICE See ATTORNEY GENERAL'S REPORT ON FEDERAL LAW ENFORCEMENT AND CRIMINAL JUSTICE ASSISTANCE ACTIVITIES **3158**

UNITED STATES. DEPT. OF JUSTICE See DEPARTMENT OF JUSTICE FINANCIAL LITIGATION ANNUAL REPORT **2959**

UNITED STATES. DEPT. OF JUSTICE See ANNUAL REPORT OF THE ATTORNEY GENERAL OF THE UNITED STATES **3139**

UNITED STATES. DEPT. OF JUSTICE. ANTITRUST DIVISION See ANTITRUST DIVISION MANUAL **3095**

UNITED STATES. DEPT. OF JUSTICE. CRIMINAL DIVISION See CRIMINAL DIVISION **3162**

UNITED STATES. DEPT. OF LABOR See TRAINING AND EMPLOYMENT REPORT OF THE SECRETARY OF LABOR **1715**

UNITED STATES. DEPT. OF LABOR See U.S. DEPARTMENT OF LABOR PROGRAM HIGHLIGHTS **1715**

UNITED STATES. DEPT. OF LABOR See NEWS / UNITED STATES DEPARTMENT OF LABOR, OFFICE OF INFORMATION **1694**

UNITED STATES. DEPT. OF LABOR See BUDGET PROPOSED FOR THE DEPARTMENT OF LABOR AND RELATED AGENCIES, THE **1656**

UNITED STATES. DEPT. OF LABOR See EMPLOYEE RETIREMENT INCOME SECURITY ACT : REPORT TO CONGRESS **3147**

UNITED STATES. DEPT. OF LABOR. OFFICE OF ADMINISTRATIVE LAW JUDGES See DECISIONS OF THE OFFICE OF ADMINISTRATIVE LAW JUDGES AND OFFICE OF ADMINISTRATIVE APPEALS **3092**

UNITED STATES. DEPT. OF LABOR. OFFICE OF THE INSPECTOR GENERAL See SEMIANNUAL REPORT - UNITED STATES. DEPT. OF LABOR. OFFICE OF THE INSPECTOR GENERAL **1710**

UNITED STATES. DEPT. OF STATE See BIOGRAPHIC REGISTER / DEPARTMENT OF STATE, U.S. FOREIGN SERVICE, INTERNATIONAL COOPERATION ADMINISTRATION, U.S. INFORMATION AGENCY, FOREIGN AGRICULTURAL SERVICE, THE **430**

UNITED STATES. DEPT. OF STATE See FOREIGN RELATIONS OF THE UNITED STATES **4522**

UNITED STATES. DEPT. OF STATE See STANDARDIZED REGULATIONS **4687**

UNITED STATES. DEPT. OF STATE. ALLOWANCES STAFF See MAXIMUM TRAVEL PER DIEM ALLOWANCES FOR FOREIGN AREAS **5484**

UNITED STATES. DEPT. OF STATE. BUREAU OF INTELLIGENCE AND RESEARCH See COMMUNIST STATES AND DEVELOPING COUNTRIES, AID AND TRADE **4541**

UNITED STATES. DEPT. OF STATE. BUREAU OF PUBLIC AFFAIRS See SELECTED STATE DEPARTMENT PUBLICATIONS / UNITED STATES DEPARTMENT OF STATE, BUREAU OF PUBLIC AFFAIRS **4685**

UNITED STATES. DEPT. OF STATE. OFFICE OF EXTERNAL RESEARCH See EXTERNAL RESEARCH STUDY **4647**

UNITED STATES. DEPT. OF STATE. OFFICE OF THE PROGRAM INSPECTOR GENERAL See ANNUAL REPORT ... PROGRAM INSPECTOR GENERAL **4464**

UNITED STATES. DEPT. OF THE AIR FORCE See CHRONOLOGY OF AMERICAN AEROSPACE EVENTS, A **16**

UNITED STATES. DEPT. OF THE AIR FORCE See AIR FORCE REPORT **4034**

UNITED STATES. DEPT. OF THE AIR FORCE See INSTRUMENT FLYING **24**

UNITED STATES. DEPT. OF THE ARMY See TRANSPORTATION AND TRAVEL : OFFICIAL TABLE OF DISTANCES, FOREIGN TRAVEL **5494**

UNITED STATES. DEPT. OF THE ARMY See INDEX OF STORAGE AND OUTLOADING DRAWINGS FOR AMMUNITION COMMODITIES **4046**

UNITED STATES. DEPT. OF THE ARMY See INDEX OF BLANK FORMS - UNITED STATES. DEPT. OF THE ARMY **4045**

UNITED STATES. DEPT. OF THE INTERIOR See DECISIONS OF THE DEPARTMENT OF THE INTERIOR (MONTHLY) **4642**

UNITED STATES. DEPT. OF THE INTERIOR See CAREERS IN THE UNITED STATES DEPARTMENT OF THE INTERIOR **4202**

UNITED STATES. DEPT. OF THE INTERIOR See DECISIONS OF THE UNITED STATES DEPARTMENT OF THE INTERIOR **4642**

UNITED STATES. DEPT. OF THE INTERIOR See INTERIOR BUDGET IN BRIEF, THE **4657**

UNITED STATES. DEPT. OF THE INTERIOR. BUDGET HIGHLIGHTS See INTERIOR BUDGET IN BRIEF, THE **4657**

UNITED STATES. DEPT. OF THE INTERIOR. OFFICE OF HEARINGS AND APPEALS See INDEX-DIGEST - UNITED STATES DEPARTMENT OF THE INTERIOR, OFFICE OF HEARINGS AND APPEALS **3081**

UNITED STATES. DEPT. OF THE INTERIOR. OFFICE OF RESEARCH AND DEVELOPMENT See ENERGY RESEARCH PROGRAM OF THE U.S. DEPARTMENT OF THE INTERIOR **1941**

UNITED STATES. DEPT. OF THE INTERIOR. WATER AND POWER RESOURCES SERVICE See WATER AND LAND RESOURCE ACCOMPLISHMENTS. FEDERAL RECLAMATION PROJECTS, SUMMARY REPORT **2208**

UNITED STATES. DEPT. OF THE TREASURY See CODE OF FEDERAL REGULATIONS. 27, ALCOHOL, TOBACCO PRODUCTS AND FIREARMS **2951**

UNITED STATES. DEPT. OF THE TREASURY See CODE OF FEDERAL REGULATIONS. 31, MONEY AND FINANCE, TREASURY **2952**

UNITED STATES. DEPT. OF THE TREASURY See FEDERAL INCOME TAX REGULATIONS (1986) **4724**

UNITED STATES. DEPT. OF THE TREASURY See OPERATION AND EFFECT OF THE DOMESTIC INTERNATIONAL SALES CORPORATION LEGISLATION ... ANNUAL REPORT, THE **848**

UNITED STATES. DEPT. OF THE TREASURY See EXPERIENCE OF FEDERAL AGENCIES UNDER THE PROGRAM OF SELF-INSURING FIDELITY LOSSES PURSUANT TO PUBLIC LAW 92-310 **2879**

UNITED STATES. DEPT. OF THE TREASURY. OFFICE OF INSPECTOR GENERAL See ANNUAL REPORT - UNITED STATES. DEPT. OF THE TREASURY. OFFICE OF THE INSPECTOR GENERAL **4711**

UNITED STATES. DEPT. OF TRANSPORTATION See FINANCIAL CONDITION OF PENN CENTRAL TRANSPORTATION COMPANY, THE **5431**

UNITED STATES. DEPT. OF TRANSPORTATION See ANNUAL REPORT / U.S. DEPARTMENT OF TRANSPORTATION **5377**

UNITED STATES. DEPT. OF TRANSPORTATION See CODE OF FEDERAL REGULATIONS. 23, HIGHWAYS **2951**

UNITED STATES. DEPT. OF TRANSPORTATION See REPORT TO THE CONGRESS OF THE UNITED STATES ON URBAN TRANSPORTATION POLICIES & ACTIVITIES **5391**

UNITED STATES. DEPT. OF TRANSPORTATION. CLIMATIC IMPACT ASSESSMENT PROGRAM OFFICE See TECHNICAL ABSTRACT REPORT - DEPT. OF TRANSPORTATION. CLIMATIC IMPACT ASSESSMENT PROGRAM **1435**

UNITED STATES. DEPT. OF TRANSPORTATION. LIBRARY SERVICES DIVISION See SELECTED LIBRARY ACQUISITIONS **3248**

UNITED STATES. DEPT. OF TRANSPORTATION. OFFICE OF HAZARDOUS MATERIALS See REPORT NO. TES **2241**

UNITED STATES. DEPT. OF TRANSPORTATION. OFFICE OF INSPECTOR GENERAL See SEMIANNUAL REPORT TO THE CONGRESS - UNITED STATES. DEPT. OF TRANSPORTATION. OFFICE OF INSPECTOR GENERAL (1981) **5392**

UNITED STATES. DEPT. OF TRANSPORTATION. OFFICE OF THE SECRETARY See FISCAL YEAR BUDGET ESTIMATES - DEPT. OF TRANSPORTATION, OFFICE OF THE SECRETARY **5382**

UNITED STATES. DEPT. OF TRANSPORTATION. OFFICE OF THE SECRETARY See DIRECTORY OF NATIONAL DEFENSE EXECUTIVE RESERVISTS ON ASSIGNMENT TO OFFICE OF SECRETARY OF TRANSPORTATION, U.S. DEPARTMENT OF TRANSPORTATION **5381**

UNITED STATES. DEPT. OF TRANSPORTATION. OFFICE OF THE SECRETARY See SECRETARY'S SEMIANNUAL REPORT TO THE CONGRESS, THE **5392**

UNITED STATES. DEPT. OF VETERANS AFFAIRS See QUADRENNIAL REPORT TO THE PRESIDENT ON THE ADEQUACY OF SPECIAL PAY FOR PHYSICIANS AND DENTISTS IN THE DEPARTMENT OF VETERANS AFFAIRS **3916**

UNITED STATES. DEPT. OF VETERANS AFFAIRS See PUBLICATIONS CATALOG, LOG 1 **4677**

UNITED STATES. DEPT. OF VETERANS AFFAIRS See DIRECTORY OF DEPARTMENT OF VETERANS AFFAIRS FACILITIES **4042**

UNITED STATES. DEPT. OF VETERANS AFFAIRS. OFFICE OF ACQUISITION AND MATERIEL MANAGEMENT See FEDERAL SUPPLY CATALOG. SECTION VII, CLASSIFICATION OF PROPERTY WITH ALPHABETICAL INDEX OF EXPENDABLE ITEMS **4837**

UNITED STATES. DEPT. OF VETERANS AFFAIRS. PUBLICATIONS SERVICE See DEPARTMENT OF VETERANS AFFAIRS PUBLICATIONS INDEX **4042**

UNITED STATES. DIGESTIVE DISEASES COORDINATING COMMITTEE See ANNUAL REPORT OF THE DIGESTIVE DISEASES COORDINATING COMMITTEE TO THE SECRETARY, U.S. DEPARTMENT OF HEALTH AND HUMAN SERVICES **3795**

UNITED STATES DIRECTORIES OF MINORITY CONTRACTORS, YELLOW PAGES, THE (US/0731-5643) [08203346] **717**

UNITED

Alphabetical Title Index

UNITED STATES DIRECTORY OF FEDERAL REGIONAL STRUCTURE (US/0730-1332) [06922593] **4692**

UNITED STATES. DISTRICT COURTS *See* FEDERAL LOCAL COURT RULES **3089**

UNITED STATES. DIVISION OF ELECTRIC ENERGY SYSTEMS. SYSTEMS MANAGEMENT & STRUCTURING *See* SYSTEMS ENGINEERING FOR POWER **2083**

UNITED STATES. DIVISION OF WATER SUPPLY AND POLLUTION CONTROL *See* WATER POLLUTION SURVEILLANCE SYSTEM : ANNUAL COMPILATION OF DATA **2247**

UNITED STATES. DIVISION OF WILDLIFE SERVICES *See* ANNUAL REPORT - UNITED STATES DEPARTMENT OF THE INTERIOR, BUREAU OF SPORT FISHERIES AND WILDLIFE, FISH AND WILDLIFE SERVICE **2187**

UNITED STATES EARTHQUAKES (US/0091-1429) [01798128] **1400**

UNITED STATES. ECONOMIC DEVELOPMENT ADMINISTRATION *See* ANNUAL REPORT - UNITED STATES. ECONOMIC DEVELOPMENT ADMINISTRATION (1969) **1598**

UNITED STATES. EMBASSY (INDONESIA) *See* INDONESIA ECONOMIC TRENDS REPORT **1567**

UNITED STATES. EMBASSY (INDONESIA). ECONOMIC-COMMERCIAL SECTION. DIRECTORY OF UNITED STATES FIRMS IN INDONESIA *See* DIRECTORY OF U.S. FIRMS AND ORGANIZATIONS IN INDONESIA **1605**

UNITED STATES. EMBASSY (SUDAN) ECONOMIC SECTION *See* KEY OFFICIALS HANDBOOK **4660**

UNITED STATES. EMPLOYEES' COMPENSATION APPEALS BOARD *See* DIGEST AND DECISIONS OF THE EMPLOYEES' COMPENSATION APPEALS BOARD **3146**

UNITED STATES. EMPLOYMENT AND TRAINING ADMINISTRATION *See* OPERATING INSTRUCTIONS HANDBOOK FOR LABOR CERTIFICATION PROGRAM FOR IMMIGRANT WORKERS. CHAPTER 1 **1700**

UNITED STATES. EMPLOYMENT AND TRAINING ADMINISTRATION *See* LISTING OF ELIGIBLE LABOR SURPLUS AREAS UNDER DEFENSE MANPOWER POLICY NO. 4A AND EXECUTIVE ORDER 10582 **1688**

UNITED STATES. EMPLOYMENT STANDARDS ADMINISTRATION *See* ESA DIRECTORY OF OFFICES / U.S. DEPARTMENT OF LABOR, EMPLOYMENT STANDARDS ADMINISTRATION **1668**

UNITED STATES. EMPLOYMENT STANDARDS ADMINISTRATION *See* BLACK LUNG BENEFITS ACT. ANNUAL REPORT ON ADMINISTRATION OF THE ACT / U.S. DEPARTMENT OF LABOR, EMPLOYMENT STANDARDS ADMINISTRATION **1655**

UNITED STATES. EMPLOYMENT STANDARDS ADMINISTRATION *See* AGE DISCRIMINATION IN EMPLOYMENT ACT OF 1967 **1642**

UNITED STATES. ENERGY INFORMATION ADMININSTRATION. OFFICE OF ENERGY DATA AND INTERPRETATION *See* NATIONAL ELECTRIC RATE BOOK **2073**

UNITED STATES. ENERGY INFORMATION ADMINISTRATION *See* ANNUAL ENERGY BALANCE (U.S.) **1931**

UNITED STATES. ENERGY INFORMATION ADMINISTRATION. OFFICE OF APPLIED ANALYSIS *See* QUARTERLY TRACKING SYSTEM, ENERGY USING AND CONSERVATION EQUIPMENT IN HOMES **1954**

UNITED STATES. ENERGY INFORMATION ADMINISTRATION. OFFICE OF STATISTICAL STANDARDS *See* DIRECTORY OF ENERGY DATA COLLECTION FORMS / ENERGY INFORMATION ADMINISTRATION, OFFICE OF STATISTICAL STANDARDS **1936**

UNITED STATES. ENERGY RESEARCH AND DEVELOPMENT ADMINISTRATION *See* FINANCIAL REPORT - ENERGY RESEARCH AND DEVELOPMENT ADMINISTRATION **1944**

UNITED STATES. ENERGY RESEARCH AND DEVELOPMENT ADMINISTRATION *See* URANIUM ENRICHMENT SERVICES ACTIVITY : FINANCIAL STATEMENTS **1630**

UNITED STATES. ENERGY RESEARCH AND DEVELOPMENT ADMINISTRATION. DIVISION OF SAFETY, STANDARDS, & COMPLIANCE *See* ENVIRONMENTAL MONITORING AT MAJOR U.S. ENERGY RESEARCH & DEVELOPMENT ADMINISTRATION CONTRACTOR SITES **2168**

UNITED STATES. ENERGY RESEARCH AND DEVELOPMENT ADMINISTRATION. FEDERAL WIND ENERGY PROGRAM *See* SUMMARY REPORT - FEDERAL WIND ENERGY PROGRAM **1958**

UNITED STATES. ENERGY RESEARCH AND DEVELOPMENT ADMINISTRATION. OFFICE OF INDUSTRY RELATIONS *See* NUCLEAR INDUSTRY, THE **2157**

UNITED STATES. ENERGY RESEARCH AND DEVELOPMENT ADMINISTRATION. SOLAR THERMAL ENERGY CONVERSION PROGRAM *See* SUMMARY REPORT - SOLAR THERMAL ENERGY CONVERSION PROGRAM **1958**

UNITED STATES. ENVIRONMENTAL DATA SERVICE *See* HOURLY PRECIPITATION DATA, TEXAS **1426**

UNITED STATES. ENVIRONMENTAL DATA SERVICE *See* HOURLY PRECIPITATION DATA, WEST VIRGINIA **1426**

UNITED STATES. ENVIRONMENTAL DATA SERVICE *See* HOURLY PRECIPITATION DATA, SOUTH CAROLINA **1425**

UNITED STATES. ENVIRONMENTAL DATA SERVICE *See* HOURLY PRECIPITATION DATA, MICHIGAN **1425**

UNITED STATES. ENVIRONMENTAL DATA SERVICE *See* HOURLY PRECIPITATION DATA, MINNESOTA **1425**

UNITED STATES. ENVIRONMENTAL DATA SERVICE *See* HOURLY PRECIPITATION DATA, PENNSYLVANIA **1425**

UNITED STATES. ENVIRONMENTAL DATA SERVICE *See* HOURLY PRECIPITATION DATA, MISSOURI **1425**

UNITED STATES. ENVIRONMENTAL DATA SERVICE *See* HOURLY PRECIPITATION DATA, ILLINOIS **1425**

UNITED STATES. ENVIRONMENTAL PROTECTION AGENCY *See* TOXIC SUBSTANCES CONTROL ACT **3116**

UNITED STATES. ENVIRONMENTAL PROTECTION AGENCY *See* ENVIRONMENTAL PROTECTION AGENCY PLANNING AND BUDGETING GUIDANCE **2229**

UNITED STATES. ENVIRONMENTAL PROTECTION AGENCY *See* EPA ACTIVITIES UNDER THE RESOURCE CONSERVATION AND RECOVERY ACT OF 1976 **2193**

UNITED STATES. ENVIRONMENTAL PROTECTION AGENCY *See* CLEAN WATER (WASHINGTON) **5532**

UNITED STATES. ENVIRONMENTAL PROTECTION AGENCY *See* COST OF CLEAN AIR AND CLEAN WATER, THE **2227**

UNITED STATES. ENVIRONMENTAL PROTECTION AGENCY *See* EPA COMPENDIUM OF REGISTERED PESTICIDES. VOLUME 1. HERBICIDES AND PLANT REGULATORS **4244**

UNITED STATES. ENVIRONMENTAL PROTECTION AGENCY *See* GRANTS ADMINISTRATION MANUAL **4652**

UNITED STATES. ENVIRONMENTAL PROTECTION AGENCY *See* ACCESS EPA **2159**

UNITED STATES. ENVIRONMENTAL PROTECTION AGENCY *See* EPA AND THE ACADEMIC COMMUNITY, PARTNERS IN RESEARCH SOLICITATION FOR GRANT PROPOSALS **2229**

UNITED STATES. ENVIRONMENTAL PROTECTION AGENCY *See* EPA COMPENDIUM OF REGISTERED PESTICIDES. VOLUME 3. INSECTICIDES, ACARICIDES, MOLLUSCICIDES AND ANTIFOULING COMPOUNDS **4244**

UNITED STATES. ENVIRONMENTAL PROTECTION AGENCY *See* PROGRESS IN THE IMPLEMENTATION OF MOTOR VEHICLE EMISSION STANDARDS **2240**

UNITED STATES. ENVIRONMENTAL PROTECTION AGENCY *See* EPA COMPENDIUM OF REGISTERED PESTICIDES. VOLUME 2. FUNGICIDES AND NEMATICIDES **4244**

UNITED STATES. ENVIRONMENTAL PROTECTION AGENCY *See* EPA COMPENDIUM OF REGISTERED PESTICIDES. VOLUME 4. RODENTICIDES AND MAMMAL, BIRD AND FISH TOXICANTS **4244**

UNITED STATES. ENVIRONMENTAL PROTECTION AGENCY *See* EPA COMPENDIUM OF REGISTERED PESTICIDES. VOLUME 5. DISINFECTANTS **4244**

UNITED STATES. ENVIRONMENTAL PROTECTION AGENCY. GRANTS ADMINISTRATION DIVISION *See* STATE AND LOCAL GRANT AWARDS **4749**

UNITED STATES. ENVIRONMENTAL PROTECTION AGENCY. LIBRARY SYSTEMS BRANCH *See* U.S. ENVIRONMENTAL PROTECTION AGENCY LIBRARY SYSTEM BOOK CATALOG **3214**

UNITED STATES. ENVIRONMENTAL PROTECTION AGENCY. NATIONAL AIR DATA BRANCH *See* NATIONAL EMISSIONS REPORT **2237**

UNITED STATES. ENVIRONMENTAL PROTECTION AGENCY. NATIONAL AIR DATA BRANCH *See* AIR QUALITY DATA - STATISTICS **2183**

UNITED STATES. ENVIRONMENTAL PROTECTION AGENCY. OFFICE OF ADMINISTRATION AND RESOURCES MANAGEMENT *See* TELEPHONE DIRECTORY - U.S. ENVIRONMENTAL PROTECTION AGENCY **2245**

UNITED STATES. ENVIRONMENTAL PROTECTION AGENCY. OFFICE OF AIR AND WATER PROGRAMS *See* OFFICE OF AIR AND WATER PROGRAMS PUBLICATION **2179**

UNITED STATES. ENVIRONMENTAL PROTECTION AGENCY. OFFICE OF AIR AND WATER PROGRAMS *See* STATE AIR POLLUTION IMPLEMENTATION PLAN PROGRESS REPORT **2182**

UNITED STATES. ENVIRONMENTAL PROTECTION AGENCY. OFFICE OF AIR QUALITY PLANNING AND STANDARDS *See* APTD **2224**

UNITED STATES. ENVIRONMENTAL PROTECTION AGENCY. OFFICE OF AIR QUALITY PLANNING AND STANDARDS *See* AIR QUALITY DATA **2223**

UNITED STATES. ENVIRONMENTAL PROTECTION AGENCY. OFFICE OF EDUCATION AND MANPOWER PLANNING *See* ABATEMENT AND POLLUTION CONTROL TRAINING AND EDUCATIONAL PROGRAMS PRESENTED BY THE UNITED STATES ENVIRONMENTAL PROTECTION AGENCY **2222**

UNITED STATES. ENVIRONMENTAL PROTECTION AGENCY. OFFICE OF GENERAL COUNSEL *See* COLLECTION OF LEGAL OPINIONS, A **3110**

UNITED STATES. ENVIRONMENTAL PROTECTION AGENCY. OFFICE OF PLANNING AND MANAGEMENT *See* END OF YEAR REPORT. REGIONAL PROGRAM PLANS ASSESSMENT **4646**

UNITED STATES. ENVIRONMENTAL PROTECTION AGENCY. OFFICE OF RADIATION PROGRAMS *See* RADIOLOGICAL QUALITY OF THE ENVIRONMENT **2240**

UNITED STATES. ENVIRONMENTAL PROTECTION AGENCY. OFFICE OF RADIATION PROGRAMS *See* RADIATION PROTECTION ACTIVITIES **2240**

UNITED STATES. ENVIRONMENTAL PROTECTION AGENCY. OFFICE OF REGIONAL AND INTERGOVERNMENTAL OPERATIONS *See* ENVIRONMENTAL PROGRAM ADMINISTRATORS **2169**

UNITED STATES. ENVIRONMENTAL PROTECTION AGENCY. OFFICE OF WATER PROGRAM OPERATIONS *See* PROGRAM REQUIREMENTS MEMORANDA FOR FISCAL YEAR ... : MUNICIPAL WASTEWATER TREATMENT WORKS CONSTRUCTION GRANTS PROGRAM / UNITED STATES ENVIRONMENTAL PROTECTION AGENCY, OFFICE OF WATER PROGRAMS OPERATIONS **2240**

UNITED STATES. ENVIRONMENTAL PROTECTION AGENCY. PERSONNEL MANAGEMENT DIVISION *See* EMPLOYMENT OPPORTUNITIES / UNITED STATES ENVIRONMENTAL PROTECTION AGENCY, PERSONNEL MANAGEMENT DIVISION **940**

UNITED STATES. ENVIRONMENTAL PROTECTION AGENCY. REGION II *See* REGION II REPORT **2203**

UNITED STATES. ENVIRONMENTAL PROTECTION AGENCY. WATER PLANNING DIVISION *See* WATER QUALITY MANAGEMENT PROGRAM SUPPLEMENTAL GUIDANCE FOR FY ... **2248**

UNITED STATES. ENVIRONMENTAL PROTECTION AGENCY. WATER SUPPLY DIVISION *See* INVENTORY OF INTERSTATE CARRIER WATER SUPPLY SYSTEMS BY STATES AND ENVIRONMENTAL PROTECTION AGENCY REGIONS **5535**

UNITED STATES. EQUAL EMPLOYMENT OPPORTUNITY COMMISSION *See* EQUAL EMPLOYMENT OPPORTUNITY COMMISSION AFFIRMATIVE ACTION PLAN **1667**

UNITED STATES. EQUAL EMPLOYMENT OPPORTUNITY COMMISSION. OFFICE OF PLANNING, RESEARCH, AND SYSTEMS *See* RESEARCH REPORT (UNITED STATES. EQUAL EMPLOYMENT OPPORTUNITY COMMISSION) **1708**

UNITED STATES. EQUAL EMPLOYMENT OPPORTUNITY COMMISSION. OFFICE OF RESEARCH. RESEARCH REPORT *See* RESEARCH REPORT (UNITED STATES. EQUAL EMPLOYMENT OPPORTUNITY COMMISSION) **1708**

UNITED STATES EXCISE TAX GUIDE (US/0083-0534) [01564344] **4757**

UNITED STATES. EXPORTS MICROFORM (FR) [10992387] **856**

UNITED

UNITED STATES. FAO INTERAGENCY COMMITTEE *See* REPORT OF THE GOVERNMENT OF THE UNITED STATES OF AMERICA TO THE FOOD AND AGRICULTURE ORGANIZATION OF THE UNITED NATIONS **126**

UNITED STATES. FARM CREDIT ADMINISTRATION *See* ANNUAL REPORT OF THE FARM CREDIT ADMINISTRATION **61**

UNITED STATES. FARM CREDIT ADMINISTRATION *See* ANNUAL REPORT OF THE FARM CREDIT ADMINISTRATION AND THE COOPERATIVE FARM CREDIT SYSTEM **61**

UNITED STATES. FARMER COOPERATIVE SERVICE *See* FCS SPECIAL REPORT **1542**

UNITED STATES. FARMERS HOME ADMINISTRATION *See* OVERVIEW - FARMERS HOME ADMINISTRATION **118**

UNITED STATES. FEDERAL AVIATION ADMINISTRATION *See* FEDERAL AVIATION REGULATIONS. PART 123. CERTIFICATION AND OPERATIONS. AIR TRAVEL CLUBS USING LARGE AIRPLANES **20**

UNITED STATES. FEDERAL AVIATION ADMINISTRATION *See* FEDERAL AVIATION REGULATIONS. PART 23. AIRWORTHINESS STANDARDS, NORMAL, UTILITY, AND ACROBATIC CATEGORY AIRPLANES **19**

UNITED STATES. FEDERAL AVIATION ADMINISTRATION *See* FEDERAL AVIATION REGULATIONS. PART 91. GENERAL OPERATING AND FLIGHT RULES **20**

UNITED STATES. FEDERAL AVIATION ADMINISTRATION *See* FEDERAL AVIATION REGULATIONS. PART 33. AIRWORTHINESS STANDARDS, AIRCRAFT ENGINES **19**

UNITED STATES. FEDERAL AVIATION ADMINISTRATION *See* FEDERAL AVIATION REGULATIONS. PART 129. OPERATIONS OF FOREIGN AIR CARRIERS **20**

UNITED STATES. FEDERAL AVIATION ADMINISTRATION *See* FEDERAL AVIATION REGULATIONS. PART 137. AGRICULTURAL AIRCRAFT OPERATIONS **20**

UNITED STATES. FEDERAL AVIATION ADMINISTRATION *See* FEDERAL AVIATION REGULATIONS. PART 121. CERTIFICATION AND OPERATIONS : DOMESTIC, FLAG, AND SUPPLEMENTAL AIR CARRIERS AND COMMERCIAL OPERATION UNITED STATES. FEDERAL AVIATION ADMINISTRATION **20**

UNITED STATES. FEDERAL AVIATION ADMINISTRATION *See* FEDERAL AVIATION REGULATIONS. PART 11. GENERAL RULE-MAKING PROCEDURES **19**

UNITED STATES. FEDERAL AVIATION ADMINISTRATION *See* FLIGHT STANDARDS INFORMATION MANUAL **21**

UNITED STATES. FEDERAL AVIATION ADMINISTRATION *See* SUMMARY OF SUPPLEMENTAL TYPE CERTIFICATES **37**

UNITED STATES. FEDERAL AVIATION ADMINISTRATION *See* FEDERAL AVIATION REGULATIONS. PART 139. CERTIFICATION AND OPERATIONS, LAND AIRPORTS SERVING CAB-CERTIFICATED SCHEDULED AIR CARRIERS **20**

UNITED STATES. FEDERAL AVIATION ADMINISTRATION *See* ACCEPTABLE METHODS, TECHNIQUES, AND PRACTICES. AIRCRAFT ALTERATIONS **3**

UNITED STATES. FEDERAL AVIATION ADMINISTRATION *See* FEDERAL AVIATION REGULATIONS. PART 61. CERTIFICATION, PILOTS AND FLIGHT INSTRUCTORS **19**

UNITED STATES. FEDERAL AVIATION ADMINISTRATION *See* FEDERAL AVIATION REGULATIONS. PART 107. AIRPORT SECURITY **20**

UNITED STATES. FEDERAL AVIATION ADMINISTRATION *See* FEDERAL AVIATION REGULATIONS. PART. 27. AIRWORTHINESS STANDARDS, NORMAL CATEGORY ROTORCRAFT **19**

UNITED STATES. FEDERAL AVIATION ADMINISTRATION *See* FEDERAL AVIATION REGULATIONS. PART 21. CERTIFICATION PROCEDURES FOR PRODUCTS AND PARTS **19**

UNITED STATES. FEDERAL AVIATION ADMINISTRATION *See* FEDERAL AVIATION REGULATIONS. PART 145. REPAIR STATIONS **20**

UNITED STATES. FEDERAL AVIATION ADMINISTRATION *See* FEDERAL AVIATION REGULATIONS. PART 31. AIRWORTHINESS STANDARDS, MANNED FREE BALLOONS **19**

UNITED STATES. FEDERAL AVIATION ADMINISTRATION *See* FEDERAL AVIATION REGULATIONS. N.PART 39, P. AIRWORTHINESS DIRECTIVES **19**

UNITED STATES. FEDERAL AVIATION ADMINISTRATION *See* SEMIANNUAL REPORT TO CONGRESS ON THE EFFECTIVENESS OF THE CIVIL AVIATION SECURITY PROGRAM / U.S. DEPARTMENT OF TRANSPORTATION, FEDERAL AVIATION ADMINISTRATION **35**

UNITED STATES. FEDERAL AVIATION ADMINISTRATION *See* FEDERAL AVIATION REGULATIONS. PART 13. ENFORCEMENT PROCEDURES **19**

UNITED STATES. FEDERAL AVIATION ADMINISTRATION *See* FEDERAL AVIATION REGULATIONS. PART 25. AIRWORTHINESS STANDARDS, TRANSPORT CATEGORY AIRPLANES **19**

UNITED STATES. FEDERAL AVIATION ADMINISTRATION *See* FEDERAL AVIATION REGULATIONS. PART 109. INDIRECT AIR CARRIER SECURITY **20**

UNITED STATES. FEDERAL AVIATION ADMINISTRATION *See* FEDERAL AVIATION REGULATIONS. PART 67. MEDICAL STANDARDS AND CERTIFICATION **20**

UNITED STATES. FEDERAL AVIATION ADMINISTRATION *See* FEDERAL AVIATION REGULATIONS. PART 1. DEFINITIONS AND ABBREVIATIONS **19**

UNITED STATES. FEDERAL AVIATION ADMINISTRATION *See* FEDERAL AVIATION REGULATIONS. PART 63. CERTIFICATION, FLIGHT CREWMEMBERS OTHER THAN PILOTS **19**

UNITED STATES. FEDERAL AVIATION ADMINISTRATION *See* FISCAL YEAR BUDGET ESTIMATES - FEDERAL AVIATION ADMINISTRATION **4726**

UNITED STATES. FEDERAL AVIATION ADMINISTRATION *See* INDEX OF FAA NATIONAL AND WA ORDERS **23**

UNITED STATES. FEDERAL AVIATION ADMINISTRATION *See* STANDARD INSTRUMENT APPROACH PROCEDURES, TAKEOFF MINIMUMS/DEPARTURES, AND FIX ACTIONS / U.S. DEPARTMENT OF TRANSPORTATION, FEDERAL AVIATION ADMINISTRATION **37**

UNITED STATES. FEDERAL AVIATION ADMINISTRATION *See* FEDERAL AVIATION REGULATIONS. PART 159. NATIONAL CAPITAL AIRPORTS **20**

UNITED STATES. FEDERAL AVIATION ADMINISTRATION *See* FEDERAL AVIATION REGULATIONS. PART 152. AIRPORT AID PROGRAM **20**

UNITED STATES. FEDERAL AVIATION ADMINISTRATION *See* NATIONAL AIRPORT SYSTEM PLAN **30**

UNITED STATES. FEDERAL AVIATION ADMINISTRATION *See* FEDERAL AVIATION REGULATIONS. PART 127. CERTIFICATION AND OPERATIONS OF SCHEDULED AIR CARRIERS AND HELICOPTERS **20**

UNITED STATES. FEDERAL AVIATION ADMINISTRATION *See* FEDERAL AVIATION REGULATIONS. PART 147. AVIATION MAINTENANCE TECHNICIAN SCHOOLS **20**

UNITED STATES. FEDERAL AVIATION ADMINISTRATION *See* FEDERAL AVIATION REGULATIONS. PART 191. WITHHOLDING SECURITY INFORMATION FROM DISCLOSURE UNDER THE AIR TRANSPORTATION SECURITY ACT OF 1974 **20**

UNITED STATES. FEDERAL AVIATION ADMINISTRATION *See* FEDERAL AVIATION REGULATIONS. PART 36. NOISE STANDARDS, AIRCRAFT TYPE AND AIRWORTHINESS CERTIFICATION **19**

UNITED STATES. FEDERAL AVIATION ADMINISTRATION *See* FEDERAL AVIATION REGULATIONS. PART 29. AIRWORTHINESS STANDARDS, TRANSPORT CATEGORY ROTORCRAFT **19**

UNITED STATES. FEDERAL AVIATION ADMINISTRATION *See* FEDERAL AVIATION REGULATIONS. PART 135. AIR TAXI OPERATORS AND COMMERCIAL OPERATORS OF SMALL AIRCRAFT **20**

UNITED STATES. FEDERAL AVIATION ADMINISTRATION *See* FEDERAL AVIATION REGULATIONS. PART 183. REPRESENTATIVES OF THE ADMINISTRATOR **20**

UNITED STATES. FEDERAL AVIATION ADMINISTRATION *See* FEDERAL AVIATION REGULATIONS. PART 93. GENERAL AIR TRAFFIC RULES AND AIRPORT TRAFFIC PATTERNS **20**

UNITED STATES. FEDERAL AVIATION ADMINISTRATION *See* FEDERAL AVIATION REGULATIONS. PART 37. TECHNICAL STANDARD ORDER AUTHORIZATION **19**

UNITED STATES. FEDERAL AVIATION ADMINISTRATION *See* NATIONAL AIRSPACE SYSTEM PLAN. ENGINEERING AND DEVELOPMENT **30**

UNITED STATES. FEDERAL AVIATION ADMINISTRATION *See* NATIONAL AVIATION SYSTEM PLAN, THE **30**

UNITED STATES. FEDERAL AVIATION ADMINISTRATION *See* FEDERAL AVIATION REGULATIONS. PART 133. ROTORCRAFT EXTERNAL-LOAD OPERATIONS **20**

UNITED STATES. FEDERAL AVIATION ADMINISTRATION *See* ANNUAL REPORT / FEDERAL AVIATION ADMINISTRATION **11**

UNITED STATES. FEDERAL AVIATION ADMINISTRATION. ANNUAL FINANCIAL REPORT *See* ANNUAL REPORT / FEDERAL AVIATION ADMINISTRATION **11**

UNITED STATES. FEDERAL AVIATION ADMINISTRATION. OFFICE OF AIRWORTHINESS *See* AIRCRAFT CERTIFICATION DIRECTORY **9**

UNITED STATES. FEDERAL AVIATION ADMINISTRATION. OFFICE OF CIVIL RIGHTS. INTERNAL PROGRAM DIVISION *See* STATUS OF EQUAL EMPLOYMENT OPPORTUNITY PROGRAM (WASHINGTON, D.C. : 1970) **4705**

UNITED STATES. FEDERAL AVIATION ADMINISTRATION. OFFICE OF THE GENERAL COUNSEL *See* STATISTICAL SUMMARY : AIR CARRIER ENFORCEMENT CASES **41**

UNITED STATES. FEDERAL AVIATION AGENCY. FLIGHT INFORMATION DIVISION. AIRMAN'S INFORMATION MANUAL *See* AIRMAN'S INFORMATION MANUAL **10**

UNITED STATES. FEDERAL COMMUNICATIONS COMMISSION *See* RULES AND REGULATIONS. PART 99, DISASTER COMMUNICATIONS SERVICE **1121**

UNITED STATES. FEDERAL COMMUNICATIONS COMMISSION *See* RULES AND REGULATIONS - FEDERAL COMMUNICATIONS COMMISSION. VOLUME 8 **1121**

UNITED STATES. FEDERAL COMMUNICATIONS COMMISSION *See* RULES AND REGULATIONS - FEDERAL COMMUNICATIONS COMMISSION. VOLUME 2 **1121**

UNITED STATES. FEDERAL COMMUNICATIONS COMMISSION *See* RULES AND REGULATIONS - FEDERAL COMMUNICATIONS COMMISSION. VOLUME 11 **1121**

UNITED STATES. FEDERAL COMMUNICATIONS COMMISSION *See* RULES AND REGULATIONS - FEDERAL COMMUNICATIONS COMMISSION. VOLUME 5 **1121**

UNITED STATES. FEDERAL COMMUNICATIONS COMMISSION *See* OVERSEAS COMMON CARRIER SECTION 214 APPLICATIONS ACCEPTED FOR FILING **1161**

UNITED STATES. FEDERAL COMMUNICATIONS COMMISSION *See* MAJOR MATTERS BEFORE THE FEDERAL COMMUNICATIONS COMMISSION **4664**

UNITED STATES. FEDERAL COMMUNICATIONS COMMISSION *See* BROADCAST ACTIONS **1127**

UNITED STATES. FEDERAL COMMUNICATIONS COMMISSION *See* COMMON CARRIER SERVICES INFORMATION **1106**

UNITED STATES. FEDERAL COMMUNICATIONS COMMISSION *See* PUBLIC NOTICE - FEDERAL COMMUNICATIONS COMMISSION. SAFETY AND SPECIAL ACTIONS **1120**

UNITED STATES. FEDERAL COMMUNICATIONS COMMISSION *See* TV BROADCAST FINANCIAL DATA **1141**

UNITED STATES. FEDERAL COMMUNICATIONS COMMISSION *See* COMMON CARRIER DOMESTIC FACILITIES APPLICATIONS **1106**

UNITED STATES. FEDERAL COMMUNICATIONS COMMISSION *See* COMMON CARRIER PUBLIC MOBILE SERVICES INFORMATION **1106**

UNITED STATES. FEDERAL COMMUNICATIONS COMMISSION *See* PUBLIC NOTICE - FEDERAL COMMUNICATIONS COMMISSION. DOMESTIC PUBLIC LAND MOBILE RADIO SERVICE **1136**

UNITED STATES. FEDERAL COMMUNICATIONS COMMISSION *See* MEMORANDUM OPINION AND ORDER **1117**

UNITED STATES. FEDERAL COMMUNICATIONS COMMISSION *See* ANNUAL REPORT / FEDERAL COMMUNICATIONS COMMISSION **1104**

UNITED STATES. FEDERAL COMMUNICATIONS COMMISSION *See* EX PARTE PRESENTATIONS IN INFORMAL RULEMAKINGS **1111**

UNITED STATES. FEDERAL COMMUNICATIONS COMMISSION *See* PUBLIC NOTICE - FEDERAL COMMUNICATIONS COMMISSION. CABLE TELEVISION AUTHORIZATION ACTIONS **1136**

UNITED STATES. FEDERAL COMMUNICATIONS COMMISSION *See* RULES AND REGULATIONS - FEDERAL COMMUNICATIONS COMMISSION. VOLUME 1 **1121**

UNITED — Alphabetical Title Index

UNITED STATES. FEDERAL COMMUNICATIONS COMMISSION *See* RULES AND REGULATIONS - FEDERAL COMMUNICATIONS COMMISSION. VOLUME 9 **1121**

UNITED STATES. FEDERAL COMMUNICATIONS COMMISSION *See* PUBLIC NOTICE - FEDERAL COMMUNICATIONS COMMISSION. CABLE TELEVISION CERTIFICATE OF COMPLIANCE ACTIONS **1136**

UNITED STATES. FEDERAL COMMUNICATIONS COMMISSION *See* RULES AND REGULATIONS **3045**

UNITED STATES. FEDERAL COMMUNICATIONS COMMISSION *See* RULES AND REGULATIONS - FEDERAL COMMUNICATIONS COMMISSION. VOLUME 3 **1121**

UNITED STATES. FEDERAL COMMUNICATIONS COMMISSION *See* RULES AND REGULATIONS - FEDERAL COMMUNICATIONS COMMISSION. VOLUME 7 **1121**

UNITED STATES. FEDERAL COMMUNICATIONS COMMISSION *See* PUBLIC NOTICE - FEDERAL COMMUNICATIONS COMMISSION. EXPERIMENTAL ACTIONS **1120**

UNITED STATES. FEDERAL COMMUNICATIONS COMMISSION *See* RULES AND REGULATIONS - FEDERAL COMMUNICATIONS COMMISSION. VOLUME 4 **1121**

UNITED STATES. FEDERAL COMMUNICATIONS COMMISSION *See* FCC CALENDAR OF EVENTS FOR WEEK OF ... **1111**

UNITED STATES. FEDERAL COMMUNICATIONS COMMISSION *See* FCC RECORD **1155**

UNITED STATES. FEDERAL COMMUNICATIONS COMMISSION *See* RULES AND REGULATIONS - FEDERAL COMMUNICATIONS COMMISSION. VOLUME 10 **1121**

UNITED STATES. FEDERAL COMMUNICATIONS COMMISSION *See* CABLE TELEVISION SERVICE REGISTRATIONS **1129**

UNITED STATES. FEDERAL COORDINATING COUNCIL FOR SCIENCE, ENGINEERING AND TECHNOLOGY *See* ACTIVITIES OF THE FEDERAL COUNCIL FOR SCIENCE AND TECHNOLOGY AND THE FEDERAL COORDINATING COUNCIL FOR SCIENCE, ENGINEERING AND TECHNOLOGY **5080**

UNITED STATES. FEDERAL COUNCIL FOR SCIENCE AND TECHNOLOGY. AD HOC COMMITTEE ON GEODYNAMICS *See* ANNUAL REPORT OF AD HOC COMMITTEE ON GEODYNAMICS TO THE FEDERAL COUNCIL FOR SCIENCE AND TECHNOLOGY **5084**

UNITED STATES. FEDERAL ENERGY REGULATORY COMMISSION *See* ORDER / UNITED STATES OF AMERICA, FEDERAL ENERGY REGULATORY COMMISSION **1952**

UNITED STATES. FEDERAL ENERGY REGULATORY COMMISSION. OFFICE OF CONGRESSIONAL AND PUBLIC AFFAIRS *See* PUBLICATIONS AND STAFF REPORTS LISTING - OFFICE OF CONGRESSIONAL AND PUBLIC AFFAIRS, FEDERAL ENERGY REGULATORY COMMISSION **1954**

UNITED STATES. FEDERAL GRAIN INSPECTION SERVICE *See* RICE CROP QUALITY **185**

UNITED STATES. FEDERAL HIGHWAY ADMINISTRATION *See* BID OPENING REPORT **5439**

UNITED STATES. FEDERAL HIGHWAY ADMINISTRATION *See* DRIVERS LICENSES **5381**

UNITED STATES. FEDERAL HIGHWAY ADMINISTRATION *See* HIGHWAY TRANSPORTATION RESEARCH AND DEVELOPMENT STUDIES **5441**

UNITED STATES. FEDERAL HIGHWAY ADMINISTRATION *See* STANDARD HIGHWAY SIGNS / AS SPECIFIED IN THE MANUAL ON UNIFORM TRAFFIC CONTROL DEVICES **5444**

UNITED STATES. FEDERAL HOME LOAN BANK BOARD *See* ANNOTATED MANUAL OF STATUTES AND REGULATIONS **3084**

UNITED STATES. FEDERAL HOME LOAN BANK BOARD *See* NEWS - FEDERAL HOME LOAN BANK BOARD **801**

UNITED STATES. FEDERAL HOUSING ADMINISTRATION *See* F H A TRENDS OF HOME MORTGAGE CHARACTERISTICS **2822**

UNITED STATES. FEDERAL HOUSING ADMINISTRATION *See* AMORTIZATION, INSURANCE PREMIUM AND OUTSTANDING PRINCIPAL BALANCE TABLES FOR HOME MORTGAGES AND LOANS INSURED UNDER THE NATIONAL HOUSING ACT **769**

UNITED STATES. FEDERAL HOUSING ADMINISTRATION. MINIMUM PROPERTY STANDARDS FOR MULTIFAMILY HOUSING *See* MINIMUM PROPERTY STANDARDS FOR MULTIFAMILY HOUSING **2828**

UNITED STATES. FEDERAL LABOR RELATIONS AUTHORITY *See* ADMINISTRATION LAW JUDGE DECISIONS REPORT **3143**

UNITED STATES. FEDERAL LABOR RELATIONS AUTHORITY *See* REPORT OF CASE DECISIONS **3153**

UNITED STATES. FEDERAL LABOR RELATIONS AUTHORITY *See* ANNUAL REPORT OF THE FEDERAL LABOR RELATIONS AUTHORITY AND THE FEDERAL SERVICE IMPASSES PANEL FOR THE FISCAL PERIOD ... **1649**

UNITED STATES. FEDERAL LABOR RELATIONS AUTHORITY *See* DECISIONS OF THE FEDERAL LABOR RELATIONS AUTHORITY **3146**

UNITED STATES. FEDERAL LABOR RELATIONS COUNCIL *See* REQUESTS FOR INTERPRETATIONS AND POLICY STATEMENTS **4705**

UNITED STATES. FEDERAL MARITIME COMMISSION *See* DECISIONS OF THE FEDERAL MARITIME COMMISSION **3180**

UNITED STATES. FEDERAL MINE SAFETY AND HEALTH REVIEW COMMISSION *See* DECISIONS - FEDERAL MINE SAFETY AND HEALTH REVIEW COMMISSION **2861**

UNITED STATES. FEDERAL POWER COMMISSION *See* FEDERAL POWER COMMISSION NEWS RELEASE. MONTHLY FUEL COST AND QUALITY INFORMATION, FPC ISSUES REPORT ON FUEL COST **4256**

UNITED STATES. FEDERAL POWER COMMISSION *See* ANNUAL REPORT - FEDERAL POWER COMMISSION **1932**

UNITED STATES. FEDERAL PREVAILING RATE ADVISORY COMMITTEE *See* ANNUAL REPORT OF FEDERAL PREVAILING RATE ADVISORY COMMITTEE **4628**

UNITED STATES. FEDERAL RAILROAD ADMINISTRATION *See* RAIL PASSENGER STATISTICS IN THE NORTHEAST CORRIDOR **5435**

UNITED STATES. FEDERAL RAILROAD ADMINISTRATION *See* FEDERAL RAILROAD ADMINISTRATION SPRING PREVIEW **5431**

UNITED STATES. FEDERAL RAILROAD ADMINISTRATION *See* AMTRAK MATRIX SYSTEM ANNUAL ORIGIN/DESTINATION PASSENGER COUNT **5429**

UNITED STATES. FEDERAL RAILROAD ADMINISTRATION. OFFICE OF SAFETY *See* RAILROAD ACCIDENT INVESTIGATION REPORTS **5435**

UNITED STATES. FEDERAL TRADE COMMISSION *See* ANNUAL REPORT OF THE FEDERAL TRADE COMMISSION **823**

UNITED STATES. FEDERAL TRADE COMMISSION *See* FEDERAL TRADE COMMISSION DECISIONS **3100**

UNITED STATES. FEDERAL TRADE COMMISSION *See* FTC FREEDOM OF INFORMATION LOG **837**

UNITED STATES FIELD HOCKEY ASSOCIATION *See* OFFICIAL FIELD HOCKEY RULES FOR SCHOOL GIRLS **4909**

UNITED STATES. FISH AND WILDLIFE SERVICE *See* WOODCOCK STATUS REPORT **5621**

UNITED STATES. FISH AND WILDLIFE SERVICE. OFFICE OF SAFETY *See* ACCIDENT CONTROL REPORT **2185**

UNITED STATES. FOOD AND DRUG ADMINISTRATION *See* PUBLIC ADVISORY COMMITTEES, AUTHORITY, STRUCTURE, FUNCTIONS, MEMBERS **4797**

UNITED STATES. FOOD AND DRUG ADMINISTRATION *See* PESTICIDE ANALYTICAL MANUAL **4246**

UNITED STATES. FOOD AND DRUG ADMINISTRATION *See* FOOD ADDITIVES ANALYTICAL MANUAL **2335**

UNITED STATES. FOOD AND DRUG ADMINISTRATION *See* FDA FREEDOM OF INFORMATION LOG **4647**

UNITED STATES. FOOD AND DRUG ADMINISTRATION *See* MEDICAL DEVICES **3608**

UNITED STATES. FOOD AND DRUG ADMINISTRATION *See* INDEX OF FDA REGULATORY LETTERS **4656**

UNITED STATES. FOOD AND DRUG ADMINISTRATION. BUREAU OF FOODS. OFFICE OF COMPLIANCE *See* PESTICIDE-PCB IN FOODS PROGRAM **4246**

UNITED STATES. FOOD AND DRUG ADMINISTRATION. OFFICE OF SCIENCE. EXTRAMURAL RESEARCH STAFF *See* EXTRAMURAL RESEARCH PROGRAMS SUPPORTED BY THE FOOD AND DRUG ADMINISTRATION **3576**

UNITED STATES. FOOD AND DRUG ADMINISTRATION. PROGRAM INFORMATION AND ANALYSIS GROUP *See* FDA QUARTERLY ACTIVITIES REPORT **4647**

UNITED STATES. FOOD AND NUTRITION SERVICE *See* FOOD STAMP PROGRAM : STATISTICAL SUMMARY OF OPERATIONS **5266**

UNITED STATES. FOOD AND NUTRITION SERVICE *See* FOOD AND NUTRITION PROGRAMS **2909**

UNITED STATES. FOOD SAFETY AND INSPECTION SERVICE *See* MEAT AND POULTRY INSPECTION **215**

UNITED STATES. FOOD SAFETY AND INSPECTION SERVICE *See* PROGRAM PLAN - UNITED STATES. FOOD SAFETY AND INSPECTION SERVICE **4198**

UNITED STATES. FOOD SAFETY AND INSPECTION SERVICE. STANDARDS AND LABELING DIVISION *See* STANDARDS AND LABELING POLICY BOOK / UNITED STATES DEPARTMENT OF AGRICULTURE, FOOD SAFETY AND INSPECTION SERVICE, REGULATORY PROGRAMS, STANDARDS AND LABELING DIVISION **2358**

UNITED STATES. FOREIGN CLAIMS SETTLEMENT COMMISSION *See* ANNUAL REPORT - UNITED STATES. FOREIGN CLAIMS SETTLEMENT COMMISSION **3123**

UNITED STATES FOREIGN TRADE *See* U.S. WATERBORNE EXPORTS AND GENERAL IMPORTS **856**

UNITED STATES FOREIGN TRADE ANNUAL (US) [08965861] **856**

UNITED STATES FOREIGN TRADE : BUNKER OIL AND COAL LADEN IN THE UNITED STATES ON VESSELS ENGAGED IN FOREIGN TRADE (US) [01768255] **856**

UNITED STATES. FOREST SERVICE *See* HIGHLIGHTS: WALLOWA-WHITMAN NATIONAL FOREST **2384**

UNITED STATES. FOREST SERVICE *See* FOREST RESOURCE REPORT - UNITED STATES. FOREST SERVICE **2381**

UNITED STATES. FOREST SERVICE *See* GENERAL TECHNICAL REPORT WO **2383**

UNITED STATES. FOREST SERVICE *See* REPORT OF THE FOREST SERVICE (WASHINGTON) **2392**

UNITED STATES. FOREST SERVICE *See* GIFFORD PINCHOT NATIONAL FOREST **2383**

UNITED STATES. FOREST SERVICE *See* FOREST SERVICE ORGANIZATIONAL DIRECTORY **2381**

UNITED STATES. FOREST SERVICE. INTERMOUNTAIN REGION *See* INTERMOUNTAIN REGION ANNUAL QUALITY PLAN **2385**

UNITED STATES. FOREST SERVICE. LAKE STATES FOREST EXPERIMENT STATION *See* STATION PAPER - U. S. FOREST SERVICE. LAKE STATES FOREST EXPERIMENT STATION, ST. PAUL **2396**

UNITED STATES. FOREST SERVICE. NORTHEASTERN AREA. STATE AND PRIVATE FORESTRY *See* FOREST PEST CONDITIONS IN THE NORTHEAST **2380**

UNITED STATES. FOREST SERVICE. NORTHERN REGION *See* FOREST INSECT AND DISEASE CONDITIONS IN THE NORTHERN REGION **2380**

UNITED STATES. FOREST SERVICE. NORTHERN REGION. DIVISION OF STATE AND PRIVATE FORESTRY *See* REPORT - USDA FOREST SERVICE, NORTHERN REGION, STATE AND PRIVATE FORESTRY **2392**

UNITED STATES. FOREST SERVICE. SOUTHEASTERN AREA. DIVISION OF FOREST PEST MANAGEMENT *See* REPORT - FOREST SERVICE. SOUTHEASTERN AREA. DIVISION OF FOREST PEST MANAGEMENT **2392**

UNITED STATES. GENERAL ACCOUNTING OFFICE *See* SUMMARIES OF CONCLUSIONS AND RECOMMENDATIONS ON DEPARTMENT OF DEFENSE OPERATIONS : REPORT TO THE HOUSE AND SENATE COMMITTEES ON APPROPRIATIONS BY THE COMPTROLLER GENERAL OF THE UNITED STATES **4058**

UNITED STATES. GENERAL ACCOUNTING OFFICE *See* EXAMINATION OF FINANCIAL STATEMENTS OF THE PENNSYLVANIA AVENUE DEVELOPMENT CORPORATION **4647**

UNITED STATES. GENERAL ACCOUNTING OFFICE *See* GENERAL ACCOUNTING OFFICE POLICY AND PROCEDURES MANUAL FOR GUIDANCE OF FEDERAL AGENCIES **4650**

UNITED STATES. GENERAL ACCOUNTING OFFICE *See* TRIENNIAL ASSESSMENT OF THE TENNESSEE VALLEY AUTHORITY **4691**

UNITED STATES. GENERAL ACCOUNTING OFFICE *See* EXAMINATION OF THE RURAL TELEPHONE BANK'S FINANCIAL STATEMENTS **743**

UNITED STATES. GENERAL ACCOUNTING OFFICE *See* POLICY AND PROCEDURES MANUAL FOR GUIDANCE OF FEDERAL AGENCIES. TITLE 4. CLAIMS **4674**

Alphabetical Title Index — UNITED

UNITED STATES. GENERAL ACCOUNTING OFFICE See AUDIT OF THE RURAL TELEPHONE BANK, DEPARTMENT OF AGRICULTURE (WASHINGTON) 1150

UNITED STATES. GENERAL ACCOUNTING OFFICE See EXAMINATION OF FINANCIAL STATEMENTS OF THE PENSION BENEFIT GUARANTY CORPORATION 1668

UNITED STATES. GENERAL ACCOUNTING OFFICE See GAO WORK INVOLVING TITLE V OF THE ENERGY POLICY AND CONSERVATION ACT OF 1975 2973

UNITED STATES. GENERAL ACCOUNTING OFFICE See FINANCIAL STATUS OF MAJOR FEDERAL ACQUISITIONS 4649

UNITED STATES. GENERAL ACCOUNTING OFFICE See EXAMINATION OF FINANCIAL STATEMENTS OF STUDENT LOAN INSURANCE FUND 1823

UNITED STATES. GENERAL ACCOUNTING OFFICE See COMPILATION OF GAO'S WORK ON TAX ADMINISTRATION ACTIVITIES 741

UNITED STATES. GENERAL ACCOUNTING OFFICE See AUDIT OF PAYMENTS FROM SPECIAL BANK ACCOUNT TO LOCKHEED AIRCRAFT CORPORATION FOR THE C-5A AIRCRAFT PROGRAM 739

UNITED STATES. GENERAL ACCOUNTING OFFICE See AMTRAK'S INVENTORY AND PROPERTY CONTROLS NEED STRENGTHENING 5429

UNITED STATES. GENERAL ACCOUNTING OFFICE See SUMMARIES OF CONCLUSIONS AND RECOMMENDATIONS ON THE OPERATIONS OF CIVIL DEPARTMENTS AND AGENCIES 4689

UNITED STATES. GENERAL ACCOUNTING OFFICE See SUMMARY OF OPEN GAO RECOMMENDATIONS FOR LEGISLATIVE ACTION 752

UNITED STATES. GENERAL ACCOUNTING OFFICE See COMPTROLLER GENERAL'S PROCUREMENT DECISIONS 949

UNITED STATES. GENERAL ACCOUNTING OFFICE See EXAMINATION OF THE FINANCIAL STATEMENTS OF FHA INSURANCE OPERATIONS 2879

UNITED STATES. GENERAL ACCOUNTING OFFICE See EXAMINATION OF FINANCIAL STATEMENTS, INTER-AMERICAN FOUNDATION 4722

UNITED STATES. GENERAL ACCOUNTING OFFICE See SOCIAL DEVELOPMENT ACTIVITIES IN LATIN AMERICA PROMOTED BY THE INTER-AMERICAN FOUNDATION 1584

UNITED STATES. GENERAL ACCOUNTING OFFICE See REPORT BY THE U. S. GENERAL ACCOUNTING OFFICE 750

UNITED STATES. GENERAL ACCOUNTING OFFICE See COMPTROLLER GENERAL'S ANNUAL REPORT 4718

UNITED STATES. GENERAL ACCOUNTING OFFICE See DECISIONS OF THE COMPTROLLER GENERAL OF THE UNITED STATES 4719

UNITED STATES. GENERAL ACCOUNTING OFFICE See EXAMINATION OF FINANCIAL STATEMENTS OF OVERSEAS PRIVATE INVESTMENT CORPORATION 897

UNITED STATES. GENERAL ACCOUNTING OFFICE See AUDIT OF THE FINANCIAL STATEMENTS OF FEDERAL CROP INSURANCE CORPORATION 2874

UNITED STATES. GENERAL ACCOUNTING OFFICE See GOVERNMENT NATIONAL MORTGAGE ASSOCIATION EXAMINATION OF FINANCIAL STATEMENTS 789

UNITED STATES. GENERAL ACCOUNTING OFFICE. OFFICE OF GENERAL COUNSEL See DIGESTS OF DECISIONS OF THE COMPTROLLER GENERAL OF THE UNITED STATES 4720

UNITED STATES. GENERAL ACCOUNTING OFFICE. OFFICE OF THE GENERAL COUNSEL See QUARTERLY DIGEST OF UNPUBLISHED DECISIONS OF THE COMPTROLLER GENERAL OF THE UNITED STATES : CONTRACTS 4677

UNITED STATES. GENERAL SERVICES ADMINISTRATION See TELEPHONE DIRECTORY, CENTRAL OFFICE AND NATIONAL CAPITAL REGION 4690

UNITED STATES. GENERAL SERVICES ADMINISTRATION See TELEPHONE DIRECTORY CENTRAL OFFICE AND REGION 3 4690

UNITED STATES. GENERAL SERVICES ADMINISTRATION See MANAGEMENT IMPROVEMENT AND COST REDUCTION GOALS 4664

UNITED STATES. GENERAL SERVICES ADMINISTRATION See MANAGEMENT REPORT - GENERAL SERVICES ADMINISTRATION 4664

UNITED STATES. GENERAL SERVICES ADMINISTRATION. OFFICE OF HUMAN RESOURCES AND ORGANIZATION See WORK FORCE PROFILE AS OF SEPTEMBER 30 ... 1718

UNITED STATES. GENERAL SERVICES ADMINISTRATION. OFFICE OF INSPECTOR GENERAL See SEMIANNUAL REPORT TO THE CONGRESS / OFFICE OF INSPECTOR GENERAL 4685

UNITED STATES GENERALIZED SYSTEM OF PREFERENCES, CARIBBEAN BASIN INITIATIVE (US) [19219061] 4757

UNITED STATES. GEOLOGICAL SURVEY See GROUND-WATER LEVELS IN THE UNITED STATES : NORTHEASTERN STATES 2090

UNITED STATES. GEOLOGICAL SURVEY See GROUND-WATER LEVELS IN THE UNITED STATES. SOUTHWESTERN STATES 5534

UNITED STATES. GEOLOGICAL SURVEY See RESEARCH AND DEVELOPMENT PROGRAM FOR OUTER CONTINENTAL SHELF OIL AND GAS OPERATIONS, TECHNICAL REPORT 4276

UNITED STATES. GEOLOGICAL SURVEY See SEISMIC ENGINEERING PROGRAM REPORT 1396

UNITED STATES. GEOLOGICAL SURVEY See GROUND-WATER LEVELS IN THE UNITED STATES. SOUTH-CENTRAL STATES 5534

UNITED STATES. GEOLOGICAL SURVEY See GROUND-WATER LEVELS IN THE UNITED STATES. NORTH-CENTRAL STATES 5534

UNITED STATES. GEOLOGICAL SURVEY See GROUND-WATER LEVELS IN THE UNITED STATES. NORTHWESTERN STATES 1413

UNITED STATES. GEOLOGICAL SURVEY See GROUND-WATER LEVELS IN THE UNITED STATES. SOUTHEASTERN STATES 1413

UNITED STATES GEOLOGICAL SURVEY IN ALASKA, ORGANIZATION AND STATUS OF PROGRAM See U.S. GEOLOGICAL SURVEY IN ALASKA ..., PROGRAMS, THE 1400

UNITED STATES. GEOLOGICAL SURVEY. NORTHWEST WATER RESOURCES DATA CENTER See MONTHLY REPORT OF WATER TEMPERATURES, TEMPERATURES IN DEGREES C. FOR SELECTED STATIONS IN THE PACIFIC NORTHWEST 1416

UNITED STATES-GERMAN ECONOMIC YEARBOOK (US/1044-4351) [18012755] 1525, 717

UNITED STATES. GODDARD SPACE FLIGHT CENTER, GREENBELT, MARYLAND See TECHNICAL ABSTRACTS - U. S. GODDARD SPACE FLIGHT CENTER 37

UNITED STATES GOLF ASSOCIATION See RULES OF GOLF FOR ... AND THE RULES FOR AMATEUR STATUS 4916

UNITED STATES GOLF ASSOCIATION. GREEN SECTION See USGA GREEN SECTION RECORD 4928

UNITED STATES GOVERNMENT ANNUAL REPORT (US/0884-1063) [11771288] 4692

UNITED STATES GOVERNMENT GRANTS UNDER THE FULBRIGHT-HAYS ACT : UNIVERSITY LECTURING, ADVANCED RESEARCH (US/0362-6792) [02141840] 4692

UNITED STATES GOVERNMENT MANUAL (1974) (US/0092-1904) [01788884] 4692

UNITED STATES GOVERNMENT ... TELEPHONE DIRECTORY. REGION 1 (US/0276-7457) [06519070] 4692

UNITED STATES GOVERNMENT TELEPHONE DIRECTORY. UTAH (US) [06778881] 4692

UNITED STATES. HEALTH CARE FINANCING ADMINISTRATION See HEALTH CARE FINANCING ADMINISTRATION RULINGS ON MEDICARE, MEDICAID, PROFESSIONAL STANDARDS REVIEW, AND RELATED MATTERS 2882

UNITED STATES. HEALTH CARE FINANCING ADMINISTRATION. OFFICE OF POLICY, PLANNING, AND RESEARCH See PROFESSIONAL STANDARDS REVIEW ORGANIZATIONS 4796

UNITED STATES. HEALTH RESOURCES ADMINISTRATION. DIVISION OF LONG-TERM CARE See ANNUAL REPORT - DIVISION OF LONG-TERM CARE 5272

UNITED STATES. HEALTH SERVICES ADMINISTRATION See REPORT OF THE ADMINISTRATOR - UNITED STATES. HEALTH SERVICES ADMINISTRATION 4798

UNITED STATES. HEALTH SERVICES ADMINISTRATION See FORWARD PLAN FOR THE HEALTH SERVICES ADMINISTRATION 4776

UNITED STATES. HEALTH SERVICES ADMINISTRATION. BUREAU OF COMMUNITY HEALTH SERVICE. DIVISION OF MONITORING AND ANALYSIS See NEIGHBORHOOD HEALTH CENTERS : SUMMARY OF PROJECT DATA. REPORT 4793

UNITED STATES. HEALTH SERVICES ADMINISTRATION. BUREAU OF COMMUNITY HEALTH SERVICES See CLINICAL PROGRAMS FOR MENTALLY RETARDED CHILDREN 3902

UNITED STATES. HEALTH SERVICES ADMINISTRATION. BUREAU OF COMMUNITY HEALTH SERVICES. DIVISION OF MONITORING AND ANALYSIS See MIGRANT HEALTH PROJECTS 4791

UNITED STATES. HEALTH SERVICES AND MENTAL HEALTH ADMINISTRATION See INDIAN HEALTH PROGRAM OF THE U.S. PUBLIC HEALTH SERVICE, THE 4784

UNITED STATES. HERITAGE CONSERVATION AND RECREATION SERVICE See YEAR-END REPORT - HERITAGE CONSERVATION AND RECREATION SERVICE 2210

UNITED STATES. HERITAGE CONSERVATION AND RECREATION SERVICE. MID-CONTINENT REGION See ANNUAL REPORT - HERITAGE CONSERVATION AND RECREATION SERVICE, MID-CONTINENT REGION 2186

UNITED STATES HOCKEY LEAGUE See U.S.H.L. YEARBOOK 4927

UNITED STATES HOLOCAUST MEMORIAL MUSEUM GUIDE (US) 5053, 5498

UNITED STATES. IMMIGRATION AND NATURALIZATION SERVICE See CITIZENSHIP DAY AND CONSTITUTION WEEK GUIDE 1918

UNITED STATES. IMMIGRATION AND NATURALIZATION SERVICE See ANNUAL REPORT OF THE IMMIGRATION AND NATURALIZATION SERVICE 1918

UNITED STATES. IMMIGRATION AND NATURALIZATION SERVICE See OPERATIONS INSTRUCTIONS, REGULATIONS, AND INTERPRETATIONS 1920

UNITED STATES. IMPORTS MICROFORM (FR) [10992374] 856

UNITED STATES. INDIAN ARTS AND CRAFTS BOARD See SOURCE DIRECTORY : NATIVE AMERICAN OWNED AND OPERATED ARTS AND CRAFTS BUSINESSES / UNITED STATES DEPARTMENT OF THE INTERIOR, INDIAN ARTS AND CRAFTS BOARD 375

UNITED STATES. INDUSTRY AND TRADE ADMINISTRATION See EXPORT MAILING LIST SERVICE; SIC RECORD COUNT, FTI PROFILE 834

UNITED STATES. INFORMATION AGENCY. OFFICE OF RESEARCH AND EVALUATION See INTERNATIONAL BROADCASTING OF ALL NATIONS; REPORT 1133

UNITED STATES. INSTITUTE FOR APPLIED TECHNOLOGY. CENTER FOR BUILDING TECHNOLOGY See PROJECT SUMMARIES OF THE CENTER FOR BUILDING TECHNOLOGY, NATIONAL BUREAU OF STANDARDS 624

UNITED STATES INSTITUTE OF PEACE JOURNAL (US/1046-7513) [17974938] 4537

UNITED STATES. INTERAGENCY ARCHEOLOGICAL SERVICES DIVISION See ARCHEOLOGICAL AND HISTORICAL DATA RECOVERY PROGRAM 258

UNITED STATES. INTERAGENCY COMMITTEE ON EMERGENCY MEDICAL SERVICES See ANNUAL REPORT - INTERAGENCY COMMITTEE ON EMERGENCY MEDICAL SERVICES, HEALTH SERVICES ADMINISTRATION 3723

UNITED STATES. INTERDEPARTMENT RADIO ADVISORY COMMITTEE See MANUAL OF REGULATIONS AND PROCEDURES FOR FEDERAL RADIO FREQUENCY MANAGEMENT 1134

UNITED STATES. INTERIM COMPLIANCE PANEL See ANNUAL REPORT - INTERIM COMPLIANCE PANEL (WASHINGTON) 2934

UNITED STATES. INTERNAL REVENUE SERVICE See LOOSELEAF REGULATIONS SYSTEM. SERVICE 3. EMPLOYMENT TAX 4736

UNITED STATES. INTERNAL REVENUE SERVICE See 1040NR FORMS AND INSTRUCTIONS 4708

UNITED STATES. INTERNAL REVENUE SERVICE See ANNUAL REPORT / COMMISSIONER OF INTERNAL REVENUE AND THE CHIEF COUNSEL FOR THE INTERNAL REVENUE SERVICE 4710

UNITED STATES. INTERNAL REVENUE SERVICE See COLLEGE GRADUATES APPOINTED BY IRS 4718

UNITED STATES. INTERNAL REVENUE SERVICE See LOOSELEAF REGULATIONS SYSTEM. SERVICE 2. ESTATE AND GIFT TAX 4736

UNITED STATES. INTERNAL REVENUE SERVICE See CODE OF FEDERAL REGULATIONS. 26, INTERNAL REVENUE 2951

UNITED STATES. INTERNAL REVENUE SERVICE See INTERNAL REVENUE CUMULATIVE BULLETIN 4732

UNITED STATES. INTERNAL REVENUE SERVICE See PACKAGE X 4740

UNITED STATES. INTERNAL REVENUE SERVICE See STATISTICS OF INCOME. SUPPLEMENTAL REPORT. INTERNATIONAL INCOME AND TAXES. DOMESTIC INTERNATIONAL SALES CORPORATION RETURNS 4700

UNITED STATES. INTERNAL REVENUE SERVICE See INTERNAL REVENUE BULLETIN 4732

UNITED STATES. INTERNAL REVENUE SERVICE See LOOSELEAF REGULATIONS SYSTEM. SERVICE 1. INCOME TAX 4736

UNITED STATES. INTERNAL REVENUE SERVICE See INSTRUCTIONS FOR FORM W-2, WAGE AND TAX STATEMENT 4732

UNITED STATES. INTERNATIONAL COOPERATION ADMINISTRATION. TECHNICAL AIDS BRANCH See INDEX OF PUBLICATIONS / TECHNICAL AIDS BRANCH, OFFICE OF INDUSTRIAL RESOURCES, INTERNATIONAL COOPERATION ADMINISTRATION 5112

UNITED STATES. INTERNATIONAL DEVELOPMENT COOPERATION AGENCY See CONGRESSIONAL PRESENTATION, FISCAL YEAR 4518

UNITED STATES. INTERNATIONAL TRADE ADMINISTRATION See SUMMARY OF U.S. EXPORT CONTROL REGULATIONS, A 852

UNITED STATES. INTERNATIONAL TRADE ADMINISTRATION See EXPORT CONTACT LIST SERVICES 834

UNITED STATES INTERNATIONAL TRADE COMMISSION See NONRUBBER FOOTWEAR : U.S. PRODUCTION, IMPORTS FOR CONSUMPTION, APPARENT U.S. CONSUMPTION, EMPLOYMENT, WHOLESALE PRICE INDEX, AND CONSUMER PRICE INDEX 1086

UNITED STATES INTERNATIONAL TRADE COMMISSION See ANNUAL REPORT / UNITED STATES INTERNATIONAL TRADE COMMISSION 823

UNITED STATES INTERNATIONAL TRADE COMMISSION. LIBRARY See OUR LIBRARY PRESENTS ... 3240

UNITED STATES. INTERSTATE COMMERCE COMMISSION See ICC NEWS 839

UNITED STATES. INTERSTATE COMMERCE COMMISSION See INTERSTATE COMMERCE COMMISSION'S REPORT TO THE PRESIDENT AND THE CONGRESS. EFFECTIVENESS OF THE ACT. AMTRAK 5432

UNITED STATES. INTERSTATE COMMERCE COMMISSION. BUREAU OF ACCOUNTS See COST OF TRANSPORTING FREIGHT BY CLASS I AND CLASS II MOTOR COMMON CARRIERS OF GENERAL COMMODITIES : MIDDLE ATLANTIC REGION, SOUTHERN (INTRA) REGION, EAST-SOUTH TERRITORY, SOUTH-CENTRAL TERRITORY 829

UNITED STATES. INTERSTATE COMMERCE COMMISSION. BUREAU OF ACCOUNTS See COST OF TRANSPORTING FREIGHT BY CLASS I AND CLASS II MOTOR COMMON CARRIERS OF GENERAL COMMODITIES, BY REGIONS OR TERRITORIES 5380

UNITED STATES. INTERSTATE COMMERCE COMMISSION. BUREAU OF ACCOUNTS See FINANCIAL AND OPERATING STATISTICS CLASS I MOTOR CARRIERS OF PASSENGERS 5401

UNITED STATES. INTERSTATE COMMERCE COMMISSION. BUREAU OF ACCOUNTS See COST OF TRANSPORTING FREIGHT BY CLASS I AND CLASS II MOTOR COMMON CARRIERS OF GENERAL COMMODITIES. TRANSCONTINENTAL TERRITORY, ROCKY MOUNTAIN REGION, MIDDLEWEST REGION, SOUTHWEST REGION, PACIFIC REGION 829

UNITED STATES. INTERSTATE COMMERCE COMMISSION. BUREAU OF ACCOUNTS See COST OF TRANSPORTING FREIGHT; CLASS I AND CLASS II MOTOR COMMON CARRIERS OF GENERAL COMMODITIES. NEW ENGLAND REGION - GROUP I, NEW ENGLAND REGION- GROUP II, CENTRAL REGION, EASTERN CENTRAL TERRITORY 830

UNITED STATES. INTERSTATE COMMERCE COMMISSION. BUREAU OF ACCOUNTS See LARGE CLASS I HOUSEHOLD GOODS CARRIERS SELECTED EARNINGS DATA 5385

UNITED STATES. INTERSTATE COMMERCE COMMISSION. BUREAU OF ACCOUNTS See LARGE CLASS I MOTOR CARRIERS OF PROPERTY SELECTED EARNINGS DATA 5385

UNITED STATES INVESTOR (US/0734-9211) [04216071] 918

UNITED STATES-ISRAEL BINATIONAL SCIENCE FOUNDATION See BIENNIAL REPORT / UNITED STATES-ISRAEL BINATIONAL SCIENCE FOUNDATION 5088

UNITED STATES JUDICIAL REPORTER CEASED. (US/0094-2553) [01789533] 3068

UNITED STATES. LABOR RESEARCH ADVISORY COUNCIL See DIRECTORY OF THE LABOR RESEARCH ADVISORY COUNCIL TO THE BUREAU OF LABOR STATISTICS 1663

UNITED STATES. LAKE STATES FOREST EXPERIMENT STATION See MISCELLANEOUS REPORT - U. S. LAKE STATES FOREST EXPERIMENT STATION, ST. PAUL 2388

UNITED STATES. LAND LOCOMOTION RESEARCH LABORATORY, CENTER LINE, MICHIGAN See RESEARCH REPORT - U. S. LAND LOCOMOTION RESEARCH LABORATORY, CENTER LINE, MICHIGAN 1994

UNITED STATES LAW WEEK, THE (US/0148-8139) [01768758] 3068

UNITED STATES LAWYERS REFERENCE DIRECTORY (US) [04226017] 3068

UNITED STATES LIFE TABLES (US) [03355052] 4560

UNITED STATES. MARINE ECOSYSTEMS ANALYSIS PROGRAM OFFICE See NOAA DATA REPORT MESA 2219

UNITED STATES. MARITIME ADMINISTRATION See INVENTORY OF AMERICAN INTERMODAL EQUIPMENT 5450

UNITED STATES. MARITIME ADMINISTRATION See INDEX OF CURRENT REGULATIONS OF THE MARITIME ADMINISTRATION, MARITIME SUBSIDY BOARD, NATIONAL SHIPPING AUTHORITY 3181

UNITED STATES. MARITIME SUBSIDY BOARD See DECISIONS OF THE MARITIME SUBSIDY BOARD, MARITIME ADMINISTRATION, DEPARTMENT OF COMMERCE 3180

UNITED STATES. MARTIN LUTHER KING, JR., FEDERAL HOLIDAY COMMISSION See ANNUAL REPORT PREPARED FOR THE PRESIDENT OF THE UNITED STATES AND THE UNITED STATES CONGRESS 4629

UNITED STATES. MATERIALS TRANSPORTATION BUREAU See PIPELINE SAFETY ADVISORY BULLETIN 4274

UNITED STATES. MATERIALS TRANSPORTATION BUREAU See ANNUAL REPORT ON HAZARDOUS MATERIALS TRANSPORTATION : HAZARDOUS MATERIALS TRANSPORTATION ACT (TITLE I, PUBLIC LAW 93-633) 2935

UNITED STATES. MEAT AND POULTRY INSPECTION PROGRAM See MEAT AND POULTRY INSPECTION MANUAL 215

UNITED STATES. MEAT AND POULTRY INSPECTION PROGRAM See MEAT AND POULTY INSPECTION REGULATIONS 215

UNITED STATES. MERIT SYSTEMS PROTECTION BOARD See DECISIONS OF THE UNITED STATES MERIT SYSTEMS PROTECTION BOARD 4702

UNITED STATES METRIC BOARD See U.S. METRIC BOARD ANNUAL REPORT 4033

UNITED STATES-MEXICO BORDER HEALTH ASSOCIATION See NEWS 4793

UNITED STATES. MIGRATORY BIRD CONSERVATION COMMISSION See REPORT OF THE MIGRATORY BIRD CONSERVATION COMMISSION 5620

UNITED STATES MILITARY ACADEMY. ASSOCIATION OF GRADUATES See ASSEMBLY (WEST POINT, N.Y.) 1101

UNITED STATES. MINING ENFORCEMENT AND SAFETY ADMINISTRATION. HEALTH AND SAFETY ANALYSIS CENTER See MESA SAFETY REVIEWS 2865

UNITED STATES. MISSOURI RIVER BASIN COMMISSION See MISSOURI RIVER BASIN, STATE AND FEDERAL WATER AND RELATED LAND RESOURCE PROGRAMS 2093

UNITED STATES. NATIONAL ADVISORY COMMITTEE ON UNIFORM TRAFFIC CONTROL DEVICES See MANUAL ON UNIFORM TRAFFIC CONTROL DEVICES FOR STREETS AND HIGHWAYS 5441

UNITED STATES. NATIONAL ADVISORY COUNCIL ON MATERNAL, INFANT, AND FETAL NUTRITION See BIENNIAL REPORT ON THE SPECIAL SUPPLEMENTAL FOOD PROGRAM FOR WOMEN, INFANTS, AND CHILDREN, AND ON THE COMMODITY SUPPLEMENTAL FOOD PROGRAM 2328

UNITED STATES. NATIONAL ADVISORY COUNCIL ON MATERNAL, INFANT, AND FETAL NUTRITION See NATIONAL ADVISORY COUNCIL ON MATERNAL, INFANT, AND FETAL NUTRITION ... BIENNIAL REPORT 3765

UNITED STATES. NATIONAL AERONAUTICS AND SPACE ADMINISTRATION See NASA TECHNICAL REPORT 29

UNITED STATES. NATIONAL AERONAUTICS AND SPACE ADMINISTRATION See NASA TECHNICAL TRANSLATION 30

UNITED STATES. NATIONAL AERONAUTICS AND SPACE ADMINISTRATION See INTEGRATED TECHNOLOGY PLAN FOR THE CIVIL SPACE PROGRAM 24

UNITED STATES. NATIONAL AERONAUTICS AND SPACE ADMINISTRATION See HEADQUARTERS TELEPHONE DIRECTORY 22

UNITED STATES. NATIONAL AERONAUTICS AND SPACE ADMINISTRATION See ANNUAL PROCUREMENT REPORT 11

UNITED STATES. NATIONAL AERONAUTICS AND SPACE ADMINISTRATION See NASA MAGAZINE 29

UNITED STATES. NATIONAL AERONAUTICS AND SPACE ADMINISTRATION. AEROSPACE SAFETY ADVISORY PANEL See REPORT TO THE ADMINISTRATOR ON THE SKYLAB PROGRAM 33

UNITED STATES. NATIONAL AERONAUTICS AND SPACE ADMINISTRATION. EARTH SCIENCE AND APPLICATIONS DIVISION See HIGHLIGHTS OF THE YEAR ... 1356

UNITED STATES NATIONAL AERONAUTICS AND SPACE ADMINISTRATION. QUALITY AND PRODUCTIVITY IMPROVEMENT PROGRAMS OFFICE See NASA TOTAL QUALITY MANAGEMENT ... ACCOMPLISHMENT REPORT 30

UNITED STATES. NATIONAL AERONAUTICS AND SPACE ADMINISTRATION. SCIENTIFIC AND TECHNICAL INFORMATION PROGRAM See NASA PATENT ABSTRACTS BIBLIOGRAPHY 29

UNITED STATES. NATIONAL AGRICULTURAL RESEARCH AND EXTENSION USERS ADVISORY BOARD See REPORT TO THE PRESIDENT AND CONGRESS / NATIONAL AGRICULTURAL RESEARCH AND EXTENSION USERS ADVISORY BOARD 126

UNITED STATES. NATIONAL ARCHIVES AND RECORDS SERVICE See CATALOG OF NATIONAL ARCHIVES MICROFILM PUBLICATIONS 2481

UNITED STATES. NATIONAL ARTHRITIS ADVISORY BOARD See CHAIRMAN'S REPORT - NATIONAL ARTHRITIS ADVISORY BOARD 3804

UNITED STATES. NATIONAL BUREAU OF STANDARDS See CONFERENCE BRIEFS - UNITED STATES. NATIONAL BUREAU OF STANDARDS 5096

UNITED STATES. NATIONAL BUREAU OF STANDARDS See APPLIED MATHEMATICS SERIES 3495

UNITED STATES. NATIONAL BUREAU OF STANDARDS See HYDRAULIC RESEARCH IN THE UNITED STATES AND CANADA 2090

UNITED STATES. NATIONAL BUREAU OF STANDARDS See NATIONAL STANDARD REFERENCE DATA SERIES 4031

UNITED STATES. NATIONAL CANCER INSTITUTE. DIVISION OF CANCER CAUSE AND PREVENTION See REPORT OF THE CARCINOGENESIS PROGRAM 3823

UNITED STATES. NATIONAL CAPITAL PLANNING COMMISSION See FEDERAL CAPITAL IMPROVEMENTS PROGRAM FOR THE NATIONAL CAPITAL REGION 898

UNITED STATES. NATIONAL CLIMATE PROGRAM OFFICE See NATIONAL CLIMATE PROGRAM : ANNUAL REPORT 1432

Alphabetical Title Index — UNITED

UNITED STATES. NATIONAL COMMISSION ON LIBRARIES AND INFORMATION SCIENCE *See* ANNUAL REPORT / NATIONAL COMMISSION ON LIBRARIES AND INFORMATION SCIENCE **3190**

UNITED STATES NATIONAL COMMITTEE FOR THE INTERNATIONAL INSTITUTE OF REFRIGERATION *See* ACTIVITIES REPORT - U.S. NATIONAL COMMITTEE FOR THE INTERNATIONAL INSTITUTE OF REFRIGERATION **2602**

UNITED STATES. NATIONAL COMMITTEE ON VITAL AND HEALTH STATISTICS *See* NATIONAL COMMITTEE ON VITAL AND HEALTH STATISTICS : [SUMMARY REPORT], THE **4810**

UNITED STATES. NATIONAL CREDIT UNION ADMINISTRATION *See* RULES AND REGULATIONS - NATIONAL CREDIT UNION ADMINISTRATION **810**

UNITED STATES. NATIONAL CREDIT UNION ADMINISTRATION *See* ANNUAL REPORT OF THE NATIONAL CREDIT UNION ADMINISTRATION **771**

UNITED STATES. NATIONAL CREDIT UNION ADMINISTRATION *See* NATIONAL CREDIT UNION ADMINISTRATION RULES AND REGULATIONS **800**

UNITED STATES. NATIONAL CRIMINAL JUSTICE INFORMATION AND STATISTICS SERVICE *See* CHILDREN IN CUSTODY **3160**

UNITED STATES. NATIONAL GALLERY OF ART *See* ANNUAL REPORT - NATIONAL GALLERY OF ART (U.S.) **336**

UNITED STATES. NATIONAL GUARD BUREAU *See* ANNUAL REVIEW / CHIEF, NATIONAL GUARD BUREAU **4035**

UNITED STATES. NATIONAL GUARD BUREAU *See* OFFICIAL ARMY NATIONAL GUARD REGISTER **4053**

UNITED STATES. NATIONAL HIGHWAY TRAFFIC SAFETY ADMINISTRATION *See* SAFETY RELATED RECALL CAMPAIGNS FOR MTOR VEHICLES AND MOTOR VEHICLE EQUIPMENT, INCLUDING TIRES: DETAILED REPORTS **5425**

UNITED STATES. NATIONAL HIGHWAY TRAFFIC SAFETY ADMINISTRATION *See* TIRES **4805**

UNITED STATES. NATIONAL HIGHWAY TRAFFIC SAFETY ADMINISTRATION *See* BRAKES **4769**

UNITED STATES. NATIONAL HIGHWAY TRAFFIC SAFETY ADMINISTRATION *See* FEDERAL MOTOR VEHICLE SAFETY STANDARDS AND REGULATIONS **5382**

UNITED STATES. NATIONAL HIGHWAY TRAFFIC SAFETY ADMINISTRATION *See* ACCELERATION AND PASSING ABILITY **5375**

UNITED STATES. NATIONAL HIGHWAY TRAFFIC SAFETY ADMINISTRATION *See* DRIVER LICENSING LAWS ANNOTATED. SUPPLEMENT **2964**

UNITED STATES. NATIONAL HIGHWAY TRAFFIC SAFETY ADMINISTRATION *See* TECHNICAL REPORTS OF THE NATIONAL HIGHWAY TRAFFIC SAFETY ADMINISTRATION **5445**

UNITED STATES. NATIONAL HIGHWAY TRAFFIC SAFETY ADMINISTRATION *See* FEDERAL MOTOR VEHICLE SAFETY STANDARDS AND REGULATIONS **4648**

UNITED STATES. NATIONAL HOUSING AGENCY *See* ANNUAL REPORT / U.S. NATIONAL HOUSING AGENCY **2815**

UNITED STATES. NATIONAL INSTITUTE OF ALLERGY AND INFECTIOUS DISEASES *See* REPORT FROM THE DIRECTOR, NATIONAL INSTITUTE OF ALLERGY AND INFECTIOUS DISEASES **3715**

UNITED STATES. NATIONAL INSTITUTE OF ALLERGY AND INFECTIOUS DISEASES. ALLERGIC AND IMMUNOLOGIC DISEASES PROGRAM *See* NIAID MANUAL OF TISSUE TYPING TECHNIQUES **3675**

UNITED STATES. NATIONAL INSTITUTE OF CHILD HEALTH AND HUMAN DEVELOPMENT. CENTER FOR POPULATION RESEARCH *See* CPR POPULATION RESEARCH **4551**

UNITED STATES. NATIONAL INSTITUTE OF DENTAL RESEARCH *See* NATIONAL INSTITUTE OF DENTAL RESEARCH PROGRAMS **1330**

UNITED STATES. NATIONAL INSTITUTE OF DENTAL RESEARCH *See* EQUAL OPPORTUNITY ASSESSMENT AND AFFIRMATIVE ACTION PLAN **1323**

UNITED STATES. NATIONAL INSTITUTE OF MENTAL HEALTH *See* PRIVATE PSYCHIATRIC HOSPITALS **3791**

UNITED STATES. NATIONAL INSTITUTE OF MENTAL HEALTH. DIVISION OF BIOMETRY. SURVEY AND REPORTS BRANCH *See* STATE AND REGIONAL DATA, FEDERALLY FUNDED COMMUNITY MENTAL HEALTH CENTERS **5311**

UNITED STATES. NATIONAL INSTITUTES OF HEALTH. CARDIOVASCULAR AND PULMONARY STUDY SECTION *See* ANNUAL REPORT - CARDIOVASCULAR AND PULMONARY STUDY SECTION, NATIONAL INSTITUTES OF HEALTH **3699**

UNITED STATES. NATIONAL INSTITUTES OF HEALTH. CENTER FOR AGING RESEARCH *See* RESEARCH HIGHLIGHTS IN AGING **3754**

UNITED STATES. NATIONAL INSTITUTES OF HEALTH DIVISION OF RESOURCES ANALYSIS *See* DHEW OBLIGATIONS TO INSTITUTIONS OF HIGHER EDUCATION AND OTHER NONPROFIT ORGANIZATIONS **1820**

UNITED STATES. NATIONAL INSTITUTES OF HEALTH. EPIDEMIOLOGY AND DISEASE CONTROL STUDY SECTION *See* ANNUAL REPORT - EPIDEMIOLOGY & DISEASE CONTROL STUDY SECTION, NATIONAL INSTITUTES OF HEALTH **3734**

UNITED STATES. NATIONAL LABOR RELATIONS BOARD *See* COURT DECISIONS RELATING TO THE NATIONAL LABOR RELATIONS ACT **3146**

UNITED STATES. NATIONAL LABOR RELATIONS BOARD *See* DECISIONS AND ORDERS OF THE NATIONAL LABOR RELATIONS BOARD **3146**

UNITED STATES. NATIONAL LABOR RELATIONS BOARD *See* CASEHANDLING MANUAL - NATIONAL LABOR RELATIONS BOARD **3145**

UNITED STATES. NATIONAL LABOR RELATIONS BOARD *See* ANNUAL REPORT OF THE NATIONAL LABOR RELATIONS BOARD **1649**

UNITED STATES. NATIONAL LABOR RELATIONS BOARD *See* RULES AND REGULATIONS ... AND STATEMENTS OF PROCEDURE / NATIONAL LABOR RELATIONS BOARD **3154**

UNITED STATES. NATIONAL LABOR RELATIONS BOARD. DIVISION OF INFORMATION *See* WEEKLY SUMMARY OF NLRB CASES **3155**

UNITED STATES. NATIONAL LIBRARY OF MEDICINE. BIBLIOGRAPHIC SERVICE DIVISON. INDEX SECTION *See* TECHNICAL NOTES : MEDLARS INDEXING INSTRUCTIONS : SUPPLEMENT **3644**

UNITED STATES. NATIONAL LIBRARY OF MEDICINE. BIOMEDICAL LIBRARY REVIEW COMMITTEE *See* ANNUAL REPORT - BIOMEDICAL LIBRARY REVIEW COMMITTEE, NATIONAL LIBRARY OF MEDICINE, NATIONAL INSTITUTES OF HEALTH **3190**

UNITED STATES. NATIONAL MARINE FISHERIES SERVICE *See* DATA REPORT - U.S. DEPARTMENT OF COMMERCE, NATIONAL OCEANIC AND ATMOSPHERIC ADMINISTRATION NATIONAL MARINE FISHERIES SERVICE **2300**

UNITED STATES. NATIONAL MARINE FISHERIES SERVICE *See* ALABAMA LANDINGS, ANNUAL SUMMARY **2293**

UNITED STATES. NATIONAL MARINE FISHERIES SERVICE *See* REPORT OF THE NATIONAL MARINE FISHERIES SERVICE **2311**

UNITED STATES. NATIONAL MARINE FISHERIES SERVICE *See* GEORGIA LANDINGS, ANNUAL SUMMARY **2304**

UNITED STATES. NATIONAL MEDIATION BOARD *See* DETERMINATIONS OF THE NATIONAL MEDIATION BOARD **3146**

UNITED STATES. NATIONAL OCEAN SERVICE *See* VFR TERMINAL AREA CHART. BALTIMORE--WASHINGTON **39**

UNITED STATES. NATIONAL OCEANIC AND ATMOSPHERIC ADMINISTRATION *See* REPORT TO THE CONGRESS ON OCEAN POLLUTION AND OFFSHORE DEVELOPMENT **1456**

UNITED STATES. NATIONAL OCEANIC AND ATMOSPHERIC ADMINISTRATION. OFFICE OF UNDERSEA RESEARCH *See* NOAA'S OFFICE OF UNDERSEA RESEARCH ... REPORT **1453**

UNITED STATES. NATIONAL PARK SERVICE *See* PUBLIC USE OF THE NATIONAL PARKS SYSTEMS (WASHINGTON) **2202**

UNITED STATES. NATIONAL PARK SERVICE *See* U.S. DEPARTMENT OF THE INTERIOR NATIONAL PARK SERVICE TRANSACTIONS AND PROCEEDINGS SERIES **2207**

UNITED STATES. NATIONAL PARK SERVICE *See* VISITOR ACCOMMODATIONS, FACILITIES, AND SERVICES FURNISHED BY CONCESSIONERS IN THE NATIONAL PARK SYSTEM **5498**

UNITED STATES. NATIONAL PARK SERVICE *See* FEDERAL RECREATION FEE REPORT **4850**

UNITED STATES. NATIONAL PARK SERVICE *See* NATIONAL PARK SERVICE SOURCE BOOK SERIES **4852**

UNITED STATES. NATIONAL PARK SERVICE *See* FEDERAL RECREATION FEE REPORT TO CONGRESS : INCLUDING FEDERAL RECREATION VISITATION AND FEE DATA WITH STATE PARK INFORMATION SUPPLEMENT **4850**

UNITED STATES. NATIONAL PARK SERVICE. FEDERAL RECREATION FEE REPORT *See* FEDERAL RECREATION FEE REPORT TO CONGRESS : INCLUDING FEDERAL RECREATION VISITATION AND FEE DATA WITH STATE PARK INFORMATION SUPPLEMENT **4850**

UNITED STATES. NATIONAL PROFESSIONAL STANDARDS REVIEW COUNCIL *See* ANNUAL REPORT - NATIONAL PROFESSIONAL STANDARDS REVIEW COUNCIL **3551**

UNITED STATES. NATIONAL RAILROAD ADJUSTMENT BOARD *See* AWARDS ... FIRST DIVISION, NATIONAL RAILROAD ADJUSTMENT BOARD **5429**

UNITED STATES. NATIONAL SCIENCE FOUNDATION *See* LISTING OF PEER REVIEWERS USED BY NSF DIVISIONS **5126**

UNITED STATES. NATIONAL SCIENCE FOUNDATION. DIVISION OF SCIENCE INFORMATION *See* FEDERAL SCIENTIFIC AND TECHNICAL COMMUNICATION ACTIVITIES : PROGRESS REPORT **5105**

UNITED STATES. NATIONAL SECURITY COUNCIL. SUBCOMMITTEE ON FOREIGN AFFAIRS RESEARCH *See* USC/FAR CONSOLIDATED PLAN FOR FOREIGN AFFAIRS RESEARCH **4537**

UNITED STATES NATIONAL STUDENT ASSOCIATION *See* NSA MAGAZINE **1838**

UNITED STATES. NATIONAL TECHNICAL INFORMATION SERVICE *See* GENERAL CATALOG OF INFORMATION SERVICES / NATIONAL TECHNICAL INFORMATION SERVICE **5107**

UNITED STATES. NATIONAL TECHNICAL INFORMATION SERVICE *See* NTIS TITLE INDEX ON MICROFICHE **5135**

UNITED STATES. NATIONAL TRANSPORTATION SAFETY BOARD *See* SAFETY EFFECTIVENESS EVALUATION : REPORT NO. NTSB-SEE **4801**

UNITED STATES. NATIONAL TRANSPORTATION SAFETY BOARD *See* BRIEFS OF AIRCRAFT ACCIDENTS INVOLVING TURBINE POWERED AIRCRAFT, U.S. GENERAL AVIATION **15**

UNITED STATES. NATIONAL TRANSPORTATION SAFETY BOARD *See* NATIONAL TRANSPORTATION SAFETY BOARD DECISIONS **5388**

UNITED STATES. NATIONAL TRANSPORTATION SAFETY BOARD *See* SAFETY RECOMMENDATIONS / NATIONAL TRANSPORTATION SAFETY BOARD **4801**

UNITED STATES. NATIONAL TRANSPORTATION SAFETY BOARD *See* BUDGET - NATIONAL TRANSPORTATION SAFETY BOARD **5378**

UNITED STATES. NATIONAL TRANSPORTATION SAFETY BOARD. BUDGET ESTIMATES *See* BUDGET - NATIONAL TRANSPORTATION SAFETY BOARD **5378**

UNITED STATES. NATIONAL WEATHER SERVICE *See* NUMERICAL WEATHER PREDICTION ACTIVITIES **1432**

UNITED STATES. NATIONAL WEATHER SERVICE. SYSTEMS DEVELOPMENT OFFICE *See* PROGRAMS & ACCOMPLISHMENTS **1433**

UNITED STATES NAVAL CIVIL ENGINEERING LABORATORY, PORT HUENEME, CALIFORNIA *See* TECHNICAL REPORT - CIVIL ENGINEERING LABORATORY, NAVAL CONSTRUCTION BATTALION CENTER, PORT HUENEME, CALIFORNIA **2032**

UNITED STATES. NAVAL FACILITIES ENGINEERING COMMAND *See* COMMAND HISTORY - UNITED STATES. NAVAL FACILITIES ENGINEERING COMMAND **4175**

UNITED STATES. NAVAL MOBILE CONSTRUCTION BATTALION FOUR *See* FOCUS ON FOUR **4176**

UNITED STATES NAVAL OBSERVATORY CIRCULAR (US/0097-0336) [01450051] **401**

UNITED STATES. NAVAL OCEANOGRAPHIC OFFICE *See* TRANSLATION - NAVAL OCEANOGRAPHIC OFFICE **1457**

UNITED
Alphabetical Title Index

UNITED STATES. NAVAL OCEANOGRAPHIC OFFICE *See* INFORMAL MANUSCRIPT - U.S. NAVAL OCEANOGRAPHIC OFFICE **1450**

UNITED STATES. NAVAL OCEANOGRAPHIC OFFICE *See* EASTERN ARCTIC ICE, THE SEASONAL OUTLOOK **1413**

UNITED STATES. NAVAL ORDNANCE SYSTEMS COMMAND *See* NAVORD OD **4180**

UNITED STATES. NAVAL SEA SYSTEMS COMMAND *See* NAVSEA JOURNAL **4180**

UNITED STATES. NAVAL TRAINING PUBLICATIONS DETACHMENT *See* COMMISSARYMAN 1 & C **4175**

UNITED STATES. NAVY DEPT *See* NAVY CONTRACTING DIRECTIVES **4180**

UNITED STATES. NAVY. MILITARY SEALIFT COMMAND *See* ANNUAL REPORT / U.S. NAVY'S MILITARY SEALIFT COMMAND **4174**

UNITED STATES-NETHERLANDS ECONOMIC YEARBOOK (US) [14574695] 717, **1587**

UNITED STATES. NORTHWEST FEDERAL REGIONAL COUNCIL *See* END OF YEAR REPORT - NORTHWEST FEDERAL REGIONAL COUNCIL **4646**

UNITED STATES. NUCLEAR REGULATORY COMMISSION *See* RULES AND REGULATIONS / UNITED STATES NUCLEAR REGULATORY COMMISSION **3045**

UNITED STATES NUCLEAR REGULATORY COMMISSION STAFF PRACTICE AND PROCEDURE DIGEST *CEASED*. (US) [04511751] 1959, **4692**

UNITED STATES. OCCUPATIONAL SAFETY AND HEALTH ADMINISTRATION *See* OCCUPATIONAL SAFETY AND HEALTH. VOLUME 4. OTHER REGULATIONS AND PROCEDURES **2867**

UNITED STATES. OCCUPATIONAL SAFETY AND HEALTH ADMINISTRATION *See* OCCUPATIONAL SAFETY AND HEALTH. VOLUME 3. CONSTRUCTION STANDARDS **2867**

UNITED STATES. OCCUPATIONAL SAFETY AND HEALTH ADMINISTRATION *See* OSHA PUBLICATIONS & TRAINING MATERIAL **2868**

UNITED STATES. OCCUPATIONAL SAFETY AND HEALTH ADMINISTRATION *See* OSHA CD-ROM **2867**

UNITED STATES. OCCUPATIONAL SAFETY AND HEALTH ADMINISTRATION *See* INDUSTRIAL HYGIENE FIELD OPERATIONS MANUAL **2863**

UNITED STATES. OCCUPATIONAL SAFETY AND HEALTH ADMINISTRATION *See* OCCUPATIONAL SAFETY AND HEALTH. VOLUME 1. GENERAL INDUSTRY STANDARDS **2867**

UNITED STATES. OCCUPATIONAL SAFETY AND HEALTH ADMINISTRATION *See* OCCUPATIONAL SAFETY AND HEALTH. VOLUME 5. FIELD OPERATIONS MANUAL **2867**

UNITED STATES. OCCUPATIONAL SAFETY AND HEALTH REVIEW COMMISSION *See* CITATOR OF THE DECISIONS OF THE OCCUPATIONAL SAFETY AND HEALTH REVIEW COMMISSION **2860**

UNITED STATES. OCCUPATIONAL SAFETY AND HEALTH REVIEW COMMISSION *See* OSAHRC REPORTS **3023**

UNITED STATES OCEANBORNE FOREIGN TRADE ROUTES (US/0161-8830) [04043773] **5458**

UNITED STATES OF ACORN (US/0890-8648) [14510555] **5313**

UNITED STATES OF AMERICA AIP, AERONAUTICAL INFORMATION PUBLICATION (US) [04791003] **38**

UNITED STATES. OFFICE OF ARCHEOLOGY AND HISTORIC PRESERVATION *See* REVIEW AND ANALYSIS OF ARCHEOLOGY PROGRAM **280**

UNITED STATES. OFFICE OF AVIATION POLICY *See* AVP BULLETIN **14**

UNITED STATES. OFFICE OF COASTAL ZONE MANAGEMENT *See* STATE COASTAL ZONE MANAGEMENT ACTIVITIES **4687**

UNITED STATES. OFFICE OF COMMUNITY PLANNING AND DEVELOPMENT *See* CPD NOTES / HEADQUARTERS, COMMUNITY PLANNING AND DEVELOPMENT **2819**

UNITED STATES. OFFICE OF CONSUMER AFFAIRS *See* STATE CONSUMER ACTION **1300**

UNITED STATES. OFFICE OF EDUCATION *See* VOCATIONAL & TECHNICAL EDUCATION; ANNUAL REPORT **1917**

UNITED STATES. OFFICE OF EDUCATION *See* RESIDENCE & MIGRATION OF COLLEGE STUDENTS **1845**

UNITED STATES. OFFICE OF EDUCATION *See* RESEARCH AND DEVELOPMENT FOR THE ADVANCEMENT OF EDUCATION **1903**

UNITED STATES. OFFICE OF EDUCATION *See* STATISTICAL REPORT, FISCAL YEAR ... : A REPORT ON THE YEAR OF TITLE I ELEMENTARY AND SECONDARY EDUCATION ACT OF 1965 **1785**

UNITED STATES. OFFICE OF EDUCATION *See* COMMISSIONER'S REPORT ON THE EDUCATION PROFESSIONS **1891**

UNITED STATES. OFFICE OF EDUCATION *See* BIENNIAL SURVEY OF EDUCATION / DEPARTMENT OF THE INTERIOR, BUREAU OF EDUCATION **1727**

UNITED STATES. OFFICE OF EDUCATION. BUREAU OF STUDENT FINANCIAL ASSISTANCE *See* APPROVAL OF AWARDS FOR INSTITUTIONS PARTICIPATING IN THE COLLEGE WORK-STUDY PROGRAM **1651**

UNITED STATES. OFFICE OF EDUCATION. DIVISION OF VOCATIONAL AND TECHNICAL EDUCATION *See* VOCATIONAL AND TECHNICAL EDUCATION SELECTED STATISTICAL TABLES **1917**

UNITED STATES. OFFICE OF ELECTRIC AND HYBRID VEHICLE SYSTEMS *See* ANNUAL REPORT TO CONGRESS ON THE IMPLEMENTATION OF PUBLIC LAW 94-413, THE ELECTRIC & HYBRID VEHICLE RESEARCH, DEVELOPMENT & DEMONSTRATION ACT OF 1976 **5377**

UNITED STATES. OFFICE OF FEDERAL CONTRACT COMPLIANCE PROGRAMS *See* FEDERAL CONTRACT COMPLIANCE MANUAL **1669**

UNITED STATES. OFFICE OF FOSSIL ENERGY *See* FOSSIL ENERGY PROGRAM REPORT **1944**

UNITED STATES. OFFICE OF FOSSIL ENERGY *See* COAL CONVERSION AND UTILIZATION. TECHNICAL REPORT **972**

UNITED STATES. OFFICE OF FOSSIL ENERGY *See* COAL DEMONSTRATION PLANTS. TECHNICAL REPORT **972**

UNITED STATES. OFFICE OF GOVERNMENT ETHICS. CONFERENCE *See* PROCEEDINGS OF THE ... ANNUAL CONFERENCES **4675**

UNITED STATES. OFFICE OF HIGHWAY PLANNING. PLANNING SERVICES BRANCH *See* NATIONAL TRUCK CHARACTERISTIC REPORT **5388**

UNITED STATES. OFFICE OF HUMAN DEVELOPMENT *See* YEAR OF ACHIEVEMENT **5314**

UNITED STATES. OFFICE OF INDIAN EDUCATION *See* INDIAN EDUCATION ACT OF 1972; REPORT OF PROGRESS, THE **1752**

UNITED STATES. OFFICE OF LIBRARIES AND LEARNING RESOURCES *See* INSTRUCTIONAL EQUIPMENT GRANTS : TITLE VI-A HIGHER EDUCATION ACT OF 1975 **1830**

UNITED STATES. OFFICE OF MANAGEMENT AND BUDGET *See* PAPERWORK AND RED TAPE **4672**

UNITED STATES. OFFICE OF MANAGEMENT AND BUDGET *See* BUDGET REVISIONS - EXECUTIVE OFFICE OF THE PRESIDENT, OFFICE OF MANAGEMENT AND BUDGET **4715**

UNITED STATES. OFFICE OF MANAGEMENT AND BUDGET *See* BUDGET OF THE UNITED STATES GOVERNMENT **4714**

UNITED STATES. OFFICE OF MANAGEMENT AND BUDGET *See* ISSUES - EXECUTIVE OFFICE OF THE PRESIDENT, OFFICE OF MANAGEMENT AND BUDGET **4734**

UNITED STATES. OFFICE OF MANAGEMENT AND BUDGET *See* MID-SESSION REVIEW : THE PRESIDENT'S BUDGET AND ECONOMIC GROWTH AGENDA OF THE ... BUDGET / EXECUTIVE OFFICE OF THE PRESIDENT, OFFICE OF MANAGEMENT AND BUDGET **4737**

UNITED STATES. OFFICE OF MANAGEMENT AND BUDGET *See* MID-SESSION REVIEW : THE PRESIDENT'S BUDGET AND ECONOMIC GROWTH AGENDA OF THE ... BUDGET / EXECUTIVE OFFICE OF THE PRESIDENT, OFFICE OF MANAGEMENT AND BUDGET **4737**

UNITED STATES. OFFICE OF MANAGEMENT AND BUDGET. STATISTICAL POLICY DIVISION *See* STATISTICAL SERVICES OF THE UNITED STATES GOVERNMENT **4700**

UNITED STATES. OFFICE OF MANAGEMENT AND BUDGET. STATISTICAL POLICY DIVISION *See* STANDARD METROPOLITAN STATISTICAL AREAS **5339**

UNITED STATES. OFFICE OF MINORITY BUSINESS ENTERPRISE *See* PROGRESS REPORT. THE MINORITY BUSINESS ENTERPRISE PROGRAM **705**

UNITED STATES. OFFICE OF OCEAN AND COASTAL RESOURCE MANAGEMENT *See* BIENNIAL REPORT TO THE CONGRESS ON COASTAL ZONE MANAGEMENT **4632**

UNITED STATES. OFFICE OF OCEAN AND COASTAL RESOURCE MANAGEMENT. OCEAN MINERALS AND ENERGY DIVISION *See* OCEAN THERMAL ENERGY CONVERSION REPORT TO CONGRESS **1952**

UNITED STATES. OFFICE OF PERSONNEL MANAGEMENT *See* DIGEST OF SIGNIFICANT CLASSIFICATION DECISIONS AND OPINIONS **939**

UNITED STATES. OFFICE OF PERSONNEL MANAGEMENT *See* ANNUAL REPORT TO CONGRESS ON THE FEDERAL EQUAL OPPORTUNITY RECRUITMENT PROGRAM **4701**

UNITED STATES. OFFICE OF PERSONNEL MANAGEMENT *See* INTERAGENCY TRAINING CATALOG OF COURSES **4704**

UNITED STATES. OFFICE OF PERSONNEL MANAGEMENT *See* INTERAGENCY TRAINING CALENDAR OF COURSES **943**

UNITED STATES. OFFICE OF PERSONNEL MANAGEMENT *See* FEDERAL EQUAL OPPORTUNITY RECRUITMENT PROGRAM (FEORP), REPORT TO CONGRESS **4702**

UNITED STATES. OFFICE OF PERSONNEL MANAGEMENT. ANNUAL REPORT TO CONGRESS ON THE FEDERAL EQUAL OPPORTUNITY RECRUITMENT PROGRAM *See* FEDERAL EQUAL OPPORTUNITY RECRUITMENT PROGRAM (FEORP), REPORT TO CONGRESS **4702**

UNITED STATES. OFFICE OF PERSONNEL MANAGEMENT. LIBRARY *See* EQUAL OPPORTUNITY IN EMPLOYMENT / OFFICE OF PERSONNEL MANAGEMENT, LIBRARY **1667**

UNITED STATES. OFFICE OF PERSONNEL MANAGEMENT. LIBRARY *See* FEDERAL CIVIL SERVICE, HISTORY, ORGANIZATION AND ACTIVITIES / OFFICE OF PERSONNEL MANAGEMENT, LIBRARY, THE **4647**

UNITED STATES. OFFICE OF PERSONNEL MANAGEMENT. LIBRARY *See* PERSONNEL MANAGEMENT IN STATE AND LOCAL GOVERNMENTS / OFFICE OF PERSONNEL MANAGEMENT **945**

UNITED STATES. OFFICE OF PERSONNEL MANAGEMENT. OFFICE OF WORKFORCE INFORMATION *See* PAY STRUCTURE OF THE FEDERAL CIVIL SERVICE **1701**

UNITED STATES. OFFICE OF PERSONNEL MANAGEMENT. PRODUCTIVITY RESEARCH DIVISION *See* PRODUCTIVITY RESEARCH PROGRAM FOR FY ..., THE **946**

UNITED STATES. OFFICE OF PERSONNEL MANAGEMENT. WORKFORCE EFFECTIVENESS AND DEVELOPMENT GROUP *See* MANAGEMENT SCIENCES TRAINING CENTER **944**

UNITED STATES. OFFICE OF PIPELINE SAFETY OPERATIONS *See* ADVISORY BULLETIN - OFFICE OF PIPELINE SAFETY OPERATIONS **5375**

UNITED STATES. OFFICE OF REFUGEE RESETTLEMENT *See* REFUGEE RESETTLEMENT PROGRAM **5304**

UNITED STATES. OFFICE OF REVENUE SHARING *See* REVENEWS **4746**

UNITED STATES. OFFICE OF REVENUE SHARING *See* ANNUAL REPORT OF THE OFFICE OF REVENUE SHARING (WASHINGTON) **4710**

UNITED STATES. OFFICE OF SCIENCE AND TECHNOLOGY POLICY *See* SCIENCE AND TECHNOLOGY : A REPORT TO THE CONGRESS **5150**

UNITED STATES. OFFICE OF SCIENCE AND TECHNOLOGY POLICY *See* SCIENCE AND TECHNOLOGY REPORT AND OUTLOOK **5151**

UNITED STATES. OFFICE OF SPACE AND TERRESTRIAL APPLICATIONS. GEODYNAMICS BRANCH *See* NASA GEODYNAMICS PROGRAM ANNUAL REPORT FOR ... / GEODYNAMICS PROGRAM OFFICE, NASA OFFICE OF SPACE AND TERRESTRIAL APPLICATIONS **29**

UNITED STATES. OFFICE OF TAX ANALYSIS *See* HIGH INCOME TAX RETURNS **4731**

UNITED STATES. OFFICE OF TELECOMMUNICATIONS POLICY *See* ACTIVITIES AND PROGRAMS - OFFICE OF TELECOMMUNICATIONS POLICY **1148**

UNITED STATES. OFFICE OF TERRITORIES *See* GENERAL INFORMATION: THE VIRGIN ISLANDS OF THE UNITED STATES **2533**

Alphabetical Title Index — UNITED

UNITED STATES. OFFICE OF THE ASSISTANT SECRETARY FOR CONSERVATION AND SOLAR ENERGY. OFFICE OF ALCOHOL FUELS *See* ANNUAL REPORT TO CONGRESS ON THE USE OF ALCOHOL IN MOTOR FUELS **1020**

UNITED STATES. OFFICE OF THE ASSISTANT SECRETARY FOR FOSSIL ENERGY *See* ENVIRONMENTAL DEVELOPMENT PLAN. COAL LIQUEFACTION **2228**

UNITED STATES. OFFICE OF THE ASSISTANT SECRETARY OF DEFENSE (MANPOWER, RESERVE AFFAIRS, AND LOGISTICS) *See* DOMESTIC BASE FACTORS REPORT **4043**

UNITED STATES. OFFICE OF THE ASSISTANT SECRETARY OF THE ARMY (CIVIL WORKS) *See* PROJECTS RECOMMENDED FOR DEAUTHORIZATION, ANNUAL REPORT **2095**

UNITED STATES. OFFICE OF THE COMPTROLLER OF THE CURRENCY *See* COMPTROLLER'S MANUAL FOR REPRESENTATIVES IN TRUSTS : REGULATIONS, INSTRUCTIONS, OPINIONS **784**

UNITED STATES. OFFICE OF THE COMPTROLLER OF THE CURRENCY *See* QUARTERLY JOURNAL / OFFICE OF THE COMPTROLLER OF THE CURRENCY **805**

UNITED STATES. OFFICE OF THE FEDERAL REGISTER *See* UNITED STATES GOVERNMENT MANUAL (1974) **4692**

UNITED STATES. OFFICE OF THE UNDER SECRETARY OF DEFENSE FOR RESEARCH AND ENGINEERING *See* DEFENSE STANDARDIZATION AND SPECIFICATION PROGRAM, POLICIES, PROCEDURES, AND INSTRUCTIONS **4042**

UNITED STATES. OFFICE OF YOUTH DEVELOPMENT *See* JUVENILE COURT STATISTICS **3168**

UNITED STATES. OFFICE OF YOUTH DEVELOPMENT *See* GRANTS - U.S. DEPARTMENT OF HEALTH, EDUCATION, AND WELFARE. OFFICE OF HUMAN DEVELOPMENT. OFFICE OF YOUTH DEVELOPMENT **5286**

UNITED STATES. OUTER CONTINENTAL SHELF ENVIRONMENTAL STUDIES ADVISORY COMMITTEE *See* ANNUAL REPORT TO THE SECRETARY, DEPARTMENT OF THE INTERIOR **1446**

UNITED STATES. PACIFIC SOUTHWEST FOREST AND RANGE EXPERIMENT STATION, BERKELEY, CALIFORNIA *See* FOREST RESEARCH NOTE **2381**

UNITED STATES. PASSPORT OFFICE *See* PASSPORT OFFICE WORKLOADS AND ACCOMPLISHMENTS **4673**

UNITED STATES PATENT AND TRADEMARK OFFICE *See* TRADEMARK RULES OF PRACTICE OF THE PATENT AND TRADEMARK OFFICE WITH FORMS AND STATUTES **1309**

UNITED STATES. PATENT AND TRADEMARK OFFICE *See* MANUAL OF PATENT EXAMINING PROCEDURE **1306**

UNITED STATES. PATENT AND TRADEMARK OFFICE *See* UNITED STATES STATUTORY INVENTION REGISTRATION [MICROFORM] **1309**

UNITED STATES PATENT AND TRADEMARK OFFICE *See* TRADEMARK MANUAL OF EXAMINING PROCEDURE (TMEP) **1309**

UNITED STATES. PATENT AND TRADEMARK OFFICE *See* PATENT AND TRADEMARK OFFICE NOTICES **1307**

UNITED STATES. PATENT AND TRADEMARK OFFICE *See* LIST OF RECENT ACCESSIONS AND FOREIGN PATENT TRANSLATIONS OF THE SCIENTIFIC LIBRARY **1306**

UNITED STATES. PATENT AND TRADEMARK OFFICE. OFFICE OF DOCUMENTATION PLANNING, SUPPORT, AND CONTROL *See* MANUAL OF CLASSIFICATION **1306**

UNITED STATES PATENTS QUARTERLY, THE (US/0041-803X) [01768767] **1309**

UNITED STATES PHARMACOPEIA DRUG INFORMATION FOR THE CONSUMER (US) [15483087] **4331**

UNITED STATES PHARMACOPEIA. NATIONAL FORMULARY. SUPPLEMENT, THE (US/0190-5384) [04662472] **4331**

UNITED STATES PHARMACOPEIA, THE (US/0195-7996) [05623396] **4331**

UNITED STATES. PLANT GENETICS AND GERMPLASM INSTITUTE. VEGETABLE LABORATORY *See* POTATO-BREEDING PROGRAM, USDA, THE **182**

UNITED STATES POLITICAL SCIENCE DOCUMENTS (US/0148-6063) [02715945] 4499, **4503**

UNITED STATES POSTAL CARD CATALOG (US/0276-7244) [07289236] **1147**

UNITED STATES POSTAL SERVICE *See* POSTAL OPERATIONS MANUAL **1146**

UNITED STATES POSTAL SERVICE *See* POSTAL CONTRACTING MANUAL **1146**

UNITED STATES POSTAL SERVICE *See* FINANCIAL MANAGEMENT MANUAL (UNITED STATES POSTAL SERVICE) **1145**

UNITED STATES POSTAL SERVICE *See* INSTRUCTIONS FOR MAILERS **1145**

UNITED STATES POSTAL SERVICE *See* POSTAL SERVICE MANUAL **1146**

UNITED STATES POSTAL SERVICE *See* ANNUAL REPORT OF THE POSTMASTER GENERAL **1144**

UNITED STATES POSTAL SERVICE *See* TELEPHONE DIRECTORY / U.S. POSTAL SERVICE **1147**

UNITED STATES POSTAL SERVICE *See* ADMINISTRATIVE SUPPORT MANUAL **1144**

UNITED STATES POSTAL SERVICE *See* DOMESTIC MAIL MANUAL **1144**

UNITED STATES POSTAL SERVICE *See* DOMESTIC AIR SERVICE INSTRUCTIONS **1144**

UNITED STATES POSTAL SERVICE *See* USPS PROCUREMENT MANUAL **1147**

UNITED STATES POSTAL SERVICE. PROCUREMENT MANUAL *See* USPS PROCUREMENT MANUAL **1147**

UNITED STATES. PRESIDENT *See* FEDERAL OCEAN PROGRAM : THE ANNUAL REPORT OF THE PRESIDENT TO THE CONGRESS ON THE NATION'S EFFORTS TO COMPREHEND, CONSERVE, AND USE THE SEA, THE **1449**

UNITED STATES. PRESIDENT *See* STATE OF THE UNION ADDRESS **4688**

UNITED STATES. PRESIDENT *See* ECONOMIC REPORT OF THE PRESIDENT TRANSMITTED TO THE CONGRESS **1484**

UNITED STATES. PRESIDENT *See* INTERNATIONAL ECONOMIC REPORT OF THE PRESIDENT **1636**

UNITED STATES. PRESIDENT *See* PUBLIC PAPERS OF THE PRESIDENTS OF THE UNITED STATES **4676**

UNITED STATES. PRESIDENT *See* CODIFICATION OF PRESIDENTIAL PROCLAMATIONS AND EXECUTIVE ORDERS **2952**

UNITED STATES. PRESIDENT *See* AERONAUTICS AND SPACE REPORT OF THE PRESIDENT. ACTIVITIES **4**

UNITED STATES. PRESIDENTIAL ADVISORY COMMITTEE ON SMALL AND MINORITY BUSINESS OWNERSHIP *See* ANNUAL REPORT / PRESIDENTIAL ADVISORY COMMITTEE ON SMALL AND MINORITY BUSINESS OWNERSHIP **639**

UNITED STATES. PRESIDENT'S CANCER PANEL *See* REPORT OF THE CHAIRMAN - UNITED STATES. PRESIDENT'S CANCER PANEL **3823**

UNITED STATES. PRESIDENT'S COMMITTEE ON EMPLOYMENT OF THE HANDICAPPED *See* HOW FEDERAL AGENCIES HAVE SERVED THE HANDICAPPED **4388**

UNITED STATES. PUBLIC HEALTH SERVICE *See* PHS GRANTS POLICY MEMORANDUM **5686**

UNITED STATES. PUBLIC HEALTH SERVICE. COMMISSIONED CORPS *See* COMMISSIONED CORPS BULLETIN **4771**

UNITED STATES. PUBLIC HEALTH SERVICE COOPERATIVE STUDY *See* PROCEEDINGS OF THE U.S. PUBLIC HEALTH SERVICE COOPERATIVE STUDIES (RENAL DISEASE AND HYPERTENSION) **3709**

UNITED STATES. RAILROAD RETIREMENT BOARD *See* ANNUAL REPORT - RAILROAD RETIREMENT BOARD **1650**

UNITED STATES. REHABILITATION SERVICES ADMINISTRATION *See* FACT SHEET BOOKLET **5285**

UNITED STATES. REHABILITATION SERVICES ADMINISTRATION *See* STATE VOCATIONAL REHABILITATION AGENCY PROGRAM DATA **5311**

UNITED STATES. REHABILITATION SERVICES ADMINISTRATION *See* PROGRAM ADMINISTRATION REVIEW OF THE SOCIAL SECURITY DISABILITY INSURANCE AND THE SUPPLEMENTAL SECURITY INCOME VOCATIONAL REHABILITATION PROGRAMS **1704**

UNITED STATES. REHABILITATION SERVICES ADMINISTRATION. ANNUAL REPORT TO THE PRESIDENT AND CONGRESS, FISCAL YEAR (US) **5313**

UNITED STATES. REHABILITATION SERVICES ADMINISTRATION. DIVISION OF PROGRAM DATA AND ANALYSIS. OFFICE OF ADMINISTRATIVE SUPPORT *See* CASELOAD STATISTICS : STATE VOCATIONAL REHABILITATION AGENCIES **5266**

UNITED STATES REPORTS (US/0891-6845) [04384322] **3068**

UNITED STATES. SCHOOL OF AEROSPACE MEDICINE *See* TECHNICAL REPORT SAM-TR **3644**

UNITED STATES. SCIENCE AND EDUCATION ADMINISTRATION. WESTERN REGION *See* ADVANCES IN AGRICULTURAL TECHNOLOGY (WESTERN SERIES) **44**

UNITED STATES. SECURITIES AND EXCHANGE COMMISSION *See* SECURITIES AND EXCHANGE COMMISSION REPORT TO CONGRESS ON THE ACCOUNTING PROFESSION AND THE COMMISSION'S OVERSIGHT ROLE / PREPARED FOR THE SUBCOMMITTEE ON GOVERNMENTAL EFFICIENCY AND THE DISTRICT OF COLUMBIA OF THE COMMITTEE ON GOVERNMENTAL AFFAIRS, UNITED STATES SENATE, BY THE SECURITIES AND EXCHANGE COMMISSION **751**

UNITED STATES. SECURITIES AND EXCHANGE COMMISSION *See* GENERAL RULES AND REGULATIONS UNDER THE INVESTMENT COMPANY ACT OF 1940 **899**

UNITED STATES. SECURITIES AND EXCHANGE COMMISSION *See* SEC DOCKET **913**

UNITED STATES. SECURITIES AND EXCHANGE COMMISSION *See* TRUST INDENTURE ACT OF 1939 RELEASE **3066**

UNITED STATES. SECURITIES AND EXCHANGE COMMISSION. OFFICE OF REPORTS AND INFORMATION SERVICES *See* CLASSIFICATION, ASSETS AND LOCATION OF REGISTERED INVESTMENT COMPANIES UNDER THE INVESTMENT COMPANY ACT OF 1940 **894**

UNITED STATES. SECURITIES AND EXCHANGE COMMISSION. OFFICE OF REPORTS AND INFORMATION SERVICES *See* SEC CORPORATION INDEX **913**

UNITED STATES. SECURITIES AND EXCHANGE COMMISSION. SEC SPEAKS *See* SEC SPEAKS IN ..., THE **3047**

UNITED STATES. SELECTIVE SERVICE SYSTEM *See* ANNUAL REPORT TO THE CONGRESS OF THE UNITED STATES FROM THE DIRECTORY OF THE SELECTIVE SERVICE SYSTEM **4035**

UNITED STATES. SELECTIVE SERVICE SYSTEM *See* LIST OF LOCAL BOARDS OF THE SELECTIVE SERVICE SYSTEM **4049**

UNITED STATES SENATE TELEPHONE DIRECTORY (US) [09629120] **4692**

UNITED STATES. SMALL BUSINESS ADMINISTRATION *See* PUBLICATIONS - SMALL BUSINESS ADMINISTRATION **705**

UNITED STATES. SMALL BUSINESS ADMINISTRATION *See* LIST OF SMALL BUSINESS CONCERNS INTERESTED IN PERFORMING RESEARCH AND DEVELOPMENT, A **690**

UNITED STATES. SMALL BUSINESS ADMINISTRATION *See* ANNUAL REPORT / SMALL BUSINESS ADMINISTRATION **639**

UNITED STATES. SMALL BUSINESS ADMINISTRATION. OFFICE OF ADVOCACY, PLANNING, AND RESEARCH *See* SMALL ENTERPRISE IN THE ECONOMY **1521**

UNITED STATES. SMALL BUSINESS ADMINISTRATION. OFFICE OF INSPECTOR GENERAL *See* SEMI-ANNUAL REPORT OF THE INSPECTOR GENERAL, U.S. SMALL BUSINESS ADMINISTRATION **3103**

UNITED STATES. SMALL BUSINESS ADMINISTRATION. OFFICE OF MANAGEMENT ASSISTANCE *See* SBA PUBLICATIONS. SBA 115A : FREE MANAGEMENT ASSISTANCE PUBLICATIONS **885**

UNITED STATES. SMALL BUSINESS ADMINISTRATION. OFFICE OF THE CHIEF COUNSEL FOR ADVOCACY *See* CATALOG OF FEDERAL PAPERWORK REQUIREMENTS, BY INDUSTRY GROUP **656**

UNITED STATES. SOCIAL AND REHABILITATION SERVICE. OFFICE OF MANAGEMENT *See* QUALITY CONTROL : STATES' CORRECTIVE ACTION ACTIVITIES **5303**

UNITED STATES. SOCIAL SECURITY ADMINISTRATION *See* LIBRARY NOTES / SOCIAL SECURITY ADMINISTRATION **5295**

UNITED STATES. SOCIAL SECURITY ADMINISTRATION *See* RULINGS. CUMULATIVE EDITION : SOCIAL SECURITY RULINGS ON FEDERAL OLD-AGE, SURVIVORS, DISABILITY, SUPPLEMENTAL SECURITY INCOME, AND BLACK LUNG BENEFITS **5306**

UNITED STATES. SOCIAL SECURITY ADMINISTRATION See ANNUAL REPORT TO THE CONGRESS FOR FISCAL YEAR ... / SOCIAL SECURITY **5273**

UNITED STATES. SOIL CONSERVATION SERVICE See REPORT OF THE CHIEF OF THE SOIL CONSERVATION SERVICE **184**

UNITED STATES. SOIL CONSERVATION SERVICE See SOIL SURVEY INVESTIGATIONS REPORT **187**

UNITED STATES. SOIL CONSERVATION SERVICE See PROGRESS REPORT OF CONSERVATION ACTIVITIES **2202**

UNITED STATES. SOIL CONSERVATION SERVICE See SCS-TP (UNITED STATES. SOIL CONSERVATION SERVICE) **185**

UNITED STATES. SOIL CONSERVATION SERVICE See INDIANA WATERSHED PROGRESS **2091**

UNITED STATES. SOUTHEAST ENVIRONMENTAL RESEARCH LABORATORY, ATHENS, GA See QUARTERLY SUMMARY - UNITED STATES. SOUTHEAST ENVIRONMENTAL RESEARCH LABORATORY, ATHENS, GA **2180**

UNITED STATES. SOUTHERN FOREST EXPERIMENT STATION, NEW ORLEANS See RESEARCH NOTE SO **2393**

UNITED STATES SPACE FOUNDATION PROCEEDINGS (US) **38**

UNITED STATES SPECIALIST, THE (US/0164-923X) [04238814] **1147**

UNITED STATES. STATE AND PRIVATE FORESTRY. NORTHEASTERN AREA See ACCOMPLISHMENTS OF FISCAL YEAR - NORTHEASTERN AREA, STATE AND PRIVATE FORESTRY **2373**

UNITED STATES STATUTORY INVENTION REGISTRATION [MICROFORM] (US) [17490819] **1309**

UNITED STATES. SUBVERSIVE ACTIVITIES CONTROL BOARD See ANNUAL REPORT / SUBVERSIVE ACTIVITIES CONTROL BOARD **4464**

UNITED STATES. SUPREME COURT See DOCKET SHEET / SUPREME COURT OF THE UNITED STATES, THE **2963**

UNITED STATES. SUPREME COURT See LANDMARK BRIEFS AND ARGUMENTS OF THE SUPREME COURT OF THE UNITED STATES : CONSTITUTIONAL LAW **3093**

UNITED STATES. SUPREME COURT See OFFICIAL REPORTS OF THE SUPREME COURT **3021**

UNITED STATES. SUPREME COURT See JUDICIAL FELLOWS PROGRAM, THE **3141**

UNITED STATES. SUPREME COURT See UNITED STATES REPORTS **3068**

UNITED STATES. SUPREME COURT See JOURNAL / SUPREME COURT OF THE UNITED STATES **3141**

UNITED STATES. SUPREME COURT See SLIP OPINION / SUPREME COURT OF THE UNITED STATES **3055**

UNITED STATES SUPREME COURT RECORDS AND BRIEFS INDEX (US) [04672027] **3068**

UNITED STATES SWIMMING RULES AND REGULATIONS (US/0742-7808) [09789188] **4927**

UNITED STATES. TAX COURT See TC REPORTED DECISIONS; CONTAINING THE FULL TEXT OF ALL REPORTED DECISIONS OF THE TAX COURT OF THE UNITED STATES **4756**

UNITED STATES. TAX COURT See REPORTS - UNITED STATES. TAX COURT **3039**

UNITED STATES. TAX COURT See TC MEMORANDUM DECISIONS : CONTAINING THE FULL TEXT OF ALL MEMORANDUM DECISIONS OF THE TAX COURT OF THE UNITED STATES RENDERED DURING ... **4756**

UNITED STATES. TAX COURT See REPORTS OF THE UNITED STATES TAX COURT **3039**

●UNITED STATES TAX REPORTER (US) **4757**

UNITED STATES TENNIS ASSOCIATION See OFFICIAL UNITED STATES TENNIS ASSOCIATION TENNIS YEARBOOK **4910**

UNITED STATES TENNIS ASSOCIATION See RECORDS OF SELECTED PLAYERS **4914**

UNITED STATES TENNIS ASSOCIATION See OFFICIAL UNITED STATES TENNIS ASSOCIATION YEARBOOK AND TENNIS GUIDE WITH THE OFFICIAL RULES, THE **4910**

UNITED STATES TENNIS CLUB REGISTRY (US/0364-8214) [02677161] **4927**

UNITED STATES TRADE AND DEVELOPMENT PROGRAM See CONGRESSIONAL PRESENTATION / UNITED STATES TRADE AND DEVELOPMENT PROGRAM **1552**

UNITED STATES TRADE ASSOCIATIONS (US/0093-6685) [01793086] **1630**

UNITED STATES TRADE FAIR (US/0742-3675) [10310738] **958**, **952**

UNITED STATES TRAVEL AND TOURISM ADMINISTRATION See PROGRAM REPORT OF THE UNITED STATES TRAVEL AND TOURISM ADMINISTRATION **5489**

UNITED STATES TRAVEL DATA CENTER See SURVEY OF STATE TRAVEL OFFICES **5491**

UNITED STATES TRAVEL DATA CENTER See NATIONAL TRAVEL EXPENDITURE STUDY **5485**

UNITED STATES. TREASURY DEPT See TREASURY DEPARTMENT TELEPHONE DIRECTORY **4691**

UNITED STATES. TREASURY DEPT. BUREAU OF GOVERNMENT FINANCIAL OPERATIONS See INVENTORY OF NONPURCHASED FOREIGN CURRENCIES **792**

UNITED STATES TREATIES AND OTHER INTERNATIONAL AGREEMENTS (US/0083-3487) [01307767] **3137**

UNITED STATES TROTTING ASSOCIATION See RACING, FARM, CORPORATE, AND STABLE NAMES **2802**

UNITED STATES TROTTING ASSOCIATION See ANNUAL YEAR BOOK - UNITED STATES TROTTING ASSOCIATION, INC **2797**

UNITED STATES TROTTING ASSOCIATION YEAR BOOK, TROTTING AND PACING See ANNUAL YEAR BOOK - UNITED STATES TROTTING ASSOCIATION, INC **2797**

UNITED STATES. U.S. DEPARTMENT OF LABOR, EMPLOYMENT STANDARDS ADMINISTRATION, WOMEN'S BUREAU See PAMPHLET - U.S. DEPARTMENT OF LABOR, EMPLOYMENT STANDARDS ADMINISTRATION, WOMEN'S BUREAU **1700**

UNITED STATES UNDERWATER FATALITY STATISTICS (US/0161-2557) [02220580] **4811**

UNITED STATES. URBAN MASS TRANSPORTATION ADMINISTRATION See REPORT TO CONGRESS CONCERNING THE DEMONSTRATION OF FARE-FREE MASS TRANSPORTATION **5391**

UNITED STATES. URBAN MASS TRANSPORTATION ADMINISTRATION. OFFICE OF TRANSIT ASSISTANCE See SUMMARY OF UMTA'S TRANSIT ASSISTANCE PROGRAM **5393**

UNITED STATES. VETERANS ADMINISTRATION See MANPOWER PLANNING DATA (WASHINGTON) **944**

UNITED STATES. VETERANS ADMINISTRATION See MEDICAL RESEARCH IN THE VETERANS' ADMINISTRATION **3611**

UNITED STATES. VETERANS ADMINISTRATION See VA EDUCATION LOAN DEFAULTS : ANNUAL REPORT **1853**

UNITED STATES. VETERANS ADMINISTRATION. DEPT. OF MEDICINE AND SURGERY See REPORT ON VISUAL IMPAIRMENT SERVICES TEAMS **4393**

UNITED STATES. VETERANS ADMINISTRATION. DEPT. OF MEDICINE AND SURGERY. MEDICAL INFORMATION RESOURCES MANAGEMENT OFFICE See DM & S ADP PLAN **3573**

UNITED STATES. VETERANS ADMINISTRATION. HEALTH PROFESSIONAL SCHOLARSHIP PROGRAM See INSTRUCTION AND CODE TABLE BOOKLET / VA HEALTH PROFESSIONAL SCHOLARSHIP PROGRAM **4046**

UNITED STATES. VETERANS ADMINISTRATION. MERIT REVIEW BOARDS See ANNUAL REPORT OF ACTIVITIES **4035**

UNITED STATES. VETERANS ADMINISTRATION. OFFICE OF FACILITIES See FIVE YEAR MEDICAL FACILITY DEVELOPMENT PLAN **3780**

UNITED STATES. VETERANS ADMINISTRATION. REPORTS AND STATISTICS SERVICE See COUNTY VETERAN POPULATION **4034**

UNITED STATES VIEWS ON MEXICO (US/0276-4709) [07368393] **2764**

UNITED STATES VOLLEYBALL ASSOCIATION See OFFICIAL ... UNITED STATES VOLLEYBALL RULES **4910**

UNITED STATES. YOUTH CONSERVATION CORPS See YOUTH CONSERVATION CORPS PROGRAM **2210**

UNITED STATES ZIP CODE MARKETING BUSINESS MAP ATLAS. NATIONAL EDITION (US/0192-4591) [05011149] **1147**

UNITED STEEL WORKERS OF AMERICA See PROCEEDINGS OF THE CONSTITUTIONAL CONVENTION OF THE UNITED STEEL WORKERS OF AMERICA **1703**

UNITED SYNAGOGUE OF AMERICA See DIRECTORY & RESOURCE GUIDE / UNITED SYNAGOGUE OF AMERICA **5047**

UNITED SYNAGOGUE REVIEW (US/0041-8153) [03953554] **5053**

UNITED TEACHER (LOS ANGELES, CALIF.) (US/0745-4163) [07379950] **1788**

UNITED TECHNOLOGIES CORPORATION See ANNUAL REPORT - UNITED TECHNOLOGIES **2096**

UNITED TECHNOLOGIES MAGAZINE (US) [06235098] **5167**

UNITED TRANSPORTATION UNION See UTU NEWS **1716**

UNITED TRANSPORTATION UNION See UTU NEWS CANADA **1716**

UNITED WAY OF AMERICA See INTERNATIONAL DIRECTORY (ALEXANDRIA, VA.) **5290**

UNITED WAY OF AMERICA. INFORMATION CENTER See DIGEST OF SELECTED REPORTS - UNITED WAY OF AMERICA **5282**

UNITED WAY OF CANADA See ANALYSE DE LA CAMPAGNE / CENTRAIDE CANADA **5271**

UNITED WAY RESEARCH SERVICES BULLETIN (CN/0843-3704) [20125165] **5313**

●UNITED YOUTH DIGEST (US/1065-5913) [26641820] **5006**

●UNITRADE CATALOGUE SPECIALISE DES TIMBRES CANADIENS (CN/1193-8838) [27996739] **2788**

●UNITRADE SPECIALIZED CATALOGUE OF CANADIAN STAMPS (CN/1193-8811) [27898461] **2788**

UNITT'S CANADIAN PRICE GUIDE TO ANTIQUES & COLLECTABLES (CN/0315-2383) [02248357] **2779**, **252**

UNITY / ASSOCIATION OF IROQUOIS AND ALLIED INDIANS (CN/0829-4216) [13263630] **2274**

UNITY DAILY WORD See DAILY WORD **4952**

UNITY DEBATE, THE *CEASED*. (CN/1183-5206) [25423811] **4692**

●UNITY IN A MULTICULTURAL U.S.A (US/1074-6250) [29698642] **4513**

UNITY (SAN FRANCISCO, CALIF. : ENGLISH/SPANISH EDITION) See UNITY IN A MULTICULTURAL U.S.A **4513**

UNITY (UNITY VILLAGE) (US/0162-3567) [01768777] **5006**

UNIVERS DU FRANCAIS SEVRES, L' (FR/1018-872X) [I1018872X] **1788**

UNIVERS DU VIVANT (FR) **401**

UNIVERS (LIMOILOU) (CN/0381-9876) [02943106] **5038**

UNIVERS MAC PARIS (FR/1161-3157) [I11613157] **1206**

●UNIVERSAL ACADEMIA (US/1064-2625) [26238856] **3472**

UNIVERSAL ALMANAC, THE (US/1045-9820) [23009612] **1929**

UNIVERSAL BUSINESS DIRECTORIES (AUST.) PTY. LTD See UBD AUSTRALIA WIDE BUSINESS AND STREET DIRECTORY: GLADSTONE **716**

UNIVERSAL BUSINESS DIRECTORIES (AUST.) PTY. LTD See UBD AUSTRALIA WIDE BUSINESS AND STREET DIRECTORY: WARWICK, STANTHORPE, GOONDIWINDI, ST. GEORGE **717**

UNIVERSAL BUSINESS DIRECTORIES (AUST.) PTY. LTD See UBD AUSTRALIA WIDE BUSINESS AND STREET DIRECTORY: TOOWOOMBA DISTRICT **717**

UNIVERSAL BUSINESS DIRECTORIES (AUST.) PTY. LTD See UBD BUSINESS & STREET DIRECTORY: BRISBANE, CITY & SUBURBAN **717**

UNIVERSAL BUSINESS DIRECTORIES (AUST.) PTY. LTD See UBD AUSTRALIA WIDE BUSINESS AND STREET DIRECTORY : GOLD COAST **716**

UNIVERSAL BUSINESS DIRECTORIES (AUST.) PTY. LTD See UBD AUSTRALIA WIDE BUSINESS AND STREET DIRECTORY: BUNDABERG **716**

UNIVERSAL BUSINESS DIRECTORIES (W.A.) PTY. LTD See UBD BUSINESS & STREET DIRECTORY, WESTERN AUSTRALIAN COUNTRY TOWNS **717**

UNIVERSAL BUSINESS DIRECTORY FOR ADELAIDE CITY & SUBURBS See BUSINESS & STREET DIRECTORY FOR ... ADELAIDE CITY & SUBURBS, INCLUDING ELIZABETH & SALISBURY **645**

UNIVERSAL BUSINESS DIRECTORY FOR SOUTH AUSTRALIAN COUNTRY (AT) [02683141] **717**

Alphabetical Title Index — UNIVERSITA

UNIVERSAL BUSINESS DIRECTORY: WESTERN AUSTRALIAN COUNTRY BUSINESS DIRECTORY *See* UBD BUSINESS & STREET DIRECTORY, WESTERN AUSTRALIAN COUNTRY TOWNS **717**

UNIVERSAL, EL (MX) [01773562] **5806**

UNIVERSAL HEALTHCARE ALMANAC, THE (US/1069-6725) [12094835] **3648**

UNIVERSAL MEDICAL DEVICE NOMENCLATURE SYSTEM (US/1059-3438) [24566070] **3648**

UNIVERSAL MESSAGE, THE (PK) [06232057] **5045**

UNIVERSAL MILITARY ABSTRACTS (II) [17242448] **4059**

UNIVERSAL POSTAL UNION. INTERNATIONAL BUREAU *See* LISTE DES DISTANCES KILOMETRIQUES, AFFERENTES AUX PARCOURS TERRITORIAUX DES DEPECHES EN TRANSIT **1145**

UNIVERSAL SERIALS AND BOOK EXCHANGE *See* USBE **427**

UNIVERSAL SERIALS AND BOOK EXCHANGE *See* USBE NEWS **3255**

UNIVERSALIA; LES EVENEMENTS, LES HOMMES, LES PROBLEMES (FR) [02403934] **1929**

UNIVERSALIST FRIENDS (US) [28988325] **5068**

UNIVERSALIST - QUAKER UNIVERSALIST GROUP (UK/0267-6648) [I02676648] **5068**

UNIVERSE (US) [21474312] **3449**

UNIVERSE IN THE CLASSROOM, THE (US/0890-6866) [12400550] 1908, **401**

UNIVERSE MANCHESTER (UK/0041-8226) [I00418226] 5006, **5813**

UNIVERSELLES (QUEBEC) (CN/0848-144X) [21102526] **5567**

UNIVERSIDAD (MX) [06343751] **2856**

UNIVERSIDAD (CL) [05041458] **1851**

UNIVERSIDAD CENTRAL DE VENEZUELA *See* PUBLICACIONES. SERIE : SEMINARIOS **1869**

UNIVERSIDAD CENTRAL DE VENEZUELA *See* COLECCION CIENCIAS SOCIALES **5195**

UNIVERSIDAD CENTRAL DE VENEZUELA. BIBLIOTECA CENTRAL *See* EDICIONES **3208**

UNIVERSIDAD CENTRAL DE VENEZUELA. FACULTAD DE AGRONOMIA *See* REVISTA DE LA FACULTAD DE AGRONOMIA **129**

UNIVERSIDAD CENTRAL DE VENEZUELA. INSTITUTO DE MATERIALES Y MODELOS ESTRUCTURALES *See* IMME BOLETIN TECNICO **2024**

UNIVERSIDAD CENTRAL DE VENEZUELA. INSTITUTO DE PRODUCCION ANIMAL *See* INFORME ANUAL / UNIVERSIDAD CENTRAL DE VENEZUELA, FACULTAD DE AGRONOMIA, INSTITUTO DE PRODUCCION ANIMAL **96**

UNIVERSIDAD COMPLUTENSE DE MADRID. INSTITUTO DE CIENCIAS DE LA EDUCACION *See* I.C.E.U.M **1896**

UNIVERSIDAD COMPLUTENSE DE MADRID. SECCION DE MATEMATICA *See* ACTAS DE LA 1.- REUNION ANUAL DE MATEMATICOS ESPANOLES **3491**

UNIVERSIDAD DE CHILE. DEPARTAMENTO DE ECONOMIA *See* OCUPACION Y DESOCUPACION, SECTORES URBANOS DE LAS REGIONES IV A X, EXCEPTO EL GRAN SANTIAGO **1699**

UNIVERSIDAD DE CHILE. FACULTAD DE AGRONOMIA *See* BOLETIN TECNICO - UNIVERSIDAD DE CHILE, FACULTAD DE AGRONOMIA **68**

UNIVERSIDAD DE COSTA RICA *See* REVISTA DE FILOLOGIA Y LINGUISTICA DE LA UNIVERSIDAD DE COSTA RICA **3316**

UNIVERSIDAD DE LA HABANA *See* UNIVERSIDAD DE LA HABANA **2553**

UNIVERSIDAD DE LA HABANA (CU/0041-8420) [01576210] **2553**

UNIVERSIDAD DE MEXICO : REVISTA DE LA UNIVERSIDAD NACIONAL AUTONOMA DE MEXICO (MX/0185-1330) [12168932] **1851**

UNIVERSIDAD DE MURCIA *See* ANALES DE CIENCIAS - UNIVERSIDAD DE MURCIA **960**

UNIVERSIDAD DE NAVARRA. FACULTAD DE FILOSOFIA Y LETRAS *See* COLECCIO HISTORICA **2684**

UNIVERSIDAD DE ORIENTE (CUMANA, VENEZUELA). INSTITUTO OCEANOGRAFICO *See* BOLETIN DEL INSTITUTO OCEANOGRAFICO DE LA UNIVERSIDAD DE ORIENTE **1447**

UNIVERSIDAD DE ORIENTE (CUMANA, VENEZUELA) INSTITUTO OCEANOGRAFICO *See* CUADERNOS OCEANOGRAFICOS **1448**

UNIVERSIDAD DE PANAMA. DIRECCION DE PLANIFICACION UNIVERSITARIA *See* BOLETIN - UNIVERSIDAD DE PANAMA, DIRECCION DE PLANIFICACION UNIVERSITARIA **1812**

UNIVERSIDAD DE SAN CARLOS DE GUATEMALA. FACULTAD DE HUMANIDADES *See* ANUARIO DE PSICOLOGIA **4574**

UNIVERSIDAD DE SEVILLA *See* HISTORIA, INSTITUCIONES, DOCUMENTOS **2691**

UNIVERSIDAD DE SONORA. DEPARTAMENTO DE GEOLOGIA *See* BOLETIN DEL DEPARTAMENTO DE GEOLOGIA, UNI-SON **1367**

UNIVERSIDAD DE VALLADOLID. FACULTAD DE FILOSOFIA Y LETRAS *See* ESTUDIOS Y DOCUMENTOS **4346**

UNIVERSIDAD DE ZARAGOZA. BIBLIOTECA UNIVERSITARIA *See* MEMORIA-INFORME / UNIVERSIDAD DE ZARAGOZA, BIBLIOTECA UNIVERSITARIA **3231**

UNIVERSIDAD DEL ZULIA. INSTITUTO DE FILOSOFIA DEL DERECHO *See* BOLETIN INFORMATIVO - INSTITUTO DE FILOSOFIA DEL DERECHO **2942**

UNIVERSIDAD LA GRAN COLOMBIA *See* REVISTA UNIVERSIDAD LA GRAN COLOMBIA **1846**

UNIVERSIDAD NACIONAL AUTONOMA DE MEXICO *See* REVISTA DE LA UNIVERSIDAD DE MEXICO **1846**

UNIVERSIDAD NACIONAL AUTONOMA DE MEXICO. DIRECCION GENERAL DE ESTUDIOS ADMINISTRATIVOS *See* INFORME / PUBLICACION COORDINADA POR LA DIRECCION GENERAL DE ESTUDIOS ADMINISTRATIVOS **1830**

UNIVERSIDAD NACIONAL AUTONOMA DE MEXICO. FACULTAD DE DERECHO *See* REVISTA DE LA FACULTAD DE DERECHO DE MEXICO **3041**

UNIVERSIDAD NACIONAL AUTONOMA DE MEXICO. INSTITUTO DE BIOLOGIA *See* ANALES DEL INSTITUTO DE BIOLOGIA, UNIVERSIDAD NACIONAL AUTONOMA DE MEXICO. SERIE ZOOLOGIA **5575**

UNIVERSIDAD NACIONAL AUTONOMA DE MEXICO. INSTITUTO DE GEOLOGIA *See* INSTITUTO DE GEOLOGIA REVISTA **1383**

UNIVERSIDAD NACIONAL AUTONOMA DE MEXICO. INSTITUTO DE GEOLOGIA *See* PALEONTOLOGIA MEXICANA **4229**

UNIVERSIDAD NACIONAL AUTONOMIA DE MEXICO. INSTITUTO DE INVESTIGACIONES ESTETICAS *See* ANALES DEL INSTITUTO DE INVESTIGACIONES ESTETICAS **336**

UNIVERSIDAD NACIONAL DE EDUCACION A DISTANCIA *See* GUIA DE LA UNIVERSIDAD NACIONAL DE EDUCACION A DISTANCIA **1826**

UNIVERSIDAD NACIONAL DE SAN AGUSTIN *See* REVISTA DE INVESTIGACION **5035**

UNIVERSIDAD NACIONAL DEL CENTRO DE LA PROVINCIA DE BUENOS AIRES *See* REVISTA DE LA UNIVERSIDAD NACIONAL DEL CENTRO DE LA PROVINCIA DE BUENOS AIRES **2552**

UNIVERSIDAD NACIONAL DEL CENTRO DEL PERU *See* ANALES CIENTIFICOS - UNIVERSIDAD NACIONAL DEL CENTRO DEL PERU **5082**

UNIVERSIDAD NACIONAL MAYOR DE SAN MARCOS. INSTITUTO VETERINARIO DE INVESTIGACIONES TROPICALES Y DE ALTURA. CENTRO DE INVESTIGACION *See* REVIEW - VETERINARY INSTITUTE FOR TROPICAL AND HIGH ALTITUDE RESEARCH, SAN MARCOS UNIVERSITY INVESTIGATION CENTRE **5520**

UNIVERSIDAD PONTIFICIA DE COMILLAS *See* MISCELANEA COMILLAS **4977**

UNIVERSIDAD PONTIFICIA DE SALAMANCA. FACULTAD DE DERECHO CANONICO *See* COLECTANEA DE JURISPRUDENCIA CANONICA **2952**

UNIVERSIDAD (SAN SALVADOR, EL SALVADOR) (ES/0041-8242) [01507480] **1851**

UNIVERSIDAD (SANTA FE) (AG/0041-8234) [01590421] **1851**

UNIVERSIDAD Y SOCIEDAD (MADRID, SPAIN) (SP) [08020419] **1788**

UNIVERSIDADE CATOLICA DE PETROPOLIS *See* REVISTA DA UNIVERSIDADE CATOLICA DE PETROPOLIS **4616**

UNIVERSIDADE DE SAO PAULO. FACULDADE DE CIENCIAS FARMACEUTICAS *See* REVISTA DE FARMACIA E BIOQUIMICA DA UNIVERSIDADE DE SAO PAULO **4328**

UNIVERSIDADE DE SAO PAULO. FACULDADE DE FILOSOFIA, CIENCIAS E LETRAS *See* PSICOLOGIA **4609**

UNIVERSIDADE DE SAO PAULO. INSTITUTO DE GEOCIENCIAS *See* BOLETIM IG-USP. SERIE CIENTIFICA / UNIVERSIDADE DE SAO PAULO, INSTITUTO DE GEOCIENCIAS **1367**

UNIVERSIDADE DE SAO PAULO. INSTITUTO OCEANOGRAFICO *See* BOLETIM DO INSTITUTO OCEANOGRAFICO **553**

UNIVERSIDADE DE UBERLANDIA FACULDADE DE DIREITO *See* REVISTA - UNIVERSIDADE DE UBERLANDIA FACULDADE DE DIREITO **3042**

UNIVERSIDADE DO AMAZONAS. CENTRO DE PESQUISAS SOCIO-ECONOMICAS *See* BOLETIM TECNICO INFORMATIVO **5193**

UNIVERSIDADE DO ESTADO DA GUANABARA. BOLETIM U.E.G *See* BOLETIM UERJ **1812**

UNIVERSIDADE DO ESTADO DO RIO DE JANEIRO *See* BOLETIM UERJ **1812**

UNIVERSIDADE FEDERAL DE MINAS GERAIS. DEPARTAMENTO DE CIENCIA POLITICA *See* CADERNOS DCP **4466**

UNIVERSIDADE FEDERAL DE MINAS GERAIS. MUSEU DE HISTORIA NATURAL *See* ARQUIVOS DO MUSEU DE HISTORIA NATURAL **4162**

UNIVERSIDADE FEDERAL DO PARANA. COMISSAO CENTRAL DO CONCURSO VESTIBULAR *See* ANALISE E INTERPRETACAO PARCIAL DAS INFORMACOES SOCIO-EDUCACIONAIS DOS CANDIDATOS AOS CONCURSOS VESTIBULARES **1808**

UNIVERSIDADE FEDERAL DO RIO GRANDE DO SUL. FACULDADE DE VETERINARIA *See* ARQUIVOS - FACULDADE DE VETERINARIA, UFRGS **5504**

UNIVERSIDADES (MX) [26491354] **1851**

UNIVERSITA CATTOLICA DEL SACRO CUORE *See* PUBBLICAZIONI DELL'UNIVERSITA CATTOLICA DEL SACRO CUORE **422**

UNIVERSITA CATTOLICA DEL SACRO CUORE *See* ANNUARIO - UNIVERSITA CATTOLICA DEL SACRO CUORE **1810**

UNIVERSITA CATTOLICA DEL SACRO CUORE *See* PUBBLICAZIONI DELL'UNIVERSITA CATTOLICA DEL SACRO CUORE. CONTRIBUTI, SERIE III. SCIENZE FILOSOFICHE **4358**

UNIVERSITA CATTOLICA DEL SACRO CUORE. FACOLTA DI AGRARIA *See* ANNALI DELLA FACOLTA DI AGRARIA UNIVERSITA CATTOLICA DEL SACRO CUORE MILANO **59**

UNIVERSITA CATTOLICA DEL SACRO CUORE. ISTITUTO DI FILOLOGIA MODERNA *See* CONTRIBUTI DELL'ISTITUTO DI FILOLOGIA MODERNA : SERIE INGLESE **3378**

UNIVERSITA DE BARI. SEMINARIO DI MATEMATICA *See* CONFERENZE DEL SEMINARIO DI MATEMATICA DELL'UNIVERSITA DI BARI **3502**

UNIVERSITA DE FIRENZE. ISTITUTO DE STORIA *See* ANNALI DELL'ISTITUTO STORIA **2674**

UNIVERSITA DEGLI STUDI DI PERUGIA. FACOLTA DI LETTERE E FILOSOFIA *See* ANNALI DELLA FACOLTA DI LETTERE E FILOSOFIA **2842**

UNIVERSITA DEGLI STUDI DI ROMA "LA SAPIENZA." *See* ANNUARIO PER GLI ANNI ACCADEMICI / UNIVERSITA DEGLI STUDI DI ROMA LA SAPIENZA **1725**

UNIVERSITA DI BARI. FACOLTA DI LITTERE E FILOSOFIA *See* ANNALI DELLA FACOLTA DI LETTERE E FILOSOFIA **4341**

UNIVERSITA DI BOLOGNA. ISTITUTO DI ENTOMOLOGIA *See* BOLLETTINO DELL'INSTITUTO DI ENTOMOLOGIA DELL'UNIVERSITA DEGLI STUDI DI BOLOGNA **5578**

UNIVERSITA DI FERRARA *See* ANNALI, NUOVA SERIE : SEZIONE 3, BIOLOGIA ANIMALE. SUPPLEMENTO **5576**

UNIVERSITA DI FIRENZE. ISTITUTO LINGUISTICO *See* STUDI DELL'ISTITUTO LINGUISTICO **3324**

UNIVERSITA DI GENOVA. ISTITUTO GEOFISICO E GEODETICO *See* RELAZIONE SULL'ATTIVITA SVOLTA NEL ... **1516**

UNIVERSITA DI PADOVA *See* ANNUARIO PER GLI ANNI ACCADEMICI ... / UNIVERSITA DEGLI STUDI DI PADOVA **1074**

UNIVERSITA DI PADOVA. ISTITUTO DI FILOLOGIA GRECA *See* BOLLETTINO DELL'ISTITUTO DI FILOLOGIA GRECA **3270**

UNIVERSITA DI PARMA. FACOLTA DI ECONOMIA E COMMERCIO *See* STUDI E RICERCHE DELLA FACOLTA DI ECONOMIA E COMMERCIO **1585**

UNIVERSITA DI PARMA. ISTITUTO DI LINGUE E LETTERATURE GERMANICHE *See* ANNALI DELL'ISTITUTO DI LINGUE E LETTERATURE GERMANICHE **3362**

UNIVERSITA — Alphabetical Title Index

UNIVERSITA DI PISA. FACOLTA DI MEDICINA VETERINARIA *See* ANNALI DELLA FACOLTA DI MEDICINA VETERINARIA DI PISA **5503**

UNIVERSITA DI SIENA. CIRCOLO GIURIDICO *See* STUDI SENESI NEL CIRCOLO GIURIDICO DELLA R. UNIVERSITA **3060**

UNIVERSITA DI TORINO. FACOLTA DI SCIENZE AGRARIE *See* ANNALI DELLA FACOLTA DI SCIENZE AGRARIE DELLA UNIVERSITA DEGLI STUDI DI TORINO **59**

UNIVERSITA J. E. PURKYNE. PRIRODOVEDECKA FAKULTA *See* SCRIPTA FACULTATIS SCIENTIARUM NATURALIUM UNIVERSITATIS PURKYNIANAE BRUNENSIS. BIOLOGIA **472**

UNIVERSITA J. E. PURKYNE. PRIRODOVEDECKA FAKULTA *See* SCRIPTA FACULTATIS SCIENTIARUM NATURALIUM UNIVERSITATIS PURKYNIANAE BRUNENSIS. GEOGRAPHIA **2576**

UNIVERSITA J.E. PURKYNE VV BRNE. KNIHOVNA *See* SOUPISY RUKOPISNYCH FONDU **425**

UNIVERSITA KARLOVA *See* ACTA. GYMNICA **1854**

UNIVERSITA KARLOVA *See* ACTA UNIVERSITATIS CAROLINAE. GEOGRAPHICA **2553**

UNIVERSITA KARLOVA *See* ACTA UNIVERSITATIS CAROLINAE. BIOLOGICA **440**

UNIVERSITA KARLOVA. LEKARSKA FAKULTA V HRADCI KRALOVE *See* SEZNAM PREDNASEK LEKARSKE FAKULTY V HRADCI KRALOVE VE STUDIJNIM ROCE ... **2522**

UNIVERSITA KARLOVA. USTAV GEOLOGICKYCH VED *See* REPORT ON RESEARCH - PRAGUE. UNIVERSITA KARLOVA. USTAV GEOLOGICKYCH VED **1360**

UNIVERSITA PALACKEHO V OLOMOUCI. PEDAGOGICKA FAKULTA *See* SBORNIK PRACI. MARXISMUS-LENINISMUS **4546**

UNIVERSITA PROGETTO *CEASED*. (IT) **1851**

UNIVERSITAET KIEL. INSTITUT FUER WELTWIRTSCHAFT. BIBLIOTHEK. STATISTISCHE UEBERSICHTEN UND BERICHT *See* STATISTISCHE UBERSICHTEN FUR DAS JAHR (UNIVERSITAT KIEL. INSTITUTS FUR WELTWIRTSCHAFT. BIBLIOTHEK) **3260**

UNIVERSITAH HA-IVRIT BI-YERUSHALAYIM *See* LIONEL COHEN LECTURES **1761**

UNIVERSITAH HA-IVRIT BI-YERUSHALAYIM *See* SCRIPTA HIEROSOLYMITANA : PUBLICATIONS OF THE HEBREW UNIVERSITY, JERUSALEM **1847**

UNIVERSITAH HA-IVRIT BI-YERUSHALAYIM. MERKAZ LE-HEKER HA-FOLKLOR *See* MEHKERE HA-MERKAZ LE-HEKER HA-FOLKLOR **2322**

UNIVERSITARIOS / PERIODICO MENSUAL PUBLICADO POR LA DIRECCION GENERAL DE DIFUSION CULTURAL, LOS (MX) [11526260] **1851**

UNIVERSITAS (GW/0341-0102) [27135534] **5167**, **367**

UNIVERSITAS (IT) [09848996] **1851**

UNIVERSITAS (ALBANY) (US/0197-1212) [04456457] **2548**

UNIVERSITAS BELGICA (BE) [04915306] **1908**

UNIVERSITAS CANONICA / PUBLICACION SEMESTRAL PREPARD A POR LA FACULTAD DE DERECHO CANONICO (CK) [08210138] **5006**

UNIVERSITAS. ENGLISH LANGUAGE EDITION (STUTTGART) *CEASED*. (GW/0341-0129) [01768793] **2856**

UNIVERSITAS HKBP NOMMENSEN. LEMBAGA PENELITIAN DAN PERENTJANNAN EKONOMI *See* BULLETIN EKONOMI DAN MANAGEMENT **1466**

UNIVERSITAS HUMANISTICA (CK/0120-4807) [03154437] **1851**

UNIVERSITAS INDONESIA. REKTOR *See* LAPORAN REKTOR PADA DIES NATALIS UNIVERSITAS INDONESIA **1834**

UNIVERSITAS KATOLIK PARAHYANGAN. LEMBAGA PENYELIDIKAN ILMIAH *See* PROFIL MAHASISWA UNIVERSITAS KATOLIK PARAHYANGAN **1842**

UNIVERSITAS NEGERI JEMBER. TEAM PELAKSANA K.K.N *See* LAPORAN PELAKSANAAN KULIAH KERJA NYATA, K.K.N **1834**

UNIVERSITAS PHILOSOPHICA (CK/0120-5323) [16066329] **4364**

UNIVERSITAS RIAU *See* WARTA UNIVERSITAS RIAU **5237**

UNIVERSITAS SRIWIJAYA *See* STATISTIK UNIVERSITAS SRIWIJAYA **1848**

UNIVERSITAS SRIWIJAYA. BADAN PELAKSANA KULIAH KERJA NYATA *See* LAPORAN PELAKSANAAN KULIAH KERJA NYATA MAHASISWA UNIVERSITAS SRIWIJAYA **1834**

UNIVERSITAS (STUTTGART) (GW/0041-9079) [02141940] **2856**

UNIVERSITAS UDAYANA *See* BULLETIN UNIVERSITAS UDAYANA **1813**

UNIVERSITAT AUGSBURG *See* FORSCHUNGSBERICHT DER UNIVERSITAT AUGSBURG **455**

UNIVERSITAT BEN-GURYON BA-NEGEV *See* DIRECTORY OF RESEARCH PERSONNEL **940**

UNIVERSITAT BERN. ARCHAEOLOGISCHES SEMINAR *See* HEFTE DES ARCHAEOLOGISCHEN SEMINARS DER UNIVERSITAT BERN **2690**

UNIVERSITAT BIELEFELD *See* INFORMATIONEN - UNIVERSITAT BIELEFELD **5113**

UNIVERSITAT BONN, PHYSIKALISCHES INSTITUT. IR (GW/0172-8741) [01728741] **4424**

UNIVERSITAT BREMEN. REKTOR *See* RECHENSCHAFTSBERICHT DES REDTORS DER UNIVERSITAT BREMEN **1843**

UNIVERSITAT DES SAARLANDES *See* ANNALES UNIVERSITATIS SARAVIENSIS. REIHE : MATHEMATISCH-NATURWISSENSCHAFTLICHE FAKULTAT **4162**

UNIVERSITAT DES SAARLANDES *See* ANNALES. RECHTS- UND WIRTSCHAFTSWISSENSCHAFTLICHE ABTEILUNG **2933**

UNIVERSITAT FRANKFURT AM MAIN *See* STUDIENFUHRER **1849**

UNIVERSITAT GOTTINGEN *See* JAHRESFORSCHUNGSBERICHT / UNIVERSITAT GOTTINGEN **1832**

UNIVERSITAT GOTTINGEN *See* GOTTINGER UNIVERSITATSREDEN **1825**

UNIVERSITAT GOTTINGEN. IBERO-AMERIKA INSTITUT FUR WIRTSCHAFTSFORSCHUNG *See* ARBEITSBERICHTE DES IBERO-AMERIKA INSTITUT FUER WIRTSCHAFTSFORSCHUNG AN DER UNIVERSITAT GOTTINGEN **1633**

UNIVERSITAT GOTTINGEN. ZENTRALSTELLE FUR WEITERBILDUNG *See* GESCHAFTSBERICHT / GEORG-AUGUST-UNIVERSITAT GOTTINGEN **1800**

UNIVERSITAT HAMBURG *See* FORSCHUNGSBERICHT. MATERIALBAND / UNIVERSITAT HAMBURG **1824**

UNIVERSITAT HAMBURG. FORSCHUNGSSTELLE FUR VOLKERRECHT UND AUSLANDISCHES OFFENTLICHES RECHT. DOKUMENTE *See* DOKUMENTE - INSTITUT FUER INTERNATIONALE ANGELEGENHEITEN DER UNIVERSITAT HAMBURG **3127**

UNIVERSITAT HANNOVER *See* UNI HANNOVER **1851**

UNIVERSITAT HEFAH *See* ACADEMIC PROGRESS OF THE UNIVERSITY; REPORT TO THE BOARD OF GOVERNORS, THE **1807**

UNIVERSITAT KARLSRUHE. INSTITUT FUR BODENMECHANIK UND FELSMECHANIK *See* VEROFFENTLICHUNGEN DES INSTITUTS FUER BODENMECHANIK UND FELSMECHANIK DER UNIVERSITAT FRIDERICIANA IN KARLSRUHE **1400**

UNIVERSITAT KIEL. INSTITUT FUER MEERESKUNDE *See* BERICHTE AUS DEM INSTITUT FUER MEERESKUNDE AN DER CHRISTIAN-ALBRECHTS-UNIVERSITAT KIEL **553**

UNIVERSITAT KOLN. ASTA. UNI-FUHRER *See* UNIFUHRER / ALLGEMEINER STUDENTENAUSSCHUSS DER UNIVERSITAT KOLN **1851**

UNIVERSITAT MUNSTER. MATHEMATISCHES INSTITUT *See* SCHRIFTENREIHE DES MATHEMATISCHEN INSTITUTS DER UNIVERSITAT MUNSTER **3533**

UNIVERSITAT TEL-AVIV. FAKULTAH LE-MISHPATIM *See* TEL AVIV UNIVERSITY STUDIES IN LAW **3063**

UNIVERSITAT TUBINGEN. UNIVERSITATSBIBLIOTHEK. ORIENTABTEILUNG *See* NEUERWERBUNGEN VORDERER ORIENT / UNIVERSITATSBIBLIOTHEK TUBINGEN, ORIENTABTEILUNG **420**

UNIVERSITAT TUBINGEN. UNIVERSITATSBIBLIOTHEK. THEOLOGISCHE ABTEILUNG *See* NEUERWERBUNGEN THEOLOGIE UND ALLGEMEINE RELIGIONSWISSENSCHAFT **4980**

UNIVERSITATEA BABES-BOLAI *See* STUDIA UNIVERSITATIS BABES-BOLYAI. BIOLOGIA **474**

UNIVERSITATEA BABES-BOLYAI *See* STUDIA UNIVERSITATIS BABES-BOLYAI. PHYSICA **4423**

UNIVERSITATEA "BABES-BOLYAI." *See* STUDIA UNIVERSITATIS BABES-BOLYAI : MATHEMATICA **3537**

UNIVERSITATEA BABES-BOLYAI *See* STUDIA UNIVERSITATIS BABES-BOLYAI. HISTORIA **2711**

UNIVERSITATEA BABES-BOLYAI *See* STUDIA UNIVERSITATIS BABES-BOLYAI. CHEMIA **993**

UNIVERSITATEA BABES-BOLYAI *See* STUDIA UNIVERSITATIS BABES-BOLYAI. PHILOLOGIA **3325**

UNIVERSITATEA DIN BRASOV *See* BULETINUL UNIVERSITATII DIN BRASOV. SERIA B : ECONOMIE FORESTIERA **2376**

UNIVERSITATEA DIN BUCURESTI *See* ANALELE UNIVERSITATII BUCURESTI : ISTORIE **2673**

UNIVERSITATEA DIN BUCURESTI *See* ANALELE UNIVERSITATII BUCURESTI : BIOLOGIE **441**

UNIVERSITATEA DIN BUCURESTI *See* ANALELE UNIVERSITATII BUCURESTI. DREPT **2933**

UNIVERSITATEA DIN BUCURESTI *See* ANALELE UNIVERSITATII BUCURESTI: PSIHOLOGIE **4573**

UNIVERSITATEA DIN BUCURESTI *See* ANALELE UNIVERSITATII BUCURESTI : LITERATURA UNIVERSALA SI COMPARATA **3361**

UNIVERSITATEA DIN BUCURESTI *See* ANALELE UNIVERSITATII BUCURESTI: SOCIOLOGIE **5239**

UNIVERSITATEA DIN BUCURESTI *See* ANALELE UNIVERSITATII BUCURESTI : FILOSOFIE **4340**

UNIVERSITATEA DIN BUCURESTI *See* ANALELE UNIVERSITATII BUCURESTI. LIMBA SI LITERATURA ROMANA **3361**

UNIVERSITATEA DIN CRAIOVA *See* ANALELE UNIVERSITATII DIN CRAIOVA: SERIA ISTORIE, GEOGRAFIE, FILOLOGIE **2673**

UNIVERSITATEA DIN CRAIOVA *See* ANALELE UNIVERSITATII DIN CRAIOVA : STIINTE FILOLOGICE **3264**

UNIVERSITATEA DIN CRAIOVA *See* ANALELE UNIVERSITATII DIN CRAIOVA. SERIA: STIINTE ECONOMICE SI GEOGRAFIE **1461**

UNIVERSITATEA DIN TIMISOARA *See* ANALELE UNIVERSITATII DIN TIMISOARA. SERIA STINTE FIZICE-CHIMICE **4396**

UNIVERSITATSBIBLIOTHEK MAINZ *See* JAHRESBERICHT ... DER UNIVERSITAETSBIBLIOTHEK MAINZ MIT VERZEICHNIS DER UNIVERSITAETSBIBLIOTHEK UEBERLASSENER SCHRIFTEN MAINZER HOCHSCHULLEHRER **3219**

UNIVERSITE CATHOLIQUE DE LOUVAIN (1425-). CENTER FOR OPERATIONS RESEARCH AND ECONOMETRICS *See* CORE DISCUSSION PAPERS **1471**

UNIVERSITE CATHOLIQUE DE LOUVAIN, LOUVAIN-LA-NEUVE, BELGIUM. INSTITUT DE LINGUISTIQUE *See* BIBLIOTHEQUE DES CAHIERS DE L'INSTITUT DE LINGUISTIQUE DE LOUVAIN **3269**

UNIVERSITE D'ABIDJAN *See* ANNALES DE L'UNIVERSITE D'ABIDJAN. SERIE F: ETHNOSOCIOLOGIE **228**

UNIVERSITE D'AIX-MARSEILLE. FACULTE DES LETTRES ET SCIENCES HUMAINES *See* TRAVAUX ET MEMOIRES **1850**

UNIVERSITE DE BESANCON CENTRE DE DOCUMENTATION ET DE BIBLIOGRAPHIE PHILOSOPHIQUES *See* TRAVAUX DU CENTRE DE DOCUMENTATION ET DE BIBLIOGRAPHIE PHILOSOPHIQUES DE BESANCON **3253**

UNIVERSITE DE CLERMONT-FERRAND. FACULTE DES SCIENCES *See* ANNALES BIOLOGIE ANIMALE **205**

UNIVERSITE DE DAKAR. FACULTE DES SCIENCES *See* ANNALES DE LA FACULTE DES SCIENCES, UNIVERSITE DE DAKAR **5083**

UNIVERSITE DE GRENOBLE *See* RECHERCHES ET TRAVAUX - UNIVERSITE DE GRENOBLE **1843**

UNIVERSITE DE GRENOBLE *See* ESSAIS ET TRAVAUX - GRENOBLE. UNIVERSITE **1823**

UNIVERSITE DE LAUSANNE *See* UNIVERSITE DE LAUSANNE EN ..., L' **1852**

UNIVERSITE DE LAUSANNE EN ..., L' (SZ) [11476428] **1852**

UNIVERSITE DE LIEGE. CENTRE D'ETUDES, DE RECHERCHES ET D'ESSAIS SCIENTIFIQUE DU GENIE CIVIL *See* MEMOIRES C.E.R.E.S **2027**

UNIVERSITE DE LIEGE. CENTRE D'ETUDES DE RECHERCHES ET D'ESSAIS SCIENTIFIQUES DES CONSTRUCTIONS DU GENIE CIVIL ET D'HYDRAULIQUE FLUVIALE *See* BULLETIN DES COURS ET DES LABORATOIRES D'ESSAIS DES CONSTRUCTIONS DU GENIE CIVIL ET D'HYDRAULIQUE FLUVIALE **2019**

Alphabetical Title Index — UNIVERSITY

UNIVERSITE DE LYON II. CENTRE D'ETUDES DU XVIIIE SIECLE *See* ETUDES SUR LA PRESSE AU XVIIIE I.E. DIX-HUITIEME **1823**

UNIVERSITE DE LYON II. CENTRE D'HISTOIRE DU CATHOLICISME *See* COLLECTION - UNIVERSITE DE LYON II. CENTRE D'HISTOIRE DU CATHOLICISME **5028**

UNIVERSITE DE METZ. CENTRE DE RECHERCHES RELATIONS INTERNATIONALES *See* TRAVAUX ET RECHERCHES - CENTRE DE RECHERCHES RELATIONS INTERNATIONALES DE L'UNIVERSITE DE METZ **4536**

UNIVERSITE DE MONCTON *See* GAZETTE DE L'UNIVERSITE DE MONCTON **1091**

UNIVERSITE DE MONCTON *See* REPERTOIRE / UNIVERSITE DE MONCTON **1844**

UNIVERSITE DE MONCTON *See* EFFECTIF ETUDIANT - UNIVERSITE DE MONCTON **1822**

UNIVERSITE DE MONTREAL. BIBLIOTHEQUE DE MEDECINE VETERINAIRE *See* NOUVELLES ACQUISITIONS - UNIVERSITE DE MONTREAL, BIBLIOTHEQUE DE MEDECINE VETERINAIRE **3237**

UNIVERSITE DE MONTREAL. BIBLIOTHEQUE DES SCIENCES HUMAINES ET SOCIALES *See* LISTE DES PERIODIQUES REGULIEREMENT RECUS - UNIVERSITE DE MONTREAL. BIBLIOTHEQUE DES SCIENCES HUMAINES ET SOCIAL **419**

UNIVERSITE DE MONTREAL. BUREAU DES ADMISSIONS *See* STATISTIQUES DE L'ADMISSION - UNIVERSITE DE MONTREAL. BUREAU DES ADMISSIONS **1848**

UNIVERSITE DE MONTREAL. BUREAU DU REGISTRAIRE *See* STATISTIQUES DE L'INSCRIPTION - UNIVERSITE DE MONTREAL, BUREAU DU REGISTRAIRE **1848**

UNIVERSITE DE MONTREAL. CENTRE DE RECHERCHE ET D'INNOVATION URBAINES *See* BULLETIN DU C. R. I. U **2816**

UNIVERSITE DE MONTREAL. DEPARTEMENT DE DEMOGRAPHIE *See* ANNUAIRE ET RAPPORT D'ACTIVITES - DEPARTEMENT DE DEMOGRAPHIE, UNIVERSITE DE MONTREAL **4549**

UNIVERSITE DE MONTREAL. ECOLE DE BIBLIOTHECONOMIE. SOCIETE DES DIPLOMES *See* BULLETIN - SOCIETE DES DIPLOMES DE L'ECOLE DE BIBLIOTHECONOMIE DE L'UNIVERSITE DE MONTREAL **3198**

UNIVERSITE DE MONTREAL. ECOLE DE RELATIONS INDUSTRIELLES *See* TIRE A PART - ECOLE DE RELATIONS INDUSTRIELLES, UNIVERSITE DE MONTREAL **947**

UNIVERSITE DE MONTREAL. ECOLE DE RELATIONS INDUSTRIELLES *See* MONOGRAPHIE - ECOLE DE RELATIONS INDUSTRIELLES, UNIVERSITE DE MONTREAL **944**

UNIVERSITE DE MONTREAL. FACULTE DE MUSIQUE *See* SFP (MONTREAL) **4152**

UNIVERSITE DE MONTREAL. INSTITUT DE BIOLOGIE *See* CONTRIBUTIONS DE L'INSTITUT DE BIOLOGIE DE L'UNIVERSITE DE MONTREAL (1948) **5581**

UNIVERSITE DE MONTREAL. INSTITUT D'ETUDES MEDIEVALES *See* PUBLICATIONS DE L'INSTITUT D'ETUDES MEDIEVALES **2626**

UNIVERSITE DE MONTREAL. SERVICE DES BIBLIOTHEQUES. DIRECTION DES SERVICES TECHNIQUES *See* SERTEK **3249**

UNIVERSITE DE NANTES *See* ANNALES LITTERAIRES **3362**

UNIVERSITE DE NEUCHATEL. FACULTE DES LETTRES *See* RECUEIL DES TRAVAUX **329**

UNIVERSITE DE PARIS I: PANTHEONSORBONNE. CENTRE DE RECHERCHES D'HISTOIRE DES MOUVEMENTS SOCIAUX ET DU SYNDICALISME *See* BULLETIN DU CENTRE DE RECHERCHES D'HISTOIRE DES MOUVEMENTS SOCIAUX ET DU SYNDICALISME **5194**

UNIVERSITE DE PARIS VII *See* ANNUAIRE - UNIVERSITE PARIS 7 **1809**

UNIVERSITE DE SHERBROOKE. BIBLIOTHEQUE GENERALE *See* GUIDE DES USAGERS / UNIVERSITE DE SHERBROOKE-BIBLIOTHEQUE GENERALE **3212**

UNIVERSITE DE SHERBROOKE. DEPARTEMENT D'ECONOMIQUE *See* COLLECTION DU DEPARTEMENT D'ECONOMIQUE **75**

UNIVERSITE DE TOULOUSE-LE MIRAIL *See* ANNALES PUBLIEES PAR L'UNIVERSITE DE TOULOUSE - LE MIRAIL **1808**

UNIVERSITE DE TOULOUSE-LE MIRAIL. INSTITUT D'ART PREHISTORIQUE *See* TRAVAUX DE L'INSTITUT D'ART PREHISTORIQUE **367**

UNIVERSITE D'OTTAWA. INFORMATHEQUE DE LINGUISTIQUE *See* LISTE DES ACQUISITIONS - INFORMATHEQUE DE LINGUISTIQUE, UNIVERSITE D'OTTAWA **3300**

UNIVERSITE DU QUEBEC *See* INVENTAIRE DE LA RECHERCHE SUBVENTIONNEE ET COMMANDITEE **1831**

UNIVERSITE DU QUEBEC A CHICOUTIMI *See* PLAN TRIENNAL DE DEVELOPPEMENT / UNIVERSITE DU QUEBEC A CHICOUTIMI **1841**

UNIVERSITE DU QUEBEC A CHICOUTIMI. BIBLIOTHEQUE *See* RAPPORT DU SERVICE DE LA BIBLIOTHEQUE DE L'UNIVERSITE DU QUEBEC A CHICOUTIMI **3243**

UNIVERSITE DU QUEBEC A HULL *See* UNISCOPE (HULL) **1851**

UNIVERSITE DU QUEBEC A MONTREAL. GROUPE DE RECHERCHE SUR LA SOCIETE MONTREALAISE AU 19E SIECLE *See* RAPPORT ET TRAVAUX - GROUPE DE RECHERCHE SUR LA SOCIETE MONTREALAISE AU 19E SIECLE **2756**

UNIVERSITE DU QUEBEC A RIMOUSKI. GROUPE DE RECHERCHE INTERDISCIPLINAIRE EN DEVELOPPEMENT DE L'EST DU QUEBEC *See* CAHIERS DU GRIDEQ **1541**

UNIVERSITE DU QUEBEC A TROIS-RIVIERES. SERVICE DE LA BIBLIOTHEQUE *See* GUIDE DE L'USAGER / UNIVERSITE DU QUEBEC A TROIS-RIVIERES, SERVICE DE LA BIBLIOTHEQUE, LE **3212**

UNIVERSITE DU QUEBEC. COORDINATION DU DOSSIER ETUDIANT *See* RELEVE DES NOUVEAUX INSCRITS **1844**

UNIVERSITE DU QUEBEC. VICE-PRESIDENCE A L'ENSEIGNEMENT ET A LA RECHERCHE *See* RELEVE DES INSCRIPTIONS **1796**

UNIVERSITE EN OUTAOUAIS, L' (CN/1181-8409) [23237129] **1852**

UNIVERSITE FRANCOPHONE D'ETE SAINTONGE-QUEBEC *See* ANNALES / UNIVERSITE FRANCOPHONE D'ETE SAINTONGE-QUEBEC **1808**

UNIVERSITE, L' (AE) [04769238] **1852**

UNIVERSITE LAVAL *See* STATISTIQUES - UNIVERSITE LAVAL **1798**

UNIVERSITE LAVAL. CENTRE D'ETUDES NORDIQUES *See* TRAVAUX ET DOCUMENTS **2763**

UNIVERSITE LIBRE DE BRUXELLES *See* PROGRAMME DES COURS / UNIVERSITE LIBRE DE BRUXELLES **1094**

UNIVERSITE LIBRE DE BRUXELLES *See* REVUE DE L'UNIVERSITE DE BRUXELLES **5148**

UNIVERSITE LIBRE DE BRUXELLS, FACULTE DE PHILOSOPHIE ET LETTRES (BE) [08289662] **4364**

UNIVERSITE LIBRE DU CONGO *See* PREVISIONS BUDGETAIRES POUR L'EXERCICE **1842**

UNIVERSITE NATIONALE DU ZAIRE. CAMPUS DE KINSHASA. FACULTE DE DROIT *See* ANNALES DE LA FACULTE DE DROIT **2933**

UNIVERSITE NATIONALE DU ZAIRE. CAMPUS DE KINSHASA. FACULTE DES SCIENCES *See* ANNALES DE LA FACULTE DES SCIENCES: SECTION MATHEMATIQUE-PHYSIQUE **3493**

UNIVERSITE NATIONALE DU ZAIRE. CAMPUS DE LUBUMBASHI *See* REVUE DE L'UNIVERSITE NATIONALE DU ZAIRE, CAMPUS DE LUBUMBASHI. SERIE A : LETTRES **1846**

UNIVERSITE NATIONALE DU ZAIRE, CAMPUS DE LUBUMBASHI *See* REVUE DE L'UNIVERSITE NATIONALE DU ZAIRE, CAMPUS DE LUBUMBASHI. SERIE B : SCIENCES **5148**

UNIVERSITE NATIONALE DU ZAIRE. CAMPUS DE LUBUMBASHI. CENTRE DE LINGUISTIQUE THEORIQUE ET APPLIQUEE *See* BULLETIN DE LIAISON - CENTRE DE LINGUISTIQUE THEORIQUE ET APPLIQUEE, UNIVERSITE NATIONALE DU ZAIRE **3270**

UNIVERSITE PARIS-SUD. INSTITUT DE PHYSIQUE NUCLEAIRE *See* ANNUAIRE **4445**

UNIVERSITE PIERRE ET MARIE CURIE *See* PUBLICATIONS MATHEMATIQUES DE L'UNIVERSITE PIERRE ET MARIE CURIE **3529**

UNIVERSITE SAINTE-ANNE *See* REVUE DE L'UNIVERSITE SAINTE-ANNE **1846**

UNIVERSITEIT EN HOGESCHOOL (NE/0566-2036) [02155428] **1852**

UNIVERSITEIT VAN AMSTERDAM. BIBLIOTHEEK *See* LIJST VAN AANWINSTEN / UNIVERSITEITSBIBLIOTHEEK VAN AMSTERDAM **3228**

UNIVERSITES (MONTREAL) (CN/0226-7454) [07865697] **1852**

UNIVERSITES (MONTREAL) (CN/0226-7454) [08187639] **1852**

UNIVERSITETET I OSLO. UNIVERSITETETS OLDSAKSAMLING *See* UNIVERSITETETS OLDSAKSAMLINGS ARSBERETNING **285**

UNIVERSITETET I OSLO. UNIVERSITETETS OLDSAKSAMLING *See* ARBOK - UNIVERSITETETS OLDSAKSAMLING **256**

UNIVERSITETET I OSLO. UNIVERSITETETS OLDSAKSAMLING *See* UNIVERSITETETS OLDSAKSAMLINGS TILVEKST **285**

UNIVERSITETET I TRONDHEIM. VITENSKAPSMUSEET *See* ARSBERETNING - UNIVERSITETET I TRONDHEIM, VITENSKAPSMUSEET **4162**

UNIVERSITETETS OLDSAKSAMLINGS ARSBERETNING (NO) [09069538] **285**

UNIVERSITETETS OLDSAKSAMLINGS TILVEKST (NO) [03266440] **285**

UNIVERSITI PERTANIAN MALAYSIA *See* BUKU PANDUAN - UNIVERSITI PERTANIAN MALAYSIA **68**

UNIVERSITI PERTANIAN MALAYSIA *See* HANDBOOK - UNIVERSITI PERTANIAN MALAYSIA **1827**

UNIVERSITIES ART ASSOCIATION OF CANADA *See* JOURNAL - UNIVERSITIES ART ASSOCIATION OF CANADA **355**

UNIVERSITIES. ENROLLMENT AND DEGREES (CN/0706-3652) [04448905] **1852**

UNIVERSITIES HANDBOOK : INDIA (II) [02245642] **1852**

UNIVERSITIES TELEPHONE DIRECTORY (CN/0847-3536) [22154861] **1852**

UNIVERSITY ADMINISTRATION. OSMANIA UNIVERSITY. HYDERABAD (II/0970-9584) [03376684] **1852**

UNIVERSITY AFFAIRS / AFFAIRES UNIVERSITAIRES (CN/0041-9257) [01604664] **1852**

UNIVERSITY AFFAIRS (DELHI) (II/0377-8029) [01797725] **1852**

UNIVERSITY AND COLLEGE LIBRARIES (US/0098-7816) [02242074] **3254, 3260**

UNIVERSITY AND COLLEGE PLACEMENT ASSOCIATION *See* U C P A JOURNAL **1851**

UNIVERSITY AND RESIDENTIAL COLLEGE FEES *See* TERTIARY AND RESIDENTIAL COLLEGE FEES **1850**

UNIVERSITY BIOMED WEEKLY (US/1078-2893) **3697**

UNIVERSITY BOOKMAN, THE (US/0041-9265) [01768797] **1852**

UNIVERSITY BULLETIN / UNIVERSITY OF RIYADH, KINGDOM OF SAUDI ARABIA (SU) [08557540] **1852**

UNIVERSITY CALENDAR SIMON FRASER. UNIVERSITY OF BC (CN) **1852, 1096**

UNIVERSITY CITY LIGHT (US/0889-8154) [14076708] **5641**

UNIVERSITY COLLEGE OF SOUTH WALES AND MONMOUTHSHIRE. LIBRARY *See* REPORT ON THE WORK OF THE LIBRARY / UNIVERSITY COLLEGE OF SOUTH WALES AND MONMOUTHSHIRE **3245**

UNIVERSITY COLLEGE, TORONTO, ONT *See* U. C. REVIEW **3449**

UNIVERSITY COMPUTING *See* AXIS: ACADEMIC COMPUTING & INFORMATION SYSTEMS **1246**

UNIVERSITY COMPUTING : THE BULLETIN OF THE IUCC (UK/0265-4385) [10970810] **1852**

UNIVERSITY DAILY KANSAN (US/0746-4967) [10078770] **5679**

UNIVERSITY DAILY, THE (US) [14392915] **5755**

UNIVERSITY DEVELOPMENT IN INDIA; BASIC FACTS AND FIGURES (II/0537-0728) [01714875] **1852**

UNIVERSITY ENTRANCE (UK) [16156126] **1852**

UNIVERSITY FILM ASSOCIATION *See* DIGEST **4067**

UNIVERSITY FINANCE, TREND ANALYSIS (CN/0829-7177) [12995049] **1852**

UNIVERSITY FOLK (UK) [01788827] **4157**

UNIVERSITY GUIDE ACCOUNTANCY (CN/1183-3297) [25423234] **753**

UNIVERSITY HERALD (SEATTLE, WASH.) (US) [17289875] **5762**

UNIVERSITY JOURNAL, THE (US/0147-6149) [03200090] **1096**

UNIVERSITY LECTURES - UNIVERSITY OF SASKATCHEWAN (CN/0080-6668) [02251929] **1852**

UNIVERSITY
Alphabetical Title Index

UNIVERSITY MONOGRAPHS (US/0883-2757) [12010770] **4281**

UNIVERSITY MUSEUM, THE UNIVERSITY OF TOKYO, THE (JA) [02243779] **4097**

UNIVERSITY NEWS (II/0566-2257) [02142013] **1852**

UNIVERSITY OF ADELAIDE *See* ANNUAL REPORT / THE UNIVERSITY OF ADELAIDE **1809**

UNIVERSITY OF ADELAIDE LIBRARY NEWS (AT/0157-3314) [I01573314] **3254**

UNIVERSITY OF AGRICULTURAL SCIENCES *See* CURRENT RESEARCH - UNIVERSITY OF AGRICULTURAL SCIENCES **78**

UNIVERSITY OF ALABAMA *See* ADMINISTRATION AND SUPPLEMENTARY INFORMATION : CATALOG - UNIVERSITY OF ALABAMA **1859**

UNIVERSITY OF ALASKA (COLLEGE) *See* SEA GRANT REPORT (COLLEGE) **2313**

UNIVERSITY OF ALASKA (COLLEGE) *See* FINANCIAL STATEMENTS WITH SUPPLEMENTAL SCHEDULES **1824**

UNIVERSITY OF ALASKA, FAIRBANKS *See* ANTHROPOLOGICAL PAPERS OF THE UNIVERSITY OF ALASKA **229**

UNIVERSITY OF ALASKA. INSTITUTE OF WATER RESOURCES *See* PUBLICATION IWR **5538**

UNIVERSITY OF ALASKA (SYSTEM) *See* BIOLOGICAL PAPERS OF THE UNIVERSITY OF ALASKA **445**

UNIVERSITY OF ALBERTA. DATA LIBRARY *See* UNIVERSITY OF ALBERTA DATA LIBRARY CATALOGUE **3255**

UNIVERSITY OF ALBERTA DATA LIBRARY CATALOGUE (CN/0713-7591) [08996022] **3255**

UNIVERSITY OF ALBERTA. FACULTY OF HOME ECONOMICS *See* RESEARCH NEWSLETTER - FACULTY OF HOME ECONOMICS, UNIVERSITY OF ALBERTA **2792**

UNIVERSITY OF ALBERTA. INSTITUTE OF LAW RESEARCH AND REFORM *See* BACKGROUND PAPER - INSTITUTE OF LAW RESEARCH AND REFORM, UNIVERSITY OF ALBERTA **2939**

UNIVERSITY OF ALBERTA. LIBRARY. SPECIAL COLLECTIONS DEPT *See* NEWS FROM THE RARE BOOK ROOM **421**

UNIVERSITY OF ALBERTA. WESTERN CANADIANA PUBLICATIONS PROJECT *See* NEWSLETTER - UNIVERSITY OF ALBERTA, WESTERN CANADIANA PUBLICATIONS PROJECT **421**

UNIVERSITY OF ARKANSAS AGRICULTURAL EXPERIMENT STATION *See* REPORT SERIES - UNIVERSITY OF ARKANSAS AGRICULTURAL EXPERIMENT STATION **126**

UNIVERSITY OF ARKANSAS AT LITTLE ROCK LAW JOURNAL (US/0162-8372) [04506486] **3068**

UNIVERSITY OF ARKANSAS (FAYETTEVILLE CAMPUS). ENGINEERING EXPERIMENT STATION *See* BULLETIN - UNIVERSITY OF ARKANSAS (FAYETTEVILLE CAMPUS). ENGINEERING EXPERIMENT STATION **1967**

UNIVERSITY OF ARKANSAS, FAYETTEVILLE. INDUSTRIAL RESEARCH AND EXTENSION CENTER *See* SUMMARY OF TAXES IN ARKANSAS, A **4751**

UNIVERSITY OF ARKANSAS MUSEUM *See* OCCASIONAL PAPERS - UNIVERSITY OF ARKANSAS MUSEUM **4094**

UNIVERSITY OF BALTIMORE JOURNAL OF ENVIRONMENTAL LAW (US/1062-6212) [24298756] **3117**

UNIVERSITY OF BALTIMORE LAW REVIEW (US/0091-5440) [01604558] **3068**

UNIVERSITY OF BALTIMORE. SCHOOL OF LAW *See* UNIVERSITY OF BALTIMORE LAW REVIEW **3068**

UNIVERSITY OF BIRMINGHAM. CENTRE FOR CONTEMPORARY CULTURAL STUDIES *See* WORKING PAPERS IN CULTURAL STUDIES **5265**

UNIVERSITY OF BIRMINGHAM. CENTRE FOR URBAN AND REGIONAL STUDIES *See* RESEARCH MEMORANDUM **4683**

UNIVERSITY OF BOMBAY *See* JOURNAL OF THE UNIVERSITY OF BOMBAY **1833**

UNIVERSITY OF BRIDGEPORT LAW REVIEW *See* BRIDGEPORT LAW REVIEW **2943**

UNIVERSITY OF BRITISH COLUMBIA *See* FACULTY & ADMINISTRATIVE DIRECTORY - THE UNIVERSITY OF BRITISH COLUMBIA **1864**

UNIVERSITY OF BRITISH COLUMBIA *See* U. B. C. REPORTS **1851**

UNIVERSITY OF BRITISH COLUMBIA *See* UNIVERSITY OF BRITISH COLUMBIA LAW REVIEW **3068**

UNIVERSITY OF BRITISH COLUMBIA. DATA LIBRARY *See* UBC DATA LIBRARY CATALOGUE. MICROFORM **3254**

UNIVERSITY OF BRITISH COLUMBIA. DEPT. OF ECONOMICS *See* RESOURCES PAPER - UNIVERSITY OF BRITISH COLUMBIA, DEPARTMENT OF ECONOMICS **1517**

UNIVERSITY OF BRITISH COLUMBIA. DEPT. OF OCEANOGRAPHY *See* ANNUAL REPORT - DEPARTMENT OF OCEANOGRAPHY. UNIVERSITY OF BRITISH COLUMBIA **1446**

UNIVERSITY OF BRITISH COLUMBIA. DIVISION OF HEALTH SERVICES RESEARCH AND DEVELOPMENT *See* REPORT - DIVISION OF HEALTH SERVICES RESEARCH AND DEVELOPMENT, UNIVERSITY OF BRITISH COLUMBIA **3917**

UNIVERSITY OF BRITISH COLUMBIA. FACULTY OF COMMERCE AND BUSINESS ADMINISTRATION *See* MONOGRAPH SERIES - FACULTY OF COMMERCE AND BUSINESS ADMINISTRATION, UNIVERSITY OF BRITISH COLUMBIA **696**

UNIVERSITY OF BRITISH COLUMBIA LAW REVIEW (CN/0068-1849) [01768802] **3068**

UNIVERSITY OF BRITISH COLUMBIA. LIBRARY *See* UBC LIBRARY BULLETIN **3254**

UNIVERSITY OF BRITISH COLUMBIA. VARSITY OUTDOOR CLUB *See* VARSITY OUTDOOR CLUB JOURNAL, THE **4880**

UNIVERSITY OF CALIFORNIA, BERKELEY *See* UNIVERSITY OF CALIFORNIA PUBLICATIONS IN GEOLOGICAL SCIENCES **1400**

UNIVERSITY OF CALIFORNIA, BERKELEY *See* PUBLICATIONS: OCCASIONAL PAPERS **1843**

UNIVERSITY OF CALIFORNIA, BERKELEY *See* UNIVERSITY OF CALIFORNIA PUBLICATIONS IN BOTANY **529**

UNIVERSITY OF CALIFORNIA, BERKELEY *See* UNIVERSITY OF CALIFORNIA PUBLICATIONS IN GEOGRAPHY **2578**

UNIVERSITY OF CALIFORNIA, BERKELEY *See* PUBLICATIONS: CLASSICAL STUDIES **1079**

UNIVERSITY OF CALIFORNIA, BERKELEY. ARCHAEOLOGICAL RESEARCH FACILITY *See* CONTRIBUTIONS OF THE UNIVERSITY OF CALIFORNIA ARCHAEOLOGICAL RESEARCH FACILITY **266**

UNIVERSITY OF CALIFORNIA, BERKELEY. CENTER FOR SOUTH AND SOUTHEAST ASIA STUDIES *See* RESEARCH MONOGRAPH - CENTER FOR SOUTH AND SOUTHEAST ASIA STUDIES, UNIVERSITY OF CALIFORNIA **2663**

UNIVERSITY OF CALIFORNIA, BERKELEY. CENTER FOR SOUTH ASIA STUDIES *See* NEWSLETTER / CENTER FOR SOUTH ASIA STUDIES, UNIVERSITY OF CALIFORNIA AT BERKELEY **2660**

UNIVERSITY OF CALIFORNIA, BERKELEY. GRADUATE SCHOOL OF BUSINESS ADMINISTRATION *See* ALUMNI DIRECTORY - UNIVERSITY OF CALIFORNIA, BERKELEY. GRADUATE SCHOOL OF BUSINESS ADMINISTRATION **1099**

UNIVERSITY OF CALIFORNIA, BERKELEY. UNIVERSITY ART MUSEUM *See* CALENDAR / UNIVERSITY ART MUSEUM BERKELEY **4086**

UNIVERSITY OF CALIFORNIA, BERKELEY, WELLNESS LETTER (US/0748-9234) [11027442] **4806**

UNIVERSITY OF CALIFORNIA, BERKELEY, WELLNESS LETTER. / AUSTRALIA (AT) **4806**

UNIVERSITY OF CALIFORNIA, DAVIS *See* ALUMNI DIRECTORY / UNIVERSITY OF CALIFORNIA, DAVIS **1100**

UNIVERSITY OF CALIFORNIA, DAVIS. COOPERATIVE EXTENSION *See* ECONOMIC AND SOCIAL ISSUES **81**

UNIVERSITY OF CALIFORNIA, DAVIS. SCHOOL OF LAW *See* U.C. DAVIS LAW REVIEW **3067**

UNIVERSITY OF CALIFORNIA, LOS ANGELES. CENTER FOR MEDIEVAL AND RENAISSANCE STUDIES *See* CONTRIBUTIONS OF THE UCLA CENTER FOR MEDIEVAL AND RENAISSANCE STUDIES **1076**

UNIVERSITY OF CALIFORNIA, LOS ANGELES. CENTER FOR THE STUDY OF EVALUATION *See* C S E MONOGRAPH SERIES IN EVALUATION **1729**

UNIVERSITY OF CALIFORNIA, LOS ANGELES. CENTER FOR THE STUDY OF EVALUATION *See* CSE REPORT **1819**

UNIVERSITY OF CALIFORNIA, LOS ANGELES. CHICANO STUDIES CENTER *See* PAMPHLET SERIES - UNIVERSITY OF CALIFORNIA, LOS ANGELES. CHICANO STUDIES CENTER **2270**

UNIVERSITY OF CALIFORNIA, LOS ANGELES. CHICANO STUDIES CENTER *See* MONOGRAPH - UNIVERSITY OF CALIFORNIA, LOS ANGELES. CHICANO STUDIES CENTER **2747**

UNIVERSITY OF CALIFORNIA, LOS ANGELES. DEPT. OF EARTH AND SPACE SCIENCES *See* ALUMNI NEWSLETTER / UNIVERSITY OF CALIFORNIA, LOS ANGELES, DEPARTMENT OF EARTH & SPACE SCIENCES **1351**

UNIVERSITY OF CALIFORNIA, LOS ANGELES. GRADUATE SCHOOL OF MANAGEMENT *See* ALUMNI DIRECTORY - UNIVERSITY OF CALIFORNIA, LOS ANGELES. GRADUATE SCHOOL OF MANAGEMENT **1100**

UNIVERSITY OF CALIFORNIA, LOS ANGELES. LABORATORY OF NUCLEAR MEDICINE AND RADIATION BIOLOGY *See* ANNUAL PROGRESS REPORT - UNIVERSITY OF CALIFORNIA, LABORATORY OF NUCLEAR MEDICINE AND RADIATION BIOLOGY **3847**

UNIVERSITY OF CALIFORNIA, LOS ANGELES. LIBRARY *See* UCLA LIBRARIAN **3254**

UNIVERSITY OF CALIFORNIA, LOS ANGELES. SCHOOL OF LAW *See* UCLA LAW REVIEW **3067**

UNIVERSITY OF CALIFORNIA, LOS ANGELES. UNIVERSITY AFFILIATED FACILITIES *See* UCLA UAF BIBLIOGRAPHY IN MENTAL RETARDATION **3662**

UNIVERSITY OF CALIFORNIA PUBLICATIONS IN ANTHROPOLOGY (US/0068-6379) [01552454] **247**

UNIVERSITY OF CALIFORNIA PUBLICATIONS IN BOTANY (US/0068-6395) [01552455] **529**

UNIVERSITY OF CALIFORNIA PUBLICATIONS IN ENTOMOLOGY (US/0068-6417) [07474332] **5614**

UNIVERSITY OF CALIFORNIA PUBLICATIONS IN GEOGRAPHY (US/0068-6441) [03714154] **2578**

UNIVERSITY OF CALIFORNIA PUBLICATIONS IN GEOLOGICAL SCIENCES (US/0068-645X) [04097047] **1400**

UNIVERSITY OF CALIFORNIA PUBLICATIONS IN LINGUISTICS *CEASED.* (US/0068-6484) [03648533] **3330**

UNIVERSITY OF CALIFORNIA PUBLICATIONS IN MODERN PHILOLOGY (US/0068-6492) [01552475] **3331**

UNIVERSITY OF CALIFORNIA PUBLICATIONS IN ZOOLOGY (US/0068-6506) [07881222] **5599**

UNIVERSITY OF CALIFORNIA PUBLICATIONS. NEAR EASTERN STUDIES (US/0068-6514) [01552477] **2667**

UNIVERSITY OF CALIFORNIA, RIVERSIDE. LATIN AMERICAN STUDIES PROGRAM *See* COMMEMORATIVE SERIES **2729**

UNIVERSITY OF CALIFORNIA, SAN DIEGO. LABORATORY OF COMPARATIVE HUMAN COGNITION *See* QUARTERLY NEWSLETTER OF THE LABORATORY OF COMPARATIVE HUMAN COGNITION, THE **4615**

UNIVERSITY OF CALIFORNIA, SAN FRANCISCO. INSTITUTE FOR HEALTH POLICY STUDIES *See* IHPS REPORT **4784**

UNIVERSITY OF CALIFORNIA (SYSTEM). SEA GRANT COLLEGE PROGRAM *See* SEA GRANT PUBLICATION (LA JOLLA) **1456**

UNIVERSITY OF CALIFORNIA. WATER RESOURCES CENTER *See* REPORT - CALIFORNIA WATER RESOURCES CENTER **5538**

UNIVERSITY OF CAMBRIDGE *See* CAMBRIDGE UNIVERSITY REPORTER **1090**

UNIVERSITY OF CAMBRIDGE *See* LIST OF MEMBERS - CAMBRIDGE UNIVERSITY **1834**

UNIVERSITY OF CAMBRIDGE *See* ORIENTAL PUBLICATIONS **2661**

UNIVERSITY OF CAMBRIDGE. AGRICULTURAL ECONOMICS UNIT *See* PIG MANAGEMENT SCHEME RESULTS **217**

UNIVERSITY OF CAMBRIDGE. DEPARTMENT OF ENGINEERING. CUED/A-TURBO (UK/0309-6521) [02907418] **2000**

Alphabetical Title Index — UNIVERSITY

UNIVERSITY OF CAMBRIDGE. DEPARTMENT OF ENGINEERING. CUED/C-MAT (UK/0309-6505) [02905821] **2000**

UNIVERSITY OF CANTERBURY *See* UNIVERSITY OF CANTERBURY PUBLICATIONS **1852**

UNIVERSITY OF CANTERBURY PUBLICATIONS (NZ/0577-991X) [03123174] **1852**

UNIVERSITY OF CAPE TOWN *See* NEW SERIES **1837**

UNIVERSITY OF CAPE TOWN. CHAMBER OF MINES PRECAMBRIAN RESEARCH UNIT *See* BULLETIN - CHAMBER OF MINES PRECAMBRIAN RESEARCH UNIT **1368**

UNIVERSITY OF CENTRAL OKLAHOMA *See* ALUMNI DIRECTORY **1097**

UNIVERSITY OF CHICAGO *See* SOCIAL SCIENCE STUDIES **5221**

UNIVERSITY OF CHICAGO. CENTER FOR CHILDREN'S BOOKS *See* BULLETIN OF THE CENTER FOR CHILDREN'S BOOKS **3370**

UNIVERSITY OF CHICAGO. CENTER FOR MIDDLE EASTERN STUDIES *See* PUBLICATIONS - UNIVERSITY OF CHICAGO. CENTER FOR MIDDLE EASTERN STUDIES **2770**

UNIVERSITY OF CHICAGO GEOGRAPHY RESEARCH PAPER (US/1054-206X) [23285894] **2578**

UNIVERSITY OF CHICAGO. GRADUATE SCHOOL OF BUSINESS *See* SELECTED PAPERS **710**

UNIVERSITY OF CHICAGO LAW REVIEW, THE (US/0041-9494) [02123921] **3068**

UNIVERSITY OF CHICAGO. LAW SCHOOL *See* ALUMNI DIRECTORY - THE UNIVERSITY OF CHICAGO LAW SCHOOL **1099**

UNIVERSITY OF CHICAGO. LAW SCHOOL *See* LAW SCHOOL RECORD **2997**

UNIVERSITY OF CHICAGO. LAW SCHOOL *See* OCCASIONAL PAPERS **3020**

UNIVERSITY OF CHICAGO. LAW SCHOOL *See* UNIVERSITY OF CHICAGO LAW REVIEW, THE **3068**

UNIVERSITY OF CHICAGO LEGAL FORUM (US/0892-5593) [13286447] **3068**

UNIVERSITY OF CHICAGO. ORIENTAL INSTITUTE *See* ORIENTAL INSTITUTE COMMUNICATIONS **3308**

UNIVERSITY OF CHICAGO. ORIENTAL INSTITUTE. RESEARCH ARCHIVES *See* ORIENTAL INSTITUTE RESEARCH ARCHIVES ACQUISITIONS LIST **2625**

UNIVERSITY OF CHICAGO SICKLE CELL CENTER HEMOGLOBIN SYMPOSIA, THE (US/0736-7406) [08622395] **3648**

UNIVERSITY OF CINCINNATI. COLLEGE OF LAW *See* UNIVERSITY OF CINCINNATI LAW REVIEW **3068**

UNIVERSITY OF CINCINNATI LAW REVIEW (US/0009-6881) [01605688] **3068**

UNIVERSITY OF CINCINNATI STUDIES IN HISTORICAL AND CONTEMPORARY EUROPE (US/0888-3882) [13557236] **2714**

UNIVERSITY OF COCHIN. DEPT. OF MARINE SCIENCES *See* BULLETIN OF THE DEPARTMENT OF MARINE SCIENCES **553**

UNIVERSITY OF COLORADO *See* UNIVERSITY OF COLORADO STUDIES. SERIES IN BIBLIOGRAPHY **427**

UNIVERSITY OF COLORADO, BOULDER. BOARD OF REGENTS *See* LAWS OF THE REGENTS, UNIVERSITY OF COLORADO **4661**

UNIVERSITY OF COLORADO (BOULDER CAMPUS). BUREAU OF BUSINESS RESEARCH. COLORADO MANUFACTURERS DIRECTORY *See* DIRECTORY OF COLORADO MANUFACTURERS **3477**

UNIVERSITY OF COLORADO (BOULDER CAMPUS). SCHOOL OF LAW *See* UNIVERSITY OF COLORADO LAW REVIEW **3068**

UNIVERSITY OF COLORADO, BOULDER. COLLEGE OF BUSINESS AND ADMINISTRATION *See* ALUMNI DIRECTORY / UNIVERSITY OF COLORADO, BOULDER, COLLEGE OF BUSINESS AND ADMINISTRATION **1100**

UNIVERSITY OF COLORADO LAW REVIEW (US/0041-9516) [08470624] **3068**

UNIVERSITY OF COLORADO STUDIES. SERIES IN BIBLIOGRAPHY (US/0588-4705) [01624044] **427**

UNIVERSITY OF COLORADO STUDIES. SERIES IN EARTH SCIENCES (US/0069-6218) [02251160] **1361**

UNIVERSITY OF CONNECTICUT. CENTER FOR REAL ESTATE AND URBAN ECONOMIC STUDIES *See* GENERAL SERIES - CENTER FOR REAL ESTATE AND URBAN ECONOMIC STUDIES, SCHOOL OF BUSINESS ADMINISTRATION, UNIVERSITY OF CONNECTICUT **4838**

UNIVERSITY OF CONNECTICUT. DEPT. OF PLANT SCIENCE *See* YANKEE NURSERY QUARTERLY **2434**

UNIVERSITY OF CONNECTICUT. INSTITUTE OF WATER RESOURCES *See* REPORT - UNIVERSITY OF CONNECTICUT. INSTITUTE OF WATER RESOURCES **5538**

UNIVERSITY OF DAR ES SALAAM. DEPT. OF EDUCATION *See* PAPERS IN EDUCATION AND DEVELOPMENT **1771**

UNIVERSITY OF DAR ES SALAAM. ECONOMIC RESEARCH BUREAU *See* ANNUAL PROGRESS REPORT / ECONOMIC RESEARCH BUREAU, UNIVERSITY OF DAR ES SALAAM **1589**

UNIVERSITY OF DAR ES SALAAM LAW JOURNAL (TZ) [30021957] **3068**

UNIVERSITY OF DAYTON *See* UNIVERSITY OF DAYTON REVIEW, THE **3355**

UNIVERSITY OF DAYTON LAW REVIEW (US/0162-9174) [04251193] **3068**

UNIVERSITY OF DAYTON. LAW SCHOOL *See* UNIVERSITY OF DAYTON LAW REVIEW **3068**

UNIVERSITY OF DAYTON REVIEW, THE (US/0041-9524) [01522016] **5006, 3355**

UNIVERSITY OF DELAWARE. COLLEGE OF MARINE STUDIES *See* TECHNICAL REPORT - COLLEGE OF MARINE STUDIES, UNIVERSITY OF DELAWARE **1457**

UNIVERSITY OF DELAWARE. LIBRARY *See* COLLECTIONS (NEWARK, DEL.) **3203**

UNIVERSITY OF DENVER *See* ALUMNI DIRECTORY / UNIVERSITY OF DENVER **1100**

UNIVERSITY OF DETROIT MERCY LAW REVIEW (US/1058-4323) [24296408] **3068**

UNIVERSITY OF DURHAM *See* DURHAM UNIVERSITY JOURNAL, THE **1822**

UNIVERSITY OF EAST ANGLIA *See* UEA PAPERS IN LINGUISTICS **3330**

UNIVERSITY OF EDINBURGH JOURNAL (UK/0041-9567) [01831427] **1852**

UNIVERSITY OF EVANSVILLE *See* ALUMNI DIRECTORY / UNIVERSITY OF EVANSVILLE **1100**

UNIVERSITY OF FLORIDA *See* MONOGRAPHS. SOCIAL SCIENCES - UNIVERSITY OF FLORIDA **5209**

UNIVERSITY OF FLORIDA *See* PAPERS DELIVERED AT THE ANNUAL CONFERENCE ON THE CARIBBEAN **2753**

UNIVERSITY OF FLORIDA *See* REVISED PLAN FOR EQUALIZING EDUCATIONAL OPPORTUNITY IN PUBLIC HIGHER EDUCATION IN FLORIDA **1846**

UNIVERSITY OF FLORIDA ACCOUNTING SERIES *CEASED*. (US) [05139580] **753**

UNIVERSITY OF FLORIDA. AGRICULTURAL EXPERIMENT STATION *See* BULLETIN - UNIVERSITY OF FLORIDA, AGRICULTURAL EXPERIMENT STATIONS **70**

UNIVERSITY OF FLORIDA. FLORIDA ALLIGATOR *See* INDEPENDENT FLORIDA ALLIGATOR, THE **1092**

UNIVERSITY OF FLORIDA. FOOD AND RESOURCE ECONOMICS DEPT *See* PUBLICATIONS OF THE FOOD AND RESOURCE ECONOMICS DEPARTMENT, UNIVERSITY OF FLORIDA **123**

UNIVERSITY OF FLORIDA. FOOD AND RESOURCE ECONOMICS DEPT *See* COSTS AND RETURNS FROM VEGETABLE CROPS IN FLORIDA, WITH COMPARISONS **168**

UNIVERSITY OF FLORIDA HUMANITIES MONOGRAPHS (US/0887-204X) [05704804] **2856**

UNIVERSITY OF FLORIDA INSTITUTE OF INTER-AMERICAN AFFAIRS *See* INTER-AMERICAN INSTITUTE SERIES **2739**

UNIVERSITY OF FLORIDA JOURNAL OF LAW AND PUBLIC POLICY (US/1047-8035) [18079099] **3068**

UNIVERSITY OF FLORIDA LATINAMERICANIST (US) [01512925] **2764**

UNIVERSITY OF FLORIDA LAW CENTER NEWS, THE (US/0502-6679) [01512978] **3068**

UNIVERSITY OF FLORIDA LAWYER : MAGAZINE OF THE UNIVERSITY OF FLORIDA COLLEGE OF LAW (US) [11057823] **3068**

UNIVERSITY OF FLORIDA. SCHOOL OF ACCOUNTING *See* UNIVERSITY OF FLORIDA ACCOUNTING SERIES **753**

UNIVERSITY OF FLORIDA. SCHOOL OF FOREST RESOURCES AND CONSERVATION *See* COOPERATIVE FOREST GENETICS RESEARCH PROGRAM **2378**

UNIVERSITY OF FLORIDA. WATER RESOURCES RESEARCH CENTER *See* PUBLICATION - FLORIDA WATER RESOURCES RESEARCH CENTER **5538**

UNIVERSITY OF GEORGIA. INSTITUTE OF COMMUNITY AND AREA DEVELOPMENT *See* PUBLICATIONS - GEORGIA. UNIVERSITY. INSTITUTE OF COMMUNITY AND AREA DEVELOPMENT **2832**

UNIVERSITY OF GEORGIA LABORATORY OF ARCHAEOLOGY SERIES (US/0433-5732) [04396363] **285**

UNIVERSITY OF GEORGIA. MARINE INSTITUTE *See* COLLECTED REPRINTS - UNIVERSITY OF GEORGIA MARINE INSTITUTE **553**

UNIVERSITY OF GHANA. INSTITUTE OF AFRICAN STUDIES *See* RESEARCH REVIEW - INSTITUTE OF AFRICAN STUDIES **2643**

UNIVERSITY OF GHANA LAW JOURNAL (GH/0041-9605) [01515689] **3068**

UNIVERSITY OF GUAM. WATER RESOURCES RESEARCH CENTER *See* TECHNICAL REPORT - WATER AND ENERGY RESEARCH INSTITUTE, UNIVERSITY OF GUAM **5540**

UNIVERSITY OF GUELPH *See* ALUMNI DIRECTORY / UNIVERSITY OF GUELPH **1100**

UNIVERSITY OF GUELPH. INDEPENDENT STUDY DIVISION *See* INDEPENDENT STUDY LINK **1830**

UNIVERSITY OF GUYANA. DEPT. OF GEOGRAPHY *See* OCCASIONAL PAPER - DEPT. OF GEOGRAPHY, UNIVERSITY OF GUYANA **2571**

UNIVERSITY OF HARTFORD OBSERVER (US/0747-3028) [10697909] **1096**

UNIVERSITY OF HARTFORD STUDIES IN LITERATURE (US/1048-9576) [21095665] **3449**

UNIVERSITY OF HAWAII AT MANOA. LIBRARY. HAWAIIAN COLLECTION *See* ACQUISITION LIST / UNIVERSITY OF HAWAII LIBRARY, HAWAIIAN COLLECTION **407**

UNIVERSITY OF HAWAII AT MANOA. SCHOOL OF LAW *See* UNIVERSITY OF HAWAII LAW REVIEW **3068**

UNIVERSITY OF HAWAII (HONOLULU). OFFICE OF THE STATE DIRECTOR FOR VOCATIONAL EDUCATION *See* STATE OF HAWAII ANNUAL ACCOUNTABILITY REPORT FOR VOCATIONAL EDUCATION FOR THE ACADEMIC YEAR ... **1916**

UNIVERSITY OF HAWAII LAW REVIEW (US/0271-9835) [05858708] **3068**

UNIVERSITY OF HAWAII. WATER RESOURCES RESEARCH CENTER *See* COLLECTED REPRINTS - WATER RESOURCES RESEARCH CENTER, UNIVERSITY OF HAWAII **5532**

UNIVERSITY OF HEALTH SCIENCES ANTIGUA. SCHOOL OF MEDICINE *See* BULLETIN / UNIVERSITY OF HEALTH SCIENCES, ANTIGUA, SCHOOL OF MEDICINE **3561**

UNIVERSITY OF HEALTH SCIENCES. COLLEGE OF OSTEOPATHIC MEDICINE *See* ALUMNI DIRECTORY / THE UNIVERSITY OF HEALTH SCIENCES, COLLEGE OF OSTEOPATHIC MEDICINE **1099**

UNIVERSITY OF HULL. DEPT. OF GEOGRAPHY *See* MISCELLANEOUS SERIES - DEPARTMENT OF GEOGRAPHY, UNIVERSITY OF HULL **2569**

UNIVERSITY OF IDAHO. FOREST, WILDLIFE, AND RANGE EXPERIMENT STATION *See* STATION NOTE - UNIVERSITY OF IDAHO FOREST, WILDLIFE AND RANGE EXPERIMENT STATION **2206**

UNIVERSITY OF IFE *See* UNIVERSITY OF IFE (NIGERIA) LAW REPORTS, THE **3068**

UNIVERSITY OF IFE (NIGERIA) LAW REPORTS, THE (NR) [04927832] **3068**

UNIVERSITY OF ILLINOIS AT CHICAGO. COLLEGE OF BUSINESS ADMINISTRATION *See* ALUMNI DIRECTORY / COLLEGE OF BUSINESS ADMINISTRATION **1098**

UNIVERSITY OF ILLINOIS AT URBANA-CHAMPAIGN. AGRICULTURAL EXPERIMENT STATION *See* FORESTRY RESEARCH REPORT **2382**

UNIVERSITY OF ILLINOIS AT URBANA-CHAMPAIGN. COLLEGE OF VETERINARY MEDICINE *See* ALUMNI DIRECTORY / UNIVERSITY OF ILLINOIS, COLLEGE OF VETERINARY MEDICINE **1100**

UNIVERSITY OF ILLINOIS AT URBANA-CHAMPAIGN. COMMUNICATIONS LIBRARY *See* NEW BOOKS IN THE COMMUNICATIONS LIBRARY **1118**

UNIVERSITY Alphabetical Title Index

UNIVERSITY OF ILLINOIS AT URBANA-CHAMPAIGN. DEPT. OF GEOGRAPHY *See* OCCASIONAL PUBLICATIONS OF THE DEPARTMENT OF GEOGRAPHY (URBANA) **2571**

UNIVERSITY OF ILLINOIS INSTITUTE OF GOVERNMENT AND PUBLIC AFFAIRS WORK PAPERS (US) **5225**

UNIVERSITY OF ILLINOIS LAW REVIEW (US/0276-9948) [07466281] **3068**

UNIVERSITY OF ISTANBUL, FACULTY OF SCIENCE, THE JOURNAL OF MATHEMATICS (TU) [24301251] **3540**

UNIVERSITY OF JAMMU *See* PROGRESS REPORT / UNIVERSITY OF JAMMU **1842**

UNIVERSITY OF JAMMU *See* ANNUAL REPORT - UNIVERSITY OF JAMMU **1809**

UNIVERSITY OF KANSAS LAW REVIEW (US/0083-4025) [01516566] **3068**

●UNIVERSITY OF KANSAS PALEONTOLOGICAL CONTRIBUTIONS (1992), THE (US/1046-8390) [20609789] **4231**

UNIVERSITY OF KANSAS PALEONTOLOGICAL CONTRIBUTIONS. ARTICLE (US/0075-5044) [02284670] **4231**

UNIVERSITY OF KANSAS PALEONTOLOGICAL CONTRIBUTIONS. MONOGRAPHS (US/0278-9744) [07936399] **4231**

UNIVERSITY OF KANSAS PALEONTOLOGICAL CONTRIBUTIONS. PAPERS (US/0075-5052) [01754995] **4231**

UNIVERSITY OF KANSAS PUBLICATIONS. HUMANISTIC STUDIES (US/0085-2473) [18701602] **2856**

UNIVERSITY OF KANSAS. SCHOOL OF LAW *See* UNIVERSITY OF KANSAS LAW REVIEW **3068**

UNIVERSITY OF KANSAS SCIENCE BULLETIN, THE (US/0022-8850) [02583598] **5167**

UNIVERSITY OF KARACHI *See* KARACHI UNIVERSITY JOURNAL OF SCIENCE **5122**

UNIVERSITY OF KENTUCKY. AGRONOMY DEPT *See* A.G.R **42**

UNIVERSITY OF KENTUCKY. COLLEGE OF AGRICULTURE *See* COLLEGE OF AGRICULTURE ALUMNI DIRECTORY / UNIVERSITY OF KENTUCKY **1101**

UNIVERSITY OF KENTUCKY. INSTITUTE FOR MINING AND MINERALS RESEARCH *See* IMMR (INSTITUTE FOR MINING AND MINERALS RESEARCH, UNIVERSITY OF KENTUCKY) **2140**

UNIVERSITY OF KENTUCKY. LIBRARIES. MAP DEPT *See* SELECTED ACQUISITIONS BULLETIN - UNIVERSITY OF KENTUCKY. LIBRARIES. MAP DEPT **2576**

UNIVERSITY OF KERALA. DEPT. OF TAMIL *See* RESEARCH PAPERS - DEPARTMENT OF TAMIL, UNIVERSITY OF KERALA **3315**

UNIVERSITY OF LEEDS. DEPARTMENT OF PHYSICAL CHEMISTRY *See* HIGH TEMPERATURE REACTION RATE DATA **1052**

UNIVERSITY OF LEEDS REVIEW, THE (UK/0041-9737) [01755701] **1096**

UNIVERSITY OF LEEDS. SCHOOL OF ENGLISH *See* LEEDS TEXTS AND MONOGRAPHS **3297**

UNIVERSITY OF LETHBRIDGE. LIBRARY *See* SERIALS RECORD FILE / UNIVERSITY OF LETHBRIDGE LIBRARY **424**

UNIVERSITY OF LONDON. INSTITUTE OF ADVANCED LEGAL STUDIES *See* ANNUAL REPORT / UNIVERSITY OF LONDON, INSTITUTE OF ADVANCED LEGAL STUDIES **2935**

UNIVERSITY OF LONDON. INSTITUTE OF ARCHAEOLOGY *See* BULLETIN OF THE INSTITUTE OF ARCHAEOLOGY / UNIVERSITY OF LONDON, INSTITUTE OF ARCHAEOLOGY **264**

UNIVERSITY OF LONDON. INSTITUTE OF CLASSICAL STUDIES *See* BULLETIN - INSTITUTE OF CLASSICAL STUDIES **1075**

UNIVERSITY OF LONDON. INSTITUTE OF HISTORICAL RESEARCH *See* ANNUAL REPORT **2610**

UNIVERSITY OF LONDON. SCHOOL OF ORIENTAL AND AFRICAN STUDIES *See* ANNUAL REPORT / SCHOOL OF ORIENTAL AND AFRICAN STUDIES, UNIVERSITY OF LONDON **2645**

UNIVERSITY OF LONDON. SCHOOL OF ORIENTAL AND AFRICAN STUDIES. LIBRARY *See* LIBRARY CATALOGUE. SUPPLEMENT **418**

●UNIVERSITY OF LOUISVILLE JOURNAL OF FAMILY LAW (US) [27254061] **3122**

UNIVERSITY OF LOUISVILLE. NATIONAL CRIME PREVENTION INSTITUTE *See* NCPI HOTLINE **3170**

UNIVERSITY OF LOUISVILLE STUDIES IN PALEONTOLOGY AND STRATIGRAPHY (US/0275-5513) [01589918] **4231**

UNIVERSITY OF MADRAS. CENTRE OF ADVANCED STUDY IN PHILOSOPHY. YEAR BOOK (II) [09150371] **4364**

UNIVERSITY OF MALAWI. LIBRARIES *See* REPORT TO SENATE / UNIVERSITY OF MALAWI LIBRARIES **3245**

UNIVERSITY OF MALAWI. UNIVERSITY LIBRARY COMMITTEE. REPORT TO THE SENATE ON THE UNIVERSITY LIBRARIES *See* REPORT TO SENATE / UNIVERSITY OF MALAWI LIBRARIES **3245**

UNIVERSITY OF MALAYA (FOUNDED 1962). DEPT. OF ENGINEERING *See* JERNAL FAKULTI KEJURUTERAAN, UNIVERSITI MALAYA **1981**

UNIVERSITY OF MANILA JOURNAL OF EAST ASIATIC STUDIES (PH) [02268966] **1852**

UNIVERSITY OF MANITOBA ANTHROPOLOGY PAPERS (CN/0227-0072) [08072058] **247**

UNIVERSITY OF MANITOBA. CENTER FOR SETTLEMENT STUDIES *See* SERIES 2 : RESEARCH REPORTS - CENTER FOR SETTLEMENT STUDIES, UNIVERSITY OF MANITOBA **5257**

UNIVERSITY OF MANITOBA. CENTRE FOR TRANSPORTATION STUDIES *See* RESEARCH REPORT - UNIVERSITY OF MANITOBA, CENTRE FOR TRANSPORTATION STUDIES **5391**

UNIVERSITY OF MANITOBA. DEPT. OF AGRICULTURAL ECONOMICS AND FARM MANAGEMENT *See* RESEARCH BULLETIN - DEPARTMENT OF AGRICULTURAL ECONOMICS AND FARM MANAGEMENT. FACULTY OF AGRICULTURE. UNIVERSITY OF MANITOBA **127**

UNIVERSITY OF MANITOBA. FACULTY OF ARTS *See* HORIZONS (WINNIPEG. 1990) **321**

UNIVERSITY OF MANITOBA ICELANDIC STUDIES (CN) [03197257] **2714**

UNIVERSITY OF MANITOBA. LIBRARIES *See* LIBRARY DIRECTIONS : A NEWSLETTER OF UNIVERSITY OF MANITOBA LIBRARIES **3225**

UNIVERSITY OF MANITOBA. UNIVERSITY RELATIONS AND INFORMATION OFFICE *See* BULLETIN - UNIVERSITY RELATIONS AND INFORMATION OFFICE, UNIVERSITY OF MANITOBA **1813**

UNIVERSITY OF MARYLAND *See* REPORT OF THE PRESIDENT - UNIVERSITY OF MARYLAND **1844**

UNIVERSITY OF MARYLAND. SCHOOL OF LIBRARY AND INFORMATION SERVICES *See* STUDENT CONTRIBUTION SERIES **3251**

UNIVERSITY OF MASSACHUSETTS AT AMHERST. COLLEGE OF ENGINEERING *See* ALUMNI DIRECTORY / COLLEGE OF ENGINEERING, UNIVERSITY OF MASSACHUSETTS AT AMHERST **1098**

UNIVERSITY OF MASSACHUSETTS AT AMHERST. DEPT. OF ANTHROPOLOGY *See* RESEARCH REPORTS / DEPARTMENT OF ANTHROPOLOGY, UNIVERSITY OF MASSACHUSETTS, AMHERST **244**

UNIVERSITY OF MASSACHUSETTS AT AMHERST. WATER RESOURCES RESEARCH CENTER *See* PUBLICATION - WATER RESOURCES RESEARCH CENTER, UNIVERSITY OF MASSACHUSETTS AT AMHERST **5538**

UNIVERSITY OF MASSACHUSETTS (SYSTEM) *See* FINANCIAL REPORT - UNIVERSITY OF MASSACHUSETTS **1824**

UNIVERSITY OF MIAMI ENTERTAINMENT & SPORTS LAW REVIEW (US/1051-2225) [20851566] **389**, **3069**

UNIVERSITY OF MIAMI INTER-AMERICAN LAW REVIEW, THE (US/0884-1756) [11359751] **3137**

UNIVERSITY OF MIAMI LAW REVIEW (US/0041-9818) [01768810] **3069**

UNIVERSITY OF MICHIGAN. CENTER FOR RESEARCH ON ECONOMIC DEVELOPMENT *See* DISCUSSION PAPER - CENTER FOR RESEARCH ON ECONOMIC DEVELOPMENT, THE UNIVERSITY OF MICHIGAN **1480**

UNIVERSITY OF MICHIGAN. DIVISION OF RESEARCH DEVELOPMENT AND ADMINISTRATION *See* RESEARCH NEWS - DIVISION OF RESEARCH DEVELOPMENT AND ADMINISTRATION **5147**

UNIVERSITY OF MICHIGAN. INSTITUTE FOR SOCIAL RESEARCH *See* ISR NEWSLETTER **5205**

UNIVERSITY OF MICHIGAN JOURNAL OF LAW REFORM (US/0363-602X) [02184008] **3069**

UNIVERSITY OF MICHIGAN. LABORATORY OF VERTEBRATE BIOLOGY *See* CONTRIBUTIONS FROM THE LABORATORY OF VERTEBRATE BIOLOGY **452**

UNIVERSITY OF MICHIGAN. LAW SCHOOL *See* UNIVERSITY OF MICHIGAN JOURNAL OF LAW REFORM **3069**

UNIVERSITY OF MICHIGAN. MUSEUM OF ANTHROPOLOGY *See* ANTHROPOLOGICAL PAPERS (UNIVERSITY OF MICHIGAN. MUSEUM OF ANTHROPOLOGY) **229**

UNIVERSITY OF MICHIGAN. MUSEUM OF ANTHROPOLOGY *See* MEMOIRS OF THE MUSEUM OF ANTHROPOLOGY, UNIVERSITY OF MICHIGAN **241**

UNIVERSITY OF MICHIGAN OCCASIONAL PAPERS / GRADUATE SCHOOL OF BUSINESS ADMINISTRATION *CEASED.* (US) [06607860] **717**, **1852**

UNIVERSITY OF MICHIGAN. SCHOOL OF INFORMATION AND LIBRARY STUDIES *See* ALUMNI DIRECTORY / THE UNIVERSITY OF MICHIGAN, SCHOOL OF INFORMATION AND LIBRARY STUDIES **1099**

UNIVERSITY OF MICHIGAN. UNIVERSITY HERBARIUM *See* CONTRIBUTIONS FROM THE UNIVERSITY OF MICHIGAN HERBARIUM **507**

UNIVERSITY OF MINNESOTA. CENTER FOR URBAN AND REGIONAL AFFAIRS *See* CURA REPORTER **2819**

UNIVERSITY OF MINNESOTA CONTINUING MEDICAL EDUCATION (US/0737-1276) [08182236] **3649**

UNIVERSITY OF MINNESOTA, DULUTH *See* UMD STATESMAN **5699**

UNIVERSITY OF MINNESOTA. IMMIGRATION HISTORY RESEARCH CENTER *See* IHRC ETHNIC BIBLIOGRAPHY **2276**

UNIVERSITY OF MINNESOTA LAW SCHOOL NEWS (US/0540-2239) [01516845] **3069**

UNIVERSITY OF MINNESOTA MEDICAL BULLETIN (US) [01714792] **3649**

UNIVERSITY OF MINNESOTA. MEDICAL SCHOOL *See* ALUMNI DIRECTORY / UNIVERSITY OF MINNESOTA MEDICAL SCHOOL **1100**

UNIVERSITY OF MINNESOTA. WATER RESOURCES RESEARCH CENTER *See* WATER NEWSLETTER **5543**

UNIVERSITY OF MISSISSIPPI STUDIES IN ENGLISH, THE (US/0278-310X) [07472060] **3449**

UNIVERSITY OF MISSOURI--COLUMBIA *See* M BOOK **1834**

UNIVERSITY OF MISSOURI-COLUMBIA. AGRICULTURAL EXPERIMENT STATION *See* RESEARCH BULLETIN - UNIVERSITY OF MISSOURI-COLUMBIA. AGRICULTURAL EXPERIMENT STATION **127**

UNIVERSITY OF MISSOURI-COLUMBIA. SCHOOL OF VETERINARY MEDICINE. FACULTY NEWSLETTER *See* VETERINARY MEDICAL REVIEW (COLUMBIA, MO.) **5525**

UNIVERSITY OF MISSOURI STUDIES (1926) (US/0076-9703) [01643579] **1852**

UNIVERSITY OF MONTANA CONTRIBUTIONS TO ANTHROPOLOGY (US/0077-118X) [01713958] **247**

UNIVERSITY OF NAIROBI. INSTITUTE OF DEVELOPMENT STUDIES *See* RESEARCH AND PUBLICATIONS **1516**

UNIVERSITY OF NATAL. AGRICULTURAL CATCHMENTS RESEARCH UNIT *See* REPORT - UNIVERSITY OF NATAL, AGRICULTURAL CATCHMENTS RESEARCH UNIT **1417**

UNIVERSITY OF NEBRASKA--LINCOLN ALUMNI ASSOCIATION *See* ALUMNI DIRECTORY / UNIVERSITY OF NEBRASKA-LINCOLN ALUMNI ASSOCIATION **1100**

UNIVERSITY OF NEBRASKA STUDIES (US/0077-6386) [01116567] **2856**

UNIVERSITY OF NEVADA, RENO. BUREAU OF GOVERNMENTAL RESEARCH *See* TECHNICAL REPORT - BUREAU OF GOVERNMENTAL RESEARCH, UNIVERSITY OF NEVADA **4690**

UNIVERSITY OF NEVADA, RENO. DESERT RESEARCH INSTITUTE *See* PREPRINT SERIES - DESERT RESEARCH INSTITUTE **1433**

UNIVERSITY OF NEVADA SYSTEM. COMMUNITY DEVELOPMENT DIVISION *See* NEVADA STATE ANNUAL PROGRAM PLAN AMENDMENT TO NEVADA STATE PLAN FOR COMMUNITY SERVICE AND CONTINUING EDUCATION PROGRAMS, TITLE I, HIGHER EDUCATION ACT, 1965 **1837**

UNIVERSITY OF NEW ENGLAND CALENDAR AND FACULTY HANDBOOK (AT) 1852

UNIVERSITY OF NEW HAMPSHIRE. COMPUTER SERVICE *See* CN-LINE (DURHAM, N.H.) 1243

UNIVERSITY OF NEW HAMPSHIRE. WATER RESOURCES RESEARCH CENTER *See* RESEARCH REPORT - WATER RESOURCES RESEARCH CENTER 5539

UNIVERSITY OF NEW HAMPSHIRE. WATER RESOURCES RESEARCH CENTER *See* BULLETIN - WATER RESOURCES RESEARCH CENTER (DURHAM) 5531

UNIVERSITY OF NEW ORLEANS. DIVISION OF BUSINESS AND ECONOMIC RESEARCH *See* RESEARCH STUDY - DIVISION OF BUSINESS AND ECONOMIC RESEARCH, COLLEGE OF BUSINESS ADMINISTRATION, UNIVERSITY OF NEW ORLEANS 1581

UNIVERSITY OF NEW SOUTH WALES LAW JOURNAL, THE (AT/0313-0096) [03333659] 3069

UNIVERSITY OF NEW SOUTH WALES. SCHOOL OF CIVIL ENGINEERING *See* UNICIV REPORT 2033

UNIVERSITY OF NEWCASTLE *See* ANNUAL REPORT / THE UNIVERSITY OF NEWCASTLE N.S.W 1809

UNIVERSITY OF NIGERIA, NSUKKA *See* REPORT FROM THE LIBRARIES - NIGERIA. UNIVERSITY, NSUKKA 3245

UNIVERSITY OF NORTH CAROLINA AT CHAPEL HILL. DEPT. OF GEOLOGY *See* ALUMNI DIRECTORY AND NEWSLETTER - UNIVERSITY OF NORTH CAROLINA AT CHAPEL HILL. DEPT. OF GEOLOGY 1097

UNIVERSITY OF NORTH CAROLINA AT CHAPEL HILL. GENERAL ALUMNI ASSOCIATION. ALUMNI OFFICE *See* ALUMNI DIRECTORY - UNIVERSITY OF NORTH CAROLINA AT CHAPEL HILL 1100

UNIVERSITY OF NORTH CAROLINA AT CHAPEL HILL. INSTITUTE OF GOVERNMENT *See* PUBLICATIONS OF THE INSTITUTE OF GOVERNMENT. CUMULATIVE SUPPLEMENT 4699

UNIVERSITY OF NORTH CAROLINA AT CHARLOTTE *See* ALUMNI DIRECTORY / THE UNIVERSITY OF NORTH CAROLINA AT CHARLOTTE 1099

UNIVERSITY OF NORTH CAROLINA AT CHARLOTTE. OFFICE OF THE CHANCELLOR *See* REPORT TO THE TRUSTEES, A 1844

UNIVERSITY OF NORTH CAROLINA (CHAPEL HILL CAMPUS) *See* UNIVERSITY OF NORTH CAROLINA STUDIES IN GERMANIC LANGUAGES AND LITERATURES. STUDIES IN THE GERMANIC LANGUAGES AND LITERATURES (CHAPEL HILL, N.C.) 3331

UNIVERSITY OF NORTH CAROLINA. STUDIES IN COMPARATIVE LITERATURE (US/0081-7775) [01760544] 3355

UNIVERSITY OF NORTH CAROLINA STUDIES IN GERMANIC LANGUAGES AND LITERATURES. STUDIES IN THE GERMANIC LANGUAGES AND LITERATURES (CHAPEL HILL, N.C.) (US/0081-8593) [01760546] 3331

UNIVERSITY OF NORTH CAROLINA (SYSTEM) HIGHWAY SAFETY RESEARCH CENTER *See* PROGRESS REPORT TO THE GOVERNOR'S HIGHWAY SAFETY OFFICE 5390

UNIVERSITY OF NORTHERN COLORADO. BUREAU OF BUSINESS AND PUBLIC RESEARCH *See* NORTHERN COLORADO BUSINESS INFORMATION FACTBOOK 700

UNIVERSITY OF NOTRE DAME. DEPARTMENT OF THEOLOGY. LITURGICAL STUDIES (US) 5006

UNIVERSITY OF NOTRE DAME STUDIES IN THE PHILOSOPHY OF RELIGION (US) [06879320] 4364, 5006

UNIVERSITY OF NOTTINGHAM MONOGRAPHS IN THE HUMANITIES (UK) [08830761] 2856

UNIVERSITY OF OREGON *See* UNIVERSITY OF OREGON ANTHROPOLOGICAL PAPERS 247

UNIVERSITY OF OREGON ANTHROPOLOGICAL PAPERS (US/0078-6071) [02635226] 247

UNIVERSITY OF OREGON. BUREAU OF GOVERNMENTAL RESEARCH AND SERVICE *See* ANNUAL REPORT / UNIVERSITY OF OREGON. BUREAU OF GOVERNMENTAL RESEARCH AND SERVICE 4630

UNIVERSITY OF OTAGO. MEDICAL SCHOOL *See* PROCEEDINGS OF THE UNIVERSITY OF OTAGO MEDICAL SCHOOL 3630

UNIVERSITY OF OTAGO STUDIES IN PREHISTORIC ANTHROPOLOGY (NZ) [07780425] 247

UNIVERSITY OF OTTAWA *See* ANNUAIRE - UNIVERSITE D'OTTAWA 1809

UNIVERSITY OF OTTAWA. DEPT. OF ECONOMICS *See* CAHIER DE RECHERCHE - FACULTE DES SCIENCES SOCIALES. DEPARTMENT DE SCIENCE ECONOMIQUE. UNIVERSITE D'OTTAWA 1467

UNIVERSITY OF OULU. DEPARTMENT OF INFORMATION PROCESSING SCIENCE. SERIES A, RESEARCH PAPERS (FI/0786-8413) [07868413] 5168

UNIVERSITY OF OXFORD. INSTITUTE OF ECONOMICS AND STATISTICS *See* ANNUAL REPORTS FOR ... / UNIVERSITY OF OXFORD, INSTITUTE OF ECONOMICS AND STATISTICS 1590

UNIVERSITY OF PENNSYLVANIA *See* PUBLICATIONS IN CONDUCT AND COMMUNICATION 1094

UNIVERSITY OF PENNSYLVANIA JOURNAL OF INTERNATIONAL BUSINESS LAW (US/0891-9895) [14639342] 3104

UNIVERSITY OF PENNSYLVANIA LAW REVIEW (US/0041-9907) [02359920] 3069

UNIVERSITY OF PENNSYLVANIA. LAW SCHOOL *See* UNIVERSITY OF PENNSYLVANIA LAW REVIEW 3069

UNIVERSITY OF PENNSYLVANIA. MEDICAL CENTER *See* UNIVERSITY OF PENNSYLVANIA MEDICAL CENTER ALUMNI DIRECTORY 1103

UNIVERSITY OF PENNSYLVANIA MEDICAL CENTER ALUMNI DIRECTORY (US) [24580676] 1103

UNIVERSITY OF PITTSBURGH *See* BUDGET PRESENTATION TO THE GENERAL ASSEMBLY OF THE COMMONWEALTH OF PENNSYLVANIA - UNIVERSITY OF PITTSBURGH 4715

UNIVERSITY OF PITTSBURGH LAW REVIEW (US/0041-9915) [01715875] 3069

UNIVERSITY OF PITTSBURGH. SCHOOL OF LAW *See* UNIVERSITY OF PITTSBURGH LAW REVIEW 3069

UNIVERSITY OF POONA *See* JOURNAL OF THE UNIVERSITY OF POONA, SCIENCE AND TECHNOLOGY 5122

UNIVERSITY OF PORTLAND REVIEW (US/0041-9923) [01645197] 2548

UNIVERSITY OF PRETORIA *See* JAARBOEK 1831

UNIVERSITY OF PRETORIA *See* DOSENTENKURSUS 1822

UNIVERSITY OF PUERTO RICO. AGRICULTURAL EXPERIMENT STATION, RIO PIEDRAS *See* BULLETIN - AGRICULTURAL EXPERIMENT STATION, RIO PIEDRAS 68

UNIVERSITY OF PUERTO RICO (MAYAGUEZ CAMPUS). DEPT. OF MARINE SCIENCES *See* CONTRIBUTIONS - UNIVERSITY OF PUERTO RICO, DEPARTMENT OF MARINE SCIENCES 554

UNIVERSITY OF PUERTO RICO (RIO PIEDRAS CAMPUS) *See* JOURNAL OF AGRICULTURE OF THE UNIVERSITY OF PUERTO RICO, THE 99

UNIVERSITY OF PUERTO RICO (RIO PIEDRAS CAMPUS). SCHOOL OF LAW *See* REVISTA JURIDICA DE LA UNIVERSIDAD DE PUERTO RICO 3042

UNIVERSITY OF PUGET SOUND LAW REVIEW (US/0161-0708) [03601474] 3069

UNIVERSITY OF PUGET SOUND. SCHOOL OF LAW *See* UNIVERSITY OF PUGET SOUND LAW REVIEW 3069

UNIVERSITY OF QUEENSLAND LAW JOURNAL, THE (AT/0083-4041) [01768814] 3069

UNIVERSITY OF QUEENSLAND. LIBRARIES *See* ANNUAL REPORT OF THE UNIVERSITY LIBRARIAN 3191

UNIVERSITY OF RAJSHANI INSTITUTE OF BANGLADESH STUDIES *See* JOURNAL OF THE INSTITUTE OF BANGLADESH STUDIES, THE 2656

UNIVERSITY OF READING. AGRICULTURAL EXTENSION AND RURAL DEVELOPMENT CENTRE *See* BULLETIN / UNIVERSITY OF READING, AGRICULTURAL EXTENSION AND RURAL DEVELOPMENT CENTRE 70

UNIVERSITY OF REDLANDS *See* ALUMNI DIRECTORY / UNIVERSITY OF REDLANDS 1100

UNIVERSITY OF REGINA. LIBRARY *See* SERIALS LIST - UNIVERSITY OF REGINA, LIBRARY 424

UNIVERSITY OF RHODESIA *See* PRINCIPAL'S REPORT TO COUNCIL - UNIVERSITY OF RHODESIA 1842

UNIVERSITY OF RICHMOND *See* UNIVERSITY OF RICHMOND LAW REVIEW 3069

UNIVERSITY OF RICHMOND LAW REVIEW (US/0566-2389) [01768815] 3069

UNIVERSITY OF ROCHESTER *See* CITY OF ROCHESTER BUDGET 4717

UNIVERSITY OF ROCHESTER *See* REPORT OF THE TREASURER (ROCHESTER) 750

UNIVERSITY OF ROCHESTER. LIBRARY *See* UNIVERSITY OF ROCHESTER LIBRARY BULLETIN 3255

UNIVERSITY OF ROCHESTER LIBRARY BULLETIN (US/0361-1272) [01910517] 3255

UNIVERSITY OF ROCHESTER. SCHOOL OF MEDICINE AND DENTISTRY *See* ALUMNI DIRECTORY - UNIVERSITY OF ROCHESTER. SCHOOL OF MEDICINE AND DENTISTRY 1100

UNIVERSITY OF SAN DIEGO. SCHOOL OF LAW *See* QUARTERLY LAW NOTES AND ALUMNI NEWS 3033

UNIVERSITY OF SAN FRANCISCO LAW REVIEW (US/0042-0018) [01587670] 3069

UNIVERSITY OF SAN FRANCISCO MARITIME LAW JOURNAL (US/1061-3331) [21021110] 3182

UNIVERSITY OF SAN FRANCISCO. SCHOOL OF LAW *See* UNIVERSITY OF SAN FRANCISCO LAW REVIEW 3069

UNIVERSITY OF SASKATCHEWAN *See* UNIVERSITY LECTURES - UNIVERSITY OF SASKATCHEWAN 1852

UNIVERSITY OF SASKATCHEWAN. ANIMAL & POULTRY SCIENCE DEPT *See* DAIRY CATTLE 210

UNIVERSITY OF SASKATCHEWAN. LIBRARY *See* SERIALS LIST MICROFORM / UNIVERSITY OF SASKATCHEWAN LIBRARY 424

UNIVERSITY OF SOUTH AFRICA *See* UNISA PSYCHOLOGIA 4621

UNIVERSITY OF SOUTH AFRICA. DEPT. OF ENGLISH *See* UNISA ENGLISH STUDIES 3449

UNIVERSITY OF SOUTH CAROLINA. INSTITUTE OF ARCHEOLOGY AND ANTHROPOLOGY *See* RESEARCH MANUSCRIPT SERIES - INSTITUTE OF ARCHEOLOGY AND ANTHROPOLOGY, UNIVERSITY OF SOUTH CAROLINA 280

UNIVERSITY OF SOUTH DAKOTA BULLETIN, THE (US/0042-0069) [03954875] 1852

UNIVERSITY OF SOUTH DAKOTA. INSTITUTE OF INDIAN STUDIES *See* UNIVERSITY OF SOUTH DAKOTA BULLETIN, THE 1852

UNIVERSITY OF SOUTHERN CALIFORNIA. AEMENIAN MUSICAL STUDIES *See* NEWSLETTER - UNIVERSITY OF SOUTHERN CALIFORNIA. ARMENIAN MUSICAL STUDIES 4141

UNIVERSITY OF SOUTHERN CALIFORNIA. COLLEGE OF LETTERS, ARTS AND SCIENCES *See* ALUMNI DIRECTORY / COLLEGE OF LETTERS, ARTS AND SCIENCES, UNIVERSITY OF SOUTHERN CALIFORNIA 1098

UNIVERSITY OF SOUTHERN CALIFORNIA, LOS ANGELES. SCHOOL OF INTERNATIONAL RELATIONS *See* FAR EASTERN AND RUSSIAN RESEARCH SERIES 4521

UNIVERSITY OF SOUTHERN CALIFORNIA. SCHOOL OF MUSIC *See* ALUMNI DIRECTORY / SCHOOL OF MUSIC, UNIVERSITY OF SOUTHERN CALIFORNIA 1099

UNIVERSITY OF STRATHCLYDE *See* RESEARCH REGISTER / UNIVERSITY OF STRATHCLYDE 5147

UNIVERSITY OF SUSSEX. INSTITUTE OF DEVELOPMENT STUDIES *See* ANNUAL REPORT ... AND ... HANDBOOK / INSTITUTE OF DEVELOPMENT STUDIES 1462

UNIVERSITY OF SUSSEX. INSTITUTE OF DEVELOPMENT STUDIES *See* IDS COMMUNICATION 1112

UNIVERSITY OF SUSSEX INSTITUTE OF DEVELOPMENT STUDIES *See* ANNUAL REPORT - INSTITUTE OF DEVELOPMENT STUDIES AT THE UNIVERSITY OF SUSSEX 5191

UNIVERSITY OF SYDNEY *See* GAZETTE / THE UNIVERSITY OF SYDNEY, THE 1091

UNIVERSITY OF SYDNEY. ARCHIVE OF AUSTRALIAN JUDAICA *See* CASUAL BULLETIN / ARCHIVE OF AUSTRALIAN JUDAICA 5046

UNIVERSITY OF TASMANIA LAW REVIEW (AT/0082-2108) [08592374] 3069

UNIVERSITY OF TENNESSEE, KNOXVILLE. COMPUTING CENTER *See* NEWSLETTER - THE UNIVERSITY OF TENNESSEE COMPUTING CENTER 1197

UNIVERSITY OF TENNESSEE, KNOXVILLE. LIBRARY *See* LIBRARY LECTURES (KNOXVILLE) 3226

UNIVERSITY OF TENNESSEE PUBLICATIONS AND CREATIVE ACHIEVEMENTS : A CATALOG OF PUBLICATIONS AND CREATIVE ACHIEVEMENTS OF THE FACULTY AND STAFF / COMPILED BY THE OFFICE OF THE VICE PRESIDENT FOR ACADEMIC AFFAIRS AND RESEARCH, THE UNIVERSITY OF TENNESSEE, THE (US) [14230760] 1788

UNIVERSITY

Alphabetical Title Index

UNIVERSITY OF TENNESSEE (SYSTEM). OFFICE OF THE VICE PRESIDENT FOR ACADEMIC AFFAIRS AND RESEARCH *See* UNIVERSITY OF TENNESSEE PUBLICATIONS AND CREATIVE ACHIEVEMENTS : A CATALOG OF PUBLICATIONS AND CREATIVE ACHIEVEMENTS OF THE FACULTY AND STAFF / COMPILED BY THE OFFICE OF THE VICE PRESIDENT FOR ACADEMIC AFFAIRS AND RESEARCH, THE UNIVERSITY OF TENNESSEE, THE **1788**

UNIVERSITY OF TEXAS AT AUSTIN. AFRICAN AND AFRO-AMERICAN STUDIES RESEARCH CENTER *See* AFRICAN AND AFRO-AMERICAN STUDIES AND RESEARCH CENTER REPRINTS **2636**

UNIVERSITY OF TEXAS AT AUSTIN. BUREAU OF BUSINESS RESEARCH *See* RESEARCH MONOGRAPH - UNIVERSITY OF TEXAS AT AUSTIN. BUREAU OF BUSINESS RESEARCH **707**

UNIVERSITY OF TEXAS AT AUSTIN. BUREAU OF ECONOMIC GEOLOGY *See* ANNUAL REPORT - BUREAU OF ECONOMIC GEOLOGY, THE UNIVERSITY OF TEXAS AT AUSTIN **1365**

UNIVERSITY OF TEXAS AT AUSTIN. BUREAU OF ECONOMIC GEOLOGY *See* GEOLOGICAL CIRCULAR **1377**

UNIVERSITY OF TEXAS AT AUSTIN. BUREAU OF ECONOMIC GEOLOGY *See* RESEARCH NOTE - BUREAU OF ECONOMIC GEOLOGY, UNIVERSITY OF TEXAS AT AUSTIN **1395**

UNIVERSITY OF TEXAS AT AUSTIN. COLLEGE OF LIBERAL ARTS *See* ALUMNI DIRECTORY / COLLEGE OF LIBERAL ARTS, THE UNIVERSITY OF TEXAS AT AUSTIN **1098**

UNIVERSITY OF TEXAS AT AUSTIN. FILM LIBRARY *See* CATALOGUE OF DEPARTMENTALLY-OWNED FILMS HOUSED WITH FILM LIBRARY / THE GENERAL LIBRARIES **3200**

UNIVERSITY OF TEXAS. BUREAU OF ECONOMIC GEOLOGY *See* PUBLICATIONS - UNIVERSITY OF TEXAS, BUREAU OF ECONOMIC GEOLOGY **1392**

UNIVERSITY OF TEXAS LIFETIME HEALTH LETTER, THE (US/1042-203X) [18968634] **4806**

UNIVERSITY OF THE DISTRICT OF COLUMBIA. WATER RESOURCES RESEARCH CENTER *See* ANNUAL REPORT / D.C. WATER RESOURCES RESEARCH CENTER **5529**

UNIVERSITY OF THE ORANGE FREE STATE. INSTITUTE FOR CONTEMPORARY HISTORY *See* ANNUAL REPORT - INSTITUTE FOR CONTEMPORARY HISTORY, UNIVERSITY OF THE ORANGE FREE STATE **2610**

UNIVERSITY OF THE STATE OF NEW YORK *See* REGENTS ... PROGRESS REPORT ON THE REGENTS STATEWIDE PLAN FOR THE DEVELOPMENT OF POSTSECONDARY EDUCATION IN NEW YORK STATE, THE **1843**

UNIVERSITY OF THE STATE OF NEW YORK *See* REGENTS ... STATEWIDE PLAN FOR HIGHER EDUCATION IN NEW YORK STATE, THE **1843**

UNIVERSITY OF THE STATE OF NEW YORK. BUREAU OF EDUCATIONAL FINANCE RESEARCH *See* FEDERAL AID PAID TO NEW YORK STATE SCHOOL DISTRICTS **1864**

UNIVERSITY OF THE STATE OF NEW YORK. BUREAU OF EDUCATIONAL FINANCE RESEARCH *See* UNDERSTANDING FINANCIAL SUPPORT OF PUBLIC SCHOOLS **1873**

UNIVERSITY OF THE STATE OF NEW YORK. BUREAU OF SCHOOL AND CATEGORICAL PROGRAMS EVALUATION *See* PROJECT OUTCOMES REPORTING **1775**

UNIVERSITY OF THE STATE OF NEW YORK. BUREAU OF SCHOOL LIBRARIES *See* PLANNING GUIDE ESEA IV, PART B: LIBRARIES AND LEARNING RESOURCES **1868**

UNIVERSITY OF THE STATE OF NEW YORK. INFORMATION CENTER ON EDUCATION *See* COLLEGE AND UNIVERSITY ADMISSIONS AND ENROLLMENT, NEW YORK STATE **1816**

UNIVERSITY OF THE STATE OF NEW YORK. INFORMATION CENTER ON EDUCATION *See* SELECTED STATISTICS ON STUDENTS AND STAFF IN NEW YORK CITY SCHOOL DISTRICTS **1797**

UNIVERSITY OF THE STATE OF NEW YORK. INFORMATION CENTER ON EDUCATION *See* ANNUAL EDUCATIONAL SUMMARY NEW YORK STATE **1724**

UNIVERSITY OF THE STATE OF NEW YORK. REGENTS STATEWIDE PLAN FOR THE DEVELOPMENT OF POSTSECONDARY EDUCATION *See* REGENTS ... STATEWIDE PLAN FOR HIGHER EDUCATION IN NEW YORK STATE, THE **1843**

UNIVERSITY OF THE WEST INDIES, CAVE HILL, BARBADOS. LAW FACULTY *See* UWI STUDENT'S LAW REVIEW **3070**

UNIVERSITY OF THE WEST INDIES PUBLISHERS' ASSOCIATION NEWSLETTER (JM) [22459477] **4820**

UNIVERSITY OF THE WEST INDIES (SAINT AUGUSTINE, TRINIDAD AND TOBAGO) *See* ANNUAL REPORT ON CACAO RESEARCH **163**

UNIVERSITY OF THE WITWATERSRAND. ECONOMIC GEOLOGY RESEARCH UNIT *See* INFORMATION CIRCULAR - UNIVERSITY OF THE WITWATERSRAND, ECONOMIC GEOLOGY RESEARCH UNIT **1383**

UNIVERSITY OF TOLEDO. COLLEGE OF LAW *See* UNIVERSITY OF TOLEDO LAW REVIEW, THE **3069**

UNIVERSITY OF TOLEDO LAW REVIEW, THE (US/0042-0190) [01517565] **3069**

UNIVERSITY OF TORONTO *See* ALUMNI DIRECTORY - UNIVERSITY OF TORONTO **1100**

UNIVERSITY OF TORONTO *See* UNIVERSITY OF TORONTO QUARTERLY **2856**

UNIVERSITY OF TORONTO *See* MEDICAL JOURNAL **3609**

UNIVERSITY OF TORONTO. CENTRE FOR URBAN AND COMMUNITY STUDIES *See* RESEARCH PAPER - CENTRE FOR URBAN AND COMMUNITY STUDIES. UNIVERSITY OF TORONTO **2833**

UNIVERSITY OF TORONTO. CENTRE FOR URBAN AND COMMUNITY STUDIES *See* MAJOR REPORT - CENTRE FOR URBAN AND COMMUNITY STUDIES, UNIVERSITY OF TORONTO **2827**

UNIVERSITY OF TORONTO. CENTRE OF CRIMINOLOGY. LIBRARY *See* ACQUISITIONS LIST - CENTRE OF CRIMINOLOGY LIBRARY, UNIVERSITY OF TORONTO **3078**

UNIVERSITY OF TORONTO DENTAL JOURNAL (CN/0843-5812) [18418486] **1337**

UNIVERSITY OF TORONTO. DEPT. OF GEOGRAPHY *See* DISCUSSION PAPER - UNIVERSITY OF TORONTO, DEPARTMENT OF GEOGRAPHY **2559**

UNIVERSITY OF TORONTO. DEPT. OF MECHANICAL ENGINEERING *See* TECHNICAL PUBLICATION SERIES - DEPARTMENT OF MECHANICAL ENGINEERING, UNIVERSITY OF TORONTO **2130**

UNIVERSITY OF TORONTO FACULTY OF LAW REVIEW (CN/0381-1638) [02585991] **3069**

UNIVERSITY OF TORONTO. FACULTY OF MANAGEMENT STUDIES. RETAILING AND INSTITUTIONAL RESEARCH PROGRAM *See* WORKING PAPER - RETAILING AND INSTITUTIONAL RESEARCH PROGRAM, FACULTY OF MANAGEMENT STUDIES, UNIVERSITY OF TORONTO **889**

UNIVERSITY OF TORONTO. FACULTY OF PHARMACY *See* CONTINUING EDUCATION (TORONTO) **4298**

UNIVERSITY OF TORONTO. FORESTRY ALUMNI ASSOCIATION *See* DIRECTORY AND NEWSLETTER - FORESTRY ALUMNI ASSOCIATION, UNIVERSITY OF TORONTO **1101**

UNIVERSITY OF TORONTO. GREAT LAKES INSTITUTE *See* REPORT - GREAT LAKES INSTITUTE, UNIVERSITY OF TORONTO **1417**

UNIVERSITY OF TORONTO. INSTITUTE FOR POLICY ANALYSIS *See* TECHNICAL PAPER SERIES - INSTITUTE FOR THE QUANTITATIVE ANALYSIS OF SOCIAL AND ECONOMIC POLICY, UNIVERSITY OF TORONTO **1523**

UNIVERSITY OF TORONTO. INSTITUTE OF AEROSPACE STUDIES *See* UTIAS TECHNICAL NOTE **39**

UNIVERSITY OF TORONTO ITALIAN STUDIES (CN) [17366917] **2714, 3449**

UNIVERSITY OF TORONTO LAW JOURNAL, THE (CN/0042-0220) [01768819] **3069**

UNIVERSITY OF TORONTO. LIBRARY AUTOMATION SYSTEMS *See* UTLAS NEWSLETTER (1979) **3255**

UNIVERSITY OF TORONTO. LIBRARY. REFERENCE DEPT *See* REFERENCE SERIES **3244**

UNIVERSITY OF TORONTO MAGAZINE (CN/0840-562X) [19281527] **1853**

UNIVERSITY OF TORONTO. MANAGEMENT STUDIES LIBRARY *See* GUIDE TO SERIAL PUBLICATIONS - MANAGEMENT STUDIES LIBRARY, UNIVERSITY OF TORONTO **730**

UNIVERSITY OF TORONTO MEDICAL JOURNAL (1965) *See* MEDICAL JOURNAL - UNIVERSITY OF TORONTO **3610**

UNIVERSITY OF TORONTO QUARTERLY (CN/0042-0247) [01585920] **2856**

UNIVERSITY OF TORONTO REVIEW (CN/0708-4382) [06272484] **3449**

UNIVERSITY OF TORONTO ROMANCE SERIES (CN/0082-5336) [01696730] **3331, 3449**

UNIVERSITY OF TORONTO. UNITED STATES ALUMNI *See* ALUMNI DIRECTORY / UNIVERSITY OF TORONTO, UNITED STATES ALUMNI **1100**

UNIVERSITY OF TULSA *See* MONOGRAPH SERIES - UNIVERSITY OF TULSA **3348**

UNIVERSITY OF TULSA ANNUAL, THE (US) [09507466] **1853**

UNIVERSITY OF UTAH PUBLICATIONS IN THE AMERICAN WEST (US/0085-5227) [01550169] **2764**

UNIVERSITY OF VICOTRIA CALENDAR (CN) **1789**

UNIVERSITY OF VIRGINIA *See* INSIDE UVA **1864**

UNIVERSITY OF VIRGINIA. ALUMNI ASSOCIATION *See* ALUMNI DIRECTORY - UNIVERSITY OF VIRGINIA. ALUMNI ASSOCIATION **1100**

UNIVERSITY OF VIRGINIA. ALUMNI ASSOCIATION *See* ALUMNI DIRECTORY / THE ALUMNI ASSOCIATION OF THE UNIVERSITY OF VIRGINIA **1099**

UNIVERSITY OF VIRGINIA. BIBLIOGRAPHICAL SOCIETY *See* STUDIES IN BIBLIOGRAPHY (CHARLOTTESVILLE, VA.) **425**

UNIVERSITY OF VIRGINIA LAW SCHOOL FOUNDATION *See* UNIVERSITY OF VIRGINIA LAW SCHOOL FOUNDATION ANNUAL REPORT, THE **3069**

UNIVERSITY OF VIRGINIA LAW SCHOOL FOUNDATION ANNUAL REPORT, THE (US/0504-3972) [02399015] **3069**

UNIVERSITY OF VIRGINIA RECORD (US/0746-5149) [08424128] **1096**

UNIVERSITY OF WALES. BOARD OF CELTIC STUDIES *See* BWLETIN Y BWRDD GWYBODAU CELTAIDD **3271**

UNIVERSITY OF WALES. MARINE SCIENCE LABORATORIES *See* CONTRIBUTIONS TO MARINE SCIENCE (MENAI BRIDGE) **554**

UNIVERSITY OF WALES REVIEW / SCIENCE & TECHNOLOGY *CEASED.* (UK) **5168**

UNIVERSITY OF WASHINGTON. ACADEMIC COMPUTER CENTER *See* NEWSLETTER-UNIVERSITY OF WASHINGTON **1197**

UNIVERSITY OF WASHINGTON. DEPARTMENT OF OCEANOGRAPHY *See* SPECIAL REPORT - UNIVERSITY OF WASHINGTON, DEPARTMENT OF OCEANOGRAPHY **1457**

UNIVERSITY OF WASHINGTON PAYROLL/PERSONNEL SYSTEM *See* SALARY STRATIFICATION REPORT / UNIVERSITY OF WASHINGTON PAYROLL/PERSONNEL SYSTEM **1709**

UNIVERSITY OF WASHINGTON PUBLICATIONS IN BIOLOGY (US/0083-7571) [01403393] **475**

UNIVERSITY OF WASHINGTON PUBLICATIONS. LANGUAGE AND LITERATURE (US/0085-7947) [08449372] **3331**

UNIVERSITY OF WASHINGTON. SCHOOL OF FISHERIES *See* RESEARCH IN FISHERIES **2311**

UNIVERSITY OF WATERLOO *See* U W GUIDELINES **1851**

UNIVERSITY OF WATERLOO BIOLOGY SERIES (CN/0317-3348) [02248174] **475**

UNIVERSITY OF WATERLOO. COMPUTER COMMUNICATIONS NETWORK GROUP *See* C C N G REPORT **1240**

UNIVERSITY OF WATERLOO. FACULTY OF ENVIRONMENTAL STUDIES *See* OCCASIONAL PAPER - FACULTY OF ENVIRONMENTAL STUDIES. UNIVERSITY OF WATERLOO **2179**

UNIVERSITY OF WATERLOO. LIBRARY *See* UNIVERSITY OF WATERLOO LIBRARY SERIALS LIST **3255**

UNIVERSITY OF WATERLOO LIBRARY SERIALS LIST (CN/0316-5949) [02247592] **3255**

UNIVERSITY OF WATERLOO. TRANSPORT GROUP *See* PUBLICATION SERIES - TRANSPORT GROUP. DEPARTMENT OF CIVIL ENGINEERING. UNIVERSITY OF WATERLOO **5793**

UNIVERSITY OF WESTERN AUSTRALIA LAW REVIEW (AT/0042-0328) [01587621] **3069**

UNIVERSITY OF WESTERN ONTARIO *See* ALUMNI DIRECTORY / UNIVERSITY OF WESTERN ONTARIO **1100**

Alphabetical Title Index — UNTERNEHMAN

UNIVERSITY OF WESTERN ONTARIO. DEPT. OF MUSIC HISTORY See STUDIES IN MUSIC FROM THE UNIVERSITY OF WESTERN ONTARIO 4155

UNIVERSITY OF WESTERN ONTARIO. SCHOOL OF BUSINESS ADMINISTRATION See WESTERN MBA PROGRAM, THE 719

UNIVERSITY OF WESTERN ONTARIO. SOCIAL SCIENCE COMPUTING LABORATORY See NEWSLETTER - SOCIAL SCIENCE COMPUTING LABORATORY 5211

UNIVERSITY OF WINDSOR See NEWSLINE - UNIVERSITY OF WINDSOR 1837

UNIVERSITY OF WINDSOR See UNIVERSITY OF WINDSOR REVIEW, THE 3449

UNIVERSITY OF WINDSOR. LIBRARY See SERIAL TITLES IN THE HUMANITIES AND SOCIAL SCIENCES (WINDSOR) 2854

UNIVERSITY OF WINDSOR. LIBRARY See SERIAL TITLES IN THE PURE AND APPLIED SCIENCES (WINDSOR) 5157

UNIVERSITY OF WINDSOR REVIEW, THE (CN/0042-0352) [01586228] 3449

UNIVERSITY OF WINDSOR. SCHOOL OF COMPUTER SCIENCE See SCHOOL OF COMPUTER SCIENCE. UNIVERSITY OF WINDSOR 1202

UNIVERSITY OF WISCONSIN See PUBLICATIONS IN MEDIEVAL SCIENCE 2704

UNIVERSITY OF WISCONSIN-EXTENSION See INDEPENDENT STUDY 1752

UNIVERSITY OF WISCONSIN--MADISON. LAND TENURE CENTER See TRAINING & METHODS SERIES 1524

UNIVERSITY OF WISCONSIN--MILWAUKEE. CENTER FOR GREAT LAKES STUDIES See SPECIAL REPORT / CENTER FOR GREAT LAKES STUDIES, UNIVERSITY OF WISCONSIN-MILWAUKEE 1847

UNIVERSITY OF WYOMING PUBLICATIONS (1935) (US/0084-3199) [01737508] 1853

UNIVERSITY OF YAOUNDE. DEPARTEMENT DES LANGUES AFRICAINES ET LINGUISTIQUE See BUDGET D'EQUIPEMENT ET DE RECHERCHE 3270

UNIVERSITY OF YAOUNDE. DEPARTMENT DES LANGUES AFRICAINES ET LINGUISTIQUE See LIVRET DU DEPARTEMENT DES LANGUES AFRICAINES ET LINGUISTIQUE 3300

UNIVERSITY OF ZAMBIA See GENERAL INFORMATION HANDBOOK 1825

UNIVERSITY OF ZAMBIA See OUTLINE OF POSTGRADUATE PROGRAMMES / UNIVERSITY OF ZAMBIA 1839

UNIVERSITY OF ZAMBIA. DEPT. OF EDUCATION See HANDBOOK / UNIVERSITY OF ZAMBIA, SCHOOL OF EDUCATION, DEPARTMENT OF EDUCATION 1827

UNIVERSITY OF ZAMBIA. DEPT. OF GEOGRAPHY See HANDBOOK FOR STUDENTS TAKING COURSES IN GEOGRAPHY / UNIVERSITY OF ZAMBIA, SCHOOL OF EDUCATION, DEPARTMENT OF GEOGRAPHY 2565

UNIVERSITY OF ZAMBIA. DEPT. OF LITERATURE & LANGUAGES See HANDBOOK / THE UNIVERSITY OF ZAMBIA, SCHOOL OF EDUCATION, DEPARTMENT OF LITERATURE & LANGUAGES 3285

UNIVERSITY OF ZAMBIA. INSTITUTE FOR AFRICAN STUDIES See COMMUNICATION - UNIVERSITY OF ZAMBIA. INSTITUTE FOR AFRICAN STUDIES 1107

UNIVERSITY OF ZAMBIA. SCHOOL OF HUMANITIES AND SOCIAL SCIENCES See ANNUAL REPORT - UNIVERSITY OF ZAMBIA. SCHOOL OF HUMANITIES & SOCIAL SCIENCES 2842

UNIVERSITY OF ZAMBIA. SCHOOL OF NATURAL SCIENCES See GUIDE BOOK FOR FIRST YEAR STUDENTS IN THE SCHOOL OF NATURAL SCIENCES 5108

UNIVERSITY OF ZAMBIA. TECHNOLOGY DEVELOPMENT AND ADVISORY UNIT See HANDBOOK AND ANNUAL REVIEW 5109

UNIVERSITY PRESS BOOK NEWS (US/1040-8991) [18565961] 427

UNIVERSITY PRESS BOOKS FOR PUBLIC AND SECONDARY SCHOOL LIBRARIES (US/1055-4173) [23169035] 3255

UNIVERSITY PRESS BOOKS FOR PUBLIC LIBRARIES (US/0731-2857) [05298179] 3255

UNIVERSITY PRINTS, BOSTON See UNIVERSITY PRINTS CATALOG 367

UNIVERSITY PRINTS CATALOG (US) [05301593] 367

UNIVERSITY PUBLISHING CEASED. (US/0191-4146) [04324773] 4833

UNIVERSITY RESEARCH IN BUSINESS AND ECONOMICS CEASED. (US/0736-8968) [08861348] 717, 1540

UNIVERSITY REVIEW OF TEXAS (US) [23150719] 4499

UNIVERSITY STATISTICS (DUBLIN, IRELAND) (IE) [20293864] 5345

UNIVERSITY STUDIES IN MEDIEVAL AND RENAISSANCE LITERATURE (US/0749-4149) [11120276] 2714, 3449

UNIVERSITY STUDIES IN PUBLIC ADMINISTRATION (II) [02422818] 4692

UNIVERSIT·A DEGLI STUDI DI TRIESTE See NOTIZIARIO - UNIVERSITA DEGLI STUDI DI TRIESTE 1838

UNIVERSO (IT/0042-0409) [02268978] 285, 2578

UNIVERSO, EL (EC) [07486717] 401

UNIVERSO [MICROFORM], L' (IT/0042-0409) [20337406] 285, 2578

UNIVERSUL CARTII / REVISTA LUNARA A MINISTERULUI CULTURII (RM) [27426983] 3449

UNIVERZITA KOMENSKEHO V BRATISLAVE. FARMACEUTICKA FAKULTA See ACTA FACULTATIS PHARMACEUTICAE UNIVERSITATIS COMENIANAE 4288

UNIVERZITA KOMENSKEHO V BRATISLAVE. PRIRODOVEDECK A FAKULTA See ACTA FACULTATIS RERUM NATURALIUM UNIVERSITATIS COMENIANAE. PHYSIOLOGIA PLANTARUM 497

UNIVERZITA KOMENSKEHO V BRATISLAVE. PRIRODOVEDECKA FAKULTA See ACTA FACULTATIS RERUM NATURALIUM UNIVERSITATIS COMENIANAE. BOTANICA 497

UNIVERZITA KOMENSKEHO V BRATISLAVE. PRIRODOVEDECKA FAKULTA See ANTHROPOLOGIA 228

UNIVERZITA KOMENSKEHO V BRATISLAVE. PRIRODOVEDECKA FAKULTA See ACTA FACULTATIS RERUM NATURALIUM UNIVERSITATIS COMENIANAE. ZOOLOGIA 5573

UNIVERZITA PALACKEHO V OLOMOUCI. LEKARSKA FAKULTA See POLYTHEMATICAL COLLECTED REPORTS OF THE MEDICAL FACULTY OF THE PALACKY UNIVERSITY 3628

UNIVERZITA PALACKEHO V OLOMOUCI. LEKARSKA FAKULTA See ACTA UNIVERSITATIS PALACKIANAE OLOMUCENSIS FACULTATIS MEDICAE SUPPLEMENTUM 3545

UNIVERZITET U BEOGRADU. ELEKTROTEHNICKI FAKULTET See PUBLIKACIJE ELEKTROTEHNICKOG FAKULTETA. UNIVERZITET U BEOGRADU. SERIJA ELEKTROENERGETIKA 2077

UNIVERZITET U SARAJEVU See PREGLED PREDAVANJA 1842

UNIVERZITET U SARAJEVU See GODISNJAK / UNIVERZITET U SARAJEVU 1825

UNIWERSYTET GDANSKI. WYDZIA MATEMATYKI, FIZYKI I CHEMII See ZESZYTY NAUKOWE WYDZIAU MATEMATYKI, FIZYKI I CHEMII. PROBLEMY DYDAKTYKI FIZYKI 4425

UNIWERSYTET JAGIELLONSKI See PRACE ARCHEOLOGICZNE 278

UNIWERSYTET JAGIELLONSKI See ZESZYTY KAUKOWE UNIWERYSTETU JAGIELLONSKIEGO. PRACE BOTANICZNE 531

UNIWERSYTET MARII CURIE-SKODOWSKIEJ See ANNALES UNIVERSITATIS MARIAE CURIE-SKODOWSKA. SECTIO C. BIOLOGIA 442

UNIWERSYTET MARII CURIE-SKODOWSKIEJ See ANNALES UNIVERSITATIS MARIAE CURIE-SKODOWSKA. SECTIO A. MATHEMATICA 3493

UNIWERSYTET MARII CURIE-SKODOWSKIEJ See ANNALES UNIVERSITATIS MARIAE CURIE-SKODOWSKA. SECTIO E AGRICULTURA 59

UNIWERSYTET MARII CURIE-SKODOWSKIEJ See ANNALES UNIVERSITATIS MARIAE CURIE-SKODOWSKA. SECTIO AAA: PHYSICA 4397

UNIWERSYTET MARII CURIE-SKODOWSKIEJ See ANNALES UNIVERSITATIS MARIAE CURIE-SKODOWSKA. SECTIO D, MEDICINA 3550

UNIWERSYTET MARII CURIE-SKODOWSKIEJ. MIEDZYUCZELNIANY INSTYTUT FILOZOFII I SOCIOLOGII See ANNALES UNIVERSITATIS MARIAE CURIE-SKLODOWSKA. SECTION I: PHILOSOPHIA-SOCIOLOGIA 4340

UNIWERSYTET MARII CURIE-SKOWDOWSKIEJ See ANNALES UNIVERSITATIS MARIAE CURIE-SKODOWSKA. SECTIO H OECONOMIA 1462

UNIWERSYTET SLASKI W KATOWICACH See PRACE Z NAUK SPOECZNYCH 5213

UNIWORLD (OTTAWA) (CN/1183-725X) [25589802] 1789

UNIX & OPEN SYSTEMS SERVICE (UK) 1206

UNIX/BUSINESS CEASED. (UK/0958-6253) [l09586253] 1239

UNIX IN THE OFFICE See OPEN INFORMATION SYSTEMS 1248

UNIX INFO (NE) 1206

UNIX MAGAZINE (JA/0913-0748) [l09130748] 1206

UNIX/MAIL (GW/0176-8654) [01768654] 1206

UNIX NEWS LONDON (UK/0956-2753) [l09562753] 1249

UNIX PRODUCTS DIRECTORY (US/0886-2575) [12878998] 1206

UNIX REVIEW (US/0742-3136) [09831601] 1239

UNIX SYSTEM PRICE PERFORMANCE GUIDE (US/1059-4159) [24584749] 1250

UNIX SYSTEM SUPPORT & UPDATE NEWS CEASED. (US/0892-8088) [15307395] 1206

UNIX SYSTEMS CEASED. (UK) 1206

UNIX TODAY! (US/1040-5038) [18432538] 1206

UNIX TOPICS FOR USERS (US/0730-255X) [07980510] 1206

UNIX USER (US/1062-5003) [25642430] 1206

UNIX/WORLD (US/0739-5922) [09776382] 1265

UNIXSYSTEM CEASED. (FR) 5168

UNIXWORLD'S OPEN COMPUTING (US/1072-4044) [28938807] 1265

UNIYA (AT) 5225

UNKNOWN PUBLIC (UK) 4157

UNLIMITED TIMES, THE (US/0738-7032) [09656331] 717

UNLISTED DRUGS (US/0042-0441) [01639749] 4331

UNLISTED DRUGS. INDEX-GUIDE (US/8755-7142) [01827481] 4331

UNMANNED SYSTEMS (US/0892-4023) [10976833] 5427, 2085

UNMANNED VEHICLE FORECAST (US) 4060

UNMUZZLED OX (US/0049-5557) [01511933] 3472

UNO (MADRID, SPAIN) CEASED. (SP) [19338830] 2553

●UNOFFICIAL GUIDE TO LAS VEGAS, THE (US/1064-5640) [26327061] 5498

UNPUBLISHED WRITINGS ON WORLD RELIGIONS (US/0149-0230) [03570120] 5007

UNREPORTED JUDGEMENTS, THE (II) [01784130] 3069

UNRESERVED PUBLIC MINI AUCTION See COLLECTABLES AUCTION / CHARLTON AUCTIONS 2772

UNRESERVED PUBLIC MINI AUCTION See NUMISMATIC AUCTION / CHARLTON AUCTIONS 2782

UNRESERVED PUBLIC MINI AUCTION See JEWELLERY AUCTION / CHARLTON AUCTIONS 2914

UNRESERVED PUBLIC MINI AUCTION See PHILATELIC AUCTION / CHARLTON AUCTIONS 2786

UNRWA : RESUME DU RAPPORT (AU) [07427214] 5313

UNSCHEDULED EVENTS (US/0042-0468) [06288317] 5264

UNSEARCHABLE RICHES (US/0042-0476) [03954905] 5020

UNSER ERMLANDBUCH See ERMLANDBUCH 2515

UNSER TSAYT (US/0042-0506) [06130308] 2494

UNSER WALD : ZEITSCRIFT DER SCHUTZGEMEINSCHAFT DEUTSCHER WALD (GW) [04124769] 2208, 2397

UNSERE HEIMAT (AU/1017-2696) [07650414] 2671

UNSERE JAGD (GW) [08178809] 4880

UNSERE JUGEND (GW/0342-5258) [06640668] 5225, 1789

UNSERE KUNSTDENKMALER (SZ/0566-263X) [02142005] 2632, 367

UNSERE STIMME (GW) [04407453] 3355

UNSERE UMWELT (GW) [01785304] 2182

UNSHAVED TRUTHS (US) 3449

UNTER DEM PFLASTER LIEGT DER STRAND (GW) [06431796] 4548

UNTERNEHMAN UND ARBEITSSTATTEN. REIHE 1.4, KOSTENSTRUKTUR IM GASTGEWERBE / HERAUSGEBER STATISTISCHES BUNDESAMT (GW) [10051539] 2809

UNTERNEHMEN Alphabetical Title Index

UNTERNEHMEN UND ARBEITSSTATTEN. REIHE 1 : DIE KOSTENSTRUKTUR IN DER WIRTSCHAFT. V. GROSSHANDEL, HANDELSVERTRETER UND HANDELSMAKLER, VERLAGSWESEN (GW/0072-3975) [02041642] **856**

UNTERNEHMEN UND ARBEITSSTATTEN. REIHE 2.2, ZAHL UND NOMINALKAPITAL DER KAPITALGESELLSCHAFTEN / HERAUSGEBER, STATISTISCHES BUNDESAMT WIESBADEN (GW) [17715432] **918**

UNTERNEHMER, DER (AU) [02268981] **1630**

UNTERNEHMUNG (SZ/0042-059X) [06663732] **856, 889**

UNTERRICHTSBLATTER DER DEUTSCHEN BUNDESPOST (GW) **1789**

UNTERRICHTSBLATTER FUER DIE BUNDESWEHRVERWALTUNG (GW) [07536807] **4060**

UNTERRICHTSPRAXIS, DIE (US/0042-062X) [02155362] 1908, **3331**

UNTERRICHTSWISSENSCHAFT (GW/0340-4099) [01789688] **1789**

UNTERRIFIED DEMOCRAT (US) [13650661] **5704**

UNTERSUCHUNGEN UBER GRUPPEN UND VERBANDE (GW/0566-2753) [01522847] **5269**

UNTERSUCHUNGEN UND MATERIALIEN ZUR VERFASSUNGS- UND LANDESGESCHICHTE (GW) [03160494] **4499**

UNTERSUCHUNGEN ZUR ANTIKEN LITERATUR UND GESCHICHTE (GW) [03160557] **2632**

UNTERSUCHUNGEN ZUR DEUTSCHEN LITERATURGESCHICHTE (GW/0083-4564) [01522915] **3449**

UNTERSUCHUNGEN ZUR GEGENWARTSKUNDE SUDOSTEUROPAS (GW/0566-2761) [01607360] **5225**

UNTERSUCHUNGEN ZUR LOGIK UND ZUR METHODOLOGIE : BEITRAEGE DES KOOPERATIONSRATES LOGIK AN DER KARL-MARX-UNIVERSITAT / HERAUSGEGEBEN IM AUFTRAG DES REKTORS DER KARL-MARX-UNIVERSITAT LEIPZIG VOM KOOPERATIONSRAT LOGIK AN DER KARL-MARX-UNIVERSITAT LEIPZIG (GW/0233-2957) [13347004] **4364**

UNTERSUCHUNGEN ZUR ROMANISCHEN PHILOLOGIE (GW/0566-2818) [01523963] **3331**

UNTERSUCHUNGEN ZUR SPRACH- UND LITERATURGESCHICHTE DER ROMANISCHEN VOLKER (GW/0083-4580) [03160535] 3331, **3449**

UNTITLED (CARMEL) *CEASED*. (US/0163-7916) [01724552] **4377**

UNUTRASNJA TRGOVINA (YU/0300-2462) [01784850] **856, 734**

UNVEILING (US/0747-931X) [10837140] **3449**

UNVNEWS / THE UNITED NATIONS VOLUNTEERS PROGRAMME (SZ) [19528365] **2912**

UNYUSHO KENKYU KIHON KEIKAKU (JA) [02554128] **2000**

UNYUSHO KOWAN GIJUTSU KENKYUJO (JAPAN) *See* KOWAN GIJUTSU KENKYUJO KOENKAI KOEN SHU **2093**

UNYUSHO KOWAN GIJUTSU KENKYUJO (JAPAN) *See* KOWAN GIJUTSU KENKYUJO HOKOKU **5535**

UNZER SHTIME / NOTRE VOIX (FR) [13658462] 4548, **5053**

UOC TUE (US) [05114399] **5022**

UOMINI E BUSINESS (IT) **717**

UOMINI E IDEE *CEASED*. (IT) [07476860] **4621**

UOMO & CULTURA (IT/0566-8794) [17668789] **247**

UOMO COLLEZIONI (IT) **1088**

UOMO HARPER'S BAZAAR (IT/1121-5496) [11215496] 3996, **1088**

UOMO, L' (IT/0391-2876) [09138267] **247**

UOMO LIBERO, L' (IT) [08901113] **2494**

UOMO MANAGER *SUSPENDED*. (IT) **3996**

UOMO MARE *CEASED*. (IT) [10842618] **596**

UOMO VOGUE, L' (IT) [07702138] 3996, **1088**

UOVO DI COLOMBO (IT) **382**

UP AGAINST THE LAW (UK) [02407331] **3069**

UP & DOWN : MENSILE DELL'ISPES DI POLITICA, ECONOMIA, CULTURA E SOCIETA (IT) [23593506] **2494**

UP-DATE - B.C. NUTRITION COUNCIL (CN/0823-8332) [12624371] **4199**

UP FROM DEPRESSION (US/1056-8042) [23858447] 4621, **2601**

UP FRONT (CN/0225-3577) [06017817] **3472**

UP HERE : LIFE IN CANADA'S NORTH (CN) [15689561] **2548**

UP INFORMATION (BE) 4537, **4499**

UP-LAND FISHING (US/0747-6493) [10757892] **2315**

UP THE GATINEAU (CN/0700-933X) [03279397] **2764**

UP TO DATE (HUMAN RESOURCE) (CN) **2856**

UP TO THE NECK (CN/0315-2944) [02247461] **5313**

UP TO THE NECK, ACTION (CN/0315-8624) [02247460] **5313**

UPCHURCH BULLETIN (US/0270-465X) [06409572] **2476**

UPCOMING (US) [06186759] **4621**

UPDATE (UK/0301-5718) [05837446] **3739**

UPDATE (CN/0847-9364) [20778045] **1908**

UPDATE (SA/1011-5544) [21009150] **5225**

UPDATE (SZ) **5007**

UPDATE - ALCOHOL-DRUG EDUCATION SERVICE (CN/0824-4839) [10638958] **1350**

UPDATE & DIALOG (DK/0906-7272) [09067272] **5007**

UPDATE AND SUPPLEMENT SERVICE (US) **1789**

UPDATE (ANNAPOLIS, MD.) (US/1041-4789) [11248746] **3069**

UPDATE (ARLINGTON) *CEASED*. (US/0162-945X) [04598425] 1908, **1917**

UPDATE (ATLANTA, GA.) (US/0731-3225) [07390187] **2159**

UPDATE CAPE TOWN (SA/0258-929X) [I0258929X] **3649**

UPDATE : CARDIOLOGY (US/0162-0975) [04083286] **3711**

UPDATE - CASH MANAGEMENT INSTITUTE (US) **815**

UPDATE CENTRAL AMERICA / INTER-RELIGIOUS TASK FORCE ON CENTRAL AMERICA (US) [20589465] **5007**

UPDATE (CENTRAL AMERICAN HISTORICAL INSTITUTE) *See* ENVIO **2732**

UPDATE - CHINOOK REGIONAL LIBRARY (CN/0828-7694) [12168371] **3255**

UPDATE / CONGRESSIONAL CAUCUS FOR WOMEN'S ISSUES (US) [11394601] 5567, **4692**

UPDATE (EASTER SEAL SOCIETY (ONTARIO) (CN/0845-1338) [20494235] **4394**

UPDATE (ELIZABETHTOWN, PA.) (US/0741-4587) [10155061] **39**

UPDATE ..., ENERGY ACTIVITIES, PROVINCE OF PRINCE EDWARD ISLAND (CN/0828-2544) [11312620] **1959**

UPDATE (EVANGELICAL WOMEN'S CAUCUS) (US) [12605419] **5007**

UPDATE - FEDERAL RESERVE BANK OF ATLANTA (US) [05458810] **815**

UPDATE - FOOD AND DRUG LAW INSTITUTE (US) 2360, **3070**

UPDATE, GCLC (US/0743-9652) [07934752] **3255**

UPDATE - GEORGIA ASSOCIATION OF EDUCATORS (US/8750-2283) [10306200] **1789**

UPDATE (HACKENSACK, N.J.) (US/0897-0939) [08526318] **4214**

UPDATE IN INTENSIVE CARE AND EMERGENCY MEDICINE *See* YEARBOOK OF INTENSIVE CARE AND EMERGENCY MEDICINE **3726**

UPDATE IN INTENSIVE CARE AND EMERGENCY MEDICINE (GW/0933-6788) [I09336788] **3649**

UPDATE IN PEDIATRIC DENTISTRY (US/0897-876X) [17653188] **1337**

UPDATE - INTERNATIONAL ASSOCIATION FOR PUBLISHING EDUCATION (CN/1180-3401) [24256739] **4820**

UPDATE - INTERNATIONAL COUNCIL FOR COMPUTERS IN EDUCATION (U.S.) (US/1040-4694) [18425559] **1225**

UPDATE / INTERPRETATION CANADA (CN/0715-3392) [09145967] 2183, **1789**

UPDATE (LIBRARY OF CONGRESS. NATIONAL LIBRARY SERVICE FOR THE BLIND AND PHYSICALLY HANDICAPPED) (US/0160-9203) [07329657] **3255**

UPDATE (LONDON. 1984) (UK/0266-7053) [I02667053] **753**

UPDATE, MARKET FORECAST, ELECTRIC ENERGY REQUIREMENTS IN THE NORTHWEST TERRITORIES (CN/0715-3740) [09157090] **1959**

UPDATE, MARKET FORECAST, ELECTRIC ENERGY REQUIREMENTS IN YUKON (CN/0821-056X) [09816212] **4762**

UPDATE - NATIONAL ASSOCIATION OF CANADIANS OF ORIGIN IN INDIA (CN/0828-5799) [12030751] **2764**

UPDATE (NATIONAL INDIAN COUNCIL ON AGING) *See* ELDER VOICES **2260**

UPDATE - NATIONAL INSTITUTE OF DYSLEXIA (U.S.) (US/0896-2669) [16991867] **1886**

UPDATE NICARAGUA (US) [04577713] **2512**

UPDATE! / NORTHWEST POWER PLANNING COUNCIL (US) [11668627] **1959**

UPDATE ON LAW-RELATED EDUCATION (US/0147-8648) [03023254] 1789, **3070**

UPDATE ON STATE LEGISLATION (US/0739-4004) [09729408] **3070**

UPDATE - ONTARIO TRUCKING ASSOCIATION (CN/0841-2472) [20136157] **5399**

UPDATE / SASKATCHEWAN ROUND TABLE ON ENVIRONMENT AND ECONOMY (CN/1185-3999) [24623956] 1525, **2183**

UPDATE (SMITHSONIAN INSTITUTION. TRAVELING EXHIBITION SERVICE) (US/0272-0345) [04968722] **4097**

UPDATE - SOCIAL SCIENCE FEDERATION OF CANADA (CN/1187-3043) [25589846] **5225**

UPDATE / SOCIAL SCIENCE FEDERATION OF CANADA (CN/1187-3043) [25589845] **5225**

UPDATE (SOCIETY OF AMERICAN TRAVEL WRITERS) *See* TRAVELWRITER MARKETLETTER **2925**

UPDATE TO THE ... CATALOG OF FEDERAL DOMESTIC ASSISTANCE (US) [02246467] **1587**

UPDATE TO THE OKLAHOMA DEVELOPMENT PLAN FOR THE OZARKS REGIONAL COMMISSION (US/0276-7015) [06172564] **1630**

UPDATE TO THE STATE OF OKLAHOMA DEVELOPMENT PLAN FOR THE OZARKS REGIONAL COMMISSION *See* UPDATE TO THE OKLAHOMA DEVELOPMENT PLAN FOR THE OZARKS REGIONAL COMMISSION **1630**

UPDATE (UKRAINIAN MUSEUM OF CANADA (SASKATOON, SASK.)) (CN/0821-5235) [09692564] **4097**

UPDATE - UNITED STATES. OFFICE OF CONVERTER REACTOR DEVELOPMENT (US/0741-9244) [10214461] **2159**

UPDATE - UNIVERSITY OF SOUTH CAROLINA. DEPT. OF MUSIC (US/8755-1233) [09087320] 1789, **4157**

UPDATE USA (UK) **1630**

UPDATE USSR (US/0884-6227) [12403912] **4499**

UPDATE (WASHINGTON, D.C. 1976) (US/0276-8909) [05023771] **4692**

UPDATE : WEEKLY DEVELOPMENTS AND INVESTMENT INSIGHTS (CN) **918**

UPDATE (WILMINGTON, N.C.) (US/0731-4809) [07608143] **5038**

UPDATE - WOMEN IN COMMUNICATIONS, INC. BOSTON PROFESSIONAL CHAPTER (US/0893-3308) [15498493] 5567, **1123**

UPDATED ECONOMICS (AT/0810-3011) [I08103011] **1525**

UPDATED OHIO EXPENDITURES (US) [11242451] **4757**

UPDATED WISCONSIN SCHOOL LAWS (US) 1789, **3070**

●UPDATES AND INFORMATION ALERTS USTTA (US) **5498**

UPDATES AND SUPPLEMENTS TO ACCOMPANY WEST'S FEDERAL TAXATION (US/0275-1119) [07088033] **4757**

UPEC *See* UPEC **2925**

UPEC (CU) [02167543] **2925**

UPHOLSTERY DESIGN & MANUFACTURING (US/1056-2052) [23586332] 2907, **3489**

UPHOLSTERY MANUFACTURING (US/0896-5935) [17209317] **2907**

●UPLINE (CHARLOTTESVILLE, VA.) (US/1062-5062) [25645568] 889, **717**

UPLINK DIRECTORY (US) [14191533] **1168**

●UPMC FORUM / UNIVERSITY OF PITTSBURGH MEDICAL CENTER (US) [26177286] **3793**

UPORIADOCHENNYE MNOZHESTVA I RESHETKI (RU) [02243248] **3540**

UPPER ARLINGTON NEWS, THE (US/0194-2131) [05361294] **5731**

UPPER CANADIAN, THE (CN/0711-0081) [08260743] **252**

Alphabetical Title Index — URGENT

UPPER CERVICAL MONOGRAPH, THE (US/0364-1953) [02555408] **4382**

UPPER COUNTY NEWS-REPORTER, THE (US) [18868297] **5657**

UPPER CUMBERLAND DEVELOPMENT DISTRICT *See* AREAWIDE ACTION PLAN OF THE UPPER CUMBERLAND DEVELOPMENT DISTRICT **2815**

UPPER MIDWEST REPORT (US/0732-3115) [07691489] **717**

UPPER OHIO VALLEY HISTORICAL REVIEW / [WHEELING AREA HISTORICAL SOCIETY] (US) [07789690] **2764**

UPPER PENINSULA CATHOLIC, THE (US/0747-1440) [10577471] **5038**

UPPER ROOM, THE (US/0042-0735) [01643904] **5007**

UPPER SHORE GENEALOGICAL SOCIETY OF MARYLAND *See* MEMBERSHIP SURNAME LIST **2460**

UPPER TEXAS COAST REPORT (US/0148-2157) [03283072] **4281**

UPPSALA RESEARCH REPORTS IN CULTURAL ANTHROPOLOGY (SW/0348-9507) [15061291] **247**

UPPSALA STUDIES IN CULTURAL ANTHROPOLOGY (SW/0348-5099) [06519928] **247**

UPPSALA UNIVERSITET. NATURGEOGRAFISKA INSTITUTIONEN *See* UNGI RAPPORT **2578**

UPPSALA UNIVERSITY, INSTITUTE OF PHYSICS (SW/0348-677X) [I0348677X] **4424**

UPPSATSER - SVERIGESLANTBRUKSUNIVERSITET, INSTITUTIONEN FOR VIRKESLARA (SW/0349-8913) [I03498913] **2397**

UPRAVLENIE I NAUCHNO-TEKHNICHESKII PROGRESS (RU/0207-6756) [10360976] **5168**

UPRAVLJAJUSCIE SISTEMY I MASINY (KIEV, 1972) (UN/0130-5395) [01791274] **1262**

UPSALA JOURNAL OF MEDICAL SCIENCES (SW/0300-9734) [01777665] **3649**

UPSALA JOURNAL OF MEDICAL SCIENCES. SUPPLEMENT (SW/0300-9726) [01639040] **3649**

UPSCALE (ATLANTA, GA.) (US/1047-2592) [20666515] **2274**

UPSHAW FAMILY JOURNAL, THE (US/0098-8960) [02241901] **435, 2476**

UPSIDE (U.S. ED.) (US/1052-0341) [22169788] **717, 1239**

● UPSIDEDOWN (WOBURN, MASS.) (US/1060-8583) [25079520] **5007**

UPSOUTH (BOWLING GREEN, KY.) (US/1069-8051) [28159798] **3449**

UPSTART CROW, THE (US/0886-2168) [06732013] **3449**

UPSTATE NEW YORK DIRECTORY OF MANUFACTURERS (US/0732-2860) [08143372] **3489**

UPTIME (APPLE II) *CEASED.* (US/0884-5646) [13034355] **1206**

UPTIME (APPLE IIGS) (US/0899-2010) [18030296] **1206**

UPTIME (COMMODORE C64 AND 128) (US/0895-8688) [16834940] **1206**

UPTIME FOR THE PC *CEASED.* (US/0894-7074) [16170932] **1206**

UPTIME (MACINTOSH) *CEASED.* (US/0895-867X) [15431971] **1206**

UPTOWN SAN DIEGO EXAMINER (US/0898-4581) [17819246] **5641**

UQACTUALITE (CN/0229-0871) [08071153] **1853**

UQAR-INFORMATION (CN/0711-2254) [08767170] **1853**

URADNI LIST REPUBLIKE SLOVENIJE (XV) [25426387] **3070**

URAL (RU) [02148832] **2524**

URAL-ALTAISCHE JAHRBUCHER (GW/0042-0786) [05057294] **3331**

URAL-ALTAISCHE JAHRBUCHER NEUE FOLGE (GW/0174-0652) [I01740652] **3331**

URAL-ALTAISCHE JAHRBUCHER (WIESBADEN, GERMANY : 1981) (GW/0042-0786) [08445696] **3331**

URANIA (IT) **3472**

URANIA (PL/0042-0794) [07865450] **401**

URANIUM AND NUCLEAR ENERGY (UK/0265-430X) [09966535] **1960**

URANIUM ENRICHMENT SERVICES ACTIVITY : FINANCIAL STATEMENTS (US) [05003704] **1630**

URANIUM INDUSTRY ANNUAL (US) [12884255] **2152**

URANIUM INSTITUTE. INTERNATIONAL SYMPOSIUM *See* URANIUM AND NUCLEAR ENERGY **1960**

URANIUM MILL TAILINGS MANAGEMENT (US/0742-8502) [07080541] **2245, 2152**

URANIUM NEWSLETTER (AU/1011-2693) [I10112693] **995**

URANIUM RESOURCES, PRODUCTION, AND DEMAND : A JOINT REPORT / BY THE EUROPEAN NUCLEAR ENERGY AGENCY AND THE INTERNATIONAL ATOMIC ENERGY AGENCY (FR) [04153064] **1630**

URANJA *See* URANIA **401**

URBA (CN/0709-9444) [06284857] **4692**

URBAN ABSTRACTS (UK/0305-103X) [05702575] **2837**

URBAN ACADEMIC LIBRARIAN (US/0276-9298) [07466485] **3255**

URBAN AFFAIRS ABSTRACTS (US/0300-6859) [01794508] **4692, 4701**

URBAN AFFAIRS ANNUAL REVIEWS (US/0083-4688) [01223662] **5265**

URBAN AFFAIRS QUARTERLY (US/0042-0816) [01768857] **2837**

● URBAN AGE, THE (US) [28694592] **2837**

URBAN AMERICA (US/0146-0544) [02851453] **2837**

URBAN AND REGIONAL INFORMATION SYSTEMS ASSOCIATION *See* URISA MEMBERSHIP DIRECTORY **2838**

URBAN AND REGIONAL RESEARCH IN CANADA (CN/0708-3823) [05133164] **2837**

URBAN AND REGIONAL STUDIES (UK/0067-8961) [01542581] **2837**

URBAN & REGIONAL TECHNOLOGY & DEVELOPMENT *See* NTIS ALERT. URBAN & REGIONAL TECHNOLOGY & DEVELOPMENT **2829**

URBAN ANTHROPOLOGY AND STUDIES OF CULTURAL SYSTEMS AND WORLD ECONOMIC DEVELOPMENT (US/0894-6019) [15079109] **247**

URBAN AREAS OF WASHINGTON (US/0360-4403) [02240774] **2578**

URBAN CANADA (SELECTED PUBLICATIONS) (CN/0709-4140) [05763333] **2837**

URBAN CENTRE, THE (CN/1187-6212) [25467759] **4692**

URBAN DESIGN & PRESERVATION QUARTERLY (US/0898-5049) [17403384] **2837**

URBAN DESIGN FORUM (UK/0141-6979) [05128910] **2837**

URBAN DESIGN UPDATE: NEWSLETTER OF THE INSTITUTE FOR URBAN DESIGN (US/0895-8076) [13120089] **2837**

URBAN DEVELOPMENT DEPARTMENT TECHNICAL PAPER (US/0253-3324) [08515720] **2837**

URBAN EDGE (ENGLISH ED.), THE (US/0163-6510) [04517656] **2837**

URBAN EDGE (ENGLISH EDITION) *See* URBAN AGE, THE **2837**

URBAN EDUCATION (BEVERLY HILLS, CALIF.) (US/0042-0859) [01768861] **1789**

URBAN ENVIRONMENT STUDY; PUBLICATION (US/0417-1233) [04841178] **2183**

● URBAN FOCUS LONDON (UK/0967-4764) [I09674764] **2714**

URBAN FORESTS (US/1052-2484) [22152255] **2397**

URBAN GEOGRAPHY (US/0272-3638) [06481550] **5225, 2578**

URBAN HEALTH *See* URBAN PRACTICE **4806**

● URBAN HISTORY (UK/0963-9268) [26451933] **2838**

URBAN HISTORY REVIEW (CN/0703-0428) [01787360] **2764**

URBAN HISTORY YEARBOOK *See* URBAN HISTORY **2838**

URBAN INDIA (II/0970-9045) [08686994] **2838**

URBAN INITIATIVES ANTI-CRIME PROGRAM (U.S.) *See* ANNUAL REPORT TO CONGRESS - URBAN INITIATIVES ANTI-CRIME PROGRAM **3157**

URBAN INSTITUTE *See* ANNUAL REPORT / THE URBAN INSTITUTE **5191**

● URBAN ISSUES IN SOCIAL WORK (US/1065-822X) [26755436] **5313**

URBAN LAND (US/0042-0891) [01715499] **2838**

URBAN LAND INSTITUTE *See* PROJECT REFERENCE FILE **624**

URBAN LAND RESEARCH FOUNDATION *See* ULRF REPORTS **2837**

URBAN LANGUAGE SERIES (US/0566-8824) [01543207] **3331**

URBAN LAWYER, THE (US/0042-0905) [01768868] **2838, 3070**

URBAN LEAGUE REVIEW, THE *CEASED.* (US/0147-1740) [01578055] **2274**

URBAN LIBRARIES COUNCIL NEWSLETTER : ULC EXCHANGE (US) **3255**

● URBAN MANAGEMENT PROGRAM (US) [26595414] **2838**

URBAN MISSION (US/1056-7216) [09902822] **5007**

URBAN NETWORK (US) **4157**

URBAN OUTLOOK (US/0732-8265) [08445335] **2838**

URBAN PLANNING QUARTERLY (US/0095-1528) [03201229] **2838**

URBAN POLICY AND RESEARCH (AT/0811-1146) [12259400] **2838**

URBAN PRACTICE (US) **4806**

URBAN REAL ESTATE MARKET IN NEW ZEALAND (NZ) [05526170] **4848**

URBAN RENEWAL PROGRESS REPORT (US/0529-0740) [03109406] **2838**

URBAN RENEWAL SERIES - DETROIT. CITY PLAN COMMISSION (US/0417-1152) [04819017] **2838**

● URBAN REPORT (WASHINGTON, D.C.), THE (US/1062-2292) [25562720] **2838**

URBAN RESEARCH REVIEW (US/0732-7277) [08407813] **2838**

URBAN REVIEW, THE (US/0042-0972) [01768869] **1789**

URBAN RING EDITION (US) **3091**

URBAN SERIES MAP (NZ/0110-8719) [08234616] **1400**

URBAN SOCIETY (US/0735-2425) [08768996] **5265**

URBAN, STATE AND LOCAL LAW NEWSLETTER (US/0195-7686) [05021031] **4692, 3070**

URBAN STREET ENVIRONMENT, THE (UK/0966-1743) [I09661743] **5446**

URBAN TRANSIT FACTS IN CANADA (CN/0821-2996) [11046519] **5399**

URBAN TRANSPORT INTERNATIONAL (UK/0953-7139) [I09537139] **5399**

URBAN TRANSPORT NEWS (US/0195-4695) [05459816] **5399**

URBAN TRANSPORTATION ABSTRACTS *See* TRANSIT RESEARCH ABSTRACTS (1992) **5395**

URBAN TRANSPORTATION MONITOR, THE (US/1040-4880) [18353617] **5399**

URBAN TRANSPORTATION OFFICIALS (US/0278-7253) [07488250] **5399**

URBAN WEST (US/0042-0999) [02269007] **2548**

URBAN WILDLIFE MANAGER'S NOTEBOOK (US/0882-584X) [11885524] **2208**

URBAN WILDLIFE NEWS (US/0882-5858) [11885575] **2208, 2222**

URBANA DAILY CITIZEN (URBANA, OHIO : 1910) (US) [17246812] **5731**

● URBANISME (FR/1240-0874) [26862549] **2838**

URBANISMES & ARCHITECTURE (FR/1145-5187) [20768882] **2838**

URBANISMO / COAM (SP/0213-9391) [16171177] **2838**

URBANISMO REVISTA *SUSPENDED.* (SP/0213-1110) [12987120] **2838**

URBANISMUS A UZEMNI PLANOVANI (XR) [02291708] **2838**

URBANISTICA *SUSPENDED.* (IT/0042-1022) [01768871] **2838**

URBANISTICA INFORMAZIONI (IT/0392-5005) [01543921] **2838**

URBANISTICAIPOTESI (IT) [02480833] **2838**

URBE (ROME, ITALY) *SUSPENDED.* (IT) [09004443] **2714**

URDU (PK) [01588431] **3449, 3331**

URDU NAMAH (PK/0042-1065) [02155240] **3449**

URETHANE ABSTRACTS (US/0149-1342) [03440418] **4460**

URETHANE PLASTICS AND PRODUCTS (US/0049-5700) [02451334] **5168**

URETHANES TECHNOLOGY (UK/0265-637X) [17428005] **4460**

URGELLIA / SOCIETAT CULTURAL URGELITANA (SP) [06777604] **2714**

URGENCES *See* TANGENCE **3444**

URGENCES MEDICALES (PARIS) (FR/0923-2524) [25292510] **3649**

URGENCIAS (SP) **3649**

URGENT ACTION BULLETIN (UK) [15686682] **4513**

URGENT — Alphabetical Title Index

URGENT ACTION BULLETIN. ECUADOR (US) [20411542] **4513**

URGENT ACTION BULLETIN. MALAYSIA (US) [20411613] **4513**

URI SASANG (KO) [25474916] **1716**

URISA MEMBERSHIP DIRECTORY (US/0898-7661) [15864122] **2838**

URISA NEWS (1982) (US/0749-9531) [09244413] **3255**

URIZEN (AG) [04327739] **367**

URJA (II/0378-9535) [03469661] 1361, **1960**

URJA OIL AND GAS INTERNATIONAL (II/0971-2038) [I09712038] **4281**

URNER BARRY'S MEAT & POULTRY DIRECTORY (US/0738-6745) [09652562] **223**

URNER BARRY'S PRICE-CURRENT (US/0273-9992) [07058647] 199, **223**

URNER BARRY'S PRICE-CURRENT. WEST COAST EDITION (US/0273-5016) [07062875] **143**

UROBOROS (US/0146-8510) [03030475] **3472**

URODA (XR/0139-6013) [I01396013] **190**

URODA WYD. POLSKIE (PL/0500-7194) [I05007194] **5567**

UROLOGE. AUSG. A, DER (GW/0340-2592) [01768873] **3993**

UROLOGE. AUSGABE B (GW/0042-1111) [01768874] **3993**

UROLOGIA (IT/0391-5603) [01695755] **3993**

UROLOGIA INTERNATIONALIS (SZ/0042-1138) [01768875] **3993**

UROLOGIA POLSKA (PL/0500-7208) [10051017] **3993**

UROLOGIC CLINICS OF NORTH AMERICA, THE (US/0094-0143) [00944385] **3993**

UROLOGIC NURSING (US/1053-816X) [19093045] 3994, **3870**

UROLOGIC RADIOLOGY (US/0171-1091) [04853185] 3947, **3994**

UROLOGIC SURGERY (MT. KISCO) (US/0193-8568) [05267024] **3977**

UROLOGICAL RESEARCH (GW/0300-5623) [01545107] **3994**

UROLOGIJA I NEFROLOGIJA (RU/0042-1154) [02451336] **3994**

UROLOGY ANNUAL (US/0889-6283) [13979206] **3994**

UROLOGY (GLENDALE, CALIF.) (US/0271-1338) [05735681] **3994**

UROLOGY (RIDGEWOOD, N.J.) (US/0090-4295) [01785123] **3994**

UROLOGY TIMES (US/0093-9722) [00937310] **3994**

URPE (US/0743-1694) [01767975] **1525**

URSS OGGI *CEASED*. (IT) [07097249] **2632**

URSUS (US) [23297246] 2208, **2222**

URUGUAY *See* LEYES PROMULGADAS **3002**

URUGUAY. ADMINISTRACION DE LAS OBRAS SANITARIAS DEL ESTADO *See* ESTADISTICA - OSE **5533**

URUGUAY. DIRECCION DE INVESTIGACIONES ECONOMICAS AGROPECUARIAS *See* PRECIOS DE PRODUCTOS E INSUMOS AGROPECUARIOS **121**

URUGUAY: ENERGIEWIRTSCHAFT (GW) [05064312] **1960**

URUGUAY, ENTWICKLUNG DER LANDWIRTSCHAFT / BUNDESSTELLE FUR AUSSENHANDELSINFORMATION (GW) [09345626] **143**

URUGUAY NEWS (US) [04459850] **2764**

URUGUAY. SERVICIO DE OCEANOGRAFIA, HIDROGRAFIA Y METEOROLOGIA *See* AVISOS A LOS NAVEGANTES **4175**

URUGUAY, WIRTSCHAFTSDATEN UND WIRTSCHAFTSDOKUMENTATION / BUNDESSTELLE FUR AUSSENHANDELSINFORMATION (GW) [09047681] **1588**

URWAH AL-WUTHQA (GENEVA, SWITZERLAND) (SZ) [11567447] **5045**

URZAD PATENTOWY POLSKIEJ RZECZYPOSPOLITEJ LUDOWEJ *See* WYKAZ PATENTOW NA WYNALAZKI UDZIELONYCH PRZEZ URZAD PATENTOWY PRL W ROKU ... **1310**

US (US/0090-158X) [01784774] **2548**

US 1 WORKSH (US/0362-7012) [02319798] **3449**

US AIR FORCE PLAN FOR DEFENSE RESEARCH SCIENCES (US/8756-5064) [10387838] **4060**

US ARCHER, THE (US/0738-9949) [09692601] **4927**

US BANKER (US) **815**

US BLACK ENGINEER (US/1058-2428) [13740914] 2000, **2274**

US CHAMBER WATCH (US) **4692**

US-CHINA REVIEW (US/0164-3886) [04698641] **4537**

US-CHINA TRADE STATISTICS (US/0732-8478) [08447756] 856, **735**

US CONGRESS DIRECTORY *See* CAPITOL ADVANTAGE **4636**

US DEPARTMENT OF STATE DISPATCH (US/1051-7693) [22105966] **4692**

US FIRE SPRINKLER REPORTER (US/0889-6038) [13990201] **2293**

US HISTORY ON CD-ROM (US) **2764**

US MAGAZINE (US/0362-4587) [02286859] **4060**

US MASTER TAX GUIDE (US/0083-1700) [06033567] **4757**

US MERGER YEARBOOK *See* MERGER YEARBOOK, THE **693**

... US MERGER YEARBOOK, THE (US) [25704461] **717**

US (NEW YORK, N.Y. 1985) (US/0147-510X) [12819655] **2548**

US PARISH (US) **5007**

US SUPREME COURT PETITIONS & BRIEFS. TAX LAW SERIES (US) 3143, **3070**

US SWIMMING NEWS *CEASED*. (US/0883-0347) [12047738] **4927**

US WURK (NE/0042-1235) [02158171] 3449, **3331**

US2U AMERICAN TECHNOLOGY REPORTER (US/1055-3436) [23157471] **5168**

USA (US) [02240773] **2764**

USA AND CANADA (UK/0956-0904) [20866345] **2578**

●USA COUNTIES [COMPUTER FILE] (US) [26605381] **2578**

USA : ENERGIEWIRTSCHAFT (GW) [04263139] **1960**

USA FACTS (US/1185-2488) [22942514] **5345**

USA FINANCIAL NEWS (US/0899-5524) [18130936] **815**

USA GYMNASTICS (US/0748-6006) [10812620] **4928**

USA-JAPAN COMPUTER CONFERENCE *See* PROCEEDINGS - USA-JAPAN COMPUTER CONFERENCE **1200**

USA KARATE FEDERATION RULES & REGULATIONS (US) **4928**

USA NEWS CATEGORY A; MAKE-UP FACE TREATMENT (FR) **406**

USA NEWS CATEGORY C, FRAGRANCES AND MENS LINES (FR) **406**

USA OUTDOORS (US/0883-6841) [12193347] 4928, **4880**

USA POLONIA (US/0199-6886) [04923273] **5722**

USA STATE FACTBOOK. CD-ROM (US) **5345**

USA TODAY (ARLINGTON, VA.) (US/0734-7456) [08799626] **5687**

●USA TODAY BASEBALL WEEKLY (US/1057-9532) [23450290] **4928**

●USA TODAY BASEBALL WEEKLY ALMANAC (US) [25363646] **4928**

USA TODAY (INTERNATIONAL ED.) (US/1745-7405) [22104222] **5722**

USA TODAY (NEW YORK, N.Y.) (US/0161-7389) [04014217] **2548**

USA VOLLEYBALL REVIEW (US) [02387135] **4928**

USA WARS: CIVIL WAR. CD-ROM (US) 2764, **4499**

USA WARS: KOREA. CD-ROM (US) **4060**

USA WARS: VIETNAM. CD-ROM (US) **4060**

USA: WIRTSCHAFT IN ZAHLEN (GW) [06267107] **1588**

USA : WIRTSCHAFTLICHE ENTWICKLUNG DER SUDOSTSTAATEN (GW) [04991274] **1588**

USA, WIRTSCHAFTLICHE ENTWICKLUNG DES BUNDESSTAATES KALIFORNIEN / UBERREICHT VON DER BUNDESSTELLE FUR AUSSENHANDELSINFORMATION (GW) [07949046] **1588**

USA, WIRTSCHAFTSPOLITIK UND -ENTWICKLUNG (GW) [01798761] **1588**

USAE (US/0894-8194) [16262228] **5687**

USAF FIGHTER WEAPONS REVIEW (US/0274-6824) [05166571] **4060**

USAF MEDICAL SERVICE DIGEST / UNITED STATES AIR FORCE (US) [14144939] **3649**

USAF WEAPONS REVIEW (US) 4060, **39**

USB MOLECULAR BIOLOGY REAGENTS/PROTOCOLS (US/1062-0370) [24873794] **475**

USBE (US/0733-1916) [08542489] **427**

USBE NEWS (US/0364-5215) [02639081] **3255**

USC COUNTRY PROFILE. INDONESIA (CN/1184-0692) [23598249] **2912**

USC COUNTRY PROFILE. LESOTHO (CN/1184-0757) [23598240] **2912**

USC COUNTRY PROFILE. MALI (CN/1184-0730) [23598230] **2912**

USC COUNTRY PROFILE. NEPAL (CN/1184-0722) [23598234] **2912**

USC COUNTRY PROFILE. SWAZILAND (CN/1184-0714) [23598561] **2912**

USC/FAR CONSOLIDATED PLAN FOR FOREIGN AFFAIRS RESEARCH (US/0093-7517) [01792228] **4537**

USC TROJAN FAMILY (US/8750-7927) [11778820] **1096**

USCSAR REPORTS / THE UNITED STATES CENTER FOR SOVIET-AMERICAN RELATIONS (US/1059-4604) [24600230] **4537**

USCTA NEWS (US/0744-0103) [07981641] **2803**

USDA FOREST SERVICE RESEARCH PAPER PSW *See* RESEARCH PAPER PSW **2393**

USDA FOREST SERVICE RESOURCE BULLETIN SE *See* FOREST SERVICE RESOURCE BULLETIN SE **2381**

USDAW TODAY : THE VOICE OF THE UNION OF SHOP, DISTRIBUTIVE AND ALLIED WORKERS (UK) [22226963] **1716**

USDC APPROVED LIST OF FISH ESTABLISHMENTS AND PRODUCTS (US/0278-9345) [07902743] 2360, **2315**

USDF BULLETIN (US/0882-5130) [11874941] **2803**

USDF CALENDAR OF COMPETITIONS (US/0882-5009) [11875355] 4928, **2803**

USDF DRESSAGE INSTRUCTORS, CLINICIANS, TRAINERS, JUDGES, TECHNICAL DELEGATES DIRECTORY (US/0882-4991) [11876087] **2803**

USE OF ENGLISH, THE (UK/0042-1243) [01715601] **1789**

●USED 4 X 4 BUYER'S GUIDE (US/1059-5775) [24639094] **5427**

USED CAR BOOK (NEW YORK, N.Y.), THE (US/0895-3899) [16619727] **5427**

USED CAR DEALER, THE (US/0279-425X) [07855546] **5427**

USED CARS INSIDER (US/1053-2552) [22496139] **5427**

USED CARS TODAY (US/0890-2291) [14177653] **5427**

USED COMPUTER GUIDE (US/0742-6089) [10386227] **1239**

USEFUL PLANTS OF WEST TROPICAL AFRICA, THE (UK) **529**

USER MODELING AND USER-ADAPTED INTERACTION (NE/0924-1868) [24925508] **1206**

USER'S GUIDE TO ARTICLE 80, A (US/1056-7135) [23819808] 2245, **2293**

USER'S GUIDE TO COMPUTER CONTRACTING (US) **1206**

USGA GOLF JOURNAL *See* GOLF JOURNAL **4896**

USGA GREEN SECTION RECORD (US/0041-5502) [02241780] **4928**

USGF TECHNICAL JOURNAL *See* TECHNIQUE (INDIANAPOLIS, IND.) **4925**

USINE NOUVELLE (FR/0042-126X) [02451392] **1588**

USINES NOUVELLE TECHNIQUE ET TECHNICIENS (FR) **3489**

USM CA RESEARCH JOURNAL, THE (PH) [24932063] **143**

USMED : ULTRASUONI IN MEDICINA (IT) **3649**

USO DE FERTILIZANTES EN LOS DISTRITOS DE RIEGO, EL (MX) [06496090] **143**

USP DI. ADVICE FOR THE PATIENT (US/0740-6916) [09594982] **4331**

USP DI. APPROVED DRUG PRODUCTS AND LEGAL REQUIREMENTS (US/1045-8298) [19491595] **4332**

USP DI. DRUG INFORMATION FOR THE HEALTH CARE PROVIDER (US/0740-4174) [08796116] **4332**

USP DI; UNITED STATES PHARMACOPOEIA DISPENSING INFORMATION (US) [06656579] **4332**

USP DI/UPDATE *CEASED*. (US/0730-1324) [05995439] **4332**

USPEHI BIOLOGICESKOJ HIMII (RU/0130-7371) [10840030] **494**

USPEHI FIZICESKIH NAUK (RU/0042-1294) [01768882] **4424**

USPEHI FIZIOLOGICESKIH NAUK (RU/0301-1798) [10815638] **587**

Alphabetical Title Index — UTAH

USPEHI MATEMATICESKIH NAUK (RU/0042-1316) [01644069] **3540**

USPEHI NA MOLEKULARNATA BIOLOGIA (BU/0205-0625) [12425733] **475**

USPEHI SOVREMENNOJ GENETIKI (RU/0566-3946) [02732256] **552**

USPEKHI KHIMII (RU/0042-1308) [01768883] **995**

USPEKHI MEKHANIKI (PL/0137-3722) [05725437] **4430**

USPEKHI MIKROBIOLOGII (RU/0566-392X) [02731996] **570**

USPEKHI NAUCHNOI FOTOGRAFII (RU) [07317763] **4377**

USPEKHI SOVREMENNOI BIOLOGII (RU/0042-1324) [02732084] **475**

USPEKHI SREDNEAZIATSKOI ARKHEOLOGII (RU/0136-7455) [06912193] **2714**

●USPS PROCUREMENT MANUAL (US) [29410160] **1147**

USQR, UNION SEMINARY QUARTERLY REVIEW (US/0362-1545) [01767984] **5007**

USSEA TAKES UP SPACE *See* SPACE AGE TIMES **35**

USSR AND EASTERN EUROPE SCIENTIFIC ABSTRACTS. BIOMEDICAL AND BEHAVIORAL SCIENCES (US) [02370927] **5168**

USSR AND EASTERN EUROPE SCIENTIFIC ABSTRACTS. CYBERNETICS, COMPUTERS, AND AUTOMATION TECHNOLOGY (US) [01597138] 1221, **1252**

USSR AND EASTERN EUROPE SCIENTIFIC ABSTRACTS. PHYSICS (US) [04212980] **4424**

USSR AND THIRD WORLD (UK/0041-5545) [01495254] **4537**

USSR BUSINESS GUIDE & DIRECTORY (RU/1055-5692) [22950371] **856**

USSR DOCUMENTS ANNUAL (US/1051-3507) [21194324] **2509**

USSR ECONOMY AND TRADE GUIDE (HK) **1641**

USSR FACTS & FIGURES ANNUAL (US/0148-7760) [03367764] **5345**

USSR : HARD CURRENCY TRADE AND PAYMENTS (US/0148-2696) [03279525] **856**

USSR IN FIGURES FOR ... / CENTRAL STATISTICAL BOARD, THE COUNCIL OF MINISTERS OF THE USSR, THE (RU) [04479409] **1588**

USSR JOURNAL OF THEORETICAL AND APPLIED MECHANICS *CEASED.* (US/1051-8045) [22123481] **2131**

USSR NEWS & INFORMATION DIGEST [COMPUTER FILE] : USSR-D / COMPILED & EDITED BY JOHN B HARLAN (US/1054-6510) [22927626] **2714**

USSR NEWS BRIEF (BE) [06894263] **4514**

USSR REPORT. ENGINEERING AND EQUIPMENT (US) [06186615] **2000**

USSR REPORT. INDUSTRIAL AFFAIRS (US) [05396454] **1630**

USSR REPORT. METEOROLOGY AND HYDROLOGY (US) [05688774] **1418**

USSR SCIENTIFIC ABSTRACTS: MATERIALS SCIENCE AND METALLURGY (US) [01944286] **4023**

USSR (SYRACUSE, N.Y.) *See* RUSSIA (SYRACUSE, N.Y.) **1595**

USSR TECHNOLOGY UPDATE *CEASED.* (US/0892-497X) [15273485] **5168**

UST CUMULATIVE INDEXING SERVICE : CUMULATIVE INDEX TO UNITED STATES TREATIES AND OTHER INTERNATIONAL AGREEMENTS (US) [04861697] **4537**

UST JOURNAL OF GRADUATE RESEARCH (PH) [16918897] **1853**

USTA COLLEGE TENNIS GUIDE / USTA EDUCATION AND RESEARCH CENTER (US) [06951941] **4928**

USTAV SKOLSKYCH INFORMACII BRATISLAVA *See* ZAVERENA SPRAVA ZO SOCIOLOGICKEHO PRIESKUMU UPLATNENIA ABSOLVENTOV POLNOHOSPODARSKYCH SMEROV STUDIA V PRAXI **148**

USTAV VEDECKOTECHNICKYCH INFORMAC PRO ZEMEDELSTVI *See* SBORNIK UVTI. ZAHRADNICTVI **2431**

USTREDNI USTAV GEOLOGICKY (PRAGUE, CZECHOSLOVAKIA) *See* VESTNIK USTEDNIHO USTAVU GEOLOGICKEHO **1401**

USTREDNI VESTNIK CESKE SOCIALISTICKE REPUBLIKY (XR) [04279136] **3070**

USTREDNY VESTNIK SLOVENSKEJ SOCIALISTICKEJ REPUBLIKY (XO) [04280042] **3070**

USUI GIJUTSU SHIRYO (JA/0917-7221) [09177221] **5541**

USYRU NEWS *See* AMERICAN SAILOR **591**

USYSA NETWORK (US) **4928**

UTAFITI (KE) [02620375] **5225**

UTAH ADVANCE REPORTS (US/0897-9227) [11680457] **3070**

UTAH. AGRICULTURAL EXPERIMENT STATION *See* RESEARCH REPORT - AGRICULTURAL EXPERIMENT STATION, UTAH STATE UNIVERSITY **127**

UTAH AGRICULTURAL STATISTICS AND UTAH DEPARTMENT OF AGRICULTURE ANNUAL REPORT (US) [18252872] **143**

UTAH ANNUAL EVALUATION REPORT; TITLE I ESEA (US/0091-3863) [01786513] **1873**

UTAH ARCHAEOLOGY (NEWSLETTER) (US/0500-7860) [06835757] **285**

UTAH BAR JOURNAL (US/0091-9691) [19580496] **3070**

UTAH BAR LETTER. ANNUAL ROSTER OF ACTIVE RESIDENT UTAH ATTORNEYS (US/0145-8558) [02792905] **3070**

UTAH BIG GAME RANGE TREND STUDIES (US/0741-9708) [10015175] 4880, **4928**

UTAH BIRDS : JOURNAL OF THE UTAH ORNITHOLOGICAL SOCIETY (US) [15483366] **5620**

UTAH BLACK BEAR HARVEST (US/0147-2380) [03131214] **2208**

UTAH BUSINESS MAGAZINE (US) **717**

UTAH CASE NAMES CITATOR (US) **3070**

UTAH. CONSTITUTIONAL REVISION COMMISSION *See* REPORT OF THE UTAH CONSTITUTIONAL REVISION COMMISSION **4681**

UTAH. CONSTITUTIONAL REVISION COMMISSION. INTERIM REPORT *See* REPORT OF THE UTAH CONSTITUTIONAL REVISION COMMISSION **4681**

UTAH COUGAR HARVEST (US) [03058305] 4880, **4928**

UTAH COUNCIL FOR HANDICAPPED AND DEVELOPMENTALLY DISABLED PERSONS *See* UTAH DEVELOPMENTAL DISABILITIES STATE PLAN **5313**

UTAH COUNCIL ON VOCATIONAL-TECHNICAL EDUCATION *See* BIENNIAL EVALUATION REPORT **1911**

UTAH COUNTY JOURNAL (US) [13404611] **5757**

UTAH DATA GUIDE : A NEWSLETTER FOR DATA USERS (US) [11927168] **1206**

UTAH. DEPT. OF EMPLOYMENT SECURITY. LABOR MARKET INFORMATION SERVICES SECTION *See* ANNUAL PLANNING INFORMATION FOR FISCAL YEAR ... / LABOR MARKET INFORMATION SERVICES SECTION, UTAH DEPARTMENT OF EMPLOYMENT SECURITY **1646**

UTAH. DEPT. OF EMPLOYMENT SECURITY. RESEARCH AND ANALYSIS SECTION *See* OCCUPATIONAL PATTERNS OF SELECTED NONMANUFACTURING INDUSTRIES IN UTAH **4207**

UTAH. DEPT. OF FINANCE *See* STATE ROAD ANNUAL REPORT **5444**

UTAH. DEPT. OF NATURAL RESOURCES *See* ANNUAL REPORT - UTAH. DEPT. OF NATURAL RESOURCES **4630**

UTAH. DEPT. OF SOCIAL SERVICES. DIVISION OF FAMILY SERVICES *See* FAMILY SERVICES IN UTAH **5285**

UTAH DEVELOPMENTAL DISABILITIES STATE PLAN (US) [04394708] **5313**

UTAH DIRECTORY OF BUSINESS AND INDUSTRY (US/8755-2841) [09917114] **1630**

UTAH. DIVISION OF WILDLIFE RESOURCES *See* UTAH COUGAR HARVEST **4928**

UTAH. DIVISION OF WILDLIFE RESOURCES *See* UTAH BLACK BEAR HARVEST **2208**

UTAH ECONOMIC AND BUSINESS REVIEW (US/0042-1405) [01545853] 717, **1525**

UTAH EDUCATION ASSOCIATION *See* UEA ACTION **1788**

UTAH ENERGY STATISTICAL ABSTRACT (US/8755-7827) [11383408] 1960, **1963**

UTAH EVANGEL, THE (US) [09879295] **5007**

●UTAH FARMER (1993) (US/1071-653X) [28680659] **143**

UTAH FARMER-STOCKMAN (US/1041-1666) [13529460] **143**

UTAH FISHING (US/0897-7283) [17605569] **4880**

UTAH. FORESTRY AND FIRE CONTROL SECTION *See* RC AND D RELEASE **2392**

UTAH GENEALOGICAL ASSOCIATION *See* NEWSLETTER / UTAH GENEALOGICAL ASSOCIATION **2464**

UTAH GEOLOGICAL AND MINERAL SURVEY *See* SURVEY NOTES - UTAH GEOLOGICAL AND MINERAL SURVEY **1399**

●UTAH HEALTH CARE IN PERSPECTIVE (US/1065-4453) [26606825] **4806**

UTAH HISTORICAL QUARTERLY (US/0042-143X) [01713705] **2764**

UTAH HOLIDAY *CEASED.* (US/0739-2311) [09706291] **5498**

UTAH-IDAHO SOUTHERN BAPTIST WITNESS (US/0746-0228) [09674670] **5068**

UTAH IN PERSPECTIVE (US/1065-5727) [26663150] **5345**

UTAH JUDICIAL BRIEFS (US/0147-3581) [03145979] **3070**

UTAH LABOR MARKET REPORT (US) [09983218] **1716**

UTAH LAW REVIEW (US/0042-1448) [01768909] **3070**

UTAH LIBRARIES/NEWS (US) [16882864] **3255**

UTAH. LIQUOR CONTROL COMMISSION *See* ANNUAL REPORT OF THE UTAH LIQUOR CONTROL COMMISSION **4629**

UTAH. LIQUOR CONTROL COMMISSION. REPORT ON OPERATIONS *See* ANNUAL REPORT OF THE UTAH LIQUOR CONTROL COMMISSION **4629**

UTAH MONTHLY LOCAL CLIMATOLOGICAL DATA. MICROFORM (US) [10863320] **1436**

UTAH MUSIC EDUCATOR (US/0502-871X) [03335144] **4157**

UTAH. OFFICE OF PLANNING AND BUDGET *See* STATE OF UTAH BIENNIAL CAPITAL BUDGET ... **4749**

UTAH. OFFICE OF THE STATE COURT ADMINISTRATOR *See* UTAH JUDICIAL BRIEFS **3070**

UTAH PRESERVATION/RESTORATION (US/0888-4331) [07893615] **2764**

UTAH PROSECUTOR, THE (US/0093-7932) [01792565] **3109**

UTAH PUBLIC LIBRARY SERVICE / PREPARED BY THE STATE LIBRARY COMMISSION OF UTAH (US) [03220288] **3255**

UTAH REPORT OF MEDICAID STATISTICS (US/0193-4252) [05182536] 5313, **5267**

UTAH SATE BAR *See* UTAH STATE BAR DIRECTORY **3070**

UTAH SCHOOL DIRECTORY (US) [08595587] **1789**

UTAH SCIENCE (US/0042-1502) [02399156] **143**

UTAH STATE BAR DIRECTORY (US/0737-9277) [08960165] **3070**

UTAH STATE BAR. REAL PROPERTY SECTION *See* REAL PROPERTY SECTION NEWS **3035**

UTAH. STATE BOARD FOR VOCATIONAL EDUCATION *See* UTAH STATE PLAN FOR THE ADMINISTRATION OF VOCATIONAL EDUCATION **1917**

UTAH STATE BOARD FOR VOCATIONAL EDUCATION *See* ANNUAL AND FIVE YEAR UTAH STATE PLAN ... FOR THE ADMINISTRATION OF VOCATIONAL EDUCATION UNDER THE VOCATIONAL EDUCATION AMENDMENTS OF 1976, PUBLIC LAW 94-482 / UTAH STATE BOARD FOR VOCATIONAL EDUCATION **1910**

UTAH. STATE BOARD OF EDUCATION *See* UTAH ANNUAL EVALUATION REPORT; TITLE I ESEA **1873**

UTAH. STATE BOARD OF EDUCATION. DIVISION OF RESEARCH AND DEVELOPMENT *See* CAREER DEVELOPMENT, DROPOUT PREVENTION PROGRAM, EXPERIMENTAL PROGRAMS, TEACHER LEADERSHIP PROGRAM, REGIONAL SERVICE UNITS **1911**

UTAH. STATE BUDGET OFFICE *See* OPERATIONS BUDGET / STATE OF UTAH **4739**

UTAH STATE BULLETIN (US/0882-4738) [11854150] **3070**

UTAH. STATE DIVISION OF HEALTH *See* UTAH STATE PLAN FOR HEALTH SERVICES **4806**

UTAH STATE HISTORICAL SOCIETY NEWSLETTER (US) [10712926] **2764**

UTAH STATE HISTORICAL SOCIETY. NEWSLETTER - UTAH STATE HISTORICAL SOCIETY *See* UTAH STATE HISTORICAL SOCIETY NEWSLETTER **2764**

UTAH — Alphabetical Title Index

UTAH. STATE LIBRARY COMMISSION *See* UTAH PUBLIC LIBRARY SERVICE / PREPARED BY THE STATE LIBRARY COMMISSION OF UTAH **3255**

UTAH STATE PLAN FOR HEALTH SERVICES (US) [02241209] **4806**

UTAH STATE PLAN FOR THE ADMINISTRATION OF VOCATIONAL EDUCATION (US/0090-7162) [01785235] **1917**

UTAH. STATE RETIREMENT OFFICE *See* ANNUAL REPORT ON THE UTAH STATE RETIREMENT SYSTEM, SCHOOL DIVISION TO THE UTAH STATE RETIREMENT BOARD **1649**

UTAH STUDIES IN LITERATURE AND LINGUISTICS (US/0171-726X) [03182072] **3331, 3450**

UTAH SYMPHONY (US/0191-1635) [04790672] **4157**

UTAH SYMPHONY ORCHESTRA *See* UTAH SYMPHONY **4157**

UTAH SYMPHONY ORCHESTRA. UTAH SYMPHONY ORCHESTRA (1968) *See* UTAH SYMPHONY **4157**

UTAH TAXPAYER (US) **4757**

UTAH, THE MORMONS AND THE WEST (US) [01548165] **2548**

UTAH WATER SUPPLY OUTLOOK AND FEDERAL-STATE-PRIVATE COOPERATIVE SNOW SURVEYS (US) [13516949] **1418**

UTAH'S VITAL STATISTICS, BIRTHS ... (US) [17967459] **5345**

UTBILDNINGSSTATISTIK (SW) [02316470] **1789**

UTBLICK LANDSKAP (SW) [I02817462] **4377, 310**

UTD PHILATELIC BULLETIN, THE (US/0732-3670) [08342248] **2788**

UTDANNINGSSTATISTIKK : GRUNNSKOLER (NO) [01798735] **1806**

UTDANNINGSSTATISTIKK : OVERSIKT (NO) [03483921] **1789, 1798**

UTDANNINGSSTATISTIKK : VAKSENOPPLRING (NO) [04212817] **1802**

UTE BULLETIN, THE (US/0300-6808) [01354325] **2274**

UTENRIKSHANDEL (NO) [01221686] **856**

UTENSIL (IT/0392-6567) [09951707] **2131**

UTIAS REPORT (CN/0082-5255) [02247281] **39**

UTIAS TECHNICAL NOTE (CN/0082-5263) [02441527] **39**

UTICA HERALD (UTICA, OHIO : 1878) (US) [11499025] **5731**

UTILISATION DES VEHICULES DE TRANSPORT ROUTIER DE MARCHANDISES EN, L' (FR) [19687866] **5399**

UTILITAS (UK/0953-8208) [20065737] **2253**

UTILITAS MATHEMATICA (CN/0315-3681) [02149601] **1206, 3540**

UTILITIES INDUSTRY LITIGATION REPORTER (US/1053-0258) [21223541] **3070**

UTILITIES LAW REVIEW (UK/0960-2356) [24130476] **4762, 3070**

UTILITIES POLICY (UK/0957-1787) [23479714] **4693**

UTILITY COMMUNICATOR'S EXCHANGE (US/0889-4248) [14047528] **4762**

UTILITY FINANCE (UK/0968-6347) [I09686347] **1630**

●UTILITY FORECASTER, THE (US/1064-5373) [26323338] **4762**

UTILITY GAS INDUSTRY IN JAPAN *See* GAS UTILITY INDUSTRY IN JAPAN **4258**

UTILITY PURCHASING AND STORES *CEASED.* (US/0042-1588) [02451398] **952**

●UTILITY REGULATORY POLICY IN THE UNITED STATES AND CANADA : COMPILATION ... OF THE NATIONAL ASSOCIATION OF REGULATORY UTILITY COMMISSIONERS (US) [26994818] **4693**

UTILITY REPORTER (SCHENECTADY, N.Y.) (US/0890-2984) [14222102] **4762**

UTILITY SPOTLIGHT (US/1065-6480) [26682030] **1525**

UTILITY SUPERVISION (1985) *CEASED.* (US/0883-8402) [12232620] **948**

●UTILITY WORKERS' LIGHT (US) [25809554] **4763**

UTILIZATION OF SHIPBUILDING AND REPAIR FACILITIES SERIES (US) [01785952] **2000, 4185**

UTILIZATION OF SHORT-TERM GENERAL AND SPECIALTY HOSPITALS IN METROPOLITAN CHICAGO FOR THE ... QUARTER OF ... (US/0748-5816) [10439121] **3793**

UTILIZATION OF SHORT-TERM GENERAL AND SPECIALTY HOSPITALS IN METROPOLITAN CHICAGO FOR THE YEAR ENDING DECEMBER 31 ... (US/0882-6943) [11846630] **3793**

UTLAS INFO TRACK (CN/0843-7521) [20141200] **427**

UTLAS NEWSLETTER (1979) (CN/0225-1760) [06511485] **3255**

UTNE READER, THE (US/8750-0256) [10669425] **2549**

UTOPIA 2 (US/0897-4357) [17502274] **5225**

UTOPIAN STUDIES (US/1045-991X) [23121633] **3450, 4548**

UTRECHT MICROPALEONTOLOGICAL BULLETINS (NE/0083-4963) [01768918] **1400, 4231**

UTRECHT MICROPALEONTOLOGICAL BULLETINS. SPECIAL PUBLICATION (NE/0165-2753) [03865751] **4231**

UTRECHT. RIJKSUNIVERSITEIT. GEOGRAFISCH INSTITUUT *See* BULLETIN ALGEMENE SOCIALE GEOGRAFIE. SERIE 1 **1549**

UTRECHT. RIJKSUNIVERSITEIT. GEOGRAFISCH INSTITUUT *See* BULLETIN SOCIALE GEOGRAFIE ONTWIKKELINGSLANDEN; SERIE 2 (UTRECHT) **5241**

UTRECHT. RIJKSUNIVERSITEIT. INSTITUUT VOOR MIZIEKWETENSCHAP *See* UTRECHTSE BIJDRAGEN TOT DE MUZIEKWETENSCHAP **4157**

UTRECHT. RIJKSUNIVERSITEIT. INSTITUUT VOOR OOSTERSE EN SLAVISCHE TALEN *See* DISPUTATIONES RHENO-TRAJECTINAE **3277**

UTRECHTSE BIJDRAGEN TOT DE MUZIEKWETENSCHAP (NE/0566-4632) [01559803] **4157**

UTRECHTSE PUBLIKATIES VOOR ALGEMENE LITERATUURWETENSCHAP (NE/0566-4640) [I05664640] **3450**

UTRIKESHANDEL. MANADSSTATISTIK (SW/0039-7288) [01607867] **856, 1641**

UTRIKESPOLITISKA INSTITUTET (SWEDEN) *See* CURRENT RESEARCH - THE SWEDISH INSTITUTE OF INTERNATIONAL AFFAIRS **4502**

UTRUHAT (TI) [11176980] **2509**

UTSUKUSHII KURASHI NO TECHO *See* KURASHI NO TECHO **1985**

UTSUNOMIYA DAIGAKU. HOKEN KANRI SENTA *See* UTSUNOMIYA DAIGAKU HOKEN KANRI SENTA NEMPO **1908**

UTSUNOMIYA DAIGAKU HOKEN KANRI SENTA NEMPO (JA) [06567414] **1908**

UTSUNOMIYA DAIGAKU. KYOIKU KOGAKU SENTA *See* UTSUNOMIYA DAIGAKU KYOIKUGAKUBU KYOIKU KOGAKU SENTA KIYO **1908**

UTSUNOMIYA DAIGAKU. KYOIKUGAKUBU *See* UTSUNOMIYA DAIGAKU KYOIKUGAKUBU KIYO **1873**

UTSUNOMIYA DAIGAKU KYOIKUGAKUBU KIYO (JA/0385-2415) [02243582] **1873**

UTSUNOMIYA DAIGAKU KYOIKUGAKUBU KYOIKU KOGAKU SENTA KIYO (JA) [06706390] **1908**

UTSUNOMIYA DAIGAKU NOGAKUBU ENSHURIN HOKOKU (JA/0286-8733) [I02868733] **2397**

UTSUNOMIYA DAIGAKU NOGAKUBU GAKUJUTSU HOKOKU (JA/0566-4691) [01604606] **143**

UTSUNOMIYA TABAKO SHIKENJO *See* GYOTEI HOKOKU - NIHON SEMBAI KOSHA UTSUNOMIYA TABAKO SHIKENJO **5373**

UTSYN (NO) [01605890] **5068**

UTTAR PRADESH (INDIA) *See* PASU PALANA PRAGATI **217**

UTTAR PRADESH JOURNAL OF ZOOLOGY (II) [12845617] **5599**

UTTARA PRADESA RAJYA SARAKA PARIVAHANA NIGAMA *See* VARSHIKA KARYA-VIVARANA / UTTARA PRADESA RAJYA SARAKA PARIVAHANA NIGAMA **5399**

UTTARA VARSHIKA (II) [02240198] **3450**

UTTARAKHANDA BHARATI (II) [02239607] **2667**

UTU NEWS (US/0098-5937) [02242159] **1716**

UTU NEWS CANADA (CN/0383-2015) [03202273] **5437, 1716**

UTUNK : ROMANIA SZOCIALISTA KOZTARSASAG IROSZOVETSEGENEK LAPJA (RM) [15502038] **3355**

UTUSAN KONSUMER (MY/0126-950X) [02166701] **1300**

UTUSAN (KUALA LUMPUR, MALAYSIA) (MY) [08150590] **2667**

UURIMUSI (ER) [07047317] **1596**

●UUSI KANSANMUSIIKKI (FI) [25482160] **4157**

UV/EB NEWS (US/0275-3901) [07123237] **4442**

UVALDE LEADER-NEWS (US) [14389774] **5755**

UVRES ET OPINIONS (RU/0473-8675) [02265402] **3450**

UW NOTES (CN/0229-9798) [08311701] **1853**

UWA NDI IGBO (NR/0189-2320) [17598637] **2325, 3450**

UWD UMWELTSCHUTZDIENST (GW) **2183**

UWI STUDENT'S LAW REVIEW (BB) [03323168] **3070**

UWLA LAW REVIEW (US/0899-7446) [09715641] **3070**

UXBRIDGE TIMES-JOURNAL (CN/0834-7336) [16402653] **5796**

UZBEK TILI VA ADABIETI MASALALARI. VOPROSY UZBEKSKOGO IAZYKA I LITERATURY (UZ) [06259911] **3450, 3331**

UZBEK TILI VA ADABIETI / UZBEKISTON SSR FANLAR AKADEMIIASI, A.S. PUSHKIN NOMIDAGI TIL VA ADABIET INSTITUTI (UZ/0134-2258) [02158190] **3450**

UZBEKISTON ADABIETI VA SANATI (TASHKENT, S.S.R. : 1956) (UZ) [14450793] **5813**

UZBEKISTON GEOLOGIIA ZHURNALI *CEASED.* (UZ) [08159886] **1400**

UZBEKISTON GEOLOGIJA ZURNALI (UZ/0042-1693) [06831682] **1400**

●UZBEKISTON RESPUBLIKASI FANLAR AKADEMIIASINING MABRUZALARI (UZ/0134-4307) [26452162] **5168**

UZBEKISTON SSR VAQTLI MATBUOT NASHRLARI SOLNOMASI VA NOTALAR / UZBEKISTON SSR NASHRIET, POLIGRAFIIA VA KITOB SAVDOSI ISHLARI DAVLAT KOMITETI [VA] UZBEKISTON SSR DAVLAT KITOB PALATASI / LETOPIS PERIODICHESKIKH IZDANII I NOT UZBEKSKOI SSR / GOSUDARSTVENNYI KOMITET UZBEKSKOI SSR PO DELAM IZDATELSTV, POLIGRAFII I KNIZHNOI TORGOVLI [I] GOSUDARSTVENNAIA KNIZHNAIA PALATA UZBEKSKOI SSR (RU) [09499229] **427**

UZBEKSKII BIOLOGICHESKII ZHURNAL (UZ/0042-1685) [01512770] **475**

UZBEKSKII KHIMICHESKII ZHURNAL (UZ/0042-1707) [04124868] **995**

V-8 TIMES (US/0274-5003) [06364345] **5427**

V-A-R-D-S REPORT, THE (US) [21264529] **918**

V & A CONSERVATION JOURNAL (UK/0967-2273) [I09672273] **4097**

V B E A NEWSLETTER (US) [01713631] **717, 1789**

V.C.O.S.S. NOTICEBOARD (AT/1031-4997) [I10314997] **5313**

V DNI ZELENYKH SVIAT (US) [02243690] **4060**

V GODINU VELIKOI VOINY *CEASED.* (RU) [19818058] **2632**

V.I.P. ADDRESS BOOK (US/1043-0261) [18438536] **435**

V.I.T.A. NEWSLETTER (WINNIPEG. 1992) (CN/1193-9532) [28061944] **1917**

V.M.E.A. NOTES (US/0733-8562) [01556133] **1908, 4157**

●V.P.I.'S IMPRINTABLES TODAY (US/1064-6868) [26373640] **4570**

V POMOSHCH MASSOVYM BIBLIOTEKAM (RU) [05792454] **3255**

V.S.T (FR/0396-8669) [04769330] **3870, 3937**

V SELSKOM KLUBE (RU) [11975927] **3450**

V2AEST2ONMUUTOKSET *See* VAESTO **4563**

VA EDUCATION LOAN DEFAULTS : ANNUAL REPORT (US/0147-3824) [03126204] **1853**

VA-NYTT (SW/0042-1995) [04124900] **2183**

VA PRACTITIONER (US/0883-5721) [12156042] **3793**

VAAD HA-LASHON HA-IVRIT BE-ERETS YISRAEL. LESHONENU LA-AM *See* LESHONENU LA-AM **3297**

VAAP (RU) [02478385] **427**

VABA EESTI SONA (US/8755-5808) [11356336] **5722**

VABA EESTLANE (CN/0837-0672) [22934978] **2476**

VABA EESTLASE TAHTRAAMAT (CN/0507-6528) [02578379] **2494**

VACACIONES EN CASAS DE LABRANZAS (SP) [05851137] **2809**

Alphabetical Title Index — VALUE

VACANCES POUR TOUS (CN/0831-3067) [14878174] **5498**

VACANT URBAN RESIDENTIAL LAND SURVEY, ... UPDATE (CN/0333-966X) [15716915] **2838**

VACATION & TRAVEL GUIDE (US/0193-9831) [03785078] **5498**

VACATION AND TRAVEL TOUR GUIDEBOOK, THE (US/1059-5996) [22330428] **5498**

●VACATION HOME REPORT (US/1049-6351) [21268370] **4855**

VACATION RENTAL MAGAZINE (US/1059-3845) [24600645] **5498**

VACATION STUDY ABROAD (FR/0083-5048) [00929754] **1789**

VACATION STUDY ABROAD (NEW YORK, N.Y.) (US/1046-2104) [17634895] **5498**

VACATION (TORONTO) (CN/0316-991X) [02247502] **5498**

VACATION TRAVEL BY CANADIANS IN THE UNITED STATES (US/0362-6040) [04800809] **5498**

VACATIONS (HOUSTON, TEX.) (US/0894-9093) [16308453] **5498**

VACATIONS UNLIMITED (US/0896-6559) [17241137] **5498**

VACAVILLE REPORTER (US) [08810877] **5641**

VACCINE (UK/0264-410X) [10399916] **3649**

●VACCINE RESEARCH (US/1056-7909) [23853547] **3677**

●VACCINE WEEKLY (US/1074-2921) **3677**

VACCINES (COLD SPRING HARBOR, N.Y.) (US/0899-4056) [13211262] **3649**

VACHER'S BIOGRAPHICAL GUIDE (UK) [20538533] **435**

VACHER'S EUROPEAN COMPANION & CONSULTANTS' REGISTER (UK/0958-0336) [09580336] **4693**

VACHER'S PARLIAMENTARY COMPANION (UK/0958-0328) [06006523] **4693**

VACUUM (UK/0042-207X) [01465970] **4430**

VACUUM CIRCUITS (US/0747-5063) [10523845] **5399**

VACUUM PHYSICS AND TECHNOLOGY (US/1069-4579) [28050710] **4424**

VAD VI GOR (SW) [10657264] **1300**

VADEMECUM DER INVESTMENTFONDS (GW) [04382596] **918**

VADEMECUM (HERGISWIL (NIEDWALDEN, SWITZERLAND)) (SZ) [11411874] **2838**

VADNAIS HEIGHTS PRESS (US) **5699**

VADO E TORNO (IT/0042-2096) [I00422096] **5399**

VAESTO (FI) [06805484] **4563**

VAESTONMUUTOKSET HELSINGISSA VUOSINA ... (FI) [19903633] **1596**

VAG-OCH VATTEN BYGGAREN (SW/0042-2177) [02933622] **2033**

VAGABONDAGES (FR/0153-9620) [04966139] **3472**

VAGARTHA (NEW DELHI) (II/0970-9916) [01781589] **3450**

VAHDAT : NASHRIYAH-I DAFTAR-I TAHKIM-I VAHDAT (IR) [10153002] **5045**

VAHITTAISKAUPAN TILINPAATOSTILASTO (FI/0784-9109) [19539015] **815**

VAICARIKI (II) [01797814] **3331**

VAIJNANIKA (II) [01790480] **5168**

VAIL TRAIL, THE (US) [11437796] **5644**

VAISSEAU DE PIERRES (FR/0981-6445) [20471676] **310**

VAJRA BODHI SEA (US/0507-6986) [02153961] **5022**

VAJRADHATU SUN, THE (US/0882-0813) [11129249] **5022**

VAKBLAD VOOR DE HANDEL IN AARDAPPELEN, GROENTEN EN FRUIT (NE/0924-7165) [14547117] 856, **190**

VAKBONDSKRANT, DE *CEASED.* (NE) [05699101] **1716**

VAKUUM IN DER PRAXIS (GW/0934-9758) [I09349758] 2000, **4424**

VAL & VE : SOCIALSTYRELSENS TIDNING (SW) [24944379] 4806, **5313**

VALARUM VELANMAI (II) [03321660] **143**

VALDERS JOURNAL, THE (US) [12361999] **5771**

VALDEZ VANGUARD (US) [17375010] **5629**

VALDOSTA DAILY TIMES, THE (US) [21188586] **5655**

VALENCIA COUNTY NEWS-BULLETIN (US/1071-3492) [26394211] **5713**

VALENCIA FRUITS (SP) 1525, **143**

VALENTIANA VALENCIENNES (FR/0989-6139) [09896139] 2714, **285**

VALENZA GIOIELLI (IT) **2915**

VALFARDS BULLETINEN / SCB (SW/0280-1418) [09968090] **5313**

VALIO, FINNISH CO-OPERATIVE DAIRIES' ASSOCIATION : [ANNUAL REPORT] (FI) [27716010] **199**

VALIO (FIRM) *See* VALIO, FINNISH CO-OPERATIVE DAIRIES' ASSOCIATION : [ANNUAL REPORT] **199**

VALIO (FIRM) *See* ANNUAL REPORT / VALIO, FINNISH CO-OPERATIVE DAIRIES' ASSOCIATION **192**

VALIS-EESTLASE KALENDER (US/0503-6291) [05232316] **1929**

VALKANIKA SYMMEIKTA (GR/1105-0136) [10728465] **2714**

VALLADOLID. UNIVERSIDAD. SEMINARIO DE ESTUDIOS DE ARTE Y ARQUEOLOGIA *See* BOLETIN DEL SEMINARIO DE ESTUDIOS DE ARTE Y ARQUEOLOGIA **262**

VALLALATSZERVEZESI ES IPARGAZDASAGI SZAKIRODALMI TAJEKOZTATO (HU/0231-0759) [16904392] **889**

VALLALATVEZETES, VALLALATSZERVEZES (II) [02487282] **1630**

VALLE D'AOSTA, BOLLETTINO ECONOMICO *See* BOLLETTINO ECONOMICO (VALLE D'AOSTA (ITALY). ASSESSORATO INDUSTRIA, COMMERCIO, ARTIGIANATO E TRASPORTI DELLA REGIONE **1549**

VALLEE DES FORTS (CN/0711-7906) [08555945] **5498**

VALLEJO BUSINESS (US/0896-7377) [17281294] **717**

VALLEJO TIMES-HERALD (US) [28492289] **5641**

VALLESIA (SZ) [02158029] **2714**

VALLEY AND FOOTHILLS NEWS *See* VALLEY-FOOTHILLS NEWS, THE **5630**

VALLEY (BURNSTOWN) (CN/1183-1847) [25423199] **2764**

VALLEY CATHOLIC, THE (US/8750-6238) [11595098] **5038**

VALLEY CITY TIMES-RECORD (VALLEY CITY, N.D. : 1964) (US) [20301709] **5726**

VALLEY COURIER (ALAMOSA, COLO.) (US/1047-1170) [14393737] **5644**

VALLEY COURIER (PORT ALBERNI, B.C. : 1988) (CN/0841-6419) [18910357] **5796**

VALLEY DAILY NEWS (US) [22261570] **5762**

VALLEY FALLS VINDICATOR, THE (US) [11910661] **5679**

VALLEY-FOOTHILLS NEWS, THE (US/0745-5321) [09276586] **5630**

VALLEY FORGE JOURNAL, THE (US/0734-5712) [08753099] **2764**

VALLEY GAZETTE, THE (US/1056-4853) [17060531] **5740**

VALLEY HORSE NEWS, THE (US/0744-2394) [08125815] **5704**

VALLEY INDEPENDENT (MONESSEN, PA. : COMBINED ED.) (US) [14251439] **5740**

VALLEY JOURNAL, THE (US/0740-4727) [09934362] **2764**

VALLEY JOURNAL, THE (US) [21656524] **5644**

VALLEY LEAVES (US/0507-6544) [07862840] **2476**

VALLEY : LEBANON VALLEY COLLEGE MAGAZINE, THE (US/0747-3672) [10765799] **1096**

VALLEY MAGAZINE (GRANADA HILLS, CALIF.) (US/8750-1430) [11036050] **1300**

VALLEY MAGAZINE (SELINSGROVE, PA.) (US/1046-0454) [19843458] **5498**

VALLEY MORNING STAR (US) [13042873] **5755**

VALLEY NEWS (US) [12348708] **5709**

VALLEY NEWS (US) [19006440] **5657**

VALLEY NEWS (APPLE VALLEY, CALIF.) (US/0745-6336) [09314604] **5641**

VALLEY NEWS DISPATCH (US) [02269127] **5740**

VALLEY NEWS (ELIZABETHTOWN, N.Y.) (US) [16954860] **5722**

VALLEY NEWS (FULTON, N.Y.), THE (US/1067-7755) [27346511] **5722**

VALLEY NEWS (MONTEBELLO) (CN/0715-4887) [09538861] **5796**

VALLEY POTATO GROWER (US/0889-4787) [11520461] **143**

VALLEY REGISTER, THE (US) [09631950] **5687**

VALLEY REPORTER (CN/0715-321X) [09099824] **5796**

VALLEY REVIEW (PEMBROKE) (CN/0711-4427) [08690337] **5796**

VALLEY SENTINEL (VALEMOUNT) (CN/0845-4183) [20103958] **5797**

VALLEY STAR (ENGLEWOOD, N.J.) (US) [12129872] **5712**

VALLEY SUN (WASILLA), THE (US/0192-8589) [05081188] **5629**

VALLEY TIMES-NEWS, THE (US) [12038379] **5628**

VALLEY TIMES (TIGARD, OR.) (US/8750-0795) [10960455] **5734**

VALLEY TRIBUNE, THE (US) [14766505] **5755**

●VALLEY VOICE (COLD SPRING, N.Y.) (US/1063-7540) [26134312] **2549**

VALMET PAPER NEWS (FI/0784-722X) [I0784722X] **4239**

VALOR (US) [17272290] **4867**

VALORE SCUOLA : AGENZIA STAMPA CGIL (IT) **1873**

VALORES Y SEGUROS / SUPERINTENDENCIA DE VALORES Y SEGUROS (CL) [10081729] **2895**

VALPARAISO (CITY). UNIVERSIDAD CATOLICA *See* ANALES DE LA UNIVERSIDAD CATOLICA DE VALPARAISO **1808**

VALPARAISO (CITY). UNIVERSIDAD CATOLICA. CENTRO DE INVESTIGACIONES DEL MARINAS *See* INVESTIGACIONES MARINAS **2306**

VALPARAISO UNIVERSITY LAW REVIEW (US/0042-2363) [01586836] **3070**

VALPARAISO UNIVERSITY. SCHOOL OF LAW *See* VALPARAISO UNIVERSITY LAW REVIEW **3070**

VALSALVA, IL (IT) **3891**

VALSUSA, LA (IT) **2494**

VALTIOLLISET VAALIT : KANSANEDUSTAJAIN VAALIT (FI) [06431946] **4503**

VALTION MENOT LAANEITTAIN (FI/0784-9745) [19587407] **4757**

VALTION VIRALLISJULKAISUT (FI/0430-5094) [01781524] **4693**

VALTION VIRKAMIESTEN PALKAT MARRASKUUSSA (FI) [02343140] **4693**

VALTIONTAKAUSLAITOS (FI) [04518422] **815**

VALUATION (AMERICAN SOCIETY OF APPRAISERS) (US/0042-238X) [06541015] 4848, **815**

VALUATION ANALYSIS FOR HOME MORTGAGE INSURANCE (US) [02924414] **2895**

VALUATION ANALYSIS FOR PROJECT MORTGAGE INSURANCE (US) [04169379] **2895**

VALUATION COMPENDIUM (BE) 5498, **856**

VALUATION CONSULTANT, THE (US/0733-8538) [01466888] **717**

VALUATION EXPLANATION NOTES (BE) 5498, **856**

VALUATION JOURNAL (US) [11691638] **717**

VALUATION JOURNAL, THE (CE) [02246232] **4848**

VALUATIONS OF SECURITIES (US) [01795876] **918**

VALUE ADDED TAXATION IN EUROPE (NE) [20578154] **4757**

VALUE ADDED TAXATION IN EUROPE. SUPPLEMENT (NE) [14284515] **4757**

VALUE ADVISOR (CN/0846-1155) [24266773] **918**

VALUE ENGINEERING & MANAGEMENT DIGEST (US/0275-4371) [07066027] **2000**

VALUE LINE CONVERTIBLES (US/0737-0717) [07754464] **918**

●VALUE LINE EARNINGS FORECASTS (US/1064-6310) [26345505] **717**

VALUE LINE INVESTMENT SURVEY (CANADIAN ED.), THE (US/1055-6354) [23295863] **918**

VALUE LINE INVESTMENT SURVEY. PART 2, SELECTION & OPINION, THE (US) [06909161] **918**

VALUE LINE INVESTMENT SURVEY. PART 3, RATINGS & REPORTS, THE (US) [06909267] **918**

VALUE LINE INVESTMENT SURVEY (U.S. ED.), THE (US/0042-2401) [01768946] **918**

VALUE LINE OPTIONS (US/0737-0709) [07754434] **918**

VALUE LINE OTC SPECIAL SITUATIONS SERVICE, THE (US/0361-2589) [02153575] **918**

VALUE OF AGRICULTURAL COMMODITIES PRODUCED, AUSTRALIA (AT) [09075155] 144, **157**

VALUE — Alphabetical Title Index

VALUE OF PUBLIC UTILITY REAL AND PERSONAL PROPERTY BY COUNTY (US/0147-6971) [03215522] 4757, **4693**

VALUE RETAIL NEWS : THE JOURNAL OF VALUE-ORIENTED RETAILING & DEVELOPMENT (US) [21480445] **1300**

VALUE TRENDS *See* INVESTMENT QUALITY TRENDS **903**

VALUE WORLD (US) [04920667] **1525**

VALUES *CEASED.* (US/0891-2904) [14701373] **1630**

●VALVE BUYERS HANDBOOK (US/0737-5727) [09401267] **2131**

VAMOS! (AG) [05068410] **1071**

VAMOS (IT) **1789**

VAN ALPHEN'S NIEUW KERKELIJK HANDBOEK (NE) [07381148] **5068**

VAN BUREN COUNTY DEMOCRAT (US) [19079312] **5632**

VAN BUREN ECHOES (US/0897-9413) [17671767] **2476**

VAN BUREN REGISTER (KEOSAUGUA, IOWA : 1982) (US) [15202813] **5673**

VAN CONVERSION BLUE BOOK OFFICIAL MARKET REPORT (US/0884-7231) [12433847] **5427**

VAN DUSEN BOTANICAL GARDEN BULLETIN (CN/0843-3461) [20365476] **529**

VAN GENDT BOOK AUCTIONS BV *See* BOOK AUCTION **4824**

VAN HOC (GARDEN GROVE, CALIF.) (US/1047-0913) [20579329] **3450**

VAN HORN ADVOCATE (US) **5755**

VAN NGHE (VM) [01798496] **3450**

VAN NGHE TIEN PHONG (US) [03473266] **2274**

VAN NGHE TRE *CEASED.* (GW) **2274**

VAN NOSTRAND'S SCIENTIFIC ENCYCLOPEDIA *CEASED.* (US) [09581960] 5168, **1929**

VAN, PICKUP, SPORT UTILITY BUYER'S GUIDE (US/1043-8270) [18904788] **5427**

VAN (RIVIERE BEAUDETTE) (CN/0824-0388) [11559864] **5007**

VAN VECHTEN REPORT, THE (US) [12067229] 1168, **937**

VAN WERT AND SURROUNDING COUNTIES, OHIO (US/0898-641X) [17866758] **2549**

VAN ZANDT RECORD, THE (US/0736-3958) [08648328] **2476**

VANADIUM / U.S. DEPARTMENT OF THE INTERIOR, BUREAU OF MINES (US) [26242056] 2152, **1630**

VANCOUVER ACADEMY OF MUSIC *See* ACADEMY NEWS! **4098**

VANCOUVER & AREA AIRPORT BUSINESS DIRECTORY (CN/0828-4504) [11856667] **39**

●VANCOUVER & AREA ... AVIATION BUSINESS DIRECTORY (CN/1188-2778) [26497543] 717, **39**

VANCOUVER ART GALLERY *See* ANNUAL REPORT - VANCOUVER ART GALLERY **336**

VANCOUVER ARTS DIRECTORY (CN/0827-3081) [11868867] **332**

VANCOUVER B.C. CITY DIRECTORY *See* VANCOUVER CITY DIRECTORY (1992) **2578**

●VANCOUVER CITY DIRECTORY (1992) (CN/1191-9396) [27809642] **2578**

VANCOUVER EAST NEWS *CEASED.* (CN/1186-7698) [24571013] **5797**

VANCOUVER EXPRESS (CN/0227-3772) [07295197] **5797**

VANCOUVER ISLAND GAS PIPELINE UPDATE (CN/1186-7973) [24623962] **4281**

VANCOUVER ISLAND REAL ESTATE BOARD *See* INDICATOR (NANAIMO) **4848**

VANCOUVER ISLAND REGIONAL LIBRARY *See* NEWSLETTER - VANCOUVER ISLAND REGIONAL LIBRARY **3236**

VANCOUVER NEWS (VANCOUVER, 1977) (CN/0715-4895) [09538903] **5797**

VANCOUVER POETRY CENTRE NEWSLETTER (CN/0228-782X) [08063683] **3472**

VANCOUVER SOUTH NEWS (1991) (CN/1186-768X) [24571017] **5797**

VANCOUVER STEP (1991) *CEASED.* (CN/1185-0310) [23598315] **332**

VANCOUVER STOCK EXCHANGE *See* OFFICIAL DAILY BULLETIN - VANCOUVER STOCK EXCHANGE **910**

VANCOUVER STOCK EXCHANGE *See* VANCOUVER STOCK EXCHANGE REVIEW **919**

VANCOUVER STOCK EXCHANGE REVIEW (CN/0049-5832) [03245053] **919**

VANCOUVER SUBURBAN DIRECTORY (CN/1185-3093) [24690765] **5498**

VANCOUVER SUN (1986) (CN/0832-1299) [14687962] **5797**

VANCOUVER (VANCOUVER, 1975) (CN/0380-9552) [12227576] **5498**

VANDANCE INTERNATIONAL (CN/1189-9808) [29604836] **1314**

VANDANCE (VANCOUVER) (CN/0705-8063) [04256130] **1314**

VANDERBILT HUSTLER, THE (US/0042-2517) [03955349] **1096**

VANDERBILT JOURNAL OF TRANSNATIONAL LAW (US/0090-2594) [01784904] **3137**

VANDERBILT LAW REVIEW (US/0042-2533) [01768951] **3070**

VANDERBILT MAGAZINE (US) [14395848] **1103**

VANDERBILT MEDICAL ALUMNI DIRECTORY (US/0740-901X) [10026850] 3649, **1103**

VANDERBILT STREET REVIEW (US/0275-7672) [10955189] **3450**

VANDERBILT TODAY (US/0279-2540) [07668236] 1103, **1096**

VANDERBILT UNIVERSITY, NASHVILLE. GRADUATE CENTER FOR LATIN AMERICAN STUDIES *See* OCCASIONAL PAPER - GRADUATE CENTER FOR LATIN AMERICAN STUDIES (VANDERBILT UNIVERSITY) **2751**

VANDERBILT UNIVERSITY PUBLICATIONS IN ANTHROPOLOGY (US) [04887492] **247**

VANDERBILT UNIVERSITY. SCHOOL OF MEDICINE *See* VANDERBILT MEDICAL ALUMNI DIRECTORY **1103**

●VANDERWICKEN'S FINANCIAL DIGEST (US/1061-3870) [25284119] **815**

VANGNET (NE/0921-2574) [14985854] **3947**

VANGUARD (US/0892-6433) [15304975] **2838**

VANGUARD ADVISER, THE (US/1056-2338) [23592287] **815**

VANGUARD (EDUCATION INFORMATION NETWORK (LOS ANGELES, CALIF.)) *CEASED.* (US/1063-2697) [24641129] **2796**

VANGUARD (VALPARAISO) (US/0042-2568) [01776824] **5007**

VANGUARD (VANCOUVER) *CEASED.* (CN/0315-5226) [02199494] **367**

VANGUARDIA ESPANOLA, LA *See* VANGUARDIA, LA **5811**

VANGUARDIA, LA (SP) **5811**

VANI (CN/0705-1867) [05761489] **2274**

VANIDADES CONTINENTAL (PN/0505-0146) [01640696] 5567, **2793**

VANIEROIS, LE (CN/0823-0153) [10082626] **1525**

VANITY FAIR (NEW YORK, N.Y.) (US/0733-8899) [08356733] **2549**

VANKITILASTO (FI) [02246916] **3178**

VANN (NO/0042-2592) [07770157] **2245**

VANTAGE POINT (KO) [04333734] **2667**

●VANTAGE (WORCESTER, MASS.) (US/1065-3473) [26578615] **2895**

VAR (CAMDEN, ME.) *CEASED.* (US/0882-0295) [11716639] **1168**

VAR FAGELVARLD (SW/0042-2649) [01624183] **5620**

VAR FODA (SW/0042-2657) [04145825] 2360, **4199**

VAR LOSEN (SW) [03331763] **5069**

VAR TRYGGHET (SW) [02239455] **5313**

VARA PALSDJUR (SW/0042-2703) [02731974] **5523**

VARAVIKSNE (LV/0506-4120) [04108157] **3450**

VARBUSINESS (US/0894-5802) [16145044] **1239**

VARD I NORDEN (NO/0107-4083) [14997584] **3870**

VARDFACKET (SW/0347-0911) [03918969] **4806**

VARESTATISTIK FOR INDUSTRI (ANNUAL) (DK/0107-7031) [10597417] **1630**

VARESTATISTIK FOR INDUSTRI. SERIE A, ANIMALSKE OG VEGETABILSKE PRODUKTER, SAMT ANDRE NRINGS OG NYDELSESMIDLER (DK/0107-0967) [08646757] **2360**

VARESTATISTIK FOR INDUSTRI. SERIE B, MINERALSKE OG KEMISKE PRODUKTER, TROG PAPIR SAMT VARER DERAF (DK/0107-0975) [08646760] **2360**

VARESTATISTIK FOR INDUSTRI. SERIE C, TEKSTILVARER, FODTJ, SPORTSARTIKLER M.V (DK/0107-0983) [08657556] **2360**

VARESTATISTIK FOR INDUSTRI. SERIE D, METALLER, METALVARER, MASKINER, APPARATER OG INSTRUMENTER, SAMT TRANSPORTMIDLER (DK/0107-0991) [08597933] **2360**

VARIA (IO/0506-4155) [02169288] **4928**

VARIA AEGYPTIACA (US/0887-4026) [13119088] **2632**

VARIA BELADIRI (US) [04792474] **4855**

VARIA (LUND, SWEDEN) (SW) [06006973] **247**

VARIA (MONTCHANIN, DEL.) (US/0888-6059) [13454370] **2549**

VARIA SOCIO-ECONOMICA / FUNDACAO DE ECONOMIA E ESTATISTICA (BL) [10292383] **1588**

VARIABLE ANNUITY / LIFE ONFLOPPY (US) **919**

VARIABLE ANNUITY/LIFE PERFORMANCE REPORT / MORNINGSTAR (US/1075-5179) [27721600] **919**

VARIABLE ANNUITY PERFORMANCE REPORT (US/1059-1435) [24417186] **919**

VARIABLE ANNUITY PERFORMANCE REPORT *See* VARIABLE ANNUITY/LIFE PERFORMANCE REPORT / MORNINGSTAR **919**

VARIABLE ANNUITY SOURCEBOOK (US/1062-3361) [25623231] **2895**

VARIASARI (MY/0506-418X) [05082052] **2509**

VARIAZIONE SEDEE NUMERO PARTITA IVA (IT) **1525**

●VARIEGATED GOSPEL (US/1061-8333) [25473912] 2274, **5007**

VARIETES DE POMMES DE TERRE AU CANADA (CN/1184-8170) [24402106] **144**

VARIETIES OF ENGLISH AROUND THE WORLD : GENERAL SERIES (GW/0172-7362) [09888043] 247, **3331**

VARIETY (US/0042-2738) [01768958] 5372, **4079**

VARIETY (US) [05250629] **5372**

VARIETY AND DAILY VARIETY TELEVISION REVIEWS (US/1064-9557) [25669594] **1142**

VARIETY CROSSPATCHES (US/0194-3278) [05395735] **4867**

VARIETY INTERNATIONAL FILM GUIDE (UK) [20871480] **4079**

VARIETY WORD-FIND PUZZLES (US/0194-3286) [05395781] **4867**

VARIETY'S VIDEO DIRECTORY PLUS (US/1066-8810) [26231669] **4377**

VARIOUS AVERAGES OF NEW JERSEY COMMERCIAL BANKS AS OF DECEMBER 31 ... ARRANGED BY GROUPS ACCORDING TO TOTAL ASSETS IN MILLIONS (US) [08873175] **815**

VARIOUS PUBLICATIONS SERIES - AARHUS UNIVERSITET. MATEMATISK INSTITUT (DK/0065-0188) [06048888] **3540**

VARKARSA, DI (II) [02245574] **1716**

VARKENS FOKKERIJMESTERIJ *See* VARKENS : MAANDBLAD VOOR FOKKERIJ & MESTERIJ **223**

VARKENS : MAANDBLAD VOOR FOKKERIJ & MESTERIJ (NE) [16635162] **223**

VARLIK (TU) [04512058] 332, **3450**

VARNANA (II) [02240212] **2509**

VAROSI KOZLEKEDES (HU/0133-0314) [I01330314] 2033, **5399**

VARSHIKA KARYA-VIVARANA / UTTARA PRADESA RAJYA SARAKA PARIVAHANA NIGAMA (II) [08697815] **5399**

VARSHIKA RIPORTA - HAINDIKRAPHTSA ENNDA HAINDALUMSA EKSAPORTASA KARPORESANA APHA INDIYA (II) [01797846] **376**

VARSHIKA VRTTANTA - MAHARASHTRA RAJYA MADHYAMIKA SIKSHANA MANDALA (II) [02240206] **1789**

VARSITY OUTDOOR CLUB JOURNAL, THE (CN/0524-5613) [02247525] 5237, **4880**

VARSITY REVIEW *See* COLUMBIA REVIEW **3340**

VARSITY (TORONTO) (CN/0042-2789) [03448400] **1096**

VARSTVO SPOMENIKOV (XV/0350-9494) [05224918] **332**

VART FORSVAR, TIDSKRIFT UTG. AF ALLMANNA FORSVARSFORENINGEN OCH FORENINGEN FOR NORRLANDS FASTA FORSVAR (SW/0042-2800) [01768935] **4060**

VAS MEGYEI KONYVTARAK ERTESITOJE, A (HU/0133-7351) [I01337351] **3255**

VASA (SZ/0301-1526) [01463487] **3802**

VASA STAR, THE (US/0746-0627) [08449169] **2274**

VASA. SUPPLEMENTUM (SZ/0251-1029) [01681159] **3802**

VASARNAP: HIREK (HU) **856**

VASCULAR FORUM *CEASED.* (US/1067-5051) [27252783] **3649**

VASCULAR MEDICINE REVIEW (UK/0954-2582) [21901089] **3802**

VASCULAR REPORTS *SUSPENDED.* (US/0748-8971) [11027733] **3977**

VASCULAR SURGERY (US/0042-2835) [01768960] **3977**

VASCULAR SURGERY OUTLOOK (US/0894-8038) [16259437] **3977**

VASCULAR VIEWS *CEASED.* (US/8756-3401) [11542810] **3649**

VASCULUM, THE (UK/0049-5891) [02733034] **4173**

VASI SZEMLE SZOMBATHELY. 1958 (HU/0505-0332) [I05050332] **2714**

VASLA (US/0042-1723) [06841997] **3255**

VASSAR PIONEER TIMES, THE (US/0193-0249) [05144582] **5694**

VASUTI KOZLEKEDESI SZAKIRODALMI TAJEKOZTATO (HU/0231-0767) [02310767] **5437**

VAT INTELLIGENCE (UK/0263-9347) [I02639947] 753, **717**

●VAT PLANNING (UK/0964-5985) [I09645985] **4757**

VAT TRIBUNALS REPORTS (UK) **4757**

VAT. VICTORIAN ASSOCIATION OF TEACHERS (AT/0156-4706) [I01564706] **1908**

VATICAN CITY. DIREZIONE GENERALE DEI MONUMENTI, MUSEI E GALLERIE PONTIFICIE *See* BOLLETTINO - MONUMENTI, MUSEI E GALLERIE PONTIFICIE **344**

VATICAN OBSERVATORY PUBLICATIONS (VC/0083-5293) [01777367] **401**

VATRA (RM) [01787478] **2524**

VATTEN (SW/0042-2886) [11445841] **5541**

VAUGHAN COURIER, THE (CN/0710-0191) [08292866] **5797**

VAUGHAN : LAW OF THE EUROPEAN COMMUNITIES SERVICE (UK) **3070**

VAUTIER *See* PICTORIAL NEW VAUTIER MAGAZINE **4375**

VAUXHALL ADVANCE, THE (CN/0706-7550) [05018224] **5797**

VAX PROFESSIONAL *See* DIGITAL SYSTEMS JOURNAL **1182**

VAX PROFESSIONAL, THE (US/8750-9628) [12130376] **1206**

VAXTODLING (SW) [01768962] **2433**

VAXTSKYDDSNOTISER (SW/0042-2169) [01640793] **4248**

VAXTSKYDDSRAPPORTER. JORDBRUK (SW/0347-3236) [04604268] **529**

VAYU MANDAL (II) [01714494] **1436**

VBA JOURNAAL (NE) **1525**

VCR LETTER, THE *See* VIDEO INVESTOR, THE **1168**

VCT *See* MMC : MEDIAS MAGNETIQUES CANADA **4444**

VCVO KNIPSELKRANT (BE) **1789**

VD NEWS (US) [05968365] **4806**

VD VOSKRESENIE *See* VOSKRESENIE **2715**

VDGSA NEWS (US/0506-306X) [02153950] **4158**

VDI-BERICHTE (GW/0083-5560) [02692629] **2000**

VDI-FORSHUNGSHEFT (GW/0042-174X) [01464471] **2000**

VDI INFORMATIONSDIENST REGELUNGSTECHNIK (GW) [05959605] **2000**

VDI NACHRICHTEN (GW/0042-1758) [08328304] **5168**

VDI-Z (GW/0042-1766) [02269137] **2131**

VDL NACHRICHTEN (GW/0340-7810) [01543724] **144**

VDLUFA KONGRESSBAND (GW) **144**

VDLUFA-SCHRIFTENREIHE (GW/0173-8712) [11092579] **144**

VDNKH SSSR (RU/0130-0911) [11421419] **144**

VDT NEWS (US/0742-938X) [10478934] 1206, **4806**

VE VENEZUELA (VE/0042-2932) [01470466] **5498**

VE6 (CN/0049-5778) [03448319] **1142**

VEA (CL) [05273147] **2553**

VEA (HATO REY, P.R.) (PR/0738-7628) [09671759] **2494**

VEA NEWS (US/0042-1790) [01769184] **1789**

VEALER, THE (US/0749-6664) [11178045] **2360**

VECERNJE NOVINE (1983) (BN/0352-261X) [I0352261X] **5779**

VECERNJI LIST (CI/0350-5006) [I03505006] **5799**

VECHE (MUNICH, GERMANY) (GW) [08583589] **2714**

VECHTAER ARBEITEN ZUR GEOGRAPHIE UND REGIONALWISSENSCHAFT (GW) [13179900] **2578**

VECKANS AFFARER (SW/0506-4406) [25639227] 1525, **717**

VECKO : B.V (XR/0862-7584) [24313972] **4060**

VECKO REVYN (SW) **5811**

VECTOR (BURLINGTON) (US/0361-8331) [02133996] **5007**

VECTOR (HARVARD, MASS.), THE (US/0738-1328) [09519774] **815**

VECTOR KLOOF (SA/0256-7008) [I02567008] 5265, **2796**

VECTOR LONDON (UK/0955-1433) [I09551433] **1206**

VECTOR PUBLIC OPINION REPORT (CN/1183-6822) [25066877] **5265**

VECTOR (READING) (UK/0505-0448) [07829021] **3450**

VECTOR (VANCOUVER) (CN/0382-0718) [02275479] **3540**

VEDA A VYSKUM PRAXI (XO/0374-1389) [09660057] **1418**

VEDA A ZIVOT (XR) [05239018] **5168**

VEDANTA KESARI, THE (II/0042-2983) [01587236] **4364**

VEDECKE PRACE / NAUCHNYE TRUDY / SCIENTIFIC STUDIES (XR) [17801685] 5541, **190**

VEDECKE PRACE OVOCNARSKE (XR/0231-6900) [10834456] **5168**

VEDECKE PRACE VYSKUMNEHO USTAVU LUK A PASIENKOV V BANSKEJ BYSTRICI (XO/0375-4928) [10041948] **5523**

VEDECKE PRACE VYSKUMNEHO USTAVU RASTLINNEJ VYROBY V PIESTANOCH. OBILNINY - STRAKOVINY / SCIENTIFIC PAPERS OF THE RESEARCH INSTITUTE FOR PLANT PRODUCTION AT PIESTANY. CEREALS - LEGUMES (XO) [06449586] 2360, **190**

VEDECKE PRACE VYSKUMNEHO USTAVU RASTLINNEJ VYROBYV PIESTANOCH. OBILNINY (XO) [08465109] **144**

VEDECKE PRACE VYSKUMNEHO USTAVU RASTLINNEJ VYYROBY V PIESTANOCH. KRMOVINY / SCIENTIFIC PAPERS OF THE RESEARCH INSTITUTE FOR PLANT PRODUCTION AT PIESTANY. FORAGE CROPS (XO) [06449592] **190**

VEDECKE PRACE VYSKUMNEHO USTAVU ZIVOCISNEJ VYROBY V NITRE (XO/0375-5010) [10769463] **5168**

VEDECKE PRACE VYZKUMNEHO USTAVU ROSTLINNE VYROBY V PRAZE-RUZYNI (XR) [12151055] **529**

VEDECKE PRACE ZEMEDELASKEHO MUZEA (XR) [05324957] **144**

VEDECKOTECHNICKY ROZVOJ V ZEMEDELSTVI *CEASED.* (CS/0862-3562) [21252936] **144**

VEDECKY CASOPIS ZEMEDELSKA EKONOMIKA (XR/0139-570X) [09867353] **144**

VEDERE *See* VEDERE INTERNATIONAL **4217**

VEDERE CONTACT INTERNATIONAL (IT/0392-0453) [03961250] **4217**

VEDERE INTERNATIONAL (IT/0302-6256) [03916323] **4217**

VEDIC LIGHT (II) [01797751] **5041**

VEDOMOSTI SEZDA NARODNYKH DEPUTATOV ROSSIISKOI FEDERATSII I VERKHOVNOGO SOVETA ROSSIISKOI FEDERATSII *CEASED.* (RU) [25727758] **3070**

VEDOMOSTI SEZDA NARODNYKH DEPUTATOV RSFSR I VERKHOVNOGO SOVETA RSFSR *See* VEDOMOSTI SEZDA NARODNYKH DEPUTATOV ROSSIISKOI FEDERATSII I VERKHOVNOGO SOVETA ROSSIISKOI FEDERATSII **3070**

VEERY (CHICAGO, ILL.) (US/1069-7144) [28146155] **3355**

VEETEELT (NE/0168-7565) [15166366] **223**

VEGETABLE GARDEN RESEARCH (CN/1181-9782) [24266311] **2433**

VEGETABLE GROWERS ASSOCIATION OF AMERICA, INC *See* ANNUAL REPORT **2409**

VEGETABLE SCIENCE (II) [08849325] **190**

VEGETABLES FOR THE HOT, HUMID TROPICS (US) [04647617] **144**

VEGETABLES (WASHINGTON) (US/0193-6603) [02925656] **190**

VEGETACE CSSR. REIHE A (XR/0506-449X) [02731506] **529**

VEGETARIAN (ALTRINCHAM, CHESHIRE : 1980) (UK/0260-3233) [08403492] **4200**

●VEGETARIAN GOURMET (US/1065-6340) [26610157] 2793, **2360**

VEGETARIAN JOURNAL (US/0885-7636 #y 0883-1165) [12747814] **4200**

VEGETARIAN TIMES (US/0164-8497) [04319263] 2360, **4200**

VEGETARIAN VOICE (US/0271-1591) [06564747] **4806**

VEGETATIO (NE/0042-3106) [01768967] **529**

VEGETATION HISTORY AND ARCHAEOBOTANY (GW/0939-6314) [I09396314] **529**

VEGETATION OF CONNECTICUT NATURAL AREAS, THE (US/0589-3747) [01321069] **529**

●VEGGIE LIFE (US/1065-2728) [26562596] **2360**

VEGPLAN *See* NORSK VEG-OG VEGTRAFIKKPLAN **5442**

VEGTATIONSMONOGRAPHIEN DER EINZELNEN GROSSRAUME (US) [01471904] **2433**

VEGYIPARI SZAKIRODALMI TAJEKOZTATO MUANYAG- ES GUMIIPARI KULONLENYOMATA (HU/0231-0775) 2017, **995**

VEHICLE AND TRAFFIC LAW (US) [05300445] 5399, **3070**

VEHICLE BUILDERS & REPAIRERS ASSOCIATION *See* DIRECTORY OF MEMBERS - VEHICLE BUILDERS & REPAIRERS ASSOCIATION **5413**

VEHICLE BUILDERS & REPAIRERS ASSOCIATION. DIRECTORY *See* DIRECTORY OF MEMBERS - VEHICLE BUILDERS & REPAIRERS ASSOCIATION **5413**

VEHICLE CODE (US) [06579412] **5427**

VEHICLE IDENTIFICATION (US/8756-940X) [11617657] **5427**

VEHICLE LEASING TODAY (US) 5427, **5399**

VEHICLE (QUEBEC) (CN/0225-5480) [08960309] **3255**

VEHICLE REGISTRATION AND MOTOR FUEL TAXES, AMOUNTS DISTRIBUTED TO LOCAL GOVERNMENTS, BY COUNTY (US/0149-0303) [03417264] **4693**

VEHICLE SYSTEM DYNAMICS (NE/0042-3114) [01641307] **2131**

VEHICLE WEIGHT AND USE DATA COLLECTED ON MINNESOTA ROADS (US) [04839751] **5399**

VEHICULES A MOTEUR NEUFS MIS EN CIRCULATION (BE) [05895482] **5427**

VEILIG BOUWEN (BE) **2871**

VEILLEUR, LE (CN/0712-6824) [09375394] **5313**

VEINTIUNO (SP) [18202630] **332**

VEJA (BL/0042-3165) [02464740] **2553**

VEJVISER FOR MASKININDUSTRIEN (DK) [05531457] **2131**

VEJVISER I DANMARKS STATISTISKE PUBLIKATIONER *See* VEJVISER I STATISTIKKEN **5345**

VEJVISER I STATISTIKKEN (DK/0109-8314) [12616075] **5345**

VEK 21 : IZDANIE NA RADIKALDEMOKRATICHESKATA PARTIIA (BU) [23472975] **4499**

VEK XX I MIR (RU/0320-8001) [19827252] **4537**

VEKER, DER (US/8750-8478) [08396609] **5265**

VEKOVE (BU/0324-0967) [01789007] **2714**

VELD & FLORA (SA/0042-3203) [02609323] **530**

VELDSTUDIES / FACULTEIT DER RUIMTELIJKE WETENSCHAPPEN. GEOGRAFISCH INSTITUUT. RIJKSUNIVERSITEIT GRONINGEN (NE/0922-9558) [I09229558] **2578**

VELDWERK AMSTERDAM (NE/0922-2782) [I09222782] **2912**

VELDWERK (AMSTERDAM) *See* INZET AMSTERDAM **2910**

VELIGER, THE (US/0042-3211) [01768969] **5599**

VELO-NEWS (US/0161-1798) [03873820] 4928, **429**

VELTRO, IL (IT/0042-3254) [02149529] **2524**

VELVET LIGHT TRAP, THE (US/0149-1830) [02587297] **4079**

VELVET TALKS (US/0274-8010) [06600939] **3996**

VEM AR DET SVENSK BIOGRAFISK HANDBOK (SW) [01681205] **2714**

VENAMCHAM'S — Alphabetical Title Index

VENAMCHAM'S EXECUTIVE NEWCOMERS GUIDE, WELCOME TO VENEZUELA *See* LIVING IN VENEZUELA **2552**

VENDING INTERNATIONAL (UK/0954-6235) [17530683] **2360**

VENDING INTERNATIONAL (UK/0954-6235) [I09546235] **937**

VENDING MACHINE OPERATORS (CN/0527-6411) [02442608] **958**

VENDING MACHINES, COIN OPERATED (US/0271-5937) [03054188] **1631**

VENDING TIMES (US/0042-3327) [01473284] **4214**

VENDING TIMES, CENSUS OF THE INDUSTRY (US) **4214**

VENDING TIMES. INTERNATIONAL BUYERS GUIDE ISSUE (US) [18277154] **4214**

VENDOR SELECTOR SERVICE (US/0748-7835) [11002188] **1631**

VENDREDI (FR/0995-0583) [24470593] **4548**

VENEREOLOGY : OFFICIAL PUBLICATION OF THE NATIONAL VENEREOLOGY COUNCIL OF AUSTRALIA (AT) [22380350] **3716**

VENETO SICUREZZA SOCIALE *SUSPENDED.* (IT) **4693**

VENEZIA ARTI : BOLLETTINO DEL DIPARTIMENTO DI STORIA E CRITICA DELLE ARTI DELL'UNIVERSITA DI VENEZIA (IT) [18062313] **367**

VENEZIA CINQUECENTO (IT) [26286412] **367**

VENEZUELA *See* LEY DE PRESUPUESTO PARA EL EJERCICIO FISCAL **4736**

VENEZUELA *See* LEGISLACION VENEZOLANA **3001**

VENEZUELA AHORA: CIENCIA (VE) [05046235] **5168**

VENEZUELA. ARCHIVO GENERAL DE LA NACION *See* BOLETIN DEL ARCHIVO GENERAL DE LA NACION (CARACAS) **2480**

VENEZUELA. DIRECCION DE GEOLOGIA *See* BOLETIN DE GEOLOGIA (CARACAS) **1367**

VENEZUELA. DIRECCION GENERAL DE ESTADISTICA Y CENSOS NACIONALES *See* ESTADISTICAS DEL COMERCIO EXTERIOR DE VENEZUELA; IMPORTACION: ARTICULO Y PAIS **728**

VENEZUELA FORESTAL : PUBLICACION CUATRIMESTRAL DE LA COMPANIA NACIONAL DE REFORESTACION, CONARE (VE) [22928844] **2398**

VENEZUELA (LONDON. 1985) (UK/0267-9957) [12985012] **2494**

VENEZUELA METALURGICA Y MINERA (VE) [02580149] **4023**

VENEZUELA. MINISTERIO DE AGRICULTURA Y CRIA. BIBLIOTECA *See* LISTA DE LIBROS Y FOLLETOS RECIBIDOS **105**

VENEZUELA. MINISTERIO DE JUSTICIA *See* REVISTA DEL MINISTERIO DE JUSTICIA **3041**

VENEZUELA. MINISTERIO DE LA DEFENSA *See* MEMORIA Y CUENTA ... QUE EL MINISTRO DE LA DEFENSA PRESENTA AL CONGRESO NACIONAL / REPUBLICA DE VENEZUELA, MINISTERIO DE LA DEFENSA **4049**

VENEZUELA. MINISTERIO DE LA DEFENSA NACIONAL *See* MEMORIA Y CUENTA ... QUE EL MINISTRO DE LA DEFENSA PRESENTA AL CONGRESO NACIONAL / REPUBLICA DE VENEZUELA, MINISTERIO DE LA DEFENSA **4049**

VENEZUELA. MINISTERIO DE RELACIONES INTERIORES *See* MRI INFORMATIVO **4666**

VENEZUELA. SECCION NACIONAL DEL INSTITUTO PANAMERICANO DE GEOGRAFIA E HISTORIA *See* INFORME ANUAL - INSTITUTO PANAMERICANO DE GEOGRAFIA E HISTORIA, SECCION NACIONAL **2566**

VENEZUELA. UNIVERSIDAD CENTRAL, CARACAS. CONSEJO DE DESARROLLO CIENTIFICO Y HUMANISTICO *See* PUBLICACION - VENEZUELA. UNIVERSIDAD CENTRAL. CONSEJO DE DESARROLLO CIENTIFICO Y HUMANISTICO **2852**

VENEZUELA. UNIVERSIDAD CENTRAL, CARACAS. DEPARTAMENTO DE ALEMAN *See* SERIE DE CUENTOS PARA LA JUVENTUD **1069**

VENEZUELA. UNIVERSIDAD CENTRAL, CARACAS. ESCUELA DE GEOLOGIA Y MINAS *See* INFORME - UNIVERSIDAD CENTRAL DE VENEZUELA, FACULTAD DE INGENIERIA, ESCUELA DE GEOLOGIA Y MINAS, LABORATORIO DE PETROGRAFIA Y GEOQUIMICA **5113**

VENEZUELA. UNIVERSIDAD CENTRAL, CARACAS. ESCUELA DE PERIODISMO *See* CUADERNOS - VENEZUELA. UNIVERSIDAD CENTRAL, CARACAS. ESCUELA DE PERIODISMO **3205**

VENEZUELA. UNIVERSIDAD CENTRAL, CARACAS. FACULTAD DE ARQUITECTURA Y URBANISMO *See* COLECCION ESPACIO Y FORMA **2818**

VENEZUELA. UNIVERSIDAD CENTRAL, CARACAS. FACULTAD DE FARMACIA *See* REVISTA DE LA FACULTAD DE FARMACIA **4328**

VENEZUELA. UNIVERSIDAD CENTRAL, CARACAS. INSTITUTO DE ANTROPOLOGIA E HISTORIA *See* ANTROPOLOGIA **230**

VENEZUELA. UNIVERSIDAD CENTRAL, CARACAS. INSTITUTO DE ANTROPOLOGIA E HISTORIA *See* FUENTES HISTORICAS **2616**

VENEZUELA. UNIVERSIDAD CENTRAL, CARACAS. INSTITUTO DE FILOSOFIA *See* COLECCION TESIS DOCTORALES **4344**

VENEZUELA. UNIVERSIDAD CENTRAL, CARACAS. INSTITUTO DE LENGUAS MODERNAS *See* LENGUAS MODERNAS **3297**

VENEZUELAN-AMERICAN CHAMBER OF COMMERCE & INDUSTRY *See* YEAR BOOK - VENEZUELAN-AMERICAN CHAMBER OF COMMERCE & INDUSTRY **821**

VENEZUELAN ECONOMIC REVIEW (VE) [07482181] **1588**

VENGERSKII MERIDIAN (HU/0865-3763) [23808962] **5225**

VENICE GONDOLIER, THE (US/0745-6263) [09314003] **5651**

VENICE. ISTITUTO DI STUDI ADRIATICI *See* MEMORIE DI BIOGEOGRAFIA ADRIATICA **2569**

VENTANA (NEW YORK, N.Y.), LA (US/0742-1818) [10261651] **2764**

VENTE AUX ENCHERES PUBLIQUES TABLEAUX MODERNES ... / GALERIE MOTTE (SW) [19482983] **367**

VENTES AUX ENCHERES PUBLIQUES (CN/0849-0465) [21914145] 252, **367**

VENTILATION DU TRAFIC COMMERCIAL (FR) [06999694] **39**

VENTILATORS & MUSCULAR DYSTROPHY (US) [18315850] **3807**

VENTILEN (SW) **3489**

VENTO DEL SUD (IT) [01787220] **1588**

VENTURA COUNTY (US/0746-9918) [10447441] **2549**

VENTURA COUNTY HISTORICAL SOCIETY *See* VENTURA COUNTY HISTORICAL SOCIETY QUARTERLY **2476**

VENTURA COUNTY HISTORICAL SOCIETY QUARTERLY (US/0042-3491) [02148987] **2476**

VENTURA COUNTY STAR *See* VENTURA COUNTY STAR-FREE PRESS **5641**

VENTURA COUNTY STAR-FREE PRESS (US) [23611105] **5641**

VENTURA FREE PRESS *See* VENTURA COUNTY STAR-FREE PRESS **5641**

VENTURE / AMERICAN NATURAL RESOURCES SYSTEM (US) [07368828] **2131**

VENTURE CAPITAL JOURNAL (US/0883-2773) [06974672] **919**

VENTURE CAPITAL JOURNAL ... YEARBOOK (US/8756-8896) [11668918] **815**

VENTURE CAPITAL YEARBOOK (US) [12691079] **919**

VENTURE (EDMONTON) (CN/0843-7904) [21101695] **1525**

VENTURE INWARD / THE MAGAZINE OF THE ASSOCIATION FOR RESEARCH AND ENLIGHTENMENT (US/0748-3406) [10927444] 4243, **5007**

VENTURE JAPAN *CEASED.* (US) [19255734] **919**

VENTURE PRODUCT NEWS (US/0738-7199) [09658221] **5168**

VENTURE ROAD (US/0883-7821) [12209801] **5498**

VENTURES IN RESEARCH (US/0092-556X) [01784454] **5168**

VENUS (US) [19472790] **3450**

VENUS; JAPANESE JOURNAL OF MALACOLOGY (JA/0042-3580) [06924925] **5599**

VERA (IT) **5567**

VERA LEX (US/0893-4851) [09848154] **2253**

VERANDA (ATLANTA, GA.) (US/1040-8150) [18541608] **2903**

VERANO, UN (US/0730-9708) [05050150] 367, **3450**

VERARBEITENDES GEWERBE IN BERLIN (WEST) (GW) [21027844] **1588**

VERARBEOTEMDES GEWERBE (GW) [10743179] **5345**

VERB (ATLANTA, GA.) (US/1060-3700) [24955953] **3450**

VERBA (SP) [02294224] **3331**

VERBAND DER BIBLIOTHEKEN DES LANDES NORDRHEIN-WESTFALEN *See* MITTEILUNGSBLATT - VERBAND DER BIBLIOTHEKEN DES LANDES NORDRHEIN WESTFALEN **3232**

VERBAND DEUTSCHER AKADEMIKER FUR LANDWIRTSCHAFT, ERNAHRUNG UND LANDESPFLEGE *See* VDL NACHRICHTEN **144**

VERBAND FUER ARBEITSSTUDIEN *See* REFA NACHRICHTEN **946**

VERBANDTECHNIK (GW/0930-3677) [22807971] **3649**

VERBATIM (US/0162-0932) [03398938] **3331**

VERBATIM REPORT (CN) [01785541] **4693**

VERBESSERUNG DER EIWEISSVERSORGUNG DER LANDWIRTSCHAFTLICHEN NUTZTIERE (GW) [06437760] **223**

VERBINDING ROTTERDAM (NE/0922-6540) [09226540] **1168**

VERBLEIB DER ABGEWIESENEN STUDIENBEWERBER (GW) [05369026] **1853**

VERBONDSNIEUWS VOOR DE BELGISCHE SIERTEELT (BE) [I07713851] **2436**

VERBORGENE WELT *See* GRENZGEBIETE DER WISSENSCHAFT **5108**

VERBREITUNGSDATEN DER SCHWEIZER PRESSE (SZ) **2925**

VERBRUIK BOUWMATERIALEN : NIEUWBOUW WONINGEN (NE) [04168565] **2033**

VERBUM (SAN DIEGO, CALIF.) *CEASED.* (US/0889-4507) [13891301] **382**

VERDAD (CORPUS CHRISTI, TEX. : 1942) (US) [05211758] **2275**

VERDAD Y VIDA (SP/0042-3718) [08378069] **5038**

VERDAUUNGSKRANKHEITEN (GW/0174-738X) [11086387] **3748**

VERDE AMBIENTE (IT) **2222**

VERDE INDEPENDENT, THE (US) [08793570] **5630**

VERDE OLVO *SUSPENDED.* (CU/0506-6913) [01498849] **4060**

VERDEDOMANI (IT) **2222**

VERDENSMARKEDET (NO) [09583950] **856**

VERDI NEWSLETTER (US/0160-2667) [03639276] **4158**

VERDICT (FALLBROOK, CALIF. : 1987) (US/0895-9951) [16881474] **5007**

VERDICTS, SETTLEMENTS & TACTICS (US/1041-0740) [18555759] **3070**

VERDIGRIS MAGAZINE (CN/0826-113X) [10926602] **2549**

VERDURE (VALLEYFIELD) (CN/0828-6841) [13143651] **2222**

VEREIN DEUTSCHER BIBLIOTHEKARE. KOMMISSION FUR EINBANDFRAGEN *See* MERKBLATTER - KOMMISSION FUR EINBANDFRAGEN VEREINS DEUTSCHER BIBLIOTHEKARE **4830**

VEREIN DEUTSCHER BIBLIOTHEKARE. KOMMISSION FUR EINBANDFRAGEN. EINBAND BUCHPFILEGE *See* MERKBLATTER - KOMMISSION FUR EINBANDFRAGEN VEREINS DEUTSCHER BIBLIOTHEKARE **4830**

VEREIN DEUTSCHER INGENIEURE *See* VDI-BERICHTE **2000**

VEREIN FUER RHEINISCHE KIRCHENGESCHICHTE *See* SCHRIFTENREIHE DES VEREINS FUER RHEINISCHE KIRCHENGESCHICHTE **4995**

VEREIN FUER WASSER-, BODEN- UND LUFTHYGIENE (GERMANY) *See* SCHRIFTENREIHE DES VEREINS FUER WASSER-, BODEN- UND LUFTHYGIENE **1360**

VEREIN FUR GESCHICHTE DER STADT WIEN *See* JAHRBUCH DES VEREINS FUER GESCHICHTE DER STADT WIEN **2694**

VEREIN FUR GESCHICHTE DES BODENSEES UND SEINER UMGEBUNG *See* SCHRIFTEN DES VEREINS FUER GESCHICHTE DES BODENSEES UND SEINER UMGEBUNG **2708**

VEREIN FUR HAMBURGISCHE GESCHICHTE *See* ZEITSCHRIFT DES VEREINS FUER HAMBURGISCHE GESCHICHTE **2634**

VEREIN FUR HESSISCHE GESCHICHTE UND LANDESKUNDE *See* ZEITSCHRIFT DES VEREINS FUER HESSISCHE GESCHICHTE UND LANDESKUNDE **2716**

VEREIN FUR LANDESKUNDE VON NIEDEROSTERREICH UND WIEN. MONATSBLATT *See* UNSERE HEIMAT **2671**

VEREIN FUR LUBECKISCHE GESCHICHTE UND ALTERTUMSKUNDE *See* ZEITSCHRIFT DES VEREINS FUER LUBECKISCHE GESCHICHTE UND ALTERTUMSKUNDE **2717**

VEREIN FUR NIEDERDEUTSCHE SPRACHFORSCHUNG *See* JAHRBUCH DES VEREINS FUER NIEDERDEUTSCHE SPRACHFORSCHUNG **3288**

VEREIN NATUR UND HEIMAT, LUBECK *See* BERICHTE DES VEREINS NATUR UND HEIMAT UND DES NATURHISTORISCHEN MUSEUMS ZU LUBECK **4163**

VEREIN ZUM SCHUTZ DER BERGWELT *See* JAHRBUCH DES VEREINS ZUM SCHUTZ DER BERGWELT **2196**

VEREINIGTE ARABISCHE EMIRATE : WIRTSCHAFTLICHE ENTWICKLUNG (GW) [03227699] **1525**

VEREINIGUNG DER FREUNDE DER MINERALOGIE UND GEOLOGIE *See* MITGLIEDERVERZEICHNIS **1388**

VEREINIGUNG DER TECHNISCHEN UBERWACHUNGS-VEREINE *See* TUV AUTO-REPORT **5427**

VEREINIGUNG SCHWEIZ. PETROLEUM-GEOLOGEN UND INGENIEURE *See* BULLETIN DER VEREINIGUNG SCHWEIZ. PETROLEUM-GEOLOGEN UND-INGENIEURE **4252**

VEREINTE NATIONEN (GW/0042-384X) [02159081] **4537**

VERFAHRENSRICHTLINIEN FUER DIE MIKROBIOLOGISCHE DIAGNOSTIK (GW/0720-9940) [I07209940] **570**

VERFASSUNG UND RECHT IN UBERSEE (GW/0506-7286) [01604312] **3094**

VERFASSUNGSSCHUTZBERICHT (GW/0343-690X) [11456267] **1309**

VERFKRONIEK (NE/0042-3904) [11713205] 4225, **4570**

VERFUGUNGEN UND MITTEILUNGEN DES MINISTERIUMS FUR VOLKSBILDUNG (GW/0323-3286) [04601251] **1789**

VERGADERACCOMMODATIEGIDS (NE) **2809**

VERGILIUS (1959) (US/0506-7294) [05808886] **1080**

VERGLEICHENDE PAEDAGOGIK *CEASED.* (GE/0042-3920) [01586141] **1789**

VERHALTENSTHERAPIE BASEL (SZ/1016-6262) [I10166262] 4621, **3937**

VERHANDELINGEN DER KONINKLIJKE NEDERLANDSE AKADEMIE VAN WETENSCHAPPEN, AFDELING NATUURKUNDE. EERSTE SECTIE (NE/0373-4668) [02255204] **5168**

VERHANDELINGEN - KONINKLIJKE ACADEMIE VOOR GENEESKUNDE VAN BELGIE (BE/0302-6469) [03593658] **3649**

VERHANDELINGEN VAN DE KONINKLIJKE ACADEMIE VOOR WETENSCHAPPEN, LETTEREN EN SCHONE KUNSTEN VAN BELGIE, KLASSE DER WETENSCHAPPEN (BE/0372-6916) [01641326] **5168**

VERHANDLUNGEN DER ANATOMISCHEN GESELLSCHAFT (GW/0066-1562) [01141511] **3680**

VERHANDLUNGEN DER DEUTSCHEN GESELLSCHAFT FUER HERZ- UND KREISLAUFFORSCHUNG (GW/0174-2817) [06508777] **3711**

VERHANDLUNGEN DER DEUTSCHEN GESELLSCHAFT FUER INNERE MEDIZIN (GW/0070-4067) [01148703] **3802**

VERHANDLUNGEN DER DEUTSCHEN GESELLSCHAFT FUER PATHOLOGIE (GW/0070-4113) [01148768] **3898**

VERHANDLUNGEN DER DEUTSCHEN GESELLSCHAFT FUER RHEUMATOLOGIE *CEASED.* (GW/0070-4121) [02320300] **3807**

VERHANDLUNGEN DER NATURFORSCHENDEN GESELLSCHAFT IN BASEL (SZ/0077-6122) [01685104] **5168**

VERHANDLUNGEN DER ORNITHOLOGISCHE GESELLSCHAFT IN BAYERN (GW) [03883824] **5520**

VERHANDLUNGEN DES DEUTSCHEN BUNDESTAGES (GW) **4499**

VERHANDLUNGEN DES DEUTSCHEN GEOGRAPHENTAGES (GW/0083-5684) [01566481] **2578**

VERHANDLUNGEN DES HISTORISCHEN VEREINS FUER NIEDERBAYERN (GW) [02093293] **2714**

VERHANDLUNGEN DES HISTORISCHEN VEREINS FUER OBERPFALZ UND REGENSBURG (GW/0342-2518) [23150358] **2714**

VERHANDLUNGEN DES NATURWISSENSCHAFTLICHEN VEREINS IN HAMBURG (1979) (GW/0173-749X) [06668518] **4173**

VERHANDLUNGEN / GESELLSCHAFT FUER OKOLOGIE (GW/0171-1113) [05313285] **2222**

VERHANDLUNGEN - INTERNATIONALE VEREINIGUNG FUER THEORETISCHE UND ANGEWANDTE LIMNOLOGIE (GW/0368-0770) [02962090] **1418**

VERHANDLUNGSBERICHT DER DEUTSCHEN GESELLSCHAFT FUER UROLOGIE (GW/0070-413X) [04849474] **3994**

VERHANDLUNGSBERICHT DER DEUTSCHEN GESELLSCHAFT FUR LASERMEDIZIN E.V. / ... TAGUNG (GW/0724-6765) [10932103] **3649**

VERHANGLUNGEN DER DEUTSCHEN ZOOLOGISCHEN GESELLSCHAFT (GW/0070-4342) [10310383] **5599**

VERIDIAN (US/0731-938X) [07901669] **3355**

VERIFICHE (IT/0391-4186) [02240781] **4364**

VERITABLE AMIE (CN/0831-0866) [13784724] **5567**

VERITAS FORUM: CORPORATE MAGAZINE OF DET NORSKE VERITAS (NO) [18507899] **5458**

VERITE STENOGRAPHIQUE, LA (FR/0246-0882) [I02460882] **718**

VERKAUF UND MARKETING (SZ/0255-7673) [I02557673] **937**

VERKAUFSLEITER-SERVICE (GW/0178-5893) [01785893] **718**

VERKEERSGEGEVENS (NE) [11758517] **4185**

VERKEHR. REIHE 6 : LUFTVERKEHR (GW) [03577620] **39**

VERKEHRSMEDIZIN UND IHRE GRENZGEBIETE (GW/0042-4021) [I00424021] **4806**

VERKEHRSWIRTSCHAFT, DIE (GW) [06360206] 5399, **5402**

VERKEHRSWIRTSCHAFTLICHE ZAHLEN (GW) [01788684] **5399**

VERKOPEN! VAKMAGAZINE VOOR COMMERCIELE AKTIE (NE) **952**

VERKORT OVERZICHT ZIEKTEVERZUIM (NE) [10786160] **1716**

VERKSAMHETEN (SW) [05626890] **631**

VERKSAMHETSBERATTELSE (SW) [15058482] **5168**

VERKSAMHETSBERATTELSE - CENTRALFORBUNDET FOR BEFALSUTBILDNING (SW) [03524478] **4060**

VERKSAMHETSBERATTELSE / ENERGIEKONOMISKA FORENINGEN (SW) [09647734] **1960**

VERKSAMHETSPLAN - STATENS RAD FOR BYGGNADSFORSKNING (SW) [02246836] **631**

VERKSTADERNA (SW/0042-4056) [07789118] **2131**

VERKUNDIGUNG UND FORSCHUNG (GW/0342-2410) [02185274] **5007**

VERLAG HOPPENSTEDT *See* VADEMECUM DER INVESTMENTFONDS **918**

VERMESSUNG, PHOTOGRAMMETRIE, KULTURTECHNIK (SZ/0252-9424) [05629939] 2578, **2000**

VERMOEGENSTEUER-HAUPTVERANLAGUNG, DIE (GW) [05277258] **3071**

VERMONT *See* VERMONT STATUTES ANNOTATED **3071**

VERMONT ADOPTIONS *See* ADOPTIONS - STATE OF VERMONT, DEPARTMENT OF SOCIAL AND REHABILITATION SERVICES **5270**

VERMONT. ALCOHOL AND DRUG ABUSE DIVISION *See* VERMONT STATE PLAN FOR DRUG ABUSE PREVENTION AND TREATMENT, THE **1350**

VERMONT BAR JOURNAL & LAW DIGEST, THE (US/0748-4925) [10043810] **3071**

VERMONT BICENTENNIAL COMMISSION *See* REPORT OF THE VERMONT BICENTENNIAL COMMISSION **2757**

VERMONT BUSINESS DIRECTORY (US/1048-7174) [21010837] **718**

VERMONT BUSINESS MAGAZINE (US/0897-7925) [17625180] **718**

VERMONT CASE NAMES CITATOR (US) **3071**

VERMONT CATHOLIC TRIBUNE (US/0042-4145) [03955453] **5038**

VERMONT COMPREHENSIVE PLAN FOR CRIMINAL JUSTICE (US) [03531619] **3178**

VERMONT. DEPT. OF EDUCATION *See* FINANCIAL STATISTICS : VERMONT SCHOOL SYSTEMS **1795**

VERMONT. DEPT. OF EDUCATION *See* ACCOUNTABILITY REPORT FOR VOCATIONAL-TECHNICAL EDUCATION / STATE OF VERMONT **1909**

VERMONT. DEPT. OF EMPLOYMENT SECURITY *See* STATISTICAL TABLES - DEPARTMENT OF EMPLOYMENT SECURITY **2898**

VERMONT. DEPT. OF FINANCE AND MANAGEMENT *See* FISCAL SUMMARY OF ... / VERMONT DEPARTMENT OF FINANCE AND MANAGEMENT **4726**

VERMONT. DEPT. OF HEALTH *See* VERMONT POPULATION ESTIMATES, STATE, COUNTY, CITIES, TOWNS, VILLAGES **4560**

VERMONT. DEPT. OF LIBRARIES *See* BIENNIAL REPORT OF THE VERMONT DEPARTMENT OF LIBRARIES **3195**

VERMONT. DEPT. OF SOCIAL AND REHABILITATION SERVICES *See* ADOPTIONS - STATE OF VERMONT, DEPARTMENT OF SOCIAL AND REHABILITATION SERVICES **5270**

VERMONT ECONOMIC ALMANAC, THE (US/0270-3955) [06400045] **1525**

VERMONT ENERGY STATISTICS (US) [09805978] 1960, **1963**

VERMONT ENIVIRONMENTAL MONITOR (US) **2183**

VERMONT ENVIRONMENTAL REPORT (US) **2183**

VERMONT FACTS AND FIGURES (US/0092-5144) [01789946] **5345**

VERMONT. FISH AND GAME DEPARTMENT *See* BULLETIN - VERMONT FISH AND GAME DEPARTMENT **2189**

VERMONT. FISH AND GAME DEPT *See* VERMONT'S FISHERIES ANNUAL **2315**

VERMONT. GENERAL ASSEMBLY. JOINT ENERGY COMMITTEE *See* REPORT OF THE JOINT ENERGY COMMITTEE **1955**

VERMONT GEOGRAPHIC INFORMATION SYSTEM : ANNUAL REPORT TO THE LEGISLATURE (US) [23065822] **2578**

VERMONT GEOLOGICAL SURVEY *See* BULLETIN / VERMONT GEOLOGICAL SURVEY **1370**

●VERMONT GOLF JOURNAL & DIRECTORY (US/1058-8442) [24398090] **4928**

VERMONT GOVERNMENT DIRECTORY (US/1056-6996) [23819745] **4693**

VERMONT. GOVERNOR'S COMMISSION ON THE ADMINISTRATION OF JUSTICE *See* VERMONT COMPREHENSIVE PLAN FOR CRIMINAL JUSTICE **3178**

●VERMONT HEALTH CARE IN PERSPECTIVE (US/1065-4461) [26606849] **4806**

VERMONT. HEALTH POLICY CORPORATION *See* ANNUAL IMPLEMENTATION PLAN (WATERBURY) **4765**

VERMONT HEALTH POLICY CORPORATION. ANNUAL IMPLEMENTATION PLAN *See* ANNUAL IMPLEMENTATION PLAN / HEALTH POLICY COUNCIL **4765**

VERMONT HISTORY (US/0042-4161) [01510194] **2764**

VERMONT HISTORY NEWS (US/0364-3387) [02337203] **2764**

VERMONT IN PERSPECTIVE (US/1065-5735) [26663295] **5345**

VERMONT INSTITUTE OF NATURAL SCIENCE *See* NEWSLETTER - VERMONT INSTITUTE OF NATURAL SCIENCE **5133**

VERMONT LABOR RELATIONS BOARD *See* ANNUAL REPORT ... OPINIONS / VERMONT LABOR RELATIONS BOARD **3144**

VERMONT LAW REVIEW (US/0145-2908) [02720915] **3071**

VERMONT LEGISLATIVE DIRECTORY AND STATE MANUAL (US/0363-3225) [01769024] **4693**

VERMONT LIBRARY DIRECTORY (US/0364-7382) [02671907] **3255**

VERMONT LIFE (US/0042-417X) [01773576] **2549**

VERMONT LOTTERY COMMISSION *See* ANNUAL REPORT / VERMONT LOTTERY **4630**

VERMONT MAGAZINE (US/1044-940X) [19951772] **2549**

VERMONT MONITOR *See* VERMONT ENIVIRONMENTAL MONITOR **2183**

VERMONT MONITOR (US/1050-6861) [21573448] **2183**

VERMONT MONTHLY LOCAL CLIMATOLOGICAL DATA. MICROFORM (US) [10858713] **1436**

VERMONT MUSIC NEWS (US/0042-4188) [01510267] **4158**

VERMONT NATURAL HISTORY (US/0270-5982) [03475257] **4173**

VERMONT NEWS GUIDE (US/0192-5261) [05053301] **5758**

VERMONT   Alphabetical Title Index

VERMONT. OFFICE OF AUDITOR OF ACCOUNTS See BIENNIAL REPORT OF THE AUDITOR OF ACCOUNTS TO THE GENERAL ASSEMBLY OF VERMONT **4713**

VERMONT. OFFICE OF GEOGRAPHIC INFORMATION SERVICES See VERMONT GEOGRAPHIC INFORMATION SYSTEM : ANNUAL REPORT TO THE LEGISLATURE **2578**

VERMONT. OFFICE OF SECRETARY OF STATE See VERMONT LEGISLATIVE DIRECTORY AND STATE MANUAL **4693**

VERMONT. OFFICE OF STATISTICAL COORDINATION See VERMONT FACTS AND FIGURES **5345**

VERMONT POPULATION ESTIMATES, STATE, COUNTY, CITIES, TOWNS, VILLAGES (US) [04476822] **4560**

VERMONT. PUBLIC SERVICE DEPT See BIENNIAL REPORT OF THE DEPARTMENT OF PUBLIC SERVICE / STATE OF VERMONT **4760**

VERMONT. RECREATION BOARD See BIENNIAL REPORT OF THE VERMONT RECREATION BOARD **4849**

VERMONT REGISTERED NURSE (US/0191-1880) [04767997] **3870**

VERMONT REPORTS CURRENT CASE SERVICE (US) **3071**

VERMONT REPORTS CURRENT CASE STUDIES (US) **3071**

VERMONT SCIENCE : RESEARCH OF THE AGRICULTURAL EXPERIMENT STATION, UNIVERSITY OF VERMONT (US) [11008793] **144**

VERMONT STANDARD, THE (US) [11509837] **5758**

VERMONT. STATE BOARD OF REGISTRATION FOR LAND SURVEYORS See REPORT OF THE PERIOD ... / VERMONT BOARD OF REGISTRATION FOR LAND SURVEYORS **2030**

VERMONT STATE DRUG PLAN See VERMONT STATE PLAN FOR DRUG ABUSE PREVENTION AND TREATMENT, THE **1350**

VERMONT. STATE GEOLOGIST See SPECIAL PUBLICATION - VERMONT GEOLOGICAL SURVEY **1398**

VERMONT. STATE GEOLOGISTS See SPECIAL BULLETIN - VERMONT GEOLOGICAL SURVEY **1397**

VERMONT STATE HOSPITAL See ANNUAL REPORT FOR FISCAL YEAR ... / VERMONT STATE HOSPITAL **3776**

VERMONT. STATE LABOR RELATIONS BOARD. OPINIONS See ANNUAL REPORT ... OPINIONS / VERMONT LABOR RELATIONS BOARD **3144**

VERMONT STATE PLAN FOR DRUG ABUSE PREVENTION AND TREATMENT, THE (US) [03347634] **1350**

VERMONT. STATE PLANNING OFFICE See A-95 CLEARINGHOUSE REPORT **2812**

VERMONT STATUTES ANNOTATED (US) [01604349] **3071**

VERMONT STUDENT ASSISTANCE CORPORATION See REPORT TO THE VERMONT GENERAL ASSEMBLY **1844**

VERMONT. UNIVERSITY. AGRICULTURAL EXTENSION SERVICE See BRIEFLET **68**

VERMONT. UNIVERSITY. GOVERNMENT RESEARCH CENTER See STATE SERIES **4688**

VERMONT YEAR BOOK (US/0083-5781) [02409709] **4693**, **718**

VERMONT'S ... BASIC COMPETENCY PROGRAM (US) [08076930] **1789**

VERMONT'S FISHERIES ANNUAL (US/0092-5810) [01791220] **2315**

VERNACULAR ARCHITECTURE (UK/0305-5477) [02390970] **310**

VERNACULAR BUILDING (UK/0267-3088) [11832168] **310**

VERNAL EXPRESS (US/0892-1091) [11300759] **5757**

VERNIEUWDESTAD (NE) [02239725] **2838**

VERNON COUNTY BROADCASTER (US) **5771**

VERNON COUNTY BROADCASTER-CENSOR (US) [11995211] **5771**

VERNON NEWS/VOICE (US/0746-8768) [10378931] **5662**

VERNON'S ... BELLEVILLE CITY DIRECTORY (CN/0849-0805) [22103383] **1123**

VERNON'S ... BRANTFORD CITY DIRECTORY (CN/0848-9203) [21492062] **2578**

VERNON'S BURLINGTON AND HAMILTON SUBURBAN DIRECTORY (CN/0701-8665) [03439603] **2578**

VERNON'S BUSINESS SOURCES, HAMILTON & NIAGARA AREA EDITION FOR SELECTED COMMUNITIES (CN/1183-5494) [24267019] **718**

VERNON'S CITY OF CAMBRIDGE (ONTARIO) DIRECTORY (CN/0317-2899) [02248044] **2578**

VERNON'S CITY OF HAMILTON (ONTARIO) DIRECTORY (CN/0316-1765) [02248020] **2578**

VERNON'S CITY OF KITCHENER-WATERLOO (ONTARIO) DIRECTORY (CN/0229-7337) [08028205] **2578**

VERNON'S CITY OF TIMMINS, ONTARIO, DIRECTORY (CN/0706-5035) [05071920] **2578**

VERNON'S ... NORTH BAY CITY DIRECTORY (CN/0849-0813) [22103373] **2578**

VERO BEACH PRESS JOURNAL (US) [01510574] **5651**

VEROEFFENTLICHUNGEN AUS DER PATHOLOGIE (GW/0340-241X) [01297285] **3898**

VEROEFFENTLICHUNGEN DER INTERNATIONALEN GESELLSCHAFT FUER GESCHICHTE DER PHARMAZIE. NEUE FOLGE, DIE (GW/0074-9729) [06529499] **4332**

VEROEFFENTLICHUNGEN DER VEREINIGING DER DEUTSCHEN STAATSRECHTSLEHRER (GW) **3071**

VEROEFFENTLICHUNGEN DES STATISTISCHEN LANDESAMTES BADEN-WUERTTEMBERG (GW) [20175737] **5345**

VEROFFENTLICHUNG AUS DER SEKTION GEOWISSENSCHAFTEN DER BERGAKADEMIE FREIBERG (GW) [04546425] **1400**

VEROFFENTLICHUNG - GESELLSCHAFT DER ORGELFREUNDE (GW/0435-8112) [01454299] **4158**

VEROFFENTLICHUNG. REIHE A, HOHERE GEODASIE / DEUTSCHE GEODATISCHE KOMMISSION BEI DER BAYERISCHEN AKADEMIE DER WISSENSCHAFTEN (GW/0065-5309) [03408751] **1412**

VEROFFENTLICHUNGEN (GW/0530-9794) [01564082] **2714**

VEROFFENTLICHUNGEN (SZ) [01765177] **3649**

VEROFFENTLICHUNGEN (GW/0568-4358) [06650998] **1080**

VEROFFENTLICHUNGEN (GW/0537-7919) [01606649] **5007**

VEROFFENTLICHUNGEN (GW) [01791616] **3071**

VEROFFENTLICHUNGEN. ABTEILUNG SUDSEE (GW/0067-5989) [03288459] **2325**

VEROFFENTLICHUNGEN AUS DEM NATURHISTORISCHEN MUSEUM WIEN (AU/0378-8202) [12122368] **4173**

VEROFFENTLICHUNGEN DER ABTEILUNG FUER SLAVISCHE SPRACHEN UND LITERATUREN DES OSTEUROPA-INSTITUTS (SLAVISCHES SEMINAR) AN DER FREIEN UNIVERSITAT BERLIN (GW/0067-592X) [08555785] **3450**

VEROFFENTLICHUNGEN DER ALTERTUMSKOMMISSION IM PROVINZIALINSTITUT FUER WESTFALISCHE LANDES- UND VOLKSFORSCHUNG, LANDSCHAFTSVERBAND WESTFALEN-LIPPE (GW) [07035053] **2714**

VEROFFENTLICHUNGEN DER ALTERTUMSKOMMISSION IM PROVINZIALINSTITUT FUR WESTFALISCHE LANDES- UND VOLKSKUNDE See VEROFFENTLICHUNGEN DER ALTERTUMSKOMMISSION IM PROVINZIALINSTITUT FUER WESTFALISCHE LANDES- UND VOLKSFORSCHUNG, LANDSCHAFTSVERBAND WESTFALEN-LIPPE **2714**

VEROFFENTLICHUNGEN DER ARBEITSGEMEINSCHAFT GETREIDEFORSCHUNG E.V., DETMOLD (GW/0342-572X) [11349688] **204**

VEROFFENTLICHUNGEN DER BUNDESANSTALT FUER ALPENLANDISCHE LANDWIRTSCHAFT GUMPENSTEIN / BUNDESMINISTERIUM FUER LAND- UND FORSTWIRTSCHAFT (AU/1010-6146) [21585396] **144**

VEROFFENTLICHUNGEN DER KOMMISSION FUER ZEITGESCHICHTE. REIHE B: FORSCHUNGEN (GW/01779470) **5038**

VEROFFENTLICHUNGEN DER KOMMISSION FUR LINGUISTIK UND KOMMUNIKATIONSFORSCHUNG (AU) [01793991] **1123**, **3331**

VEROFFENTLICHUNGEN DER KOMMISSION FUR ZEITGESCHICHTE. REIHE A : QUELLEN (GW) [01590564] **5038**

VEROFFENTLICHUNGEN DER SCHWEIZERISCHEN KARTELLKOMMISSION (SZ) [03336063] **3071**

VEROFFENTLICHUNGEN DER SENATSKOMMISSION FUER HUMANISMUS-FORSCHUNG (GW) [04800250] **2714**

VEROFFENTLICHUNGEN DER STERNWARTE IN SONNEBERG (GW) [02068597] **401**

VEROFFENTLICHUNGEN DER URGESCHICHTLICHEN SAMMLUNGEN DES LANDESMUSEUMS ZU HANNOVER (GW/0931-6280) [I09316280] **4097**

VEROFFENTLICHUNGEN DES ARCHIVES DER STADT STUTTGART (GW) [01640726] **2714**

VEROFFENTLICHUNGEN DES DEUTSCHEN HISTORISCHEN INSTITUTS IN LONDON (GW) [05068726] **2714**

VEROFFENTLICHUNGEN DES GEOBOTANISCHEN INSTITUTS DER ETH, STIFTUNG RUBEL, ZURICH (SW/0254-9433) [10919357] **530**

VEROFFENTLICHUNGEN DES HESSISCHEN STATISTISCHEN LANDESAMTES (GW) [01795928] **5345**

VEROFFENTLICHUNGEN DES INSTITUTS FUER BODENMECHANIK UND FELSMECHANIK DER UNIVERSITAT FRIDERICIANA IN KARLSRUHE (GW/0453-3267) [05511027] **1400**

VEROFFENTLICHUNGEN DES INSTITUTS FUER KUSTEN- UND BINNENFISCHEREI HAMBURG (GW/0343-2203) [I03432203] **2315**

VEROFFENTLICHUNGEN DES INSTITUTS FUER NEUE MUSIK UND MUSIKERZIEHUNG DARMSTADT (GW/0418-3827) [01625060] **4158**

VEROFFENTLICHUNGEN DES INSTITUTS FUER WASSERFORSCHUNG GMBH DORTMUND UND DER HYDROLOGISCHEN ABTEILUNG DER DORTMUNDER STADTWERKE AG (GW/0342-474X) [04853539] **5541**

VEROFFENTLICHUNGEN DES LANDESAMTES FUER DATENVERARBEITUNG UND STATISTIK NORDRHEIN-WESTFALEN (GW) [02880704] **5346**

VEROFFENTLICHUNGEN DES LEIBNIZ-ARCHIVS (GW) [01801517] **3540**

VEROFFENTLICHUNGEN DES MUSEUMS FUER UR- UND FRUHGESCHICHTE POTSDAM (GE/0079-4376) [02486338] **285**

VEROFFENTLICHUNGEN DES OSTEUROPA-INSTITUTES MUNCHEN. REIHE: WIRTSCHAFT UND GESELLSCHAFT (GW/0580-2008) [02497666] **1588**

VEROFFENTLICHUNGEN DES STAATSARCHIVS POTSDAM (GW) [05803944] **2714**

VEROFFENTLICHUNGEN DES TIROLER LANDESMUSEUM FERDINANDEUM (AU/0379-0231) [21370395] **2714**

VEROFFENTLICHUNGEN DES ZENTRALINSTITUTS FUER ALTE GESCHICHTE UND ARCHAEOLOGIE DER AKADEMIE DER WISSENSCHAFTEN DER DDR (GW) [03278656] **285**

VEROFFENTLICHUNGEN DES ZENTRALINSTITUTS FUER PHYSIK DER ERDE (GW/0514-8790) [04062855] **1412**

VEROFFENTLICHUNGEN FUER NATURSCHUTZ UND LANDSCHAFTSPFLEGE IN BADEN-WURTTEMBERG (GW/0342-684X) [07407620] **2208**, **4173**

VEROFFENTLICHUNGEN - MAX-PLANCK-INSTITUT FUER GESCHICHTE (GW/0436-1180) [01437255] **2632**

VEROFFENTLICHUNGEN. NEUE FOLGE, REIHE 4. SCHRIFTEN ZUR BEETHOVENFORSCHUNG (GW) [02618418] **4158**

VEROFFENTLICHUNGSVERZEICHNIS / STATISTISCHES BUNDESAMT (GW) [11363574] **427**

VEROHALLINNON KASIKIRJA: MAATILATALOUDEN VEROTUS (FI) [03394177] **4757**

VEROHALLITUKSEN YHTENAISTAMISOHJEET VUODELTA ... TOIMITETTAVAA VEROTUSIA VARTEN (FI) [19029787] **4757**

VERONA FATHER MISSIONS See VERONA MISSIONS **5007**

VERONA ILLUSTRATA : RIVISTA DEL MUSEO DI CASTELVECCHIO (IT/1120-3226) [21925497] **367**

VERONA MISSIONS (US/0164-4211) [04722056] **5007**

VERONA PRESS, THE (US) [11853167] **5771**

VERORDNUNGSBLATT DES LANDESSCHULRATES FUER OBEROESTERREICH (AU) [02468032] **1789**

VERORDNUNGSBLATT FUR DIE BRITISCHE ZONE See BUNDESGESETZBLATT **2945**

VERPACKUNG (GW/0042-4269) [07582819] **4222**

Alphabetical Title Index — VESELYE

VERPAKKEN (NE) **4222**

VERPAKKING (NE) [07607279] **4222**

VERPAKKINGS MANAGEMENT (NE) **4217**

VERPLEEGKUNDE (NE/0920-3273) [29879194] **3870**

VERPLEEGKUNDIGE STUDIES (NE/0167-4706) [04680413] **3870**

VERPLEEGKUNDIGEN EN GEMEENSCHAPSZORG (BE) **3870**

VERRE ACTUALITES (FR/0180-0078) [I01800078] **2595**

VERRE (PARIS, FRANCE) (FR/0984-7979) [17454029] **2595**

VERRI, IL (IT/0506-7715) [01624196] 332, **3450**

VERS DEMAIN (EDITION FRANCAISE) (CN/0317-8471) [02304213] **5225**

VERS L'EDUCATION NOUVELLE (FR/0151-1904) [16788118] **1789**

VERS UN DEVELOPPEMENT SOLIDAIRE (SZ) **4537**

VERSAILLES POLICY, THE (US) [17278040] **5731**

VERSAILLES PREGNY-CHAMBERY (SZ/0505-3668) [I05053668] **2714**

VERSAILLES REPUBLICAN (VERSAILLES, IND. : 1893) (US) [11880122] **5668**

VERSANTS (SZ) [09681761] 3355, **3331**

VERSATILITY (US/0893-3537) [15494010] **4424**

VERSE (OXFORD, OXFORDSHIRE) (US/0268-3830) [11882511] **3473**

VERSICHERUNGSMEDIZIN (GW/0933-4548) [17726184] 2895, **3649**

VERSICHERUNGSRECHT (GW) [01643048] **2895**

VERSICHERUNGSWIRTSCHAFT (GW/0042-4358) [06754885] **2895**

VERSION (SIDNEY, N.S.W.) (AT) [09594947] **2511**

VERSLAE VAN DIE GEKOSE KOMITEE OOR DIE MORATORIUMWYSIGINGSWETSONT WERP. REPORTS OF THE SELECT COMMITTEE ON THE MORATORIUM AMENDMENT BILL (SA) [06245874] **3071**

VERSLAE VAN DIE GEKOSE KOMITEE OOR DIE WETSONTWERP OP OUTEURSREG. REPORTS OF THE SELECT COMMITTEE ON THE COPYRIGHT BILL (SA) [05896083] **1309**

VERSLAE VAN DIE GEKOSE KOMITEE VOOR DIE BOSWETSONTWERP (SA) [06268524] 2398, **3071**

VERSLAE VAN DIE GEKOSE KOMITEE VOOR PENSIOENE (SA) [05810178] 2895, **1716**

VERSLAE VAN DIE GEKOSE KOMITEE VOOR STAATSGROND (SA) [05913200] **4693**

VERSLAG - BOSBOURAAD (SA) [03308150] **2398**

VERSLAG DEUR DIE VOORSITTER OOR DIE RAAD SE BEDRYWIGHEDE (SA) [03991521] **4693**

VERSLAG / KAMER VAN KOOPHANDEL EN FABRIEKEN VOOR AMSTERDAM (NE) [07797093] **856**

VERSLAG LEVENSMIDDELEN EN KEURING VAN WAREN (NE) [02359554] **2360**

VERSLAG ONDERZOEK KWALITEIT OPPERVLAKTEWATER IN ZEELAND (NE) [01793768] 5541, **2245**

VERSLAG OVER HET BOEKJAAR ... (NE) [12851934] **815**

VERSLAG OVER HET BOEKJAAR ... / GAK (NE) [09400034] **1631**

VERSLAG OVER HET JAAR ... / STICHTING FONDS VOOR DE LETTEREN (NE) [10478264] **3450**

VERSLAG / PROEFSTATION VOOR DE AKKERBOUW ON DE GROENTETEELT IN DE VOLLEGROND (NE) [21344890] 2433, **2360**

VERSLAG VAN DE DELEGATIE VAN HET KONINKRIJK DER NEDERLANDEN NAAR DE WERELDGEZONDHEIDSVERGADERING (NE) [03127720] **4806**

VERSLAG VAN DE HOOFDCONSULENT VOOR DE MUSEA (NE) [04215728] **4097**

VERSLAG VAN DE RAAD VAN BEHEER OVER DE VERRICHTINGEN (BE) [04517453] **2838**

VERSLAG VAN DE STAND DER ZIEKENGELDVERZEKERING *See* STAND ZIEKENGELDVERZEKERING VERSLAG OVER ... / SOCIALE VERZEKERINGSRAAD **2894**

VERSLAG VAN DE VERZEKERINGSKAMER INGEVOLGE DE WET OP HET SCHADEVERZEKERINGSBEDRIJF OVER HET JAAR ... (NE) [08656275] **2895**

VERSLAG VAN DE WERKZAAMHEDEN - COMMISSIE VOOR DE BESTUURSHERVORMING (NE) [06742012] **1853**

VERSLAG VAN DE WERKZAAMHEDEN VAN DE SOCIALE VERZEKERINGSRAAD *See* JAARVERSLAG - SOCIALE VERZEKERINGSRAAAD **5291**

VERSLAG VAN DIE DIREKTEUR-GENERAAL, GEMEENSKAPSONTWIKKELING VIR DIE TYDPERK ... (SA) [09330815] **2839**

VERSLAG VAN DIE GEKOSE KOMITEE OOR POS- EN TELEKOMMUNIKASIEWESE. REPORT OF THE SELECT COMMITTEE ON POSTS AND TELECOMMUNICATIONS (SA) [05805977] 1168, **1147**

VERSLAG VAN DIE OUDITEUR-GENERAAL OOR DIE REKENINGS VAN DIE ONTWIKKELINGSRAAD SUID-ORANJE-VRYSTAAT-GEBIED VIR DIE BOEKJAAR ... / REPORT OF THE AUDITOR-GENERAL ON THE ACCOUNTS OF THE SOUTHERN ORANGE FREE STATE AREA DEVELOPMENT BOARD FOR THE FINANCIAL YEAR ... (SA) [15321679] **4757**

VERSLAG VAN DIE OUDITEUR-GENERAAL OOR DIE REKENINGS VAN DIE RAAD VIR INMAAKVRUGTE VIR DIE BOEKJAAR ... (SA) [17574171] 4758, **2360**

VERSLAG VAN DIE OUDITEUR-GENERAAL OOR DIE REKENINGS VAN DIE SYBOKHAARRAAD. REPORT OF THE AUDITOR-GENERAL ON THE ACCOUNTS OF THE MOHAIR BOARD (SA) [06280974] **4693**

VERSLAG VAN DIE OUDITEUR-GENERAAL VOOR DIE REKENINGS VAN DIE SIGOREIRRAAD (SA) [06005145] **753**

VERSLAG VAN DIE OUDITEUR-GENERAAL VOOR DIE SUIDWES-AFRIKAREKENING WAT DEEL UITMAAK VAN DIE STAATSINKOMSTEFONDS VAN DIE REPUBLIEK VAN SUID-AFRIKA (SA) [06644165] **4758**

VERSLAG VAN DIE RAAD VAN SUID-AFRIKAANSE VERVOERDIENSTE VIR DIE JAAR GEEINDIG ... (SA) [09103787] **5399**

VERSLAG VIR DIE TYDPERK. DEPARTEMENT VAN JUSTISIE VAN DIE REPUBLIEK VAN SUID-AFRIKA (SA) [16269986] **4693**

VERSLAGEN EN MEDEDEELINGEN VAN DE PLANTENZIEKTENKUNDIGE DIENST, WAGENINGEN (NE/0169-8346) [I01698346] **530**

VERSLAGEN EN MEDEDELING - PLANTENZIEKTENKUNDIGE DIENST (NE) [01642313] **144**

VERSLAGEN EN MEDEDELINGEN - COMMISSIE VOOR HYDROLOGISCH ONDERZOEK T.N.O (NE/0548-1228) [03799607] **1418**

VERSLAGEN EN MEDEDELINGEN - KONINKLIJKE ACADEMIE VOOR NEDERLANDSE TAAL - EN LETTERKUNDE (BE) [01794030] 3450, **3331**

VERSLAGEN VAN LANDBOUWKUNDIGE ONDERZOEKINGEN DER RIJKSLANDBOUWPROEFSTATIONS *CEASED.* (NE/0372-6223) [06663805] **144**

VERSTANDLICHE WISSENSCHAFT (GW/0083-5846) [01514909] 5225, **2632**

VERSUCHSANSTALT FUER WASSERBAU, HYDROLOGIE UND GLAZIOLOGIE *See* MITTEILUNGEN DER VERSUCHSANSTALT FUER WASSERBAU, HYDROLOGIE UND GLAZIOLOGIE **1416**

VERSUS *CEASED.* (NE/0168-2121) [I01682121] **4079**

VERSUS (MILAN, ITALY) (IT/0393-8255) [02160796] **3331**

VERTEGENWOORDIGINGEN VAN HET KONINKRIJK DER NEDERLANDEN IN HET BUITENLAND / MINISTERIE VAN BUITENLANDSE ZAKEN (NE) [04424786] **4499**

VERTEGENWOORDIGINGEN VAN NEDERLAND IN HET BUITENLAND *See* VERTEGENWOORDIGINGEN VAN HET KONINKRIJK DER NEDERLANDEN IN HET BUITENLAND / MINISTERIE VAN BUITENLANDSE ZAKEN **4499**

VERTEX (LOS ANGELES) (US/0091-7257) [01788014] **3450**

VERTICAL APPLICATION RESELLER (US) **1245**

VERTICAL FILE INDEX (US/0042-4439) [04769693] **427**

VERTICE (LISBOA) (PO/0042-4447) [03191756] **3355**

VERTIFLITE (US/0042-4455) [06999043] **39**

VERTIGO (CN/1188-0511) [25796519] **376**

VERTIGO (PARIS, FRANCE) (FR/0985-1402) [20073232] **4079**

VERWALTUNG (BERLIN), DIE (GW/0042-4498) [04016327] **4693**

VERWALTUNG UND FORTBILDUNG (GW) [06177591] **4693**

VERWALTUNGSARCHIV (GW/0042-4501) [05021191] **3071**

VERWALTUNGSBERICHT DES BEZIRKS BONN DER BERGBAU-BERUFSGENOSSENSCHAFT / HERAUSGEGEBEN VON DER BEZIRKSVERWALTUNG BONN DER BERGBAU-BERUFSGENOSSENSCHAFT (GW) [11455009] 2895, **2871**

VERWALTUNGSBERICHT DES BEZIRKS CLAUSTHAL-ZELLERFELD DER BERGBAU-BERUFSGENOSSENSCHAFT (GW) [06570871] 4023, **2152**

VERWALTUNGSRECHTSPRECHUNG IN DEUTSCHLAND (GW) [01769040] **3071**

VERWALTUNGSRUNDSCHAU (GW/0342-5592) [07113718] **889**

VERWALTUNGSWIRT, DER (GW/0174-6162) [I01746162] **3071**

VERWARMING EN VENTILATIE (NE/0042-451X) [07786366] **2608**

VERY BEGINNING (LYNN-MAR COMMUNITY SCHOOL DISTRICT ED.), THE (US/0747-4989) [10737767] **1789**

VERY SMALL COMPANY AUDIT SYSTEM (UK) **753**

VERZAMELDE OVERDRUKKEN - PLANTENZIEKTENKUNDIGE DIENST (NE/0466-9959) [01704726] **2433**

VERZEICHNIS DER ALLGEMEINBILDENDEN SCHULEN (GW) [07040843] 1789, **1798**

VERZEICHNIS DER BERUFSBILDENDEN SCHULEN (GW) [06968321] **1917**

VERZEICHNIS DER MITGLIEDER / DEUTSCHES ARCHAEOLOGISCHES INSTITUT (GW) [20402868] **285**

VERZEICHNIS DER NEUERWERBUNGEN - JOHN F. KENNEDY-INSTITUT FUER NORDAMERIKASTUDIEN, FREIE UNIVERSITAT BERLIN BIBLIOTHEK (GW/0936-384X) [19915833] **427**

VERZEICHNIS DER ORIENTALISCHEN HANDSCHRIFTEN IN DEUTSCHLAND (GW/0506-7936) [01605464] **2667**

VERZEICHNIS DER ORIENTALISCHEN HANDSCHRIFTEN IN DEUTSCHLAND. SUPPLEMENTBAND (GW/0506-7944) [03171547] **3336**

●VERZEICHNIS DER VEROFFENTLICHUNGEN / STATISTISCHES BUNDESAMT (GW) [24932158] **4820**

VERZEICHNIS DER WISSENSCHAFTLICHEN FILME. TEILVERZEICHNIS B (GW/0174-1993) [05771004] 2245, **144**

VERZEICHNIS DER WISSENSCHAFTLICHEN VEROFFENTLICHUNGEN (GW) [05505452] **4811**

VERZEICHNIS LEIFERBARER BUCHER. EERGANZUNGSBAND (GW/0067-8899) [03192923] **4822**

VERZEICHNIS LEIFERBARER BUCHER. SCHLAGWORT-VERZEICHNIS (GW) [04540130] **3255**

VERZEICHNIS LIEFERBARER BUCHER. ISBN-REGISTER (GW) [04554622] **4833**

VERZEICHNIS RHEINLAND-PFALZISCHER RECHTS- UND VERWALTUNGSVORSCHRIFTEN (GW) [10224921] **3094**

VERZEICHNIS WISSENSCHAFTLICHER PUBLIKATIONEN (GW) [07053410] **4332**

VERZEKERINGS ARCHIEF, HET (NE) **2895**

VERZEKERINGS MAGAZINE (NE/0925-3440) [I09253440] **2856**

VERZEKERINGS MAGAZINE VVP (NE) **2895**

VERZINKEN *See* FEUERVERZINKEN **4002**

VES SVET (RU) [03495021] **3450**

●VESCI AKADEMII NAVUK BELARUSI. SERYA BIALAGICNYH NAVUK (BW) [26977768] **494**

●VESCI AKADEMII NAVUK BELARUSI. SERYA FIZIKA-ENERGETYCNYH NAVUK (BW) [27206177] **2108**

●VESCI AKADEMII NAVUK BELARUSI. SERYA HIMICNYH NAVUK (BW) [27206062] 4424, **995**

VESELKA (US/0300-6379) [01779158] **1071**

VESELYE KARTINKI (RU/0504-0523) [02733006] **1071**

VESEOIUZNOE

VESEOIUZNOE MINERALOGICHESKOE OBSHCHESTVO See ZAPISKI VSESOIUZNOGO MINERALOGICHESKOGO OBSHCHESTVA **1445**

VESNIK / VOJNI MUZEJ, BEOGRAD (YU/0067-5660) [24490088] **4060**

VESNIK (VOJNI MUZEJ JUGOSLOVENSKE NARODNE ARMIJE (BELGRADE, SERBIA)) See VESNIK / VOJNI MUZEJ, BEOGRAD **4060**

●VESTAL PRESS RESOURCE CATALOGUE, THE (US/1066-4823) [26949675] **427**

VESTIBULLES (MONTREAL) (CN/1186-1258) [24267113] **382**

VESTIGIA (GW/0506-8010) [01516637] **2632**

VESTIRAMA (SP) **1088**

VESTNIK (AU) **4499**

VESTNIK (US/0574-8526) [01553774] **1921**

●VESTNIK AKADEMIE VED CESKE REPUBLIKY (XR) [30405037] **3649**

●VESTNIK AKADEMIE ZEMEDELSKYCH VED CSFR (XR) [26387533] **144**

VESTNIK AKADEMII MEDITSINSKIKH NAUK SSSR (RU/0002-3027) [01478757] **3649**

VESTNIK AKADEMII NAUK KAZAKHSKOI SSR See VESTNIK AKADEMII NAUK RESPUBLIKI KAZAKHSTAN / QAZAQSTAN RESPUBLIKASY GHYLYM AKADEMIIASYNYNG KHABARSHYSY **5168**

VESTNIK AKADEMII NAUK RESPUBLIKI KAZAKHSTAN See VESTNIK NATSIONALNOI AKADEMII NAUK RESPUBLIKI KAZAKHSTAN / QAZAQSTAN RESPUBLIKASY ULTTYQ GHYLYM AKADEMIIASYNYNG KHABARSHYSY **5168**

VESTNIK AKADEMII NAUK RESPUBLIKI KAZAKHSTAN / QAZAQSTAN RESPUBLIKASY GHYLYM AKADEMIIASYNYNG KHABARSHYSY (KZ) [26676765] **5168**

VESTNIK AKADEMII NAUK SSSR (RU/0002-3442) [01141537] **5168**

VESTNIK AKADEMII NAUK SSSR. ENGLISH. HERALD OF THE USSR ACADEMY OF SCIENCES See HERALD OF THE RUSSIAN ACADEMY OF SCIENCES **5109**

VESTNIK CESKOSLOVENSKE AKADEMIE VED (XR/0009-0492) [08635775] **3649**

VESTNIK CESKOSLOVENSKE AKADEMIE ZEMEDELSKE See VESTNIK AKADEMIE ZEMEDELSKYCH VED CSFR **144**

VESTNIK CESKOSLOVENSKYCH SPOLKU V MONTREALE (CN/0700-8171) [03589148] **2764**

VESTNIK DERMATOLOGII I VENEROLOGII (RU/0042-4609) [01697223] **3723**

VESTNIK DOPRAVY (XR) [05951676] **5399**

VESTNIK DREVNEJ ISTORII (RU/0321-0391) [01478836] **2632**

VESTNIK FEDERALNIHO URADU PRO VYNALEZY. CAST A, VYNALEZY (XR/0231-9942) [19958730] **1309**

VESTNIK FEDERALNIHO URADU PRO VYNALEZY. CAST B, OCHRANNE ZNAMKY, PRUMYSLOVE UZORY (XR/0231-9985) [19976548] **1309**

VESTNIK HIRURGII IM. I.I. GREKOVA (RU/0042-4625) [01765583] **3994**

VESTNIK ISTORII MIROVOI KULTURY *CEASED.* (RU/0505-3862) [05235878] **2632**

VESTNIK KIEVSKOGO POLITEKHNICHESKOGO INSTITUTA. SERIIA PRIBOROSTROENIIA (UN/0321-2211) [03217116] **3489**

VESTNIK KIEVSKOGO POLITEKHNICHESKOGO INSTITUTA. SERIIA RADIOELEKTRONIKA (UN) [11478243] **4442**

VESTNIK KIEVSKOGO UNIVERSITETA. ASTRONOMIIA (UN/0321-3927) [07789534] **401**

VESTNIK KIEVSKOGO UNIVERSITETA. FIZIKA / MINISTERSTVO VYSSHEGO I SREDNEGO SPETSIALNOGO OBRAZOVANIIA USSR (UN/0372-607X) [16127620] **4424**

VESTNIK KIEVSKOGO UNIVERSITETA. ROMANO-GERMANSKAIA FILOLOGIIA (UN/0135-1117) [08334116] **3331**

VESTNIK, LE MESSAGER (FR/0767-7294) [02163413] **2524**

VESTNIK LENINGRAD UNIVERSITY: MATHEMATICS See VESTNIK ST. PETERSBURG UNIVERSITY: MATHEMATICS **3540**

VESTNIK LENINGRADSKOGO UNIVERSITETA. MATEMATIKA, MEKHANIKA, ASTRONOMIIA (US/0883-623X) [12183910] **2131**

VESTNIK LENINGRADSKOGO UNIVERSITETA. SERIIA 1, MATEMATIKA, MEKHANIKA, ASTRONOMIIA See VESTNIK SANKT-PETERBURGSKOGO UNIVERSITETA. SERIIA 1, MATEMATIKA, MEKHANIKA, ASTRONOMIIA **3540**

VESTNIK LENINGRADSKOGO UNIVERSITETA. SERIIA 2, ISTORIIA, IAZYKOZNANIE, LITERATUROVEDENIE See VESTNIK SANKT-PETERBURGSKOGO UNIVERSITETA. SERIIA 2, ISTORIIA, IAZYKOZNANIE, LITERATUROVEDENIE **2632**

VESTNIK LENINGRADSKOGO UNIVERSITETA. SERIIA 3, BIOLOGIIA See VESTNIK SANKT-PETERBURGSKOGO UNIVERSITETA. SERIIA 3, BIOLOGIIA **475**

VESTNIK LENINGRADSKOGO UNIVERSITETA. SERIIA 5, EKONOMIKA See VESTNIK SANKT-PETERBURGSKOGO UNIVERSITETA. SERIIA 5, EKONOMIKA **1525**

VESTNIK LENINGRADSKOGO UNIVERSITETA. SERIIA 7, GEOLOGIIA, GEOGRAFIIA See VESTNIK SANKT-PETERBURGSKOGO UNIVERSITETA. SERIIA 7, GEOLOGIIA, GEOGRAFIIA **1400**

VESTNIK MASINOSTROENIJA (RU/0042-4633) [11161804] **2152**

●VESTNIK MINISTERSTVA SKOLSTVI, MLADEZE A TELOVYCHOVY CESKE REPUBLIKY (XR) [30684081] **1886**

VESTNIK MINISTERSTVA VNESHNIKH SNOSHENII SSSR See DIPLOMATICHESKII VESTNIK **3127**

VESTNIK MORKOVSKOGO UNIVERSITETA. SERIIA IX : PRAVO (RU) [03930172] **3071**

VESTNIK MOSKOVSKOGO UNIVERSITETA SERIA 14 PSIHOLOGIA (RU/0137-0936) [01370936] **4621**

VESTNIK MOSKOVSKOGO UNIVERSITETA. SERIA 16. BIOLOGIA (RU/0137-0952) [03863708] **475**

VESTNIK MOSKOVSKOGO UNIVERSITETA. SERIA IX : FILOLOGIIA (RU/0130-0075) [04589128] **3331**

VESTNIK MOSKOVSKOGO UNIVERSITETA. SERIIA 12, SOTSIALNO-POLITICHESKIE ISSLEDOVANIIA (RU) [22526428] **4548**

VESTNIK MOSKOVSKOGO UNIVERSITETA SERIIA I, MATEMATIKA, MEKHANIKA (RU/0579-9368) [08920169] **2131, 3540**

VESTNIK MOSKOVSKOGO UNIVERSITETA. SERIIA II. KHIMIIA (RU/0579-9384) [04647939] **995**

VESTNIK MOSKOVSKOGO UNIVERSITETA. SERIIA III, FIZIKA, ASTRONOMIIA (RU/0579-9392) [04681614] **4424**

VESTNIK MOSKOVSKOGO UNIVERSITETA. SERIIA V, GEOGRAFIIA (RU/0579-9414) [01758746] **2579**

VESTNIK MOSKOVSKOGO UNIVERSITETA. SERIIA VI, EKONOMIKA (RU/0130-0105) [03592710] **1525**

VESTNIK MOSKOVSKOGO UNIVERSITETA. SERIIA VII : FILOSOFIIA (RU/0130-0091) [03406980] **4364**

VESTNIK MOSKOVSKOGO UNIVERSITETA. SERIIA VIII: ISTORIIA (RU) [07349757] **2632**

VESTNIK MOSKOVSKOGO UNIVERSITETA. SERIIA X : ZHURNALISTIKA (RU) [04782594] **2925**

VESTNIK MOSKOVSKOGO UNIVERSITETA. SERIIA XIV : PSIKHOLOGIIA (RU/0137-0936) [03925733] **4621**

VESTNIK MOSKOVSKOGO UNIVERSITETA. SERIIA XV : VYCHISLITELNAIA MATEMATIKA I KIBERNETIKA (RU/0137-0782) [03937033] **1252, 1262**

VESTNIK MOSKOVSKOGO UNIVERSITETA. SERIIA XV, VYCHISLITELNAIA MATEMATIKA I KIBERNETIKA. ENGLISH (US/0278-6419) [05098198] **3540, 1252**

VESTNIK MOSKOVSKOGO UNIVERSITETA. SERIJA 4: GEOLOGIJA (RU/0579-9406) [04474335] **1400**

VESTNIK NATSIONALNOI AKADEMII NAUK RESPUBLIKI KAZAKHSTAN / QAZAQSTAN RESPUBLIKASY ULTTYQ GHYLYM AKADEMIIASYNYNG KHABARSHYSY (KZ) [30411330] **5168**

VESTNIK OFTALMOLOGII (RU/0042-465X) [04128023] **3879**

VESTNIK OTORINOLARINGOLOGII (RU/0042-4668) [01777883] **3891**

VESTNIK (OWINGS MILLS, MD.) (US/1055-2278) [23116358] **2275**

VESTNIK RENTGENOLOGII I RADIOLOGII (RU/0042-4676) [01589137] **3947**

●VESTNIK ROSSIISKOI AKADEMII MEDITSINSKIKH NAUK / ROSSIISKAIA AKADEMIIA MEDITSINSKIKH NAUK (RU) [26850483] **3649**

●VESTNIK ROSSIISKOI AKADEMII NAUK (RU) [25918528] **5169**

●VESTNIK SANKT-PETERBURGSKOGO UNIVERSITETA. SERIIA 1, MATEMATIKA, MEKHANIKA, ASTRONOMIIA (RU) [29348902] **401, 3540**

●VESTNIK SANKT-PETERBURGSKOGO UNIVERSITETA. SERIIA 2, ISTORIIA, IAZYKOZNANIE, LITERATUROVEDENIE (RU) [25931936] **3332, 2632**

●VESTNIK SANKT-PETERBURGSKOGO UNIVERSITETA. SERIIA 3, BIOLOGIIA (RU) [26461624] **475**

●VESTNIK SANKT-PETERBURGSKOGO UNIVERSITETA. SERIIA 5, EKONOMIKA (RU) [26725306] **1525**

●VESTNIK SANKT-PETERBURGSKOGO UNIVERSITETA. SERIIA 7, GEOLOGIIA, GEOGRAFIIA (RU) [26779043] **2579, 1400**

VESTNIK SELSKOHOZJAJSTVENNOJ NAUKI (RU/0206-6335) [01769043] **144**

VESTNIK SELSKOHOZJAJSTVENNOJ NAUKI KAZAHSTANA (KZ/0042-4684) [10634697] **144**

VESTNIK SLOVENSKEGA KEMIJSKEGA DRUSTVA (XV/0560-3110) [09522936] **995**

●VESTNIK ST. PETERSBURG UNIVERSITY: MATHEMATICS (US/1063-4541) [26040002] **3540**

VESTNIK STATISTIKI (RU/0042-4692) [02176631] **5346**

VESTNIK STATISTIKI : ORGAN TSSU SSSR (RU/0320-8168) [01961021] **5346**

VESTNIK USTEDNIHO USTAVU GEOLOGICKEHO (XR/0042-1359) [05002417] **1401**

VESTNIK USTREDNIHO USTAVU GEOLOGICKEHO (XR/0042-4730) [18854557] **1401**

VESTNIK VSESOJUZNOGO NAUCNO-ISSLEDOVATELSKOGO INSTITUTA ZELEZNODOROZNOGO TRANSPORTA (RU/0042-4749) [10074451] **5399**

VESTNIK ZOOLOGII (UN/0084-5604) [02030622] **5599**

VESTSI AKADEMII NAVUK BELARUSKAI SSR. SERYIA SELSKAHASPADARCHYKH NAVUK (BW) [28613640] **144**

VESTSI AKADEMII NAVUK BSSR. SERYIA BIIALAHICHNYKH NAVUK See VESCI AKADEMII NAVUK BELARUSI. SERYA BIALAGICNYH NAVUK **494**

VESTSI AKADEMII NAVUK BSSR. SERYIA FIZIKA-ENERHETYCHNYKH NAVUK See VESCI AKADEMII NAVUK BELARUSI. SERYA FIZIKA-ENERGETYCNYH NAVUK **2108**

VESTSI AKADEMII NAVUK BSSR. SERYIA KHIMICHNYKH NAVUK See VESCI AKADEMII NAVUK BELARUSI. SERYA HIMICNYH NAVUK **995**

VESTURES INSTITUTS (LATVIJAS PSR ZINATNU AKADEMIJA) See ZINATNISKAS ATSKAITES SESIJAS MATERIALI PAR ARHEOLOGU UN ETNOGRAFU PETIJUMU REZULTATIEM **248**

VET MHOW (II/0970-7573) [109707573] **5523**

VETDOC (UK) **5523, 5528**

VETENSKAPS-SOCIETETEN I LUND See ARSBOK - VETENSKAPSSOCIETETEN I LUND **1074**

VETENSKAPSAKADEMIEN (SW) [01794273] **5169**

VETERA CHRISTIANORUM (IT/1121-9696) [111219696] **5007**

VETERA CHRISTIANORUM (IT/0506-8126) [02001884] **5020**

VETERAN (WASHINGTON, D.C.) (US/0893-8547) [15682061] **4060**

VETERANOTES (US/0278-7156) [07610976] **4060**

VETERANS ADMINISTRATION See SUMMARY OF MEDICAL PROGRAMS **3643**

VETERANS ADVOCATE (WASHINGTON, D.C.), THE (US/1046-3429) [20383656] **3071**

VETERANS BENEFITS UNDER CURRENT EDUCATIONAL PROGRAMS. INFORMATION BULLETIN (US/0196-2655) [05757758] **1789**

VETERANS IN NEBRASKA (US) [04986789] **4060**

VETERANS NEWSLETTER (CINEMA & TELEVISION VETERANS) (UK) [20148329] **1142, 4079**

VETERANS OF FOREIGN WARS OF THE UNITED STATES See VFW, VETERANS OF FOREIGN WARS MAGAZINE **4060**

Alphabetical Title Index VICHE

VETERANS READJUSTMENT APPOINTMENTS IN THE FEDERAL GOVERNMENT (US/0278-5803) [07798007] **4705**

VETERANS' VOICE (US) [10929333] **4514**

VETERANS' VOICES (US/0504-0779) [02242955] **3450**

VETERINARIA ARGENTINA (AG/0326-4629) [11042483] **5523**

VETERINARIA CREMONA (IT/0394-3151) [I03943151] **5523**

VETERINARIA E ZOOTECNIA (BL/0102-5716) [17293222] **5599, 5523**

VETERINARIA (MEXICO) (MX/0301-5092) [07359632] **5523**

VETERINARIA (SARAJEVO) (BN/0372-6827) [01769056] **5524**

VETERINARIA TROPICAL (VE/0379-8275) [04090174] **5524**

VETERINARIAN MAGAZINE *CEASED.* (CN/0849-5009) [21205817] **5524**

VETERINARIANS' PRODUCT & THERAPEUTIC REFERENCE (US) [01777373] **5524**

VETERINARIIA (UKRAINE. MINISTERSTVO SILSKOHO HOSPODARSTVA) (UN/0321-0502) [03813156] **5524**

VETERINARIJA (MOSKVA) (RU/0042-4846) [10884201] **5524**

VETERINARIUM (TU) [24600739] **5524**

VETERINARNA SBIRKA (BU/0205-3829) [03813181] **5524**

VETERINARNAIA NAUKA-PROIZVODSTVU (BW) [03049289] **5524**

VETERINARNI MEDICINA (XR/0375-8427) [05585047] **5524**

VETERINARNO-MEDICINSKI NAUKI (BU/0324-1068) [I03241068] **5524**

VETERINARSKA STANICA (YU/0350-7149) [I03507149] **5524**

VETERINARSKI ARHIV (CI/0372-5480) [01714865] **5524**

VETERINARSKI GLASNIK (YU/0350-2457) [01714291] **5524**

VETERINARSTVI (XR/0506-8231) [01769060] **5524**

VETERINARY ACUPUNCTURE NEWSLETTER (US) [10118324] **5524**

●VETERINARY & COMPARATIVE OPHTHALMOLOGY (US/1076-4607) [30426782] **5524**

VETERINARY AND COMPARATIVE ORTHOPAEDICS AND TRAUMATOLOGY (GW/0932-0814) [18203645] **5524**

VETERINARY AND HUMAN TOXICOLOGY (US/0145-6296) [02765341] **3984, 5524**

VETERINARY ANNUAL, THE (UK/0083-5870) [01769061] **5525**

VETERINARY BIOLOGICAL PRODUCTS. LICENSEES (US) [07603805] **5525**

VETERINARY BIOTECHNOLOGY NEWSLETTER / OFFICE INTERNATIONAL DES EPIZOOTIES (FR/1018-533X) [26187952] **5525**

VETERINARY BULLETIN (LONDON) (UK/0042-4854) [01769063] **5525, 5528**

VETERINARY CANCER SOCIETY, ... ANNUAL CONFERENCE (US) [25963402] **5525**

VETERINARY CANCER SOCIETY. CONFERENCE *See* VETERINARY CANCER SOCIETY, ... ANNUAL CONFERENCE **5525**

●VETERINARY CLINICAL NUTRITION (US/1076-3872) [30468343] **5525**

VETERINARY CLINICAL PATHOLOGY (US/0275-6382) [05118950] **5525**

VETERINARY CLINICS OF NORTH AMERICA. EQUINE PRACTICE, THE (US/0749-0739) [11078671] **5525**

VETERINARY CLINICS OF NORTH AMERICA. FOOD ANIMAL PRACTICE, THE (US/0749-0720) [11078622] **5525**

VETERINARY CLINICS OF NORTH AMERICA. SMALL ANIMAL PRACTICE, THE (US/0195-5616) [04683654] **5525**

VETERINARY DERMATOLOGY (UK/0959-4493) [22177744] **5525**

VETERINARY DRUG REGISTRATION NEWSLETTER (FR/1010-3538) [20006147] **5525**

VETERINARY ECONOMICS (US/0042-4862) [01769065] **5525**

VETERINARY FORUM (US/1047-6326) [13984002] **5525**

VETERINARY HERITAGE: BULLETIN OF THE AMERICAN VETERINARY HISTORY SOCIETY (US) [10555231] **5525**

VETERINARY HISTORY (UK/0301-6943) [05883299] **5525**

VETERINARY IMMUNOLOGY AND IMMUNOPATHOLOGY (NE/0165-2427) [05867096] **5525**

VETERINARY MANAGEMENT UPDATE (US/1042-1696) [18958787] **5525**

VETERINARY MEDICAL JOURNAL GIZA (UA/1110-1423) [23234889] **227**

VETERINARY MEDICAL REVIEW (COLUMBIA, MO.) (US/1059-0994) [07482307] **5525**

VETERINARY MEDICAL SCHOOL ADMISSION REQUIREMENTS IN THE UNITED STATES AND CANADA. / SPONSORED BY THE ASSOCIATION OF AMERICAN VETERINARY MEDICAL COLLEGES (US) [13369679] **5525**

VETERINARY MEDICINE (1985) (US/8750-7943) [11631608] **5526**

VETERINARY MEDICINE REPORT *CEASED.* (US/0895-7703) [16793901] **5526**

VETERINARY MICROBIOLOGY (NE/0378-1135) [02786044] **570, 5526**

VETERINARY NEWS (ALBANY) (US/0360-1730) [01713578] **5526**

VETERINARY NURSING JOURNAL (UK) **5526, 3870**

VETERINARY PARASITOLOGY (NE/0304-4017) [01939255] **5526**

VETERINARY PATHOLOGY (US/0300-9858) [00932839] **5526**

VETERINARY PHARMACEUTICALS & BIOLOGICALS (US/0272-4669) [06904145] **5526**

VETERINARY PRACTICE (UK/0042-4897) [02371062] **5526**

VETERINARY PRACTICE MANAGEMENT (EPSOM AND EWELL, SURREY) (UK/0268-9189) [15319568] **5526**

VETERINARY PRACTICE NURSE (UK) **5526**

VETERINARY PRACTICE STAFF (US/1047-8639) [20805821] **5526**

VETERINARY QUARTERLY, THE (NE/0165-2176) [05393794] **5526**

VETERINARY RADIOLOGY *See* VETERINARY RADIOLOGY & ULTRASOUND **5526**

●VETERINARY RADIOLOGY & ULTRASOUND (US/1058-8183) [24384362] **3947, 5526**

VETERINARY RECORD (UK/0042-4900) [01769072] **5526**

VETERINARY REGISTER (US) [04625541] **5526**

VETERINARY REPORTS (US) [17804320] **5526**

●VETERINARY RESEARCH (FR/0928-4249) [27944714] **5526**

VETERINARY RESEARCH COMMUNICATIONS (NE/0165-7380) [06845473] **5527**

VETERINARY REVIEW (SYDNEY, N.S.W.) (AT) [10281574] **5527**

VETERINARY SCOPE (US) [01769076] **5527**

VETERINARY SURGERY (US/0161-3499) [03905443] **5527**

VETERINARY TECHNICIAN (US/8750-8990) [10470681] **5527**

VETERINARY TIMES (UK/1352-9374) [11467098] **5527**

VETERINARY UPDATE (US) [17535595] **5527**

●VETERINARY UPDATE (LARGE ANIMALS) (US/1059-8456) [25652278] **2803, 5527**

VETERINARY UPDATE (LARGE ANIMALS (EQUINE)) *See* VETERINARY UPDATE (LARGE ANIMALS) **5527**

VETERINARY UPDATE (LARGE ANIMALS (FOOD)) *See* VETERINARY UPDATE (LARGE ANIMALS) **5527**

VETERINER FAKULTESI DERGISI (TU/0003-3685) [01236117] **5527**

VETERINER FAKULTESI DERGISI. SELCUK UNIVERSITESI (TU/1011-2057) [I10112057] **5527**

VETERINER HEKIMLER DERNEGI DERGISI (TU/0377-6395) [01342999] **5527**

VETMARK INTERNATIONAL POULTRY PRACTICE (UK) **223**

VETO WARSZAWA (PL/0209-0554) [I02090554] **718**

VETRINA (IT/0391-5840) [I03915840] **857**

VETRINA *See* ESPRESSIONI IN VETRINA **833**

VETROINFORMAZIONE (IT) [11301204] **2595**

VETSKAP (SW/0283-8708) **1096**

VETTE (US/0199-7890) [06158591] **5427**

VETTE VUES MAGAZINE (US/0279-8476) [07331159] **5427**

VETTE'N USA (US/0194-3294) [05395844] **5427**

VETUS LATINA. AUS DER GESCHICHTE DER LATEINISCHEN BIBEL (GW/0571-9070) [I05719070] **5020**

VETUS LATINA DIE RESTE DER ALTLATEINISCHEN BIBEL (GW) **5020**

VETUS TESTAMENTUM (NE/0042-4935) [01769078] **5020**

VEUX-TU-SAVOIR (CN/0227-0722) [08327365] **1873**

VEVAY REVEILLE-ENTERPRISE, THE (US) [11832508] **5668**

VEZETESTUDOMANY (HU) [02452740] **718**

VFDB ZEITSCHRIFT (GW/0042-1084) [03170116] **2017**

VFR TERMINAL AREA CHART. BALTIMORE--WASHINGTON (US) [25468302] **39**

VFW MAGAZINE *See* VFW, VETERANS OF FOREIGN WARS MAGAZINE **4060**

VFW, VETERANS OF FOREIGN WARS MAGAZINE (US/0161-8598) [04044051] **4060**

VGB-KRAFTWERKSTECHNIK (GW/0372-5715) [02693756] **2000**

VGB-TB (GW/0722-3951) [09832072] **1960**

VHF COMMUNICATIONS (GW/0177-7505) [I01777505] **1123**

VI (SW/0346-4180) [01769079] **2524**

VIA (IT) [19968923] **2245**

VIA (BERKELEY) (US/0147-8184) [03234853] **3450**

VIA (CAMB.) (US/0506-8347) [01586541] **310**

VIA DOMITIA *CEASED.* (FR/0563-9786) [02166627] **2714**

●VIA INTERNATIONAL PORT OF NEW YORK-NEW JERSEY (US) [25850889] **5399**

VIA PENSACOLA (US/0505-4176) [01519940] **5458**

VIA PORT OF NEW YORK-NEW JERSEY *See* VIA INTERNATIONAL PORT OF NEW YORK-NEW JERSEY **5399**

VIA RAIL CANADA *See* ANNUAL REPORT / VIA RAIL CANADA INC **5429**

VIAGGI DI ERODOTO (IT) **2632**

VIANDES ET PRODUITS CARNES AUBIERE (FR/0241-0389) [I02410389] **2360**

VIATA ARMATEI : REVISTA ILUSTRATA DE LITERATURA SI ARTA EDITATA DE MINISTERUL APARARII NATIONALE (RM/0042-5044) [23231292] **4060**

VIATA MEDICALA (RM/0042-5036) [02417802] **3650**

VIATA ROMANEASCA : REVISTA A UNIUNII SCRIITORILOR DIN R.P.R (RM) [12671761] **3355**

VIATEURS EN MISSION (CN/0226-7861) [06515574] **5007**

VIATKA (UN) [02665316] **2715**

VIATOR (BERKELEY) (US/0083-5897) [01769080] **1080**

●VIBE (NEW YORK, N.Y.) (US/1070-4701) [28385131] **2494**

VIBES (NEW YORK) (US/0270-6350) [06449561] **4158**

VIBORG STIFTSMUSEUM *See* MIV: MUSEERNE I VIBORG AMT **2699**

VIBRANT LIFE (US/0749-3509) [11123688] **5069, 2601**

VIBRATIONAL SPECTRA AND STRUCTURE (NE/0090-1911) [01783664] **1058, 4442**

VIBRATIONS (CLARENDON HILLS, ILL.) (US/1066-8268) [16205019] **4424**

VIBRATIONS (MONTREAL) (CN/0703-9883) [03890096] **4158**

VIBRATIONS (OTTAWA. 1975) (CN/0382-9227) [03210066] **2839**

VIBRATIONS (TORONTO) (CN/0227-6755) [08071684] **4394**

VIC LIBRARY *See* FILM AND VIDEO CATALOGUE / VIENNA INTERNATIONAL CENTRE LIBRARY **1944**

VIC LIBRARY *See* FILM CATALOGUE ... / VIENNA INTERNATIONAL CENTRE LIBRARY **4447**

VIC LIBRARY FILM CATALOGUE *See* FILM CATALOGUE ... / VIENNA INTERNATIONAL CENTRE LIBRARY **4447**

VICA JOURNAL (US/1044-0151) [19645414] **4209**

VICAKSANA (CE) [02177439] **3450**

VICARA (NP) [01790475] **2509**

VICARIA DE LA SOLIDARIDAD (CL) [11333598] **5038**

VICE VERSA (MONTREAL, QUEBEC) (CN/0829-2299) [15059417] **2549**

VICENZA ECONOMICA (1984) (IT) [12629213] **857**

●VICHE (RU) [26273636] **4499**

VICINO — Alphabetical Title Index

VICINO ORIENTE (IT) [08178035] **2779**

VICKERS BOND TRADERS GUIDE (US/1044-6834) [19822124] **919**

VICKERS DIRECTORY OF INSTITUTIONAL INVESTORS (US/1046-5340) [20400064] **919**

VICKERS STOCK TRADERS GUIDE (US/1044-6850) [19822789] **919**

VICKERS WEEKLY INSIDER REPORT (US) **919**

VICKSBURG EVENING POST (US/0884-8912) [10307676] **5702**

VICTIMOLOGY (US/0361-5170) [02381340] **3178**

VICTIMS OF VIOLENCE REPORT (CN) [22421815] **3178, 5313**

VICTOR VALLEY MAGAZINE (US/0738-8586) [09660750] **2549**

VICTORIA ADVOCATE (VICTORIA, TEX. : DAILY) (US) [13698588] **5755**

VICTORIA, AUSTRALIA. COMMITTEE OF PUBLIC ACCOUNTS *See* REPORT FROM THE PUBLIC ACCOUNTS COMMITTEE UPON UNPAID ACCOUNTS **4744**

VICTORIA, AUSTRALIA. DEPT. OF AGRICULTURE. LIBRARY SERVICES *See* BIBLIOGRAPHY OF PUBLICATIONS **66**

VICTORIA, AUSTRALIA. DEPT. OF AGRICULTURE. SHEEP INDUSTRY BRANCH *See* SHEEP INDUSTRY REVIEW VICTORIA **221**

VICTORIA, AUSTRALIA. ENVIRONMENT PROTECTION AUTHORITY *See* ANNUAL REPORT - VICTORIA, AUSTRALIA. ENVIRONMENT PROTECTION AUTHORITY **3109**

VICTORIA, AUSTRALIA. LAW CALENDAR *See* LAW CALENDAR **2995**

VICTORIA, AUSTRALIA. LAW DEPT *See* LAW CALENDAR **2995**

VICTORIA, AUSTRALIA. NATIONAL GALLERY, MELBOURNE. COUNCIL OF TRUSTEES *See* ART BULLETIN OF VICTORIA **338**

VICTORIA, AUSTRALIA. NATIONAL PARKS ADVISORY COMMITTEE *See* REPORT - VICTORIA, AUSTRALIA. NATIONAL PARKS ADVISORY COMMITTEE **2203**

VICTORIA, AUSTRALIA. WORKERS COMPENSATION BOARD *See* DECISIONS - WORKERS COMPENSATION BOARD (VICTORIA) **3146**

VICTORIA BOULEVARD (CN/1184-7573) [24256692] **332**

VICTORIA BUSINESS REVIEW (CN/0824-4472) [10526426] **1631**

VICTORIA COUNTY RECORD (CN/0703-8747) [03959998] **5797**

VICTORIA, CROSSROADS OF SOUTH TEXAS (US/0277-4569) [07563582] **2476**

VICTORIA. DEPT. OF COMMUNITY SERVICES *See* REPORT OF THE DEPARTMENT OF COMMUNITY SERVICES FOR THE YEAR ENDED 30 JUNE **5305**

VICTORIA. DEPT. OF MANUFACTURING AND INDUSTRY DEVELOPMENT *See* ANNUAL REPORT / DEPARTMENT OF MANUFACTURING AND INDUSTRY DEVELOPMENT, VICTORIA, AUSTRALIA **2133**

VICTORIA. DEPT. OF PLANNING AND HOUSING *See* ANNUAL REPORT / DEPARTMENT OF PLANNING AND HOUSING **2814**

VICTORIA EDUCATION GAZETTE AND TEACHERS' AID (AT) [07616023] **1789**

VICTORIA. EQUAL OPPORTUNITY BOARD *See* ANNUAL REPORT OF THE EQUAL OPPORTUNITY BOARD **4504**

VICTORIA. FORESTS COMMISSION *See* BULLETIN - FORESTS COMMISSION, VICTORIA **2376**

VICTORIA GOVERNMENT GAZETTE (AT) [08322750] **4693**

VICTORIA HISTORY OF THE COUNTY OF GLOUCESTER (UK) [07380791] **2715**

VICTORIA HUMANIST *See* HUMANIST IN CANADA **4348**

VICTORIA INSIDER *CEASED.* (CN/0843-4395) [20443297] **2765**

VICTORIA. LIQUOR CONTROL COMMISSION *See* REPORT AND STATEMENT OF ACCOUNTS - LIQUOR CONTROL COMMISSION **3174**

VICTORIA. MINES DEPT. GROUNDWATER INVESTIGATION PROGRAM REPORT *See* GROUNDWATER INVESTIGATION PROGRAM **1414**

VICTORIA. MINISTRY OF EMPLOYMENT AND TRAINING *See* ANNUAL REPORT **1648**

VICTORIA. MINISTRY OF HOUSING AND CONSTRUCTION *See* REPORT OF THE DIRECTOR GENERAL OF HOUSING AND CONSTRUCTION FOR THE PERIOD FROM ... **2833**

VICTORIA. MOTOR ACCIDENTS BOARD *See* ANNUAL REPORT OF THE MOTOR ACCIDENTS BOARD FOR THE YEAR ENDED 30 JUNE ... (VICTORIA) **5438**

VICTORIA NATURALIST, THE (CN/0049-612X) [02284690] **4173**

VICTORIA (NEW YORK, N.Y.) (US/1040-6883) [18513873] **5567**

VICTORIA. OFFICE OF THE REGISTRAR OF FRIENDLY SOCIETIES *See* REPORT OF THE REGISTRAR OF FRIENDLY SOCIETIES FOR THE YEAR ENDED 30 JUNE **5236**

VICTORIA. PLANNING CONSULTATIVE COUNCIL *See* ANNUAL REPORT OF THE PLANNING CONSULTATIVE COUNCIL FOR THE YEAR ENDED 30 JUNE ... (VICTORIA) **1546**

VICTORIA. PUBLIC RECORD OFFICE *See* ANNUAL REPORT, YEAR ENDED 30 JUNE ... / PUBLIC RECORD OFFICE **2479**

VICTORIA (SAN DIEGO, CALIF) (US/8750-2534) [11189460] **5007**

VICTORIA. STATE EMPLOYEES RETIREMENT BENEFITS BOARD *See* REPORT OF THE STATE EMPLOYEES RETIREMENT BENEFITS BOARD FOR THE YEAR ENDED 30 JUNE ... **4681**

VICTORIA STATUS OF WOMEN ACTION GROUP. CONFERENCE *See* FOCUS WOMEN **5557**

VICTORIA. SUPREME COURT *See* VICTORIAN REPORTS **3071**

VICTORIA TIMES COLONIST (CN) **5797**

VICTORIA TIMES COLONIST / BY CARRIER (CN) **5797**

VICTORIA. TREASURY DEPT *See* FINANCE **4724**

VICTORIA. TREASURY DEPT *See* BUDGET SPEECH / PRESENTED BY THE TREASURER OF VICTORIA ON THE OCCASION OF THE BUDGET **4715**

VICTORIA. TREASURY DEPT *See* BUDGET SUMMARY AND PROGRAM BUDGET EXPENDITURES / PRESENTED BY THE TREASURER OF VICTORIA FOR THE INFORMATION OF HONOURABLE MEMBERS ON THE OCCASION OF THE BUDGET **4715**

VICTORIA UNIVERSITY OF MANCHESTER. AGRICULTURAL ECONOMICS DEPT *See* BULLETIN - DEPARTMENT OF AGRICULTURAL ECONOMICS **69**

VICTORIA UNIVERSITY OF WELLINGTON. LIBRARY *See* ANNUAL REPORT OF THE UNIVERSITY LIBRARIAN FOR ... VICTORIA UNIVERSITY OF WELLINGTON, THE LIBRARY **3191**

VICTORIA. VICTORIAN MINISTRY OF IMMIGRATION & ETHNIC AFFAIRS *See* ANNUAL REPORT / VICTORIAN MINISTRY OF IMMIGRATION & ETHNIC AFFAIRS **1918**

VICTORIAN ACCIDENT COMPENSATION PRACTICE GUIDE (AT) **3071**

VICTORIAN BAR NEWS (AT/0159-3285) [I01593285] **3071**

VICTORIAN BEE JOURNAL *See* AUSTRALIAN BEE JOURNAL **63**

VICTORIAN BRANCH NEWS (AT/0813-6394) [08136394] **3650**

VICTORIAN BULLETIN (AT) **1225**

VICTORIAN DAIRY INDUSTRY AUTHORITY *See* REPORT FOR YEAR ENDED 30TH JUNE ... / VICTORIAN DAIRY INDUSTRY AUTHORITY **198**

VICTORIAN ETHNIC AFFAIRS COMMISSION *See* ANNUAL REPORT / VICTORIAN ETHNIC AFFAIRS COMMISSION **4630**

VICTORIAN FICTION RESEARCH GUIDES (AT/0158-3921) [08982246] **3450**

VICTORIAN GOVERNMENT DIRECTORY (AT/0158-1589) [07186213] **4693**

VICTORIAN GOVERNMENT PUBLICATIONS RECEIVED BY THE STATE LIBRARY OF VICTORIA (AT) [08770531] **4693**

VICTORIAN HISTORICAL JOURNAL (AT) [16403248] **2671**

VICTORIAN HOMES (AT) 635, **2903**

VICTORIAN HOMES (US/0744-415X) [08256866] 2903, **310**

VICTORIAN LITERATURE & CULTURE (US/1060-1503) [24883363] **3450**

VICTORIAN NATIONAL PARKS ASSOCIATION JOURNAL *See* PARKWATCH **2202**

VICTORIAN NATURALIST (AT/0042-5184) [01586391] **4173**

VICTORIAN NETBALLER (AT) **4928**

VICTORIAN NEWSLETTER, THE (US/0042-5192) [01638972] **3355**

VICTORIAN ORGAN JOURNAL (AT/0310-4834) [I03104834] **4158**

VICTORIAN PERIODICALS REVIEW (US/0709-4698) [05339718] 2856, **3355**

VICTORIAN POETRY (US/0042-5206) [01624422] **3450**

VICTORIAN REAL ESTATE JOURNAL (AT/0815-3132) [I08153132] **4848**

VICTORIAN REPORTS (AT/0505-4435) [01769090] **3071**

VICTORIAN REVIEW (CN/0848-1512) [20549139] **3450**

VICTORIAN SAMPLER (US/1047-3947) [20689902] **2903**

VICTORIAN SOCIETY IN AMERICA *See* VICTORIAN TRAVELER'S COMPANION **5498**

VICTORIAN STUDIES (US/0042-5222) [01769095] 1080, **3450**

VICTORIAN STUDIES BULLETIN (US/0275-8660) [03678154] **3450**

VICTORIAN TEACHER (AT/0810-056X) [I0810056X] **1908**

VICTORIAN TRADES HALL COUNCIL *See* VICTORIAN TRADES HALL COUNCIL OFFICIAL TRADE UNION DIRECTORY & DIGEST **1716**

VICTORIAN TRADES HALL COUNCIL OFFICIAL TRADE UNION DIRECTORY & DIGEST (AT) [03454513] **1716**

VICTORIAN TRAVELER'S COMPANION (US/0198-9626) [06263000] **5498**

VICTORIAN VEGETABLE GROWER, THE (AT) [02810309] **190**

VICTORIAN YEAR-BOOK (AT/0067-1223) [01640846] **4701**

VICTORIANS INSTITUTE *See* VICTORIANS INSTITUTE JOURNAL **5237**

VICTORIANS INSTITUTE JOURNAL (US/0886-3865) [01458163] **5237**

VICTORIA'S ERA (US/1040-6972) [18503744] **2632**

VICTORY LANE (US/0887-1426) [13110196] **4928**

VICTORY MUSIC REVIEW (US) **4158**

VICTORY (SAN DIEGO, CALIF.) (US/0745-9173) [09591211] **5007**

VIDA DAS ARTES (BL) [02244477] **332**

VIDA HISPANICA (1972) (UK/0308-4957) [05080705] **3332**

VIDA NEUVA (SP) **5007**

VIDA RELIGIOSA (SP) **5007**

VIDA RURAL (SP) **144**

VIDA VALENCIANA, LA (SP) [02441098] **2715**

VIDA Y PENSAMIENTO (CR) [09276687] **5007**

VIDAS SECAS (BL) [07192101] **2667**

VIDE, LES COUCHES MINCES, LE (FR/0223-4335) [05684782] 995, **4424**

VIDEAZIMUT CLIPS (CN) **4537**

VIDEO AGE INTERNATIONAL (US/0278-5013) [07817679] 718, **1142**

VIDEO & AUDIO REPORT (NE) **1123**

VIDEO AND FILM CATALOGUE (CN) 4377, **4079**

VIDEO & TELEVISION (US/1046-3860) [17937214] **1142**

VIDEO ANNUAL, THE (US/1055-0267) [23059962] 4377, **3255**

VIDEO BROADCAST (FR) 4377, **1142**

VIDEO BUSINESS (US/0279-571X) [07102477] **4377**

VIDEO. BUYER'S GUIDE *See* VIDEO TEST ANNUAL AND BUYER'S GUIDE **2085**

VIDEO CAMERA (UK) **1123**

VIDEO CHOICE (US/0896-2871) [16978456] 1168, **4079**

VIDEO COMPUTING *SUSPENDED.* (US/8756-5250) [11594485] **1142**

VIDEO CONFERENCING : ANALYSIS OF AN EMERGING TECHNOLOGY (US/1057-140X) [23954847] **1123**

VIDEO DISK MONITOR *See* MULTIMEDIA MONITOR **1619**

VIDEO EVENT (US/1045-2885) [20074135] **4079**

VIDEO EXTRA (US/0888-0492) [13452102] **1168**

VIDEO GAMES & COMPUTER ENTERTAINMENT (US/1059-2938) [20968997] 1867, **1231**

VIDEO GAMES : THE ULTIMATE GAMING MAGAZINE (US) **4867**

VIDEO GUIDE (VANCOUVER) *CEASED.* (CN/0228-6726) [08003289] **1142**

VIDEO INDUSTRY DIRECTORY (US/0730-6180) [07119868] **1142**

VIDEO INK (US/1059-2245) [24571889] **332**

Alphabetical Title Index

VIERTELJAHRSHEFTE

VIDEO INSIDER (US/1046-0837) [15789465] 4079, **1142**

VIDEO INVESTOR (US/1042-7694) [19212288] **4377**

VIDEO INVESTOR, THE (US/1046-6045) 4079, **1168**

VIDEO JOURNAL OF COLOR FLOW IMAGING (US/1052-2182) [22221440] **3947**

VIDEO JOURNAL OF ECHOCARDIOGRAPHY (US/1052-2174) [22221383] **3711**

VIDEO LAW MONTHLY (US/0741-5125) [09215252] 3071, **1123**

VIDEO LIBRARIAN, THE (US/0887-6851) [13306621] 3255, **4377**

VIDEO MAGAZINE (US/1044-7288) [18425064] **1142**

VIDEO MAGAZINE (IT) [09594974] **2085**

VIDEO MAKER *CEASED.* (UK/0268-0750) [21207399] **4079**

VIDEO MANAGEMENT *CEASED.* (US/1047-7713) [20575959] 4079, **889**

VIDEO MARKETING NEWS (US) [23244083] **4377**

VIDEO MARKETING SURVEYS AND FORECASTS (US/0740-4247) [09934512] **2085**

VIDEO MONITOR (SILVER SPRING, MD.) (US/0888-9538) [13754425] **1168**

VIDEO MOVIE GUIDE (US) [13274840] **4079**

VIDEO MOVIES (BREMERTON, WASH.) *CEASED.* (US/1063-5106) [26048471] **1142**

VIDEO NETWORKS (US/0738-7563) [08519373] **1142**

VIDEO NOW (US/8755-7290) [11453219] **1168**

VIDEO-PRESSE (CN/0315-3975) [02489653] **1071**

VIDEO PRODUCT NEWS (US/0271-5953) [06663118] **4079**

VIDEO PRODUCTION TECHNIQUES (UK) **4079**

VIDEO PROGRAMS INDEX, THE (US/0272-1236) [06038720] **4377**

VIDEO PROPHILES *CEASED.* (US/1055-6060) [23239434] 2779, **1142**

VIDEO RATING GUIDE FOR LIBRARIES (US/1045-3393) [20074892] 4079, **3255**

VIDEO REGISTER AND TELECONFERENCING RESOURCES DIRECTORY, THE *CEASED.* (US/0887-3836) [13205052] 1168, **2085**

VIDEO RETAILER (UK) **4377**

VIDEO REVIEW (NEW YORK, N.Y.) (US/0196-8793) [05914050] **4377**

VIDEO : REVISTA DE CIRURGIA (SP) **3977**

VIDEO (SAN FRANCISCO, CALIF.) (US/0276-0835) [07313610] 1142, **4079**

VIDEO SCENE (CN/0838-9586) [18314790] **4079**

VIDEO SERVICES NEWS *See* PHILLIPS BUSINESS INFORMATION'S INTERACTIVE VIDEO NEWS **4372**

VIDEO SERVICES NEWS / PHILLIPS BUSINESS INFORMATION, INC (US/1067-3849) [27195371] **4377**

VIDEO SHOPPER (US/1057-8250) [24124126] **1142**

VIDEO SOFTWARE DEALERS ASSOCIATION *See* VSDA MEMBERSHIP DIRECTORY **1143**

VIDEO SOFTWARE MAGAZINE (US/1046-607X) [20482127] **4377**

VIDEO SOURCE BOOK, THE (US/0748-0881) [05998038] **4377**

VIDEO STORE (US/0195-1750) [05331939] **1142**

VIDEO (STUTTGART, GERMANY) (GW) [11537593] **4378**

VIDEO SYSTEMS (US/0361-0942) [02245120] **1142**

VIDEO TECHNOLOGY NEWSLETTER (US/1040-2772) [18367367] **4378**

VIDEO TEST ANNUAL AND BUYER'S GUIDE (US/0736-2587) [09079261] **2085**

VIDEO THE MAGAZINE (UK) **4079**

VIDEO TIMES (SKOKIE, ILL.) *CEASED.* (US/0742-8111) [11854134] **4378**

● VIDEO TOASTER USER (US/1075-8704) [28249123] **1235**

VIDEO TODAY *CEASED.* (UK) **4079**

VIDEO TRIAL REPORT *CEASED.* (US) **3071**

VIDEO UIT EN THUIS (NE) 2286, **1080**

VIDEO VISION *CEASED.* (US/0888-3297) [13586967] **1142**

VIDEO WATCHDOG (US/1070-9991) [26042506] 4378, **4079**

VIDEO WEEK (US/0196-5905) [05851622] **1142**

VIDEO X (US/0277-3481) [07543236] **1142**

VIDEOCAMERA AND ELECTRONIC IMAGING (AT/1035-9508) [I10359508] **1142**

VIDEODISC BOOK, THE (US) [11638153] **1206**

VIDEODISC COMPENDIUM FOR EDUCATION AND TRAINING *See* MULTIMEDIA AND VIDEODISC COMPENDIUM FOR EDUCATION AND TRAINING **1801**

VIDEODISC COMPENDIUM FOR EDUCATION AND TRAINING, THE (US/1047-921X) [20149084] **1790**

VIDEOGRAPHY (US/0363-1001) [02409346] **1143**

VIDEOHOUND'S GOLDEN MOVIE RETRIEVER (US) [23806790] **4079**

VIDEOLOG (US/0746-7699) [09629829] **4079**

VIDEOLOG : PROGRAMS FOR GENERAL INTEREST AND ENTERTAINMENT, THE (US/0193-9602) [04828800] 5320, **1143**

VIDEOLOG : PROGRAMS FOR THE HEALTH SCIENCES, THE (US/0195-7295) [05135148] **4806**

VIDEOMAKER (US/0889-4973) [13992449] **1168**

VIDEOMANIA (CN/0711-7914) [08555970] **4867**

VIDEONEWS INTERNATIONAL (HOLLYWOOD, CALIF.) (US/1044-6354) [19855732] **1143**

VIDEOPHILE, THE (US/0164-5862) [04513037] **1143**

VIDEOPLAYER (US/0090-3922) [01783697] **5320**

VIDEOS FOR BUSINESS AND TRAINING *CEASED.* (US/1043-9759) [19620026] **1143**

VIDEOSCOPIC SURGERY *CEASED.* (US/1058-7357) [24364577] **3977**

VIDEOSOCIOLOGY (US/0099-1384) [02242845] **5265**

VIDEOTEL INTERNATIONAL REVIEW (IT) **1143**

VIDEOTEX & RNIS MAGAZINE *See* SOLUTIONS TELEMATIQUES PARIS **1121**

VIDEOTEX & RNIS MAGAZINE (FR/1143-6360) [I11436360] **1123**

VIDEOTEX PARIS (FR/0247-4352) [I02474352] **1235**

VIDEOVISIE (NE) **1143**

VIDESA MANTRALAYA KI ANUDANOM KI MANGEM (II) [02421871] **4693**

VIDESA VYAPARA MANTRALAYA KI ANUDANOM KI MANGEM (II) [02422546] **857**

VIDURA (II) [01769097] **1123**

VIDYA KARYA (IO) [01790722] **1790**

VIDYA (SANTA BARBARA, CALIF.) (US/1049-2526) [21185382] **5045**

VIDYAJYOTI (DELHI) (II/0970-1222) [02993099] **5038**

VIE CHRETIENNE, LA (FR/0382-0181) [02285050] **5007**

VIE (CLAYTON, MO.), LA (US/0886-1846) [12824938] **3332**

VIE COMMUNALE ET DEPARTEMENTALE, LA (FR/0042-5400) [17269587] **4693**

VIE CONSACREE (BE) [05933294] **5007**

VIE CONTINUE, LA *CEASED.* (CN/1181-8328) [23230652] **5182**

VIE DE FEMME (CN/0703-9875) [07817984] **5567**

VIE DES ARTS (CN/0042-5435) [06188006] **332**

VIE DES BETES, LA (FR) [04524582] **4173**

VIE DES COMMUNAUTES RELIGIEUSES (CN) **5007**

VIE DU RAIL PARIS, LA (FR/0042-5478) [I00425478] **5437**

VIE DU TIERS-MONDE (CG/0506-8894) [05217644] **2912**

VIE E TRASPORTI (IT) [07344717] **5399**

VIE ECONOMIQUE (BERNE), LA (SZ/0253-3987) [06461738] **1526**

VIE ELECTRIQUE SODEL (FR) **2085**

VIE EN ESTRIE (CN/0832-7238) [15809171] **2549**

VIE EN PLEIN AIR (CN/0844-1804) [19759468] 4928, **5427**

VIE EN ROSE, LA *CEASED.* (CN/0228-5479) [07822871] **5567**

VIE ET MILIEU (1980) (FR/0240-8759) [07816187] 1458, **2222**

VIE ET SANTE DAMMARIE-LES-LYS (FR/0042-5524) [I00425524] **4806**

VIE ETUDIANTE *CEASED.* (CN/1183-6369) [25066755] **1853**

VIE FAMILIALE (RW) [02387343] **2286**

VIE FRANCAISE (PARIS, FRANCE: 1978) (FR/0220-5858) [06759358] 815, **1588**

VIE FRANCAISE (QUEBEC) (CN/0382-0262) [02211054] **2549**

VIE LITURGIQUE (CN/0380-8254) [02585049] **5038**

VIE MARINE *See* MARINE LIFE **556**

VIE MEDICALE, LA *CEASED.* (FR/0042-5583) [11452373] **3650**

VIE MUNICIPALE A JONQUIERE, LA (CN/0712-3248) [08890797] **4693**

VIE MUSICALE EN FRANCE SOUS LES ROIS BOURBONS. 2EME SERIE. RECHERCHES SUR LA MUSIQUE FRANCAISE CLASSIQUE, LA (FR/0080-0139) [01642023] **4158**

VIE MUSICALE EN FRANCE SOUS LES ROIS BOURBONS. ETUDES (FR/0083-6109) [01538658] **4158**

VIE OBLATE (CN/0318-9392) [02441905] **5038**

VIE OUVRIERE (MONTREAL, QUEBEC) (CN/0229-3803) [08185772] 5007, **1716**

VIE PARIS. 1976, LA (FR/0151-2323) [I01512323] **5038**

VIE PEDAGOGIQUE (CN/0707-2511) [05026439] **1790**

VIE SANS FRONTIERES (CN/1180-3258) [23242497] **4621**

VIE SERVITE (CN/0709-8812) [06033537] **5007**

VIE SOCIALE (FR/0042-5605) [05523993] **5225**

VIE SPIRITUELLE, LA (FR/0042-5613) [01769106] **5007**

VIE WALLONNE (BE/0042-5648) [02153914] **2715**

VIEH- UND FLEISCHKOMMISSION *See* JAHRESBERICHT DER VIEH- UND FLEISCHKOMMISSION BEIM BUNDESMINISTERIUM FUER LAND- UND FORSTWIRTSCHAFT **2345**

VIEIL ART, LE (CN/0228-2623) [07313899] 367, **5182**

VIEILLES MAISONS FRANCAISES PARIS (FR/0049-6316) [I00496316] **310**

VIENNA *See* AMTSBLATT DER STADT WIEN **4625**

VIENNA, AUSTRIA. MAGISTRAT ABTEILUNG WIRTSCHAFTSANGELEGENHEITEN *See* KONJUNKTURBERICHT **1502**

VIENNA CIRCLE COLLECTION (NE) [01538787] **2524**

VIENNA. FORSCHUNGSINSTITUT FUER TECHNIKGESCHICHTE *See* BLAETTER FUER TECHNIKGESCHICHTE **5089**

VIENNA. FORSTLICHE BUNDES-VERSUCHSANSTALT MARIABRUNN *See* LAWINENEREIGNISSE UND WITTERUNGSABLAUF IN OSTERREICH **1386**

VIENNA PRESSE- UND INFORMATIONSDIENST *See* BUDGET DER BUNDESHAUPTSTADT WIEN **780**

VIENNA. VERSUCHSSTATION FUER DAS GARUNGSGEWERBE *See* MITTEILUNGEN DER VERSUCHSSTATION FUER DAS GARUNGSGEWERBE IN WIEN **1027**

VIER BULLETIN (AT) **1790**

VIERAEA (SP/0210-945X) [05249016] 475, **4173**

VIERTE WELT AKTUELL (GW) [15313124] **4514**

VIERTELJAHRES-SCHRIFTENREIHE - OSTERREICHISCHES FORSCHUNGSINSTITUT FUR SPARKASSENWESEN (AU) [03462390] **815**

VIERTELJAHRESBERICHTE PROBLEMS OF INTERNATIONAL COOPERATION (GW/0936-451X) [I0936451X] **4537**

VIERTELJAHRESHEFT ZUR AUSLANDSSTATISTIK / STATISTISCHES BUNDESAMT (GW) [24208970] **1588**

VIERTELJAHRESSCHRIFT (AU/0001-799X) [01893197] **3451**

VIERTELJAHRESSCHRIFT FUER HEILPADAGOGIK UND IHRE NACHBARGEBIETE (SZ/0017-9655) [I00179655] **1790**

VIERTELJAHRSCHRIFT FUER SOZIAL- UND WIRTSCHAFTSGESCHICHTE (GW/0042-5699) [02153518] 5225, **1588**

VIERTELJAHRSCHRIFT FUR SOZIAL- UND WIRTSCHAFTSGESCHICHTE BEIHEFTE (GW) [13727008] **5225**

VIERTELJAHRSHEFT DER CHRISTLICHEN WISSENSCHAFT. BIBELLEKTIONEN (US/0145-7411) [02775837] **5020**

VIERTELJAHRSHEFTE FUER ZEITGESCHICHTE (GW/0042-5702) [01717063] **2632**

VIERTELJAHRSHEFTE Alphabetical Title Index

VIERTELJAHRSHEFTE FUER ZEITGESCHICHTE. SCHRIFTENREIHE (GW/0506-9408) [03215697] **2632**

VIERTELJAHRSHEFTE ZUR KONJUNKTURFORSCHUNG *See* VIERTELJAHRSHEFTE ZUR WIRTSCHAFTSFORSCHUNG **815**

VIERTELJAHRSHEFTE ZUR WIRTSCHAFTSFORSCHUNG (GW/0340-1707) [07613397] 1526, **815**

VIES-A-VIES (MONTREAL. 1988) (CN/0842-1838) [19915513] **4621**

●VIESAGE (MONTREAL) (CN/1191-1077) [25796526] **2895**

VIET NAM HAI NGOAI (US/1055-4610) [05037427] **1929**

VIETNAM (VM/0042-5710) [03247740] **2667**

VIETNAM BULLETIN (NE/0506-9661) [02153941] **2667**

VIETNAM BUSINESS DIRECTORY OF SOUTHERN CALIFORNIA (US) [16798750] **718**

VIETNAM BUSINESS REPORT (US) [I13419425] **718**

VIETNAM BUSINESS REPORT (UK) [I13519425] **718**

VIETNAM COMMENTARY / INFORMATION & RESOURCE CENTER *SUSPENDED.* (SI/0218-1169) [19470921] **2667**

VIETNAM COURIER *SUSPENDED.* (VM/0506-9696) [01779162] **2509**

VIETNAM DIGEST (BERKELEY) (US/0272-3344) [05880111] **2667**

VIETNAM FORUM, THE (US/0735-3855) [08917168] **2667**

VIETNAM GENERATION (US/1042-7597) [19133343] **2765**

VIETNAM ILLUSTRATED (VM) **2667**

VIETNAM INSIGHT (US/1061-7310) [22842881] **4514**

VIETNAM (IVRY, FRANCE) (FR) [07804923] **2667**

●VIETNAM JOURNAL : PROJECT OF THE VIETNAM HUMAN RIGHTS GROUP (US) [28624953] 2667, **4514**

VIETNAM (LEESBURG, VA.) (US/1046-2902) [17941016] **2632**

VIETNAM MAGAZINE (US/0506-9777) [01542867] **2667**

●VIETNAM MARKET WATCH (US/1071-7900) [28731188] **718**

VIETNAM. NHA GIAM-DOC KHI-TUONG *See* THOI TIET NGUYET SAN **1436**

VIETNAM OIL AND GAS REPORT (UK) [I09686029] **4281**

VIETNAM QUARTERLY (US/0364-9407) [02568361] **2667**

VIETNAM REPORT (VM) [05239177] **4537**

VIETNAM STUDIES BULLETIN (US/1047-3475) [03574147] **2667**

VIETNAM (SYRACUSE, N.Y.) (US/1058-3831) [24281439] **4499**

VIETNAM TODAY (AT/1030-9985) [05255294] **4537**

VIETNAM UPDATE (US/0899-6601) [18140352] **2632**

VIETNAM WAR NEWSLETTER (US/0743-2496) [09652329] **4060**

VIETNAM YOUTH (VM) [01799392] 5265, **1071**

VIETNAMESE STUDIES. HANOI, VIETNAM (1966) (VM/0085-7823) [01542949] **2667**

VIEUX MARLY, LE (FR/0988-1808) [I09881808] **2715**

●VIEW (BEDFORD, N.H.) (US/1070-1362) [28281635] 889, **735**

VIEW FROM SPRINGFIELD (US/0277-4844) [04709614] 3071, **4693**

VIEW (OAKLAND) (US/0163-9706) [04544851] **367**

●VIEW POINTS (FULLERTON, CALIF.) (US/1063-0325) [25896176] **1123**

VIEWCAMERA (SACRAMENTO, CALIF.) (US/1066-6958) [20285618] **4378**

●VIEWFINDER (LEWISTON, MAINE) (US/1064-4520) [26065950] **1143**

VIEWPOINT (PK) [02246801] **2667**

VIEWPOINT (UK) [04661586] **5007**

VIEWPOINT (US/1049-9199) [21353977] **2632**

VIEWPOINT / ASSOCIATION OF REHABILITATION PROGRAMS IN DATA PROCESSING (US/0890-2658) [14201866] 1886, **5313**

VIEWPOINT (COLUMBUS) (US/0361-2678) [02246167] **332**

VIEWPOINT - INSURANCE BUREAU OF CANADA *CEASED.* (CN/0827-2654) [11825532] **2896**

VIEWPOINT (MARLOW HEIGHTS) (US/0194-5289) [04796222] **5568**

VIEWPOINT (NEW YORK. 1968) (US/0190-3535) [04635815] 3650, **2896**

VIEWPOINT (TORONTO. 1961) (CN/0702-8547) [03520224] **1588**

VIEWPOINTS (ATLANTA, GA.) (US/1064-5063) [04216853] **5069**

VIEWPOINTS (MONTREAL) (CN/0042-5818) [02184654] **4499**

VIEWPOINTS ON DIGESTIVE DISEASES *CEASED.* (US) [01777888] **3748**

VIEWS AND ESTIMATES OF THE COMMITTEE ON FOREIGN AFFAIRS ON THE BUDGET (US/0278-4939) [05047810] **3137**

VIEWS & VISIONS (US/0882-469X) [11874470] **3879**

VIEWS (BOSTON, MASS.) (US/0743-8044) [05281985] **4378**

VIEWTRON MAGAZINE & GUIDE *CEASED.* (US/0749-0186) [11052576] **2549**

VIF EXPRESS, LE (BE) [20406191] **718**

VIGENCIA (AG) [01543042] **2856**

VIGIL (UK/0954-0881) [19082225] **3451**

VIGILANCE (FR/0398-9399) [I03989399] **1790**

VIGILANZA IGIENICO SANITARIA (IT) **4806**

VIGILE URBANO, IL (IT) **3178**

VIGILIA (HU/0042-6024) [04994514] **5038**

VIGILIAE CHRISTIANAE *CEASED.* (NE/0042-6032) [01640835] **3451**

VIGNANA BHARATHI (II/0377-8487) [02160734] 2000, **5169**

VIGNE A A, LA (CN/0708-6377) [05257294] **1350**

VIGNE PARIS, LA (FR/1145-5799) [I11455799] **2371**

VIGNERON CHAMPENOIS, LE (FR) [04149210] **2371**

VIGNETTES (US/0091-3456) [01786370] **1096**

VIGNEVINI (IT/0390-0479) [02087684] **2371**

VIJANDEN VAN GEWASSEN EN HUN BESTRIJDING (BE) [17235243] **4248**

VIJAYA (NP) [02239615] **3451**

VIJESTI MUZEALACA I KONZERVATORA HRVATSKE (CI/0042-6083) [03593672] **4097**

VIJNANA PARISHAD ANUSANDHAN PATRIKA (II) [18188585] **3540**

VIJNANA SARASVATI (II) [11805588] **3255**

VIKALPA (II/0256-0909) [04220479] **889**

VIKASA DARPANA (NP) [08620659] **1588**

VIKING COLLECTION, THE (DK/0108-8408) [17276056] **2715**

VIKING COLLEGE CATALOG (US/0362-997X) [02396064] **4820**

VIKING (INKSTER, MICH.), THE (US/1061-3498) [25259906] **1096**

VIKING (OSLO) (NO/0332-608X) [02215024] **2715**

VIKING PRESS, INC., NEW YORK *See* VIKING COLLEGE CATALOG **4820**

VIKING SOCIETY FOR NORTHERN RESEARCH, LONDON *See* SAGA-BOOK **3432**

VIKING TOURIST GUIDE (CN/0828-4849) [12035491] **5498**

VIKING UPDATE (US/1046-7823) [20519797] **4928**

VIKRAM UNIVERSITY. INSTITUTE OF GEOLOGY *See* JOURNAL OF THE INSTITUTE OF GEOLOGY, VIKRAM UNIVERSITY **1385**

VIKRANT (II) [01783600] **4060**

VILAG ES NYELV (HU) [04814976] **3332**

VILAGTORTENET (HU/0083-6265) [05502586] **2632**

VILAS COUNTY NEWS-REVIEW (US) [12058083] **5771**

VILLA DE MADRID : REVISTA DEL EXMO. AYUNTAMIENTO (SP/0042-6164) [05526907] **2715**

VILLA RICA BREEZE *See* VILLA RICAN, THE **5655**

VILLA RICAN, THE (US/0895-7312) [16758100] **5655**

VILLAGE CRIER *See* NEW JERSEY 50 PLUS **5711**

VILLAGE CRIER (TOMS RIVER, N.J.), THE (US/1066-1204) [04927042] **5712**

VILLAGE LAW (US/0148-8015) [03377329] **3071**

VILLAGE NEPAL (NP) [07783008] **5225**

VILLAGE OF YORKVILLE VOICE, THE (CN/1186-1525) [24280014] **5797**

VILLAGE REPORT SERIES (BG) [13087458] **2839**

VILLAGE TIMES, THE (US/0889-8677) [11151058] **5722**

VILLAGE VIEWS (US/0893-9543) [13720863] **310**

VILLAGE VOICE (NEW YORK), THE (US/0042-6180) [01696813] **2549**

VILLAGEOIS, LE (CN/0711-3439) [08605205] **5797**

VILLAGER (BRONXVILLE, N.Y.), THE (US/0042-6199) [03955609] **2549**

VILLAGER (MISSISSAUGA) (CN/0226-5907) [06859065] **5797**

VILLAGER (MOSCOW, PA.) (US) [16314862] **5740**

VILLAGER, THE (US) [19608540] **5644**

VILLAGER, THE (US) [13988074] **2275**

VILLAGER (TORONTO. 1982) (CN/0834-745X) [17636324] **5797**

VILLAMOSSAG (HU/0042-6210) [08237399] **2085**

VILLANOVA ENVIRONMENTAL LAW JOURNAL, THE (US/1049-2631) [20436895] **3117**

VILLANOVA LAW REVIEW (US/0042-6229) [01769143] **3071**

VILLE DE HAMPSTEAD REPERTOIRE (CN/0227-8626) [06859407] **2579**

VILLE DE JONQUIERE, VILLE A CONGRES ET TOURISTIQUE (CN/0828-6183) [12069292] **2765**

VILLE E GIARDINI *See* VILLE GIARDINI **2433**

VILLE GIARDINI (IT/0042-6237) [04601086] **2433**

VILLE (MONTREAL), EN (CN/0826-7731) [13569247] **5498**

VILLE PLATTE GAZETTE, THE (US/8750-6785) [11671537] **5684**

VIM & VIGOR (US/0886-6554) [12966194] **2601**

VIMAN DAIJIST (PK) [02239402] **3451**

VIN VALDATAIN, PIEMONTEIS, LIGURE (IT) [02243193] **2371**

VINAVER STUDIES IN FRENCH (UK/0264-5564) [13941189] 2715, **3451**

VINCENNES SUN-COMMERCIAL, THE (US) [13105284] **5668**

VINCENT-CURTIS EDUCATION REGISTER, THE (US) [05332403] **1790**

VINCENT-CURTIS (FIRM) *See* VINCENT-CURTIS EDUCATION REGISTER, THE **1790**

VINCENT VOICES (US/1057-9761) [24203196] **2476**

VINCULO (BL) [01795417] **4364**

VINCULOS (CR/0304-3703) [01377341] **247**

VINCULUM (AT/0157-759X) [I0157759X] 1908, **3540**

VINDICATOR (LIBERTY, TEX.) (US/0746-6838) [10210634] **5755**

VINDICATOR (YOUNGSTOWN, OHIO) (US/0890-9857) [12961328] **5731**

VINDUET (NO/0042-6288) [01607120] **3451**

VINE. VERY INFORMAL NEWSLETTER ON LIBRARY AUTOMATION (UK/0305-5728) [03683330] **3255**

VINELAM MOTI (II) [02239583] **2509**

VINELAND TIMES JOURNAL (US) [15370889] **5712**

VINES OBSERVER (US) [28030329] **5169**

VINEYARD ALMANAC & WINE GAZETTEER, THE (US/0276-4687) [07370985] **2371**

VINEYARD & WINERY MANAGEMENT (US/1047-4951) [13817628] **2371**

VINEYARD GAZETTE, THE (US) [09397107] **5690**

VINEYARD VIEW (US) [08520117] **2371**

VINGNANAM (CE) [24236832] **5169**

VINGTIEME SIECLE (PARIS, FRANCE : 1984) (FR/0294-1759) [11817686] **2632**

VINI D'ITALIA *CEASED.* (IT/0042-630X) [01730094] **2371**

VINIFERA WINE GROWERS JOURNAL, THE *CEASED.* (US/0095-3563) [01796080] 2372, **190**

VINITA DAILY JOURNAL (US) [13676514] **5733**

VINIYOGA (SP) **2856**

VINIYOJANA LEKHE, UTTARA PRADESA SARAKARA (II) [07216087] **4758**

VINO, IL (IT) **2372**

VINO Y GASTRONOMIA (SP/1131-5997) [I11315997] **190**

VINOHRAD (XR/0042-6326) [09917724] **2372**

VINS D'ALSACE (FR) **2372**

VINTAGE '45 *CEASED.* (US/0742-1494) [10266866] **5568**

Alphabetical Title Index — VIRGINIA

VINTAGE AIRCRAFT DIRECTORY (UK) [03734139] **39**

VINTAGE AIRPLANE, THE (US/0091-6943) [01788070] 252, **39**

VINTAGE BUYERS GUIDE (US/0737-6626) [09444522] **2372**

VINTAGE CAR ANNUAL (UK) [07418580] **5427**

VINTAGE FASHIONS **CEASED.** (US/1047-4420) [20695247] 2779, **1088**

VINTAGE FORD, THE (US/0042-6350) [03955644] **5427**

●VINTAGE GUITAR (US/1056-8581) [23881638] **4158**

VINTAGE JAZZ MART (UK/0042-6369) [13061412] 5320, **4158**

VINTAGE LORRY ANNUAL (UK) [07181280] **5427**

VINTAGE (NEW YORK, N.Y. 1971) **CEASED.** (US/0049-6456) [01792227] **2360**

VINTAGE TRIUMPH, THE (US/0147-9695) [03257595] **5427**

VINTON COUNTY COURIER, THE (US) [16896497] **5731**

VINTON MESSENGER, THE (US/8750-7919) [11779194] **5760**

VINUM (SZ/0177-2570) [16539275] **2372**

VINYAR TENGWAR (US/1054-7606) [22968305] **3332**

VINYL EDITION, THE (US/0278-5455) [07786036] 5320, **4158**

VIOLA DA GAMBA SOCIETY OF AMERICA See VDGSA NEWS **4158**

VIOLA DA GAMBA SOCIETY OF AMERICA See JOURNAL OF THE VIOLA DA GAMBA SOCIETY OF AMERICA **4127**

VIOLA GRANGE (FIRM), THE See APPLICATIONS PROGRAMS **1278**

VIOLA : JAHRBUCH DER INTERNATIONALEN VIOLA-FORSCHUNGSGESELLSCHAFT, DIE (GW/0172-9098) [06679505] 389, **4158**

VIOLATIONS OF HUMAN RIGHTS IN SOVIET OCCUPIED LITHUANIA, THE (US/0360-7453) [02240328] **4514**

VIOLENCE, AGGRESSION TERRORISM (US/0891-5172) [14874789] **5265**

●VIOLENCE AND ABUSE ABSTRACTS (US/1077-2197) 5313, **5267**

VIOLENCE AND TERRORISM (US) [20741361] **4060**

VIOLENCE AND VICTIMS (US/0886-6708) [12956058] **3178**

VIOLENCE UPDATE **CEASED.** (US/1052-2689) [22246309] **4621**

VIOLENT KIN! (US/1064-5071) [20707972] **3178**

VIOLEXCHANGE, THE (US/0892-5437) [15246759] **4158**

VIOLIN SOCIETY OF AMERICA See JOURNAL OF THE VIOLIN SOCIETY OF AMERICA **4127**

VIOLONCELLO SOCIETY INC., NEWSLETTER (US/0507-7281) [07096641] **4158**

VIOMECHANIKE EPITHEORESIS (GR) [01794004] **1588**

VIOTECHNIKON EPIMELETERION ATHENON See EKTHESIS PEPRAGMEN VIOTECHNIKON EPIMELETERION ATHENON **833**

VIP NEWSLETTER (US/0738-7091) [09656459] **4394**

VIP. VAKBLAD VOOR IMAGE PROCESSING (NE/0926-3241) [I09263241] **1221**

VIP VIEWS INSIGHTS AND PERSPECTIVES (US) **1790**

VIRAL IMMUNOLOGY (US/0882-8245) [12004000] **3677**

VIRCHOWS ARCHIV (GW) **3898**

VIRCHOWS ARCHIV. A, PATHOLOGICAL ANATOMY AND HISTOPATHOLOGY (GW/0174-7398) [09418260] 541, **3898**

VIRCHOWS ARCHIV. B, CELL PATHOLOGY (GW/0340-6075) [07806507] **3898**

VIRCHOWS ARCHIV. SECTION A, PATHOLOGICAL ANATOMY AND HISTOPATHOLOGY See VIRCHOWS ARCHIV **3898**

VIRCHOWS ARCHIV. SECTION B, CELL PATHOLOGY See VIRCHOWS ARCHIV **3898**

VIREO (CN/0823-6127) [09816396] **4820**

VIRGIL SOCIETY See PROCEEDINGS OF THE VIRGIL SOCIETY **5235**

VIRGIN ISLANDS ARCHAEOLOGICAL SOCIETY See JOURNAL OF THE VIRGIN ISLANDS ARCHAEOLOGICAL SOCIETY **272**

VIRGIN ISLANDS BUREAU OF LIBRARIES, MUSEUMS, AND ARCHAEOLOGICAL SERVICES See ANNUAL REPORT FOR FISCAL YEAR ... / BUREAU OF LIBRARIES, MUSEUMS, AND ARCHAEOLOGICAL SERVICES **3190**

●VIRGIN ISLANDS COURT RULES ANNOTATED (US) [25237671] **3071**

VIRGIN ISLANDS DAILY NEWS, THE (VI) [10531523] **5813**

VIRGIN ISLANDS DIRECTORY OF SERVICES FOR THE AGING (VI) [11226486] **5313**

VIRGIN ISLANDS GOVERNMENT DOCUMENTS: A QUARTERLY CHECKLIST (VI) [04836778] **4693**

VIRGIN ISLANDS GUIDANCE NEWSLETTER (VI/0505-625X) [01548117] **1917**

VIRGIN ISLANDS LABOR MARKET REVIEW (VI/8756-1638) [11439723] **1716**

VIRGIN ISLANDS OF THE UNITED STATES See SESSION LAWS OF THE VIRGIN ISLANDS **3048**

VIRGIN ISLANDS OF THE UNITED STATES. BUREAU OF LIBRARIES, MUSEUMS AND ARCHAEOLOGICAL SERVICES See VIRGIN ISLANDS GOVERNMENT DOCUMENTS: A QUARTERLY CHECKLIST **4693**

VIRGIN ISLANDS OF THE UNITED STATES. GOVERNOR See VIRGIN ISLANDS OF THE UNITED STATES. GOVERNOR. BUDGET **4758**

VIRGIN ISLANDS OF THE UNITED STATES. GOVERNOR. BUDGET (VI/0735-9926) [09027332] **4758**

VIRGIN ISLANDS OF THE UNITED STATES. LAWS, STATUTES, ETC See VIRGIN ISLANDS RULES AND REGULATIONS. VIRGIN ISLANDS REGISTER **3071**

VIRGIN ISLANDS REPORTS (US) [01769157] **3071**

VIRGIN ISLANDS RULES AND REGULATIONS. VIRGIN ISLANDS REGISTER (US) [01607370] **3071**

VIRGIN ISLANDS VITAL STATISTICS ... DEATHS (VI) [20147271] **4563**

VIRGINIA See VIRGINIA LAW REPORTS **3071**

●VIRGINIA ACQUACULTURE MARKET NEWS REPORT (US/1064-4768) [26319408] **2315**

VIRGINIA AGRICULTURAL DEVELOPMENT AUTHORITY See ANNUAL REPORT / VIRGINIA AGRICULTURAL DEVELOPMENT AUTHORITY **61**

VIRGINIA AGRICULTURAL FOUNDATION See ANNUAL REPORT / VIRGINIA AGRICULTURAL FOUNDATION **61**

VIRGINIA AGRICULTURAL STATISTICS (US/0360-3830) [02243674] 5346, **157**

VIRGINIA ANNUAL ACCOUNTABILITY REPORT FOR VOCATIONAL EDUCATION (US) [10854135] **1917**

VIRGINIA APPALACHIAN NOTES (US/0739-3482) [07468058] **2476**

VIRGINIA ASSESSMENT/SALES RATIO STUDY (US/0099-2186) [02243686] **4758**

VIRGINIA ASSOCIATION OF COMMUNITY SERVICES BOARDS See ANNUAL REPORT / VIRGINIA ASSOCIATION OF COMMUNITY SERVICES BOARDS, INC **5273**

VIRGINIA. ATHLETIC COMMISSION See REPORT OF THE VIRGINIA ATHLETIC COMMISSION TO THE GOVERNOR OF VIRGINIA **4915**

VIRGINIA. ATTORNEY GENERAL'S OFFICE See VIRGINIA MAGISTRATE, THE **3143**

VIRGINIA AVIFAUNA (US/0505-7043) [01321223] **5620**

VIRGINIA BANKERS' ASSOCIATION See OFFICIAL DIRECTORY - VIRGINIA BANKERS ASSOCIATION **802**

VIRGINIA BAPTIST REGISTER, THE (US/0083-6311) [01798626] **5069**

VIRGINIA BAR ASSOCIATION See VIRGINIA BAR ASSOCIATION JOURNAL, THE **3071**

VIRGINIA BAR ASSOCIATION JOURNAL, THE (US/0360-3857) [02244167] **3071**

●VIRGINIA (BERRYVILLE, VA.) (US/1064-5691) [26248235] **2765**

VIRGINIA. BUREAU OF FINANCIAL INSTITUTIONS See ANNUAL REPORT OF THE BUREAU OF FINANCIAL INSTITUTIONS, STATE CORPORATION COMMISSION, COMMONWEALTH OF VIRGINIA **771**

VIRGINIA. BUREAU OF FRUIT, VEGETABLE, AND PEANUT MARKETING SERVICES See ANNUAL REPORT / BUREAU OF FRUIT, VEGETABLE, AND PEANUT MARKETING SERVICES **2327**

VIRGINIA BUSINESS (US/0888-1340) [13517153] **718**

VIRGINIA CAVALCADE (US/0042-6474) [01549497] **2765**

VIRGINIA CLIMATE ADVISORY (US/0743-6785) [05297626] **1436**

VIRGINIA. COMMISSION OF OUTDOOR RECREATION See BIENNIAL REPORT - VIRGINIA COMMISSION OF OUTDOOR RECREATION **4869**

VIRGINIA. COMMISSION OF OUTDOOR RECREATION See VIRGINIA OUTDOORS PLAN. EXECUTIVE SUMMARY, THE **4880**

VIRGINIA COMMUNITY COLLEGE SYSTEM See FINANCIAL REPORT - VIRGINIA COMMUNITY COLLEGE SYSTEM **1824**

VIRGINIA CONTINUING LEGAL EDUCATION See VIRGINIA CONTINUING LEGAL EDUCATION BULLETIN **3071**

VIRGINIA CONTINUING LEGAL EDUCATION BULLETIN (US/0196-5174) [03170712] 1790, **3071**

VIRGINIA CONTRACTOR (US/0273-6861) [06824876] **2033**

VIRGINIA COOPERATIVE CROP REPORTING SERVICE See VIRGINIA AGRICULTURAL STATISTICS **157**

VIRGINIA COOPERATIVE EXTENSION SERVICE See VIRGINIA GARDENER NEWSLETTER / DEPARTMENT OF HORTICULTURE, COOPERATIVE EXTENSION DIVISION, VIRGINIA TECH **2433**

VIRGINIA. COUNCIL FOR THE DEAF See PROGRESS IN COMMUNICATION **4392**

VIRGINIA COUNCIL OF HIGHWAY INVESTIGATION AND RESEARCH See REPRINT **5443**

VIRGINIA COUNCIL ON INDIANS See REPORT OF THE VIRGINIA COUNCIL ON INDIANS TO THE GOVERNOR AND THE GENERAL ASSEMBLY **2757**

VIRGINIA COUNTRY (US/0734-6603) [07586950] **2549**

VIRGINIA. COURT OF APPEALS See VIRGINIA COURT OF APPEALS REPORTS **3071**

VIRGINIA COURT OF APPEALS REPORTS (US) [14298087] **3071**

VIRGINIA DENTAL JOURNAL (US/0049-6472) [08226368] **1337**

VIRGINIA. DEPT. OF ACCOUNTS See REPORT OF THE COMPTROLLER TO THE GOVERNOR OF VIRGINIA **4745**

VIRGINIA. DEPT. OF AGRICULTURE AND CONSUMER SERVICES See ANNUAL REPORT. PLANNING AND DEVELOPMENT **61**

VIRGINIA. DEPT. OF AGRICULTURE AND CONSUMER SERVICES See YEAR IN REVIEW (RICHMOND, VA.), THE **2361**

VIRGINIA. DEPT. OF AVIATION See OPERATIONS REPORT / VIRGINIA DEPARTMENT OF AVIATION **31**

VIRGINIA. DEPT. OF COMMUNITY COLLEGES. FINANCIAL REPORT See FINANCIAL REPORT - VIRGINIA COMMUNITY COLLEGE SYSTEM **1824**

VIRGINIA. DEPT. OF CORRECTIONS See ... REPORTS / DEPARTMENT OF CORRECTIONS AND PAROLE BOARD, COMMONWEALTH OF VIRGINIA, THE **3175**

VIRGINIA. DEPT. OF CORRECTIONS See REPORT OF PERSONS DISCHARGED FROM PAROLE AND PERSONS VIOLATING PAROLE **3174**

VIRGINIA. DEPT. OF CORRECTIONS See STATISTICAL DATA ON PERSONS RELEASED FROM PAROLE BY DISCHARGE AND VIOLATION **3083**

VIRGINIA. DEPT. OF CORRECTIONS. BUREAU OF MANAGEMENT INFORMATION See REPORT OF PROBATION SUPERVISION WORKLOAD **3174**

VIRGINIA. DEPT. OF CORRECTIONS. BUREAU OF MANAGEMENT INFORMATION See REPORT OF RECIDIVISTS COMMITTED TO THE VIRGINIA STATE PENAL SYSTEM **3174**

VIRGINIA. DEPT. OF CORRECTIONS. BUREAU OF MANAGEMENT INFORMATION See CHILDREN'S CASES DISPOSED OF BY THE JUVENILE COURTS **3160**

VIRGINIA. DEPT. OF CORRECTIONS. BUREAU OF RESEARCH, REPORTING, AND EVALUATION See REPORT OF PROBATION SUPERVISION WORKLOAD **3174**

VIRGINIA. DEPT. OF CORRECTIONS. RESEARCH AND REPORTING UNIT See JAIL COMMITMENTS AND CONFINEMENTS **3166**

VIRGINIA. DEPT. OF EDUCATION See TITLE I IN ACTION **1788**

VIRGINIA. DEPT. OF EMERGENCY SERVICES See ANNUAL REPORT / COMMONWEALTH OF VIRGINIA, DES, DEPARTMENT OF EMERGENCY SERVICES **4765**

VIRGINIA — Alphabetical Title Index

VIRGINIA. DEPT. OF FINANCE. DIVISION OF ACCOUNTS AND CONTROL. REPORT OF COMPTROLLER *See* REPORT OF THE COMPTROLLER TO THE GOVERNOR OF VIRGINIA **4745**

VIRGINIA. DEPT. OF HEALTH PROFESSIONS *See* REPORT OF THE DEPARTMENT OF HEALTH PROFESSIONS, COMMONWEALTH OF VIRGINIA FOR THE ... BIENNIUM **4798**

VIRGINIA. DEPT. OF HEALTH REGULATORY BOARDS *See* BIENNIAL REPORT / COMMONWEALTH OF VIRGINIA, DEPARTMENT OF HEALTH REGULATORY BOARDS **4768**

VIRGINIA. DEPT. OF LABOR AND INDUSTRY *See* BIENNIAL REPORT / VIRGINIA DEPARTMENT OF LABOR AND INDUSTRY **1655**

VIRGINIA. DEPT. OF MENTAL HEALTH AND MENTAL RETARDATION *See* SUMMARY OF GENERAL STATISTICS **4811**

VIRGINIA. DEPT. OF MENTAL HEALTH AND MENTAL RETARDATION *See* COMPREHENSIVE STATE PLAN FOR DRUG ABUSE CONTROL (VIRGINIA) **1342**

VIRGINIA. DEPT. OF MILITARY AFFAIRS *See* ANNUAL REPORT / COMMONWEALTH OF VIRGINIA, DEPARTMENT OF MILITARY AFFAIRS **4035**

VIRGINIA. DEPT. OF PERSONNEL AND TRAINING *See* ANNUAL REPORT - VIRGINIA DEPARTMENT OF PERSONNEL AND TRAINING **4701**

VIRGINIA. DEPT. OF PLANNING AND BUDGET *See* EXECUTIVE BUDGET / COMMONWEALTH OF VIRGINIA **4722**

VIRGINIA. DEPT. OF PLANNING AND BUDGET. ECONOMIC RESEARCH SECTION *See* ASSESSMENT OF THE COMMONWEALTH **4711**

VIRGINIA. DEPT. OF TAXATION *See* TAXABLE SALES IN VIRGINIA COUNTIES & CITIES BASED ON RETAIL SALES TAX REVENUES **4754**

VIRGINIA. DEPT. OF TAXATION *See* VIRGINIA ASSESSMENT/SALES RATIO STUDY **4758**

VIRGINIA. DEPT. OF TRANSPORTATION *See* BULLETIN : A VDOT MONTHLY NEWSPAPER **5378**

VIRGINIA. DEPT. OF WELFARE AND INSTITUTIONS. STATISTICAL DATA ON PERSONS RELEASED FROM PAROLE BY DISCHARGE AND VIOLATION *See* STATISTICAL DATA ON PERSONS RELEASED FROM PAROLE BY DISCHARGE AND VIOLATION **3083**

VIRGINIA DISC [COMPUTER FILE] (US) [24478608] **1206**

VIRGINIA. DIVISION OF AERONAUTICS *See* OPERATIONS REPORT - STATE CORPORATION COMMISSION, DIVISION OF AERONAUTICS **31**

VIRGINIA. DIVISION OF EDUCATIONAL RESEARCH AND STATISTICS *See* VIRGINIA HIGH SCHOOL DROPOUTS **1798**

VIRGINIA. DIVISION OF EDUCATIONAL RESEARCH AND STATISTICS *See* PILOT STUDIES APPROVED FOR STATE AID IN PUBLIC SCHOOL SYSTEMS IN VIRGINIA **1902**

VIRGINIA. DIVISION OF MARKETS *See* PRODUCT PROMOTION **1622**

VIRGINIA. DIVISION OF MARKETS *See* MARKET NEWS (RICHMOND) **107**

VIRGINIA. DIVISION OF MINERAL RESOURCES *See* LIST OF PUBLICATIONS AND MAPS **1386**

VIRGINIA DIVISION OF MINERAL RESOURCES PUBLICATION (US/0160-4643) [03672808] **1445**

VIRGINIA. DIVISION OF MOTOR VEHICLES *See* BIENNIAL REPORT - VIRGINIA DIVISION OF MOTOR VEHICLES **5407**

VIRGINIA. DIVISION OF TRAFFIC & SAFETY *See* SURVEY OF OUT-OF-STATE PASSENGER CARS AND OUT-OF-STATE CAMPER VEHICLES ON INTERSTATE, ARTERIAL AND PRIMARY HIGHWAYS IN VIRGINIA, A **5445**

VIRGINIA. DIVISION OF TRAFFIC & SAFETY *See* SUMMARY OF ACCIDENT DATA (RICHMOND) **5445**

VIRGINIA. DIVISION OF TRAFFIC & SAFETY *See* TRAFFIC DATA FROM AUTOMATIC TRAFFIC RECORDER STATIONS **5446**

VIRGINIA EDUCATION ASSOCIATION *See* VEA NEWS **1789**

VIRGINIA EDUCATIONAL DIRECTORY (US/0083-6354) [02243389] **1790**

VIRGINIA EMPLOYMENT COMMISSION *See* LABOR MARKET INFORMATION DIRECTORY FOR VIRGINIA EMPLOYMENT COMMISSION **1683**

VIRGINIA EMPLOYMENT COMMISSION. LABOR MARKET INFORMATION UNIT *See* SPECIAL REPORT ON VETERANS **4057**

VIRGINIA EMPLOYMENT COMMISSION. MANPOWER RESEARCH DIVISION *See* MANPOWER INFORMATION FOR AFFIRMATIVE ACTION PROGRAMS **1689**

VIRGINIA EMPLOYMENT COMMISSION. MANPOWER RESEARCH DIVISION *See* WAGE & FRINGE BENEFITS FOR SELECTED OCCUPATIONS PAID BY VIRGINIA MANUFACTURERS **1717**

VIRGINIA EMPLOYMENT COMMISSION. MANPOWER RESEARCH DIVISION *See* AFFIRMATIVE ACTION INFORMATION **1642**

VIRGINIA. EMPLOYMENT COMMISSION. MANPOWER RESEARCH DIVISION *See* AREA MANPOWER REVIEW : RICHMOND, VIRGINIA STANDARD METROPOLITAN STATISTICAL AREA **1652**

VIRGINIA EMPLOYMENT COMMISSION. MANPOWER RESEARCH DIVISION *See* LABOR MARKET INFORMATION FOR AFFIRMATIVE ACTION PROGRAMS **1683**

VIRGINIA. EMPLOYMENT COMMISSION. MANPOWER RESEARCH DIVISION *See* AREA MANPOWER REVIEW : ROANOKE, VIRGINIA AREA **1652**

VIRGINIA EMPLOYMENT LAW LETTER (US/1042-461X) [19057111] **3155**

VIRGINIA ENGINEER (1974), THE (US/0504-4251) [05095872] **2000**

VIRGINIA ENGLISH BULLETIN (US/0504-426X) [06148289] 3451, **3332**

●VIRGINIA ENVIRONMENTAL COMPLIANCE UPDATE (US/1068-9516) [27866853] **3117**

VIRGINIA ENVIRONMENTAL ENDOWMENT *See* ANNUAL REPORT - VIRGINIA ENVIRONMENTAL ENDOWMENT **2161**

VIRGINIA ENVIRONMENTAL LAW JOURNAL (US/1045-5183) [19769977] **3117**

VIRGINIA EXTENSION (US/0745-7200) [09400841] **1543**

VIRGINIA EXTENSION NEWS *See* VIRGINIA EXTENSION **1543**

VIRGINIA FACTS (DALLAS, TEX.) (US/1054-8351) [22980647] **2765**

VIRGINIA FAMILY PHYSICIAN NEWSLETTER (US) [23110576] **3739**

VIRGINIA FARMER (BALTIMORE, MD.) (US/0746-1186) [09772899] **144**

VIRGINIA FORESTS (1974) (US/0740-011X) [09860187] **2398**

VIRGINIA FRUIT (US/0097-1782) [01799546] **2433**

●VIRGINIA FRUIT AND VEGETABLE MARKET INFORMATION (US/1064-4083) [26319358] 144, **2360**

VIRGINIA GAME & FISH (US/0897-8794) [17647967] **4880**

VIRGINIA GARDENER *See* VIRGINIA GARDENER NEWSLETTER / DEPARTMENT OF HORTICULTURE, COOPERATIVE EXTENSION DIVISION, VIRGINIA TECH **2433**

●VIRGINIA GARDENER NEWSLETTER / DEPARTMENT OF HORTICULTURE, COOPERATIVE EXTENSION DIVISION, VIRGINIA TECH (US) [26618842] **2433**

VIRGINIA GARDENER, THE (US/1057-3003) [08547620] **2433**

VIRGINIA GAZETTE (1930) (US/0049-6480) [01769187] **5760**

VIRGINIA GAZETTE (VIRGINIA, ILL.) (US) [13483931] **5760**

VIRGINIA GENEALOGICAL SOCIETY *See* MEMBERSHIP LIST - VIRGINIA GENEALOGICAL SOCIETY **2460**

VIRGINIA GENEALOGIST, THE (US/0300-645X) [01769189] **2476**

VIRGINIA. GENERAL ASSEMBLY *See* MANUAL OF THE SENATE AND HOUSE OF DELEGATES **4664**

VIRGINIA. GENERAL ASSEMBLY *See* DIGEST OF ACTS OF THE GENERAL ASSEMBLY OF VIRGINIA **2961**

VIRGINIA. GENERAL ASSEMBLY. HOUSE OF DELEGATES *See* HOUSE BILL SUMMARIES **4654**

VIRGINIA GEOGRAPHER, THE (US/0042-6512) [01550288] **2579**

VIRGINIA. GOVERNOR *See* BUDGET. SUPPLEMENT (VIRGINIA. GOVERNOR) **4715**

VIRGINIA. GOVERNOR'S OFFICE *See* EXECUTIVE ORDER - VIRGINIA **2968**

VIRGINIA. GOVERNOR'S YOUTH COUNCIL *See* REPORT OF THE GOVERNOR'S YOUTH COUNCIL (RICHMOND) **1068**

VIRGINIA GUARDPOST (US/0360-5876) [02631345] **4060**

●VIRGINIA HEALTH CARE IN PERSPECTIVE (US/1065-447X) [26606873] **4806**

VIRGINIA HIGH SCHOOL DROPOUTS (US/0091-5149) [01783740] **1798**

VIRGINIA HIGH SCHOOL LEAGUE *See* DIRECTORY / VIRGINIA HIGH SCHOOL LEAGUE, INC **1736**

VIRGINIA HIGH SCHOOL LEAGUE. LEAGUE DIRECTORY *See* DIRECTORY / VIRGINIA HIGH SCHOOL LEAGUE, INC **1736**

VIRGINIA HISTORICAL ABSTRACTS (US/0734-5089) [08755536] **2765**

VIRGINIA HISTORICAL SOCIETY *See* DOCUMENTS - VIRGINIA HISTORICAL SOCIETY **2731**

VIRGINIA. HOUSING STUDY COMMISSION *See* REPORT OF THE VIRGINIA HOUSING STUDY COMMISSION **2833**

VIRGINIA INDUSTRIAL DIRECTORY (US/0882-3219) [07421942] **1631**

VIRGINIA INSTITUTE OF MARINE SCIENCE *See* SPECIAL REPORT IN APPLIED MARINE SCIENCE AND OCEAN ENGINEERING **2095**

VIRGINIA INSTITUTE OF MARINE SCIENCE, GLOUCESTER POINT *See* CONTRIBUTION - VIRGINIA INSTITUTE OF MARINE SCIENCE **554**

VIRGINIA INTERMONT COLLEGE *See* ALUMNI DIRECTORY / VIRGINIA INTERMONT COLLEGE **1100**

VIRGINIA JOURNAL OF EDUCATION (1980) (US/0270-837X) [06492079] **1908**

VIRGINIA JOURNAL OF INTERNATIONAL LAW (US/0042-6571) [01769192] **3137**

VIRGINIA JOURNAL OF SCIENCE (US/0042-658X) [01589393] **5169**

VIRGINIA JOURNAL, THE (US/0739-4586) [06148314] **1859**

●VIRGINIA LABOR MARKET REVIEW / VIRGINIA EMPLOYMENT COMMISSION, ECONOMIC INFORMATION SERVICES DIVISION (US) [28354366] **1716**

VIRGINIA LAND USE DIGEST (US) **4848**

VIRGINIA LAW REPORTS (US/8750-3247) [11251236] **3071**

VIRGINIA LAW REVIEW (US/0042-6601) [00826179] **3071**

VIRGINIA LAW WEEKLY (US/0042-661X) [01606665] **3072**

VIRGINIA LAWYER (US/0899-9473) [18153938] **3072**

VIRGINIA LEGAL DESKBOOK : THE COMMON SENSE APPROACH (US/1060-4065) [24649700] **3072**

VIRGINIA LEGAL STUDIES (US) [01555955] **3072**

VIRGINIA LIBRARY ASSOCIATION *See* OCCASIONAL PAPERS - VIRGINIA LIBRARY ASSOCIATION **3238**

VIRGINIA LIFELINE (US/0279-6023) [07114597] **3650**

VIRGINIA LMI DIRECTORY (US) [12348727] **1716**

VIRGINIA, LOCAL TAXES ON MANUFACTURERS (US) [17966261] **4758**

VIRGINIA MAGAZINE OF HISTORY AND BIOGRAPHY, THE (US/0042-6636) [01642879] 435, **2765**

VIRGINIA MAGISTRATE, THE (US) [04396878] **3143**

●VIRGINIA MANUFACTURERS DIRECTORY (US/1065-2493) [26537737] **3489**

VIRGINIA MARITIMER (US) [13438519] **5458**

VIRGINIA MASON CLINIC BULLETIN (US) [15682461] **3650**

VIRGINIA MEDICAL QUARTERLY : VMQ (US/1052-4231) [22214331] **3650**

VIRGINIA. MILK COMMISSION *See* STATISTICAL SUMMARY - COMMONWEALTH OF VIRGINIA, STATE MILK COMMISSION **2362**

VIRGINIA MINERALS (US/0042-6652) [01555983] **1445**

VIRGINIA MUNICIPAL LEAGUE *See* TAX RATES IN VIRGINIA TOWNS **4754**

VIRGINIA MUNICIPAL LEAGUE DIRECTORY (US) [07368668] **4693**

VIRGINIA MUSEUM OF FINE ARTS *See* BULLETIN - VIRGINIA MUSEUM OF FINE ARTS **4086**

VIRGINIA MUSEUM OF FINE ARTS *See* PUBLICATIONS - VIRGINIA MUSEUM OF FINE ARTS, RICHMOND **4095**

VIRGINIA MUSEUM OF NATURAL HISTORY MEMOIR (US) [22589930] 4231, **4173**

VIRGINIA MUSIC EDUCATORS ASSOCIATION *See* V.M.E.A. NOTES **4157**

VIRGINIA NUMISMATIST, THE (US) [04934519] **2783**

VIRGINIA NURSE (US/0270-7780) [04286851] **3870**

VIRGINIA NURSES TODAY (US) [28441694] **3870**

VIRGINIA OUTDOORS PLAN. EXECUTIVE SUMMARY, THE (US) [07040510] **4880**

VIRGINIA PHARMACIST, THE (US/0042-6717) [01556198] **4332**

VIRGINIA POLYTECHNIC INSTITUTE AND STATE UNIVERSITY. SCHOOL OF FORESTRY AND WILDLIFE RESOURCES *See* FWS **2383**

VIRGINIA POSTMASTER, THE (US/0744-2297) [08119428] **1148**

VIRGINIA POULTRYMAN, THE (US/0042-6733) [02718633] **223**

VIRGINIA. PROPRIETARY SCHOOL SERVICE *See* PROPRIETARY SCHOOL DIRECTORY **1775**

VIRGINIA PTA BULLETIN (US/0042-6709) [04052739] **1874**

VIRGINIA QUARTERLY REVIEW, THE (US/0042-675X) [01769202] **3355**

VIRGINIA REGISTER OF REGULATIONS, THE (US) [11383778] **4693**, **3072**

VIRGINIA REPORT ON PLANNING FOR INFORMATION TECHNOLOGY RESOURCES (US) [23978405] **3255**

VIRGINIA RESEARCHER (CHARLOTTESVILLE VA) (US/0049-6499) [03956537] **3072**

VIRGINIA REVIEW (US/0732-9156) [08309756] **4693**

●VIRGINIA REVIEW OF SOCIOLOGY (US) [26492520] **5265**

VIRGINIA SAGE'S MANAGEMENT TECHNOLOGY (US/0882-6307) [11905112] **889**

VIRGINIA. SECRETARY OF THE COMMONWEALTH *See* REPORT OF THE SECRETARY OF THE COMMONWEALTH TO THE GOVERNOR AND GENERAL ASSEMBLY OF VIRGINIA **4681**

VIRGINIA SETTLERS (QUARTERLY) (US/0885-2626) [12598268] **2476**

VIRGINIA SOCIAL SCIENCE JOURNAL (US/0507-1305) [04691481] **5225**

VIRGINIA SOCIETY OF ORNITHOLOGY *See* VSO NEWSLETTER **5620**

VIRGINIA STATE APPLE COMMISSION *See* ACTIVITY REPORT OF THE VIRGINIA STATE APPLE COMMISSION **2407**

VIRGINIA STATE APPLE COMMISSION *See* ANNUAL REPORT / VIRGINIA STATE APPLE COMMISSION **1598**

VIRGINIA STATE BAR. YOUNGER MEMBERS CONFERENCE *See* NEWSLETTER - VIRGINIA STATE BAR. YOUNGER MEMBERS CONFERENCE **3017**

VIRGINIA. STATE BOARD OF EDUCATION *See* REPORT ON PUBLIC EDUCATION IN VIRGINIA **1778**

VIRGINIA. STATE BOARD OF EDUCATION. EDUCATIONAL DIRECTORY *See* VIRGINIA EDUCATIONAL DIRECTORY **1790**

VIRGINIA STATE BOARD OF MEDICINE *See* ROSTER OF REGISTERED PRACTITIONERS OF THE HEALING ARTS LICENSED AND REGISTERED IN THE STATE OF VIRGINIA **3917**

VIRGINIA. STATE BOARD OF NURSING *See* REPORT - VIRGINIA. STATE BOARD OF NURSING **3868**

VIRGINIA. STATE BOARD OF VOCATIONAL EDUCATION *See* VIRGINIA ANNUAL ACCOUNTABILITY REPORT FOR VOCATIONAL EDUCATION **1917**

VIRGINIA STATE LIBRARY PUBLICATIONS (US/0083-6524) [01559122] **2765**

VIRGINIA. STATE OFFICE ON VOLUNTEERISM *See* ANNUAL REPORT - VIRGINIA STATE OFFICE ON VOLUNTEERISM **5273**

VIRGINIA. STATE PORT AUTHORITY. RESEARCH DEPT *See* FOREIGN TRADE ANNUAL REPORT; VIRGINIA PORTS **836**

VIRGINIA STATE RAIL PLAN ... UPDATE (US) [06242580] **5438**

VIRGINIA. SUPREME COURT *See* CASES DECIDED IN THE SUPREME COURT OF VIRGINIA **2949**

VIRGINIA. SUPREME COURT *See* STATE OF THE JUDICIARY REPORT **3143**

VIRGINIA. SUPREME COURT. OFFICE OF THE EXECUTIVE SECRETARY. STATE OF THE JUDICIARY REPORT *See* STATE OF THE JUDICIARY REPORT **3143**

VIRGINIA TAX REVIEW (US/0735-9004) [07753500] **4758**, **3072**

VIRGINIA TIDEWATER GENEALOGY (US/0099-2496) [02242597] **2476**

VIRGINIA TOWN & CITY (US/0042-6784) [01769208] **4693**

VIRGINIA. TRUCK EXPERIMENT STATION, NORFOLK *See* BULLETIN - VIRGINIA. TRUCK EXPERIMENT STATION, NORFOLK **2411**

VIRGINIA UNION UNIVERSITY (RICHMOND, VA). *See* ALUMNI DIRECTORY - VIRGINIA UNION UNIVERSITY (RICHMOND, VA.) **1100**

VIRGINIA UNITED METHODIST ADVOCATE (US/0891-5598) [14971562] **5069**

VIRGINIA. UNIVERSITY *See* FINANCIAL REPORT - UNIVERSITY OF VIRGINIA **1824**

VIRGINIA. WATER COMMISSION *See* ANNUAL REPORT OF THE VIRGINIA WATER COMMISSION TO THE GOVERNOR AND THE GENERAL ASSEMBLY OF VIRGINIA **5529**

VIRGINIA WATER RESOURCES RESEARCH CENTER *See* ANNUAL REPORT - VIRGINIA WATER RESOURCES RESEARCH CENTER **5530**

VIRGINIA/WEST VIRGINIA QUERIES (US/0890-9423) [14472191] **2476**

VIRGINIA WILDLIFE (US/0042-6792) [01769210] **2208**

VIRGINIA WOOLF MISCELLANY (US/0736-251X) [03736064] **3355**

VIRGINIAN-PILOT, THE (US/0889-6127) [12227724] **5760**

VIRGINIAN (STAUNTON, VA.), THE (US/0743-4243) [10574174] **2549**

VIRGINIA'S APPROPRIATIONS FOR HIGHER EDUCATION (US/0094-8241) [01795110] **1853**

VIRGINIAS, MARYLAND, DELAWARE AND DISTRICT OF COLUMBIA LEGAL DIRECTORY, THE (US/0507-1348) [01482858] **3072**

VIRITTAJA (FI/0042-6806) [01769212] **3332**

VIRKSOMHEDEN VED SYGEHUSE ... / SUNDHEDSSTYRELSEN (DK/0903-8086) [18307959] **3793**

VIROLOGY & AIDS ABSTRACTS (US/0896-5919) [17204729] **3677**, **3662**

VIROLOGY (NEW YORK, N.Y.) (US/0042-6822) [01769213] **570**

●VIRTUAL REALITY MARKET PLACE (US/1065-271X) [26562616] 1239, **1217**

VIRTUAL REALITY REPORT *CEASED*. (US/1052-6242) [22338649] 1217, **1283**

●VIRTUAL REALITY SPECIAL REPORT (US/1074-1038) [29592732] **1206**

●VIRTUAL REALITY WORLD (US/1060-9547) [25124905] 1221, **1217**

VIRTUE (US/0164-7288) [04373782] 5568, **5007**

VIRUS BULLETIN (UK/0956-9979) [22216935] **1227**

VIRUS GENES (US/0920-8569) [17390370] 552, **571**

VIRUS INFORMATION EXCHANGE NEWSLETTER FOR SOUTH-EAST ASIA AND THE WESTERN PACIFIC *CEASED*. (AT/0813-5444) [19962795] **571**

●VIRUS NEWS AND REVIEWS (US/1061-8384) [25472808] **1206**

VIRUS RESEARCH (NE/0168-1702) [10694473] **571**

VIRUS RESEARCH. SUPPLEMENT (NE/0921-2590) [12686717] **571**

VIRUSES IN WASTE, RENOVATED, AND OTHER WATERS (US/0736-6647) [04384058] 571, **2245**

VISALIA TIMES-DELTA (US) [08786446] **5641**

VISAO *SUSPENDED*. (BL/0042-6873) [01769216] **2553**

VISCOCHIRURGIA (IT/0394-6134) [I03946134] **3977**

VISHAYA VASTU (II) [08359935] **3451**

VISHVESHVARANAND INDOLOGICAL JOURNAL (II/0507-1410) [01770966] **3332**

VISIBILITIES *CEASED*. (US/0892-7375) [15249551] **2796**

VISIBLE GRAIN SUPPLIES AND DISPOSITION (CN/0380-8718) [01791391] **204**

VISIBLE LANGUAGE (US/0022-2224) [01387812] **4570**

VISIBLE RELIGION / INSTITUTE OF RELIGIOUS INCONOGRAPHY, STATE UNIVERSITY GRONINGEN *CEASED*. (NE/0169-5606) [09901701] **5008**

VISIER (SZ) [03511317] **4928**

VISION (UK/0142-8543) [05881770] 4079, **1143**

VISION (US) **5008**

VISION (UK) 2275, 5053, **5568**

VISION (MX/0042-6911) [02160941] **3355**

VISION (PH/0042-692X) [02185046] **332**

VISION (US) **5008**

VISION (US/0274-6581) [05032078] **5008**

VISION AND VISUAL HEALTH CARE (UK/0892-9726) [15229877] **3879**

VISION BOLIVIANA (BO) [02240864] **2765**

VISION DU YOGA, LA (HT) [05627281] **2601**

VISION FOR AMERICA'S FUTURE: AN AGENDA FOR THE 1990S, A (US/1055-9213) **5313**

VISION (KARACHI, PAKISTAN) (PK) [01769219] **2509**

VISION LETTER, THE *SUSPENDED*. (US/0042-6962) [01796064] **4499**

VISION (MONTREAL) (CN/0382-0424) [02289395] **4461**

VISION (PASADENA, CALIF.) (US/0882-6609) [11927052] 1790, **5008**

VISION QUARTERLY (US) **3489**

VISION RESEARCH (OXFORD) (UK/0042-6989) [01589794] **3879**

VISION RESOURCE UPDATE (US) **4394**

VISION (SAN ANTONIO, TEX.) (US/0733-1460) [06934563] **5755**

●VISION TECNOLOGICA / PUBLICACION DE INTEVEP, S.A (VE/1315-0855) [29617632] **4281**

VISION, TERRE ET FORET (CN/0848-3809) [21101955] 144, **2398**

VISIONES DE LA RAZA (US) [08608784] **2494**

VISIONMONDAY (NEW YORK, N.Y.) (US/1054-7665) [22968575] 3880, **4217**

VISIONS (US/1043-4194) [19484081] 1314, **2601**

VISIONS / CANADIAN MENTAL HEALTH ASOCIATION, B.C. DIVISION (CN/1185-5940) [25127588] 5313, **4806**

VISIONS DE GUERRA I DE RETAGUARDA (SP) [01713954] **2715**

VISIONS IN LEISURE AND BUSINESS (US/0277-5204) [07586864] 718, **4855**

VISIONS-INTERNATIONAL (US) 3473, **3451**

VISIONS (KINGSTON, N.Y.) (US/0736-7686) [09198504] **332**

VISIONS MAGAZINE (BOSTON, MASS.) (US/1064-8658) [26432537] 1143, **4378**

VISIONS (MORAINE, OHIO) (US/0744-9178) [08651882] **5038**

VISIONS OF NEW MEXICO *CEASED*. (US/1042-2161) [18975899] **2765**

VISIONS (VICTORIA) (CN/0848-7324) [23263333] **4708**

VISITANDIN, LE (CN/0714-3230) [08985250] **5797**

VISITANTE DOMINICAL, EL (US/0194-9160) [05110007] **5038**

VISITANTE, EL (PR) [20948707] **5008**

VISITOR ACCOMMODATIONS, FACILITIES, AND SERVICES FURNISHED BY CONCESSIONERS IN THE NATIONAL PARK SYSTEM (US) [04061712] **5498**

VISITOR BEHAVIOR (US/0892-4996) [15273662] **4621**

VISITOR DUBLIN (IE/0790-6056) [I07906056] **5498**

VISITOR GUIDE TO FRONTIER VISTA TRAVEL REGION (CN/0823-6615) [09951448] **5498**

VISITOR GUIDE TO PRAIRIE VALLEYS TRAVEL REGION (CN/0823-6607) [09951452] **5499**

VISITOR GUIDE TO WOODLAND PARK TRAVEL REGION (CN/0823-6593) [09951440] **5499**

VISITOR (KITCHENER, ONT.) (CN/0839-1335) [18805570] **5499**

VISITORS & CONVENTION SERVICES NEWSLETTER (CN/0713-7613) [08985152] **5499**

VISLESHANA (II) [03525628] **1588**

VISNIK KIIVSKOGO UNIVERSITETU. SERIJA HIMII (UN/0372-6088) [03067050] **995**

VISNIK LVIVSKOGO ORDENA LENINA DERZARNOGO UNIVERSITETU IM. IV. FRANKA. SERIJA MEHANIKO-MATEMATICNA (UN/0320-6572) [06399772] **3540**

VISNYK (US/0042-7004) [03956671] **4499**

VISNYK AKADEMII NAUK UKRAINY : NAUKOVYI TA HROMADSKO-POLITYCHNYI ZHURNAL PREZYDII AKADEMII NAUK UKRAINY (UN) [26126151] **5169**

VISNYK KYIVSKOHO UNIVERSITETU. SERIIA FIZYKY (UN) [03057107] **4424**

VISNYK L'VIVS'KOHO ORDENA LENINA DERZHAVNOHO UNIVERSYTETU IM IVANA FRANKA. SERIIA KHIMICHNA (UN/0460-0509) [01210296] **995**

VISNYK REPRESIJ V UKRAINI (US/0749-8624) [10595808] **4499**

VISNYK. SERIIA FILOLOHICHNA (UN/0460-0452) [04287650] **3332**

VISOKE

VISOKE SKOLE (BOSNIA AND HERCEGOVINA. REPUBLICKI ZAVOD ZA STATISTIKU) (BN) [07624068] **1853**

VISPAC NEWSLETTER (CN/0712-7170) [08693664] **2085**

VISSA GEODEZIJA (BU/0324-1114) [02436901] **2579**

VISSH KHIMIKO-TEKHNOLOGICHESKI INSTITUT (SOFIA, BULGARIA) See GODISNIK NA VISSIJA HIMIKO-TEHNOLOGICESKI INSTITUT--SOFIJA **2012**

VISTA DE MEXICO, LA (US/0895-6464) [16729136] **5499**

VISTA (EDMONTON) (CN/1183-7128) [25468215] **1790**

VISTA PRESS, THE (US/0893-3464) [15513446] **5641**

VISTA (SASKATOON) (CN/0382-0289) [02230996] **1790**

VISTA/U.S.A (US/0507-1577) [04795336] **5499**

VISTAS IN ASTRONOMY (UK/0083-6656) [01573793] **401**

VISTAS IN PLANT SCIENCES (II/0378-9454) [03789454] **530**

VISTAS (LUBBOCK, TEX.) (US/1055-9159) [23368966] **5313**

VISTAS (MERION, PA.) (US/0278-7660) [07500154] **367**

VISTAS (MIAMI, FLA.) (US/0733-9720) [08029807] **2549**

VISTAZO (EC) [06615833] **5800**

VISTI - INSTYTUTU SV. VOLODYMYRA (CN/0380-0369) [02443238] **2275**

VISTI / (OSEREDOK UKRAINSKOI KULTURY I OSVITY (CN/0824-5991) [10845183] **2765**

VISTO (IT/1120-4486) [I11204486] **2494**

VISUAL ANTHROPOLOGY (JOURNAL) (UK/0894-9468) [16318487] **247**

VISUAL ANTHROPOLOGY REVIEW (US/1058-7187) [24300330] 4378, **247**

VISUAL ARTS AND CRAFTS COMMUNICATION COUNCIL OF ALBERTA See NEWSLETTER - VISUAL ARTS & CRAFTS COMMUNICATION COUNCIL OF ALBERTA **374**

VISUAL ARTS. FELLOWSHIPS (US) [18423909] **367**

VISUAL ARTS HANDBOOK (CN/0380-5743) [02627442] **367**

VISUAL ARTS NEWS (CN/0704-0512) [03960139] **368**

VISUAL ARTS. ORGANIZATIONS See VISUAL ARTS. VISUAL ARTISTS ORGANIZATIONS, VISUAL ARTISTS PUBLIC PROJECTS, SPECIAL PROJECTS / NATIONAL ENDOWMENT FOR THE ARTS **368**

VISUAL ARTS. ORGANIZATIONS / NATIONAL ENDOWMENT FOR THE ARTS (US) [18154792] **332**

VISUAL ARTS RESEARCH (US/0736-0770) [09069635] **368**

●VISUAL ARTS. VISUAL ARTISTS ORGANIZATIONS, VISUAL ARTISTS PUBLIC PROJECTS, SPECIAL PROJECTS / NATIONAL ENDOWMENT FOR THE ARTS (US) [28323049] **368**

●VISUAL BASIC DEVELOPER (US) **1206**

●VISUAL C++ DEVELOPER (US) **1206**

●VISUAL COGNITION (UK/1350-6285) **4621**

VISUAL COMMUNICATIONS JOURNAL (US/0507-1658) [02244223] **4570**

VISUAL COMMUNICATIONS NEWSLETTER See VIEW POINTS (FULLERTON, CALIF.) **1123**

VISUAL COMPUTER, THE (GW/0178-2789) [13104790] **1235**

VISUAL DIALOG (US/0360-4225) [02244577] **368**

VISUAL MEDIA (CN/0840-4313) [19491692] **4079**

VISUAL MERCHANDISING & STORE DESIGN (US/0745-4295) [09093674] **958**

VISUAL NEUROSCIENCE (US/0952-5238) [17700144] **3847**

VISUAL OBSERVATIONS OF ARTIFICIAL EARTH SATELLITES IN FINLAND (FI) [02246600] **39**

VISUAL RESOURCES (US/0197-3762) [06017386] **368**

VISUAL RESOURCES ASSOCIATION BULLETIN (US/1046-9001) [19653660] 4378, **368**

VISUAL SOCIOLOGY (US/1067-1684) [27155770] **5265**

VISUM NIEUWS CEASED. (NE/0925-8275) **1853**

VISVA-BHARATI JOURNAL OF PHILOSOPHY, THE (II/0042-7187) [01608251] **4364**

VISVA-BHARATI QUARTERLY (II/0042-7195) [01769229] **1309**

VISVA HINDI DARSANA (II) [06483306] **3332**

VITA DEL POPOLO, LA (IT) **2495**

VITA DELL'INFANZIA (IT) [05885657] **1790**

VITA E PENSIERO (IT/0042-725X) [01623935] **4364**

VITA E SALUTE (IT/0042-7268) [I00427268] **2495**

VITA EVANGELICA (ENGLISH EDITION) (CN/0507-1690) [02996490] **5008**

VITA IN CAMPAGNA (IT/1120-3005) [12800458] **144**

VITA ITALIANA (IT/0507-1712) [02159089] **2524**

VITA JOURNAL See V.I.T.A. NEWSLETTER (WINNIPEG. 1992) **1917**

VITA LATINA (FR/0042-7306) [01588452] **3332**

VITA MATHEMATICA (GW) [17892835] **3541**

VITA MONASTICA (IT) **5008**

VITA SANA CEASED. (CN/0826-2756) [11073590] **4806**

VITA SOCIALE (IT/0042-7365) [05985968] **5038**

VITAE SCHOLASTICAE (US/0735-1909) [08892132] 1798, **1790**

VITAL (FR) **2602**

VITAL AND HEALTH STATISTICS. SERIES 1: PROGRAMS AND COLLECTION PROCEDURES (US/0083-2014) [01590095] **4806**

VITAL AND HEALTH STATISTICS. SERIES 2, DATA EVALUATION AND METHODS RESEARCH (US/0083-2057) [01471638] **4806**

VITAL & HEALTH STATISTICS. SERIES 3, ANALYTICAL AND EPIDEMIOLOGICAL STUDIES (US/0886-4691) [10816303] **4811**

VITAL AND HEALTH STATISTICS. SERIES 4, DOCUMENTS AND COMMITTEE REPORTS (US/0083-2073) [01471658] **5346**

VITAL & HEALTH STATISTICS. SERIES 5, COMPARATIVE INTERNATIONAL VITAL AND HEALTH STATISTICS REPORTS (US/0892-8959) [11120379] **4806**

VITAL AND HEALTH STATISTICS. SERIES 10, DATA FROM THE NATIONAL HEALTH SURVEY (US/0083-1972) [01967685] **4806**

VITAL AND HEALTH STATISTICS. SERIES 11, DATA FROM THE NATIONAL HEALTH SURVEY (US/0083-1980) [01773549] **4806**

VITAL & HEALTH STATISTICS. SERIES 14, DATA FROM THE NATIONAL HEALTH SURVEY (US) [09771052] **4807**

VITAL & HEALTH STATISTICS. SERIES 15, DATA FROM THE NATIONAL HEALTH SURVEY (US/0895-4925) [07995708] **4807**

VITAL AND HEALTH STATISTICS. SERIES 16, COMPILATIONS OF ADVANCE DATA FROM VITAL AND HEALTH STATISTICS (US) [19891866] **4807**

VITAL AND HEALTH STATISTICS. SERIES 20, DATA FROM THE NATIONAL VITAL STATISTICS SYSTEM (US/0083-2022) [01768532] **4806**

VITAL AND HEALTH STATISTICS. SERIES 21. DATA ON NATALITY, MARRIAGE, AND DIVORCE (US/1057-7629) [23266043] **4563**

VITAL AND HEALTH STATISTICS. SERIES 23. DATA FROM THE NATIONAL SURVEY OF FAMILY GROWTH (US/0278-5234) [03582966] **4560**

VITAL AND HEALTH STATISTICS. SERIES 24, COMPILATIONS OF DATA ON NATALITY, MORTALITY, MARRIAGE, DIVORCE, AND INDUCED TERMINATIONS OF PREGNANCY (US) [19818846] **4807**

VITAL CHRISTIANITY (1994) (US/1077-6982) [30858908] **5008**

VITAL CONNECTIONS (US/0890-832X) [14472948] 2286, **5269**

VITAL ISSUES (WASHINGTON, D.C.) (US/1056-6368) [23379245] **2275**

VITAL LEGAL DOCUMENTS IN THE NEW PEOPLE'S GOVERNMENT (PH) [16850855] **3072**

VITAL NEXUS (CN/1180-1395) [24256732] **2253**

VITAL SIGNS (US) **3650**

VITAL SIGNS PHARMACY SERVICES NEWSLETTER (US/0739-9588) [09899165] **4332**

VITAL SIGNS (STORRS, CONN.) (US/0749-856X) [11190967] **4621**

●VITAL SIGNS : THE TRENDS THAT ARE SHAPING OUR FUTURE / LESTER R. BROWN, ET. AL (US) [27128822] **1596**

VITAL SPEECHES OF THE DAY (US/0042-742X) [01769234] **2495**

VITAL STATISTICS ANNUAL REVIEW (CN/0707-7548) [04801264] **4807**

VITAL STATISTICS (CONCORD, N.H.) (US/0737-1896) [09286613] **5346**

VITAL STATISTICS (EUGENE) (US/0164-0151) [04553104] **5346**

VITAL STATISTICS IN CORRECTIONS (US) [11656808] 3178, **3084**

VITAL STATISTICS OF NEW YORK STATE (US/0097-9449) [01799421] **5346**

VITAL STATISTICS OF THE UNITED STATES (US/0083-6710) [01168068] **5346**

VITAL STATISTICS ON CONGRESS (US/0896-9469) [10270504] **4693**

VITAL STATISTICS. PRELIMINARY ANNUAL REPORT (OTTAWA) (CN/0317-3143) [02443739] 4560, **4563**

VITAL STATISTICS REPORT (PH/0116-2675) [20682155] **5346**

VITAL TIMES (US/1056-4020) [23714203] **5182**

VITALITE (CN/1185-1988) [24257279] **2253**

VITALITY CEASED. (CN/0829-6014) [13512718] 5568, **2602**

VITALITY (DALLAS, TEX.) (US/1074-5831) [22427661] **2602**

VITAMIN CONNECTION CEASED. (UK/0957-6436) [I09576436] **4200**

VITAMIN D (GW/0721-7110) [08093870] **4200**

VITAMIN E ... ABSTRACTS (US/0736-9158) [09247457] **4200**

VITAMINE, MINERALSTOFFE, SPURENELEMENTE IN MEDIZIN, ERNAHRUNG UND UMWELT (GW/0930-4827) [23045554] **4200**

VITAMINS AND HORMONES; ADVANCES IN RESEARCH AND APPLICATIONS (US/0083-6729) [01587931] **3733**

VITCHYZNA; LITERATURNO-KHUDOZHNII ZHURNAL (UN/0042-7470) [03250594] **3355**

VITCYZNA (KIIV) (UN/0131-2561) [10082172] **3451**

VITI (FR/0399-3558) [15094500] **190**

VITICULTURA ENOLOGIA PROFESIONAL (SP) **145**

VITIS (GW/0042-7500) [01769236] **475**

VITIS, VITICULTURE AND ENOLOGY ABSTRACTS (GW/0175-8292) [11334941] 2372, **2362**

VITO (SEATTLE, WASH.), LA (US/0735-3154) [08939508] **2275**

VITREOUS ENAMELLER (UK/0042-7519) [02451456] **2017**

VITRIINI (FI/0357-749X) [09694598] 5073, **2810**

VITRINE (NE) **4097**

VITRO TECHNICAL JOURNAL (US/1054-481X) [10244045] **2000**

VITUTALAIPPULIKAL : TAMILILA VITUTALAIPPULUKALIN ATIKARAPURVAMANA ETU (II) [11795587] **2667**

VIVA (KE) [02435139] **5568**

VIVA MT. LAWLEY CEASED. (AT/1035-4859) [I10354859] 4514, **2275**

VIVA (NEW YORK) (NE/0149-4473) [01242013] **2549**

VIVA ORIGINO (JA) [10377377] **4173**

VIVA VIRUS (CN/0824-8214) [10451559] **389**

VIVANT UNIVERS (BE/0042-7527) [01786177] **2579**

VIVARIUM (NE/0042-7543) [01769243] **4364**

VIVARIUM (LAKESIDE, CALIF.), THE (US/1047-2665) [18161076] **5599**

VIVCHARSTVO / MINISTERSTVO SIL'SKOHO HOPODARSTVA, UKRAINS'KOI RSR (UN) [12069764] **223**

VIVECANA (BOMBAY, INDIA) (II) [11805414] **3451**

VIVEREOGGI (IT) **5265**

VIVIENDA (MX) [06993356] **2839**

VIVIR CON SALUD (SP) **4807**

VIVLIO TES CHRONIAS (GR) [10003728] **2632**

VIVLIOGRAPHIKA (GR) [01792552] **3255**

VIVRE + (CN/0228-5517) [07805580] **5182**

VIVRE A PIERREFONDS (CN/1187-4988) [25652337] **2765**

VIVRE A PIERREFONDS (CN/1187-4988) [25652340] **2549**

VIVRE ENSEMBLE LILLE (FR/0291-1795) [I02911795] **5008**

VIVRE ENSEMBLE PARIS (FR/1152-6653) [I11526653] **1790**

VOICE

VIVRE (GRANBY) (CN/0226-7772) [06515296] **5008**

VIVRE LE PRIMAIRE (CN/0835-5169) [18047583] **1806**

●VIZ (HATTIESBURG, MISS.) (US/1064-153X) [26227122] **3451**

VIZANTIJSKIJ VREMENNIK (RU/0253-2581) [I02532581] **2633**

VIZGAZDALKODAS ES KORNYEZETVEDELEM (HU) [01798836] 2245, **5541**

VIZIONS (CAMDEN, ME.) (US/1053-6256) [22590202] **1124**

VIZUGYI KOZLEMENYEK (HU/0042-7616) [04268364] **2096**

●VJESNIK (CI) [28366082] **5799**

VJESNIK ARHEOLOSKOG MUZEJA U ZAGREBU (CI/0350-7165) [I03507165] **285**

VJESNIK SOCIJALISTICOG SAVEZA RADNOG NARODA HRVATSKE *See* NOVI VJESNIK **5799**

VJESNIK ZA ARHEOLOGIJU I HISTORIJU DALMATINSKU (CI/0350-8447) [05246717] **285**

VLA NEWSLETTER (US/0896-0720) [15337928] **3255**

VLAAMS DIERGENEESKUNDIG TIJDSCHRIFT (BE/0303-9021) [01769246] **5527**

VLAAMSE GIDS, DE (BE) [09407427] **2856**

VLAAMSE TOERISTISCHE BIBLIOTHEEK (NE/0772-8425) [21014940] **5499**

VLAANDEREN (BE/0042-7683) [02538944] **332**

VLAANSE ACADEMIE VOOR WETENSCHAPPEN, LETTEREN EN SCHONE KUSTEN VAN BELGIE. KLASSE DER LETTEREN *See* MEDEDELINGEN VAN DE KONINKLIJKE ACADEMIE VOOR WETENSCHAPPEN, LETTEREN EN SCHONE KUSTEN VAN BELGIE, KLASSE DER LETTEREN **2850**

VLASTIVEDNE LISTY (XR) [06712676] **2715**

VLASTIVEDNY CASOPIS (XO/0508-1976) [02173958] **2715**

VLASTIVEDNY VESTNIK MORAVSKY (XR) [05247511] **2715**

●VLDB JOURNAL, THE (US/1066-8888) [27078023] **1255**

VLEES EN VLEESWAREN (NE) **2360**

VLEIS / MEAT (SA) [08115609] **223**

VLEISRAADFOKUS (SA) [04140904] **223**

VLIEGENDE HOLLANDER, DE (NE) **39**

VLIESSTOFF NONWOVEN INTERNATIONAL (GW/0935-6347) [I09356347] **5359**

VLSI DESIGN *See* VLSI DESIGN **2085**

●VLSI DESIGN (US/1063-9667) [26182680] **2085**

●VLSI DESIGN (PHILADELPHIA, PA.) (US/1065-514X) [26621523] **1206**

VLSI UPDATE (US/0270-8507) [06508882] 1230, 1265, **1239**

VM/370 CMS EXEC USER'S GUIDE (CN/0229-124X) [08010323] **1281**

VM UPDATE (UK) **1281**

VMEBUS HANDBOOK : VMEBUS USER GROUP INTERNATIONAL (BE) **857**

VMEBUS SYSTEMS (US/0884-1357) [12308365] **1273**

VMR; VETERINARY MEDICAL REVIEW (GW/0341-9851) [07003229] **5527**

VNESHNIAIA TORGOVLIA (RU/0134-8469) [01782064] **857**

VNESHNIE EKONOMICHESKIE SVIAZI SSSR *CEASED*. (RU) [20411750] **857**

VNESNJAJA TORGOVLJA (RU/0321-057X) [02269272] **857**

VNITRNI LEKARSTVI (XR/0042-773X) [01642134] **3802**

VNR NEW MATHEMATICS LIBRARY (US) [07780731] **3541**

VO. VIE OUVRIERE (CN/0849-035X) [I0849035X] **1716**

VOCABLE (ENGLISH ED.) (FR/0763-9686) [I07639686] **2856**

VOCACIONES (SP) **4209**

VOCAL MAJORITY, THE (US/0148-4230) [02269273] **5568**

VOCATION REHABILITATION ANNUAL REPORT FOR ... (US) [10801596] **1716**

VOCATIONAL & TECHNICAL EDUCATION; ANNUAL REPORT (US/0083-2898) [05230397] **1917**

VOCATIONAL AND TECHNICAL EDUCATION SELECTED STATISTICAL TABLES (US) [03371583] **1917**

VOCATIONAL ASPECT OF EDUCATION, THE (UK/0305-7879) [01769253] **1917**

●VOCATIONAL CAREERS SOURCEBOOK (US/1060-5630) [25036755] **4209**

VOCATIONAL EDUCATION; ANNUAL REPORT (US) [04444251] **1917**

VOCATIONAL EDUCATION EVALUATION REPORT (US/0363-650X) [02522229] **1917**

VOCATIONAL EDUCATION FOR YOUNG PERSONS AND ADULTS IN SCHOOL BOARDS (CN/1187-1490) [24690650] **1917**

VOCATIONAL EDUCATION IN OREGON (US/0474-3636) [02245189] **1917**

VOCATIONAL EDUCATION IN RHODE ISLAND, ... ANNUAL PROGRAM PLAN (US) [10297888] **1917**

VOCATIONAL EDUCATION IN WEST VIRGINIA *See* ANNUAL REPORT / WEST VIRGINIA STATE ADVISORY COUNCIL ON VOCATIONAL EDUCATION **1910**

VOCATIONAL EDUCATION JOURNAL (US/0884-8009) [12359089] **1917**

VOCATIONAL EDUCATION PROGRAM DIRECTORY, SECONDARY, POSTSECONDARY, ADULT / STATE OF INDIANA, STATE BOARD OF VOCATIONAL AND TECHNICAL EDUCATION (US) [08240324] **1917**

VOCATIONAL EDUCATION - SECRETARY OF EDUCATION TO THE CONGRESS (US) [09930741] **1917**

VOCATIONAL EDUCATION WEEKLY (US) [23245423] **1917**

VOCATIONAL EVALUATION AND WORK ADJUSTMENT BULLETIN (US/0160-8312) [02269274] **4395**

VOCATIONAL REHABILITATION IN GEORGIA (US) [08556854] **1716**

VOCATIONAL REHABILITATION INDEX (US/0096-1426) [03185083] **5313**

●VOCATIONAL SEARCH (US/1071-2747) [28599859] 1917, **1798**

VOCATIONAL TRAINING (GW/0378-5068) [05690755] **1917**

VOCATIONAL TRAINING NEWS (US/0047-5785) [10610894] **1917**

VOCE DEGLI ITALO CANADESI (CN/0842-9715) [19901379] **5797**

VOCE DEI BERICI, LA (IT) **2495**

VOCE DEI VIGILI URBANI, LA (IT) **1073**

VOCE DI MILANO, LA (IT) **2495**

VOCE EVANGELICA (CN/0708-2479) [05018652] **5008**

VOCEADOR, EL (US/0742-101X) [10266606] **1790**

●VOCES DEL TIEMPO : REVISTA DE RELIGION Y SOCIEDAD (GT) [26790996] 5265, **5008**

VODNI HOSPODARSTVI (PN/0322-8231) [22932942] **5541**

VODNYE RESURSY (RU/0321-0596) [01594948] 1418, **5541**

VODOHOSPODARSKY CASOPIS (XO/0042-790X) [01599742] **1418**

VODOSNABZENIE I SANITARNAJA TEHNIKA (RU/0321-4044) [07647970] **2245**

VOEDING (NE/0042-7926) [01599862] **4200**

VOEDING & MILiEU (NE/0926-0447) [I09260447] **1300**

VOEDINGSMIDDELEN TECHNOLOGIE (NE/0042-7934) [09534363] **2361**

VOENNAIA MYSL (RU) [24130760] **4060**

VOENNO-ISTORICHESKI SBORNIK (BU/0204-4080) [05312775] **4060**

VOENNO-ISTORICHESKII ZHURNAL : ORGAN MINISTERSTVA OBORONY SOIUZA SSR (RU) [01599940] 2633, **4060**

VOENNO-MEDICINSKIJ ZURNAL (RU/0026-9050) [01777892] **3650**

VOENNYE STRANITSY (RU) [25384500] **3451**

VOENNYE ZNANIIA (RU) [05687680] 4060, **1073**

VOENNYJ VESTNIK *CEASED*. (RU/0320-0752) [05464669] **4060**

VOETBAL INTERNATIONAL SPECIAL (NE/0923-2486) [I09232486] **4928**

VOGELJAAR, HET (NE) [10488052] **5599**

VOGELWARTE, DIE (GW/0049-6650) [01769260] **5599**

VOGELWELT. BEIHEFT (GW) [01715724] **5600**

VOGELWELT, DIE (GW/0042-7993) [05686154] 2208, **5620**

VOGTLAND-JAHRBUCH ... FUER SOZIALISTISCHE HEIMATGESCHICHTE UND HEIMATKUNDE (GW) [20478251] **4548**

VOGUE (IT/0042-8027) [03331959] 406, 1088, **5568**

VOGUE. (BRITISH EDITION) (UK) 406, 1088, **5568**

VOGUE DECORATION (FR/0767-0508) [I07670508] **2903**

VOGUE ENFANTS (FR) [18762393] **1088**

VOGUE GIOIELLO (IT) **2915**

VOGUE HOMMES (FR/0750-3628) [10633917] **1088**

VOGUE ITALIA. BAMBINI (MILAN, ITALY : 1982) (IT/1120-7787) [10549566] **1088**

VOGUE KNITTING INTERNATIONAL (US/0890-9237) [14273949] 5568, **5186**

VOGUE MUNCHEN (GW/0176-6104) [I01766104] 406, 1088, **5568**

VOGUE (NEW YORK) (US/0042-8000) [01769261] 406, 1088, **5568**

VOGUE PARIS (FR) [10474517] 406, 1088, **5568**

VOGUE PATTERNS (US/0095-2788) [01796524] **5186**

VOGUE PATTERNS (BRITISH EDITION) (UK/0142-338X) [04422875] 5568, **5186**

VOGUE PELLE (IT/1120-7795) [08442013] 3186, **1088**

VOGUE SPOSA (IT) **5568**

VOICE (DALLAS, TEX.), THE (US/0888-2517) [13534461] **4395**

VOICE (EAST LANSING, MICH.) (US/0883-573X) [10975877] 3072, 4694, **1790**

VOICE FOR EDUCATION, THE (US/0896-6605) [17241800] **1790**

VOICE FOR THE DEFENSE (US/0364-2232) [02617082] **3109**

VOICE (FRANKLIN, WIS.), THE (US/0889-3543) [08710156] 4758, **3793**

VOICE INTERNATIONAL (UK/0967-2052) [28461432] **1168**

VOICE LITERARY SUPPLEMENT (US) [08167551] **3355**

●VOICE LONDON. 1992 (UK/0966-789X) [I0966789X] **3891**

VOICE M.A.N, THE (US/0505-8708) [07325740] **2433**

VOICE NEWS (US/0886-2087) [10969400] 1265, **1168**

VOICE OF BUSINESS (US/0042-8108) [03956743] **718**

VOICE OF CHORUS AMERICA, THE (US/1074-0805) [24620697] **4158**

VOICE OF EGYPT (KE) [02244198] 4538, **2667**

VOICE OF EVANGELICAL METHODISM, THE (US/0164-3606) [04632963] **5069**

VOICE OF FREEDOM (DALLAS, TEX.) (US/0042-8116) [01609116] **5008**

VOICE OF ISLAM, THE (PK/0042-8132) [01773591] **5045**

VOICE OF MISSIONS (US/0042-8175) [03956785] **5069**

VOICE OF NORTH CAROLINA SCHOOL BOARDS ASSOCIATION (US/0744-4583) [08289789] **1874**

VOICE OF SANKARA, THE (II) [06504993] **4364**

VOICE OF SMALL BUSINESS, THE (US/0037-7198) [05459601] **718**

VOICE OF THE ARAB WORLD. INTELLIGENCE REPORT (UK/0954-5697) [18502094] **2509**

VOICE OF THE CEMENT, LIME, GYPSUM AND ALLIED WORKERS (US/0042-8191) [01609626] **1717**

VOICE OF THE DIABETIC (US/1041-8490) [18901069] **3733**

VOICE OF THE ELGIN FARMER (CN/0227-8480) [06858649] **145**

VOICE OF THE ESSEX FARMER, THE (CN/0703-8852) [03979783] **145**

VOICE OF THE HAWKEYES, THE (US/0892-7421) [15249976] **4928**

VOICE OF THE HOSPITALITY ASSOCIATION (UK) 5073, **2810**

VOICE OF THE HURON FARMER, THE (CN/0715-4372) [09146017] **145**

VOICE OF THE MIDDLESEX FARMER, THE (CN/0709-1915) [05586204] **145**

VOICE OF THE PEDESTRIAN, THE *SUSPENDED*. (NE) [05123395] 5399, **2839**

VOICE OF THE PHARMACIST (US/0507-2379) [01609744] **4332**

VOICE OF THE TENNESSEE WALKING HORSE (US/0505-8813) [01782202] **2803**

VOICE OF THE TRAPPER (US/0194-6927) [04948474] **4880**

VOICE OF THE TURTLE (SAN DIEGO, CALIF.) (US/0739-9324) [09835907] **5237**

VOICE OF THE VALLEY (WARDSVILLE) (CN/0820-7577) [10330445] **1790**

VOICE OF THE WORKING WOMAN, THE (II) [08294416] 5568, **1717**

VOICE — Alphabetical Title Index

VOICE OF THE YOUTH (CN/0229-4834) [08036568] **4548**

VOICE OF UNITED SENIOR CITIENS OF ONTARIO, INC (CN/0382-0068) [02287959] **5182**

VOICE OF WALDEN, THE (US/0898-6193) [14340697] **2208**

VOICE OF WASHINGTON MUSIC EDUCATORS (US/0147-4367) [01611007] 1908, **4158**

VOICE OF YOUTH ADVOCATES (US/0160-4201) [03678027] 1071, **3451**

VOICE OF YOUTH (CHICAGO, ILL.), THE (US/0042-8256) [01779168] **1921**

VOICE. OFFICIAL PUBLICATION OF MICHIGAN ASSOCIATION OF NURSEYMEN (US) **2433**

VOICE (ORLAND PARK, ILL), THE (US/0742-4302) [10360888] **145**

VOICE (OTTAWA) (CN/0713-0333) [08734191] **3178**

VOICE PROCESSING (US/0884-6685) [11750422] 1283, **1168**

VOICE PROCESSING MAGAZINE (US/1042-0460) [18922915] **1206**

VOICE TECHNOLOGY NEWS (US/1045-1498) [20021381] 5169, **2131**

VOICE, THE (US/1040-1121) [18325757] **2293**

VOICE, THE (US) **2433**

VOICE (VANCOUVER. 1983) (CN/0822-7896) [10446075] **5797**

VOICE (WESTCHESTER) (US/0049-6669) [03956727] **5008**

VOICEBOOK *See* T-GUIDE **852**

VOICEPOWER REVIEW, THE (CN/1181-8204) [23243220] **1168**

VOICES (AMERICAN ACADEMY OF PSYCHOTHERAPISTS) (US/0042-8272) [01611184] **3937**

VOICES (DEERFIELD, ILL.) **CEASED.** (US/0891-3420) [09928496] **5008**

VOICES (EDMONTON) (CN/0832-8315) [16517503] **3332**

VOICES FROM THE ATTIC (US/1062-628X) [25115569] **5568**

●VOICES FROM THE MIDDLE (US/1074-4762) [29716939] 3332, **1908**

VOICES FROM THE THIRD WORLD (II) [20938881] **5008**

VOICES IN ITALIAN AMERICANA (US/1048-292X) [20911218] **3451**

VOICES INTERNATIONAL (US/0042-8280) [03423019] **3473**

VOICES ISRAEL (IS) [07784430] **3473**

VOICES OF MEXICO **CEASED.** (MX/0186-9418) [14155186] **2512**

VOICES OF THE AFRICAN DIASPORA (US/1054-4283) [22881664] **2275**

VOICES OF THE PAST (UK) [05244252] **4158**

●VOICES (RENO, NEV.) (US/1065-2914) [26572392] **2796**

VOICES (SOUTHBURY) (US/0193-1474) [05122660] **5646**

VOICES (SURREY) (CN/0840-4003) [19751896] **3451**

VOICES : THE QUARTERLY JOURNAL OF THE NATIONAL LIBRARY OF AUSTRALIA (AT/1036-1561) [24868211] **3255**

VOICES (TORONTO, ONT.) (CN/0838-7176) [18111209] **4705**

●VOICES (WASHINGTON, D.C.) (US/1066-2944) [26915738] 3769, **3870**

VOICI PARIS (FR/0986-7481) [I09867481] **5568**

VOIE D'AVALLON, LA (FR/0241-6646) [I02416646] **5008**

VOIE LACTEE (CN/0710-5479) [08713724] **3769**

●VOIE NAVIGABLE TRENT-SEVERN, PLANIFICATION DE GESTION (CN/1191-4742) [26758076] **4694**

VOIES FERREES (FR/0249-4914) [I02494914] **857**

VOILA (US) **1071**

●VOILA LUXEMBOURG (LU/1017-2947) [24888687] **2524**

VOILA QUEBEC (CN/0228-698X) [07821012] **5499**

VOILE LIBRE (MONTREAL, QUEBEC) **CEASED.** (CN/0826-4511) [11197196] **4928**

VOILES ET VOILIERS PARIS (FR/0751-5405) [I07515405] **596**

VOIR DIRE (MONTREAL) (CN/0826-4503) [11197192] **4395**

●VOIR (QUEBEC) (CN/1188-5017) [26497753] **332**

VOIX D'AFRIQUE (IV) [04224429] **2500**

VOIX DE L'A.M.S.A, LA (CN/0704-7770) [08063845] **4694**

VOIX DES JEUNES (TORONTO. 1979) (CN/0229-4842) [08036574] **4548**

VOIX DES PRAIRIES, LA (US/0743-1848) [08604156] **2476**

VOIX DU PEUPLE (TORONTO) (CN/0824-247X) [10057328] **4548**

VOIX DU RETRAITE (FR) **3755**

VOIX DU SANCTUAIRE (CN/0700-9313) [03291410] **5008**

VOIX ET IMAGES (CN/0318-9201) [02442278] **3451**

VOIX FRANCO-ONTARIENNE, LA (CN/0713-8040) [08996213] **2765**

VOIX MULTICULTURELLE, LA (CN/0227-2067) [06563021] **2765**

VOIX SEFARAD (CN/0704-5352) [09456962] **2275**

VOJENSKE ZDRAVOTNICKE LISTY (XR/0372-7025) [I03727025] **3650**

VOJNO-ISTORISKI GLASNIK (YU/0042-8442) [05232217] **4060**

VOJNOSANITETSKI PREGLED (YU/0042-8450) [01777893] 4060, **3650**

VOJVOANSKA AKADEMIJA NAUKA I UMETNOSTI *See* GODISNJAK ZA ... / VOJVOANSKA AKADEMIJA NAUKA I UMETNOSTI **5231**

VOKRUG SVIETA (RU/0321-0669) [14990976] **2579**

VOLARE ROZZANO (IT/1121-5607) [I11215607] **39**

VOLE (UK/0140-4571) [03423032] **310**

VOLGA (RU/0507-2573) [02172520] **2524**

VOLGA TRIBUNE, THE (US/0163-6154) [04417171] **5744**

VOLITVE (XV) [07038142] **4694**

VOLK "CLIP BOOK." (US) [09152413] **382**

VOLK + RECHT : ORGAN DER DEMOKRATISCHEN JURISTEN DER SCHWEIZ (SZ) [07329698] **3072**

VOLK UND KULTUR : ZEITSCHRIFT DES RATES FUER KULTUR UND SOZIALISTISCHE ERZIEHUNG (RM) [06405871] **2715**

VOLKS-CALENDAR FUR DIE DEUTSCHEN IN WEST-CANADA (MICROFICHE) (CN/0383-1930) [02879602] **2495**

VOLKSBOTE; UNABHANGIGE WOCHENZEITUNG DER VERTRIEBENEN (MICROFICHE) (GW) [04434249] **2715**

VOLKSKRANT, DE (NE) [10707527] **5807**

VOLKSKUNDE (1940) (BE/0775-3128) [09770326] **2325**

VOLKSKUNDIG BULLETIN (NE) [03738972] **2325**

VOLKSMUSIK, DIE (AU) [07612263] **4158**

VOLKSREPUBLIC KONGO, WIRTSCHAFTSDATEN *See* VOLKSREPUBLIK KONGO, WIRTSCHAFTSDATEN UND WIRTSCHAFTSDOKUMENTATION / BUNDESSTELLE FUR AUSSENHANDELSINFORMATION **1588**

VOLKSREPUBLIK KONGO : WIRTSCHAFTLICHE ENTWICKLUNG (GW) [02515895] **1588**

VOLKSREPUBLIK KONGO, WIRTSCHAFTSDATEN UND WIRTSCHAFTSDOKUMENTATION / BUNDESSTELLE FUR AUSSENHANDELSINFORMATION (GW) [09099688] **1588**

VOLKSWAGEN DO BRASIL, S.A *See* ANNUAL REPORT / VOLKSWAGEN DO BRASIL, S.A **1598**

VOLKSWAGEN GREATS (US/0049-6723) [02943537] **5427**

VOLKSWAGENSTIFTUNG *See* BERICHT (VOLKSWAGENSTIFTUNG) **2485**

VOLKSWIRTSCHAFTLICHE GESAMTRECHNUNGEN. REIHE 3, VIERTELJAHRESERGEBNISSE DER SOZIALPRODUKTSBERECHUNG (GW) [18445438] **1631**

VOLKSWIRTSCHAFTLICHE SCHRIFTEN (GW/0505-9372) [01613928] **1526**

VOLLEY BALL (FR) **4928**

VOLLEYBALL (GW/0323-5211) [I03235211] **4928**

VOLLEYBALL (UK) **4928**

VOLLEYBALL CASE BOOK AND OFFICIALS MANUAL (US/0749-1832) [11069850] **4928**

VOLLEYBALL COACHES JOURNAL (CN/0842-2958) [19276432] **4928**

VOLLEYBALL MAGAZINE (US/0274-6662) [03476012] **4928**

VOLLEYBALL MONTHLY (US/0889-1990) [13808998] 4867, **4928**

VOLLEYBALL ROME (IT/1012-1730) [I10121730] **4928**

VOLLEYBALL RULE BOOK (US/0882-1372) [06124440] **4928**

VOLLEYBALL TRAINING (GW) **4928**

VOLLEYBALL WORLD (UK/0955-8047) [I09558047] **4928**

VOLLEYWORLD (SZ) [22256074] **4928**

VOLTA REVIEW, THE (US/0042-8639) [02501390] **4395**

VOLUME OF PAPERS - ANNUAL CONFERENCE AUSTRALIAN INSTITUTE OF HEALTH SURVEYORS SOUTH AUSTRALIAN DIVISION (AT/0312-1267) [05080336] **4807**

... VOLUME OF THE WALPOLE SOCIETY, THE (UK/0141-0016) [07374030] **368**

VOLUME OF TRAFFIC ON THE PRIMARY ROAD SYSTEM OF IOWA (US) [09541733] **5446**

VOLUMEZERO (US) [14388678] **310**

VOLUNTARY ACTION LEADERSHIP (US/0149-6492) [03511276] **5313**

VOLUNTARY ACTION NEWS *See* VOLUNTARY ACTION LEADERSHIP **5313**

VOLUNTARY EFFORT QUARTERLY (US/0193-2179) [05105763] **3650**

VOLUNTARY FUNDS ADMINISTERED BY THE UNITED NATIONS HIGH COMMISSIONER FOR REFUGEES ACCOUNTS, AND REPORT OF THE BOARD OF AUDITORS (US) [01640785] **3137**

VOLUNTARY HOUSING (UK) [07728026] **2839**

VOLUNTARY INDUSTRIAL ENERGY CONSERVATION (US/0192-5016) [05015267] **1960**

VOLUNTARY SUPPORT OF AMERICA'S COLLEGES AND UNIVERSITIES *See* VOLUNTARY SUPPORT OF EDUCATION **1853**

VOLUNTARY SUPPORT OF EDUCATION (US/0363-3683) [02412283] **1853**

VOLUNTAS : INTERNATIONAL JOURNAL OF VOLUNTARY AND NON-PROFIT ORGANISATIONS (UK/0957-8765) [22945479] **4339**

VOLUNTEER & VISITOR'S GUIDE (US) 5182, **3755**

VOLUNTEER CENTRE *See* INFORMATION FROM THE VOLUNTEER CENTRE MEDIA PROJECT : THE ... YEAR REPORT OF THE MEDIA PROJECT **1113**

VOLUNTEER HAPPENINGS (US) [22995844] **4758**

VOLUNTEER LAKE MONITORING PROGRAM (US) [17668172] **2245**

VOLUNTEER LEADER, THE (US/0005-1861) [01777382] **3793**

VOLUNTEER NEWSPAPER / CALIFORNIA HOSPITAL ASSOCIATION, DIVISION OF VOLUNTEER SERVICES (US) [09949649] **3793**

VOLUNTEER OPPORTUNITIES (CN/0828-6566) [12069354] **5313**

VOLUNTEER UPDATE (US) [24914422] **4807**

VOLUNTEERING (US/0275-3030) [07087605] **5313**

VOLUNTEERISM (NEW YORK, N.Y.) (US/0000-1325) [21321403] **5267**

VOLUNTEERS IN ACTION (CN/0824-1848) [11825330] **5313**

VOLUNTEERS IN FIRE PREVENTION (US) [09027737] **2293**

VOLUNTEERS WHO PRODUCE BOOKS (US/0193-113X) [05116203] **4395**

VOLVO, AKTIEBOLAGET *See* ANNUAL REPORT - VOLVO **5403**

VOLWASSENEN EDUCATIE *See* PROFIEL VAN BEROEPSONDERWIJS EN VOLWASSENENEDUCATIE **1775**

VOM WASSER (GW/0083-6915) [01769283] **5541**

VON DER HEYDT-MUSEUM *See* JAHRESBERICHT / VON DER HEYDT-MUSEUM KUNST- UND MUSEUMSVEREIN **354**

VON KARMAN INSTITUTE FOR FLUID DYNAMICS *See* LECTURE SERIES - VON KARMAN INSTITUTE FOR FLUID DYNAMICS **2093**

VOORAZIATISCH-EGYPTISCH GENOOTSCHAP EX ORIENTE LUX *See* JAARBERICHT VAN HET VOORAZIATISCH-EGYPTISCH GENOOTSCHAP EX ORIENTE LUX **2769**

VOPROSY ADYGEISKOGO IAZYKOZNANIIA / ADYGEISKII NAUCHNO-ISSLEDOVATELSKII INSTITUT, EKONOMIKI, IAZYKA, LITERATURY I ISTORII (RU) [08828599] **3332**

VOPROSY AKUSHERSTVA I PEDIATRII (RU/0137-0162) [05735070] **3912**

VOPROSY ALGEBRY / GOMELSKIFI GOSUDARSTVENNYI UNIVERSITET (BW/0234-4823) [15210227] **3541**

Alphabetical Title Index

VOPROSY ATOMNOI NAUKI I TEKHNIKI. SERIIA OBSHCHAIA I IADERNAIA FIZIKA (RU/0207-0472) [10128623] **4451**

VOPROSY ATOMNOI NAUKI I TEKHNIKI. SERIIA TEKHNIKA FIZICHESKOGO EKSPERIMENTA (RU/0207-0480) [10148784] **4451**

VOPROSY ATOMNOJ NAUKI I TEHNIKI. FIZIKA RADIACIONNYH POVREZDENIJ I RADIACIONNOE MATERIALOVEDENIE (RU/0134-5400) [10128930] **4442**

VOPROSY ATOMNOJ NAUKI I TEHNIKI. RADIACIONNAJA TEHNIKA (RU) [11050366] **4442**

VOPROSY BIBLIOGRAFOVEDENIIA (RU) [05515093] **427**

VOPROSY BOTANIKI IUGO-VOSTOKA (RU) [03458547] **530**

VOPROSY EKOLOGII I OKHRANY PRIPRODY (RU/0206-4731) [08524022] **2208**

VOPROSY EKONOMIKI (RU/0042-8736) [01838451] 1526, **718**

VOPROSY EKONOMIKI I KONVERSII / NAUCHNYI SOVET MEZHOTRASLEVOI EKONOMIKI I KONVERSII (RU) [29664965] **1526**

VOPROSY ELEKTRODINAMIKI I MEKHANIKI SPLOSHNYKH SRED (LV) [06034641] 2085, **4445**

VOPROSY EPIDEMIOLOGII ZLOKACHESTVENNYKH OPUKHOLEI (RU) [06130846] **3825**

VOPROSY FILOLOGII (RU) [02520766] **3332**

VOPROSY FILOSOFII (RU/0042-8744) [01465913] 4548, **4364**

VOPROSY FINNO-UGORSKOI FILOLOGII / LENINGRADSKII GOSUDARSTVENNYI UNIVERSITET IMENI A.A. ZHDANOVA (RU) [05259566] **3332**

VOPROSY FIZICHESKOI GEOGRAFII LATVIISKOI SSR (LV) [05218624] **2579**

VOPROSY FONETIKI I FONOLOGII (RU) [12783980] **3332**

VOPROSY GEOGRAFII TURKMENISTANA (TK) [03739597] **4173**

VOPROSY GEOKHIMII I TIPOMORFIZM MINERALOV (RU/0136-1813) [06553792] **1401**

VOPROSY GERMANSKOI FILOLOGII (RU) [06153767] **3332**

VOPROSY GIDRODINAMIKI I TEPLOOBMENA V KRIOGENNYH SISTEMAH (UN/0320-8702) [02244889] **2096**

VOPROSY IAPONSKOI FILOLOGII (FU) [02206186] **3332**

VOPROSY IAZYKOZNANIIA (RU/0373-658X) [01769286] **3332**

VOPROSY IKHTIOLOGII (RU/0042-8752) [01769287] **2315**

VOPROSY INFEKCIONNOJ PATOLOGII I IMMUNOLOGII (RU/0372-5952) [05670484] **3716**

VOPROSY INFORMATSIONNOI TEKHNOLOGII (RU) [19218501] **1262**

VOPROSY INZHENERNOI GEOLGII I GRUNTOVEDENIIA (RU) [05818664] **2000**

VOPROSY ISTOCHNIKOVEDENIIA I ISTORIOGRAFII (RU) [04508537] **2633**

VOPROSY ISTORII (BW) [04767274] **2715**

VOPROSY ISTORII (RU/0042-8779) [01769288] **2633**

VOPROSY ISTORII ESTESTVOZNANIJA I TEHNIKI (RU/0507-3367) [07695384] **5169**

VOPROSY ISTORII I TEORII ESTETIKI (RU) [05255478] **332**

VOPROSY ISTORII KPSS. NEKOTORYE VOPROSY ORGANIZATORSKOI I IDEOLOGICHESKOI DEIATELNOSTI KPSS, NA MATERIALAKH BELORUSSKOI SSR (BW) [02773050] **4694**

VOPROSY ISTORII RELIGII I ATEIZMA (RU/0506-0044) [05422827] **5008**

VOPROSY IZUCHENIIA I PREPODAVANIIA SOVETSKOI LITERATURY (RU) [05906549] 3451, **1908**

VOPROSY KHUDOZHESTVENNOGO OBRAZOVANIIA (RU) [05521812] **332**

VOPROSY KIBERNETIKI (TASKENT) (UZ/0321-2769) [06021451] **1252**

VOPROSY KINETIKI I KATALIZA (RU/0320-0027) [02608882] **1058**

VOPROSY KLASSICHESKOI FILOLOGII (RU/0507-3529) [02172332] **3332**

VOPROSY KLINICESKOJ MEDICINY (DUSANBE) (RU/0137-0618) [06458923] **3650**

VOPROSY KURORTOLOGII, FIZIOTERAPII I LECEBNOJ FIZICESKOJ KULTURY (RU/0042-8787) [10185800] **3650**

VOPROSY KVANTOVOI TEORII ATOMOV I MOLEKUL (RU) [06493186] **4430**

VOPROSY LITERATURY (RU/0042-8795) [01616709] **3451**

VOPROSY LITERATURY NARODOV SSSR (UN) [02987092] **3451**

VOPROSY MEDICINSKOJ HIMII (RU/0042-8809) [03547889] **494**

VOPROSY METODOLOGII (RU) [25223827] **4364**

VOPROSY MUZYKALNOI FORMY (RU/0507-3723) [04077666] **4158**

VOPROSY NEJROHIRURGII (RU/0042-8817) [04683497] **3977**

VOPROSY OBRABOTKI I INTERPRETATSII GEOFIZICHESKIKH NABLIUDENII (RU) [02556291] **1412**

VOPROSY OKHRANY MATERINSTVA I DETSTVA *See* MATERINSTVO I DETSTVO / MINISTERSTVO ZDRAVOOKHRANENIIA ROSSIISKOI FEDERATSII **3906**

VOPROSY ONKOLOGIJ (RU/0507-3758) [05692988] **3825**

VOPROSY OPTOELEKTRONIKI I SPEKTROSKOPII (RU) [07220699] **4442**

VOPROSY PITANIIA (RU/0042-8833) [01608262] **4200**

VOPROSY PRIKLADNOI MATEMATIKI I MEKHANIKI (KZ) [02641885] **3541**

VOPROSY PSIHOLOGII (RU/0042-8841) [01769291] **4621**

VOPROSY PSIKHOLOGII OBSHCHENIIA I POZNANIIA LIUDMI DRUG DRUGA / MINISTERSTVO VYSSHEGO I SREDNEGO SPETSIALNOGO OBRAZOVANIIA RSFSR, KUBANSKII GOSUDARSTVENNYI UNIVERSITET (RU) [07626123] **1124**

VOPROSY RADIOBIOLOGII I BIOLOGICHESKOGO DEISTVIIA TSITOSTATICHESKIKH PREPARATOV (RU) [01784560] **3825**

VOPROSY RASCHETA ELEMENTOV AVIATSIONNYKH KONSTRUKTSII SBORNIK STATEI (RU) [20291964] **39**

VOPROSY REGIONALNOJ GEOLOGII (RU/0202-2478) [05140495] **1401**

VOPROSY RUSSKOGO IAZYKOZNANIIA (RU/0385-4324) **3332**

VOPROSY RUSSKOI LITERATURY (UN/0507-3871) [01605577] **3451**

VOPROSY SISTEMOTEKHNIKI (RU/0206-4715) [16751854] **1255**

VOPROSY SIUZHETOSLOZHENIIA (LV) [04374194] **3451**

VOPROSY SLOVOOBRAZOVANIIA V INDOEVROPEISKIKH IAZYKAKH (RU) [04624047] **3332**

VOPROSY SOTSIALNO-POLITICHESKOGO RAZVITIIA SOVETSKOGO OBSHCHESTVA (RU) [02522094] **4499**

VOPROSY SOVREMENNOGO KAPITALIZMA (RU) [05699448] **1588**

VOPROSY STRATIGRAFII (RU) [02518541] **1401**

VOPROSY STRATIGRAFII I PALEONTOLOGII (RU) [03615946] **1401**

VOPROSY STRUKTURY GERMANSKIKH IAZYKOV (RU) [05461203] **3332**

VOPROSY TATRSKOGO IAZYKOZNANIIA (RU) [19909168] **3332**

VOPROSY TEORETICHESKOI I IADERNOI FIZIKI (RU) [02414076] **4451**

VOPROSY TEORII PLAZMY (RU/0507-4045) [09647516] **4445**

VOPROSY TEORII PLAZMY (US/0080-2050) [01908566] **4424**

VOPROSY TEORII SISTEM AVTOMATICESKOGO UPRAVLENIIA (RU/0130-0415) [02244546] 3451, **2131**

VOPROSY TRAVMATOLOGII, TOSIKOLOGII, SKOROPOSTIZHNOI SMERTI I DEONTOLOGII V EKSPERTNOI PRAKTIKE (RU) [07078393] **3742**

VOPROSY VIRUSOLOGII (US/0734-0311) [07929554] **571**

VOPROSY VIRUSOLOGII (RU/0507-4088) [01769293] **571**

VOPROSY VIRUSOLOGII. ENGLISH. SOVIET PROGRESS IN VIROLOGY *See* RUSSIAN PROGRESS IN VIROLOGY **570**

VORARLBERG (AUSTRIA) *See* RECHNUNGSABSCHLUSS DES LANDES VORARLBERG **4744**

VORGANGE (GW/0507-4150) [05222671] **2524**

VORMEN UIT VUUR (NE/0927-748X) [I0927748X] **2595**

VORTEX (TORONTO) (CN/0823-7034) [10199132] **4867**

VORTICE (MX) [04556787] **3451**

VORTRAGE (GW/0537-7927) [02130963] **2715**

VORTRAGE FUER PFLANZENZUCHTUNG (GW/0723-7812) [09787277] 552, **530**

VORTRAGE - RHEINISCH-WESTFALISCHE AKADEMIE DER WISSENSCHAFTEN, N, NATUR-, INGENIEUR- UND WIRTSCHAFTSWISSENSCHAFTEN (GW/0066-5754) [05177781] **5169**

VORTRAGE UND AUFSATZE (GW/0509-6065) [01637028] **1526**

VORWARTS (NEW YORK, N.Y.) (US/0746-7869) [09836450] **5722**

VOS AFFAIRES MUNICIPALES (CN/0713-6714) [08916548] **4694**

●VOSKRESENIE (RU) [25798247] **2715**

VOSPITANIE SHKOLNIKOV (RU/0042-8957) [02167744] **1790**

VOSTOK AFRO AZIATSKIE OBSHCHESTVA ISTORIA I SOVREMENNOST (URR) **2644**

VOSTOK / AKADEMIIA NAUK SSSR, INSTITUT VOSTOKOVEDENIIA [I] INSTITUT AFRIKI (RU/0869-1908) [24189679] **2667**

VOSTOK--ZAPAD (RU) [14162002] **2633**

VOTERS AND CANDIDATES PAMPHLET (US) [04947885] **4499**

VOTES AND PROCEEDINGS OF THE HOUSE OF REPRESENTATIVES (AT) [01518751] **4694**

VOTES AND PROCEEDINGS OF THE LEGISLATIVE ASSEMBLY OF MANITOBA (CN/0319-3020) [02443882] **4694**

VOTES AND PROCEEDINGS (OTTAWA) (CN/0384-224X) [03254623] **4694**

VOTING INFORMATION NEWS : A MONTHLY ROUNDUP OF VOTING NEWS AND ISSUES FROM THE FEDERAL VOTING ASSISTANCE PROGRAM (FVAP) (US) [24233990] **4499**

VOTRE AFFAIRE, C'EST NOTRE AFFAIRE (CN/0708-613X) [02872063] **815**

VOTRE BEAUTE *See* VOTRE BEAUTE, VOTRE SANTE **406**

VOTRE BEAUTE, VOTRE SANTE (FR/0042-8965) [10490929] **406**

VOTRE BOTTIN DE CROSSE (CN/0712-757X) [08724013] 4867, **4928**

VOTRE GUIDE QUOTIDIEN (CN/1184-1842) [23686558] **3541**

VOTRE HOROSCOPE (MONTREAL. 1982) (CN/0820-8891) [09551499] **391**

VOTRE MAISON (IT) **2903**

VOTRE REGIME DER RENTES DU QUEBEC (1973) (CN/0315-6575) [02248236] **718**

VOTRE SANTE (TORONTO), A (CN/1183-3025) [25608112] **2602**

VOTRE SUCCES *CEASED.* (CN/0843-6665) [20377699] **718**

VOVSKOE GEOLOGICHESKOE OBSHCHESTVO, L' *See* MINERALOGICHESKII SBORNIK **1388**

VOX (UK) **4158**

VOX BENEDICTINA (CN/0715-8726) [10453283] 5568, **5038**

VOX CANBERRA (AT/1032-0458) [I10320458] 3332, **1790**

VOX EVANGELICA (UK/0263-6786) [01777103] **5008**

VOX JURIS TRABALHISTA (BL) [02243814] **3155**

VOX LATINA (GW/0172-5300) [09045856] **3332**

VOX MAGAZINE (NEW YORK, N.Y. 1990) (US/1052-8814) [22407224] 332, **3451**

VOX MEDIAEVALIS (US/0743-927X) [10706810] **1080**

VOX PATRUM (PL) [10969152] **5008**

VOX REFORMATA (AT/0728-0912) [02451469] **5008**

VOX ROMANICA (SZ/0042-899X) [01200600] **3332**

VOX SANGUINIS (SZ/0042-9007) [01769301] **3774**

VOX (VIENNA, AUSTRIA) (AU) [07140126] 5320, **4158**

VOYAGE EN GROUPE (CN/0711-6136) [11100317] **5499**

VOYAGER (US) [06062511] **5651**

VOYAGER INTERNATIONAL (US/1040-8541) [18553638] **2579**

VOYAGES D'AFFAIRES PARIS (FR/0995-4228) [I0995-4228] **718**

VOYAGES TO THE INLAND SEA (US/0095-5388) [01783476] **3473**

VOYAGEUR (US/0042-904X) [01586231] **2765**

VOYAGEUR (GREEN BAY, WIS.) (US/1062-7634) [11325918] **2633**

VOYEUR, THE (US) [03423154] **3451**

VOZ DE HOUSTON, LA (US) [15127068] **5755**

VOZ DE LA CULTURA, LA (SP) **332**

VOZ DE LA MAYORIA, LA (UY) [11911984] **1717**

VOZ DE LA VALDERIA, LA (SP) **2524**

VOZ DE PORTUGAL (US/0746-0279) [09694214] **2549**

VOZ (DENVER, COLO.) (US/0746-0988) [09747738] **5644**

VOZ, LA (US) [02253029] **2495**

VOZ LAJERA : ORGANO OFICIAL DEL MUNICIPIO DE SAN JOSE DE LAS LAJAS EN EL EXILIO, LA (US) [09551697] **4499**

VOZ LIBRE, LA (US) [15064308] **5641**

VOZ (SEATTLE, WASH.) (US) [09779925] **2495**

VOZAC See VOZAC I SAOBRACAJ **5427**

VOZAC I SAOBRACAJ (CI) [03338383] **5427**

VOZES (BL) [01619432] **2495**

● VOZES CULTURA (BL) [26990282] **5225**

VOZVRASHCHENIE (RU) [25759443] **3451**

● VPM MAGAZINE (CN) [28166276] **4079**

VPU NEWS See TAGLINE (OLNEY) **4820**

VR & KLIMA (NO/0803-3293) [I08033293] **1436**

VR. VERMESSUNGSWESEN UND RAUMORDNUNG (GW/0340-5141) [07824053] 2001, **2579**

VR. VERPACKUNGS-RUNDSCHAU (GW/0341-7131) [03015474] **4222**

VR VIDEOREGISTRARE (IT/0394-2384) [I03942384] **4079**

VRA BULLETIN BOARD (US/0090-4465) [01785325] 5314, **4694**

VRA ECONOMIC DIGEST (US/0747-7996) [10787522] **5073**

VRAC, EN (CN/0706-1048) [08036604] **4538**

VRANJSKI GLASNIK (YU/0507-4428) [05235926] **2715**

VREMENNIK PUSHKINSKOI KOMISSII / AKADEMII NAUK SSSR, OTDELENIE LITERATURY I IAZYKA PUCHKINSKAIA KOMMISSIIA (RU) [01478859] **3451**

VREMIA I MY (RU) [25004225] **5053**

VRIJ NEDERLAND : VN (NE) [09210055] **2524**

VRIJE FRIES, DE (NE) [02184014] 3332, **3451**

VRIJETIJD EN SAMENLEVING (NE/0167-966X) [I0167966X] **4855**

VROUWENBELANGEN LEIDEN (NE/0925-482X) [I0925482X] **5568**

VRUCHTBARE AARDE (NE) 145, **476**

VS NEWS *CEASED.* (US/0748-7886) [11012842] **1273**

VSAM UPDATE (UK) **1281**

VSB: VIDEOTEX STRATEGIES AND BUSINESS (IT) **938**

VSDA MEMBERSHIP DIRECTORY (US/1062-8894) [24145729] **1143**

VSE BUSINESS REPORT (CN/0846-1031) [24256958] **919**

VSE UPDATE (UK) **1281**

● VSEMIRNYI UGOLOVNYI ARKHIV (RU) [26629337] **3109**

VSESOIUZNAIA AKADEMIIA SELSKOKHOZIA ISTVENNYKH NAUK. SOVIET AGRICULTURE SCIENCES See SOVIET AGRICULTURAL SCIENCES **136**

VSESOIUZNOE AGENTSTVO PO AVTORSKIM PRAVAM See VAAP **427**

VSESOIUZNOE ENTOMOLOGICHESKOE OBSHCHESTVO See TRUDY VSESOIUZNOGO ENTOMOLOGICHESKOGO OBSHCHESTVA **5599**

VSESOIUZNOE KHIMICHESKOE OBSHCHESTVO IM. D.I. MENDELEEVA See ZHURNAL VSESOIUZNOGO KHIMICHESKOGO OBSHCHESTVA IM. D.I. MENDELEEVA **996**

VSESOIUZNOE MINERALOGICHESKOE OBSHCHESTVO. ZAPADNO-SIBIRSKOE OTDELENIE See ZAPISKI ZAPADNO-SIBIRSKOGO OTDELENIIA **1445**

VSESOIUZNOE OBEDINENIE MASHPRIBORINTORG See MASHPRIBORINTORG **3484**

VSESOIUZNOE OBEDINENIE TRAKTOROEKSPORT See TRACTOROEXPORT **161**

VSESOIUZNOE OBSHCHESTVO POCHVOVEDOV (SOVIET UNION) See INFORMATSIONNYI MATERIAL / AKADEMIIA NAUK SSSR, NAUCHNYI TSENTR BIOLOGICHESKIKH ISSLEDOVANII ... ET AL **174**

VSESOIUZNOE PALEONTOLOGICHESKOE OBSHCHESTVO See EZHEGODNIK **4227**

VSESOIUZNOE PALEONTOLOGICHESKOE OBSHCHESTVO. SESSIIA See TRUDY ... SESSII VSESOIUZNOGO PALEONTOLOGICHESKOGO OBSHCHESTVA **4231**

VSESOIUZNYI NAUCHNO-ISSLEDOVATELSKII I PROEKTNO-KONSTRUKTORSKII UGOLNYI INSTITUT See NAUCHNYE TRUDY **2147**

VSESOIUZNYI NAUCHNO-ISSLEDOVATELSKII INSTITUT FIZICHESKOI KULTURY See NAUCHNYE TRUDY **1857**

VSESOIUZNYI NAUCHNO-ISSLEDOVATELSKII INSTITUT FIZIOLOGII, BIOKHIMII I PITANIIA SELSKOKHOZIAISTVENNYKH ZHIVOTNYKH (SOVIET UNION) See NAUCNYE TRUDY - VSESOJUZNYJ NAUCNO-ISSLEDOVATELSKIJ INSTITUT FIZIOLOGII BIOHIMII I PITANIJA SELSKO-HOZJAJSTEVENNYH ZIVOTNYH **5516**

VSESOIUZNYI NAUCHNO-ISSLEDOVATELSKII INSTITUT LIUMINOFOROV I OSOBO CHISTYKH VESHCHESTV See LIUMINESTSENTNYE MATERIALY I OSOBO CHISTYE VSHCHESTVA **4438**

VSESOIUZNYI NAUCHNO-ISSLEDOVATELSKII INSTITUT PO PERERABOTKE NEFTI See TRUDY - VSESOIUZNYI NAUCHNO-ISSLEDOVATELSKII INSTITUT PO PERERABOTKE NEFTI **4280**

VSESOIUZNYI NAUCHNO-ISSLEDOVATELSKII INSTITUT RISA See BIULLETEN NAUCNO-TEHNICESKOJ INFORMACII VSESOUZNOGO NAUCNO-ISSLEDOVATELSKOGO INSTITUTA RISA **164**

VSESOIUZNYI NAUCHNO-ISSLEDOVATELSKII INSTITUT VAGONSTROENIIA See TRUDY **5437**

VSESOIUZNYI NAUCHNO-ISSLEDOVATELSKII INSTITUT ZERNOBOBOVYKH I KRUPIANYKH KULTUR See BIULLETIN NAUCHNO-TEKHNICHESKOI INFORMATSII VSESOIUZNOGO NAUCHNO-ISSLEDOVATELSKOGO INSTITUTA ZERNOBOBOVYKH I KRUPIANYKH KULTUR **200**

VSESOIUZNYI NAUCHNO-ISSLEDOVATELSKII INSTITUT ZERNOVOGO KHOZIAISTVA See TRUDY VSESOIUZNOGO NAUCNO-ISSLEDOVATELSKOGO INSTITUTA ZERNOVOGO HOZAJSTVA **143**

VSESOIUZNYI NAUCHNO-ISSLEDOVATELSLOI INSTITUT FIZIOLOGII, BIOKHIMII I PITANIIA SELSKOKHOZIAISTVENNYKH ZHIVOTNYKH (SOVIET UNION) See BIULLETIN VSESOIUZNOGO NAUCHNO-ISSLEDOVATELSKOGO INSTITUTA FIZIOLOGII, BIOKHIMII I PITANIIA SELSKOKHOZIAISTVENNYKH ZHIVOTNYKH **5506**

VSESOIUZNYI SEZDA PROFESSIONALNYKH SOIUZOV See MATERIALY SEZDA PROFESSIONALNYKH SOIUZOV SSSR **1690**

VSESVIT (KIIV) (UN/0320-8370) [05378927] **2524**

VSMF-ASSEM INFORMATION / VERBAND SCHWEIZERISCHER MARKTFORSCHER (SZ) [07715337] **938**

VSO NEWSLETTER (US) [06467797] **5620**

VSPOMOGATELNYE ISTORICHESKIE DISTSIPLINY (RU/0507-5238) [01641213] **2633**

VST REVUE See TT REVUE / HERAUSGEBER, VERBAND OFFENTLICHER VERKEHR VOV ... ET AL **5398**

VSTA NEWSDATA (AT/0729-2546) [I07292546] **1790**

VSTRECHA (RU) [27377473] **3451**

VSTRECI (PHILADELPHIA, PA.) (US/0888-5257) [10636563] **3473**

VT RESEARCH SERIES (US/0090-5283) [03201509] **1917**

V+T. VERKEHR UND TECHNIK (GW/0340-4536) [07567331] **5399**

VT WONEN (NE) **2907**

VTAE JOURNAL (US) [04798178] **1917**

VTB. VERFAHRENSTECHNISCHE BERICHTE (GW/0042-3890) [I00423890] **2001**

VTT JULKAISUJA (FI/1235-0613) [I12350613] **5169**

VTT SYMPOSIUM (FI/0357-9387) [25812225] **5169**

VTT TIEDOTTEITA (FI/1235-0605) [I12350605] **5169**

VUELTA (MX/0185-1586) [03366962] **2512**

VUES NOUVELLES (FR) [02246663] **39**

VUES SUR L'ECONOMIE D'AQUITAINE (FR/0395-9473) [06247277] **5346**

VULKANOLOGIIA I SEISMOLOGIA (US/0742-0463) [10259290] **1412**

VULKANOLOGIIA I SEISMOLOGIIA (RU) [05871649] **1412**

VUODEN LUONNONKUVAT ... (FI) [09849699] **4378**

VUOTO, SCIENZA E TECNOLOGIA (IT/0391-3155) [02245770] **2131**

VVS (DK/0346-4636) [07770200] **2608**

VVS BULLETIN (NE) **5346**

VW TRENDS (US/8750-3301) [11256847] **5428**

VWA (SZ) [10285492] 3451, **3473**

VWD CHEMIE KAUTSCHUK (GW) **1030**

VWD-STAHL (GW) **4028**

VXI JOURNAL (US/1072-9933) [28934878] **1206**

VYCHISLITELNAIA I PRIKLADNAIA MATEMATIKA (RU/0321-4117) [00957904] **3541**

VYCHISLITELNAIA TEKHNIKA (RU) [02242018] **1262**

VYCHISLITELNAIA TEKHNIKA SOTSIALISTICHESKIKH STRAN (RU) [05202322] **1262**

VYCHISLITELNYE METODY I PROGRAMMIROVANIE (RU/0507-5386) [03818267] **1281**

VYCHISLITELNYE PROTSESSY I SISTEMY (RU) [10815872] **1262**

VYCHISLITELNYE SISTEMY (MOSCOW, R.S.F.S.R.) (RU) [07592389] **1207**

VYCHODOSLOVENSKY KRAJ V TLACI (XO) [03215690] **2636**

VYIAULENCHAE MASTATSTVA BELARUSI (BW) [04801651] **368**

VYROBNI DRUZSTEVNICTVI (XR) [02243660] **1631**

VYROCNI ZPRAVA HYDROMETEOROLOGICKEHO USTAVU (XR) [02458137] **1418**

VYSKUMNE PRACE Z ODBORU PAPIERA A CELULOZY (XO/0139-5033) [11576525] **4239**

VYSKUMNY USTAV CHOVU A SLACHTENIA HYDINY See HYDINARSTVO **212**

VYSOKA SKOLA BANSKA V OSTRAVE See SBORNIK VEDECKYCH PRACI. RADA HUTNICKA. DOKLADY. SERIIA METALLURGICHESKAIA. TRANSACTIONS. METALLURGICAL SERIES **4018**

VYSOKA SKOLA BANSKA V OSTRAVIE See SBORNIK VEDECKYCH PRACI. VYSOKA SKOLA BANSKA, OSTRAVA. RADA HORNICKO-GEOLOGICKA **1396**

VYSOKA SKOLA CHEMICKO-TECHNOLOGICKA V PRAZE See SBORNIK VYSOKE SKOLY CHEMICKO-TECHNOLOGICKE V PRAZE. FIZIKALNI CHEMIE. SBORNIK PRAZHSKOGO KHIMIKO-TECHNOLOGICHESKOGO INSTITUTA. FIZICHESKAIA KHIMIIA. SCIENTIFIC PAPERS OF THE PRAGUE INSTITUTE OF CHEMICAL TECHNOLOGY. PHYSICAL CHEMISTRY **1057**

VYSOKA SKOLA CHEMICKO-TECHNOLOGICKA V PRAZE See SBORNIK VYSOKE SKOLY CHEMICKO-TECHNOLOGICKE V PRAZE. AUTOMATIZOVANE SYSTEMY RIZENI A VYPOCETNI METODY. SBORNIK PRAZHSKOGO KHIMIKO-TEKHNOLOGICHESKOGO INSTITUTA. AVTOMATIZIROVANNYE SISTEMY UPRAVLENIIA I VYCHISLITELNYE METODY. SCIENTIFIC PAPERS OF THE PRAGUE INSTITUTE OF CHEMICAL TECHNOLOGY. AUTOMATIC CONTROL SYSTEMS AND COMPUTING METHODS **2017**

VYSOKA SKOLA CHEMICKO-TECHNOLOGICKA V PRAZE See SBORNIK. CHEMICKE INZENYRSTVI A AUTOMATIZACE **2017**

VYSOKA SKOLA CHEMICKO-TECHNOLOGICKA V PRAZE See SBORNIK VYSOKE SKOLY CHEMICKO-TECHNOLOGICKE V PRAZE. FIZIKA MATERIALU A MERICI TECHNIKA. SBORNIK PRAZHSKOGO KHIMIKO-TECHNOLOGICHESKOGO INSTITUTA. FIZIKA MATERIALOV I IZMERITELNAIA TEKHNIKA. SCIENTIFIC PAPERS OF THE PRAGUE INSTITUTE OF CHEMICAL TECHNOLOGY. MATERIAL SCIENCE AND MEASUREMENT TECHNIQUE **2108**

VYSOKA SKOLA CHEMICKO-TECHNOLOGICKA V PRAZE See SBORNIK VYSOKE SKOLY CHEMICKO-TECHNOLOGICKE V PRAZE. POLYMERY-CHEMIE, VLASTNOSTI A ZPRACOVANI **1047**

Alphabetical Title Index — WAKAYAMA

VYSOKA SKOLA ZEMEDELSKA V BRNE. FAKULTA AGRONOMICKA See ACTA UNIVERSITATIS AGRICULTURAE. FACULTAS AGRONOMICA **44**

VYSOKOCHISTYE VESHCHESTVA / AKADEMIIA NAUK SSSR (RU/0235-0122) [16749232] **995**

VYSOKOMOLEKULARNYE SOEDINENA. SERIA A (RU/0507-5475) [05979501] **995**

● VYSOKOMOLEKULIARNYE SOEDINENIIA. SERIIA A I SERIIA B (RU) [28716136] **995**

VYSOKOMOLEKULIARNYE SOEDINENIIA. SERIIA B (RU/0042-9368) [05322853] **995**

VYSOKOMOLEKULIARNYE SOEDINENIIA. SERIIA B, KRATKIE SOOBSHCHENIIA See VYSOKOMOLEKULIARNYE SOEDINENIIA. SERIIA A I SERIIA B **995**

VYSOKOTEMPERATURNAIA SVERKHPROVODIMOST / LENINGRADSKII GOSUDARSTVENNYI UNIVERSITET (RU) [22721172] **4432**

VYSTAVKA DOSTIZHENII NARODNOGO KHOZIIAISTVA SSSR (MOSCOW, R.S.F.S.R.). INFORMATSIONNYI BIULLETEN See VDNKH SSSR **144**

VYTIS (US/0042-9384) [03956867] **5237**

VYTVARNA KULTURA (XR/0139-9365) [23007434] 2001, **368**

VYTVARNA VYCHOVA (XR) [19986242] **368**

VYTVARNY ZIVOT (XO/0139-7214) [I01397214] **368**

VYZANTINOS DOMOS (GR) [20376646] **2715**

VYZKUM V CHOVU SKOTU (CS/0139-7265) [I01397265] **145**

VYZKUMNY USTAV CKD See TECHNICKY SBORNIK - VYZKUMNY USTAV CKD **2130**

VYZKUMNY USTAV GEOLOGICKEHO INZENYRSTVI See PRACE VYZKUMNEHO USTAVU GEOLOGICKEHO INZENYRSTVI **4275**

VYZKUMNY USTAV RYBARSKY A HYDROBIOLOGICKY See PRACE VURH VODNANY **2310**

VYZKUMY V CECHACH (XR/0862-2930) [02239890] **2715**

VYZKUMY V CECHACH. SUPPLEMENTUM (XR/0231-956X) [I0231956X] **2715**

VYZVOLNYI SHLIAKH (UK/0042-9422) [05732609] **3355**

VZGOJNOVARSTVENE ORGANIZACIJE V SOLSKOM LETU ... SEZNAMON POROCEVALSKIH ENOT (ZAVOD SR SLOVENIJE ZA STATISTIKO : 1979) (XV) [08731190] **145**

VZRYVNOE DELO (RU/0372-7009) [02187108] **1030**

W (US/0162-9115) [01781845] **1088**

W.A. PRIMARY PRINCIPAL (AT/0729-9435) [I07299435] 1874, **1806**

W. ATLEE BURPEE COMPANY See BURPEE GARDENS **2411**

W. ATLEE BURPEE COMPANY See BURPEE SPRING FLOWERING BULBS : ... PRE-SEASON SALE CATALOG **2411**

W. ATLEE BURPEE COMPANY See BURPEE'S IMPORTED DUTCH BULBS : ... WHOLESALE PRICES FOR THE TRADE **2411**

W DRODZE (PL/0137-480X) [I0137480X] **5008**

W.E. UPJOHN INSTITUTE FOR EMPLOYMENT RESEARCH See INSTITUTE REPORT (KALAMAZOO, MICH.), THE **1680**

W H M I S COMPLIANCE MANUAL (CN) **2871**

W. K. KELLOGG FOUNDATION See W.K. KELLOGG FOUNDATION ANNUAL REPORT **4339**

W.K. KELLOGG FOUNDATION ANNUAL REPORT (US/0889-7956) [14066290] **4339**

W-MEMO (US/0163-8300) [04508096] 5314, **4694**

W. STRUVE NIMELINE TARTU ASTROFUUSIKA OBSERVATOORIUM See TARTU TAHETORNI KALENDER **401**

W.W. 1 AERO (US/0736-198X) [09055024] 2779, **39**

WA EDUCATION NEWS (AT/0729-2104) [I07292104] **1790**

WAAC MEMBERSHIP DIRECTORY / WESTERN ASSOCIATION FOR ART CONSERVATION (US) [21237824] **368**

WAATL CIRCULAR (AT/1036-3858) [I10363858] **3256**

WABASH PLAIN DEALER (WABASH, IND. : DAILY : 1937) (US) [15299227] **5668**

WABOLU-HEFTE (GW/0175-4211) [24124722] **2183**

WACKY WORLD OF PEAFOWL REPORT, THE (US/1056-6759) [23844930] 4288, **5620**

WACO CITIZEN, THE (US) [15170636] **5755**

WACO FARM AND LABOR JOURNAL (1986) (US/0889-3233) [13856629] 1717, **145**

WACO LABOR JOURNAL See WACO FARM AND LABOR JOURNAL (1986) **145**

WACO MESSENGER, THE (US) [15788967] **5755**

WACO TRIBUNE-HERALD (US) [14642207] **5755**

WACONDA ROOTS AND BRANCHES (US/8755-2167) [11229722] **2477**

WACONIA PATRIOT (US) [01716080] **5699**

WAD-AL-HAYARA (SP) [02184116] **332**

WADE WORLD (US/0898-5421) [13311495] **4275**

WADENA NEWS [MICROFORM], THE (CN) [15465819] **5797**

WADENA PIONEER JOURNAL (US) [01769330] **5699**

WADI AL-NIL (UA) [12120879] **2667**

WAERME- UND STOFFUEBERTRAGUNG See HEAT AND MASS TRANSFER **4430**

WAFERNEWS CONFIDENTIAL (US) **2085**

WAFFEN- UND KOSTUMKUNDE (GW/0042-9945) [08392109] **252**

WAFL BOOK, THE (US/0160-872X) [03777587] **4079**

WAGA KUNI KIGYO NO KAIGAI JIGYO KATSUDO, SONO GENJO TO MONDAITEN (JA) [01797374] **919**

WAGA KUNI KIGYO NO KEIEI BUNSEKI. KIGYOBETSU TOKEI HEN (JA) [01799685] **815**

WAGA KUNI NO KOGOYO: TEKKO HEN (JA) [01797404] **4023**

WAGA KUNI NO KOKOGYO: KAGAKU KOGYO HEN, GOMU SEIHIN HEN, PURASUCHIKKU SEIHIN HEN, YOGYO KENZAI HEN (JA) [01797403] **1631**

WAGA KUNI NO KOKOGYO: KAMI PARUPU KOGYO HEN (JA) [01797400] **4239**

WAGA KUNI NO KOKOGYO : KIKAI KOGYO HEN; CHU-TANZOGYO HEN (JA) [01797406] **1631**

WAGA KUNI NO KOKOGYO : SENI KOGYO HEN; SENI RYUTSU HEN (JA) [01797402] **5359**

WAGA KUNI SEKIYU KAIHATSU NO GENJO (JA) [03116445] **4281**

WAGA KUNI SHOHIN BOEKI NO GENJO: TOKEI; KAIGAI SHIJO HAKUSHO (JA) [01796931] **857**

WAGE & FRINGE BENEFITS FOR SELECTED OCCUPATIONS PAID BY VIRGINIA MANUFACTURERS (US/0099-2054) [02239327] **1717**

WAGE & SALARY HANDBOOK (US/0191-3433) [04840963] **1717**

WAGE AND SALARY SURVEY. ANNUAL (CN) [01589676] **1717**

WAGE BULLETIN (US) [03371537] **1717**

WAGE CHRONOLOGY : BERKSHIRE HATHAWAY AND THE CLOTHING AND TEXTILE WORKERS (US/0272-9024) [06949566] **1717**

WAGE CHRONOLOGY. BERKSHIRE HATHAWAY INC. AND THE TEXTILE WORKERS UNION OF AMERICA, TWUA See WAGE CHRONOLOGY : BERKSHIRE HATHAWAY AND THE CLOTHING AND TEXTILE WORKERS **1717**

WAGE CHRONOLOGY SERIES. SER 4, THE (US) [07040876] **1717**

WAGE CHRONOLOGY: THE BOEING CO. (WASHINGTON PLANTS) See WAGE CHRONOLOGY : THE BOEING CO., WASHINGTON PLANTS, AND INTERNATIONAL ASSOCIATION OF MACHINISTS **1717**

WAGE CHRONOLOGY : THE BOEING CO., WASHINGTON PLANTS, AND INTERNATIONAL ASSOCIATION OF MACHINISTS (US/0362-7233) [02327094] **1717**

WAGE DIFFERENCES AMONG LARGE CITY GOVERNMENTS AND COMPARISONS WITH INDUSTRY AND FEDERAL PAY / U.S. DEPARTMENT OF LABOR, BUREAU OF LABOR STATISTICS (US) [08293264] 1717, **1540**

WAGE DIFFERENCES AMONG METROPOLITAN AREAS : SUMMARY (US/0272-8109) [06922464] **1717**

WAGE-PRICE LAW & ECONOMICS REVIEW (US/0361-6665) [02247065] **1526**

WAGENINGEN AGRICULTURAL UNIVERSITY PAPERS (NE) [21480209] **145**

WAGENINGSE SOCIOLOGISCHE STUDIES : WSS (NE/0923-4365) [20716726] 145, **5265**

WAGES AND HOURS (US/0149-2691) [03464153] **1717**

WAGES AND SALARIES PAID SUPPORT PERSONNEL IN PUBLIC SCHOOLS (US/0742-0870) [04378283] **1874**

WAGES AND WORKING CONDITIONS BY OCCUPATION (CN/0706-4926) [04632295] **1717**

WAGES FOR HOUSEWORK : CAMPAIGN BULLETIN, THE (CN/0229-1967) [08028029] **1717**

WAGES, HOURS OF WORK AND OVERTIME PAY PROVISIONS IN SELECTED INDUSTRIES. ONTARIO (CN/0318-4013) [02239688] **1717**

WAGES IN NEW YORK CITY (US/0364-3883) [02624017] **1717**

WAGES, SALARIES AND HOURS OF LABOUR, NEW BRUNSWICK (CN/0383-3569) [08286346] **1717**

WAGNER (UK) [07984816] **4158**

WAGNER LATIN AMERICAN NEWSLETTER, THE (US/0198-7496) [04173677] **2765**

WAGNER NEWS (LONDON, ENGLAND) (UK/0261-3468) [09337350] **389**

WAGONER (JOURNAL) (US) [07933704] **2477**

WAGS RAG (US/1048-9150) [21105746] **2477**

WAHDAH (CAIRO, EGYPT) (UA) [09483106] **2667**

WAHDAH (JUBA, SUDAN) (SJ) [08029829] **2644**

WAHDAH (PARIS, FRANCE) (MR) [11859311] **2526**

WAHKAW, THE (US/0743-6483) [10620214] **2477**

WAHKIAKUM COUNTY EAGLE (US) [17377207] **5763**

WAHL ZUM ... DEUTSCHEN BUNDESTAG AM ... IN NIEDERSACHSEN (GW) [10624830] **4499**

WAHL ZUM NIEDERSACHSISCHEN LANDTAG DER ... (GW) [10484888] **4503**

WAHYU (IO) [07099731] **5045**

WAI KUO CHE HSUEH SHIH YEN CHIU CHI KAN – CHUNG-KUO SHE HUI KO HSUEH YUAN CHE HSUEH YEN CHIU SO, HSI FANG CHE HSUEH YEN CHIU CHIU SHIH PIEN (CC) [06227427] **4365**

WAI KUO SHIH CHIH SHIH (CH) [10624850] **2633**

WAI KUO WEN HSUEH YEN CHIU (WU-CHANG, HUPEH PROVINCE, CHINA) (CC) [07442970] **3451**

WAI KUO WEN HSUEH / [PEI-CHING WAI KUO YU HSUEH YUAN, WAI KUO WEN HSUEH YEN CHIU SO] (CC) [19003282] **3451**

WAI KUO WEN I SSU CHAO / CHUNG-KUO SHE HUI KO HSUEH YUAN CHING PAO YEN CHIU SO PIEN I (CC) [11863798] **332**

WAI KUO YU (CC) [11150239] **3332**

WAIBLINGEN IN VERGANGENHEIT UND GEGENWART (GW) [02479714] **2715**

WAIKATO DAIRY CO-OPERATIVE LIMITED See ANNUAL REPORT & ACCOUNTS / WAIKATO DAIRY CO-OPERATIVE LIMITED **191**

WAITOMO NEWS (NZ) **5807**

WAITSBURG TIMES See TIMES (WAITSBURG, WASH.) **5762**

WAKALAT AL-SUDAN LIL-ANBA See WEEKLY REVIEW - SUDAN NEWS AGENCY **2644**

WAKALAT AL-SUDAN LIL-ANBA See AROUND THE GLOBE **2611**

WAKALAT AL-SUDAN LIL-ANBA See SUNA **2644**

WAKAN IYAKU GAKKAISHI (JA/0289-730X) [I0289730X] 4332, **3650**

WAKAN-YAKU KENKYUJO NEMPO (JA) [02246554] **4332**

WAKARIYASUI KOSEI NENKIN HOKEN HO : KAISETSU TO SODAN (JA) [07678485] **5314**

WAKARUSA TRIBUNE, THE (US) [15648839] **5668**

WAKAYAMA IGAKU (JA/0043-0013) [09773931] **3650**

WAKAYAMA-KEN EISEI KOGAI KENKYU SENTA NENPO (JA/0915-3179) [27422641] 4807, **2183**

WAKAYAMA-KEN KOGYO SHIKENJO See WAKAYAMA-KEN KOGYO SHIKENJO HOKOKU **1631**

WAKAYAMA-KEN KOGYO SHIKENJO HOKOKU (JA) [07604156] **1631**

WAKAYAMA KENRITSU HAKUBUTSUKAN See WAKAYAMA KENRITSU HAKUBUTSUKAN NEMPO **4097**

WAKAYAMA — Alphabetical Title Index

WAKAYAMA KENRITSU HAKUBUTSUKAN NEMPO (JA) [08448307] **4097**

WAKAYAMA KOGYO KOTO SENMON GAKKO KENKYU KIYO (JA) [21572749] **1096, 5169**

WAKAYAMA MEDICAL REPORTS (JA/0511-084X) [01356221] **3650**

WAKE FOREST LAW REVIEW (US/0043-003X) [01696576] **3072**

WAKE FOREST UNIVERSITY. OVERSEAS RESEARCH CENTER See DEVELOPING NATIONS MONOGRAPH SERIES **1555**

WAKE TREASURES (US/1055-7857) [23308052] **2477**

WAKEFORD MANUAL EMPLOYEE TAXATION (UK) **4758**

WAKITA HERALD, THE (US) [13673984] **5733**

WAKONDA TIMES (US/1054-3449) [22855682] **5744**

WAKOU TOULOUSE (FR/0998-2221) [I09982221] **1790**

WAKULLA COUNTY NEWS (US) [01635855] **5651**

WAKUSEI KAGAKU (JA) [09262459] **401**

WALCOT FAMILY BULLETIN (UK/0307-028X) [06989150] **2477**

WALDARBEIT, DIE (GW/0043-0048) [10097451] **2398**

WALDENBOOKS BESTSELLERS *CEASED.* (US/0738-9973) [09707352] **4833**

WALDEN'S ABC GUIDE AND PAPER PRODUCTION YEARBOOK (US/0731-2571) [07004495] **4239**

WALDEN'S FIBER AND BOARD REPORT (US) **4239**

WALDEN'S PAPER CATALOG (US) [10815421] **4239**

WALDEN'S PAPER REPORT (US) **4239**

WALDHYGIENE (GW/0511-0939) [10097472] **2398**

WALKER COUNTY MESSENGER (US) [20150395] **5655**

WALKER'S MANUAL OF WESTERN CORPORATIONS (US/0894-153X) [04697654] **718**

WALKER'S WORLD NEWSLETTER (US/0888-3491) [13562678] **4928**

WALKING HORSE REPORT (US/0093-6928) [03974320] **2803**

WALKING HORSE WORLD (US/8750-8109) [11799560] **2803**

WALKING MAGAZINE, THE (US/1042-2102) [15034240] **2602**

WALKING TOURS & RESTAURANT MENU GUIDE (PR) [28118791] **2765**

WALKING TOURS OF SAN JUAN See WALKING TOURS & RESTAURANT MENU GUIDE **2765**

WALL PAPER (NEW YORK, N.Y.), THE (US/0273-6837) [06820822] **2903**

WALL SAFETY POSTER (US) **2871**

WALL ST. U.S.A (US/0090-9335) [01784423] **919**

●WALL STREET & TECHNOLOGY (US/1060-989X) [25147997] **919**

WALL STREET COMPUTER REVIEW (US/0738-4343) [09600094] **919**

WALL STREET DIGEST, THE (US/0899-0530) [12993087] **919**

WALL STREET FINAL, THE (US/0270-9910) [06539962] **718**

WALL STREET JOURNAL ADVERTISING REPORT (US/0883-4792) [12157221] **767**

WALL STREET JOURNAL. EASTERN EDITION, THE (US/0099-9660) [04299067] **5690**

WALL STREET JOURNAL (EUROPE) (BE/0921-9986) [09524653] **5778**

WALL STREET JOURNAL MAGAZINE, THE (US/0277-352X) [07536521] **2549**

WALL STREET JOURNAL. MIDWEST EDITION, THE (US) [03374576] **5690**

WALL STREET JOURNAL ONDISC COMPUTER FILE, THE (US) [25809149] **718**

WALL STREET JOURNAL. SOUTHWEST EDITION, THE (US/0193-225X) [05166090] **816**

WALL STREET JOURNAL. WESTERN EDITION, THE (US/0193-2241) [03787143] **5690**

WALL STREET LETTER (US/0277-4992) [02451479] **919**

WALL STREET MICRO INVESTOR (US/0740-8919) [12404135] **1273, 919**

WALL STREET NETWORK NEWS *CEASED.* (US/1063-3839) [25993326] **1244**

WALL STREET REPORTS (US/0043-0099) [01624050] **919**

WALL STREET TRANSCRIPT, THE (US/0043-0102) [01769367] **919**

WALLA WALLA UNION-BULLETIN (US) [17390524] **5763**

WALLACE ENTERPRISE (US) **5724**

WALLACE-HOMESTEAD PRICE GUIDE TO DOLLS (US/8755-3813) [11264328] **2585**

WALLACE-HOMESTEAD PRICE GUIDE TO PATTERN GLASS (US) [15876285] **2595**

WALLACE MINER, THE (US/0883-671X) [12069700] **5658**

WALLACE STEVENS JOURNAL, THE (US/0148-7132) [03092707] **3473**

WALLACEANA (MY) [03719929] **2222**

WALLACES FARMER (1959) (US/0043-0129) [14234443] **145**

WALLCOVERINGS, WINDOWS & INTERIOR FASHION (US/1055-4394) [23184064] **2903**

WALLEYE (US/0744-1266) [08042279] **2208, 4880**

WALLEYE IN-SIDER (US/1068-1220) [27471118] **4880, 2315**

WALLRAF-RICHARTZ-JAHRBUCH (GW/0083-7105) [01160213] **368**

WALLS & CEILINGS (US/0043-0161) [02246127] **631**

WALNUT COUNCIL BULLETIN (US/1041-5769) [18692013] **2398**

WALPOLE SOCIETY NOTE BOOK, THE (US/1045-4349) [05133782] **332**

WALPOLE SOCIETY (U.S.) See WALPOLE SOCIETY NOTE BOOK, THE **332**

WALSH COUNTY FREE PRESS (US) [01769375] **5726**

●WALSH COUNTY RECORD (1992), THE (US/1067-5922) [27305001] **5726**

WALT DISNEY PRODUCTIONS See DISNEY MAGAZINE **1063**

WALT DISNEY UNCLE SCROOGE (US/0894-5268) [10920161] **4867**

WALT DISNEY'S COMICS AND STORIES (US/0894-5284) [08630804] **4867**

WALT DISNEY'S DONALD DUCK ADVENTURES (US/1041-3170) [17378082] **4867**

WALT DISNEY'S GOOFY ADVENTURES (US/1050-2580) [21432344] **1071**

WALT DISNEY'S HOLIDAY PARADE (US/1055-4882) [23190929] **4867**

WALT DISNEY'S MICKEY & DONALD (US/1041-1615) [18666499] **4867**

WALT DISNEY'S MICKEY MOUSE (US/0894-525X) [16126509] **1071**

WALT DISNEY'S MICKEY MOUSE MAGAZINE (US/0895-285X) [16544956] **1071**

WALT DISNEY'S SUMMER FUN (US/1057-817X) [24122362] **4867**

WALT WHITMAN QUARTERLY REVIEW (US/0737-0679) [09307854] **3452**

WALTER EUCKEN INSTITUT See VORTRAGE UND AUFSATZE **1526**

WALTER PRESCOTT WEBB MEMORIAL LECTURES (US/0083-713X) [01637099] **3452**

WALTERS ART GALLERY (BALTIMORE, MD.) See WALTERS (BALTIMORE, MD.), THE **368**

WALTERS ART GALLERY (BALTIMORE, MD.) See JOURNAL OF THE WALTERS ART GALLERY **4090**

WALTERS (BALTIMORE, MD.), THE (US/1044-8683) [19501237] **368**

WALTHAM INTERNATIONAL FOCUS (UK/0964-7082) [23289841] **5527**

WALTHILL CITIZEN, THE (US/8750-3484) [11269528] **5707**

WALTON TRIBUNE, THE (US/0893-410X) [15543077] **5655**

WAMEGO TIMES (WAMEGO, KAN. : 1917) (US) [12362332] **5679**

WANDERING VOLHYNIANS (CN/1180-2901) [24368538] **2715**

WANG IN THE NEWS (US/0896-2111) [16954598] **1239**

WANGAR (CN/0712-1865) [09021834] **5797**

WANI : UNA REVISTA SOBRE LA COSTA ATLANTICA (NQ) [12043078] **3332**

WANT ADVERTISER (US) **2495, 2779**

WANTED MISSING PERSONS (US/8756-0399) [11713115] **5314**

WANTOK (PP) [05902295] **2511**

WANT'S FEDERAL-STATE COURT DIRECTORY (US/0742-1095) [10296033] **3143**

●WANT'S THEATRE DIRECTORY (US/1064-1300) [26210436] **5372**

WAPAKONETA DAILY NEWS, THE (US) [17062504] **5731**

WAPATO INDEPENDENT (US) [17416334] **5763**

WAPITI (CN/0713-0546) [08716931] **3256**

WAPITI (FR) **4173**

WAPITI MAASTRICHT (NE/0923-4764) [I09234764] **3452**

WAR & SOCIETY (AT/0729-2473) [09655660] **5265, 2633**

WAR AND SOCIETY NEWSLETTER (GW/0344-3086) [02380825] **4060**

WAR ANNUAL (UK) [15242148] **4060**

WAR CRY (UK) **4499**

WAR CRY (NEW YORK, N.Y.), THE (US/0043-0234) [01644508] **5314**

WAR CRY (OAKVILLE) *CEASED.* (CN/0043-0218) [02275940] **5008**

WAR IN HISTORY (UK/0968-3445) **2633**

WAR, LITERATURE, AND THE ARTS (US/1046-6967) [20306659] **333, 3452**

WAR RESEARCH INFO SERVICE (US/1058-6283X) [24394735] **4060**

WARASAN KROMKANPAET LAE ANAMAI (TH/0125-1643) [01197228] **3650**

WARASAN PHESATCHESAT MAHA WITTHAYALAI MAHIDON (TH/0125-1570) [11455584] **4332**

WARBIRDS (US/0744-6624) [08486053] **39**

WARBLER (TORONTO) (CN/1183-6830) [25067053] **4708**

WARD COUNTY HERITAGE (US) **2477**

WARD-PHILLIPS LECTURES IN ENGLISH LANGUAGE AND LITERATURE (US/0083-7210) [01646640] **3452, 3332**

WARDAIR WORLD (1983) (CN/0822-9678) [11100314] **5499**

WARDEN'S ... ANNUAL REPORT ON THE RONDEVLEI BIRD SANCTUARY FOR THE YEAR ... / RONDEVLEI BIRD SANCTUARY, THE (SA) [09538683] **2208**

WARD'S AUTO WORLD (US/0043-0315) [02244862] **5428**

WARD'S AUTOMOTIVE INTERNATIONAL (US/0895-2191) [15567210] **5428**

WARD'S AUTOMOTIVE REPORTS (US/0886-5175) [02451484] **5402**

WARD'S AUTOMOTIVE YEARBOOK (US/0083-7229) [02222623] **5428**

WARD'S BUSINESS DIRECTORY (US) **718**

WARD'S BUSINESS DIRECTORY OF U.S. PRIVATE AND PUBLIC COMPANIES (US/1048-8707) [21096593] **718**

WARD'S ENGINE AND VEHICLE TECHNOLOGY UPDATE (US) **5428**

●WARD'S PRIVATE COMPANY PROFILES (US/1071-9555) [28774902] **718**

●WARD'S SALES PROSPECTOR (US/1059-9266) [24813346] **718**

WARD'S SPECIAL REPORTS (US) **5428**

WARD'S TAX LAW AND PLANNING. INFORMATION CIRCULARS AND RULINGS (CN/1184-7468) [24256634] **4758**

WARD'S TAX LAW AND PLANNING. INTERPRETATION BULLETINS (CN/1184-745X) [24256672] **4758**

WARD'S TAX TREATIES (CN/1184-1494) [23598667] **4758**

WARD'S WHO'S WHO AMONG U.S. MOTOR VEHICLE MANUFACTURERS (US/0147-9822) [03263269] **435**

WAREHOUSE SUPERVISOR'S BULLETIN (US) **889**

WAREHOUSE SUPERVISOR'S DEVELOPMENT PROGRAM (US) **889**

WAREHOUSES LICENSED UNDER U.S. WAREHOUSE ACT (US/0738-0348) [09381379] **718**

●WAREHOUSING / DISTRIBUTION DIRECTORY (US/1075-0282) [26296284] **857**

WAREHOUSING REVIEW (US/8750-8710) [11878630] **719**

WAREHOUSING SUPERVISOR'S BULLETIN (US/0744-8864) [08622985] **719**

WARENVERZEICHNIS FUER DIE AUSSENHANDELSSTATISTIK (GW) [10097036] **719, 1929**

WARENZEICHEN- UND MUSTERBLATT *CEASED.* (GW) [02242128] **1309**

WARENZEICHENBLATT See WARENZEICHEN- UND MUSTERBLATT **1309**

WARENZEICHENBLATT. TEIL 1, (ANGEMELDETE ZEICHEN). AUSGABE A (GW/0043-0331) [I00430331] **719, 1929**

Alphabetical Title Index — WASHINGTON

WARENZEICHENBLATT. TEIL 2, (EINGETRAGENE ZEICHEN). AUSGABE A (GW/0043-034X) [I0043034X] 719, **1930**

WARFIELD'S *See* WARFIELD'S BUSINESS RECORD **719**

●WARFIELD'S BUSINESS RECORD (US/1061-1622) [25058141] **719**

●WARLOCK AND THE INFINITY WATCH (US/1062-3248) [25586509] **382**

WARM SPRINGS STATE HOSPITAL *See* ANNUAL REPORT **3776**

WARMAN'S AMERICANA & COLLECTIBLES (US/0739-6457) [09804352] **2779**

WARMAN'S ANTIQUES AND THEIR PRICES (US/0196-2272) [03921145] **252**

WARME- UND STOFFUBERTRAGUNG (GW/0042-9929) [01715556] **2131**

WARMER BULLETIN (UK) [20881397] **2245**

WARMETECHNIK (GW/0720-3438) [08478979] **2608**

●WARNING LETTER BULLETIN (US/1069-4218) [28036684] 3650, **4332**

WARNOCK HERSEY APPRAISAL COMPANY (CN/0821-2120) [09457143] **4848**

WARP AND WEFT (MCMINNVILLE, OR.) (US/0732-6890) [08741712] **5359**

WARPATH (OTTAWA) (CN/0315-2871) [02247230] **333**

WARRANTY WATCH (US/0363-9517) [02560724] 1300, **3072**

WARREN-NEWPORT PRESS (US/0745-8118) [09477172] **5662**

WARREN PUBLISHING'S CABLE & STATION COVERAGE ATLAS (US/1047-9902) [19785059] **1168**

WARREN REPORT, THE (US/0738-9140) [09705364] **889**

WARREN SHEAF (US) [01696330] **5699**

WARREN SPRING LABORATORY (STEVENAGE, ENGLAND) *See* INVESTIGATION OF AIR POLLUTION; NATIONAL SURVEY, SMOKE AND SULPHUR DIOXIDE, THE **2233**

WARREN-TEED G.I. TRACT (US/0360-7666) [01932009] **3748**

●WARREN'S CABLE REGULATION MONITOR (US/1067-6252) [27345171] **1168**

WARREN'S MOVIE POSTER PRICE GUIDE (US/0884-3791) [12541409] 2779, **4079**

WARRENTON CLIPPER (WARRENTON, GA. : 1876) (US) [13212041] **5655**

WARRIOR (SHEARWATER. 1978) (CN/0707-8056) [04875825] **4060**

WARROAD PIONEER (US) [01769397] **5699**

WARSAW AUTUMN (PL) [19897928] **4158**

WARSAW. INSTYTUT TECHNIKI BUDOWLANEJ *See* BIULETYN INFORMACYJNY **2019**

WARSAW. INSTYTUTU TECHNIKI BUDOWLANEJ *See* PRACE INSTYTUTU TECHNIKI BUDOWLANEJ **2028**

WARSAW VOICE, THE (PL/0860-7591) [22723790] **5808**

WARSHIP INTERNATIONAL (US/0043-0374) [01647131] **4185**

WARSHIPS FORECAST (US) **4061**

WARTA BEA CUKA (IO) [0224669C] **4758**

WARTA DEMOGRAFI (IO) [02245654] **4560**

WARTA EKSIM (IO) [01794255] **857**

WARTA GEOLOGI (MY/0126-5539) [02943502] **1401**

WARTA GPEI / GABUNGAN PERUSAHAAN EKSPOR INDONESIA (IO) [27132665] 958, **857**

WARTA HINDU DHARMA (IO) [02514326] **5041**

WARTA IMIGRASI (IO) [03278030] **1921**

WARTA KESEHATAN (IO/0377-6549) [02243758] **4807**

WARTA PASARAN LADA / PEPPER MARKET BULLETIN (MY/0126-5903) [02244569] **2361**

WARTA UNIVERSITAS RIAU (IO) [02245657] **5237**

WARTIME ROAD NOTE (UK) [20304523] **5446**

WARUNKI SRODOWISKOWE POLSKIEJ STREFY POLUDNIOWEGO BALTYKU-MATERIALY ODDZIALU MORSKIEGO (PL) **1458**

WARWICK BEACON (US) [26109211] **5741**

WARWICKSHIRE HISTORY (UK) [02183988] **2715**

WARY CANARY, THE (US/0899-1405) [18005580] 4807, **2183**

WAS TUN (GW/0043-0404) [08182855] **4499**

WAS UND WIE (GW) [01786658] **4694**

WAS, WESTERN APICULTURAL SOCIETY JOURNAL (US/0199-221X) [05212642] **5600**

WASAFIRI (UK/0269-0055) [14929302] **3452**

WASAGA BEACH NEWS (1979) (CN/0704-4895) [06136308] **5797**

WASAGA BEACH TIMES (CN/0712-4945) [09137656] **2549**

WASAGA STAR TIMES (CN/1185-4901) [25589860] **5797**

WASATCH WAVE, THE (US) [12260840] 1096, **5757**

WASCANA REVIEW (CN/0043-0412) [01588220] **3452**

WASCANA WITNESS (CN/0382-8379) [02775621] **5797**

WASECA COUNTY, MINNESOTA. AUDITOR *See* FINANCIAL STATEMENT **4725**

WASECA COUNTY NEWS (US/0745-8177) [09485301] **5699**

WASEDA BULLETIN OF COMPARATIVE LAW (JA/0285-9211) [08526017] **3137**

WASEDA BUSINESS & ECONOMIC STUDIES (JA/0388-1008) [02176723] **1588**

WASEDA DAIGAKU DAIGAKUIN RIKOGAKU KENKYU IHO (JA) [04523837] 1853, **2001**

WASEDA DAIGAKU RIKOGAKU KENKYUJO HOKOKU (JA/0372-7181) [02320472] **2001**

WASEDA DAIGAKU. SHISUTEMU KAGAKU KENKYUJO *See* WASEDA DAIGAKU SHISUTEMU KAGAKU KENKYUJO KIYO **2001**

WASEDA DAIGAKU SHISUTEMU KAGAKU KENKYUJO KIYO (JA) [04316061] **2001**

WASEDA DAIGAKU, TOKYO. DAIGAKUIN. RIKOGAKU KENKYUKA *See* WASEDA DAIGAKU DAIGAKUIN RIKOGAKU KENKYU IHO **2001**

WASEDA DAIGAKU, TOKYO. IMONO KENKYUJO *See* CHUKEN HOKOKU **4000**

WASEDA DAIGAKU, TOKYO. RIKOGAKU KENKYUJO *See* WASEDA DAIGAKU RIKOGAKU KENKYUJO HOKOKU **2001**

WASEDA DAIGAKU, TOKYO. RIKOGAKUBU *See* MEMOIRS OF THE SCHOOL OF SCIENCE AND ENGINEERING. WASEDA UNIVERSITY **1987**

WASEDA DAIGAKU. TOSHOKAN *See* CHUGOKUBUN CHOSENBUN TOSHO MOKUROKU **413**

WASEDA DAIGAKU. TOSHOKAN *See* CHIKUJI KANKOBUTSU UKEIRE MOKUROKU **413**

WASEDA ECONOMIC PAPERS (JA/0511-1943) [01647184] **1526**

WASEDA FORAMU (JA/0287-2323) [11471968] **1853**

WASEDA JINBUN SHIZEN KAGAKU KENKYU (JA/0286-1275) [11646564] **5169**

WASEDA SHAKAI KAGAKU KENKYU (JA/0286-1283) [07028910] **5225**

WASEDA SHOGAKU (JA) [02243654] **857**

WASHBURN COUNTY REGISTER (SHELL LAKE, WIS. : 1928) (US/8755-0520) [11243423] **5771**

WASHBURN LAW JOURNAL (US/0043-0420) [01769410] **3072**

WASHBURN UNIVERSITY OF TOPEKA. SCHOOL OF LAW *See* WASHBURN UNIVERSITY SCHOOL OF LAW ALUMNI DIRECTORY **1103**

WASHBURN UNIVERSITY SCHOOL OF LAW ALUMNI DIRECTORY (US/0278-7652) [07861835] 3072, **1103**

WASHINGTON (US/0083-7393) [01137226] **4499**

WASHINGTON (US/0083-7393) [01137266] 5225, **719**

WASHINGTON ACADEMY OF SCIENCES, WASHINGTON, D.C *See* JOURNAL OF THE WASHINGTON ACADEMY OF SCIENCES **5122**

WASHINGTON ACTION REPORTER (US/0195-5233) [05590215] **4694**

WASHINGTON AFRO-AMERICAN AND THE WASHINGTON TRIBUNE (US) [07383870] **5687**

WASHINGTON AGRICULTURAL RECORD, THE (US/0195-0673) [02468964] **145**

WASHINGTON AGRICULTURAL STATISTICS (US/0095-4330) [01796743] 5346, **157**

WASHINGTON AND JEFFERSON LITERARY JOURNAL (US/0043-0455) [01656738] **3452**

WASHINGTON AND LEE LAW REVIEW (US/0043-0463) [01769418] **3072**

WASHINGTON APPLE PI (US/1056-7682) [18369439] **1207**

WASHINGTON AREA FILMMAKERS LEAGUE *See* WAFL BOOK, THE **4079**

WASHINGTON-AREA MICROCOMPUTER DIRECTORY, THE (US/0882-8962) [11124312] **1273**

WASHINGTON BEVERAGE INSIGHT (US/0890-8060) [13238249] **2372**

●WASHINGTON BEVERAGE JOURNAL (US/1058-9341) [24439111] **2372**

WASHINGTON BUSINESS JOURNAL (US/0737-3147) [09337854] **719**

WASHINGTON BUSINESS LAW REPORTER (US/0735-8350) [09050525] **3104**

WASHINGTON CALENDAR MAGAZINE (US/0161-0260) [03801407] **5499**

WASHINGTON CENTER FOR METROPOLITAN STUDIES *See* WASHINGTON REGION **4560**

WASHINGTON CENTER OF FOREIGN POLICY RESEARCH *See* STUDIES IN INTERNATIONAL AFFAIRS **4536**

WASHINGTON CEO (US/1048-4981) [20959468] **719**

WASHINGTON CITY AND COUNTY EMPLOYEE SALARIES AND BENEFIT SURVEY (US) [02244515] **1717**

WASHINGTON COACH, THE (US/0043-0501) [09864000] **4928**

WASHINGTON COASTAL CURRENTS (US) [09404486] 2222, **2208**

WASHINGTON COMMUNITY COLLEGES FACTBOOK. ADDENDUM A, STUDENT ENROLLMENTS, ACADEMIC YEAR (US) [05795598] **1853**

WASHINGTON COMMUNITY COLLEGES FALL QUARTER REPORT / PREPARED BY THE DIVISION FOR INFORMATION SERVICES, RESEARCH & EVALUATION (US) [07957118] **1853**

WASHINGTON CONSUMER'S CHECKBOOK (US/0272-0469) [06746986] **1300**

WASHINGTON COUNSELETTER (US/0740-8501) [08961842] **1790**

WASHINGTON COUNTS (US/1063-0155) [25123814] **145**

WASHINGTON COUNTY BULLETIN, THE (US) [01769422] **5699**

WASHINGTON COUNTY NEWS (US) **5628**

WASHINGTON COUNTY NEWS (CHIPLEY, FLA.) (US/0279-795X) [07260886] **5651**

WASHINGTON COUNTY NEWS (WASHINGTON, KAN.) (US) [12868350] **5679**

WASHINGTON COUNTY REPORTS (US) [01769425] **3072**

WASHINGTON COURT RULES. FEDERAL (US/1052-8385) [18725990] **3072**

WASHINGTON COURT RULES. STATE (US/1052-8377) [18725985] **3072**

WASHINGTON CREDIT LETTER *CEASED.* (US/0742-2008) [10114679] **816**

WASHINGTON CREDIT LETTER DIGEST (US/0195-959X) [05667964] **3072**

WASHINGTON CREDIT LETTER PRIVACY REPORT *SUSPENDED.* (US/0195-9581) [05668170] **3072**

WASHINGTON CRIME NEWS SERVICES' CORPORATE SECURITY DIGEST (US/0894-3826) [16074782] **3178**

WASHINGTON CRIME NEWS SERVICES' CRIMINAL JUSTICE DIGEST (US/0889-5724) [11834248] **3072**

WASHINGTON CRIME NEWS SERVICES' NARCOTICS CONTROL DIGEST (US/0889-5708) [04705626] 1350, **3178**

WASHINGTON CRIME NEWS SERVICES' NARCOTICS DEMAND REDUCTION DIGEST (US/1043-8572) [19582892] **1350**

WASHINGTON CRIME NEWS SERVICES' ORGANIZED CRIME DIGEST (US/0889-5716) [05981224] **3178**

WASHINGTON CRIME NEWS SERVICES' TRAINING AIDS DIGEST (US/0889-5732) [05896054] **3179**

WASHINGTON CRIMINAL JUSTICE REPORT'S CRIME VICTIMS DIGEST (US/0884-5107) [10584464] **3179**

WASHINGTON CROP AND LIVESTOCK REPORTING SERVICE *See* WASHINGTON AGRICULTURAL STATISTICS **157**

WASHINGTON — Alphabetical Title Index

WASHINGTON D.C. AREA BUSINESS DIRECTORY (US/1048-7077) [21012852] **719**

WASHINGTON, D.C. COMPUTER CURRENTS (US/0897-9316) [17387925] **1207**

● WASHINGTON, D.C. INTERNSHIP DIRECTORY (US/1061-379X) [25278301] **1790**

WASHINGTON, D.C. MARKETING DIRECTORY (US/1058-3173) [23195210] **938**

WASHINGTON D. C. METROPOLITAN AREA FOUNDATION DIRECTORY, THE (US/0192-5342) [05019421] **4694**

WASHINGTON, D.C. MINI-MICRO COMPUTER REPORT, THE *CEASED.* (US/0363-7905) [02515211] **1265, 1292, 1273**

WASHINGTON, D.C. ON $ ... AND $ ... A DAY (US) [07482266] **5499**

WASHINGTON DANCEVIEW *See* DANCEVIEW **1312**

WASHINGTON DRUG LETTER (WASHINGTON. 1979) (US/0194-1291) [05320071] **3072, 4332**

WASHINGTON EDUCATION DIRECTORY (US) [04197032] **1790**

WASHINGTON EDUCATIONAL DIRECTORY *See* WASHINGTON EDUCATION DIRECTORY **1790**

● WASHINGTON EMPLOYMENT LAW LETTER (US/1072-0588) [28855595] **3155**

● WASHINGTON ENVIRONMENTAL COMPLIANCE UPDATE (US/1072-0596) [28855635] **3117**

WASHINGTON ENVIRONMENTAL QUALITY PROFILE / UNITED STATES, ENVIRONMENTAL PROTECTION AGENCY, REGION) (US) [07065169] **2245**

WASHINGTON EVENING JOURNAL, THE (US/0894-2552) [15803403] **5673**

WASHINGTON EXECUTIVE TRAVEL REPORT *CEASED.* (US/0897-8328) [17636960] **719, 5499**

WASHINGTON FACT BOOK (US/0275-0597) [05205076] **2549**

WASHINGTON FARMER-STOCKMAN *See* PACIFIC FARMER-STOCKMAN **118**

WASHINGTON FARMLETTER *See* WEBSTER AGRICULTURAL LETTER, THE **145**

WASHINGTON FEDERAL SCIENCE NEWSLETTER (US/0740-0535) [09856842] **5169**

WASHINGTON FLYER MAGAZINE (US/1046-3089) [20376960] **5499**

WASHINGTON FOOD DEALER MAGAZINE, THE (US/0043-0560) [03958528] **2361**

WASHINGTON GEOLOGY (US/1058-2134) [23373745] **1401**

● WASHINGTON GREEN (US/1060-5665) [25037664] **1526**

● WASHINGTON HEALTH CARE IN PERSPECTIVE (US/1065-4488) [26606893] **4807**

WASHINGTON HEALTH RECORD (US/0164-1514) [04588063] **4807**

WASHINGTON HISTORY (US/1042-9719) [19264991] **2765**

WASHINGTON IN PERSPECTIVE (US/1065-5751) [26665752] **5346**

WASHINGTON INFORMATION DIRECTORY (US/0887-8064) [02243002] **4694**

WASHINGTON INFORMER, THE (US/0741-9414) [10269159] **2275**

WASHINGTON INQUIRER (US/0749-1050) [10988617] **1526, 4538**

WASHINGTON INSIGHT (US/0899-7241) [18211602] **476**

WASHINGTON INTERNATIONAL ARTS LETTER (US/0043-0609) [01769429] **4339, 2856**

WASHINGTON INTERNATIONAL BUSINESS REPORT (US/0049-691X) [05878177] **1641, 719**

WASHINGTON INTERNATIONAL ORGANIZATIONAL GUIDE (US/0273-0049) [06987506] **857**

WASHINGTON ISLAND OBSERVER (US) [23020849] **5771**

WASHINGTON JAILS : A REPORT TO THE LEGISLATURE (US) [02787416] **3179**

WASHINGTON JEWISH WEEK (US/0746-9373) [10392429] **5053**

● WASHINGTON JOB SOURCE, THE (US/1067-0769) [27129230] **4209**

WASHINGTON JOURNAL OF HEALTH, PHYSICAL EDUCATION, RECREATION AND DANCE (US/0889-3551) [12444203] **1859**

WASHINGTON JOURNALISM REVIEW (1983) *See* AMERICAN JOURNALISM REVIEW **2917**

WASHINGTON JOURNALISM REVIEW (1983) (US/0741-8876) [10218965] **2925**

WASHINGTON LABOR MARKET (US) **1717**

WASHINGTON LAW REVIEW (1967) (US/0043-0617) [01769430] **3072**

WASHINGTON LAWYER, THE (US/0890-8761) [14440051] **3072**

WASHINGTON LETTER (AMERICAN BAR ASSOCIATION) (US/0516-9968) [01661464] **3072**

WASHINGTON LETTER / JOINT MARITIME CONGRESS (US) [09949792] **5458**

WASHINGTON LETTER OF OCEANOGRAPHY (US) [02305811] **1458**

WASHINGTON LETTER ON LATIN AMERICA *CEASED.* (UK/0278-2618) [07753634] **1526**

WASHINGTON LETTER ON TRANSPORTATION (US) **5399**

WASHINGTON LIBRARIES. DIRECTORY OF LIBRARIES IN WASHINGTON STATE (US) [14633401] **3256**

WASHINGTON LIVING (US/0744-6373) [08462598] **2549**

WASHINGTON LOBBYISTS & LAWYERS DIRECTORY, THE (US/0741-9295) [08592862] **3072**

WASHINGTON LOCAL GOVERNMENT PERSONNEL INSTITUTE *See* WASHINGTON CITY AND COUNTY EMPLOYEE SALARIES AND BENEFIT SURVEY **1717**

WASHINGTON MANUFACTURERS REGISTER (US/0148-5687) [03734723] **952, 3489**

WASHINGTON MASONIC TRIBUNE : THE OFFICIAL MAGAZINE OF THE MASONIC GRAND LODGE OF WASHINGTON (US/1060-393X) [24956814] **5237**

WASHINGTON MEMO (US/0739-4179) [04109535] **3122**

WASHINGTON MEMO - NATIONAL COUNCIL OF SAVINGS INSTITUTIONS (U.S.) (US/0882-2247) [11780617] **816**

WASHINGTON MISSOURIAN (US/0743-8052) [10675155] **5704**

WASHINGTON MONITOR *See* WEEKLY REGULATORY MONITOR, THE **3073**

WASHINGTON MONTHLY, THE (US/0043-0633) [01604513] **4499**

WASHINGTON MUNICIPAL SALARIES AND FRINGE BENEFITS (US) [06756224] **4694, 1717**

WASHINGTON NEWSLETTER (US) [01769433] **3256**

WASHINGTON NEWSLINES (US/0363-1214) [02175205] **2549**

WASHINGTON NOTES ON AFRICA (US/0512-610X) [06558058] **2500**

WASHINGTON NURSE, THE (US/0734-5666) [04730333] **3871**

WASHINGTON OPERA MAGAZINE, THE (US/0196-3236) [05782340] **4158**

WASHINGTON PACIFIC REPORT, THE (US/0748-6359) [09207953] **4499**

WASHINGTON PAPERS, THE (US/0278-937X) [01662322] **919**

WASHINGTON PARK ARBORETUM BULLETIN (US/1046-8749) [14927850] **2433**

WASHINGTON PHARMACIST, THE (US/0745-7413) [09420467] **4332**

WASHINGTON PHYSICIANS DIRECTORY, THE (US/0161-7176) [03996848] **3917**

WASHINGTON POLICY CHOICES / INSTITUTE FOR PUBLIC POLICY AND MANAGEMENT, UNIVERSITY OF WASHINGTON (US) [24445814] **4694**

WASHINGTON POST BOOK WORLD, THE (US) [11056395] **4833**

WASHINGTON POST INDEX (ANN ARBOR, MICH.) (US/1041-1534) [18662750] **5694**

WASHINGTON POST (WASHINGTON, D.C. : 1974) (US/0190-8286) [02269358] **5648**

WASHINGTON PROPERTY LAW REPORTER (US) [16932449] **4848, 3072**

WASHINGTON PSYCHIATRIC SOCIETY DIRECTORY, THE (US/0196-6537) [05826543] **3937**

WASHINGTON PSYCHIATRIC SOCIETY, WASHINGTON, DC *See* WASHINGTON PSYCHIATRIC SOCIETY DIRECTORY, THE **3937**

WASHINGTON PUBLIC LIBRARY STATISTICS / WASHINGTON STATE LIBRARY (US) [27818568] **3256, 3260**

WASHINGTON PUBLIC POWER SUPPLY SYSTEM *See* WASHINGTON PUBLIC POWER SUPPLY SYSTEM ANNUAL REPORT **1960**

WASHINGTON PUBLIC POWER SUPPLY SYSTEM ANNUAL REPORT (US/0191-2631) [04819297] **1960**

WASHINGTON PURCHASER *SUSPENDED.* (US/0043-0706) [05065256] **952**

WASHINGTON QUARTERLY, THE (US/0163-660X) [04413219] **4538**

WASHINGTON RADIOLOGY REPORT *See* MEDICAL DEVICES REPORT **3608**

WASHINGTON REGION (US/0099-2046) [02243748] **4560**

WASHINGTON REMOTE SENSING LETTER (US/0739-6538) [07712033] **2579, 1361**

WASHINGTON REPORT (US/0043-0722) [01674706] **5314**

WASHINGTON REPORT (AMERICAN ADVERTISING FEDERATION) (US/0195-5322) [05590057] **767**

WASHINGTON REPORT - AMERICAN ASSOCIATION OF HOMES FOR THE AGING (US) [05575849] **5314**

WASHINGTON REPORT (COUNCIL OF THE AMERICAS) (US) [15545704] **719**

WASHINGTON REPORT INGAA *CEASED.* (US) **4281**

WASHINGTON REPORT (INTERSTATE CONFERENCE ON WATER PROBLEMS) *SUSPENDED.* (US/0737-3503) [09359033] **4694**

WASHINGTON REPORT ON AFRICA (US/0733-8104) [08645708] **1526, 4499**

WASHINGTON REPORT ON LATIN AMERICA & THE CARIBBEAN (US/0893-1232) [15364395] **4538, 857**

WASHINGTON REPORT ON LONG TERM CARE (US/0091-7311) [02252089] **3793**

WASHINGTON REPORT ON MIDDLE EAST AFFAIRS, THE (US/8755-4917) [08664762] **4538, 2526**

WASHINGTON REPORT ON THE HEMISPHERE (US/0275-5599) [07181723] **2912**

WASHINGTON REPORTER (WASHINGTON, D.C.), THE (US/1052-696X) [22351478] **5648**

WASHINGTON REPORTS. 2D SERIES (US/0889-8162) [01769465] **3072**

WASHINGTON REPRESENTATIVES (US/0192-060X) [04889287] **4499**

WASHINGTON RETAIL REPORT (US/0882-4207) [08156607] **958**

WASHINGTON RETAIL WEEKLY (US/1058-4757) [24310920] **958**

WASHINGTON REVIEW (US/0163-903X) [04526135] **3452, 333**

WASHINGTON RICELETTER *CEASED.* (US) [02904686] **2361**

WASHINGTON SCIENCE TEACHERS' ASSOCIATION *See* WASHINGTON SCIENCE TEACHERS' JOURNAL **5169**

WASHINGTON SCIENCE TEACHERS' JOURNAL (US/0164-7369) [04409472] **1908, 5169**

WASHINGTON SEA GRANT PUBLICATION (US) [01677776] **1458**

WASHINGTON SERVICE BUREAU *See* WASHINGTON SERVICE BUREAU SUPREME COURT BRIEF SERVICE. SECURITIES **3072**

WASHINGTON SERVICE BUREAU *See* WASHINGTON SERVICE BUREAU SUPREME COURT BRIEF SERVICE. ANTITRUST AND SECURITIES **3104**

WASHINGTON SERVICE BUREAU SUPREME COURT BRIEF SERVICE. ANTITRUST AND SECURITIES (US/0164-4610) [04743876] **3104**

WASHINGTON SERVICE BUREAU SUPREME COURT BRIEF SERVICE. SECURITIES *CEASED.* (US/0199-1507) [05657160] **3072**

WASHINGTON SOCIAL LEGISLATION BULLETIN (US/0149-2578) [02270798] **4694**

WASHINGTON SOUNDS (US/0043-0757) [01663401] **4395**

WASHINGTON SPECTATOR (1985), THE (US/0887-428X) [13000927] **2549**

WASHINGTON STATE (US/0092-380X) [01789150] **4694**

WASHINGTON (STATE). ADULT CORRECTIONS DIVISION *See* WASHINGTON JAILS : A REPORT TO THE LEGISLATURE **3179**

● WASHINGTON STATE ADVANCED TECHNOLOGY : THE ANNUAL SURVEY OF THE STATE'S TECHNOLOGY COMPANIES (US) [27721177] **5169**

WASHINGTON STATE BAR NEWS (US/0886-5213) [01769448] **3073**

WASHINGTON STATE BIENNIAL REPORT ON STATE AGENCIES (US) [25193662] **4694**

WASHINGTON (STATE). BOARD OF ACCOUNTANCY *See* REGISTER - WASHINGTON STATE BOARD OF ACCOUNTANCY **750**

WASHINGTON (STATE). COMMISSION FOR VOCATIONAL EDUCATION *See* WASHINGTON STATE PLAN FOR VOCATIONAL EDUCATION **1917**

WASHINGTON (STATE). COMMISSION FOR VOCATIONAL EDUCATION *See* ANNUAL PROGRAM PLAN / WASHINGTON STATE, COMMISSION FOR VOCATIONAL EDUCATION **1910**

Alphabetical Title Index

WASHINGTON (STATE). COUNCIL FOR POSTSECONDARY EDUCATION *See* MOBILITY OF UNDERGRADUATE COLLEGE STUDENTS BETWEEN WASHINGTON COLLEGES AND UNIVERSITIES **1836**

WASHINGTON (STATE). COUNCIL FOR POSTSECONDARY EDUCATION *See* LEGISLATIVE ACTIONS AFFECTING HIGHER EDUCATION, WASHINGTON STATE LEGISLATURE **1865**

WASHINGTON (STATE). COUNCIL FOR POSTSECONDARY EDUCATION. FINANCIAL ANALYSIS SECTION *See* REVIEW AND RECOMMENDATIONS ... OPERATING BUDGET REQUEST FOR WASHINGTON PUBLIC HIGHER EDUCATION **1845**

WASHINGTON STATE DENTAL ASSOCIATION *See* WSDA MEMBERSHIP DIRECTORY & RESOURCE GUIDE **1337**

WASHINGTON (STATE). DEPT. OF ECOLOGY *See* ANNUAL AGENCY PLAN **2160**

WASHINGTON (STATE). DEPT. OF ECOLOGY. PLANNING AND DEVELOPMENT DIVISION *See* STATE WATER PROGRAM; BIENNIAL REPORT (WASHINGTON (STATE)) **5539**

WASHINGTON (STATE). DEPT. OF GAME *See* TRAPPING SEASONS AND REGULATIONS / STATE OF WASHINGTON, DEPARTMENT OF GAME **4879**

WASHINGTON (STATE). DEPT. OF MOTOR VEHICLES. RESEARCH AND TECHNOLOGY *See* RESEARCH REPORT - DEPARTMENT OF MOTOR VEHICLES. RESEARCH AND TECHNOLOGY DIVISION (OLYMPIA) **5424**

WASHINGTON (STATE). DEPT. OF SOCIAL AND HEALTH SERVICES *See* REPORT : DRUG ABUSE PREVENTION PLAN **1348**

WASHINGTON (STATE). DEPT. OF SOCIAL AND HEALTH SERVICES *See* DRUG ABUSE PREVENTION PLAN **1343**

WASHINGTON (STATE). DEPT. OF SOCIAL AND HEALTH SERVICES *See* PROPOSED COMPREHENSIVE ANNUAL SOCIAL SERVICES PROGRAM PLAN FOR THE STATE OF WASHINGTON **5302**

WASHINGTON (STATE). DEPT. OF SOCIAL AND HEALTH SERVICES *See* OVERVIEW / STATE OF WASHINGTON, DEPARTMENT OF SOCIAL & HEALTH SERVICES, AN **4795**

WASHINGTON (STATE). DEPT. OF SOCIAL AND HEALTH SERVICES. OVERVIEW OF SOCIAL AND HEALTH SERVICES *See* OVERVIEW / STATE OF WASHINGTON, DEPARTMENT OF SOCIAL & HEALTH SERVICES, AN **4795**

WASHINGTON (STATE). DIVISION OF GEOLOGY AND EARTH RESOURCES *See* BULLETIN - WASHINGTON DEPARTMENT OF NATURAL RESOURCES, DIVISION OF GEOLOGY AND EARTH RESOURCES **1371**

WASHINGTON (STATE). DIVISION OF GEOLOGY AND EARTH RESOURCES *See* BULLETIN - DIVISION OF GEOLOGY AND EARTH RESOURCES (OLYMPIA) **1369**

WASHINGTON (STATE). DIVISION OF POWER RESOURCES *See* BULLETIN - STATE OF WASHINGTON DIVISION OF POWER RESOURCES **1934**

WASHINGTON (STATE) DIVISION OF VOCATIONAL REHABILITATION STATE FACILITIES PLAN (US) **5314**

WASHINGTON (STATE). EMPLOYMENT SECURITY DEPT *See* ANNUAL PLANNING REPORT : SEATTLE-EVERETT, WASHINGTON AREA **1648**

WASHINGTON STATE ENERGY USE PROFILE (US/0734-7294) [06910427] **1960**

WASHINGTON STATE ENTOMOLOGICAL SOCIETY *See* PROCEEDINGS OF THE WASHINGTON STATE ENTOMOLOGICAL SOCIETY **5613**

WASHINGTON (STATE). ENVIRONMENTAL PROTECTION SECTION *See* STATE OF WASHINGTON ENVIRONMENTAL RADIATION PROGRAM ... ANNUAL REPORT **2244**

WASHINGTON (STATE). GOVERNOR *See* GOVERNOR'S PROPOSED ... OPERATING BUDGET SUPPORTING DATA, STATEWIDE SUMMARY TABLES **4729**

WASHINGTON (STATE). GOVERNOR *See* GOVERNOR'S PROPOSED SUPPORTING DATA AND ... OPERATING BUDGET **4729**

WASHINGTON (STATE). GOVERNOR. CURRENT LAW OPERATING BUDGET *See* GOVERNOR'S PROPOSED SUPPORTING DATA AND ... OPERATING BUDGET **4729**

WASHINGTON (STATE). GOVERNOR. GOVERNOR'S PROPOSED SUPPORTING DATA AND ... OPERATING BUDGET *See* GOVERNOR'S PROPOSED ... OPERATING BUDGET SUPPORTING DATA, STATEWIDE SUMMARY TABLES **4729**

WASHINGTON STATE HIGHWAY ACCIDENT REPORT (US) [19660965] **5446**

WASHINGTON STATE HORTICULTURAL ASSOCIATION *See* PROCEEDINGS, ANNUAL MEETING - WASHINGTON STATE HORTICULTURAL ASSOCIATION **2428**

WASHINGTON STATE HOSPITAL COMMISSION *See* ANNUAL REPORT OF THE WASHINGTON STATE HOSPITAL COMMISSION **3776**

WASHINGTON (STATE). INDIAN ASSISTANCE DIVISION *See* INDIAN ECONOMIC EMPLOYMENT ASSISTANCE PROGRAM, PROGRESS REPORT **5289**

WASHINGTON (STATE). JUDICIAL COUNCIL *See* ANNUAL REPORT OF THE JUDICIAL COUNCIL OF THE STATE OF WASHINGTON **3139**

WASHINGTON STATE LABOR MARKET AND ECONOMIC REPORT / C. LABOR MARKET AND ECONOMIC ANALYSIS BRANCH, WASHINGTON STATE EMPLOYMENT SECURITY (US) [22270748] **1717**

WASHINGTON (STATE). LEGISLATIVE. BUDGET COMMITTEE. REPORT *See* PERFORMANCE AUDIT **4740**

WASHINGTON (STATE). LEGISLATURE *See* LEGISLATIVE MANUAL, STATE OF WASHINGTON **4661**

WASHINGTON (STATE). LEGISLATURE. JOINT COMMITTEE ON EDUCATION *See* EDUCATION IN WASHINGTON **1739**

WASHINGTON STATE LOTTERY *See* ANNUAL REPORT / WASHINGTON STATE LOTTERY **772**

WASHINGTON STATE MEDIA DIRECTORY (US/0196-8572) [14220335] **1124**

WASHINGTON STATE MONTHLY ELECTRICAL STATUS REPORT (US/0732-5045) [07325461] **2085**

WASHINGTON (STATE). OFFICE OF BOATING WATER SAFETY *See* ANNUAL REPORT - OFFICE OF BOATING WATER SAFETY (WASHINGTON (STATE)) **591**

WASHINGTON (STATE). OFFICE OF THE ATTORNEY GENERAL *See* CHARITABLE TRUST DIRECTORY, OFFICE OF ATTORNEY GENERAL **3140**

WASHINGTON (STATE). OFFICE OF THE SECRETARY OF STATE *See* OFFICIAL CANDIDATES PAMPHLET **4485**

WASHINGTON (STATE). OFFICE OF THE SECRETARY OF STATE *See* VOTERS AND CANDIDATES PAMPHLET **4499**

WASHINGTON (STATE). OFFICE OF THE STATE TREASURER *See* CERTIFICATION OF CONSTITUTIONAL LIMITATION ON THE BONDED DEBT OF THE STATE OF WASHINGTON **4717**

WASHINGTON (STATE). OFFICE OF THE STATE TREASURER *See* ANNUAL REPORT FOR THE FISCAL YEAR ... TO THE GOVERNOR AND LEGISLATURE OF THE STATE OF WASHINGTON **4710**

WASHINGTON STATE PATROL *See* SUMMARY OF ACCIDENTS INVOLVING THE DRINKING DRIVER **5445**

WASHINGTON STATE PATROL *See* TEEN-AGE DRIVERS (OLYMPIA) **5445**

WASHINGTON (STATE) PERSONNEL APPEALS BOARD *See* SUMMARY OF DECISIONS / WASHINGTON STATE PERSONNEL APPEALS BOARD **4705**

WASHINGTON STATE PLAN FOR VOCATIONAL EDUCATION (US) [04258336] **1917**

WASHINGTON STATE PROGRAM FOR MIGRANT CHILDREN'S EDUCATION (US/0093-1691) [01791738] **1790**

WASHINGTON (STATE). PUBLIC DISCLOSURE COMMISSION *See* REPORT/TECHNICAL STUDY : REPORTED LOBBYING EXPENDITURES **4682**

WASHINGTON STATE REGISTER (US/0164-6389) [04412911] **4694**

WASHINGTON STATE RESOURCE DIRECTORY FOR LOCAL JURISDICTIONS (US) [05688035] **4758**

WASHINGTON (STATE). STATE BOARD FOR COMMUNITY COLLEGE EDUCATION *See* PROFESSIONAL PERSONNEL CHARACTERISTICS **1842**

WASHINGTON (STATE). STATE BOARD OF EDUCATION *See* SCHOOL BUILDING CONSTRUCTION NEEDS **1904**

WASHINGTON (STATE). STATE EMPLOYMENT DEVELOPMENT SERVICES COUNCIL *See* REPORT TO THE GOVERNOR - WASHINGTON (STATE). STATE EMPLOYMENT DEVELOPMENT SERVICES COUNCIL **1707**

WASHINGTON (STATE). SUPERINTENDENT OF PUBLIC INSTRUCTION *See* DEMOGRAPHIC PROFILES, SOCIOECONOMIC PROFILES, AND PER CAPITA INCOMES OF THE RESIDENT POPULATIONS OF WASHINGTON STATE SCHOOL DISTRICTS **4552**

WASHINGTON (STATE). SUPREME COURT *See* WASHINGTON REPORTS. 2D SERIES **3072**

WASHINGTON (STATE). TOXICS CLEANUP PROGRAM *See* SITE REGISTER / TOXICS CLEANUP PROGRAM, WASHINGTON STATE DEPARTMENT OF ECOLOGY **2243**

WASHINGTON (STATE). TRAFFIC SAFETY COMMISSION *See* ANNUAL WORK PROGRAM - WASHINGTON TRAFFIC SAFETY COMMISSION **4767**

WASHINGTON (STATE). TRAFFIC SAFETY COMMISSION *See* HIGHWAY SAFETY PLAN - WASHINGTON (STATE). TRAFFIC SAFETY COMMISSION **5441**

WASHINGTON (STATE). UNIVERSITY. DIVISION OF MARINE RESOURCES *See* WASHINGTON SEA GRANT PUBLICATION **1458**

WASHINGTON (STATE). UNIVERSITY. INSTITUTE FOR COMPARATIVE AND FOREIGN AREA STUDIES *See* PUBLICATIONS ON ASIA **2662**

WASHINGTON (STATE). UNIVERSITY. INSTITUTE FOR COMPARATIVE AND FOREIGN AREA STUDIES *See* PUBLICATIONS ON RUSSIA AND EASTERN EUROPE **4492**

WASHINGTON (STATE). VOCATIONAL REHABILITATION SERVICES DIVISION *See* STATE FACILITIES PLAN (OLYMPIA) **5311**

WASHINGTON STATE VOTER (US/0043-0846) [03958397] **4500**

WASHINGTON STATE WORK INJURY AND ILLNESS SUMMARY (US) [08664004] **2871**

WASHINGTON STATE YEARBOOK (US/0736-3850) [09114030] **4694**

WASHINGTON STATE'S WATER (US/0161-5912) [02289655] **5541**

WASHINGTON TARIFF AND TRADE LETTER (US/0276-8275) [07445352] **857**

WASHINGTON TECHNOLOGY (US/1058-9163) [15620011] **5169**

●WASHINGTON TELECOM NEWS (US/1069-7500) [28170303] **1168**

WASHINGTON TELECOMMUNICATIONS DIRECTORY (US) [16820415] **1169**

WASHINGTON TIMES-HERALD (WASHINGTON, IND.) (US) [11891070] **5668**

WASHINGTON TIMES (WASHINGTON, D.C. : 1982), THE (US/0732-8494) [08472624] **5648**

WASHINGTON TRANSPORTATION NEWSLETTER (US/0091-5734) [01786226] **5399**

WASHINGTON UNIVERSITY JOURNAL OF URBAN AND CONTEMPORARY LAW (US/8756-0801) [09588381] **2839, 3073**

WASHINGTON UNIVERSITY LAW QUARTERLY (US/0043-0862) [01587560] **3073**

WASHINGTON UNIVERSITY LIBRARY STUDIES (US/0508-1165) [01664510] **3256**

WASHINGTON UNIVERSITY (SAINT LOUIS, MO.). SCHOOL OF LAW *See* WASHINGTON UNIVERSITY LAW QUARTERLY **3073**

WASHINGTON UNIVERSITY, ST. LOUIS. LIBRARIES *See* WASHINGTON UNIVERSITY LIBRARY STUDIES **3256**

WASHINGTON UNIVERSITY (ST. LOUIS, MO.). LIBRARIES *See* REPORT - WASHINGTON UNIVERSITY (ST. LOUIS, MO.) **3245**

WASHINGTON UNIVERSITY, ST. LOUIS, MO. LIBRARIES. LIBRARY OF THE SCHOOL OF MEDICINE *See* PHILSOM/S : PERIODICAL HOLDINGS IN THE LIBRARY OF THE SCHOOL OF MEDICINE BY SUBJECT **3241**

WASHINGTON VIEW (US/1042-4229) [19038295] **2549**

WASHINGTON WATCH (FOREST HILLS, NEW YORK, N.Y.) (US/0275-1216) [07087879] **4500**

WASHINGTON WEEKLY (WASHINGTON, D.C. 1989) (US/1054-1683) [22777341] **5073**

WASHINGTON WOMAN (ARLINGTON, VA.) (US/0887-2627) [13201481] **5568**

WASHINGTON WOMAN NEWS (US/1055-4912) [23078035] **5568**

WASHINGTONIAN (WASHINGTON, D.C.), THE (US/0043-0897) [01680831] **2549**

WASHINGTON'S HEALTH (US/0043-0900) [01645305] **4807**

WASHINGTON'S LAND & PEOPLE (US/0891-6373) [14939038] **145**

WASHOUT REVIEW (US/0149-6077) [03494400] **3356**

WASHTUCNA WORLD (US) [16993204] **5763**

WASI WRITER *See* WASI : [BULLETIN] **3452**

●WASI : [BULLETIN] (MW) [27954593] **2925, 3452**

WASMANN JOURNAL OF BIOLOGY, THE (US/0043-0927) [06322423] **476**

WASSAJA (1982) **SUSPENDED.** (US/0745-1520) [08869241] **2765**

WASSER, ENERGIE, LUFT (SZ/0377-905X) [02536446] **2096**

WASSER-KALENDER (BERLIN) (GW/0511-3520) [02176666] **5541**

WASSER, LUFT UND BODEN. HANDBUCH UMWELTTECHNIK (GW) [21379545] 2001, **2183**

WASSER, LUFT UND BODEN : WLB (GW/0341-2679) [21009464] **2245**

WASSER UND ABWASSER IN FORSCHUNG UND PRAXIS (GW/0512-5030) [02813488] **5541**

WASSER UND ABWASSER (VIENNA) (AU/0508-122X) [01769482] **2245**

WASSER UND BODEN (GW/0043-0951) [04149362] **145**

WASSERVERSORGUNG UND ABWASSERBESEITIGUNG IN DER WIRTSCHAFT (GW) [10498553] 2245, **5541**

WASSERWIRTSCHAFT (GW/0043-0978) [06484267] **5541**

WASSERWIRTSCHAFT-WASSERTECHNIK (BERLIN, DDR) (GW/0043-0986) [01664730] **2096**

WASTE AGE (US/0043-1001) [01623800] **2245**

WASTE AGE'S RECYCLING TIMES (US/1042-0614) [18927089] **2246**

●WASTE & ENVIRONMENT TODAY. BIBLIOGRAPHIC JOURNAL (UK/0965-4496) [25742948] **2246**

●WASTE & ENVIRONMENT TODAY. NEWS JOURNAL (UK/0965-4488) [25742901] **2246**

WASTE BUSINESS WEST (CN/1185-4731) [25127479] **2246**

WASTE DISPOSAL AND WATER MANAGEMENT IN AUSTRALIA (AT/0311-3558) [I03113558] 5541, **2246**

WASTE DISPOSAL STATISTICS BASED ON ESTIMATES (UK) [03910198] 2246, **2185**

WASTE DISPOSAL STATISTICS ... ESTIMATES / CIPFA, STATISTICAL INFORMATION SERVICE (UK) [07909347] 2246, **2185**

WASTE INFORMATION DIGESTS (US/1050-3153) [21456664] **2246**

WASTE MANAGEMENT (UK) **2246**

WASTE MANAGEMENT (US/0275-6196) [07193151] **2246**

WASTE MANAGEMENT & ENVIRONMENT (AT) **2246**

WASTE MANAGEMENT & RESEARCH (UK/0734-242X) [08702026] **2246**

WASTE MANAGEMENT BULLETIN (UK) [20650132] **2246**

WASTE MANAGEMENT (ELMSFORD) (US/0956-053X) [19565194] **2246**

●WASTE MANAGEMENT NEWS (WACO, TEX.) (US/1062-7529) [25728256] **2246**

WASTE MANAGEMENT RESEARCH ABSTRACTS : INFORMATION ON RESEARCH IN PROGRESS (AU) [09096953] **2246**

WASTE MANAGEMENT RESEARCH REPORT. NEWS FROM STATE UNIVERSITY OF NEW YORK AT BUFFALO AND STONY BROOK AND CORNELL UNIVERSITY (US) [21590640] **2246**

WASTE MANAGEMENT TODAY. BIBLIOGRAPHIC JOURNAL *See* WASTE & ENVIRONMENT TODAY. BIBLIOGRAPHIC JOURNAL **2246**

WASTE MANAGEMENT TODAY. NEWS JOURNAL *See* WASTE & ENVIRONMENT TODAY. NEWS JOURNAL **2246**

WASTE MINIMIZATION UPDATE (US/1064-6140) [26341499] **2246**

WASTE PAPER NEWS (UK/0956-4683) [I09564683] **4239**

WASTE PLANNING (UK/0965-3147) [I09653147] **2246**

WASTE RECOVERY REPORT (US/0889-0072) [12380130] **2246**

WASTE TREATMENT TECHNOLOGY NEWS (US/0885-0003) [12565263] **2246**

WASTELANDS (CN/0228-1937) [07970502] **3452**

WASTELANDS NEWS : A QQUARTERLY NEWSLETTER OF SOCIETY FOR PROMOTION OF WASTELANDS DEVELOPMENT (II) [21289481] **2246**

WASTELINES (US/0112-398X) [I0112398X] **2183**

WASTES MANAGEMENT (UK) [08288469] **2246**

WASTEWATER TECHNOLOGY CENTRE (CANADA) *See* PROGRAM OVERVIEW - WASTEWATER TECHNOLOGY CENTRE, CANADA **2240**

WATAKUSHI NO RIREKISHO (JA) [01800311] **435**

WATAN (SANA, YEMEN) (YE) [07919414] **2667**

WATASHITACHI NO SENKYO; SENKYO HAKUSHO UNDO NO TAIKEN KIROKU (JA) [03403621] **4500**

WATASHITACHI NO SHIZEN. NATURE (JA) [07016878] 5620, **2208**

WATAUGA ASSOCIATION OF GENEALOGISTS *See* BULLETIN - WATAUGA ASSOCIATION OF GENEALOGISTS **2441**

WATAUGA DEMOCRAT (US/0745-1903) [08924309] **5724**

WATCH & CLOCK REVIEW (US/0279-6198) [07120926] **2916**

WATCH REVIEW (HK) **2916**

WATCHING AND WAITING (UK) **5008**

WATCHMAKER, JEWELLER & SILVERSMITH (1941) **CEASED.** (UK/0043-1079) [I00431079] **2915**

WATCHMAN, THE (US) [17500356] **5684**

WATCHTOWER, THE (US/0043-1087) [02284893] **5069**

WATCHWORDS GCSE ENGLISH REVIEW **CEASED.** (UK/0960-877X) **3332**

WATCOM NEWS (CN/0828-5624) [12577391] **1282**

WATDOC NEWSLETTER (CN/0820-0211) [02248601] **5541**

WATER ACTIVITIES TRADE REPORT (US) 5541, **2096**

WATER, AIR, AND SOIL POLLUTION (NE/0049-6979) [00991730] **2247**

WATER & ENVIRONMENT INTERNATIONAL (UK/0956-0157) [27690295] 2183, **5541**

●WATER & ENVIRONMENT MANAGEMENT (UK/0968-3321) [I09683321] 2183, **5542**

WATER AND ENVIRONMENTAL MANAGEMENT : JOURNAL OF THE INSTITUTION OF WATER AND ENVIRONMENTAL MANAGEMENT (UK/0951-7359) [16907351] 5542, **2247**

WATER & IRRIGATION REVIEW *See* INTERNATIONAL WATER & IRRIGATION REVIEW **175**

WATER AND LAND RESOURCE ACCOMPLISHMENTS. FEDERAL RECLAMATION PROJECTS, SUMMARY REPORT (US/0271-8049) [06239421] 5542, **2208**

WATER & SEWAGE INTERNATIONAL (UK/0956-0157) [23088520] **5542**

WATER AND SEWER PROGRAMS FOR OHIO (US/0148-2785) [03279504] **5542**

WATER AND SOIL MANAGEMENT PUBLICATION (NZ/0110-4691) [08932922] **190**

WATER & SOIL MISCELLANEOUS PUBLICATION (NZ/0110-4705) [05090166] **190**

WATER AND WASTE NEWS *See* WASTE MANAGEMENT NEWS (WACO, TEX.) **2246**

WATER & WASTE TREATMENT (1985) (UK/0950-6551) [12579608] 5542, **2247**

WATER AND WASTES DIGEST (US/0043-1141) [00930815] 2247, **5542**

WATER & WASTEWATER DIGEST (US/0748-2612) [08270110] 5542, **2247**

WATER & WASTEWATER INTERNATIONAL (US/0891-5385) [14902659] **5542**

WATER AND WATER RIGHTS (US) [09618094] **3182**

WATER AUTHORITY OF WESTERN AUSTRALIA *See* ANNUAL REPORT / WATER AUTHORITY OF WESTERN AUSTRALIA **5530**

WATER (BRUSSEL) (BE/0770-7193) [14766429] **5542**

WATER BULLETIN (EAST LANSING) (US/0543-8926) [01152304] **1418**

WATER CHEMISTRY OF NUCLEAR REACTOR SYSTEMS (UK/0950-8686) [11294209] 1031, **5542**

WATER CHLORINATION (US/0272-9210) [12904013] **5542**

WATER CIRCULAR (US/0502-8450) [01148718] **5542**

WATER CONDITIONING & PURIFICATION (US/0746-4029) [09834511] **5542**

WATER CONDITIONS AND FLOOD EVENTS IN CALIFORNIA *See* CALIFORNIA HIGH WATER (1979-80) **1413**

WATER CONNECTION : THE NEW ENGLAND INTERSTATE WATER POLLUTION CONTROL COMMISSION NEWSLETTER (US) [11462663] **5542**

WATER DATA - GREAT BRITAIN. DEPT. OF THE ENVIRONMENT. WATER DATA UNIT (UK) [03779072] **5542**

WATER DESALINATION REPORT (US) [08443736] **5542**

WATER ENGINEERING & MANAGEMENT (US/0273-2238) [07023071] **2096**

WATER ENVIRONMENT & TECHNOLOGY (US/1044-9493) [19957465] **2247**

●WATER ENVIRONMENT LABORATORY SOLUTIONS (US/1074-2972) [29689843] 5542, **2247**

WATER ENVIRONMENT REGULATION WATCH (US) **5542**

●WATER ENVIRONMENT RESEARCH MICROFORM: A RESEARCH PUBLICATION OF THE WATER ENVIRONMENT FEDERATION (US) [25308854] **5542**

WATER EQUIPMENT NEWS (US/0194-1194) [05320713] **5542**

WATER FARMING JOURNAL (US/1051-0583) [14387727] **2315**

WATER FLYING (US/0733-1754) [08550687] **39**

WATER FLYING ANNUAL (US/0193-4198) [05182870] **39**

WATER FOR WESTERN ENERGY DEVELOPMENT UPDATE (US/0163-5883) [04396505] **1960**

WATER IMPACTS (US) **5542**

WATER-IN-PLANTS BIBLIOGRAPHY **CEASED.** (NE) [03618372] **427**

WATER INDUSTRY STATISTICAL PROFILE, A (US/0149-029X) [03417347] **5549**

WATER INDUSTRY. UNITED KINGDOM SERVICE AND COSTS ... AND CHARGES FOR SERVICE ... (UK) [21493515] 2247, **5542**

WATER INFORMATION BULLETIN (BOISE) (US/0511-3598) [01149054] **5542**

WATER INTERNATIONAL (US/0250-8060) [02244031] **5542**

WATER INTERNATIONAL : OFFICIAL JOURNAL OF THE INTERNATIONAL WATER RESOURCES ASSOCIATION **CEASED.** (US) [10318774] **5543**

WATER INVENTORY REPORT (US) [03973765] **5543**

WATER JOURNAL (US/0892-9548) [02255980] 4694, **5543**

WATER LAW (UK/0959-9754) [25701950] **5543**

WATER LAW NEWSLETTER (BOULDER, COLO. : 1976) (US/0737-044X) [03751849] **3182**

WATER LEVELS AND ARTESIAN PRESSURE IN OBSERVATION WELLS IN THE UNITED STATES *See* GROUND-WATER LEVELS IN THE UNITED STATES. NORTH-CENTRAL STATES **5534**

WATER LEVELS AND ARTESIAN PRESSURE IN OBSERVATION WELLS IN THE UNITED STATES *See* GROUND-WATER LEVELS IN THE UNITED STATES. NORTHWESTERN STATES **1413**

WATER LEVELS AND ARTESIAN PRESSURE IN OBSERVATION WELLS IN THE UNITED STATES *See* GROUND-WATER LEVELS IN THE UNITED STATES. SOUTHEASTERN STATES **1413**

WATER LINE NEWSLETTER (US/0196-075X) [03476246] **5543**

WATER MANAGEMENT TECHNICAL REPORT (US) [03173964] **5543**

WATER (MELBOURNE) (AT/0310-0367) [11007121] 5543, **2247**

WATER NEWS **CEASED.** (US) [04238579] **5543**

WATER NEWS (CAMBRIDGE) (CN/0821-0233) [09658192] **5543**

WATER NEWSLETTER (US/0043-1273) [01769493] 2183, **5543**

WATER NEWSLETTER (US/0544-3482) [01758090] **5543**

WATER OPERATION AND MAINTENANCE BULLETIN (US/0145-2800) [02602859] **5543**

WATER POLLUTION CONTROL ASSOCIATION OF PENNSYLVANIA MAGAZINE (US/0890-4553) [02451517] **2247**

WATER POLLUTION CONTROL FEDERATION *See* YEARBOOK - WATER POLLUTION CONTROL FEDERATION **2248**

WATER POLLUTION CONTROL NEWS (US) 5543, **2247**

WATER POLLUTION CONTROL PLAN (SPRINGFIELD) (US/0091-4541) [01787046] 2247, **5543**

Alphabetical Title Index

WATER-RESOURCES

WATER POLLUTION REPORT (VI) [01785217] 2247, **5543**

WATER POLLUTION RESEARCH JOURNAL OF CANADA (CN/0197-9140) [06158834] 5543, **2247**

WATER POLLUTION RESEARCH (OXFORD) (UK) [02409724] **2247**

WATER POLLUTION SURVEILLANCE SYSTEM : ANNUAL COMPILATION OF DATA (US/0502-0395) [01485474] 5543, **2247**

WATER PROTECTION, CONSERVATION, MANAGEMENT (US/1057-2163) [21354229] **5543**

WATER QUALITY AND POLLUTION CONTROL IN MICHIGAN (US) [06258085] 5543, **2247**

WATER QUALITY ASSOCIATION NEWSLETTER (US/0745-1512) [08869093] 5543, **2247**

WATER QUALITY CONTROL DIGEST *CEASED.* (US/0043-1346) [01667241] 2247, **5543**

WATER QUALITY COUNCIL OF QUEENSLAND *See* ANNUAL REPORT - THE WATER QUALITY COUNCIL OF QUEENSLAND **5530**

WATER QUALITY INSTRUMENTATION (US/0096-6304) [01367855] **5543**

WATER QUALITY INTERNATIONAL (UK/0892-211X) [15118359] **2247**

WATER QUALITY MANAGEMENT DIRECTORY (US/0148-1797) [03276577] **5543**

WATER QUALITY MANAGEMENT PROGRAM SUPPLEMENTAL GUIDANCE FOR FY ... (US) [09910482] **2248**

WATER QUALITY MONITORING DATA FOR GEORGIA STREAMS (US/0097-7519) [01798505] 2248, **5543**

WATER QUALITY SERIES (LOGAN) (US/0270-9503) [04403983] **5543**

WATER REACTOR SAFETY RESEARCH DIVISION QUARTERLY PROGRESS REPORT / DEPARTMENT OF NUCLEAR ENERGY, BROOKHAVEN NATIONAL LABORATORY (US) [09416556] **2159**

WATER-RELATED DISEASE OUTBREAKS SURVEILLANCE. ANNUAL SUMMARY (US/0275-7249) [06623954] 5543, **2248**

WATER REPORTER, THE (US) [13452374] **5543**

WATER RESEARCH CENTRE *See* ANNUAL REPORT AND ACCOUNTS - WATER RESEARCH CENTRE **2224**

WATER RESEARCH COMMISSION *See* REPORT - WATER RESEARCH COMMISSION **5538**

WATER RESEARCH (OXFORD) (UK/0043-1354) [01769499] **5543**

WATER RESEARCH TOPICS (UK/0730-9619) [07871481] **5543**

WATER RESOURCE DATA FOR INDIANA (US/0364-4340) [09705714] **5543**

WATER RESOURCES (US/0097-8078) [01799472] **1419**

WATER RESOURCES ABSTRACTS (COLLEGE PARK, MD.) *See* WATER RESOURCES ABSTRACTS. VOLUME 1 **5544**

WATER RESOURCES ABSTRACTS (COLLEGE PARK, MD.) (US/1040-9009) [18568753] **5544**

WATER RESOURCES ABSTRACTS. VOLUME 1 (US/1053-5624) [22577530] **5544**

WATER RESOURCES ABSTRACTS [COMPUTER FILE] (US) [25404650] **5544**

WATER RESOURCES ACTIVITIES IN FLORIDA / U.S. GEOLOGICAL SURVEY (US) [15535720] **5544**

WATER-RESOURCES ACTIVITIES OF THE U.S. GEOLOGICAL SURVEY IN ILLINOIS (US) [19854531] 1419, **5544**

WATER-RESOURCES ACTIVITIES OF THE U.S. GEOLOGICAL SURVEY IN NEW MEXICO (US) [14449771] 1419, **5544**

WATER RESOURCES BASIC RECORDS REPORT (US/0731-7638) [04692349] **5544**

WATER RESOURCES BULLETIN : GROUND WATER SERIES (CN/0383-5456) [05932800] **5544**

WATER-RESOURCES BULLETIN (SALT LAKE CITY) (US/0094-7636) [05116514] **5544**

WATER RESOURCES BULLETIN (URBANA) (US/0043-1370) [01240574] **5544**

WATER RESOURCES COORDINATION DIRECTORY (US/0270-0034) [06298555] **5544**

WATER RESOURCES DATA. ALASKA (US/0741-0689) [10069054] **5544**

WATER RESOURCES DATA. ARIZONA (US) [10035447] **5544**

WATER RESOURCES DATA. CALIFORNIA (US) [09607588] **5544**

WATER RESOURCES DATA. COLORADO (US/0741-0697) [09094575] **5544**

WATER RESOURCES DATA FOR FLORIDA (US/0275-2689) [09519641] **5544**

WATER RESOURCES DATA FOR ILLINOIS (US/0364-4332) [08808462] **5544**

WATER RESOURCES DATA FOR IOWA *See* WATER RESOURCES DATA. IOWA **5545**

WATER RESOURCES DATA FOR MASSACHUSETTS AND RHODE ISLAND *See* WATER RESOURCES DATA. MASSACHUSETTS AND RHODE ISLAND **5545**

WATER RESOURCES DATA FOR MICHIGAN (US/0364-4375) [09050589] **5544**

WATER RESOURCES DATA FOR MINNESOTA (US/0364-4383) [09288997] **5544**

WATER RESOURCES DATA FOR MISSISSIPPI (US/0364-510X) [02277809] **5544**

WATER RESOURCES DATA FOR NEW MEXICO (US/0364-4065) [09752130] **5544**

WATER RESOURCES DATA FOR NORTH CAROLINA *See* WATER RESOURCES DATA. NORTH CAROLINA **5545**

WATER RESOURCES DATA FOR NORTH DAKOTA *See* WATER RESOURCES DATA. NORTH DAKOTA **5545**

WATER RESOURCES DATA FOR PENNSYLVANIA (US/0197-0755) [09107571] **5544**

WATER RESOURCES DATA FOR TEXAS *See* WATER RESOURCES DATA. TEXAS **5546**

WATER RESOURCES DATA FOR VIRGINIA *See* WATER RESOURCES DATA. VIRGINIA **5546**

WATER RESOURCES DATA FOR WEST VIRGINIA (US/0364-4421) [09247168] **5545**

WATER RESOURCES DATA. IDAHO (US/0364-4324) [10142193] **5545**

WATER RESOURCES DATA. IOWA (US/0364-4359) [08941279] **5545**

WATER RESOURCES DATA. KANSAS (US/0741-4803) [09379946] **5545**

WATER RESOURCES DATA. KENTUCKY (US/0364-4081) [10307502] **5545**

WATER RESOURCES DATA. LOUISIANA (US) [08913791] **5545**

WATER RESOURCES DATA. MARYLAND AND DELAWARE (US/0364-4367) [08942231] **5545**

WATER RESOURCES DATA. MASSACHUSETTS AND RHODE ISLAND (US) [12545247] **5545**

WATER RESOURCES DATA. MISSOURI (US/0741-6296) [09290627] **5545**

WATER RESOURCES DATA. MONTANA (US/0364-4073) [09499409] **5545**

WATER RESOURCES DATA. NEBRASKA (US/0363-1974) [09604921] **5545**

WATER RESOURCES DATA. NEVADA (US) [10544523] **5545**

WATER RESOURCES DATA. NEW HAMPSHIRE AND VERMONT (US) [10526776] **5545**

WATER RESOURCES DATA. NEW JERSEY (US) [08938847] **5545**

WATER RESOURCES DATA. NEW YORK (US) [13769377] **5545**

WATER RESOURCES DATA. NORTH CAROLINA (US/0734-5747) [08752255] **5545**

WATER RESOURCES DATA. NORTH DAKOTA (US) [09290674] **5545**

WATER RESOURCES DATA. OHIO (US) [13578214] **5545**

WATER RESOURCES DATA. OKLAHOMA (US) [10037293] **5545**

WATER RESOURCES DATA. OREGON (US) [09609648] **5545**

WATER RESOURCES DATA. PUERTO RICO AND THE U.S. VIRGIN ISLANDS (US/8756-9809) [11682996] **5545**

WATER RESOURCES DATA. SOUTH CAROLINA (US/0732-9997) [10518184] **5545**

WATER RESOURCES DATA. SOUTH DAKOTA (US/0741-451X) [09093986] **5545**

WATER RESOURCES DATA SUMMARY (US) [07336616] **5545**

WATER RESOURCES DATA. TENNESSEE (US/0163-9447) [10114908] **5545**

WATER RESOURCES DATA. TEXAS (US/0742-1575) [09564843] **5546**

WATER RESOURCES DATA. VIRGINIA (US/0276-1319) [08901716] **5546**

WATER RESOURCES DATA. WASHINGTON (US/0364-3557) [10027808] **5546**

WATER RESOURCES DATA. WISCONSIN (US/0740-8803) [09752030] **5546**

WATER RESOURCES DATA. WYOMING (US/0364-3565) [09607652] **5546**

WATER RESOURCES DEVELOPMENT BY THE U.S. ARMY CORPS OF ENGINEERS IN ARKANSAS (1979) (US) [06205111] **5546**

WATER RESOURCES DEVELOPMENT BY THE U.S. ARMY CORPS OF ENGINEERS IN IDAHO (1979) (US) [05357795] **5546**

WATER RESOURCES DEVELOPMENT BY THE U.S. ARMY CORPS OF ENGINEERS IN ILLINOIS (US) [07769474] **5546**

WATER RESOURCES DEVELOPMENT BY THE U.S. ARMY CORPS OF ENGINEERS IN NORTH CAROLINA (US) [07786047] **5546**

WATER RESOURCES DEVELOPMENT BY THE U.S. ARMY CORPS OF ENGINEERS IN TEXAS (US) [07756218] **5546**

WATER RESOURCES DEVELOPMENT BY THE US ARMY CORPS OF ENGINEERS IN KANSAS / US ARMY CORPS OF ENGINEERS, SOUTHWESTERN DIVISION (US) [07841937] **5546**

WATER RESOURCES DEVELOPMENT BY THE US ARMY CORPS OF ENGINEERS IN OKLAHOMA (US/0744-0480) [07769419] **5546**

WATER RESOURCES DEVELOPMENT IN IOWA (US/0732-6408) [08324834] **5546**

WATER RESOURCES DEVELOPMENT IN LOUISIANA (UNITED STATES. ARMY. CORPS OF ENGINEERS. LOWER MISSISSIPPI VALLEY DIVISION : 1981) (US) [09085702] **5546**

WATER RESOURCES DEVELOPMENT IN MICHIGAN (1981) (US/0278-5781) [07688124] **5546**

WATER RESOURCES DEVELOPMENT IN MINNESOTA (US/0278-5447) [04854368] **5546**

WATER RESOURCES DEVELOPMENT IN WISCONSIN (UNITED STATES. ARMY. CORPS OF ENGINEERS. NORTH CENTRAL DIVISION : 1981) (US) [07910550] **5546**

WATER RESOURCES DIVISION TRAINING BULLETIN (US) [08044448] **5546**

WATER RESOURCES. INFORMATION SERIES. REPORT - NEVADA (US/0548-3557) [01147987] **5546**

WATER-RESOURCES INVESTIGATIONS IN ARIZONA / UNITED STATES GEOLOGICAL SURVEY, WATER RESOURCES DIVISION, IN COOPERATION WITH THE ARIZONA WATER COMMISSION AND OTHER STATE, MUNICIPAL, AND FEDERAL AGENCIES (US) [08843766] **5546**

WATER-RESOURCES INVESTIGATIONS IN MISSOURI / DEPARTMENT OF THE INTERIOR, UNITED STATES GEOLOGICAL SURVEY IN COOPERATION WITH THE MISSOURI DIVISION OF GEOLOGY AND LAND SURVEY, AND OTHER STATE, MUNICIPAL, AND FEDERAL AGENCIES (US) [08935094] **5546**

WATER-RESOURCES INVESTIGATIONS IN NEVADA (US/0277-9293) [07643845] **5546**

WATER RESOURCES INVESTIGATIONS IN NORTH CAROLINA *See* WATER-RESOURCES INVESTIGATIONS IN NORTH CAROLINA / DEPARTMENT OF THE INTERIOR, UNITED STATES GEOLOGICAL SURVEY, IN COOPERATION WITH NORTH CAROLINA DEPARTMENT OF NATURAL AND ECONOMIC RESOURCES AND OTHER STATE, MUNICIPAL, AND FEDERAL AGENCIES **5546**

WATER-RESOURCES INVESTIGATIONS IN NORTH CAROLINA / DEPARTMENT OF THE INTERIOR, UNITED STATES GEOLOGICAL SURVEY, IN COOPERATION WITH NORTH CAROLINA DEPARTMENT OF NATURAL AND ECONOMIC RESOURCES AND OTHER STATE, MUNICIPAL, AND FEDERAL AGENCIES (US) [08934647] **5546**

WATER-RESOURCES INVESTIGATIONS IN OREGON / DEPARTMENT OF THE INTERIOR, UNITED STATES GEOLOGICAL SURVEY IN COOPERATION WITH THE OREGON WATER RESOURCES DEPARTMENT AND OTHER STATE, MUNICIPAL, AND FEDERAL AGENCIES (US) [08938222] **5546**

WATER-RESOURCES — Alphabetical Title Index

WATER-RESOURCES INVESTIGATIONS IN SOUTH CAROLINA / DEPARTMENT OF THE INTERIOR, UNITED STATES GEOLOGICAL SURVEY IN COOPERATION WITH THE SOUTH CAROLINA WATER RESOURCES COMMISSION AND OTHER STATE, MUNICIPAL, AND FEDERAL AGENCIES (US) [08934855] **5547**

WATER-RESOURCES INVESTIGATIONS IN TEXAS (US) [03334829] **5547**

WATER-RESOURCES INVESTIGATIONS OF THE U.S. GEOLOGICAL SURVEY IN MISSOURI (US) [06829925] **5547**

WATER-RESOURCES INVESTIGATIONS OF THE U.S. GEOLOGICAL SURVEY NEW MEXICO DISTRICT (US/0196-1357) [05150414] 1419, **5547**

WATER-RESOURCES INVESTIGATIONS REPORT / U.S. GEOLOGICAL SURVEY (US) [11036945] 1419, **5547**

WATER RESOURCES JOURNAL (US/0377-8053) [01437501] **5547**

WATER RESOURCES MANAGEMENT (DORDRECHT, NETHERLANDS) (NE/0920-4741) [15694082] **5547**

WATER RESOURCES MONOGRAPH (US/0270-9600) [01715827] **5547**

WATER RESOURCES PLANNING SERIES (US/0270-9481) [04404037] **5547**

WATER RESOURCES REPORT (ROLLA) (US/0076-9614) [02891040] **5547**

WATER RESOURCES RESEARCH (US/0043-1397) [01171541] **5547**

WATER RESOURCES RESEARCH INSTITUTE OF THE UNIVERSITY OF NORTH CAROLINA *See* NEWS - WATER RESOURCES RESEARCH INSTITUTE OF THE UNIVERSITY OF NORTH CAROLINA **5536**

WATER RESOURCES RESEARCH SERIES (NASHVILLE) (US/0092-3699) [05535951] **5547**

WATER RESOURCES SERIES (US/0501-2953) [01605705] **5547**

WATER RESOURCES SERIES (LARAMIE) (US/0084-3210) [01543175] **5547**

WATER RESOURCES SERIES (NASHVILLE, TENN.) (US/0495-1026) [01543281] **5547**

WATER RESOURCES SPECIAL REPORT (US/0161-2867) [03889058] **5547**

WATER RESOURCES SUMMARY (LITTLE ROCK) (US/0518-6374) [01203322] **5547**

WATER RESOURCES SYMPOSIUM (US/0083-7709) [01674655] **5547**

WATER REUSE (US) [05905575] **5547**

WATER RIGHTS RESUME. DIVISION 6 (US) **5547**

WATER S. A (SA/0378-4738) [03789177] **5547**

WATER SAFETY JOURNAL (US) [15722586] **4807**

WATER SCIENCE AND TECHNOLOGY (UK/0273-1223) [07004034] **5548**

WATER SCIENCE REVIEWS *CEASED.* (UK/0266-4615) [13367351] 5548, **1038**

WATER SCOOTER (US/0899-9775) [18300135] **596**

WATER SCOOTER BUSINESS (US/1061-3196) [25250707] **596**

WATER SERVICES (UK/0301-7028) [01792564] **2248**

WATER SERVICES YEARBOOK (UK/0307-1782) [06226707] 2248, **5548**

WATER SEWAGE & EFFLUENT (SA/0257-8700) [I02578700] 2248, **5548**

WATER SKIER (WINTER HAVEN), THE (US/0049-7002) [01667485] **4928**

WATER SPACE (UK/0306-2775) [I03062775] **5548**

WATER SPOUTS (US) [05217783] **145**

WATER SUPPLY (UK/0735-1917) [08891448] **5548**

WATER SUPPLY & MANAGEMENT *CEASED.* (UK/0364-7714) [03712128] 2033, **5548**

WATER SUPPLY OUTLOOK ... FOR THE NORTHEASTERN UNITED STATES (US/0732-5312) [03169949] 5548, **1419**

WATER SUPPLY OUTLOOK FOR THE WESTERN UNITED STATES (US) [06163175] 5548, **1419**

WATER SUPPLY OUTLOOK FOR UTAH AND FEDERAL-STATE-PRIVATE COOPERATIVE SNOW SURVEYS *See* UTAH WATER SUPPLY OUTLOOK AND FEDERAL-STATE-PRIVATE COOPERATIVE SNOW SURVEYS **1418**

WATER SUPPLY PAPERS OF THE INSTITUTE OF GEOLOGICAL SCIENCES. RESEARCH REPORT (UK) [06794385] 1401, **5548**

WATER SURVEY OF CANADA *See* SURFACE WATER DATA. BRITISH COLUMBIA **5540**

WATER SURVEY OF CANADA *See* SURFACE WATER DATA. ONTARIO **1418**

WATER SURVEY OF CANADA *See* SURFACE WATER DATA : SASKATCHEWAN **1418**

WATER SURVEY OF CANADA DIRECTORATE *See* HISTORICAL STREAMFLOW SUMMARY: SASKATCHEWAN **1414**

WATER SYSTEMS NEWS AND HOME WATER REPORT (US) **5548**

WATER TECHNOLOGY (US/0192-3633) [05054990] **5548**

WATER TREATMENT (CC/0921-2639) [21929944] **5548**

WATER TREATMENT INSTITUTE NEWSLETTER (US/0889-7123) [14064397] **2248**

WATER UTILITY OPERATING DATA (US/0276-7481) [07411768] **5548**

WATER, WASTEWATER-CHEMICAL AND RADIOLOGICAL ANALYSES : TABULATION (US/0192-3374) [04986883] **5548**

WATER WELL JOURNAL (US/0043-1443) [01769510] **5548**

WATER WELL RECORDS FOR ONTARIO (CN/0226-4552) [04519156] **5548**

WATER WORKS AND SEWER BOARD OF THE CITY OF BIRMINGHAM *See* ANNUAL REPORT / WATER WORKS AND SEWER BOARD OF THE CITY OF BIRMINGHAM **5530**

WATERBORNE & HIGH SOLIDS COATINGS BULLETIN (UK/0140-8798) [I01408798] **4225**

WATERBULLETIN (UK/0262-9909) [08447804] 719, **5548**

WATERBURY REPUBLICAN-AMERICAN (US) [27347801] **4500**

WATERCOLOR : AN AMERICAN ARTIST PUBLICATION (US) [22411531] **368**

WATERCRAFT DEALER (US) [23197048] **596**

WATERFOWLER'S WORLD (US/0739-0327) [07336781] **2208**

WATERFRONT NEWS (US/8756-0038) [11455814] **596**

WATERFRONT WORLD (US/0733-0677) [08255083] **2839**

WATERKAMPIOEN, DE (NE) [08582346] **4929**

WATERLINE (WINDSOR) (CN/1183-6377) [24690675] **4929**

WATERLINES (UK/0262-8104) [09565114] **5548**

WATERLOO CHRONICLE (CN) **5797**

WATERLOO COURIER CEDAR FALLS (US/8750-0868) [10961312] **5673**

WATERLOO HISTORICAL SOCIETY (CN/0315-5021) [02443159] **2765**

WATERLOO POTTERS' WORKSHOP *See* NEWSLETTER - WATERLOO POTTERS' WORKSHOP **374**

WATERMASTER SERVICE IN THE WEST COAST BASIN, LOS ANGELES COUNTY (US) [06150162] **5548**

WATERSCHAPSBELANGEN (NE/0043-1486) [07818194] **5548**

WATERSHED SENTINEL, THE (CN/1188-360X) [25882963] **2208**

WATERSKI (WINTER PARK, FLA.) (US/0883-7813) [12210539] **4929**

WATERSPORTS BUSINESS (US) [20159822] 719, **4929**

WATERTOWN DAILY TIMES (WATERTOWN, N.Y. : 1929) (US/0891-009X) [14523504] **5722**

WATERTOWN DAILY TIMES (WATERTOWN, WIS.) (US/0885-680X) [12719099] **5771**

WATERTOWN PUBLIC OPINION (US) [11193768] **5744**

WATERTOWN STANDARD *See* WATERTOWN DAILY TIMES (WATERTOWN, N.Y. : 1929) **5722**

WATERVILLE TELEGRAPH (WATERVILLE, KAN. : 1880) (US) [11978083] **5679**

WATERVILLE TIMES (WATERVILLE, N.Y.) (US) [10967998] **5722**

WATERWAY GUIDE (GREAT LAKES EDITION) (US) [08140108] **596**

WATERWAY GUIDE. MID-ATLANTIC EDITION (US/0509-917X) [02175272] **597**

WATERWAY GUIDE. NORTHERN EDITION (US/0090-712X) [02604801] 4185, **597**

WATERWAY GUIDE. SOUTHERN EDITION (US/0511-3806) [02497094] **5458**

WATERWAYS EXPERIMENT STATION (U.S.) *See* TECHNICAL REPORT - U. S. WATERWAYS EXPERIMENT STATION, VICKSBURG, MISS **2095**

WATERWAYS JOURNAL, THE (US/0043-1524) [01714538] **5399**

WATERWAYS (NEW YORK, N.Y.) (US/0197-4777) [06036674] **3473**

WATERWHEEL (SILVER SPRING, MD.) (US/0898-6606) [17869562] 2253, **5008**

WATERWORKER *CEASED.* (US/0894-5942) [16146131] **1401**

WATERWORLD NEWS (US/0747-9735) [10842029] 5548, **2248**

● WATERWORLD REVIEW (US/1068-5839) [27393019] **5548**

WATFORD BUSINESS DIRECTORY (UK/0957-1124) [I09571124] **719**

WATHENA TIMES, THE FRIDAY TROY REPUBLICAN, THE (US) [11085258] **5679**

WATI/TS-VIEW [COMPUTER FILE] (US) [25809410] **145**

WATKINS REPORT ON CONSULTANTS' MARKETING STRATEGIES, THE (US/0894-1041) [15797372] **889**

WATKINS REVIEW & EXPRESS, THE (US/1041-6250) [18235506] **5722**

WATNO DUR, THE (CN/0700-8163) [03399838] **2765**

WATSONIA (UK/0043-1532) [01769517] **530**

WATSONVILLE REGISTER-PAJARONIAN (US) [27931202] **5641**

WATT MILANO (IT/1121-208X) [I1121208X] **5169**

WAUKESHA COUNTY FREEMAN *See* FREEMAN (WAUKESHA, WIS.), THE **5767**

WAUKESHA COUNTY FREEMAN, THE (US/0895-6391) [16725294] **5771**

WAUKESHA FREEMAN (WAUKESHA, WIS. : DAILY) *See* WAUKESHA COUNTY FREEMAN, THE **5771**

WAUKON DEMOCRAT (WAUKON, IOWA : 1945) (US) [14938619] **5673**

WAUKON REPUBLICAN-STANDARD (US) [14983383] **5673**

WAUPACA COUNTY POST (US) [13210508] **5771**

WAUPUN LEADER-NEWS, THE (US) [13240792] **5771**

WAURIKA NEWS-DEMOCRAT (US/8750-0701) [10960022] **5733**

WAUSAU DAILY HERALD (US/0887-4271) [13221197] **5771**

WAUSHARA ARGUS, THE (US) [11833202] **5771**

WAUWATOSA NEWS-TIMES (US) [13770973] **5771**

WAVE (US) **5647**

WAVE MOTION (NE/0165-2125) [04589517] **3541**

WAVE (ROCKAWAY BEACH, N.Y.), THE (US/0882-7028) [11929591] **5722**

WAVELENGTH (NEW ORLEANS, LA.) (US/0741-2460) [07252995] **4158**

WAVELENGTHS NORTH RYDE (AT/1038-6793) [I10386793] **1361**

WAVERLY DEMOCRAT, THE (US) [16077380] **5673**

WAVERLY GAZETTE (WAVERLY, KAN. : 1898) (US) [10250759] **5679**

WAVERLY GENEALOGICAL AND HISTORICAL SOCIETY NEWSLETTER (US) 2765, **2477**

WAVES (US) [06029789] **3473**

WAVES IN RANDOM MEDIA (UK/0959-7174) [23156565] 3541, **4424**

WAVES (SEATTLE, WASH.) *CEASED.* (US) [15239357] **3356**

WAVES (SPRING VALLEY, CALIF.) *See* UNDERWATER NEWS & TECHNOLOGY **1458**

WAVES (SPRING VALLEY, CALIF.) (US/1055-0348) [23063290] **2096**

WAWASAN (IO) [06779992] **2667**

WAWATAY NEWS (CN/0703-9387) [03951241] **2275**

WAX DATA (US/0887-5456) [13308127] **1631**

WAXAHACHIE DAILY LIGHT, THE (US/0896-0291) [14950021] **5755**

WAY AL-ARABI (YE) [09520634] **2667**

WAY MAGAZINE, THE (US/0277-0431) [07485293] **5020**

WAY MARKINGS (US/0273-3765) [05366758] **1148**

WAY OF ST. FRANCIS (1980) (US/0273-8295) [06954923] **5008**

WAY OF THE ZEPHYR, THE (US/0748-1683) [10884134] **5428**

WAY, THE (UK/0043-1575) [01668563] **5008**

Alphabetical Title Index — WEEKLY

WAYCROSS JOURNAL-HERALD (US) [19787082] **5655**

WAYNE CO., MICH. AIR POLLUTION CONTROL DIVISION *See* PROGRESS IN AIR POLLUTION CONTROL **2240**

WAYNE CO., MICH. AIR POLLUTION CONTROL DIVISION. AIR POLLUTION CONTROL PROGRESS REPORT *See* PROGRESS IN AIR POLLUTION CONTROL **2240**

WAYNE CO., MICH. DEPT. OF SOCIAL SERVICES *See* ANNUAL REPORT - WAYNE COUNTY DEPARTMENT OF SOCIAL SERVICES **5273**

WAYNE COUNTY MAIL (US/0745-7685) [09434363] **5722**

WAYNE COUNTY NEWS, THE (US) [10479164] **5702**

WAYNE COUNTY NEWS (WAYNE, W.VA.) (US) [13297732] **5765**

WAYNE COUNTY OUTLOOK, THE (US) [14231039] **5683**

WAYNE INDEPENDENT, THE (US/0899-479X) [10173953] **5740**

WAYNE LAW REVIEW (US/0043-1621) [01604882] **3073**

WAYNE STATE UNIVERSITY. LIBRARIES *See* NEWSLETTER - WAYNE STATE UNIVERSITY LIBRARIES **3236**

WAYNEDALE NEWS (US) [15615662] **5668**

WAYNESBURG REPUBLICAN (WAYNESBURG, PA. : 1870) (US) [16954937] **5740**

WAYS *See* NEW WAYS (EVANSTON, ILL.) **3931**

WAYS & MEANS (WASHINGTON, D.C.) (US/0193-4716) [05062699] **4694**

WAYZGOOSE (CN/0715-4720) [09313019] **4570**

WAZA / MARKAZ DIRASAT AL-FULKLUR (SJ) [07617719] **2325**

● WAZO WEUSI (US/1065-5883) [26650028] **2275**

● WB (GREENDALE, WIS.) (US/1078-2958) [31037816] **4929**

WBA NEWSLETTER (BOSTON, MASS.) (US/0272-1201) [06745787] **3073**

WBAI FOLIO (US) [04732456] **1143**

WBAI (RADIO STATION) NEW YORK (CITY) *See* WBAI FOLIO **1143**

WBF BODYBUILDING LIFESTYLES : THE OFFICIAL PUBLICATION OF THE WORLD BODYBUILDING FEDERATION (US/1062-4368) [25622310] **4929, 2602**

● WBF IN ACTION (US/1061-1444) [25186920] **1717**

WCA NATIONAL UPDATE (US) [25842517] **5568, 333**

WCAT IN FOCUS (CN/1180-2588) [23659202] **3073**

● WCB UPDATE (CN/1191-6885) [27194011] **1717**

WCBB 10 PULSE *See* VIEWFINDER (LEWISTON, MAINE) **1143**

WCCI FORUM (US/0116-5461) [19744726] **1908**

WCI : WESTERN CONSTRUCTION AND INDUSTRY MAGAZINE (CN/0043-3624) [10441239] **631**

WCOE (CARMICHAEL, CALIF.) (US/1059-6712) [24624401] **5568, 631**

WCW COLLECTORS EDITIONS *CEASED.* (US/1062-3752) [25602550] **4929**

WDA JOURNAL (US/1046-9338) [19070722] **1337**

WDS FORUM (US/0275-9748) [07286158] **3452**

WE REPRESENT IN ISRAEL AND ABROAD (IS) [01792856] **719**

● WE THE PEOPLE (NORTH READING, MASS.) (US/1064-0568) [26208934] **4500**

● WE THE PEOPLE (WASHINGTON, D.C. : 1992) (US/1061-2564) [25222671] **3073**

WEA NEWS (US) [09221825] **1790**

WEALTH AND RICHES NEWSLETTER (US/0899-8396) [18235902] **816**

WEALTH FORMULA, THE (US/0749-8071) [11177269] **4758**

● WEALTH RANKINGS (US/1066-7903) [27049356] **719**

WEANS NEWSLETTER (CN/0847-5741) [24368314] **1917**

WEAPONS COMPLEX MONITOR (US/1047-8957) [20808172] **2248, 4061**

WEAPONS SYSTEMS RESEARCH LABORATORY (AUSTRALIA) *See* ANNUAL REPORT / DEPARTMENT OF DEFENCE, DEFENCE SCIENCE AND TECHNOLOGY ORGANISATION, WEAPONS SYSTEMS RESERCH LABORATORY **4035**

WEAR (US/0199-4018) [05842176] **857**

WEAR (SZ/0043-1648) [01769532] **2132**

WEAR OF MATERIALS (US/0192-4990) [05015782] **2132**

● WEARABLE CRAFTS (US/1073-0680) [29306971] **5186**

WEARABLE WONDERS *See* WEARABLE CRAFTS **5186**

WEATHER (UK/0043-1656) [01769533] **1436**

WEATHER ALMANAC, THE (US/0731-5627) [03564790] **1436**

WEATHER & CLIMATE REPORT (US/0730-8256) [04205670] **1436**

WEATHER AND FORECASTING (US/0882-8156) [11984782] **1436**

WEATHER REVIEW: NEW SOUTH WALES *See* MONTHLY WEATHER REVIEW : NEW SOUTH WALES **1432**

WEATHER TRENDS *CEASED.* (US) [05767633] **1436**

WEATHER VANE *See* WEST VIRGINIA NURSE **3871**

WEATHER VANE (CHARLESTON, W. VA.), THE (US/0043-1664) [03959447] **3871**

WEATHERCOCK, THE (US) [06999685] **2765**

WEATHERFORD DEMOCRAT (WEATHERFORD, TX) (US) [14985014] **5755**

WEATHERWISE (US/0043-1672) [01714187] **1436**

WEAVER'S (SIOUX FALLS, S.D.) (US/1042-7643) [18928354] **5359**

WEAVINGS (US/0890-6491) [14340241] **5008**

WEB (CN/0704-7355) [03887292] **1790**

WEB ABBOTSFORD (AT/1036-3912) [I10363912] **1908**

WEB OF SPIDER-MAN (US/0887-9702) [12671266] **4867**

WEB (SANTA CRUZ, CALIF.), THE (US/1055-6907) [23271367] **1071, 3452**

WEB, THE (US) [08303475] **3452**

WEB (WALTHAM) (US/0093-6170) [01792690] **4158**

WEBB REPORT : A NEWSLETTER ON SEXUAL HARASSMENT BY SUSAN L. WEBB, THE (US/1053-0932) [22454933] **1717, 3179**

WEBBER'S (AT) [21719988] **3452**

WEBBIA (IT/0083-7792) [01769536] **530**

WEBB'S POSTAL STATIONERY CATALOGUE OF CANADA AND NEWFOUNDLAND (CN/0841-6001) [19027434] **1148**

WEBER STUDIES (US/0891-8899) [11872924] **2856**

● WEBSTER AGRICULTURAL LETTER, THE (US/1073-4813) [29417376] **145**

WEBSTER HERALD, THE (US/0745-1377) [08695682] **5722**

WEBSTER POST, THE (US/0745-3663) [08471746] **5722**

WEBSTER PROGRESS-TIMES, THE (US) [15122667] **5702**

WEBSTER REPUBLICAN, THE (US) [13291777] **5765**

WEBSTER REVIEW (US/0363-1230) [02175232] **3452**

WEBSTERS NINTH NEW COLLEGIATE DICTIONARY. CD-ROM (US) **1930**

WEBSTER'S WAGON WHEEL (US/1067-523X) [20308837] **2477**

WECHSEL- UND SCHECKRECHT ALLER LANDER, DAS *SUSPENDED.* (GW) [01765097] **816**

WEDGE (WILLOW STREET, PA.), THE (US/1060-4650) [24998575] **2477**

WEDGWOOD SOCIETY *See* PROCEEDINGS **2593**

● WEDKARSTWO I TY (PL/0867-4663) [I08674663] **4880**

WEDKARZ POLSKI (PL/0867-3195) [I08673195] **2315**

WEE GIANT (CN/0702-4894) [03960014] **3452**

WEE WISDOM; YOUNG FOLKS MAGAZINE DEVOTED TO PRACTICAL CHRISTIANITY *CEASED.* (US/0043-1710) [01588838] **1071**

WEED ABSTRACTS (UK/0043-1729) [01645073] **190, 157**

WEED CONTROL IN SUMMER CROPS (AT/1033-3061) [I10333061] **145**

WEED CONTROL MANUAL (US/0741-9856) [02758303] **2433**

WEED PRESS (US/1064-6469) [26348068] **5641**

WEED RESEARCH (UK/0043-1737) [01769537] **530**

WEED SCIENCE (US/0043-1745) [02441164] **145**

WEED SCIENCE SOCIETY OF AMERICA *See* WSSA ABSTRACTS : MEETING OF THE WEED SCIENCE SOCIETY OF AMERICA **157**

WEED SCIENCE SOCIETY OF AMERICA *See* ABSTRACTS, MEETING OF THE WEED SCIENCE SOCIETY OF AMERICA **161**

WEED TECHNOLOGY (US/0890-037X) [14122699] **145**

WEEDMAN NEWSLETTER (US/0883-7791) [11682855] **2477**

WEEDWATCHER (IO/0215-1367) [I02151367] **2433**

WEEK-END BIG RED *See* BIG RED NEWS **5714**

WEEK-END NATIONAL, LE (CN/0823-6011) [09796261] **2550**

WEEK IN EUROPE, THE (UK) [19039341] **2524**

WEEK IN GERMANY, THE (US) [04660708] **719**

WEEKBLAD VOOR FISCAL RECHT (NE) **3073**

WEEKBLAD VOOR LERAREN (NE) **1908**

WEEKBLAD VOOR PRIVAATRECHT, NOTARIS-AMBT EN REGISTRATIE *See* WPNR, WEEKBLAD VOOR PRIVAATRECHT, NOTARIAAT EN REGISTRATIE **3076**

WEEKDAY HOMILY HELPS (US) **5038**

WEEKEND (IT) [02241827] **4929**

WEEKEND DESERT POST (US/8750-4316) [11392717] **5641**

WEEKEND MAGAZINE INDEX CARDS MICROFORM (CN) [10615566] **5797**

WEEKEND WOOD PROJECTS (US/1058-3750) [24282789] **635**

● WEEKEND WOODCRAFTS (US/1058-9821) [24450728] **2907**

WEEKEND WOODWORKER ANNUAL, THE (US/1058-4072) [23599756] **635**

WEEKEND WOODWORKING PROJECTS (US/1042-6094) [19094938] **635, 2779**

WEEKENDS (US) **5499**

WEEKLY ADVISORY / COMMODITY FUTURES TRADING COMMISSION (US) [21578131] **857**

WEEKLY AMERICAN (POPLAR BLUFF, MO.) (US/0893-6048) [15601773] **5704**

WEEKLY ANALYSIS OF ECUADOREAN ISSUES (EC/0252-2659) [05002573] **4500, 1526**

WEEKLY BANK CLEARINGS (US/0734-8924) [08441532] **816**

WEEKLY BPN PROPANE NEWSLETTER (US/0193-4724) [05069963] **4281**

WEEKLY BULLET, THE (US/0743-460X) [10607601] **4880, 4929**

WEEKLY BULLETIN (US) [07541360] **3117**

WEEKLY BULLETIN - CALIFORNIA. STATE BANKING DEPT (US/1064-5918) [06189220] **816**

WEEKLY BULLETIN (DILLSBURG, PA.) (US) [13499297] **5740**

WEEKLY BULLETIN - HUNGARIAN NEWS AGENCY (BUDAPEST, 1970) (HU/0024-8495) [18533826] **2524**

WEEKLY BULLETIN LEATHER SHOE NEWS CO *See* WEEKLY BULLETIN - WEEKLY BULLETIN LEATHER SHOE NEWS CO **3186**

WEEKLY BULLETIN - NEW YORK (STATE). BANKING DEPT (US/0276-8488) [05016344] **816**

WEEKLY BULLETIN OF LEATHER & SHOE NEWS *See* WEEKLY BULLETIN - WEEKLY BULLETIN LEATHER SHOE NEWS CO **3186**

WEEKLY BULLETIN. PORT OF NEW ORLEANS *CEASED.* (US/0192-382X) [05013113] **5458**

WEEKLY BULLETIN - WEEKLY BULLETIN LEATHER SHOE NEWS CO *CEASED.* (US/ 03756340] **3186**

WEEKLY CABLE ACTION UPDATE (US) [08903759] **1143**

WEEKLY CALIFORNIA CITATOR (US/0092-2560) [01788347] **3073**

WEEKLY CHALLENGER (US) [01670430] **5651**

WEEKLY CHECKLIST OF CANADIAN GOVERNMENT PUBLICATIONS (CN/0706-4659) [04678199] **4694**

WEEKLY COAL PRODUCTION (US/0733-0545) [08517081] **2153**

WEEKLY COAL REPORT *See* WEEKLY COAL PRODUCTION **2153**

WEEKLY COLLEGIAN (US) [11912577] **5740**

WEEKLY COMMERCIAL NEWS (LOS ANGELES, CALIF.) (US/0888-0670) [12898350] **719**

WEEKLY — Alphabetical Title Index

WEEKLY COMPILATION OF PRESIDENTIAL DOCUMENTS (US/0511-4187) [01769543] **4701**

WEEKLY CONDITION REPORT OF LARGE COMMERCIAL BANKS AND DOMESTIC SUBSIDIARIES *See* WEEKLY CONSOLIDATED CONDITION REPORT OF LARGE COMMERCIAL BANKS AND DOMESTIC SUBSIDIARIES **816**

WEEKLY CONGRESSIONAL MONITOR, THE (US/0197-8403) [04914907] **4694**

WEEKLY CONSOLIDATED CONDITION REPORT OF LARGE COMMERCIAL BANKS AND DOMESTIC SUBSIDIARIES (US) [05527165] **816**

WEEKLY COTTON MARKET REVIEW (US/0145-0360) [02586039] **5359, 190**

WEEKLY CRIMINAL BULLETIN (CN/0703-1319) [06264331] **3109**

WEEKLY DECISIONS SUMMARY (AT) **1631**

WEEKLY DIGEST OF CIVIL PROCEDURE, THE (CN/0827-4266) [12847228] **3091**

WEEKLY DIGEST OF FAMILY LAW (CN/0713-7907) [09246113] **3122**

WEEKLY EPIDEMIOLOGICAL RECORD (SZ/0049-8114) [04393595] **4807, 3736, 3716**

WEEKLY EUROBOND GUIDE (UK) **816**

WEEKLY EUROPEAN LPG REPORT (UK) **4281**

WEEKLY FLORIDA TIMES UNION, THE (US) [13002147] **5651**

WEEKLY FOB PRICE SUMMARY, PAST SALES, INLAND MILLS *See* MONTHLY F.O.B. PRICE SUMMARY PAST SALES. INLAND MILLS **2403**

WEEKLY HARDWOOD REVIEW (US/1063-9314) [26187510] **2405**

WEEKLY HERALD (MADISON, IND. : 1974) (US) [12485082] **5668**

WEEKLY HERALD (MONTREAL) (CN/1184-0374) [23231246] **5797**

WEEKLY INDIA TRIBUNE (US/0744-4524) [08275729] **5662**

WEEKLY INFORMATION BULLETIN - HOUSE OF COMMONS (UK) [04941870] **4694**

WEEKLY INFORMATION REPORT - U.S. NUCLEAR REGULATORY COMMISSION (US/1056-9065) [09917635] **2159**

WEEKLY INSIDERS DAIRY & EGG LETTER (US/0270-4153) [06416190] **199**

WEEKLY INSIDERS POULTRY REPORT (US/0160-4872) [02760974] **223, 157**

WEEKLY INSIDERS TURKEY LETTER (US/0160-4910) [02760948] **223, 157**

WEEKLY INSURED UNEMPLOYMENT REPORT (US) **1717, 2896**

WEEKLY INTERNATIONAL MARKET ALERT (US/1051-807X) [22124143] **857**

WEEKLY JAPAN DIGEST, THE (US/1060-2259) [23320259] **719, 4500**

WEEKLY LAW REPORTS (UK) [01769548] **3073**

WEEKLY LEGISLATIVE SUMMARY (US) [06661862] **3073**

WEEKLY LETTING REPORT - IOWA. HIGHWAY DIVISION (US) [06048031] **2033**

WEEKLY LIST OF MONTANA STATE PUBLICATIONS RECEIVED BY MONTANA STATE LIBRARY (US) [06506570] **4694**

WEEKLY LIVESTOCK REPORTER, THE (US/0043-1842) [03959665] **223**

WEEKLY MAIL (JOHANNESBURG, SOUTH AFRICA) (SA) [12685336] **5810**

WEEKLY MARKET BULLETIN (CONCORD) (US/0043-1850) [03959749] **145**

WEEKLY MARKET REPORT - ENGLAND (UK) **5359**

WEEKLY MESSENGER (JEWETT, TEX.) (US) [14256938] **5755**

WEEKLY MINEOLA MONITOR, THE (US) [14472641] **5755**

WEEKLY NEWS LETTER - ILLINOIS STATE AFL-CIO (US/0019-2279) [02262156] **1717**

WEEKLY NEWS (MIAMI, FLA.), THE (US/0199-4395) [05867151] **2796**

WEEKLY NEWS QUIZ GAME (US) **1790**

WEEKLY NEWS (STRATFORD) (CN/0712-3043) [08781481] **5797**

WEEKLY OF BUSINESS AVIATION, THE (US/0509-9528) [08322439] **39**

WEEKLY OFFICIAL INTELLIGENCE (UK) [27321349] **919**

WEEKLY PETROLEUM ARGUS (UK/0268-7844) [02687844] **4282**

WEEKLY PETROLEUM STATUS REPORT / U.S. DEPARTMENT OF ENERGY, ENERGY INFORMATION ADMINISTRATION (US/1057-5790) [09978225] **4282**

WEEKLY PHARMACY REPORTS (US/0043-1893) [01769556] **4332**

WEEKLY PRODUCTION AND DRILLING STATISTICS, ALBERTA OIL AND GAS INDUSTRY *See* ALBERTA DRILLING PROGRESS AND PIPELINE RECEIPTS WEEKLY REPORT **4249**

WEEKLY PSYCHIATRY UPDATE SERIES (US/0161-4568) [03900637] **3937**

●WEEKLY PUZZLER, THE (US/1060-779X) [25060564] **4867**

WEEKLY QUIZ BOWL QUESTIONS *CEASED.* (US) **1790**

WEEKLY RATES SUMMARY (AT) **816**

WEEKLY RAW COTTON REPORT (UK) [13829413] **145**

WEEKLY READER. EDITION 1 (US/0890-3220) [14201781] **1790**

WEEKLY READER. EDITION 2 (US/0890-3212) [14201746] **1790**

WEEKLY READER. EDITION 3 (US/0890-3204) [14201695] **1790**

WEEKLY READER. EDITION 4 (US/0890-3190) [14201247] **1791**

WEEKLY READER. EDITION 5 (US/0890-3182) [14201196] **1791**

WEEKLY READER. EDITION K (US/0890-3166) [14201061] **1791**

WEEKLY READER (LOS ANGELES, CALIF.) *See* REFLECTIONS (LOS ANGELES) **3725**

WEEKLY READER OF HOUSING AND COMMUNITY NEWS, THE (US/1056-9545) [23899255] **2839**

WEEKLY READER. PRE-K EDITION (US/0890-3174) [14201142] **1791**

WEEKLY READER. SENIOR EDITION (US/0890-3239) [14201834] **1791**

WEEKLY READER. SUMMER EDITION B (US/0899-6113) [18154320] **1791**

WEEKLY READER. SUMMER EDITION C (US/0899-6121) [18154518] **1071**

WEEKLY RECORDER, THE (US) [17249487] **5740**

WEEKLY REGISTER-CALL (CENTRAL CITY, COLO. : 1861) (US) [13162014] **5644**

WEEKLY REGULATORY MONITOR, THE (US/0161-2972) [03884961] **3073**

WEEKLY REPORT (HK) **919**

WEEKLY REPORT OF CERTIFICATED STOCK IN LICENSED WAREHOUSES/ U.S. DEPARTMENT OF AGRICULTURE, AGRICULTURAL MARKETING SERVICE, COTTON DIVISION (US) [09740353] **145**

WEEKLY REVIEW (EMMONS, MINN.), THE (US/1059-4744) [24603504] **5699**

WEEKLY REVIEW - SUDAN NEWS AGENCY (SJ) [01791715] **2644**

WEEKLY REVIEW, THE (KE) [02241306] **4538**

WEEKLY REVIEW (VIKING) (CN/0710-0175) [08289428] **5797**

WEEKLY RIVER SUMMARY AND FORECAST (US) [18265597] **1401**

WEEKLY SALE & DISCOUNT MAGAZINE (LOS ANGELES ED.) (US/1055-8535) [23359919] **719**

WEEKLY STATISTICAL BULLETIN (AMERICAN PETROLEUM INSTITUTE. STATISTICS DEPT.) (US) [15334463] **4282, 4285**

WEEKLY STATISTICAL SUGAR TRADE JOURNAL (US/0043-1923) [02758358] **2361, 2362**

WEEKLY STOCK CHARTS. CANADIAN AND U.S. INDUSTRIAL COMPANIES (CN/0830-1972) [15287395] **919**

WEEKLY STOCK CHARTS. ... CANADIAN RESOURCE COMPANIES (CN/0829-3139) [15152835] **919**

WEEKLY SUMMARY - BRITISH COLUMBIA SECURITIES COMMISSION (1989) (CN/1187-1733) [26290570] **919**

WEEKLY SUMMARY OF NLRB CASES (US/0364-8109) [07389475] **3155**

WEEKLY TELEVISION ACTION UPDATE (US) [08899749] **1143**

WEEKLY TIMES (PRESCOTT, ARK.) *See* TIMES-PICAYUNE, THE **5632**

WEEKLY TIMES TECHNICAL ANNUAL *SUSPENDED.* (AT/1031-4695) [19651087] **161**

WEEKLY WEATHER AND CROP BULLETIN (US/0043-1974) [01388055] **145, 1437**

WEEKLY WESTPORT REPORTER, THE (US/0738-8055) [09690878] **5704**

WEEKLY WOOL INTERNATIONAL (AT/1320-4122) **5359**

WEEKLY WORLD NEWS (US/0199-574X) [06010349] **5651**

WEEKLY WRAP-UP / MINNESOTA HOUSE OF REPRESENTATIVES (US) [04997658] **3073**

WEGE DER FORSCHUNG (GW/0509-9609) [03195943] **3332**

WEGE ZUM MENSCHEN (GW/0043-2040) [06569422] **5008**

WEGEN (NE/0043-2067) [07818164] **2033**

WEGVERVOER (NE) **5446**

WEGWEISER ZUR VOLKERKUNDE (GW/0511-4225) [03199032] **2325**

WEGWIJS (NE) **2839**

WEHLING (A. VICTOR) BUCHGROSSHANDLUNG-ZEITSCHRIFTEN-GROSSVERTRIEB *See* LAGERKATALOG **418**

WEHRAUSBILDUNG (GW/0178-3084) [12877819] **4061**

WEHRAUSBILDUNG IN WORT UND BILD *See* WEHRAUSBILDUNG **4061**

WEHRMACHT IM KAMPF, DIE (GW/0511-4233) [01714796] **2633**

WEHRMEDIZIN UND WEHRPHARMAZIE (GW) [02242593] **4332**

WEHRMEDIZINISCHE MONATSSCHRIFT (GW/0043-2156) [11341035] **3650**

WEHRTECHNIK (GW/0043-2172) [02885614] **4061**

WEI HSING CHI SUAN CHI (CH) [10591236] **1273**

WEI LAI YU FA CHAN FUTURE AND DEVELOPMENT (CC) [09590429] **2633**

WEI SHENG CHING CHI (CC) [11414106] **1526**

WEI SHENG WU HSUEH PAO (CC/0001-6209) [01778432] **571**

WEIGHING & MEASUREMENT (US/0095-537X) [01793358] **4033**

WEIGHT CONTROL DIGEST (CONSUMER ED.) *See* WEIGHT CONTROL DIGEST (DALLAS, TEX. 1992), THE **4200**

WEIGHT CONTROL DIGEST (CONSUMER ED.), THE (US/1053-1459) [22464731] **4200**

●WEIGHT CONTROL DIGEST (DALLAS, TEX. 1992), THE (US/1075-2889) [29949355] **4200**

WEIGHT CONTROL DIGEST (PROFESSIONAL ED.) *See* WEIGHT CONTROL DIGEST (DALLAS, TEX. 1992), THE **4200**

WEIGHT ENGINEERING (US) [02451535] **2001**

WEIGHT WATCHERS (US/0043-2180) [01605102] **2602**

WEIGHT WATCHERS WOMEN'S HEALTH AND FITNESS NEWS *CEASED.* (US/0896-4696) [16795258] **5568, 4807**

WEIGHTWATCHERS (UK) **4200**

WEIMAR. HOCHSCHULE FUER ARCHITEKTUR UND BAUWESEN *See* WISSENSCHAFTLICHE ZEITSCHRIFT **311**

WEIMARER BEITRAEGE (AU/0043-2199) [I00432199] **3452**

WEIMARER BEITRAEGE (GW/0323-4223) [00851926] **3452**

WEIN & SEKT JOURNAL *CEASED.* (GW) **1300**

WEIN-WISSENSCHAFT, DIE (GW/0375-8818) [03902693] **2361**

WEINBURG & BLACK ON TAKE-OVERS AND MERGERS (UK) **719**

WEINWIRTSCHAFT, DIE (GW/0341-6364) [02680584] **2372**

WEINWIRTSCHAFT. MARKT, DIE (GW/0723-1350) [09345548] **2372**

WEINWIRTSCHAFT. TECHNIK, DIE (GW/0723-1369) [09345574] **2372**

WEIRD TALES (US/0898-5073) [05712942] **3452**

WEIRDBOOK (US/8755-7452) [11479385] **3452, 5075**

WEIRTON DAILY TIMES, THE (US) [02269409] **5765**

WEISER SIGNAL-AMERICAN, THE (US) [20379307] **5658**

WEISHENGWUXUE TONGBAO (CC/0253-2654) [04486215] **571**

WEISHENGWUXUE ZAZHI (CC/1002-056X) [I1002056X] **571**

●WEISS RESEARCH'S INSURANCE SAFETY DIRECTORY (US/1074-2158) [26524571] **2896**

WEITERENTWICKLUNG DER PSYCHOANALYSE UND IHRER ANWENDUNGEN (GW) [03294861] **4621**

WELCOME BACK STUDENT GUIDE (CN/0839-1483) [18805648] **1791**

WELCOME HOME (US/8750-9563) [11951989] **2286**

WELCOME TO CZECHOSLOVAKIA *CEASED.* (CS/0043-2210) [01769572] **5499**

WELCOME TO NORWAY (NO) [19074414] **2525**

WELCOME TO THE TAX REVOLT (US/0271-6119) [06583301] **4758**

● WELCOME TO THE USA (US/1059-0021) [24458050] **5499**

WELDALERT (UK) **4028**

WELDASEARCH INDUSTRY NEWS (UK) **3490**

WELDASEARCH SELECT (UK) **4028**

WELDING ABSTRACTS / WELDING INSTITUTE (UK/0952-0287) [22245737] **4028**

WELDING & FABRICATING DATA BOOK (US/0278-7067) [06323991] **4028**

WELDING AND METAL FABRICATION (UK/0043-2245) [06121787] **4028**

WELDING-BRAZING-SOLDERING DIGEST (US/1050-3013) [15233339] **4028**

WELDING DATA BOOK (US/0511-4365) [01629583] **4028**

WELDING DESIGN & FABRICATION (US/0043-2253) [01606070] **4028**

WELDING DISTRIBUTOR, THE *See* GASES AND WELDING DISTRIBUTOR, THE **4027**

WELDING DISTRIBUTOR (1966) (US/0192-7671) [05138511] **938**

WELDING IN THE WORLD (UK/0043-2288) [02451540] **4028**

WELDING INTERNATIONAL (UK/0950-7116) [16664267] **4028**

WELDING JOURNAL (US/0043-2296) [02602789] **4028**

WELDING QUARTERLY *See* WHAT'S NEW IN WELDING **4023**

WELDING RESEARCH ABROAD (US/0043-2318) [01623916] **4028**

WELDING RESEARCH (MIAMI) (US/0096-7629) [01780699] **4028**

WELDING RESEARCH NEWS (US/0511-4381) [01780700] **4028**

WELDING REVIEW *See* WELDING REVIEW INTERNATIONAL **4029**

WELDING REVIEW INTERNATIONAL (UK/0262-642X) **4029**

WELDON TIMES, THE (CN/0702-8989) [03782117] **3073**

WELEDA KORRESPONDENZBLATTER FUR ARZTE (GW/0379-7031) [04794725] **4332**

WELEETKAN, THE (US/0746-4339) [10037237] **5733**

WELFARE IN AUSTRALIA (AT/0310-4869) [I03104869] **5314**

WELFARE MANCHESTER (UK/0269-879X) [I0269879X] **5314**

WELFARE RIGHTS BULLETIN (UK/0263-2098) [20018926] **5314**

● WELFARE TO WORK (US/1060-5622) [25036719] **5314**

WELL-BEING *See* VEGETARIAN TIMES **4200**

WELL SERVICE MARKET REPORT (US/1058-0646) [24189145] **2248**

WELL SERVICING (US/0043-2393) [05137935] **4282**

WELLAND & PELHAM BUSINESS BOOK, THE (CN/1189-069X) [25314212] **719**

WELLAND CANALS SOCIETY *See* REPORT / WELLAND CANALS SOCIETY **1625**

WELLAND NEWS MAGAZINE (CN/0712-1806) [08724171] **5797**

WELLAND TOURISM NEWS / TOURISM OF WELLAND NIAGARA (CN/1185-9369) [25423423] **5499**

WELLCOME TRENDS IN OPHTHALMOLOGY (US) [05300091] **3880**

WELLESBOURNE, ENG. NATIONAL VEGETABLE RESEARCH STATION *See* ANNUAL REPORT - NATIONAL VEGETABLE RESEARCH STATION **163**

WELLESLEY EDITION, THE (US/0083-7881) [01630166] **4158**

WELLESLEY TOWNSMAN, THE (US) [11189972] **5690**

WELLINGTON DAILY NEWS, THE (US) [12686472] **5679**

WELLINGTON ENTERPRISE (WELLINGTON, OHIO : 1901) (US) [11686893] **5731**

WELLINGTON LEADER (WELLINGTON, TEX.) (US) [14267249] **5755**

WELLINGTON'S WORRY-FREE INVESTING *CEASED*. (US/0891-1258) [14638854] **919**

WELLNESS DIGEST, THE (US) [13343551] **4807**

WELLNESS ENCYCLOPEDIA OF FOOD AND NUTRITION (US) **4807**

WELLNESS JOURNAL, THE *CEASED*. (US/0739-4411) [09737263] **4807**

WELLNESS MANAGEMENT (US/1062-1156) [15508956] **4807**

WELLNESS : MAXIMUM PHYSICAL & MENTAL HEALTH (AT) **4621**, **2602**

WELLNESS MEDIA *CEASED*. (US) [15738147] **4807**

WELLNESS NEW MEXICO (US/8756-5048) [11692882] **2602**

WELLNESS NEWSLETTER, THE *CEASED*. (US/0740-8498) [09712165] **2602**

WELLNESS PERSPECTIVES (US/0748-1764) [10474238] **4807**

WELLS MIRROR (US) [01769586] **5699**

WELLSBORO GAZETTE (WELLSBORO, PA. : 1984) (US) [13171438] **5740**

WELLSIAN (EDWALTON, NOTTINGHAMSHIRE : 1976) (UK/0263-1776) [04416505] **3452**

WELLSPRING: A JOURNAL FOR UNITED METHODIST CLERGYMAN (US) **5069**

WELLSPRING (EDMONTON) (CN/1187-7472) [25796443] **2602**

WELLSPRING (LONG LAKE, MINN.) (US/1045-2974) [20085645] **3452**

WELLSTON SENTRY, THE (US) [16823535] **5731**

WELLWOMAN (US/0275-6528) [04533748] **5069**

WELSH AGRICULTURAL STATISTICS / WELSH OFFICE / YSTADEGAU AMAETHYDDOL CYMRU / Y SWYDDFA GYMREIG (UK/0262-8325) [06152983] **145**

WELSH ECONOMIC TRENDS (UK) [02247053] **1526**

WELSH HOSPITAL WAITING LIST BULLETIN / WELSH OFFICE / BWLETIN RHESTR AROS YSBYTAI CYMRU / Y SWYDDFA GYMREIG (UK/0266-0776) [18790682] **3793**

WELSH HOUSING STATISTICS / WELSH OFFICE / YSTADEGAU TAI CYMRU / Y SWYDDFA GYMREIG (UK/0262-8333) [12369066] **2839**

WELSH JOURNAL OF EDUCATION, THE (UK/0957-297X) [21546235] **1791**

WELSH POLITICAL ARCHIVE LECTURE, THE (UK) [20081321] **4500**

WELSH SOCIAL TRENDS / WELSH OFFICE / TUEDDIADAU CYMDEITHASOL / Y SWYDDFA GYMREIG (UK/0140-9018) [06150647] **1526**

WELSH SOILS DISCUSSION GROUP *See* REPORT - WELSH SOILS DISCUSSION GROUP **184**

WELSH TRANSPORT STATISTICS / YSTADEGAU TRAFNIDIAETH CYMRU (UK/0267-8160) [15719365] **5399**

WELT DER ARBEIT *CEASED*. (AU/0043-2482) [05152322] **1717**

WELT DER SLAVEN (GW/0043-2520) [01769590] **3332**

WELT DER TIERE, DIE (GW) [04397883] **5600**

WELT DES ISLAMS, DIE (NE/0043-2539) [02175211] **3452**, **5045**

WELT DES ORIENTS, DIE (GW/0043-2547) [01586576] **3332**

WELT, DIE (GW) [03212170] **5802**

WELTBUHNE, DIE *CEASED*. (GW/0043-2598) [04562048] **2525**

WELTGESCHEHEN (GW/0020-9465) [04631820] **4538**

WELTKUNST, DIE (GW/0043-261X) [05510033] **252**, **368**

WELTMISSION, DIE (GW/0723-6204) [25565517] **5008**

WELTMISSION (EVANGELISCHES MISSIONSWERK IM BEREICH DER BUNDESREPUBLIK DEUTSCHLAND UND BERLIN WEST) *See* WELTMISSION, DIE **5008**

WELTMISSION (EVANGELISCHES MISSIONSWERK IN DER BUNDESREPUBLIK DEUTSCHLAND UND BERLIN WEST) (GW/0341-082X) [09554161] **5008**

WELTWIRTSCHAFT (TUBINGEN), DIE (GW/0043-2652) [02236542] **1588**

WELTWIRTSCHAFTLICHES ARCHIV (GW/0043-2636) [01640929] **5225**

WELTWOCHE, DIE (SZ) [08341688] **2525**

WELZIJNSWERK KRONIEK *See* TIJDSCHRIFT VOOR WELZIJNSWERK **5312**

WELZYNSWEEKBLAD 1981 (NE/0169-0639) [01690639] **5314**

WEMTA JOURNAL *See* PROFESSIONALS **3725**

WEN, I *See* SHIH CHIEH WEN HSUEH **3436**

WEN HSUEH CHIEH (CH) [09514275] **3452**

WEN HSUEH LUN TSUNG / HO-NAN SHENG SHE HUI KO HSUEH YUAN, WEN HSUEH YEN CHIU SO, HO-NAN SHENG WEN HSUEH HSUEH HUI PIEN (CC) [11886122] **3452**

WEN HSUEH YUEH PAO (CHANG-SHA SHIH, CHINA) (CC) [11281876] **3452**

WEN HUA YU SHENG HUO (CC) [05392719] **2668**

WEN HUI PAO SO YIN (CC) [07186149] **427**

WEN HUI YUEH KAN / WEN HUI YUEH KAN PIEN CHI PU (CC) [10756476] **333**

WEN I LI LUN YEN CHIU (CC) [08408330] **333**

WEN-LAI KUNG SHANG NIEN CHIEN (MY) [02246235] **1631**

WEN SHIH CHE HSUEH PAO / KUO LI TAIWAN TA HSUEH (CH/0508-3052) [01769603] **2856**

WEN SHIH TZU LIAO HSUAN CHI (SHANTUNG PROVINCE, CHINA) (CC) [10591744] **2668**

WEN TZU YU WEN HUA (CH) [08910220] **3333**

WEN WU (CC/0511-4772) [01769606] **5269**

WEN WU TIEN TI (CC) [08393776] **2668**, **285**

WENATCHEE WORLD, THE (US) [14402267] **5763**

WENCO INTERNATIONAL TRADE DIRECTORY, THE (US/0091-9705) [01788917] **857**

WENDELL'S REPORT FOR CONTROLLERS (US/1067-7313) [27340830] **753**

WENDING (NE/0043-2695) [07119020] **5009**

WENNER-GREN CENTER INTERNATIONAL SYMPOSIUM SERIES (US/0083-7989) [01632425] **5169**

WENTWORTH BYGONES (CN/0083-8004) [02443327] **2765**

WENWU (CC/0511-4772) [08101360] **5225**

WENZLICK (ROY) AND COMPANY *See* REAL ESTATE ANALYST, THE **4843**

WEPS [COMPUTER FILE] : ARCHIVAL OF WORLD ENERGY PROJECTION SYSTEM (US) [25362578] **1960**

WER IST WER? (GW) [01769609] **435**

WER LIEFERT WAS? CD-ROM (GW) **938**

WER SCHREIBT WORUBER? JOURNALISTEN-HANDBUCH *See* JOURNALISTEN-HANDBUCH **2921**

WER SPIELTE WAS? (GW) [08287711] **4158**, **5372**

WERBEN UND VERKAUFEN : W & V (GW/0042-9538) [24126034] **938**

WERBUNG IN DEUTSCHLAND (GW) [21317066] **767**

WE'RE LIVING IN FUNNY TIMES (US/1045-0491) [20010976] **3452**

WERELD EN ZENDING (NE/0165-988X) [02181003] **5009**

WERELD VAN HET JONGE KIND, DE *See* JONGE KIND **1755**

WERELDWIJD (BE) **5009**

WERK, BAUEN + WOHNEN (GERMAN ED.) (GW/0005-6529) [08704752] **310**

WERKBLAD NEDERLANDSE DIDACTIEK (BE) **3333**, **1791**

WERKE DER KUNST IN HEIDELBERG : EINE SCHRIFTENREIHE IM AUFTRAG DER JOSEPHINE UND EDVARD VON PORTHEIM-STIFTUNG FUR WISSENSCHAFT UND KUNST (GW/0083-8039) [08504260] **333**

WERKE JOSEPH HAYDN (US) **4158**

WERKEN - GHENT. RIJKSUNIVERSITEIT. HOGERE SCHOOL VOOR HANDELS- EN ECONOMISCHE WETENSCHAPPEN (BE/0435-9577) [01457710] **1853**

WERKEN UITGEGEVEN DOOR DE LINSCHOTEN-VEREENIGING (NE) [01645770] **5237**

WERKER, DE (BE) [07810570] **1717**

WERKGROEP INTEGRATIE NEDERLANDSTALIGE KERKMUZIEK *See* WINEK INFO **4159**

WERKING (BEUSICHEM) *See* PROFIEL VAN BEROEPSONDERWIJS EN VOLWASSENENEDUCATIE **1775**

WERKLIKE EN VERWAGTE KAPITAALBESTEDING VAN DIE OPENBARE SEKTOR (SA) [19739157] **4758**

WERKSTATT UND BETRIEB (GW/0043-2792) [09067942] **2132**

WERKSTOFF UND INNOVATION (GW/0934-7321) [I09347321] **631**

WERKSTOFFE, BETRIEBSLEITUNG + TECHNIK (GW) [11065121] **2033**

WERKSTOFFE + TECHNIK *See* WERKSTOFFE, BETRIEBSLEITUNG + TECHNIK **2033**

WERKSTOFFE UND KONSTRUKTION (GW) [20584623] **2001**

WERKSTOFFE — Alphabetical Title Index

WERKSTOFFE UND KORROSION (GW/0043-2822) [01587137] **4023**

WERKZEUG MASCHINEN FUER DIE METALLBEARBEITUNG, HANDBUCH (GW/0173-6396) [11903205] **4023**

WERNER-HEISENBERG-INSTITUT FUER PHYSIK *See* JAHRESBERICHT / MAX-PLANCK-INSTITUT FUER PHYSIK UND ASTROPHYSIK, WERNER-HEISENBERG-INSTITUT FUER PHYSIK **4407**

WERTE DER DEUTSCHEN HEIMAT *See* WERTE UNSERER HEIMAT **2525**

WERTE UNSERER HEIMAT (GW) [03195992] **2525**

WERTPAPIER-MITTLEILUNGEN. TEIL 4. ZEITSCHRIFT FUER WIRTSCHAFTS- UND BANKRECHT (GW/0342-6971) [06157967] **3088**

WESCON CONFERENCE RECORD (1979) (US/1044-6036) [06128128] **2085**

WESCONN (US/0360-9189) [02239879] **1853**

WESLEY W. SPINK LECTURES ON COMPARATIVE MEDICINE (US) [01641829] **3650**

WESLEYAN ADVOCATE, THE (US/0043-289X) [02395732] **5069**

WESLEYAN CHRISTIAN ADVOCATE (US/0190-6097) [02395692] **5069**

WESLEYAN (MIDDLETOWN) (US/0148-4249) [03303295] **1103**

WESLEYAN NEW POETS (US) **3473**

WESLEYAN POETRY (US) **3473**

WESLEYAN POETRY IN TRANSLATION (US) **3473**

WESLEYAN POETRY PROGRAM *See* WESLEYAN POETRY **3473**

WESLEYAN POETRY PROGRAM *See* WESLEYAN POETRY IN TRANSLATION **3473**

WESLEYAN POETRY PROGRAM *See* WESLEYAN NEW POETS **3473**

WESLEYAN POETRY PROGRAM, THE (US) [01633493] **3473**

WESLEYAN THEOLOGICAL JOURNAL (US/0092-4245) [01789816] **5009**

WESLEYAN WORLD (US/0739-0440) [08535896] **5009**

WESSEX GEOGRAPHER (UK) [05623035] **2579**

WEST AFRICA (LONDON) (UK/0043-2962) [01639542] **2500**

WEST AFRICA OIL SERVICE (UK) **4282**

WEST AFRICA OIL SERVICE (UK) **4282**

WEST AFRICA RICE DEVELOPMENT ASSOCIATION *See* RETROSPECTIVE INDEX - WEST AFRICA RICE DEVELOPMENT ASSOCIATION **128**

WEST AFRICA RICE DEVELOPMENT ASSOCIATION *See* ANNUAL REPORT - WEST AFRICA RICE DEVELOPMENT ASSOCIATION **163**

WEST AFRICA SERIES (US/0066-1058) [01795899] **2644**

WEST AFRICA (SOUTH YARRA, VIC.) (US) [18897173] **5499**

WEST AFRICAN JOURNAL OF ARCHAEOLOGY (NR/0083-8160) [01633851] 247, **285**

WEST AFRICAN JOURNAL OF BIOLOGICAL AND APPLIED CHEMISTRY (NR/0043-2989) [05161172] 476, **995**

WEST AFRICAN JOURNAL OF MEDICINE (NR/0189-160X) [09483650] **3650**

WEST AFRICAN JOURNAL OF MODERN LANGUAGES (NR/0331-0531) [03199069] **3333**

WEST AFRICAN JOURNAL OF PHARMACOLOGY AND DRUG RESEARCH (NR/0303-691X) [00978796] **4332**

WEST AFRICAN JOURNAL OF SOCIOLOGY AND POLITICAL SCIENCE, THE (UK/0308-4450) [02014734] **5265**

WEST AFRICAN JOURNAL OF SURGERY (NR/0331-054X) [02759796] **3977**

WEST ALLIS ENTERPRISE (WEST ALLIS, WIS. 1967) (US/1062-4902) [25638527] **5771**

● WEST ALLIS POST (1992), THE (US/1067-1862) [27159696] **5772**

WEST ALLIS POST-ENTERPRISE *See* WEST ALLIS POST (1992), THE **5772**

WEST ALLIS POST-ENTERPRISE, THE (US/1062-483X) [25638380] **5772**

WEST ALLIS POST/STAR *See* WEST ALLIS POST-ENTERPRISE, THE **5772**

WEST ALLIS POST-STAR *See* WEST ALLIS STAR **5772**

WEST ALLIS STAR (US) **5772**

WEST & EAST (CH/0043-3047) [01554630] **2668**

WEST ART (US) **368**

WEST AUSTRALIAN TRADE & EXPORT GUIDE (AT) [16857377] **857**

WEST BEND DAILY NEWS (US/0899-2444) [18044661] **5772**

WEST BENGAL. BUREAU OF APPLIED ECONOMICS AND STATISTICS *See* MONTHLY STATISTICAL DIGEST, WEST BENGAL **1536**

WEST BENGAL. BUREAU OF APPLIED ECONOMICS AND STATISTICS *See* STATISTICS OF EMPLOYMENT IN LOCAL BODIES IN WEST BENGAL **1539**

WEST BENGAL. BUREAU OF APPLIED ECONOMICS AND STATISTICS *See* STATISTICAL HANDBOOK - WEST BENGAL. BUREAU OF APPLIED ECONOMICS AND STATISTICS **5340**

WEST BENGAL (INDIA). FINANCE DEPT *See* STATEMENT SHOWING FINANCIAL RESULTS OF IMPORTANT SCHEMES OF GOVERNMENT INVOLVING TRANSACTIONS OF A COMMERCIAL OR SEMI-COMMERCIAL NATURE **713**

WEST BENGAL (INDIA). FINANCE DEPT *See* EXPLANATORY MEMORANDUM ON THE BUDGET OF THE GOVERNMENT OF WEST BENGAL **4723**

WEST BENGAL (INDIA). FINANCE DEPT *See* DETAILED CIVIL BUDGET ESTIMATES. GOVERNMENT OF WEST BENGAL **4720**

WEST BENGAL (INDIA). FINANCE DEPT. CIVIL BUDGET ESTIMATE *See* DETAILED CIVIL BUDGET ESTIMATES. GOVERNMENT OF WEST BENGAL **4720**

WEST BENGAL (INDIA). LEGISLATURE. LEGISLATIVE ASSEMBLY. COMMITTEE ON PUBLIC ACCOUNTS *See* REPORT OF THE COMMITTEE ON PUBLIC ACCOUNTS **4745**

WEST BENGAL INFORMATION DIRECTORY (II) [07228173] **2509**

WEST BENGAL LABOUR GAZETTE (II) [01680970] **3155**

WEST BENGAL. LEGISLATURE. LEGISLATIVE ASSEMBLY. COMMITTEE ON RULES *See* REPORT OF THE COMMITTEE ON RULES **3038**

WEST BENGAL STATE ELECTRICITY BOARD *See* PERFORMANCE BUDGET - WEST BENGAL STATE ELECTRICITY BOARD **4673**

WEST BENGAL. STATE STATISTICAL BUREAU. STATISTICAL HAND BOOK *See* STATISTICAL HANDBOOK - WEST BENGAL. BUREAU OF APPLIED ECONOMICS AND STATISTICS **5340**

WEST BRANCH (US/0149-6441) [03519907] **3452**

WEST BRANCH TIMES (WEST BRANCH, IOWA : 1889) (US) [12047380] **5673**

WEST CANADIAN RESEARCH PUBLICATIONS OF GEOLOGY AND RELATED SCIENCES. SERIES 1 (CN/0511-5604) [02940806] **1361**

WEST CARLETON BANNER (CN/0229-6713) [08023765] **5797**

WEST COAST LIFELINER (CN/0225-4255) [09234457] **4807**

WEST COAST LINE (CN/1182-4271) [22147748] **3452**

WEST COAST PEDDLAR (US/0199-3356) [05796888] **2550**

WEST COAST STUDIES (US/1041-4037) [18759983] **4560**

WEST COUNTY TIMES (US/0746-6323) [10195185] **5641**

WEST EDMONTON EXAMINER (CN/0707-509X) [04754907] **5797**

WEST ENDER (CN/0229-6012) [08010328] **5797**

WEST ESSEX TRIBUNE (US) [13211305] **5712**

WEST EUROPE REPORT (US) [05392416] **1143**

WEST EUROPEAN POLITICS (UK/0140-2382) [04161094] **4500**

WEST FARGO PIONEER (US) [04105475] **5726**

WEST FLORIDA PAINTBALL PRESS *See* FLORIDA PAINTBALL PRESS **4895**

WEST FORTY-NINTH (CN/1183-2681) [24690665] **3452**

WEST GEORGIA COLLEGE *See* STUDIES IN THE SOCIAL SCIENCES (CARROLLTON, GA.) **5223**

WEST GEORGIA COLLEGE *See* ALUMNI DIRECTORY - WEST GEORGIA COLLEGE **1100**

WEST GEORGIA COLLEGE *See* WEST GEORGIA COLLEGE REVIEW **1853**

WEST GEORGIA COLLEGE REVIEW (US/0043-3136) [01448757] **1853**

WEST GERMANY *CEASED*. (US) [08398319] **4758**

WEST GERMANY (ERNST & ERNST) *See* WEST GERMANY **4758**

WEST GROUP FORECAST OF POWER LOADS AND RESOURCES FOR . *See* NORTHWEST REGIONAL FORECAST OF POWER LOADS AND RESOURCES FOR ... / COMPILED BY PACIFIC NORTHWEST UTILITIES CONFERENCE COMMITTEE, SYSTEM PLANNING OFFICE **1951**

WEST HARTFORD NEWS (US/1057-1272) [07846039] **5646**

WEST HAVEN NEWS (US) [28088184] **5646**

WEST HAWAII TODAY (US/0744-4591) [08289852] **5656**

WEST HILL NEWS (CN/0841-2588) [20135322] **5797**

WEST HILLS REVIEW *SUSPENDED*. (US/0890-9024) [05510515] 3356, **3452**

WEST HILLSBOROUGH TIMES *See* ST. PETERSBURG TIMES **5651**

WEST INDIAN LAW JOURNAL (JM/0253-7370) [03976859] **3073**

WEST INDIAN MEDICAL JOURNAL, THE (JM/0043-3144) [04969229] **3650**

WEST INDIAN (TORONTO) (CN/0824-3328) [10335094] **4500**

WEST INDIES MONTHLY LOCAL CLIMATOLOGICAL DATA. MICROFORM (US) [10858579] **1437**

WEST JAPAN RAILWAY COMPANY *See* ANNUAL REPORT / WEST JAPAN RAILWAY COMPANY **5429**

WEST KENTUCKY NEWS (US) [15482550] **5683**

WEST LIBERTY STATE COLLEGE *See* ALUMNI DIRECTORY / WEST LIBRARY STATE COLLEGE **1100**

WEST LYON HERALD, THE (US) [16394304] **5673**

WEST MICHIGAN BOWLER (US/0895-5387) [16687306] **4929**

WEST MICHIGAN PROFILE (US/0890-4391) [14233678] **2550**

WEST MIDDLESEX FAMILY HISTORY SOCIETY JOURNAL (UK/0142-517X) [16220517] **2477**

WEST MIDLANDS DIRECTORY FOR TRADE AND INDUSTRY, THE (UK) [19247743] **1631**

WEST MIFFLIN AREA RECORD (US/0747-4024) [10810604] **5740**

WEST MILTON RECORD, THE (US) [17420204] **5731**

WEST NEWS, THE (US) [14980866] **5756**

WEST OESTLICHE SPIEGELUNGEN (GW) **4538**

WEST OF ENGLAND MEDICAL JOURNAL (UK) [22098387] **3650**

WEST ORANGE TIMES (US) **5651**

WEST OST JOURNAL (AU) 1526, **4500**

WEST PLAINS DAILY QUILL (US) [13741040] **5704**

WEST PRINCE GRAPHIC (CN/0710-6416) [08368473] **5797**

WEST RICHLANDER, THE (US) [16996288] **5763**

WEST SEATTLE HERALD (US) [17293408] **5763**

WEST SEDGWICK COUNTY NEWS-SENTINEL, THE (US) [12574311] **5679**

WEST SIDE MESSENGER (BROWNSBURG, IND.) (US) [15097052] **5668**

WEST SIDE SPIRIT (CITY EDITION) (US/0885-9531) [12813346] **5722**

WEST SURREY FAMILY HISTORY SOCIETY RECORD SERIES (UK/0261-5681) [11546754] **2633**

WEST-TAX PREPARER TO ACCOMPANY WEST'S FEDERAL TAXATION (US/1043-3961) [19356825] **4758**

WEST TENNESSEE HISTORICAL SOCIETY, MEMPHIS *See* PAPERS - WEST TENNESSEE HISTORICAL SOCIETY **2753**

WEST TEXAS GEOLOGICAL SOCIETY *See* GUIDEBOOK - WEST TEXAS GEOLOGICAL SOCIETY **1382**

WEST TEXAS HISTORICAL ASSOCIATION, ABILENE *See* WEST TEXAS HISTORICAL ASSOCIATION YEAR BOOK, THE **2765**

WEST TEXAS HISTORICAL ASSOCIATION YEAR BOOK, THE (US/0886-6155) [01586955] **2765**

WEST TEXAS STATE UNIVERSITY *See* FINANCIAL REPORT - WEST TEXAS STATE UNIVERSITY **1824**

WEST TOLEDOHERALD (US/8750-1872) [11097319] **5731**

WEST TORONTO NEWS-EXPRESS, THE (CN/0821-5197) [09606611] **5797**

WEST VALLEY NEWS, THE (US/0747-1726) [10617492] **5694**

WEST VANCOUVER (B.C.) *See* WEST VANCOUVER REPORT **2839**

Alphabetical Title Index — WESTCOAST

WEST VANCOUVER REPORT (CN/0836-4397) [17235776] 4694, **2839**

WEST VIRGINIA ACADEMY OF SCIENCE *See* PROCEEDINGS OF THE WEST VIRGINIA ACADEMY OF SCIENCE **5142**

WEST VIRGINIA ADVOCATE, THE (US/0891-9240) [15040524] **5765**

WEST VIRGINIA AGRICULTURAL STATISTICS / WEST VIRGINIA CROP REPORTING SERVICE (US) [08187486] 145, **157**

WEST VIRGINIA BLUE BOOK (US) [01589048] **4694**

WEST VIRGINIA BOARD OF EXAMINERS FOR REGISTERED PROFESSIONAL NURSES *See* REPORT OF THE WEST VIRGINIA BOARD OF EXAMINERS FOR REGISTERED PROFESSIONAL NURSES TO THE GOVERNOR .. FOR THE BIENNIUM PERIOD ENDING DECEMBER 31 ... **3868**

WEST VIRGINIA. BOARD OF REGENTS *See* ANNUAL REPORT / WEST VIRGINIA BOARD OF REGENTS **1809**

WEST VIRGINIA BOARD OF REGENTS *See* FACT BOOK AND REPORT OF THE WEST VIRGINIA STATE SYSTEM OF HIGHER EDUCATION **1823**

WEST VIRGINIA BOARD OF REGENTS *See* WEST VIRGINIA'S STATE SYSTEM OF HIGHER EDUCATION **1853**

WEST VIRGINIA BOARD OF REGENTS *See* PHYSICAL FACILITIES AT INSTITUTIONS OF HIGHER EDUCATION IN WEST VIRGINIA **1841**

WEST VIRGINIA. BOARD OF REGENTS. PLANNING AND MANAGEMENT INFORMATION SYSTEMS SECTION *See* FACULTY CHARACTERISTICS, PUBLIC COLLEGES AND UNIVERSITIES IN WEST VIRGINIA **1823**

WEST VIRGINIA. BUREAU OF EMPLOYMENT PROGRAMS *See* ANNUAL REPORT TO THE GOVERNOR / WEST VIRGINIA BUREAU OF EMPLOYMENT PROGRAMS **1650**

WEST VIRGINIA BUSINESS INDEX (US/0195-4644) [05459457] **719**

WEST VIRGINIA. CIVIL SERVICE COMMISSION *See* WEST VIRGINIA CIVIL SERVICE SYSTEM; ANNUAL REPORT **4705**

WEST VIRGINIA CIVIL SERVICE SYSTEM; ANNUAL REPORT (US) [06705301] **4705**

WEST VIRGINIA COAL BELL (US) [07198997] **2153**

WEST VIRGINIA COAL FACTS (US/0091-5513) [01787531] **2153**

WEST VIRGINIA CPA (US) **753**

WEST VIRGINIA DAILY NEWS, THE (US) [12789500] **5765**

WEST VIRGINIA DENTAL JOURNAL (US/0043-3225) [01769677] **1337**

WEST VIRGINIA. DEPT. OF EMPLOYMENT SECURITY. LABOR AND ECONOMIC RESEARCH *See* DEBIT BALANCES, WEST VIRGINIA'S UNEMPLOYMENT COMPENSATION LAW **1662**

WEST VIRGINIA. DEPT. OF EMPLOYMENT SECURITY. LABOR AND ECONOMIC RESEARCH SECTION *See* EMPLOYMENT AND EARNINGS TRENDS; ANNUAL SUMMARY (WEST VIRGINIA) **1532**

WEST VIRGINIA. DEPT. OF EMPLOYMENT SECURITY. RESEARCH AND STATISTICS DIVISION *See* WEST VIRGINIA WORK FORCE ANNUAL AVERAGES **1717**

WEST VIRGINIA. DEPT. OF EMPLOYMENT SECURITY. RESEARCH AND STATISTICS DIVISION *See* WEST VIRGINIA LABOR FORCE ANNUAL AVERAGES HOURS & EARNINGS : WEST VIRGINIA STANDARD METROPOLITAN STATISTICAL AREAS **1540**

WEST VIRGINIA. DEPT. OF EMPLOYMENT SECURITY. RESEARCH AND STATISTICS DIVISION. RS *See* RS-SERIES **1709**

WEST VIRGINIA. DEPT. OF EMPLOYMENT SECURITY. RESEARCH AND STATISTICS SECTION *See* RS-SERIES **1709**

WEST VIRGINIA. DEPT. OF NATURAL RESOURCES *See* ANNUAL REPORT ON THE COMPREHENSIVE WATER RESOURCES PLAN **5529**

WEST VIRGINIA. DEPT. OF NATURAL RESOURCES *See* ANNUAL REPORT / WEST VIRGINIA DEPARTMENT OF NATURAL RESOURCES **2187**

WEST VIRGINIA. DIVISION ENERGY. HEALTH, SAFETY AND TRAINING (SECTION) *See* ANNUAL REPORT AND DIRECTORY OF MINES / STATE OF WEST VIRGINIA, DIVISION OF ENERGY, HEALTH SAFETY AND TRAINING, MINES AND MINERALS **2133**

WEST VIRGINIA. DIVISION OF PROFESSIONAL DEVELOPMENT SYSTEMS *See* TEACHER EDUCATION CENTERS IN WEST VIRGINIA **1906**

WEST VIRGINIA DOCTORS OF MEDICINE (US/0743-1333) [10502153] **3917**

WEST VIRGINIA FOLKLORE JOURNAL (US/0196-2175) [05766019] **2325**

WEST VIRGINIA FORESTRY NOTES (US/0197-1387) [03866539] **2398**

WEST VIRGINIA GAME & FISH (US/0897-9162) [17664688] **4880**

WEST VIRGINIA GEOLOGICAL AND ECONOMIC SURVEY *See* REPORT OF INVESTIGATIONS / STATE OF WEST VIRGINIA, GEOLOGICAL AND ECONOMIC SURVEY **1395**

WEST VIRGINIA GEOLOGICAL AND ECONOMIC SURVEY *See* BULLETIN - WEST VIRGINIA GEOLOGICAL AND ECONOMIC SURVEY **1371**

WEST VIRGINIA GEOLOGICAL AND ECONOMIC SURVEY *See* CIRCULAR - WEST VIRGINIA GEOLOGICAL AND ECONOMIC SURVEY **1372**

WEST VIRGINIA. GEOLOGICAL AND ECONOMIC SURVEY. CIRCULAR SERIES *See* CIRCULAR - WEST VIRGINIA GEOLOGICAL AND ECONOMIC SURVEY **1372**

WEST VIRGINIA. GEOLOGICAL SURVEY *See* CURRENT GEOLOGICAL RESEARCH IN WEST VIRGINIA **1372**

WEST VIRGINIA. GEOLOGICAL SURVEY *See* PUBLICATIONS OF THE WEST VIRGINIA GEOLOGICAL SURVEY **1392**

WEST VIRGINIA. GEOLOGICAL SURVEY. LIST OF PUBLICATIONS *See* PUBLICATIONS OF THE WEST VIRGINIA GEOLOGICAL SURVEY **1392**

WEST VIRGINIA. GOVERNOR'S COMMITTEE ON CRIME, DELINQUENCY, AND CORRECTIONS *See* ANNUAL REPORT - GOVERNOR'S COMMITTEE ON CRIME, DELINQUENCY AND CORRECTIONS (CHARLESTON) **3157**

WEST VIRGINIA. GOVERNOR'S HIGHWAY SAFETY ADMINISTRATION *See* ANNUAL REPORT - WEST VIRGINIA GOVERNOR'S HIGHWAY SAFETY ADMINISTRATION **4630**

● WEST VIRGINIA HEALTH CARE IN PERSPECTIVE (US/1065-4496) [26606924] **4807**

WEST VIRGINIA HILLBILLY (RICHWOOD, W.VA. : 1986) (US/0888-0409) [13448141] **5765**

WEST VIRGINIA HILLS & STREAMS (US/0279-0580) [07483253] **2208**

WEST VIRGINIA HISTORICAL ASSOCIATION *See* JOURNAL OF THE WEST VIRGINIA HISTORICAL ASSOCIATION, THE **2743**

WEST VIRGINIA HISTORY (US/0043-325X) [01769679] **2765**

WEST VIRGINIA IN PERSPECTIVE (US/1065-576X) [26665804] **5346**

WEST VIRGINIA LABOR FORCE ANNUAL AVERAGES HOURS & EARNINGS : WEST VIRGINIA STANDARD METROPOLITAN STATISTICAL AREAS (US/0097-7837) [01798746] **1540**

WEST VIRGINIA LAW REVIEW (US/0043-3268) [01769680] **3073**

WEST VIRGINIA LIBRARIES (US/0043-3276) [02451566] **3256**

WEST VIRGINIA LIBRARY COMMISSION *See* WVLC NEWSLETTER **3256**

WEST VIRGINIA MANUFACTURERS REGISTER (US/0893-2824) [15472145] **3489**

WEST VIRGINIA MEDICAL JOURNAL (US/0043-3284) [01696771] **3650**

WEST VIRGINIA MINING DIRECTORY (US/0743-5282) [10586917] **2153**

● WEST VIRGINIA NURSE (US/1074-8091) [29837562] **3871**

WEST VIRGINIA PHARMACIST, THE (US/0043-3292) [08582438] **4332**

WEST VIRGINIA RAILROAD MAINTENANCE AUTHORITY *See* STATE RAIL PLAN, ANNUAL UPDATE **5437**

WEST VIRGINIA REGISTER : RULES OF GOVERNMENTAL AGENCIES / SECRETARY OF STATE'S OFFICE, ADMINISTRATIVE LAW DIVISION (US) [10703473] **3073**

WEST VIRGINIA. REHABILITATION SERVICES *See* ANNUAL REPORT / RS, REHABILITATION SERVICES, WEST VIRGINIA STATE BOARD OF REHABILITATION **5273**

WEST VIRGINIA. SAFETY RESPONSIBILITY DIVISION *See* STATISTICAL REPORT OF ACCIDENTS (CHARLESTON) **5402**

WEST VIRGINIA SCHOOL JOURNAL (1990) (US/1056-733X) [23711446] **1791**

WEST VIRGINIA SOUTHERN BAPTIST, THE (US/1049-8443) [11474018] **5069**

WEST VIRGINIA SPELEOLOGICAL SURVEY *See* BULLETIN - WEST VIRGINIA SPELEOLOGICAL SURVEY **1403**

WEST VIRGINIA STATE ADVISORY COUNCIL ON VOCATIONAL EDUCATION *See* ANNUAL REPORT / WEST VIRGINIA STATE ADVISORY COUNCIL ON VOCATIONAL EDUCATION **1910**

WEST VIRGINIA STATE BAR *See* WEST VIRGINIA STATE BAR JOURNAL **3073**

WEST VIRGINIA STATE BAR *See* WEST VIRGINIA STATE BAR CONTINUING LEGAL EDUCATION BULLETIN **3073**

WEST VIRGINIA STATE BAR CONTINUING LEGAL EDUCATION BULLETIN (US/0161-1909) [03855080] **3073**

WEST VIRGINIA STATE BAR JOURNAL *CEASED*. (US/0364-3425) [02630880] **3073**

WEST VIRGINIA. STATE BOARD EDUCATION *See* PLAN FOR THE ADMINISTRATION OF VOCATIONAL EDUCATION, A **1915**

WEST VIRGINIA. STATE BOARD OF EDUCATION *See* VOCATIONAL EDUCATION; ANNUAL REPORT **1917**

WEST VIRGINIA. STATE BOARD OF EDUCATION *See* RECOMMENDATIONS OF THE WEST VIRGINIA BOARD OF EDUCATION FOR LEGISLATIVE ACTION **3036**

WEST VIRGINIA. STATE BOARD OF REGISTRATION FOR PROFESSIONAL ENGINEERS *See* BIENNIAL ROSTER OF REGISTRANTS FOR THE YEAR ENDING JUNE 30 ... : REPORT OF THE STATE BOARD OF REGISTRATION FOR PROFESSIONAL ENGINEERS OF WEST VIRGINIA **1966**

WEST VIRGINIA. STATE COMMISSION ON MENTAL RETARDATION *See* PLANNING FOR THE DEVELOPMENTALLY DISABLED **5301**

WEST VIRGINIA UNION LIST (US/0512-4743) [16707530] **3256**

WEST VIRGINIA. UNIVERSITY. COLLEGE OF LAW *See* CLE BULLETIN **2951**

WEST VIRGINIA UNIVERSITY. WATER RESEARCH INSTITUTE *See* BULLETIN - WATER RESEARCH INSTITUTE (MORGANTOWN) **5531**

WEST VIRGINIA WILDLIFE RESEARCH (US/0276-3834) [05023779] **2208**

WEST VIRGINIA. WILDLIFE RESOURCES DIVISION *See* BULLETIN - WEST VIRGINIA DEPARTMENT OF NATURAL RESOURCES, WILDLIFE RESOURCES DIVISION **2189**

WEST VIRGINIA WORK FORCE ANNUAL AVERAGES (US/0095-6112) [01784536] **1717**

WEST VIRGINIA'S STATE SYSTEM OF HIGHER EDUCATION (US/0091-6196) [01787254] **1853**

WESTAF'S NATIONAL ARTS JOBBANK (US/1046-7718) [19769605] **333**

WESTBOROUGH NEWS, THE (US/0893-3782) [15511802] **5690**

● WESTBRIDGE ART MARKET REPORT (CN/1191-3371) [26497808] **368**

WESTBROOK COLLEGE *See* ALUMNI DIRECTORY / WESTBROOK COLLEGE **1100**

WESTCHESTER BAR JOURNAL (US/0746-1844) [09833273] **3073**

WESTCHESTER COMMERCE (US/0888-3459) [12622194] **857**

WESTCHESTER COMMUNITY COLLEGE *See* ALUMNI DIRECTORY / WESTCHESTER COMMUNITY COLLEGE **1100**

WESTCHESTER CONNECTIONS : JOURNAL OF THE WESTCHESTER COUNTY GENEALOGICAL SOCIETY (US) [23460990] **2477**

WESTCHESTER COUNTY BUSINESS JOURNAL (US/1057-686X) [24096107] **719**

WESTCHESTER COUNTY PRESS, THE (US/0043-3373) [03961369] **2550**

WESTCHESTER FAMILY (US/1043-6774) [19532359] **1071**

WESTCHESTER HISTORIAN, THE (US/0049-7266) [06678795] **2477, 2765**

WESTCHESTER HUMAN SERVICES DIRECTORY (US/8755-4534) [11287128] **5314**

WESTCHESTER LAW JOURNAL (US/0049-7274) [03961404] **3073**

WESTCHESTER PLANNING (US/0363-356X) [02180506] **4694**

WESTCOAST LOGGER (CN/1189-3575) [26066455] **2405**

WESTCOAST LOGGER *See* LOGGER (VANCOUVER) **2402**

WESTCOAST MARINER (CN/0844-5567) [20001526] **5458**

WESTCOAST MUSIC (CN/0228-8168) [07805800] **4158**

WESTCOAST
Alphabetical Title Index

WESTCOAST READER, THE (CN/0822-7225) [10768400] **2550**

WESTCOAST REFLECTIONS (CN/1184-7832) [24368288] **5182**

WESTCOAST WOMEN'S NETWORK *See* DIRECTORY / WESTCOASTS WOMEN'S NETWORK **5554**

WESTDEUTSCHER HANDWERKSKAMMERTAG *See* HANDWERK IM LANDE NORDRHEIN-WESTFALEN, DAS **679**

WESTERHEEM (NE/0166-4301) [I01664301] **285**

WESTERLY (AT/0043-342X) [02254692] **3452**

WESTERLY SUN, THE (US/1065-1209) [11912123] **5741**

WESTERMARCK SOCIETY *See* TRANSACTIONS OF THE WESTERMARCK SOCIETY **5264**

WESTERN AMERICA VACATION TRAVELER (US/1058-8493) [24404802] **5499**

WESTERN AMERICAN LITERATURE (US/0043-3462) [01586008] **3453**

WESTERN AND CENTRAL NEW YORK FRUIT AND VEGETABLE REPORT (US/0744-4508) [08274304] **190**

WESTERN & EASTERN TREASURES (US/0890-0876) [07213233] **4880**

WESTERN ANGLER (AT/1035-493X) [I1035493X] **2316**

WESTERN APICULTURAL SOCIETY OF NORTH AMERICA *See* WAS, WESTERN APICULTURAL SOCIETY JOURNAL **5600**

WESTERN ASSOCIATION FOR ART CONSERVATION *See* WAAC MEMBERSHIP DIRECTORY / WESTERN ASSOCIATION FOR ART CONSERVATION **368**

WESTERN ASSOCIATION OF FISH AND WILDLIFE AGENCIES (U.S.) *See* PROCEEDINGS OF THE WESTERN ASSOCIATION OF FISH AND WILDLIFE AGENCIES AND THE WESTERN DIVISION AMERICAN FISHERIES ASSOCIATION **2202**

WESTERN ASSOCIATION OF MAP LIBRARIES *See* INFORMATION BULLETIN / WESTERN ASSOCIATION OF MAP LIBRARIES **3215**

WESTERN ASSOCIATION OF MAP LIBRARIES *See* OCCASIONAL PAPER / WESTERN ASSOCIATION OF MAP LIBRARIES **2582**

WESTERN ASSOCIATION OF SCHOOLS AND COLLEGES (U.S.) *See* DIRECTORY OF ACCREDITED INSTITUTIONS, CANDIDATES FOR ACCREDITATION **1820**

WESTERN AUSTRALIA *See* SUPPLEMENTARY BUDGET INFORMATION / WESTERN AUSTRALIA **4751**

WESTERN AUSTRALIA *See* PROGRAM STATEMENTS / WESTERN AUSTRALIA **4742**

WESTERN AUSTRALIA. ABORIGINAL AFFAIRS PLANNING AUTHORITY *See* ANNUAL REPORT FOR THE YEAR ENDED 30TH JUNE ... / ABORIGINAL AFFAIRS PLANNING AUTHORITY **4627**

WESTERN AUSTRALIA. BUREAU OF CONSUMER AFFAIRS *See* ANNUAL REPORT OF THE COMMISSIONER FOR CONSUMER AFFAIRS FOR THE YEAR ENDED JUNE 30 ... / GOVERNMENT OF WESTERN AUSTRALIA **1293**

WESTERN AUSTRALIA. CORPORATE AFFAIRS DEPT *See* ANNUAL REPORT / CORPORATE AFFAIRS DEPARTMENT, WESTERN AUSTRALIA **4627**

WESTERN AUSTRALIA. DEPARTMENT OF AGRICULTURE *See* BULLETIN - DEPT. OF AGRICULTURE **69**

WESTERN AUSTRALIA. DEPT. FOR YOUTH, SPORT, AND RECREATION *See* ANNUAL REPORT OF THE DEPARTMENT FOR YOUTH, SPORT, AND RECREATION / GOVERNMENT OF WESTERN AUSTRALIA **4848**

WESTERN AUSTRALIA. DEPT. OF AGRICULTURE. MARKETING & ECONOMICS BRANCH *See* REPORT ON THE MARKET MILK INDUSTRY IN WESTERN AUSTRALIA **1625**

WESTERN AUSTRALIA. DEPT. OF COMPUTING & INFORMATION TECHNOLOGY *See* ANNUAL REPORT / GOVERNMENT OF WESTERN AUSTRALIA, DEPARTMENT OF COMPUTING & INFORMATION TECHNOLOGY **4627**

WESTERN AUSTRALIA. DEPT. OF CONSERVATION AND LAND MANAGEMENT *See* ANNUAL REPORT / DEPARTMENT OF CONSERVATION AND LAND MANAGEMENT **2186**

WESTERN AUSTRALIA. DEPT. OF INDUSTRIAL DEVELOPMENT *See* BASIC INFORMATION FOR INDUSTRIALISTS **892**

WESTERN AUSTRALIA. DEPT. OF LANDS ADMINISTRATION *See* ANNUAL REPORT / DEPARTMENT OF LANDS ADMINISTRATION **4627**

WESTERN AUSTRALIA. DEPT. OF MINES *See* STATISTICAL SUMMARY / DEPARTMENT OF MINES, WESTERN AUSTRALIA **2151**

WESTERN AUSTRALIA. DEPT. OF OCCUPATIONAL HEALTH, SAFETY & WELFARE *See* ANNUAL REPORT / DEPARTMENT OF OCCUPATIONAL HEALTH, SAFETY & WELFARE **2859**

WESTERN AUSTRALIA. DEPT. OF RESOURCES DEVELOPMENT *See* REPORT ON ACTIVITIES / DEPARTMENT OF RESOURCES DEVELOPMENT, GOVERNMENT OF WESTERN AUSTRALIA **2203**

WESTERN AUSTRALIA. DEPT. OF RESOURCES DEVELOPMENT *See* ANNUAL REPORT / DEPARTMENT OF RESOURCES DEVELOPMENT **2186**

WESTERN AUSTRALIA. DEPT. OF TRANSPORT *See* ANNUAL REPORT OF THE DEPARTMENT OF TRANSPORT FOR THE YEAR ENDED JUNE 30 ... **5376**

WESTERN AUSTRALIA. EDUCATION DEPT *See* SCHOOLS & STAFFING **1782**

WESTERN AUSTRALIA. EGG MARKETING BOARD *See* OFFICIAL NEWSLETTER - WESTERN AUSTRALIAN EGG MARKETING BOARD **934**

WESTERN AUSTRALIA. ENVIRONMENTAL PROTECTION AUTHORITY *See* ANNUAL REPORTS / ENVIRONMENTAL PROTECTION AUTHORITY AND CONSERVATION AND ENVIRONMENT COUNCIL **2161**

WESTERN AUSTRALIA. ENVIRONMENTAL PROTECTION AUTHORITY. ENVIRONMENTAL PROTECTION AUTHORITY ANNUAL REPORT INCORPORATING CONSERVATION & ENVIRONMENT COUNCIL ANNUAL REPORT *See* ANNUAL REPORTS / ENVIRONMENTAL PROTECTION AUTHORITY AND CONSERVATION AND ENVIRONMENT COUNCIL **2161**

WESTERN AUSTRALIA. EQUAL OPPORTUNITY COMMISSION *See* ANNUAL REPORT / COMMISSIONER FOR EQUAL OPPORTUNITY **1648**

WESTERN AUSTRALIA. FORESTS DEPT *See* BULLETIN - FORESTS DEPARTMENT **2376**

WESTERN AUSTRALIA. GEOLOGICAL SURVEY *See* REPORT / GEOLOGICAL SURVEY OF WESTERN AUSTRALIA **1394**

WESTERN AUSTRALIA. GREAT SOUTHERN DEVELOPMENT AUTHORITY *See* ANNUAL REPORT FOR THE YEAR ENDING 30TH JUNE ... / GREAT SOUTHERN DEVELOPMENT AUTHORITY **4627**

WESTERN AUSTRALIA IN BRIEF (AT/0727-2022) [I07272022] **3073**

WESTERN AUSTRALIA. LAWS, STATUTES, ETC *See* REPRINTED ACTS OF THE PARLIAMENT OF WESTERN AUSTRALIA **3039**

WESTERN AUSTRALIA. MENTAL HEALTH SERVICES *See* REPORT OF THE DIRECTOR OF MENTAL HEALTH SERVICES **4798**

WESTERN AUSTRALIA. NATIONAL PARKS AUTHORITY *See* REPORT - NATIONAL PARKS AUTHORITY OF W.A **2203**

WESTERN AUSTRALIA. OFFICE OF INDUSTRIAL RELATIONS *See* ANNUAL REPORT / OFFICE OF INDUSTRIAL RELATIONS **1597**

WESTERN AUSTRALIA. PARLIAMENT *See* PARLIAMENT OF WESTERN AUSTRALIA DIGEST, THE **3025**

WESTERN AUSTRALIA. PARLIAMENT. LEGISLATIVE ASSEMBLY. PUBLIC ACCOUNTS AND EXPENDITURE REVIEW COMMITTEE *See* ANNUAL REPORT FOR ... / WESTERN AUSTRALIA, LEGISLATIVE ASSEMBLY, PUBLIC ACCOUNTS AND EXPENDITURE REVIEW COMMITTEE **4710**

WESTERN AUSTRALIA. PUBLIC SERVICE BOARD *See* ANNUAL REPORT - PUBLIC SERVICE BOARD (PERTH) **4701**

WESTERN AUSTRALIA PUBLIC SERVICE BOARD. ANNUAL REPORT - PUBLIC SERVICE BOARD *See* ANNUAL REPORT / PUBLIC SERVICE COMMISSION OF WESTERN AUSTRALIA **4701**

WESTERN AUSTRALIA. REAL ESTATE AND BUSINESS AGENTS SUPERVISORY BOARD *See* ANNUAL REPORT OF THE REAL ESTATE AND BUSINESS AGENTS SUPERVISORY BOARD FOR THE PERIOD 1ST JULY ... TO 30TH JUNE ... (WESTERN AUSTRALIA) **4834**

WESTERN AUSTRALIA. SETTLEMENT AGENTS SUPERVISORY BOARD *See* ANNUAL REPORT / SETTLEMENT AGENTS SUPERVISORY BOARD **4834**

WESTERN AUSTRALIA. SUPREME COURT. LAW LIBRARY *See* ANNUAL REPORT / LAW LIBRARY, SUPREME COURT OF WESTERN AUSTRALIA **3190**

WESTERN AUSTRALIA. TECHNICAL EDUCATION DIVISION *See* TECHNICAL AND FURTHER EDUCATION. APPLIED SCIENCES : TAFE **5162**

WESTERN AUSTRALIA. TECHNICAL EDUCATION DIVISION *See* TECHNICAL AND FURTHER EDUCATION. ART, DESIGN AND FASHION **366**

WESTERN AUSTRALIA. TECHNICAL EDUCATION DIVISION *See* TECHNICAL AND FURTHER EDUCATION. HEALTH AND COMMUNITY CARE **4804**

WESTERN AUSTRALIA. TECHNICAL EDUCATION DIVISION *See* TECHNICAL AND FURTHER EDUCATION. ENGINEERING **1998**

WESTERN AUSTRALIA. TECHNICAL EDUCATION DIVISION *See* TECHNICAL AND FURTHER EDUCATION. DETAILS OF SUBJECTS **1916**

WESTERN AUSTRALIA. TECHNICAL EDUCATION DIVISION *See* TECHNICAL AND FURTHER EDUCATION. GENERAL STUDIES **1787**

WESTERN AUSTRALIA. TECHNICAL EDUCATION DIVISION *See* TECHNICAL AND FURTHER EDUCATION. HOSPITALITY AND TOURISM **5492**

WESTERN AUSTRALIA. TECHNICAL EDUCATION DIVISION *See* TECHNICAL AND FURTHER EDUCATION. ARCHITECTURAL AND BUILDING STUDIES **309**

WESTERN AUSTRALIA. TECHNICAL EDUCATION DIVISION *See* TECHNICAL AND FURTHER EDUCATION. MANAGEMENT, BUSINESS AND COMMERCIAL STUDIES **715**

WESTERN AUSTRALIA. TERTIARY EDUCATION COMMISSION *See* REPORT ON NEW ENROLMENTS IN WESTERN AUSTRALIAN TERTIARY EDUCATION INSTITUTIONS **1844**

WESTERN AUSTRALIA. TRAFFIC BOARD *See* ANNUAL REPORT OF THE TRAFFIC BOARD FOR THE YEAR ENDING JUNE 30 ... (WESTERN AUSTRALIA) **5438**

WESTERN AUSTRALIA. UNIVERSITY. DEPT. OF GEOGRAPHY *See* THESES AND DISSERTATIONS PRESENTED AND CURRENTLY BEING UNDERTAKEN IN GEOGRAPHY **2577**

WESTERN AUSTRALIA. WORKERS' COMPENSATION AND REHABILITATION COMMISSION *See* ANNUAL REPORT FOR THE YEAR ENDING JUNE 30 ... OF THE WORKERS' COMPENSATION AND REHABILITATION COMMISSION **1649**

WESTERN AUSTRALIAN COASTAL SHIPPING COMMISSION *See* ANNUAL REPORT - WESTERN AUSTRALIAN COASTAL SHIPPING COMMISSION **5447**

WESTERN AUSTRALIAN ECONOMIC REVIEW (AT/0726-6685) [I07266685] **1631**

WESTERN AUSTRALIAN ECONOMY, THE (AT) [05658372] **1526**

WESTERN AUSTRALIAN EGG MARKETING BOARD *See* ANNUAL REPORT / WESTERN AUSTRALIAN EGG MARKETING BOARD **2327**

WESTERN AUSTRALIAN HERBARIUM *See* WESTERN AUSTRALIAN HERBARIUM ANNUAL REPORT **530**

WESTERN AUSTRALIAN HERBARIUM ANNUAL REPORT (AT) [04802091] **530**

WESTERN AUSTRALIAN INDUSTRIAL GAZETTE, THE (AT) [01769700] **1631**

WESTERN AUSTRALIAN INSTITUTE OF TECHNOLOGY GAZETTE (AT/0049-7347) [I00497347] **5169**

WESTERN AUSTRALIAN LABOUR MARKET, THE (AT) [16836622] **1717**

WESTERN AUSTRALIAN MANUFACTURERS DIRECTORY (AT) [07661135] **3489**

WESTERN AUSTRALIAN MEAT INDUSTRY AUTHORITY *See* SUMMARY OF ACTIVITIES OF THE WESTERN AUSTRALIAN MEAT INDUSTRY AUTHORITY FOR THE YEAR ENDED ... **222**

WESTERN AUSTRALIAN MUSEUM *See* RECORDS OF THE WESTERN AUSTRALIAN MUSEUM **4171**

WESTERN AUSTRALIAN NATURALIST, THE (AT/0508-4865) [01660674] **4173**

WESTERN AUSTRALIAN PARENT & CITIZEN (AT) **1874**

WESTERN AUSTRALIAN POST SECONDARY EDUCATION COMMISSION *See* ANNUAL REPORT OF THE WESTERN AUSTRALIAN POST SECONDARY EDUCATION COMMISSION FOR THE PERIOD ... TO ... **1809**

WESTERN

WESTERN AUSTRALIAN POTATO MARKETING BOARD See ANNUAL REPORT AND ACCOUNTS / WESTERN AUSTRALIAN POTATO MARKETING BOARD **162**

WESTERN AUSTRALIAN REPORTS (AT/0083-8764) [01769702] **3073**

WESTERN AUSTRALIAN SCHOOL OF MINES See ANNUAL MAGAZINE / WESTERN AUSTRALIAN SCHOOL OF MINES **2133**

WESTERN AUSTRALIAN URBAN LANDS COUNCIL See REVIEW OF OPERATIONS - WESTERN AUSTRALIAN URBAN LANDS COUNCIL **1518**

WESTERN AUSTRALIAN YEAR BOOK / COMMONWEALTH BUREAU OF CENSUS AND STATISTICS, WESTERN AUSTRALIAN OFFICE (AT/0083-8772) [08261989] **1930**

WESTERN AUTOBODY *SUSPENDED.* (CN/0842-9855) [19746232] **5428**

WESTERN BACKCOUNTRY MAGAZINE (US/0194-4398) [04654502] **4880**

WESTERN BANK DIRECTORY (US/0272-5371) [04257159] **816**

WESTERN BANKERS DIRECTORY (US) **816**

WESTERN BIOETHICS NETWORK (US) [16115564] 3650, **2253**

WESTERN BIRDS (US/0160-1121) [02623069] **5620**

WESTERN BLUE CHIP ECONOMIC FORECAST (US/1042-6795) [18964989] **1526**

WESTERN BOWHUNTER (US/0274-7219) [06537319] **4880**

WESTERN BOWLER (US/0746-7060) [10221080] **4929**

WESTERN BUILDER (US/0043-3535) [03961500] **631**

WESTERN BULLETIN (DK) [01788974] **4158**

WESTERN CANADA : ALASKA CAMPING (US/0146-6585) [02996464] **4880**

WESTERN CANADA OUTDOORS (ALBERTA EDITION) (CN/0836-446X) [17236760] **2208**

WESTERN CANADA OUTDOORS (SASKATCHEWAN EDITION) (CN/0836-4451) [17236771] **2208**

WESTERN CANADA WATER AND SEWAGE CONFERENCE See PAPERS PRESENTED AT THE ANNUAL CONVENTION **2238**

WESTERN CANADIAN ANTHROPOLOGIST, THE *CEASED.* (CN/0829-0547) [11687132] **247**

WESTERN CANADIAN ANTIQUE & ART DEALERS YEARBOOK (CN/0705-310X) [03797368] 368, **252**

WESTERN CANADIAN LUMBER WORKER, THE (CN/0049-7371) [02231097] **2405**

WESTERN CANADIAN SOCIETY FOR HORTICULTURE. MEETING See REPORTS OF PROCEEDINGS OF ANNUAL MEETING - WESTERN CANADIAN SOCIETY FOR HORTICULTURE **2430**

WESTERN CANADIAN STEAM LOCOMOTIVE DIRECTORY (CN/0085-8188) [02443291] **5438**

WESTERN CATHOLIC REPORTER (CN/0512-5235) [02703108] **5038**

WESTERN CITY (SACRAMENTO, CALIF. : 1976) (US/0279-5337) [05140814] **4694**

WESTERN CIVILIZATION (US/0735-0392) [07972626] 5225, **2633**

WESTERN CLEANER & LAUNDERER (US/0049-741X) [05130501] **1031**

WESTERN COLLEGE READING & LEARNING ASSOCIATION NEWSLETTER (US/0746-1305) [09787598] **1853**

WESTERN COLLEGE READING ASSOCIATION See PROCEEDINGS OF THE ANNUAL CONFERENCE OF THE WESTERN COLLEGE READING ASSOCIATION **1842**

WESTERN COMMERCE & INDUSTRY MAGAZINE (CN) 719, **2361**

WESTERN CONCEPT, THE (US) [02252662] **5726**

WESTERN CONTRACTOR See MID-WEST CONTRACTOR **621**

WESTERN ELECTRONIC SHOW AND CONVENTION See TECHNICAL PAPERS **2083**

WESTERN ENERGY (US/1062-4147) [25614776] **1960**

WESTERN EUROPE (UK/0953-6906) [18081458] **2525**

WESTERN EUROPE (WASHINGTON, D.C. : 1982) (US/0084-2338) [08275645] **2715**

WESTERN EUROPEAN AIRPORT ASSOCIATION See STATISTIQUES DE TRAFIC **41**

WESTERN EUROPEAN SPECIALISTS SECTION NEWSLETTER (US/0734-4503) [08745440] **3333**

WESTERN EXPLORER, THE (US/0511-7445) [02385120] **2765**

WESTERN EXPRESS (US/0510-2332) [07746662] **2788**

WESTERN FARMER AND GRAZIER. WESTERN FARM WEEKLY (AT) [01945060] **145**

WESTERN FINANCIAL JOURNAL (US/0008-106X) [05795128] **4758**

WESTERN FISHERIES See PACIFIC FISHING **2310**

WESTERN FISHERIES MAGAZINE (AT/1033-4149) [19927230] **2316**

WESTERN FLOORS (US/0049-7398) [05130709] 2405, **2904**

WESTERN FOLKLORE (US/0043-373X) [05910334] **2325**

WESTERN FORESTRY NURSERY COUNCIL (U.S.). CONFERENCE See CONFERENCE PROCEEDINGS - WESTERN FORESTRY COUNCIL (U.S.) CONFERENCE **2378**

WESTERN FOUNDATION OF VERTEBRATE ZOOLOGY See OCCASIONAL PAPERS OF THE WESTERN FOUNDATION OF VERTEBRATE ZOOLOGY **5593**

WESTERN FOUNDATION OF VERTEBRATE ZOOLOGY See MONOGRAPHS OF THE WESTERN FOUNDATION OF VERTEBRATE ZOOLOGY **5592**

WESTERN FRONT (US/0043-3748) [01695692] **5763**

WESTERN FRONTIER LIBRARY, THE (US/0083-887X) [01661666] **2765**

WESTERN FRONTIERSMAN SERIES (US/0083-8888) [01661694] **2765**

WESTERN FRUIT GROWER (US/0164-6001) [04213516] 2361, **146**

WESTERN GEOGRAPHER *CEASED.* (AT/0313-8860) [05969491] **2579**

WESTERN GEOGRAPHICAL SERIES (CN/0315-2022) [03221032] **2579**

WESTERN GEOGRAPHY (CN/1187-1121) [22477842] **2579**

WESTERN GERMAN/EEC AND WORLD MARKETS. ANNUAL REVIEW (GW) [19872496] **199**

WESTERN GROCER MAGAZINE (1977) (CN/0705-906X) [04097995] **2361**

WESTERN GROWER & SHIPPER (US/0043-3799) [01661758] **190**

WESTERN HISTORICAL QUARTERLY (US/0043-3810) [01769730] 2765, **2636**

WESTERN HOG JOURNAL (CN/0225-3488) [06032815] **223**

WESTERN HORSEMAN, THE (US/0043-3837) [01769731] **2803**

WESTERN HUMANITIES REVIEW (US/0043-3845) [02419692] **3453**

WESTERN HVACR NEWS (US/0273-5687) [07079039] **2608**

WESTERN ILLINOIS REGIONAL STUDIES *CEASED.* (US/0192-1355) [04302438] 3453, **2766**

WESTERN INDUSTRIAL CONNECTION See CHRYSALIS CONNECTION **5279**

WESTERN INTERSTATE COMMISSION FOR HIGHER EDUCATION See WICHE REPORTS ON HIGHER EDUCATION IN THE WEST **1853**

WESTERN JOURNAL OF AGRICULTURAL ECONOMICS See JOURNAL OF AGRICULTURAL AND RESOURCE ECONOMICS **99**

WESTERN JOURNAL OF APPLIED FORESTRY (US/0885-6095) [12681760] **2398**

WESTERN JOURNAL OF BLACK STUDIES, THE (US/0197-4327) [02986838] 5225, **2275**

● WESTERN JOURNAL OF COMMUNICATION (US/1057-0314) [23915926] **1124**

WESTERN JOURNAL OF MEDICINE, THE (US/0093-0415) [01799362] **3650**

WESTERN JOURNAL OF NURSING RESEARCH (US/0193-9459) [04946643] **3871**

WESTERN JOURNAL OF SPEECH COMMUNICATION See WESTERN JOURNAL OF COMMUNICATION **1124**

WESTERN KANSAS WORLD (US) [08817652] **5679**

● WESTERN KENTUCKY JOURNAL (US/1072-6756) [29176513] **2766**

WESTERN LABOUR ARBITRATION CASES *CEASED.* (CN/0317-6924) [02569633] **3155**

WESTERN LANDS AND WATER SERIES (US/0083-8934) [01662060] **2766**

WESTERN LEGAL HISTORY (US/0896-2189) [16960875] 2633, **3073**

WESTERN LINKS (HILTON HEAD ISLAND, S.C.) (US/1052-3219) [22258011] 5499, **4929**

WESTERN LIVESTOCK JOURNAL. CENTRAL EDITION (US/0094-6710) [03802098] **223**

WESTERN LIVESTOCK REPORTER (US) [03383695] **223**

WESTERN LIVESTOCK ROUND-UP (US) [03383711] **223**

WESTERN LIVING (CALGARY ED.) (CN/0829-4046) [16877860] **2550**

WESTERN LIVING (EDMONTON ED.) (CN/0824-0612) [16877546] **2550**

WESTERN LIVING (VANCOUVER ED.) (CN/0824-0604) [16877590] **2904**

WESTERN LIVING (VICTORIA ED.) (CN/0829-4038) [16877884] **2550**

WESTERN LOS ANGELES COUNTY APARTMENT OWNER/BUILDER (US/0192-1576) [04751233] **2839**

WESTERN LUMBER FACTS (US/0511-7704) [05740271] **2405**

WESTERN MACHINERY AND STEEL WORLD. BUYERS GUIDE (US/0732-8540) [08440888] **2132**

WESTERN MANAGEMENT GROUP See SALARY SURVEY (LOS GATOS) **1709**

WESTERN MARYLAND GENEALOGY (US/0747-7805) [10807414] **2477**

WESTERN MBA PROGRAM, THE (CN) [11434819] 1853, **719**

WESTERN METALWORKING DIRECTORY (US) [18690119] **4023**

WESTERN MINING DIRECTORY (US/0162-9026) [04244383] **2153**

WESTERN MINING NEWS (US/0300-662X) [01356099] **919**

WESTERN MONTANA GENEALOGICAL SOCIETY BULLETIN (US/0748-2515) [10899893] **2477**

WESTERN NEW ENGLAND LAW REVIEW (US/0190-6593) [04187612] **3073**

WESTERN NEW YORK *CEASED.* (US/0149-5070) [03503136] **719**

WESTERN NEW YORK FAMILY MAGAZINE (US) **2286**

WESTERN NEW YORK GENEALOGICAL SOCIETY See JOURNAL - WESTERN NEW YORK GENEALOGICAL SOCIETY **2456**

WESTERN NEWS (LIBBY, MONT.), THE (US/0745-0362) [08737628] **5706**

WESTERN NEWS (LONDON) (CN/0316-8654) [02247244] **1853**

● WESTERN OBLATE STUDIES (US/1065-4011) [26612108] **2766**

WESTERN OBSERVER (ANSON, TEX. : 1945) (US) [13880757] **5756**

WESTERN OIL AND GAS WORLD (US/1070-6100) [28298820] **4282**

WESTERN OIL WORLD (US/0884-7592) [12423929] **4282**

WESTERN OUTDOOR NEWS (US/0049-7479) [03076117] **4880**

WESTERN OUTDOORS (US/0043-4000) [02250612] **4880**

WESTERN OUTFITTER (US/0049-7487) [05066157] **1088**

WESTERN PACKING NEWS See NATIONAL PACKING NEWS **2351**

WESTERN PENNSYLVANIA BLUEGRASS COMMITTEE See NEWSLETTER - WESTERN PENNSYLVANIA BLUEGRASS COMMITTEE **4141**

WESTERN PENNSYLVANIA GENEALOGICAL QUARTERLY See WESTERN PENNSYLVANIA GENEALOGICAL SOCIETY QUARTERLY **2477**

WESTERN PENNSYLVANIA GENEALOGICAL SOCIETY QUARTERLY (US/0278-7431) [07864303] **2477**

WESTERN PETROLEUM REGISTER (US/0273-1762) [05705501] **4282**

WESTERN PHARMACOLOGY SOCIETY See PROCEEDINGS OF THE WESTERN PHARMACOLOGY SOCIETY **4326**

WESTERN PHOTOGRAPHER (US/0738-8039) [09690675] **4378**

WESTERN PLANNER, THE (US/0279-0602) [07297540] **4695**

WESTERN POLITICAL QUARTERLY See POLITICAL RESEARCH QUARTERLY **4489**

WESTERN POLITICAL QUARTERLY, THE (US/0043-4078) [01769755] **4500**

WESTERN PREHISTORIC RESEARCH ARCHEOLOGICAL MONOGRAPH (US/0739-1080) [09688749] **285**

WESTERN PREMIERS' TASK FORCE ON CONSTITUTIONAL TRENDS See REPORT / WESTERN PREMIERS' TASK FORCE ON CONSTITUTIONAL TRENDS **4682**

WESTERN PRODUCER (CN/0043-4094) [03341794] **146**

WESTERN QUEENS GAZETTE, THE (US) [17724297] **5722**

WESTERN — Alphabetical Title Index

WESTERN RACING NEWS (US/0510-2626) [10722280] 4929, **5428**

WESTERN RAILROADER AND WESTERN RAILFAN (US/0149-4996) [03502986] **5438**

WESTERN RECORDER (MIDDLETOWN) (US/0043-4132) [03961730] **5009**

WESTERN REGIONAL AGRICULTURAL ENGINEERING SERVICE *See* WRAES QUARTERLY **147**

WESTERN REPORT (CN/0831-8891) [15246727] **2766**

WESTERN RESOURCES WRAP-UP CEASED. (US/1065-0806) [06395220] **2208**

WESTERN RETAILER (US/1044-7768) [19899527] **889**

WESTERN RETAILER NEWS (US/0279-2311) [07663762] **958**

WESTERN RIDER (1987) (CN/0820-571X) [16861084] **2803**

WESTERN ROADS : OFFICIAL JOURNAL OF THE MAIN ROADS DEPARTMENT, WESTERN AUSTRALIA (AT) [07234729] **5446**

WESTERN ROOFING INSULATION AND SIDING (US/0164-5803) [04508633] 310, **631**

WESTERN ROUNDUP COUNTRY MUSIC TRADE DIRECTORY & NEWS REPORT (US/0273-1991) [06991730] **4158**

WESTERN ROUNDUP : WESTERN NEW YORK'S COUNTRY MUSIC GUIDE (US) [03922921] **4159**

WESTERN RURAL DEVELOPMENT CENTER *See* WESTERN WIRE **5314**

WESTERN SAMOA. DEPT. OF ECONOMIC DEVELOPMENT *See* WESTERN SAMOA'S ... DEVELOPMENT PLAN / GOVERNMENT OF WESTERN SAMOA **1526**

WESTERN SAMOA'S ... DEVELOPMENT PLAN / GOVERNMENT OF WESTERN SAMOA (WS) [19225957] **1526**

WESTERN SIKH SAMACHAR (CN/0709-0455) [05359794] **2766**

WESTERN SKIER (CN/1184-2679) [24265574] **4929**

WESTERN SOCIALIST, THE (US/0043-4191) [01589457] **4548**

WESTERN SOCIETY FOR FRENCH HISTORY *See* PROCEEDINGS OF THE ANNUAL MEETING OF THE WESTERN SOCIETY FOR FRENCH HISTORY **2703**

WESTERN SOCIETY OF WEED SCIENCE *See* RESEARCH PROGRESS REPORT - WESTERN SOCIETY OF WEED SCIENCE **185**

WESTERN SOCIETY OF WEED SCIENCE *See* PROCEEDINGS OF THE WESTERN SOCIETY OF WEED SCIENCE **183**

WESTERN SPECTRUM (CN/0317-333X) [02248131] **1853**

WESTERN SPORTSMAN (CN/0709-1532) [05527962] **4929**

WESTERN STAR (BESSEMER, ALA.), THE (US/0889-0080) [13787251] **5628**

WESTERN STAR (COLDWATER, KAN.) (US) [10435159] **5679**

WESTERN STATE LIBRARY *See* ANNUAL REPORT - WESTERN STATE LIBRARY **3191**

WESTERN STATE, NIGERIA. MINISTRY OF ECONOMIC PLANNING AND RECONSTRUCTION. STATISTICS DIVISION *See* SUMMARY OF CURRENT INCOME TAX STATISTICS **4701**

WESTERN STATE UNIVERSITY LAW REVIEW (US/0362-8892) [03185162] **3073**

WESTERN STATES JEWISH HISTORY (US/0749-5471) [10139066] 5053, **2275**

WESTERN STATES WATER COUNCIL *See* WATER FOR WESTERN ENERGY DEVELOPMENT UPDATE **1960**

WESTERN STATES WATER COUNCIL *See* ANNUAL REPORT - WESTERN STATES WATER COUNCIL **5530**

● WESTERN STYLES (US/1075-8917) [30416616] **2550**

WESTERN TAX (US/0734-9904) [08871619] 4758, **3074**

WESTERN TAX REVIEW (US/8755-0083) [08571832] **4758**

WESTERN TEACHER (AT/0310-5369) [03105369] **1908**

WESTERN TIMES ANNUAL (II) [10590944] **4758**

WESTERN TIMES (SHARON SPRINGS, KAN. : 1934) (US) [12727165] **5679**

WESTERN TRAILS NEWSLETTER (US) **2477**

WESTERN TRUCK NEWS (CN/0229-6268) [08401420] **5399**

WESTERN VIKING (US) [02252104] **2275**

WESTERN WALLA WALLA COUNTY ARGUS (US) [17377436] **5763**

WESTERN WASHINGTON HORTICULTURAL ASSOCIATION *See* PROCEEDINGS OF THE ANNUAL MEETING, WESTERN WASHINGTON HORTICULTURAL ASSOCIATION **2429**

WESTERN WATER (US/0735-5424) [03813086] **5548**

WESTERN WEATHER (US/0890-0000) [14224940] 1364, **1437**

WESTERN WEEKLY REPORTS (CN/0049-7525) [01769774] **3074**

WESTERN WHEEL (CN/0701-1571) [03406505] **2550**

WESTERN WILDLANDS SUSPENDED. (US/0363-6690) [01781590] **2208**

WESTERN WIRE (US) [03172460] **5314**

WESTERN WOOD PRODUCTS ASSOCIATION *See* QUARTERLY INJURY & ILLNESS INCIDENCE REPORT **2868**

WESTERN WOOD PRODUCTS ASSOCIATION *See* BAROMETER (PORTLAND) **2399**

WESTERN WOOD PRODUCTS ASSOCIATION *See* MONTHLY F.O.B. PRICE SUMMARY PAST SALES. INLAND MILLS **2403**

WESTERN WORLD AVON COLLECTORS NEWSLETTER CEASED. (US/8750-295X) [11253930] **2779**

WESTERN WORLD REVIEW (US/0043-4299) [03498453] **3356**

WESTERNER, THE (US/0279-3628) [06800896] **1096**

WESTERNERS. SAN DIEGO CORRAL *See* WRANGLER **2766**

WESTEUROPA QUELLEN ZUM KRAFTFAHRZEUGMARKT (GW) [06211749] **5428**

WESTEUROPA : QUELLEN ZUM MARKT FUR ELEKTROHAUSGERATE (GW) [06550924] **2812**

WESTFAELISCHE ZEITSCHRIFT (GW/0083-9043) [07064955] **2715**

WESTFALEN (MUNSTER) (GW/0043-4337) [02180407] **2715**

WESTFALISCHE FORSCHUNGEN (GW/0083-9027) [02178877] **2715**

WESTFIELD ENTERPRISE (US) [13803764] **5668**

WESTFIELD LEADER, THE (US) [11958153] **5712**

WESTFIELD REPUBLICAN (US) [10035175] **5722**

WESTFIELD STATE COLLEGE *See* ALUMNI DIRECTORY / WESTFIELD STATE COLLEGE **1100**

WESTFORD EAGLE (US/0744-7957) [08560438] **5690**

WESTHOPE STANDARD (US) [01769779] **5726**

WESTIGAN REVIEW OF POETRY, THE (US) [03499185] **3356**

WESTIN (CN/0826-2349) [10862212] **2550**

WESTINDIAN DIGEST SUSPENDED. (UK/0143-6619) [07393426] **2525**

WESTINE REPORT (US/0749-6990) [11165739] **5772**

WESTIR'S WESTERN SYDNEY LETTER (AT/0726-0075) [07260075] **2511**

WESTLAKER TIMES, THE (US/0746-9802) [10442933] **5731**

WESTLAND EAGLE, THE (US/0192-6497) [05060877] **5694**

WESTMINISTER WINDOW (US) **5644**

WESTMINISTER RECORD (UK) **5009**

WESTMINSTER REVIEW (NEW WILMINGTON, PA.), THE (US/1057-9559) [24171731] **3453**

WESTMINSTER STUDIES IN EDUCATION (UK/0140-6728) [05039102] **1791**

WESTMINSTER THEOLOGICAL JOURNAL, THE (US/0043-4388) [01715830] **5009**

WESTMORELAND RECORDER (WESTMORELAND, KAN. : 1919) (US) [12378160] **5679**

WESTMORLAND HISTORICAL SOCIETY (N.B.) *See* NEWSLETTER - WESTMORLAND HISTORICAL SOCIETY **2750**

WESTMOUNT BULLETIN (1990) (CN/1184-017X) [23230849] **4695**

WESTMOUNT BULLETIN (1990) (CN/1184-017X) [23230856] **4695**

WESTON DEMOCRAT, THE (US) [11200866] **5765**

WESTON FORUM, THE (US) [28013693] **5646**

WESTON TIMES REVIEW (CN/0316-5434) [02247484] **2550**

WESTOSHA REPORT (US/0192-9356) [05135333] **5772**

WESTPAC MELBOURNE INSTITUTE OF INDEXES OF ECONOMIC ACTIVITY (AT) **1526**

WESTPREUSSE, DER (GW) [07897909] **2715**

WESTPREUSSEN-JAHRBUCH (GW/0511-8484) [02178857] **2715**

WEST'S ANNOTATED CALIFORNIA CODES (US) [01552414] **3074**

WEST'S ARIZONA DIGEST 2D LAW FINDER (US) [23200952] **3074**

● WEST'S ARIZONA LAW FINDER (US) [27599402] **3074**

WEST'S ATLANTIC DIGEST 2D (US) [02351098] **3074**

WEST'S BANKRUPTCY REPORTER (US/0199-5782) [05932198] **3088**

WEST'S CALIFORNIA REPORTER (US/8750-2623) [12427331] **3074**

WEST'S CALIFORNIA RULES OF COURT: STATE AND FEDERAL *See* CALIFORNIA RULES OF COURT. FEDERAL **3139**

WEST'S CRIMINAL LAW NEWS (US/8750-2607) [10812681] **3109**

WEST'S EDUCATION LAW DIGEST (US/0741-5346) [09337111] 1791, **3074**

WEST'S EDUCATION LAW REPORTER (US/0744-8716) [08458969] 1791, **3074**

WEST'S EDUCATION LAW REPORTER. SPECIAL PAMPHLET / NATIONAL ASSOCIATION OF COLLEGE AND UNIVERSITY ATTORNEYS (US) [09291901] 1853, **3074**

WEST'S FEDERAL CASE NEWS (US/0162-2005) [03858048] **3074**

WEST'S FEDERAL FORMS (US) [01604461] **3074**

WEST'S FEDERAL RULES DECISIONS (US/1048-4906) [17786688] **3074**

WEST'S FEDERAL TAX MANUAL WITH WESTLAW (US/0749-1034) [11078757] 4758, **3074**

WEST'S FEDERAL TAX SYSTEM (US/0277-5158) [07213870] 4758, **3074**

WEST'S FEDERAL TAXATION. CORPORATION, S CORPORATION, AND PARTNERSHIP PRACTICE SETS (US/1054-1918) [22730744] **719**

WEST'S FEDERAL TAXATION. CORPORATIONS, PARTNERSHIPS, ESTATES AND TRUSTS (US/0270-5265) [04973676] **4758**

WEST'S FEDERAL TAXATION. FEDERAL TAX FORMS (US/0741-532X) [10149072] **4758**

WEST'S FEDERAL TAXATION. INDIVIDUAL INCOME TAXES (US/0272-0329) [04973624] **4758**

WEST'S FEDERAL TAXATION. INDIVIDUAL PRACTICE SETS (US/1068-8943) [27817253] **4758**

WEST'S FEDERAL TAXATION. PRACTICE SETS *See* WEST'S FEDERAL TAXATION. INDIVIDUAL PRACTICE SETS **4758**

WEST'S FLORIDA DIGEST 2D (US) [11197376] **2550**

WEST'S ILLINOIS DECISIONS (US/8750-2615) [03081188] **3074**

WEST'S INDIANA DIGEST 2D LAW FINDER (US) [24487383] **3074**

WEST'S LOUISIANA SESSION LAW SERVICE (US/0148-1991) [03276536] **3074**

WEST'S LOUISIANA STATUTES ANNOTATED (US) [01642855] **3074**

WEST'S MCKINNEY'S FORMS (US) [02846652] **3074**

WEST'S MILITARY JUSTICE DIGEST (US/0272-9334) [06955932] **3183**

WEST'S MILITARY JUSTICE REPORTER (US/0147-7315) [03220026] **3183**

WEST'S MISSISSIPPI CASES REPORTED IN SOUTHERN REPORTER, SECOND SERIES (US/1053-5322) [22404037] **3074**

WEST'S NEW HAMPSHIRE DIGEST, 1760 TO DATE, COVERING CASES FROM STATE AND FEDERAL COURTS (US) [01642378] **3074**

WEST'S NEW JERSEY DIGEST (US) [02256461] **3074**

WEST'S NEW YORK SUPPLEMENT (US/1048-3624) [18498875] **3074**

WEST'S OKLAHOMA DECISIONS (US/1041-6730) [18765294] **3074**

WEST'S OREGON CASES REPORTED IN PACIFIC REPORTER, SECOND SERIES (US) [19898109] **3074**

WEST'S PERSONAL INJURY NEWS (US/0746-1526) [09485613] **3074**

WEST'S RHODE ISLAND DIGEST, 1783 TO DATE (US) [02250962] **3074**

WEST'S SOCIAL SECURITY REPORTING SERVICE. SOCIAL SECURITY CASES FROM U.S. SUPREME COURT, U.S. COURT OF APPEALS, U.S. DISTRICT COURTS, U.S. CLAIMS COURT, U.S. BANKRUPTCY COURTS, STATE APPELLATE COURTS (US) [10288522] 2896, **3074**

WEST'S SOUTH WESTERN REPORTER (US/1048-3780) [17592356] **3075**

WEST'S SOUTHERN REPORT (US/1048-3799) [17592899] **3075**

●WEST'S TAX LAW DICTIONARY (US) [26367323] 4758, **3075**

WEST'S VETERANS APPEALS REPORTER (US) [24947747] 3075, **4061**

WEST'S WYOMING DIGEST, A DIGEST OF WYOMING LEGAL AUTHORITIES, STATE AND FEDERAL (US) [01696435] **3075**

WESTSIDE ENTERPRISE, THE (US) [16459672] **5668**

●WESTSIDE GAZETTE. THURSDAY (US) **5651**

WESTSIDE MESSENGER (US/0891-2297) [14702908] **5731**

WESTVILLE INDICATOR (US) [13199196] **5668**

WESTWARD INTO NEBRASKA (US/0738-0380) [03974018] **2477**

WESTWAYS (US/0043-4434) [08439424] **5428**

WESTWIND (LOS ANGELES, CALIF.) (US/0508-6191) [03499220] **333**

WESTWIND WEATHER BULLETIN (UK) **1437**

WESTWORD (US/0194-7710) [03597337] **5644**

WESTWORD (EDMONTON) (CN/1184-678X) [24267022] **2925**

WESTWORDS (SAN MARINO, CALIF.) (US/1056-5531) [23737607] **2484**

WESTWORLD MAGAZINE (BRITISH COLUMBIA ED.) (CN/0843-3356) [20243216] **2495**

WETA (WASHINGTON, D.C.) (US/1041-2700) [18699656] **1143**

WETCHASAN SATTAWAPHAET (TH/0125-6491) [10890319] **5527**

WETENSCHAP EN SAMENLEVING (NE/0043-4442) [07818251] **146**

WETENSCHAPPELIJKE MEDEDELINGEN KNNV (NE) [05047104] **4174**

WETENSCHAPPELIJKE TIJDINGEN (BE) [06577441] **2715**

WETHERSFIELD POST (US) [27972842] **5646**

WETLANDS (AT/0725-0312) [I07250312] 558, **1361**

WETLANDS ECOLOGY AND MANAGEMENT (NE/0923-4861) [19330678] **2222**

WETLANDS : JOURNAL OF THE COAST AND WETLANDS SOCIETY (AT) [09883685] **2511**

WETLANDS RESEARCH UPDATE (US) [23850449] **2222**

WETLANDS (WILMINGTON, N.C.) (US/0277-5212) [07586818] 476, **2208**

WETTANK. WOMENS ECONOMIC THINK TANK (AT) **1526**

WETTBEWERB IN RECHT UND PRAXIS MIT KARTELLRECHT *See* WETTBEWERB IN RECHT UND PRAXIS : WRP **3104**

WETTBEWERB IN RECHT UND PRAXIS : WRP (GW/0172-049X) [07824949] **3104**

WETTER UND LEBEN (AU/0043-4450) [02776821] **1437**

WETTERAUER GESCHICHTSBLAETTER (GW/0509-6213) [02178850] **2715**

WETUMPKA HERALD, THE (US) [12038508] **5628**

WETZEL CHRONICLE (US) [13306335] **5765**

WEYBURN REVIEW [MICROFORM] (CN) [15504246] **5797**

WEYERHAEUSER SCIENCE SYMPOSIUM (US/0191-2984) [04848641] **2398**

WEYER'S FLOTTENASCHENBUCH (NORTH AMERICAN ED.) (US/0741-000X) [01666550] **4185**

WEYERS FLOTTENTASCHENBUCH (GW) [03200739] **4185**

WFCD COMMUNICATOR (CN/0822-8183) [10522273] **146**

WFS QUARTERLY (US/1071-1767) [16513825] 5568, **2293**

WG & L REAL ESTATE OUTLOOK *CEASED.* (US/0277-8475) [07641407] **4848**

WG & L TAX PLANNING ANNUAL (US/0898-9516) [17957866] **4758**

WG&L PENSION AND BENEFITS FACT BOOK *CEASED.* (US/1040-0036) [18287025] **919**

WG&L TAX PLANNING CHECKLISTS (US/1056-6554) [23763875] **4758**

●WGL TAX JOURNAL DIGEST, THE (US/1075-0223) [28328112] **4758**

WGO MONATSHEFTE FUER OSTEUROPAISCHES RECHT (GW/0042-9678) [01789857] **3075**

WHALEWATCHER (US/0273-4419) [05389549] 2208, **5600**

WHARTON AGRICULTURE SERVICE (US/0749-5854) [11129533] **146**

WHARTON ECONOMETRIC FORECASTING ASSOCIATES. MIDDLE EAST ECONOMIC SERVICE *See* DATA BANKS **4254**

WHARTON INTERNATIONAL AGRICULTURE SERVICE. LONG-TERM FORECAST (US/0749-579X) [11139021] **146**

WHARTON INTERNATIONAL AGRICULTURE SERVICE. MEDIUM TERM FORECAST (US/0749-5803) [11139009] **146**

WHARTON JOURNAL-SPECTATOR, THE (US/1076-7266) [14950389] **5756**

WHARTON LONG-TERM FORECAST *See* LONG-TERM FORECAST **1573**

WHARTON LONG-TERM FORECAST EXTENSION TO THE YEAR ... (US/0749-6494) [11147476] **1526**

WHARTON REPORT (UK/0950-1800) [I09501800] 719, **1207**

WHAT CAR? (UK) [01794825] **5428**

WHAT COLOR IS YOUR PARACHUTE? (US/8755-4658) [04603518] **4210**

WHAT DO I READ NEXT? (US/1052-2212) [22218965] **3256**

WHAT EVERY ENGINEER SHOULD KNOW (US/0892-4015) [07787128] **2001**

WHAT EVERY VETERAN SHOULD KNOW (US/0083-9108) [03342036] **4061**

WHAT HI-FI? (UK) **5320**

WHAT IT COSTS (US/0193-9718) [05273603] **2896**

WHAT IT COSTS TO RUN AN AGENCY (US) [04780988] **719**

WHAT KEYBOARD? (UK/0266-030X) [I0266030X] **4159**

WHAT MICRO? (UK/0264-441X) [I0264441X] **1273**

WHAT PC? (UK) **1273**

WHAT RESEARCH SAYS TO THE SCIENCE AND MATHEMATICS TEACHER (AT/1033-3738) [I10333738] 5169, 3541, **1908**

WHAT SATELLITE (UK/0956-2362) [I09562362] **1124**

WHAT THEY SAID (US/0512-5804) [00928164] **2633**

WHAT TO BUY (UK) **4214**

WHAT TO BUY FOR BUSINESS (UK/0265-296X) [I0265296X] **4214**

WHAT TO BUY FOR BUSINESS (U.S. ED.) (US/0886-6163) [08374446] **4214**

WHAT TO DO ABOUT PERSONNEL PROBLEMS IN NEW YORK STATE (US) [16786293] **948**

WHAT VIDEO? LONDON. 1980 (UK/0260-7530) [I02607530] **4079**

WHAT WHERE WHEN *See* SIOUXLAND EVENTS **4854**

WHAT'S AHEAD IN HUMAN RESOURCES (US) **948**

WHATS AHEAD IN PERSONNEL *See* WHAT'S AHEAD IN HUMAN RESOURCES **948**

WHAT'S BREWING (CN/0714-2056) [09340442] **2372**

WHAT'S BREWING? *CEASED.* (US/0279-9707) [07492374] **4929**

WHAT'S COOKING (CN/0702-7338) [03409613] **2793**

WHAT'S HAPPENING IN WASHINGTON (US/0732-8362) [08445430] **1874**

WHAT'S HAPPENING MAGAZINE (BELLEVILLE. 1991) (CN/1185-345X) [24690893] **389**

WHAT'S LINE (US/0882-472X) [11183803] 4395, **3256**

WHAT'S NEW FOR FAMILY FUN CENTERS (US) **719**

WHAT'S NEW IN ACCOUNTING CANADA (CN/0826-094X) [10785398] **753**

WHAT'S NEW IN ADVERTISING AND MARKETING (US/0043-4558) [02451607] **767**

WHAT'S NEW IN ARIZONA (US) **2550**

WHAT'S NEW IN BUILDING (UK) **631**

WHAT'S NEW IN BUILDING SINGAPORE (SI/0217-1260) [I02171260] **631**

WHAT'S NEW IN BUSINESS INFORMATION (UK/0952-7001) [I09527001] **719**

WHAT'S NEW IN COLLECTIVE BARGAINING NEGOTIATIONS & CONTRACTS (US/0190-5244) [02451609] **3155**

WHAT'S NEW IN COMPUTING *CEASED.* (UK/0262-2734) [I02622734] **1207**

WHAT'S NEW IN COMPUTING (SI) **1245**

WHAT'S NEW IN COMPUTING (AT) **1207**

WHAT'S NEW IN DESIGN (UK) 2001, **3489**

WHAT'S NEW IN ELECTRONICS (UK) **2085**

WHAT'S NEW IN ELECTRONICS EUROPE (UK) **2085**

WHAT'S NEW IN FARMING (UK) [04156546] **146**

WHAT'S NEW IN FOREST RESEARCH (NZ/0110-1048) [02255983] **2398**

WHAT'S NEW IN HOME ECONOMICS (US/0043-4590) [01769801] **2793**

WHAT'S NEW IN INDUSTRY (UK) **1631**

WHAT'S NEW IN INSTRUMENTATION (UK) **1221**

WHAT'S NEW IN MARKETING (UK/0269-2058) [I02692058] **938**

WHAT'S NEW IN PROCESSING (UK/0268-523X) [I0268523X] **1263**

WHAT'S NEW IN PUBLICATIONS (EDMONTON) (CN/0706-8662) [04520835] **427**

WHAT'S NEW IN SOLID STATE (AT) [01769802] **2085**

●WHAT'S NEW IN WELDING (CN/1191-9833) [27809707] **4023**

WHAT'S ON IN LONDON (UK) **5499**

WHAT'S ON VIDEO AND CINEMA *SUSPENDED.* (AT) [13563080] **4378**

WHAT'S WORKING (US) **719**

WHAT'S WORKING FOR NONPROFIT FUNDRAISING (US) **938**

WHAT'S WORKING IN PARENT INVOLVEMENT (US/1053-2609) [22495620] **1791**

WHEAT AUSTRALIA INTERNATIONAL (AT/0814-9267) [12821723] **191**

WHEAT, BARLEY AND TRITICALE ABSTRACTS (UK/0265-7880) [10719013] 204, **5178**

WHEAT GROWER (WASHINGTON, D.C.), THE (US/0882-9691) [06899199] **146**

WHEAT INFORMATION SERVICE (JA/0510-3517) [01769803] **146**

WHEAT LIFE (US/0043-4701) [03961807] **146**

WHEAT MARKET REPORT. PMR (UK) [02938951] **204**

WHEAT RIDGE JEFFERSON SENTINEL, THE (US/1060-5223) [24473938] **5644**

WHEATGROWER (REGINA) (CN/0829-4763) [13435716] **191**

WHEEL CLICKS (US/0043-4744) [04238102] **5438**

WHEEL EXTENDED, THE (JA) [01667782] **5399**

WHEEL-O-RAMA (US/0882-6676) [11910844] **5428**

WHEEL (SAN FRANCISCO, CALIF.) (US/0888-1103) [13506345] **5428**

WHEEL, THE (CE/0049-7541) [01781485] **5022**

WHEELER TIMES, THE (US) [14389634] **5756**

WHEELER'S DESERT LETTER (US/0164-629X) [04442106] 1526, **719**

●WHEELER'S INLAND EMPIRE (US/1064-1610) [26346999] 720, **1526**

WHEELERS RV RESORT & CAMPGROUND GUIDE (US/0194-0384) [05153068] **4880**

WHEELER'S TRAILER RESORT AND CAMPGROUND GUIDE. SUN BELT EDITION (US/0090-600X) [01785155] **4880**

WHEELING & TRANSMISSION MONTHLY (US) **952**

WHEELING LIFE (US/0192-0286) [05079498] **5662**

WHEELING NEWS-REGISTER (US) [02269511] **5765**

WHEELMEN, THE (US/0195-7023) [05535351] **429**

WHEELOCK COLLEGE *See* ALUMNI DIRECTORY / WHEELOCK COLLEGE **1100**

WHEELS (AUSTRALIA) (AT/0043-4779) **5399**

WHEELS (DETROIT, MICH.) (US/1047-3165) [11096469] **5428**

WHEELS ETC (US) **5399**

WHEELS — Alphabetical Title Index

WHEELS OF TIME (US/0738-565X) [07346571] **5399**

WHEELWRIGHTINGS (US/0192-5865) [05069220] **3453**

WHEN YOU GET SSI : WHAT YOU NEED TO KNOW (US) [25512797] **5314**

WHERE AMERICA'S LARGE FOUNDATIONS MAKE THEIR GRANTS *CEASED.* (US/0083-9167) [03214713] **2856**

WHERE CALGARY (CN/1182-1981) [23242632] **4867**

WHERE ROCKY MOUNTAINS (CN/0849-309X) [23238154] **2579**

WHERE THE TRAILS CROSS (US/0092-4164) [01788666] 5237, **2477**

WHERE TO BUY BUSINESS INFORMATION (UK/0967-6406) [I09676406] **720**

WHERE TO BUY CHEMICALS AND CHEMICAL PLANT (UK/0308-0021) **995**

WHERE TO BUY CONSTRUCTION & MAINTENANCE SERVICES FOR BUILDINGS *CEASED.* (UK/0268-6325) [16150863] **631**

WHERE TO EAT IN CANADA (CN/0315-3088) [02441769] **5073**

WHERE TO EAT IN HAMPSHIRE (UK) [16561338] **5073**

WHERE TO EAT IN SCOTLAND (UK) [20524540] **5073**

WHERE TO GO IN MINNEAPOLIS & ST. PAUL (US/0739-9693) [09840129] **5499**

WHERE TO LEARN ENGLISH IN GREAT BRITAIN (UK/0143-2214) [07398309] 1791, **3333**

● WHERE TO RETIRE (US/1060-0094) [24877864] **5182**

WHERE TO STAY IN SCOTLAND, BED AND BREAKFAST (UK) [07867100] 5499, **2810**

WHERE TO WRITE FOR VITAL RECORDS (US/0738-2340) [08738425] **2477**

WHERE VANCOUVER (CN/1180-9671) [23295930] **5499**

WHEREVER IN THE WORLD, FOR JESUS' SAKE (US/0889-0781) [04444598] **5009**

WHETSTONE (LETHBRIDGE) (CN/0318-1065) [03039952] 368, **3453**

WHICH CAMERA? (UK/0263-9106) [I02639106] **4378**

WHICH CD? (UK) [21438212] **1207**

WHICH COMPUTER? *CEASED.* (UK/0140-3435) [08546143] **1207**

WHICH EUROPEAN DATABASE? (UK/0960-5061) [I09605061] **1255**

WHICH? (LONDON) (UK/0043-4841) [04182393] **1300**

WHICH LONDON SCHOOL? (UK/0959-7271) [I09597271] **1791**

WHICH SCHOOL? (UK) [13563698] **1791**

● WHICH SCHOOL? FOR A LEVELS (UK) **1853**

● WHICH SCHOOL? FOR SPECIAL NEEDS (UK/0965-1004) [I09651004] **1886**

WHICH VAN? (UK/0267-1816) [I02671816] **5428**

WHICH? WAY TO HEALTH (UK/0957-1728) [I09571728] **2602**

WHIDBEY NEWS-TIMES (US/1060-7161) [17196050] **5763**

WHIDDEN LECTURES (UK/0083-9248) [01667821] **2856**

WHILLAN'S TAX TABLES (UK) **4758**

WHIPPET, THE (US/0164-6478) [04456577] **4288**

WHISKEY, WOMEN, AND ... *CEASED.* (US/0091-7664) [01788195] **4159**

WHISPERING WIND (US/0300-6565) [01355769] 2766, **2275**

WHISTLE PUNK (CN/0825-477X) [11240746] **2398**

WHISTLE (VANCOUVER) (CN/0227-0862) [08773950] **4929**

WHISTLER QUESTION (CN/0383-820X) [03230478] **5797**

WHITAKER'S BOOK LIST *CEASED.* (UK/0953-041X) [18148802] **427**

WHITAKER'S BOOKBANK CD-ROM SERVICE (UK/0951-8711) [I09518711] **3256**

WHITAKER'S BOOKS IN PRINT (UK/0953-0398) [18786493] **427**

WHITAKER'S BOOKS IN PRINT [MICROFORM] (UK/0953-0401) [17465245] **427**

WHITAKER'S BOOKS NOW OP. MICROFORM (UK) [18346150] **4833**

WHITAKER'S BOOKS OF THE MONTH & BOOKS TO COME *CEASED.* (UK/0043-4868) [01644150] **4833**

WHITAKER'S ISBN LISTING (UK/0265-7775) [18492688] **4833**

WHITAKER'S NEW AND FORTHCOMING BOOKS. [MICROFORM] (US) [28823490] **4833**

WHITAKER'S PUBLISHERS IN THE UNITED KINGDOM AND THEIR ADDRESSES (UK) [10399395] **4820**

WHITBY COMMUNITY SERVICES DIRECTORY (CN/1185-6238) [25066761] **5314**

WHITBY FREE PRESS (CN/0844-398X) [22570264] **5797**

WHITBY FREE PRESS (CN/0844-398X) [19747163] **5797**

WHITE BEAR PRESS, THE (US/0892-1326) [01587595] **5699**

WHITE BOOK OF SKI AREAS. U.S. AND CANADA, THE (US/0163-9684) [04543680] **4929**

WHITE COLLAR (US/0043-4876) [01589989] **1717**

WHITE-COLLAR CRIME REPORTER, THE (US/0891-6721) [14960487] **3179**

WHITE COLLAR MANAGEMENT *See* MANAGEMENT POLICIES AND PERSONNEL LAW **3151**

WHITE-COLLAR PAY. PRIVATE GOODS-PRODUCING INDUSTRIES (US) [22914814] **1718**

WHITE COUNTY HERITAGE (US/0043-4906) [02194893] **2766**

WHITE COUNTY RECORD (JUDSONIA, ARK.) (US/8750-5177) [11484615] **5632**

WHITE DWARF (UK/0265-8712) [I02658712] **2779**

WHITE FLOWER FARM *See* GARDEN BOOK / WHITE FLOWER FARM, THE **2415**

WHITE HOUSE FELLOWSHIPS, THE (US/0149-2837) [03173117] **4705**

WHITE HOUSE HISTORY (US/0748-8114) [10672536] **2633**

WHITE HOUSE NEWS PHOTOGRAPHERS ANNUAL AWARDS (US/0163-3430) [04336152] **4378**

WHITE HOUSE WEEKLY (US/0737-9218) [09476280] **2766**

WHITE LEADER, THE (US/0899-9805) [13555584] **5744**

WHITE LIGHT, THE (US/0742-8820) [10518080] **4243**

WHITE LIST OF CUSTOMS OFFICERS IN CANADA, THE *CEASED.* (CN/0703-5926) [04130185] **4695**

WHITE, NEW YORK CORPORATIONS: BCL, N-PCL AND RELATED STATUTES (US) [04407049] **3104**

WHITE PAPER ON INTERNATIONAL TRADE: JAPAN (JA) [01792741] 857, **735**

WHITE PAPER ON JAPANESE ECONOMY (JA) [02052957] **1588**

WHITE PAPER ON JAPANESE TRADE (JA) [05080233] **857**

WHITE PAPER ON TRANSPORTATION SAFETY IN JAPAN / TRAFFIC SAFETY POLICY OFFICE, PRIME MINISTER'S OFFICE (JA) [10063995] **5400**

WHITE PAPERS OF JAPAN (JA) [01064154] **1526**

WHITE PINE (US) [03500541] **3473**

WHITE RIVER JOURNAL (US) [20314254] **5632**

WHITE RIVER VALLEY HISTORICAL QUARTERLY (US/0510-372X) [04598153] **2766**

WHITE ROCKER (1990), THE (US/1049-3387) [21204451] **5756**

WHITE TOPS, THE (US/0043-499X) [03961947] **4867**

WHITE TRIANGLE NEWS (US/0164-5145) [04583786] **5237**

WHITE WALL REVIEW (CN/0712-8991) [11245886] **3453**

WHITE WING MESSENGER (US/0043-5007) [03967089] **5009**

WHITE WOLF MAGAZINE (US/0897-9391) [17671701] **4867**

WHITEACRE REPORT, THE (US) **631**

WHITECOURT FREE PRESS, THE (CN/0821-5553) [09670596] **5798**

WHITECOURT STAR (CN/0847-8597) [20665644] **5798**

WHITEFISH PILOT, THE (US) [13337044] **5706**

● WHITEHALL COMPANION, THE (UK) [27697780] **4695**

WHITEHALL TIMES (WHITEHALL, N.Y. : 1927) (US) [16955143] **5722**

WHITEHALL TIMES (WHITEHALL, WIS. : 1924) (US) [11985740] **5772**

WHITEMAN AND WHEATCROFT ON INCOME TAX *CEASED.* (UK) [02424098] **4758**

WHITEMAN ON CAPITAL GAINS TAX *CEASED.* (UK) **4758**

WHITESBORO NEWS *See* WHITESBORO NEWS-RECORD **5756**

WHITESBORO NEWS-RECORD (US) [14962193] **5756**

WHITESBORO RECORD *See* WHITESBORO NEWS-RECORD **5756**

WHITEWALLS (CHICAGO, ILL.) (US/0190-9835) [06741708] **368**

WHITEWOOD CENTENNIAL *See* LAWRENCE COUNTY CENTENNIAL **5744**

WHITEWRIGHT SUN, THE (US) [17542521] **5756**

WHITLEY REPUBLICAN, THE (US) [14217372] **5683**

WHITLOCK'S WESSEX (UK) [02550319] **2715**

WHITNEY MESSENGER, THE (US) [14950081] **5756**

WHITNEY REVIEW (US/0511-8824) [01645072] 368, **4097**

WHITSUN FOUNDATION *See* ANNUAL REPORT AND ACCOUNTS / THE WHITSUN FOUNDATION **1546**

WHITTIER DAILY NEWS (US/1069-2819) [27967112] **5641**

WHITTIER LAW REVIEW (US/0195-7643) [04596003] **3075**

WHITTIER NEWSLETTER (US/0511-8832) [01769818] 3356, **435**

WHIZ FUNNIES (CN/0229-0804) [08008231] **3453**

WHMIS HANDBOOK, THE (CN) **2871**

WHO AIDS SERIES (SZ/1011-5773) [17757295] **3677**

WHO AUDITS AMERICA (US/0149-0281) [03417295] **753**

WHO AUDITS AUSTRALIA? (1987) (AT/1035-2015) [I10352015] 4759, **753**

WHO DRUG INFORMATION (SZ/1010-9609) [16392428] **4332**

WHO DRUG REFERENCE LIST (SW) **4332**

WHO FOOD ADDITIVES SERIES (UK/0300-0923) [01786864] **2361**

WHO GOES WHERE (UK) [01784426] **5499**

WHO GOT IN? (US/1077-0739) [27764107] **1853**

WHO IS DOING WHAT IN HISTORIC PRESERVATION (CN/0229-1738) [06213896] **310**

WHO IS WHO (II) [01784213] **435**

WHO IS WHO, GOVERNMENT, POLITICS, BANKING AND INDUSTRY IN LATIN AMERICA *See* WHO'S WHO IN LATIN AMERICA (NEW YORK, N.Y.) **437**

WHO IS WHO IN KENYA (KE) [09136975] **435**

WHO IS WHO IN RECYCLING WORLDWIDE / TREND (SZ) [25175682] **2248**

WHO IS WHO (WAYNESVILLE, N.C.) (US/1055-0852) [23070597] **2183**

WHO KNOWS, A GUIDE TO WASHINGTON EXPERTS (US/0894-8801) [13592118] 720, **4695**

WHO KNOWS, A GUIDE TO WASHINGTON EXPERTS *See* WHO KNOWS WHAT, A GUIDE TO EXPERTS / BY WASHINGTON RESEARCHERS, LTD **4695**

● WHO KNOWS WHAT, A GUIDE TO EXPERTS / BY WASHINGTON RESEARCHERS, LTD (US) [30545736] 591, **4695**

WHO KNOWS WHO (US) **720**

WHO MAKES MACHINERY AND PLANT (GW) [19949148] **2132**

● WHO MAKES MACHINERY IN GERMANY (GW) [27875224] **2132**

● WHO OWNS CORPORATE AMERICA (US/1061-1258) [25184469] **919**

WHO OWNS WHAT IN WORLD BANKING *CEASED.* (UK) [03825480] **816**

● WHO OWNS WHOM (UK) [28573035] **720**

WHO OWNS WHOM: AUSTRALASIA AND FAR EAST (UK/0302-4091) [01792919] **720**

WHO OWNS WHOM: CONTINENTAL EUROPE (UK/0140-6582) [03742380] **720**

WHO OWNS WHOM. NORTH AMERICA (UK/0308-8502) [04246582] **720**

WHO OWNS WHOM: UNITED KINGDOM AND REPUBLIC OF IRELAND (UK/0140-4040) [03691966] **720**

WHO PAYS WHAT (CN/1193-6665) [27202863] **4820**

WHO PUT THE BOMP! (US/0039-7873) [02439003] **4159**

WHO REGIONAL PUBLICATIONS. EUROPEAN SERIES (DK/0378-2255) [02606799] **4807**

WHO? (SHERBROOKE) (CN/0700-9534) [03399849] **2766**

Alphabetical Title Index

WHO WAS WHO (US/0083-9345) [01589583] **435**

WHO WAS WHO, A COMPANION TO WHO'S WHO, CONTAINING THE BIOGRAPHIES OF THOSE WHO DIED (UK) [04049930] **435**

WHO WAS WHO IN AMERICA (US/0146-8081) [01713564] **435**

WHO WEEKLY (AT/1037-812X) [I1037812X] **2511**

WHO, WHAT, & WHERE IN COMMUNICATIONS SECURITY (US/0730-3033) [07979419] **1169**

WHO WRITES WHAT IN LIFE AND HEALTH INSURANCE (US/0363-1036) [03544729] **2896**

●WHODUZZIT? (NEW YORK, N.Y.) (US/1062-0427) [25512462] **4373**

WHOLE AGAIN RESOURCE GUIDE, THE (US/0734-9033) [08822837] **4621, 5265**

WHOLE ARTS DIRECTORY (US) [18474584] **333**

WHOLE CLASSROOM PUBLISHING GROUP *See* WHOLE CLASSROOM, THE **1791**

WHOLE CLASSROOM, THE (US/0193-3884) [05216651] **1791**

WHOLE EARTH NEWSLETTER (US/0361-1930) [01714777] **5009**

WHOLE EARTH REVIEW (US/0749-5056) [11128532] **2495**

WHOLE FOODS (US/0193-1504) [05122605] **2361**

WHOLE LIFE (US/0888-2061) [13611116] **4807**

WHOLE LIFE TIMES (US/0279-5604) [07097053] **4200**

WHOLE WORLD OIL DIRECTORY, THE *CEASED.* (US/0148-3609) [05210873] **4282**

WHOLESALE-BY-MAIL CATALOG, THE (US/1049-0116) [24488797] **767**

WHOLESALE DRUGS MAGAZINE (US/0743-3778) [05816421] **4332**

WHOLESALE PRICE AND ORDER SHEET / APPLEWOOD SEED CO (US) [12068617] **2433**

WHOLESALE PRICE LIST / BULK'S NURSERIES (US) [11967437] **2433**

WHOLESALE TRADE (CN/0380-7894) [02586000] **857**

WHOLESALE TRADE STATISTICS. WHOLESALE MERCHANTS, AGENTS AND BROKERS (CN/0823-1214) [11081579] **857**

WHOLESALER (ELMHURST), THE (US/0032-1680) [05052373] **2609**

WHOLESALER PRODUCTS CATALOG (US/0276-7813) [07409672] **631**

WHOM NEWSLETTER / WOMEN HISTORIANS OF THE MIDWEST (US/1046-1000) [02395120] **2633**

WHOOPER, THE (CN/0049-7592) [03520248] **2208**

WHOOT (US/8750-4057) [11382741] **2550**

WHOOT. CASINO GUIDE *See* WHOOT **2550**

WHO'S DOING WHAT? (US/1059-4175) [24583682] **2912**

WHO'S DRILLING (AT/0159-1878) [I01591878] 2153, **4282**

WHO'S INVENTING WHAT? (US/1049-8168) [21316010] **1309**

WHO'S MAILING WHAT! (US/8755-2671) [11258232] 938, **767**

WHO'S PEGGING (AT/0817-6353) 2153, **4282**

WHO'S PRINTING WHAT (DIRECTORY) (US/1057-803X) [24119108] **4570**

WHO'S PRINTING WHAT? (NEWSLETTER) (US/1056-6376) [23751284] **4570**

WHO'S WEALTHY IN AMERICA (US/1048-809X) [21067329] **720**

WHO'S WHAT IN FLORIDA GOVERNMENT (US) [01669958] **4695**

WHO'S WHO (UK) **435**

WHO'S WHO AMONG AMERICAN HIGH SCHOOL STUDENTS (US) [01940085] **436**

WHO'S WHO AMONG AMERICAN LAW STUDENTS (US/0278-6478) [07845638] **436, 3075**

WHO'S WHO AMONG BLACK AMERICANS (US/0362-5753) [02304283] **436**

WHO'S WHO AMONG BLACK WOMEN IN CALIFORNIA (US/0734-5720) [08752727] **436**

●WHO'S WHO AMONG HISPANIC AMERICANS (US/1052-7354) [22363965] **2275**

WHO'S WHO AMONG STUDENTS IN AMERICAN JUNIOR COLLEGES (US) [01769826] **436**

WHO'S WHO AMONG STUDENTS IN AMERICAN UNIVERSITIES AND COLLEGES (US) [02252109] **436**

WHO'S WHO AND GUIDE TO THE ELECTRICAL INDUSTRY (UK) [03572908] 2085, **436**

WHO'S WHO AT THE ABA (US/0191-8184) [04965318] **436**

WHO'S WHO AT THE FRANKFURT BOOK FAIR (GW) [05703332] 4820, **4833**

WHO'S WHO BUYERS GUIDE TO ELECTRONIC SOURCES (MIDWESTERN ED.) *See* WHO'S WHO ELECTRONICS BUYERS GUIDE (MIDWESTERN ED.) **2086**

WHO'S WHO BUYERS GUIDE TO ELECTRONIC SOURCES (MIDWESTERN ED.) (US/1057-6304) [24083478] **2085**

WHO'S WHO BUYERS GUIDE TO ELECTRONIC SOURCES (NORTHEASTERN ED.) *See* WHO'S WHO ELECTRONICS BUYERS GUIDE (NORTHEASTERN ED.) **2086**

WHO'S WHO BUYERS GUIDE TO ELECTRONIC SOURCES (NORTHEASTERN ED.) (US/1057-6347) [24083516] **2086**

WHO'S WHO BUYERS GUIDE TO ELECTRONIC SOURCES (SOUTHEASTERN ED.) *See* WHO'S WHO ELECTRONICS BUYERS GUIDE (SOUTHEASTERN ED.) **2086**

WHO'S WHO BUYERS GUIDE TO ELECTRONIC SOURCES (SOUTHEASTERN ED.) (US/1057-6339) [24083570] **2086**

WHO'S WHO BUYERS GUIDE TO ELECTRONIC SOURCES (SOUTHWESTERN ED.) *See* WHO'S WHO ELECTRONICS BUYERS GUIDE (SOUTHWESTERN ED.) **2086**

WHO'S WHO BUYERS GUIDE TO ELECTRONIC SOURCES (SOUTHWESTERN ED.) (US/1057-6320) [24083669] **2086**

WHO'S WHO (CHICAGO) (US/0148-3773) [03288647] **436**

WHO'S WHO, CHICANO OFFICEHOLDERS *SUSPENDED.* (US/0738-4637) [09573829] **436**

WHO'S WHO - COMMONWEALTH BROADCASTING ASSOCIATION (UK) [07041181] **1143**

WHO'S WHO DANS L'INDUSTRIE PHARMACEUTIQUE (FR) **4332**

WHO'S WHO DIRECTORY OF SPORTS, RECREATION AND PHYSICAL EDUCATION (CN/0229-611X) [10595536] **4929**

●WHO'S WHO ELECTRONICS BUYERS GUIDE (MIDWESTERN ED.) (US/1066-7601) [27043955] **2086**

●WHO'S WHO ELECTRONICS BUYERS GUIDE (NORTHEASTERN ED.) (US/1066-761X) [27044028] **2086**

●WHO'S WHO ELECTRONICS BUYERS GUIDE (SOUTHEASTERN ED.) (US/1066-7628) [27044146] **2086**

●WHO'S WHO ELECTRONICS BUYERS GUIDE (SOUTHWESTERN ED.) (US/1066-7644) [27044170] **2086**

WHO'S WHO, EUROPEAN COMMUNITIES AND OTHER EUROPEAN ORGANIZATIONS *See* EURO WHO'S WHO: WHO'S WHO IN THE EUROPEAN COMMUNITIES AND IN THE OTHER EUROPEAN ORGANIZATIONS **432**

WHO'S WHO FOR ACCU, A (JA) [09300925] **436**

WHO'S WHO GUIDE OF PETROCHEMICAL & PLASTICS COMPANIES (US) [22379184] **4282, 4461**

WHO'S WHO IN AMERICA (US/0083-9396) [01141571] **436**

WHO'S WHO IN AMERICA (JUNIOR & SENIOR HIGH SCHOOL VERSION) (US/1049-8540) [21316000] **427**

WHO'S WHO IN AMERICAN ART (US/0000-0191) [01607194] **335**

WHO'S WHO IN AMERICAN EDUCATION (OWINGS MILLS, MD.) (US/1046-7203) [18482532] 436, **1791**

WHO'S WHO IN AMERICAN LAW (US/0162-7880) [03473804] 436, **3075**

WHO'S WHO IN AMERICAN LAW ENFORCEMENT (US/0277-3511) [07036539] **436**

WHO'S WHO IN AMERICAN POLITICS (US/0000-0205) [01135742] 4695, **436**

WHO'S WHO IN AMERICA'S RESTAURANTS (US/0743-6122) [10623102] **436**

WHO'S WHO IN ASIAN AND AUSTRALASIAN POLITICS (UK) [24801756] **4500**

WHO'S WHO IN ASSOCIATION MANAGEMENT (US/0360-7038) [01738546] **436**

WHO'S WHO IN ATHLETICS IN AMERICAN COLLEGES AND UNIVERSITIES (US/1044-9906) [19964219] 1853, **4929**

WHO'S WHO IN ATHLETICS IN AMERICAN HIGH SCHOOLS (US/1049-9229) [21354244] **436**

●WHO'S WHO IN ATHLETICS IN AMERICAN JUNIOR COLLEGES (US/1049-9237) [21354260] **436**

WHO'S WHO IN AUSTRALASIA AND THE FAR EAST *CEASED.* (UK) [19621375] **436**

WHO'S WHO IN AUSTRALIA (AT) [08961714] **436**

WHO'S WHO IN AUSTRIA (IT) **436**

WHO'S WHO IN BLACK CORPORATE AMERICA (US/0277-5336) [07586656] **436**

WHO'S WHO IN BLACK DENTISTRY IN AMERICA (US) [18424519] **1337**

WHO'S WHO IN CALIFORNIA (1956) (US/0511-8948) [03507572] **436**

WHO'S WHO IN CALIFORNIA BUSINESS AND FINANCE (US/0195-539X) [05509763] 720, **436**

WHO'S WHO IN CANADIAN BUSINESS (CN/0227-3411) [07821141] **436**

WHO'S WHO IN CANADIAN HOLSTEIN SIRES (CN) **224**

WHO'S WHO IN CANADIAN LITERATURE (CN/0715-9366) [10380751] 436, **3453**

WHO'S WHO IN CHIROPRACTIC, INTERNATIONAL *SUSPENDED.* (US/0147-8265) [03234916] **436**

WHO'S WHO IN COLLECTIBLES AND ANTIQUES (US/1043-8173) [19566819] **252**

WHO'S WHO IN COMPUTERS AND DATA PROCESSING (US) [01588039] **1263**

WHO'S WHO IN COMPUTING (UK) [02244346] **436**

WHO'S WHO IN COMPUTING (EASTERN EDITION) *See* WHO'S WHO (PQ/ATLANTIC ED.) **1263**

WHO'S WHO IN COMPUTING (WESTERN EDITION) *See* WHO'S WHO (WESTERN CANADA ED.) **1263**

WHO'S WHO IN CONSUMER ELECTRONICS (US/0883-7317) [12223912] **436**

WHO'S WHO IN COSTA RICA (CR) [05929426] **436**

WHO'S WHO IN DENTAL TECHNOLOGY (US) [30899094] **1337**

WHO'S WHO IN DIRECT MARKETING CREATIVE SERVICES (US) [17640941] **938**

WHO'S WHO IN DISPLAY HOLOGRAPHY (US/0161-3669) [03905431] **436**

WHO'S WHO IN ECOLOGY (US/0091-3154) [01784437] **436**

WHO'S WHO IN ELECTRONIC COMMERCE (US) **1207**

WHO'S WHO IN ELECTRONICS SOURCES (MIDWESTERN ED.) *See* WHO'S WHO BUYERS GUIDE TO ELECTRONIC SOURCES (MIDWESTERN ED.) **2085**

WHO'S WHO IN ELECTRONICS SOURCES (NORTHEASTERN ED.) *See* WHO'S WHO BUYERS GUIDE TO ELECTRONIC SOURCES (NORTHEASTERN ED.) **2086**

WHO'S WHO IN ELECTRONICS SOURCES (SOUTHEASTERN ED.) *See* WHO'S WHO BUYERS GUIDE TO ELECTRONIC SOURCES (SOUTHEASTERN ED.) **2086**

WHO'S WHO IN ELECTRONICS SOURCES (SOUTHWESTERN ED.) *See* WHO'S WHO BUYERS GUIDE TO ELECTRONIC SOURCES (SOUTHWESTERN ED.) **2086**

WHO'S WHO IN ENGINEERING (NEW YORK. 1977) (US/0149-7537) [03534794] 2001, **436**

WHO'S WHO IN ENTERTAINMENT *CEASED.* (US/1044-0887) [19003710] **335**

●WHO'S WHO IN EUROPEAN INSTITUTIONS AND ENTERPRISES (SZ) [27902165] **4500**

WHO'S WHO IN EUROPEAN INSTITUTIONS, ORGANIZATIONS, AND ENTERPRISES (IT) [12679535] **4500**

WHO'S WHO IN EUROPEAN INTEGRATION STUDIES (GW) [20782281] **1526**

WHO'S WHO IN FASHION (SZ) [09264741] **1088**

WHO'S WHO IN FEDERAL GOVERNMENT DIRECTORY (AT) **4695**

WHO'S WHO IN FEDERAL GOVERNMENT PRIME CONTRACTORS (US/0882-0260) [11718566] 4695, **437**

WHO'S WHO IN FINANCE AND INDUSTRY (US/0083-9523) [01228020] 437, **720**

WHO'S WHO IN FLORICULTURE (US/0511-8964) [02784243] **437**

WHO'S WHO IN FLORIDA (US/0094-7784) [01784468] **437**

WHO'S WHO IN FRANCE (FR/0083-9531) [01604694] **437**

WHO'S WHO IN FRESNO (US/0364-7196) [02658606] **437**

WHO'S WHO IN GEORGIA (US/0093-1233) [01784463] **437**

WHO'S WHO IN GOLF COURSE MANAGEMENT : DIRECTORY & SOURCE BOOK (US) [13152652] **4929**

WHO'S WHO IN GRAPHIC ART (SZ) [01672907] **382**, **437**

WHO'S WHO IN HR (US/1047-3130) [20665286] **948**, **437**

WHO'S WHO IN INDIA (BOMBAY, INDIA) (II) [12533614] **437**

WHO'S WHO IN INDIAN ENGINEERING & INDUSTRY (II) [03762095] **437**

WHO'S WHO IN INDIAN RELICS (US/0747-7538) [08185183] **2275**, **437**

WHO'S WHO IN INDIAN SCIENCE (II) [01639007] **437**

WHO'S WHO IN INSURANCE (US/0083-9574) [01769837] **437**

WHO'S WHO IN INTELLECTUAL PROPERTY (US/0899-1766) [18010261] **1309**

WHO'S WHO IN INTERIOR DESIGN (US/0897-5914) [17559770] **2904**

WHO'S WHO IN INTERIOR LANDSCAPING (US/0733-2440) [08016394] **437**

WHO'S WHO IN INTERNATIONAL AFFAIRS *SUSPENDED*. (UK) [23182965] **4538**

WHO'S WHO IN INTERNATIONAL BANKING (UK) [12565591] **816**

WHO'S WHO IN IRAN / [IRAN RESEARCH GROUP] (GW) [21487104] **437**

WHO'S WHO IN LANDSCAPE CONTRACTING (1979) (US/0730-7225) [07312579] **2433**

●WHO'S WHO IN LATIN AMERICA (NEW YORK, N.Y.) (US/1068-7696) [27827184] **437**

WHO'S WHO IN LEBANON (LE/0083-9612) [01586183] **437**

WHO'S WHO IN LIVE ANIMAL TRADE & TRANSPORT (US/1042-2633) [18980966] **224**

WHO'S WHO IN LOCAL GOVERNMENT MANAGEMENT (US) [12484013] **889**

WHO'S WHO IN MALAYSIA & SINGAPORE (PETALING JAYA, SELANGOR) (MY/0217-1910) [10921939] **2509**, **437**

WHO'S WHO IN MEDICINE (GW) **437**

WHO'S WHO IN MUSIC (TUSCALOOSA) (US/0191-264X) [04819190] **437**

WHO'S WHO IN NATIONAL ATHLETICS HIGH SCHOOL FOOTBALL (US/0094-954X) [01795990] **437**

WHO'S WHO IN NEW ZEALAND (NZ) [05254294] **437**

WHO'S WHO IN NORTH CAROLINA (US/0093-4178) [01784466] **437**

WHO'S WHO IN NORTH DAKOTA (US/0742-6038) [10386173] **437**

WHO'S WHO IN P/M (US/0361-6304) [02170276] **437**

●WHO'S WHO IN PHOTOGRAPHY (PLYMOUTH, VT.) (US/1052-4037) [22283988] **4378**

WHO'S WHO IN PIPELINING (US) **4282**

WHO'S WHO IN PIPELINING (US/0742-020X) [10232243] **437**

WHO'S WHO IN POLAND (ZURICH, SWITZERLAND) (SZ) [09270335] **437**

WHO'S WHO IN PROFESSIONAL PEST CONTROL (US/0272-4219) [06782357] **4248**, **437**

WHO,S WHO IN PROFESSIONAL PHOTOGRAPHY (US/1048-2563) [18462083] **4378**

WHO'S WHO IN RAILROADING IN NORTH AMERICA *CEASED*. (US) [01773007] **437**

WHO'S WHO IN RELIGION (US/0160-3728) [02393813] **437**, **5009**

WHO'S WHO IN RICHMOND BUSINESS (US/0198-6953) [05200224] **437**

WHO'S WHO IN RISK MANAGEMENT (US) [03972062] **2896**, **437**

WHO'S WHO IN SAUDI ARABIA (SU) [03583153] **437**

WHO'S WHO IN SCANDINAVIA (GW) [08075207] **437**

●WHO'S WHO IN SCIENCE AND ENGINEERING (US/1063-5599) [25646125] **437**, **5169**

WHO'S WHO IN SCOTLAND (UK) [23926537] **437**

WHO'S WHO IN SINGAPORE (SI) [08010012] **437**

WHO'S WHO IN SPECIAL LIBRARIES (US/0278-842X) [07593795] **3256**, **437**

WHO'S WHO IN STAINED GLASS (US/0742-6321) [10379591] **437**

WHO'S WHO IN STEEL AND METALS (US/0511-9049) [01189048] **4023**, **438**

WHO'S WHO IN SWITZERLAND, INCLUDING THE PRINCIPALITY OF LIECHTENSTEIN (SZ/0083-9736) [01606220] **438**

WHO'S WHO IN SYSTEMS (ONTARIO ED.) *See* WHO'S WHO (ONTARIO ED.) **1263**

WHO'S WHO IN TEXAS (US/0094-6680) [01784501] **438**

WHO'S WHO IN THAILAND (TH) [01788083] **438**

WHO'S WHO IN THE ARAB WORLD (LE/0083-9752) [01604140] **438**

WHO'S WHO IN THE ARTS (GW) [03348335] **438**

WHO'S WHO IN THE ARTS AND LITERATURE (GW/0722-916X) [11479293] **333**, **3453**

WHO'S WHO IN THE CITY / STOCK EXCHANGE PRESS (UK/0956-3016) [20243848] **816**, **920**

WHO'S WHO IN THE COSMETIC INDUSTRY (US) [04697734] **438**

WHO'S WHO IN THE DENTAL LABORATORY INDUSTRY (US/0195-6221) [04717442] **1337**

WHO'S WHO IN THE EAST (US/0083-9760) [01769843] **438**

WHO'S WHO IN THE EGG AND POULTRY INDUSTRIES IN THE UNITED STATES AND CANADA (US/1044-5528) [16448360] **224**

WHO'S WHO IN THE EMERGENCY & RESCUE SERVICES (UK) **4807**

WHO'S WHO IN THE FISH INDUSTRY (US/0270-160X) [06348923] **2316**

WHO'S WHO IN THE FISH INDUSTRY, CANADA (US/1040-7804) [18525080] **2316**

WHO'S WHO IN THE FISH INDUSTRY, CENTRAL & SOUTH AMERICA (US/1064-931X) [26464020] **2316**

●WHO'S WHO IN THE INTERNATIONAL PERSONNEL MANAGEMENT ASSOCIATION (US/1064-1653) [25985054] **948**

WHO'S WHO IN THE LABOUR MOVEMENT (MY) [02510139] **438**

WHO'S WHO IN THE MIDWEST (US/0083-9787) [01142593] **438**

WHO'S WHO IN THE MOTION PICTURE INDUSTRY (US/0278-6516) [07845742] **438**

●WHO'S WHO IN THE PEACE CORPS (US/1065-8459) [26776897] **438**

WHO'S WHO IN THE PICTURE FRAMING INDUSTRY (US/0147-2119) [03118033] **958**, **438**

WHO'S WHO IN THE SECURITIES INDUSTRY (US/0090-418X) [01785214] **438**

WHO'S WHO IN THE SOUTH AND SOUTHWEST (US/0083-9809) [01157737] **438**

WHO'S WHO IN THE STONE BUSINESS (US/0884-0229) [12180593] **631**

WHO'S WHO IN THE WATER INDUSTRY. YEARBOOK (UK) **438**, **5548**

WHO'S WHO IN THE WEST (1971) (US/0896-7709) [05282690] **438**

WHO'S WHO IN THE WORLD (US/0083-9825) [01133198] **438**

WHO'S WHO IN TOBACCO / CONFECTIONERY DISTRIBUTION (US/0734-208X) [08671992] **438**

WHO'S WHO IN TRAINING AND DEVELOPMENT (US/0092-4598) [01789772] **438**

WHO'S WHO IN TRINIDAD AND TOBAGO (TR) [01792947] **438**

WHO'S WHO IN U.S. BUSINESS IN AUSTRALIA (AT) [02600539] **857**

WHO'S WHO IN UNITED STATES POLITICS AND AMERICAN POLITICAL ALMANAC (US) [02488952] **4500**, **438**

WHO'S WHO IN WASHINGTON (US/0732-5673) [08384574] **438**

WHO'S WHO IN WEST VIRGINIA (CLARKSBURG, W. VA.) (US/0742-8510) [10441867] **438**

WHO'S WHO IN WESTERN EUROPE *CEASED*. (UK) [07749817] **438**

WHO'S WHO IN WORLD PETROCHEMICAL & PLASTICS (US) [22334494] **438**

WHO'S WHO IN WORLD PETROCHEMICALS *See* WHO'S WHO IN WORLD PETROCHEMICAL & PLASTICS **438**

WHO'S WHO IN WRITERS, EDITORS & POETS, UNITED STATES & CANADA (US/1049-8621) [20974776] **427**

WHO'S WHO, JAMAICA (JM) [10346984] **438**

WHO'S WHO (LONDON. 1849) (UK/0083-937X) [01162806] **438**

WHO'S WHO OF AMERICAN BUSINESS LEADERS (US/1056-6147) [23747751] **720**

WHO'S WHO OF AMERICAN HIGH SCHOOL BASKETBALL COACHES (US/1040-7464) [18516684] **438**, **4929**

WHO'S WHO OF AMERICAN WOMEN (US/0083-9841) [01111931] **5568**, **438**

WHO'S WHO OF AUSTRALIAN WRITERS (AT) **438**, **3453**

WHO'S WHO OF CALIFORNIA EXECUTIVE WOMEN (US/0748-0601) [10881426] **438**

WHO'S WHO OF CANADIAN WOMEN *CEASED*. (CN/0823-5015) [10638808] **439**

WHO'S WHO OF COMMONWEALTH UNIVERSITY VICE-CHANCELLORS, PRESIDENTS AND RECTORS *See* WHO'S WHO OF VICE-CHANCELLORS, PRESIDENTS AND RECTORS OF COMMONWEALTH UNIVERSITIES **1853**

WHO'S WHO OF CONSUMER CREDIT MANAGEMENT, A (US/0512-5847) [03818529] **439**

WHO'S WHO OF EMERGING LEADERS IN AMERICA *CEASED*. (US/0895-965X) [16395697] **439**

WHO'S WHO OF SOUTHERN AFRICA (SA) [01769850] **439**

●WHO'S WHO OF THE ASIAN PACIFIC RIM (US/1059-5392) [24622774] **2509**

●WHO'S WHO OF VICE-CHANCELLORS, PRESIDENTS AND RECTORS OF COMMONWEALTH UNIVERSITIES (UK) [29660220] **1853**

WHO'S WHO (ONTARIO ED.) (CN/1193-073X) [I1193073X] **1263**

●WHO'S WHO (PQ/ATLANTIC ED.) (CN/1193-3593) [27019156] **1263**

WHO'S WHO, SARAWAK (MY) [11628981] **439**

●WHO'S WHO (WESTERN CANADA ED.) (CN/1193-3607) [27019154] **1263**

WHO'S WHO WORLDWIDE REGISTRY (US/1056-6708) [23845020] **439**

WHRO MAGAZINE (US/1058-9384) [24438901] **1143**

WHSTC LIBRARY CATALOG (CN/0712-9297) [09670591] **3256**

WHY ECONOMIC POLICIES CHANGE COURSE (FR) **1596**

WHY? MAGAZINE (CN/0710-3492) [08934607] **1806**

WHY - WORLD HUNGER YEAR (US/1046-7548) [20480901] **2912**

●WI CPA (US/1062-2209) [24986040] **753**

WIADOMOSCI ARCHEOLOGICZNE (PL/0043-5082) [02184264] **285**

WIADOMOSCI BOTANICZNE (PL/0043-5090) [02778401] **530**

WIADOMOSCI CHEMICZNE (PL/0043-5104) [04163896] **995**

WIADOMOSCI EKOLOGICZNE (PL/0013-2969) [01769853] **2222**

WIADOMOSCI HISTORYCZNE (PL/0511-9162) [05146227] **2633**

WIADOMOSCI HUTNICZE (PL/0043-5139) [11466070] **4023**

WIADOMOSCI HUTNICZE *See* HUTNIK, WIADOMOSCI HUTNICZE **4003**

WIADOMOSCI INSTYTUTU MELORACJI I UZYTKOW ZIELONYCH (PL/0509-6677) [11449962] **2001**

WIADOMOSCI INSTYTUTU METEOROLOGII I GOSPODARKI WODNEJ (PL/0208-6263) [07355622] **1419**, **1437**

WIADOMOSCI LEKARSKIE (1960) (PL/0043-5147) [11465555] **3651**

WIADOMOSCI MELIORACYJNE I LAKARSKIE (PL/0510-4262) [04164512] **3651**

WIADOMOSCI NUMIZMATYCZNE (PL) [05907219] **2783**

WIADOMOSCI PARAZYTOLOGICZNE (PL/0043-5163) [02844792] **571**

WIADOMO'SCI POLSKIE (US) [05686667] **2275**

WIADOMOSCI SPORTOWE (PL/0137-8112) [I01378112] **4929**

WIADOMOSCI STATYSTYCZNE (WARSAW, POLAND : 1956) (PL) [11625376] **5346**

WIADOMOSCI TYTONIOWE (PL) [04164568] **5374**

WIADOMOSCI ZIELARSKIE (PL/0137-3838) [04164598] **146**

WIBAUX PIONEER-GAZETTE, THE (US) [12756999] **5706**

WICAZO SA REVIEW (US/0749-6427) [11166842] **2766**

WICHE REPORTS ON HIGHER EDUCATION IN THE WEST (US) [06167277] **1853**

WICHITA BUSINESS JOURNAL (US/0894-4032) [13545829] **720**

WICHITA COMMERCE *CEASED*. (US/1048-8782) [21058206] **857**

WILDLIFE

WICHITA EAGLE (1989), THE (US/1046-3127) [20386511] **5679**

WICHITA JOURNAL (US/1048-3365) [12650159] **5679**

WICKS SUBJECT INDEX TO COMMONWEALTH LEGISLATION (AT) [20786179] **3075**

WIDE ANGLE (US/0160-6840) [02757185] **4080**

WIDE AREA COMMUNICATIONS (UK) **1124**

WIDE-SCREEN *See* 35/70: JOURNAL OF THE FEATURE FILM INDUSTRY **4062**

WIDE SMILES (US/1056-7402) [23841292] **5314**

WIDE WORLD OF CANOEING (US/0273-0111) [06964275] **597**

WIDE WORLD OF TAXIDERMY *See* TAXIDERMY REVIEW **2778**

●WIDENER JOURNAL OF PUBLIC LAW (US/1064-5012) [26319717] **3075**

WIDENING HORIZONS (UK/0049-7614) [02253030] **5568**

WIDER WORKING PAPERS (FI/0782-8233) [17869174] **1588**

WIDERSPRUCH (SZ) [08598754] **4548**

WIDERSPRUCH. SONDERBAND (SZ) [21016314] **4548**

WIDEWORLD OXFORD (UK/0956-5353) [l09565353] **2495**

WIDYA (MY) [01790713] **2509**

WIDYAPURA (IO) [05810040] **2839**

WIECZOR KATOWICE (PL/0137-9364) [l01379364] **5808**

WIECZOR WROCAWIA (PL/0137-9372) [l01379372] **5808**

WIECZOR WYBRZEZA (PL/0137-9380) [l01379380] **5808**

WIEDERHALL (NE/0920-1629) [22340453] **310**

WIEDZA I ZYCIE (PL) [05394386] **2525**

WIEDZA OBRONNA : DWUMIESIECZNIK TOWARZYSTWA WIEDZY OBRONNEJ (PL/0209-0031) [09850668] **4061**

WIEK OSWIECENIA (PL) [06034760] **2715**

WIEL (SA/0257-5426) [l02575426] **5428**

WIELAND-STUDIEN (GW) [23888232] **3453**

WIEN AKTUELL (AU/0043-5279) [01788375] **2525**

WIEN KURIER (AU) **5778**

WIENER (GW) **2495**

WIENER ABENDPOST (AU) [20448527] **5778**

WIENER ARBEITEN ZUR DEUTSCHEN LITERATUR (AU) [01682382] **3453**

WIENER ARCHIV FUR GESCHICHTE DES SLAWENTUMS UND OSTEUROPAS (AU) [01605539] **2715**

WIENER BEITRAEGE ZUR ENGLISCHEN PHILOLOGIE (AU/0083-9914) [01587192] **3333**

WIENER BEITRAGE ZUR KULTURGESCHICHTE UND LINGUISTIK (AU/0083-9922) [01769857] **3333**, **247**

WIENER BEITRAGE ZUR THEOLOGIE (AU) [01769858] **5009**

WIENER ETHNOHISTORISCHE BLATTER (AU) [02184254] **247**

WIENER ETHNOHISTORISCHE BLATTER. BEIHEFT (AU) [03201729] **247**

WIENER GEOGRAPHISCHE SCHRIFTEN (AU/0083-9957) [01769861] **2579**

WIENER GESCHICHTSBLATTER (AU/0043-5317) [01769862] **2716**

WIENER HUMANISTISCHE BLATTER (AU/0083-9965) [02184245] **1081**

WIENER JAHRBUCH FUR PHILOSOPHIE (AU/0083-999X) [02191354] **4365**

WIENER KLINISCHE WOCHENSCHRIFT (AU/0043-5325) [01587509] **3651**

WIENER KLINISCHE WOCHENSCHRIFT. SUPPLEMENTUM (AU/0300-5178) [01587970] **3651**

WIENER LIBRARY *See* WIENER LIBRARY BULLETIN, THE **3256**

WIENER LIBRARY BULLETIN, THE **SUSPENDED.** (UK/0043-5333) [01586579] **3256**

WIENER LINGUISTISCHE GAZETTE (GW) [02859672] **3333**

WIENER MEDIZINISCHE WOCHENSCHRIFT (AU/0043-5341) [01695447] **3651**

WIENER MITTEILUNGEN, WASSER, ABWASSER, GEWASSER (AU/0379-5349) [11009464] **5549**

WIENER MUSIKWISSENSCHAFTLICHE BEITRAGE (AU/0511-9294) [01682634] **4159**

WIENER RICHTER, DER (AU) [10640966] **3143**

WIENER SLAVISTISCHES JAHRBUCH (AU/0084-0041) [01641976] **3333**

WIENER SLAWISTISCHER ALMANACH (GW/0258-6819) [04668662] **3333**

WIENER STADTWERKE *See* GESCHAFTSBERICHT **4650**

WIENER STUDIEN (AU/0084-005X) [01160436] **3333**

WIENER STUDIEN (AU) [07110166] **2716**

WIENER TAG, DER (AU) [20360860] **5778**

WIENER TIERARZTLICHE MONATSSCHRIFT (AU/0043-535X) [01696180] **5527**

WIENER VOLKERKUNDLICHE MITTEILUNGEN (AU/0084-0068) [02191440] **247**

WIENER WIRTSCHAFTS- UND FINANZWISSENSCHAFTLICHE UNTERSUCHUNGEN (GW) [03201749] **1526**

WIENER WIRTSCHAFTS-WOCHE (AU) [20070782] **5778**

WIENER ZEITSCHRIFT FUER DIE KUNDE DES MORGENLANDES (AU/0084-0076) [01589789] **3333**, **2633**

WIENER ZEITSCHRIFT FUER SUCHTFORSCHUNG (AU/0250-4936) [06409144] **1350**

WIENER ZEITSCHRIFT FUR DIE KUNDE SUDASIENS UND ARCHIV FUR INDISCHE PHILOSOPHIE (NE/0084-0084) [01780637] **4365**

WIES I PANSTWO (PL/1230-0659) [l12300659] **146**

WIES WSPOCZESNA; PISMO RUCHU LUDOWEGO (PL/0511-9375) [02771384] **5265**

WIESENBERGER MUTUAL FUNDS INVESTMENT REPORT *See* CDA/WIESENBERGER MUTUAL FUNDS UPDATE **894**

WIEZ (PL) [12853626] **5009**

WIGGINS ENTERPRISE *See* STONE COUNTY ENTERPRISE **5702**

WIJSGERIG PERSPECTIEF OP MAATSCHAPPIJ EN WETENSCHAP (NE) [17966823] **4365**

WIK. ZEITSCHRIFT FUER WIRTSCHAFT, KRIMINALITAT UND SICHERHEIT (GW/0935-5758) [l09355758] **720**, **5177**

WILBUR REGISTER, THE (US) [17319591] **5763**

WILCOX PROGRESSIVE ERA (US) [16693875] **5628**

WILD BLUEBERRY GROWER (US/0890-3786) [14227185] **2433**

WILD CAT (UK) [05704291] **2208**

WILD EARTH (US/1055-1166) [23077499] **2183**

WILD FLOWER NOTES / NEW ENGLAND WILD FLOWER SOCIETY (US) [13449396] **2433**

WILD FOREST REVIEW (US/1074-3650) [29690306] **2398**

WILD GOOSE ASSOCIATION *See* RADIONAVIGATION JOURNAL **4182**

WILD GOOSE ASSOCIATION. TECHNICAL SYMPOSIUM *See* PROCEEDINGS OF THE ANNUAL TECHNICAL SYMPOSIUM - WILD GOOSE ASSOCIATION. TECHNICAL SYMPOSIUM **2202**

WILD OATS (WINNIPEG) (CN/1185-2194) [24570930] **204**

WILD OREGON (US) [06676863] **2208**

WILD PRAHRAN (AT/1030-469X) [l1030469X] **4880**

WILD ROSE CHRONICLE (CN/0706-5094) [04518985] **5798**

●WILD STEELHEAD AND ATLANTIC SALMON (US/1072-558X) [29009737] **4855**

WILD WEST (LEESBURG, VA.) (US/1046-4638) [18654422] **2766**

WILDBIRD (US/0892-5534) [15214312] **5621**

WILDE TIMES (CN/0712-4279) [08720642] **2796**

WILDERNESS (AT) **2208**

WILDERNESS ALBERTA (CN/0830-8284) [15483187] **4174**, **2209**

WILDERNESS ARTS AND RECREATION (1977) (CN/0705-3150) [03890114] **4880**

WILDERNESS MEDICINE LETTER : THE OFFICIAL NEWSLETTER OF THE WILDERNESS MEDICAL SOCIETY (US) [23110559] **4880**, **3651**

WILDERNESS NEWS *See* WILDERNESS **2208**

WILDERNESS RECORD (US/0194-3030) [05469611] **2209**

●WILDERNESS SERIES (US/1056-3318) [23664193] **4880**

WILDERNESS TRAILS 'N' TALES (CN/0828-9654) [12045243] **2209**, **4880**

WILDERNESS (WASHINGTON, D.C.) (US/0736-6477) [08894009] **2209**

WILDFIRE NEWS AND NOTES / SPONSORED BY NATIONAL FIRE PROTECTION ASSOCIATION ... [ET AL.] (US) [22651164] **2293**

WILDFIRE STATISTICS (US/0360-8034) [02245042] **2293**, **2398**, **2399**

WILDFLOWER (CN/0842-5132) [13726664] **530**, **2209**

WILDFLOWER (AUSTIN, TEX. 1984) (US/0898-8803) [12547027] **2433**, **530**

WILDFLOWER (AUSTIN, TEX. 1988) **SUSPENDED.** (US/0896-4858) [17162027] **2433**, **530**

WILDFLOWERS (US) [01320744] **2433**

WILDFOWL (ADEL, IOWA) (US/0886-0637) [12827681] **4880**

WILDFOWL CARVING AND COLLECTING (US/0886-3407) [12868758] **2779**, **376**

WILDFOWL (SLIMBRIDGE) (UK/0954-6324) [01644905] **2183**, **5621**

WILDFOWL TRUST *See* WILDFOWL (SLIMBRIDGE) **5621**

WILDHALTUNG (GW) [25511216] **5600**

WILDLAND NEWS (CN/0316-3350) [02199064] **2209**

WILDLAND/URBAN INTERFACE (US/1056-702X) [23819788] **2293**

WILDLIFE ABSTRACTS (US/0499-4175) [01561529] **2209**

WILDLIFE & FISH WORLDWIDE. VOLUME 1 (US/1046-6479) [20512020] **2316**, **2209**

WILDLIFE & FISH WORLDWIDE. VOLUME 1 *See* WILDLIFE WORLDWIDE **2210**

WILDLIFE & FISH WORLDWIDE. VOLUME 1 *See* WILDLIFE REVIEW & FISHERIES REVIEW **2209**

WILDLIFE ART NEWS (US/0746-9640) [10426763] **368**

WILDLIFE AUSTRALIA (AT/0043-5481) [11143782] **2209**

WILDLIFE BEHAVIOR AND ECOLOGY SERIES (US/0084-0122) [01606687] **2222**

WILDLIFE CLUBS OF KENYA ASSOCIATION *See* NEWSLETTER - THE WILDLIFE CLUBS OF KENYA ASSOCIATION **5593**

WILDLIFE COLLECTABLES JOURNAL, THE (CN/0827-2409) [11607534] **368**, **2209**

WILDLIFE CONSERVATION (US/1048-4949) [20872335] **5600**, **2209**

WILDLIFE CONSERVATION REPORT (US/0891-2734) [14687594] **2209**

WILDLIFE DISEASE NEWSLETTER (US) [09614187] **5527**

WILDLIFE DISEASE REVIEW **SUSPENDED.** (US/0736-6094) [09171219] **5527**

WILDLIFE HARVEST (US/0886-3458) [05208413] **2209**, **4880**

WILDLIFE IN NORTH CAROLINA (US/0043-549X) [02401003] **2209**

WILDLIFE JOURNAL *See* JOURNAL OF WILDLIFE REHABILITATION **2196**

WILDLIFE JOURNAL (US/0893-6560) [15626400] **2209**

WILDLIFE MANAGEMENT LEAFLET (US/0148-9461) [02778382] **2209**

WILDLIFE MONOGRAPHS (US/0084-0173) [01623949] **5600**

WILDLIFE NEWS / AFRICAN WILDLIFE LEADERSHIP FOUNDATION (US) [04609669] **2209**

WILDLIFE PAMPHLET (PROVIDENCE) (US/0511-9480) [01343486] **2209**

WILDLIFE POPULATIONS AND RESEARCH UNIT PROJECT DESCRIPTIONS (US/0734-5518) [08303230] **2209**

WILDLIFE PRESERVATION TRUST ... ANNUAL REPORT (US) [09363089] **2209**

WILDLIFE PUBLICATION (WELLINGTON) (NZ) [01586426] **2209**

WILDLIFE REHABILITATION (US) [22523006] **2209**

WILDLIFE REHABILITATION TODAY (US/1044-2618) [19720688] **2183**, **227**

WILDLIFE RESEARCH (AT/1035-3712) [23740383] **5600**

WILDLIFE RESEARCH (US/0361-1256) [02245272] **2209**

WILDLIFE RESEARCH CENTER, DENVER *See* RESEARCH ACCOMPLISHMENTS - WILDLIFE RESEARCH CENTER (DENVER) **2203**

WILDLIFE RESEARCH REPORT (DENVER, COLO.) (US/0277-4070) [06440303] **2209**

WILDLIFE

Alphabetical Title Index

●WILDLIFE REVIEW & FISHERIES REVIEW (US/1070-499X) [26656905] 2316, **2209**

WILDLIFE REVIEW (FORT COLLINS) (US/0043-5511) [01769882] 2209, **2185**

WILDLIFE SOCIETY See MEMBERSHIP DIRECTORY AND CERTIFICATION REGISTRY **2198**

WILDLIFE SOCIETY See WILDLIFE SOCIETY BULLETIN **2209**

WILDLIFE SOCIETY BULLETIN (US/0091-7648) [01788203] **2209**

WILDLIFE TECHNICAL BULLETIN (US) [20414442] **2210**

WILDLIFE VIEWS See ARIZONA WILDLIFE VIEWS **2187**

●WILDLIFE WORLDWIDE (US/1070-5007) [27129095] **2210**

WILDROWS (US/0278-1603) [07714907] **2766**

WILDWOOD ECHOES See JOURNAL OF HEALTH & HEALING (WILDWOOD, GA.) **2599**

●WILEY BUSINESS INTELLIGENCE REPORTS. ALGERIA (UK/1073-3213) [29401103] **720**

●WILEY BUSINESS INTELLIGENCE REPORTS. ANGOLA (UK/1073-3221) [29401128] **720**

●WILEY BUSINESS INTELLIGENCE REPORTS. ARGENTINA (UK/1073-323X) [29401316] **720**

●WILEY BUSINESS INTELLIGENCE REPORTS. AUSTRALIA (UK/1073-3256) [29401849] **720**

●WILEY BUSINESS INTELLIGENCE REPORTS. AUSTRIA (UK/1073-3248) [29401817] **720**

●WILEY BUSINESS INTELLIGENCE REPORTS. AZERBAIJAN (UK/1073-3264) [29401910] **720**

●WILEY BUSINESS INTELLIGENCE REPORTS. BAHAMAS (UK/1073-3272) [29401968] **720**

●WILEY BUSINESS INTELLIGENCE REPORTS. BAHRAIN (UK/1073-3299) [29402051] **720**

●WILEY BUSINESS INTELLIGENCE REPORTS. BANGLADESH (UK/1073-3302) [29402073] **720**

●WILEY BUSINESS INTELLIGENCE REPORTS. BELGIUM (UK/1073-3280) [29402013] **720**

●WILEY BUSINESS INTELLIGENCE REPORTS. BOLIVIA (UK/1073-3310) [29402093] **720**

●WILEY BUSINESS INTELLIGENCE REPORTS. BOTSWANA (UK/1073-3329) [29402132] **720**

●WILEY BUSINESS INTELLIGENCE REPORTS. BRAZIL (UK/1073-3345) [29403284] **720**

●WILEY BUSINESS INTELLIGENCE REPORTS. BRUNEI (UK/1073-3337) [29403253] **720**

●WILEY BUSINESS INTELLIGENCE REPORTS. CAMEROON (UK/1073-337X) [29403397] **720**

●WILEY BUSINESS INTELLIGENCE REPORTS. CANADA (UK/1073-3361) [29403361] **721**

●WILEY BUSINESS INTELLIGENCE REPORTS. CHINA (UK/1073-3396) [29403956] **721**

●WILEY BUSINESS INTELLIGENCE REPORTS. COLOMBIA (UK/1073-340X) [29403981] **721**

●WILEY BUSINESS INTELLIGENCE REPORTS. COSTA RICA (UK/1073-3418) [29404018] **721**

●WILEY BUSINESS INTELLIGENCE REPORTS. CUBA (UK/1073-3426) [29404043] **721**

●WILEY BUSINESS INTELLIGENCE REPORTS. CZECH REPUBLIC (UK/1073-3434) [29404066] **721**

●WILEY BUSINESS INTELLIGENCE REPORTS. ECUADOR (UK/1073-3450) [29418423] **721**

●WILEY BUSINESS INTELLIGENCE REPORTS. EGYPT (UK/1073-3469) [29418448] **721**

●WILEY BUSINESS INTELLIGENCE REPORTS. EL SALVADOR (UK/1073-3477) [29418475] **721**

●WILEY BUSINESS INTELLIGENCE REPORTS. ESTONIA (UK/1073-3485) [29418494] **721**

●WILEY BUSINESS INTELLIGENCE REPORTS. FINLAND (UK/1073-3493) [29418518] **721**

●WILEY BUSINESS INTELLIGENCE REPORTS. FRANCE (UK/1073-3507) [29418531] **721**

●WILEY BUSINESS INTELLIGENCE REPORTS. GABON (UK/1073-3515) [29418554] **721**

●WILEY BUSINESS INTELLIGENCE REPORTS. GERMANY (UK/1073-3523) [29418571] **721**

●WILEY BUSINESS INTELLIGENCE REPORTS. GHANA (UK/1073-3531) [29418591] **721**

●WILEY BUSINESS INTELLIGENCE REPORTS. GREECE (UK/1073-354X) [29418706] **721**

●WILEY BUSINESS INTELLIGENCE REPORTS. GUATEMALA (UK/1073-3558) [29418728] **721**

●WILEY BUSINESS INTELLIGENCE REPORTS. GUYANA (UK/1073-3566) [29418757] **721**

●WILEY BUSINESS INTELLIGENCE REPORTS. HAITI (UK/1073-3574) [29418783] **721**

●WILEY BUSINESS INTELLIGENCE REPORTS. HONDURAS (UK/1073-3604) [29418936] **721**

●WILEY BUSINESS INTELLIGENCE REPORTS. HONG KONG (UK/1073-3590) [29418916] **721**

●WILEY BUSINESS INTELLIGENCE REPORTS. HUNGARY (UK/1073-3582) [29418890] **721**

●WILEY BUSINESS INTELLIGENCE REPORTS. INDIA (UK/1073-3620) [29419598] **721**

●WILEY BUSINESS INTELLIGENCE REPORTS. INDONESIA (UK/1073-3612) [29419575] **721**

●WILEY BUSINESS INTELLIGENCE REPORTS. IRAN (UK/1073-3647) [29419632] **721**

●WILEY BUSINESS INTELLIGENCE REPORTS. IRAQ (UK/1073-3655) [29419654] **721**

●WILEY BUSINESS INTELLIGENCE REPORTS. IRELAND (UK/1073-3639) [29419615] **721**

●WILEY BUSINESS INTELLIGENCE REPORTS. ISRAEL (UK/1073-3663) [29419666] **721**

●WILEY BUSINESS INTELLIGENCE REPORTS. ITALY (UK/1073-3671) [29419702] **721**

●WILEY BUSINESS INTELLIGENCE REPORTS. JAMAICA (UK/1073-3698) [29419856] **721**

●WILEY BUSINESS INTELLIGENCE REPORTS. JAPAN (UK/1073-3701) [29419880] **721**

●WILEY BUSINESS INTELLIGENCE REPORTS. JORDAN (UK/1073-371X) [29419957] **721**

●WILEY BUSINESS INTELLIGENCE REPORTS. KAZAKHSTAN (UK/1073-3728) [29419994] **721**

●WILEY BUSINESS INTELLIGENCE REPORTS. KENYA (UK/1073-3736) [29420021] **722**

●WILEY BUSINESS INTELLIGENCE REPORTS. KOREA (UK/1073-3744) [29420051] **722**

●WILEY BUSINESS INTELLIGENCE REPORTS. KUWAIT (UK/1073-3752) [29420098] **722**

●WILEY BUSINESS INTELLIGENCE REPORTS. LEBANON (UK/1073-3760) [29420122] **722**

●WILEY BUSINESS INTELLIGENCE REPORTS. LIBYA (UK/1073-3779) [29420195] **722**

●WILEY BUSINESS INTELLIGENCE REPORTS. LUXEMBOURG (UK/1073-3787) [29420671] **722**

●WILEY BUSINESS INTELLIGENCE REPORTS. MALAYSIA (UK/1073-3795) [29420690] **722**

●WILEY BUSINESS INTELLIGENCE REPORTS. MEXICO (UK/1073-4236) [29420704] **722**

●WILEY BUSINESS INTELLIGENCE REPORTS. MOROCCO (UK/1073-3809) [29420722] **722**

●WILEY BUSINESS INTELLIGENCE REPORTS. MOZAMBIQUE (UK/1073-3817) [29420751] **722**

●WILEY BUSINESS INTELLIGENCE REPORTS. NETHERLANDS (UK/1073-3841) [29420839] **722**

●WILEY BUSINESS INTELLIGENCE REPORTS. NEW ZEALAND (UK/1073-3868) [29423568] **722**

●WILEY BUSINESS INTELLIGENCE REPORTS. NICARAGUE (UK/1073-3833) [29420809] **722**

●WILEY BUSINESS INTELLIGENCE REPORTS. NIGERIA (UK/1073-3825) [29420774] **722**

●WILEY BUSINESS INTELLIGENCE REPORTS. NORWAY (UK/1073-385X) [29420878] **722**

●WILEY BUSINESS INTELLIGENCE REPORTS. OMAN (UK/1073-3876) [29423599] **722**

●WILEY BUSINESS INTELLIGENCE REPORTS. PAKISTAN (UK/1073-3884) [29423634] **722**

●WILEY BUSINESS INTELLIGENCE REPORTS. PARAGUAY (UK/1073-3914) [29452848] **722**

●WILEY BUSINESS INTELLIGENCE REPORTS. PERU (UK/1073-3957) [29452923] **722**

●WILEY BUSINESS INTELLIGENCE REPORTS. PHILIPPINES (UK/1073-3922) [29452863] **722**

●WILEY BUSINESS INTELLIGENCE REPORTS. POLAND (UK/1073-3930) [29452885] **722**

●WILEY BUSINESS INTELLIGENCE REPORTS. PORTUGAL (UK/1073-3949) [29452909] **722**

●WILEY BUSINESS INTELLIGENCE REPORTS. PUERTO RICO (UK/1073-3965) [29452940] **722**

●WILEY BUSINESS INTELLIGENCE REPORTS. RUSSIA (UK/1073-3973) [29453108] **722**

●WILEY BUSINESS INTELLIGENCE REPORTS. SAUDI ARABIA (UK/1073-399X) [29453146] **722**

●WILEY BUSINESS INTELLIGENCE REPORTS. SENEGAL (UK/1073-4007) [29453155] **722**

●WILEY BUSINESS INTELLIGENCE REPORTS. SINGAPORE (UK/1073-4023) [29453211] **722**

●WILEY BUSINESS INTELLIGENCE REPORTS. SLOVAK REPUBLIC (UK/1073-4015) [29453191] **722**

●WILEY BUSINESS INTELLIGENCE REPORTS. SOUTH AFRICA (UK/1073-3981) [29453129] **722**

●WILEY BUSINESS INTELLIGENCE REPORTS. SPAIN (UK/1073-4031) [29453240] **722**

●WILEY BUSINESS INTELLIGENCE REPORTS. SRI LANKA (UK/1073-404X) [29453259] **722**

●WILEY BUSINESS INTELLIGENCE REPORTS. SUDAN (UK/1073-4058) [29453285] **722**

●WILEY BUSINESS INTELLIGENCE REPORTS. SWEDEN (UK/1073-4260) [29453344] **723**

●WILEY BUSINESS INTELLIGENCE REPORTS. SWITZERLAND (UK/1073-4066) [29453374] **723**

●WILEY BUSINESS INTELLIGENCE REPORTS. SYRIA (UK/1073-4074) [29453496] **723**

●WILEY BUSINESS INTELLIGENCE REPORTS. TAIWAN (UK/1073-4082) [29453515] **723**

●WILEY BUSINESS INTELLIGENCE REPORTS. TAJIKISTAN (UK/1073-4090) [29453534] **723**

●WILEY BUSINESS INTELLIGENCE REPORTS. TANZANIA (UK/1073-4112) [29453574] **723**

●WILEY BUSINESS INTELLIGENCE REPORTS. THAILAND (UK/1073-4104) [29453557] **723**

●WILEY BUSINESS INTELLIGENCE REPORTS. TUNISIA (UK/1073-4120) [29453593] **723**

●WILEY BUSINESS INTELLIGENCE REPORTS. TURKEY (UK/1073-4139) [29453614] **723**

WILEY CONSTRUCTION LAW UPDATE (US/1054-9331) [23023961] **631**

WILEY EMPLOYMENT LAW UPDATE (US/1054-402X) [22877063] **3155**

WILEY LIBRARIANS' NEWSLETTER (US/1063-0686) [25305807] **4833**

WILEY MONOGRAPHS IN CHEMICAL PHYSICS (US/0277-2477) [07540139] **4425**

WILEY MONOGRAPHS IN CRYSTALLOGRAPHY (US/0277-2507) [07540178] **1033**

WILEY/RONALD-NATIONAL ASSOCIATION OF ACCOUNTANTS PROFESSIONAL BOOK SERIES (US/0743-1090) [10509981] **753**

WILEY SEARCH UPDATE USER NETWORK (US/0734-6182) [08774224] **1244**

WILEY SERIES IN COMPUTING (UK/0277-2647) [07556525] **1207**

WILEY SERIES IN DIAGNOSTIC AND THERAPEUTIC RADIOLOGY (US/0277-2566) [07546208] **3947**

WILEY SERIES IN MANAGEMENT (US/0271-6046) [06684443] **889**

WILEY SERIES IN MARKETING (US/0273-2955) [07037435] **938**

WILEY SERIES IN PLASMA PHYSICS (US/0271-602X) [06684505] **4425**

WILEY SERIES IN PSYCHOLOGY AND PRODUCTIVITY AT WORK (UK/0738-0860) [09511254] **4621**

WILEY SERIES IN PURE AND APPLIED OPTICS (US/0277-2493) [07540149] **4442**

WILEY SERIES IN URBAN RESEARCH, THE (US/0190-1109) [04629196] **2839**

WILEY SERIES OF PRACTICAL CONSTRUCTION GUIDES (US/0271-6011) [06684479] **631**

WILEY SERIES ON CANCER INVESTIGATION AND MANAGEMENT (UK/0749-5935) [09562219] **3825**

WILEY SERIES ON DEVELOPMENTS IN NURSING RESEARCH (UK/0737-6065) [08968492] **3871**

WILEY SERIES ON MOLECULAR PHARMACOLOGY OF CELL REGULATION (UK) [22893137] **476**

WILEY SERIES ON NEW HORIZONS IN ONCOLOGY (UK/0737-7290) [08404713] **3825**

WILEY SERIES ON PERSONALITY PROCESSES (US/0195-4008) [05470901] **4621**

WILEY SERIES ON STUDIES IN ENVIRONMENTAL MANAGEMENT AND RESOURCE DEVELOPMENT (UK/0272-4022) [06833327] **948**

WILEY SERIES ON SYSTEMS ENGINEERING AND ANALYSIS (US/0084-019X) [06833020] **2001**

WILEY SERVICE MANAGEMENT SERIES (US/0273-2963) [07037911] **889**

WILEY WORD PROCESSING SERIES (US/0277-268X) [07556570] **1292**

WILFRID LAURIER UNIVERSITY. LIBRARY *See* SERIALS HOLDINGS MICROFORM / WILFRID LAURIER UNIVERSITY **424**

WILKAMITE RECORD, THE (US) [15153599] **5702**

WILKERSON'S HEALTH CARE STRATEGIST *See* WINDHOVER'S HEALTH CARE STRATEGIST **3651**

WILKIE COLLINS SOCIETY JOURNAL (US/0897-2982) [07807352] **3453**

WILL-GRUNDY COUNTIES GENEALOGICAL SOCIETY QUARTERLY (US/8756-6931) [09614197] **2477**

WILLA CATHER PIONEER MEMORIAL AND EDUCATIONAL FOUNDATION *See* WILLA CATHER PIONEER MEMORIAL NEWSLETTER **3453**

WILLA CATHER PIONEER MEMORIAL NEWSLETTER (US/0197-663X) [04560752] **3453**

WILLA CATHER YEARBOOK, THE (US/1048-8618) [21068078] **3453**

●WILLA / WOMEN IN LITERATURE AND LIFE ASSEMBLY (US/1065-9080) [26790585] 5568, **3453**

WILLAMETTE JOURNAL OF THE LIBERAL ARTS (US/0740-6789) [09991958] 2856, 3453, **333**

WILLAMETTE LAW REVIEW (US/0191-9822) [04821100] **3075**

WILLAMETTE NATIONAL FOREST *See* WILLAMETTE, THE **2398**

WILLAMETTE, THE (US) [01784024] **2398**

WILLAMETTE WEEK (US) [11515525] **5734**

WILLAPA HARBOR HERALD, THE (US/1065-3805) [17331133] **5763**

WILLDENOWIA (GW/0511-9618) [07988328] **530**

●WILLIAM AND MARY BILL OF RIGHTS JOURNAL, THE (US/1065-8254) [26282285] 4514, **3075**

WILLIAM AND MARY BUSINESS REVIEW (US/0160-5232) [03690757] **723**

WILLIAM AND MARY LAW REVIEW (US/0043-5589) [01640594] **3075**

WILLIAM AND MARY QUARTERLY, THE (US/0043-5597) [01607858] **2766**

WILLIAM AND MARY REVIEW, THE (US/0043-5600) [01714846] **1854**

WILLIAM CARLOS WILLIAMS REVIEW (US/0196-6286) [05864218] **3356**

WILLIAM E. SIMON GRADUATE SCHOOL OF BUSINESS ADMINISTRATION *See* ALUMNI DIRECTORY / WILLIAM E. SIMON GRADUATE SCHOOL OF BUSINESS ADMINISTRATION, UNIVERSITY OF ROCHESTER **1100**

WILLIAM J. COOPER FOUNDATION LECTURES (US) [01741701] **4500**

WILLIAM L. HUTCHESON MEMORIAL FOREST BULLETIN (US/0485-764X) [01588578] **2398**

WILLIAM MARSH RICE UNIVERSITY, HOUSTON, TEX. OFFICE OF DEVELOPMENT *See* RICE UNIVERSITY ALUMNI DIRECTORY **1102**

WILLIAM MITCHELL ENVIRONMENTAL LAW JOURNAL **SUSPENDED.** (US/0737-2795) [09342217] **3117**

WILLIAM MITCHELL LAW REVIEW (US/0270-272X) [02180199] **3075**

WILLIAM T. GRANT FOUNDATION *See* ANNUAL REPORT - WILLIAM T. GRANT FOUNDATION **5273**

WILLIAM WINTER COMMENTS (1976) (US/0274-5852) [04071114] **4538**

WILLIAMS COLLEGE *See* ALUMNI DIRECTORY / WILLIAMS COLLEGE **1100**

WILLIAMS, DOUG *See* AUTOMOTIVE Q & A **5407**

WILLIAMS' FAMILY BULLETIN, THE (US/0043-5627) [08380475] **2477**

WILLIAMS NEWS (US) [08840569] **5630**

WILLIAMS NORTHERN LIGHT (US/0744-7582) [01769897] **5699**

WILLIAMS REPORT (US/1075-8550) [20376617] 948, **1124**

WILLIAMSBURG JOURNAL TRIBUNE WILLIAMSBURG, IOWA 1972 (US) [12239038] **5674**

WILLIAMSBURG RESEARCH STUDIES (US) [01743795] **2766**

WILLIAMSBURG'S PUBLICK OBSERVER (US) [06518405] **2550**

WILLIAMSON COUNTY SUN, THE (US) [13476673] **5756**

WILLIAMSON DAILY NEWS (US/0883-1602) [12120688] **5765**

WILLIAMSPORT SUN-GAZETTE (US/1056-3083) [13870659] **5740**

WILLING'S PRESS GUIDE (UK/0000-0213) [06246233] **767**

WILLISTON DAILY HERALD (US) [01769899] **5726**

WILLIWAW **CEASED.** (US/0894-8488) [16270312] **3473**

WILLOW GROVE GUIDE (US/0746-4592) [10053133] **5741**

WILLOW SPRINGS (US/0739-1277) [09692524] **3356**

WILLOW TRANSFER QUARTERLY (CN/0826-2098) [11564254] 2779, **2595**

WILLOWS JOURNAL (US) [28408199] **5641**

WILLS (US) [02239704] **3119**

WILLS FOR ALBERTA (CN/0824-1406) [11816161] **3119**

WILMER RETINA UPDATE, THE (US) **3651**

WILMETTE LIFE (US/0745-0044) [08711178] **5662**

WILMETTE NEWS/VOICE (US/0745-9750) [09650213] **5662**

WILMINGTON JOURNAL (WILMINGTON, N.C.), THE (US/0049-7649) [03962050] **5724**

WILMOT ENTERPRISE, THE (US) [13555616] **5744**

WILSHIRE CENTER'S LARCHMONT CHRONICLE (US/0192-1932) [05133366] **5641**

WILSON AND WILSON'S COMPREHENSIVE ANALYTICAL CHEMISTRY (NE) [07068294] **1020**

WILSON BULLETIN (WILSON ORNITHOLOGICAL SOCIETY), THE (US/0043-5643) [02397807] **5621**

WILSON BUSINESS ABSTRACTS (US/1057-6533) [24083590] 723, **735**

WILSON COUNTY CITIZEN (US) [12770481] **5679**

WILSON LIBRARY BULLETIN (US/0043-5651) [01604318] **3256**

WILSON QUARTERLY (WASHINGTON), THE (US/0363-3276) [02757163] **2495**

WILSON WAREHOUSE (US/0734-953X) [08819224] **2477**

WILSON WORLD, THE (US) [11149517] **5679**

WILTON BULLETIN (US) [28013685] **5646**

WILTON-DURANT ADVOCATE NEWS (US/0746-6315) [10195150] **5674**

WILTON PARK PAPERS (UK/0953-8542) [21263211] **4538**

WILTSHIRE ARCHAEOLOGICAL AND NATURAL HISTORY MAGAZINE (1982) (UK/0262-6608) [08877384] 4174, **285**

WILTSHIRE FOLKLIFE (UK) [06220089] **2325**

WIMBLEDON : LA GENTE CHE LEGGE **CEASED.** (IT) [22102728] **3256**

WIN FDM'S WOODWORKING INDUSTRY NEWSLETTER (US) **635**

WIN MAGAZINE (VAN NUYS, CALIF.) (US/1047-854X) [20794964] **4867**

WIN NEWS (US/0145-7985) [02694733] **5568**

WINAK (GT/0257-6449) [13348288] 247, **1791**

WINCHENDON COURIER, THE (US) [23031555] **5690**

WINCHESTER CATHEDRAL RECORD (UK/0308-6321) [103086321] **2716**

WINCHESTER CHRONICLE *See* HERALD-CHRONICLE (WINCHESTER, TENN.), THE **5745**

WINCHESTER EVENING STAR *See* WINCHESTER STAR (WINCHESTER, VA.) **5760**

WINCHESTER HERALD-TIMES *See* HERALD-CHRONICLE (WINCHESTER, TENN.), THE **5745**

WINCHESTER STAR (WINCHESTER, VA.) (US/1064-0665) [14201561] **5760**

WINCHESTER SUN (WINCHESTER, KY. : 1912) (US) [13591075] **5683**

WINCHESTER TIMES (WINCHESTER, ILL. : 1865 : WEEKLY) (US) [12622142] **5662**

WINCKELMANNSPROGRAMM DER ARCHAOLOGISCHEN GESELLSCHAFT ZU BERLIN (GW) [01894767] 285, **368**

WIND ENERGY ABSTRACTS (US/0277-2140) [07525338] **1960**

WIND ENERGY NEWS (US/0886-2818) [12876826] **1960**

WIND ENERGY REPORT (US/0162-8623) [04242513] **1960**

WIND ENERGY TECHNOLOGY (US/0896-5102) [17197263] **1960**

WIND ENGINEERING (UK/0309-524X) [03603853] **1437**

WIND ENGINEERING ABSTRACTS (UK/0263-0915) [09006948] **2001**

WIND KRAFT JOURNAL (GW/0720-8073) [09129225] **1960**

WIND (PIKEVILLE, KY.) (US/0361-2481) [01746180] **3453**

WIND RIVER NEWS (US) [13698774] **5773**

WIND RIVER RENDEZVOUS, THE (US/0739-232X) [08427103] **2766**

WIND ROSE, THE (US/0049-7657) [05669128] **4097**

WIND STATS NEWSLETTER (DK) **1361**

WIND SURFING (US/1057-0799) [23174579] **4929**

WIND TURBINE WORLDWIDE CATALOG (US/0899-4013) [18082661] **2001**

WINDER NEWS, THE (US) [19113468] **5655**

WINDHAM JOURNAL, THE (US) [11714946] **5722**

WINDHAM PHOENIX (US/0888-0832) [13117466] **2550**

WINDHOVER'S HEALTH CARE STRATEGIST (US) [28089888] 4332, **3651**

WINDIRECTIONS (UK/0950-0642) [I09500642] **1960**

WINDLESS ORCHARD, THE (US/0043-5716) [02460528] **3473**

WINDMILL HERALD (CN/0712-6417) [09538884] **5798**

WINDMILL HERALD (CENTRAL-EASTERN CANADA ED.) (CN/0837-3299) [18310475] **5798**

WINDOS *See* WINDOWS KONKRET **1207**

WINDOS (GW/0940-8029) [I09408029] **1207**

WINDOW & WALL DECORATING IDEAS *See* BETTER HOMES AND GARDENS DECORATING IDEAS. WINDOW & WALL IDEAS **2899**

WINDOW (BETHESDA, MD.) (US/0275-2166) [03503146] **3453**

WINDOW FASHIONS (US/0886-9669) [13079568] **2904**

WINDOW INDUSTRIES (UK/0263-1784) [I02631784] **2595**

WINDOW LETTER, THE (US) **1292**

●WINDOW MARKETPLACE (US/1062-418X) [25614832] **1631**

●WINDOW ON CHEMOMETRICS (UK/0966-9086) **1031**

●WINDOW ON DRUG MONITORING (UK/0966-9094) 476, **5169**

WINDOW ON THE ARTS, LITERATURE, AND SOCIETY, THE (US/1055-1719) [23102250] 3453, **333**

WINDOWS & DOS USER'S GUIDE **CEASED.** (US/1064-5993) [26335206] **1207**

WINDOWS (AUSTIN, TEX.) (US/1056-0556) [23366157] **5009**

WINDOWS (COLLEGE STATION, TEX.) (US/0745-0729) [08799180] **5169**

WINDOWS/DOS DEVELOPER'S JOURNAL (US/1059-2407) [24516191] **1273**

●WINDOWS KONKRET (GW) **1207**

WINDOWS LETTER (US) **1292**

WINDOWS MAGAZINE (FR) **2904**

WINDOWS MAGAZINE (NE) **1207**

WINDOWS MAGAZINE (US/1060-1066) [24867227] **1282**

WINDOWS MAGAZINE (UK) **1207**

●WINDOWS REPORT, THE (US/1065-3627) [26593575] **1292**

WINDOWS SHOPPER'S GUIDE, THE **CEASED.** (US/1049-071X) [21120646] **1207**

●WINDOWS SOFTWARE CONNECTION (US/1065-0784) [26515618] **1292**

●WINDOWS SOURCES (US/1065-9641) [26820342] **1207**

●WINDOWS TECH JOURNAL (US/1061-3501) [25259853] **1282**

WINDOWS USER **CEASED.** (US/1065-3481) [26578095] **1207**

WINDPOWER MONTHLY (DK/0109-7318) [12415595] **1960**

WINDRIDER (US/0279-4659) [07889702] **4929**

WINDS — Alphabetical Title Index

WINDS OF CHANGE (BOULDER, COLO.) (US/0888-8612) [13725387] **5169**

WINDSCRIPT (CN/0822-2363) [10235776] 368, **3453**

WINDSOR CHRONICLE, THE (US/0746-2336) [09869006] **5758**

WINDSOR JOURNAL, THE (US) [27994808] **5646**

WINDSOR LOCKS JOURNAL, THE (US) [27994793] **5647**

WINDSOR REVIEW (CN) **3453**

WINDSOR REVIEW OF LEGAL AND SOCIAL ISSUES (CN/0838-3596) [20710619] **3075**

WINDSOR STAR MICROFORM, THE (CN/0839-2277) [10082683] **5798**

WINDSOR THIS MONTH **SUSPENDED.** (CN/0318-2460) [02441776] **2550**

WINDSOR YEARBOOK OF ACCESS TO JUSTICE, THE (CN/0710-0841) [07801274] **3075**

WINDSPEAKER (CN/0834-177X) [16206216] **5798**

WINDSPORT (CN/0826-5003) [11377335] **4929**

WINDSTORM (US/0737-7789) [09455669] **4159**

WINDSURF AND BOARD SAILING (UK) **597**

WINDSURF MAGAZINE (UK) **597**

WINDSURFING CALIFORNIA (US/1063-8172) [26142481] **4929**

WINDY CITY SPELEONEWS, THE (US/0148-2823) [03286229] **1412**

WINDY TIMES (US) **2477**

WINE (UK/0043-5791) [05014098] **2372**

WINE ADVOCATE, THE (US/0887-8463) [10588319] **2372**

WINE & DINE (CN/0227-3837) [06858736] 2372, **2361**

WINE AND FOOD MAGAZINE See HOUSE & GARDEN (BRITISH EDITION, 1948) **2901**

WINE & LIQUOR SALES (US) [01320986] **2372**

WINE AND SPIRIT GAZETTE (HARPER'S WEEKLY) See HARPERS WINE AND SPIRIT GAZETTE **2367**

WINE & SPIRIT INTERNATIONAL (UK) [21433538] **2372**

WINE & SPIRIT TRADE REVIEW See OFF LICENCE NEWS **2370**

WINE & SPIRITS (BERKELEY, CALIF.) (US/0890-0299) [14145399] **2372**

WINE AND SPIRITS WHOLESALERS OF AMERICA See ROSTER/INDUSTRY DIRECTORY **2370**

WINE AND SPIRITS WHOLESALERS OF AMERICA See ANNUAL PERFORMANCE STUDY - WINE AND SPIRITS WHOLESALERS OF AMERICA **2363**

WINE BUSINESS INSIDER (US/1057-8544) [24130585] **2372**

WINE COUNTRY INTERNATIONAL (US/1048-0455) [20784338] **2372**

WINE EAST (US/0892-662X) [15266757] **2372**

WINE EDUCATOR, THE (US/1046-6851) [20496189] **2372**

WINE INVESTOR. EXECUTIVE EDITION, THE (US/0889-4256) [14047251] **2372**

WINE NEWS (CORAL GABLES, FLA.), THE (US/1065-4895) [24325808] **2372**

WINE NEWS, THE (US) **2372**

WINE NOW (US/0094-5153) [01794633] **2372**

WINE ON LINE (US/1053-4776) [22537669] 2361, **2372**

WINE PRODUCTION, AUSTRALIA AND STATES / AUSTRALIAN BUREAU OF STATISTICS (AT) [07298342] 2372, **2362**

WINE QUARTERLY REVIEW See WINE **2372**

WINE SPECTATOR, THE (US/0193-497X) [05229172] **2372**

WINE SPECTATOR ULTIMATE GUIDE TO BUYING WINE, THE (US/1058-5729) [24333556] **2372**

WINE SPECTATOR'S GUIDE TO SELECTED WINES, THE (US/0749-033X) [11036045] **2372**

WINE SPECTATOR'S ULTIMATE GUIDE TO BUYING WINE See ULTIMATE GUIDE TO BUYING WINE / THE WINE SPECTATOR **2371**

WINE SPECTATOR'S WINE COUNTRY GUIDE TO CALIFORNIA, THE (US/0897-8492) [17641242] **2372**

WINE TIDINGS (CN/0228-6157) [07822712] **2372**

WINE TRADE (SAN FRANCISCO), THE (US/0196-1381) [05753305] **2373**

WINE WORLD (US/0199-7483) [01714619] **2373**

WINEGAR TREE, THE (US/0742-6356) [06573436] **2477**

WINEK INFO (NE) [03078434] **4159**

WINES AND VINES (US/0043-583X) [06671904] 146, **2373**

WINES & VINES. BUYER'S GUIDE ISSUE (US/0043-583X) [08913464] **2373**

WINESBURG EAGLE, THE (US/0147-3166) [03139958] 3356, **439**

WINESTATE (AT/0156-6490) [01566490] **2373**

WINFIELD DAILY COURIER (1931), THE (US/0889-6747) [10445352] **5679**

WINFIELD PRESS, THE (US/0273-6993) [06825972] **5662**

WING & SHOT (US/0892-1849) [15115643] **4880**

WING FOOT CLAN, THE (US/0043-5872) [06023670] **5078**

WING NEWSLETTER (JA/0388-1032) [03881032] **39**

WING SPAN (MOONEE PONDS) (AT/1036-7810) [23961486] **5621**

WING WORLD (US/0745-273X) [09013376] **4083**

WINGFOOT LIGHTER-THAN-AIR SOCIETY. BULLETIN See BUOYANT FLIGHT **15**

WINGING IT (US/1042-511X) [19073826] **5600**

WINGS (AT) **39**

WINGS & AERONEWS (SA) [02439016] **39**

WINGS (CALGARY) (CN/0701-1369) [03406404] **39**

WINGS MAGAZINE (CN) **39**

WINGS (MANLIUS) (US/0197-1174) [05965234] **1886**

WINGS (NEVADA CITY) (US/0161-6331) [03978407] **39**

WINGS OF ALOHA (US) 5499, **39**

WINGS OF GOLD (PENSACOLA, FLA.) (US/0274-7405) [06549438] **39**

WINGS OF PROGRESS (US) [08177710] **1908**

WINGS OVER AFRICA See WINGS & AERONEWS **39**

WINGS : WOMEN IN NEWS GATHERING (CN/1186-8872) [24690633] 5568, **2925**

WINGSPAN (US/0892-2659) [14763994] **1791**

WINGSPAN HIGH WYCOMBE (UK/0955-9000) [I09559000] **40**

WINGTIPS (LANSING, N.Y.) **CEASED.** (US/8756-4505) [11561422] **5600**

WINK BULLETIN (US) [14389748] **5756**

WINKLER COUNTY NEWS, THE (US/1048-2997) [14185276] **5756**

WINKLER PRINS JAARBOEK (NE) [06362330] **2716**

WINN PARISH COURIER (US/0743-7102) [10649295] **2477**

WINNEBAGO INDIAN NEWS (US/1060-3026) [24607794] **5707**

WINNECONNE NEWS, THE (US) [12170861] **5772**

WINNEPEG, (MAN.) See CURRENT ESTIMATES - CITY OF WINNIPEG **4719**

WINNEPEG WOMAN (CN/0709-6844) [05696340] **5568**

WINNER CURRICULUM OUTLINE AND TEACHING GUIDES (US) 1806, **1908**

WINNER (NAGS HEAD, N. C.) (US/1058-773X) [24370424] **4621**

WINNER (WASHINGTON, D.C.), THE (US/0043-5937) [03962793] 1071, **1350**

WINNETKA NEWS/VOICE (US/0745-9742) [09650326] **5662**

WINNICOTT STUDIES (UK/0267-3142) [16521305] **4621**

WINNIE (FR/0296-8576) [I02968576] **1071**

WINNING (ALLENTOWN, PA.) (US/1055-7830) [23306930] **429**

WINNING EDGE, THE (US) [20840179] **4929**

WINNING EXPORTS (AT) [01793520] **857**

WINNING HOOPS (US/0893-6439) [15626267] **4929**

WINNING SWEEPSTAKES NEWSLETTER (US/0738-0143) [09495702] **2779**

WINNING (TULSA, OKLA.) (US/0744-2467) [08135657] **4867**

WINNIPEG CHAMBER OF COMMERCE See DIRECTORY/BUYERS' GUIDE AND DAILY PLANNER **819**

WINNIPEG FOLK FESTIVAL See WINNIPEG FOLK FESTIVAL NEWSLETTER **4159**

WINNIPEG FOLK FESTIVAL NEWSLETTER (CN/0700-3129) [03264447] **4159**

WINNIPEG FREE PRESS (CN/0828-1785) [01607085] **5798**

WINNIPEG GUIDE, THE (CN/0703-5292) [05785078] **5798**

WINNIPEG MAGAZINE (CN/0707-6185) [04747042] **2550**

WINNIPEG SUN (1980) (CN/0711-3773) [08489199] **5798**

WINNIPEG TRIBUNE (CN) [01640037] **5798**

WINNSBORO NEWS (WINNSBORO, TEX. : 1908) (US/8755-948X) [11429689] **5756**

WINONA COURIER (US) [01769931] **5699**

WINONA DAILY NEWS (US/0273-9941) [01696879] **5699**

WINONA TIMES, THE (US) [16579494] **5702**

WINSLOW MAIL, THE (US/8750-5711) [11446658] **5630**

WINSTED JOURNAL (US) [01769948] **5699**

WINSTON COUNTY JOURNAL, THE (US/8750-9385) [10931379] **5702**

WINSTON CUP ILLUSTRATED (US/1048-6119) [20981040] **4930**

WINSTON CUP SCENE (US/1053-461X) [22605749] **4930**

WINSTON-SALEM CHRONICLE (US) [12156348] **5724**

WINSTON-SALEM JOURNAL (US) [12156422] **5724**

WINSTON-SALEM MAGAZINE (US/8755-9587) [11456913] **2550**

WINSTON'S TRAVEL DELUXE **CEASED.** (US/0897-7313) [17605767] **5499**

WINTER FUELS REPORT / ENERGY INFORMATION ADMINSTRATION, OFFICE OF OIL AND GAS, U.S. DEPT. OF ENERGY (US) [23231578] **1960**

WINTER HAVEN DAILY CHIEF (US) [13020774] **5651**

WINTER HAVEN DAILY NEWS-CHIEF (US) [01746535] **5651**

WINTER PARK-MAITLAND OBSERVER (US/1064-3613) [26271684] **5651**

WINTER PARK MANIFEST (US) [23117652] **5644**

WINTER PARK OUTLOOK (US/0745-9203) [09591510] **5651**

WINTER PARK SUN HERALD (US) [01746899] **5651**

WINTER PARK SUN OUTLOOK (US/1051-967X) [22161201] **5651**

WINTER RECREATION DIRECTORY (CN/0825-4044) [11250670] **4855**

WINTER WHEAT AND RYE SEEDINGS (US/0191-1090) [02693051] **191**

WINTERS ENTERPRISE, THE (US) [14277969] **5756**

WINTERS EXPRESS (US) [08773426] **5641**

WINTERSPORT (NE) [06140690] **4855**

WINTERTHUR PORTFOLIO (US/0084-0416) [01332742] **368**

WINTERTHURER JAHRBUCH (SZ/0508-8410) [06660207] **2716**

WINZER : FACHBLATT DES OSTERREICHISCHE WEINHAUS, DER (AU/0043-5953) [13518990] **2373**

WIP FUN (CN/0824-4782) [10522263] **3256**

WIPO NEWSLETTER **CEASED.** (SZ) [21589545] **1309**

WIRAZU, NA (CN/1188-8377) [26714786] **4930**

WIRE (GW/0043-5996) [02451621] **4023**

WIRE AND WIRE PRODUCTS MANUFACTURERS (PRELIMINARY ED.) **SUSPENDED.** (CN/0384-4781) [03418322] **4023**

WIRE INDUSTRY (UK/0043-6011) [02451624] **2086**

WIRE INDUSTRY YEARBOOK (UK/0084-0424) [I00840424] **4023**

WIRE JOURNAL DIRECTORY/CATALOG (US/0091-3162) [01786837] **4023**

WIRE JOURNAL INTERNATIONAL (US/0277-4275) [07485314] **4023**

WIRE (LONDON, ENGLAND) (UK/0952-0686) [11941257] **4159**

WIRE : OFFICIAL ORGAN OF THE ROYAL SIGNALS ASSOCIATION, THE (UK) **5237**

WIRE PRODUCTION See WIRE WORLD INTERNATIONAL **2086**

WIRE ROPE NEWS See WIRE ROPE NEWS & SLING TECHNOLOGY **3489**

Alphabetical Title Index — WISCONSIN

WIRE ROPE NEWS & SLING TECHNOLOGY (US/0740-1809) [09901905] **3489**

WIRE TECHNOLOGY BUYER'S GUIDE (US/0145-2886) [02720539] **4023**

WIRE TECHNOLOGY INTERNATIONAL (US/0898-9850) [16417295] **4023**

WIRE WORLD INTERNATIONAL (GW/0043-6046) [02451627] **2086**

WIRED LIBRARIAN'S NEWSLETTER **SUSPENDED.** (US/0884-593X) [11137747] **3256**

●WIRED (SAN FRANCISCO, CALIF.) (US/1059-1028) [24479723] **1169, 1207**

●WIRELESS BUSINESS & FINANCE (US) **816, 1169**

●WIRELESS CABLE INVESTOR (US/1075-1483) [29947246] **1169**

WIRELESS CELLULAR (US/1058-6717) [24356835] **1124**

WIRELESS COMPUTING (US/1056-4977) [23725695] **1207**

●WIRELESS DATA NEWS (US/1069-3416) [27994748] **1124**

WIRELESS DESIGN & DEVELOPMENT (US/1076-4240) [30482912] **1169**

WIRELESS FOR THE CORPORATE USER (US) **1169**

WIRELESS INDUSTRY DIRECTORY (US) **1169**

WIRELESS INVESTOR (US/1054-6960) [22940387] **857, 1169**

●WIRELESS MEDIA & MESSAGING (US) **1207, 1169**

WIRELESS MESSAGING REPORT (US) **1169**

WIRELESS NETWORKS (NE/1022-0038) **2086**

WIRELESS PCN TELECOMMUNICATIONS (US/1058-6725) [24356869] **1169**

WIRELESS PERSONAL COMMUNICATIONS (NE/0929-6212) **1124**

WIRELESS REGISTER. WORLD WIDE EDITION, THE (US/0277-2825) [07518550] **1143**

WIRELESS SATELLITE & BROADCASTING (US/1058-6695) [24356658] **1143**

WIRELESS SPECTRUM MANAGEMENT (US/1058-6709) [24356704] **1124**

●WIRELESS TELECOM INVESTOR (US/1075-413X) [30047184] **1169**

WIRELESS TELECOMMUNICATIONS (US/1057-5391) [24072552] **1169**

●WIRELINE (DALLAS, TEX.) (US/1062-8746) [25776297] **1337**

WIREWORLD (GW/0934-5906) [20401227] **2001**

WIRING DEVICES AND SUPPLIES (US/0741-8221) [03060271] **2086**

WIRKENDES WORT (ZEITSCHRIFT) (GW/0043-6089) [01258417] **3333**

WIRKUNG DER LITERATUR (GW/0084-0467) [01747147] **3453**

WIRTSCHAFT, DIE (GW/0508-8550) [03221870] **1526, 723**

WIRTSCHAFT IM SUDWESTERN (GW) [06684277] **1588**

WIRTSCHAFT IN ZAHLEN / STATISTISCHES BUNDESAMT (GW) [10653195] **1526**

WIRTSCHAFT UDSSR INTERN (GW) **1526**

WIRTSCHAFT UND ERZIEHUNG (GW/0174-6170) [01746170] **1791**

WIRTSCHAFT UND GESELLSCHAFT (AU/0378-5130) [04235706] **1588**

WIRTSCHAFT UND GESELLSCHAFT IM GETEILTEN DEUTSCHLAND **CEASED.** (GW) [18366230] **4500**

WIRTSCHAFT UND RECHT (SZ/0043-6135) [02557213] **1631**

WIRTSCHAFT UND STATISTIK (GW/0043-6143) [01644252] **5346**

WIRTSCHAFT UND WETTBEWERB (GW/0043-6151) [05284713] **857**

WIRTSCHAFTLICHE ENTWICKLUNG: AFGHANISTAN (GW) [01787732] **1588**

WIRTSCHAFTLICHE ENTWICKLUNG : AGYPTEN (GW) [01787737] **1588**

WIRTSCHAFTLICHE ENTWICKLUNG : GUATEMALA (GW) [01787739] **1588**

WIRTSCHAFTLICHE ENTWICKLUNG : KUWAIT (GW) [01787736] **1588**

WIRTSCHAFTLICHE ENTWICKLUNG: MADAGASKAR (GW) [01787731] **1588**

WIRTSCHAFTLICHE ENTWICKLUNG : MOCAMBIQUE (GW) [01789760] **1589**

WIRTSCHAFTLICHE ENTWICKLUNG : NICARAGUA (GW) [01787742] **1589**

WIRTSCHAFTLICHE ENTWICKLUNG : VENEZUELA (GW) [01787740] **1589**

WIRTSCHAFTLICHE ENTWICKLUNG : ZYPERN (GW) [01789761] **1589**

WIRTSCHAFTS-GEOGRAPHISCHE STUDIEN (AU/1017-0510) [05301241] **2579**

WIRTSCHAFTSBERICHT UBER DIE LATEINAMERIKANISCHEN LAENDER SOWIE SPANIEN UND PORTUGAL (GW/0415-6285) [05059546] **1589**

WIRTSCHAFTSBERICHTE (VIENNA, AUSTRIA) See CA QUARTERLY **1467**

WIRTSCHAFTSDIENST (HAMBURG) (GW/0043-6275) [07083456] **1526**

WIRTSCHAFTSEIGENE FUTTER (GW/0049-7711) [03802223] **224**

WIRTSCHAFTSINFORMATIK (GW/0937-6429) [21718039] **1263**

WIRTSCHAFTSPOLITISCHE BLAETTER (AU/0043-6291) [02269561] **1526**

WIRTSCHAFTSPRUFUNG, DIE (GW/0043-6313) [02558977] **753**

WIRTSCHAFTSRECHT (GW/0512-6320) [06344485] **3104**

WIRTSCHAFTSRECHTLICHE BLAETTER : WBL (AU/0930-3855) [15906774] **3104**

WIRTSCHAFTSREVUE See BILANZ **1464**

WIRTSCHAFTSRUCKBLICK IN ZAHLEN / BAYERISCHES STAATSMINISTERIUM FUER WIRTSCHAFT UND VERKEHR (GW) [19816082] **1526**

WIRTSCHAFTSSCHUTZ + SICHERHEITSTECHNIK (GW/0173-3303) [07955405] **3179**

WIRTSCHAFTSWISSENSCHAFTLICHE UND WIRTSCHAFTSRECHTLICHE UNTERSUCHUNGEN (GW) [01769957] **3075, 1526**

WIRTSCHAFTSWISSENSCHAFTLICHE VEROFFENTLICHUNGEN (GW/0067-5938) [02763668] **1526**

WIRTSCHAFTSWOCHE (GW) [02240911] **857**

WISCONSERVATION (US/0164-3649) [04634320] **2210**

WISCONSIN See WISCONSIN ADMINISTRATIVE CODE; ADMINISTRATIVE RULES OF STATE AGENCIES PUBLISHED PURSUANT TO CHAP. 227 WISCONSIN STATUTES **4695**

WISCONSIN See WISCONSIN STATUTES **3075**

WISCONSIN See WORKERS' COMPENSATION LAW OF THE STATE OF WISCONSIN **3155**

WISCONSIN ACADEMY OF SCIENCES, ARTS AND LETTERS See TRANSACTIONS OF THE WISCONSIN ACADEMY OF SCIENCES, ARTS, AND LETTERS **5167**

WISCONSIN ACADEMY REVIEW (US/0512-1175) [01770019] **2856**

WISCONSIN ADMINISTRATIVE CODE; ADMINISTRATIVE RULES OF STATE AGENCIES PUBLISHED PURSUANT TO CHAP. 227 WISCONSIN STATUTES (US) [01769986] **4695**

WISCONSIN ADMINISTRATIVE LAW DIGEST, THE (US) [10713495] **3094**

WISCONSIN ADMINISTRATIVE REGISTER (US) [04309928] **3075**

WISCONSIN AGRICULTURAL STATISTICS (US/0512-1329) [02791267] **146, 157**

WISCONSIN AGRICULTURE REPORTING SERVICE See WISCONSIN FARM REPORTER : DAIRY, CROPS, LIVESTOCK **146**

WISCONSIN AGRICULTURIST (US/0043-6356) [04178599] **146**

WISCONSIN ALMANAC, THE (US/0734-0982) [08664613] **2766**

WISCONSIN ANNUAL HIGHWAY SAFETY WORK PROGRAM (US/0148-7728) [03369194] **4807, 5446**

WISCONSIN ARBORIST, THE (US/0887-8927) [13441032] **2433, 2183**

WISCONSIN ARCHEOLOGIST, THE (US/0043-6364) [00852007] **285**

WISCONSIN ARCHITECT (US) [02253943] **310**

WISCONSIN. ARTS BOARD See BIENNIAL REPORT - WISCONSIN ARTS BOARD **316**

WISCONSIN ASTROPHYSICS (US/0363-3675) [02186942] **40**

WISCONSIN. ATTORNEY GENERAL'S OFFICE See OPINIONS OF THE ATTORNEY GENERAL OF THE STATE OF WISCONSIN **3142**

WISCONSIN AUTOMOBILE AND TRUCK DEALERS ASSOCIATION See OFFICIAL WISCONSIN AUTOMOBILE VALUATION GUIDE **5422**

WISCONSIN BALTIC STUDIES (US/0743-7218) [10656362] **2766**

WISCONSIN. BANKING DEPT. ANNUAL REPORT See ANNUAL REPORT OF THE OFFICE OF COMMISSIONER OF BANKING **772**

WISCONSIN BLUE BOOK, THE (US) [03212585] **4695**

WISCONSIN. BUREAU OF HEALTH STATISTICS See HOSPITAL UTILIZATION DATA, WISCONSIN **3785**

WISCONSIN. BUREAU OF LOCAL FINANCIAL ASSISTANCE See INDEBTEDNESS / BUREAU OF LOCAL FINANCIAL ASSISTANCE **790**

WISCONSIN. BUREAU OF LOCAL FINANCIAL ASSISTANCE See BULLETIN (WISCONSIN. BUREAU OF LOCAL FINANCIAL ASSISTANCE) **4715**

WISCONSIN BUSINESS WOMAN, THE (US/0508-9921) [05389974] **5568, 723**

WISCONSIN CAREER DIRECTIONS (US/1056-5558) [23737686] **4210**

WISCONSIN CENTER FOR EDUCATION RESEARCH See BIBLIOGRAPHY OF PUBLICATIONS / WISCONSIN CENTER FOR EDUCATION RESEARCH **1793**

WISCONSIN CHINA SERIES (US/0084-053X) [06575326] **3453**

WISCONSIN. CONSERVATION WORK PROJECTS BOARD See BIENNIAL REPORT - STATE OF WISCONSIN, CONSERVATION WORK PROJECTS BOARD **2188**

WISCONSIN COOPERATIVE PEST SURVEY BULLETIN (US) [06927389] **4248, 146**

WISCONSIN COUNTIES (US/0749-6818) [01770023] **4695**

WISCONSIN COURT RULES AND PROCEDURE. FEDERAL (US) [20443209] **3075**

WISCONSIN COURT RULES AND PROCEDURE. STATE (US) [20443216] **3075**

WISCONSIN COURT RULES AND PROCEDURE..., STATE AND FEDERAL See WISCONSIN COURT RULES AND PROCEDURE. STATE **3075**

WISCONSIN COURT RULES AND PROCEDURE..., STATE AND FEDERAL See WISCONSIN COURT RULES AND PROCEDURE. FEDERAL **3075**

WISCONSIN. CRIME INFORMATION BUREAU See WISCONSIN CRIMINAL JUSTICE INFORMATION, CRIME AND ARRESTS **3084**

WISCONSIN. CRIME INFORMATION BUREAU See LAW ENFORCEMENT BULLETIN **3168**

WISCONSIN CRIMINAL JUSTICE INFORMATION, CRIME AND ARRESTS (US) [01774201] **3084**

WISCONSIN CROP WEATHER (US) **146**

WISCONSIN DAIRY FACTS (US/0092-0304) [01787267] **199**

WISCONSIN DEER AND BEAR HARVEST SUMMARY (US) [04521107] **4880**

WISCONSIN. DEPT. OF AGRICULTURE, TRADE, AND CONSUMER PROTECTION See BIENNIAL REPORT - WISCONSIN. DEPT. OF AGRICULTURE, TRADE AND CONSUMER PROTECTION **66**

WISCONSIN. DEPT. OF AGRICULTURE, TRADE AND CONSUMER PROTECTION. PLANT INDUSTRY DIVISION See WISCONSIN COOPERATIVE PEST SURVEY BULLETIN **146**

WISCONSIN. DEPT. OF DEVELOPMENT See BIENNIAL REPORT / STATE OF WISCONSIN, DEPARTMENT OF DEVELOPMENT **1548**

WISCONSIN. DEPT. OF EMPLOYMENT RELATIONS See BIENNIAL REPORT - STATE OF WISCONSIN, DEPARTMENT OF EMPLOYMENT RELATIONS **4701**

WISCONSIN. DEPT. OF HEALTH AND SOCIAL SERVICES See BIENNIAL BUDGET REQUEST - WISCONSIN DEPARTMENT OF HEALTH AND SOCIAL SERVICES **5274**

WISCONSIN. DEPT. OF INDUSTRY, LABOR AND HUMAN RELATIONS See BIENNIAL REPORT - STATE OF WISCONSIN, DEPARTMENT OF INDUSTRY, LABOR AND HUMAN RELATIONS **1655**

WISCONSIN. DEPT. OF INDUSTRY, LABOR AND HUMAN RELATIONS See WISCONSIN LABOR FORCE **1718**

WISCONSIN. DEPT. OF INDUSTRY, LABOR AND HUMAN RELATIONS. BUREAU OF RESEARCH AND STATISTICS. EMPLOYMENT SECURITY SECTION See WISCONSIN LABOR FORCE **1718**

WISCONSIN. DEPT. OF INDUSTRY, LABOR AND HUMAN RELATIONS. BUREAU OF RESEARCH AND STATISTICS. RISK MANAGEMENT SECTION See WORKMEN'S COMPENSATION DATA **1719**

WISCONSIN. DEPT. OF JUSTICE See PROSECUTORS' BULLETIN, THE **3108**

WISCONSIN — Alphabetical Title Index

WISCONSIN. DEPT. OF NATURAL RESOURCES *See* WISCONSIN WATER QUALITY ... REPORT TO CONGRESS **5549**

WISCONSIN. DEPT. OF NATURAL RESOURCES *See* WISCONSIN DEER AND BEAR HARVEST SUMMARY **4880**

WISCONSIN. DEPT. OF NATURAL RESOURCES *See* WISCONSIN OUTDOORS AND CONSERVATION NEWS **4880**

WISCONSIN. DEPT. OF NATURAL RESOURCES *See* RESEARCH REPORT - WISCONSIN. DEPT. OF NATURAL RESOURCES **2204**

WISCONSIN. DEPT. OF REGULATION AND LICENSING *See* FINANCIAL REPORT ON REGISTERED CHARITABLE ORGANIZATIONS **5285**

WISCONSIN. DEPT. OF REGULATION AND LICENSING *See* BIENNIAL REPORT - STATE OF WISCONSIN, DEPARTMENT OF REGULATION AND LICENSING **4632**

WISCONSIN. DEPT. OF REVENUE *See* ANNUAL ECONOMIC REPORT - WISCONSIN DEPARTMENT OF REVENUE **4709**

WISCONSIN. DEPT. OF REVENUE *See* BIENNIAL REPORT - DEPARTMENT OF REVENUE (WISCONSIN) **4713**

WISCONSIN. DEPT. OF REVENUE. DIVISION OF RESEARCH AND ANALYSIS *See* SUMMARY OF TAX EXEMPTION DEVICES / DIVISION OF RESEARCH AND ANALYSIS, DEPARTMENT OF REVENUE **4751**

WISCONSIN. DEPT. OF TRANSPORTATION. DIVISION OF PLANNING *See* STATE OF WISCONSIN STATE SUMMARY. TYPE AND AMOUNT OF AIDS PAID TO ALL GOVERNMENTAL UNITS AND COUNTIES **5444**

WISCONSIN. DEPT. OF VETERANS AFFAIRS *See* BIENNIAL REPORT - STATE OF WISCONSIN, DEPARTMENT OF VETERANS AFFAIRS **4038**

WISCONSIN DIALOGUE : A FACULTY JOURNAL FOR THE UNIVERSITY OF WISCONSIN-EAU CLAIRE (US) [07682674] **5237**

WISCONSIN. DIVISION FOR HANDICAPPED CHILDREN *See* BUREAU MEMORANDUM **4385**

WISCONSIN. DIVISION FOR LIBRARY SERVICES *See* WISCONSIN LIBRARY SERVICE RECORD **3256**

WISCONSIN. DIVISION OF BUILDINGS AND GROUNDS *See* ENERGY USE, STATE OFFICE BUILDINGS **1942**

WISCONSIN. DIVISION OF CORRECTIONS. OFFICE OF SYSTEMS AND EVALUATION *See* RESIDENTS IN WISCONSIN ADULT CORRECTIONAL INSTITUTIONS **3175**

WISCONSIN. DIVISION OF CORRECTIONS. OFFICE OF SYSTEMS AND EVALUATION *See* ADULT PROBATION ADMISSIONS **3156**

WISCONSIN. DIVISION OF HEALTH *See* ACCIDENTAL POISONING IN WISCONSIN **4763**

WISCONSIN. DIVISION OF HEALTH *See* FINANCIAL REPORT - DEPARTMENT OF HEALTH & SOCIAL SERVICES, DIVISION OF HEALTH **4775**

WISCONSIN. DIVISION OF HIGHWAY SAFETY COORDINATION *See* WISCONSIN ANNUAL HIGHWAY SAFETY WORK PROGRAM **5446**

WISCONSIN DRUGGIST *See* WISCONSIN PHARMACIST, THE **4332**

WISCONSIN ECONOMIC INDICATORS (US) [11686498] **1589**

WISCONSIN. EDUCATIONAL COMMUNICATIONS BOARD *See* BIENNIAL REPORT - EDUCATIONAL COMMUNICATIONS BOARD **1889**

WISCONSIN. EDUCATIONAL COMMUNICATIONS BOARD *See* PROGRAM BUDGET REQUEST - EDUCATIONAL COMMUNICATIONS BOARD **1842**

WISCONSIN EDUCATIONAL RADIO NETWORK *See* RADIO GUIDE (MADISON) **1137**

●WISCONSIN EMPLOYMENT LAW LETTER (US/1059-5066) [24609823] **3155**

WISCONSIN. EMPLOYMENT SECURITY DIVISION *See* EMPLOYMENT AND WAGES COVERED BY WISCONSIN'S U. C. LAW **3147**

WISCONSIN. ENERGY DEVELOPMENT AND DEMONSTRATION PROGRAM *See* ENERGY DEVELOPMENT AND DEMONSTRATION PROGRAM : YEAR END REPORT **1940**

WISCONSIN ENGINEER (US/0043-6453) [02451631] **2001**

WISCONSIN ENGLISH JOURNAL (US) [01770026] 1908, **3333**

●WISCONSIN ENVIRONMENTAL COMPLIANCE UPDATE (US/1072-9151) [29236682] **3117**

WISCONSIN ESCAPE (US/0273-9755) [07048763] **5499**

WISCONSIN. ETHICS BOARD *See* BIENNIAL REPORT - STATE OF WISCONSIN ETHICS BOARD **2249**

WISCONSIN FARM REPORTER : DAIRY, CROPS, LIVESTOCK (US) [04475244] **146**

WISCONSIN. FEDERAL PROPERTY PROGRAM *See* PROPERTY HIGHLIGHTS **4675**

WISCONSIN GEOGRAPHER (US/0892-5224) [14388315] **2579**

WISCONSIN GEOLOGICAL AND NATURAL HISTORY SURVEY *See* BULLETIN - WISCONSIN GEOLOGICAL AND NATURAL HISTORY SURVEY **1371**

WISCONSIN GOLF (US/1042-6620) [19103865] **4930**

WISCONSIN. GOVERNOR *See* EXECUTIVE BUDGET MESSAGE / STATE OF WISCONSIN **4723**

WISCONSIN. GOVERNOR'S ADVOCACY COMMITTEE FOR CHILDREN AND YOUTH *See* BIENNIAL REPORT - GOVERNOR'S ADVOCACY COMMITTEE FOR CHILDREN AND YOUTH **5274**

●WISCONSIN HEALTH CARE IN PERSPECTIVE (US/1065-450X) [26606953] **4807**

WISCONSIN. HIGHER EDUCATIONAL AIDS BOARD *See* STUDENT FINANCIAL AID ACTIVITY REPORT **1848**

WISCONSIN HOLIDAY NEWS *See* WISCONSIN ESCAPE **5499**

WISCONSIN HOLSTEIN NEWS (US/0194-4401) [04656534] **199**

WISCONSIN HOME GALLERY MAGAZINE (US/0888-6822) [13695113] 311, **2904**

WISCONSIN IN PERSPECTIVE (US/1065-5778) [26665876] **5346**

WISCONSIN INTERNATIONAL LAW JOURNAL (US/0743-7951) [10030538] **3138**

WISCONSIN. INVESTMENT BOARD *See* BIENNIAL REPORT - STATE OF WISCONSIN, INVESTMENT BOARD **4713**

WISCONSIN ISSUES (US) 816, **753**

WISCONSIN JEWISH CHRONICLE, THE (US/0043-6488) [03963149] **5053**

WISCONSIN JOURNAL OF PUBLIC INSTRUCTION (US/0098-6976) [02241118] **1791**

WISCONSIN LABOR FORCE (US/0095-3644) [01796599] **1718**

WISCONSIN LABOR HISTORY SOCIETY *See* NEWSLETTER - WISCONSIN LABOR HISTORY SOCIETY **1695**

WISCONSIN LAW REVIEW (US/0043-650X) [01607158] **3075**

WISCONSIN LAWYER (US/1043-0490) [19082211] **4695**

WISCONSIN LEGAL DIRECTORY, THE (US) [06483515] **3075**

WISCONSIN. LEGISLATIVE COUNCIL *See* DIGEST OF COUNCIL BILLS - WISCONSIN. LEGISLATIVE COUNCIL **2961**

WISCONSIN. LEGISLATIVE COUNCIL *See* GENERAL REPORT OF THE LEGISLATIVE COUNCIL TO THE LEGISLATURE **4650**

WISCONSIN. LEGISLATURE. JOINT COMMITTEE FOR REVIEW OF ADMINISTRATIVE RULES *See* BIENNIAL REPORT / JOINT COMMITTEE FOR REVIEW OF ADMINISTRATIVE RULES **2941**

WISCONSIN LIBRARY SERVICE RECORD (US/0361-2848) [02246403] **3256**

WISCONSIN LIVE STOCK BREEDERS' ASSOCIATION *See* BULLETIN FROM WISCONSIN LIVE STOCK BREEDERS' ASSOCIATION, THE **208**

WISCONSIN LUTHERAN QUARTERLY (US/0362-5648) [01645762] **5009**

WISCONSIN MAGAZINE OF HISTORY (US/0043-6534) [01642391] **2766**

WISCONSIN MANUFACTURERS REGISTER (US/0738-0070) [09506810] **3489**

WISCONSIN MASTER PLUMBER (US/0199-1639) [05688939] **2609**

WISCONSIN MEDICAL ALUMNI QUARTERLY (US/8755-1519) [08677465] 3793, **1103**

WISCONSIN MEDICAL JOURNAL (US/0043-6542) [01770034] **3651**

WISCONSIN NEWMONTH (US/1059-0935) [24479081] **2550**

WISCONSIN. OFFICE OF COMMISSIONER OF BANKING *See* ANNUAL REPORT OF THE OFFICE OF COMMISSIONER OF BANKING **772**

WISCONSIN. OFFICE OF CONSUMER PROTECTION *See* CONSUMER PROTECTION REPORT **1295**

WISCONSIN. OFFICE OF CONSUMER PROTECTION. ANNUAL REPORT *See* CONSUMER PROTECTION REPORT **1295**

WISCONSIN. OFFICE OF EMERGENCY ENERGY ASSISTANCE *See* BIENNIAL REPORT OF THE OFFICE OF EMERGENCY ENERGY ASSISTANCE **1933**

WISCONSIN. OFFICE OF THE COMMISSIONER OF CREDIT UNIONS *See* BIENNIAL REPORT OF OFFICE OF THE COMMISSIONER OF CREDIT UNIONS **778**

WISCONSIN. OFFICE OF THE COMMISSIONER OF SECURITIES *See* WISCONSIN SECURITIES BULLETIN **920**

WISCONSIN OUTDOOR JOURNAL (US/0893-5769) [15585348] **4880**

WISCONSIN OUTDOORS AND CONSERVATION NEWS (US) [03929735] 2210, **4880**

WISCONSIN. PERSONNEL COMMISSION *See* BIENNIAL REPORT - STATE OF WISCONSIN, PERSONNEL COMMISSION **4701**

WISCONSIN PHARMACIST, THE (US/0043-6585) [07147716] **4332**

WISCONSIN PHYSICIANS : DESCRIPTION AND DISTRIBUTION (US/0361-817X) [02247024] **3917**

WISCONSIN PUBLIC EMPLOYMENT DECISIONS DIGEST (US/0145-8655) [02803382] **1718**

WISCONSIN PUBLIC/PRIVATE SCHOOL DIRECTORY *See* WISCONSIN SCHOOL DIRECTORY / WISCONSIN DPI **1791**

WISCONSIN PUBLICATIONS IN THE HISTORY OF SCIENCE AND MEDICINE (US/0736-4318) [09034126] **3651**

WISCONSIN REA NEWS *See* WISCONSIN REC NEWS **1543**

WISCONSIN REALTOR, THE (US/0279-2583) [07686598] **4848**

WISCONSIN REC NEWS (US) [08733834] 2086, **1543**

WISCONSIN REGIONAL WRITER (US) [08680396] **3453**

WISCONSIN REGISTERED LICENSED VETERINARIANS. BULLETIN (US) [01788063] **5527**

WISCONSIN REHABILITATION ASSOCIATION *See* GOAL, THE **1676**

WISCONSIN REPORTER (US/0746-150X) [09709791] **3075**

WISCONSIN RESEARCH AND DEVELOPMENT CENTER FOR COGNITIVE LEARNING *See* INDIVIDUALLY GUIDED EDUCATION **1896**

WISCONSIN RESEARCH AND DEVELOPMENT CENTER FOR COGNITIVE LEARNING *See* WORKING PAPER **5265**

WISCONSIN. RESETTLEMENT ASSISTANCE OFFICE *See* THANG-TIEN **4059**

WISCONSIN RESTAURATEUR, THE (US/0274-7472) [06549884] 723, **5073**

WISCONSIN REVIEW (OSHKOSH) (US/0043-6631) [02441297] **3453**

●WISCONSIN SCHOOL DIRECTORY / WISCONSIN DPI (US) [24834235] **1791**

WISCONSIN SCHOOL MUSICIAN, THE (US/0043-6658) [01748667] 1791, **4159**

WISCONSIN SCHOOL NEWS (US) [02253458] **1874**

WISCONSIN SECURITIES BULLETIN (US) [04730893] **920**

WISCONSIN SERVICES DIRECTORY / WISCONSIN MANUFACTURERS & COMMERCE (US) [14926854] **1631**

WISCONSIN SILENT SPORTS (US/0882-9640) [12046553] **4930**

WISCONSIN SMALL BUSINESS COUNSELOR (US/0897-5116) [17010973] **889**

WISCONSIN SNOW FROST (US) **1437**

WISCONSIN SOCIOLOGIST *See* SOCIOLOGICAL IMAGINATION **5260**

WISCONSIN SOCIOLOGIST, THE (US/0043-6666) [01640812] **5265**

WISCONSIN SPANISH TEACHER (US) [06322768] 1908, **3333**

WISCONSIN SPORTSMAN (US/0361-9451) [02441473] **4880**

WISCONSIN. STATE BOARD OF VOCATIONAL, TECHNICAL AND ADULT EDUCATION *See* VTAE JOURNAL **1917**

WISCONSIN. STATE BOARD OF VOCATIONAL, TECHNICAL AND ADULT EDUCATION *See* STAFF NOTES - WISCONSIN BOARD OF VOCATIONAL, TECHNICAL AND ADULT EDUCATION **1916**

WISCONSIN. STATE BUDGET OFFICE *See* EXECUTIVE BUDGET POLICY ISSUE PAPERS **4647**

WISCONSIN STATE BUILDING COMMISSION See BUILDING PROJECTS STATUS REPORT : A REPORT TO THE WISCONSIN LEGISLATURE **604**

WISCONSIN. STATE ELECTIONS BOARD See BIENNIAL REPORT OF WISCONSIN STATE ELECTIONS BOARD **4632**

WISCONSIN STATE JOURNAL (MADISON, WIS. : 1862) (US/0749-405X) [05025315] **5772**

WISCONSIN STATE NURSES' ASSOCIATION. BULLETIN See STAT **3869**

WISCONSIN STATE READING ASSOCIATION See JOURNAL - WISCONSIN STATE READING ASSOCIATION **1899**

WISCONSIN STATUTES (US) [01769988] **3075**

WISCONSIN STUDIES IN LITERATURE (US) [02558922] **3453**

WISCONSIN TAX APPEALS COMMISSION See DECISIONS - WISCONSIN TAX APPEALS COMMISSION **4719**

WISCONSIN TAX BULLETIN (US) [04734693] **4759**

WISCONSIN TAXPAYER, THE (US/0043-6720) [01714582] **4759**

WISCONSIN TRAILS (US/0095-4314) [01796750] **2550**

WISCONSIN. UNIVERSITY. BUREAU OF BUSINESS RESEARCH AND SERVICE See RESEARCH IN THE SCHOOL OF BUSINESS (MADISON) **1517**

WISCONSIN. UNIVERSITY--MADISON. INSTITUTE FOR RESEARCH ON POVERTY See RESEARCH REPORT - INSTITUTE FOR RESEARCH ON POVERTY (MADISON) **5215**

WISCONSIN. UNIVERSITY--MADISON. SEA GRANT COLLEGE PROGRAM See ADVISORY REPORT - UNIVERSITY OF WISCONSIN SEA GRANT COLLEGE PROGRAM **1807**

WISCONSIN. UNIVERSITY, MILWAUKEE. CENTER FOR LATIN AMERICA See DISCUSSION PAPER - CENTER FOR LATIN AMERICA IN THE UNIVERSITY OF WISCONSIN, MILWAUKEE **1821**

WISCONSIN VETERINARY MEDICAL ASSOCIATION See BULLETIN - WISCONSIN VETERINARY MEDICAL ASSOCIATION **5506**

WISCONSIN VOCATIONAL EDUCATOR, THE **CEASED.** (US) [07145120] **1917**

WISCONSIN WATER QUALITY ... REPORT TO CONGRESS (US/0740-4700) [08721273] **5549**

WISCONSIN WOMEN'S LAW JOURNAL (US/1052-3421) [12192424] 5568, **3075**

WISCONSIN WOOD MARKETING BULLETIN (US) [04233071] 938, **2405**

WISCONSIN WOODS & WATER (US/1041-1291) [18650855] **4881**

WISCONSIN WORK FORCE See WISCONSIN LABOR FORCE **1718**

WISCONSIN ZIP+4 STATE DIRECTORY (US) [11636522] **1148**

WISDEN'S CRICKETERS ALMANAC (UK) **4930**

WISE COUNTY MESSENGER (US/0746-8679) [10351580] **5756**

WISE GIVING GUIDE (US/0275-0031) [07069071] **4339**

WISE OWL NEWS (TORONTO) (CN/0705-7814) [04518907] **2871**

WISE WOMAN, THE (US/0883-119X) [12067355] **5568**

WISENET (AT/0815-0753) [I08150753] 5170, **5568**

●WISER NOW (US/1071-2275) [28577147] **3755**

WISH LETTER / GRIGSBY CACTUS GARDENS (US) [11521561] **2433**

WISHEK STAR (US) [01770046] **5726**

WISLEY HANDBOOK (UK) [04413087] **2433**

WISPAS (NZ/0110-0815) [I01100815] **5549**

WISSENSCHAFT UND FORTSCHRITT (GW/0510-6966) [01080817] **5170**

WISSENSCHAFT UND GEGENWART. GEISTESWISSENSCHAFTLICHE REIHE (GW) [06841468] **5170**

WISSENSCHAFT UND GEGENWART. JURISTISCHE REIHE (GW) [07095681] **3076**

WISSENSCHAFT UND GESELLSCHAFT (GW/0512-1426) [01807608] **2857**

WISSENSCHAFT UND WEISHEIT (GW/0043-678X) [02186360] **5009**

WISSENSCHAFT UND WELTBILD; ZEITSCHRIFT FUER GRUNDFRAGEN DER FORSCHUNG UND WELTANSCHAUUNG (AU/0043-6798) [02186378] **4365**

WISSENSCHAFTEN IN DER DDR (GW) [03703418] **5170**

WISSENSCHAFTLICH-TECHNISCHER BERICHT / BEREICH WISSENSCHAFTLICH-TECHNISCHE BETRIEBSEINRICHTUNGEN (GW) [11001600] **40**

WISSENSCHAFTLICHE ABHANDLUNGEN (GW/0417-1411) [04886270] **146**

WISSENSCHAFTLICHE BEITRAEGE AUS EUROPAISCHEN HOCHSCHULEN REIHE 11 MATHEMATIK (GW/0934-0505) [I09340505] **3541**

WISSENSCHAFTLICHE BERICHTE AUS DER HOCHMAGNETFELDANLAGE DER TECHNISCHEN UNIVERSITAT BRAUNSCHWEIG (GW/0723-9459) [20518428] **1854**

WISSENSCHAFTLICHE BERICHTE - ZENTRALINSTITUT FUER FESTKORPERPHYSIK UND WERKSTOFFORSCHUNG (GW/0138-2179) [06435930] **4425**

WISSENSCHAFTLICHE MITTEILUNGEN (GW/0936-7195) [12636472] **2579**

WISSENSCHAFTLICHE MITTEILUNGEN DES BOSNISCH-HERZEGOWINISCHEN LANDESMUSEUMS. HEFT A : ARCHAOLOGIE (YU/0352-1990) [I03521990] **285**

WISSENSCHAFTLICHE MONOGRAPHIEN ZUM ALTEN UND NEUEN TESTAMENT (GW/0512-1582) [05222675] **5009**

WISSENSCHAFTLICHE REIHE / ZENTRALINSTITUT FUER DIE KASSENARZTLICHE VERSORGUNG IN DER BUNDESREPUBLIK DEUTSCHLAND (GW/0932-4658) [10407458] **2896**

WISSENSCHAFTLICHE SCHRIFTENREIHE (GW/0435-7523) [02028229] **1527**

WISSENSCHAFTLICHE TAGUNG; VORTRAGE (GW/0419-0041) [05109197] **530**

WISSENSCHAFTLICHE TAGUNGEN DER TECHNISCHEN UNIVERSITAT KARL-MARX-STADT (GW/0863-5544) [I08635544] **5170**

WISSENSCHAFTLICHE UND ANGEWANDTE PHOTOGRAPHIE, DIE (AU/0084-0998) [01770048] **4378**

WISSENSCHAFTLICHE UNTERSUCHUNGEN ZUM NEUEN TESTAMENT (GW/0512-1604) [03209439] **5020**

WISSENSCHAFTLICHE VEREINIGUNG FUER AUGENOPTIK UND OPTOMETRIE (GER.) See FACHVORTRAGE DES WVAO-JAHRESKONGRESSES, DIE **4215**

WISSENSCHAFTLICHE ZEITSCHRIFT (GW/0040-1528) [02253972] **2495**

WISSENSCHAFTLICHE ZEITSCHRIFT (GE/0509-9773) [01672802] **311**

WISSENSCHAFTLICHE ZEITSCHRIFT DER ELEKTROTECHNIK (GW/0373-9953) [08579937] **2086**

WISSENSCHAFTLICHE ZEITSCHRIFT DER HOCHSCHULE FUER ARCHITEKTUR UND BAUWESEN WEIMAR AUSGABE A (GW/0863-0712) [I08630712] **311**

WISSENSCHAFTLICHE ZEITSCHRIFT DER HOCHSCHULE FUER ARCHITEKTUR UND BAUWESEN WEIMAR AUSGABE B (GW/0863-0720) [I08630720] **311**

WISSENSCHAFTLICHE ZEITSCHRIFT DER HOCHSCHULE FUER BAUWESEN LEIPZIG (SZ/0457-3943) [05012915] **311**

WISSENSCHAFTLICHE ZEITSCHRIFT DER HOCHSCHULE FUER OEKONOMIE (GW/0067-5954) [04148709] **1527**

WISSENSCHAFTLICHE ZEITSCHRIFT DER HUMBOLDT-UNIVERSITAT ZU BERLIN. GEISTES- UND SOZIALWISSENSCHAFTEN (GW) [24453130] **5225**

WISSENSCHAFTLICHE ZEITSCHRIFT DER HUMBOLDT-UNIVERSITAT ZU BERLIN REIHE AGRARWISSENSCHAFTEN (GW/0863-0658) [I08630658] **146**

WISSENSCHAFTLICHE ZEITSCHRIFT DER HUMBOLDT-UNIVERSITAT ZU BERLIN. REIHE MATHEMATIK/NATURWISSENSCHAFT EN (GW/0863-0631) [21098053] **5170**

WISSENSCHAFTLICHE ZEITSCHRIFT DER PADAGOGISCHEN HOCHSCHULE "KARL LIEBKNECHT" POTSDAM (GW/0138-290X) [01715317] **5170**

WISSENSCHAFTLICHE ZEITSCHRIFT DER TECHNISCHE HOCHSCHULE LEIPZIG (GW/0323-6129) [03501755] **5170**

WISSENSCHAFTLICHE ZEITSCHRIFT DER TECHNISCHEN UNIVERSITAT CHEMNITZ (GW/0941-9950) [I09419950] **995**

WISSENSCHAFTLICHE ZEITSCHRIFT DER TECHNISCHEN UNIVERSITAT DRESDEN (GW/0043-6925) [05012740] **5170**

WISSENSCHAFTLICHE ZEITSCHRIFT DER UNIVERSITAT ROSTOCK. NATURWISSENSCHAFTLICHE REIHE (GW/0863-1204) [09570294] **5170**

WISSENSCHAFTLICHE ZEITSCHRIFT - ERNST-MORITZ-ARNDT-UNIVERSITAT GRIEFSWALD. MEDIZINISCHE REIHE (GW/0138-1067) [01598062] **3651**

WISSENSCHAFTLICHE ZEITSCHRIFT - MARTIN-LUTHER-UNIV. HALLE-WITTENBERG. MATHEMATISCH-NATURWISSENSCH AFTLICHE REIHE (GW/0138-1504) [08632732] **5170**

WISSENSCHAFTLICHER BUCH BESPRECHUNGSDIENST : WIBB (GW/0179-0080) [19705975] 4365, **5009**

WISSENSCHAFTLISCHE ZEITSCHRIFT DER TECHNISCHEN UNIVERSITAT OTTO VON GUERICKE MAGDEBURG (GW/0863-0925) [18461877] **2033**

WISSENSCHAFTSRECHT, WISSENSCHAFTSVERWALTUNG, WISSENSCHAFTSFORDERUNG (GW/0443-6976) [05135421] 1854, **3076**

WIST. WIRTSCHAFTSWISSENSCHAFTLICHE S STUDIUM (GW/0340-1650) [I03401650] 1641, **1596**

WISTAR INSTITUTE OF ANATOMY AND BIOLOGY See WISTAR SYMPOSIUM SERIES **587**

WISTAR SYMPOSIUM SERIES (US/0271-9347) [06578154] **587**

WISTRA (GW/0721-6890) [09515678] **3109**

WISU. DAS WIRTSCHAFTSSTUDIUM (GW/0340-3084) [I03403084] **1854**

WITCH AND THE CHAMELEON, THE (CN/0382-0246) [03079378] **3453**

WITHERBY AND COMPANY, LONDON See REFERENCE BOOK OF MARINE INSURANCE CLAUSES **2891**

WITHIN ASAE (US/0741-0387) [10076035] 146, **2001**

WITHIN ASAE See RESOURCE (SAINT JOSEPH, MICH.) **1994**

WITHOUT PREJUDICE **CEASED.** (US/0892-9408) [15296763] **4514**

WITHOUT PREJUDICE (EDMONTON) (CN/0706-5574) [04589591] **2896**

WITNESS (AMBLER), THE (US/0197-8896) [03476349] **5069**

WITNESS (FARMINGTON HILLS, MICH.) (US/0891-1371) [14627910] **3453**

WITNESS FOR PEACE NEWSLETTER (US) [15125889] 4365, **4500**

WITTENBERG ENTERPRISE AND BIRNAMWOOD NEWS (WITTENBERG, WIS. : 1982) (US/0885-081X) [12210671] **5772**

WITTENBERG HISTORY JOURNAL, THE (US/0147-9873) [03260379] **2633**

WITTENBERG REVIEW OF LITERATURE & ART (US/0147-0868) [03106041] **3356**

WITTENBERG'S PRODUCTS LIABILITY: THE LAW IN MISSISSIPPI (US) **3076**

WITTERUNG IN UBERSEE, DIE (GW/0043-7085) [01808864] **1437**

WITTHAYASAN KASETSART (TH/0075-5192) [02255383] **146**

WITTHAYASAN KASETSART. SAKHA THAMMACHT / KASETSART JOURNAL. NATURAL SCIENCES (TH) [11922409] **146**

WITTHAYASAN KASETSAT. SAKHA SANGKHOMMASAT (TH/0125-8370) [11967414] **5226**

WITTYWORLD (US/0892-9807) [15307754] **376**

●WITZ (PENNGROVE, CALIF.) (US/1061-4583) [25312404] **3453**

WIZARD: THE GUIDE TO COMICS (US) **2779**

●WJC REPORT : WORLD JEWISH CONGRESS PUBLICATION, THE (US) [26122153] **5053**

●WJCT MAGAZINE (US/1065-8564) [26778470] **1143**

WLB. WASSER, LUFT UND BETRIEB See WASSER, LUFT UND BODEN : WLB **2245**

WLN PARTICIPANT (US/0278-6303) [05430795] **3256**

WLW JOURNAL **CEASED.** (US/0272-1996) [06182031] **3256**

WMS REPORT (US) [16316793] **5549**

WN TRENDS, HEALTH CARE AND MANAGEMENT (US/0742-1052) [10295886] **4808**

WNC BUSINESS JOURNAL See ORIGINAL WNC BUSINESS JOURNAL, THE **701**

Alphabetical Title Index

WNC BUSINESS JOURNAL (US/1049-7145) [16961399] **723**

WNY MOTORIST (US/0149-3175) [03454034] **5428**

WNYF (US/0042-9775) [06135294] **2293**

WO MEN AI KO HSUEH (CC) [07820066] **5170**

WOCHE IN AUSTRALIEN, DIE (AT) **5777**

WOCHE (ZURICH, SWITZERLAND) (SZ) [08605525] **2525**

WOCHEN PRESSE, DIE (AU) [13346373] **5778**

WOCHENBERICHT - DEUTSCHES INSTITUT FUER WIRTSCHAFTSFORSCHUNG (GW/0012-1304) [02258272] **1589**

WOCHENBLATT FUER PAPIERFABRIKATION (GW/0043-7131) [04167519] **4240**

WOHNBAU (AU) [03920786] **2839**

WOHNBAUFORSCHUNG IN OSTERREICH (AU) [03522734] **2839**

WOHNGELD IN NORDRHEIN-WESTFALEN (GW) [03641228] 2839, **2841**

WOHNMOBIL & CARAVAN (GW) **5499**

WOHNRECHTLICHE BLAETTER (AU/0933-2766) [I09332766] 2839, **3076**

WOHNUNGEN, DIE (AU) [01799925] **2839**

WOJSKO I WYCHOWANIE : PISMO ZONIERZY ZAWODOWYCH WP (PL) [22894834] **4061**

WOJSKOWY PRZEGLAD HISTORYCZNY (PL/0043-7182) [03219176] **2716**

WOKNA CHEMICZNE (PL/0208-7499) [10049167] **995**

WOLF! (CLIFTON HEIGHTS, PA.) (US/1042-6426) [19097342] **4881**

WOLF PARK NEWS (US) [13441489] **5600**

WOLFE CITY MIRROR, THE (US/0746-536X) [10125403] **5756**

WOLFE COUNTY NEWS, THE (US) [14473042] **5683**

WOLFENBUETTELER STUDIEN ZUR AUFKLAERUNG (GW/0342-5940) [02242556] **4365**

WOLFENBUTTELER ABHANDLUNGEN ZUR RENAISSANCEFORSCHUNG (GW/0724-956X) [14055292] 3453, **2716**

WOLFENBUTTELER BAROCK-NACHRICHTEN (GW/0340-6318) [03220012] **3454**

WOLFENBUTTELER BEITRAEGE (GW/0300-2012) [02194673] **3256**

WOLFENBUTTELER NOTIZEN ZUR BUCHGESCHICHTE (GW/0341-2253) [03679878] **4833**

WOLFENBUTTELER RENAISSANCE MITTEILUNGEN (GW/0342-4340) [03887927] **2716**

WOLFMAN REPORT ON THE PHOTOGRAPHIC & IMAGING INDUSTRY IN THE UNITED STATES (US/0897-5132) [12043787] **4378**

WOLGAN CHOSON (KO) [07386827] **2509**

WOLGAN CHUNGANG (KO) [05162211] **2509**

WOLGAN HANUIYAK CHONGBO (KO) [05167746] **3651**

WOLGAN KOMPYUTO HAKSUP (KO) [10728319] **1207**

WOLGAN KONCHUK MUNHWA (KO) [07707209] **311**

WOLGAN KONSOL (KO) [09079009] 631, 2033, **311**

WOLGAN KOSIN (KO) [11360928] **5009**

WOLGAN KWAHAK (CH) [12379855] **5170**

WOLGAN KYOBO (KO) [10083668] **2896**

WOLGAN KYONGJE TONGHYANG (KO) [07963138] **1527**

WOLGAN KYONGNI (KO) [11325646] 889, **753**

WOLGAN MOKHOE (KO) [11356680] **5009**

WOLGAN MOT (KO) [11459758] **1088**

WOLGAN MUNHAK (KO) [05227154] **3454**

WOLGAN MUNHWAJAE (KO) [05133172] **2668**

WOLGAN NAKKSI (KO) [10833216] **4881**

WOLGAN PADA (KO) [10187835] **1458**

WOLGAN PANGSONG (KO) [08948575] **1143**

WOLGAN POJANG SANOP (KO) [11768797] **4222**

WOLGAN SEDAE (KO) [05160222] **2510**

WOLGAN SOMYU (KO) [09223379] **5359**

WOLGAN SSIRUM (KO) [11311640] **4930**

WOLGAN TOKSO (KO) [05224757] **4833**

WOLGAN TONGSO MUNHWA (KO) [05236766] 333, **2633**

WOLGAN UMAK (KO) [05167386] **4159**

WOLGAN UNJON SEGYE (KO) [10728461] **5428**

WOLSLEY BULLETIN, THE (CN/0842-084X) [19043300] **5798**

WOLVERINE (US/1044-453X) [19022153] **4867**

WOLVERINE (ANN ARBOR, MICH.), THE (US/1048-9940) [21102269] **4930**

WOLVES AND RELATED CANIDS (US/0899-9317) [18276702] **5600**

WOMACK COURIER (US/0743-7099) [10649236] **2477**

WOMAN (CH) **5568**

WOMAN *CEASED.* (US/1042-4849) [19069953] **5568**

WOMAN ACTIVIST, THE (US/0049-7770) [02269587] 5568, **4500**

WOMAN ALIVE (UK/0962-2152) [I09622152] **5009**

WOMAN & HOME (UK) **5568**

WOMAN BOWLER *See* WB (GREENDALE, WIS.) **4929**

WOMAN BOWLER, THE (US/0043-7255) [02252120] **4930**

WOMAN CONSTITUTIONALIST (US/0043-728X) [01775456] **5568**

WOMAN DIVER (US/1054-8580) [22996446] 5569, **4930**

WOMAN ENGINEER. (GREENLAWN, N.Y.), THE (US/0887-2120) [08705153] 5569, **2001**

WOMAN ENGINEER, THE (UK) [01812040] 5569, **2001**

WOMAN IN HISTORY (US/0195-9743) [05732161] **5569**

WOMAN LOCALLY (US/0163-3244) [05883779] **5569**

WOMAN OF POWER (US/0743-2596) [10546363] **5569**

WOMAN POET (US/0195-6183) [05526987] **3473**

WOMAN WRITER (AT/0313-6485) [I03136485] **3454**

WOMANEWS (US) [11483997] **5569**

WOMANIST (OTTAWA) (CN/0849-4975) [21201063] **5569**

WOMAN'S ART JOURNAL (US/0270-7993) [06497852] 5569, **368**

WOMAN'S DAY (US/0043-7336) [01770065] **5569**

WOMAN'S DAY (AUSTRALIA) (AT) **5569**

WOMAN'S DAY COOKING FOR TWO (US/0198-0297) [06157202] **2793**

WOMAN'S DAY CROSSWORDS (US/0732-054X) [08297341] **4867**

WOMAN'S DAY DESSERT LOVER'S COOKBOOK (US/0278-1026) [07696359] **2793**

WOMAN'S DAY GREAT HOLIDAY BAKING IDEAS (US/0195-6299) [05513934] **2793**

WOMAN'S DAY HELPFUL HINTS LETTER (US/1056-7836) [23853216] **2793**

WOMAN'S DAY VEGETABLE GARDENING, CANNING & FREEZING (US/0161-2344) [03861804] **2433**

WOMAN'S ENTERPRI$E (US/0898-6126) [17859043] **5569**

WOMAN'S EXECUTIVE BULLETIN *CEASED.* (US/0164-9515) [04251113] 5569, **723**

WOMAN'S GUIDE TO WASHINGTON, D.C, A (US/0090-080X) [01784648] **5499**

WOMAN'S HOME COMPANION (PH) [02197008] **5569**

WOMAN'S JOURNAL (UK/0043-7344) **5569**

● WOMAN'S LIFE (NEW YORK, N.Y. 1993) (US/1065-0733) [26498596] **5569**

WOMAN'S NEWSPAPER (US) [14095785] **5712**

WOMAN'S OWN (UK) **5569**

WOMAN'S PULPIT, THE (US/0043-7379) [02147152] 5569, **5009**

WOMAN'S RELIEF CORPS. JOURNAL OF THE ... NATIONAL CONVENTION *See* JOURNAL OF THE ... CONVENTION - NATIONAL WOMAN'S RELIEF CORP **5559**

WOMAN'S TOUCH (US/0190-4620) [04720302] 5069, **5569**

WOMAN'S VOICE (NAIROBI, KENYA) (KE) [08008136] **5569**

WOMAN'S WEEKLY LONDON. (1961) (UK/0043-7417) [I00437417] **5569**

WOMAN'S WORLD (ENGLEWOOD, N.J.) (US/0272-961X) [06968463] **5569**

WOMANSPEAK (AT/0311-8479) [05249751] **5569**

WOMBAT *SUSPENDED.* (US) [03503384] **1071**

WOMBLE, CARLYLE, SANDRIDGE & RICE'S NORTH CAROLINA ENVIRONMENTAL LAW LETTER (US/1047-4633) [20697256] 2183, **3076**

WOMEN (UK/0957-4042) [22349229] 333, **5569**

● WOMEN AGAINST SEXUAL HARASSMENT RAG, THE (US/1068-2449) [27482625] **5569**

WOMEN ALIVE (US/0890-3395) [14227773] 5569, **5009**

WOMEN & CRIMINAL JUSTICE (US/0897-4454) [17501958] 5569, **3179**

WOMEN AND ENVIRONMENTS (CN/0229-480X) [07966485] **5569**

WOMEN & GUNS (US/1045-7704) [20239317] **5569**

WOMEN & HEALTH (US/0363-0242) [02337206] 5569, **3769**

WOMEN AND HEALTH ROUNDTABLE *See* ROUNDTABLE REPORT **4800**

WOMEN AND INTERNATIONAL DEVELOPMENT ANNUAL, THE (US/1045-893X) [20282701] **5569**

WOMEN AND LANGUAGE (US/8755-4550) [11313029] **3333**

WOMEN & LITERATURE *CEASED.* (US/0147-1759) [02715989] 5569, **3454**

WOMEN AND MINORITIES IN SCIENCE AND ENGINEERING (US/0739-666X) [08192908] 5569, **5170**

WOMEN AND MINORITY MANPOWER STATISTICS (US/0149-8959) [03574025] 1718, **1540**

WOMEN & PERFORMANCE (US/0740-770X) [09855579] 4080, **5372**

WOMEN & POLITICS (US/0195-7732) [05661577] 5569, **4500**

WOMEN AND REVOLUTION (US) [02269598] **5569**

WOMEN AND THE LABOR FORCE : STATE OF ILLINOIS (US) [06155250] 5569, **1718**

WOMEN AND THE LAW (FREDERICTON) (CN/0847-5253) [23263376] 5569, **3076**

WOMEN & THE LAW REPORT (US/0741-4102) [09722735] **3076**

WOMEN & THERAPY (US/0270-3149) [06394106] **5569**

WOMEN & WORK *CEASED.* (US/0196-8394) [01780645] 5569, **1718**

WOMEN AND WORK (BEVERLY HILLS, CALIF.) (US/0882-0910) [11751015] 5569, **1718**

WOMEN ARTISTS NEWS (US/0149-7081) [03534670] 5569, **333**

WOMEN ARTISTS NEWSLETTER *See* WOMEN ARTISTS NEWS **333**

WOMEN ARTISTS SLIDE LIBRARY JOURNAL *See* WOMEN'S ART MAGAZINE **369**

WOMEN AS MANAGERS (US) 889, **5569**

WOMEN (BOCA RATON) (US/0273-0014) [04453880] **5570**

WOMEN CAN (CN/0319-0994) [02442111] **5798**

WOMEN IN ACTION (IT) [11845476] **5570**

WOMEN IN BUSINESS (CN/0714-6795) [09666885] 5570, **723**

WOMEN IN BUSINESS (KANSAS CITY, MO.) (US/0043-7441) [03967391] 5570, **723**

WOMEN IN COMMUNICATIONS, INC *See* NATIONAL MEMBERSHIP DIRECTORY - WOMEN IN COMMUNICATIONS, INC **1118**

WOMEN IN DESIGN INTERNATIONAL COMPENDIUM (US/0735-3421) [08904140] 5570, **376**

WOMEN IN EDUCATION (VENTURA, CALIF.) (US) [07848922] 5570, **1791**

● WOMEN IN HIGHER EDUCATION (US/1060-8303) [25065894] 5570, **1854**

WOMEN IN MANAGEMENT (CN/1185-4863) [24360407] **889**

● WOMEN IN MANAGEMENT REVIEW (UK/0964-9425) [26122156] 889, 5570, **735**

WOMEN IN MANAGEMENT REVIEW & ABSTRACTS *See* WOMEN IN MANAGEMENT REVIEW **735**

WOMEN IN MEDICAL ACADEMIA (US/0162-6892) [04139545] 5570, **3651**

WOMEN IN NATURAL RESOURCES (US) [17846791] 2398, **5570**

WOMEN IN NEBRASKA; A LABOR FORCE ANALYSIS (US) [05052950] 5570, **1718**

WOMEN IN PUBLIC SERVICE : A QUARTERLY OF THE CENTER FOR WOMEN IN GOVERNMENT (US) [25261041] **5570**

WOMEN IN THE ARTS BULLETIN (US) [03718194] 5570, **369**

WOMEN IN THE ARTS / THE NATIONAL MUSEUM OF WOMEN IN THE ARTS (US/1058-7217) [24330533] 5570, **369**

WOMEN IN THE COAST GUARD (US) [25806570] **5570**

WOMEN IN THE LABOUR FORCE (CN) [02444054] 1718, **5570**

WOMEN IN THE LABOUR FORCE. FACTS AND FIGURES (CN/0382-2192) [01783749] 5570, **1718**

WOMEN IN THE UNIVERSITY GRADUATING POPULATION (CN/0713-3332) [08741258] 5570, **1854**

WOMEN IN THE WORKING WORLD (US/0145-7802) [02782901] **5570**

WOMEN LAW REPORTER (US/0095-1188) [02241700] 5570, **3076**

WOMEN LAWYERS' JOURNAL (US/0043-7468) [01770072] 5570, **3076**

WOMEN LIBRARY WORKERS (U.S.) See WLW JOURNAL **3256**

WOMEN LIKE ME (CN/0821-4794) [09631087] 5570, **723**

WOMEN OF CHINA (CC) [05050439] **5570**

WOMEN OF EUROPE (BE/0258-6169) [07448493] **5570**

WOMEN OF KOREA (KO/0512-1817) [02187132] **5570**

WOMEN OF THE EAST, INC (US/1068-8501) [27827904] **5570**

WOMEN ORGANIZING *CEASED*. (US/0732-992X) [08500985] **5570**

WOMEN/PAY EQUITY EMPLOYMENT LAW (CN) [22689618] **3155**

WOMEN POLICE MAGAZINE (US) **3179**

WOMEN STUDIES ABSTRACTS (US/0049-7835) [01770074] 5570, **5572**

WOMEN TO BY OF FOR AND ABOUT *CEASED*. (US/0043-7492) [01789287] **5570**

WOMEN TODAY (BEETON, CN/0711-4435) [08534452] **5570**

WOMEN TODAY (WASHINGTON, D.C. : 1982) (US) [09015017] **5570**

WOMEN UNLIMITED (US) [19804520] **5570**

WOMEN (WASHINGTON) (US/0095-1536) [01800094] **5570**

WOMEN, WATER AND SANITATION (US/1053-1432) [22461307] **2248**

WOMEN WITH WHEELS (US/1043-979X) [19638054] 5570, **5428**

WOMEN, WORK AND DEVELOPMENT (SZ/0253-2042) [09241483] **5570**

● WOMEN WRITERS OF ITALY (US/1056-4535) [23712147] 5570, **3454**

WOMEN'S AD REVIEW (US/0164-7911) [04348452] **5570**

WOMEN'S ADVOCATE (NEW YORK, N.Y.) (US) [08995670] **3122**

WOMEN'S AND CHILDREN'S WEAR AND FASHION ACCESSORIES BUYERS See WOMEN'S & CHILDREN'S WEAR AND FASHION ACCESSORIES BUYERS **1088**

WOMEN'S & CHILDREN'S WEAR AND FASHION ACCESSORIES BUYERS (US/0741-0735) [05188134] **1088**

WOMEN'S ART MAGAZINE (UK) [24481379] 5570, **369**

WOMEN'S ART MAGAZINE (UK) **369**

WOMENS ART REGISTER BULLETIN (AT) **333**

WOMEN'S BAR ASSOCIATION OF MASSACHUSETTS See WBA NEWSLETTER (BOSTON, MASS.) **3073**

WOMEN'S BUSINESS NETWORK (OTTAWA, ONT.) See WOMEN IN BUSINESS **723**

WOMEN'S CAUCUS FOR ART See NATIONAL NETWORK DIRECTORY **359**

WOMEN'S CAUCUS FOR ART See WCA NATIONAL UPDATE **333**

WOMEN'S CAUCUS-RELIGIOUS STUDIES (ORGANIZATION) See NEWSLETTER - WOMEN'S CAUCUS-RELIGIOUS STUDIES **4982**

WOMEN'S CIRCLE (US/0509-089X) [05396555] 376, **5186**

WOMENS CIRCLE CROCHET (US/0279-1978) [07624661] **5186**

WOMEN'S CIRCLE HOME COOKING See HOME COOKING **2790**

WOMEN'S COACHING CLINIC (US/0146-1133) [03500946] 5570, **4930**

WOMEN'S CONCERNS (CN/0827-2263) [11830245] 5570, **5009**

WOMEN'S DIRECTORY FOR THE CEDAR RAPIDS AND IOWA CITY AREA, A (US/0736-4784) [09205343] **5570**

WOMEN'S EDUCATION (CN/0714-9786) [09457228] 5570, **1791**

WOMEN'S EDUCATIONAL EQUITY ACT PROGRAM See REPORT OF ACTIVITIES / WOMEN'S EDUCATIONAL EQUITY ACT PROGRAM **1778**

WOMEN'S EDUCATIONAL EQUITY ACT PROGRAM (U.S.) See REPORT OF ACTIVITIES / WOMEN'S EDUCATIONAL EQUITY ACT PROGRAM **1778**

WOMEN'S FASTPITCH WORLD (US/0899-5508) [18130501] **4930**

WOMENS GLOBAL NETWORK FOR REPRODUCTIVE RIGHTS NEWSLETTER (NE) **5570**

WOMEN'S GUIDE TO BOOKS, THE (US) [04753033] **5570**

WOMEN'S HEALTH (UK) 5570, **2602**

WOMEN'S HEALTH ADVISER POSTER (US/1047-2800) [20666820] 4808, **5570**

WOMEN'S HEALTH ISSUES (US/1049-3867) [21214029] 2602, **5571**

● WOMEN'S HEALTH JOURNAL (US) 5571, **3651**

● WOMEN'S HEALTH LETTER (US/1062-4163) [25559003] 5571, **3651**

● WOMEN'S HEALTH NURSING SCAN (1993) (US/1070-308X) [27392677] 3769, **3871**

WOMEN'S HEALTH UPDATE *CEASED*. (US/8756-7849) [11654756] **5571**

● WOMEN'S HISTORY REVIEW (UK/0961-2025) [25943278] **5571**

WOMEN'S HOUSEHOLD (US/0510-7385) [03967518] **5571**

WOMEN'S HOUSEHOLD CROCHET (US/0745-0575) [08770658] 376, **5186**

● WOMEN'S INFORMATION DIRECTORY (US/1063-0554) [25848948] **5571**

WOMEN'S INTER-CHURCH COUNCIL OF CANADA See NEWSLETTER - WOMEN'S INTER-CHURCH COUNCIL OF CANADA **4982**

WOMEN'S INTERNATIONAL BOWLING CONGRESS See BYLAWS, RULES, AND SPECIFICATIONS - WOMEN'S INTERNATIONAL BOWLING CONGRESS **4888**

WOMEN'S INTERNATIONAL BOWLING CONGRESS See PLAYING RULES **4912**

WOMEN'S INTERNATIONAL NETWORK See WIN NEWS **5568**

WOMEN'S INVESTMENT NETWORK NEWSLETTER (CN/0821-5596) [09666913] 5571, **920**

WOMEN'S LARGE & HALF SIZE SPECIALTY STORES (US/0743-3972) [10513516] **1088**

WOMEN'S LEAGUE OUTLOOK (US/0043-7557) [03967580] 5571, **5053**

WOMEN'S LEGAL DEFENSE FUND NEWSLETTER, THE (US/0736-9433) [06631141] 5571, **3076**

WOMEN'S LETTER, THE (US/0889-549X) [13919572] **5571**

WOMEN'S MUSIC PLUS (US) [11057635] 333, **5571**

WOMEN'S ORGANIZATIONS & LEADERS DIRECTORY (US/0092-6639) [01783661] **5571**

WOMEN'S ORGANIZATIONS IN HAMILTON-WENTWORTH (CN/0823-9142) [11579892] **5571**

WOMEN'S POLITICAL REPORTER / GEORGIA WOMEN'S POLITICAL CAUCUS (US/0735-6927) [08681297] 5571, **4500**

WOMEN'S POLITICAL TIMES (US/0195-1688) [04041910] 5571, **4500**

WOMEN'S PROGRAM (US/0360-4780) [02243954] 4514, **5571**

WOMEN'S QUARTERLY REVIEW (US/0882-1135) [11965205] **5571**

WOMEN'S RECORD See TWR'S INSIDER REPORT **5567**

WOMEN'S RECORD, THE (US/0888-4609) [13613974] **5571**

WOMEN'S RECOVERY NETWORK (US/1052-1763) [22202780] **5571**

WOMEN'S REPORT (UK/0306-1426) [01789271] **5571**

WOMEN'S RESEARCH NETWORK NEWS : A NEWSLETTER OF THE NATIONAL COUNCIL FOR RESEARCH ON WOMEN (US) [23208599] **5571**

WOMEN'S REVIEW OF BOOKS, THE (US/0738-1433) [09529447] 5571, **3356**

WOMEN'S RIGHTS BULLETIN (CN/0711-463X) [08569916] 1718, **5571**

WOMEN'S RIGHTS LAW REPORTER (US/0085-8269) [01795817] 5571, **3076**

WOMEN'S SPORTS AND FITNESS (US/8750-653X) [10817239] 5571, **4930**

● WOMEN'S SPORTS EXPERIENCE, THE (US/1061-1568) [25193726] 5571, **4930**

WOMEN'S STUDIES (US/0049-7878) [01791887] **5571**

WOMEN'S STUDIES IN COMMUNICATION (US/0749-1409) [08848461] 5571, **1124**

WOMEN'S STUDIES INDEX (US/1058-6369) [22964764] **5571**

WOMEN'S STUDIES INTERNATIONAL FORUM (UK/0277-5395) [07590245] **5571**

WOMEN'S STUDIES JOURNAL (NZ) [14929028] **5571**

WOMEN'S STUDIES QUARTERLY (US/0732-1562) [07387895] **5571**

WOMEN'S STUDIES QUARTERLY INDEX (US) **5572**

WOMEN'S TRAVEL CONNECTIONS (US/0882-8458) [12004668] 5572, **5499**

WOMEN'S TRAVELLER (US) 2796, **5499**

WOMEN'S WORK (MONTESANO, WASH.) (US/1058-4870) [24322879] 5572, **1718**

WOMEN'S WORK (WASHINGTON) (US/0360-1986) [02244342] 5572, **1718**

WOMEN'S WORLD / ISIS-WICCE (SZ) [11845413] **5572**

WOMEN'S WORLD (WASHINGTON, D.C.) (US/0043-759X) [03967624] 5053, **5572**

WOMEN'S YELLOW PAGES, THE (US) [04221045] **5572**

WOMENWISE (US/0890-9695) [11325926] 5572, **4808**

WONDER MAN (US/1060-7595) [25058247] **4867**

WONDER (SOUND BEACH, N.Y.) (US/1057-2821) [23996891] **2550**

WONDER WOMAN (US) [14907050] **4867**

WONDERFUL WEST VIRGINIA (US/0030-7157) [02241231] 4881, **2210**

WONDERSCIENCE : FUN PHYSICAL SCIENCE ACTIVITIES FOR CHILDREN AND ADULTS TO DO TOGETHER (US) [19414583] **5170**

WONJARYOK ANJON CHONGBO (KO) [04985565] **2159**

WONJARYOK KISUL CHONGBO (KO) [04940362] **4451**

WONJARYOK SANOP (KO) [09050800] **2159**

WONJARYOK YONGU (KO) [09351371] **1960**

WOOD ANALYSIS CENTRE NEWSLETTER (AT) **2405**

WOOD AND EQUIPMENT NEWS (UK) **2405**

WOOD & EQUIPMENT NEWS + WOODWORKING MATERIALS (UK/0263-1180) [I02631180] **2405**

WOOD AND FIBER SCIENCE (US/0735-6161) [08950455] **2406**

WOOD & WOOD PRODUCTS (US/0043-7662) [05362616] **2406**

WOOD & WOOD PRODUCTS. RED BOOK (US) [22301666] **2406**

WOOD BASED PANELS INTERNATIONAL (UK/0040-7798) [11081626] 631, **2406**

WOOD DESIGN FOCUS (US) [24385744] 2001, **311**

WOOD DIGEST (US/1045-7348) [20180454] **635**

WOOD IBIS (US/0275-6773) [03503457] **3473**

WOOD INDUSTRIES (CN/0835-0078) [16955755] **2406**

WOOD INDUSTRIES OF NEW MEXICO (US) **2406**

WOOD LAKE NEWS (US) [01770078] **5699**

WOOD MACHINING NEWS (US/0743-5231) [10609745] **2406**

● WOOD MAGAZINE'S SUPER SCROLLSAW PATTERNS (US/1063-7893) [26139440] **635**

WOOD 'N ENERGY (CONCORD, N.H. : 1980) (US/0273-5695) [07079509] **1960**

WOOD PRODUCTS, INTERNATIONAL TRADE AND FOREIGN MARKETS (US) [16146975] **2406**

WOOD PRODUCTS TRADE AND FOREIGN MARKETS / UNITED STATES DEPARTMENT OF AGRICULTURE, FOREIGN AGRICULTURAL SERVICE (US) [28247138] **2406**

WOOD PROJECTS (NEW YORK, N.Y. 1991) (US/1058-3815) [24282374] 376, **635**

WOOD PULP AND FIBER STATISTICS *CEASED*. (US) [02253038] **4240**

WOOD RESEARCH (JA/0372-719X) [02245270] **2406**

WOOD RIVER JOURNAL (US) [19716205] **5658**

WOOD SCIENCE AND TECHNOLOGY (US/0043-7719) [01770079] **2406**

WOOD — Alphabetical Title Index

●WOOD TECHNOLOGY (US/1067-1064) [27049616] **2406**

WOOD TECHNOLOGY NOTES (CN/0227-1001) [08871311] **2406**

WOOD-WOODS FAMILY MAGAZINE, THE (US/0091-6706) [01786345] **2477**

WOODALL PUBLISHING COMPANY *See* WOODALL'S RV BUYER'S CATALOG **5400**

WOODALL PUBLISHING COMPANY *See* WOODALL'S RV BUYER'S GUIDE **5400**

WOODALL'S BETTER CAMPING (US/0091-2018) [01786637] **4881**

WOODALL'S CAMPGROUND DIRECTORY. EASTERN EDITION (US/0162-7406) [03301153] **4881**

WOODALL'S CAMPGROUND DIRECTORY. NORTH AMERICAN EDITION (US/0146-1362) [02865861] **4881**

WOODALL'S CAMPGROUND DIRECTORY. WESTERN EDITION (US/0162-7414) [03301125] **4881**

WOODALL'S CAMPGROUND MANAGEMENT (US/0162-3796) [04164000] **889**

WOODALL'S DIRECTORY OF MOBILE HOME COMMUNITIES (US/0094-1891) [01794212] **2839**

WOODALL'S FLORIDA & SOUTHERN STATES RETIREMENT AND RESORT COMMUNITIES (US/0163-4313) [04376427] **4855**

WOODALL'S FLORIDA CAMPGROUND DIRECTORY (US/0090-5151) [01785154] **4881**

WOODALL'S FLORIDA (GERMAN ED.) (US/0198-1110) [06177421] **5499**

WOODALL'S MISSOURI/ARKANSAS CAMPGROUND DIRECTORY (US/0163-5328) [04401396] **4881**

WOODALL'S MOBILE HOME LIFESTYLE (US/0091-5505) [01787493] **2839**

WOODALL'S MOBILE MODULAR HOUSING TODAY *See* WOODALL'S MOBILE HOME LIFESTYLE **2839**

WOODALL'S MOBILE/MODULAR LIVING (US/0093-7274) [01793066] **2839**

WOODALL'S RETIREMENT AND RESORT COMMUNITIES. EASTERN EDITION (US/0145-577X) [02761298] **4855**

WOODALL'S RETIREMENT AND RESORT COMMUNITIES. NATIONAL EDITION (US/0146-4892) [02953732] **4855**

WOODALL'S ... RETIREMENT DIRECTORY *CEASED*. (US/0731-6526) [08205709] **5182**

WOODALL'S RV BUYER'S CATALOG (US/0162-7015) [04196762] **5400**

WOODALL'S RV BUYER'S GUIDE (US/0162-7368) [04221850] **5400**

WOODALL'S RV OWNER'S HANDBOOK (US/0192-4532) [05044643] **5400**

WOODALL'S ... TENT CAMPING GUIDE. EASTERN EDITION (US/0742-3969) [17763228] **4881**

WOODALL'S ... TENT CAMPING GUIDE. WESTERN REGION (US/0742-3950) [17640865] **5499**

WOODALL'S THE TENTING DIRECTORY. CENTRAL REGION (US/0742-3977) [10340920] **4881**

WOODALL'S TRAILERING PARKS & CAMPGROUNDS. CANADIAN EDITION (US/0362-3823) [02311970] **5499**

WOODALL'S TRAILERING PARKS AND CAMPGROUNDS DIRECTORY (US) [01793923] **4881**

WOODALL'S TRAILERING PARKS & CAMPGROUNDS. WESTERN EDITION (US/0095-9243) [01798768] 5499, **4881**

WOODBOOK, THE (US/0161-7893) [03894927] **2406**

WOODBROOKE INTERNATIONAL JOURNAL, THE (UK) [09198523] **1854**

WOODCHUCK, THE (US) [02057266] **2406**

WOODCOCK STATUS REPORT (US) [03215056] **5621**

WOODENBOAT, THE (US/0095-067X) [01796154] **597**

WOODFORD SUN (US) [11224480] **5683**

WOODLAKE ECHO AND THE THREE RIVERS CURRENT (US/1072-1819) [28877262] **5641**

WOODLAND DUNES DUNESLETTER (US) [08733775] **2210**

WOODLANDS SECTION NEWS BULLETIN (CN) [03519054] **4240**

WOODMEN OF THE WORLD MAGAZINE (US/0043-7751) [03967662] **2896**

WOODS HOLE OCEANOGRAPHIC INSTITUTION *See* REPORTS ON RESEARCH - WOODS HOLE OCEANOGRAPHIC INSTITUTION **1456**

WOODS HOLE OCEANOGRAPHIC INSTITUTION. SEA GRANT PROGRAM *See* SEA GRANT PROGRAM REPORT **1456**

WOODS 'N' WATER (US/0194-8253) [05038497] **4881**

WOODSHOP NEWS. NORTHEAST (US/0894-5403) [16126237] **2406**

WOODSIDE HERALD (US) [11425129] **5722**

WOODSIDE REPORT, THE (CN/1192-2958) [29206032] 4282, **1960**

WOODSMAN (US) [17376291] **5756**

WOODSMITH (US/0164-4114) [04713102] **635**

WOODSON WATCHER PLUS ALLIED LINES (US/0741-6881) [10083436] **2477**

WOODSTOCK SERIES, THE (US/0891-9585) [15048250] **4159**

WOODSTOCK TIMES (US) [22747737] **5722**

WOODSTOVE FIREPLACE AND EQUIPMENT DIRECTORY (US/0160-3299) [03657166] **2812**

WOODTURNING (UK) **635**

WOODVILLE LEADER AND DUNN COUNTY PICTORIAL MESSENGER, THE (US/0748-6812) [11001853] **5772**

WOODVILLE REPUBLICAN (WOODVILLE, MISS. : 1861) (US) [16582724] **5702**

WOODWARD NEWS (US/0883-8755) [12292939] **5733**

WOODWORK (ROSS, CALIF.) (US/1045-3040) [20068029] **635**

WOODWORKER AND ART CRAFTSMAN *See* WOODWORKER (HEMEL HEMPSTEAD. (1910)) **635**

WOODWORKER (HEMEL HEMPSTEAD. (1910)) (UK/0043-776X) [06699055] **635**

WOODWORKER (NEW YORK, N.Y. 1980) (US/0197-4149) [05896610] **635**

WOODWORKER, THE *CEASED*. (US/0894-7481) [16218528] **5734**

WOODWORKER'S JOURNAL (NEW MILFORD), THE (US/0199-1892) [05699485] **635**

WOODWORKING INTERNATIONAL (UK) [17541729] **635**

WOODWORKING INTERNATIONAL NURNBERG (GW/0177-7114) [01777114] **635**

WOODWORKING (MARKHAM) (CN/0838-4185) [18609069] **2406**

WOODWORKING SOURCER (CN/1180-5862) [23237149] **635**

WOODWORKS (UK) **635**

WOOL & CARPET REVIEW (PK) [09964672] **5359**

WOOL AND MOHAIR / CROP REPORTING BOARD, ECONOMICS AND STATISTICS SERVICE, U.S. DEPARTMENT OF AGRICULTURE (US) [02687889] **5359**

WOOL & WOOLLENS OF INDIA (II/0043-7808) [02794621] **5359**

WOOL INTERNATIONAL INSIGHT (AT/1322-3992) **5359**

WOOL MARKET NEWS MONTHLY PERSPECTIVE (AT) [09725950] **5360**

WOOL MARKET NEWS. WEEKLY MARKET SUMMARY (AT) [09569071] **5360**

WOOL MARKET REVIEW (NZ/1171-9672) [111719672] **5360**

WOOL (PALMERSTON NORTH) (NZ/0110-6015) [02832472] 146, **5360**

WOOL QUARTERLY (UK/0142-1921) [05025404] 5360, **5361**

WOOL RECORD (BRADFORD, WEST YORKSHIRE : 1982) (UK/0263-6131) [09389218] **5360**

WOOL RECORD WEEKLY MARKET REPORT (UK) [07546188] **5360**

WOOL REPORT NEW ZEALAND (NZ/0112-6059) [25565398] **5360**

WOOL SACK, THE (US/0043-7840) [03967678] **224**

WOOL SCIENCE REVIEW (UK/0043-7859) [01589587] **5360**

WOOL STATISTICS (UK) [02832509] **5361**

WOOL TECHNOLOGY AND SHEEP BREEDING (AT/0043-7875) [06245366] **224**

WOONSTEDE DOOR DE EEUWEN HEEN, DE (BE) [10138301] **311**

WOORD EN DAAD WOORD AND ACTION (SA/0257-8921) [17966695] **5009**

WOORDENBOEK DER NEDERLANDSCHE TAAL (NE) [05390364] **3333**

WOOSTER DAILY RECORD *See* DAILY RECORD (WOOSTER, OHIO), THE **5728**

WORCESTER BUSINESS JOURNAL (US/1063-6595) [23283619] **723**

WORCESTER COUNTY MESSENGER (US) [19027068] **5687**

WORCESTER MAGAZINE (WORCESTER) (US/0191-4960) [04936296] **4855**

WORCESTER MEDICINE (US/1055-6370) [21538196] **3651**

WORCESTER POLYTECHNIC INSTITUTE STUDIES IN SCIENCE, TECHNOLOGY, AND CULTURE (US/0897-926X) [17664873] **5170**

WORCESTER POLYTECHNIC INSTITUTE, WORCESTER, MASS *See* WPI JOURNAL **5171**

WORCESTER REVIEW, THE (US/8756-5277) [11607681] **3473**

WORCESTERSHIRE HISTORICAL SOCIETY *See* WORCESTERSHIRE HISTORICAL SOCIETY (PUBLICATIONS) **5237**

WORCESTERSHIRE HISTORICAL SOCIETY (PUBLICATIONS) (UK/0141-4577) [01770098] **5237**

WORD AMONG US, THE (US/0742-4639) [08745838] **5038**

WORD & IMAGE (LONDON. 1985) (UK/0266-6286) [11856748] **1124**

WORD AND SPIRIT (US/0193-9211) [05269709] **5038**

WORD AND WAY (US/0049-7959) [03967695] **5009**

WORD & WITNESS (US/1047-2339) [07846441] **5069**

WORD & WORLD (US/0275-5270) [07148874] **5009**

WORD (BROOKLYN), THE (US/0043-7964) [01950817] **5009**

WORD FOR WORD *CEASED*. (US/0896-7717) [17286822] 1239, **1273**

WORD FROM WASHINGTON (US/0738-8012) [09689781] **5314**

WORD IN ACTION (UK) [01588044] 5020, **5813**

WORD IN LIFE (AT) 1908, **5009**

WORD LOOM (CN/0714-3257) [09021852] **3454**

WORD OF LIFE FELLOWSHIP, INC *See* WORD OF LIFE LIFE LINES **5009**

WORD OF LIFE LIFE LINES (US/0194-6684) [04935590] **5009**

WORD OF MOUTH (SAN ANTONIO, TEX.) (US/1048-3950) [20939163] **1886**

WORD ON WORSHIP (US/0888-1316) [13527192] **5010**

WORD PLAYS *CEASED*. (US/0749-7768) [09703913] **5372**

WORD PROCESSING (FRANKLIN LAKES) (US/0196-8114) [03511033] **1292**

WORD PROCESSING NEWS *See* AOR OBSERVER, THE **4210**

WORD PROCESSING, QUALITY CLINIC (US/0895-0628) [16438573] **1292**

WORD PROCESSING SKILLS PROGRAM (US) **1292**

●WORD SEARCH CHALLENGE (US/1065-2930) [26572224] **4868**

WORD (ST. JOHN'S) (CN/1180-5145) [24368363] 3454, **2925**

WORD WAYS (US/0043-7980) [01604435] **3333**

WORD WIZE (US/1048-6852) [21000886] **4868**

WORD (WORCESTER) (US/0043-7956) [01995240] **3333**

WORDENS PAST (US/0740-9516) [10032176] **2478**

WORDPERFECT (UK) [l09677216] **1292**

WORDPERFECT FOR THE LAW OFFICE (US/1070-3896) [27994639] 1292, **3076**

●WORDPERFECT FOR WINDOWS MAGAZINE (US/1058-9783) [24450744] **1292**

WORDPERFECT (OREM, UTAH) (US/1042-5152) [19048756] **1292**

WORDPERFECT REPORT (US/1053-9638) [22712416] **1292**

●WORDPERFECT SOFTWARE CONNECTION (US/1063-2719) [25955234] **1292**

WORDPERFECTIONIST, THE (US) [15078892] **1292**

WORDS & PHRASES LEGALLY DEFINED (UK) **3076**

WORDS AND WINDMILLS (AT/0311-1784) [l03111784] **1908**

WORDS BY SPECIALISTS (US) **1791**

●WORDS ON CASSETTE (US) [25242617] **427**

WORDS ON TAPE *See* WORDS ON CASSETTE **427**

WORDS (WILLOW GROVE) *CEASED*. (US/0164-4742) [03594017] **4214**

WORDS WORTH (UK/0140-346X) [l0140346X] **1908**

WORDSWORTH CIRCLE (US/0006-8006) [01187141] **3356**

WORDWATCHING *CEASED.* (US/0731-9290) [08268816] **1791**

WORK : A JOURNAL OF PREVENTION, ASSESSMENT, AND REHABILITATION (US/1051-9815) [22161995] **4808**

WORK ABROAD *CEASED.* (US/0714-7503) [10611455] **4210**

WORK & FAMILY LIFE (US/1040-0958) [18319876] **2287**

WORK & FAMILY SOURCEBOOK, THE (US) [18588373] 948, **2287**

WORK AND OCCUPATIONS (US/0730-8884) [08077859] **4210**

WORK AND PEOPLE (AT/0312-455X) [02244850] **948**

WORK AND STRESS (UK/0267-8373) [15606717] 1718, **4621**

WORK BOAT, THE (US/0043-8014) [01822078] **597**

WORK BOAT WORLD (UK/1037-3748) [I10373748] 5458, **597**

WORK (BOCA RATON) (US/0273-0022) [04454026] **1718**

WORK DIGEST (US/0822-2711) [10516374] **1718**

WORK, EMPLOYMENT AND SOCIETY (UK/0950-0170) [15514983] **1718**

WORK EXPERIENCE OF THE POPULATION (US/0162-0592) [04077893] **1718**

WORK-FAMILY ROUNDTABLE (US/1060-930X) [25113719] **2287**

WORK FORCE PROFILE AS OF SEPTEMBER 30 ... (US/0276-9247) [07436386] **1718**

WORK HEALTH SAFETY (FI/0783-6899) [I07836899] **2871**

WORK IN AMERICA (US/0892-5488) [15070940] **948**

WORK IN AMERICA INSTITUTE STUDIES IN PRODUCTIVITY *CEASED.* (US/0149-869X) [03568442] **1631**

WORK IN FLORIDA (US/0149-3329) [06720131] **1718**

WORK IN PROGRESS (JOHANNESBURG, SOUTH AFRICA) *CEASED.* (SA) [10503230] 1718, **4500**

WORK IN PROGRESS (STONE CENTER FOR DEVELOPMENTAL SERVICES AND STUDIES) (US/1046-3674) [10449115] **4622**

WORK IN PROGRESS - UNIVERSITY OF EDINBURGH. DEPARTMDENT OF LINGUISTICS (UK/0959-6569) [10423398] **3333**

WORK INJURIES (CN/0835-233X) [15686283] **2871**

WORK INJURY MANAGEMENT (US) 1718, **2896**

WORK OF THE STOCKHOLM PUBLIC LIBRARY IN ..., THE (SW) [10616822] **3256**

WORK PROGRAM / FERIC (CN/0713-7826) [06293996] **2398**

WORK PROGRAMME AND BUDGET (ET) [01792377] **146**

WORK RELATED ABSTRACTS (US/0273-3234) [02486546] 1718, **1540**

WORK RELEASE FOR MISDEMEANANTS IN MINNESOTA (US/0160-5240) [01607099] **3179**

WORK REPORTS - EARLY SITES RESEARCH SOCIETY (US) [04367241] **5237**

WORK STOPPAGES IN GOVERNMENT (US/0147-9547) [03253731] **1718**

WORK STOPPAGES IN NEW YORK STATE (ANNUAL : 1982) (US) [13783863] **1718**

WORK STUDY (UK/0043-8022) [07049136] **889**

WORK, STUDY, TRAVEL ABROAD (US/0749-453X) [10514483] **1791**

WORK TIMES (US/0736-9166) [09271202] 4210, **723**

WORK YEARS AND PERSONNEL COSTS, EXECUTIVE BRANCH, UNITED STATES GOVERNMENT (US/0277-3325) [06654936] 4695, **1718**

WORKAMERICA (US/0740-4077) [09935587] **1718**

WORKAMPER NEW$ (US/0895-3678) [16577328] **1718**

WORKBASKET *See* WORKBASKET AND HOME ARTS MAGAZINE, THE **376**

WORKBASKET AND HOME ARTS MAGAZINE, THE (US/0162-9123) [05396033] **376**

WORKBENCH (US/0043-8057) [01645005] **635**

WORKBOAT INTERNATIONAL (UK) [I0268733X] **597**

WORKBOOK (LOS ANGELES, CALIF.) (US) [10471910] **382**

WORKBOOK, THE (US/0195-4636) [03476431] **1300**

WORKBOOK'S SINGLE IMAGE (US/1065-6103) [24656937] **382**

WORKCAMPS PROGRAMME. PROGRAMME DE CHANTIERS. PROGRAMA DE CAMPAMENTOS (FR) [03283120] **1718**

WORKER CO-OPS (TORONTO. 1980) (CN/0829-576X) [16079748] 1718, **1543**

WORKER ESPERANTIST, THE (UK) [24308208] **3333**

WORKER FOR THE MARYLAND-D.C.-VIRGINIA AREA, THE (US/0273-4680) [05735090] **1718**

WORKER FOR THE NORTHWEST, THE (US/0273-4672) [05735106] **1718**

WORKERS' ADVOCATE SUPPLEMENT, THE (US/0882-6366) [11930068] **4500**

WORKER'S ADVOCATE, THE (US/0276-363X) [07353726] **4548**

WORKERS' COMP ADVISOR (CALIFORNIA ED.) (US/1054-7819) [22969763] **2896**

WORKERS' COMP ADVISOR (OHIO ED.) (US/1058-7179) [24370388] **1719**

WORKERS COMP INSURANCE AND LAW (US) 3088, **2896**

●WORKERS' COMP MANAGED CARE (US/1066-2669) [26906876] **2896**

WORKERS' COMP YEARBOOK (US) **3088**

WORKERS COMPENSATION (UK) **1719**

WORKERS' COMPENSATION BOARD OF BRITISH COLUMBIA *See* WORKERS' COMPENSATION REPORTER **1719**

WORKERS COMPENSATION BOARD OF MANITOBA. UPDATE, COMPENSATION NEWS FOR MANITOBA EMPLOYERS *See* WCB UPDATE **1717**

WORKERS' COMPENSATION BOARD OF NEWFOUNDLAND AND LABRADOR *See* ANNUAL REPORT / WORKERS' COMPENSATION BOARD, NEWFOUNDLAND AND LABRADOR **1650**

WORKERS COMPENSATION CASE MANAGEMENT (US) **3088**

WORKERS' COMPENSATION DESK BOOK (US) 5314, **2896**

WORKERS COMPENSATION HEALTH CARE COST CONTAINMENT (US) **3088**

WORKERS' COMPENSATION JOURNAL OF OHIO (US/0886-9162) [13033431] **1719**

WORKER'S COMPENSATION LAW BULLETIN (US/0748-7878) [05634846] **3155**

WORKERS' COMPENSATION LAW OF THE STATE OF ARKANSAS (US) [07021343] **3155**

WORKERS' COMPENSATION LAW OF THE STATE OF CONNECTICUT (US) [06976490] **3155**

WORKERS' COMPENSATION LAW OF THE STATE OF HAWAII (US) [06967788] **3155**

WORKERS' COMPENSATION LAW OF THE STATE OF WISCONSIN (US) [07020969] **3155**

WORKERS' COMPENSATION LAW REVIEW (US/1050-9836) [20709658] 1719, **3076**

WORKERS' COMPENSATION LAWS OF CALIFORNIA, THE (US/0748-4135) [05572996] **3155**

WORKERS' COMPENSATION LEGISLATION IN AUSTRALIA / DEPARTMENT OF SOCIAL SECURITY (AT) [08038796] **3076**

WORKERS' COMPENSATION MANAGING CLAIMS (CN/0847-5857) [24368313] 1719, **2896**

WORKERS' COMPENSATION MANUAL FOR UNION REPRESENTATIVES (US/0195-671X) [05528363] **3155**

WORKERS COMPENSATION OUTLOOK (BOSTON, MASS.) (US/1052-6358) [22343675] 2896, **1719**

WORKERS COMPENSATION REPORT (AT/0816-2107) [I08162107] **1719**

WORKERS' COMPENSATION REPORTER (CN/0826-4198) [11807695] **1719**

WORKERS' COMPENSATION REPORTS *SUSPENDED.* (AT) [01759978] 2896, **3076**

WORKERS' COMPENSATION REPORTS, WESTERN AUSTRALIA (AT) [22853700] **2896**

WORKERS' COMPENSATION STATISTICS (PP/0377-6522) [02240604] 1719, **1540**

WORKERS COMPENSATION STRATEGIES FOR LOWERING COSTS (US) **3088**

WORKERS COMPENSATION. VICTORIA *See* ACCIDENT COMPENSATION. VICTORIA **2872**

WORKERS COVERED BY KENTUCKY UNEMPLOYMENT INSURANCE LAW BY COUNTY (US/0149-371X) [03469060] 1719, **2896**

WORKERS EDUCATION (II) [01784207] 5226, **1719**

WORKERS' EDUCATIONAL ASSOCIATION *See* STUDIES FOR TRADE UNIONISTS **1712**

WORKERS HEALTH INTERNATIONAL NEWSLETTER (UK) **2871**

WORKERS LIFE : THE MAGAZINE FOR WORKERS (IE) [12061690] **1719**

WORKERS NEWS (UK) **1719**

WORKERS TIME (JM) [03267574] **4500**

WORKERS' UNITY (UK) [24299096] **1719**

WORKERS VANGUARD (NEW YORK, N.Y.) (US/0276-0746) [03880717] **1719**

WORKERS VOICE, THE (BM) [05712552] **1719**

WORKERS WORLD *See* WORKERS WORLD WW **4500**

WORKERS WORLD WW (US/1070-4205) [28359687] **4500**

WORKFORCE (AT/0811-9023) [I08119023] **1719**

WORKFORCE INDUSTRIAL REGISTER (AT) **1719**

WORKFORCE STRATEGIES (US/1062-8991) [22480994] **948**

●WORKFORCE (WASHINGTON, D.C.) (US/1063-4363) [26032719] 2896, **1719**

●WORKGROUP COMPUTING REPORT (US/1068-9699) [27662226] **4214**

●WORKGROUP COMPUTING SERIES. DESKTOP APPLICATIONS (US) [26321736] 1292, **1273**

●WORKGROUP COMPUTING SERIES. DIRECTORY OF MICROCOMPUTER HARDWARE (US) [26666642] **1239**

WORKGROUP COMPUTING SERIES. HARDWARE PRODUCT DIRECTORY (US) [26208612] 1273, **1239**

WORKGROUP COMPUTING SERIES. HARDWARE VENDOR DIRECTORY (US) [26208848] **1239**

●WORKGROUP COMPUTING SERIES. INFORMATION DELIVERY / DATAPRO (US) [26222610] **1263**

●WORKGROUP COMPUTING SERIES. MULTIMEDIA SOLUTIONS / DATAPRO (US) [26222819] **1263**

●WORKGROUP COMPUTING SERIES. PERIPHERALS (US) [26321754] 1240, **1273**

●WORKGROUP COMPUTING SERIES. SYSTEMS (US) [26321744] **1273**

●WORKGROUP COMPUTING SERIES. SYSTEMS SOFTWARE (OS/NOS/GUI) (US) [26321759] **1292**

WORKING (US/0270-0417) [05161892] **1719**

WORKING BRIEF - UNEMPLOYMENT UNIT (UK/0956-6120) [I09566120] **1719**

WORKING CLASS OPPOSITION : MONTHLY NEWSPAPER OF THE INTERNATIONALIST WORKERS PARTY (US) [17204227] **1719**

WORKING CLASS, THE (II) [01784066] **1719**

WORKING COMMUNICATOR (US) **1124**

WORKING CONDITIONS IN BRITISH COLUMBIA INDUSTRY (CN) [01783849] **1719**

WORKING FOR WILDLIFE (CN/0229-7183) [10330374] **2210**

WORKING HOLIDAYS (LONDON, ENGLAND) (UK) [08564578] 5499, **1791**

WORKING HOLIDAYS. SUPPLEMENT FOR NORTH AMERICAN READERS (CN/0828-8070) [09379223] **5499**

●WORKING IT OUT (US/1064-489X) [26296575] 2796, **1719**

WORKING MOTHER (NEW YORK, N.Y. 1981) (US/0278-193X) [07728388] **2287**

WORKING NOTES ON COMMUNITY RIGHT TO KNOW (US) **2248**

WORKING PAPER / CAIRO DEMOGRAPHIC CENTRE (UA) [17726111] **4560**

WORKING PAPER - CANADIAN ENERGY RESEARCH INSTITUTE (CN/0225-3828) [06033285] **1960**

WORKING PAPER ... / CO-OPERATIVE FUTURE DIRECTIONS PROJECT (CN/0712-1490) [08581261] **1543**

WORKING PAPER / DEPARTMENT OF AGRICULTURAL ECONOMICS AND BUSINESS, UNIVERSITY OF GUELPH (CN) [15607165] **146**

WORKING PAPER - DEPARTMENT OF ECONOMICS. UNIVERSITY OF NEW BRUNSWICK (CN/0711-5326) [08422743] **1527**

WORKING PAPER - DEVELOPMENT STUDY UNIT, DEPARTMENT OF SOCIAL ANTHROPOLOGY, UNIVERSITY OF STOCKHOLM (SW/0284-9224) [I02849224] **247**

WORKING — Alphabetical Title Index

WORKING PAPER - FACULTY OF ADMINISTRATION, UNIVERSITY OF OTTAWA (CN/0701-3086) [05072043] 4695, **723**

WORKING PAPER - FLORIDA STATE UNIVERSITY. CENTER FOR THE STUDY OF POPULATION (US/0740-9095) [10048165] **4561**

WORKING PAPER / HELEN KELLOGG INSTITUTE FOR INTERNATIONAL STUDIES, UNIVERSITY OF NOTRE DAME (US) [13173535] **2913**

WORKING PAPER (INTERNATIONAL CENTRE FOR DIARRHOEAL DISEASE RESEARCH, BANGLADESH) (BG/0254-959X) [09518158] **4808**

WORKING PAPER (INTERNATIONAL FOOD POLICY RESEARCH INSTITUTE) (PH) [10164091] 2361, **2096**

WORKING PAPER - JOINT CENTER FOR HOUSING STUDIES OF MIT AND HARVARD UNIVERSITY (US/0883-9689) [12267301] **2839**

WORKING PAPER (LAW REFORM COMMISSION OF CANADA) (CN/0708-2827) [02248723] **3076**

WORKING PAPER / MULTINATIONAL ENTERPRISES PROGRAMME (SZ) [07216255] **1527**

WORKING PAPER / NATIONAL CENTRE FOR DEVELOPMENT STUDIES, AUSTRALIAN NATIONAL UNIVERSITY (AT/0815-7596) [13119155] **146**

●WORKING PAPER / NATURAL HAZARDS RESEARCH AND APPLICATIONS INFORMATION CENTER, INSTITUTE OF BEHAVIORAL SCIENCE, UNIVERSITY OF COLORADO (US) [26971050] **1437**

WORKING PAPER. POLICY BRANCH, AGRICULTURE CANADA (CN) [24899423] **146**

WORKING PAPER (QUEEN'S UNIVERSITY (KINGSTON, ONT.). CENTRE FOR RESOURCE STUDIES) (CN/0226-7616) [06512159] **2153**

WORKING PAPER - RETAILING AND INSTITUTIONAL RESEARCH PROGRAM, FACULTY OF MANAGEMENT STUDIES, UNIVERSITY OF TORONTO (CN/0381-8985) [02604012] **889**

WORKING PAPER - ROLE OF THE AUTOMOBILE STUDY, TRANSPORT CANADA (CN/0228-2011) [06758512] **5428**

WORKING PAPER / SCHOOL OF GEOGRAPHY, UNIVERSITY OF LEEDS (UK) [07244127] **2579**

WORKING PAPER - SCHOOL OF URBAN & REGIONAL PLANNING. UNIVERSITY OF WATERLOO (CN/0713-8466) [09067695] **2839**

WORKING PAPER SERIES - DEPARTMENT OF BUSINESS, SCHOOL OF BUSINESS AND ECONOMICS, WILFRID LAURIER UNIVERSITY (CN/0714-7228) [09204496] **723**

WORKING PAPER SERIES - HEALTH SERVICES MANAGEMENT UNIT. DEPARTMENT OF SOCIAL ADMINISTRATION. UNIVERSITY OF MANCHESTER (UK/0141-2647) [06445230] **4808**

WORKING PAPER SERIES / THE CENTER FOR INTERNATIONAL AFFAIRS, HARVARD UNIVERSITY (US) [23568290] **4538**

WORKING PAPER SERIES - UNIVERSITY OF ARIZONA. MEXICAN AMERICAN STUDIES AND RESEARCH CENTER (US/0732-7749) [08426516] **5226**

WORKING PAPER SERIES (UNIVERSITY OF CHICAGO. CENTER FOR RESEARCH IN SECURITY PRICES) (US) [05696560] **723**

WORKING PAPER SERIES (UNIVERSITY OF TORONTO. STRUCTURAL ANALYSIS PROGRAMME) (CN/0226-1774) [09050356] **5265**

WORKING PAPER / SWEDISH UNIVERSITY OF AGRICULTURAL SCIENCES, INTERNATIONAL RURAL DEVELOPMENT CENTRE (SW/1100-8679) [24578209] **147**

WORKING PAPER / THE GEORGE MORRIS CENTRE (CN) [22656409] **147**

WORKING PAPER / UNIVERSITY OF MINNESOTA, CENTER FOR NATURAL RESOURCE POLICY AND MANAGEMENT STUDIES (US) [11227266] **2210**

WORKING PAPER - UNIVERSITY OF NEWCASTLE, FACULTY OF MEDICINE (AT/0813-4472) [09473047] **3651**

WORKING PAPER (UNIVERSITY OF TEXAS AT AUSTIN. CENTER FOR ENERGY STUDIES) (US) [09121426] **1960**

WORKING PAPER / UNIVERSITY OF TORONTO, DEVELOPMENT STUDIES PROGRAMME (CN/0829-9277) [13784643] **1527**

WORKING PAPER (UNIVERSITY OF WATERLOO. ACCOUNTING GROUP) (CN/0821-4069) [09864036] **753**

WORKING PAPER (UNIVERSITY OF WESTERN ONTARIO.) CENTRE FOR THE STUDY OF INTERNATIONAL ECONOMIC RELATIONS (CN/0228-4235) [08499800] **1641**

WORKING PAPER (UNIVERSITY OF ZIMBABWE. DEPT. OF AGRICULTURAL ECONOMICS & EXTENSION) (RH) [19105048] **147**

WORKING PAPER - WORLD EMPLOYMENT PROGRAMME RESEARCH (SZ/0251-0251) [02510251] **1719**

WORKING PAPERS (US) **1527**

WORKING PAPERS / ANNUAL SEMINARS ON AFRICAN GOVERNANCE (US) **4500**

WORKING PAPERS - CENTRE FOR APPLIED ECONOMIC RESEARCH. UNIVERSITY OF NEW SOUTH WALES (AT/0157-4701) [01574701] **1527**

●WORKING PAPERS / ECONOMICS DEPARTMENT, OECD (FR) [26227489] **1527**

WORKING PAPERS IN AFRICAN STUDIES (SW/0281-6814) [11410369] **2644**

WORKING PAPERS IN BAKER LIBRARY *CEASED.* (US/0364-6645) [02222694] **723**

WORKING PAPERS IN CULTURAL STUDIES (UK/0049-7991) [02216335] **5265**

WORKING PAPERS IN DEMOGRAPHY (AT) [08555921] **4561**

WORKING PAPERS IN ECONOMICS HAMILTON (NZ/0112-8191) [01128191] **1527**

WORKING PAPERS IN IRISH STUDIES (US/0732-2674) [08338011] **2716**

WORKING PAPERS IN LINGUISTICS (COLUMBUS, OHIO) (US/0473-9604) [03889333] **3333**

WORKING PAPERS IN LINGUISTICS (HONOLULU, HAWAII) (US/0884-0458) [06646397] **3333**

WORKING PAPERS IN LINGUISTICS (SEATTLE, WASH.) (US/0892-8886) [03632839] **3333**

WORKING PAPERS IN LINGUISTICS / UNIVERSITY OF TRONDHEIM (NO/0802-3956) [17816811] **3333**

WORKING PAPERS IN TRADE AND DEVELOPMENT (AT/0816-5181) [17275875] **2913**

WORKING PAPERS INDEX *CEASED.* (US) [24494291] **5226**

WORKING PAPERS (KBENHAVNS DEIVERSITET. CENTER FOR AFRIKASTUDIER) (DK/0902-9621) [19651329] **2501**

WORKING PAPERS - LUND UNIVERSITY, DEPARTMENT OF LINGUISTICS, GENERAL LINGUISTICS, PHONETICS (SW/0280-526X) [0280526X] **3333**

WORKING PAPERS OF THE JAPANESE STUDIES CENTRE (AT/0813-9733) [19907640] **2668**

WORKING PAPERS ON COMMERCIALIZATION OF AGRICULTURE AND NUTRITION / INTERNATIONAL FOOD POLICY RESEARCH INSTITUTE (US) [14392557] **191**

WORKING PAPERS ON FOOD SUBSIDIES / INTERNATIONAL FOOD POLICY RESEARCH INSTITUTE (US) [14392578] **2361**

WORKING PAPERS ON LANGUAGE, GENDER & SEXISM (AT/1036-4099) [I10364099] **3333**

WORKING PAPERS (ORGANISATION FOR ECONOMIC CO-OPERATION AND DEVELOPMENT. DEPT. OF ECONOMICS AND STATISTICS) (FR) [09513315] **1527**

WORKING PAPERS (ORGANISATION FOR ECONOMIC CO-OPERATION AND DEVELOPMENT. DEPT. OF ECONOMICS AND STATISTICS *See* WORKING PAPERS / ECONOMICS DEPARTMENT, OECD **1527**

WORKING PAPERS / ROCHESTER CENTER FOR ECONOMIC RESEARCH (US) **1527**

WORKING PAPERS / RODNEY L. WHITE CENTER FOR FINANCIAL RESEARCH (US) **1527**

WORKING PAPERS SERIES / INSTITUTE OF SOCIAL STUDIES, NETHERLANDS (NE) [15154849] **5226**

WORKING PAPERS / SHLRC (AT/0313-7791) [15514768] **3333**

WORKING PAPERS (UNIVERSITY OF SYDNEY. CENTRE FOR ASIAN STUDIES) (AT) [16949287] **2633**

WORKING PARENTS *SUSPENDED.* (US/0747-6140) [10763757] **2287**

WORKING PEOPLE'S DAILY MICROFORM, THE (BR) [09824578] **5779**

WORKING PRESS OF THE NATION, THE (US/0084-1323) [04224567] 1124, 2925, **2926**

WORKING SMART (NEW YORK, N.Y.) (US/1049-4855) [21244869] **889**

WORKING TEACHER (CN/0705-2022) [05761462] **1791**

WORKING TITLE (CN/1180-3819) [23004968] **333**

WORKING TOGETHER FOR YESTERDAY, TODAY, AND TOMORROW (LINCOLN, NEB.) (US/0733-4826) [08566924] **5572**

WORKING TOGETHER (SEATTLE, WASH.) (US/1064-8585) [26435517] **5314**

WORKING WOMAN (US/0145-5761) [02761141] **5572**

WORKING WOMEN IN CANADA (CN/0384-0654) [03245108] 1719, **5572**

WORKLIFE : A PUBLICATION ON EMPLOYMENT AND PERSONS WITH DISABILITIES (US) [17946245] **4395**

WORKLIFE REPORT, THE (CN/0834-292X) [16349435] **1719**

WORKLOAD RECORDING METHOD & PERSONNEL MANAGEMENT MANUAL (US) [30024810] **3898**

WORKMENS' COMP NEWSLETTER (US) [1719, **2896**

WORKMEN'S COMPENSATION DATA (US/0097-9163) [01799435] 2896, **1719**

WORKMEN'S COMPENSATION FOR OCCUPATIONAL INJURIES AND DEATH (US) [05620778] 2896, **1719**

WORKMEN'S COMPENSATION LAW OF THE STATE OF ARKANSAS *See* WORKERS' COMPENSATION LAW OF THE STATE OF ARKANSAS **3155**

WORKMEN'S COMPENSATION LAW OF THE STATE OF WISCONSIN *See* WORKERS' COMPENSATION LAW OF THE STATE OF WISCONSIN **3155**

WORKPAPERS OF THE SUMMER INSTITUTE OF LINGUISTICS, UNIVERSITY OF NORTH DAKOTA (US/0361-4700) [02015736] **3333**

WORKPLACE AND THE LAW, THE (US/1056-4683) [23716448] 3076, **1719**

WORKPLACE CHANGE (AT) [19547263] **1719**

WORKPLACE HEALTH (US) **2871**

WORKPLACE HEALTH & SAFETY MANUAL (AU) **2871**

WORKPLACE INJURY REPORTER (US/1054-7312) [22947496] 3076, **1719**

●WORKPLACE ISSUES & ANSWERS (US/1061-8643) [25482277] **2253**

WORKPLACE MELBOURNE (AT/1036-5117) [I10365117] **1719**

●WORKPLACE SAFETY AWARENESS PROGRAM (US/1059-1044) [24479702] **2871**

WORKPLACE TRENDS (US/1047-4447) [20696411] **948**

●WORKPLACE VITALITY (US/1074-4452) [29709543] **2871**

WORKPLAN (TORONTO) (CN/1182-4506) [23259462] **2210**

WORKS (ALTADENA, CALIF.) (US/1055-0909) [23070828] **5010**

WORKS AND DAYS (US/0886-2060) [11121933] **333**

WORKS ISSUED BY THE HAKLUYT SOCIETY (UK/0951-6158) [01607733] **2579**

WORKS ISSUED BY THE HAKLUYT SOCIETY. EXTRA SERIES (UK) [01775759] **5237**

WORKS (LOS ANGELES, CALIF.) (US/0884-9013) [12539895] **2550**

WORKS MANAGEMENT (UK/0374-4795) [07678392] **889**

WORKS OF ART (CHICAGO, ILL.) (US/1058-0409) [24198966] **333**

WORKS OF JOHN WESLEY, THE (UK) **5069**

WORKSHEET MAGAZINE *See* TEACHER'S HELPER MAGAZINE : KINDERGARTEN EDITION **1906**

WORKSHOP CONFERENCES HOECHST (NE/0259-7284) [04822051] **3651**

WORKSHOP (LOUISVILLE, KY.) *CEASED.* (US/0895-4372) [16639237] **1292**

WORKSHOP ON INTERACTIVE COMPUTING *See* PROCEEDINGS / ... ANNUAL WORKSHOP ON INTERACTIVE COMPUTING, CAD/CAM, ELECTRICAL ENGINEERING EDUCATION **1991**

WORKSHOP REPORT - UNESCO. INTERGOVERNMENTAL OCEANOGRAPHIC COMMISSION (FR/0251-9569) [03690429] **1458**

WORKSHOP SUMMARIES : A PUBLICATION OF THE AMERICAN SOCIETY OF PLANT PHYSIOLOGISTS *CEASED.* (US/0743-1589) [08906034] **587**

WORKSHOP YEARBOOK AND PRODUCTION ENGINEERING MANUAL, THE (UK) [20316571] **2132**

WORKSHOPS FOR LEGAL ASSISTANTS. BANKRUPTCY (US/1071-9067) [28716836] **3076**

WORKSHOPS FOR LEGAL ASSISTANTS. EMPLOYEE BENEFITS (US/1071-9059) [26146641] **3076**

WORKSHOPS FOR LEGAL ASSISTANTS. LITIGATION, LEGAL RESEARCH AND WRITING, ENVIRONMENTAL LAW AND TOXIC TORT LITIGATION (US/1071-9075) [26145954] **3769**

●WORKSIGHT (EDMONTON) (CN/1188-4126) [26290464] **1719**

WORKSITE WELLNESS WORKS (US/1053-492X) [22545489] 4808, **4200**

WORKSTATION ADVISORY SERVICE (US) **1207**

WORKSTATION (AUSTIN, TEX.) (US/1059-9959) [24841761] **1207**

WORKSTATION NEWS *CEASED.* (US/1049-491X) [21237768] **1207**

WORKSTATION REPORT *See* DESIGNNETWORK'S WORKSTATION REPORT **4211**

WORKSTATION REPORT, THE (US/1040-7472) [18516741] **4214**

WORKSTATION REPORT'S ... BUYER' GUIDE TO OFFICE FURNITURE, THE (US/1062-7650) [25669298] 952, **4214**

●WORKWATCH (BELLINGHAM, WASH.) (US/1062-9742) [25826615] **1719**

WORLD ACCOUNTING REPORT; A MONTHLY BULLETIN ON DEVELOPMENTS IN INTERNATIONAL ACCOUNTING (UK) [06803007] **753**

WORLD ACROBATICS (AT/1038-6963) [I10386963] **389**

WORLD ADVERTISING REVIEW (UK/0950-4540) [12963872] 767, **382**

WORLD AEROSPACE & DEFENSE INTELLIGENCE (US) 4061, **40**

WORLD AEROSPACE PROFILE : THE INTERNATIONAL REVIEW OF AEROSPACE DESIGN AND DEVELOPMENT (UK/0268-8670) [14922394] **40**

WORLD AFFAIRS (II) [24222346] **4538**

WORLD AFFAIRS (BOCA RATON, FLA.) (US/1058-1766) [24233528] **4538**

WORLD AFFAIRS JOURNAL (US/0731-4728) [08190110] **4538**

WORLD AFFAIRS QUARTERLY (US/8755-0687) [01589643] **4538**

WORLD AFFAIRS (WASHINGTON) (US/0043-8200) [01641796] **4538**

WORLD AGRICULTURAL ECONOMICS AND RURAL SOCIOLOGY ABSTRACTS (US/0043-8219) [01770119] 147, **157**

WORLD AGRICULTURAL PRODUCTION (US/1052-0279) [17846849] **147**

WORLD AGRICULTURAL STATISTICS (IT) [11328599] **147**

WORLD AGRICULTURAL SUPPLY AND DEMAND ESTIMATES (US/0277-3139) [07092807] **147**

WORLD AGRICULTURE (WASHINGTON, D.C. 1991) (US/1060-9741) [23899113] 2361, **147**

WORLD AIR POWER JOURNAL (UK/0959-7050) [21216449] **40**

WORLD AIRLINE ACCIDENT SUMMARY (UK) **40**

WORLD AIRLINE FLEETS (UK) [04625420] **40**

WORLD AIRLINE FLEETS NEWS (UK/0951-8673) [16828323] **5400**

●WORLD AIRLINE MAINTENANCE FORECAST (US) **40**

WORLD AIRLINE NEWS (US/1059-4183) [24585271] **40**

WORLD AIRNEWS (SA) [01788592] **40**

WORLD AIRNEWS (SA/0261-2399) [I02612399] **40**

WORLD AIRSHOW NEWS (US/0888-5265) [13651713] **40**

WORLD ALLIANCE OF YMCAS. EXECUTIVE COMMITTEE *See* REPORT AND RESOLUTIONS OF THE ... MEETING OF THE EXECUTIVE COMMITTEE **4992**

WORLD ALMANAC AND BOOK OF FACTS, THE (US/0084-1382) [01770120] **1930**

WORLD ALMANAC GUIDE TO PRO HOCKEY, THE (US/0095-7240) [01798582] **4930**

WORLD ALMANAC OF U.S. POLITICS, THE (US/1043-1535) [19329774] **4500**

WORLD ALUMINIUM DATABOOK (UK/0951-2233) **4023**

WORLD ALUMINUM ABSTRACTS *See* ALUMINIUM INDUSTRY ABSTRACTS **4025**

WORLD AMATEUR BOXING MAGAZINE (GW) **4930**

WORLD & I, THE (US/0887-9346) [13486032] **2495**

WORLD AND PRESS (GW/0509-1632) [I05091632] **3334**

●WORLD & SCIENCE, THE (US/1059-1931) [24506948] **5170**

WORLD AND THE SCHOOL, THE (UK/0043-8235) [01606683] **2633**

WORLD AND UNITED STATES AVIATION AND SPACE RECORDS AS OF ... (US/0890-510X) [12074946] **40**

WORLD ANIMAL REVIEW / REVUE MONDIALE DE ZOOTECHNIE / REVISTA MUNDIAL DE ZOOTECNIA (IT/1014-6954) [28385347] **224**

WORLD ANIMAL SCIENCE. B, DISCIPLINARY APPROACH (NE) [08471796] **5527**

WORLD ANTI-COMMUNIST LEAGUE. WACL BULLETIN *See* FREEDOM DIGEST **4522**

WORLD AQUACULTURE (US/1041-5602) [18800397] **2316**

WORLD ARBITRATION & MEDIATION REPORT (UK/0960-0949) [22212424] **3138**

WORLD ARCHAEOLOGY (UK/0043-8243) [02243103] **285**

WORLD ARCHITECTURE (LONDON. 1989) (UK/0956-9758) [22379084] **311**

WORLD AROUND YOU, THE (US/0199-8293) [06192254] **4395**

WORLD ART TRENDS (US/0739-537X) [09724610] **369**

WORLD (ASHEVILLE, N.C.) (US/0888-157X) [13492496] 5010, **2550**

WORLD ASSOCIATION OF VETERINARY FOOD HYGIENISTS *See* PROCEEDINGS--SYMPOSIUM OF THE WORLD ASSOCIATION OF VETERINARY HYGIENISTS **5519**

WORLD AT LARGE, THE (US/1060-3816) [24949382] **2550**

WORLD AUTOMOTIVE ALTERNATIVE ENERGY & FUELS BULLETIN (US) 5428, 4282, **1960**

WORLD AUTOMOTIVE ENVIRONMENT & SAFETY BULLETIN (US) 2871, **5428**

WORLD AUTOMOTIVE INDUSTRY WEEKLY (US) **5428**

WORLD AUTOMOTIVE MARKET *See* WORLD AUTOMOTIVE MARKET REPORT **5428**

WORLD AUTOMOTIVE MARKET REPORT (US) [27052146] 858, **5428**

WORLD AUTOMOTIVE MARKET, THE (US) [13439557] **5428**

WORLD AUTOMOTIVE MATERIALS & COMPOSITES BULLETIN (US) **5428**

WORLD AUTOMOTIVE NEWS SERVICE (US) **5428**

WORLD AUTOMOTIVE TECHNOLOGY TRACKING (US) **5428**

WORLD AVIATION BUYER'S GUIDE *See* WORLD AVIATION DIRECTORY. BUYER'S GUIDE **40**

WORLD AVIATION DIRECTORY (US/0043-826X) [02413063] **40**

●WORLD AVIATION DIRECTORY. BUYER'S GUIDE (US/1064-0509) [25610909] **40**

WORLD BADMINTON (UK/0255-4429) [I02554429] **4930**

WORLD BALLET AND DANCE (UK) [21317939] 389, **1314**

WORLD BANK (US) **816**

WORLD BANK *See* TELEPHONE DIRECTORY / THE WORLD BANK **813**

WORLD BANK *See* TAQRIR AN AL-TANMIYAH FI AL-ALAM **1586**

WORLD BANK ATLAS (US/0085-8293) [02255743] **816**

WORLD BANK CATALOG. ACCESSION LIST (US/0303-9463) [01798002] **816**

WORLD BANK CATALOG OF PUBLICATIONS, THE (US/0253-7389) [08530122] **1540**

WORLD BANK DISCUSSION PAPERS (US/0259-210X) [14155986] **1527**

WORLD BANK ECONOMIC REVIEW, THE (US/0258-6770) [13534968] **1631**

WORLD BANK GROUP DIRECTORY, THE (US) [22339140] **1169**

WORLD BANK POLICY RESEARCH BULLETIN (US/1014-8590) [21344789] 1641, **816**

WORLD BANK REPRINT SERIES (US/0253-2131) [05796705] **816**

WORLD BANK RESEARCH OBSERVER, THE (US/0257-3032) [12303480] **1631**

WORLD BANK RESEARCH PROGRAM (1986), THE (US/0258-3143) [13204681] **1631**

WORLD BANK STUDIES IN WATER SUPPLY AND SANITATION (UK) [08970118] 2248, **5549**

WORLD BANK TECHNICAL PAPER (US/0253-7494) [09103701] 147, **5170**

WORLD BANK WATCH, THE *CEASED.* (US/1054-4313) [20336317] **816**

WORLD BANKING ABSTRACTS (UK/0265-9484) [19052006] **816**

WORLD BASEBALL MAGAZINE (US/1040-5216) [18435231] **4930**

WORLD BEER REVIEW (US/1071-1090) [28554315] **2373**

WORLD BIBLIOGRAPHICAL SERIES (UK) [04694425] **427**

WORLD BIO LICENSING & PATENT REPORT (US/1047-4730) [20423585] **3697**

WORLD BIOTECH REPORT (UK) **3697**

WORLD BIRDWATCH : THE NEWSLETTER OF THE INTERNATIONAL COUNCIL FOR BIRD PRESERVATION (UK) [17051730] 5621, **2210**

WORLD BOOK & TRAVEL REPORT (US/0146-4248) [02958320] **5499**

WORLD BOOK HEALTH & MEDICAL ANNUAL, THE (US/0890-4480) [14229102] 4808, **3651**

WORLD BOOK YEAR BOOK, THE (US/0084-1439) [01833861] **1930**

WORLD (BOSTON, MASS.), THE (US/0892-2462) [15062337] **5010**

WORLD BOWLS (UK/0966-9884) [I09669884] **4930**

WORLD BOXING (US/1051-9033) [12025897] **4930**

WORLD BROADCASTING INFORMATION (UK) **1143**

WORLD BUDDHISM (CE/0043-8286) [01770125] **5022**

WORLD BUDDHISM (CE/0084-1447) [01640957] **5022**

WORLD BUSINESS ACADEMY PERSPECTIVES (US/1061-9917) [25513076] **723**

WORLD BUSINESS & ECONOMIC REVIEW / COMPILED BY WALDEN PUBLISHING (UK/1351-4725) [30450244] 723, **1527**

WORLD BUSINESS DIGEST (US/0731-003X) [08106346] **723**

●WORLD BUSINESS DIRECTORY (DETROIT, MICH.) (US/1062-1172) [26799290] **723**

WORLD BUSINESS (MENLO PARK, CALIF.) (US/0732-734X) [08398190] **858**

WORLD BUSINESS (OTTAWA) (CN/1182-0993) [22281362] **723**

WORLD CALENDAR (UK) [08102014] **4023**

WORLD CARTOGRAPHY (US/0084-1471) [01770127] **2583**

WORLD CEMENT (UK/0263-6050) [08570518] 2017, **631**

WORLD CEMENT DIRECTORY (FR) [04754292] **1031**

WORLD CERAMICS ABSTRACTS (UK/0957-8897) [19959904] **2595**

WORLD CERAMICS & REFRACTORIES (UK/0959-6127) [22212911] **2595**

WORLD CHAMBER OF COMMERCE DIRECTORY (US/1048-2849) [19900575] **821**

WORLD CHAMPIONSHIP WRESTLING MAGAZINE : WCW *CEASED.* (US/1057-1396) [23954787] **4930**

WORLD CHRISTIAN : TODAY'S MISSION MAGAZINE (US/0743-2399) [09245267] **5010**

●WORLD CLASS DESIGN TO MANUFACTURE : WCDM (UK/1352-3074) [30629194] **3489**

WORLD CLASS ENTERTAINMENT (US/1048-0862) [20850364] **2495**

WORLD CLINIC YEARBOOK / AMERICAN SWIMMING COACHES ASSOCIATION (US/0747-5853) [16669508] **4930**

WORLD CLOTHING MANUFACTURER (UK/1350-6773) **1088**

●WORLD COAL DORKING (UK/0968-3224) [I09683224] **2153**

WORLD COAL LETTER *See* INTERNATIONAL COAL LETTER **2140**

WORLD COCOA SITUATION (US) [15522800] **147**

WORLD COFFEE & TEA (US/0043-8340) [02187101] **2373**

WORLD COFFEE SITUATION *See* TROPICAL PRODUCTS, WORLD MARKETS AND TRADE / UNITED STATES DEPARTMENT OF AGRICULTURE, FOREIGN AGRICULTURAL SERVICE **189**

WORLD COFFEE SITUATION / UNITED STATES DEPARTMENT OF AGRICULTURE, FOREIGN AGRICULTURAL SERVICE (US) [15249261] **147**

WORLD COGENERATION (US/1053-5802) [22581908] **2132**

WORLD COIN NEWS (US/0145-9090) [02801177] **2783**

WORLD COLLECTORS ANNUARY (NE/0084-1498) [01770130] **369**

WORLD COMMERCIAL AIRCRAFT / ENGINES ORDERS & OPTIONS (US) **40**

WORLD

WORLD COMMODITY FORECASTS *See* WORLD COMMODITY FORECASTS. FOOD, FEEDSTUFFS AND BEVERAGES **1527**

WORLD COMMODITY FORECASTS *See* WORLD COMMODITY FORECASTS. INDUSTRIAL RAW MATERIALS **1527**

WORLD COMMODITY FORECASTS. FOOD, FEEDSTUFFS AND BEVERAGES (UK) 2361, **1527**

WORLD COMMODITY FORECASTS. INDUSTRIAL RAW MATERIALS (UK) **1527**

WORLD COMMODITY FORECASTS / THE ECONOMIST INTELLIGENCE UNIT (UK/0267-6303) [23200005] **1527**

WORLD COMMODITY REPORT (UK) **724**

WORLD COMPETITION (SZ/1011-4548) [17020461] **3104**

WORLD COMPETITIVENESS REPORT (SZ/1015-5449) [15178540] **1641**

WORLD CONFEDERATION OF ORGANIZATIONS OF THE TEACHING PROFESSION *See* HANDBOOK - WORLD CONFEDERATION OF ORGANIZATIONS OF THE TEACHING PROFESSION **1895**

WORLD CONFEDERATION OF ORGANIZATIONS OF THE TEACHING PROFESSION *See* BIENNIAL REPORT - WORLD CONFEDERATION OF ORGANIZATIONS OF THE TEACHING PROFESSION **1889**

WORLD CONVENTION DATES. EVENT PLANNER'S GUIDE (US) [08547989] **2793**

WORLD (COOS BAY, OR.), THE (US/1062-8495) [23861115] **5734**

WORLD COPPER DATABOOK (UK/0950-2262) [15307651] **4024**

WORLD COTTON SITUATION (US) [15188529] **147**

WORLD COUNCIL OF CHURCHES. CENTRAL COMMITTEE *See* MINUTES OF THE ... MEETING / CENTRAL COMMITTEE OF THE WORLD COUNCIL OF CHURCHES **4977**

WORLD COUNCIL OF CHURCHES. COMMISSION ON THE CHURCHES' PARTICIPATION IN DEVELOPMENT *See* CCPD ACTIVITY REPORT **4943**

WORLD COUNCIL OF CREDIT UNIONS *See* YEARBOOK - WORLD COUNCIL OF CREDIT UNIONS **1544**

WORLD COUNCIL OF PEACE *See* LIST OF MEMBERS - WORLD PEACE COUNCIL **3132**

WORLD COUNTERTRADE & BARTER NEWS (UK/0960-0248) [I09600248] **858**

WORLD COUNTERTRADE AND BARTER NEWS *See* WORLD NEWS **1527**

WORLD COUNTRY REPORT SERVICE (US) [12997128] **920**

WORLD CRICKET ANNUAL (PK) [08004176] **4930**

WORLD CROPS : PRODUCTION, UTILIZATION, AND DESCRIPTION (NE/0167-1782) [07711411] 191, **530**

WORLD CULTURES (US/1045-0564) [18578455] **5269**

WORLD CURRENCY CHARTS *CEASED.* (US/0090-2810) [01783009] **920**

WORLD CURRENCY YEARBOOK (US/0743-5363) [10601518] **816**

WORLD DAIRY SITUATION *See* DAIRY, LIVESTOCK, AND POULTRY. DAIRY, WORLD MARKETS AND TRADE / UNITED STATES DEPARTMENT OF AGRICULTURE, FOREIGN AGRICULTURAL SERVICE **193**

WORLD DAIRY SITUATION / UNITED STATES DEPARTMENT OF AGRICULTURE, FOREIGN AGRICULTURAL SERVICE (US) [18386065] **199**

WORLD DATA : BOOK OF THE YEAR (AUSTRALIA) (AT) **1930**

WORLD DATA CENTER A: METEOROLOGY *See* DATA REPORT, HIGH ALTITUDE METEOROLOGICAL DATA. INTERNATIONAL DELAYED DATA ISSUE **1425**

WORLD DATA CENTER A--OCEANOGRAPHY *See* CATALOGUE OF ACCESSIONED PUBLICATIONS. SUPPLEMENT **1447**

WORLD DATA CENTER A--OCEANOGRAPHY *See* OCEANOGRAPHIC DATA EXCHANGE **1454**

WORLD DATA CENTER C2 FOR GEOMAGNETISM *See* DATA CATALOGUE - WORLD DATA CENTER C2 FOR GEOMAGNETISM **4443**

WORLD DEBT TABLES (US/0253-2859) [04571388] 1641, **1540**

WORLD DEFENCE ALMANAC : THE BALANCE OF MILITARY POWER (GW) [16827433] 4538, **4061**

WORLD DEFENSE FORCES *SUSPENDED.* (US/0891-4850) [14868195] **4061**

WORLD DEVELOPMENT (UK/0305-750X) [01787937] **1641**

WORLD DEVELOPMENT FORUM *CEASED.* (US/0883-1556) [11081684] **1527**

WORLD DEVELOPMENT INDICATORS [COMPUTER FILE] (US) [18229208] **1589**

WORLD DEVELOPMENT (NEW YORK, N.Y.) *See* CHOICES : THE HUMAN DEVELOPMENT MAGAZINE / UNDP **2908**

WORLD DEVELOPMENT REPORT (US/0163-5085) [04227367] **1589**

WORLD DICTIONARIES IN PRINT *CEASED.* (US/0000-0604) [10093104] **1930**

WORLD DIESEL & OFF-HIGHWAY NEWS (US) **5428**

WORLD DIRECTORY : LEAD & ZINC MINES & PRIMARY METALLURGICAL WORKS (UK) **4024**

WORLD DIRECTORY OF AL-ANON FAMILY GROUPS AND ALATEENS (US/0512-2716) [03461690] **1350**

●WORLD DIRECTORY OF DIPLOMATIC REPRESENTATION (UK/0965-3783) [25986007] **4705**

●WORLD DIRECTORY OF ENERGY CONSERVATION AND RENEWABLE ENERGY SOFTWARE FOR MICROCOMPUTERS (US/1048-2288) [20874553] **1960**

WORLD DIRECTORY OF ENVIRONMENTAL ORGANIZATIONS (US/0092-0908) [01784388] **2210**

●WORLD DIRECTORY OF FERTILIZER MANUFACTURERS (UK) 3489, **147**

WORLD DIRECTORY OF FERTILIZER PRODUCTS (UK) [09015084] 1031, **147**

WORLD DIRECTORY OF FREIGHT CONFERENCES (UK) **5458**

WORLD DIRECTORY OF HISTORIANS OF MATHEMATICS (CN/0315-1700) [02239816] **3541**

WORLD DIRECTORY OF MATHEMATICIANS / PUBLISHED UNDER THE AUSPICES OF THE INTERNATIONAL MATHEMATICAL UNION (II/0512-2740) [01773052] **3541**

WORLD DIRECTORY OF MEDICAL SCHOOLS (SZ/0512-2759) [02220818] **3651**

WORLD DIRECTORY OF NEUROLOGICAL SURGEONS. PART 1, UNITED STATES OF AMERICA AND CANADA (US/0276-5306) [07312311] **3977**

WORLD DIRECTORY OF PHYSIOLOGISTS / INTERNATIONAL UNION OF PHYSIOLOGICAL SCIENCES (US) [08005554] **587**

WORLD DIRECTORY: SECONDARY LEAD PLANTS (UK) **4024**

WORLD DIRECTORY: SECONDARY ZINC PLANTS (UK) **4024**

WORLD DREDGING, MINING & CONSTRUCTION (US/1045-0343) [18543563] **2153**

WORLD DRUG MARKET ANNUAL (UK) **4333**

WORLD EAGLE (US/0193-7871) [05246558] 5226, **5228**

WORLD ECONOMIC AND BUSINESS REVIEW (US) [22001700] 724, **1527**

WORLD ECONOMIC AND FINANCIAL SURVEYS (US/0258-7440) [13610664] 816, **1527**

●WORLD ECONOMIC AND SOCIAL SURVEY / DEPARTMENT OF ECONOMIC AND SOCIAL INFORMATION AND POLICY ANALYSIS (US) [30879082] 1527, **1641**

WORLD ECONOMIC BULLETIN (US/0197-811X) [06112933] **1589**

WORLD ECONOMIC CONDITIONS IN RELATION TO AGRICULTURAL TRADE (US/0364-7234) [05022136] **1641**

WORLD ECONOMIC DATA (US/0891-4125) [14766048] **1527**

WORLD ECONOMIC OUTLOOK (PHILADELPHIA, PA.) (US/0749-6125) [10292110] **1527**

WORLD ECONOMIC OUTLOOK (WASHINGTON) (US/0256-6877) [07621785] **1641**

WORLD ECONOMIC REVIEW (PHILADELPHIA, PA.) (US/0197-7466) [06098900] **1527**

WORLD ECONOMIC SERVICE DATA BANKS *See* WORLD SERVICE DATA BANKS **1641**

WORLD ECONOMIC SURVEY (NEW YORK, N.Y.) (US/0084-1714) [01188668] 1527, **1641**

WORLD ECONOMIC SURVEY (NEW YORK, N.Y.) *See* WORLD ECONOMIC AND SOCIAL SURVEY / DEPARTMENT OF ECONOMIC AND SOCIAL INFORMATION AND POLICY ANALYSIS **1641**

WORLD ECONOMIC SURVEY (NEW YORK, N.Y.). READER *See* WORLD ECONOMIC SURVEY. STUDENT EDITION / DEPARTMENT OF INTERNATIONAL ECONOMIC AND SOCIAL AFFAIRS **1589**

●WORLD ECONOMIC SURVEY. STUDENT EDITION / DEPARTMENT OF INTERNATIONAL ECONOMIC AND SOCIAL AFFAIRS (US) [26971623] **1589**

WORLD ECONOMY, THE (UK/0378-5920) [03601984] **1641**

WORLD EDUCATION NEWS & REVIEWS (US/0897-6724) [17604720] **1791**

WORLD EDUCATION REPORT (FR) [25061473] **1792**

WORLD EDUCATION REPORTS (US/0300-7006) [01355819] 2287, **1792**

WORLD ELECTRONICS COMPANIES FILE (UK/0951-5747) [I09515747] **2086**

WORLD ELECTRONICS COMPANIES FILE 1990/91 (UK) [20523222] **2086**

WORLD EMPLOYMENT PROGRAMME RESEARCH WORKING PAPER. WEP-2-22 (US) [17352559] **5170**

WORLD ENERGY AND NUCLEAR DIRECTORY : ORGANIZATIONS AND RESEARCH ACTIVITIES IN ATOMIC AND NON-ATOMIC ENERGY (UK) [22665935] **1960**

WORLD ENERGY NEWS (CALGARY) (CN/0843-2295) [20243277] 1961, **4282**

WORLD ENERGY OUTLOOK (US/0197-789X) [04577996] **1961**

WORLD ENGLISHES (UK/0883-2919) [12101053] **3334**

●WORLD ENVIRONMENT REPORT (US/0098-8235) [25160815] **2248**

WORLD ENVIRONMENTAL DIRECTORY (US/0094-4742) [01790813] **2183**

WORLD EQUITY (UK) **816**

WORLD EVANGELIZATION (CHARLOTTE, N.C.) (US) [15799419] **5010**

WORLD EXCELLENCE IN CORRUGATED GRAPHICS (UK) [23077524] **382**

WORLD EXECUTIVES DIGEST (HK) **724**

WORLD FACTBOOK (WASHINGTON, D.C.) (US/0277-1527) [07390695] **2579**

●WORLD FAITHS ENCOUNTER (UK) [25535837] **5010**

WORLD FAITHS INSIGHT *See* WORLD FAITHS ENCOUNTER **5010**

WORLD FARMERS' TIMES : A WORLD FARMERS' TIMES FOUNDATION PUBLICATION (SZ) [15480734] **147**

WORLD FEDERALIST (ARLINGTON, VA.) (US/0749-4793) [10592009] **4501**

WORLD FEDERATION FOR MENTAL HEALTH *See* NEWSLETTER - WORLD FEDERATION FOR MENTAL HEALTH **3931**

WORLD FEDERATION OF ADVERTISERS *See* REPORT & REVIEW / WORLD FEDERATION OF ADVERTISERS, WFA **765**

WORLD FEDERATION OF INTERNATIONAL MUSIC COMPETITIONS *See* PREMIERS PRIX ... DES CONCOURS MEMBRES DE LA FEDERATION, LES **4147**

WORLD FEDERATION OF TRADE UNIONS *See* TNC'S BULLETIN **1714**

WORLD FERTILIZER PLANT LIST AND ATLAS (UK) **147**

WORLD FERTILIZER REVIEW (UK) **191**

WORLD FIBRE NEWS (UK) [01788295] **5360**

WORLD FINANCE (WASHINGTON, D.C.) (US/1055-1573) [23096259] **1641**

WORLD FINANCIAL MARKETS (US/0190-2083) [01160218] **816**

WORLD FISHING (UK/0043-8480) [01844467] **2316**

WORLD FOCUS (II) [07250981] **4501**

●WORLD FOOD CHEMICAL NEWS (US/1073-2357) [29368064] **2361**

WORLD FOOD PROBLEMS (IT/0084-179X) [01432703] **2361**

WORLD FOOD PROGRAMME JOURNAL (IT/1010-9099) [15748411] **2913**

WORLD FOOD REGULATION REVIEW (UK/0963-4894) [24194929] 3076, **2361**

WORLD FOOD SURVEY (IT) [01317647] 2361, **147**

WORLD FOOTWEAR (US/0894-3079) [15993588] **1088**

WORLD FREE FLIGHT REVIEW (US/0191-3247) [04836196] **40**

Alphabetical Title Index

WORLD

WORLD FREIGHT SHIPPER **CEASED.** (UK) **5458**

WORLD FUTURE SOCIETY (US/0732-7676) [08428019] **5237**

WORLD FUTURE SOCIETY. WASHINGTON D.C. CHAPTER **See** WORLD FUTURE SOCIETY **5237**

WORLD FUTURES (US/0260-4027) [07288633] **4365**

WORLD GAS INTELLIGENCE : PIW'S GAS MARKET REPORT (US) [21927293] **4282**

WORLD GAS REPORT **See** INTERNATIONAL GAS REPORT **4261**

WORLD GEOPHYSICAL NEWS (US/1053-9859) [22714419] **4282**

WORLD GOODWILL **See** WORLD GOODWILL NEWSLETTER **2913**

WORLD GOODWILL NEWSLETTER (UK/0161-2352) [03880538] **2913**

WORLD GRAIN (US/0745-8991) [09551776] **204**

WORLD GRAIN LIST (CN/0846-3212) [25066639] 858, **147**

WORLD GRAIN SITUATION AND OUTLOOK (US/0898-3399) [15325111] **204**

WORLD GRAIN STATISTICS (UK) [25901430] **204**

WORLD GUIDE TO ABBREVIATIONS OF ORGANIZATIONS (UK) [03244052] **1930**

WORLD GUIDE TO FOREIGN SERVICES (US) [16914565] **4538**

WORLD GUIDE TO LIBRARIES (GW/0000-0221) [01840686] **3256**

WORLD GUIDE TO LIBRARIES (GW/0936-0085) [20437336] **3260**

WORLD GUIDE TO SCIENTIFIC ASSOCIATIONS AND LEARNED SOCIETIES (US) [04635328] **5176**

WORLD GUIDE TO SPECIAL LIBRARIES (GW/0724-8717) [10412451] **3260**

●WORLD GUIDE TO TELEVISION & FILM (US/1072-6144) [29049760] 4080, **1143**

WORLD GUIDE TO TELEVISION & PROGRAMMING (US/1058-1944) [24238591] **1143**

WORLD GUIDE TO TRADE ASSOCIATIONS (US/0094-1611) [01794001] **858**

WORLD GUIDE TO UNIVERSITIES. INTERNATIONALES UNIVERSITATS-HANDBUCH (US) [02256635] **1930**

WORLD HANDBALL MAGAZINE (SZ/0255-884X) [I0255884X] **4930**

WORLD HARP CONGRESS REVIEW : OFFICIAL PUBLICATION OF THE WORLD HARP CONGRESS, INC (US) [16531897] **4159**

WORLD HARVEST (US) [04075384] **147**

WORLD HEALTH (SZ/0043-8502) [01770145] **4808**

WORLD HEALTH FORUM (SZ/0251-2432) [06812919] **4808**

WORLD HEALTH ORGANIZATION **See** WORLD HEALTH ORGANIZATION TECHNICAL REPORT SERIES **4808**

WORLD HEALTH ORGANIZATION **See** WORLD HEALTH STATISTICS QUARTERLY **4811**

WORLD HEALTH ORGANIZATION **See** BASIC DOCUMENTS **4768**

WORLD HEALTH ORGANIZATION **See** INTERNATIONAL NONPROPRIETARY NAMES (INN) FOR PHARMACEUTICAL SUBSTANCES / DENOMINATIONS COMMUNES INTERNATIONALES (DCI) POUR LES SUBSTANCES PHARMACEUTIQUES **4309**

WORLD HEALTH ORGANIZATION **See** PORTS DESIGNATED IN APPLICATION OF THE INTERNATIONAL HEALTH REGULATIONS **5454**

WORLD HEALTH ORGANIZATION **See** YELLOW-FEVER VACCINATING CENTRES FOR INTERNATIONAL TRAVEL **4808**

WORLD HEALTH ORGANIZATION **See** BULLETIN OF THE WORLD HEALTH ORGANIZATION **3560**

WORLD HEALTH ORGANIZATION. EXECUTIVE BOARD **See** RESOLUTIONS AND DECISIONS, ANNEXES / WORLD HEALTH ORGANIZATION, EXECUTIVE BOARD **4799**

WORLD HEALTH ORGANIZATION TECHNICAL REPORT SERIES (SZ/0512-3054) [01770148] **4808**

WORLD HEALTH STATISTICS ANNUAL (SZ/0250-3794) [00997974] **4811**

WORLD HEALTH STATISTICS QUARTERLY (SZ/0379-8070) [04360123] **4811**

WORLD HELICOPTER ACCIDENT SUMMARY & BINDERS **See** WORLD AIRLINE ACCIDENT SUMMARY **40**

WORLD HERITAGE WORLD (US/0270-1995) [06345714] **2478**

WORLD HIGHWAYS (US/0043-8529) [01770154] **5446**

WORLD HISTORY BULLETIN (US/0886-117X) [12920178] **2633**

WORLD HOCKEY (UK/0964-0681) [I09640681] **4930**

●WORLD HORTICULTURAL TRADE & U.S. EXPORT OPPORTUNITIES / UNITED STATES DEPARTMENT OF AGRICULTURE, FOREIGN AGRICULTURAL SERVICE (US) [30317686] **2433**

WORLD HOSPITALS (UK/0512-3135) [01641311] **3793**

WORLD IN FIGURES **See** ECONOMIST BOOK OF VITAL WORLD STATISTICS, THE **5326**

WORLD INDUSTRIAL REPORTER (US/0043-8561) **4538**

WORLD INSURANCE REPORT (UK) [14269212] **2896**

WORLD INSURANCE REPORT CORPORATE (UK/0955-4823) [I09554823] **2896**

WORLD INTELLECTUAL PROPERTY ORGANIZATION **See** LIST OF SELECTED WIPO MEETINGS **1306**

WORLD INTELLECTUAL PROPERTY REPORT (UK/0952-7613) [17278716] **1309**

●WORLD INTELLIGENCE REVIEW (US/1076-9285) [30642096] **3356**

●WORLD INTERMODAL FREIGHT MARKET (US) 858, **5458**

●WORLD INVESTMENT DIRECTORY. VOL. 1, ASIA AND THE PACIFIC (US) [26066394] **920**

WORLD INVESTMENT REPORT (US) [24861531] **920**

WORLD ISLAMIC TIMES (PK) [09425350] **5045**

●WORLD IVHS MARKET (US) **5400**

WORLD JOURNAL OF MICROBIOLOGY & BIOTECHNOLOGY (UK/0959-3993) [22201215] 3697, **571**

WORLD JOURNAL OF PSYCHOSYNTHESIS (US/0043-860X) [03519738] **3937**

WORLD JOURNAL OF SURGERY (US/0364-2313) [02991729] **3977**

WORLD JOURNAL OF UROLOGY (GW/0724-4983) [09791303] **3994**

WORLD JURIST, THE (US/0043-8618) [01793262] **4501**

WORLD LABOUR REPORT (SZ/0255-5514) [22123317] **1720**

WORLD LAW DIRECTORY **See** WORLD LEGAL DIRECTORY **3076**

WORLD LEASING YEARBOOK (UK/0264-0732) [09293367] **1631**

WORLD LEATHER (US/0894-3087) [15993442] **3186**

WORLD LEGAL DIRECTORY (US) [01784494] **3076**

WORLD LEISURE & RECREATION (US) [11950996] **4855**

WORLD LETTER (IOWA CITY, IOWA) (US/1054-8823) [23004571] **3454**

WORLD LINK (UK) [18097771] **1589**

WORLD LIST OF FAMILY PLANNING ADDRESSES / INTERNATIONAL PLANNED PARENTHOOD FEDERATION (UK/0535-1774) [19897723] **591**

WORLD LIST OF SOCIAL SCIENCE PERIODICALS (FR/0251-4877) [01775445] **5226**

WORLD LIST OF UNIVERSITIES, OTHER INSTITUTIONS OF HIGHER EDUCATION AND UNIVERSITY ORGANISATIONS. LISTE MONDIALE DES UNIVERSITES, AUTRES ETABLISSEMENTS D'ENSEIGNEMENT SUPERIEUR ET ORGANISATIONS UNIVERSITAIRES (GW/0084-1889) [05868884] 1854, **1930**

WORLD LITERATURE TODAY (US/0196-3570) [02805697] **3454**

WORLD LITERATURE WRITTEN IN ENGLISH (CN/0093-1705) [01791888] **3356**

WORLD LONG-TERM ECONOMIC OUTLOOK (US/0749-5838) [10497533] **1527**

WORLD MAGAZINE (LONDON, ENGLAND) **CEASED.** (UK/0951-2195) [18157028] **2579**

WORLD M&A NETWORK (US/1046-4778) [20425845] **816**

WORLD MANUFACTURING (US/0091-8407) [01788294] **4024**

WORLD MAP DIRECTORY, THE **CEASED.** (US/1040-1687) [18338040] **2583**

WORLD MARKET FOR DAIRY PRODUCTS, THE (SZ/0259-8213) [08878946] **199**

WORLD MARKET PERSPECTIVE **CEASED.** (US/0229-4044) [08071356] 1589, **817**

WORLD MARXIST REVIEW **CEASED.** (UK) [04877185] **4501**

WORLD MEDIA REPORT (WASHINGTON, D.C) (US/0887-4182) [13222057] **1124**

WORLD MEDICAL JOURNAL (GW/0049-8122) [01770169] **3651**

●WORLD MEDICAL REVIEWS IN GLAUCOMA (US/1062-774X) [25738230] **3880**

WORLD MEDICAL REVIEWS IN PARKINSON'S DISEASE **CEASED.** (US/1062-7731) [25738204] **3651**

WORLD MEDICAL REVIEWS IN PERINATOLOGY (US/0892-614X) [15248223] 3769, **3912**

WORLD MEETINGS. MEDICINE (US/0161-2875) [03831681] **3651**

WORLD MEETINGS OUTSIDE UNITED STATES AND CANADA (US/0043-8677) [00933135] **5170**

WORLD MEETINGS. SOCIAL & BEHAVIORAL SCIENCES, HUMAN SERVICES & MANAGEMENT (US/0194-6161) [03566837] 1183, 1792, **5226**

WORLD MEETINGS: UNITED STATES AND CANADA (US/0043-8693) [02246743] **5170**

WORLD METAL STATISTICS (UK/0043-8758) [06160564] 4024, **4026**

WORLD METAL STATISTICS (UK) **4024**

WORLD METAL STATISTICS YEARBOOK (UK/0266-7355) [10820783] **4024**

WORLD METEOROLOGICAL ORGANIZATION **See** SPECIAL ENVIRONMENTAL REPORT - WORLD METEOROLOGICAL ORGANIZATION **1434**

WORLD METEOROLOGICAL ORGANIZATION **See** CLIMATIC ATLAS OF EUROPE **1422**

WORLD METEOROLOGICAL ORGANIZATION **See** TECHNICAL NOTE - WORLD METEOROLOGICAL ORGANIZATION **1435**

WORLD METEOROLOGICAL ORGANIZATION **See** COMPOSITION OF THE WMO **1424**

WORLD METEOROLOGICAL ORGANIZATION **See** CATALOGUE OF PUBLICATIONS - WORLD METEOROLOGICAL ORGANIZATION **1421**

WORLD METEOROLOGICAL ORGANIZATION **See** WORLD WEATHER WATCH : THE PLAN AND IMPLEMENTATION PROGRAMME **1437**

WORLD METEOROLOGICAL ORGANIZATION **See** REPORT - WORLD METEOROLOGICAL ORGANIZATION **1434**

WORLD METEOROLOGICAL ORGANIZATION. COMMISSION FOR AGRICULTURAL METEOROLOGY **See** ABRIDGED FINAL REPORT - WORLD METEOROLOGICAL ORGANIZATION. COMMISSION FOR AGRICULTURAL METEOROLOGY **1419**

WORLD MILITARY & CIVIL AIRCRAFT BRIEFING (US) 4061, **40**

WORLD MILITARY AND SOCIAL EXPENDITURES (US/0363-4795) [02469505] 4061, 4759, **4062**

WORLD MILITARY EXPENDITURES AND ARMS TRANSFERS (US/0897-4667) [03736163] **4061**

WORLD MINE PRODUCTION OF GOLD (US) [18211363] **2153**

WORLD MINE PRODUCTION OF SILVER (US/1044-7482) [19872413] 1631, **4024**

WORLD MINERAL STATISTICS (UK) [04144075] 1445, **1364**

WORLD MINING EQUIPMENT (US/0746-729X) [10219207] **2153**

WORLD MISSILE FORECAST **See** MISSILE FORECAST **4051**

WORLD MISSION JOURNAL **See** MISSIONS TODAY (MEMPHIS, TENN.) **4978**

WORLD MISSLES BRIEFING (US) **4061**

WORLD MODEL HISTORICAL DATA (US/0749-5846) [10384994] **1589**

WORLD MONEY ANALYST (HK) **1527**

WORLD MONEY OUTLOOK (FR/1016-1546) [02225977] **817**

WORLD MONITOR **CEASED.** (US/0897-9472) [17671741] **2495**

WORLD MOTOR VEHICLE DATA (US/0085-8307) [01784678] 3489, **5428**

WORLD MUSEUM PUBLICATIONS (US/0000-0698) [08943831] **4097**

WORLD MUSIC CONNECTIONS (US/1049-0140) [21108724] **4159**

WORLD NAPHTHA SURVEY : REGIONAL ANALYSIS, THE (US) [04823478] 1031, **1631**

WORLD NAPHTHA SURVEY : WORLD SUMMARY (SZ) [04961829] **1631**

WORLD NATURAL GAS (US/0195-6965) [03941210] **4282**

WORLD — Alphabetical Title Index

WORLD NEIGHBORS IN ACTION (US) **2913**

WORLD NEUROLOGY (UK/0899-9465) [18305929] **3847**

WORLD (NEW YORK, N.Y. 1967) (US/0512-2295) [02250623] **753**

WORLD (NEW YORK, N.Y. : 1967), THE (US/0043-8154) [01380595] **3473**

WORLD NEWS (UK) **1527**

WORLD NEWS DIGEST (US) [07344745] 2633, **858**

WORLD NEWSMAP OF THE WEEK (US/1046-1434) [08738680] **1792**

WORLD NICKEL STATISTICS (UK/0965-0830) [I09650830] **4024**

WORLD NICKEL STATISTICS MONTHLY BULLETIN (NE) 4024, **4026**

WORLD NUCLEAR INDUSTRY HANDBOOK (UK) [14913323] **2159**

WORLD NUCLEAR PERFORMANCE (US/0891-4435) [14958017] **1961**

WORLD OF ANIMALS (US) **5600**

WORLD OF ASP (CN/0380-4712) [02039844] **4808**

WORLD OF BANKING, THE (US/0730-8736) [08077525] 889, **817**

WORLD OF BEER, THE (IT/1121-158X) [I1121158X] **2373**

●WORLD OF CO-OPERATIVE ENTERPRISE, THE (UK) [29698131] **1543**

WORLD OF GYMNASTICS (SZ) **4930**

WORLD OF HOUSE PLANTS, THE (US/0148-9089) [03383491] **2434**

WORLD OF INTERIORS, THE (UK/0264-083X) [10853678] 311, **2904**

●WORLD OF INVENTION (US/1071-0973) [28551977] **5170**

WORLD OF IRISH NURSING (IE/0332-3056) [02256383] **3871**

WORLD OF LEARNING, THE (UK/0084-2117) [01112439] **1854**

WORLD OF LUBAVITCH (CN/0824-7420) [11463160] **5053**

WORLD OF MUSIC (WILHELMSHAVEN) (SZ/0043-8774) [01642050] **4159**

WORLD OF PERSONNEL **CEASED.** (US/0892-6247) [15248728] **1720**

WORLD OF POLITICS (US/0094-2316) [01793180] **4501**

WORLD OF PUMPS (US/0744-8643) [08605453] **2132**

●WORLD OF SCIENTIFIC DISCOVERY (US/1071-0981) [28551986] **5171**

WORLD OF WHEELS (CN/0824-5487) [10680985] **5428**

WORLD OF WINNERS (US/1041-3529) [18731720] **1124**

●WORLD OF WORK : THE MAGAZINE OF THE ILO (SZ/1020-0029) [27163827] **1720**

WORLD OIL (HOUSTON, TEX.) (US/0043-8790) [02397256] **4282**

WORLD OIL MARKET ANALYSIS (CN/0824-5533) [10680976] 1527, **4282**

WORLD OIL TRADE (UK/0950-1029) [I09501029] **4282**

WORLD OILSEED SITUATION AND OUTLOOK *See* OILSEEDS, WORLD MARKETS AND TRADE / UNITED STATES DEPARTMENT OF AGRICULTURE, FOREIGN AGRICULTURE SERVICE **1620**

WORLD OILSEED SITUATION AND OUTLOOK (US/1076-4976) [22881532] **1631**

WORLD OPERA SCHEDULE (US/1042-931X) [19213407] **4159**

WORLD OPINION UPDATE (US/0193-3329) [03571304] **4538**

WORLD ORCHID CONFERENCE *See* PROCEEDINGS - WORLD ORCHID CONFERENCE **2429**

WORLD ORDER (US/0043-8804) [06608942] 4365, **5010**

WORLD OUTLOOK / EIU (UK/0424-3331) [01788706] **1527**

●WORLD OUTLOOK / SHIH CHIEH CHAN WANG (CH) [25686067] **4501**

●WORLD PAPER (TONBRIDGE) (UK/1353-2677) [29591576] **4240**

WORLD PARISH (US/0043-8839) [01786858] **5010**

WORLD PATENT INFORMATION (UK/0172-2190) [06600800] **1309**

WORLD PATENT LAW AND PRACTICE (US) [01519270] **1309**

WORLD PATENT LAW AND PRACTICE: PATENT STATUTES, REGULATION AND TREATIES. COMPILED BY JOHN P. SINNOTT (US) [02395443] **1310**

WORLD PATENTS ABSTRACTS: EUROPEAN PATENTS REPORT. CHEMICAL (UK) **1310**

WORLD PATENTS ABSTRACTS: UNITED STATES PATENTS ABSTRACTS. CHEMICAL (UK) **1310**

WORLD PEACE (NR) [01784842] **4538**

WORLD PEACE COUNCIL *See* PROGRAMME OF ACTION / WORLD PEACE COUNCIL **4532**

WORLD PEACE NEWS (US/0049-8130) [01640265] **4538**

WORLD PENTECOST (UK) [01786128] **5069**

WORLD PERSPECTIVES (MADISON, WIS.) **SUSPENDED.** (US/1058-1022) [20938954] **4501**

WORLD PETROCHEMICALS *See* CHEMICAL MATTERS **1022**

WORLD PHARMACEUTICAL STANDARDS REVIEW (UK/0961-1118) [23988462] **4333**

WORLD PHARMACEUTICALS DIRECTORY (US/0276-2277) [07254878] **4333**

●WORLD PHARMACEUTICALS REPORT (UK/0966-7687) [I09667687] **4333**

WORLD PHEASANT ASSOCIATION *See* JOURNAL - WORLD PHEASANT ASSOCIATION **2196**

WORLD PLASTICS & RUBBER TECHNOLOGY (UK) 5078, **4461**

WORLD PLASTICS MONITOR (US/0895-9099) [16854915] **4461**

WORLD POLICY (CN/0229-6942) [09543137] 1641, **4538**

WORLD POLICY GUIDE (UK) [18671034] **2896**

WORLD POLICY JOURNAL (US/0740-2775) [09902768] **4538**

WORLD POLITICS (US/0043-8871) [01770184] **4538**

WORLD POLITICS (GUILFORD) (US/0198-0300) [06157898] **4501**

WORLD POLLEN AND SPORE FLORA (SW/0346-4601) [02251842] **530**

WORLD POPULATION. ADVANCE REPORT / U.S. DEPARTMENT OF COMMERCE, BUREAU OF THE CENSUS (US) [10172353] **4561**

WORLD POPULATION DATA SHEET OF THE POPULATION REFERENCE BUREAU, INC (US/0085-8315) [03012616] **4561**

WORLD POPULATION ESTIMATES (US/0163-2361) [04318778] **4561**

WORLD PORT CONSTRUCTION & OCEAN TECHNOLOGY *See* PORT ENGINEERING MANAGEMENT **624**

WORLD PORT INDEX (US/0502-3343) [06928389] **5458**

WORLD PORTS (1978) (US/0194-4681) [04684084] **5458**

WORLD POULTRY INDUSTRY (UK) [06671929] **224**

WORLD POWER SYSTEMS INTELLIGENCE (US) **2086**

WORLD PRESS DIGEST (CN/0225-5790) [06141461] **2925**

WORLD PRESS REVIEW (US/0195-8895) [05701324] **4539**

WORLD PRODUCTIVITY NEWS **SUSPENDED.** (US/0730-1537) [07957012] **724**

WORLD PROGRESS (US/0043-8901) [03968652] **2550**

WORLD PROGRESS YEARBOOK (US/0091-1852) [01786554] **2633**

WORLD PUBLISHING MONITOR (UK/0960-653X) [23274847] 4820, **4822**

WORLD PULSE (US/1063-7931) [26137341] **5010**

WORLD PUMPS (UK/0262-1762) [08419474] **2132**

WORLD RABBIT SCIENCES (FR) **476**

WORLD RADIO REPORT (US/0892-2640) [15139661] **1143**

WORLD RADIO TV HANDBOOK (UK/0144-7750) [04244995] **1143**

WORLD RECORD GAME FISHES (US/0194-3340) [05356122] **2316**

WORLD REFUGEE SURVEY (US/0197-5439) [06063918] **1921**

WORLD REPORT (WHITESTONE, N.Y.) (US/1043-8343) [17629430] **3454**

WORLD RESOURCE REVIEW (US/1042-8011) [19224179] **2210**

WORLD RESOURCES (US/0887-0403) [13066297] **2210**

WORLD RESOURCES DATA DISKETTE [COMPUTER FILE] (US) [24596761] **1589**

WORLD REVIEW **CEASED.** (AT/0043-8960) [03243703] **4501**

WORLD REVIEW OF ANIMAL PRODUCTION (IT/0043-8979) [01642088] **147**

WORLD REVIEW OF NUTRITION AND DIETETICS (SZ/0084-2230) [01770190] **4200**

WORLD RIVERS REVIEW (US) **5549**

WORLD ROAD STATISTICS (SZ) [07806027] **5446**

WORLD SATELLITE ALMANAC (US/0885-1611) [12580109] **1169**

WORLD SATELLITE ANNUAL, THE (US/1052-7842) [20215265] **1169**

WORLD SATELLITE DIRECTORY (POTOMAC, MD.), THE (US/1046-0950) [19366782] **1169**

WORLD SATELLITE TRANSPONDER LOADING REPORT (US) **1143**

WORLD SCANNER REPORT : A JOURNAL OF VHF-UHF SCANNER TECHNOLOGY & ENGINEERING, THE (US/1061-9240) [25492608] **2001**

WORLD SCIENTIFIC LECTURE NOTES IN PHYSICS (SI) [14507391] **4425**

WORLD SCOUTING (SZ/0043-8995) [01608104] **5237**

WORLD SCOUTING NEWS (SZ) **1071**

WORLD SCREEN NEWS (US/1051-2896) [21769321] **389**

WORLD SERVICE DATA BANKS (US/0749-5811) [11139112] **1641**

WORLD SHIPPING STATISTICS (UK) [03317989] **5402**

WORLD SHRIMP FARMING (BIMONTHLY REPORT) (US/1047-5672) [19575719] **2316**

WORLD SHRIMP FARMING (BIMONTHLY REPORT) *See* SHRIMP NEWS INTERNATIONAL **2313**

WORLD SMOKING & HEALTH (US/0161-7672) [03990949] 4808, **5374**

WORLD SOCCER (UK) [03761041] **4930**

WORLD SOCCER NEWS (CN/0711-3919) [08690339] **4930**

WORLD SOIL RESOURCES REPORTS (IT/0532-0488) [02995780] **191**

WORLD SOLID FUELS, ELECTRICITY, GAS, IRON AND STEEL AND PETROLEUM STATISTICS (UK) [01216521] 4282, **1961**

WORLD SPACE DIRECTORY *See* WORLD AVIATION DIRECTORY **40**

WORLD SPACE INDUSTRY SURVEY. TEN YEAR OUTLOOK (FR) **40**

WORLD SPACE SYSTEMS BRIEFING (US) **40**

WORLD SPACEFLIGHT NEWS (US/0737-8548) [09468622] **40**

WORLD STAINLESS STEEL STATISTICS (UK) [04424693] 1631, **4026**

WORLD STATISTICAL DIRECTORY OF VOLUNTEER AND DEVELOPMENT SERVICE ORGANISATIONS (SZ) [01796127] 5314, **5267**

WORLD STATISTICS IN BRIEF (US) [02801820] **5346**

WORLD STATUS MAP (US/0887-9559) [11760587] **5499**

WORLD STEEL (GW) **4024**

WORLD STEEL EXPORTS : QUANTITY (UK) [03304699] 4024, **1631**

WORLD STRENGTH OF THE COMMUNIST PARTY ORGANIZATIONS (US/0084-2257) [02211149] **4548**

WORLD STUDENT NEWS (XR/0014-2255) [01725431] **1792**

WORLD SUGAR JOURNAL (UK) [04107391] **147**

WORLD SUGAR SITUATION AND OUTLOOK / UNITED STATES DEPARTMENT OF AGRICULTURE, FOREIGN AGRICULTURAL SERVICE (US) [19869064] 2361, **858**

WORLD SULPHUR AND SULPHURIC ACID PLANT LIST (UK) **1031**

WORLD SURFACE COATINGS ABSTRACTS (UK/0043-9088) [02246763] 4225, **4226**

WORLD TABLES (BALTIMORE, MD.) (US/1043-5573) [01726858] **1641**

WORLD TANKER FLEET REVIEW (UK) [08913767] **5458**

WORLD TAX REPORT (UK) [05723253] **4759**

WORLD TEA SITUATION / UNITED STATES DEPARTMENT OF AGRICULTURE, FOREIGN AGRICULTURAL SERVICE (US) [17273854] **1632**

WORLD TECHNOLOGY PATENT LICENSING GAZETTE (US/0278-8047) [03829229] **1310**

WORLD TELECOMMUNICATIONS DIRECTORY (US/0364-3360) [02625538] **1169**

WORLD TELECOMMUNICATIONS MARKETFILE SERVICES (UK) **1169**

WORLD TELECOMS DAILY (UK) **1169**

WORLD TELEMEDIA (UK/0961-6284) [I09616284] **1169**

WORLD TEXTILE ABSTRACTS (UK/0043-9118) [01770193] 5360, **5361**

WORLD TEXTILES (UK) **5360**

Alphabetical Title Index — WOW

WORLD THIS YEAR, THE (US/0364-8575) [01727149] **4501**

WORLD TIN STATISTICS (UK/0965-0822) **4024**

WORLD TOBACCO (UK/0043-9126) [07680573] **5374**

WORLD TOBACCO DIRECTORY (UK/0084-2273) [02177475] **5374**

WORLD TOBACCO SITUATION *See* TOBACCO, WORLD MARKETS & TRADE / UNITED STATES DEPARTMENT OF AGRICULTURE, FOREIGN AGRICULTURAL SERVICE **5374**

WORLD TOBACCO SITUATION / UNITED STATES DEPARTMENT OF AGRICULTURE, FOREIGN AGRICULTURAL SERVICE (US) [15203820] **5374**

WORLD TODAY, THE (UK/0043-9134) [01770196] 1527, **4539**

WORLD TOPICS YEAR BOOK (US) [04424164] **2633**

WORLD TOY NEWS (UK) **2585**

●WORLD TRADE AND ARBITRATION MATERIALS (SZ) **858**

WORLD TRADE ANNUAL (US/0512-3739) [01213196] **858**

WORLD TRADE IN LEAD AND ZINC (UK) **4024**

WORLD TRADE IN LIQUIFIED PETROLEUM GASES (US/0890-2976) [10563733] **4282**

WORLD TRADE INDEX *SUSPENDED*. (UK) [08463333] **858**

WORLD TRADE (IRVINE, CALIF.) (US/1054-8637) [18342158] **858**

WORLD TRADE LINK (UK) **858**

WORLD TRADE MATERIALS (SZ/1013-4514) [19503252] **858**

WORLD TRADE NEWS (CLEVELAND, OHIO) (US/1071-1775) [09484979] **858**

WORLD TRADE NEWSPAPER (CN/0843-4174) [20659322] **858**

●WORLD TRADE RESOURCES GUIDE (US/1058-1618) [24233749] 5458, **858**

WORLD TRADE STAINLESS, HIGH SPEED AND OTHER ALLOY STEEL (UK/0952-5742) [I09525742] **4026**

WORLD TRADE STEEL (UK/0952-5734) [16220280] **1540**

WORLD TRADE STEEL (UK/0952-5734) [I09525734] **1632**

WORLD TRADE UNION MOVEMENT *CEASED*. (CS) [05663394] **1720**

WORLD TRADERS (JA) **858**

WORLD TRANSLATIONS INDEX : A JOINT PUBLICATION OF INTERNATIONAL TRANSLATIONS CENTRE [AND] CENTRE NATIONAL DE LA RECHERCHE SCIENTIFIQUE IN CO-OPERATION WITH THE NATIONAL TRANSLATIONS CENTER AT THE JOHN CRERAR LIBRARY OF THE UNIVERSITY OF CHICAGO (NE/0259-8264) [14958659] **5171**

●WORLD TRANSPORT POLICY & PRACTICE (UK/1355-2554) **5400**

WORLD TRAVEL AND TOURISM REVIEW *CEASED*. (UK) [23806854] **5500**

WORLD TRAVELING (US/0163-1780) [04315623] **5500**

WORLD TRIBUNE (US/0049-8165) [03968716] **4378**

WORLD TUNNELLING & SUBSURFACE EXCAVATION (UK) **2153**

WORLD UNION (II) [09555147] **4539**

WORLD VIEW (NEW YORK, N.Y.) (US/0264-0872) [09229886] **2633**

WORLD VIEW (TORONTO) (CN/0713-3391) [09313115] **5010**

WORLD VISION (US) [03172234] **2913**

WORLD WAR I AEROPLANES *See* W.W. 1 AERO **39**

WORLD WAR II (US/0898-4204) [13545127] **2633**

WORLD WAR II INVESTIGATOR *CEASED*. (UK/0953-4857) [17979801] **2633**

WORLD WARSHIPS FORECAST (US/0882-5610) [11618615] **4185**

WORLD WASTES (US/1064-8429) [25055413] **2248**

WORLD WATCH (WASHINGTON, D.C.) (US/0896-0615) [16898592] **1596**

WORLD WATER AND ENVIRONMENTAL ENGINEER (UK) [22614444] 2248, **5549**

WORLD WEATHER WATCH PLANNING REPORT (SZ/0084-2451) [03342424] **1437**

WORLD WEATHER WATCH : THE PLAN AND IMPLEMENTATION PROGRAMME (SZ) [02441066] **1437**

WORLD WEATHERDISC. CD-ROM (US) **1437**

WORLD WEIGHTLIFTING (HU/0230-3035) [16904678] 4930, **2602**

WORLD WHO'S WHO OF WOMEN IN EDUCATION, THE (UK) [05018310] **439**

WORLD WHO'S WHO OF WOMEN, THE (UK) [01793488] 5572, **439**

WORLD-WIDE GOLF DIRECTORY (US/0093-2477) [01784480] **4930**

WORLD-WIDE OFFICIAL ORGAN BLUE BOOK (US/0277-4135) [07546281] **4159**

WORLD-WIDE PRINTER (GW/0147-4804) [04118261] **4570**

WORLD WIDE SHIPPING (US/1060-7900) [12358744] **5458**

WORLD WILDLIFE FUND *See* YEARBOOK / WWF, WORLD WILDLIFE FUND **2210**

WORLD WILDLIFE NEWS *See* WWF NEWS **2210**

WORLD WINE ALMANAC & WINE ATLAS (US/0145-9848) [02920396] **2373**

WORLD WOOD (US/0043-9258) [01770201] **2406**

WORLD WRESTLING FEDERATION BATTLEMANIA (US/1056-3946) [23703594] **4930**

WORLD WROUGHT COPPER STATISTICS (UK/0266-7347) [I02667347] **4024**

WORLD YEARBOOK OF EDUCATION (UK/0084-2508) [05192606] 1792, **1874**

WORLD YEARBOOK OF ROBOTICS RESEARCH AND DEVELOPMENT, THE *CEASED*. (UK) [12061317] **1217**

WORLD YOUTH (US) [02269723] **1071**

WORLDAIDS (UK/0954-6510) [19598969] **3677**

WORLDBOOK OF IABC (US) [22431592] **767**

WORLDCASTS. PRODUCT (US/0163-6723) [04432406] **1632**

WORLDCASTS. REGIONAL (US/0163-6731) [04432571] **1632**

WORLDLAW (US/0748-9692) [11041876] **3138**

WORLDLETTER *CEASED*. (US/0891-1649) [14687356] **5265**

WORLDLIT (CN/0820-6686) [09403344] **1887**

WORLDMARK ENCYCLOPEDIA OF THE NATIONS (US) [06100239] **1930**

WORLDRADIO, INC (US) 2086, **1169**

WORLDRADIO NEWS (US) **1143**

WORLD'S FAIR (CORTE MADERA, CALIF.) (US/0273-480X) [07062660] **5226**

WORLD'S FAIR, THE (UK) [06212726] **4868**

●WORLD'S LATEST TECHNOLOGIES AND NEW PRODUCTS (II) [25651224] **5171**

WORLD'S NEW PRODUCTS (UK) **724**

WORLD'S POULTRY SCIENCE JOURNAL (UK/0043-9339) [01644586] **224**

WORLD'S WORD (US/8756-0631) [11633047] **3454**

WORLDWATCH PAPER (US/0270-8019) [02140248] **2210**

WORLDWIDE ACCOUNTING, BUSINESS, AND EDUCATION JOURNAL, THE (US/1055-2103) [23121969] **753**

WORLDWIDE BIOMEDICAL MEETINGS, CONFERENCES, AND EXHIBITIONS (US/0190-0617) [03941699] **3651**

WORLDWIDE BRANCH LOCATIONS OF MULTINATIONAL COMPANIES (US) **724**

WORLDWIDE BROCHURES (PRINT ED.) (US/1053-9158) [22599383] **5500**

WORLDWIDE BUSINESS CONNECTION (US/0892-9424) [15296836] **724**

●WORLDWIDE BUSINESS PRACTICES REPORT (US/1069-4447) [28049167] **724**

WORLDWIDE CHALLENGE (SAN BERNARDINO, CALIF.) (US/0746-9241) [10401839] **5010**

WORLDWIDE DIRECTORY OF AGROBIOLOGICALS, THE (UK) [25651104] **476**

WORLDWIDE DIRECTORY OF EAST INDIANS QUARTERLY (US/0748-223X) [10911228] **2495**

WORLDWIDE EDUCATIONAL DIRECTORY (PK) [09805894] **1792**

WORLDWIDE FINANCIAL REGULATIONS (UK) [18386453] **1641**

WORLDWIDE FRANCHISE DIRECTORY *CEASED*. (US/1056-456X) [23719054] **958**

●WORLDWIDE GOVERNMENT DIRECTORY, REGIONAL EDITION. THE FORMER SOVIET BLOC (US/1063-1259) [25882046] **2716**

WORLDWIDE GOVERNMENT DIRECTORY, WITH INTERNATIONAL ORGANIZATIONS (US/0894-1521) [16727954] 4501, **4695**

●WORLDWIDE GOVERNMENT REPORT (US/1065-1098) [26508574] **4695**

WORLDWIDE GUIDE TO MEDICAL ELECTRONICS MARKETING REPRESENTATION, THE (US/0146-8014) [03876699] 3651, **3256**

WORLDWIDE HOTEL INDUSTRY (US/0894-6027) [14939976] **2810**

WORLDWIDE HUNTING ANNUAL (US/0276-4865) [07356002] **4881**

WORLDWIDE LODGING INDUSTRY. DIGEST / HORWATH & HORWATH INTERNATIONAL (US) [08712822] **2810**

WORLDWIDE MANPOWER DISTRIBUTION BY GEOGRAPHICAL AREA (US/1058-0328) [07853323] 4061, **4062**

WORLDWIDE MISSIONS (US/0199-0292) [01777115] **5010**

WORLDWIDE NATURAL GAS INDUSTRY DIRECTORY (US/1051-3973) [21952655] **4282**

WORLDWIDE OFFSHORE CONTRACTORS & EQUIPMENT DIRECTORY (US/1058-9686) [15715362] 4282, **4285**

WORLDWIDE PETROCHEMICAL DIRECTORY (US/0084-2583) [03586015] **4282**

WORLDWIDE PETROLEUM PHONE/FAX/TELEX DIRECTORY (US/1054-7959) [22973255] **4282**

WORLDWIDE PRODUCT DIRECTORY *See* MULTILINGUAL COMPUTING **1196**

●WORLDWIDE PROJECTS (US/0192-5512) [27351701] 724, **2001**

WORLDWIDE REFINING AND GAS PROCESSING DIRECTORY (1978) (US/0277-0962) [05703343] **4283**

WORLDWIDE REGISTER OF ADULT EDUCATION (US/0084-2486) [02517543] **1802**

WORLDWIDE REPORT. NUCLEAR DEVELOPMENT AND PROLIFERATION (US) [05387832] **1961**

WORLDWIDE SURVEY OF MOTOR GASOLINE QUALITY (UK) [08746562] **4283**

WORLDWIDE TANKER NOMINAL FREIGHT SCALE / JOINTLY SPONSORED AND ISSUED BY WORLDSCALE ASSOCIATION (LONDON) LIMITED [AND] WORLDSCALE ASSOCIATION (NYC) INC (UK) [11094135] **5458**

●WORLDWIDE TRAVEL INFORMATION CONTACT BOOK (US/1051-6247) [21996904] **5500**

WORLDWIDE TRAVEL PLANNER *CEASED*. (US/0890-4766) [14256377] **5500**

WORLDWIDE U.S. ACTIVE DUTY MILITARY PERSONNEL CASUALTIES / DEPARTMENT OF DEFENSE (US) [11052574] **4061**

WORLDWIND (CN/0707-2279) [06054474] **1071**

WORLDWISE (HANOVER, N.H.) (US/1053-1572) [22466927] **5709**

WORMWOOD REVIEW, THE (US/0043-9401) [01639726] 3473, **3454**

WORSHIP (US/0043-941X) [01770212] **5010**

WORSHIP AND ARTS *CEASED*. (US/0890-5754) [01697055] **5010**

WORSHIP AND PREACHING (UK/0032-7407) [02156889] **5010**

WORSHIP IN INDIA SERIES (II) [07232948] **5010**

WORSHIP (NASHVILLE, TENN.) (US/1046-381X) [20403127] **5069**

WORSHIP TIMES *CEASED*. (US/0164-6303) [04442946] **5010**

WORSHIP WORKS (US/1051-9653) [18646930] **5010**

WORTERBUCH DER KLASSISCHEN ARABISCHEN SPRACHE (GW) **3334**

●WORTH (BOSTON, MASS.) (US/1060-5967) [25039992] **920**

WORTHINGTON DESCENDANTS (US/8755-5344) [11358835] **2478**

WORTHWHILE PRICE GUIDE, THE (US/0192-9666) [05140029] **4833**

WOSINSKY MOR MUZEUM EVKONYVE, A (HU/0865-5464) [I08655464] **4097**

WOUND & SKIN CARE (CN/1187-1164) [25066887] **3723**

WOUND BALLISTICS REVIEW (US/1055-0305) [23062944] 3743, **3179**

●WOUND REPAIR AND REGENERATION (US/1067-1927) [27159397] **3651**

WOUNDS (KING OF PRUSSIA, PA.) (US/1044-7946) [19904471] **3652**

WOW! (NEW YORK, N.Y. 1987) (US/0897-4721) [17513612] **389**

WPA — Alphabetical Title Index

WPA, WRITING PROGRAM ADMINISTRATION (US/0196-4682) [05815339] **3454**

WPAS MUSELETTER See MUSELETTER (WASHINGTON, D.C.) **4132**

WPI JOURNAL (US/0148-6128) [03335789] **5171**

WPIX EDITORIALS (US/0197-7474) [06099280] **1143**

WPNR, WEEKBLAD VOOR PRIVAATRECHT, NOTARIAAT EN REGISTRATIE (NE) [03196831] **3076**

● WPROST (PL) [25566327] **2525**

WRAES QUARTERLY (US) [02566091] **147**

WRANGELL SENTINEL (US) **5629**

WRANGLER (US) [07861093] **2766**

WRAP CEASED. (US/0896-1697) [16943815] **1124**

WRAP (UK) **4808**

WRAP UP (NORWOOD, N.J.) (US/0741-8523) [10222668] **3652**

WRAP UP ON LATIN AMERICAN AGRICULTURE, FOOD, FISHING & LIVESTOCK (US/0741-8531) [10221341] **1589**

WRAY GAZETTE, THE (US) [19468832] **5644**

WRC RESEARCH REPORT (US/0073-5442) [01707052] **5549**

WRD INFORMATION GUIDE (US) [08978527] **5549, 1419**

WRECKING AND SALVAGE JOURNAL (US/0043-9460) **631**

WREE-VIEW OF WOMEN FOR RACIAL AND ECONOMIC EQUALITY, THE (US/0892-3116) [11063772] **5572, 4514**

WREP (US/1057-2465) [05540214] **147**

WRESTLER (ROCKVILLE CENTRE, N.Y.), THE (US/1052-0899) [09771394] **4930**

WRESTLING ALL STARS, HEROES & VILLAINS (US/0885-8551) [12763514] **4931**

WRESTLING EYE CEASED. (US/1059-0706) [24469608] **4931**

WRESTLING FURY CEASED. (US/1059-0714) [19044689] **4931**

WRESTLING MASTERS (US/8755-3767) [11135538] **4931**

WRESTLING SUPERSTARS (US/1042-5284) [19076533] **4931**

WRESTLING USA (LAHABRA) (US/0199-6258) [06031607] **4931**

WRESTLING (VERNON CENTER, MINN.) (US/0891-0707) [14561217] **4931**

WRESTLING'S MAIN EVENT (US/0278-9612) [07936631] **4931**

WRF COMMENT (CN/0821-1248) [10003775] **1527**

WRI PAPER (US/0886-1447) [12849389] **1527**

WRIGHT/CHAMBERS REPORT, THE (US/0897-5256) [17538944] **4570**

WRIGHT COUNTY JOURNAL-PRESS (US) [01770221] **5699**

WRIGHT COUNTY MONITOR (US) [10860499] **5674**

WRIGHT FAMILY WORKBOOK (US/8756-7229) [10310978] **2478**

● WRIGHT STUDIES (US/1045-7992) [20237125] **311**

WRIGHTSVILLE HEADLIGHT, THE (US/0747-3737) [10788451] **5655**

WRIGLEY'S HOTEL DIRECTORY (CN/0316-8298) [02247181] **2810**

WRIT, THE (US) [01606533] **3076**

WRIT (TORONTO) (CN/0316-3768) [02996386] **3454**

WRIT (WASHINGTON), THE (US/0198-8107) [06184087] **3076**

WRITE ANGLES (CN/1182-901X) [23599130] **3454, 2925**

WRITE NOW! (US) **3454**

WRITE-OFF (US/0272-2739) [06830094] **4759**

WRITE TO FAME (US/0884-6049) [12402197] **3454**

WRITER AND ILLUSTRATOR : QUARTERLY JOURNAL OF THE ASSOCIATION OF WRITERS AND ILLUSTRATORS FOR CHILDREN (II) [08756635] **1071, 3454**

WRITER (BOSTON) (US/0043-9517) [01189621] **3454**

WRITERS' & ARTISTS' YEARBOOK (UK) [15603118] **333**

WRITER'S & PHOTOGRAPHER'S GUIDE TO NEWSPAPER MARKETS (US/0277-6162) [07612169] **4378**

WRITERS AT WORK (US/0510-9671) [06411418] **3454**

WRITER'S DIGEST, THE (US/0043-9525) [05626706] **3473, 3454**

WRITERS DIRECTORY, THE (UK/0084-2699) [01776757] **2925**

WRITER'S FORUM (CINCINNATI, OHIO) (US/1057-0756) [23935177] **3454**

WRITERS FORUM (COLORADO SPRINGS) (US/0163-9072) [04300613] **3454**

WRITER'S GUIDELINES (PITTSBURG, MO.) (US/1053-1793) [22469197] **2925**

WRITERS GUILD DIRECTORY (US/0196-5611) [04272248] **2925**

WRITERS GUILD OF AMERICA, WEST See NEWSLETTER-WRITERS GUILD OF AMERICA, WEST **3417**

WRITER'S HANDBOOK (LONDON, ENGLAND) (UK) [19006379] **4820**

WRITER'S HANDBOOK, THE (US/0084-2710) [01780656] **2926**

WRITERS' JOURNAL (SAINT PAUL, MINN.) (US/0891-8759) [15025544] **3454**

WRITER'S LIFELINE (CN/0225-610X) [06183558] **2926**

WRITER'S MARKET, THE (US/0084-2729) [01361183] **4820**

WRITER'S N.W (US/1053-833X) [21768468] **4820**

WRITER'S NETWORK, THE (US/1054-2299) [22787073] **3454, 2926**

WRITER'S NEWSLETTER CEASED. (US) [04161490] **3454**

WRITER'S NORTHWEST HANDBOOK (US/0896-7946) [13744111] **4820**

WRITER'S NOTES & QUOTES (US/0043-955X) [03500268] **3454**

WRITERS' UNION OF CANADA See NEWSLETTER - WRITERS' UNION OF CANADA **3417**

WRITERS' WORKSHOP (US/1055-0224) [23059549] **2926**

WRITERS WORKSHOP, CALCUTTA See LITERARY READER **3406**

WRITER'S WORLD (BIG STONE GAP, VA.) (US/1057-0772) [23931817] **3454, 2926**

WRITER'S YEARBOOK (US/0084-2737) [01732923] **3454**

WRITING ABOUT WOMEN (US/1053-7937) [22646810] **3454**

● WRITING AND EDITING FOR SCIENCE AND TECHNOLOGY (US/1062-0168) [25505454] **5171**

WRITING AWARDS : REMINDER LIST OF ELIGIBLE RELEASES (US) [06298146] **4080**

WRITING CENTER JOURNAL, THE (US) [08660829] **1854**

WRITING CONCEPTS (US/1050-4788) [21499235] **2926**

● WRITING FOR OUR LIVES (US/1062-3434) [25589811] **3454**

WRITING (HIGHLAND PARK, ILL.) (US/0279-7208) [07238674] **2926, 1792**

● WRITING IN OHIO (US/1060-4448) [25028003] **3455**

WRITING IN PEEL (CN/0714-413X) [09054267] **3455**

WRITING INSTRUCTOR, THE (US/0277-7789) [07639733] **1908, 3334**

● WRITING IT RIGHT (US/1065-6154) [26648881] **3455, 2926**

WRITING LAB NEWSLETTER (US/1040-3779) [10226128] **1908, 3334**

WRITING (NELSON) (CN/0706-1889) [07101850] **3473**

WRITING NOTEBOOK (US) **1225, 1908, 1292**

WRITING ON THE EDGE (US/1064-6051) [22162414] **1908, 3455**

● WRITING RIGHT NEWSLETTER (US/1062-8770) [25776398] **3473**

WRITING TEACHER (SAN ANTONIO, TEX.) (US/0894-5837) [16149620] **1908**

WRITING (TORONTO) (CN/0712-1385) [08581300] **3455**

WRITINGS ... FROM THE GREAT PLAINS (US) [06412005] **3455**

WRITINGS ON IRISH HISTORY (PRINT COPY) (IE) [17691237] **2716**

● WRITTEN AND SPOKEN HINDI (US/1065-2442) [26537604] **3334**

WRITTEN COMMUNICATION (US/0741-0883) [10084338] **1124**

WRITTEN WORD, THE (US/0738-8004) [09662792] **1792**

WRONGFUL DEATH ACTIONS: THE LAW IN ALABAMA (US) **3076**

WRONGFUL DISCHARGE REPORT (US/1053-0274) [18094764] **3155**

WRONGFUL DISMISSAL EMPLOYMENT LAW (CN/0827-4673) [13232000] **3155**

WROVA REPORTER, THE (US/0747-2838) [10688343] **5662**

WRP. WASCHEREI- & REINIGUNGSPRAXIS 1990 (GW/0938-9067) [09389067] **1632**

WRRC BULLETIN (US/0544-3466) [01758089] **5549**

WRRI (US/0163-9765) [01711524] **5549**

WRRI BULLETIN (US/0097-5729) [01518588] **5549**

WRRI REPORT (US/0731-7557) [01711542] **5549**

WRU NEWS & ABSTRACTS (UK/0960-2615) [09602615] **1207**

WRU NEWS & ABSTRACTS See QWL NEWS & ABSTRACTS / WORK RESEARCH UNIT **946**

● WSDA MEMBERSHIP DIRECTORY & RESOURCE GUIDE (US) [26181578] **1337**

WSDA MEMBERSHIP ROSTER See WSDA MEMBERSHIP DIRECTORY & RESOURCE GUIDE **1337**

WSI MITTEILUNGEN (GW/0342-300X) [02059554] **1720**

WSN EXPRESS (US/1056-7925) [23853597] **40**

WSSA ABSTRACTS : MEETING OF THE WEED SCIENCE SOCIETY OF AMERICA (US) [12642190] **2434, 157**

WSTB NEWSLETTER (US) **5549**

WT PRODUKTION UND MANAGEMENT (GW/0941-2360) **1632**

WT. WERKSTATTSTECHNIK (GW/0340-4544) [09062903] **2132**

WTF TAEKWONDO (KO) [19832138] **4931**

WTO NEWS (SP/1014-7276) [27206639] **5500**

WU-HAN TA HSUEH HSUEH PAO. SHE HUI KO HSUEH PAN (CH) [10964946] **1854**

WU-HAN TA HSUEH HSUEH PAO. TZU JAN KO HSUEH PAN (CC) [10036586] **5171**

WU-HAN TA HSUEH TZU JAN K'O HSUEH PAO See WUHAN DAXUE XUEBAO. ZIRAN. KEXUE **5171**

WU HSIA SHIH CHIEH (CH) [01790397] **3455**

WU HSIEN TIEN (CH) [09330751] **2086**

WU HSIEN TIEN YUEH KAN (CH) [01797482] **2086**

WU LI (CC) [01799785] **4425**

WU LI HSUEH CHIN CHAN / CHUNG-KUO WU LI HSUEH HUI CHU PAN (CC) [09937831] **4425**

WU MING WEN HSUEH (CH) [10991980] **3455**

WU TZU KUAN LI (CH) [10568767] **889**

WU YU NIEN CHIEN (HK) [11513714] **2839**

WUFA (PK) [13156375] **2668**

WUHAN DAXUE XUEBAO. ZIRAN. KEXUE (CH/0253-9888) [02206273] **5171**

WUHAN GONGYE DAXUE XUEBAO (CC/1000-2405) [I10002405] **5171**

WUJI HUAXUE XUEBAO (CC/1001-4861) [I10014861] **1038**

WULI HUAXUE XUEBAO (CC/1000-6818) [21663502] **4425, 995**

WULI XUEBAO (CC/1000-3290) [06159430] **4425**

WURTTEMBERGISCHES WOCHENBLATT FUR LANDWIRTSCHAFT (GW) [07931921] **147**

WURZBURG HEUTE : ZEITSCHRIFT FUER KULTUR UND WIRTSCHAFT (GW) [05238958] **1528**

WURZBURGER GEOGRAPHISCHE ARBEITEN (GW/0510-9833) [06263438] **2579**

WURZBURGER JAHRBUCHER FUR DIE ALTERTUMSWISSENSCHAFT (GW/0342-5932) [03548742] **3334, 1081**

WURZBURGER UNIVERSITATSREDEN (GW) [07080562] **1854**

WUSUN JIANCE (CC/1000-6656) [13695863] **2001**

WUYI KEXUE (CC/1001-4276) [11898829] **4174**

WVC DOCUMENTATIE / MINISTERIE VAN WELZIJN, VOLKSGEZONDHEID EN CULTUUR (NE) [10617192] **5314**

WVLC NEWSLETTER (US/0149-0567) [03417393] **3256**

WWD (US/0149-5380) [03504983] **1088**

WWF MAGAZINE (US/8756-7792) [11654678] **4931**

WWF NEWS (SZ/0254-3893) [09274092] **2210**

WWIM. WHO'S WHERE IN MUSIC (US/0146-1966) [02881713] **4159**

WWS, WORLD WIDE SHIPPING GUIDE (US/0162-0088) [04067967] **5458**

WXXI PROGRAM GUIDE (1985) (US/0883-1106) [12055755] **1143**

Alphabetical Title Index

WXXI PROGRAM GUIDE (ROCHESTER, N.Y. : 1985) *See* WXXI (ROCHESTER, N.Y.) **1143**

WXXI (ROCHESTER, N.Y.) (US/1055-2960) [23132829] **1143**

WYANDOTTE WEST (US) [13049146] **5679**

WYCHOWANIE FIZYCZNE I SPORT (PL/0043-9630) [I00439630] **2602**

WYKAZ PATENTOW NA WYNALAZKI UDZIELONYCH PRZEZ URZAD PATENTOWY PRL W ROKU ... (PL/0477-1826) [19862693] **1310**

WYKAZ PATENTOW UDZIELONYCH PRZEZ URZAD PATENTOWY RZ.P. W LATACH . *See* WYKAZ PATENTOW NA WYNALAZKI UDZIELONYCH PRZEZ URZAD PATENTOWY PRL W ROKU ... **1310**

WYLIE NEWS, THE (US) [17376448] **5756**

WYNALAZCZOSC I RACJONALIZACJA *See* TEMAT **5165**

WYNALAZCZOSC I RACJONALIZACJA (MICROFORM) (US) [06714665] **1632**

WYNBOER (SA/0043-9657) [095423C0] **2373**

WYNIKI OCENY SWIN NA PODSTAWIE BADAN PRZEPROWADZONYCH W STACJACH KONTROLI UZYTKOWOSCI RZEZNEJ TRZODY CHLEWNEJ INSTYTUTU ZOOTECHNIKI ZA ROK ... (PL) [10966396] **224**

WYNIKI POMIAROW PIONOWEGO ROZKLADU OZONU W ATMOSFERZE (PL) **1437**

WYNIKI SPISU ROLNICZEGO (PL) [06551117] **147**

WYNNE PROGRESS, THE (US) [21920719] **5632**

WYOMING *See* SCHOOL LAWS OF THE STATE OF WYOMING **1871**

WYOMING. AD VALOREM TAX DIVISION *See* ANNUAL REPORT - DEPARTMENT OF REVENUE AND TAXATION. AD VALOREM TAX DIVISION (CHEYENNE) **4710**

WYOMING ADULT EDUCATION : ADULT EDUCATION PLAN (US/0361-2171) [02246283] **1802**

WYOMING AGRICULTURAL EXPERIMENT STATION *See* SCIENCE MONOGRAPH **132**

WYOMING AGRICULTURAL STATISTICS (US/0363-9339) [02570926] 147, **157**

WYOMING ANNUAL PLANNING REPORT (US/0749-7512) [09962891] **1720**

WYOMING ARCHAEOLOGIST, THE (US/0043-9665) [03385880] **285**

WYOMING ASSOCIATION OF SCHOOL ADMINISTRATORS *See* SALARIES & WAGES IN WYOMING PUBLIC SCHOOLS **1709**

WYOMING CASE NAMES CITATOR (US) **3076**

WYOMING CATHOLIC REGISTER, THE (US/0746-5580) [10129634] **5038**

WYOMING CONTRIBUTIONS TO ANTHROPOLOGY (US/0196-1500) [04711363] **247**

WYOMING COURTS; NEWSLETTER OF THE WYOMING COURT SYSTEM (US) [06157200] **3143**

WYOMING COVERED EMPLOYMENT AND WAGE DATA BY INDUSTRY AND COUNTY / PREPARED BY RESEARCH & ANALYSIS SECTION, EMPLOYMENT SECURITY COMMISSION OF WYOMING (US) [06044946] 1720, **1540**

WYOMING. DEPT. OF ADMINISTRATION AND FISCAL CONTROL. STATISTICS AND RESEARCH DIVISION *See* WYOMING POPULATION AND EMPLOYMENT FORECAST REPORT **4561**

WYOMING DIRECTORY OF MANUFACTURING AND MINING (US/0511-0289) [02047416] 2153, **3489**

WYOMING EAGLE *See* WYOMING TRIBUNE-EAGLE **5773**

WYOMING EAGLE, THE (US/8750-0825) [10960765] **5773**

WYOMING EDUCATOR, THE (US/0043-969X) [03968782] **1792**

WYOMING. ENERGY CONSERVATION OFFICE *See* ANNUAL REPORT - WYOMING ENERGY CONSERVATION OFFICE **1932**

WYOMING. GAME AND FISH COMMISSION. FISHERIES MANAGEMENT ANNUAL PROGRESS REPORT ON PROJECTS IN THE WORK SCHEDULE *See* FISHERIES MANAGEMENT ANNUAL PROGRESS REPORT ON PROJECTS IN THE ... WORK SCHEDULE **2302**

WYOMING. GAME AND FISH DEPARTMENT *See* FISHERIES MANAGEMENT ANNUAL PROGRESS REPORT ON PROJECTS IN THE ... WORK SCHEDULE **2302**

WYOMING GEO-NOTES (US/8756-0348) [06522451] 1528, **1401**

WYOMING GEOLOGICAL ASSOCIATION *See* GUIDEBOOK - WYOMING GEOLOGICAL ASSOCIATION **1382**

WYOMING. GOVERNOR *See* WYOMING STATE BUDGET. SUPPLEMENT **4759**

●WYOMING HEALTH CARE IN PERSPECTIVE (US/1065-4518) [26606992] **4808**

WYOMING IN PERSPECTIVE (US/1065-5786) [26665935] **5346**

WYOMING INCOME AND EMPLOYMENT REPORT (US) [07936091] 948, **1720**

WYOMING ISSUES (US/0163-5433) [04397274] **1589**

WYOMING. JUDICIAL PLANNING COMMITTEE *See* WYOMING COURTS; NEWSLETTER OF THE WYOMING COURT SYSTEM **3143**

WYOMING LABOR FORCE TRENDS (US/0512-4409) [05040279] **1720**

WYOMING. LEGISLATIVE SERVICE OFFICE *See* ANNUAL REPORT / LEGISLATIVE SERVICE OFFICE - WYOMING **4627**

WYOMING MINERAL AND ENERGY YEARBOOK (US) [23450982] **1445**

WYOMING MINERAL YEARBOOK *See* WYOMING MINERAL AND ENERGY YEARBOOK **1445**

WYOMING NURSE (US) **3871**

WYOMING. OFFICE OF INFORMATION PRACTICES *See* INFORMATION PRACTICES IN WYOMING STATE GOVERNMENT **4656**

WYOMING OFFICIAL DIRECTORY (US/0146-700X) [03013886] **4695**

WYOMING OIL AND GAS CONSERVATION COMMISSION *See* WYOMING OIL AND GAS STATISTICS **4285**

WYOMING OIL AND GAS STATISTICS (US/0360-2923) [02243602] 4283, **4285**

WYOMING POPULATION AND EMPLOYMENT FORECAST REPORT (US) [05282846] **4561**

WYOMING PUBLIC SCHOOLS FUND ACCOUNTING AND REPORTING (US) [06743762] **753**

WYOMING. RECREATION COMMISSION *See* ANNUAL STATE HISTORIC PRESERVATION PLAN (WYOMING) **2721**

WYOMING RURAL ELECTRIC NEWS (US/0043-9770) [03968818] **2086**

WYOMING. SECRETARY OF STATE'S OFFICE *See* WYOMING OFFICIAL DIRECTORY **4695**

WYOMING. STATE AUDITOR *See* REPORT TO THE STOCKHOLDERS **4746**

WYOMING. STATE BOARD OF NURSING *See* ANNUAL REPORT - WYOMING STATE BOARD OF NURSING **3851**

WYOMING STATE BUDGET. SUPPLEMENT (US) [05053268] **4759**

WYOMING. STATE DEPT. OF EDUCATION *See* WYOMING ADULT EDUCATION : ADULT EDUCATION PLAN **1802**

WYOMING. STATE DEPT. OF EDUCATION *See* FY ... ACCOUNTABILITY REPORT FOR VOCATIONAL EDUCATION (WYOMING) **1913**

WYOMING. STATE DEPT. OF EDUCATION *See* WYOMING EDUCATOR, THE **1792**

WYOMING. STATE DEPT. OF EDUCATION. DIVISION OF ADMINISTRATIVE SERVICES *See* WYOMING PUBLIC SCHOOLS FUND ACCOUNTING AND REPORTING **753**

WYOMING STATE PLAN (US/0098-0846) [01799253] 2248, **5549**

WYOMING STATE TRIBUNE (CHEYENNE, WYO. : 1937) (US/8750-0817) [10745699] **5773**

WYOMING STATE TRIBUNE (CHEYENNE, WYO. : 1937) *See* WYOMING TRIBUNE-EAGLE **5773**

WYOMING STATISTICAL REVIEW (US) [01770245] **5346**

WYOMING STOCKMAN FARMER (US/0043-9800) [03968835] **147**

WYOMING, THE HUB OF THE WHEEL (US/0884-2930) [12357839] **2857**

WYOMING TRADE WINDS (US/0512-4611) [01737357] **1528**

●WYOMING TRIBUNE-EAGLE (US) [30087687] **5773**

WYOMING. UNIVERSITY. OFFICE OF REGISTRATION AND RECORDS *See* STATISTICAL SUMMARY OF THE OFFICE OF REGISTRATION AND RECORDS **1798**

WYOMING URBAN AREAS ... ANNUAL REPORT (US) [10859880] **5400**

WYOMING. WATER PLANNING PROGRAM *See* REPORT - STATE ENGINEER'S OFFICE, WYOMING WATER PLANNING PROGRAM **5538**

WYOMING WATER POLLUTION CONTROL PROGRAM PLAN (US/0147-4197) [03161583] **5549**

WYOMING. WATER QUALITY DIVISION *See* WYOMING STATE PLAN **5549**

WYOMING. WATER QUALITY DIVISION *See* WYOMING WATER POLLUTION CONTROL PROGRAM PLAN **5549**

WYOMING WILDLIFE (US/0043-9819) [01770262] **2210**

WYOMING WOOL GROWER (US/0043-9827) [03968854] 5360, **224**

WYOMING'S COMPREHENSIVE REPORT ON TRAFFIC ACCIDENTS (US/0747-8771) [10797014] **5446**

WYSIWYG **SUSPENDED.** (US/0890-0981) [14153667] **4820**

WYTHE COUNTY HISTORICAL REVIEW (US/0275-9179) [05867836] **2766**

WYZSZA SZKOA PEDAGOGICZNA W GDANSKU. WYDZIA HUMANISTYCZNY *See* ZESZYTY NAUKOWE **2857**

WYZSZA SZKOA PEDAGOGICZNA W KRAKOWIE *See* PRACE JEZYKOZNAWCZE **3311**

WYZSZA SZKOA PEDAGOGICZNA W KRAKOWIE *See* PRACE ZOOLOGICZNE **5594**

X-6 ACTIVITY REPORT (US) [08678965] **858**

X BILINMEYEN (TU) **3541**

X-FACTOR (US/0894-6604) [13637262] **4868**

X-FORCE (NEW YORK, N.Y.) (US/1057-6800) [24102651] **4868**

X-IT (CN/0824-2178) [10768369] 333, **3455**

X MAGAZINE (US/1051-4155) [21956634] 2316, 5078, **2495**

X-MEN CLASSIC (US/1049-7382) [21289663] **4868**

X-MEN (NEW YORK, N.Y.) (US/1057-6819) [24098492] **4868**

X-RAY (UK) [02641840] **5265**

X-RAY DIFFRACTION ABSTRACTS (UK) [01788062] **4442**

X-RAY SPECTROMETRY (UK/0049-8246) [01604130] **1020**

●X RESOURCE, THE (US/1058-5591) [24329477] **1207**

X-SEN BUNSEKI NO SHINPO (JA/0911-7806) [28103151] **4442**

●X, THE FUTURE OF SEX (US/1061-6977) [25405919] **5188**

XALMAN; ALMA CHICANA DE AZTLAN (US/0748-6189) [04609567] **3455**

XALOC (MX) [01793361] **2716**

XANADU (WANTAGH) (US/0146-0463) [02846886] **3473**

XAVIER INSTITUTE. FOOD MARKETING CENTRE *See* JOURNAL OF THE FOOD MARKETING CENTRE **2347**

XAVIER REVIEW (US/0887-6681) [08146729] **3356**

XENHARMONIKON (US/0098-3330) [02241528] **4159**

XENIA DAILY GAZETTE, THE (US/8750-4650) [11460719] **5731**

XENIA (ROMA) (IT/0394-4859) [07522968] **285**

XENOBIOTICA (UK/0049-8254) [01588798] 494, **3984**

XENOPHILIA (CN/1050-5334) [21533492] **3473**

●XENOTRANSPLANTATION (DK/0908-665X) **3652**

XEROGRAMMATA; HOCHSCHULSCHRIFTEN ZUR PHILOSOPHIE (GW/0512-6614) [01432264] **4365**

XEROX DISCLOSURE JOURNAL (US/0361-4190) [02246522] **1310**

XIANDAI HUAGONG (CH/0253-4320) [09034286] **1031**

XIANGTAN DAXUE ZIRAN KEXUE XUEBAO (CC/1000-5900) [21707890] 1096, **5171**

XIB (SAN DIEGO, CALIF.) (US/1058-420X) [24301370] **3473**

XIBAO SHENGWUXUE ZAZHI (CC/0253-9977) [09232120] **541**

XIBEI DAXUE XUEBAO ZIRAN KEXUE BAN (CC/1000-274X) [I1000274X] **1096**

XIBEI GONGYE DAXUE XUEBAO (CC/1000-2758) [I10002758] **5171**

XIBEI QINGGONGYE XUEYUAN XUEBAO (CC/1000-5811) [I10005811] **5171**

XIBEI SHI-DI (CH/1000-4076) [10571169] **2668**

XIBEI SHIFAN XUEYUAN XUEBAO. ZIRAN KEXUE BAN (CC/0254-6167) [10345067] **5171**

Alphabetical Title Index

XIII MAGAZINE (BRUXELLES) (BE/1017-6950) [23823840] **1169**

XIII MAGAZINE NEWS REVIEW (BE) [23823828] **1124**

XIN GINGNIAN KEXUE (SI/0303-089X) [01797542] **5171**

XIN SHENG (SI/0438-0797) [01797539] **3455**

XING GUANG (SI/0303-0881) [01797554] **2510**

XINJIANG DIZHI (CC/1000-8845) [I10008845] **1401**

XINY IYAOXUE ZAZHI (CC/0376-656X) [06311546] **5171**

XIYOU JINSHU (CC/0258-7076) [09579002] **4024**

XUESHU JIKAN *CEASED.* (CH/0439-8017) [01752367] **1528**

XUMU SHOUYI XUEBAO (CH/0257-5574) [I02575574] **5527**

XYZ *See* XYZ DIRECTION **369**

● XYZ DIRECTION (UK/0965-3848) [25684466] **369**

XYZ (MONTREAL, QUEBEC) (CN/0828-5608) [13435655] **3455**

Y.E.S. QUARTERLY (US/0884-6677) [11782123] **5600**

Y-NOT ANTIQUE & FLEA MARKET DIRECTORY, THE (US/0192-8821) [05080942] **252**

Y U L SERIALS LIST (CN/0225-5081) [06136584] **3256**

Y WEEKLY, THE (US/0883-3133) [10054220] **5756**

YA-CHOU HSIEN TAI SHIH CHI / PAI TI, CHEN, CHIEN-WO HO PIEN (CH) [08664153] **3473**

YA-CHOU JEN (CH) [08215828] **2510**

YA-CHOW SHU TS'AI YEN CHIU FA CHAN CHUNG HSIN *See* PROGRESS REPORT / ASIAN VEGETABLE RESEARCH AND DEVELOPMENT CENTER **123**

YA HOTLINE (CN/0701-8894) [03956511] 3455, **1071**

YA-LU CHIANG (CC) [04664142] **3455**

YA SPAIN (SP) **5811**

YA VEREMOS (NQ) [07397845] **2766**

YACHT (GW/0043-9932) [I00439932] **597**

YACHT PREMIERE ENGLISH ED (IT/1120-2424) [I11202424] **4856**

YACHTING BOAT OWNERS BUYERS GUIDE *See* YACHTING'S BOAT BUYERS GUIDE **597**

YACHTING MONTHLY, THE (UK/0043-9983) [08961492] **597**

YACHTING (NEW YORK, N.Y.) (US/0043-9940) [01770269] **597**

YACHTING NEWS (US/0192-1649) [05120739] **597**

YACHTING WORLD (UK/0043-9991) [08961538] **597**

YACHTING YEAR BOOK OF NORTHERN CALIFORNIA (US/0094-8136) [01795302] **597**

YACHTING'S BOAT BUYERS GUIDE *CEASED.* (US/0740-7483) [08037449] **597**

YACHTS AND YACHTING (UK/0044-0000) [I00440000] **597**

YACHTSMAN'S GUIDE TO THE GREATER ANTILLES (US/0162-7635) [04213102] **5500**

YACHTSMAN'S GUIDE TO THE VIRGIN ISLANDS & PUERTO RICO (US/0735-9020) [08986397] **5500**

YACHTSMAN'S POCKET ALMANAC, THE (US/0276-8917) [07426996] **597**

YAD BE-YAD (IS) [01794751] **1071**

YAD-I BAIZA : ASRI ADAB MEN JADID RAVIYYON KA TARJUMAN (PK) [24396303] **3455**

YAD LAKORE (IS) **3256**

YAD VASHEM STUDIES (IS/0084-3296) [03953641] **2716**

YADAM KWA SIRHWA (KO) [05156577] **5075**

YADORIGA (JA/0513-417X) [02844771] **5600**

YADUIN NO HOSHU SHOYO CHOSA HOKOKUSHO (JA) [02245174] **1720**

YAERSA MEREMER ENESTIYUT. SOCIO-ECONOMICS DEPT *See* SOCIO-ECONOMICS DEPARTMENT RESEARCH PROGRAMME **136**

YAEYAMA YORAN (JA) [04097332] **1589**

YAGHAG-HOI-JI (KO/0377-9556) [01924863] **4333**

YAGL-AMBU; PAPUA NEW GUINEA JOURNAL OF THE SOCIAL SCIENCES AND HUMANITIES (PP) [01156033] **5226**

YAHADUT (IS) [01784343] **5054**

YAITYOPYA BEHERAWI BANK *See* ANNUAL REPORT / NATIONAL BANK OF ETHIOPIA **771**

YAITYOPYA NEGD BANK *See* TRADE DIRECTORY - COMMERCIAL BANK OF ETHIOPIA S. C **854**

YAITYOPYA NEGD BANK. MARKET RESEARCH DEPT *See* MARKET REPORT - YAITYOPYA NEGD BANK **1574**

YAKCHE HAKHOE CHI. JOURNAL OF KOREAN PHARMACEUTICAL SCIENCES (KO) [05320729] **4333**

YAKIMA & KLICKITAT FISHERIES / YAKIMA/KLICKITAT PRODUCTION PROJECT (US) [24005374] **2316**

YAKIMA HERALD-REPUBLIC (US) [17416231] **5763**

YAKIMA VALLEY GENEALOGICAL SOCIETY *See* BULLETIN - YAKIMA VALLEY GENEALOGICAL SOCIETY **2441**

YAKKYOKU (JA/0044-0035) [I00440035] **4333**

YAKUBUTSU DOTAI (JA/0916-1139) [I09161139] **4200**

YAKUBUTSU, SEISHIN, KODO (JA/0285-5313) [08683692] 4333, **4622**

YAKUGAKU TOSHOKAN. PHARMACEUTICAL LIBRARY BULLETIN (JA/0386-2062) [02511186] 4333, **3256**

YAKUGAKU ZASSHI (JA/0031-6903) [01762192] **4333**

YAKUIN NO HOSHU SHOYO CHOSA HOKOKOKUSHO *See* YAKUIN NO HOSHU SHOYO TO KIMEKATA **1589**

YAKUIN NO HOSHU SHOYO NENSHU (JA) [05691162] **4759**

YAKUIN NO HOSHU SHOYO TO KIMEKATA (JA) [07062675] **1589**

YAKUIN SHIKI HO (JA) [06148716] **724**

YAKUJI KOGYO SEISAN DOTAI TOKEI NEMPO (JA) [02551379] **4333**

YAKURI TO CHIRYO (JA/0386-3603) [01193970] **4333**

YAKUZAIGAKU (JA/0372-7629) [09769792] **4333**

YALE ALUMNI MAGAZINE (1984) (US/8750-409X) [11388812] **1103**

YALE CLASSICAL MONOGRAPHS (US) [04910522] **1081**

YALE CLASSICAL STUDIES (UK/0084-330X) [01715507] **1081**

YALE COLLEGE SERIES (US/0084-3318) [01446265] **1096**

YALE DAILY NEWS (US/0890-2240) [14184532] **5647**

YALE EDITIONS OF THE PRIVATE PAPERS OF JAMES BOSWELL. RESEARCH EDITION : CORRESPONDENCE, THE (US) [01446341] **1854**

YALE FOREST SCHOOL NEWS (US/0148-5741) [01447097] **2398**

YALE FRENCH STUDIES (US/0044-0078) [01770272] **2716**

YALE GERMANIC STUDIES *CEASED.* (US/0084-3334) [01770276] **2716**

YALE HISTORICAL PUBLICATIONS. HISTORY OF ART *See* YALE PUBLICATIONS IN THE HISTORY OF ART **369**

YALE HISTORICAL PUBLICATIONS. MANUSCRIPTS AND EDITED TEXTS (US/0084-3342) [01775990] **2633**

YALE JOURNAL OF BIOLOGY AND MEDICINE, THE (US/0044-0086) [01641751] 476, **3652**

YALE JOURNAL OF CRITICISM, THE (US/0893-5378) [15565288] **3356**

YALE JOURNAL OF INTERNATIONAL LAW, THE (US/0889-7743) [12626339] **3138**

YALE JOURNAL OF LAW AND FEMINISM (US/1043-9366) [19571969] 5572, **3076**

YALE JOURNAL OF LAW AND LIBERATION, THE *SUSPENDED.* (US/1051-7022) [20874566] **4514**

YALE JOURNAL OF LAW & THE HUMANITIES (US/1041-6374) [18775720] 2857, **3076**

YALE JOURNAL ON REGULATION (US/0741-9457) [10212254] **3076**

YALE JUDAICA SERIES (US/0084-3369) [01770275] **5054**

YALE LAW & POLICY REVIEW (US/0740-8048) [09586836] **3077**

YALE LAW JOURNAL, THE (US/0044-0094) [01770276] **3077**

YALE LAW REPORT (US/0513-1391) [01447152] **3077**

YALE LITERARY MAGAZINE, THE (US) [27042472] 3473, **3455**

YALE POLITICAL MONTHLY (US/0736-6175) [09157520] **4501**

YALE PUBLICATIONS IN THE HISTORY OF ART (US/0084-3415) [01770279] **369**

YALE REVIEW, THE (US/0044-0124) [01590252] **5226**

YALE SCIENTIFIC (US/0091-0287) [04025668] **5171**

YALE SERIES IN ECONOMIC HISTORY (US) [01447248] **1528**

YALE SERIES OF YOUNGER POETS, THE (US/0084-3458) [01605127] **3473**

YALE STUDIES IN ENGLISH (US/0084-3482) [01770282] 3455, **3334**

YALE STUDIES IN POLITICAL SCIENCE (US/0084-3490) [01640870] **4501**

YALE UNIVERSITY. DEPARTMENT OF ANTHROPOLOGY *See* YALE UNIVERSITY PUBLICATIONS IN ANTHROPOLOGY **247**

YALE UNIVERSITY. ECONOMIC GROWTH CENTER *See* CENTER PAPER (PRINCETON, N.J.) **4551**

YALE UNIVERSITY. LIBRARY *See* YALE UNIVERSITY LIBRARY GAZETTE, THE **3256**

YALE UNIVERSITY LIBRARY GAZETTE, THE (US/0044-0175) [01586270] **3256**

YALE UNIVERSITY. MUSIC EXECUTIVE COMMITTEE *See* MUSIC AT YALE **4133**

YALE UNIVERSITY. PEABODY MUSEUM OF NATURAL HISTORY *See* BULLETIN - PEABODY MUSEUM OF NATURAL HISTORY **4164**

YALE UNIVERSITY PUBLICATIONS IN ANTHROPOLOGY (US) [01167057] **247**

YALE WEEKLY BULLETIN AND CALENDAR (US/0740-0233) [03252829] **1096**

YALE WESTERN AMERICANA SERIES (US/0084-3563) [01607994] **2766**

YALKUT LE-SIVIM, TEKHNOLOGYAH U-MINHAL SHEL TEKSTIL (IS/0372-7777) [I03727777] **5360**

YALKUT MORESHET (IS/0513-4617) [05700286] **5054**

YALOBUSHA PIONEER (US/0742-7638) [08038510] **2766**

YAMAGATA DAIGAKU *See* YAMAGATA DAIGAKU KIYO: SHIZEN KAGAKU **5171**

YAMAGATA DAIGAKU *See* YAMAGATA DAIGAKU KIYO : NOGAKU **147**

YAMAGATA DAIGAKU *See* YAMAGATA DAIGAKU KIYO : KYOIKU DAGAKU **5171**

YAMAGATA DAIGAKU KIYO : KYOIKU DAGAKU (JA) [05755363] 1792, **5171**

YAMAGATA DAIGAKU KIYO : NOGAKU (JA/0513-4676) [02830168] **147**

YAMAGATA DAIGAKU KIYO: SHIZEN KAGAKU (JA/0513-4692) [05504717] **5171**

YAMAGATA-KEN EISEI KENKYUJO HO (JA/0513-4706) [10400844] **4808**

YAMAGATA NORIN GAKKAI *See* KAIHO **102**

YAMAGUCHI DAIGAKU *See* TECHNOLOGY REPORTS OF THE YAMAGUCHI UNIVERSITY **5164**

YAMAGUCHI DAIGAKU KOGAKUBU KENKYU HOKOKU (JA/0372-7661) [04162291] **2001**

YAMAGUCHI DAIGAKU NOGAKUBU GAKUJUTSU HOKOKU (JA/0513-1715) [02841083] **148**

YAMAGUCHI DAIGAKU. NOGAKUBU SHIMONOSEKI *See* YAMAGUCHI DAIGAKU NOGAKUBU GAKUJUTSU HOKOKU **148**

YAMAGUCHI DAIGAKU. KOGAKUBU *See* YAMAGUCHI DAIGAKU KOGAKUBU KENKYU HOKOKU **2001**

YAMAGUCHI IGAKU (JA/0513-1731) [09769011] **3652**

YAMAGUCHI JUIGAKU ZASSHI (JA/0388-9335) [12901252] **5527**

YAMAGUCHI-KEN CHIKUSAN SHIKENJO *See* GYOMU HOKOKU **211**

YAMAGUCHI-KEN EISEI KENKYUJO *See* YAMAGUCHI-KEN EISEI KENKYUJO NEMPO **4808**

YAMAGUCHI-KEN EISEI KENKYUJO NEMPO (JA) [08134486] **4808**

YAMAGUCHI-KEN GAIKAI SAIBAI GYOGYO SENTA *See* YAMAGUCHI-KEN GAIKAI SAIBAI GYOGYO SENTA HOKOKU **2316**

YAMAGUCHI-KEN GAIKAI SAIBAI GYOGYO SENTA HOKOKU (JA) [06792282] **2316**

YAMAGUCHI-KEN GAIKAI SUISAN SHIKENJO KENKYU HOKOKU (JA/0386-3816) [07242857] **2316**

YAMAGUCHI-KEN KOGAI SENTA *See* YAMAGUCHI-KEN KOGAI SENTA NENPO **2248**

YAMAGUCHI-KEN KOGAI SENTA NENPO (JA) [06484714] **2248**

YAMAGUCHI-KEN NAIKAI SUISAN SHIKENJO HOKOKU (JA) [07243398] **2316**

YAMAGUCHI-KEN NAIKAI SUISAN SHIKENJO NEMPO (JA) [07243320] **2316**

Alphabetical Title Index — YEAR

YAMANASHI DAIGAKU KYOIKU GAKUBU KENKYU HOKOKU. DAI 2 BUNSATSU, SHIZEN KAGAKU KEI (JA/0385-8766) [12821375] 4174, **5171**

YAMANASHI IKA DAIGAKU ZASSHI (JA/0912-0025) [28100433] **3652**

YAMANASHI-KEN EISEI KOGAI KENKYUJO *See* YAMANASHI-KEN EISEI KOGAI KENKYUJO NENPO **4808**

YAMANASHI-KEN EISEI KOGAI KENKYUJO NENPO (JA/0915-437X) [25339604] **4808**

YAMANASHI-KEN KOGYO GIJUTSU SENTA KENKYU HOKOKU (JA/0914-711X) [24362674] **5171**

YAMASHINA CHORUI KENKYUJO, KENKYU HOKOKU (JA/0044-0183) [02830183] **5621**

YAMASHINA CHORUI KENKYUJO, TOKYO *See* YAMASHINA CHORUI KENKYUJO, KENKYU HOKOKU **5621**

YANG CHI SHU, HAI (CC) [13364683] **1458**

YANG SHUI CHAN YEN CHIU, HAI (CH) [10049545] **2316**

YANG YAO WU, HAI (CC) [18007503] **4333**

YANGBONGGYE (KO) [10125693] **5600**

YANKE XUEBAO (CC/1000-4432) [13678494] **3880**

YANKEE DOODLER MAGAZINE, THE (US/1056-8506) [23880526] **2550**

YANKEE (DUBLIN, N.H.) (US/0044-0191) [01607446] **2550**

YANKEE FOOD SERVICE (US/0195-2552) [05424024] **2361**

YANKEE HOMES *CEASED.* (US/8756-0259) [11454896] **4848**

YANKEE HORSETRADER *CEASED.* (US/0192-5210) [05053553] 5527, **2803**

YANKEE MAGAZINE'S TRAVEL GUIDE TO NEW ENGLAND (US) [24393723] **5500**

YANKEE NURSERY QUARTERLY (US) [25366642] **2434**

YANKEE OILMAN (US/0044-0205) [04256692] 2609, **4283**

YANKEE TRAVELER (DUBLIN, N.H.), THE (US/1061-4699) [25364791] **5500**

YANKEES MAGAZINE (US/0744-0006) [07966946] **4931**

YANKTON DAILY PRESS & DAKOTAN (US) [13417490] **5744**

YANKUANG CESHI (CC/0254-5357) [09382876] **1445**

YANSHI KUANGWUXUE ZAZHI (CC/1000-6524) [21663544] 1459, **1445**

YAO HSUEH HSUEH PAO (CC/0513-4870) [10377970] 476, **4333**

YAOWU FENXI ZAZHI (CC/0254-1793) [08335135] **4333**

YARD & GARDEN (US/0896-6834) [17251407] **2434**

YARDSTICKS FOR COSTING (CN/0319-3438) [02443079] **631**

YARHON HA-STATISTI LE-YISRAEL, HA- (IS/0021-1982) [01798097] **5346**

YARHON HA-STATISTI LE-YISRAEL. MUSAF, HA- (IS) [01798077] **5346**

YARHON LI-STATISTIKAH SHEL MEHIRIM (IS) [01796553] 1528, **1541**

YARHON STATISTI LE-TAYARUT ULE-SERUTE HARAHAH *See* TOURISM AND HOTEL SERVICES STATISTICS QUARTERLY **5501**

YARN MARKET NEWS *CEASED.* (US/0882-7982) [11987020] 1632, **5360**

YARNCRAFT (US/0730-7640) [08069534] 376, **5186**

YASAI CHAGYO SHIKENJO KENKYU HOKOKU. A, YASAI, KAKI (JA/0916-684X) [24357256] **2434**

YASAI CHAGYO SHIKENJO KENKYU HOKOKU. B, CHAGYO (JA/0916-6858) [24395808] **2373**

YASASHII BUSINESS EIGO (JA) **724**

YASO / CHUGOKU BUNGEI KENKYUKAI (JA) [12072431] **3455**

YASURAGI (JA) [02246929] **5269**

YATES CENTER NEWS (YATES CENTER, KAN. : 1948) (US) [12952713] **5679**

YAUTUKA (BG) [08272996] **2287**

YAVARAN-I INQILAB (IR) [10080553] **2510**

YAWMIYAT WA-WATHAIQ AL-WAHDAH AL-ARABIYAH / MARKAZ DIRASAT AL-WAHDAH AL-ARABIYAH (LY) [09528525] **2668**

YAXKIN (HO) [02553787] **248**

YAYA (CN/0824-1457) [11807830] **3257**

YAYASAN TENAGA KERJA INDONESIA *See* LAPORAN KEGIATAN YAYASAN TENAGA KERJA INDONESIA **1687**

YAZOO HERALD, THE (US) [16068959] **5702**

YEAR BOOK (UK/0305-0998) [04911886] **821**

YEAR BOOK (UA) [01800323] **1528**

YEAR BOOK - AMERICAN ACADEMY OF ACTUARIES (US/0569-2032) [02250773] **2896**

YEAR BOOK (AMERICAN SOCIETY OF BOOKPLATE COLLECTORS AND DESIGNERS) (US/0275-1569) [08909719] **2779**

YEAR BOOK AND CLERICAL DIRECTORY *See* CLERICAL DIRECTORY / CHURCH OF THE PROVINCE OF SOUTHERN AFRICA **4948**

YEAR-BOOK AND DIGEST, THE (II) [07712034] **4759**

YEAR BOOK AND DIRECTORY OF MEMBERS - INSTITUTE OF BUILDING (UK) [01784932] **631**

YEAR BOOK & DIRECTORY - SOCIETY OF AIRWAY PIONEERS (US) [06130823] **40**

YEAR BOOK AND DIRECTORY - UNITED CHURCH OF CANADA (CN/0848-4449) [22478244] **5010**

YEAR BOOK AND LIST OF MEMBERS (INSTITUTE OF HOUSING (GREAT BRITAIN)) *See* INSTITUTE OF HOUSING YEAR BOOK, THE **2825**

YEAR BOOK AND PROCEEDINGS OF THE GENERAL ASSEMBLY - PRESBYTERIAN CHURCH OF NEW ZEALAND (NZ/0110-0416) [02243477] **5069**

YEAR BOOK & REGISTER OF MEMBERS / CLARINET AND SAXOPHONE SOCIETY (UK/0260-1702) [08819380] **4159**

YEAR BOOK - ANDHRA PRADESH AKADEMI OF SCIENCES (II) [03269597] **5171**

YEAR BOOK - ASSOCIATION OF COUNTY COUNCILS (UK) [06179522] **4695**

YEAR BOOK - ASSOCIATION OF IRON AND STEEL ENGINEERS (US) [06309422] **2086**

YEAR BOOK, AUSTRALIA (AT/0810-8633) [04703377] **5346**

YEAR BOOK / AUSTRALIAN ACADEMY OF SCIENCE (AT/0067-1584) [13958708] **5171**

YEAR BOOK - BANARAS HINDU UNIVERSITY. CENTRE OF ADVANCED STUDY IN PHILOSOPHY (II) [01784264] **4365**

YEAR BOOK - BRITISH FEDERATION OF MUSIC FESTIVALS (UK/0309-8044) [04553480] **389**

YEAR BOOK / CALIFORNIA COMMUNITY FOUNDATION (US) [11897945] **4695**

YEAR BOOK - CANADIAN RACING PIGEON UNION (CN/0316-2559) [02247247] **4931**

YEAR BOOK - CARNEGIE INSTITUTION OF WASHINGTON (US/0069-066X) [01116801] **5171**

YEAR BOOK - CINCINNATI SYMPHONY ORCHESTRA (US/0190-8685) [04059042] **4159**

YEAR BOOK COLOR ATLAS SERIES (US/0147-9784) [03269236] **2583**

YEAR BOOK / DUTCHESS COUNTY HISTORICAL SOCIETY (US/0739-8565) [09832837] **2766**

YEAR BOOK - FLORIDA GENEALOGICAL SOCIETY, TAMPA, FLA (US/0428-7282) [01405654] **2478**

YEAR BOOK - FLORIDA STATE BOARD OF ENGINEER EXAMINERS (US) [01304511] **2001**

YEAR BOOK FOR NORWEGIAN PETROLEUM SOCIETY (NO) [06524256] **4283**

YEAR BOOK - HISTORICAL SOCIETY OF HOPKINS COUNTY (US/0197-0291) [05206199] **2766**

YEAR BOOK - INSURANCE ACCOUNTING AND STATISTICAL ASSOCIATION (US/0534-4352) [02730906] **2896**

YEAR BOOK (LEO BAECK INSTITUTE) (UK/0075-8744) [01035634] **2275**

YEAR BOOK - NATIONAL AURICULA & PRIMULA SOCIETY (NORTHERN SECTION) (UK) [05690518] **148**

YEAR BOOK - NATIONAL AURICULA & PRIMULA SOCIETY (SOUTHERN SECTION) (UK) [05285493] **2434**

YEAR BOOK OF ADULT EDUCATION (UK/0084-3601) [01456898] **1802**

YEAR BOOK OF ANESTHESIA *See* YEAR BOOK OF ANESTHESIA AND PAIN MANAGEMENT, THE **3684**

YEAR BOOK OF ANESTHESIA AND PAIN MANAGEMENT, THE (US/1073-5437) [26566507] **3684**

YEAR BOOK OF ANESTHESIOLOGY AND PAIN MANAGEMENT, THE (US) [31029495] **3684**

YEAR BOOK OF CARDIOLOGY, THE (US/0145-4145) [02529628] **3711**

● YEAR BOOK OF CHIROPRACTIC (US) [26949754] **3807**

YEAR BOOK OF CLINICAL MICROBIOLOGY (US/1054-772X) [22969393] 3652, **571**

YEAR BOOK OF CLINICAL PHARMACY, THE (US/0271-7956) [06699588] **4333**

YEAR BOOK OF CRITICAL CARE MEDICINE, THE (US/0734-3299) [08724105] **3652**

YEAR BOOK OF DENTISTRY, THE (US/0084-3717) [01770311] **1337**

● YEAR BOOK OF DERMATOLOGIC SURGERY (US/1059-0587) [24467023] **3723**

YEAR BOOK OF DERMATOLOGY, THE (US/0093-3619) [03940168] **3723**

YEAR BOOK OF DIAGNOSTIC RADIOLOGY, THE (US/0098-1672) [02240976] **3947**

YEAR BOOK OF DIGESTIVE DISEASES, THE (US/0739-5930) [09772978] **3802**

YEAR BOOK OF DRUG THERAPY, THE (US/0084-3733) [01770299] **4333**

YEAR BOOK OF EMERGENCY MEDICINE, THE (US/0271-7964) [06699558] **3726**

YEAR BOOK OF ENDOCRINOLOGY, THE (US/0084-3741) [01640717] **3733**

YEAR BOOK OF FAMILY PRACTICE, THE (US/0147-1996) [03499609] **3739**

YEAR BOOK OF GERIATRICS AND GERONTOLOGY (US/0894-2757) [15965058] **3755**

YEAR BOOK OF HAND SURGERY, THE (US/0739-5949) [09772942] **3977**

YEAR BOOK OF HEALTH CARE MANAGEMENT (US/1050-995X) [21742721] **4808**

YEAR BOOK OF HEMATOLOGY, THE (US/0882-5998) [11902771] **3774**

YEAR BOOK OF INFECTIOUS DISEASES, THE (US/0743-9261) [10718918] **3716**

YEAR BOOK OF INFERTILITY, THE (US/0896-4475) [17154595] **3652**

YEAR-BOOK OF LABOUR STATISTICS / INTERNATIONAL LABOUR OFFICE (SZ/0084-3857) [01753615] **1541**

YEAR BOOK OF MEDICINE, THE (US/0084-3873) [01587659] **3652**

YEAR BOOK OF NEONATAL AND PERINATAL MEDICINE, THE (US/1044-4890) [19823038] **3769**

● YEAR BOOK OF NEPHROLOGY, THE (US/1046-6266) [20511456] **3994**

YEAR BOOK OF NEUROLOGY AND NEUROSURGERY, THE (US/0513-5117) [01623676] **3847**

● YEAR BOOK OF NEURORADIOLOGY, THE (US/1062-337X) [25587216] **3947**

YEAR BOOK OF NUCLEAR MEDICINE, THE (US/0084-3903) [01770322] 3947, **3849**

... YEAR BOOK OF OBSTETRICS AND GYNECOLOGY, THE (US/0084-3911) [01770323] **3769**

YEAR BOOK OF OCCUPATIONAL AND ENVIRONMENTAL HEALTH (US/0899-8035) [18229246] **2871**

YEAR BOOK OF ONCOLOGY (US/1040-1741) [18339206] **3825**

YEAR BOOK OF OPHTHALMOLOGY, THE (US/0084-392X) [01770324] **3880**

YEAR BOOK OF ORTHOPEDICS, THE (US/0276-1092) [06988268] **3885**

YEAR BOOK OF OTOLARYNGOLOGY. HEAD AND NECK SURGERY, THE (US/1041-892X) [12673354] **3977**

YEAR BOOK OF PATHOLOGY AND CLINICAL PATHOLOGY, THE (US/0084-3946) [01770325] **3898**

YEAR BOOK OF PEDIATRICS, THE (US/0084-3954) [01640200] **3912**

YEAR BOOK OF PLASTIC, RECONSTRUCTIVE, AND AESTHETIC SURGERY (US/1040-175X) [18339196] **3977**

YEAR BOOK OF PODIATRIC MEDICINE AND SURGERY (CHICAGO, ILL.), THE (US/0742-194X) [10294849] **3918**

YEAR BOOK OF PSYCHIATRY AND APPLIED MENTAL HEALTH, THE (US/0084-3970) [01770326] **3937**

YEAR BOOK OF PULMONARY DISEASE, THE (US/8756-3452) [11539142] **3952**

YEAR BOOK OF REHABILITATION, THE *CEASED.* (US/8756-3460) [11539211] 1930, **3652**

YEAR BOOK OF SPORTS MEDICINE, THE (US/0162-0908) [04098761] **3957**

YEAR BOOK OF SURGERY, THE (US/0090-3671) [01784992] **3977**

... YEAR BOOK OF THE CANADIAN BAR ASSOCIATION AND THE MINUTES OF PROCEEDINGS OF THE ... ANNUAL MEETING, THE (CN/0318-4935) [02740750] **3077**

YEAR — Alphabetical Title Index

YEAR BOOK OF THE INDIAN NATIONAL SCIENCE ACADEMY, THE (II/0073-6619) [02241242] **5171**

YEAR BOOK OF THE NATIONAL INSTITUTE OF SCIENCES OF INDIA *See* YEAR BOOK OF THE INDIAN NATIONAL SCIENCE ACADEMY, THE **5171**

YEAR BOOK OF THE ROYAL SOCIETY OF EDINBURGH (UK/0080-4576) [01645178] **5237**

YEAR-BOOK OF THE ROYAL SOCIETY OF LONDON (UK/0080-4673) [01681097] **5237**

YEAR BOOK OF THE UNITED BAPTIST CONVENTION OF THE ATLANTIC PROVINCES (CN/0082-7843) [02248106] **5069**

● YEAR BOOK OF TRANSPLANTATION (US/1060-2968) [24916935] **3978**

YEAR BOOK OF ULTRASOUND, THE (US/1050-4443) [21489314] **4453**

YEAR BOOK OF UROLOGY, THE (US/0084-4071) [06569531] **3994**

YEAR BOOK OF VASCULAR SURGERY, THE (US/0749-4041) [11120658] **3978**

YEAR BOOK - PERQUIMANS COUNTY HISTORICAL SOCIETY (US/0196-8866) [05592761] **2766**

YEAR BOOK (QATAR. WIZARAT AL-ILAM) (QA) [09649883] **2668**

YEAR BOOK - ROYAL SOCIETY OF TROPICAL MEDICINE AND HYGIENE (UK/0080-4711) [01439147] **3987**

YEAR BOOK - ROYAL YACHTING ASSOCIATION (UK/0307-868X) [01799026] **597**

YEAR BOOK / SOCIETY OF ACTUARIES (US) [03535237] **2896**

YEAR BOOK - THE AMERICAN PHILOSOPHICAL SOCIETY (US/0065-9762) [01480559] **4365**

YEAR BOOK / THE LIBRARY ASSOCIATION (UK) [08405719] **3257**

YEAR BOOK - THE ROYAL INSTITUTION OF CHARTERED SURVEYORS (UK/0308-1451) [02243578] **2579**

YEAR BOOK - ULSTER FOLK AND TRANSPORT MUSEUM (UK) [03170726] **4097**

YEAR BOOK - UNITED REFORMED CHURCH (UK) [01794018] **5069**

YEAR BOOK - VENEZUELAN-AMERICAN CHAMBER OF COMMERCE & INDUSTRY (VE) [03739090] **821**

YEAR BOOK ... (... YEAR OF ISSUE) / THE CHURCH OF SCOTLAND (UK/0069-3995) [10217979] **5010**

YEAR-END REGULATORY REVIEW (US/0749-4017) [07840951] **724**

YEAR-END REPORT - HERITAGE CONSERVATION AND RECREATION SERVICE (US/0192-4621) [04987172] **2210**

YEAR END REPORT - KANSAS ECONOMIC OPPORTUNITY OFFICE (US/0160-0869) [03135005] 2839, **1528**

YEAR IN BRIEF, THE (US/0748-2086) [10895008] **4061**

YEAR IN IMMUNOLOGY, THE *CEASED.* (SZ/0256-2308) [10642806] **3677**

YEAR IN PICTURES, THE (US/0161-7141) [03997016] **2633**

YEAR IN REVIEW / AIR FORCE SYSTEMS COMMAND, THE (US) [24239808] **4061**

YEAR IN REVIEW - CRANBROOK INSTITUTE OF SCIENCE (US/1060-5037) [23303140] 5171, **4097**

YEAR IN REVIEW (RECREATION VEHICLE INDUSTRY ASSOCIATION (U.S.) (US) [18447803] **1632**

YEAR IN REVIEW (RICHMOND, VA.), THE (US/0748-0423) [10538499] 148, **2361**

YEAR LEFT, THE *CEASED.* (UK) [13346120] **4548**

YEAR OF ACHIEVEMENT (US/0148-8570) [03133592] **5314**

YEAR REPORT - TEMPORARY STATE COMMISSION ON THE WATER SUPPLY NEEDS OF SOUTHEASTERN NEW YORK (US/0092-2676) [01786490] **5549**

YEAR-ROUND EDUCATION ACTIVITIES IN THE UNITED STATES (US/0149-3302) [03460997] **1792**

YEARBOOK (CN/0710-4707) [08486269] **5069**

YEARBOOK - AFRICANA SOCIETY OF PRETORIA (SA) [03604000] **2644**

YEARBOOK / AMERICAN GOAT SOCIETY (US/0065-8456) [01479935] **224**

YEARBOOK - AMERICAN SOCIETY OF PENSION ACTUARIES (US/0194-3979) [05359999] 2897, **1720**

YEARBOOK - AMERICAN SOCIETY OF SANITARY ENGINEERING (US/0066-068X) [01480841] **2248**

YEARBOOK AND CHURCH DIRECTORY OF THE ORTHODOX CHURCH IN AMERICA (US/0145-7950) [02365781] **5040**

YEARBOOK AND DIRECTORY OF OSTEOPATHIC PHYSICIANS (US/0084-358X) [04031993] **3652**

YEARBOOK & DIRECTORY OF THE CHRISTIAN CHURCH (DISCIPLES OF CHRIST) (US/0731-5392) [08201548] **5010**

YEARBOOK AND DIRECTORY / SEMICONDUCTOR INDUSTRY ASSOCIATION (US) [06664870] **2086**

YEARBOOK AND MINUTES OF THE ANNUAL CONFERENCE - EVANGELICAL FREE CHURCH OF AMERICA *See* YEARBOOK / EVANGELICAL FREE CHURCH OF AMERICA **5069**

YEARBOOK AND MINUTES OF THE ANNUAL CONFERENCE - EVANGELICAL FREE CHURCH OF AMERICA (US/0092-4660) [01789011] **5069**

YEARBOOK AND PHILATELIC SOCIETIES' DIRECTORY (UK/0260-1265) [07557920] **2788**

YEARBOOK & REGISTER OF MEMBERS / INCORPORATED SOCIETY OF MUSICIANS (UK) [12268990] **4159**

YEARBOOK / ASSOCIATION FOR SUPERVISION AND CURRICULUM DEVELOPMENT OF THE NATIONAL EDUCATION ASSOCIATION (US/1042-9018) [08162172] **1909**

YEARBOOK (ASSOCIATION OF EUROPEAN AIRLINES) (BE) [13320243] **40**

YEARBOOK - ASSOCIATION OF PACIFIC COAST GEOGRAPHERS (US/0066-9628) [01518443] **2579**

YEARBOOK - AUSTRALIAN ACADEMY OF SCIENCE (AT) [01814680] **5171**

YEARBOOK - AUSTRALIAN SOCIETY OF EDUCATIONAL TECHNOLOGY (AT/0313-4202) [03134202] **1792**

YEARBOOK - BAPTIST UNION OF WESTERN CANADA (CN/0067-4087) [02593550] **5069**

YEARBOOK - CALIFORNIA MACADAMIA SOCIETY (US/0068-5720) [05380149] 2361, **2434**

YEARBOOK - CANADIAN INSTITUTE OF ACTUARIES (CN/0068-8975) [02441942] **2897**

YEARBOOK - CASUALTY ACTUARIAL SOCIETY (US/0895-6022) [04020177] **2897**

YEARBOOK / CLAREMONT READING CONFERENCE (US/0886-6880) [01554821] **3334**

YEARBOOK : COMMERCIAL ARBITRATION (NE) [02741309] **3104**

YEARBOOK, CONTAINING HISTORICAL DOCUMENTS AND TABLES *See* YEARBOOK OF THE AMERICAN BAPTIST CHURCHES IN THE U.S.A **5069**

YEARBOOK (COUNCIL ON TECHNOLOGY TEACHER EDUCATION (U.S.) (US/1048-4779) [15960431] **1917**

YEARBOOK - CREDIT UNION NATIONAL ASSOCIATION (US) [06452782] **817**

YEARBOOK DE PEDIATRIA (SP) **3912**

YEARBOOK - ENSIGN CLASS ASSOCIATION (US/0146-2458) [02915968] **4931**

YEARBOOK / EVANGELICAL FREE CHURCH OF AMERICA (US/1049-8591) [01568485] **5069**

YEARBOOK / EVANGELICAL LUTHERAN CHURCH IN AMERICA (US) [17457095] **5069**

YEARBOOK FOR TRADITIONAL MUSIC (US/0740-1558) [08717450] **4159**

YEARBOOK / GENERAL SOCIETY OF COLONIAL WARS (US/0882-2328) [07901702] **2766**

YEARBOOK / GRUPPO IRI (IT) [09612739] **1632**

YEARBOOK - IFA (NE/0377-6662) [02243204] **4759**

YEARBOOK - ILLINOIS CREDIT UNION LEAGUE (1988) (US/1046-2996) [20333796] **817**

YEARBOOK - INDEPENDENT SCHOOLS ASSOCIATION (UK) [05918430] **1792**

YEARBOOK / INDIANA DENTAL ASSOCIATION (US/0733-5784) [06221034] **1337**

YEARBOOK / INSTITUTE OF MANAGEMENT CONSULTANTS (US/0260-373X) [08743115] **889**

YEARBOOK - INSTITUTION OF CIVIL ENGINEERS (UK) [02888276] **2034**

YEARBOOK / INTERNATIONAL COURT OF JUSTICE (NE/0074-445X) [01714864] **3138**

YEARBOOK - INTERNATIONAL MARITIME COMMITTEE (BE) [05049039] **4185**

YEARBOOK. (INTERNATIONAL WORK GROUP FOR INDIGENOUS AFFAIRS) (DK/0902-6266) [22340092] **4514**

YEARBOOK / LUTHERAN CHURCH IN AMERICA (US) [01586479] **5069**

YEARBOOK - NATIONAL ASSOCIATION OF CONGREGATIONAL CHRISTIAN CHURCHES, THE (US/0272-5339) [06836625] **5010**

YEARBOOK - NATIONAL COUNCIL OF TEACHERS OF MATHEMATICS (US/0077-4103) [01759166] **3541**

YEARBOOK - NATIONAL COUNCIL OF WOMEN OF CANADA (MICROFICHE) (CN) [05018061] **5572**

YEARBOOK - NATIONAL SOCIETY OF PUBLIC ACCOUNTANTS (US/0547-9193) [04127016] **753**

YEARBOOK - NEW YORK COUNTY LAWYERS' ASSOCIATION (US/0548-8729) [02349975] **3077**

YEARBOOK - NEW YORK YEARLY MEETING, RELIGIOUS SOCIETY OF FRIENDS (US/0148-3013) [03282942] **5069**

YEARBOOK OF AGRICULTURAL STATISTICS (NE) **158**

YEARBOOK OF AGRICULTURE (1980), THE *CEASED.* (US/0886-7690) [07094188] **148**

YEARBOOK OF AMERICAN AND CANADIAN CHURCHES (US/0195-9034) [01798538] **5010**

YEARBOOK OF ANESTHESIA AND PAIN MANAGEMENT *See* YEAR BOOK OF ANESTHESIOLOGY AND PAIN MANAGEMENT, THE **3684**

YEARBOOK OF ASTRONOMY *CEASED.* (US/0084-3660) [01645379] **401**

YEARBOOK OF BLOW MOLDED PACKAGING, THE (US/1058-4358) [24252889] **4461**

YEARBOOK OF CO-OPERATIVE ENTERPRISE (UK/0952-5556) [18178697] **1544**

YEARBOOK OF COMPARATIVE AND GENERAL LITERATURE (US/0084-3695) [01770310] **3356**

YEARBOOK OF COMPARATIVE AND GENERAL LITERATURE (SZ) **3455**

YEARBOOK OF CONSTRUCTION ARTICLES *CEASED.* (US/0747-8399) [10192268] **631**

YEARBOOK OF CONTEMPORARY POETRY, THE (US) [01457736] **3473**

YEARBOOK OF EDUCATION LAW, THE (US/1049-0264) [18820565] **1874**

YEARBOOK OF ENGLISH STUDIES / ARISTOTLE UNIVERSITY OF THESSALONIKI, FACULTY OF PHILOSOPHY, SCHOOL OF ENGLISH (GR) [23113852] **3334**

YEARBOOK OF ENGLISH STUDIES, THE (UK/0306-2473) [01681221] **3334**

YEARBOOK OF EUROPEAN LAW (UK) [09214712] **3077**

YEARBOOK OF EUROPEAN STUDIES (NE/0920-4792) [18633936] **2525**

YEARBOOK OF EXPERTS, AUTHORITIES & SPOKESPERSONS. AN ENCYCLOPEDIA OF SOURCES (US/1051-4058) [21952886] **1930**

YEARBOOK OF FINNISH FOREIGN POLICY (FI/0355-0079) [01796595] **4539**

YEARBOOK OF FISHERY STATISTICS (IT/0084-375X) [01770315] 2316, **2318**

YEARBOOK OF GERMAN-AMERICAN STUDIES (US/0741-2827) [08802101] **2766**

YEARBOOK OF HERPETOLOGY (US/0098-2644) [02240315] **5600**

● YEARBOOK OF INTENSIVE CARE AND EMERGENCY MEDICINE (GW) [26671809] **3726**

YEARBOOK OF INTERNATIONAL ORGANIZATIONS (BE/0084-3814) [05826589] **1930**

YEARBOOK OF INTERNATIONAL ORGANIZATIONS (BE/0084-3814) [01371384] **4539**

YEARBOOK OF INVESTMENT STATISTICS (HU/0230-418X) [09381326] 920, **735**

YEARBOOK OF ITALIAN STUDIES (IT/0826-9661) [01713655] **3455**

YEARBOOK OF JEHOVAH'S WITNESSES (US/0084-3849) [01715769] **5010**

YEARBOOK OF LABOR STATISTICS (MANILA) (US/0115-1851) [02607386] 1720, **1541**

YEARBOOK OF LANGLAND STUDIES, THE (US/0890-2917) [14196017] **3473**

YEARBOOK OF LAW, COMPUTERS, AND TECHNOLOGY *See* INTERNATIONAL YEARBOOK OF LAW, COMPUTERS, AND TECHNOLOGY **2984**

YEARBOOK OF MORPHOLOGY (NE/0922-3495) [19338895] **3334**

YEARBOOK OF NORDIC STATISTICS (SW/0078-1088) [01117462] **5346**

YEARBOOK OF PHYSICAL ANTHROPOLOGY (WASHINGTON) (US/0096-848X) [01367782] **248**

YEARBOOK OF PODIATRIC MEDICINE AND SURGERY (US/0276-6744) [07373380] **3918**

YEARBOOK OF POPULATION RESEARCH IN FINLAND (FI/0506-3590) [05246444] **4561**

YEARBOOK OF PROCUREMENT ARTICLES (US) [05635811] **3077**

YEARBOOK OF ROMANIAN STUDIES (US/0149-7219) [03531951] **2716**

YEARBOOK OF SCIENCE AND THE FUTURE (US/0096-3291) [01798584] **5171**

YEARBOOK OF STATISTICS: SINGAPORE (SI/0583-3655) [02024669] **5347**

YEARBOOK OF THE AMERICAN BAPTIST CHURCHES IN THE U.S.A (US/0092-3478) [01789601] **5069**

YEARBOOK OF THE AMERICAN READING FORUM (US/0895-3562) [11184793] **3334**

YEARBOOK OF THE CALIFORNIA AVOCADO SOCIETY (US/0096-5960) [09997597] **2434**

... YEARBOOK OF THE CANADIAN BAR ASSOCIATION AND THE MINUTES OF PROCEEDINGS OF THE ... ANNUAL MEETING, THE (CN/0318-4935) [02729618] **3077**

YEARBOOK OF THE ESTONIAN LEARNED SOCIETY IN AMERICA *CEASED.* (US/0425-3329) [01607497] **1854**

YEARBOOK OF THE EUROPEAN CONVENTION ON HUMAN RIGHTS, THE EUROPEAN COMMISSION AND EUROPEAN COURT OF HUMAN RIGHTS (NE) [04375454] **4514**

YEARBOOK OF THE HEATHER SOCIETY (UK/0440-5757) [02447352] **5237**

YEARBOOK OF THE INTERNATIONAL ASSOCIATION FOR CHILD AND ADOLESCENT PSYCHIATRY AND ALLIED PROFESSIONS (US/0277-6790) [07106408] **3937**

YEARBOOK OF THE INTERNATIONAL LAW COMMISSION (US/0082-8289) [01242842] **3138**

YEARBOOK OF THE NATIONAL CONFERENCE OF STATE LEGISLATIVE LEADERS (US/0547-521X) [01589329] **4695**

... YEARBOOK OF THE NATIONAL SOCIETY FOR THE STUDY OF EDUCATION, THE (US/0077-5762) [04330481] **1792**

YEARBOOK OF THE SOCIETY FOR PIRANDELLO STUDIES, THE (UK) [25988566] 3455, **5372**

YEARBOOK OF THE UNITED NATIONS (US/0082-8521) [01768016] **3138**

●YEARBOOK OF WOMEN STUDIES, A (US/1048-8626) [21068056] **5572**

YEARBOOK OF WORLD ELECTRONICS DATA ... VOL. 1, WEST EUROPE (UK/0954-0180) [22227379] **2086**

YEARBOOK OF WORLD ELECTRONICS DATA ... VOL. 2, AMERICA, JAPAN & ASIA PACIFIC (UK/0954-0172) [22227389] **2086**

YEARBOOK ON HUMAN RIGHTS FOR ... (US/0251-6519) [01770335] **4514**

YEARBOOK ON INDIA'S FOREIGN POLICY (II/8756-5307) [11580394] **4539**

YEARBOOK ON SOCIALIST LEGAL SYSTEMS *CEASED.* (US/0887-9117) [13414782] **3138**

YEARBOOK (ROYAL BALLET) (UK/0144-1205) [13026357] **1314**

YEARBOOK - ROYAL CANADIAN COLLEGE OF ORGANISTS (1978) (CN/0228-9539) [07966390] **4159**

YEARBOOK - SALMON AND TROUT ASSOCIATION (UK/0969-1405) [09691405] **2316**

YEARBOOK, SHIPYARDS, BOATBUILDERS, AND MARINE ENGINEERS (NO) [07845900] **4185**

YEARBOOK - SOCIETY OF WIRELESS PIONEERS (US/0098-5910) [02239491] **2087**

YEARBOOK / TIRE AND RIM ASSOCIATION, INC (US/0362-6725) [10978836] 5429, **5400**

YEARBOOK (TIRE AND RIM ASSOCIATION OF AMERICA) *See* YEARBOOK / TIRE AND RIM ASSOCIATION, INC **5400**

YEARBOOK / UNITED NATIONS COMMISSION ON INTERNATIONAL TRADE LAW (US/0251-4265) [01276996] **3138**

YEARBOOK - WATER POLLUTION CONTROL FEDERATION (US) [04922123] **2248**

YEARBOOK, WITH HISTORICAL AND GENEALOGICAL JOURNAL (US/0519-3117) [02703236] **2767**

YEARBOOK (WORLD CONFEDERATION OF JEWISH COMMUNITY CENTERS) (US) [08581812] **5054**

YEARBOOK - WORLD COUNCIL OF CREDIT UNIONS (US/0147-7803) [03225877] 817, **1544**

YEARBOOK / WWF, WORLD WILDLIFE FUND (SZ) [07592525] **2210**

YEARLY ALL INDIA CRIMINAL DIGEST (II/0377-6719) [01790643] **3109**

YEARLY BULLETIN OF PRICE STATISTICS. WHOLESALE / MINISTRY OF PLANNING, CENTRAL STATISTICAL OFFICE (KU) [13323907] **724**

YEARLY REVIEW (II) [18946898] **3356**

YEARS AHEAD, THE (US/0513-2096) [01588745] **5010**

YEAR'S BEST FANTASY AND HORROR (US) [22157591] **3455**

YEAR'S BEST MYSTERY & SUSPENSE STORIES, THE (US/0741-0212) [08796361] **3455**

YEAR'S BEST SCIENCE FICTION (NEW YORK, N.Y.), THE (US/0743-1740) [10530019] **3455**

YEAR'S WORK IN ENGLISH STUDIES (UK/0084-4144) [01770338] 3334, **3455**

YEAR'S WORK IN MODERN LANGUAGE STUDIES (UK/0084-4152) [01770339] **3334**

YEAR'S WORK IN MUSIC, THE (UK) [01463647] **4159**

YEAR'S WORK - INSURANCE INSTITUTE FOR HIGHWAY SAFETY, THE (US/0276-7325) [07414403] 2897, **5446**

YEAST CHICHESTER (WEST SUSSEX) (UK/0749-503X) [11128931] **1048**

YEAST (DAVIS, CALIF.) (CN/0513-5222) [06960649] **571**

YEATS (US/0742-6224) [10268100] **3455**

YEATS ANNUAL (LONDON, ENGLAND) (UK/0278-7687) [08913760] **3455**

YEATS ELIOT REVIEW (CN/0704-5700) [04814057] **3455**

YECHONG PAEKSO (KO) [09179024] **333**

YEDA LE-MEDA (IS) [05900185] **4759**

YEDDA IAM (IS/0334-4053) [02291687] **2325**

YEDION (IS) [05975891] **5458**

YEDION LE-TEKNOLOGYAH SEL MEDA U-MAHSEVIM (IS/0303-1381) [01793546] **1263**

YEDI'OT GENAZIM (IS/0513-5230) [02158178] **5054**

YEH CHIN FEN HSI (CC) [10013747] **4024**

YEH TSAO (US/0094-0097) [01797550] **2510**

YEJIN FENXI (CC/1000-7571) [I10007571] **4024**

YELL COUNTY HISTORICAL & GENEALOGICAL SOCIETY BULLETIN *See* BULLETIN - YELL COUNTY HISTORICAL & GENEALOGICAL ASSOCIATION (ARK.) **2441**

YELLOW BRICK ROAD (ROCHESTER, N.Y.) *CEASED.* (US/0888-5745) [13675078] **1071**

YELLOW BRICK ROAD (TEMPE, ARIZ.) (US/0361-8552) [02142087] **3455**

YELLOW-FEVER VACCINATING CENTRES FOR INTERNATIONAL TRAVEL (SZ/0510-8675) [05816481] **4808**

YELLOW PAGES AND DIRECTORY REPORT (US) **4820**

YELLOW PAGES AND DIRECTORY REPORT (US) **4820**

YELLOW PAGES INDUSTRY SOURCEBOOK (US) **4820**

YELLOW PAGES MARKET FORECAST (US) [17408205] 938, **4820**

YELLOW PAGES OF ROCK / THE ALBUM NETWORK (US) [15135793] **4159**

YELLOW PAGES SALES & MARKETING (US) 768, **938**

YELLOW PAPERS, THE (CN/0714-6892) [09250145] **1792**

YELLOW SILK (US/0736-9212) [08853950] 333, **3455**

YELLOW SPRINGS NEWS (US) [16619613] **5731**

YELLOWBACK LIBRARY (US) [08523968] 1071, 2779, **3455**

YELLOWED PAGES (US/1050-7361) [05713279] **2478**

YELLOWHEAD REGIONAL LIBRARY *See* NEWSLETTER OF THE YELLOWHEAD REGIONAL LIBRARY **3235**

YELLOWHEAD STAR (CN/1182-6096) [23226711] **5798**

YELLOWJACKET (QUINCY, ILL.) (US/0277-9668) [07581481] **2478**

YELLOWSTONE GRIZZLY BEAR INVESTIGATIONS (US/0192-8031) [04845264] **5600**

YELMO *SUSPENDED.* (SP/0006-6966) [01534613] **3334**

YEN CHIU HUI PAO (CH/0255-5905) [13568163] **148**

YEN CHIU HUI PAO (TAI-WAN SHENG TAI-NAN CHU NUNG YEH KAI LIANG CHANG) (CH) [11094069] **148**

YEN CHIU HUI PAO / TAI-WAN TANG YEH YEN CHIU SO (CH/0372-2414) [02583139] **191**

YEN CHIU PAO KAO (CH/0077-5819) [02564498] **148**

YEN CHIU SHIH YEN PAO KAO - TAI-WAN TANG YEH KU FEN YU HSIEN KUNG SSU HSU CHAN YEN CHIU SO (CH) [06907534] **224**

YEN KAO YUEH KAN (CH) [08924683] **4695**

YEN SHIH HSUEH PAO (CC) [13830290] **1459**

YEN SHIH KUANG WU CHI TSE SHIH *See* YANSHI KUANGWUXUE ZAZHI **1445**

YENCHING JOURNAL OF SOCIAL STUDIES, THE (CH) [01466083] **5226**

YENI UFUKLAR (TU) [02242101] **5237**

YEO WON (KO) **5572**

YERMO (SP/0513-5311) [05667212] **5010**

YERUSHILTON (IS) [03097409] **2668**

YERUSHOLAYMER ALMANAKH (IS) [02244449] **3455**

YES (LONDON, ENGLAND) (UK) [09271979] **5010**

YESTERDAYS (US/0278-3924) [07782553] **2478**

YESTERDAYS (GONZALES (TX)) (US) [08006134] **2478**

YESTERDAY'S MEMORIES (US/0098-1796) [01799603] **4159**

YESTERDAY'S NEWS (CN/0318-5494) [02442124] **2767**

YESTERYEAR (PRINCETON) (US/0194-9349) [05123093] **252**

YESTERYEARS (US/0044-037X) [02218383] **2478**

YESUL KWA PIPYONG (KO) [10944010] **333**

YESUL PYONGNON (HANGUK YESUL PYONGNONGA HYOBUIHOE) (KO) [08122058] **333**

YETMINSTER LOCAL HISTORY SOCIETY (UK) [19117859] **2716**

YHA ACCOMODATION GUIDE. ENGLAND & WALES / YHA (UK) [19876404] **5314**

YHTEENVETO TIELIIKENNEVAHINGOISTA (FI) [02243048] **5446**

YIBIAO CAILIAO (CC/1001-3725) [I10013725] **5171**

YICHUAN (CC/0253-9772) [05337861] **552**

YICHUAN XUEBAO (CC/0379-4172) [I03794172] **552**

YIDDISH (US/0364-4308) [02723738] **3455**

YIDDISHE KULTUR (US/0044-0426) [02269773] **3456**

YIDDISHKEIT (IS/0792-044X) [I0792044X] **5054**

YIDISHE SHPRAKH (US/0044-0442) [01796374] **3334**

YIELDS, COSTS, PRICES (KE) [08498721] **148**

YIHUA BAO (US/0745-2322) [08968579] **5763**

YILLIK BULTENI - KAVAK VE HIZLI GELISEN YABANCI TUR ORMAN AGACLARI ARASTIRMA ENSTITUSU (TU) [05520188] **2398**

YIN HSIANG CHIH NAN (CH) [07031583] **5320**

YIN MU CHU TSO (CH) [08914542] **4080**

YIN YEAH SHENG HUO TSA CHIH (CH) **4159**

YIN YUEH SHENG HUO (HK) [01790384] **4159**

YIN YUEH YU YIN HSIANG (CH) [01797505] **5320**

YING CHUN HUA (CH) [08808105] **369**

YING SHIH CHUN CHIU (CC) [11844232] **4080**

YING TSAO CHIEN TSAI TSUNG LAN (CH) [11541725] 631, **2034**

YING YUNG HUA HSUEH (CHANG-CHUN SHIH, CHINA) (CC) [13590713] **995**

YING YUNG SHENG HSUEH (CC) [09449222] 4453, **2001**

YING — Alphabetical Title Index

YING YUNG SHU HSUEH HO LI HSUEH (CC/1000-0887) [08602897] **3541**

YINGYONG KEXUE XUEBAO (CC/0255-8297) [10389044] **5171**

YINGYONG QIXIANG XUEBAO (CC/1001-7313) [I10017313] **1437**

YINGYONG SHUXUE XUEBAO (CC) [04312320] **3541**

YIQI YIBIAO XUEBAO (CC/0254-3087) [10476921] **5171**

YISRAEL SELLANU (US/0279-182X) [07546416] **2770**

YIVO ANNUAL (US/1050-8864) [21719126] 2275, **5054**

YIVO BLETER (US/0084-4217) [02210881] 2275, **3456**

YIVO NEWS (US/0898-8358) [15686693] 2275, **5054**

YLEISISSA ALIOIKEUKSISSA SYYTETYT JA TUOMITUT (FI) [10569536] 3077, **3084**

YLLI (AA/0513-5486) [05436004] **2495**

YLLKAT (AA) **1071**

YM (US/0888-5842) [13567884] **1071**

YMCA DIRECTORY (US) 2602, **5314**

YMCA WORLD (SZ) 2602, **4856**

YMCA YEAR BOOK AND OFFICIAL ROSTERS *See* YMCA DIRECTORY **5314**

YMER (SW/0044-0477) [01644580] **248**

YO YO TIMES (US/0897-7704) [17623585] 4868, **1071**

YODAESAENG (KO) [10845201] 5572, **1854**

YOGA AND HEALTH (UK/0953-2161) **4365**

YOGA INTERNATIONAL (US/1055-7911) [23326285] **4186**

YOGA JOURNAL (US/0191-0965) [04790082] 4622, **2602**

YOGA LIFE (1982) (CN/0824-2526) [10036633] **4365**

YOGA-MIMAMSA (II/0044-0507) [01606875] **4186**

YOGA RESEARCH (US/0191-3298) [04836059] **4186**

YOGA TODAY *See* YOGA AND HEALTH **4365**

YOGYAKARTA, INDONESIA (DAERAH ISTIMEWA) *See* PERATURAN DAERAH DAERAH ISTIMEWA YOGYAKARTA **3026**

YOGYAKARTA, INDONESIA (DAERAH ISTIMEWA). DINAS PERINDUSTRIAN *See* LAPORAN DINAS PERINDUSTRIAN DAERAH ISTIMEWA YOGYAKARTA **1572**

YOGYAKARTA, INDONESIA (DAERAH ISTIMEWA). DINAS TENAGA KERJA *See* LAPORAN TAHUNAN DINAS TENAGA KERJA DAERAH ISTIMEWA YOGYAKARTA **1687**

YOJANA (II/0044-0515) [01642870] **4695**

YOKOHAMA IGAKU (JA/0372-7726) [09498330] **3652**

YOKOHAMA KOKURITSU DAIGAKU. KANKYO KAGAKU KENKYU SENTA *See* YOKOHAMA KOKURITSU DAIGAKU KANKYO KAGAKU KENKYU SENTA KIYO BULLETIN: INSTITUTE OF ENVIRONMENTAL SCIENCE AND TECHNOLOGY, YOKOHAMA NATIONAL UNIVERSITY **2248**

YOKOHAMA KOKURITSU DAIGAKU KANKYO KAGAKU KENKYU SENTA KIYO BULLETIN: INSTITUTE OF ENVIRONMENTAL SCIENCE AND TECHNOLOGY, YOKOHAMA NATIONAL UNIVERSITY (JA) [06656036] 2222, **2248**

YOKOHAMA KOKURITSU DAIGAKU. KYOIKU GAKUBU. SCIENCE REPORTS OF THE YOKOHAMA NATIONAL UNIVERSITY. SECTION II: BIOLOGICAL AND GEOLOGICAL SCIENCES *See* SCIENCE REPORTS OF THE YOKOHAMA NATIONAL UNIVERSITY. SECTION II: BIOLOGY AND GEOLOGY / FACULTY OF EDUCATION, YOKOHAMA NATIONAL UNIVERSITY **472**

YOKOHAMA KOKURITSU DAIGAKU. KYOIKUGAKUBU *See* SCIENCE REPORTS OF THE YOKOHAMA NATIONAL UNIVERSITY. SECTION I : MATHEMATICS, PHYSICS, CHEMISTRY **5153**

YOKOHAMA MATHEMATICAL JOURNAL, THE (JA/0044-0523) [01715735] **3541**

YOKOHAMA MEDICAL BULLETIN (JA/0044-0531) [01586146] **3652**

YOKOHAMA SHIRITSU DAIGAKU SOGO KENKYU (JA) [09865849] **2248**

YOKOSUKA-SHI HAKUBUTSUKAN *See* YOKOSUKA-SHI HAKUBUTSUKAN SHIRYOSHU **4097**

YOKOSUKA-SHI HAKUBUTSUKAN SHIRYOSHU (JA/0386-4286) [06567276] **4097**

YOKSA MINSOKHAK / HANGUK YOKSA MINSOK HAKHOE (KO) [25490902] **2770**

YOKSO (KUNGNIP CHONMUNDAE (KOREA)) (KO) [07473266] **401**

YOKYUJO KAINAN TOKEI (JA) [02245282] **4185**

YOLMAE (SEOUL, KOREA) (KO) [11339492] **2510**

YOMAN HA-PATENTIM VEHA-MIDGAMIN (IS/0334-3332) [01795658] **1310**

YOMIURI SHIMBUN (NEW YORK, N.Y.) (US/0890-8710) [07826824] **5641**

YON YONCHO (KO) [04904388] **5374**

YONAGO ACTA MEDICA (JA/0513-5710) [01770348] **3652**

YONAGO IGAKU ZASSHI (JA/0044-0558) [I00440558] **3652**

YONBO (KO) [10600659] **5172**

YONBO (KO) [09059593] **3794**

YONCHA POGOSO - KUNGMIN UNHAENG (KO) [04372210] **817**

YONG REIDI (KO) [07981524] **2510**

YONGHAK NONJIP (KO) [05199196] 3456, **3334**

YONGS NONCHONG (KO) [05199281] **5226**

YON'GU NONJIP - IHWA YOJA TAEHAKKYO, TAEHAGWON (KO) [05026463] **5237**

YONGU NONMUNJIP (KO) [16932905] 996, **4425**

YONGU NONMUNJIP (HANGUK ENOJI YONGUSO) (KO) [09152104] **5172**

YONGU NONMUNJIP (HANGUK KWAHAK KISURWON) (KO) [12279271] **2001**

YONGU NONMUNJIP (HANGUK WONJARYOK YONGUSO) *See* YONGU NONMUNJIP (HANGUK ENOJI YONGUSO) **5172**

YONGU NONMUNJIP (PUSAN TAEHAKKYO. MULSONG YONGUSO) (KO) [10137242] **4430**

YON'GU NONMUNJIP - TAEPYONGYANG CHANGHAK MUNHWA CHAEDAN (KO) [05026836] **5237**

YONGU NONMUNJIP (ULSAN KONGKWA TAEHAK. PYONGSOL KONGOP CHONMUN TAEHAK) (KO) [09372880] **5172**

YONGU POGO (IMOP SIHOMJANG (KOREA). SUWON YUKCHONG CHIJANG) *See* YONGU POGO / SALLIMCHONG, SUWON YUKCHONG CHIJANG **2398**

YON'GU POGO - KUNGNIP K ONGOP PYOJUN SIHOMSO (KO) [05425706] **5172**

YONGU POGO / SALLIMCHONG, SUWON YUKCHONG CHIJANG (KO) [19949870] **2398**

YONHAP (TAEGU, KOREA) (KO) [13410861] **2495**

YONHAP YONGAM (KO) [08027064] **2668**

YONKERS HISTORICAL BULLETIN (US/0513-2673) [06678828] **2767**

YONSE OMUNHAK (KO) [05529814] **3334**

YONSE TAEHAKKYO, SEOUL, KOREA. SANOP KISUL YON'GUSO *See* SANOP KISUL YON'GUSO NONMUNJIP **1995**

YONSEI MEDICAL JOURNAL (KO/0513-5796) [01586556] **3652**

YONSEI REPORTS ON TROPICAL MEDICINE (KO/0375-5207) [01586459] **3987**

YONTEV BLETER (SA) [03623775] **5054**

YOOP HAKHOE CHI. JOURNAL OF THE KOREAN CERAMIC SOCIETY (KO) [04798641] **2595**

YORAN - HOKKAIDO KOGYO KAIHATSU (JA) [02441383] **5172**

YORAN - HOKKAIDO ZAIMUKYOKU (JA) [02622599] **4759**

YORAN - KOGYO GIJUTSUIN OSAKA KOGYO GIJUTSU SHIKENJO (JA) [01799682] **996**

YORAN - KOKURITSU BOSAI KAGAKU GIJUTSU SENTA (JA) [02376538] **2579**

YORAN - KOKURITSU KOSHU EISEIIN (JA) [03415510] **4808**

YORAN- [TOHOKU KOGYO GIJUTSU SHIKENJO] (JA) [01797234] **5172**

YORK COUNTY COAST STAR (US) **5685**

YORK COUNTY GENEALOGICAL SOCIETY JOURNAL (US) **2478**

YORK DAILY RECORD (YORK, PA. : 1973) (US/1043-4313) [13647456] **5741**

YORK DISPATCH, THE (US/1050-267X) [11148520] **5741**

YORK GEORGIAN SOCIETY *See* ANNUAL REPORT - YORK GEORGIAN SOCIETY **5228**

YORK HISTORIAN (UK/0309-3743) [03575915] 2633, **311**

YORK PAPERS IN LINGUISTICS (UK/0307-3238) [02199758] **3334**

YORK PIONEER, THE (CN/0513-2711) [02441859] **2767**

YORK REGIONAL TOPIC, THE (CN/0710-2011) [08418979] **5798**

YORK RIVER UPLANDS COUNTRY ROADS (CN) [30714894] **5500**

YORK RIVER UPLANDS DIRECTORY *See* YORK RIVER UPLANDS COUNTRY ROADS **5500**

YORK UNIVERSITY, (TORONTO, ONT.) *See* BRIEF TO THE ONTARIO COUNCIL ON UNIVERSITY AFFAIRS (YORK UNIVERSITY) **1812**

YORK UNIVERSITY (TORONTO, ONT.). CENTRE FOR RESEARCH IN EXPERIMENTAL SPACE SCIENCE *See* C R E S S SPECTROSCOPIC REPORT **4399**

YORK UNIVERSITY (TORONTO, ONT.). FACULTY OF ENVIRONMENTAL STUDIES *See* STUDENT DISCUSSION PAPER **2221**

YORK UNIVERSITY (TORONTO, ONT.) INSTITUTE FOR BEHAVIOURAL RESEARCH *See* BULLETIN - YORK UNIVERSITY, TORONTO. INSTITUTE FOR BEHAVIOURAL RESEARCH **4579**

YORK UNIVERSITY (TORONTO, ONT.). INSTITUTE FOR BEHAVIOURAL RESEARCH. SOCIAL PSYCHOLOGY RESEARCH PROGRAMME *See* RESEARCH REPORT - YORK UNIVERSITY. SOCIAL PSYCHOLOGY RESEARCH PROGRAMME. INSTITUTE FOR BEHAVIOURAL RESEARCH **5256**

YORK UNIVERSITY, TORONTO, ONT. LIBRARIES *See* Y U L SERIALS LIST **3256**

YORKIE TALES (US/0883-7686) [12207181] **4288**

YORKSHIRE ARCHAEOLOGICAL JOURNAL, THE (UK/0084-4276) [06569551] **285**

YORKSHIRE ARCHAEOLOGICAL SOCIETY *See* RECORD SERIES / YORKSHIRE ARCHAEOLOGICAL SOCIETY **280**

YORKSHIRE DIALECT SOCIETY *See* TRANSACTIONS OF THE YORKSHIRE DIALECT SOCIETY **3329**

YORKSHIRE GEOLOGICAL SOCIETY *See* PROCEEDINGS OF THE YORKSHIRE GEOLOGICAL SOCIETY **1391**

YORKSHIRE JOURNAL (US/0044-0612) [01770354] **5527**

YORKSHIRE TERRIER QUARTERLY, THE (US) [01789804] **4288**

YORKTON THIS WEEK & ENTERPRISE (CN/1186-429X) [I1186429X] **5798**

YORKVIEW (CN/0822-2517) [10669124] **2767**

YORKVILLE ENQUIRER (US) [10749176] **5743**

YOSAN JIMU TEIYO (JA) [02377907] **4759**

YOSETSU GAKKAI *See* TRANSACTIONS OF THE JAPAN WELDING SOCIETY **4028**

YOSETSU GAKKAI RONBUNSHU (JA/0288-4771) [11596570] **4029**

YOSETSU GIJUTSU. WELDING TECHNIQUE (JA) **4029**

YOSETSU SHOTOKUZEIHO (JA) [02741304] **4759**

YOSHA (JA/0916-6076) [I09166076] **1031**

YOSHOKU KENKYUJO KENKYU HOKOKU (JA/0389-5858) [08724007] **2316**

YOSONG (KO) [09208534] **5572**

YOSONG (KO) [10240577] **2510**

YOSONG CHUNGANG (KO) [05157237] **2510**

YOSONG MUNHAK (KO) [10707029] **3456**

YOSONG TONGA (KO) [10884511] **427**

YOSUI TO HAISUI (JA/0513-5907) [10412952] **2248**

YOU! (AGOURA HILLS, CALIF.) (US/1064-8682) [23988519] **5038**

YOU & THE LAW (US/0731-1109) [04355021] 724, **3077**

YOU AND YOUR BUSINESS (US/0736-4865) [09142683] **724**

YOU (NEW YORK. 1976) (US/0146-2318) [02908437] **4622**

YOU TORONTO. 1990 (CN/1189-4695) [11894695] 5572, **1088**

YOU (VANCOUVER) (CN/0705-3037) [03900315] **406**

YOUJI HUAXUE (CC/0253-2786) [08901954] **1049**

YOUNG (CN/0702-1755) [03466173] **1096**

Alphabetical Title Index — YOUTHWORKER

YOUNG ALLIANCE (II/0049-836X) [01770360] **724**

YOUNG AMERICA SINGS... ANTHOLOGY OF PRIVATE SECONDARY SCHOOL POETRY (US) [01441807] **3473**

YOUNG AND ALIVE (US/0738-8101) [09703006] **4395**

YOUNG AUTHOR'S MAGAZINE (US/0741-7594) [10219092] 3456, **2926**

YOUNG BUDDHIST, THE (SI/0377-8088) [01783608] **5022**

YOUNG CHILDREN (US/0044-0728) [01590294] **1806**

YOUNG EAST *CEASED*. (JA/0513-5974) [02199751] 2668, **5022**

YOUNG EXECUTIVE (US/0735-9063) [08997237] **889**

YOUNG FABIAN PAMPHLET (UK/0513-5982) [01639050] **4501**

YOUNG FARMER *See* NATIONAL NEWS FOR THE YOUTH MOVEMENT FOR THE COUNTRYSIDE **1067**

YOUNG FASHIONS MAGAZINE *CEASED*. (US/0884-7630) [12488690] **1088**

YOUNG GENERATION (SI) **1071**

YOUNG INDIAN (II/0049-8378) [02240185] **2668**

YOUNG INDIANA JONES CHRONICLES, THE *CEASED*. (US/1061-4966) [25325081] **3456**

YOUNG ISRAEL VIEWPOINT *See* VIEWPOINT **2632**

YOUNG JUDAEAN (US/0044-0817) [03970165] **5054**

YOUNG LAWYERS NEWSLETTER (US/0147-6777) [03213717] **3077**

YOUNG MARCH, THE (II/0377-6727) [01797757] 4501, **1071**

YOUNG MUSICIANS (US/0044-0841) [01781987] **4159**

YOUNG PEOPLE NOW (UK) [15173797] **5314**

YOUNG PEOPLE TODAY *SUSPENDED*. (US/0738-887X) [09699486] **2495**

YOUNG SALVATIONIST (US/0746-861X) [10352233] **5010**

YOUNG SOCIALIST (NEW YORK. 1972) *SUSPENDED*. (US/0360-0157) [02241738] 4548, **3356**

YOUNG SOLDIER (AT/0300-3264) [01424310] **1071**

YOUNG SPARTACUS (US/0162-2692) [03452252] **1071**

YOUNG SUPERSTARS (US/0196-092X) [05753097] **1072**

YOUNG VOICES (OLYMPIA, WASH.) (US/1046-8404) [20408420] **1072**

YOUNG VOICES, YOUR VOICES (CN/1182-4980) [23237381] **3456**

YOUNG WINTER'S TALES (UK) [05175084] **1072**

YOUNG WOMAN (US/0278-3932) [07782623] **5572**

YOUNG WORKER (US) [05315151] **1720**

YOUNG WRESTLER, THE (US/0160-5771) [03699930] **4931**

YOUNGER ELEMENTARY CLASS PACKET, THE (US/0160-4287) [03685856] **1792**

YOUNKIN FAMILY NEWS BULLETIN (US/1058-2045) [24123657] **2478**

YOUR ASSOCIATE IN SACRAMENTO FOR SPECIAL EDUCATION (US/1065-0873) [26498047] **1887**

YOUR BIG BACKYARD (US/0886-5299) [07382807] **1072**

YOUR BUSINESS AND THE LAW (BUSINESS RESEARCH PUBLICATIONS, INC.) *See* MANAGEMENT POLICIES AND PERSONNEL LAW **3151**

YOUR BUSINESS (SMITHS FALLS) (CN/0832-1647) [15535114] **724**

YOUR CANADA PENSION PLAN (CN/0317-8951) [02604430] **4759**

●YOUR CHICAGO EXPRESS (US/1065-495X) [26614362] **2897**

YOUR CHILD'S HEALTH AND DEVELOPMENT (US/1055-6036) [23237431] 2602, **2287**

YOUR CHURCH (US/0049-8394) [01779511] **5010**

YOUR CLASSIC (UK/0957-6525) [I09576525] **5429**

YOUR COLLEGE-BOUND STUDENTS (US/0097-6571) [01799897] **1854**

YOUR COMPLETE OFFICE (AT) **4214**

YOUR COMPUTER (AT/0263-0885) [I02630885] **1273**

YOUR COMPUTER CAREER *CEASED*. (US/0884-4615) [12423672] 1207, **4210**

YOUR COMPUTER MOSMAN (AT/0725-3931) [I07253931] **1207**

YOUR DAILY CYCLE GUIDE (CN/0711-1231) [08767161] **401**

●YOUR DOG (US/1078-0343) [30998547] **5527**

YOUR EDMUNDITE MISSIONS NEWS LETTER (US/0044-1015) [04052985] **5011**

YOUR FAMILY PET *CEASED*. (US/0278-744X) [07862634] **4288**

YOUR FAVORITE COUNTRY STARS (US/1042-0843) [18936152] 2495, **4160**

YOUR FEDERAL INCOME TAX FOR INDIVIDUALS / DEPARTMENT OF THE TREASURY, INTERNAL REVENUE SERVICE (US) [10317068] **4759**

YOUR GARDEN CLAYTON (AT/0044-1031) [I00441031] **2434**

YOUR GUIDE TO ARRANGING BANK & DEBT FINANCING FOR YOUR OWN BUSINESS IN CANADA (CN/1191-0542) [25652292] **817**

YOUR GUIDE TO CANADIAN EXPORT FINANCING (CN/1191-047X) [25652301] **858**

YOUR GUIDE TO FINANCIAL ASSISTANCE FOR BUSINESS IN ATLANTIC CANADA (CN/1191-0356) [25652241] **724**

YOUR GUIDE TO FINANCIAL ASSISTANCE FOR BUSINESS IN ONTARIO (CN/1191-0348) [25652240] **817**

YOUR GUIDE TO FINANCIAL ASSISTANCE FOR BUSINESS IN QUEBEC (CN/1191-0526) [25652299] **817**

YOUR GUIDE TO FINANCIAL ASSISTANCE FOR BUSINESS IN WESTERN CANADA *See* YOUR GUIDE TO GOVERNMENT FINANCIAL ASSISTANCE FOR BUSINESS IN ALBERTA **724**

YOUR GUIDE TO FINANCIAL ASSISTANCE FOR BUSINESS IN WESTERN CANADA (CN/1191-050X) [25652303] **817**

YOUR GUIDE TO FINANCIAL ASSISTANCE FOR BUSINESS IN WESTERN CANADA *See* YOUR GUIDE TO GOVERNMENT FINANCIAL ASSISTANCE FOR BUSINESS IN THE YUKON **725**

YOUR GUIDE TO FINANCING BUSINESS GROWTH BY SELLING A PIECE OF THE PIE (CN/1191-0488) [25652290] **817**

YOUR GUIDE TO FLORIDA SCHOLARSHIPS (US) **1854**

YOUR GUIDE TO FLORIDA SCHOLARSHIPS AND OTHER FINANCIAL ASSISTANCE PROGRAMS (US/1070-7824) [23349304] **1854**

●YOUR GUIDE TO GOVERNMENT FINANCIAL ASSISTANCE FOR BUSINESS IN ALBERTA (CN/1198-046X) [30842286] **724**

●YOUR GUIDE TO GOVERNMENT FINANCIAL ASSISTANCE FOR BUSINESS IN THE YUKON (CN/1198-0575) [30842273] **725**

YOUR GUIDE TO PREPARING A PLAN TO RAISE MONEY FOR YOUR OWN BUSINESS (CN/1191-0496) [25652289] **725**

YOUR GUIDE TO RAISING VENTURE CAPITAL FOR YOUR OWN BUSINESS IN CANADA (CN/1191-0534) [25652295] **725**

YOUR GUIDE TO STARTING & SELF-FINANCING YOUR OWN BUSINESS IN CANADA (CN/1191-0518) [25652293] **725**

YOUR HEALTH & FITNESS (US/0279-9324) [07365069] **4808**

YOUR HEALTH & SAFETY (US/8750-8842) [11884875] **4808**

YOUR HIGHWAY DEPARTMENT, ARKANSAS (US/0094-9914) [01795309] **5446**

YOUR INCOME TAX (US) [01755552] **4759**

YOUR MEDICARE HANDBOOK FOR RAILROAD RETIREMENT BENEFICIARIES (US) [21943265] **2897**

YOUR MONEY (CHICAGO, ILL.) (US/1057-123X) [23958475] **920**

YOUR MONEY WEEKLY (AT) **4759**

YOUR MONEY WEEKLY (AT/0158-2836) [I01582836] **817**

YOUR MORTGAGE MAGAZINE (AT/1039-0081) **817**

YOUR NEW ECONOMY HOME PLANS (US/0275-2174) [07089936] **311**

YOUR NEWS (CN/0833-2908) [15561755] 2478, **5798**

●YOUR PATIENT & FITNESS IN ENDOCRINOLOGY (US/1062-371X) [25602136] **3733**

YOUR PERSONAL BEST *CEASED*. (US/1040-7057) [18506042] **4622**

YOUR PHARMACY (AT/0817-2455) [I08172455] 938, 952, **4333**

YOUR PRESENCE (US/1056-3806) [23675042] **5269**

YOUR PUBLIC SCHOOLS (US) [06895913] **1792**

YOUR QUEBEC PENSION PLAN (CN/0317-3429) [02248140] **5314**

YOUR RETIREMENT CHIPPENDALE (AT/1031-6620) [I10316620] 920, **5182**

YOUR SCHOOL & THE LAW (US/0094-0399) [02253953] 1792, **3077**

YOUR TELEPHONE PERSONALITY (US) **725**

YOUR TOMORROW (UK) [17015884] **5011**

YOUR UNION MATTERS (CN/0844-3750) [20121269] **1720**

YOUR WORLD (WASHINGTON, D.C.) (US/0894-1335) [15807354] **2495**

YOUR YANKEE HERITAGE (US) [05536524] **2478**

YOUSE JINSHU (CC/0513-3424) [08863343] **4024**

YOUTH & ADULTS TOGETHER (CN/0713-3634) [09743332] **5011**

YOUTH AND NATION *SUSPENDED*. (US) [01641776] **5722**

YOUTH AND POLICY (UK/0262-9970) [12259652] **1072**

YOUTH & SOCIETY (US/0044-118X) [01770384] **5265**

YOUTH (BOCA RATON) (US/0273-2610) [05163648] **1072**

YOUTH CONSERVATION CORPS (US/0276-9271) [07440670] **2210**

YOUTH CONSERVATION CORPS PILOT PROGRAM *See* YOUTH CONSERVATION CORPS PROGRAM **2210**

YOUTH CONSERVATION CORPS PROGRAM (US/0190-8367) [04744307] **2210**

YOUTH COURT REPORT / MISSISSIPPI DEPARTMENT OF YOUTH SERVICES (US) [12110845] **3077**

YOUTH EXCHANGE PROGRAMS (CN/1186-0480) [24265560] **1792**

YOUTH FISHERIES EDUCATION PROGRAM : [NEWSLETTER] (CN/1186-2394) [24401865] **2316**

YOUTH (FREDERICTON, N.B.) (CN/0712-1768) [08781419] **1072**

YOUTH HAPPINESS *See* YOUNG AND ALIVE **4395**

YOUTH ILLUSTRATOR, THE (US/1053-1815) [22469277] **5011**

YOUTH IN ACTION. BIBLE STUDY CARDS (US/1057-0209) [23915234] **5020**

YOUTH IN DISCOVERY. BIBLE STUDY CARDS (US/1057-0195) [23915156] **5020**

YOUTH IN NEBRASKA; A LABOR FORCE ANALYSIS (US) [04973685] **1720**

YOUTH IN SOCIETY *CEASED*. (UK/0307-1790) [01798566] **5314**

YOUTH LAW NEWS (US/0882-8520) [10525368] **3122**

YOUTH LEADER (SPRINGFIELD, MO.), THE (US/0190-4566) [04720120] 1072, **5011**

YOUTH LIBRARY REVIEW (UK/0269-4859) [I02694859] **3257**

YOUTH MARKETING REPORT (US) **938**

YOUTH MARKETS ALERT (US/1041-7516) [18839358] **938**

YOUTH MINISTRY QUARTERLY *CEASED*. (US/1047-1642) [20618680] 5070, **1072**

YOUTH MINISTRY QUARTERLY (US/1054-7126) [22949981] **5038**

YOUTH ORGANISATIONS OF GREAT BRITAIN (UK) [11396905] **5265**

YOUTH (PASADENA, CALIF.) (US/0279-6651) [07151271] 5011, **1072**

YOUTH POLICY (US) [08722516] **5314**

YOUTH PROGRAMS (WALTHAM, MASS.) (US) [09984059] 1072, **5314**

YOUTH-SERVING ORGANIZATIONS DIRECTORY (US/0196-9668) [05278798] **5314**

YOUTH SPORTS (US/0894-4377) [16074161] 1072, **4931**

YOUTH THEATRE JOURNAL (US/0892-9092) [15141409] 1072, **5372**

YOUTH UPDATE (US) **5038**

YOUTH UPDATE (REXDALE, ONT.) (CN/0830-9221) [14708417] 5314, **3179**

YOUTH'S LIVING IDEALS (US/0274-7707) [06575063] **1072**

YOUTH'S WEEKLY (HK) **1072**

YOUTHWALK (US) 5011, **1072**

YOUTHWORKER JOURNAL (US/0747-3486) [10762885] 1072, **5011**

YOUTHWORKER UPDATE (US/0889-5058) [13912862] **1720**

YOYUEN OYOBI KOON KAGAKU (JA/0916-1589) [I09161589] **996**

YPSILANTI PRESS (US) **5694**

YPSILON : REVISTA CENTROAMERICA DE PLANIFICACION (CR) [24992362] **5226**

YRL NEWS & VIEWS (CN/1188-0384) [25314018] **3257**

YSB (WASHINGTON, D.C.) (US/1056-6198) [23748171] **2275**

YU HANG HSUEH PAO (CC/1000-1328) [21601031] **40**

YU KUAN CHUNG-HUA MIN KUO TU SHU HSUAN MU (CH) [06993354] **427**

YU TIEN KAI FA LUN WEN CHI / CHUNG-KUO SHIH YU HSUEH HUI SHIH YU KUNG CHENG HSUEH HUI PIEN (CC) [09649969] **4283**

YU WEN CHIAO HSUEH TUNG HSUN / YUWEN JIAOXUE TONGXUN (CC) [11394944] **3334**

YU WEN CHIAO YEN / YUWEN JIAOYAN (CC) [10592000] **3334**

YU WEN CHIH SHIH TSUNG KAN / PEI-CHING SHIH YU YEN HSUEH HUI PIEN (CH) [08909509] **3334**

YU WEN HSUEH HSI (JEN MIN CHIAO YU CHU PAN SHE) (CH) [09237419] **3334**

YU WEN LUN TSUNG / SHANG-HAI SHIH YU WEN HSUEH HUI PIEN (CC) [08734336] **3334**

YU WEN YUEH KAN (CH) [10991927] **3456, 3334**

YU YEH NIEN CHIEN / CHUNG-HUA YEH TSA CHIH SHE PIEN (CH) [08324176] **2316**

YU YEH SHENG WU SHIH YEN SO, TAI-PEI See JINGJI-BU GUOLI TAIWAN DAXUE HEBANYUVE SHENGWU SHIYAN-SUO YANJIU BAOGAO **2306**

YU YEN CHIAO HSUEH YU YEN CHIU (CC) [06241372] **3334**

YU YEN YEN CHIU / HUA CHUNG KUNG HSUEH YUAN CHUNG-KUO YU YEN CHIU SO (CC) [08963964] **3334**

YU YEN YEN CHIU LUN TSUNG / NAN KAI TA HSUEH CHUNG WEN HSI YU YEN HSUEH CHIAO YEN SHIH PIEN (CC) [11591753] **3334**

YUAN I HSUEH PAO (CC/0372-784X) [09458566] **2434**

YUAN MING YUAN / CHUNG-KUO YUAN MING YUAN HSUEH HUI CHOU PEI WEI YUAN HUI (CH) [09331426] **2668**

YUANZIHE WULI *CEASED.* (CC/0253-3790) [08966903] **4451**

YUANZINENG KEXUE JISHU (CC/1000-6931) [15586537] 1961, **2159**

YUANZINENG NONGYE YINGYONG (CC/0253-3596) [08691117] 148, **1961**

YUASA AND HARA PATENT NEWS (JA) [03247584] **1310**

YUASA JIHO / YUASA DENCHI KABUSHIKI KAISHA (JA/0513-6342) [10452841] **2087**

YUBAL GOBES MEHQARIM SEL HA-MERKAZ LE-HEQER HA-MUSIQAH HA-YHUDIT (IS/0084-439X) [02191211] 5054, **4160**

YUBIN CHOKIN (JA) [01797319] **817**

YUBIN CHOKIN KEIEI SHIRYO (JA) [02246966] **817**

YUBIN CHOKIN TO NI KANSURU SERON CHOSA KEKKA HOKOKUSHO (JA) [04116632] **817**

YUBIN GAIMU NO KISO (JA) [01797377] **1148**

YUCAIPA VALLEY FAMILY FINDERS QUARTERLY See YVGS FAMILY FINDERS **2478**

YUCAIPA VALLEY FAMILY FINDERS QUARTERLY / YUCAIPA VALLEY GENEALOGICAL SOCIETY (US) [12852992] **2478**

YUEH CHI. YUEQI (CC) [11461171] **4160**

YUEH TAN. YUETAN (CC) [11479609] **4160**

YUGE SHOSEN KOTO SEMMON GAKKO See KIYO - YUGE SHOSEN KOTO SEMMON GAKKO **4178**

YUGNTRUF (US/0098-3640) [02241400] 5054, **3456**

YUGONG / YUKONG (KO) [10257814] **1632**

YUGOPAYOGI (II) [11349207] **3456**

YUGOSLAV ECONOMIC REVIEW *SUSPENDED.* (YU/0352-3543) [11143900] **1528**

YUGOSLAV INFORMATION BULLETIN OF THE LEAGUE OF COMMUNISTS OF YUGOSLAVIA & THE SOCIALIST ALLIANCE OF WORKING PEOPLE OF YUGOSLAVIA (YU) [01380564] **4548**

YUGOSLAV JOURNAL OF OPERATIONS RESEARCH (YU/0354-0243) [I03540243] **1632**

YUGOSLAV LAW (YU/0350-2252) [04291924] **3077**

YUGOSLAV REVIEW [A MONTHLY MAGAZINE OF THE SERBS, CROATS AND SLOVENES], THE (YU/0512-9907) [01443661] **2525**

YUGOSLAV SERBO-CROATIAN--ENGLISH CONTRASTIVE PROJECT See PRILOZI I GRAA **3311**

YUGOSLAV SURVEY (YU/0044-1341) [01770396] **2716**

YUGOSLAV TOURIST NEWS AND COMMERCIAL INFORMATION (YU) [05381244] **5500**

YUGOSLAVIA See SLUZBENI LIST SAVEZNE REPUBLIKE JUGOSLAVIJE **3055**

YUGOSLAVIA ECHO : ECONOMY, FINANCE, TRADE (XV) [06694116] **1528**

YUGOSLAVIA EXPORT (CI/0044-1368) [02269803] **858**

YUGOSLAVIA; HOTEL AND TOURIST DIRECTORY (YU) [02246620] **2810**

YUGOSLAVIA. HOTELSKE CENE (YU) [11105890] **2810**

YUGOSLAVIA. LAWS, ETC See SLUZBENI LIST SAVEZNE REPUBLIKE JUGOSLAVIJE **3055**

YUGOSLAVIA. SAVEZNI ZAVOD ZA STATISTIKU See UNUTRASNJA TRGOVINA **734**

YUGOSLAVIA. SAVEZNI ZAVOD ZA STATISTIKU See SAOBRACAJNE NEZGODE NA PUTEVIMA **5402**

YUGOSLAVIA (SYRACUSE, N.Y.) See UKRAINE (SYRACUSE, N.Y.) **1587**

YUGOSLAVIA TRAVEL AGENTS' MANUAL / ASSOCIATION OF YUGOSLAV (YU) [11774885] **5500**

YUKAGAKU (JA/0513-398X) [08947212] **1031**

YUKI GOSEI KAGAKU KYOKAI See YUKI GOSEI KAGAKU KYOKAISHI **1049**

YUKI GOSEI KAGAKU KYOKAISHI (JA/0037-9980) [01434548] **1049**

YUKIJIRUSHI NYUGYO KENKYUJO HOKOKU (JA/0082-4763) [18170640] **199**

YUKON DATA BOOK (CN/0829-0652) [18452079] **2550**

YUKON KOMIX (CN/0229-0383) [08023718] **4868**

YUKON NEWS (1972) (CN/0318-1952) [02441721] **5798**

YUKON TERRITORY See STATUTES OF THE YUKON TERRITORY **3059**

YUKON TERRITORY. BUDGET BUREAU See MAIN ESTIMATES - BUDGET BUREAU **4736**

YUKRANDA (II) [01784259] **5041**

YUMA DAILY SUN, THE (US/1048-2237) [10668796] **5712**

YUMA PIONEER, THE (US) [19250815] **5644**

YUN CHOU HSUEH TSA CHIH (CC) [10013976] **3541**

YUNHWAL KWALLI (KO) [10225426] **2132**

YUNNAN ZHIWU YANJIU (CC/0253-2700) [08115877] **530**

YUNYU TOKEI HIMMOKU HYO (JA) [03954420] 858, **735**

YUSEI GYOSEI ROPPO (JA) [18358174] **1148**

YUSEI SHIZAI (JA) [01797378] **1148**

YUSHI (JA) [10423446] **1031**

YUSHU NENKAN (JA) [01797255] **2788**

YUSHUTSU SENI TOKEI KYOKAI (JAPAN) See TEXTILE EXPORTS OF JAPAN : COUNTRY BY COMMODITY **5357**

YUSHUTSU TOKEI HIMMOKU HYO. / EXPORT STATISTICAL SCHEDULE: JAPAN (JA) [03354870] 858, **735**

YUSHUTSUNYU BUKKA SHISU NEMPO (JA) [01796939] **1528**

YUSHUTSUNYU TOKEI HIMMOKU HYO (JA) [01797317] **858**

YUVA AVAJA (NP) [01790470] **2510**

YUVA BHARATI (II) [01790603] **1072**

YUVA PRAGATI (II) [02240232] **2287**

YUVAKA (II) [01800039] **2510**

YUVAKA (NP) [02239610] **2287**

YUWON (KO) [10257845] **1632**

●YVGS FAMILY FINDERS (US/1069-9333) [28187101] **2478**

YWN (IS/0021-3306) [02262838] **4365**

Z BADAN KLASY ROBOTNICZEJ I INTELIGENCJI (PL/0084-4403) [01470756] **1720**

Z BIBLIA NA CO DZIEN (PL) [05122625] **5011**

Z DZIEJOW FORM ARTYSTYCZNYCH W LITERATURZE POLSKIEJ (PL/0084-4411) [03762201] **3456**

Z DZIEJOW MUZYKI POLSKIEJ (PL) [04314772] **4160**

Z KNIHOVNICKE PRAXE (XR) [19366020] **3257**

Z MAGAZINE (ZA) [01466045] **2644**

Z MAGAZINE (BOSTON, MASS.) (US/1056-5507) [20864508] **4501**

Z MISCELLANEOUS (US/0892-9696) [15305144] 369, **3456**

Z (OSLO, NORWAY) (NO/0800-1464) [11608417] **4080**

Z OTCHANI WIEKOW (PL/0044-1481) [02208400] **285**

●Z PAPERS (US/1060-2070) [24886387] **4548**

Z POLA WALKI (PL/0044-149X) [01473629] **4548**

Z PROBLEMATYKI PRAWA PRACY I POLITYKI SOCJALNEJ / UNIWERSYTET SLASKI (PL) [07384309] **3155**

Z-REPORT (AU) **817**

ZA IGURU (JA) [10488898] **889**

ZA NETWORK NEWS REPORTS (US/0748-9560) [11036344] **1143**

ZA RIDNU CERKVU (CN/0318-1642) [02578852] **5038**

ZA RUBEZHOM (RU) [06204056] **4539**

ZA RULEM (RU/0321-4249) [24614575] **5458**

●ZA ZAGOLOVKAMI (US/1060-6092) [25052390] 725, **3077**

ZABAN O ADAB : BIHAR URDU AKADMI KA SIHMAHI JARIDAH (II) [11407342] **3456**

ZABS REVIEW : A PUBLICATION OF THE ZAMBIA BUREAU OF STANDARDS (ZA) [22361482] **4033**

ZAC, ZEITSCHRIFT FUER ANTIMIKROBIELLE, ANTINEOPLASTISCHE CHEMOTHERAPIE (GW/0724-9004) [11876311] 494, **3652**

ZACCHIA (IT/0044-1570) [09531223] **3652**

ZACKS PROFIT GUIDE (US) **920**

ZAGADNIENIA BIOFIZYKI WSPOCZESNEJ (PL/0137-9690) [03029169] **496**

ZAGADNIENIA EKONOMIKI ROLNEJ (PL/0044-1600) [02848327] **148**

ZAGADNIENIA EKSPLOATACJI MASZYN (PL/0137-5474) [01789743] **2132**

ZAGADNIENIA NAUKOZNAWSTWA (PL/0044-1619) [02199661] **5172**

ZAGADNIENIA RODZAJOW LITERACKICH (PL/0084-4446) [01639683] **3456**

ZAGADNIENIA TRANSPORTU (PL) [02243123] **5400**

ZAGADNIENIA WYCHOWAWCZE A ZDROWIE PSYCHICZNE (PL/0324-8526) [02243122] 3937, **3912**

ZAGAT LOS ANGELES, SO. CALIFORNIA RESTAURANT SURVEY (US/1062-2403) [23742232] **5073**

ZAGAT UNITED STATES TRAVEL SURVEY. CENTRAL STATES (US/1060-720X) [25051768] 5500, **2810**

ZAGAT UNITED STATES TRAVEL SURVEY. WESTERN STATES (US/1060-7196) [23245112] **2810**

ZAGREB. UNIVERZITET. FAKULTET STROJARSTVA I BRODOGRADNJE See ZBORNIK RADOVA **2132**

ZAGREB. UNIVERZITET. PRAVNI FAKULTET See ZBORNIK PRAVNOG FAKULTETA U ZAGREBU **3077**

ZAHLEN AUS DER DEUTSCHEN SCHWEINEPRODUKTION (GW) [12041529] **224**

ZAHLEN AUS OESTERREICHS LAND- UND FORSTWIRTSCHAFT (AU) [01789856] **2398**

ZAHLEN ZUR KOHLENWIRTSCHAFT (GW/0723-0036) [07468047] **1632**

ZAHLENSPIEGEL (GW) [05432180] **5172**

ZAHLENSPIEGEL (GW) [05234771] **5347**

ZAHLENWERTE UND FUNKTIONEN AUS NATURWISSENSCHAFTEN UND TECHNIK GRUPPE 2. ATOM- UND MOLEKULARPHYSIK (GW/0075-7918) [06107734] **4425**

ZAHLENWERTE UND FUNKTIONEN AUS NATURWISSENSCHAFTEN UND TECHNIK GRUPPE 3. KRISTALL- UND FESTKORPERPHYSIK (GW/0075-787X) [06107777] **4425**

ZAHLENWERTE UND FUNKTIONEN AUS NATURWISSENSCHAFTEN UND TECHNIK GRUPPE 6. ASTRONOMIE, ASTROPHYSIK UND WELTRAUMFORSCHUNG (GW/0075-7896) [06107526] **401**

ZAHLENWERTE UND FUNKTIONEN AUS NATURWISSENSCHAFTEN UND TECHNIK, NEUE SERIE (GW) [06290346] **4425**

Alphabetical Title Index — ZAVERENA

ZAHLENWERTE UND FUNKTIONEN AUS NATURWISSENSCHAFTEN UND TECHNIK NEUE SERIE, GRUPPE VII, BIOPHYSIK (GW) [20087739] **4425**

ZAHLUNGSBILANZ DER SCHWEIZ IM JAHRE ... / KOMMISSION FUER KONJUNKTURFRAGEN, DIE (SZ) [18733840] **4501**

ZAHNAERZTLICHE MITTEILUNGEN (GW/0044-1643) [07579408] **1337**

ZAHNARTZLICHER GESUNDHEITSDIENST (GW/0340-5478) [09109545] **1337**

ZAHNARZT JOURNAL **CEASED.** (GW/0344-3736) [09034180] **1337**

ZAHNARZTEBLATT BADEN-WURTTEMBERG (GW/0340-3017) [05269086] **1337**

ZAHNTECHNIK (SZ) **1337**

ZAHRANICNI OBCHOD (XR) [03760724] **858**

ZAHRAT AL-KHALIJ (TS) [07511781] **2510**

ZAIKAI (JA) [08174385] **889**

ZAIKAI KANSOKU. FINANCIAL WORLD OBSERVING (JA) **725**

ZAIKAI NAGOYA (JA) [01799670] **817, 890**

ZAIKEN HOKOKU (JA/0916-4456) [24252778] **5172**

ZAINICHI CHOSENJIN SHI KENKYU (JA) [04187802] **2668**

ZAINICHI GAISHI KIGYO YORAN / NIHON KOGYO SHINBUN HENSHUKYOKU HEN (JA) [12075161] **725**

ZAIRE *See* JOURNAL OFFICIEL **2990**

ZAIRE-AFRIQUE (CG/0251-298X) [01476849] **2644**

ZAIRE BUSINESS (CG/0377-810X) [01794403] **1589**

ZAIRE. CONSEIL LEGISLATIF NATIONAL *See* COMPTE RENDU ANALYTIQUE - REPUBLIQUE DU ZAIRE, CONSEIL LEGISLATIF NATIONAL **4639**

ZAIRE : ENERGIEWIRTSCHAFT (GW) [05691264] **1961**

ZAIRE : LUFTVERKEHR (GW) [04383402] **40**

ZAIRE : WIRTSCHAFTLICHE ENTWICKLUNG (GW) [05140917] **1589**

ZAIRYO (JA/0514-5163) [10118957] **2001**

ZAIRYO GIJUTSU NO GENJO TO TEMBO; SOGO REBYU (JA) [02246418] **2002**

ZAIRYO KAGAKU (JA/0388-3930) [10418753] **5172**

ZAIRYO TO KANKYO (JA/0917-0480) [23282203] **2002**

ZAIRYO TO PUROSESU (JA/0914-6628) [l09146628] **2002**

ZAISEI SHOROPPO (JA) [03083787] **4759**

ZAISEI TO JICHI (JA) [04443561] **4759**

ZAJEDNICA KULTURE (YU) [03394118] **2716**

ZAKBOEK ONDERWIJSSTATISTIEKEN / HOOFDAFDELING STATISTIEKEN VAN ONDERWIJS EN WETENSCHAPPEN (NE) [08339666] 1792, **1798**

ZAKON : ZHURNAL DLIA DELOVYKH LIUDEI (RU/0869-4400) [27153655] 920, **3077**

● ZAKONNOST (RU) [25919595] 4695, **3179**

ZAKONOMERNOSTI RAZMESENIA POLEZNYH ISKOPAEMYH (RU/0514-1958) [02270775] 2153, **1445**

● ZALE CORPORATION BANKRUPTCY NEWS (US/1061-3161) [25249995] **817**

ZAMBEZIA (RH/0379-0622) [01785804] **5226**

ZAMBIA. AUDITOR-GENERAL *See* REPORT OF THE AUDITOR-GENERAL FOR ... ON THE ACCOUNTS OF PARASTATAL BODIES **4680**

ZAMBIA. CABINET OFFICE. MANAGEMENT SERVICES SECTION *See* ANNUAL REPORT OF THE MANAGEMENT SERVICES SECTION FOR THE YEARS ... **4628**

ZAMBIA. CENTRAL STATISTICAL OFFICE *See* MONTHLY DIGEST OF STATISTICS **5333**

ZAMBIA. CENTRAL STATISTICAL OFFICE *See* ZAMBIA IN FIGURES **5347**

ZAMBIA DAILY MAIL MICROFORM (ZA) [11674078] **5813**

ZAMBIA. DEPT. OF AGRICULTURE *See* "HOW TO GROW" SERIES **93**

ZAMBIA. DEPT. OF MARKETING AND COOPERATIVES *See* ANNUAL REPORT - REPUBLIC OF ZAMBIA, MINISTRY OF RURAL DEVELOPMENT, DEPARTMENT OF MARKETING AND COOPERATIVES **1598**

ZAMBIA. DEPT. OF TOWN AND COUNTRY PLANNING *See* ANNUAL REPORT OF THE DEPARTMENT OF TOWN AND COUNTRY PLANNING **2814**

ZAMBIA DIRECTORY, THE (ZA) [05064210] **2501**

ZAMBIA ENTERPRISE (ZA) [08066519] **1632**

ZAMBIA. GEOLOGICAL SURVEY DEPT *See* ANNUAL REPORT OF THE GEOLOGICAL SURVEY DEPARTMENT (LUSAKA) **1365**

ZAMBIA IN FIGURES (ZA) [06956436] **5347**

ZAMBIA INDUSTRIAL CASES REPORTS / REPUBLIC OF ZAMBIA, MINISTRY OF LABOUR AND SOCIAL SERVICES, INDUSTRIAL RELATIONS COURT, THE (ZA) [11446298] **3155**

ZAMBIA. INDUSTRIAL RELATIONS COURT *See* ZAMBIA INDUSTRIAL CASES REPORTS / REPUBLIC OF ZAMBIA, MINISTRY OF LABOUR AND SOCIAL SERVICES, INDUSTRIAL RELATIONS COURT, THE **3155**

ZAMBIA. INDUSTRIAL RELATIONS COURT *See* ANNUAL REPORTS FOR THE YEARS ... / REPUBLIC OF ZAMBIA, MINISTRY OF LABOUR AND SOCIAL SERVICES, INDUSTRIAL RELATIONS COURT **3144**

ZAMBIA JOURNAL OF SCIENCE AND TECHNOLOGY (ZA/0378-8857) [02641270] **5172**

ZAMBIA LAW JOURNAL (ZA) [01770409] **3077**

ZAMBIA LAW REPORTS (ZA) [04227625] **3077**

ZAMBIA LIBRARY ASSOCIATION *See* JOURNAL - ZAMBIA LIBRARY ASSOCIATION **3221**

ZAMBIA MINING YEAR BOOK (ZA) [01798384] **2153**

ZAMBIA. MINISTRY OF EDUCATION *See* STATISTICAL PROFILE OF ZAMBIAN EDUCATION **1797**

ZAMBIA. MINISTRY OF HOME AFFAIRS *See* ANNUAL REPORT FOR THE YEAR ... / REPUBLIC OF ZAMBIA, MINISTRY OF HOME AFFAIRS **4627**

ZAMBIA. MINISTRY OF LEGAL AFFAIRS *See* ANNUAL REPORT FOR THE YEARS ... / REPUBLIC OF ZAMBIA, MINISTRY OF LEGAL AFFAIRS **4627**

ZAMBIA. MINISTRY OF RURAL DEVELOPMENT. STATISTICS SECTION *See* QUARTERLY AGRICULTURAL STATISTICAL BULLETIN **156**

ZAMBIA. MINISTRY OF RURAL DEVELOPMENT. STATISTICS SECTION. STATISTICAL BULLETIN *See* QUARTERLY AGRICULTURAL STATISTICAL BULLETIN **156**

ZAMBIA MUSEUMS JOURNAL (ZA) [05284273] **4097**

ZAMBIA. NATIONAL ASSEMBLY. COMMITTEE ON FOREIGN AFFAIRS *See* REPORT OF THE COMMITTEE ON FOREIGN AFFAIRS FOR THE ... SESSION OF THE ... NATIONAL ASSEMBLY APPOINTED ON ... / REPUBLIC OF ZAMBIA **4533**

ZAMBIA. NATIONAL ASSEMBLY. COMMITTEE ON GOVERNMENT ASSURANCES *See* REPORT OF THE COMMITTEE ON GOVERNMENT ASSURANCES FOR THE ... SESSION OF THE ... NATIONAL ASSEMBLY, APPOINTED ON ... / REPUBLIC OF ZAMBIA **4681**

ZAMBIA. NATIONAL COMMISSION FOR DEVELOPMENT PLANNING *See* ECONOMIC REVIEW AND ANNUAL PLAN **1484**

ZAMBIA. NATIONAL PARKS AND WILDLIFE SERVICE *See* ANNUAL REPORT - NATIONAL PARKS AND WILDLIFE SERVICE (ZAMBIA) **2186**

ZAMBIA NURSE (KITWE, ZAMBIA : 1978) (ZA/0044-1740) [09639553] **3871**

ZAMBIA. OFFICE OF THE PRIME MINISTER *See* LUSAKA PROVINCE ANNUAL REPORT FOR THE YEAR ... / REPUBLIC OF ZAMBIA, OFFICE OF THE PRIME MINISTER **4663**

ZAMBIA. PROVINCIAL AND LOCAL GOVERNMENT ADMINISTRATION DIVISION. EASTERN PROVINCE *See* ANNUAL REPORT / REPUBLIC OF ZAMBIA, OFFICE OF THE PRIME MINISTER, PROVINCIAL AND LOCAL GOVERNMENT ADMINISTRATION DIVISION, EASTERN PROVINCE **4629**

ZAMBIA. PUBLIC ACCOUNTS COMMITTEE *See* REPORT OF THE PUBLIC ACCOUNTS COMMITTEE **4746**

ZAMBIA. WORKMEN'S COMPENSATION FUND CONTROL BOARD *See* COMPENSATION MIRROR **1660**

ZAMBIAN GEOGRAPHICAL JOURNAL (ZA) [03738346] **2579**

ZAMBIAN INDUSTRIAL DIRECTORY (ZA) [01791236] **1632**

ZAMBIAN ORNITHOLOGICAL SOCIETY *See* BULLETIN - ZAMBIAN ORNITHOLOGICAL SOCIETY **5616**

ZAMBIAN ORNITHOLOGICAL SOCIETY NEWSLETTER (ZA/0378-4533) [I03784533] **5621**

ZAMLUNGEN (US) [07466094] **3456**

ZANCO : THE SCIENTIFIC JOURNAL OF SALAHADDIN UNIVERSITY (IQ) [20053635] **5172**

ZANY WORD SEARCH & FIND PUZZLES (US/0732-5649) [08413659] **4868**

ZANZIBAR NEWSLETTER (UK) [21916377] **4501**

ZANZIBAR. WIZARA YA ELIMU *See* RIPOTI YA UTEKELEZAJI WA MPANGO WA MAENDELEO / SERIKALI YA MAPINDUZI YA ZANZIBAR, WIZARA YA ELIMU **1781**

ZANZIBAR. WIZARA YA HABARI, UTAMADUNI, NA MICHEZO *See* RIPOTI YA UTEKELEZAJI WA MPANGO WA MAENDELEO / SERIKALI YA MAPINDUZI YA ZANZIBAR, WIZARA YA HABARI, UTAMADUNI, NA MICHEZO **4684**

ZAPAD (CN/0226-3068) [06461270] **2275**

● ZAPAD TODAY (CN) [26668906] **2275**

ZAPADNE KARPATY. MINERALOGIA, PETROGRAFIA, GEOCHEMIA, METALOGENEZA (XO/0139-8946) [04448999] **1401**

ZAPADNE KARPATY. SERIA GEOLOGIA (XO/0139-8288) [05508087] **1401**

ZAPADNE KARPATY. SERIA HYDROGEOLOGIA A INZINIERSKA GEOLOGIA (XO/0139-7583) [02821996] **1419**

ZAPISKI HISTORYCZNE (PL/0044-1791) [02098337] **2716**

ZAPISKI RUSSKOI AKADEMICHESKOI GRUPPY V SSHA (US) [10687031] **1854**

● ZAPISKI VSEROSSIISKOGO MINERALOGICHESKOGO OBSHCHESTVA / ROSSIISKAIA AKADEMIIA NAUK (RU/0869-6055) [26751281] **1445**

ZAPISKI VSESOIUZNOGO MINERALOGICHESKOGO OBSHCHESTVA (RU/0042-9260) [01769310] **1445**

ZAPISKI ZAPADNO-SIBIRSKOGO OTDELENIIA (RU) [04058566] **1445**

ZAPISNAIA KNIZHKA PARTINOGO AKTIVISTA *See* KNIZHKA PARTIINOGO AKTIVISTA **4660**

ZAPISY BELARUSKAHA INSTYTUTU NAVUKI I MASTATSVA (US/0510-3746) [02269520] **2716**

ZAPOSLENI PO OBCINAH (XV) [01785917] **1720**

ZAPOSLENO OSOBLJE (YU) [01785883] **1720**

ZAPOSLENO OSOBLJE I NETO LICNI DOHOCI PO GRUPAMA DELATNOSTI (YU) [01784852] **1720**

ZAPOVEDNIKI BELORUSSII / GOSUDARSTVENNOE ZAPOVEDNO-OKHOTNICHE KHOZIAISTVO BELOVEZHSKAIA PUSHCHA (BW/0136-7595) [08542452] **4174**

ZARUBEZHNOE VOENNOE OBOZRENIE (RU) [07566456] **4061**

ZARUBEZHNYE ZAPISKI (RU/0514-2210) [01470125] **2525**

ZARUBEZHNYI VOSTOK (RU) [21072321] **3456**

● ZARUBEZNAA PERIODICESKAA PECAT NA RUSSKOM AZYKE (US/1066-4858) [26961992] **2525**

ZASCITA METALLOV (RU/0044-1856) [01477508] **4024**

ZASCITA RASTENIJ (RU/0044-1864) [10433619] **191**

ZASHCHITA RASTENII (RU/0044-1864) [01770412] 4248, **530**

ZASHCHITNYE POKRYTIIA NA METALLAKH / AKADEMIIA NAUK UKRAINSKOI SSR, INSTITUT PROBLEM MATERIALOVEDENIIA (UN/0514-5864) [27366619] **4024**

ZASSHI KIJI SAKUIN, JINBUN SHAKAI HEN (JA) [01799726] **2857**

ZASSHI KIJI SAKUIN. JINBUN SHAKAI HEN (CUMULATIVE EDITION) (JA) [10470475] **2857**

ZASSHI KIJI SAKUIN. KAGAKU GIJUTSU HEN (JA) [01799740] **5176**

ZASSHI SHINBUN SOKATAROGU. PERIODICALS IN PRINT (JA) [04864337] **5805**

ZASSO KENKYU (JA/0372-798X) [10476073] **148**

ZASTITA BILJA (YU/0514-5872) [02830203] **530**

ZASTOSOWANIA MATEMATYKI (PL/0044-1899) [01466221] **3541**

ZAVALA COUNTY SENTINEL (LA PRYOR, TEX. : 1913) (US) [14109098] **5756**

ZAVERENA SPRAVA ZO SOCIOLOGICKEHO PRIESKUMU UPLATNENIA ABSOLVENTOV POLNOHOSPODARSKYCH SMEROV STUDIA V PRAXI (BL) [08370317] **148**

ZAVOD

ZAVOD SR SLOVENIJE ZA STATISTIKO
See KULTURNO-UMETNISKA IN PROSVETNA DEJAVNOST **5330**

ZAVOD SR SLOVENIJE ZA STATISTIKO
See OSNOVNE IN SREDNJE SOLE **1771**

ZAVOD SR SLOVENIJE ZA STATISTIKO
See ZAPOSLENI PO OBCINAH **1720**

ZAVOD SR SLOVENIJE ZA STATISTIKO
See OSNOVNE SOLE PO KRAJEVNIH SKUPNOSTIH **1771**

ZAVOD SR SLOVENIJE ZA STATISTIKO
See TELESNA VZGOJA, SPORT IN SPORTNA REKREACIJA **1859**

ZAVOD SR SLOVENIJE ZA STATISTIKO
See LETNI PREGLED PROMETA IN ZVEZ **5385**

ZAVOD SR SLOVENIJE ZA STATISTIKO
See DELAVCI V ZDRUZENEM DELU IN SAMOSTOJNEM OSEBNEM DELU, PRIPRAVNIKI TER FLUKTUACIJA DELAVCEV **1662**

ZAVOD SR SLOVENIJE ZA STATISTIKO
See DESEZONIRANE CASOVNE VRSTE SR SLOVENIJE **1662**

ZAVOD SR SLOVENIJE ZA STATISTIKO
See VOLITVE **4694**

ZAVOD SR SLOVENIJE ZA STATISTIKO
See DRUZBENA PREHRANA **2334**

ZAVODSKAJA LABORATORIJA (RU/0321-4265) [02407625] **1020**

ZB, ZEIT IM BILD (SZ) [06316998] **2525**

ZB. ZIERPFLANZENBAU (GW/0342-6556) [I03426556] **2434**

ZBIERKA ZAKONOV, CESKOSLOVENSKA SOCIALISTICKA REPUBLIKA (XR) [07116640] **4549**

ZBIERKA ZAKONOV REPUBLIKY CESKOSLOVENSKEJ See ZBIERKA ZAKONOV, CESKOSLOVENSKA SOCIALISTICKA REPUBLIKA **4549**

ZBIRNYK PRATS ... NAUKOVYKH SHEVCHENKIVSKIKH KONFERENTSII / AKADEMIIA NAUK UKRAINSSKOI RSR, INSTYTUT LITERATURY IM. T.H. SHEVCHENKA (UN) [04736956] **3456**

ZBLIZENIA KOSZALIN (PL/0138-0745) [I01380745] **2525**

ZBORNIK - ARHEOLOSKI MUZEJ NA MAKEDONIJA. RECUEIL DES TRAVAUX (XN/0560-222X) [04816838] **286**

ZBORNIK AVSTRALSKIH SLOVENCEV (AT) [18286731] **2275**

ZBORNIK FILOZOFICKEJ FAKULTY. PHILOSOPHICA (XO) [08512886] **4365**

ZBORNIK FILOZOFICKEJ FAKULTY UNIVERZITY KOMENSKEHO. ETHNOLOGIA SLAVICA (XO/0083-4106) [02302149] **248**

ZBORNIK FILOZOFSKE FAKULTETE / UNIVERZA V LJUBLJANI, FILOZOFSKA FAKULTETA (XV/0350-848X) [08187953] **3456**

ZBORNIK GOZDARSTVA IN LESARSTVA (XV) [04849198] **2398**

ZBORNIK ISTORIJE KNJIZEVNOSTI (YU/0084-5183) [02514783] **3456**

ZBORNIK MATICE SRPSKE ZA DRUSTVENE NAUKE (YU) [12227075] **5226**

ZBORNIK MATICE SRPSKE ZA FILOLOGIJU I LINGVISTIKU / MATICA SRPSKA, ODELJENJE ZA KNJIZEVNOST I JEZIK (YU/0514-6143) [12764669] **3335**

ZBORNIK MATICE SRPSKE ZA ISTORIJU / MATICA SRPSKA, ODELJENJE ZA DRUSTVENE NAUKE (YU/0352-5716) [12771899] **2633**

ZBORNIK MATICE SRPSKE ZA LIKOVNE UMETNOSTI / MATICA SRPSKA, ODELJENJE ZA LIKOVNE UMETNOSTI (YU/0352-6844) [21057533] **369**

ZBORNIK MATICE SRPSKE ZA PRIRODNE NAUKE (XN/0352-4906) [I03524906] **5172**

ZBORNIK MATICE SRPSKE ZA SLAVISTIKU / MATICA SRPSKA, ODELJENJE ZA KNJIZEVNOST I JEZIK (YU/0350-0470) [11692122] **3335**

ZBORNIK NARODNOG MUZEJA U BEOGRADU (YU/0522-8352) [12546411] **286**

ZBORNIK PRAC USTAVU EXPERIMENTALNEJ FARMAKOLOGIE SAV (CZ/0231-7834) [10043213] **4333**

ZBORNIK PRAVNOG FAKULTETA U ZAGREBU (CI) [01770401] **3077**

ZBORNIK RADOVA (YU) [05514687] **3541**

ZBORNIK RADOVA (CI) [05352136] **2132**

ZBORNIK RADOVA ETNOGRAFSKOG INSTITUTA (YU) [02243419] **248**

ZBORNIK RADOVA O ENTOMOFAUNI SR SRBIJE (YU) [06970638] **5614**

ZBORNIK RADOVA - POLJOPRIVREDNI FAKULTET. INSTITUT ZA STOCARSTVO, NOVI SAD (YU/0350-8005) [I03508005] **224**

ZBORNIK RADOVA POLJOPRIVREDNOG FAKULTETA (YU/0522-8530) [01519460] **1854**

ZBORNIK RADOVA PRIRODNO-MATEMATICKOG FAKULTETA. SERIJA ZA BIOLOGIJU (YU/0352-1788) [11070667] **3652**, **476**

ZBORNIK RADOVA PRIRODNO-MATEMATICKOG FAKULTETA. SERIJA ZA FIZIKU (YU/0352-0889) [11071163] **4425**

ZBORNIK RADOVA VIZANTOLOSKOG INSTITUTA (YU/0584-9888) [01766386] **1081**, **2634**

ZBORNIK SLOVENSKEHO BANSKEHO MUZEA (XO) [09850760] **2153**

ZBORNIK SLOVENSKEHO NARODNEHO MUZEA (XO/0524-2223) [02788879] **4097**

ZBORNIK SLOVENSKEHO NARODNEHO MUZEA. HISTORIA. ANNALES MUSEI NATIONALIS SLOVACI (XO/0139-5378) [02240424] **2716**

ZBORNIK UNIVERZITY KOMENSKEHO. HISTORICA (XO) [17736131] **2716**

ZBORNIK VEDECKYCH PRAC DREVARSKEJ FAKULTY VYSOKEJ SKOLY LESNICKEJ A DREVARSKEJ VO ZVOLENE (XO) [01779173] **2398**

ZBORNIK VEDECKYCH PRAC ELEKTROTECHNICKEJ FAKULTY SVST BRATISLAVA (XO) [08924497] **2087**

ZBORNIK VEDECKYCH PRAC VYSOKEJ SKOLY TECHNICKEJ V KOSICIACH (XO/0371-4616) [07949223] **5172**

ZBORNIK VETERINARSKE FAKULTETE, UNIVERZA LJUBLJANA (XV/0353-8044) [25108234] **5527**

ZBORNIK VYCHODOSLOVENSKEHO MUZEA V KOSICIACH. PIRIODNE VEDY (XO) [08949527] **4174**

ZBORNIK ZA JEZIK I KNJIZEVNOST (YU) [02244367] **3335**

ZBORNIK ZA UMETNOSTNO ZGODOVINO. ARCHIVES D'HISTOIRE DE L'ART (XV/0351-224X) [02323978] **369**, **2716**

ZBORNIK ZASTITE SPOMENIKA KULTURE. RECUEIL DES TRAVAUX SUR LA PROTECTION DES MONUMENTS HISTORIQUES (YU/0514-616X) [01477656] **2716**, **369**

ZBORNIK ZAVODA ZA POVIJESNE ZNANOSTI ISTRAZIVACKOG CENTRA JUGOSLAVENSKE AKADEMIJE ZNANOSTI I UMJETNOSTI (CI/0351-2681) [08383898] **2716**

ZCLA JOURNAL (US/0360-991X) [02155734] **5022**

ZDB FORDERUNGEN, ZIELVORSTELLUNGEN FUER DIE ... LEGISLATURPERIODE DES DEUTSCHEN BUNDESTAGES (GW/0342-7943) [11881207] **631**, **1720**

● ZDES I TEPER (RU/0131-3266) [26332134] **3456**

ZDM. ZENTRALBLATT FUER DIDAKTIK DER MATHEMATIK (GW) [07785322] **3541**

ZDOROVE (RU/0044-1945) [06269567] **3652**

ZDRAVOOHRANENIE (KISINEV) (MV/0513-8728) [07588323] **4808**

ZDRAVOOHRANENIE TADZIKISTANA (TA/0514-2415) [08800063] **3652**

ZDRAVOOKHRANENIE BELORUSSII (BW/0044-1961) [10124270] **3652**

ZDRAVOOKHRANENIE KAZAKHSTANA (KZ/0372-8277) [08804316] **4808**

ZDRAVOOKHRANENIE KYRGYZSTANA / MINISTERSTVO ZDRAVOOKHRANENIIA RESPUBLIKI KYRGYZSTAN (KG) [25861795] **4809**

ZDRAVOOKHRANENIE ROSSIJSKOJ FEDERACII (RU/0044-197X) [02235221] **4809**

ZDRAVOOKHRANENIE TURKMENISTANA / ORGAN MINISTERSTVA ZDRAVOOKHRANENIIA TSSR (TK/0513-8736) [08523085] **4809**

ZDRAVOTNICKE AKTUALITY (XR) **4809**

ZDRAVSTVENI VESTNIK (XV/0350-0063) [I03500063] **3652**

ZDROWIE (PL) [16185254] **4809**

ZDROWIE PUBLICZNE (PL/0044-2011) [05518520] **4809**

ZDRUZENO PREDUZECE MASINOGRADNJA See MAG **2121**

ZEAL (US/0514-2482) [04053256] **5011**

ZEALAND. PROVINCIALE WATERSTAATSDIENST See VERSLAG ONDERZOEK KWALITEIT OPPERVLAKTEWATER IN ZEELAND **2245**

● ZEBRA MUSSEL WATCH (CN/1188-4584) [26758293] **5600**

ZED. ZIMBABWE ENVIRONMENT & DESIGN (RH/1016-152X) [10113908] **311**

ZEEVAARTVERWANTE BEDRIJVEN / CENTRAAL BUREAU VOOR DE STATISTIEK, HOOFDAFDELING STATISTIEKEN VAN VERKEER EN VERVOER (NE/0168-3187) [12003997] **5458**

ZEGGENSCHAP (NE) **4695**

ZEICHEN DER ZEIT (BERLIN, GERMANY) (GW/0044-2038) [07449516] **5011**

ZEIHOGAKU (JA/0494-8262) [19893140] **4759**

ZEIMU TOKEI KARA MITA MINKAN KYUYO NO JITTAI (JA) [02453546] **1720**

ZEIMU TOKEISHO See FUKUOKA KOKUZEIKYOKU TOKEISHO **4727**

ZEISS INFORMATION (ENGLISH ED.) See ZEISS INFORMATION WITH JENA REVIEW **4442**

● ZEISS INFORMATION WITH JENA REVIEW (GW/0941-7567) [27941631] **4442**

ZEIT, DIE (CN) [01643321] **5798**

ZEITGEMASSE SCHAFHALTUNG : MIT EINEM KAPITEL UBER MILCHSCHAFHALTUNG (AU) [19055683] **199**

ZEITGENOSSISCHES MUSIKSCHAFFEN IN DER DEUTSCHEN DEMOKRATISCHEN REPUBLIK (GW/0232-9387) [10548866] **4160**

ZEITGESCHICHTE (AU/0256-5250) [01791153] **2634**

ZEITSCHRIFT DER ARBEITSGEMEINSCHAFT OSTERREICHISCHER ENTOMOLOGEN (GW) [01494804] **5600**

ZEITSCHRIFT DER DEUTSCHEN GEMMOLOGISCHEN GESELLSCHAFT (GW) [04656341] **2915**

ZEITSCHRIFT DER DEUTSCHEN GEOLOGISCHEN GESELLSCHAFT (GW/0012-0189) [01566378] **1401**

ZEITSCHRIFT DER DEUTSCHEN MORGENLANDISCHEN GESELLSCHAFT (GW/0341-0137) [01566426] **3456**, **3335**

ZEITSCHRIFT DER SAVIGNY-STIFTUNG FUER RECHTSGESCHICHTE. GERMANISTISCHE ABTEILUNG (GW/0323-4045) [02210922] **3077**

ZEITSCHRIFT DER SAVIGNY-STIFTUNG FUER RECHTSGESCHICHTE. KANONISTISCHE ABTEILUNG (GW/0323-4142) [02210909] **3077**

ZEITSCHRIFT DER SAVIGNY-STIFTUNG FUER RECHTSGESCHICHTE. ROMANISTISCHE ABTEILUNG (AU/0323-4096) [I03234096] **3456**

ZEITSCHRIFT DER SAVIGNY-STIFTUNG FUER RECHTSGESCHICHTE. ROMANISTISCHE ABTEILUNG (AU) [02210889] **3077**

ZEITSCHRIFT DES AACHENER GESCHICHTSVEREINS (GW/0065-0137) [01585710] **2716**

ZEITSCHRIFT DES BAYERISCHEN STATISTISCHEN LANDESAMTS (GW) [04388507] **5347**

ZEITSCHRIFT DES BERNISCHEN JURISTENVEREINS (SZ/0044-2127) [09392059] **3077**

ZEITSCHRIFT DES BREISGAU-GESCHICHTSVEREINS SCHAUINSLAND (GW) [06825162] **2716**

ZEITSCHRIFT DES DEUTSCHEN PALASTINA-VEREINS (1953) (GW/0012-1169) [06291473] **2634**

ZEITSCHRIFT DES DEUTSCHER VEREINS FUER KUNSTWISSENSCHAFT (1963) (GW/0044-2135) [05034121] **333**

ZEITSCHRIFT DES HISTORISCHEN VEREINES FUER STEIERMARK (AU) [02086406] **2671**

ZEITSCHRIFT DES HISTORISCHEN VEREINS FUER SCHWABEN (GW/0342-3131) [02134167] **2634**

ZEITSCHRIFT DES KONIGLICH BAYERISCHEN STATISTISCHEN BUREAU See ZEITSCHRIFT DES BAYERISCHEN STATISTISCHEN LANDESAMTS **5347**

ZEITSCHRIFT DES VERBANDES DER NAMENSTRAGER (AU) [10713573] **2478**

ZEITSCHRIFT DES VEREINS FUER HAMBURGISCHE GESCHICHTE (GW/0083-5587) [02174044] **2634**

ZEITSCHRIFT DES VEREINS FUER HESSISCHE GESCHICHTE UND LANDESKUNDE (GW) [02159146] **2716**

ZEITSCHRIFT DES VEREINS FUER LUBECKISCHE GESCHICHTE UND ALTERTUMSKUNDE (GW/0083-5609) [01713691] **2717**

Alphabetical Title Index — ZEITSCHRIFT

ZEITSCHRIFT FEUR METEOROLOGIE *See* METEOROLOGISCHE ZEITSCHRIFT / HERAUSGEGEBEN VON DER DEUTSCHEN METEOROLOGISCHEN GESELLSCHAFT, OSTERREICHISCHEN GESELLSCHAFT FEUR METEOROLOGIE, SCHWEIZERISCHEN GESELLSCHAFT FUER GEOPHYSIK **1431**

ZEITSCHRIFT FUER ACKER- UND PFLANZENBAU (GW/0931-2250) [11131127] **148**

ZEITSCHRIFT FUER AGRARGESCHICHTE UND AGRARSOZIOLOGIE (GW/0044-2194) [02269835] **148**

ZEITSCHRIFT FUER AGYPTISCHE SPRACHE UND ALTERTUMSKUNDE (GW/0044-216X) [01607529] **286**

ZEITSCHRIFT FUER ALTHEBRAISTIK (GW/0932-4461) [17821456] **3335**

ZEITSCHRIFT FUER ANALYSIS UND IHRE ANWENDUNGEN (GW/0232-2064) [09834540] **3541**

ZEITSCHRIFT FUER ANGEWANDTE ENTOMOLOGIE (GW/0044-2240) [01770418] 148, **5614**

ZEITSCHRIFT FUER ANGEWANDTE MATHEMATIK UND MECHANIK (GW/0044-2267) [01590219] 2002, **3541**

ZEITSCHRIFT FUER ANGEWANDTE MATHEMATIK UND PHYSIK : ZAMP (SZ/0044-2275) [01587079] 4425, **3541**

ZEITSCHRIFT FUER ANGEWANDTE METEOROLOGIE (GW) **1437**

ZEITSCHRIFT FUER ANGEWANDTE UMWELTFORSCHUNG (GW/0933-9027) **2183**

ZEITSCHRIFT FUER ANGEWANDTE ZOOLOGIE (GW/0044-2291) [01770422] 4248, **5600**

ZEITSCHRIFT FUER ANGEWANDTE ZOOLOGIE. BEIHEFTE (GW/0514-2563) [01490963] **5600**

ZEITSCHRIFT FUER ANGLISTIK UND AMERIKANISTIK *CEASED.* (GW/0044-2305) [01641977] **3456**

ZEITSCHRIFT FUER ANORGANISCHE UND ALLGEMEINE CHEMIE (GW/0044-2313) [01770423] **1038**

ZEITSCHRIFT FUER ANTIMIKROBIELLE ANTINEOPLASTISCHE CHEMOTHERAPIE *See* ANTIINFECTIVE DRUGS AND CHEMOTHERAPY **3551**

ZEITSCHRIFT FUER ARABISCHE LINGUISTIK (GW/0170-026X) [04706126] **3335**

ZEITSCHRIFT FUER ARBEITS- UND ORGANISATIONSPSYCHOLOGIE (GW) [16267778] **4622**

ZEITSCHRIFT FUER ARBEITSRECHT UND SOZIALRECHT (AU/0044-2321) [01639053] **3155**

ZEITSCHRIFT FUER ARBEITSWISSENSCHAFT (GW/0340-2444) [02082938] 2871, **1720**

ZEITSCHRIFT FUER ARCHAEOLOGIE (GW/0044-233X) [01770424] **286**

ZEITSCHRIFT FUER ARCHAEOLOGIE DES MITTELALTERS (GW/0340-0824) [01798599] **286**

ZEITSCHRIFT FUER ARZTLICHE FORTBILDUNG (GW/0044-2178) [01778450] **3739**

ZEITSCHRIFT FUER ASSYRIOLOGIE UND VORDERASIATISCHE ARCHAEOLOGIE (GW/0084-5299) [05955279] **286**

ZEITSCHRIFT FUER ASTHETIK UND ALLGEMEINE KUNSTWISSENSCHAFT (BONN, GERMANY) (GW/0044-2186) [05662998] **369**

ZEITSCHRIFT FUER AUSLAENDISCHES OEFFENTLICHES RECHT UND VOELKERRECHT (GW/0044-2348) [01715354] 4695, **3138**

ZEITSCHRIFT FUER AUSLANDERRECHT UND AUSLANDERPOLITIK : ZAR (GW) [08971639] **3077**

ZEITSCHRIFT FUER AUSLANDISCHE LANDWIRTSCHAFT (GW/0049-8599) [06833801] **148**

ZEITSCHRIFT FUER AUSLANDISCHES UND INTERNATIONALES ARBEITS UND SOZIALRECHT (GW/0930-861X) [20312728] **3155**

ZEITSCHRIFT FUER BADER- UND KLIMAHEILKUNDE (GW/0720-0587) [06691206] **3652**

ZEITSCHRIFT FUER BALKANOLOGIE (GW/0044-2356) [01643552] **2717**

ZEITSCHRIFT FUER BAYERISCHE KIRCHENGESCHICHTE (GW) [02216306] **5070**

ZEITSCHRIFT FUER BAYERISCHE LANDESGESCHICHTE (GW/0044-2364) [01770428] **2717**

ZEITSCHRIFT FUER BERUFS- UND WIRTSCHAFTSPADAGOGIK 1980 (GW/0172-2875) [01722875] **1918**

ZEITSCHRIFT FUER BETRIEBSWIRTSCHAFT (GW/0044-2372) [01770429] **1632**

ZEITSCHRIFT FUER BEVOELKERUNGSWISSENSCHAFT (GW/0340-2398) [02728797] **4561**

ZEITSCHRIFT FUER BEWASSERUNGSWIRTSCHAFT (GW/0049-8602) [02640846] **148**

ZEITSCHRIFT FUER BIBLIOTHEKSWESEN UND BIBLIOGRAPHIE (GW/0044-2380) [01645087] **3257**

ZEITSCHRIFT FUER BIBLIOTHEKSWESEN UND BIBLIOGRAPHIE. SONDERHEFT (GW/0514-6364) [04267237] **3257**

ZEITSCHRIFT FUER CELTISCHE PHILOLOGIE (GW/0084-5302) [02451724] 3456, **3335**

ZEITSCHRIFT FUER DAS GESAMTE FAMILIENRECHT (GW/0044-2410) [01588723] **3122**

ZEITSCHRIFT FUER DAS GESAMTE HANDELSRECHT UND WIRTSCHAFTSRECHT (GW/0044-2437) [01770437] **3078**

ZEITSCHRIFT FUER DAS GESAMTE KREDITWESEN (GW/0340-8485) [01640669] **817**

ZEITSCHRIFT FUER DAS GESAMTE KREDITWESEN. SCHRIFTENREIHE (GW/0044-2445) [01508495] **817**

ZEITSCHRIFT FUER DAS GESANTE GENOSSENSCHAFTSWESEN (GW/0044-2429) [05308188] **1544**

ZEITSCHRIFT FUER DEN ERDKUNDEUNTERRICHT (GW/0044-2461) [03720331] **2579**

ZEITSCHRIFT FUER DEUTSCHE PHILOLOGIE (GW/0044-2496) [01590460] **3335**

ZEITSCHRIFT FUER DEUTSCHE PHILOLOGIE. BEIHEFT (GW) [01770444] **3335**

ZEITSCHRIFT FUER DEUTSCHES ALTERTUM UND DEUTSCHE LITERATUR (GW/0044-2518) [08246148] 3456, **3335**

ZEITSCHRIFT FUER DIALEKTOLOGIE UND LINGUISTIK (GW/0044-1449) [01770449] **3335**

ZEITSCHRIFT FUER DIE ALTTESTAMENTLICHE WISSENSCHAFT (GW/0044-2526) [01607310] **5020**

ZEITSCHRIFT FUER DIE ALTTESTAMENTLICHE WISSENSCHAFT. BEIHEFTE (GW) [01697009] **5020**

ZEITSCHRIFT FUER DIE GESAMTE HYGIENE UND IHRE GRENZGEBIETE *CEASED.* (GW/0049-8610) [01770452] **4809**

ZEITSCHRIFT FUER DIE GESAMTE INNERE MEDIZIN UND IHRE GRENZGEBIETE *CEASED.* (GW/0044-2542) [01770453] **3652**

ZEITSCHRIFT FUER DIE GESAMTE STRAFRECHTSWISSENSCHAFT (GW/0084-5310) [01589743] **3109**

ZEITSCHRIFT FUER DIE GESAMTE VERSICHERUNGS-WISSENSCHAFT (GW/0044-2585) [05308613] **2897**

ZEITSCHRIFT FUER DIE GESCHICHTE DER SAARGEGEND (GW/0513-9058) [02215019] **2717**

ZEITSCHRIFT FUER DIE GESCHICHTE DES OBERRHEINS (GW) [02214955] **2717**

ZEITSCHRIFT FUER DIE NEUTESTAMENTLICHE WISSENSCHAFT UND DIE KUNDE DER ALTEREN KIRCHE (GW/0044-2615) [01773087] **5011**

ZEITSCHRIFT FUER DIFFERENTIELLE UND DIAGNOSTISCHE PSYCHOLOGIE (SZ/0170-1789) [17063571] **4622**

ZEITSCHRIFT FUER EISENBAHNWESEN UND VERKEHRSTECHNIK (GW/0373-322X) [02451718] **5438**

ZEITSCHRIFT FUER ENERGIEWIRTSCHAFT (GW/0343-5377) [05717214] **1961**

ZEITSCHRIFT FUER ENTWICKLUNGSPSYCHOLOGIE UND PADAGOGISCHE PSYCHOLOGIE (GW/0049-8637) [02847697] 4622, **1792**

ZEITSCHRIFT FUER ERKRANKUNGEN DER ATMUNGSORGANE *CEASED.* (GW/0303-657X) [01141085] **3952**

ZEITSCHRIFT FUER ERNAEHRUNGSWISSENSCHAFT. SUPPLEMENTUM (GW/0084-5337) [01491261] **4200**

ZEITSCHRIFT FUER ERNAHRUNGSWISSENSCHAFT (GW/0044-264X) [01770461] **4200**

ZEITSCHRIFT FUER ETHNOLOGIE (GW/0044-2666) [01770462] **248**

ZEITSCHRIFT FUER EVANGELISCHE ETHIK (GW/0044-2674) [01589796] 2253, **5070**

ZEITSCHRIFT FUER EVANGELISCHES KIRCHENRECHT (GW/0044-2690) [02214898] **5070**

ZEITSCHRIFT FUER EXPERIMENTELLE UND ANGEWANDTE PSYCHOLOGIE (GW/0044-2712) [01357278] **4622**

ZEITSCHRIFT FUER FLUGWISSENSCHAFTEN UND WELTRAUMFORSCHUNG (GW/0342-068X) [03150219] **40**

ZEITSCHRIFT FUER FRANZOSISCHE SPRACHE UND LITERATUR (GW/0044-2747) [06115039] 3456, **3335**

ZEITSCHRIFT FUER FREMDSPRACHENFORSCHUNG : ZFF: ORGAN DER DEUTSCHEN GESELLSCHAFT FUER FREMDSPRACHENFORSCHUNG (DGFF) (GW) [24161046] **3335**

ZEITSCHRIFT FUER GASTROENTEROLOGIE (GW/0044-2771) [01778452] **3748**

ZEITSCHRIFT FUER GEBURTSHILFE UND PERINATOLOGIE (GW/0300-967X) [01785172] **3769**

ZEITSCHRIFT FUER GEMEINWIRTSCHAFT (AU) **1589**

ZEITSCHRIFT FUER GEOLOGISCHE WISSENSCHAFTEN (GW/0303-4534) [01791558] **1401**

ZEITSCHRIFT FUER GEOMORPHOLOGIE (GW/0372-8854) [01607040] 2579, **1401**

ZEITSCHRIFT FUER GEOMORPHOLOGIE. SUPPLEMENTBAND (GW/0044-2798) [03809514] **1401**

ZEITSCHRIFT FUER GERONTOLOGIE (GW/0044-281X) [01790987] **3755**

ZEITSCHRIFT FUER GERONTOPSYCHOLOGIE & -PSYCHIATRIE (SZ/1011-6877) [24538326] 3937, 4622, **3755**

ZEITSCHRIFT FUER GESCHICHTE DER ARABISCH-ISLAMISCHEN WISSENSCHAFTEN (GW/0179-4639) [13881364] **1792**

ZEITSCHRIFT FUER GESCHICHTSWISSENSCHAFT (GW/0044-2828) [01770474] **2634**

ZEITSCHRIFT FUER GESETZGEBUNG : ZG *CEASED.* (GW/0179-4051) [20438130] 4695, **3078**

● ZEITSCHRIFT FUER GESUNDHEITSPSYCHOLOGIE (GW/0943-8149) **4622**

ZEITSCHRIFT FUER GLETSCHERKUNDE UND GLAZIALGEOLOGIE (AU/0044-2836) [01779517] **1401**

ZEITSCHRIFT FUER HEERESKUNDE (GW/0044-2852) [08622169] **4061**

ZEITSCHRIFT FUER HEILPAEDAGOGIK (GW) [08045168] **1859**

ZEITSCHRIFT FUER HERZ THORAX UND GEFAESSCHIRURGIE (GW/0930-9225) [24538387] 3711, **3978**

ZEITSCHRIFT FUER HISTORISCHE FORSCHUNG (GW/0340-0174) [02240584] **2634**

ZEITSCHRIFT FUER INDIVIDUALPSYCHOLOGIE (GW/0342-393X) [I0342393X] **4622**

ZEITSCHRIFT FUER INTERNATIONALE ERZIEHUNGS- UND SOZIALWISSENSCHAFTLICHE FORSCHUNG (GW/0930-9381) [27204733] **1792**

ZEITSCHRIFT FUER JAGDWISSENSCHAFT (GW/0044-2887) [01643663] **4931**

ZEITSCHRIFT FUER KARDIOLOGIE (GW/0300-5860) [01773091] **3711**

ZEITSCHRIFT FUER KATALANISTIK (GW/0932-2221) [19117832] **3335**

ZEITSCHRIFT FUER KATHOLISCHE THEOLOGIE (AU/0044-2895) [01774234] **5038**

ZEITSCHRIFT FUER KINDER- UND JUGENDPSYCHIATRIE (SZ/0301-6811) [I03016811] **3937**

ZEITSCHRIFT FUER KIRCHENGESCHICHTE (GW/0044-2925) [00949350] **5011**

ZEITSCHRIFT FUER KLASSISCHE HOMOOPATHIE : KH (GW) [19962318] **3775**

ZEITSCHRIFT FUER KLINISCHE PSYCHOLOGIE (GW/0084-5345) [04849543] **4622**

ZEITSCHRIFT FUER KLINISCHE PSYCHOLOGIE, PSYCHOPATHOLOGIE UND PSYCHOTHERAPIE (GW/0723-6557) [09764270] **4622**

ZEITSCHRIFT FUER KRISTALLOGRAPHIE (GW) [04734421] **1033**

ZEITSCHRIFT FUER KULTUR, POLITIK, KIRCHE (SZ/1017-7620) [I10177620] **5011**

ZEITSCHRIFT FUER KULTUR, POLITIK, KIRCHE (SZ) [21202831] **5226**

ZEITSCHRIFT FUER KULTURAUSTAUSCH (GW/0044-2976) [06621272] **2717**

ZEITSCHRIFT — Alphabetical Title Index

ZEITSCHRIFT FUER KULTURTECHNIK UND LANDENWICKLUNG (GW/0934-666X) [19255854] **148**

ZEITSCHRIFT FUER KUNSTGESCHICHTE (GW/0044-2992) [00930029] **369**

ZEITSCHRIFT FUER KUNSTTECHNOLOGIE UND KONSERVIERUNG (GW/0931-7198) [18427157] **369**

ZEITSCHRIFT FUER LARMBEKAMPFUNG (GW/0174-1098) [06633106] **2248**

ZEITSCHRIFT FUER LATEINAMERIKA (AU) [02229054] **2767**

ZEITSCHRIFT FUER LEBENSMITTEL-UNTERSUCHUNG UND -FORSCHUNG (GW/0044-3026) [01578486] **2361**

ZEITSCHRIFT FUER LOGISTIK (GW/0173-8062) [I01738062] **890**

ZEITSCHRIFT FUER LUFT- UND WELTRAUMRECHT (GW/0340-8329) [02255994] 40, **3078**

ZEITSCHRIFT FUER LYMPHOLOGIE (GW/0343-8554) [04556891] **3653**

ZEITSCHRIFT FUER MATHEMATISCHE LOGIK UND GRUNDLAGEN DER MATHEMATIK (GW/0044-3050) [01770494] **3541**

ZEITSCHRIFT FUER MENSCHENKUNDE (AU/0379-4458) [I03794458] **248**

ZEITSCHRIFT FUER METALLKUNDE (STUTTGART, GERMANY) (GW/0044-3093) [08208635] **4024**

ZEITSCHRIFT FUER MIKROSKOPISCH-ANATOMISCHE FORSCHUNG *CEASED.* (GW/0044-3107) [01770496] **574**

ZEITSCHRIFT FUER MILITARMEDIZIN (SZ/0514-8782) [07895483] **3653**

ZEITSCHRIFT FUER MISSION (GW) [02217384] **5011**

ZEITSCHRIFT FUER MISSIONSWISSENSCHAFT UND RELIGIONSWISSENSCHAFT (GW/0044-3123) [01774235] **5011**

ZEITSCHRIFT FUER MORPHOLOGIE UND ANTHROPOLOGIE (GW/0044-314X) [01714241] **248**

ZEITSCHRIFT FUER MYKOLOGIE (GW/0170-110X) [04219364] **576**

ZEITSCHRIFT FUER NATIONALOKONOMIE. SUPPLEMENTUM (AU/0084-537X) [01483640] 1528, **3542**

ZEITSCHRIFT FUER NATURFORSCHUNG (GW/0932-0784) [15599360] 1059, **4425**

ZEITSCHRIFT FUER NEUERE RECHTSGESCHICHTE (AU/0250-6459) [06672588] **3078**

ZEITSCHRIFT FUER NEUERE THEOLOGIEGESCHICHTE (GW) **5011**

ZEITSCHRIFT FUER NEUROPSYCHOLOGIE (SZ/1016-264X) [I1016264X] 3847, **4622**

ZEITSCHRIFT FUER ORTHOPADIE UND IHRE GRENZGEBIETE (GW/0044-3220) [01606978] **3885**

ZEITSCHRIFT FUER OSTFORSCHUNG (GW/0044-3239) [01624049] **2717**

ZEITSCHRIFT FUER PAEDAGOGIK (GW/0044-3247) [02269867] **1792**

ZEITSCHRIFT FUER PAEDAGOGISCHE PSYCHOLOGIE (SZ/1010-0652) [21531032] **4622**

ZEITSCHRIFT FUER PAPYROLOGIE UND EPIGRAPHIK (GW/0084-5388) [01466587] **3456**

ZEITSCHRIFT FUER PARAPSYCHOLOGIE UND GRENZGEBIETE DER PSYCHOLOGIE (GW/0028-3479) [02269870] **4243**

ZEITSCHRIFT FUER PARLAMENTSFRAGEN (GW/0340-1758) [02216469] **4695**

ZEITSCHRIFT FUER PFLANZENERHARUNG UND BODENKUNDE (GW/0044-3263) [02549878] **530**

ZEITSCHRIFT FUER PFLANZENKRANKHEITEN UND PFLANZENSCHUTZ (1970) (GW/0340-8159) [01620051] **531**

ZEITSCHRIFT FUER PFLANZENKRANKHEITEN UND PFLANZENSCHUTZ. SONDERHEFT (GW) [10570426] **531**

ZEITSCHRIFT FUER PHILOSOPHISCHE FORSCHUNG (GW/0044-3301) [02216464] **4365**

ZEITSCHRIFT FUER PHONETIK, SPRACHWISSENSCHAFT UND KOMMUNIKATIONSFORSCHUNG (GW/0044-331X) [05948040] **3335**

ZEITSCHRIFT FUER PHOTOGRAMMETRIE UND FERNERKUNDUNG (GW/0934-0351) [18235926] **2580**

ZEITSCHRIFT FUER PHYSIK. A, HADRONS AND NUCLEI (GW/0939-7922) [23089680] **4451**

ZEITSCHRIFT FUER PHYSIK. B, CONDENSED MATTER (GW/0722-3277) [06631419] **4425**

ZEITSCHRIFT FUER PHYSIK. C, PARTICLES AND FIELDS (GW/0170-9739) [04763456] **4425**

ZEITSCHRIFT FUER PHYSIK. D, ATOMS, MOLECULES AND CLUSTERS (GW/0178-7683) [13304143] **4425**

ZEITSCHRIFT FUER PHYSIKALISCHE CHEMIE (GW) [06125091] **1059**

ZEITSCHRIFT FUER PHYSIKALISCHE CHEMIE (NEUE FOLGE) (GW/0044-3336) [01770520] **1059**

ZEITSCHRIFT FUER PHYSIKALISCHE CHEMIE. SUPPLEMENTHEFT (NEUE FOLGE) (GW/0724-410X) [09315686] **1059**

ZEITSCHRIFT FUER PHYSIKALISCHE MEDIZIN, BALNEOLOGIE, MED. KLIMATOLOGIE (GW/0720-9762) [08460747] **3653**

ZEITSCHRIFT FUER PHYSIOTHERAPIE (GW/0003-9357) [01778461] **4382**

ZEITSCHRIFT FUER PHYTOTHERAPIE (GW/0722-348X) [08964378] **531**

ZEITSCHRIFT FUER PLANUNG : ZP (GW/0936-8787) [23150118] **890**

ZEITSCHRIFT FUER POLITIK (GW/0044-3360) [01607137] **4501**

ZEITSCHRIFT FUER POLITISCHE, OEKONOMIE UND SOZIALISTISCHE POLITIK (GW) 1528, **4501**

ZEITSCHRIFT FUER PSYCHOLOGIE MIT ZEITSCHRIFT FUER ANGEWANDTE PSYCHOLOGIE (GW/0044-3409) [09407093] **4622**

ZEITSCHRIFT FUER PSYCHOSOMATISCHE MEDIZIN UND PSYCHOANALYSE (GW/0340-5613) [02269880] **3653**

ZEITSCHRIFT FUER RECHTSPOLITIK (GW/0514-6496) [01770529] **4501**

ZEITSCHRIFT FUER RECHTSSOZIOLOGIE (GW/0174-0202) [07809249] **5265**

ZEITSCHRIFT FUER RELIGIONS- UND GEISTESGESCHICHTE (GW/0044-3441) [01639767] **5011**

ZEITSCHRIFT FUER RHEUMATOLOGIE (GW/0340-1855) [01607176] **3807**

ZEITSCHRIFT FUER ROMANISCHE PHILOLOGIE (GW/0049-8661) [01200233] **3335**

ZEITSCHRIFT FUER SAUGETIERKUNDE (GW/0044-3468) [01643768] 5600, **476**

ZEITSCHRIFT FUER SCHADENSRECHT : ZFS / HERAUSGEGEBEN VON DEN RECHTSANWAELTEN ALFRED FLEISCHMANN, HANAU ... [ET AL.] (GW/0173-0568) [07232482] **3078**

ZEITSCHRIFT FUER SCHWEIZERISCHE ARCHAEOLOGIE UND KUNSTGESCHICHTE (SZ/0044-3476) [01770534] **286**

ZEITSCHRIFT FUER SCHWEIZERISCHES RECHT (SZ/0084-540X) [01770536] **3078**

ZEITSCHRIFT FUER SEMIOTIK (GW/0170-6241) [05149011] **5172**

ZEITSCHRIFT FUER SEXUALFORSCHUNG (GW/0932-8114) [18485470] **5188**

ZEITSCHRIFT FUER SLAVISCHE PHILOLOGIE (GW/0044-3492) [01770538] **3335**

ZEITSCHRIFT FUER SLAWISTIK (GW/0044-3506) [01189564] **3335**

ZEITSCHRIFT FUER SOZIALISATIONSFORSCHUNG UND ERZIEHUNGSSOZIOLOGIE (GW/0720-4361) [I07204361] **5265**

ZEITSCHRIFT FUER SOZIALPSYCHOLOGIE (SZ/0044-3514) [02216531] 5265, **4622**

ZEITSCHRIFT FUER SOZIOLOGIE (GW/0340-1804) [02269886] **5265**

ZEITSCHRIFT FUER SPIELMUSIK (GW) [09025904] **4160**

ZEITSCHRIFT FUER SPIELMUSIK AUF ALLERLEI INSTRUMENTEN *See* ZEITSCHRIFT FUER SPIELMUSIK **4160**

ZEITSCHRIFT FUER SPRACHWISSENSCHAFT : ORGAN DER DEUTSCHEN GESELLSCHAFT FUER SPRACHWISSENSCHAFT (GW/0721-9067) [09026607] **3335**

ZEITSCHRIFT FUER STOMATOLOGIE (AU/0175-7784) [10974266] **3716**

ZEITSCHRIFT FUER THEOLOGIE UND KIRCHE (GW/0044-3549) [01770542] **5011**

ZEITSCHRIFT FUER THEOLOGIE UND KIRCHE. BEIHEFT (GW) [05797719] **5011**

ZEITSCHRIFT FUER TIERPHYSIOLOGIE, TIERERNAHRUNG UND FUTTERMITTELKUNDE (GW/0044-3565) [06852189] **5600**

ZEITSCHRIFT FUER TRANSPLANTATIONSMEDIZIN (GW) **3653**

ZEITSCHRIFT FUER TURKEISTUDIEN : ZFTS (GW/0934-0696) [21016094] **2668**

ZEITSCHRIFT FUER UMWELTPOLITIK & UMWELTRECHT (GW/0931-0983) [13772001] **3117**

ZEITSCHRIFT FUER UNFALLCHIRURGIE UND VERSICHERUNGSMEDIZIN (SZ/1017-1584) [21901060] **3653**

ZEITSCHRIFT FUER UNTERNEHMENS- UND GESELLSCHAFTSRECHT (GW) [02341374] **3104**

ZEITSCHRIFT FUER UNTERNEHMENSGESCHICHTE (GW/0342-2852) [03467762] **725**

ZEITSCHRIFT FUER VERGLEICHENDE RECHTSWISSENSCHAFT (GW/0044-3638) [01770553] **3138**

ZEITSCHRIFT FUER VERGLEICHENDE SPRACHFORSCHUNG. ERGANZUNGSHEFTE (GW) [01696733] **3335**

ZEITSCHRIFT FUER VERKEHRSWISSENSCHAFT (GW/0044-3670) [01770555] 1124, **5400**

ZEITSCHRIFT FUER VERMESSUNGSWESEN. ZFV (GW/0340-4560) [03281751] **2034**

ZEITSCHRIFT FUER VERWALTUNG (AU) [02650996] **3094**

ZEITSCHRIFT FUER VOLKSKUNDE (GW/0044-3700) [01586819] **2325**

ZEITSCHRIFT FUER WASSER- UND ABWASSER FORSCHUNG (GW/0044-3727) [01770559] 2248, **1419**

ZEITSCHRIFT FUER WIRTSCHAFTS- UND SOZIALWISSENSCHAFTEN (GW/0342-1783) [01472331] **1528**

ZEITSCHRIFT FUER WIRTSCHAFTSGEOGRAPHIE (GW/0044-3751) [01770560] **2580**

ZEITSCHRIFT FUER WIRTSCHAFTSPOLITIK (GW/0721-3808) [12067741] **1528**

ZEITSCHRIFT FUER WIRTSCHAFTSRECHT (GW/0723-9416) [09376756] **3088**

ZEITSCHRIFT FUER WURTTEMBERGISCHE LANDESGESCHICHTE (GW/0044-3786) [01607097] **2717**

ZEITSCHRIFT FUER ZAHNARZTLICHE IMPLANTOLOGIE (GW/0177-3348) [28226223] **1337**

ZEITSCHRIFT FUER ZIVILPROZESS (GW/0342-3468) [01770564] **3078**

ZEITSCHRIFT FUER ZOLLE UND VERBRAUCHSTEUERN *See* ZEITSCHRIFT FUER ZOLLE + VERBRAUCHSTEUERN : ZFZ **4759**

ZEITSCHRIFT FUER ZOLLE + VERBRAUCHSTEUERN : ZFZ (GW) [07697064] **4759**

ZEITSCHRIFT FUER ZOOLOGISCHE SYSTEMATIK UND EVOLUTIONSFORSCHUNG (GW/0044-3808) [01770565] **5600**

ZEITSCHRIFT FUHRUNG + ORGANISATION : ZFO (GW/0722-7485) [10237276] **725**

ZEITSCHRIFT FUR ARZTLICHE FORTBILDUNG (BERLIN) *See* BERLINER ARZTEBLATT **3555**

ZEITSCHRIFT FUR DATENERARBEITUNG (GW) [06660873] **1207**

ZEITSCHRIFT FUR GANZHEITSFORSCHUNG (AU) [01785471] 5265, **4365**

ZEITSCHRIFT FUR GESETZGEBUNG UND RECHTSPRECHUNG IN GRAUBUNDEN (SZ) [11466324] **3078**

ZEITSCHRIFT FUR KULTUR, POLITIK, KIRCHE (SW) **5070**

ZEITSCHRIFT FUR KUNSTPADAGOGIK (GW) [01785470] **369**

ZEITSCHRIFT FUR NATURFORSCHUNG (GW/0939-5075) [15666516] **476**

ZEITSCHRIFT FUR NATURFORSCHUNG (GW/0932-0776) [15363854] **996**

ZEITSCHRIFT FUR PHONETIK, SPRACHWISSENSCHAFT UND KOMMUNIKATIONSFORSCHUNG *See* SPRACHTYPOLOGIE UND UNIVERSALIENFORSCHUNG **3323**

ZEITSCHRIFT FUR PSYCHOANALYTISCHE THEORIE UND PRAXIS (NE/0169-3395) [I01693395] **4622**

ZEITSCHRIFT FUR SCHWEIZERISCHE KIRCHENGESCHICHTE. REVUE D'HISTOIRE ECCLESIASTIQUE SUISSE (SZ/0044-3484) [02218375] **5011**

ZEITSCHRIFT FUR TIERZUCHTUNG UND ZUCHTUNGSBIOLOGIE (HAMBURG, GERMANY : 1939) (GW/0044-3581) [08405606] **224**

Alphabetical Title Index ZESZYTY

ZEITSCHRIFT FUR VERKEHRSRECHT (AU) [08235833] **5400**

ZEITSCHRIFT FUR VERKEHRSSICHERHET (GW/0044-3654) [08252250] **4809, 5446**

ZEITSCHRIFT FUR WASSER- UND ABWASSER FORSCHUNG See ACTA HYDROCHIMICA ET HYDROBIOLOGICA **1412**

ZEITSCHRIFT INTERNE REVISION (GW/0044-3816) [04305996] **725**

ZEITSCHRIFTEN-DATENBANK : ZDB (GW/0171-8932) [06066713] **427**

ZEITSCHRIFTENDIENST (GW/0417-2957) [05001869] **3257**

ZEITSCHRIFTENINHALTSDIENST THEOLOGIE (GW/0340-8361) [03082085] **5011**

ZEITSCRIFT FUR KLINISCHE MEDIZIN (BERLIN, DDR) CEASED. (GW/0233-1608) [12182970] **3653**

ZEITUNG FUER KOMMUNALE WIRTSCHAFT (GW) [05988693] **4695**

ZEITUNG FUR HISTORISCHE WERTPAPIERE (GW) [08002156] **920**

ZEITUNGS-INDEX (GW/0340-0107) [01830161] **5802**

ZEITWEISER DER GALIZIENDEUTSCHEN (GW) [02432255] **2717**

ZEITWENDE (GW/0341-7166) [07052827] **3356**

ZEITZEICHEN ZEITUNG DER KATHOLISCHEN ARBEITERBEWEGUNG OESTERREICHS (AU) **5038**

ZELLSTOFF UND PAPIER (GW/0044-3867) [02451747] **4240**

ZELLULOID (GW/0724-7656) [I07247656] **4080**

ZEMALJSKI MUZEJ BOSNE I HERCEGOVINE See GLASNIK ZEMALJSKOG MUZEJA BOSNE I HERCEGOVINE U SARAJEVU. ARHEOLOGIJA **269**

ZEMANIM (IS) [06966089] **2634**

ZEMEDELSKA TECHNIKA (XR/0044-3883) [07124674] **161**

ZEMEDELSKE MUZEUM See VEDECKE PRACE ZEMEDELASKEHO MUZEA **144**

ZEMENT UND BETON (AU/0514-2946) [07898133] **5172**

ZEMLEDELIE (RU/0044-3913) [01770570] **148**

ZEMLIA I LIUDI (RU/0514-2989) [02230828] **2580**

ZEMLIA I LIUDY UKRAINY (UN/0869-1487) [24031426] **148**

●ZEMLIA SIBIR (RU/0869-3382) [26849075] **2580**

ZEMLIA SIBIRSKAIA, DAL'NEVOSTOCHNAIA (RU) [02030543] **149**

ZEMLJA I VSELENNAJA (RU/0044-3948) [02235173] **401**

ZEMLJISTE I BILJKA (YU/0514-6658) [01644289] **149**

ZEN BUNKA (JA) [01586652] **5011**

ZEN CENTER OF LOS ANGELES See ZCLA JOURNAL **5022**

ZENAIR NEWS (US/0889-4353) [14047507] **40**

ZENIT (NE) [03425617] **401, 41**

ZENITH (UK/0084-5442) [05925711] **5172**

ZENKOKU GINKO SHOKUINROKU (JA) [01799739] **817**

ZENKOKU KACHIKU HOKEN EISEI GYOSEKI SHOROKU (JA) [02246974] **224**

ZENKOKU KIKAI KOJO MEIBO (JA) [02717074] **2132**

ZENKOKU KOGAIKEN KAISHI (JA/0385-1028) [10417983] **2183**

ZENKOKU KYOSHINKEI SETCHI JOKYO ICHIRAN (JA) [03955982] **1412**

ZENKOKU SHAKAI FUKUSHI KYOGIKAI See SHAKAI FUKUSHI NO DOKO **5307**

ZENKOKU SHIGAICHI KAKAKU SHISU (JA) [07335066] **4848**

ZENKOKU SHIMBUN MAIKUROFIRUMU SEISAKU SHOZO ICHIRAN (JA) [01790096] **5805**

ZENKOKU SHIYU BUKKEN SAIGAI KYOSAIKAI. BOSAI SEMMON TOSHOKAN See KOGAI KANKEI TOSHO MOKUROKU. TSUIROKU **2235**

ZENKOKU TANKI DAIGAKU KIYO RONBUN SAKUIN. GOGAKU BUNGAKU HEN / HENSHU, TOSHOKAN KAGAKKAI (JA) [09567306] **3335**

ZENKOKU TANKI DAIGAKU KIYO RONBUN SAKUIN. KASEIGAKU HEN (JA) [09567353] **2793**

ZENKUKU HAIGAN KANJA TOROKU (JA) [08459172] **3825**

ZENTRALAFRIKANISCHE REPUBLIK, WIRTSCHAFTLICHE ENTWICKLUNG / BUNDESSTELLE FUER AUSSENHANDELSINFORMATION (GW) [11580659] **1589**

ZENTRALAFRIKANISHCHES KAISERREICH: WIRTSCHAFTLICHE ENTWICKLUNG (GW) [04486234] **1589**

ZENTRALASIATISCHE STUDIEN DES SEMINARS FUER SPRACH- UND KULTURWISSENSCHAFT ZENTRALASIENS DER UNIVERSITAT BONN (GW/0514-857X) [01607214] **2668**

ZENTRALBIBLIOTHEK DER BUNDESWEHR See MILITARWISSENSCHAFTLICHE QUELLENKUNDE **4062**

ZENTRALBLATT FUER ARBEITSMEDIZIN, ARBEITSSCHUTZ, PROPHYLAXE UND ERGONOMIE (GW/0173-3338) [06598356] **3653**

ZENTRALBLATT FUER BAKTERIOLOGIE (GW/0934-8840) [25361026] **571**

ZENTRALBLATT FUER BAKTERIOLOGIE. SUPPLEMENT (GW/0941-018X) [22457399] **571**

ZENTRALBLATT FUER CHIRURGIE (GW/0044-409X) [01770586] **3978**

ZENTRALBLATT FUER CHIRURGIE. SONDERBAND (GW/0044-409X) [01641140] **3978**

ZENTRALBLATT FUER GEOLOGIE UND PALAEONTOLOGIE. TEIL 1: ALLGEMEINE, ANGEWANDTE, REGIONALE UND HISTORISCHE GEOLOGIE (GW/0340-5109) [05086215] **4231, 1401**

ZENTRALBLATT FUER GEOLOGIE UND PALAONTOLOGIE. TEIL II: PALAONTOLOGIE (GW/0044-4189) [05747947] **4231**

ZENTRALBLATT FUER GYNAKOLOGIE (GW/0044-4197) [01770600] **3769**

ZENTRALBLATT FUER HYGIENE UND UMWELTMEDIZIN (GW/0934-8859) [19959110] **4809**

ZENTRALBLATT FUER JUGENDRECHT (GW/0176-6449) [13715563] **3122**

ZENTRALBLATT FUER MATHEMATIK UND IHRE GRENZGEBIETE (GW/0044-4235) [01770606] **3542, 3543**

ZENTRALBLATT FUER MECHANIK (GW) [01770607] **2132**

ZENTRALBLATT FUER MIKROBIOLOGIE (GW/0232-4393) [08440321] **571**

ZENTRALBLATT FUER MINERALOGIE. TEIL I, KRISTALLOGRAPHIE UND MINERALOGIE (GW/0514-7115) [01604365] **1445**

ZENTRALBLATT FUER MINERALOGIE. TEIL II. PETROGRAPHIE, TECHNISCHE MINERALOGIE, GEOCHEMIE UND LAGERSTATTENKUNDE (GW/0514-7123) [01494887] **1401**

ZENTRALBLATT FUER NEUROCHIRURGIE (GW/0044-4251) [01770609] **3978**

ZENTRALBLATT FUER PATHOLOGIE : GENERAL PATHOLOGY/PATHOLOGICAL ANATOMY (GW/0863-4106) [23587004] **3899**

ZENTRALBLATT FUER PHARMAZIE, PHARMAKOTHERAPIE UND LABORATORIUMSDIAGNOSTIK CEASED. (SZ/0049-8696) [01777898] **4333**

ZENTRALBLATT FUER SOZIALVERSICHERUNG, SOZIALHILFE UND VERSORGUNG (GW/0044-4278) [01770611] **5315**

ZENTRALBLATT FUER VETERINARMEDIZIN. REIHE A (GW/0514-7158) [01770613] **5528**

ZENTRALBLATT HALS- NASEN- OHRENHEILKUNDE, PLASTISCHE CHIRURGIE AN KOPF UND HALS (GW/0340-5214) [08967046] **3891, 3978**

ZENTRALBLATT HAUT- UND GESCHLECHTSKRANKHEITEN (GW/0343-3048) [04343389] **3717, 3723**

ZENTRALBLATT INNERE MEDIZIN CEASED. (GW) [14819769] **3802**

ZENTRALBLATT KINDERHEILKUNDE (GW/0722-8953) [08731439] **3912**

ZENTRALBLATT NEUROLOGIE, PSYCHIATRIE (GW/0722-3064) [08406403] **3938, 3847**

ZENTRALBLATT OPHTHALMOLOGIE (GW/0722-9933) [08535344] **3880**

ZENTRALBLATT RADIOLOGIE (GW/0722-3072) [08403123] **3947**

ZENTRALBLATT RECHTSMEDIZIN (GW/0722-3056) [08405601] **3743**

ZENTRALE MARKT- UND PREISBERICHTELLE FUR ERZEUGNISSE DER LAND-, FORST- UND ERNAHRUNGSWIRTSCHAFT See BILANZ GETREIDE-FUTTERMITTEL : BR DEUTSCHLAND, EG UND WELTMARKT **200**

ZENTRALE MARKT- UND PREISBERICHTSTELLE FUR ERZEUGNISSE DER LAND-, FORST- UND ERNAHRUNGSWIRTSCHAFT See AGRARMARKTE BR DEUTSCHLAND, EWG UND WELTMARKT : EIER UND GEFLUGEL, DIE **204**

ZENTRALE MARKT- UND PREISBERICHTSTELLE FUR ERZEUGNISSE DER LAND-, FORST- UND ERNAHRUNGSWIRTSCHAFT See ZMP BILANZ **2361**

ZENTRALINSTITUT FUR FESTKORPERPHYSIK UND WERKSTOFFORSCHUNG See WISSENSCHAFTLICHE BERICHTE - ZENTRALINSTITUT FUER FESTKORPERPHYSIK UND WERKSTOFFORSCHUNG **4425**

ZENTRALINSTITUT FUR VERSUCHSTIERZUCHT See ANNUAL REPORT / ZENTRALINSTITUT FUER VERSUCHSTIERZUCHT **5503**

ZENTRALORGAN CHIRURGIE (GW/0722-6985) [08546577] **3978**

ZEOLITES (US/0144-2449) [07518623] **1033, 1038**

ZEPHYRHILLS NEWS (US) [01491638] **5651**

ZEPHYRUS (SP/0514-7336) [05062765] **286**

ZERNOVOE HOZAJSTVO (RU/0372-9893) [01795116] **191**

ZERNOVYE KULTURY (RU/0235-2532) [18197413] **149**

ZERO CEASED. (UK) [22513495] **4549, 5572**

ZERO POPULATION GROWTH NEWSLETTER (US) [05931875] **4561**

ZERO TO THREE (US/0736-8038) [07557754] **3912**

ZEROUNO (IT) **1207**

ZEROWORK (US/0148-8902) [03383582] **1720**

ZEST (NELSON) (CN/0824-3492) [11197200] **5458**

ZESZYT NAUKOWY. BUDOWNICTWO WODNE I INZYNIERIA SANITARNA (PL) [18923827] **2096**

ZESZYT NAUKOWY - POLITECHNIKA KRAKOWSKA. BUDOWNICTWO LADOWE (PL/0454-4862) [I04544862] **631**

ZESZYTY HISTORYCZNE (FR/0044-4391) [02226124] **2717**

ZESZYTY KAUKOWE UNIWERYSTETU JAGIELLONSKIEGO. PRACE BOTANICZNE (PL/0302-8585) [02256546] **531**

ZESZYTY LITERACKIE : ZL (FR) [09820914] **3456**

ZESZYTY NAUKOWE (PL) [04865543] **2857**

ZESZYTY NAUKOWE (AKADEMIA EKONOMICZNA W KRAKOWIE) (PL/0208-7944) [02325135] **1528**

ZESZYTY NAUKOWE. AKADEMIA ROLNICZA W KRAKOWIE, ZOOTECHNIKA (PL/0137-1916) [01495462] **224**

ZESZYTY NAUKOWE - AKADEMIA ROLNICZA W SZCZECINIE (PL) [03184857] **149**

ZESZYTY NAUKOWE - AKADEMIA TECHNICZNO-ROLNICZA IM. JANA I JEDRZEJA SNIADECKICH W BYDGOSZCZY. CHEMIA I TECHNOLOGIA CHEMICZNA (PL/0208-6360) [18769888] **5172, 996**

ZESZYTY NAUKOWE AKADEMII EKONOMICZNEJ W KRAKOWIE (PL) **1528**

ZESZYTY NAUKOWE AKADEMII GORNICZO-HUTNICZEJ IM. STANISAWA STASZICA. CHEMIA (PL/0860-1100) [15470148] **996**

ZESZYTY NAUKOWE AKADEMII GORNICZO-HUTNICZEJ IM. STANISAWA STASZICA. GORNICTWO (PL/0372-9400) [19980284] **5172, 1445**

ZESZYTY NAUKOWE AKADEMII GORNICZO-HUTNICZEJ IM. STANISAWA STASZICA. MECHANIKA (PL/0239-5320) [22328587] **4024**

ZESZYTY NAUKOWE AKADEMII GORNICZO-HUTNICZEJ IM. STANISAWA STASZICA. METALURGIA I ODLEWNICTWO (PL/0372-9443) [01757194] **4024**

ZESZYTY NAUKOWE AKADEMII ROLNICZEJ IM. H. KOATAJA W KRAKOWIE LESNICTWO (PL/0239-930X) [I0239930X] **149**

ZESZYTY NAUKOWE AKADEMII ROLNICZEJ W KRAKOWIE. ROLNICTWO (PL/0137-1886) [12498611] **149**

ZESZYTY NAUKOWE AKADEMII ROLNICZEJ WE WROCAWIU. ROLNICTWO (PL/0137-1959) [I01371959] **149**

ZESZYTY NAUKOWE AKADEMII ROLNICZEJ WE WROCAWIU. ROZPRAWA HABILITACYJNA (PL/0867-1427) [24357616] **149**

ZESZYTY NAUKOWE AKADEMII ROLNICZEJ WE WROCAWIU. ZOOTECHNIKA (PL/0137-2017) [12117981] **149**

ZESZYTY

Alphabetical Title Index

ZESZYTY NAUKOWE AKADEMII ROLNICZO-TECHNICZNEJ W OLSZTYNIE. GEODEZJA I URZADZENIA ROLNE (PL/0324-9174) [04447218] 149, **2002**

● ZESZYTY NAUKOWE. BIOLOGIA / UNIWERSYTET GDANSKI (PL/0867-3357) [29458598] **476**

ZESZYTY NAUKOWE INSTYTUTU BADANIA PRAWA SADOWEGO (PL) [04322254] **3078**

ZESZYTY NAUKOWE KATOLICKIEGO UNIWERSYTETU LUBELSKIEGO (PL/0044-4405) [02263705] **5172**

ZESZYTY NAUKOWE NAUK SPOECZNYCH I EKONOMICZNYCH (PL/0208-7669) [10969070] **5226**

ZESZYTY NAUKOWE. OCEANOGRAFIA / UNIWERSYTET GDANSKI (PL) [28650122] **1458**

ZESZYTY NAUKOWE - POLITECHNIKA IODZKA. TECHNOLOGIA I CHEMIA SPOZYWCZA (PL/0209-0600) [09588224] **1031**

ZESZYTY NAUKOWE - POLITECHNIKA SLASKA. MATEMATYKA. FIZYKA (PL/0072-470X) [11009036] 4425, **3542**

ZESZYTY NAUKOWE POLITECHNIKI CZESTOCHOWSKIEJ. NAUKI TECHNICZNE. HUTNICTWO (PL/0372-9524) [11446286] **5172**

ZESZYTY NAUKOWE POLITECHNIKI GDANSKIEJ. CHEMIA (PL/0416-7341) [10074435] **5172**

ZESZYTY NAUKOWE POLITECHNIKI SLASKIEJ. CHEMIA (PL/0372-9494) [09947185] **996**

ZESZYTY NAUKOWE POLITECHNIKI SLASKIEJ. ENERGETYKA (PL/0372-9796) [10789760] 2002, **1961**

ZESZYTY NAUKOWE POLITECHNIKI SLASKIEJ. GORNICTWO (PL/0372-9508) [11009244] **2153**

ZESZYTY NAUKOWE POLITECHNIKI SLASKIEJ. MATEMATYKA-FIZYKA GEOCHRONOMETRIA (PL) [20112580] **3542**

ZESZYTY NAUKOWE. SERIA I (PL/0208-4902) [02246421] **1528**

ZESZYTY NAUKOWE. SERIA SPECJALNA: MONOGRAFIE (PL) **1528**

ZESZYTY NAUKOWE UNIWERSYTETU JAGIELLONSKIEGE. UNIVERSITATIS IAGELLONICAE ACTA CHIMICA (PL/0867-1095) [I08671095] **996**

ZESZYTY NAUKOWE UNIWERSYTETU JAGIELLONSKIEGO. ACTA COSMOLOGICA (PL/0137-2386) [03637560] **401**

ZESZYTY NAUKOWE UNIWERSYTETU JAGIELLONSKIEGO. PRACE INFORMATYCZNE (PL/0860-0295) [16114987] **1207**

ZESZYTY NAUKOWE UNIWERSYTETU JAGIELLONSKIEGO. PRACE SOCJOLOGICZNE (PL) [08153574] **5265**

ZESZYTY NAUKOWE UNIWERSYTETU JAGIELLONSKIEGO. PRACE Z BIOLOGII MOLEKULARNEJ (PL/0137-2351) [02359786] **476**

ZESZYTY NAUKOWE UNIWERSYTETU JAGIELLONSKIEGO. PRACE Z HISTORII SZTUKI (PL/0083-4424) [I00834424] **2634**

ZESZYTY NAUKOWE UNIWERSYTETU JAGIELLONSKIEGO. PRACE Z NAUK POLITYCZNYCH (PL/0137-2378) [02830395] **4501**

ZESZYTY NAUKOWE UNIWERSYTETU JAGIELLONSKIEGO. UNIVERSITATIS IAGELLONICAE FOLIA PHYSICA (PL) [29019272] **4425**

ZESZYTY NAUKOWE. WETERYNARIA (PL/0137-1975) [03641152] **5528**

ZESZYTY NAUKOWE WYDZIAU BIOLOGII, GEOGRAFII I OCEANOLOGII. BIOLOGIA *See* ZESZYTY NAUKOWE. BIOLOGIA / UNIWERSYTET GDANSKI **476**

ZESZYTY NAUKOWE WYDZIAU BIOLOGII I NAUK O ZIEMI. OCEANOGRAFIA *See* ZESZYTY NAUKOWE. OCEANOGRAFIA / UNIWERSYTET GDANSKI **1458**

ZESZYTY NAUKOWE WYDZIAU MATEMATYKI, FIZYKI I CHEMII. PROBLEMY DYDAKTYKI FIZYKI (PL) [02354000] **4425**

ZESZYTY NAUKOWE WYZSZEJ SZKOY PEDAGOGICZNEJ W BYDGOSZCZY. STUDIA TECHNICZNE (PL/0239-5061) [11463876] **476**

ZESZYTY NAUKOWE WYZSZEJ SZKOY ROLNICZEJ WE WROCAWIU *See* ZESZYTY NAUKOWE AKADEMII ROLNICZEJ WE WROCAWIU. ZOOTECHNIKA **149**

ZESZYTY NAUKOWY - POLITECHNIKA KRAKOWSKA. CHEMIA (PL/0075-7055) [10325332] **1020**

ZESZYTY PRASOZNAWCZE (PL) [02239199] **3456**

ZESZYTY PROBLEMOWE POSTEPOW NAUK ROLNICZYCH (PL/0084-5477) [02847681] **149**

ZET M OP (NE) 3938, **1072**

ZETA (BOLOGNA, ITALY) (IT) [19496224] **4365**

ZETA PHI BETA SORORITY *See* ALUMNAE DIRECTORY / ZETA PHI BETA SORORITY, INC **1808**

ZETA PSI FRATERNITY *See* DIRECTORY OF MEMBERS / ZETA PSI FRATERNITY OF NORTH AMERICA **1821**

ZETA TAU ALPHA *See* ALUMNAE DIRECTORY / ZETA TAU ALPHA FRATERNITY **1808**

ZETA (UDINE) (IT/0393-2362) [10568935] **3473**

ZETETIC SCHOLAR (US/0741-6229) [04656210] **4243**

ZEV, DET, GLASERS ANNALEN, DIE EISENBAHNTECHNIK (GW/0941-0589) [I09410589] **5438**

ZEVENTIENDE EEUW, DE (NE/0921-142X) [15596085] **2634**

ZFA. ZEITSCHRIFT FUER ALLGEMEINMEDIZIN (GW/0341-9835) [02668794] **3739**

ZFA, ZEITSCHRIFT FUER ARBEITSRECHT (GW) [01794311] **3156**

ZFBR, ZEITSCHRIFT FUER DEUTSCHES UND INTERNATIONALES BAURECHT (GW) [06315304] 631, **3078**

ZFI-MITTEILUNGEN (GW/0323-8776) [11124595] **3947**

ZFL : INTERN. ZEITSCHRIFT FUER LEBENSMITTEL-TECHNOLOGIE UND -VERFAHRENSTECHNIK (GW/0722-5733) [26011205] **2361**

ZGL. ZEITSCHRIFT FUER GERMANISTISCHE LINGUISTIK (GW/0301-3294) [01795549] **3335**

ZGODA / UNITY (US) [08814641] **2275**

ZGODOVINSKI CASOPIS (XV/0350-5774) [02226054] **2634**

ZHEJIANG GONGXUEYUAN XUEBAO (CC/1000-209X) [I1000209X] **2002**

ZHEJIANG LINYE KE JI (CC/1001-3776) [20742358] **2398**

ZHEJIANG YIKE DAXUE XUEBAO (CC/1000-1743) [I0810743] **3653**

ZHEJIANG ZHONGYI ZAZHI (CC/0411-8421) [I04118421] **3653**

ZHELEZNODOROZHNYI TRANSPORT (RU/0044-4448) [05464168] **5438**

ZHELEZNYE DOROGI SSSR (RU) [19690702] **5438**

ZHENCI YANJIU (CC/1000-0607) [12532521] **3653**

ZHENGLUN ZHOUKAN (CH/0528-9688) [10091822] **3356**

ZHENJUN XUEBAO (CC/0256-1883) [09231686] **576**

ZHENKONG KEXUE YU JISHU (CC/0253-9748) [09224968] **5172**

ZHENSHCHINAKH, O (RU) [11982367] **5372**

ZHENSHCHINY MIRA (RU/0044-4456) [02236072] **5572**

ZHILENG XUEBAO (CC/0253-4339) [09030968] **2609**

ZHILISHCHNOE I KOMMUNALNOE KHOZIAISTVO (RU/0044-4464) [11570292] **149**

ZHILISHCHNOE STROITELSTVO (RU/0044-4472) [02223003] **631**

ZHINKA (UN) [17485431] **5572**

● ZHINKA (UN) [25000707] **5572**

ZHIVOTNOVUDNI NAUKI (BU/0514-7441) [01789945] 224, **5528**

ZHIWU BAOHU (CC/0529-1542) [22154032] **531**

ZHIZN (RU) [12652359] **2525**

ZHONG HUA YI XUE ZA ZHI (CC/0376-2491) [01385509] **3653**

ZHONG SHAN YIXUEYUAN XUEBAO (CC/0254-1440) [08325341] **3653**

ZHONG XI LIAO WANG TAI (US/0892-7456) [15249995] **2668**

ZHONGCAOYAO (CC/0253-2670) [09034129] **4333**

ZHONGGUO CHUBAN NIANJIAN / CHINA PUBLISHING YEARBOOK (CC/1001-8859) [I10018859] **4820**

ZHONGGUO DIANJI GONGCHENG XUEBAO (CC/0258-8013) [15191980] **2087**

ZHONGGUO DIZHI KEXUEYUAN, YICHANG DIZHI KUANGCHAN YANJIUSUO SUOKAN (CC/0254-5063) [09977837] **1402**

ZHONGGUO DIZHI KEXUEYUAN YUANBAO (CH/0254-3176) [08473113] **1402**

ZHONGGUO DIZHI XUEHUI ZHUANKAN (CH/0578-1825) [04634061] **1402**

ZHONGGUO FANGZHI DAXUE XUEBAO (CC/1000-1476) [16167825] **5360**

ZHONGGUO GUOSHU (CH/1000-8047) [I10008047] 2361, **191**

ZHONGGUO HANGTIAN (CC/1002-7742) [I10027742] **41**

ZHONGGUO HUANJING KEXUE (CC/1000-6923) [09590467] **2183**

ZHONGGUO JIGUANG (CC/0258-7025) [11594519] **4442**

ZHONGGUO JISHENGCHONGBING FANGZHI ZAZHI (CC/1001-6627) [I10016627] **3653**

ZHONGGUO JISHENGCHONGXUE YU JISHENGCHONGPING ZAZHI (CC/1000-7423) [16742612] **3653**

ZHONGGUO JIXIE GONGCHENG XUEKAN (CH/0257-9731) [09149157] **2132**

ZHONGGUO KANGSHENGSU ZAZHI (CC/1001-8689) [I10018689] 572, 3697, **4333**

ZHONGGUO KEXUE. A, SHUXUE, WULIXUE, TIANWENXUE, JISHUKEXUE (CC/0254-5896) [10065285] **5172**

ZHONGGUO KEXUE. B, HUAXUE, SHENGWUXUE, NONGXUE, YIXUE, DIXUE (CC/0254-590X) [10366687] **5172**

ZHONGGUO KEXUE JISHU DAXUE XUEBAO (CC/0253-2778) [08888912] **5172**

ZHONGGUO KONGJIAN KEXUE JISHU (CC/1000-758X) [I1000758X] 5172, **41**

ZHONGGUO MIANHUA (CC/1000-632X) [I1000632X] **5360**

ZHONGGUO MIANYIXUE ZAZHI (CC/1000-484X) [I1000484X] **3677**

ZHONGGUO NIANGZAO (CC/0254-5071) [09770839] **2373**

ZHONGGUO PIGE (CC/1001-6813) [I10016813] **3186**

ZHONGGUO SHOUYI KE-JI (CH/1000-6419) [I10006419] **5528**

ZHONGGUO SHOUYI ZAZHI (CC/0529-6005) [09857071] **5528**

ZHONGGUO SHUIDAO KEXUE (CH/1001-7216) [I10017216] 191, **2361**

ZHONGGUO TIAOWEIPIN (CC/1000-9973) [I10009973] **2361**

ZHONGGUO TUDI KEXUE (CC/1001-8158) [I10018158] **1361**

ZHONGGUO XITU XUEBAO (CC/1000-4343) [20949506] **4024**

ZHONGGUO XUMU ZAZHI (CC/0258-7033) [10476895] **5528**

ZHONGGUO YAOFANG (CH/1001-0408) [I10010408] **4333**

ZHONGGUO YAOKE DAXUE XUEBAO (CC/1000-5048) [I10005048] **4333**

ZHONGGUO YAOLI XUEBAO (CC/0253-9756) [07233495] **4333**

ZHONGGUO YAOLIXUE YU DULIXUE ZAZHI (CC/1000-3002) [21979422] 4334, **3984**

ZHONGGUO YAOXUE ZAZHI (1989) (CC/1001-2494) [20818523] **4334**

ZHONGGUO YIKE DAXUE XUEBAO (CC/0258-4646) [17725085] **3653**

ZHONGGUO YIXUE KEXUEYUAN XUEBAO (CC/0253-3774) [06565468] **3653**

ZHONGGUO YIXUE WENZHAI. ZHONGYI (CC/0254-9042) [08750695] **3653**

ZHONGGUO YIYAO GONGYE ZAZHI (CC/1001-8255) [24851980] **4334**

ZHONGGUO YUNDONG YIXUE ZAZHI (CC/1000-6710) [12365352] **3957**

ZHONGGUO YUWEN (TAIPEI) (CH/1017-2300) [I10172300] **3336**

ZHONGGUO ZAOZHI (CC/0254-508X) [09770706] **4240**

ZHONGGUO ZHENJIU (CC/0255-2930) [08611257] **3653**

ZHONGGUO ZHI CHUN (US/0735-8237) [09025967] **2668**

ZHONGGUO ZHONGLIU LINCHUANG (CC/1000-8179) [21979279] **3825**

ZHONGGUO ZHONGYAO ZAZHI (CC/1001-5302) [20223454] **3653**

ZHONGHUA FANGSHE YIXUE YU FANGHU ZAZHI (CC/0254-5098) [08661768] 4809, **3947**

ZHONGHUA GUKE ZAZHI (CC/0253-2352) [08006678] **3885**

ZHONGHUA HEYIXUE ZAZHI (CC/0253-9780) [08563269] **3849**

ZHONGHUA HULI ZAZHI (CC/0254-1769) [08392678] **3871**

ZHONGHUA JIEHE HE HUXI ZAZHI (CC/1001-0939) [17356090] **3952**

ZHONGHUA LAODONG WEISHENG ZHIYEBING ZAZHI (CC/1001-9391) [11320242] **2871**

ZHONGHUA LAONIAN YIXUE ZAZHI (CC/0254-9026) [09109235] **3755**

ZHONGHUA LILIAO ZAZHI (CC/0254-1408) [08422049] **4382**

Alphabetical Title Index ZKG

ZHONGHUA LINXUE JIKAN (CH/0578-1345) [01638957] **2398**

ZHONGHUA LIUXINGBING ZAZHI (CC/0254-6450) [08617360] 3736, **3717**

ZHONGHUA MAZUIXUE ZAZHI (CC/0254-1416) [08404736] **3684**

ZHONGHUA MINGUO SHOUYI XUEHUI ZAZHI (CH/0253-9179) [02863853] **5528**

ZHONGHUA MINGUO WAIKE YIXUE HUI ZAZHI (CH/1011-6788) [I10116788] **3978**

ZHONGHUA MINGUO WEI SHENGWU JI MIANYIXUE ZAZHI (CH/0253-2662) [06803344] **572**

ZHONGHUA MINGUO XIAOERKE YIXUEHUI ZAZHI (CH/0001-6578) [11077347] **3912**

ZHONGHUA MINGUO XIAOHUA XIYI XUEHUI ZAZHI (CH/1013-7696) [I10137696] **3748**

ZHONGHUA MINGUO XINZANGXUE HUI ZAZHI (CH/1011-6842) [I10116842] **3711**

ZHONGHUA NEIFENMI DAIXIE ZAZHI (CC/1000-6699) [I10006699] **3733**

ZHONGHUA WEISHENGWUXUE HE MIANYIXUE ZAZHI (CC/0254-5101) [08233562] 572, **3677**

ZHONGHUA WULIYIXUE ZAZHI (CC/0254-1424) [08398595] **3654**

ZHONGHUA WUSHU (CC/1000-3525) [11513641] **2602**

ZHONGHUA XIAOHUA ZAZHI (CC/0254-1432) [08323068] **3748**

ZHONGHUA XUEYEXUE ZAZHI (CC/0253-2727) [08719853] **3774**

ZHONGHUA YISHI ZAZHI (CC/0255-7053) [09639752] **3654**

ZHONGHUA YIXUE JIANYAN ZAZHI (CC/0253-973X) [05370234] **5172**

ZHONGHUA YUFANG-YIXUE ZAZHI (CC/0253-9624) [05188943] **3654**

ZHONGHUA ZHENGXING SHAOSHANG WAIKE ZAZHI (CC/1000-7806) [12901787] **3978**

ZHONGHUA ZHENJUNXUEHUI HUIKAN (CH/1013-2732) [I10132732] **577**

ZHONGHUA ZHONGLIU ZAZHI (CC/0253-3766) [05827861] **3825**

ZHONGHVA KUNCHONG (CH/0258-462X) [10784897] **5600**

ZHONGNAN KUANGYE XUEYUAN XUEBAO (CH/0253-4347) [09034201] 4024, **2153**

ZHONGUA MINGUO MAZUI XUEHUI ZAZHI (CH/0529-5769) [08341938] **3654**

ZHONGWAI ZAZHI (CH/1016-4162) [I10164162] **3356**

ZHONGYANG YANJIUYUAN LISHI YUYAN YANJIUSUO JIKAN (CH/1012-4195) [03776932] 3336, **2510**

ZHONGYAOCAI (CH/1001-4454) [I10014454] **3654**

Z'HUITRES (CN/0824-2445) [11245750] **2634**

ZHUJI (CN/0824-6017) [10845147] **5798**

ZHULDYZ (KZ/0134-3580) [14920555] **3456**

ZHURNAL EVOLIUTSIONNOI BIOKHIMII I FIZIOLOGII (RU/0044-4529) [02465684] 587, **494**

ZHURNAL FIZICHESKOI KHIMII (RU/0044-4537) [01770625] **1059**

ZHURNAL FIZICHESKOI KHIMII. MICROFORM (RU) [08546300] **1059**

ZHURNAL MIKROBIOLOGII, EPIDEMIOLOGII I IMMUNOBIOLOGII (RU/0372-9311) [01770627] 3736, **3678**

ZHURNAL NAUCHNOI I PRIKLADNOI FOTOGRAFII I KINEMATOGRAFII (US/0734-1504) [08682084] **4378**

ZHURNAL NAUCHNOI I PRIKLADNOI FOTOGRAFII I KINEMATOGRAFII See ZHURNAL NAUCHNOI I PRIKLADNOI FOTOGRAFII / ROSSIISKAIA AKADEMIIA NAUK **4378**

ZHURNAL NAUCHNOI I PRIKLADNOI FOTOGRAFII I KINEMATOGRAFII. ENGLISH. SCIENTIFIC & APPLIED PHOTOGRAPHY & CINEMATOGRAPHY See SCIENTIFIC & APPLIED PHOTOGRAPHY **4376**

● ZHURNAL NAUCHNOI I PRIKLADNOI FOTOGRAFII / ROSSIISKAIA AKADEMIIA NAUK (RU) [27903113] **4378**

ZHURNAL NEORGANICHESKOI KHIMII (RU/0044-457X) [01714292] **1038**

ZHURNAL ORGANICHESKOI KHIMII. ENGLISH. JOURNAL OF ORGANIC CHEMISTRY OF THE USSR See JOURNAL OF ORGANIC CHEMISTRY OF THE USSR **1043**

ZHURNAL STRUKTURNOJ HIMII (RU/0136-7463) [02275685] **1059**

ZHURNAL VSESOIUZNOGO KHIMICHESKOGO OBSHCHESTVA IM. D.I. MENDELEEVA (RU/0373-0247) [11488153] **996**

ZHURNAL VYSSHEI NERVNOI DEIATELNOSTI IMENI I. P. PAVLOVA (RU/0044-4677) [01770633] **3847**

ZHURNALIST (RU/0130-3589) [02230863] **2926**

ZHURNALIST, PRESSA, AUDITORIIA / LENINGRADSKII GOSUDARSTVENNYI UNIVERSITET IM. A.A. ZHDANOVA (RU/0134-8442) [09227592] **2926**

ZHURNALIST UKRAINY (UN/0132-8425) [03151098] **2926**

ZHUZAO (CC/1001-4977) [21767608] **4024**

ZHUZAO JISHU (CC/1000-8365) [I10008365] **4024**

ZHUZI YANJIU HUIKAN (CC/1000-6567) [08748681] **191**

ZI INTERNATIONAL (GW/0341-0552) [02885728] **631**

ZIBALDONE (MUNCHEN) (GW/0930-8997) [15748511] **3456**

ZIBRANNIA POSTANOV URIADU UKRAINY (UN/0130-884X) [26668784] **3078**

ZIEGENFUSS FAMILIES, THE (US) [09990424] **2478**

ZIEKENHUIS, HET (NE/0044-4715) [01357858] **3794**

ZIEKENHUIS MANAGEMENT MAGAZINE (NE) 890, **3794**

ZIEKENHUISFARMACIE (NE/0169-2720) [25996032] 3794, **4334**

ZIEKENHUISHYGIENE EN INFEKTIEPREVENTIE See TIJDSCHRIFT VOOR HYGIENE EN INFEKTIEPREVENTIE **3793**

ZIEKENHUISHYGIENE EN INFEKTIEPREVENTIE (NE/0168-6976) [01686976] **3794**

ZIEKTEVERZUIM IN ..., HET (NE) [11843567] **1720**

ZIELONY SZTANDAR (PL/0137-9359) [I01379399] **2525**

ZIELSPRACHE DEUTSCH (GW/0341-5864) [01770636] **3336**

ZIELSPRACHE ENGLISCH (GW/0342-6173) [04928439] **3336**

ZIELSPRACHE RUSSISCH CEASED. (GW/0173-9522) [06952634] **3336**

ZIEMIA GORZOWSKA (PL/0208-6999) [I02086999] **2525**

ZIEMIA KALISKA (PL/0208-7421) [I02087421] **5808**

ZIEMIE ZACHODNIE (PL/0084-5507) [01493286] **2717**

ZIEMNIAK (PL/0302-7716) [01792558] 2361, **191**

ZIEN See BLIND (AMSTERDAM, NETHERLANDS) **344**

ZIGZAG'S MONDAY MORNING QUARTERBACK (US/1064-3575) [26267471] 1632, **2907**

ZIKNA (IS) [01784362] **5182**

ZILLIONS (MOUNT VERNON, N.Y.) (US/1050-8163) [21626048] 1072, **1300**

ZIMBABWE See ESTIMATES OF EXPENDITURE FOR THE YEAR ENDING JUNE 30 - ZIMBABWE **4721**

ZIMBABWE AGRICULTURAL JOURNAL (RH/1017-5156) [06561978] **149**

ZIMBABWE. AGRICULTURAL RESEARCH COUNCIL See TECHNICAL REPORT / AGRICULTURAL RESEARCH COUNCIL OF ZIMBABWE RHODESIA **140**

ZIMBABWE AT WORK (RH) [15683959] **1632**

ZIMBABWE. DEPT. OF PHYSICAL PLANNING See ANNUAL REVIEW / DEPARTMENT OF PHYSICAL PLANNING, MINISTRY OF LOCAL GOVERNMENT, RURAL AND URBAN DEVELOPMENT **2815**

ZIMBABWE. DIVISION OF LIVESTOCK AND PASTURES See ANNUAL REPORT FOR THE YEAR ENDED - ZIMBABWE. DIVISION OF LIVESTOCK AND PASTURES **205**

ZIMBABWE ENGINEER (1992) (RH/1019-6404) [I10196404] **2002**

ZIMBABWE GOVERNMENT GAZETTE (RH) **4696**

ZIMBABWE INDUSTRY AND COMMERCE (RH) [08862698] **858**

ZIMBABWE JOURNAL OF AGRICULTURAL RESEARCH, THE (RH/0251-1045) [06645893] **149**

ZIMBABWE JOURNAL OF EDUCATIONAL RESEARCH : ZJER (RH/1013-3445) [19681635] **1792**

ZIMBABWE LAW REVIEW (RH) [13139210] **3078**

ZIMBABWE LIBRARIAN, THE (RH/1015-6828) [07148929] **3257**

ZIMBABWE. MINISTRY OF HIGHER EDUCATION See ANNUAL REPORT OF THE SECRETARY FOR HIGHER EDUCATION FOR THE YEAR ENDED ... **1809**

ZIMBABWE NATIONAL BIBLIOGRAPHY (RH) [06740584] **427**

ZIMBABWE NEWS, THE (ZA) [03249703] **2501**

ZIMBABWE NURSE, THE (RH/1012-9103) [11535270] **3871**

ZIMBABWE PATENT AND TRADE MARKS JOURNAL (RH) **1310**

ZIMBABWE PEOPLE'S VOICE : OFFICIAL ORGAN OF THE ZIMBABWE AFRICAN PEOPLE'S UNION (ZAPU), THE (ZA) [07261452] **2644**

ZIMBABWE. REGISTRAR OF BANKS AND FINANCIAL INSTITUTIONS See REPORT OF THE REGISTRAR OF BANKS AND FINANCIAL INSTITUTIONS AND REGISTRAR OF BUILDING SOCIETIES FOR THE YEAR ENDED DECEMBER 31 ... - (ZIMBABWE) **808**

ZIMBABWE RESEARCH INDEX (RH) [07500873] **427**

ZIMBABWE SCIENCE NEWS, THE (RH/1016-1503) [06575677] **5172**

ZIMBABWE TOBACCO NEWS (RH) **5374**

ZIMBABWE TOBACCO TODAY See ZIMBABWE TOBACCO NEWS **5374**

ZIMBABWE TOBACCO TODAY See TOBACCO NEWS **5374**

ZIMBABWE VETERINARY JOURNAL (RH/1016-1511) [07193763] **5528**

ZIMBABWEA (RH/0250-3018) [11567667] 248, **2644**

ZIMBABWEAN HISTORY : THE JOURNAL OF THE HISTORICAL ASSOCIATION OF ZIMBABWE (RH) [11795800] **2644**

ZIMBABWEAN PREHISTORY : JOURNAL OF THE PREHISTORY SOCIETY OF ZIMBABWE (RH) [10659431] **248**

ZIMMERMAN CASH FLOW LETTER, THE (US/1065-3600) [26593461] **817**

ZIMMER'S QUICK & EASY COMPUTER TAX PROGRAM (CN/0842-3946) [19486545] **4759**

ZINATNISKAS ATSKAITES SESIJAS MATERIALI PAR ARHEOLOGU UN ETNOGRAFU PETIJUMU REZULTATIEM (LV) [02441070] 286, 2275, **248**

ZINC (CN/0319-6631) [02442849] **4024**

● ZINC IN ... / PREPARED IN THE BRANCH OF METALS AND BRANCH OF DATA COLLECTION AND COORDINATION (US) [29656833] **4025**

ZINC INDUSTRY IN . See ZINC IN ... / PREPARED IN THE BRANCH OF METALS AND BRANCH OF DATA COLLECTION AND COORDINATION **4025**

ZINC INDUSTRY IN ... / U.S. DEPARTMENT OF THE INTERIOR, BUREAU OF MINES (US) [16349614] **4025**

ZINC TODAY (AT/0158-7765) [I01587765] **2153**

ZINCSCAN (UK/0950-1592) [15064554] **4025**

ZINOCYY SVIT (CN/0513-9856) [01796594] **5572**

ZINOTAJS (CN/0227-2423) [03896455] 3356, **2717**

ZIONIST IDEAS (IS) [11027272] **5054**

ZIONIST RECORD AND SA JEWISH CHRONICLE (SA) [03075327] **5054**

ZION'S HERALD (1975) (US/0098-9282) [02242891] **5070**

ZIONSVILLE TIMES SENTINEL (US/0886-4330) [12886489] **5668**

ZIP + 4 CODE STATE DIRECTORY (US) **1148**

ZIRAN KEXUESHI YANJIU (CC/1000-0224) [I10000224] **1361**

ZIRAN ZAZHI (CC/0253-9608) [04873827] **5172**

ZIRRAT FAKULTESI DERGISI. SERI: A (TU) [03149265] **149**

ZITO HLEB (YU/0351-0999) [10033181] **5172**

ZIVA (XR/0044-4812) [03807815] **4174**

ZIVA ANTIKA (XN/0514-7727) [04288125] **1081**

ZIVILDIENST, DER (GW) [03523386] **4696**

ZIVILSCHUTZ AKTUELL (AU) [18704807] **1073**

ZIVOCISNA VYROBA (XR/0044-4847) [09531421] **224**

ZIVOT (SARAJEVO) (BN/0514-776X) [02269917] **3456**

ZIVOT WARSAWA (PL/0514-0188) [I05140188] **2275**

ZIZANIOLOGIA (GR/0255-7940) [12670958] **531**

ZKG INTERNATIONAL (GW/0722-4397) [I07224397] **632**

ZKG INTERNATIONAL. EDITION B (GW/0722-4400) [I07224400] **632**

ZLODZENIE

ZLODZENIE POLSKIEJ STREFY PRZYBRZEZNEJ-MATERIALY ODDZIALU MORSKIEGO (PL) **1458**

ZLR, ZEITSCHRIFT FUER DAS GESAMTE LEBENSMITTELRECHT (GW/0342-3476) [01798462] **2361, 3078**

ZMIANY CEN W GOSPODARCE NARODOWEJ ... (PL) [29396031] **5347**

ZMP BILANZ (GW) [03741624] **2361**

ZMP BILANZ. GEMUSE (GW) [07500309] **191**

ZMP BILANZ. GETREIDE-FUTTERMITTEL (GW/0170-7809) [08790909] **204**

ZMP-BILANZ : KARTOFFELN (GW) [08148598] **191**

ZMP. BILANZ. OBST (GW) [07500312] **191**

ZMP MARKTBERICHT: SCHLACHTVIEH (GW) [05318690] **224**

ZNACAJNIJI PROIZVODI U IZVOZU I UVOZU SR HRVATSKE / SOCIJALISTICKA REPUBLIKA HRVATSKA, REPUBLICKI ZAVOD ZA STATISTIKU (CI) [10279110] **858**

ZNAK (PL/0044-488X) [03250101] **5011**

ZNAKI CZASU (FR/0984-8274) [I09848274] **5011**

ZNAMENOSETS *CEASED*. (RU) [01795199] **4061**

ZNAMJA (MOSKVA) (RU/0130-1616) [01770640] **3356**

ZNAMJA ROSSII (US/0044-4901) [02235149] **2717**

ZNANIE--SILA (RU/0130-1640) [08057369] **5173**

ZNANOST I PRAKSA U POLJOPRIVREDI I PREHRAMBENOJ TEHNOLOGIJI / OOUR POLJOPRIVREDNI INSTITUT (CI/0352-1346) [22697961] **552, 531**

ZNANSTVENOISTRAZIVACKE I RAZVOJNE ORGANIZACIJE (CI) [02479367] **5173**

ZODAK CENTRE FOR RELIGIOUS RESEARCH PUBLICATIONS (AT) **5011**

ZODCHESTVO (RU) [02244992] **311**

ZODIAC (MILAN, ITALY : 1988) (IT/0394-9249) [20961830] **311**

ZODIAQUE *CEASED*. (FR/0044-4952) [01774239] **369**

ZOEN ZASSHI (JA) [08133995] **2434**

ZOGRAF : CASOPIS ZA SREDNJOVEKOVNU UMETNOST (YU/0514-7867) [02314997] **2717**

ZOLDFELULETGAZDALKODAS (HU) [01261904] **2434**

ZOLDSEGTERMESZTESI KUTATO INTEZET *See* ZOLDSEGTERMESZTESI KUTATO INTEZET BULLETINJE **2434**

ZOLDSEGTERMESZTESI KUTATO INTEZET BULLETINJE (HU/0133-3682) [08725218] **149, 2434**

ZOLDSEGTERMESZTESI KUTATO INTEZET BULLETINJE (HU) [02848289] **149, 2434**

ZOLL UND HANDELSINFORMATION (GW) **3078**

ZOLLDIENST (GW) [03679966] **3078**

ZONA ABIERTA (SP/0210-2692) [02242928] **5226**

ZONA FRANCA *SUSPENDED*. (VE/0044-4987) [02269920] **3456**

ZONA TORRIDA (VE) [01314303] **2553**

ZONE (BROOKLYN) (US/0162-1904) [04118018] **3456**

ZONE FRANC, LA (FR) [02244271] **817**

ZONE HEATING NEWS (CN/0842-9693) [19491014] **2609**

ZONE LIBRE (CN/0705-3606) [03900612] **2550**

ZONIERZ POLSKI (PL/0044-4979) [I00444979] **4061**

ZONING AND LAND USE CONTROLS / BY PATRICK J. ROHAN ; CONTRIBUTORS, GARY I. COHEN ... [ET AL.] (US) [09485104] **2839**

ZONING AND PLANNING LAW HANDBOOK (US/0731-5791) [07627494] **2839, 3078**

ZONING AND PLANNING LAW REPORT (US/0161-8113) [04016701] **2839, 3078**

ZONING BULL. (BOSTON, MASS.) (US/0514-7905) [01495243] **2839**

ZONING NEWS (US/8755-3856) [10580093] **2839**

ZONING REPORT (MARGATE, FL.), THE (US/0748-0083) [10890980] **2839**

ZONTIAN (US/0279-3229) [01770646] **5572**

ZOO ANVERS (BE/0044-5029) [04557856] **5601**

ZOO BIOLOGY (US/0733-3188) [08563882] **5601**

ZOO GOER, THE (US/0163-416X) [04376420] **5601**

ZOO ONE *See* A TO Z **2185**

ZOO-SANITARY SITUATION IN MEMBER COUNTRIES IN ... / OFFICE INTERNATIONAL DES EPIZOOTIES (FR) [11410230] **5528**

ZOO VIEW (US/0276-3303) [04823347] **5601**

ZOOBOOKS (SAN DIEGO, CALIF.) (US/0737-9005) [09477981] **5601**

ZOOLOGICA (GW/0044-5088) [01770653] **5601**

ZOOLOGICA AFRICANA (SA/0044-5096) [01020208] **5601**

ZOOLOGICA POLONIAE; ARCHIVUM SOCIETATIS ZOOLOGORUM POLONIAE (PL/0044-510X) [01469223] **5601**

ZOOLOGICA RECORD / SECTION 13. INSECTA. SECTION A, GENERAL INSECTA AND SMALLER ORDERS (US) **5601**

ZOOLOGICA SCRIPTA (UK/0300-3256) [01496343] **5601**

ZOOLOGICAL JOURNAL OF THE LINNEAN SOCIETY (UK/0024-4082) [01799617] **5601**

ZOOLOGICAL PARKS AND AQUARIUMS IN THE AMERICAS (US/0740-7610) [04702129] **5601**

ZOOLOGICAL RECORD (CH) **5601**

ZOOLOGICAL RECORD : BEING RECORDS OF ZOOLOGICAL LITERATURE, SECTION 7. BRACHIOPODA (UK) [01643372] **5601**

ZOOLOGICAL RECORD: BEING RECORDS OF ZOOLOGICAL LITERATURE, SECTION 10. CRUSTACEA (UK) [01770658] **5601**

ZOOLOGICAL RECORD (LONDON) (UK/0144-3607) [06344527] **5601, 5604**

● ZOOLOGICAL RECORD ON CD (US/1072-1983) [28885165] **5601, 5604**

ZOOLOGICAL RECORD SEARCH GUIDE, THE (US/1053-802X) [12208441] **5601**

ZOOLOGICAL RECORD / SECTION 1. COMPREHENSIVE ZOOLOGY (US) **5601**

ZOOLOGICAL RECORD / SECTION 2. PROTOZOA (US) **5601**

ZOOLOGICAL RECORD / SECTION 3. PORIFERA & ARCHAEOCYATHA (US) **5601**

ZOOLOGICAL RECORD / SECTION 4. COELENTERATA & CTENOPHORA (US) **5601**

ZOOLOGICAL RECORD / SECTION 5. ECHINODERMATA (US) **5601**

ZOOLOGICAL RECORD / SECTION 6. WORMS AND FOSSIL MISCELLANEA, SECTION A. PLATYHELMINTHES AND NEMATODA TOGETHER WITH NEMERTINEA, MESOZOA, NEMATOMORPHA, ACANTHOCEPHALA AND PLACOZOA (US) **5601**

ZOOLOGICAL RECORD / SECTION 6. WORMS AND FOSSIL MISCELLANEA, SECTION B. ANNELIDA TOGETHER WITH ROTIFERA, CHAETOGNATHA, ECHIURA, SIPUNCULA, GASTROTRICHA, KINORHYNCHA, PRIAPULIDA, GNATHOSTOMULIDA AND POGONOPHORA (US) **5602**

ZOOLOGICAL RECORD / SECTION 6. WORMS AND FOSSIL MISCELLANEA, SECTION C. CONODONTA AND FOSSIL MISCELLANEA (US) **5602**

ZOOLOGICAL RECORD / SECTION 8. BRYOZOA (POLYZOA) AND ENTROPROCTA (US) **5602**

ZOOLOGICAL RECORD / SECTION 9. MOLLUSCA (US) **5602**

ZOOLOGICAL RECORD / SECTION 11. TRILOBITOMORPHA (US) **5602**

ZOOLOGICAL RECORD / SECTION 12. ARACHNIDA TOGETHER WITH MYRIAPODA, MEROSTOMATA, PANTOPODA, TARDIGRADA, SYMPHYLIDA, PAUROPODA, ONYCHOPHORA, ARTHROPLEURIDA AND PENTASTOMIDA (US) **5602**

ZOOLOGICAL RECORD / SECTION 13. INSECTA. SECTION B, COLEOPTERA (US) **5602**

ZOOLOGICAL RECORD / SECTION 13. INSECTA. SECTION C, DIPTERA (US) **5602**

ZOOLOGICAL RECORD / SECTION 13. INSECTA. SECTION D, LEPIDOPTERA (US) **5602**

ZOOLOGICAL RECORD / SECTION 13. INSECTA. SECTION E, HYMENOPTERA (US) **5602**

ZOOLOGICAL RECORD / SECTION 13. INSECTA. SECTION F, HEMIPTERA (US) **5602**

ZOOLOGICAL RECORD / SECTION 14. PROTOCHORDATA (US) **5602**

ZOOLOGICAL RECORD / SECTION 15. PISCES (US) **5602**

ZOOLOGICAL RECORD / SECTION 16. AMPHIBIA (US) **5602**

ZOOLOGICAL RECORD / SECTION 17. REPTILIA (US) **5602**

ZOOLOGICAL RECORD / SECTION 18. AVES (US) **5602**

ZOOLOGICAL RECORD / SECTION 19. MAMMALIA (US) **5602**

ZOOLOGICAL RECORD / SECTION 20. LIST OF NEW GENERIC AND SUBGENERIC NAMES (US) **5602**

ZOOLOGICAL RECORD SERIAL SOURCES (US/1041-4657) [18774527] **5602**

ZOOLOGICAL SCIENCE (JA/0289-0003) [10860200] **5602**

ZOOLOGICAL SOCIETY (CALCUTTA, INDIA) *See* PROCEEDINGS OF THE ZOOLOGICAL SOCIETY **5595**

ZOOLOGICAL SOCIETY OF INDIA *See* JOURNAL OF THE ZOOLOGICAL SOCIETY OF INDIA **5589**

ZOOLOGICAL STUDIES (CH/1021-5506) **5602**

ZOOLOGICAL SURVEY OF INDIA *See* RECORDS OF THE ZOOLOGICAL SURVEY OF INDIA. MISCELLANEOUS PUBLICATION. OCCASIONAL PAPER **5596**

ZOOLOGICAL SURVEY OF INDIA *See* BULLETIN OF THE ZOOLOGICAL SURVEY OF INDIA **5580**

ZOOLOGICAL SURVEY OF INDIA *See* MEMOIRS OF THE ZOOLOGICAL SURVEY OF INDIA **5591**

ZOOLOGICESKIJ ZURNAL (RU/0044-5134) [10460307] **5602**

ZOOLOGISCHE ABHANDLUNGEN / STAATLICHES MUSEUM FUER TIERKUNDE IN DRESDEN (GW/0375-5231) [01624171] **5602**

ZOOLOGISCHE BEITRAEGE (GW/0044-5150) [01770664] **5602**

ZOOLOGISCHE BIJDRAGEN *SUSPENDED*. (NE/0459-1801) [02448283] **5602**

ZOOLOGISCHE DOCUMENTATIE (BE/0563-1750) [01420298] **5603**

ZOOLOGISCHE GARTEN; ZEITSCHRIFT FUER DIE GESAMTE TIERGARTNEREI (GW/0044-5169) [01773095] **5603**

ZOOLOGISCHE JAHRBUCHER. ABTEILUNG FUER ALLGEMEINE ZOOLOGIE UND PHYSIOLOGIE DER TIERE (GW/0044-5185) [01770665] **5603**

ZOOLOGISCHE JAHRBUCHER. ABTEILUNG FUER ANATOMIE UND ONTOGENIE DER TIERE (GW/0044-5177) [01645063] **5603**

ZOOLOGISCHE JAHRBUCHER. ABTEILUNG FUER SYSTEMATIK, OKOLOGIE UND GEOGRAPHIE DER TIERE (GW/0044-5193) [01770666] **5603**

ZOOLOGISCHE JAHRBUECHER. ABTEILUNG FUER ALLGEMEINE ZOOLOGIE UND PHYSIOLOGIE DER TIERE *See* ZOOLOGY : ANALYSIS OF COMPLEX SYSTEMS, ZACS **5603**

ZOOLOGISCHE JAHRBUECHER. ABTEILUNG FUER ANATOMIE UND ONTOGIENIE DER TIERE *See* ZOOLOGY : ANALYSIS OF COMPLEX SYSTEMS, ZACS **5603**

ZOOLOGISCHE MEDEDELINGEN (NE/0024-0672) [01589398] **5603**

ZOOLOGISCHE VERHANDELINGEN (NE/0024-1652) [02448284] **5603**

ZOOLOGISCHE WETENSCHAPPEN / KONINKLIJK MUSEUM VOOR MIDDEN-AFRIKA / SCIENCES ZOOLOGIQUES / MUSEE ROYAL DE L'AFRIQUE CENTRALE (BE) [16679246] **5603**

ZOOLOGISCHER ANZEIGER (GW/0044-5231) [01770668] **5603**

ZOOLOGISCHES MUSEUM IN BERLIN *See* MITTEILUNGEN AUS DEM ZOOLOGISCHEN MUSEUM IN BERLIN **5591**

● ZOOLOGY : ANALYSIS OF COMPLEX SYSTEMS, ZACS (GW/0944-2006) [30690413] **5603**

ZOOM *CEASED*. (US) [03808926] **4378**

ZOOM IN : NEW FILMS AND VIDEOS FROM THE NATIONAL FILM BOARD OF CANADA (CN/1186-9240) [25351914] **4080**

ZOOM (MILAN, ITALY) (IT) [09355057] **4378**

ZOOM ON THE NFB (CN/0848-7138) [23247452] **4080**

ZOOMER & CO *CEASED*. (US/1051-7804) [22121488] **2287**

ZOOMIN' (US) [25396382] **5603**

ZOOMORPHOLOGY (GW/0720-213X) [07121937] **476, 5603**

ZOON (SA/0044-5274) [I00445274] **5603**

ZOONOOZ (US) [06139244] **5603**

ZOONOSES (AG/0514-7972) [05770634] **3654**

ZOOPHYSIOLOGY (GW/0720-1842) [05973653] **587, 5603**

ZOOSCAPE (LOS ANGELES, CALIF.) (US/1060-3859) [24955957] **5603**

Alphabetical Title Index

ZOOSOUNDS (US/0276-329X) [04823664] **5603**

ZOOTECHNIKA See ZESZYTY NAUKOWE. AKADEMIA ROLNICZA W KRAKOWIE, ZOOTECHNIKA **224**

ZOOTECHNIKA / AKADEMIA ROLNICZA W SZCZECINIE (PL/0137-1940) [10970037] **224**

ZOOTECNIA INTERNATIONAL (IT/0392-0593) [I03920593] **5603**

ZOOTECNIA TROPICAL (VE) [17349244] **224**

ZOOTECNICA E NUTRIZIONE ANIMALE (IT/0390-0487) [01360939] **224**

ZOOTECNICA INTERNATIONAL (IT) [07408039] **225**

ZOOTEHNIE SI MEDICINA VETERINARA See MEDICINA VETERINARA SI CRESTEREA ANIMALELOR **5516**

ZOOTEKHNIIA (RU/0235-2478) [19564066] **225**

ZOR. ZEITSCHRIFT FUER OPERATIONS-RESEARCH (GW/0340-9422) [01779519] **5173**

ZOR, ZEITSCHRIFT FUER OPERATIONS RESEARCH : METHODS AND MODELS OF OPERATIONS RESEARCH (GW/0340-9422) [19293305] **3542**

ZORA NEALE HURSTON FORUM, THE (US/1051-6867) [15610848] **3456**

ZORYAN BULLETIN, THE (US/0748-464X) [10952872] **2668**

ZOSEN GIJUTSU (JA/0387-2203) [08699149] **4185**

ZOSEN KANKEI GIJUTSU SHIRYO SOKUHO See SENPAKU KAIYO KOGAKU GIJUTSU BUNKEN SOKUHO **4185**

ZOSUI GIJUTSU (JA/0385-1001) [10417911] **5549**

ZOUNDS (CN/0703-4709) [03520225] **4160**

ZPA. ZEITSCHRIFT FUER PRAKTISCHE AUGENHEILKUNDE (GW/0173-2595) [07505620] **3880**

ZPG REPORTER (US/0199-0071) [05513938] **4561**, **2287**

ZPRAVA O SCHUZI SNEMOVNY NARODU / FEDERALNI SHROMAZDENI CESKOLOVENSKE SOCIALISTICKE REPUBLIKY (XR) [10191240] **4501**

ZPRAVA O SPOLECNE SCHUZI SNEMOVNY LIDU A SNEMOVNY NARODU / FEDERALNI SHROMAZDENI CESKOLOVENSKE SOCIALISTICKE REPUBLIKY (XR) [10190483] **4696**

ZPRAVA VZLU (XR) [09841038] **41**

ZPRAVODAJ - CESKOSLOVENSKE NARODNI SDRUZENI V KANADE, ODBOCKA VANCOUVER (CN/0701-0109) [03406207] **2550**

ZPRAVODAJ - FEDERALNI MINISTERSTVO PRO TECHNICKY A INVESTICNI ROZVOJ, MINISTERSTVO VYSTAVBY A TECHNIKY CSR, MINISTERSTVO VYSTAVBY A TECHNIKY SSR (XR) [06291228] **5173**

ZPRAVODAJ KOORDINOVANE SITE VEDECKYCH INFORMACI PRO ETNOGRAFII A FOLKLORISTIKU (XR) [20155863] 2325, **2276**

ZPRAVODAJ MINISTERSTVA STAVEBNICTVI CESKE SOCIALISTICKE REPUBLIKY (XR) [06049174] **632**

ZPRAVODAJ VZLU (XR/0044-5355) [I00445355] **5173**

ZPRAVY CSAV (XR) [02909651] **2525**

ZPRAVY GEOGRAFICKENO USTAVU CSAV (XR/0375-6122) [04812146] **2580**

ZPRAVY - SVU (US/0036-2050) [01565761] **2857**

ZRELISHCHNYE ISKUSSTVA (RU/0207-9739) [10450972] **389**

ZRV : ZEITSCHRIFT FUER RECHTSVERGLEICHUNG, INTERNAT. PRIVATRECHT UND EUROPARECHT (AU) [26713466] **3138**

ZU FRAGEN DES SOZIALISTISCHEN WELTSYSTEMS; AUSWAHLBIBLIOGRAPHIE (GW) [06871221] **4503**

ZUCHTUNGSKUNDE (GW/0044-5401) [01772770] 5603, **476**

ZUCKER- UND SUSSWAREN WIRTSCHAFT (GW/0373-0204) [01785305] **2362**

ZUCKERINDUSTRIE (GW/0344-8657) [03994841] **1031**

ZUCKERRUEBE, DIE (GW/0044-5398) [04171747] **191**

ZUCKERWIRTSCHAFT (GW) **149**

ZUERCHER WIRTSCHAFTSBRIEF (SZ) **1528**

ZUGAKU KENKYU (JA/0387-5512) [10426034] **5173**

ZUIDAFRIKAANSE KOERIER (SZ/0167-9767) [17459919] **4501**

ZUIDELIJK AFRIKA NIEUWS (NE) [03219249] **2644**

ZUIVELINDUSTRIE (NE/0168-518X) [12407889] **199**

ZUIVELZICHT (NE/0165-8573) [02846732] **199**

ZUKUNFTSORIENTIERTE BILDUNGSPOLITIK : DOKUMENTATION DES ... REGENSBURGER KONGRESSES FREIE SCHULE EINE NOTWENDIGE ALTERNATIVE ZUM HERKOMMLICHEN SCHULSYSTEM (GW) [20475475] **1792**

ZULIA, VENEZUELA. UNIVERSIDAD See MEMORIA Y CUENTA **1835**

ZUM NACHDENKEN (GW) [07887286] **4501**

ZUM : ZEITSCHRIFT FUER URHEBER- UND MEDIENRECHT/FILM UND RECHT (GW/0177-6762) [12936736] 1310, **4080**

ZUMAQUE (VE) [04199707] **4283**

ZUPFMUSIK MAGAZIN (GW/0176-0971) [28196954] **4160**

ZUPNI VJESNIK NASE GOSPE KRALJICE HRVATA, TORONTO, HRVATSKIH MUCENIKA, MISSISSAUGA (CN/0820-6449) [09428151] **5038**

ZUR POLITIK UND ZEITGESCHICHTE (GW/0514-8294) [01498321] **4501**

ZUR PRAXIS DER VOLKSSCHULE (SZ) [19479546] **1792**

ZURCHER BEITRAGE ZUR DEUTSCHEN LITERATUR- UND GEISTESGESCHICHTE *CEASED*. (SW) [03259718] **3456**

ZURICH. SCHWEIZERISCHES LANDESMUSEUM See JAHRESBERICHT - SCHWEIZERISCHES LANDESMUSEUM ZURICH **4089**

ZURNAL ANALITICHESKOI HIMII (RU/0044-4502) [01642749] **1020**

ZURNAL EKSPERIMENTALNOJ I TEORETICESKOJ FIZIKI (RU/0044-4510) [10917256] **4426**

ZURNAL MOSKOVSKOJ PATRIARHII (RU/0132-862X) [01645718] **5040**

ZURNAL NEVROPATOLOGII I PSIHIATRII IM S.S. KORSAKOVA *CEASED*. (RU/0044-4588) [01585884] 3938, **3847**

ZURNAL OBSCEJ BIOLOGI (RU/0044-4596) [01770628] **476**

ZURNAL OBSEJ HIMII (RU/0044-460X) [06903195] **996**

ZURNAL ORGANICESKOJ HIMII (RU/0514-7492) [02276562] **1049**

ZURNAL PRIKLADNOI HIMII (RU/0044-4618) [01623884] **996**

ZURNAL PRIKLADNOI SPEKTROSKOPII (MINSK) (RU/0514-7506) [02235249] **4442**

ZURNAL TEHNICESKOJ FIZIKI (RU/0044-4642) [01770632] **4426**

ZURNAL USNYH, NOSOVYH I GORLOVYH BOLEZNEJ (UN/0044-4650) [07789435] **3891**

ZURNAL VYCISLITELNOJ MATEMATIKI I MATEMATICESKOJ FIZIKI (RU/0044-4669) [01640629] 1208, 3542, **4426**

ZURNALS (LITTLETON, MASS.) (US/0277-9811) [07674153] **2276**

ZUSAMMEN MONATSZEITSCHRIFT FUR JUNGE LEUTE (IT) **1792**

ZUSAMMENSTELLUNG DER STATISTISCHEN ANGABEN DER GASVERSORGUNGSUNTERNEHMEN IN DER BUNDESREPUBLIK DEUTSCHLAND UND IN WEST-BERLIN See GASSTATISTIK FUR DIE BUNDESREPUBLIK DEUTSCHLAND **4283**

ZUSETSU EPOKA TOKEI SHIRYO (JA) [01799700] **5347**

●ZUZU'S PETALS QUARTERLY (US/1060-9571) [25124778] **3456**

ZVAIGZNOTA DEBESS (LV/0135-129X) [06099782] **401**

ZVARACSKE SPRAVY (XO/0322-9785) [11586085] **4029**

ZVARTNOTS (AI/0033-1163) [24070527] **5173**

ZVAZAJ (CN/0700-5172) [03403013] **2767**

ZVEZDA *CEASED*. (RU/0321-1878) [01507146] **2525**

ZVEZDA VOSTOKA; LITERATURNO-KHUDOZHESTVENNYI I OBSHCHESTVENNO-POLITICHESKII ZHURNAL (RU) [02235136] **2525**

ZVUK (BEOGRAD) (YU/0044-555X) [03250222] **4160**

ZWEIG FORECAST (US) **725**

●ZWEIG LETTER, THE (US/1068-1310) [27449817] **890**

ZWF CIM (GW/0932-0482) [15815201] **2132**

ZWIASTUN (PL/0514-4655) [07419126] **5011**

ZWIAZKOWIEC (CN) [13446844] **5798**

ZWIERCIADO (PL/0514-0994) [I05140994] **5572**

ZWIERZETA LABORATORYJNE (PL/0084-5825) [05729456] 5528, **5604**

ZWINGLIANA (SZ/0254-4407) [02287528] **5011**

ZWINGLIANA: BEITRAEGE ZUR GESCHICHTE ZWINGLIS DER REFORMATION UND DES PROTESTANTISMUS IN DER SEHWEIZ (SZ) **5011**

ZWO : PLAATS EN PERSPEKTIEF (NE) [06466343] **5173**

ZWOLSE DRUKKEN EN HERDRUKKEN VOOR DER MAATSCHAPPIJ DER NEDERLANDSE LETTERKUNDE TE LEIDEN (NE/0514-4787) [01499019] **3456**

ZWR (GW/0044-166X) [01777608] **1337**

ZYCIE CZESTOCHOWY (PL/0137-9410) [I01379410] **5808**

ZYCIE GOSPODARCZE (PL) [01506645] **1589**

ZYCIE I MYSL (PL/0044-5584) [03246556] **5011**

ZYCIE I ZDROWIE (PL) [01793159] **4809**

ZYCIE KATOLICKIE W POLSCE (PL) [17568566] **5012**

ZYCIE OTTAWY (CN/0707-3976) [04746990] **5266**

ZYCIE PRZEMYSKIE (PL/0208-6964) [I02086964] **2525**

ZYCIE SZKOY WYZSZEJ (PL/0591-2377) [05518749] **1792**

ZYCIE WARSZAWY (PL) [10310530] **5808**

ZYCIE WETERYNARYJNE (PL/0137-6810) [02185215] **5528**

ZYDOWSKI INSTYTUT HISTROYCZNY W POLSCE See BIULETYN ZYDOWSKIEGO INSTYTUTU HISTORYCZNEGO W POLSCE **5046**

ZYGON (UK/0591-2385) [01814793] **5012**

ZYGOS (ATHENS, GREECE : 1982) *CEASED*. (GR/0252-8150) [08620555] **369**

●ZYGOTE (UK/0967-1994) [28037956] **476**

ZYMURGY (US/0196-5921) [05850150] **2373**

ZYPERN : ENERGIEWIRTSCHAFT (GW) [05145905] **1961**

ZYPERN, TURKISCH VERWALTETER TEIL : WIRTSCHAFTLICHE ENTWICKLUNG (GW) [06211664] **1589**

ZYWIENIE CZOWIEKA I METABOLIZM (PL/0209-164X) [14360666] **4200**

ZYZZYVA (US/8756-5633) [11585815] 369, **3457**

ZZAP! 64 See COMMODORE FORCE **1244**

ZZAP! 64 (UK/0954-867X) [I0954867X] 4868, **1245**